holy BIBLE

NEW INTERNATIONAL VERSION

Cross Reference Edition
With Concordance

Hodder & Stoughton
LONDON SYDNEY AUCKLAND

NIV Cross Reference Edition with Concordance
first published in Great Britain 1986
0 340 36338 X
This impression 1998

You will be pleased to know that a portion of the purchase price of your new NIV Bible has been allocated to the International Bible Society to help spread the Gospel of Jesus Christ around the world.

This publication is not included under licences issued by the Copyright Licensing Agency. Photoset by Rowland Phototypesetting Ltd., Bury St Edmunds, Suffolk. Printed for Hodder & Stoughton Ltd, a division of Hodder Headline PLC, 338 Euston Road, London NW1 3BH by Clays Ltd, St Ives plc.

CONTENTS

THE BOOKS OF THE OLD TESTAMENT

THE BOOKS OF THE NEW TESTAMENT

INTRODUCTION

It has often been noted that the best commentary on the Bible is the Bible itself. In this cross reference edition of the NIV, the Bible text is supplemented by a centre column of references, which direct the reader to further passages that expand, clarify or reinforce the meaning of the verses being read. A comprehensive concordance and a short Bible atlas add to the usefulness of this Bible as an invaluable but compact resource for biblical study.

History

The NIV Cross Reference Bible began with a vision of one individual more than a decade ago. By the time the project was completed it involved more than forty individuals and half a dozen computers.

Dr. Donald Madvig, then of Bethel Theological Seminary in St. Paul, U.S.A., began work on the *NIV Cross Reference Bible* in 1973, shortly after the first text edition of the NIV New Testament was published. His method was to refine and rearrange material drawn from the best available study Bibles. The New Testament was completed in essence in 1980. As Madvig began his work on the Old Testament, he realised the poor quality of the content and organisation of the study Bibles on which he had been basing his work. However, ill health prevented his continued involvement with the project. In 1981 Zondervan Bible Publishers invited John Kohlenberger of Portland, Oregon, to continue the work on the Old Testament. Because of the amount of research and collation required, five Old Testament scholars were called in to help. These men, most of whom had served as translators of the NIV, gathered teams of students from their respective educational institutions to collate and evaluate Old Testament cross references as Madvig had done for the New Testament.

Since an enormous amount of sorting of data was necessary for the Old Testament, it was apparent that this could best be done by computers; therefore the Control Data Corporation was asked to develop the software needed for this undertaking.

The material the contributors accumulated amounted to nearly 5,000 hand-written pages that were edited and keyed into a massive computer database. By June of 1982 the input was completed and the material was sorted into biblical order. This was then edited for obvious errors, corrected, re-sorted and sent back to the original contributors in October of 1982 for further editing.

During this process the New Testament materials were re-worked to match the format that had by now been adopted for the Old Testament. The Old Testament contributors' references to the New Testament were also evaluated in order to tie them into New Testament "chains", further assuring the cohesiveness of the two Testaments. During 1983 the references were organised into "chains", which after a final phase of thorough examination and editing totalled just over 82,000 references—without any loss of information.

There followed the process of typesetting the references and incorporating them into the anglicised NIV text, to produce the format of the present edition.

Features of the NIV Cross Reference Bible

Because of the exacting manual work combined with the precision of the computer process, the *NIV Cross Reference Bible* is one of the most thorough, accurate and best organised reference Bibles available. The primary features are the text of the New International Version and the cross reference system itself.

Before examining each feature independently, you should become familiar with the general layout of the page. The first pages of Matthew will serve this purpose well. Most important is the text of the NIV. You will notice that it is not laid out verse-by-verse in each of the two columns of text. Verse numbers still appear as raised figures preceding the words that start each verse, but the text is organised in **paragraph** form, a more meaningful way of dividing the text.

Further, the structure of the text is pointed out by **special indentations**. The structure of chapter 1, as explained in verse 17, is emphasised by double spacing between the three groups of genealogical materials and by indenting each of the fourteen generations in their sections: Abraham (vv. 2–6a), David (vv. 6b–11) and the exile to Babylon (vv. 12–16). Other examples of special indentations include poetry (Mt 2:6,18), letters (Ac 15:23–29) and lists (Ne 7:8–63).

Paragraphs show the logical organisation of the verses or sentences of the text: **Subheadings** show the logical organisation of the paragraphs. The section of Matthew 1:1–17 is therefore entitled "The Genealogy of Jesus".

Footnotes to the NIV text are indicated by raised, bold-faced letters following the words or phrases they explain. They point out such things as alternative translations (Mt 2:2[b]), meanings of Hebrew and Greek terms (Mt 1:17[b], 21[c]), Old Testament quotations (Mt 2:6[d], 15[f], 18[g],) and alternative readings in ancient biblical manuscripts (Mt 5:22[b], 44[i]). These footnotes appear at the bottom of the right-hand column, preceded by the footnote letter and verse number.

Cross References are also indicated by raised letters, but this system employs a different typeface than the one for footnotes: NIV footnotes use a **bold** typeface, while cross reference footnotes use a *light italic* typeface. When a single word is addressed by both types of footnotes, the bold NIV raised letter comes first, as in Matthew 1:21, "Jesus,[c t]".

Further, although the cross references normally appear in the centre column, some passages are so rich in references that there is insufficient space in the centre column alone. The first page of Genesis is an example. In such cases they continue at the bottom of the right-hand column *preceding* the NIV footnotes.

To locate the cross references for any word or phrase, first find the **chapter and verse** in the centre column. Then, match the *raised italic* letter in the section for that verse in the centre column. It is important to begin with the chapter and verse designation, because each footnote letter can be repeated two or three times on each *page* but can be used only once in a single *verse*.

One final feature of the page is the system of **Parallel and Reference passages**. When two or more passages of Scripture are nearly identical or deal with the same event, this "parallel" is noted at the subheadings for those passages. At Matthew 1:1, verses 1–17 are noted as "parallel" (*pp*) to Luke 3:23–38, as are verses 3–6 to Ruth 4:18–22 and 7–11 to 1 Chronicles 3:10–17. Similar events in the Gospels and narrative portions of the Old Testament are noted as "reference passages" and are indicated by the abbreviation "*Ref*", as at Matthew 8:23.

The Cross Reference System

As you begin to use the reference system, you will notice that some of the references are picked out in bold type. References not in bold require no further explanation. The bold references, however, indicate a location where further references on the same theme may be found. This location is the key entry for that theme.

Two points must immediately be made about this basic scheme. First, because of limits of space, the initial reference is not always the key entry. Second, where there are a large number of entries on one theme, there may be more than one key entry.

An example of the first instance occurs in Matthew 1:20, where the reference to the word "angel" is listed in the centre column as **"Ac 5:19"**. The key entry relating to angels is in Acts, not in its first appearance in Matthew (otherwise the books of Genesis and Matthew would be all references and little text). An example of the second occurs in Matthew 1:1 where the phrase "Son of David" is referenced to seven locations as well as to **"Mt 9:27"**. At Matthew 9:27 "Son of David" is referenced to an additional eight locations.

A further examination of this "Son of David" theme would reveal that the subdivision is generally based on specific subject matter. The references at Matthew 1:1 relate to the Old Testament background of Jesus' descent from David while the references at Matthew 9:27 are all statements or confessions proclaiming Jesus as the son of David. This is also true of the "angel" list at Acts 5:19. The texts listed in the centre column relate to the "angel of the Lord", or the "angel of God", while the texts listed at **"Jn 20:12"** refer to angels in general.

Because of these subdivisions, you will want to work through *all* of the references and all of *their* references, to whatever degree you desire. Whether they are bold references or not, they all have significant points of contact with the words and concepts you are studying.

A good example of the resources of the *NIV Cross Reference Bible* is provided by the material at Genesis 1:1. There are four lists of references to the first verse of the Bible. All relate to creation, but from different perspectives. Note *a* deals with creation as having taken place "in the beginning". Note *b* lists the three other occurrences of the word "created" in Genesis 1–2. Note *c* focuses on "the heavens" as God's creation. Note *d*, because it is attached to the end of the verse as well as to the word "earth", deals with the word "earth", the phrase "the heavens and the earth" and with creation itself (the whole verse).

Just as all of these facets and elements of creation are contained in this verse, so they will be in others. The various chains will intersect and diverge; your perspectives will be sharpened as well as broadened as you work through the cross reference system. This will be true of any subject you study. The resources of the *NIV Cross Reference Bible* are virtually inexhaustible—but you must decide how far you wish to work through each study.

There are several additional features regarding the lists of references that you should note. First, as you work through each list, you will find that they are in biblical order with one exception. If reference is made to a verse within the same chapter you are studying, that "ver" reference is first in the list, regardless of biblical order (see note *b* at Matthew 9:26). Second, if an Old Testament verse is quoted in the New Testament, the New Testament reference is marked with an asterisk (*). Third, if a reference leads from a textual variant in a footnote to the NIV text, the abbreviation *fn* appears **before** the reference. If it leads to a footnote, *fn* appears **after** the reference.

Parallel and Reference Passages

When two or more passages of Scripture are nearly identical or deal with the same event, this "parallel" is noted at the subheadings for those passages. These passages are especially common in the Gospels and in Samuel, Kings and Chronicles. (Parallel passages in the Psalms are noted directly after the Psalm number, as in Psalm 14. Parallels in Obadiah simply precede verse 1, as there are no subheadings in the book).

When the two (or more) passages are identical or nearly identical, as at Ezra 1:1, this "parallel" is noted with *"pp"*. When the passages are similar, though not the same event, as at Genesis 12:10, this similarity is noted with *"Ref"*. Both types of passages always extend to several verses. Individual parallel verses, such as Judges 17:6 and 21:25, are connected in the cross references, but are not marked as parallel passages.

Two things should be kept in mind when studying parallel and reference passages. First, these passages are noted at the subheadings but do not necessarily cover the entire range of verses covered by that subheading. For example, at 2 Chronicles 36:15 the subheading "The Fall of Jerusalem" covers verses 15–23, but the first parallel covers only verses 17–20 and the second, verses 22–23.

Second, when a parallel or reference passage is noted at a subheading *no further parallels are listed in the cross reference system*. This was done to conserve space and avoid repetition. Thus, whenever you are studying any verse in any passage of Scripture, check the subheading to see if there are parallel passages to include in your study for further illumination and further references.

Concordance

Alongside the cross reference system and the parallel and reference passages, this Bible contains a comprehensive short concordance.

The Concordance may be used to find remembered or half-remembered verses by looking up their key words. If you wanted to find the verse that states "iron sharpens iron", you could locate it under either the word "iron" or "sharpens". But if you wanted to locate the verse that states that the word of God is "sharper than any double-edged sword", you would have to be more selective with your words, for neither "than" nor "any" are listed. For more information on the Concordance see the separate Introduction on page 1143.

Maps

The sixteen-page Bible atlas contains full-colour maps especially adapted for the NIV, and covers both Old and New Testaments.

The contributors and editors of this Bible hope that the NIV Cross Reference Bible will assist you through a lifetime of enriching biblical study.

PREFACE

THE NEW INTERNATIONAL VERSION is a completely new translation of the Holy Bible made by over a hundred scholars working directly from the best available Hebrew, Aramaic and Greek texts. It had its beginning in 1965 when, after several years of exploratory study by committees from the Christian Reformed Church and the National Association of Evangelicals, a group of scholars met at Palos Heights, Illinois, and concurred in the need for a new translation of the Bible in contemporary English. This group, though not made up of official church representatives, was transdenominational. Its conclusion was endorsed by a large number of leaders from many denominations who met in Chicago in 1966.

Responsibility for the new version was delegated by the Palos Heights group to a self-governing body of fifteen, the Committee on Bible Translation, composed for the most part of biblical scholars from colleges, universities and seminaries. In 1967 the New York Bible Society (now the International Bible Society) generously undertook the financial sponsorship of the project—a sponsorship that made it possible to enlist the help of many distinguished scholars. The fact that participants from the United States, Great Britain, Canada, Australia and New Zealand worked together gave the project its international scope. That they were from many denominations—including Anglican, Assemblies of God, Baptist, Brethren, Christian Reformed, Church of Christ, Evangelical Free, Lutheran, Mennonite, Methodist, Nazarene, Presbyterian, Wesleyan and other churches—helped to safeguard the translation from sectarian bias.

How it was made helps to give the New International Version its distinctiveness. The translation of each book was assigned to a team of scholars. Next, one of the Intermediate Editorial Committees revised the initial translation, with constant reference to the Hebrew, Aramaic or Greek. Their work then went to one of the General Editorial Committees, which checked it in detail and made another thorough revision. This revision in turn was carefully reviewed by the Committee on Bible Translation, which made further changes and then released the final version for publication. In this way the entire Bible underwent three revisions, during each of which the translation was examined for its faithfulness to the original languages and for its English style.

All this involved many thousands of hours of research and discussion regarding the meaning of the texts and the precise way of putting them into English. It may well be that no other translation has been made by a more thorough process of review and revision from committee to committee than this one.

From the beginning of the project, the Committee on Bible Translation held to certain goals for the New International Version: that it would be an accurate translation and one that would have clarity and literary quality and so prove suitable for public and private reading, teaching, preaching, memorising and liturgical use. The Committee also sought to preserve some measure of continuity with the long tradition of translating the Scriptures into English.

In working towards these goals, the translators were united in their commitment to the authority and infallibility of the Bible as God's Word in written form. They believe that it contains the divine answer to the deepest needs of humanity, that it sheds unique light on our path in a dark world, and that it sets forth the way to our eternal well-being.

The first concern of the translators has been the accuracy of the translation and its fidelity to the thought of the biblical writers. They have weighed the significance of the lexical and grammatical details of the Hebrew, Aramaic and Greek texts. At the same time, they have striven for more than a word-for-word translation. Because thought patterns and syntax differ from language to language, faithful communication of the meaning of the writers of the Bible demands frequent modifications in sentence structure and constant regard for the contextual meanings of words.

A sensitive feeling for style does not always accompany scholarship. Accordingly the Committee on Bible Translation submitted the developing version to a number of stylistic consultants. Two of them read every book of both Old and New Testaments twice—once before and once after the last major revision—and made invaluable suggestions. Samples of the translation were tested for clarity and ease of reading by various kinds of people—young and old, highly educated and less well educated, ministers and laymen.

Concern for clear and natural English—that the New International Version should be idiomatic but not idiosyncratic, contemporary but not dated—motivated the translators and consultants. At the same time, they tried to reflect the differing styles of the biblical writers. In view of the international use of English, the translators sought to avoid obvious Americanisms on the one hand and obvious Anglicisms on the other. A British edition reflects the comparatively few differences of significant idiom and of spelling.

As for the traditional pronouns "thou", "thee" and "thine" in reference to the Deity, the translators judged that to use these archaisms (along with old verb forms such as "doest", "wouldest" and "hadst") would violate accuracy in translation. Neither Hebrew, Aramaic nor Greek uses special pronouns for the persons of the Godhead. A present-day translation is not enhanced by forms that in the time of the King James Version were used in everyday speech, whether referring to God or man.

For the Old Testament the standard Hebrew text, the Masoretic Text as published in the latest editions of *Biblia Hebraica*, was used throughout. The Dead Sea Scrolls contain material bearing on an earlier stage of the Hebrew text. They were consulted, as were the Samaritan Pentateuch and the ancient scribal traditions relating to textual changes. Sometimes a variant Hebrew reading in the margin of the Masoretic Text was followed instead of the text itself. Such instances, being variants within the Masoretic tradition, are not specified by footnotes. In rare cases, words in the consonantal text were divided differently from the way they appear in the Masoretic Text. Footnotes indicate this. The translators also consulted the more important early versions—the Septuagint; Aquila, Symmachus and Theodotion; the Vulgate; the Syriac Peshitta; the Targums; and for the Psalms the *Juxta Hebraica* of Jerome. Readings from these versions were occasionally followed where the Masoretic Text seemed doubtful and where accepted principles of textual criticism showed that one or more of these textual witnesses appeared to provide the correct reading. Such instances are footnoted. Sometimes vowel letters and vowel signs did not, in the judgment of the translators, represent the correct vowels for the original consonantal text. Accordingly some words were read with a different set of vowels. These instances are usually not indicated by footnotes.

The Greek text used in translating the New Testament was an eclectic one. No other piece of ancient literature has such an abundance of manuscript witnesses as does the New Testament. Where existing manuscripts differ, the translators made their choice of readings according to accepted principles of New Testament textual criticism. Footnotes call attention to places where there was uncertainty about what the original text was. The best current printed texts of the Greek New Testament were used.

There is a sense in which the work of translation is never wholly finished. This applies to all great literature and uniquely so to the Bible. In 1973 the New Testament in the New International Version was published. Since then, suggestions for corrections and revisions have been received from various sources. The Committee on Bible Translation carefully considered the suggestions and adopted a number of them. These were incorporated in the first printing of the entire Bible in 1978. Additional revisions were made by the Committee on Bible Translation in 1983 and appear in printings after that date.

As in other ancient documents, the precise meaning of the biblical texts is sometimes uncertain. This is more often the case with the Hebrew and Aramaic texts than with the Greek text. Although archaeological and linguistic discoveries in this century aid in understanding difficult passages, some uncertainties remain. The more significant of these have been called to the reader's attention in the footnotes.

In regard to the divine name *YHWH*, commonly referred to as the *Tetragrammaton*, the translators adopted the device used in most English versions of rendering that name as "LORD" in capital letters to distinguish it from *Adonai*, another Hebrew word rendered "Lord", for which small letters are used. Wherever the two names stand together in the Old Testament as a compound name of God, they are rendered "Sovereign LORD".

Because for most readers today the phrases "the LORD of hosts" and "God of hosts" have little meaning, this version renders them "the LORD Almighty" and "God Almighty". These renderings convey the sense of the Hebrew, namely, "he who is sovereign over all the 'hosts' (powers) in heaven and on earth, especially over the 'hosts' (armies) of Israel." For readers unacquainted with Hebrew this does not make clear the distinction between *Sabaoth* ("hosts" or "Almighty") and *Shaddai* (which can also be translated "Almighty"), but the latter occurs infrequently and is always footnoted. When *Adonai* and *YHWH Sabaoth* occur together, they are rendered "the Lord, the LORD Almighty".

As for other proper nouns, the familiar spellings of the Authorised Version are generally retained. Names traditionally spelled with "ch", except where it is final, are usually spelled in this translation with "k" or "c", since the biblical languages do not have the sound that "ch" frequently indicates in English—for example, in *chant*. For well-known names such as Zechariah, however, the traditional spelling has been retained. Variation in the spelling of names in the original languages has usually not been indicated. Where a person or place has two or more different names in the Hebrew, Aramaic or Greek texts, the more familiar one has generally been used, with footnotes where needed.

To achieve clarity the translators sometimes supplied words not in the original texts but required by the context. If there was uncertainty about such material, it is enclosed in brackets. Also for the sake of clarity or style, nouns, including some proper nouns, are sometimes substituted for pronouns, and vice versa. And though the Hebrew writers often shifted back and forth between first, second and third personal pronouns without change of antecedent, this translation often makes them uniform, in accordance with English style and without the use of footnotes.

Poetical passages are printed as poetry, that is, with indentation of lines and with separate stanzas. These are generally designed to reflect the structure of Hebrew poetry. This poetry is normally characterised by parallelism in balanced lines. Most of the poetry in the Bible is in the Old Testament, and scholars differ regarding the scansion of Hebrew lines. The translators determined the stanza divisions for the most part by analysis of the subject matter. The stanzas therefore serve as poetic paragraphs.

As an aid to the reader, italicised sectional headings are inserted in most of the books. They are not to be regarded as part of the NIV text, are not for oral reading, and are not intended to dictate the interpretation of the sections they head.

The footnotes in this version are of several kinds, most of which need no explanation. Those giving alternative translations begin with "Or" and generally introduce the alternative with the last word preceding it in the text, except when it is a single-word alternative; in poetry quoted in a footnote a slant mark indicates a line division. Footnotes introduced by "Or" do not have uniform significance. In some cases two possible translations were considered to have about equal validity. In other cases, though the translators were convinced that the translation in the text was correct, they judged that another interpretation was possible and of sufficient importance to be represented in a footnote.

In the New Testament, footnotes that refer to uncertainty regarding the original text are introduced by "Some manuscripts" or similar expressions. In the Old Testament, evidence for the reading chosen is given first and evidence for the alternative is added after a semicolon (for example: Septuagint; Hebrew *father*). In such notes the term "Hebrew" refers to the Masoretic Text.

It should be noted that minerals, flora and fauna, architectural details, articles of clothing and jewellery, musical instruments and other articles cannot always be identified with precision. Also measures of capacity in the biblical period are particularly uncertain (see the table of weights and measures following the text).

Like all translations of the Bible, made as they are by imperfect man, this one undoubtedly falls short of its goals. Yet we are grateful to God for the extent to which he has enabled us to realise these goals and for the strength he has given us and our colleagues to complete our task. We offer this version of the Bible to him in whose name and for whose glory it has been made. We pray that it will lead many into a better understanding of the Holy Scriptures and a fuller knowledge of Jesus Christ the incarnate Word, of whom the Scriptures so faithfully testify.

The Committee on Bible Translation

June 1978
(Revised August 1983)

Names of the translators and editors may be secured
from the International Bible Society
1820 Jet Stream Drive, Colorado Springs, CO 80921-3696, U.S.A.

ABBREVIATIONS FOR THE BOOKS OF THE BIBLE

Genesis	Ge	Nahum	Na
Exodus	Ex	Habakkuk	Hab
Leviticus	Lev	Zephaniah	Zep
Numbers	Nu	Haggai	Hag
Deuteronomy	Dt	Zechariah	Zec
Joshua	Jos	Malachi	Mal
Judges	Jdg	Matthew	Mt
Ruth	Ru	Mark	Mk
1 Samuel	1Sa	Luke	Lk
2 Samuel	2Sa	John	Jn
1 Kings	1Ki	Acts	Ac
2 Kings	2Ki	Romans	Ro
1 Chronicles	1Ch	1 Corinthians	1Co
2 Chronicles	2Ch	2 Corinthians	2Co
Ezra	Ezr	Galatians	Gal
Nehemiah	Ne	Ephesians	Eph
Esther	Est	Philippians	Php
Job	Job	Colossians	Col
Psalms	Ps	1 Thessalonians	1Th
Proverbs	Pr	2 Thessalonians	2Th
Ecclesiastes	Ecc	1 Timothy	1Ti
Song of Songs	SS	2 Timothy	2Ti
Isaiah	Isa	Titus	Tit
Jeremiah	Jer	Philemon	Phm
Lamentations	La	Hebrews	Heb
Ezekiel	Eze	James	Jas
Daniel	Da	1 Peter	1Pe
Hosea	Hos	2 Peter	2Pe
Joel	Joel	1 John	1Jn
Amos	Am	2 John	2Jn
Obadiah	Ob	3 John	3Jn
Jonah	Jnh	Jude	Jude
Micah	Mic	Revelation	Rev

THE
OLD TESTAMENT

Genesis

The Beginning

1 In the beginning[a] God created[b]
the heavens[c] and the earth.[d] 2Now
the earth was[a] formless[e] and
empty,[f] darkness was over the
surface of the deep,[g] and the Spirit
of God[h] was hovering[i] over the
waters.

3And God said,[j] "Let there be light,"
and there was light.[k] 4God saw that
the light was good,[l] and he separ-
ated the light from the darkness.[m]
5God called[n] the light "day", and
the darkness he called "night".[o]
And there was evening, and there
was morning[p]—the first day.
6And God said,[q] "Let there be an ex-
panse[r] between the waters[s] to sep-
arate water from water." 7So God
made the expanse and separated
the water under the expanse from
the water above it.[t] And it was so.[u]
8God called[v] the expanse "sky".[w]
And there was evening, and there
was morning[x]—the second day.
9And God said, "Let the water under
the sky be gathered to one place,[y]
and let dry ground[z] appear." And it
was so.[a] 10God called[b] the dry
ground "land", and the gathered
waters[c] he called "seas".[d] And God
saw that it was good.[e]
11Then God said, "Let the land
produce vegetation:[f] seed-bearing
plants and trees on the land that
bear fruit with seed in it, according
to their various kinds.[g]" And it was
so.[h] 12The land produced vegeta-
tion: plants bearing seed according
to their kinds[i] and trees bearing
fruit with seed in it according to
their kinds. And God saw that
it was good.[j] 13And there was
evening, and there was morning[k]
—the third day.
14And God said, "Let there be lights[l] in
the expanse of the sky to separate
the day from the night,[m] and let
them serve as signs[n] to mark sea-
sons[o] and days and years,[p] 15and let
them be lights in the expanse of the
sky to give light on the earth." And
it was so.[q] 16God made two great
lights—the greater light[r] to govern[s]
the day and the lesser light to gov-
ern[t] the night.[u] He also made the
stars.[v] 17God set them in the ex-
panse of the sky to give light on the
earth, 18to govern the day and the
night,[w] and to separate light from
darkness. And God saw that it was
good.[x] 19And there was evening,
and there was morning[y]—the
fourth day.
20And God said, "Let the water teem
with living creatures,[z] and let birds
fly above the earth across the
expanse of the sky."[a] 21So God
created[b] the great creatures of the
sea[c] and every living and moving
thing with which the water teems,[d]
according to their kinds, and every
winged bird according to its kind.[e]
And God saw that it was good.[f]
22God blessed them and said, "Be
fruitful and increase in number and
fill the water in the seas, and let the
birds increase on the earth."[g] 23And
there was evening, and there was
morning[h]—the fifth day.
24And God said, "Let the land produce
living creatures[i] according to their

Ch. 1

1 [a]Ps 102:25; Pr 8:23; Isa 40:21; 41:4,26; Jn 1:1–2; [b]ver 21,27; Ge 2:3; [c]ver 6; Ne 9:6; Job 9:8; 37:18; Ps 96:5; 104:2; 115:15; 121:2; 136:5; Isa 40:22; 42:5; 51:13; Jer 10:12; 51:15; [d]Ge 14:19; 2Ki 19:15; Ne 9:6; Job 38:4; Ps 90:2; 136:6; 146:6; Isa 37:16; 40:28; 42:5; 44:24; 45:12,18; Jer 27:5; 32:17; Ac 14:15; 17:24; Eph 3:9; Col 1:16; Heb 3:4; 11:3; Rev 4:11; 10:6
2 [e]Isa 23:1; 24:10; 27:10; 32:14; 34:11; [f]Isa 45:18; Jer 4:23; [g]Ge 8:2; Job 7:12; 26:8; 38:9; Ps 36:6; 42:7; 104:6; 107:24; Pr 30:4; [h]Ge 2:7; Job 33:4; Ps 104:30; Isa 32:15; [i]Dt 32:11; Isa 31:5
3 [j]ver 6; Ps 33:6,9; 148:5; Heb 11:3; [k]2Co 4:6*; 1Jn 1:5–7
4 [l]ver 10,12,18, 21,25,31; Ps 104:31; 119:68; Jer 31:35; [m]ver 14; Ex 10:21–23; Job 26:10; 38:19; Ps 18:28; 104:20; 105:28; Isa 42:16; 45:7
5 [n]ver 8,10; Ge 2:19,23; [o]Ps 74:16; [p]ver 8, 13,19,23,31
6 [q]**ver 3**; [r]**ver 1**; Isa 44:24; 2Pe 3:5; [s]ver 9; Ps 24:2; 136:6
7 [t]Ge 7:11; Job 26:10; 38:8–11,16; Ps 68:33; 148:4; Pr 8:28; [u]ver 9,11,15,24
8 [v]**ver 5**; [w]Job 9:8; 37:18; Ps 19:1; 104:2; Isa 40:22; 44:24; 45:12; Jer 10:12; Zec 12:1; [x]**ver 5**
9 [y]Job 38:8–11; Ps 33:7; 104:6–9; Pr 8:29; Jer 5:22; 2Pe 3:5; [z]Ps 95:5; Jnh 1:9; Hag 2:6; [a]**ver 7**
10 [b]**ver 5**; [c]Ps 33:7; [d]Job 38:8; Ps 90:2; 95:5; [e]**ver 4**
11 [f]Ps 65:9–13; 104:14; [g]ver 12,21,24–25; Ge 2:5; 6:20; 7:14; Lev 11:14,19,22; Dt 14:13,18; 1Co 15:38; [h]**ver 7**
12 [i]**ver 11**; [j]**ver 4** *13* [k]**ver 5**
14 [l]Ps 74:16; 136:7; [m]**ver 4**; [n]Jer 10:2; [o]Ps 104:19; [p]Ge 8:22; Jer 31:35–36; 33:20,25 *15* [q]**ver 7**
16 [r]Dt 17:3; Job 31:26; Jer 43:13; Eze 8:16; [s]Ps 136:8; [t]Ps 136:9; [u]Job 38:33; Ps 74:16; 104:19; Jer 31:35; Jas 1:17; [v]Dt 4:19; Job 9:9; 38:7,31–32; Ps 8:3; 33:6; Ecc 12:2; Isa 40:26; Jer 8:2; Am 5:8
18 [w]Jer 33:20,25; [x]**ver 4** *19* [y]**ver 5**
20 [z]Ps 146:6; [a]Ge 2:19
21 [b]**ver 1**; [c]Job 3:8; 7:12; Ps 74:13; 148:7; Isa 27:1; Eze 32:2; [d]Ps 104:25–26; [e]**ver 11**; [f]**ver 4**
22 [g]ver 28; Ge 8:17; 9:1,7,19; 47:27; Lev 26:9; Eze 36:11
23 [h]**ver 5** *24* [i]Ge 2:19

---

[a]2 Or possibly *became*

kinds:[j] livestock, creatures that
move along the ground, and wild
animals, each according to its
kind." And it was so.[k] 25God made
the wild animals[l] according to their
kinds, the livestock according to
their kinds, and all the creatures
that move along the ground accord-
ing to their kinds.[m] And God saw
that it was good.[n]
26Then God said, "Let us[o] make
man[p] in our image,[q] in our like-
ness,[r] and let them rule[s] over the
fish of the sea and the birds of the
air,[t] over the livestock, over all the
earth,[b] and over all the creatures
that move along the ground."

27So God created[u] man[v]
in his own image,[w]
in the image of God[x]
he created him;
male and female[y]
he created them.[z]

28God blessed them and said to
them,[a] "Be fruitful and increase in
number;[b] fill the earth[c] and subdue
it. Rule over[d] the fish of the sea and
the birds of the air and over every
living creature that moves on the
ground."[e]
29Then God said, "I give you
every seed-bearing plant on the
face of the whole earth and every
tree that has fruit with seed in it.
They will be yours for food.[f] 30And
to all the beasts of the earth and all
the birds of the air and all the crea-
tures that move on the ground—
everything that has the breath of
life[g] in it—I give every green plant
for food.[h]" And it was so.
31God saw all that he had made,[i]
and it was very good.[j] And there
was evening, and there was morn-
ing[k]—the sixth day.

2

Thus the heavens and the earth
were completed in all their vast
array.[a]

2By the seventh day[b] God had finished
the work he had been doing; so on
the seventh day he rested[a] from all
his work.[c] 3And God blessed the
seventh day and made it holy,[d] be-
cause on it he rested[e] from all the
work of creating[f] that he had done.

Adam and Eve

4This is the account[g] of the heavens
and the earth when they were created.[h]

24 [j]ver 11; [k]**ver 7**
25 [l]Ge 7:21–22; Jer 27:5; [m]**ver 11**; [n]**ver 4**
26 [o]Ge 3:5,22; 11:7; Ps 100:3; Isa 6:8; [p]Isa 45:18; [q]ver 27; Ge 5:3; 9:6; Ps 8:5; 82:6; 89:6; 1Co 11:7; 2Co 4:4; Col 1:15; 3:10; Jas 3:9; [r]Ac 17:28–29; [s]Ge 9:2; Ps 8:6–8; [t]Ps 8:8
27 [u]**ver 1**; [v]Ge 2:7; Ps 103:14; 119:73; [w]**ver 26**; [x]Ge 5:1; [y]Ge 5:2; Mt 19:4*; Mk 10:6*; Gal 3:28; [z]Dt 4:32
28 [a]Ge 33:5; Jos 24:3; Ps 113:9; 127:3,5; [b]**Ge 17:6**; [c]**ver 22**; Ge 6:1; Ac 17:26; [d]ver 26; Ps 115:16; [e]Ps 8:6–8
29 [f]Ge 9:3; Dt 12:15; Ps 104:14; 1Ti 4:3
30 [g]Ge 2:7; 7:22; [h]Job 38:41; Ps 78:25; 104:14,27; 111:5; 136:25; 145:15; 147:9
31 [i]Ps 104:24; 136:5; Pr 3:19; Jer 10:12; [j]**ver 4**; 1Ti 4:4; [k]**ver 5**

Ch. 2

1 [a]Dt 4:19; 17:3; 2Ki 17:16; 21:3; Ps 104:2; Isa 44:24; 45:12; 48:13; 51:13
2 [b]Dt 5:14; [c]ver 2–3; Ex 20:11; 31:17; 34:21; Jn 5:17; Heb 4:4*
3 [d]Ex 16:23; 20:10; 23:12; 31:15; 35:2; Lev 23:3; Ne 9:14; Isa 58:13; Jer 17:22; [e]Ps 95:11; Heb 4:1–11; [f]**Ge 1:1**
4 [g]Ge 5:1; 6:9; 10:1; 11:10,27; 25:12,19; 36:1,9; 37:2; [h]Ge 1:1; Job 38:8–11
5 [i]**Ge 1:11**; [j]Job 38:28; Ps 65:9–10; Jer 10:13

When the LORD God made the earth
and the heavens—5and no shrub of the
field had yet appeared on the earth[b] and
no plant of the field had yet sprung up,[i]
for the LORD God had not sent rain on
the earth[b][j] and there was no man to
work the ground, 6but streams[c] came up
from the earth and watered the whole
surface of the ground—7the LORD God
formed[k] the man[d][l] from the dust[m] of the
ground[n] and breathed into his nostrils
the breath[o] of life,[p] and the man became
a living being.[q]
8Now the LORD God had planted a
garden in the east, in Eden;[r] and there
he put the man he had formed. 9And the
LORD God made all kinds of trees grow
out of the ground—trees[s] that were
pleasing to the eye and good for food. In
the middle of the garden were the tree
of life[t] and the tree of the knowledge of
good and evil.[u]
10A river[v] watering the garden flowed
from Eden;[w] from there it was separated
into four headwaters. 11The name of the
first is the Pishon; it winds through the
entire land of Havilah,[x] where there is
gold. 12(The gold of that land is good;
aromatic resin[e][y] and onyx are also
there.) 13The name of the second river is
the Gihon; it winds through the entire
land of Cush.[f] 14The name of the third
river is the Tigris;[z] it runs along the east
side of Asshur. And the fourth river is
the Euphrates.[a]
15The LORD God took the man and put
him in the Garden of Eden[b] to work it
and take care of it. 16And the LORD God
commanded the man, "You are free
to eat from any tree in the garden;[c]
17but you must not eat from the tree
of the knowledge of good and evil,[d]

7 [k]Isa 29:16; 43:1,21; 44:2; [l]**Ge 1:27**; [m]Ge 3:19; 18:27; Job 4:19; 10:9; 17:16; 34:15; Ps 90:3; Ecc 3:20; 12:7; [n]Ge 3:23; 4:2; Ps 103:14; Jer 18:6; 1Co 15:47; [o]**Ge 1:2**; Job 27:3; Isa 2:22; [p]**Ge 1:30**; Isa 42:5; Ac 17:25; [q]Job 12:10; 32:8; 33:4; 34:14; Ps 104:29; Isa 57:16; Eze 37:5; 1Co 15:45*
8 [r]ver 10,15; Ge 3:23–24; 4:16; 13:10; Isa 51:3; Eze 28:13; 31:9,16; 36:35; Joel 2:3
9 [s]Eze 31:8; [t]Ge 3:22,24; Pr 3:18; 11:30; **Rev 2:7**; [u]Eze 47:12
10 [v]Nu 24:6; Ps 46:4; Eze 47:5; [w]**ver 8**
11 [x]Ge 10:7; 25:18
12 [y]Nu 11:7
14 [z]Ge 41:1; Da 10:4; [a]Ge 15:18; 31:21; Ex 23:31; Nu 22:5; Dt 1:7; 11:24; Jos 1:4; 2Sa 8:3; 1Ki 4:21; 2Ki 23:29; 24:7; 1Ch 5:9; 18:3; 2Ch 35:20; Jer 13:4; 46:2; 51:63; **Rev 9:14**
15 [b]**ver 8**
16 [c]Ge 3:1–2
17 [d]Ge 3:11,17

b26 Hebrew; Syriac *all the wild animals*
a2 Or *ceased*; also in verse 3
b5 Or *land*; also in verse 6
c6 Or *mist*
d7 The Hebrew for *man* (*adam*) sounds like and may be related to the Hebrew for *ground* (*adamah*); it is also the name *Adam* (see Gen. 2:20).
e12 Or *good; pearls*
f13 Possibly south-east Mesopotamia

for when you eat of it you will surely
die."[e]
18The LORD God said, "It is not good
for the man to be alone. I will make a
helper suitable for him."[f]
19Now the LORD God had formed out
of the ground all the beasts of the field[g]
and all the birds of the air.[h] He brought
them to the man to see what he would
name them; and whatever the man
called[i] each living creature,[j] that was its
name. 20So the man gave names to all
the livestock, the birds of the air and all
the beasts of the field.
But for Adam[g] no suitable helper[k] was
found. 21So the LORD God caused the
man to fall into a deep sleep;[l] and while
he was sleeping, he took one of the
man's ribs[h] and closed up the place with
flesh. 22Then the LORD God made a
woman from the rib[i][m] he had taken out
of the man, and he brought her to the
man.
23The man said,

"This is now bone of my bones
and flesh of my flesh;[n]
she shall be called[o] 'woman',[j]
for she was taken out of man.[p]"

24For this reason a man will leave his
father and mother and be united[q] to his
wife, and they will become one flesh.[r]
25The man and his wife were both
naked,[s] and they felt no shame.

The Fall of Man

3 Now the serpent[a] was more crafty
than any of the wild animals the
LORD God had made. He said to the
woman, "Did God really say, 'You must
not eat from any tree in the garden'?[b]"
2The woman said to the serpent, "We
may eat fruit from the trees in the
garden,[c] 3but God did say, 'You must
not eat fruit from the tree that is in the
middle of the garden, and you must not
touch it, or you will die.'"[d]
4"You will not surely die," the ser-
pent said to the woman.[e] 5"For God
knows that when you eat of it your eyes
will be opened, and you will be like
God,[f] knowing good and evil."
6When the woman saw that the fruit
of the tree was good for food and pleas-
ing to the eye, and also desirable[g] for
gaining wisdom, she took some and ate
it. She also gave some to her husband,[h]
who was with her, and he ate it.[i] 7Then
the eyes of both of them were opened,
and they realised that they were naked;[j]
so they sewed fig leaves together and
made coverings for themselves.[k]

8Then the man and his wife heard
the sound of the LORD God as he was
walking[l] in the garden in the cool of the
day, and they hid[m] from the LORD God
among the trees of the garden. 9But the
LORD God called to the man, "Where are
you?"[n]
10He answered, "I heard you in the
garden, and I was afraid[o] because I was
naked;[p] so I hid."
11And he said, "Who told you that
you were naked?[q] Have you eaten from
the tree from which I commanded you
not to eat?"[r]
12The man said, "The woman you put
here with me[s]—she gave me some fruit
from the tree, and I ate it."
13Then the LORD God said to the
woman, "What is this you have done?"
The woman said, "The serpent de-
ceived me,[t] and I ate."
14So the LORD God said to the serpent,
"Because you have done this,

"Cursed[u] are you above all the
livestock
and all the wild animals!
You will crawl on your belly
and you will eat dust[v]
all the days of your life.
15And I will put enmity
between you and the woman,
and between your offspring[a][w] and
hers;[x]
he will crush[b] your head,[y]
and you will strike his heel."

16To the woman he said,

"I will greatly increase your pains in
childbearing;
with pain you will give birth to
children.[z]
Your desire will be for your husband,
and he will rule over you."[a]

17To Adam he said, "Because you lis-
tened to your wife and ate from the tree
about which I commanded you, 'You
must not eat of it,'[b]

"Cursed[c] is the ground[d] because of
you;

17 [e]Ge 3:1,3; 5:5; 9:29; Dt 30:15, 19; Jer 42:16; Eze 3:18; **Ro 5:12; 6:23**
18 [f]Pr 31:11; 1Co 11:9; 1Ti 2:13
19 [g]Ps 8:7; [h]**Ge 1:20**; [i]**Ge 1:5**; [j]Ge 1:24
20 [k]Ge 3:20; 4:1
21 [l]Ge 15:12; 1Sa 26:12; Job 33:15
22 [m]1Co 11:8–9, 12; 1Ti 2:13
23 [n]Ge 29:14; Eph 5:28–30; [o]**Ge 1:5**; [p]1Co 11:8
24 [q]Mal 2:15; [r]Mt 19:5*; Mk 10:7–8*; 1Co 6:16*; Eph 5:31*
25 [s]Ge 3:7, 10–11; Isa 47:3; La 1:8

Ch. 3

1 [a]Job 1:7; 2:2; 2Co 11:3; Rev 12:9; 20:2; [b]**Ge 2:17**
2 [c]Ge 2:16
3 [d]**Ge 2:17**
4 [e]**Jn 8:44**; 2Co 11:3
5 [f]**Ge 1:26**; 14:18–19; Ps 7:8; Isa 14:14; Eze 28:2
6 [g]Jas 1:14–15; 1Jn 2:16; [h]Nu 30:7–8; Jer 44:15,19,24; [i]2Co 11:3; 1Ti 2:14
7 [j]Ge 2:25; [k]ver 21
8 [l]Lev 26:12; Dt 23:14; [m]Job 13:16; 23:7; 31:33; 34:22–23; Ps 5:5; 139:7–12; Isa 29:15; Jer 16:17; 23:24; 49:10; Rev 6:15–16
9 [n]Ge 4:9; 16:8; 18:9; 1Ki 19:9,13
10 [o]Ex 19:16; 20:18; Dt 5:5; 1Sa 12:18; [p]Ge 2:25
11 [q]Ge 2:25; [r]**Ge 2:17**
12 [s]Ge 2:22
13 [t]Ro 7:11; 2Co 11:3; 1Ti 2:14
14 [u]Dt 28:15–20; [v]Ps 72:9; Isa 49:23; 65:25; Mic 7:17
15 [w]Jn 8:44; Ac 13:10; 1Jn 3:8; [x]Ge 16:11; Jdg 13:5; Isa 7:14; 8:3; 9:6; Mt 1:23; Lk 1:31; Gal 4:4; Rev 12:17; [y]Ro 16:20; Heb 2:14
16 [z]Ps 48:5–6; Isa 13:8; 21:3; 26:17; Jer 4:31; 6:24; Mic 4:9; 1Ti 2:15; [a]1Co 11:3; **Eph 5:22**
17 [b]**Ge 2:17**; [c]Ge 5:29; Nu 35:33; Ps 106:39; Isa 24:5; Jer 3:1; Ro 8:20–22; [d]Ge 6:13; 8:21; Isa 54:9

g20 Or *the man* h21 Or *took part of the man's side*
i22 Or *part*
j23 The Hebrew for *woman* sounds like the Hebrew for *man*. a15 Or *seed* b15 Or *strike*

through painful toil[e] you will eat of it
all the days of your life.[f]
18It will produce thorns and thistles[g] for you,
and you will eat the plants of the field.[h]
19By the sweat of your brow[i]
you will eat your food[j]
until you return to the ground,
since from it you were taken;
for dust you are
and to dust you will return."[k]

20Adam[c] named his wife Eve,[d][l] be-
cause she would become the mother of
all the living.
21The LORD God made garments of
skin for Adam and his wife and clothed
them.[m] 22And the LORD God said, "The
man has now become like one of us,[n]
knowing good and evil. He must not be
allowed to reach out his hand and take
also from the tree of life[o] and eat, and
live for ever." 23So the LORD God
banished him from the Garden of Eden[p]
to work the ground[q] from which he had
been taken. 24After he drove the man
out, he placed on the east side[e] of the
Garden of Eden[r] cherubim[s] and a
flaming sword[t] flashing back and forth
to guard the way to the tree of life.[u]

Cain and Abel

4 Adam[a] lay with his wife[a] Eve,[b] and
she became pregnant and gave
birth to Cain.[b][c] She said, "With the help
of the LORD I have brought forth[c] a
man." 2Later she gave birth to his
brother Abel.[d]
Now Abel kept flocks, and Cain
worked the soil.[e] 3In the course of time
Cain brought some of the fruits of the
soil as an offering[f] to the LORD.[g] 4But
Abel brought fat portions[h] from some of
the firstborn of his flock.[i] The LORD
looked with favour on Abel and his
offering,[j] 5but on Cain and his offering
he did not look with favour. So Cain
was very angry, and his face was down-
cast.
6Then the LORD said to Cain, "Why
are you angry?[k] Why is your face down-
cast? 7If you do what is right, will you
not be accepted? But if you do not do
what is right, sin is crouching at your
door;[l] it desires to have you, but you
must master it."[m]
8Now Cain said to his brother Abel,
"Let's go out to the field."[d] And while
they were in the field, Cain attacked his
brother Abel and killed him.[n]
9Then the LORD said to Cain, "Where
is your brother Abel?"[o]
"I don't know,[p]" he replied. "Am I
my brother's keeper?"
10The LORD said, "What have you
done? Listen! Your brother's blood cries
out to me from the ground.[q] 11Now you
are under a curse[r] and driven from the
ground, which opened its mouth to re-
ceive your brother's blood from your
hand. 12When you work the ground, it
will no longer yield its crops for you.[s]
You will be a restless wanderer[t] on the
earth.[u]"
13Cain said to the LORD, "My punish-
ment is more than I can bear. 14Today
you are driving me from the land, and I
will be hidden from your presence;[v]
I will be a restless wanderer on the
earth,[w] and whoever finds me will kill
me."[x]
15But the LORD said to him, "Not so;[e]
if anyone kills Cain[y], he will suffer
vengeance[z] seven times over.[a]" Then
the LORD put a mark on Cain so that
no-one who found him would kill him.
16So Cain went out from the LORD's
presence[b] and lived in the land of Nod,[f]
east of Eden.[c]
17Cain lay with his wife,[d] and she
became pregnant and gave birth to
Enoch. Cain was then building a city,[e]
and he named it after his son[f] Enoch.
18To Enoch was born Irad, and Irad was
the father of Mehujael, and Mehujael
was the father of Methushael, and
Methushael was the father of Lamech.
19Lamech married[g] two women,[h] one
named Adah and the other Zillah.
20Adah gave birth to Jabal; he was the
father of those who live in tents and
raise livestock. 21His brother's name
was Jubal; he was the father of all who
play the harp[i] and flute.[j] 22Zillah also

17 [e]Ge 29:32; 31:42; Ex 3:7; Ps 66:11; 127:2; Ecc 1:13; [f]Ge 47:9; Job 5:7; 7:1; 14:1; Ecc 2:23; Jer 20:18
18 [g]Job 31:40; Isa 5:6; Heb 6:8; [h]Ps 104:14
19 [i]Ps 104:23; [j]Ge 14:18; Dt 8:3,9; 23:4; Ru 1:6; 2:14; 2Th 3:10; [k]Ge 2:7; Job 7:21; Ps 146:4; 1Co 15:47; Heb 9:27
20 [l]Ge 2:20; 2Co 11:3; 1Ti 2:13
21 [m]ver 7
22 [n]Ge 1:26; [o]Ge 2:9; Rev 2:7
23 [p]Ge 2:8; [q]Ge 2:7
24 [r]Ge 2:8; [s]Ex 25:18–22; 1Sa 4:4; 2Sa 6:2; 22:11; 1Ki 6:27; 8:6; 2Ki 19:15; 2Ch 5:8; Ps 18:10; 80:1; 99:1; Isa 37:16; Eze 10:1; 28:16; [t]Job 40:19; Ps 104:4; Isa 27:1; [u]Ge 2:9

Ch. 4

1 [a]ver 17,25; [b]Ge 2:20; [c]Heb 11:4; 1Jn 3:12; Jude 11
2 [d]Mt 23:35; Lk 11:51; Heb 11:4; 12:24; [e]Ge 2:7
3 [f]Lev 2:1–2; Isa 43:23; Jer 41:5; [g]Nu 18:12
4 [h]Lev 3:16; 2Ch 29:35; [i]Ex 13:2,12; Dt 15:19; [j]Heb 11:4
6 [k]Jnh 4:4
7 [l]Ge 44:16; Nu 32:23; Isa 59:12; [m]Job 11:15; 22:27; Ps 27:3; 46:2; Ro 6:16
8 [n]Mt 23:35; Lk 11:51; 1Jn 3:12; Jude 11
9 [o]Ge 3:9; [p]Jn 8:44
10 [q]Ge 9:5; 37:20,26; Ex 21:12; Nu 35:33; Dt 21:7,9; 2Sa 4:11; Job 16:18; 24:2; 31:38; Ps 9:12; 106:38; Heb 12:24; Rev 6:9–10
11 [r]Dt 11:28; 2Ki 2:24
12 [s]Dt 28:15–24; [t]Ps 37:25; 59:15; 109:10; [u]ver 14
14 [v]2Ki 17:18; Ps 51:11; 139:7–12; Jer 7:15; 52:3; [w]ver 12; Dt 28:64–67; [x]Ge 9:6; Ex 21:12,14; Lev 24:17; Nu 35:19,21,27,33; 1Ki 2:32; 2Ki 11:16
15 [y]Eze 9:4,6; [z]Ex 21:20; [a]ver 24; Lev 26:21; Ps 79:12
16 [b]Jude 11; [c]Ge 2:8 17 [d]ver 1; [e]Ps 55:9; [f]Ps 49:11
19 [g]Ge 6:2; [h]Ge 29:28; Dt 21:15; Ru 4:11; 1Sa 1:2
21 [i]Ge 31:27; Ex 15:20; 1Sa 16:16; 1Ch 25:3; Ps 33:2; 43:4; Isa 16:11; Da 3:5; [j]Job 21:12; 30:31; Ps 150:4

[c]20 Or *The man*
[d]20 *Eve* probably means *living*.
[e]24 Or *placed in front*
[a]1 Or *The man*
[b]1 *Cain* sounds like the Hebrew for *brought forth* or *acquired*.
[c]1 Or *have acquired*
[d]8 Samaritan Pentateuch, Septuagint, Vulgate and Syriac; Masoretic Text does not have "*Let's go out to the field.*"
[e]15 Septuagint, Vulgate and Syriac; Hebrew *Very well*
[f]16 *Nod* means *wandering* (see verses 12 and 14).

had a son, Tubal-Cain, who forged[k] all
kinds of tools out of[g] bronze and iron.
Tubal-Cain's sister was Naamah.
23Lamech said to his wives,

"Adah and Zillah, listen to me;
wives of Lamech, hear my words.
I have killed[h l] a man for wounding
me,
a young man for injuring me.
24If Cain is avenged[m] seven times,[n]
then Lamech seventy-seven
times.[o]"

25Adam lay with his wife[p] again, and
she gave birth to a son and named him
Seth,[i q] saying, "God has granted me
another child in place of Abel, since
Cain killed him."[r] 26Seth also had a son,
and he named him Enosh.[s]
At that time men began to call on[j] the
name of the LORD.[t]

From Adam to Noah

5 This is the written account[a] of
Adam's line.[b]

When God created man, he made him
in the likeness of God.[c] 2He created
them[d] male and female[e] and blessed
them. And when they were created, he
called them "man".[a]
3When Adam had lived 130 years, he
had a son in his own likeness, in his
own image;[f] and he named him Seth.[g]
4After Seth was born, Adam lived 800
years and had other sons and daugh-
ters. 5Altogether, Adam lived 930 years,
and then he died.[h]
6When Seth had lived 105 years, he
became the father[b] of Enosh.[i] 7And after
he became the father of Enosh, Seth
lived 807 years and had other sons and
daughters. 8Altogether, Seth lived 912
years, and then he died.
9When Enosh had lived 90 years, he
became the father of Kenan.[j] 10And after
he became the father of Kenan, Enosh
lived 815 years and had other sons and
daughters. 11Altogether, Enosh lived
905 years, and then he died.
12When Kenan had lived 70 years, he
became the father of Mahalalel.[k] 13And
after he became the father of Mahalalel,
Kenan lived 840 years and had other
sons and daughters. 14Altogether,
Kenan lived 910 years, and then he
died.
15When Mahalalel had lived 65 years,
he became the father of Jared.[l] 16And
after he became the father of Jared,
Mahalalel lived 830 years and had other
sons and daughters. 17Altogether, Ma-
halalel lived 895 years, and then he
died.
18When Jared had lived 162 years, he
became the father of Enoch.[m] 19And
after he became the father of Enoch,
Jared lived 800 years and had other sons
and daughters. 20Altogether, Jared lived
962 years, and then he died.
21When Enoch had lived 65 years, he
became the father of Methuselah.[n]
22And after he became the father of
Methuselah, Enoch walked with God[o]
300 years and had other sons and
daughters. 23Altogether, Enoch lived
365 years. 24Enoch walked with God;[p]
then he was no more, because God took
him away.[q]
25When Methuselah had lived 187
years, he became the father of Lamech.[r]
26And after he became the father of
Lamech, Methuselah lived 782 years
and had other sons and daughters.
27Altogether, Methuselah lived 969
years, and then he died.
28When Lamech had lived 182 years,
he had a son. 29He named him Noah[c s]
and said, "He will comfort us in the
labour and painful toil of our hands
caused by the ground the LORD has
cursed."[t] 30After Noah was born,
Lamech lived 595 years and had other
sons and daughters. 31Altogether,
Lamech lived 777 years, and then he
died.
32After Noah was 500 years old,[u] he
became the father of Shem,[v] Ham and
Japheth.[w]

The Flood

6 When men began to increase in
number on the earth[a] and daugh-
ters were born to them, 2the sons of
God[b] saw that the daughters of men[c]
were beautiful,[d] and they married[e] any
of them they chose. 3Then the LORD
said, "My Spirit[f] will not contend with[a]
man for ever,[g] for he is mortal;[b h] his
days will be a hundred and twenty
years."
4The Nephilim[i] were on the earth in

22 [k]Ex 35:35; 1Sa 13:19; 2Ki 24:14
23 [l]Ge 9:5–6; Ex 20:13; 21:12; 23:7; Lev 19:18; 24:17; Dt 27:24; 32:35
24 [m]Dt 32:35; 2Ki 9:7; Ps 18:47; 94:1; Isa 35:4; Jer 51:56; Na 1:2; [n]**ver 15**; [o]Mt 18:22
25 [p]ver 1; [q]Ge 5:3; 1Ch 1:1; [r]ver 8
26 [s]Ge 5:6; 1Ch 1:1; Lk 3:38; [t]Ge 12:8; 13:4; 21:33; 22:9; 26:25; 33:20; 35:1; Ex 17:15; 1Ki 18:24; Ps 116:17; Joel 2:32; Zep 3:9; **Ac 2:21**

Ch. 5

1 [a]Ge 2:4; [b]1Ch 1:1; [c]**Ge 1:27**; Col 3:10
2 [d]Ge 1:28; [e]**Ge 1:27**; Mt 19:4; Mk 10:6; Gal 3:28
3 [f]**Ge 1:26**; 1Co 15:49; [g]**Ge 4:25**; Lk 3:38
5 [h]**Ge 2:17**; Heb 9:27
6 [i]**Ge 4:26**; Lk 3:38
9 [j]1Ch 1:2; Lk 3:37
12 [k]1Ch 1:2; Lk 3:37
15 [l]1Ch 1:2; Lk 3:37
18 [m]1Ch 1:3; Lk 3:37; Jude 14
21 [n]1Ch 1:3; Lk 3:37
22 [o]ver 24; Ge 6:9; 17:1; 24:40; 48:15; 2Ki 20:3; Ps 116:9; Mic 6:8; Mal 2:6
24 [p]**ver 22**; [q]2Ki 2:1,11; Ps 49:15; 73:24; 89:48; Heb 11:5
25 [r]1Ch 1:3; Lk 3:36
29 [s]1Ch 1:3; Lk 3:36; [t]**Ge 3:17**; Ro 8:20
32 [u]Ge 7:6,11; 8:13; [v]Lk 3:36; [w]Ge 6:10; 9:18; 10:1; 1Ch 1:4; Isa 65:20

Ch. 6

1 [a]**Ge 1:28**
2 [b]Job 1:6 *fn*; 2:1 *fn*; [c]ver 4; [d]Dt 21:11; [e]**Ge 4:19**
3 [f]Job 34:14; Gal 5:16–17; [g]Isa 57:16; 1Pe 3:20; [h]Job 10:9; Ps 78:39; 103:14; Isa 40:6
4 [i]Nu 13:33

g22 Or *who instructed all who work in*
h23 Or *I will kill*
i25 *Seth* probably means *granted*.
j26 Or *to proclaim*
a2 Hebrew *adam*
b6 *Father* may mean *ancestor*; also in verses 7–26.
c29 *Noah* sounds like the Hebrew for *comfort*.
a3 Or *My spirit will not remain in*
b3 Or *corrupt*

those days—and also afterwards—when the sons of God went to the daughters of men[j] and had children by them. They were the heroes of old, men of renown.[k]

5The LORD saw how great man's wickedness on the earth had become,[l] and that every inclination of the thoughts of his heart was only evil all the time.[m] 6The LORD was grieved[n] that he had made man on the earth, and his heart was filled with pain. 7So the LORD said, "I will wipe mankind, whom I have created, from the face of the earth[o]—men and animals, and creatures that move along the ground, and birds of the air—for I am grieved that I have made them.[p]" 8But Noah[q] found favour in the eyes of the LORD.[r]

9This is the account[s] of Noah.

Noah was a righteous man, blameless[t] among the people of his time,[u] and he walked with God.[v] 10Noah had three sons: Shem,[w] Ham and Japheth.[x]

11Now the earth was corrupt[y] in God's sight and was full of violence.[z] 12God saw how corrupt[a] the earth had become, for all the people on earth had corrupted their ways.[b] 13So God said to Noah, "I am going to put an end to all people, for the earth is filled with violence because of them. I am surely going to destroy[c] both them and the earth.[d] 14So make yourself an ark of cypress[c] wood;[e] make rooms in it and coat it with pitch[f] inside and out. 15This is how you are to build it: The ark is to be 450 feet long, 75 feet wide and 45 feet high.[d] 16Make a roof for it and finish[e] the ark to within 18 inches[f] of the top. Put a door in the side of the ark and make lower, middle and upper decks. 17I am going to bring floodwaters[g] on the earth to destroy all life under the heavens, every creature that has the breath of life in it. Everything on earth will perish.[h] 18But I will establish my covenant with you,[i] and you will enter the ark[j]—you and your sons and your wife and your sons' wives with you. 19You are to bring into the ark two of all living creatures, male and female, to keep them alive with you.[k] 20Two[l] of every kind of bird, of every kind of animal and of every kind[m] of creature that moves along the ground will come to you to be kept alive.[n] 21You are to take every kind of food that is to be eaten and store it away as food for you and for them."

22Noah did everything just as God commanded him.[o]

4 [j]ver 2; [k]Ge 11:4
5 [l]Ge 38:7; Job 34:26; Jer 1:16; 44:5; Eze 3:19; [m]Ge 8:21; Ps 14:1–3
6 [n]Ex 32:14; 1Sa 15:11,35; 2Sa 24:16; 1Ch 21:15; Isa 63:10; Jer 18:7–10; Eph 4:30
7 [o]Eze 33:28; Zep 1:2,18; [p]ver 17; Ge 7:4,21; Dt 28:63; 29:20
8 [q]Eze 14:14; [r]Ge 19:19; 39:4; Ex 33:12–13,17; 34:9; Nu 11:15; Ru 2:2; Lk 1:30; Ac 7:46
9 [s]**Ge 2:4**; [t]Ge 17:1; Dt 18:13; 2Sa 22:24; Job 1:1; 4:6; 9:21; 12:4; 31:6; Ps 15:2; 18:23; 19:13; 37:37; Pr 2:7; [u]Ge 7:1; Ps 37:39; Jer 15:1; Eze 14:14,20; Da 10:11; **Lk 1:6**; Heb 11:7; 2Pe 2:5; [v]**Ge 5:22**
10 [w]Lk 3:36; [x]**Ge 5:32**
11 [y]Dt 31:29; Jdg 2:19; [z]Ps 7:9; 73:6; Eze 7:23; 8:17; 28:16; Mal 2:16
12 [a]Ex 32:7; Dt 4:16; 9:12,24; [b]Ps 14:1–3
13 [c]Dt 28:63; 2Ki 8:19; Ezr 9:14; Jer 44:11; [d]ver 17; Ge 7:4,21–23; Job 34:15; Isa 5:6; 24:1–3; Jer 44:27; Eze 7:2–3
14 [e]Heb 11:7; 1Pe 3:20; [f]Ex 2:3
17 [g]Ps 29:10; [h]**ver 7,13**; 2Pe 2:5
18 [i]Ge 9:9–16; 17:7; 19:12; Ex 6:4; 34:10, 27; Dt 29:13, 14–15; Ps 25:10; 74:20; 106:45; Isa 55:3; Jer 32:40; Eze 16:60; Hag 2:5; 1Pe 3:20; [j]Ge 7:1, 7,13
19 [k]Ge 7:15
20 [l]Ge 7:15; [m]**Ge 1:11**; [n]Ge 7:3

7 The LORD then said to Noah, "Go into the ark, you and your whole family,[a] because I have found you righteous[b] in this generation. 2Take with you seven[a] of every kind of clean[c] animal, a male and its mate, and two of every kind of unclean animal, a male and its mate, 3and also seven of every kind of bird, male and female, to keep their various kinds alive[d] throughout the earth. 4Seven days from now I will send rain[e] on the earth[f] for forty days[g] and forty nights,[h] and I will wipe from the face of the earth every living creature I have made.[i]"

5And Noah did all that the LORD commanded him.[j]

6Noah was six hundred years old[k] when the floodwaters came on the earth. 7And Noah and his sons and his wife and his sons' wives entered the ark[l] to escape the waters of the flood. 8Pairs of clean and unclean[m] animals, of birds and of all creatures that move along the ground, 9male and female, came to Noah and entered the ark, as God had commanded Noah.[n] 10And after the seven days[o] the floodwaters came on the earth.

11In the six hundredth year of Noah's life,[p] on the seventeenth day of the second month[q]—on that day all the springs of the great deep[r] burst forth, and the floodgates of the heavens[s] were opened. 12And rain fell on the earth for forty days and forty nights.[t]

13On that very day Noah and his sons,[u] Shem, Ham and Japheth, together with his wife and the wives of his three sons, entered the ark.[v] 14They had with them every wild animal according

22 [o]Ge 7:5,9,16; Ex 7:6; 39:43; 40:16,19,21,23,25,27,29, 32

Ch. 7
1 [a]**Ge 6:18**; Mt 24:38; Lk 17:26–27; Heb 11:7; 1Pe 3:20; 2Pe 2:5; [b]**Ge 6:9**; Eze 14:14
2 [c]ver 8; Ge 8:20; Lev 10:10; 11:1–47; Dt 14:3–20; Eze 44:23; Hag 2:12; Ac 10:14–15 **3** [d]Ge 6:20
4 [e]Ge 8:2; [f]1Ki 13:34; Jer 28:16; [g]Nu 13:25; Dt 9:9; 1Sa 17:16; 1Ki 19:8; [h]ver 12,17; Ex 24:18; 32:1; 34:28; Dt 9:9,11,18,25; 10:10; Job 37:6,13; Mt 4:2; [i]**Ge 6:7,13**
5 [j]**Ge 6:22** **6** [k]**Ge 5:32** **7** [l]**Ge 6:18**
8 [m]**ver 2** **9** [n]**Ge 6:22** **10** [o]**ver 4**
11 [p]**Ge 5:32**; [q]Ge 8:4,14; [r]**Ge 1:7**; Job 28:11; Ps 36:6; 42:7; Pr 8:24; Isa 51:10; Eze 26:19; [s]Ge 8:2; 2Ki 7:2; Ps 78:23; Isa 24:18; Mal 3:10
12 [t]**ver 4; 1Sa 12:17; Job 28:26**
13 [u]Ge 8:16; 1 Pe 3:20; 2Pe 2:5; [v]**Ge 6:18**

c14 The meaning of the Hebrew for this word is uncertain.
d15 Hebrew *300 cubits long, 50 cubits wide and 30 cubits high* (about 140 metres long, 23 metres wide and 13.5 metres high)
e16 Or *Make an opening for light by finishing*
f16 Hebrew *a cubit* (about 0.5 metre)
a2 Or *seven pairs*; also in verse 3

to its kind, all livestock according to their kinds, every creature that moves along the ground according to its kind and every bird according to its kind,[w] everything with wings. 15Pairs of all creatures that have the breath of life in them came to Noah and entered the ark.[x] 16The animals going in were male and female of every living thing, as God had commanded Noah.[y] Then the LORD shut him in.

17For forty days[z] the flood kept coming on the earth, and as the waters increased they lifted the ark high above the earth. 18The waters rose and increased greatly on the earth, and the ark floated on the surface of the water. 19They rose greatly on the earth, and all the high mountains under the entire heavens were covered.[a] 20The waters rose and covered the mountains to a depth of more than twenty feet.[b,c][b] 21Every living thing that moved on the earth perished—birds, livestock, wild animals, all the creatures that swarm over the earth, and all mankind.[c] 22Everything on dry land that had the breath of life[d] in its nostrils died. 23Every living thing on the face of the earth was wiped out; men and animals and the creatures that move along the ground and the birds of the air were wiped from the earth.[e] Only Noah was left, and those with him in the ark.[f]

24The waters flooded the earth for a hundred and fifty days.[g]

8 But God remembered[a] Noah and all the wild animals and the livestock that were with him in the ark, and he sent a wind over the earth,[b] and the waters receded. 2Now the springs of the deep and the floodgates of the heavens[c] had been closed, and the rain[d] had stopped falling from the sky. 3The water receded steadily from the earth. At the end of the hundred and fifty days[e] the water had gone down, 4and on the seventeenth day of the seventh month[f] the ark came to rest on the mountains[g] of Ararat.[h] 5The waters continued to recede until the tenth month, and on the first day of the tenth month the tops of the mountains became visible.

6After forty days[i] Noah opened the window he had made in the ark 7and sent out a raven,[j] and it kept flying back and forth until the water had dried up from the earth.[k] 8Then he sent out a dove[l] to see if the water had receded from the surface of the ground. 9But the dove could find no place to set its feet because there was water over all the surface of the earth; so it returned to Noah in the ark. He reached out his hand and took the dove and brought it back to himself in the ark. 10He waited seven more days and again sent out the dove from the ark. 11When the dove returned to him in the evening, there in its beak was a freshly plucked olive leaf! Then Noah knew that the water had receded from the earth.[m] 12He waited seven more days and sent the dove out again, but this time it did not return to him.

13By the first day of the first month of Noah's six hundred and first year,[n] the water had dried up from the earth. Noah then removed the covering from the ark and saw that the surface of the ground was dry. 14By the twenty-seventh day of the second month[o] the earth was completely dry.

15Then God said to Noah, 16"Come out of the ark, you and your wife and your sons and their wives.[p] 17Bring out every kind of living creature that is with you—the birds, the animals, and all the creatures that move along the ground—so they can multiply on the earth and be fruitful and increase in number upon it."[q]

18So Noah came out, together with his sons and his wife and his sons' wives.[r] 19All the animals and all the creatures that move along the ground and all the birds—everything that moves on the earth—came out of the ark, one kind after another.

20Then Noah built an altar to the LORD[s] and, taking some of all the clean animals and clean[t] birds, he sacrificed burnt offerings[u] on it. 21The LORD smelled the pleasing aroma[v] and said in his heart: "Never again will I curse the ground[w] because of man, even though[a] every inclination of his heart is evil from childhood.[x] And never again will I destroy[y] all living creatures,[z] as I have done.

22"As long as the earth endures,
seedtime and harvest,[a]
cold and heat,
summer and winter,[b]
day and night
will never cease."[c]

14 [w]**Ge 1:11**
15 [x]ver 8–9; Ge 6:19
16 [y]**Ge 6:22**
17 [z]**ver 4**
19 [a]Ps 104:6
20 [b]Ge 8:4–5; 2Pe 3:6
21 [c]**Ge 6:7**,13; 2Pe 3:6
22 [d]Ge 1:30
23 [e]Job 14:19; 21:18; 22:11, 16; Ps 90:5; Isa 28:2; Mt 24:39; Lk 17:27; 1Pe 3:20; 2Pe 2:5; [f]Heb 11:7
24 [g]Ge 8:3; Job 12:15

Ch. 8

1 [a]Ge 9:15; 19:29; 21:1; 30:22; Ex 2:24; Nu 10:9; Ru 4:13; 1Sa 1:11, 19; 2Ki 20:3; 1Ch 16:15; Ne 1:8; 5:19; 13:14,22,31; Job 14:13; Ps 105:42; 106:4; Lk 1:54,72; [b]Ex 14:21; Jos 2:10; 3:16; Job 12:15; Ps 66:6; Isa 11:15; 44:27; Na 1:4
2 [c]**Ge 7:11**; [d]**Ge 7:4**
3 [e]**Ge 7:24**
4 [f]**Ge 7:11**; [g]Ge 7:20; [h]2Ki 19:37; Jer 51:27
6 [i]Ge 7:12
7 [j]Lev 11:15; Dt 14:14; 1Ki 17:4,6; Job 38:41; Ps 147:9; Pr 30:17; Isa 34:11; Lk 12:24; [k]ver 11
8 [l]Job 30:31; Ps 55:6; 74:19; SS 2:12,14; Isa 38:14; 59:11; 60:8; Jer 48:28; Eze 7:16; Hos 7:11; 11:11; Na 2:7; Mt 3:16; 10:16; Jn 1:32
11 [m]ver 7
13 [n]**Ge 5:32**
14 [o]**Ge 7:11**
16 [p]**Ge 7:13**
17 [q]**Ge 1:22**
18 [r]1Pe 3:20; 2Pe 2:5

20 [s]Ge 12:7–8; 13:18; 22:9; 26:25; 33:20; 35:7; Ex 17:15; 24:4; [t]**Ge 7:8**; [u]Ge 22:2,13; Ex 10:25; 20:24; 40:29; Lev 1:3; 4:29; 6:8–13; Nu 6:11; Jdg 6:26; 11:31; 1Sa 20:29; Job 1:5; 42:8
21 [v]Ex 29:18,25; Lev 1:9,13; 2:9; 4:31; Nu 15:3,7; 2Co 2:15; [w]**Ge 3:17**; [x]Ge 6:5; Ps 51:5; Jer 17:9; Mt 15:19; Ro 1:21; [y]Jer 44:11; [z]Ge 9:11,15; Isa 54:9
22 [a]Jos 3:15; Ps 67:6; Jer 5:24; [b]Ps 74:17; Zec 14:8; [c]**Ge 1:14**

[b]20 Hebrew *fifteen cubits* (about 6.9 metres)
[c]20 Or *rose more than twenty feet, and the mountains were covered*
[a]21 Or *man, for*

God's Covenant With Noah

9 Then God blessed Noah and his sons, saying to them, "Be fruitful and increase in number and fill the earth.[a] 2The fear and dread of you will fall upon all the beasts of the earth and all the birds of the air, upon every creature that moves along the ground, and upon all the fish of the sea; they are given into your hands.[b] 3Everything that lives and moves will be food for you.[c] Just as I gave you the green plants, I now give you everything.[d]

4"But you must not eat meat that has its lifeblood still in it.[e] 5And for your lifeblood I will surely demand an accounting.[f] I will demand an accounting from every animal.[g] And from each man, too, I will demand an accounting for the life of his fellow man.[h]

6"Whoever sheds the blood of man,
by man shall his blood be shed;[i]
for in the image of God[j]
has God made man.

7As for you, be fruitful and increase in number; multiply on the earth and increase upon it."[k]

8Then God said to Noah and to his sons with him: 9"I now establish my covenant with you[l] and with your descendants after you 10and with every living creature that was with you—the birds, the livestock and all the wild animals, all those that came out of the ark with you—every living creature on earth. 11I establish my covenant[m] with you:[n] Never again will all life be cut off by the waters of a flood; never again will there be a flood to destroy the earth."[o]

12And God said, "This is the sign of the covenant[p] I am making between me and you and every living creature with you, a covenant for all generations to come:[q] 13I have set my rainbow[r] in the clouds, and it will be the sign of the covenant between me and the earth. 14Whenever I bring clouds over the earth and the rainbow[s] appears in the clouds, 15I will remember my covenant[t] between me and you and all living creatures of every kind. Never again will the waters become a flood to destroy all life.[u] 16Whenever the rainbow[v] appears in the clouds, I will see it and remember the everlasting covenant[w] between God and all living creatures of every kind on the earth."

17So God said to Noah, "This is the sign of the covenant[x] I have established between me and all life on the earth."

The Sons of Noah

18The sons of Noah who came out of the ark were Shem, Ham and Japheth.[y] (Ham was the father of Canaan.)[z] 19These were the three sons of Noah,[a] and from them came the people who were scattered over the earth.[b]

20Noah, a man of the soil, proceeded[a] to plant a vineyard. 21When he drank some of its wine,[c] he became drunk and lay uncovered inside his tent. 22Ham, the father of Canaan, saw his father's nakedness[d] and told his two brothers outside. 23But Shem and Japheth took a garment and laid it across their shoulders; then they walked in backwards and covered their father's nakedness. Their faces were turned the other way so that they would not see their father's nakedness.

24When Noah awoke from his wine and found out what his youngest son had done to him, 25he said,

"Cursed[e] be Canaan![f]
The lowest of slaves
will he be to his brothers."[g]

26He also said,

"Blessed be the LORD, the God of
Shem![h]
May Canaan be the slave[i] of Shem.[b]
27May God extend the territory of
Japheth;[c][j]
may Japheth live in the tents of
Shem,[k]
and may Canaan be his[d] slave."

28After the flood Noah lived 350 years. 29Altogether, Noah lived 950 years, and then he died.[l]

The Table of Nations

10 This is the account[a] of Shem, Ham and Japheth,[b] Noah's sons,[c] who themselves had sons after the flood.

Ch. 9
1 [a]Ge 1:22
2 [b]Ge 1:26
3 [c]Ge 1:29; [d]Ac 10:15; Col 2:16
4 [e]Lev 3:17; 7:26; 17:10–14; 19:26; Dt 12:16, 23–25; 15:23; 1Sa 14:33; Eze 33:25; Ac 15:20,29
5 [f]Ge 42:22; 50:15; 1Ki 2:32; 2Ch 24:22; Ps 9:12; [g]Ex 21:28–32; [h]Ge 4:10
6 [i]Ge 4:14; Jdg 9:24; Mt 26:52; [j]Ge 1:26
7 [k]Ge 1:22
9 [l]ver 11; Ge 6:18
11 [m]ver 16; Isa 24:5; 33:8; Hos 6:7; [n]ver 9; [o]Ge 8:21
12 [p]ver 17; Ge 17:11; [q]Ge 17:12; Ex 12:14; Lev 3:17; 6:18; 17:7; Nu 10:8
13 [r]ver 14; Eze 1:28; Rev 4:3; 10:1
14 [s]ver 13
15 [t]Ge 8:1; Ex 2:24; 6:5; 34:10; Lev 26:42,45; Dt 7:9; Ps 89:34; 103:18; 105:8; 106:45; Eze 16:60; [u]Ge 8:21
16 [v]ver 13; [w]ver 11; Ge 17:7,13,19; 2Sa 7:13; 23:5; Ps 105:9–10; Isa 9:7; 54:10; 55:3; 59:21; 61:8; Jer 31:31–34; 32:40; 33:21; Eze 16:60; 37:26; Heb 13:20
17 [x]ver 12
18 [y]Ge 5:32; Lk 3:36; [z]ver 25–27; Ge 10:6,15
19 [a]Ge 5:32; [b]Ge 1:22; 10:32; 11:4,8–9
21 [c]Ge 19:35
22 [d]Hab 2:15
25 [e]Ge 27:12; [f]ver 18; Ex 20:5; Ps 79:8; Isa 14:21; Jer 31:29; 32:18; [g]Ge 25:23; 27:29,37,40; 37:10; 49:8; Nu 24:18; Jos 9:23
26 [h]Ge 14:20; Ex 18:10; Ps 7:17; [i]1Ki 9:21
27 [j]Ge 10:2–5; [k]Eph 2:13–14; 3:6
29 [l]Ge 2:17

Ch. 10
1 [a]Ge 2:4; [b]Ge 5:32; [c]ver 32; 1Ch 1:4

[a]20 Or *soil, was the first*
[b]26 Or *be his slave*
[c]27 *Japheth* sounds like the Hebrew for *extend.*
[d]27 Or *their*

The Japhethites

10:2–5pp—1Ch 1:5–7

2The sons[a] of Japheth:
Gomer,[d] Magog,[e] Madai, Javan,[f]
Tubal,[g] Meshech[h] and Tiras.
3The sons of Gomer:
Ashkenaz,[i] Riphath and Togar-
mah.[j]
4The sons of Javan:
Elishah,[k] Tarshish,[l] the Kittim[m]
and the Rodanim.[b] 5(From these
the maritime peoples spread out
into their territories by their clans
within their nations, each with
its own language.)[n]

The Hamites

10:6–20pp—1Ch 1:8–16

6The sons of Ham:
Cush,[o] Mizraim,[c] Put[p] and
Canaan.[q]
7The sons of Cush:
Seba,[r] Havilah,[s] Sabtah, Raamah[t]
and Sabtecah.
The sons of Raamah:
Sheba[u] and Dedan.[v]

8Cush was the father[d] of Nimrod,[w]
who grew to be a mighty warrior on the
earth. 9He was a mighty[x] hunter[y] before
the LORD; that is why it is said, "Like
Nimrod, a mighty hunter before the
LORD." 10The first centres of his king-
dom were Babylon,[z] Erech,[a] Akkad and
Calneh,[b] in[e] Shinar.[f][c] 11From that land
he went to Assyria,[d] where he built
Nineveh,[e] Rehoboth Ir,[g] Calah 12and
Resen, which is between Nineveh and
Calah; that is the great city.

13Mizraim was the father of
the Ludites, Anamites, Lehab-
ites, Naphtuhites, 14Pathrusites,
Casluhites (from whom the Phil-
istines[f] came) and Caphtorites.[g]
15Canaan[h] was the father of
Sidon[i] his firstborn,[h][j] and of the
Hittites,[k] 16Jebusites,[l] Amorites,[m]
Girgashites,[n] 17Hivites,[o] Arkites,
Sinites, 18Arvadites,[p] Zemarites
and Hamathites.[q]

Later the Canaanite[r] clans scattered
19and the borders of Canaan[s] reached
from Sidon[t] towards Gerar[u] as far as
Gaza,[v] and then towards Sodom,
Gomorrah, Admah and Zeboiim,[w] as far
as Lasha.
20These are the sons of Ham by their
clans and languages, in their territories
and nations.

The Semites

10:21–31pp—Ge 11:10–27; 1Ch 1:17–27

21Sons were also born to Shem, whose
older brother was[i] Japheth; Shem was
the ancestor of all the sons of Eber.[x]
22The sons of Shem:
Elam,[y] Asshur,[z] Arphaxad,[a] Lud
and Aram.[b]
23The sons of Aram:
Uz,[c] Hul, Gether and Meshech.[j]
24Arphaxad was the father of[k]
Shelah,
and Shelah the father of Eber.[d]
25Two sons were born to Eber:
One was named Peleg,[l] because
in his time the earth was divided;
his brother was named Joktan.
26Joktan was the father of
Almodad, Sheleph, Hazar-
maveth, Jerah, 27Hadoram,
Uzal,[e] Diklah, 28Obal, Abimael,
Sheba,[f] 29Ophir,[g] Havilah and
Jobab. All these were sons of
Joktan.

30The region where they lived stretched
from Mesha towards Sephar, in the
eastern hill country.

2 [d]Eze 38:6; [e]Eze 38:2; 39:6; Rev 20:8; [f]Eze 27:19; [g]Isa 66:19; Eze 27:13; 32:26; [h]Eze 39:1
3 [i]Jer 51:27; [j]Eze 27:14; 38:6
4 [k]Eze 27:7; [l]Ps 48:7; 72:10; Isa 2:16; 23:1,6, 10,14; 60:9; 66:19; Jer 10:9; Eze 27:12,25; 38:13; Jnh 1:3; [m]Nu 24:24; Isa 23:12; Jer 2:10; Eze 27:6; Da 11:30
5 [n]Ge 9:27
6 [o]2Ki 19:9; 2Ch 12:3; 16:8; Isa 11:11; 18:1; 20:3; 43:3; Jer 46:9; Eze 30:4, 9; 38:5; Na 3:9; Zep 2:12; 3:10; [p]Eze 27:10; 38:5; [q]**Ge 9:18**
7 [r]Isa 43:3; [s]**Ge 2:11**; [t]Eze 27:22; [u]Ge 25:3; 1Ki 10:1; 2Ch 9:1; Job 1:15; 6:19; 16:11; Ps 72:10,15; Isa 60:6; Jer 6:20; Eze 27:22; 38:13; Joel 3:8; [v]1Ch 1:32; Isa 21:13; Jer 25:23–24; 49:8; Eze 27:15,20; 38:13
8 [w]Mic 5:6
9 [x]2Ch 14:9; 16:8; Isa 18:2; [y]Ge 25:27; 27:3
10 [z]Ge 11:9; 2Ch 36:17; Isa 13:1; 47:1; Jer 21:2; 25:12; 50:1; [a]Ezr 4:9; [b]Isa 10:9; Am 6:2; [c]Ge 11:2; 14:1; Zec 5:11
11 [d]Ps 83:8; Mic 5:6; [e]2Ki 19:36; Isa 37:37; Jnh 1:2; 3:2–3; 4:11; Na 1:1; Zep 2:13
14 [f]Ge 21:32,34; 26:1,8; Jos 13:2; Jdg 3:3; Isa 14:31; Jer 47:1,4; Am 9:7; [g]Dt 2:23; 1Ch 1:12
15 [h]**Ge 9:18**; [i]ver 19; Jos 11:8; Jdg 10:6; Isa 23:2,4; Jer 25:22; 27:3; 47:4; Eze 28:21; 32:30; Joel 3:4; Zec 9:2; [j]Ex 4:22; Nu 1:20; 3:2; 18:15; 26:5; 33:4; [k]Ge 15:20; 23:3,20; 25:10; 26:34; 27:46; 49:32; Nu 13:29; Jos 1:4; 1Sa 26:6; Eze 16:3
16 [l]Jdg 19:10; 1Ch 11:4; Ezr 9:1; [m]Ex 3:8; Nu 13:29; 21:13; 32:39; Dt 1:4; Jos 2:10; 2Ch 8:7; [n]Ge 15:18–21; Dt 7:1
17 [o]Ge 34:2; 36:2; Ex 3:8; Dt 7:1; Jdg 3:3
18 [p]Eze 27:8; [q]1Ch 18:3; [r]Ge 12:6; 13:7; 50:11; Ex 13:11; Nu 13:29; 14:25; 21:3; 33:40; Dt 1:7; Jdg 1:1
19 [s]Ge 11:31; 12:1; 13:12; 17:8; 24:3; 26:34; 27:46; 28:1, 6,8; 31:18; 35:6; 37:1; Lev 25:38; [t]**ver 15**; Ge 49:13; Jos 19:28; Jdg 1:31; 18:28; 2Sa 24:6; [u]2Ch 14:13; [v]Dt 2:23; Jos 10:41; 11:22; 15:47; Jdg 1:18; 6:4; 16:1,21; 1Sa 6:17; Jer 25:20; 47:1; Am 1:6; Zep 2:4; [w]Ge 14:2; Dt 29:23
21 [x]ver 24; Nu 24:24
22 [y]Ge 14:1; Isa 11:11; 21:2; Jer 25:25; 49:34; Eze 32:24; Da 8:2; [z]Nu 24:22,24; Eze 27:23; [a]Lk 3:36; [b]Jdg 3:10; 1Ki 11:25; 19:15; 20:34; 22:31; 2Ki 5:1; 8:7
23 [c]Ge 22:21; Job 1:1; Jer 25:20; La 4:21
24 [d]**ver 21**; Lk 3:35
27 [e]Eze 27:19
28 [f]1Ki 10:1; Job 6:19; Ps 72:10,15; Isa 60:6; Eze 27:22
29 [g]1Ki 9:28; 10:11; 1Ch 29:4; Job 22:24; 28:16; Ps 45:9; Isa 13:12

---

[a]2 *Sons* may mean *descendants* or *successors* or *nations;* also in verses 3, 4, 6, 7, 20–23, 29 and 31.
[b]4 Some manuscripts of the Masoretic Text and Samaritan Pentateuch (see also Septuagint and 1 Chron. 1:7); most manuscripts of the Masoretic Text *Dodanim*
[c]6 That is, Egypt; also in verse 13
[d]8 *Father* may mean *ancestor* or *predecessor* or *founder;* also in verses 13, 15, 24 and 26.
[e]10 Or *Erech and Akkad—all of them in*
[f]10 That is, Babylonia
[g]11 Or *Nineveh with its city squares*
[h]15 Or *of the Sidonians, the foremost*
[i]21 Or *Shem, the older brother of*
[j]23 See Septuagint and 1 Chron. 1:17; Hebrew *Mash.*
[k]24 Hebrew; Septuagint *father of Cainan, and Cainan was the father of*
[l]25 *Peleg* means *division.*

31 These are the sons of Shem by their
clans and languages, in their territories
and nations.

32 These are the clans of Noah's sons,[h]
according to their lines of descent, with-
in their nations. From these the nations
spread out over the earth[i] after the
flood.

The Tower of Babel

11 Now the whole world had
one language[a] and a common
speech. 2 As men moved eastward,[a]
they found a plain in Shinar[b][b] and
settled there.
3 They said to each other, "Come, let's
make bricks[c] and bake them thorough-
ly." They used brick instead of stone,[d]
and bitumen[e] for mortar. 4 Then they
said, "Come, let us build ourselves a
city, with a tower that reaches to the
heavens,[f] so that we may make a name[g]
for ourselves and not be scattered[h] over
the face of the whole earth."[i]
5 But the LORD came down[j] to see the
city and the tower that the men were
building. 6 The LORD said, "If as one
people speaking the same language[k]
they have begun to do this, then no-
thing they plan to do will be impossible
for them. 7 Come, let us[l] go down[m] and
confuse their language so they will not
understand each other."[n]
8 So the LORD scattered them from
there over all the earth,[o] and they
stopped building the city. 9 That is why
it was called Babel[c][p]—because there
the LORD confused the language[q] of
the whole world.[r] From there the LORD
scattered[s] them over the face of the
whole earth.

From Shem to Abram

11:10–27pp—Ge 10:21–31; 1Ch 1:17–27

10 This is the account[t] of Shem.

Two years after the flood, when Shem
was 100 years old, he became the father[d]
of Arphaxad.[u] 11 And after he became
the father of Arphaxad, Shem lived 500
years and had other sons and daugh-
ters.
12 When Arphaxad had lived 35 years,
he became the father of Shelah.[v] 13 And
after he became the father of Shelah,
Arphaxad lived 403 years and had other
sons and daughters.[e]
14 When Shelah had lived 30 years, he
became the father of Eber.[w] 15 And after
he became the father of Eber, Shelah
lived 403 years and had other sons and
daughters.
16 When Eber had lived 34 years, he
became the father of Peleg.[x] 17 And after
he became the father of Peleg, Eber
lived 430 years and had other sons and
daughters.
18 When Peleg had lived 30 years, he
became the father of Reu.[y] 19 And after
he became the father of Reu, Peleg lived
209 years and had other sons and
daughters.
20 When Reu had lived 32 years, he
became the father of Serug.[z] 21 And after
he became the father of Serug, Reu lived
207 years and had other sons and
daughters.
22 When Serug had lived 30 years, he
became the father of Nahor.[a] 23 And after
he became the father of Nahor, Serug
lived 200 years and had other sons and
daughters.
24 When Nahor had lived 29 years, he
became the father of Terah.[b] 25 And after
he became the father of Terah, Nahor
lived 119 years and had other sons and
daughters.
26 After Terah had lived 70 years, he
became the father of Abram,[c] Nahor[d]
and Haran.[e]

27 This is the account[f] of Terah.

Terah became the father of Abram,
Nahor[g] and Haran. And Haran became
the father of Lot.[h] 28 While his father
Terah was still alive, Haran died in Ur of
the Chaldeans,[i] in the land of his birth.
29 Abram and Nahor[j] both married. The
name of Abram's wife was Sarai,[k] and
the name of Nahor's wife was Milcah;[l]
she was the daughter of Haran, the
father of both Milcah and Iscah. 30 Now
Sarai was barren; she had no children.[m]
31 Terah took his son Abram, his
grandson Lot[n] son of Haran, and his
daughter-in-law[o] Sarai, the wife of his
son Abram, and together they set out

32 [h]**ver 1**; [i]Ge 9:19
Ch. 11
1 [a]ver 6
2 [b]**Ge 10:10**
3 [c]Ex 1:14; 5:7; Jer 43:9; [d]Isa 9:10; Am 5:11; [e]Ge 14:10
4 [f]Dt 1:28; 6:10; 9:1; Job 20:6; Jer 51:53; [g]Ge 6:4; [h]Dt 30:3; 1Ki 22:17; Est 3:8; Ps 44:11; Jer 31:10; 40:15; Eze 6:8; Joel 3:2; [i]Ge 9:19; Dt 4:27
5 [j]ver 7; Ge 18:21; Ex 3:8; 19:11,18,20; Ps 18:9; 144:5
6 [k]**ver 1**
7 [l]**Ge 1:26**; [m]**ver 5**; [n]Ge 42:23; Dt 28:49; Isa 28:11; 33:19; Jer 5:15; 1Co 14:2,11
8 [o]**Ge 9:19**; Dt 32:8; **Lk 1:51**
9 [p]**Ge 10:10**; [q]Ps 55:9; [r]Ac 2:5–11; [s]Isa 2:10,21; 13:14; 24:1
10 [t]**Ge 2:4**; [u]Lk 3:36
12 [v]Lk 3:35
14 [w]Lk 3:35
16 [x]Lk 3:35
18 [y]Lk 3:35
20 [z]Lk 3:35
22 [a]Lk 3:34
24 [b]Lk 3:34
26 [c]Lk 3:34; [d]Jos 24:2; [e]2Ki 19:12; Isa 37:12; Eze 27:23
27 [f]**Ge 2:4**; [g]ver 29; Ge 31:53; [h]ver 31; Ge 12:4; 13:1,5, 8,12; 14:12; 19:1; Lk 17:28; 2Pe 2:7
28 [i]ver 31; Ge 15:7; Ne 9:7; Job 1:17; 16:11; Eze 23:23; Ac 7:4
29 [j]**ver 27**,31; Ge 22:20,23; 24:10,15,24; 29:5; [k]Ge 12:5,11; 16:1; 17:15; [l]Ge 22:20
30 [m]Ge 16:1; 18:11; 25:21; 29:31; 30:1,22; Jdg 13:2; 1Sa 1:5; Ps 113:9; Lk 1:7,36
31 [n]**ver 27**; [o]Ge 38:11; Lev 18:15; 20:12; Ru 1:6,22; 2:20; 4:15; 1Sa 4:19; 1Ch 2:4; Eze 22:11; Mic 7:6

a2 Or *from the east;* or *in the east*
b2 That is, Babylonia
c9 That is, Babylon; *Babel* sounds like the Hebrew for *confused.*
d10 *Father* may mean *ancestor;* also in verses 11–25.
e12,13 Hebrew; Septuagint (see also Luke 3:35, 36 and note at Gen. 10:24) *35 years, he became the father of Cainan. 13And after he became the father of Cainan, Arphaxad lived 430 years and had other sons and daughters, and then he died. When Cainan had lived 130 years, he became the father of Shelah. And after he became the father of Shelah, Cainan lived 330 years and had other sons and daughters*

from Ur of the Chaldeans[p] to go to Canaan.[q] But when they came to Haran,[r] they settled there.

32 Terah[s] lived 205 years, and he died in Haran.

The Call of Abram

12 The LORD had said to Abram, "Leave your country, your people and your father's household[a] and go to the land[b] I will show you.[c]

2 "I will make you into a great nation[d]
and I will bless you;[e]
I will make your name great,
and you will be a blessing.[f]
3 I will bless those who bless you,
and whoever curses you I will
curse;[g]
and all peoples on earth
will be blessed through you.[h]"

4 So Abram left, as the LORD had told him; and Lot[i] went with him. Abram was seventy-five years old[j] when he set out from Haran.[k] 5 He took his wife Sarai,[l] his nephew Lot, all the possessions they had accumulated[m] and the people[n] they had acquired in Haran, and they set out for the land of Canaan,[o] and they arrived there.

6 Abram travelled through the land[p] as far as the site of the great tree of Moreh[q] at Shechem.[r] At that time the Canaanites[s] were in the land. 7 The LORD appeared to Abram[t] and said, "To your offspring[a] I will give this land.[u]"[v] So he built an altar there to the LORD,[w] who had appeared to him.

8 From there he went on towards the hills east of Bethel[x] and pitched his tent,[y] with Bethel on the west and Ai[z] on the east. There he built an altar to the LORD and called on the name of the LORD.[a] 9 Then Abram set out and continued towards the Negev.[b]

Abram in Egypt

12:10–20Ref—Ge 20:1–18; 26:1–11

10 Now there was a famine in the land,[c] and Abram went down to Egypt to live there for a while because the famine was severe.[d] 11 As he was about to enter Egypt, he said to his wife Sarai,[e] "I know what a beautiful woman[f] you are. 12 When the Egyptians see you, they will say, 'This is his wife.' Then they will kill me but will let you live. 13 Say you are my sister,[g] so that I will be treated well for your sake and my life will be spared because of you."

14 When Abram came to Egypt, the Egyptians saw that she was a very beautiful woman.[h] 15 And when Pharaoh's officials saw her, they praised her to Pharaoh, and she was taken into his palace. 16 He treated Abram well for her sake, and Abram acquired sheep and cattle, male and female donkeys, menservants and maidservants, and camels.[i]

17 But the LORD inflicted[j] serious diseases on Pharaoh and his household[k] because of Abram's wife Sarai. 18 So Pharaoh summoned Abram. "What have you done to me?"[l] he said. "Why didn't you tell me she was your wife?[m] 19 Why did you say, 'She is my sister,'[n] so that I took her to be my wife? Now then, here is your wife. Take her and go!" 20 Then Pharaoh gave orders about Abram to his men, and they sent him on his way, with his wife and everything he had.

Abram and Lot Separate

13 So Abram went up from Egypt[a] to the Negev,[b] with his wife and everything he had, and Lot[c] went with him. 2 Abram had become very wealthy[d] in livestock[e] and in silver and gold.

3 From the Negev[f] he went from place to place until he came to Bethel,[g] to the place between Bethel and Ai[h] where his tent had been earlier 4 and where he had first built an altar.[i] There Abram called on the name of the LORD.[j]

31 [p]**ver 28**; Ac 7:4; [q]**Ge 10:19**; [r]**ver 29**; Ge 12:4; 27:43; 28:5,10; 29:4; 2Ki 19:12; Eze 27:23
32 [s]Jos 24:2

Ch. 12

1 [a]Ge 20:13; 24:4,27,40; [b]**Ge 10:19**; [c]Ge 15:7; 26:2; Jos 24:3; Ac 7:3*; Heb 11:8
2 [d]Ge 13:16; 15:5; 17:2,4; 18:18; 22:17; 26:4; 28:3,14; 32:12; 35:11; 41:49; 46:3; 47:27; 48:4, 16,19; Ex 1:7; 5:5; 32:13; Dt 1:10; 10:22; 13:17; 26:5; Jos 11:4; 24:3; 2Sa 17:11; 1Ki 3:8; 4:20; 1Ch 27:23; 2Ch 1:9; Ne 9:23; Ps 107:38; Isa 6:13; 10:22; 48:19; 51:2; 54:3; 60:22; Jer 33:22; Mic 4:7; [e]Ge 24:1, 35; 25:11; 26:3; 28:4; Ex 20:24; Nu 22:12; 23:8,20; 24:9; Ps 67:6; 115:12; Isa 44:3; 61:9; 65:23; Mal 3:12; [f]Ge 22:18; Isa 19:24; Jer 4:2; Hag 2:19; Zec 8:13
3 [g]Ge 27:29; Ex 23:22; Nu 24:9; Dt 30:7; [h]Ge 15:5; 18:18; 22:18; 26:4; 28:4,14; Dt 9:5; Ps 72:17; Isa 19:25; Ac 3:25; Gal 3:8*
4 [i]**Ge 11:27**; [j]Ge 16:3,16; 17:1, 17,24; 21:5; [k]**Ge 11:31**
5 [l]**Ge 11:29**; [m]ver 16; Ge 13:2,6; 31:18; 46:6; [n]Ge 14:14; 15:3; 17:23; Ecc 2:7; [o]Ge 11:31; 16:3; Heb 11:8
6 [p]Heb 11:9; [q]Ge 35:4; Dt 11:30; Jos 24:26; Jdg 7:1; 9:6; [r]Ge 33:18; 37:12; Jos 17:7; 20:7; 24:1; Jdg 8:31; 21:19; 1Ki 12:1; Ps 60:6; 108:7; [s]**Ge 10:18**
7 [t]Ge 17:1; 18:1; 26:2; 35:1; Ex 6:3; Ac 7:2; [u]Ex 3:8; Nu 10:29; Dt 30:5; Heb 11:8; [v]Ge 13:15,17; 15:18; 17:8; 23:18; 24:7; 26:3–4; 28:13; 35:12; 48:4; 50:24; Ex 6:4,8; 13:5,11; 32:13; 33:1; Nu 11:12; Dt 1:8; 2:31; 9:5; 11:9; 34:4; 2Ki 25:21; 1Ch 16:16; 2Ch 20:7; Ps 105:9–11; Jer 25:5; Eze 47:14; Ac 7:5; Ro 4:13; Gal 3:16*; [w]**Ge 8:20**; 13:4
8 [x]Ge 13:3; 28:11,19; 35:1,8,15; Jos 7:2; 8:9; 1Sa 7:16; 1Ki 12:29; Hos 12:4; Am 3:14; 4:4; [y]Ge 26:25; 33:19; Heb 11:9; [z]Jos 7:2; 12:9; Ezr 2:28; Ne 7:32; Jer 49:3; [a]**Ge 4:26**; **8:20**
9 [b]Ge 13:1,3; 20:1; 24:62; Nu 13:17; 33:40; Dt 34:3; Jos 10:40
10 [c]Ge 41:27,57; 42:5; 43:1; 47:4,13; Ru 1:1; 2Sa 21:1; 2Ki 8:1; Ps 105:19; [d]Ge 41:30,54,56; 47:20; Ps 105:16
11 [e]**Ge 11:29**; [f]ver 14; Ge 24:16; 26:7; 29:17; 39:6
13 [g]Ge 20:2; 26:7 *14* [h]**ver 11**
16 [i]**ver 5**; Ge 24:35; 26:14; 30:43; 32:5; 34:23; 47:17; Job 1:3; 31:25
17 [j]2Ki 15:5; Job 30:11; Isa 53:4,10; [k]1Ch 16:21; Ps 105:14
18 [l]Ge 20:9; 26:10; 29:25; 31:26; 44:15; [m]Isa 43:27; 51:2; Eze 16:3 *19* [n]Ge 20:5; 26:9

Ch. 13

1 [a]Ge 45:25; [b]**Ge 12:9**; [c]**Ge 11:27**
2 [d]**Ge 12:5**; 26:13; Pr 10:22; [e]Ge 32:15; Job 1:3; 42:12
3 [f]**Ge 12:9**; [g]**Ge 12:8**; [h]Jos 7:2
4 [i]**Ge 12:7**; [j]**Ge 4:26**

[a]7 Or *seed*

5Now Lot,[k] who was moving about
with Abram, also had flocks and herds
and tents. 6But the land could not sup-
port them while they stayed together,
for their possessions were so great that
they were not able to stay together.[l]
7And quarrelling[m] arose between
Abram's herdsmen and the herdsmen
of Lot. The Canaanites[n] and Perizzites[o]
were also living in the land[p] at that time.
8So Abram said to Lot,[q] "Let's not
have any quarrelling between you and
me,[r] or between your herdsmen and
mine, for we are brothers.[s] 9Is not the
whole land before you? Let's part com-
pany. If you go to the left, I'll go to the
right; if you go to the right, I'll go to the
left."[t]
10Lot looked up and saw that the
whole plain[u] of the Jordan[v] was well
watered, like the garden of the LORD,[w]
like the land of Egypt,[x] towards Zoar.[y]
(This was before the LORD destroyed
Sodom[z] and Gomorrah.)[a] 11So Lot chose
for himself the whole plain of the Jordan
and set out towards the east. The two
men parted company: 12Abram lived in
the land of Canaan,[b] while Lot[c] lived
among the cities of the plain[d] and
pitched his tents near Sodom.[e] 13Now
the men of Sodom[f] were wicked and
were sinning greatly against the LORD.[g]
14The LORD said to Abram after Lot
had parted from him, "Lift up your eyes
from where you are and look north and
south, east and west.[h] 15All the land that
you see I will give to you and your
offspring[a] for ever.[i] 16I will make your
offspring like the dust of the earth, so
that if anyone could count the dust,
then your offspring could be counted.[j]
17Go, walk through the length and
breadth of the land,[k] for I am giving it to
you."[l]
18So Abram moved his tents and went
to live near the great trees of Mamre[m] at
Hebron,[n] where he built an altar to the
LORD.[o]

Abram Rescues Lot

14 At this time Amraphel king of
Shinar,[a][a] Arioch king of Ellasar,
Kedorlaomer[b] king of Elam[c] and Tidal
king of Goiim 2went to war against Bera
king of Sodom, Birsha king of Gomor-
rah, Shinab king of Admah, Shemeber
king of Zeboiim,[d] and the king of Bela
(that is, Zoar).[e] 3All these latter kings
joined forces in the Valley of Siddim[f]
(the Salt Sea[b][g]). 4For twelve years they
had been subject to Kedorlaomer,[h] but
in the thirteenth year they rebelled.
5In the fourteenth year, Kedorlaomer[i]
and the kings allied with him went out
and defeated the Rephaites[j] in Ashter-
oth Karnaim, the Zuzites in Ham, the
Emites[k] in Shaveh Kiriathaim 6and the
Horites[l] in the hill country of Seir,[m] as
far as El Paran[n] near the desert. 7Then
they turned back and went to En Mish-
pat (that is, Kadesh),[o] and they con-
quered the whole territory of the
Amalekites,[p] as well as the Amorites[q]
who were living in Hazezon Tamar.[r]
8Then the king of Sodom, the king of
Gomorrah,[s] the king of Admah, the
king of Zeboiim[t] and the king of Bela
(that is, Zoar)[u] marched out and drew
up their battle lines in the Valley of
Siddim[v] 9against Kedorlaomer[w] king of
Elam,[x] Tidal king of Goiim, Amraphel
king of Shinar and Arioch king of Ella-
sar—four kings against five. 10Now the
Valley of Siddim[y] was full of tar[z] pits,
and when the kings of Sodom and
Gomorrah[a] fled, some of the men fell
into them and the rest fled to the hills.[b]
11The four kings seized all the goods[c] of
Sodom and Gomorrah and all their
food; then they went away. 12They also
carried off Abram's nephew Lot[d] and
his possessions, since he was living in
Sodom.
13One who had escaped came and
reported this to Abram the Hebrew.[e]
Now Abram was living near the great
trees of Mamre[f] the Amorite, a brother[c]
of Eshcol[g] and Aner, all of whom were
allied with Abram. 14When Abram
heard that his relative[h] had been taken
captive, he called out the 318 trained[i]
men born in his household[j] and went in
pursuit as far as Dan.[k] 15During the

5 *k*Ge 11:27
6 *l*Ge 12:5; 33:9; 36:7
7 *m*Ge 26:20–21; Nu 20:3; *n*Ge 10:18; *o*Ge 15:20; 34:30; Ex 3:8; Jdg 1:4; *p*Ge 12:6; 34:30
8 *q*Ge 11:27; *r*Pr 15:18; 20:3; *s*Ge 19:9; Ex 2:14; Nu 16:13; Ps 133:1
9 *t*Ge 20:15; 34:10; 47:6; Jer 40:4
10 *u*1Ki 7:46; 2Ch 4:17; *v*Nu 13:29; 33:48; *w*Ge 2:8–10; Isa 51:3; Eze 31:8–9; *x*Ge 46:7; *y*Ge 14:2; 19:22,30; Dt 34:3; Isa 15:5, Jer 48:34; *z*Dt 29:23; Job 39:6; Ps 107:34; Jer 4:26; *a*Ge 14:8; 19:17–29
12 *b*Ge 10:19; *c*Ge 11:27; *d*ver 10; Ge 19:17,25,29; *e*Ge 14:12
13 *f*Ge 19:4; Isa 1:10; 3:9; *g*Ge 18:20; 19:5; 20:6; 39:9; Nu 32:23; 1Sa 12:23; 2Sa 12:13; Ps 51:4; Eze 16:49–50; 2Pe 2:8
14 *h*Ge 28:14; 32:12; 48:16; Dt 3:27; 13:17; Isa 54:3
15 *i*Ge 12:7; Gal 3:16*
16 *j*Ge 12:2; 16:10; 17:20; 21:13,18; 25:16; Nu 23:10
17 *k*ver 15; Nu 13:17–25; *l*Ge 12:7; 15:7
18 *m*Ge 14:13,24; 18:1; 23:17,19; 25:9; 49:30; 50:13; *n*Ge 23:2; 35:27; 37:14; Nu 13:22; Jos 10:3,36; Jdg 1:10; 1Sa 30:31; 2Sa 2:1,3,11; 1Ch 11:1; *o*Ge 8:20

Ch. 14

1 *a*Ge 10:10; *b*ver 4,9,17; *c*Ge 10:22
2 *d*Ge 10:19; *e*Ge 13:10
3 *f*ver 8,10; *g*Nu 34:3,12; Dt 3:17; Jos 3:16; 12:3; 15:2,5; 18:19
4 *h*ver 1
5 *i*ver 1; *j*Ge 15:20; Dt 2:11,20; 3:11,13; Jos 12:4; 13:12; 17:15; 1Ch 20:4; *k*Dt 2:10
6 *l*Ge 36:20; Dt 2:12,22; *m*Ge 32:3; 33:14,16; 36:8; Dt 1:2; 2:1,5,22; Jos 11:17; 24:4; 1Ch 4:42; Isa 34:5; Eze 25:8; 35:2; Am 1:6; *n*Ge 21:21; Nu 10:12; 12:16; 13:3,26; Hab 3:3
7 *o*Ge 16:14; 20:1; Nu 13:26; 20:1; 32:8; Dt 1:2; Jos 10:41; Jdg 11:16; Ps 29:8; *p*Ex 17:8; Nu 13:29; 14:25; 24:20; Dt 25:17; Jdg 3:13; 6:3; 10:12; 12:15; 1Sa 14:48; 15:2; 28:18; 2Sa 1:1; 1Ch 4:43; Ps 83:7; *q*Nu 13:29; Dt 1:4; Jos 2:10; 13:4; *r*2Ch 20:2; Eze 48:28
8 *s*Ge 13:10; *t*Dt 29:23; Hos 11:8; *u*Ge 13:10; *v*ver 3
9 *w*ver 1; *x*Ge 10:22
10 *y*ver 3; *z*Ge 11:3; *a*ver 17,21; *b*Ge 19:17,30; Jos 2:16; Ps 11:1
11 *c*ver 16,21
12 *d*Ge 11:27
13 *e*Ge 37:28; 39:14,17; 40:15; 41:12; 43:32; Ex 3:18; 1Sa 4:6; 14:11; *f*Ge 13:18; *g*Nu 13:23; 32:9; Dt 1:24
14 *h*ver 12; *i*Dt 4:9; Pr 22:6; *j*Ge 12:5; *k*Dt 34:1; Jdg 18:29; 1Ki 15:20

a15 Or *seed;* also in verse 16
a1 That is, Babylonia; also in verse 9
b3 That is, the Dead Sea
c13 Or *a relative;* or *an ally*

night Abram divided his men[l] to attack
them and he routed them, pursuing
them as far as Hobah, north of Damas-
cus.[m] 16He recovered[n] all the goods[o] and
brought back his relative Lot and his
possessions, together with the women
and the other people.
17After Abram returned from defeat-
ing Kedorlaomer[p] and the kings allied
with him, the king of Sodom[q] came out
to meet him in the Valley of Shaveh
(that is, the King's Valley).[r]
18Then Melchizedek[s] king of Salem[d][t]
brought out bread[u] and wine.[v] He was
priest of God Most High,[w] 19and he
blessed Abram,[x] saying,

"Blessed be Abram by God Most
High,[y]
Creator[e] of heaven and earth.[z]
20And blessed be[f] God Most High,[a]
who delivered your enemies into
your hand."

Then Abram gave him a tenth of every-
thing.[b]
21The king of Sodom[c] said to Abram,
"Give me the people and keep the
goods[d] for yourself."
22But Abram said to the king of
Sodom,[e] "I have raised my hand[f] to
the LORD, God Most High,[g] Creator of
heaven and earth,[h] and have taken an
oath 23that I will accept nothing belong-
ing to you,[i] not even a thread or the
thong of a sandal, so that you will never
be able to say, 'I made Abram rich.' 24I
will accept nothing but what my men
have eaten and the share that belongs to
the men who went with me—to Aner,
Eshcol and Mamre.[j] Let them have their
share."

15 [l]Jdg 7:16; [m]Ge 15:2; 2Sa 8:5; 1Ki 20:34; 2Ki 16:9; Isa 7:8; 8:4; 10:9; 17:1; Jer 49:23, 27; Eze 27:18; Am 1:3–5
16 [n]1Sa 30:8,18; [o]ver 11
17 [p]ver 1; [q]ver 10; [r]2Sa 18:18
18 [s]Ps 110:4; Heb 5:6; 7:17,21; [t]Ps 76:2; Heb 7:2; [u]**Ge 3:19;** [v]Jdg 9:13; 19:19; Est 1:10; Ps 104:15; Pr 31:6; Ecc 10:19; SS 1:2; [w]ver 22; Ps 7:8,17; Da 7:27
19 [x]Heb 7:6; [y]ver 18; [z]ver 22; **Ge 1:1;** 24:3; Jos 2:11; Ps 148:5; Mt 11:25
20 [a]**Ge 9:26; 24:27;** [b]Ge 28:22; Dt 14:22; 26:12; Lk 18:12; Heb 7:4
21 [c]**ver 10;** [d]**ver 11**
22 [e]**ver 10;** [f]Ex 6:8; Nu 14:30; Dt 32:40; Ne 9:15; Eze 20:5; Da 12:7; Rev 10:5–6; [g]**ver 18;** [h]**ver 19**
23 [i]1Sa 15:3,19; 2Ki 5:16; Est 8:11; 9:10,15
24 [j]**Ge 13:18**

God's Covenant With Abram

15

After this, the word of the LORD
came to Abram[a] in a vision:[b]

"Do not be afraid,[c] Abram.
I am your shield,[a][d]
your very great reward."[b][e]

2But Abram said, "O Sovereign LORD,[f]
what can you give me since I remain
childless[g] and the one who will inherit[c]
my estate is Eliezer of Damascus?[h]"
3And Abram said, "You have given me
no children; so a servant[i] in my house-
hold[j] will be my heir."
4Then the word of the LORD came to
him: "This man will not be your heir,
but a son coming from your own body
will be your heir.[k]" 5He took him out-
side and said, "Look up at the heavens
and count the stars[l]—if indeed you can
count them." Then he said to him, "So
shall your offspring be."[m]
6Abram believed the LORD, and he
credited it to him as righteousness.[n]
7He also said to him, "I am the LORD,
who brought you out[o] of Ur of the Chal-
deans[p] to give you this land to take
possession of it."[q]
8But Abram said, "O Sovereign
LORD,[r] how can I know[s] that I shall gain
possession of it?"[t]
9So the LORD said to him, "Bring me a
heifer,[u] a goat and a ram, each three
years old,[v] along with a dove and a
young pigeon."[w]
10Abram brought all these to him, cut
them in two and arranged the halves
opposite each other;[x] the birds, how-
ever, he did not cut in half.[y] 11Then birds
of prey came down on the carcasses,[z]
but Abram drove them away.
12As the sun was setting, Abram fell
into a deep sleep,[a] and a thick and
dreadful darkness came over him.
13Then the LORD said to him, "Know for
certain that your descendants will be
strangers in a country not their own,
and they will be enslaved[b] and ill-
treated four hundred years.[c] 14But I will
punish the nation they serve as slaves,
and afterwards they will come out[d] with
great possessions.[e] 15You, however, will
go to your fathers[f] in peace and be
buried at a good old age.[g] 16In the fourth
generation[h] your descendants will come
back here,[i] for the sin of the Amorites[j]
has not yet reached its full measure."

Ch. 15

1 [a]1Sa 15:10; 2Sa 7:4; 1Ki 6:11; 12:22; Jer 1:13; Eze 3:16; Da 10:1; [b]Ge 46:2; Nu 12:6; 24:4; Ru 1:20; Job 33:15; [c]Ge 21:17; 26:24; 46:3; Ex 14:13; 20:20; 2Ki 6:16; 2Ch 20:15,17; Ps 27:1; Isa 7:4; 41:10,13–14; 43:1,5; Jer 1:8; Hag 2:5; [d]Dt 33:29; 2Sa 22:3,31; Ps 3:3; 5:12; 18:2; 28:7; 33:20; 84:11; 119:114; 144:2; Pr 2:7; 30:5; [e]Ps 18:20; 37:25; 58:11; Isa 3:10
2 [f]ver 8; Isa 49:22; Jer 44:26; Eze 5:11; 16:48; [g]Ac 7:5; [h]**Ge 14:15**
3 [i]Ge 24:2,34; [j]**Ge 12:5**
4 [k]Gal 4:28
5 [l]Job 11:8; 35:5; Ps 8:3; 147:4; Jer 33:22; [m]**Ge 12:2; Jer 30:19;** Ro 4:18*; Heb 11:12
6 [n]Ps 106:31; Ro 4:3*; 20–24*; Gal 3:6*; Jas 2:23*
7 [o]Ge 12:1; Ex 20:2; Ac 7:3; Heb 11:8; [p]**Ge 11:28;** Ac 7:4; [q]**Ge 13:17;** 17:8; 28:4; 35:12; 48:4; Ex 6:8; Dt 9:5
8 [r]**ver 2;** [s]Lk 1:18; [t]Dt 12:20; 19:8
9 [u]Nu 19:2; Dt 21:3; Hos 4:16; Am 4:1; [v]1Sa 1:24; [w]Lev 1:14; 5:7,11; 12:8
10 [x]ver 17; Jer 34:18; [y]Lev 1:17; 5:8
11 [z]Dt 28:26; Jer 7:33
12 [a]**Ge 2:21**
13 [b]Ex 1:11; 3:7; 5:6,10–14,18; 6:5; Dt 5:15; Job 3:18; [c]ver 16; Ex 12:40; Nu 20:15; Ac 7:6,17; Gal 3:17
14 [d]Ge 50:24; Ex 3:8; 6:6–8; 12:25; Nu 10:29; Jos 1:2; Ac 7:7*; [e]Ex 12:32–38
15 [f]Ge 47:30; 49:29; Dt 31:16; 2Sa 7:12; 1Ki 1:21; Ps 49:19; [g]Ge 25:8; 35:29; Ex 23:26; Dt 34:7; Jos 14:11; Jdg 8:32; 1Ch 29:28; Job 5:26; 21:23; 42:17; Ps 91:16; Pr 3:16; 9:11; Isa 65:20
16 [h]**ver 13;** Ex 12:40; [i]Ge 28:15; 46:4; 48:21; 50:24; Ex 3:8,17; [j]Lev 18:28; Jos 13:4; Jdg 10:11; 1Ki 21:26; 2Ki 16:3; 21:11; Eze 16:3

[d]18 That is, Jerusalem
[e]19 Or *Possessor;* also in verse 22
[f]20 Or *And praise be to*
[a]1 Or *sovereign*
[b]1 Or *shield; / your reward will be very great*
[c]2 The meaning of the Hebrew for this phrase is uncertain.

17When the sun had set and darkness had fallen, a smoking brazier with a blazing torch[k] appeared and passed between the pieces.[l] 18On that day the LORD made a covenant with Abram[m] and said, "To your descendants I give this land,[n] from the river[d] of Egypt[o] to the great river, the Euphrates[p]—19the land of the Kenites,[q] Kenizzites, Kadmonites, 20Hittites,[r] Perizzites,[s] Rephaites,[t] 21Amorites, Canaanites, Girgashites and Jebusites."[u]

Hagar and Ishmael

16 Now Sarai,[a] Abram's wife, had borne him no children.[b] But she had an Egyptian maidservant[c] named Hagar;[d] 2so she said to Abram, "The LORD has kept me from having children.[e] Go, sleep with my maidservant; perhaps I can build a family through her."[f]

Abram agreed to what Sarai said. 3So after Abram had been living in Canaan[g] ten years,[h] Sarai his wife took her Egyptian maidservant Hagar and gave her to her husband to be his wife. 4He slept with Hagar,[i] and she conceived.

When she knew she was pregnant, she began to despise her mistress.[j] 5Then Sarai said to Abram, "You are responsible for the wrong I am suffering. I put my servant in your arms, and now that she knows she is pregnant, she despises me. May the LORD judge between you and me."[k]

6"Your servant is in your hands,[l]" Abram said. "Do with her whatever you think best." Then Sarai ill-treated[m] Hagar; so she fled from her.

7The angel of the LORD[n] found Hagar near a spring[o] in the desert; it was the spring that is beside the road to Shur.[p] 8And he said, "Hagar,[q] servant of Sarai, where have you come from, and where are you going?"[r]

"I'm running away from my mistress Sarai," she answered.

9Then the angel of the LORD told her, "Go back to your mistress and submit to her." 10The angel added, "I will so increase your descendants that they will be too numerous to count."[s]

11The angel of the LORD[t] also said to her:

"You are now with child
and you will have a son.[u]
You shall name him[v] Ishmael,[a][w]
for the LORD has heard of your
misery.[x]
12He will be a wild donkey[y] of a man;
his hand will be against everyone
and everyone's hand against him,
and he will live in hostility
towards[b] all his brothers."[z]

13She gave this name to the LORD who spoke to her: "You are the God who sees me,"[a] for she said, "I have now seen[c] the One who sees me."[b] 14That is why the well[c] was called Beer Lahai Roi;[d][d] it is still there, between Kadesh[e] and Bered.

15So Hagar[f] bore Abram a son,[g] and Abram gave the name Ishmael[h] to the son she had borne. 16Abram was eighty-six years old[i] when Hagar bore him Ishmael.

The Covenant of Circumcision

17 When Abram was ninety-nine years old,[a] the LORD appeared to him[b] and said, "I am God Almighty;[a][c] walk before me and be blameless.[d] 2I will confirm my covenant between me and you[e] and will greatly increase your numbers."[f]

3Abram fell face down,[g] and God said to him, 4"As for me, this is my covenant with you:[h] You will be the father of many nations.[i] 5No longer will you be called Abram;[b] your name will be Abraham,[c][j] for I have made you a father of many nations.[k] 6I will make you very fruitful;[l] I will make nations of you, and kings will come from you.[m] 7I will

15:17 [k]Jdg 7:16,20; 15:4–5; [l]**ver 10**
18 [m]Ge 17:2,4,7; Ex 6:4; 34:10, 27; 1Ch 16:16; Ps 105:9; [n]**Ge 12:7**; [o]Nu 34:5; Jos 15:4, 47; 1Ki 8:65; 2Ki 24:7; 2Ch 7:8; Isa 27:12; Jer 37:5; 46:2; La 4:17; Eze 30:22; 47:19; [p]**Ge 2:14**
19 [q]Nu 24:21; Jdg 1:16; 4:11,17; 5:24; 1Sa 15:6; 27:10; 30:29; 1Ch 2:55
20 [r]**Ge 10:15; Dt 7:1**; [s]**Ge 13:7**; [t]**Ge 14:5**
21 [u]**Ge 10:16**; Jos 3:10; 24:11; Ne 9:8

Ch. 16

1 [a]**Ge 11:29**; [b]**Ge 11:30**; Lk 1:7,36; Gal 4:24–25; [c]Ge 24:61; 29:24, 29; 31:33; 46:18; [d]ver 3–4,8,15; Ge 21:14; 25:12
2 [e]Ge 29:31; 30:2; [f]Ge 19:32; 30:3–4, 9–10
3 [g]**Ge 12:5**; [h]**Ge 12:4**
4 [i]**ver 1**; [j]Ge 30:1; 1Sa 1:6
5 [k]Ge 31:53; Ex 5:21; Jdg 11:27; 1Sa 24:12,15; 26:10,23; Ps 50:6; 75:7
6 [l]Jos 9:25; [m]Ge 31:50
7 [n]ver 11; Ge 21:17; 22:11, 15; 24:7,40; 31:11; 48:16; Ex 3:2; 14:19; 23:20,23; 32:34; 33:2; Nu 22:22; Jdg 2:1; 6:11; 13:3; 2Sa 24:16; 1Ki 19:5; 2Ki 1:3; 19:35; Ps 34:7; Zec 1:11; **Ac 5:19**; [o]ver 14; Ge 21:19; [p]Ge 20:1; 25:18; Ex 15:22; 1Sa 15:7; 27:8
8 [q]**ver 1**; [r]**Ge 3:9**
10 [s]**Ge 13:16**
11 [t]**ver 7; Ac 5:19**; [u]**Ge 3:15**; [v]Ge 12:2–3; 18:19; Ne 9:7; Isa 44:1; Am 3:2; Mt 1:21; Lk 1:13,31; [w]Ge 17:19; 21:3; 37:25,28; 39:1; Jdg 8:24; [x]Ge 29:32; 31:42; Ex 2:24; 3:7,9; 4:31; Nu 20:16; Dt 26:7; 1Sa 9:16
12 [y]Job 6:5; 11:12; 24:5; 39:5; Ps 104:11; Jer 2:24; Hos 8:9; [z]Ge 25:18
13 [a]Ps 139:1–12; [b]Ge 32:30; 33:10; Ex 24:10; 33:20,23; Nu 12:8; Jdg 6:22; 13:22; Isa 6:5
14 [c]**ver 7**; [d]Ge 24:62; 25:11; [e]**Ge 14:7**
15 [f]**ver 1**; [g]Ge 21:9; Gal 4:22; [h]Ge 17:18; 25:12; 28:9
16 [i]**Ge 12:4**

Ch. 17

1 [a]**Ge 12:4**; [b]**Ge 12:7**; [c]Ge 28:3; 35:11; 43:14; 48:3; 49:25; Ex 6:3; Ru 1:20; Job 5:17; 6:4,14; 22:21; 33:19; 36:16; Isa 13:6; Joel 1:15; Mic 6:9; [d]**Ge 5:22**; 20:5; Dt 18:13; 1Ki 3:6; 9:4; Job 1:1; Ps 15:2; 18:23; 78:72; 101:2
2 [e]**Ge 15:18; 22:16–18**; [f]**Ge 12:2**
3 [g]ver 17; Ge 18:2; 19:1; 33:3; Ex 18:7; Nu 14:5; Jos 5:14; 7:6; Jdg 13:20; Eze 1:28; 3:23
4 [h]**Ge 15:18**; [i]ver 16; **Ge 12:2**; 25:23
5 [j]ver 15; Ge 32:28; 35:10; 37:3,13; 43:6; 46:2; 1Ki 18:31; 2Ki 17:34; 1Ch 1:34; Ne 9:7; Isa 48:1; **Jn 1:42**; [k]Ro 4:17*
6 [l]Ge 1:28; 22:17; 26:22; 28:3; 35:11; 41:52; 47:27; 48:4; 49:22; Lev 26:9; Dt 7:13; [m]ver 16,19; Ge 18:10; 21:1; 36:31; Isa 51:2; Mt 1:6

---

d18 Or *Wadi* a11 *Ishmael* means *God hears.*
b12 Or *live to the east / of* c13 Or *seen the back of*
d14 *Beer Lahai Roi* means *well of the Living One who sees me.* a1 Hebrew *El-Shaddai*
b5 *Abram* means *exalted father.*
c5 *Abraham* means *father of many.*

establish my covenant[n][o] as an ever-
lasting covenant[p][q] between me and you
and your descendants after you for the
generations to come, to be your God[r]
and the God of your descendants after
you.[s] 8The whole land of Canaan,[t]
where you are now an alien,[u] I will give
as an everlasting possession to you and
your descendants after you;[v] and I will
be their God.[w]"

9Then God said to Abraham, "As for
you, you must keep my covenant,[x] you
and your descendants after you for the
generations to come.[y] 10This is my cov-
enant with you and your descendants
after you, the covenant you are to keep:
Every male among you shall be circum-
cised.[z] 11You are to undergo circum-
cision,[a] and it will be the sign of the
covenant[b] between me and you. 12For
the generations to come[c] every male
among you who is eight days old must
be circumcised,[d] including those born in
your household or bought with money
from a foreigner—those who are not
your offspring. 13Whether born in your
household or bought with your money,
they must be circumcised.[e] My cov-
enant in your flesh is to be an everlast-
ing covenant.[f] 14Any uncircumcised
male, who has not been circumcised[g]
in the flesh, will be cut off from his
people;[h] he has broken my covenant.[i]"

15God also said to Abraham, "As for
Sarai[j] your wife, you are no longer to call
her Sarai; her name will be Sarah.[k] 16I
will bless her and will surely give you a
son by her.[l] I will bless her so that she
will be the mother of nations;[m] kings of
peoples will come from her."

17Abraham fell face down;[n] he
laughed[o] and said to himself, "Will a
son be born to a man a hundred years
old?[p] Will Sarah bear a child at the age
of ninety?"[q] 18And Abraham said to
God, "If only Ishmael[r] might live under
your blessing!"[s]

19Then God said, "Yes, but your wife
Sarah will bear you a son,[t] and you will
call him Isaac.[d][u] I will establish my cov-
enant with him[v] as an everlasting cov-
enant[w] for his descendants after him.
20And as for Ishmael, I have heard you: I
will surely bless him; I will make him
fruitful and will greatly increase his
numbers.[x] He will be the father of
twelve rulers,[y] and I will make him into
a great nation.[z] 21But my covenant[a] I will
establish with Isaac, whom Sarah will
bear to you[b] by this time next year."[c]
22When he had finished speaking with
Abraham, God went up from him.[d]

23On that very day Abraham took his

7 [n]**Ge 15:18**; Lev 26:9,15; [o]**Ge 6:18**; [p]**Heb 13:20**; [q]**Ge 9:16**; [r]Ex 6:7; 20:2; 29:45–46; Lev 11:44–45; 18:2; 22:33; 25:38; 26:12, 45; Nu 15:41; Dt 4:20; 7:6, 21; 29:13; 2Sa 7:24; Jer 14:9; Rev 21:7; [s]Ro 9:8; Gal 3:16
8 [t]**Ge 10:19**; [u]Ge 23:4; 28:4; 35:27; 37:1; Ex 6:4; 1Ch 29:15; [v]**Ge 12:7**; **15:7**; [w]**ver 7**; Jer 31:1
9 [x]Ge 22:18; Ex 19:5; Dt 5:2; [y]Ge 18:19
10 [z]ver 23; Ge 21:4; Lev 12:3; Jos 5:2,5,7; Jn 7:22; Ac 7:8; Ro 4:11
11 [a]Ex 12:48; Dt 10:16; [b]**Ge 9:12**; Ro 4:11
12 [c]**Ge 9:12**; [d]Ge 21:4; Lev 12:3; Jos 5:2; **Lk 1:59**
13 [e]Ex 12:44,48; [f]**Ge 9:16**
14 [g]ver 23; [h]Ex 4:24–26; 12:15,19; 30:33; Lev 7:20,25; 17:4; 18:29; 19:8; 20:17; Nu 9:13; 15:30; 19:13; Dt 17:12; Jos 5:2–8; Job 38:15; Ps 37:28; [i]Eze 44:7
15 [j]**Ge 11:29**; [k]**ver 5**
16 [l]**ver 6**; **Isa 29:22**; [m]**ver 4**; Ge 24:60; Gal 4:31
17 [n]**ver 3**; [o]Ge 18:12; 21:6; [p]**Ge 12:4**; [q]Ge 18:11,13; 21:7; 24:1,36; Jer 20:15; Lk 1:18; Ro 4:19; Gal 4:23; Heb 11:11
18 [r]**Ge 16:15**; [s]Ge 21:11
19 [t]**ver 6,21**; Ge 18:14; 21:2; 1Sa 1:20; [u]**Ge 16:11**; Mt 1:21; Lk 1:13,31; [v]Ge 26:3; 50:24; Ex 13:11; Dt 1:8; [w]**Ge 9:16**; **Gal 3:16**

son Ishmael and all those born in his
household[e] or bought with his money,
every male in his household, and cir-
cumcised them, as God told him.[f]
24Abraham was ninety-nine years old[g]
when he was circumcised,[h] 25and his
son Ishmael[i] was thirteen; 26Abraham
and his son Ishmael were both circum-
cised on that same day. 27And every
male in Abraham's household,[j] includ-
ing those born in his household or
bought from a foreigner, was circum-
cised with him.

The Three Visitors

18 The LORD appeared to Abra-
ham[a] near the great trees of
Mamre[b] while he was sitting at the en-
trance to his tent[c] in the heat of the day.
2Abraham looked up[d] and saw three
men[e] standing nearby. When he saw
them, he hurried from the entrance of
his tent to meet them and bowed low to
the ground.[f]

3He said, "If I have found favour in
your eyes,[g] my lord,[a] do not pass your
servant[h] by. 4Let a little water be
brought, and then you may all wash
your feet[i] and rest under this tree. 5Let
me get you something to eat,[j] so you can
be refreshed and then go on your way
—now that you have come to your
servant."

"Very well," they answered, "do as
you say."

6So Abraham hurried into the tent to
Sarah. "Quick," he said, "get three
seahs[b] of fine flour and knead it and
bake some bread."[k]

7Then he ran to the herd and selected
a choice, tender calf[l] and gave it to a
servant, who hurried to prepare it. 8He
then brought some curds[m] and milk[n]
and the calf that had been prepared,
and set these before them.[o] While they
ate, he stood near them under a tree.

20 [x]**Ge 13:16**; [y]Ge 25:12–16; [z]Ge 25:18; 48:19
21 [a]Ex 34:10; [b]**ver 19**; [c]Ge 18:10,14
22 [d]Ge 18:33; 35:13; Nu 12:9 *23* [e]**Ge 12:5**; [f]**ver 10,14**
24 [g]**Ge 12:4**; [h]Ro 4:11 *25* [i]Ge 16:16
27 [j]Ge 14:14

Ch. 18

1 [a]**Ge 12:7**; Ac 7:2; [b]**Ge 13:18**; [c]Ge 19:1; 23:10,18; 34:20,24; Ru 4:1; Ps 69:12; Heb 11:9
2 [d]Ge 24:63; [e]ver 16,22; Ge 19:1,10; 32:24; Jos 5:13; Jdg 13:6–11; Hos 12:3–4; Heb 13:2; [f]**Ge 17:3**; **43:28**
3 [g]Ge 19:19; 39:4; Ru 2:2,10,13; 1Sa 1:18; Est 2:15; [h]Ge 32:4,18,20; 33:5
4 [i]Ge 19:2; 24:32; 43:24; Jdg 19:21; 2Sa 11:8; **Lk 7:44**
5 [j]Jdg 13:15; 19:5 *6* [k]Ge 19:3; 2Sa 13:8
7 [l]1Sa 28:24; Lk 15:23
8 [m]Isa 7:15,22; [n]Jdg 4:19; 5:25; [o]Jdg 6:19

d19 *Isaac* means *he laughs*. a3 Or *O Lord*
b6 That is, probably about 39 pints (about 22 litres)

9"Where is your wife Sarah?"[p] they
asked him.
"There, in the tent,[q]" he said.
10Then the LORD[c] said, "I will surely
return to you about this time next year,[r]
and Sarah your wife will have a son."[s]
Now Sarah was listening at the en-
trance to the tent, which was behind
him. 11Abraham and Sarah were already
old and well advanced in years,[t] and
Sarah was past the age of childbearing.[u]
12So Sarah laughed[v] to herself as she
thought, "After I am worn out and my
master[d][w] is old, will I now have this
pleasure?"
13Then the LORD said to Abraham,
"Why did Sarah laugh and say, 'Will I
really have a child, now that I am old?'[x]
14Is anything too hard for the LORD?[y] I
will return to you at the appointed time
next year[z] and Sarah will have a son."[a]
15Sarah was afraid, so she lied and
said, "I did not laugh."
But he said, "Yes, you did laugh."

Abraham Pleads for Sodom

16When the men[b] got up to leave, they
looked down towards Sodom, and
Abraham walked along with them to
see them on their way. 17Then the LORD
said, "Shall I hide from Abraham[c] what
I am about to do?[d] 18Abraham will surely
become a great and powerful nation,[e]
and all nations on earth will be blessed
through him. 19For I have chosen him,[f]
so that he will direct his children[g] and
his household after him to keep the way
of the LORD[h] by doing what is right and
just,[i] so that the LORD will bring about
for Abraham what he has promised
him."[j]
20Then the LORD said, "The outcry
against Sodom[k] and Gomorrah is so
great[l] and their sin so grievous[m] 21that I
will go down[n] and see if what they have
done is as bad as the outcry that has
reached me. If not, I will know."
22The men[o] turned away and went
towards Sodom,[p] but Abraham re-
mained standing before the LORD.[e][q]
23Then Abraham approached him and
said: "Will you sweep away the right-
eous with the wicked?[r] 24What if there
are fifty righteous people in the city?
Will you really sweep it away and not
spare[f] the place for the sake of the fifty
righteous people in it?[s] 25Far be it from
you to do such a thing[t]—to kill the
righteous with the wicked, treating the
righteous[u] and the wicked alike.[v] Far be
it from you! Will not the Judge[g][w] of all
the earth do right?"[x]
26The LORD said, "If I find fifty right-
eous people in the city of Sodom, I will
spare the whole place for their sake."[y]
27Then Abraham spoke up again:
"Now that I have been so bold as to
speak to the Lord, though I am nothing
but dust and ashes,[z] 28what if the num-
ber of the righteous is five less than
fifty? Will you destroy the whole city
because of five people?"
"If I find forty-five there," he said, "I
will not destroy it."
29Once again he spoke to him, "What
if only forty are found there?"
He said, "For the sake of forty, I will
not do it."
30Then he said, "May the Lord not be
angry,[a] but let me speak. What if only
thirty can be found there?"
He answered, "I will not do it if I find
thirty there."
31Abraham said, "Now that I have
been so bold as to speak to the Lord,
what if only twenty can be found
there?"
He said, "For the sake of twenty, I
will not destroy it."
32Then he said, "May the Lord not be
angry, but let me speak just once more.[b]
What if only ten can be found there?"
He answered, "For the sake of ten,[c] I
will not destroy it."
33When the LORD had finished
speaking[d] with Abraham, he left,[e] and
Abraham returned home.[f]

Sodom and Gomorrah Destroyed

19 The two angels[a] arrived at
Sodom[b] in the evening, and
Lot[c] was sitting in the gateway of the
city.[d] When he saw them, he got up to
meet them and bowed down with his
face to the ground.[e] 2"My lords," he
said, "please turn aside to your ser-
vant's house. You can wash your feet[f]
and spend the night and then go on
your way early in the morning."
"No," they answered, "we will
spend the night in the square."[g]
3But he insisted[h] so strongly that they
did go with him and entered his house.[i]

9 [p]**Ge 3:9;** [q]Ge 24:67; Heb 11:9
10 [r]**Ge 17:21;** 21:2; 2Ki 4:16; [s]**Ge 17:6;** Ro 9:9*
11 [t]**Ge 17:17;** Lk 1:18; [u]**Ge 11:30;** Ro 4:19; Heb 11:11–12
12 [v]**Ge 17:17;** [w]1Pe 3:6
13 [x]**Ge 17:17**
14 [y]Job 42:2; Isa 40:29; 50:2; 51:9; Jer 32:17,27; **Mt 19:26;** Ro 4:21; [z]**ver 10;** [a]**Ge 17:19;** Ro 9:9*; Gal 4:23
16 [b]**ver 2**
17 [c]Am 3:7; [d]Ge 19:24; Job 1:16; Ps 107:34
18 [e]**Ge 12:2;** Gal 3:8*
19 [f]Ge 17:9; [g]Dt 4:9–10; 6:7; [h]Jos 24:15; Eph 6:4; [i]Ge 22:12,18; 26:5; 2Sa 8:15; Ps 17:2; 99:4; Jer 23:5; [j]**Ge 16:11; Isa 14:1**
20 [k]Isa 1:10; Jer 23:14; Eze 16:46; [l]Ge 19:13; [m]**Ge 13:13**
21 [n]**Ge 11:5**
22 [o]**ver 2;** [p]Ge 19:1; [q]Ge 19:27
23 [r]Ex 23:7; Lev 4:3,22,27; Nu 16:22; Dt 27:25; 2Sa 24:17; Ps 11:4–7; 94:21; Eze 18:4; 2Pe 2:9
24 [s]ver 26; Jer 5:1
25 [t]Ge 44:7,17; Dt 8:3–7; 34:10; [u]Isa 5:20; Am 5:15; Mal 2:17; 3:18; [v]Dt 1:16–17; [w]Jdg 11:27; Job 9:15; Ps 7:11; 94:2; Heb 12:23; [x]Ge 20:4; Dt 32:4; 2Ch 19:7; Ezr 9:15; Ne 9:33; Job 8:3, 20; 34:10; 36:23; Ps 58:11; 75:7; 94:2; 119:137; Isa 3:10–11; Eze 18:25; Da 4:37; 9:14; Mal 2:17; Ro 3:6
26 [y]**ver 24**
27 [z]**Ge 2:7; Job 2:8**
30 [a]ver 32; Ge 44:18; Ex 32:22
32 [b]**ver 30;** Jdg 6:39; [c]Jer 5:1
33 [d]Ex 31:18; [e]**Ge 17:22;** [f]Ge 31:55

Ch. 19
1 [a]**Ge 18:2;** Heb 13:2; [b]Ge 18:22; [c]**Ge 11:27;** [d]**Ge 18:1;** [e]**Ge 17:3;** 48:12; Ru 2:10; 1Sa 25:23; 2Sa 14:33; 2Ki 2:15
2 [f]**Ge 18:4;** Lk 7:44; [g]Jdg 19:15,20
3 [h]Ge 33:11; [i]Job 31:32

[c]10 Hebrew *Then he* [d]12 Or *husband*
[e]22 Masoretic Text; an ancient Hebrew scribal tradition *but the LORD remained standing before Abraham*
[f]24 Or *forgive;* also in verse 26 [g]25 Or *Ruler*

He prepared a meal for them, baking bread without yeast,[j] and they ate.[k] 4Before they had gone to bed, all the men from every part of the city of Sodom[l]—both young and old—surrounded the house. 5They called to Lot, "Where are the men who came to you tonight? Bring them out to us so that we can have sex with them."[m]

6Lot went outside to meet them[n] and shut the door behind him 7and said, "No, my friends. Don't do this wicked thing. 8Look, I have two daughters who have never slept with a man. Let me bring them out to you, and you can do what you like with them. But don't do anything to these men, for they have come under the protection of my roof."[o]

9"Get out of our way," they replied. And they said, "This fellow came here as an alien,[p] and now he wants to play the judge![q] We'll treat you worse than them." They kept bringing pressure on Lot and moved forward to break down the door.

10But the men[r] inside reached out and pulled Lot back into the house and shut the door. 11Then they struck the men who were at the door of the house, young and old, with blindness[s] so that they could not find the door.

12The two men said to Lot, "Do you have anyone else here—sons-in-law, sons or daughters, or anyone else in the city who belongs to you?[t] Get them out of here, 13because we[u] are going to destroy this place. The outcry to the LORD against its people is so great[v] that he has sent us to destroy it."[w]

14So Lot went out and spoke to his sons-in-law, who were pledged to marry[a] his daughters. He said, "Hurry and get out of this place, because the LORD is about to destroy the city![x]" But his sons-in-law thought he was joking.[y]

15With the coming of dawn, the angels urged Lot, saying, "Hurry! Take your wife and your two daughters who are here, or you will be swept away[z] when the city is punished.[a]"

16When he hesitated, the men grasped his hand and the hands of his wife and of his two daughters[b] and led them safely out of the city, for the LORD was merciful to them.[c] 17As soon as they had brought them out, one of them said, "Flee for your lives![d] Don't look back,[e] and don't stop anywhere in the plain![f] Flee to the mountains[g] or you will be swept away!"

18But Lot said to them, "No, my lords,[b] please! 19Your[c] servant has found favour in your[c] eyes,[h] and you[c] have shown great kindness[i] to me in sparing my life. But I can't flee to the mountains;[j] this disaster will overtake me, and I'll die. 20Look, here is a town near enough to run to, and it is small. Let me flee to it—it is very small, isn't it? Then my life will be spared."

21He said to him, "Very well, I will grant this request[k] too; I will not overthrow the town you speak of. 22But flee there quickly, because I cannot do anything until you reach it." (That is why the town was called Zoar.[d][l])

23By the time Lot reached Zoar,[m] the sun had risen over the land. 24Then the LORD rained down burning sulphur[n] on Sodom and Gomorrah[o]—from the LORD out of the heavens.[p] 25Thus he overthrew those cities[q] and the entire plain,[r] including all those living in the cities—and also the vegetation in the land.[s] 26But Lot's wife looked back,[t] and she became a pillar of salt.[u]

27Early the next morning Abraham got up and returned to the place where he had stood before the LORD.[v] 28He looked down towards Sodom and Gomorrah, towards all the land of the plain, and he saw dense smoke rising from the land, like smoke from a furnace.[w]

29So when God destroyed the cities of the plain,[x] he remembered[y] Abraham, and he brought Lot out of the catastrophe[z] that overthrew the cities where Lot had lived.[a]

Lot and His Daughters

30Lot and his two daughters left Zoar[b] and settled in the mountains,[c] for he was afraid to stay in Zoar. He and his two daughters lived in a cave. 31One day the older daughter said to the younger, "Our father is old, and there is no man around here to lie with us, as is the custom all over the earth. 32Let's get our father to drink wine and then lie with him and preserve our family line[d] through our father."[e]

33That night they got their father to drink wine, and the older daughter went in and lay with him. He was not aware of it when she lay down or when she got up.[f]

3 jEx 12:39; kGe 18:6
4 lGe 13:13
5 mGe 13:13; Lev 18:22; Dt 23:18; Jdg 19:22; Ro 1:24–27
6 nJdg 19:23
8 oJdg 19:24; 2 Pe 2:7–8
9 pGe 23:4; qGe 13:8; Ac 7:27
10 rGe 18:2
11 sDt 28:28–29; 2Ki 6:18; Ac 13:11
12 tGe 6:18
13 uEx 12:29; 2Sa 24:16; 2Ki 19:35; 1Ch 21:12; 2Ch 32:21; vGe 18:20; w1Ch 21:15; Ps 78:49; Jer 21:12; 25:18; 44:22; 51:45
14 xNu 16:21; Rev 18:4; yEx 9:21; 1Ki 13:18; Jer 5:12; 43:2; Lk 17:28
15 zNu 16:26; Job 21:18; Ps 58:9; 73:19; 90:5; aRev 18:4
16 b2Pe 2:7; cEx 34:6; Ps 33:18–19
17 d1Ki 19:3; Jer 48:6; ever 26; fGe 13:12; gver 19; Ge 14:10; Mt 24:16
19 hGe 6:8; 18:3; iGe 24:12; 39:21; 40:14; 47:29; Ru 1:8; 2:20; 3:10; jver 17,30
21 k1Sa 25:35; 2Sa 14:8; Job 42:9
22 lGe 13:10
23 mGe 13:10
24 nJob 18:15; Ps 11:6; Isa 30:33; 34:9; Eze 38:22; oDt 29:23; Isa 1:9; 13:19; Jer 49:18; 50:40; Am 4:11; pGe 18:17; Lev 10:2; Mt 10:15; Lk 17:29
25 qver 24; Eze 26:16; Zep 3:8; Hag 2:22; rGe 13:12; sPs 107:34; Isa 1:10; Jer 20:16; 23:14; La 4:6; Eze 16:48
26 tver 17; uLk 17:32
27 vGe 18:22
28 wGe 15:17; Ex 19:18; Rev 9:2; 18:9
29 xGe 13:12; yGe 8:1; z2Pe 2:7; aGe 14:12; Eze 14:16
30 bver 22; Ge 13:10; cver 19; Ge 14:10
32 dGe 16:2; ever 34,36; Ge 38:18
33 fver 35

a14 Or *were married to*
b18 Or *No, Lord;* or *No, my lord*
c19 The Hebrew is singular.
d22 *Zoar* means *small.*

34The next day the older daughter
said to the younger, "Last night I lay
with my father. Let's get him to drink
wine again tonight, and you go in and
lie with him so we can preserve our
family line through our father."[g] 35So
they got their father to drink wine[h] that
night also, and the younger daughter
went and lay with him. Again he was
not aware of it when she lay down or
when she got up.[i]

36So both of Lot's daughters became
pregnant by their father.[j] 37The older
daughter had a son, and she named him
Moab;[e][k] he is the father of the Moabites[l]
of today. 38The younger daughter also
had a son, and she named him Ben-
Ammi;[f] he is the father of the Ammo-
nites[m] of today.

Abraham and Abimelech

20:1–18Ref—Ge 12:10–20; 26:1–11

20 Now Abraham moved on from
there[a] into the region of the
Negev[b] and lived between Kadesh[c] and
Shur.[d] For a while[e] he stayed in Gerar,[f]
2and there Abraham said of his wife
Sarah, "She is my sister."[g] Then
Abimelech[h] king of Gerar sent for Sarah
and took her.[i]

3But God came to Abimelech[j] in a
dream[k] one night and said to him, "You
are as good as dead[l] because of the
woman you have taken; she is a married
woman."[m]

4Now Abimelech had not gone near
her, so he said, "Lord, will you destroy
an innocent nation?[n] 5Did he not say to
me, 'She is my sister,'[o] and didn't she
also say, 'He is my brother'? I have done
this with a clear conscience[p] and clean
hands."[q]

6Then God said to him in the dream,
"Yes, I know you did this with a clear
conscience, and so I have kept[r] you
from sinning against me.[s] That is why I
did not let you touch her. 7Now return
the man's wife, for he is a prophet,[t] and
he will pray for you[u] and you will live.
But if you do not return her, you may be
sure that you and all yours will die."[v]

8Early the next morning Abimelech
summoned all his officials, and when he
told them all that had happened, they
were very much afraid. 9Then Abi-
melech called Abraham in and said,
"What have you done to us? How have I
wronged you that you have brought
such great guilt upon me and my king-
dom? You have done things to me that
should not be done."[w] 10And Abimelech
asked Abraham, "What was your
reason for doing this?"

11Abraham replied, "I said to myself,
'There is surely no fear of God[x] in this
place, and they will kill me because of
my wife.'[y] 12Besides, she really is my
sister,[z] the daughter of my father
though not of my mother; and she be-
came my wife. 13And when God had me
wander[a] from my father's household,[b] I
said to her, 'This is how you can show
your love to me: Everywhere we go, say
of me, "He is my brother."'"

14Then Abimelech[c] brought sheep
and cattle and male and female slaves
and gave them to Abraham,[d] and he
returned Sarah his wife to him. 15And
Abimelech said, "My land is before you;
live wherever you like."[e]

16To Sarah he said, "I am giving your
brother a thousand shekels[a] of silver.
This is to cover the offence against you
before all who are with you; you are
completely vindicated."

17Then Abraham prayed to God,[f] and
God healed Abimelech, his wife and his
slave girls so they could have children
again, 18for the LORD had closed up
every womb in Abimelech's household
because of Abraham's wife Sarah.[g]

The Birth of Isaac

21 Now the LORD was gracious to
Sarah[a] as he had said, and the
LORD did for Sarah what he had prom-
ised.[b] 2Sarah became pregnant and bore
a son[c] to Abraham in his old age,[d] at the
very time God had promised him.[e]
3Abraham gave the name Isaac[a][f] to the
son Sarah bore him. 4When his son Isaac
was eight days old, Abraham circum-
cised him,[g] as God commanded him.
5Abraham was a hundred years old[h]
when his son Isaac was born to him.

6Sarah said, "God has brought me

34 [g]**ver 32**
35 [h]Ge 9:21; [i]ver 33
36 [j]**ver 32**
37 [k]Ge 36:35; Ex 15:15; Nu 25:1; Isa 15:1; 25:10; Jer 25:21; 48:1; Eze 25:8; Zep 2:9; [l]Nu 22:4; 24:17; Dt 2:9; Jdg 3:28; Ru 1:4,22; 1Sa 14:47; 22:3–4; 2Sa 8:2; 2Ki 1:1; 3:4; Ezr 9:1; Ps 108:9; Jer 48:1
38 [m]Nu 21:24; Dt 2:19; 23:3; Jos 12:2; Jdg 3:13; 10:6–7; 1Sa 11:1–11; 14:47; 1Ch 19:1; 2Ch 20:23; 26:8; 27:5; Ne 2:19; 4:3; Jer 25:21; 40:14; 49:1; Eze 21:28; 25:2; Am 1:13

Ch. 20

1 [a]Ge 18:1; [b]**Ge 12:9**; [c]**Ge 14:7**; [d]**Ge 16:7**; [e]Ge 26:3; [f]Ge 26:1,6,17
2 [g]**Ge 12:13**; [h]ver 14; Ge 21:22; 26:1; [i]**Ge 12:15**
3 [j]Nu 22:9,20; [k]Ge 28:12; 31:10,24; 37:5,9; 40:5; 41:1; Nu 12:6; Dt 13:1; Job 33:15; Da 2:1; 4:5; [l]Ex 10:7; 12:33; Ps 105:38; [m]ver 7; Ge 26:11; 1Ch 16:21; Ps 105:14
4 [n]**Ge 18:25**
5 [o]**Ge 12:19**; [p]**Ge 17:1**; [q]Ps 7:8; 25:21; 26:6; 41:12
6 [r]1Sa 25:26,34; [s]**Ge 13:13**; Ps 41:4; 51:4
7 [t]Dt 18:18; 34:10; 2Ki 3:11; 5:3; 1Ch 16:22; Ps 105:15; [u]ver 17; Ex 8:8; Nu 11:2; 12:13; 1Sa 7:5; 1Ki 13:6; Job 42:8; Jer 18:20; 37:3; 42:2; [v]**ver 3**; **Ps 9:5**
9 [w]**Ge 12:18**; 34:7
11 [x]Ge 42:18; Ne 5:15; Job 31:23; Ps 36:1; Pr 16:6; [y]**Ge 12:12**; 31:31
12 [z]**Ge 12:13**
13 [a]Dt 26:5; 1Ch 16:20; Isa 30:28; 63:17; [b]**Ge 12:1**
14 [c]**ver 2**; [d]**Ge 12:16**
15 [e]**Ge 13:9**; **45:18**
17 [f]**ver 7**; Job 42:9
18 [g]Ge 12:17

Ch. 21

1 [a]1Sa 2:21; [b]**Ge 8:1**; **17:6**,21; 18:14; Gal 4:23; Heb 11:11
2 [c]**Ge 17:19**; **30:6**; [d]Gal 4:22; Heb 11:11; [e]**Ge 18:10**
3 [f]**Ge 16:11**; **17:19**; Jos 24:3
4 [g]**Ge 17:10**,12; Ac 7:8
5 [h]**Ge 12:4**; Heb 6:15

[e]37 *Moab* sounds like the Hebrew for *from father*.
[f]38 *Ben-Ammi* means *son of my people*.
[a]16 That is, about 25 pounds (about 11.5 kilograms)
[a]3 *Isaac* means *he laughs*.

laughter,[i] and everyone who hears
about this will laugh with me." 7And
she added, "Who would have said to
Abraham that Sarah would nurse chil-
dren? Yet I have borne him a son in his
old age."[j]

Hagar and Ishmael Sent Away

8The child grew and was weaned,[k]
and on the day Isaac was weaned Abra-
ham held a great feast. 9But Sarah saw
that the son whom Hagar the Egyptian
had borne to Abraham[l] was mocking,[m]
10 and she said to Abraham, "Get rid of
that slave woman[n] and her son, for that
slave woman's son will never share in
the inheritance with my son Isaac."[o]
11The matter distressed Abraham
greatly because it concerned his son.[p]
12But God said to him, "Do not be so
distressed about the boy and your maid-
servant. Listen to whatever Sarah tells
you, because it is through Isaac that
your offspring[b] will be reckoned.[q] 13I
will make the son of the maidservant
into a nation[r] also, because he is your
offspring."
14Early the next morning Abraham
took some food and a skin of water and
gave them to Hagar.[s] He set them on her
shoulders and then sent her off with the
boy. She went on her way and wan-
dered in the desert of Beersheba.[t]
15When the water in the skin was
gone, she put the boy under one of the
bushes. 16Then she went off and sat
down nearby, about a bow-shot away,
for she thought, "I cannot watch the
boy die." And as she sat there nearby,
she[c] began to sob.[u]
17God heard the boy crying,[v] and the
angel of God[w] called to Hagar from
heaven[x] and said to her, "What is the
matter, Hagar? Do not be afraid;[y] God
has heard the boy crying as he lies there.
18Lift the boy up and take him by the
hand, for I will make him into a great
nation."[z]
19Then God opened her eyes[a] and she
saw a well of water.[b] So she went and
filled the skin with water and gave the
boy a drink.
20God was with the boy[c] as he grew
up. He lived in the desert and became
an archer. 21While he was living in the
Desert of Paran,[d] his mother got a wife
for him[e] from Egypt.

The Treaty at Beersheba

22At that time Abimelech[f] and Phicol
the commander of his forces[g] said to
Abraham, "God is with you in every-
thing you do.[h] 23Now swear[i] to me here
before God that you will not deal falsely
with me or my children or my descend-
ants.[j] Show to me and the country
where you are living as an alien the
same kindness that I have shown to
you."[k]
24Abraham said, "I swear it."
25Then Abraham complained to
Abimelech about a well of water that
Abimelech's servants had seized.[l] 26But
Abimelech said, "I don't know who has
done this. You did not tell me, and I
heard about it only today."
27So Abraham brought sheep and
cattle and gave them to Abimelech, and
the two men made a treaty.[m] 28Abraham
set apart seven ewe lambs from the
flock, 29and Abimelech asked Abraham,
"What is the meaning of these seven
ewe lambs you have set apart by them-
selves?"
30He replied, "Accept these seven
lambs from my hand as a witness[n] that I
dug this well."[o]
31So that place was called Beer-
sheba,[d][p] because the two men swore an
oath[q] there.
32After the treaty[r] had been made at
Beersheba,[s] Abimelech and Phicol the
commander of his forces[t] returned to
the land of the Philistines.[u] 33Abraham
planted a tamarisk tree[v] in Beersheba,
and there he called upon the name of
the LORD,[w] the Eternal God.[x] 34And
Abraham stayed in the land of the Phil-
istines[y] for a long time.

Abraham Tested

22 Some time later God tested[a]
Abraham. He said to him,
"Abraham!"
"Here I am," [b] he replied.
2Then God said, "Take your son[c],
your only son, Isaac, whom you love,
and go to the region of Moriah.[d] Sac-
rifice him there as a burnt offering[e] on
one of the mountains I will tell you
about."[f]

6 [i]Ge 17:17; Job 8:21; Ps 126:2; Isa 12:6; 35:2; 44:23; 52:9; 54:1
7 [j]**Ge 17:17**
8 [k]1Sa 1:23
9 [l]**Ge 16:15**; [m]Ge 39:14; Gal 4:29
10 [n]Ge 39:17; [o]Ge 25:6; Gal 4:30*
11 [p]Ge 17:18
12 [q]Mt 1:2; Ro 9:7*; Heb 11:18*
13 [r]**Ge 13:16**
14 [s]**Ge 16:1**; [t]ver 31–32; Ge 22:19; 26:33; 28:10; 46:1,5; Jos 15:28; 19:2; Jdg 20:1; 1Sa 3:20; 1Ch 4:28; Ne 11:27
16 [u]Jer 6:26; Am 8:10; Zec 12:10
17 [v]Ex 3:7; Nu 20:16; Dt 26:7; Ps 6:8; [w]**Ge 16:7**; [x]Ge 22:11,15; [y]**Ge 15:1**
18 [z]**Ge 17:20**
19 [a]Nu 22:31; [b]**Ge 16:7**
20 [c]Ge 26:3,24; 28:15; 39:2,21, 23; Lk 1:66
21 [d]**Ge 14:6**; [e]Ge 24:4,38; 28:2; 34:4,8; Jdg 14:2
22 [f]**Ge 20:2**; [g]ver 32; Ge 26:26; [h]ver 23; Ge 26:28; 28:15; 31:3,5,42; 39:2–3; 1Sa 3:19; 16:18; 2Ch 1:1; Ps 46:7; Isa 7:14; 8:8,10; 41:10; 43:5
23 [i]ver 31; Ge 25:33; 26:31; 31:53; Jos 2:12; 1Ki 2:8; [j]1Sa 24:21; [k]**ver 22**; Jos 2:12
25 [l]Ge 26:15,18, 20–22
27 [m]ver 31–32; Ge 26:28,31; 31:44,53
30 [n]Ge 31:44, 47–48,50,52; Jos 22:27–28, 34; 24:27; Isa 19:20; Mal 2:14; [o]ver 25; Ge 26:25,32
31 [p]**ver 14**; [q]**ver 23,27**
32 [r]**ver 27**; [s]**ver 14**; [t]**ver 22**; [u]**Ge 10:14**
33 [v]1Sa 22:6; 31:13; [w]**Ge 4:26**; [x]Ex 15:18; Dt 32:40; 33:27; Job 36:26; Ps 10:16; 45:6; 90:2; 93:2; 102:24; 103:19; 146:10; Isa 40:28; Jer 10:10; Hab 1:12; 3:6; Heb 13:8
34 [y]**Ge 10:14**

Ch. 22

1 [a]Ex 15:25; 16:4; 20:20; Dt 8:2,16; 13:3; Jdg 2:22; 3:1; 2Ch 32:31; Ps 66:10; Heb 11:17; Jas 1:12–13; [b]ver 11; Ge 31:11; 46:2; 1Sa 3:4,6,8; Isa 6:8
2 [c]ver 12,16; Jn 3:16; Heb 11:17; 1Jn 4:9; [d]2Ch 3:1; [e]**Ge 8:20**; [f]ver 9

b12 Or *seed*
c16 Hebrew; Septuagint *the child*
d31 *Beersheba* can mean *well of seven* or *well of the oath*.

3Early the next morning[g] Abraham got up and saddled his donkey. He took with him two of his servants and his son Isaac. When he had cut enough wood for the burnt offering, he set out for the place God had told him about. 4On the third day Abraham looked up and saw the place in the distance. 5He said to his servants, "Stay here with the donkey while I and the boy go over there. We will worship and then we will come back to you.[h]"

6Abraham took the wood for the burnt offering and placed it on his son Isaac,[i] and he himself carried the fire and the knife.[j] As the two of them went on together, 7Isaac spoke up and said to his father Abraham, "Father?"

"Yes, my son?" Abraham replied.

"The fire and wood are here," Isaac said, "but where is the lamb[k] for the burnt offering?"

8Abraham answered, "God himself will provide[l] the lamb[m] for the burnt offering, my son." And the two of them went on together.

9When they reached the place God had told him about,[n] Abraham built an altar[o] there and arranged the wood[p] on it. He bound his son Isaac and laid him on the altar,[q] on top of the wood. 10Then he reached out his hand and took the knife[r] to slay his son.[s] 11But the angel of the LORD[t] called out to him from heaven,[u] "Abraham! Abraham!"[v]

"Here I am,"[w] he replied.

12"Do not lay a hand on the boy," he said. "Do not do anything to him. Now I know that you fear God,[x] because you have not withheld from me your son, your only son.[y]"

13Abraham looked up and there in a thicket he saw a ram[a] caught by its horns.[z] He went over and took the ram and sacrificed it as a burnt offering instead of his son.[a] 14So Abraham called[b] that place The LORD[c] Will Provide. And to this day it is said, "On the mountain of the LORD it will be provided.[d]"

15The angel of the LORD[e] called to Abraham from heaven[f] a second time 16and said, "I swear by myself,[g] declares the LORD, that because you have done this and have not withheld your son, your only son,[h] 17I will surely bless you[i] and make your descendants[j] as numerous as the stars in the sky[k] and as the sand on the seashore.[l] Your descendants will take possession of the cities of their enemies,[m] 18and through your offspring[b] all nations on earth will be blessed,[n] because you have obeyed me."[o]

3 [g]Jos 8:10
5 [h]Ex 24:14
6 [i]Jn 19:17; [j]ver 10; Jdg 19:29
7 [k]Ex 29:38–42; Lev 1:10; Rev 13:8
8 [l]ver 14; [m]ver 13; **Jn 1:29**
9 [n]ver 2; [o]**Ge 4:26; 8:20;** [p]Lev 1:7; 1Ki 18:33; [q]Heb 11:17–19; Jas 2:21
10 [r]**ver 6;** [s]ver 3; **Ge 18:19**
11 [t]**Ge 16:7;** [u]**Ge 21:17;** [v]Ge 46:2; [w]**ver 1**
12 [x]**Ge 18:19;** 42:18; Ex 18:21; 1Sa 15:22; Job 1:1; 37:24; Pr 8:13; Jas 2:21–22; [y]**ver 2;** Jn 3:16; 1Jn 4:9
13 [z]**ver 8;** [a]**Ge 8:20;** Ro 8:32
14 [b]Ex 17:15; Jdg 6:24; [c]Isa 30:29; [d]ver 8
15 [e]**Ge 16:7;** [f]**Ge 21:17**
16 [g]Ex 13:11; 32:13; 33:1; Isa 45:23; 62:8; Jer 22:5; 44:26; 49:13; 51:14; Am 6:8; Lk 1:73; Heb 6:13; [h]**ver 2**
17 [i]**Ge 12:2;** [j]Heb 6:14*; [k]**Ge 15:5;** Ex 32:13; Dt 7:7; 28:62; [l]**Ge 12:2; 26:24;** Hos 1:10; Ro 9:27; Heb 11:12; [m]Ge 24:60; Est 9:2
18 [n]**Ge 12:2,**3; Ac 3:25*; Gal 3:8*; [o]**ver 10;** Ge 17:2,9; Ps 105:9
19 [p]Ge 21:14; 26:23; 28:10
20 [q]**Ge 11:29**
21 [r]**Ge 10:23;** [s]Job 32:2; Jer 25:23
22 [t]Ge 24:15,47; 25:20
23 [u]Ge 24:15; [v]**Ge 11:29**
24 [w]Ge 25:6; 35:22; 36:12; Jdg 8:31; 2Sa 3:7; 1Ki 2:22; 11:3; 1Ch 1:32; SS 6:8

Ch. 23

2 [a]Jos 14:15; 15:13; 20:7; 21:11; [b]**Ge 13:18;** [c]Ge 24:67

19Then Abraham returned to his servants, and they set off together for Beersheba.[p] And Abraham stayed in Beersheba.

Nahor's Sons

20Some time later Abraham was told, "Milcah is also a mother; she has borne sons to your brother Nahor:[q] 21Uz[r] the firstborn, Buz[s] his brother, Kemuel (the father of Aram), 22Kesed, Hazo, Pildash, Jidlaph and Bethuel.[t]" 23Bethuel became the father of Rebekah.[u] Milcah bore these eight sons to Abraham's brother Nahor.[v] 24His concubine,[w] whose name was Reumah, also had sons: Tebah, Gaham, Tahash and Maacah.

The Death of Sarah

23 Sarah lived to be a hundred and twenty-seven years old. 2She died at Kiriath Arba[a] (that is, Hebron)[b] in the land of Canaan, and Abraham went to mourn for Sarah and to weep over her.[c]

3Then Abraham rose from beside his dead wife and spoke to the Hittites.[a][d] He said, 4"I am an alien and a stranger[e] among you. Sell me some property for a burial site here so that I can bury my dead.[f]"

5The Hittites replied to Abraham, 6"Sir, listen to us. You are a mighty prince[g] among us. Bury your dead in the choicest of our tombs. None of us will refuse you his tomb for burying your dead."

7Then Abraham rose and bowed down before the people of the land, the Hittites. 8He said to them, "If you are willing to let me bury my dead, then listen to me and intercede with Ephron son of Zohar[h] on my behalf 9so that he will sell me the cave of Machpelah,[i] which belongs to him and is at the end of his field. Ask him to sell it to me for the full price as a burial site among you."

3 [d]Ge 10:15
4 [e]**Ge 17:8;** 19:9; Ex 2:22; Lev 25:23; Ps 39:12; 105:12; 119:19; Heb 11:9,13; [f]Ge 49:30; Ac 7:16
6 [g]Ge 14:14–16; 24:35 8 [h]Ge 25:9
9 [i]ver 17,19; Ge 25:9; 47:30; 49:30; 50:13

[a]13 Many manuscripts of the Masoretic Text, Samaritan Pentateuch, Septuagint and Syriac; most manuscripts of the Masoretic Text *a ram behind* ⌞*him*⌟
[b]18 Or *seed*
[a]3 Or *the sons of Heth;* also in verses 5, 7, 10, 16, 18, and 20

10Ephron the Hittite was sitting among his people and he replied to Abraham in the hearing of all the Hittites[j] who had come to the gate[k] of his city. 11"No, my lord," he said. "Listen to me; I give[b][l] you the field, and I give[b] you the cave that is in it. I give[b] it to you in the presence of my people. Bury your dead."

12Again Abraham bowed down before the people of the land 13and he said to Ephron in their hearing, "Listen to me, if you will. I will pay the price of the field. Accept it from me so that I can bury my dead there."

14Ephron answered Abraham, 15"Listen to me, my lord; the land is worth four hundred shekels[c] of silver,[m] but what is that between me and you? Bury your dead."

16Abraham agreed to Ephron's terms and weighed out for him the price he had named in the hearing of the Hittites: four hundred shekels of silver,[n] according to the weight current among the merchants.[o]

17So Ephron's field in Machpelah[p] near Mamre[q]—both the field and the cave in it, and all the trees within the borders of the field—was legally made over 18to Abraham as his property[r] in the presence of all the Hittites[s] who had come to the gate[t] of the city. 19Afterwards Abraham buried his wife Sarah in the cave in the field of Machpelah[u] near Mamre (which is at Hebron[v]) in the land of Canaan.[w] 20So the field and the cave in it were legally made over[x] to Abraham by the Hittites as a burial site.[y]

Isaac and Rebekah

24 Abraham was now old and well advanced in years,[a] and the LORD had blessed[b] him in every way.[c] 2He said to the chief[a] servant[d] in his household, the one in charge of all that he had,[e] "Put your hand under my thigh.[f] 3I want you to swear[g] by the LORD, the God of heaven[h] and the God of earth,[i] that you will not get a wife for my son[j] from the daughters of the Canaanites,[k] among whom I am living,[l] 4but will go to my country and my own relatives[m] and get a wife for my son Isaac.[n]"

5The servant asked him, "What if the woman is unwilling to come back with me to this land?[o] Shall I then take your son back to the country you came from?[p]"

6"Make sure that you do not take my son back there,"[q] Abraham said. 7"The LORD, the God of heaven,[r] who brought me out of my father's household and my native land[s] and who spoke to me and promised me on oath, saying, 'To your offspring[b][t] I will give this land'[u]—he will send his angel before you[v] so that you can get a wife for my son from there. 8If the woman is unwilling to come back with you, then you will be released from this oath[w] of mine. Only do not take my son back there."[x] 9So the servant put his hand under the thigh[y] of his master[z] Abraham and swore an oath to him concerning this matter.

10Then the servant took ten of his master's camels[a] and left, taking with him all kinds of good things[b] from his master. He set out for Aram Naharaim[c][c] and made his way to the town of Nahor.[d] 11He made the camels kneel down near the well[e] outside the town; it was towards evening, the time the women go out to draw water.[f]

12Then he prayed, "O LORD, God of my master Abraham,[g] give me success[h] today, and show kindness[i] to my master Abraham. 13See, I am standing beside this spring, and the daughters of the townspeople are coming out to draw water.[j] 14May it be that when I say to a girl, 'Please let down your jar that I may have a drink,' and she says, 'Drink,[k] and I'll water your camels too'[l]—let her be the one you have chosen for your servant Isaac.[m] By this I will know[n] that you have shown kindness to my master."

15Before he had finished praying,[o] Rebekah[p] came out with her jar on her shoulder. She was the daughter of Bethuel[q] son of Milcah,[r] who was the wife of Abraham's brother Nahor.[s] 16The girl was very beautiful,[t] a virgin;[u] no man had ever lain with her. She went down to the spring, filled her jar and came up again.

17The servant hurried to meet her and said, "Please give me a little water from your jar."[v]

18"Drink,[w] my lord," she said, and

10 [j]ver 18; [k]**Ge 18:1**; Dt 22:15; 25:7; Jos 20:4; Ru 4:11; 2Sa 15:2; 2Ki 15:35; Ps 127:5; Pr 31:23; Jer 26:10; 36:10
11 [l]2Sa 24:23
15 [m]Eze 45:12
16 [n]2Sa 24:24; Jer 32:9; Zec 11:12; [o]2Sa 14:26
17 [p]**ver 9**; [q]**Ge 13:18**
18 [r]Ge 12:7; [s]ver 10; [t]**Ge 18:1**
19 [u]**ver 9**; [v]**Ge 13:18**; Jos 14:13; 1Ch 29:27; [w]Ge 49:31
20 [x]Jer 32:10; [y]**Ge 10:15**; 35:29; 47:30; 49:30; 50:5,13

Ch. 24

1 [a]**Ge 17:17**; Jos 23:1; [b]Ge 12:2; Gal 3:9; [c]ver 35
2 [d]**Ge 15:3**; [e]Ge 39:4–6; [f]ver 9; Ge 47:29
3 [g]Ge 47:31; 50:25; [h]ver 7; [i]**Ge 14:19**; **Nu 20:14**; [j]Dt 7:3; 2Co 6:14–17; [k]**Ge 10:15–19**; [l]ver 37
4 [m]**Ge 12:1**; Jdg 14:3; [n]**ver 29**; **Ge 21:21**
5 [o]ver 39; [p]Heb 11:15
6 [q]ver 8
7 [r]ver 3; [s]Ge 12:1; [t]Ro 4:13; Gal 3:16*; [u]**Ge 12:7**; [v]**Ge 16:7**
8 [w]ver 41; Jos 2:12,17,20; 9:20; [x]**ver 6**
9 [y]**ver 2**; [z]Ge 32:4; 33:8
10 [a]ver 19; 1Ki 10:2; 1Ch 12:40; Isa 30:6; [b]ver 22, 30,47,53; Ge 43:11; 45:23; [c]Nu 23:7; Dt 23:4; Jdg 3:8; [d]**Ge 11:29**
11 [e]Ex 2:15; [f]ver 13; Ge 29:2, 9–10; Ex 2:16; 1Sa 9:11; Jn 4:7
12 [g]ver 27,42,48; Ge 26:24; 28:13; 31:42,53; 32:9; 43:23; 46:3; Ex 3:6,15–16; 4:5; 1Ki 18:36; Ps 75:9; 94:7; [h]ver 21,40,51,56; Ge 27:20; Ne 1:11; [i]**Ge 19:19**; Jos 2:12; Job 10:12
13 [j]**ver 11**,43; Ge 29:8
14 [k]ver 18,46; [l]ver 19; [m]ver 44; [n]Jos 2:12; Jdg 6:17,37; 1Sa 14:10; 1Ki 13:3; Ps 86:17; Isa 38:7; Jer 44:29
15 [o]ver 45; [p]**Ge 22:23**; [q]**Ge 22:22**; [r]**Ge 11:29**; [s]**Ge 11:29**
16 [t]**Ge 12:11**; [u]Dt 22:15–21
17 [v]ver 45; 1Ki 17:10; Jn 4:7
18 [w]**ver 14**

b11 Or *sell*
c15 That is, about 10 pounds (about 4.5 kilograms)
a2 Or *oldest* b7 Or *seed*
c10 That is, North-west Mesopotamia

quickly lowered the jar to her hands and
gave him a drink.
19After she had given him a drink, she
said, "I'll draw water for your camels[x]
too,[y] until they have finished drinking."
20So she quickly emptied her jar into the
trough, ran back to the well to draw
more water, and drew enough for all his
camels.[z] 21Without saying a word, the
man watched her closely to learn
whether or not the LORD had made his
journey successful.[a]
22When the camels had finished
drinking, the man took out a gold nose
ring[b] weighing a beka[d] and two gold
bracelets[c] weighing ten shekels.[e] 23Then
he asked, "Whose daughter are you?[d]
Please tell me, is there room in your
father's house for us to spend the
night?[e]"
24She answered him, "I am the
daughter of Bethuel, the son that Milcah
bore to Nahor.[f]" 25And she added, "We
have plenty of straw and fodder,[g] as
well as room for you to spend the
night."
26Then the man bowed down and
worshipped the LORD,[h] 27saying,
"Praise be to the LORD,[i] the God of my
master Abraham,[j] who has not aban-
doned his kindness and faithfulness[k] to
my master. As for me, the LORD has led
me on the journey[l] to the house of my
master's relatives."[m]
28The girl ran and told her mother's
household about these things.[n] 29Now
Rebekah had a brother named Laban,[o]
and he hurried out to the man at the
spring. 30As soon as he had seen the
nose ring, and the bracelets on his sis-
ter's arms,[p] and had heard Rebekah tell
what the man said to her, he went out to
the man and found him standing by the
camels near the spring. 31"Come, you
who are blessed by the LORD,"[q] he said.
"Why are you standing out here? I have
prepared the house and a place for the
camels."
32So the man went to the house, and
the camels were unloaded. Straw and
fodder[r] were brought for the camels,
and water for him and his men to wash
their feet.[s] 33Then food was set before
him, but he said, "I will not eat until I
have told you what I have to say."
"Then tell us," ⌊Laban⌋ said.
34So he said, "I am Abraham's ser-
vant.[t] 35The LORD has blessed[u] my mas-
ter abundantly,[v] and he has become
wealthy.[w] He has given him sheep and
cattle, silver and gold, menservants and
maidservants, and camels and donk-
eys.[x] 36My master's wife Sarah has
borne him a son in her[f] old age,[y] and he
has given him everything he owns.[z]
37And my master made me swear an
oath,[a] and said, 'You must not get a wife
for my son from the daughters of the
Canaanites, in whose land I live,[b] 38but
go to my father's family and to my own
clan, and get a wife for my son.'[c]
39"Then I asked my master, 'What if
the woman will not come back with
me?'[d]
40"He replied, 'The LORD, before
whom I have walked,[e] will send his
angel with you[f] and make your journey
a success,[g] so that you can get a wife for
my son from my own clan and from my
father's family.[h] 41Then, when you go to
my clan, you will be released from my
oath even if they refuse to give her to
you—you will be released from my
oath.'[i]
42"When I came to the spring today, I
said, 'O LORD, God of my master Abra-
ham, if you will, please grant success[j] to
the journey on which I have come.
43See, I am standing beside this spring;[k]
if a maiden[l] comes out to draw water
and I say to her, "Please let me drink a
little water from your jar,"[m] 44and if she
says to me, "Drink, and I'll draw water
for your camels too," let her be the one
the LORD has chosen for my master's
son.'[n]
45"Before I finished praying in my
heart,[o] Rebekah came out, with her jar
on her shoulder.[p] She went down to the
spring and drew water, and I said to
her, 'Please give me a drink.'[q]
46"She quickly lowered her jar from
her shoulder and said, 'Drink, and I'll
water your camels too.'[r] So I drank, and
she watered the camels also.[s]
47"I asked her, 'Whose daughter are
you?'[t]
"She said, 'The daughter of Bethuel[u]
son of Nahor, whom Milcah bore to
him.'[v]
"Then I put the ring in her nose[w] and
the bracelets on her arms,[x] 48and I
bowed down and worshipped the
LORD.[y] I praised the LORD, the God
of my master Abraham,[z] who had led
me on the right road to get the grand-
daughter of my master's brother for his
son.[a] 49Now if you will show kindness
and faithfulness[b] to my master, tell me;
and if not, tell me, so I may know which
way to turn."
50Laban and Bethuel[c] answered,

19 [x]ver 10; [y]ver 14
20 [z]ver 46
21 [a]**ver 12**
22 [b]ver 47; Ge 41:42; Isa 3:21; Eze 16:11–12; [c]**ver 10**
23 [d]ver 47; [e]Jdg 19:15; 20:4
24 [f]ver 29,47; **Ge 11:29**
25 [g]ver 32; Jdg 19:19
26 [h]ver 48,52; Ex 4:31; 12:27; 1Ch 29:20; 2Ch 20:18
27 [i]Ge 14:20; Ex 18:10; Ru 4:14; 1Sa 25:32; 2Sa 18:28; 1Ki 1:48; 8:56; Ps 28:6; 41:13; 68:19; 106:48; Lk 1:68; [j]**ver 12**; [k]ver 49; Ge 32:10; 47:29; Jos 2:14; Ps 98:3; [l]ver 21; [m]**ver 12**,48; **Ge 12:1**
28 [n]Ge 29:12
29 [o]ver 4; Ge 25:20; 27:43; 28:2,5; 29:5, 12–13
30 [p]**ver 10**; Eze 23:42
31 [q]Ge 26:29; Ps 115:15
32 [r]**ver 25**; [s]**Ge 18:4**
34 [t]**Ge 15:3**
35 [u]**Ge 12:2**; [v]ver 1; [w]**Ge 23:6**; [x]**Ge 12:16**
36 [y]**Ge 17:17**; [z]Ge 25:5; 26:14
37 [a]Ge 50:5,25; [b]ver 3
38 [c]**Ge 21:21**
39 [d]**ver 5**
40 [e]**Ge 5:22**; [f]**Ge 16:7**; [g]**ver 12**; [h]**Ge 12:1**
41 [i]**ver 8**
42 [j]**ver 12**
43 [k]**ver 13**; [l]Pr 30:19; Isa 7:14; [m]**ver 14**
44 [n]ver 14
45 [o]1Sa 1:13; [p]ver 15; [q]**ver 17**; Jn 4:7
46 [r]ver 18–19; [s]ver 20
47 [t]ver 23; [u]**Ge 22:22**; [v]**ver 24**; [w]**ver 22**; [x]**ver 10**; Isa 3:19; Eze 16:11–12
48 [y]**ver 26**; [z]**ver 12**; [a]**ver 27**
49 [b]**ver 27**
50 [c]Ge 22:22

[d]22 That is, about 1/5 ounce (about 6 grams)
[e]22 That is, about 4 ounces (about 115 grams)
[f]36 Or *his*

"This is from the LORD;[d] we can say nothing to you one way or the other.[e] 51Here is Rebekah; take her and go, and let her become the wife of your master's son, as the LORD has directed.[f]"

52When Abraham's servant heard what they said, he bowed down to the ground before the LORD.[g] 53Then the servant brought out gold and silver jewellery and articles of clothing[h] and gave them to Rebekah; he also gave costly gifts[i] to her brother and to her mother. 54Then he and the men who were with him ate and drank and spent the night there.

When they got up the next morning, he said, "Send me on my way[j] to my master."

55But her brother and her mother replied, "Let the girl remain with us ten days or so;[k] then you[g] may go."

56But he said to them, "Do not detain me, now that the LORD has granted success[l] to my journey. Send me on my way[m] so I may go to my master."

57Then they said, "Let's call the girl and ask her about it."[n] 58So they called Rebekah and asked her, "Will you go with this man?"

"I will go,"[o] she said.

59So they sent their sister Rebekah on her way,[p] along with her nurse[q] and Abraham's servant and his men. 60And they blessed[r] Rebekah and said to her,

"Our sister, may you increase
to thousands upon thousands;[s]
may your offspring possess
the gates of their enemies."[t]

61Then Rebekah and her maids[u] got ready and mounted their camels and went back with the man. So the servant took Rebekah and left.

62Now Isaac had come from Beer Lahai Roi,[v] for he was living in the Negev.[w] 63He went out to the field one evening to meditate,[h][x] and as he looked up,[y] he saw camels approaching. 64Rebekah also looked up and saw Isaac. She got down from her camel[z] 65and asked the servant, "Who is that man in the field coming to meet us?"

"He is my master," the servant answered. So she took her veil[a] and covered herself.

66Then the servant told Isaac all he had done. 67Isaac brought her into the tent[b] of his mother Sarah,[c] and he married Rebekah.[d] So she became his wife, and he loved her;[e] and Isaac was comforted after his mother's death.[f]

50 [d] Ps 118:23; [e] Ge 31:7,24,29,42; 48:16
51 [f] **ver 12**
52 [g] **ver 26**
53 [h] Ge 45:22; Ex 3:22; 12:35; 2Ki 5:5; [i] **ver 10**
54 [j] ver 56,59; Ge 30:25
55 [k] Jdg 19:4
56 [l] **ver 12**; [m] **ver 54**
57 [n] Jdg 19:3
58 [o] Ru 1:16
59 [p] **ver 54**; [q] Ge 35:8
60 [r] Ge 27:4,19; 28:1; 31:55; 48:9,15,20; Jos 22:6; [s] **Ge 17:16**; [t] Ge 22:17; Ps 127:5; Pr 27:11
61 [u] **Ge 16:1**; 30:3; 46:25
62 [v] **Ge 16:14**; [w] **Ge 12:9**
63 [x] Jos 1:8; Ps 1:2; 77:12; 119:15,27,48,97,148; 143:5; 145:5; [y] Ge 18:2
64 [z] Ge 31:17,34; 1Sa 30:17
65 [a] Ge 38:14; SS 1:7; 4:1,3; 6:7; Isa 47:2
67 [b] Ge 31:33; [c] **Ge 18:9**; [d] Ge 25:20; 49:31; [e] Ge 29:18,20; 34:3; Jdg 16:4; [f] Ge 23:1–2

Ch. 25

2 [a] Jer 25:25; [b] Ge 36:35; 37:28,36; Ex 2:15; Nu 22:4; 25:6,18; 31:2; Jos 13:21; Jdg 6:1,3; 7:1; 8:1, 22,24; 9:17; 1Ki 11:18; Ps 83:9; Isa 9:4; 10:26; 60:6; Hab 3:7; [c] Job 2:11; 8:1
3 [d] **Ge 10:7**; [e] **Ge 10:7**
4 [f] Isa 60:6
5 [g] **Ge 24:36**
6 [h] **Ge 22:24**; [i] **Ge 21:10**; [j] Ge 29:1; Jdg 6:3, 33; 1Ki 4:30; Job 1:3; Eze 25:4
7 [k] ver 26; Ge 12:4; 35:28; 47:9,28; 50:22,26; Job 42:16
8 [l] **Ge 15:15**; [m] ver 17; Ge 35:29; 49:29, 33; Nu 20:24; 31:2; Dt 31:14; 32:50; 34:5

The Death of Abraham

25:1–4pp—1Ch 1:32–33

25 Abraham took[a] another wife, whose name was Keturah. 2She bore him Zimran,[a] Jokshan, Medan, Midian,[b] Ishbak and Shuah.[c] 3Jokshan was the father of Sheba[d] and Dedan;[e] the descendants of Dedan were the Asshurites, the Letushites and the Leummites. 4The sons of Midian were Ephah,[f] Epher, Hanoch, Abida and Eldaah. All these were descendants of Keturah.

5Abraham left everything he owned to Isaac.[g] 6But while he was still living, he gave gifts to the sons of his concubines[h] and sent them away from his son Isaac[i] to the land of the east.[j]

7Altogether, Abraham lived a hundred and seventy-five years.[k] 8Then Abraham breathed his last and died at a good old age,[l] an old man and full of years; and he was gathered to his people.[m] 9His sons Isaac and Ishmael buried him[n] in the cave of Machpelah[o] near Mamre,[p] in the field of Ephron[q] son of Zohar the Hittite,[r] 10the field Abraham had bought from the Hittites.[b][s] There Abraham was buried with his wife Sarah. 11After Abraham's death, God blessed his son Isaac,[t] who then lived near Beer Lahai Roi.[u]

Ishmael's Sons

25:12–16pp—1Ch 1:29–31

12This is the account[v] of Abraham's son Ishmael, whom Sarah's maidservant, Hagar[w] the Egyptian, bore to Abraham.[x]

13These are the names of the sons of Ishmael, listed in the order of their birth: Nebaioth[y] the firstborn of Ishmael, Kedar,[z] Adbeel, Mibsam, 14Mishma, Dumah,[a] Massa, 15Hadad, Tema,[b] Jetur,[c] Naphish and Kedemah. 16These were the sons of Ishmael, and these are the names of the twelve tribal rulers[d] according to their settlements and camps.[e] 17Altogether, Ishmael lived

9 [n] Ge 35:29; 47:30; 49:31; [o] **Ge 23:9**; [p] **Ge 13:18**; [q] Ge 23:8; [r] Ge 49:29; 50:13 **10** [s] **Ge 10:15**
11 [t] **Ge 12:2**; [u] **Ge 16:14**
12 [v] **Ge 2:4**; [w] **Ge 16:1**; [x] **Ge 17:20**; 21:18
13 [y] Ge 28:9; 36:3; [z] Ps 120:5; SS 1:5; Isa 21:16; 42:11; 60:7; Jer 2:10; 49:28; Eze 27:21
14 [a] Jos 15:52; Isa 21:11; Ob 1
15 [b] Job 6:19; Isa 21:14; Jer 25:23; [c] 1Ch 5:19
16 [d] Ge 17:20; [e] **Ge 13:16**; Ps 83:6

g55 Or *she*
h63 The meaning of the Hebrew for this word is uncertain. a1 Or *had taken*
b10 Or *the sons of Heth*

a hundred and thirty-seven years. He breathed his last and died, and he was gathered to his people.[f] 18His descendants[g] settled in the area from Havilah to Shur,[h] near the border of Egypt, as you go towards Asshur. And they lived in hostility towards[c] all their brothers.[i]

Jacob and Esau

19This is the account[j] of Abraham's son Isaac.

Abraham became the father of Isaac, 20and Isaac was forty years old[k] when he married Rebekah[l] daughter of Bethuel[m] the Aramean from Paddan Aram[d][n] and sister of Laban[o] the Aramean.[p]

21Isaac prayed to the LORD on behalf of his wife, because she was barren.[q] The LORD answered his prayer,[r] and his wife Rebekah became pregnant. 22The babies jostled each other within her, and she said, "Why is this happening to me?" So she went to enquire of the LORD.[s]

23The LORD said to her,

"Two nations[t] are in your womb,
  and two peoples from within you
    will be separated;
one people will be stronger than the
    other,
  and the older will serve the
    younger.[u]"

24When the time came for her to give birth,[v] there were twin boys in her womb.[w] 25The first to come out was red,[x] and his whole body was like a hairy garment;[y] so they named him Esau.[e][z] 26After this, his brother came out,[a] with his hand grasping Esau's heel;[b] so he was named Jacob.[f][c] Isaac was sixty years old[d] when Rebekah gave birth to them.

27The boys grew up, and Esau became a skilful hunter,[e] a man of the open country,[f] while Jacob was a quiet man, staying among the tents. 28Isaac, who had a taste for wild game,[g] loved Esau, but Rebekah loved Jacob.[h]

29Once when Jacob was cooking some stew,[i] Esau came in from the open country,[j] famished. 30He said to Jacob, "Quick, let me have some of that red stew![k] I'm famished!" (That is why he was also called Edom.[g])[l]

31Jacob replied, "First sell me your birthright.[m]"

32"Look, I am about to die," Esau said. "What good is the birthright to me?"

33But Jacob said, "Swear[n] to me first." So he swore an oath to him, selling his birthright[o] to Jacob.

34Then Jacob gave Esau some bread and some lentil stew.[p] He ate and drank, and then got up and left.

So Esau despised his birthright.

Isaac and Abimelech

26:1–11Ref—Ge 12:10–20; 20:1–18

26 Now there was a famine in the land[a]—besides the earlier famine of Abraham's time—and Isaac went to Abimelech king of the Philistines[b] in Gerar.[c] 2The LORD appeared[d] to Isaac and said, "Do not go down to Egypt;[e] live in the land where I tell you to live.[f] 3Stay in this land for a while,[g] and I will be with you[h] and will bless you.[i] For to you and your descendants I will give all these lands[j] and will confirm the oath I swore to your father Abraham.[k] 4I will make your descendants[l] as numerous as the stars in the sky[m] and will give them all these lands,[n] and through your offspring[a] all nations on earth will be blessed,[o] 5because Abraham obeyed me[p] and kept my requirements, my commands, my decrees[q] and my laws.[r]" 6So Isaac stayed in Gerar.[s]

7When the men of that place asked him about his wife, he said, "She is my sister,[t]" because he was afraid to say, "She is my wife." He thought, "The men of this place might kill me on account of Rebekah, because she is beautiful."

8When Isaac had been there a long time, Abimelech king of the Philistines[u] looked down from a window and saw Isaac caressing his wife Rebekah. 9So Abimelech summoned Isaac and said, "She is really your wife! Why did you say, 'She is my sister'?[v]"

Isaac answered him, "Because I thought I might lose my life on account of her."

17 [f]ver 8
18 [g]**Ge 17:20;** 21:18; [h]**Ge 16:7;** [i]Ge 16:12
19 [j]**Ge 2:4**
20 [k]ver 26; Ge 26:34; 35:28; [l]**Ge 24:67;** [m]**Ge 22:22;** [n]Ge 28:2,5–6; 30:20; 31:18; 33:18; 35:9,26; 46:15; 48:7; [o]**Ge 24:29;** [p]Ge 31:20,24; Dt 26:5
21 [q]**Ge 11:30;** [r]Ge 30:17,22; 1Sa 1:17,23; 1Ch 5:20; 2Ch 33:13; Ezr 8:23; Ps 127:3
22 [s]Ex 18:15; 28:30; 33:7; Lev 24:12; Nu 9:6–8; 27:5,21; Dt 17:9; Jdg 18:5; 1Sa 9:9; 10:22; 14:36; 22:10; 1Ki 22:8; 2Ki 3:11; 22:13; Isa 30:2; Jer 21:2; 37:7, 17; Eze 14:7; 20:1,3
23 [t]**Ge 17:4;** [u]**Ge 9:25;** 48:14,19; Ro 9:11–12*
24 [v]Lk 1:57; 2:6; [w]Ge 38:27
25 [x]1Sa 16:12; [y]Ge 27:11; [z]Ge 27:1,15
26 [a]Ge 38:29; [b]Hos 12:3; [c]Ge 27:36; 32:27; Dt 23:7; Jos 24:4; Ob 10,12; [d]**ver 7,20**
27 [e]**Ge 10:9;** [f]ver 29; Ge 27:3,5
28 [g]Ge 27:3–4,9, 14,19; [h]Ge 27:6; 37:3
29 [i]2Ki 4:38–40; [j]**ver 27**
30 [k]ver 34; [l]Ge 32:3; 36:1,8–9, 19; Nu 20:14; Dt 23:7; Ps 137:7; Jer 25:21; 40:11; 49:7
31 [m]Dt 21:16–17; 1Ch 5:1–2
33 [n]**Ge 21:23; 47:31;** [o]Ge 27:36; Heb 12:16
34 [p]ver 30

Ch. 26

1 [a]**Ge 12:10; Dt 32:24;** [b]**Ge 10:14;** Jdg 10:6; [c]**Ge 20:1**
2 [d]**Ge 12:7;** [e]Ge 46:3; [f]**Ge 12:1**
3 [g]Ge 20:1; [h]**Ge 21:20;** 27:45; 31:3,5; 32:9; 35:3; 48:21; Ex 3:12; 33:14–16; Nu 23:21; Dt 31:23; Jos 1:5; Isa 43:2; Jer 1:8,19; Hag 1:13; [i]ver 12; **Ge 12:2;** [j]**Ge 12:7;** Ac 7:5; [k]**Ge 17:19**
4 [l]ver 24; Ge 48:4; [m]**Ge 12:2; Nu 10:36;** [n]**Ge 12:7;** [o]**Ge 12:3;** Ac 3:25*; Gal 3:8
5 [p]**Ge 18:19;** [q]Ps 119:80,112; Eze 18:21; [r]Lev 18:4–5,26; 19:19,37; 20:8,22; 25:18; 26:3; Nu 15:40; Dt 4:40; 6:2; 11:1; 1Ki 2:3 *6* [s]**Ge 20:1** *7* [t]**Ge 12:13**
8 [u]**Ge 10:14** *9* [v]**Ge 12:19**

[c]18 Or *lived to the east of*
[d]20 That is, North-west Mesopotamia
[e]25 *Esau* may mean *hairy*; he was also called Edom, which means *red*.
[f]26 *Jacob* means *he grasps the heel* (figuratively, *he deceives*). [g]30 *Edom* means *red*.
[a]4 Or *seed*

10Then Abimelech said, "What is this you have done to us?[w] One of the men might well have slept with your wife, and you would have brought guilt upon us."

11So Abimelech gave orders to all the people: "Anyone who molests[x] this man or his wife shall surely be put to death."[y]

12Isaac planted crops in that land and the same year reaped a hundredfold,[z] because the LORD blessed him.[a] 13The man became rich, and his wealth continued to grow until he became very wealthy.[b] 14He had so many flocks and herds and servants[c] that the Philistines envied him.[d] 15So all the wells[e] that his father's servants had dug in the time of his father Abraham, the Philistines stopped up,[f] filling them with earth.

16Then Abimelech said to Isaac, "Move away from us;[g] you have become too powerful for us.[h]"

17So Isaac moved away from there and encamped in the Valley of Gerar[i] and settled there. 18Isaac reopened the wells[j] that had been dug in the time of his father Abraham, which the Philistines had stopped up after Abraham died, and he gave them the same names his father had given them.

19Isaac's servants dug in the valley and discovered a well of fresh water there. 20But the herdsmen of Gerar quarrelled[k] with Isaac's herdsmen and said, "The water is ours!"[l] So he named the well Esek,[b] because they disputed with him. 21Then they dug another well, but they quarrelled[m] over that one also; so he named it Sitnah.[c] 22He moved on from there and dug another well, and no-one quarrelled over it. He named it Rehoboth,[d][n] saying, "Now the LORD has given us room[o] and we will flourish[p] in the land."

23From there he went up to Beersheba.[q] 24That night the LORD appeared to him and said, "I am the God of your father Abraham.[r] Do not be afraid,[s] for I am with you;[t] I will bless you and will increase the number of your descendants[u] for the sake of my servant Abraham."[v]

25Isaac built an altar[w] there and called on the name of the LORD.[x] There he pitched his tent, and there his servants dug a well.[y]

26Meanwhile, Abimelech had come to him from Gerar, with Ahuzzath his personal adviser and Phicol the commander of his forces.[z] 27Isaac asked them, "Why have you come to me, since you were hostile to me and sent me away?[a]"

28They answered, "We saw clearly that the LORD was with you;[b] so we said, 'There ought to be a sworn agreement between us'—between us and you. Let us make a treaty[c] with you 29that you will do us no harm,[d] just as we did not molest you but always treated you well and sent you away in peace. And now you are blessed by the LORD."[e]

30Isaac then made a feast[f] for them, and they ate and drank. 31Early the next morning the men swore an oath[g] to each other. Then Isaac sent them on their way, and they left him in peace.

32That day Isaac's servants came and told him about the well[h] they had dug. They said, "We've found water!" 33He called it Shibah,[e] and to this day the name of the town has been Beersheba.[f][i]

34When Esau was forty years old,[j] he married Judith daughter of Beeri the Hittite, and also Basemath daughter of Elon the Hittite.[k] 35They were a source of grief to Isaac and Rebekah.[l]

Jacob Gets Isaac's Blessing

27 When Isaac was old and his eyes were so weak that he could no longer see,[a] he called for Esau his older son[b] and said to him, "My son."

"Here I am," he answered.

2Isaac said, "I am now an old man and don't know the day of my death.[c] 3Now then, get your weapons—your quiver and bow—and go out to the open country[d] to hunt some wild game for me. 4Prepare me the kind of tasty food I like[e] and bring it to me to eat, so that I may give you my blessing[f] before I die."[g]

5Now Rebekah was listening as Isaac spoke to his son Esau. When Esau left for the open country[h] to hunt game and bring it back, 6Rebekah said to her son Jacob,[i] "Look, I overheard your father say to your brother Esau, 7'Bring me some game and prepare me some tasty food to eat, so that I may give you my blessing in the presence of the LORD before I die.'[j] 8Now, my son, listen carefully and do what I tell you:[k] 9Go out to the flock and bring me two choice young goats,[l] so that I can prepare some tasty food for your father, just the way he likes it.[m] 10Then take it to your father

10 [w]**Ge 12:18**
11 [x]1Sa 24:6; 26:9; Ps 105:15; [y]**Ge 20:3**
12 [z]Mt 13:8; [a]**ver 3**
13 [b]**Ge 13:2; Dt 8:18**
14 [c]**Ge 12:16; 24:36**; 32:23; [d]Ge 37:11
15 [e]**Ge 21:30**; [f]**Ge 21:25**
16 [g]ver 27; Jdg 11:7; [h]Ex 1:9; Ps 105:24–25
17 [i]**Ge 20:1**
18 [j]**Ge 21:30**
20 [k]**Ge 13:7**; [l]Ge 21:25
21 [m]**Ge 13:7**
22 [n]Ge 36:37; [o]Ps 18:19; Isa 33:20; 54:2; Am 9:11; [p]**Ge 17:6**
23 [q]**Ge 22:19**
24 [r]**Ge 24:12**; [s]**Ge 15:1; Jos 8:1**; [t]**Ge 21:20**; [u]**ver 4**; [v]ver 4; Ge 17:7; **22:17**; 28:14; 30:27; 39:5; Dt 13:17
25 [w]**Ge 8:20**; [x]**Ge 4:26; Ac 2:21**; [y]**Ge 21:30**
26 [z]**Ge 21:22**
27 [a]**ver 16**
28 [b]**Ge 21:22**; [c]**Ge 21:27**; Jos 9:6
29 [d]Ge 31:29,52; [e]**Ge 24:31**
30 [f]Ge 31:54; Ex 18:12; 24:11; 1Sa 20:27
31 [g]**Ge 21:23,27**
32 [h]**Ge 21:30**
33 [i]**Ge 21:14**
34 [j]**Ge 25:20**; [k]**Ge 10:15**; 28:9; 36:2; Jos 3:10; 1Sa 26:6; 1Ki 10:29
35 [l]Ge 27:46; 28:8; Job 7:16

Ch. 27

1 [a]Ge 48:10; Dt 34:7; 1Sa 3:2; [b]**Ge 25:25**
2 [c]Ge 47:29; 1Ki 2:1
3 [d]**Ge 25:27**
4 [e]**Ge 25:28**; [f]ver 10,25,31; **Ge 24:60**; 49:28; Dt 33:1; Heb 11:20; [g]ver 7
5 [h]**Ge 25:27**
6 [i]**Ge 25:28**
7 [j]ver 4
8 [k]ver 13,43
9 [l]1Sa 16:20; [m]**Ge 25:28**

b20 *Esek* means *dispute.*
c21 *Sitnah* means *opposition.*
d22 *Rehoboth* means *room.*
e33 *Shibah* can mean *oath* or *seven.*
f33 *Beersheba* can mean *well of the oath* or *well of seven.*

to eat, so that he may give you his blessing[n] before he dies."

11Jacob said to Rebekah his mother, "But my brother Esau is a hairy man,[o] and I'm a man with smooth skin. 12What if my father touches me?[p] I would appear to be tricking him and would bring down a curse[q] on myself rather than a blessing."

13His mother said to him, "My son, let the curse fall on me.[r] Just do what I say;[s] go and get them for me."

14So he went and got them and brought them to his mother, and she prepared some tasty food, just the way his father liked it.[t] 15Then Rebekah took the best clothes[u] of Esau her older son,[v] which she had in the house, and put them on her younger son Jacob. 16She also covered his hands and the smooth part of his neck with the goatskins.[w] 17Then she handed to her son Jacob the tasty food and the bread she had made.

18He went to his father and said, "My father."

"Yes, my son," he answered. "Who is it?"[x]

19Jacob said to his father, "I am Esau your firstborn.[y] I have done as you told me. Please sit up and eat some of my game[z] so that you may give me your blessing."[a]

20Isaac asked his son, "How did you find it so quickly, my son?"

"The LORD your God gave me success,[b]" he replied.

21Then Isaac said to Jacob, "Come near so I can touch you,[c] my son, to know whether you really are my son Esau or not."

22Jacob went close to his father Isaac,[d] who touched[e] him and said, "The voice is the voice of Jacob, but the hands are the hands of Esau." 23He did not recognise him, for his hands were hairy like those of his brother Esau;[f] so he blessed him. 24"Are you really my son Esau?" he asked.

"I am," he replied.

25Then he said, "My son, bring me some of your game to eat, so that I may give you my blessing."[g]

Jacob brought it to him and he ate; and he brought some wine and he drank. 26Then his father Isaac said to him, "Come here, my son, and kiss me."

27So he went to him and kissed[h] him.[i] When Isaac caught the smell of his clothes,[j] he blessed him and said,

"Ah, the smell of my son
is like the smell of a field
that the LORD has blessed.[k]
28May God give you of heaven's dew[l]
and of earth's richness[m]—
an abundance of grain[n] and new
wine.[o]
29May nations serve you
and peoples bow down to you.[p]
Be lord over your brothers,
and may the sons of your mother
bow down to you.[q]
May those who curse you be cursed
and those who bless you be
blessed."[r]

30After Isaac finished blessing him and Jacob had scarcely left his father's presence, his brother Esau came in from hunting. 31He too prepared some tasty food and brought it to his father. Then he said to him, "My father, sit up and eat some of my game, so that you may give me your blessing."[s]

32His father Isaac asked him, "Who are you?"[t]

"I am your son," he answered, "your firstborn, Esau."[u]

33Isaac trembled violently and said, "Who was it, then, that hunted game and brought it to me?[v] I ate it just before you came and I blessed him—and indeed he will be blessed!"[w]

34When Esau heard his father's words, he burst out with a loud and bitter cry[x] and said to his father, "Bless[y] me—me too, my father!"

35But he said, "Your brother came deceitfully[z] and took your blessing."[a]

36Esau said, "Isn't he rightly named Jacob?[a][b] He has deceived[c] me these two times: He took my birthright,[d] and now he's taken my blessing!"[e] Then he asked, "Haven't you reserved any blessing for me?"

37Isaac answered Esau, "I have made him lord over you and have made all his relatives his servants, and I have sustained him with grain and new wine.[f] So what can I possibly do for you, my son?"

38Esau said to his father, "Do you have only one blessing, my father? Bless me too, my father!" Then Esau wept aloud.[g]

39His father Isaac answered him,[h]

"Your dwelling will be
away from the earth's richness,

10 [n]**ver 4**
11 [o]Ge 25:25
12 [p]ver 22; [q]**Ge 9:25**
13 [r]Mt 27:25; [s]**ver 8**
14 [t]**Ge 25:28**
15 [u]ver 27; SS 4:11; [v]**Ge 25:25**
16 [w]ver 22–23
18 [x]ver 32
19 [y]ver 32; [z]**Ge 25:28;** [a]**ver 4**
20 [b]**Ge 24:12**
21 [c]ver 12
22 [d]Ge 45:4; [e]ver 12
23 [f]ver 16
25 [g]**ver 4**
27 [h]Ge 31:28,55; 33:4; 48:10; Ex 4:27; 18:7; Ru 1:9; 1Sa 20:41; 2Sa 14:33; 19:39; [i]Heb 11:20; [j]**ver 15;** [k]Ps 65:9–13
28 [l]Dt 33:13; 2Sa 1:21; Job 18:16; 29:19; Pr 3:20; Isa 26:19; Hos 14:5; Hag 1:10; Zec 8:12; [m]ver 39; Ge 49:25; Lev 26:20; Dt 33:13; [n]Ps 65:9; 72:16; [o]ver 37; Nu 18:12; Dt 7:13; 33:28; 2Ki 18:32; Ps 4:7; Isa 36:17; Jer 31:12; 40:10
29 [p]2Sa 8:14; Ps 68:31; 72:11; Isa 19:21,23; 27:13; 45:14, 23; 49:7,23; 60:12,14; 66:23; Jer 12:17; Da 2:44; Zec 14:17–18; [q]**Ge 9:25; 25:23; 37:7;** [r]ver 33; Ge 12:3
31 [s]**ver 4**
32 [t]ver 18; [u]ver 19
33 [v]ver 35; [w]**ver 29**
34 [x]Heb 12:17; [y]Ex 12:32
35 [z]Jer 9:4; 12:6; [a]ver 19,45
36 [b]**Ge 25:26;** [c]Ge 29:25; 31:20,26; 34:13; 1Sa 28:12; [d]**Ge 25:33;** [e]Heb 12:16–17
37 [f]**ver 28;** Dt 16:13; Ezr 6:9; Isa 16:10; Jer 40:12
38 [g]Ge 29:11; Nu 14:1; Jdg 2:4; 21:2; Ru 1:9; 1Sa 11:4; 30:4; Heb 12:17 **39** [h]Heb 11:20

[a]36 *Jacob* means *he grasps the heel* (figuratively, *he deceives*).

away from the dew[i] of heaven
above.[j]
40You will live by the sword
and you will serve[k] your brother.[l]
But when you grow restless,
you will throw his yoke
from off your neck."[m]

Jacob Flees to Laban

41Esau held a grudge[n] against Jacob[o] because of the blessing his father had given him. He said to himself, "The days of mourning[p] for my father are near; then I will kill[q] my brother Jacob."[r]

42When Rebekah was told what her older son Esau[s] had said, she sent for her younger son Jacob and said to him, "Your brother Esau is consoling himself with the thought of killing you.[t] 43Now then, my son, do what I say:[u] Flee at once to my brother Laban[v] in Haran.[w] 44Stay with him for a while[x] until your brother's fury subsides. 45When your brother is no longer angry with you and forgets what you did to him,[y] I'll send word for you to come back from there.[z] Why should I lose both of you in one day?"

46Then Rebekah said to Isaac, "I'm disgusted with living because of these Hittite[a] women. If Jacob takes a wife from among the women of this land,[b] from Hittite women like these, my life will not be worth living."[c]

28 So Isaac called for Jacob and blessed[a][a] him and commanded him: "Do not marry a Canaanite woman.[b] 2Go at once to Paddan Aram,[b][c] to the house of your mother's father Bethuel.[d] Take a wife for yourself there, from among the daughters of Laban, your mother's brother.[e] 3May God Almighty[c][f] bless[g] you and make you fruitful[h] and increase your numbers[i] until you become a community of peoples. 4May he give you and your descendants the blessing given to Abraham,[j] so that you may take possession of the land[k] where you now live as an alien,[l] the land God gave to Abraham." 5Then Isaac sent Jacob on his way,[m] and he went to Paddan Aram,[n] to Laban son of Bethuel the Aramean,[o] the brother of Rebekah,[p] who was the mother of Jacob and Esau.

6Now Esau learned that Isaac had blessed Jacob and had sent him to Paddan Aram to take a wife from there, and that when he blessed him he commanded him, "Do not marry a Canaanite woman,"[q] 7and that Jacob had obeyed his father and mother and had gone to Paddan Aram. 8Esau then realised how displeasing the Canaanite women[r] were to his father Isaac;[s] 9so he went to Ishmael[t] and married Mahalath, the sister of Nebaioth[u] and daughter of Ishmael son of Abraham, in addition to the wives he already had.[v]

Jacob's Dream at Bethel

10Jacob left Beersheba[w] and set out for Haran.[x] 11When he reached a certain place,[y] he stopped for the night because the sun had set. Taking one of the stones there, he put it under his head[z] and lay down to sleep. 12He had a dream[a] in which he saw a stairway[d] resting on the earth, with its top reaching to heaven, and the angels of God were ascending and descending on it.[b] 13There above it[e] stood the LORD,[c] and he said: "I am the LORD, the God of your father Abraham and the God of Isaac.[d] I will give you and your descendants the land[e] on which you are lying.[f] 14Your descendants will be like the dust of the earth, and you[g] will spread out to the west and to the east, to the north and to the south.[h] All peoples on earth will be blessed through you and your offspring.[i] 15I am with you[j] and will watch over you[k][l] wherever you go,[m] and I will bring you back to this land.[n] I will not leave you[o] until I have done what I have promised you."[p][q]

16When Jacob awoke from his sleep,[r] he thought, "Surely the LORD is in this place, and I was not aware of it." 17He was afraid and said, "How awesome is this place![s] This is none other than the house of God;[t] this is the gate of heaven."

18Early the next morning Jacob took the stone he had placed under his head[u] and set it up as a pillar[v] and poured oil on top of it.[w] 19He called that place Bethel,[f][x] though the city used to be called Luz.[y]

39 [i]ver 28; [j]Ge 36:6
40 [k]2Sa 8:14; [l]**Ge 9:25;** [m]2Ki 8:20–22
41 [n]Ge 37:4; 49:23; 50:15; 1Sa 17:28; [o]Ge 31:17; 32:11; Hos 10:14; [p]Ge 50:4,10; Nu 20:29; [q]ver 42; [r]Ob 10
42 [s]Ge 32:3,11; 33:4; [t]ver 41
43 [u]**ver 8;** [v]Ge 24:29; [w]**Ge 11:31**
44 [x]Ge 31:38,41
45 [y]ver 35; [z]Ge 26:3
46 [a]**Ge 10:15;** [b]**Ge 10:15–19;** [c]Ge 26:35; **Job 7:7**

Ch. 28

1 [a]Ge 24:60; [b]Ge 24:3
2 [c]Ge 25:20; [d]Ge 25:20; [e]**Ge 21:21; 24:29**
3 [f]**Ge 17:1;** [g]Ge 48:16; Nu 6:24; Ru 2:4; Ps 129:8; 134:3; Jer 31:23; [h]**Ge 17:6;** [i]**Ge 12:2**
4 [j]**Ge 12:2,3;** [k]**Ge 15:7;** [l]**Ge 17:8**
5 [m]**Ge 11:31;** [n]Hos 12:12; [o]Ge 25:20; [p]Ge 24:29
6 [q]**ver 1**
8 [r]**Ge 10:15–19;** [s]Ge 26:35
9 [t]Ge 16:15; [u]Ge 25:13; [v]Ge 26:34
10 [w]Ge 21:14; [x]Ge 11:31
11 [y]**Ge 12:8;** [z]ver 18
12 [a]Ge 20:3; 37:19; [b]Jn 1:51
13 [c]**Ge 12:7;** 35:7,9; 48:3; [d]**Ge 24:12;** 48:16; 49:25; 50:17; [e]**Ge 12:7;** [f]Ge 46:4; 48:21
14 [g]Ge 26:4; [h]**Ge 12:2; 13:14; 26:24;** [i]**Ge 12:3;** Ac 3:25; Gal 3:8
15 [j]**Ge 21:20;** [k]Ps 121:5,7–8; [l]ver 20; [m]ver 22; Ge 35:3; [n]ver 21; **Ge 15:16;** 30:25; 31:30; [o]Dt 31:6,8; Jos 1:5; Ne 4:14; Ps 9:10; [p]Lev 26:42; [q]Ps 105:10
16 [r]1Ki 3:15; Jer 31:26
17 [s]Ex 3:5; 19:21; Jos 5:15; Ps 68:24,35; [t]ver 22; Ge 32:2; 1Ch 22:1; 2Ch 3:1
18 [u]ver 11; [v]ver 22; Ge 31:13,45,51; 35:14; Ex 24:4; Jos 24:26–27; Isa 19:19; [w]Lev 8:11; Jos 4:9
19 [x]**Ge 12:8;** [y]Ge 35:6; 48:3; Jos 16:2; 18:13; Jdg 1:23,26

[a]1 Or *greeted*
[b]2 That is, North-west Mesopotamia; also in verses 5, 6 and 7
[c]3 Hebrew *El-Shaddai*
[d]12 Or *ladder*
[e]13 Or *There beside him*
[f]19 *Bethel* means *house of God*.

20 Then Jacob made a vow,[z] saying, "If God will be with me and will watch over me[a] on this journey I am taking and will give me food to eat and clothes to wear[b] 21 so that I return safely[c] to my father's house,[d] then the LORD[g] will be my God[e] 22 and[h] this stone that I have set up as a pillar[f] will be God's house,[g] and of all that you give me I will give you a tenth.[h]"

Jacob Arrives in Paddan Aram

29 Then Jacob continued on his journey and came to the land of the eastern peoples.[a] 2 There he saw a well in the field, with three flocks of sheep lying near it because the flocks were watered from that well.[b] The stone[c] over the mouth of the well was large. 3 When all the flocks were gathered there, the shepherds would roll the stone[d] away from the well's mouth and water the sheep.[e] Then they would return the stone to its place over the mouth of the well.

4 Jacob asked the shepherds, "My brothers, where are you from?"[f]

"We're from Haran,[g]" they replied.

5 He said to them, "Do you know Laban, Nahor's grandson?"[h]

"Yes, we know him," they answered.

6 Then Jacob asked them, "Is he well?"

"Yes, he is," they said, "and here comes his daughter Rachel[i] with the sheep.[j]"

7 "Look," he said, "the sun is still high; it is not time for the flocks to be gathered. Water the sheep and take them back to pasture."

8 "We can't," they replied, "until all the flocks are gathered and the stone[k] has been rolled away from the mouth of the well. Then we will water[l] the sheep."

9 While he was still talking with them, Rachel came with her father's sheep,[m] for she was a shepherdess. 10 When Jacob saw Rachel[n] daughter of Laban, his mother's brother, and Laban's sheep, he went over and rolled the stone[o] away from the mouth of the well and watered[p] his uncle's sheep.[q] 11 Then Jacob kissed[r] Rachel and began to weep aloud.[s] 12 He had told Rachel that he was a relative[t] of her father and a son of Rebekah.[u] So she ran and told her father.[v]

13 As soon as Laban[w] heard the news about Jacob, his sister's son, he hurried to meet him. He embraced him[x] and kissed him and brought him to his home, and there Jacob told him all these things. 14 Then Laban said to him, "You are my own flesh and blood."[y]

Jacob Marries Leah and Rachel

After Jacob had stayed with him for a whole month, 15 Laban said to him, "Just because you are a relative[z] of mine, should you work for me for nothing? Tell me what your wages[a] should be."

16 Now Laban had two daughters; the name of the older was Leah,[b] and the name of the younger was Rachel.[c] 17 Leah had weak[a] eyes, but Rachel[d] was lovely in form, and beautiful.[e] 18 Jacob was in love with Rachel[f] and said, "I'll work for you seven years in return for your younger daughter Rachel."[g]

19 Laban said, "It's better that I give her to you than to some other man. Stay here with me." 20 So Jacob served seven years to get Rachel,[h] but they seemed like only a few days to him because of his love for her.[i]

21 Then Jacob said to Laban, "Give me my wife. My time is completed, and I want to lie with her.[j]"

22 So Laban brought together all the people of the place and gave a feast.[k] 23 But when evening came, he took his daughter Leah[l] and gave her to Jacob, and Jacob lay with her. 24 And Laban gave his servant girl Zilpah[m] to his daughter as her maidservant.[n]

25 When morning came, there was Leah! So Jacob said to Laban, "What is this you have done to me?[o] I served you for Rachel, didn't I? Why have you deceived me?[p]"

26 Laban replied, "It is not our custom here to give the younger daughter in marriage before the older one.[q] 27 Finish this daughter's bridal week;[r] then we will give you the younger one also, in return for another seven years of work.[s]"

28 And Jacob did so. He finished the week with Leah, and then Laban gave him his daughter Rachel to be his wife.[t] 29 Laban gave his servant girl Bilhah[u] to his daughter Rachel as her maidservant.[v] 30 Jacob lay with Rachel also, and he loved Rachel more than Leah.[w] And he worked for Laban another seven years.[x]

20 [z]Ge 31:13; Lev 7:16; 22:18; 23:38; 27:2,9; Nu 6:2; 15:3; Dt 12:6; Jdg 11:30; 1Sa 1:21; 2Sa 15:8; [a]**ver 15;** [b]1Ti 6:8
21 [c]Jdg 11:31; [d]**ver 15;** [e]Ex 15:2; Dt 26:17; Jos 24:18; Ps 48:14; 118:28
22 [f]**ver 18;** 1Sa 7:12; [g]**ver 17;** [h]**Ge 14:20; Nu 18:21;** Lk 18:12

Ch. 29

1 [a]**Ge 25:6**
2 [b]**Ge 24:11;** [c]ver 3,8,10
3 [d]**ver 2;** [e]ver 8
4 [f]Ge 42:7; Jdg 19:17; [g]**Ge 11:31**
5 [h]**Ge 11:29**
6 [i]Ge 30:22–24; 35:16; 46:19, 22; [j]Ex 2:16
8 [k]**ver 2;** [l]**Ge 24:13**
9 [m]Ex 2:16
10 [n]ver 16; [o]**ver 2;** [p]**Ge 24:11;** [q]ver 3; Ex 2:17
11 [r]ver 13; [s]Ge 33:4; 42:24; 43:30; 45:2, 14–15; 46:29; 50:1,17; Ru 1:9
12 [t]ver 15; [u]**Ge 24:29;** [v]Ge 24:28
13 [w]**Ge 24:29;** [x]Ge 33:4; 45:14–15; 48:10; Ex 4:27; 18:7; Lk 15:20
14 [y]Ge 2:23; 37:27; Jdg 9:2; 2Sa 5:1; 19:12–13; 20:1; Ne 5:5; Isa 58:7
15 [z]ver 12; [a]Ge 30:28,32; 31:7,41
16 [b]ver 17,23, 28,30; Ge 30:9; 35:23; 47:30; 49:31; Ru 4:11; [c]ver 9–10
17 [d]**ver 16;** [e]**Ge 12:11**
18 [f]**Ge 24:67;** [g]ver 20,27,30; Ge 30:26; Hos 12:12
20 [h]**ver 18;** Ge 31:15; [i]SS 8:7; Hos 12:12
21 [j]Jdg 15:1
22 [k]Jdg 14:10; Isa 25:6; Jn 2:1–2
23 [l]**ver 16**
24 [m]Ge 30:9; [n]**Ge 16:1**
25 [o]**Ge 12:18;** [p]**Ge 27:36**
26 [q]Jdg 15:2; 1Sa 14:49; 18:17,20; 2Sa 6:23
27 [r]Jdg 14:12; [s]**ver 18;** Ge 31:41
28 [t]**ver 16; Ge 4:19**
29 [u]Ge 30:3; 35:22; 49:4; Dt 22:30; 1Ch 5:1; [v]**Ge 16:1**
30 [w]**ver 16;** [x]**ver 20**

[g]20,21 Or *Since God . . . father's house, the* LORD
[h]21,22 Or *house, and the* LORD *will be my God,* [22]*then*
[a]17 Or *delicate*

Jacob's Children

31 When the LORD saw that Leah was not loved,[y] he opened her womb,[z] but Rachel was barren. 32 Leah became pregnant and gave birth to a son.[a] She named him Reuben,[b][b] for she said, "It is because the LORD has seen my misery.[c] Surely my husband will love me now."

33 She conceived again, and when she gave birth to a son she said, "Because the LORD heard that I am not loved,[d] he gave me this one too." So she named him Simeon.[c][e]

34 Again she conceived, and when she gave birth to a son she said, "Now at last my husband will become attached to me,[f] because I have borne him three sons." So he was named Levi.[d][g]

35 She conceived again, and when she gave birth to a son she said, "This time I will praise the LORD." So she named him Judah.[e][h] Then she stopped having children.[i]

30 When Rachel saw that she was not bearing Jacob any children,[a] she became jealous of her sister.[b] So she said to Jacob, "Give me children, or I'll die!"

2 Jacob became angry with her and said, "Am I in the place of God,[c] who has kept you from having children?"[d]

3 Then she said, "Here is Bilhah,[e] my maidservant.[f] Sleep with her so that she can bear children for me and that through her I too can build a family."[g]

4 So she gave him her servant Bilhah as a wife.[h] Jacob slept with her,[i] 5 and she became pregnant and bore him a son. 6 Then Rachel said, "God has vindicated me;[j] he has listened to my plea and given me a son."[k] Because of this she named him Dan.[a][l]

7 Rachel's servant Bilhah[m] conceived again and bore Jacob a second son. 8 Then Rachel said, "I have had a great struggle with my sister, and I have won."[n] So she named him Naphtali.[b][o]

9 When Leah[p] saw that she had stopped having children,[q] she took her maidservant Zilpah[r] and gave her to Jacob as a wife.[s] 10 Leah's servant Zilpah[t] bore Jacob a son. 11 Then Leah said, "What good fortune!"[c] So she named him Gad.[d][u]

12 Leah's servant Zilpah bore Jacob a second son. 13 Then Leah said, "How happy I am! The women will call me[v] happy."[w] So she named him Asher.[e][x]

14 During wheat harvest,[y] Reuben went out into the fields and found some mandrake plants,[z] which he brought to his mother Leah. Rachel said to Leah, "Please give me some of your son's mandrakes."

15 But she said to her, "Wasn't it enough[a] that you took away my husband? Will you take my son's mandrakes too?"

"Very well," Rachel said, "he can sleep with you tonight in return for your son's mandrakes."[b]

16 So when Jacob came in from the fields that evening, Leah went out to meet him. "You must sleep with me," she said. "I have hired you with my son's mandrakes."[c] So he slept with her that night.

17 God listened to Leah,[d] and she became pregnant and bore Jacob a fifth son. 18 Then Leah said, "God has rewarded me for giving my maidservant to my husband."[e] So she named him Issachar.[f][f]

19 Leah conceived again and bore Jacob a sixth son. 20 Then Leah said, "God has presented me with a precious gift. This time my husband will treat me with honour,[g] because I have borne him six sons." So she named him Zebulun.[g][h]

21 Some time later she gave birth to a daughter and named her Dinah.[i]

22 Then God remembered Rachel;[j] he listened to her[k] and opened her womb.[l] 23 She became pregnant and gave birth to a son[m] and said, "God has taken away my disgrace."[n] 24 She named him

31 [y]ver 33; Dt 21:15–17; [z]**Ge 11:30; 16:2**; Ru 4:13; 1Sa 1:19; Ps 127:3
32 [a]Ge 30:23; Ru 4:13; 1Sa 1:20; [b]Ge 37:21; 46:8; 48:5,14; 49:3; Ex 6:14; Nu 1:5,20; 26:5; Dt 33:6; Jos 4:12; 1Ch 5:1,3; [c]**Ge 16:11**
33 [d]**ver 31**; [e]Ge 34:25; 46:10; 48:5; 49:5; Ex 6:15; Nu 1:6,22; 34:20; 1Ch 4:24; Eze 48:24
34 [f]Ge 30:20; 1Sa 1:2–4; [g]Ge 34:25; 46:11; 49:5–7; Ex 2:1; 6:16,19; Nu 1:47; 3:17–20; 26:57; Dt 33:8; 1Ch 6:1,16; 23:6–24, 13–14
35 [h]Ge 35:23; 37:26; 38:1; 43:8; 44:14,18; 46:12; 49:8; 1Ch 2:3; 4:1; Isa 48:1; Mt 1:2–3; [i]Ge 30:9

Ch. 30

1 [a]**Ge 11:30**; Isa 49:21; 54:1; [b]**Ge 16:4**; Lev 18:18
2 [c]Ge 50:19; Dt 32:35; 2Ki 5:7; [d]**Ge 16:2**
3 [e]ver 7; **Ge 29:29**; [f]**Ge 24:61**; [g]Ge 16:2
4 [h]ver 9,18; [i]Ge 16:3–4
6 [j]Ps 35:24; 43:1; [k]ver 23; Ge 21:2; Ru 4:13; 1Sa 1:20; [l]Ge 46:23; 49:16–17; Nu 26:42–43; Jos 19:40–48; Jdg 1:34; 13:2; 18:2; Jer 4:15; 8:16; Eze 48:1
7 [m]**ver 3**
8 [n]Ge 32:28; Hos 12:3–4; [o]Ge 35:25; 46:24; 49:21; Nu 1:42; 26:48; Dt 33:23; Jdg 4:6; 5:18; 1Ch 7:13
9 [p]**Ge 29:16**; [q]Ge 29:35; [r]Ge 29:24; [s]**ver 4**
10 [t]Ge 46:18
11 [u]Ge 35:26; 46:16; 49:19; Ex 1:4; Nu 1:24; 26:18; Jos 4:12; 1Ch 5:11; 12:8; Jer 49:1
13 [v]Ps 127:3; [w]Ru 4:14; Ps 127:4–5; Lk 1:48; [x]Ge 35:26; 46:17; 49:20; Nu 1:40; 26:47; Dt 33:24; Jos 19:24–31; 1Ch 7:30–31
14 [y]Ex 34:22; Jdg 15:1; Ru 2:23; 1Sa 6:13; 12:17; [z]ver 15–16; SS 7:13
15 [a]Nu 16:9,13; Isa 7:13; Eze 34:18; [b]Ge 38:16; Eze 16:33; Hos 9:1
16 [c]**ver 14**
17 [d]**Ge 25:21**
18 [e]**ver 4**; [f]Ge 46:13; 49:14; Nu 1:8,28–29; 26:25; Dt 27:12; 33:18; Jos 17:10; 19:17; 21:6,28; Jdg 5:15; 10:1; 1Ch 7:1
20 [g]**Ge 29:34**; 1Pe 3:7; [h]Ge 35:23; 46:14; 49:13; Nu 1:30; 26:27; 34:25; Dt 33:18; Jdg 5:18
21 [i]Ge 34:1; 46:15
22 [j]**Ge 8:1**; [k]**Ge 25:21**; [l]**Ge 11:30**
23 [m]**ver 6; Ge 29:32**; [n]Isa 4:1; 25:8; 45:17; 54:4; Lk 1:25

b32 *Reuben* sounds like the Hebrew for *he has seen my misery;* the name means *see, a son.*
c33 *Simeon* probably means *one who hears.*
d34 *Levi* sounds like and may be derived from the Hebrew for *attached.*
e35 *Judah* sounds like and may be derived from the Hebrew for *praise.*
a6 *Dan* here means *he has vindicated.*
b8 *Naphtali* means *my struggle.*
c11 Or *"A troop is coming!"*
d11 *Gad* can mean *good fortune* or *a troop.*
e13 *Asher* means *happy.*
f18 *Issachar* sounds like the Hebrew for *reward.*
g20 *Zebulun* probably means *honour.*

Joseph,[h][o] and said, "May the LORD add to me another son."[p]

Jacob's Flocks Increase

25After Rachel gave birth to Joseph, Jacob said to Laban, "Send me on my way[q] so that I can go back to my own homeland.[r] 26Give me my wives and children, for whom I have served you,[s] and I will be on my way. You know how much work I've done for you."

27But Laban said to him, "If I have found favour in your eyes,[t] please stay. I have learned by divination[u] that[i] the LORD has blessed me because of you."[v] 28He added, "Name your wages,[w] and I will pay them."

29Jacob said to him, "You know how I have worked for you[x] and how your livestock has fared under my care.[y] 30The little you had before I came has increased greatly, and the LORD has blessed you wherever I have been.[z] But now, when may I do something for my own household?"[a]

31"What shall I give you?" he asked.

"Don't give me anything," Jacob replied. "But if you will do this one thing for me, I will go on tending your flocks and watching over them: 32Let me go through all your flocks today and remove from them every speckled or spotted sheep, every dark-coloured lamb and every spotted or speckled goat.[b] They will be my wages.[c] 33And my honesty will testify for me in the future, whenever you check on the wages you have paid me. Any goat in my possession that is not speckled or spotted, or any lamb that is not dark-coloured,[d] will be considered stolen."[e]

34"Agreed," said Laban. "Let it be as you have said." 35That same day he removed all the male goats that were streaked or spotted, and all the speckled or spotted female goats (all that had white on them) and all the dark-coloured lambs,[f] and he placed them in the care of his sons.[g] 36Then he put a three-day journey[h] between himself and Jacob, while Jacob continued to tend the rest of Laban's flocks.

37Jacob, however, took fresh-cut branches from poplar, almond[i] and plane trees[j] and made white stripes on them by peeling the bark and exposing the white inner wood of the branches.[k] 38Then he placed the peeled branches[l] in all the watering troughs,[m] so that they would be directly in front of the flocks when they came to drink. When the flocks were in heat[n] and came to drink, 39they mated in front of the branches.[o] And they bore young that were streaked or speckled or spotted.[p] 40Jacob set apart the young of the flock by themselves, but made the rest face the streaked and dark-coloured animals[q] that belonged to Laban. Thus he made separate flocks for himself and did not put them with Laban's animals. 41Whenever the stronger females were in heat,[r] Jacob would place the branches in the troughs in front of the animals so that they would mate near the branches,[s] 42but if the animals were weak, he would not place them there. So the weak animals went to Laban and the strong ones to Jacob.[t] 43In this way the man grew exceedingly prosperous and came to own large flocks, and maidservants and menservants, and camels and donkeys.[u]

Jacob Flees From Laban

31 Jacob heard that Laban's sons[a] were saying, "Jacob has taken everything our father owned and has gained all this wealth from what belonged to our father."[b] 2And Jacob noticed that Laban's attitude towards him was not what it had been.[c]

3Then the LORD said to Jacob, "Go back[d] to the land of your fathers and to your relatives, and I will be with you."[e]

4So Jacob sent word to Rachel and Leah to come out to the fields where his flocks were. 5He said to them, "I see that your father's[f] attitude towards me is not what it was before,[g] but the God of my father has been with me.[h] 6You know that I've worked for your father with all my strength,[i] 7yet your father has cheated[j] me by changing my wages[k] ten times.[l] However, God has not allowed him to harm me.[m] 8If he said, 'The speckled ones will be your wages,' then all the flocks gave birth to speckled young; and if he said, 'The streaked ones will be your wages,'[n] then all the flocks bore streaked young. 9So God has taken away your father's livestock[o] and has given them to me.[p]

10"In the breeding season I once had a dream[q] in which I looked up and saw that the male goats mating with the flock were streaked, speckled or spotted. 11The angel of God[r] said to me in the dream,[s] 'Jacob.' I answered, 'Here I am.'[t] 12And he said, 'Look up and see that all the male goats mating with the

24 [o]**Ge 29:6**; 32:22; 33:2,7; 35:24; 37:2; 39:1; 49:22–26; Dt 33:13; [p]Ge 35:17; 1Sa 4:20
25 [q]**Ge 24:54**; [r]**Ge 28:15**
26 [s]**Ge 29:18**
27 [t]Ge 33:10; 50:4; Est 2:15; [u]Ge 44:5,15; Lev 19:26; Nu 22:7; 23:23; 24:1; Jos 13:22; 2Ki 17:17; Jer 27:9; [v]ver 30; **Ge 26:24**; 31:38; Dt 28:11; 2Sa 6:11
28 [w]**Ge 29:15**
29 [x]Ge 31:6; [y]Ge 31:38–40
30 [z]**ver 27**; [a]1Ti 5:8
32 [b]ver 33,35, 39–40; Ge 31:8,12; [c]**Ge 29:15**
33 [d]**ver 32**; [e]Ge 31:39
35 [f]**ver 32**; [g]Ge 31:1
36 [h]Ge 31:22; Ex 3:18; 5:3; 8:27
37 [i]Jer 1:11; [j]Eze 31:8; [k]ver 38,41
38 [l]**ver 37**; [m]Ex 2:16; [n]ver 41; Jer 2:24
39 [o]ver 41; [p]**ver 32**
40 [q]**ver 32**
41 [r]**ver 38**; [s]**ver 37**
42 [t]Ge 31:1,9, 16,43
43 [u]**Ge 12:16**

Ch. 31

1 [a]Ge 30:35; [b]**Ge 30:42**
2 [c]ver 5
3 [d]ver 13; Ge 32:9; Dt 30:3; Isa 10:21; 35:10; Jer 30:3; 42:12; [e]**Ge 21:22; 26:3**
5 [f]ver 29,42,53; Ge 43:23; Da 2:23; [g]ver 2; [h]**Ge 21:22; 26:3**
6 [i]Ge 30:29
7 [j]Lev 6:2; Am 8:5; [k]**Ge 29:15**; [l]ver 41; Nu 14:22; Job 19:3; [m]ver 52; **Ge 24:50**
8 [n]**Ge 30:32**
9 [o]Job 39:2; Eze 31:6; [p]**Ge 30:42**
10 [q]**Ge 20:3**
11 [r]**Ge 16:7**; [s]**Ge 20:3**; [t]**Ge 22:1; Ex 3:4**

h24 *Joseph* means *may he add.*
i27 Or possibly *have become rich and*

flock are streaked, speckled or spotted,[u]
for I have seen all that Laban has been
doing to you.[v] 13I am the God of Bethel,[w]
where you anointed a pillar[x] and where
you made a vow[y] to me. Now leave this
land at once and go back to your native
land.[z]' "

14Then Rachel and Leah replied, "Do
we still have any share[a] in the inherit-
ance of our father's estate? 15Does he
not regard us as foreigners?[b] Not only
has he sold us, but he has used up what
was paid for us.[c] 16Surely all the wealth
that God took away from our father
belongs to us and our children.[d] So do
whatever God has told you."

17Then Jacob put his children and his
wives[e] on camels,[f] 18and he drove all his
livestock ahead of him, along with all
the goods he had accumulated[g] in Pad-
dan Aram,[a][h] to go to his father Isaac[i] in
the land of Canaan.[j]

19When Laban had gone to shear
his sheep,[k] Rachel stole her father's
household gods.[l] 20Moreover, Jacob
deceived[m] Laban the Aramean[n] by not
telling him he was running away.[o]
21So he fled[p] with all he had, and cross-
ing the River,[b][q] he headed for the hill
country of Gilead.[r]

Laban Pursues Jacob

22On the third day[s] Laban was told
that Jacob had fled.[t] 23Taking his rel-
atives[u] with him[v], he pursued Jacob for
seven days and caught up with him in
the hill country of Gilead.[w] 24Then God
came to Laban the Aramean[x] in a dream
at night and said to him,[y] "Be careful not
to say anything to Jacob, either good or
bad."[z]

25Jacob had pitched his tent in the hill
country of Gilead[a] when Laban over-
took him, and Laban and his relatives
camped there too. 26Then Laban said to
Jacob, "What have you done?[b] You've
deceived me,[c] and you've carried off my
daughters like captives in war.[d] 27Why
did you run off secretly and deceive me?
Why didn't you tell me,[e] so that I could
send you away with joy and singing to
the music of tambourines[f] and harps?[g]
28You didn't even let me kiss my grand-
children and my daughters good-bye.[h]
You have done a foolish thing. 29I have
the power to harm you;[i] but last night
the God of your father[j] said to me, 'Be
careful not to say anything to Jacob,
either good or bad.'[k] 30Now you have
gone off because you longed to return to
your father's house.[l] But why did you
steal[m] my gods?"[n]

31Jacob answered Laban, "I was
afraid, because I thought you would
take your daughters away from me by
force.[o] 32But if you find anyone who has
your gods, he shall not live.[p] In the
presence of our relatives, see for your-
self whether there is anything of yours
here with me; and if so, take it." Now
Jacob did not know that Rachel had
stolen the gods.[q]

33So Laban went into Jacob's tent and
into Leah's tent[r] and into the tent of
the two maidservants,[s] but he found
nothing.[t] After he came out of Leah's
tent, he entered Rachel's tent. 34Now
Rachel had taken the household gods[u]
and put them inside her camel's saddle[v]
and was sitting on them. Laban
searched[w] through everything in the
tent but found nothing.

35Rachel said to her father, "Don't be
angry, my lord, that I cannot stand up
in your presence;[x] I'm having my
period.[y]" So he searched but could not
find the household gods.[z]

36Jacob was angry and took Laban to
task. "What is my crime?" he asked
Laban. "What sin have I committed[a]
that you hunt me down?[b] 37Now that
you have searched through all my
goods, what have you found that be-
longs to your household?[c] Put it here
in front of your relatives[d] and mine, and
let them judge between the two of us.[e]

38"I have been with you for twenty
years now.[f] Your sheep and goats have
not miscarried,[g] nor have I eaten rams
from your flocks. 39I did not bring you
animals torn by wild beasts; I bore the
loss myself. And you demanded pay-
ment from me for whatever was stolen[h]
by day or night.[i] 40This was my situa-
tion: The heat consumed me in the day-
time and the cold at night, and sleep
fled from my eyes.[j] 41It was like this for
the twenty years[k] I was in your house-
hold. I worked for you fourteen years
for your two daughters[l] and six years for
your flocks,[m] and you changed my
wages[n] ten times.[o] 42If the God of my
father,[p] the God of Abraham[q] and the
Fear of Isaac,[r] had not been with me,[s]

12 [u]**Ge 30:32;** [v]Ex 3:7
13 [w]Ge 28:10–22; [x]**Ge 28:18;** [y]**Ge 28:20;** [z]**ver 3**
14 [a]2Sa 20:1; 1Ki 12:16
15 [b]Dt 15:3; 23:20; Ru 2:10; 2Sa 15:19; 1Ki 8:41; Ob 11; [c]**Ge 29:20**
16 [d]**Ge 30:42**
17 [e]**Ge 27:41;** [f]**Ge 24:63–64**
18 [g]**Ge 12:5;** [h]**Ge 25:20;** [i]Ge 35:27; [j]**Ge 10:19**
19 [k]Ge 38:12–13; 1Sa 25:2,4,7; 2Sa 13:23; [l]ver 30,32, 34–35; Ge 35:2; Jos 24:14; Jdg 17:5; 18:14, 17,24,30; 1Sa 7:3; 19:13; 2Ki 23:24; Hos 3:4
20 [m]**Ge 27:36;** [n]**Ge 25:20;** [o]ver 27
21 [p]ver 22; Ex 2:15; 14:5; 1Ki 18:46; 19:3; Jer 26:21; [q]**Ge 2:14;** [r]ver 23, 25; Ge 37:25; Nu 26:30; 32:1; Dt 3:10; Jos 12:2; Jer 22:6
22 [s]**Ge 30:36;** [t]**ver 21**
23 [u]ver 37; [v]Ex 14:9; [w]**ver 21**
24 [x]**Ge 25:20;** [y]**Ge 20:3;** [z]**Ge 24:50**
25 [a]**ver 21**
26 [b]**Ge 12:18;** [c]**Ge 27:36;** [d]Ge 34:29; 1Sa 30:2–3
27 [e]ver 20; [f]Ex 15:20; Jdg 11:34; 1Sa 10:5; 2Sa 6:5; Ps 68:25; Isa 24:8; Jer 31:4; [g]**Ge 4:21**
28 [h]**Ge 27:27;** Ru 1:14; Ac 20:37
29 [i]**ver 7; Ge 26:29;** [j]**ver 5;** [k]**Ge 24:50**
30 [l]**Ge 28:15;** Job 29:2; [m]Ge 44:8; [n]**ver 19**
31 [o]**Ge 20:11**
32 [p]Ge 44:9; [q]**ver 19**
33 [r]Ge 24:67; [s]**Ge 16:1;** [t]ver 37
34 [u]**ver 19;** [v]**Ge 24:63–64;** [w]ver 37; Ge 44:12
35 [x]Ex 20:12; Lev 19:3,32; Dt 21:18; 27:16; Jer 35:18; [y]Lev 15:19–23; [z]ver 19
36 [a]1Sa 19:5; 20:32; [b]1Sa 23:23; 24:11
37 [c]ver 33; [d]ver 23; [e]Dt 1:16; 16:18
38 [f]**Ge 27:44;** [g]**Ge 30:27**
39 [h]Ge 30:33; [i]Ex 22:13
40 [j]Ps 132:4; 2Co 11:27
41 [k]**Ge 27:44;** [l]Ge 29:30; [m]**Ge 30:32;** [n]**Ge 29:15;** [o]**ver 7**
42 [p]**ver 5; Ex 3:15;** [q]**Ge 24:12;** [r]ver 53; Ge 46:1; [s]**Ge 21:22;** Ps 124:1–2

[a]*18* That is, North-west Mesopotamia
[b]*21* That is, the Euphrates

you would surely have sent me away empty-handed. But God has seen my hardship and the toil of my hands,[t] and last night he rebuked you."[u]"

43Laban answered Jacob, "The women are my daughters, the children are my children, and the flocks are my flocks.[v] All you see is mine. Yet what can I do today about these daughters of mine, or about the children they have borne? 44Come now, let's make a covenant,[w] you and I, and let it serve as a witness between us."[x]

45So Jacob took a stone and set it up as a pillar.[y] 46He said to his relatives, "Gather some stones." So they took stones and piled them in a heap,[z] and they ate there by the heap. 47Laban called it Jegar Sahadutha,[c] and Jacob called it Galeed.[d][a]

48Laban said, "This heap[b] is a witness between you and me today."[c] That is why it was called Galeed. 49It was also called Mizpah,[e][d] because he said, "May the LORD keep watch between you and me when we are away from each other. 50If you ill-treat[e] my daughters or if you take any wives besides my daughters, even though no-one is with us, remember that God is a witness[f] between you and me."[g]

51Laban also said to Jacob, "Here is this heap,[h] and here is this pillar[i] I have set up between you and me. 52This heap is a witness,[j] and this pillar is a witness, that I will not go past this heap to your side to harm you and that you will not go past this heap[k] and pillar to my side to harm me.[l] 53May the God of Abraham[m] and the God of Nahor,[n] the God of their father, judge between us."[o]

So Jacob took an oath[p] in the name of the Fear of his father Isaac.[q] 54He offered a sacrifice[r] there in the hill country and invited his relatives to a meal.[s] After they had eaten, they spent the night there.

55Early the next morning Laban kissed his grandchildren and his daughters[t] and blessed[u] them. Then he left and returned home.[v]

Jacob Prepares to Meet Esau

32 Jacob also went on his way, and the angels of God[a] met him. 2When Jacob saw them, he said, "This is the camp of God!"[b] So he named that place Mahanaim.[a][c]

3Jacob sent messengers[d] ahead of him to his brother Esau[e] in the land of Seir,[f] the country of Edom.[g] 4He instructed them: "This is what you are to say to my master[h] Esau: 'Your servant[i] Jacob says, I have been staying with Laban[j] and have remained there till now. 5I have cattle and donkeys, sheep and goats, menservants and maidservants.[k] Now I am sending this message to my lord,[l] that I may find favour in your eyes.[m]' "

6When the messengers returned to Jacob, they said, "We went to your brother Esau, and now he is coming to meet you, and four hundred men are with him."[n]

7In great fear[o] and distress[p] Jacob divided the people who were with him into two groups,[b][q] and the flocks and herds and camels as well. 8He thought, "If Esau comes and attacks one group,[c] the group[c] that is left may escape."

9Then Jacob prayed, "O God of my father Abraham,[r] God of my father Isaac,[s] O LORD, who said to me, 'Go back to your country and your relatives, and I will make you prosper,'[t] 10I am unworthy of all the kindness and faithfulness[u] you have shown your servant. I had only my staff[v] when I crossed this Jordan, but now I have become two groups.[w] 11Save me, I pray, from the hand of my brother Esau, for I am afraid[x] he will come and attack me,[y] and also the mothers with their children.[z] 12But you have said, 'I will surely make you prosper and will make your descendants like the sand[a] of the sea, which cannot be counted.[b]' "

13He spent the night there, and from what he had with him he selected a gift[c] for his brother Esau: 14two hundred female goats and twenty male goats, two hundred ewes and twenty rams,[d] 15thirty female camels with their young, forty cows and ten bulls, and twenty female donkeys and ten male donkeys.[e] 16He put them in the care of his servants, each herd by itself, and said to his servants, "Go ahead of me, and keep some space between the herds."[f]

17He instructed the one in the lead: "When my brother Esau meets you and asks, 'To whom do you belong, and where are you going, and who owns all

42 [t]Ge 3:17; [u]Ge 24:50
43 [v]Ge 30:32,42
44 [w]Ge 21:27; [x]Ge 21:30
45 [y]Ge 28:18
46 [z]ver 48,51–52
47 [a]Ge 21:30
48 [b]ver 46; [c]Ge 21:30; Jer 29:23; 42:5
49 [d]Jos 11:3; Jdg 10:17; 11:29
50 [e]Ge 16:6; [f]Dt 31:19; Jos 24:27; Jdg 11:10; 1Sa 12:5; 20:14,23,42; Job 16:19; Jer 29:23; 42:5; Mic 1:2; [g]Ge 21:30; Dt 4:26; Jer 7:11
51 [h]ver 46; [i]Ge 28:18
52 [j]Ge 21:30; [k]ver 46; [l]ver 7; Ge 26:29
53 [m]Ge 24:12; [n]Ge 11:27; [o]Ge 16:5; [p]Ge 21:23,27; [q]ver 42
54 [r]Ge 46:1; Ex 24:5; Lev 3:1; [s]Ge 26:30
55 [t]ver 28; Ru 1:9; [u]Ge 24:60; Ex 39:43; [v]Ge 18:33

Ch. 32

1 [a]Ge 16:11; 2Ki 6:16–17; 1Ch 21:15; Ps 34:7; 35:5; 91:11; Da 6:22
2 [b]Ge 28:17; [c]Jos 13:26,30; 21:38; 2Sa 2:8, 29; 17:24; 19:32; 1Ki 2:8; 4:14; 1Ch 6:80
3 [d]Nu 21:21; Jdg 11:17; [e]Ge 27:41–42; [f]Ge 14:6; Nu 24:18; [g]Ge 25:30; 36:16
4 [h]Ge 24:9; [i]Ge 18:3; [j]Ge 31:41
5 [k]Ge 12:16; [l]Ge 24:9; [m]Ge 33:8,10,15; 34:11; 47:25, 29; 50:4; Ru 2:13
6 [n]Ge 33:1
7 [o]ver 11; [p]Ge 35:3; Ps 4:1; 77:2; 107:6; [q]ver 10; Ge 33:1
9 [r]Ge 24:12; [s]Ge 28:13; [t]Ge 26:3; 31:13
10 [u]Ge 24:27; [v]Ge 38:18; 47:31; Nu 17:2; [w]ver 7
11 [x]ver 7; [y]Ge 43:18; Ps 59:2; [z]Ge 27:41
12 [a]Ge 22:17; 1Ki 4:20,29; [b]Ge 12:2; 13:14; Hos 1:10; Ro 9:27
13 [c]ver 13–15,18,20–21; Ge 33:10; 43:11,15,25–26; 1Sa 16:20; Pr 18:16; 21:14
14 [d]Nu 7:88
15 [e]Ge 13:2; 42:26; 45:23
16 [f]Ge 33:8

c47 The Aramaic *Jegar Sahadutha* means *witness heap.*
d47 The Hebrew *Galeed* means *witness heap.*
e49 *Mizpah* means *watchtower.*
a2 *Mahanaim* means *two camps.*
b7 Or *camps;* also in verse 10
c8 Or *camp*

these animals in front of you?' 18then
you are to say, 'They belong to your
servant[g] Jacob. They are a gift[h] sent to
my lord Esau, and he is coming behind
us.'"
19He also instructed the second, the
third and all the others who followed
the herds: "You are to say the same
thing to Esau when you meet him.
20And be sure to say, 'Your servant[i]
Jacob is coming behind us.'" For he
thought, "I will pacify him with these
gifts[j] I am sending on ahead;[k] later,
when I see him, perhaps he will receive
me."[l] 21So Jacob's gifts[m] went on ahead
of him, but he himself spent the night in
the camp.

Jacob Wrestles with God

22That night Jacob got up and took his
two wives, his two maidservants and
his eleven sons[n] and crossed the ford of
the Jabbok.[o] 23After he had sent them
across the stream, he sent over all his
possessions.[p] 24So Jacob was left alone,[q]
and a man[r] wrestled with him till day-
break. 25When the man saw that he
could not overpower him, he touched
the socket of Jacob's hip[s] so that his hip
was wrenched as he wrestled with the
man. 26Then the man said, "Let me go,
for it is daybreak."
But Jacob replied, "I will not let you
go unless you bless me."[t]
27The man asked him, "What is your
name?"
"Jacob,"[u] he answered.
28Then the man said, "Your name[v]
will no longer be Jacob, but Israel,[d][w]
because you have struggled with God
and with men and have overcome."[x]
29Jacob said, "Please tell me your
name."[y]
But he replied, "Why do you ask my
name?"[z] Then he blessed[a] him there.
30So Jacob called the place Peniel,[e]
saying, "It is because I saw God face to
face,[b] and yet my life was spared."
31The sun rose above him as he
passed Peniel,[f][c] and he was limping
because of his hip. 32Therefore to this
day the Israelites do not eat the tendon
attached to the socket of the hip,[d]
because the socket of Jacob's hip was
touched near the tendon.

Jacob Meets Esau

33 Jacob looked up and there was
Esau, coming with his four
hundred men;[a] so he divided the chil-
dren among Leah, Rachel and the two
maidservants.[b] 2He put the maid-
servants and their children[c] in front,
Leah and her children next, and Rachel
and Joseph[d] in the rear. 3He himself
went on ahead and bowed down to the
ground[e] seven times[f] as he approached
his brother.
4But Esau[g] ran to meet Jacob and
embraced him; he threw his arms
around his neck and kissed him.[h] And
they wept.[i] 5Then Esau looked up and
saw the women and children. "Who are
these with you?" he asked.
Jacob answered, "They are the
children God has graciously given your
servant.[j]"
6Then the maidservants and their
children[k] approached and bowed
down.[l] 7Next, Leah and her children[m]
came and bowed down.[n] Last of all
came Joseph and Rachel,[o] and they too
bowed down.
8Esau asked, "What do you mean by
all these droves I met?"[p]
"To find favour in your eyes, my
lord,"[q] he said.
9But Esau said, "I already have
plenty,[r] my brother. Keep what you
have for yourself."
10"No, please!" said Jacob. "If I have
found favour in your eyes,[s] accept this
gift[t] from me. For to see your face is like
seeing the face of God,[u] now that you
have received me favourably.[v] 11Please
accept the present[w] that was brought to
you, for God has been gracious to me[x]
and I have all I need."[y] And because
Jacob insisted,[z] Esau accepted it.
12Then Esau said, "Let us be on our
way; I'll accompany you."
13But Jacob said to him, "My lord[a]
knows that the children are tender and
that I must care for the ewes and cows
that are nursing their young.[b] If they are
driven hard just one day, all the animals
will die. 14So let my lord go on ahead of
his servant, while I move along slowly
at the pace of the droves[c] before me and
that of the children, until I come to my
lord in Seir.[d]"
15Esau said, "Then let me leave some
of my men with you."
"But why do that?" Jacob asked. "Just
let me find favour in the eyes of my
lord."[e]
16So that day Esau started on his way
back to Seir.[f] 17Jacob, however, went to
Succoth,[g] where he built a place for him-
self and made shelters for his livestock.
That is why the place is called Succoth.[a]

18 g**Ge 18:3;** h**ver 13**
20 i**Ge 18:3;** j**ver 13**; 1Sa 9:7; 2Ki 8:8; Jer 40:5; k1Sa 25:19; lGe 33:10; Ex 28:38; Lev 1:4; Mal 1:8
21 m**ver 13**
22 n**Ge 30:24;** oNu 21:24; Dt 2:37; 3:16; Jos 12:2
23 p**Ge 26:14**
24 qDa 10:8; r**Ge 18:2**
25 sver 32
26 tHos 12:4
27 u**Ge 25:26**
28 vIsa 1:26; 56:5; 60:14; 62:2,4,12; 65:15; w**Ge 17:5;** x**Ge 30:8**
29 yEx 3:13; 6:3; Jdg 13:17; zJdg 13:18; aGe 25:11; 35:9; 48:3
30 b**Ge 16:13;** 1Co 13:12
31 cJdg 8:9
32 dver 25

Ch. 33

1 a**Ge 32:6;** b**Ge 32:7**
2 cver 6; d**Ge 30:24**
3 ever 6–7; Ge 17:3; 37:7–10; 42:6; 43:26; 44:14; 48:12; 1Sa 20:41; f2Ki 5:10,14
4 g**Ge 27:41–42;** h**Ge 29:11;** Lk 15:20; i**Ge 27:27**
5 jGe 18:3; 48:9; Ps 127:3; Isa 8:18
6 kver 2; l**ver 3**
7 mver 2; n**ver 3;** o**Ge 30:24**
8 pGe 32:14–16; q**Ge 24:9; 32:5**
9 rver 11; **Ge 13:6**
10 s**Ge 30:27; 32:5;** t**Ge 32:13;** u**Ge 16:13;** v**Ge 32:20**
11 w1Sa 25:27; 30:26; xGe 30:43; y**ver 9;** zGe 19:3
13 aver 8; bIsa 40:11; Jer 31:8
14 cEx 12:38; d**Ge 14:6**
15 e**Ge 32:5**
16 f**Ge 14:6**
17 gJos 13:27; Jdg 8:5–6,8, 14–16; 1Ki 7:46; 2Ch 4:17; Ps 60:6; 108:7

d28 *Israel* means *he struggles with God.*
e30 *Peniel* means *face of God.*
f31 Hebrew *Penuel*, a variant of *Peniel*
a17 *Succoth* means *shelters.*

18After Jacob came from Paddan
Aram,[b][h] he arrived safely at the[c] city of
Shechem[i] in Canaan and camped within
sight of the city. 19For a hundred pieces
of silver,[d] he bought from the sons of
Hamor,[j] the father of Shechem,[k] the plot
of ground[l] where he pitched his tent.[m]
20There he set up an altar[n] and called it
El Elohe Israel.[e]

Dinah and the Shechemites

34 Now Dinah,[a] the daughter Leah
had borne to Jacob, went out to
visit the women of the land. 2When
Shechem[b] son of Hamor[c] the Hivite,[d] the
ruler of that area, saw her, he took her
and raped her.[e] 3His heart was drawn
to Dinah[f] daughter of Jacob,[g] and he
loved[h] the girl and spoke tenderly[i] to
her. 4And Shechem said to his father
Hamor, "Get me this girl as my wife."[j]
5When Jacob heard that his daughter
Dinah had been defiled,[k] his sons were
in the fields with his livestock; so he
kept quiet about it until they came
home.
6Then Shechem's father Hamor went
out to talk with Jacob.[l] 7Now Jacob's
sons had come in from the fields as soon
as they heard what had happened.
They were filled with grief[m] and fury,[n]
because Shechem had done a disgrace-
ful thing in[a] Israel[o] by lying with Jacob's
daughter—a thing that should not be
done.[p]
8But Hamor said to them, "My son
Shechem has his heart set on your
daughter. Please give her to him as his
wife.[q] 9Intermarry with us; give us your
daughters and take our daughters for
yourselves.[r] 10You can settle among us;[s]
the land is open to you.[t] Live in it, trade[b]
in it,[u] and acquire property in it.[v]"
11Then Shechem said to Dinah's
father and brothers, "Let me find favour
in your eyes,[w] and I will give you what-
ever you ask. 12Make the price for the
bride[x] and the gift I am to bring as great
as you like, and I'll pay whatever you
ask me. Only give me the girl as my
wife."
13Because their sister Dinah had been
defiled,[y] Jacob's sons replied deceitful-
ly[z] as they spoke to Shechem and his
father Hamor. 14They said to them, "We
can't do such a thing; we can't give our
sister to a man who is not circumcised.[a]
That would be a disgrace to us. 15We will
give our consent to you on one con-
dition[b] only: that you become like us by
circumcising all your males.[c] 16Then we
will give you our daughters and take
your daughters for ourselves.[d] We'll
settle among you and become one
people with you.[e] 17But if you will not
agree to be circumcised, we'll take our
sister[c] and go."
18Their proposal seemed good to
Hamor and his son Shechem. 19The
young man, who was the most hon-
oured[f] of all his father's household, lost
no time in doing what they said, be-
cause he was delighted with Jacob's
daughter.[g] 20So Hamor and his son
Shechem went to the gate of their city[h]
to speak to their fellow townsmen.
21"These men are friendly towards us,"
they said. "Let them live in our land and
trade in it;[i] the land has plenty of room
for them. We can marry their daughters
and they can marry ours.[j] 22But the men
will consent to live with us as one peo-
ple only on the condition that our males
be circumcised,[k] as they themselves are.
23Won't their livestock, their property
and all their other animals become
ours?[l] So let us give our consent to
them, and they will settle among us."[m]
24All the men who went out of the city
gate[n] agreed with Hamor and his son
Shechem, and every male in the city
was circumcised.
25Three days later, while all of them
were still in pain,[o] two of Jacob's sons,
Simeon[p] and Levi,[q] Dinah's brothers,
took their swords[r] and attacked the un-
suspecting city,[s] killing every male.[t]
26They put Hamor and his son Shechem
to the sword[u] and took Dinah[v] from
Shechem's house and left. 27The sons of
Jacob came upon the dead bodies and
looted the city[w] where[d] their sister had
been defiled.[x] 28They seized their flocks
and herds and donkeys[y] and everything
else of theirs in the city and out in the
fields.[z] 29They carried off all their wealth
and all their women and children,[a]
taking as plunder[b] everything in the
houses.[c]
30Then Jacob said to Simeon and Levi,
"You have brought trouble[d] on me by
making me a stench[e] to the Canaanites
and Perizzites, the people living in this
land.[f] We are few in number,[g] and if

18 [h]**Ge 25:20;** [i]**Ge 12:6**
19 [j]Ge 34:2; Jdg 9:28; Ac 7:16; [k]Ge 34:2; Jos 24:32; [l]Ge 34:10,16,21; 47:27; Jn 4:5; [m]**Ge 12:8**
20 [n]**Ge 4:26; 8:20**

Ch. 34

1 [a]**Ge 30:21**
2 [b]**Ge 33:19;** [c]**Ge 33:19;** [d]**Ge 10:17;** [e]Dt 21:14; 2Sa 13:14
3 [f]ver 26; [g]ver 19; [h]**Ge 24:67;** [i]Ge 50:21; Isa 14:1; 40:2
4 [j]**Ge 21:21**
5 [k]ver 2,13,27; Ge 35:22; 49:4; Dt 27:20; 33:6; 1Ch 5:1
6 [l]Jdg 14:2–5
7 [m]1Co 5:2; [n]Ge 39:19; 49:6–7; 2Sa 12:5; 13:21; Est 7:7; Pr 6:34; [o]Dt 22:21; Jdg 19:23; 20:6; 2Sa 13:12; Jer 29:23; [p]**Ge 20:9**
8 [q]**Ge 21:21;** Dt 21:11
9 [r]ver 16,21; Dt 7:3; Jos 23:12
10 [s]ver 23; Ge 46:34; 47:6,27; [t]**Ge 13:9;** [u]Ge 42:34; [v]**Ge 33:19**
11 [w]**Ge 32:5**
12 [x]Ex 22:16; Dt 22:29; 1Sa 18:25
13 [y]**ver 5;** [z]**Ge 27:36**
14 [a]Ge 17:14; Jdg 14:3; 1Sa 31:4; Isa 52:1
15 [b]1Sa 11:2; [c]ver 22; Ex 12:48
16 [d]**ver 9;** [e]**Ge 33:19**
19 [f]Ge 49:3; 1Ch 11:21; [g]ver 3
20 [h]**Ge 18:1**
21 [i]**Ge 33:19;** [j]**ver 9**
22 [k]**ver 15**
23 [l]ver 28; **Ge 12:16;** [m]**ver 10**
24 [n]**Ge 18:1**
25 [o]Jos 5:8; [p]**Ge 29:33;** [q]**Ge 29:34;** [r]Ge 49:5; Mal 2:16; [s]Jdg 18:7,10,27; Eze 38:11; [t]Ge 49:7
26 [u]**ver 7;** Ge 48:22; [v]ver 3
27 [w]2Ki 21:14; [x]**ver 5**
28 [y]Ge 43:18; [z]**ver 23**
29 [a]**Ge 31:26;** [b]Nu 14:3; 31:9,53; Dt 2:35; Jos 7:21; [c]2Ki 8:12; Isa 13:16; La 5:11; Am 1:13; Zec 14:2
30 [d]Ge 43:6; Ex 5:23; Nu 11:11; [e]Ex 5:21; 6:9; 1Sa 13:4; 27:12; 2Sa 10:6; 1Ch 19:6; [f]**Ge 13:7;** [g]Ge 35:26; 46:27; Ex 1:5; Dt 10:22; 26:5; 1Ch 16:19; Ps 105:12

b*18* That is, North-west Mesopotamia
c*18* Or *arrived at Shalem, a*
d*19* Hebrew *hundred kesitahs;* a kesitah was a unit of money of unknown weight and value.
e*20* *El Elohe Israel* can mean *God, the God of Israel* or *mighty is the God of Israel.*
a*7* Or *against*
b*10* Or *move about freely;* also in verse 21
c*17* Hebrew *daughter*
d*27* Or *because*

they join forces against me and attack me, I and my household will be destroyed."

31But they replied, "Should he have treated our sister like a prostitute?[h]"

Jacob Returns to Bethel

35 Then God said to Jacob, "Go up to Bethel[a] and settle there, and build an altar[b] there to God,[c] who appeared to you[d] when you were fleeing from your brother Esau."[e]

2So Jacob said to his household[f] and to all who were with him, "Get rid of the foreign gods[g] you have with you, and purify yourselves and change your clothes.[h] 3Then come, let us go up to Bethel, where I will build an altar to God,[i] who answered me in the day of my distress[j] and who has been with me wherever I have gone.[k]" 4So they gave Jacob all the foreign gods they had and the rings in their ears,[l] and Jacob buried them under the oak[m] at Shechem.[n] 5Then they set out, and the terror of God[o] fell upon the towns all around them so that no-one pursued them.[p]

6Jacob and all the people with him came to Luz[q] (that is, Bethel) in the land of Canaan.[r] 7There he built an altar,[s] and he called the place El Bethel,[a][t] because it was there that God revealed himself to him[u] when he was fleeing from his brother.[v]

8Now Deborah, Rebekah's nurse,[w] died and was buried under the oak[x] below Bethel.[y] So it was named Allon Bacuth.[b]

9After Jacob returned from Paddan Aram,[c][z] God appeared to him again and blessed him.[a] 10God said to him, "Your name is Jacob,[d] but you will no longer be called Jacob; your name will be Israel."[e][b] So he named him Israel.

11And God said to him, "I am God Almighty;[f][c] be fruitful and increase in number.[d] A nation[e] and a community of nations will come from you, and kings will come from your body.[f] 12The land I gave to Abraham and Isaac I also give to you, and I will give this land to your descendants after you.[g]"[h] 13Then God went up from him[i] at the place where he had talked with him.

14Jacob set up a stone pillar[j] at the place where God had talked with him, and he poured out a drink offering[k] on it; he also poured oil on it.[l] 15Jacob called the place where God had talked with him Bethel.[g][m]

31 [h]ver 2

Ch. 35

1 [a]**Ge 12:8;** [b]**Ge 4:26;** 8:20; [c]ver 3; [d]**Ge 12:7;** [e]ver 7; Ge 27:43
2 [f]Ge 18:19; Jos 24:15; [g]**Ge 31:19; Jos 24:14;** [h]Ex 19:10,14; Nu 8:7,21; 19:19
3 [i]ver 1; [j]**Ge 32:7; Jdg 2:15;** [k]**Ge 26:3**
4 [l]Ge 24:22; Ex 32:3; 35:22; Jdg 8:24; Pr 25:12; [m]ver 8; [n]**Ge 12:6**
5 [o]Ex 15:16; 23:27; Dt 2:25; Jos 2:9; 1Sa 7:10; 13:7; 14:15; 2Ch 14:14; 17:10; 20:29; Ps 9:20; Isa 19:17; Zec 14:13; [p]Ps 105:14
6 [q]**Ge 28:19;** [r]**Ge 10:19**
7 [s]**Ge 8:20;** [t]Ge 28:19; [u]**Ge 28:13;** [v]**ver 1**
8 [w]Ge 24:59; [x]ver 4; [y]**Ge 12:8;** 1Sa 10:3
9 [z]**Ge 25:20;** [a]**Ge 28:13; 32:29**
10 [b]**Ge 17:5**
11 [c]**Ge 17:1;** [d]**Ge 12:2;** [e]**Ge 12:2;** [f]**Ge 17:6**
12 [g]**Ge 28:13;** [h]**Ge 12:7; 15:7**
13 [i]**Ge 17:22**
14 [j]**Ge 28:22;** [k]Ex 29:40; Lev 23:13; Nu 6:15,17; 15:5; 28:7,14; 2Sa 23:16; 2Ch 29:35; [l]**Ge 28:18**
15 [m]**Ge 12:8**
16 [n]ver 19; Ge 48:7; Ru 1:2; 4:11; 1Sa 17:12; Mic 5:2; [o]**Ge 29:6**
17 [p]Ge 38:28; Ex 1:15; [q]**Ge 30:24**
18 [r]1Sa 4:21; 14:3; [s]ver 24; Ge 42:4; 43:16,29; 45:12,14; 49:27; Nu 1:36; Dt 33:12
19 [t]**ver 16;** [u]Ge 48:7; Jos 19:15; Jdg 12:8; 17:7; 19:1,18; Ru 1:1,19; 1Sa 17:12; Mic 5:2

The Deaths of Rachel and Isaac

35:23–26pp—1Ch 2:1–2

16Then they moved on from Bethel. While they were still some distance from Ephrath,[n] Rachel[o] began to give birth and had great difficulty. 17And as she was having great difficulty in childbirth, the midwife[p] said to her, "Don't be afraid, for you have another son."[q] 18As she breathed her last—for she was dying—she named her son Ben-Oni.[h][r] But his father named him Benjamin.[i][s]

19So Rachel died and was buried on the way to Ephrath[t] (that is, Bethlehem[u]). 20Over her tomb Jacob set up a pillar, and to this day[v] that pillar marks Rachel's tomb.[w]

21Israel moved on again and pitched his tent beyond Migdal Eder.[x] 22While Israel was living in that region, Reuben went in and slept with his father's concubine[y] Bilhah,[z] and Israel heard of it.

Jacob had twelve sons:

23The sons of Leah:[a]

Reuben the firstborn[b] of Jacob,
Simeon, Levi, Judah,[c] Issachar
and Zebulun.[d]

24The sons of Rachel:

Joseph[e] and Benjamin.[f]

25The sons of Rachel's maidservant Bilhah:[g]

Dan and Naphtali.[h]

26The sons of Leah's maidservant Zilpah:[i]

Gad[j] and Asher.[k]

These were the sons of Jacob,[l] who were born to him in Paddan Aram.[m]

27Jacob came home to his father Isaac[n] in Mamre,[o] near Kiriath Arba[p] (that is, Hebron),[q] where Abraham and Isaac had stayed.[r] 28Isaac lived a hundred and eighty years.[s] 29Then he breathed his

20 [v]Jos 4:9; 7:26; 8:28; 10:27; 1Sa 6:18; [w]1Sa 10:2
21 [x]Jos 15:21
22 [y]**Ge 22:24;** [z]**Ge 29:29; 34:5; Lev 18:8**
23 [a]**Ge 29:16;** [b]Ge 43:33; 46:8; [c]**Ge 29:35;** [d]**Ge 30:20**
24 [e]**Ge 30:24;** [f]**ver 18** 25 [g]Ge 37:2; [h]**Ge 30:8**
26 [i]Ge 37:2; [j]**Ge 30:11;** [k]**Ge 30:13;** [l]**Ge 34:30;** 46:8; Ex 1:1–4; [m]**Ge 25:20**
27 [n]Ge 31:18; [o]**Ge 13:18;** [p]Ge 23:2; Jos 15:54; Jdg 1:10; Ne 11:25; [q]**Ge 13:18;** [r]**Ge 17:8** 28 [s]**Ge 25:7**,20

[a]7 *El Bethel* means *God of Bethel.*
[b]8 *Allon Bacuth* means *oak of weeping.*
[c]9 That is, North-west Mesopotamia; also in verse 26
[d]10 *Jacob* means *he grasps the heel* (figuratively, *he deceives*).
[e]10 *Israel* means *he struggles with God.*
[f]11 Hebrew *El-Shaddai*
[g]15 *Bethel* means *house of God.*
[h]18 *Ben-Oni* means *son of my trouble.*
[i]18 *Benjamin* means *son of my right hand.*

last and died and was gathered to his
people,[t] old and full of years.[u] And his
sons Esau and Jacob buried him.[v]

Esau's Descendants

36:10–14pp—1Ch 1:35–37
36:20–28pp—1Ch 1:38–42

36 This is the account[a] of Esau (that
is, Edom).[b]

2Esau took his wives from the
women of Canaan:[c] Adah daughter
of Elon the Hittite,[d] and Oholiba-
mah[e] daughter of Anah[f] and grand-
daughter of Zibeon the Hivite[g]—
3also Basemath[h] daughter of
Ishmael and sister of Nebaioth.[i]
4Adah bore Eliphaz to Esau,
Basemath bore Reuel,[j] 5and Oholi-
bamah bore Jeush, Jalam and
Korah.[k] These were the sons of
Esau, who were born to him in
Canaan.

6Esau took his wives and sons
and daughters and all the members
of his household, as well as his
livestock and all his other animals
and all the goods he had acquired
in Canaan,[l] and moved to a land
some distance from his brother
Jacob.[m] 7Their possessions were too
great for them to remain together;
the land where they were staying
could not support them both be-
cause of their livestock.[n] 8So Esau[o]
(that is, Edom)[p] settled in the hill
country of Seir.[q]

9This is the account[r] of Esau the father
of the Edomites[s] in the hill country of
Seir.

10These are the names of Esau's sons:
Eliphaz, the son of Esau's wife
Adah, and Reuel, the son of
Esau's wife Basemath.[t]
11The sons of Eliphaz:[u]
Teman,[v] Omar, Zepho, Gatam
and Kenaz.[w]
12Esau's son Eliphaz also had a
concubine[x] named Timna, who
bore him Amalek.[y] These were
grandsons of Esau's wife Adah.[z]
13The sons of Reuel:
Nahath, Zerah, Shammah and
Mizzah. These were grandsons
of Esau's wife Basemath.[a]
14The sons of Esau's wife Oholiba-
mah[b] daughter of Anah and grand-
daughter of Zibeon, whom she
bore to Esau:
Jeush, Jalam and Korah.[c]

29 [t]Ge 25:8; [u]Ge 15:15; [v]Ge 23:20; 25:9

Ch. 36

1 [a]Ge 2:4; [b]Ge 25:30
2 [c]Ge 28:8–9; [d]Ge 26:34; [e]ver 14,18; [f]ver 25; 1Ch 1:40; [g]ver 24; Ge 10:17; 1Ch 1:40
3 [h]ver 4,10,13, 17; [i]Ge 25:13
4 [j]ver 3; 1Ch 1:35
5 [k]ver 14,18; 1Ch 1:35
6 [l]Ge 12:5; [m]Ge 27:39
7 [n]Ge 13:6
8 [o]Dt 2:4; [p]Ge 25:30; [q]Ge 14:6
9 [r]Ge 2:4; [s]ver 1,43
10 [t]ver 3
11 [u]ver 15–16; 1Ch 1:45; Job 2:11; 4:1; [v]Jer 49:7,20; Eze 25:13; Am 1:12; Ob 9; Hab 3:3; [w]ver 15
12 [x]Ge 22:24; [y]Ex 17:8,16; Nu 24:20; Dt 25:17,19; 1Sa 15:2; 27:8; [z]ver 16
13 [a]ver 3
14 [b]ver 2; [c]ver 5
15 [d]ver 19,40; Ex 15:15; [e]Job 2:11; Jer 49:7; Eze 25:13; Am 1:12; Hab 3:3; [f]ver 11
16 [g]ver 11; [h]Ge 32:3; Ex 15:15; Nu 20:14; 33:37; [i]ver 12
17 [j]1Ch 1:37; [k]ver 3
18 [l]ver 2; [m]ver 5
19 [n]1Ch 1:35; [o]Ge 25:30; [p]ver 15
20 [q]Ge 14:6; [r]ver 29
21 [s]ver 30
24 [t]ver 2; [u]Jos 15:19; [v]Job 1:14
25 [w]ver 2; [x]ver 2
29 [y]ver 20

15These were the chiefs[d] among
Esau's descendants:
The sons of Eliphaz the firstborn of
Esau:
Chiefs Teman,[e] Omar, Zepho,
Kenaz,[f] 16Korah,[a] Gatam and
Amalek. These were the chiefs
descended from Eliphaz[g] in
Edom;[h] they were grandsons of
Adah.[i]
17The sons of Esau's son Reuel:[j]
Chiefs Nahath, Zerah, Shammah
and Mizzah. These were the
chiefs descended from Reuel in
Edom; they were grandsons of
Esau's wife Basemath.[k]
18The sons of Esau's wife Oholiba-
mah:[l]
Chiefs Jeush, Jalam and Korah.[m]
These were the chiefs descended
from Esau's wife Oholibamah
daughter of Anah.
19These were the sons of Esau[n] (that
is, Edom),[o] and these were their chiefs.[p]

20These were the sons of Seir the Hor-
ite,[q] who were living in the region:
Lotan, Shobal, Zibeon, Anah,[r]
21Dishon, Ezer and Dishan.
These sons of Seir in Edom were
Horite chiefs.[s]
22The sons of Lotan:
Hori and Homam.[b] Timna was
Lotan's sister.
23The sons of Shobal:
Alvan, Manahath, Ebal, Shepho
and Onam.
24The sons of Zibeon:[t]
Aiah and Anah. This is the Anah
who discovered the hot springs[c][u]
in the desert while he was graz-
ing the donkeys[v] of his father
Zibeon.
25The children of Anah:[w]
Dishon and Oholibamah[x] daugh-
ter of Anah.
26The sons of Dishon:[d]
Hemdan, Eshban, Ithran and
Keran.
27The sons of Ezer:
Bilhan, Zaavan and Akan.
28The sons of Dishan:
Uz and Aran.
29These were the Horite chiefs:
Lotan, Shobal, Zibeon, Anah,[y]

---

[a]16 Masoretic Text; Samaritan Pentateuch (see also Gen. 36:11 and 1 Chron. 1:36) does not have *Korah.*
[b]22 Hebrew *Hemam,* a variant of *Homam* (see 1 Chron. 1:39)
[c]24 Vulgate; Syriac *discovered water;* the meaning of the Hebrew for this word is uncertain.
[d]26 Hebrew *Dishan,* a variant of *Dishon*

30Dishon, Ezer and Dishan.
These were the Horite chiefs,[z]
according to their divisions, in
the land of Seir.

The Rulers of Edom

36:31–43pp—1Ch 1:43–54

31These were the kings who reigned
in Edom before any Israelite king[a]
reigned:[e]
32Bela son of Beor became king of
Edom. His city was named
Dinhabah.
33When Bela died, Jobab son of Zerah
from Bozrah[b] succeeded him as
king.
34When Jobab died, Husham from
the land of the Temanites[c] suc-
ceeded him as king.
35When Husham died, Hadad son of
Bedad, who defeated Midian[d] in
the country of Moab,[e] succeeded
him as king. His city was named
Avith.
36When Hadad died, Samlah from
Masrekah succeeded him as
king.
37When Samlah died, Shaul from Re-
hoboth[f] on the river[f] succeeded
him as king.
38When Shaul died, Baal-Hanan son
of Acbor succeeded him as king.
39When Baal-Hanan son of Acbor
died, Hadad[g] succeeded him as
king. His city was named Pau,
and his wife's name was Mehet-
abel daughter of Matred, the
daughter of Me-Zahab.

40These were the chiefs[g] descended
from Esau, by name, according to their
clans and regions:
Timna, Alvah, Jetheth, 41Oholi-
bamah, Elah, Pinon, 42Kenaz,
Teman, Mibzar, 43Magdiel and
Iram. These were the chiefs of
Edom, according to their settle-
ments in the land they occupied.

This was Esau the father of the
Edomites.[h]

Joseph's Dreams

37 Jacob lived in the land where
his father had stayed,[a] the land
of Canaan.[b]

2This is the account[c] of Jacob.

Joseph,[d] a young man of seventeen,[e]
was tending the flocks[f] with his
brothers, the sons of Bilhah[g] and the
sons of Zilpah,[h] his father's wives, and
he brought their father a bad report[i]
about them.
3Now Israel[j] loved Joseph more than
any of his other sons,[k] because he had
been born to him in his old age;[l] and he
made a richly ornamented[a] robe[m] for
him.[n] 4When his brothers saw that their
father loved him more than any of
them, they hated him[o] and could not
speak a kind word to him.
5Joseph had a dream,[p] and when he
told it to his brothers,[q] they hated him
all the more.[r] 6He said to them, "Listen
to this dream I had: 7We were binding
sheaves[s] of corn out in the field when
suddenly my sheaf rose and stood up-
right, while your sheaves gathered
round mine and bowed down to it."[t]
8His brothers said to him, "Do you
intend to reign over us? Will you actual-
ly rule us?"[u] And they hated him all the
more[v] because of his dream and what he
had said.
9Then he had another dream,[w] and he
told it to his brothers. "Listen," he said,
"I had another dream, and this time the
sun and moon and eleven stars[x] were
bowing down to me."[y]
10When he told his father as well as
his brothers,[z] his father rebuked[a] him
and said, "What is this dream you had?
Will your mother and I and your
brothers actually come and bow down
to the ground before you?"[b] 11His
brothers were jealous of him,[c] but his
father kept the matter in mind.[d]

Joseph Sold by His Brothers

12Now his brothers had gone to graze
their father's flocks near Shechem,[e]
13and Israel[f] said to Joseph, "As you
know, your brothers are grazing the
flocks near Shechem.[g] Come, I am going
to send you to them."
"Very well," he replied.
14So he said to him, "Go and see if all
is well with your brothers[h] and with the
flocks, and bring word back to me."
Then he sent him off from the Valley of
Hebron.[i]
When Joseph arrived at Shechem, 15a
man found him wandering around in

---

30 [z]ver 21
31 [a]**Ge 17:6**
33 [b]Isa 34:6; 63:1; Jer 49:13,22
34 [c]Jer 49:7; Eze 25:13; Ob 9
35 [d]**Ge 25:2**; [e]**Ge 19:37**; Nu 21:11; 22:1; Dt 1:5; Jdg 3:30; Ru 1:1,6
37 [f]Ge 26:22
40 [g]**ver 15**
43 [h]**ver 9**

Ch. 37

1 [a]**Ge 17:8**; [b]**Ge 10:19**
2 [c]**Ge 2:4**; [d]**Ge 30:24**; [e]Ge 41:46; 2Sa 5:4; [f]Ge 46:32; 1Sa 16:11; 17:15; Ps 78:71; Am 7:15; [g]Ge 35:25; [h]Ge 35:26; [i]1Sa 2:24
3 [j]**Ge 17:5**; [k]**Ge 25:28**; [l]Ge 43:27; 44:20; [m]ver 23, 31–32; 2Sa 13:18–19; [n]Ge 43:34; 45:22; 1Sa 1:4–5; Est 2:9
4 [o]**ver 24; Ge 27:41**; Ac 7:9
5 [p]**Ge 20:3; 28:12**; [q]ver 10; [r]ver 8
7 [s]Ru 2:7,15; [t]ver 9–10; Ge 27:29; 42:6,9; 43:26,28; 44:14; 50:18; 2Sa 1:2; 9:6
8 [u]Ge 41:44; 42:10; 44:16, 18; 48:22; 49:26; Dt 33:16; [v]ver 5
9 [w]**ver 7**; Ge 28:12; [x]Rev 12:1; [y]Dt 4:19; 17:3
10 [z]ver 5; [a]Ru 2:16; Ps 9:5; 68:30; 106:9; 119:21; Isa 17:13; 54:9; Zec 3:2; [b]**ver 7; Ge 9:25; 33:3**
11 [c]Ge 26:14; Ac 7:9; [d]Lk 2:19,51
12 [e]**Ge 12:6**
13 [f]**Ge 17:5**; [g]Ge 33:19
14 [h]1Sa 17:18; [i]**Ge 13:18**

---

[e]31 Or *before an Israelite king reigned over them*
[f]37 Possibly the Euphrates
[g]39 Many manuscripts of the Masoretic Text, Samaritan Pentateuch and Syriac (see also 1 Chron. 1:50); most manuscripts of the Masoretic Text *Hadar*
[a]3 The meaning of the Hebrew for *richly ornamented* is uncertain; also in verses 23 and 32.

the fields and asked him, "What are you
looking for?"
16 He replied, "I'm looking for my
brothers. Can you tell me where they
are grazing their flocks?"
17 "They have moved on from here,"
the man answered. "I heard them say,
'Let's go to Dothan.'[j]"
So Joseph went after his brothers and
found them near Dothan. 18 But they
saw him in the distance, and before he
reached them, they plotted to kill him.[k]
19 "Here comes that dreamer!" they
said to each other. 20 "Come now, let's
kill him and throw him into one of these
cisterns[m] and say that a ferocious ani-
mal[n] devoured him.[o] Then we'll see
what comes of his dreams."[p]
21 When Reuben[q] heard this, he tried
to rescue him from their hands. "Let's
not take his life," he said.[r] 22 "Don't shed
any blood. Throw him into this cistern[s]
here in the desert, but don't lay a hand
on him." Reuben said this to rescue him
from them and take him back to his
father.[t]
23 So when Joseph came to his
brothers, they stripped him of his robe
—the richly ornamented robe[u] he was
wearing—24 and they took him and
threw him into the cistern.[v] Now the
cistern was empty; there was no water
in it.
25 As they sat down to eat their meal,
they looked up and saw a caravan of
Ishmaelites[w] coming from Gilead.[x]
Their camels were loaded with spices,
balm[y] and myrrh,[z] and they were on
their way to take them down to Egypt.[a]
26 Judah[b] said to his brothers, "What
will we gain if we kill our brother and
cover up his blood?[c] 27 Come, let's sell
him to the Ishmaelites and not lay our
hands on him; after all, he is our
brother,[d] our own flesh and blood.[e]"
His brothers agreed.
28 So when the Midianite[f] merchants
came by, his brothers pulled Joseph up
out of the cistern[g] and sold[h] him for
twenty shekels[b] of silver[i] to the
Ishmaelites,[j] who took him to Egypt.[k]
29 When Reuben returned to the cis-
tern and saw that Joseph was not there,
he tore his clothes.[l] 30 He went back to
his brothers and said, "The boy isn't
there! Where can I turn now?"[m]
31 Then they got Joseph's robe,[n]
slaughtered a goat and dipped the robe
in the blood.[o] 32 They took the
ornamented robe[p] back to their father
and said, "We found this. Examine it to
see whether it is your son's robe."
33 He recognised it and said, "It is my
son's robe! Some ferocious animal[q] has
devoured him. Joseph has surely been
torn to pieces."[r]
34 Then Jacob tore his clothes,[s] put on
sackcloth[t] and mourned for his son
many days.[u] 35 All his sons and daugh-
ters came to comfort him,[v] but he re-
fused to be comforted.[w] "No," he said,
"in mourning will I go down to the
grave[c][x] to my son.[y]" So his father wept
for him.
36 Meanwhile, the Midianites[d][z] sold
Joseph[a] in Egypt to Potiphar, one of
Pharaoh's officials, the captain of the
guard.[b]

Judah and Tamar

38 At that time, Judah[a] left his
brothers and went down to stay
with a man of Adullam[b] named Hirah.[c]
2 There Judah met the daughter of a
Canaanite man named Shua.[d] He mar-
ried her and lay with her; 3 she became
pregnant and gave birth to a son, who
was named Er.[e] 4 She conceived again
and gave birth to a son and named him
Onan.[f] 5 She gave birth to still another
son and named him Shelah.[g] It was at
Kezib that she gave birth to him.
6 Judah got a wife for Er, his firstborn,
and her name was Tamar.[h] 7 But Er,
Judah's firstborn, was wicked in the
LORD's sight;[i] so the LORD put him to
death.[j]
8 Then Judah said to Onan, "Lie with
your brother's wife and fulfil your duty
to her as a brother-in-law to produce
offspring for your brother."[k] 9 But Onan
knew that the offspring would not be
his; so whenever he lay with his
brother's wife, he spilled his semen on
the ground to keep from producing
offspring for his brother. 10 What he did
was wicked in the LORD's sight; so he
put him to death also.[l]

17 [j]2Ki 6:13
18 [k]1Sa 19:1; 2Ch 24:21; Ps 31:13,20; 37:12,32; **Mt 12:14**; Mk 14:1; Ac 23:12
19 [l]**Ge 28:12**
20 [m]ver 22; Jer 38:6,9; [n]ver 33; Lev 26:6, 22; Dt 32:24; 2Ki 17:25; Eze 34:25; [o]ver 31–33; **Ge 4:10**; [p]Ge 50:20
21 [q]**Ge 29:32**; [r]Ge 42:22
22 [s]**ver 20**; [t]ver 29–30
23 [u]ver 3
24 [v]**ver 4**; Ge 49:23; Jer 38:6; 41:7; Eze 22:27
25 [w]**Ge 16:11**; [x]**Ge 31:21**; **SS 4:1**; [y]Jer 8:22; 22:6; 46:11; [z]Ge 43:11; Ex 30:23; Ps 45:8; Pr 7:17; SS 1:13; Mt 2:11; [a]ver 28; Ge 39:1; Ps 105:17
26 [b]**Ge 29:35**; [c]**Ge 4:10**
27 [d]Ge 42:21; [e]**Ge 29:14**
28 [f]**Ge 25:2**; [g]Jer 38:13; [h]Ex 21:16; [i]Lev 27:5; Mt 26:15; [j]**Ge 16:11**; [k]ver 36; Ge 39:1; 45:4–5; Ps 105:17; Jer 12:6; Ac 7:9
29 [l]ver 34; Ge 44:13; Nu 14:6; Jos 7:6; 2Sa 1:11; 2Ki 2:12; 5:7; 11:14; 22:11; Job 1:20; 2:12; Isa 36:22; 37:1; Jer 36:24; 41:5; Joel 2:13
30 [m]ver 22
31 [n]**ver 3**; [o]Rev 19:13
32 [p]**ver 3**
33 [q]**ver 20**; [r]Ge 42:13,38; 44:20,28
34 [s]**ver 29**; [t]2Sa 3:31; 1Ki 20:31; 21:27; 2Ki 6:30; 19:1, 2; Job 16:15; Ps 69:11; Isa 3:24; 15:3; 22:12; 32:11; 37:1; Jer 48:37; 49:3; Joel 1:13; [u]Ge 50:3,10, 11; Nu 20:29; Dt 34:8
35 [v]Job 2:11; 15:11; 16:5; 42:11; [w]2Sa 12:17; Ps 77:2; Jer 31:15; [x]Ge 42:38; 44:22,29,31; [y]2Sa 12:23
36 [z]**Ge 25:2**; [a]**ver 28**; [b]Ge 39:1; 40:3; 41:10,12; 1Sa 22:14

Ch. 38
1 [a]**Ge 29:35**; [b]Jos 12:15; 15:35; 1Sa 22:1; 2Sa 23:13; 2Ch 11:7; [c]ver 12,20 *2* [d]ver 12; 1Ch 2:3
3 [e]ver 6; Ge 46:12; Nu 26:19
4 [f]ver 8–9; Ge 46:12; Nu 26:19
5 [g]Nu 26:20; 1Ch 2:3; 4:21 *6* [h]ver 11,13
7 [i]**Ge 6:5**; [j]ver 10; Ge 46:12; Lev 10:1–2; 1Ch 2:3
8 [k]Dt 25:5–6; Ru 4:5; Mt 22:24–28
10 [l]**ver 7**; Dt 25:7–10

b28 That is, about 8 ounces (about 0.2 kilogram)
c35 Hebrew *Sheol*
d36 Samaritan Pentateuch, Septuagint, Vulgate and Syriac (see also verse 28); Masoretic Text *Medanites*

11 Judah then said to his daughter-in-law[m] Tamar,[n] "Live as a widow in your father's house[o] until my son Shelah[p] grows up."[q] For he thought, "He may die too, just like his brothers." So Tamar went to live in her father's house.

12 After a long time Judah's wife, the daughter of Shua,[r] died. When Judah had recovered from his grief, he went up to Timnah,[s] to the men who were shearing his sheep,[t] and his friend Hirah the Adullamite[u] went with him.

13 When Tamar[v] was told, "Your father-in-law is on his way to Timnah to shear his sheep,"[w] 14 she took off her widow's clothes,[x] covered herself with a veil[y] to disguise herself, and then sat down[z] at the entrance to Enaim, which is on the road to Timnah.[a] For she saw that, though Shelah[b] had now grown up, she had not been given to him as his wife.

15 When Judah saw her, he thought she was a prostitute,[c] for she had covered her face. 16 Not realising[d] that she was his daughter-in-law,[e] he went over to her by the roadside and said, "Come now, let me sleep with you."[f]

"And what will you give me to sleep with you?"[g] she asked.

17 "I'll send you a young goat[h] from my flock," he said.

"Will you give me something as a pledge[i] until you send it?" she asked.

18 He said, "What pledge should I give you?"

"Your seal[j] and its cord, and the staff[k] in your hand," she answered. So he gave them to her and slept with her, and she became pregnant by him.[l] 19 After she left, she took off her veil and put on her widow's clothes[m] again.

20 Meanwhile Judah sent the young goat by his friend the Adullamite[n] in order to get his pledge[o] back from the woman, but he did not find her. 21 He asked the men who lived there, "Where is the shrine-prostitute[p] who was beside the road at Enaim?"

"There hasn't been any shrine-prostitute here," they said.

22 So he went back to Judah and said, "I didn't find her. Besides, the men who lived there said, 'There hasn't been any shrine-prostitute here.'"

23 Then Judah said, "Let her keep what she has,[q] or we will become a laughing-stock.[r] After all, I did send her this young goat, but you didn't find her."

24 About three months later Judah was told, "Your daughter-in-law Tamar is guilty of prostitution, and as a result she is now pregnant."

Judah said, "Bring her out and have her burned to death!"[s]

25 As she was being brought out, she sent a message to her father-in-law. "I am pregnant by the man who owns these," she said. And she added, "See if you recognise whose seal and cord and staff these are."[t]

26 Judah recognised them and said, "She is more righteous than I,[u] since I wouldn't give her to my son Shelah.[v]" And he did not sleep with her again.

27 When the time came for her to give birth, there were twin boys in her womb.[w] 28 As she was giving birth, one of them put out his hand; so the midwife[x] took a scarlet thread and tied it on his wrist[y] and said, "This one came out first." 29 But when he drew back his hand, his brother came out,[z] and she said, "So this is how you have broken out!" And he was named Perez.[a][a] 30 Then his brother, who had the scarlet thread on his wrist,[b] came out and he was given the name Zerah.[b][c]

Joseph and Potiphar's Wife

39 Now Joseph[a] had been taken down to Egypt. Potiphar, an Egyptian who was one of Pharaoh's officials, the captain of the guard,[b] bought him from the Ishmaelites who had taken him there.[c]

2 The LORD was with Joseph[d] and he prospered, and he lived in the house of his Egyptian master. 3 When his master saw that the LORD was with him[e] and that the LORD gave him success in everything he did,[f] 4 Joseph found favour in his eyes[g] and became his attendant. Potiphar put him in charge of his household,[h] and he entrusted to his care everything he owned.[i] 5 From the time he put him in charge of his household and of all that he owned, the LORD blessed the household[j] of the Egyptian because of Joseph.[k] The blessing of the LORD was on everything Potiphar had, both in the house and in the field.[l] 6 So he left in Joseph's care everything he had;[m] with Joseph in charge, he did not concern himself with anything except the food he ate.

11 [m]Ge 11:31; [n]ver 6; [o]Ru 1:8; [p]ver 14, 26; [q]Ru 1:13
12 [r]ver 2; [s]ver 14; Jos 15:10, 57; 19:43; Jdg 14:1–2; 2Ch 28:18; [t]Ge 31:19; [u]ver 1
13 [v]ver 6; [w]Ge 31:19
14 [x]ver 19; [y]Ge 24:65; [z]Jer 3:2; [a]ver 12; [b]ver 11
15 [c]Jdg 11:1; 16:1
16 [d]Ge 42:23; [e]Lev 18:15; 20:12; Ru 1:6; [f]Ge 39:7,12; 2Sa 13:11; [g]Ge 30:15
17 [h]Jdg 15:1; [i]ver 20
18 [j]ver 25; 1Ki 21:8; Est 3:12; 8:8; SS 8:6; Isa 49:16; Jer 22:24; Hag 2:23; 2Co 1:22; Eph 1:13; [k]Ge 32:10; Ex 4:2; [l]Ge 19:32
19 [m]ver 14
20 [n]ver 1; [o]ver 17
21 [p]Ge 19:5; Lev 19:29; Dt 22:21; 23:17; 2Ki 23:7; Hos 4:14
23 [q]ver 18; [r]Ex 32:25; Job 12:4; Jer 20:7; La 3:14
24 [s]Lev 20:10,14; 21:9; Dt 22:21, 22; Jos 7:25; Jdg 15:6; 1Sa 31:12; Job 31:11,28; Eze 16:38
25 [t]ver 18
26 [u]1Sa 24:17; [v]ver 11
27 [w]Ge 25:24
28 [x]Ge 35:17; [y]ver 30
29 [z]Ge 25:26; [a]Ge 46:12; Nu 26:20–21; Ru 4:12,18; 2Sa 5:20; 6:8; 1Ch 2:4; 9:4; Isa 28:21; Mt 1:3
30 [b]ver 28; [c]Ge 46:12; 1Ch 2:4; Ne 11:24

Ch. 39

1 [a]Ge 30:24; [b]Ge 37:36; [c]Ge 37:25
2 [d]Ge 21:20,22; Jos 1:5; 6:27; Jdg 1:19; 1Sa 18:14; Ac 7:9
3 [e]Ge 21:22; [f]ver 23; 1Sa 18:14; 2Ki 18:7; 2Ch 20:20; Ps 1:3; 128:2; Isa 33:6
4 [g]Ge 6:8; 18:3; [h]Ge 47:6; 1Ki 11:28; Pr 22:29; [i]ver 8,22; Ge 40:4; 42:37
5 [j]2Sa 6:11; [k]Ge 26:24; [l]Dt 28:3; Ps 128:4
6 [m]Ge 24:2

[a]29 *Perez* means *breaking out*.
[b]30 *Zerah* can mean *scarlet* or *brightness*.

Now Joseph was well-built and hand-
some,[n] 7and after a while his master's
wife took notice of Joseph and said,
"Come to bed with me!"[o]
8But he refused.[p] "With me in
charge," he told her, "my master does
not concern himself with anything in
the house; everything he owns he has
entrusted to my care.[q] 9No-one is
greater in this house than I am.[r] My
master has withheld nothing from me
except you, because you are his wife.
How then could I do such a wicked
thing and sin against God?"[s] 10And
though she spoke to Joseph day after
day, he refused[t] to go to bed with her
or even to be with her.
11One day he went into the house to
attend to his duties,[u] and none of the
household servants[v] was inside. 12She
caught him by his cloak[w] and said,
"Come to bed with me!"[x] But he left his
cloak in her hand and ran out of the
house.[y]
13When she saw that he had left his
cloak in her hand and had run out of the
house, 14she called her household ser-
vants.[z] "Look," she said to them, "this
Hebrew[a] has been brought to us to make
sport of us![b] He came in here to sleep
with me, but I screamed.[c] 15When he
heard me scream for help, he left his
cloak beside me and ran out of the
house."[d]
16She kept his cloak beside her until
his master came home. 17Then she told
him this story:[e] "That Hebrew[f] slave[g]
you brought us came to me to make
sport of me. 18But as soon as I screamed
for help, he left his cloak beside me and
ran out of the house."
19When his master heard the story his
wife told him, saying, "This is how your
slave treated me," he burned with
anger.[h] 20Joseph's master took him and
put him in prison,[i] the place where the
king's prisoners were confined.
But while Joseph was there in the
prison, 21the LORD was with him;[j] he
showed him kindness[k] and granted him
favour in the eyes of the prison warder.[l]
22So the warder put Joseph in charge of
all those held in the prison, and he was
made responsible for all that was done
there.[m] 23The warder paid no attention
to anything under Joseph's[n] care, be-
cause the LORD was with Joseph and
gave him success in whatever he did.[o]

The Cupbearer and the Baker

40 Some time later, the cupbearer[a]
and the baker[b] of the king of
Egypt offended their master, the king of

6 [n]**Ge 12:11;** Ex 2:2; 1Sa 9:2; 16:12; 17:42; Est 2:7; Da 1:4
7 [o]**Ge 38:16;** Pr 7:15–18
8 [p]Pr 6:23–24; [q]**ver 4**
9 [r]Ge 41:33,40; [s]**Ge 13:13; Nu 22:34**
10 [t]Est 3:4
11 [u]Ex 18:20; Dt 1:18; [v]ver 14
12 [w]2Sa 13:11; Pr 7:13; [x]**Ge 38:16;** [y]ver 15; Pr 5:8; 2Ti 2:22
14 [z]ver 11; [a]**Ge 14:13;** [b]**Ge 21:9;** [c]Dt 22:24,27
15 [d]**ver 12**
17 [e]Ex 20:16; 23:1,7; Dt 5:20; Ps 101:5; [f]**Ge 14:13;** [g]Ge 21:10
19 [h]**Ge 34:7; Est 1:12**
20 [i]Ge 40:3; 41:10; Ps 105:18
21 [j]**Ge 21:20;** [k]**Ge 19:19;** [l]Ex 3:21; 11:3; 12:36; Est 2:9; Ps 106:46; Pr 16:7; Da 1:9
22 [m]**ver 4**
23 [n]**Ge 21:20; Nu 14:43;** [o]**ver 3**

Ch. 40

1 [a]ver 9,13,21; Ne 1:11; [b]ver 16,20
2 [c]Pr 16:14–15; 19:12; [d]Ge 41:10; Est 2:21
3 [e]**Ge 37:36; 39:20**
4 [f]**Ge 37:36;** [g]**Ge 39:4;** [h]ver 7; Ge 42:17
5 [i]**Ge 20:3;** [j]Ge 41:11
7 [k]**ver 4;** [l]Ne 2:2
8 [m]Ge 41:8,15; [n]Ge 41:16,25, 28,32; Dt 29:29; Da 2:22,28,47
9 [o]**ver 1**
10 [p]Isa 27:6; 35:1–2; Hos 14:7
12 [q]ver 16; Ge 41:12,15,25; Da 2:36; 4:19; [r]ver 18
13 [s]ver 19–20; Jos 1:11; 3:2; Ezr 8:32; Ne 2:11; [t]ver 19; [u]**ver 1**
14 [v]1Sa 25:31; Lk 23:42; [w]**Ge 19:19;** 1Sa 20:14,42; 2Sa 9:1; 1Ki 2:7; [x]ver 23; Ge 41:9; Ecc 9:15

Egypt. 2Pharaoh was angry[c] with his
two officials,[d] the chief cupbearer and
the chief baker, 3and put them in
custody in the house of the captain of
the guard,[e] in the same prison where
Joseph was confined. 4The captain of
the guard[f] assigned them to Joseph,[g]
and he attended them.
After they had been in custody[h] for
some time, 5each of the two men—the
cupbearer and the baker of the king of
Egypt, who were being held in prison
—had a dream[i] the same night, and
each dream had a meaning of its own.[j]
6When Joseph came to them the next
morning, he saw that they were de-
jected. 7So he asked Pharaoh's officials
who were in custody[k] with him in his
master's house, "Why are your faces so
sad today?"[l]
8"We both had dreams," they
answered, "but there is no-one to inter-
pret them."[m]
Then Joseph said to them, "Do not
interpretations belong to God?[n] Tell me
your dreams."
9So the chief cupbearer[o] told Joseph
his dream. He said to him, "In my
dream I saw a vine in front of me, 10and
on the vine were three branches.
As soon as it budded, it blossomed,[p]
and its clusters ripened into grapes.
11Pharaoh's cup was in my hand, and I
took the grapes, squeezed them into
Pharaoh's cup and put the cup in his
hand."
12"This is what it means,[q]" Joseph
said to him. "The three branches are
three days.[r] 13Within three days[s] Phar-
aoh will lift up your head[t] and restore
you to your position, and you will put
Pharaoh's cup in his hand, just as you
used to do when you were his cup-
bearer.[u] 14But when all goes well with
you, remember me[v] and show me kind-
ness;[w] mention me to Pharaoh[x] and
get me out of this prison. 15For I was
forcibly carried off from the land of the
Hebrews,[y] and even here I have done
nothing to deserve being put in a
dungeon."[z]
16When the chief baker[a] saw that
Joseph had given a favourable interpret-
ation,[b] he said to Joseph, "I too had a
dream: On my head were three baskets[c]
of bread.[a] 17In the top basket were all
kinds of baked goods for Pharaoh, but
the birds were eating them out of the
basket on my head."

15 [y]**Ge 14:13;** [z]Ge 39:20; Job 13:27
16 [a]**ver 1;** [b]**ver 12;** [c]Am 8:1–2

[a]16 Or *three wicker baskets*

18"This is what it means," Joseph
said. "The three baskets are three days.[d]
19Within three days[e] Pharaoh will lift off
your head[f] and hang you on a tree.[b][g]
And the birds will eat away your
flesh."[h]
20Now the third day[i] was Pharaoh's
birthday,[j] and he gave a feast for all his
officials.[k] He lifted up the heads of the
chief cupbearer and the chief baker[l] in
the presence of his officials: 21He re-
stored the chief cupbearer[m] to his pos-
ition,[n] so that he once again put the cup
into Pharaoh's hand,[o] 22but he hanged[c]
the chief baker,[p] just as Joseph had said
to them in his interpretation.[q]
23The chief cupbearer, however, did
not remember Joseph; he forgot him.[r]

Pharaoh's Dreams

41 When two full years had
passed, Pharaoh had a dream:[a]
He was standing by the Nile,[b] 2when
out of the river there came up seven
cows, sleek and fat,[c] and they grazed
among the reeds.[d] 3After them, seven
other cows, ugly and gaunt, came up
out of the Nile and stood beside those
on the riverbank. 4And the cows that
were ugly and gaunt ate up the seven
sleek, fat cows. Then Pharaoh woke
up.[e]
5He fell asleep again and had a second
dream: Seven ears of corn,[f] healthy and
good, were growing on a single stalk.
6After them, seven other ears of corn
sprouted—thin and scorched by the
east wind.[g] 7The thin ears of corn swal-
lowed up the seven healthy, full ears.
Then Pharaoh woke up;[h] it had been a
dream.
8In the morning his mind was
troubled,[i] so he sent for all the
magicians[j] and wise men of Egypt.
Pharaoh told them his dreams, but no-
one could interpret them for him.[k]
9Then the chief cupbearer said to
Pharaoh, "Today I am reminded of my
shortcomings.[l] 10Pharaoh was once
angry with his servants,[m] and he im-
prisoned me and the chief baker in the
house of the captain of the guard.[n]
11Each of us had a dream the same
night, and each dream had a meaning of
its own.[o] 12Now a young Hebrew[p] was
there with us, a servant of the captain of
the guard.[q] We told him our dreams,
and he interpreted them for us, giving
each man the interpretation of his
dream.[r] 13And things turned out exactly
as he interpreted them to us: I was re-
stored to my position, and the other
man was hanged."[a][s]
14So Pharaoh sent for Joseph, and
he was quickly brought from the
dungeon.[t] When he had shaved[u] and
changed his clothes,[v] he came before
Pharaoh.
15Pharaoh said to Joseph, "I had a
dream, and no-one can interpret it.[w] But
I have heard it said of you that when
you hear a dream you can interpret it."[x]
16"I cannot do it," Joseph replied to
Pharaoh, "but God will give Pharaoh
the answer he desires."[y]
17Then Pharaoh said to Joseph, "In
my dream I was standing on the bank of
the Nile,[z] 18when out of the river there
came up seven cows, fat and sleek, and
they grazed among the reeds.[a] 19After
them, seven other cows came up—
scrawny and very ugly and lean. I had
never seen such ugly cows in all the
land of Egypt. 20The lean, ugly cows ate
up the seven fat cows that came up first.
21But even after they ate them, no-one
could tell that they had done so; they
looked just as ugly as before. Then I
woke up.
22"In my dreams I also saw seven ears
of corn, full and good, growing on a
single stalk. 23After them, seven other
ears sprouted—withered and thin and
scorched by the east wind. 24The thin
ears of corn swallowed up the seven
good ears. I told this to the magicians,
but none could explain it to me."[b]
25Then Joseph said to Pharaoh, "The
dreams of Pharaoh are one and the
same.[c] God has revealed to Pharaoh
what he is about to do.[d] 26The seven
good cows[e] are seven years, and the
seven good ears of corn are seven years;
it is one and the same dream. 27The
seven lean, ugly cows that come up
afterwards are seven years, and so are
the seven worthless ears of corn
scorched by the east wind: They are
seven years of famine.[f]
28"It is just as I said to Pharaoh: God
has shown Pharaoh what he is about to
do.[g] 29Seven years of great abundance[h]
are coming throughout the land of
Egypt, 30but seven years of famine[i] will
follow them. Then all the abundance in
Egypt will be forgotten, and the famine
will ravage the land.[j] 31The abundance
in the land will not be remembered,
because the famine that follows it will be
so severe. 32The reason the dream was

18 [d]ver 12
19 [e]ver 13; [f]**ver 13**; [g]ver 22; Dt 21:22–23; Est 2:23; 7:10; [h]Dt 28:26; 1Sa 17:44; 2Sa 21:10; 1Ki 14:11; 16:4; 21:24; Eze 39:4
20 [i]ver 13; [j]Mt 14:6–10; [k]Est 2:18; Mk 6:21; [l]**ver 1**
21 [m]**ver 1**; [n]2Ki 25:27; Jer 52:31; [o]ver 13
22 [p]**ver 19**; [q]Ge 41:13; Ps 105:19
23 [r]**ver 14**; **Ecc 1:11**

Ch. 41

1 [a]Ge 20:3; [b]ver 17; **Ge 2:14**; Ex 1:22; 2:5; 7:15
2 [c]ver 26; Jer 5:28; [d]ver 18; Ex 2:3; Job 40:21; Isa 19:6
4 [e]ver 7
5 [f]Jos 13:3; 2Ki 4:42; 1Ch 13:5; Isa 23:3; Jer 2:18
6 [g]Ex 10:13; 14:21; Job 6:26; 11:2; 15:2; Ps 11:6; 48:7; Isa 11:15; 27:8; Jer 4:11; 18:17; Eze 19:12; 27:26; Hos 12:1; 13:15; Jnh 4:8
7 [h]ver 4
8 [i]Job 7:14; Da 2:1,3; 4:5,19; [j]Ex 7:11,22; Da 1:20; 2:2, 27; 4:7; 5:7; [k]ver 24; **Ge 40:8**; Da 4:18
9 [l]**Ge 40:14**
10 [m]**Ge 40:2**; [n]**Ge 37:36**; **39:20**
11 [o]Ge 40:5
12 [p]**Ge 14:13**; 39:17; [q]**Ge 37:36**; 40:4; [r]**Ge 40:12**
13 [s]**Ge 40:22**
14 [t]Ps 105:20; [u]Isa 18:2,7; [v]**Ge 35:2**; 45:22; Ru 3:3; 2Sa 12:20
15 [w]**Ge 40:8**; [x]**Ge 40:12**; Da 4:18; 5:16
16 [y]**Ge 40:8**
17 [z]**ver 1**
18 [a]**ver 2**
24 [b]**ver 8**
25 [c]**Ge 40:12**; [d]**Ge 40:8**; Isa 46:11; Da 2:45
26 [e]**ver 2**
27 [f]**Ge 12:10**
28 [g]**Ge 40:8** **29** [h]ver 47
30 [i]ver 54; Ge 45:6,11; 47:13; Ps 105:16; [j]ver 56; **Ge 12:10**

[b]19 Or *and impale you on a pole* [c]22 Or *impaled*
[a]13 Or *impaled*

given to Pharaoh in two forms is that
the matter has been firmly decided[k] by
God, and God will do it soon.[l]
33"And now let Pharaoh look for a
discerning and wise man[m] and put him
in charge of the land of Egypt.[n] 34Let
Pharaoh appoint commissioners[o] over
the land to take a fifth[p] of the harvest of
Egypt during the seven years of abun-
dance.[q] 35They should collect all the
food of these good years that are coming
and store up the grain under the author-
ity of Pharaoh, to be kept in the cities for
food.[r] 36This food should be held in
reserve for the country, to be used dur-
ing the seven years of famine that will
come upon Egypt,[s] so that the country
may not be ruined by the famine."
37The plan seemed good to Pharaoh
and to all his officials.[t] 38So Pharaoh
asked them, "Can we find anyone like
this man, one in whom is the spirit of
God?"[b][u]
39Then Pharaoh said to Joseph, "Since
God has made all this known to you,[v]
there is no-one so discerning and wise
as you.[w] 40You shall be in charge of my
palace,[x] and all my people are to submit
to your orders.[y] Only with respect to the
throne will I be greater than you."[z]

Joseph in Charge of Egypt

41So Pharaoh said to Joseph, "I hereby
put you in charge of the whole land of
Egypt."[a] 42Then Pharaoh took his signet
ring[b] from his finger and put it on
Joseph's finger. He dressed him in
robes[c] of fine linen[d] and put a gold chain
around his neck.[e] 43He had him ride in a
chariot[f] as his second-in-command,[c][g]
and men shouted before him, "Make
way!"[d][h] Thus he put him in charge of
the whole land of Egypt.[i]
44Then Pharaoh said to Joseph, "I am
Pharaoh, but without your word no-one
will lift hand or foot in all Egypt."[j]
45Pharaoh gave Joseph[k] the name
Zaphenath-Paneah and gave him Ase-
nath daughter of Potiphera, priest[l] of
On,[e][m] to be his wife.[n] And Joseph went
throughout the land of Egypt.
46Joseph was thirty years old[o] when
he entered the service[p] of Pharaoh king
of Egypt. And Joseph went out from
Pharaoh's presence and travelled
throughout Egypt. 47During the seven
years of abundance[q] the land produced
plentifully. 48Joseph collected all the
food produced in those seven years of
abundance in Egypt and stored it in the
cities.[r] In each city he put the food
grown in the fields surrounding it.
49Joseph stored up huge quantities of
grain, like the sand of the sea;[s] it was so
much that he stopped keeping records
because it was beyond measure.
50Before the years of famine came,
two sons were born to Joseph by Ase-
nath daughter of Potiphera, priest of
On.[t] 51Joseph named his firstborn[u]
Manasseh[f][v] and said, "It is because
God has made me forget all my trouble
and all my father's household." 52The
second son he named Ephraim[g][w] and
said, "It is because God has made me
fruitful[x] in the land of my suffering."
53The seven years of abundance in
Egypt came to an end, 54and the seven
years of famine[y] began,[z] just as Joseph
had said. There was famine in all the
other lands, but in the whole land of
Egypt there was food. 55When all Egypt
began to feel the famine,[a] the people
cried to Pharaoh for food. Then Pharaoh
told all the Egyptians, "Go to Joseph
and do what he tells you."[b]
56When the famine had spread over
the whole country, Joseph opened the
storehouses and sold grain to the
Egyptians,[c] for the famine[d] was severe
throughout Egypt.[e] 57And all the coun-
tries came to Egypt to buy grain from
Joseph,[f] because the famine was severe
in all the world.[g]

Joseph's Brothers Go to Egypt

42 When Jacob learned that there
was grain in Egypt,[a] he said to
his sons, "Why do you just keep look-
ing at each other?" 2He continued, "I
have heard that there is grain in Egypt.
Go down there and buy some for us,[b] so
that we may live and not die."[c]
3Then ten of Joseph's brothers went
down to buy grain[d] from Egypt. 4But
Jacob did not send Benjamin,[e] Joseph's
brother, with the others, because he

32 [k]Da 2:5; [l]**Ge 40:8**
33 [m]ver 39; [n]**Ge 39:9**
34 [o]Est 2:3; [p]Ge 47:24,26; 1Sa 8:15; [q]ver 48; Ge 47:14
35 [r]ver 48
36 [s]ver 56; Ge 42:6; 47:14
37 [t]Ge 45:16; Est 2:4; Isa 19:11
38 [u]Nu 27:18; Dt 34:9; Da 2:11; 4:8–9,18; 5:11,14
39 [v]Da 2:11; 5:11; [w]ver 33
40 [x]1Ki 4:6; 2Ki 15:5; Isa 22:15; 36:3; [y]**Ge 39:9**; Ps 105:21–22; Ac 7:10; [z]Est 10:3
41 [a]ver 43,55; Ge 42:6; 45:8,13, 26; Est 8:2; Jer 40:7; Da 6:3
42 [b]**Ge 24:22**; Est 3:10; 8:2,8; [c]1Sa 17:38; 18:4; 1Ki 19:19; Est 6:8, 11; Da 5:29; Zec 3:4; [d]Ex 25:4; Est 8:15; Da 5:29; [e]Ps 73:6; SS 4:9; Isa 3:18; Eze 16:11; Da 5:7, 16,29
43 [f]Ge 46:29; 50:9; Isa 2:7; 22:18; [g]Est 10:3; [h]Est 6:9; [i]**ver 41**
44 [j]**Ge 37:8**; Est 10:2; Ps 105:22
45 [k]Est 2:7; [l]Ex 2:16; [m]Eze 30:17; [n]ver 50; Ge 46:20,27
46 [o]**Ge 37:2**; [p]1Sa 8:11; 16:21; Pr 22:29; Da 1:19
47 [q]ver 29
48 [r]**ver 34**
49 [s]**Ge 12:2**
50 [t]**ver 45**
51 [u]Ge 48:14,18, 20; 49:3; [v]Ge 46:20; 48:1; 50:23; Nu 1:34; Dt 33:17; Jos 4:12; 17:1; 1Ch 7:14
52 [w]Ge 46:20; 48:1,5; 50:23; Nu 1:32; 26:28; Dt 33:17; Jos 14:4; Jdg 5:14; 1Ch 7:20; 2Ch 30:1; Ps 60:7; Jer 7:15; Ob 19; [x]**Ge 17:6**
54 [y]**Ge 12:10**; [z]Ac 7:11
55 [a]Dt 32:24; 2Ch 20:9; Isa 51:19; Jer 5:12; 27:8; 42:16; 44:27; [b]ver 41; Jn 2:5
56 [c]ver 36; [d]**Ge 12:10**; [e]ver 30
57 [f]Ge 42:5; 47:15; [g]**Ge 12:10**

Ch. 42
1 [a]Ac 7:12
2 [b]Ge 43:2,4; 44:25; [c]ver 19,33; Ge 43:8; 47:19; Ps 33:18–19 *3* [d]ver 10; Ge 43:20
4 [e]**Ge 35:18**

b38 Or *of the gods*
c43 Or *in the chariot of his second-in-command*; or *in his second chariot* d43 Or *Bow down*
e45 That is, Heliopolis; also in verse 50
f51 *Manasseh* sounds like and may be derived from the Hebrew for *forget*.
g52 *Ephraim* sounds like the Hebrew for *twice fruitful*.

was afraid that harm might come to
him.[f] 5So Israel's sons were among
those who went to buy grain,[g] for the
famine was in the land of Canaan[h] also.[i]
6Now Joseph was the governor of the
land,[j] the one who sold grain to all its
people.[k] So when Joseph's brothers ar-
rived, they bowed down to him with
their faces to the ground.[l] 7As soon as
Joseph saw his brothers, he recognised
them, but he pretended to be a stranger
and spoke harshly to them.[m] "Where do
you come from?"[n] he asked.
"From the land of Canaan," they re-
plied, "to buy food."
8Although Joseph recognised his
brothers, they did not recognise him.[o]
9Then he remembered his dreams[p]
about them and said to them, "You are
spies![q] You have come to see where our
land is unprotected."[r]
10"No, my lord,[s]" they answered.
"Your servants have come to buy food.[t]
11We are all the sons of one man. Your
servants[u] are honest men,[v] not spies.[w]"
12"No!" he said to them. "You have
come to see where our land is unprotec-
ted."[x]
13But they replied, "Your servants[y]
were twelve brothers, the sons of one
man, who lives in the land of Canaan.[z]
The youngest is now with our father,
and one is no more."[a]
14Joseph said to them, "It is just as I
told you: You are spies![b] 15And this is
how you will be tested: As surely as
Pharaoh lives,[c] you will not leave this
place unless your youngest brother
comes here.[d] 16Send one of your number
to get your brother;[e] the rest of you will
be kept in prison,[f] so that your words
may be tested to see if you are telling the
truth.[g] If you are not, then as surely as
Pharaoh lives, you are spies![h]" 17And he
put them all in custody[i] for three days.
18On the third day, Joseph said to
them, "Do this and you will live, for I
fear God:[j] 19If you are honest men,[k]
let one of your brothers stay here in
prison,[l] while the rest of you go and
take grain back for your starving
households.[m] 20But you must bring
your youngest brother to me,[n] so that
your words may be verified and that
you may not die." This they proceeded
to do.
21They said to one another, "Surely
we are being punished because of our
brother.[o] We saw how distressed he was
when he pleaded with us for his life, but
we would not listen; that's why this
distress[p] has come upon us."
22Reuben replied, "Didn't I tell you
not to sin against the boy?[q] But you
wouldn't listen! Now we must give an
accounting[r] for his blood."[s] 23They did
not realise[t] that Joseph could under-
stand them,[u] since he was using an
interpreter.
24He turned away from them and be-
gan to weep,[v] but then turned back and
spoke to them again. He had Simeon
taken from them and bound before their
eyes.[w]
25Joseph gave orders to fill their bags
with grain,[x] to put each man's silver
back in his sack,[y] and to give them pro-
visions[z] for their journey.[a] After this
was done for them, 26they loaded their
grain on their donkeys[b] and left.
27At the place where they stopped for
the night one of them opened his sack to
get feed for his donkey,[c] and he saw his
silver in the mouth of his sack.[d] 28"My
silver has been returned," he said to his
brothers. "Here it is in my sack."
Their hearts sank[e] and they turned to
each other trembling[f] and said, "What is
this that God has done to us?"[g]
29When they came to their father
Jacob in the land of Canaan,[h] they told
him all that had happened to them.[i]
They said, 30"The man who is lord over
the land spoke harshly to us[j] and treated
us as though we were spying on the
land.[k] 31But we said to him, 'We are
honest men; we are not spies.[l] 32We
were twelve brothers, sons of one
father. One is no more, and the
youngest is now with our father in
Canaan.'[m]
33"Then the man who is lord over the
land said to us, 'This is how I will know
whether you are honest men: Leave one
of your brothers here with me, and take
food for your starving households and
go.[n] 34But bring your youngest brother
to me so I will know that you are not
spies but honest men.[o] Then I will give
your brother back to you,[p] and you can
trade[a] in the land.[q]'"
35As they were emptying their sacks,
there in each man's sack was his pouch
of silver![r] When they and their father
saw the money pouches, they were
frightened.[s] 36Their father Jacob said to
them, "You have deprived me of my
children. Joseph is no more and Simeon
is no more,[t] and now you want to take
Benjamin.[u] Everything is against me![v]"
37Then Reuben said to his father,

4 [f]ver 38
5 [g]**Ge 41:57**; [h]ver 13,29; Ge 31:18; 45:17; [i]**Ge 12:10; Dt 32:24**; Ac 7:11
6 [j]**Ge 41:41; Ne 5:14**; [k]**Ge 41:36**; [l]**Ge 33:3**
7 [m]ver 30; [n]**Ge 29:4**
8 [o]Ge 37:2
9 [p]**Ge 37:7**; [q]ver 14,16,30; Dt 1:22; Jos 2:1; 6:22; [r]ver 12
10 [s]**Ge 37:8**; [t]**ver 3**
11 [u]ver 13; Ge 44:7,9,16,19, 21,31; 46:34; 47:3; [v]ver 15–16,19–20, 34; [w]ver 31
12 [x]ver 9
13 [y]**ver 11**; [z]**ver 5**; Ge 46:31; 47:1; [a]ver 24, 32,36; **Ge 37:33**; 43:7, 29,33; 44:8; Jer 31:15
14 [b]**ver 9**
15 [c]1Sa 17:55; [d]**ver 11**; Ge 43:3,5,7; 44:21,23
16 [e]ver 15; [f]ver 19; [g]**ver 11**; [h]**ver 9**
17 [i]**Ge 40:4**
18 [j]**Ge 20:11; 22:12**; Lev 19:14; 25:43; 2Sa 23:3
19 [k]**ver 11**; [l]ver 16; [m]**ver 2**
20 [n]**ver 15**
21 [o]Ge 37:26–28; [p]Ge 45:5
22 [q]Ge 37:21–22; [r]**Ge 9:5**; [s]Ge 45:24
23 [t]Ge 38:16; [u]**Ge 11:7**
24 [v]**Ge 29:11**; [w]**ver 13**; Ge 43:14,23
25 [x]Ge 43:2; [y]ver 27,35; Ge 43:12,18,21; 44:1,8; [z]Jer 40:5; [a]Ge 45:21,23
26 [b]**Ge 32:15**; 44:13; 45:17; 1Sa 25:18; Isa 30:6
27 [c]Jdg 19:19; Job 39:9; Isa 1:3; [d]**ver 25**
28 [e]Jos 2:11; 5:1; 7:5; [f]Mk 5:33; [g]Ge 43:23
29 [h]ver 5; [i]Ge 44:24
30 [j]ver 7; [k]**ver 9**
31 [l]ver 11
32 [m]**ver 13**
33 [n]**ver 2**
34 [o]**ver 11**; [p]**ver 24**; [q]Ge 34:10
35 [r]ver 25; [s]Ge 43:18
36 [t]ver 13; [u]ver 24; [v]Job 3:25; Pr 10:24; Ro 8:31

[a]34 Or *move about freely*

"You may put both of my sons to death if I do not bring him back to you. Entrust him to my care,[w] and I will bring him back."[x]

38But Jacob said, "My son will not go down there with you; his brother is dead[y] and he is the only one left. If harm comes to him[z] on the journey you are taking, you will bring my grey head down to the grave[b][a] in sorrow.[b]"

The Second Journey to Egypt

43 Now the famine was still severe in the land.[a] 2So when they had eaten all the grain they had brought from Egypt,[b] their father said to them, "Go back and buy us a little more food."[c]

3But Judah[d] said to him, "The man warned us solemnly, 'You will not see my face again unless your brother is with you.'[e] 4If you will send our brother along with us, we will go down and buy food for you.[f] 5But if you will not send him, we will not go down, because the man said to us, 'You will not see my face again unless your brother is with you.[g]'"

6Israel[h] asked, "Why did you bring this trouble[i] on me by telling the man you had another brother?"

7They replied, "The man questioned us closely about ourselves and our family. 'Is your father still living?'[j] he asked us. 'Do you have another brother?'[k] We simply answered his questions. How were we to know he would say, 'Bring your brother down here'?"[l]

8Then Judah[m] said to Israel[n] his father, "Send the boy along with me and we will go at once, so that we and you and our children may live and not die.[o] 9I myself will guarantee his safety; you can hold me personally responsible for him.[p] If I do not bring him back to you and set him here before you, I will bear the blame[q] before you all my life.[r] 10As it is, if we had not delayed,[s] we could have gone and returned twice."

11Then their father Israel[t] said to them, "If it must be, then do this: Put some of the best products[u] of the land in your bags and take them down to the man as a gift[v]—a little balm[w] and a little honey, some spices[x] and myrrh,[y] some pistachio nuts and almonds. 12Take double the amount[z] of silver with you, for you must return the silver that was put back into the mouths of your sacks.[a] Perhaps it was a mistake. 13Take your brother also and go back to the man at once.[b] 14And may God Almighty[a][c] grant you mercy[d] before the man so that he will let your other brother and Benjamin come back with you.[e] As for me, if I am bereaved, I am bereaved."[f]

15So the men took the gifts and double the amount of silver,[g] and Benjamin also. They hurried[h] down to Egypt and presented themselves[i] to Joseph. 16When Joseph saw Benjamin[j] with them, he said to the steward of his house,[k] "Take these men to my house, slaughter an animal and prepare dinner;[l] they are to eat with me at noon."

17The man did as Joseph told him and took the men to Joseph's house.[m] 18Now the men were frightened[n] when they were taken to his house.[o] They thought, "We were brought here because of the silver that was put back into our sacks[p] the first time. He wants to attack us[q] and overpower us and seize us as slaves[r] and take our donkeys.[s]"

19So they went up to Joseph's steward[t] and spoke to him at the entrance to the house. 20"Please, sir," they said, "we came down here the first time to buy food.[u] 21But at the place where we stopped for the night we opened our sacks and each of us found his silver—the exact weight—in the mouth of his sack. So we have brought it back with us.[v] 22We have also brought additional silver with us to buy food. We don't know who put our silver in our sacks."

23"It's all right," he said. "Don't be afraid. Your God, the God of your father,[w] has given you treasure in your sacks;[x] I received your silver." Then he brought Simeon out to them.[y]

24The steward took the men into Joseph's house,[z] gave them water to wash their feet[a] and provided fodder for their donkeys. 25They prepared their gifts[b] for Joseph's arrival at noon,[c] because they had heard that they were to eat there.

26When Joseph came home,[d] they presented to him the gifts[e] they had brought into the house, and they bowed down before him to the ground.[f] 27He asked them how they were, and then he said, "How is your aged father[g] you told me about? Is he still living?"[h]

28They replied, "Your servant our father[i] is still alive and well." And they bowed low[j] to pay him honour.[k]

29As he looked about and saw his

37 [w]Ge 39:4; [x]Ge 43:9; 44:32
38 [y]Ge 37:33; [z]ver 4; [a]Ge 37:35; [b]Ge 44:29,34; 48:7

Ch. 43

1 [a]Ge 12:10
2 [b]Ge 42:25; [c]Ge 42:2
3 [d]ver 8; Ge 44:14,18; 46:28; [e]Ge 42:15
4 [f]Ge 42:2
5 [g]Ge 42:15; 44:26; 2Sa 3:13
6 [h]ver 8,11; Ge 17:5; [i]Ge 34:30
7 [j]ver 27; Ge 45:3; [k]Ge 42:13; 44:19; [l]Ge 42:15
8 [m]ver 3; Ge 29:35; [n]ver 6; [o]Ge 42:2; Ps 33:18–19
9 [p]1Sa 23:20; [q]Ge 44:10,17; [r]Ge 42:37; Phm 1:18–19
10 [s]Ge 45:9
11 [t]ver 6; [u]Ge 24:10; [v]Ge 32:13; [w]Ge 37:25; Eze 27:17; [x]Ex 30:23; 1Ki 10:2; Eze 27:22; [y]Ge 37:25
12 [z]ver 15; Ex 22:4,7; Pr 6:31; [a]Ge 42:25
13 [b]ver 3
14 [c]Ge 17:1; [d]Dt 13:17; Ps 25:6; [e]Ge 42:24; [f]2Sa 18:33; Est 4:16
15 [g]ver 12; [h]Ge 45:9,13; [i]Ge 47:2,7; Mt 2:11
16 [j]Ge 35:18; [k]ver 17,24,26; Ge 44:1,4,12; 2Sa 19:17; Isa 22:15; [l]ver 31; Lk 15:23
17 [m]ver 16
18 [n]Ge 42:35; [o]Ge 44:14; [p]Ge 42:25; [q]Ge 32:11; [r]Ge 44:9,16, 33; 50:18; [s]Ge 34:28
19 [t]ver 16
20 [u]Ge 42:3
21 [v]ver 15; Ge 42:25
23 [w]Ge 24:12; 31:5; Ex 3:6; [x]Ge 42:28; [y]Ge 42:24
24 [z]ver 16; [a]Ge 18:4
25 [b]Ge 32:13; [c]ver 16
26 [d]ver 16; [e]Ge 32:13; Mt 2:11; [f]Ge 33:3
27 [g]Ge 37:3; [h]ver 7
28 [i]Ge 44:24,27,30; [j]Ge 18:2; Ex 18:7; [k]Ge 37:7

b38 Hebrew *Sheol* a14 Hebrew *El-Shaddai*

brother Benjamin, his own mother's
son,[l] he asked, "Is this your youngest
brother, the one you told me about?"[m]
And he said, "God be gracious to you,[n]
my son." 30 Deeply moved[o] at the sight
of his brother, Joseph hurried out and
looked for a place to weep. He went into
his private room and wept[p] there.
31 After he had washed his face, he
came out and, controlling himself,[q]
said, "Serve the food."[r]

32 They served him by himself, the
brothers by themselves, and the Egyp-
tians who ate with him by themselves,
because Egyptians could not eat with
Hebrews,[s] for that is detestable to Egyp-
tians.[t] 33 The men had been seated be-
fore him in the order of their ages, from
the firstborn[u] to the youngest;[v] and they
looked at each other in astonishment.
34 When portions were served to them
from Joseph's table, Benjamin's portion
was five times as much as anyone
else's.[w] So they feasted[x] and drank
freely with him.

A Silver Cup in a Sack

44 Now Joseph gave these instruc-
tions to the steward of his
house:[a] "Fill the men's sacks with as
much food as they can carry, and put
each man's silver in the mouth of his
sack.[b] 2 Then put my cup,[c] the silver
one,[d] in the mouth of the youngest
one's sack, along with the silver for his
grain." And he did as Joseph said.

3 As morning dawned, the men were
sent on their way with their donkeys.[e]
4 They had not gone far from the city
when Joseph said to his steward,[f] "Go
after those men at once, and when you
catch up with them, say to them, 'Why
have you repaid good with evil?[g] 5 Isn't
this the cup[h] my master drinks from
and also uses for divination?[i] This is a
wicked thing you have done.'"

6 When he caught up with them, he
repeated these words to them. 7 But they
said to him, "Why does my lord say
such things? Far be it from your ser-
vants[j] to do anything like that![k] 8 We
even brought back to you from the land
of Canaan[l] the silver[m] we found inside
the mouths of our sacks.[n] So why would
we steal[o] silver or gold from your mas-
ter's house? 9 If any of your servants[p]
is found to have it, he will die;[q] and
the rest of us will become my lord's
slaves."[r]

10 "Very well, then," he said, "let it be
as you say. Whoever is found to have it[s]
will become my slave;[t] the rest of you
will be free from blame."[u]

11 Each of them quickly lowered his
sack to the ground and opened it.
12 Then the steward[v] proceeded to
search,[w] beginning with the oldest and
ending with the youngest.[x] And the cup
was found in Benjamin's sack.[y] 13 At
this, they tore their clothes.[z] Then they
all loaded their donkeys[a] and returned
to the city.

14 Joseph was still in the house[b] when
Judah[c] and his brothers came in, and
they threw themselves to the ground
before him.[d] 15 Joseph said to them,
"What is this you have done?[e] Don't
you know that a man like me can find
things out by divination?"[f]

16 "What can we say to my lord?"[g]
Judah[h] replied. "What can we say? How
can we prove our innocence?[i] God has
uncovered your servants'[j] guilt. We are
now my lord's slaves[k]—we ourselves
and the one who was found to have the
cup."[l]

17 But Joseph said, "Far be it from me
to do such a thing![m] Only the man who
was found to have the cup will become
my slave.[n] The rest of you, go back to
your father in peace."[o]

18 Then Judah[p] went up to him and
said: "Please, my lord,[q] let your servant
speak a word to my lord. Do not be
angry[r] with your servant, though you
are equal to Pharaoh himself. 19 My
lord asked his servants,[s] 'Do you have
a father or a brother?'[t] 20 And we
answered, 'We have an aged father, and
there is a young son born to him in his
old age.[u] His brother is dead,[v] and he is
the only one of his mother's sons left,
and his father loves him.'[w]

21 "Then you said to your servants,[x]
'Bring him down to me so I can see him
for myself.'[y] 22 And we said to my lord,[z]
'The boy cannot leave his father; if he
leaves him, his father will die.'[a] 23 But
you told your servants, 'Unless your
youngest brother comes down with
you, you will not see my face again.'[b]
24 When we went back to your servant
my father,[c] we told him what my lord[d]
had said.[e]

25 "Then our father said, 'Go back and
buy a little more food.'[f] 26 But we said,
'We cannot go down. Only if our
youngest brother is with us will we go.
We cannot see the man's face unless our
youngest brother is with us.'[g]

27 "Your servant my father[h] said to us,
'You know that my wife bore me two
sons.[i] 28 One of them went away from

29 [l]**Ge 35:18;** [m]**Ge 42:13;** [n]Nu 6:25; Ps 67:1; 119:58; Isa 30:18–19; 33:2
30 [o]Jn 11:33,38; [p]**Ge 29:11**
31 [q]Ge 45:1; Isa 30:18; 42:14; 63:15; 64:12; [r]**ver 16**
32 [s]**Ge 14:13;** Gal 2:12; [t]Ge 46:34; Ex 8:26
33 [u]**Ge 35:23;** [v]**Ge 42:13;** 44:12
34 [w]**Ge 37:3;** **2Ki 25:30;** [x]Lk 15:23

Ch. 44

1 [a]**Ge 43:16;** [b]**Ge 42:25**
2 [c]ver 5,10,12, 16; [d]ver 8
3 [e]Jdg 19:9
4 [f]**Ge 43:16;** [g]Ps 35:12; 38:20; 109:5; Pr 17:13; Jer 18:20
5 [h]**ver 2;** [i]Ge 30:27; Dt 18:10–14
7 [j]Ge 42:11; [k]Ge 18:25
8 [l]Ge 42:13; [m]ver 2; [n]Ge 42:25; 43:15; [o]Ge 31:30
9 [p]**Ge 42:11;** [q]Ge 31:32; [r]**ver 10;** **Ge 43:18**
10 [s]**ver 2;** [t]ver 9,17,33; [u]**Ge 43:9**
12 [v]**Ge 43:16;** [w]Ge 31:34; [x]**Ge 43:33;** [y]ver 2
13 [z]Ge 37:29; [a]**Ge 42:26**
14 [b]Ge 43:18; [c]ver 16; **Ge 29:35; 43:3;** [d]Ge 33:3
15 [e]**Ge 12:18;** [f]**Ge 30:27**
16 [g]ver 22,24; **Ge 37:8;** [h]**ver 14;** [i]Ps 26:6; 73:13; [j]**Ge 42:11;** [k]**Ge 43:18;** [l]**ver 2**
17 [m]**Ge 18:25;** [n]**ver 10;** [o]**Ge 43:9**
18 [p]**Ge 29:35;** [q]**ver 16;** [r]**Ge 18:30**
19 [s]**Ge 42:11;** [t]**Ge 43:7**
20 [u]**Ge 37:3;** [v]**Ge 37:33;** [w]**Ge 42:13**
21 [x]**Ge 42:11;** [y]**Ge 42:15**
22 [z]**ver 16;** [a]**Ge 37:35**
23 [b]**Ge 42:15; 43:5**

24 [c]**Ge 43:28;** [d]**ver 16;** [e]**Ge 42:29** **25** [f]**Ge 42:2**
26 [g]**Ge 43:5** **27** [h]**Ge 43:28;** [i]**Ge 46:19**

me, and I said, "He has surely been torn to pieces."[j] And I have not seen him since.[k] 29If you take this one from me too and harm comes to him, you will bring my grey head down to the grave[a][l] in misery.'[m]

30"So now, if the boy is not with us when I go back to your servant my father[n] and if my father, whose life is closely bound up with the boy's life,[o] 31sees that the boy isn't there, he will die.[p] Your servants[q] will bring the grey head of our father down to the grave[r] in sorrow. 32Your servant guaranteed the boy's safety to my father. I said, 'If I do not bring him back to you, I will bear the blame before you, my father, all my life!'[s]

33"Now then, please let your servant remain here as my lord's slave[t] in place of the boy,[u] and let the boy return with his brothers. 34How can I go back to my father if the boy is not with me? No! Do not let me see the misery[v] that would come upon my father."[w]

Joseph Makes Himself Known

45 Then Joseph could no longer control himself[a] before all his attendants, and he cried out, "Make everyone leave my presence!"[b] So there was no-one with Joseph when he made himself known to his brothers. 2And he wept[c] so loudly that the Egyptians heard him, and Pharaoh's household heard about it.[d]

3Joseph said to his brothers, "I am Joseph! Is my father still living?"[e] But his brothers were not able to answer him,[f] because they were terrified at his presence.[g]

4Then Joseph said to his brothers, "Come close to me."[h] When they had done so, he said, "I am your brother Joseph, the one you sold into Egypt![i] 5And now, do not be distressed[j] and do not be angry with yourselves for selling me here,[k] because it was to save lives that God sent me ahead of you.[l] 6For two years now there has been famine[m] in the land, and for the next five years there will not be ploughing and reaping. 7But God sent me ahead of you to preserve for you a remnant[n] on earth and to save your lives by a great deliverance.[a][o]

8"So then, it was not you who sent me here, but God.[p] He made me father[q] to Pharaoh, lord of his entire household and ruler of all Egypt.[r] 9Now hurry[s] back to my father and say to him, 'This is what your son Joseph says: God has made me lord of all Egypt. Come down to me; don't delay.[t] 10You shall live in the region of Goshen[u] and be near me—you, your children and grandchildren, your flocks and herds, and all you have.[v] 11I will provide for you there,[w] because five years of famine[x] are still to come. Otherwise you and your household and all who belong to you will become destitute.'[y]

12"You can see for yourselves, and so can my brother Benjamin,[z] that it is really I who am speaking to you.[a] 13Tell my father about all the honour accorded me in Egypt[b] and about everything you have seen. And bring my father down here quickly."[c]

14Then he threw his arms around his brother Benjamin and wept, and Benjamin[d] embraced him,[e] weeping. 15And he kissed[f] all his brothers and wept over them.[g] Afterwards his brothers talked with him.[h]

16When the news reached Pharaoh's palace that Joseph's brothers had come,[i] Pharaoh and all his officials[j] were pleased.[k] 17Pharaoh said to Joseph, "Tell your brothers, 'Do this: Load your animals[l] and return to the land of Canaan,[m] 18and bring your father and your families back to me. I will give you the best of the land of Egypt[n] and you can enjoy the fat of the land.'[o]

19"You are also directed to tell them, 'Do this: Take some carts[p] from Egypt for your children and your wives, and get your father and come. 20Never mind about your belongings,[q] because the best of all Egypt[r] will be yours.' "

21So the sons of Israel did this. Joseph gave them carts,[s] as Pharaoh had commanded, and he also gave them provisions for their journey.[t] 22To each of them he gave new clothing,[u] but to Benjamin he gave three hundred shekels[b] of silver and five sets of clothes.[v] 23And this is what he sent to his father: ten donkeys[w] loaded with the best things[x] of Egypt, and ten female donkeys loaded with grain and bread and other provisions for his journey.[y] 24Then he sent his brothers away, and as they

28 [j]Ge 37:33; [k]Ge 45:26,28; 46:30; 48:11
29 [l]Ge 37:35; [m]**Ge 42:38**
30 [n]**Ge 43:28;** [o]1Sa 18:1; 2Sa 1:26
31 [p]**ver 22;** [q]**Ge 42:11;** [r]**Ge 37:35**
32 [s]**Ge 42:37**
33 [t]**ver 10;** **Ge 43:18;** [u]Jn 15:13
34 [v]**Ge 42:38;** [w]Est 8:6

Ch. 45

1 [a]Ge 43:31; [b]2Sa 13:9
2 [c]Ge 29:11; [d]ver 16; Ac 7:13
3 [e]Ge 43:7; [f]ver 15; [g]Ge 44:20; Job 21:6; 23:15; Mt 17:6; Mk 6:49–50
4 [h]Ge 27:21–22; [i]Ge 37:28
5 [j]Ge 42:21; [k]Ge 42:22; [l]ver 7–8; Ge 50:20; Job 10:12; Ps 105:17
6 [m]**Ge 41:30**
7 [n]2Ki 19:4,30, 31; Ezr 9:8, 13; Isa 1:9; 10:20–21; 11:11,16; 46:3; Jer 6:9; 42:2; 50:20; Mic 4:7; 5:7; Zep 2:7; [o]**ver 5;** Ge 49:18; Ex 15:2; 1Sa 14:45; 2Ki 13:5; Est 4:14; Isa 25:9; Mic 7:7
8 [p]ver 5; [q]Jdg 17:10; 2Ki 6:21; 13:14; [r]**Ge 41:41**
9 [s]**Ge 43:15;** [t]Ge 43:10; Ac 7:14
10 [u]Ge 46:28,34; 47:1,11,27; 50:8; Ex 8:22; 9:26; 10:24; [v]Ge 46:6–7
11 [w]Ge 47:12; 50:21; [x]**Ge 41:30;** [y]Ps 102:17
12 [z]**Ge 35:18;** [a]Mk 6:50
13 [b]**Ge 41:41;** [c]**Ge 43:15;** Ac 7:14
14 [d]Ge 35:18; [e]**Ge 29:13**
15 [f]**Ge 29:11;** Lk 15:20; [g]**Ge 29:11,13; 46:4;** [h]ver 3
16 [i]ver 2; Ac 7:13; [j]Ge 50:7; [k]**Ge 41:37**
17 [l]Ge 42:26; [m]**Ge 42:5**
18 [n]ver 20; Ge 20:15; 46:34; 47:6,11,27; Jer 40:4; [o]Ezr 9:12; Ps 37:19; Isa 1:19
19 [p]ver 21,27; Ge 46:5; Nu 7:3–8
20 [q]Ge 46:6,32; [r]**ver 18** *21* [s]**ver 19;** [t]**Ge 42:25**
22 [u]**Ge 24:53;** [v]**Ge 37:3; 41:14;** Jdg 14:12–13; 2Ki 5:22
23 [w]**Ge 42:26;** [x]**Ge 24:10;** [y]**Ge 42:25**

[a]29 Hebrew *Sheol;* also in verse 31
[a]7 Or *save you as a great band of survivors*
[b]22 That is, about 7½ pounds (about 3.5 kilograms)

were leaving he said to them, "Don't
quarrel on the way!"[z]
25So they went up out of Egypt[a] and
came to their father Jacob in the land of
Canaan.[b] 26They told him, "Joseph is
still alive! In fact, he is ruler of all
Egypt."[c] Jacob was stunned; he did not
believe them.[d] 27But when they told him
everything Joseph had said to them,
and when he saw the carts[e] Joseph had
sent to carry him back, the spirit of their
father Jacob revived. 28And Israel said,
"I'm convinced![f] My son Joseph is still
alive. I will go and see him before I
die."[g]

Jacob Goes to Egypt

46 So Israel[a] set out with all that
was his, and when he reached
Beersheba,[b] he offered sacrifices[c] to the
God of his father Isaac.[d]
2And God spoke to Israel[e] in a vision
at night[f] and said, "Jacob! Jacob!"
"Here I am,"[g] he replied.
3"I am God, the God of your father,"[h]
he said. "Do not be afraid[i] to go down to
Egypt,[j] for I will make you into a great
nation[k] there.[l] 4I will go down to Egypt
with you, and I will surely bring you
back again.[m] And Joseph's own hand
will close your eyes.[n]"
5Then Jacob left Beersheba,[o] and
Israel's[p] sons took their father Jacob and
their children and their wives in the
carts[q] that Pharaoh had sent to transport
him. 6They also took with them their
livestock and the possessions[r] they had
acquired[s] in Canaan, and Jacob and all
his offspring went to Egypt.[t] 7He took
with him to Egypt[u] his sons and grand-
sons and his daughters and grand-
daughters—all his offspring.[v]

8These are the names of the sons of
Israel[w] (Jacob and his descendants) who
went to Egypt:

Reuben the firstborn[x] of Jacob.
9The sons of Reuben:[y]
Hanoch, Pallu,[z] Hezron and
Carmi.[a]
10The sons of Simeon:[b]
Jemuel,[c] Jamin, Ohad, Jakin,
Zohar[d] and Shaul the son of a
Canaanite woman.
11The sons of Levi:[e]
Gershon,[f] Kohath[g] and Merari.[h]
12The sons of Judah:[i]
Er,[j] Onan,[k] Shelah, Perez[l] and
Zerah[m] (but Er and Onan had
died in the land of Canaan).[n]
The sons of Perez:[o]
Hezron and Hamul.[p]
13The sons of Issachar:[q]
Tola, Puah,[a][r] Jashub[b][s] and Shim-
ron.
14The sons of Zebulun:[t]
Sered, Elon and Jahleel.
15These were the sons Leah bore to
Jacob in Paddan Aram,[c][u] besides his
daughter Dinah.[v] These sons and
daughters of his were thirty-three in all.

16The sons of Gad:[w]
Zephon,[d][x] Haggi, Shuni, Ezbon,
Eri, Arodi and Areli.
17The sons of Asher:[y]
Imnah, Ishvah, Ishvi and Beriah.
Their sister was Serah.
The sons of Beriah:
Heber and Malkiel.
18These were the children born to
Jacob by Zilpah,[z] whom Laban had
given to his daughter Leah[a]—sixteen in
all.

19The sons of Jacob's wife Rachel:[b]
Joseph and Benjamin.[c] 20In
Egypt, Manasseh[d] and Ephraim[e]
were born to Joseph[f] by Asenath
daughter of Potiphera, priest of
On.[e][g]
21The sons of Benjamin:[h]
Bela, Beker, Ashbel, Gera,
Naaman, Ehi, Rosh, Muppim,
Huppim and Ard.[i]
22These were the sons of Rachel[j] who
were born to Jacob—fourteen in all.

23The son of Dan:[k]
Hushim.[l]
24The sons of Naphtali:[m]
Jahziel, Guni, Jezer and Shillem.
25These were the sons born to Jacob
by Bilhah,[n] whom Laban had given to
his daughter Rachel[o]—seven in all.

26All those who went to Egypt with
Jacob—those who were his direct de-
scendants, not counting his sons' wives
—numbered sixty-six persons.[p] 27With

24 [z]Ge 42:21–22
25 [a]Ge 13:1; [b]Ge 42:29
26 [c]Ge 41:41; [d]Ge 44:28; 1Ki 10:7
27 [e]ver 19
28 [f]Lk 16:31; [g]Ge 44:28

Ch. 46

1 [a]ver 5; [b]Ge 21:14; [c]Ge 31:54; [d]Ge 31:42
2 [e]Ge 17:5; [f]Ge 15:1; [g]Ge 22:1
3 [h]Ge 28:13; [i]Ge 15:1; [j]Ge 26:2; [k]Ge 12:2; [l]Ex 1:7
4 [m]Ge 15:16; 28:13; [n]ver 29; Ge 45:14–15; 50:1
5 [o]Ge 21:14; [p]ver 1; [q]Ge 45:19
6 [r]Ge 45:20; [s]Ge 12:5; [t]Nu 20:15; Dt 26:5; Jos 24:4; 1Sa 12:8; Ps 105:23; Isa 52:4; Ac 7:15
7 [u]Ge 13:10; [v]ver 6; Ge 45:10
8 [w]Ge 35:26; Ex 1:1; Nu 26:4; [x]Ge 29:32
9 [y]Ex 6:14; Nu 1:20; 26:7; 1Ch 5:3; [z]Nu 26:5; 1Ch 5:3; [a]Nu 26:6
10 [b]Ge 29:33; Nu 26:14; [c]Ex 6:15; Nu 26:12; [d]Nu 26:13
11 [e]Ge 29:34; Nu 3:17; [f]Ex 6:16; Nu 3:21; 4:38; [g]Ex 6:16; Nu 3:27; 1Ch 23:12; [h]Ex 6:19; Nu 3:20,33; 4:29; 26:57; 1Ch 6:19
12 [i]Ge 29:35; [j]Ge 38:3; [k]Ge 38:4; [l]Ge 38:29; [m]Ge 38:30; [n]Ge 38:7; Nu 26:19; [o]1Ch 2:5; Mt 1:3; [p]Nu 26:21
13 [q]Ge 30:18; [r]Nu 26:23; Jdg 10:1; 1Ch 7:1; [s]Nu 26:24
14 [t]Ge 30:20
15 [u]Ge 25:20; 29:31–35; [v]Ge 30:21
16 [w]Ge 30:11; Nu 1:25; [x]Nu 26:15
17 [y]Ge 30:13
18 [z]Ge 30:10; [a]Ge 16:1
19 [b]Ge 29:6; [c]Ge 44:27
20 [d]Ge 41:51; [e]Ge 41:52; [f]Nu 26:28–37; [g]Ge 41:45
21 [h]Nu 26:38–41; 1Ch 7:6–12; 8:1; [i]Nu 26:40; 1Ch 8:3
22 [j]Ge 29:6 *23* [k]Ge 30:6; [l]Nu 26:42
24 [m]Ge 30:8 *25* [n]Ge 30:8; [o]Ge 24:61
26 [p]ver 5–7; Ex 1:5; Dt 10:22

[a]*13* Samaritan Pentateuch and Syriac (see also 1 Chron. 7:1); Masoretic Text *Puvah*
[b]*13* Samaritan Pentateuch and some Septuagint manuscripts (see also Num. 26:24 and 1 Chron. 7:1); Masoretic Text *Job*
[c]*15* That is, North-west Mesopotamia
[d]*16* Samaritan Pentateuch and Septuagint (see also Num. 26:15); Masoretic Text *Ziphion*
[e]*20* That is, Heliopolis

the two sons[f] who had been born to
Joseph in Egypt,[q] the members of Jacob's
family, which went to Egypt, were
seventy[g] in all.[r]

28Now Jacob sent Judah[s] ahead of him
to Joseph to get directions to Goshen.[t]
When they arrived in the region of
Goshen, 29Joseph had his chariot[u] made
ready and went to Goshen to meet
his father Israel.[v] As soon as Joseph
appeared before him, he threw his arms
around his father[h] and wept[w] for a long
time.[x]
30Israel[y] said to Joseph, "Now I am
ready to die, since I have seen for myself
that you are still alive."[z]
31Then Joseph said to his brothers and
to his father's household, "I will go up
and speak to Pharaoh and will say to
him, 'My brothers and my father's
household, who were living in the land
of Canaan,[a] have come to me.[b] 32The
men are shepherds;[c] they tend live-
stock,[d] and they have brought along
their flocks and herds and everything
they own.'[e] 33When Pharaoh calls you in
and asks, 'What is your occupation?'[f]
34you should answer, 'Your servants[g]
have tended livestock from our boy-
hood on, just as our fathers did.'[h] Then
you will be allowed to settle[i] in the re-
gion of Goshen,[j] for all shepherds are
detestable to the Egyptians.[k]"

47 Joseph went and told Pharaoh,
"My father and brothers, with
their flocks and herds and everything
they own, have come from the land of
Canaan[a] and are now in Goshen."[b] 2He
chose five of his brothers and presented
them[c] before Pharaoh.
3Pharaoh asked the brothers, "What
is your occupation?"[d]
"Your servants[e] are shepherds,[f]" they
replied to Pharaoh, "just as our fathers
were." 4They also said to him, "We
have come to live here awhile,[g] because
the famine is severe in Canaan[h] and
your servants' flocks have no pasture.[i]
So now, please let your servants settle
in Goshen."[j]
5Pharaoh said to Joseph, "Your father
and your brothers have come to you,
6and the land of Egypt is before you;
settle[k] your father and your brothers in
the best part of the land.[l] Let them live
in Goshen. And if you know of any
among them with special ability,[m] put
them in charge of my own livestock.[n]"
7Then Joseph brought his father Jacob
in and presented him[o] before Pharaoh.
After Jacob blessed[a] Pharaoh,[p] 8Pharaoh
asked him, "How old are you?"

9And Jacob said to Pharaoh, "The
years of my pilgrimage are a hundred
and thirty.[q] My years have been few and
difficult,[r] and they do not equal the
years of the pilgrimage of my fathers.[s]"
10Then Jacob blessed[b] Pharaoh[t] and
went out from his presence.
11So Joseph settled his father and his
brothers in Egypt and gave them prop-
erty in the best part of the land,[u]
the district of Rameses,[v] as Pharaoh
directed. 12Joseph also provided his
father and his brothers and all his
father's household with food, according
to the number of their children.[w]

Joseph and the Famine

13There was no food, however, in the
whole region because the famine was
severe; both Egypt and Canaan wasted
away because of the famine.[x] 14Joseph
collected all the money that was to be
found in Egypt and Canaan in payment
for the grain they were buying,[y] and he
brought it to Pharaoh's palace.[z] 15When
the money of the people of Egypt and
Canaan was gone,[a] all Egypt came to
Joseph[b] and said, "Give us food. Why
should we die before your eyes?[c] Our
money is used up."
16"Then bring your livestock,[d]" said
Joseph. "I will sell you food in exchange
for your livestock, since your money is
gone.[e]" 17So they brought their livestock
to Joseph, and he gave them food in
exchange for their horses,[f] their sheep
and goats, their cattle and donkeys.[g]
And he brought them through that year
with food in exchange for all their live-
stock.
18When that year was over, they came
to him the following year and said, "We
cannot hide from our lord the fact that
since our money is gone[h] and our live-
stock belongs to you,[i] there is nothing
left for our lord except our bodies and
our land. 19Why should we perish be-
fore your eyes[j]—we and our land as
well? Buy us and our land in exchange
for food,[k] and we with our land will be
in bondage to Pharaoh.[l] Give us seed so
that we may live and not die,[m] and that
the land may not become desolate."
20So Joseph bought all the land in
Egypt for Pharaoh. The Egyptians, one
and all, sold their fields, because the

27 [q]**Ge 41:45;** [r]**Ge 34:30;** Ac 7:14
28 [s]**Ge 43:3;** [t]**Ge 45:10**
29 [u]**Ge 41:43;** [v]ver 1,30; **Ge 32:28;** 47:29,31; [w]**Ge 29:11;** [x]**ver 4;** Lk 15:20
30 [y]**ver 29;** [z]**Ge 44:28**
31 [a]**Ge 42:13;** [b]**Ge 45:10**
32 [c]**Ge 47:3;** [d]**Ge 37:2;** [e]**Ge 45:20**
33 [f]Ge 47:3
34 [g]**Ge 42:11;** [h]**Ge 47:3;** [i]**Ge 34:10;** [j]**Ge 45:10;** [k]**Ge 43:32**

Ch. 47

1 [a]**Ge 42:13;** [b]**Ge 46:31**
2 [c]**Ge 43:15**
3 [d]Ge 46:33; [e]**Ge 42:11;** [f]Ge 46:32
4 [g]Ru 1:1; [h]**Ge 12:10;** [i]1Ki 18:5; Jer 14:5–6; Joel 1:18; [j]Ge 46:34
6 [k]**Ge 34:10;** [l]**Ge 13:9; 45:18;** [m]Ex 18:21,25; Dt 1:13,15; 2Ch 19:5; Ps 15:2; [n]**Ge 39:4**
7 [o]**Ge 43:15;** [p]ver 10; 2Sa 14:22; 19:39; 1Ki 8:66
9 [q]**Ge 25:7;** [r]**Ge 3:17;** Ps 39:4; 89:47; [s]Job 8:9; Ps 39:12
10 [t]**ver 7**
11 [u]**Ge 45:10,**18; [v]Ex 1:11; 12:37; Nu 33:3,5
12 [w]**Ge 45:11**
13 [x]**Ge 12:10; 41:30**
14 [y]**Ge 41:36;** [z]**Ge 41:34;** Ex 7:23; 8:24; Jer 43:9
15 [a]ver 16,18; [b]**Ge 41:57;** [c]ver 19; Ex 16:3
16 [d]ver 18–19; [e]ver 15
17 [f]Ex 14:9; [g]**Ge 12:16**
18 [h]**ver 15;** [i]**ver 16**
19 [j]**ver 15;** [k]**ver 16;** [l]ver 21, 25; [m]**Ge 42:2**

f27 Hebrew; Septuagint *the nine children*
g27 Hebrew (see also Exodus 1:5 and footnote); Septuagint (see also Acts 7:14) *seventy-five*
h29 Hebrew *around him*
a7 Or *greeted*
b10 Or *said farewell to*

famine was too severe[n] for them. The land became Pharaoh's, 21and Joseph reduced the people to servitude,[c o] from one end of Egypt to the other. 22However, he did not buy the land of the priests,[p] because they received a regular allotment from Pharaoh and had food enough from the allotment[q] Pharaoh gave them. That is why they did not sell their land.

23Joseph said to the people, "Now that I have bought you and your land today for Pharaoh, here is seed[r] for you so you can plant the ground.[s] 24But when the crop comes in, give a fifth[t] of it to Pharaoh. The other four-fifths you may keep as seed for the fields and as food for yourselves and your households and your children."

25"You have saved our lives," they said. "May we find favour in the eyes of our lord;[u] we will be in bondage to Pharaoh."[v]

26So Joseph established it as a law concerning land in Egypt—still in force today—that a fifth[w] of the produce belongs to Pharaoh. It was only the land of the priests that did not become Pharaoh's.[x]

27Now the Israelites settled in Egypt in the region of Goshen.[y] They acquired property there[z] and were fruitful and increased greatly in number.[a]

28Jacob lived in Egypt[b] seventeen years, and the years of his life were a hundred and forty-seven.[c] 29When the time drew near for Israel[d] to die,[e] he called for his son Joseph and said to him, "If I have found favour in your eyes,[f] put your hand under my thigh[g] and promise that you will show me kindness[h] and faithfulness.[i] Do not bury me in Egypt, 30but when I rest with my fathers,[j] carry me out of Egypt and bury me where they are buried."[k]

"I will do as you say," he said.

31"Swear to me,"[l] he said. Then Joseph swore to him,[m] and Israel[n] worshipped as he leaned on the top of his staff.[d o]

Manasseh and Ephraim

48 Some time later Joseph was told, "Your father is ill." So he took his two sons Manasseh and Ephraim[a] along with him. 2When Jacob was told, "Your son Joseph has come to you," Israel[b] rallied his strength and sat up on the bed.

3Jacob said to Joseph, "God Almighty[a c] appeared to me at Luz[d] in the land of Canaan, and there he blessed me[e] 4and said to me, 'I am going to make you fruitful and will increase your numbers.[f] I will make you a community of peoples, and I will give this land[g] as an everlasting possession to your descendants after you.'[h]

5"Now then, your two sons born to you in Egypt[i] before I came to you here will be reckoned as mine; Ephraim and Manasseh will be mine,[j] just as Reuben[k] and Simeon[l] are mine. 6Any children born to you after them will be yours; in the territory they inherit they will be reckoned under the names of their brothers. 7As I was returning from Paddan,[b m] to my sorrow[n] Rachel died in the land of Canaan while we were still on the way, a little distance from Ephrath. So I buried her there beside the road to Ephrath" (that is, Bethlehem).[o]

8When Israel[p] saw the sons of Joseph,[q] he asked, "Who are these?"

9"They are the sons God has given me here,"[r] Joseph said to his father.

Then Israel said, "Bring them to me so that I may bless[s] them."

10Now Israel's eyes were failing because of old age, and he could hardly see.[t] So Joseph brought his sons close to him, and his father kissed them[u] and embraced them.[v]

11Israel[w] said to Joseph, "I never expected to see your face again,[x] and now God has allowed me to see your children too."[y]

12Then Joseph removed them from Israel's knees[z] and bowed down with his face to the ground.[a] 13And Joseph took both of them, Ephraim on his right towards Israel's left hand and Manasseh on his left towards Israel's right hand,[b] and brought them close to him. 14But Israel[c] reached out his right hand and put it on Ephraim's head,[d] though he was the younger,[e] and crossing his arms, he put his left hand on Manasseh's head, even though Manasseh was the firstborn.[f]

15Then he blessed[g] Joseph and said,

"May the God before whom my
fathers
Abraham and Isaac walked,[h]

20 nGe 12:10
21 over 19
22 pver 26; qDt 14:28–29
23 rIsa 55:10; 61:11; sNe 5:3
24 tGe 41:34
25 uGe 32:5; vver 19
26 wGe 41:34; xver 22
27 yGe 45:10,18; zGe 33:19; aGe 1:22; 12:2; 17:6
28 bPs 105:23; cGe 25:7
29 dGe 46:29; eGe 27:2; fGe 32:5; gGe 24:2; hGe 19:19; iGe 24:27; Jdg 1:24; 2Sa 2:6
30 jGe 15:15; kGe 23:20; 25:9; 29:16; 50:25; Ex 13:19; Jos 24:32; Ac 7:15–16
31 lGe 21:23; Jos 2:20; Jdg 15:12; 1Sa 24:21; 30:15; mGe 24:3; nGe 46:29; oGe 32:10; Heb 11:21 *fn*; 1Ki 1:47

Ch. 48

1 aGe 41:52; Heb 11:21
2 bver 8–9,11, 14,20
3 cGe 17:1; dGe 28:19; eGe 28:13; 32:29
4 fGe 12:2; 17:6; gGe 12:7; 28:13; hGe 15:7
5 iGe 41:50–52; j1Ch 5:1; kGe 29:32; lGe 29:33
7 mGe 25:20; nGe 42:38; oGe 35:19; Ru 1:2; 1Sa 16:4
8 pver 2; qver 10
9 rGe 33:5; sGe 24:60
10 tGe 27:1; uGe 27:27; vGe 29:13
11 wver 2; xGe 44:28; yGe 50:23; Job 42:16; Ps 103:17; 128:6
12 zGe 50:23; Job 3:12; aGe 19:1; 33:3; 37:10
13 bPs 16:8; 73:23; 110:1; Mt 25:33
14 cver 2; dver 17–18; eGe 25:23; fGe 29:32; 41:51

15 gGe 24:60; hGe 5:22

c21 Samaritan Pentateuch and Septuagint (see also Vulgate); Masoretic Text *and he moved the people into the cities*
d31 Or *Israel bowed down at the head of his bed*
a3 Hebrew *El-Shaddai*
b7 That is, North-west Mesopotamia

the God who has been my
shepherd[i]
all my life to this day,
16the Angel[j] who has delivered me
from all harm[k]
—may he bless[l] these boys.[m]
May they be called by my name
and the names of my fathers
Abraham and Isaac,[n]
and may they increase greatly
upon the earth."[o]

17When Joseph saw his father placing
his right hand[p] on Ephraim's head[q] he
was displeased; so he took hold of his
father's hand to move it from Ephraim's
head to Manasseh's head. 18Joseph said
to him, "No, my father, this one is the
firstborn; put your right hand on his
head."[r]

19But his father refused and said, "I
know, my son, I know. He too will
become a people, and he too will be-
come great.[s] Nevertheless, his younger
brother will be greater than he,[t] and his
descendants will become a group of
nations."[u] 20He blessed[v] them that day[w]
and said,

"In your[c] name will Israel[x] pronounce
this blessing:[y]
'May God make you like Ephraim[z]
and Manasseh.'[a]"

So he put Ephraim ahead of Manasseh.
21Then Israel said to Joseph, "I am
about to die, but God will be with you[d][b]
and take you[d] back to the land of your[d]
fathers.[c] 22And to you, as one who is
over your brothers,[d] I give the ridge of
land[e][e] I took from the Amorites with my
sword[f] and my bow."

Jacob Blesses His Sons

49:1–28Ref—Dt 33:1–29

49 Then Jacob called for his sons
and said: "Gather round so that
I can tell you what will happen to you in
days to come.[a]

2"Assemble[b] and listen, sons of Jacob;
listen to your father Israel.[c]

3"Reuben, you are my firstborn,[d]
my might, the first sign of my
strength,[e]
excelling in honour,[f] excelling in
power.
4Turbulent as the waters,[g] you will no
longer excel,
for you went up onto your father's
bed,
onto my couch and defiled it.[h]

5"Simeon[i] and Levi[j] are brothers—
their swords[a] are weapons of
violence.[k]
6Let me not enter their council,
let me not join their assembly,[l]
for they have killed men in their
anger[m]
and hamstrung[n] oxen as they
pleased.
7Cursed be their anger, so fierce,
and their fury,[o] so cruel![p]
I will scatter them in Jacob
and disperse them in Israel.[q]

8"Judah,[b][r] your brothers will praise
you;
your hand will be on the neck[s] of
your enemies;
your father's sons will bow down to
you.[t]
9You are a lion's[u] cub,[v] O Judah;[w]
you return from the prey,[x] my son.
Like a lion he crouches and lies down,
like a lioness—who dares to rouse
him?
10The sceptre will not depart from
Judah,[y]
nor the ruler's staff from between
his feet,
until he comes to whom it belongs[c][z]
and the obedience of the nations is
his.[a]
11He will tether his donkey[b] to a vine,
his colt to the choicest branch;[c]
he will wash his garments in wine,
his robes in the blood of grapes.[d]
12His eyes will be darker than wine,
his teeth whiter than milk.[d][e]

13"Zebulun[f] will live by the seashore
and become a haven for ships;
his border will extend towards
Sidon.[g]

14"Issachar[h] is a scrawny[e] donkey
lying down between two
saddlebags.[f][i]

15 [i]Ge 49:24; 2Sa 5:2; Ps 23:1; 80:1; Isa 40:11; Jer 23:4 *16* [j]**Ge 16:7;** [k]**Ge 24:50;** 2Sa 4:9; Ps 71:4; Jer 15:21; Da 3:17; [l]**Ge 28:3;** [m]1Ch 5:1; Eze 47:13; Heb 11:21; [n]**Ge 28:13;** [o]**Ge 12:2; 13:14** *17* [p]ver 13; [q]**ver 14** *18* [r]**ver 14** *19* [s]**Ge 17:20;** [t]**Ge 25:23;** [u]**Ge 12:2** *20* [v]**Ge 24:60;** [w]Heb 11:21; [x]**ver 2;** [y]Lev 9:22; Nu 6:23; Dt 10:8; 21:5; [z]Nu 2:18; Jer 31:9; [a]**Ge 41:51;** Nu 2:20; 10:23; Ru 4:11 *21* [b]**Ge 26:3;** [c]**Ge 15:16; 28:13;** Dt 30:3; Ps 126:1; Jer 29:14; Eze 34:13 *22* [d]**Ge 37:8;** [e]Jos 24:32; Jn 4:5; [f]**Ge 34:26**

Ch. 49

1 [a]Nu 24:14; Dt 31:29; Jer 23:20; Da 2:28,45 *2* [b]Jos 24:1; [c]ver 16,28; Ps 34:11 *3* [d]**Ge 29:32; 41:51;** [e]Dt 21:17; Ps 78:51; 105:36; [f]**Ge 34:19** *4* [g]Isa 57:20; Jer 49:23; [h]**Ge 29:29; 34:5** *5* [i]**Ge 29:33;** [j]Ge 29:34; [k]**Ge 34:25; Pr 4:17** *6* [l]Ps 1:1; Pr 1:15; Eph 5:11; [m]**Ge 34:26;** [n]Jos 11:6,9; 2Sa 8:4; 1Ch 18:4 *7* [o]Ge 34:7; [p]Ge 34:25; [q]Jos 19:1,9; 21:1–42 *8* [r]**Ge 29:35;** [s]Dt 28:48; [t]**Ge 9:25;** 1Ch 5:2 *9* [u]Nu 24:9; Ps 7:2; 10:9; Eze 19:5; Mic 5:8; [v]Eze 19:2; [w]Rev 5:5; [x]ver 27; Nu 23:24; Job 38:39; Ps 17:12; 22:13; 104:21

10 [y]Nu 24:17,19; Jdg 1:1–2; 20:18; 1Ch 5:2; 28:4; Ps 60:7; 108:8; [z]Eze 21:27; [a]Ps 2:9; 72:8–11; 98:3; 110:2; Isa 2:4; 26:18; 42:1,4; 45:22; 48:20; 49:6; 51:5 *11* [b]Jdg 5:10; 10:4; Zec 9:9; [c]Dt 8:8; 2Ki 18:32; [d]Dt 32:14; Isa 63:2 *12* [e]SS 5:12 *13* [f]**Ge 30:20;** [g]**Ge 10:19** *14* [h]**Ge 30:18;** [i]Jdg 5:16; Ps 68:13

c20 The Hebrew is singular.
d21 The Hebrew is plural.
e22 Or *And to you I give one portion more than to your brothers—the portion*
a5 The meaning of the Hebrew for this word is uncertain.
b8 *Judah* sounds like and may be derived from the Hebrew for *praise.*
c10 Or *until Shiloh comes;* or *until he comes to whom tribute belongs*
d12 Or *will be dull from wine, / his teeth white from milk*
e14 Or *strong* f14 Or *campfires*

15When he sees how good is his resting
place
and how pleasant is his land,[j]
he will bend his shoulder to the
burden[k]
and submit to forced labour.[l]

16"Dan[g] [m] will provide justice for his
people
as one of the tribes of Israel.[n]
17Dan[o] will be a serpent by the roadside,
a viper along the path,[p]
that bites the horse's heels[q]
so that its rider tumbles backwards.

18"I look for your deliverance,[r] O LORD.[s]

19"Gad[h] [t] will be attacked by a band of
raiders,
but he will attack them at their
heels.[u]

20"Asher's[v] food will be rich;[w]
he will provide delicacies fit for a
king.[x]

21"Naphtali[y] is a doe set free
that bears beautiful fawns.[i] [z]

22"Joseph[a] is a fruitful vine,[b]
a fruitful vine near a spring,
whose branches[c] climb over a wall.[j]
23With bitterness archers attacked him;[d]
they shot at him with hostility.[e]
24But his bow remained steady,[f]
his strong arms[g] stayed[k] supple,
because of the hand of the Mighty One
of Jacob,[h]
because of the Shepherd,[i] the Rock
of Israel,[j]
25because of your father's God,[k] who
helps[l] you,
because of the Almighty,[l] [m] who
blesses you
with blessings of the heavens above,
blessings of the deep that lies
below,[n]
blessings of the breast[o] and womb.[p]
26Your father's blessings are greater
than the blessings of the ancient
mountains,
than[m] the bounty of the age-old
hills.[q]
Let all these rest on the head of
Joseph,[r]
on the brow of the prince among[n]
his brothers.[s]

27"Benjamin[t] is a ravenous wolf;[u]
in the morning he devours the
prey,[v]
in the evening he divides the
plunder."[w]

15 [j]Jos 19:17–23; [k]Eze 29:18; [l]1Ki 4:6; 5:13; 9:21; Isa 14:2; 31:8
16 [m]Ge 30:6; [n]**ver 2**
17 [o]Jdg 18:27; [p]Jer 8:17; Am 9:3; [q]ver 19
18 [r]**Ge 45:7**; Ps 40:1–3; [s]Ps 119:166,174
19 [t]**Ge 30:11**; [u]ver 17
20 [v]**Ge 30:13**; [w]Isa 25:6; [x]Job 29:6
21 [y]**Ge 30:8**; [z]Job 39:1
22 [a]Ge 30:24; [b]**Ge 17:6**; Ps 128:3; Eze 19:10; [c]Ps 80:10
23 [d]1Ch 10:3; [e]**Ge 27:41; 37:24**
24 [f]Job 29:20; [g]Ps 18:34; Isa 63:12; [h]Ps 132:2,5; Isa 1:24; 10:34; 49:26; 60:16; [i]**Ge 48:15**; [j]Dt 32:4,15,18,31; 1Sa 2:2; 2Sa 22:32; Ps 18:2,31; 19:14; 78:35; 89:26; 144:1; Isa 17:10; 26:4; 30:29; 44:8; Hab 1:12
25 [k]**Ge 28:13**; [l]Ex 18:4; Ps 27:9; [m]**Ge 17:1**; [n]**Ge 27:28**; [o]Isa 66:11; [p]Dt 7:13; 28:4; Ps 107:38; Pr 10:22
26 [q]Hab 3:6; [r]1Ch 5:1; Eze 47:13; [s]**Ge 37:8**
27 [t]Ge 35:18; Jdg 20:12–13; [u]Hab 1:8; Zep 3:3; [v]**ver 9**; [w]Nu 31:11; Dt 2:35; Jos 7:21; 8:2; 22:8; Jdg 8:24
28 [x]**ver 2**; [y]**Ge 27:4**
29 [z]Ge 50:16; [a]**Ge 25:8**; [b]**Ge 15:15**; 50:25; 2Sa 2:32; 19:37; [c]**Ge 25:9**
30 [d]**Ge 23:9**; [e]**Ge 13:18**; [f]**Ge 23:4**; [g]**Ge 23:20**
31 [h]Ge 25:9; [i]Ge 23:19; [j]**Ge 24:67**; [k]**Ge 23:20; 29:16**
32 [l]**Ge 10:15**
33 [m]**Ge 25:8**; Ac 7:15

28All these are the twelve tribes of
Israel,[x] and this is what their father said
to them when he blessed them, giving
each the blessing[y] appropriate to him.

The Death of Jacob

29Then he gave them these instruc-
tions:[z] "I am about to be gathered to my
people.[a] Bury me with my fathers[b] in the
cave in the field of Ephron the Hittite,[c]
30the cave in the field of Machpelah,[d]
near Mamre[e] in Canaan, which Abra-
ham bought as a burial place[f] from
Ephron the Hittite, along with the
field.[g] 31There Abraham[h] and his wife
Sarah[i] were buried, there Isaac and his
wife Rebekah[j] were buried, and there I
buried Leah.[k] 32The field and the cave in
it were bought from the Hittites.[o] [l]"
33When Jacob had finished giving in-
structions to his sons, he drew his feet
up into the bed, breathed his last and
was gathered to his people.[m]

50 Joseph threw himself upon his
father and wept over him and
kissed him.[a] 2Then Joseph directed the
physicians in his service to embalm
his father Israel. So the physicians
embalmed him,[b] 3taking a full forty
days, for that was the time required
for embalming. And the Egyptians
mourned for him seventy days.[c]
4When the days of mourning[d] had
passed, Joseph said to Pharaoh's court,[e]
"If I have found favour in your eyes,[f]
speak to Pharaoh for me. Tell him, 5'My
father made me swear an oath[g] and
said, "I am about to die;[h] bury me in the
tomb I dug for myself[i] in the land of
Canaan."[j] Now let me go up and bury
my father;[k] then I will return.'"
6Pharaoh said, "Go up and bury your
father, as he made you swear to do."
7So Joseph went up to bury his father.
All Pharaoh's officials[l] accompanied
him—the dignitaries of his court[m] and

Ch. 50
1 [a]**Ge 29:11; 46:4**
2 [b]ver 26; 2Ch 16:14; Mt 26:12; Mk 16:1; Jn 19:39–40
3 [c]**Ge 37:34; Dt 1:3**
4 [d]**Ge 27:41**; [e]ver 7; [f]**Ge 30:27; 32:5**
5 [g]**Ge 24:37**; [h]ver 24; [i]2Sa 18:18; 2Ch 16:14; Isa 22:16; Mt 27:60; [j]Ge 47:31; [k]Mt 8:21
7 [l]Ge 45:16; [m]ver 4

[g]16 *Dan* here means *he provides justice.*
[h]19 *Gad* can mean *attack* and *band of raiders.*
[i]21 Or *free; / he utters beautiful words*
[j]22 Or *Joseph is a wild colt, / a wild colt near a spring, / a wild donkey on a terraced hill*
[k]23,24 Or *archers will attack . . . will shoot . . . will remain . . . will stay*
[l]25 Hebrew *Shaddai*
[m]26 Or *of my progenitors, / as great as*
[n]26 Or *the one separated from*
[o]32 Or *the sons of Heth*

all the dignitaries of Egypt—8besides all
the members of Joseph's household and
his brothers and those belonging to his
father's household.[n] Only their children
and their flocks and herds were left in
Goshen.[o] 9Chariots[p] and horsemen[a] also
went up with him. It was a very large
company.
10When they reached the threshing-
floor[q] of Atad, near the Jordan, they
lamented loudly and bitterly;[r] and there
Joseph observed a seven-day period[s] of
mourning[t] for his father.[u] 11When the
Canaanites[v] who lived there saw the
mourning at the threshing-floor of
Atad, they said, "The Egyptians are
holding a solemn ceremony of mourn-
ing."[w] That is why that place near the
Jordan is called Abel Mizraim.[b]
12So Jacob's sons did as he had com-
manded them:[x] 13They carried him to
the land of Canaan and buried him in
the cave in the field of Machpelah,[y] near
Mamre,[z] which Abraham had bought as
a burial place from Ephron the Hittite,[a]
along with the field.[b] 14After burying
his father, Joseph returned to Egypt,
together with his brothers and all the
others who had gone with him to bury
his father.[c]

Joseph Reassures His Brothers

15When Joseph's brothers saw that
their father was dead, they said, "What
if Joseph holds a grudge[d] against us and
pays us back for all the wrongs we did to
him?"[e] 16So they sent word to Joseph,
saying, "Your father left these instruc-
tions[f] before he died: 17'This is what you
are to say to Joseph: I ask you to forgive
your brothers the sins[g] and the wrongs
they committed in treating you so
badly.'[h] Now please forgive the sins
of the servants of the God of your
father."[i] When their message came to
him, Joseph wept.[j]
18His brothers then came and threw
themselves down before him.[k] "We are
your slaves,"[l] they said.
19But Joseph said to them, "Don't be
afraid. Am I in the place of God?[m]
20You intended to harm me,[n] but God
intended[o] it for good[p] to accomplish
what is now being done, the saving of
many lives.[q] 21So then, don't be afraid.
I will provide for you and your
children."[r] And he reassured them
and spoke kindly[s] to them.

The Death of Joseph

22Joseph stayed in Egypt, along with
all his father's family. He lived a hun-
dred and ten years[t] 23and saw the third
generation[u] of Ephraim's[v] children.[w]
Also the children of Makir[x] son of
Manasseh[y] were placed at birth on
Joseph's knees.[c][z]
24Then Joseph said to his brothers, "I
am about to die.[a] But God will surely
come to your aid[b] and take you up out of
this land to the land[c] he promised on
oath to Abraham,[d] Isaac[e] and Jacob."[f]
25And Joseph made the sons of Israel
swear an oath[g] and said, "God will sure-
ly come to your aid, and then you must
carry my bones[h] up from this place."[i]
26So Joseph died[j] at the age of a hun-
dred and ten.[k] And after they embalmed
him,[l] he was placed in a coffin in Egypt.

8 [n]ver 14; [o]**Ge 45:10**
9 [p]**Ge 41:43**
10 [q]Nu 15:20; Ru 3:2; 2Sa 24:18; 1Ki 22:10; [r]2Sa 1:17; 3:33; 2Ch 35:25; Eze 32:16; Ac 8:2; [s]1Sa 31:13; Job 2:13; Eze 3:15; [t]**Ge 27:41; Lev 10:6;** [u]**Ge 37:34**
11 [v]**Ge 10:18;** [w]**Ge 37:34**
12 [x]Ge 49:29
13 [y]**Ge 23:9;** [z]**Ge 13:18;** [a]**Ge 25:9;** [b]**Ge 23:20**
14 [c]ver 8
15 [d]**Ge 27:41;** [e]ver 17; Ge 9:5; 37:28; Zep 3:11; 1Pe 3:9
16 [f]Ge 49:29
17 [g]**Mt 6:14;** [h]**ver 15;** [i]**Ge 28:13;** [j]**Ge 29:11**
18 [k]**Ge 37:7;** [l]**Ge 43:18**
19 [m]**Ge 30:2; Ex 32:34;** Ro 12:19; Heb 10:30
20 [n]Ge 37:20; [o]Isa 10:7; Mic 4:11–12; [p]Ro 8:28; [q]**Ge 45:5;** Est 4:14
21 [r]**Ge 45:11;** [s]**Ge 34:3;** Eph 4:32
22 [t]**Ge 25:7;** Jos 24:29

23 [u]Job 42:16; [v]**Ge 41:52;** [w]**Ge 48:11;** [x]Nu 26:29; 27:1; 32:39–40; 36:1; Dt 3:15; Jos 13:31; 17:1; Jdg 5:14; [y]**Ge 41:51;** [z]**Ge 48:12**
24 [a]ver 5; [b]Ru 1:6; Ps 35:2; 106:4; Isa 38:14; [c]**Ge 15:14;** [d]**Ge 13:17;** [e]**Ge 17:19;** [f]**Ge 12:7; 15:16**
25 [g]**Ge 24:37;** [h]**Ge 49:29;** [i]**Ge 47:29–30;** Heb 11:22
26 [j]Ex 1:6; [k]**Ge 25:7;** [l]**ver 2**

a9 Or *charioteers*
b11 *Abel Mizraim* means *mourning of the Egyptians.*
c23 That is, were counted as his

Exodus

The Israelites Oppressed

1 These are the names of the sons of
Israel[a] who went to Egypt with
Jacob, each with his family: 2Reuben,
Simeon, Levi and Judah; 3Issachar,
Zebulun and Benjamin; 4Dan and
Naphtali; Gad and Asher.[b] 5The de-
scendants of Jacob numbered seventy[a]
in all;[c] Joseph was already in Egypt.
6Now Joseph and all his brothers and
all that generation died,[d] 7but the
Israelites were fruitful and multiplied
greatly and became exceedingly numer-
ous,[e] so that the land was filled with
them.
8Then a new king, who did not know
about Joseph, came to power in Egypt.[f]
9"Look," he said to his people, "the
Israelites have become much too
numerous[g] for us.[h] 10Come, we must
deal shrewdly[i] with them or they will
become even more numerous and, if
war breaks out, will join our enemies,
fight against us and leave the country."[j]
11So they put slave masters[k] over
them to oppress them with forced
labour,[l] and they built Pithom and
Rameses[m] as store cities[n] for Pharaoh.
12But the more they were oppressed, the
more they multiplied and spread; so the
Egyptians came to dread the Israelites
13and worked them ruthlessly.[o] 14They
made their lives bitter with hard labour[p]
in brick[q] and mortar and with all kinds
of work in the fields; in all their hard
labour the Egyptians used them ruth-
lessly.[r]
15The king of Egypt said to the He-
brew midwives,[s] whose names were
Shiphrah and Puah, 16"When you help
the Hebrew women in childbirth and
observe them on the delivery stool, if it
is a boy, kill him; but if it is a girl, let
her live."[t] 17The midwives, however,
feared[u] God and did not do what the
king of Egypt had told them to do;[v] they
let the boys live. 18Then the king of
Egypt summoned the midwives and
asked them, "Why have you done this?
Why have you let the boys live?"
19The midwives answered Pharaoh,
"Hebrew women are not like Egyptian
women; they are vigorous and give
birth before the midwives arrive."[w]
20So God was kind to the midwives[x]
and the people increased and became
even more numerous. 21And because
the midwives feared[y] God, he gave
them families[z] of their own.
22Then Pharaoh gave this order to all
his people: "Every boy that is born[b] you
must throw into the Nile,[a] but let every
girl live."[b]

The Birth of Moses

2 Now a man of the house of Levi[a]
married a Levite woman,[b] 2and she
became pregnant and gave birth to a
son. When she saw that he was a fine[c]
child, she hid him for three months.[d]
3But when she could hide him no lon-
ger, she got a papyrus[e] basket for him
and coated it with tar and pitch.[f] Then
she placed the child in it and put it
among the reeds[g] along the bank of the
Nile. 4His sister[h] stood at a distance to
see what would happen to him.
5Then Pharaoh's daughter went
down to the Nile to bathe, and her
attendants were walking along the river
bank.[i] She saw the basket among the
reeds and sent her slave girl to get it.
6She opened it and saw the baby. He
was crying, and she felt sorry for him.
"This is one of the Hebrew babies," she
said.
7Then his sister asked Pharaoh's
daughter, "Shall I go and get one of the
Hebrew women to nurse the baby for
you?"
8"Yes, go," she answered. And the

Ch. 1

1 [a]**Ge 46:8**
4 [b]Ge 35:22–26; Nu 1:20–43
5 [c]**Ge 46:26**
6 [d]Ge 50:26; Ac 7:15
7 [e]ver 9; **Ge 12:2**; Dt 7:13; Eze 16:7
8 [f]Jer 43:11; 46:2
9 [g]**ver 7**; [h]**Ge 26:16**
10 [i]Ge 15:13; Ex 3:7; 18:11; Ps 64:2; 71:10; 83:3; Isa 53:3; [j]Ps 105:24–25; Ac 7:17–19
11 [k]Ex 3:7; 5:10, 13–14; [l]**Ge 15:13**; Ex 2:11; 5:4; 6:6–7; Jos 9:27; 1Ki 9:21; 1Ch 22:2; Isa 60:10; [m]**Ge 47:11**; [n]1Ki 9:19; 2Ch 8:4
13 [o]ver 14; Ge 15:13–14; Ex 5:21; 16:3; Lev 25:43,46,53; Dt 4:20; 26:6; 1Ki 8:51; Ps 129:1; Isa 30:6; 48:10; Jer 11:4
14 [p]Dt 26:6; Ezr 9:9; Isa 14:3; [q]**Ge 11:3**; [r]Ex 2:23; 3:9; Nu 20:15; 1Sa 10:18; 2Ki 13:4; Ps 66:11; 81:6; Ac 7:19
15 [s]**Ge 35:17**
16 [t]ver 22
17 [u]ver 21; Pr 16:6; [v]1Sa 22:17; Da 3:16–18; Ac 4:18–20; 5:29
19 [w]Lev 19:11; Jos 2:4–6; 1Sa 19:14; 2Sa 17:20
20 [x]Pr 11:18; 22:8; Ecc 8:12; Isa 3:10; Heb 6:10
21 [y]**ver 17**; [z]1Sa 2:35; 2Sa 7:11, 27–29; 1Ki 11:38; 14:10
22 [a]**Ge 41:1**; [b]ver 16; Ac 7:19

Ch. 2

1 [a]**Ge 29:34**; [b]ver 2; Ex 6:20; Nu 26:59
2 [c]**Ge 39:6**; [d]Heb 11:23
3 [e]Isa 18:2; [f]Ge 6:14; [g]**Ge 41:2**; **Job 8:11**; Ac 7:21
4 [h]Ex 15:20 *5* [i]Ex 7:15; 8:20

[a]5 Masoretic Text (see also Gen. 46:27); Dead Sea Scrolls and Septuagint (see also Acts 7:14 and note at Gen. 46:27) *seventy-five*
[b]22 Masoretic Text; Samaritan Pentateuch, Septuagint and Targums *born to the Hebrews*

girl went and got the baby's mother.
9Pharaoh's daughter said to her, "Take
this baby and nurse him for me, and I
will pay you." So the woman took the
baby and nursed him. 10When the child
grew older, she took him to Pharaoh's
daughter and he became her son. She
named[j] him Moses,[a] saying, "I drew[k]
him out of the water."

Moses Flees to Midian

11One day, after Moses had grown
up, he went out to where his own peo-
ple[l] were and watched them at their
hard labour.[m] He saw an Egyptian beat-
ing a Hebrew, one of his own people.
12Glancing this way and that and seeing
no-one, he killed the Egyptian and hid
him in the sand. 13The next day he went
out and saw two Hebrews fighting. He
asked the one in the wrong, "Why are
you hitting your fellow Hebrew?"[n]
14The man said, "Who made you ruler
and judge over us?[o] Are you thinking of
killing me as you killed the Egyptian?"
Then Moses was afraid and thought,
"What I did must have become
known."
15When Pharaoh heard of this, he
tried to kill[p] Moses, but Moses fled[q]
from Pharaoh and went to live in
Midian,[r] where he sat down by a well.
16Now a priest of Midian[s] had seven
daughters, and they came to draw
water[t] and fill the troughs[u] to water
their father's flock. 17Some shepherds
came along and drove them away, but
Moses got up and came to their rescue[v]
and watered their flock.[w]
18When the girls returned to Reuel[x]
their father, he asked them, "Why have
you returned so early today?"
19They answered, "An Egyptian res-
cued us from the shepherds. He even
drew water for us and watered the
flock."
20"And where is he?" he asked his
daughters. "Why did you leave him?
Invite him to have something to eat."[y]
21Moses agreed to stay with the man,
who gave his daughter Zipporah[z] to
Moses in marriage. 22Zipporah gave
birth to a son, and Moses named him
Gershom,[b][a] saying, "I have become an
alien[b] in a foreign land."
23During that long period,[c] the king of
Egypt died.[d] The Israelites groaned in
their slavery[e] and cried out, and their
cry[f] for help because of their slavery
went up to God. 24God heard their
groaning and he remembered[g] his
covenant[h] with Abraham, with Isaac
and with Jacob. 25So God looked on the
Israelites and was concerned[i] about
them.

Moses and the Burning Bush

3 Now Moses was tending the flock
of Jethro[a] his father-in-law, the
priest of Midian,[b] and he led the flock to
the far side of the desert and came to
Horeb,[c] the mountain[d] of God. 2There
the angel of the LORD[e] appeared to him
in flames of fire[f] from within a bush.[g]
Moses saw that though the bush was on
fire it did not burn up. 3So Moses
thought, "I will go over and see this
strange sight—why the bush does not
burn up."
4When the LORD saw that he had gone
over to look, God called[h] to him from
within the bush,[i] "Moses! Moses!"
And Moses said, "Here I am."[j]
5"Do not come any closer,"[k] God
said. "Take off your sandals, for the
place where you are standing is holy
ground."[l] 6Then he said, "I am the God
of your father, the God of Abraham, the
God of Isaac and the God of Jacob."[m] At
this, Moses hid[n] his face, because he
was afraid to look at God.[o]
7The LORD said, "I have indeed seen[p]
the misery[q] of my people in Egypt. I
have heard them crying out because of
their slave drivers, and I am concerned[r]
about their suffering.[s] 8So I have come
down[t] to rescue them from the hand of
the Egyptians and to bring them up out
of that land into a good and spacious
land,[u] a land flowing with milk and
honey[v]—the home of the Canaanites,
Hittites, Amorites, Perizzites, Hivites[w]
and Jebusites.[x] 9And now the cry of
the Israelites has reached me, and I
have seen the way the Egyptians are
oppressing[y] them. 10So now, go. I am
sending[z] you to Pharaoh to bring my
people the Israelites out of Egypt."[a]
11But Moses said to God, "Who am I,[b]

10 [j]1Sa 1:20; [k]2Sa 22:17
11 [l]Ac 7:23; Heb 11:24–26; [m]**Ex 1:11**
13 [n]Ac 7:26
14 [o]**Ge 13:8**; Ac 7:27*
15 [p]Ex 4:19; [q]**Ge 31:21**; [r]Heb 11:27
16 [s]Ex 3:1; 18:1; [t]**Ge 24:11**; [u]**Ge 30:38**
17 [v]1Sa 30:8; Ps 31:2; [w]**Ge 29:10**
18 [x]Ex 3:1; 4:18; 18:1,5,12; Nu 10:29
20 [y]Ge 31:54
21 [z]Ex 4:25; 18:2; Nu 12:1
22 [a]Jdg 18:30; [b]**Ge 23:4**; Heb 11:13
23 [c]Ac 7:30; [d]Ex 4:19; [e]**Ex 1:14**; [f]ver 24; Ex 3:7,9; 6:5; Nu 20:15–16; Dt 26:7; Jdg 2:18; 1Sa 12:8; Ps 5:2; 18:6; 39:12; 81:7; 102:1; Jas 5:4
24 [g]**Ge 8:1**; [h]**Ge 9:15**; 15:15; 17:4; 22:16–18; 26:3; 28:13–15; Ex 32:13; 2Ki 13:23; Ps 105:10,42; Jer 14:21
25 [i]Ex 3:7; 4:31; Lk 1:25

Ch. 3

1 [a]**Ex 2:18**; Jdg 1:16; [b]**Ex 2:16**; [c]ver 12; Ex 17:6; 19:1–11,5; 33:6; Dt 1:2, 6; 4:10; 5:2; 29:1; 1Ki 19:8; Mal 4:4; [d]Ex 4:27; 18:5; 24:13; Dt 4:11,15
2 [e]**Ge 16:7; Ex 12:23; Ac 5:19**; [f]Ex 19:18; 1Ki 19:12; [g]ver 4; Ex 2:2–6; Dt 33:16; Mk 12:26; Lk 20:37; Ac 7:30
4 [h]Ex 19:3; Lev 1:1; [i]Ex 4:5; [j]Ge 31:11; 1Sa 3:4; Isa 6:8
5 [k]Jer 30:21; [l]**Ge 28:17**; Ac 7:33*
6 [m]**Ge 24:12; Ex 4:5**; Mt 22:32*; Mk 12:26*; Lk 20:37*; Ac 3:13; 7:32*; [n]1Ki 19:13; [o]Ex 24:11; 33:20; Jdg 13:22; Job 13:11; 23:16; 30:15; Isa 6:5
7 [p]1Sa 9:16; [q]ver 16; **Ge 16:11**; 1Sa 1:11; Ne 9:9; Ps 106:44; [r]**Ex 2:25**; Ac 7:34*; [s]**Ex 1:10**
8 [t]**Ge 11:5**; Ac 7:34*; [u]**Ge 12:7; 15:14**; [v]ver 17; Ex 13:5; 33:3; Lev 20:24; Nu 13:27; Dt 1:25; 6:3; 8:7–9; 11:9; 26:9; 27:3; Jos 5:6; Jer 11:5; 32:22; Eze 20:6; [w]Jos 11:3; Jdg 3:3; 2Sa 24:7; [x]**Ge 15:18–21**; Ezr 9:1
9 [y]**Ex 1:14; Nu 10:9**
10 [z]Ex 4:12; Jos 24:5; 1Sa 12:8; Ps 105:26; Ac 7:34*; [a]Ex 6:13,26; 12:41,51; 20:2; Dt 4:20; 1Sa 12:6; 1Ki 8:16; Mic 6:4
11 [b]Ex 4:10; 6:12,30; Jdg 6:15; 1Sa 9:21; 15:17; 18:18; 2Sa 7:18; 2Ch 2:6; Isa 6:5; Jer 1:6

[a]10 *Moses* sounds like the Hebrew for *draw out*.
[b]22 *Gershom* sounds like the Hebrew for *an alien there*.

that I should go to Pharaoh and bring
the Israelites out of Egypt?"
12And God said, "I will be with you.[c]
And this will be the sign[d] to you that it is
I who have sent you: When you have
brought the people out of Egypt, you[a]
will worship God on this mountain."[e]
13Moses said to God, "Suppose I go to
the Israelites and say to them, 'The God
of your fathers has sent me to you,' and
they ask me, 'What is his name?'[f] Then
what shall I tell them?"
14God said to Moses, "I AM WHO I
AM.[b] This is what you are to say to the
Israelites: 'I AM[g] has sent me to you.'"
15God also said to Moses, "Say to the
Israelites, 'The LORD,[c] the God of your
fathers[h]—the God of Abraham, the God
of Isaac and the God of Jacob[i]—has sent
me to you.' This is my name[j] for ever,
the name by which I am to be remem-
bered from generation to generation.[k]
16"Go, assemble the elders[l] of Israel
and say to them, 'The LORD, the God of
your fathers—the God of Abraham,
Isaac and Jacob[m]—appeared to me and
said: I have watched over you and have
seen[n] what has been done to you in
Egypt. 17And I have promised to bring
you up out of your misery in Egypt[o] into
the land of the Canaanites, Hittites,
Amorites, Perizzites, Hivites and Jebu-
sites—a land flowing with milk and
honey.'[p]
18"The elders of Israel will listen[q] to
you. Then you and the elders are to go
to the king of Egypt and say to him, 'The
LORD, the God of the Hebrews,[r] has met[s]
with us. Let us take a three-day journey[t]
into the desert to offer sacrifices[u] to the
LORD our God.' 19But I know that the
king of Egypt will not let you go unless a
mighty hand[v] compels him. 20So I will
stretch out my hand[w] and strike the
Egyptians with all the wonders[x] that I
will perform among them. After that, he
will let you go.[y]
21"And I will make the Egyptians
favourably disposed[z] towards this peo-
ple, so that when you leave you will not
go empty-handed.[a] 22Every woman is to
ask her neighbour and any woman liv-
ing in her house for articles of silver[b] and
gold[c] and for clothing, which you will
put on your sons and daughters. And so
you will plunder[d] the Egyptians."[e]

Signs for Moses

4 Moses answered, "What if they do
not believe me or listen[a] to me and
say, 'The LORD did not appear to you'?"
2Then the LORD said to him, "What is
that in your hand?"
"A staff,"[b] he replied.
3The LORD said, "Throw it on the
ground."
Moses threw it on the ground and it
became a snake,[c] and he ran from it.
4Then the LORD said to him, "Reach out
your hand and take it by the tail." So
Moses reached out and took hold of the
snake and it turned back into a staff in
his hand. 5"This," said the LORD, "is so
that they may believe[d] that the LORD, the
God of their fathers—the God of Abra-
ham, the God of Isaac and the God of
Jacob—has appeared to you."
6Then the LORD said, "Put your hand
inside your cloak." So Moses put his
hand into his cloak, and when he took it
out, it was leprous,[a] like snow.[e]
7"Now put it back into your cloak,"
he said. So Moses put his hand back into
his cloak, and when he took it out, it
was restored,[f] like the rest of his flesh.
8Then the LORD said, "If they do not
believe[g] you or pay attention to the first
miraculous sign,[h] they may believe the
second. 9But if they do not believe these
two signs or listen to you, take some
water from the Nile and pour it on the
dry ground. The water you take from
the river will become blood[i] on the
ground."
10Moses said to the LORD, "O Lord, I
have never been eloquent, neither in
the past nor since you have spoken to
your servant. I am slow of speech and
tongue."[j]
11The LORD said to him, "Who gave
man his mouth? Who makes him deaf or
mute?[k] Who gives him sight or makes
him blind?[l] Is it not I, the LORD? 12Now
go;[m] I will help you speak and will teach
you what to say."[n]

12 [c]**Ge 26:3; Ex 14:22**; Ro 8:31; [d]Nu 26:10; Jos 2:12; Jdg 6:17; Ps 86:17; Isa 7:14; 8:18; 20:3; Jer 44:29; [e]**ver 1**; Ac 7:7
13 [f]**Ge 32:29**
14 [g]Ex 6:2–3; Jn 8:58; Heb 13:8; Rev 1:8; 4:8
15 [h]Ge 31:42; Da 2:23; [i]**Ge 24:12**; [j]Ex 6:3, 7; 15:3; 23:21; 34:5–7; Lev 24:11; Dt 28:58; Ps 30:4; 83:18; 96:2; 97:12; 135:13; 145:21; Isa 42:8; Jer 16:21; 33:2; Hos 12:5; [k]Ps 45:17; 72:17; 102:12
16 [l]Ex 4:29; 17:5; Lev 4:15; Nu 11:16; 16:25; Dt 5:23; 19:12; Jdg 8:14; Ru 4:2; Pr 31:23; Eze 8:11; [m]**Ge 24:12**; [n]Ex 4:31; 2Ki 19:16; 2Ch 6:20; Ps 33:18; 66:7
17 [o]**Ge 15:16**; 46:4; Ex 6:6; [p]**ver 8**
18 [q]Ex 4:1,8,31; 6:12,30; [r]**Ge 14:13**; [s]Nu 23:4,16; [t]**Ge 30:36**; [u]Ex 4:23; 5:1,3; 6:11; 7:16; 8:20,27; 9:13; 10:9,26
19 [v]Ex 4:21; 6:6; 7:3; 10:1; 11:9; Dt 4:34; 2Ch 6:32
20 [w]Ex 6:1,6; 7:4–5; 9:15; 13:3,9,14,16; 15:6,12; Dt 4:34,37; 5:15; 7:8; 26:8; 2Ki 17:36; 2Ch 6:32; Ps 118:15–16; 136:12; Isa 41:10; 63:12; Jer 21:5; 51:25; Da 9:15; [x]Ex 4:21; 7:3; 11:9–10; 15:11; 34:10; Nu 14:11; Dt 3:24; 4:34; 6:22; Ne 9:10; Ps 71:19; 72:18; 77:14; 78:43; 86:10; 105:27; 106:22; 135:9; 136:4; Jer 32:20; Mic 7:15; Ac 7:36; [y]Ex 11:1; 12:31–33
21 [z]**Ge 39:21**; [a]Ex 11:2; 2Ch 30:9; Ne 1:11; Ps 105:37; 106:46; Jer 42:12
22 [b]Job 27:16–17; [c]Ex 11:2; 12:35; Ezr 1:4,6; 7:16; Ps 105:37; [d]**Ge 15:14**; Eze 39:10; [e]Eze 29:10

Ch. 4

1 [a]**Ex 3:18**
2 [b]ver 17,20; Ge 38:18; Ex 7:19; 8:5,16; 14:16,21; 17:5–6, 9; Nu 17:2; 20:8; Jos 8:18; Jdg 6:21; 1Sa 14:27; 2Ki 4:29
3 [c]Ex 7:8–12,15 *5* [d]ver 31; **Ex 3:6**; 14:31; 19:9
6 [e]Lev 13:2,11; Nu 12:10; Dt 24:9; 2Ki 5:1,27; 2Ch 26:21
7 [f]2Ki 5:14; Mt 8:3; Lk 17:12–14
8 [g]**Ex 3:18**; [h]ver 30; Jdg 6:17; 1Ki 13:3; Isa 7:14; Jer 44:29 *9* [i]Ex 7:17–21 *10* [j]**Ex 3:11**
11 [k]Lk 1:20,64; [l]Ps 94:9; 146:8; Mt 11:5; Jn 10:21
12 [m]**Ex 3:10**; [n]ver 15–16; Nu 23:5; Dt 18:15,18; Isa 50:4; 51:16; Jer 1:9; Mt 10:19–20; Mk 13:11; **Lk 12:12**

[a]*12* The Hebrew is plural.
[b]*14* Or *I WILL BE WHAT I WILL BE*
[c]*15* The Hebrew for *LORD* sounds like and may be derived from the Hebrew for *I AM* in verse 14.
[a]*6* The Hebrew word was used for various diseases affecting the skin—not necessarily leprosy.

13But Moses said, "O Lord, please send someone else to do it."[o]

14Then the LORD's anger burned[p] against Moses and he said, "What about your brother, Aaron the Levite? I know he can speak well. He is already on his way to meet[q] you, and his heart will be glad when he sees you. 15You shall speak to him and put words in his mouth;[r] I will help both of you speak and will teach you what to do. 16He will speak to the people for you, and it will be as if he were your mouth[s] and as if you were God to him.[t] 17But take this staff[u] in your hand[v] so that you can perform miraculous signs[w] with it."

Moses Returns to Egypt

18Then Moses went back to Jethro his father-in-law and said to him, "Let me go back to my own people in Egypt to see if any of them are still alive."

Jethro said, "Go, and I wish you well."

19Now the LORD had said to Moses in Midian, "Go back to Egypt, for all the men who wanted to kill[x] you are dead."[y] 20So Moses took his wife and sons,[z] put them on a donkey and started back to Egypt. And he took the staff[a] of God in his hand.

21The LORD said to Moses, "When you return to Egypt, see that you perform before Pharaoh all the wonders[b] I have given you the power to do. But I will harden his heart[c] so that he will not let the people go.[d] 22Then say to Pharaoh, 'This is what the LORD says: Israel is my firstborn son,[e] 23and I told you, "Let my son go,[f] so that he may worship[g] me." But you refused to let him go; so I will kill your firstborn son.'"[h]

24At a lodging place on the way, the LORD met ⌊Moses⌋[b] and was about to kill[i] him. 25But Zipporah[j] took a flint knife, cut off her son's foreskin[k] and touched ⌊Moses'⌋ feet with it.[c] "Surely you are a bridegroom of blood to me," she said. 26So the LORD let him alone. (At that time she said "bridegroom of blood", referring to circumcision.)

27The LORD said to Aaron, "Go into the desert to meet Moses." So he met Moses at the mountain[l] of God and kissed[m] him. 28Then Moses told Aaron everything the LORD had sent him to say,[n] and also about all the miraculous signs he had commanded him to perform.

29Moses and Aaron brought together all the elders[o] of the Israelites, 30and Aaron told them everything the LORD had said to Moses. He also performed the signs[p] before the people, 31and they believed.[q] And when they heard that the LORD was concerned[r] about them and had seen their misery,[s] they bowed down and worshipped.[t]

13 [o]Jnh 1:1–3
14 [p]Nu 11:1,10, 33; 12:9; 16:15; 22:22; 24:10; 32:13; Dt 7:25; Jos 7:1; Job 17:8; [q]ver 27; 1Sa 10:2–5
15 [r]ver 30; Nu 23:5,12,16; Dt 18:18; Jos 1:8; Isa 51:16; 59:21; Jer 1:9; 31:33
16 [s]Ex 7:1–2; Jer 15:19; 36:6; [t]Nu 33:1; Ps 77:20; 105:26; Mic 6:4
17 [u]**ver 2**; [v]ver 20; Ex 17:9; [w]Ex 7:9–21; 8:5,16; 9:22; 10:12–15, 21–23; 14:15–18,26; Nu 14:11; Dt 4:34; Ps 74:9; 78:43; 105:27
19 [x]Ex 2:15; [y]Ex 2:23; Mt 2:20
20 [z]Ex 2:22; 18:3; Ac 7:29; [a]**ver 2**
21 [b]**Ex 3:19**,20; [c]Ex 7:3,13; 8:15; 9:12,35; 10:1,20,27; 11:10; 14:4,8; Dt 2:30; Jos 11:20; 1Sa 6:6; Ps 105:25; Isa 6:10; 63:17; Jn 12:40; Ro 9:18; [d]Ex 8:32; 9:17
22 [e]**Ge 10:15**; Dt 32:6; Isa 9:6; 63:16; 64:8; Jer 3:19; 31:9; Hos 11:1; Mal 2:10; Ro 9:4; 2Co 6:18
23 [f]Ex 5:1; 7:16; [g]**Ex 3:18**; [h]Ge 49:3; Ex 11:5; 12:12,29; Nu 8:17; 33:4; Ps 78:51; 105:36; 135:8; 136:10
24 [i]Nu 22:22
25 [j]**Ex 2:21**; [k]Ge 17:14; Jos 5:2–3
27 [l]**Ex 3:1**; [m]**Ge 27:27; 29:13**
28 [n]ver 16
29 [o]**Ex 3:16**
30 [p]**ver 8**
31 [q]**Ex 3:18**; [r]**Ex 2:25**; [s]**Ge 16:11**; [t]**Ge 24:26**

Bricks Without Straw

5 Afterwards Moses and Aaron went to Pharaoh and said, "This is what the LORD, the God of Israel, says: 'Let my people go,[a] so that they may hold a festival[b] to me in the desert.'"

2Pharaoh said, "Who is the LORD,[c] that I should obey him and let Israel go? I do not know the LORD and I will not let Israel go."[d]

3Then they said, "The God of the Hebrews has met with us. Now let us take a three-day journey[e] into the desert to offer sacrifices to the LORD our God, or he may strike us with plagues[f] or with the sword."

4But the king of Egypt said, "Moses and Aaron, why are you taking the people away from their labour?[g] Get back to your work!" 5Then Pharaoh said, "Look, the people of the land are now numerous,[h] and you are stopping them from working."

6That same day Pharaoh gave this order to the slave drivers[i] and foremen in charge of the people: 7"You are no longer to supply the people with straw for making bricks;[j] let them go and gather their own straw. 8But require them to make the same number of bricks as before; don't reduce the quota.[k] They are lazy;[l] that is why they are crying out, 'Let us go and sacrifice to our God.'[m] 9Make the work harder for the men so that they keep working and pay no attention to lies."

10Then the slave drivers[n] and the foremen went out and said to the people, "This is what Pharaoh says: 'I will not give you any more straw. 11Go and get your own straw wherever you can find it, but your work will not be reduced[o] at all.'" 12So the people scattered all over

Ch. 5
1 [a]**Ex 4:23**; [b]**Ex 3:18**
2 [c]Jdg 2:10; Job 21:15; Mal 3:14; [d]Ex 3:19
3 [e]**Ge 30:36**; [f]Lev 26:25; Nu 14:12; Dt 28:21; 2Sa 24:13
4 [g]**Ex 1:11**; 6:6–7 *5* [h]**Ge 12:2** *6* [i]**Ge 15:13**
7 [j]**Ge 11:3** *8* [k]ver 14,18; [l]ver 17; [m]Ex 10:11
10 [n]ver 13; Ex 1:11 *11* [o]ver 19

[b]24 Or *Moses' son*; Hebrew *him*
[c]25 Or *and drew near ⌊Moses'⌋ feet*

Egypt to gather stubble to use for straw.
13The slave drivers kept pressing them,
saying, "Complete the work required
of you for each day, just as when you
had straw." 14The Israelite foremen
appointed by Pharaoh's slave drivers
were beaten[p] and were asked, "Why
didn't you meet your quota of bricks
yesterday or today, as before?"
15Then the Israelite foremen went and
appealed to Pharaoh: "Why have you
treated your servants this way? 16Your
servants are given no straw, yet we are
told, 'Make bricks!' Your servants are
being beaten, but the fault is with your
own people."
17Pharaoh said, "Lazy, that's what
you are—lazy![q] That is why you keep
saying, 'Let us go and sacrifice to the
LORD.' 18Now get to work.[r] You will not
be given any straw, yet you must
produce your full quota of bricks."
19The Israelite foremen realised they
were in trouble when they were told,
"You are not to reduce the number of
bricks required of you for each day."
20When they left Pharaoh, they found
Moses and Aaron waiting to meet them,
21and they said, "May the LORD look
upon you and judge[s] you! You have
made us a stench[t] to Pharaoh and his
officials and have put a sword[u] in their
hand to kill us."[v]

God Promises Deliverance

22Moses returned to the LORD and
said, "O Lord, why have you brought
trouble upon this people?[w] Is this why
you sent me? 23Ever since I went to
Pharaoh to speak in your name, he has
brought trouble upon this people, and
you have not rescued[x] your people at
all."

6 Then the LORD said to Moses,
"Now you will see what I will do to
Pharaoh: Because of my mighty hand[a]
he will let them go;[b] because of my
mighty hand he will drive them out of
his country."[c]
2God also said to Moses, "I am the
LORD.[d] 3I appeared to Abraham, to Isaac
and to Jacob as God Almighty,[a][e] but by
my name[f] the LORD[b][g] I did not make
myself known to them.[c] 4I also estab-
lished my covenant[h] with them to give
them the land[i] of Canaan, where they
lived as aliens.[j] 5Moreover, I have heard
the groaning[k] of the Israelites, whom
the Egyptians are enslaving, and I have
remembered my covenant.[l]
6"Therefore, say to the Israelites: 'I
am the LORD, and I will bring you out
from under the yoke of the Egyptians.[m] I
will free you from being slaves to them,
and I will redeem[n] you with an out-
stretched arm[o] and with mighty acts of
judgment.[p] 7I will take you as my own
people, and I will be your God.[q] Then
you will know[r] that I am the LORD your
God, who brought you out from under
the yoke of the Egyptians. 8And I will
bring you to the land[s] I swore[t] with
uplifted hand[u] to give to Abraham, to
Isaac and to Jacob.[v] I will give it to you as
a possession. I am the LORD.'"[w]
9Moses reported this to the Israelites,
but they did not listen to him because
of their discouragement and cruel
bondage.[x]
10Then the LORD said to Moses, 11"Go,
tell[y] Pharaoh king of Egypt to let the
Israelites go out of his country."[z]
12But Moses said to the LORD, "If the
Israelites will not listen[a] to me, why
would Pharaoh listen to me, since I
speak with faltering lips[d]?"[b]

Family Record of Moses and Aaron

13Now the LORD spoke to Moses and
Aaron about the Israelites and Pharaoh
king of Egypt, and he commanded them
to bring the Israelites out of Egypt.[c]

14These were the heads of their
families:[e][d]

The sons of Reuben[e] the firstborn
son of Israel were Hanoch and
Pallu, Hezron and Carmi. These
were the clans of Reuben.
15The sons of Simeon[f] were
Jemuel, Jamin, Ohad, Jakin, Zohar
and Shaul the son of a Canaanite
woman. These were the clans of
Simeon.
16These were the names of the
sons of Levi[g] according to their
records: Gershon,[h] Kohath and
Merari.[i] Levi lived 137 years.

14 [p]ver 16; Isa 10:24
17 [q]ver 8
18 [r]**Ge 15:13**
21 [s]**Ge 16:5**; [t]**Ge 34:30**; [u]Ex 16:3; Nu 14:3; 20:3; [v]**Ex 1:13; 14:11**
22 [w]Nu 11:11; Dt 1:12; Jos 7:7
23 [x]Jer 4:10; 20:7; Eze 14:9

Ch. 6

1 [a]**Ex 3:20; Dt 5:15**; [b]**Ex 3:20**; [c]Ex 11:1; 12:31,33,39
2 [d]ver 6–8,29; Ex 3:14–15; 7:5,17; 8:22; 10:2; 12:12; 14:4,18; 16:12; Lev 11:44; 18:21; 20:7; Isa 25:3; 41:20; 43:11; 49:23; 60:16; Eze 13:9; 25:17; 36:38; 37:6,13; Joel 2:27
3 [e]**Ge 17:1**; [f]**Ex 3:15**; 2Sa 7:26; Ps 48:10; 61:5; 68:4; 83:18; 99:3; Isa 52:6; [g]Ex 3:14; Jn 8:58
4 [h]**Ge 6:18; 15:18**; [i]**Ge 12:7**; Ac 7:5; Ro 4:13; Gal 3:16; Heb 11:8–10; [j]**Ge 17:8**
5 [k]**Ex 2:23**; Ac 7:34; [l]**Ge 9:15**
6 [m]ver 7; Ex 3:8; 12:17,51; 16:1, 6; 18:1; 19:1; 20:2; 29:46; Lev 22:33; 26:13; Dt 6:12; Ps 81:10; 136:11; Jer 2:6; Hos 13:4; Am 2:10; Mic 6:4; [n]Ex 15:13; Dt 7:8; 9:26; 1Ch 17:21; Job 19:25; Ps 19:14; 34:22; 74:2; 77:15; 107:2; Isa 29:22; 35:9; 43:1; 44:23; 48:20; Jer 15:21; 31:11; 50:34; [o]**Ex 3:19,20; Jer 32:21**; Ac 13:17; [p]Ex 3:20; Ps 9:16; 105:27
7 [q]**Ge 17:7; Ex 34:9**; Eze 11:19–20; Ro 9:4; [r]**ver 2**; 1Ki 20:13,28; Isa 43:10; 48:7; Eze 39:6; Joel 3:17
8 [s]**Ge 12:7**; Ex 3:8; [t]Jer 11:5; Eze 20:6; [u]**Ge 14:22**; Rev 10:5–6; [v]Ps 136:21–22; [w]Lev 18:21
9 [x]**Ge 34:30**; Ex 2:23 **11** [y]ver 29; [z]**Ex 3:18**
12 [a]**Ex 3:18**; [b]Ex 4:10 **13** [c]Ex 3:10
14 [d]Ex 13:3; Nu 1:1; 26:4; [e]**Ge 29:32** **15** [f]**Ge 29:33**
16 [g]**Ge 29:34**; [h]**Ge 46:11**; [i]Nu 3:17; Jos 21:7; 1Ch 6:1,16

a3 Hebrew *El-Shaddai*
b3 See note at Exodus 3:15.
c3 Or *Almighty, and by my name the LORD did I not let myself be known to them?*
d12 Hebrew *I am uncircumcised of lips;* also in verse 30
e14 The Hebrew for *families* here and in verse 25 refers to units larger than clans.

17 The sons of Gershon, by clans, were Libni and Shimei.[j]

18 The sons of Kohath[k] were Amram, Izhar, Hebron and Uzziel.[l] Kohath lived 133 years.

19 The sons of Merari were Mahli and Mushi.[m]

These were the clans of Levi according to their records.

20 Amram[n] married his father's sister Jochebed, who bore him Aaron and Moses.[o] Amram lived 137 years.

21 The sons of Izhar[p] were Korah, Nepheg and Zicri.

22 The sons of Uzziel were Mishael, Elzaphan[q] and Sithri.

23 Aaron married Elisheba, daughter of Amminadab[r] and sister of Nahshon,[s] and she bore him Nadab and Abihu,[t] Eleazar[u] and Ithamar.[v]

24 The sons of Korah[w] were Assir, Elkanah and Abiasaph. These were the Korahite clans.

25 Eleazar son of Aaron married one of the daughters of Putiel, and she bore him Phinehas.[x]

These were the heads of the Levite families, clan by clan.

26 It was this same Aaron and Moses to whom the LORD said, "Bring the Israelites out of Egypt[y] by their divisions."[z] 27 They were the ones who spoke to Pharaoh[a] king of Egypt about bringing the Israelites out of Egypt. It was the same Moses and Aaron.[b]

Aaron to Speak for Moses

28 Now when the LORD spoke to Moses in Egypt, 29 he said to him, "I am the LORD.[c] Tell Pharaoh king of Egypt everything I tell you."

30 But Moses said to the LORD, "Since I speak with faltering lips,[d] why would Pharaoh listen to me?"

7 Then the LORD said to Moses, "See, I have made you like God[a] to Pharaoh, and your brother Aaron will be your prophet.[b] 2 You are to say everything I command you, and your brother Aaron is to tell Pharaoh to let the Israelites go out of his country. 3 But I will harden Pharaoh's heart,[c] and though I multiply my miraculous signs and wonders[d] in Egypt, 4 he will not listen[e] to you. Then I will lay my hand on Egypt and with mighty acts of judgment[f] I will bring out my divisions,[g] my people the Israelites. 5 And the Egyptians will know that I am the LORD[h] when I stretch out my hand[i] against Egypt and bring the Israelites out of it."

6 Moses and Aaron did just as the LORD commanded[j] them. 7 Moses was eighty years old[k] and Aaron eighty-three when they spoke to Pharaoh.

Aaron's Staff Becomes a Snake

8 The LORD said to Moses and Aaron, 9 "When Pharaoh says to you, 'Perform a miracle,'[l] then say to Aaron, 'Take your staff and throw it down before Pharaoh,' and it will become a snake."[m]

10 So Moses and Aaron went to Pharaoh and did just as the LORD commanded. Aaron threw his staff down in front of Pharaoh and his officials, and it became a snake. 11 Pharaoh then summoned the wise men and sorcerers,[n] and the Egyptian magicians[o] also did the same things by their secret arts:[p] 12 Each one threw down his staff and it became a snake. But Aaron's staff swallowed up their staffs. 13 Yet Pharaoh's heart[q] became hard and he would not listen[r] to them, just as the LORD had said.

The Plague of Blood

14 Then the LORD said to Moses, "Pharaoh's heart is unyielding;[s] he refuses to let the people go. 15 Go to Pharaoh in the morning as he goes out to the water.[t] Wait on the bank of the Nile[u] to meet him, and take in your hand the staff that was changed into a snake. 16 Then say to him, 'The LORD, the God of the Hebrews, has sent me to say to you: Let my people go, so that they may worship[v] me in the desert. But until now you have not listened.[w] 17 This is what the LORD says: By this you will know that I am the LORD:[x] With the staff that is in my hand I will strike the water of the Nile, and it will be changed into blood.[y] 18 The fish in the Nile will die, and the river will stink;[z] the Egyptians will not be able to drink its water.'"[a]

19 The LORD said to Moses, "Tell Aaron, 'Take your staff[b] and stretch out your hand[c] over the waters of Egypt—over the streams and canals, over the ponds and all the reservoirs'—and they will turn to blood. Blood will be

17 [j]Nu 3:18; 1Ch 6:17
18 [k]Nu 3:27; 1Ch 23:12; [l]Nu 3:19; 1Ch 6:2,18
19 [m]Nu 3:20,33; 1Ch 6:19; 23:21
20 [n]1Ch 23:13; [o]Ex 2:1–2; Nu 26:59
21 [p]1Ch 6:38
22 [q]Lev 10:4; Nu 3:30; 1Ch 15:8; 2Ch 29:13
23 [r]Ru 4:19–20; 1Ch 2:10; [s]Nu 1:7; 2:3; Mt 1:4; [t]Ex 24:1; 28:1; Lev 10:1; [u]Lev 10:6; Nu 3:2,32; 16:37, 39; Dt 10:6; Jos 14:1; [v]Ex 28:1; Lev 10:12,16; Nu 3:2; 4:28; 26:60; 1Ch 6:3; 24:1
24 [w]ver 21; Nu 16:1; 1Ch 6:22,37
25 [x]Nu 25:7,11; 31:6; Jos 24:33; Ps 106:30
26 [y]**Ex 3:10;** [z]Ex 7:4; 12:17, 41,51
27 [a]Ex 5:1; [b]Nu 3:1; Ps 77:20
29 [c]**ver 2**
30 [d]**Ex 3:11**

Ch. 7

1 [a]**Ex 4:16;** [b]Ex 4:15; Ac 14:12
3 [c]**Ex 4:21;** Ro 9:18; [d]**Ex 3:20; 10:1;** Ac 7:36
4 [e]ver 13,16,22; Ex 8:15,19; 9:12; 11:9; [f]**Ex 3:20;** Ac 7:36; [g]**Ex 6:26**
5 [h]**Ex 6:2;** [i]Ex 3:20; Ps 138:7; Eze 6:14; 25:13
6 [j]ver 2,10,20; Ge 6:22
7 [k]Dt 31:2; 34:7; Ac 7:23,30
9 [l]Dt 6:22; 2Ki 19:29; Ps 78:43; 86:17; 105:27; 135:9; Isa 7:11; 37:30; 38:7–8; 55:13; **Jn 2:11;** [m]Ex 4:2–5
11 [n]Ex 22:18; Dt 18:10; 1Sa 6:2; 2Ki 21:6; Isa 2:6; 47:12; Jer 27:9; Mal 3:5; [o]**Ge 41:8;** 2Ti 3:8; [p]ver 22; Ex 8:7,18; **Mt 24:24**
13 [q]**Ex 4:21;** [r]**ver 4**

14 [s]ver 22; Ex 8:15,32; 9:7; 10:1,20,27
15 [t]Ex 8:20; [u]**Ge 41:1** *16* [v]**Ex 3:18;** [w]**ver 4**
17 [x]**Ex 6:2;** 14:25; [y]ver 19–21; Ex 4:9; Rev 11:6; 16:4
18 [z]Isa 19:6; [a]ver 21,24; Ps 78:44
19 [b]**Ex 4:2;** [c]Ex 14:21; 2Ki 5:11

everywhere in Egypt, even in the wooden buckets and stone jars."

20Moses and Aaron did just as the LORD had commanded.[d] He raised his staff in the presence of Pharaoh and his officials and struck the water of the Nile,[e] and all the water was changed into blood.[f] 21The fish in the Nile died, and the river smelled so bad that the Egyptians could not drink its water. Blood was everywhere in Egypt.

22But the Egyptian magicians[g] did the same things by their secret arts,[h] and Pharaoh's heart[i] became hard; he would not listen to Moses and Aaron, just as the LORD had said. 23Instead, he turned and went into his palace, and did not take even this to heart. 24And all the Egyptians dug along the Nile to get drinking water,[j] because they could not drink the water of the river.

The Plague of Frogs

25Seven days passed after the LORD struck the Nile.

8 1Then the LORD said to Moses, "Go to Pharaoh and say to him, 'This is what the LORD says: Let my people go, so that they may worship[a] me. 2If you refuse to let them go, I will plague your whole country with frogs.[b] 3The Nile will teem with frogs. They will come up into your palace and your bedroom and onto your bed, into the houses of your officials and on your people,[c] and into your ovens and kneading troughs.[d] 4The frogs will go up on you and your people and all your officials.'"

5Then the LORD said to Moses, "Tell Aaron, 'Stretch out your hand with your staff[e] over the streams and canals and ponds, and make frogs[f] come up on the land of Egypt.'"

6So Aaron stretched out his hand over the waters of Egypt, and the frogs[g] came up and covered the land. 7But the magicians did the same things by their secret arts;[h] they also made frogs come up on the land of Egypt.

8Pharaoh summoned Moses and Aaron and said, "Pray[i] to the LORD to take the frogs away from me and my people, and I will let your people go to offer sacrifices[j] to the LORD."

9Moses said to Pharaoh, "I leave to you the honour of setting the time[k] for me to pray for you and your officials and your people that you and your houses may be rid of the frogs, except for those that remain in the Nile."

10"Tomorrow," Pharaoh said.

Moses replied, "It will be as you say, so that you may know there is no-one like the LORD our God.[l] 11The frogs will leave you and your houses, your officials and your people; they will remain only in the Nile."

12After Moses and Aaron left Pharaoh, Moses cried out to the LORD about the frogs he had brought on Pharaoh. 13And the LORD did what Moses asked.[m] The frogs died in the houses, in the courtyards and in the fields. 14They were piled into heaps, and the land reeked of them. 15But when Pharaoh saw that there was relief,[n] he hardened his heart[o] and would not listen to Moses and Aaron, just as the LORD had said.

The Plague of Gnats

16Then the LORD said to Moses, "Tell Aaron, 'Stretch out your staff[p] and strike the dust of the ground,' and throughout the land of Egypt the dust will become gnats." 17They did this, and when Aaron stretched out his hand with the staff and struck the dust of the ground, gnats[q] came upon men and animals. All the dust throughout the land of Egypt became gnats. 18But when the magicians[r] tried to produce gnats by their secret arts,[s] they could not. And the gnats were on men and animals.

19The magicians said to Pharaoh, "This is the finger[t] of God." But Pharaoh's heart[u] was hard and he would not listen,[v] just as the LORD had said.

The Plague of Flies

20Then the LORD said to Moses, "Get up early in the morning[w] and confront Pharaoh as he goes to the water and say to him, 'This is what the LORD says: Let my people go, so that they may worship[x] me. 21If you do not let my people go, I will send swarms of flies on you and your officials, on your people and into your houses. The houses of the Egyptians will be full of flies, and even the ground where they are.

22" 'But on that day I will deal differently with the land of Goshen,[y] where my people live;[z] no swarms of flies will be there, so that you will know[a] that I, the LORD, am in this land. 23I will make a distinction[**a**] between my people and your people.[b] This miraculous sign will occur tomorrow.' "

24And the LORD did this. Dense

20 [d]ver 6; [e]Ex 17:5; [f]Ps 78:44; 105:29; 114:3; Hab 3:8
22 [g]**Ge 41:8;** [h]**ver 11; Mt 24:24;** [i]ver 13,**14**; Ex 8:19; Ps 105:28
24 [j]**ver 18**

Ch. 8

1 [a]Ex 3:12; 4:23; 5:1; 9:1
2 [b]Ps 78:45; 105:30; Rev 16:13
3 [c]Ex 10:6; [d]Ex 12:34
5 [e]**Ex 4:2;** 7:9–20; 9:23; 10:13,21–22; 14:27; [f]**Ex 4:17**
6 [g]Ps 78:45; 105:30
7 [h]**Ex 7:11; Mt 24:24**
8 [i]ver 28; Ex 9:28; 10:17; Nu 21:7; 1Sa 12:19; 1Ki 13:6; Jer 42:2; Ac 8:24; [j]ver 25; Ex 10:8, 24; 12:31
9 [k]Ex 9:5
10 [l]Ex 9:14; 15:11; Dt 3:24; 4:35; 33:26; 2Sa 7:22; 1Ki 8:23; 1Ch 17:20; 2Ch 6:14; Ps 71:19; 86:8; 89:6; 113:5; Isa 40:18; 42:8; 46:9; Jer 10:6; 49:19; Mic 7:18
13 [m]Jas 5:16–18
15 [n]Ecc 8:11; [o]**Ex 7:14**
16 [p]**Ex 4:2**
17 [q]Ps 105:31
18 [r]Ex 9:11; Da 5:8; [s]**Ex 7:11**
19 [t]Ex 7:5; 10:7; 12:33; 31:18; 1Sa 6:9; Ne 9:6; Ps 8:3; 33:6; Lk 11:20; [u]**Ex 7:22;** [v]**Ex 7:4**
20 [w]Ex 7:15; 9:13; [x]**Ex 3:18**
22 [y]**Ge 45:10;** [z]Ex 9:4,6,26; 10:23; 11:7; 12:13; 19:5; Dt 4:20; 7:6; 14:2; 26:18; 1Ki 8:36; Job 36:11; Ps 33:12; 135:4; Mal 3:17; [a]Ex 7:5; 9:29
23 [b]Ex 9:4,6; 10:23; 11:7; 12:13,23,27

a23 Septuagint and Vulgate; Hebrew *will put a deliverance*

swarms of flies poured into Pharaoh's
palace and into the houses of his of-
ficials, and throughout Egypt the land
was ruined by the flies.[c]
25Then Pharaoh summoned[d] Moses
and Aaron and said, "Go, sacrifice to
your God here in the land."
26But Moses said, "That would not be
right. The sacrifices we offer the LORD
our God would be detestable to the
Egyptians.[e] And if we offer sacrifices
that are detestable in their eyes, will
they not stone us? 27We must take a
three-day journey[f] into the desert to
offer sacrifices[g] to the LORD our God, as
he commands us."
28Pharaoh said, "I will let you go to
offer sacrifices to the LORD your God in
the desert, but you must not go very far.
Now pray[h] for me."
29Moses answered, "As soon as I
leave you, I will pray to the LORD, and
tomorrow the flies will leave Pharaoh
and his officials and his people. Only be
sure that Pharaoh does not act deceit-
fully[i] again by not letting the people go
to offer sacrifices to the LORD."
30Then Moses left Pharaoh and
prayed to the LORD,[j] 31and the LORD did
what Moses asked: The flies left Phar-
aoh and his officials and his people; not
a fly remained. 32But this time also
Pharaoh hardened his heart[k] and would
not let the people go.

The Plague on Livestock

9 Then the LORD said to Moses, "Go
to Pharaoh and say to him, 'This is
what the LORD, the God of the Hebrews,
says: "Let my people go, so that they
may worship[a] me." 2If you refuse to let
them go and continue to hold them
back, 3the hand[b] of the LORD will bring a
terrible plague[c] on your livestock in the
field—on your horses and donkeys and
camels and on your cattle and sheep
and goats. 4But the LORD will make a
distinction between the livestock of
Israel and that of Egypt,[d] so that no
animal belonging to the Israelites will
die.'"
5The LORD set a time and said,
"Tomorrow the LORD will do this in the
land." 6And the next day the LORD did
it: All the livestock[e] of the Egyptians
died, but not one animal belonging to
the Israelites died.[f] 7Pharaoh sent men
to investigate and found that not even
one of the animals of the Israelites had
died. Yet his heart[g] was unyielding and
he would not let the people go.[h]

The Plague of Boils

8Then the LORD said to Moses and
Aaron, "Take handfuls of soot from a
furnace and have Moses toss it into the
air in the presence of Pharaoh. 9It will
become fine dust over the whole land of
Egypt, and festering boils[i] will break out
on men and animals throughout the
land."
10So they took soot from a furnace and
stood before Pharaoh. Moses tossed it
into the air, and festering boils broke
out on men and animals. 11The ma-
gicians[j] could not stand before Moses
because of the boils that were on them
and on all the Egyptians. 12But the LORD
hardened Pharaoh's heart[k] and he
would not listen[l] to Moses and Aaron,
just as the LORD had said to Moses.

The Plague of Hail

13Then the LORD said to Moses, "Get
up early in the morning, confront Phar-
aoh and say to him, 'This is what the
LORD, the God of the Hebrews, says: Let
my people go, so that they may wor-
ship[m] me, 14or this time I will send the
full force of my plagues against you and
against your officials and your people,
so you may know[n] that there is no-one
like[o] me in all the earth. 15For by now I
could have stretched out my hand and
struck you and your people[p] with a
plague that would have wiped you off
the earth. 16But I have raised you up[a] for
this very purpose,[q] that I might show
you my power[r] and that my name might
be proclaimed in all the earth. 17You still
set yourself against my people and will
not let them go. 18Therefore, at this time
tomorrow I will send the worst hail-
storm[s] that has ever fallen on Egypt,
from the day it was founded till now.[t]
19Give an order now to bring your live-
stock and everything you have in the
field to a place of shelter, because the
hail will fall on every man and animal
that has not been brought in and is still
out in the field, and they will die.'"
20Those officials of Pharaoh who
feared[u] the word of the LORD hurried to
bring their slaves and their livestock
inside. 21But those who ignored[v] the
word of the LORD left their slaves and
livestock in the field.
22Then the LORD said to Moses,
"Stretch out your hand towards the sky
so that hail will fall all over Egypt—on

24 [c]Ps 78:45; 105:31
25 [d]ver 8; Ex 9:27; 10:16; 12:31
26 [e]Ge 43:32
27 [f]Ge 30:36; [g]Ex 3:18
28 [h]ver 8; Jer 37:3; Ac 8:24
29 [i]ver 15; Ex 9:30; 10:11; Isa 26:10
30 [j]ver 12; Ex 9:33; 10:18
32 [k]Ex 7:14

Ch. 9

1 [a]Ex 8:1
3 [b]Ex 7:4; 1Sa 5:6; Job 13:21; Ps 32:4; 39:10; Ac 13:11; [c]Lev 26:25; Ps 78:50; Am 4:10
4 [d]ver 26; Ex 8:23
6 [e]ver 19–21; Ex 11:5; 12:29; [f]Ps 78:48–50
7 [g]Ex 7:22; [h]Ex 7:14; 8:32
9 [i]Lev 13:18–19; Dt 28:27,35; 2Ki 20:7; Job 2:7; Isa 38:21; Rev 16:2
11 [j]Ex 8:18
12 [k]Ex 4:21; [l]Ex 7:4
13 [m]Ex 3:18
14 [n]Ex 8:10; [o]Ex 15:11; 1Sa 2:2; 2Sa 7:22; 1Ki 8:23; 1Ch 17:20; Ps 35:10; 71:19; 86:8; 89:6; Isa 46:9; Jer 10:6; Mic 7:18
15 [p]Ex 3:20
16 [q]Pr 16:4; [r]Ex 14:4,17,31; Ps 20:6; 25:11; 68:28; 71:18; 106:8; 109:21; Ro 9:17*
18 [s]ver 23; Jos 10:11; Ps 78:47–48; 105:32; 148:8; Isa 30:30; Eze 38:22; Hag 2:17; [t]ver 24; Ex 10:6
20 [u]Pr 13:13
21 [v]Ge 19:14; Eze 33:4–5

[a]16 *Or have spared you*

men and animals and on everything growing in the fields of Egypt." 23When Moses stretched out his staff towards the sky, the LORD sent thunder[w] and hail,[x] and lightning flashed down to the ground. So the LORD rained hail on the land of Egypt; 24hail fell and lightning flashed back and forth. It was the worst storm in all the land of Egypt since it had become a nation.[y] 25Throughout Egypt hail struck everything in the fields—both men and animals; it beat down everything growing in the fields and stripped every tree.[z] 26The only place it did not hail was the land of Goshen,[a] where the Israelites were.[b]

27Then Pharaoh summoned Moses and Aaron. "This time I have sinned,"[c] he said to them. "The LORD is in the right,[d] and I and my people are in the wrong. 28Pray[e] to the LORD, for we have had enough thunder and hail. I will let you go;[f] you don't have to stay any longer."

29Moses replied, "When I have gone out of the city, I will spread out my hands[g] in prayer to the LORD. The thunder will stop and there will be no more hail, so you may know that the earth[h] is the LORD's. 30But I know that you and your officials still do not fear[i] the LORD God."

31(The flax and barley[j] were destroyed, since the barley was in the ear and the flax was in bloom. 32The wheat and spelt,[k] however, were not destroyed, because they ripen later.)

33Then Moses left Pharaoh and went out of the city. He spread out his hands towards the LORD; the thunder and hail stopped, and the rain no longer poured down on the land. 34When Pharaoh saw that the rain and hail and thunder had stopped, he sinned again: He and his officials hardened their hearts. 35So Pharaoh's heart[l] was hard and he would not let the Israelites go, just as the LORD had said through Moses.

The Plague of Locusts

10 Then the LORD said to Moses, "Go to Pharaoh, for I have hardened his heart[a] and the hearts of his officials so that I may perform these miraculous signs[b] of mine among them 2that you may tell your children[c] and grandchildren how I dealt harshly[d] with the Egyptians and how I performed my signs among them, and that you may know that I am the LORD."[e]

3So Moses and Aaron went to Pharaoh and said to him, "This is what the LORD, the God of the Hebrews, says: 'How long will you refuse to humble[f] yourself before me? Let my people go, so that they may worship me. 4If you refuse[g] to let them go, I will bring locusts[h] into your country tomorrow. 5They will cover the face of the ground so that it cannot be seen. They will devour what little you have left[i] after the hail, including every tree that is growing in your fields.[j] 6They will fill your houses[k] and those of all your officials and all the Egyptians—something neither your fathers nor your forefathers have ever seen from the day they settled in this land till now.'"[l] Then Moses turned and left Pharaoh.

7Pharaoh's officials said to him, "How long will this man be a snare[m] to us? Let the people go, so that they may worship the LORD their God. Do you not yet realise that Egypt is ruined?"[n]

8Then Moses and Aaron were brought back to Pharaoh. "Go, worship[o] the LORD your God," he said. "But just who will be going?"

9Moses answered, "We will go with our young and old, with our sons and daughters, and with our flocks and herds, because we are to celebrate a festival[p] to the LORD."

10Pharaoh said, "The LORD be with you—if I let you go, along with your women and children! Clearly you are bent on evil.[a] 11No! Let only the men go; and worship the LORD, since that's what you have been asking for." Then Moses and Aaron were driven out of Pharaoh's presence.

12And the LORD said to Moses, "Stretch out your hand[q] over Egypt so that locusts will swarm over the land and devour everything growing in the fields, everything left by the hail."

13So Moses stretched out his staff[r] over Egypt, and the LORD made an east wind blow across the land all that day and all that night. By morning the wind had brought the locusts;[s] 14they invaded all Egypt and settled down in every area of the country in great numbers. Never before had there been such a plague of locusts,[t] nor will there ever be again. 15They covered all the ground until it

23 [w]Ex 20:18; 1Sa 7:10; 12:17; Ps 18:13; 29:3; 68:33; 77:17; 104:7; [x]**ver 18**; Rev 8:7; 16:21
24 [y]**ver 18**
25 [z]Ps 105:32–33; Eze 13:13
26 [a]**ver 4**; Isa 32:18–20; [b]Ex 10:23; 11:7; 12:13; Am 4:7
27 [c]ver 34; Ex 10:16; Nu 14:40; Dt 1:41; Jos 7:11; Jdg 10:10; 1Sa 15:24; 24:17; 26:21; [d]Ps 11:7; 116:5; 119:137; 129:4; 145:17; Jer 12:1; La 1:18
28 [e]**Ex 8:8**; Ac 8:24; [f]**Ex 8:8**
29 [g]ver 33; 1Ki 8:22,38; Job 11:13; Ps 77:2; 88:9; 143:6; Isa 1:15; [h]Ex 19:5; Job 41:11; Ps 24:1; 50:12; 1Co 10:26
30 [i]**Ex 8:29**
31 [j]Dt 8:8; Ru 1:22; 2:23; 2Sa 14:30; 17:28; Isa 28:25; Eze 4:9; Joel 1:11
32 [k]Isa 28:25
35 [l]**Ex 4:21**

Ch. 10

1 [a]**Ex 4:21**; [b]**Ex 3:19; 7:3**; Jos 24:17; Ne 9:10; Ps 74:9; 105:26–36
2 [c]Ex 12:26–27; 13:8,14; Dt 4:9; 6:20; 32:7; Jos 4:6; Ps 44:1; 71:18; 78:4–5; Joel 1:3; [d]1Sa 6:6; [e]**Ex 6:2**
3 [f]1Ki 21:29; 2Ki 22:19; 2Ch 7:14; 12:7; 33:23; 34:27; Job 42:6; Isa 58:3; Da 5:22; Jas 4:10; 1Pe 5:6
4 [g]Ex 8:2; 9:2; [h]Dt 28:38; Ps 105:34; Pr 30:27; Joel 1:4; Rev 9:3
5 [i]Ex 9:32; Joel 1:4; [j]ver 15
6 [k]Joel 2:9; [l]**Ex 9:18**
7 [m]Ex 23:33; 34:12; Dt 7:16; 12:30; 20:18; Jos 23:7–13; Jdg 2:3; 8:27; 16:5; 1Sa 18:21; Ps 106:36; Ecc 7:26; [n]**Ge 20:3; Ex 8:19**
8 [o]**Ex 8:8**
9 [p]**Ex 3:18**
12 [q]Ex 7:19
13 [r]ver 21–22; Ex 4:17; 8:5,17; 9:23; 14:15–16,26–27; 17:5; Nu 20:8; [s]ver 4; 1Ki 8:37; Ps 78:46; 105:34; Am 4:9; Na 3:16
14 [t]Dt 28:38; Ps 78:46; Isa 33:4; Joel 1:4; 2:1–11,25; **Am 4:9**

[a]*10* Or *Be careful, trouble is in store for you!*

was black. They devoured[u] all that was left after the hail—everything growing in the fields and the fruit on the trees. Nothing green remained on tree or plant in all the land of Egypt.

16Pharaoh quickly summoned[v] Moses and Aaron and said, "I have sinned[w] against the LORD your God and against you. 17Now forgive[x] my sin once more and pray[y] to the LORD your God to take this deadly plague away from me."

18Moses then left Pharaoh and prayed to the LORD.[z] 19And the LORD changed the wind to a very strong west wind, which caught up the locusts and carried them into the Red Sea.[b] Not a locust was left anywhere in Egypt. 20But the LORD hardened Pharaoh's heart,[a] and he would not let the Israelites go.

The Plague of Darkness

21Then the LORD said to Moses, "Stretch out your hand towards the sky so that darkness[b] will spread over Egypt—darkness that can be felt." 22So Moses stretched out his hand towards the sky, and total darkness[c] covered all Egypt for three days. 23No-one could see anyone else or leave his place for three days. Yet all the Israelites had light in the places where they lived.[d]

24Then Pharaoh summoned Moses and said, "Go,[e] worship the LORD. Even your women and children[f] may go with you; only leave your flocks and herds behind."[g]

25But Moses said, "You must allow us to have sacrifices and burnt offerings[h] to present to the LORD our God. 26Our livestock too must go with us; not a hoof is to be left behind. We have to use some of them in worshipping the LORD our God, and until we get there we will not know what we are to use to worship the LORD."

27But the LORD hardened Pharaoh's heart,[i] and he was not willing to let them go. 28Pharaoh said to Moses, "Get out of my sight! Make sure you do not appear before me again! The day you see my face you will die."

29"Just as you say," Moses replied, "I will never appear[j] before you again."

The Plague on the Firstborn

11 Now the LORD said to Moses, "I will bring one more plague on Pharaoh and on Egypt. After that, he will let you go[a] from here, and when he does, he will drive you out completely.[b] 2Tell the people that men and women alike are to ask their neighbours for articles of silver and gold."[c] 3(The LORD made the Egyptians favourably disposed[d] towards the people, and Moses himself was highly regarded[e] in Egypt by Pharaoh's officials and by the people.)

4So Moses said, "This is what the LORD says: 'About midnight[f] I will go throughout Egypt.[g] 5Every firstborn[h] son in Egypt will die, from the firstborn son of Pharaoh, who sits on the throne, to the firstborn son of the slave girl, who is at her hand mill,[i] and all the firstborn of the cattle as well. 6There will be loud wailing[j] throughout Egypt—worse than there has ever been or ever will be again. 7But among the Israelites not a dog will bark at any man or animal.' Then you will know that the LORD makes a distinction[k] between Egypt and Israel. 8All these officials of yours will come to me, bowing down before me and saying, 'Go,[l] you and all the people who follow you!' After that I will leave."[m] Then Moses, hot with anger, left Pharaoh.

9The LORD had said to Moses, "Pharaoh will refuse to listen[n] to you—so that my wonders[o] may be multiplied in Egypt." 10Moses and Aaron performed all these wonders before Pharaoh, but the LORD hardened Pharaoh's heart,[p] and he would not let the Israelites go out of his country.

The Passover

12:14–20pp—Lev 23:4–8; Nu 28:16–25; Dt 16:1–8

12 The LORD said to Moses and Aaron in Egypt, 2"This month is to be for you the first month,[a] the first month of your year. 3Tell the whole community of Israel that on the tenth day of this month each man is to take a lamb[a][b] for his family, one for each household.[c] 4If any household is too small for a whole lamb, they must share one with their nearest neighbour, having taken into account the number of people there are. You are to determine the amount of lamb needed in accordance with what each person will eat. 5The animals you choose must be year-old males without defect,[d] and you may take them from the sheep or the goats. 6Take care of them until the fourteenth day of the month,[e] when all the people

15 [u]Dt 28:38; Ps 105:34–35; Joel 1:4; Am 7:2; Mal 3:11
16 [v]**Ex 8:25;** [w]**Ex 9:27**
17 [x]1Sa 15:25; [y]**Ex 8:8**
18 [z]**Ex 8:30**
20 [a]**Ex 4:21**
21 [b]Dt 28:29
22 [c]Ps 105:28; Isa 13:10; 45:7; 50:3; Rev 16:10
23 [d]**Ex 8:22;** Am 4:7
24 [e]**Ex 8:8;** [f]ver 8–10; [g]**Ge 45:10**
25 [h]**Ge 8:20;** **Ex 18:12**
27 [i]**Ex 4:21**
29 [j]Ex 11:8; Heb 11:27

Ch. 11

1 [a]Ex 3:20; [b]Ex 6:1
2 [c]**Ex 3:21,22**
3 [d]**Ge 39:21;** [e]Dt 34:11; 2Sa 7:9; 8:13; 22:44; 23:1; Est 9:4; Ps 89:27
4 [f]Ex 12:29; Job 34:20; [g]Ex 12:23; Ps 81:5
5 [h]**Ex 4:23;** [i]Isa 47:2
6 [j]Ex 12:30; Pr 21:13; Am 5:17
7 [k]**Ex 8:22**
8 [l]Ex 12:31–33; [m]Heb 11:27
9 [n]**Ex 7:4;** [o]**Ex 3:20**
10 [p]**Ex 4:21;** Ro 2:5

Ch. 12

2 [a]ver 18; Ex 13:4; 23:15; 34:18; 40:2; Dt 16:1
3 [b]Mk 14:12; 1Co 5:7; [c]ver 21
5 [d]Ex 29:1; Lev 1:3; 3:1; 4:3; 22:18–21; 23:12; Nu 6:14; 15:8; 28:3; Dt 15:21; 17:1; Heb 9:14; 1Pe 1:19
6 [e]ver 19; Lev 23:5; Nu 9:1–3,5,11; Jos 5:10; 2Ch 30:2

[b]19 Hebrew *Yam Suph*; that is, Sea of Reeds
[a]3 The Hebrew word can mean both *lamb* or *kid*; also in verse 4.

of the community of Israel must slaughter them at twilight.[f] 7Then they are to take some of the blood[g] and put it on the sides and tops of the door-frames of the houses where they eat the lambs. 8That same night[h] they are to eat the meat roasted[i] over the fire, along with bitter herbs,[j] and bread made without yeast.[k] 9Do not eat the meat raw or cooked in water, but roast it over the fire—head, legs and inner parts.[l] 10Do not leave any of it till morning;[m] if some is left till morning, you must burn it. 11This is how you are to eat it: with your cloak tucked into your belt, your sandals on your feet and your staff in your hand. Eat it in haste; it is the LORD's Passover.[n o]

12"On that same night I will pass through[p] Egypt and strike down[q] every firstborn[r]—both men and animals—and I will bring judgment on all the gods[s] of Egypt. I am the LORD.[t] 13The blood will be a sign for you on the houses where you are; and when I see the blood, I will pass over[u] you. No destructive plague will touch you when I strike Egypt.[v]

14"This is a day you are to commemorate;[w] for the generations to come you shall celebrate it as a festival to the LORD—a lasting ordinance.[x] 15For seven days you are to eat bread made without yeast.[y] On the first day remove the yeast from your houses, for whoever eats anything with yeast in it from the first day until the seventh must be cut off[z] from Israel. 16On the first day hold a sacred assembly, and another one on the seventh day. Do no work[a] at all on these days, except to prepare food for everyone to eat—that is all you may do.

17"Celebrate the Feast of Unleavened Bread,[b] because it was on this very day that I brought your divisions out of Egypt.[c] Celebrate this day as a lasting ordinance for the generations to come.[d] 18In the first month[e] you are to eat bread made without yeast, from the evening of the fourteenth day until the evening of the twenty-first day. 19For seven days no yeast is to be found in your houses. And whoever eats anything with yeast in it must be cut off[f] from the community of Israel, whether he is an alien[g] or native-born. 20Eat nothing made with yeast. Wherever you live[h], you must eat unleavened bread."[i]

21Then Moses summoned all the elders of Israel and said to them, "Go at once and select the animals for your families and slaughter the Passover[j] lamb. 22Take a bunch of hyssop,[k] dip it into the blood in the basin and put some of the blood[l] on the top and on both sides of the door-frame. Not one of you shall go out of the door of his house until morning. 23When the LORD goes through the land to strike[m] down the Egyptians, he will see the blood[n] on the top and sides of the door-frame and will pass over[o] that doorway, and he will not permit the destroyer[p] to enter your houses and strike you down.

24"Obey these instructions as a lasting ordinance[q] for you and your descendants. 25When you enter the land[r] that the LORD will give you as he promised, observe this ceremony. 26And when your children[s] ask you, 'What does this ceremony mean to you?' 27then tell them, 'It is the Passover[t] sacrifice to the LORD, who passed over the houses of the Israelites in Egypt and spared our homes when he struck down the Egyptians.' "[u] Then the people bowed down and worshipped.[v] 28The Israelites did just what the LORD commanded[w] Moses and Aaron.

29At midnight[x] the LORD[y] struck down all the firstborn[z] in Egypt, from the firstborn of Pharaoh, who sat on the throne, to the firstborn of the prisoner, who was in the dungeon, and the firstborn of all the livestock[a] as well. 30Pharaoh and all his officials and all the Egyptians got up during the night, and there was loud wailing[b] in Egypt, for there was not a house without someone dead.

The Exodus

31During the night Pharaoh summoned Moses and Aaron and said, "Up! Leave my people, you and the Israelites! Go, worship[c] the LORD as you have requested. 32Take your flocks and herds,[d] as you have said, and go. And also bless[e] me."

33The Egyptians urged the people to hurry[f] and leave[g] the country. "For otherwise," they said, "we will all die!"[h] 34So the people took their dough before the yeast was added, and carried it on their shoulders in kneading troughs[i] wrapped in clothing. 35The Israelites did as Moses instructed and asked the

6 [f]Ex 16:12; Dt 16:4,6
7 [g]ver 13,23; Eze 9:6
8 [h]ver 10; Ex 16:19; 23:18; 34:25; Lev 7:15; Nu 9:12; [i]Dt 16:7; 2Ch 35:13; [j]Nu 9:11; [k]ver 19–20; Ex 13:3; Dt 16:3–4; 1Co 5:8
9 [l]Ex 29:13,17, 22; Lev 3:3
10 [m]**ver 8**; Ex 13:7; 29:34; Lev 22:30; Dt 16:4
11 [n]ver 33; Dt 16:3; Isa 48:20; 52:12; [o]ver 13, 21,27,43; Lev 23:5; Nu 9:2, 4; 28:16; Dt 16:1; Jos 5:10; 2Ki 23:21,23; 2Ch 30:1; Ezr 6:19; Isa 31:5; Eze 45:21
12 [p]Am 5:17; [q]Isa 10:33; 31:8; 37:36; [r]ver 29; **Ex 4:23**; 13:15; [s]Ex 15:11; 18:11; Nu 33:4; 2Ch 2:5; Ps 95:3; 97:9; 135:5; Isa 19:1; Jer 43:12; 44:8; [t]**Ex 6:2**
13 [u]**ver 11**,23; Heb 11:28; [v]**Ex 8:23**
14 [w]Ex 13:9; 23:14; 32:5; [x]ver 17,24; Ex 13:5,10; 27:21; Lev 3:17; 10:9; 16:29; 17:7; 23:14; 24:3; Nu 18:23
15 [y]Ex 13:6–7; 23:15; 34:18; Lev 23:6; Nu 28:17; Dt 16:3; 1Co 5:7; [z]**Ge 17:14**
16 [a]Nu 29:35
17 [b]Ex 23:15; 34:18; Dt 16:16; 2Ch 8:13; 30:21; Ezr 6:22; Mt 26:17; Lk 22:1; Ac 12:3; [c]ver 41; **Ex 6:6**,26; 13:3; Lev 19:36; [d]Lev 3:17
18 [e]**ver 2**
19 [f]**Ge 17:14**; [g]Nu 9:14; 15:14; 35:15; Dt 1:16; Jos 8:33
20 [h]Lev 3:17; Nu 35:29; Eze 6:6; [i]Ex 13:6
21 [j]**ver 11**; Mk 14:12–16

22 [k]Lev 14:4,6; Nu 19:18; Ps 51:7; [l]Heb 11:28
23 [m]Isa 19:22; [n]**ver 7**; Rev 7:3; [o]**ver 13**; [p]**Ge 16:7**; Isa 37:36; Jer 6:26; 48:8; 1Co 10:10; Heb 11:28
24 [q]**ver 14**
25 [r]**Ge 15:14**; Ex 3:17
26 [s]Ex 10:2
27 [t]**ver 11**; [u]**Ex 8:23**; [v]**Ge 24:26**
28 [w]ver 50
29 [x]**Ex 11:4**; [y]**Ge 19:13**; [z]**Ex 4:23**; [a]**Ex 9:6**
30 [b]**Ex 11:6**
31 [c]**Ex 8:8**
32 [d]Ex 10:9,26; [e]Ge 27:34
33 [f]**ver 11**; [g]**Ex 6:1**; 1Sa 6:6; [h]**Ge 20:3**; **Ex 8:19**
34 [i]Ex 8:3

Egyptians for articles of silver and gold[j]
and for clothing.[k] 36The LORD had made
the Egyptians favourably disposed[l]
towards the people, and they gave
them what they asked for; so they
plundered[m] the Egyptians.
37The Israelites journeyed from
Rameses[n] to Succoth.[o] There were about
six hundred thousand men[p] on foot,
besides women and children. 38Many
other people[q] went up with them, as
well as large droves of livestock, both
flocks and herds. 39With the dough they
had brought from Egypt, they baked
cakes of unleavened bread. The dough
was without yeast because they had
been driven out[r] of Egypt and did not
have time to prepare food for them-
selves.
40Now the length of time the Israelite
people lived in Egypt[b] was 430 years.[s]
41At the end of the 430 years, to the very
day, all the LORD's divisions[t] left Egypt.[u]
42Because the LORD kept vigil that night
to bring them out of Egypt, on this
night all the Israelites are to keep vigil
to honour the LORD for the generations
to come.[v]

Passover Restrictions

43The LORD said to Moses and Aaron,
"These are the regulations for the Pass-
over:[w]
"No foreigner[x] is to eat of it. 44Any
slave you have bought may eat of it after
you have circumcised[y] him, 45but a tem-
porary resident and a hired worker[z]
may not eat of it.
46"It must be eaten inside one house;
take none of the meat outside the
house. Do not break any of the bones.[a]
47The whole community of Israel must
celebrate it.
48"An alien living among you who
wants to celebrate the LORD's Passover
must have all the males in his house-
hold circumcised; then he may take part
like one born in the land.[b] No uncircum-
cised[c] male may eat of it. 49The same law
applies to the native-born and to the
alien[d] living among you."
50All the Israelites did just what the
LORD had commanded[e] Moses and
Aaron. 51And on that very day the LORD
brought the Israelites out of Egypt[f] by
their divisions.[g]

Consecration of the Firstborn

13 The LORD said to Moses, 2"Con-
secrate to me every firstborn
male.[a] The first offspring of every womb
among the Israelites belongs to me,
whether man or animal."
3Then Moses said to the people,
"Commemorate this day, the day you
came out of Egypt,[b] out of the land of
slavery, because the LORD brought you
out of it with a mighty hand.[c] Eat no-
thing containing yeast.[d] 4Today, in the
month of Abib,[e] you are leaving. 5When
the LORD brings you into the land of the
Canaanites,[f] Hittites, Amorites, Hivites
and Jebusites[g]—the land he swore to
your forefathers to give you, a land
flowing with milk and honey[h]—you are
to observe this ceremony[i] in this month:
6For seven days eat bread made without
yeast and on the seventh day hold a
festival[j] to the LORD. 7Eat unleavened
bread during those seven days; nothing
with yeast in it is to be seen among you,
nor shall any yeast be seen anywhere
within your borders. 8On that day tell
your son,[k] 'I do this because of what the
LORD did for me when I came out of
Egypt.' 9This observance will be for you
like a sign on your hand[l] and a reminder
on your forehead[m] that the law of the
LORD is to be on your lips. For the LORD
brought you out of Egypt with his
mighty hand.[n] 10You must keep this
ordinance[o] at the appointed time[p] year
after year.
11"After the LORD brings you into the
land of the Canaanites[q] and gives it to
you, as he promised on oath[r] to you and
your forefathers,[s] 12you are to give over
to the LORD the first offspring of every
womb. All the firstborn males of your
livestock belong to the LORD.[t] 13Redeem
with a lamb every firstborn donkey,[u]
but if you do not redeem it, break its
neck.[v] Redeem[w] every firstborn among
your sons.[x]
14"In days to come when your son[y]
asks you, 'What does this mean?' say to
him, 'With a mighty hand the LORD
brought us out of Egypt, out of the land
of slavery.[z] 15When Pharaoh stubbornly
refused to let us go, the LORD killed
every firstborn in Egypt, both man and
animal. This is why I sacrifice to the
LORD the first male offspring of every
womb and redeem each of my firstborn
sons.'[a] 16And it will be like a sign on
your hand and a symbol on your

35 [j]Ex 3:22; [k]Ge 24:53
36 [l]Ge 39:21; [m]Ex 3:22
37 [n]Ge 47:11; [o]Ex 13:20; Nu 33:3–5; [p]Ge 12:2; Ex 38:26; Nu 1:46; 2:32; 11:13,21; 26:51
38 [q]Nu 11:4; Jos 8:35
39 [r]Ex 3:20; 11:1
40 [s]Ge 15:13; Ac 7:6; Gal 3:17
41 [t]Ex 6:26; [u]Ex 3:10
42 [v]Ex 13:10; Lev 3:17; Nu 9:3; Dt 16:1,6
43 [w]ver 11; [x]ver 48; Nu 9:14; 15:14; 2Ch 6:32–33; Isa 14:1; 56:3, 6; 60:10
44 [y]Ge 17:12–13
45 [z]Lev 22:10
46 [a]Nu 9:12; Ps 22:14; 34:20; 51:8; Pr 17:22; Jn 19:36*
48 [b]ver 49; Lev 19:18,34; 24:22; Nu 9:14; 10:32; [c]Eze 44:7
49 [d]Lev 24:22; Nu 15:15–16, 29; Dt 1:16
50 [e]ver 28
51 [f]Ex 3:10; 6:6; [g]Ex 6:26

Ch. 13

2 [a]ver 12,13,15; Ex 22:29; 34:20; Lev 27:26; Nu 3:13; 8:17; 18:15; Dt 15:19; Ne 10:36; Lk 2:23*
3 [b]ver 14: Ex 7:4; Lev 26:13; Nu 1:1; 9:1; 22:5; 26:4; Dt 4:45; 5:6; Ps 81:10; 114:1; [c]Ex 3:20; [d]Ex 12:8
4 [e]Ex 12:2
5 [f]ver 11; [g]Ex 3:8; [h]Ex 3:8; [i]Ex 12:25–26
6 [j]Ex 12:15–20
8 [k]Ex 10:2; Ps 78:5–6
9 [l]Isa 44:5; [m]ver 16; Dt 6:8; 11:18; Pr 3:3; Mt 23:5; [n]Ex 3:20
10 [o]Ex 12:14; [p]Ps 75:2; 102:13
11 [q]ver 5; [r]Ge 22:16; Dt 1:8; [s]Ge 12:7; 17:19; Ps 105:42–45
12 [t]Ge 4:4; Lev 27:26; Nu 3:13; 18:15,17; Lk 2:23*
13 [u]ver 15; Lev 27:11; [v]Ex 34:20; Isa 66:3; [w]Nu 3:46–47; [x]Nu 18:15
14 [y]Ex 10:2; [z]Ex 20:2; Dt 7:8; 28:68
15 [a]ver 2

b40 Masoretic Text; Samaritan Pentateuch and Septuagint *Egypt and Canaan*

forehead[b] that the LORD brought us out of Egypt with his mighty hand."

Crossing the Sea

17When Pharaoh let the people go, God did not lead them on the road through the Philistine country, though that was shorter. For God said, "If they face war, they might change their minds and return to Egypt."[c] 18So God led[d] the people around by the desert road towards the Red Sea.[a] The Israelites went up out of Egypt armed for battle.[e]

19Moses took the bones of Joseph[f] with him because Joseph had made the sons of Israel swear an oath. He had said, "God will surely come to your aid, and then you must carry my bones up with you from this place."[b][g]

20After leaving Succoth[h] they camped at Etham on the edge of the desert.[i] 21By day the LORD went ahead[j] of them in a pillar of cloud[k] to guide them on their way and by night in a pillar of fire to give them light, so that they could travel by day or night. 22Neither the pillar of cloud by day nor the pillar of fire by night left[l] its place in front of the people.

14

Then the LORD said to Moses, 2"Tell the Israelites to turn back and camp near Pi Hahiroth, between Migdol[a] and the sea. They are to camp by the sea, directly opposite Baal Zephon.[b] 3Pharaoh will think, 'The Israelites are wandering around the land in confusion, hemmed in by the desert.' 4And I will harden Pharaoh's heart,[c] and he will pursue them.[d] But I will gain glory[e] for myself through Pharaoh and all his army, and the Egyptians will know that I am the LORD."[f] So the Israelites did this.

5When the king of Egypt was told that the people had fled,[g] Pharaoh and his officials changed their minds[h] about them and said, "What have we done? We have let the Israelites go and have lost their services!" 6So he had his chariot made ready and took his army with him. 7He took six hundred of the best chariots,[i] along with all the other chariots of Egypt, with officers over all of them. 8The LORD hardened the heart[j] of Pharaoh king of Egypt, so that he pursued the Israelites, who were marching out boldly[k]. 9The Egyptians—all Pharaoh's horses[l] and chariots, horsemen[a] and troops[m]—pursued the Israelites and overtook[n] them as they camped by the sea near Pi Hahiroth, opposite Baal Zephon.[o]

10As Pharaoh approached, the Israelites looked up, and there were the Egyptians, marching after them. They were terrified and cried[p] out to the LORD. 11They said to Moses, "Was it because there were no graves in Egypt that you brought us to the desert to die?[q] What have you done to us by bringing us out of Egypt? 12Didn't we say to you in Egypt, 'Leave us alone; let us serve the Egyptians'? It would have been better for us to serve the Egyptians than to die in the desert!"[r]

13Moses answered the people, "Do not be afraid.[s] Stand firm and you will see[t] the deliverance the LORD will bring you today. The Egyptians you see today you will never see[u] again. 14The LORD will fight[v] for you; you need only to be still."[w]

15Then the LORD said to Moses, "Why are you crying out to me?[x] Tell the Israelites to move on. 16Raise your staff[y] and stretch out your hand over the sea to divide the water[z] so that the Israelites can go through the sea on dry ground. 17I will harden the hearts[a] of the Egyptians so that they will go in after them.[b] And I will gain glory through Pharaoh and all his army, through his chariots and his horsemen. 18The Egyptians will know that I am the LORD[c] when I gain glory through Pharaoh, his chariots and his horsemen."

19Then the angel of God,[d] who had been travelling in front of Israel's army, withdrew and went behind them. The pillar of cloud[e] also moved from in front and stood behind[f] them, 20coming between the armies of Egypt and Israel. Throughout the night the cloud brought darkness[g] to the one side and light to the other; so neither went near the other all night long.

21Then Moses stretched out his hand[h] over the sea,[i] and all that night the LORD drove the sea back with a strong east wind[j] and turned it into dry land.[k] The waters were divided,[l] 22and the Israelites went through the sea[m] on dry

16 [b]**ver 9**
17 [c]Ex 14:11; Nu 14:1–4; Dt 17:16; Hos 11:5
18 [d]Ex 15:22; Ps 136:16; Eze 20:10; [e]Jos 1:14; 4:13
19 [f]Jos 24:32; Ac 7:16; Heb 11:22; [g]**Ge 47:29–30**
20 [h]**Ex 12:37;** [i]Nu 33:6
21 [j]Ex 32:1; 33:14; Dt 2:7; 31:8; Jdg 4:14; 5:4; Ps 68:7; 77:20; Jer 2:2; Hab 3:13; [k]Ex 14:19, 24; 24:16; 33:9–10; 34:5; 40:38; Nu 9:16; 12:5; 14:14; Dt 1:33; Ne 9:12, 19; Ps 78:14; 99:7; 105:39; Isa 4:5; 1Co 10:1
22 [l]Ne 9:19

Ch. 14

2 [a]Nu 33:7; Jer 44:1; Eze 29:10; [b]ver 9
4 [c]**Ex 4:21;** [d]ver 8,17,23; Ps 71:11; [e]**Ex 9:16;** Ro 9:17, 22–23; [f]**Ex 6:2;** Eze 32:15
5 [g]**Ge 31:21;** [h]Ps 105:25
7 [i]Ex 15:4
8 [j]**Ex 11:10;** [k]Nu 33:3; Ac 13:17
9 [l]Ge 47:17; [m]ver 6–7,25; Jos 24:6; Isa 43:17; [n]Ex 15:9; [o]ver 2
10 [p]Ex 15:25; Jos 24:7; Ne 9:9; Ps 5:2; 34:17; 50:15; 107:6,28
11 [q]**Ex 5:21;** 16:3; 17:3; Nu 11:1; 14:22; 20:4; 21:5; Dt 9:7
12 [r]**Ex 5:21;** 15:24; 17:2; Ps 106:7–8
13 [s]**Ge 15:1;** [t]1Sa 12:16; 2Ch 20:17; [u]ver 30
14 [v]ver 25; Ex 15:3; Dt 1:30; 3:22; 20:4; Jos 10:14; 23:3,10; 2Sa 5:24; 2Ch 20:29; Ne 4:20; Ps 24:8; 35:1; Isa 42:13; Jer 41:12; [w]1Sa 12:16; Ps 37:7; 46:10; 116:7; Isa 28:12; 30:15; Zec 2:13

15 [x]Jos 7:10 *16* [y]**Ex 4:2;** [z]ver 27; Isa 10:26
17 [a]Ex 4:21; [b]**ver 4** *18* [c]**Ex 6:2;** Eze 32:15
19 [d]**Ge 16:7;** Isa 63:9; [e]**Ex 13:21;** 1Co 10:1; [f]Isa 26:7; 42:16; 49:10; 52:12; 58:8 *20* [g]Jos 24:7
21 [h]**Ex 7:19;** [i]**Ex 4:2;** Job 26:12; Isa 14:27; 23:11; 51:15; Jer 31:35; Ac 7:36; [j]**Ge 41:6;** Ex 15:8; 2Sa 22:16; 1Ki 19:11; Job 38:1; 40:6; Jer 23:19; Na 1:3; [k]**ver 22; Ge 8:1;** [l]2Ki 2:8; Ps 74:13; 78:13; 114:5; 136:13; Isa 63:12
22 [m]ver 16; Nu 33:8; Jos 24:6; Isa 43:16; 63:11; 1Co 10:1

[a]18 Hebrew *Yam Suph;* that is, Sea of Reeds
[b]19 See Gen. 50:25.
[a]9 Or *charioteers;* also in verses 17, 18, 23, 26 and 28

ground,[n] with a wall[o] of water on their
right and on their left.
23The Egyptians pursued them, and
all Pharaoh's horses and chariots and
horsemen[p] followed them into the sea.
24During the last watch of the night the
LORD looked down from the pillar of fire
and cloud[q] at the Egyptian army and
threw it into confusion.[r] 25He made the
wheels of their chariots come off[b] so
that they had difficulty driving. And the
Egyptians said, "Let's get away from
the Israelites! The LORD is fighting[s] for
them against Egypt."[t]
26Then the LORD said to Moses,
"Stretch out your hand over the sea so
that the waters may flow back over the
Egyptians and their chariots and horse-
men." 27Moses stretched out his hand
over the sea, and at daybreak the sea
went back to its place.[u] The Egyptians
were fleeing towards[c] it, and the LORD
swept them into the sea.[v] 28The water
flowed back and covered the chariots
and horsemen—the entire army of
Pharaoh that had followed the Israelites
into the sea.[w] Not one of them sur-
vived.[x]
29But the Israelites went through the
sea on dry ground,[y] with a wall[z] of
water on their right and on their left.
30That day the LORD saved[a] Israel from
the hands of the Egyptians, and Israel
saw the Egyptians lying dead on the
shore. 31And when the Israelites saw
the great power[b] the LORD displayed
against the Egyptians, the people
feared[c] the LORD and put their trust[d] in
him and in Moses his servant.

The Song of Moses and Miriam

15 Then Moses and the Israelites
sang this song[a] to the LORD:

"I will sing[b] to the LORD,
for he is highly exalted.
The horse and its rider[c]
he has hurled into the sea.[d]
2The LORD is my strength[e] and my
song;
he has become my salvation.[f]
He is my God,[g] and I will praise him,
my father's God, and I will exalt[h]
him.
3The LORD is a warrior;[i]
the LORD is his name.[j]
4Pharaoh's chariots and his army[k]
he has hurled into the sea.
The best of Pharaoh's officers
are drowned in the Red Sea.[a]
5The deep waters[l] have covered them;
they sank to the depths like a
stone.[m]
6"Your right hand,[n] O LORD,
was majestic in power.
Your right hand,[o] O LORD,
shattered[p] the enemy.
7In the greatness of your majesty[q]
you threw down those who
opposed you.
You unleashed your burning anger;[r]
it consumed[s] them like stubble.
8By the blast of your nostrils[t]
the waters piled up.[u]
The surging waters stood firm like a
wall;[v]
the deep waters congealed in the
heart of the sea.[w]

9"The enemy boasted,
'I will pursue,[x] I will overtake them.
I will divide the spoils;[y]
I will gorge myself on them.
I will draw my sword
and my hand will destroy them.'
10But you blew with your breath,[z]
and the sea covered them.
They sank like lead
in the mighty waters.[a]

11"Who among the gods is like you,[b] O
LORD?
Who is like you—
majestic in holiness,[c]
awesome in glory,[d]
working wonders?[e]
12You stretched out[f] your right hand
and the earth swallowed them.[g]

13"In your unfailing love you will lead[h]
the people you have redeemed.[i]

22 [n]ver 21,29; **Ex 3:12**; 15:19; Dt 31:6–8; Jos 3:16,17; 4:22; Ne 9:11; Ps 66:6; 77:19; 106:9; Isa 11:15; 41:10; 43:5; 44:27; 50:2; 51:10; 63:13; Jer 46:28; Na 1:4; Heb 11:29; [o]Ex 15:8; Jos 3:13; Ps 78:13
23 [p]ver 7
24 [q]**Ex 13:21**; 1Co 10:1; [r]Ex 23:27; Jos 10:10; 1Sa 5:9; 7:10; 14:15; 2Sa 5:24; 2Ki 7:6; 19:7
25 [s]**ver 14**; [t]ver 9; Dt 32:31; 1Sa 2:2; 4:8
27 [u]Jos 4:18; [v]ver 28; Ex 15:1,21; Dt 1:40; 2:1; 11:4; Ps 78:53; 106:11; 136:15; Heb 11:29
28 [w]ver 23; Ex 15:19; Jos 24:7; [x]**ver 27**; Ex 15:5; Jdg 4:16; Ne 9:11
29 [y]ver 21,**22**; Jos 24:11; 2Ki 2:8; Ps 74:15; [z]Ps 78:13
30 [a]ver 29; 1Sa 14:23; 1Ch 11:14; Ps 44:7; 106:8,10,21; Isa 43:3; 50:2; 51:9–10; 60:16; 63:8,11
31 [b]**Ex 9:16**; Ps 147:5; [c]Ex 20:18; Dt 31:13; Jos 4:24; 1Sa 12:18; Ps 76:7; 112:1; [d]**Ex 4:5**; Ps 22:4; 40:3; 106:12; Jn 2:11; 11:45

Ch. 15

1 [a]Nu 21:17; Jdg 5:1; 2Sa 22:1; 1Ch 16:9; Job 36:24; Ps 59:16; 105:2; Rev 15:3; [b]Jdg 5:3; Ps 13:6; 21:13; 27:6; 61:8; 104:33; 106:12; Isa 12:5,6; 42:10–11; 44:23; [c]Dt 11:4; Ps 76:6; Jer 51:21; [d]**Ex 14:27**
2 [e]Ps 18:1; 59:17; [f]**Ge 45:7**; Ex 14:13; Ps 18:2,46; 25:5; 27:1; 62:2; 118:14; Isa 12:2; 33:2; Jnh 2:9; Hab 3:18; [g]**Ge 28:21**; [h]Dt 10:21; 2Sa 22:47; Ps 22:3; 30:1; 34:3; 35:27; 99:5; 103:19; 107:32; 108:5; 109:1; 118:28; 145:11; 148:14; Isa 24:15; 25:1; Jer 17:14; Da 4:37
3 [i]**Ex 14:14**; Rev 19:11; [j]**Ex 3:15**
4 [k]Ex 14:6–7; Jer 51:21
5 [l]**Ex 14:28**; [m]ver 10; Ne 9:11
6 [n]Ps 16:11; 17:7; 21:8; 63:8; 74:11; 77:10; 89:13; 98:1; 118:15; 138:7; [o]**Ex 3:20**; **Job 40:14**; [p]Nu 24:8; 1Sa 2:10; Ps 2:9
7 [q]Dt 33:26; Ps 150:2; [r]Ps 2:5; 78:49–50; Jer 12:13; 25:38; [s]Ex 24:17; Dt 4:24; 9:3; Ps 18:8; 59:13; Heb 12:29
8 [t]**Ex 14:21**; Ps 18:15; [u]Jos 3:13; Ps 78:13; Isa 43:16; [v]**Ex 14:22**; [w]Ps 46:2
9 [x]Ex 14:5–9; Dt 28:45; Ps 7:5; La 1:3; [y]Jdg 5:30; Isa 9:3; 53:12; Lk 11:22
10 [z]Job 4:9; 15:30; Isa 11:4; 30:33; 40:7; [a]ver 5; Ne 9:11; Ps 29:3; 32:6; 77:19
11 [b]**Ex 8:10**; Ps 77:13; **Isa 46:5**; [c]Lev 19:2; 1Sa 2:2; 1Ch 16:29; Ps 99:3; 110:3; Isa 6:3; Rev 4:8; [d]**Ex 14:4**; Ps 4:2; 8:1; 26:8; Isa 35:2; 40:5; [e]**Ex 3:20**
12 [f]**Ex 7:5**; [g]Nu 16:32; 26:10; Dt 11:6; Ps 106:17
13 [h]Ne 9:12; Ps 77:20; [i]**Ex 6:6**; Job 33:28; Ps 71:23; 106:10; Isa 1:27; 41:14; 43:14; 44:22–24; 51:10; 63:9; Tit 2:14

[b]25 Or *He jammed the wheels of their chariots* (see Samaritan Pentateuch, Septuagint and Syriac)
[c]27 Or *from*
[a]4 Hebrew *Yam Suph;* that is, Sea of Reeds; also in verse 22

In your strength you will guide them
to your holy dwelling.[j]
14 The nations will hear and tremble;[k]
anguish[l] will grip the people of
Philistia.[m]
15 The chiefs[n] of Edom[o] will be terrified,
the leaders of Moab will be seized
with trembling,[p]
the people[b] of Canaan will melt[q] away;
16 terror[r] and dread will fall upon
them.
By the power of your arm
they will be as still as a stone[s]—
until your people pass by, O LORD,
until the people you bought[c][t] pass
by.[u]
17 You will bring[v] them in and plant
them[w]
on the mountain[x] of your
inheritance—
the place, O LORD, you made for your
dwelling,[y]
the sanctuary,[z] O LORD, your hands
established.
18 The LORD will reign
for ever and ever."[a]

19 When Pharaoh's horses, chariots
and horsemen[d] went into the sea,[b] the
LORD brought the waters of the sea back
over them, but the Israelites walked
through the sea on dry ground.[c] 20 Then
Miriam[d] the prophetess,[e] Aaron's sister,
took a tambourine in her hand, and
all the women followed her, with
tambourines[f] and dancing.[g] 21 Miriam
sang[h] to them:

"Sing to the LORD,
for he is highly exalted.
The horse and its rider[i]
he has hurled into the sea."[j]

The Waters of Marah and Elim

22 Then Moses led Israel from the Red
Sea and they went into the Desert[k] of
Shur.[l] For three days they travelled in
the desert without finding water.[m]
23 When they came to Marah, they could
not drink its water because it was
bitter. (That is why the place is called
Marah.[e][n]) 24 So the people grumbled[o]
against Moses, saying, "What are we to
drink?"[p]
25 Then Moses cried out[q] to the LORD,
and the LORD showed him a piece of
wood. He threw[r] it into the water, and
the water became sweet.
There the LORD made a decree and a
law for them, and there he tested[s] them.
26 He said, "If you listen carefully to the
voice of the LORD your God and do what

13 [j]ver 17; Ps 68:16; 76:2; 78:54
14 [k]ver 16; Ex 23:27; Dt 2:25; Jos 2:9; 5:1; 9:24; 1Sa 4:7; Est 8:17; Ps 48:6; 96:9; 99:1; 114:7; Eze 38:20; [l]Isa 13:8; [m]Ps 83:7
15 [n]**Ge 36:15;** [o]Dt 2:4; [p]Nu 22:3; Ps 114:7; [q]Jos 2:9,24
16 [r]**ver 14; Ge 35:5;** [s]1Sa 25:37; [t]Ps 74:2; 2Pe 2:1; [u]Dt 2:4
17 [v]Ex 23:20; 32:34; 33:12; [w]2Sa 7:10; Ps 44:2; 80:8,15; Isa 5:2; 60:21; Jer 2:21; 11:17; 24:6; Am 9:15; [x]Dt 33:19; Ps 2:6; 3:4; 15:1; 78:54,68; 133:3; Da 9:16; Joel 2:1; Ob 16; Zep 3:11; [y]**ver 13;** Ps 132:13–14; [z]Ps 78:69; 114:2
18 [a]**Ge 21:33;** Ps 9:7; 29:10; 55:19; 66:7; 80:1; 102:12; 145:13; La 5:19
19 [b]**Ex 14:28;** [c]**Ex 14:22**
20 [d]ver 21; Ex 2:4; Nu 12:1; 20:1; 26:59; 1Ch 4:17; 6:3; [e]Jdg 4:4; 2Ki 22:14; 2Ch 34:22; Ne 6:14; Isa 8:3; Eze 13:17; [f]**Ge 31:27;** 1Sa 18:6; Ps 81:2; Isa 30:32; [g]**Ge 4:21;** Jdg 11:34; 21:21; 1Sa 18:6; 2Sa 6:5,14,16; Ps 30:11; 149:3; 150:4; SS 6:13; Jer 31:4,13
21 [h]1Sa 18:7; [i]Am 2:15; Hag 2:22; [j]**Ex 14:27**
22 [k]Ps 78:52; [l]**Ge 16:7;** [m]Ex 17:1,3; Nu 20:2,5; 33:14; Ps 107:5
23 [n]Nu 33:8; Ru 1:20
24 [o]**Ex 14:12;** 16:2; 17:3; Nu 14:2; Jos 9:18; Ps 78:18,42; 106:13,25; Eze 16:43; [p]Mt 6:31

is right in his eyes, if you pay attention
to his commands and keep[t] all his de-
crees,[u] I will not bring on you any of the
diseases[v] I brought on the Egyptians,
for I am the LORD, who heals[w] you."
27 Then they came to Elim, where
there were twelve springs and seventy
palm trees, and they camped[x] there
near the water.

Manna and Quail

16 The whole Israelite community
set out from Elim and came to
the Desert of Sin,[a] which is between
Elim and Sinai, on the fifteenth day of
the second month after they had come
out of Egypt.[b] 2 In the desert the whole
community grumbled[c] against Moses
and Aaron. 3 The Israelites said to them,
"If only we had died by the LORD's hand
in Egypt![d] There we sat round pots of
meat and ate all the food[e] we wanted,
but you have brought us out into this
desert to starve this entire assembly to
death."[f]
4 Then the LORD said to Moses, "I will
rain down bread from heaven[g] for you.
The people are to go out each day and
gather enough for that day. In this way I
will test[h] them and see whether they
will follow my instructions. 5 On the
sixth day they are to prepare what they
bring in, and that is to be twice[i] as much
as they gather on the other days."
6 So Moses and Aaron said to all the
Israelites, "In the evening you will
know that it was the LORD who brought
you out of Egypt,[j] 7 and in the morning
you will see the glory[k] of the LORD,
because he has heard your grumbling[l]
against him. Who are we, that you
should grumble against us?"[m] 8 Moses

25 [q]**Ex 14:10;** [r]2Ki 2:21; 4:41; 6:6; [s]**Ge 22:1;** Jdg 3:4; Job 23:10; Ps 81:7; Isa 48:10
26 [t]Ex 23:22; Dt 11:13; 15:5; 28:1; Jer 11:6; [u]Ex 19:5–6; 20:2–17; Dt 7:12; [v]Dt 7:15; 28:27,58–60; 32:39; 1Sa 5:6; Ps 30:2; 41:3–4; 103:3; [w]Ex 23:25–26; 2Ki 20:5; Ps 25:11; 103:3; 107:20; Jer 30:17; Hos 11:3
27 [x]Nu 33:9

Ch. 16

1 [a]Ex 17:1; Nu 33:11–12; [b]**Ex 6:6;** 12:1–2
2 [c]**Ex 15:24;** 1Co 10:10
3 [d]Ex 17:3; Nu 14:2; 20:3; [e]Nu 11:4,34; Dt 12:20; Ps 78:18; 106:14; Jer 44:17; [f]**Ge 47:15;** Dt 8:3
4 [g]ver 14–15; Dt 8:3; Ne 9:15; Ps 78:24; 105:40; **Jn 6:31***; [h]**Ge 22:1** 5 [i]ver 22; Lev 25:21 6 [j]**Ex 6:6**
7 [k]ver 10; Ex 24:16; 29:43; 33:18,22; 40:34; Lev 9:6; Nu 16:19,42; Dt 5:24; 1Ki 8:11; Ps 63:2; Isa 6:3; 35:2; 40:5; 44:23; 60:1; 66:18; Eze 1:28; 10:4; 43:5; Hab 2:14; Hag 2:7; Jn 11:40; [l]ver 12; Nu 11:1,18; 14:2,27–28; 17:5; [m]Nu 16:11

b15 Or *rulers* c16 Or *created*
d19 Or *charioteers* e23 *Marah* means *bitter*.

also said, "You will know that it was the
LORD when he gives you meat to eat in
the evening and all the bread you want
in the morning, because he has heard
your grumbling against him. Who are
we? You are not grumbling[n] against us,
but against the LORD."[o]
9Then Moses told Aaron, "Say to the
entire Israelite community, 'Come
before the LORD, for he has heard your
grumbling.'"
10While Aaron was speaking to the
whole Israelite community, they looked
towards the desert, and there was the
glory[p] of the LORD appearing in the
cloud.[q]
11The LORD said to Moses, 12"I have
heard the grumbling[r] of the Israelites.
Tell them, 'At twilight you will eat meat,
and in the morning you will be filled
with bread. Then you will know that I
am the LORD your God.'"[s]
13That evening quail[t] came and cov-
ered the camp, and in the morning there
was a layer of dew[u] around the camp.
14When the dew was gone, thin flakes
like frost[v] on the ground appeared on
the desert floor. 15When the Israelites
saw it, they said to each other, "What is
it?" For they did not know[w] what it was.
Moses said to them, "It is the bread[x]
the LORD has given you to eat. 16This is
what the LORD has commanded: 'Each
one is to gather as much as he needs.
Take an omer[a][y] for each person you
have in your tent.'"
17The Israelites did as they were told;
some gathered much, some little. 18And
when they measured it by the omer, he
who gathered much did not have too
much, and he who gathered little did
not have too little.[z] Each one gathered as
much as he needed.
19Then Moses said to them, "No-one
is to keep any of it until morning."[a]
20However, some of them paid no
attention to Moses; they kept part of it
until morning, but it was full of maggots
and began to smell.[b] So Moses was
angry[c] with them.
21Each morning everyone gathered as
much as he needed, and when the sun
grew hot, it melted away. 22On the sixth
day, they gathered twice[d] as much—
two omers[b] for each person—and the
leaders of the community[e] came and
reported this to Moses. 23He said to
them, "This is what the LORD com-
manded: 'Tomorrow is to be a day of
rest, a holy Sabbath[f] to the LORD. So
bake what you want to bake and boil
what you want to boil. Save whatever is
left and keep it until morning.'"
24So they saved it until morning, as
Moses commanded, and it did not stink
or get maggots in it. 25"Eat it today,"
Moses said, "because today is a Sabbath
to the LORD. You will not find any of it
on the ground today. 26Six days you are
to gather it, but on the seventh day, the
Sabbath,[g] there will not be any."
27Nevertheless, some of the people
went out on the seventh day to gather it,
but they found none. 28Then the LORD
said to Moses, "How long will you[c]
refuse to keep my commands[h] and my
instructions? 29Bear in mind that the
LORD has given you the Sabbath; that is
why on the sixth day he gives you bread
for two days. Everyone is to stay where
he is on the seventh day; no-one is to go
out." 30So the people rested on the
seventh day.
31The people of Israel called the bread
manna.[d][i] It was white like coriander
seed and tasted like wafers made with
honey. 32Moses said, "This is what the
LORD has commanded: 'Take an omer of
manna and keep it for the generations to
come, so they can see the bread I gave
you to eat in the desert when I brought
you out of Egypt.'"
33So Moses said to Aaron, "Take a jar
and put an omer of manna[j] in it. Then
place it before the LORD to be kept for the
generations to come."
34As the LORD commanded Moses,
Aaron put the manna in front of the
Testimony,[k] that it might be kept. 35The
Israelites ate manna[l] for forty years,[m]
until they came to a land that was
settled; they ate manna until they
reached the border of Canaan.[n]
36(An omer[o] is one tenth of an
ephah.)[p]

Water From the Rock

17 The whole Israelite community
set out from the Desert of Sin,[a]
travelling from place to place as the
LORD commanded. They camped at
Rephidim,[b] but there was no water[c] for
the people to drink. 2So they quarrelled
with Moses and said, "Give us water[d] to
drink."[e]
Moses replied, "Why do you quarrel
with me? Why do you put the LORD to
the test?"[f]

8 [n]ver 7; [o]Nu 23:21; Dt 33:5; Jdg 8:23; 1Sa 8:7; 12:12; **Mt 10:40**; Ro 13:2; 1Th 4:8
10 [p]**ver 7**; Jn 11:4; [q]Ex 13:21; 40:34–35; 1Ki 8:10; 2Ch 7:1; Eze 10:4
12 [r]**ver 7**; [s]**Ex 6:2; 20:2**
13 [t]Nu 11:31; Ps 78:27–28; 105:40; 106:15; [u]Nu 11:9
14 [v]ver 31; Nu 11:7–9; Dt 8:3, 16; Ps 105:40
15 [w]Dt 8:16; [x]**ver 4**; Ne 9:20; **Jn 6:31**
16 [y]ver 32,36
18 [z]2Co 8:15*
19 [a]ver 23; Ex 12:10
20 [b]ver 24; [c]Ex 32:19
22 [d]**ver 5**; [e]Ex 34:31
23 [f]**Ge 2:3; Ex 20:8**; Dt 5:13–14
26 [g]ver 23
28 [h]Jos 9:14; Ps 78:10; 106:13; 107:11; 119:1; Jer 32:23
31 [i]**ver 14**
33 [j]Heb 9:4; Rev 2:17
34 [k]Ex 25:16,21, 22; 27:21; 31:18; 40:20; Lev 16:13; Nu 1:50; 7:89; 10:11; 17:4,10; Dt 10:2; 1Ki 8:9; 2Ch 5:10
35 [l]Jn 6:31,49; [m]Nu 14:33; 33:38; Dt 1:3; 2:7; 8:2–4; Jos 5:6; Jdg 3:11; Ne 9:21; Ps 95:10; Am 5:25; [n]Jos 5:12
36 [o]**ver 16**; [p]Lev 5:11; 6:20; Nu 5:15; 15:4; 28:5

Ch. 17

1 [a]**Ex 16:1**; [b]ver 8; Ex 19:2; Nu 33:15; [c]Nu 20:5; 21:5; 33:14
2 [d]Nu 20:2; 33:14; Ps 107:5; [e]**Ex 14:12**; [f]Dt 6:16; Ps 78:18, 41; 106:14; Mt 4:7; 1Co 10:9

[a]*16* That is, probably about 4 pints (about 2 litres); also in verses 18, 32, 33 and 36
[b]*22* That is, probably about 7½ pints (about 4.5 litres) [c]*28* The Hebrew is plural.
[d]*31* *Manna* means *What is it?* (see verse 15).

3 But the people were thirsty[g] for water there, and they grumbled[h] against Moses. They said, "Why did you bring us up out of Egypt to make us and our children and livestock die[i] of thirst?"

4 Then Moses cried out to the LORD, "What am I to do with these people? They are almost ready to stone[j] me."

5 The LORD answered Moses, "Walk on ahead of the people. Take with you some of the elders of Israel and take in your hand the staff[k] with which you struck the Nile,[l] and go. 6 I will stand there before you by the rock at Horeb.[m] Strike[n] the rock, and water[o] will come out of it for the people to drink." So Moses did this in the sight of the elders of Israel. 7 And he called the place Massah[a][p] and Meribah[b][q] because the Israelites quarrelled and because they tested the LORD saying, "Is the LORD among us or not?"

The Amalekites Defeated

8 The Amalekites[r] came and attacked the Israelites at Rephidim.[s] 9 Moses said to Joshua,[t] "Choose some of our men and go out to fight the Amalekites. Tomorrow I will stand on top of the hill with the staff[u] of God in my hands."

10 So Joshua fought the Amalekites as Moses had ordered, and Moses, Aaron and Hur[v] went to the top of the hill. 11 As long as Moses held up his hands, the Israelites were winning,[w] but whenever he lowered his hands, the Amalekites were winning. 12 When Moses' hands grew tired, they took a stone and put it under him and he sat on it. Aaron and Hur held his hands up—one on one side, one on the other—so that his hands remained steady till sunset.[x] 13 So Joshua overcame the Amalekite[y] army with the sword.

14 Then the LORD said to Moses, "Write[z] this on a scroll as something to be remembered and make sure that Joshua hears it, because I will completely blot out[a] the memory of Amalek[b] from under heaven."

15 Moses built an altar[c] and called[d] it The LORD is my Banner. 16 He said, "For hands were lifted up to the throne of the LORD. The[c] LORD will be at war against the Amalekites[e] from generation to generation."[f]

Jethro Visits Moses

18 Now Jethro,[a] the priest of Midian[b] and father-in-law of Moses, heard of everything God had done for Moses and for his people Israel, and how the LORD had brought Israel out of Egypt.[c]

2 After Moses had sent away his wife Zipporah,[d] his father-in-law Jethro received her 3 and her two sons.[e] One son was named Gershom,[a] for Moses said, "I have become an alien in a foreign land";[f] 4 and the other was named Eliezer,[b][g] for he said, "My father's God was my helper;[h] he saved me from the sword of Pharaoh."

5 Jethro, Moses' father-in-law, together with Moses' sons and wife, came to him in the desert, where he was camped near the mountain[i] of God. 6 Jethro had sent word to him, "I, your father-in-law Jethro, am coming to you with your wife and her two sons."

7 So Moses went out to meet his father-in-law and bowed down[j] and kissed[k] him. They greeted each other and then went into the tent. 8 Moses told his father-in-law about everything the LORD had done to Pharaoh and the Egyptians for Israel's sake and about all the hardships[l] they had met along the way and how the LORD had saved[m] them.

9 Jethro was delighted to hear about all the good things[n] the LORD had done for Israel in rescuing them from the hand of the Egyptians. 10 He said, "Praise be to the LORD,[o] who rescued you from the hand of the Egyptians and of Pharaoh, and who rescued the people from the hand of the Egyptians. 11 Now I know that the LORD is greater than all other gods,[p] for he did this to those who had treated Israel arrogantly."[q] 12 Then Jethro, Moses' father-in-law,[r] brought a burnt offering[s] and other sacrifices[t] to God, and Aaron came with all the elders of Israel to eat bread[u] with Moses' father-in-law in the presence[v] of God.

13 The next day Moses took his seat to serve as judge for the people, and they stood round him from morning till evening. 14 When his father-in-law saw all that Moses was doing for the people, he said, "What is this you are doing for the people? Why do you alone sit as judge,

3 [g]**Ex 15:22;** [h]**Ex 15:24;** [i]**Ex 14:11**
4 [j]Nu 14:10; 1Sa 30:6; **Jn 8:59**
5 [k]**Ex 4:2; 10:12–13;** [l]Ex 7:20
6 [m]**Ex 3:1;** [n]Nu 20:8; [o]Nu 20:11; Dt 8:15; Jdg 15:19; 2Ki 3:20; Ne 9:15; Ps 74:15; 78:15–16; 105:41; 107:35; 114:8; Isa 30:25; 35:6; 43:19; 48:21; 1Co 10:4
7 [p]Dt 6:16; 9:22; 33:8; Ps 95:8; [q]Nu 20:13,24; 27:14; Ps 81:7; 106:32
8 [r]**Ge 36:12;** [s]**ver 1**
9 [t]Ex 24:13; 32:17; 33:11; Nu 11:28; 27:22; Dt 1:38; Jos 1:1; Ac 7:45; [u]**Ex 4:17**
10 [v]ver 10–12; Ex 24:14; 31:2
11 [w]Jas 5:16
12 [x]Jos 8:26
13 [y]ver 8
14 [z]Ex 24:4; 34:27; Nu 33:2; Dt 31:9; Job 19:23; Isa 30:8; Jer 36:2; 45:1; 51:60; [a]Ex 32:33; Dt 29:20; Job 18:17; Ps 9:5; 34:16; 109:15; Eze 18:4; [b]ver 13; **Ge 36:12;** Nu 24:7; Jdg 3:13; 1Sa 30:17–18; Ps 83:7
15 [c]**Ge 8:20;** [d]**Ge 22:14**
16 [e]Nu 24:7; 1Sa 15:8,32; 1Ch 4:43; Est 3:1; 8:3; 9:24; [f]Est 9:5

Ch. 18

1 [a]**Ex 2:18;** [b]**Ex 2:16;** [c]**Ex 6:6**
2 [d]**Ex 2:21**
3 [e]**Ex 4:20;** Ac 7:29; [f]**Ex 2:22**
4 [g]**1Ch 23:15;** [h]**Ge 49:25; Dt 33:29**
5 [i]**Ex 3:1**
7 [j]**Ge 17:3; 43:28;** [k]**Ge 29:13**
8 [l]**Nu 20:14;** Ne 9:32; [m]**Ex 15:6,** 16; Ps 81:7
9 [n]Jos 21:45; 1Ki 8:66; Ne 9:25; Ps 145:7; Isa 63:7
10 [o]**Ge 9:26; 24:27**
11 [p]**Ex 12:12; 1Ch 16:25;** [q]**Ex 1:10; Lk 1:51**
12 [r]Ex 3:1; [s]Ex 10:25; 20:24; Lev 1:2–9; [t]Ge 31:54; Ex 24:5; [u]**Ge 26:30;** [v]Dt 12:7

[a]7 *Massah* means *testing*.
[b]7 *Meribah* means *quarrelling*.
[c]16 Or *"Because a hand was against the throne of the* LORD, *the*
[a]3 *Gershom* sounds like the Hebrew for *an alien there*.
[b]4 *Eliezer* means *my God is helper*.

while all these people stand round you from morning till evening?"

15Moses answered him, "Because the people come to me to seek God's will.[w] 16Whenever they have a dispute,[x] it is brought to me, and I decide between the parties and inform them of God's decrees and laws."[y]

17Moses' father-in-law replied, "What you are doing is not good. 18You and these people who come to you will only wear yourselves out. The work is too heavy for you; you cannot handle it alone.[z] 19Listen now to me and I will give you some advice, and may God be with you.[a] You must be the people's representative before God and bring their disputes[b] to him. 20Teach them the decrees and laws,[c] and show them the way to live[d] and the duties they are to perform.[e] 21But select capable men[f] from all the people—men who fear[g] God, trustworthy men who hate dishonest gain[h]—and appoint them as officials[i] over thousands, hundreds, fifties and tens. 22Have them serve as judges for the people at all times, but have them bring every difficult case[j] to you; the simple cases they can decide themselves. That will make your load lighter, because they will share[k] it with you. 23If you do this and God so commands, you will be able to stand the strain, and all these people will go home satisfied."

24Moses listened to his father-in-law and did everything he said. 25He chose capable men from all Israel and made them leaders[l] of the people, officials over thousands, hundreds, fifties and tens.[m] 26They served as judges[n] for the people at all times. The difficult cases[o] they brought to Moses, but the simple ones they decided themselves.[p]

27Then Moses sent his father-in-law on his way, and Jethro returned to his own country.[q]

At Mount Sinai

19 In the third month after the Israelites left Egypt[a]—on the very day—they came to the Desert of Sinai.[b] 2After they set out from Rephidim,[c] they entered the Desert of Sinai, and Israel camped there in the desert in front of the mountain.[d]

3Then Moses went up to God,[e] and the LORD called[f] to him from the mountain and said, "This is what you are to say to the house of Jacob and what you are to tell the people of Israel: 4'You yourselves have seen what I did to Egypt,[g] and how I carried you on eagles' wings[h] and brought you to myself.[i] 5Now if you obey me fully[j] and keep my covenant,[k] then out of all nations you will be my treasured possession.[l] Although the whole earth[m] is mine, 6you[a] will be for me a kingdom of priests[n] and a holy nation.'[o] These are the words you are to speak to the Israelites."

7So Moses went back and summoned the elders[p] of the people and set before them all the words the LORD had commanded him to speak.[q] 8The people all responded together, "We will do everything the LORD has said."[r] So Moses brought their answer back to the LORD.

9The LORD said to Moses, "I am going to come to you in a dense cloud,[s] so that people will hear me speaking[t] with you and will always put their trust[u] in you." Then Moses told the LORD what the people had said.

10And the LORD said to Moses, "Go to the people and consecrate[v] them today and tomorrow. Make them wash their clothes[w] 11and be ready by the third day,[x] because on that day the LORD will come down[y] on Mount Sinai[z] in the sight of all the people. 12Put limits[a] for the people around the mountain and tell them, 'Be careful that you do not go up the mountain or touch the foot of it. Whoever touches the mountain shall surely be put to death. 13He shall surely be stoned[b] or shot with arrows; not a hand is to be laid on him. Whether man or animal, he shall not be permitted to live.' Only when the ram's horn[c] sounds a long blast may they go up to the mountain."[d]

14After Moses had gone down the mountain to the people, he consecrated them, and they washed their clothes.[e] 15Then he said to the people, "Prepare yourselves for the third day. Abstain[f] from sexual relations."

16On the morning of the third day there was thunder[g] and lightning, with a thick cloud[h] over the mountain, and a very loud trumpet blast.[i] Everyone in

15 [w]**ver 19; Ge 25:22**
16 [x]Ex 24:14; [y]ver 15; Lev 24:12; Nu 15:34; Dt 1:17; 2Ch 19:7; Pr 24:23; Mal 2:9
18 [z]Nu 11:11,14, 17; Dt 1:9,12
19 [a]Ex 3:12; [b]ver 15; Nu 27:5
20 [c]Dt 4:1,5; 5:1; Ps 119:12,26, 68; [d]Ps 143:8; [e]**Ge 39:11**
21 [f]**Ge 47:6**; Ac 6:3; [g]**Ge 22:12**; [h]Ex 23:8; Dt 16:19; 1Sa 12:3; Ps 15:5; Pr 17:23; 28:8; Ecc 7:7; Eze 18:8; 22:12; [i]Nu 1:16; 7:2; 10:4; Dt 16:18; Ezr 7:25
22 [j]Lev 24:11; Dt 1:17–18; [k]Nu 11:17; Dt 1:9
25 [l]Nu 1:16; 7:2; 11:16; Dt 16:18; [m]Dt 1:13–15
26 [n]Dt 16:18; 2Ch 19:5; Ezr 7:25; [o]Dt 1:17; [p]ver 22
27 [q]Nu 10:29–30

Ch. 19

1 [a]**Ex 6:6**; [b]Nu 1:1; 3:14; 33:15
2 [c]**Ex 17:1**; [d]**ver 17; Ex 3:1**; Dt 5:2–4
3 [e]Ex 20:21; [f]**Ex 3:4; 25:22**; Ac 7:38
4 [g]Dt 29:2; Jos 24:7; [h]Dt 32:11; Ps 103:5; Isa 40:31; Jer 4:13; 48:40; Rev 12:14; [i]Dt 33:12; Isa 31:5; Eze 16:6
5 [j]Ex 15:26; Dt 6:3; Ps 78:10; Jer 7:23; [k]**Ge 17:9; Ex 3:1**; [l]**Ex 8:22; 34:9; Dt 8:1; Tit 2:14**; [m]**Ex 9:29**; 1Co 10:26
6 [n]Isa 61:6; 66:21; **1Pe 2:5**; [o]Ge 18:19; Lev 11:44–45; Dt 4:37; 7:6; 26:19; 28:9; 29:13; 33:3; Isa 4:3; 62:12; Jer 2:3; Am 3:2
7 [p]Ex 18:12; Lev 4:15; 9:1; Nu 16:25; [q]Ex 4:30; 1Sa 8:10
8 [r]Ex 24:3,7; Dt 5:27; 26:17
9 [s]ver 16; Ex 20:21; 24:15–16; 33:9; 34:5; Dt 4:11; 2Sa 22:10,12; 2Ch 6:1; Ps 18:11; 97:2; 99:7; Mt 17:5; [t]Dt 4:12,36; Jn 12:29–30; [u]**Ex 4:5**
10 [v]ver 14,22; Lev 11:44; Nu 11:18; 1Sa 16:5; Joel 2:16; Heb 10:22; [w]**Ge 35:2**; Rev 22:14
11 [x]ver 16; [y]**Ge 11:5**; [z]ver 3,20; **Ex 3:1**; 24:16; 31:18; 34:2,4,29,32; Lev 7:38; 26:46; 27:34; Nu 3:1; Dt 10:5; Ne 9:13; Gal 4:24–25 *12* [a]ver 23
13 [b]Heb 12:20*; [c]Jos 6:4; 1Ch 15:28; Ps 81:3; 98:6; [d]ver 21; Ex 34:3 *14* [e]**Ge 35:2**
15 [f]1Sa 21:4; 1Co 7:5
16 [g]1Sa 2:10; Isa 29:6; [h]**ver 9**; [i]Heb 12:18–19; Rev 4:1

[a]5,6 Or *possession, for the whole earth is mine.* [6]*You*

the camp trembled.[j] 17Then Moses led
the people out of the camp to meet
with God, and they stood at the foot
of the mountain.[k] 18Mount Sinai was
covered with smoke,[l] because the LORD
descended on it in fire.[m] The smoke
billowed up from it like smoke
from a furnace,[n] the whole mountain[b]
trembled[o] violently, 19and the sound
of the trumpet grew louder and louder.
Then Moses spoke and the voice[p] of
God answered[q] him.[c]
20The LORD descended to the top of
Mount Sinai[r] and called Moses to the
top of the mountain. So Moses went up
21and the LORD said to him, "Go down
and warn the people so they do not
force their way through to see the[s] LORD
and many of them perish.[t] 22Even the
priests, who approach[u] the LORD, must
consecrate[v] themselves, or the LORD will
break out against them."[w]
23Moses said to the LORD, "The people
cannot come up Mount Sinai,[x] because
you yourself warned us, 'Put limits[y]
around the mountain and set it apart as
holy.'"
24The LORD replied, "Go down and
bring Aaron[z] up with you. But the
priests and the people must not force
their way through to come up to the
LORD, or he will break out against
them."[a]
25So Moses went down to the people
and told them.

The Ten Commandments

20:1–17pp—Dt 5:6–21

20 And God spoke[a] all these
words:[b]
2"I am the LORD your God,[c] who
brought you out[d] of Egypt,[e]
out of the land of slavery.[f]
3"You shall have no other gods
before[a] me.[g]
4"You shall not make for yourself
an idol[h] in the form of any-
thing in heaven above or on
the earth beneath or in the
waters below. 5You shall not
bow down to them or wor-
ship[i] them; for I, the LORD
your God,[j] am a jealous God,
punishing the children for the
sin of the fathers[k] to the third
and fourth generation[l] of
those who hate me, 6but
showing love to a thousand[m]
⌊generations⌋ of those who
love me and keep my
commandments.
7"You shall not misuse the name of
the LORD your God, for the
LORD will not hold anyone
guiltless who misuses his
name.[n]
8"Remember the Sabbath[o] day by
keeping it holy. 9Six days you
shall labour and do all your
work,[p] 10but the seventh day
is a Sabbath[q] to the LORD your
God. On it you shall not do
any work, neither you, nor
your son or daughter, nor
your manservant or maid-
servant, nor your animals,
nor the alien within your
gates. 11For in six days the
LORD made the heavens and
the earth,[r] the sea, and all that
is in them, but he rested[s] on
the seventh day.[t] Therefore
the LORD blessed the Sabbath
day and made it holy.
12"Honour your father and your
mother,[u] so that you may live
long[v] in the land[w] the LORD
your God is giving you.
13"You shall not murder.[x]
14"You shall not commit adultery.[y]
15"You shall not steal.[z]
16"You shall not give false testimony[a]
against your neighbour.[b]
17"You shall not covet[c] your neigh-
bour's house. You shall not
covet your neighbour's wife,
or his manservant or maid-
servant, his ox or donkey, or

16 [j]**Ge 3:10**; 1Sa 13:7; 14:15; 28:5; Ps 99:1; Heb 12:21
17 [k]**ver 2**; Dt 4:11
18 [l]Ex 20:18; Ps 104:32; Isa 6:4; Rev 15:8; [m]**Ex 3:2**; 24:17; Lev 9:24; Dt 4:11, 24,33,36; 5:4; 9:3; 1Ki 18:24, 38; 1Ch 21:26; 2Ch 7:1; Ps 18:8; Heb 12:18; [n]**Ge 19:28**; Rev 9:2; [o]Jdg 5:5; 2Sa 22:8; Ps 18:7; 68:8; Isa 2:19; 5:25; 41:15; 64:1; Jer 4:24; 10:10; Mic 1:4; Na 1:5; Hab 3:6, 10; Hag 2:6
19 [p]**ver 9**; Dt 4:33; Ne 9:13; [q]Ps 81:7
20 [r]**ver 11**
21 [s]Ex 24:10–11; Nu 4:20; 1Sa 6:19; [t]**ver 13**
22 [u]Lev 10:3; [v]1Sa 16:5; 2Ch 29:5; Joel 2:16; [w]ver 24; 2Sa 6:7
23 [x]ver 11; [y]ver 12
24 [z]Ex 24:1,9; [a]ver 22

Ch. 20

1 [a]Dt 10:4; [b]Ne 9:13; Ps 119:9; 147:19; Mal 4:4
2 [c]**Ge 17:7**; Ex 16:12; Lev 19:2; 20:7; Isa 43:3; Eze 20:19; [d]**Ge 15:7**; [e]**Ex 6:6**; [f]Ex 13:3; Eze 20:6
3 [g]ver 23; Ex 34:14; Dt 6:14; 13:10; 2Ki 17:35; Ps 44:20; 81:9; Jer 1:16; 7:6,9; 11:13; 19:4; 25:6; 35:15
4 [h]ver 5,23; Ex 32:8; 34:17; Lev 19:4; 26:1; Dt 4:15–19, 23; 27:15; 2Sa 7:22; 1Ki 14:9; 2Ki 17:12; Isa 40:19; 42:8; 44:9
5 [i]Ex 23:13,24; Jos 23:7; Jdg 6:10; 2Ki 17:35; Isa 44:15, 17,19; 46:6; [j]Ex 34:14; Dt 4:24; Jos 24:19; Na 1:2; [k]**Ge 9:25**; **Lev 26:39**; [l]Ex 34:7; Nu 14:18; Jer 32:18
6 [m]Ex 34:7; Nu 14:18; Dt 7:9; Jer 32:18; Lk 1:50; Ro 11:28
7 [n]Ex 22:28; Lev 18:21; 19:12; 22:2; 24:11,16; Dt 6:13; 10:20; Job 2:5,9; Ps 63:11; Isa 8:21; Eze 20:39; 39:7; **Mt 5:33**
8 [o]**Ex 16:23**; 31:13–16; 35:3; Lev 19:3,30; 26:2; Isa 56:2; Jer 17:21–27; Eze 22:8
9 [p]Ex 23:12; 31:13–17; 34:21; 35:2–3; Lev 23:3; Lk 13:14
10 [q]**Ge 2:3**; Ex 31:14; Lev 23:38; Nu 28:9; Isa 56:2; Eze 20:12,20
11 [r]Ge 1:3–2:1; [s]**Ge 2:2**; [t]Ex 31:17; Heb 4:4
12 [u]**Ge 31:35**; **Dt 5:16**; Mt 15:4*; 19:19*; Mk 7:10*; 10:19*; Lk 18:20*; Eph 6:2; [v]Dt 6:2; Eph 6:3; [w]Dt 11:9; 25:15; Jer 35:7
13 [x]**Ge 4:23**; Mt 5:21*; 19:18*; Mk 10:19*; Lk 18:20*; Ro 13:9*; Jas 2:11*
14 [y]Lev 18:20; 20:10; Nu 5:12,13,29; Pr 6:29,32; Mt 5:27*; 19:18*; Mk 10:19*; Lk 18:20*; Ro 13:9*; Jas 2:11*
15 [z]Lev 19:11,13; Eze 18:7; Mt 19:18*; Mk 10:19*; Lk 18:20*; Ro 13:9*
16 [a]Lev 19:11; Jer 9:3,5; [b]Ex 23:1,7; Lev 19:18; Ps 50:20; 101:5; 119:29; Mt 19:18*; Mk 10:19; Lk 3:14*; 18:20*
17 [c]Lk 12:15; Ro 7:7*; 13:9*; Eph 5:3; Heb 13:5

[b]18 Most Hebrew manuscripts; a few Hebrew manuscripts and Septuagint *all the people*
[c]19 Or *and God answered him with thunder*
[a]3 Or *besides*

anything that belongs to your
neighbour."

18When the people saw the thunder
and lightning and heard the trumpet[d]
and saw the mountain in smoke,[e] they
trembled with fear.[f] They stayed at a
distance 19and said to Moses, "Speak to
us yourself and we will listen. But do
not have God speak[g] to us or we will
die."[h]

20Moses said to the people, "Do not
be afraid.[i] God has come to test[j] you, so
that the fear[k] of God will be with you to
keep you from sinning."[l]

21The people remained at a distance,
while Moses approached the thick
darkness[m] where God was.

Idols and Altars

22Then the LORD said to Moses, "Tell
the Israelites this: 'You have seen for
yourselves that I have spoken to you
from heaven:[n] 23Do not make any gods
to be alongside me;[o] do not make for
yourselves gods of silver or gods of
gold.[p]

24" 'Make an altar[q] of earth for me and
sacrifice on it your burnt offerings[r] and
fellowship offerings,[b] your sheep and
goats and your cattle. Wherever I cause
my name[s] to be honoured, I will come to
you and bless[t] you. 25If you make an
altar of stones for me, do not build it
with dressed stones, for you will defile
it if you use a tool[u] on it. 26And do not
go up to my altar on steps, lest your
nakedness[v] be exposed on it.'

21

"These are the laws[a] you are to
set before them:

Hebrew Servants

21:2–6pp—Dt 15:12–18
21:2–11Ref—Lev 25:39–55

2"If you buy a Hebrew servant,[b] he is
to serve you for six years. But in the
seventh year, he shall go free,[c] without
paying anything. 3If he comes alone, he
is to go free alone; but if he has a wife
when he comes, she is to go with him.
4If his master gives him a wife and she
bears him sons or daughters, the
woman and her children shall belong to
her master, and only the man shall go
free.

5"But if the servant declares, 'I love
my master and my wife and children
and do not want to go free,'[d] 6then his
master must take him before the
judges.[a][e] He shall take him to the door
or the door-post and pierce[f] his ear
with an awl. Then he will be his servant
for life.[g]

7"If a man sells his daughter as a
servant, she is not to go free as men-
servants do. 8If she does not please the
master who has selected her for him-
self,[b] he must let her be redeemed. He
has no right to sell her to foreigners,
because he has broken faith with her. 9If
he selects her for his son, he must grant
her the rights of a daughter. 10If he
marries another woman, he must not
deprive the first one of her food, cloth-
ing and marital rights.[h] 11If he does not
provide her with these three things, she
is to go free, without any payment of
money.

Personal Injuries

12"Anyone who strikes a man and
kills him shall surely be put to death.[i]
13However, if he does not do it inten-
tionally, but God lets it happen, he is to
flee to a place[j] I will designate. 14But if a
man schemes and kills another man de-
liberately,[k] take him away from my altar
and put him to death.[l]

15"Anyone who attacks[c] his father or
his mother must be put to death.

16"Anyone who kidnaps another and
either sells[m] him or still has him when
he is caught must be put to death.[n]

17"Anyone who curses his father or
mother must be put to death.[o]

18"If men quarrel and one hits the
other with a stone or with his fist[d] and
he does not die but is confined to bed,
19the one who struck the blow will not
be held responsible if the other gets up
and walks around outside with his staff;
however, he must pay the injured man
for the loss of his time and see that he is
completely healed.

20"If a man beats his male or female
slave with a rod and the slave dies as a
direct result, he must be punished, 21but
he is not to be punished if the slave gets
up after a day or two, since the slave is
his property.[p]

22"If men who are fighting hit a

18 [d]Ex 19:16–19; Dt 4:36; Isa 58:1; Jer 6:17; Eze 33:3; Heb 12:18–19; Rev 1:10; [e]**Ex 19:18;** [f]**Ge 3:10; Ex 14:31; 19:16**
19 [g]Job 37:4,5; 40:9; Ps 29:3–4; [h]Dt 5:5,23–27; 18:16; Gal 3:19
20 [i]**Ge 15:1;** [j]**Ge 22:1;** [k]Dt 4:10; 6:2,24; 10:12; Ps 111:10; 128:1; Pr 1:7; Ecc 12:13; Isa 8:13; [l]Job 1:8; 2:3; 28:28; Pr 3:7; 8:13; 14:16; 16:6
21 [m]**Ex 19:9;** Dt 5:22; Ps 18:9; 68:4; 97:2; Isa 19:1
22 [n]Dt 5:24,26; Ne 9:13
23 [o]**ver 3;** [p]Ex 22:20; 32:4, 8,31; 34:17; Dt 29:17–18; Ne 9:18
24 [q]Ex 27:1; 40:29; Nu 16:38; Dt 27:5; Jos 8:30; 2Ki 16:14; 2Ch 4:1; Ezr 3:2; Eze 43:13; [r]**Ge 8:20; Ex 18:12;** [s]Dt 12:5; 16:6,11; 26:2; 1Ki 9:3; 2Ki 21:4,7; 2Ch 6:6; 12:13; Ezr 6:12; [t]**Ge 12:2;** 22:17
25 [u]Jos 8:31; 1Ki 6:7
26 [v]Eze 43:17

Ch. 21

1 [a]Ex 24:3; 34:32; Dt 4:14; 6:1
2 [b]Ex 22:3; [c]ver 7; Jer 34:8,14
5 [d]Dt 15:16
6 [e]Ex 22:8–9; Dt 17:9; 19:17; 25:1; [f]Ps 40:6; [g]Job 39:9; 41:4
10 [h]1Co 7:3–5
12 [i]ver 15,17; **Ge 4:14,**23; Ex 31:15; Lev 20:9,10; 24:16; 27:29; Nu 1:51; 35:16,30–31; Dt 13:5; 19:11; 22:22; 27:16; Job 31:11; Pr 20:20; **Mt 26:52**
13 [j]Nu 35:10–34; Dt 4:42; 19:2–13; Jos 20:9
14 [k]Ge 4:8; Nu 35:20; 2Sa 3:27; 20:10; Heb 10:26; [l]Dt 19:11–12; 1Ki 2:28–34
16 [m]Ge 37:28; [n]Ex 22:4; Dt 24:7
17 [o]**ver 12; Dt 5:16;** Mt 15:4*; Mk 7:10*
21 [p]Lev 25:44–46

[b]24 Traditionally *peace offerings*
[a]6 Or *before God*
[b]8 Or *master so that he does not choose her*
[c]15 Or *kills*
[d]18 Or *with a tool*

pregnant woman and she gives• birth prematurely[e] but there is no serious injury, the offender must be fined whatever the woman's husband demands[q] and the court allows. 23But if there is serious injury, you are to take life for life,[r] 24eye for eye, tooth for tooth,[s] hand for hand, foot for foot, 25burn for burn, wound for wound, bruise for bruise.

26"If a man hits a manservant or maidservant in the eye and destroys it, he must let the servant go free to compensate for the eye. 27And if he knocks out the tooth of a manservant or maidservant, he must let the servant go free to compensate for the tooth.

28"If a bull gores a man or a woman to death, the bull must be stoned to death,[t] and its meat must not be eaten. But the owner of the bull will not be held responsible. 29If, however, the bull has had the habit of goring and the owner has been warned but has not kept it penned up[u] and it kills a man or woman, the bull must be stoned and the owner also must be put to death. 30However, if payment is demanded of him, he may redeem his life by paying whatever is demanded.[v] 31This law also applies if the bull gores a son or a daughter. 32If the bull gores a male or female slave, the owner must pay thirty shekels[f][w] of silver to the master of the slave, and the bull must be stoned.

33"If a man uncovers a pit[x] or digs one and fails to cover it and an ox or a donkey falls into it, 34the owner of the pit must pay for the loss; he must pay its owner, and the dead animal will be his.

35"If a man's bull injures the bull of another and it dies, they are to sell the live one and divide both the money and the dead animal equally. 36However, if it was known that the bull had the habit of goring, yet the owner did not keep it penned up,[y] the owner must pay, animal for animal, and the dead animal will be his.

Protection of Property

22 "If a man steals an ox or a sheep and slaughters it or sells it, he must pay back[a] five head of cattle for the ox and four sheep for the sheep.

2"If a thief is caught breaking in[b] and is struck so that he dies, the defender is not guilty of bloodshed;[c] 3but if it happens[a] after sunrise, he is guilty of bloodshed.

"A thief must certainly make restitution,[d] but if he has nothing, he must be sold[e] to pay for his theft.

4"If the stolen animal is found alive in his possession[f]—whether ox or donkey or sheep—he must pay back double.[g]

5"If a man grazes his livestock in a field or vineyard and lets them stray and they graze in another man's field, he must make restitution[h] from the best of his own field or vineyard.

6"If a fire breaks out and spreads into thornbushes so that it burns shocks[i] of grain or standing corn or the whole field, the one who started the fire must make restitution.[j]

7"If a man gives his neighbour silver or goods for safekeeping[k] and they are stolen from the neighbour's house, the thief, if he is caught, must pay back double.[l] 8But if the thief is not found, the owner of the house must appear before the judges[b][m] to determine whether he has laid his hands on the other man's property. 9In all cases of illegal possession of an ox, a donkey, a sheep, a garment, or any other lost property about which somebody says, 'This is mine,' both parties are to bring their cases before the judges.[n] The one whom the judges declare[c] guilty must pay back double to his neighbour.

10"If a man gives a donkey, an ox, a sheep or any other animal to his neighbour for safekeeping[o] and it dies or is injured or is taken away while no-one is looking, 11the issue between them will be settled by the taking of an oath[p] before the LORD that the neighbour did not lay hands on the other person's property. The owner is to accept this, and no restitution is required. 12But if the animal was stolen from the neighbour, he must make restitution[q] to the owner. 13If it was torn to pieces by a wild animal, he shall bring in the remains as evidence and he will not be required to pay for the torn animal.[r]

14"If a man borrows an animal from his neighbour and it is injured or dies while the owner is not present, he must make restitution.[s] 15But if the owner is with the animal, the borrower will not have to pay. If the animal was hired, the money paid for the hire covers the loss.[t]

Social Responsibility

16"If a man seduces a virgin[u] who is not pledged to be married and sleeps

22 [q]ver 30
23 [r]Lev 24:19; Dt 19:21
24 [s]**ver 23**; Mt 5:38*
28 [t]ver 32; Ge 9:5
29 [u]ver 36
30 [v]ver 22
32 [w]Ge 37:28; Zec 11:12–13; Mt 26:15; 27:3,9
33 [x]Lk 14:5
36 [y]ver 29

Ch. 22

1 [a]Lev 6:1–7; 2Sa 12:6; Pr 6:31; **Lk 19:8**
2 [b]Job 24:16; Jer 2:34; Hos 7:1; Mt 6:19–20; 24:43; [c]Nu 35:27
3 [d]ver 1; [e]**Ex 21:2; Mt 18:25**
4 [f]1Sa 12:5; [g]**Ge 43:12**
5 [h]ver 1
6 [i]Jdg 15:5; [j]ver 1
7 [k]ver 10; Lev 6:2; [l]**Ge 43:12**
8 [m]**Ex 21:6**
9 [n]ver 8; Dt 25:1
10 [o]**ver 7**
11 [p]Lev 6:3; 1Ki 8:31; 2Ch 6:22; Heb 6:16
12 [q]ver 1
13 [r]Ge 31:39
14 [s]ver 1
15 [t]Lev 19:13; Job 17:5
16 [u]Dt 22:28

[e]22 Or *she has a miscarriage*
[f]32 That is, about 12 ounces (about 0.3 kilogram)
[a]3 Or *if he strikes him*
[b]8 Or *before God*; also in verse 9
[c]9 Or *whom God declares*

with her, he must pay the bride-price,[v]
and she shall be his wife. 17If her father
absolutely refuses to give her to him, he
must still pay the bride-price for virgins.
18"Do not allow a sorceress[w] to live.
19"Anyone who has sexual relations
with an animal[x] must be put to death.
20"Whoever sacrifices to any god[y]
other than the LORD must be de-
stroyed.[d][z]
21"Do not ill-treat an alien[a] or oppress
him, for you were aliens[b] in Egypt.
22"Do not take advantage of a widow
or an orphan.[c] 23If you do and they cry
out[d] to me, I will certainly hear their
cry.[e] 24My anger will be aroused, and I
will kill you with the sword; your wives
will become widows and your children
fatherless.[f]
25"If you lend money to one of my
people among you who is needy, do not
be like a money-lender; charge him no
interest.[e][g] 26If you take your neigh-
bour's cloak as a pledge,[h] return it to
him by sunset, 27because his cloak is
the only covering he has for his body.
What else will he sleep in?[i] When he
cries out to me, I will hear, for I am
compassionate.[j]
28"Do not blaspheme God[f][k] or curse[l]
the ruler of your people.[m]
29"Do not hold back offerings[n] from
your granaries or your vats.[g]
"You must give me the firstborn of
your sons.[o] 30Do the same with your
cattle and your sheep.[p] Let them stay
with their mothers for seven days, but
give them to me on the eighth day.[q]
31"You are to be my holy people.[r] So
do not eat the meat of an animal torn by
wild beasts;[s] throw it to the dogs.

Laws of Justice and Mercy

23 "Do not spread false reports.[a]
Do not help a wicked man by
being a malicious witness.[b]
2"Do not follow the crowd in doing
wrong. When you give testimony in a
lawsuit, do not pervert justice[c] by siding
with the crowd,[d] 3and do not show
favouritism[e] to a poor man in his law-
suit.
4"If you come across your enemy's[f] ox
or donkey wandering off, be sure to
take it back to him.[g] 5If you see the
donkey[h] of someone who hates you
fallen down under its load, do not leave
it there; be sure you help him with it.
6"Do not deny justice[i] to your poor
people in their lawsuits. 7Have nothing
to do with a false charge[j] and do not put
an innocent[k] or honest person to death,[l]
for I will not acquit the guilty.[m]
8"Do not accept a bribe,[n] for a bribe
blinds those who see and twists the
words of the righteous.
9"Do not oppress an alien;[o] you
yourselves know how it feels to be
aliens, because you were aliens in
Egypt.

Sabbath Laws

10"For six years you are to sow your
fields and harvest the crops, 11but
during the seventh year let the land
lie unploughed and unused.[p] Then
the poor among your people may get
food from it, and the wild animals may
eat what they leave. Do the same with
your vineyard and your olive grove.
12"Six days do your work,[q] but on the
seventh day do not work, so that your
ox and your donkey may rest and the
slave born in your household, and the
alien as well, may be refreshed.[r]
13"Be careful[s] to do everything I have
said to you. Do not invoke the names of
other gods;[t] do not let them be heard on
your lips.[u]

The Three Annual Festivals

14"Three times[v] a year you are to
celebrate a festival to me.
15"Celebrate the Feast of Unleavened
Bread;[w] for seven days eat bread made
without yeast, as I commanded you. Do

16 [v]**Ge 34:12**
18 [w]**Ex 7:11**; Lev 19:26,31; 20:27; Dt 18:11; 1Sa 28:3; 2Ch 33:6; Isa 57:3
19 [x]Lev 18:23; 20:15; Dt 27:21
20 [y]**Ex 20:23**; 34:15; Lev 17:7; Nu 25:2; Dt 32:17; Ps 106:37; [z]Lev 27:29; Dt 13:5; 17:2–5; 18:20; 1Ki 18:40; 19:1; 2Ki 10:25; 23:20; 2Ch 15:13
21 [a]Ex 23:9; Lev 19:33; 24:22; Nu 15:14; Dt 1:16; 24:17; Eze 22:29; [b]Dt 10:19; 27:19; Zec 7:10; Mal 3:5
22 [c]ver 26; Dt 10:18; 24:6,10, 12,17; Job 22:6,9; 24:3, 21; Ps 68:5; 146:9; Pr 23:10; Isa 1:17; Jer 7:5, 6; 21:12; 22:3; Eze 18:5–9,12; Zec 7:9–10; Mal 3:5; Jas 1:27
23 [d]Lk 18:7; [e]Dt 10:18; 15:9; 24:15; Job 34:28; 35:9; Ps 10:14,17; 12:5; 18:6; 34:15; Jas 5:4
24 [f]Ps 109:9; La 5:3
25 [g]Lev 25:35–37; Dt 15:7–11; 23:20; Ne 5:7, 10; Ps 15:5; Eze 18:8
26 [h]**ver 22**; Pr 20:16; Eze 33:15; Am 2:8
27 [i]Dt 24:13,17; Job 22:6; 24:7; 29:11; 31:19–20; Eze 18:12,16; [j]Ex 34:6; Dt 4:31; 2Ch 30:9; Ne 9:17; Ps 99:8; 103:8; 116:5; 145:8; Joel 2:13; Jnh 4:2
28 [k]**Ex 20:7**; [l]2Sa 16:5,9; 19:21; 1Ki 21:10; 2Ki 2:23; Ps 102:8; [m]Ecc 10:20; Ac 23:5*
29 [n]Ex 23:15,16,19; 34:20,26; Lev 19:24; 23:10; Nu 18:13; 28:26; Dt 18:4; 26:2,10; 1Sa 6:3; Ne 10:35; Pr 3:9; Mal 3:10; [o]**Ex 13:2**; Nu 8:16–17; Lk 2:23
30 [p]Ex 34:19; Dt 15:19; [q]Ge 17:12; Lev 12:3; 22:27
31 [r]Ex 19:6; Lev 19:2; 22:31; Ezr 9:2; [s]Lev 7:24; 17:15; 22:8; Dt 14:21; Eze 4:14; 44:31

Ch. 23
1 [a]**Ge 39:17**; Mt 19:18; Lk 3:14; [b]**Ex 20:16**; Dt 5:20; 19:16–21; Ps 27:12; 35:11; Pr 19:5; Ac 6:11
2 [c]ver 3,6,9; Lev 19:15,33; Dt 1:17; 16:19; 24:17; 27:19; 1Sa 8:3; [d]Job 31:34
3 [e]Dt 1:17
4 [f]Ro 12:20; [g]Lev 6:3; 19:11; Dt 22:1–3
5 [h]Dt 22:4
6 [i]ver 2; Dt 23:16; Pr 22:22
7 [j]**Ex 20:16**; **Eph 4:25**; [k]Mt 27:4; [l]**Ge 18:23**; [m]Ex 34:7; Dt 19:18; 25:1
8 [n]**Ex 18:21**; Lev 19:15; Dt 10:17; 27:25; Job 15:34; 36:18; Ps 26:10; Pr 6:35; 15:27; 17:8; Isa 1:23; 5:23; Mic 3:11; 7:3
9 [o]**ver 2**; **Ex 22:21**; Lev 19:33–34; Eze 22:7
11 [p]Lev 25:1–7; Ne 10:31
12 [q]**Ex 20:9**; Lk 13:14; [r]Ge 2:2–3
13 [s]Dt 4:9,23; 1Ti 4:16; [t]ver 32; Dt 12:3; Jos 23:7; Ps 16:4; Zec 13:2; [u]Dt 18:20; Jos 23:7; Ps 16:4; Hos 2:17
14 [v]ver 17; **Ex 12:14**; 34:23,24; Dt 16:16; 1Ki 9:25; 2Ch 8:13; Eze 46:9
15 [w]**Ex 12:17**; Mt 26:17; Lk 22:1; Ac 12:3

[d]20 The Hebrew term refers to the irrevocable giving over of things or persons to the LORD, often by totally destroying them.
[e]25 Or *excessive interest*
[f]28 Or *Do not revile the judges*
[g]29 The meaning of the Hebrew for this phrase is uncertain.

this at the appointed time in the month of Abib,[x] for in that month you came out of Egypt.

"No-one is to appear before me empty-handed.[y]

16"Celebrate the Feast of Harvest[z] with the firstfruits[a] of the crops you sow in your field.

"Celebrate the Feast of Ingathering[b] at the end of the year, when you gather in your crops from the field.[c]

17"Three times[d] a year all the men are to appear before the Sovereign LORD.

18"Do not offer the blood of a sacrifice to me along with anything containing yeast.[e]

"The fat of my festival offerings must not be kept until morning.[f]

19"Bring the best of the firstfruits[g] of your soil to the house of the LORD your God.

"Do not cook a young goat in its mother's milk.[h]

God's Angel to Prepare the Way

20"See, I am sending an angel[i] ahead of you to guard you along the way and to bring you to the place I have prepared.[j] 21Pay attention to him and listen[k] to what he says. Do not rebel against him; he will not forgive[l] your rebellion,[m] since my Name[n] is in him. 22If you listen carefully to what he says and do[o] all that I say, I will be an enemy[p] to your enemies and will oppose those who oppose you. 23My angel will go ahead of you and bring you into the land of the Amorites, Hittites, Perizzites, Canaanites, Hivites and Jebusites,[q] and I will wipe them out. 24Do not bow down before their gods or worship[r] them or follow their practices.[s] You must demolish[t] them and break their sacred stones[u] to pieces. 25Worship the LORD your God,[v] and his blessing[w] will be on your food and water. I will take away sickness[x] from among you, 26and none will miscarry or be barren[y] in your land. I will give you a full life span.[z]

27"I will send my terror[a] ahead of you and throw into confusion[b] every nation you encounter. I will make all your enemies turn their backs and run.[c] 28I will send the hornet[d] ahead of you to drive the Hivites, Canaanites and Hittites[e] out of your way. 29But I will not drive them out in a single year, because the land would become desolate and the wild animals[f] too numerous for you. 30Little by little I will drive them out before you, until you have increased enough to take possession[g] of the land.

31"I will establish your borders from the Red Sea[a] to the Sea of the Philistines,[b] and from the desert to the River.[c] [h] I will hand over to you the people who live in the land and you will drive them out[i] before you. 32Do not make a covenant[j] with them or with their gods. 33Do not let them live in your land, or they will cause you to sin against me, because the worship of their gods will certainly be a snare[k] to you."

The Covenant Confirmed

24 Then he said to Moses, "Come up to the LORD, you and Aaron,[a] Nadab and Abihu,[b] and seventy of the elders[c] of Israel. You are to worship at a distance, 2but Moses alone is to approach[d] the LORD; the others must not come near. And the people may not come up with him."

3When Moses went and told the people all the LORD's words and laws,[e] they responded with one voice, "Everything the LORD has said we will do."[f] 4Moses then wrote[g] down everything the LORD had said.

He got up early the next morning and built an altar[h] at the foot of the mountain and set up twelve stone pillars[i] representing the twelve tribes of Israel. 5Then he sent young Israelite men, and they offered burnt offerings[j] and sacrificed young bulls as fellowship offerings[a] [k] to the LORD. 6Moses[l] took half of the blood[m] and put it in bowls, and the other half he sprinkled[n] on the altar. 7Then he took the Book of the Covenant[o] and read it to the people. They responded, "We will do everything the LORD has said; we will obey."[p]

8Moses then took the blood, sprinkled it on the people[q] and said,

15 [x]**Ex 12:2;** [y]**Ex 22:29**
16 [z]Lev 23:15–21; Nu 28:26; Dt 16:9; 2Ch 8:13; [a]**Ex 22:29; 34:22;** [b]Ex 34:22; Lev 23:34,42; Dt 16:16; 31:10; Ezr 3:4; Ne 8:14; Zec 14:16; [c]Lev 23:39; Dt 16:13; Jer 40:10
17 [d]**ver 14**
18 [e]Ex 34:25; Lev 2:11; [f]**Ex 12:8**
19 [g]**Ex 22:29; 34:22; Nu 18:12;** [h]Ex 34:26; Dt 14:21
20 [i]**Ge 16:7;** [j]Ex 15:17
21 [k]Dt 18:19; Jer 13:15; [l]Dt 29:20; 2Ki 24:4; La 1:17; [m]Nu 17:10; Dt 9:7; 31:27; Jos 24:19; Ps 25:7; 78:8,40, 56; 106:33; 107:11; 1Jn 5:16; [n]**Ex 3:15**
22 [o]**Ex 15:26;** [p]**Ge 12:3;** Isa 41:11; Jer 30:20
23 [q]Nu 13:29; 21:21; Jos 3:10; 24:8,11; Ezr 9:1; Ps 135:11
24 [r]**Ex 20:5;** [s]Lev 18:3; 20:23; Dt 9:4; 12:30–31; Jer 10:2; [t]Ex 34:13; Nu 33:52; Dt 7:5; 12:3; Jdg 2:2; 2Ki 18:4; 23:14; [u]Lev 26:1; Dt 16:22; 1Ki 14:23; 2Ki 3:2; 10:26; 17:10; 2Ch 14:3; Isa 27:9
25 [v]Mt 4:10; [w]Lev 26:3–13; Dt 7:12–15; 28:1–14; [x]**Ex 15:26**
26 [y]Lev 26:3–4; Dt 7:14; 28:4; Mal 3:11; [z]**Ge 15:15;** Dt 4:1, 40; 32:47; Ps 90:10
27 [a]**Ge 35:5; Ex 15:14;** [b]**Ex 14:24;** Dt 7:23; [c]2Sa 22:41; Ps 18:40; 21:12
28 [d]Dt 7:20; Jos 24:12; [e]Ex 33:2; 34:11,24; Nu 13:29; Dt 4:38; 11:23; 18:12; Jos 3:10; 24:11; Ps 78:55
29 [f]Dt 7:22 *30* [g]Jos 23:5
31 [h]**Ge 2:14;** Dt 34:2; Ezr 4:20; [i]Dt 7:24; 9:3; Jos 21:44; 24:12,18; Ps 80:8
32 [j]**Ge 26:28;** Ex 34:12; Dt 7:2; Jos 9:7; Jdg 2:2; 1Sa 11:1; 1Ki 15:19; 20:34; Eze 17:13 *33* [k]**Ex 10:7**

Ch. 24
1 [a]**Ex 19:24;** [b]**Ex 6:23;** [c]ver 9; Nu 11:16
2 [d]Nu 12:6–8
3 [e]**Ex 21:1;** Gal 3:19; [f]**Ex 19:8;** Jos 24:24
4 [g]**Ex 17:14;** [h]**Ge 8:20;** [i]**Ge 28:18; Dt 27:2**
5 [j]Lev 1:3; [k]**Ge 31:54**
6 [l]Ex 14:15; 32:31; Ps 99:6; [m]Heb 9:18; [n]Lev 1:11; 3:2, 8,13; 5:9; Mt 26:28
7 [o]2Ki 23:2,21; Heb 9:19; [p]Ex 19:8; Jer 40:3; 42:6,21; 43:2 *8* [q]Heb 9:19; 1Pe 1:2

[a]31 Hebrew *Yam Suph*; that is, Sea of Reeds
[b]31 That is, the Mediterranean
[c]31 That is, the Euphrates
[a]5 Traditionally *peace offerings*

"This is the blood of the covenant[r] that the LORD has made with you in accordance with all these words."

9Moses and Aaron, Nadab and Abihu, and the seventy elders[s] of Israel went up 10and saw[t] the God of Israel. Under his feet was something like a pavement made of sapphire,[b][u] clear as the sky[v] itself. 11But God did not raise his hand against these leaders of the Israelites; they saw[w] God, and they ate and drank.[x]

12The LORD said to Moses, "Come up to me on the mountain and stay here, and I will give you the tablets of stone,[y] with the law and commands I have written for their instruction."

13Then Moses set out with Joshua[z] his assistant, and Moses went up on the mountain[a] of God. 14He said to the elders, "Wait here for us until we come back to you. Aaron and Hur[b] are with you, and anyone involved in a dispute[c] can go to them."

15When Moses went up on the mountain, the cloud[d] covered it, 16and the glory[e] of the LORD settled on Mount Sinai.[f] For six days the cloud covered the mountain, and on the seventh day the LORD called to Moses from within the cloud.[g] 17To the Israelites the glory of the LORD looked like a consuming fire[h] on top of the mountain. 18Then Moses entered the cloud as he went on up the mountain. And he stayed on the mountain forty[i] days and forty nights.[j]

Offerings for the Tabernacle

25:1–7pp—Ex 35:4–9

25 The LORD said to Moses, 2"Tell the Israelites to bring me an offering. You are to receive the offering for me from each man whose heart prompts[a] him to give. 3These are the offerings you are to receive from them: gold, silver and bronze; 4blue, purple and scarlet yarn[b] and fine linen; goat hair; 5ram skins dyed red and hides of sea cows;[a][c] acacia wood;[d] 6olive oil[e] for the light; spices for the anointing oil and for the fragrant incense;[f] 7and onyx stones and other gems to be mounted on the ephod[g] and breastpiece.[h]

8"Then have them make a sanctuary[i] for me, and I will dwell[j] among them. 9Make this tabernacle and all its furnishings exactly like the pattern[k] I will show you.

The Ark

25:10–20pp—Ex 37:1–9

10"Have them make a chest[l] of acacia wood—two and a half cubits long, a cubit and a half wide, and a cubit and a half high.[b] 11Overlay[m] it with pure gold, both inside and out, and make a gold moulding around it. 12Cast four gold rings for it and fasten them to its four feet, with two rings[n] on one side and two rings on the other. 13Then make poles of acacia wood and overlay them with gold.[o] 14Insert the poles[p] into the rings on the sides of the chest to carry it. 15The poles are to remain in the rings of this ark; they are not to be removed.[q] 16Then put in the ark the Testimony,[r] which I will give you.

17"Make an atonement cover[c][s] of pure gold—two and a half cubits long and a cubit and a half wide.[d] 18And make two cherubim[t] out of hammered gold at the ends of the cover. 19Make one cherub on one end and the second cherub on the other; make the cherubim of one piece with the cover, at the two ends. 20The cherubim[u] are to have their wings spread upwards, overshadowing[v] the cover with them. The cherubim are to face each other, looking towards the cover. 21Place the cover on top of the ark[w] and put in the ark the Testimony,[x] which I will give you. 22There, above the cover between the two cherubim[y] that are over the ark of the Testimony, I will meet[z] with you and give you all my commands for the Israelites.[a]

The Table

25:23–29pp—Ex 37:10–16

23"Make a table[b] of acacia wood—two cubits long, a cubit wide and a cubit and a half high.[e] 24Overlay it with pure gold

8 [r]Lev 26:3; Dt 5:2–3; Jos 24:25; 2Ki 11:17; Jer 11:4,8; 31:32; 34:13; Zec 9:11; **Mt 26:28; Lk 22:20;** Heb 9:20*
9 [s]**ver 1**
10 [t]**Ge 16:13**; Nu 12:6; Isa 6:1; Eze 1:1; 8:3; 40:2; **Jn 1:18**; [u]Job 28:16; Isa 54:11; Eze 1:26; 10:1; [v]Rev 4:3
11 [w]**ver 10; Ex 3:6; 19:21;** [x]Eze 44:3; Mt 26:29
12 [y]Ex 31:18; 32:15–16; 34:1,28,29; Dt 4:13; 5:22; 8:3; 9:9–11; 10:4; 2Co 3:3
13 [z]**Ex 17:9;** [a]**Ex 3:1**
14 [b]**Ex 17:10;** [c]Ex 18:16
15 [d]**Ex 19:9**; Mt 17:5
16 [e]**Ex 16:7**; Lev 9:23; Nu 14:10; 1Sa 4:21,22; Eze 8:4; 11:22; [f]**Ex 19:11;** [g]Ps 99:7
17 [h]**Ex 15:7; 19:18**; Heb 12:18,29
18 [i]1Ki 19:8; [j]**Ge 7:4**; Mt 4:2

Ch. 25

2 [a]Ex 35:21–22, 26–27,29; 36:2; 2Ki 12:4; 1Ch 29:5,7,9; 2Ch 24:10; 29:31; Ezr 2:68; Ne 7:70–72; 2Co 8:11–12; 9:7
4 [b]Ex 28:4–8
5 [c]Nu 4:6,10; [d]Dt 10:3
6 [e]Ex 27:20; 30:22–32; 35:28; 39:37; Nu 4:16; [f]Ex 30:1,7,35; 31:11; 35:28; Lev 16:12; Nu 4:16; 7:14; 2Ch 13:11
7 [g]Ex 28:4,6–14; 29:5; Jdg 8:27; Hos 3:4; [h]Lev 8:8
8 [i]Ex 36:1–5; Lev 4:6; 10:4, 7; 21:12,23; Nu 3:28; Heb 9:1–2; [j]Ex 29:45; Lev 26:11–12; Nu 5:3; Dt 12:11; 1Ki 6:13; Zec 2:10; 2Co 6:16
9 [k]ver 40; Ex 26:30; 27:8; 31:11; 39:32,42–43; Nu 8:4; 1Ch 28:11,19; Ac 7:44; Heb 8:5
10 [l]Dt 10:1–5; 1Ki 6:19; Heb 9:4
11 [m]ver 24; Ex 30:3 *12* [n]ver 26; Ex 30:4
13 [o]ver 28; Ex 27:6; 30:5; 37:28
14 [p]Ex 27:7; 40:20; 1Ch 15:15 *15* [q]1Ki 8:8
16 [r]**Ex 16:34**; Heb 9:4 *17* [s]ver 21; Lev 16:13; Ro 3:25
18 [t]Ex 26:1,31; 36:35; 1Ki 6:23,27; 8:6; 2Ch 3:10–13; Heb 9:5
20 [u]**Ge 3:24**; [v]Ex 37:9; 1Ki 8:7; 1Ch 28:18; Heb 9:5
21 [w]ver 10–15; Ex 26:34; 40:20; Dt 10:5; [x]**Ex 16:34**; Heb 9:4
22 [y]Nu 7:89; 1Sa 4:4; 2Sa 6:2; 22:11; 2Ki 19:15; 1Ch 13:6; 28:18; Ps 18:10; 80:1; 99:1; Isa 37:16; [z]**Ex 19:3**; 29:42; 30:6,36; Lev 1:1; 16:2; Nu 17:4; [a]Jer 3:16
23 [b]ver 30; Ex 26:35; 40:4,22; Lev 24:6; Nu 3:31; 1Ki 7:48; 1Ch 28:16; 2Ch 4:8,19; Eze 41:22; 44:16; Heb 9:2

b10 Or *lapis lazuli* **a**5 That is, dugongs
b10 That is, about 3¾ feet (about 1.1 metres) long and 2¼ feet (about 0.7 metre) wide and high
c17 Traditionally *a mercy seat*
d17 That is, about 3¾ feet (about 1.1 metres) long and 2¼ feet (about 0.7 metre) wide
e23 That is, about 3 feet (about 0.9 metre) long and 1½ feet (about 0.5 metre) wide and 2¼ feet (about 0.7 metre) high

and make a gold moulding around it.
25Also make around it a rim a hand-
breadth[f] wide and put a gold moulding
on the rim. 26Make four gold rings for
the table and fasten them to the four
corners, where the four legs are. 27The
rings are to be close to the rim to hold
the poles used in carrying the table.
28Make the poles of acacia wood,
overlay them with gold[c] and carry the
table with them. 29And make its plates
and dishes of pure gold, as well as its
pitchers and bowls for the pouring
out of offerings.[d] 30Put the bread of the
Presence[e] on this table to be before
me at all times.

The Lampstand

25:31–39pp—Ex 37:17–24

31"Make a lampstand[f] of pure gold
and hammer it out, base and shaft; its
flowerlike cups, buds and blossoms
shall be of one piece with it. 32Six
branches are to extend from the sides of
the lampstand—three on one side and
three on the other. 33Three cups shaped
like almond flowers with buds and
blossoms are to be on one branch,
three on the next branch, and the same
for all six branches extending from the
lampstand. 34And on the lampstand
there are to be four cups shaped like
almond flowers with buds and
blossoms. 35One bud shall be under the
first pair of branches extending from the
lampstand, a second bud under the
second pair, and a third bud under the
third pair—six branches in all. 36The
buds and branches shall all be of one
piece with the lampstand, hammered
out of pure gold.[g]
37"Then make its seven lamps[h] and
set them up on it so that they light the
space in front of it. 38Its wick trimmers
and trays[i] are to be of pure gold. 39A
talent[g] of pure gold is to be used for the
lampstand and all these accessories.
40See that you make them according to
the pattern[j] shown you on the moun-
tain.

The Tabernacle

26:1–37pp—Ex 36:8–38

26 "Make the tabernacle[a] with ten
curtains of finely twisted linen
and blue, purple and scarlet yarn, with
cherubim[b] worked into them by a skilled
craftsman. 2All the curtains are to be the
same size[c]—twenty-eight cubits long
and four cubits wide.[a] 3Join five of the
curtains together, and do the same with
the other five. 4Make loops of blue
material along the edge of the end
curtain in one set, and do the same with
the end curtain in the other set. 5Make
fifty loops on one curtain and fifty loops
on the end curtain of the other set, with
the loops opposite each other. 6Then
make fifty gold clasps and use them to
fasten the curtains together so that the
tabernacle is a unit.[d]
7"Make curtains of goat hair for
the tent over the tabernacle—eleven
altogether. 8All eleven curtains are to be
the same size[e]—thirty cubits long and
four cubits wide.[b] 9Join five of the cur-
tains together into one set and the other
six into another set. Fold the sixth cur-
tain double at the front of the tent.
10Make fifty loops along the edge of the
end curtain in one set and also along the
edge of the end curtain in the other set.
11Then make fifty bronze clasps and put
them in the loops to fasten the tent
together as a unit.[f] 12As for the addition-
al length of the tent curtains, the half
curtain that is left over is to hang down
at the rear of the tabernacle. 13 The tent
curtains will be a cubit[c] longer on both
sides; what is left will hang over the
sides of the tabernacle so as to cover it.
14Make for the tent a covering[g] of ram
skins dyed red, and over that a covering
of hides of sea cows.[d][h]
15"Make upright frames of acacia
wood for the tabernacle. 16Each frame is
to be ten cubits long and a cubit and a
half wide,[e] 17with two projections set
parallel to each other. Make all the
frames of the tabernacle in this way.
18Make twenty frames for the south side
of the tabernacle 19and make forty silver
bases[i] to go under them—two bases for
each frame, one under each projection.
20For the other side, the north side of the
tabernacle, make twenty frames 21and
forty silver bases[j]—two under each
frame. 22Make six frames for the far end,
that is, the west end of the tabernacle,
23and make two frames for the corners at
the far end. 24At these two corners they
must be double from the bottom all the
way to the top, and fitted into a single
ring; both shall be like that. 25So there

28 [c]ver 13
29 [d]Nu 4:7
30 [e]Ex 35:13; 39:36; 40:4,23; Lev 24:5–9; Nu 4:7; 1Sa 21:4–6; 1Ki 7:48; 1Ch 23:29
31 [f]Ex 26:35; 31:8; 35:14; 39:37; 40:4,24; Lev 24:4; Nu 3:31; 1Ki 7:49; 2Ch 4:7; Zec 4:2; Heb 9:2; Rev 1:12
36 [g]ver 18; Nu 8:4
37 [h]Ex 27:21; 30:8; Lev 24:3–4; Nu 8:2; 1Sa 3:3; 2Ch 13:11
38 [i]ver 37; Nu 4:9
40 [j]ver 9; Ac 7:44; Heb 8:5*

Ch. 26

1 [a]Ex 29:42; 40:2; Lev 8:10; Nu 1:50; Jos 22:19,29; 2Sa 7:2; 1Ki 1:39; Ac 7:44; Heb 8:2,5; 13:10; **Rev 21:3;** [b]**Ex 25:18**
2 [c]ver 8
6 [d]ver 11
8 [e]ver 2
11 [f]ver 6
14 [g]Nu 3:25; [h]Nu 4:25
19 [i]ver 21,25,32; Ex 38:27
21 [j]**ver 19**

[f]*25* That is, about 3 inches (about 8 centimetres)
[g]*39* That is, about 75 pounds (about 34 kilograms)
[a]*2* That is, about 42 feet (about 13 metres) long and 6 feet (about 1.8 metres) wide
[b]*8* That is, about 45 feet (about 13.5 metres) long and 6 feet (about 1.8 metres) wide
[c]*13* That is, about 1½ feet (about 0.5 metre)
[d]*14* That is, dugongs
[e]*16* That is, about 15 feet (about 4.5 metres) long and 2¼ feet (about 0.7 metre) wide

will be eight frames and sixteen silver bases—two under each frame.

26"Also make crossbars of acacia wood: five for the frames on one side of the tabernacle, 27five for those on the other side, and five for the frames on the west, at the far end of the tabernacle. 28The centre crossbar is to extend from end to end at the middle of the frames. 29Overlay the frames with gold and make gold rings to hold the crossbars. Also overlay the crossbars with gold.

30"Set up the tabernacle[k] according to the plan[l] shown you on the mountain.

31"Make a curtain[m] of blue, purple and scarlet yarn and finely twisted linen, with cherubim[n] worked into it by a skilled craftsman. 32Hang it with gold hooks on four posts of acacia wood overlaid with gold and standing on four silver bases.[o] 33Hang the curtain from the clasps and place the ark of the Testimony behind the curtain.[p] The curtain will separate the Holy Place from the Most Holy Place.[q] 34Put the atonement cover[r] on the ark of the Testimony in the Most Holy Place. 35Place the table[s] outside the curtain on the north side of the tabernacle and put the lampstand[t] opposite it on the south side.

36"For the entrance to the tent make a curtain[u] of blue, purple and scarlet yarn and finely twisted linen—the work of an embroiderer.[v] 37Make gold hooks for this curtain and five posts of acacia wood overlaid with gold. And cast five bronze bases for them.

The Altar of Burnt Offering

27:1–8pp—Ex 38:1–7

27 "Build an altar[a] of acacia wood, three cubits[a] high; it is to be square, five cubits long and five cubits wide.[b] 2Make a horn[b] at each of the four corners, so that the horns and the altar are of one piece, and overlay the altar with bronze. 3Make all its utensils of bronze—its pots to remove the ashes, and its shovels, sprinkling bowls,[c] meat forks and firepans.[d] 4Make a grating for it, a bronze network, and make a bronze ring at each of the four corners of the network. 5Put it under the ledge of the altar so that it is halfway up the altar. 6Make poles of acacia wood for the altar and overlay them with bronze.[e] 7The poles are to be inserted into the rings so they will be on two sides of the altar when it is carried.[f] 8Make the altar hollow, out of boards. It is to be made just as you were shown[g] on the mountain.

30 [k]Ex 40:2; Nu 9:15; [l]**Ex 25:9**
31 [m]Nu 4:5; 2Ch 3:14; Mt 27:51; Lk 23:45; Heb 9:3; [n]**Ex 25:18**
32 [o]**ver 19**
33 [p]Ex 27:21; 35:12; 40:3, 21; Lev 16:2; Nu 3:31; 4:5; 2Ch 3:14; [q]Lev 16:2,16; 1Ki 6:16; 7:50; 8:6; 2Ch 3:8; 5:7; Eze 41:4; Heb 9:2–3
34 [r]Ex 25:21; 30:6; 37:6; Lev 16:2; Heb 9:5
35 [s]**Ex 25:23;** Heb 9:2; [t]**Ex 25:31**
36 [u]Ex 35:15; 40:5,28; [v]Ps 45:14; Eze 16:10; 26:16; 27:7

Ch. 27

1 [a]**Ex 20:24; 40:6; 1Ki 8:64**
2 [b]Ex 29:12; 30:2; 37:25; Lev 4:7; 1Ki 1:50; 2:28; Ps 118:27; Jer 17:1; Eze 43:15; Am 3:14; Zec 9:15
3 [c]Nu 7:13; 1Ki 7:40,45; 2Ki 12:13; [d]Nu 4:14; 1Ch 28:17; Jer 52:18
6 [e]**Ex 25:13**
7 [f]Ex 25:14,28
8 [g]**Ex 25:9**
9 [h]Ex 35:17; 40:8,33; Lev 6:16,26; Eze 40:14; 42:1
16 [i]Ex 40:33; [j]Ex 36:37
20 [k]**Ex 25:6**
21 [l]Ex 28:43; 29:42; 30:36; 33:7; Lev 1:1; 6:26; 8:3,31; Nu 1:1; 31:54; Jos 18:1; 1Ki 1:39; [m]**Ex 16:34**

The Courtyard

27:9–19pp—Ex 38:9–20

9"Make a courtyard[h] for the tabernacle. The south side shall be a hundred cubits[c] long and is to have curtains of finely twisted linen, 10with twenty posts and twenty bronze bases and with silver hooks and bands on the posts. 11The north side shall also be a hundred cubits long and is to have curtains, with twenty posts and twenty bronze bases and with silver hooks and bands on the posts.

12"The west end of the courtyard shall be fifty cubits[d] wide and have curtains, with ten posts and ten bases. 13On the east end, towards the sunrise, the courtyard shall also be fifty cubits wide. 14Curtains fifteen cubits[e] long are to be on one side of the entrance, with three posts and three bases, 15and curtains fifteen cubits long are to be on the other side, with three posts and three bases.

16"For the entrance to the courtyard, provide a curtain[i] twenty cubits[f] long, of blue, purple and scarlet yarn and finely twisted linen—the work of an embroiderer[j]—with four posts and four bases. 17All the posts around the courtyard are to have silver bands and hooks, and bronze bases. 18The courtyard shall be a hundred cubits long and fifty cubits wide,[g] with curtains of finely twisted linen five cubits[h] high, and with bronze bases. 19All the other articles used in the service of the tabernacle, whatever their function, including all the tent pegs for it and those for the courtyard, are to be of bronze.

Oil for the Lampstand

27:20–21pp—Lev 24:1–3

20"Command the Israelites to bring you clear oil[k] of pressed olives for the light so that the lamps may be kept burning. 21In the Tent of Meeting,[l] outside the curtain that is in front of the Testimony,[m] Aaron and his sons are to

[a]*1* That is, about 4½ feet (about 1.4 metres)
[b]*1* That is, about 7½ feet (about 2.3 metres) long and wide
[c]*9* That is, about 150 feet (about 46 metres); also in verse 11
[d]*12* That is, about 75 feet (about 23 metres); also in verse 13
[e]*14* That is, about 22½ feet (about 6.9 metres); also in verse 15
[f]*16* That is, about 30 feet (about 9 metres)
[g]*18* That is, about 150 feet (about 46 metres) long and 75 feet (about 23 metres) wide
[h]*18* That is, about 7½ feet (about 2.3 metres)

keep the lamps[n] burning before the LORD from evening till morning. This is to be a lasting ordinance[o] among the Israelites for the generations to come.

The Priestly Garments

28 "Have Aaron[a] your brother brought to you from among the Israelites, with his sons Nadab and Abihu,[b] Eleazar and Ithamar,[c] so that they may serve me as priests.[d] 2Make sacred garments[e] for your brother Aaron, to give him dignity and honour.[f] 3Tell all the skilled men[g] to whom I have given wisdom[h] in such matters that they are to make garments for Aaron, for his consecration, so that he may serve me as priest. 4These are the garments they are to make: a breastpiece,[i] an ephod,[j] a robe,[k] a woven tunic,[l] a turban[m] and a sash. They are to make these sacred garments for your brother Aaron and his sons, so that they may serve me as priests. 5Make them use gold, and blue, purple and scarlet yarn, and fine linen.[n]

The Ephod

28:6–14pp—Ex 39:2–7

6"Make the ephod[o] of gold, and of blue, purple and scarlet yarn, and of finely twisted linen—the work of a skilled craftsman. 7It is to have two shoulder pieces attached to two of its corners, so that it can be fastened. 8Its skilfully woven waistband[p] is to be like it—of one piece with the ephod and made with gold, and with blue, purple and scarlet yarn, and with finely twisted linen.

9"Take two onyx stones and engrave[q] on them the names of the sons of Israel 10in the order of their birth—six names on one stone and the remaining six on the other. 11Engrave the names of the sons of Israel on the two stones the way a gem cutter engraves a seal. Then mount the stones in gold filigree settings 12and fasten them on the shoulder pieces of the ephod as memorial stones for the sons of Israel. Aaron is to bear the names on his shoulders[r] as a memorial[s] before the LORD. 13Make gold filigree settings 14and two braided chains of pure gold, like a rope, and attach the chains to the settings.

The Breastpiece

28:15–28pp—Ex 39:8–21

15"Fashion a breastpiece[t] for making decisions—the work of a skilled craftsman. Make it like the ephod: of gold, and of blue, purple and scarlet yarn, and of finely twisted linen. 16It is to be square—a span[a] long and a span wide—and folded double. 17Then mount four rows of precious stones[u] on it. In the first row there shall be a ruby, a topaz and a beryl; 18in the second row a turquoise, a sapphire[b] and an emerald; 19in the third row a jacinth, an agate and an amethyst; 20in the fourth row a chrysolite,[v] an onyx and a jasper.[c] Mount them in gold filigree settings. 21There are to be twelve stones, one for each of the names of the sons of Israel,[w] each engraved like a seal with the name of one of the twelve tribes.[x]

22"For the breastpiece make braided chains of pure gold, like a rope. 23Make two gold rings for it and fasten them to two corners of the breastpiece. 24Fasten the two gold chains to the rings at the corners of the breastpiece, 25and the other ends of the chains to the two settings, attaching them to the shoulder pieces of the ephod at the front. 26Make two gold rings and attach them to the other two corners of the breastpiece on the inside edge next to the ephod. 27Make two more gold rings and attach them to the bottom of the shoulder pieces on the front of the ephod, close to the seam just above the waistband of the ephod. 28The rings of the breastpiece are to be tied to the rings of the ephod with blue cord, connecting it to the waistband, so that the breastpiece will not swing out from the ephod.

29"Whenever Aaron enters the Holy Place,[y] he will bear the names of the sons of Israel over his heart on the breastpiece of decision as a continuing memorial before the LORD. 30Also put the Urim and the Thummim[z] in the breastpiece, so they may be over Aaron's heart whenever he enters the presence of the LORD. Thus Aaron will always bear the means of making decisions for the Israelites over his heart before the LORD.

Other Priestly Garments

28:31–43pp—Ex 39:22–31

31"Make the robe of the ephod entirely of blue cloth, 32with an opening for the head in its centre. There shall be a

21 [n]Ex **25:37**; [o]Ex 29:9; 30:21; Lev 3:17; 16:34; 17:7; Nu 18:23; 19:21; 1Sa 30:25

Ch. 28

1 [a]Lev 8:30; Ps 99:6; Heb 5:4; [b]**Ex 6:23**; 24:9; [c]**Ex 6:23**; [d]Lev 8:2; 21:1; Nu 18:1–7; Dt 18:5; 1Sa 2:28; Heb 5:1
2 [e]Ex 29:5,29; 31:10; 35:19; 39:1; Lev 8:7–9,30; 16:32; Nu 20:26–28; [f]ver 40
3 [g]Ex 31:6; 35:10,25,35; 36:1; [h]Ex 31:3; Dt 34:9; Isa 11:2; 1Co 12:8; **Eph 1:17**
4 [i]ver 15–30; [j]**Ex 25:7**; [k]ver 31–35; [l]ver 39; Lev 10:5; [m]ver 37
5 [n]Ex 25:4
6 [o]**Ex 25:7**
8 [p]Ex 29:5
9 [q]SS 8:6; Isa 49:16; Hag 2:23
12 [r]Dt 33:12; Job 31:36; [s]ver 29; Ex 30:16; Nu 10:10; 31:54; Jos 4:7; Zec 6:14
15 [t]**Ex 25:7**
17 [u]Eze 28:13; Rev 21:19–20
20 [v]Eze 1:16; 10:9; Da 10:6
21 [w]Jos 4:8; [x]Rev 21:12
29 [y]ver 43
30 [z]Lev 8:8; Nu 27:21; Dt 33:8; 1Sa 28:6; Ezr 2:63; Ne 7:65

[a]*16* That is, about 9 inches (about 23 centimetres)
[b]*18* Or *lapis lazuli*
[c]*20* The precise identification of some of these precious stones is uncertain.

woven edge like a collar[d] around this opening, so that it will not tear. 33 Make pomegranates[a] of blue, purple and scarlet yarn around the hem of the robe, with gold bells between them. 34 The gold bells and the pomegranates are to alternate around the hem of the robe. 35 Aaron must wear it when he ministers. The sound of the bells will be heard when he enters the Holy Place before the LORD and when he comes out, so that he will not die.

36 "Make a plate[b] of pure gold and engrave on it as on a seal: HOLY TO THE LORD.[c] 37 Fasten a blue cord to it to attach it to the turban; it is to be on the front of the turban. 38 It will be on Aaron's forehead, and he will bear the guilt[d] involved in the sacred gifts the Israelites consecrate, whatever their gifts may be. It will be on Aaron's forehead continually so that they will be acceptable[e] to the LORD.

39 "Weave the tunic[f] of fine linen and make the turban[g] of fine linen. The sash is to be the work of an embroiderer. 40 Make tunics, sashes and headbands for Aaron's sons,[h] to give them dignity and honour.[i] 41 After you put these clothes[j] on your brother Aaron and his sons, anoint[k] and ordain them. Consecrate them so they may serve me as priests.[l]

42 "Make linen undergarments[m] as a covering for the body, reaching from the waist to the thigh. 43 Aaron and his sons must wear them whenever they enter the Tent of Meeting[n] or approach the altar to minister in the Holy Place,[o] so that they will not incur guilt and die.[p]

"This is to be a lasting ordinance[q] for Aaron and his descendants.

Consecration of the Priests

29:1–37pp—Lev 8:1–36

29 "This is what you are to do to consecrate[a] them, so that they may serve me as priests: Take a young bull and two rams without defect.[b] 2 And from fine wheat flour, without yeast, make bread, and cakes mixed with oil, and wafers spread with oil.[c] 3 Put them in a basket and present them in it—along with the bull and the two rams.[d] 4 Then bring Aaron and his sons to the entrance to the Tent of Meeting and wash them with water.[e] 5 Take the garments[f] and dress Aaron with the tunic, the robe of the ephod, the ephod itself and the breastpiece. Fasten the ephod on him by its skilfully woven waistband.[g] 6 Put the turban[h] on his head and attach the sacred diadem[i] to the turban. 7 Take the anointing oil[j] and anoint him by pouring it on his head. 8 Bring his sons and dress them in tunics[k] 9 and put headbands on them. Then tie sashes on Aaron and his sons.[a][l] The priesthood is theirs by a lasting ordinance.[m] In this way you shall ordain Aaron and his sons.

10 "Bring the bull to the front of the Tent of Meeting, and Aaron and his sons shall lay their hands on its head.[n] 11 Slaughter it in the LORD's presence[o] at the entrance to the Tent of Meeting. 12 Take some of the bull's blood and put it on the horns[p] of the altar with your finger, and pour out the rest of it at the base of the altar.[q] 13 Then take all the fat[r] around the inner parts,[s] the covering of the liver, and both kidneys with the fat around them, and burn them on the altar. 14 But burn the bull's flesh and its hide and its offal[t] outside the camp. It is a sin offering.[u]

15 "Take one of the rams,[v] and Aaron and his sons shall lay their hands on its head.[w] 16 Slaughter it and take the blood and sprinkle it against the altar on all sides. 17 Cut the ram into pieces and wash[x] the inner parts and the legs, putting them with the head and the other pieces. 18 Then burn the entire ram on the altar. It is a burnt offering to the LORD, a pleasing aroma,[y] an offering made to the LORD by fire.

19 "Take the other ram,[z] and Aaron and his sons shall lay their hands on its head.[a] 20 Slaughter it, take some of its blood and put it on the lobes of the right ears of Aaron and his sons, on the thumbs of their right hands, and on the big toes of their right feet.[b] Then sprinkle blood against the altar on all sides.[c] 21 And take some of the blood[d] on the altar and some of the anointing oil[e] and sprinkle it on Aaron and his garments and on his sons and their garments. Then he and his sons and their garments will be consecrated.[f]

33 [a]Nu 13:23; 1Sa 14:2; 1Ki 7:18; SS 4:3; Jer 52:22; Joel 1:12; Hag 2:19
36 [b]ver 37; Ex 29:6; Lev 8:9; [c]Zec 14:20
38 [d]Lev 5:1; 10:17; 16:22; 22:9,16; Nu 18:1; Isa 53:5, 6,11; Eze 4:4–6; Heb 9:28; 1Pe 2:24; [e]**Ge 32:20**; Lev 22:20,27; 23:11; Isa 56:7
39 [f]ver 4; [g]Ex 29:6; Lev 16:4; Eze 24:17,23; 44:18
40 [h]ver 4; Ex 29:8–9; 39:41; 40:14; Lev 8:13; [i]ver 2
41 [j]Ex 40:13; [k]Ex 29:7; Lev 6:20; 10:7; 21:12; Nu 35:25; [l]Ex 29:7–9; 30:30; 40:15; Lev 4:3; 6:22; 8:1–36; Nu 3:3; Heb 7:28
42 [m]Lev 6:10; 16:4,23; Eze 44:18
43 [n]**Ex 27:21**; [o]ver 29; [p]Ex 30:20,21; Lev 16:13; 22:9; Nu 1:51; 4:15, 20; 18:22; [q]**Ex 27:21**

Ch. 29

1 [a]ver 21,44; Lev 20:7; Jos 3:5; 1Ch 15:12; [b]Eze 43:23
2 [c]ver 23; Lev 2:1,4; 6:19–23; Nu 6:15
3 [d]ver 15,19
4 [e]Ex 40:12; Lev 14:8; 16:4; Heb 10:22
5 [f]**Ex 28:2**; [g]Ex 28:8
6 [h]Ex 28:39; Isa 3:23; Zec 3:5; [i]**Ex 28:36**
7 [j]ver 21; **Ex 28:41**; 30:25,30–31; 37:29; 40:9; Lev 21:10; 1Sa 10:1; 1Ki 1:39; Ps 89:20; 133:2; 141:5
8 [k]**Ex 28:4**; Lev 16:4
9 [l]Ex 28:40; [m]**Ex 27:21**; 40:15; Nu 3:10; 18:7; 25:13; Dt 18:5; Jdg 17:5; 1Sa 2:30; 1Ki 12:31
10 [n]ver 19; Lev 1:4; 4:15; 16:21; Nu 8:12
11 [o]Lev 1:5,11; 4:24; 6:16,25; 14:13
12 [p]**Ex 27:2**; [q]Lev 4:7; 9:9
13 [r]ver 22; Lev 1:8; 3:3,5,9; 4:10; 6:12; 7:3,5,31; 9:10; Nu 18:17; 1Sa 2:15; 1Ki 8:64; 2Ch 7:7; 29:35; 35:14; Isa 43:24; Eze 44:15; [s]**Ex 12:9**
14 [t]Na 3:6; Mal 2:3; [u]Lev 4:12,21; 16:27; Nu 19:3–5; Heb 13:11
15 [v]**ver 3**; [w]ver 10; Lev 3:2; 2Ch 29:23
17 [x]Lev 1:9,13 **18** [y]**Ge 8:21**; 2Co 2:15
19 [z]**ver 3**; [a]**ver 10**
20 [b]Lev 14:14,25; [c]ver 16; Lev 1:5,11; 3:2
21 [d]Heb 9:22; [e]**ver 7**; [f]**ver 1**

[d]32 The meaning of the Hebrew for this word is uncertain. [a]9 Hebrew; Septuagint *on them*

22"Take from this ram the fat,[g] the fat
tail, the fat around the inner parts, the
covering of the liver, both kidneys with
the fat around them, and the right
thigh. (This is the ram for the ordina-
tion.) 23From the basket of bread made
without yeast, which is before the LORD,
take a loaf, and a cake made with oil,
and a wafer. 24Put all these in the hands
of Aaron and his sons and wave them
before the LORD as a wave offering.[h]
25Then take them from their hands and
burn them on the altar along with the
burnt offering for a pleasing aroma to
the LORD, an offering made to the LORD
by fire.[i] 26After you take the breast of the
ram for Aaron's ordination, wave it
before the LORD as a wave offering, and
it will be your share.[j]
27"Consecrate those parts of the
ordination ram that belong to Aaron
and his sons:[k] the breast that was waved
and the thigh that was presented. 28This
is always to be the regular share from
the Israelites for Aaron and his sons. It
is the contribution the Israelites are to
make to the LORD from their fellowship
offerings.[b] [l]
29"Aaron's sacred garments[m] will
belong to his descendants so that
they can be anointed and ordained in
them.[n] 30The son[o] who succeeds him
as priest and comes to the Tent of
Meeting to minister in the Holy Place
is to wear them seven days.
31"Take the ram[p] for the ordination
and cook the meat in a sacred place.[q]
32At the entrance to the Tent of Meeting,
Aaron and his sons are to eat the meat of
the ram and the bread[r] that is in the
basket. 33They are to eat these offerings
by which atonement was made for their
ordination and consecration. But no-
one else may eat[s] them, because they
are sacred. 34And if any of the meat of
the ordination ram or any bread is left
over till morning,[t] burn it up. It must
not be eaten, because it is sacred.
35"Do for Aaron and his sons every-
thing I have commanded you, taking
seven days to ordain them. 36Sacrifice a
bull each day[u] as a sin offering to make
atonement.[v] Purify the altar by making
atonement for it, and anoint it to conse-
crate[w] it. 37For seven days make atone-
ment for the altar and consecrate it.
Then the altar will be most holy, and
whatever touches it will be holy.[x]
38"This is what you are to offer on the
altar regularly each day:[y] two lambs a
year old. 39Offer one in the morning and
the other at twilight.[z] 40With the first
lamb offer a tenth of an ephah[c] of fine
flour mixed with a quarter of a hin[d] of
oil[a] from pressed olives, and a quarter of
a hin of wine as a drink offering.[b]
41Sacrifice the other lamb at twilight[c]
with the same grain offering[d] and its
drink offering as in the morning—a
pleasing aroma, an offering made to the
LORD by fire.
42"For the generations to come[e] this
burnt offering is to be made regularly[f] at
the entrance to the Tent of Meeting[g]
before the LORD. There I will meet you
and speak to you;[h] 43there also I will
meet with the Israelites, and the place
will be consecrated by my glory.[i]
44"So I will consecrate the Tent of
Meeting and the altar and will conse-
crate Aaron and his sons to serve me as
priests.[j] 45Then I will dwell[k] among the
Israelites and be their God.[l] 46They will
know that I am the LORD their God, who
brought them out of Egypt[m] so that I
might dwell among them. I am the LORD
their God.[n]

The Altar of Incense

30:1-5pp—Ex 37:25-28

30 "Make an altar[a] of acacia wood
for burning incense.[b] 2It is to be
square, a cubit long and a cubit wide,
and two cubits high[a]—its horns[c] of one
piece with it. 3Overlay the top and all
the sides and the horns with pure gold,
and make a gold moulding around it.[d]
4Make two gold rings[e] for the altar
below the moulding—two on opposite
sides—to hold the poles used to carry it.
5Make the poles of acacia wood and
overlay them with gold.[f] 6Put the altar in
front of the curtain that is before the ark
of the Testimony—before the atone-
ment cover[g] that is over the Testimony
—where I will meet with you.
7"Aaron must burn fragrant incense[h]
on the altar every morning when he
tends the lamps. 8He must burn incense

22 [g]**ver 13**
24 [h]Lev 7:30; 9:21; 10:15; 14:12; 23:11, 20; Nu 6:20; 8:11,13,15
25 [i]ver 18
26 [j]Lev 7:31-34
27 [k]Ex 22:29; Lev 7:31,34; Nu 18:11,12; Dt 18:3
28 [l]ver 22-27; Lev 7:30,34; 10:15
29 [m]**Ex 28:2; Lev 16:4;** [n]Nu 20:28
30 [o]Lev 6:22; Nu 3:3; 20:28
31 [p]Lev 7:37; 2Ch 13:9; [q]Lev 10:14; Nu 19:9; Eze 42:13
32 [r]Mt 12:4
33 [s]Lev 22:10,13
34 [t]**Ex 12:10**
36 [u]Heb 10:11; [v]ver 33,37; Ex 30:10; Lev 1:4; 4:20; 16:16; Nu 6:11; 8:12,19; 16:46; 25:13; 2Ch 29:24; [w]Ex 40:10; Nu 7:10
37 [x]Ex 30:28-29; 40:10; Eze 43:25; Mt 23:19
38 [y]Lev 23:2; Nu 28:3-8; 1Ch 16:40; 2Ch 8:13; Eze 46:13-15; Da 12:11
39 [z]Nu 28:4,8; 1Ki 18:36; 2Ch 13:11; Ezr 3:3; Ps 141:2; Da 9:21
40 [a]Ex 30:24; Nu 15:4; 28:5; [b]**Ge 35:14;** Lev 23:37; 2Ki 16:13
41 [c]1Ki 18:29,36; 2Ki 3:20; 16:15; Ezr 9:4, 5; Ps 141:2; Da 9:21; [d]Lev 2:1; 5:13; 10:12; Nu 4:16; 6:17; 1Ki 8:64; Isa 43:23
42 [e]Ex 30:8,10, 21,31; 31:13; [f]Eze 46:15; [g]**Ex 26:1; 27:21;** [h]ver 43; Ex 25:22; 33:9, 11; Nu 7:89
43 [i]Ex 33:18; 40:34; Lev 9:6; 1Ki 8:11; 2Ch 5:14; 7:2; Ps 26:8; 85:9; Eze 1:28; 43:5; Hag 1:8; 2:7
44 [j]**ver 1**
45 [k]**Ex 25:8**; Nu 35:34; Jn 14:17; **Ro 8:10;** [l]**Ge 17:7**; 2Co 6:16
46 [m]**Ex 6:6**; 19:4-6; Dt 5:6; Ps 114:1; Hag 2:5; [n]**Ge 17:7**
Ch. 30
1 [a]Ex 40:5,26; Nu 4:11; 1Ki 6:20; Eze 41:22; [b]**Ex 25:6**; 37:29; Lk 1:11; Heb 9:4; Rev 8:3
2 [c]**Ex 27:2**; Rev 9:13 **3** [d]**Ex 25:11**
4 [e]**Ex 25:12** **5** [f]**Ex 25:13** **6** [g]Ex 25:22; **26:34**
7 [h]**Ex 25:6**; 40:27; Nu 3:10; Dt 33:10; 1Sa 2:28; 1Ch 6:49; 2Ch 2:4; 26:18; 29:7

[b]28 Traditionally *peace offerings*
[c]40 That is, probably about 4 pints (about 2 litres)
[d]40 That is, probably about 1½ pints (about 1 litre)
[a]2 That is, about 1½ feet (about 0.5 metre) long and wide and about 3 feet (about 0.9 metre) high

again when he lights the lamps at twilight so that incense will burn regularly before the LORD for the generations to come.[i] 9Do not offer on this altar any other incense[j] or any burnt offering or grain offering, and do not pour a drink offering on it. 10Once a year[k] Aaron shall make atonement[l] on its horns. This annual atonement must be made with the blood of the atoning sin offering[m] for the generations to come.[n] It is most holy to the LORD."

Atonement Money

11Then the LORD said to Moses, 12"When you take a census[o] of the Israelites to count them, each one must pay the LORD a ransom[p] for his life at the time he is counted. Then no plague[q] will come on them when you number them. 13Each one who crosses over to those already counted is to give a half shekel,[b] according to the sanctuary shekel,[r] which weighs twenty gerahs. This half shekel is an offering to the LORD. 14All who cross over, those twenty years old or more,[s] are to give an offering to the LORD. 15The rich are not to give more than a half shekel and the poor are not to give less[t] when you make the offering to the LORD to atone for your lives. 16Receive the atonement[u] money from the Israelites and use it for the service of the Tent of Meeting.[v] It will be a memorial[w] for the Israelites before the LORD, making atonement for your lives."

Basin for Washing

17Then the LORD said to Moses, 18"Make a bronze basin,[x] with its bronze stand, for washing. Place it between the Tent of Meeting and the altar, and put water in it. 19Aaron and his sons are to wash their hands and feet[y] with water[z] from it. 20Whenever they enter the Tent of Meeting, they shall wash with water so that they will not die.[a] Also, when they approach the altar to minister by presenting an offering made to the LORD by fire, 21they shall wash their hands and feet so that they will not die. This is to be a lasting ordinance[b] for Aaron and his descendants for the generations to come."[c]

Anointing Oil

22Then the LORD said to Moses, 23"Take the following fine spices:[d] 500 shekels[c] of liquid myrrh,[e] half as much (that is, 250 shekels) of fragrant cinnamon,[f] 250 shekels of fragrant cane,[g] 24500 shekels[h] of cassia[i]—all according to the sanctuary shekel—and a hin[d] of olive oil. 25Make these into a sacred anointing oil, a fragrant blend, the work of a perfumer.[j] It will be the sacred anointing oil.[k] 26Then use it to anoint[l] the Tent of Meeting, the ark of the Testimony, 27the table and all its articles, the lampstand and its accessories, the altar of incense, 28the altar of burnt offering and all its utensils, and the basin with its stand. 29You shall consecrate them[m] so they will be most holy, and whatever touches them will be holy.[n]

30"Anoint Aaron and his sons and consecrate[o] them so they may serve me as priests.[p] 31Say to the Israelites, 'This is to be my sacred anointing oil[q] for the generations to come.[r] 32Do not pour it on men's bodies and do not make any oil with the same formula. It is sacred, and you are to consider it sacred.[s] 33Whoever makes perfume like it and whoever puts it on anyone other than a priest must be cut off[t] from his people.' "

Incense

34Then the LORD said to Moses, "Take fragrant spices[u]—gum resin, onycha and galbanum—and pure frankincense, all in equal amounts, 35and make a fragrant blend of incense,[v] the work of a perfumer.[w] It is to be salted and pure and sacred. 36Grind some of it to powder and place it in front of the Testimony in the Tent of Meeting, where I will meet[x] with you. It shall be most holy[y] to you. 37Do not make any incense with this formula for yourselves; consider it holy[z] to the LORD. 38Whoever makes any like it to enjoy its fragrance must be cut off[a] from his people."

Bezalel and Oholiab

31:2–6pp—Ex 35:30–35

31 Then the LORD said to Moses, 2"See I have chosen Bezalel[a] son of Uri, the son of Hur,[b] of the tribe of

8 [i]**Ex 25:37; 29:42**
9 [j]Lev 10:1; Nu 16:7,40
10 [k]Lev 16:2; [l]Lev 9:7; 16:18–19,30; 23:27,28; 25:9; [m]Ex 29:14; Lev 4:3; 6:25; 7:7; 8:2,14; Nu 6:11; [n]**Ex 29:42**
12 [o]Ex 38:25; Nu 1:2,49; 4:2,29; 14:29; 26:2; 31:26; 2Sa 24:1; 2Ki 12:4; [p]Ex 38:26; Nu 31:50; **Mt 20:28;** [q]Nu 14:12; Dt 28:58–61; 2Sa 24:13; 1Ki 8:37
13 [r]ver 24; Ex 38:24,26; Lev 5:15; 27:3,25; Nu 3:47; 7:13; 18:16; Eze 4:10; 45:12; Mt 17:24
14 [s]Ex 38:26; Nu 1:3,18; 14:29; 26:2; 32:11; 2Ch 25:5
15 [t]Pr 22:2; Eph 6:9
16 [u]ver 12; [v]Ex 38:25–28; 2Ch 24:5; [w]Nu 31:54
18 [x]Ex 31:9; 35:16; 38:8; 39:39; 40:7,30; 1Ki 7:38; 2Ch 4:6
19 [y]Ex 40:31–32; Jn 13:10; [z]Ex 29:4; 40:12; Lev 8:6; Ps 26:6; Heb 10:22
20 [a]**Ex 28:43**
21 [b]**Ex 27:21;** [c]Ex 29:42
23 [d]**Ge 43:11;** [e]**Ge 37:25;** [f]Pr 7:17; SS 4:14; [g]SS 4:14; Isa 43:24; Jer 6:20
24 [h]**ver 13**; [i]Ps 45:8; Eze 27:19
25 [j]ver 35; Ex 37:29; 1Ch 9:30; [k]**Ex 29:7; 1Sa 9:16**
26 [l]Ex 40:9; Lev 8:10; Nu 7:1
29 [m]Lev 8:10–11; [n]Ex 29:37; Lev 6:18,27; Mt 23:17
30 [o]Ex 29:7; Lev 8:2,12,30; 10:7; 16:32; 21:10,12; 1Ch 15:12; Ps 133:2; [p]**Ex 28:41**
31 [q]Ex 29:7; [r]**Ex 29:42**
32 [s]ver 25,37
33 [t]ver 38; **Ge 17:14**
34 [u]SS 3:6
35 [v]Ex 25:6; [w]**ver 25**
36 [x]**Ex 25:22;** [y]ver 32; Ex 29:37; Lev 2:3
37 [z]**ver 32**
38 [a]**ver 33**

Ch. 31

2 [a]Ex 36:1–2; 37:1; 38:22; 1Ch 2:20; 2Ch 1:5; [b]**Ex 17:10**

[b]13 That is, about ⅕ ounce (about 6 grams); also in verse 15
[c]23 That is, about 12½ pounds (about 6 kilograms)
[d]24 That is, probably about 6½ pints (about 4 litres)

Judah, 3and I have filled him with the
Spirit of God, with skill, ability and
knowledge[c] in all kinds of crafts[d]—4to
make artistic designs for work in gold,
silver and bronze, 5to cut and set stones,
to work in wood, and to engage in all
kinds of craftsmanship. 6Moreover, I
have appointed Oholiab[e] son of Ahisa-
mach, of the tribe of Dan,[f] to help him.
Also I have given skill to all the crafts-
men[g] to make everything I have com-
manded you: 7the Tent of Meeting,[h] the
ark of the Testimony[i] with the atone-
ment cover[j] on it, and all the other fur-
nishings of the tent—8the table[k] and its
articles, the pure gold lampstand[l] and
all its accessories, the altar of incense,[m]
9the altar of burnt offering[n] and all its
utensils, the basin[o] with its stand—
10and also the woven garments[p], both
the sacred garments for Aaron the priest
and the garments for his sons when
they serve as priests, 11and the anoint-
ing oil[q] and fragrant incense[r] for the
Holy Place. They are to make them just
as I commanded[s] you."

The Sabbath

12Then the LORD said to Moses, 13"Say
to the Israelites, 'You must observe my
Sabbaths.[t] This will be a sign[u] between
me and you for the generations to
come,[v] so that you may know that I
am the LORD, who makes you holy.[a][w]
14" 'Observe the Sabbath, because it is
holy to you. Anyone who desecrates it
must be put to death;[x] whoever does
any work on that day must be cut off
from his people. 15For six days, work[y] is
to be done, but the seventh day is a
Sabbath of rest,[z] holy to the LORD. Who-
ever does any work on the Sabbath day
must be put to death. 16The Israelites are
to observe the Sabbath,[a] celebrating it
for the generations to come as a lasting
covenant. 17It will be a sign[b] between
me and the Israelites for ever, for in six
days the LORD made the heavens and
the earth, and on the seventh day he
abstained from work and rested.[c]' "[d]
18When the LORD finished speaking to
Moses on Mount Sinai,[e] he gave him the
two tablets of the Testimony, the tablets
of stone[f] inscribed by the finger of God.[g]

The Golden Calf

32 When the people saw that
Moses was so long in coming
down from the mountain,[a] they
gathered round Aaron and said,
"Come, make us gods[a] who will go be-
fore[b] us. As for this fellow Moses who
brought us up out of Egypt, we don't
know what has happened to him."[c]
2Aaron answered them, "Take off the
gold ear-rings[d] that your wives, your
sons and your daughters are wearing,
and bring them to me." 3So all the peo-
ple took off their ear-rings and brought
them to Aaron. 4He took what they
handed him and made it into an idol[e]
cast in the shape of a calf,[f] fashioning it
with a tool. Then they said, "These are
your gods,[b][g] O Israel, who brought you
up out of Egypt."[h]
5When Aaron saw this, he built an
altar in front of the calf and announced,
"Tomorrow there will be a festival[i] to
the LORD." 6So the next day the people
rose early and sacrificed burnt offerings[j]
and presented fellowship offerings.[c]
Afterwards they sat down to eat and
drink[k] and got up to indulge in revelry.[l]
7Then the LORD said to Moses, "Go
down, because your people, whom you
brought up out of Egypt,[m] have become
corrupt.[n] 8They have been quick to turn
away[o] from what I commanded them
and have made themselves an idol[p] cast
in the shape of a calf.[q] They have bowed
down to it and sacrificed[r] to it and have
said, 'These are your gods, O Israel,
who brought you up out of Egypt.'[s]
9"I have seen these people," the LORD
said to Moses, "and they are a stiff-
necked[t] people. 10Now leave me alone[u]
so that my anger may burn against them
and that I may destroy[v] them. Then I
will make you into a great nation."[w]
11But Moses sought the favour[x] of the
LORD his God. "O LORD," he said, "why
should your anger burn against your
people, whom you brought out of Egypt
with great power and a mighty hand?[y]
12Why should the Egyptians say, 'It was
with evil intent that he brought them

3 [c]**Ex 28:3**; [d]1Ki 7:14; 1Co 12:4
6 [e]Ex 36:1–2; 38:23; [f]1Ki 7:14; 2Ch 2:14; [g]**Ex 28:3**
7 [h]Ex 36:8–38; [i]Ex 37:1–5; [j]Ex 37:6; 40:20
8 [k]Ex 37:10–16; [l]Ex 37:17–24; Lev 24:4; [m]Ex 37:25–28
9 [n]Ex 38:3; Nu 4:14; [o]**Ex 30:18**
10 [p]**Ex 28:2**
11 [q]Ex 30:22–32; 37:29; [r]**Ex 25:6**; [s]**Ex 25:9**
13 [t]**Ex 20:8**; [u]ver 17; Isa 56:4; Eze 20:12,20; [v]**Ex 29:42**; [w]Lev 11:44; 20:8; 21:8; Eze 37:28
14 [x]Ex 35:2; Nu 15:32–36
15 [y]**Ex 20:8**, 9–11; 35:2; Lev 16:29; 23:3; Nu 29:7; [z]**Ge 2:3**
16 [a]**Ex 20:8**
17 [b]**ver 13**; [c]**Ge 2:2–3**; [d]**Ge 2:2**; **Ex 20:9**; Isa 56:2; 58:13; 66:23; Jer 17:21–22; Eze 20:12,20
18 [e]**Ex 19:11**; [f]**Ex 24:12**; 2Co 3:3; Heb 9:4; [g]Ex 32:15–16; 34:1,28; Dt 4:13; 9:10

Ch. 32

1 [a]Ge 7:4; Dt 9:9–12; [b]**Ex 13:21**; [c]ver 23; Ac 7:40*
2 [d]Jdg 8:24–27
4 [e]**Ex 20:23**; Jdg 17:3–4; Isa 30:22; [f]ver 8, 24,35; Dt 9:16; Ne 9:18; Ps 106:19; Ac 7:41; [g]Ex 20:23; Isa 42:17; [h]1Ki 12:28; 14:9; 2Ki 10:29; 17:16; 2Ch 13:8; Hos 8:6; 10:5
5 [i]Lev 23:2,37; 2Ki 10:20; Joel 2:15
6 [j]Ex 20:24; 34:15; Lev 3:1; 4:10; 6:12; 9:4; 22:21; Nu 6:14; 25:2; Dt 27:7; Jdg 20:26; Eze 43:27; Ac 7:41; [k]Jdg 19:4; Ru 3:3; 1Sa 1:9; 2Sa 11:11; 1Ki 13:23; 18:42; Ne 8:12; Job 1:4; Ecc 5:18; 8:15; Jer 16:8; [l]ver 17–19; 1Co 10:7*
7 [m]ver 4,11; Ex 33:1; [n]**Ge 6:11–12**; Eze 20:8
8 [o]Jer 7:26; 16:12; Mal 2:8; 3:7; [p]**Ex 20:4**; [q]**ver 4**; [r]Ex 22:20; [s]1Ki 12:28; Eze 23:8
9 [t]Ex 33:3,5; 34:9; Dt 9:6,13; 10:16; 31:27; Jdg 2:19; 2Ki 17:14; 2Ch 30:8; 36:13; Ne 9:16; Ps 78:8; Pr 29:1; Isa 46:12; 48:4; Jer 7:26; Eze 2:4; Hos 4:16; Ac 7:51
10 [u]1Sa 2:25; Jer 7:16; 11:14; 14:11; [v]Ex 22:24; 33:3,5; Nu 16:21,45; Dt 9:14,19; Ps 106:23; Jer 14:12; Eze 20:13; [w]Nu 14:12; Dt 9:14
11 [x]Dt 9:18; 2Sa 21:1; 2Ch 15:2; Ps 9:10; 34:4; 106:23; Isa 9:13; Jer 15:1; [y]ver 13; Dt 9:26; 1Sa 7:9; Ne 1:10; Ps 136:12

[a]13 Or *who sanctifies you*; or *who sets you apart as holy*
[a]1 Or *a god*; also in verses 23 and 31
[b]4 Or *This is your god*; also in verse 8
[c]6 Traditionally *peace offerings*

out, to kill them in the mountains and to
wipe them off the face of the earth'?[z]
Turn from your fierce anger; relent and
do not bring disaster[a] on your people.
13Remember[b] your servants Abraham,
Isaac and Israel, to whom you swore by
your own self:[c] 'I will make your descen-
dants as numerous as the stars[d] in the
sky and I will give your descendants all
this land[e] I promised them, and it will be
their inheritance for ever.'" 14Then the
LORD relented[f] and did not bring on his
people the disaster he had threatened.
15Moses turned and went down the
mountain with the two tablets of the
Testimony[g] in his hands.[h] They were
inscribed[i] on both sides, front and back.
16The tablets were the work of God;
the writing was the writing of God,
engraved on the tablets.[j]
17When Joshua[k] heard the noise of the
people shouting, he said to Moses,
"There is the sound of war in the
camp."
18Moses replied:

"It is not the sound of victory,
it is not the sound of defeat;
it is the sound of singing that I
hear."

19When Moses approached the camp
and saw the calf[l] and the dancing,[m] his
anger burned[n] and he threw the tablets
out of his hands, breaking them to
pieces[o] at the foot of the mountain.
20And he took the calf they had made
and burned[p] it in the fire; then he
ground it to powder,[q] scattered it on the
water[r] and made the Israelites drink it.
21He said to Aaron, "What did these
people do to you, that you led them into
such great sin?"
22"Do not be angry,[s] my lord," Aaron
answered. "You know how prone these
people are to evil.[t] 23They said to me,
'Make us gods who will go before us. As
for this fellow Moses who brought us up
out of Egypt, we don't know what has
happened to him.'[u] 24So I told them,
'Whoever has any gold jewellery, take it
off.' Then they gave me the gold, and I
threw it into the fire, and out came this
calf!"[v]
25Moses saw that the people were
running wild and that Aaron had let
them get out of control and so become a
laughing-stock[w] to their enemies. 26So
he stood at the entrance to the camp and
said, "Whoever is for the LORD, come to
me." And all the Levites rallied to him.
27Then he said to them, "This is what
the LORD, the God of Israel, says: 'Each
man strap a sword to his side. Go back
and forth through the camp from one
end to the other, each killing his brother
and friend and neighbour.'"[x] 28The
Levites did as Moses commanded,
and that day about three thousand of
the people died. 29Then Moses said,
"You have been set apart to the LORD
today, for you were against your own
sons and brothers, and he has blessed
you this day."
30The next day Moses said to the
people, "You have committed a great
sin.[y] But now I will go up to the LORD;
perhaps I can make atonement[z] for your
sin."
31So Moses went back to the LORD and
said, "Oh, what a great sin these people
have committed![a] They have made
themselves gods of gold.[b] 32But now,
please forgive their sin[c]—but if not,
then blot me[d] out of the book[e] you have
written."
33The LORD replied to Moses, "Who-
ever has sinned against me I will blot
out[f] of my book. 34Now go, lead[g] the
people to the place[h] I spoke of, and my
angel[i] will go before you. However,
when the time comes for me to punish, I
will punish[j] them for their sin."
35And the LORD struck the people
with a plague because of what they did
with the calf[k] Aaron had made.

33 Then the LORD said to Moses,
"Leave this place, you and the
people you brought up out of Egypt,
and go up to the land I promised on
oath[a] to Abraham, Isaac and Jacob,
saying, 'I will give it to your descend-
ants.'[b] 2I will send an angel[c] before you
and drive out the Canaanites, Amorites,
Hittites, Perizzites, Hivites and Jebu-
sites.[d] 3Go up to the land flowing with
milk and honey.[e] But I will not go with
you, because you are a stiff-necked[f]
people and I might destroy[g] you on the
way."
4When the people heard these dis-
tressing words, they began to mourn[h]
and no-one put on any ornaments. 5For
the LORD had said to Moses, "Tell the
Israelites, 'You are a stiff-necked
people.[i] If I were to go with you even
for a moment, I might destroy[j] you.
Now take off your ornaments and I
will decide what to do with you.'"
6So the Israelites stripped off their
ornaments at Mount Horeb.[k]

12 [z]Nu 14:13–16; Dt 9:28; [a]ver 14; Ex 33:13
13 [b]**Ex 2:24**; 33:13; [c]**Ge 22:16**; Heb 6:13; [d]Ge 15:5; 22:17; [e]**Ge 12:7**
14 [f]Dt 9:19; 1Sa 15:11; 2Sa 24:16; 1Ki 21:29; 1Ch 21:15; Ps 106:45; Jer 18:8; 26:3, 19; Am 7:3,6; Jnh 3:10
15 [g]Ex 31:18; Heb 9:4; [h]**Ex 19:18**; 34:4,29; Dt 9:15; [i]2Co 3:3
16 [j]**Ex 24:12**
17 [k]**Ex 17:9**
19 [l]Dt 9:16; [m]ver 6; 1Co 10:7; [n]Ezr 9:3; Ps 119:53,158; [o]Ex 34:1; Dt 9:17
20 [p]Dt 7:25; 12:3; Jos 7:1; 2Ki 23:6; 1Ch 14:12; [q]2Ch 34:7; Mic 1:7; [r]Dt 9:21
22 [s]**Ge 18:30**; [t]Dt 9:24; 28:20; 2Ki 21:15; Ezr 9:13; Ne 9:28; Jer 4:4; 44:3; Eze 6:9
23 [u]**ver 1**; Ac 7:40
24 [v]**ver 4**
25 [w]**Ge 38:23**
27 [x]Nu 25:3,5; Dt 33:9; Eze 9:5
30 [y]1Sa 12:20; Ps 25:11; 85:2; [z]Lev 1:4; 4:20, 26; 5:6,10,13; 6:7
31 [a]Ex 34:9; Dt 9:18; [b]**Ex 20:23**
32 [c]Nu 14:19; [d]Ro 9:3; [e]Ps 69:28; Eze 13:9; Da 7:10; 12:1; Mal 3:16; **Lk 10:20**
33 [f]**Ex 17:14; Job 21:20**; Rev 3:5
34 [g]**Ex 15:17**; [h]Ex 3:17; [i]**Ex 14:19**; [j]**Ge 50:19**; Dt 32:35; Ps 89:32; 94:23; 99:8; 109:20; Isa 27:1; Jer 5:9; 11:22; 23:2; 44:13,29; Hos 12:2; Ro 2:5–6
35 [k]**ver 4**

Ch. 33
1 [a]**Ex 13:11; Nu 14:23**; Heb 6:13; [b]**Ge 12:7**
2 [c]**Ex 14:19**; [d]**Ex 23:28**
3 [e]**Ex 3:8**; [f]Ex 32:9; Ac 7:51; [g]**Ex 32:10**
4 [h]Nu 14:39; Ezr 9:3; Est 4:1; Ps 119:53
5 [i]**Ex 32:9**; [j]**Ex 32:10** *6* [k]**Ex 3:1**

The Tent of Meeting

7Now Moses used to take a tent and
pitch it outside the camp some distance
away, calling it the "tent of meeting".[l]
Anyone enquiring[m] of the LORD would
go to the tent of meeting outside the
camp. 8And whenever Moses went out
to the tent, all the people rose and stood
at the entrances to their tents,[n] watch-
ing Moses until he entered the tent. 9As
Moses went into the tent, the pillar of
cloud[o] would come down and stay at the
entrance, while the LORD spoke[p] with
Moses. 10Whenever the people saw the
pillar of cloud standing at the entrance
to the tent, they all stood and wor-
shipped, each at the entrance to his
tent.[q] 11The LORD would speak to Moses
face to face,[r] as a man speaks with his
friend. Then Moses would return to the
camp, but his young assistant Joshua[s]
son of Nun did not leave the tent.

Moses and the Glory of the LORD

12Moses said to the LORD, "You have
been telling me, 'Lead these people,'[t]
but you have not let me know whom
you will send with me. You have said, 'I
know you by name[u] and you have
found favour[v] with me.' 13If you are
pleased with me, teach me your ways[w]
so I may know you and continue to find
favour with you. Remember that this
nation is your people."[x]
14The LORD replied, "My Presence[y]
will go with you, and I will give you
rest."[z]
15Then Moses said to him, "If your
Presence[a] does not go with us, do not
send us up from here. 16How will
anyone know that you are pleased with
me and with your people unless you
go with us?[b] What else will distinguish
me and your people from all the other
people on the face of the earth?"[c]
17And the LORD said to Moses, "I will
do the very thing you have asked,[d]
because I am pleased with you and I
know you by name."[e]
18Then Moses said, "Now show me
your glory."[f]
19And the LORD said, "I will cause all
my goodness to pass[g] in front of you,
and I will proclaim my name,[h] the LORD,
in your presence. I will have mercy on
whom I will have mercy, and I will have
compassion on whom I will have com-
passion.[i] 20But," he said, "you cannot
see my face, for no-one may see[j] me and
live."
21Then the LORD said, "There is a
place near me where you may stand on
a rock. 22When my glory passes by, I will
put you in a cleft in the rock[k] and cover
you with my hand[l] until I have passed
by. 23Then I will remove my hand and
you will see my back; but my face must
not be seen."

The New Stone Tablets

34 The LORD said to Moses,
"Chisel out two stone tablets
like the first ones,[a] and I will write on
them the words that were on the first
tablets,[b] which you broke.[c] 2Be ready in
the morning, and then come up on
Mount Sinai.[d] Present yourself to me
there on top of the mountain. 3No-one is
to come with you or be seen anywhere
on the mountain;[e] not even the flocks
and herds may graze in front of the
mountain."
4So Moses chiselled[f] out two stone
tablets like the first ones and went up
Mount Sinai early in the morning, as the
LORD had commanded him; and he
carried the two stone tablets in his
hands.[g] 5Then the LORD came down in
the cloud[h] and stood there with him and
proclaimed his name, the LORD.[i] 6And
he passed in front of Moses, proclaim-
ing, "The LORD, the LORD, the com-
passionate[j] and gracious God, slow to
anger,[k] abounding in love[l] and faithful-
ness,[m] 7maintaining love to thousands,[n]
and forgiving wickedness, rebellion
and sin.[o] Yet he does not leave the guilty
unpunished;[p] he punishes the children
and their children for the sin of the
fathers to the third and fourth gener-
ation."[q]
8Moses bowed to the ground at once
and worshipped. 9"O Lord, if I have
found favour[r] in your eyes," he said,
"then let the Lord go with us.[s] Although
this is a stiff-necked[t] people, forgive our
wickedness and our sin,[u] and take us as
your inheritance."[v]
10Then the LORD said: "I am making a
covenant[w] with you. Before all your
people I will do wonders[x] never before

7 [l]**Ex 27:21;** [m]**Ge 25:22; 1Ki 22:5**
8 [n]ver 10; Nu 16:27
9 [o]Ex 13:21; **19:9;** Dt 31:15; 1Co 10:1; [p]**Ex 29:42;** 31:18; Ps 99:7
10 [q]**ver 8**
11 [r]Nu 12:8; Dt 5:4; 34:10; [s]**Ex 17:9**
12 [t]Ex 3:10; **15:17;** [u]ver 17; Isa 43:1; 45:3; 49:1; Jn 10:14–15; 2Ti 2:19; [v]**Ge 6:8**
13 [w]Ps 25:4; 27:11; 51:13; 86:11; 103:7; 143:8; [x]Ex 3:7; Dt 9:26,29; Ps 77:15
14 [y]**Ex 13:21;** Dt 4:37; Isa 63:9; Hag 1:13; 2:4; [z]Dt 12:9,10; 25:19; Jos 1:13; 11:23; 21:44; 22:4; 23:1; 1Ki 8:56; Isa 63:14; Jer 31:2; Mt 11:28; Heb 4:1–11
15 [a]ver 3; Ex 34:9; 2Ki 13:23; 17:18; 23:27; 24:20; Ps 51:11; 80:3, 7,19; Jer 7:15; 52:3
16 [b]Ex 34:5; 40:34–35; Nu 9:15; 14:14; [c]Ex 34:10; Lev 20:24,26; Nu 23:9; Dt 4:7,32,34; 32:9; 33:28
17 [d]Ex 34:28; Dt 9:18,25; 10:10; Jas 5:16; [e]**Ge 6:8**
18 [f]**Ex 16:7;** Jn 1:14; 12:41; 1Ti 6:16; Rev 15:8
19 [g]1Ki 19:11; [h]Ex 6:3; 34:5–7; [i]Ro 9:15*
20 [j]**Ge 16:13; Ex 3:6; Dt 5:26; Jn 1:18**
22 [k]Ge 49:24; 1Ki 19:9; Ps 27:5; 31:20; 62:7; 91:1; Isa 2:21; Jer 4:29; [l]Ps 91:4; Isa 49:2; 51:16

Ch. 34

1 [a]**Ex 24:12;** [b]Dt 10:2,4; [c]**Ex 32:19**
2 [d]**Ex 19:11**
3 [e]**Ex 19:13**

4 [f]Dt 10:3; [g]**Ex 32:15**
5 [h]**Ex 13:21; 19:9;** [i]Ex 6:3; 33:19
6 [j]**Ex 22:27; Nu 14:20; Ps 86:15;** [k]Nu 14:18; Ps 78:38; Jer 15:15; Ro 2:4; [l]**Ge 19:16;** [m]Ps 61:7; 108:4; 115:1; 138:2; 143:1; La 3:23; Jas 5:11
7 [n]**Ex 20:6;** Dt 5:10; [o]1Ki 8:30; Ps 86:5; 103:3; 130:4,8; Isa 43:25; Da 9:9; 1Jn 1:9; [p]Ex 23:7; Jos 24:19; Job 7:20–21; 9:28; 10:14; Mic 6:1–16; Na 1:3; [q]**Ex 20:5**
9 [r]Ex 33:13; Nu 11:15; [s]**Ex 33:15;** [t]Ex 32:9; [u]Nu 14:19; 1Ki 8:30; 2Ch 6:21; Ps 19:12; 25:11; Jer 33:8; Hos 14:2; [v]**Ex 6:7;** 19:5; Dt 4:20; 7:6; 9:26,29; 14:2; 26:18; 32:9; 1Sa 10:1; 2Sa 14:16; 1Ki 8:51,53; Ps 28:9; 33:12; 74:2; 79:1; 94:14; 106:5,40; Isa 19:25; 63:17; Jer 10:16; 51:19; Mic 7:18; Zec 2:12
10 [w]**Ge 6:18; 9:15; 15:18;** Dt 5:2–3; [x]**Ex 3:20**

done in any nation in all the world.[y] The
people you live among will see how
awesome is the work that I, the LORD,
will do for you. 11Obey what I com-
mand[z] you today. I will drive out before
you the Amorites, Canaanites, Hittites,
Perizzites, Hivites and Jebusites.[a] 12Be
careful not to make a treaty[b] with those
who live in the land where you are
going, or they will be a snare[c] among
you. 13Break down their altars, smash
their sacred stones and cut down their
Asherah poles.[a][d] 14Do not worship any
other god,[e] for the LORD, whose name[f]
is Jealous, is a jealous God.[g]
15"Be careful not to make a treaty[h]
with those who live in the land; for
when they prostitute[i] themselves to
their gods and sacrifice to them, they
will invite you and you will eat their
sacrifices.[j] 16And when you choose
some of their daughters as wives[k] for
your sons and those daughters
prostitute themselves to their gods,[l]
they will lead your sons to do the
same.
17"Do not make cast idols.[m]
18"Celebrate the Feast of Unleavened
Bread.[n] For seven days eat bread made
without yeast,[o] as I commanded you.
Do this at the appointed time in the
month of Abib,[p] for in that month you
came out of Egypt.
19"The first offspring[q] of every womb
belongs to me, including all the
firstborn males of your livestock,
whether from herd or flock. 20Redeem
the firstborn donkey with a lamb, but if
you do not redeem it, break its neck.[r]
Redeem all your firstborn sons.[s]
"No-one is to appear before me
empty-handed.[t]
21"Six days you shall labour, but on
the seventh day you shall rest;[u] even
during the ploughing season and
harvest[v] you must rest.
22"Celebrate the Feast of Weeks with
the firstfruits[w] of the wheat harvest, and
the Feast of Ingathering[x] at the turn of
the year.[b] 23Three times[y] a year all your
men are to appear before the Sovereign
LORD, the God of Israel. 24I will drive out
nations[z] before you and enlarge your
territory,[a] and no-one will covet your
land when you go up three times each
year to appear before the LORD your
God.
25"Do not offer the blood of a sacrifice
to me along with anything containing
yeast,[b] and do not let any of the sacrifice
from the Passover Feast remain until
morning.[c]
26"Bring the best of the firstfruits[d] of
your soil to the house of the LORD your
God.
"Do not cook a young goat in its
mother's milk."[e]
27Then the LORD said to Moses,
"Write[f] down these words, for in
accordance with these words I have
made a covenant[g] with you and with
Israel." 28Moses was there with the
LORD forty days and forty nights[h]
without eating bread or drinking
water.[i] And he wrote on the tablets[j]
the words of the covenant—the Ten
Commandments.[k]

The Radiant Face of Moses

29When Moses came down from
Mount Sinai[l] with the two tablets of the
Testimony in his hands,[m] he was not
aware that his face was radiant[n] because
he had spoken with the LORD. 30When
Aaron and all the Israelites saw Moses,
his face was radiant, and they were
afraid to come near him. 31But Moses
called to them; so Aaron and all the
leaders of the community[o] came back
to him, and he spoke to them.
32Afterwards all the Israelites came
near him, and he gave them all the
commands[p] the LORD had given him
on Mount Sinai.
33When Moses finished speaking to
them, he put a veil[q] over his face. 34But
whenever he entered the LORD's pres-
ence to speak with him, he removed the
veil until he came out. And when he
came out and told the Israelites what he
had been commanded, 35they saw that
his face was radiant.[r] Then Moses
would put the veil back over his face
until he went in to speak with the LORD.

Sabbath Regulations

35 Moses assembled the whole
Israelite community and said to
them, "These are the things the LORD
has commanded[a] you to do: 2For six
days, work is to be done, but the
seventh day shall be your holy day, a
Sabbath[b] of rest to the LORD. Whoever
does any work on it must be put to
death.[c] 3Do not light a fire in any of your
dwellings on the Sabbath day."[d]

10 [y]**Ex 33:16**
11 [z]Dt 6:25; Jos 11:15; [a]**Ex 23:28**
12 [b]Jdg 2:2; [c]**Ex 10:7**
13 [d]**Ex 23:24**; Nu 33:52; Dt 7:5; 12:3; Jdg 6:26; 1Ki 15:13; 2Ch 15:16; 17:6; 34:3–4; Mic 5:14
14 [e]**Ex 20:3**; [f]Isa 9:6; [g]**Ex 20:5**
15 [h]ver 12; Dt 23:6; Ezr 9:12; [i]Ex 22:20; 32:8; Dt 31:16; Jdg 2:17; 2Ki 17:8; 1Ch 5:25; 2Ch 11:15; Am 2:4; [j]**Ex 32:6**; 1Co 8:4
16 [k]Dt 7:3; 17:17; Jos 23:12; Jdg 3:6; 14:3; 1Ki 11:1,2; 16:31; Ezr 9:2; 10:3; Ne 10:30; 13:25–26; [l]Dt 7:4; 12:31; 20:18; 1Ki 11:4; 2Ki 21:3–15; Ps 106:34–41; Mal 2:11
17 [m]**Ex 20:4**
18 [n]**Ex 12:17**; Mt 26:17; Lk 22:1; Ac 12:3; [o]**Ex 12:15**; [p]**Ex 12:2**
19 [q]Ex 13:2
20 [r]**Ex 13:13**; [s]**Ex 13:2**; [t]**Ex 22:29**; Dt 16:16; Eze 46:9
21 [u]Ge 2:2–3; [v]Ne 13:15; Isa 56:2; 58:13
22 [w]ver 26; Ex 23:19; Lev 2:12,14; 7:13; 23:10,17; Nu 28:26; [x]**Ex 23:16**
23 [y]**Ex 23:14**
24 [z]**Ex 23:28**; [a]Dt 12:20; 19:8; Job 12:23
25 [b]**Ex 23:18**; [c]**Ex 12:8**
26 [d]**Ex 22:29**; **Nu 18:12**; [e]**Ex 23:19**
27 [f]**Ex 17:14**; [g]**Ge 6:18; 15:18**
28 [h]**Ge 7:4**; Mt 4:2; Lk 4:2; [i]Dt 9:9,18; Ezr 10:6; [j]ver 1; Ex 31:18; [k]Dt 4:13; 10:4
29 [l]**Ex 19:11**; [m]**Ex 32:15**; [n]ver 35; Ps 34:5; Isa 60:5; Mt 17:2; 2Co 3:7,13
31 [o]Ex 16:22
32 [p]**Ex 21:1**; 35:1,4
33 [q]2Co 3:13
35 [r]ver 29

Ch. 35
1 [a]**Ex 34:32**
2 [b]**Ge 2:3**; Ex 34:21; Dt 5:13–14; [c]**Ex 31:14**
3 [d]Ex 16:23

[a]13 That is, symbols of the goddess Asherah
[b]22 That is, in the autumn

Materials for the Tabernacle

35:4–9pp—Ex 25:1–7
35:10–19pp—Ex 39:32–41

4Moses said to the whole Israelite
community, "This is what the LORD has
commanded: 5From what you have,
take an offering for the LORD. Everyone
who is willing is to bring to the LORD an
offering of gold, silver and bronze;
6blue, purple and scarlet yarn and fine
linen; goat hair; 7ram skins dyed red and
hides of sea cows;[a] acacia wood; 8olive
oil[e] for the light; spices for the anointing
oil and for the fragrant incense; 9and
onyx stones and other gems to be
mounted on the ephod and breastpiece.
10"All who are skilled among you are
to come and make everything the LORD
has commanded:[f] 11the tabernacle[g] with
its tent and its covering, clasps, frames,
crossbars, posts and bases; 12the ark[h]
with its poles and the atonement cover
and the curtain[i] that shields it; 13the
table[j] with its poles and all its articles
and the bread of the Presence; 14the
lampstand[k] that is for light with its
accessories, lamps and oil for the light;
15the altar[l] of incense with its poles, the
anointing oil[m] and the fragrant incense;[n]
the curtain for the doorway at the en-
trance to the tabernacle;[o] 16the altar[p] of
burnt offering with its bronze grating,
its poles and all its utensils; the bronze
basin[q] with its stand; 17the curtains of
the courtyard with its posts and bases,
and the curtain for the entrance to the
courtyard;[r] 18the tent pegs[s] for the
tabernacle and for the courtyard, and
their ropes; 19the woven garments worn
for ministering in the sanctuary—both
the sacred garments[t] for Aaron the
priest and the garments for his sons
when they serve as priests."
20Then the whole Israelite community
withdrew from Moses' presence, 21and
everyone who was willing and whose
heart moved him came and brought an
offering to the LORD for the work on the
Tent of Meeting, for all its service, and
for the sacred garments. 22All who were
willing, men and women alike, came
and brought gold jewellery of all kinds:
brooches, ear-rings, rings and orna-
ments. They all presented their gold as a
wave offering to the LORD. 23Everyone
who had blue, purple or scarlet yarn[u] or
fine linen, or goat hair, ram skins dyed
red or hides of sea cows brought them.
24Those presenting an offering of silver
or bronze brought it as an offering to the
LORD, and everyone who had acacia
wood for any part of the work brought
it. 25Every skilled woman[v] spun with
her hands and brought what she had
spun—blue, purple or scarlet yarn or
fine linen. 26And all the women who
were willing and had the skill spun the
goat hair. 27The leaders[w] brought onyx
stones and other gems[x] to be mounted
on the ephod and breastpiece. 28They
also brought spices and olive oil for the
light and for the anointing oil and for
the fragrant incense.[y] 29All the Israelite
men and women who were willing[z]
brought to the LORD freewill offerings[a]
for all the work the LORD through Moses
had commanded them to do.

Bezalel and Oholiab

35:30–35pp—Ex 31:2–6

30Then Moses said to the Israelites,
"See, the LORD has chosen Bezalel son
of Uri, the son of Hur, of the tribe of
Judah, 31and he has filled him with the
Spirit of God, with skill, ability and
knowledge in all kinds of crafts[b]—32to
make artistic designs for work in gold,
silver and bronze, 33to cut and set
stones, to work in wood and to engage
in all kinds of artistic craftsmanship.
34And he has given both him and
Oholiab[c] son of Ahisamach, of the tribe
of Dan, the ability to teach[d] others. 35He
has filled them with skill to do all kinds
of work[e] as craftsmen, designers,
embroiderers in blue, purple and scarlet
yarn and fine linen, and weavers—all of
them master craftsmen and designers.

36

1So Bezalel, Oholiab and every
skilled person[a] to whom the
LORD has given skill and ability to know
how to carry out all the work of
constructing the sanctuary[b] are to
do the work just as the LORD has
commanded."
2Then Moses summoned Bezalel[c] and
Oholiab[d] and every skilled person to
whom the LORD had given ability and
who was willing[e] to come and do the
work. 3They received from Moses all the
offerings[f] the Israelites had brought to
carry out the work of constructing the
sanctuary. And the people continued to
bring freewill offerings morning after
morning. 4So all the skilled craftsmen
who were doing all the work on the
sanctuary left their work 5and said to
Moses, "The people are bringing more
than enough[g] for doing the work the
LORD commanded to be done."
6Then Moses gave an order and they

8 [e]**Ex 25:6**
10 [f]Ex 31:6; 39:43
11 [g]Ex 26:1–37; 36:8–38
12 [h]Ex 25:10–22; 37:1–9; [i]**Ex 26:33**
13 [j]Ex 25:23–30; 37:10–16
14 [k]**Ex 25:31**
15 [l]Ex 30:1–6; 37:25–28; [m]Ex 30:25; [n]Ex 30:34–38; [o]**Ex 26:36**
16 [p]Ex 27:1–8; 38:1–7; [q]**Ex 30:18**
17 [r]**Ex 27:9**; 38:9–20
18 [s]Ex 27:19; 38:20
19 [t]**Ex 28:2**
23 [u]Ex 39:1
25 [v]**Ex 28:3**
27 [w]**Ex 25:2**; 1Ch 29:6; [x]1Ch 29:8
28 [y]**Ex 25:6**
29 [z]**Ex 25:2**; [a]ver 4–9; Ex 25:1–7; 36:3; 2Ki 12:4
31 [b]ver 35; 2Ch 2:7,14
34 [c]**Ex 31:6**; [d]2Ch 2:14
35 [e]ver 31

Ch. 36

1 [a]Ex 28:3; [b]Ex 25:8
2 [c]**Ex 31:2**; [d]**Ex 31:6**; [e]**Ex 25:2**
3 [f]**Ex 35:29**
5 [g]2Ch 24:14; 31:10; 2Co 8:2–3

[a]7 That is, dugongs; also in verse 23

sent this word throughout the camp:
"No man or woman is to make anything
else as an offering for the sanctuary."
And so the people were restrained from
bringing more, 7because what they
already had was more[h] than enough to
do all the work.

The Tabernacle

36:8–38pp—Ex 26:1–37

8All the skilled men among the work-
men made the tabernacle with ten cur-
tains of finely twisted linen and blue,
purple and scarlet yarn, with cherubim
worked into them by a skilled crafts-
man. 9All the curtains were the same
size—twenty-eight cubits long and four
cubits wide.[a] 10They joined five of the
curtains together and did the same with
the other five. 11Then they made loops
of blue material along the edge of the
end curtain in one set, and the same was
done with the end curtain in the other
set. 12They also made fifty loops on one
curtain and fifty loops on the end cur-
tain of the other set, with the loops
opposite each other. 13Then they made
fifty gold clasps and used them to fasten
the two sets of curtains together so that
the tabernacle was a unit.[i]
14They made curtains of goat hair for
the tent over the tabernacle—eleven all
together. 15All eleven curtains were the
same size—thirty cubits long and four
cubits wide.[b] 16They joined five of the
curtains into one set and the other six
into another set. 17Then they made fifty
loops along the edge of the end curtain
in one set and also along the edge of the
end curtain in the other set. 18They
made fifty bronze clasps to fasten the
tent together as a unit.[j] 19Then they
made for the tent a covering of ram
skins dyed red, and over that a covering
of hides of sea cows.[c]
20They made upright frames of acacia
wood for the tabernacle. 21Each frame
was ten cubits long and a cubit and a
half wide,[d] 22with two projections set
parallel to each other. They made all the
frames of the tabernacle in this way.
23They made twenty frames for the
south side of the tabernacle 24and made
forty silver bases to go under them—
two bases for each frame, one under
each projection. 25For the other side, the
north side of the tabernacle, they made
twenty frames 26and forty silver bases
—two under each frame. 27They made
six frames for the far end, that is, the
west end of the tabernacle, 28and two
frames were made for the corners of the
tabernacle at the far end. 29At these two
corners the frames were double from
the bottom all the way to the top and
fitted into a single ring; both were made
alike. 30So there were eight frames and
sixteen silver bases—two under each
frame.
31They also made crossbars of acacia
wood: five for the frames on one side of
the tabernacle, 32five for those on the
other side, and five for the frames on the
west, at the far end of the tabernacle.
33They made the centre crossbar so that
it extended from end to end at the
middle of the frames. 34They overlaid
the frames with gold and made gold
rings to hold the crossbars. They also
overlaid the crossbars with gold.
35They made the curtain[k] of blue,
purple and scarlet yarn and finely
twisted linen, with cherubim worked
into it by a skilled craftsman. 36They
made four posts of acacia wood for it
and overlaid them with gold. They
made gold hooks for them and cast their
four silver bases. 37For the entrance to
the tent they made a curtain of blue,
purple and scarlet yarn and finely
twisted linen—the work of an
embroiderer;[l] 38and they made five
posts with hooks for them. They over-
laid the tops of the posts and their bands
with gold and made their five bases of
bronze.

The Ark

37:1–9pp—Ex 25:10–20

37 Bezalel[a] made the ark[b] of acacia
wood—two and a half cubits
long, a cubit and a half wide, and a cubit
and a half high.[a] 2He overlaid it with
pure gold,[c] both inside and out, and
made a gold moulding around it. 3He
cast four gold rings for it and fastened
them to its four feet, with two rings on
one side and two rings on the other.
4Then he made poles of acacia wood and
overlaid them with gold. 5And he
inserted the poles into the rings on
the sides of the ark to carry it.
6He made the atonement cover[d] of
pure gold—two and a half cubits long

7 [h]1Ki 7:47
13 [i]ver 18
18 [j]ver 13
35 [k]Ex 39:38; Mt 27:51; Lk 23:45; Heb 9:3
37 [l]Ex 27:16

Ch. 37

1 [a]**Ex 31:2;** [b]Ex 30:6; 39:35; Dt 10:3
2 [c]ver 11,26
6 [d]**Ex 26:34;** 31:7; Heb 9:5

[a]*9* That is, about 42 feet (about 13 metres) long and 6 feet (about 1.8 metres) wide

[b]*15* That is, about 45 feet (about 13.5 metres) long and 6 feet (about 1.8 metres) wide

[c]*19* That is, dugongs

[d]*21* That is, about 15 feet (about 4.5 metres) long and 2¼ feet (about 0.7 metre) wide

[a]*1* That is, about 3¾ feet (about 1.1 metres) long and 2¼ feet (about 0.7 metre) wide and high

and a cubit and a half wide.[b] 7Then he
made two cherubim[e] out of hammered
gold at the ends of the cover. 8He made
one cherub on one end and the second
cherub on the other; at the two ends he
made them of one piece with the cover.
9The cherubim had their wings spread
upwards, overshadowing[f] the cover
with them. The cherubim faced each
other, looking towards the cover.[g]

The Table

37:10–16pp—Ex 25:23–29

10They[c] made the table[h] of acacia
wood—two cubits long, a cubit wide,
and a cubit and a half high.[d] 11Then they
overlaid it with pure gold[i] and made a
gold moulding around it. 12They also
made around it a rim a handbreadth[e]
wide and put a gold moulding on the
rim. 13They cast four gold rings for the
table and fastened them to the four
corners, where the four legs were. 14The
rings[j] were put close to the rim to hold
the poles used in carrying the table.
15The poles for carrying the table were
made of acacia wood and were overlaid
with gold. 16And they made from pure
gold the articles for the table—its plates
and dishes and bowls and its pitchers
for the pouring out of drink offerings.

The Lampstand

37:17–24pp—Ex 25:31–39

17They made the lampstand[k] of pure
gold and hammered it out, base and
shaft; its flowerlike cups, buds and
blossoms were of one piece with it.
18Six branches extended from the sides
of the lampstand—three on one side
and three on the other. 19Three cups
shaped like almond flowers with buds
and blossoms were on one branch,
three on the next branch and the same
for all six branches extending from the
lampstand. 20And on the lampstand
were four cups shaped like almond
flowers with buds and blossoms. 21One
bud was under the first pair of branches
extending from the lampstand, a
second bud under the second pair, and
a third bud under the third pair—six
branches in all. 22The buds and the
branches were all of one piece with the
lampstand, hammered out of pure
gold.[l]
23They made its seven lamps,[m] as well
as its wick trimmers and trays, of pure
gold. 24They made the lampstand and
all its accessories from one talent[f] of
pure gold.

7 [e]Eze 41:18
9 [f]Heb 9:5; [g]Dt 10:3
10 [h]Heb 9:2
11 [i]ver 2
14 [j]ver 27
17 [k]Heb 9:2; Rev 1:12
22 [l]ver 17; Nu 8:4
23 [m]Ex 40:4,25
25 [n]Ex 30:34–36; Lk 1:11; Heb 9:4; Rev 8:3; [o]Ex 27:2; Rev 9:13
27 [p]ver 14
28 [q]Ex 25:13
29 [r]Ex 31:11; [s]Ex 30:1,25; 39:38

Ch. 38

2 [a]2Ch 1:5
3 [b]Ex 31:9
8 [c]Ex 30:18; 40:7; [d]Dt 23:17; 1Sa 2:22; 1Ki 14:24

The Altar of Incense

37:25–28pp—Ex 30:1–5

25They made the altar of incense[n] out
of acacia wood. It was square, a cubit
long and a cubit wide, and two cubits
high[g]—its horns[o] of one piece with it.
26They overlaid the top and all the sides
and the horns with pure gold, and made
a gold moulding around it. 27They made
two gold rings[p] below the moulding
—two on opposite sides—to hold the
poles used to carry it. 28They made the
poles of acacia wood and overlaid them
with gold.[q]
29They also made the sacred anoint-
ing oil[r] and the pure, fragrant incense[s]
—the work of a perfumer.

The Altar of Burnt Offering

38:1–7pp—Ex 27:1–8

38 They[a] built the altar of burnt
offering of acacia wood, three
cubits[b] high; it was square, five cubits
long and five cubits wide.[c] 2They made
a horn at each of the four corners, so
that the horns and the altar were of one
piece, and they overlaid the altar with
bronze.[a] 3They made all its utensils[b] of
bronze—its pots, shovels, sprinkling
bowls, meat forks and firepans. 4They
made a grating for the altar, a bronze
network, to be under its ledge, halfway
up the altar. 5They cast bronze rings to
hold the poles for the four corners of the
bronze grating. 6They made the poles of
acacia wood and overlaid them with
bronze. 7They inserted the poles into
the rings so they would be on the sides
of the altar for carrying it. They made it
hollow, out of boards.

Basin for Washing

8They made the bronze basin[c] and its
bronze stand from the mirrors of the
women[d] who served at the entrance to
the Tent of Meeting.

---

[b]6 That is, about 3¾ feet (about 1.1 metres) long and 2¼ feet (about 0.7 metre) wide
[c]10 Or *He*; also in verses 11–29
[d]10 That is, about 3 feet (about 0.9 metre) long, 1½ feet (about 0.5 metre) wide, and 2¼ feet (about 0.7 metre) high
[e]12 That is, about 3 inches (about 8 centimetres)
[f]24 That is, about 75 pounds (about 34 kilograms)
[g]25 That is, about 1½ feet (about 0.5 metre) long and wide, and about 3 feet (about 0.9 metre) high
[a]1 Or *He*; also in verses 2–9
[b]1 That is, about 4½ feet (about 1.4 metres)
[c]1 That is, about 7½ feet (about 2.3 metres) long and wide

The Courtyard

38:9–20pp—Ex 27:9–19

9Next they made the courtyard. The south side was a hundred cubits[d] long and had curtains of finely twisted linen, 10with twenty posts and twenty bronze bases, and with silver hooks and bands on the posts. 11The north side was also a hundred cubits long and had twenty posts and twenty bronze bases, with silver hooks and bands on the posts.

12The west end was fifty cubits[e] wide and had curtains, with ten posts and ten bases, with silver hooks and bands on the posts. 13The east end, towards the sunrise, was also fifty cubits wide. 14Curtains fifteen cubits[f] long were on one side of the entrance, with three posts and three bases, 15and curtains fifteen cubits long were on the other side of the entrance to the courtyard, with three posts and three bases. 16All the curtains around the courtyard were of finely twisted linen. 17The bases for the posts were bronze. The hooks and bands on the posts were silver, and their tops were overlaid with silver; so all the posts of the courtyard had silver bands.

18The curtain for the entrance to the courtyard was of blue, purple and scarlet yarn and finely twisted linen—the work of an embroiderer. It was twenty cubits[g] long and, like the curtains of the courtyard, five cubits[h] high, 19with four posts and four bronze bases. Their hooks and bands were silver, and their tops were overlaid with silver. 20All the tent pegs[e] of the tabernacle and of the surrounding courtyard were bronze.

The Materials Used

21These are the amounts of the materials used for the tabernacle, the tabernacle of the Testimony,[f] which were recorded at Moses' command by the Levites under the direction of Ithamar[g] son of Aaron, the priest. 22(Bezalel[h] son of Uri, the son of Hur, of the tribe of Judah, made everything the LORD commanded Moses; 23with him was Oholiab[i] son of Ahisamach, of the tribe of Dan—a craftsman and designer, and an embroiderer in blue, purple and scarlet yarn and fine linen.) 24The total amount of the gold from the wave offering used for all the work on the sanctuary[j] was 29 talents and 730 shekels,[i] according to the sanctuary shekel.[k]

25The silver obtained from those of the community who were counted in the census[l] was 100 talents and 1,775 shekels,[j] according to the sanctuary shekel—26one beka per person,[m] that is, half a shekel,[k] according to the sanctuary shekel,[n] from everyone who had crossed over to those counted, twenty years old or more,[o] a total of 603,550 men.[p] 27The 100 talents[l] of silver were used to cast the bases[q] for the sanctuary and for the curtain—100 bases from the 100 talents, one talent for each base. 28They used the 1,775 shekels[m] to make the hooks for the posts, to overlay the tops of the posts, and to make their bands.

29The bronze from the wave offering was 70 talents and 2,400 shekels.[n] 30They used it to make the bases for the entrance to the Tent of Meeting, the bronze altar with its bronze grating and all its utensils, 31the bases for the surrounding courtyard and those for its entrance and all the tent pegs for the tabernacle and those for the surrounding courtyard.

The Priestly Garments

39 From the blue, purple and scarlet yarn[a] they made woven garments for ministering in the sanctuary.[b] They also made sacred garments[c] for Aaron, as the LORD commanded Moses.

The Ephod

39:2–7pp—Ex 28:6–14

2They[a] made the ephod of gold, and of blue, purple and scarlet yarn, and of finely twisted linen. 3They hammered out thin sheets of gold and cut strands to be worked into the blue, purple and scarlet yarn and fine linen—the work of a skilled craftsman. 4They made shoulder pieces for the ephod, which were attached to two of its corners, so that it could be fastened. 5Its skilfully woven waistband was like it—of one piece with the ephod and made with gold, and with blue, purple and scarlet yarn, and with finely twisted linen, as the LORD commanded Moses.

20 *e*Ex 35:18
21 *f*Nu 1:50,53; 8:24; 9:15; 10:11; 17:7; 1Ch 23:32; 2Ch 24:6; Ac 7:44; Rev 15:5; *g*Nu 4:28,33
22 *h*Ex 31:2
23 *i*Ex 31:6
24 *j*Ex 30:16; *k*Ex 30:13
25 *l*Ex 30:12
26 *m*Ex 30:12; *n*Ex 30:13; *o*Ex 30:14; *p*Ex 12:37
27 *q*Ex 26:19

Ch. 39

1 *a*Ex 35:23; *b*Ex 35:19; *c*ver 41; Ex 28:2

d9 That is, about 150 feet (about 46 metres)
e12 That is, about 75 feet (about 23 metres)
f14 That is, about 22½ feet (about 6.9 metres)
g18 That is, about 30 feet (about 9 metres)
h18 That is, about 7½ feet (about 2.3 metres)
i24 The weight of the gold was about one ton (about 1 metric ton).
j25 The weight of the silver was a little over 3⅓ tons (about 3.4 metric tons).
k26 That is, about ⅕ ounce (about 6 grams)
l27 That is, about 3⅓ tons (about 3.4 metric tons)
m28 That is, about 45 pounds (about 20 kilograms)
n29 The weight of the bronze was about 2⅓ tons (about 2.4 metric tons).
a2 Or *He*; also in verses 7, 8, and 22

6They mounted the onyx stones in gold filigree settings and engraved them like a seal with the names of the sons of Israel. 7Then they fastened them on the shoulder pieces of the ephod as memorial[d] stones for the sons of Israel, as the LORD commanded Moses.

The Breastpiece

39:8–21pp—Ex 28:15–28

8They fashioned the breastpiece[e]—the work of a skilled craftsman. They made it like the ephod: of gold, and of blue, purple and scarlet yarn, and of finely twisted linen. 9It was square—a span[b] long and a span wide—and folded double. 10Then they mounted four rows of precious stones on it. In the first row there was a ruby, a topaz and a beryl; 11in the second row a turquoise, a sapphire[c] and an emerald; 12in the third row a jacinth, an agate and an amethyst; 13in the fourth row a chrysolite, an onyx and a jasper.[d] They were mounted in gold filigree settings. 14There were twelve stones, one for each of the names of the sons of Israel, each engraved like a seal with the name of one of the twelve tribes.[f]

15For the breastpiece they made braided chains of pure gold, like a rope. 16They made two gold filigree settings and two gold rings, and fastened the rings to two of the corners of the breastpiece. 17They fastened the two gold chains to the rings at the corners of the breastpiece, 18and the other ends of the chains to the two settings, attaching them to the shoulder pieces of the ephod at the front. 19They made two gold rings and attached them to the other two corners of the breastpiece on the inside edge next to the ephod. 20Then they made two more gold rings and attached them to the bottom of the shoulder pieces on the front of the ephod, close to the seam just above the waistband of the ephod. 21They tied the rings of the breastpiece to the rings of the ephod with blue cord, connecting it to the waistband so that the breastpiece would not swing out from the ephod—as the LORD commanded Moses.

Other Priestly Garments

39:22–31pp—Ex 28:31–43

22They made the robe of the ephod entirely of blue cloth—the work of a weaver—23with an opening in the centre of the robe like the opening of a collar,[e] and a band around this opening, so that it would not tear. 24They made pomegranates of blue, purple and scarlet yarn and finely twisted linen around the hem of the robe. 25And they made bells of pure gold and attached them around the hem between the pomegranates. 26The bells and pomegranates alternated around the hem of the robe to be worn for ministering, as the LORD commanded Moses.

27For Aaron and his sons, they made tunics of fine linen[g]—the work of a weaver—28and the turban[h] of fine linen, the linen headbands and the undergarments of finely twisted linen. 29The sash was of finely twisted linen and blue, purple and scarlet yarn—the work of an embroiderer—as the LORD commanded Moses.

30They made the plate, the sacred diadem, out of pure gold and engraved on it, like an inscription on a seal: HOLY TO THE LORD.[i] 31Then they fastened a blue cord to it to attach it to the turban,[j] as the LORD commanded Moses.

Moses Inspects the Tabernacle

39:32–41pp—Ex 35:10–19

32So all the work on the tabernacle, the Tent of Meeting, was completed. The Israelites did everything just as the LORD commanded Moses.[k] 33Then they brought the tabernacle[l] to Moses: the tent and all its furnishings, its clasps, frames, crossbars, posts and bases; 34the covering of ram skins dyed red, the covering of hides of sea cows[f] and the shielding curtain; 35the ark of the Testimony[m] with its poles and the atonement cover; 36the table[n] with all its articles and the bread of the Presence;[o] 37the pure gold lampstand[p] with its row of lamps and all its accessories,[q] and the oil[r] for the light; 38the gold altar,[s] the anointing oil,[t] the fragrant incense,[u] and the curtain[v] for the entrance to the tent; 39the bronze altar[w] with its bronze grating, its poles and all its utensils; the basin[x] with its stand; 40the curtains of the courtyard with its posts and bases, and the curtain for the entrance to the courtyard;[y] the ropes and tent pegs for the courtyard; all the furnishings for the tabernacle, the Tent of Meeting; 41and the woven garments[z] worn for ministering in the sanctuary, both the sacred garments for

7 [d]Lev 24:7; Jos 4:7
8 [e]Lev 8:8
14 [f]Rev 21:12
27 [g]Lev 6:10; 8:2
28 [h]ver 31; **Ex 28:4**; Lev 8:9; Isa 61:10
30 [i]Isa 23:18; Zec 14:20
31 [j]**ver 28**
32 [k]**Ex 25:9**
33 [l]Ex 25:8–40; 36:8–38
35 [m]**Ex 37:1**
36 [n]Ex 25:23–30; 37:10–16; [o]**Ex 25:30**
37 [p]**Ex 25:31**; [q]Ex 25:31–39; [r]**Ex 25:6**
38 [s]Ex 30:1–10; 37:25–28; [t]Ex 30:22–32; 37:29; [u]Ex 30:34–38; **37:29**; [v]**Ex 36:35**
39 [w]Ex 27:1–8; 38:1–7; [x]**Ex 30:18**
40 [y]Ex 27:9–19; 38:9–20
41 [z]**ver 1**

b9 That is, about 9 inches (about 23 centimetres)
c11 Or *lapis lazuli*
d13 The precise identification of some of these precious stones is uncertain.
e23 The meaning of the Hebrew for this word is uncertain.
f34 That is, dugongs

Aaron the priest and the garments for
his sons when serving as priests.
42The Israelites had done all the work
just as the LORD had commanded
Moses.[a] 43Moses inspected the work
and saw that they had done it just as
the LORD had commanded.[b] So Moses
blessed[c] them.

Setting Up the Tabernacle

40 Then the LORD said to Moses:
2"Set up[a] the tabernacle, the
Tent of Meeting,[b] on the first day of the
first month.[c] 3Place the ark[d] of the Testi-
mony in it and shield the ark with the
curtain. 4Bring in the table[e] and set out
what belongs on it.[f] Then bring in the
lampstand[g] and set up its lamps. 5Place
the gold altar[h] of incense in front of the
ark of the Testimony and put the curtain
at the entrance to the tabernacle.
6"Place the altar[i] of burnt offering in
front of the entrance to the tabernacle,
the Tent of Meeting; 7place the basin[j]
between the Tent of Meeting and the
altar and put water in it. 8Set up the
courtyard[k] around it and put the curtain
at the entrance to the courtyard.
9"Take the anointing oil and anoint[l]
the tabernacle and everything in it; con-
secrate it and all its furnishings,[m] and it
will be holy. 10Then anoint the altar of
burnt offering and all its utensils; con-
secrate[n] the altar, and it will be most
holy. 11Anoint the basin and its stand
and consecrate them.
12"Bring Aaron and his sons to the
entrance to the Tent of Meeting[o] and
wash them with water.[p] 13Then dress
Aaron in the sacred garments,[q] anoint
him and consecrate[r] him so that he may
serve me as priest. 14Bring his sons and
dress them in tunics.[s] 15Anoint them
just as you anointed their father, so that
they may serve me as priests. Their
anointing will be to a priesthood that
will continue for all generations to
come.[t]" 16Moses did everything just as
the LORD commanded[u] him.
17So the tabernacle[v] was set up on the
first day of the first month[w] in the
second year. 18When Moses[x] set up the
tabernacle, he put the bases in place,
erected the frames,[y] inserted the cross-
bars and set up the posts. 19Then he
spread the tent over the tabernacle and
put the covering[z] over the tent, as the
LORD commanded[a] him.
20He took the Testimony[b] and placed
it in the ark,[c] attached the poles to the
ark and put the atonement cover[d] over
it. 21Then he brought the ark into the
tabernacle and hung the shielding
curtain[e] and shielded the ark of the
Testimony, as the LORD commanded[f]
him.
22Moses placed the table[g] in the Tent
of Meeting on the north side of the
tabernacle outside the curtain 23and set
out the bread[h] on it before the LORD, as
the LORD commanded[i] him.
24He placed the lampstand[j] in the
Tent of Meeting opposite the table on
the south side of the tabernacle 25and set
up the lamps[k] before the LORD, as the
LORD commanded[l] him.
26Moses placed the gold altar[m] in the
Tent of Meeting in front of the curtain
27and burned fragrant incense on it, as
the LORD commanded[n] him. 28Then he
put up the curtain[o] at the entrance to the
tabernacle.
29He set the altar[p] of burnt offering
near the entrance to the tabernacle, the
Tent of Meeting, and offered on it burnt
offerings and grain offerings,[q] as the
LORD commanded[r] him.
30He placed the basin[s] between the
Tent of Meeting and the altar and put
water in it for washing, 31and Moses
and Aaron and his sons used it to wash[t]
their hands and feet. 32They washed
whenever they entered the Tent of
Meeting or approached the altar,[u] as the
LORD commanded[v] Moses.
33Then Moses set up the courtyard[w]
around the tabernacle and altar and put
up the curtain[x] at the entrance to the
courtyard. And so Moses finished the
work.

The Glory of the LORD

34Then the cloud[y] covered the Tent of
Meeting, and the glory[z] of the LORD
filled the tabernacle. 35Moses could not
enter the Tent of Meeting because the
cloud had settled upon it, and the glory[a]
of the LORD filled the tabernacle.[b]
36In all the travels of the Israelites,
whenever the cloud lifted from above
the tabernacle, they would set out;[c]
37but if the cloud did not lift, they did
not set out—until the day it lifted. 38So
the cloud[d] of the LORD was over the
tabernacle by day, and fire was in the
cloud by night, in the sight of all the
house of Israel during all their travels.

42 aEx 25:9
43 bEx 25:9; 35:10; cGe 31:55; Lev 9:22–23; Nu 6:23–27; Dt 21:5; 26:15; 2Sa 6:18; 1Ki 8:14,55; 1Ch 16:2; 2Ch 30:27

Ch. 40

2 aEx 26:30; bver 34,35; Lev 1:1; 3:2; 6:26; 9:23; 16:16; Nu 1:1; 7:89; 11:16; 17:4; 20:6; Jos 18:1; 19:51; Jer 7:12; cver 17; Ex 12:2; Nu 9:1
3 dEx 26:33
4 eEx 25:23; fEx 25:30; gEx 25:31
5 hEx 30:1
6 iEx 27:1; 2Ki 16:14; 2Ch 4:1
7 jEx 30:18
8 kEx 27:9
9 lEx 30:26; mNu 7:1
10 nEx 29:36
12 oNu 8:9; pEx 29:4; 30:19
13 qEx 28:41; rLev 8:12
14 sEx 28:40; Lev 10:5
15 tEx 29:9
16 uGe 6:22
17 vNu 7:1; wver 2
18 x2Ch 1:3; yEx 36:20–34
19 zEx 36:19; aGe 6:22
20 bEx 16:34; Heb 9:4; cEx 25:21; dEx 25:17–22; 26:34; 31:7
21 eEx 26:33; fGe 6:22
22 gEx 25:23
23 hEx 25:30; Lev 24:5–8; iGe 6:22
24 jEx 25:31
25 kEx 37:23; lGe 6:22
26 mEx 30:1
27 nGe 6:22
28 oEx 26:36
29 pEx 20:24; qEx 29:38–42; rGe 6:22
30 sver 7; Ex 30:18
31 tEx 30:19–21
32 uEx 30:20; vGe 6:22
33 wEx 27:9; 38:9–20; xEx 27:16

34 yEx 19:16; Lev 16:2; Nu 9:15–23; 1Ki 8:12; 2Ch 5:13; Isa 6:4; Eze 10:4; zEx 16:7; Jn 1:14; 12:41; Rev 15:8
35 aEx 16:10; b1Ki 8:11; 2Ch 5:13–14; 7:2
36 cNu 9:17–23; 10:13
38 dEx 13:21; 1Co 10:1

Leviticus

The Burnt Offering

1 The LORD called to Moses[a] and spoke to him from the Tent of Meeting.[b] He said, 2"Speak to the Israelites and say to them: 'When any of you brings an offering to the LORD,[c] bring as your offering an animal from either the herd or the flock.[d]

3" 'If the offering is a burnt offering[e] from the herd,[f] he is to offer a male without defect.[g] He must present it at the entrance to the Tent[h] of Meeting so that it[a] will be acceptable[i] to the LORD. 4He is to lay his hand on the head[j] of the burnt offering,[k] and it will be accepted[l] on his behalf to make atonement[m] for him. 5He is to slaughter[n] the young bull[o] before the LORD, and then Aaron's sons[p] the priests shall bring the blood and sprinkle it against the altar on all sides[q] at the entrance to the Tent of Meeting. 6He is to skin[r] the burnt offering and cut it into pieces.[s] 7The sons of Aaron the priest are to put fire on the altar and arrange wood[t] on the fire. 8Then Aaron's sons the priests shall arrange the pieces, including the head and the fat,[u] on the burning wood[v] that is on the altar. 9He is to wash the inner parts and the legs with water,[w] and the priest is to burn all of it[x] on the altar.[y] It is a burnt offering,[z] an offering made by fire,[a] an aroma pleasing to the LORD.[b]

10" 'If the offering is a burnt offering from the flock, from either the sheep[c] or the goats,[d] he is to offer a male without defect. 11He is to slaughter it at the north side of the altar[e] before the LORD, and Aaron's sons the priests shall sprinkle its blood against the altar on all sides.[f] 12He is to cut it into pieces, and the priest shall arrange them, including the head and the fat,[g] on the burning wood that is on the altar. 13He is to wash the inner parts and the legs with water,[h] and the priest is to bring all of it and burn it[i] on the altar.[j] It is a burnt offering,[k] an offering made by fire, an aroma pleasing to the LORD.

14" 'If the offering to the LORD is a burnt offering of birds, he is to offer a dove or a young pigeon.[l] 15The priest shall bring it to the altar, wring off the head[m] and burn it on the altar; its blood shall be drained out on the side of the altar.[n] 16He is to remove the crop with its contents[b] and throw it to the east side of the altar, where the ashes[o] are. 17He shall tear it open by the wings, not severing it completely,[p] and then the priest shall burn it on the wood[q] that is on the fire on the altar. It is a burnt offering, an offering made by fire, an aroma pleasing to the LORD.

The Grain Offering

2 " 'When someone brings a grain offering[a] to the LORD, his offering is to be of fine flour.[b] He is to pour oil[c] on it,[d] put incense on it[e] 2and take it to Aaron's sons the priests. The priest shall take a handful of the fine flour[f] and oil, together with all the incense,[g] and burn this as a memorial portion[h] on the altar, an offering made by fire,[i] an aroma pleasing to the LORD.[j] 3The rest of the grain offering belongs to Aaron and his sons;[k] it is a most holy[l] part of the offerings made to the LORD by fire.

4" 'If you bring a grain offering baked in an oven,[m] it is to consist of fine flour: cakes made without yeast and mixed with oil, or[a] wafers[n] made without yeast and spread with oil.[o] 5If your grain offering is prepared on a griddle,[p] it is to be made of fine flour mixed with oil, and without yeast. 6Crumble it and pour oil on it; it is a grain offering. 7If your grain

Ch. 1

1 [a]**Ex 3:4; 25:22;** [b]**Ex 27:21; 40:2**
2 [c]Lev 7:16,38; 22:21; 23:38; 27:9; [d]Lev 22:18–19; Nu 15:3
3 [e]**Ge 8:20;** [f]ver 10; Lev 22:27; Ezr 8:35; Mal 1:8; [g]**ver 5; Ex 12:5; Lev 22:19,**20; Heb 9:14; 1Pe 1:19; [h]Lev 6:25; 17:9; Nu 6:16; Dt 12:5–6,11; [i]Isa 58:5
4 [j]**Ex 29:10,**15; [k]ver 3; Lev 4:29; 6:25; Eze 45:15; [l]**Ge 32:20;** [m]**Ex 29:36; 32:30**
5 [n]Ex 29:11; Lev 3:2,8; [o]**ver 3;** Ex 29:1; Nu 15:8; Dt 18:3; Ps 50:9; 69:31; [p]Lev 8:2; 10:6; 21:1; [q]**Ex 29:20;** Heb 12:24; 1Pe 1:2
6 [r]Lev 7:8; [s]Ex 29:17
7 [t]ver 17; **Ge 22:9;** Lev 3:5; 6:12
8 [u]ver 12; **Ex 29:13;** Lev 8:20; [v]Lev 9:13
9 [w]**Ex 29:17;** [x]Lev 6:22; [y]ver 13; Ex 29:18; Lev 9:14; [z]ver 3; [a]Lev 23:8,25, 36; Nu 28:6, 19; [b]ver 13; Ge 8:21; Lev 2:2; 3:5,16; 17:6; Nu 18:17; 28:11–13; Eph 5:2
10 [c]**Ge 22:7;** [d]**ver 3;** Ex 12:5; Lev 3:12; 4:23,28; 5:6; Nu 15:11
11 [e]**Ex 29:11;** [f]**Ex 29:20**
12 [g]**ver 8**
13 [h]**Ex 29:17;** [i]Lev 6:22; [j]**ver 9;** [k]Dt 12:27
14 [l]Ge 15:9; Lk 2:24
15 [m]Lev 5:8; [n]Lev 5:9
16 [o]Lev 4:12; 6:10; Nu 4:13
17 [p]**Ge 15:10;** [q]**ver 7**

Ch. 2

1 [a]**Ex 29:41;** Lev 6:14–18; [b]Ex 29:2,40; Lev 5:11; [c]Nu 15:4; 28:5; [d]**Ex 29:2;** Lev 7:12; [e]ver 2,15–16; Lev 24:7; Ne 13:9; Isa 43:23
2 [f]Lev 5:11; [g]Lev 6:15; Isa 1:13; 65:3; 66:3; [h]ver 9,16; Lev 5:12; 6:15; 24:7; Nu 5:26; 18:8; Ps 16:5; 73:26; Isa 53:12; [i]ver 16; [j]**Lev 1:9**
3 [k]ver 10; Lev 6:16; 10:12–13; [l]**Ex 30:36**
4 [m]Lev 7:9; 26:26; [n]Lev 7:12; 8:26; [o]**Ex 29:2**
5 [p]Lev 6:21; 7:9; Eze 4:3

---

[a]3 Or *he*
[b]16 Or *crop and the feathers;* the meaning of the Hebrew for this word is uncertain.
[a]4 Or *and*

offering is cooked in a pan,[q] it is to be made of fine flour and oil. 8Bring the grain offering made of these things to the LORD; present it to the priest, who shall take it to the altar. 9He shall take out the memorial portion[r] from the grain offering and burn it on the altar as an offering made by fire, an aroma pleasing to the LORD.[s] 10The rest of the grain offering belongs to Aaron and his sons;[t] it is a most holy part of the offerings made to the LORD by fire.[u]

11" 'Every grain offering you bring to the LORD must be made without yeast,[v] for you are not to burn any yeast or honey in an offering made to the LORD by fire. 12You may bring them to the LORD as an offering of the firstfruits,[w] but they are not to be offered on the altar as a pleasing aroma. 13Season all your grain offerings with salt.[x] Do not leave the salt of the covenant[y] of your God out of your grain offerings; add salt to all your offerings.

14" 'If you bring a grain offering of firstfruits[z] to the LORD, offer crushed heads of new grain roasted in the fire. 15Put oil and incense[a] on it; it is a grain offering. 16The priest shall burn the memorial portion[b] of the crushed grain and the oil, together with all the incense,[c] as an offering made to the LORD by fire.[d]

The Fellowship Offering

3 " 'If someone's offering is a fellowship offering,[a a] and he offers an animal from the herd, whether male or female, he is to present before the LORD an animal without defect.[b] 2He is to lay his hand on the head[c] of his offering and slaughter it[d] at the entrance to the Tent of Meeting.[e] Then Aaron's sons the priests shall sprinkle[f] the blood against the altar[g] on all sides.[h] 3From the fellowship offering he is to bring a sacrifice made to the LORD by fire: all the fat[i] that covers the inner parts[j] or is connected to them, 4both kidneys[k] with the fat around them near the loins, and the covering of the liver, which he will remove with the kidneys. 5Then Aaron's sons[l] are to burn it on the altar[m] on top of the burnt offering[n] that is on the burning wood,[o] as an offering made by fire, an aroma pleasing to the LORD.[p]

6" 'If he offers an animal from the flock as a fellowship offering[q] to the LORD, he is to offer a male or female without defect. 7If he offers a lamb,[r] he is to present it before the LORD.[s] 8He is to lay his hand on the head of his offering and slaughter it[t] in front of the Tent of Meeting. Then Aaron's sons shall sprinkle its blood against the altar on all sides. 9From the fellowship offering he is to bring a sacrifice[u] made to the LORD by fire: its fat, the entire fat tail cut off close to the backbone, all the fat that covers the inner parts or is connected to them, 10both kidneys with the fat on them near the loins, and the covering of the liver, which he will remove with the kidneys. 11The priest shall burn them on the altar[v] as food,[w] an offering made to the LORD by fire.[x]

12" 'If his offering is a goat,[y] he is to present it before the LORD. 13He is to lay his hand on its head and slaughter it in front of the Tent of Meeting. Then Aaron's sons shall sprinkle[z] its blood against the altar on all sides.[a] 14From what he offers he is to make this offering to the LORD by fire: all the fat that covers the inner parts or is connected to them, 15both kidneys with the fat on them near the loins, and the covering of the liver, which he will remove with the kidneys.[b] 16The priest shall burn them on the altar[c] as food,[d] an offering made by fire, a pleasing aroma.[e] All the fat[f] is the LORD's.[g]

17" 'This is a lasting ordinance[h] for the generations to come,[i] wherever you live:[j] You must not eat any fat or any blood.[k]' "

The Sin Offering

4 The LORD said to Moses, 2"Say to the Israelites: 'When anyone sins unintentionally[a] and does what is forbidden in any of the LORD's commands[b]—

3" 'If the anointed priest[c] sins,[d] bringing guilt on the people, he must bring to the LORD a young bull[e] without defect[f] as a sin offering[g] for the sin he has committed.[h] 4He is to present the bull at the entrance to the Tent of Meeting before the LORD.[i] He is to lay his hand on its head and slaughter it before the LORD. 5Then the anointed priest shall take some of the bull's blood[j] and carry it into the Tent of Meeting. 6He is to dip his finger into the blood and sprinkle[k]

7 [q]Lev 7:9
9 [r]ver 2; [s]Ge 8:21
10 [t]ver 3; [u]Ezr 2:63
11 [v]Ex 23:18; Lev 6:16
12 [w]Ex 34:22
13 [x]Mk 9:49; [y]Nu 18:19; 2Ch 13:5; Eze 43:24
14 [z]Ex 34:22; Nu 15:20; Dt 16:13; 26:2; Ru 3:2
15 [a]ver 1
16 [b]ver 2; [c]ver 1; [d]Nu 4:16; Jer 14:12

Ch. 3

1 [a]ver 6; Ex 32:6; Lev 7:11–34; 17:5; [b]Ex 12:5
2 [c]Ex 29:15; Nu 8:10; [d]Lev 1:5; [e]Ex 40:2; [f]Ex 24:6; [g]Lev 17:6; Nu 18:17; [h]Ex 29:20
3 [i]Ex 29:13; [j]Ex 12:9
4 [k]ver 10; Ex 29:13; Lev 4:9
5 [l]Lev 7:29–34; [m]ver 11,16; [n]Ex 29:13, 38–42; Nu 28:3–10; [o]Lev 1:7; [p]Lev 1:9
6 [q]ver 1; Lev 22:21; Nu 15:3,8
7 [r]Lev 17:3; Nu 15:5; 28:5,7–8; [s]Lev 17:8–9; 1Ki 8:62
8 [t]Lev 1:5
9 [u]Isa 34:6; Jer 46:10; Eze 39:19; Zep 1:7
11 [v]ver 5; [w]ver 16; Lev 21:6, 17; Nu 28:2; [x]Lev 9:18
12 [y]Lev 1:10; 4:3
13 [z]Ex 24:6; [a]Lev 1:5
15 [b]Lev 7:4
16 [c]ver 5; Lev 7:31; [d]ver 11; [e]Lev 1:9; [f]Ge 4:4; [g]1Sa 2:16
17 [h]Ex 12:14; 27:21; [i]Ge 9:12; [j]Ex 12:20; [k]Ge 9:4; Lev 7:25–26; 17:10–16; Dt 12:16; Ac 15:20

Ch. 4

2 [a]ver 13,27; Lev 5:15–18; 22:14; Nu 15:24–29; 35:11–15; Jos 20:3,9; Heb 9:7; [b]ver 22; Nu 15:22
3 [c]Ex 28:41; [d]Ge 18:23; [e]ver 14; Lev 3:12; 8:14; 10:16; 16:3,5; Nu 15:27; Ps 66:15; Eze 43:19,23; [f]Ex 12:5; [g]ver 24; Ex 30:10; Lev 5:6–13; 9:2–22; Heb 9:13–14; [h]ver 32
4 [i]ver 15,24; Lev 1:3; Nu 8:12
5 [j]ver 16; Lev 16:14
6 [k]Ex 24:8

[a]*1* Traditionally *peace offering;* also in verses 3, 6 and 9

some of it seven times before the LORD,[l]
in front of the curtain of the sanctuary.[m]
7The priest shall then put some of the
blood on the horns[n] of the altar of frag-
rant incense that is before the LORD in
the Tent of Meeting. The rest of the
bull's blood he shall pour out at the base
of the altar[o] of burnt offering[p] at the
entrance to the Tent of Meeting. 8He
shall remove all the fat[q] from the bull of
the sin offering—the fat that covers the
inner parts or is connected to them,
9both kidneys with the fat on them near
the loins, and the covering of the liver,
which he will remove with the kidneys[r]
—10just as the fat is removed from the
ox[a][s] sacrificed as a fellowship offering.[b][t]
Then the priest shall burn them on the
altar of burnt offering.[u] 11But the hide of
the bull and all its flesh, as well as the
head and legs, the inner parts and offal[v]
—12that is, all the rest of the bull—he
must take outside the camp[w] to a place
ceremonially clean,[x] where the ashes[y]
are thrown, and burn it[z] in a wood fire
on the ash heap.[a]

13"'If the whole Israelite community
sins unintentionally[b] and does what is
forbidden in any of the LORD's com-
mands, even though the community is
unaware of the matter, they are guilty.
14When they become aware of the sin
they committed, the assembly must
bring a young bull[c] as a sin offering[d] and
present it before the Tent of Meeting.
15The elders[e] of the community are to lay
their hands[f] on the bull's head[g] before
the LORD, and the bull shall be slaugh-
tered before the LORD.[h] 16Then the
anointed priest is to take some of the
bull's blood[i] into the Tent of Meeting.
17He shall dip his finger into the blood
and sprinkle[j] it before the LORD[k] seven
times in front of the curtain. 18He is to
put some of the blood[l] on the horns of
the altar that is before the LORD[m] in the
Tent of Meeting. The rest of the blood
he shall pour out at the base of the altar[n]
of burnt offering at the entrance to the
Tent of Meeting. 19He shall remove all
the fat[o] from it and burn it on the altar,[p]
20and do with this bull just as he did
with the bull for the sin offering. In this
way the priest will make atonement[q] for
them, and they will be forgiven.[r] 21Then
he shall take the bull outside the camp[s]
and burn it as he burned the first
bull. This is the sin offering for the
community.[t]

22"'When a leader[u] sins uninten-
tionally[v] and does what is forbidden in
any of the commands of the LORD his
God, he is guilty. 23When he is made
aware of the sin he committed, he must
bring as his offering a male goat[w] with-
out defect. 24He is to lay his hand on the
goat's head and slaughter it at the place
where the burnt offering is slaughtered
before the LORD.[x] It is a sin offering.[y]
25Then the priest shall take some of the
blood of the sin offering with his finger
and put it on the horns of the altar[z] of
burnt offering and pour out the rest of
the blood at the base of the altar.[a] 26He
shall burn all the fat on the altar as he
burned the fat of the fellowship offer-
ing. In this way the priest will make
atonement[b] for the man's sin, and he
will be forgiven.[c]

27"'If a member of the community
sins unintentionally[d] and does what is
forbidden in any of the LORD's com-
mands, he is guilty. 28When he is made
aware of the sin he committed, he must
bring as his offering[e] for the sin he com-
mitted a female goat[f] without defect.
29He is to lay his hand on the head[g] of
the sin offering[h] and slaughter it at the
place of the burnt offering.[i] 30Then the
priest is to take some of the blood with
his finger and put it on the horns of the
altar of burnt offering[j] and pour out the
rest of the blood at the base of the altar.
31He shall remove all the fat, just as
the fat is removed from the fellowship
offering, and the priest shall burn it
on the altar[k] as an aroma pleasing to the
LORD.[l] In this way the priest will make
atonement[m] for him, and he will be
forgiven.[n]

32"'If he brings a lamb[o] as his sin
offering, he is to bring a female without
defect.[p] 33He is to lay his hand on its
head and slaughter it[q] for a sin offering[r]
at the place where the burnt offering is
slaughtered.[s] 34Then the priest shall
take some of the blood of the sin offer-
ing with his finger and put it on the
horns of the altar of burnt offering and
pour out the rest of the blood at the base
of the altar.[t] 35He shall remove all the
fat, just as the fat is removed from the
lamb of the fellowship offering, and the
priest shall burn it on the altar[u] on top of
the offerings made to the LORD by fire.
In this way the priest will make atone-
ment for him for the sin he has commit-
ted, and he will be forgiven.

6 [l]ver 17; Lev 16:14,19; [m]**Ex 25:8**
7 [n]**Ex 27:2;** [o]ver 34; **Ex 29:12;** Lev 8:15; [p]ver 18,30; Lev 5:9; 9:9; 16:18
8 [q]ver 19
9 [r]**Lev 3:4**
10 [s]Lev 9:4; [t]**Ex 32:6;** [u]**Ex 29:13**
11 [v]Ex 29:14; Lev 8:17; 9:11; Nu 19:5
12 [w]**Ex 29:14;** Lev 8:17; 9:11; Heb 13:11; [x]Lev 6:11; 10:14; Nu 19:9; [y]**Lev 1:16;** [z]Lev 6:30; [a]Lev 16:3
13 [b]**ver 2**
14 [c]**ver 3;** [d]Nu 15:24
15 [e]**Ex 3:16; 19:7;** [f]2Ch 29:23; [g]**Ex 29:10;** Lev 8:14,22; Nu 8:10; [h]**ver 4**
16 [i]**ver 5**
17 [j]Nu 19:4,18; [k]**ver 6**
18 [l]Lev 8:15; 17:6; 2Ch 29:22; [m]ver 7; Lev 6:30; 10:18; [n]Lev 5:9
19 [o]ver 8; [p]ver 26
20 [q]**Ex 29:36; 32:30; Ro 3:25;** Heb 10:10–12; [r]ver 26,31, 35; Nu 15:25
21 [s]**ver 12;** [t]Lev 16:5,15; 2Ch 29:21
22 [u]Nu 31:13; [v]ver 2
23 [w]**ver 3; Lev 1:10**
24 [x]**ver 4;** [y]**ver 3;** Lev 6:25
25 [z]Lev 16:18; Eze 43:20,22; [a]Lev 9:9
26 [b]**Ex 32:30;** [c]Lev 5:10; 12:8
27 [d]**ver 2**
28 [e]Lev 5:6; Eze 40:39; 44:27; [f]**ver 3; Lev 1:10**
29 [g]ver 4,24; [h]**Lev 1:4;** [i]**Ge 8:20**
30 [j]**ver 7**
31 [k]ver 35; [l]**Ge 8:21;** [m]Lev 1:4; [n]**ver 20**
32 [o]Ex 29:38; Lev 9:3; 14:10; [p]Lev 1:3
33 [q]Lev 1:5; [r]Lev 1:4; [s]ver 29
34 [t]**ver 7**
35 [u]ver 31

[a]*10* The Hebrew word can include both male and female.
[b]*10* Traditionally *peace offering;* also in verses 26, 31 and 35

5 "'If a person sins because he does not speak up when he hears a public charge to testify[a] regarding something he has seen or learned about, he will be held responsible.[b]

2"'Or if a person touches anything ceremonially unclean—whether the carcasses of unclean wild animals or of unclean livestock or of unclean creatures that move along the ground[c]—even though he is unaware of it, he has become unclean[d] and is guilty.

3"'Or if he touches human uncleanness[e]—anything that would make him unclean[f]—even though he is unaware of it, when he learns of it he will be guilty.

4"'Or if a person thoughtlessly takes an oath[g] to do anything, whether good or evil[h]—in any matter one might carelessly swear about—even though he is unaware of it, in any case when he learns of it he will be guilty.

5"'When anyone is guilty in any of these ways, he must confess[i] in what way he has sinned 6and, as a penalty for the sin he has committed, he must bring to the LORD a female lamb or goat[j] from the flock as a sin offering;[k] and the priest shall make atonement[l] for him for his sin.

7"'If he cannot afford[m] a lamb,[n] he is to bring two doves or two young pigeons[o] to the LORD as a penalty for his sin—one for a sin offering and the other for a burnt offering. 8He is to bring them to the priest, who shall first offer the one for the sin offering. He is to wring its head from its neck,[p] not severing it completely,[q] 9and is to sprinkle[r] some of the blood of the sin offering against the side of the altar;[s] the rest of the blood must be drained out at the base of the altar.[t] It is a sin offering. 10The priest shall then offer the other as a burnt offering in the prescribed way[u] and make atonement[v] for him for the sin he has committed, and he will be forgiven.[w]

11"'If, however, he cannot afford[x] two doves or two young pigeons,[y] he is to bring as an offering for his sin a tenth of an ephah[a][z] of fine flour[a] for a sin offering. He must not put oil or incense on it, because it is a sin offering. 12He is to bring it to the priest, who shall take a handful of it as a memorial portion[b] and burn it on the altar[c] on top of the offerings made to the LORD by fire. It is a sin offering. 13In this way the priest will make atonement[d] for him for any of these sins he has committed, and he will be forgiven. The rest of the offering will belong to the priest,[e] as in the case of the grain offering.[f]'"

The Guilt Offering

14The LORD said to Moses: 15"When a person commits a violation and sins unintentionally[g] in regard to any of the LORD's holy things, he is to bring to the LORD as a penalty[h] a ram[i] from the flock, one without defect and of the proper value in silver, according to the sanctuary shekel.[b][j] It is a guilt offering.[k] 16He must make restitution[l] for what he has failed to do in regard to the holy things, add a fifth of the value[m] to that and give it all to the priest, who will make atonement for him with the ram as a guilt offering, and he will be forgiven.

17"If a person sins and does what is forbidden in any of the LORD's commands, even though he does not know it,[n] he is guilty and will be held responsible.[o] 18He is to bring to the priest as a guilt offering[p] a ram from the flock, one without defect and of the proper value. In this way the priest will make atonement for him for the wrong he has committed unintentionally, and he will be forgiven.[q] 19It is a guilt offering; he has been guilty of[c] wrongdoing against the LORD."[r]

6 The LORD said to Moses: 2"If anyone sins and is unfaithful to the LORD[a] by deceiving his neighbour[b] about something entrusted to him or left in his care[c] or stolen, or if he cheats[d] him, 3or if he finds lost property and lies about it,[e] or if he swears falsely,[f] or if he commits any such sin that people may do—4when he thus sins and becomes guilty, he must return[g] what he has stolen or taken by extortion, or what was entrusted to him, or the lost property he found, 5or whatever it was he swore falsely about. He must make restitution[h] in full, add a fifth of the value to it and give it all to the owner on the day he presents his guilt offering.[i] 6And as a penalty he must bring to the priest, that is, to the LORD, his guilt offering,[j] a ram from the flock, one without defect and of the proper value.[k] 7In this way the priest will make atonement[l]

Ch. 5

1 [a]Pr 29:24; Mt 26:63; [b]ver 17; **Ex 28:38;** Lev 7:18; 17:16; 19:8; 20:17; 24:15; Nu 5:31; 9:13; 15:31; 19:20; 30:15
2 [c]Lev 11:11, 24–40; Dt 14:8; Isa 52:11; [d]ver 3; Lev 7:21; 11:8,24; 13:45; Nu 19:22; Job 15:16; Ps 51:5; Isa 6:5; 64:6; Eze 36:17; Hag 2:13
3 [e]Nu 19:11–16; [f]Lev 7:20; 11:25; 14:19; 21:1; Nu 5:2; 9:6; 19:7; Eze 44:25
4 [g]Nu 30:6,8; [h]Isa 41:23
5 [i]Lev 16:21; 26:40; Nu 5:7; Jos 7:19; 1Ki 8:47; Pr 28:13
6 [j]**Lev 1:10; 4:3;** [k]**Lev 4:28;** [l]**Ex 32:30**
7 [m]ver 11; Lev 12:8; 14:21; 27:8; [n]Lev 12:8; 14:22,30; [o]**Ge 15:9;** Nu 6:10
8 [p]Lev 1:15; [q]Lev 1:17
9 [r]**Ex 24:6;** [s]Lev 1:15; [t]**Lev 4:7**
10 [u]Lev 1:14–17; 1Ch 15:13; [v]**Ex 32:30;** [w]**Lev 4:26**
11 [x]**ver 7;** [y]**Ge 15:9;** [z]**Ex 16:36;** [a]**Lev 2:1**
12 [b]**Lev 2:2;** [c]Lev 2:9
13 [d]**Ex 32:30;** [e]Lev 2:3; [f]**Ex 29:41**
15 [g]**Lev 4:2;** [h]Lev 22:14; [i]**Ex 29:3;** Lev 6:6; Nu 5:8; 6:14; 15:6; 28:11; [j]**Ex 30:13;** [k]ver 16, 18; Lev 6:5–6; 7:1,6–10; 14:12–17; 19:21–22; Nu 6:12; 18:9; 1Sa 6:3; Ezr 10:19; Isa 53:10
16 [l]Lev 6:4; [m]ver 15; Lev 27:13; Nu 5:7
17 [n]ver 15; [o]**ver 1**
18 [p]Lev 6:6; 14:12; [q]**ver 15**
19 [r]2Ki 12:16

Ch. 6

2 [a]Nu 5:6; Ps 73:27; Ac 5:4; Col 3:9; [b]Lev 19:11; Jer 9:4–5; [c]**Ex 22:7;** [d]**Ge 31:7**
3 [e]**Ex 23:4;** [f]**Ex 22:11**
4 [g]Lev 5:16; Eze 33:15; **Lk 19:8**
5 [h]Nu 5:7; [i]**Lev 5:15**
6 [j]**Lev 5:15;** [k]Nu 5:8
7 [l]**Ex 32:30**

[a]*11* That is, probably about 4 pints (about 2 litres)
[b]*15* That is, about ⅔ ounce (about 11.5 grams)
[c]*19* Or *has made full expiation for his*

for him before the LORD, and he will be forgiven for any of these things he did that made him guilty."

The Burnt Offering

8The LORD said to Moses: 9"Give Aaron and his sons this command: 'These are the regulations for the burnt offering[m]: The burnt offering is to remain on the altar hearth throughout the night, till morning, and the fire must be kept burning on the altar.[n] 10The priest shall then put on his linen clothes,[o] with linen undergarments next to his body,[p] and shall remove the ashes[q] of the burnt offering that the fire has consumed on the altar and place them beside the altar. 11Then he is to take off these clothes and put on others, and carry the ashes outside the camp to a place that is ceremonially clean.[r] 12The fire on the altar must be kept burning; it must not go out. Every morning the priest is to add firewood[s] and arrange the burnt offering on the fire and burn the fat[t] of the fellowship offerings[a][u] on it. 13The fire must be kept burning on the altar continuously; it must not go out.

The Grain Offering

14" 'These are the regulations for the grain offering:[v] Aaron's sons are to bring it before the LORD, in front of the altar. 15The priest is to take a handful of fine flour and oil, together with all the incense[w] on the grain offering,[x] and burn the memorial portion[y] on the altar as an aroma pleasing to the LORD. 16Aaron and his sons[z] shall eat the rest[a] of it, but it is to be eaten without yeast[b] in a holy place;[c] they are to eat it in the courtyard[d] of the Tent of Meeting.[e] 17It must not be baked with yeast; I have given it as their share[f] of the offerings made to me by fire.[g] Like the sin offering and the guilt offering, it is most holy.[h] 18Any male descendant of Aaron may eat it.[i] It is his regular share[j] of the offerings made to the LORD by fire for the generations to come.[k] Whatever touches it will become holy.[b][l] ' "

19The LORD also said to Moses, 20"This is the offering Aaron and his sons are to bring to the LORD on the day he[c] is anointed:[m] a tenth of an ephah[d][n] of fine flour[o] as a regular grain offering,[p] half of it in the morning and half in the evening. 21Prepare it with oil on a griddle;[q] bring it well-mixed and present the grain offering broken[e] in pieces as an aroma pleasing to the LORD. 22The son who is to succeed him as anointed priest[r] shall prepare it. It is the LORD's regular share and is to be burned completely.[s] 23Every grain offering of a priest shall be burned completely; it must not be eaten."

The Sin Offering

24The LORD said to Moses, 25"Say to Aaron and his sons: 'These are the regulations for the sin offering:[t] The sin offering is to be slaughtered before the LORD[u] in the place[v] where the burnt offering is slaughtered; it is most holy. 26The priest who offers it shall eat it; it is to be eaten in a holy place,[w] in the courtyard[x] of the Tent of Meeting.[y] 27Whatever touches any of the flesh will become holy,[z] and if any of the blood is spattered on a garment, you must wash it in a holy place. 28The clay pot[a] that the meat is cooked in must be broken; but if it is cooked in a bronze pot, the pot is to be scoured and rinsed with water. 29Any male in a priest's family may eat it;[b] it is most holy.[c] 30But any sin offering whose blood is brought into the Tent of Meeting to make atonement[d] in the Holy Place[e] must not be eaten; it must be burned.[f]

The Guilt Offering

7 " 'These are the regulations for the guilt offering,[a] which is most holy: 2The guilt offering is to be slaughtered in the place where the burnt offering is slaughtered, and its blood is to be sprinkled against the altar on all sides. 3All its fat[b] shall be offered: the fat tail and the fat that covers the inner parts, 4both kidneys with the fat on them near the loins, and the covering of the liver, which is to be removed with the kidneys.[c] 5The priest shall burn them on the altar[d] as an offering made to the LORD by fire. It is a guilt offering. 6Any male in a priest's family may eat it,[e] but it must be eaten in a holy place; it is most holy.[f]

7" 'The same law applies to both the sin offering[g] and the guilt offering:[h] They belong to the priest[i] who makes atonement with them.[j] 8The priest who offers a burnt offering for anyone may

6:9 [m]Lev 7:37; [n]ver 12
6:10 [o]Ex 39:27; [p]Ex 28:39–43; 39:28; [q]Lev 1:16
6:11 [r]Lev 4:12
6:12 [s]Lev 1:7; [t]Ex 29:13; [u]Ex 32:6
6:14 [v]Lev 2:1; Nu 6:15; 15:4; 28:13
6:15 [w]Lev 2:1; [x]Lev 2:9; [y]Lev 2:2
6:16 [z]Lev 2:3; [a]Eze 44:29; [b]Lev 2:11; [c]ver 26; Ex 29:11; Lev 10:13; 16:24; 24:9; Nu 18:10; [d]Ex 27:9; [e]Ex 29:31; Lev 8:31
6:17 [f]Nu 5:9; [g]Ex 29:28; Lev 7:7; 10:16–18; [h]ver 29; Ex 40:10; Lev 10:12; 21:22; 24:9; Nu 18:9–10
6:18 [i]ver 29; Lev 2:3; 7:6; Nu 18:9–10; [j]Nu 5:9; [k]Ge 9:12; [l]Ex 30:29
6:20 [m]Ex 28:41; [n]Ex 16:36; [o]Nu 5:15; 28:5; [p]Ex 29:2; Lev 23:13; Nu 4:16
6:21 [q]Lev 2:5
6:22 [r]Ex 28:41; 29:30; [s]Lev 1:9
6:25 [t]Ex 30:10; Lev 4:24; [u]Lev 1:3; [v]Ex 29:11
6:26 [w]ver 16; [x]Ex 27:9; [y]Ex 27:21; 40:2
6:27 [z]Ex 29:37; Lev 10:10; Eze 44:19; 46:20; Hag 2:12
6:28 [a]Lev 11:33; 15:12; Nu 19:15
6:29 [b]ver 18; [c]ver 17; Eze 42:13
6:30 [d]Eze 45:15; [e]Lev 4:18; [f]Lev 4:12

Ch. 7

7:1 [a]Lev 5:15; Eze 40:39
7:3 [b]Ex 29:13
7:4 [c]Lev 3:15
7:5 [d]Ex 29:13
7:6 [e]Lev 6:18; [f]Eze 42:13
7:7 [g]Ex 30:10; [h]Lev 5:15; [i]ver 6; Lev 2:3; 6:17,26; 14:13; 2Ki 12:16; 1Co 9:13; 10:18; [j]Nu 5:8

[a]12 Traditionally *peace offerings*
[b]18 Or *Whoever touches them must be holy;* similarly in verse 27
[c]20 Or *each*
[d]20 That is, probably about 4 pints (about 2 litres)
[e]21 The meaning of the Hebrew for this word is uncertain.

keep its hide[k] for himself. 9Every grain offering baked in an oven[l] or cooked in a pan[m] or on a griddle[n] belongs to the priest who offers it, 10and every grain offering, whether mixed with oil or dry, belongs equally to all the sons of Aaron.

The Fellowship Offering

11"'These are the regulations for the fellowship offering[a] a person may present to the LORD:

12"'If he offers it as an expression of thankfulness, then along with this thank-offering[o] he is to offer cakes[p] of bread made without yeast[q] and mixed with oil, wafers[r] made without yeast and spread with oil,[s] and cakes of fine flour well-kneaded and mixed with oil. 13Along with his fellowship offering of thanksgiving[t] he is to present an offering with cakes of bread made with yeast.[u] 14He is to bring one of each kind as an offering, a contribution to the LORD; it belongs to the priest who sprinkles the blood of the fellowship offerings. 15The meat of his fellowship offering of thanksgiving must be eaten on the day it is offered; he must leave none of it till morning.[v]

16"'If, however, his offering is the result of a vow[w] or is a freewill offering,[x] the sacrifice shall be eaten on the day he offers it, but anything left over may be eaten on the next day.[y] 17Any meat of the sacrifice left over till the third day must be burned up.[z] 18If any meat of the fellowship offering[a] is eaten on the third day, it will not be accepted.[b] It will not be credited[c] to the one who offered it, for it is impure; the person who eats any of it will be held responsible.[d]

19"'Meat that touches anything ceremonially unclean must not be eaten; it must be burned up. As for other meat, anyone ceremonially clean may eat it. 20But if anyone who is unclean[e] eats any meat of the fellowship offering belonging to the LORD, that person must be cut off from his people.[f] 21If anyone touches something unclean[g]—whether human uncleanness or an unclean animal or any unclean, detestable thing—and then eats any of the meat of the fellowship offering belonging to the LORD, that person must be cut off from his people.'"

Eating Fat and Blood Forbidden

22The LORD said to Moses, 23"Say to the Israelites: 'Do not eat any of the fat of cattle, sheep or goats.[h] 24The fat of an animal found dead or torn by wild animals[i] may be used for any other purpose, but you must not eat it. 25Anyone who eats the fat of an animal from which an offering by fire may be[b] made to the LORD must be cut off from his people. 26And wherever you live, you must not eat the blood[j] of any bird or animal. 27If anyone eats blood,[k] that person must be cut off from his people.'"

The Priests' Share

28The LORD said to Moses, 29"Say to the Israelites: 'Anyone who brings a fellowship offering to the LORD is to bring part of it as his sacrifice to the LORD. 30With his own hands he is to bring the offering made to the LORD by fire; he is to bring the fat, together with the breast, and wave the breast before the LORD as a wave offering.[l] 31The priest shall burn the fat on the altar,[m] but the breast belongs to Aaron and his sons.[n] 32You are to give the right thigh of your fellowship offerings to the priest as a contribution.[o] 33The son of Aaron who offers the blood and the fat of the fellowship offering shall have the right thigh as his share. 34From the fellowship offerings of the Israelites, I have taken the breast that is waved and the thigh[p] that is presented and have given them to Aaron the priest and his sons[q] as their regular share from the Israelites.'"

35This is the portion of the offerings made to the LORD by fire that were allotted to Aaron and his sons on the day they were presented to serve the LORD as priests. 36On the day they were anointed,[r] the LORD commanded that the Israelites give this to them as their regular share for the generations to come.

37These, then, are the regulations for the burnt offering,[s] the grain offering,[t] the sin offering, the guilt offering, the ordination offering[u] and the fellowship offering, 38which the LORD gave Moses[v] on Mount Sinai[w] on the day he commanded the Israelites to bring their offerings to the LORD,[x] in the Desert of Sinai.

The Ordination of Aaron and His Sons

8:1-36pp—Ex 29:1-37

8 The LORD said to Moses, 2"Bring Aaron and his sons,[a] their garments,[b] the anointing oil,[c] the bull for

---

8 [k]Lev 1:6
9 [l]Lev 2:4; [m]Lev 2:7; [n]Lev 2:5
12 [o]ver 13,15; Lev 22:29; Ps 50:14; 54:6; 107:22; 116:17; Jer 33:11; [p]Jer 44:19; [q]Nu 6:19; [r]Lev 2:4; [s]Lev 2:1
13 [t]ver 12; Ex 34:22; [u]Lev 23:17; Am 4:5
15 [v]Ex 12:10
16 [w]Ge 28:20; Lev 1:2; Dt 23:21–23; [x]Ex 35:29; Lev 22:18,21; 23:38; Nu 15:3; 29:39; Dt 12:6; Ps 54:6; Eze 46:12; [y]Lev 19:5–8
17 [z]Ex 12:10; Lev 19:6
18 [a]2Ch 33:16; [b]Lev 19:7; [c]Nu 18:27; [d]Lev 5:1
20 [e]Lev 5:3; [f]Ge 17:14; Lev 22:3–7
21 [g]Lev 5:2
23 [h]Lev 17:3; Dt 14:4
24 [i]Ex 22:31
26 [j]Ge 9:4
27 [k]Ge 9:4
30 [l]Ex 29:24
31 [m]Ex 29:13; [n]Ex 29:27
32 [o]Ex 29:27; Lev 10:14–15; Nu 5:9; 6:20; 18:18
34 [p]Ex 29:22; Lev 10:15; Nu 6:20; 1Sa 9:24; [q]Ex 29:27
36 [r]Lev 8:12,30
37 [s]Lev 6:9; [t]Lev 6:14; [u]Ex 29:31
38 [v]Lev 26:46; Nu 36:13; Dt 4:5; 29:1; [w]Ex 19:11; [x]Lev 1:2

Ch. 8

2 [a]Ex 28:1; Lev 1:5; [b]Ex 28:2, 4,43; 39:27; [c]Ex 30:23–25, 30

---

a11 Traditionally *peace offering;* also in verses 13–37
b25 Or *fire is*

the sin offering,[d] the two rams[e] and the basket containing bread made without yeast,[f] 3and gather the entire assembly[g] at the entrance to the Tent of Meeting." 4Moses did as the LORD commanded him, and the assembly gathered at the entrance to the Tent of Meeting.

5Moses said to the assembly, "This is what the LORD has commanded to be done.[h]" 6Then Moses brought Aaron and his sons forward and washed them with water.[i] 7He put the tunic on Aaron, tied the sash around him, clothed him with the robe and put the ephod on him. He also tied the ephod to him by its skilfully woven waistband; so it was fastened on him.[j] 8He placed the breastpiece[k] on him and put the Urim and Thummim[l] in the breastpiece. 9Then he placed the turban[m] on Aaron's head and set the gold plate, the sacred diadem,[n] on the front of it, as the LORD commanded Moses.[o]

10Then Moses took the anointing oil[p] and anointed[q] the tabernacle[r] and everything in it, and so consecrated them. 11He sprinkled some of the oil on the altar seven times, anointing the altar and all its utensils and the basin with its stand, to consecrate them.[s] 12He poured some of the anointing oil on Aaron's head and anointed[t] him to consecrate him.[u] 13Then he brought Aaron's sons[v] forward, put tunics[w] on them, tied sashes around them and put headbands on them, as the LORD commanded Moses.[x]

14He then presented the bull[y] for the sin offering,[z] and Aaron and his sons laid their hands on its head.[a] 15Moses slaughtered the bull and took some of the blood,[b] and with his finger he put it on all the horns of the altar[c] to purify the altar.[d] He poured out the rest of the blood at the base of the altar. So he consecrated it to make atonement for it.[e] 16Moses also took all the fat around the inner parts, the covering of the liver, and both kidneys and their fat, and burned it on the altar. 17But the bull with its hide and its flesh and its offal[f] he burned up outside the camp,[g] as the LORD commanded Moses.

18He then presented the ram[h] for the burnt offering, and Aaron and his sons laid their hands on its head. 19Then Moses slaughtered the ram and sprinkled the blood against the altar on all sides. 20He cut the ram into pieces and burned the head, the pieces and the fat.[i] 21He washed the inner parts and the legs with water and burned the whole ram on the altar as a burnt offering, a pleasing aroma, an offering made to the LORD by fire, as the LORD commanded Moses.

22He then presented the other ram, the ram for the ordination,[j] and Aaron and his sons laid their hands on its head.[k] 23Moses slaughtered the ram and took some of its blood and put it on the lobe of Aaron's right ear, on the thumb of his right hand and on the big toe of his right foot.[l] 24Moses also brought Aaron's sons forward and put some of the blood on the lobes of their right ears, on the thumbs of their right hands and on the big toes of their right feet. Then he sprinkled blood against the altar on all sides.[m] 25He took the fat[n], the fat tail, all the fat around the inner parts, the covering of the liver, both kidneys and their fat and the right thigh. 26Then from the basket of bread made without yeast, which was before the LORD, he took a cake of bread, and one made with oil, and a wafer;[o] he put these on the fat portions and on the right thigh. 27He put all these in the hands of Aaron and his sons and waved them before the LORD[p] as a wave offering. 28Then Moses took them from their hands and burned them on the altar on top of the burnt offering as an ordination offering, a pleasing aroma, an offering made to the LORD by fire. 29He also took the breast —Moses' share of the ordination ram[q] —and waved it before the LORD as a wave offering, as the LORD commanded Moses.

30Then Moses[r] took some of the anointing oil and some of the blood from the altar and sprinkled them on Aaron and his garments[s] and on his sons and their garments. So he consecrated[t] Aaron and his garments and his sons and their garments.

31Moses then said to Aaron and his sons, "Cook the meat at the entrance to the Tent of Meeting[u] and eat it there with the bread from the basket of ordination offerings, as I commanded, saying,[a] 'Aaron and his sons are to eat it.' 32Then burn up the rest of the meat and the bread. 33Do not leave the entrance to the Tent of Meeting for seven days, until the days of your ordination are completed, for your ordination will last seven days.[v] 34What has been done today was commanded by the LORD[w] to make atonement for you. 35You must stay at the entrance to the Tent of Meeting day and night for seven days and do what the LORD requires,[x] so that

2 [d]Ex 30:10; [e]ver 18,22; [f]Ex 29:2–3
3 [g]Nu 8:9
5 [h]Ex 29:1
6 [i]Ex 29:4; 30:19; Ac 22:16
7 [j]Ex 28:4
8 [k]Ex 25:7; [l]Ex 28:30
9 [m]Ex 39:28; [n]Ex 28:36; [o]Ex 28:2; Lev 21:10
10 [p]ver 2; [q]Ex 30:26; [r]Ex 26:1
11 [s]Ex 30:29
12 [t]Lev 7:36; [u]Ex 30:30
13 [v]Ex 28:40; [w]Ex 28:4,39; 39:27; [x]Lev 21:10
14 [y]Lev 4:3; [z]Ex 30:10; [a]Lev 4:15
15 [b]Lev 4:18; [c]Lev 4:7; [d]Heb 9:22; [e]Eze 43:20
17 [f]Lev 4:11; [g]Lev 4:12
18 [h]ver 2
20 [i]Lev 1:8
22 [j]ver 2; [k]Lev 4:15
23 [l]Lev 14:14,25
24 [m]Heb 9:18–22
25 [n]Lev 3:3–5
26 [o]Lev 2:4
27 [p]Nu 5:25
29 [q]Lev 7:31–34
30 [r]Ex 28:1; [s]Ex 28:2; [t]Lev 7:36
31 [u]Lev 6:16
33 [v]Lev 14:8; 15:13,28; Nu 19:11; Eze 43:25
34 [w]Heb 7:16
35 [x]Lev 18:30; 22:9; Nu 3:7; 9:19; Dt 11:1; 1Ki 2:3; Eze 48:11; Zec 3:7

[a]31 Or *I was commanded:*

you will not die; for that is what I have been commanded." 36So Aaron and his sons did everything the LORD commanded through Moses.

The Priests Begin Their Ministry

9 On the eighth day[a] Moses summoned Aaron and his sons and the elders[b] of Israel. 2He said to Aaron, "Take a bull calf for your sin offering and a ram for your burnt offering, both without defect, and present them before the LORD. 3Then say to the Israelites: 'Take a male goat[c] for a sin offering,[d] a calf[e] and a lamb[f]—both a year old and without defect—for a burnt offering, 4and an ox[a] [g] and a ram for a fellowship offering[b] [h] to sacrifice before the LORD, together with a grain offering mixed with oil. For today the LORD will appear to you.[i]' "

5They took the things Moses commanded to the front of the Tent of Meeting, and the entire assembly came near and stood before the LORD. 6Then Moses said, "This is what the LORD has commanded you to do, so that the glory of the LORD[j] may appear to you."

7Moses said to Aaron, "Come to the altar and sacrifice your sin offering and your burnt offering and make atonement for yourself and the people;[k] sacrifice the offering that is for the people and make atonement for them, as the LORD has commanded.[l]"

8So Aaron came to the altar and slaughtered the calf as a sin offering[m] for himself. 9His sons brought the blood to him,[n] and he dipped his finger into the blood and put it on the horns of the altar; the rest of the blood he poured out at the base of the altar.[o] [p] 10On the altar he burned the fat, the kidneys and the covering of the liver from the sin offering, as the LORD commanded Moses; 11the flesh and the hide[q] he burned up outside the camp.[r]

12Then he slaughtered the burnt offering.[s] His sons handed him the blood,[t] and he sprinkled it against the altar on all sides. 13They handed him the burnt offering piece by piece, including the head, and he burned them on the altar.[u] 14He washed the inner parts and the legs and burned them on top of the burnt offering on the altar.[v]

15Aaron then brought the offering that was for the people.[w] He took the goat for the people's sin offering and slaughtered it and offered it for a sin offering as he did with the first one.

16He brought the burnt offering and offered it in the prescribed way.[x] 17He also brought the grain offering, took a handful of it and burned it on the altar in addition to the morning's burnt offering.[y]

18He slaughtered the ox and the ram as the fellowship offering for the people.[z] His sons handed him the blood, and he sprinkled it against the altar on all sides. 19But the fat portions of the ox and the ram—the fat tail, the layer of fat, the kidneys and the covering of the liver—20these they laid on the breasts, and then Aaron burned the fat on the altar. 21Aaron waved the breasts and the right thigh before the LORD as a wave offering,[a] as Moses commanded.

22Then Aaron lifted his hands towards the people and blessed them.[b] And having sacrificed the sin offering, the burnt offering and the fellowship offering, he stepped down.

23Moses and Aaron then went into the Tent of Meeting.[c] When they came out, they blessed the people; and the glory of the LORD[d] appeared to all the people. 24Fire[e] came out from the presence of the LORD and consumed the burnt offering and the fat portions on the altar. And when all the people saw it, they shouted for joy and fell face down.[f]

The Death of Nadab and Abihu

10 Aaron's sons Nadab and Abihu[a] took their censers,[b] put fire in them[c] and added incense;[d] and they offered unauthorised fire before the LORD,[e] contrary to his command.[f] 2So fire came out[g] from the presence of the LORD and consumed them,[h] and they died before the LORD.[i] 3Moses then said to Aaron, "This is what the LORD spoke of when he said:

" 'Among those who approach me[j]
I will show myself holy;[k]
in the sight of all the people
I will be honoured.[l]' "

Aaron remained silent.

4Moses summoned Mishael and Elzaphan,[m] sons of Aaron's uncle Uzziel,[n] and said to them, "Come here; carry your cousins outside the camp,[o] away from the front of the sanctuary.[p]" 5So they came and carried them, still in their tunics,[q] outside the camp, as Moses ordered.

Ch. 9

1 [a]Eze 43:27; [b]**Lev 4:15**
3 [c]**Lev 4:3;** [d]ver 15; Lev 10:16; [e]ver 8; [f]**Lev 4:32**
4 [g]Lev 4:10; [h]**Ex 32:6;** [i]Ex 29:43
6 [j]**Ex 16:7**
7 [k]Lev 16:6; [l]**Ex 30:10;** Heb 5:1,3; 7:27
8 [m]Lev 4:1–12; 10:19
9 [n]ver 12,18; [o]**Ex 29:12;** [p]Eze 43:20
11 [q]**Lev 4:11;** [r]**Lev 4:12**
12 [s]Lev 10:19; [t]**ver 9**
13 [u]**Lev 1:8**
14 [v]**Lev 1:9**
15 [w]Lev 4:27–31
16 [x]Lev 1:1–13
17 [y]Lev 3:5
18 [z]Lev 3:1–11
21 [a]**Ex 29:24,26**
22 [b]**Ge 48:20;** Ex **39:43;** Lk 24:50
23 [c]**Ex 40:2;** [d]**Ex 24:16**
24 [e]**Ex 19:18;** Jdg 6:21; 13:20; [f]1Ki 18:39

Ch. 10

1 [a]Ex 6:23; 24:1; 28:1; Nu 3:2–4; 26:61; 1Ch 6:3; [b]Nu 16:46; 1Ki 7:50; 2Ki 25:15; 2Ch 4:22; Jer 52:19; Eze 8:11; [c]Lev 16:12; Nu 16:7,18; Isa 6:6; [d]**Ex 30:9;** [e]ver 2; Lev 16:1; [f]Ex 30:9
2 [g]Ps 106:18; [h]Nu 11:1; 16:35; Ps 2:12; 50:3; Isa 29:6; [i]**Ge 19:24; 38:7;** Nu 16:35; 1Ch 24:2; Job 1:16
3 [j]Ex 19:22; [k]Ex 30:29; Lev 21:6; 22:32; Nu 16:5; 20:13; Isa 5:16; Eze 28:22; 38:16; [l]Ex 14:4; Isa 44:23; 49:3; 55:5; 60:21
4 [m]**Ex 6:22;** [n]Ex 6:18; [o]Ac 5:6, 9–10; [p]**Ex 25:8**
5 [q]**Lev 8:13**

a4 The Hebrew word can include both male and female; also in verses 18 and 19.

b4 Traditionally *peace offering*; also in verses 18 and 22

6 Then Moses said to Aaron and his sons Eleazar and Ithamar,[r] "Do not let your hair become unkempt,[a][s] and do not tear your clothes,[t] or you will die and the LORD will be angry with the whole community.[u] But your relatives, all the house of Israel, may mourn[v] for those the LORD has destroyed by fire. 7 Do not leave the entrance to the Tent of Meeting[w] or you will die, because the LORD's anointing oil[x] is on you." So they did as Moses said.

8 Then the LORD said to Aaron, 9 "You and your sons are not to drink wine[y] or other fermented drink[z] whenever you go into the Tent of Meeting, or you will die. This is a lasting ordinance[a] for the generations to come. 10 You must distinguish between the holy and the common, between the unclean and the clean,[b] 11 and you must teach[c] the Israelites all the decrees the LORD has given them through Moses.[d]"

12 Moses said to Aaron and his remaining sons, Eleazar and Ithamar, "Take the grain offering[e] left over from the offerings made to the LORD by fire and eat it prepared without yeast beside the altar,[f] for it is most holy. 13 Eat it in a holy place,[g] because it is your share and your sons' share of the offerings made to the LORD by fire; for so I have been commanded.[h] 14 But you and your sons and your daughters may eat the breast[i] that was waved and the thigh that was presented. Eat them in a ceremonially clean place;[j] they have been given to you and your children as your share of the Israelites' fellowship offerings.[b] 15 The thigh[k] that was presented and the breast that was waved must be brought with the fat portions of the offerings made by fire, to be waved before the LORD as a wave offering.[l] This will be the regular share for you and your children, as the LORD has commanded."

16 When Moses enquired about the goat of the sin offering[m] and found that it had been burned up, he was angry with Eleazar and Ithamar, Aaron's remaining sons, and asked, 17 "Why didn't you eat the sin offering[n] in the sanctuary area? It is most holy; it was given to you to take away the guilt[o] of the community by making atonement for them before the LORD. 18 Since its blood was not taken into the Holy Place,[p] you should have eaten the goat in the sanctuary area, as I commanded.[q]"

19 Aaron replied to Moses, "Today they sacrificed their sin offering and their burnt offering[r] before the LORD, but such things as this have happened to me. Would the LORD have been pleased if I had eaten the sin offering today?" 20 When Moses heard this, he was satisfied.

Clean and Unclean Food

11:1–23pp—Dt 14:3–20

11 The LORD said to Moses and Aaron, 2 "Say to the Israelites: 'Of all the animals that live on land, these are the ones you may eat:[a] 3 You may eat any animal that has a split hoof completely divided and that chews the cud.

4 " 'There are some that only chew the cud or only have a split hoof, but you must not eat them.[b] The camel, though it chews the cud, does not have a split hoof; it is ceremonially unclean for you. 5 The coney,[a] though it chews the cud, does not have a split hoof; it is unclean for you. 6 The rabbit, though it chews the cud, does not have a split hoof; it is unclean for you. 7 And the pig,[c] though it has a split hoof completely divided, does not chew the cud; it is unclean for you. 8 You must not eat their meat or touch their carcasses; they are unclean for you.[d]

9 " 'Of all the creatures living in the water of the seas and the streams, you may eat any that have fins and scales. 10 But all creatures in the seas or streams that do not have fins and scales—whether among all the swarming things or among all the other living creatures in the water—you are to detest.[e] 11 And since you are to detest them, you must not eat their meat and you must detest their carcasses.[f] 12 Anything living in the water that does not have fins and scales is to be detestable to you.[g]

13 " 'These are the birds you are to detest and not eat because they are detestable: the eagle, the vulture, the black vulture, 14 the red kite, any kind[h] of black kite, 15 any kind of raven,[i] 16 the horned owl, the screech owl, the gull, any kind of hawk, 17 the little owl, the cormorant, the great owl, 18 the white owl,[j] the desert owl, the osprey, 19 the stork,[k] any kind[l] of heron, the hoopoe and the bat.[b][m]

20 " 'All flying insects that walk on all fours are to be detestable to you.[n]

6 [r]**Ex 6:23**; [s]Lev 13:45; 21:10; Nu 5:18; [t]Jer 41:5; **Mk 14:63**; [u]Nu 1:53; 16:22; Jos 7:1; 22:18; [v]Ge 50:3,10; Nu 20:29; 1Sa 25:1
7 [w]**Ex 25:8**; [x]**Ex 28:41**
9 [y]Ge 9:21; Ex 29:40; Lev 23:13; Nu 15:5; Dt 28:39; Isa 5:22; 22:13; 28:1; 29:9; 56:12; Jer 35:6; Hos 4:11; Hab 2:15–16; [z]Nu 6:3; 28:7; Dt 14:26; 29:6; Jdg 13:4; Pr 20:1; 23:29–35; 31:4–7; Isa 28:7; Eze 44:21; Mic 2:11; Lk 1:15; **Eph 5:18**; 1Ti 3:3; Tit 1:7; [a]**Ex 12:14**
10 [b]**Ge 7:2**; **Lev 6:27**; 14:57; 20:25; Eze 22:26
11 [c]2Ch 15:3; 17:7; Ezr 7:25; Ne 8:7; Mal 2:7; [d]Dt 17:10–11; 24:8; 25:1; 33:10; Pr 4:27; Hag 2:11; Mal 2:7
12 [e]**Ex 29:41**; [f]Lev 6:14–18
13 [g]**Lev 6:16**; [h]Eze 42:13
14 [i]Nu 5:9; [j]**Ex 29:31**; **Lev 4:12**
15 [k]**Lev 7:34**; [l]**Ex 29:28**
16 [m]**Lev 9:3**
17 [n]Lev 6:24–30; Eze 42:13; [o]**Ex 28:38**
18 [p]**Lev 4:18**; 6:26; [q]**Lev 6:17**
19 [r]Lev 9:12

Ch. 11

2 [a]Ac 10:12–14
4 [b]Ac 10:14
7 [c]Isa 65:4; 66:3,17
8 [d]**Lev 5:2**; Heb 9:10
10 [e]ver 12
11 [f]**Lev 5:2**
12 [g]ver 10
14 [h]**Ge 1:11**
15 [i]**Ge 8:7**
18 [j]Isa 13:21; 14:23; 34:11, 13; Zep 2:14
19 [k]Zec 5:9; [l]**Ge 1:11**; [m]Isa 2:20
20 [n]Ac 10:14

[a]6 Or *Do not uncover your heads*
[b]14 Traditionally *peace offerings*
[a]5 That is, the hyrax or rock badger
[b]19 The precise identification of some of the birds, insects and animals in this chapter is uncertain.

21There are, however, some winged creatures that walk on all fours that you may eat: those that have jointed legs for hopping on the ground. 22Of these you may eat any kind of locust,[o] katydid, cricket or grasshopper. 23But all other winged creatures that have four legs you are to detest.

24" 'You will make yourselves unclean by these;[p] whoever touches their carcasses will be unclean till evening.[q] 25Whoever picks up one of their carcasses must wash his clothes,[r] and he will be unclean till evening.[s]

26" 'Every animal that has a split hoof not completely divided or that does not chew the cud is unclean for you; whoever touches ⌞the carcass of⌟ any of them will be unclean. 27Of all the animals that walk on all fours, those that walk on their paws are unclean for you; whoever touches their carcasses will be unclean till evening. 28Anyone who picks up their carcasses must wash his clothes, and he will be unclean till evening.[t] They are unclean for you.

29" 'Of the animals that move about on the ground, these are unclean for you:[u] the weasel, the rat,[v] any kind of great lizard, 30the gecko, the monitor lizard, the wall lizard, the skink and the chameleon. 31Of all those that move along the ground, these are unclean for you. Whoever touches them when they are dead will be unclean till evening. 32When one of them dies and falls on something, that article, whatever its use, will be unclean, whether it is made of wood, cloth, hide or sackcloth.[w] Put it in water; it will be unclean till evening, and then it will be clean. 33If one of them falls into a clay pot, everything in it will be unclean, and you must break the pot.[x] 34Any food that could be eaten but has water on it from such a pot is unclean, and any liquid that could be drunk from it is unclean. 35Anything that one of their carcasses falls on becomes unclean; an oven or cooking pot must be broken up. They are unclean, and you are to regard them as unclean. 36A spring, however, or a cistern for collecting water remains clean, but anyone who touches one of these carcasses is unclean. 37If a carcass falls on any seeds that are to be planted, they remain clean. 38But if water has been put on the seed and a carcass falls on it, it is unclean for you.

39" 'If an animal that you are allowed to eat dies,[y] anyone who touches the carcass[z] will be unclean till evening. 40Anyone who eats some of the carcass[a] must wash his clothes, and he will be unclean till evening.[b] Anyone who picks up the carcass must wash his clothes, and he will be unclean till evening.

41" 'Every creature that moves about on the ground is detestable; it is not to be eaten. 42You are not to eat any creature that moves about on the ground, whether it moves on its belly or walks on all fours or on many feet; it is detestable. 43Do not defile yourselves by any of these creatures.[c] Do not make yourselves unclean by means of them or be made unclean by them. 44I am the LORD your God;[d] consecrate yourselves[e] and be holy,[f] because I am holy.[g] Do not make yourselves unclean by any creature that moves about on the ground.[h] 45I am the LORD who brought you up out of Egypt[i] to be your God;[j] therefore be holy, because I am holy.[k]

46" 'These are the regulations concerning animals, birds, every living thing that moves in the water and every creature that moves about on the ground. 47You must distinguish between the unclean and the clean, between living creatures that may be eaten and those that may not be eaten.[l] "

Purification After Childbirth

12 The LORD said to Moses, 2"Say to the Israelites: 'A woman who becomes pregnant and gives birth to a son will be ceremonially unclean for seven days, just as she is unclean during her monthly period.[a] 3On the eighth day[b] the boy is to be circumcised.[c] 4Then the woman must wait thirty-three days to be purified from her bleeding. She must not touch anything sacred or go to the sanctuary until the days of her purification are over. 5If she gives birth to a daughter, for two weeks the woman will be unclean, as during her period. Then she must wait sixty-six days to be purified from her bleeding.

6" 'When the days of her purification for a son or daughter are over,[d] she is to bring to the priest at the entrance to the Tent of Meeting a year-old lamb[e] for a burnt offering and a young pigeon or a dove for a sin offering.[f] 7He shall offer them before the LORD to make atonement for her, and then she will be ceremonially clean from her flow of blood.

" 'These are the regulations for the woman who gives birth to a boy or a girl. 8If she cannot afford a lamb, she is to bring two doves or two young

22 [o]Mt 3:4; Mk 1:6
24 [p]**Lev 5:2;** [q]ver 27-40; Lev 13:3; 14:46; 15:5; 22:6; Nu 19:7,19
25 [r]ver 28; **Ex 19:10;** Lev 13:6; 14:8,47; 15:5; 16:26; Nu 8:7; 19:7; [s]Lev 13:34; Nu 19:8; 31:24
28 [t]Heb 9:10
29 [u]ver 41; [v]Isa 66:17
32 [w]Lev 15:12; Nu 19:18; 31:20
33 [x]**Lev 6:28**
39 [y]Lev 17:15; 22:8; Dt 14:21; Eze 4:14; 44:31; [z]ver 40; Lev 22:4; Nu 19:11
40 [a]**ver 39;** [b]ver 25; Lev 14:8; 17:15; 22:8; Eze 44:31; Heb 9:10
43 [c]ver 44; Lev 20:25; 22:5
44 [d]**Ex 6:2,7;** 20:2; Isa 43:3; 51:15; Eze 20:5; [e]**Ex 19:10;** Lev 20:7; Nu 15:40; Jos 3:5; 7:13; 1Ch 15:12; 2Ch 29:5; 35:6; [f]**Ex 22:31; Dt 14:2;** [g]**Ex 31:13;** Lev 19:2; 20:7; Jos 24:19; 1Sa 2:2; Job 6:10; Ps 99:3; Eph 1:4; 1Th 4:7; 1Pe 1:15-16*; [h]**ver 43**
45 [i]Lev 25:38,55; [j]**Ge 17:7;** [k]**Ex 19:6;** 1Pe 1:16*
47 [l]Lev 10:10

Ch. 12

2 [a]Lev 15:19; 18:19; Isa 64:6; Eze 18:6; 22:10; 36:17
3 [b]**Ex 22:30;** [c]**Ge 17:10; Lk 1:59**
6 [d]Lk 2:22; [e]Ex 29:38; Lev 23:12; Nu 6:12,14; 7:15; [f]Lev 5:7

pigeons,[g] one for a burnt offering and
the other for a sin offering.[h] In this way
the priest will make atonement for her,
and she will be clean.[i]"

Regulations About Infectious Skin Diseases

13 The LORD said to Moses and
Aaron, 2"When anyone has a
swelling[a] or a rash or a bright spot[b] on
his skin that may become an infectious
skin disease,[a][c] he must be brought to
Aaron the priest[d] or to one of his sons[b]
who is a priest. 3The priest is to examine
the sore on his skin, and if the hair in the
sore has turned white and the sore
appears to be more than skin deep,[c] it is
an infectious skin disease. When the
priest examines him, he shall pro-
nounce him ceremonially unclean.[e] 4If
the spot[f] on his skin is white but does
not appear to be more than skin deep
and the hair in it has not turned white,
the priest is to put the infected person in
isolation for seven days.[g] 5On the
seventh day[h] the priest is to examine
him,[i] and if he sees that the sore is
unchanged and has not spread in the
skin, he is to keep him in isolation
another seven days. 6On the seventh
day the priest is to examine him again,
and if the sore has faded and has not
spread in the skin, the priest shall pro-
nounce him clean;[j] it is only a rash. The
man must wash his clothes,[k] and he will
be clean.[l] 7But if the rash does spread in
his skin after he has shown himself to
the priest to be pronounced clean, he
must appear before the priest again.[m]
8The priest is to examine him, and if the
rash has spread in the skin, he shall
pronounce him unclean; it is an infec-
tious disease.

9"When anyone has an infectious
skin disease, he must be brought to the
priest. 10The priest is to examine him,
and if there is a white swelling in the
skin that has turned the hair white and
if there is raw flesh in the swelling, 11it is
a chronic skin disease[n] and the priest
shall pronounce him unclean. He is not
to put him in isolation, because he is
already unclean.

12"If the disease breaks out all over his
skin and, so far as the priest can see, it
covers all the skin of the infected person
from head to foot, 13the priest is to
examine him, and if the disease has
covered his whole body, he shall pro-
nounce that person clean. Since it has all
turned white, he is clean. 14But when-
ever raw flesh appears on him, he will
be unclean. 15When the priest sees the
raw flesh, he shall pronounce him un-
clean. The raw flesh is unclean; he has
an infectious disease.[o] 16Should the raw
flesh change and turn white, he must go
to the priest. 17The priest is to examine
him, and if the sores have turned white,
the priest shall pronounce the infected
person clean;[p] then he will be clean.

18"When someone has a boil[q] on his
skin and it heals, 19and in the place
where the boil was, a white swelling or
reddish-white[r] spot[s] appears, he must
present himself to the priest. 20The
priest is to examine it, and if it appears
to be more than skin deep and the hair
in it has turned white, the priest shall
pronounce him unclean. It is an infec-
tious skin disease[t] that has broken out
where the boil was. 21But if, when the
priest examines it, there is no white hair
in it and it is not more than skin deep
and has faded, then the priest is to put
him in isolation for seven days. 22If it is
spreading in the skin, the priest shall
pronounce him unclean; it is infectious.
23But if the spot is unchanged and has
not spread, it is only a scar from the boil,
and the priest shall pronounce him
clean.[u]

24"When someone has a burn on his
skin and a reddish-white or white spot
appears in the raw flesh of the burn,
25the priest is to examine the spot, and if
the hair in it has turned white, and it
appears to be more than skin deep, it is
an infectious disease that has broken
out in the burn. The priest shall pro-
nounce him unclean; it is an infectious
skin disease.[v] 26But if the priest ex-
amines it and there is no white hair in
the spot and if it is not more than skin
deep and has faded, then the priest is to
put him in isolation for seven days.[w]
27On the seventh day the priest is to
examine him,[x] and if it is spreading in
the skin, the priest shall pronounce him
unclean; it is an infectious skin disease.
28If, however, the spot is unchanged
and has not spread in the skin but has
faded, it is a swelling from the burn, and
the priest shall pronounce him clean; it
is only a scar from the burn.[y]

29"If a man or woman has a sore on
the head[z] or on the chin, 30the priest is to
examine the sore, and if it appears to be
more than skin deep and the hair in it is

8 [g]**Ge 15:9**; Lev 14:22; [h]Lev 5:7; Lk 2:22–24*; [i]**Lev 4:26**

Ch. 13

2 [a]ver 10,19, 28,43; [b]ver 4, 38–39; Lev 14:56; [c]ver 3, 9,15; **Ex 4:6**; Lev 14:3,32; Nu 5:2; Dt 24:8; [d]Dt 24:8
3 [e]ver 8,11,20, 30; Lev 21:1; Nu 9:6
4 [f]**ver 2**; [g]ver 5, 21,26,33,46; Lev 14:38; Nu 12:14–15; Dt 24:9
5 [h]Lev 14:9; [i]ver 27,32, 34,51
6 [j]ver 13,17,23, 28,34; Mt 8:3; Lk 5:12–14; [k]**Lev 11:25**; [l]Lev 11:25; 14:8–9,20,48; 15:8; Nu 8:7
7 [m]Lk 5:14
11 [n]**Ex 4:6; Lev 14:8; Nu 12:10**; Mt 8:2
15 [o]**ver 2**
17 [p]**ver 6**
18 [q]**Ex 9:9**
19 [r]ver 24,42; Lev 14:37; [s]**ver 2**
20 [t]ver 2
23 [u]**ver 6**
25 [v]ver 11
26 [w]**ver 4**
27 [x]**ver 5**
28 [y]**ver 2**
29 [z]ver 43–44

[a]2 Traditionally *leprosy*; the Hebrew word was used for various diseases affecting the skin—not necessarily leprosy; also elsewhere in this chapter.
[b]2 Or *descendants*
[c]3 Or *be lower than the rest of the skin*; also elsewhere in this chapter

yellow and thin, the priest shall pronounce that person unclean; it is an itch, an infectious disease of the head or chin. 31But if, when the priest examines this kind of sore, it does not seem to be more than skin deep and there is no black hair in it, then the priest is to put the infected person in isolation for seven days.[a] 32On the seventh day the priest is to examine the sore,[b] and if the itch has not spread and there is no yellow hair in it and it does not appear to be more than skin deep, 33he must be shaved except for the diseased area, and the priest is to keep him in isolation another seven days. 34On the seventh day the priest is to examine the itch,[c] and if it has not spread in the skin and appears to be no more than skin deep, the priest shall pronounce him clean. He must wash his clothes, and he will be clean.[d] 35But if the itch does spread in the skin after he is pronounced clean, 36the priest is to examine him, and if the itch has spread in the skin, the priest does not need to look for yellow hair; the person is unclean.[e] 37If, however, in his judgment it is unchanged and black hair has grown in it, the itch is healed. He is clean, and the priest shall pronounce him clean.

38"When a man or woman has white spots on the skin, 39the priest is to examine them, and if the spots are dull white, it is a harmless rash that has broken out on the skin; that person is clean.

40"When a man has lost his hair and is bald,[f] he is clean. 41If he has lost his hair from the front of his scalp and has a bald forehead, he is clean. 42But if he has a reddish-white sore on his bald head or forehead, it is an infectious disease breaking out on his head or forehead. 43The priest is to examine him, and if the swollen sore on his head or forehead is reddish-white like an infectious skin disease, 44the man is diseased and is unclean. The priest shall pronounce him unclean because of the sore on his head.

45"The person with such an infectious disease must wear torn clothes,[g] let his hair be unkempt,[d] cover the lower part of his face[h] and cry out, 'Unclean! Unclean!'[i] 46As long as he has the infection he remains unclean. He must live alone; he must live outside the camp.[j]

Regulations About Mildew

47"If any clothing is contaminated with mildew—any woollen or linen clothing, 48any woven or knitted material of linen or wool, any leather or anything made of leather—49and if the contamination in the clothing, or leather, or woven or knitted material, or any leather article, is greenish or reddish, it is a spreading mildew and must be shown to the priest.[k] 50The priest is to examine the mildew[l] and isolate the affected article for seven days. 51On the seventh day he is to examine it,[m] and if the mildew has spread in the clothing, or the woven or knitted material, or the leather, whatever its use, it is a destructive mildew; the article is unclean.[n] 52He must burn up the clothing, or the woven or knitted material of wool or linen, or any leather article that has the contamination in it, because the mildew is destructive; the article must be burned up.[o]

53"But if, when the priest examines it, the mildew has not spread in the clothing, or the woven or knitted material, or the leather article, 54he shall order that the contaminated article be washed. Then he is to isolate it for another seven days. 55After the affected article has been washed, the priest is to examine it, and if the mildew has not changed its appearance, even though it has not spread, it is unclean. Burn it with fire, whether the mildew has affected one side or the other. 56If, when the priest examines it, the mildew has faded after the article has been washed, he is to tear the contaminated part out of the clothing, or the leather, or the woven or knitted material. 57But if it reappears in the clothing, or in the woven or knitted material, or in the leather article, it is spreading, and whatever has the mildew must be burned with fire. 58The clothing, or the woven or knitted material, or any leather article that has been washed and is rid of the mildew, must be washed again, and it will be clean."

59These are the regulations concerning contamination by mildew in woollen or linen clothing, woven or knitted material, or any leather article, for pronouncing them clean or unclean.

Cleansing From Infectious Skin Diseases

14 The LORD said to Moses, 2"These are the regulations for the diseased person at the time of his ceremonial cleansing, when he is brought to the priest:[a] 3The priest is to

31 [a]ver 4
32 [b]**ver 5**
34 [c]**ver 5**; [d]**Lev 11:25**
36 [e]ver 30
40 [f]Lev 21:5; 2Ki 2:23; Isa 3:24; 15:2; 22:12; Eze 27:31; 29:18; Am 8:10; Mic 1:16
45 [g]**Lev 10:6**; [h]Eze 24:17,22; Mic 3:7; [i]**Lev 5:2**; La 4:15; Lk 17:12
46 [j]Nu 5:1–4; 12:14; 2Ki 7:3; 15:5
49 [k]Mk 1:44
50 [l]Eze 44:23
51 [m]**ver 5**; [n]Lev 14:44
52 [o]ver 55,57

Ch. 14

2 [a]Lev 13:57; Dt 24:8; Mt 8:2–4; Mk 1:40–44; Lk 5:12–14; 17:14

d45 Or *clothes, uncover his head*

go outside the camp and examine him.[b] If the person has been healed of his infectious skin disease,[a][c] 4the priest shall order that two live clean birds and some cedar wood, scarlet yarn and hyssop[d] be brought for the one to be cleansed.[e] 5Then the priest shall order that one of the birds be killed over fresh water in a clay pot.[f] 6He is then to take the live bird and dip it, together with the cedar wood, the scarlet yarn and the hyssop, into the blood of the bird that was killed over the fresh water.[g] 7Seven times[h] he shall sprinkle[i] the one to be cleansed of the infectious disease and pronounce him clean. Then he is to release the live bird in the open fields.[j]

8"The person to be cleansed must wash his clothes,[k] shave off all his hair and bathe with water;[l] then he will be ceremonially clean.[m] After this he may come into the camp,[n] but he must stay outside his tent for seven days. 9On the seventh day[o] he must shave off all his hair;[p] he must shave his head, his beard, his eyebrows and the rest of his hair. He must wash his clothes and bathe himself with water, and he will be clean.[q]

10"On the eighth day[r] he must bring two male lambs and one ewe lamb[s] a year old, each without defect, along with three-tenths of an ephah[b][t] of fine flour mixed with oil for a grain offering,[u] and one log[c] of oil.[v] 11The priest who pronounces him clean shall present[w] both the one to be cleansed and his offerings before the LORD at the entrance to the Tent of Meeting.[x]

12"Then the priest is to take one of the male lambs and offer it as a guilt offering,[y] along with the log of oil; he shall wave them before the LORD as a wave offering.[z] 13He is to slaughter the lamb in the holy place[a] where the sin offering and the burnt offering are slaughtered. Like the sin offering, the guilt offering belongs to the priest;[b] it is most holy. 14The priest is to take some of the blood of the guilt offering and put it on the lobe of the right ear of the one to be cleansed, on the thumb of his right hand and on the big toe of his right foot.[c] 15The priest shall then take some of the log of oil, pour it in the palm of his own left hand,[d] 16dip his right forefinger into the oil in his palm, and with his finger sprinkle some of it before the LORD seven times.[e] 17The priest is to put some of the oil remaining in his palm on the lobe of the right ear of the one to be cleansed, on the thumb of his right hand and on the big toe of his right foot, on top of the blood of the guilt offering.[f] 18The rest of the oil in his palm the priest shall put on the head of the one to be cleansed[g] and make atonement for him before the LORD.

19"Then the priest is to sacrifice the sin offering and make atonement for the one to be cleansed from his uncleanness.[h] After that, the priest shall slaughter the burnt offering 20and offer it on the altar, together with the grain offering, and make atonement for him,[i] and he will be clean.[j]

21"If, however, he is poor[k] and cannot afford these,[l] he must take one male lamb as a guilt offering to be waved to make atonement for him, together with a tenth of an ephah[d] of fine flour mixed with oil for a grain offering, a log of oil, 22and two doves or two young pigeons,[m] which he can afford, one for a sin offering and the other for a burnt offering.[n]

23"On the eighth day he must bring them for his cleansing to the priest at the entrance to the Tent of Meeting,[o] before the LORD.[p] 24The priest is to take the lamb for the guilt offering,[q] together with the log of oil,[r] and wave them before the LORD as a wave offering.[s] 25He shall slaughter the lamb for the guilt offering and take some of its blood and put it on the lobe of the right ear of the one to be cleansed, on the thumb of his right hand and on the big toe of his right foot.[t] 26The priest is to pour some of the oil into the palm of his own left hand,[u] 27and with his right forefinger sprinkle some of the oil from his palm seven times before the LORD. 28Some of the oil in his palm he is to put on the same places he put the blood of the guilt offering—on the lobe of the right ear of the one to be cleansed, on the thumb of his right hand and on the big toe of his right foot. 29The rest of the oil in his palm the priest shall put on the head of the one to be cleansed, to make atonement for him before the LORD.[v] 30Then he shall sacrifice the doves or the young pigeons, which the person can afford,[w] 31one[e] as a sin offering and the other as a burnt offering,[x] together with the grain offering. In this way the priest will make

3 [b]Lev 13:46; [c]**Lev 13:2**
4 [d]**Ex 12:22;** [e]ver 6,49, 51–52; Nu 19:6; Ps 51:7
5 [f]ver 50
6 [g]**ver 4**
7 [h]ver 51; [i]2Ki 5:10,14; Isa 52:15; Eze 36:25; [j]ver 53
8 [k]**Lev 11:25;** [l]ver 9; **Ex 29:4;** Lev 15:5; 17:15; 22:6; Nu 19:7–8; [m]ver 20; [n]**Lev 13:11;** Nu 5:2–3; 12:14–15; 19:20; 31:24; 2Ch 26:21
9 [o]**Lev 13:5;** [p]Nu 6:9; Dt 21:12; [q]**Lev 13:6**
10 [r]Nu 6:10; Mt 8:4; Mk 1:44; Lk 5:14; [s]**Lev 4:32;** [t]Nu 15:9; 28:20; [u]Lev 2:1; [v]ver 12, 15,21,24
11 [w]Nu 6:16; [x]Nu 6:10
12 [y]**Lev 5:18;** [z]**Ex 29:24**
13 [a]**Ex 29:11;** [b]Lev 6:24–30; **7:7**
14 [c]**Ex 29:20**
15 [d]ver 26
16 [e]ver 27
17 [f]ver 28
18 [g]ver 31; Lev 15:15
19 [h]ver 31; **Lev 5:3;** 15:15
20 [i]Lev 15:30; [j]ver 8
21 [k]**Lev 5:7;** [l]ver 22,32
22 [m]**Lev 5:7;** [n]Lev 15:30
23 [o]Lev 15:14,29; [p]**ver 10–11**
24 [q]Nu 6:14; [r]**ver 10;** [s]ver 12
25 [t]**Ex 29:20**
26 [u]ver 15
29 [v]ver 18
30 [w]**Lev 5:7**
31 [x]ver 22; Lev 5:7; 15:15,30

[a]*3* Traditionally *leprosy*; the Hebrew word was used for various diseases affecting the skin—not necessarily leprosy; also elsewhere in this chapter.
[b]*10* That is, probably about 11½ pints (about 6.5 litres)
[c]*10* That is, probably about ½ pint (about 0.3 litre); also in verses 12, 15, 21 and 24
[d]*21* That is, probably about 4 pints (about 2 litres)
[e]*31* Septuagint and Syriac; Hebrew [31]*such as the person can afford, one*

atonement before the LORD on behalf of the one to be cleansed.[y]"

32These are the regulations for anyone who has an infectious skin disease[z] and who cannot afford the regular offerings[a] for his cleansing.

Cleansing From Mildew

33The LORD said to Moses and Aaron, 34"When you enter the land of Canaan,[b] which I am giving you as your possession,[c] and I put a spreading mildew in a house in that land, 35the owner of the house must go and tell the priest, 'I have seen something that looks like mildew in my house.' 36The priest is to order the house to be emptied before he goes in to examine the mildew, so that nothing in the house will be pronounced unclean. After this the priest is to go in and inspect the house. 37He is to examine the mildew on the walls, and if it has greenish or reddish[d] depressions that appear to be deeper than the surface of the wall, 38the priest shall go out of the doorway of the house and close it up for seven days.[e] 39On the seventh day[f] the priest shall return to inspect the house. If the mildew has spread on the walls, 40he is to order that the contaminated stones be torn out and thrown into an unclean place outside the town.[g] 41He must have all the inside walls of the house scraped and the material that is scraped off dumped into an unclean place outside the town. 42Then they are to take other stones to replace these and take new clay and plaster the house.

43"If the mildew reappears in the house after the stones have been torn out and the house scraped and plastered, 44the priest is to go and examine it and, if the mildew has spread in the house, it is a destructive mildew; the house is unclean.[h] 45It must be torn down—its stones, timbers and all the plaster—and taken out of the town to an unclean place.

46"Anyone who goes into the house while it is closed up will be unclean till evening.[i] 47Anyone who sleeps or eats in the house must wash his clothes.[j]

48"But if the priest comes to examine it and the mildew has not spread after the house has been plastered, he shall pronounce the house clean,[k] because the mildew is gone. 49To purify the house he is to take two birds and some cedar wood, scarlet yarn and hyssop.[l] 50He shall kill one of the birds over fresh water in a clay pot.[m] 51Then he is to take the cedar wood, the hyssop,[n] the scarlet yarn and the live bird, dip them into the blood of the dead bird and the fresh water, and sprinkle the house seven times.[o] 52He shall purify the house with the bird's blood, the fresh water, the live bird, the cedar wood, the hyssop and the scarlet yarn. 53Then he is to release the live bird in the open fields[p] outside the town. In this way he will make atonement for the house, and it will be clean.[q]"

54These are the regulations for any infectious skin disease,[r] for an itch, 55for mildew[s] in clothing or in a house, 56and for a swelling, a rash or a bright spot,[t] 57to determine when something is clean or unclean.

These are the regulations for infectious skin diseases and mildew.[u]

Discharges Causing Uncleanness

15 The LORD said to Moses and Aaron, 2"Speak to the Israelites and say to them: 'When any man has a bodily discharge,[a] the discharge is unclean. 3Whether it continues flowing from his body or is blocked, it will make him unclean. This is how his discharge will bring about uncleanness:

4" 'Any bed the man with a discharge lies on will be unclean, and anything he sits on will be unclean. 5Anyone who touches his bed must wash his clothes[b] and bathe with water,[c] and he will be unclean till evening.[d] 6Whoever sits on anything that the man with a discharge sat on must wash his clothes and bathe with water, and he will be unclean till evening.

7" 'Whoever touches the man[e] who has a discharge[f] must wash his clothes and bathe with water, and he will be unclean till evening.

8" 'If the man with the discharge spits[g] on someone who is clean, that person must wash his clothes and bathe with water, and he will be unclean till evening.

9" 'Everything the man sits on when riding will be unclean, 10and whoever touches any of the things that were under him will be unclean till evening; whoever picks up those things[h] must wash his clothes and bathe with water, and he will be unclean till evening.

11" 'Anyone the man with a discharge touches without rinsing his hands with water must wash his clothes and bathe with water, and he will be unclean till evening.

12" 'A clay pot[i] that the man touches must be broken, and any wooden article[j] is to be rinsed with water.

31 [y]**ver 18–19**
32 [z]**Lev 13:2;** [a]**ver 21**
34 [b]Ge 12:5; Ex 6:4; Nu 13:2; [c]Ge 17:8; 48:4; Nu 27:12; 32:22; Dt 3:27; 7:1; 32:49
37 [d]**Lev 13:19**
38 [e]**Lev 13:4**
39 [f]Lev 13:5
40 [g]ver 45
44 [h]Lev 13:51
46 [i]**Lev 11:24**
47 [j]**Lev 11:25**
48 [k]**Lev 13:6**
49 [l]1Ki 4:33
50 [m]ver 5
51 [n]ver 6; Ps 51:7; [o]**ver 4**,7
53 [p]**ver 7;** [q]ver 20
54 [r]Lev 13:2
55 [s]Lev 13:47–52
56 [t]Lev 13:2
57 [u]**Lev 10:10**

Ch. 15

2 [a]ver 16,32; Lev 22:4; Nu 5:2; 2Sa 3:29; Mt 9:20
5 [b]**Lev 11:25;** [c]Lev 14:8; [d]**Lev 11:24**
7 [e]ver 19; Lev 22:5; [f]ver 16; Lev 22:4
8 [g]Nu 12:14
10 [h]Nu 19:10
12 [i]**Lev 6:28;** [j]**Lev 11:32**

13"'When a man is cleansed from his
discharge, he is to count off seven days[k]
for his ceremonial cleansing; he must
wash his clothes and bathe himself with
fresh water, and he will be clean.[l] 14On
the eighth day he must take two doves
or two young pigeons[m] and come before
the LORD to the entrance to the Tent of
Meeting and give them to the priest.
15The priest is to sacrifice them, the one
for a sin offering[n] and the other for a
burnt offering.[o] In this way he will make
atonement before the LORD for the man
because of his discharge.[p]
16"'When a man has an emission of
semen,[q] he must bathe his whole body
with water, and he will be unclean till
evening.[r] 17Any clothing or leather that
has semen on it must be washed with
water, and it will be unclean till eve-
ning. 18When a man lies with a woman
and there is an emission of semen,[s] both
must bathe with water, and they will be
unclean till evening.
19"'When a woman has her regular
flow of blood, the impurity of her
monthly period[t] will last seven days,
and anyone who touches her will be
unclean till evening.
20"'Anything she lies on during her
period will be unclean, and anything
she sits on will be unclean. 21Whoever
touches her bed must wash his clothes
and bathe with water, and he will be un-
clean till evening.[u] 22Whoever touches
anything she sits on must wash his
clothes and bathe with water, and he
will be unclean till evening. 23Whether
it is the bed or anything she was sitting
on, when anyone touches it, he will be
unclean till evening.
24"'If a man lies with her and her
monthly flow[v] touches him, he will be
unclean for seven days; any bed he lies
on will be unclean.
25"'When a woman has a discharge of
blood for many days at a time other than
her monthly period[w] or has a discharge
that continues beyond her period, she
will be unclean as long as she has the
discharge, just as in the days of her
period. 26Any bed she lies on while her
discharge continues will be unclean, as
is her bed during her monthly period,
and anything she sits on will be un-
clean, as during her period. 27Whoever
touches them will be unclean; he must
wash his clothes and bathe with water,
and he will be unclean till evening.
28"'When she is cleansed from her
discharge, she must count off seven
days, and after that she will be cere-
monially clean. 29On the eighth day she
must take two doves or two young
pigeons[x] and bring them to the priest at
the entrance to the Tent of Meeting.
30The priest is to sacrifice one for a
sin offering and the other for a burnt
offering. In this way he will make
atonement for her before the LORD for
the uncleanness of her discharge.[y]
31"'You must keep the Israelites
separate from things that make them
unclean, so they will not die in their
uncleanness for defiling my dwelling-
place,[a][z] which is among them.'"
32These are the regulations for a man
with a discharge, for anyone made un-
clean by an emission of semen,[a] 33for a
woman in her monthly period, for a
man or a woman with a discharge, and
for a man who lies with a woman who is
ceremonially unclean.[b]

The Day of Atonement

16:2–34pp—Lev 23:26–32; Nu 29:7–11

16 The LORD spoke to Moses after
the death of the two sons of
Aaron who died when they approached
the LORD.[a] 2The LORD said to Moses:
"Tell your brother Aaron not to come
whenever he chooses[b] into the Most
Holy Place[c] behind the curtain[d] in front
of the atonement cover[e] on the ark, or
else he will die, because I appear[f] in the
cloud[g] over the atonement cover.
3"This is how Aaron is to enter the
sanctuary area:[h] with a young bull[i] for a
sin offering and a ram for a burnt offer-
ing.[j] 4He is to put on the sacred linen
tunic,[k] with linen undergarments next
to his body; he is to tie the linen sash
around him and put on the linen tur-
ban.[l] These are sacred garments;[m] so he
must bathe himself with water[n] before
he puts them on.[o] 5From the Israelite
community[p] he is to take two male
goats[q] for a sin offering and a ram for a
burnt offering.
6"Aaron is to offer the bull for his own
sin offering to make atonement for him-
self and his household.[r] 7Then he is to
take the two goats and present them
before the LORD at the entrance to the
Tent of Meeting. 8He is to cast lots[s] for
the two goats—one lot for the LORD and
the other for the scapegoat.[a][t] 9Aaron
shall bring the goat whose lot falls to the
LORD and sacrifice it for a sin offering.
10But the goat chosen by lot as the
scapegoat shall be presented alive

13 [k]**Lev 8:33;** [l]ver 5
14 [m]Lev 14:22
15 [n]Lev 5:7; [o]Lev 14:31; [p]**Lev 14:18,**19
16 [q]**ver 2;** Dt 23:10; [r]ver 5; Dt 23:11
18 [s]1Sa 21:4
19 [t]**ver 24**
21 [u]ver 27
24 [v]ver 19; Lev 12:2; 18:19; 20:18; Eze 18:6
25 [w]Mt 9:20; Mk 5:25; Lk 8:43
29 [x]Lev 14:22
30 [y]Lev 5:10; 14:20,31; 18:19; 2Sa 11:4; Mk 5:25; Lk 8:43
31 [z]Lev 20:3; Nu 5:3; 19:13,20; 2Sa 15:25; 2Ki 21:7; Ps 33:14; 74:7; 76:2; Eze 5:11; 23:38
32 [a]**ver 2**
33 [b]ver 19,24–25

Ch. 16

1 [a]**Lev 10:1**
2 [b]Ex 30:10; Heb 9:7; [c]**Ex 26:33;** Heb 9:25; 10:19; [d]**Ex 26:33;** Heb 6:19; [e]**Ex 26:34;** [f]**Ex 25:22;** [g]**Ex 40:34; 2Sa 22:10**
3 [h]ver 6; Lev 4:1–12; Heb 9:24–25; [i]**Lev 4:3;** [j]ver 5
4 [k]**Lev 8:13;** [l]**Ex 28:39;** [m]ver 32; **Ex 28:42;** 29:29–30; Lev 21:10; Nu 20:26,28; [n]**Ex 29:4;** Heb 10:22; [o]Eze 9:2; 44:17–18
5 [p]**Lev 4:13–21;** [q]ver 20; **Lev 4:3;** 2Ch 29:23; Ps 50:9
6 [r]Lev 9:7; Heb 7:27; 9:7,12
8 [s]Nu 26:55–56; 33:54; 34:13; Jos 14:2; 18:6; Jdg 20:9; Ne 10:34; Est 3:7; 9:24; Ps 22:18; Pr 16:33; [t]ver 10,26

[a]31 Or *my tabernacle*

[a]8 That is, the goat of removal; Hebrew *azazel;* also in verses 10 and 26

before the LORD to be used for making atonement[u] by sending it into the desert as a scapegoat.

11"Aaron shall bring the bull for his own sin offering to make atonement for himself and his household,[v] and he is to slaughter the bull for his own sin offering. 12He is to take a censer full of burning coals[w] from the altar before the LORD and two handfuls of finely ground fragrant incense[x] and take them behind the curtain. 13He is to put the incense on the fire before the LORD, and the smoke of the incense will conceal the atonement cover[y] above the Testimony, so that he will not die.[z] 14He is to take some of the bull's blood[a] and with his finger sprinkle it on the front of the atonement cover; then he shall sprinkle some of it with his finger seven times before the atonement cover.[b]

15"He shall then slaughter the goat for the sin offering for the people[c] and take its blood behind the curtain[d] and do with it as he did with the bull's blood: He shall sprinkle[e] it on the atonement cover and in front of it. 16In this way he will make atonement[f] for the Most Holy Place[g] because of the uncleanness and rebellion of the Israelites, whatever their sins have been. He is to do the same for the Tent of Meeting,[h] which is among them in the midst of their uncleanness. 17No-one is to be in the Tent of Meeting from the time Aaron goes in to make atonement in the Most Holy Place until he comes out, having made atonement for himself, his household and the whole community of Israel.

18"Then he shall come out to the altar[i] that is before the LORD and make atonement for it. He shall take some of the bull's blood and some of the goat's blood and put it on all the horns of the altar.[j] 19He shall sprinkle some of the blood on it with his finger seven times to cleanse it and consecrate it from the uncleanness of the Israelites.[k]

20"When Aaron has finished making atonement for the Most Holy Place, the Tent of Meeting and the altar, he shall bring forward the live goat.[l] 21He is to lay both hands on the head of the live goat[m] and confess[n] over it all the wickedness and rebellion of the Israelites—all their sins—and put them on the goat's head. He shall send the goat away into the desert in the care of a man appointed for the task. 22The goat will carry on itself all their sins[o] to a solitary place; and the man shall release it in the desert.

23"Then Aaron is to go into the Tent of Meeting and take off the linen garments[p] he put on before he entered the Most Holy Place, and he is to leave them there.[q] 24He shall bathe himself with water in a holy place[r] and put on his regular garments.[s] Then he shall come out and sacrifice the burnt offering for himself and the burnt offering for the people,[t] to make atonement for himself and for the people.[u] 25He shall also burn the fat of the sin offering on the altar.

26"The man who releases the goat as a scapegoat[v] must wash his clothes[w] and bathe himself with water;[x] afterwards he may come into the camp. 27The bull and the goat for the sin offerings, whose blood was brought into the Most Holy Place to make atonement, must be taken outside the camp;[y] their hides, flesh and offal are to be burned up. 28The man who burns them must wash his clothes and bathe himself with water; afterwards he may come into the camp.[z]

29"This is to be a lasting ordinance[a] for you: On the tenth day of the seventh month[b] you must deny yourselves[b][c] and not do any work[d]—whether native-born[e] or an alien living among you—30because on this day atonement will be made[f] for you, to cleanse you. Then, before the LORD, you will be clean from all your sins.[g] 31It is a sabbath of rest, and you must deny yourselves;[h] it is a lasting ordinance.[i] 32The priest who is anointed and ordained[j] to succeed his father as high priest is to make atonement. He is to put on the sacred linen garments[k] 33and make atonement for the Most Holy Place, for the Tent of Meeting and the altar, and for the priests and all the people of the community.[l]

34"This is to be a lasting ordinance[m] for you: Atonement is to be made once a year[n] for all the sins of the Israelites."

And it was done, as the LORD commanded Moses.

Eating Blood Forbidden

17 The LORD said to Moses, 2"Speak to Aaron and his sons[a] and to all the Israelites and say to them: 'This is what the LORD has commanded: 3Any Israelite who sacrifices an ox,[a] a lamb[b] or a goat[c] in the camp or outside of it 4instead of bringing it to the entrance to the Tent of Meeting[d] to present it as an offering to the LORD in front of the

10 [u]**Isa 53:4–10; Ro 3:25**
11 [v]**ver 6**,24,33
12 [w]**Lev 10:1;** Rev 8:5; [x]**Ex 25:6; 30:34–38**
13 [y]**Ex 25:17;** [z]**Ex 28:43**
14 [a]**Lev 4:5;** Heb 9:7,13,25; [b]**Lev 4:6**
15 [c]**Lev 4:13–21;** Heb 7:27; 9:7,12; 13:11; [d]Heb 9:3; [e]**Lev 4:17;** Nu 19:19; Isa 52:15; Eze 36:25
16 [f]**Ex 29:36; Ro 3:25;** [g]**Ex 26:33;** Heb 9:25; [h]Ex 29:4; **40:2**
18 [i]**Lev 4:7;** [j]**Lev 4:25**
19 [k]Eze 43:20
20 [l]**ver 5**
21 [m]**Ex 29:10;** [n]**Lev 5:5**
22 [o]**Ex 28:38;** Isa 53:12
23 [p]**Ex 28:42;** [q]Eze 42:14
24 [r]**Lev 6:16;** [s]ver 3–5; [t]Lev 1:3; [u]**ver 11**
26 [v]**ver 8;** [w]**Lev 11:25;** [x]Lev 14:8
27 [y]**Ex 29:14**
28 [z]Nu 19:8,10
29 [a]**Ex 12:14;** [b]Lev 25:9; [c]ver 31; Lev 23:27, 32; Nu 29:7; Isa 58:3; [d]**Ex 31:15; Lev 23:28;** [e]Ex 12:19
30 [f]**Ex 30:10;** [g]Ps 51:2; Jer 33:8; Eze 36:33; Zec 13:1; Eph 5:26
31 [h]Ezr 8:21; Isa 58:3,5; Da 10:12; [i]Ac 27:9
32 [j]**Ex 30:30;** [k]**ver 4; Ex 28:2**
33 [l]**ver 11**,16–18; Eze 45:18
34 [m]**Ex 27:21;** [n]Heb 9:7,25

Ch. 17

2 [a]Lev 10:6,12
3 [b]**Lev 3:7;** [c]**Lev 7:23**
4 [d]ver 9; 1Ki 8:4; 2Ch 1:3

[b]29 Or *must fast;* also in verse 31
[a]3 The Hebrew word can include both male and female.

tabernacle of the LORD[e]—that man shall
be considered guilty of bloodshed; he
has shed blood and must be cut off from
his people.[f] 5This is so that the Israelites
will bring to the LORD the sacrifices they
are now making in the open fields. They
must bring them to the priest, that is,
to the LORD, at the entrance to the Tent
of Meeting and sacrifice them as
fellowship offerings.[b][g] 6The priest is to
sprinkle the blood against the altar[h] of
the LORD[i] at the entrance to the Tent of
Meeting and burn the fat as an aroma
pleasing to the LORD[j]. 7They must no
longer offer any of their sacrifices to the
goat idols[c][k] to whom they prostitute
themselves.[l] This is to be a lasting
ordinance[m] for them and for the
generations to come.'[n]
8"Say to them: 'Any Israelite or any
alien living among them who offers a
burnt offering or sacrifice 9and does not
bring it to the entrance to the Tent[o] of
Meeting[p] to sacrifice it to the LORD[q]—
that man must be cut off from his
people.
10" 'Any Israelite or any alien living
among them who eats any blood—I will
set my face against that person who eats
blood[r] and will cut him off from his
people. 11For the life of a creature is in
the blood,[s] and I have given it to you to
make atonement for yourselves on the
altar; it is the blood that makes atone-
ment for one's life.[t] 12Therefore I say to
the Israelites, "None of you may eat
blood, nor may an alien living among
you eat blood."
13" 'Any Israelite or any alien living
among you who hunts any animal or
bird that may be eaten must drain out
the blood and cover it with earth,[u]
14because the life of every creature is its
blood. That is why I have said to the
Israelites, "You must not eat the blood
of any creature, because the life of every
creature is its blood; anyone who eats it
must be cut off."[v]
15" 'Anyone, whether native-born or
alien, who eats anything[w] found dead
or torn by wild animals[x] must wash his
clothes and bathe with water,[y] and he
will be ceremonially unclean till eve-
ning;[z] then he will be clean. 16But if he
does not wash his clothes and bathe
himself, he will be held responsible.[a]' "

Unlawful Sexual Relations

18 The LORD said to Moses,
2"Speak to the Israelites and say
to them: 'I am the LORD your God.[a] 3You
must not do as they do in Egypt, where
you used to live, and you must not do as
they do in the land of Canaan, where I
am bringing you. Do not follow their
practices.[b] 4You must obey my laws[c] and
be careful to follow my decrees.[d] I am
the LORD your God.[e] 5Keep my decrees
and laws,[f] for the man who obeys them
will live by them.[g] I am the LORD.
6" 'No-one is to approach any close
relative to have sexual relations. I am
the LORD.
7" 'Do not dishonour your father[h] by
having sexual relations with your
mother.[i] She is your mother; do not
have relations with her.
8" 'Do not have sexual relations
with your father's wife;[j] that would
dishonour your father.[k]
9" 'Do not have sexual relations
with your sister,[l] either your father's
daughter or your mother's daughter,
whether she was born in the same
home or elsewhere.[m]
10" 'Do not have sexual relations with
your son's daughter or your daughter's
daughter; that would dishonour you.
11" 'Do not have sexual relations with
the daughter of your father's wife, born
to your father; she is your sister.
12" 'Do not have sexual relations with
your father's sister;[n] she is your father's
close relative.
13" 'Do not have sexual relations with
your mother's sister,[o] because she is
your mother's close relative.
14" 'Do not dishonour your father's
brother by approaching his wife to have
sexual relations; she is your aunt.[p]
15" 'Do not have sexual relations with
your daughter-in-law.[q] She is your son's
wife; do not have relations with her.[r]
16" 'Do not have sexual relations
with your brother's wife;[s] that would
dishonour your brother.
17" 'Do not have sexual relations with
both a woman and her daughter.[t] Do
not have sexual relations with either her
son's daughter or her daughter's
daughter; they are her close relatives.
That is wickedness.
18" 'Do not take your wife's[u] sister as a
rival wife and have sexual relations with
her while your wife is living.
19" 'Do not approach a woman to have
sexual relations during the unclean-
ness[v] of her monthly period.[w]
20" 'Do not have sexual relations with
your neighbour's wife[x] and defile
yourself with her.

4 [e]Dt 12:5–21; [f]**Ge 17:14**
5 [g]**Lev 3:1**; Eze 43:27
6 [h]**Lev 4:18**; [i]**Lev 3:2**; [j]**Lev 1:9**
7 [k]**Ex 22:20**; [l]**Ex 34:15**; Jer 3:6, 9; Eze 23:3; 1Co 10:20; [m]**Ex 12:14**; [n]**Ge 9:12**
9 [o]**Lev 1:3**; [p]**ver 4**; [q]**Lev 3:7**
10 [r]**Ge 9:4**
11 [s]ver 14; [t]Heb 9:22
13 [u]Lev 7:26; Eze 24:7; 33:25; Ac 15:20
14 [v]**Ge 9:4**
15 [w]**Lev 7:24**; [x]**Ex 22:31**; [y]**Lev 14:8**; [z]**Lev 11:40**
16 [a]**Lev 5:1**

Ch. 18

2 [a]**Ge 17:7**
3 [b]ver 24–30; **Ex 23:24**; Dt 18:9; 2Ki 16:3; 17:8; 1Ch 5:25
4 [c]Ge 26:5; [d]Dt 4:1; 1Ki 11:11; Jer 44:10,23; Eze 11:12; [e]ver 2
5 [f]Ge 26:5; [g]Dt 4:1; Ne 9:29; Isa 55:3; Eze 18:9; 20:11; Am 5:4–6; Mt 19:17; **Ro 10:5***; Gal 3:12*
7 [h]ver 8; Lev 20:11; Dt 27:20; [i]Eze 22:10
8 [j]1Co 5:1; [k]Ge 35:22; Lev 20:11; Dt 22:30; 27:20
9 [l]ver 11; Lev 20:17; Dt 27:22; [m]Lev 20:17; Dt 27:22; 2Sa 13:13; Eze 22:11
12 [n]ver 13; Lev 20:19
13 [o]ver 12,14; Lev 20:20
14 [p]**ver 13**
15 [q]**Ge 11:31**; **38:16**; [r]Eze 22:11
16 [s]Lev 20:21; Mt 14:4; Mk 6:18
17 [t]Lev 20:14; Dt 27:23
18 [u]**Ge 30:1**
19 [v]**Lev 15:25–30**; [w]**Lev 15:24**
20 [x]**Ex 20:14**; Mt 5:27–28; 1Co 6:9; Heb 13:4

[b]5 Traditionally *peace offerings*
[c]7 Or *demons*

21“‘Do not give any of your children[y]
to be sacrificed[a] to Molech,[z] for you
must not profane the name of your
God.[a] I am the LORD.[b]
22“‘Do not lie with a man as one lies
with a woman;[c] that is detestable.[d]
23“‘Do not have sexual relations with
an animal and defile yourself with it. A
woman must not present herself to an
animal to have sexual relations with it;
that is a perversion.[e]
24“‘Do not defile yourselves in any of
these ways, because this is how the
nations that I am going to drive out
before you[f] became defiled.[g] 25Even
the land was defiled;[h] so I punished it
for its sin,[i] and the land vomited out its
inhabitants.[j] 26But you must keep my
decrees and my laws.[k] The native-born
and the aliens living among you must
not do any of these detestable things,
27for all these things were done by the
people who lived in the land before you,
and the land became defiled. 28And if
you defile the land,[l] it will vomit you
out[m] as it vomited out the nations that
were before you.
29“‘Everyone who does any of these
detestable things—such persons must
be cut off from their people. 30Keep my
requirements[n] and do not follow any
of the detestable customs that were
practised before you came and do not
defile yourselves with them. I am the
LORD your God.[o]’ ”

Various Laws

19 The LORD said to Moses,
2“Speak to the entire assembly
of Israel[a] and say to them: ‘Be holy be-
cause I, the LORD your God,[b] am holy.[c]
3“‘Each of you must respect his
mother and father,[d] and you must
observe my Sabbaths.[e] I am the LORD
your God.[f]
4“‘Do not turn to idols or make gods
of cast metal for yourselves.[g] I am the
LORD your God.[h]
5“‘When you sacrifice a fellowship
offering[a] to the LORD, sacrifice it in such
a way that it will be accepted on your
behalf. 6It shall be eaten on the day you
sacrifice it or on the next day; anything
left over until the third day must be
burned up.[i] 7If any of it is eaten on the
third day, it is impure and will not be
accepted.[j] 8Whoever eats it will be held
responsible[k] because he has desecrated
what is holy[l] to the LORD; that person
must be cut off from his people.[m]
9“‘When you reap the harvest of your
land, do not reap to the very edges[n] of
your field or gather the gleanings of
your harvest.[o] 10Do not go over your
vineyard a second time[p] or pick up the
grapes that have fallen.[q] Leave them for
the poor and the alien.[r] I am the LORD
your God.
11“‘Do not steal.[s]
“‘Do not lie.[t]
“‘Do not deceive one another.[u]
12“‘Do not swear falsely[v] by my
name[w] and so profane[x] the name of your
God. I am the LORD.
13“‘Do not defraud your neighbour[y]
or rob[z] him.[a]
“‘Do not hold back the wages of a
hired man[b] overnight.[c]
14“‘Do not curse the deaf or put a
stumbling-block in front of the blind,[d]
but fear your God.[e] I am the LORD.
15“‘Do not pervert justice;[f] do not
show partiality[g] to the poor or
favouritism to the great,[h] but judge
your neighbour fairly.[i]
16“‘Do not go about spreading
slander[j] among your people.
“‘Do not do anything that endangers
your neighbour’s life.[k] I am the LORD.
17“‘Do not hate your brother in your
heart.[l] Rebuke your neighbour frankly[m]
so that you will not share in his guilt.
18“‘Do not seek revenge[n] or bear a
grudge[o] against one of your people,[p] but
love your neighbour[q] as yourself.[r] I am
the LORD.
19“‘Keep my decrees.[s]
“‘Do not mate different kinds of
animals.
“‘Do not plant your field with two
kinds of seed.[t]
“‘Do not wear clothing woven of two
kinds of material.[u]
20“‘If a man sleeps with a woman who
is a slave girl promised to another man[v]
but who has not been ransomed or
given her freedom, there must be due
punishment. Yet they are not to be put
to death, because she had not been

21 [y]Dt 12:31; 18:10; 2Ki 16:3; 17:17; 21:6; 23:10; 2Ch 28:1-4; 33:6; Ps 106:37–38; Isa 57:5; Jer 7:30–31; 19:5; 32:35; Eze 16:20; Mic 6:7; [z]Lev 20:2–5; Dt 9:4; 1Ki 11:5,7,33; Isa 57:9; Jer 32:35; 49:1; Zep 1:5; [a]Lev 19:12; 21:6; Isa 48:11; Eze 22:26; 36:20; Am 2:7; Mal 1:12; [b]**Ex 6:2**
22 [c]Lev 20:13; Dt 23:18; Ro 1:27; 1Co 6:9; [d]**Ge 19:5**
23 [e]Ex 22:19; Lev 20:15; Dt 27:21
24 [f]ver 3,27,30; Lev 20:23; [g]Dt 9:4; 18:12
25 [h]Nu 35:34; Dt 21:23; [i]Lev 20:23; Dt 9:5; 12:31; 18:12; [j]ver 28; Lev 20:22; Job 20:15; Jer 51:34
26 [k]**Ge 26:5**
28 [l]Lev 20:22; Ezr 9:11; La 1:17; [m]**ver 25**
30 [n]**Lev 8:35**; [o]ver 2

Ch. 19

2 [a]Nu 14:5; Ps 68:26; [b]**Ex 20:2**; [c]**Ex 15:11**; 1Pe 1:16*; **Lev 11:44**; **20:26**
3 [d]Ex 20:12; [e]**Ex 20:8**; [f]Lev 11:44
4 [g]**Ex 20:4**; Jdg 17:3; Ps 96:5; 115:4–7; 135:15; [h]Lev 11:44
6 [i]Lev 7:16–17
7 [j]Lev 7:18
8 [k]**Lev 5:1**; [l]Lev 22:2,15–16; Nu 18:32; [m]**Ge 17:14**
9 [n]Ru 2:2–3,7, 16–17; [o]Lev 23:10,22; Dt 24:19–22; Job 24:10
10 [p]Dt 24:20; [q]ver 9; [r]Dt 24:19,21
11 [s]Ex 20:15; **23:4**; Lk 3:14; [t]**Ex 20:16; Eph 4:25**; [u]**Lev 6:2**
12 [v]Jer 5:2; 7:9; Mal 3:5; [w]Ex 3:13; 20:7; Dt 18:19; Pr 18:10; Isa 42:8; Jer 44:16,26; **Mt 5:33**; [x]Jer 34:16
13 [y]Lev 25:14,17; [z]**Ex 20:15**; [a]**Ex 22:15**,25–27; [b]Job 7:2; 24:12; 31:39; Isa 16:14; Mal 3:5; [c]Dt 24:15; Jer 22:13; Mt 20:8; 1Ti 5:18; Jas 5:4
14 [d]**Ex 4:11**; Lev 21:18; Dt 27:18; [e]ver 32; Lev 25:17,36
15 [f]**Ex 23:2**; [g]Dt 24:17; Job 13:8,10; 32:21; Pr 28:21; [h]Job 34:19; [i]**Ex 23:8**; Pr 24:23; Mal 2:9; Jas 2:1–4
16 [j]Ps 15:3; 31:13; 41:6; 101:5; Jer 6:28; 9:4; Eze 22:9; [k]Ex 23:7; Dt 10:17; 27:25; Ps 15:5; Eze 22:12
17 [l]**1Jn 2:9**; [m]**Mt 18:15**
18 [n]**Ge 4:23**; Ro 12:19; Heb 10:30; [o]Ps 103:9; [p]**Ex 12:48**; [q]**Ex 20:16**; [r]ver 34; **Mt 5:43***; 19:16*; 22:39*; Mk 12:21*; Lk 10:27*; Jn 13:34; Ro 13:9*; Gal 5:14*; Jas 2:8*
19 [s]**Ge 26:5**; [t]Dt 22:9; [u]Dt 22:11
20 [v]Dt 22:23–27

[a]21 Or *to be passed through ⌊the fire⌋*
[a]5 Traditionally *peace offering*

freed. 21The man, however, must bring a ram to the entrance to the Tent of Meeting for a guilt offering to the LORD.[w] 22With the ram of the guilt offering the priest is to make atonement for him before the LORD for the sin he has committed, and his sin will be forgiven.[x]

23"'When you enter the land and plant any kind of fruit tree, regard its fruit as forbidden.[b] For three years you are to consider it forbidden;[b] it must not be eaten. 24In the fourth year all its fruit will be holy,[y] an offering of praise to the LORD. 25But in the fifth year you may eat its fruit. In this way your harvest will be increased. I am the LORD your God.

26"'Do not eat any meat with the blood still in it.[z]

"'Do not practise divination[a] or sorcery.[b]

27"'Do not cut the hair at the sides of your head or clip off the edges of your beard.[c]

28"'Do not cut[d] your bodies for the dead or put tattoo marks on yourselves. I am the LORD.

29"'Do not degrade your daughter by making her a prostitute,[e] or the land will turn to prostitution and be filled with wickedness.[f]

30"'Observe my Sabbaths[g] and have reverence for my sanctuary. I am the LORD.[h]

31"'Do not turn to mediums[i] or seek out spiritists,[j] for you will be defiled by them. I am the LORD your God.

32"'Rise in the presence of the aged, show respect[k] for the elderly[l] and revere your God.[m] I am the LORD.[n]

33"'When an alien lives with you in your land, do not ill-treat him. 34The alien living with you must be treated as one of your native-born.[o] Love him as yourself,[p] for you were aliens[q] in Egypt.[r] I am the LORD your God.

35"'Do not use dishonest standards when measuring length, weight or quantity.[s] 36Use honest scales[t] and honest weights, an honest ephah[c][u] and an honest hin.[d][v] I am the LORD your God, who brought you out of Egypt.[w]

37"'Keep all my decrees[x] and all my laws[y] and follow them. I am the LORD.'"

Punishments for Sin

20 The LORD said to Moses, 2"Say to the Israelites: 'Any Israelite or any alien living in Israel who gives[a] any of his children to Molech must be put to death.[a] The people of the community are to stone him.[b] 3I will set my face against that man and I will cut him off from his people;[c] for by giving his children to Molech, he has defiled[d] my sanctuary[e] and profaned my holy name.[f] 4If the people of the community close their eyes when that man gives one of his children to Molech and they fail to put him to death,[g] 5I will set my face against that man and his family and will cut off from their people both him and all who follow him in prostituting themselves to Molech.

6"'I will set my face against the person who turns to mediums and spiritists to prostitute himself by following them, and I will cut him off from his people.[h]

7"'Consecrate yourselves[i] and be holy,[j] because I am the LORD your God.[k] 8Keep my decrees[l] and follow them. I am the LORD, who makes you holy.[b][m]

9"'If anyone curses his father[n] or mother,[o] he must be put to death.[p] He has cursed his father or his mother, and his blood will be on his own head.[q]

10"'If a man commits adultery with another man's wife[r]—with the wife of his neighbour—both the adulterer and the adulteress must be put to death.[s]

11"'If a man sleeps with his father's wife, he has dishonoured his father.[t] Both the man and the woman must be put to death; their blood will be on their own heads.[u]

12"'If a man sleeps with his daughter-in-law,[v] both of them must be put to death. What they have done is a perversion; their blood will be on their own heads.

13"'If a man lies with a man as one lies with a woman, both of them have done what is detestable.[w] They must be put to death; their blood will be on their own heads.

14"'If a man marries both a woman and her mother,[x] it is wicked. Both he and they must be burned in the fire,[y] so that no wickedness will be among you.[z]

15"'If a man has sexual relations with an animal,[a] he must be put to death,[b] and you must kill the animal.

16"'If a woman approaches an animal

21 [w]**Lev 5:15**
22 [x]**Lev 5:15**
24 [y]**Ex 22:29**
26 [z]**Ge 9:4;** [a]**Ge 30:27; Isa 44:25;** [b]**Ex 22:18;** 2Ki 17:17
27 [c]Lev 21:5; Dt 14:1; 2Sa 10:4; Jer 41:5; 48:37
28 [d]Lev 21:5; Dt 14:1; 1Ki 18:28; Jer 16:6; 41:5; 47:5
29 [e]Lev 21:9; Dt 23:18; [f]Ge 34:7; Lev 21:9
30 [g]**Ex 20:8;** [h]Lev 26:2
31 [i]**Ex 22:18;** 1Sa 28:7–20; 1Ch 10:13; [j]Lev 20:6; 2Ki 21:6; 23:24; Isa 8:19; 19:3; 29:4; 47:12; 65:4
32 [k]1Ki 12:8; [l]Job 32:4; Pr 23:22; La 5:12; 1Ti 5:1; [m]**ver 14**; Job 29:8; [n]Lev 11:44; 25:17
34 [o]**Ex 12:48;** [p]**ver 18;** [q]**Ex 22:21;** [r]Ex 23:9; Dt 10:19; 23:7; Ps 146:9
35 [s]Dt 25:13–16
36 [t]Job 31:6; Pr 11:1; Hos 12:7; Mic 6:11; [u]Jdg 6:19; Ru 2:17; 1Sa 1:24; 17:17; Eze 45:10; [v]Dt 25:13–15; Pr 20:10; Eze 45:11; [w]**Ex 12:17**
37 [x]2Ki 17:37; 2Ch 7:17; Ps 119:5; Eze 18:9; [y]**Ge 26:5**

Ch. 20

2 [a]ver 10; Ge 26:11; Ex 19:12; [b]ver 27; Lev 24:14; Nu 15:35–36; Dt 21:21; Jos 7:25
3 [c]ver 5–6; Lev 23:30; [d]Ps 74:7; 79:1; Jer 7:30; Eze 5:11; [e]**Lev 15:31;** [f]**Lev 18:21**
4 [g]Dt 17:2–5
6 [h]**ver 3; Lev 19:31**
7 [i]**Lev 11:44;** [j]**Ex 29:1;** 31:13; Lev 11:45; Eph 1:4; 1Pe 1:16*; [k]**Ex 6:2; 20:2**
8 [l]**Ge 26:5;** [m]**Ex 31:13;** Eze 20:12
9 [n]Ex 20:12; Jer 35:16; Mal 1:6; 2:10; [o]**Ex 20:12;** Dt 27:16; Eze 22:7; [p]Ex 21:17; Dt 21:20–21; Mt 15:4*; Mk 7:10*; [q]ver 11; Dt 22:30; Jos 2:19; 2Sa 1:16; 3:29; 1Ki 2:37; Eze 18:13; 33:4–5
10 [r]Ex 20:14; Dt 5:18; 22:22; Jn 8:5; [s]**Ge 38:24; Ex 21:12**
11 [t]**Lev 18:7;** [u]**ver 9; Lev 18:8**
12 [v]**Ge 11:31; 38:16**
13 [w]Lev 18:22
14 [x]**Lev 18:17;** [y]Lev 21:9; Nu 16:39; Jdg 14:15; 15:6; [z]**Lev 18:8;** Dt 27:23
15 [a]**Ex 22:19;** [b]ver 10

b23 Hebrew *uncircumcised*
c36 An ephah was a dry measure.
d36 A hin was a liquid measure.
a2 Or *sacrifices;* also in verses 3 and 4
b8 Or *who sanctifies you;* or *who sets you apart as holy*

to have sexual relations with it, kill both the woman and the animal. They must be put to death; their blood will be on their own heads.

17"'If a man marries his sister,[c] the daughter of either his father or his mother, and they have sexual relations, it is a disgrace. They must be cut off before the eyes[d] of their people. He has dishonoured his sister and will be held responsible.[e]

18"'If a man lies with a woman during her monthly period[f] and has sexual relations with her, he has exposed the source of her flow, and she has also uncovered it. Both of them must be cut off from their people.[g]

19"'Do not have sexual relations with the sister of either your mother or your father,[h] for that would dishonour a close relative; both of you would be held responsible.

20"'If a man sleeps with his aunt,[i] he has dishonoured his uncle. They will be held responsible; they will die childless.[j]

21"'If a man marries his brother's wife,[k] it is an act of impurity; he has dishonoured his brother. They will be childless.[l]

22"'Keep all my decrees and laws[m] and follow them, so that the land[n] where I am bringing you to live may not vomit you out. 23You must not live according to the customs of the nations[o] I am going to drive out before you.[p] Because they did all these things, I abhorred them.[q] 24But I said to you, "You will possess their land; I will give it to you as an inheritance, a land flowing with milk and honey."[r] I am the LORD your God, who has set you apart from the nations.[s]

25"'You must therefore make a distinction between clean and unclean animals and between unclean and clean birds.[t] Do not defile yourselves by any animal or bird or anything that moves along the ground—those which I have set apart as unclean for you. 26You are to be holy to me[c][u] because I, the LORD, am holy,[v] and I have set you apart from the nations[w] to be my own.

27"'A man or woman who is a medium[x] or spiritist among you must be put to death.[y] You are to stone them;[z] their blood will be on their own heads.'"

Rules for Priests

21 The LORD said to Moses, "Speak to the priests, the sons of Aaron,[a] and say to them: 'A priest must not make himself ceremonially unclean[b] for any of his people who die,[c] 2except for a close relative, such as his mother or father,[d] his son or daughter, his brother, 3or an unmarried sister who is dependent on him since she has no husband—for her he may make himself unclean.[e] 4He must not make himself unclean for people related to him by marriage,[a] and so defile himself.

5"'Priests must not shave[f] their heads or shave off the edges of their beards[g] or cut their bodies.[h] 6They must be holy to their God[i] and must not profane the name of their God.[j] Because they present the offerings made to the LORD by fire,[k] the food of their God,[l] they are to be holy.[m]

7"'They must not marry women defiled by prostitution or divorced from their husbands,[n] because priests are holy to their God.[o] 8Regard them as holy,[p] because they offer up the food of your God.[q] Consider them holy, because I the LORD am holy—I who make you holy.[b][r]

9"'If a priest's daughter defiles herself by becoming a prostitute, she disgraces her father; she must be burned in the fire.[s]

10"'The high priest, the one among his brothers who has had the anointing oil poured on his head[t] and who has been ordained to wear the priestly garments,[u] must not let his hair become unkempt[c] or tear his clothes.[v] 11He must not enter a place where there is a dead body.[w] He must not make himself unclean,[x] even for his father or mother,[y] 12nor leave the sanctuary[z] of his God or desecrate it, because he has been dedicated by the anointing oil[a] of his God. I am the LORD.

13"'The woman he marries must be a virgin.[b] 14He must not marry a widow, a divorced woman, or a woman defiled by prostitution, but only a virgin from his own people, 15so that he will not defile his offspring among his people. I am the LORD, who makes him holy.'"[d]

16The LORD said to Moses, 17"Say to Aaron: 'For the generations to come none of your descendants who has a defect[c] may come near to offer the food of his God.[d] 18No man who has any defect[e] may come near: no man who is blind[f] or lame,[g] disfigured or deformed;

17 [c]**Lev 18:9;** [d]**Ge 17:14;** [e]**Lev 5:1**
18 [f]**Lev 15:24;** [g]Eze 18:6
19 [h]**Lev 18:12**
20 [i]**Lev 18:13;** [j]ver 21; Ge 15:2
21 [k]**Lev 18:16;** Mt 14:4; Mk 6:18; [l]**ver 20**
22 [m]**Ge 26:5;** [n]**Lev 18:25–28**
23 [o]**Lev 18:3;** [p]**Lev 18:24;** [q]**Lev 18:25**
24 [r]**Ex 3:8;** Nu 14:8; 16:14; [s]**Ex 33:16**
25 [t]Lev 10:10; Dt 14:3–21; Ac 10:14
26 [u]Dt 14:2; [v]ver 8; Lev 19:2; Jos 24:19; 2Ki 19:22; Ps 99:3; [w]**Ex 33:16**
27 [x]**Ex 22:18;** [y]**Lev 19:31;** [z]**ver 2; Lev 24:14**

Ch. 21

1 [a]**Ex 28:1; Lev 1:5;** [b]**Lev 5:3; 13:3;** [c]ver 11; Nu 5:2; 6:6; 19:11; 31:19
2 [d]ver 11
3 [e]Nu 6:6
5 [f]Lev 13:40; Jer 7:29; 16:6; [g]Eze 5:1; 44:20; [h]**Lev 19:28**
6 [i]ver 8; Ezr 8:28; [j]Lev 18:21; [k]**Lev 3:11;** [l]ver 17, 22; Lev 22:25; [m]**Ex 19:22; Lev 10:3**
7 [n]ver 13–14; [o]Eze 44:22
8 [p]ver 6; [q]Lev 3:11; [r]**Ex 31:13**
9 [s]**Ge 38:24; Lev 19:29**
10 [t]**Ex 29:7;** [u]**Lev 8:7–9,** 13; **Lev 16:4;** [v]**Lev 10:6**
11 [w]Nu 5:2; 6:6; 9:6; 19:11, 13–14; 31:19; [x]Lev 19:28; [y]ver 2
12 [z]**Ex 25:8;** [a]**Ex 28:41**
13 [b]Eze 44:22
17 [c]ver 18,21,23; [d]**ver 6**
18 [e]Lev 22:19–25; [f]**Lev 19:14;** [g]2Sa 4:4; 9:3; 19:26

[c]26 Or *be my holy ones*
[a]4 Or *unclean as a leader among his people*
[b]8 Or *who sanctify you;* or *who set you apart as holy*
[c]10 Or *not uncover his head*
[d]15 Or *who sanctifies him;* or *who sets him apart as holy*

19no man with a crippled foot or hand, 20or who is hunchbacked or dwarfed, or who has any eye defect, or who has festering or running sores or damaged testicles.[h] 21No descendant of Aaron the priest who has any defect[i] is to come near to present the offerings made to the LORD by fire.[j] He has a defect; he must not come near to offer the food of his God.[k] 22He may eat the most holy food of his God,[l] as well as the holy food; 23yet because of his defect,[m] he must not go near the curtain or approach the altar, and so desecrate my sanctuary.[n] I am the LORD, who makes them holy.[e][o]'"

24So Moses told this to Aaron and his sons and to all the Israelites.

22

The LORD said to Moses, 2"Tell Aaron and his sons to treat with respect the sacred offerings[a] the Israelites consecrate to me, so that they will not profane my holy name.[b] I am the LORD.[c]

3"Say to them: 'For the generations to come, if any of your descendants is ceremonially unclean and yet comes near the sacred offerings that the Israelites consecrate to the LORD,[d] that person must be cut off from my presence.[e] I am the LORD.

4"'If a descendant of Aaron has an infectious skin disease[a] or a bodily discharge,[f] he may not eat the sacred offerings until he is cleansed. He will also be unclean if he touches something defiled by a corpse[g] or by anyone who has an emission of semen, 5or if he touches any crawling thing[h] that makes him unclean, or any person[i] who makes him unclean, whatever the uncleanness may be. 6The one who touches any such thing will be unclean[j] till evening.[k] He must not eat any of the sacred offerings unless he has bathed himself with water.[l] 7When the sun goes down, he will be clean, and after that he may eat the sacred offerings, for they are his food.[m] 8He must not eat anything found dead[n] or torn by wild animals,[o] and so become unclean[p] through it. I am the LORD.[q]

9"'The priests are to keep my requirements[r] so that they do not become guilty[s] and die[t] for treating them with contempt. I am the LORD, who makes them holy.[b][u]

10"'No-one outside a priest's family may eat the sacred offering, nor may the guest of a priest or his hired worker eat it.[v] 11But if a priest buys a slave with money, or if a slave is born in his household, that slave may eat his food.[w] 12If a priest's daughter marries anyone other than a priest, she may not eat any of the sacred contributions. 13But if a priest's daughter becomes a widow or is divorced, yet has no children, and she returns to live in her father's house as in her youth, she may eat of her father's food. No unauthorised person, however, may eat any of it.

14"'If anyone eats a sacred offering by mistake,[x] he must make restitution to the priest for the offering and add a fifth of the value[y] to it. 15The priests must not desecrate the sacred offerings[z] the Israelites present to the LORD[a] 16by allowing them to eat[b] the sacred offerings and so bring upon them guilt[c] requiring payment.[d] I am the LORD, who makes them holy.[e]'"

Unacceptable Sacrifices

17The LORD said to Moses, 18"Speak to Aaron and his sons and to all the Israelites and say to them: 'If any of you—either an Israelite or an alien living in Israel[f]—presents a gift[g] for a burnt offering to the LORD, either to fulfil a vow[h] or as a freewill offering,[i] 19you must present a male without defect[j] from the cattle, sheep or goats in order that it may be accepted on your behalf.[k] 20Do not bring anything with a defect,[l] because it will not be accepted on your behalf.[m] 21When anyone brings from the herd or flock[n] a fellowship offering[c][o] to the LORD to fulfil a special vow or as a freewill offering,[p] it must be without defect or blemish[q] to be acceptable.[r] 22Do not offer to the LORD the blind, the injured or the maimed, or anything with warts or festering or running sores. Do not place any of these on the altar as an offering made to the LORD by fire. 23You may, however, present as a freewill offering an ox[d] or a sheep that is deformed or stunted, but it will not be accepted in fulfilment of a vow. 24You must not offer to the LORD an animal whose testicles are bruised, crushed, torn or cut.[s] You must not do this in

20 [h]Lev 22:24; Dt 23:1; Isa 56:3
21 [i]ver 17; [j]Lev 3:11; [k]Lev 22:19
22 [l]1Co 9:13
23 [m]ver 17; [n]Ex 25:8; [o]Lev 20:8

Ch. 22

2 [a]Lev 19:8; [b]Ex 20:7; Mt 5:33; [c]Eze 44:8
3 [d]Ezr 8:28; [e]Lev 7:20–21; Nu 19:13
4 [f]Lev 15:2–15; [g]Lev 11:24–28, 39
5 [h]Lev 11:24–28, 43; [i]Lev 15:7
6 [j]Hag 2:13; [k]Lev 11:24; [l]Lev 14:8
7 [m]Nu 18:11
8 [n]Lev 11:39; [o]Ex 22:31; [p]Lev 11:40; [q]Lev 11:44
9 [r]Lev 8:35; [s]Ex 28:38; [t]ver 16; Ex 28:43; [u]Lev 20:8
10 [v]ver 13; Ex 12:45; 29:33
11 [w]Ge 17:13; Ex 12:44
14 [x]Lev 4:2; [y]Lev 5:15
15 [z]Lev 19:8; [a]Nu 18:32
16 [b]Nu 18:11; [c]Ex 28:38; [d]ver 9; [e]Lev 20:8
18 [f]Nu 15:16; 19:10; Jos 8:33; [g]Lev 1:2; [h]ver 21; Ge 28:20; Nu 15:8; Ps 22:25; 76:11; 116:18; [i]Lev 7:16
19 [j]Lev 1:3; 21:18–21; Nu 28:11; Dt 15:21; [k]Lev 1:2
20 [l]Lev 1:3; Dt 15:21; 17:1; Eze 43:23; 45:18; 46:6; Mal 1:8; Heb 9:14; 1Pe 1:19; [m]Ex 28:38
21 [n]Lev 1:2; [o]Ex 32:6; Lev 3:6; [p]Lev 7:16; [q]Ex 12:5; Mal 1:14; [r]Am 4:5
24 [s]Lev 21:20

[e]23 Or *who sanctifies them;* or *who sets them apart as holy*
[a]4 Traditionally *leprosy;* the Hebrew word was used for various diseases affecting the skin—not necessarily leprosy.
[b]9 Or *who sanctifies them;* or *who sets them apart as holy;* also in verse 16
[c]21 Traditionally *peace offering*
[d]23 The Hebrew word can include both male and female.

your own land, 25and you must not
accept such animals from the hand of a
foreigner and offer them as the food of
your God.[t] They will not be accepted on
your behalf, because they are deformed
and have defects.[u]' "
26The LORD said to Moses, 27"When a
calf, a lamb or a goat[v] is born, it is to
remain with its mother for seven days.[w]
From the eighth day[x] on, it will be
acceptable[y] as an offering made to the
LORD by fire. 28Do not slaughter a cow or
a sheep and its young on the same day.[z]
29"When you sacrifice a thank-
offering[a] to the LORD, sacrifice it in such
a way that it will be accepted on your
behalf. 30It must be eaten that same day;
leave none of it till morning.[b] I am the
LORD.[c]
31"Keep[d] my commands and follow
them.[e] I am the LORD. 32Do not profane
my holy name.[f] I must be acknowledged
as holy by the Israelites.[g] I am the LORD,
who makes[e] you holy[f][h] 33and who
brought you out of Egypt[i] to be your
God.[j] I am the LORD."

23

The LORD said to Moses,
2"Speak to the Israelites and say
to them: 'These are my appointed
feasts, the appointed feasts[a] of the
LORD, which you are to proclaim as
sacred assemblies.[b]

The Sabbath

3" 'There are six days when you may
work,[c] but the seventh day is a Sabbath
of rest,[d] a day of sacred assembly. You
are not to do any work;[e] wherever you
live, it is a Sabbath to the LORD.

The Passover and Unleavened Bread

23:4–8pp—Ex 12:14–20; Nu 28:16–25; Dt 16:1–8

4" 'These are the LORD's appointed
feasts, the sacred assemblies you are to
proclaim at their appointed times:[f] 5The
LORD's Passover[g] begins at twilight on
the fourteenth day of the first month.[h]
6On the fifteenth day of that month the
LORD's Feast of Unleavened Bread[i]
begins; for seven days[j] you must eat
bread made without yeast. 7On the first
day hold a sacred assembly[k] and do no
regular work. 8For seven days present
an offering made to the LORD by fire.[l]
And on the seventh day hold a sacred
assembly and do no regular work.' "

Firstfruits

9The LORD said to Moses, 10"Speak to
the Israelites and say to them: 'When
you enter the land I am going to give
you[m] and you reap its harvest,[n] bring to
the priest a sheaf[o] of the first grain you
harvest.[p] 11He is to wave the sheaf be-
fore the LORD[q] so that it will be accepted[r]
on your behalf; the priest is to wave it on
the day after the Sabbath. 12On the day
you wave the sheaf, you must sacrifice
as a burnt offering to the LORD a lamb
a year old[s] without defect,[t] 13together
with its grain offering[u] of two-tenths of
an ephah[a][v] of fine flour mixed with oil
—an offering made to the LORD by fire, a
pleasing aroma—and its drink offering[w]
of a quarter of a hin[b] of wine.[x] 14You
must not eat any bread, or roasted or
new grain,[y] until the very day you bring
this offering to your God.[z] This is to be a
lasting ordinance for the generations to
come,[a] wherever you live.[b]

Feast of Weeks

23:15–22pp—Nu 28:26–31; Dt 16:9–12

15" 'From the day after the Sabbath,
the day you brought the sheaf of the
wave offering, count off seven full
weeks. 16Count off fifty days up to the
day after the seventh Sabbath,[c] and
then present an offering of new grain to
the LORD. 17From wherever you live,
bring two loaves made of two-tenths of
an ephah[d] of fine flour, baked with
yeast, as a wave offering of firstfruits[e] to
the LORD. 18Present with this bread
seven male lambs, each a year old and
without defect, one young bull and two
rams. They will be a burnt offering to
the LORD, together with their grain
offerings and drink offerings[f]—an
offering made by fire, an aroma
pleasing to the LORD. 19Then sacrifice
one male goat for a sin offering and two
lambs, each a year old, for a fellowship
offering.[c] 20The priest is to wave the two
lambs before the LORD as a wave offer-
ing,[g] together with the bread of the
firstfruits. They are a sacred offering to
the LORD for the priest. 21On that same
day you are to proclaim a sacred
assembly[h] and do no regular work.[i] This
is to be a lasting ordinance for the
generations to come, wherever you live.
22" 'When you reap the harvest[j] of
your land, do not reap to the very edges
of your field or gather the gleanings

25 [t]Lev 21:6; [u]Lev 1:3; 3:1; Nu 19:2
27 [v]Lev 1:3; [w]Ex 22:30; [x]Ex 22:30; [y]Ex 28:38
28 [z]Dt 22:6–7
29 [a]Lev 7:12
30 [b]Lev 7:15; [c]Lev 11:44
31 [d]Dt 4:2,40; Ps 105:45; [e]Ex 22:31
32 [f]Lev 18:21; [g]Lev 10:3; [h]Lev 20:8
33 [i]Ex 6:6; [j]Ge 17:7

Ch. 23

2 [a]ver 4,37,44; Nu 29:39; Eze 44:24; Col 2:16; [b]ver 21,27
3 [c]Ex 20:9; [d]Ex 20:10; Heb 4:9–10; [e]ver 7,21,35; Nu 28:26
4 [f]Na 1:15
5 [g]Ex 12:11; [h]Ex 12:6
6 [i]Ex 12:17; [j]Ex 12:19
7 [k]ver 3,8
8 [l]Lev 1:9
10 [m]Nu 15:2,18; [n]Lev 19:9; [o]Lev 19:9; [p]Ex 22:29; 34:22; Ro 11:16
11 [q]Ex 29:24; [r]Ex 28:38
12 [s]Lev 12:6; [t]Ex 12:5
13 [u]Lev 2:14–16; 6:20; [v]ver 17; Lev 24:5; Nu 15:6; 28:9; [w]Ge 35:14; [x]Lev 10:9
14 [y]Jos 5:11; Ru 2:14; 1Sa 17:17; 25:18; 2Sa 17:28; [z]Ex 34:26; [a]Lev 3:17; Nu 10:8; 15:21; [b]Jer 2:3
16 [c]Ac 2:1; 20:16
17 [d]ver 13; [e]Ex 34:22
18 [f]ver 13; Ex 29:41; 30:9; 37:16; Jer 19:13; 44:18
20 [g]Ex 29:24
21 [h]ver 2; Ex 32:5; [i]ver 3
22 [j]Lev 19:9

[e]32 Or *made*
[f]32 Or *who sanctifies you;* or *who sets you apart as holy*
[a]13 That is, probably about 7½ pints (about 4.5 litres); also in verse 17
[b]13 That is, probably about 1½ pints (about 1 litre)
[c]19 Traditionally *peace offering*

of your harvest.[k] Leave them for the poor and the alien.[l] I am the LORD your God.' "

Feast of Trumpets

23:23–25pp—Nu 29:1–6

23The LORD said to Moses, 24"Say to the Israelites: 'On the first day of the seventh month you are to have a day of rest, a sacred assembly[m] commemorated with trumpet blasts.[n] 25Do no regular work,[o] but present an offering made to the LORD by fire.[p]' "

Day of Atonement

23:26–32pp—Lev 16:2–34; Nu 29:7–11

26The LORD said to Moses, 27"The tenth day of this seventh month[q] is the Day of Atonement.[r] Hold a sacred assembly[s] and deny yourselves,[d] and present an offering made to the LORD by fire. 28Do no work[t] on that day, because it is the Day of Atonement, when atonement is made for you before the LORD your God. 29Anyone who does not deny himself on that day must be cut off from his people.[u] 30I will destroy from among his people[v] anyone who does any work on that day. 31You shall do no work at all. This is to be a lasting ordinance[w] for the generations to come, wherever you live. 32It is a sabbath of rest[x] for you, and you must deny yourselves. From the evening of the ninth day of the month until the following evening you are to observe your sabbath."[y]

Feast of Tabernacles

23:33–43pp—Nu 29:12–39; Dt 16:13–17

33The LORD said to Moses, 34"Say to the Israelites: 'On the fifteenth day of the seventh[z] month the LORD's Feast of Tabernacles[a] begins, and it lasts for seven days. 35The first day is a sacred assembly;[b] do no regular work.[c] 36For seven days present offerings made to the LORD by fire, and on the eighth day hold a sacred assembly[d] and present an offering made to the LORD by fire.[e] It is the closing assembly; do no regular work.

37(" 'These are the LORD's appointed feasts, which you are to proclaim as sacred assemblies for bringing offerings made to the LORD by fire—the burnt offerings and grain offerings, sacrifices and drink offerings[f] required for each day. 38These offerings[g] are in addition to those for the LORD's Sabbaths[h] and[e] in addition to your gifts and whatever you have vowed and all the freewill offerings[i] you give to the LORD.)

39" 'So beginning with the fifteenth day of the seventh month, after you have gathered the crops of the land, celebrate the festival[j] to the LORD for seven days;[k] the first day is a day of rest, and the eighth day also is a day of rest. 40On the first day you are to take choice fruit from the trees, and palm fronds, leafy branches[l] and poplars,[m] and rejoice[n] before the LORD your God for seven days. 41Celebrate this as a festival to the LORD for seven days each year. This is to be a lasting ordinance for the generations to come; celebrate it in the seventh month. 42Live in booths[o] for seven days: All native-born Israelites are to live in booths 43so that your descendants will know[p] that I made the Israelites live in booths when I brought them out of Egypt. I am the LORD your God.' "

44So Moses announced to the Israelites the appointed feasts of the LORD.

Oil and Bread Set Before the LORD

24:1–3pp—Ex 27:20–21

24

The LORD said to Moses, 2"Command the Israelites to bring you clear oil of pressed olives for the light so that the lamps may be kept burning continually. 3Outside the curtain of the Testimony in the Tent of Meeting, Aaron is to tend the lamps before the LORD from evening till morning, continually. This is to be a lasting ordinance[a] for the generations to come. 4The lamps on the pure gold lampstand[b] before the LORD must be tended continually.

5"Take fine flour and bake twelve loaves of bread,[c] using two-tenths of an ephah[a][d] for each loaf. 6Set them in two rows, six in each row, on the table of pure gold[e] before the LORD. 7Along each row put some pure incense[f] as a memorial portion[g] to represent the bread and to be an offering made to the LORD by fire. 8This bread is to be set out before the LORD regularly,[h] Sabbath after Sabbath,[i] on behalf of the Israelites, as a lasting covenant. 9It belongs to Aaron and his sons,[j] who are to eat it in a holy place,[k] because it is a most

---

22 [k]**Lev 19:10**; Dt 24:19–21; Ru 2:15; [l]Ru 2:2
24 [m]ver 27,36; Ezr 3:1; [n]Lev 25:9; Nu 10:9–10; 29:1; 31:6; 2Ki 11:14; 2Ch 13:12; Ps 98:6
25 [o]ver 21; [p]**Lev 1:9**
27 [q]**Lev 16:29**; [r]**Ex 30:10**; [s]**ver 2,24**
28 [t]ver 31
29 [u]Ge 17:14; Lev 7:20; Nu 5:2
30 [v]**Lev 20:3**
31 [w]Lev 3:17
32 [x]**Lev 16:31**; [y]Ne 13:19
34 [z]1Ki 8:2; Hag 2:1; [a]**Ex 23:16**; Jn 7:2
35 [b]ver 2; [c]ver 3
36 [d]**ver 24**; 1Ki 8:2; 2Ch 7:9; Ne 8:18; Jn 7:37; [e]**Lev 1:9**
37 [f]ver 13
38 [g]**Lev 1:2**; [h]**Ex 20:10**; 2Ch 2:4; Eze 45:17; [i]**Lev 7:16**
39 [j]Isa 62:9; [k]**Ex 23:16**
40 [l]Ps 118:27; [m]Ne 8:14–17; Ps 137:2; Isa 44:4; [n]Dt 12:7; 14:26; 28:47; Ne 8:10; Ps 9:2; 66:6; 105:43; Joel 2:26
42 [o]**Ex 23:16**
43 [p]Ps 78:5

Ch. 24

3 [a]**Ex 12:14**
4 [b]**Ex 25:31**
5 [c]**Ex 25:30**; Heb 9:2; [d]**Lev 23:13**
6 [e]Ex 25:23–30; Nu 4:7
7 [f]**Lev 2:1**; [g]**Lev 2:2**
8 [h]Ex 25:30; Nu 4:7; 1Ch 9:32; 2Ch 2:4; [i]Mt 12:5
9 [j]Mt 12:4; Mk 2:26; Lk 6:4; [k]**Lev 6:16**

---

[d]27 Or *and fast*; also in verses 29 and 32
[e]38 Or *These feasts are in addition to the LORD's Sabbaths, and these offerings are*
[a]5 That is, probably about 7½ pints (about 4.5 litres)

holy[l] part of their regular share of the
offerings made to the LORD by fire."

A Blasphemer Stoned

10Now the son of an Israelite mother
and an Egyptian father went out among
the Israelites, and a fight broke out in
the camp between him and an Israelite.
11The son of the Israelite woman
blasphemed the Name[m] with a curse;[n]
so they brought him to Moses.[o] (His
mother's name was Shelomith, the
daughter of Dibri the Danite.)[p] 12They
put him in custody until the will of the
LORD should be made clear to them.[q]
13Then the LORD said to Moses:
14"Take the blasphemer outside the
camp. All those who heard him are to
lay their hands on his head, and the
entire assembly is to stone him.[r] 15Say to
the Israelites: 'If anyone curses his
God,[s] he will be held responsible;[t]
16anyone who blasphemes[u] the name of
the LORD must be put to death.[v] The
entire assembly must stone him.
Whether an alien or native-born, when
he blasphemes the Name, he must be
put to death.
17"'If anyone takes the life of a human
being, he must be put to death.[w]
18Anyone who takes the life of some-
one's animal must make restitution[x]—
life for life. 19If anyone injures his
neighbour, whatever he has done must
be done to him: 20fracture for fracture,
eye for eye, tooth for tooth.[y] As he has
injured the other, so he is to be injured.
21Whoever kills an animal must make
restitution,[z] but whoever kills a man
must be put to death.[a] 22You are to have
the same law for the alien[b] and the
native-born.[c] I am the LORD your God.'"
23Then Moses spoke to the Israelites,
and they took the blasphemer outside
the camp and stoned him.[d] The
Israelites did as the LORD commanded
Moses.

The Sabbath Year

25 The LORD said to Moses on
Mount Sinai,[a] 2"Speak to the
Israelites and say to them: 'When you
enter the land I am going to give you,
the land itself must observe a sabbath to
the LORD. 3For six years sow your fields,
and for six years prune your vineyards
and gather their crops.[b] 4But in the
seventh year the land is to have a
sabbath of rest,[c] a sabbath to the LORD.
Do not sow your fields or prune your
vineyards.[d] 5Do not reap what grows of
itself[e] or harvest the grapes[f] of your
untended vines.[g] The land is to have a
year of rest. 6Whatever the land yields
during the sabbath year[h] will be food for
you—for yourself, your manservant
and maidservant, and the hired worker
and temporary resident who live among
you, 7as well as for your livestock and
the wild animals[i] in your land. What-
ever the land produces may be eaten.

The Year of Jubilee

25:8–38Ref—Dt 15:1–11
25:39–55Ref—Ex 21:2–11; Dt 15:12–18

8"'Count off seven sabbaths of years
—seven times seven years—so that the
seven sabbaths of years amount to a
period of forty-nine years. 9Then have
the trumpet[j] sounded everywhere on
the tenth day of the seventh month;[k] on
the Day of Atonement[l] sound the trum-
pet throughout your land. 10Consecrate
the fiftieth year and proclaim liberty[m]
throughout the land to all its inhabi-
tants. It shall be a jubilee[n] for you; each
one of you is to return to his family
property[o] and each to his own clan.
11The fiftieth year shall be a jubilee[p] for
you; do not sow and do not reap what
grows of itself or harvest the untended
vines.[q] 12For it is a jubilee and is to be
holy for you; eat only what is taken
directly from the fields.
13"'In this Year of Jubilee[r] everyone is
to return to his own property.
14"'If you sell land to one of your
countrymen or buy any from him, do
not take advantage of each other.[s] 15You
are to buy from your countryman on the
basis of the number of years since the
Jubilee. And he is to sell to you on the
basis of the number of years[t] left for
harvesting crops. 16When the years are
many, you are to increase the price, and
when the years are few, you are to
decrease the price,[u] because what he is
really selling you is the number of
crops. 17Do not take advantage of each
other,[v] but fear your God.[w] I am the
LORD your God.[x]
18"'Follow my decrees and be careful
to obey my laws,[y] and you will live
safely in the land.[z] 19Then the land will
yield its fruit,[a] and you will eat your fill
and live there in safety.[b] 20You may ask,

9 [l]**Lev 6:17**
11 [m]**Ex 3:15;** [n]**Ex 20:7; 2Ki 6:33; Job 1:11;** [o]**Ex 18:22;** [p]Ex 31:2; Nu 1:4; 7:2; 10:15; 13:2; 17:2; Jos 7:18; 1Ki 7:14
12 [q]**Ex 18:16**
14 [r]ver 23; **Lev 20:2;** Dt 13:9; 17:5,7; Ac 7:58
15 [s]**Ex 22:28;** [t]**Lev 5:1**
16 [u]**Ex 22:28;** [v]**Ex 21:12;** 1Ki 21:10,13; Mt 26:66; Mk 14:64; Jn 10:33; 19:7; Ac 7:58
17 [w]ver 21; Ge 9:6; **Ex 21:12;** Dt 27:24
18 [x]ver 21
20 [y]**Ex 21:24;** Mt 5:38*
21 [z]**ver 18;** [a]**ver 17**
22 [b]**Ex 12:49; 22:21;** Eze 47:22; [c]Nu 9:14
23 [d]**ver 14**

Ch. 25

1 [a]Ex 19:11
3 [b]Ex 23:10
4 [c]ver 5–6,20; Lev 26:35; 2Ch 36:21; [d]Isa 36:16; 37:30
5 [e]2Ki 19:29; [f]Ge 40:10; Nu 6:3; 13:20; Dt 23:24; Ne 13:15; Isa 5:2; [g]ver 4,11
6 [h]**ver 4**
7 [i]Ex 23:11
9 [j]Lev 23:24; Nu 10:8; Jos 6:4; Jdg 3:27; 7:16; 1Sa 13:3; Isa 27:13; Zec 9:14; [k]**Lev 16:29;** [l]**Ex 30:10**
10 [m]Isa 61:1; Jer 34:8,15,17; **Lk 4:19;** [n]ver 11,28,50; Lev 27:17,21; Nu 36:4; Eze 46:17; [o]ver 27
11 [p]ver 10; [q]ver 5
13 [r]ver 10
14 [s]**Lev 19:13;** 1Sa 12:3–4; 1Co 6:8
15 [t]ver 27; Lev 27:18,23
16 [u]ver 27,51–52

17 [v]**Lev 19:13;** Job 31:16; Pr 22:22; Jer 7:5–6; 21:12; 22:3, 15; Zec 7:9–10; 1Th 4:6; [w]**Lev 19:14;** [x]**Lev 19:32**
18 [y]**Ge 26:5;** [z]ver 19; Lev 26:4–5; Dt 12:10; 33:28; Job 5:22; Ps 4:8; Jer 23:6; 30:10; 32:37; 33:16; Eze 28:26; 34:25; 38:14
19 [a]Lev 26:4; Dt 11:14; 28:12; Isa 55:10; [b]**ver 18**

"What will we eat in the seventh year[c] if we do not plant or harvest our crops?" 21I will send you such a blessing[d] in the sixth year that the land will yield enough for three years.[e] 22While you plant during the eighth year, you will eat from the old crop and will continue to eat from it until the harvest of the ninth year comes in.[f]

23" 'The land[g] must not be sold permanently, because the land is mine[h] and you are but aliens[i] and my tenants. 24Throughout the country that you hold as a possession, you must provide for the redemption[j] of the land.

25" 'If one of your countrymen becomes poor and sells some of his property, his nearest relative[k] is to come and redeem[l] what his countryman has sold. 26If, however, a man has no-one to redeem it for him but he himself prospers[m] and acquires sufficient means to redeem it, 27he is to determine the value for the years[n] since he sold it and refund the balance to the man to whom he sold it; he can then go back to his own property.[o] 28But if he does not acquire the means to repay him, what he sold will remain in the possession of the buyer until the Year of Jubilee. It will be returned[p] in the Jubilee, and he can then go back to his property.[q]

29" 'If a man sells a house in a walled city, he retains the right of redemption a full year after its sale. During that time he may redeem it. 30If it is not redeemed before a full year has passed, the house in the walled city shall belong permanently to the buyer and his descendants. It is not to be returned in the Jubilee. 31But houses in villages without walls round them are to be considered as open country. They can be redeemed, and they are to be returned in the Jubilee.

32" 'The Levites always have the right to redeem their houses in the Levitical towns,[r] which they possess. 33So the property of the Levites is redeemable —that is, a house sold in any town they hold—and is to be returned in the Jubilee, because the houses in the towns of the Levites are their property among the Israelites. 34But the pasture-land belonging to their towns must not be sold; it is their permanent possession.[s]

35" 'If one of your countrymen becomes poor[t] and is unable to support himself among you, help him[u] as you would an alien or a temporary resident, so that he can continue to live among you. 36Do not take interest[v] of any kind[a] from him, but fear your God,[w] so that your countryman may continue to live among you. 37You must not lend him money at interest[x] or sell him food at a profit. 38I am the LORD your God, who brought you out of Egypt to give you the land of Canaan[y] and to be your God.[z]

39" 'If one of your countrymen becomes poor among you and sells himself to you, do not make him work as a slave.[a] 40He is to be treated as a hired worker[b] or a temporary resident among you; he is to work for you until the Year of Jubilee. 41Then he and his children are to be released, and he will go back to his own clan and to the property[c] of his forefathers.[d] 42Because the Israelites are my servants, whom I brought out of Egypt,[e] they must not be sold as slaves. 43Do not rule over them ruthlessly,[f] but fear your God.[g]

44" 'Your male and female slaves are to come from the nations around you; from them you may buy slaves. 45You may also buy some of the temporary residents living among you and members of their clans born in your country, and they will become your property. 46You can will them to your children as inherited property and can make them slaves for life, but you must not rule over your fellow Israelites ruthlessly.

47" 'If an alien or a temporary resident among you becomes rich and one of your countrymen becomes poor and sells himself[h] to the alien living among you or to a member of the alien's clan, 48he retains the right of redemption[i] after he has sold himself. One of his relatives[j] may redeem him: 49An uncle or a cousin or any blood-relative in his clan may redeem him. Or if he prospers,[k] he may redeem himself. 50He and his buyer are to count the time from the year he sold himself up to the Year of Jubilee.[l] The price for his release is to be based on the rate paid to a hired man[m] for that number of years. 51If many years remain, he must pay for his redemption a larger share of the price paid for him. 52If only a few years remain until the Year of Jubilee, he is to compute that and pay for his redemption accordingly.[n] 53He is to be treated as a man hired from year to year; you must see to it that his owner does not rule over him ruthlessly.[o]

54" 'Even if he is not redeemed in any of these ways, he and his children are to be released in the Year of Jubilee, 55for the Israelites belong to me as servants.

20 [c]**ver 4**
21 [d]Dt 28:8,12; Ps 133:3; 134:3; 147:13; Eze 44:30; Hag 2:19; Mal 3:10; [e]**Ex 16:5**
22 [f]Lev 26:10
23 [g]Nu 36:7; 1Ki 21:3; Eze 46:18; [h]Ex 19:5; [i]**Ge 23:4; Heb 11:13**
24 [j]ver 29,48; Ru 4:7; Jer 32:8
25 [k]ver 48; Ru 2:20; Jer 32:7; [l]Lev 27:13, 19,31; Ru 4:4
26 [m]ver 49
27 [n]**ver 15**; [o]ver 10
28 [p]Lev 27:24; [q]**ver 10**
32 [r]Nu 35:1–8; Jos 21:2
34 [s]Nu 35:2–5; Eze 48:14
35 [t]Dt 24:14–15; [u]Dt 15:8; Ps 37:21,26; Pr 21:26; Lk 6:35
36 [v]**Ex 22:25**; Jer 15:10; [w]**Lev 19:32**
37 [x]**Ex 22:25**
38 [y]**Ge 10:19**; [z]**Ge 17:7**
39 [a]1Ki 5:13; 9:22; Jer 34:14
40 [b]ver 53
41 [c]ver 28; [d]Jer 34:8
42 [e]ver 38
43 [f]**Ex 1:13**; Eze 34:4; Col 4:1; [g]**Ge 42:18**
47 [h]Ne 5:5; Job 24:9
48 [i]**ver 24**; [j]**ver 25**
49 [k]ver 26
50 [l]**ver 10**; [m]Job 7:1; 14:6; Isa 16:14; 21:16
52 [n]**ver 16**
53 [o]Col 4:1

[a]36 Or *take excessive interest*; similarly in verse 37

They are my servants, whom I brought out of Egypt.[p] I am the LORD your God.[q]

Reward for Obedience

26 "'Do not make idols[a] or set up an image[b] or a sacred stone[c] for yourselves, and do not place a carved stone[d] in your land to bow down before it. I am the LORD your God.

2 "'Observe my Sabbaths[e] and have reverence for my sanctuary.[f] I am the LORD.

3 "'If you follow my decrees and are careful to obey[g] my commands, 4 I will send you rain[h] in its season,[i] and the ground will yield its crops and the trees of the field their fruit.[j] 5 Your threshing will continue until grape harvest and the grape harvest will continue until planting, and you will eat all the food you want[k] and live in safety in your land.[l]

6 "'I will grant peace in the land,[m] and you will lie down[n] and no-one will make you afraid.[o] I will remove savage beasts[p] from the land, and the sword will not pass through your country. 7 You will pursue your enemies,[q] and they will fall by the sword before you. 8 Five[r] of you will chase a hundred, and a hundred of you will chase ten thousand, and your enemies will fall by the sword before you.[s]

9 "'I will look on you with favour and make you fruitful and increase your numbers,[t] and I will keep my covenant[u] with you. 10 You will still be eating last year's harvest when you will have to move it out to make room for the new.[v] 11 I will put my dwelling-place[a][w] among you, and I will not abhor you.[x] 12 I will walk[y] among you and be your God,[z] and you will be my people.[a] 13 I am the LORD your God,[b] who brought you out of Egypt[c] so that you would no longer be slaves to the Egyptians; I broke the bars of your yoke[d] and enabled you to walk with heads held high.

Punishment for Disobedience

14 "'But if you will not listen to me and carry out all these commands,[e] 15 and if you reject my decrees and abhor my laws[f] and fail to carry out all my commands and so violate my covenant,[g] 16 then I will do this to you: I will bring upon you sudden terror, wasting diseases and fever[h] that will destroy your sight and drain away your life.[i] You will plant seed in vain, because your enemies will eat it.[j] 17 I will set my face[k] against you so that you will be defeated[l] by your enemies;[m] those who hate you will rule over you,[n] and you will flee even when no-one is pursuing you.[o]

18 "'If after all this you will not listen to me,[p] I will punish[q] you for your sins seven times over.[r] 19 I will break down your stubborn pride[s] and make the sky above you like iron and the ground beneath you like bronze.[t] 20 Your strength will be spent in vain,[u] because your soil will not yield its crops, nor will the trees of the land yield their fruit.[v]

21 "'If you remain hostile[w] towards me and refuse to listen to me, I will multiply your afflictions seven times over,[x] as your sins deserve. 22 I will send wild animals[y] against you, and they will rob you of your children, destroy your cattle and make you so few[z] in number that your roads will be deserted.[a]

23 "'If in spite of these things you do not accept my correction[b] but continue to be hostile towards me, 24 I myself will be hostile[c] towards you and will afflict you for your sins seven times over. 25 And I will bring the sword[d] upon you to avenge[e] the breaking of the covenant. When you withdraw into your cities, I will send a plague[f] among you, and you will be given into enemy hands. 26 When I cut off your supply of bread,[g] ten women will be able to bake your bread in one oven, and they will dole out the bread by weight. You will eat, but you will not be satisfied.

27 "'If in spite of this you still do not listen to me[h] but continue to be hostile towards me, 28 then in my anger[i] I will be hostile[j] towards you, and I myself will punish you for your sins seven times over.[k] 29 You will eat[l] the flesh of your

55 [p]**Lev 11:45;** [q]Lev 11:44

Ch. 26

1 [a]**Ex 20:4;** [b]Ps 97:7; Isa 48:5; Jer 44:19; Hab 2:18; [c]**Ex 23:24;** [d]Nu 33:52
2 [e]**Ex 20:8;** [f]Lev 19:30
3 [g]**Ge 26:5; Ex 24:8;** Dt 6:17; 7:12; 11:13,22; 28:1,9
4 [h]Dt 11:14; 28:12; Ps 68:9; Jer 5:24; Hos 6:3; Joel 2:23; Zec 10:1; [i]Job 5:10; Ps 65:9; 104:13; 147:8; Jer 5:24; [j]**Ex 23:26; Lev 25:19; Job 14:9;** Ps 67:6
5 [k]Dt 6:11; 11:15; Eze 36:29–30; Joel 2:19,26; [l]**Lev 25:18**
6 [m]Ps 29:11; 37:11; 85:8; 147:14; Isa 26:3; 54:13; 60:18; Hag 2:9; [n]Ps 3:5; 4:8; Pr 3:24; [o]Job 11:18–19; Isa 17:2; Jer 30:10; Mic 4:4; Zep 3:13; [p]**ver 22; Ge 37:20**
7 [q]Ps 18:37; 44:5
8 [r]Isa 30:17; [s]Dt 28:7; 32:30; Jos 23:10; Jdg 15:15; 1Ch 12:14
9 [t]**Ge 1:22; 17:6;** Ne 9:23; [u]**Ge 17:7**
10 [v]Lev 25:22
11 [w]Ex 25:8; Ps 74:7; 76:2; Eze 37:27; [x]ver 15,43–44; Dt 31:6; 1Sa 12:22; 1Ki 6:13; 2Ki 17:15
12 [y]**Ge 3:8;** [z]**Ge 17:7;** [a]Ex 6:7; Jer 7:23; 11:4; 24:7; 30:22; 31:1; Zec 13:9; 2Co 6:16*
13 [b]Lev 11:44; [c]**Ex 6:6; 13:3;** [d]Isa 10:27; Jer 2:20; 27:2; 28:10; 30:8; Eze 30:18; 34:27; Hos 11:4
14 [e]Dt 28:15–68; Mal 2:2
15 [f]**ver 11;** [g]**Ge 17:7**
16 [h]Dt 28:22,35; Ps 78:33; [i]ver 39; 1Sa 2:33; Ps 107:17; Eze 4:17; 24:23; 33:10; [j]Jdg 6:3–6; Job 31:8
17 [k]Lev 17:10; Eze 15:7; [l]Dt 28:48; Jos 7:12; Jdg 2:15; 1Ki 8:33; 2Ch 6:24; [m]Jos 7:4; Jer 19:7; 21:7; [n]Ps 106:41; [o]ver 36–37; Dt 28:7,25; Ps 53:5; Pr 28:1; Isa 30:17
18 [p]ver 14; [q]Ps 99:8; Jer 21:14; Am 3:14; [r]ver 21
19 [s]Ps 10:4; 73:6; Isa 16:6; 25:11; 28:1–3; Jer 13:9; 48:29; Eze 24:21; Am 6:8; Zep 3:11; [t]Dt 28:23; Job 38:38
20 [u]Dt 28:38; Ps 127:1; Isa 17:11; 49:4; Jer 12:13; Mic 6:15; Hag 1:6; [v]Dt 11:17; 28:24
21 [w]ver 41; [x]ver 18; **Ge 4:15**
22 [y]**Ge 37:20;** [z]Dt 28:62; Jer 42:2; [a]Jer 5:6; 14:16; 15:3; 16:4; Eze 14:15
23 [b]Jer 2:30; 5:3; 7:28; 17:23; 32:33; Zep 3:2
24 [c]2Sa 22:27
25 [d]Jer 5:17; 15:3; 47:6; Eze 11:8; 14:17; 21:4; 33:2; [e]Jer 50:28; 51:6,11; [f]**Ex 5:3; 9:3;** Nu 16:46; 1Ki 8:37; Hab 3:5
26 [g]1Ki 8:37; 18:2; 2Ki 4:38; 6:25; 8:1; 25:3; Ps 105:16; Isa 3:1; 9:20; Jer 37:21; 52:6; Eze 4:16–17; 5:16; 14:13; Hos 4:10; Mic 6:14
27 [h]ver 14
28 [i]Dt 32:19; Jdg 2:14; Ps 78:59; 106:40; [j]Dt 7:10; Job 34:11; Isa 59:18; 65:6–7; 66:6; Jer 17:10; 25:29; Joel 3:4; [k]ver 18
29 [l]2Ki 6:29; Jer 19:9; La 4:10; Eze 5:10

[a]11 Or *my tabernacle*

sons and the flesh of your daughters.[m]
30I will destroy your high places,[n] cut
down your incense altars[o] and pile your
dead bodies on the lifeless forms of your
idols,[p] and I will abhor[q] you. 31I will turn
your cities into ruins[r] and lay waste[s]
your sanctuaries,[t] and I will take no
delight in the pleasing aroma of your
offerings.[u] 32I will lay waste the land,[v] so
that your enemies who live there will be
appalled.[w] 33I will scatter[x] you among
the nations[y] and will draw out my
sword[z] and pursue you. Your land will
be laid waste,[a] and your cities will lie in
ruins.[b] 34Then the land will enjoy its
sabbath years all the time that it lies
desolate[c] and you are in the country of
your enemies;[d] then the land will rest
and enjoy its sabbaths. 35All the time
that it lies desolate, the land will have
the rest[e] it did not have during the
sabbaths you lived in it.

36"'As for those of you who are left, I
will make their hearts so fearful in the
lands of their enemies that the sound of
a wind-blown leaf[f] will put them to
flight.[g] They will run as though fleeing
from the sword, and they will fall, even
though no-one is pursuing them.[h]
37They will stumble over one another[i] as
though fleeing from the sword, even
though no-one is pursuing them. So
you will not be able to stand before your
enemies.[j] 38You will perish[k] among the
nations; the land of your enemies will
devour you.[l] 39Those of you who are left
will waste away in the lands of their
enemies because of their sins; also
because of their fathers'[m] sins they will
waste away.[n]

40"'But if they will confess[o] their sins[p]
and the sins of their fathers[q]—their
treachery against me and their hostility
towards me, 41which made me hostile[r]
towards them so that I sent them
into the land of their enemies—then
when their uncircumcised hearts[s] are
humbled[t] and they pay[u] for their sin, 42I
will remember my covenant with Jacob[v]
and my covenant with Isaac[w] and my
covenant with Abraham,[x] and I will re-
member the land. 43For the land will be
deserted[y] by them and will enjoy its
sabbaths while it lies desolate without
them. They will pay for their sins
because they rejected[z] my laws and
abhorred my decrees.[a] 44Yet in spite of
this, when they are in the land of their
enemies,[b] I will not reject them or abhor[c]
them so as to destroy them completely,[d]
breaking my covenant[e] with them. I am
the LORD their God. 45But for their sake I
will remember[f] the covenant with their
ancestors whom I brought out of Egypt[g]
in the sight of the nations to be their
God. I am the LORD.'"

46These are the decrees, the laws and
the regulations that the LORD estab-
lished on Mount Sinai[h] between himself
and the Israelites through Moses.[i]

Redeeming What Is the LORD's

27 The LORD said to Moses,
2"Speak to the Israelites and say
to them: 'If anyone makes a special vow[a]
to dedicate persons to the LORD by giv-
ing equivalent values, 3set the value of a
male between the ages of twenty and
sixty at fifty shekels[a] of silver, according
to the sanctuary shekel;[b][b] 4and if it is a
female, set her value at thirty shekels.[c]
5If it is a person between the ages of five
and twenty, set the value of a male at
twenty shekels[d][c] and of a female at ten
shekels.[e] 6If it is a person between one
month and five years, set the value of a
male at five shekels[f][d] of silver and that
of a female at three shekels[g] of silver. 7If
it is a person sixty years old or more, set
the value of a male at fifteen shekels[h]
and of a female at ten shekels. 8If any-
one making the vow is too poor to pay[e]
the specified amount, he is to present
the person to the priest, who will set the
value[f] for him according to what the
man making the vow can afford.

9"'If what he vowed is an animal that
is acceptable as an offering to the LORD,[g]
such an animal given to the LORD be-
comes holy.[h] 10He must not exchange it

29 [m]Dt 28:53
30 [n]Dt 12:2; 1Sa 9:12; 10:5; 1Ki 3:2,4; 12:31; 13:2,32; 2Ki 17:29; 23:20; 2Ch 34:3; Ps 78:58; Eze 6:3; 16:16; Am 7:9; [o]2Ch 34:4; Isa 17:8; 27:9; Eze 6:6; [p]Isa 21:9; Jer 50:2; Eze 6:13; [q]Ps 106:40; Am 6:8
31 [r]Ne 1:3; Isa 1:7; 3:8,26; 6:11; 24:12; 61:4; Jer 4:7; 9:11; 25:11; 34:22; 44:2,6, 22; Eze 36:33; Mic 2:4; 3:12; Zep 2:5; 3:6; [s]2Ki 22:19; [t]Ps 74:3–7; Isa 63:18; 64:11; La 2:7; Eze 24:21; Am 7:9; [u]Am 5:21–22; 8:10
32 [v]Isa 5:6; Jer 9:11; 12:11; 25:11; 26:9; 33:10; 34:22; 44:22; [w]1Ki 9:8; 2Ch 29:8; Isa 52:14; Jer 18:16; 19:8; 48:39; Eze 5:14; 26:16; 27:35; 28:19
33 [x]Jer 40:15; 50:17; Eze 34:6; Joel 3:2; [y]Dt 4:27; 28:64; Ne 1:8; Ps 44:11; 106:27; Jer 4:11; 9:16; 13:24; 31:10; Eze 5:10; 12:15; 17:21; 20:23; 22:15; Zec 7:14; [z]Jer 42:16; Eze 5:2,12; Am 9:4; [a]Isa 49:19; Jer 7:34; [b]ver 31; 1Sa 15:22; Job 36:11; Jer 40:3
34 [c]Isa 1:7; Jer 7:34; 25:11; 44:6; Eze 33:29; [d]ver 43; 2Ch 36:21
35 [e]**Lev 25:4**
36 [f]Job 13:25; [g]2Ki 25:5; Ps 58:7; La 1:3,6; 4:19; Eze 21:7; [h]**ver 17**
37 [i]Jer 6:21; 13:16; 46:16; Eze 3:20; Na 3:3; [j]Jos 7:12
38 [k]Job 4:9; 36:12; Ps 1:6; Isa 1:28; Jer 16:4; 44:27; [l]Dt 4:26
39 [m]Ex 20:5; Isa 14:21; [n]**ver 16**; Isa 24:16
40 [o]**Lev 5:5**; [p]Ps 32:5; 38:18; [q]Ne 9:2; Ps 106:6; Jer 3:12–15; 14:20; Hos 5:15; Lk 15:18; 1Jn 1:9
41 [r]**ver 21**; [s]Dt 10:16; 30:6; Jer 4:4; 9:25–26; Eze 44:7,9; Ac 7:51; [t]2Ch 7:14; 12:6; Eze 20:43; [u]Isa 6:7; 33:24; 40:2; 53:5–6,11
42 [v]Ge 28:15; 35:11–12; [w]**Ge 26:5**; [x]**Ex 2:24**
43 [y]Ps 69:25; Isa 6:11; 32:14; 62:4; Jer 2:15; 44:2; La 1:1; Eze 36:4; [z]Nu 11:20; 14:31; 1Sa 8:7; Ps 106:24; [a]**ver 11**; Eze 20:13
44 [b]**ver 33**; 2Ki 17:20; 25:11; 2Ch 6:36; 36:20; [c]**ver 11**; Ro 11:2; [d]Dt 4:31; Jer 4:27; 5:10; 30:11; [e]Jdg 2:1; Jer 31:37; 33:26; 51:5
45 [f]Dt 4:31; [g]Ex 6:8; Lev 25:38
46 [h]**Ex 19:11**; [i]**Lev 7:38**; 27:34

Ch. 27

2 [a]**Ge 28:20** *3* [b]**Ex 30:13** *5* [c]**Ge 37:28**
6 [d]Nu 3:47; 18:16 *8* [e]**Lev 5:11**; [f]ver 12,14
9 [g]**Ge 28:20**; **Lev 1:2**; [h]ver 21,26,28; Ex 40:9; Nu 6:20; 18:17; Dt 15:19

---

a3 That is, about 1¼ pounds (about 0.6 kilogram); also in verse 16
b3 That is, about ⅖ ounce (about 11.5 grams); also in verse 25
c4 That is, about 12 ounces (about 0.3 kilogram)
d5 That is, about 8 ounces (about 0.2 kilogram)
e5 That is, about 4 ounces (about 115 grams); also in verse 7
f6 That is, about 2 ounces (about 55 grams)
g6 That is, about 1¼ ounces (about 35 grams)
h7 That is, about 6 ounces (about 170 grams)

or substitute a good one for a bad one,
or a bad one for a good one;[i] if he should
substitute one animal for another, both
it and the substitute become holy. 11If
what he vowed is a ceremonially
unclean animal[j]—one that is not
acceptable as an offering to the LORD
—the animal must be presented to the
priest, 12who will judge its quality as
good or bad. Whatever value the priest
then sets, that is what it will be. 13If the
owner wishes to redeem[k] the animal, he
must add a fifth to its value.[l]
14" 'If a man dedicates his house as
something holy to the LORD, the priest
will judge its quality as good or bad.
Whatever value the priest then sets,
so it will remain. 15If the man who
dedicates his house redeems it,[m] he
must add a fifth to its value, and the
house will again become his.
16" 'If a man dedicates to the LORD
part of his family land, its value is to be
set according to the amount of seed
required for it—fifty shekels of silver to
a homer[i] of barley seed. 17If he dedicates
his field during the Year of Jubilee, the
value that has been set remains. 18But if
he dedicates his field after the Jubilee,[n]
the priest will determine the value
according to the number of years that
remain[o] until the next Year of Jubilee,
and its set value will be reduced. 19If the
man who dedicates the field wishes to
redeem it,[p] he must add a fifth to its
value, and the field will again become
his. 20If, however, he does not redeem
the field, or if he has sold it to someone
else, it can never be redeemed. 21When
the field is released in the Jubilee,[q] it will
become holy,[r] like a field devoted to the
LORD;[s] it will become the property of the
priests.[j]
22" 'If a man dedicates to the LORD a
field he has bought, which is not part of
his family land, 23the priest will deter-
mine its value up to the Year of Jubilee,[t]
and the man must pay its value on that
day as something holy to the LORD. 24In
the Year of Jubilee the field will revert to
the person from whom he bought it,[u]
the one whose land it was. 25Every value
is to be set according to the sanctuary
shekel,[v] twenty gerahs[w] to the shekel.
26" 'No-one, however, may dedicate
the firstborn of an animal, since the
firstborn already belongs to the LORD;[x]
whether a cow[k] or a sheep, it is the
LORD's. 27If it is one of the unclean
animals,[y] he may buy it back at its set
value, adding a fifth of the value to it. If
he does not redeem it, it is to be sold at
its set value.
28" 'But nothing that a man owns and
devotes[l] [z] to the LORD—whether man or
animal or family land—may be sold or
redeemed; everything so devoted is
most holy[a] to the LORD.
29" 'No person devoted to destruc-
tion[m] may be ransomed; he must be put
to death.[b]
30" 'A tithe[c] of everything from the
land, whether grain from the soil or fruit
from the trees, belongs to the LORD; it is
holy[d] to the LORD. 31If a man redeems[e]
any of his tithe, he must add a fifth of
the value[f] to it. 32The entire tithe of the
herd and flock—every tenth animal that
passes under the shepherd's rod[g]—will
be holy to the LORD. 33He must not
pick out the good from the bad or make
any substitution. If he does make a
substitution,[h] both the animal and its
substitute become holy and cannot be
redeemed.[i] ' "

34These are the commands the LORD
gave Moses on Mount Sinai[j] for the
Israelites.[k]

10 [i]ver 33
11 [j]ver 27; Ex 13:13; Nu 18:15
13 [k]**Lev 25:25**; [l]**Lev 5:16**
15 [m]ver 13,20
18 [n]Lev 25:10; [o]Lev 25:15
19 [p]**Lev 25:25**
21 [q]**Lev 25:10**; [r]**ver 9**; [s]ver 28; Nu 18:14; Eze 44:29
23 [t]**Lev 25:15**
24 [u]Lev 25:28
25 [v]**Ex 30:13**; [w]Nu 3:47; Eze 45:12
26 [x]**Ex 13:12**
27 [y]**ver 11**
28 [z]Nu 18:14; Jos 6:17–19; [a]**ver 9**
29 [b]Dt 7:26
30 [c]Nu 18:26; Dt 12:6,17; 14:22, 28; 2Ch 31:6; Ne 10:37; 12:44; 13:5; Mal 3:8; [d]Dt 7:6; Ezr 9:2; Isa 6:13
31 [e]**Lev 25:25**; [f]Lev 5:16
32 [g]Ps 89:32; Jer 33:13; Eze 20:37
33 [h]ver 10; [i]Nu 18:21
34 [j]**Ex 19:11**; [k]**Lev 7:38**; Ac 7:38

i*16* That is, probably about 6 bushels (about 220 litres) j*21* Or *priest*
k*26* The Hebrew word can include both male and female.
l*28* The Hebrew term refers to the irrevocable giving over of things or persons to the LORD.
m*29* The Hebrew term refers to the irrevocable giving over of things or persons to the LORD, often by totally destroying them.

Numbers

The Census

1 The LORD spoke to Moses in the
Tent of Meeting[a] in the Desert of
Sinai[b] on the first day of the second
month[c] of the second year after the
Israelites came out of Egypt.[d] He said:
2"Take a census[e] of the whole Israelite
community by their clans and families,[f]
listing every man by name,[g] one by one.
3You and Aaron[h] are to number by their
divisions all the men in Israel twenty
years old or more[i] who are able to serve
in the army.[j] 4One man from each tribe,[k]
each the head of his family,[l] is to help
you.[m] 5These are the names[n] of the men
who are to assist you:

from Reuben,[o] Elizur son of Shedeur;[p]
6from Simeon,[q] Shelumiel son of Zurishaddai;[r]
7from Judah,[s] Nahshon son of Amminadab;[t]
8from Issachar,[u] Nethanel son of Zuar;[v]
9from Zebulun,[w] Eliab son of Helon;[x]
10from the sons of Joseph:
from Ephraim,[y] Elishama son of Ammihud;[z]
from Manasseh,[a] Gamaliel son of Pedahzur;[b]
11from Benjamin,[c] Abidan son of Gideoni;[d]
12from Dan,[e] Ahiezer son of Ammishaddai;[f]
13from Asher,[g] Pagiel son of Ocran;[h]
14from Gad,[i] Eliasaph son of Deuel;[j]
15from Naphtali,[k] Ahira son of Enan.[l]"

16These were the men appointed from
the community, the leaders[m] of their
ancestral tribes.[n] They were the heads
of the clans of Israel.[o]
17Moses and Aaron took these men
whose names had been given, 18and
they called the whole community
together on the first day of the second
month.[p] The people indicated their
ancestry[q] by their clans and families,[r]
and the men twenty years old or more[s]
were listed by name, one by one, 19as
the LORD commanded Moses. And so he
counted[t] them in the Desert of Sinai:

20From the descendants of Reuben[u] the
firstborn son[v] of Israel:
All the men twenty years old or
more who were able to serve in
the army were listed by name,
one by one, according to the rec-
ords of their clans and families.
21The number from the tribe of
Reuben[w] was 46,500.

22From the descendants of Simeon:[x]
All the men twenty years old or
more who were able to serve in
the army were counted and listed
by name, one by one, according
to the records of their clans and
families. 23The number from the
tribe of Simeon was 59,300.[y]

24From the descendants of Gad:[z]
All the men twenty years old or
more who were able to serve in
the army were listed by name,
according to the records of their
clans and families. 25The number
from the tribe of Gad[a] was 45,650.

26From the descendants of Judah:[b]
All the men twenty years old or
more who were able to serve in
the army were listed by name,
according to the records of their
clans and families. 27The number
from the tribe of Judah[c] was
74,600.

28From the descendants of Issachar:[d]
All the men twenty years old or
more who were able to serve in
the army were listed by name,
according to the records of their

Ch. 1

1 [a]**Ex 27:21; 40:2**; [b]**Ex 19:1**; [c]ver 18; [d]**Ex 6:14**
2 [e]Ex 30:11–16; [f]ver 18; [g]Nu 3:40
3 [h]Ex 4:14; Nu 17:3; [i]**Ex 30:14**; [j]ver 20; Nu 26:2; Jos 5:4; 1Ch 5:18
4 [k]**Lev 24:11; Jos 7:1**; [l]ver 16; Nu 7:2; 30:1; 31:26; [m]Ex 18:21; Nu 34:18; Dt 1:15; Jos 22:14
5 [n]Nu 17:2; [o]**Ge 29:32**; Rev 7:5; [p]Nu 2:10; 7:30; 10:18
6 [q]ver 22; Nu 25:14; [r]Nu 2:12; 7:36,41; 10:19
7 [s]ver 26; **Ge 29:35**; Ps 78:68; [t]Ex 6:23; Nu 7:12; Ru 4:20; 1Ch 2:10; Mt 1:4; Lk 3:32
8 [u]**Ge 30:18**; Nu 10:15; [v]Nu 2:5; 7:18
9 [w]ver 30; Nu 10:16; [x]Nu 2:7; 7:24
10 [y]ver 32; [z]Nu 2:18; 7:48,53; 10:22; [a]ver 34; Nu 10:23; [b]Nu 2:20; 7:54
11 [c]Nu 10:24; [d]Nu 2:22; 7:60; Ps 68:27
12 [e]ver 38; [f]Nu 2:25; 7:66; 10:25
13 [g]ver 40; Nu 10:26; [h]Nu 2:27; 7:72
14 [i]ver 24; Nu 10:20; [j]Nu 2:14; 7:42
15 [k]ver 42; Nu 10:27; [l]Nu 2:29; 7:78
16 [m]**Ex 18:25**; [n]Nu 32:28; [o]**ver 4**
18 [p]ver 1; [q]Ezr 2:59; Heb 7:3; [r]ver 2; [s]**Ex 30:14**

19 [t]Ex 30:12; Nu 26:63; 31:49
20 [u]**Ge 29:32; 46:9**; Rev 7:5; [v]**Ge 10:15**
21 [w]Nu 26:7 *22* [x]**Ge 29:33**; Rev 7:7
23 [y]Nu 26:14 *24* [z]**Ge 30:11; Jos 13:24–28**; Rev 7:5
25 [a]Ge 46:16; Nu 26:18; 1Ch 5:11
26 [b]**ver 7**; Mt 1:2; Rev 7:5 *27* [c]Nu 26:22
28 [d]**Ge 30:18**; Rev 7:7

clans and families. 29The number
from the tribe of Issachar[e] was
54,400.[f]

30From the descendants of Zebulun:[g]
All the men twenty years old or
more who were able to serve in
the army were listed by name,
according to the records of their
clans and families. 31The number
from the tribe of Zebulun was
57,400.[h]

32From the sons of Joseph:[i]
From the descendants of Ephraim:[j]
All the men twenty years old or
more who were able to serve in
the army were listed by name,
according to the records of their
clans and families. 33The number
from the tribe of Ephraim[k] was
40,500.

34From the descendants of Manasseh:[l]
All the men twenty years old or
more who were able to serve in
the army were listed by name,
according to the records of their
clans and families. 35The number
from the tribe of Manasseh was
32,200.

36From the descendants of Benjamin:[m]
All the men twenty years old or
more who were able to serve in
the army were listed by name,
according to the records of their
clans and families. 37The number
from the tribe of Benjamin[n] was
35,400.

38From the descendants of Dan:[o]
All the men twenty years old or
more who were able to serve in
the army were listed by name,
according to the records of their
clans and families. 39The number
from the tribe of Dan was
62,700.[p]

40From the descendants of Asher:[q]
All the men twenty years old or
more who were able to serve in
the army were listed by name,
according to the records of their
clans and families. 41The number
from the tribe of Asher[r] was
41,500.

42From the descendants of Naphtali:[s]
All the men twenty years old or
more who were able to serve in
the army were listed by name,
according to the records of their
clans and families. 43The number
from the tribe of Naphtali[t] was
53,400.[u]

44These were the men counted by
Moses and Aaron[v] and the twelve
leaders of Israel, each one representing
his family. 45All the Israelites twenty
years old or more[w] who were able to
serve in Israel's army were counted
according to their families.[x] 46The total
number was 603,550.[y]

47The families of the tribe of Levi,[z]
however, were not counted[a] along with
the others. 48The LORD had said to
Moses: 49"You must not count the tribe
of Levi or include them in the census of
the other Israelites. 50Instead, appoint
the Levites to be in charge of the taber-
nacle[b] of the Testimony[c]—over all its
furnishings[d] and everything belonging
to it. They are to carry the tabernacle
and all its furnishings; they are to
take care of it and encamp round it.
51Whenever the tabernacle[e] is to move,[f]
the Levites are to take it down, and
whenever the tabernacle is to be set up,
the Levites shall do it.[g] Anyone else
who goes near it shall be put to death.[h]
52The Israelites are to set up their tents
by divisions, each man in his own camp
under his own standard.[i] 53The Levites,
however, are to set up their tents round
the tabernacle[j] of the Testimony so that
wrath will not fall[k] on the Israelite
community. The Levites are to be
responsible for the care of the tabernacle
of the Testimony.[l]"
54The Israelites did all this just as the
LORD commanded Moses.

The Arrangement of the Tribal Camps

2 The LORD said to Moses and Aaron:
2"The Israelites are to camp round
the Tent of Meeting some distance from
it, each man under his standard[a] with
the banners of his family."

3On the east, towards the
sunrise, the divisions of the camp
of Judah are to encamp under
their standard. The leader of the
people of Judah is Nahshon son
of Amminadab.[b] 4His division
numbers 74,600.
5The tribe of Issachar[c] will camp
next to them. The leader of the
people of Issachar is Nethanel son
of Zuar.[d] 6His division numbers
54,400.
7The tribe of Zebulun will be

29 [e]**Ge 30:18**; [f]Nu 26:25
30 [g]**Ge 30:20**; Rev 7:8
31 [h]Nu 26:27
32 [i]Ge 49:26; [j]**Ge 41:52**
33 [k]Nu 26:37; 1Ch 7:20
34 [l]**Ge 41:51**; Rev 7:6
36 [m]**Ge 35:18**; 2Ch 17:17; Jer 32:44; Ob 19; Rev 7:8
37 [n]Nu 26:41
38 [o]Ge 30:6; Dt 33:22
39 [p]Nu 26:43
40 [q]**Ge 30:13**; Nu 26:44; Rev 7:6
41 [r]Nu 26:47
42 [s]**Ge 30:8**; Rev 7:6
43 [t]Nu 26:50; [u]**Ex 1:1-4**
44 [v]Nu 26:64
45 [w]ver 3; Nu 14:29; [x]Nu 2:32
46 [y]**Ex 12:37**; 2Sa 24:9
47 [z]**Nu 3:17-20**; [a]Nu 4:3,49
50 [b]Ex 25:9; **26:1**; [c]**Ex 16:34**; Ac 7:44; Rev 15:5; [d]Nu 3:31
51 [e]**Ex 26:1**; [f]Nu 4:5; [g]Nu 3:38; 4:15; [h]**Ex 21:12**
52 [i]Nu 10:14; Ps 20:5; SS 2:4; 6:4
53 [j]Nu 2:10; 3:23,29,38; [k]Lev 10:6; Nu 16:46; 18:5; Dt 9:22; [l]**Ex 38:21**; Nu 18:2-4

Ch. 2

2 [a]Ps 74:4; Isa 31:9; Jer 4:21
3 [b]**Ex 6:23**
5 [c]Nu 10:15; [d]**Nu 1:8**

next. The leader of the people of Zebulun is Eliab son of Helon.[e] 8His division numbers 57,400.

9All the men assigned to the camp of Judah, according to their divisions, number 186,400. They will set out first.[f]

10On the south[g] will be the divisions of the camp of Reuben under their standard. The leader of the people of Reuben is Elizur son of Shedeur.[h] 11His division numbers 46,500.

12The tribe of Simeon[i] will camp next to them. The leader of the people of Simeon is Shelumiel son of Zurishaddai.[j] 13His division numbers 59,300.

14The tribe of Gad[k] will be next. The leader of the people of Gad is Eliasaph son of Deuel.[a][l] 15His division numbers 45,650.

16All the men assigned to the camp of Reuben,[m] according to their divisions, number 151,450. They will set out second.

17Then the Tent of Meeting and the camp of the Levites[n] will set out in the middle of the camps. They will set out in the same order as they encamp, each in his own place under his standard.

18On the west[o] will be the divisions of the camp of Ephraim[p] under their standard. The leader of the people of Ephraim is Elishama son of Ammihud.[q] 19His division numbers 40,500.

20The tribe of Manasseh[r] will be next to them. The leader of the people of Manasseh is Gamaliel son of Pedahzur.[s] 21His division numbers 32,200.

22The tribe of Benjamin[t] will be next. The leader of the people of Benjamin is Abidan son of Gideoni.[u] 23His division numbers 35,400.

24All the men assigned to the camp of Ephraim,[v] according to their divisions, number 108,100. They will set out third.[w]

25On the north[x] will be the divisions of the camp of Dan, under their standard.[y] The leader of the people of Dan is Ahiezer son of Ammishaddai.[z] 26His division numbers 62,700.

27The tribe of Asher will camp next to them. The leader of the people of Asher is Pagiel son of Ocran.[a] 28His division numbers 41,500.

29The tribe of Naphtali[b] will be next. The leader of the people of Naphtali is Ahira son of Enan.[c] 30His division numbers 53,400.

31All the men assigned to the camp of Dan number 157,600. They will set out last,[d] under their standards.

32These are the Israelites, counted according to their families.[e] All those in the camps, by their divisions, number 603,550.[f] 33The Levites, however, were not counted[g] along with the other Israelites, as the LORD commanded Moses.

34So the Israelites did everything the LORD commanded Moses; that is the way they encamped under their standards, and that is the way they set out, each with his clan and family.

The Levites

3 This is the account of the family of Aaron and Moses[a] at the time the LORD talked with Moses on Mount Sinai.[b]

2The names of the sons of Aaron were Nadab the firstborn[c] and Abihu, Eleazar and Ithamar.[d] 3Those were the names of Aaron's sons, the anointed priests,[e] who were ordained to serve as priests. 4Nadab and Abihu, however, fell dead before the LORD[f] when they made an offering with unauthorised fire before him in the Desert of Sinai.[g] They had no sons; so only Eleazar and Ithamar[h] served as priests during the lifetime of their father Aaron.[i]

5The LORD said to Moses, 6"Bring the tribe of Levi[j] and present them to Aaron the priest to assist him.[k] 7They are to perform duties for him and for the whole community[l] at the Tent of Meeting by doing the work[m] of the tabernacle. 8They are to take care of all the furnishings of the Tent of Meeting, fulfilling the obligations of the Israelites by doing the work of the tabernacle. 9Give the Levites to Aaron and his sons;[n] they are the Israelites who are to

---

7 [e]Nu 1:9; 10:16
9 [f]Nu 10:14; Jdg 1:1
10 [g]**Nu 1:53;** [h]Nu 1:5
12 [i]Nu 10:19; [j]**Nu 1:6**
14 [k]Nu 10:20; [l]Nu 1:14; 10:20
16 [m]Nu 10:18
17 [n]Nu 1:50; 10:21
18 [o]**Nu 1:53;** [p]**Ge 48:20;** Jer 31:18–20; [q]Nu 1:10
20 [r]**Ge 48:20;** [s]**Nu 1:10**
22 [t]Nu 10:24; [u]**Nu 1:11**
24 [v]Nu 10:22; [w]Ps 80:2
25 [x]**Nu 1:53;** [y]Nu 10:25; [z]**Nu 1:12**
27 [a]Nu 1:13; 10:26
29 [b]Nu 10:27; [c]Nu 1:15; 10:27
31 [d]Nu 10:25; Jos 6:9
32 [e]Nu 1:45; [f]**Ex 12:37**
33 [g]Nu 1:47; 26:57–62

Ch. 3

1 [a]**Ex 6:27;** [b]**Ex 19:11**
2 [c]Nu 1:20; [d]**Ex 6:23**
3 [e]**Ex 28:41; 29:30**
4 [f]**Lev 10:2;** [g]**Lev 10:1;** [h]Lev 10:6,12; Nu 4:28; [i]1Ch 24:1
6 [j]Dt 10:8; 31:9; 1Ch 15:2; [k]Nu 8:6–22; 18:1–7; 2Ch 29:11
7 [l]Nu 1:53; 8:19; [m]**Lev 8:35**
9 [n]ver 12,45; Nu 8:19; 18:6

---

[a]*14* Many manuscripts of the Masoretic Text, Samaritan Pentateuch and Vulgate (see also Num. 1:14); most manuscripts of the Masoretic Text *Reuel*

be given wholly to him.[a] 10 Appoint Aaron[o] and his sons to serve as priests;[p] anyone else who approaches the sanctuary must be put to death."[q]

11 The LORD also said to Moses, 12 "I have taken the Levites[r] from among the Israelites in place of the first male offspring[s] of every Israelite woman. The Levites are mine,[t] 13 for all the firstborn are mine.[u] When I struck down all the firstborn in Egypt, I set apart for myself every firstborn in Israel, whether man or animal. They are to be mine. I am the LORD."[v]

14 The LORD said to Moses in the Desert of Sinai,[w] 15 "Count[x] the Levites by their families and clans. Count every male a month old or more."[y] 16 So Moses counted them, as he was commanded by the word of the LORD.

17 These were the names of the sons of Levi:[z]
Gershon,[a] Kohath[b] and Merari.[c]
18 These were the names of the Gershonite clans:
Libni and Shimei.[d]
19 The Kohathite clans:
Amram, Izhar, Hebron and Uzziel.[e]
20 The Merarite clans:[f]
Mahli and Mushi.[g]
These were the Levite clans, according to their families.

21 To Gershon[h] belonged the clans of the Libnites and Shimeites;[i] these were the Gershonite clans. 22 The number of all the males a month old or more who were counted was 7,500. 23 The Gershonite clans were to camp on the west, behind the tabernacle.[j] 24 The leader of the families of the Gershonites was Eliasaph son of Lael. 25 At the Tent of Meeting the Gershonites were responsible for the care of the tabernacle[k] and tent, its coverings,[l] the curtain at the entrance[m] to the Tent of Meeting,[n] 26 the curtains of the courtyard,[o] the curtain at the entrance to the courtyard surrounding the tabernacle and altar,[p] and the ropes[q]—and everything[r] related to their use.

27 To Kohath[s] belonged the clans of the Amramites, Izharites, Hebronites and Uzzielites;[t] these were the Kohathite[u] clans. 28 The number of all the males a month old or more[v] was 8,600.[b] The Kohathites were responsible[w] for the care of the sanctuary.[x] 29 The Kohathite clans were to camp on the south side[y] of the tabernacle. 30 The leader of the families of the Kohathite clans was Elizaphan[z] son of Uzziel. 31 They were responsible for the care of the ark,[a] the table,[b] the lampstand,[c] the altars,[d] the articles[e] of the sanctuary used in ministering, the curtain,[f] and everything related to their use.[g] 32 The chief leader of the Levites was Eleazar[h] son of Aaron, the priest. He was appointed over those who were responsible[i] for the care of the sanctuary.[j]

33 To Merari belonged the clans of the Mahlites and the Mushites;[k] these were the Merarite clans.[l] 34 The number of all the males a month old or more[m] who were counted was 6,200. 35 The leader of the families of the Merarite clans was Zuriel son of Abihail; they were to camp on the north side of the tabernacle.[n] 36 The Merarites were appointed[o] to take care of the frames of the tabernacle,[p] its crossbars,[q] posts,[r] bases, all its equipment, and everything related to their use,[s] 37 as well as the posts of the surrounding courtyard[t] with their bases, tent pegs[u] and ropes.

38 Moses and Aaron and his sons were to camp to the east[v] of the tabernacle, towards the sunrise, in front of the Tent of Meeting.[w] They were responsible for the care of the sanctuary[x] on behalf of the Israelites. Anyone else who approached the sanctuary was to be put to death.[y]

39 The total number of Levites counted[z] at the LORD's command by Moses and Aaron according to their clans, including every male a month old or more, was 22,000.[a]

40 The LORD said to Moses, "Count all the firstborn Israelite males who are a month old or more[b] and make a list of their names.[c] 41 Take the Levites for me in place of all the firstborn of the Israelites,[d] and the livestock of the Levites in place of all the firstborn of the livestock of the Israelites. I am the LORD."[e]

42 So Moses counted all the firstborn of the Israelites, as the LORD commanded him. 43 The total number of firstborn males a month old or more,[f] listed by name, was 22,273.[g]

10 [o]**Ex 30:7**; [p]**Ex 29:9**; [q]Nu 1:51
12 [r]Ne 13:29; Mal 2:4; [s]ver 41; Nu 8:16, 18; [t]**ver 9**; Ex 13:2; Nu 8:14; 16:9
13 [u]**Ex 13:12**; [v]Lev 11:44
14 [w]**Ex 19:1**
15 [x]ver 39; **Nu 1:19**; [y]ver 22; Nu 18:16; 26:62
17 [z]**Ge 29:34; 46:11**; Nu 1:47; 1Ch 15:4; 23:6; 2Ch 29:12; [a]Jos 21:6; [b]Jos 21:4; [c]**Ex 6:16**
18 [d]Ex 6:17
19 [e]**Ex 6:18**
20 [f]**Ge 46:11**; [g]**Ex 6:19**
21 [h]**Ge 46:11**; [i]Ex 6:17
23 [j]**Nu 2:18**
25 [k]Ex 25:9; Nu 7:1; [l]Ex 26:14; [m]Ex 26:36; Nu 4:25; [n]Ex 40:2
26 [o]Ex 27:9; [p]ver 31; [q]Ex 35:18; [r]Nu 4:26
27 [s]**Ge 46:11; Ex 6:18**; [t]Ex 6:18; 1Ch 26:23; [u]Nu 4:15,37
28 [v]ver 15; [w]Nu 4:4,15; [x]**Ex 25:8**; 30:13; 2Ch 30:19; Ps 15:1; 20:2; Eze 44:27
29 [y]**Nu 1:53**
30 [z]**Ex 6:22**
31 [a]**Ex 25:10–22**; Dt 10:1–8; 2Ch 5:2; Jer 3:16; [b]**Ex 25:23**; [c]**Ex 25:31**; 1Ch 28:15; Jer 52:19; [d]ver 26; [e]Nu 1:50; [f]**Ex 26:33**; Nu 4:5; [g]Nu 4:15; 18:3
32 [h]**Ex 6:23**; [i]ver 28; [j]Nu 4:19; 18:3
33 [k]**Ex 6:19**; [l]**Ge 46:11**
34 [m]ver 15
35 [n]**Nu 2:25**
36 [o]Nu 4:32; [p]Ex 26:15–25; 35:20–29; [q]Ex 26:26–29; [r]Ex 36:36; [s]Nu 18:3
37 [t]Ex 27:10–17; [u]Ex 27:19
38 [v]Nu 2:3; [w]**Nu 1:53**; 1Ch 9:27; 23:32; [x]ver 7; Nu 18:5; [y]ver 10; Nu 1:51
39 [z]**ver 15**; [a]Nu 26:62
40 [b]ver 15; [c]Nu 1:2
41 [d]ver 12; [e]Lev 11:44
43 [f]ver 15; [g]ver 39

[a]9 Most manuscripts of the Masoretic Text; some manuscripts of the Masoretic Text, Samaritan Pentateuch and Septuagint (see also Num. 8:16) *to me*
[b]28 Hebrew; some Septuagint manuscripts *8,300*

44The LORD also said to Moses, 45"Take the Levites in place of all the firstborn of Israel, and the livestock of the Levites in place of their livestock. The Levites are to be mine.[h] I am the LORD.[i] 46To redeem[j] the 273 firstborn Israelites who exceed the number of the Levites, 47collect five shekels[c][k] for each one, according to the sanctuary shekel,[l] which weighs twenty gerahs.[m] 48Give the money for the redemption[n] of the additional Israelites to Aaron and his sons."[o]

49So Moses collected the redemption money[p] from those who exceeded the number redeemed by the Levites. 50From the firstborn of the Israelites[q] he collected silver weighing 1,365 shekels,[d][r] according to the sanctuary shekel. 51Moses gave the redemption money to Aaron and his sons, as he was commanded by the word of the LORD.

The Kohathites

4 The LORD said to Moses and Aaron: 2"Take a census[a] of the Kohathite branch of the Levites by their clans and families. 3Count[b] all the men from thirty to fifty years of age[c] who come to serve in the work in the Tent of Meeting.

4"This is the work[d] of the Kohathites[e] in the Tent of Meeting: the care of the most holy things.[f] 5When the camp is to move,[g] Aaron and his sons are to go in and take down the shielding curtain[h] and cover the ark of the Testimony with it.[i] 6Then they are to cover this with hides of sea cows,[a][j] spread a cloth of solid blue over that and put the poles[k] in place.

7"Over the table of the Presence[l] they are to spread a blue cloth and put on it the plates, dishes and bowls, and the jars for drink offerings;[m] the bread that is continually there[n] is to remain on it. 8Over these they are to spread a scarlet cloth, cover that with hides of sea cows and put its poles[o] in place.

9"They are to take a blue cloth and cover the lampstand that is for light, together with its lamps, its wick trimmers and trays,[p] and all its jars for the oil used to supply it. 10Then they are to wrap it and all its accessories in a covering of hides of sea cows and put it on a carrying frame.[q]

11"Over the gold altar[r] they are to spread a blue cloth and cover that with hides of sea cows and put its poles[s] in place.

12"They are to take all the articles[t] used for ministering in the sanctuary, wrap them in a blue cloth, cover that with hides of sea cows and put them on a carrying frame.[u]

13"They are to remove the ashes[v] from the bronze altar[w] and spread a purple cloth over it. 14Then they are to place on it all the utensils[x] used for ministering at the altar, including the firepans,[y] meat forks,[z] shovels[a] and sprinkling bowls.[b] Over it they are to spread a covering of hides of sea cows and put its poles[c] in place.

15"After Aaron and his sons have finished covering the holy furnishings and all the holy articles, and when the camp is ready to move,[d] the Kohathites[e] are to come to do the carrying.[f] But they must not touch the holy things[g] or they will die.[h][i] The Kohathites are to carry those things that are in the Tent of Meeting.

16"Eleazar[j] son of Aaron, the priest, is to have charge of the oil for the light,[k] the fragrant incense,[l] the regular grain offering[m] and the anointing oil. He is to be in charge of the entire tabernacle and everything in it, including its holy furnishings and articles."

17The LORD said to Moses and Aaron, 18"See that the Kohathite tribal clans are not cut off from the Levites. 19So that they may live and not die when they come near the most holy things,[n] do this for them: Aaron and his sons[o] are to go into the sanctuary and assign to each man his work and what he is to carry.[p] 20But the Kohathites must not go in to look[q] at the holy things, even for a moment, or they will die."

The Gershonites

21The LORD said to Moses, 22"Take a census also of the Gershonites by their families and clans. 23Count all the men from thirty to fifty years of age[r] who come to serve in the work at the Tent of Meeting.

24"This is the service of the Gershonite clans as they work and carry burdens: 25They are to carry the curtains of the tabernacle,[s] the Tent of Meeting,[t] its covering[u] and the outer covering of hides of sea cows, the curtains for the entrance to the Tent of Meeting, 26the curtains of the courtyard surrounding the tabernacle and altar,[v] the curtain for the entrance,[w] the ropes

45 hver 9; iLev 11:44
46 jEx 13:13; Nu 18:15
47 kLev 27:6; lEx 30:13; mLev 27:25
48 nver 51; over 50
49 pver 48
50 qver 41,45; rver 46–48

Ch. 4

2 aEx 30:12
3 bNu 1:47; cver 23; Nu 8:25; 1Ch 23:3,24, 27; Ezr 3:8
4 dNu 3:28; eNu 7:9; fver 19
5 gNu 1:51; hEx 26:31,33; i1Ch 23:26
6 jEx 25:5; kEx 25:13–15; 1Ki 8:7; 2Ch 5:8
7 lLev 24:6; mEx 39:36; Jer 52:19; nEx 25:30
8 oEx 26:26–28
9 pEx 25:38
10 qver 12
11 rEx 30:1; sEx 30:4
12 tNu 3:31; uver 10
13 vLev 1:16; wEx 27:1–8; Nu 3:31
14 xEx 31:9; yEx 27:3; z1Ch 28:17; 2Ch 4:16; a2Ch 4:11; bEx 27:3; Nu 7:84; 2Ch 4:8; Jer 52:18; cEx 27:6
15 dver 5; eNu 3:27; fNu 7:9; gver 4; hEx 28:43; iNu 1:51; 2Sa 6:6–7
16 jLev 10:6; Nu 3:32; kEx 25:6; lEx 25:6; mEx 29:41; Lev 6:14–23
19 nver 15; over 27; pNu 3:32
20 qEx 19:21
23 rver 3
25 sEx 27:10–18; tNu 3:25; uEx 26:14
26 vEx 27:9; wEx 27:16

c47 That is, about 2 ounces (about 55 grams)
d50 That is, about 35 pounds (about 15.5 kilograms)
a6 That is, dugongs; also elsewhere in this chapter

and all the equipment[x] used in its service. The Gershonites are to do all that needs to be done with these things. 27All their service, whether carrying or doing other work, is to be done under the direction of Aaron and his sons.[y] You shall assign to them as their responsibility[z] all they are to carry. 28This is the service of the Gershonite clans[a] at the Tent of Meeting. Their duties are to be under the direction of Ithamar[b] son of Aaron, the priest.

The Merarites

29"Count[c] the Merarites by their clans and families.[d] 30Count all the men from thirty to fifty years of age who come to serve in the work at the Tent of Meeting. 31This is their duty as they perform service at the Tent of Meeting: to carry the frames of the tabernacle, its crossbars, posts and bases,[e] 32as well as the posts of the surrounding courtyard with their bases, tent pegs, ropes,[f] all their equipment and everything related to their use. Assign to each man the specific things he is to carry. 33This is the service of the Merarite clans as they work at the Tent of Meeting under the direction of Ithamar[g] son of Aaron, the priest."

The Numbering of the Levite Clans

34Moses, Aaron and the leaders of the community counted the Kohathites[h] by their clans and families. 35All the men from thirty to fifty years of age[i] who came to serve in the work in the Tent of Meeting, 36counted by clans, were 2,750. 37This was the total of all those in the Kohathite clans[j] who served in the Tent of Meeting. Moses and Aaron counted them according to the LORD's command through Moses.

38The Gershonites[k] were counted by their clans and families. 39All the men from thirty to fifty years of age who came to serve in the work at the Tent of Meeting, 40counted by their clans and families, were 2,630. 41This was the total of those in the Gershonite clans who served at the Tent of Meeting. Moses and Aaron counted them according to the LORD's command.

42The Merarites were counted by their clans and families. 43All the men from thirty to fifty years of age[l] who came to serve in the work at the Tent of Meeting, 44counted by their clans, were 3,200. 45This was the total of those in the Merarite clans.[m] Moses and Aaron counted them according to the LORD's command through Moses.

46So Moses, Aaron and the leaders of Israel counted[n] all the Levites by their clans and families. 47All the men from thirty to fifty years of age[o] who came to do the work of serving and carrying the Tent of Meeting 48numbered 8,580.[p] 49At the LORD's command through Moses, each was assigned his work and told what to carry.

Thus they were counted,[q] as the LORD commanded Moses.

The Purity of the Camp

5 The LORD said to Moses, 2"Command the Israelites to send away from the camp anyone who has an infectious skin disease[a][a] or a discharge[b] of any kind, or who is ceremonially unclean[c] because of a dead body.[d] 3Send away male and female alike; send them outside the camp so that they will not defile their camp, where I dwell among them.[e]" 4The Israelites did this; they sent them outside the camp. They did just as the LORD had instructed Moses.

Restitution for Wrongs

5The LORD said to Moses, 6"Say to the Israelites: 'When a man or woman wrongs another in any way[b] and so is unfaithful[f] to the LORD, that person is guilty[g] 7and must confess[h] the sin he has committed. He must make full restitution[i] for his wrong, add one fifth to it and give it all to the person he has wronged. 8But if that person has no close relative to whom restitution can be made for the wrong, the restitution belongs to the LORD and must be given to the priest, along with the ram[j] with which atonement is made for him.[k] 9All the sacred contributions the Israelites bring to a priest will belong to him.[l] 10Each man's sacred gifts are his own, but what he gives to the priest will belong to the priest.[m]' "

The Test for an Unfaithful Wife

11Then the LORD said to Moses, 12"Speak to the Israelites and say to them: 'If a man's wife goes astray[n] and is unfaithful to him 13by sleeping with another man,[o] and this is hidden from

26 [x]Nu 3:26
27 [y]ver 19; [z]Nu 3:25–26
28 [a]Nu 7:7; [b]Ex 6:23
29 [c]Ex 30:12; [d]Ge 46:11
31 [e]Nu 3:36
32 [f]Nu 3:37
33 [g]Ex 38:21
34 [h]ver 2
35 [i]ver 3
37 [j]Nu 3:27
38 [k]Ge 46:11
43 [l]ver 3
45 [m]ver 29
46 [n]Nu 1:19
47 [o]ver 3
48 [p]Nu 3:39
49 [q]Nu 1:47

Ch. 5

2 [a]Lev 13:2; [b]Lev 15:2; Mt 9:20; [c]Lev 13:3; Nu 9:6–10; [d]Lev 21:11
3 [e]Ex 29:45; Lev 26:12; 2Co 6:16
6 [f]Lev 6:2; [g]Lev 5:14–6:7
7 [h]Lev 5:5; Lk 19:8; [i]Lev 5:16
8 [j]Lev 5:15; [k]Lev 6:6–7
9 [l]Lev 6:17
10 [m]Lev 7:29–34
12 [n]ver 19–21; Ex 20:14
13 [o]Ex 20:14

[a]2 Traditionally *leprosy;* the Hebrew word was used for various diseases affecting the skin—not necessarily leprosy.

[b]6 Or *woman commits any wrong common to mankind*

her husband and her impurity is undetected (since there is no witness against her and she has not been caught in the act), 14and if feelings of jealousy[p] come over her husband and he suspects his wife and she is impure—or if he is jealous and suspects her even though she is not impure—15then he is to take his wife to the priest. He must also take an offering of a tenth of an ephah[c][q] of barley flour[r] on her behalf. He must not pour oil on it or put incense on it, because it is a grain offering for jealousy,[s] a reminder[t] offering to draw attention to guilt.

16"'The priest shall bring her and make her stand before the LORD. 17Then he shall take some holy water in a clay jar and put some dust from the tabernacle floor into the water. 18After the priest has made the woman stand before the LORD, he shall loosen her hair[u] and place in her hands the reminder offering, the grain offering for jealousy,[v] while he himself holds the bitter water that brings a curse.[w] 19Then the priest shall put the woman under oath and say to her, "If no other man has slept with you and you have not gone astray[x] and become impure while married to your husband, may this bitter water that brings a curse[y] not harm you. 20But if you have gone astray[z] while married to your husband and you have defiled yourself by sleeping with a man other than your husband"—21here the priest is to put the woman under this curse of the oath[a]—"may the LORD cause your people to curse and denounce you when he causes your thigh to waste away and your abdomen to swell.[d] 22May this water[b] that brings a curse[c] enter your body so that your abdomen swells and your thigh wastes away."[e]

"'Then the woman is to say, "Amen. So be it.[d]"

23"'The priest is to write these curses on a scroll[e] and then wash them off into the bitter water. 24He shall make the woman drink the bitter water that brings a curse, and this water will enter her and cause bitter suffering. 25The priest is to take from her hands the grain offering for jealousy, wave it before the LORD[f] and bring it to the altar. 26The priest is then to take a handful of the grain offering as a memorial offering[g] and burn it on the altar; after that, he is to make the woman drink the water. 27If she has defiled herself and been unfaithful to her husband, then when she is made to drink the water that brings a curse, it will go into her and cause bitter suffering; her abdomen will swell and her thigh waste away,[f] and she will become accursed[h] among her people. 28If, however, the woman has not defiled herself and is free from impurity, she will be cleared of guilt and will be able to have children.

29"'This, then, is the law of jealousy when a woman goes astray[i] and defiles herself while married to her husband, 30or when feelings of jealousy[j] come over a man because he suspects his wife. The priest is to make her stand before the LORD and is to apply this entire law to her. 31The husband will be innocent of any wrongdoing, but the woman will bear the consequences[k] of her sin.'"

The Nazirite

6 The LORD said to Moses, 2"Speak to the Israelites and say to them: 'If a man or woman wants to make a special vow,[a] a vow of separation[b] to the LORD as a Nazirite,[c] 3he must abstain from wine[d] and other fermented drink and must not drink vinegar[e] made from wine or from other fermented drink. He must not drink grape juice or eat grapes[f] or raisins. 4As long as he is a Nazirite, he must not eat anything that comes from the grapevine, not even the seeds or skins.

5"'During the entire period of his vow of separation no razor[g] may be used on his head.[h] He must be holy until the period of his separation to the LORD is over; he must let the hair of his head grow long. 6Throughout the period of his separation to the LORD he must not go near a dead body.[i] 7Even if his own father or mother or brother or sister dies, he must not make himself ceremonially unclean[j] on account of them, because the symbol of his separation to God is on his head. 8Throughout the period of his separation he is consecrated to the LORD.

9"'If someone dies suddenly in his presence, thus defiling the hair he has dedicated,[k] he must shave his head on the day of his cleansing[l]—the seventh day. 10Then on the eighth day[m] he must

14 [p]ver 30; Pr 6:34; 27:4; SS 8:6
15 [q]**Ex 16:36**; [r]**Lev 6:20**; [s]ver 18,25; [t]Eze 21:23; 29:16
18 [u]**Lev 10:6**; 1Co 11:6; [v]ver 15; [w]ver 19
19 [x]ver 12,29; [y]ver 18
20 [z]ver 12
21 [a]Jos 6:26; 1Sa 14:24; Ne 10:29
22 [b]Ps 109:18; [c]ver 18; [d]Dt 27:15
23 [e]Jer 45:1
25 [f]Lev 8:27
26 [g]**Lev 2:2**
27 [h]Isa 43:28; 65:15; Jer 26:6; 29:18; 42:18; 44:12,22; Zec 8:13
29 [i]**ver 19**
30 [j]**ver 14**
31 [k]**Lev 5:1**

Ch. 6

2 [a]ver 5; **Ge 28:20**; Ac 21:23; [b]ver 6; [c]Jdg 13:5; 16:17
3 [d]**Lev 10:9**; **Lk 1:15**; [e]Ru 2:14; Ps 69:21; Pr 10:26; [f]**Lev 25:5**
5 [g]Ps 52:2; 57:4; 59:7; Isa 7:20; Eze 5:1; [h]1Sa 1:11
6 [i]**Lev 21:1-3**; Nu 19:11-22
7 [j]Nu 9:6
9 [k]ver 18; [l]**Lev 14:9**
10 [m]**Lev 14:10**

c15 That is, probably about 4 pints (about 2 litres)
d21 Or *causes you to have a miscarrying womb and barrenness*
e22 Or *body and cause you to be barren and have a miscarrying womb*
f27 Or *suffering; she will have barrenness and a miscarrying womb*

bring two doves or two young pigeons[n]
to the priest at the entrance to the Tent
of Meeting.[o] 11The priest is to offer one
as a sin offering[p] and the other as a burnt
offering[q] to make atonement[r] for him
because he sinned by being in the
presence of the dead body. That same
day he is to consecrate his head. 12He
must dedicate himself to the LORD for
the period of his separation and must
bring a year-old male lamb[s] as a guilt
offering.[t] The previous days do not
count, because he became defiled dur-
ing his separation.
13" 'Now this is the law for the Naz-
irite when the period of his separation
is over.[u] He is to be brought to the en-
trance to the Tent of Meeting.[v] 14There
he is to present his offerings to the LORD:
a year-old male lamb without defect[w] for
a burnt offering, a year-old ewe lamb
without defect for a sin offering,[x] a
ram[y] without defect for a fellowship
offering,[a][z] 15together with their grain
offerings[a] and drink offerings,[b] and a
basket of bread made without yeast—
cakes made of fine flour mixed with oil,
and wafers spread with oil.[c]
16" 'The priest is to present them[d] be-
fore the LORD[e] and make the sin offering
and the burnt offering.[f] 17He is to pre-
sent the basket of unleavened bread and
is to sacrifice the ram as a fellowship
offering[g] to the LORD, together with its
grain offering[h] and drink offering.[i]
18" 'Then at the entrance to the Tent of
Meeting, the Nazirite must shave off the
hair that he dedicated.[j] He is to take the
hair and put it in the fire that is under
the sacrifice of the fellowship offering.
19" 'After the Nazirite has shaved off
the hair of his dedication, the priest is to
place in his hands a boiled shoulder of
the ram, and a cake and a wafer from the
basket, both made without yeast.[k] 20The
priest shall then wave them before the
LORD as a wave offering;[l] they are holy[m]
and belong to the priest, together with
the breast that was waved and the thigh
that was presented.[n] After that, the
Nazirite may drink wine.[o]
21" 'This is the law of the Nazirite[p]
who vows his offering to the LORD in
accordance with his separation, in addi-
tion to whatever else he can afford. He
must fulfil the vow[q] he has made,
according to the law of the Nazirite.' "

The Priestly Blessing

22The LORD said to Moses, 23"Tell
Aaron and his sons, 'This is how you are
to bless[r] the Israelites. Say to them:

24" ' "The LORD bless you[s]
and keep you;[t]
25the LORD make his face shine upon
you[u]
and be gracious to you;[v]
26the LORD turn his face[w] towards you
and give you peace.[x]" ' "

27"So they will put my name[y] on the
Israelites, and I will bless them."

Offerings at the Dedication of the Tabernacle

7 When Moses finished setting up
the tabernacle,[a] he anointed[b] it and
consecrated it and all its furnishings.[c]
He also anointed and consecrated the
altar and all its utensils.[d] 2Then the
leaders of Israel,[e] the heads of families
who were the tribal leaders in charge
of those who were counted,[f] made
offerings. 3They brought as their gifts
before the LORD six covered carts[g] and
twelve oxen—an ox from each leader
and a cart from every two. These they
presented before the tabernacle.
4The LORD said to Moses, 5"Accept
these from them, that they may be used
in the work at the Tent of Meeting. Give
them to the Levites as each man's work
requires."
6So Moses took the carts and oxen and
gave them to the Levites. 7He gave two
carts and four oxen to the Gershonites,[h]
as their work required, 8and he gave
four carts and eight oxen to the
Merarites,[i] as their work required. They
were all under the direction of Ithamar
son of Aaron, the priest. 9But Moses did
not give any to the Kohathites,[j] because
they were to carry on their shoulders[k]
the holy things, for which they were
responsible.
10When the altar was anointed,[l] the
leaders brought their offerings for its
dedication[m] and presented them before
the altar. 11For the LORD had said to
Moses, "Each day one leader is to bring
his offering for the dedication of the
altar."

12The one who brought his offering on
the first day was Nahshon[n] son of
Amminadab of the tribe of Judah.
13His offering was one silver plate
weighing a hundred and thirty
shekels,[a] and one silver sprinkling

10 [n]**Lev 5:7;** [o]Lev 14:11
11 [p]**Ex 30:10;** [q]**Ge 8:20;** [r]**Ex 29:36**
12 [s]**Lev 12:6;** [t]**Lev 5:15**
13 [u]Ac 21:26; [v]Lev 14:11
14 [w]**Ex 12:5;** [x]ver 11; Lev 4:3; 14:10; [y]**Lev 5:15;** [z]Lev 3:1
15 [a]Lev 2:1; **6:14;** [b]**Ge 35:14;** [c]**Ex 29:2**
16 [d]Lev 1:3; [e]ver 10; [f]ver 11
17 [g]Lev 3:1; [h]**Ex 29:41;** [i]Lev 23:13
18 [j]ver 9; Ac 21:24
19 [k]Lev 7:12
20 [l]Lev 7:30; [m]**Lev 27:9;** [n]**Lev 7:34;** [o]Ecc 9:7
21 [p]ver 13; [q]ver 2
23 [r]Dt 21:5; 1Ch 23:13
24 [s]**Ge 28:3;** Dt 28:3–6; Ps 28:9; 128:5; [t]1Sa 2:9; Ps 17:8
25 [u]Job 29:24; Ps 4:6; 31:16; 80:3; 119:135; [v]Ge 43:29; Ps 25:16; 86:16; 119:29
26 [w]Ps 4:6; 44:3; [x]Ps 4:8; 29:11; 37:11, 37; 127:2; Isa 14:7; Jer 33:6; Jn 14:27
27 [y]Dt 28:10; 2Sa 7:23; 2Ch 7:14; Ne 9:10; Jer 25:29; Eze 36:23

Ch. 7

1 [a]Ex 40:17; [b]**Ex 30:26;** [c]**Ex 40:9;** [d]ver 84, 88; Ex 40:10; 2Ch 7:9
2 [e]Nu 1:5–16; [f]Nu 1:19
3 [g]Ge 45:19; 1Sa 6:7–14; 1Ch 13:7
7 [h]Nu 4:24–26, 28
8 [i]Nu 4:31–33
9 [j]Nu 4:4; [k]Nu 4:15
10 [l]ver 1; **Ex 29:36;** [m]2Ch 7:9
12 [n]**Nu 1:7**

[a]*14* Traditionally *peace offering;* also in verses 17 and 18
[a]*13* That is, about 3¼ pounds (about 1.5 kilograms); also elsewhere in this chapter

bowl[o] weighing seventy shekels,[b][p]
both according to the sanctuary
shekel,[q] each filled with fine flour
mixed with oil as a grain offering;[r]
14one gold dish[s] weighing ten
shekels,[c][t] filled with incense;[u]
15one young bull,[v] one ram and one
male lamb a year old, for a burnt
offering;[w] 16one male goat for a sin
offering;[x] 17and two oxen, five
rams, five male goats and five male
lambs a year old, to be sacrificed as
a fellowship offering.[d][y] This was
the offering of Nahshon son of
Amminadab.[z]

18On the second day Nethanel son of
Zuar,[a] the leader of Issachar, brought
his offering.
19The offering he brought was one
silver plate weighing a hundred
and thirty shekels, and one silver
sprinkling bowl weighing seventy
shekels, both according to the sanc-
tuary shekel, each filled with fine
flour mixed with oil as a grain offer-
ing; 20one gold dish[b] weighing ten
shekels, filled with incense; 21one
young bull, one ram and one male
lamb a year old, for a burnt offer-
ing; 22one male goat for a sin offer-
ing; 23and two oxen, five rams, five
male goats and five male lambs
a year old, to be sacrificed as a
fellowship offering. This was the
offering of Nethanel son of Zuar.

24On the third day, Eliab son of Helon,[c]
the leader of the people of Zebulun,
brought his offering.
25His offering was one silver plate
weighing a hundred and thirty
shekels, and one silver sprinkling
bowl weighing seventy shekels,
both according to the sanctuary
shekel, each filled with fine flour
mixed with oil as a grain offering;
26one gold dish weighing ten
shekels, filled with incense; 27one
young bull, one ram and one male
lamb a year old, for a burnt offer-
ing; 28one male goat for a sin offer-
ing; 29and two oxen, five rams, five
male goats and five male lambs a
year old, to be sacrificed as a fellow-
ship offering. This was the offering
of Eliab son of Helon.

30On the fourth day Elizur son of
Shedeur,[d] the leader of the people of
Reuben, brought his offering.
31His offering was one silver plate
weighing a hundred and thirty
shekels, and one silver sprinkling
bowl weighing seventy shekels,
both according to the sanctuary
shekel, each filled with fine flour
mixed with oil as a grain offering;
32one gold dish weighing ten
shekels, filled with incense; 33one
young bull, one ram and one male
lamb a year old, for a burnt offer-
ing; 34one male goat for a sin offer-
ing; 35and two oxen, five rams, five
male goats and five male lambs a
year old, to be sacrificed as a fellow-
ship offering. This was the offering
of Elizur son of Shedeur.

36On the fifth day Shelumiel son of
Zurishaddai,[e] the leader of the people of
Simeon, brought his offering.
37His offering was one silver plate
weighing a hundred and thirty
shekels, and one silver sprinkling
bowl weighing seventy shekels,
both according to the sanctuary
shekel, each filled with fine flour
mixed with oil as a grain offering;
38one gold dish weighing ten
shekels, filled with incense; 39one
young bull, one ram and one male
lamb a year old, for a burnt offer-
ing; 40one male goat for a sin offer-
ing; 41and two oxen, five rams, five
male goats and five male lambs a
year old, to be sacrificed as a fellow-
ship offering. This was the offering
of Shelumiel son of Zurishaddai.

42On the sixth day Eliasaph son of
Deuel,[f] the leader of the people of Gad,
brought his offering.
43His offering was one silver plate
weighing a hundred and thirty
shekels, and one silver sprinkling
bowl weighing seventy shekels,
both according to the sanctuary
shekel, each filled with fine flour
mixed with oil as a grain offering;
44one gold dish weighing ten
shekels, filled with incense; 45one
young bull, one ram and one male
lamb a year old, for a burnt offer-
ing; 46one male goat for a sin offer-
ing; 47and two oxen, five rams, five
male goats and five male lambs a
year old, to be sacrificed as a fellow-
ship offering. This was the offering
of Eliasaph son of Deuel.

13 [o]**Ex 27:3**; [p]ver 85; [q]**Ex 30:13**; Lev 27:3–7; [r]Lev 2:1; Nu 6:15; 15:4
14 [s]ver 20; 1Ki 7:50; 2Ki 25:14; 2Ch 4:22; 24:14; [t]ver 86; [u]**Ex 25:6**
15 [v]Ex 24:5; 29:3; Nu 28:11; [w]Lev 1:3
16 [x]Lev 4:3
17 [y]Lev 3:1; [z]Nu 1:7
18 [a]**Nu 1:8**
20 [b]**ver 14**
24 [c]**Nu 1:9**
30 [d]**Nu 1:5**
36 [e]**Nu 1:6**
42 [f]**Nu 1:14**

b*13* That is, about 1¾ pounds (about 0.8 kilogram); also elsewhere in this chapter
c*14* That is, about 4 ounces (about 115 grams); also elsewhere in this chapter
d*17* Traditionally *peace offering;* also elsewhere in this chapter

48 On the seventh day Elishama son of
Ammihud,[g] the leader of the people of
Ephraim, brought his offering.
49 His offering was one silver plate
weighing a hundred and thirty
shekels, and one silver sprinkling
bowl weighing seventy shekels,
both according to the sanctuary
shekel, each filled with fine flour
mixed with oil as a grain offering;
50 one gold dish weighing ten
shekels, filled with incense; 51 one
young bull, one ram and one male
lamb a year old, for a burnt offer-
ing; 52 one male goat for a sin offer-
ing; 53 and two oxen, five rams, five
male goats and five male lambs a
year old, to be sacrificed as a fellow-
ship offering. This was the offering
of Elishama son of Ammihud.[h]

54 On the eighth day Gamaliel son of
Pedahzur,[i] the leader of the people of
Manasseh, brought his offering.
55 His offering was one silver plate
weighing a hundred and thirty
shekels, and one silver sprinkling
bowl weighing seventy shekels,
both according to the sanctuary
shekel, each filled with fine flour
mixed with oil as a grain offering;
56 one gold dish weighing ten
shekels, filled with incense; 57 one
young bull, one ram and one male
lamb a year old, for a burnt offer-
ing; 58 one male goat for a sin offer-
ing; 59 and two oxen, five rams, five
male goats and five male lambs a
year old, to be sacrificed as a fellow-
ship offering. This was the offering
of Gamaliel son of Pedahzur.

60 On the ninth day Abidan son of
Gideoni,[j] the leader of the people of
Benjamin, brought his offering.
61 His offering was one silver plate
weighing a hundred and thirty
shekels, and one silver sprinkling
bowl weighing seventy shekels,
both according to the sanctuary
shekel, each filled with fine flour
mixed with oil as a grain offering;
62 one gold dish weighing ten
shekels, filled with incense; 63 one
young bull, one ram and one male
lamb a year old, for a burnt offer-
ing; 64 one male goat for a sin offer-
ing; 65 and two oxen, five rams, five
male goats and five male lambs a
year old, to be sacrificed as a fellow-
ship offering. This was the offering
of Abidan son of Gideoni.

48 [g]Nu 1:10
53 [h]Nu 1:10
54 [i]Nu 1:10
60 [j]Nu 1:11
66 [k]Nu 1:12
72 [l]Nu 1:13
78 [m]Nu 1:15

66 On the tenth day Ahiezer son of
Ammishaddai,[k] the leader of the people
of Dan, brought his offering.
67 His offering was one silver plate
weighing a hundred and thirty
shekels, and one silver sprinkling
bowl weighing seventy shekels,
both according to the sanctuary
shekel, each filled with fine flour
mixed with oil as a grain offering;
68 one gold dish weighing ten
shekels, filled with incense; 69 one
young bull, one ram and one male
lamb a year old, for a burnt offer-
ing; 70 one male goat for a sin offer-
ing; 71 and two oxen, five rams, five
male goats and five male lambs a
year old, to be sacrificed as a fellow-
ship offering. This was the offering
of Ahiezer son of Ammishaddai.

72 On the eleventh day Pagiel son of
Ocran,[l] the leader of the people of
Asher, brought his offering.
73 His offering was one silver plate
weighing a hundred and thirty
shekels, and one silver sprinkling
bowl weighing seventy shekels,
both according to the sanctuary
shekel, each filled with fine flour
mixed with oil as a grain offering;
74 one gold dish weighing ten
shekels, filled with incense; 75 one
young bull, one ram and one male
lamb a year old, for a burnt offer-
ing; 76 one male goat for a sin offer-
ing; 77 and two oxen, five rams, five
male goats and five male lambs a
year old, to be sacrificed as a fellow-
ship offering. This was the offering
of Pagiel son of Ocran.

78 On the twelfth day Ahira son of
Enan,[m] the leader of the people of
Naphtali, brought his offering.
79 His offering was one silver plate
weighing a hundred and thirty
shekels, and one silver sprinkling
bowl weighing seventy shekels,
both according to the sanctuary
shekel, each filled with fine flour
mixed with oil as a grain offering;
80 one gold dish weighing ten
shekels, filled with incense; 81 one
young bull, one ram and one male
lamb a year old, for a burnt offer-
ing; 82 one male goat for a sin offer-
ing; 83 and two oxen, five rams, five
male goats and five male lambs a
year old, to be sacrificed as a fellow-
ship offering. This was the offering
of Ahira son of Enan.

84These were the offerings of the Israelite leaders for the dedication of the altar when it was anointed:[n] twelve silver plates, twelve silver sprinkling bowls[o] and twelve gold dishes.[p] 85Each silver plate weighed a hundred and thirty shekels, and each sprinkling bowl seventy shekels. Altogether, the silver dishes weighed two thousand four hundred shekels,[e] according to the sanctuary shekel.[q] 86The twelve gold dishes filled with incense weighed ten shekels each, according to the sanctuary shekel.[r] Altogether, the gold dishes weighed a hundred and twenty shekels.[f] 87The total number of animals for the burnt offering[s] came to twelve young bulls, twelve rams and twelve male lambs a year old, together with their grain offering.[t] Twelve male goats were used for the sin offering.[u] 88The total number of animals for the sacrifice of the fellowship offering[v] came to twenty-four oxen, sixty rams, sixty male goats and sixty male lambs[w] a year old. These were the offerings for the dedication of the altar after it was anointed.[x]

89When Moses entered the Tent of Meeting[y] to speak with the LORD,[z] he heard the voice speaking to him from between the two cherubim above the atonement cover[a] on the ark of the Testimony.[b] And he spoke with him.

Setting Up the Lamps

8 The LORD said to Moses, 2"Speak to Aaron and say to him, 'When you set up the seven lamps, they are to light the area in front of the lampstand.[a]' "

3Aaron did so; he set up the lamps so that they faced forward on the lampstand, just as the LORD commanded Moses. 4This is how the lampstand was made: It was made of hammered gold[b]—from its base to its blossoms. The lampstand was made exactly like the pattern[c] the LORD had shown Moses.

The Setting Apart of the Levites

5The LORD said to Moses: 6"Take the Levites from among the other Israelites and make them ceremonially clean.[d] 7To purify them, do this: Sprinkle the water of cleansing[e] on them; then make them shave their whole bodies[f] and wash their clothes,[g] and so purify themselves.[h] 8Make them take a young bull with its grain offering of fine flour mixed with oil;[i] then you are to take a second young bull for a sin offering.[j] 9Bring the Levites to the front of the Tent of Meeting[k] and assemble the whole Israelite community.[l] 10You are to bring the Levites before the LORD, and the Israelites are to lay their hands on them.[m] 11Aaron is to present the Levites before the LORD as a wave offering[n] from the Israelites, so that they may be ready to do the work of the LORD.

12"After the Levites lay their hands on the heads of the bulls,[o] use the one for a sin offering[p] to the LORD and the other for a burnt offering,[q] to make atonement[r] for the Levites. 13Make the Levites stand in front of Aaron and his sons and then present them as a wave offering[s] to the LORD. 14In this way you are to set the Levites apart from the other Israelites, and the Levites will be mine.[t]

15"After you have purified the Levites and presented them as a wave offering,[u] they are to come to do their work at the Tent of Meeting.[v] 16They are the Israelites who are to be given wholly to me. I have taken them as my own in place of the firstborn,[w] the first male offspring[x] from every Israelite woman. 17Every firstborn male in Israel, whether man or animal,[y] is mine. When I struck down all the firstborn in Egypt, I set them apart for myself.[z][a] 18And I have taken the Levites in place of all the firstborn sons in Israel.[b] 19Of all the Israelites, I have given the Levites as gifts to Aaron and his sons[c] to do the work at the Tent of Meeting on behalf of the Israelites[d] and to make atonement for them[e] so that no plague will strike the Israelites when they go near the sanctuary."

20Moses, Aaron and the whole Israelite community did with the Levites just as the LORD commanded Moses. 21The Levites purified themselves and washed their clothes.[f] Then Aaron presented them as a wave offering before the LORD and made atonement[g] for them to purify them.[h] 22After that, the Levites came to do their work[i] at the Tent of Meeting under the supervision of Aaron and his sons. They did with the Levites just as the LORD commanded Moses.

23The LORD said to Moses, 24"This applies to the Levites: Men twenty-five years old or more[j] shall come to take part in the work at the Tent of Meeting,[k] 25but at the age of fifty,[l] they must retire from their regular service and work no longer. 26They may assist their brothers

84 [n]ver 1,10; [o]**Nu 4:14;** [p]ver 14
85 [q]ver 13
86 [r]ver 13
87 [s]ver 15; [t]ver 13; [u]ver 16
88 [v]ver 17; [w]Ge 32:14; [x]**ver 1,**10
89 [y]**Ex 40:2;** [z]**Ex 29:42;** [a]**Ex 16:34;** Ps 80:1; 99:1; [b]Nu 3:31

Ch. 8

2 [a]Ex 25:37
4 [b]**Ex 25:36;** [c]**Ex 25:9**
6 [d]Lev 22:2; Isa 1:16; 52:11
7 [e]Nu 19:9,17; 31:23; [f]**Lev 14:9;** Nu 6:9; Dt 21:12; [g]**Ge 35:2;** Lev 14:8; [h]**Ge 35:2**
8 [i]Lev 2:1; Nu 15:8–10; [j]Lev 4:3
9 [k]Ex 40:12; [l]Lev 8:3
10 [m]**Lev 3:2;** Ac 6:6
11 [n]**Ex 29:24**
12 [o]**Ex 29:10;** [p]Lev 4:3; Nu 6:11; [q]Lev 1:3; [r]**Ex 29:36**
13 [s]**Ex 29:24**
14 [t]**Nu 3:12**
15 [u]**Ex 29:24;** [v]Ex 40:2
16 [w]Nu 1:20; [x]**Nu 3:12**
17 [y]**Ex 4:23;** [z]**Ex 22:29;** [a]**Ex 13:2**
18 [b]**Nu 3:12**
19 [c]**Nu 3:9;** [d]**Nu 3:7;** [e]Nu 16:46
21 [f]ver 7; **Ge 35:2;** [g]Nu 16:47; [h]ver 12
22 [i]ver 11
24 [j]1Ch 23:3; [k]**Ex 38:21**
25 [l]**Nu 4:3**

[e]85 That is, about 61 pounds (about 28 kilograms)
[f]86 That is, about 3 pounds (about 1.4 kilograms)

in performing their duties at the Tent of Meeting, but they themselves must not do the work.[m] This, then, is how you are to assign the responsibilities of the Levites."

The Passover

9 The LORD spoke to Moses in the Desert of Sinai in the first month[a] of the second year after they came out of Egypt.[b] He said, 2"Make the Israelites celebrate the Passover[c] at the appointed time.[d] 3Celebrate it at the appointed time, at twilight on the fourteenth day of this month,[e] in accordance with all its rules and regulations.[f]"

4So Moses told the Israelites to celebrate the Passover,[g] 5and they did so in the Desert of Sinai[h] at twilight on the fourteenth day of the first month.[i] The Israelites did everything just as the LORD commanded Moses.[j]

6But some of them could not celebrate the Passover on that day because they were ceremonially unclean[k] on account of a dead body.[l] So they came to Moses and Aaron[m] that same day 7and said to Moses, "We have become unclean because of a dead body, but why should we be kept from presenting the LORD's offering with the other Israelites at the appointed time?[n]"

8Moses answered them, "Wait until I find out what the LORD commands concerning you."[o]

9Then the LORD said to Moses, 10"Tell the Israelites: 'When any of you or your descendants are unclean because of a dead body[p] or are away on a journey, they may still celebrate[q] the LORD's Passover. 11They are to celebrate it on the fourteenth day of the second month[r] at twilight. They are to eat the lamb, together with unleavened bread and bitter herbs.[s] 12They must not leave any of it till morning[t] or break any of its bones.[u] When they celebrate the Passover, they must follow all the regulations.[v] 13But if a man who is ceremonially clean and not on a journey fails to celebrate the Passover, that person must be cut off from his people[w] because he did not present the LORD's offering at the appointed time. That man will bear the consequences of his sin.

14" 'An alien[x] living among you who wants to celebrate the LORD's Passover must do so in accordance with its rules and regulations. You must have the same regulations for the alien and the native-born.' "

The Cloud Above the Tabernacle

15On the day the tabernacle, the Tent of the Testimony,[y] was set up,[z] the cloud[a] covered it. From evening till morning the cloud above the tabernacle looked like fire.[b] 16That is how it continued to be; the cloud covered it, and at night it looked like fire.[c] 17Whenever the cloud lifted from above the Tent, the Israelites set out;[d] wherever the cloud settled, the Israelites encamped.[e] 18At the LORD's command the Israelites set out, and at his command they encamped. As long as the cloud stayed over the tabernacle, they remained[f] in camp. 19When the cloud remained over the tabernacle a long time, the Israelites obeyed the LORD's order[g] and did not set out.[h] 20Sometimes the cloud was over the tabernacle only a few days; at the LORD's command they would encamp, and then at his command they would set out. 21Sometimes the cloud stayed only from evening till morning, and when it lifted in the morning, they set out. Whether by day or by night, whenever the cloud lifted, they set out. 22Whether the cloud stayed over the tabernacle for two days or a month or a year, the Israelites would remain in camp and not set out; but when it lifted, they would set out. 23At the LORD's command they encamped, and at the LORD's command they set out. They obeyed the LORD's order, in accordance with his command through Moses.

The Silver Trumpets

10 The LORD said to Moses: 2"Make two trumpets[a] of hammered silver, and use them for calling the community[b] together and for having the camps set out.[c] 3When both are sounded, the whole community is to assemble before you at the entrance to the Tent of Meeting. 4If only one is sounded, the leaders[d]—the heads of the clans of Israel—are to assemble before you. 5When a trumpet blast is sounded, the tribes camping on the east are to set out.[e] 6At the sounding of a second blast, the camps on the south are to set out.[f] The blast will be the signal for setting out. 7To gather the assembly, blow the trumpets,[g] but not with the same signal.[h]

8"The sons of Aaron, the priests, are to blow the trumpets. This is to be a lasting ordinance for you and the generations to come.[i] 9When you go into battle in your own land against an

26 [m]ver 11

Ch. 9

1 [a]Ex 40:2; [b]Nu 1:1
2 [c]Ex 12:11; [d]ver 7
3 [e]Ex 12:6,42; [f]Ex 12:2–11, 43–49; Lev 23:5–8; Dt 16:1–8
4 [g]ver 2; Ex 12:11
5 [h]ver 1; [i]Ex 12:6; [j]ver 3
6 [k]Lev 5:3; 13:3; [l]Lev 21:11; [m]Ex 18:15; Nu 27:2
7 [n]ver 2
8 [o]Ex 18:15; Lev 24:12; Nu 15:34; 27:5,21; Ps 85:8
10 [p]ver 6; [q]2Ch 30:2
11 [r]Ex 12:6; [s]Ex 12:8
12 [t]Ex 12:8; [u]Ex 12:46; Jn 19:36*; [v]ver 3
13 [w]Ge 17:14
14 [x]Ex 12:19,43
15 [y]Ex 38:21; [z]Ex 26:30; [a]Ex 33:16; [b]Ex 13:21
16 [c]Ex 40:38
17 [d]ver 21; [e]1Co 10:1
18 [f]Ex 40:37
19 [g]Lev 8:35; [h]Ex 40:37

Ch. 10

2 [a]ver 8–9; Nu 31:6; Ne 12:35; Ps 47:5; 98:6; 150:3; [b]Ne 4:18; Jer 4:5, 19; 6:1; Hos 5:8; 8:1; Joel 2:1,15; Am 3:6; [c]Nu 33:3
4 [d]Ex 18:21
5 [e]ver 14
6 [f]ver 18
7 [g]Jer 4:5; 6:1; Eze 33:3; Joel 2:1; [h]1Co 14:8
8 [i]Ge 9:12; Nu 15:14; 35:29

enemy who is oppressing you,[j] sound a blast on the trumpets.[k] Then you will be remembered[l] by the LORD your God and rescued from your enemies.[m] 10Also at your times of rejoicing—your appointed feasts and New Moon festivals[n]—you are to sound the trumpets[o] over your burnt offerings[p] and fellowship offerings,**[a]**[q] and they will be a memorial for you before your God. I am the LORD your God.[r]"

The Israelites Leave Sinai

11On the twentieth day of the second month of the second year,[s] the cloud lifted[t] from above the tabernacle of the Testimony.[u] 12Then the Israelites set out from the Desert of Sinai and travelled from place to place until the cloud came to rest in the Desert of Paran.[v] 13They set out, this first time, at the LORD's command through Moses.[w]

14The divisions of the camp of Judah went first, under their standard.[x] Nahshon son of Amminadab[y] was in command. 15Nethanel son of Zuar was over the division of the tribe[z] of Issachar,[a] 16and Eliab son of Helon[b] was over the division of the tribe of Zebulun.[c] 17Then the tabernacle was taken down, and the Gershonites and Merarites, who carried it, set out.[d]

18The divisions of the camp of Reuben[e] went next, under their standard.[f] Elizur son of Shedeur[g] was in command. 19Shelumiel son of Zurishaddai was over the division of the tribe of Simeon,[h] 20and Eliasaph son of Deuel was over the division of the tribe of Gad.[i] 21Then the Kohathites[j] set out, carrying the holy things.[k] The tabernacle was to be set up before they arrived.[l]

22The divisions of the camp of Ephraim[m] went next, under their standard. Elishama son of Ammihud[n] was in command. 23Gamaliel son of Pedahzur was over the division of the tribe of Manasseh,[o] 24and Abidan son of Gideoni was over the division of the tribe of Benjamin.[p]

25Finally, as the rear guard[q] for all the units, the divisions of the camp of Dan set out, under their standard. Ahiezer son of Ammishaddai[r] was in command. 26Pagiel son of Ocran was over the division of the tribe of Asher,[s] 27and Ahira son of Enan was over the division of the tribe of Naphtali.[t] 28This was the order of march for the Israelite divisions as they set out.

29Now Moses said to Hobab[u] son of Reuel[v] the Midianite, Moses' father-in-law,[w] "We are setting out for the place about which the LORD said, 'I will give it to you.'[x] Come with us and we will treat you well, for the LORD has promised good things to Israel."

30He answered, "No, I will not go;[y] I am going back to my own land and my own people.[z]"

31But Moses said, "Please do not leave us. You know where we should camp in the desert, and you can be our eyes.[a] 32If you come with us, we will share with you[b] whatever good things the LORD gives us.[c]"

33So they set out[d] from the mountain of the LORD and travelled for three days. The ark of the covenant of the LORD[e] went before them during those three days to find them a place to rest.[f] 34The cloud of the LORD was over them by day when they set out from the camp.[g]

35Whenever the ark set out, Moses said,

"Rise up,[h] O LORD!
May your enemies be scattered;[i]
may your foes flee before you.[j]"[k]

36Whenever it came to rest, he said,

"Return,[l] O LORD,
to the countless thousands of Israel.[m]"

Fire From the LORD

11

Now the people complained[a] about their hardships in the hearing of the LORD,[b] and when he heard them his anger was aroused.[c] Then fire from the LORD burned among them[d] and consumed[e] some of the outskirts of the camp. 2When the people cried out to Moses, he prayed[f] to the LORD[g] and the fire died down. 3So that place was called Taberah,**[a]**[h] because fire from the LORD had burned among them.[i]

Quail From the LORD

4The rabble with them began to crave other food,[j] and again the Israelites started wailing[k] and said, "If only we

9 [j]Ex 3:9; Jdg 2:18; 6:9; 1Sa 10:18; 2Ki 13:4; Ps 106:42; [k]**Lev 23:24**; [l]**Ge 8:1**; [m]2Ch 13:12; Ps 106:4
10 [n]Nu 28:11; 1Sa 20:5,24; 2Ki 4:23; 2Ch 8:13; Ps 81:3; Isa 1:13; Eze 45:17; 46:6; Am 8:5; [o]**Lev 23:24**; [p]Lev 1:3; [q]Lev 3:1; Nu 6:14; [r]Lev 11:44
11 [s]Ex 40:17; [t]Nu 9:17; [u]**Ex 38:21**
12 [v]**Ge 14:6**; Dt 1:1; 33:2
13 [w]Dt 1:6
14 [x]**Nu 1:52; 2:3–9**; [y]Nu 1:7
15 [z]**Lev 24:11**; [a]**Nu 1:8**
16 [b]**Nu 2:7**; [c]**Nu 1:9**
17 [d]ver 21; Nu 4:21–32
18 [e]Nu 2:16; [f]Nu 2:10–16; [g]**Nu 1:5**
19 [h]Nu 1:6
20 [i]**Nu 1:14**
21 [j]**Nu 2:17**; [k]Nu 4:20; [l]**ver 17**
22 [m]Nu 2:24; [n]**Nu 1:10**
23 [o]**Nu 1:10**
24 [p]Nu 1:11
25 [q]**Nu 2:31**; [r]**Nu 1:12**
26 [s]**Nu 1:13**
27 [t]**Nu 1:15**
29 [u]Jdg 4:11; [v]**Ex 2:18**; [w]**Ex 3:1**; [x]**Ge 12:7; 15:14**
30 [y]Mt 21:29; [z]**Ex 18:27**
31 [a]Job 29:15
32 [b]**Ex 12:48**; Dt 10:18; [c]Ps 22:27–31; 67:5–7
33 [d]ver 12; Dt 1:33; [e]Dt 10:8; 31:9; Jos 3:3; Jdg 20:27; 2Sa 15:24; [f]Jer 31:2
34 [g]Nu 9:15–23
35 [h]2Ch 6:41; Ps 17:13; 44:26; 94:2; 132:8; [i]Jdg 5:31; 1Sa 2:1; Ps 68:1; 92:9; [j]Dt 5:9; 7:10; 32:41; Ps 68:2; Isa 17:12–14; [k]Isa 59:18
36 [l]Isa 52:8; 63:17; [m]Ge 15:5; 26:4; Dt 1:10; 10:22; Ne 9:23

Ch. 11
1 [a]**Ex 14:11; 16:7**; La 3:39; [b]Nu 12:2; Dt 1:34; [c]**Ex 4:14**; [d]**Lev 10:2**; [e]Nu 21:28; Ps 78:63; Isa 26:11
2 [f]Dt 9:19; 1Sa 2:25; 12:23; Ps 106:23; [g]**Ge 20:7**; Nu 21:7; Dt 9:20; Jnh 2:1
3 [h]Dt 9:22; [i]Nu 16:35; Job 1:16; Isa 10:17
4 [j]**Ex 16:3**; [k]ver 18

a10 Traditionally *peace offerings*
a3 *Taberah* means *burning*.

had meat to eat! 5We remember the fish we ate in Egypt at no cost—also the cucumbers, melons, leeks, onions and garlic.[l] 6But now we have lost our appetite; we never see anything but this manna!"[m]'

7The manna was like coriander seed[n] and looked like resin.[o] 8The people went around gathering it,[p] and then ground it in a hand mill or crushed it in a mortar. They cooked it in a pot or made it into cakes. And it tasted like something made with olive oil. 9When the dew[q] settled on the camp at night, the manna also came down.

10Moses heard the people of every family wailing,[r] each at the entrance to his tent. The LORD became exceedingly angry, and Moses was troubled. 11He asked the LORD, "Why have you brought this trouble[s] on your servant? What have I done to displease you that you put the burden of all these people on me?[t] 12Did I conceive all these people? Did I give them birth? Why do you tell me to carry them in my arms, as a nurse carries an infant,[u] to the land you promised on oath[v] to their forefathers?[w] 13Where can I get meat for all these people?[x] They keep wailing to me, 'Give us meat to eat!' 14I cannot carry all these people by myself; the burden is too heavy for me.[y] 15If this is how you are going to treat me, put me to death[z] right now[a]—if I have found favour in your eyes—and do not let me face my own ruin."

16The LORD said to Moses: "Bring me seventy of Israel's elders[b] who are known to you as leaders and officials among the people.[c] Make them come to the Tent of Meeting,[d] that they may stand there with you. 17I will come down and speak with you[e] there, and I will take of the Spirit that is on you and put the Spirit on them.[f] They will help you carry the burden of the people so that you will not have to carry it alone.[g]

18"Tell the people: 'Consecrate yourselves[h] in preparation for tomorrow, when you will eat meat. The LORD heard you when you wailed,[i] "If only we had meat to eat! We were better off in Egypt!"[j] Now the LORD will give you meat,[k] and you will eat it. 19You will not eat it for just one day, or two days, or five, ten or twenty days, 20but for a whole month—until it comes out of your nostrils and you loathe it[l]—because you have rejected the LORD,[m] who is among you, and have wailed before him, saying, "Why did we ever leave Egypt?"'"[n]

5 [l]**Ex 16:3**; Nu 21:5
6 [m]Ex 16:14
7 [n]**Ex 16:31**; [o]Ge 2:12
8 [p]Ex 16:16
9 [q]Ex 16:13
10 [r]ver 4
11 [s]**Ge 34:30**; [t]**Ex 5:22**; **18:18**
12 [u]Isa 40:11; 49:23; 66:11–12; [v]Nu 14:16; [w]**Ge 12:7**; Ex 13:5
13 [x]**Ex 12:37**; Jn 6:5–9
14 [y]**Ex 18:18**
15 [z]Ex 32:32; [a]1Ki 19:4; Job 6:9; 7:15–16; 9:21; 10:1; Isa 38:12; Jnh 4:3
16 [b]**Ex 3:16**; [c]**Ex 18:25**; [d]**Ex 40:2**
17 [e]Ex 19:20; [f]ver 25,29; 1Sa 10:6; 2Ki 2:9, 15; 3:12; Isa 32:15; 40:5; 63:11; Joel 2:28; Hag 2:5; [g]**Ex 18:18**; Jer 19:1
18 [h]**Ex 19:10**; [i]**Ex 16:7**; [j]ver 5; Ac 7:39; [k]Ps 78:20
20 [l]Ps 78:29; 106:14–15; [m]**Lev 26:43**; Jos 24:27; Jdg 8:23; 1Sa 10:19; Job 31:28; Isa 59:13; Hos 13:11; [n]ver 33; Job 20:13,23
21 [o]**Ex 12:37**
22 [p]Mt 15:33
23 [q]Isa 50:2; 59:1; [r]Nu 23:19; 1Sa 15:29; Eze 12:25; 24:14
25 [s]**Ex 19:9**; Nu 12:5; [t]ver 17; [u]ver 29; 1Sa 10:6; 19:23; [v]**Ac 2:17**; [w]ver 26; Nu 24:2; Jdg 3:10; 1Sa 10:10; 19:20; 2Ch 15:1
26 [x]**ver 25**; 1Ch 12:18; Rev 1:10
28 [y]Ex 17:9; Nu 13:8; 26:65; Jos 14:10; [z]Ex 33:11; Jos 1:1; [a]Mk 9:38–40
29 [b]1Sa 10:5; 19:20; 2Ch 24:19; Jer 7:25; 44:4; 1Co 14:5; [c]**ver 17**; [d]Nu 27:18
31 [e]**Ex 16:13**; Ps 78:26–28

21But Moses said, "Here I am among six hundred thousand men[o] on foot, and you say, 'I will give them meat to eat for a whole month!' 22Would they have enough if flocks and herds were slaughtered for them? Would they have enough if all the fish in the sea were caught for them?"[p]

23The LORD answered Moses, "Is the LORD's arm too short?[q] You will now see whether or not what I say will come true for you."[r]

24So Moses went out and told the people what the LORD had said. He brought together seventy of their elders and made them stand round the Tent. 25Then the LORD came down in the cloud[s] and spoke with him,[t] and he took of the Spirit[u] that was on him and put the Spirit on the seventy elders.[v] When the Spirit rested on them, they prophesied,[w] but they did not do so again.[b]

26However, two men, whose names were Eldad and Medad, had remained in the camp. They were listed among the elders, but did not go out to the Tent. Yet the Spirit also rested on them,[x] and they prophesied in the camp. 27A young man ran and told Moses, "Eldad and Medad are prophesying in the camp."

28Joshua son of Nun,[y] who had been Moses' assistant[z] since youth, spoke up and said, "Moses, my lord, stop them!"[a]

29But Moses replied, "Are you jealous for my sake? I wish that all the LORD's people were prophets[b] and that the LORD would put his Spirit[c] on them!"[d] 30Then Moses and the elders of Israel returned to the camp.

31Now a wind went out from the LORD and drove quail[e] in from the sea. It brought them[c] down all around the camp to about three feet[d] above the ground, as far as a day's walk in any direction. 32All that day and night and all the next day the people went out and gathered quail. No-one gathered less than ten homers.[e] Then they spread them out all around the camp. 33But while the meat was still between their teeth[f] and before it could be consumed, the anger[g] of the LORD burned against the people, and he struck them with a severe plague.[h] 34Therefore the place

33 [f]Ps 78:30; [g]Nu 14:18; Dt 9:7; Jdg 2:12; 2Ki 22:17; Ps 106:29; Jer 44:3; Eze 8:17; [h]**ver 18–20**; Ps 106:15; Isa 10:16

[b]25 Or *prophesied and continued to do so*
[c]31 Or *They flew*
[d]31 Hebrew *two cubits* (about 0.9 metre)
[e]32 That is, probably about 60 bushels (about 2.2 kilolitres)

was named Kibroth Hattaavah,[f] [i]
because there they buried the people
who had craved other food.
35From Kibroth Hattaavah the people
travelled to Hazeroth[j] and stayed there.

Miriam and Aaron Oppose Moses

12 Miriam[a] and Aaron began to
talk against Moses because of
his Cushite wife,[b] for he had married a
Cushite. 2"Has the LORD spoken only
through Moses?" they asked. "Hasn't
he also spoken through us?"[c] And the
LORD heard this.[d]
3(Now Moses was a very humble
man,[e] more humble than anyone else on
the face of the earth.)
4At once the LORD said to Moses,
Aaron and Miriam, "Come out to the
Tent of Meeting, all three of you." So
the three of them came out. 5Then the
LORD came down in a pillar of cloud;[f] he
stood at the entrance to the Tent and
summoned Aaron and Miriam. When
both of them stepped forward, 6he said,
"Listen to my words:

"When a prophet of the LORD is
among you,
I reveal[g] myself to him in visions,[h]
I speak to him in dreams.[i]
7But this is not true of my servant
Moses;[j]
he is faithful in all my house.[k]
8With him I speak face to face,
clearly and not in riddles;[l]
he sees the form of the LORD.[m]
Why then were you not afraid
to speak against my servant
Moses?"[n]

9The anger of the LORD burned
against them,[o] and he left them.[p]
10When the cloud lifted from above
the Tent,[q] there stood Miriam—
leprous,[a] like snow.[r] Aaron turned
towards her and saw that she had
leprosy;[s] 11and he said to Moses,
"Please, my lord, do not hold against us
the sin we have so foolishly committed.[t]
12Do not let her be like a stillborn infant
coming from its mother's womb with its
flesh half eaten away."
13So Moses cried out to the LORD, "O
God, please heal her![u]"
14The LORD replied to Moses, "If her
father had spat in her face,[v] would she
not have been in disgrace for seven
days? Confine her outside the camp[w] for
seven days; after that she can be
brought back." 15So Miriam was
confined outside the camp[x] for seven
days,[y] and the people did not move on
till she was brought back.
16After that, the people left Hazeroth[z]
and encamped in the Desert of Paran.[a]

Exploring Canaan

13 The LORD said to Moses, 2"Send
some men to explore[a] the land
of Canaan,[b] which I am giving to the
Israelites.[c] From each ancestral tribe[d]
send one of its leaders."
3So at the LORD's command Moses
sent them out from the Desert of Paran.
All of them were leaders of the
Israelites.[e] 4These are their names:

from the tribe of Reuben,
Shammua son of Zaccur;
5from the tribe of Simeon, Shaphat
son of Hori;
6from the tribe of Judah, Caleb son
of Jephunneh;[f]
7from the tribe of Issachar, Igal son
of Joseph;
8from the tribe of Ephraim,
Hoshea son of Nun;[g]
9from the tribe of Benjamin, Palti
son of Raphu;
10from the tribe of Zebulun,
Gaddiel son of Sodi;
11from the tribe of Manasseh (a tribe
of Joseph), Gaddi son of Susi;
12from the tribe of Dan, Ammiel son
of Gemalli;
13from the tribe of Asher, Sethur
son of Michael;
14from the tribe of Naphtali, Nahbi
son of Vophsi;
15from the tribe of Gad, Geuel son
of Maki.

16These are the names of the men Moses
sent to explore[h] the land. (Moses gave
Hoshea son of Nun[i] the name Joshua.)[j]
17When Moses sent them to explore
Canaan,[k] he said, "Go up through the
Negev[l] and on into the hill country.[m]
18See what the land is like and whether
the people who live there are strong or
weak, few or many. 19What kind of land
do they live in? Is it good or bad? What
kind of towns do they live in? Are they
unwalled or fortified? 20How is the soil?
Is it fertile or poor? Are there trees on it
or not? Do your best to bring back some
of the fruit of the land."[n] (It was the
season for the first ripe grapes.)[o]

34 [i]Nu 33:16; Dt 9:22
35 [j]Nu 33:17

Ch. 12

1 [a]**Ex 15:20;** [b]**Ex 2:21**
2 [c]Nu 16:3; [d]**Nu 11:1**
3 [e]Mt 11:29
5 [f]**Ex 13:21; Nu 11:25**
6 [g]1Sa 3:7,21; [h]**Ge 15:1;** [i]**Ge 20:3; Mt 27:19;** Heb 1:1
7 [j]Dt 34:5; Jos 1:1–2; Ps 105:26; [k]Heb 3:2,5
8 [l]Jdg 14:12; 1Ki 10:1; Ps 49:4; Pr 1:6; Da 5:12; [m]Ex 20:4; Job 19:26; Ps 17:15; 140:13; Isa 6:1; [n]Ex 24:2
9 [o]**Ex 4:14;** [p]**Ge 17:22**
10 [q]Ex 40:2; [r]**Ex 4:6;** Dt 24:9; [s]**Lev 13:11;** 2Ki 5:1,27; 2Ch 16:12; 21:12–15; 26:19
11 [t]2Sa 19:19; 24:10
13 [u]Ex 15:26; Ps 6:2; 147:3; Isa 1:6; 30:26; 53:5; Jer 17:14; Hos 6:1
14 [v]Dt 25:9; Job 17:6; 30:9–10; Isa 50:6; [w]**Lev 13:46**
15 [x]**Lev 14:8;** [y]**Lev 13:4**
16 [z]Nu 11:35; [a]Ge 21:21; Nu 10:12; 15:32

Ch. 13

2 [a]ver 16; Dt 1:22; [b]**Lev 14:34;** [c]Jos 1:3; [d]**Lev 24:11**
3 [e]Nu 1:16
6 [f]ver 30; Nu 14:6,24; 34:19; Dt 1:36; Jdg 1:12–15
8 [g]**Nu 11:28**
16 [h]**ver 2;** [i]ver 8; [j]Dt 32:44
17 [k]ver 2; Jos 14:7; [l]**Ge 12:9;** [m]Dt 1:7; Jos 9:1; Jdg 1:9
20 [n]Dt 1:25; [o]**Lev 25:5**

[f]34 *Kibroth Hattaavah* means *graves of craving*.
[a]10 The Hebrew word was used for various diseases affecting the skin—not necessarily leprosy.

21So they went up and explored the land from the Desert of Zin[p] as far as Rehob,[q] towards Lebo[a] Hamath.[r] 22They went up through the Negev and came to Hebron,[s] where Ahiman, Sheshai and Talmai,[t] the descendants of Anak,[u] lived. (Hebron had been built seven years before Zoan in Egypt.)[v] 23When they reached the Valley of Eshcol,[b][w] they cut off a branch bearing a single cluster of grapes. Two of them carried it on a pole between them, along with some pomegranates[x] and figs.[y] 24That place was called the Valley of Eshcol because of the cluster of grapes the Israelites cut off there. 25At the end of forty days[z] they returned from exploring the land.[a]

Report on the Exploration

26They came back to Moses and Aaron and the whole Israelite community at Kadesh[b] in the Desert of Paran.[c] There they reported to them[d] and to the whole assembly and showed them the fruit of the land.[e] 27They gave Moses this account: "We went into the land to which you sent us, and it does flow with milk and honey![f] Here is its fruit.[g] 28But the people who live there are powerful, and the cities are fortified and very large.[h] We even saw descendants of Anak[i] there.[j] 29The Amalekites[k] live in the Negev; the Hittites,[l] Jebusites[m] and Amorites[n] live in the hill country;[o] and the Canaanites[p] live near the sea and along the Jordan.[q]"

30Then Caleb[r] silenced the people before Moses and said, "We should go up and take possession of the land, for we can certainly do it."

31But the men who had gone up with him said, "We can't attack those people; they are stronger than we are."[s] 32And they spread among the Israelites a bad report[t] about the land they had explored. They said, "The land we explored devours[u] those living in it. All the people we saw there are of great size.[v] 33We saw the Nephilim[w] there (the descendants of Anak[x] come from the Nephilim). We seemed like grasshoppers[y] in our own eyes, and we looked the same to them."

The People Rebel

14 That night all the people of the community raised their voices and wept aloud.[a] 2All the Israelites grumbled[b] against Moses and Aaron, and the whole assembly said to them, "If only we had died in Egypt![c] Or in this desert![d] 3Why is the LORD bringing us to this land only to let us fall by the sword?[e] Our wives and children[f] will be taken as plunder.[g] Wouldn't it be better for us to go back to Egypt?[h]" 4And they said to each other, "We should choose a leader and go back to Egypt.[i]"

5Then Moses and Aaron fell face down[j] in front of the whole Israelite assembly[k] gathered there. 6Joshua son of Nun[l] and Caleb son of Jephunneh, who were among those who had explored the land, tore their clothes[m] 7and said to the entire Israelite assembly, "The land we passed through and explored is exceedingly good.[n] 8If the LORD is pleased with us,[o] he will lead us into that land, a land flowing with milk and honey,[p] and will give it to us.[q] 9Only do not rebel[r] against the LORD. And do not be afraid[s] of the people of the land,[t] because we will swallow them up. Their protection is gone, but the LORD is with[u] us.[v] Do not be afraid of them."[w]

10But the whole assembly talked about stoning[x] them. Then the glory of the LORD[y] appeared at the Tent of Meeting to all the Israelites. 11The LORD said to Moses, "How long will these people treat me with contempt?[z] How long will they refuse to believe in me,[a] in spite of all the miraculous signs[b] I have performed among them? 12I will strike them down with a plague[c] and destroy them, but I will make you into a nation[d] greater and stronger than they."[e]

13Moses said to the LORD, "Then the Egyptians will hear about it! By your power you brought these people up from among them.[f] 14And they will tell the inhabitants of this land about it. They have already heard[g] that you, O LORD, are with these people[h] and that

21 [p]Nu 20:1; 27:14; 33:36; Dt 32:51; Jos 15:1; [q]Jos 19:28; Jdg 1:31; 18:28; 2Sa 10:6; 1Ch 6:75; [r]Nu 34:8; Jos 13:5; Jdg 3:3; 1Ki 8:65; 2Ki 14:25; 1Ch 13:5; 2Ch 7:8; Jer 52:9; Eze 47:16,20; Am 6:14
22 [s]**Ge 13:18; 23:19**; [t]Jos 15:14; Jdg 1:10; [u]ver 28; Dt 2:10; 9:2; Jos 11:21; 15:13; Jdg 1:20; [v]Ps 78:12,43; Isa 19:11,13; 30:4; Eze 30:14
23 [w]**Ge 14:13**; [x]**Ex 28:33**; [y]Ge 3:7; Nu 20:5; Dt 8:8; 2Ki 18:31; Ne 13:15
25 [z]**Ge 7:4**; [a]Nu 14:34
26 [b]**Ge 14:7**; [c]**Ge 14:6**; [d]Nu 32:8; [e]Dt 1:25
27 [f]**Ex 3:8**; [g]Dt 1:25; Jer 2:7
28 [h]Dt 1:28; 9:1–2; [i]**ver 22**; [j]Jos 14:12
29 [k]**Ge 14:7**; [l]**Ge 10:15**; Dt 7:1; 20:17; 1Ki 9:20; 10:29; 2Ki 7:6; [m]**Ex 3:8**; [n]**Ge 10:16**; [o]ver 17; [p]**Ge 10:18**; [q]**Ge 13:10**; Nu 22:1; 32:5; Dt 1:1; Jos 1:2; Jdg 3:28; Ps 42:6
30 [r]**ver 6**
31 [s]Dt 9:1; Jos 14:8
32 [t]Nu 14:36–37; [u]Eze 36:13–14; [v]Dt 1:28; Am 2:9
33 [w]Ge 6:4; [x]ver 28; Dt 1:28; Jos 11:22; 14:12; [y]Ecc 12:5; Isa 40:22

Ch. 14

1 [a]**Ge 27:38**; Ex 33:4; Nu 25:6; Dt 1:45; Jdg 20:23,26; 2Sa 3:32; Job 31:29
2 [b]**Ex 15:24**; Heb 3:16; [c]**Ex 16:3**; [d]**Nu 11:1**; 16:13; 20:4; 21:5
3 [e]**Ex 5:21**; [f]ver 31; [g]**Ge 34:29**;Dt 1:39; Ps 109:11; Isa 33:4; Eze 7:21; 25:7; 26:5; [h]Ac 7:39
4 [i]Ne 9:17
5 [j]**Lev 9:24**; Nu 16:4,22,45; 20:6; Jos 5:14; 2Sa 14:4; 1Ch 21:16; Eze 1:28; [k]**Lev 19:2**
6 [l]Nu 11:28; [m]**Ge 37:29**,34; Jdg 11:35; 2Sa 13:31; 2Ki 19:1; Ezr 9:3; Est 4:1; **Mk 14:63**
7 [n]Nu 13:27; Dt 1:25
8 [o]Dt 7:8; 10:15; Ps 18:19; 22:8; 37:23; 41:11; 56:9; 147:11; Pr 11:20; Isa 62:4; Mal 2:17; [p]Nu 13:27; [q]Dt 1:21
9 [r]Dt 1:26; 9:7,23–24; [s]Ge 26:24; 2Ch 32:7; Ps 118:6; Jer 41:18; 42:11; [t]Dt 1:21; 7:18; 20:1; [u]Hag 2:4; [v]**Ge 21:22**; Dt 1:30; 2Ch 13:12; Jer 15:20; 46:28; Hag 1:13; [w]ver 24
10 [x]**Ex 17:4**; [y]**Ex 24:16**
11 [z]Ex 23:21; Nu 15:31; 16:30; 1Sa 2:17; Eze 31:14; Mal 1:13; [a]Dt 1:32; Ps 78:22; 106:24; Jn 3:15; [b]**Ex 3:20; 4:17; 10:1**
12 [c]**Ex 5:3; 30:12**; [d]**Ex 32:10**; [e]Dt 9:14; 29:20; 32:26; Ps 109:13
13 [f]Ex 32:11–14; Ps 106:23
14 [g]Ex 15:14; [h]Nu 5:3; 16:3; Jos 2:9

[a]21 Or *towards the entrance to*
[b]23 *Eshcol* means *cluster*; also in verse 24.

you, O LORD, have been seen face to face,[i] that your cloud stays over them,[j] and that you go before them in a pillar of cloud by day and a pillar of fire by night.[k] 15If you put these people to death all at one time, the nations who have heard this report about you will say, 16'The LORD was not able to bring these people into the land he promised them on oath;[l] so he slaughtered them in the desert.'[m]

17"Now may the Lord's strength be displayed, just as you have declared: 18'The LORD is slow to anger, abounding in love and forgiving sin and rebellion.[n] Yet he does not leave the guilty unpunished; he punishes the children for the sin of the fathers to the third and fourth generation.'[o] 19In accordance with your great love, forgive[p] the sin of these people,[q] just as you have pardoned them from the time they left Egypt until now."[r]

20The LORD replied, "I have forgiven them,[s] as you asked. 21Nevertheless, as surely as I live[t] and as surely as the glory of the LORD[u] fills the whole earth,[v] 22not one of the men who saw my glory and the miraculous signs[w] I performed in Egypt and in the desert but who disobeyed me and tested me ten times[x]—23not one of them will ever see the land I promised on oath[y] to their forefathers. No-one who has treated me with contempt[z] will ever see it.[a] 24But because my servant Caleb[b] has a different spirit and follows me wholeheartedly,[c] I will bring him into the land he went to, and his descendants will inherit it.[d] 25Since the Amalekites[e] and Canaanites[f] are living in the valleys, turn[g] back tomorrow and set out towards the desert along the route to the Red Sea."[a][h]

26The LORD said to Moses and Aaron: 27"How long will this wicked community grumble against me? I have heard the complaints of these grumbling Israelites.[i] 28So tell them, 'As surely as I live,[j] declares the LORD, I will do to you[k] the very things I heard you say: 29In this desert your bodies will fall[l]—every one of you twenty years old or more[m] who was counted in the census[n] and who has grumbled against me. 30Not one of you will enter the land[o] I swore with uplifted hand[p] to make your home, except Caleb son of Jephunneh[q] and Joshua son of Nun.[r] 31As for your children that you said would be taken as plunder, I will bring them in to enjoy the land you have rejected.[s] 32But you—your bodies will fall[t] in this desert. 33Your children will be shepherds here for forty years,[u] suffering for your unfaithfulness, until the last of your bodies lies in the desert. 34For forty years[v]—one year for each of the forty days you explored the land[w]—you will suffer for your sins and know what it is like to have me against you.' 35I, the LORD, have spoken, and I will surely do these things[x] to this whole wicked community, which has banded together against me. They will meet their end in this desert; here they will die."[y]

36So the men Moses had sent[z] to explore the land, who returned and made the whole community grumble[a] against him by spreading a bad report[b] about it—37these men responsible for spreading the bad report[c] about the land were struck down and died of a plague[d] before the LORD. 38Of the men who went to explore the land,[e] only Joshua son of Nun and Caleb son of Jephunneh survived.[f]

39When Moses reported this[g] to all the Israelites, they mourned[h] bitterly. 40Early the next morning they went up towards the high hill country.[i] "We have sinned[j]," they said. "We will go up to the place the LORD promised."

41But Moses said, "Why are you disobeying the LORD's command? This will not succeed![k] 42Do not go up, because the LORD is not with you. You will be defeated by your enemies,[l] 43for the Amalekites[m] and Canaanites[n] will face you there. Because you have turned away from the LORD, he will not be with you[o] and you will fall by the sword."

44Nevertheless, in their presumption they went up[p] towards the high hill country, though neither Moses nor the ark of the LORD's covenant moved from the camp.[q] 45Then the Amalekites and Canaanites[r] who lived in that hill country[s] came down and attacked them and beat them down all the way to Hormah.[t]

Supplementary Offerings

15 The LORD said to Moses, 2"Speak to the Israelites and say to them: 'After you enter the land I am

14 [i]Dt 5:4; 34:10; [j]**Ex 33:16**; [k]**Ex 13:21**
16 [l]Nu 11:12; [m]Ex 32:12; Jos 7:7
18 [n]**Ex 20:6**; 34:6; Ps 145:8; Jnh 4:2; Jas 5:11; [o]Ex 20:5
19 [p]**Ex 34:9**; 1Ki 8:34; Ps 85:2; 103:3; [q]Ps 106:45; [r]Ps 78:38
20 [s]Ex 34:6; Ps 99:8; 106:23; Mic 7:18–20
21 [t]ver 28; Dt 32:40; Jdg 8:19; Ru 3:13; 1Sa 14:39; 19:6; Isa 49:18; Jer 4:2; Eze 5:11; Zep 2:9; [u]Lev 9:6; [v]Ps 72:19; Isa 6:3; 40:5; Hab 2:14
22 [w]ver 11; [x]**Ex 14:11**; 17:7; 32:1; Ps 81:7; 1Co 10:5
23 [y]ver 16; **Ex 33:1**; Nu 32:11; Dt 1:34; Ps 95:11; 106:26; [z]ver 11; [a]Heb 3:18
24 [b]Nu 13:6; [c]ver 6–9; Dt 1:36; Jos 14:8,14; [d]Nu 26:65; 32:12; Ps 25:13; 37:9,11
25 [e]**Ge 14:7**; [f]**Ge 10:18**; [g]Dt 1:40; [h]Ex 23:31; Nu 21:4; 1Ki 9:26
27 [i]Ex 16:12; Dt 1:34–35
28 [j]**ver 21**; [k]Nu 33:56
29 [l]ver 23,30,32; Nu 26:65; 32:13; 1Co 10:5; Heb 3:17; Jude 5; [m]**Nu 1:45**; [n]**Ex 30:12**
30 [o]**ver 29**; [p]Ex 6:8; Dt 32:40; Ne 9:15; Ps 106:26; Eze 20:5; 36:7; [q]Nu 13:6; [r]Nu 11:28
31 [s]**Lev 26:43**
32 [t]**ver 29**,35
33 [u]ver 34; **Ex 16:35**; Ac 13:18; Heb 3:9
34 [v]**ver 33**; [w]Nu 13:25
35 [x]Nu 23:19; [y]**ver 32**
36 [z]Nu 13:4–16; [a]ver 2; [b]**Nu 13:32**
37 [c]Nu 13:32; 1Co 10:10; Heb 3:17; [d]Nu 16:49; 25:9; 26:1; 31:16; Dt 4:3
38 [e]ver 30; Nu 13:4–16; [f]ver 24; Jos 14:6
39 [g]ver 28–35; [h]**Ex 33:4**
40 [i]ver 45; Nu 13:17; [j]**Ex 9:27**
41 [k]2Ch 24:20
42 [l]Dt 1:42
43 [m]Jdg 3:13; [n]ver 45; Nu 13:29; [o]**Ge 39:23**; Dt 31:8; Jos 6:27; Jdg 1:19; 6:16; 1Sa 3:19; 18:14; 2Ch 1:1
44 [p]Dt 1:43; [q]Nu 31:6
45 [r]**ver 43**; [s]**ver 40**; [t]Nu 21:3; Dt 1:44; Jos 12:14; 15:30; 19:4; Jdg 1:17; 1Sa 30:30; 1Ch 4:30

[a]25 Hebrew *Yam Suph*; that is, Sea of Reeds

giving you[a] as a home 3and you present to the LORD offerings made by fire, from the herd or the flock,[b] as an aroma pleasing to the LORD[c]—whether burnt offerings[d] or sacrifices, for special vows or freewill offerings[e] or festival offerings[f]—4then the one who brings his offering shall present to the LORD a grain offering[g] of a tenth of an ephah[a] of fine flour[h] mixed with a quarter of a hin[b] of oil. 5With each lamb[i] for the burnt offering or the sacrifice, prepare a quarter of a hin of wine[j] as a drink offering.[k]

6" 'With a ram[l] prepare a grain offering[m] of two-tenths of an ephah[c][n] of fine flour mixed with a third of a hin[d] of oil,[o] 7and a third of a hin of wine[p] as a drink offering.[q] Offer it as an aroma pleasing to the LORD.[r]

8" 'When you prepare a young bull[s] as a burnt offering or sacrifice, for a special vow[t] or a fellowship offering[e][u] to the LORD, 9bring with the bull a grain offering[v] of three-tenths of an ephah[f][w] of fine flour mixed with half a hin[g] of oil. 10Also bring half a hin of wine[x] as a drink offering.[y] It will be an offering made by fire, an aroma pleasing to the LORD.[z] 11Each bull or ram, each lamb or young goat, is to be prepared in this manner. 12Do this for each one, for as many as you prepare.[a]

13" 'Everyone who is native-born[b] must do these things in this way when he brings an offering made by fire as an aroma pleasing to the LORD.[c] 14For the generations to come,[d] whenever an alien[e] or anyone else living among you presents an offering[f] made by fire[g] as an aroma pleasing to the LORD, he must do exactly as you do. 15The community is to have the same rules for you and for the alien living among you; this is a lasting ordinance for the generations to come.[h] You and the alien shall be the same before the LORD: 16The same laws and regulations will apply both to you and to the alien living among you.[i]' "

17The LORD said to Moses, 18"Speak to the Israelites and say to them: 'When you enter the land to which I am taking you[j] 19and you eat the food of the land,[k] present a portion as an offering to the LORD.[l] 20Present a cake from the first of your ground meal[m] and present it as an offering from the threshing-floor.[n][o] 21Throughout the generations to come[p] you are to give this offering to the LORD from the first of your ground meal.[q]

Offerings for Unintentional Sins

22" 'Now if you unintentionally fail to keep any of these commands the LORD gave Moses[r]—23any of the LORD's commands to you through him, from the day the LORD gave them and continuing through the generations to come[s]—24and if this is done unintentionally[t] without the community being aware of it,[u] then the whole community is to offer a young bull for a burnt offering[v] as an aroma pleasing to the LORD,[w] along with its prescribed grain offering[x] and drink offering,[y] and a male goat for a sin offering.[z] 25The priest is to make atonement for the whole Israelite community, and they will be forgiven,[a] for it was not intentional[b] and they have brought to the LORD for their wrong an offering made by fire[c] and a sin offering.[d] 26The whole Israelite community and the aliens living among them will be forgiven, because all the people were involved in the unintentional wrong.[e]

27" 'But if just one person sins unintentionally,[f] he must bring a year-old female goat for a sin offering.[g] 28The priest is to make atonement[h] before the LORD for the one who erred by sinning unintentionally, and when atonement has been made for him, he will be forgiven.[i] 29One and the same law applies to everyone who sins unintentionally, whether he is a native-born Israelite or an alien.[j]

30" 'But anyone who sins defiantly,[k] whether native-born or alien,[l] blasphemes the LORD,[m] and that person must be cut off from his people.[n] 31Because he has despised[o] the LORD's word and broken his commands,[p] that person must surely be cut off; his guilt remains on him.[q]' "

The Sabbath-Breaker Put to Death

32While the Israelites were in the desert,[r] a man was found gathering wood on the Sabbath day.[s] 33Those who found him gathering wood brought him to Moses and Aaron and the whole assembly, 34and they kept him in

Ch. 15
2 [a]**Lev 23:10**
3 [b]**Lev 1:2;** [c]ver 24; **Lev 1:9;** [d]Lev 1:3; Nu 28:13; [e]**Lev 7:16; Ezr 1:4;** [f]Lev 23:1–44
4 [g]**Lev 6:14;** [h]**Ex 16:36**
5 [i]**Lev 3:7;** [j]**Lev 10:9;** [k]**Ge 35:14**
6 [l]**Lev 5:15;** [m]Nu 28:12; 29:14; [n]**Lev 23:13;** [o]Eze 46:14
7 [p]ver 5; [q]Lev 23:13; Nu 28:14; 29:18; [r]**Lev 1:9**
8 [s]**Ex 12:5; Lev 1:5;** [t]**Lev 22:18;** [u]**Lev 3:6**
9 [v]Lev 2:1; [w]**Lev 14:10**
10 [x]Nu 28:14; [y]Lev 23:13; [z]Lev 1:9
12 [a]Ezr 7:17
13 [b]**Lev 16:29;** [c]Lev 1:9
14 [d]Lev 3:17; Nu 10:8; [e]**Ex 12:19**,43; **22:21;** [f]**Lev 22:18;** [g]ver 25
15 [h]ver 14,21
16 [i]Ex 12:49; **Lev 22:18;** Nu 9:14
18 [j]**Lev 23:10**
19 [k]Jos 5:11–12; [l]Nu 18:8
20 [m]**Lev 23:14;** [n]**Lev 2:14; Nu 18:27;** [o]**Ge 50:10**
21 [p]**Lev 23:14;** [q]Eze 44:30; Ro 11:16
22 [r]**Lev 4:2**
23 [s]ver 21
24 [t]ver 25–26; [u]**Lev 5:15;** [v]Lev 4:14; [w]**ver 3;** [x]Lev 2:1; [y]Lev 23:13; Nu 6:15; [z]Lev 4:3
25 [a]Lev 4:20; **Ro 3:25;** [b]ver 22, 24; [c]ver 14; [d]Lev 4:3
26 [e]**ver 24**
27 [f]Lev 4:27; [g]Lev 4:3; Nu 6:14
28 [h]Nu 8:12; 28:22; [i]Lev 4:20
29 [j]**Ex 12:49**
30 [k]Nu 14:40–44; Dt 1:43; 17:13; Ps 19:13; [l]ver 14; [m]2Ki 19:6,20; Isa 37:6,23; Eze 20:27; [n]**Ge 17:14; Job 31:22**
31 [o]**Nu 14:11;** [p]1Sa 15:23,26; 2Sa 11:27; 12:9; Ps 119:126; Pr 13:13; [q]**Lev 5:1;** Eze 18:20
32 [r]**Nu 12:16;** [s]Ex 31:14–15; 35:2–3

[a]4 That is, probably about 4 pints (about 2 litres)
[b]4 That is, probably about 1½ pints (about 1 litre); also in verse 5
[c]6 That is, probably about 7½ pints (about 4.5 litres)
[d]6 That is, probably about 2¼ pints (about 1.2 litres); also in verse 7
[e]8 Traditionally *peace offering*
[f]9 That is, probably about 11½ pints (about 6.5 litres)
[g]9 That is, probably about 3 pints (about 2 litres); also in verse 10

custody, because it was not clear what
should be done to him.[t] 35Then the
LORD said to Moses, "The man must
die.[u] The whole assembly must stone
him outside the camp.[v]" 36So the
assembly took him outside the camp
and stoned him[w] to death,[x] as the
LORD commanded Moses.[y]

Tassels on Garments

37The LORD said to Moses, 38"Speak to
the Israelites and say to them:
'Throughout the generations to come[z]
you are to make tassels on the corners of
your garments,[a] with a blue cord on
each tassel. 39You will have these tassels
to look at and so you will remember[b] all
the commands of the LORD, that you
may obey them and not prostitute
yourselves[c] by going after the lusts of
your own hearts[d] and eyes. 40Then you
will remember to obey all my
commands[e] and will be consecrated to
your God.[f] 41I am the LORD your God,
who brought you out of Egypt to be
your God.[g] I am the LORD your God.[h]'"

Korah, Dathan and Abiram

16 Korah[a] son of Izhar, the son of
Kohath, the son of Levi, and
certain Reubenites—Dathan and
Abiram,[b] sons of Eliab,[c] and On son of
Peleth—became insolent[a] 2and rose up
against Moses.[d] With them were 250
Israelite men, well-known community
leaders who had been appointed
members of the council.[e] 3They came as
a group to oppose Moses and Aaron[f]
and said to them, "You have gone too
far! The whole community is holy,[g]
every one of them, and the LORD is with
them.[h] Why then do you set yourselves
above the LORD's assembly?"[i]
4When Moses heard this, he fell face
down.[j] 5Then he said to Korah and all
his followers: "In the morning the LORD
will show who belongs to him and who
is holy,[k] and he will make that person
come near him.[l] The man he chooses[m]
he will cause to come near him. 6You,
Korah, and all your followers[n] are to do
this: Take censers[o] 7and tomorrow put
fire[p] and incense[q] in them before the
LORD. The man the LORD chooses[r] will
be the one who is holy.[s] You Levites
have gone too far!"
8Moses also said to Korah, "Now
listen, you Levites! 9Isn't it enough[t] for
you that the God of Israel has separated
you from the rest of the Israelite com-
munity and brought you near himself to
do the work at the LORD's tabernacle
and to stand before the community and
minister to them?[u] 10He has brought you
and all your fellow Levites near himself,
but now you are trying to get the priest-
hood too.[v] 11It is against the LORD that
you and all your followers have banded
together. Who is Aaron that you should
grumble[w] against him?[x]"
12Then Moses summoned Dathan
and Abiram,[y] the sons of Eliab. But they
said, "We will not come![z] 13Isn't it
enough that you have brought us up out
of a land flowing with milk and honey[a]
to kill us in the desert?[b] And now you
also want to lord it over us?[c]
14Moreover, you haven't brought us
into a land flowing with milk and
honey[d] or given us an inheritance of
fields and vineyards.[e] Will you gouge
out the eyes of[b] these men?[f] No, we
will not come![g]"
15Then Moses became very angry[h]
and said to the LORD, "Do not accept
their offering. I have not taken so much
as a donkey[i] from them, nor have I
wronged any of them."
16Moses said to Korah, "You and all
your followers are to appear before the
LORD tomorrow—you and they and
Aaron.[j] 17Each man is to take his censer
and put incense in it—250 censers in
all—and present it before the LORD. You
and Aaron are to present your censers
also.[k]" 18So each man took his censer,[l]
put fire and incense in it, and stood with
Moses and Aaron at the entrance to the
Tent of Meeting. 19When Korah had
gathered all his followers in opposition
to them[m] at the entrance to the Tent
of Meeting, the glory of the LORD[n]
appeared to the entire assembly. 20The
LORD said to Moses and Aaron,
21"Separate yourselves[o] from this
assembly so that I can put an end to
them at once."[p]
22But Moses and Aaron fell face
down[q] and cried out, "O God, God of
the spirits of all mankind,[r] will you be
angry with the entire assembly[s] when
only one man sins?"[t]

34 [t]Nu 9:8
35 [u]Ex 31:14-15; [v]**Lev 20:2**; Lk 4:29; Ac 7:58
36 [w]**Lev 20:2**; [x]**Ex 31:14**; [y]Jer 17:21
38 [z]Lev 3:17; Nu 10:8; [a]Dt 22:12; Mt 23:5
39 [b]Dt 4:23; 6:12; Ps 73:27; [c]**Lev 17:7**; Jdg 2:17; Ps 106:39; Jer 3:2; Hos 4:12; [d]Ps 78:37; Jer 7:24; Eze 20:16
40 [e]**Ge 26:5**; Dt 11:13; Ps 103:18; 119:56; [f]**Lev 11:44**; Ro 12:1; Col 1:22; 1Pe 1:15
41 [g]**Ge 17:7**; [h]**Ex 20:2**

Ch. 16

1 [a]**Ex 6:24**; Jude 11; [b]ver 24; Ps 106:17; [c]Nu 26:8; Dt 11:6
2 [d]Nu 27:3; [e]Nu 1:16; 26:9
3 [f]ver 7; Ps 106:16; [g]Ex 19:6; [h]**Nu 14:14**; [i]Nu 12:2
4 [j]Nu 14:5
5 [k]**Lev 10:3**; 2Ti 2:19*; [l]Jer 30:21; [m]Nu 17:5; Ps 65:4; 105:26; Jer 50:44
6 [n]ver 7,16; [o]**Lev 10:1**; Rev 8:3
7 [p]**Lev 10:1**; [q]**Ex 30:9**; [r]**ver 6**; [s]ver 5
9 [t]**Ge 30:15**; [u]Nu 3:6; Dt 10:8; 17:12; 21:5; 1Sa 2:11; Ps 134:1; Eze 44:11
10 [v]Nu 3:10; 18:7; Jdg 17:5,12
11 [w]ver 41; 1Co 10:10; [x]**Ex 16:7**
12 [y]**ver 1**,27; [z]ver 14
13 [a]Nu 13:27; [b]Nu 14:2; [c]**Ge 13:8**; Ac 7:27,35
14 [d]**Lev 20:24**; [e]Ex 22:5; 23:11; Nu 20:5; 1Ki 4:25; Ne 13:15; Ps 105:33; Jer 5:17; Hos 2:12; Joel 2:22; Hag 2:19; Zec 3:10; [f]Jdg 16:21; 1Sa 11:2; Jer 39:7; [g]ver 12
15 [h]**Ex 4:14**; [i]1Sa 12:3 **16** [j]**ver 6**
17 [k]Eze 8:11 **18** [l]Lev 10:1
19 [m]ver 42; Nu 20:2; [n]**Ex 16:7**; Nu 14:10; 20:6
21 [o]ver 24; [p]**Ge 19:14**; **Ex 32:10**
22 [q]**Nu 14:5**; [r]Nu 27:16; Job 12:10; 27:8; 33:4; 34:14; Jer 32:27; Eze 18:4; Heb 12:9; [s]**Lev 10:6**; [t]**Ge 18:23**; **Job 21:20**

a1 Or *Peleth—took* ⌊*men*⌋
b14 Or *you make slaves of*; or *you deceive*

23Then the LORD said to Moses, 24"Say to the assembly, 'Move away from the tents of Korah, Dathan and Abiram.'"

25Moses got up and went to Dathan and Abiram, and the elders of Israel[u] followed him. 26He warned the assembly, "Move back from the tents of these wicked men![v] Do not touch anything belonging to them, or you will be swept away[w] because of all their sins.[x]" 27So they moved away from the tents of Korah, Dathan and Abiram.[y] Dathan and Abiram had come out and were standing with their wives, children[z] and little ones at the entrances to their tents.[a]

28Then Moses said, "This is how you will know[b] that the LORD has sent me[c] to do all these things and that it was not my idea: 29If these men die a natural death and experience only what usually happens to men, then the LORD has not sent me.[d] 30But if the LORD brings about something totally new, and the earth opens its mouth[e] and swallows them, with everything that belongs to them, and they go down alive into the grave,[c][f] then you will know that these men have treated the LORD with contempt.[g]"

31As soon as he finished saying all this, the ground under them split apart[h] 32and the earth opened its mouth and swallowed them,[i] with their households and all Korah's men and all their possessions. 33They went down alive into the grave,[j] with everything they owned; the earth closed over them, and they perished and were gone from the community. 34At their cries, all the Israelites around them fled, shouting, "The earth is going to swallow us too!"

35And fire came out from the LORD[k] and consumed[l] the 250 men who were offering the incense.

36The LORD said to Moses, 37"Tell Eleazar[m] son of Aaron, the priest, to take the censers[n] out of the smouldering remains and scatter the coals some distance away, for the censers are holy —38the censers of the men who sinned at the cost of their lives.[o] Hammer the censers into sheets to overlay the altar,[p] for they were presented before the LORD and have become holy. Let them be a sign[q] to the Israelites."

39So Eleazar the priest[r] collected the bronze censers brought by those who had been burned up,[s] and he had them hammered out to overlay the altar, 40as the LORD directed him through Moses. This was to remind the Israelites that no-one except a descendant of Aaron should come to burn incense[t] before the LORD,[u] or he would become like Korah and his followers.[v]

41The next day the whole Israelite community grumbled against Moses and Aaron. "You have killed the LORD's people," they said.

42But when the assembly gathered in opposition[w] to Moses and Aaron and turned towards the Tent of Meeting, suddenly the cloud covered it and the glory of the LORD[x] appeared. 43Then Moses and Aaron went to the front of the Tent of Meeting, 44and the LORD said to Moses, 45"Get away from this assembly so that I can put an end[y] to them at once." And they fell face down.

46Then Moses said to Aaron, "Take your censer[z] and put incense in it, along with fire from the altar, and hurry to the assembly[a] to make atonement[b] for them. Wrath has come out from the LORD;[c] the plague[d] has started." 47So Aaron did as Moses said, and ran into the midst of the assembly. The plague had already started among the people,[e] but Aaron offered the incense and made atonement for them. 48He stood between the living and the dead, and the plague stopped.[f] 49But 14,700 people died from the plague, in addition to those who had died because of Korah.[g] 50Then Aaron returned to Moses at the entrance to the Tent of Meeting, for the plague had stopped.

The Budding of Aaron's Staff

17 The LORD said to Moses, 2"Speak to the Israelites and get twelve staffs[a] from them, one from the leader of each of their ancestral tribes.[b] Write the name of each man on his staff. 3On the staff of Levi write Aaron's name,[c] for there must be one staff for the head of each ancestral tribe. 4Place them in the Tent of Meeting[d] in front of the Testimony,[e] where I meet with you.[f] 5The staff belonging to the man I choose[g] will sprout,[h] and I will rid myself of this constant grumbling[i] against you by the Israelites."

6So Moses spoke to the Israelites, and their leaders gave him twelve staffs, one for the leader of each of their ancestral tribes, and Aaron's staff was among them. 7Moses placed the staffs before the LORD in the Tent of the Testimony.[j]

8The next day Moses entered the Tent of the Testimony[k] and saw that Aaron's

---

25 [u]**Ex 19:7**
26 [v]Isa 52:11; [w]**Ge 19:15;** [x]Jer 51:6
27 [y]**ver 12;** [z]ver 32; Jos 7:24; Isa 13:16; 14:21; [a]**Ex 33:8**
28 [b]1Ki 18:36; [c]Ex 3:12; Jn 5:36; 6:38
29 [d]Nu 24:13; Job 31:2; Ecc 3:19
30 [e]Ps 141:7; Isa 5:14; [f]ver 33; **Ge 37:35;** 1Sa 2:6; Job 5:26; 21:13; Ps 9:17; 16:10; 55:15; Isa 14:11; 38:18; [g]**Nu 14:11; Eze 26:20**
31 [h]Isa 64:1–2; Eze 47:1–12; Mic 1:3–4; Zec 14:4
32 [i]**Ex 15:12**
33 [j]**ver 30; Ecc 9:10**
35 [k]**Nu 11:1–3;** 26:10; Rev 11:5; [l]**Lev 10:2**
37 [m]**Ex 6:23;** [n]ver 6
38 [o]Lev 10:1; Pr 20:2; [p]**Ex 20:24;** 38:1–7; [q]Nu 26:10; Dt 28:46; Jer 44:29; Eze 14:8; 2Pe 2:6
39 [r]2Ch 26:18; [s]**Lev 20:14**
40 [t]**Ex 30:1;** 2Ki 12:3; Isa 1:13; 66:3; Jer 41:5; 44:3; [u]**Ex 30:9;** 2Ch 26:18; [v]**Nu 3:10**
42 [w]**ver 19;** [x]Ex 16:7; Nu 14:10
45 [y]**Ex 32:10**
46 [z]**Lev 10:1;** [a]Lev 10:6; [b]**Ex 29:36;** [c]**Nu 1:53;** [d]**Lev 26:25;** Nu 8:19; Ps 106:29
47 [e]Nu 25:6–8
48 [f]Nu 25:8; Ps 106:30
49 [g]ver 32

Ch. 17

2 [a]**Ge 32:10;** Ex 4:2; [b]Nu 1:4
3 [c]**Nu 1:3**
4 [d]**Ex 40:2;** [e]ver 7; **Ex 16:34;** [f]Ex 25:22
5 [g]**Nu 16:5;** [h]ver 8; [i]**Ex 16:7**
7 [j]**Ex 38:21**
8 [k]ver 7; Nu 1:50

---

[c]30 Hebrew *Sheol;* also in verse 33

staff,[l] which represented the house of
Levi, had not only sprouted but had
budded, blossomed and produced
almonds.[m] 9Then Moses brought out all
the staffs[n] from the LORD's presence to
all the Israelites. They looked at them,
and each man took his own staff.
10The LORD said to Moses, "Put back
Aaron's staff[o] in front of the Testimony,
to be kept as a sign to the rebellious.[p]
This will put an end to their grumbling
against me, so that they will not die."
11Moses did just as the LORD
commanded him.
12The Israelites said to Moses, "We
shall die! We are lost, we are all lost![q]
13Anyone who even comes near the
tabernacle of the LORD will die.[r] Are we
all going to die?"

Duties of Priests and Levites

18 The LORD said to Aaron, "You,
your sons and your father's
family are to bear the responsibility for
offences against the sanctuary,[a] and you
and your sons alone are to bear the
responsibility for offences against the
priesthood. 2Bring your fellow Levites
from your ancestral tribe to join you and
assist you when you and your sons
minister[b] before the Tent of the Testi-
mony. 3They are to be responsible to
you[c] and are to perform all the duties of
the Tent,[d] but they must not go near the
furnishings of the sanctuary or the altar,
or both they and you will die.[e] 4They are
to join you and be responsible for the
care of the Tent of Meeting—all the
work at the Tent—and no-one else may
come near where you are.[f]
5"You are to be responsible for the
care of the sanctuary and the altar,[g] so
that wrath will not fall on the Israelites
again. 6I myself have selected your fel-
low Levites from among the Israelites as
a gift to you,[h] dedicated to the LORD to
do the work at the Tent of Meeting.[i] 7But
only you and your sons may serve as
priests in connection with everything at
the altar and inside the curtain.[j] I am
giving you the service of the priesthood
as a gift.[k] Anyone else who comes near
the sanctuary must be put to death.[l]"

Offerings for Priests and Levites

8Then the LORD said to Aaron, "I
myself have put you in charge of the
offerings presented to me; all the holy
offerings the Israelites give me I give to
you and your sons as your portion[m] and
regular share.[n] 9You are to have the part
of the most holy offerings[o] that is kept
from the fire. From all the gifts they
bring me as most holy offerings,
whether grain[p] or sin[q] or guilt offerings,[r]
that part belongs to you and your sons.
10Eat it as something most holy; every
male shall eat it.[s] You must regard it as
holy.[t]
11"This also is yours: whatever is set
aside from the gifts of all the wave
offerings[u] of the Israelites. I give this to
you and your sons and daughters as
your regular share.[v] Everyone in your
household who is ceremonially clean[w]
may eat it.
12"I give you all the finest olive oil and
all the finest new wine and grain[x] they
give to the LORD[y] as the firstfruits of
their harvest.[z] 13All the land's firstfruits
that they bring to the LORD will be
yours.[a] Everyone in your household
who is ceremonially clean may eat it.[b]
14"Everything in Israel that is
devoted[a] to the LORD[c] is yours. 15The
first offspring of every womb, both man
and animal, that is offered to the LORD is
yours.[d] But you must redeem[e] every
firstborn[f] son and every firstborn male
of unclean animals.[g] 16When they are a
month old,[h] you must redeem them at
the redemption price set at five
shekels[b][i] of silver, according to the
sanctuary shekel,[j] which weighs twenty
gerahs.[k]
17"But you must not redeem the
firstborn of an ox, a sheep or a goat; they
are holy.[l] Sprinkle their blood[m] on the
altar and burn their fat[n] as an offering
made by fire, an aroma pleasing to the
LORD.[o] 18Their meat is to be yours, just
as the breast of the wave offering[p] and
the right thigh are yours.[q] 19Whatever is
set aside from the holy[r] offerings the
Israelites present to the LORD I give to
you and your sons and daughters as
your regular share. It is an everlasting
covenant of salt[s] before the LORD for
both you and your offspring."
20The LORD said to Aaron, "You will
have no inheritance in their land, nor
will you have any share among them;[t] I
am your share and your inheritance[u]
among the Israelites.
21"I give to the Levites all the tithes[v] in
Israel as their inheritance[w] in return for
the work they do while serving at the

8 [l]ver 2,10; [m]Eze 17:24; Heb 9:4
9 [n]ver 2
10 [o]**ver 8**; [p]**Ex 23:21**; Dt 9:24; Ps 66:7; 68:18; Pr 24:21
12 [q]Jdg 13:22; Isa 6:5; 15:1
13 [r]Nu 1:51

Ch. 18

1 [a]**Ex 28:38**
2 [b]Nu 3:10
3 [c]**Nu 3:32**; [d]Nu 1:51; [e]ver 7
4 [f]**Nu 3:38**
5 [g]ver 3; Lev 6:12
6 [h]**Nu 3:9**; [i]Nu 3:8
7 [j]Heb 9:3,6; [k]ver 20; Ex 29:9; 40:13; Heb 5:4; [l]ver 3; Nu 3:10
8 [m]**Lev 2:2**; [n]Lev 6:16; 7:6,31–34,36; Dt 18:1; 2Ch 31:4
9 [o]**Lev 6:17**; [p]Lev 2:1; [q]Lev 6:25; [r]**Lev 5:15**
10 [s]**Lev 6:16**; [t]Lev 6:17–18
11 [u]Ex 29:26; Lev 7:30; Nu 6:20; [v]Lev 7:31–34; [w]Lev 13:3; 22:1–16
12 [x]Dt 7:13; 11:14; 12:17; 28:51; 2Ki 18:32; 2Ch 31:5; Ne 10:37; Jer 31:12; Eze 23:41; Hos 2:8; Joel 1:10; Hag 1:11; [y]**Ge 4:3**; [z]Ex 23:19; 34:26; Ne 10:35
13 [a]**Ex 29:27**; [b]ver 11
14 [c]**Lev 27:21**; Jos 6:17–19
15 [d]Ex 13:2; [e]**Nu 3:46**; [f]**Ge 10:15**; [g]**Ex 13:13**
16 [h]**Nu 3:15**; [i]Lev 27:6; [j]**Ex 30:13**; [k]Nu 3:47
17 [l]**Lev 27:9**; [m]**Lev 3:2**; [n]**Ex 29:13**; [o]**Lev 1:9**
18 [p]Lev 7:30; [q]ver 11
19 [r]2Ki 12:4; [s]**Lev 2:13**
20 [t]Nu 26:62; Dt 12:12; [u]ver 24; Dt 10:9; 14:27; 18:1–2; Jos 13:33; Eze 44:28
21 [v]ver 24; **Ge 28:22**; Nu 31:28; Dt 14:22; Ne 10:37; 13:5; Mal 3:8; [w]Lev 27:30–33; Heb 7:5

[a]*14* The Hebrew term refers to the irrevocable giving over of things or persons to the LORD, often by totally destroying them.
[b]*16* That is, about 2 ounces (about 55 grams)

Tent of Meeting.[x] 22From now on the
Israelites must not go near the Tent of
Meeting, or they will bear the conse-
quences of their sin and will die.[y] 23It is
the Levites who are to do the work at the
Tent of Meeting and bear the responsi-
bility for offences against it. This is a
lasting ordinance[z] for the generations to
come.[a] They will receive no inheritance[b]
among the Israelites.[c] 24Instead, I give to
the Levites as their inheritance the
tithes that the Israelites present as an
offering to the LORD.[d] That is why I said
concerning them: 'They will have no
inheritance among the Israelites.' "
25The LORD said to Moses, 26"Speak to
the Levites and say to them: 'When you
receive from the Israelites the tithe I give
you[e] as your inheritance, you must
present a tenth of that tithe as the
LORD's offering.[f] 27Your offering will be
reckoned[g] to you as grain from the
threshing-floor[h] or juice from the
winepress.[i] 28In this way you also will
present an offering to the LORD from
all the tithes[j] you receive from the
Israelites. From these tithes you must
give the LORD's portion to Aaron the
priest. 29You must present as the LORD's
portion the best and holiest part of
everything given to you.'
30"Say to the Levites: 'When you pre-
sent the best part, it will be reckoned to
you as the product of the threshing-
floor or the winepress.[k] 31You and your
households may eat the rest of it
anywhere, for it is your wages for
your work at the Tent of Meeting.[l] 32By
presenting the best part[m] of it you will
not be guilty in this matter;[n] then you
will not defile the holy offerings[o] of the
Israelites, and you will not die.' "

The Water of Cleansing

19 The LORD said to Moses and
Aaron: 2"This is a requirement
of the law that the LORD has comman-
ded: Tell the Israelites to bring you a red
heifer[a] without defect or blemish[b] and
that has never been under a yoke.[c] 3Give
it to Eleazar[d] the priest; it is to be taken
outside the camp[e] and slaughtered in
his presence. 4Then Eleazar the priest is
to take some of its blood on his finger
and sprinkle[f] it seven times towards the
front of the Tent of Meeting. 5While he
watches, the heifer is to be burned—its
hide, flesh, blood and offal.[g] 6The priest
is to take some cedar wood, hyssop[h] and
scarlet wool[i] and throw them onto the
burning heifer. 7After that, the priest
must wash his clothes and bathe him-
self with water.[j] He may then come into
the camp, but he will be ceremonially
unclean till evening. 8The man who
burns it must also wash his clothes and
bathe with water, and he too will be
unclean till evening.
9"A man who is clean shall gather up
the ashes of the heifer[k] and put them in a
ceremonially clean place[l] outside the
camp. They shall be kept by the Israelite
community for use in the water of
cleansing;[m] it is for purification from
sin.[n] 10The man who gathers up[o] the
ashes of the heifer must also wash
his clothes, and he too will be unclean
till evening.[p] This will be a lasting
ordinance[q] both for the Israelites and
for the aliens living among them.[r]
11"Whoever touches the dead body[s]
of anyone will be unclean for seven
days.[t] 12He must purify himself with the
water on the third day and on the
seventh day;[u] then he will be clean. But
if he does not purify himself on the third
and seventh days, he will not be clean.[v]
13Whoever touches the dead body[w] of
anyone and fails to purify himself
defiles the LORD's tabernacle.[x] That
person must be cut off from Israel.[y]
Because the water of cleansing has not
been sprinkled on him, he is unclean;[z]
his uncleanness remains on him.
14"This is the law that applies when
a person dies in a tent: Anyone who
enters the tent and anyone who is in it
will be unclean for seven days, 15and
every open container[a] without a lid
fastened on it will be unclean.
16"Anyone out in the open who
touches someone who has been killed
with a sword or someone who has died
a natural death,[b] or anyone who touches
a human bone[c] or a grave,[d] will be
unclean for seven days.[e]
17"For the unclean person, put some
ashes[f] from the burned purification
offering into a jar and pour fresh water[g]
over them. 18Then a man who is cere-
monially clean is to take some hyssop,[h]
dip it in the water and sprinkle[i] the tent
and all the furnishings and the people
who were there. He must also sprinkle
anyone who has touched a human bone
or a grave[j] or someone who has been
killed or someone who has died a
natural death. 19The man who is clean
is to sprinkle[k] the unclean person on
the third and seventh days, and on the
seventh day he is to purify him.[l] The
person being cleansed must wash his
clothes[m] and bathe with water, and that
evening he will be clean. 20But if a

21 [x]Nu 1:53
22 [y]**Ex 28:43**
23 [z]**Ex 12:14; 27:21**; [a]Nu 10:8; [b]ver 20; Nu 26:62; Dt 10:9; [c]Eze 44:10
24 [d]Lev 27:30; Dt 26:12
26 [e]ver 21; [f]ver 28; Ne 10:38
27 [g]Lev 7:18; [h]Ge 50:10; Dt 15:14; Jdg 6:37; Ru 3:3, 6,14; 1Sa 23:1; [i]ver 12,30
28 [j]Mal 3:8
30 [k]**ver 27**
31 [l]ver 23
32 [m]Lev 22:15; [n]ver 29; [o]**Lev 19:8**

Ch. 19

2 [a]**Ge 15:9**; Heb 9:13; [b]**Lev 22:19–25**; [c]Dt 21:3; 1Sa 6:7
3 [d]Nu 3:4; [e]**Ex 29:14**
4 [f]**Lev 4:17**
5 [g]**Ex 29:14**
6 [h]ver 18; Ps 51:7; [i]**Lev 14:4**
7 [j]**Lev 11:25; 14:8**
9 [k]Heb 9:13; [l]**Ex 29:31; Lev 4:12**; [m]ver 13; Nu 8:7; [n]**Ge 35:2**
10 [o]Lev 15:10; [p]Lev 14:46; [q]Lev 3:17; [r]**Lev 22:18**
11 [s]**Lev 21:1**; [t]**Lev 8:33**; Nu 31:19
12 [u]ver 19; Nu 31:19; [v]ver 20; 2Ch 26:21
13 [w]**Lev 21:11**; [x]**Lev 15:31**; 2Ch 36:14; Ps 79:1; [y]Lev 7:20; 22:3; [z]ver 22; Hag 2:13
15 [a]**Lev 6:28**
16 [b]Nu 31:19; [c]1Ki 13:2; 2Ki 23:14; Eze 6:5; [d]2Ki 23:6; Mt 23:27; [e]**Lev 5:3**
17 [f]ver 9; [g]**Nu 8:7**
18 [h]**ver 6; Ex 12:22**; [i]**Lev 4:17**; [j]ver 16
19 [k]**Lev 16:14–15**; [l]Nu 31:19; Eze 36:25; Heb 10:22; [m]**Ge 35:2**

person who is unclean does not purify himself, he must be cut off from the community, because he has defiled[n] the sanctuary of the LORD.[o] The water of cleansing has not been sprinkled on him, and he is unclean.[p] 21This is a lasting ordinance[q] for them.

"The man who sprinkles the water of cleansing must also wash his clothes, and anyone who touches the water of cleansing will be unclean till evening. 22Anything that an unclean[r] person touches becomes unclean, and anyone who touches it becomes unclean till evening."

Water From the Rock

20 In the first month the whole Israelite community arrived at the Desert of Zin,[a] and they stayed at Kadesh.[b] There Miriam[c] died and was buried.

2Now there was no water[d] for the community,[e] and the people gathered in opposition[f] to Moses and Aaron. 3They quarrelled[g] with Moses and said, "If only we had died when our brothers fell dead[h] before the LORD![i] 4Why did you bring the LORD's community into this desert,[j] that we and our livestock should die here?[k] 5Why did you bring us up out of Egypt to this terrible place? It has no grain or figs, grapevines or pomegranates.[l] And there is no water to drink!"[m]

6Moses and Aaron went from the assembly to the entrance to the Tent of Meeting[n] and fell face down,[o] and the glory of the LORD[p] appeared to them. 7The LORD said to Moses, 8"Take the staff,[q] and you and your brother Aaron gather the assembly together. Speak to that rock before their eyes and it will pour out its water.[r] You will bring water out of the rock for the community so that they and their livestock can drink."

9So Moses took the staff[s] from the LORD's presence,[t] just as he commanded him. 10He and Aaron gathered the assembly together[u] in front of the rock and Moses said to them, "Listen, you rebels, must we bring you water out of this rock?"[v] 11Then Moses raised his arm and struck the rock twice with his staff. Water[w] gushed out, and the community and their livestock drank.

12But the LORD said to Moses and Aaron, "Because you did not trust in me enough to honour me as holy[x] in the sight of the Israelites, you will not bring this community into the land I give them."[y]

20 [n]Ps 74:7; [o]**Lev 15:31**; [p]**ver 12; Lev 14:8**
21 [q]**Ex 27:21**
22 [r]**Lev 5:2**; 15:4–12

Ch. 20

1 [a]Nu 13:21; [b]ver 14; Nu 13:26; 33:36; Dt 1:46; Jdg 11:17; Ps 29:8; [c]**Ex 15:20**
2 [d]**Ex 15:22**; [e]Ex 17:1; [f]**Nu 16:19**
3 [g]ver 13; **Ge 13:7**; Ex 17:2; 21:18; [h]**Ex 5:21**; [i]**Nu 14:2**; 16:31–35
4 [j]**Nu 14:2**; [k]**Ex 14:11**; Nu 14:3; 16:13
5 [l]Nu 13:23; 16:14; [m]**Ex 17:1**
6 [n]**Ex 40:2**; [o]Nu 14:5; [p]**Nu 16:19**
8 [q]**Ex 4:2**; **10:12–13**; [r]Ex 17:6; Isa 41:18; 43:20; Jer 31:9
9 [s]Nu 17:2; [t]Nu 17:10
10 [u]ver 8; [v]Ps 106:32–33
11 [w]**Ex 17:6; Isa 33:21**
12 [x]Nu 27:14; Dt 32:51; Isa 5:16; 8:13; [y]ver 24; Dt 1:37; 3:27
13 [z]**Ex 17:7**; [a]**ver 3**; [b]**Lev 10:3**
14 [c]**ver 1**; [d]**ver 16; Ge 25:30; 36:16**; [e]Ge 24:3; Dt 4:39; Jos 2:11; 9:9; [f]**Ex 18:8**
15 [g]**Ge 46:6**; [h]**Ge 15:13**; [i]**Ex 1:14**
16 [j]**Ge 16:11; 21:17; Ex 2:23**; [k]Ex 14:19; [l]Ex 12:42; Dt 26:8; [m]ver 14, 23; Nu 33:37
17 [n]ver 20; Nu 21:22; Dt 2:27; Jdg 11:17
18 [o]ver 14; [p]Nu 21:23
19 [q]Ex 12:38; [r]Dt 2:6,28
20 [s]**ver 17–18**; [t]ver 14
21 [u]Nu 21:23; [v]Nu 21:4; Dt 2:8; Jdg 11:18
22 [w]Dt 1:46; [x]Nu 33:37; 34:7; Dt 32:50

13These were the waters of Meribah,[a][z] where the Israelites quarrelled[a] with the LORD and where he showed himself holy among them.[b]

Edom Denies Israel Passage

14Moses sent messengers from Kadesh[c] to the king of Edom,[d] saying:

"This is what your brother Israel says: You know[e] about all the hardships[f] that have come upon us. 15Our forefathers went down into Egypt,[g] and we lived there many years.[h] The Egyptians ill-treated[i] us and our fathers, 16but when we cried out to the LORD, he heard our cry[j] and sent an angel[k] and brought us out of Egypt.[l]

"Now we are here at Kadesh, a town on the edge of your territory.[m] 17Please let us pass through your country. We will not go through any field or vineyard, or drink water from any well. We will travel along the king's highway and not turn to the right or to the left until we have passed through your territory."[n]

18But Edom[o] answered:

"You may not pass through here; if you try, we will march out and attack you with the sword."[p]

19The Israelites replied:

"We will go along the main road, and if we or our livestock[q] drink any of your water, we will pay for it.[r] We only want to pass through on foot—nothing else."

20Again they answered:

"You may not pass through."[s]

Then Edom[t] came out against them with a large and powerful army. 21Since Edom refused to let them go through their territory,[u] Israel turned away from them.[v]

The Death of Aaron

22The whole Israelite community set out from Kadesh[w] and came to Mount Hor.[x] 23At Mount Hor, near the border

---

[a]13 *Meribah* means *quarrelling*.

of Edom,[y] the LORD said to Moses and
Aaron, 24"Aaron will be gathered to his
people.[z] He will not enter the land I give
the Israelites, because both of you
rebelled against my command[a] at the
waters of Meribah.[b] 25Call Aaron and
his son Eleazar and take them up
Mount Hor.[c] 26Remove Aaron's
garments[d] and put them on his son
Eleazar, for Aaron will be gathered to
his people;[e] he will die there."

27Moses did as the LORD commanded:
They went up Mount Hor[f] in the sight
of the whole community. 28Moses
removed Aaron's garments and put
them on his son Eleazar.[g] And Aaron
died there[h] on top of the mountain.
Then Moses and Eleazar came down
from the mountain, 29and when the
whole community learned that Aaron
had died,[i] the entire house of Israel
mourned for him[j] thirty days.

Arad Destroyed

21 When the Canaanite king of
Arad,[a] who lived in the Negev,[b]
heard that Israel was coming along the
road to Atharim, he attacked the
Israelites and captured some of them.
2Then Israel made this vow[c] to the LORD:
"If you will deliver these people into our
hands, we will totally destroy[a][d] their
cities." 3The LORD listened to Israel's
plea and gave the Canaanites[e] over to
them. They completely destroyed them[f]
and their towns; so the place was
named Hormah.[b][g]

The Bronze Snake

4They travelled from Mount Hor[h]
along the route to the Red Sea,[c][i] to go
round Edom.[j] But the people grew
impatient on the way;[k] 5they spoke
against God[l] and against Moses, and
said, "Why have you brought us up
out of Egypt[m] to die in the desert?[n]
There is no bread! There is no water![o]
And we detest this miserable food!"[p]

6Then the LORD sent venomous
snakes[q] among them; they bit the
people and many Israelites died.[r] 7The
people came to Moses[s] and said, "We
sinned[t] when we spoke against the
LORD and against you. Pray that the
LORD[u] will take the snakes away from
us." So Moses prayed[v] for the people.

8The LORD said to Moses, "Make a
snake and put it up on a pole;[w] anyone
who is bitten can look at it and live." 9So
Moses made a bronze snake[x] and put it
up on a pole. Then when anyone was
bitten by a snake and looked at the
bronze snake, he lived.[y]

The Journey to Moab

10The Israelites moved on and
camped at Oboth.[z] 11Then they set out
from Oboth and camped in Iye Abarim,
in the desert that faces Moab[a] towards
the sunrise. 12From there they moved
on and camped in the Zered Valley.[b]
13They set out from there and camped
alongside the Arnon,[c] which is in the
desert extending into Amorite territory.
The Arnon is the border of Moab,
between Moab and the Amorites.[d]
14That is why the Book of the Wars[e] of
the LORD says:

"... Waheb in Suphah[d] and the
ravines,
the Arnon 15and[e] the slopes of the
ravines
that lead to the site of Ar[f]
and lie along the border of Moab."

16From there they continued on to Beer,[g]
the well where the LORD said to Moses,
"Gather the people together and I will
give them water."

17Then Israel sang this song:[h]

"Spring up, O well!
Sing about it,
18about the well that the princes dug,
that the nobles of the people sank—
the nobles with sceptres and staffs."

Then they went from the desert to
Mattanah, 19from Mattanah to Nahaliel,
from Nahaliel to Bamoth, 20and from
Bamoth to the valley in Moab where the
top of Pisgah[i] overlooks the wasteland.

Defeat of Sihon and Og

21Israel sent messengers[j] to say to
Sihon[k] king of the Amorites:[l]

22"Let us pass through your coun-
try. We will not turn aside into any

23 [y]**ver 16**
24 [z]**Ge 25:8**; [a]**ver 10**; [b]**Ex 17:7**
25 [c]Nu 33:38
26 [d]Ex 28:1–4; 40:13; **Lev 16:4**; [e]ver 24; Nu 27:13; 31:2
27 [f]Nu 33:38
28 [g]**Ex 29:29**; [h]ver 26; Nu 33:38; Dt 10:6; 32:50
29 [i]Dt 32:50; [j]**Ge 27:41**; **Lev 10:6**; **Dt 34:8**

Ch. 21

1 [a]Nu 33:40; Jos 12:14; [b]**Ge 12:9**; Nu 13:17; Dt 1:7; Jdg 1:9,16
2 [c]Lev 7:16; [d]ver 3; Ex 22:20; Dt 2:34; Jos 2:10; 8:26; Jer 25:9; 50:21
3 [e]**Ge 10:18**; [f]**ver 2**; [g]**Nu 14:45**
4 [h]Nu 20:22; [i]Nu 14:25; Dt 2:1; 11:4; [j]**Nu 20:21**; [k]Dt 2:8; Jdg 11:18
5 [l]Ps 78:19; [m]Nu 11:20; [n]**Ex 14:11**; Nu 14:2–3; [o]Nu 20:5; [p]**Nu 11:5**
6 [q]ver 7; Dt 8:15; 32:33; Job 20:14; Ps 58:4; 140:3; Jer 8:17; [r]1Co 10:9
7 [s]Ps 78:34; Hos 5:15; [t]Nu 14:40; [u]Ex 8:8; 1Sa 7:8; Jer 27:18; 37:3; Ac 8:24; [v]**Nu 11:2**
8 [w]Jn 3:14
9 [x]2Ki 18:4; [y]Jn 3:14–15
10 [z]Nu 33:43
11 [a]**Ge 36:35**; Nu 33:44; Dt 34:8; Jer 40:11
12 [b]Dt 2:13–14
13 [c]Nu 22:36; Dt 2:24; Jos 12:1; Jdg 11:13,18; 2Ki 10:33; Isa 16:2; Jer 48:20; [d]**Ge 10:16**
14 [e]1Sa 17:47; 18:17; 25:28
15 [f]ver 28; Dt 2:9,18; Isa 15:1
16 [g]Nu 25:1; 33:49; Jdg 9:21; Isa 15:8
17 [h]**Ex 15:1**
20 [i]Nu 23:14; Dt 3:17,27; 34:1; Jos 12:3; 13:20
21 [j]**Ge 32:3**; [k]Nu 32:33; Dt 1:4; Jos 2:10; 12:2,4; 13:10; Jdg 11:19–21; 1Ki 4:19; Ne 9:22; Ps 135:11; 136:19; Jer 48:45; [l]**Ex 23:23**

[a]2 The Hebrew term refers to the irrevocable giving over of things or persons to the LORD, often by totally destroying them; also in verse 3.
[b]3 *Hormah* means *destruction*.
[c]4 Hebrew *Yam Suph*; that is, Sea of Reeds
[d]14 The meaning of the Hebrew for this phrase is uncertain.
[e]14,15 Or *"I have been given from Suphah and the ravines / of the Arnon*[15]*to*

field or vineyard, or drink water
from any well. We will travel along
the king's highway until we have
passed through your territory.[m]"
23But Sihon would not let Israel pass
through his territory.[n] He mustered his
entire army and marched out into the
desert against Israel. When he reached
Jahaz,[o] he fought with Israel.[p] 24Israel,
however, put him to the sword[q] and
took over his land[r] from the Arnon to
the Jabbok,[s] but only as far as the
Ammonites,[t] because their border was
fortified. 25Israel captured all the cities
of the Amorites[u] and occupied them,[v]
including Heshbon[w] and all its sur-
rounding settlements. 26Heshbon was
the city of Sihon[x] king of the Amorites,[y]
who had fought against the former king
of Moab[z] and had taken from him all his
land as far as the Arnon.[a]
27That is why the poets say:

"Come to Heshbon and let it be
  rebuilt;
 let Sihon's city be restored.

28"Fire went out from Heshbon,
 a blaze from the city of Sihon.[b]
It consumed[c] Ar[d] of Moab,
 the citizens of Arnon's heights.[e]
29Woe to you, O Moab![f]
 You are destroyed, O people of
  Chemosh![g]
He has given up his sons as fugitives[h]
 and his daughters as captives[i]
 to Sihon king of the Amorites.

30"But we have overthrown them;
 Heshbon is destroyed all the way to
  Dibon.[j]
We have demolished them as far as
  Nophah,
 which extends to Medeba.[k]"

31So Israel settled in the land of the
Amorites.[l]
32After Moses had sent spies[m] to
Jazer,[n] the Israelites captured its
surrounding settlements and drove out
the Amorites who were there. 33Then
they turned and went up along the road
towards Bashan[o],[p] and Og king of
Bashan and his whole army marched
out to meet them in battle at Edrei.[q]
34The LORD said to Moses, "Do not be
afraid of him, for I have handed him
over to you, with his whole army and
his land. Do to him what you did to
Sihon king of the Amorites, who
reigned in Heshbon.[r]"
35So they struck him down, together

22 [m]**Nu 20:17**
23 [n]Nu 20:21; [o]Dt 2:32; Jos 13:18; 21:36; Jdg 11:20; Isa 15:4; Jer 48:21,34; [p]Nu 20:18
24 [q]Dt 2:33; 3:3; 29:7; Ps 135:10–11; Am 2:9; [r]ver 35; Dt 3:4; [s]**Ge 32:22**; Nu 32:33; Jdg 11:13,22; [t]**Ge 19:38**; Dt 2:37; Jos 13:10
25 [u]Nu 13:29; Jdg 10:11; Am 2:10; [v]Jdg 11:26; [w]ver 30; Nu 32:3; Dt 1:4; 29:7; Jos 9:10; 12:2; Isa 15:4; 16:8; Jer 48:2,34
26 [x]ver 21; Dt 29:7; Ps 135:11; [y]Nu 13:29; [z]ver 11; [a]ver 13
28 [b]Jer 48:45; [c]**Nu 11:1**; [d]**ver 15**; [e]Nu 22:41; Dt 12:2; Jos 13:17; Isa 15:2; Jer 19:5
29 [f]Nu 24:17; 2Sa 8:2; 1Ch 18:2; Ps 60:8; Isa 25:10; Jer 48:46; [g]Jdg 10:6; 11:24; Ru 1:15; 1Ki 11:7,33; 2Ki 23:13; Jer 48:7,46; [h]Isa 15:5; [i]Isa 16:2
30 [j]Nu 32:3; Jos 13:9,17; Ne 11:25; Isa 15:2; Jer 48:18,22; [k]Jos 13:16; 1Ch 19:7
31 [l]Nu 13:29
32 [m]Jos 2:1; 6:22; 7:2; Jdg 18:2; 2Sa 10:3; 1Ch 19:3; [n]Nu 32:1,3,35; Jos 13:25; 2Sa 24:5; 1Ch 6:81; Isa 16:8; Jer 48:32
33 [o]Nu 32:33; Dt 3:3; 31:4; Jos 2:10; 12:4; 13:30; 1Ki 4:19; Ne 9:22; Ps 135:11; 136:20; [p]Dt 3:4; 32:14; Jos 9:10; 1Ki 4:13; [q]Dt 1:4; 3:1,10; Jos 12:4; 13:12,31; 19:37
34 [r]Dt 3:2
35 [s]Jos 9:10; [t]**ver 24**

with his sons and his whole army,
leaving them no survivors.[s] And they
took possession of his land.[t]

Balak Summons Balaam

22 Then the Israelites travelled to
the plains of Moab[a] and camped
along the Jordan[b] across from Jericho.[a c]
2Now Balak son of Zippor[d] saw all
that Israel had done to the Amorites,
3and Moab was terrified because there
were so many people. Indeed, Moab
was filled with dread[e] because of the
Israelites.
4The Moabites[f] said to the elders of
Midian,[g] "This horde is going to lick up
everything[h] around us, as an ox licks up
the grass of the field.[i]"
So Balak son of Zippor, who was king
of Moab at that time, 5sent messengers
to summon Balaam son of Beor,[j] who
was at Pethor, near the River,[b k] in his
native land. Balak said:

"A people has come out of
Egypt;[l] they cover the face of the
land and have settled next to me.
6Now come and put a curse[m] on
these people, because they are too
powerful for me. Perhaps then I
will be able to defeat them and
drive them out of the country.[n] For
I know that those you bless are
blessed, and those you curse are
cursed."

7The elders of Moab and Midian left,
taking with them the fee for divination.[o]
When they came to Balaam, they told
him what Balak had said.
8"Spend the night here," Balaam said
to them, "and I will bring you back the
answer the LORD gives me.[p]" So the
Moabite princes stayed with him.
9God came to Balaam[q] and asked,[r]
"Who are these men with you?"
10Balaam said to God, "Balak son of

Ch. 22
1 [a]**Nu 21:11**; [b]**Nu 13:29**; **Jos 2:7**; [c]Nu 31:12; 33:48; Dt 32:49; Jos 2:1
2 [d]Nu 23:1–3; Jos 24:9; Jdg 11:25; Mic 6:5; Rev 2:14
3 [e]**Ex 15:15**
4 [f]**Ge 19:37**; [g]**Ge 25:2**; [h]Nu 32:17–18,29; [i]Job 5:25; Ps 72:16
5 [j]ver 7; Nu 24:25; 31:8,16; Dt 23:4; Jos 13:22; Ne 13:2; Mic 6:5; **2Pe 2:15**; [k]**Ge 2:14**; [l]**Ex 13:3**
6 [m]ver 12,17; Nu 23:7,11,13; 24:9–10; [n]ver 11
7 [o]Ge 30:27 *8* [p]ver 19
9 [q]**Ge 20:3**; [r]ver 20; Nu 23:5; 24:4,16

[a]1 Hebrew *Jordan of Jericho;* possibly an ancient name for the Jordan River
[b]5 That is, the Euphrates

Zippor, king of Moab, sent me this message: 11'A people that has come out of Egypt covers the face of the land. Now come and put a curse on them for me. Perhaps then I will be able to fight them and drive them away.' "

12But God said to Balaam, "Do not go with them. You must not put a curse on those people, because they are blessed.[s]"

13The next morning Balaam got up and said to Balak's princes, "Go back to your own country, for the LORD has refused to let me go with you."

14So the Moabite princes returned to Balak and said, "Balaam refused to come with us."

15Then Balak sent other princes, more numerous and more distinguished than the first. 16They came to Balaam and said:

> "This is what Balak son of Zippor says: Do not let anything keep you from coming to me, 17because I will reward you handsomely[t] and do whatever you say. Come and put a curse[u] on these people for me."

18But Balaam answered them, "Even if Balak gave me his palace filled with silver and gold, I could not do anything great or small to go beyond the command of the LORD my God.[v] 19Now stay here tonight as the others did, and I will find out what else the LORD will tell me.[w]"

20That night God came to Balaam[x] and said, "Since these men have come to summon you, go with them, but do only what I tell you."[y]

Balaam's Donkey

21Balaam got up in the morning, saddled his donkey and went with the princes of Moab. 22But God was very angry[z] when he went, and the angel of the LORD[a] stood in the road to oppose him. Balaam was riding on his donkey, and his two servants were with him. 23When the donkey saw the angel of the LORD standing in the road with a drawn sword[b] in his hand, she turned off the road into a field. Balaam beat her[c] to get her back on the road.

24Then the angel of the LORD stood in a narrow path between two vineyards, with walls on both sides. 25When the donkey saw the angel of the LORD, she pressed close to the wall, crushing Balaam's foot against it. So he beat her again.

26Then the angel of the LORD moved on ahead and stood in a narrow place where there was no room to turn, either to the right or to the left. 27When the donkey saw the angel of the LORD, she lay down under Balaam, and he was angry[d] and beat her with his staff. 28Then the LORD opened the donkey's mouth,[e] and she said to Balaam, "What have I done to you to make you beat me these three times?[f]"

29Balaam answered the donkey, "You have made a fool of me! If I had a sword in my hand, I would kill you right now.[g]"

30The donkey said to Balaam, "Am I not your own donkey, which you have always ridden, to this day? Have I been in the habit of doing this to you?"

"No," he said.

31Then the LORD opened Balaam's eyes,[h] and he saw the angel of the LORD standing in the road with his sword drawn. So he bowed low and fell face down.

32The angel of the LORD asked him, "Why have you beaten your donkey these three times? I have come here to oppose you because your path is a reckless one before me.[c] 33The donkey saw me and turned away from me these three times. If she had not turned away, I would certainly have killed you by now,[i] but I would have spared her."

34Balaam said to the angel of the LORD, "I have sinned.[j] I did not realise you were standing in the road to oppose me. Now if you are displeased, I will go back."

35The angel of the LORD said to Balaam, "Go with the men, but speak only what I tell you." So Balaam went with the princes of Balak.

36When Balak[k] heard that Balaam was coming, he went out to meet him at the Moabite town on the Arnon[l] border, at the edge of his territory. 37Balak said to Balaam, "Did I not send you an urgent summons? Why didn't you come to me? Am I really not able to reward you?"

38"Well, I have come to you now," Balaam replied. "But can I say just anything? I must speak only what God puts in my mouth."[m]

39Then Balaam went with Balak to Kiriath Huzoth. 40Balak sacrificed cattle and sheep,[n] and gave some to Balaam

12 [s]**Ge 12:2**
17 [t]ver 37; Nu 24:11; [u]**ver 6**
18 [v]ver 38; Nu 23:12,26; 24:13; 1Ki 22:14; 2Ch 18:13; Jer 42:4
19 [w]ver 8
20 [x]**Ge 20:3**; [y]ver 35,38; Nu 23:5,12, 16,26; 24:13; 2Ch 18:13
22 [z]**Ex 4:14**; [a]**Ge 16:7**; Jdg 13:3,6,13
23 [b]Jos 5:13; [c]ver 25,27
27 [d]Nu 11:1; Jas 1:19
28 [e]2Pe 2:16; [f]ver 32
29 [g]ver 33; Dt 25:4; Pr 12:10; 27:23–27; Mt 15:19
31 [h]Ge 21:19
33 [i]**ver 29**
34 [j]Ge 39:9; Nu 14:40; 1Sa 15:24,30; 2Sa 12:13; 24:10; Job 33:27; Ps 51:4
36 [k]ver 2; [l]**Nu 21:13**
38 [m]Nu 23:5, 16,26
40 [n]Nu 23:1,14, 29; Eze 45:23

[c]32 The meaning of the Hebrew for this clause is uncertain.

and the princes who were with him.
41 The next morning Balak took Balaam
up to Bamoth Baal,[o] and from there he
saw part of the people.[p]

Balaam's First Oracle

23 Balaam said, "Build me seven
altars here, and prepare seven
bulls and seven rams[a] for me." 2 Balak
did as Balaam said, and the two of them
offered a bull and a ram on each altar.[b]
3 Then Balaam said to Balak, "Stay
here beside your offering while I go
aside. Perhaps the LORD will come to
meet with me.[c] Whatever he reveals to
me I will tell you." Then he went off to a
barren height.
4 God met with him,[d] and Balaam said,
"I have prepared seven altars, and on
each altar I have offered a bull and a
ram."
5 The LORD put a message in Balaam's
mouth[e][f] and said, "Go back to Balak and
give him this message."[g]
6 So he went back to him and found
him standing beside his offering, with
all the princes of Moab.[h] 7 Then Balaam[i]
uttered his oracle:[j]

"Balak brought me from Aram,[k]
the king of Moab from the eastern
mountains.[l]
'Come,' he said, 'curse Jacob for me;
come, denounce Israel.'[m]
8 How can I curse
those whom God has not cursed?[n]
How can I denounce
those whom the LORD has not
denounced?[o]
9 From the rocky peaks I see them,
from the heights I view them.[p]
I see people who live apart
and do not consider themselves
one of the nations.[q]
10 Who can count the dust of Jacob[r]
or number the fourth part of Israel?
Let me die the death of the righteous,[s]
and may my end be like theirs![t]"

11 Balak said to Balaam, "What have
you done to me? I brought you to curse
my enemies,[u] but you have done
nothing but bless them!"[v]
12 He answered, "Must I not speak
what the LORD puts in my mouth?"[w]

Balaam's Second Oracle

13 Then Balak said to him, "Come with
me to another place[x] where you can see
them; you will see only a part but not all
of them.[y] And from there, curse them
for me.[z]" 14 So he took him to the field of
Zophim on the top of Pisgah,[a] and there
he built seven altars and offered a bull
and a ram on each altar.[b]
15 Balaam said to Balak, "Stay here
beside your offering while I meet with
him over there."
16 The LORD met with Balaam and put a
message in his mouth[c] and said, "Go
back to Balak and give him this
message."
17 So he went to him and found him
standing beside his offering, with the
princes of Moab.[d] Balak asked him,
"What did the LORD say?"
18 Then he uttered his oracle:[e]

"Arise, Balak, and listen;
hear me, son of Zippor.[f]
19 God is not a man,[g] that he should lie,[h]
nor a son of man, that he should
change his mind.[i]
Does he speak and then not act?
Does he promise[j] and not fulfil?
20 I have received a command to bless;[k]
he has blessed,[l] and I cannot
change it.[m]

21 "No misfortune is seen in Jacob,[n]
no misery observed in Israel.[a][o]
The LORD their God is with them;[p]
the shout of the King[q] is among
them.
22 God brought them out of Egypt;[r]
they have the strength of a wild ox.[s]
23 There is no sorcery against Jacob,
no divination[t] against Israel.
It will now be said of Jacob
and of Israel, 'See what God has
done!'
24 The people rise like a lioness;[u]
they rouse themselves like a lion[v]
that does not rest till he devours his
prey
and drinks the blood[w] of his
victims."

25 Then Balak said to Balaam, "Neither
curse them at all nor bless them at all!"
26 Balaam answered, "Did I not tell
you I must do whatever the LORD
says?"[x]

41 [o]**Nu 21:28;** [p]Nu 23:13

Ch. 23

1 [a]**Nu 22:40**
2 [b]ver 14,30
3 [c]ver 15
4 [d]ver 16
5 [e]**Ex 4:12;** Isa 59:21; [f]**Ex 4:15;** [g]**Nu 22:20**
6 [h]ver 17
7 [i]Nu 22:5; Jos 24:9; [j]ver 18; Nu 24:3,21; 2Sa 23:1; [k]2Ki 5:1; [l]**Ge 24:10;** [m]**Nu 22:6;** Ne 13:2
8 [n]Nu 22:12; [o]ver 20; Isa 43:13
9 [p]Nu 22:41; [q]**Ex 33:16; Dt 32:8**
10 [r]**Ge 13:16;** [s]Ps 16:3; 116:15; Isa 57:1; [t]Ps 37:37
11 [u]**Nu 22:6;** [v]Nu 24:10; Jos 24:10; Ne 13:2
12 [w]**Nu 22:18**,20
13 [x]ver 27; [y]Nu 22:41; [z]**Nu 22:6**
14 [a]**Nu 21:20;** 27:12; [b]**ver 2**
16 [c]**Ex 4:15; Nu 22:38**
17 [d]ver 6
18 [e]**ver 7;** [f]Nu 22:2
19 [g]Job 9:32; Isa 55:9; Hos 11:9; [h]**Nu 11:23;** [i]1Sa 15:29; Job 12:13; 36:5; Ps 33:11; 89:34; 102:27; 110:4; Jer 4:28; 7:16; Mal 3:6; Tit 1:2; Heb 6:18; 7:21; Jas 1:17; [j]2Sa 7:25; Ps 119:38
20 [k]ver 5,16; Nu 24:1; [l]Ge 22:17; Nu 22:12; [m]**ver 8; Job 9:12**
21 [n]Ps 32:2,5; 85:2; Ro 4:7–8; [o]Isa 33:24; 40:2; Jer 50:20; [p]**Ge 26:3;** Ex 29:45–46; Dt 4:7; Ps 34:17–18; 145:18; Zec 2:10; [q]Dt 32:15; 33:5; Ps 89:15–18; Isa 44:2
22 [r]Nu 24:8; Jos 2:10; 9:9; [s]Dt 33:17; Job 39:9; Ps 22:21; 29:6; 92:10; Isa 34:7
23 [t]ver 3; **Ge 30:27;** Nu 24:1
24 [u]Nu 24:9; Eze 19:2; Na 2:11; [v]**Ge 49:9;** [w]Isa 49:26
26 [x]**Nu 22:18**,20

[a]21 Or *He has not looked on Jacob's offences / or on the wrongs found in Israel.*

Balaam's Third Oracle

27Then Balak said to Balaam, "Come,
let me take you to another place.[y]
Perhaps it will please God to let you
curse them for me[z] from there." 28And
Balak took Balaam to the top of Peor,[a]
overlooking the wasteland.
29Balaam said, "Build me seven altars
here, and prepare seven bulls and seven
rams for me." 30Balak did as Balaam had
said, and offered a bull and a ram on
each altar.[b]

24 Now when Balaam saw that it
pleased the LORD to bless
Israel,[a] he did not resort to sorcery[b] as at
other times, but turned his face towards
the desert.[c] 2When Balaam looked out
and saw Israel encamped tribe by tribe,
the Spirit of God came upon him[d] 3and
he uttered his oracle:

"The oracle of Balaam son of Beor,
the oracle of one whose eye sees
clearly,[e]
4the oracle of one who hears the words
of God,[f]
who sees a vision from the
Almighty,[a][g]
who falls prostrate, and whose
eyes are opened:

5"How beautiful are your tents,[h] O
Jacob,
your dwelling-places, O Israel!

6"Like valleys they spread out,
like gardens beside a river,[i]
like aloes[j] planted by the LORD,
like cedars beside the waters.[k]
7Water will flow from their buckets;
their seed will have abundant
water.

"Their king will be greater than
Agag;[l]
their kingdom will be exalted.[m]

8"God brought them out of Egypt;
they have the strength of a wild ox.
They devour hostile nations
and break their bones in pieces;[n]
with their arrows they pierce
them.[o]
9Like a lion they crouch and lie down,
like a lioness[p]—who dares to rouse
them?

"May those who bless you be
blessed[q]
and those who curse you be
cursed!"[r]

10Then Balak's anger burned[s] against
Balaam. He struck his hands together[t]
and said to him, "I summoned you to
curse my enemies,[u] but you have
blessed them[v] these three times.[w]
11Now leave at once and go home![x] I said
I would reward you handsomely,[y] but
the LORD has kept you from being
rewarded."
12Balaam answered Balak, "Did I not
tell the messengers you sent me,[z]
13'Even if Balak gave me his palace filled
with silver and gold, I could not do
anything of my own accord, good or
bad, to go beyond the command of the
LORD[a]—and I must say only what the
LORD says'?[b] 14Now I am going back to
my people, but come, let me warn you
of what this people will do to your
people in days to come."[c]

Balaam's Fourth Oracle

15Then he uttered his oracle:

"The oracle of Balaam son of Beor,
the oracle of one whose eye sees
clearly,
16the oracle of one who hears the words[d]
of God,
who has knowledge from the Most
High,[e]
who sees a vision from the Almighty,
who falls prostrate, and whose eyes
are opened:

17"I see him, but not now;
I behold him, but not near.[f]
A star will come out of Jacob;[g]
a sceptre will rise out of Israel.[h]
He will crush the foreheads of Moab,[i]
the skulls[b][j] of[c] all the sons of
Sheth.[d]
18Edom[k] will be conquered;
Seir,[l] his enemy, will be
conquered,[m]
but Israel[n] will grow strong.
19A ruler will come out of Jacob[o]
and destroy the survivors of the
city."

Balaam's Final Oracles

20Then Balaam saw Amalek[p] and
uttered his oracle:

"Amalek was first among the nations,
but he will come to ruin at last."[q]

27 [y]ver 13; [z]Nu 24:10
28 [a]Nu 25:3,18; 31:16; Dt 3:29; 4:3; Jos 22:17; Ps 106:28; Hos 9:10
30 [b]ver 2

Ch. 24

1 [a]Nu 23:20; [b]Nu 23:23; [c]Nu 23:28
2 [d]Nu 11:25–26
3 [e]ver 15
4 [f]Nu 22:9; [g]Ge 15:1
5 [h]Jer 4:20; 30:18; Mal 2:12
6 [i]Ge 2:10; [j]Ps 45:8; SS 4:14; [k]Job 29:19; Ps 1:3; 104:16; Eze 31:5
7 [l]Ex 17:8–16; [m]Dt 28:1; 2Sa 5:12; 1Ch 14:2; Ps 89:27; 145:11–13
8 [n]Ex 15:6; Jer 50:17; [o]2Sa 18:14; Ps 45:5
9 [p]Nu 23:24; [q]Ge 12:2; [r]Ge 12:3
10 [s]Ex 4:14; [t]Job 27:23; 34:37; La 2:15; Eze 21:14; 22:13; 25:6; [u]Nu 22:6; [v]Nu 23:11; Dt 23:5; [w]ver 3–9; Nu 23:7–10, 18–24
11 [x]ver 14,25; [y]Nu 22:17
12 [z]Nu 22:18
13 [a]Nu 22:18; [b]Nu 22:20
14 [c]Ge 49:1; Nu 31:8,16; Mic 6:5
16 [d]Nu 22:9; [e]Ge 14:18; Isa 14:14
17 [f]Rev 1:7; [g]Mt 2:2; [h]Ge 49:10; [i]Ge 19:37; Nu 21:29; Dt 23:6; Isa 15:1– 16:14; [j]Jer 48:45
18 [k]2Sa 8:12; 1Ch 18:11; Ps 60:8; Isa 11:14; Am 9:12; [l]Ge 14:6; Dt 1:44; Jos 12:7; 15:10; Jdg 5:4; [m]Ob 2; [n]Ge 9:25
19 [o]Ge 49:10; Mic 5:2
20 [p]Ge 14:7; Ex 17:14; [q]Dt 25:19; 1Sa 15:20; 30:17–20; 2Sa 8:12; 1Ch 18:11

a4 Hebrew *Shaddai*; also in verse 16
b17 Samaritan Pentateuch (see also Jer. 48:45); the meaning of the word in the Masoretic Text is uncertain. c17 Or possibly *Moab, / batter*
d17 Or *all the noisy boasters*

21Then he saw the Kenites[r] and
uttered his oracle:

"Your dwelling-place is secure,[s]
your nest is set in a rock;
22yet you Kenites will be destroyed
when Asshur[t] takes you captive."

23Then he uttered his oracle:

"Ah, who can live when God does
this?[e]
24 Ships will come from the shores of
Kittim;[u]
they will subdue Asshur[v] and Eber,[w]
but they too will come to ruin.[x]"

25Then Balaam[y] got up and returned
home and Balak went his own way.

Moab Seduces Israel

25 While Israel was staying in
Shittim,[a] the men began to
indulge in sexual immorality[b] with
Moabite[c] women,[d] 2who invited them to
the sacrifices[e] to their gods.[f] The people
ate and bowed down before these gods.
3So Israel joined in worshipping[g] the
Baal of Peor.[h] And the LORD's anger
burned against them.
4The LORD said to Moses, "Take all the
leaders[i] of these people, kill them and
expose[j] them in broad daylight before
the LORD,[k] so that the LORD's fierce
anger[l] may turn away from Israel."
5So Moses said to Israel's judges,
"Each of you must put to death[m] those
of your men who have joined in
worshipping the Baal of Peor."[n]
6Then an Israelite man brought to his
family a Midianite[o] woman right before
the eyes of Moses and the whole
assembly of Israel while they were
weeping[p] at the entrance to the Tent of
Meeting. 7When Phinehas[q] son of
Eleazar, the son of Aaron, the priest,
saw this, he left the assembly, took a
spear[r] in his hand 8and followed the
Israelite into the tent. He drove the
spear through both of them—through
the Israelite and into the woman's body.
Then the plague against the Israelites
was stopped;[s] 9but those who died in
the plague[t] numbered 24,000.[u]
10The LORD said to Moses,
11"Phinehas son of Eleazar, the son of
Aaron, the priest, has turned my anger
away from the Israelites;[v] for he was as
zealous as I am for my honour[w] among
them, so that in my zeal I did not put an
end to them. 12Therefore tell him I am
making my covenant of peace[x] with
him. 13He and his descendants will have
a covenant of a lasting priesthood,[y]
because he was zealous[z] for the honour[a]
of his God and made atonement[b] for the
Israelites."[c]
14The name of the Israelite who was
killed with the Midianite woman[d] was
Zimri son of Salu, the leader of a
Simeonite family.[e] 15And the name of
the Midianite woman who was put to
death was Cozbi[f] daughter of Zur, a
tribal chief of a Midianite family.[g]
16The LORD said to Moses,[h] 17"Treat
the Midianites[i] as enemies[j] and kill
them,[k] 18because they treated you as
enemies when they deceived you in
the affair of Peor[l] and their sister Cozbi,
the daughter of a Midianite leader, the
woman who was killed when the
plague came as a result of Peor."

The Second Census

26 After the plague[a] the LORD said
to Moses and Eleazar son of
Aaron, the priest, 2"Take a census[b] of
the whole Israelite community by fam-
ilies—all those twenty years old or more
who are able to serve in the army[c] of
Israel." 3So on the plains of Moab[d] by
the Jordan across from Jericho,[a][e] Moses
and Eleazar the priest spoke with them
and said, 4"Take a census of men
twenty years old or more, as the LORD
commanded Moses."

These were the Israelites who came
out of Egypt:[f]

5The descendants of Reuben,[g] the
firstborn son of Israel, were:
through Hanoch,[h] the Hanochite
clan;
through Pallu,[i] the Palluite clan;
6through Hezron,[j] the Hezronite clan;
through Carmi,[k] the Carmite clan.
7These were the clans of Reuben; those
numbered were 43,730.
8The son of Pallu was Eliab, 9and the

21 [r]**Ge 15:19**; [s]Ps 37:27; Pr 1:33; Isa 32:18; Eze 34:27
22 [t]**Ge 10:22**
24 [u]**Ge 10:4**; [v]ver 22; [w]**Ge 10:21**; [x]ver 20
25 [y]**Nu 22:5**

Ch. 25

1 [a]**Nu 21:16**; Jos 2:1; Isa 66:11; Joel 3:18; Mic 6:5; [b]Jer 5:7; 7:9; 9:2; 1Co 10:8; Rev 2:14; [c]**Ge 19:37**; [d]Nu 31:16
2 [e]**Ex 32:6**; [f]Ex 20:5; Dt 32:38; 1Co 10:20
3 [g]Dt 4:19; Jdg 2:19; 1Ki 9:9; Jer 1:16; 44:3; [h]**Nu 23:28**
4 [i]Nu 7:2; 13:3; [j]2Sa 21:6; [k]Dt 4:3; [l]Ex 32:12; Dt 13:17; Jos 7:26; 2Ki 23:26; 2Ch 28:11; 29:10; 30:8; Ezr 10:14; Jer 44:3
5 [m]**Ex 32:27**; [n]Hos 9:10
6 [o]**Ge 25:2**; [p]**Nu 14:1**; Jdg 2:4; Ru 1:9; 1Sa 11:4; 2Sa 15:30; Ezr 10:1; Ps 126:6; Jer 41:6
7 [q]**Ex 6:25**; Jos 22:13; Jdg 20:28; [r]Jdg 5:8; 1Sa 13:19,22; 1Ki 18:28; Ps 35:3; 46:9; Joel 3:10; Mic 4:3
8 [s]Ps 106:30
9 [t]**Nu 14:37**; 1Co 10:8; [u]Nu 31:16
11 [v]Ps 106:30; [w]Ex 20:5; Dt 32:16,21; Ps 78:58
12 [x]Isa 11:9; 54:10; Eze 34:25; 37:26; Mal 2:4–5
13 [y]**Ex 29:9**; [z]1Ki 19:10; 2Ki 10:16; [a]ver 11; [b]**Ex 29:36**; **Ro 3:25**; [c]Ps 106:31; Jer 33:18
14 [d]ver 6; [e]**Nu 1:6**
15 [f]ver 18; [g]Nu 31:8; Jos 13:21; Hab 3:7
16 [h]Nu 31:7
17 [i]Nu 31:1–3; [j]Ex 23:22; Jdg 2:16–18; Ne 9:27; Ps 8:2; 21:8; 74:23; [k]Dt 21:1; 1Sa 17:9,35; 2Ki 9:27; 10:25
18 [l]**Nu 23:28**

Ch. 26

1 [a]**Nu 14:37**; 25:8 **2** [b]Ex 30:11–16; [c]**Nu 1:3**
3 [d]ver 63; Nu 33:48; Jos 13:32; [e]Nu 22:1
4 [f]**Ex 6:14**; **13:3** **5** [g]Nu 1:20; [h]**Ge 46:9**; [i]1Ch 5:3
6 [j]1Ch 5:3; [k]Ge 46:9

[e]23 Masoretic Text; with a different word division of the Hebrew *A people will gather from the north.*
[a]3 Hebrew *Jordan of Jericho*; possibly an ancient name for the Jordan River; also in verse 63

sons of Eliab[l] were Nemuel, Dathan and
Abiram. The same Dathan and Abiram
were the community[m] officials who
rebelled against Moses and Aaron and
were among Korah's followers when
they rebelled against the LORD.[n] 10The
earth opened its mouth and swallowed
them[o] along with Korah, whose
followers died when the fire devoured
the 250 men.[p] And they served as a
warning sign.[q] 11The line of Korah,[r]
however, did not die out.[s]

12The descendants of Simeon by their clans were:
through Nemuel,[t] the Nemuelite clan;
through Jamin,[u] the Jaminite clan;
through Jakin, the Jakinite clan;
13through Zerah,[v] the Zerahite clan;
through Shaul, the Shaulite clan.
14These were the clans of Simeon;[w] there were 22,200 men.[x]

15The descendants of Gad by their clans were:
through Zephon,[y] the Zephonite clan;
through Haggi, the Haggite clan;
through Shuni, the Shunite clan;
16through Ozni, the Oznite clan;
through Eri, the Erite clan;
17through Arodi,[b] the Arodite clan;
through Areli, the Arelite clan.
18These were the clans of Gad;[z] those numbered were 40,500.

19Er[a] and Onan[b] were sons of Judah, but they died[c] in Canaan.
20The descendants of Judah by their clans were:
through Shelah,[d] the Shelanite clan;
through Perez,[e] the Perezite clan;
through Zerah, the Zerahite clan.[f]
21The descendants of Perez[g] were:
through Hezron,[h] the Hezronite clan;
through Hamul, the Hamulite clan.
22These were the clans of Judah;[i] those numbered were 76,500.

23The descendants of Issachar by their clans were:
through Tola,[j] the Tolaite clan;
through Puah, the Puite[c] clan;
24through Jashub,[k] the Jashubite clan;
through Shimron, the Shimronite clan.
25These were the clans of Issachar;[l] those numbered were 64,300.

26The descendants of Zebulun[m] by their clans were:
through Sered, the Seredite clan;
through Elon, the Elonite clan;
through Jahleel, the Jahleelite clan.
27These were the clans of Zebulun;[n] those numbered were 60,500.

28The descendants of Joseph[o] by their clans through Manasseh and Ephraim[p] were:

29The descendants of Manasseh:[q]
through Makir,[r] the Makirite clan (Makir was the father of Gilead[s]);
through Gilead, the Gileadite clan.
30These were the descendants of Gilead:[t]
through Iezer,[u] the Iezerite clan;
through Helek, the Helekite clan;
31through Asriel, the Asrielite clan;
through Shechem, the Shechemite clan;
32through Shemida, the Shemidaite clan;
through Hepher, the Hepherite clan.
33(Zelophehad[v] son of Hepher had no sons;[w] he had only daughters, whose names were Mahlah, Noah, Hoglah, Milcah and Tirzah.)[x]
34These were the clans of Manasseh; those numbered were 52,700.[y]

35These were the descendants of Ephraim[z] by their clans:
through Shuthelah, the Shuthelahite clan;
through Beker, the Bekerite clan;
through Tahan, the Tahanite clan.
36These were the descendants of Shuthelah:
through Eran, the Eranite clan.
37These were the clans of Ephraim;[a] those numbered were 32,500.

These were the descendants of Joseph by their clans.

38The descendants of Benjamin[b] by their clans were:
through Bela, the Belaite clan;
through Ashbel, the Ashbelite clan;
through Ahiram, the Ahiramite clan;
39through Shupham,[d] the Shuphamite clan;

9 [l]Nu 16:1; [m]Nu 1:16; [n]**Nu 16:2**
10 [o]**Ex 15:12;** [p]**Nu 16:35;** [q]**Ex 3:12; Nu 16:38**
11 [r]Ex 6:24; [s]Nu 16:33; Dt 5:9; 24:16; 2Ki 14:6; 2Ch 25:4; Eze 18:20
12 [t]**Ge 46:10;** [u]1Ch 4:24
13 [v]**Ge 46:10**
14 [w]**Ge 46:10;** [x]Nu 1:23
15 [y]Ge 46:16
18 [z]**Ge 30:11; Nu 1:25; Jos 13:24–28**
19 [a]**Ge 38:3;** [b]**Ge 38:4;** [c]Ge 38:7
20 [d]**Ge 38:5;** [e]**Ge 38:29;** [f]Jos 7:17
21 [g]**Ge 38:29;** [h]Ru 4:19; 1Ch 2:9
22 [i]Nu 1:27
23 [j]**Ge 46:13**
24 [k]Ge 46:13
25 [l]**Ge 30:18**
26 [m]Nu 1:30
27 [n]**Ge 30:20**
28 [o]Nu 1:32; 36:1; [p]**Ge 41:52**
29 [q]Nu 1:34; [r]Ge 50:23; [s]Jdg 11:1
30 [t]Nu 27:1; 36:1; 1Ch 7:14, 17; [u]Jos 17:2; Jdg 6:11; 8:2
33 [v]Nu 27:1; 36:2; Jos 17:3; 1Ch 7:15; [w]Nu 27:3; [x]Nu 36:11
34 [y]Nu 1:35
35 [z]Nu 1:32
37 [a]**Nu 1:33**
38 [b]Ge 46:21; Nu 1:36; 1Ch 8:40

[b]17 Samaritan Pentateuch and Syriac (see also Gen. 46:16); Masoretic Text *Arod*
[c]23 Samaritan Pentateuch, Septuagint, Vulgate and Syriac (see also 1 Chron. 7:1); Masoretic Text *through Puvah, the Punite*
[d]39 A few manuscripts of the Masoretic Text, Samaritan Pentateuch, Vulgate and Syriac (see also Septuagint); most manuscripts of the Masoretic Text *Shephupham*

through Hupham, the Huphamite
clan.
40The descendants of Bela through Ard[c]
and Naaman were:
through Ard,[e] the Ardite clan;
through Naaman, the Naamite
clan.
41These were the clans of Benjamin;[d]
those numbered were 45,600.

42These were the descendants of Dan[e]
by their clans:[f]
through Shuham,[g] the Shuhamite
clan.
These were the clans of Dan: 43All of
them were Shuhamite clans; and those
numbered were 64,400.

44The descendants of Asher[h] by their
clans were:
through Imnah, the Imnite clan;
through Ishvi, the Ishvite clan;
through Beriah, the Beriite clan;
45and through the descendants of
Beriah:
through Heber, the Heberite clan;
through Malkiel, the Malkielite
clan.
46(Asher had a daughter named Serah.)
47These were the clans of Asher;[i] those
numbered were 53,400.

48The descendants of Naphtali[j] by their
clans were:
through Jahzeel, the Jahzeelite clan;
through Guni, the Gunite clan;
49through Jezer, the Jezerite clan;
through Shillem, the Shillemite clan.
50These were the clans of Naphtali;[k]
those numbered were 45,400.[l]

51The total number of the men of Israel
was 601,730.[m]

52The LORD said to Moses, 53"The
land is to be allotted to them as an
inheritance based on the number of
names.[n] 54To a larger group give a larger
inheritance, and to a smaller group a
smaller one; each is to receive its inheri-
tance according to the number[o] of those
listed.[p] 55Be sure that the land is distri-
buted by lot.[q] What each group inherits
will be according to the names for its
ancestral tribe. 56Each inheritance is to
be distributed by lot among the larger
and smaller groups."

57These were the Levites[r] who were
counted by their clans:
through Gershon, the Gershonite
clan;
through Kohath, the Kohathite clan;
through Merari, the Merarite clan.
58These also were Levite clans:
the Libnite clan,
the Hebronite clan,
the Mahlite clan,
the Mushite clan,
the Korahite clan.
(Kohath was the forefather of
Amram;[s] 59the name of Amram's
wife was Jochebed,[t] a descendant
of Levi, who was born to the
Levites[f] in Egypt. To Amram she
bore Aaron, Moses[u] and their sis-
ter[v] Miriam.[w] 60Aaron was the
father of Nadab and Abihu, Eleazar
and Ithamar.[x] 61But Nadab and
Abihu[y] died when they made an
offering before the LORD with un-
authorised fire.)[z]

62All the male Levites a month old or
more numbered 23,000.[a] They were not
counted[b] along with the other Israelites
because they received no inheritance[c]
among them.[d]

63These are the ones counted[e] by
Moses and Eleazar the priest when they
counted the Israelites on the plains of
Moab[f] by the Jordan across from
Jericho.[g] 64Not one of them was among
those counted[h] by Moses and Aaron[i] the
priest when they counted the Israelites
in the Desert of Sinai. 65For the LORD had
told those Israelites they would surely
die in the desert,[j] and not one of them
was left except Caleb[k] son of Jephunneh
and Joshua son of Nun.[l]

Zelophehad's Daughters

27:1–11pp—Nu 36:1–12

27 The daughters of Zelophehad[a]
son of Hepher,[b] the son of
Gilead,[c] the son of Makir,[d] the son
of Manasseh, belonged to the clans of
Manasseh son of Joseph. The names
of the daughters were Mahlah, Noah,
Hoglah, Milcah and Tirzah. They
approached 2the entrance to the Tent of
Meeting[e] and stood before Moses,[f]
Eleazar the priest, the leaders[g] and the
whole assembly, and said, 3"Our father
died in the desert.[h] He was not among
Korah's followers, who banded
together against the LORD,[i] but he died
for his own sin and left no sons.[j] 4Why

40 [c]**Ge 46:21**
41 [d]Nu 1:37
42 [e]Nu 1:38; [f]Jdg 18:19; [g]Ge 46:23
44 [h]**Nu 1:40**
47 [i]Nu 1:41
48 [j]**Ge 30:8**
50 [k]Nu 1:43; [l]Nu 1:42
51 [m]**Ex 12:37**
53 [n]ver 55; Jos 11:23; 14:1; Eze 45:8
54 [o]Nu 33:54; [p]Nu 35:8
55 [q]**Lev 16:8**
57 [r]**Ge 46:11**
58 [s]Ex 6:20
59 [t]**Ex 2:1**; [u]**Ex 6:20**; [v]**Ex 2:4**; [w]**Ex 15:20**
60 [x]Ex 6:23
61 [y]**Lev 10:1–2**; [z]Nu 3:4
62 [a]Nu 3:39; [b]Nu 1:47; [c]**Nu 18:23**; [d]**Nu 2:33**
63 [e]**Nu 1:19**; [f]**ver 3**; [g]Nu 22:1
64 [h]**Nu 14:29**; [i]Nu 1:44
65 [j]Nu 14:28; 1Co 10:5; [k]Nu 13:6; [l]**Nu 11:28**

Ch. 27

1 [a]**Nu 26:33**; [b]Jos 17:2–3; [c]**Nu 26:30**; [d]**Ge 50:23**; 1Ch 2:21
2 [e]Ex 40:2,17; [f]**Nu 9:6**; [g]Nu 1:16; 31:13; 32:2; 36:1
3 [h]Nu 26:65; [i]Nu 16:2; [j]Nu 26:33

[e]40 Samaritan Pentateuch and Vulgate (see also Septuagint); Masoretic Text does not have *through Ard,*
[f]59 Or *Jochebed, a daughter of Levi, who was born to Levi*

should our father's name disappear
from his clan because he had no son?
Give us property among our father's
relatives."
5So Moses brought their case[k] before
the LORD[l] 6and the LORD said to him,
7"What Zelophehad's daughters are
saying is right. You must certainly give
them property as an inheritance[m]
among their father's relatives and give
their father's inheritance over to them.[n]
8"Say to the Israelites, 'If a man dies
and leaves no son, give his inheritance
over to his daughter. 9If he has no
daughter, give his inheritance to his
brothers. 10If he has no brothers, give
his inheritance to his father's brothers.
11If his father had no brothers, give his
inheritance to the nearest relative in his
clan, that he may possess it. This is to be
a legal requirement[o] for the Israelites, as
the LORD commanded Moses.'"

Joshua to Succeed Moses

12Then the LORD said to Moses, "Go
up this mountain[p] in the Abarim Range[q]
and see the land[r] I have given the
Israelites.[s] 13After you have seen it, you
too will be gathered to your people,[t] as
your brother Aaron[u] was, 14for when
the community rebelled at the waters
in the Desert of Zin,[v] both of you
disobeyed my command to honour
me as holy[w] before their eyes." (These
were the waters of Meribah[x] Kadesh,
in the Desert of Zin.)
15Moses said to the LORD, 16"May the
LORD, the God of the spirits of all
mankind,[y] appoint a man over this
community 17to go out and come in
before them, one who will lead them
out and bring them in, so that the
LORD's people will not be like sheep
without a shepherd."[z]
18So the LORD said to Moses, "Take
Joshua son of Nun, a man in whom is
the spirit,[a][a] and lay your hand on him.[b]
19Make him stand before Eleazar the
priest and the entire assembly and com-
mission him[c] in their presence.[d] 20Give
him some of your authority so that the
whole Israelite community will obey
him.[e] 21He is to stand before Eleazar the
priest, who will obtain decisions for him
by enquiring[f] of the Urim[g] before the
LORD. At his command he and the entire
community of the Israelites will go out,
and at his command they will come in."
22Moses did as the LORD commanded
him. He took Joshua and made him
stand before Eleazar the priest and the
whole assembly. 23Then he laid his
hands on him and commissioned him,[h]
as the LORD instructed through Moses.

Daily Offerings

28 The LORD said to Moses, 2"Give
this command to the Israelites
and say to them: 'See that you present to
me at the appointed time[a] the food[b] for
my offerings made by fire, as an aroma
pleasing to me.'[c] 3Say to them: 'This is
the offering made by fire that you are to
present to the LORD: two lambs a year
old without defect,[d] as a regular burnt
offering each day.[e] 4Prepare one lamb in
the morning and the other at twilight,[f]
5together with a grain offering[g] of a
tenth of an ephah[a] of fine flour[h] mixed
with a quarter of a hin[b] of oil[i] from
pressed olives. 6This is the regular burnt
offering[j] instituted at Mount Sinai[k] as a
pleasing aroma, an offering made to the
LORD by fire.[l] 7The accompanying drink
offering[m] is to be a quarter of a hin of
fermented drink[n] with each lamb. Pour
out the drink offering to the LORD at the
sanctuary.[o] 8Prepare the second lamb at
twilight,[p] along with the same kind of
grain offering and drink offering that
you prepare in the morning.[q] This is an
offering made by fire, an aroma
pleasing to the LORD.[r]

Sabbath Offerings

9"'On the Sabbath[s] day, make an
offering of two lambs a year old without
defect,[t] together with its drink offering
and a grain offering of two-tenths of an
ephah[c][u] of fine flour mixed with oil.[v]
10This is the burnt offering for every
Sabbath,[w] in addition to the regular
burnt offering[x] and its drink offering.

Monthly Offerings

11"'On the first of every month,[y] pre-
sent to the LORD a burnt offering of two
young bulls,[z] one ram[a] and seven male
lambs a year old, all without defect.[b]
12With each bull there is to be a grain
offering[c] of three-tenths of an ephah[d][d]
of fine flour mixed with oil; with the
ram, a grain offering of two-tenths[e] of

5 [k]**Ge 25:22**; Ex **18:19**; [l]**Nu 9:8**
7 [m]Job 42:15; [n]ver 8; Jos 17:4
11 [o]Nu 35:29
12 [p]Nu 23:14; [q]Nu 33:47; Jer 22:20; [r]Dt 3:23–27; 32:48–52; [s]**Lev 14:34**
13 [t]Nu 20:12; 31:2; Dt 4:22; 31:14; 32:50; 1Ki 2:1; [u]Nu 20:28
14 [v]**Nu 20:1**,2–5; [w]**Nu 20:12**; [x]**Ex 17:7**
16 [y]**Nu 16:22**; **Job 21:20**
17 [z]1Ki 22:17; 2Ch 18:16; Eze 34:5; Zec 10:2; **Mt 9:36**
18 [a]**Ge 41:38**; Nu 11:25–29; [b]ver 23; Dt 34:9; Ac 6:6
19 [c]ver 23; Dt 3:28; 31:14,23; [d]Dt 31:7
20 [e]Jos 1:16–17
21 [f]**Ge 25:22**; Jos 9:14; Ps 106:13; Isa 8:19; Hag 1:13; Mal 2:7; 3:1; [g]**Ex 28:30**
23 [h]**ver 19**

Ch. 28

2 [a]Lev 23:1–44; [b]**Lev 3:11**; [c]Lev 1:9
3 [d]**Ex 12:5**; [e]Ex 29:38; Am 4:4
4 [f]**Ex 29:39**
5 [g]Nu 29:6; [h]Lev 6:20; [i]**Lev 2:1**
6 [j]Lev 1:3; [k]Ex 19:3; [l]**Lev 1:9**
7 [m]Nu 6:15; [n]**Lev 10:9**; **23:13**; [o]**Lev 3:7**; Nu 3:28
8 [p]**Ex 29:39**; [q]**Lev 3:7**; [r]ver 2; Lev 1:9
9 [s]**Ex 20:10**; Mt 12:5; [t]ver 3; [u]**Lev 23:13**; [v]ver 5
10 [w]**Lev 23:38**; [x]ver 3
11 [y]**Nu 10:10**; [z]**Nu 7:15**; [a]**Lev 5:15**; [b]Lev 1:3
12 [c]**Nu 15:6**; **29:3**; [d]Nu 15:9; [e]ver 20

[a]18 Or *Spirit*
[a]5 That is, probably about 4 pints (about 2 litres); also in verses 13, 21 and 29
[b]5 That is, probably about 1½ pints (about 1 litre); also in verses 7 and 14
[c]9 That is, probably about 7½ pints (about 4.5 litres); also in verses 12, 20 and 28
[d]12 That is, probably about 11½ pints (about 6.5 litres); also in verses 20 and 28

an ephah of fine flour mixed with oil;
13and with each lamb, a grain offering[f]
of a tenth[g] of an ephah of fine flour
mixed with oil. This is for a burnt
offering,[h] a pleasing aroma, an offering
made to the LORD[i] by fire. 14With each
bull there is to be a drink offering[j] of half
a hin[e] of wine; with the ram, a third of a
hin;[f] and with each lamb, a quarter of a
hin. This is the monthly burnt offering
to be made at each new moon[k] during
the year. 15Besides the regular burnt
offering[l] with its drink offering, one
male goat[m] is to be presented to the
LORD as a sin offering.[n]

The Passover

28:16–25pp—Ex 12:14–20; Lev 23:4–8; Dt 16:1–8

16"'On the fourteenth day of the first
month the LORD's Passover[o] is to be
held. 17On the fifteenth day of this
month there is to be a festival; for seven
days[p] eat bread made without yeast.[q]
18On the first day hold a sacred
assembly and do no regular work.[r]
19Present to the LORD an offering made
by fire,[s] a burnt offering of two young
bulls, one ram and seven male lambs a
year old, all without defect.[t] 20With each
bull prepare a grain offering of three-
tenths of an ephah[u] of fine flour mixed
with oil; with the ram, two-tenths;[v]
21and with each of the seven lambs,
one-tenth.[w] 22Include one male goat as a
sin offering[x] to make atonement for
you.[y] 23Prepare these in addition to the
regular morning burnt offering. 24In this
way prepare the food for the offering
made by fire every day for seven days as
an aroma pleasing to the LORD;[z] it is to be
prepared in addition to the regular
burnt offering and its drink offering.
25On the seventh day hold a sacred
assembly and do no regular work.

Feast of Weeks

28:26–31pp—Lev 23:15–22; Dt 16:9–12

26"'On the day of firstfruits,[a] when
you present to the LORD an offering of
new grain during the Feast of Weeks,[b]
hold a sacred assembly and do no regu-
lar work.[c] 27Present a burnt offering of
two young bulls, one ram and seven
male lambs a year old as an aroma
pleasing to the LORD.[d] 28With each bull
there is to be a grain offering of three-
tenths of an ephah of fine flour mixed
with oil; with the ram, two-tenths;[e]
29and with each of the seven lambs,
one-tenth.[f] 30Include one male goat[g] to
make atonement for you. 31Prepare
these together with their drink offer-
ings, in addition to the regular burnt
offering[h] and its grain offering. Be sure
the animals are without defect.

Feast of Trumpets

29:1–6pp—Lev 23:23–25

29 "'On the first day of the
seventh month hold a sacred
assembly and do no regular work.[a] It is a
day for you to sound the trumpets. 2As
an aroma pleasing to the LORD,[b] prepare
a burnt offering[c] of one young bull, one
ram and seven male lambs a year old,[d]
all without defect.[e] 3With the bull pre-
pare a grain offering[f] of three-tenths of
an ephah[a] of fine flour mixed with oil;
with the ram, two-tenths;[b] 4and with
each of the seven lambs, one-tenth.[c][g]
5Include one male goat[h] as a sin offering
to make atonement for you. 6These are
in addition to the monthly[i] and daily
burnt offerings[j] with their grain offer-
ings[k] and drink offerings[l] as specified.
They are offerings made to the LORD by
fire—a pleasing aroma.[m]

Day of Atonement

29:7–11pp—Lev 16:2–34; 23:26–32

7"'On the tenth day of this seventh
month hold a sacred assembly. You
must deny yourselves[d][n] and do no
work.[o] 8Present as an aroma pleasing to
the LORD a burnt offering of one young
bull, one ram and seven male lambs a
year old, all without defect.[p] 9With the
bull prepare a grain offering[q] of three-
tenths of an ephah of fine flour mixed
with oil; with the ram, two-tenths;[r]
10and with each of the seven lambs,
one-tenth.[s] 11Include one male goat[t] as a
sin offering, in addition to the sin
offering for atonement and the regular
burnt offering[u] with its grain offering,
and their drink offerings.[v]

Feast of Tabernacles

29:12–39pp—Lev 23:33–43; Dt 16:13–17

12"'On the fifteenth day of the
seventh[w] month,[x] hold a sacred assem-
bly and do no regular work. Celebrate a

13 [f]**Lev 6:14;** [g]ver 21; [h]**Nu 15:3;** [i]Lev 1:9
14 [j]**Nu 15:7;** [k]ver 11; 2Ch 2:4; Ezr 3:5
15 [l]ver 3,23–24, [m]ver 30; [n]Lev 4:3; Nu 29:16,19
16 [o]**Ex 12:11;** 2Ch 30:13; 35:1
17 [p]**Ex 12:19;** [q]**Ex 12:15**
18 [r]**Ex 12:16**
19 [s]**Lev 1:9;** [t]ver 11
20 [u]**Lev 14:10;** [v]ver 12
21 [w]ver 13
22 [x]Lev 4:3; Ro 8:3; [y]**Nu 15:28**
24 [z]Lev 1:9
26 [a]**Ex 34:22;** [b]**Ex 23:16;** [c]ver 18
27 [d]ver 19
28 [e]ver 12
29 [f]ver 13
30 [g]ver 15
31 [h]ver 3,19

Ch. 29

1 [a]Nu 28:18
2 [b]Nu 28:2; [c]Lev 1:9; Nu 28:11; [d]ver 36; [e]Lev 1:3; Nu 28:3
3 [f]ver 14; Nu 28:12
4 [g]Nu 28:13
5 [h]Nu 28:15
6 [i]Nu 28:11; [j]Nu 28:3; [k]Nu 28:5; [l]Nu 28:7; [m]Lev 1:9; Nu 28:2
7 [n]Ac 27:9; [o]**Ex 31:15**
8 [p]ver 2
9 [q]**ver 3**,18; [r]Nu 28:12
10 [s]Nu 28:13
11 [t]ver 5; Nu 28:15; [u]**Lev 16:3;** [v]**ver 6**
12 [w]1Ki 8:2; 12:32; [x]**Lev 23:24**

[e]*14* That is, probably about 3 pints (about 2 litres)
[f]*14* That is, probably about 2¼ pints (about 1.2 litres)
[a]*3* That is, probably about 11½ pints (about 6.5 litres); also in verses 9 and 14
[b]*3* That is, probably about 7½ pints (about 4.5 litres); also in verses 9 and 14
[c]*4* That is, probably about 4 pints (about 2 litres); also in verses 10 and 15
[d]*7* Or *must fast*

festival to the LORD for seven days.
13Present an offering made by fire as an
aroma pleasing to the LORD,[y] a burnt
offering of thirteen young bulls, two
rams and fourteen male lambs a year
old, all without defect.[z] 14With each of
the thirteen bulls prepare a grain
offering[a] of three-tenths of an ephah
of fine flour mixed with oil; with each
of the two rams, two-tenths; 15and
with each of the fourteen lambs,
one-tenth.[b] 16Include one male goat as a
sin offering,[c] in addition to the regular
burnt offering with its grain offering
and drink offering.[d]

17" 'On the second day[e] prepare
twelve young bulls, two rams and four-
teen male lambs a year old, all without
defect.[f] 18With the bulls, rams and
lambs, prepare their grain offerings[g]
and drink offerings[h] according to the
number specified.[i] 19Include one male
goat as a sin offering,[j] in addition to the
regular burnt offering[k] with its grain
offering, and their drink offerings.[l]

20" 'On the third day prepare eleven
bulls, two rams and fourteen male
lambs a year old, all without defect.[m]
21With the bulls, rams and lambs,
prepare their grain offerings and drink
offerings according to the number
specified.[n] 22Include one male goat as
a sin offering, in addition to the regular
burnt offering with its grain offering
and drink offering.

23" 'On the fourth day prepare ten
bulls, two rams and fourteen male
lambs a year old, all without defect.
24With the bulls, rams and lambs,
prepare their grain offerings and drink
offerings according to the number
specified. 25Include one male goat as
a sin offering, in addition to the regular
burnt offering with its grain offering
and drink offering.

26" 'On the fifth day prepare nine
bulls, two rams and fourteen male
lambs a year old, all without defect.
27With the bulls, rams and lambs,
prepare their grain offerings and drink
offerings according to the number
specified. 28Include one male goat as
a sin offering, in addition to the regular
burnt offering with its grain offering
and drink offering.

29" 'On the sixth day prepare eight
bulls, two rams and fourteen male
lambs a year old, all without defect.
30With the bulls, rams and lambs,
prepare their grain offerings and drink
offerings according to the number
specified. 31Include one male goat as
a sin offering, in addition to the regular
burnt offering with its grain offering
and drink offering.

32" 'On the seventh day prepare seven
bulls, two rams and fourteen male
lambs a year old, all without defect.
33With the bulls, rams and lambs,
prepare their grain offerings and drink
offerings according to the number
specified. 34Include one male goat as
a sin offering, in addition to the regular
burnt offering with its grain offering
and drink offering.

35" 'On the eighth day hold an
assembly[o] and do no regular work.
36Present an offering made by fire as
an aroma pleasing to the LORD,[p] a burnt
offering of one bull, one ram and seven
male lambs a year old,[q] all without
defect. 37With the bull, the ram and
the lambs, prepare their grain offerings
and drink offerings according to the
number specified. 38Include one male
goat as a sin offering, in addition to the
regular burnt offering with its grain
offering and drink offering.

39" 'In addition to what you vow[r]
and your freewill offerings,[s] prepare
these for the LORD at your appointed
feasts:[t] your burnt offerings,[u] grain
offerings, drink offerings and fellow-
ship offerings.' "[e][v]

40Moses told the Israelites all that the
LORD commanded him.

Vows

30 Moses said to the heads of the
tribes of Israel:[a] "This is what
the LORD commands: 2When a man
makes a vow to the LORD or takes an
oath to bind himself by a pledge, he
must not break his word but must do
everything he said.[b]

3"When a young woman still living in
her father's house makes a vow to the
LORD or binds herself by a pledge 4and
her father hears about her vow or
pledge but says nothing to her, then all
her vows and every pledge by which
she bound herself will stand.[c] 5But if her
father forbids her[d] when he hears about
it, none of her vows or the pledges by
which she bound herself will stand; the
LORD will release her because her father
has forbidden her.

6"If she marries after she makes a
vow[e] or after her lips utter a rash
promise by which she binds herself
7and her husband hears about it but
says nothing to her, then her vows or

13 [y]ver 2; Nu 28:2; [z]Nu 28:3
14 [a]**ver 3; Nu 15:6**
15 [b]ver 4; Nu 28:13
16 [c]ver 5; **Nu 28:15**; [d]ver 6
17 [e]Lev 23:36; [f]ver 2; Nu 28:3
18 [g]**ver 9**; [h]Nu 28:7; [i]Nu 15:4–12
19 [j]**Nu 28:15**; [k]Nu 28:3; [l]ver 6
20 [m]**ver 17**
21 [n]**ver 18**
35 [o]**Lev 23:36**
36 [p]Lev 1:9; [q]ver 2
39 [r]Nu 6:2; [s]**Lev 7:16**; [t]**Lev 23:2**; [u]Lev 1:3; 1Ch 23:31; 2Ch 31:3; [v]Lev 3:1

Ch. 30

1 [a]**Nu 1:4**
2 [b]Dt 23:21–23; Jdg 11:35; Job 22:27; Ps 22:25; 50:14; 61:5,8; 76:11; 116:14; Pr 20:25; Ecc 5:4–5; Isa 19:21; Jnh 1:16; 2:9
4 [c]ver 7
5 [d]ver 8,12,15
6 [e]**Lev 5:4**

[e]39 Traditionally *peace offerings*

the pledges by which she bound herself will stand. 8But if her husband[f] forbids her when he hears about it, he nullifies the vow that binds her or the rash promise by which she binds herself, and the LORD will release her.[g]

9"Any vow or obligation taken by a widow or divorced woman will be binding on her.

10"If a woman living with her husband makes a vow or binds herself by a pledge under oath 11and her husband hears about it but says nothing to her and does not forbid her, then all her vows or the pledges by which she bound herself will stand. 12But if her husband nullifies them when he hears about them, then none of the vows or pledges that came from her lips will stand.[h] Her husband has nullified them, and the LORD will release her. 13Her husband may confirm or nullify any vow she makes or any sworn pledge to deny herself. 14But if her husband says nothing to her about it from day to day, then he confirms all her vows or the pledges binding on her. He confirms them by saying nothing to her when he hears about them. 15If, however, he nullifies them[i] some time after he hears about them, then he is responsible for her guilt."

16These are the regulations the LORD gave Moses concerning relationships between a man and his wife, and between a father and his young daughter still living in his house.

Vengeance on the Midianites

31 The LORD said to Moses, 2"Take vengeance on the Midianites[a] for the Israelites. After that, you will be gathered to your people.[b]"

3So Moses said to the people, "Arm some of your men to go to war against the Midianites and to carry out the LORD's vengeance[c] on them. 4Send into battle a thousand men from each of the tribes of Israel." 5So twelve thousand men armed for battle,[d] a thousand from each tribe, were supplied from the clans of Israel. 6Moses sent them into battle,[e] a thousand from each tribe, along with Phinehas[f] son of Eleazar, the priest, who took with him articles from the sanctuary[g] and the trumpets[h] for signalling.

7They fought against Midian, as the LORD commanded Moses,[i] and killed every man.[j] 8Among their victims were Evi, Rekem, Zur, Hur and Reba[k]—the five kings of Midian.[l] They also killed Balaam son of Beor[m] with the sword.[n] 9The Israelites captured the Midianite women[o] and children and took all the Midianite herds, flocks and goods as plunder.[p] 10They burned[q] all the towns where the Midianites had settled, as well as all their camps.[r] 11They took all the plunder and spoils, including the people and animals,[s] 12and brought the captives, spoils[t] and plunder to Moses and Eleazar the priest and the Israelite assembly[u] at their camp on the plains of Moab, by the Jordan across from Jericho.[a][v]

13Moses, Eleazar the priest and all the leaders of the community went to meet them outside the camp. 14Moses was angry with the officers of the army[w]—the commanders of thousands and commanders of hundreds—who returned from the battle.

15"Have you allowed all the women to live?" he asked them. 16"They were the ones who followed Balaam's advice[x] and were the means of turning the Israelites away from the LORD in what happened at Peor,[y] so that a plague[z] struck the LORD's people. 17Now kill all the boys. And kill every woman who has slept with a man,[a] 18but save for yourselves every girl who has never slept with a man.

19"All of you who have killed anyone or touched anyone who was killed[b] must stay outside the camp seven days.[c] On the third and seventh days you must purify yourselves[d] and your captives. 20Purify every garment[e] as well as everything made of leather, goat hair or wood.[f]"

21Then Eleazar the priest said to the soldiers who had gone into battle,[g] "This is the requirement of the law that the LORD gave Moses: 22Gold, silver, bronze, iron,[h] tin, lead 23and anything else that can withstand fire must be put through the fire,[i] and then it will be clean. But it must also be purified with the water of cleansing.[j] And whatever cannot withstand fire must be put through that water. 24On the seventh day wash your clothes and you will be clean.[k] Then you may come into the camp.[l]"

Dividing the Spoils

25The LORD said to Moses, 26"You and Eleazar the priest and the family heads[m] of the community are to count

[a]12 Hebrew *Jordan of Jericho;* possibly an ancient name for the Jordan River

8 [f]**Ge 3:6;** [g]ver 5
12 [h]Eph 5:22; Col 3:18
15 [i]**ver 5**

Ch. 31

2 [a]**Ge 25:2;** [b]**Nu 20:26**
3 [c]Jdg 11:36; 1Sa 24:12; 2Sa 4:8; 22:48; Ps 94:1; 149:7; Isa 34:8; Jer 11:20; 46:10; Eze 25:17
5 [d]ver 6,21
6 [e]**ver 5;** [f]**Ex 6:25;** [g]Nu 14:44; [h]**Nu 10:2**
7 [i]Nu 25:16; [j]Dt 20:13; Jdg 21:11; 1Ki 11:15–16
8 [k]Jos 13:21; [l]**Nu 25:15;** [m]**Nu 22:5; 24:14;** [n]Jos 13:22
9 [o]ver 15; [p]**Ge 34:29**
10 [q]Jos 6:24; 8:28; 11:11; Jdg 18:27; [r]Ge 25:16; 1Ch 6:54; Ps 69:25; Eze 25:4
11 [s]ver 26; Dt 20:14; 2Ch 28:8
12 [t]ver 32,53; Ge 49:27; Ex 15:9; [u]**Nu 27:2;** [v]Nu 22:1
14 [w]ver 48; Ex 18:21; Dt 1:15; 2Sa 18:1
16 [x]**Nu 22:5; 24:14; 2Pe 2:15;** [y]**Nu 23:28;** 25:1–9; [z]**Nu 14:37**
17 [a]Dt 7:2; 20:16–18; Jdg 21:11
19 [b]Nu 19:16; [c]**Lev 21:1;** [d]Nu 19:12
20 [e]Nu 19:19; [f]**Lev 11:32**
21 [g]**ver 5**
22 [h]Jos 6:19; 22:8
23 [i]**1Co 3:13;** [j]**Nu 8:7**
24 [k]**Lev 11:25;** [l]**Lev 14:8**
26 [m]**Nu 1:4**

all the people[n] and animals that were captured.[o] 27Divide[p] the spoils between the soldiers who took part in the battle and the rest of the community. 28From the soldiers who fought in the battle, set apart as tribute for the LORD[q] one out of every five hundred, whether persons, cattle, donkeys, sheep or goats. 29Take this tribute from their half share and give it to Eleazar the priest as the LORD's part. 30From the Israelites' half, select one out of every fifty, whether persons, cattle, donkeys, sheep, goats or other animals. Give them to the Levites, who are responsible for the care of the LORD's tabernacle."[r] 31So Moses and Eleazar the priest did as the LORD commanded Moses.

32The plunder remaining from the spoils[s] that the soldiers took was 675,000 sheep, 3372,000 cattle, 3461,000 donkeys 35and 32,000 women who had never slept with a man.

36The half share of those who fought in the battle was:

> 337,500 sheep, 37of which the tribute for the LORD[t] was 675;
> 3836,000 cattle, of which the tribute for the LORD was 72;
> 3930,500 donkeys, of which the tribute for the LORD was 61;
> 4016,000 people, of which the tribute for the LORD was 32.

41Moses gave the tribute to Eleazar the priest as the LORD's part,[u] as the LORD commanded Moses.[v]

42The half belonging to the Israelites, which Moses set apart from that of the fighting men— 43the community's half —was 337,500 sheep, 4436,000 cattle, 4530,500 donkeys 46and 16,000 people. 47From the Israelites' half, Moses selected one out of every fifty persons and animals, as the LORD commanded him, and gave them to the Levites, who were responsible for the care of the LORD's tabernacle.

48Then the officers[w] who were over the units of the army—the commanders of thousands and commanders of hundreds—went to Moses 49and said to him, "Your servants have counted[x] the soldiers under our command, and not one is missing.[y] 50So we have brought as an offering to the LORD the gold articles each of us acquired—armlets, bracelets, signet rings, ear-rings and necklaces—to make atonement for ourselves[z] before the LORD."

51Moses and Eleazar the priest accepted from them the gold—all the handcrafted articles. 52All the gold from the commanders of thousands and commanders of hundreds that Moses and Eleazar presented as a gift to the LORD weighed 16,750 shekels.[b] 53Each soldier had taken plunder[a] for himself. 54Moses and Eleazar the priest accepted the gold from the commanders of thousands and commanders of hundreds and brought it into the Tent of Meeting[b] as a memorial[c] for the Israelites before the LORD.

The Transjordan Tribes

32 The Reubenites and Gadites, who had very large herds and flocks,[a] saw that the lands of Jazer[b] and Gilead[c] were suitable for livestock.[d] 2So they came to Moses and Eleazar the priest and to the leaders of the community,[e] and said, 3"Ataroth,[f] Dibon,[g] Jazer,[h] Nimrah,[i] Heshbon,[j] Elealeh,[k] Sebam,[l] Nebo[m] and Beon[n]—4the land the LORD subdued[o] before the people of Israel—are suitable for livestock,[p] and your servants have livestock. 5If we have found favour in your eyes," they said, "let this land be given to your servants as our possession. Do not make us cross the Jordan.[q]"

6Moses said to the Gadites and Reubenites, "Shall your countrymen go to war while you sit here? 7Why do you discourage the Israelites from going over into the land the LORD has given them?[r] 8This is what your fathers did when I sent them from Kadesh Barnea to look over the land.[s] 9After they went up to the Valley of Eshcol[t] and viewed the land, they discouraged the Israelites from entering the land the LORD had given them. 10The LORD's anger was aroused[u] that day and he swore this oath:[v] 11'Because they have not followed me wholeheartedly, not one of the men twenty years old or more[w] who came up out of Egypt[x] will see the land I promised on oath[y] to Abraham, Isaac and Jacob[z]—12not one except Caleb son of Jephunneh the Kenizzite and Joshua son of Nun, for they followed the LORD wholeheartedly.'[a] 13The LORD's anger burned against Israel[b] and he made them wander in the desert for forty years, until the whole generation of those who had done evil in his sight was gone.[c]

14"And here you are, a brood of sinners, standing in the place of your fathers and making the LORD even more angry with Israel.[d] 15If you turn away

26 [n]**Nu 1:19;** [o]**ver 11–12**
27 [p]Jos 22:8; 1Sa 25:13; 30:24
28 [q]ver 37–41; **Nu 18:21**
30 [r]Nu 3:7; 18:3
32 [s]**ver 12**
37 [t]ver 38–41
41 [u]Nu 5:9; 18:8; [v]ver 21,28
48 [w]**ver 14**
49 [x]**Nu 1:19;** [y]Jer 23:4
50 [z]**Ex 30:16**
53 [a]**Ge 34:29;** Dt 20:14
54 [b]**Ex 27:21;** 40:2; [c]**Ex 28:12**

Ch. 32

1 [a]ver 24,36; Jdg 5:16; [b]**Nu 21:32;** [c]**Ge 31:21;** [d]Ex 12:38
2 [e]Lev 4:22; Nu 27:2
3 [f]ver 34; Jos 16:2,7; 18:13; [g]ver 34; **Nu 21:30;** [h]ver 1; [i]ver 36; Jos 13:27; [j]Nu 21:25; [k]ver 37; Isa 15:4; 16:9; Jer 48:34; [l]Jos 13:19; Isa 16:8–9; Jer 48:32; [m]Nu 33:47; Dt 32:49; 34:1; 1Ch 5:8; [n]ver 38; Jos 13:17; Eze 25:9
4 [o]Nu 21:34; [p]Ex 12:38
5 [q]**Nu 13:29**
7 [r]Nu 13:27–14:4
8 [s]Nu 13:3,26; Dt 1:19–25
9 [t]Nu 13:23; Dt 1:24
10 [u]Nu 11:1; [v]**Nu 14:20–23**
11 [w]**Ex 30:14;** [x]Nu 1:1; [y]**Nu 14:23;** [z]Nu 14:28–30
12 [a]Nu 14:24,30; Ps 63:8
13 [b]**Ex 4:14;** [c]Nu 14:28–35; 26:64–65
14 [d]**ver 10;** Dt 1:34; Ps 78:59

b52 That is, about 420 pounds (about 190 kilograms)

from following him, he will again leave all this people in the desert, and you will be the cause of their destruction.[e]"

16Then they came up to him and said, "We would like to build pens[f] here for our livestock[g] and cities for our women and children. 17But we are ready to arm ourselves and go ahead of the Israelites[h] until we have brought them to their place.[i] Meanwhile our women and children will live in fortified cities, for protection from the inhabitants of the land. 18We will not return to our homes until every Israelite has received his inheritance.[j] 19We will not receive any inheritance with them on the other side of the Jordan, because our inheritance[k] has come to us on the east side of the Jordan."[l]

20Then Moses said to them, "If you will do this—if you will arm yourselves before the LORD for battle,[m] 21and if all of you will go armed over the Jordan before the LORD until he has driven his enemies out before him[n]—22then when the land is subdued before the LORD, you may return[o] and be free from your obligation to the LORD and to Israel. And this land will be your possession[p] before the LORD.[q]

23"But if you fail to do this, you will be sinning against the LORD; and you may be sure that your sin will find you out.[r] 24Build cities for your women and children, and pens for your flocks,[s] but do what you have promised.[t]"

25The Gadites and Reubenites said to Moses, "We your servants will do as our lord commands.[u] 26Our children and wives, our flocks and herds will remain here in the cities of Gilead.[v] 27But your servants, every man armed for battle, will cross over to fight[w] before the LORD, just as our lord says."

28Then Moses gave orders about them[x] to Eleazar the priest and Joshua son of Nun[y] and to the family heads of the Israelite tribes.[z] 29He said to them, "If the Gadites and Reubenites, every man armed for battle, cross over the Jordan with you before the LORD, then when the land is subdued before you,[a] give them the land of Gilead as their possession.[b] 30But if they do not cross over[c] with you armed, they must accept their possession with you in Canaan.[d]"

31The Gadites and Reubenites answered, "Your servants will do what the LORD has said.[e] 32We will cross over before the LORD into Canaan armed,[f] but the property we inherit will be on this side of the Jordan.[g]"

33Then Moses gave to the Gadites,[h] the Reubenites and the half-tribe of Manasseh[i] son of Joseph the kingdom of Sihon king of the Amorites[j] and the kingdom of Og king of Bashan[k]—the whole land with its cities and the territory around them.[l]

34The Gadites built up Dibon, Ataroth, Aroer,[m] 35Atroth Shophan, Jazer,[n] Jogbehah,[o] 36Beth Nimrah[p] and Beth Haran as fortified cities, and built pens for their flocks.[q] 37And the Reubenites rebuilt Heshbon,[r] Elealeh[s] and Kiriathaim,[t] 38as well as Nebo[u] and Baal Meon (these names were changed) and Sibmah.[v] They gave names to the cities they rebuilt.

39The descendants of Makir[w] son of Manasseh went to Gilead,[x] captured it and drove out the Amorites[y] who were there. 40So Moses gave Gilead to the Makirites,[z] the descendants of Manasseh, and they settled there. 41Jair,[a] a descendant of Manasseh, captured their settlements and called them Havvoth Jair.**[a]**[b] 42And Nobah captured Kenath[c] and its surrounding settlements and called it Nobah[d] after himself.[e]

Stages in Israel's Journey

33 Here are the stages in the journey[a] of the Israelites when they came out of Egypt[b] by divisions under the leadership of Moses and Aaron.[c] 2At the LORD's command Moses recorded[d] the stages in their journey.[e] This is their journey by stages:

3The Israelites set out[f] from Rameses[g] on the fifteenth day of the first month, the day after the Passover.[h] They marched out boldly[i] in full view of all the Egyptians, 4who were burying all their firstborn,[j] whom the LORD had struck down among them; for the LORD had brought judgment[k] on their gods.[l]

5The Israelites left Rameses and camped at Succoth.[m]

6They left Succoth and camped at Etham, on the edge of the desert.[n]

7They left Etham, turned back to Pi Hahiroth, to the east of Baal

15 [e]Dt 30:17–18; 2Ch 7:20
16 [f]ver 24,36; 1Sa 24:3; Ps 50:9; 78:70; [g]Ex 12:38; Dt 3:19
17 [h]Dt 3:18; Jos 4:12–13; [i]**Nu 22:4**; Dt 3:20
18 [j]Jos 22:1–4
19 [k]ver 22,29; [l]Nu 21:33; Jos 12:1; 22:7
20 [m]ver 17
21 [n]ver 17
22 [o]Jos 22:4; [p]**Lev 14:34**; [q]Dt 3:18–20
23 [r]**Ge 4:7; Isa 3:9**
24 [s]**ver 1**,16; [t]Nu 30:2
25 [u]ver 29; Jos 1:16,18; 22:2
26 [v]ver 16,24; Jos 1:14; 12:2; 22:9; 2Sa 2:9; 1Ch 5:9
27 [w]ver 17,21
28 [x]ver 29; Dt 3:18–20; Jos 1:13; [y]Nu 11:28; [z]Nu 1:16
29 [a]**Nu 22:4**; [b]**ver 19**
30 [c]ver 23; [d]ver 29,32
31 [e]ver 29
32 [f]ver 17; [g]**ver 30**; Jos 12:6
33 [h]Jos 13:24–28; 1Sa 13:7; [i]Jos 1:12; [j]Nu 21:21; Dt 2:26; [k]**ver 19; Jos 12:5**; [l]**Nu 21:24**; 34:14; Dt 2:36; Jos 12:6
34 [m]Dt 2:36; 3:12; 4:48; Jos 12:2; 13:9; Jdg 11:26; 1Sa 30:28; 1Ch 5:8; Jer 48:19
35 [n]ver 3; [o]Jdg 8:11
36 [p]**ver 3**; [q]**ver 1**
37 [r]Nu 21:25; [s]**ver 3**; [t]Jos 13:19; 1Ch 6:76; Jer 48:1, 23; Eze 25:9
38 [u]**ver 3**; Isa 15:2; Jer 48:1, 22; [v]**ver 3**
39 [w]**Ge 50:23**; [x]Nu 26:29; Dt 2:36; [y]**Ge 10:16**
40 [z]**Ge 50:23**; Dt 3:15
41 [a]1Ki 4:13; [b]Dt 3:14; Jos 13:30; Jdg 10:4; 1Ch 2:23
42 [c]1Ch 2:23; [d]Jdg 8:11; [e]1Sa 15:12; 2Sa 18:18; Ps 49:11; Isa 22:16; 56:5

Ch. 33
1 [a]Ex 17:1; 40:36; [b]Nu 1:1; [c]**Ex 4:16**; 6:26
2 [d]**Ex 17:14**; [e]**ver 1**
3 [f]Nu 10:2; [g]**Ge 47:11**; [h]Jos 5:10; [i]**Ex 14:8**
4 [j]**Ex 4:23**; [k]2Ch 24:24; Jer 15:3; Eze 14:21; [l]**Ex 12:12**
5 [m]Ex 12:37 *6* [n]Ex 13:20

[a]41 Or *them the settlements of Jair*

Zephon,[o] and camped near
Migdol.[p]
8They left Pi Hahiroth[a][q] and
passed through the sea[r] into the
desert, and when they had
travelled for three days in the
Desert of Etham, they camped at
Marah.[s]
9They left Marah and went to
Elim, where there were twelve
springs and seventy palm trees,
and they camped[t] there.
10They left Elim[u] and camped by
the Red Sea.[b]
11They left the Red Sea and
camped in the Desert of Sin.[v]
12They left the Desert of Sin and
camped at Dophkah.
13They left Dophkah and camped
at Alush.
14They left Alush and camped at
Rephidim, where there was no
water for the people to drink.[w]
15They left Rephidim[x] and
camped in the Desert of Sinai.[y]
16They left the Desert of Sinai and
camped at Kibroth Hattaavah.[z]
17They left Kibroth Hattaavah
and camped at Hazeroth.[a]
18They left Hazeroth and camped
at Rithmah.
19They left Rithmah and camped
at Rimmon Perez.
20They left Rimmon Perez and
camped at Libnah.[b]
21They left Libnah and camped at
Rissah.
22They left Rissah and camped at
Kehelathah.
23They left Kehelathah and
camped at Mount Shepher.
24They left Mount Shepher and
camped at Haradah.
25They left Haradah and camped
at Makheloth.
26They left Makheloth and
camped at Tahath.
27They left Tahath and camped at
Terah.
28They left Terah and camped at
Mithcah.
29They left Mithcah and camped
at Hashmonah.
30They left Hashmonah and
camped at Moseroth.[c]
31They left Moseroth and camped
at Bene Jaakan.[d]
32They left Bene Jaakan and
camped at Hor Haggidgad.
33They left Hor Haggidgad and
camped at Jotbathah.[e]
34They left Jotbathah and camped
at Abronah.
35They left Abronah and camped
at Ezion Geber.[f]
36They left Ezion Geber and
camped at Kadesh, in the Desert of
Zin.[g]
37They left Kadesh and camped
at Mount Hor,[h] on the border of
Edom.[i] 38At the LORD's command
Aaron the priest went up Mount
Hor, where he died[j] on the first day
of the fifth month of the fortieth
year[k] after the Israelites came out of
Egypt.[l] 39Aaron was a hundred and
twenty-three years old when he
died on Mount Hor.
40The Canaanite king[m] of Arad,[n]
who lived in the Negev[o] of Canaan,
heard that the Israelites were
coming.
41They left Mount Hor and
camped at Zalmonah.
42They left Zalmonah and
camped at Punon.
43They left Punon and camped at
Oboth.[p]
44They left Oboth and camped at
Iye Abarim, on the border of
Moab.[q]
45They left Iyim[c] and camped at
Dibon Gad.
46They left Dibon Gad and
camped at Almon Diblathaim.
47They left Almon Diblathaim
and camped in the mountains of
Abarim,[r] near Nebo.[s]
48They left the mountains of
Abarim[t] and camped on the plains
of Moab[u] by the Jordan[v] across from
Jericho.[d][w] 49There on the plains of
Moab they camped along the
Jordan from Beth Jeshimoth[x] to
Abel Shittim.[y]

50On the plains of Moab by the Jordan
across from Jericho[z] the LORD said to
Moses, 51"Speak to the Israelites and
say to them: 'When you cross the
Jordan into Canaan,[a] 52drive out all the
inhabitants of the land before you.
Destroy all their carved images and
their cast idols, and demolish all their
high places.[b] 53Take possession of the
land and settle in it, for I have given you
the land to possess.[c] 54Distribute the
land by lot,[d] according to your clans.[e] To

7 [o]Ex 14:9; [p]**Ex 14:2**
8 [q]Ex 14:2; [r]**Ex 14:22**; [s]**Ex 15:23**
9 [t]Ex 15:27
10 [u]Ex 16:1
11 [v]**Ex 16:1**
14 [w]**Ex 15:22; 17:2**
15 [x]**Ex 17:1**; [y]**Ex 19:1**
16 [z]**Nu 11:34**
17 [a]Nu 11:35
20 [b]Jos 10:29; 12:15; 15:42; 21:13; 2Ki 8:22; 19:8; 23:31; 1Ch 6:57; 2Ch 21:10; Isa 37:8; Jer 52:1
30 [c]Dt 10:6
31 [d]Dt 10:6
33 [e]Dt 10:7
35 [f]Dt 2:8; 1Ki 9:26; 22:48
36 [g]**Nu 13:21**
37 [h]**Nu 20:22**; [i]**Ge 36:16; Nu 20:16**
38 [j]**Nu 27:13**; [k]**Ex 16:35**; [l]Nu 20:25–28
40 [m]**Ge 10:18**; [n]**Nu 21:1**; [o]**Ge 12:9**
43 [p]Nu 21:10
44 [q]**Nu 21:11**
47 [r]Nu 27:12; [s]Nu 32:3
48 [t]Nu 27:12; [u]**Nu 26:3**; [v]**Ge 13:10**; [w]Nu 22:1; Jos 12:9
49 [x]Jos 12:3; 13:20; Eze 25:9; [y]**Nu 21:16**
50 [z]ver 48
51 [a]Nu 34:2; Jos 3:17
52 [b]**Lev 26:1**; Ps 106:34–36
53 [c]Dt 11:31; 17:14; Jos 1:11; 21:43
54 [d]**Lev 16:8**; Nu 36:2; [e]Nu 26:54

[a]8 Many manuscripts of the Masoretic Text, Samaritan Pentateuch and Vulgate; most manuscripts of the Masoretic Text *left from before Hahiroth*
[b]10 Hebrew *Yam Suph*; that is, Sea of Reeds; also in verse 11
[c]45 That is, Iye Abarim
[d]48 Hebrew *Jordan of Jericho*; possibly an ancient name for the Jordan River; also in verse 50

a larger group give a larger inheritance, and to a smaller group a smaller one.[f] Whatever falls to them by lot will be theirs. Distribute it according to your ancestral tribes.[g]

55" 'But if you do not drive out the inhabitants of the land, those you allow to remain will become barbs in your eyes and thorns[h] in your sides. They will give you trouble in the land where you will live. 56And then I will do to you what I plan to do to them.[i]' "

Boundaries of Canaan

34 The LORD said to Moses, 2"Command the Israelites and say to them: 'When you enter Canaan,[a] the land that will be allotted to you as an inheritance[b] will have these boundaries:[c]

3" 'Your southern side will include some of the Desert of Zin[d] along the border of Edom. On the east, your southern boundary will start from the end of the Salt Sea,[a][e] 4cross south of Scorpion[b] Pass,[f] continue on to Zin and go south of Kadesh Barnea.[g] Then it will go to Hazar Addar and over to Azmon,[h] 5where it will turn, join the Wadi of Egypt[i] and end at the Sea.[c]

6" 'Your western boundary will be the coast of the Great Sea.[j] This will be your boundary on the west.[k]

7" 'For your northern boundary,[l] run a line from the Great Sea to Mount Hor[m] 8and from Mount Hor to Lebo[d] Hamath.[n] Then the boundary will go to Zedad, 9continue to Ziphron and end at Hazar Enan. This will be your boundary on the north.

10" 'For your eastern boundary,[o] run a line from Hazar Enan to Shepham. 11The boundary will go down from Shepham to Riblah[p] on the east side of Ain[q] and continue along the slopes east of the Sea of Kinnereth.[e][r] 12Then the boundary will go down along the Jordan and end at the Salt Sea.

" 'This will be your land, with its boundaries on every side.' "

13Moses commanded the Israelites: "Assign this land by lot[s] as an inheritance.[t] The LORD has ordered that it be given to the nine and a half tribes, 14because the families of the tribe of Reuben, the tribe of Gad and the half-tribe of Manasseh have received their inheritance.[u] 15These two and a half tribes have received their inheritance on the east side of the Jordan of Jericho,[f] towards the sunrise."

16The LORD said to Moses, 17"These are the names of the men who are to assign the land for you as an inheritance: Eleazar the priest and Joshua[v] son of Nun. 18And appoint one leader from each tribe to help[w] assign the land.[x] 19These are their names:[y]

Caleb[z] son of Jephunneh,
from the tribe of Judah;[a]
20Shemuel son of Ammihud,
from the tribe of Simeon;[b]
21Elidad son of Kislon,
from the tribe of Benjamin;[c]
22Bukki son of Jogli,
the leader from the tribe of Dan;
23Hanniel son of Ephod,
the leader from the tribe of Manasseh[d] son of Joseph;
24Kemuel son of Shiphtan,
the leader from the tribe of Ephraim[e] son of Joseph;
25Elizaphan son of Parnach,
the leader from the tribe of Zebulun;[f]
26Paltiel son of Azzan,
the leader from the tribe of Issachar;
27Ahihud son of Shelomi,
the leader from the tribe of Asher;[g]
28Pedahel son of Ammihud,
the leader from the tribe of Naphtali."

29These are the men the LORD commanded to assign the inheritance to the Israelites in the land of Canaan.[h]

Towns for the Levites

35 On the plains of Moab by the Jordan across from Jericho,[a][a] the LORD said to Moses, 2"Command the Israelites to give the Levites towns to live in[b] from the inheritance the Israelites will possess. And give them pasture-lands[c] around the towns. 3Then they will have towns to live in and pasture-lands for their cattle, flocks and all their other livestock.[d]

4"The pasture-lands around the towns that you give the Levites will extend out fifteen hundred feet[b] from the town wall. 5Outside the town,

54 [f]Nu 35:8; [g]Jos 18:10
55 [h]Jos 23:13; Jdg 2:3; Ps 106:36; Isa 55:13; Eze 2:6; 28:24; Mic 7:4; 2Co 12:7
56 [i]Nu 14:28

Ch. 34

2 [a]**Nu 33:51;** [b]Ge 17:8; Dt 1:7–8; Jos 23:4; Ps 78:54–55; 105:11; [c]Eze 47:15
3 [d]Nu 13:21; Jos 15:1–3; [e]**Ge 14:3**
4 [f]Jos 15:3; Jdg 1:36; [g]Nu 32:8; [h]Jos 15:4
5 [i]Ge 15:18
6 [j]Jos 1:4; 9:1; 15:12,47; 23:4; Eze 47:10,15; 48:28; [k]Eze 47:19–20
7 [l]Eze 47:15–17; [m]**Nu 20:22**
8 [n]Nu 13:21; Jos 13:5
10 [o]Jos 15:5
11 [p]2Ki 23:33; 25:6,21; Jer 39:5; 52:9,27; [q]Jos 15:32; 21:16; 1Ch 4:32; [r]Dt 3:17; Jos 11:2; 13:27
13 [s]**Lev 16:8;** Jos 18:10; Mic 2:5; [t]Jos 13:6; 14:1–5; Isa 49:8; 65:9; Eze 45:1
14 [u]Nu 32:19; Dt 33:21; Jos 14:3
17 [v]Nu 11:28; Dt 1:38
18 [w]**Nu 1:4;** [x]Jos 14:1
19 [y]ver 29; [z]**Nu 26:65;** [a]Ge 29:35; Dt 33:7; Ps 60:7
20 [b]**Ge 29:33**
21 [c]Ge 49:27; Jdg 5:14; Ps 68:27
23 [d]Nu 1:34
24 [e]Nu 1:32
25 [f]**Ge 30:20**
27 [g]Nu 1:40
29 [h]ver 19

Ch. 35

1 [a]Nu 22:1
2 [b]Lev 25:32–34; Jos 14:3–4; [c]Jos 21:1–42
3 [d]Dt 18:6; Jos 14:4; 21:2

[a]3 That is, the Dead Sea; also in verse 12
[b]4 Hebrew *Akrabbim*
[c]5 That is, the Mediterranean; also in verses 6 and 7
[d]8 Or *to the entrance to* [e]11 That is, Galilee
[f]15 *Jordan of Jericho* was possibly an ancient name for the Jordan River.
[a]1 Hebrew *Jordan of Jericho;* possibly an ancient name for the Jordan River
[b]4 Hebrew *a thousand cubits* (about 450 metres)

measure three thousand feet[c][e] on the east side, three thousand on the south side, three thousand on the west and three thousand on the north, with the town in the centre. They will have this area as pasture-land for the towns.[f]

Cities of Refuge

35:6–34Ref—Dt 4:41–43; 19:1–14; Jos 20:1–9

6"Six of the towns you give the Levites will be cities of refuge, to which a person who has killed someone may flee.[g] In addition, give them forty-two other towns. 7In all you must give the Levites forty-eight towns, together with their pasture-lands. 8The towns you give the Levites from the land the Israelites possess are to be given in proportion to the inheritance of each tribe: Take many towns from a tribe that has many, but few from one that has few."[h]

9Then the LORD said to Moses: 10"Speak to the Israelites and say to them: 'When you cross the Jordan into Canaan,[i] 11select some towns to be your cities of refuge, to which a person who has killed someone[j] accidentally[k] may flee. 12They will be places of refuge from the avenger,[l] so that a person accused of murder[m] may not die before he stands trial before the assembly.[n] 13These six towns you give will be your cities of refuge.[o] 14Give three on this side of the Jordan and three in Canaan as cities of refuge. 15These six towns will be a place of refuge for Israelites, aliens and any other people living among them, so that anyone who has killed another accidentally can flee there.

16" 'If a man strikes someone with an iron object so that he dies, he is a murderer; the murderer shall be put to death.[p] 17Or if anyone has a stone in his hand that could kill, and he strikes someone so that he dies, he is a murderer; the murderer shall be put to death. 18Or if anyone has a wooden object in his hand that could kill, and he hits someone so that he dies, he is a murderer; the murderer shall be put to death. 19The avenger of blood[q] shall put the murderer to death; when he meets him, he shall put him to death.[r] 20If anyone with malice aforethought pushes another or throws something at him intentionally[s] so that he dies 21or if in hostility he hits him with his fist so that he dies, that person shall be put to death;[t] he is a murderer. The avenger of blood[u] shall put the murderer to death when he meets him.

5 [e]Jos 3:4; [f]Lev 25:34; 2Ch 11:14; 13:9; 23:2; 31:19
6 [g]ver 11; Jos 21:13
8 [h]Nu 26:54; 33:54
10 [i]Nu 33:51; Dt 9:1; Jos 1:2,11
11 [j]ver 22–25; [k]**Ex 21:13**
12 [l]ver 19; Dt 19:6; Jos 20:3; 2Sa 14:11; [m]ver 26–28; [n]ver 24–25
13 [o]ver 6,14
16 [p]**Ex 21:12**
19 [q]**ver 12**; [r]ver 21
20 [s]**Ex 21:14**
21 [t]Ex 21:14; [u]ver 19
22 [v]**Ex 21:13**
24 [w]**ver 12**
25 [x]ver 32; [y]**Ex 28:41**; [z]**Ex 29:7**
29 [a]Nu 27:11; [b]Nu 10:8; [c]**Ex 12:20**
30 [d]Dt 17:6; 19:15; **Mt 18:16**; Jn 7:51
31 [e]Ex 21:30; Job 6:22; Ps 49:8; Pr 13:8
33 [f]**Ge 4:10**
34 [g]Lev 18:24–25; [h]**Ex 29:45**

Ch. 36

1 [a]**Nu 26:30**; [b]Ge 50:23; [c]**Nu 26:28**; [d]**Nu 27:2**

22" 'But if without hostility someone suddenly pushes another or throws something at him unintentionally[v] 23or, without seeing him, drops a stone on him that could kill him, and he dies, then since he was not his enemy and he did not intend to harm him, 24the assembly[w] must judge between him and the avenger of blood according to these regulations. 25The assembly must protect the one accused of murder from the avenger of blood and send him back to the city of refuge to which he fled. He must stay there until the death of the high priest,[x] who was anointed[y] with holy oil.[z]

26" 'But if the accused ever goes outside the limits of the city of refuge to which he has fled 27and the avenger of blood finds him outside the city, the avenger of blood may kill the accused without being guilty of murder. 28The accused must stay in his city of refuge until the death of the high priest; only after the death of the high priest may he return to his own property.

29" 'These are to be legal requirements[a] for you throughout the generations to come,[b] wherever you live.[c]

30" 'Anyone who kills a person is to be put to death as a murderer only on the testimony of witnesses. But no-one is to be put to death on the testimony of only one witness.[d]

31" 'Do not accept a ransom[e] for the life of a murderer, who deserves to die. He must surely be put to death.

32" 'Do not accept a ransom for anyone who has fled to a city of refuge and so allow him to go back and live on his own land before the death of the high priest.

33" 'Do not pollute the land where you are. Bloodshed pollutes the land,[f] and atonement cannot be made for the land on which blood has been shed, except by the blood of the one who shed it. 34Do not defile the land[g] where you live and where I dwell,[h] for I, the LORD, dwell among the Israelites.' "

Inheritance of Zelophehad's Daughters

36:1–12pp—Nu 27:1–11

36 The family heads of the clan of Gilead[a] son of Makir,[b] the son of Manasseh, who were from the clans of the descendants of Joseph,[c] came and spoke before Moses and the leaders,[d]

[c]5 Hebrew *two thousand cubits* (about 900 metres)

the heads of the Israelite families. 2They
said, "When the LORD commanded my
lord to give the land as an inheritance to
the Israelites by lot,[e] he ordered you to
give the inheritance of our brother
Zelophehad[f] to his daughters. 3Now
suppose they marry men from other
Israelite tribes; then their inheritance
will be taken from our ancestral
inheritance and added to that of the
tribe they marry into. And so part of
the inheritance allotted to us will be
taken away. 4When the Year of Jubilee[g]
for the Israelites comes, their
inheritance will be added to that of the
tribe into which they marry, and their
property will be taken from the tribal
inheritance of our forefathers."

5Then at the LORD's command Moses
gave this order to the Israelites: "What
the tribe of the descendants of Joseph
is saying is right. 6This is what the
LORD commands for Zelophehad's
daughters: They may marry anyone
they please as long as they marry
within the tribal clan of their father. 7No
inheritance[h] in Israel is to pass from
tribe to tribe, for every Israelite shall
keep the tribal land inherited from his
forefathers. 8Every daughter who
inherits land in any Israelite tribe
must marry someone in her father's
tribal clan,[i] so that every Israelite will
possess the inheritance of his fathers.
9No inheritance may pass from tribe to
tribe, for each Israelite tribe is to keep
the land it inherits."

10So Zelophehad's daughters did
as the LORD commanded Moses.
11Zelophehad's daughters—Mahlah,
Tirzah, Hoglah, Milcah and Noah[j]—
married their cousins on their father's
side. 12They married within the clans of
the descendants of Manasseh son of
Joseph, and their inheritance remained
in their father's clan and tribe.[k]

13These are the commands and regu-
lations the LORD gave through Moses[l] to
the Israelites on the plains of Moab by
the Jordan across from Jericho.[a][m]

2 [e]Nu 33:54; [f]Nu 26:33
4 [g]Lev 25:10
7 [h]Lev 25:23
8 [i]1Ch 23:22
11 [j]Nu 26:33
12 [k]1Ch 7:15
13 [l]Lev 7:38; 27:34; [m]Nu 22:1

[a]13 Hebrew *Jordan of Jericho*; possibly an ancient name for the Jordan River

Deuteronomy

The Command to Leave Horeb

1 These are the words Moses spoke
to all Israel in the desert east of the
Jordan[a]—that is, in the Arabah[b]—
opposite Suph, between Paran[c] and
Tophel, Laban, Hazeroth and Dizahab.
2(It takes eleven days to go from Horeb[d]
to Kadesh Barnea[e] by the Mount Seir[f]
road.)[g]
3In the fortieth year,[h] on the first day
of the eleventh month,[i] Moses pro-
claimed[j] to the Israelites all that the
LORD had commanded him concerning
them. 4This was after he had defeated
Sihon[k] king of the Amorites,[l] who
reigned in Heshbon,[m] and at Edrei had
defeated Og[n] king of Bashan, who
reigned in Ashtaroth.[o]
5East of the Jordan in the territory of
Moab,[p] Moses began to expound this
law, saying:

6The LORD our God said to us[q] at
Horeb,[r] "You have stayed long enough[s]
at this mountain. 7Break camp and ad-
vance into the hill country of the Amor-
ites;[t] go to all the neighbouring peoples
in the Arabah,[u] in the mountains, in the
western foothills, in the Negev[v] and
along the coast, to the land of the
Canaanites[w] and to Lebanon,[x] as far as
the great river, the Euphrates.[y] 8See, I
have given you this land[z].[a] Go in and
take possession of the land that the
LORD swore[b] he would give to your
fathers—to Abraham, Isaac and Jacob
—and to their descendants after them."

The Appointment of Leaders

9At that time I said to you, "You are
too heavy a burden[c] for me to carry
alone.[d] 10The LORD your God has in-
creased[e] your numbers[f] so that today
you are as many[g] as the stars in the sky.[h]
11May the LORD, the God of your
fathers, increase[i] you a thousand times
and bless you as he has promised![j]
12But how can I bear your problems
and your burdens and your disputes
all by myself?[k] 13Choose some wise,
understanding and respected men[l]
from each of your tribes, and I will set
them over you."
14You answered me, "What you pro-
pose to do is good."
15So I took[m] the leading men of your
tribes,[n] wise and respected men,[o] and
appointed them to have authority over
you—as commanders[p] of thousands, of
hundreds, of fifties and of tens and as
tribal officials.[q] 16And I charged your
judges at that time: Hear the disputes
between your brothers and judge[r]
fairly,[s] whether the case is between
brother Israelites or between one of
them and an alien.[t] 17Do not show par-
tiality[u] in judging; hear both small and
great alike. Do not be afraid of any
man,[v] for judgment belongs to God.
Bring me any case too hard for you, and
I will hear it.[w] 18And at that time I told
you everything you were to do.[x]

Spies Sent Out

19Then, as the LORD our God com-
manded us, we set out from Horeb and
went towards the hill country of the
Amorites[y] through all that vast and
dreadful desert[z] that you have seen, and
so we reached Kadesh Barnea.[a] 20Then I
said to you, "You have reached the hill
country of the Amorites, which the
LORD our God is giving us. 21See, the
LORD your God has given you the land.
Go up and take possession[b] of it as the
LORD, the God of your fathers, told you.
Do not be afraid;[c] do not be dis-
couraged."[d]
22Then all of you came to me and said,
"Let us send men ahead to spy[e] out the
land[f] for us and bring back a report
about the route we are to take and the
towns we will come to."

Ch. 1

1 [a]**Nu 13:29**; Dt 4:46; [b]ver 7; Dt 2:8; 3:17; Jos 3:16; 8:14; 11:2; Eze 47:8; [c]**Nu 10:12**
2 [d]**Ex 3:1**; [e]**Ge 14:7**; Dt 2:14; 9:23; Jos 15:3; [f]**Nu 24:18**; [g]ver 19
3 [h]Nu 14:33; 32:13; Dt 8:2; Heb 3:7–9; [i]Ge 50:3; Dt 34:8; Jos 4:19; [j]Dt 4:1–2
4 [k]Nu 21:21–26; [l]**Ge 10:16; 14:7**; [m]**Nu 21:25**; [n]Nu 21:33–35; Dt 3:10; [o]Jos 9:10; 12:4; 1Ch 11:44
5 [p]**Nu 21:11**
6 [q]Nu 10:13; [r]**Ex 3:1**; [s]Dt 2:3
7 [t]ver 19; Dt 2:24; 7:1; Jos 10:5; [u]**ver 1**; [v]**Nu 21:1**; Jos 11:16; 12:8; 2Sa 24:7; [w]**Ge 10:18**; [x]Dt 11:24; [y]**Ge 2:14**
8 [z]**Jos 23:13**; [a]**Nu 34:2**; [b]**Ex 13:11; Nu 14:23**; Heb 6:13–14
9 [c]**Nu 11:14**; Ps 38:4; [d]**Ex 18:18**
10 [e]ver 11; Eze 16:7; [f]**Dt 7:13**; [g]**Ge 15:5**; Isa 51:2; 60:22; Eze 33:24; [h]**Ge 22:17; Nu 10:36**
11 [i]**ver 10**; [j]ver 8; Ex 32:13; 2Sa 24:3; 1Ch 21:3
12 [k]**Ex 5:22; 18:18**
13 [l]**Ge 47:6**
15 [m]Ex 18:25; [n]Ex 5:14; Nu 11:16; Jos 1:10; 3:2; [o]**Ge 47:6**; [p]Nu 31:14; 1Sa 8:12; 22:7; 1Ki 14:27; [q]**Nu 1:4**
16 [r]1Ki 3:9; Ps 72:1; Pr 2:9; [s]**Ge 31:37**; Jn 7:24; [t]**Ex 12:19, 49; 22:21**
17 [u]**Ex 18:16; Lev 19:15**; Ac 10:34; Jas 2:1; [v]Pr 29:25; [w]Ex 18:26 *18* [x]**Ge 39:11**
19 [y]**ver 7**; [z]Dt 2:7; 8:15; 32:10; Ps 136:16; Jer 2:2,6; Hos 13:5; [a]ver 2; Nu 13:26
21 [b]Dt 9:23; [c]**Nu 14:9**; Jos 1:6,9,18; 2Sa 10:12; Ps 27:14; [d]Dt 7:18; Jos 8:1; 10:8 *22* [e]Nu 13:1–3; [f]**Ge 42:9**

23The idea seemed good to me; so I
selected[g] twelve of you, one man from
each tribe. 24They left and went up into
the hill country, and came to the Valley
of Eshcol[h] and explored it. 25Taking with
them some of the fruit of the land, they
brought it down to us and reported,[i] "It
is a good land[j] that the LORD our God is
giving us."[k]

Rebellion Against the LORD

26But you were unwilling to go up;[l]
you rebelled[m] against the command of
the LORD your God. 27You grumbled[n] in
your tents and said, "The LORD hates us;
so he brought us out of Egypt to deliver
us into the hands of the Amorites to
destroy us. 28Where can we go? Our
brothers have made us lose heart. They
say, 'The people are stronger and taller[o]
than we are; the cities are large, with
walls up to the sky. We even saw the
Anakites[p] there.'"

29Then I said to you, "Do not be ter-
rified; do not be afraid[q] of them.[r] 30The
LORD your God, who is going before
you, will fight[s] for you, as he did for you
in Egypt, before your very eyes, 31and in
the desert. There you saw how the LORD
your God carried[t] you, as a father carries
his son, all the way you went until you
reached this place."[u]

32In spite of this,[v] you did not trust[w] in
the LORD your God, 33who went ahead
of you on your journey, in fire by night
and in a cloud by day,[x] to search[y] out
places for you to camp and to show you
the way you should go.

34When the LORD heard[z] what you
said, he was angry[a] and solemnly
swore:[b] 35"Not a man of this evil genera-
tion shall see the good land[c] I swore to
give your forefathers, 36except Caleb[d]
son of Jephunneh. He will see it, and I
will give him and his descendants the
land he set his feet on, because he
followed the LORD wholeheartedly.[e]"

37Because of you the LORD became
angry[f] with me also and said, "You shall
not enter[g] it, either. 38But your assistant,
Joshua[h] son of Nun, will enter it.
Encourage[i] him, because he will lead[j]
Israel to inherit[k] it. 39And the little ones
that you said would be taken captive,[l]
your children who do not yet know[m]
good from bad—they will enter the
land. I will give it to them and they will
take possession of it. 40But as for you,
turn round and set out towards the
desert along the route to the Red
Sea."[a] [n]

41Then you replied, "We have sinned
against the LORD. We will go up and
fight, as the LORD our God commanded
us." So every one of you put on his
weapons, thinking it easy to go up into
the hill country.

42But the LORD said to me, "Tell them,
'Do not go up and fight, because I will
not be with you. You will be defeated by
your enemies.'"[o]

43So I told you, but you would not
listen. You rebelled against the LORD's
command and in your arrogance you
marched up into the hill country. 44The
Amorites who lived in those hills came
out against you; they chased you like a
swarm of bees[p] and beat you down from
Seir[q] all the way to Hormah.[r] 45You
came back and wept before the LORD,[s]
but he paid no attention[t] to your weep-
ing and turned a deaf ear[u] to you. 46And
so you stayed in Kadesh[v] many days
—all the time you spent there.

Wanderings in the Desert

2 Then we turned back and set out
towards the desert along the route
to the Red Sea,[a] [a] as the LORD had
directed me. For a long time we made
our way around the hill country of Seir.[b]

2Then the LORD said to me, 3"You
have made your way around this hill
country long enough;[c] now turn north.
4Give the people these orders:[d] 'You are
about to pass through the territory of
your brothers the descendants of Esau,[e]
who live in Seir.[f] They will be afraid[g] of
you, but be very careful. 5Do not pro-
voke them to war, for I will not give you
any of their land, not even enough to
put your foot on. I have given Esau the
hill country of Seir as his own.[h] 6You are
to pay them in silver for the food you eat
and the water you drink.'"

7The LORD your God has blessed you
in all the work of your hands. He has
watched[i] over your journey through
this vast desert.[j] These forty years[k] the
LORD your God has been with you, and
you have not lacked anything.[l]

8So we went on past our brothers the
descendants of Esau, who live in Seir.
We turned from[m] the Arabah[n] road,
which comes up from Elath and Ezion
Geber,[o] and travelled along the desert
road of Moab.[p]

9Then the LORD said to me, "Do not
harass the Moabites or provoke them to

23 [g]Nu 13:1–3
24 [h]Nu 13:21–25; **32:9**
25 [i]**Nu 13:27;** [j]**Nu 14:7;** [k]Jos 1:2
26 [l]Nu 14:1–4; [m]**Nu 14:9**
27 [n]Dt 9:28; Ps 106:25
28 [o]**Nu 13:32** [p]**Nu 13:33;** Dt 9:1–3
29 [q]Dt 3:22; 20:3; Ne 4:14; [r]Dt 7:18; 20:1; 31:6
30 [s]**Ex 14:14**
31 [t]Ex 19:4; Dt 32:10–12; Ps 28:9; Isa 46:3–4; 63:9; Hos 11:3; Ac 13:18; [u]Jer 31:32
32 [v]**Nu 14:11;** [w]Dt 9:23; Ps 78:22; 106:24; Zep 3:2; Heb 3:19; Jude 5
33 [x]Ex 13:21; Nu 9:15–23; Ne 9:12; Ps 78:14; [y]**Nu 10:33**
34 [z]**Nu 11:1;** [a]**Nu 32:14;** [b]**Nu 14:23**,28–30; Eze 20:15; Heb 3:11
35 [c]**Nu 14:29**
36 [d]**Nu 13:6;** [e]**Nu 14:24**
37 [f]Ps 106:32; [g]**Nu 27:13**
38 [h]**Nu 11:28;** [i]Dt 31:7; [j]Dt 3:28; [k]Jos 11:23; Ps 78:55; 136:21
39 [l]**Nu 14:3;** [m]Isa 7:15–16
40 [n]**Ex 14:27;** Jdg 11:16
42 [o]**Nu 14:41–43**
44 [p]Ps 118:12; [q]**Nu 24:18;** [r]**Nu 14:45**
45 [s]**Nu 14:1;** [t]Job 27:9; 35:13; Ps 18:41; 66:18; Pr 1:28; Isa 1:15; Jer 14:12; La 3:8; Mic 3:4; **Jn 9:31;** [u]Ps 28:1; 39:12; Pr 28:9
46 [v]**Nu 20:1**

Ch. 2

1 [a]**Ex 14:27; Nu 21:4;** [b]**Nu 24:18**
3 [c]Dt 1:6
4 [d]Nu 20:14–21; [e]Ge 36:8; [f]ver 1; [g]Ex 15:16
5 [h]Jos 24:4
7 [i]Dt 8:2–4; [j]**Ex 13:21; Dt 1:19;** [k]ver 14; **Nu 14:33;** 32:13; Jos 5:6; [l]Ne 9:21; Am 2:10
8 [m]**Nu 20:21;** [n]**Dt 1:1;** [o]Nu 33:35; 1Ki 9:26; [p]**Nu 21:4**

[a]40 Hebrew *Yam Suph;* that is, Sea of Reeds
[a]1 Hebrew *Yam Suph;* that is, Sea of Reeds

war, for I will not give you any part of their land. I have given Ar[q] to the descendants of Lot[r] as a possession."

10(The Emites[s] used to live there—a people strong and numerous, and as tall as the Anakites.[t] 11Like the Anakites, they too were considered Rephaites,[u] but the Moabites called them Emites. 12Horites[v] used to live in Seir, but the descendants of Esau drove them out. They destroyed the Horites from before them and settled in their place, just as Israel did[w] in the land the LORD gave them as their possession.)

13And the LORD said, "Now get up and cross the Zered Valley.[x]" So we crossed the valley.

14Thirty-eight years[y] passed from the time we left Kadesh Barnea[z] until we crossed the Zered Valley. By then, that entire generation[a] of fighting men had perished from the camp, as the LORD had sworn to them.[b] 15The LORD's hand was against them until he had completely eliminated[c] them from the camp.

16Now when the last of these fighting men among the people had died, 17the LORD said to me, 18"Today you are to pass by the region of Moab at Ar.[d] 19When you come to the Ammonites,[e] do not harass them or provoke them to war,[f] for I will not give you possession of any land belonging to the Ammonites. I have given it as a possession to the descendants of Lot.[g]"

20(That too was considered a land of the Rephaites,[h] who used to live there; but the Ammonites called them Zamzummites. 21They were a people strong and numerous, and as tall as the Anakites.[i] The LORD destroyed them from before the Ammonites, who drove them out and settled in their place. 22The LORD had done the same for the descendants of Esau, who lived in Seir,[j] when he destroyed the Horites from before them. They drove them out and have lived in their place to this day. 23And as for the Avvites[k] who lived in villages as far as Gaza,[l] the Caphtorites[m] coming out from Caphtor[b][n] destroyed them and settled in their place.)

Defeat of Sihon King of Heshbon

24"Set out now and cross the Arnon Gorge.[o] See, I have given into your hand Sihon the Amorite,[p] king of Heshbon, and his country. Begin to take possession of it and engage[q] him in battle. 25This very day I will begin to put the terror[r] and fear[s] of you on all the nations under heaven. They will hear reports of you and will tremble[t] and be in anguish because of you."

26From the desert of Kedemoth[u] I sent messengers to Sihon[v] king of Heshbon offering peace[w] and saying, 27"Let us pass through your country. We will stay on the main road; we will not turn aside to the right or to the left.[x] 28Sell us food to eat[y] and water to drink for their price in silver. Only let us pass through on foot[z]—29as the descendants of Esau, who live in Seir, and the Moabites, who live in Ar, did for us—until we cross the Jordan into the land the LORD our God is giving us." 30But Sihon king of Heshbon refused to let us pass through. For the LORD[a] your God had made his spirit stubborn[b] and his heart obstinate[c] in order to give him into your hands,[d] as he has now done.

31The LORD said to me, "See, I have begun to deliver Sihon and his country over to you. Now begin to conquer and possess his land."[e]

32When Sihon and all his army came out to meet us in battle[f] at Jahaz, 33the LORD our God delivered[g] him over to us and we struck him down,[h] together with his sons and his whole army. 34At that time we took all his towns and completely destroyed[c][i] them—men, women and children. We left no survivors. 35But the livestock[j] and the plunder[k] from the towns we had captured we carried off for ourselves. 36From Aroer[l] on the rim of the Arnon Gorge, and from the town in the gorge, even as far as Gilead,[m] not one town was too strong for us. The LORD our God gave[n] us all of them. 37But in accordance with the command of the LORD our God,[o] you did not encroach on any of the land of the Ammonites,[p] neither the land along the course of the Jabbok[q] nor that around the towns in the hills.

Defeat of Og King of Bashan

3 Next we turned and went up along the road towards Bashan, and Og king of Bashan[a] with his whole army marched out to meet us in battle at Edrei.[b] 2The LORD said to me, "Do not be afraid[c] of him, for I have handed him over to you with his whole army and his land. Do to him what you did to Sihon king of the Amorites, who reigned in Heshbon."

9 [q]**Nu 21:15**; [r]Ge 19:38; Ps 83:8
10 [s]Ge 14:5; [t]**Nu 13:22,33**
11 [u]**Ge 14:5**
12 [v]**Ge 14:6**; [w]Nu 21:25,35
13 [x]**Nu 21:12**
14 [y]**ver 7**; [z]**Dt 1:2**; [a]Nu 14:29–35; [b]Dt 1:34–35; Jos 5:6
15 [c]Ps 106:26; Jude 5
18 [d]**Nu 21:15**
19 [e]**Ge 19:38**; [f]2Ch 20:10; [g]**ver 9**
20 [h]**Ge 14:5**
21 [i]ver 10
22 [j]**Ge 14:6**
23 [k]Jos 13:3; 18:23; 2Ki 17:31; [l]**Ge 10:19**; [m]**Ge 10:14**; [n]Jer 47:4; Am 9:7
24 [o]Nu 21:13–14; Jdg 11:13,18; [p]**Dt 1:7**; [q]Dt 3:6
25 [r]**Ge 35:5**; Dt 11:25; [s]Jos 2:9, 11; 1Ch 14:17; 2Ch 14:14; 17:10; 20:29; Isa 2:19; 13:13; 19:16; [t]Ex 15:14–16
26 [u]Jos 13:18; 1Ch 6:79; [v]Dt 1:4; Jdg 11:21–22; [w]Dt 20:10; Jdg 21:13; 2Sa 20:19
27 [x]Nu 21:21–22
28 [y]Dt 23:4; [z]**Nu 20:19**
30 [a]Jdg 14:4; 1Ki 12:15; [b]**Ex 4:21**; Ro 9:18; [c]**Ex 14:17**; [d]La 3:65
31 [e]**Ge 12:7**
32 [f]**Nu 21:23**
33 [g]Ex 23:31; Dt 7:2; 31:5; [h]**Nu 21:24**
34 [i]**Nu 21:2**; Dt 3:6; 7:2; Ps 106:34
35 [j]Dt 3:7; [k]**Ge 34:29; 49:27**
36 [l]**Nu 32:34**; [m]**Nu 32:39**; [n]Ps 44:3
37 [o]ver 18–19; [p]**Nu 21:24**; [q]**Ge 32:22**

Ch. 3

1 [a]**Nu 32:19**; [b]**Nu 21:33**
2 [c]Jos 10:8; 2Ki 19:6; Isa 7:4

[b]23 That is, Crete
[c]34 The Hebrew term refers to the irrevocable giving over of things or persons to the LORD, often by totally destroying them.

3So the LORD our God also gave into our hands Og king of Bashan and all his army. We struck them down,[d] leaving no survivors.[e] 4At that time we took all his cities.[f] There was not one of the sixty cities that we did not take from them —the whole region of Argob, Og's kingdom[g] in Bashan.[h] 5All these cities were fortified with high walls and with gates and bars, and there were also a great many unwalled villages. 6We completely destroyed[a] them, as we had done with Sihon king of Heshbon, destroying[a][i] every city—men, women and children. 7But all the livestock[j] and the plunder from their cities we carried off for ourselves.

8So at that time we took from these two kings of the Amorites[k] the territory east of the Jordan, from the Arnon Gorge as far as Mount Hermon.[l] 9(Hermon is called Sirion[m] by the Sidonians; the Amorites call it Senir.)[n] 10We took all the towns on the plateau, and all Gilead, and all Bashan as far as Salecah[o] and Edrei, towns of Og's kingdom in Bashan. 11(Only Og king of Bashan was left of the remnant of the Rephaites.[p] His bed[b] was made of iron and was more than thirteen feet long and six feet wide.[c] It is still in Rabbah[q] of the Ammonites.)

Division of the Land

12Of the land that we took over at that time, I gave the Reubenites and the Gadites the territory north of Aroer[r] by the Arnon Gorge, including half the hill country of Gilead, together with its towns. 13The rest of Gilead and also all of Bashan, the kingdom of Og, I gave to the half-tribe of Manasseh.[s] (The whole region of Argob in Bashan used to be known as a land of the Rephaites.[t] 14Jair,[u] a descendant of Manasseh, took the whole region of Argob as far as the border of the Geshurites and the Maacathites;[v] it was named[w] after him, so that to this day Bashan is called Havvoth Jair.[d]) 15And I gave Gilead to Makir.[x] 16But to the Reubenites and the Gadites I gave the territory extending from Gilead down to the Arnon Gorge (the middle of the gorge being the border) and out to the Jabbok River,[y] which is the border of the Ammonites. 17Its western border was the Jordan in the Arabah,[z] from Kinnereth[a] to the Sea of the Arabah[b] (the Salt Sea[e][c]), below the slopes of Pisgah.

18I commanded you at that time: "The LORD your God has given[d] you this land to take possession of it. But all your able-bodied men, armed for battle, must cross over ahead of your brother Israelites.[e] 19However, your wives,[f] your children and your livestock[g] (I know you have much livestock) may stay in the towns I have given you, 20until the LORD gives rest to your brothers as he has to you, and they too have taken over the land that the LORD your God is giving them, across the Jordan. After that, each of you may go back to the possession I have given you."

Moses Forbidden to Cross the Jordan

21At that time I commanded Joshua: "You have seen with your own eyes all that the LORD your God has done to these two kings. The LORD will do the same to all the kingdoms over there where you are going. 22Do not be afraid[h] of them;[i] the LORD your God himself will fight[j] for you."

23At that time I pleaded[k] with the LORD: 24"O Sovereign LORD, you have begun to show to your servant your greatness[l] and your strong hand. For what god[m] is there in heaven or on earth who can do the deeds and mighty works[n] you do?[o] 25Let me go over and see the good land[p] beyond the Jordan —that fine hill country and Lebanon.[q]"

26But because of you the LORD was angry[r] with me and would not listen to me. "That is enough," the LORD said. "Do not speak to me any more about this matter. 27Go up to the top of Pisgah[s] and look west and north and south and east.[t] Look at the land with your own eyes, since you are not going to cross[u] this Jordan.[v] 28But commission[w] Joshua, and encourage[x] and strengthen him, for he will lead this people across[y] and will cause them to inherit the land that you will see." 29So we stayed in the valley near Beth Peor.[z]

Obedience Commanded

4 Hear now, O Israel, the decrees[a] and laws I am about to teach[b] you. Follow them so that you may live[c] and

3 [d]Nu 21:24; [e]Nu 21:35
4 [f]**Nu 21:24;** [g]ver 13; [h]**Nu 21:33**
6 [i]Dt 2:24
7 [j]Dt 2:35
8 [k]Nu 32:33; Jos 13:8–12; [l]Dt 4:48; Jos 11:3, 17; 12:1; 13:5; Jdg 3:3; 1Ch 5:23; Ps 42:6; 89:12; 133:3; SS 4:8
9 [m]Ps 29:6; [n]1Ch 5:23; SS 4:8; Eze 27:5
10 [o]Jos 12:5; 1Ch 5:11
11 [p]Ge 14:5; [q]Jos 13:25; 15:60; 2Sa 11:1; 12:26; 17:27; 1Ch 20:1; Jer 49:2; Eze 21:20; 25:5; Am 1:14
12 [r]Dt 2:36
13 [s]Dt 29:8; [t]**Ge 14:5**
14 [u]**Nu 32:41;** [v]Jos 12:5; 13:11,13; 2Sa 10:6; 23:34; 2Ki 25:23; 1Ch 4:19; Jer 40:8; [w]Jos 19:47; Ps 49:11
15 [x]**Ge 50:23;** Nu 32:39–40
16 [y]**Nu 21:24**
17 [z]2Sa 2:29; 4:7; Eze 47:8; [a]**Nu 34:11;** [b]**Dt 1:1;** [c]**Ge 14:3**
18 [d]Jos 1:13; [e]**Nu 32:17**
19 [f]Jos 1:14; [g]**Nu 32:16**
22 [h]**Dt 1:29;** [i]Dt 7:18; 20:1; 31:6; 2Ch 32:8; Ps 23:4; Isa 41:10; [j]**Ex 14:14**
23 [k]Dt 1:37; 31:2; 32:52; 34:4
24 [l]Dt 5:24; 11:2; 32:3; [m]**Ex 8:10;** [n]Ps 71:16; 106:2; 145:12; 150:2; [o]2Sa 7:22
25 [p]Dt 4:22; [q]Dt 1:7; Jos 1:4; 9:1; 11:17; 12:7; 13:5; Jdg 3:3; 9:15; 1Ki 4:33
26 [r]ver 27; Dt 1:37; 31:2
27 [s]**Nu 21:20;** [t]**Ge 13:14;** [u]**ver 26; Nu 20:12;** Dt 32:52; [v]**Nu 27:12**
28 [w]Nu 27:18–23; [x]Dt 31:7; [y]Dt 1:38; 31:3,23
29 [z]**Nu 23:28;** Dt 4:46; 34:6; Jos 13:20

Ch. 4
1 [a]**Lev 18:4;** [b]Dt 1:3; [c]**Lev 18:5;** Dt 30:15–20; **Ro 10:5**

[a]*6* The Hebrew term refers to the irrevocable giving over of things or persons to the LORD, often by totally destroying them.
[b]*11* Or *sarcophagus*
[c]*11* Hebrew *nine cubits long and four cubits wide* (about 4 metres long and 1.8 metres wide)
[d]*14* Or *called the settlements of Jair*
[e]*17* That is, the Dead Sea

may go in and take possession of the land that the LORD, the God of your fathers, is giving you. 2Do not add[d] to what I command you and do not subtract[e] from it, but keep[f] the commands[g] of the LORD your God that I give you.

3You saw with your own eyes what the LORD did at Baal Peor.[h] The LORD your God destroyed from among you everyone who followed the Baal of Peor, 4but all of you who held fast to the LORD your God are still alive today.

5See, I have taught[i] you decrees and laws[j] as the LORD my God commanded[k] me, so that you may follow them in the land you are entering[l] to take possession of it. 6Observe[m] them carefully, for this will show your wisdom[n] and understanding to the nations, who will hear about all these decrees and say, "Surely this great nation is a wise and understanding people."[o] 7What other nation is so great[p] as to have their gods near[q] them the way the LORD our God is near us whenever we pray to him? 8And what other nation is so great as to have such righteous decrees and laws[r] as this body of laws I am setting before you today?

9Only be careful,[s] and watch yourselves closely so that you do not forget the things your eyes have seen or let them slip from your heart as long as you live. Teach[t] them to your children[u] and to their children after them. 10Remember the day you stood before the LORD your God at Horeb,[v] when he said to me, "Assemble the people before me to hear my words so that they may learn[w] to revere[x] me as long as they live in the land[y] and may teach[z] them to their children." 11You came near and stood at the foot of the mountain[a] while it blazed with fire[b] to the very heavens, with black clouds and deep darkness.[c] 12Then the LORD spoke[d] to you out of the fire. You heard the sound of words but saw no form;[e] there was only a voice.[f] 13He declared to you his covenant,[g] the Ten Commandments,[h] which he commanded you to follow and then wrote them on two stone tablets. 14And the LORD directed me at that time to teach you the decrees and laws[i] you are to follow in the land that you are crossing the Jordan to possess.

Idolatry Forbidden

15You saw no form[j] of any kind the day the LORD spoke to you at Horeb[k] out of the fire. Therefore watch yourselves very carefully,[l] 16so that you do not become corrupt[m] and make for yourselves an idol,[n] an image of any shape, whether formed like a man or a woman, 17or like any animal on earth or any bird that flies in the air,[o] 18or like any creature that moves along the ground or any fish in the waters below. 19And when you look up to the sky and see the sun,[p] the moon and the stars[q]—all the heavenly array[r]—do not be enticed[s] into bowing down to them and worshipping[t] things the LORD your God has apportioned to all the nations under heaven. 20But as for you, the LORD took you and brought you out of the iron-smelting furnace,[u] out of Egypt,[v] to be the people of his inheritance,[w] as you now are.

21The LORD was angry with me[x] because of you, and he solemnly swore that I would not cross the Jordan and enter the good land the LORD your God is giving you as your inheritance. 22I will die in this land;[y] I will not cross the Jordan; but you are about to cross over and take possession of that good land.[z] 23Be careful not to forget the covenant[a] of the LORD your God that he made with you; do not make for yourselves an idol[b] in the form of anything the LORD your God has forbidden. 24For the LORD your God is a consuming fire,[c] a jealous God.[d]

25After you have had children and grandchildren and have lived in the land a long time—if you then become corrupt[e] and make any kind of idol,[f] doing evil[g] in the eyes of the LORD your God and provoking him to anger, 26I call heaven and earth as witnesses[h] against you[i] this day that you will quickly perish[j] from the land that you are crossing the Jordan to possess. You will not live there long but will certainly be destroyed. 27The LORD will scatter[k] you among the peoples, and only a few of you will survive[l] among the nations to which the LORD will drive you. 28There you will worship man-made gods[m] of wood and stone,[n] which cannot see or hear or eat or smell.[o] 29But if from there you seek[p] the LORD your God, you will

2 [d]Dt 12:32; Jos 1:7; Pr 30:6; Rev 22:18–19; [e]Jer 26:2; [f]**Lev 22:31**; [g]Dt 10:12–13; Ecc 12:13
3 [h]Nu 25:1–9; Ps 106:28
5 [i]Ps 71:17; 119:102; Jer 32:33; [j]**Ex 18:20**; [k]**Lev 27:34**; [l]Ezr 9:11
6 [m]Dt 29:9; 1Ki 2:3; [n]Dt 30:19–20; 32:46–47; Ps 19:7; 119:98; Pr 1:7; 2Ti 3:15; [o]Job 1:1; 28:28; Ps 111:10; Pr 2:5; 3:7; 9:10; Ecc 12:13; Eze 5:5
7 [p]ver 32–34; 2Sa 7:23; [q]**Nu 23:21; Ps 46:1**; Ac 17:27
8 [r]Ps 89:14; 97:2; 119:7, 62,144,160, 172; Ro 3:2
9 [s]**Ex 23:13**; [t]**Ge 14:14**; 18:19; Dt 6:20–25; Eph 6:4; [u]**Ex 10:2**
10 [v]**Ex 3:1**; [w]Dt 14:23; 17:19; 31:12–13; Ps 2:11; 111:10; 147:11; Isa 8:13; Jer 32:40; [x]**Ex 20:20**; [y]Dt 12:1; [z]ver 9
11 [a]**Ex 3:1; 19:17**; [b]**Ex 19:18**; [c]**Ex 19:9**; Ps 18:11; 97:2
12 [d]Ex 20:22; Dt 5:4,22; **Mt 3:17**; Heb 12:19; [e]Jn 5:37; [f]**Ex 19:9**
13 [g]Dt 9:9; Ro 9:4; [h]**Ex 24:12**
14 [i]**Ex 21:1**
15 [j]Isa 40:18; 41:22–24; [k]**Ex 3:1**; [l]Jos 23:11; Mal 2:15
16 [m]**Ge 6:11–12**; Dt 9:12; 31:29; 32:5; Jdg 2:19; [n]Ex 20:4–5; Ro 1:23
17 [o]Ro 1:23
19 [p]Dt 17:3; 2Ki 23:11; Job 31:26; Jer 8:2; 43:13; Eze 8:16; [q]**Ge 1:16**; [r]**Ge 2:1; 37:9**; Ro 1:25; [s]Dt 13:5; [t]**Nu 25:3**
20 [u]**Ex 1:13**; [v]**Ex 3:10**; [w]**Ge 17:7; Ex 8:22; 34:9**; Tit 2:14
21 [x]Nu 20:12; Dt 1:37
22 [y]Nu 27:13–14; [z]Dt 3:25
23 [a]ver 9; [b]**Ex 20:4**
24 [c]**Ex 15:7; 19:18**; Heb 12:29; [d]**Ex 20:5**
25 [e]ver 16; [f]ver 23; [g]1Ki 11:6; 15:26; 16:25,30; 2Ki 17:2, 17; 21:2
26 [h]Ge 31:50; Pr 14:5; [i]Dt 30:18–19; 31:28; 32:1; Ps 50:4; Isa 1:2; 34:1; Jer 6:19; Mic 6:2; [j]Dt 6:15; 7:4
27 [k]**Lev 26:33**; Dt 28:36,64; 29:28; 1Ki 8:46; 2Ki 17:6; Ps 44:11; 106:27; Jer 3:8; Mic 1:16; [l]Isa 17:6; 21:17; Ob 5
28 [m]Dt 13:2; 28:36,64; 1Sa 26:19; Jer 5:19; 16:13; Ac 19:26; [n]Dt 29:17; [o]Ps 115:4–8; 135:15–18; Isa 8:19; 26:14; 44:17–20; Rev 9:20
29 [p]1Sa 13:12; 2Ki 13:4; 2Ch 7:14; 15:4; 33:12; Ps 78:34; 119:58; Isa 45:19,22; 55:6; Jer 26:19; Da 9:13; Hos 3:5; Am 5:4

find him if you look for him with all your
heart[q] and with all your soul.[r] 30When
you are in distress[s] and all these things
have happened to you, then in later
days[t] you will return[u] to the LORD your
God and obey him. 31For the LORD your
God is a merciful[v] God; he will not aban-
don[w] or destroy[x] you or forget[y] the cov-
enant with your forefathers, which he
confirmed to them by oath.

The LORD Is God

32Ask[z] now about the former days,
long before your time, from the day God
created man on the earth;[a] ask from one
end of the heavens to the other.[b] Has
anything so great[c] as this ever hap-
pened, or has anything like it ever been
heard of? 33Has any other people heard
the voice of God[a] speaking out of fire, as
you have, and lived?[d] 34Has any god
ever tried to take for himself one nation
out of another nation,[e] by testings,[f] by
miraculous signs[g] and wonders,[h] by
war, by a mighty hand and an out-
stretched arm,[i] or by great and awe-
some deeds,[j] like all the things the LORD
your God did for you in Egypt before
your very eyes?
35You were shown these things so
that you might know that the LORD is
God; besides him there is no other.[k]
36From heaven he made you hear his
voice[l] to discipline[m] you. On earth he
showed you his great fire, and you
heard his words from out of the fire.
37Because he loved[n] your forefathers
and chose their descendants after them,
he brought you out of Egypt by his
Presence and his great strength,[o] 38to
drive out before you nations greater and
stronger than you and to bring you into
their land to give it to you for your
inheritance,[p] as it is today.
39Acknowledge[q] and take to heart this
day that the LORD is God in heaven
above and on the earth below. There is
no other.[r] 40Keep[s] his decrees and com-
mands,[t] which I am giving you today,
so that it may go well[u] with you and
your children after you and that you
may live long[v] in the land the LORD your
God gives you for all time.

Cities of Refuge

4:41–43Ref—Nu 35:6–34; Dt 19:1–14; Jos 20:1–9

41Then Moses set aside three cities
east of the Jordan, 42to which anyone
who had killed a person could flee if he
had unintentionally[w] killed his neigh-
bour without malice aforethought. He
could flee into one of these cities and
save his life. 43The cities were these:
Bezer in the desert plateau, for the
Reubenites; Ramoth[x] in Gilead, for
the Gadites; and Golan in Bashan,
for the Manassites.

Introduction to the Law

44This is the law Moses set before the
Israelites. 45These are the stipulations,
decrees and laws Moses gave them
when they came out of Egypt 46and
were in the valley near Beth Peor east of
the Jordan, in the land of Sihon[y] king of
the Amorites, who reigned in Heshbon
and was defeated by Moses and the
Israelites as they came out of Egypt.
47They took possession of his land and
the land of Og king of Bashan, the two
Amorite kings east of the Jordan. 48This
land extended from Aroer[z] on the rim of
the Arnon Gorge to Mount Siyon[b][a] (that
is, Hermon[b]), 49and included all the
Arabah east of the Jordan, as far as the
Sea of the Arabah,[c] below the slopes of
Pisgah.

The Ten Commandments

5:6–21pp—Ex 20:1–17

5 Moses summoned all Israel and
said:
Hear, O Israel, the decrees and the
laws[a] I declare in your hearing today.
Learn them and be sure to follow them.
2The LORD our God made a covenant[b]
with us at Horeb.[c] 3It was not with our
fathers that the LORD made this cov-
enant, but with us,[d] with all of us who
are alive here today.[e] 4The LORD spoke[f]
to you face to face[g] out of the fire[h] on the
mountain. 5(At that time I stood be-
tween[i] the LORD and you to declare to
you the word of the LORD, because you
were afraid[j] of the fire and did not go up
the mountain.) And he said:

6"I am the LORD your God, who
brought you out of Egypt,[k] out
of the land of slavery.[l]

29 [q]1Sa 7:3; 1Ki 8:48; Jer 29:13; [r]Dt 6:5; 30:1–3,10
30 [s]Lev 26:41; Dt 31:17,21; Ps 4:1; 18:6; 46:1; 59:16; 107:6; [t]Dt 31:29; Jer 23:20; Hos 3:5; Heb 1:2; [u]Dt 30:2; 1Ki 8:48; Ne 1:9; Jer 3:1,12,22; 4:1; 18:11; Joel 2:12
31 [v]Ex 34:6; Ne 9:31; Ps 111:4; [w]Dt 31:6,8; Jos 1:5; 1Ki 8:57; 1Ch 28:9,20; Ps 9:10; 27:9; 71:9; Isa 42:16; Heb 13:5; [x]**Lev 26:44**; [y]Lev 26:45
32 [z]Dt 32:7; [a]**Ge 1:27**; Isa 45:12; [b]Dt 28:64; 30:1; Jer 9:16; Mt 24:31; [c]ver 7; 2Sa 7:23
33 [d]Ex 20:22; Dt 5:24–26
34 [e]Ex 14:30; [f]Isa 7:12; [g]**Ex 4:17**; [h]Dt 7:19; 26:8; 29:3; 1Ch 16:12; Ps 9:1; 40:5; Jer 32:20; [i]**Ex 3:20**; Dt 5:15; 6:21; 15:15; [j]Ex 15:11; Dt 34:12; Ps 45:4; 65:5
35 [k]ver 39; Ex 8:10; Dt 7:9; 32:4,12; 1Sa 2:2; 1Ki 8:60; 2Ki 19:19; Isa 43:10; Mk 12:32
36 [l]**Ex 19:19**; Heb 12:25; [m]Dt 8:5
37 [n]Dt 7:8; 10:15; 23:5; 33:3; Ps 44:3; Jer 31:3; Hos 11:1; Mal 1:2; 2:11; [o]**Ex 3:20; 33:14**
38 [p]Nu 34:14–15; Dt 7:1; 9:5
39 [q]Ex 8:10; [r]**ver 35**; Ex 15:11
40 [s]**Lev 22:31**; [t]ver 1; **Ge 26:5**; Dt 5:29; 11:1; Ps 105:45; Isa 48:18; [u]Dt 5:16; 12:25; Isa 3:10; [v]**Ex 23:26**; Eph 6:2–3
42 [w]**Ex 21:13**
43 [x]Jos 21:38; 1Ki 22:3; 2Ki 8:28; 9:14
46 [y]Nu 21:26
48 [z]Dt 2:36; [a]Dt 3:9; [b]**Dt 3:8**

Ch. 5

1 [a]**Ex 18:20**
2 [b]Ex 19:5; Jer 11:2; Heb 9:15; 10:15–17; [c]**Ge 17:9; Ex 3:1**
3 [d]Dt 11:2–7; [e]Nu 26:63–65; Heb 8:9
4 [f]**Dt 4:12**; [g]**Nu 14:14**; [h]**Ex 19:18**
5 [i]Gal 3:19; [j]**Ge 3:10**; Heb 12:18–21
6 [k]**Ex 13:3; 29:46**; [l]Lev 26:1; Dt 6:4; Ps 81:10

[a]33 Or *of a god*
[b]48 Hebrew; Syriac (see also Deut. 3:9) *Sirion*
[c]49 That is, the Dead Sea

7"You shall have no other gods be-
fore[a] me.
8"You shall not make for yourself
an idol in the form of anything
in heaven above or on the
earth beneath or in the waters
below.[m] 9You shall not bow
down to them or worship
them; for I, the LORD your
God, am a jealous God,
punishing the children for the
sin of the fathers[n] to the third
and fourth generation of
those who hate me,[o] 10but
showing love to a thousand[p]
⌞generations⌟ of those who
love me and keep my com-
mandments.[q]
11"You shall not misuse the name[r] of
the LORD your God, for the
LORD will not hold anyone
guiltless who misuses his
name.[s]
12"Observe the Sabbath day by
keeping it holy,[t] as the LORD
your God has commanded
you. 13Six days you shall
labour and do all your work,
14but the seventh day[u] is a
Sabbath to the LORD your
God. On it you shall not do
any work, neither you, nor
your son or daughter, nor
your manservant or maid-
servant,[v] nor your ox, your
donkey or any of your ani-
mals, nor the alien within your
gates, so that your man-
servant and maidservant may
rest, as you do.[w] 15Remember
that you were slaves[x] in Egypt
and that the LORD your God
brought you out of there
with a mighty hand[y] and an
outstretched arm.[z] Therefore
the LORD your God has com-
manded you to observe the
Sabbath day.
16"Honour your father[a] and your
mother,[b] as the LORD your
God has commanded you, so
that you may live long[c] and
that it may go well with you in
the land the LORD your God is
giving you.
17"You shall not murder.[d]
18"You shall not commit adultery.[e]
19"You shall not steal.[f]
20"You shall not give false testimony
against your neighbour.[g]
21"You shall not covet your neigh-
bour's wife. You shall not
set your desire on your
neighbour's house or land, his
manservant or maidservant,
his ox or donkey, or anything
that belongs to your neigh-
bour."[h]

22These are the commandments the
LORD proclaimed in a loud voice to your
whole assembly there on the mountain
from out of the fire, the cloud and the
deep darkness;[i] and he added nothing
more. Then he wrote them on two stone
tablets[j] and gave them to me.
23When you heard the voice out of the
darkness, while the mountain was
ablaze with fire, all the leading men of
your tribes and your elders[k] came to me.
24And you said, "The LORD our God has
shown us[l] his glory and his majesty,[m]
and we have heard his voice from the
fire. Today we have seen that a man can
live even if God speaks with him.[n] 25But
now, why should we die? This great fire
will consume us, and we will die if we
hear the voice of the LORD our God any
longer.[o] 26For what mortal man has ever
heard the voice of the living God speak-
ing out of fire, as we have, and sur-
vived?[p] 27Go near and listen to all that
the LORD our God says.[q] Then tell us
whatever the LORD our God tells you.
We will listen and obey."[r]
28The LORD heard you when you
spoke to me and the LORD said to me, "I
have heard what this people said to
you. Everything they said was good.[s]
29Oh, that their hearts would be inclined
to fear me[t] and keep all my commands[u]
always, so that it might go well with
them and their children for ever![v]
30"Go, tell them to return to their
tents. 31But you stay here[w] with me so
that I may give you all the commands,
decrees and laws that you are to teach
them to follow in the land I am giving
them to possess."
32So be careful to do what the LORD
your God has commanded you;[x] do not
turn aside to the right or to the left.[y]
33Walk in all the way that the LORD your
God has commanded you,[z] so that you
may live and prosper and prolong your
days[a] in the land that you will possess.

Love the LORD Your God

6 These are the commands, decrees
and laws the LORD your God
directed me to teach you to observe in

8 [m]Lev 26:1; Dt 4:15–18; Ps 78:58; 97:7
9 [n]**Nu 26:11;** [o]Ex 34:7; **Nu 10:35;** 14:18
10 [p]**Ex 34:7;** [q]Nu 14:18; Dt 7:9; Ne 1:5; Jer 32:18; Da 9:4
11 [r]Ps 139:20; [s]Lev 19:12; Dt 10:20; Mt 5:33–37
12 [t]Ex 16:23–30; 31:13–17; Mk 2:27–28
14 [u]**Ge 2:2;** Mt 12:2; Mk 2:27; Heb 4:4; [v]Job 31:13; Jer 34:9–11; [w]Jer 17:21,24
15 [x]**Ge 15:13;** [y]Ex 6:1; Ps 108:6; Jer 32:21; [z]**Dt 4:34**
16 [a]Mal 1:6; [b]Ex 21:17; Lev 19:3; Eze 22:7; Mt 15:4*; 19:19*; Mk 7:10*; 10:9*; Lk 18:20*; Eph 6:2–3*; [c]**Dt 4:40;** 11:9; Pr 3:1–2
17 [d]Ge 9:6; Lev 24:17; Ecc 3:3; Jer 40:15; 41:3; Mt 5:21–22*; 19:19*; Mk 10:19*; Lk 18:20*; Ro 13:9*; Jas 2:11*
18 [e]Lev 20:10; Mt 5:27–30; 19:18*; Mk 10:19*; Lk 18:20*; Ro 13:9*; Jas 2:11*
19 [f]Lev 19:11; Mt 19:19*; Mk 10:19*; Lk 18:20*; Ro 13:9*
20 [g]**Ex 23:1;** Mt 19:18*; Mk 10:19*; Lk 18:20*
21 [h]Ro 7:7*; 13:9*
22 [i]**Ex 20:21;** [j]**Ex 24:12**
23 [k]**Ex 3:16**
24 [l]Dt 4:34; 8:5; 11:2; Isa 53:4; [m]**Dt 3:24;** [n]Ex 19:19
25 [o]Ex 20:18–19; Dt 18:16; Heb 12:19
26 [p]**Ex 33:20;** Dt 4:33; Jdg 6:22–23; 13:22; Isa 6:5
27 [q]**Ex 19:8;** [r]**Ex 24:7**
28 [s]Dt 18:17
29 [t]Ps 81:8,13; [u]Jos 22:5; Ps 78:7; [v]ver 33; **Dt 4:1**,40; 12:25; 22:7 *31* [w]Ex 24:12
32 [x]**Dt 4:29;** 10:12; [y]Dt 17:11,20; 28:14; Jos 1:7; 1Ki 15:5; 2Ki 22:2; Pr 4:27
33 [z]Isa 3:10; Jer 7:23; 38:20; **Lk 1:6;** [a]**ver 29**

[a]7 Or *besides*

the land that you are crossing the Jordan
to possess, 2so that you, your children
and their children after them may fear[a]
the LORD your God as long as you live[b]
by keeping all his decrees and com-
mands[c] that I give you, and so that you
may enjoy long life.[d] 3Hear, O Israel,
and be careful to obey[e] so that it may go
well with you and that you may increase
greatly[f] in a land flowing with milk and
honey,[g] just as the LORD, the God of
your fathers, promised[h] you.
4Hear, O Israel: The LORD our God,
the LORD is one.[a][i] 5Love[j] the LORD your
God with all your heart[k] and with all
your soul and with all your strength.[l]
6These commandments that I give you
today are to be upon your hearts.[m]
7Impress them on your children. Talk
about them when you sit at home and
when you walk along the road, when
you lie down and when you get up.[n]
8Tie them as symbols on your hands and
bind them on your foreheads.[o] 9Write
them on the door-frames of your houses
and on your gates.[p]
10When the LORD your God brings
you into the land he swore to your
fathers, to Abraham, Isaac and Jacob, to
give you—a land with large, flourishing
cities you did not build,[q] 11houses filled
with all kinds of good things you did not
provide, wells you did not dig,[r] and
vineyards and olive groves you did not
plant—then when you eat and are sat-
isfied,[s] 12be careful that you do not
forget[t] the LORD, who brought you out
of Egypt, out of the land of slavery.
13Fear the LORD[u] your God, serve him
only[v] and take your oaths[w] in his name.[x]
14Do not follow other gods, the gods of
the peoples around you; 15for the LORD
your God[y], who is among you, is a
jealous God and his anger will burn
against you, and he will destroy you
from the face of the land. 16Do not test
the LORD your God[z] as you did at Mas-
sah. 17Be sure to keep[a] the commands of
the LORD your God and the stipulations
and decrees he has given you.[b] 18Do
what is right and good in the LORD's
sight,[c] so that it may go well[d] with you
and you may go in and take over the
good land that the LORD promised on
oath to your forefathers, 19thrusting out
all your enemies[e] before you, as the
LORD said.
20In the future, when your son asks
you,[f] "What is the meaning of the
stipulations, decrees and laws the LORD
our God has commanded you?" 21tell
him: "We were slaves of Pharaoh in
Egypt, but the LORD brought us out of
Egypt with a mighty hand.[g] 22Before our
eyes the LORD sent miraculous signs and
wonders—great and terrible—upon
Egypt and Pharaoh and his whole
household. 23But he brought us out
from there to bring us in and give us the
land that he promised on oath to our
forefathers. 24The LORD commanded us
to obey all these decrees and to fear the
LORD our God,[h] so that we might always
prosper and be kept alive, as is the case
today.[i] 25And if we are careful to obey all
this law[j] before the LORD our God, as he
has commanded us, that will be our
righteousness."[k]

Driving Out the Nations

7 When the LORD your God brings
you into the land you are entering
to possess[a] and drives out before you
many nations[b]—the Hittites,[c] Girgash-
ites,[d] Amorites,[e] Canaanites, Perizzites,[f]
Hivites[g] and Jebusites,[h] seven nations
larger and stronger than you—2and
when the LORD your God has delivered[i]
them over to you and you have defeated
them, then you must destroy[j] them
totally.[a][k] Make no treaty[l] with them,
and show them no mercy.[m] 3Do not
intermarry with them.[n] Do not give
your daughters to their sons or take
their daughters for your sons, 4for they
will turn your sons away from following
me to serve other gods,[o] and the LORD's
anger will burn against you and will
quickly destroy[p] you. 5This is what you
are to do to them: Break down their
altars, smash their sacred stones, cut
down their Asherah poles[b][q] and burn
their idols in the fire.[r] 6For you are a
people holy[s] to the LORD your God.[t] The
LORD your God has chosen[u] you out of
all the peoples on the face of the earth to
be his people, his treasured posses-
sion[v].

Ch. 6

2 [a]**Ex 20:20; 1Sa 12:24;** [b]Dt 4:9; [c]**Ge 26:5;** [d]**Ex 20:12**
3 [e]**Ex 19:5;** [f]Ge 15:5; Dt 5:33; [g]**Ex 3:8;** Dt 32:13–14; [h]Ex 13:5
4 [i]Dt 4:35,39; Ne 9:6; Ps 86:10; Isa 44:6; Zec 14:9; Mk 12:29*; Jn 10:30; 1Co 8:4; Eph 4:6; Jas 2:19
5 [j]Dt 11:1,22; Mt 22:37*; Mk 12:30*; Lk 10:27*; [k]1Sa 12:24; [l]Dt 4:29; 10:12; Jos 22:5
6 [m]ver 8; Dt 11:18; 30:14; 32:46; Ps 26:2; 37:31; 40:8; 119:11; Pr 3:3; Isa 51:7; Jer 17:1; 31:33; Eze 40:4
7 [n]Dt 4:9; 11:19; Pr 22:6; Eph 6:4
8 [o]**ver 6; Ex 13:9;** Mt 23:5
9 [p]Dt 11:20
10 [q]**Ge 11:4;** Dt 12:29; 19:1; Jos 24:13; Ps 105:44
11 [r]Jer 2:13; [s]**Lev 26:5;** Dt 8:10; 14:29; 31:20
12 [t]Dt 4:9,23; 2Ki 17:38; Ps 44:17; 78:7; 103:2
13 [u]Ps 33:8; 34:9; [v]Dt 13:4; 1Sa 7:3; Jer 44:10; Mt 4:10*; Lk 4:4*,8; [w]1Sa 20:3; [x]**Ex 20:7; Mt 5:33**
15 [y]Dt 4:24; 5:9
16 [z]**Ex 17:2;** Mt 4:7*; Lk 4:12*
17 [a]**Lev 26:3;** [b]Dt 11:22; Ps 119:4,56,100, 134,168
18 [c]2Ki 18:6; Isa 36:7; 38:3; [d]Dt 4:40
19 [e]Ex 23:27; Jos 21:44; Ps 78:53; 107:2; 136:24
20 [f]**Ex 10:2**
21 [g]**Dt 4:34**
24 [h]Dt 10:12; 30:6; Ps 86:11; Jer 32:39; [i]Ps 27:12; 41:2; **Ro 10:5**
25 [j]Ps 103:18; 119:34,55; [k]Dt 24:13; **Ro 9:31**

Ch. 7

1 [a]**Lev 14:34; Dt 4:38;** [b]Dt 20:16–18; 31:3; [c]Ge 15:20; [d]**Ge 10:16;** [e]**Dt 1:7;** [f]Ge 13:7; [g]**Ge 10:17;** [h]Jos 3:10,
2 [i]**Dt 2:33;** [j]**Dt 2:34;** [k]Nu 31:17; Dt 33:27; Jos 11:11; [l]**Ex 23:32;** [m]ver 16; Dt 13:8; 19:13; 25:12
3 [n]Ex 34:15–16; Jos 22:16; Da 9:7
4 [o]Jdg 3:6; [p]**Dt 4:26**
5 [q]**Ex 34:13;** Dt 16:21; [r]**Ex 23:24**
6 [s]Ex 19:6; **Lev 27:30;** [t]Dt 26:19; Ps 30:4; 37:28; 50:5; 52:9; [u]Dt 14:2; 1Ki 3:8; Isa 41:9; Eze 20:5; [v]**Ge 17:7; Ex 8:22; 34:9;** Isa 43:1; Ro 9:4; Tit 2:14

---

[a]4 Or *The LORD our God is one LORD;* or *The LORD is our God, the LORD is one;* or *The LORD is our God, the LORD alone*

[a]2 The Hebrew term refers to the irrevocable giving over of things or persons to the LORD, often by totally destroying them; also in verse 26.

[b]5 That is, symbols of the goddess Asherah; here and elsewhere in Deuteronomy

7The LORD did not set his affection on you and choose you because you were more numerous[w] than other peoples, for you were the fewest[x] of all peoples.[y] 8But it was because the LORD loved[z] you and kept the oath he swore[a] to your forefathers that he brought you out with a mighty hand[b] and redeemed[c] you from the land of slavery,[d] from the power of Pharaoh king of Egypt. 9Know therefore that the LORD your God is God;[e] he is the faithful God,[f] keeping his covenant of love[g] to a thousand generations[h] of those who love him and keep his commands.[i] 10But

those who hate him he will repay to
  their face by destruction;
he will not be slow to repay to their
  face those who hate him.[j]

11Therefore, take care to follow the commands, decrees and laws I give you today.

12If you pay attention to these laws and are careful to follow them, then the LORD your God will keep his covenant of love with you, as he swore to your forefathers.[k] 13He will love you and bless you[l] and increase your numbers.[m] He will bless the fruit of your womb,[n] the crops of your land—your grain, new wine[o] and oil[p]—the calves of your herds and the lambs of your flocks in the land that he swore to your forefathers to give you.[q] 14You will be blessed more than any other people; none of your men or women will be childless, nor any of your livestock without young.[r] 15The LORD will keep you free from every disease.[s] He will not inflict on you the horrible diseases you knew in Egypt,[t] but he will inflict them on all who hate you.[u] 16You must destroy all the peoples the LORD your God gives over to you.[v] Do not look on them with pity[w] and do not serve their gods,[x] for that will be a snare[y] to you.

17You may say to yourselves, "These nations are stronger than we are. How can we drive them out?[z]" 18But do not be afraid[a] of them; remember well what the LORD your God did to Pharaoh and to all Egypt.[b] 19You saw with your own eyes the great trials, the miraculous signs and wonders, the mighty hand[c] and outstretched arm, with which the LORD your God brought you out. The LORD your God will do the same to all the peoples you now fear.[d] 20Moreover, the LORD your God will send the hornet[e] among them until even the survivors who hide from you have perished. 21Do not be terrified by them, for the LORD your God, who is among you,[f] is a great and awesome God.[g] 22The LORD your God will drive out those nations before you, little by little.[h] You will not be allowed to eliminate them all at once, or the wild animals will multiply around you. 23But the LORD your God will deliver them over to you, throwing them into great confusion until they are destroyed.[i] 24He will give their kings[j] into your hand,[k] and you will wipe out their names from under heaven. No-one will be able to stand up against you;[l] you will destroy them.[m] 25The images of their gods you are to burn[n] in the fire. Do not covet[o] the silver and gold on them, and do not take it for yourselves, or you will be ensnared[p] by it, for it is detestable[q] to the LORD your God. 26Do not bring a detestable thing into your house or you, like it, will be set apart for destruction.[r] Utterly abhor and detest it, for it is set apart for destruction.

Do Not Forget the LORD

8 Be careful to follow every command I am giving you today, so that you may live[a] and increase and may enter and possess the land that the LORD promised on oath to your forefathers.[b] 2Remember how the LORD your God led[c] you all the way in the desert these forty years, to humble you and to test[d] you in order to know what was in your heart, whether or not you would keep his commands. 3He humbled[e] you, causing you to hunger and then feeding you with manna,[f] which neither you nor your fathers had known, to teach[g] you that man does not live on bread[h] alone but on every word that comes from the mouth[i] of the LORD.[j] 4Your clothes did not wear out and your feet did not swell during these forty years.[k] 5Know then in your heart that as a man disciplines his son, so the LORD your God disciplines you.[l]

6Observe the commands of the LORD your God, walking in his ways[m] and revering him.[n] 7For the LORD your God is bringing you into a good land[o]—a

7 [w]**Ge 22:17;** [x]Ge 34:30; [y]Dt 4:37; 10:22
8 [z]**Dt 4:37;** 1Ki 10:9; 2Ch 2:11; Ps 44:3; [a]Ex 32:13; **Nu 14:8;** Ro 11:28; [b]**Ex 3:20;** [c]**Ex 6:6;** [d]**Ex 13:14**
9 [e]**Dt 4:35;** [f]Ps 18:25; 33:4; 108:4; 145:13; 146:6; Isa 49:7; Jer 42:5; Hos 11:12; **1Co 1:9;** [g]ver 12; 1Ki 8:23; 2Ch 6:14; Ne 1:5; 9:32; [h]**Ex 20:6;** [i]**Dt 5:10**
10 [j]**Lev 26:28; Nu 10:35;** Na 1:2
12 [k]Lev 26:3–13; Dt 28:1–14; Ps 105:8–9; Mic 7:20
13 [l]Ps 11:5; 146:8; Pr 15:9; Isa 51:1; Jn 14:21; [m]**Ge 17:6;** Ex 1:7; Dt 1:10; 13:17; 30:5; Ps 107:38; [n]**Ge 49:25;** [o]**Ge 27:28;** [p]**Nu 18:12;** [q]Dt 28:4
14 [r]Ex 23:26
15 [s]**Ex 15:26;** [t]**Ex 9:9;** [u]**Ex 23:25;** Dt 30:8–10
16 [v]ver 24; Jos 6:2; 10:26; [w]**ver 2;** [x]Jdg 3:6; Ezr 9:1; Ps 106:36; [y]ver 25; **Ex 10:7**
17 [z]Nu 33:53
18 [a]**Nu 14:9; Dt 1:21,29;** [b]Ps 105:5; 119:52
19 [c]Ps 136:12; [d]Dt 4:34
20 [e]**Ex 23:28**
21 [f]**Ge 17:7;** Jos 3:10; [g]Dt 10:17; Ne 1:5; 9:32; Ps 47:2; 66:3; 68:35; Isa 9:6; Da 9:4
22 [h]Ex 23:28–30
23 [i]Ex 23:27; Jos 10:10
24 [j]Jos 10:24; Ps 110:5; [k]**ver 16;** [l]**Ex 23:31;** Dt 11:25; Jos 1:5; 10:8; 23:9; [m]Jos 21:44
25 [n]**Ex 4:14; 32:20;** [o]Ex 20:17; Jos 7:21; [p]**ver 16;** [q]Dt 17:1
26 [r]Lev 27:28–29

Ch. 8
1 [a]Dt 4:1; [b]**Ex 19:5;** Job 36:11; Ps 16:11; Eze 20:19
2 [c]Dt 29:5; Ps 136:16; Am 2:10; [d]**Ge 22:1**
3 [e]2Ch 36:12; Ps 44:9; Pr 18:12; Isa 2:11; Jer 44:10; [f]**Ex 16:4;** [g]1Ki 8:36; Ps 25:5; 94:12; 119:171; [h]ver 9; **Ge 3:19;** Job 23:12; Ps 104:15; Pr 28:21; Isa 51:14; Jer 42:14; [i]Job 22:22; Ps 119:13; 138:4; [j]**Ex 16:2–3;** Mt 4:4*; Lk 4:4*
4 [k]Dt 29:5; Ne 9:21
5 [l]Dt 4:36; 2Sa 7:14; Job 5:17; 33:19; Pr 3:11–12; Heb 12:5–11; Rev 3:19
6 [m]**Ex 33:13;** 1Ki 3:14; Ps 81:13; 95:10; [n]Dt 5:33
7 [o]Ps 106:24; Jer 3:19; Eze 20:6

land with streams and pools of water,
with springs flowing in the valleys and
hills;[p] 8a land with wheat and barley,[q]
vines[r] and fig-trees,[s] pomegranates,
olive oil and honey;[t] 9a land where
bread[u] will not be scarce and you will
lack nothing;[v] a land where the rocks are
iron and you can dig copper out of the
hills.[w]
10When you have eaten and are satis-
fied,[x] praise the LORD your God for the
good land he has given you. 11Be careful
that you do not forget[y] the LORD your
God, failing to observe his commands,
his laws and his decrees that I am giving
you this day. 12Otherwise, when you
eat and are satisfied, when you build
fine houses and settle down,[z] 13and
when your herds and flocks grow large
and your silver and gold increase and all
you have is multiplied, 14then your
heart will become proud and you will
forget[a] the LORD your God, who brought
you out of Egypt, out of the land of
slavery. 15He led you through the vast
and dreadful desert,[b] that thirsty and
waterless land, with its venomous
snakes[c] and scorpions. He brought you
water out of hard rock.[d] 16He gave you
manna[e] to eat in the desert, something
your fathers had never known,[f] to hum-
ble and to test[g] you so that in the end it
might go well with you. 17You may say
to yourself,[h] "My power and the
strength of my hands[i] have produced
this wealth for me." 18But remember the
LORD your God, for it is he who gives
you the ability to produce wealth,[j] and
so confirms his covenant, which he
swore to your forefathers, as it is today.
19If you ever forget the LORD your God
and follow other gods[k] and worship and
bow down to them, I testify against you
today that you will surely be destroyed.[l]
20Like the nations[m] the LORD destroyed
before you, so you will be destroyed for
not obeying the LORD your God.[n]

Not Because of Israel's Righteousness

9 Hear, O Israel. You are now about
to cross the Jordan[a] to go in and
dispossess nations greater and stronger
than you,[b] with large cities[c] that have
walls up to the sky.[d] 2The people are
strong and tall—Anakites! You know
about them and have heard it said:
"Who can stand up against the Ana-
kites?"[e] 3But be assured today that the
LORD your God is the one who goes
across ahead of you[f] like a devouring
fire.[g] He will destroy them; he will sub-
due them before you. And you will
drive them out and annihilate them
quickly,[h] as the LORD has promised you.
4After the LORD your God has driven
them out before you, do not say to
yourself,[i] "The LORD has brought me
here to take possession of this land be-
cause of my righteousness." No, it is on
account of the wickedness[j] of these na-
tions[k] that the LORD is going to drive
them out before you. 5It is not because
of your righteousness or your integrity[l]
that you are going in to take possession
of their land; but on account of the
wickedness[m] of these nations,[n] the
LORD your God will drive them out[o]
before you, to accomplish what he
swore[p] to your fathers, to Abraham,
Isaac and Jacob.[q] 6Understand, then,
that it is not because of your righteous-
ness that the LORD your God is giving
you this good land to possess, for you
are a stiff-necked people.[r]

The Golden Calf

7Remember this and never forget how
you provoked[s] the LORD your God to
anger in the desert. From the day you
left Egypt until you arrived here, you
have been rebellious[t] against the LORD.[u]
8At Horeb you aroused the LORD's
wrath[v] so that he was angry enough to
destroy you.[w] 9When I went up on the
mountain to receive the tablets of stone,
the tablets of the covenant[x] that the
LORD had made with you, I stayed on
the mountain forty days[y] and forty
nights; I ate no bread and drank no
water.[z] 10The LORD gave me two stone
tablets inscribed by the finger of God.[a]
On them were all the commandments
the LORD proclaimed to you on the
mountain out of the fire, on the day of
the assembly.[b]
11At the end of the forty days and
forty nights,[c] the LORD gave me the two
stone tablets,[d] the tablets of the cov-
enant. 12Then the LORD told me, "Go
down from here at once, because your
people whom you brought out of Egypt
have become corrupt.[e] They have
turned away quickly[f] from what I com-
manded them and have made a cast idol
for themselves."
13And the LORD said to me, "I have
seen this people[g], and they are a stiff-
necked people indeed! 14Let me alone,[h]

7 [p]Dt 11:9–12; Jer 2:7
8 [q]**Ex 9:31**; [r]**Ge 49:11**; [s]**Nu 13:23; 1Ki 4:25**; [t]Dt 32:13; Ps 81:16
9 [u]**ver 3**; [v]Jdg 18:10; [w]Job 28:2
10 [x]Dt 6:10–12
11 [y]Dt 4:9
12 [z]Pr 30:9; Hos 13:6
14 [a]ver 11; Ps 78:7; 106:21
15 [b]**Dt 1:19; 32:10**; [c]Nu 21:6; Isa 14:29; 30:6; [d]Ex 17:6; Dt 32:13; Job 28:9; Ps 78:15; 114:8
16 [e]**Ex 16:14**; [f]Ex 16:15; [g]**Ge 22:1**
17 [h]Dt 9:4,7,24; 31:27; [i]Jdg 7:2; Ps 44:3; Isa 10:13
18 [j]Ge 26:13; Dt 26:10; 28:4; 1Sa 2:7; Ps 25:13; 112:3; Pr 8:18; 10:22; Ecc 9:11; Hos 2:8
19 [k]Dt 6:14; Ps 16:4; Jer 7:6; 13:10; 25:6; [l]Dt 4:26; 30:18
20 [m]2Ki 21:2; Ps 10:16; [n]Eze 5:5–17

Ch. 9

1 [a]**Nu 35:10**; [b]Dt 4:38; [c]**Nu 13:28**; [d]**Ge 11:4**
2 [e]Nu 13:22; Jos 11:22
3 [f]Dt 31:3; Jos 3:11; [g]**Ex 15:7; 19:18**; Heb 12:29; [h]**Ex 23:31**
4 [i]**Dt 8:17**; [j]2Ki 16:3; 17:8; 21:2; Ezr 9:11; [k]**Ex 23:24; Lev 18:21,24–30**; Dt 18:9–14
5 [l]**Eph 2:9**; [m]Dt 18:9; [n]**Lev 18:25**; [o]Dt 4:38; 11:23; [p]**Ge 12:7**; [q]Eze 36:32
6 [r]**Ex 32:9**; Ac 7:51
7 [s]**Nu 11:33**; [t]**Ex 23:21**; [u]**Ex 14:11**

8 [v]Nu 16:46; 1Sa 28:18; Job 20:28; Ps 2:12; 7:11; 69:24; 110:5; Isa 9:19; Eze 20:13; [w]Ex 32:7–10; Ezr 9:14; Ps 106:19
9 [x]**Dt 4:13**; [y]**Ge 7:4**; [z]**Ex 24:12**
10 [a]**Ex 31:18**; [b]Dt 10:4; 18:16
11 [c]**Ge 7:4**; [d]**Ex 24:12**
12 [e]**Dt 4:16**; [f]Jdg 2:17
13 [g]ver 6; Dt 10:16
14 [h]Ex 32:10

so that I may destroy them and blot out[i]
their name from under heaven.[j] And I
will make you into a nation stronger and
more numerous than they."
15So I turned and went down from the
mountain while it was ablaze with fire.
And the two tablets of the covenant
were in my hands.[a][k] 16When I looked, I
saw that you had sinned against the
LORD your God; you had made for
yourselves an idol cast in the shape of a
calf.[l] You had turned aside quickly from
the way that the LORD had commanded
you. 17So I took the two tablets and
threw them out of my hands, breaking
them to pieces before your eyes.
18Then once again I fell[m] prostrate be-
fore the LORD for forty days and forty
nights; I ate no bread and drank no
water,[n] because of all the sin you had
committed,[o] doing what was evil in the
LORD's sight and so provoking him to
anger. 19I feared the anger and wrath of
the LORD, for he was angry enough with
you to destroy you.[p] But again the LORD
listened to me.[q] 20And the LORD was
angry enough with Aaron to destroy
him, but at that time I prayed for Aaron
too. 21Also I took that sinful thing of
yours, the calf you had made, and
burned it in the fire. Then I crushed it
and ground it to powder as fine as dust[r]
and threw the dust into a stream that
flowed down the mountain.[s]
22You also made the LORD angry[t] at
Taberah,[u] at Massah[v] and at Kibroth
Hattaavah.[w]
23And when the LORD sent you out
from Kadesh Barnea,[x] he said, "Go up
and take possession[y] of the land I have
given you." But you rebelled[z] against
the command of the LORD your God.
You did not trust[a] him or obey him.
24You have been rebellious against the
LORD ever since I have known you.[b]
25I lay prostrate before the LORD those
forty days and forty nights[c] because the
LORD had said he would destroy you.[d]
26I prayed to the LORD and said, "O
Sovereign LORD, do not destroy your
people,[e] your own inheritance[f] that you
redeemed[g] by your great power and
brought out of Egypt with a mighty
hand.[h] 27Remember your servants
Abraham, Isaac and Jacob. Overlook
the stubbornness[i] of this people, their
wickedness and their sin. 28Otherwise,
the country[j] from which you brought us
will say, 'Because the LORD was not able
to take them into the land he had prom-
ised them, and because he hated them,[k]
he brought them out to put them to
death in the desert.'[l] 29But they are your
people,[m] your inheritance[n] that you
brought out by your great power and
your outstretched arm."[o]

Tablets Like the First Ones

10 At that time the LORD said to
me, "Chisel out two stone
tablets[a] like the first ones and come up
to me on the mountain. Also make a
wooden chest.[a] 2I will write on the tab-
lets the words that were on the first
tablets, which you broke. Then you are
to put them in the chest."[b]
3So I made the ark out of acacia wood[c]
and chiselled[d] out two stone tablets like
the first ones, and I went up on the
mountain with the two tablets in my
hands. 4The LORD wrote on these tablets
what he had written before, the Ten
Commandments[e] he had proclaimed[f] to
you on the mountain, out of the fire, on
the day of the assembly.[g] And the LORD
gave them to me. 5Then I came back
down the mountain[h] and put the tablets
in the ark[i] I had made,[j] as the LORD
commanded me, and they are there
now.[k]
6(The Israelites travelled from the
wells of the Jaakanites to Moserah.[l]
There Aaron died[m] and was buried, and
Eleazar[n] his son succeeded him as
priest.[o] 7From there they travelled to
Gudgodah and on to Jotbathah, a
land with streams of water.[p] 8At that
time the LORD set apart the tribe of
Levi[q] to carry the ark of the covenant[r] of
the LORD, to stand before the LORD to
minister[s] and to pronounce blessings[t]
in his name, as they still do today.[u]
9That is why the Levites have no share
or inheritance among their brothers;
the LORD is their inheritance,[v] as the
LORD your God told them.)
10Now I had stayed on the mountain
forty days and nights, as I did the first
time, and the LORD listened to me at this
time also. It was not his will to destroy
you.[w] 11"Go," the LORD said to me, "and
lead the people on their way, so that
they may enter and possess the land
that I swore to their fathers to give
them."

Fear the LORD

12And now, O Israel, what does the
LORD your God ask of you[x] but to fear[y]
the LORD your God, to walk[z] in all his
ways, to love him,[a] to serve the LORD[b]

14 [i]**Nu 14:12**; [j]Jer 7:16
15 [k]**Ex 32:15**
16 [l]**Ex 32:4**
18 [m]**Ex 34:28**; [n]ver 9; [o]**Ex 32:31**
19 [p]**Ex 32:14**; Heb 12:21*; [q]ver 26; Ex 34:10; **Nu 11:2**; 1Sa 7:9; Jer 15:1
21 [r]Ps 18:42; Isa 29:5; 40:15; [s]Ex 32:20; Isa 2:18; Mic 1:7
22 [t]**Nu 1:53**; [u]Nu 11:3; [v]**Ex 17:7**; [w]Nu 11:34
23 [x]**Dt 1:2**; [y]Dt 1:21; [z]**Nu 14:9**; [a]**Dt 1:32**; Ps 106:24
24 [b]**Dt 8:17**
25 [c]**Ge 7:4**; [d]ver 18; **Ex 33:17**
26 [e]**Ex 33:13**; [f]**Ex 34:9**; [g]**Ex 6:6**; Dt 15:15; 2Sa 7:23; Ps 78:35; [h]**ver 19**; **Ex 32:11**
27 [i]ver 6; **Ex 32:9**
28 [j]Dt 32:27; [k]**Dt 1:27**; [l]**Ex 32:12**; Jos 7:9
29 [m]**Ex 33:13**; [n]**Ex 34:9**; Dt 32:9; [o]Dt 4:34; Ne 1:10; Jer 27:5; 32:17

Ch. 10

1 [a]Ex 34:1–2
2 [b]Ex 25:16,21; 2Ch 5:10; 6:11
3 [c]Ex 37:1–9; [d]Ex 34:4
4 [e]**Ex 24:12**; **34:28**; [f]Ex 20:1; [g]**Dt 9:10**
5 [h]**Ex 19:11**; [i]**Ex 25:10**; **1Sa 3:3**; [j]**Ex 25:21**; [k]1Ki 8:9
6 [l]Nu 33:30; [m]**Nu 27:13**; [n]Ex 6:23; [o]**Nu 20:25–28**
7 [p]Nu 33:32–34; Ps 42:1; SS 5:12; Isa 32:2
8 [q]**Nu 3:6**; [r]**Nu 10:33**; [s]**Nu 16:9**; [t]**Ge 48:20**; [u]1Ch 23:26
9 [v]**Nu 18:20**
10 [w]**Ex 33:17**
12 [x]Mic 6:8; [y]**Ex 20:20**; [z]1Ki 2:3; 3:3; 9:4; [a]Dt 5:33; 6:13; Mt 22:37; 1Ti 1:5; [b]Dt 11:13; 28:47; Ps 100:2

[a]*15* Or *And I had the two tablets of the covenant with me, one in each hand* [a]*1* That is, an ark

your God with all your heart[c] and with
all your soul,[d] 13and to observe the
LORD's commands[e] and decrees that I
am giving you today for your own
good?[f]
14To the LORD your God belong the
heavens,[g,h,i] even the highest heavens,[j,k]
the earth and everything in it.[l] 15Yet the
LORD set his affection on your fore-
fathers and loved[m] them, and he chose
you,[n] their descendants, above all the
nations, as it is today.[o] 16Circumcise[p]
your hearts,[q] therefore, and do not be
stiff-necked[r] any longer. 17For the LORD
your God is God of gods[s] and Lord of
lords,[t] the great God, mighty and awe-
some,[u] who shows no partiality[v] and
accepts no bribes.[w] 18He defends the
cause of the fatherless and the widow,[x]
and loves the alien, giving him food and
clothing.[y] 19And you are to love[z] those
who are aliens,[a] for you yourselves were
aliens in Egypt.[b] 20Fear the LORD your
God and serve him.[c] Hold fast[d] to him
and take your oaths in his name.[e] 21He is
your praise;[f] he is your God, who per-
formed for you those great[g] and awe-
some wonders[h] you saw with your own
eyes. 22Your forefathers who went
down into Egypt were seventy in all,[i]
and now the LORD your God has made
you as numerous as the stars in the sky.[j]

Love and Obey the LORD

11 Love[a] the LORD your God and
keep his requirements, his de-
crees, his laws and his commands
always.[b] 2Remember today that your
children[c] were not the ones who saw
and experienced the discipline of the
LORD your God:[d] his majesty,[e] his
mighty hand, his outstretched arm;[f]
3the signs he performed and the things
he did in the heart of Egypt, both to
Pharaoh king of Egypt and to his whole
country;[g] 4what he did to the Egyptian
army, to its horses and chariots,[h] how
he overwhelmed them with the waters
of the Red Sea[a][i] as they were pursuing
you, and how the LORD brought lasting
ruin on them. 5It was not your children
who saw what he did for you in the
desert until you arrived at this place,
6and what he did[j] to Dathan and Abir-
am, sons of Eliab the Reubenite, when
the earth opened[k] its mouth right in the
middle of all Israel and swallowed them
up with their households, their tents
and every living thing that belonged to
them. 7But it was your own eyes that
saw all these great things the LORD has
done.[l]
8Observe therefore all the com-
mands[m] I am giving you today, so that
you may have the strength to go in and
take over the land that you are crossing
the Jordan to possess,[n] 9and so that you
may live long[o] in the land that the LORD
swore[p] to your forefathers to give to
them and their descendants, a land
flowing with milk and honey.[q] 10The
land you are entering to take over is not
like the land of Egypt,[r] from which you
have come, where you planted your
seed and irrigated it by foot as in a
vegetable garden. 11But the land you are
crossing the Jordan to take possession
of is a land of mountains and valleys[s]
that drinks rain from heaven.[t] 12It is a
land the LORD your God cares for; the
eyes[u] of the LORD your God are con-
tinually on it from the beginning of the
year to its end.
13So if you faithfully obey[v] the com-
mands I am giving you today—to love[w]
the LORD your God and to serve him
with all your heart and with all your
soul[x]—14then I will send rain[y] on your
land in its season, both autumn and
spring rains,[z] so that you may gather
in your grain, new wine and oil. 15I
will provide grass[a] in the fields for
your cattle, and you will eat and be
satisfied.[b]
16Be careful, or you will be enticed to
turn away and worship other gods and
bow down to them.[c] 17Then the LORD's
anger[d] will burn against you, and he will
shut[e] the heavens so that it will not rain
and the ground will yield no produce,[f]
and you will soon perish[g] from the good
land the LORD is giving you. 18Fix these
words of mine in your hearts and
minds; tie them as symbols on your
hands and bind them on your fore-
heads.[h] 19Teach them to your children,[i]
talking about them when you sit at
home and when you walk along the
road, when you lie down and when you
get up.[j] 20Write them on the door-
frames of your houses and on your
gates,[k] 21so that your days and the days

12 [c]**Dt 6:5**; Ps 119:2; [d]**Dt 5:32**
13 [e]**Dt 4:2**; [f]Dt 5:33; 6:24
14 [g]Ps 148:4; Isa 19:1; Hab 3:8; [h]Ne 9:6; Job 35:5; Ps 8:3; 89:11; 104:3; [i]Dt 33:26; [j]Ps 115:16; [k]1Ki 8:27; [l]Ex 19:5; Ps 24:1; Ac 17:24
15 [m]**Dt 4:37**; [n]Ps 105:6; 135:4; [o]**Nu 14:8**; Ro 11:28; 1Pe 2:9
16 [p]**Ge 17:11**; [q]**Lev 26:41**; Dt 30:6; Jer 32:39; [r]**Ex 32:9**; **Dt 9:13**
17 [s]Jos 22:22; Ps 135:5; 136:2; Da 2:47; 11:36; [t]Ps 136:3; **1Ti 6:15**; [u]**Dt 7:21**; [v]Dt 1:17; Mal 2:9; [w]**Ex 23:8**; **Lev 19:16**
18 [x]Ex 22:21–24; 23:9; Lev 19:33; Dt 27:19; Job 29:13; Ps 94:6; Isa 10:2; Jer 49:11; [y]**Nu 10:32**
19 [z]Dt 7:12; [a]**Ex 22:21**; **Dt 24:19**; [b]**Lev 19:34**; Eze 47:22–23
20 [c]Mt 4:10; [d]Dt 11:22; 13:4; 30:20; Jos 23:8; Ru 1:14; 2Ki 18:6; Ps 119:31; Isa 38:3; [e]**Ex 20:7**
21 [f]**Ex 15:2**; [g]1Sa 12:24; Ps 126:2; [h]2Sa 7:23
22 [i]**Ge 34:30**; **46:26**; Ac 7:14; [j]**Ge 12:2**; **Nu 10:36**

Ch. 11

1 [a]**Dt 6:5**; [b]**Lev 8:35**
2 [c]Dt 31:13; Ps 78:6; [d]**Dt 5:24**; [e]**Dt 3:24**; [f]Ps 136:12
3 [g]Ex 7:8–21
4 [h]**Ex 15:1**; [i]**Ex 14:27**; **Nu 21:4**
6 [j]Nu 16:1–35; Ps 106:16–18; [k]Isa 24:19
7 [l]Dt 5:3
8 [m]Ezr 9:10; [n]Dt 31:6–7, 23; Jos 1:7
9 [o]**Dt 5:16**; [p]Dt 9:5; [q]**Ex 3:8**
10 [r]Isa 11:15; 37:25
11 [s]Eze 36:4; [t]Dt 8:7; Ne 9:25
12 [u]1Ki 8:29; 9:3
13 [v]**Dt 6:17**; [w]**Dt 10:12**; [x]Dt 4:29; Jer 17:24
14 [y]**Lev 26:4**; Ac 14:17; [z]Ps 147:8; Jer 3:3; 5:24; Joel 2:23; Jas 5:7
15 [a]Ps 104:14; [b]**Lev 26:5**
16 [c]Dt 4:19; 8:19; 29:18; Job 31:9,27
17 [d]Dt 6:15; 9:19; [e]1Ki 17:1; 2Ch 6:26; 7:13; [f]**Lev 26:20**; [g]Dt 4:26; 28:12,24
18 [h]**Ex 13:9**; Dt 6:6–8
19 [i]**Ex 12:26**; Dt 6:7; Ps 145:4; Isa 38:19; Jer 32:39; [j]Dt 4:9–10
20 [k]Dt 6:9

[a]4 Hebrew *Yam Suph*; that is, Sea of Reeds

of your children may be many[l] in the land that the LORD swore to give your forefathers, as many as the days that the heavens are above the earth.[m]

22 If you carefully observe[n] all these commands I am giving you to follow —to love[o] the LORD your God, to walk in all his ways and to hold fast[p] to him —23 then the LORD will drive out[q] all these nations[r] before you, and you will dispossess nations larger and stronger than you.[s] 24 Every place where you set your foot will be yours:[t] Your territory will extend from the desert to Lebanon, and from the Euphrates River[u] to the western sea.[b] 25 No man will be able to stand against you. The LORD your God, as he promised you, will put the terror[v] and fear of you on the whole land, wherever you go.[w]

26 See, I am setting before you today a blessing[x] and a curse[y]—27 the blessing[z] if you obey the commands of the LORD your God that I am giving you today; 28 the curse if you disobey[a] the commands of the LORD your God and turn from the way that I command you today by following other gods,[b] which you have not known. 29 When the LORD your God has brought you into the land you are entering to possess, you are to proclaim on Mount Gerizim[c] the blessings, and on Mount Ebal[d] the curses.[e] 30 As you know, these mountains are across the Jordan, west of the road,[c] towards the setting sun, near the great trees of Moreh,[f] in the territory of those Canaanites living in the Arabah in the vicinity of Gilgal.[g] 31 You are about to cross the Jordan to enter and take possession[h] of the land the LORD your God is giving[i] you. When you have taken it over and are living there, 32 be sure that you obey all the decrees and laws I am setting before you today.

The One Place of Worship

12 These are the decrees[a] and laws you must be careful to follow in the land that the LORD, the God of your fathers, has given you to possess—as long as you live in the land.[b] 2 Destroy completely all the places on the high mountains[c] and on the hills and under every spreading tree[d] where the nations you are dispossessing worship their gods. 3 Break down their altars, smash[e] their sacred stones and burn[f] their Asherah[g] poles in the fire; cut down the idols of their gods and wipe out their names[h] from those places.

4 You must not worship the LORD your God in their way.[i] 5 But you are to seek the place the LORD your God will choose from among all your tribes to put his Name[j] there for his dwelling.[k] To that place you must go; 6 there bring your burnt offerings and sacrifices, your tithes[l] and special gifts, what you have vowed[m] to give and your freewill offerings, and the firstborn of your herds and flocks.[n] 7 There, in the presence[o] of the LORD your God, you and your families shall eat and shall rejoice[p] in everything you have put your hand to, because the LORD your God has blessed you.

8 You are not to do as we do here today, everyone as he sees fit,[q] 9 since you have not yet reached the resting place[r] and the inheritance[s] the LORD your God is giving you. 10 But you will cross the Jordan and settle in the land the LORD your God is giving[t] you as an inheritance, and he will give you rest[u] from all your enemies around you so that you will live in safety. 11 Then to the place the LORD your God will choose as a dwelling for his Name[v]—there you are to bring everything I command you: your burnt offerings and sacrifices, your tithes and special gifts, and all the choice possessions you have vowed to the LORD.[w] 12 And there rejoice[x] before the LORD your God, you, your sons and daughters, your menservants and maidservants, and the Levites[y] from your towns, who have no allotment or inheritance[z] of their own. 13 Be careful not to sacrifice your burnt offerings anywhere you please.[a] 14 Offer them only at the place the LORD will choose[b] in one of your tribes, and there observe everything I command you.

15 Nevertheless, you may slaughter your animals in any of your towns and eat as much of the meat as you want, as if it were gazelle or deer,[c] according to the blessing the LORD your God gives you. Both the ceremonially unclean and the clean may eat it. 16 But you must not eat the blood;[d] pour[e] it out on the ground like water.[f] 17 You must not eat

21 [l]Job 5:26; Pr 3:2; 4:10; 9:11; [m]Ps 72:5
22 [n]**Dt 6:17**; [o]**Dt 6:5**; [p]**Dt 10:20**
23 [q]**Dt 9:5**; [r]**Ex 23:28**; [s]Dt 9:1
24 [t]Ge 15:18; Dt 1:36; 12:20; 19:8; Jos 1:3; 14:9; [u]**Ge 2:14**
25 [v]**Dt 2:25**; [w]Ex 23:27; Dt 7:24
26 [x]Ps 24:5; [y]Lev 26:14–17; Dt 27:13–26; 30:1,15,19; La 2:17; Da 9:11; Hag 1:11; Mal 2:2; 3:9; 4:6
27 [z]Dt 28:1–14; Ps 24:5
28 [a]2Ch 24:20; Jer 42:13; 44:16; [b]**Dt 4:28**; 13:6,13; 29:26; 1Sa 26:19
29 [c]Jdg 9:7; [d]Dt 27:4; Jos 8:30; [e]Dt 27:12–13; Jos 8:33; Jn 4:20
30 [f]**Ge 12:6**; [g]Jos 4:19; 5:9; 9:6; 10:6; 14:6; 15:7; Jdg 2:1; 2Ki 2:1; Mic 6:5
31 [h]**Nu 33:53**; [i]Dt 12:10; Jos 11:23

Ch. 12

1 [a]Ps 119:5; [b]Dt 4:9–10; 6:15; 1Ki 8:40; Eze 20:19
2 [c]**Nu 21:28**; [d]1Ki 14:23; 2Ki 17:10; Isa 57:5; Jer 2:20; 3:6,13
3 [e]2Ki 11:18; [f]**Ex 32:20**; [g]Ex 34:13; 1Ki 14:15,23; [h]**Ex 23:13**
4 [i]ver 30; 2Ki 17:15; Jer 10:2
5 [j]**Ex 20:24**; **2Sa 7:13**; [k]ver 11, 13; Dt 14:23; 15:20; 16:2,11; 18:6; 26:2; 1Sa 2:29; 1Ki 5:5; 8:16; 9:3; 2Ch 2:4; 6:6; 7:12, 16; Ezr 6:12; 7:15; Ps 26:8; 78:68; Zec 2:12
6 [l]**Lev 27:30**; [m]**Ge 28:20**; [n]Jos 22:27; Isa 66:20
7 [o]**Ex 18:12**; [p]**Lev 23:40**; Ecc 3:12–13; 5:18–20; **Isa 62:9**
8 [q]Jdg 17:6; 21:25
9 [r]**Ex 33:14**; Dt 3:20; Ps 95:11; Mic 2:10; [s]Dt 4:21
10 [t]**Dt 11:31**; [u]**Ex 33:14**
11 [v]**ver 5**; [w]**Lev 1:3**; Jos 22:23
12 [x]ver 7; [y]Dt 26:11–13; [z]**Nu 18:20**
13 [a]**ver 5**
14 [b]ver 11
15 [c]ver 22; Dt 14:5; 15:22
16 [d]**Ge 9:4**; Ac 15:20; [e]ver 23–24; **Ge 35:14**; 1Ch 11:18; Jer 7:18; [f]**Lev 17:13**; **Dt 15:23**; Jn 19:34

[b]24 That is, the Mediterranean
[c]30 Or *Jordan, westward*

in your own towns the tithe[g] of your grain and new wine and oil,[h] or the firstborn of your herds and flocks, or whatever you have vowed to give,[i] or your freewill offerings or special gifts.[j] 18Instead, you are to eat[k] them in the presence of the LORD your God at the place the LORD your God will choose[l]—you, your sons and daughters, your menservants and maidservants, and the Levites from your towns—and you are to rejoice[m] before the LORD your God in everything you put your hand to. 19Be careful not to neglect the Levites[n] as long as you live in your land.[o]

20When the LORD your God has enlarged your territory[p] as he promised[q] you, and you crave meat[r] and say, "I would like some meat," then you may eat as much of it as you want. 21If the place where the LORD your God chooses to put his Name[s] is too far away from you, you may slaughter animals from the herds and flocks the LORD has given you, as I have commanded you, and in your own towns you may eat as much of them as you want.[t] 22Eat them as you would gazelle or deer.[u] Both the ceremonially unclean and the clean may eat. 23But be sure you do not eat the blood,[v] because the blood is the life, and you must not eat the life with the meat.[w] 24You must not eat the blood; pour it out on the ground like water.[x] 25Do not eat it, so that it may go well[y] with you and your children after you, because you will be doing what is right[z] in the eyes of the LORD.

26But take your consecrated things and whatever you have vowed to give,[a] and go to the place the LORD will choose. 27Present your burnt offerings[b] on the altar of the LORD your God, both the meat and the blood. The blood of your sacrifices must be poured beside the altar of the LORD your God, but you may eat[c] the meat. 28Be careful to obey all these regulations I am giving you, so that it may always go well[d] with you and your children after you, because you will be doing what is good and right in the eyes of the LORD your God.

29The LORD your God will cut off[e] before you the nations you are about to invade and dispossess. But when you have driven them out and settled in their land,[f] 30and after they have been destroyed before you, be careful not to be ensnared[g] by enquiring about their gods, saying, "How do these nations serve their gods? We will do the same."[h] 31You must not worship the LORD your God in their way, because in worshipping their gods, they do all kinds of detestable things the LORD hates.[i] They even burn their sons[j] and daughters in the fire as sacrifices to their gods.[k]

32See that you do all I command you; do not add[l] to it or take away from it.

Worshipping Other Gods

13 If a prophet,[a] or one who foretells by dreams,[b] appears among you and announces to you a miraculous sign or wonder, 2and if the sign[c] or wonder of which he has spoken takes place, and he says, "Let us follow other gods"[d] (gods you have not known) "and let us worship them," 3you must not listen to the words of that prophet[e] or dreamer.[f] The LORD your God is testing[g] you to find out whether you love[h] him with all your heart and with all your soul. 4It is the LORD your God you must follow,[i] and him you must revere.[j] Keep his commands and obey him; serve him and hold fast[k] to him. 5That prophet or dreamer must be put to death,[l] because he preached rebellion against the LORD your God, who brought you out of Egypt and redeemed you from the land of slavery; he has tried to turn[m] you from the way the LORD your God commanded you to follow. You must purge the evil[n] from among you.

6If your very own brother, or your son or daughter, or the wife you love, or your closest friend secretly entices[o] you, saying, "Let us go and worship other gods"[p] (gods that neither you nor your fathers have known, 7gods of the peoples around you, whether near or far, from one end of the land to the other), 8do not yield[q] to him or listen to him. Show him no pity.[r] Do not spare him or shield him. 9You must certainly put him to death.[s] Your hand[t] must be the first in putting him to death, and then the hands of all the people. 10Stone him to death, because he tried to turn you away[u] from the LORD your God, who brought you out of Egypt, out of the land of slavery. 11Then all Israel will hear and be afraid,[v] and no-one among you will do such an evil thing again.

12If you hear it said about one of the towns the LORD your God is giving you to live in 13that wicked men[w] have arisen among you and have led the people of their town astray, saying, "Let us go

17 [g]**Lev 27:30;** [h]**Nu 18:12;** [i]ver 26; Nu 18:19; [j]Dt 14:23; 15:20
18 [k]Dt 14:23; 15:20; [l]ver 5; [m]ver 7,12; Dt 14:26; Ne 8:10; Ecc 3:12–13; 5:18–20
19 [n]ver 12; Dt 14:27; Ne 13:10; [o]Mal 3:8
20 [p]**Ex 34:24;** [q]**Ge 15:8; Dt 11:24;** [r]**Ex 16:3**
21 [s]Dt 14:24; [t]Lev 17:4
22 [u]**ver 15**
23 [v]**Lev 7:26;** [w]Eze 33:25
24 [x]ver 16
25 [y]**Dt 4:40;** [z]ver 28; Ex 15:26; Dt 13:18; 1Ki 11:38; 2Ki 12:2
26 [a]**ver 17;** Nu 5:9–10
27 [b]**Lev 1:13;** [c]Lev 3:1–17
28 [d]Dt 4:40; Ecc 8:12
29 [e]Jos 23:4; [f]**Dt 6:10**
30 [g]**Ex 10:7;** [h]**ver 4**
31 [i]**Lev 18:25;** [j]**Lev 18:21;** [k]**2Ki 3:27**
32 [l]**Dt 4:2;** Rev 22:18–19

Ch. 13

1 [a]Mt 24:24; Mk 13:22; 2Th 2:9; [b]**Ge 20:3;** Jer 23:25; 27:9; 29:8
2 [c]Dt 18:22; 1Sa 2:34; 10:9; 2Ki 19:29; 20:9; Isa 7:11; [d]**Dt 11:28**
3 [e]2Pe 2:1; [f]1Sa 28:6,15; [g]**Ge 22:1;** 1Ki 13:18; 22:22–23; Jer 29:31; 43:2; Eze 13:9; 1Co 11:19; [h]Dt 6:5
4 [i]2Ki 23:3; 2Ch 34:31; 2Jn 1:6; [j]**Dt 6:13; Ps 5:7;** [k]**Dt 10:20**
5 [l]**Ex 21:12; 22:20;** [m]ver 10; Dt 4:19; [n]Dt 17:7,12; 19:19; 24:7; Jdg 20:13; **1Co 5:13**
6 [o]Dt 17:2–7; 29:18; [p]**Dt 11:28**
8 [q]Pr 1:10; [r]**Dt 7:2**
9 [s]ver 5; [t]**Lev 24:14**
10 [u]**Ex 20:3**
11 [v]Dt 17:13; 19:20; 21:21; 1Ti 5:20
13 [w]Jdg 19:22; 20:13; 1Sa 2:12; 10:27; 11:12; 25:17; 1Ki 21:10

and worship other gods" (gods you have not known), 14then you must enquire, probe and investigate it thoroughly.[x] And if it is true and it has been proved that this detestable thing has been done among you,[y] 15you must certainly put to the sword all who live in that town. Destroy it completely,[a][z] both its people and its livestock.[a] 16Gather all the plunder of the town into the middle of the public square and completely burn the town[b] and all its plunder as a whole burnt offering to the LORD your God.[c] It is to remain a ruin[d] for ever, never to be rebuilt. 17None of those condemned things[a] shall be found in your hands, so that the LORD will turn from his fierce anger;[e] he will show you mercy,[f] have compassion[g] on you, and increase your numbers,[h] as he promised[i] on oath to your forefathers, 18because you obey the LORD your God, keeping all his commands that I am giving you today and doing what is right[j] in his eyes.

Clean and Unclean Food

14:3–20pp—Lev 11:1–23

14 You are the children[a] of the LORD your God. Do not cut yourselves or shave the front of your heads for the dead, 2for you are a people holy[b] to the LORD your God.[c] Out of all the peoples on the face of the earth, the LORD has chosen you to be his treasured possession.[d]

3Do not eat any detestable thing.[e] 4These are the animals you may eat:[f] the ox, the sheep, the goat,[g] 5the deer,[h] the gazelle, the roe deer, the wild goat,[i] the ibex, the antelope and the mountain sheep.[a] 6You may eat any animal that has a split hoof divided in two and that chews the cud. 7However, of those that chew the cud or that have a split hoof completely divided you may not eat the camel, the rabbit or the coney.[b] Although they chew the cud, they do not have a split hoof; they are ceremonially unclean for you. 8The pig is also unclean; although it has a split hoof, it does not chew the cud. You are not to eat their meat or touch their carcasses.[j]

9Of all the creatures living in the water, you may eat any that has fins and scales. 10But anything that does not have fins and scales you may not eat; for you it is unclean.

11You may eat any clean bird. 12But these you may not eat: the eagle, the vulture, the black vulture, 13the red kite, the black kite, any kind[k] of falcon,[l] 14any kind of raven,[m] 15the horned owl, the screech owl, the gull, any kind of hawk, 16the little owl, the great owl, the white owl, 17the desert owl,[n] the osprey, the cormorant, 18the stork, any kind of heron, the hoopoe and the bat.

19All flying insects that swarm are unclean to you; do not eat them. 20But any winged creature that is clean you may eat.[o]

21Do not eat anything you find already dead.[p] You may give it to an alien living in any of your towns, and he may eat it, or you may sell it to a foreigner. But you are a people holy to the LORD your God.[q]

Do not cook a young goat in its mother's milk.[r]

Tithes

22Be sure to set aside a tenth[s] of all that your fields produce each year. 23Eat[t] the tithe of your grain, new wine[u] and oil, and the firstborn of your herds and flocks in the presence of the LORD your God at the place he will choose as a dwelling for his Name,[v] so that you may learn[w] to revere[x] the LORD your God always. 24But if that place is too distant and you have been blessed by the LORD your God and cannot carry your tithe (because the place where the LORD will choose to put his Name is so far away), 25then exchange[y] your tithe for silver, and take the silver with you and go to the place the LORD your God will choose. 26Use the silver to buy whatever you like: cattle, sheep, wine or other fermented drink,[z] or anything you wish. Then you and your household shall eat there in the presence of the LORD your God and rejoice.[a] 27And do not neglect the Levites[b] living in your towns, for they have no allotment or inheritance of their own.[c]

28At the end of every three years, bring all the tithes[d] of that year's produce and store it in your towns,[e] 29so that the Levites (who have no allotment[f] or inheritance[g] of their own) and the aliens,[h] the fatherless and the widows who live in your towns may come and eat and be satisfied,[i] and so that the

---

13:14 [x]Jdg 20:12; [y]Dt 17:4
15 [z]Isa 24:6; 34:5; 43:28; 47:6; La 2:6; Da 9:11; Zec 8:13; Mal 4:6; [a]Ex 22:20
16 [b]2Ki 25:9; Jer 39:8; 52:13; Eze 16:41; [c]Dt 7:25–26; Jos 6:24; [d]Jos 8:28; Isa 7:16; 17:1; 24:10; 25:2; 27:10; 32:14,19; 37:26; Jer 49:2; Mic 1:6
17 [e]Ex 32:12; Nu 25:4; [f]Ge 43:14; [g]Dt 30:3; [h]Dt 7:13; [i]Ge 12:2; 13:14; 26:24
18 [j]Dt 12:25

Ch. 14

1 [a]Jn 1:12; Ro 8:14; 9:8
2 [b]Ge 28:14; Ex 22:31; Isa 6:13; Mal 2:15; [c]Lev 20:26; Ro 12:1; [d]Ex 8:22; Dt 7:6
3 [e]Eze 4:14
4 [f]Ac 10:14; [g]Lev 7:23
5 [h]Dt 12:15; [i]Job 39:1; Ps 104:18
8 [j]Lev 5:2
13 [k]Ge 1:11; [l]Isa 34:15
14 [m]Ge 8:7
17 [n]Ps 102:6; Isa 13:21; 14:23; 34:11; Zep 2:14
20 [o]Lev 20:25
21 [p]Lev 11:39; [q]ver 2; [r]Ex 23:19
22 [s]Ge 14:20; Lev 27:30; Nu 18:21
23 [t]Dt 12:17–18; [u]Ps 4:7; [v]Dt 12:5; 1Ki 3:2; [w]Dt 4:10; [x]Ps 22:23; 33:8; Mal 2:5
25 [y]Mt 21:12; Jn 2:14
26 [z]Lev 10:9; Ecc 10:16–17; [a]Lev 23:40; Dt 12:18
27 [b]Dt 12:19; [c]Nu 18:20; 26:62; Dt 18:1–2
28 [d]Lev 27:30; [e]Dt 26:12
29 [f]Ge 47:22; [g]Nu 26:62; [h]Dt 16:11; 24:19–21; Ps 94:6; Isa 1:17; 58:6; [i]Dt 6:11

---

[a]*15* The Hebrew term refers to the irrevocable giving over of things or persons to the LORD, often by totally destroying them; also in verse 17.
[a]*5* The precise identification of some of the birds and animals in this chapter is uncertain.
[b]*7* That is, the hyrax or rock badger

LORD your God may bless[j] you in all the work of your hands.

The Year for Cancelling Debts

15:1–11Ref—Lev 25:8–38

15 At the end of every seven years you must cancel debts.[a] 2This is how it is to be done: Every creditor shall cancel the loan he has made to his fellow Israelite. He shall not require payment from his fellow Israelite or brother, because the LORD's time for cancelling debts has been proclaimed. 3You may require payment from a foreigner,[b] but you must cancel any debt your brother owes you. 4However, there should be no poor among you, for in the land the LORD your God is giving you to possess as your inheritance, he will richly bless[c] you, 5if only you fully obey the LORD your God and are careful to follow[d] all these commands I am giving you today. 6For the LORD your God will bless you as he has promised, and you will lend to many nations but will borrow from none. You will rule over many nations but none will rule over you.[e]

7If there is a poor man[f] among your brothers in any of the towns of the land that the LORD your God is giving you, do not be hard-hearted or tight-fisted[g] towards your poor brother. 8Rather be open-handed[h] and freely lend him whatever he needs. 9Be careful not to harbour this wicked thought: "The seventh year, the year for cancelling debts,[i] is near," so that you do not show ill will[j] towards your needy brother and give him nothing. He may then appeal to the LORD against you, and you will be found guilty of sin.[k] 10Give generously to him and do so without a grudging heart;[l] then because of this the LORD your God will bless[m] you in all your work and in everything you put your hand to. 11There will always be poor people[n] in the land. Therefore I command you to be open-handed towards your brothers and towards the poor and needy in your land.[o]

Freeing Servants

15:12–18pp—Ex 21:2–6
15:12–18Ref—Lev 25:38–55

12If a fellow Hebrew, a man or woman, sells himself to you and serves you six years, in the seventh year you must let him go free.[p] 13And when you release him, do not send him away empty-handed. 14Supply him liberally from your flock, your threshing-floor[q] and your winepress. Give to him as the LORD your God has blessed you. 15Remember that you were slaves[r] in Egypt and the LORD your God redeemed you.[s] That is why I give you this command today.

16But if your servant says to you, "I do not want to leave you," because he loves you and your family and is well off with you, 17then take an awl and push it through his ear lobe into the door, and he will become your servant for life. Do the same for your maidservant.

18Do not consider it a hardship to set your servant free, because his service to you these six years has been worth twice as much as that of a hired hand. And the LORD your God will bless you in everything you do.

The Firstborn Animals

19Set apart for the LORD[t] your God every firstborn male[u] of your herds and flocks.[v] Do not put the firstborn of your oxen to work, and do not shear the firstborn of your sheep.[w] 20Each year you and your family are to eat them in the presence of the LORD your God at the place he will choose.[x] 21If an animal has a defect,[y] is lame or blind, or has any serious flaw, you must not sacrifice it to the LORD your God.[z] 22You are to eat it in your own towns. Both the ceremonially unclean and the clean may eat it, as if it were gazelle or deer.[a] 23But you must not eat the blood; pour it out on the ground like water.[b]

Passover

16:1–8pp—Ex 12:14–20; Lev 23:4–8; Nu 28:16–25

16 Observe the month of Abib[a] and celebrate the Passover[b] of the LORD your God, because in the month of Abib he brought you out of Egypt by night. 2Sacrifice as the Passover to the LORD your God an animal from your flock or herd at the place the LORD will choose as a dwelling for his Name.[c] 3Do not eat it with bread made with yeast, but for seven days eat unleavened bread, the bread of affliction,[d] because you left Egypt in haste[e]—so that all the days of your life you may remember the time of your departure from Egypt.[f] 4Let no yeast be found in your possession in all your land for seven days. Do not let any of the meat you sacrifice on the evening[g] of the first day remain until morning.[h]

---

29 [j]Dt 15:10; Ps 41:1; Pr 22:9; Mal 3:10

Ch. 15

1 [a]Dt 31:10; Ne 10:31
3 [b]**Ge 31:15**; Dt 23:20; 28:12; Ru 2:10
4 [c]Dt 28:8
5 [d]**Ex 15:26**; Dt 7:12; 28:1
6 [e]Dt 28:12–13, 44
7 [f]ver 11; Mt 26:11; [g]1Jn 3:17
8 [h]Mt 5:42; Lk 6:34; **Ac 24:17**
9 [i]ver 1; [j]Mt 20:15; [k]**Ex 22:23; Job 5:15**; Jas 5:4
10 [l]2Co 9:5; [m]**Dt 14:29**
11 [n]**ver 7**; [o]Mt 26:11; Mk 14:7; Jn 12:8
12 [p]Jer 34:14
14 [q]**Nu 18:27**
15 [r]Ex 13:3; Jer 34:13; [s]Ex 20:2; **Dt 4:34; 9:26**; 16:12; 24:18; Jer 16:14; 23:7
19 [t]**Lev 27:9**; [u]**Ex 13:2**; [v]**Ge 4:4**; [w]**Ex 22:30**
20 [x]**Lev 7:15–18**; Dt 12:5–7, 17–18
21 [y]**Ex 12:5**; [z]**Lev 22:19–25**; Dt 17:1; Mal 1:8,13
22 [a]**Dt 12:15**
23 [b]**Ge 9:4**; Dt 12:16; Eze 33:25

Ch. 16

1 [a]**Ex 12:2**; [b]**Ex 12:11**; 2Ki 23:21; Mt 26:17–29
2 [c]Dt 12:5,26
3 [d]Ex 12:8,39; 34:18; 1Co 5:8; [e]**Ex 12:11**; [f]Dt 4:9
4 [g]**Ex 12:6**; [h]**Ex 12:8**; Mk 14:12

5You must not sacrifice the Passover
in any town the LORD your God gives
you 6except in the place he will choose
as a dwelling for his Name. There you
must sacrifice the Passover in the eve-
ning, when the sun goes down, on the
anniversary[a][i] of your departure from
Egypt. 7Roast[j] it and eat it at the place
the LORD your God will choose. Then in
the morning return to your tents. 8For
six days eat unleavened bread and on
the seventh day hold an assembly[k] to
the LORD your God and do no work.[l]

Feast of Weeks

16:9–12pp—Lev 23:15–22; Nu 28:26–31

9Count off seven weeks[m] from the
time you begin to put the sickle to the
standing corn.[n] 10Then celebrate the
Feast of Weeks to the LORD your God by
giving a freewill offering in proportion
to the blessings the LORD your God has
given you. 11And rejoice[o] before the
LORD your God at the place he will
choose as a dwelling for his Name[p]—
you, your sons and daughters, your
menservants and maidservants, the
Levites[q] in your towns, and the aliens,[r]
the fatherless and the widows living
among you.[s] 12Remember that you were
slaves in Egypt,[t] and follow carefully
these decrees.

Feast of Tabernacles

16:13–17pp—Lev 23:33–43; Nu 29:12–39

13Celebrate the Feast of Tabernacles
for seven days after you have gathered
the produce of your threshing-floor[u]
and your winepress.[v] 14Be joyful[w] at
your Feast—you, your sons and
daughters, your menservants and
maidservants, and the Levites, the
aliens, the fatherless and the widows
who live in your towns. 15For seven
days celebrate the Feast to the LORD
your God at the place the LORD will
choose. For the LORD your God will
bless you in all your harvest and in all
the work of your hands, and your joy[x]
will be complete.

16Three times a year all your men
must appear[y] before the LORD your God
at the place he will choose: at the Feast
of Unleavened Bread,[z] the Feast of
Weeks and the Feast of Tabernacles.[a]
No man should appear before the LORD
empty-handed:[b] 17Each of you must
bring a gift in proportion to the way the
LORD your God has blessed you.

Judges

18Appoint judges[c] and officials for
each of your tribes in every town the
LORD your God is giving you, and they
shall judge the people fairly.[d] 19Do not
pervert justice[e] or show partiality.[f] Do
not accept a bribe,[g] for a bribe blinds the
eyes of the wise and twists the words of
the righteous. 20Follow justice and jus-
tice alone, so that you may live and
possess the land the LORD your God is
giving you.

Worshipping Other Gods

21Do not set up any wooden Asherah
pole[b][h] beside the altar you build to the
LORD your God,[i] 22and do not erect a
sacred stone,[j] for these the LORD your
God hates.

17 Do not sacrifice to the LORD
your God an ox or a sheep that
has any defect[a] or flaw in it, for that
would be detestable[b] to him.[c]

2If a man or woman living among you
in one of the towns the LORD gives you is
found doing evil in the eyes of the LORD
your God in violation of his covenant,[d]
3and contrary to my command[e] has wor-
shipped other gods,[f] bowing down to
them or to the sun[g] or the moon or the
stars of the sky,[h] 4and this has been
brought to your attention, then you
must investigate it thoroughly. If it is
true[i] and it has been proved that this
detestable thing has been done in
Israel,[j] 5take the man or woman who has
done this evil deed to your city gate and
stone that person to death.[k] 6On the
testimony of two or three witnesses a
man shall be put to death, but no-one
shall be put to death on the testimony of
only one witness.[l] 7The hands of the
witnesses must be the first in putting
him to death,[m] and then the hands of all
the people.[n] You must purge the evil[o]
from among you.

Law Courts

8If cases come before your courts that
are too difficult for you to judge[p]—
whether bloodshed, lawsuits or
assaults[q]—take them to the place the
LORD your God will choose.[r] 9Go to
the priests, who are Levites,[s] and to the
judge[t] who is in office at that time.
Enquire of them and they will give you
the verdict.[u] 10You must act according

6 [i]**Ex 12:42**
7 [j]**Ex 12:8**
8 [k]**Lev 23:8;** [l]Mt 26:17; Lk 2:41; 22:7; Jn 2:13
9 [m]Ac 2:1; [n]**Ex 23:16**
11 [o]Dt 12:7; [p]**Ex 20:24; 2Sa 7:13;** [q]Dt 12:12; [r]**Dt 14:29;** [s]Ne 8:10
12 [t]**Dt 15:15**
13 [u]**Lev 2:14;** [v]**Ge 27:37; Ex 23:16**
14 [w]**ver 11**
15 [x]Job 38:7; Ps 4:7; 28:7; 30:11
16 [y]Dt 31:11; Ps 84:7; [z]**Ex 12:17;** [a]**Ex 23:14,16;** Ezr 3:4; [b]**Ex 34:20**
18 [c]**Ex 18:21,26;** [d]Ge 31:37
19 [e]**Ex 23:2;** [f]**Lev 19:15;** [g]**Ex 18:21; 1Sa 8:3**
21 [h]**Dt 7:5;** [i]Ex 34:13; 1Ki 14:15; 2Ki 17:16; 21:3; 2Ch 33:3
22 [j]**Ex 23:24**

Ch. 17

1 [a]**Ex 12:5; Lev 22:20;** [b]Dt 7:25; [c]**Dt 15:21**
2 [d]Dt 13:6–11
3 [e]Jer 7:31; [f]Ex 22:20; [g]**Ge 1:16;** [h]**Ge 2:1; 37:9**
4 [i]Dt 22:20; [j]Dt 13:12–14
5 [k]**Lev 24:14**
6 [l]Nu 35:30; Dt 19:15; **Mt 18:16**
7 [m]Jn 8:7; [n]**Lev 24:14;** Ac 7:58; [o]**Dt 13:5;** 1Co 5:13*
8 [p]Ex 21:6; [q]2Ch 19:10; [r]Dt 12:5; Ps 122:3–5
9 [s]Dt 24:8; 27:9; [t]**Ex 21:6;** [u]**Ge 25:22;** Dt 19:17; Eze 44:24; Hag 2:11

[a]6 *Or down, at the time of day*
[b]21 *Or Do not plant any tree dedicated to Asherah*

to the decisions they give you at the
place the LORD will choose. Be careful to
do everything they direct you to do.
11 Act according to the law they teach
you and the decisions they give you. Do
not turn aside from what they tell you,
to the right or to the left.[v] 12 The man
who shows contempt[w] for the judge or
for the priest who stands ministering[x]
there to the LORD your God must be put
to death.[y] You must purge the evil from
Israel.[z] 13 All the people will hear and be
afraid, and will not be contemptuous
again.[a]

The King

14 When you enter the land the LORD
your God is giving you and have taken
possession[b] of it and settled in it,[c] and
you say, "Let us set a king over us like
all the nations around us,"[d] 15 be sure to
appoint[e] over you the king the LORD
your God chooses. He must be from
among your own brothers.[f] Do not place
a foreigner over you, one who is not a
brother Israelite. 16 The king, moreover,
must not acquire great numbers of
horses[g] for himself[h] or make the people
return to Egypt[i] to get more of them,[j] for
the LORD has told you, "You are not to
go back that way again."[k] 17 He must not
take many wives,[l] or his heart will be led
astray.[m] He must not accumulate[n] large
amounts of silver and gold.[o]
18 When he takes the throne[p] of his
kingdom, he is to write[q] for himself on a
scroll a copy[r] of this law, taken from that
of the priests, who are Levites. 19 It is to
be with him, and he is to read it all the
days of his life[s] so that he may learn to
revere the LORD his God and follow
carefully all the words of this law and
these decrees[t] 20 and not consider him-
self better than his brothers and turn
from the law[u] to the right or to the left.[v]
Then he and his descendants will reign
a long time over his kingdom in Israel.[w]

Offerings for Priests and Levites

18 The priests, who are Levites[a]
—indeed the whole tribe of
Levi—are to have no allotment or in-
heritance with Israel. They shall live on
the offerings[b] made to the LORD by fire,
for that is their inheritance.[c] 2 They shall
have no inheritance among their
brothers; the LORD is their inheritance,[d]
as he promised them.[e]
3 This is the share due to the priests[f]
from the people who sacrifice a bull[g] or a
sheep: the shoulder, the jowls and the
inner parts.[h] 4 You are to give them the
firstfruits of your grain, new wine and
oil, and the first wool from the shearing
of your sheep,[i] 5 for the LORD your God
has chosen them[j] and their descendants
out of all your tribes to stand and minis-
ter[k] in the LORD's name always.[l]
6 If a Levite moves from one of your
towns anywhere in Israel where he is
living, and comes in all earnestness to
the place the LORD will choose,[m] 7 he
may minister in the name[n] of the LORD
his God like all his fellow Levites who
serve there in the presence of the LORD.
8 He is to share equally in their benefits
even though he has received money
from the sale of family possessions.[o]

Detestable Practices

9 When you enter the land the LORD
your God is giving you, do not learn to
imitate[p] the detestable ways[q] of the
nations there. 10 Let no-one be found
among you who sacrifices his son or
daughter in[a] the fire,[r] who practises divi-
nation[s] or sorcery,[t] interprets omens,
engages in witchcraft,[u] 11 or casts spells,[v]
or who is a medium or spiritist[w] or who
consults the dead. 12 Anyone who does
these things is detestable to the LORD,
and because of these detestable prac-
tices the LORD your God will drive out
those nations before you.[x] 13 You must
be blameless[y] before the LORD your
God.[z]

The Prophet

14 The nations you will dispossess
listen to those who practise sorcery or
divination.[a] But as for you, the LORD
your God has not permitted you to do
so. 15 The LORD your God will raise up for
you a prophet like me from among your
own brothers.[b] You must listen to him.
16 For this is what you asked of the LORD
your God at Horeb on the day of the
assembly when you said, "Let us not
hear the voice of the LORD our God nor
see this great fire any more, or we will
die."[c]
17 The LORD said to me: "What they
say is good. 18 I will raise up for them a

11 [v]**Lev 10:11; Dt 5:32** *12* [w]Nu 15:30; [x]**Nu 16:9;** [y]ver 13; **Ge 17:14;** Dt 13:11; 18:20; 19:20; 1Ki 18:40; Jer 14:14; Hos 4:4; Zec 13:3; [z]**Dt 13:5** *13* [a]**ver 12** *14* [b]**Nu 33:53;** [c]Jos 21:43; [d]1Sa 8:5, 19–20; 10:19 *15* [e]1Sa 16:3; 2Sa 5:3; [f]Jer 30:21 *16* [g]Isa 2:7; 30:16; [h]1Sa 8:11; 1Ki 4:26; 9:19; 10:26; 2Ch 1:14; Ps 20:7; [i]1Ki 10:29; Isa 31:1; Jer 42:14; [j]1Ki 10:28; Isa 31:1; Eze 17:15; [k]**Ex 13:17** *17* [l]**Ex 34:16;** 2Sa 5:13; 12:11; 1Ki 11:3; 2Ch 11:21; [m]1Ki 11:2; Pr 31:3; [n]1Ki 10:27; [o]2Ch 1:11; Isa 2:7 *18* [p]1Ki 1:46; 1Ch 29:23; [q]Dt 31:22,24; Jos 24:26; 1Sa 10:25; [r]2Ch 23:11 *19* [s]Dt 4:9–10; Jos 1:8; [t]Dt 11:13; 1Ki 3:3; 11:38; 2Ki 22:2 *20* [u]Jos 23:6; Job 23:12; Ps 119:102; [v]**Dt 5:32; 1Ki 9:4;** [w]1Sa 8:5; 10:25; 1Ki 2:3; 1Ch 28:8

Ch. 18

1 [a]Jer 33:18,21; [b]**Nu 18:8;** [c]**Nu 18:20;** 1Co 9:13 *2* [d]Nu 18:20; [e]Jos 13:14 *3* [f]**Ex 29:27;** [g]**Lev 1:5;** [h]Lev 7:28–34; Nu 18:12 *4* [i]Ex 22:29; Nu 18:12 *5* [j]Ex 28:1; [k]Dt 10:8; [l]**Ex 29:9** *6* [m]**Nu 35:2–3; Dt 12:5** *7* [n]ver 19; 1Ki 18:32; 22:16; Ps 118:26 *8* [o]Nu 18:24; 2Ch 31:4; Ne 12:44,47; 13:12

9 [p]Dt 9:5; 12:29–31; [q]**Lev 18:3;** 2Ki 21:2; 2Ch 28:3; 33:2; 34:33; Ezr 6:21; 9:11; Jer 44:4
10 [r]**Lev 18:21;** [s]1Sa 15:23; [t]**Ex 7:11;** [u]**Lev 19:31**
11 [v]Isa 47:9; [w]**Ex 22:18; 1Sa 28:13** *12* [x]**Lev 18:24**
13 [y]**Ge 6:9;** Ps 119:1; [z]Mt 5:48 *14* [a]2Ki 21:6
15 [b]**Mt 21:11;** Lk 2:25–35; Jn 1:21; Ac 3:22*; 7:37*
16 [c]**Ex 20:19;** Dt 5:23–27

[a]*10* Or *who makes his son or daughter pass through*

prophet[d] like you from among their
brothers; I will put my words[e] in his
mouth,[f] and he will tell them everything
I command him.[g] 19If anyone does not
listen[h] to my words that the prophet
speaks in my name,[i] I myself will call
him to account.[j] 20But a prophet who
presumes to speak in my name any-
thing I have not commanded him to say,
or a prophet who speaks in the name of
other gods,[k] must be put to death."[l]
21You may say to yourselves, "How
can we know when a message has not
been spoken by the LORD?" 22If what a
prophet proclaims in the name of the
LORD does not take place or come true,[m]
that is a message the LORD has not
spoken.[n] That prophet has spoken pre-
sumptuously.[o] Do not be afraid of him.

Cities of Refuge

19:1–14Ref—Nu 35:6–34; Dt 4:41–43; Jos 20:1–9

19 When the LORD your God has
destroyed the nations whose
land he is giving you, and when you
have driven them out and settled in
their towns and houses,[a] 2then set aside
for yourselves three cities centrally
located in the land the LORD your God is
giving you to possess. 3Build roads to
them and divide into three parts the
land the LORD your God is giving you as
an inheritance, so that anyone who kills
a man may flee there.
4This is the rule concerning the man
who kills another and flees there to save
his life—one who kills his neighbour
unintentionally, without malice afore-
thought. 5For instance, a man may go
into the forest with his neighbour to cut
wood, and as he swings his axe to fell a
tree, the head may fly off and hit his
neighbour and kill him. That man may
flee to one of these cities and save his
life. 6Otherwise, the avenger of blood[b]
might pursue him in a rage, overtake
him if the distance is too great, and kill
him even though he is not deserving of
death, since he did it to his neighbour
without malice aforethought. 7This is
why I command you to set aside for
yourselves three cities.
8If the LORD your God enlarges your
territory,[c] as he promised[d] on oath to
your forefathers, and gives you the
whole land he promised them, 9because
you carefully follow all these laws I com-
mand you today—to love the LORD your
God and to walk always in his ways[e]
—then you are to set aside three more
cities. 10Do this so that innocent blood[f]
will not be shed in your land, which the
LORD your God is giving you as your
inheritance, and so that you will not be
guilty of bloodshed.[g]
11But if a man hates his neighbour and
lies in wait for him, assaults and kills
him,[h] and then flees to one of these
cities, 12the elders of his town shall send
for him, bring him back from the city,
and hand him over to the avenger of
blood to die. 13Show him no pity.[i] You
must purge from Israel the guilt of shed-
ding innocent blood,[j] so that it may go
well with you.
14Do not move your neighbour's
boundary stone set up by your prede-
cessors in the inheritance you receive in
the land the LORD your God is giving
you to possess.[k]

Witnesses

15One witness is not enough to con-
vict a man accused of any crime or of-
fence he may have committed. A matter
must be established by the testimony of
two or three witnesses.[l]
16If a malicious witness[m] takes the
stand to accuse a man of a crime, 17the
two men involved in the dispute must
stand in the presence of the LORD before
the priests and the judges[n] who are in
office at the time. 18The judges must
make a thorough investigation,[o] and if
the witness proves to be a liar, giving
false testimony against his brother,
19then do to him as he intended to do to
his brother.[p] You must purge the evil
from among you. 20The rest of the
people will hear of this and be afraid,[q]
and never again will such an evil thing
be done among you. 21Show no pity:[r]
life for life, eye for eye, tooth for tooth,
hand for hand, foot for foot.[s]

Going to War

20 When you go to war against
your enemies and see horses
and chariots and an army greater than
yours,[a] do not be afraid[b] of them,[c] be-
cause the LORD your God, who brought
you up out of Egypt, will be with[d] you.
2When you are about to go into battle,
the priest shall come forward and
address the army. 3He shall say: "Hear,
O Israel, today you are going into battle
against your enemies. Do not be faint-
hearted[e] or afraid; do not be terrified or
give way to panic before them. 4For the
LORD your God is the one who goes with
you[f] to fight[g] for you against your
enemies to give you victory.[h]"
5The officers shall say to the army:

18 [d]Ge 20:7; [e]Isa 2:3; 26:8; 51:4; Mic 4:2; [f]Ex 4:12; [g]Jn 4:25–26; 14:24; Ac 3:22*
19 [h]Ex 23:21; [i]ver 7; Lev 19:12; 2Ki 2:24; [j]Jos 22:23; Ac 3:23*; Heb 12:25
20 [k]Ex 23:13; [l]Dt 13:1–5; 17:12
22 [m]Dt 13:2; 1Sa 3:20; [n]1Ki 22:28; Jer 28:9; [o]ver 20

Ch. 19

1 [a]Dt 6:10–11
6 [b]Nu 35:12
8 [c]Ex 34:24; [d]Ge 15:8; Dt 11:24
9 [e]Dt 6:5
10 [f]Pr 6:17; Jer 7:6; 26:15; [g]Dt 21:1–9
11 [h]Ex 21:12; 1Jn 3:15
13 [i]Dt 7:2; [j]Dt 21:9; 1Ki 2:31
14 [k]Dt 27:17; Job 24:2; Ps 16:6; Pr 15:25; 22:28; 23:10; Isa 1:23; Hos 5:10
15 [l]Dt 17:6; Mt 18:16*; 26:60; 2Co 13:1*
16 [m]Ex 23:1; Pr 6:19
17 [n]Ex 21:6
18 [o]Ex 23:7
19 [p]Pr 19:5,9; 1Co 5:13*
20 [q]Dt 13:11
21 [r]ver 13; [s]Ex 21:24; Mt 5:38*

Ch. 20

1 [a]Ps 20:7; Isa 31:1; [b]Nu 14:9; [c]Dt 3:22; 1Sa 17:45; [d]Isa 41:10
3 [e]1Sa 17:32; Job 23:16; Ps 22:14; Isa 7:4; 35:4; Jer 51:46
4 [f]2Ch 20:14–22; [g]Ex 14:14; 1Ch 5:22; Ne 4:20; [h]Jdg 12:3; 15:18; Ps 44:7; 144:10

"Has anyone built a new house and not
dedicated[i] it? Let him go home, or he
may die in battle and someone else may
dedicate it. 6 Has anyone planted[j] a
vineyard and not begun to enjoy it?[k] Let
him go home, or he may die in battle
and someone else enjoy it. 7 Has anyone
become pledged to a woman and not
married her? Let him go home, or he
may die in battle and someone else marry
her.[l]" 8 Then the officers shall add, "Is
any man afraid or fainthearted? Let him
go home so that his brothers will not
become disheartened too."[m] 9 When the
officers have finished speaking to the
army, they shall appoint commanders
over it.

10 When you march up to attack a city,
make its people an offer of peace.[n] 11 If
they accept and open their gates, all the
people in it shall be subject[o] to forced
labour[p] and shall work for you. 12 If they
refuse to make peace and they engage
you in battle, lay siege to that city.
13 When the LORD your God delivers it
into your hand, put to the sword all the
men in it.[q] 14 As for the women, the
children, the livestock[r] and everything
else in the city,[s] you may take these as
plunder[t] for yourselves. And you may
use the plunder the LORD your God
gives you from your enemies. 15 This is
how you are to treat all the cities that are
at a distance[u] from you and do not
belong to the nations nearby.

16 However, in the cities of the nations
the LORD your God is giving you as an
inheritance, do not leave alive anything
that breathes.[v] 17 Completely destroy[a]
them—the Hittites, Amorites, Canaan-
ites, Perizzites, Hivites and Jebusites—
as the LORD your God has commanded
you. 18 Otherwise, they will teach you to
follow all the detestable things they do
in worshipping their gods,[w] and you
will sin[x] against the LORD your God.

19 When you lay siege to a city for a
long time, fighting against it to capture
it, do not destroy its trees by putting an
axe to them, because you can eat their
fruit. Do not cut them down. Are the
trees of the field people, that you should
besiege them?[b] 20 However, you may cut
down trees that you know are not fruit
trees[y] and use them to build siege works
until the city at war with you falls.

Atonement for an Unsolved Murder

21 If a man is found slain, lying in a
field in the land the LORD your
God is giving you to possess, and it is
not known who killed him,[a] 2 your
elders and judges shall go out and mea-
sure the distance from the body to the
neighbouring towns. 3 Then the elders
of the town nearest the body shall take a
heifer that has never been worked and
has never worn a yoke[b] 4 and lead her
down to a valley that has not been
ploughed or planted and where there is
a flowing stream. There in the valley
they are to break the heifer's neck. 5 The
priests, the sons of Levi, shall step for-
ward, for the LORD your God has chosen
them to minister and to pronounce
blessings[c] in the name of the LORD and
to decide all cases of dispute and
assault.[d] 6 Then all the elders of the town
nearest the body shall wash their hands[e]
over the heifer whose neck was broken
in the valley, 7 and they shall declare:
"Our hands did not shed this blood, nor
did our eyes see it done. 8 Accept this
atonement for your people Israel,
whom you have redeemed, O LORD,
and do not hold your people guilty of
the blood of an innocent man." And the
bloodshed will be atoned for.[f] 9 So you
will purge[g] from yourselves the guilt of
shedding innocent blood, since you
have done what is right in the eyes of
the LORD.

Marrying a Captive Woman

10 When you go to war against your
enemies and the LORD your God deliv-
ers them into your hands[h] and you take
captives,[i] 11 if you notice among the cap-
tives a beautiful[j] woman and are
attracted to her,[k] you may take her as
your wife. 12 Bring her into your home
and make her shave her head,[l] trim her
nails 13 and put aside the clothes she was
wearing when captured. After she has
lived in your house and mourned her
father and mother for a full month,[m]
then you may go to her and be her
husband and she shall be your wife. 14 If
you are not pleased with her, let her go
wherever she wishes. You must not sell
her or treat her as a slave, since you
have dishonoured her.[n]

The Right of the Firstborn

15 If a man has two wives,[o] and he
loves one but not the other, and both
bear him sons but the firstborn is the

5 [i]Ne 12:27
6 [j]Jer 31:5; Eze 28:26; Mic 1:6; [k]1Co 9:7
7 [l]Dt 24:5; Pr 5:18
8 [m]Jdg 7:3
10 [n]**Dt 2:26**; Lk 14:31–32
11 [o]ver 15; 2Ki 6:22; [p]1Ki 9:21; 1Ch 22:2; Isa 31:8
13 [q]Nu 31:7
14 [r]Jos 8:2; 22:8; [s]**Nu 31:11**; [t]**Nu 31:53**
15 [u]**ver 11**; Jos 9:9
16 [v]Ex 23:31–33; Nu 21:2–3; **Dt 7:2**; Jos 6:21; 10:1; 11:14
18 [w]**Ex 34:16**; [x]**Ex 10:7**
20 [y]Jer 6:6

Ch. 21

1 [a]**Nu 25:17**
3 [b]**Nu 19:2**
5 [c]**Ge 48:20**; **Ex 39:43**; [d]Dt 17:8–11
6 [e]Mt 27:24
8 [f]Nu 35:33–34
9 [g]Dt 19:13
10 [h]Jos 21:44; [i]1Ki 8:46; 1Ch 9:1; Ezr 5:12; Jer 40:1; Eze 1:1; 17:12; Da 2:25; Mic 4:10
11 [j]Ge 6:2; [k]**Ge 24:8**
12 [l]**Lev 14:9**; **Nu 8:7**; 1Co 11:5
13 [m]Ps 45:10
14 [n]**Ge 34:2**
15 [o]**Ge 4:19**

[a]17 The Hebrew term refers to the irrevocable giving over of things or persons to the LORD, often by totally destroying them.

[b]19 Or *down to use in the siege, for the fruit trees are for the benefit of man.*

son of the wife he does not love,[p] 16when he wills his property to his sons, he must not give the rights of the firstborn to the son of the wife he loves in preference to his actual firstborn, the son of the wife he does not love.[q] 17He must acknowledge the son of his unloved wife as the firstborn by giving him a double[r] share of all he has. That son is the first sign of his father's strength.[s] The right of the firstborn belongs to him.[t]

A Rebellious Son

18If a man has a stubborn and rebellious[u] son[v] who does not obey his father and mother[w] and will not listen to them when they discipline him, 19his father and mother shall take hold of him and bring him to the elders at the gate of his town. 20They shall say to the elders, "This son of ours is stubborn and rebellious. He will not obey us. He is a profligate and a drunkard." 21Then all the men of his town shall stone him to death.[x] You must purge the evil[y] from among you. All Israel will hear of it and be afraid.[z]

Various Laws

22If a man guilty of a capital offence[a] is put to death and his body is hung on a tree, 23you must not leave his body on the tree overnight.[b] Be sure to bury[c] him that same day, because anyone who is hung on a tree is under God's curse.[d] You must not desecrate[e] the land the LORD your God is giving you as an inheritance.

22 If you see your brother's ox or sheep straying, do not ignore it but be sure to take it back to him.[a] 2If the brother does not live near you or if you do not know who he is, take it home with you and keep it until he comes looking for it. Then give it back to him. 3Do the same if you find your brother's donkey or his cloak or anything he loses. Do not ignore it.

4If you see your brother's donkey[b] or his ox fallen on the road, do not ignore it. Help him to get it to its feet.[c]

5A woman must not wear men's clothing, nor a man wear women's clothing, for the LORD your God detests anyone who does this.

6If you come across a bird's nest beside the road, either in a tree or on the ground, and the mother is sitting on the young or on the eggs, do not take the mother with the young.[d] 7You may take the young, but be sure to let the mother go,[e] so that it may go well with you and you may have a long life.[f]

8When you build a new house, make a parapet around your roof so that you may not bring the guilt of bloodshed on your house if someone falls from the roof.[g]

9Do not plant two kinds of seed in your vineyard;[h] if you do, not only the crops you plant but also the fruit of the vineyard will be defiled.[a]

10Do not plough with an ox and a donkey yoked together.[i]

11Do not wear clothes of wool and linen woven together.[j]

12Make tassels on the four corners of the cloak you wear.[k]

Marriage Violations

13If a man takes a wife and, after lying with her[l], dislikes her 14and slanders her and gives her a bad name, saying, "I married this woman, but when I approached her, I did not find proof of her virginity," 15then the girl's father and mother shall bring proof that she was a virgin to the town elders at the gate.[m] 16The girl's father will say to the elders, "I gave my daughter in marriage to this man, but he dislikes her. 17Now he has slandered her and said, 'I did not find your daughter to be a virgin.' But here is the proof of my daughter's virginity." Then her parents shall display the cloth before the elders of the town, 18and the elders[n] shall take the man and punish him. 19They shall fine him a hundred shekels of silver[b] and give them to the girl's father, because this man has given an Israelite virgin a bad name. She shall continue to be his wife; he must not divorce her as long as he lives.

20If, however, the charge is true[o] and no proof of the girl's virginity can be found, 21she shall be brought to the door of her father's house and there the men of her town shall stone her to death. She has done a disgraceful thing[p] in Israel by being promiscuous while still in her father's house. You must purge the evil from among you.

22If a man is found sleeping with another man's wife, both the man who slept[q] with her and the woman must die.[r] You must purge the evil from Israel.

23If a man happens to meet in a town a virgin pledged to be married and he

15 [p]Ge 29:33
16 [q]1Ch 26:10
17 [r]2Ki 2:9; Isa 40:2; 61:7; Zec 9:12; [s]**Ge 49:3;** [t]Ge 25:31; Lk 15:12
18 [u]Ps 78:8; Jer 5:23; Zep 3:1; [v]Pr 30:17; [w]**Ge 31:35;** Pr 1:8; Isa 30:1; Eph 6:1–3
21 [x]**Lev 20:9;** [y]Dt 19:19; [z]**Dt 13:11**
22 [a]Dt 22:26; Mt 26:66; Mk 14:64; Ac 23:29
23 [b]Jos 8:29; 10:27; Jn 19:31; [c]Eze 39:12; [d]Ezr 6:11; Est 2:23; 7:9; 8:7; 9:13, 25; Isa 50:11; Gal 3:13*; [e]**Lev 18:25**

Ch. 22

1 [a]Ex 23:4–5; Pr 27:10; Zec 7:9
4 [b]Ex 23:5; [c]1Co 9:9
6 [d]Lev 22:28
7 [e]**Lev 22:28;** [f]**Dt 5:29**
8 [g]Jos 2:8; 1Sa 9:25; 2Sa 11:2
9 [h]Lev 19:19
10 [i]2Co 6:14
11 [j]Lev 19:19
12 [k]Nu 15:37–41; Mt 23:5
13 [l]Dt 24:1
15 [m]**Ge 23:10**
18 [n]Ex 18:21; Dt 1:9–18
20 [o]Dt 17:4
21 [p]**Ge 34:7; 38:24; Lev 19:29;** Dt 23:17–18; 1Co 5:13*
22 [q]2Sa 11:4; [r]**Ge 38:24; Ex 21:12;** Mt 5:27–28; Jn 8:5; 1Co 6:9; Heb 13:4

[a]9 Or *be forfeited to the sanctuary*
[b]19 That is, about 2½ pounds (about 1 kilogram)

sleeps with her, 24you shall take both of
them to the gate of that town and stone
them to death—the girl because she
was in a town and did not scream for
help, and the man because he violated
another man's wife. You must purge
the evil from among you.[s]
25But if out in the country a man hap-
pens to meet a girl pledged to be mar-
ried and rapes her, only the man who
has done this shall die. 26Do nothing to
the girl; she has committed no sin de-
serving death. This case is like that of
someone who attacks and murders his
neighbour, 27for the man found the girl
out in the country, and though the
betrothed girl screamed,[t] there was
no-one to rescue her.
28If a man happens to meet a virgin
who is not pledged to be married and
rapes her and they are discovered,[u] 29he
shall pay the girl's father fifty shekels of
silver.[c] He must marry the girl, for he
has violated her. He can never divorce
her as long as he lives.
30A man is not to marry his father's
wife; he must not dishonour his father's
bed.[v]

Exclusion From the Assembly

23 No-one who has been emascu-
lated[a] by crushing or cutting
may enter the assembly of the LORD.
2No-one born of a forbidden mar-
riage[a] nor any of his descendants may
enter the assembly of the LORD, even
down to the tenth generation.
3No Ammonite[b] or Moabite or any of
his descendants may enter the assembly
of the LORD, even down to the tenth
generation.[c] 4For they did not come to
meet you with bread and water[d] on your
way when you came out of Egypt, and
they hired Balaam[e] son of Beor from
Pethor in Aram Naharaim[b][f] to pro-
nounce a curse on you.[g] 5However, the
LORD your God would not listen to
Balaam but turned the curse[h] into a
blessing for you, because the LORD your
God loves[i] you. 6Do not seek a treaty[j] of
friendship with them as long as you
live.[k]
7Do not abhor an Edomite,[l] for he is
your brother.[m] Do not abhor an Egyp-
tian, because you lived as an alien in
his country.[n] 8The third generation of
children born to them may enter the
assembly of the LORD.

Uncleanness in the Camp

9When you are encamped against
your enemies, keep away from every-
thing impure.[o] 10If one of your men
is unclean because of a nocturnal
emission, he is to go outside the
camp and stay there.[p] 11But as evening
approaches he is to wash himself, and at
sunset[q] he may return to the camp.[r]
12Designate a place outside the camp
where you can go to relieve yourself.
13As part of your equipment have some-
thing to dig with, and when you relieve
yourself, dig a hole and cover up your
excrement. 14For the LORD your God
moves[s] about in your camp to protect
you and to deliver your enemies to you.
Your camp must be holy,[t] so that he will
not see among you anything indecent
and turn away from you.

Miscellaneous Laws

15If a slave has taken refuge[u] with
you, do not hand him over to his mas-
ter.[v] 16Let him live among you wherever
he likes and in whatever town he
chooses. Do not oppress[w] him.
17No Israelite man[x] or woman is to
become a shrine-prostitute.[y] 18You must
not bring the earnings of a female
prostitute or of a male prostitute[c] into
the house of the LORD your God to pay
any vow, because the LORD your God
detests them both.[z]
19Do not charge your brother interest,
whether on money or food or anything
else that may earn interest.[a] 20You may
charge a foreigner[b] interest, but not a
brother Israelite, so that the LORD your
God may bless[c] you in everything you
put your hand to in the land you are
entering to possess.
21If you make a vow to the LORD your
God, do not be slow to pay it,[d] for the
LORD your God will certainly demand it
of you and you will be guilty of sin.[e]
22But if you refrain from making a vow,
you will not be guilty.[f] 23Whatever your
lips utter you must be sure to do, be-
cause you made your vow freely to the
LORD your God with your own mouth.
24If you enter your neighbour's
vineyard, you may eat all the grapes
you want, but do not put any in your
basket. 25If you enter your neighbour's
cornfield, you may pick the ears with
your hands, but you must not put a
sickle to his standing corn.[g]
24 If a man marries a woman who
becomes displeasing to him[a]
because he finds something indecent
about her; and he writes her a certificate

24 [s]1Co 5:13*
27 [t]**Ge 39:14**
28 [u]Ex 22:16
30 [v]**Ge 29:29; Lev 18:8; 20:9;** 1Co 5:1

Ch. 23

1 [a]**Lev 21:20**
3 [b]**Ge 19:38;** [c]ver 4; Ne 13:2
4 [d]Dt 2:28; [e]**Nu 23:7; 2Pe 2:15;** [f]**Ge 24:10;** [g]**ver 3**
5 [h]Nu 24:10; Jos 24:10; Pr 26:2; [i]**Dt 4:37**
6 [j]**Nu 24:17;** Isa 15:1; 25:10; Jer 25:21; 27:3; 48:1; Eze 25:8; Zep 2:9; [k]Ezr 9:12; Mt 5:43
7 [l]**Ge 25:30;** [m]**Ge 25:26;** [n]**Lev 19:34**
9 [o]Lev 15:1–33
10 [p]Lev 15:16
11 [q]**Lev 15:16;** [r]1Sa 21:5
14 [s]**Ge 3:8;** [t]Ex 3:5
15 [u]2Sa 22:3; Ps 2:12; 71:1; [v]1Sa 30:15
16 [w]Ex 22:21; **23:6**
17 [x]1Ki 14:24; 15:12; 22:46; 2Ki 23:7; Job 36:14; [y]**Ge 38:21**
18 [z]**Ge 19:5; Lev 20:13;** Rev 22:15
19 [a]**Lev 25:35–37;** Ne 5:2–7
20 [b]**Ge 31:15; Dt 15:3;** [c]Dt 15:10
21 [d]**Nu 6:21;** Jdg 11:35; Ps 15:4; [e]Nu 30:1–2; Job 22:27; Ps 61:8; 65:1; 76:11; Ecc 5:4–5; Isa 19:21; **Mt 5:33;** Ac 5:3
22 [f]Ac 5:4
25 [g]Mt 12:1; Mk 2:23; Lk 6:1

Ch. 24

1 [a]Dt 22:13

c29 That is, about 1¼ pounds (about 0.6 kilogram)
a2 Or *one of illegitimate birth*
b4 That is, North-west Mesopotamia
c18 Hebrew *of a dog*

of divorce,[b] gives it to her and sends her
from his house, 2and if after she leaves
his house she becomes the wife of
another man, 3and her second husband
dislikes her and writes her a certificate
of divorce, gives it to her and sends her
from his house, or if he dies, 4then her
first husband, who divorced her, is not
allowed to marry her again after she has
been defiled. That would be detestable
in the eyes of the LORD. Do not bring sin
upon the land the LORD[c] your God is
giving you as an inheritance.

5If a man has recently married, he
must not be sent to war or have any
other duty laid on him. For one year he
is to be free to stay at home and bring
happiness to the wife he has married.[d]

6Do not take a pair of millstones—not
even the upper one—as security for a
debt, because that would be taking a
man's livelihood as security.[e]

7If a man is caught kidnapping one of
his brother Israelites and treats him as a
slave or sells him, the kidnapper must
die.[f] You must purge the evil from
among you.[g]

8In cases of leprous[a] diseases be very
careful to do exactly as the priests, who
are Levites,[h] instruct you. You must fol-
low carefully what I have commanded
them.[i] 9Remember what the LORD your
God did to Miriam along the way after
you came out of Egypt.[j]

10When you make a loan of any kind
to your neighbour, do not go into his
house to get what he is offering as a
pledge.[k] 11Stay outside and let the man
to whom you are making the loan bring
the pledge out to you. 12If the man is
poor, do not go to sleep with his pledge[l]
in your possession. 13Return his cloak to
him by sunset[m] so that he may sleep in
it.[n] Then he will thank you, and it will be
regarded as a righteous act in the sight
of the LORD your God.[o]

14Do not take advantage of a hired
man who is poor and needy, whether
he is a brother Israelite or an alien living
in one of your towns[p]. 15Pay him his
wages each day before sunset, because
he is poor[q] and is counting on it.[r] Other-
wise he may cry to the LORD against
you, and you will be guilty of sin.[s]

16Fathers shall not be put to death for
their children, nor children put to death
for their fathers; each is to die for his
own sin.[t]

17Do not deprive the alien or the
fatherless[u] of justice,[v] or take the cloak
of the widow as a pledge. 18Remember
that you were slaves in Egypt[w] and the
LORD your God redeemed you from
there. That is why I command you to do
this.

19When you are harvesting in your
field and you overlook a sheaf, do not
go back to get it.[x] Leave it for the alien,[y]
the fatherless and the widow,[z] so that
the LORD your God may bless[a] you in all
the work of your hands. 20When you
beat the olives from your trees, do not
go over the branches a second time.[b]
Leave what remains for the alien, the
fatherless and the widow. 21When you
harvest the grapes in your vineyard, do
not go over the vines again. Leave what
remains for the alien, the fatherless and
the widow. 22Remember that you were
slaves in Egypt. That is why I command
you to do this.[c]

25

When men have a dispute, they
are to take it to court and the
judges[a] will decide the case,[b] acquitting[c]
the innocent and condemning the
guilty.[d] 2If the guilty man deserves to be
beaten,[e] the judge shall make him lie
down and have him flogged in his pres-
ence with the number of lashes his
crime deserves, 3but he must not give
him more than forty lashes.[f] If he is
flogged more than that, your brother
will be degraded in your eyes.[g]

4Do not muzzle an ox while it is tread-
ing out the grain.[h]

5If brothers are living together and
one of them dies without a son, his
widow must not marry outside the fam-
ily. Her husband's brother shall take her
and marry her and fulfil the duty of a
brother-in-law to her.[i] 6The first son she
bears shall carry on the name of the
dead brother so that his name will not
be blotted out from Israel.[j]

7However, if a man does not want to
marry his brother's wife,[k] she shall go to
the elders at the town gate[l] and say,
"My husband's brother refuses to carry
on his brother's name in Israel. He will
not fulfil the duty of a brother-in-law to
me."[m] 8Then the elders of his town shall
summon him and talk to him. If he
persists in saying, "I do not want to
marry her," 9his brother's widow shall
go up to him in the presence of the
elders, take off one of his sandals,[n] spit
in his face[o] and say, "This is what is
done to the man who will not build up
his brother's family line." 10That man's

1 [b]ver 3; 2Ki 17:6; Isa 50:1; Jer 3:8; Mal 2:16; Mt 1:19; 5:31*; 19:7–9; Mk 10:4–5
4 [c]Jer 3:1
5 [d]**Dt 20:7**
6 [e]**Ex 22:22**
7 [f]**Ex 21:16;** [g]1Co 5:13*
8 [h]**Dt 17:9;** [i]Lev 13:1–46; **14:2**
9 [j]**Nu 12:10**
10 [k]Ex 22:25–27
12 [l]**Ex 22:26**
13 [m]Ex 22:26; [n]**Ex 22:27;** [o]Dt 6:25; Ps 106:31; Da 4:27
14 [p]Lev 19:13; 25:35–43; Dt 15:12–18; Job 24:4; Pr 14:31; 19:17; Am 4:1; 1Ti 5:18
15 [q]**Lev 25:35;** [r]**Lev 19:13;** Mt 20:8; [s]**Ex 22:23; Job 12:19;** Jas 5:4
16 [t]**Nu 26:11;** Jer 31:29–30
17 [u]Ex 22:22; Job 6:27; 24:9; 29:12; Ps 10:18; 82:3; Pr 23:10; Eze 22:7; [v]**Ex 22:21; 23:2; Dt 10:18**
18 [w]**Dt 15:15**
19 [x]**Lev 19:9;** [y]Dt 10:19; 27:19; Eze 47:22; Zec 7:10; Mal 3:5; [z]ver 20; Dt 14:29; [a]**Dt 14:29;** Pr 19:17; 28:27; Ecc 11:1
20 [b]Lev 19:10
22 [c]ver 18

Ch. 25

1 [a]**Ex 21:6;** [b]Dt 17:8–13; 19:17; Ac 23:3; [c]1Ki 8:32; [d]**Ex 23:7;** Dt 1:16–17
2 [e]Pr 10:13; 19:29; Lk 12:47–48
3 [f]Mt 27:26; Jn 19:1; 2Co 11:24; [g]Jer 20:2
4 [h]**Nu 22:29;** 1Co 9:9*; 1Ti 5:18*
5 [i]Ru 4:10,13; Mt 22:24; Mk 12:19; Lk 20:28
6 [j]Ge 38:9; Ru 4:5,10
7 [k]Ru 1:15; [l]**Ge 23:10;** [m]Ru 4:1–2,5–6
9 [n]Jos 24:22; Ru 4:7–8,11; [o]Nu 12:14; Job 17:6; 30:10; Isa 50:6

[a]8 The Hebrew word was used for various diseases affecting the skin—not necessarily leprosy.

line shall be known in Israel as The Family of the Unsandalled.

11If two men are fighting and the wife of one of them comes to rescue her husband from his assailant, and she reaches out and seizes him by his private parts, 12you shall cut off her hand. Show her no pity.[p]

13Do not have two differing weights in your bag—one heavy, one light.[q] 14Do not have two differing measures in your house—one large, one small. 15You must have accurate and honest weights and measures, so that you may live long[r] in the land the LORD your God is giving you. 16For the LORD your God detests anyone who does these things, anyone who deals dishonestly.[s]

17Remember what the Amalekites[t] did to you along the way when you came out of Egypt. 18When you were weary and worn out, they met you on your journey and cut off all who were lagging behind; they had no fear of God.[u] 19When the LORD your God gives you rest[v] from all the enemies[w] around you in the land he is giving you to possess as an inheritance, you shall blot out the memory of Amalek[x] from under heaven. Do not forget!

Firstfruits and Tithes

26 When you have entered the land that the LORD your God is giving you as an inheritance and have taken possession of it and settled in it, 2take some of the firstfruits[a] of all that you produce from the soil of the land that the LORD your God is giving you and put them in a basket. Then go to the place that the LORD your God will choose as a dwelling for his Name[b] 3and say to the priest in office at the time, "I declare today to the LORD your God that I have come to the land that the LORD swore to our forefathers to give us." 4The priest shall take the basket from your hands and set it down in front of the altar of the LORD your God. 5Then you shall declare before the LORD your God: "My father was a wandering[c] Aramean,[d] and he went down into Egypt with a few people[e] and lived there and became a great nation,[f] powerful and numerous. 6But the Egyptians ill-treated us and made us suffer,[g] putting us to hard labour.[h] 7Then we cried out to the LORD, the God of our fathers, and the LORD heard our voice[i] and saw[j] our misery,[k] toil and oppression.[l] 8So the LORD brought us out of Egypt[m] with a mighty hand and an outstretched arm,[n] with great terror and with miraculous signs and wonders.[o] 9He brought us to this place and gave us this land, a land flowing with milk and honey;[p] 10and now I bring the firstfruits of the soil that you, O LORD, have given me.[q]" Place the basket before the LORD your God and bow down before him. 11And you and the Levites[r] and the aliens among you shall rejoice[s] in all the good things the LORD your God has given to you and your household.

12When you have finished setting aside a tenth[t] of all your produce in the third year, the year of the tithe,[u] you shall give it to the Levite, the alien, the fatherless and the widow, so that they may eat in your towns and be satisfied. 13Then say to the LORD your God: "I have removed from my house the sacred portion and have given it to the Levite, the alien, the fatherless and the widow, according to all you commanded. I have not turned aside from your commands nor have I forgotten any of them.[v] 14I have not eaten any of the sacred portion while I was in mourning, nor have I removed any of it while I was unclean,[w] nor have I offered any of it to the dead. I have obeyed the LORD my God; I have done everything you commanded me. 15Look down from heaven,[x] your holy dwelling-place, and bless[y] your people Israel and the land you have given us as you promised on oath to our forefathers, a land flowing with milk and honey."

Follow the LORD's Commands

16The LORD your God commands you this day to follow these decrees and laws; carefully observe them with all your heart and with all your soul.[z] 17You have declared this day that the LORD is your God and that you will walk in his ways, that you will keep his decrees, commands and laws, and that you will obey him.[a] 18And the LORD has declared this day that you are his people, his treasured possession[b] as he promised, and that you are to keep all his commands. 19He has declared that he will set you in praise,[c] fame and honour high above all the nations[d] he has made and that you will be a people holy[e] to the LORD your God, as he promised.

The Altar on Mount Ebal

27 Moses and the elders of Israel commanded the people: "Keep all these commands[a] that I give you

12 [p]**Dt 7:2**
13 [q]Pr 11:1; 20:23; Mic 6:11
15 [r]**Ex 20:12**
16 [s]Pr 11:1
17 [t]**Ge 36:12**
18 [u]Ps 36:1; Ro 3:18
19 [v]Ex 33:14; Heb 3:18–19; [w]Est 9:16; [x]**Ge 36:12**

Ch. 26

2 [a]**Ex 22:29**; [b]**Ex 20:24; Dt 12:5**
5 [c]**Ge 20:13**; [d]**Ge 25:20**; [e]**Ge 34:30**; 43:14; [f]**Ge 12:2**
6 [g]**Nu 20:15**; [h]**Ex 1:13**
7 [i]**Ge 21:17**; [j]Ex 3:9; 2Ki 13:4; 14:26; [k]**Ge 16:11**; [l]Ps 42:9; 44:24; 72:14
8 [m]**Nu 20:16**; [n]**Ex 3:20**; [o]**Dt 4:34**; 34:11–12
9 [p]**Ex 3:8**
10 [q]**Dt 8:18**
11 [r]Dt 12:12; [s]**Dt 16:11**
12 [t]**Ge 14:20**; [u]**Nu 18:24**; Dt 14:28–29; Heb 7:5,9
13 [v]Ps 119:141, 153,176
14 [w]Lev 7:20; Hos 9:4
15 [x]Ps 68:5; 80:14; 102:19; Isa 63:15; Zec 2:13; [y]**Ex 39:43**
16 [z]Dt 4:29
17 [a]Ex 19:8; Ps 48:14
18 [b]Ex 6:7; Dt 7:6
19 [c]Isa 62:7; Zep 3:20; [d]Dt 4:7–8; 28:1, 13,44; 1Ch 14:2; Ps 148:14; Isa 40:11; [e]**Dt 7:6**

Ch. 27

1 [a]Ps 78:7

today. 2When you have crossed the Jor-
dan[b] into the land the LORD your God is
giving you, set up some large stones[c]
and coat them with plaster.[d] 3Write on
them all the words of this law when you
have crossed over to enter the land the
LORD your God is giving you, a land
flowing with milk and honey,[e] just as
the LORD, the God of your fathers,
promised you. 4And when you have
crossed the Jordan, set up these stones
on Mount Ebal,[f] as I command you to-
day, and coat them with plaster. 5Build
there an altar[g] to the LORD your God, an
altar of stones. Do not use any iron tool[h]
upon them. 6Build the altar of the LORD
your God with stones from the field and
offer burnt offerings on it to the LORD
your God. 7Sacrifice fellowship offer-
ings[a] [i] there, eating them and rejoicing[j]
in the presence of the LORD your God.[k]
8And you shall write very clearly all the
words of this law on these stones[l] you
have set up."[m]

Curses From Mount Ebal

9Then Moses and the priests, who are
Levites,[n] said to all Israel, "Be silent, O
Israel, and listen! You have now become
the people of the LORD your God.[o]
10Obey the LORD your God and follow
his commands and decrees that I give
you today."
11On the same day Moses comman-
ded the people:
12When you have crossed the Jordan,
these tribes shall stand on Mount Ger-
izim[p] to bless the people: Simeon, Levi,
Judah, Issachar,[q] Joseph and Benjamin.[r]
13And these tribes shall stand on Mount
Ebal[s] to pronounce curses: Reuben,
Gad, Asher, Zebulun, Dan and Naph-
tali.
14The Levites shall recite to all the
people of Israel in a loud voice:

15"Cursed is the man who carves
an image or casts an idol[t]—a thing
detestable[u] to the LORD, the work of
the craftsman's hands—and sets it
up in secret."
Then all the people shall say,
"Amen!"[v]
16"Cursed is the man who dis-
honours his father or his mother."[w]
Then all the people shall say,
"Amen!"
17"Cursed is the man who moves
his neighbour's boundary stone."[x]
Then all the people shall say,
"Amen!"
18"Cursed is the man who leads
the blind astray on the road."[y]
Then all the people shall say,
"Amen!"
19"Cursed is the man who with-
holds justice from the alien,[z] the
fatherless or the widow."[a]
Then all the people shall say,
"Amen!"
20"Cursed is the man who sleeps
with his father's wife, for he dis-
honours his father's bed."[b]
Then all the people shall say,
"Amen!"
21"Cursed is the man who has
sexual relations with any animal."[c]
Then all the people shall say,
"Amen!"
22"Cursed is the man who sleeps
with his sister, the daughter of his
father or the daughter of his
mother."[d]
Then all the people shall say,
"Amen!"
23"Cursed is the man who sleeps
with his mother-in-law."[e]
Then all the people shall say,
"Amen!"
24"Cursed is the man who kills[f]
his neighbour secretly."[g]
Then all the people shall say,
"Amen!"
25"Cursed is the man who
accepts a bribe to kill an innocent
person."[h]
Then all the people shall say,
"Amen!"
26"Cursed is the man who does
not uphold the words of this law by
carrying them out."[i]
Then all the people shall say,
"Amen!"[j]

Blessings for Obedience

28 If you fully obey the LORD your
God and carefully follow[a] all his
commands[b] that I give you today, the
LORD your God will set you high above
all the nations on earth.[c] 2All these
blessings will come upon you[d] and
accompany you if you obey the LORD
your God:

3You will be blessed[e] in the city
and blessed in the country.[f]
4The fruit of your womb will be
blessed, and the crops of your land
and the young of your livestock

2 [b]Jos 4:1; [c]Ex 24:4; Jos 24:26; 1Sa 7:12; [d]Jos 8:31
3 [e]Ex 3:8
4 [f]Dt 11:29
5 [g]Ex 20:24; [h]Ex 20:25
7 [i]Ex 32:6; [j]Dt 16:11; [k]Jos 8:31
8 [l]Isa 8:1; 30:8; Hab 2:2; [m]Jos 8:32
9 [n]Dt 17:9; [o]Dt 26:18
12 [p]Dt 11:29; [q]Ge 30:18; [r]Jos 8:35
13 [s]Dt 11:29
15 [t]Ex 20:4; [u]1Ki 11:5,7; 2Ki 23:13; Isa 44:19; 66:3; [v]Nu 5:22; 1Co 14:16
16 [w]Ge 31:35; Ex 21:12; Dt 5:16
17 [x]Dt 19:14
18 [y]Lev 19:14
19 [z]Ex 22:21; Dt 24:19; [a]Ex 23:2; Dt 10:18
20 [b]Ge 34:5; Lev 18:7
21 [c]Ex 22:19
22 [d]Lev 18:9
23 [e]Lev 20:14
24 [f]Ge 4:23; [g]Ex 21:12
25 [h]Ex 23:7–8; Lev 19:16
26 [i]Lev 26:14; Dt 28:15; Ps 119:21; Jer 11:3; Gal 3:10*; [j]Jer 11:5

Ch. 28

1 [a]Dt 15:5; [b]Lev 26:3; [c]Nu 24:7; Dt 26:19
2 [d]Jer 32:24; Zec 1:6
3 [e]Ps 144:15; [f]Ge 39:5

[a]7 Traditionally *peace offerings*

—the calves of your herds and the
lambs of your flocks.[g]
5 Your basket and your kneading
trough will be blessed.
6 You will be blessed when you
come in and blessed when you go
out.[h]

7 The LORD will grant that the enemies[i]
who rise up against you will be defeated
before you. They will come at you from
one direction but flee from you in
seven.[j]
8 The LORD will send a blessing on
your barns and on everything you put
your hand to. The LORD your God will
bless[k] you in the land he is giving you.
9 The LORD will establish you as his
holy people,[l] as he promised you on
oath, if you keep the commands[m] of the
LORD your God and walk in his ways.
10 Then all the peoples on earth will see
that you are called by the name[n] of the
LORD, and they will fear you. 11 The LORD
will grant you abundant prosperity—in
the fruit of your womb, the young of
your livestock[o] and the crops of your
ground—in the land he swore to your
forefathers to give you.[p]
12 The LORD will open the heavens, the
storehouse[q] of his bounty,[r] to send rain[s]
on your land in season and to bless[t] all
the work of your hands. You will lend to
many nations but will borrow from
none.[u] 13 The LORD will make you the
head, not the tail. If you pay attention to
the commands of the LORD your God
that I give you this day and carefully
follow[v] them, you will always be at the
top, never at the bottom.[w] 14 Do not turn
aside from any of the commands I give
you today, to the right or to the left,[x]
following other gods and serving them.

Curses for Disobedience

15 However, if you do not obey[y] the
LORD your God and do not carefully
follow all his commands and decrees I
am giving you today,[z] all these curses
will come upon you and overtake you:[a]

16 You will be cursed in the city
and cursed in the country.[b]
17 Your basket and your kneading
trough will be cursed.[c]
18 The fruit of your womb will be
cursed, and the crops of your land,
and the calves of your herds and
the lambs of your flocks.[d]
19 You will be cursed when you
come in and cursed when you go
out.[e]

20 The LORD will send on you curses,[f]
confusion and rebuke[g] in everything
you put your hand to, until you are
destroyed and come to sudden ruin[h]
because of the evil[i] you have done
in forsaking him.[a] 21 The LORD will
plague you with diseases until he has
destroyed you from the land you are
entering to possess.[j] 22 The LORD will
strike you with wasting disease,[k] with
fever and inflammation, with scorching
heat and drought,[l] with blight[m] and mil-
dew, which will plague[n] you until you
perish.[o] 23 The sky over your head will be
bronze, the ground beneath you iron.[p]
24 The LORD will turn the rain[q] of your
country into dust and powder; it will
come down from the skies until you are
destroyed.
25 The LORD will cause you to be de-
feated[r] before your enemies. You will
come at them from one direction but flee
from them in seven,[s] and you will be-
come a thing of horror[t] to all the king-
doms on earth.[u] 26 Your carcasses will be
food for all the birds of the air[v] and the
beasts of the earth, and there will be
no-one to frighten them away.[w] 27 The
LORD will afflict you with the boils of
Egypt[x] and with tumours, festering
sores and the itch, from which you can-
not be cured. 28 The LORD will afflict you
with madness, blindness and confusion
of mind. 29 At midday you will grope[y]
about like a blind man in the dark. You
will be unsuccessful in everything you
do; day after day you will be oppressed
and robbed, with no-one to rescue[z] you.
30 You will be pledged to be married to
a woman, but another will take her and
ravish her.[a] You will build a house, but
you will not live in it.[b] You will plant a
vineyard, but you will not even begin to
enjoy its fruit.[c] 31 Your ox will be slaugh-
tered before your eyes, but you will eat
none of it. Your donkey will be forcibly
taken from you and will not be re-
turned. Your sheep will be given to your
enemies, and no-one will rescue them.
32 Your sons and daughters will be given
to another nation,[d] and you will wear
out your eyes watching for them day

4 [g]**Ge 49:25; Dt 8:18**
6 [h]Ps 121:8
7 [i]2Ch 6:34; [j]**Lev 26:8**,17
8 [k]Dt 15:4
9 [l]**Ex 19:6**; [m]**Lev 26:3**
10 [n]**Nu 6:27**; 1Ki 8:43; Jer 25:29; Da 9:18
11 [o]**Ge 30:27**; [p]ver 4; Dt 30:9
12 [q]Job 38:22; Ps 135:7; Jer 10:13; 51:16; [r]Ps 65:11; 68:10; Jer 31:12; [s]**Lev 26:4**; 1Ki 8:35–36; 18:1; Ps 104:13; Isa 5:6; 30:23; 32:20; [t]Isa 61:9; 65:23; Jer 32:38–41; Mal 3:12; [u]ver 44; **Lev 25:19**; **Dt 15:3**,6; Eze 34:26
13 [v]Jer 11:6; [w]**Dt 26:19**
14 [x]**Dt 5:32**; Jos 1:7
15 [y]1Ki 9:6; 2Ch 7:19; [z]**Dt 27:26**; [a]Dt 29:27; Jos 23:15; 2Ch 12:5; Da 9:11; Mal 2:2
16 [b]ver 3
17 [c]ver 5
18 [d]ver 4
19 [e]ver 6
20 [f]ver 8,15; Lev 26:16; Jer 42:18; Mal 2:2; 3:9; 4:6; [g]Ps 39:11; 76:6; 80:16; Isa 17:13; 51:20; 54:9; 66:15; Eze 5:15; [h]Dt 4:26; [i]**Ex 32:22**
21 [j]Lev 26:25; Nu 14:12; Jer 24:10; Am 4:10
22 [k]ver 48; Dt 32:24; [l]Lev 26:16; 2Ki 8:1; Job 12:15; Ps 105:16; Jer 14:1; Hag 1:11; Mal 3:9; [m]Hag 2:17; [n]**Lev 26:25**; [o]Dt 4:26; Am 4:9
23 [p]**Lev 26:19**
24 [q]Lev 26:19; Dt 11:17; 1Ki 8:35; 17:1; Isa 5:6; Jer 14:1; Hag 1:10
25 [r]1Sa 4:10; Ps 78:62; [s]**Lev 26:17**; [t]ver 37; [u]2Ch 29:8; 30:7; Jer 15:4; 24:9; 26:6; 29:18; 44:12; Eze 23:46
26 [v]**Ge 40:19**; [w]Ps 79:2; Isa 18:6; Jer 7:33; 12:9; 15:2; 16:4; 19:7; 34:20
27 [x]Dt 7:15
29 [y]Ge 19:11; Ex 10:21; Job 5:14; 12:25; 24:13; 38:15; Isa 59:10; [z]Jdg 3:9; 2Ki 13:5; Est 4:14; Isa 19:20; 43:11; Hos 13:4; Ob 21
30 [a]Job 31:10; [b]Isa 65:22; Am 5:11; [c]Jer 12:13
32 [d]ver 41

[a]20 Hebrew *me*

after day, powerless to lift a hand. 33A
people that you do not know will eat
what your land and labour produce,
and you will have nothing but cruel
oppression[e] all your days.[f] 34The sights
you see will drive you mad.[g] 35The LORD
will afflict your knees and legs with
painful boils[h] that cannot be cured,
spreading from the soles of your feet to
the top of your head.[i]

36The LORD will drive you and the
king[j] you set over you to a nation un-
known to you or your fathers.[k] There
you will worship other gods, gods of
wood and stone.[l] 37You will become a
thing of horror[m] and an object of scorn[n]
and ridicule[o] to all the nations where the
LORD will drive you.[p]

38You will sow much seed in the field
but you will harvest little,[q] because
locusts[r] will devour[s] it. 39You will plant
vineyards and cultivate them but you
will not drink the wine[t] or gather the
grapes, because worms will eat[u] them.[v]
40You will have olive trees throughout
your country but you will not use the
oil, because the olives will drop off.[w]
41You will have sons and daughters but
you will not keep them, because they
will go into captivity.[x] 42Swarms of
locusts[y] will take over all your trees and
the crops of your land.

43The alien who lives among you will
rise above you higher and higher, but
you will sink lower and lower.[z] 44He will
lend to you, but you will not lend to
him.[a] He will be the head, but you will
be the tail.[b]

45All these curses will come upon
you. They will pursue you and overtake
you[c] until you are destroyed,[d] because
you did not obey the LORD your God
and observe the commands and decrees
he gave you. 46They will be a sign and a
wonder to you and your descendants
for ever.[e] 47Because you did not serve[f]
the LORD your God joyfully and gladly[g]
in the time of prosperity, 48therefore in
hunger and thirst,[h] in nakedness and
dire poverty, you will serve the enemies
the LORD sends against you. He will put
an iron yoke[i] on your neck[j] until he has
destroyed you.

49The LORD will bring a nation against
you[k] from far away, from the ends of the
earth,[l] like an eagle[m] swooping down, a
nation whose language you will not
understand,[n] 50a fierce-looking nation
without respect for the old[o] or pity for
the young. 51They will devour the
young of your livestock and the crops of
your land until you are destroyed. They
will leave you no grain, new wine[p] or
oil,[q] nor any calves of your herds or
lambs of your flocks until you are
ruined.[r] 52They will lay siege[s] to all the
cities throughout your land until the
high fortified walls in which you trust
fall down. They will besiege all the cities
throughout the land the LORD your God
is giving you.[t]

53Because of the suffering that your
enemy will inflict on you during the
siege, you will eat the fruit of the womb,
the flesh of the sons and daughters the
LORD your God has given you.[u] 54Even
the most gentle and sensitive man
among you will have no compassion on
his own brother or the wife he loves or
his surviving children, 55and he will not
give to one of them any of the flesh of
his children that he is eating. It will be
all he has left because of the suffering
that your enemy will inflict on you dur-
ing the siege of all your cities.[v] 56The
most gentle and sensitive[w] woman
among you—so sensitive and gentle
that she would not venture to touch the
ground with the sole of her foot—will
begrudge the husband she loves and
her own son or daughter[x] 57the after-
birth from her womb and the children
she bears. For she intends to eat them[y]
secretly during the siege and in the dis-
tress that your enemy will inflict on you
in your cities.

58If you do not carefully follow all the
words of this law,[z] which are written in
this book, and do not revere[a] this glo-
rious and awesome name[b]—the LORD
your God—59the LORD will send fearful
plagues on you and your descendants,
harsh and prolonged disasters, and
severe and lingering illnesses. 60He will
bring upon you all the diseases of
Egypt[c] that you dreaded, and they will
cling to you. 61The LORD will also bring
on you every kind of sickness and disas-
ter not recorded in this Book of the
Law,[d] until you are destroyed.[e] 62You
who were as numerous as the stars in
the sky[f] will be left but few[g] in number,
because you did not obey the LORD your
God. 63Just as it pleased[h] the LORD to
make you prosper and increase in num-
ber, so it will please[i] him to ruin and

33 [e]Jer 6:6; 22:17; [f]Jer 5:15–17; Eze 25:4
34 [g]ver 67
35 [h]Dt 7:15; Rev 16:2; [i]Job 2:7; 7:5; 13:28; 30:17,30; Isa 1:6
36 [j]1Sa 12:25; [k]**Dt 4:27;** 2Ki 24:14; 25:7,11; 2Ch 33:11; 36:21; Ezr 5:12; Jer 15:14; 16:13; 27:20; 39:1–9; 52:28; La 1:3; [l]**Dt 4:28**
37 [m]ver 25; Jer 42:18; Eze 5:15; [n]Ps 22:7; 39:8; 44:13; 64:8; Jer 18:16; 48:27; Mic 6:16; [o]2Ch 7:20; Ezr 9:7; Jer 44:8; [p]1Ki 9:7; Ps 44:14; Jer 19:8; 24:9; 25:9,18; 29:18; La 2:15
38 [q]Lev 26:20; Ps 129:7; Isa 5:10; Jer 12:13; Hos 8:7; Mic 6:15; Hag 1:6, 9; 2:16; [r]**Ex 10:4;** [s]**Ex 10:15**
39 [t]**Lev 10:9;** [u]Joel 1:4; 2:25; Mal 3:11; [v]Isa 5:10; 17:10–11; Zep 1:13
40 [w]Jer 11:16; Mic 6:15
41 [x]ver 32
42 [y]ver 38; Jdg 6:5; 7:12; Jer 46:23
43 [z]ver 13
44 [a]**ver 12;** [b]**Dt 26:19**
45 [c]**Ex 15:9;** [d]ver 15; Dt 4:25–26
46 [e]**Nu 16:38;** Ps 71:7; Isa 8:18; 20:3; Eze 5:15; Zec 3:8
47 [f]**Dt 10:12;** [g]**Lev 23:40;** Ne 9:35
48 [h]Jer 14:3; La 4:4; [i]Jer 28:13–14; La 1:14; [j]Ge 49:8
49 [k]**Lev 26:44;** [l]Isa 5:26–30; 7:18–20; 39:3; Jer 4:16; 5:15; 6:22; 25:32; 31:8; Hab 1:6; [m]2Sa 1:23; Jer 4:13; 48:40; 49:22; La 4:19; Eze 17:3; Hos 8:1; [n]**Ge 11:7;** 1Co 14:21*
50 [o]Isa 47:6
51 [p]Ps 4:7; Isa 36:17; Hag 1:11; [q]**Nu 18:12;** [r]ver 33; Jdg 6:4
52 [s]2Ki 6:24; [t]Jer 10:18; Eze 6:10; Zep 1:14–17
53 [u]ver 57; Lev 26:29; 2Ki 6:28–29; La 2:20
55 [v]2Ki 6:29 *56* [w]Isa 47:1; [x]La 4:10
57 [y]**ver 53**
58 [z]Dt 31:24; [a]Ps 96:4; Jer 5:22; Mal 1:14; 2:5; 3:5,16; 4:2; [b]**Ex 3:15; Jos 7:9** *60* [c]Ex 15:26
61 [d]Dt 29:21; 30:10; 31:26; Jos 1:8; 8:34; 23:6; 24:26; 2Ki 14:6; 22:8; 2Ch 17:9; 25:4; Ne 8:1,18; Mal 4:4; [e]Dt 4:25–26 *62* [f]**Ge 22:17;** Dt 4:27; 10:22; [g]**Lev 26:22**
63 [h]Dt 30:9; Isa 62:5; 65:19; Jer 32:41; Zep 3:17; [i]Pr 1:26

destroy you.[j] You will be uprooted[k]
from the land you are entering to
possess.
64Then the LORD will scatter[l] you
among all nations,[m] from one end of the
earth to the other.[n] There you will
worship other gods—gods of wood and
stone, which neither you nor your
fathers have known.[o] 65Among those
nations you will find no repose, no rest-
ing place[p] for the sole of your foot. There
the LORD will give you an anxious mind,
eyes[q] weary with longing, and a de-
spairing heart.[r] 66You will live in con-
stant suspense, filled with dread both
night and day, never sure of your life.
67In the morning you will say, "If only it
were evening!" and in the evening, "If
only it were morning!"—because of the
terror that will fill your hearts and the
sights that your eyes will see.[s] 68The
LORD will send you back in ships to
Egypt on a journey I said you should
never make again.[t] There you will offer
yourselves for sale to your enemies as
male and female slaves, but no-one will
buy you.

Renewal of the Covenant

29 These are the terms of the cov-
enant the LORD commanded
Moses to make with the Israelites in
Moab,[a] in addition to the covenant he
had made with them at Horeb.[b]
2Moses summoned all the Israelites
and said to them:

Your eyes have seen all that the LORD
did in Egypt to Pharaoh, to all his of-
ficials and to all his land.[c] 3With your
own eyes you saw those great trials,
those miraculous signs and great won-
ders.[d] 4But to this day the LORD has not
given you a mind that understands or
eyes that see or ears that hear.[e] 5During
the forty years that I led[f] you through
the desert, your clothes did not wear
out, nor did the sandals on your feet.[g]
6You ate no bread and drank no wine or
other fermented drink.[h] I did this so that
you might know that I am the LORD your
God.[i]
7When you reached this place, Sihon[j]
king of Heshbon[k] and Og king of
Bashan came out to fight against us, but
we defeated them.[l] 8We took their land
and gave it as an inheritance[m] to the
Reubenites, the Gadites and the half-
tribe of Manasseh.[n]
9Carefully follow[o] the terms of this
covenant,[p] so that you may prosper in
everything you do.[q] 10All of you are
standing today in the presence of the
LORD your God—your leaders and chief
men, your elders and officials, and all
the other men of Israel, 11together with
your children and your wives, and the
aliens living in your camps who chop
your wood and carry your water.[r] 12You
are standing here in order to enter into a
covenant with the LORD your God, a
covenant the LORD is making with you
this day and sealing with an oath, 13to
confirm you this day as his people,[s] that
he may be your God[t] as he promised
you and as he swore to your fathers,
Abraham, Isaac and Jacob. 14I am
making this covenant,[u] with its oath,
not only with you 15who are standing
here with us today in the presence of the
LORD our God but also with those who
are not here today.[v]
16You yourselves know how we lived
in Egypt and how we passed through
the countries on the way here. 17You
saw among them their detestable im-
ages and idols of wood and stone, of
silver and gold.[w] 18Make sure there is no
man or woman, clan or tribe among you
today whose heart turns[x] away from the
LORD our God to go and worship the
gods of those nations; make sure there
is no root among you that produces
such bitter poison.[y]
19When such a person hears the
words of this oath, he invokes a bless-
ing[z] on himself and therefore thinks, "I
will be safe, even though I persist in
going my own way."[a] This will bring
disaster on the watered land as well as
the dry.[a] 20The LORD will never be will-
ing to forgive[b] him; his wrath and zeal[c]
will burn[d] against that man. All the
curses written in this book will fall upon
him, and the LORD will blot[e] out his
name from under heaven. 21The LORD
will single him out from all the tribes of
Israel for disaster,[f] according to all the
curses of the covenant written in this
Book of the Law.[g]
22Your children who follow you in
later generations and foreigners who
come from distant lands will see the
calamities that have fallen on the land
and the diseases with which the LORD
has afflicted it.[h] 23The whole land will be
a burning waste[i] of salt[j] and sulphur

63 [j]**Ge 6:7**; [k]Ps 52:5; Jer 12:14; 31:28; 45:4
64 [l]**Dt 4:27**; Ezr 9:7; Isa 6:12; Jer 32:23; 43:11; 52:27; [m]Ne 1:8; Ps 44:11; Jer 13:24; 18:17; 22:22; [n]**Dt 4:32**; **Jer 8:19**; [o]Dt 11:28; 32:17
65 [p]La 1:3; [q]Job 11:20; [r]Lev 26:16,36; Hos 9:17
67 [s]ver 34
68 [t]**Ex 13:14**

Ch. 29

1 [a]**Lev 7:38**; [b]**Ex 3:1**
2 [c]Ex 19:4
3 [d]**Dt 4:34**
4 [e]Isa 6:10; 32:3; 48:8; Jer 5:21; Eze 12:2; **Mt 13:15**; Ro 11:8*; Eph 4:18
5 [f]**Dt 8:2**; [g]**Dt 8:4**
6 [h]**Lev 10:9**; [i]Dt 8:3
7 [j]**Nu 21:26**; [k]**Nu 21:25**; [l]Nu 21:21–24, 33–35; Dt 2:26–3:11
8 [m]Ps 78:55; 135:12; 136:22; [n]Nu 32:33; Dt 3:12–13
9 [o]**Dt 4:6**; **Jos 1:7**; [p]Ex 19:5; Ps 25:10; 103:18; [q]Jos 1:8; 2Ch 31:21
11 [r]Jos 9:21,23, 27; 1Ch 20:3
13 [s]**Ge 6:18**; **Ex 19:6**; [t]**Ge 17:7**
14 [u]Ex 19:5; Isa 59:21; Jer 31:31; 32:40; 50:5; Eze 16:62; 37:26; Heb 8:7–8
15 [v]**Ge 6:18**; Ac 2:39
17 [w]Ex 20:23; Dt 4:28
18 [x]**Dt 13:6**; [y]**Dt 11:16**; Heb 12:15
19 [z]Ps 72:17; Isa 65:16; [a]Ps 36:2
20 [b]**Ex 23:21**; [c]Ex 34:14; Eze 23:25; Zep 1:18; [d]Ps 74:1; 79:5; 80:4; Eze 36:5; [e]2Ki 13:23; 14:27; Rev 3:5
21 [f]Dt 32:23; Eze 7:26; [g]**Dt 28:61**
22 [h]Jer 19:8; 49:17; 50:13
23 [i]Isa 1:7; 6:11; 9:18; 64:10; Jer 12:11; 44:2,6; Mic 5:11; [j]**Ge 13:10**; Eze 47:11

[a]19 Or *way, in order to add drunkenness to thirst."*

—nothing planted, nothing sprouting, no vegetation growing on it. It will be like the destruction of Sodom and Gomorrah,[k] Admah and Zeboiim, which the LORD overthrew in fierce anger.[l] 24 All the nations will ask: "Why has the LORD done this to this land?[m] Why this fierce, burning anger?"

25 And the answer will be: "It is because this people abandoned the covenant of the LORD, the God of their fathers, the covenant he made with them when he brought them out of Egypt.[n] 26 They went off and worshipped other gods and bowed down to them, gods they did not know, gods he had not given them. 27 Therefore the LORD's anger burned against this land, so that he brought on it all the curses written in this book.[o] 28 In furious anger and in great wrath[p] the LORD uprooted[q] them from their land and thrust them into another land, as it is now."

29 The secret things belong to the LORD our God,[r] but the things revealed belong to us and to our children for ever, that we may follow all the words of this law.[s]

Prosperity After Turning to the LORD

30 When all these blessings and curses[a] I have set before you come upon you and you take them to heart wherever the LORD your God disperses you among the nations,[b] 2 and when you and your children return[c] to the LORD your God and obey him with all your heart[d] and with all your soul according to everything I command you today, 3 then the LORD your God will restore your fortunes[a][e] and have compassion[f] on you and gather[g] you again from all the nations where he scattered[h] you.[i] 4 Even if you have been banished to the most distant land under the heavens,[j] from there the LORD your God will gather[k] you and bring you back.[l] 5 He will bring[m] you to the land that belonged to your fathers, and you will take possession of it. He will make you more prosperous and numerous[n] than your fathers. 6 The LORD your God will circumcise your hearts and the hearts of your descendants,[o] so that you may love[p] him with all your heart and with all your soul, and live. 7 The LORD your God will put all these curses[q] on your enemies who hate and persecute you.[r] 8 You will again obey the LORD and follow all his commands I am giving you today. 9 Then the LORD your God will make you most prosperous in all the work of your hands and in the fruit of your womb, the young of your livestock and the crops of your land.[s] The LORD will again delight[t] in you and make you prosperous, just as he delighted in your fathers, 10 if you obey the LORD your God and keep his commands and decrees that are written in this Book of the Law[u] and turn to the LORD your God with all your heart and with all your soul.[v]

The Offer of Life or Death

11 Now what I am commanding you today is not too difficult for you or beyond your reach.[w] 12 It is not up in heaven, so that you have to ask, "Who will ascend into heaven[x] to get it and proclaim it to us so that we may obey it?"[y] 13 Nor is it beyond the sea,[z] so that you have to ask, "Who will cross the sea to get it and proclaim it to us so that we may obey it?"[a] 14 No, the word is very near you; it is in your mouth and in your heart so that you may obey it.[b]

15 See, I set before you today life[c] and prosperity,[d] death[e] and destruction.[f] 16 For I command you today to love[g] the LORD your God, to walk in his ways, and to keep his commands, decrees and laws; then you will live[h] and increase, and the LORD your God will bless you in the land you are entering to possess.

17 But if your heart turns away and you are not obedient, and if you are drawn away to bow down to other gods and worship them, 18 I declare to you this day that you will certainly be destroyed.[i] You will not live long in the land you are crossing the Jordan to enter and possess.

19 This day I call heaven and earth as witnesses against you[j] that I have set before you life and death, blessings and curses.[k] Now choose life, so that you and your children may live 20 and that you may love[l] the LORD your God, listen to his voice, and hold fast to him. For the LORD is your life,[m] and he will give[n] you many years in the land[o] he swore to give to your fathers, Abraham, Isaac and Jacob.

23 [k]**Ge 19:24–25**; Zep 2:9; **Mt 10:15**; Ro 9:29; [l]**Ge 14:8**
24 [m]1Ki 9:8; 2Ch 36:19; Jer 16:10; 22:8–9; 52:13
25 [n]2Ki 17:23; 2Ch 36:21
27 [o]**Dt 28:15**
28 [p]Ps 7:11; [q]1Ki 14:15; 2Ch 7:20; Ps 9:6; 52:5; Pr 2:22; Jer 12:14; 31:28; 42:10; Eze 19:12
29 [r]Ac 1:7; [s]Jn 5:39; Ac 17:11; 2Ti 3:16

Ch. 30

1 [a]**Dt 11:26**; [b]Lev 26:40–45; **Dt 4:32**; 29:28
2 [c]**Dt 4:30**; [d]Dt 4:29; Ps 119:2
3 [e]Ps 14:7; 53:6; 85:1; 126:4; Jer 30:18; 33:11; Eze 16:53; Joel 3:1; Zep 2:7; [f]Dt 13:17; [g]**Ge 48:21**; [h]**Ge 11:4**; Dt 4:27; [i]Isa 11:11; Jer 12:15; 16:15; 24:6; 29:14; 48:47; 49:6
4 [j]Ps 19:6; [k]Isa 17:6; 24:13; 27:12; 40:11; 49:5; 56:8; Eze 20:34,41; 34:13; [l]Ne 1:8–9; Isa 11:12; 41:5; 42:10; 43:6; 48:20; 62:11; Jer 31:8,10; 50:2
5 [m]Jer 29:14; [n]**Dt 7:13**
6 [o]**Dt 6:24**; **10:16**; [p]Dt 6:5
7 [q]**Ge 12:3**; [r]Dt 7:15
9 [s]Jer 1:10; 24:6; 31:28; 32:41; 42:10; 45:4; [t]**Dt 28:63**
10 [u]**Dt 28:61**; [v]**Dt 4:29**
11 [w]Ps 19:8; Isa 45:19,23; 63:1
12 [x]Pr 30:4; [y]Ro 10:6*
13 [z]Job 28:14; [a]Ro 10:7*
14 [b]**Dt 6:6**; Ro 10:8*
15 [c]Pr 10:16; 11:19; 12:28; Jer 21:8; [d]Dt 28:11; Job 36:11; Ps 25:13; 106:5; Pr 3:1–2; [e]**Ge 2:17**; [f]**Dt 11:26**
16 [g]Dt 6:5; [h]ver 19; Dt 4:1; 32:47; Ne 9:29
18 [i]**Dt 8:19**
19 [j]Dt 4:26; [k]**Dt 11:26**
20 [l]Dt 6:5; [m]Dt 4:1; **8:3**; 32:47; Ps 27:1; Pr 3:22; **Jn 5:26**; Ac 17:28; [n]Ge 12:7; [o]Ps 37:3

[a]3 Or *will bring you back from captivity*

Joshua to Succeed Moses

31 Then Moses went out and
spoke these words to all Israel:
2"I am now a hundred and twenty years
old[a] and I am no longer able to lead
you.[b] The LORD has said to me, 'You
shall not cross the Jordan.'[c] 3The LORD
your God himself will cross[d] over ahead
of you.[e] He will destroy these nations[f]
before you, and you will take posses-
sion of their land. Joshua also will cross[g]
over ahead of you, as the LORD said.
4And the LORD will do to them what he
did to Sihon and Og,[h] the kings of the
Amorites, whom he destroyed along
with their land. 5The LORD will deliver[i]
them to you, and you must do to them
all that I have commanded you. 6Be
strong and courageous.[j] Do not be
afraid or terrified[k] because of them, for
the LORD your God goes with you;[l] he
will never leave you[m] nor forsake[n] you."
7Then Moses summoned Joshua and
said[o] to him in the presence of all Israel,
"Be strong and courageous, for you
must go with this people into the land
that the LORD swore to their forefathers
to give them,[p] and you must divide it
among them as their inheritance. 8The
LORD himself goes before you and will
be with you;[q] he will never leave you nor
forsake you.[r] Do not be afraid; do not be
discouraged."

The Reading of the Law

9So Moses wrote[s] down this law and
gave it to the priests, the sons of Levi,
who carried[t] the ark of the covenant of
the LORD, and to all the elders of Israel.
10Then Moses commanded them: "At
the end of every seven years, in the year
for cancelling debts,[u] during the Feast of
Tabernacles,[v] 11when all Israel comes to
appear[w] before the LORD your God at the
place he will choose,[x] you shall read this
law[y] before them in their hearing.
12Assemble the people—men, women
and children, and the aliens living in
your towns—so that they can listen and
learn[z] to fear[a] the LORD your God and
follow carefully all the words of this
law. 13Their children,[b] who do not know
this law, must hear it and learn to fear
the LORD your God as long as you live in
the land you are crossing the Jordan to
possess."

Israel's Rebellion Predicted

14The LORD said to Moses, "Now the
day of your death[c] is near. Call Joshua[d]
and present yourselves at the Tent of
Meeting, where I will commission
him."[e] So Moses and Joshua came and
presented themselves at the Tent of
Meeting.[f]
15Then the LORD appeared at the Tent
in a pillar of cloud, and the cloud stood
over the entrance to the Tent.[g] 16And the
LORD said to Moses: "You are going
to rest with your fathers,[h] and these
people will soon prostitute[i] themselves
to the foreign gods of the land they are
entering. They will forsake[j] me and
break the covenant I made with them.
17On that day I will become angry[k] with
them and forsake[l] them; I will hide[m] my
face[n] from them, and they will be des-
troyed. Many disasters[o] and difficulties
will come upon them, and on that day
they will ask, 'Have not these disasters
come upon us because our God is not
with us?'[p] 18And I will certainly hide my
face on that day because of all their
wickedness in turning to other gods.
19"Now write[q] down for yourselves
this song and teach it to the Israelites
and make them sing it, so that it may be
a witness[r] for me against them. 20When I
have brought them into the land flow-
ing with milk and honey, the land I
promised on oath to their forefathers,[s]
and when they eat their fill and thrive,
they will turn to other gods[t] and
worship them,[u] rejecting me and break-
ing my covenant.[v] 21And when many
disasters and difficulties come upon
them,[w] this song will testify against
them, because it will not be forgotten by
their descendants. I know what they are
disposed to do,[x] even before I bring
them into the land I promised them on
oath." 22So Moses wrote[y] down this
song that day and taught it to the
Israelites.
23The LORD gave this command[z] to
Joshua son of Nun: "Be strong and
courageous,[a] for you will bring the
Israelites into the land I promised them
on oath, and I myself will be with you."
24After Moses finished writing[b] in a
book the words of this law[c] from begin-
ning to end, 25he gave this command to
the Levites who carried[d] the ark of the
covenant of the LORD: 26"Take this Book
of the Law and place it beside the ark of
the covenant of the LORD your God.
There it will remain as a witness against

Ch. 31
2 [a]Ex 7:7; [b]Nu 27:17; 1Ki 3:7; [c]Dt 3:23,26
3 [d]Nu 27:18; [e]Dt 9:3; [f]Dt 7:1; [g]Dt 3:28
4 [h]Nu 21:33
5 [i]Dt 2:33
6 [j]ver 7,23; Jos 1:6,9,18; 10:25; 1Ch 22:13; 28:20; 2Ch 32:7; [k]Jer 1:8,17; Eze 2:6; [l]Ge 28:15; Dt 1:29; 20:4; Mt 28:20; [m]Ps 56:9; 118:6; [n]Dt 4:31; 1Sa 12:22; 1Ki 6:13; Ps 94:14; Isa 41:17; Heb 13:5*
7 [o]ver 23; Nu 27:23; [p]Jos 1:6
8 [q]Ex 13:21; [r]Ge 28:15; Dt 4:31
9 [s]Ex 17:14; [t]ver 25; 1Ch 15:2
10 [u]Dt 15:1; [v]Ex 23:16; Dt 16:13
11 [w]Dt 16:16; [x]Dt 12:5; [y]Jos 8:34–35; 2Ki 23:2; Ne 8:2
12 [z]Dt 4:10; [a]Hag 1:12; Mal 1:6; 3:5,16
13 [b]Dt 11:2
14 [c]Ge 25:8; Nu 27:13; [d]Nu 27:23; Dt 34:9; Jos 1:1–9; [e]Nu 27:19; [f]Ex 33:9–11
15 [g]Ex 33:9
16 [h]Ge 15:15; [i]Ex 34:15; Dt 4:25–28; Jdg 2:12; [j]Jdg 10:6, 13; 1Ki 9:9; 18:18; 19:10; Jer 2:13; 5:19; 19:4
17 [k]Dt 32:16; Jdg 2:14,20; 10:7; 2Ki 13:3; 22:13; Ps 106:29,40; Jer 7:18; 21:5; 36:7; [l]Jdg 6:13; 2Ch 15:2; 24:20; Ezr 8:22; Ps 44:9; Isa 2:6; [m]Dt 32:20; Isa 1:15; 45:15; 53:3; 54:8; [n]Job 13:24; Ps 13:1; 27:9; 30:7; 104:29; Isa 50:6; Jer 33:5; Eze 39:29; Mic 3:4; [o]Jer 4:20; Eze 7:26; [p]Nu 14:42; Hos 9:12
19 [q]ver 22; [r]Ge 31:50
20 [s]Dt 6:10–12; [t]Ps 4:2; 16:4; 40:4; Jer 13:25; Da 3:28; Am 2:4; [u]Dt 8:19; 11:16–17; [v]ver 16
21 [w]Dt 4:30; [x]1Ch 28:9; Hos 5:3; Jn 2:24–25
22 [y]ver 19 **23** [z]ver 7; [a]Jos 1:6
24 [b]Dt 17:18; 2Ki 22:8; [c]Dt 28:58 **25** [d]ver 9

you.[e] 27For I know how rebellious[f] and
stiff-necked[g] you are. If you have been
rebellious against the LORD while I am
still alive and with you, how much more
will you rebel after I die! 28Assemble
before me all the elders of your tribes
and all your officials, so that I can speak
these words in their hearing and call
heaven and earth to testify against
them.[h] 29For I know that after my death
you are sure to become utterly corrupt[i]
and to turn from the way I have com-
manded you. In days to come, disaster[j]
will fall upon you because you will do
evil in the sight of the LORD and provoke
him to anger by what your hands have
made."

The Song of Moses

30And Moses recited the words of this
song from beginning to end in the hear-
ing of the whole assembly of Israel:

32 Listen,[a] O heavens,[b] and I will
speak;
hear, O earth, the words of my
mouth.[c]
2Let my teaching fall like rain[d]
and my words descend like dew,[e][f]
like showers[g] on new grass,
like abundant rain on tender plants.

3I will proclaim[h] the name of the LORD.[i]
Oh, praise the greatness[j] of our
God!
4He is the Rock,[k] his works are perfect,[l]
and all his ways are just.
A faithful God[m] who does no wrong,
upright[n] and just is he.[o]

5They have acted corruptly towards
him;
to their shame they are no longer his
children,
but a warped and crooked
generation.[a][p]
6Is this the way you repay[q] the LORD,
O foolish[r] and unwise people?[s]
Is he not your Father,[t] your Creator,[b]
who made you and formed you?[u]

7Remember the days of old;[v]
consider the generations long past.[w]
Ask your father and he will tell you,
your elders, and they will explain to
you.[x]
8When the Most High[y] gave the nations
their inheritance,
when he divided all mankind,[z]
he set up boundaries[a] for the peoples
according to the number of the sons
of Israel.[c][b]

26 [e]ver 19
27 [f]**Ex 23:21**; [g]**Dt 9:27**
28 [h]Dt 4:26; 30:19; 32:1; Job 20:27; Isa 26:21
29 [i]**Dt 4:16**; Rev 9:20; [j]1Ki 9:9; 22:23; 2Ki 22:16

Ch. 32

1 [a]Ps 49:1; Mic 1:2; [b]Jer 2:12; [c]**Dt 4:26**
2 [d]2Sa 23:4; [e]Ps 107:20; Isa 9:8; 55:11; [f]Mic 5:7; [g]Ps 65:10; 68:9; 72:6; 147:8
3 [h]Ps 118:17; 145:6; [i]Ex 33:19; 34:5–6; [j]**Dt 3:24**
4 [k]**Ge 49:24**; [l]2Sa 22:31; Ps 18:30; 19:7; [m]**Dt 4:35**; [n]Ps 92:15; [o]**Ge 18:25**
5 [p]ver 20; Mt 17:17; Lk 9:41; Ac 2:40
6 [q]Ps 116:12; [r]Ps 94:8; Jer 5:21; [s]ver 28; [t]**Ex 4:22**; 2Sa 7:24; [u]ver 15
7 [v]Ps 44:1; 74:2; 77:5; Isa 51:9; 63:9; [w]Dt 4:32; Job 8:8; 20:4; Ps 78:4; Isa 46:9; [x]**Ex 10:2**; Job 15:18
8 [y]Ps 7:8; [z]**Ge 11:8**; Ac 8:1; [a]Ps 74:17; [b]Nu 23:9; Dt 33:12,28; Jer 23:6
9 [c]Ps 16:5; 73:26; 119:57; 142:5; Jer 10:16; [d]**Dt 9:29; 1Sa 26:19**
10 [e]**Dt 1:19**; [f]Dt 8:15; Job 12:24; Ps 107:40; [g]Ps 32:10; Jer 31:22; [h]Ps 17:8; Pr 7:2; Hos 13:5; Zec 2:8
11 [i]**Ex 19:4**; [j]Ps 17:8; 18:10–19; 61:4
12 [k]Ps 106:9; Isa 63:13; Jer 31:32; [l]Dt 4:35; [m]ver 39; Jdg 2:12; Ps 18:31; 81:9; Isa 43:12; 45:5

9For the LORD's portion[c] is his people,
Jacob his allotted inheritance.[d]

10In a desert[e] land he found him,
in a barren and howling waste.[f]
He shielded[g] him and cared for him;
he guarded him as the apple of his
eye,[h]
11like an eagle that stirs up its nest
and hovers over its young,[i]
that spreads its wings to catch them
and carries them on its pinions.[j]
12The LORD alone led[k] him;[l]
no foreign god was with him.[m]

13He made him ride on the heights[n] of
the land
and fed him with the fruit of the
fields.
He nourished him with honey from
the rock,[o]
and with oil[p] from the flinty crag,
14with curds and milk from herd and
flock
and with fattened lambs and goats,
with choice rams of Bashan[q]
and the finest grains of wheat.[r]
You drank the foaming blood of the
grape.[s]

15Jeshurun[d][t] grew fat[u] and kicked;
filled with food, he became heavy
and sleek.
He abandoned[v] the God who made
him
and rejected the Rock[w] his Saviour.
16They made him jealous[x] with their
foreign gods
and angered[y] him with their
detestable idols.
17They sacrificed[z] to demons,[a] which are
not God—
gods they had not known,[b]
gods that recently appeared,[c]
gods your fathers did not fear.
18You deserted the Rock, who fathered
you;
you forgot[d] the God who gave you
birth.

13 [n]Dt 33:29; 2Sa 22:34; Ps 18:33; Isa 33:16; 58:14; Eze 36:2; Hab 3:19; [o]**Dt 8:8**; [p]Dt 33:24; Job 29:6
14 [q]**Nu 21:33**; [r]Ps 65:9; 81:16; 147:14; [s]**Ge 49:11**
15 [t]Dt 33:5,26; Isa 44:2; [u]Dt 31:20; Jer 5:28; [v]Dt 31:16; Isa 1:4,28; 58:2; 65:11; Jer 15:6; Eze 14:5; [w]**Ge 49:24**
16 [x]**Nu 25:11; 1Co 10:22**; [y]**Dt 31:17; 1Ki 14:9**
17 [z]**Ex 32:8**; [a]**Ex 22:20**; 1Co 10:20; [b]**Dt 28:64**; [c]Jdg 5:8
18 [d]Jdg 3:7; 1Sa 12:9; Ps 44:17,20; 106:21; Jer 2:32; Eze 23:35; Hos 8:14; 13:6

[a]5 Or *Corrupt are they and not his children, / a generation warped and twisted to their shame*
[b]6 Or *Father, who bought you*
[c]8 Masoretic Text; Dead Sea Scrolls (see also Septuagint) *sons of God*
[d]15 *Jeshurun* means *the upright one,* that is, Israel.

19The LORD saw this and rejected them[e]
because he was angered by his sons
and daughters.[f]
20"I will hide my face[g] from them," he
said,
"and see what their end will be;
for they are a perverse generation,[h]
children who are unfaithful.[i]
21They made me jealous[j] by what is no
god
and angered me with their
worthless idols.[k]
I will make them envious by those
who are not a people;
I will make them angry by a nation
that has no understanding.[l]
22For a fire has been kindled by my
wrath,[m]
one that burns to the realm of death[e]
below.[n]
It will devour[o] the earth and its
harvests[p]
and set on fire the foundations of
the mountains.[q]

23"I will heap calamities[r] upon them
and expend my arrows[s] against
them.
24I will send wasting famine[t] against
them,
consuming pestilence[u] and deadly
plague;[v]
I will send against them the fangs of
wild beasts,[w]
the venom of vipers[x] that glide in
the dust.[y]
25In the street the sword will make them
childless;
in their homes terror[z] will reign.[a]
Young men and young women will
perish,
infants and grey-haired men.[b]
26I said I would scatter[c] them
and blot out their memory from
mankind,[d]
27but I dreaded the taunt of the enemy,
lest the adversary misunderstand[e]
and say, 'Our hand has triumphed;
the LORD has not done all this.'"[f]

28They are a nation without sense,
there is no discernment[g] in them.
29If only they were wise and would
understand this[h]
and discern what their end will be![i]
30How could one man chase a thousand,
or two put ten thousand to flight,[j]
unless their Rock had sold them,[k]
unless the LORD had given them
up?[l]
31For their rock is not like our Rock,[m]
as even our enemies concede.[n]

19 [e]Lev 26:30; Ps 78:59; [f]Am 6:8
20 [g]Dt 31:17,29; Ps 4:6; 44:24; [h]**ver 5**; [i]Dt 9:23
21 [j]**Nu 25:11; 1Co 10:22**; [k]ver 17; 1Ki 16:13,26; 2Ki 17:15; Ps 31:6; Jer 2:5; 8:19; 10:8; 16:19; Jnh 2:8; [l]Ro 10:19*
22 [m]Ps 7:11; [n]Nu 16:31–35; Ps 18:7–8; Jer 15:14; La 4:11; [o]Am 7:4; [p]Lev 26:20; [q]Ps 83:14
23 [r]**Dt 29:21**; [s]ver 42; 2Sa 22:15; Job 6:4; Ps 7:13; 18:14; 45:5; 77:17; 120:4; Isa 5:28; 49:2; Eze 5:16; Hab 3:9,11
24 [t]Ge 26:1; **41:55**; 42:5; 2Sa 24:13; 1Ch 21:12; [u]**Dt 28:22**; [v]Ps 91:6; [w]**Ge 37:20**; [x]ver 33; Job 20:16; Ps 58:4; Jer 8:17; Am 5:18–19; Mic 7:17; [y]Job 20:16
25 [z]Isa 24:17; [a]Jer 14:18; La 1:20; Eze 7:15; 2Co 7:5; [b]2Ch 36:17; Isa 13:18; Jer 4:31; La 2:21
26 [c]Dt 4:27; [d]**Nu 14:12**; Job 18:17; Ps 34:16; 37:28; 109:15; Isa 14:20
27 [e]Dt 9:26–28; [f]Ps 140:8; Isa 10:13; Jer 40:2–3
28 [g]Isa 1:3; 5:13; 27:11; Jer 8:7
29 [h]Dt 5:29; Ps 81:13; [i]Isa 47:7; La 1:9
30 [j]**Lev 26:8**; [k]Jdg 2:14; 3:8; 4:2; 10:7; 1Sa 12:9; [l]Nu 21:34; 1Sa 23:7; Ps 31:8; 44:12; 106:41; Isa 50:1; 54:6
31 [m]**Ge 49:24**; [n]**Ex 14:25**
32 [o]Jer 23:14; [p]Job 6:4; 20:16; [q]Dt 29:18
33 [r]**ver 24**
34 [s]Job 14:17; Jer 2:22; Hos 13:12

32Their vine comes from the vine of
Sodom[o]
and from the fields of Gomorrah.
Their grapes are filled with poison,[p]
and their clusters with bitterness.[q]
33Their wine is the venom of serpents,
the deadly poison of cobras.[r]

34"Have I not kept this in reserve
and sealed it in my vaults?[s]
35It is mine to avenge;[t] I will repay.[u]
In due time their foot will slip;[v]
their day of disaster is near
and their doom rushes upon
them."[w]

36The LORD will judge his people[x]
and have compassion[y] on his
servants[z]
when he sees their strength is gone
and no-one is left, slave[a] or free.
37He will say: "Now where are their
gods,
the rock they took refuge in,[b]
38the gods who ate the fat of their
sacrifices
and drank the wine of their drink
offerings?[c]
Let them rise up to help you!
Let them give you shelter!

39"See now that I myself am He![d]
There is no god besides me.[e]
I put to death[f] and I bring to life,[g]
I have wounded and I will heal,[h]
and no-one can deliver out of my
hand.[i]
40I lift my hand[j] to heaven and declare:
As surely as I live for ever,[k]
41when I sharpen my flashing sword[l]
and my hand grasps it in judgment,
I will take vengeance[m] on my
adversaries
and repay those who hate me.[n]
42I will make my arrows drunk with
blood,[o]
while my sword devours flesh:[p]

35 [t]**ver 41; Ge 4:24; Jer 51:6**; [u]**Ge 30:2; Ex 32:34; Ps 54:5; Ro 12:19***; Heb 10:30*; [v]Ps 17:5; 35:6; 37:31; 38:16; 66:9; 73:2,18; 94:18; 121:3; Pr 4:19; Jer 23:12; [w]Eze 7:8–9
36 [x]Heb 10:30*; [y]Am 7:3; [z]Lev 26:43–45; Dt 30:1–3; Jdg 2:18; Ps 90:13; 102:13; 103:13; 106:45; 135:14; Joel 2:14; [a]1Ki 14:10; 21:21; 2Ki 9:8
37 [b]Jdg 10:14; Jer 2:28; 11:12
38 [c]Nu 25:1–2; Jer 11:12; 44:8,25
39 [d]Isa 41:4; 43:10; 44:7; 46:4; 48:12; [e]**ver 12**; [f]1Sa 2:6; [g]1Sa 2:6; 2Ki 5:7; Ps 68:20; Jn 11:25–26; [h]Ex 15:26; Job 5:18; 15:11; Ps 147:3; Isa 6:10; 19:22; 30:26; 53:5; 57:18; Jer 33:6; Hos 6:1; Mal 4:2; 1Pe 2:24; [i]Job 9:12; 10:7; Ps 7:2; 50:22; Isa 43:13; Da 4:35; Hos 5:14
40 [j]**Ge 14:22**; [k]**Ge 21:33**; Rev 1:18
41 [l]Jdg 7:20; Ps 7:12; 45:3; Isa 27:1; 34:6; 66:16; Jer 12:12; Eze 21:9–10; [m]ver 35; Ps 149:7; Jer 46:10; Na 1:2; [n]Ps 137:8; Jer 25:14; 50:29; 51:24,56
42 [o]**ver 23**; [p]2Sa 2:26; Jer 12:12; 44:1; 46:10,14

---

[e]22 Hebrew *to Sheol*

the blood of the slain and the captives,
the heads of the enemy leaders."

43Rejoice,[q] O nations, with his people,[f,g]
for he will avenge the blood of his
servants;[r]
he will take vengeance on his enemies[s]
and make atonement for his land
and people.[t]

44Moses came with Joshua[h][u] son of
Nun and spoke all the words of this
song in the hearing of the people.
45When Moses finished reciting all these
words to all Israel, 46he said to them,
"Take to heart all the words I have
solemnly declared to you this day,[v] so
that you may command[w] your children
to obey carefully all the words of this
law. 47They are not just idle words for
you—they are your life.[x] By them you
will live long[y] in the land you are
crossing the Jordan to possess."

Moses to Die on Mount Nebo

48On that same day the LORD told
Moses,[z] 49"Go up into the Abarim[a]
Range to Mount Nebo[b] in Moab, across
from Jericho,[c] and view Canaan,[d] the
land I am giving the Israelites as their
own possession. 50There on the moun-
tain that you have climbed you will die[e]
and be gathered to your people, just as
your brother Aaron died[f] on Mount
Hor[g] and was gathered to his people.
51This is because both of you broke faith
with me in the presence of the Israelites
at the waters of Meribah Kadesh[h] in the
Desert of Zin[i] and because you did
not uphold my holiness among the
Israelites.[j] 52Therefore, you will see the
land only from a distance;[k] you will not
enter[l] the land I am giving to the people
of Israel."

Moses Blesses the Tribes

33:1–29Ref—Ge 49:1–28

33 This is the blessing[a] that Moses
the man of God[b] pronounced on
the Israelites before his death. 2He said:

"The LORD came from Sinai[c]
and dawned over them from Seir;[d]
he shone forth[e] from Mount Paran.[f]
He came with[a] myriads of holy ones[g]
from the south, from his mountain
slopes.[b]
3Surely it is you who love[h] the people;
all the holy ones are in your hand.[i]
At your feet they all bow down,[j]
and from you receive instruction,
4the law that Moses gave us,[k]
the possession of the assembly of
Jacob.[l]
5He was king[m] over Jeshurun[c][n]
when the leaders of the people
assembled,
along with the tribes of Israel.

6"Let Reuben live and not die,
nor[d] his men be few."[o]

7And this he said about Judah:[p]

"Hear, O LORD, the cry of Judah;
bring him to his people.
With his own hands he defends his
cause.
Oh, be his help against his foes!"

8About Levi[q] he said:

"Your Thummim and Urim[r] belong
to the man you favoured.[s]
You tested[t] him at Massah;
you contended with him at the
waters of Meribah.[u]
9He said of his father and mother,[v]
'I have no regard for them.'
He did not recognise his brothers
or acknowledge his own children,
but he watched over your word
and guarded your covenant.[w]
10He teaches[x] your precepts to Jacob
and your law to Israel.[y]
He offers incense before you[z]
and whole burnt offerings on your
altar.[a]
11Bless all his skills, O LORD,
and be pleased with the work of his
hands.[b]
Smite the loins of those who rise up
against him;
strike his foes till they rise no more."

12About Benjamin[c] he said:

"Let the beloved of the LORD rest
secure in him,[d]
for he shields him all day long,[e]
and the one the LORD loves[f] rests
between his shoulders.[g]"

43 [q]Ps 137:6; Isa 25:9; 65:18; 66:10; Ro 15:10*; [r]2Ki 9:7; Rev 6:10; [s]Isa 1:24; Jer 9:9; [t]Ps 65:3; 79:9
44 [u]Nu 13:8,16
46 [v]Dt 6:6; Jn 1:17; 7:19; [w]Dt 6:7
47 [x]Dt 30:20; [y]Ex 23:26; Dt 33:25; Isa 65:22
48 [z]Nu 27:12
49 [a]Nu 27:12; [b]Nu 32:3; [c]Nu 22:1; [d]Lev 14:34
50 [e]Ge 25:8; Nu 27:13; [f]Nu 20:29; [g]Nu 20:22
51 [h]Eze 47:19; [i]Nu 13:21; 20:11–13; [j]Nu 27:14
52 [k]Dt 34:1–3; [l]Dt 3:27

Ch. 33

1 [a]Ge 27:4; [b]Jos 14:6; 1Sa 2:27; 9:6; 1Ki 12:22; 13:1; 2Ki 1:9–13; 5:8; Jer 35:4
2 [c]Ex 19:18; Ps 68:8; [d]Jos 11:17; Jdg 5:4; [e]Ps 50:2; 80:1; 94:1; [f]Nu 10:12; [g]Ps 89:7; Da 4:13; 7:10; 8:13; Zec 14:5; Ac 7:53; Gal 3:19; Heb 2:2; Rev 5:11
3 [h]Dt 4:37; [i]Dt 7:6; [j]Lk 10:39; Rev 4:10
4 [k]Dt 4:2; Jn 1:17; 7:19; [l]Ps 119:111
5 [m]Ex 16:8; 1Sa 10:19; Ps 10:16; 149:2; [n]Nu 23:21; Dt 32:15
6 [o]Ge 34:5
7 [p]Ge 49:10
8 [q]Ge 29:34; [r]Ex 28:30; [s]Ps 106:16; [t]Nu 14:22; [u]Ex 17:7
9 [v]Ex 32:26–29; [w]Ps 61:5; Mal 2:5
10 [x]Ezr 7:10; Ne 8:18; Ps 119:151; Jer 23:22; Mal 2:6; [y]Lev 10:11; Dt 17:8–11; 31:9–13; [z]Ex 30:7; Lev 16:12–13; [a]Ps 51:19
11 [b]2Sa 24:23; Ps 20:3; 51:19
12 [c]Ge 35:18; [d]Dt 4:37–38; 12:10; 32:8; [e]Ex 19:4; [f]Ps 60:5; 127:2; Isa 5:1; [g]Ex 28:12

f43 Or *Make his people rejoice, O nations*
g43 Masoretic Text; Dead Sea Scrolls (see also Septuagint) *people, / and let all the angels worship him /*
h44 Hebrew *Hoshea*, a variant of *Joshua*
a2 Or *from*
b2 The meaning of the Hebrew for this phrase is uncertain.
c5 *Jeshurun* means *the upright one*, that is, Israel; also in verse 26.
d6 Or *but let*

13About Joseph[h] he said:

"May the LORD bless his land
with the precious dew from heaven above
and with the deep waters that lie below;[i]
14with the best the sun brings forth
and the finest the moon can yield;
15with the choicest gifts of the ancient mountains[j]
and the fruitfulness of the everlasting hills;
16with the best gifts of the earth and its fulness
and the favour of him who dwelt in the burning bush.[k]
Let all these rest on the head of Joseph,
on the brow of the prince among[e] his brothers.[l]
17In majesty he is like a firstborn bull;
his horns[m] are the horns of a wild ox.[n]
With them he will gore[o] the nations,
even those at the ends of the earth.
Such are the ten thousands of Ephraim;[p]
such are the thousands of Manasseh.[q]"

18About Zebulun[r] he said:

"Rejoice, Zebulun, in your going out,
and you, Issachar,[s] in your tents.
19They will summon peoples to the mountain[t]
and there offer sacrifices of righteousness;[u]
they will feast on the abundance of the seas,[v]
on the treasures hidden in the sand."

20About Gad[w] he said:

"Blessed is he who enlarges Gad's domain![x]
Gad lives there like a lion,
tearing at arm or head.
21He chose the best land for himself;[y]
the leader's portion was kept for him.[z]
When the heads of the people assembled,
he carried out the LORD's righteous will,[a]
and his judgments concerning Israel."

22About Dan[b] he said:

"Dan is a lion's cub,
springing out of Bashan."

23About Naphtali[c] he said:

"Naphtali is abounding with the favour of the LORD
and is full of his blessing;
he will inherit southward to the lake."

24About Asher[d] he said:

"Most blessed of sons is Asher;
let him be favoured by his brothers,
and let him bathe his feet in oil.[e]
25The bolts of your gates will be iron and bronze,[f]
and your strength will equal your days.[g]

26"There is no-one like the God of Jeshurun,[h]
who rides[i] on the heavens to help you[j]
and on the clouds[k] in his majesty.[l]
27The eternal[m] God is your refuge,[n]
and underneath are the everlasting[o] arms.
He will drive out your enemy before you,[p]
saying, 'Destroy him!'[q]
28So Israel will live in safety alone;[r]
Jacob's spring is secure
in a land of grain and new wine,
where the heavens drop dew.[s]
29Blessed are you, O Israel![t]
Who is like you,[u]
a people saved by the LORD?[v]
He is your shield and helper[w]
and your glorious sword.
Your enemies will cower before you,
and you will trample down their high places.[f] [x]"

The Death of Moses

34 Then Moses climbed Mount
Nebo[a] from the plains of Moab
to the top of Pisgah,[b] across from
Jericho.[c] There the LORD showed[d] him
the whole land—from Gilead to Dan,[e]
2all of Naphtali, the territory of Ephraim
and Manasseh, all the land of Judah as
far as the western sea,[a] [f] 3the Negev[g]
and the whole region from the Valley of
Jericho, the City of Palms,[h] as far as
Zoar.[i] 4Then the LORD said to him, "This

13 [h]**Ge 30:24;** [i]Ge 27:28; Ps 148:7
15 [j]Hab 3:6
16 [k]**Ex 3:2;** [l]**Ge 37:8**
17 [m]1Sa 2:10; 2Sa 22:3; Eze 34:21; [n]**Nu 23:22;** [o]1Ki 22:11; Ps 44:5; [p]**Ge 41:52;** [q]**Ge 41:51**
18 [r]**Ge 30:20;** [s]**Ge 30:18**
19 [t]**Ex 15:17;** Ps 48:1; Isa 2:3; 65:11; 66:20; Jer 31:6; [u]Ps 4:5; 51:19; [v]Isa 18:7; 23:18; 45:14; 60:5,11; 61:6; Hag 2:7; Zec 14:14
20 [w]Ge 30:11; [x]Dt 3:12–17
21 [y]Nu 32:1–5, 31–32; [z]**Nu 34:14;** [a]Jos 22:1–3
22 [b]Ge 49:16; **Nu 1:38**
23 [c]**Ge 30:8**
24 [d]**Ge 30:13;** [e]**Ge 49:20; Dt 32:13**
25 [f]Ne 3:3; 7:3; Ps 147:13; [g]**Dt 32:47**
26 [h]**Dt 32:15;** [i]Ps 18:10; 68:33; [j]**Dt 10:14; Ps 104:3;** [k]2Sa 22:10; Ps 18:9; 68:4; Da 7:13; [l]**Ex 15:7**
27 [m]Ex 15:18; Isa 40:28; 57:15; [n]Ps 9:9; 84:1; 90:1; 91:9; [o]**Ge 21:33;** [p]Ex 34:11; Jos 24:18; [q]**Dt 7:2**
28 [r]**Ex 33:16; Lev 25:18; Dt 32:8;** Ps 16:9; Pr 1:33; Isa 14:30; [s]ver 13; Ge 27:28
29 [t]Ps 1:1; 32:1–2; 144:15; [u]2Sa 22:45; Ps 18:44; 66:3; 81:15; [v]Dt 4:7; [w]Ge 15:1; Ex 18:4; Ps 10:14; 18:1; 27:1,9; 30:10; 54:4; 70:5; 115:9–11; 118:7; Isa 45:24; Hos 13:9; Hab 3:19; [x]**Nu 33:52; Dt 32:13**

Ch. 34
1 [a]**Nu 32:3;** [b]**Nu 21:20;** [c]Dt 32:49; [d]Dt 32:52; [e]**Ge 14:14**
2 [f]**Ex 23:31**
3 [g]**Ge 12:9;** [h]Jdg 1:16; 3:13; 2Ch 28:15; [i]**Ge 13:10**

[e]16 Or *of the one separated from*
[f]29 Or *will tread upon their bodies*
[a]2 That is, the Mediterranean

is the land I promised on oath[j] to Abra-
ham, Isaac and Jacob[k] when I said, 'I will
give it[l] to your descendants.' I have let
you see it with your eyes, but you will
not cross[m] over into it."
5And Moses the servant of the LORD[n]
died[o] there in Moab, as the LORD had
said. 6He buried him[b] in Moab, in the
valley opposite Beth Peor,[p] but to this
day no-one knows where his grave is.[q]
7Moses was a hundred and twenty
years old[r] when he died, yet his eyes
were not weak[s] nor his strength gone.[t]
8The Israelites grieved for Moses in the
plains of Moab[u] thirty days,[v] until the
time of weeping and mourning[w] was
over.
9Now Joshua son of Nun was filled
with the spirit[c] of wisdom[x] because
Moses had laid his hands on him.[y] So
the Israelites listened to him and did
what the LORD had commanded Moses.
10Since then, no prophet[z] has risen in
Israel like Moses,[a] whom the LORD knew
face to face,[b] 11who did all those miracu-
lous signs and wonders[c] the LORD sent
him to do in Egypt—to Pharaoh and to
all his officials[d] and to his whole land.
12For no-one has[e] ever shown the
mighty power or performed the awe-
some deeds[f] that Moses did in the sight
of all Israel.

4 [j]Ge 28:13; [k]Jos 21:43; [l]Ge 12:7; [m]Dt 3:23
5 [n]Nu 12:7; [o]Ge 25:8
6 [p]Dt 3:29; [q]Jude 9
7 [r]Ex 7:7; [s]Ge 27:1; [t]Ge 15:15
8 [u]Nu 21:11; [v]Ge 37:34; Dt 1:3; [w]2Sa 11:27
9 [x]Ge 41:38; Ex 28:3; Isa 11:2; [y]Dt 31:14; Ac 6:6
10 [z]Ge 20:7; [a]Dt 18:15,18; [b]Ex 33:11
11 [c]Dt 4:34; [d]Ex 11:3
12 [e]Heb 3:1–6; [f]Dt 4:34

[b]6 Or *He was buried*
[c]9 Or *Spirit*

Joshua

The LORD Commands Joshua

1 After the death of Moses the servant of the LORD,[a] the LORD said to Joshua[b] son of Nun, Moses' assistant: 2"Moses my servant is dead. Now then, you and all these people, get ready to cross the Jordan River[c][d] into the land[e] I am about to give to them[f]—to the Israelites. 3I will give you every place where you set your foot,[g] as I promised Moses.[h] 4Your territory will extend from the desert to Lebanon,[i] and from the great river, the Euphrates[j]—all the Hittite[k] country—to the Great Sea[a] on the west.[l] 5No-one will be able to stand up against you[m] all the days of your life. As I was with[n] Moses, so I will be with you; I will never leave you nor forsake[o] you.

6"Be strong[p] and courageous,[q] because you will lead these people to inherit the land I swore to their forefathers[r] to give them. 7Be strong and very courageous. Be careful to obey[s] all the law[t] my servant Moses[u] gave you; do not turn from it to the right or to the left,[v] that you may be successful wherever you go.[w] 8Do not let this Book of the Law[x] depart from your mouth;[y] meditate[z] on it day and night, so that you may be careful to do everything written in it. Then you will be prosperous and successful.[a] 9Have I not commanded you? Be strong and courageous. Do not be terrified;[b] do not be discouraged,[c] for the LORD your God will be with you wherever you go."[d]

10So Joshua ordered the officers of the people:[e] 11"Go through the camp[f] and tell the people, 'Get your supplies[g] ready. Three days[h] from now you will cross the Jordan[i] here to go in and take possession[j] of the land the LORD your God is giving you for your own.'"

12But to the Reubenites, the Gadites and the half-tribe of Manasseh,[k] Joshua said, 13"Remember the command that Moses the servant of the LORD gave you: 'The LORD your God is giving you rest[l] and has granted you this land.' 14Your wives,[m] your children and your livestock may stay in the land[n] that Moses gave you east of the Jordan, but all your fighting men, fully armed,[o] must cross over ahead of your brothers.[p] You are to help your brothers 15until the LORD gives them rest, as he has done for you, and until they too have taken possession of the land that the LORD your God is giving them. After that, you may go back and occupy your own land, which Moses the servant of the LORD gave you east of the Jordan towards the sunrise."[q]

16Then they answered Joshua, "Whatever you have commanded us we will do, and wherever you send us we will go.[r] 17Just as we fully obeyed Moses, so we will obey you.[s] Only may the LORD your God be with you as he was with Moses. 18Whoever rebels against your word and does not obey[t] your words, whatever you may command them, will be put to death. Only be strong and courageous!"[u]

Rahab and the Spies

2 Then Joshua son of Nun secretly sent two spies[a] from Shittim.[b] "Go, look over[c] the land," he said, "especially Jericho.[d]" So they went and entered the house of a prostitute[a] named Rahab[e] and stayed there.

2The king of Jericho was told, "Look! Some of the Israelites have come here tonight to spy out the land." 3So the king of Jericho sent this message to Rahab:[f] "Bring out the men who came to you and entered your house, because they have come to spy out the whole land."

Ch. 1

1 [a]Ex 14:31; Dt 34:5; Rev 15:3; [b]**Ex 17:9**
2 [c]**Nu 13:29;** [d]**Nu 35:10;** [e]**Ge 15:14;** [f]Ge 12:7; Dt 1:25
3 [g]**Dt 11:24;** [h]Ge 50:24; Nu 13:2; Dt 1:8
4 [i]**Dt 3:25;** [j]**Ge 2:14;** [k]**Ge 10:15;** 23:10; Ex 3:8; [l]Nu 34:2–12; Ezr 4:20
5 [m]**Dt 7:24;** [n]ver 17; **Ge 26:3; 39:2;** Jdg 6:12; 1Sa 10:7; Jer 1:8; 30:11; [o]**Ge 28:15; Dt 4:31**
6 [p]2Sa 2:7; 1Ki 2:2; Isa 41:6; Joel 3:9–10; [q]**Dt 1:21; 31:6; Jdg 5:21;** [r]Jer 3:18; 7:7
7 [s]Dt 29:9; 1 Ki 2:3; 3:3; [t]Ezr 7:26; Ps 78:10; 119:136; Isa 42:24; Jer 26:4–6; 32:23; 44:10; [u]ver 2,15; **Nu 12:7;** Job 1:8; 42:7; [v]**Dt 5:32;** Jos 23:6; [w]ver 9; **Dt 4:2;** 5:33; **11:8;** Jos 11:15
8 [x]**Dt 28:61; Ps 147:19;** [y]**Ex 4:15;** Isa 59:21; [z]**Ge 24:63;** [a]Dt 29:9; 1Sa 18:14; Ps 1:1–3; Isa 52:13; 53:10; Jer 23:5
9 [b]**Dt 31:6;** Jos 10:8; 2Ki 19:6; Isa 35:4; 37:6; [c]**Dt 1:21;** Job 4:5; [d]**ver 7;** Dt 31:8; Jer 1:8
10 [e]**Dt 1:15**
11 [f]Jos 3:2; [g]1Sa 17:22; Isa 10:28; [h]**Ge 40:13;** [i]**Nu 35:10;** [j]**Nu 33:53**
12 [k]Nu 32:33
13 [l]**Ex 33:14;** Ps 55:6; Isa 11:10; 28:12; 30:15; 32:18; 40:31; Jer 6:16; 45:3; La 5:5
14 [m]Dt 3:19; [n]**Nu 32:26;** [o]**Ex 13:18;** [p]Jos 4:12
15 [q]Nu 32:20–22; Jos 22:1–4
16 [r]**Nu 27:20; 32:25**
17 [s]**Nu 27:20**
18 [t]**Nu 32:25;** [u]**Dt 1:21; 31:6**

Ch. 2

1 [a]**ver 4; Ge 42:9;** [b]**Nu 25:1;** Jos 3:1; Joel 3:18; [c]**Nu 21:32;** Jdg 18:2; [d]**Nu 33:48;** [e]Jos 6:17,25; **Heb 11:31**
3 [f]Jos 6:23

[a]4 That is, the Mediterranean
[a]1 Or possibly *an innkeeper*

4But the woman had taken the two men[g] and hidden them.[h] She said, "Yes, the men came to me, but I did not know where they had come from. 5At dusk, when it was time to close the city gate,[i] the men left. I don't know which way they went. Go after them quickly. You may catch up with them."[j] 6(But she had taken them up to the roof and hidden them under the stalks of flax[k] she had laid out on the roof.)[l] 7So the men set out in pursuit of the spies on the road that leads to the fords of the Jordan,[m] and as soon as the pursuers[n] had gone out, the gate was shut.

8Before the spies lay down for the night, she went up on the roof[o] 9and said to them, "I know that the LORD has given this land to you and that a great fear[p] of you has fallen on us, so that all who live in this country are melting in fear because of you. 10We have heard how the LORD dried up[q] the water of the Red Sea[b] for you when you came out of Egypt,[r] and what you did to Sihon and Og,[s] the two kings of the Amorites[t] east of the Jordan,[u] whom you completely destroyed.[c v] 11When we heard of it, our hearts sank[d w] and everyone's courage failed[x] because of you,[y] for the LORD your God[z] is God in heaven above and on the earth[a] below. 12Now then, please swear to me[b] by the LORD that you will show kindness[c] to my family, because I have shown kindness to you. Give me a sure sign[d] 13that you will spare the lives of my father and mother, my brothers and sisters, and all who belong to them,[e] and that you will save us from death."

14"Our lives for your lives!"[f] the man assured her. "If you don't tell what we are doing, we will treat you kindly and faithfully[g] when the LORD gives us the land."

15So she let them down by a rope[h] through the window,[i] for the house she lived in was part of the city wall. 16Now she had said to them, "Go to the hills[j] so that the pursuers[k] will not find you. Hide yourselves there three days[l] until they return, and then go on your way."[m]

17The men said to her, "This oath[n] you made us swear will not be binding on us 18unless, when we enter the land, you have tied this scarlet cord[o] in the window[p] through which you let us down, and unless you have brought your father and mother, your brothers and all your family[q] into your house. 19If anyone goes outside your house into the street, his blood will be on his own head;[r] we will not be responsible. As for anyone who is in the house with you, his blood will be on our head[s] if a hand is laid on him. 20But if you tell what we are doing, we will be released from the oath you made us swear.[t]"

21"Agreed," she replied. "Let it be as you say." So she sent them away and they departed. And she tied the scarlet cord[u] in the window.[v]

22When they left, they went into the hills and stayed there three days,[w] until the pursuers[x] had searched all along the road and returned without finding them. 23Then the two men started back. They went down out of the hills, forded the river and came to Joshua son of Nun and told him everything that had happened to them. 24They said to Joshua, "The LORD has surely given the whole land into our hands;[y] all the people are melting in fear[z] because of us."

Crossing the Jordan

3 Early in the morning Joshua and all the Israelites set out from Shittim[a] and went to the Jordan,[b] where they camped before crossing over. 2After three days[c] the officers[d] went throughout the camp,[e] 3giving orders to the people: "When you see the ark of the covenant[f] of the LORD your God, and the priests,[g] who are Levites,[h] carrying it, you are to move out from your positions and follow it. 4Then you will know which way to go, since you have never been this way before. But keep a distance of about a thousand yards[a i] between you and the ark; do not go near it."

5Joshua told the people, "Consecrate yourselves,[j] for tomorrow the LORD will do amazing things[k] among you."

6Joshua said to the priests, "Take up the ark of the covenant and pass on ahead of the people." So they took it up and went ahead of them.

7And the LORD said to Joshua, "Today I will begin to exalt you[l] in the eyes of all Israel, so that they may know that I am with you as I was with Moses.[m] 8Tell the

4 [g]ver 1; Jos 6:22; [h]Jos 6:17
5 [i]Jdg 5:8; 9:35; 16:2; [j]**Heb 11:31**
6 [k]Jdg 15:14; Pr 31:13; Isa 19:9; [l]**Ex 1:19**; Jos 6:25; 2Sa 17:19
7 [m]Nu 22:1; Jdg 3:28; 7:24; 12:5–6; Isa 16:2; [n]ver 16,22
8 [o]**Dt 22:8**; Jdg 16:27; 2Sa 16:22; Ne 8:16; Isa 15:3; 22:1; Jer 32:29
9 [p]**Ge 35:5; Ex 15:14**
10 [q]**Ge 8:1**; Ex 14:21; Jos 3:17; Ps 74:15; [r]**Nu 23:22**; [s]**Nu 21:21**; [t]**Ge 10:16; 14:7**; [u]Jos 9:10; [v]**Nu 21:2**
11 [w]**Ge 42:28**; [x]**Dt 2:25**; Ps 107:26; Jnh 1:5; [y]**Ex 15:14**; Jos 5:1; 7:5; 2Sa 4:1; Ps 22:14; Isa 13:7; 19:1; Jer 51:30; Na 2:10; [z]2Ki 5:15; 19:15; Da 6:26; [a]**Ge 14:19; Nu 20:14**
12 [b]**Ge 24:8; 47:31**; [c]**Ge 24:12**; Ru 3:10; [d]**Ge 24:14; Ex 3:12**; Jos 4:6; 1Sa 2:34; 2Ki 19:29
13 [e]ver 18; Jos 6:23
14 [f]1Ki 20:39,42; 2Ki 10:24; [g]**Ge 47:29**
15 [h]Jer 38:6,11; [i]ver 18,21; Ge 26:8; Jdg 5:28; 1Sa 19:12
16 [j]**Ge 14:10**; [k]**ver 7**; [l]ver 22; [m]**Heb 11:31**
17 [n]**Ge 24:8**
18 [o]ver 21; [p]**ver 15**; [q]**ver 13**
19 [r]**Lev 20:9**; [s]Mt 27:25
20 [t]**Ge 24:8; 47:31**
21 [u]ver 18; [v]**ver 15**
22 [w]ver 16; [x]**ver 7**
24 [y]Jos 10:8; 11:6; Jdg 3:28; 7:9,14; 20:28; 1Sa 14:10; [z]**Ex 15:15**

Ch. 3
1 [a]**Jos 2:1**; [b]**Ge 13:10**; Job 40:23
2 [c]**Ge 40:13**; Jos 2:16; [d]**Dt 1:15**; [e]Jos 1:11
3 [f]**Nu 10:33**; [g]ver 8,17; Nu 4:15; Dt 31:9; 1Ki 8:3; [h]1Sa 6:15 *4* [i]Nu 35:5
5 [j]**Ex 29:1; Lev 11:44**; [k]Jdg 6:13; 1Ch 16:9,24; Ps 26:7; 75:1 *7* [l]Jos 4:14; 1Ch 29:25; [m]Jos 1:5

b10 Hebrew *Yam Suph*; that is, Sea of Reeds
c10 The Hebrew term refers to the irrevocable giving over of things or persons to the LORD, often by totally destroying them. d11 Hebrew *melted*
a4 Hebrew *about two thousand cubits* (about 900 metres)

priests[n] who carry the ark of the covenant: 'When you reach the edge of the Jordan's waters, go and stand in the river.'"

9Joshua said to the Israelites, "Come here and listen to the words of the LORD your God. 10This is how you will know that the living God[o] is among you[p] and that he will certainly drive out before you the Canaanites, Hittites,[q] Hivites, Perizzites,[r] Girgashites, Amorites and Jebusites.[s] 11See, the ark of the covenant of the Lord of all the earth[t] will go into the Jordan ahead of you.[u] 12Now then, choose twelve men[v] from the tribes of Israel, one from each tribe. 13And as soon as the priests who carry the ark of the LORD—the Lord of all the earth[w]—set foot in the Jordan, its waters flowing downstream[x] will be cut off[y] and stand up in a heap.[z]"

14So when the people broke camp to cross the Jordan, the priests carrying the ark of the covenant[a] went ahead[b] of them. 15Now the Jordan[c] is in flood[d] all during harvest.[e] Yet as soon as the priests who carried the ark reached the Jordan and their feet touched the water's edge, 16the water from upstream stopped flowing.[f] It piled up in a heap[g] a great distance away, at a town called Adam in the vicinity of Zarethan,[h] while the water flowing down[i] to the Sea of the Arabah[j] (the Salt Sea[b][k]) was completely cut off.[l] So the people crossed over opposite Jericho.[m] 17The priests[n] who carried the ark of the covenant of the LORD stood firm on dry ground in the middle of the Jordan,[o] while all Israel passed by until the whole nation had completed the crossing on dry ground.[p]

4 When the whole nation had finished crossing the Jordan,[a] the LORD said to Joshua, 2"Choose twelve men[b] from among the people, one from each tribe, 3and tell them to take up twelve stones[c] from the middle of the Jordan[d] from right where the priests stood and to carry them over with you and put them down at the place where you stay tonight.[e]"

4So Joshua called together the twelve men[f] he had appointed from the Israelites, one from each tribe, 5and said to them, "Go over before the ark of the LORD your God into the middle of the Jordan.[g] Each of you is to take up a stone on his shoulder, according to the number of the tribes of the Israelites, 6to serve as a sign[h] among you. In the future, when your children[i] ask you, 'What do these stones mean?'[j] 7tell them that the flow of the Jordan was cut off[k] before the ark of the covenant of the LORD. When it crossed the Jordan, the waters of the Jordan were cut off. These stones are to be a memorial[l] to the people of Israel for ever."

8So the Israelites did as Joshua commanded them. They took twelve stones[m] from the middle of the Jordan,[n] according to the number of the tribes of the Israelites, as the LORD had told Joshua;[o] and they carried them over with them to their camp, where they put them down. 9Joshua set up the twelve stones[p] that had been[a] in the middle of the Jordan at the spot where the priests who carried the ark of the covenant had stood. And they are there to this day.[q]

10Now the priests who carried the ark remained standing in the middle of the Jordan until everything the LORD had commanded Joshua was done by the people, just as Moses had directed Joshua. The people hurried over, 11and as soon as all of them had crossed, the ark of the LORD and the priests came to the other side while the people watched. 12The men of Reuben,[r] Gad[s] and the half-tribe of Manasseh[t] crossed over, armed, in front of the Israelites,[u] as Moses had directed them.[v] 13About forty thousand armed for battle[w] crossed over[x] before the LORD to the plains of Jericho for war.

14That day the LORD exalted[y] Joshua in the sight of all Israel; and they revered him all the days of his life, just as they had revered Moses.

15Then the LORD said to Joshua, 16"Command the priests carrying the ark of the Testimony[z] to come up out of the Jordan."

17So Joshua commanded the priests, "Come up out of the Jordan."

18And the priests came up out of the river carrying the ark of the covenant of the LORD. No sooner had they set their feet on the dry ground than the waters of the Jordan returned to their place[a] and ran in flood[b] as before.

19On the tenth day of the first month the people went up from the Jordan and camped at Gilgal[c] on the eastern border of Jericho. 20And Joshua set up at Gilgal the twelve stones[d] they had taken out of the Jordan. 21He said to the Israelites, "In the future when your descendants

8 [n]ver 3
10 [o]Dt 5:26; 1Sa 17:26,36; 2Ki 19:4,16; Ps 18:46; 42:2; 84:2; Isa 37:4,17; Jer 10:10; 23:36; Da 6:26; Hos 1:10; **Mt 16:16**; [p]**Dt 7:21**; [q]**Ge 26:34**; [r]Jos 17:15; 24:11; Jdg 1:4; 3:5; [s]**Ex 3:8; 23:23; Dt 7:1**; Jos 9:1; 11:3; 12:8; Jdg 19:11; 1Ch 11:4
11 [t]ver 13; Ex 19:5; Dt 10:14; Job 9:10; 28:24; 41:11; Ps 50:12; 97:5; Zec 6:5; [u]**Dt 9:3**
12 [v]Jos 4:2,4
13 [w]**ver 11**; [x]ver 16; [y]Jos 4:7; [z]**Ex 14:22; Isa 11:15**
14 [a]Ps 132:8; [b]Ac 7:44–45
15 [c]2Ki 2:6; [d]Jos 4:18; 1Ch 12:15; Isa 8:7; [e]**Ge 8:22**
16 [f]Ps 66:6; 74:15; 114:3; [g]Job 38:37; Ps 33:7; [h]1Ki 4:12; 7:46; [i]ver 13; [j]**Dt 1:1**; [k]**Ge 14:3**; [l]**Ge 8:1; Ex 14:22**; [m]2Ki 2:4
17 [n]**ver 3**; [o]Jos 4:3,5,8–10; [p]**Ex 14:22; Jos 2:10**

Ch. 4

1 [a]Dt 27:2
2 [b]**Jos 3:12**
3 [c]ver 20; [d]**Jos 3:17**; [e]ver 19
4 [f]**Jos 3:12**
5 [g]**Jos 3:17**
6 [h]**Jos 2:12**; [i]**Ex 10:2**; [j]ver 21; Ex 12:26; **13:14**
7 [k]Jos 3:13; [l]**Ex 28:12**
8 [m]Ex 28:21; [n]**Jos 3:17**; [o]ver 20
9 [p]**Ge 28:18**; Jos 24:26; 1Sa 7:12; [q]**Ge 35:20**
12 [r]**Ge 29:32**; [s]**Ge 30:11**; [t]**Ge 41:51**; [u]**Nu 32:27**; [v]Nu 32:29
13 [w]**Ex 13:18**; [x]**Nu 32:17**
14 [y]**Jos 3:7**
16 [z]Ex 25:22
18 [a]Ex 14:27; [b]**Jos 3:15**
19 [c]**Dt 11:30**
20 [d]ver 3,8

[b]16 That is, the Dead Sea
[a]9 Or *Joshua also set up twelve stones*

ask their fathers, 'What do these stones
mean?'[e] 22 tell them, 'Israel crossed the
Jordan on dry ground.'[f] 23 For the LORD
your God dried up the Jordan before
you until you had crossed over. The
LORD your God did to the Jordan just
what he had done to the Red Sea[b] when
he dried it up before us until we had
crossed over.[g] 24 He did this so that all
the peoples of the earth might know[h]
that the hand of the LORD is powerful[i]
and so that you might always fear the
LORD your God.[j]"

Circumcision at Gilgal

5 Now when all the Amorite kings
west of the Jordan and all the
Canaanite kings along the coast[a] heard
how the LORD had dried up the Jordan
before the Israelites until we had
crossed over, their hearts sank[a][b] and
they no longer had the courage to face
the Israelites.
2 At that time the LORD said to Joshua,
"Make flint knives[c] and circumcise[d] the
Israelites again." 3 So Joshua made flint
knives and circumcised the Israelites at
Gibeath Haaraloth.[b]
4 Now this is why he did so: All those
who came out of Egypt—all the men of
military age[e]—died in the desert on the
way after leaving Egypt.[f] 5 All the people
that came out had been circumcised, but
all the people born in the desert during
the journey from Egypt had not. 6 The
Israelites had moved about in the des-
ert[g] forty years[h] until all the men who
were of military age when they left
Egypt had died, since they had not
obeyed the LORD. For the LORD had
sworn to them that they would not see
the land that he had solemnly promised
their fathers to give us,[i] a land flowing
with milk and honey.[j] 7 So he raised up
their sons in their place, and these were
the ones Joshua circumcised. They were
still uncircumcised because they had
not been circumcised on the way. 8 And
after the whole nation had been circum-
cised, they remained where they were
in camp until they were healed.[k]
9 Then the LORD said to Joshua, "To-
day I have rolled away the reproach of
Egypt from you." So the place has been
called Gilgal[c][l] to this day.
10 On the evening of the fourteenth
day of the month,[m] while camped at
Gilgal on the plains of Jericho, the
Israelites celebrated the Passover.[n]
11 The day after the Passover, that very
day, they ate some of the produce of the
land:[o] unleavened bread[p] and roasted
grain.[q] 12 The manna stopped the day
after[d] they ate this food from the land;
there was no longer any manna for the
Israelites, but that year they ate of the
produce of Canaan.[r]

The Fall of Jericho

13 Now when Joshua was near Jericho,
he looked up and saw a man[s] standing
in front of him with a drawn sword[t] in
his hand. Joshua went up to him and
asked, "Are you for us or for our
enemies?"
14 "Neither," he replied, "but as com-
mander of the army of the LORD I have
now come." Then Joshua fell face
down[u] to the ground[v] in reverence, and
asked him, "What message does my
Lord[e] have for his servant?"
15 The commander of the LORD's army
replied, "Take off your sandals, for the
place where you are standing is holy."[w]
And Joshua did so.

6 Now Jericho[a] was tightly shut up
because of the Israelites. No-one
went out and no-one came in.
2 Then the LORD said to Joshua, "See, I
have delivered[b] Jericho into your hands,
along with its king and its fighting men.
3 March around the city once with all the
armed men. Do this for six days. 4 Make
seven priests carry trumpets of rams'
horns[c] in front of the ark. On the
seventh day, march around the city
seven times, with the priests blowing
the trumpets.[d] 5 When you hear them
sound a long blast[e] on the trumpets,
make all the people give a loud shout;[f]
then the wall of the city will collapse and
the people will go up, every man
straight in."
6 So Joshua son of Nun called the
priests and said to them, "Take up the
ark of the covenant of the LORD and
make seven priests carry trumpets in
front of it."[g] 7 And he ordered the
people, "Advance[h]! March around the
city, with the armed guard going ahead
of the ark[i] of the LORD."
8 When Joshua had spoken to the
people, the seven priests carrying the
seven trumpets before the LORD went
forward, blowing their trumpets, and
the ark of the LORD's covenant followed
them. 9 The armed guard marched

21 [e]ver 6
22 [f]**Ex 14:22**
23 [g]Ex 14:19–22
24 [h]1Ki 8:60; 18:36; 2Ki 5:15; Ps 67:2; 83:18; 106:8; Isa 37:20; 52:10; [i]Ex 15:16; 1Ch 29:12; Ps 44:3; 89:13; 98:1; 118:15–16; [j]**Ex 14:31**

Ch. 5

1 [a]**Nu 13:29;** [b]**Ge 42:28**
2 [c]**Ex 4:25;** [d]**Ge 17:10**,12,14
4 [e]**Nu 1:3;** [f]Dt 2:14
6 [g]Nu 32:13; Jos 14:10; Ps 107:4; [h]**Ex 16:35;** [i]Nu 14:23,29–35; Dt 2:14; [j]**Ex 3:8**
8 [k]Ge 34:25
9 [l]**Dt 11:30**
10 [m]**Ex 12:6;** [n]**Ex 12:11**
11 [o]**Nu 15:19;** [p]Ex 12:15; [q]**Lev 23:14**
12 [r]Ex 16:35
13 [s]**Ge 18:2;** [t]Nu 22:23
14 [u]**Ge 17:3;** [v]**Ge 19:1**
15 [w]**Ge 28:17;** Ex 3:5; Ac 7:33

Ch. 6

1 [a]Jos 24:11
2 [b]ver 16; Dt 7:24; Jos 8:1
4 [c]**Ex 19:13;** [d]**Lev 25:9**
5 [e]Ex 19:13; [f]ver 20; 1Sa 4:5; 2Sa 6:15; Ezr 3:11; 10:12; Ps 42:4; 95:1; Isa 8:9; 42:13
6 [g]ver 4
7 [h]Ex 14:15; [i]Nu 10:35; 1Sa 4:3; 7:1

b23 Hebrew *Yam Suph;* that is, Sea of Reeds
a1 Hebrew *melted*
b3 *Gibeath Haaraloth* means *hill of foreskins.*
c9 *Gilgal* sounds like the Hebrew for *roll.*
d12 Or *the day* e14 Or *lord*

ahead of the priests who blew the trum-
pets, and the rear guard[j] followed the
ark. All this time the trumpets were
sounding. 10But Joshua had command-
ed the people, "Do not give a war cry,
do not raise your voices, do not say a
word until the day I tell you to shout.
Then shout![k]" 11So he had the ark of the
LORD carried around the city, circling it
once. Then the people returned to camp
and spent the night there.

12Joshua got up early the next morn-
ing and the priests took up the ark of the
LORD. 13The seven priests carrying the
seven trumpets went forward, march-
ing before the ark of the LORD and
blowing the trumpets. The armed men
went ahead of them and the rear guard
followed the ark of the LORD, while the
trumpets kept sounding. 14So on the
second day they marched around the
city once and returned to the camp.
They did this for six days.

15On the seventh day, they got up at
daybreak and marched around the city
seven times in the same manner, except
that on that day they circled the city
seven times.[l] 16The seventh time
around, when the priests sounded the
trumpet blast, Joshua commanded the
people, "Shout! For the LORD has given
you the city![m] 17The city and all that is in
it are to be devoted[a][n] to the LORD. Only
Rahab the prostitute[b][o] and all who are
with her in her house shall be spared,
because she hid[p] the spies we sent. 18But
keep away from the devoted things,[q] so
that you will not bring about your own
destruction by taking any of them.
Otherwise you will make the camp of
Israel liable to destruction[r] and bring
trouble[s] on it. 19All the silver and gold
and the articles of bronze and iron[t] are
sacred to the LORD and must go into his
treasury."

20When the trumpets sounded,[u] the
people shouted, and at the sound of the
trumpet, when the people gave a loud
shout,[v] the wall collapsed; so every man
charged straight in, and they took the
city.[w] 21They devoted[x] the city to the
LORD and destroyed[y] with the sword
every living thing in it—men and
women, young and old, cattle, sheep
and donkeys.

22Joshua said to the two men[z] who
had spied out[a] the land, "Go into the
prostitute's house and bring her out and
all who belong to her, in accordance
with your oath to her.[b]" 23So the young
men who had done the spying went in
and brought out Rahab, her father and
mother and brothers and all who
belonged to her.[c] They brought out her
entire family and put them in a place
outside the camp of Israel.

24Then they burned the whole city[d]
and everything in it, but they put the
silver and gold and the articles of bronze
and iron[e] into the treasury of the LORD's
house.[f] 25But Joshua spared[g] Rahab the
prostitute,[h] with her family and all who
belonged to her, because she hid the
men Joshua had sent as spies to Jericho[i]
—and she lives among the Israelites to
this day.

26At that time Joshua pronounced this
solemn oath:[j] "Cursed[k] before the LORD
is the man who undertakes to rebuild
this city, Jericho:

"At the cost of his firstborn son
    will he lay its foundations;
at the cost of his youngest
    will he set up its gates."[l]

27So the LORD was with Joshua,[m] and
his fame spread[n] throughout the land.

Achan's Sin

7 But the Israelites acted unfaithfully
in regard to the devoted things[a];[a]
Achan[b] son of Carmi, the son of Zimri,[b]
the son of Zerah,[c] of the tribe of Judah,[d]
took some of them. So the LORD's anger
burned[e] against Israel.[f]

2Now Joshua sent men from Jericho to
Ai,[g] which is near Beth Aven[h] to the east
of Bethel,[i] and told them, "Go up and
spy out[j] the region." So the men went
up and spied out Ai.

3When they returned to Joshua, they
said, "Not all the people will have to
go up against Ai. Send two or three
thousand men to take it and do not
weary all the people, for only a few men
are there." 4So about three thousand
men went up; but they were routed by
the men of Ai,[k] 5who killed about thirty-
six[l] of them. They chased the Israelites
from the city gate as far as the stone
quarries[c] and struck them down on the
slopes. At this the hearts of the people
melted[m] and became like water.

6Then Joshua tore his clothes[n] and fell

9 [j]ver 13; **Nu 2:31**; Isa 52:12
10 [k]ver 20; 1Sa 4:5; Ezr 3:11
15 [l]1Ki 18:44; 2Ki 4:35; 5:14
16 [m]**ver 2**
17 [n]ver 21; Lev 27:28; Dt 20:17; Isa 13:5; 24:1; 34:2,5; Mal 4:6; [o]**Jos 2:1**; [p]ver 25; Jos 2:4
18 [q]Jos 7:1; 1Ch 2:7; [r]Jos 7:12; [s]Jos 7:25–26
19 [t]ver 24; Nu 31:22
20 [u]Lev 25:9; Jdg 6:34; 7:22; 1Ki 1:41; Isa 18:3; 27:13; Jer 4:21; 42:14; Am 2:2; [v]**ver 5,10**; [w]Heb 11:30
21 [x]**ver 17**; [y]**Dt 20:16**
22 [z]**Ge 42:9; Jos 2:4**; [a]**Nu 21:32**; [b]Jos 2:14; Heb 11:31
23 [c]**Jos 2:13**
24 [d]**Nu 31:10**; [e]**ver 19**; [f]**Dt 13:16**
25 [g]Jdg 1:25; [h]**Jos 2:1**; [i]**ver 17; Jos 2:6**
26 [j]1Sa 14:24; [k]**Nu 5:21**; [l]1Ki 16:34
27 [m]**Ge 39:2; Nu 14:43**; [n]Jos 9:1; 1Ch 14:17

Ch. 7

1 [a]**Jos 6:18**; [b]ver 26; 1Ch 2:7; [c]Jos 22:20; [d]ver 18; Nu 1:4; [e]**Ex 4:14; 32:20**; [f]**Lev 10:6**
2 [g]**Ge 12:8; Jos 8:1,28**; [h]Jos 18:12; 1Sa 13:5; 14:23; Hos 4:15; 5:8; 10:5; [i]Ge 12:8; Jos 12:16; 16:1; Jdg 1:22; 1Sa 30:27; 2Ki 23:15; Jer 48:13; Am 3:14; 4:4; 5:5–6; 7:10,13; [j]**Nu 21:32**
4 [k]**Lev 26:17; Dt 28:25**
5 [l]Jos 22:20; [m]**Ge 42:28**; Ps 22:14; Isa 13:7; Eze 21:7; Na 2:10
6 [n]**Ge 37:29**

[a]*17* The Hebrew term refers to the irrevocable giving over of things or persons to the LORD, often by totally destroying them; also in verses 18 and 21.
[b]*17* Or possibly *innkeeper*; also in verses 22 and 25
[a]*1* The Hebrew term refers to the irrevocable giving over of things or persons to the LORD, often by totally destroying them; also in verses 11, 12, 13 and 15.
[b]*1* See Septuagint and 1 Chron. 2:6; Hebrew *Zabdi*; also in verses 17 and 18.
[c]*5* Or *as far as Shebarim*

face down[o] to the ground before the ark
of the LORD, remaining there till eve-
ning.[p] The elders of Israel[q] did the same,
and sprinkled dust[r] on their heads.
7And Joshua said, "Ah, Sovereign
LORD, why[s] did you ever bring this peo-
ple across the Jordan to deliver us into
the hands of the Amorites to destroy
us?[t] If only we had been content to stay
on the other side of the Jordan! 8O Lord,
what can I say, now that Israel has been
routed by its enemies? 9The Canaanites
and the other people of the country will
hear about this and they will surround
us and wipe out our name from the
earth.[u] What then will you do for your
own great name?[v]"
10The LORD said to Joshua, "Stand up!
What are you doing down on your face?
11Israel has sinned;[w] they have violated
my covenant,[x] which I commanded
them to keep. They have taken some of
the devoted things; they have stolen,
they have lied,[y] they have put them
with their own possessions.[z] 12That is
why the Israelites cannot stand against
their enemies;[a] they turn their backs[b]
and run[c] because they have been made
liable to destruction.[d] I will not be
with you any more[e] unless you destroy
whatever among you is devoted to
destruction.
13"Go, consecrate the people. Tell
them, 'Consecrate yourselves[f] in prepa-
ration for tomorrow; for this is what the
LORD, the God of Israel, says: That
which is devoted is among you, O
Israel. You cannot stand against your
enemies until you remove it.
14" 'In the morning, present[g] your-
selves tribe by tribe. The tribe that the
LORD takes[h] shall come forward clan by
clan; the clan that the LORD takes shall
come forward family by family; and the
family that the LORD takes shall come
forward man by man. 15He who is
caught with the devoted things[i] shall be
destroyed by fire,[j] along with all that
belongs to him.[k] He has violated the
covenant[l] of the LORD and has done a
disgraceful thing in Israel!' "[m]
16Early the next morning Joshua had
Israel come forward by tribes, and
Judah was taken. 17The clans of Judah
came forward, and he took the Zera-
hites.[n] He had the clan of the Zerahites
come forward by families, and Zimri
was taken. 18Joshua had his family come
forward man by man, and Achan son of
Carmi, the son of Zimri, the son of
Zerah, of the tribe of Judah,[o] was
taken.[p]
19Then Joshua said to Achan, "My
son, give glory[q] to the LORD,[d] the God of
Israel, and give him the praise.[e] Tell[r] me
what you have done; do not hide it from
me."
20Achan replied, "It is true! I have
sinned against the LORD, the God of
Israel. This is what I have done: 21When
I saw in the plunder[s] a beautiful robe
from Babylonia,[f] two hundred shekels[g]
of silver and a wedge of gold weighing
fifty shekels,[h] I coveted[t] them and
took them. They are hidden in the
ground inside my tent, with the silver
underneath."
22So Joshua sent messengers, and
they ran to the tent, and there it was,
hidden in his tent, with the silver
underneath. 23They took the things
from the tent, brought them to Joshua
and all the Israelites and spread them
out before the LORD.
24Then Joshua, together with all
Israel, took Achan son of Zerah, the
silver, the robe, the gold wedge, his
sons[u] and daughters, his cattle, don-
keys and sheep, his tent and all that he
had, to the Valley of Achor.[v] 25Joshua
said, "Why have you brought this
trouble[w] on us? The LORD will bring
trouble on you today."
Then all Israel stoned him,[x] and after
they had stoned the rest, they burned
them.[y] 26Over Achan they heaped[z] up a
large pile of rocks, which remains to this
day.[a] Then the LORD turned from his
fierce anger.[b] Therefore that place has
been called the Valley of Achor[i][c] ever
since.

Ai Destroyed

8 Then the LORD said to Joshua, "Do
not be afraid;[a] do not be dis-
couraged.[b] Take the whole army[c] with
you, and go up and attack Ai.[d] For I
have delivered[e] into your hands the
king of Ai, his people, his city and his
land. 2You shall do to Ai and its king as
you did to Jericho and its king, except
that you may carry off their plunder[f]
and livestock for yourselves.[g] Set an
ambush[h] behind the city."

6 [o]**Ge 17:3**; 1Ch 21:16; Eze 9:8; [p]Jdg 20:23; [q]Jos 8:10; 9:11; 20:4; 23:2; [r]1Sa 4:12; 2Sa 13:19; 15:32; Ne 9:1; Job 2:12; La 2:10; Eze 27:30; Rev 18:19
7 [s]1Sa 4:3; [t]**Ex 5:22; Nu 14:16**
9 [u]Ex 32:12; **Dt 9:28**; [v]Dt 28:58; 1Sa 12:22; Ps 48:10; 106:8; Jer 14:21
11 [w]**Ex 9:27**; Dt 29:27; Jos 24:16–27; 2Ki 17:7; Hos 10:9; [x]ver 15; Jos 6:17–19; 23:16; Jdg 2:20; 1Sa 15:24; Ps 78:10; [y]Ac 5:1–2; [z]ver 21
12 [a]Lev 26:37; [b]Ps 18:40; 21:12; [c]**Lev 26:17**; [d]Jos 6:18; [e]Ps 44:9; 60:10
13 [f]**Lev 11:44**
14 [g]1Sa 10:19; [h]Pr 16:33
15 [i]Jos 6:18; [j]Dt 7:25; 2Ki 25:9; 1Ch 14:12; Isa 37:19; Jer 43:12; Eze 30:16; [k]1Sa 14:39; [l]**ver 11**; [m]Ge 34:7
17 [n]Nu 26:20
18 [o]**ver 1; Lev 24:11**; [p]Jnh 1:7
19 [q]Ex 14:17; 1Sa 6:5; Ps 96:8; Isa 42:12; Jer 13:16; Jn 9:24*; [r]**Lev 5:5**; 1Sa 14:43
21 [s]**Ge 34:29; 49:27**; [t]**Dt 7:25**; Eph 5:5; 1Ti 6:10
24 [u]**Nu 16:27**; [v]ver 26; Jos 15:7; Isa 65:10; Hos 2:15
25 [w]**Jos 6:18**; [x]**Lev 20:2**; Dt 17:5; 1Ki 12:18; 2Ch 10:18; 24:21; Ne 9:26; [y]**Ge 38:24**
26 [z]2Sa 18:17; [a]**Ge 35:20**; [b]**Nu 25:4**; [c]**ver 24**

Ch. 8
1 [a]Ge 26:24; Dt 31:6; [b]**Nu 14:9; Dt 1:21**; [c]Jos 10:7; [d]Jos 7:2; 9:3; 10:1; 12:9; [e]**Jos 6:2**
2 [f]**Ge 49:27**; [g]ver 27; Dt 20:14; [h]ver 4,12; Jdg 9:43; 20:29

---

d19 A solemn charge to tell the truth
e19 Or *and confess to him*
f21 Hebrew *Shinar*
g21 That is, about 5 pounds (about 2.3 kilograms)
h21 That is, about 1¼ pounds (about 0.6 kilogram)
i26 *Achor* means *trouble.*

3So Joshua and the whole army
moved out to attack Ai. He chose thirty
thousand of his best fighting men and
sent them out at night 4with these
orders: "Listen carefully. You are to set
an ambush behind the city. Don't go
very far from it. All of you be on the
alert. 5I and all those with me will ad-
vance on the city, and when the men
come out against us, as they did before,
we will flee from them. 6They will pur-
sue us until we have lured them away
from the city, for they will say, 'They are
running away from us as they did be-
fore.' So when we flee from them, 7you
are to rise up from ambush and take the
city. The LORD your God will give it into
your hand.[i] 8When you have taken the
city, set it on fire.[j] Do what the LORD has
commanded.[k] See to it; you have my
orders."

9Then Joshua sent them off, and they
went to the place of ambush[l] and lay in
wait between Bethel and Ai, to the west
of Ai—but Joshua spent that night with
the people.

10Early the next morning[m] Joshua
mustered his men, and he and the lead-
ers of Israel[n] marched before them to Ai.
11The entire force that was with him
marched up and approached the city
and arrived in front of it. They set up
camp north of Ai, with the valley be-
tween them and the city. 12Joshua had
taken about five thousand men and set
them in ambush between Bethel and Ai,
to the west of the city. 13They had the
soldiers take up their positions—all
those in the camp to the north of the city
and the ambush to the west of it. That
night Joshua went into the valley.

14When the king of Ai saw this, he
and all the men of the city hurried out
early in the morning to meet Israel in
battle at a certain place overlooking the
Arabah.[o] But he did not know[p] that an
ambush had been set against him be-
hind the city. 15Joshua and all Israel let
themselves be driven back[q] before
them, and they fled towards the desert.[r]
16All the men of Ai were called to pursue
them, and they pursued Joshua and
were lured away[s] from the city. 17Not a
man remained in Ai or Bethel who did
not go after Israel. They left the city
open and went in pursuit of Israel.

18Then the LORD said to Joshua, "Hold
out towards Ai the javelin[t] that is in
your hand,[u] for into your hand I will
deliver the city." So Joshua held out his
javelin[v] towards Ai. 19As soon as he
did this, the men in the ambush rose
quickly[w] from their position and rushed
forward. They entered the city and cap-
tured it and quickly set it on fire.[x]

20The men of Ai looked back and saw
the smoke of the city rising against the
sky,[y] but they had no chance to escape
in any direction, for the Israelites who
had been fleeing towards the desert had
turned back against their pursuers.
21For when Joshua and all Israel saw
that the ambush had taken the city and
that smoke was going up from the city,
they turned round[z] and attacked the
men of Ai. 22The men of the ambush
also came out of the city against them,
so that they were caught in the middle,
with Israelites on both sides. Israel cut
them down, leaving them neither survi-
vors nor fugitives.[a] 23But they took the
king of Ai alive[b] and brought him to
Joshua.

24When Israel had finished killing all
the men of Ai in the fields and in the
desert where they had chased them,
and when every one of them had been
put to the sword, all the Israelites re-
turned to Ai and killed those who were
in it. 25Twelve thousand men and
women fell that day—all the people of
Ai.[c] 26For Joshua did not draw back the
hand that held out his javelin[d] until he
had destroyed[a][e] all who lived in Ai.[f]
27But Israel did carry off for themselves
the livestock and plunder of this city, as
the LORD had instructed Joshua.[g]

28So Joshua burned[h] Ai[i] and made it a
permanent heap of ruins,[j] a desolate
place to this day.[k] 29He hung the king of
Ai on a tree and left him there until
evening. At sunset,[l] Joshua ordered
them to take his body from the tree and
throw it down at the entrance of the city
gate. And they raised a large pile of
rocks[m] over it, which remains to this
day.

The Covenant Renewed at Mount Ebal

30Then Joshua built on Mount Ebal[n]
an altar[o] to the LORD, the God of Israel,
31as Moses the servant of the LORD had
commanded the Israelites. He built it
according to what is written in the Book
of the Law of Moses—an altar of uncut
stones, on which no iron tool[p] had been
used. On it they offered to the LORD
burnt offerings and sacrificed fellow-
ship offerings.[b][q] 32There, in the pres-
ence of the Israelites, Joshua copied on

7 [i]Jdg 7:7; 1Sa 23:4
8 [j]Jdg 20:29–38; [k]ver 19
9 [l]2Ch 13:13
10 [m]Ge 22:3; [n]**Jos 7:6**
14 [o]**Dt 1:1**; [p]Jdg 20:34
15 [q]Jdg 20:36; [r]Jos 15:61; 16:1; 18:12
16 [s]Jdg 20:31
18 [t]Job 41:26; Ps 35:3; [u]**Ex 4:2**; 17:9–12; [v]ver 26
19 [w]Jdg 20:33; [x]**ver 8**
20 [y]Jdg 20:40
21 [z]Jdg 20:41
22 [a]Dt 7:2; Jos 10:1
23 [b]1Sa 15:8
25 [c]Dt 20:16–18
26 [d]ver 18; [e]**Nu 21:2**; [f]Ex 17:12
27 [g]**ver 2**
28 [h]**Nu 31:10**; [i]Jos 7:2; Jer 49:3; [j]**Dt 13:16**; Jos 10:1; [k]**Ge 35:20**
29 [l]**Dt 21:23**; Jn 19:31; [m]2Sa 18:17
30 [n]ver 33; **Dt 11:29**; [o]**Ex 20:24**
31 [p]**Ex 20:25**; [q]Dt 27:6–7

[a]*26* The Hebrew term refers to the irrevocable giving over of things or persons to the LORD, often by totally destroying them.
[b]*31* Traditionally *peace offerings*

stones the law of Moses, which he had
written.[r] 33All Israel, aliens and citizens[s]
alike, with their elders, officials and
judges, were standing on both sides of
the ark of the covenant of the LORD,
facing those who carried it—the priests,
who were Levites.[t] Half of the people
stood in front of Mount Gerizim and
half of them in front of Mount Ebal,[u] as
Moses the servant of the LORD had
formerly commanded when he gave in-
structions to bless the people of Israel.
34Afterwards, Joshua read all the
words of the law—the blessings and the
curses—just as it is written in the Book
of the Law.[v] 35There was not a word of
all that Moses had commanded that
Joshua did not read to the whole assem-
bly of Israel, including the women and
children, and the aliens who lived
among them.[w]

The Gibeonite Deception

9 Now when all the kings west of the
Jordan heard about these things
—those in the hill country,[a] in the west-
ern foothills, and along the entire coast
of the Great Sea[a][b] as far as Lebanon[c]
(the kings of the Hittites, Amorites,
Canaanites, Perizzites,[d] Hivites[e] and
Jebusites)[f]—2they came together to
make war against Joshua and Israel.
3However, when the people of Gib-
eon[g] heard what Joshua had done to
Jericho and Ai,[h] 4they resorted to a ruse:
They went as a delegation whose don-
keys were loaded[b] with worn-out sacks
and old wineskins, cracked and mend-
ed. 5The men put worn and patched
sandals on their feet and wore old
clothes. All the bread of their food sup-
ply was dry and mouldy. 6Then they
went to Joshua in the camp at Gilgal[i]
and said to him and the men of Israel,
"We have come from a distant country;[j]
make a treaty[k] with us."
7The men of Israel said to the Hivites,[l]
"But perhaps you live near us. How
then can we make a treaty[m] with you?"
8"We are your servants,"[n] they said to
Joshua.
But Joshua asked, "Who are you and
where do you come from?"
9They answered: "Your servants have
come from a very distant country[o] be-
cause of the fame of the LORD your God.
For we have heard reports[p] of him: all
that he did in Egypt,[q] 10and all that he
did to the two kings of the Amorites east
of the Jordan—Sihon king of Heshbon,[r]
and Og king of Bashan,[s] who reigned in
Ashtaroth.[t] 11And our elders and all
those living in our country said to us,
'Take provisions for your journey; go
and meet them and say to them, "We
are your servants; make a treaty with
us." ' 12This bread of ours was warm
when we packed it at home on the day
we left to come to you. But now see how
dry and mouldy it is. 13And these wine-
skins that we filled were new, but see
how cracked they are. And our clothes
and sandals are worn out by the very
long journey."
14The men of Israel sampled their pro-
visions but did not enquire[u] of the LORD.
15Then Joshua made a treaty of peace[v]
with them to let them live,[w] and the
leaders of the assembly ratified it by
oath.
16Three days after they made the trea-
ty with the Gibeonites, the Israelites
heard that they were neighbours, living
near[x] them. 17So the Israelites set out
and on the third day came to their cities:
Gibeon, Kephirah, Beeroth[y] and Kiriath
Jearim.[z] 18But the Israelites did not
attack them, because the leaders of the
assembly had sworn an oath[a] to them by
the LORD, the God of Israel.
The whole assembly grumbled[b]
against the leaders, 19but all the leaders
answered, "We have given them our
oath by the LORD, the God of Israel, and
we cannot touch them now. 20This is
what we will do to them: We will let
them live, so that wrath will not fall on
us for breaking the oath[c] we swore to
them." 21They continued, "Let them
live,[d] but let them be woodcutters and
water-carriers[e] for the entire com-
munity." So the leaders' promise to
them was kept.
22Then Joshua summoned the
Gibeonites and said, "Why did you de-
ceive us by saying, 'We live a long way[f]
from you,' while actually you live near[g]
us? 23You are now under a curse:[h] You
will never cease to serve as woodcutters
and water-carriers for the house of my
God."
24They answered Joshua, "Your ser-
vants were clearly told[i] how the LORD
your God had commanded his servant
Moses to give you the whole land and to
wipe out all its inhabitants from before
you. So we feared for our lives because
of you, and that is why we did this. 25We
are now in your hands.[j] Do to us what-
ever seems good and right[k] to you."

32 [r]Dt 27:8
33 [s]**Lev 16:29;** [t]Dt 31:12; [u]Dt 11:29; Jn 4:20
34 [v]**Dt 28:61;** 31:11
35 [w]**Ex 12:38;** Dt 31:12

Ch. 9

1 [a]**Nu 13:17;** [b]**Nu 34:6;** [c]**Dt 3:25;** [d]Ge 13:7; **Jos 3:10;** [e]ver 7; Jos 11:19; [f]**Jos 3:10**
3 [g]ver 17; Jos 10:10; 11:19; 18:25; 21:17; 2Sa 2:12; 5:25; 20:8; 1Ki 3:4; 9:2; 1Ch 8:29; 14:16; 16:39; 21:29; 2Ch 1:3; Ne 3:7; Isa 28:21; Jer 28:1; 41:12; [h]Ge 12:8; **Jos 8:1**
6 [i]**Dt 11:30;** [j]ver 22; [k]**Ge 26:28**
7 [l]**ver 1;** [m]**Ex 23:32; 1Ki 5:12**
8 [n]2Ki 10:5
9 [o]**Dt 20:15;** [p]ver 24; [q]**Nu 23:22**
10 [r]**Nu 21:25;** [s]**Nu 21:33;** [t]**Nu 21:24**,35; Jos 2:10
14 [u]**Ex 16:28; Nu 27:21**
15 [v]**ver 3**,7; Jos 10:1,4; 11:19; 2Sa 21:2; 24:1; [w]ver 21; Jdg 1:21; Ps 106:34
16 [x]ver 22
17 [y]Jos 18:25; 2Sa 4:2; 23:37; [z]Jos 15:9,60; 18:14–15; Jdg 18:12; 1Sa 6:21; 7:2; Ps 132:6; Jer 26:20
18 [a]ver 15; Jdg 21:1,7,18; 1Sa 20:17; Ps 15:4; [b]**Ex 15:24**
20 [c]**Ge 24:8**
21 [d]**ver 15;** [e]**Dt 29:11**
22 [f]ver 6; [g]ver 16
23 [h]**Ge 9:25**
24 [i]ver 9
25 [j]Ge 16:6; [k]Jer 26:14

[a]1 That is, the Mediterranean
[b]4 Most Hebrew manuscripts; some Hebrew manuscripts, Vulgate and Syriac (see also Septuagint) *They prepared provisions and loaded their donkeys*

26So Joshua saved them from the
Israelites, and they did not kill them.
27That day he made the Gibeonites[l]
woodcutters and water-carriers[m] for the
community and for the altar of the LORD
at the place the LORD would choose.[n]
And that is what they are to this day.

The Sun Stands Still

10 Now Adoni-Zedek[a] king of
Jerusalem[b] heard that Joshua
had taken Ai[c] and totally destroyed[a][d] it,
doing to Ai and its king as he had done
to Jericho and its king, and that the
people of Gibeon[e] had made a treaty of
peace[f] with Israel and were living near
them. 2He and his people were very
much alarmed at this, because Gibeon
was an important city, like one of the
royal cities; it was larger than Ai, and all
its men were good fighters. 3So Adoni-
Zedek king of Jerusalem appealed to
Hoham king of Hebron,[g] Piram king of
Jarmuth,[h] Japhia king of Lachish[i] and
Debir[j] king of Eglon.[k] 4"Come up and
help me attack Gibeon," he said, "be-
cause it has made peace[l] with Joshua
and the Israelites."
5Then the five kings[m] of the Amor-
ites[n]—the kings of Jerusalem, Hebron,
Jarmuth, Lachish and Eglon—joined
forces. They moved up with all their
troops and took up positions against
Gibeon and attacked it.
6The Gibeonites then sent word to
Joshua in the camp at Gilgal:[o] "Do not
abandon your servants. Come up to us
quickly and save us! Help us, because
all the Amorite kings from the hill coun-
try have joined forces against us."
7So Joshua marched up from Gilgal
with his entire army,[p] including all the
best fighting men. 8The LORD said to
Joshua, "Do not be afraid[q] of them; I
have given them into your hand.[r] Not
one of them will be able to withstand
you."[s]
9After an all-night march from Gilgal,
Joshua took them by surprise. 10The
LORD threw them into confusion[t] before
Israel,[u] who defeated them in a great
victory at Gibeon.[v] Israel pursued them
along the road going up to Beth Horon[w]
and cut them down all the way to Aze-
kah[x] and Makkedah.[y] 11As they fled be-
fore Israel on the road down from Beth
Horon to Azekah, the LORD hurled large
hailstones[z] down on them from the
sky,[a] and more of them died from the
hailstones than were killed by the
swords of the Israelites.

12On the day the LORD gave the Amor-
ites[b] over to Israel, Joshua said to the
LORD in the presence of Israel:

"O sun, stand still over Gibeon,
O moon, over the Valley of
Aijalon."[c]
13So the sun stood still,[d]
and the moon stopped,
till the nation avenged itself on[b] its
enemies,

as it is written in the Book of Jashar.[e]
The sun stopped[f] in the middle of the
sky and delayed going down about a
full day. 14There has never been a day
like it before or since, a day when the
LORD listened to a man. Surely the LORD
was fighting[g] for Israel!
15Then Joshua returned with all Israel
to the camp at Gilgal.[h]

Five Amorite Kings Killed

16Now the five kings had fled[i] and
hidden in the cave at Makkedah.
17When Joshua was told that the five
kings had been found hiding in the cave
at Makkedah, 18he said, "Roll large
rocks up to the mouth of the cave, and
post some men there to guard it. 19But
don't stop! Pursue your enemies, attack
them from the rear and don't let them
reach their cities, for the LORD your God
has given them into your hand."
20So Joshua and the Israelites de-
stroyed them completely[j]—almost to a
man—but the few who were left
reached their fortified cities.[k] 21The
whole army then returned safely to
Joshua in the camp at Makkedah, and
no-one uttered a word against the
Israelites.
22Joshua said, "Open the mouth of
the cave and bring those five kings out
to me." 23So they brought the five kings
out of the cave—the kings of Jerusalem,
Hebron, Jarmuth, Lachish and Eglon.
24When they had brought these kings[l] to
Joshua, he summoned all the men of
Israel and said to the army commanders
who had come with him, "Come here
and put your feet[m] on the necks of these
kings." So they came forward and
placed their feet[n] on their necks.
25Joshua said to them, "Do not be

27 [l]Ex 1:11; [m]Dt 29:11; [n]Dt 12:5

Ch. 10

1 [a]ver 3; [b]Jos 12:10; 15:8,63; 18:28; Jdg 1:7; [c]Jos 8:1; [d]Dt 20:16; Jos 8:22; [e]Jos 9:3; [f]Jos 9:15
3 [g]Ge 13:18; [h]ver 5; Jos 12:11; 15:35; 21:29; Ne 11:29; [i]ver 5, 31; Jos 12:11; 15:39; 2Ki 14:19; 2Ch 11:9; 25:27; 32:9; Ne 11:30; Isa 36:2; 37:8; Jer 34:7; Mic 1:13; [j]ver 38; Jos 11:21; 12:13; 13:26; 15:7,49; 21:15; Jdg 1:11; 1Ch 6:58; [k]ver 23,34,36; Jos 12:12; 15:39
4 [l]Jos 9:15
5 [m]ver 16; [n]Nu 13:29; Dt 1:7
6 [o]Dt 11:30
7 [p]Jos 8:1
8 [q]Dt 3:2; Jos 1:9; [r]Jos 2:24; [s]Dt 7:24
10 [t]Ex 14:24; [u]Dt 7:23; [v]Jos 9:3; [w]Jos 16:3,5; 18:13–14; 21:22; 1Sa 13:18; 1Ki 9:17; 1Ch 6:68; 7:24; 2Ch 8:5; 25:13; [x]Jos 15:35; 1Sa 17:1; 2Ch 11:9; Ne 11:30; Jer 34:7; [y]ver 16–17,21; Jos 12:16; 15:41
11 [z]Ex 9:18; Ps 18:12; Isa 28:2,17; 32:19; Eze 13:11,13; [a]Jdg 5:20
12 [b]Am 2:9; [c]Jos 19:42; 21:24; Jdg 1:35; 12:12; 1Sa 14:31; 1Ch 6:69; 8:13; 2Ch 11:10; 28:18
13 [d]Hab 3:11; [e]2Sa 1:18; [f]Isa 38:8
14 [g]ver 42; Ex 14:14; Ps 106:43; 136:24; Isa 63:10; Jer 21:5
15 [h]ver 43
16 [i]Ps 68:12
20 [j]Dt 20:16; [k]2Ch 11:10; Jer 4:5; 5:17; 8:14; 35:11
24 [l]Dt 7:24; [m]Mal 4:3; [n]2Sa 22:40; Ps 110:1; Isa 51:23

[a]1 The Hebrew term refers to the irrevocable giving over of things or persons to the LORD, often by totally destroying them; also in verses 28, 35, 37, 39 and 40. [b]13 Or *nation triumphed over*

afraid; do not be discouraged. Be strong
and courageous.[o] This is what the LORD
will do to all the enemies you are going
to fight." 26Then Joshua struck and
killed the kings and hung them on five
trees, and they were left hanging on the
trees until evening.
27At sunset[p] Joshua gave the order
and they took them down from the trees
and threw them into the cave where
they had been hiding. At the mouth of
the cave they placed large rocks, which
are there to this day.[q]
28That day Joshua took Makkedah.
He put the city and its king to the sword
and totally destroyed everyone in it. He
left no survivors.[r] And he did to the
king of Makkedah as he had done to the
king of Jericho.[s]

Southern Cities Conquered

29Then Joshua and all Israel with him
moved on from Makkedah to Libnah[t]
and attacked it. 30The LORD also gave
that city and its king into Israel's hand.
The city and everyone in it Joshua put to
the sword. He left no survivors there.
And he did to its king as he had done to
the king of Jericho.
31Then Joshua and all Israel with him
moved on from Libnah to Lachish;[u] he
took up positions against it and attacked
it. 32The LORD handed Lachish over to
Israel, and Joshua took it on the second
day. The city and everyone in it he put
to the sword, just as he had done to
Libnah. 33Meanwhile, Horam king of
Gezer[v] had come up to help Lachish,
but Joshua defeated him and his army
—until no survivors were left.
34Then Joshua and all Israel with him
moved on from Lachish to Eglon;[w] they
took up positions against it and attacked
it. 35They captured it that same day and
put it to the sword and totally destroyed
everyone in it, just as they had done to
Lachish.
36Then Joshua and all Israel with him
went up from Eglon to Hebron[x] and
attacked it. 37They took the city and put
it to the sword, together with its king,
its villages and everyone[y] in it. They
left no survivors. Just as at Eglon, they
totally destroyed it and everyone in it.
38Then Joshua and all Israel with him
turned round and attacked Debir.[z]
39They took the city, its king and its
villages, and put them to the sword.
Everyone in it they totally destroyed.
They left no survivors. They did to
Debir and its king as they had done to
Libnah and its king and to Hebron.[a]
40So Joshua subdued the whole
region, including the hill country, the
Negev,[b] the western foothills and the
mountain slopes,[c] together with all their
kings.[d] He left no survivors. He totally
destroyed all who breathed, just as the
LORD, the God of Israel, had com-
manded.[e] 41Joshua subdued them from
Kadesh Barnea[f] to Gaza[g] and from the
whole region of Goshen[h] to Gibeon.
42All these kings and their lands Joshua
conquered in one campaign, because
the LORD, the God of Israel, fought[i] for
Israel.
43Then Joshua returned with all Israel
to the camp at Gilgal.[j]

Northern Kings Defeated

11 When Jabin[a] king of Hazor[b]
heard of this, he sent word to
Jobab king of Madon, to the kings of
Shimron[c] and Acshaph,[d] 2and to the
northern kings who were in the moun-
tains, in the Arabah[e] south of Kin-
nereth,[f] in the western foothills and in
Naphoth Dor[a][g] on the west; 3to the
Canaanites in the east and west; to the
Amorites, Hittites, Perizzites[h] and Jebu-
sites in the hill country;[i] and to the
Hivites[j] below Hermon[k] in the region of
Mizpah.[l] 4They came out with all their
troops and a large number of horses and
chariots—a huge army, as numerous as
the sand on the seashore.[m] 5All these
kings joined forces[n] and made camp
together at the Waters of Merom,[o] to
fight against Israel.
6The LORD said to Joshua, "Do not be
afraid of them, because by this time
tomorrow I will hand all of them over[p] to
Israel, slain. You are to hamstring[q] their
horses and burn their chariots."[r]
7So Joshua and his whole army came
against them suddenly at the Waters of
Merom and attacked them, 8and the
LORD gave them into the hand of Israel.
They defeated them and pursued them
all the way to Greater Sidon,[s] to Mis-
rephoth Maim,[t] and to the Valley of
Mizpah on the east, until no survivors
were left. 9Joshua did to them as the
LORD had directed: He hamstrung their
horses and burned their chariots.
10At that time Joshua turned back and
captured Hazor and put its king to the
sword.[u] (Hazor had been the head of
all these kingdoms.) 11Everyone in it
they put to the sword. They totally

25 oDt 31:6
27 pDt 21:23; qGe 35:20
28 rDt 20:16; sver 30,32,35, 39; Jos 6:21
29 tNu 33:20
31 uver 3
33 vJos 12:12; 16:3,10; 21:21; Jdg 1:29; 2Sa 5:25; 1Ki 9:15; 1Ch 6:67
34 wver 3
36 xGe 13:18; Jos 14:13; 15:13; 20:7; 21:11; Jdg 16:3
37 yver 28
38 zver 3
39 aver 28
40 bGe 12:9; Jos 12:8; 15:19,21; 18:25; 19:8; 1Sa 30:27; cDt 1:7; dDt 7:24; eDt 20:16–17
41 fGe 14:7; gGe 10:19; hJos 11:16; 15:51
42 iver 14
43 jver 15; Jos 5:9; 1Sa 7:16; 10:8; 11:14; 13:12

Ch. 11

1 aJdg 4:2,7,23; Ps 83:9; bver 10; Jos 12:19; 15:23,25; 19:36; Jdg 4:2,17; 1Sa 12:9; 1Ki 9:15; 2Ki 15:29; Ne 11:33; Jer 49:28,33; cJos 19:15; dJos 12:20; 19:25
2 ever 16; Dt 1:1; Jos 12:1; 18:18; fNu 34:11; Dt 3:17; Jos 19:35; 1Ki 15:20; gJos 12:23; 17:11; Jdg 1:27; 1Ki 4:11; 1Ch 7:29
3 hJos 3:10; iNu 13:17; jEx 3:8; Dt 7:1; Jdg 3:3,5; 1Ki 9:20; kDt 3:8; lver 8; Ge 31:49; Jos 15:38; 18:26; Jdg 11:11; 20:1; 21:1; 1Sa 7:5–6; 1Ki 15:22; 2Ki 25:23
4 mGe 12:2; Jdg 7:12; 1Sa 13:5
5 nJdg 5:19; over 7
6 pJos 2:24; qGe 49:6; rver 9
8 sGe 10:15; Jdg 18:7; tJos 13:6
10 uIsa 3:25; Jer 41:2; 44:18

a2 Or *in the heights of Dor*

destroyed[b] them,[v] not sparing anything
that breathed,[w] and he burned up[x]
Hazor itself.
12Joshua took all these royal cities and
their kings and put them to the sword.
He totally destroyed them, as Moses the
servant of the LORD had commanded.[y]
13Yet Israel did not burn any of the cities
built on their mounds—except Hazor,
which Joshua burned. 14The Israelites
carried off for themselves all the plun-
der and livestock of these cities, but all
the people they put to the sword until
they completely destroyed them, not
sparing anyone that breathed.[z] 15As the
LORD commanded his servant Moses, so
Moses commanded Joshua, and Joshua
did it; he left nothing undone of all that
the LORD commanded Moses.[a]
16So Joshua took this entire land: the
hill country,[b] all the Negev,[c] the whole
region of Goshen, the western foot-
hills,[d] the Arabah and the mountains of
Israel with their foothills, 17from Mount
Halak, which rises towards Seir,[e] to Baal
Gad[f] in the Valley of Lebanon[g] below
Mount Hermon.[h] He captured all their
kings and struck them down, putting
them to death.[i] 18Joshua waged war
against all these kings for a long time.
19Except for the Hivites[j] living in
Gibeon,[k] not one city made a treaty of
peace[l] with the Israelites, who took
them all in battle. 20For it was the LORD
himself who hardened their hearts[m] to
wage war against Israel, so that he
might destroy them totally, extermina-
ting them without mercy, as the LORD
had commanded Moses.[n]
21At that time Joshua went and de-
stroyed the Anakites[o] from the hill coun-
try: from Hebron, Debir[p] and Anab,[q]
from all the hill country of Judah, and
from all the hill country of Israel. Joshua
totally destroyed them and their towns.
22No Anakites were left in Israelite terri-
tory; only in Gaza,[r] Gath[s] and Ashdod[t]
did any survive. 23So Joshua took the
entire land,[u] just as the LORD had
directed Moses, and he gave it as an
inheritance[v] to Israel according to their
tribal divisions.[w x]
Then the land had rest[y] from war.[z]

List of Defeated Kings

12 These are the kings of the land
whom the Israelites had de-
feated and whose territory they took[a]
over east of the Jordan,[b] from the
Arnon[c] Gorge to Mount Hermon,[d]
including all the eastern side of the
Arabah:[e]

2Sihon king of the Amorites,
who reigned in Heshbon.[f] He ruled
from Aroer[g] on the rim of the
Arnon Gorge—from the middle of
the gorge—to the Jabbok River,[h]
which is the border of the Ammo-
nites.[i] This included half of Gilead.[j]
3He also ruled over the eastern Ara-
bah from the Sea of Kinnereth[a][k] to
the Sea of the Arabah (the Salt
Sea[b][l]), to Beth Jeshimoth,[m] and
then southward below the slopes
of Pisgah.[n]

4And the territory of Og king of
Bashan,[o]
one of the last of the Rephaites,[p]
who reigned in Ashtaroth[q] and
Edrei. 5He ruled over Mount Her-
mon, Salecah,[r] all of Bashan[s] to the
border of the people of Geshur[t] and
Maacah,[u] and half of Gilead[v] to the
border of Sihon king of Heshbon.

6Moses, the servant of the LORD, and
the Israelites conquered them.[w] And
Moses the servant of the LORD gave their
land to the Reubenites, the Gadites and
the half-tribe of Manasseh to be their
possession.[x]
7These are the kings of the land that
Joshua and the Israelites conquered on
the west side of the Jordan, from Baal
Gad in the Valley of Lebanon[y] to Mount
Halak, which rises towards Seir (their
lands Joshua gave as an inheritance
to the tribes of Israel according to
their tribal divisions—8the hill country,
the western foothills, the Arabah, the
mountain slopes, the desert and the
Negev[z]—the lands of the Hittites, Amo-
rites, Canaanites, Perizzites, Hivites
and Jebusites):[a]

9the king of Jericho[b] one
the king of Ai[c] (near
Bethel[d]) one
10the king of Jerusalem[e] one
the king of Hebron one
11the king of Jarmuth one
the king of Lachish[f] one
12the king of Eglon[g] one
the king of Gezer[h] one

11 [v]**Dt 7:2**; [w]Dt 20:16–17; [x]**Nu 31:10**
12 [y]Nu 33:50–52; Dt 7:2
14 [z]**Dt 20:16**
15 [a]Ex 34:11; Dt 7:2; **Jos 1:7**
16 [b]Nu 13:17; [c]**Dt 1:7**; [d]**Jos 10:41**
17 [e]**Ge 14:6; Nu 24:18; Dt 33:2**; [f]Jos 13:5; [g]**Dt 3:25**; Jos 12:7; [h]Dt 3:9; Jos 12:8; [i]Dt 7:24
19 [j]**Jos 9:1**; [k]**Jos 9:3**; [l]**Jos 9:15**
20 [m]**Ex 4:21; 14:17**; Ro 9:18; [n]Dt 7:16; Jdg 14:4
21 [o]**Nu 13:22**,33; [p]**Jos 10:3**; [q]Jos 15:50
22 [r]**Ge 10:19**; [s]Jos 12:17; 19:13; 1Sa 5:8; 17:4; 1Ki 2:39; 2Ki 14:25; 1Ch 8:13; Am 6:2; [t]Jos 15:47; 1Sa 5:1; Isa 20:1
23 [u]Jos 21:43–45; Ne 9:24; [v]**Dt 1:38**; 12:9–10; **25:19**; **Jos 13:7**; [w]**Nu 26:53**; [x]Ps 105:44; [y]**Ex 33:14**; [z]Jos 14:15

Ch. 12

1 [a]Ps 136:21; [b]**Nu 32:19**; [c]**Nu 21:13**; [d]Dt 3:8; [e]**Jos 11:2**
2 [f]ver 5; **Nu 21:21**,25; Jos 13:10; Jdg 11:19; [g]**Nu 32:34**; **Jos 13:16**; [h]**Ge 32:22**; [i]**Ge 19:38**; [j]Ge 31:21; **Nu 32:26**; Dt 2:36; **3:15**; Jos 13:11,25; 17:1; 20:8; 21:38; Jdg 5:17; 7:3; 10:8
3 [k]Jos 11:2; [l]**Ge 14:3**; [m]**Nu 33:49**; Jos 13:20; [n]**Nu 21:20**
4 [o]**Nu 21:21**,33; Jos 13:30; [p]**Ge 14:5**; [q]**Dt 1:4**
5 [r]**Dt 3:10**; [s]Nu 32:33; Jos 17:1; 20:8; 21:27; 22:7; [t]Jos 13:2,13; 1Sa 27:8; [u]**Dt 3:14**; [v]ver 2
6 [w]**Dt 3:8**; [x]Nu 32:29,33; Jos 13:8
7 [y]**Jos 11:17**
8 [z]**Dt 1:7**; [a]**Jos 3:10; 11:17**; Ezr 9:1
9 [b]**Nu 33:48**; [c]**Ge 12:8; Jos 8:1**; [d]**Jos 7:2**; 8:9; 18:13; Jdg 1:23; 4:5; 20:18; 21:2; Ne 11:31
10 [e]**Jos 10:1**
11 [f]**Jos 10:3**
12 [g]**Jos 10:3**; [h]**Jos 10:33**

[b]11 The Hebrew term refers to the irrevocable giving over of things or persons to the LORD, often by totally destroying them; also in verses 12, 20 and 21.
[a]3 That is, Galilee
[b]3 That is, the Dead Sea

13 the king of Debir[i] one
the king of Geder one
14 the king of Hormah[j] one
the king of Arad[k] one
15 the king of Libnah[l] one
the king of Adullam[m] one
16 the king of Makkedah[n] one
the king of Bethel[o] one
17 the king of Tappuah[p] one
the king of Hepher[q] one
18 the king of Aphek[r] one
the king of Lasharon one
19 the king of Madon one
the king of Hazor[s] one
20 the king of Shimron
Meron one
the king of Acshaph[t] one
21 the king of Taanach[u] one
the king of Megiddo[v] one
22 the king of Kedesh[w] one
the king of Jokneam[x] in
Carmel[y] one
23 the king of Dor
(in Naphoth Dor[c] [z]) one
the king of Goyim in
Gilgal one
24 the king of Tirzah[a] one
thirty-one kings in all.[b]

Land Still to Be Taken

13 When Joshua was old and well
advanced in years,[a] the LORD
said to him, "You are very old, and
there are still very large areas of land to
be taken over.

2 "This is the land that remains: all
the regions of the Philistines[b] and
Geshurites:[c] 3 from the Shihor
River[d] on the east of Egypt to the
territory of Ekron[e] on the north, all
of it counted as Canaanite (the terri-
tory of the five Philistine rulers[f] in
Gaza, Ashdod,[g] Ashkelon,[h] Gath
and Ekron—that of the Avvites);[i]
4 from the south, all the land of the
Canaanites, from Arah of the Sido-
nians as far as Aphek,[j] the region of
the Amorites,[k] 5 the area of the
Gebalites[a];[l] and all Lebanon[m] to the
east, from Baal Gad below Mount
Hermon[n] to Lebo[b] Hamath.[o]

6 "As for all the inhabitants of the
mountain regions from Lebanon to Mis-
rephoth Maim,[p] that is, all the Sido-
nians, I myself will drive them out[q] be-
fore the Israelites. Be sure to allocate
this land to Israel for an inheritance, as I
have instructed you,[r] 7 and divide it as
an inheritance[s] among the nine tribes
and half of the tribe of Manasseh."

Division of the Land East of the Jordan

8 The other half of Manasseh,[c] the Reu-
benites and the Gadites had received
the inheritance that Moses had given
them east of the Jordan, as he, the ser-
vant of the LORD, had assigned[t] it to
them.[u]

9 It extended from Aroer[v] on the rim
of the Arnon Gorge, and from the
town in the middle of the gorge,
and included the whole plateau[w] of
Medeba as far as Dibon,[x] 10 and all
the towns of Sihon king of the
Amorites, who ruled in Heshbon,[y]
out to the border of the Ammo-
nites.[z] 11 It also included Gilead,[a]
the territory of the people of
Geshur and Maacah, all of Mount
Hermon and all Bashan as far as
Salecah[b]—12 that is, the whole king-
dom of Og in Bashan,[c] who had
reigned in Ashtaroth[d] and Edrei[e]
and had survived as one of the last
of the Rephaites.[f] Moses had de-
feated them and taken over their
land.[g] 13 But the Israelites did not
drive out the people of Geshur[h] and
Maacah,[i] so they continue to live
among the Israelites to this day.[j]

14 But to the tribe of Levi he gave no
inheritance, since the offerings made by
fire to the LORD, the God of Israel, are
their inheritance, as he promised them.[k]

15 This is what Moses had given to the
tribe of Reuben, clan by clan:

16 The territory from Aroer[l] on the
rim of the Arnon Gorge, and from
the town in the middle of the gorge,
and the whole plateau past Mede-
ba[m] 17 to Heshbon and all its towns
on the plateau,[n] including Dibon,[o]
Bamoth Baal,[p] Beth Baal Meon,[q]
18 Jahaz,[r] Kedemoth,[s] Mephaath,[t]
19 Kiriathaim,[u] Sibmah,[v] Zereth
Shahar on the hill in the valley,
20 Beth Peor,[w] the slopes of Pisgah,
and Beth Jeshimoth 21—all the

12:13 [i]Jos 10:3
14 [j]Nu 14:45; [k]Nu 21:1
15 [l]Nu 33:20; [m]Ge 38:1; Jos 15:35; Mic 1:15
16 [n]Jos 10:10; [o]Jos 7:2
17 [p]Jos 15:34; 16:8; 17:8; [q]Jos 11:22; 1Ki 4:10
18 [r]Jos 13:4; 19:30; Jdg 1:31; 1Sa 4:1; 29:1
19 [s]Jos 11:1
20 [t]Jos 11:1
21 [u]Jos 17:11; 21:25; [v]Jdg 1:27; 5:19; 1Ki 4:12
22 [w]Jos 15:23; 19:37; 20:7; 21:32; Jdg 4:6,9; [x]Jos 19:11; 21:34; [y]Jos 15:55; 19:26; 1Sa 15:12; 2Sa 23:35
23 [z]Jos 11:2
24 [a]1Ki 14:17; 15:33; 16:8,23; SS 6:4; [b]Ps 135:11; 136:18

Ch. 13

1 [a]Ge 24:1; Jos 14:10; 23:1–2; 1Ki 1:1
2 [b]Ge 10:14; Jdg 3:31; [c]Jos 12:5
3 [d]1Ch 13:5; Isa 23:3; Jer 2:18; [e]Jos 15:11,45; 19:43; Jdg 1:18; 1Sa 5:10; 7:14; [f]Jdg 3:3; 16:5,18; 1Sa 6:4,17; Isa 14:29; Jer 25:20; Eze 25:15; [g]Jos 11:22; Am 3:9; [h]Jdg 1:18; 14:19; 2Sa 1:20; [i]Dt 2:23
4 [j]Jos 12:18; [k]Ge 14:7; 15:16; Am 2:10
5 [l]1Ki 5:18; Ps 83:7; Eze 27:9; [m]Jos 11:17; [n]Dt 3:8; [o]Nu 13:21; 34:8; Jdg 3:3
6 [p]Jos 11:8; [q]Ps 80:8; [r]Nu 33:54; 34:13
7 [s]Jos 11:23; Ps 78:55
8 [t]Jos 12:6; [u]Jos 18:7
9 [v]ver 16; Nu 32:34; Dt 2:36; Jdg 11:26; 2Sa 24:5; [w]ver 17,21; Jer 48:8,21; [x]Nu 21:30; 32:3; Isa 15:2; Jer 48:18,22
10 [y]Jos 12:2; [z]Nu 21:24
11 [a]Jos 12:2; [b]Jos 12:5
12 [c]Dt 1:4; [d]Jos 12:4; [e]Nu 21:33; [f]Ge 14:5; [g]Dt 3:8
13 [h]Jos 12:5; [i]Dt 3:14; [j]Dt 3:12
14 [k]ver 33; Dt 18:1–2; Jos 14:3
16 [l]ver 9; Jos 12:2; 1Sa 30:28; [m]Nu 21:30; Isa 15:2
17 [n]ver 9; [o]Nu 32:3; [p]Nu 22:41; [q]1Ch 5:8; Jer 48:23; Eze 25:9
18 [r]Nu 21:23; [s]Dt 2:26; [t]Jos 21:37; Jer 48:21
19 [u]Nu 32:37; [v]Nu 32:3
20 [w]Dt 3:29

[c]12:23 Or *in the heights of Dor*
[a]13:5 That is, the area of Byblos
[b]5 Or *to the entrance to*
[c]8 Hebrew *With it* (that is, with the other half of Manasseh)

towns on the plateau[x] and the entire realm of Sihon king of the Amorites, who ruled at Heshbon. Moses had defeated him and the Midianite chiefs,[y] Evi, Rekem, Zur, Hur and Reba[z]—princes allied with Sihon—who lived in that country. 22 In addition to those slain in battle, the Israelites had put to the sword Balaam son of Beor,[a] who practised divination.[b] 23 The boundary of the Reubenites was the bank of the Jordan. These towns and their villages were the inheritance of the Reubenites, clan by clan.[c]

24 This is what Moses had given to the tribe of Gad, clan by clan:

25 The territory of Jazer,[d] all the towns of Gilead[e] and half the Ammonite country as far as Aroer, near Rabbah;[f] 26 and from Heshbon[g] to Ramath Mizpah and Betonim, and from Mahanaim[h] to the territory of Debir;[i] 27 and in the valley, Beth Haram, Beth Nimrah,[j] Succoth[k] and Zaphon[l] with the rest of the realm of Sihon king of Heshbon (the east side of the Jordan, the territory up to the end of the Sea of Kinnereth[d m]). 28 These towns and their villages were the inheritance of the Gadites,[n] clan by clan.

29 This is what Moses had given to the half-tribe of Manasseh, that is, to half the family of the descendants of Manasseh, clan by clan:

30 The territory extending from Mahanaim[o] and including all of Bashan,[p] the entire realm of Og king of Bashan[q]—all the settlements of Jair[r] in Bashan, sixty towns, 31 half of Gilead, and Ashtaroth and Edrei (the royal cities of Og in Bashan).[s] This was for the descendants of Makir[t] son of Manasseh—for half of the sons of Makir, clan by clan.[u]

32 This is the inheritance Moses had given when he was in the plains of Moab[v] across the Jordan east of Jericho.[w] 33 But to the tribe of Levi, Moses had given no inheritance;[x] the LORD, the God of Israel, is their inheritance,[y] as he promised them.[z]

Division of the Land West of the Jordan

14 Now these are the areas the Israelites received as an inheritance[a] in the land of Canaan, which Eleazar[b] the priest, Joshua son of Nun and the heads of the tribal clans of Israel[c] allotted[d] to them.[e] 2 Their inheritances were assigned by lot[f] to the nine-and-a-half tribes,[g] as the LORD had commanded through Moses. 3 Moses had granted the two-and-a-half tribes their inheritance east of the Jordan[h] but had not granted the Levites an inheritance among the rest,[i] 4 for the sons of Joseph had become two tribes—Manasseh and Ephraim.[j] The Levites received no share of the land but only towns to live in, with pasture-lands for their flocks and herds.[k] 5 So the Israelites divided the land, just as the LORD had commanded Moses.[l]

Hebron Given to Caleb

6 Now the men of Judah approached Joshua at Gilgal,[m] and Caleb son of Jephunneh[n] the Kenizzite said to him, "You know what the LORD said to Moses the man of God[o] at Kadesh Barnea[p] about you and me.[q] 7 I was forty years old when Moses the servant of the LORD sent me from Kadesh Barnea[r] to explore the land.[s] And I brought him back a report according to my convictions,[t] 8 but my brothers who went up with me made the hearts of the people sink.[a u] I, however, followed the LORD my God wholeheartedly.[v] 9 So on that day Moses swore to me, 'The land on which your feet have walked will be your inheritance[w] and that of your children[x] for ever, because you have followed the LORD my God wholeheartedly.'[b]

10 "Now then, just as the LORD promised,[y] he has kept me alive for forty-five years since the time he said this to Moses, while Israel moved[z] about in the desert. So here I am today, eighty-five years old![a] 11 I am still as strong[b] today as the day Moses sent me out; I'm just as vigorous[c] to go out to battle now as I was then. 12 Now give me this hill country that the LORD promised me that day.[d] You yourself heard then that the Anakites[e] were there and their cities were large and fortified,[f] but, the LORD helping me, I will drive them out just as he said."

13 Then Joshua blessed[g] Caleb son of Jephunneh[h] and gave him Hebron[i] as his inheritance.[j] 14 So Hebron has belonged to Caleb son of Jephunneh the

21 x ver 9; y Ge 25:2; Nu 25:15; z Nu 31:8
22 a Nu 22:5; b Ge 30:27; Nu 23:23
23 c 1Ch 5:7
25 d Nu 21:32; Jos 21:39; e Jos 12:2; f Dt 3:11
26 g Nu 21:25; Jer 49:3; h Ge 32:2; i Jos 10:3
27 j Nu 32:3; k Ge 33:17; l Jdg 12:1; Ps 48:2; m Nu 34:11
28 n Ge 46:16; Nu 32:33; Eze 48:27
30 o Ge 32:2; p Nu 21:33; q Jos 12:4; r Nu 32:41
31 s Nu 21:33; t Ge 50:23; u Jos 17:5
32 v Nu 26:3; w Nu 22:1
33 x Nu 26:62; y Nu 18:20; z ver 14; Jos 18:7; Eze 44:28

Ch. 14

1 a Jos 11:23; Ps 16:6; 136:21; b Ex 6:23; c Jos 21:1; d Nu 26:53; e Nu 34:17–18; Jos 19:51
2 f Lev 16:8; g Nu 34:13
3 h Nu 32:33; 34:14; i Nu 35:2; Jos 13:14
4 j Ge 41:52; Jdg 1:29; k Nu 35:2–3; Jos 21:2
5 l Nu 34:13
6 m Dt 11:30; n Nu 13:6; 14:30; o Dt 33:1; p Nu 13:26; q Nu 14:38
7 r Jos 15:3; s Nu 13:17; t Nu 13:30; 14:6–9
8 u Nu 13:31; v Nu 14:24; 32:12
9 w Dt 11:24; x Nu 14:24
10 y Nu 11:28; 14:30; z Jos 5:6; a Jos 13:1
11 b Dt 34:7; c Ge 15:15
12 d Nu 14:24; e Nu 13:33; f Nu 13:28
13 g Jos 22:6–7; h 1Sa 25:3; 30:14; i Ge 23:19; Jos 10:36; j Jdg 1:20; 1Ch 6:56

d 27 That is, Galilee
a 8 Hebrew *melt*
b 9 Deut. 1:36

Kenizzite ever since, because he followed the LORD, the God of Israel, wholeheartedly.[k] 15(Hebron used to be called Kiriath Arba[l] after Arba,[m] who was the greatest man among the Anakites.)

Then the land had rest[n] from war.

Allotment for Judah

15:15–19pp—Jdg 1:11–15

15 The allotment for the tribe of Judah, clan by clan, extended down to the territory of Edom,[a] to the Desert of Zin[b] in the extreme south.[c]

2Their southern boundary started from the bay at the southern end of the Salt Sea,[a][d] 3crossed south of Scorpion[b] Pass,[e] continued on to Zin and went over to the south of Kadesh Barnea.[f] Then it ran past Hezron up to Addar and curved around to Karka. 4It then passed along to Azmon[g] and joined the Wadi of Egypt,[h] ending at the sea. This is their[c] southern boundary.

5The eastern boundary[i] is the Salt Sea[j] as far as the mouth of the Jordan.

The northern boundary[k] started from the bay of the sea at the mouth of the Jordan, 6went up to Beth Hoglah[l] and continued north of Beth Arabah[m] to the Stone of Bohan[n] son of Reuben. 7The boundary then went up to Debir[o] from the Valley of Achor[p] and turned north to Gilgal,[q] which faces the Pass of Adummim south of the gorge. It continued along to the waters of En Shemesh[r] and came out at En Rogel.[s] 8Then it ran up the Valley of Ben Hinnom[t] along the southern slope of the Jebusite[u] city (that is, Jerusalem[v]). From there it climbed to the top of the hill west of the Hinnom Valley[w] at the northern end of the Valley of Rephaim.[x] 9From the hilltop the boundary headed towards the spring of the waters of Nephtoah,[y] came out at the towns of Mount Ephron and went down towards Baalah[z] (that is, Kiriath Jearim).[a] 10Then it curved westward from Baalah[b] to Mount Seir,[c] ran along the northern slope of Mount Jearim (that is, Kesalon), continued down to Beth Shemesh[d] and crossed to Timnah.[e] 11It went to the northern slope of Ekron,[f] turned towards Shikkeron, passed along to Mount Baalah[g] and reached Jabneel.[h] The boundary ended at the sea.

12The western boundary is the coastline of the Great Sea.[d][i]

These are the boundaries around the people of Judah by their clans.

13In accordance with the LORD's command to him, Joshua gave to Caleb[j] son of Jephunneh a portion in Judah—Kiriath Arba,[k] that is, Hebron.[l] (Arba was the forefather of Anak.)[m] 14From Hebron Caleb drove out the three Anakites[n]—Sheshai, Ahiman and Talmai[o]—descendants of Anak.[p] 15From there he marched against the people living in Debir (formerly called Kiriath Sepher). 16And Caleb said, "I will give my daughter Acsah[q] in marriage to the man who attacks and captures Kiriath Sepher." 17Othniel[r] son of Kenaz, Caleb's brother, took it; so Caleb gave his daughter Acsah to him in marriage.

18One day when she came to Othniel, she urged him[e] to ask her father for a field. When she got off her donkey, Caleb asked her, "What can I do for you?"

19She replied, "Do me a special favour. Since you have given me land in the Negev,[s] give me also springs of water." So Caleb gave her the upper and lower springs.[t]

20This is the inheritance of the tribe of Judah, clan by clan:

21The southernmost towns of the tribe of Judah in the Negev[u] towards the boundary of Edom were:

Kabzeel,[v] Eder,[w] Jagur, 22Kinah, Dimonah, Adadah, 23Kedesh,[x] Hazor,[y] Ithnan, 24Ziph,[z] Telem, Bealoth, 25Hazor Hadattah, Kerioth Hezron (that is, Hazor),[a] 26Amam, Shema, Moladah,[b] 27Hazar Gaddah, Heshmon, Beth Pelet, 28Hazar Shual,[c] Beersheba,[d] Biziothiah, 29Baalah,[e] Iim, Ezem,[f] 30Eltolad,[g] Kesil, Hormah,[h] 31Ziklag,[i] Madmannah,[j] Sansannah, 32Lebaoth,

14 [k]**Nu 14:24**
15 [l]**Ge 23:2;** [m]Jos 15:13; [n]Jos 11:23; Jdg 3:11; 1Ki 4:24; 5:4; 1Ch 22:9

Ch. 15

1 [a]Nu 34:3; [b]**Nu 13:21;** [c]Jos 18:5
2 [d]**Ge 14:3**
3 [e]**Nu 34:4;** [f]**Dt 1:2**
4 [g]Nu 34:4; [h]**Ge 15:18**
5 [i]Nu 34:10; [j]**Ge 14:3;** [k]Jos 18:15–19
6 [l]Jos 18:19,21; [m]ver 61; Jos 18:18; [n]Jos 18:17
7 [o]**Jos 10:3;** [p]**Jos 7:24;** [q]**Dt 11:30;** [r]Jos 18:17; [s]Jos 18:16; 2Sa 17:17; 1Ki 1:9
8 [t]2Ch 28:3; Jer 19:6; [u]ver 63; Jos 18:16,28; Jdg 1:21; 19:10; 2Sa 5:6; 1Ch 11:4; Ezr 9:1; [v]**Jos 10:1;** [w]2Ki 23:10; Jer 7:31; 19:2; [x]2Sa 5:18,22; 1Ch 14:9; Isa 17:5
9 [y]Jos 18:15; [z]ver 10–11,29; 2Sa 6:2; 1Ch 13:6; [a]**Jos 9:17**
10 [b]**ver 9;** [c]**Nu 24:18;** [d]Jos 19:22,38; 21:16; Jdg 1:33; 1Sa 6:9; 1Ki 4:9; 2Ki 14:11; [e]**Ge 38:12**
11 [f]**Jos 13:3;** [g]**ver 9;** [h]Jos 19:33
12 [i]**Nu 34:6**
13 [j]1Sa 25:3; 30:14; [k]**Ge 23:2;** [l]**Jos 10:36;** 21:12; 1Ch 6:56; [m]**Nu 13:22**
14 [n]**Nu 13:33;** [o]**Nu 13:22;** [p]Jdg 1:10,20
16 [q]1Ch 2:49
17 [r]Jdg 3:9,11; 1Ch 4:13; 27:15
19 [s]**Jos 10:40;** [t]Ge 36:24
21 [u]**Jos 10:40;** [v]2Sa 23:20; 1Ch 11:22; [w]Ge 35:21
23 [x]**Jos 12:22;** [y]**Jos 11:1**
24 [z]ver 55; 1Sa 23:14; 2Ch 11:8
25 [a]**Jos 11:1**
26 [b]Jos 19:2; 1Ch 4:28; Ne 11:26
28 [c]Jos 19:3; 1Ch 4:28; [d]**Ge 21:14**
29 [e]**ver 9;** [f]Jos 19:3; 1Ch 4:29
30 [g]Jos 19:4; [h]**Nu 14:45**
31 [i]Jos 19:5; 1Sa 27:6; 1Ch 4:30; 12:1; Ne 11:28; [j]1Ch 2:49

[a]2 That is, the Dead Sea; also in verse 5
[b]3 Hebrew *Akrabbim*
[c]4 Hebrew *your*
[d]12 That is, the Mediterranean; also in verse 47
[e]18 Hebrew and some Septuagint manuscripts; other Septuagint manuscripts (see also note at Judges 1:14) *Othniel, he urged her*

Shilhim, Ain[k] and Rimmon[l]—a total of twenty-nine towns and their villages.

33 In the western foothills:
Eshtaol,[m] Zorah,[n] Ashnah,[o] 34 Zanoah,[p] En Gannim,[q] Tappuah,[r] Enam, 35 Jarmuth,[s] Adullam,[t] Socoh,[u] Azekah,[v] 36 Shaaraim,[w] Adithaim and Gederah[x] (or Gederothaim)[f]—fourteen towns and their villages.
37 Zenan, Hadashah, Migdal Gad, 38 Dilean, Mizpah,[y] Joktheel,[z] 39 Lachish,[a] Bozkath,[b] Eglon,[c] 40 Cabbon, Lahmas, Kitlish, 41 Gederoth,[d] Beth Dagon,[e] Naamah and Makkedah[f]—sixteen towns and their villages.
42 Libnah,[g] Ether, Ashan,[h] 43 Iphtah, Ashnah,[i] Nezib, 44 Keilah,[j] Aczib[k] and Mareshah[l]—nine towns and their villages.
45 Ekron,[m] with its surrounding settlements and villages; 46 west of Ekron, all that were in the vicinity of Ashdod,[n] together with their villages; 47 Ashdod,[o] its surrounding settlements and villages; and Gaza, its settlements and villages, as far as the Wadi of Egypt[p] and the coastline of the Great Sea.[q]

48 In the hill country:
Shamir,[r] Jattir,[s] Socoh,[t] 49 Dannah, Kiriath Sannah (that is, Debir[u]), 50 Anab,[v] Eshtemoh,[w] Anim, 51 Goshen,[x] Holon[y] and Giloh[z]—eleven towns and their villages.
52 Arab, Dumah,[a] Eshan, 53 Janim, Beth Tappuah, Aphekah, 54 Humtah, Kiriath Arba[b] (that is, Hebron) and Zior—nine towns and their villages.
55 Maon,[c] Carmel,[d] Ziph,[e] Juttah,[f] 56 Jezreel,[g] Jokdeam, Zanoah,[h] 57 Kain, Gibeah[i] and Timnah[j]—ten towns and their villages.
58 Halhul, Beth Zur,[k] Gedor,[l] 59 Maarath, Beth Anoth and Eltekon—six towns and their villages.
60 Kiriath Baal[m] (that is, Kiriath Jearim[n]) and Rabbah[o]—two towns and their villages.

61 In the desert:[p]
Beth Arabah,[q] Middin, Secacah, 62 Nibshan, the City of Salt and En Gedi[r]—six towns and their villages.
63 Judah could not[s] dislodge the Jebusites,[t] who were living in Jerusalem;[u] to this day the Jebusites live there with the people of Judah.[v]

32 [k]Nu 34:11; [l]Jos 19:7; Jdg 20:45; 21:13; Zec 14:10
33 [m]Jos 19:41; Jdg 13:25; 16:31; 18:2; [n]Jdg 13:2; 18:11; 2Ch 11:10; Ne 11:29; [o]ver 43
34 [p]ver 56; 1Ch 4:18; Ne 3:13; 11:30; [q]Jos 19:21; 21:29; [r]**Jos 12:17**
35 [s]**Jos 10:3**; [t]**Ge 38:1**; [u]ver 48; 1Ki 4:10; [v]**Jos 10:10**
36 [w]1Sa 17:52; 1Ch 4:31; [x]1Ch 12:4
38 [y]**Jos 11:3**; [z]2Ki 14:7
39 [a]**Jos 10:3**; [b]2Ki 22:1; [c]**Jos 10:3**
41 [d]2Ch 28:18; [e]Jos 19:27; [f]**Jos 10:10**
42 [g]**Nu 33:20**; [h]Jos 19:7; 1Sa 30:30; 1Ch 4:32; 6:59
43 [i]ver 33
44 [j]1Sa 23:1–2; 1Ch 4:19; Ne 3:17–18; [k]Jos 19:29; Jdg 1:31; Mic 1:14; [l]Mic 1:15
45 [m]**Jos 13:3**
46 [n]Jos 11:22
47 [o]**Jos 11:22**; [p]**Ge 15:18**; [q]**Nu 34:6**
48 [r]Jdg 10:1; [s]Jos 21:14; 1Sa 30:27; 1Ch 6:57; [t]**ver 35**
49 [u]**Jos 10:3**
50 [v]Jos 11:21; [w]Jos 21:14; 1Sa 30:28
51 [x]**Jos 10:41**; [y]Jos 21:15; Jer 48:21; [z]2Sa 15:12
52 [a]**Ge 25:14**
54 [b]**Ge 35:27**
55 [c]Jdg 10:12; 1Sa 23:24–25; 25:1–2; 1Ch 2:45; [d]**Jos 12:22**; [e]**ver 24**; [f]Jos 21:16
56 [g]Jos 17:16; 19:18; Jdg 6:33; 1Sa 25:43; 1Ki 18:45; 1Ch 3:1; Hos 1:5; [h]**ver 34**
57 [i]Jos 18:28; 24:33; Jdg 19:12; 20:4; 2Sa 23:29; 1Ch 11:31; [j]**Ge 38:12**
58 [k]1Ch 2:45; 2Ch 11:7; Ne 3:16; [l]1Ch 4:39; 12:7

Allotment for Ephraim and Manasseh

16 The allotment for Joseph began at the Jordan of Jericho,[a] east of the waters of Jericho, and went up from there through the desert[a] into the hill country of Bethel.[b] 2 It went on from Bethel (that is, Luz[c]),[b] crossed over to the territory of the Arkites[d] in Ataroth,[e] 3 descended westward to the territory of the Japhletites as far as the region of Lower Beth Horon[f] and on to Gezer,[g] ending at the sea.
4 So Manasseh and Ephraim, the descendants of Joseph, received their inheritance.[h]

5 This was the territory of Ephraim, clan by clan:
The boundary of their inheritance went from Ataroth Addar[i] in the east to Upper Beth Horon[j] 6 and continued to the sea. From Micmethath[k] on the north it curved eastward to Taanath Shiloh, passing by it to Janoah[l] on the east. 7 Then it went down from Janoah[m] to Ataroth[n] and Naarah, touched Jericho and came out at the Jordan. 8 From Tappuah[o] the border went west to the Kanah Ravine[p] and ended at the sea. This was the inheritance of the tribe of the Ephraimites, clan by clan. 9 It also included all the towns and their villages that were set aside for the Ephraimites within the inheritance of the Manassites.[q]
10 They did not dislodge the Canaanites living in Gezer; to this day the Canaanites live among the people of Ephraim but are required to do forced labour.[r]

60 [m]ver 9; [n]**Jos 9:17**; [o]**Dt 3:11** *61* [p]**Jos 8:15**; [q]**ver 6**
62 [r]1Sa 23:29; 24:1; Eze 47:10
63 [s]Jos 16:10; 17:12; Jdg 1:21; 1Ki 9:21; [t]**ver 8**; [u]**Jos 10:1**; [v]Eze 48:7

Ch. 16

1 [a]**Jos 8:15**; [b]**Jos 12:9**
2 [c]**Ge 28:19**; [d]2Sa 15:32; [e]**ver 5**; **Nu 32:3**
3 [f]**Jos 10:10**; [g]**Jos 10:33** *4* [h]Jos 18:5
5 [i]ver 2; Jos 18:13; [j]**Jos 10:10**
6 [k]Jos 17:7; [l]ver 7; 2Ki 15:29 *7* [m]**ver 6**; [n]**Nu 32:3**
8 [o]**Jos 12:17**; [p]Jos 17:9; 19:28 *9* [q]Eze 48:5
10 [r]**Jos 15:63**; 17:13; Jdg 1:28–29; 1Ki 9:16

---

f36 Or *Gederah and Gederothaim*
a1 *Jordan of Jericho* was possibly an ancient name for the Jordan River.
b2 Septuagint; Hebrew *Bethel to Luz*

17

This was the allotment for the
tribe of Manasseh[a] as Joseph's
firstborn,[b] that is, for Makir,[c] Ma-
nasseh's firstborn. Makir was the ances-
tor of the Gileadites, who had received
Gilead[d] and Bashan[e] because the Maki-
rites were great soldiers. 2So this allot-
ment was for the rest of the people of
Manasseh[f]—the clans of Abiezer,[g]
Helek, Asriel,[h] Shechem, Hepher[i] and
Shemida.[j] These are the other male de-
scendants of Manasseh son of Joseph by
their clans.
3Now Zelophehad son of Hepher,[k]
the son of Gilead, the son of Makir, the
son of Manasseh, had no sons but only
daughters,[l] whose names were Mahlah,
Noah, Hoglah, Milcah and Tirzah.
4They went to Eleazar the priest, Joshua
son of Nun, and the leaders and said,
"The LORD commanded Moses to give
us an inheritance among our brothers."
So Joshua gave them an inheritance
along with the brothers of their father,
according to the LORD's command.[m]
5Manasseh's share consisted of ten
tracts of land besides Gilead and Bashan
east of the Jordan,[n] 6because the daugh-
ters of the tribe of Manasseh received an
inheritance among the sons. The land
of Gilead belonged to the rest of the
descendants of Manasseh.
7The territory of Manasseh ex-
tended from Asher[o] to Mic-
methath[p] east of Shechem.[q] The
boundary ran southward from
there to include the people living at
En Tappuah. 8(Manasseh had the
land of Tappuah, but Tappuah[r] it-
self, on the boundary of Manasseh,
belonged to the Ephraimites.)
9Then the boundary continued
south to the Kanah Ravine.[s] There
were towns belonging to Ephraim
lying among the towns of
Manasseh, but the boundary of
Manasseh was the northern side
of the ravine and ended at the sea.
10On the south the land belonged
to Ephraim, on the north to
Manasseh. The territory of Ma-
nasseh reached the sea and
bordered Asher[t] on the north and
Issachar[u] on the east.[v]
11Within Issachar[w] and Asher,
Manasseh also had Beth Shan,[x]
Ibleam[y] and the people of Dor,[z] En-
dor,[a] Taanach[b] and Megiddo,[c]
together with their surrounding
settlements (the third in the list is
Naphoth[a]).[d]
12Yet the Manassites were not able[e] to
occupy these towns, for the Canaanites
were determined to live in that region.
13However, when the Israelites grew
stronger, they subjected the Canaanites
to forced labour but did not drive them
out completely.[f]
14The people of Joseph said to Joshua,
"Why have you given us only one allot-
ment and one portion for an inherit-
ance? We are a numerous people and
the LORD has blessed us abundantly."[g]
15"If you are so numerous," Joshua
answered, "and if the hill country of
Ephraim is too small for you, go up into
the forest[h] and clear land for yourselves
there in the land of the Perizzites[i] and
Rephaites.[j]"
16The people of Joseph replied, "The
hill country is not enough for us, and all
the Canaanites who live in the plain
have iron chariots,[k] both those in Beth
Shan[l] and its settlements and those in
the Valley of Jezreel."[m]
17But Joshua said to the house of
Joseph—to Ephraim and Manasseh—
"You are numerous and very powerful.
You will have not only one allotment[n]
18but the forested hill country[o] as well.
Clear it, and its farthest limits will be
yours; though the Canaanites have iron
chariots[p] and though they are strong,
you can drive them out."

Division of the Rest of the Land

18

The whole assembly of the
Israelites gathered at Shiloh[a]
and set up the Tent of Meeting[b] there.
The country was brought under their
control, 2but there were still seven
Israelite tribes who had not yet received
their inheritance.
3So Joshua said to the Israelites:
"How long will you wait before you
begin to take possession of the land that
the LORD, the God of your fathers, has
given you? 4Appoint three men from
each tribe. I will send them out to make
a survey of the land and to write a
description of it,[c] according to the in-
heritance of each.[d] Then they will return
to me. 5You are to divide the land into
seven parts. Judah is to remain in its
territory on the south[e] and the house of
Joseph in its territory on the north.[f]
6After you have written descriptions of
the seven parts of the land, bring them
here to me and I will cast lots[g] for you in
the presence of the LORD our God. 7The
Levites, however, do not get a portion
among you, because the priestly service

Ch. 17

1 [a]Nu 1:34; 1Ch 7:14; [b]**Ge 41:51**; [c]**Ge 50:23**; [d]**Jos 12:2**; [e]**Jos 12:5**
2 [f]Jos 22:7; [g]**Nu 26:30**; Jdg 6:11,34; 8:2; 1Ch 7:18; [h]1Ch 7:14; [i]**Nu 27:1**; [j]1Ch 7:19
3 [k]**Nu 27:1**; [l]**Nu 26:33**
4 [m]Nu 27:5–7
5 [n]Jos 13:30–31
7 [o]ver 10; Jos 19:24,31; 21:6,30; Jdg 1:31; 5:17; 6:35; 7:23; [p]Jos 16:6; [q]**Ge 12:6**; Jos 21:21; 24:25; Jdg 9:1
8 [r]**Jos 12:17**
9 [s]**Jos 16:8**
10 [t]**ver 7**; [u]**Ge 30:18**; [v]Eze 48:5
11 [w]ver 10; [x]ver 16; Jdg 1:27; 1Sa 31:10; 2Sa 21:12; 1Ki 4:12; 1Ch 7:29; [y]2Ki 9:27; [z]**Jos 11:2**; [a]1Sa 28:7; Ps 83:10; [b]**Jos 12:21**; [c]1Ki 9:15; [d]Eze 48:4
12 [e]**Jos 15:63**
13 [f]Jdg 1:27–28
14 [g]Nu 26:28–37
15 [h]2Sa 18:6; [i]**Jos 3:10**; [j]**Ge 14:5**; Jos 15:8; 18:16; 2Sa 5:18; 23:13; Isa 17:5
16 [k]ver 18; Jdg 1:19; 4:3,13; [l]**ver 11**; [m]**Jos 15:56**; **1Sa 29:1**
17 [n]Eze 48:5
18 [o]1Sa 1:1; [p]**ver 16**

Ch. 18

1 [a]ver 8; Jos 19:51; 21:2; Jdg 18:31; 21:12,19; 1Sa 1:3; 3:21; 4:3; 1Ki 14:2; Ps 78:60; Jer 7:12; 26:6; 41:5; [b]**ver 10**; **Ex 27:21**; **40:2**; Ac 7:45
4 [c]ver 8; [d]Mic 2:5
5 [e]Jos 15:1; [f]Jos 16:1–4
6 [g]**Lev 16:8**

[a]*11* That is, Naphoth Dor

of the LORD is their inheritance.[h] And Gad, Reuben and the half-tribe of Manasseh have already received their inheritance on the east side of the Jordan. Moses the servant of the LORD gave it to them.[i]"

8As the men started on their way to map out the land, Joshua instructed them, "Go and make a survey of the land and write a description of it.[j] Then return to me, and I will cast lots for you here at Shiloh[k] in the presence of the LORD." 9So the men left and went through the land. They wrote its description on a scroll, town by town, in seven parts, and returned to Joshua in the camp at Shiloh. 10Joshua then cast lots[l] for them in Shiloh in the presence[m] of the LORD, and there he distributed the land to the Israelites according to their tribal divisions.[n]

Allotment for Benjamin

11The lot came up for the tribe of Benjamin, clan by clan. Their allotted territory lay between the tribes of Judah and Joseph:

12On the north side their boundary began at the Jordan, passed the northern slope of Jericho and headed west into the hill country, coming out at the desert[o] of Beth Aven.[p] 13From there it crossed to the south slope of Luz[q] (that is, Bethel[r]) and went down to Ataroth Addar[s] on the hill south of Lower Beth Horon.

14From the hill facing Beth Horon[t] on the south the boundary turned south along the western side and came out at Kiriath Baal (that is, Kiriath Jearim),[u] a town of the people of Judah. This was the western side.

15The southern side began at the outskirts of Kiriath Jearim on the west, and the boundary came out at the spring of the waters of Nephtoah.[v] 16The boundary went down to the foot of the hill facing the Valley of Ben Hinnom, north of the Valley of Rephaim.[w] It continued down the Hinnom Valley[x] along the southern slope of the Jebusite city and so to En Rogel.[y] 17It then curved north, went to En Shemesh, continued to Geliloth,[z] which faces the Pass of Adummim,[a] and ran down to the Stone of Bohan[b] son of Reuben. 18It continued to the northern slope of Beth Arabah[a][c] and on down into the Arabah.[d] 19It then went to the northern slope of Beth Hoglah[e] and came out at the northern bay of the Salt Sea,[b][f] at the mouth of the Jordan in the south. This was the southern boundary.

20The Jordan formed the boundary on the eastern side.

These were the boundaries that marked out the inheritance of the clans of Benjamin on all sides.[g]

21The tribe of Benjamin, clan by clan, had the following cities:

Jericho, Beth Hoglah,[h] Emek Keziz, 22Beth Arabah,[i] Zemaraim,[j] Bethel,[k] 23Avvim,[l] Parah, Ophrah,[m] 24Kephar Ammoni, Ophni and Geba[n]—twelve towns and their villages.

25Gibeon,[o] Ramah,[p] Beeroth,[q] 26Mizpah,[r] Kephirah,[s] Mozah, 27Rekem, Irpeel, Taralah, 28Zelah,[t] Haeleph, the Jebusite city[u] (that is, Jerusalem[v]), Gibeah[w] and Kiriath—fourteen towns and their villages.[x]

This was the inheritance of Benjamin for its clans.[y]

Allotment for Simeon

19:2–10pp—1Ch 4:28–33

19 The second lot came out for the tribe of Simeon, clan by clan. Their inheritance lay within the territory of Judah.[a] 2It included:

Beersheba[b] (or Sheba),[a] Moladah,[c] 3Hazar Shual,[d] Balah, Ezem,[e] 4Eltolad,[f] Bethul, Hormah,[g] 5Ziklag,[h] Beth Marcaboth, Hazar Susah, 6Beth Lebaoth and Sharuhen—thirteen towns and their villages;

7Ain, Rimmon,[i] Ether and Ashan[j]—four towns and their villages—8and all the villages around these towns as far as Baalath Beer (Ramah in the Negev).[k]

This was the inheritance of the tribe of the Simeonites, clan by clan. 9The inheritance of the Simeonites was taken from the share of Judah,[l] because Judah's portion was more than they needed. So the Simeonites received their inheritance within the territory of Judah.[m]

7 [h]Jos 13:33; [i]Jos 13:8
8 [j]ver 4; [k]ver 1
10 [l]Nu 34:13; [m]ver 1; Jer 7:12; [n]Nu 33:54; Jos 19:51
12 [o]Jos 8:15; [p]Jos 7:2
13 [q]Ge 28:19; [r]Jos 12:9; [s]Nu 32:3; Jos 16:5
14 [t]Jos 10:10; [u]Jos 9:17
15 [v]Jos 15:9
16 [w]Jos 17:15; [x]Jos 15:8; [y]Jos 15:7
17 [z]Jos 22:10; [a]Jos 15:7; [b]Jos 15:6
18 [c]Jos 15:6; [d]Jos 11:2
19 [e]Jos 15:6; [f]Ge 14:3
20 [g]1Sa 9:1
21 [h]Jos 15:6
22 [i]Jos 15:6; [j]2Ch 13:4; [k]Jos 16:1
23 [l]Dt 2:23; [m]Jdg 6:11,24; 8:27,32; 9:5; 1Sa 13:17
24 [n]Jos 21:17; 1Sa 13:3,16; 14:5; 1Ki 15:22; 2Ki 23:8; Isa 10:29
25 [o]Jos 9:3; [p]Jos 10:40; Jdg 4:5; 19:13; 1Sa 1:1,19; 2:11; 7:17; 25:1; 1Ki 15:17,21; Ezr 2:26; Ne 11:33; Isa 10:29; Jer 31:15; 40:1; [q]Jos 9:17; Ezr 2:25; Ne 7:29
26 [r]Jos 11:3; [s]Jos 9:17; Ezr 2:25; Ne 7:29
28 [t]2Sa 21:14; [u]Jos 15:8; [v]Jos 10:1; [w]Jos 15:57; [x]Jos 9:17; [y]Eze 48:23

Ch. 19

1 [a]Ge 49:7
2 [b]Ge 21:14; 1Ki 19:3; [c]Jos 15:26
3 [d]Jos 15:28; [e]Jos 15:29
4 [f]Jos 15:30; [g]Nu 14:45
5 [h]Jos 15:31
7 [i]Jos 15:32; [j]Jos 15:42
8 [k]Jos 10:40
9 [l]Ge 49:7; [m]Eze 48:24

[a]18 Septuagint; Hebrew *slope facing the Arabah*
[b]19 That is, the Dead Sea
[a]2 Or *Beersheba, Sheba*; 1 Chron. 4:28 does not have *Sheba*.

Allotment for Zebulun

10The third lot came up for Zebulun,[n]
clan by clan:
The boundary of their inherit-
ance went as far as Sarid.[o] 11Going
west it ran to Maralah, touched
Dabbesheth, and extended to the
ravine near Jokneam.[p] 12It turned
east from Sarid[q] towards the sun-
rise to the territory of Kisloth Tabor
and went on to Daberath[r] and up to
Japhia. 13Then it continued east-
ward to Gath Hepher[s] and Eth
Kazin; it came out at Rimmon[t] and
turned towards Neah. 14There the
boundary went round on the north
to Hannathon and ended at the
Valley of Iphtah El.[u] 15Included
were Kattath, Nahalal,[v] Shimron,[w]
Idalah and Bethlehem.[x] There were
twelve towns and their villages.
16These towns and their villages were
the inheritance of Zebulun,[y] clan by
clan.[z]

Allotment for Issachar

17The fourth lot came out for Issachar,[a]
clan by clan. 18Their territory included:
Jezreel,[b] Kesulloth, Shunem,[c]
19Hapharaim, Shion, Anaharath,
20Rabbith, Kishion,[d] Ebez,
21Remeth, En Gannim,[e] En Haddah
and Beth Pazzez. 22The boundary
touched Tabor,[f] Shahazumah and
Beth Shemesh,[g] and ended at the
Jordan. There were sixteen towns
and their villages.
23These towns and their villages were
the inheritance of the tribe of Issachar,[h]
clan by clan.[i]

Allotment for Asher

24The fifth lot came out for the tribe of
Asher,[j] clan by clan. 25Their territory
included:
Helkath, Hali, Beten, Acshaph,[k]
26Allammelech, Amad and Mishal.[l]
On the west the boundary touched
Carmel[m] and Shihor Libnath. 27It
then turned east towards Beth
Dagon,[n] touched Zebulun[o] and the
Valley of Iphtah El,[p] and went
north to Beth Emek and Neiel, pass-
ing Cabul[q] on the left. 28It went to
Abdon,[b][r] Rehob,[s] Hammon[t] and
Kanah,[u] as far as Greater Sidon.[v]
29The boundary then turned back
towards Ramah[w] and went to the
fortified city of Tyre,[x] turned to-
wards Hosah and came out at the
sea[y] in the region of Aczib,[z] 30Um-
mah, Aphek[a] and Rehob.[b] There
were twenty-two towns and their
villages.
31These towns and their villages were
the inheritance of the tribe of Asher,[c]
clan by clan.

Allotment for Naphtali

32The sixth lot came out for Naphtali,
clan by clan:
33Their boundary went from
Heleph and the large tree in
Zaanannim,[d] passing Adami
Nekeb and Jabneel[e] to Lakkum and
ending at the Jordan. 34The bound-
ary ran west through Aznoth Tabor
and came out at Hukkok.[f] It
touched Zebulun[g] on the south,
Asher on the west and the Jordan[c]
on the east. 35The fortified cities
were Ziddim, Zer, Hammath,[h]
Rakkath, Kinnereth,[i] 36Adamah,
Ramah,[j] Hazor,[k] 37Kedesh,[l] Edrei,[m]
En Hazor, 38Iron, Migdal El,
Horem, Beth Anath[n] and Beth
Shemesh.[o] There were nineteen
towns and their villages.
39These towns and their villages were
the inheritance of the tribe of Naphtali,
clan by clan.[p]

Allotment for Dan

40The seventh lot came out for the tribe
of Dan, clan by clan. 41The territory of
their inheritance included:
Zorah, Eshtaol,[q] Ir Shemesh,
42Shaalabbin, Aijalon,[r] Ithlah,
43Elon, Timnah,[s] Ekron,[t] 44Eltekeh,
Gibbethon,[u] Baalath,[v] 45Jehud,
Bene Berak, Gath Rimmon,[w] 46Me
Jarkon and Rakkon, with the area
facing Joppa.[x]
47(But the Danites had difficulty
taking possession of their territory,[y]
so they went up and attacked Le-
shem[z], took it, put it to the sword and
occupied it. They settled in Leshem and
named[a] it Dan after their forefather.)[b]
48These towns and their villages were
the inheritance of the tribe of Dan,[c] clan
by clan.

Allotment for Joshua

49When they had finished dividing
the land into its allotted portions, the
Israelites gave Joshua son of Nun an
inheritance among them, 50as the LORD

10 [n]ver 16,27,34; Jos 21:7,34; [o]ver 12
11 [p]**Jos 12:22**
12 [q]ver 10; [r]Jos 21:28; 1Ch 6:72
13 [s]**Jos 11:22**; [t]Jos 15:32
14 [u]ver 27
15 [v]Jos 21:35; [w]Jos 11:1; [x]**Ge 35:19**
16 [y]**ver 10**; [z]Eze 48:26
17 [a]**Ge 30:18**
18 [b]**Jos 15:56**; [c]1Sa 28:4; 1Ki 1:3; 2Ki 4:8
20 [d]Jos 21:28
21 [e]**Jos 15:34**
22 [f]Jdg 4:6,12; 8:18; Ps 89:12; Jer 46:18; [g]**Jos 15:10**
23 [h]Jos 17:10; [i]Ge 49:15; Eze 48:25
24 [j]**Jos 17:7**
25 [k]**Jos 11:1**
26 [l]Jos 21:30; [m]**Jos 12:22**; 1Ki 18:19; 2Ki 2:25
27 [n]Jos 15:41; [o]**ver 10**; [p]ver 14; [q]1Ki 9:13
28 [r]Jos 21:30; 1Ch 6:74; [s]ver 30; Nu 13:21; Jos 21:31; Jdg 1:31; [t]1Ch 6:76; [u]**Jos 16:8**; [v]**Ge 10:19**
29 [w]Jos 18:25; [x]2Sa 5:11; 24:7; Ezr 3:7; Ps 45:12; Isa 23:1; Jer 25:22; Eze 26:2; [y]Jdg 5:17; [z]**Jos 15:44**
30 [a]**Jos 12:18**; [b]**ver 28**
31 [c]**Ge 30:13; Jos 17:7; Eze 48:2**
33 [d]Jdg 4:11; [e]Jos 15:11
34 [f]1Ch 6:75; [g]**ver 10**
35 [h]1Ch 2:55; [i]**Jos 11:2**
36 [j]Jos 18:25; [k]**Jos 11:1**
37 [l]**Jos 12:22**; [m]**Nu 21:33**
38 [n]Jdg 1:33; [o]**Jos 15:10**
39 [p]Eze 48:3
41 [q]**Jos 15:33**
42 [r]**Jos 10:12**
43 [s]**Ge 38:12**; [t]**Jos 13:3**
44 [u]Jos 21:23; 1Ki 15:27; 16:15; [v]1Ki 9:18; 2Ch 8:6
45 [w]Jos 21:24; 1Ch 6:69
46 [x]2Ch 2:16; Ezr 3:7; Jnh 1:3; Ac 9:36
47 [y]Jdg 18:1; [z]Jdg 18:7,14; [a]**Dt 3:14**; [b]Jdg 18:27,29
48 [c]**Ge 30:6**

b28 Some Hebrew manuscripts (see also Joshua 21:30); most Hebrew manuscripts *Ebron*
c34 Septuagint; Hebrew *west, and Judah, the Jordan,*

had commanded. They gave him the
town he asked for—Timnath Serah[d][d] in
the hill country of Ephraim. And he
built up the town and settled there.
51These are the territories that Eleazar
the priest, Joshua son of Nun and the
heads of the tribal clans of Israel
assigned by lot at Shiloh in the presence
of the LORD at the entrance to the Tent of
Meeting. And so they finished dividing[e]
the land.[f]

Cities of Refuge

20:1–9Ref—Nu 35:9–34; Dt 4:41–43; 19:1–14

20 Then the LORD said to Joshua:
2"Tell the Israelites to designate
the cities of refuge, as I instructed you
through Moses, 3so that anyone who
kills a person accidentally and un-
intentionally[a] may flee there and find
protection from the avenger of blood.[b]
4"When he flees to one of these cities,
he is to stand in the entrance of the city
gate[c] and state his case before the
elders[d] of that city. Then they are to
admit him into their city and give him a
place to live with them. 5If the avenger
of blood pursues him, they must not
surrender the one accused, because he
killed his neighbour unintentionally
and without malice aforethought. 6He is
to stay in that city until he has stood trial
before the assembly[e] and until the death
of the high priest who is serving at that
time. Then he may go back to his own
home in the town from which he fled."
7So they set apart Kedesh[f] in Galilee in
the hill country of Naphtali, Shechem[g]
in the hill country of Ephraim, and
Kiriath Arba[h] (that is, Hebron[i]) in the
hill country of Judah.[j] 8On the east side
of the Jordan of Jericho[a] they designated
Bezer[k] in the desert on the plateau in the
tribe of Reuben, Ramoth in Gilead[l][m] in
the tribe of Gad, and Golan in Bashan[n]
in the tribe of Manasseh. 9Any of the
Israelites or any alien living among
them who killed someone accidentally[o]
could flee to these designated cities and
not be killed by the avenger of blood
prior to standing trial before the
assembly.[p]

Towns for the Levites

21:4–39pp—1Ch 6:54–80

21 Now the family heads of the
Levites approached Eleazar the
priest, Joshua son of Nun, and the
heads of the other tribal families of
Israel[a] 2at Shiloh[b] in Canaan and said to
them, "The LORD commanded through
Moses that you give us towns[c] to live in,
with pasture-lands for our livestock."[d]

50 dJos 24:30; Jdg 2:9
51 eJos 23:4; fJos 14:1; 18:10; Ac 13:19

Ch. 20

3 aLev 4:2; bNu 35:12
4 cGe 23:10; Jer 38:7; dJos 7:6
6 eNu 35:12
7 fJos 12:22; gGe 12:6; hGe 35:27; iJos 10:36; jLk 1:39
8 kJos 21:36; 1Ch 6:78; l1Ch 6:80; mJos 12:2; nJos 12:5; 1Ch 6:71
9 oLev 4:2; pEx 21:13

Ch. 21

1 aJos 14:1
2 bJos 18:1; cLev 25:32; dNu 35:2–3; Jos 14:4
4 eNu 3:17; fver 19
5 gver 26
6 hNu 3:17; iGe 30:18; jJos 17:7
7 kEx 6:16; lver 40; mJos 19:10
11 nGe 23:2; oJos 10:36
12 pJos 15:13
13 qNu 35:6; rNu 33:20
14 sJos 15:48; tJos 15:50
15 uJos 15:51; vJos 10:3
16 wNu 34:11; xJos 15:55; yJos 15:10
17 zJos 9:3; aJos 18:24; Ne 11:31
18 b2Sa 23:27; 1Ki 2:26; Ezr 2:23; Ne 7:27; 11:32; Isa 10:30; Jer 1:1; 11:21; 32:7
19 c2Ch 31:15; dver 4

3So, as the LORD had commanded, the
Israelites gave the Levites the following
towns and pasture-lands out of their
own inheritance:
4The first lot came out for the
Kohathites,[e] clan by clan. The Levites
who were descendants of Aaron the
priest were allotted thirteen towns from
the tribes of Judah, Simeon and Ben-
jamin.[f] 5The rest of Kohath's descend-
ants were allotted ten towns from the
clans of the tribes of Ephraim, Dan and
half of Manasseh.[g]
6The descendants of Gershon[h] were
allotted thirteen towns from the clans of
the tribes of Issachar,[i] Asher,[j] Naphtali
and the half-tribe of Manasseh in
Bashan.
7The descendants of Merari,[k] clan by
clan, received twelve[l] towns from the
tribes of Reuben, Gad and Zebulun.[m]
8So the Israelites allotted to the Le-
vites these towns and their pasture-
lands, as the LORD had commanded
through Moses.

9From the tribes of Judah and Simeon
they allotted the following towns by
name 10(these towns were assigned to
the descendants of Aaron who were
from the Kohathite clans of the Levites,
because the first lot fell to them):
11They gave them Kiriath Arba[n]
(that is, Hebron[o]), with its sur-
rounding pasture-land, in the hill
country of Judah. (Arba was the
forefather of Anak.) 12But the fields
and villages around the city they
had given to Caleb son of Jephun-
neh as his possession.[p]
13So to the descendants of Aaron
the priest they gave Hebron (a city
of refuge[q] for one accused of mur-
der), Libnah,[r] 14Jattir,[s] Eshtemoa,[t]
15Holon,[u] Debir,[v] 16Ain,[w] Juttah[x]
and Beth Shemesh,[y] together with
their pasture-lands—nine towns
from these two tribes.
17And from the tribe of Benjamin
they gave them Gibeon,[z] Geba,[a]
18Anathoth[b] and Almon, together
with their pasture-lands—four
towns.
19All the towns[c] for the priests, the de-
scendants of Aaron, were thirteen,
together with their pasture-lands.[d]

20The rest of the Kohathite clans of the
Levites were allotted towns from the
tribe of Ephraim:

---

d50 Also known as *Timnath Heres* (see Judges 2:9)
a8 *Jordan of Jericho* was possibly an ancient name for the Jordan River.

21In the hill country of Ephraim
they were given Shechem[e] (a city of
refuge for one accused of mur-
der) and Gezer,[f] 22Kibzaim and
Beth Horon,[g] together with their
pasture-lands—four towns.[h]
23Also from the tribe of Dan they
received Eltekeh, Gibbethon,[i]
24Aijalon[j] and Gath Rimmon,[k]
together with their pasture-lands
—four towns.
25From half the tribe of Manasseh
they received Taanach[l] and Gath
Rimmon, together with their
pasture-lands—two towns.
26All these ten towns and their pasture-
lands were given to the rest of the
Kohathite clans.[m]

27The Levite clans of the Gershonites
were given:
from the half-tribe of Manasseh,
Golan in Bashan[n] (a city of refuge
for one accused of murder[o]) and
Be Eshtarah, together with their
pasture-lands—two towns;
28from the tribe of Issachar,[p]
Kishion,[q] Daberath,[r] 29Jarmuth[s]
and En Gannim,[t] together with
their pasture-lands—four towns;
30from the tribe of Asher,[u]
Mishal,[v] Abdon,[w] 31Helkath and
Rehob,[x] together with their pas-
ture-lands—four towns;
32from the tribe of Naphtali,
Kedesh[y] in Galilee (a city of refuge
for one accused of murder[z]), Ham-
moth Dor and Kartan, together
with their pasture-lands—three
towns.
33All the towns of the Gershonite[a] clans
were thirteen, together with their
pasture-lands.

34The Merarite clans (the rest of the
Levites) were given:
from the tribe of Zebulun,[b]
Jokneam,[c] Kartah, 35Dimnah and
Nahalal,[d] together with their
pasture-lands—four towns;
36from the tribe of Reuben,
Bezer,[e] Jahaz,[f] 37Kedemoth and
Mephaath,[g] together with their
pasture-lands—four towns;
38from the tribe of Gad,
Ramoth[h] in Gilead[i] (a city of refuge
for one accused of murder), Maha-
naim,[j] 39Heshbon and Jazer,[k]
together with their pasture-lands
—four towns in all.
40All the towns allotted to the Merarite
clans, who were the rest of the Levites,
were twelve.[l]
41The towns of the Levites in the
territory held by the Israelites were
forty-eight in all, together with their
pasture-lands.[m] 42Each of these towns
had pasture-lands surrounding it; this
was true for all these towns.

43So the LORD gave Israel all the land
he had sworn to give their forefathers,[n]
and they took possession[o] of it and set-
tled there.[p] 44The LORD gave them rest[q]
on every side, just as he had sworn to
their forefathers. Not one of their ene-
mies[r] withstood them; the LORD handed
all their enemies[s] over to them.[t] 45Not
one of all the LORD's good promises[u] to
the house of Israel failed; every one was
fulfilled.

Eastern Tribes Return Home

22 Then Joshua summoned the
Reubenites, the Gadites and the
half-tribe of Manasseh 2and said to
them, "You have done all that Moses
the servant of the LORD commanded,[a]
and you have obeyed me in everything I
commanded. 3For a long time now—to
this very day—you have not deserted
your brothers but have carried out the
mission the LORD your God gave you.
4Now that the LORD your God has given
your brothers rest[b] as he promised, re-
turn to your homes[c] in the land that
Moses the servant of the LORD gave you
on the other side of the Jordan.[d] 5But be
very careful to keep the commandment[e]
and the law that Moses the servant of
the LORD gave you: to love the LORD[f]
your God, to walk in all his ways, to
obey his commands,[g] to hold fast to him
and to serve him with all your heart and
all your soul.[h]"
6Then Joshua blessed[i] them and sent
them away, and they went to their
homes. 7(To the half-tribe of Manasseh
Moses had given land in Bashan,[j] and to
the other half of the tribe Joshua gave
land on the west side[k] of the Jordan with
their brothers.) When Joshua sent them
home, he blessed them,[l] 8saying, "Re-
turn to your homes with your great
wealth—with large herds of livestock,[m]
with silver, gold, bronze and iron,[n] and
a great quantity of clothing—and div-
ide[o] with your brothers the plunder[p]
from your enemies."
9So the Reubenites, the Gadites and
the half-tribe of Manasseh left the
Israelites at Shiloh[q] in Canaan to return
to Gilead,[r] their own land, which they
had acquired in accordance with the
command of the LORD through Moses.
10When they came to Geliloth[s] near

21 [e]Jos 17:7; [f]Jos 10:33
22 [g]Jos 10:10; [h]1Sa 1:1
23 [i]Jos 19:44
24 [j]Jos 10:12; [k]Jos 19:45
25 [l]Jos 12:21
26 [m]ver 5
27 [n]Jos 12:5; [o]Nu 35:6
28 [p]Ge 30:18; [q]Jos 19:20; [r]Jos 19:12
29 [s]Jos 10:3; [t]Jos 15:34
30 [u]Jos 17:7; [v]Jos 19:26; [w]Jos 19:28
31 [x]Jos 19:28
32 [y]Jos 12:22; [z]Nu 35:6
33 [a]ver 6
34 [b]Jos 19:10; [c]Jos 12:22
35 [d]Jos 19:15
36 [e]Jos 20:8; [f]Nu 21:23; Dt 2:32; Jdg 11:20
37 [g]Jos 13:18
38 [h]Dt 4:43; [i]Jos 12:2; [j]Ge 32:2
39 [k]Jos 13:25
40 [l]ver 7
41 [m]Nu 35:7
43 [n]Dt 34:4; [o]Dt 11:31; [p]Dt 17:14
44 [q]Ex 33:14; [r]Dt 6:19; [s]Ex 23:31; [t]Dt 21:10
45 [u]Jos 23:14; Ne 9:8

Ch. 22

2 [a]Nu 32:25
4 [b]Ex 33:14; [c]Nu 32:22; Dt 3:20; [d]Nu 32:18; Jos 1:13–15
5 [e]Isa 43:22; Mal 3:14; [f]Jos 23:11; [g]Dt 5:29; [h]Dt 6:5
6 [i]Ge 24:60; Ex 39:43
7 [j]Nu 32:19; Jos 12:5; [k]Jos 17:2; [l]Jos 14:13; Lk 24:50
8 [m]Dt 20:14; [n]Nu 31:22; [o]Nu 31:27; [p]Ge 49:27; 1Sa 30:16; 2Sa 1:1; Isa 9:3
9 [q]Jos 18:1; [r]Nu 32:26
10 [s]Jos 18:17

the Jordan in the land of Canaan, the
Reubenites, the Gadites and the half-
tribe of Manasseh built an imposing
altar[t] there by the Jordan. 11And when
the Israelites heard that they had built
the altar on the border of Canaan at
Geliloth near the Jordan on the Israelite
side, 12the whole assembly of Israel
gathered at Shiloh[u] to go to war against
them.

13So the Israelites sent Phinehas[v] son
of Eleazar,[w] the priest, to the land of
Gilead—to Reuben, Gad and the half-
tribe of Manasseh. 14With him they sent
ten of the chief men, one for each of the
tribes of Israel, each the head of a family
division among the Israelite clans.[x]

15When they went to Gilead—to
Reuben, Gad and the half-tribe of Ma-
nasseh—they said to them: 16"The whole
assembly of the LORD says: 'How could
you break faith[y] with the God of Israel
like this? How could you turn away
from the LORD and build yourselves an
altar in rebellion[z] against him now?
17Was not the sin of Peor[a] enough for
us? Up to this very day we have not
cleansed ourselves from that sin, even
though a plague fell on the community
of the LORD! 18And are you now turning
away from the LORD?

"'If you rebel against the LORD today,
tomorrow he will be angry with the
whole community[b] of Israel. 19If the
land you possess is defiled, come over
to the LORD's land, where the LORD's
tabernacle[c] stands, and share the land
with us. But do not rebel against the
LORD or against us by building an altar[d]
for yourselves, other than the altar of
the LORD our God. 20When Achan son of
Zerah acted unfaithfully regarding the
devoted things,[a][e] did not wrath[f] come
upon the whole community[g] of Israel?
He was not the only one who died for
his sin.'"[h]

21Then Reuben, Gad and the half-
tribe of Manasseh replied to the heads
of the clans of Israel: 22"The Mighty
One, God, the LORD! The Mighty One,
God,[i] the LORD![j] He knows![k] And let
Israel know! If this has been in rebellion
or disobedience to the LORD, do not
spare us this day. 23If we have built our
own altar to turn away from the LORD
and to offer burnt offerings and grain
offerings,[l] or to sacrifice fellowship
offerings[b] on it, may the LORD himself
call us to account.[m]

24"No! We did it for fear that some day
your descendants might say to ours,
'What do you have to do with the LORD,
the God of Israel? 25The LORD has made
the Jordan a boundary between us and
you—you Reubenites and Gadites! You
have no share in the LORD.' So your
descendants might cause ours to stop
fearing the LORD.

26"That is why we said, 'Let us get
ready and build an altar—but not for
burnt offerings or sacrifices.' 27On the
contrary, it is to be a witness[n] between
us and you and the generations that
follow, that we will worship the LORD at
his sanctuary with our burnt offerings,
sacrifices and fellowship offerings.[o]
Then in the future your descendants
will not be able to say to ours, 'You have
no share in the LORD.'

28"And we said, 'If they ever say this
to us, or to our descendants, we will
answer: Look at the replica of the LORD's
altar, which our fathers built, not for
burnt offerings and sacrifices, but as a
witness[p] between us and you.'

29"Far be it from us to rebel[q] against
the LORD and turn away from him today
by building an altar for burnt offerings,
grain offerings and sacrifices, other
than the altar of the LORD our God that
stands before his tabernacle.[r]"

30When Phinehas the priest and the
leaders of the community—the heads of
the clans of the Israelites—heard what
Reuben, Gad and Manasseh had to say,
they were pleased. 31And Phinehas son
of Eleazar, the priest, said to Reuben,
Gad and Manasseh, "Today we know
that the LORD is with us,[s] because you
have not acted unfaithfully towards the
LORD in this matter. Now you have res-
cued the Israelites from the LORD's
hand."

32Then Phinehas son of Eleazar, the
priest, and the leaders returned to
Canaan from their meeting with the
Reubenites and Gadites in Gilead and
reported to the Israelites.[t] 33They were
glad to hear the report and praised
God.[u] And they talked no more about
going to war against them to devastate
the country where the Reubenites and
the Gadites lived.

34And the Reubenites and the Gadites
gave the altar this name: A Witness[v]
Between Us that the LORD is God.

Joshua's Farewell to the Leaders

23 After a long time had passed
and the LORD had given Israel
rest[a] from all their enemies around

10 [t]ver 19,26–27; Isa 19:19; 56:7
12 [u]Jos 18:1
13 [v]**Nu 25:7;** [w]Nu 3:32; Jos 24:33
14 [x]ver 32; **Nu 1:4**
16 [y]**Dt 7:3;** 1Sa 13:13; 15:11; [z]Dt 12:13–14
17 [a]**Nu 23:28;** 25:1–9
18 [b]**Lev 10:6**
19 [c]**Ex 26:1;** [d]**ver 10**
20 [e]Jos 7:1; [f]Ps 7:11; [g]Lev 10:6; [h]Jos 7:5
22 [i]**Dt 10:17;** [j]Ps 50:1; [k]1Sa 2:3; 16:7; 1Ki 8:39; 1Ch 28:9; Ps 11:4; 40:9; 44:21; 139:4; Jer 17:10
23 [l]Jer 41:5; [m]**Dt 12:11; 18:19;** 1Sa 20:16
27 [n]**Ge 21:30;** Jos 24:27; Isa 19:20; [o]**Dt 12:6**
28 [p]**Ge 21:30**
29 [q]Jos 24:16; [r]**Ex 26:1**
31 [s]2Ch 15:2
32 [t]**ver 14**
33 [u]1Ch 29:20; Da 2:19; Lk 2:28
34 [v]**Ge 21:30**

Ch. 23

1 [a]**Dt 12:9;** Jos 21:44

[a]20 The Hebrew term refers to the irrevocable giving over of things or persons to the LORD, often by totally destroying them.
[b]23 Traditionally *peace offerings;* also in verse 27

them, Joshua, by then old and well ad-
vanced in years,[b] 2summoned all Israel
—their elders,[c] leaders, judges and
officials[d]—and said to them: "I am old
and well advanced in years.[e] 3You
yourselves have seen everything the
LORD your God has done to all these
nations for your sake; it was the LORD
your God who fought for you.[f]
4Remember how I have allotted[g] as an
inheritance[h] for your tribes all the land
of the nations that remain—the nations
I conquered—between the Jordan and
the Great Sea[a][i] in the west. 5The LORD
your God himself will drive them out[j] of
your way. He will push them out[k] be-
fore you, and you will take possession
of their land, as the LORD your God
promised you.[l]
6"Be very strong; be careful to obey all
that is written in the Book of the Law[m] of
Moses, without turning aside[n] to the
right or to the left.[o] 7Do not associate
with these nations that remain among
you; do not invoke the names of their
gods or swear[p] by them. You must not
serve them or bow down[q] to them. 8But
you are to hold fast to the LORD[r] your
God, as you have until now.
9"The LORD has driven out before you
great and powerful nations;[s] to this day
no-one has been able to withstand you.[t]
10One of you routs a thousand,[u] because
the LORD your God fights for you,[v] just
as he promised. 11So be very careful[w] to
love the LORD[x] your God.
12"But if you turn away and ally
yourselves with the survivors of these
nations that remain among you and if
you intermarry with them[y] and associ-
ate with them,[z] 13then you may be sure
that the LORD your God will no longer
drive out[a] these nations before you. In-
stead, they will become snares[b] and
traps for you, whips on your backs and
thorns in your eyes,[c] until you perish
from this good land,[d] which the LORD
your God has given you.
14"Now I am about to go the way of all
the earth.[e] You know with all your heart
and soul that not one of all the good
promises the LORD your God gave you
has failed. Every promise[f] has been ful-
filled; not one has failed.[g] 15But just as
every good promise[h] of the LORD your
God has come true, so the LORD will
bring on you all the evil[i] he has
threatened, until he has destroyed you[j]
from this good land he has given you.[k]
16If you violate the covenant of the LORD
your God, which he commanded you,
and go and serve other gods and bow
down to them, the LORD's anger will
burn against you, and you will quickly
perish from the good land he has given
you.'"

The Covenant Renewed at Shechem

24 Then Joshua assembled[a] all the
tribes of Israel at Shechem.[b] He
summoned[c] the elders,[d] leaders, judges
and officials of Israel,[e] and they pre-
sented themselves before God.
2Joshua said to all the people, "This is
what the LORD, the God of Israel, says:
'Long ago your forefathers, including
Terah the father of Abraham and
Nahor,[f] lived beyond the River[a] and
worshipped other gods.[g] 3But I took
your father Abraham from the land
beyond the River and led him through-
out Canaan[h] and gave him many de-
scendants.[i] I gave him Isaac,[j] 4and to
Isaac I gave Jacob and Esau.[k] I assigned
the hill country of Seir[l] to Esau, but
Jacob and his sons went down to
Egypt.[m]
5" 'Then I sent Moses and Aaron,[n]
and I afflicted the Egyptians by what I
did there, and I brought you out.[o]
6When I brought your fathers out of
Egypt, you came to the sea,[p] and the
Egyptians pursued them with chariots
and horsemen[b][q] as far as the Red Sea.[c][r]
7But they cried[s] to the LORD for help, and
he put darkness[t] between you and the
Egyptians; he brought the sea over
them and covered them.[u] You saw with
your own eyes what I did to the Egyp-
tians.[v] Then you lived in the desert for a
long time.[w]
8" 'I brought you to the land of the
Amorites[x] who lived east of the Jordan.
They fought against you, but I gave
them into your hands. I destroyed them
from before you, and you took posses-
sion of their land.[y] 9When Balak son of
Zippor,[z] the king of Moab, prepared to
fight against Israel, he sent for Balaam
son of Beor[a] to put a curse on you.[b] 10But
I would not listen to Balaam, so he
blessed you[c] again and again, and I
delivered you out of his hand.
11" 'Then you crossed the Jordan[d]
and came to Jericho.[e] The citizens of
Jericho fought against you, as did also
the Amorites, Perizzites,[f] Canaanites,

1 [b]Jos 13:1
2 [c]Jos 7:6; [d]Jos 24:1; [e]Jos 13:1
3 [f]Ex 14:14; Dt 20:4
4 [g]Jos 19:51; [h]Nu 34:2; Ps 78:55; [i]Nu 34:6
5 [j]ver 13; Jdg 2:21; [k]Ps 44:5; Jer 46:15; [l]Ex 23:30
6 [m]Dt 28:61; [n]Dt 17:20; [o]Jos 1:7
7 [p]Ex 23:13; Jer 5:7; 12:16; [q]Ex 20:5
8 [r]Dt 10:20
9 [s]Dt 11:23; [t]Dt 7:24
10 [u]Lev 26:8; Jdg 3:31; [v]Ex 14:14
11 [w]Dt 4:15; [x]Jos 22:5
12 [y]Ge 34:9; [z]Ex 34:16; Ps 106:34–35
13 [a]ver 5; [b]Ex 10:7; [c]Nu 33:55; [d]Dt 1:8; 1Ki 9:7; 2Ki 25:21
14 [e]1Ki 2:2; [f]Ps 119:140; 145:13; [g]Jos 21:45
15 [h]1Ki 8:56; Jer 33:14; [i]1Ki 14:10; 2Ki 22:16; Isa 24:6; 34:5; 43:28; Jer 6:19; 11:8; 35:17; 39:16; Mal 4:6; [j]Jos 24:20; [k]Lev 26:17; Dt 28:15; Jer 40:2
16 [l]Dt 4:25–26

Ch. 24

1 [a]Ge 49:2; [b]Ge 12:6; [c]1Sa 12:7; 1Ki 8:14; [d]Jos 7:6; [e]Jos 23:2
2 [f]Ge 11:26; [g]Ge 11:32
3 [h]Ge 12:1; [i]Ge 1:28; 12:2; [j]Ge 21:3
4 [k]Ge 25:26; [l]Ge 14:6; Nu 24:18; [m]Ge 46:5–6
5 [n]Ex 3:10; [o]Ex 12:51
6 [p]Ex 14:22; [q]Ex 14:9; [r]Ex 14:23
7 [s]Ex 14:10; [t]Ex 14:20; [u]Ex 14:28; [v]Ex 19:4; [w]Dt 1:46
8 [x]Ex 23:23; [y]Nu 21:31
9 [z]Nu 22:2; [a]Nu 23:7; [b]Nu 22:6
10 [c]Nu 23:11; Dt 23:5
11 [d]Ex 14:29; [e]Jos 6:1; [f]Jos 3:10

[a]4 That is, the Mediterranean
[a]2 That is, the Euphrates; also in verses 3, 14 and 15
[b]6 Or *charioteers*
[c]6 Hebrew *Yam Suph*; that is, Sea of Reeds

Hittites, Girgashites, Hivites and Jebu-
sites,[g] but I gave them into your hands.[h]
12 I sent the hornet[i] ahead of you, which
drove them out[j] before you—also the
two Amorite kings. You did not do it
with your own sword and bow.[k] 13 So I
gave you a land[l] on which you did not
toil and cities you did not build; and you
live in them and eat from vineyards and
olive groves that you did not plant.'[m]
14 "Now fear the LORD[n] and serve him
with all faithfulness.[o] Throw away the
gods[p] your forefathers worshipped
beyond the River and in Egypt,[q] and
serve the LORD. 15 But if serving the LORD
seems undesirable to you, then choose
for yourselves this day whom you will
serve, whether the gods your fore-
fathers served beyond the River, or the
gods of the Amorites,[r] in whose land
you are living. But as for me and my
household,[s] we will serve the LORD."[t]
16 Then the people answered, "Far be
it from us to forsake[u] the LORD to serve
other gods! 17 It was the LORD our God
himself who brought us and our fathers
up out of Egypt, from that land of
slavery,[v] and performed those great
signs[w] before our eyes. He protected us
on our entire journey and among all the
nations through which we travelled.
18 And the LORD drove out[x] before us all
the nations,[y] including the Amorites,
who lived in the land.[z] We too will serve
the LORD, because he is our God.[a]"
19 Joshua said to the people, "You are
not able to serve the LORD. He is a holy
God;[b] he is a jealous God.[c] He will not
forgive[d] your rebellion[e] and your sins.
20 If you forsake the LORD[f] and serve
foreign gods, he will turn[g] and bring
disaster[h] on you and make an end of
you,[i] after he has been good to you."
21 But the people said to Joshua, "No!
We will serve the LORD."
22 Then Joshua said, "You are wit-
nesses[j] against yourselves that you
have chosen[k] to serve the LORD."
"Yes, we are witnesses,[l]" they
replied.
23 "Now then," said Joshua, "throw
away the foreign gods[m] that are among
you and yield your hearts[n] to the LORD,
the God of Israel."

11 [g]**Ge 15:18–21**; [h]Ex 23:23; Dt 7:1
12 [i]**Ex 23:28**; Ps 44:3,6–7; [j]**Ex 23:31**; [k]Ps 135:11
13 [l]Ex 6:8; [m]Dt 6:10–11
14 [n]1Sa 12:14; Job 23:15; Ps 19:9; 119:120; [o]Dt 10:12; 18:13; 1Sa 12:24; 2Co 1:12; [p]ver 23; **Ge 31:19**; Ex 12:12; 18:11; 20:3; Nu 25:2; Dt 11:28; Jdg 10:16; Ru 1:15; Isa 55:7; [q]Eze 23:3
15 [r]Jdg 6:10; Ru 1:15; [s]**Ge 35:2**; [t]Ru 1:16; 2:12; 1Ki 18:21; Da 3:18
16 [u]Jos 22:29
17 [v]Jdg 6:8; [w]**Ex 10:1**
18 [x]**Ex 23:31**; [y]**Dt 33:27**; [z]Ac 7:45; [a]**Ge 28:21**
19 [b]**Lev 11:44**; **20:26**; [c]**Ex 20:5**; [d]**Ex 34:7**; [e]**Ex 23:21**
20 [f]1Ch 28:9,20; 2Ch 24:18; [g]Ac 7:42; [h]1Sa 12:25; Hos 13:11; [i]Jos 23:15
22 [j]ver 27; Ru 4:10; Isa 8:2; 43:10; 44:8; Jer 42:5; Mal 2:14; [k]Ps 119:30, 173; [l]**Dt 25:9**
23 [m]**ver 14**; [n]1Ki 8:58; Ps 119:36; 141:4; Jer 31:33
24 [o]Ex 19:8; Jer 42:6
25 [p]**Ex 24:8**; [q]**Jos 17:7**; [r]Ex 15:25
26 [s]**Dt 17:18**; [t]**Dt 28:61; 31:24**; [u]**Ge 28:18; Dt 27:2**; [v]**Ge 12:6; Jdg 4:11**
27 [w]**Ge 28:18**; Hab 2:11; [x]**ver 22; Ge 21:30; Jos 22:27**; [y]**Jos 7:11**; [z]**Nu 11:20; Pr 30:9**
28 [a]Jdg 21:23–24

24 And the people said to Joshua, "We
will serve the LORD our God and obey
him."[o]
25 On that day Joshua made a cov-
enant[p] for the people, and there at
Shechem[q] he drew up for them decrees
and laws.[r] 26 And Joshua recorded[s] these
things in the Book of the Law of God.[t]
Then he took a large stone[u] and set it up
there under the oak[v] near the holy place
of the LORD.
27 "See!" he said to all the people.
"This stone[w] will be a witness[x] against
us. It has heard all the words the LORD
has said to us. It will be a witness
against you if you are untrue[y] to your
God."[z]

Buried in the Promised Land

24:29–31pp—Jdg 2:6–9

28 Then Joshua sent the people away,
each to his own inheritance.[a]
29 After these things, Joshua son of
Nun, the servant of the LORD, died[b] at
the age of a hundred and ten.[c] 30 And
they buried him in the land of his inherit-
ance, at Timnath Serah[d][d] in the hill
country of Ephraim, north of Mount
Gaash.[e]
31 Israel served the LORD throughout
the lifetime of Joshua and of the elders[f]
who outlived him and who had experi-
enced everything the LORD had done for
Israel.
32 And Joseph's bones,[g] which the
Israelites had brought up from Egypt,[h]
were buried at Shechem in the tract of
land[i] that Jacob bought for a hundred
pieces of silver[e] from the sons of Hamor,
the father of Shechem. This became the
inheritance of Joseph's descendants.
33 And Eleazar son of Aaron[j] died and
was buried at Gibeah,[k] which had been
allotted to his son Phinehas[l] in the hill
country[m] of Ephraim.

29 [b]Jdg 1:1; [c]**Ge 50:22**
30 [d]**Jos 19:50**; [e]2Sa 23:30
31 [f]Jos 7:6
32 [g]Heb 11:22; [h]**Ge 47:29–30**; [i]Ge 33:19; Jn 4:5; Ac 7:16
33 [j]**Jos 22:13**; [k]**Jos 15:57**; [l]**Ex 6:25**; [m]1Sa 9:4; 1Ki 4:8

[d]30 Also known as *Timnath Heres* (see Judges 2:9)
[e]32 Hebrew *hundred kesitahs*; a kesitah was a unit of money of unknown weight and value.

Judges

Israel Fights the Remaining Canaanites

1:11–15pp—Jos 15:15–19

1 After the death[a] of Joshua, the Israelites asked the LORD, "Who will be the first[b] to go up and fight for us against the Canaanites?[c]"

2The LORD answered, "Judah[d] is to go; I have given the land into their hands.[e]"

3Then the men of Judah said to the Simeonites their brothers, "Come up with us into the territory allotted to us, to fight against the Canaanites. We in turn will go with you into yours." So the Simeonites[f] went with them.

4When Judah attacked, the LORD gave the Canaanites and Perizzites[g] into their hands and they struck down ten thousand men at Bezek.[h] 5It was there that they found Adoni-Bezek[i] and fought against him, putting to rout the Canaanites and Perizzites. 6Adoni-Bezek fled, but they chased him and caught him, and cut off his thumbs and big toes.

7Then Adoni-Bezek said, "Seventy kings with their thumbs and big toes cut off have picked up scraps under my table. Now God has paid me back[j] for what I did to them." They brought him to Jerusalem,[k] and he died there.

8The men of Judah attacked Jerusalem[l] also and took it. They put the city to the sword and set it on fire.

9After that, the men of Judah went down to fight against the Canaanites living in the hill country,[m] the Negev[n] and the western foothills. 10They advanced against the Canaanites living in Hebron[o] (formerly called Kiriath Arba[p]) and defeated Sheshai, Ahiman and Talmai.[q]

11From there they advanced against the people living in Debir[r] (formerly called Kiriath Sepher). 12And Caleb said, "I will give my daughter Acsah in marriage to the man who attacks and captures Kiriath Sepher." 13Othniel son of Kenaz, Caleb's younger brother, took it; so Caleb gave his daughter Acsah to him in marriage.

14One day when she came to Othniel, she urged him[a] to ask her father for a field. When she got off her donkey, Caleb asked her, "What can I do for you?"

15She replied, "Do me a special favour. Since you have given me land in the Negev, give me also springs of water." Then Caleb gave her the upper and lower springs.[s]

16The descendants of Moses' father-in-law,[t] the Kenite,[u] went up from the City of Palms[b] [v] with the men of Judah to live among the people of the Desert of Judah in the Negev near Arad.[w]

17Then the men of Judah went with the Simeonites[x] their brothers and attacked the Canaanites living in Zephath, and they totally destroyed[c] the city. Therefore it was called Hormah.[d] [y] 18The men of Judah also took[e] Gaza,[z] Ashkelon[a] and Ekron—each city with its territory.

19The LORD was with[b] the men of Judah. They took possession of the hill country,[c] but they were unable to drive the people from the plains, because they had iron chariots.[d] 20As Moses had promised, Hebron[e] was given to Caleb, who drove from it the three sons of Anak.[f] 21The Benjamites, however, failed[g] to dislodge the Jebusites, who were living in Jerusalem;[h] to this day the Jebusites live there with the Benjamites.

22Now the house of Joseph[i] attacked Bethel,[j] and the LORD was with them. 23When they sent men to spy out Bethel (formerly called Luz),[k] 24the spies saw a man coming out of the city and they said to him, "Show us how to get into the city and we will see that you are treated well.[l]" 25So he showed them, and they put the city to the sword but spared[m] the man and his whole family. 26He then went to the land of the Hittites,[n] where he built a city and called it Luz,[o] which is its name to this day.

Ch. 1

1 [a]Jos 24:29; [b]**Nu 2:3–9;** Jdg 20:18; 1Ki 20:14; [c]ver 27; **Ge 10:18;** Jdg 3:1–6
2 [d]**Ge 49:10;** [e]ver 4; Jdg 3:28; 4:7,14; 7:9
3 [f]ver 17
4 [g]**Ge 13:7; Jos 3:10;** [h]1Sa 11:8
5 [i]ver 6–7
7 [j]Lev 24:19; Jer 25:12; [k]**Jos 10:1**
8 [l]ver 21; Jos 15:63; 2Sa 5:6
9 [m]**Nu 13:17;** [n]**Ge 12:9; Nu 21:1;** Isa 30:6
10 [o]**Ge 13:18;** [p]**Ge 35:27;** [q]ver 20; **Nu 13:22;** Jos 15:14
11 [r]Jos 10:38
15 [s]**Nu 13:6**
16 [t]Nu 10:29; [u]**Ge 15:19;** [v]Dt 34:3; Jdg 3:13; 2Ch 28:15; [w]Nu 21:1; Jos 12:14
17 [x]ver 3; [y]**Nu 14:45**
18 [z]Jos 11:22; [a]**Jos 13:3**
19 [b]**Nu 14:43;** [c]Nu 13:17; [d]**Jos 17:16**
20 [e]Jos 10:36; [f]**ver 10; Jos 14:13**
21 [g]**Jos 9:15; 15:63;** [h]**ver 8**
22 [i]Jdg 10:9; [j]**Jos 7:2**
23 [k]**Ge 28:19**
24 [l]**Ge 47:29**
25 [m]Jos 6:25
26 [n]**Dt 7:1;** Eze 16:3; [o]**Ge 28:19**

[a]14 Hebrew; Septuagint and Vulgate *Othniel, he urged her* [b]16 That is, Jericho
[c]17 The Hebrew term refers to the irrevocable giving over of things or persons to the LORD, often by totally destroying them.
[d]17 *Hormah* means *destruction.*
[e]18 Hebrew; Septuagint *Judah did not take*

27But Manasseh did not[p] drive out the people of Beth Shan or Taanach or Dor[q] or Ibleam[r] or Megiddo[s] and their surrounding settlements, for the Canaanites[t] were determined to live in that land. 28When Israel became strong, they pressed the Canaanites into forced labour but never drove them out completely.[u] 29Nor did Ephraim[v] drive out the Canaanites living in Gezer,[w] but the Canaanites continued to live there among them.[x] 30Neither did Zebulun drive out the Canaanites living in Kitron or Nahalol, who remained among them; but they did subject them to forced labour. 31Nor did Asher[y] drive out those living in Acco or Sidon[z] or Ahlab or Aczib[a] or Helbah or Aphek[b] or Rehob,[c] 32and because of this the people of Asher lived among the Canaanite inhabitants of the land. 33Neither did Naphtali drive out those living in Beth Shemesh[d] or Beth Anath[e]; but the Naphtalites too lived among the Canaanite inhabitants of the land, and those living in Beth Shemesh and Beth Anath became forced labourers for them. 34The Amorites[f] confined the Danites[g] to the hill country, not allowing them to come down into the plain.[h] 35And the Amorites were determined also to hold out in Mount Heres,[i] Aijalon[j] and Shaalbim,[k] but when the power of the house of Joseph increased, they too were pressed into forced labour. 36The boundary of the Amorites was from Scorpion[f] Pass[l] to Sela[m] and beyond.[n]

The Angel of the LORD at Bokim

2 The angel of the LORD[a] went up from Gilgal[b] to Bokim[c] and said, "I brought you up out of Egypt[d] and led you into the land that I swore to give to your forefathers.[e] I said, 'I will never break my covenant with you,[f] 2and you shall not make a covenant with the people of this land,[g] but you shall break down their altars.[h]' Yet you have disobeyed[i] me. Why have you done this? 3Now therefore I tell you that I will not drive them out before you;[j] they will be ⌞thorns⌟[k] in your sides and their gods will be a snare[l] to you."

4When the angel of the LORD had spoken these things to all the Israelites, the people wept aloud,[m] 5and they called that place Bokim.[a][n] There they offered sacrifices to the LORD.

Disobedience and Defeat

2:6–9pp—Jos 24:29–31

6After Joshua had dismissed the Israelites, they went to take possession of the land, each to his own inheritance. 7The people served the LORD throughout the lifetime of Joshua and of the elders who outlived him and who had seen all the great things the LORD had done for Israel.[o]

8Joshua son of Nun,[p] the servant of the LORD, died at the age of a hundred and ten. 9And they buried him in the land of his inheritance, at Timnath Heres[b][q] in the hill country of Ephraim, north of Mount Gaash.

10After that whole generation had been gathered to their fathers, another generation grew up, who knew neither the LORD nor what he had done for Israel.[r] 11Then the Israelites did evil[s] in the eyes of the LORD[t] and served the Baals.[u] 12They forsook the LORD, the God of their fathers, who had brought them out of Egypt. They followed and worshipped various gods[v] of the peoples around them.[w] They provoked[x] the LORD to anger[y] 13because they forsook[z] him and served Baal and the Ashtoreths.[a] 14In his anger[b] against Israel the LORD handed them over[c] to raiders who plundered[d] them. He sold them[e] to their enemies all around, whom they were no longer able to resist.[f] 15Whenever Israel went out to fight, the hand of the LORD was against them[g] to defeat them, just as he had sworn to them. They were in great distress.[h]

16Then the LORD raised up judges,[c][i] who saved[j] them out of the hands of these raiders. 17Yet they would not listen to their judges but prostituted[k] themselves to other gods[l] and worshipped them.[m] Unlike their fathers, they quickly turned[n] from the way in which their fathers had walked, the way of obedience to the LORD's commands.[o] 18Whenever the LORD raised up a judge for them, he was with the judge and saved[p] them out of the hands of their enemies as long as the judge lived; for the LORD had compassion[q] on them as they groaned[r] under those who oppressed and afflicted[s] them. 19But when the

27 [p]1Ki 9:21; [q]**Jos 11:2;** [r]**Jos 17:11;** [s]**Jos 12:21;** [t]**ver 1**
28 [u]Jos 17:12–13
29 [v]Jos 14:4; Jdg 5:14; [w]**Jos 10:33;** [x]Jos 16:10
31 [y]**Jos 17:7;** [z]**Ge 49:13;** [a]**Jos 15:44;** [b]**Jos 12:18;** [c]**Nu 13:21**
33 [d]**Jos 15:10;** [e]Jos 19:38
34 [f]Nu 13:29; Jdg 10:11; 1Sa 7:14; [g]**Ge 30:6;** [h]Jdg 18:1
35 [i]Jdg 8:13; [j]Jos 19:42; [k]1Ki 4:9
36 [l]Jos 15:3; [m]2Ki 14:7; Isa 16:1; 42:11; [n]Ps 106:34

Ch. 2

1 [a]**Ge 16:7;** [b]**Dt 11:30;** [c]ver 5; [d]Ex 20:2; Jdg 6:8; [e]Ge 17:8; [f]**Lev 26:42–44;** Dt 7:9
2 [g]**Ex 23:32; 34:12;** Dt 7:2; [h]**Ex 23:24;** 34:13; Dt 7:5; 2Ch 14:3; [i]Jer 7:28
3 [j]Jos 23:13; [k]**Nu 33:55;** [l]**Ex 10:7**
4 [m]**Ge 27:38; Nu 25:6;** 2Ki 17:13
5 [n]ver 1
7 [o]ver 17
8 [p]Jos 1:1
9 [q]**Jos 19:50**
10 [r]**Ex 5:2;** Gal 4:8
11 [s]1Ki 15:26; [t]Jdg 3:12; 4:1; 6:1; 10:6; [u]Jdg 3:7; 8:33; 1Ki 16:31; 22:53; 2Ki 10:18; 17:16
12 [v]**Dt 32:12;** Ps 106:36; [w]**Dt 31:16;** Jdg 10:6; [x]**Nu 11:33;** [y]Dt 4:25; Ps 78:58; 106:40
13 [z]1Sa 7:3; 1Ki 11:5,33; 2Ki 23:13; [a]Jdg 3:7; 5:8; 6:25; 8:33; 10:6; 1Sa 31:10; Ne 9:26; Ps 78:56; Jer 11:10
14 [b]**Dt 31:17;** [c]Ne 9:27; Ps 106:41; [d]Ps 44:10; 89:41; Eze 34:8; [e]**Dt 32:30; Jdg 3:8;** [f]**Dt 28:25**
15 [g]Ru 1:13; Job 19:21; Ps 32:4; [h]Ge 35:3; 2Sa 22:7; 2Ch 15:4; Job 5:5; 20:22; Ps 4:1; 18:6
16 [i]Ru 1:1; 1Sa 4:18; 7:6,15; 2Sa 7:11; 1Ch 17:10; Ac 13:20; [j]1Sa 11:3; Ps 106:43
17 [k]**Ex 34:15; Nu 15:39;** [l]**Ps 4:2;** [m]Ne 9:28; Ps 106:36; [n]Dt 9:12; [o]ver 7
18 [p]1Sa 7:3; 2Ki 13:5; Isa 19:20; 43:3,11; 45:15,21; 49:26; 60:16; 63:8; [q]**Dt 32:36;** [r]**Ex 2:23;** [s]**Nu 10:9**

f36 Hebrew *Akrabbim*
a5 *Bokim* means *weepers*.
b9 Also known as *Timnath Serah* (see Joshua 19:50 and 24:30)
c16 Or *leaders*; similarly in verses 17–19

judge died, the people returned to ways
even more corrupt[t] than those of their
fathers,[u] following other gods and
serving and worshipping them.[v] They
refused to give up their evil practices
and stubborn[w] ways.
20Therefore the LORD was very angry[x]
with Israel and said, "Because this
nation has violated the covenant[y] that I
laid down for their forefathers and has
not listened to me, 21I will no longer
drive out[z] before them any of the
nations Joshua left when he died.
22I will use them to test[a] Israel and see
whether they will keep the way of the
LORD and walk in it as their forefathers
did." 23The LORD had allowed those
nations to remain; he did not drive
them out at once by giving them into the
hands of Joshua.[b]

3 These are the nations the LORD left
to test[a] all those Israelites who had
not experienced any of the wars in Ca-
naan 2(he did this only to teach warfare
to the descendants of the Israelites who
had not had previous battle experience):
3the five[b] rulers of the Philistines,[c] all the
Canaanites, the Sidonians, and the Hiv-
ites[d] living in the Lebanon mountains
from Mount Baal Hermon[e] to Lebo[a]
Hamath.[f] 4They were left to test[g] the
Israelites to see whether they would
obey the LORD's commands, which he
had given their forefathers through
Moses.
5The Israelites lived[h] among the
Canaanites, Hittites, Amorites, Periz-
zites,[i] Hivites and Jebusites.[j] 6They took
their daughters[k] in marriage and gave
their own daughters to their sons, and
served their gods.[l m]

Othniel

7The Israelites did evil in the eyes of
the LORD; they forgot the LORD[n] their
God and served the Baals and the
Asherahs.[o] 8The anger of the LORD
burned against Israel so that he sold[p]
them into the hands of Cushan-
Rishathaim[q] king of Aram Naharaim,[b r]
to whom the Israelites were subject for
eight years. 9But when they cried out[s] to
the LORD, he raised up for them a de-
liverer,[t] Othniel[u] son of Kenaz, Caleb's
younger brother, who saved them.
10The Spirit of the LORD came upon
him,[v] so that he became Israel's judge[c]
and went to war. The LORD gave
Cushan-Rishathaim[w] king of Aram[x]
into the hands of Othniel, who over-
powered him. 11So the land had peace[y]
for forty years,[z] until Othniel son of
Kenaz[a] died.

Ehud

12Once again the Israelites did evil in
the eyes of the LORD[b], and because they
did this evil the LORD gave Eglon king of
Moab[c] power over Israel. 13Getting the
Ammonites[d] and Amalekites[e] to join
him, Eglon came and attacked Israel,
and they took possession of the City of
Palms.[d f] 14The Israelites were subject to
Eglon king of Moab[g] for eighteen years.
15Again the Israelites cried out to the
LORD, and he gave them a deliverer[h]
—Ehud,[i] a left-handed man,[j] the son of
Gera the Benjamite. The Israelites sent
him with tribute[k] to Eglon king of Moab.
16Now Ehud[l] had made a double-edged
sword about a foot and a half[e] long,
which he strapped to his right thigh
under his clothing. 17He presented the
tribute[m] to Eglon king of Moab, who
was a very fat man.[n] 18After Ehud had
presented the tribute, he sent on their
way the men who had carried it. 19At the
idols[f] near Gilgal he himself turned
back and said, "I have a secret message
for you, O king."
The king said, "Quiet!" And all his
attendants left him.
20Ehud then approached him while
he was sitting alone in the upper room
of his summer palace[g o] and said, "I have
a message from God for you." As the
king rose[p] from his seat, 21Ehud reached
with his left hand, drew the sword[q]
from his right thigh and plunged it into
the king's belly. 22Even the handle sank
in after the blade, which came out of his
back. Ehud did not pull the sword out,
and the fat closed in over it. 23Then
Ehud went out to the porch;[h] he shut
the doors of the upper room behind him
and locked them.
24After he had gone, the servants
came and found the doors of the upper
room locked. They said, "He must be
relieving himself[r] in the inner room of
the house." 25They waited to the point
of embarrassment,[s] but when he did not

19 [t]**Ge 6:11; Dt 4:16;** [u]Dt 32:17; Ne 9:2; Ps 78:57; Jer 44:3,9; [v]Jdg 4:1; 8:33; [w]**Ex 32:9**
20 [x]**Dt 31:17;** Jos 23:16; [y]**Jos 7:11; 2Ki 17:15**
21 [z]**Jos 23:5**
22 [a]**Ge 22:1;** Ex 15:25
23 [b]Jdg 1:1

Ch. 3

1 [a]Ex 15:25
3 [b]**Jos 13:3;** [c]**Ge 10:14;** [d]**Ge 10:17; Ex 3:8;** [e]**Dt 3:8;** [f]**Nu 13:21**
4 [g]**Ex 15:25**
5 [h]Ps 106:35; [i]**Jos 3:10;** [j]**Jos 11:3;** Ezr 9:1
6 [k]Ezr 10:18; Ne 13:23; Mal 2:11; [l]**Ex 34:16;** Dt 7:3–4; [m]**Dt 7:16**
7 [n]Dt 4:9; **32:18;** Jdg 8:34; Ps 78:11,42; 106:7; Jer 23:27; [o]**Ex 34:13; Jdg 2:11,13;** 1Ki 16:33; 2Ch 34:7; Isa 17:8
8 [p]Jdg 2:14; Ps 44:12; Isa 50:1; 52:3; [q]ver 10; [r]**Ge 24:10**
9 [s]ver 15; Jdg 6:6–7; 10:10; 1Sa 12:10; Ps 106:44; 107:13; [t]**Dt 28:29;** Ne 9:27; [u]**Jos 15:17**
10 [v]**Nu 11:25;** Jdg 6:34; 11:29; 13:25; 14:6,19; 15:14; 1Sa 11:6; 16:13; 1Ki 18:46; 1Ch 12:18; 2Ch 24:20; Isa 11:2; [w]ver 8; [x]**Ge 10:22**
11 [y]ver 30; **Jos 14:15;** Jdg 5:31; 8:28; [z]**Ex 16:35;** [a]**Jos 15:17**
12 [b]**Jdg 2:11;** [c]1Sa 12:9
13 [d]**Ge 19:38;** Jdg 10:11; [e]**Ge 14:7;** [f]**Jdg 1:16**
14 [g]Jer 48:1

15 [h]**ver 9;** [i]ver 16; Jdg 4:1; [j]Jdg 20:16; 1Ch 12:2; [k]ver 17–18; 2Sa 8:2,6; 1Ki 4:21; 2Ki 17:3; Est 10:1; Ps 68:29; 72:10; 89:22; Ecc 2:8; Isa 60:5; Hos 10:6
16 [l]**ver 15** **17** [m]**ver 15;** [n]Job 15:27; Ps 73:4
20 [o]Am 3:15; [p]Ne 8:5 **21** [q]2Sa 2:16; 3:27; 20:10
24 [r]1Sa 24:3 **25** [s]2Ki 2:17; 8:11

[a]3 Or *to the entrance to*
[b]8 That is, North-west Mesopotamia
[c]10 Or *leader* [d]13 That is, Jericho
[e]16 Hebrew *a cubit* (about 0.5 metre)
[f]19 Or *the stone quarries;* also in verse 26
[g]20 The meaning of the Hebrew for this phrase is uncertain.
[h]23 The meaning of the Hebrew for this word is uncertain.

open the doors of the room, they took a
key and unlocked them. There they saw
their lord fallen to the floor, dead.
26While they waited, Ehud got away.
He passed by the idols and escaped to
Seirah. 27When he arrived there, he
blew a trumpet[t] in the hill country of
Ephraim, and the Israelites went down
with him from the hills, with him
leading them.
28"Follow me," he ordered, "for the
LORD has given Moab,[u] your enemy,
into your hands.[v]" So they followed
him down and, taking possession of the
fords of the Jordan[w] that led to Moab,
they allowed no-one to cross over. 29At
that time they struck down about ten
thousand Moabites, all vigorous and
strong; not a man escaped. 30That day
Moab[x] was made subject to Israel, and
the land had peace[y] for eighty years.

Shamgar

31After Ehud came Shamgar son of
Anath,[z] who struck down six hundred[a]
Philistines[b] with an ox-goad. He too
saved Israel.

Deborah

4 After Ehud[a] died, the Israelites
once again did evil[b] in the eyes of
the LORD.[c] 2So the LORD sold them[d] into
the hands of Jabin, a king of Canaan,
who reigned in Hazor.[e] The commander
of his army was Sisera,[f] who lived in
Harosheth Haggoyim. 3Because he had
nine hundred iron chariots[g] and had
cruelly oppressed[h] the Israelites for
twenty years, they cried to the LORD for
help.
4Deborah,[i] a prophetess,[j] the wife of
Lappidoth, was leading[a] Israel at that
time. 5She held court[k] under the Palm of
Deborah between Ramah[l] and Bethel[m]
in the hill country of Ephraim, and the
Israelites came to her to have their dis-
putes decided. 6She sent for Barak son
of Abinoam[n] from Kedesh[o] in Naphtali
and said to him, "The LORD, the God of
Israel, commands you: 'Go, take with
you ten thousand men of Naphtali[p] and
Zebulun[q] and lead the way to Mount
Tabor.[r] 7I will lure Sisera, the comman-
der of Jabin's[s] army, with his chariots
and his troops to the Kishon River[t] and
give him into your hands.[u]' "
8Barak said to her, "If you go with me,
I will go; but if you don't go with me, I
won't go."
9"Very well," Deborah said, "I will go
with you. But because of the way you
are going about this,[b] the honour will
not be yours, for the LORD will hand
Sisera over to a woman." So Deborah
went with Barak to Kedesh,[v] 10where
he summoned[w] Zebulun and Naphtali.
Ten thousand men followed him, and
Deborah also went with him.
11Now Heber the Kenite had left the
other Kenites,[x] the descendants of
Hobab,[y] Moses' brother-in-law,[c] and
pitched his tent by the great tree[z] in
Zaanannim[a] near Kedesh.
12When they told Sisera that Barak
son of Abinoam had gone up to Mount
Tabor,[b] 13Sisera gathered together his
nine hundred iron chariots[c] and all the
men with him, from Harosheth Hag-
goyim to the Kishon River.[d]
14Then Deborah said to Barak, "Go!
This is the day the LORD has given Sisera
into your hands.[e] Has not the LORD gone
ahead[f] of you?" So Barak went down
Mount Tabor, followed by ten thousand
men. 15At Barak's advance, the LORD
routed[g] Sisera and all his chariots and
army by the sword, and Sisera aban-
doned his chariot and fled on foot. 16But
Barak pursued the chariots and army as
far as Harosheth Haggoyim. All the
troops of Sisera fell by the sword; not a
man was left.[h]
17Sisera, however, fled on foot to the
tent of Jael,[i] the wife of Heber the
Kenite,[j] because there were friendly
relations between Jabin king of Hazor[k]
and the clan of Heber the Kenite.
18Jael[l] went out to meet Sisera and
said to him, "Come, my lord, come
right in. Don't be afraid." So he entered
her tent, and she put a covering over
him.
19"I'm thirsty," he said. "Please give
me some water." She opened a skin of
milk,[m] gave him a drink, and covered
him up.
20"Stand in the doorway of the tent,"
he told her. "If someone comes by and
asks you, 'Is anyone here?' say 'No.'"
21But Jael,[n] Heber's wife, picked up a
tent peg and a hammer and went
quietly to him while he lay fast
asleep,[o] exhausted. She drove the peg
through his temple into the ground,
and he died.[p]
22Barak came by in pursuit of Sisera,
and Jael[q] went out to meet him.
"Come," she said, "I will show you the
man you're looking for." So he went in

27 [t]Lev 25:9; Jdg 6:34; 7:18; 2Sa 2:28; Isa 18:3; Jer 42:14
28 [u]Ge 19:37; [v]Jos 2:24; Jdg 1:2; [w]Nu 13:29; Jos 2:7
30 [x]Ge 36:35; [y]ver 11
31 [z]Jdg 5:6; [a]Jos 23:10; [b]Jos 13:2; Jdg 10:11; 13:1; 1Sa 5:1; 31:1; 2Sa 8:1; Jer 25:20; 47:1

Ch. 4

1 [a]Jdg 3:15; [b]Jdg 2:19; [c]Jdg 2:11
2 [d]Dt 32:30; [e]Jos 11:1; [f]1Sa 12:9; Ps 83:9
3 [g]Jos 17:16; [h]Jdg 10:12; Ps 106:42
4 [i]Jdg 5:1,7,12,15; [j]Ex 15:20
5 [k]1Sa 14:2; 22:6; [l]Jos 18:25; [m]Jos 12:9
6 [n]Jdg 5:1,12,15; 1Sa 12:11; Heb 11:32; [o]Jos 12:22; [p]Ge 30:8; [q]Jdg 5:18; 6:35; [r]Jos 19:22
7 [s]Jos 11:1; [t]ver 13; Jdg 5:21; 1Ki 18:40; Ps 83:9; [u]Jdg 1:2
9 [v]Jos 12:22
10 [w]2Ch 36:23; Ezr 1:2; Isa 41:2; 42:6; 45:3; 46:11; 48:15
11 [x]Ge 15:19; [y]Nu 10:29; [z]Jos 24:26; Jdg 9:6; [a]Jos 19:33
12 [b]Jos 19:22
13 [c]Jos 17:16; [d]ver 7; Jdg 5:19
14 [e]Jdg 1:2; [f]Dt 9:3; 1Sa 8:20; 2Sa 5:24; Ps 68:7
15 [g]Ex 14:24; Ps 18:14
16 [h]Ex 14:28; Ps 83:9
17 [i]ver 18,21–22; Jdg 5:6,24; [j]Ge 15:19; [k]Jos 11:1
18 [l]ver 17
19 [m]Ge 18:8
21 [n]ver 17; [o]Ge 2:21; 15:12; 1Sa 26:12; Isa 29:10; Jnh 1:5; [p]Jdg 5:26
22 [q]ver 17

a4 Traditionally *judging*
b9 Or *But on the expedition you are undertaking*
c11 Or *father-in-law*

with her, and there lay Sisera with the tent peg through his temple—dead.[r]
23On that day God subdued[s] Jabin,[t]
the Canaanite king, before the
Israelites. 24And the hand of the
Israelites grew stronger and stronger against Jabin, the Canaanite king, until they destroyed him.[u]

The Song of Deborah

5 On that day Deborah[a] and Barak son of Abinoam[b] sang this song:[c]

2"When the princes in Israel take the lead,
 when the people willingly offer[d] themselves—
 praise the LORD![e]

3"Hear this, you kings! Listen, you rulers!
 I will sing to[a] the LORD, I will sing;[f]
 I will make music to[b] the LORD, the God of Israel.[g]

4"O LORD, when you went out[h] from Seir,[i]
 when you marched from the land of Edom,
the earth shook,[j] the heavens poured,
 the clouds poured down water.[k]
5The mountains quaked[l] before the LORD, the One of Sinai,
 before the LORD, the God of Israel.

6"In the days of Shamgar son of Anath,[m]
 in the days of Jael,[n] the roads[o] were abandoned;
 travellers took to winding paths.[p]
7Village life[c] in Israel ceased,
 ceased until I,[d] Deborah,[q] arose,
 arose a mother in Israel.
8When they chose new gods,[r]
 war came to the city gates,[s]
and not a shield or spear[t] was seen
 among forty thousand in Israel.
9My heart is with Israel's princes,
 with the willing volunteers[u] among the people.
 Praise the LORD!

10"You who ride on white donkeys,[v]
 sitting on your saddle blankets,
 and you who walk along the road,
consider 11the voice of the singers[e] at the watering places.
 They recite the righteous acts[w] of the LORD,
 the righteous acts of his warriors[f] in Israel.

"Then the people of the LORD
 went down to the city gates.[x]
12'Wake up,[y] wake up, Deborah![z]
 Wake up, wake up, break out in song!
Arise, O Barak![a]
 Take captive your captives,[b] O son of Abinoam.'

13"Then the men who were left
 came down to the nobles;
the people of the LORD
 came to me with the mighty.
14Some came from Ephraim,[c] whose roots were in Amalek;[d]
 Benjamin[e] was with the people who followed you.
From Makir[f] captains came down,
 from Zebulun those who bear a commander's staff.
15The princes of Issachar[g] were with Deborah;[h]
 yes, Issachar was with Barak,[i]
 rushing after him into the valley.
In the districts of Reuben
 there was much searching of heart.
16Why did you stay among the campfires[g][j]
 to hear the whistling for the flocks?[k]
In the districts of Reuben
 there was much searching of heart.
17Gilead[l] stayed beyond the Jordan.
 And Dan, why did he linger by the ships?
Asher[m] remained on the coast[n]
 and stayed in his coves.
18The people of Zebulun[o] risked their very lives;
 so did Naphtali[p] on the heights of the field.[q]

19"Kings came,[r] they fought;
 the kings of Canaan fought
at Taanach by the waters of Megiddo,[s]
 but they carried off no silver, no plunder.[t]
20From the heavens[u] the stars fought,
 from their courses they fought against Sisera.
21The river Kishon[v] swept them away,
 the age-old river, the river Kishon.
 March on, my soul; be strong![w]
22Then thundered the horses' hoofs—
 galloping, galloping go his mighty steeds.[x]
23'Curse Meroz,' said the angel of the LORD.

22 [r]Jdg 5:27
23 [s]Ne 9:24; Ps 18:47; 44:2; 47:3; 144:2; [t]Jos 11:1
24 [u]Ps 83:9; 106:43

Ch. 5

1 [a]Jdg 4:4; [b]Jdg 4:6; [c]Ex 15:1; Ps 32:7
2 [d]2Ch 17:16; Ps 110:3; [e]ver 9
3 [f]Ex 15:1; [g]Ps 27:6
4 [h]Ex 13:21; [i]Nu 24:18; Dt 33:2; [j]2Sa 22:8; Ps 18:7; 77:18; 82:5; Isa 2:19,21; 13:13; 24:18; 64:3; Jer 10:10; 50:46; 51:29; Joel 3:16; Na 1:5; Hab 3:6; [k]Ps 68:8; 77:17
5 [l]Ex 19:18; Ps 29:6; 46:3; 77:18; 114:4; Isa 64:3
6 [m]Jdg 3:31; [n]Jdg 4:17; [o]Lev 26:22; Isa 33:8; [p]Ps 125:5; Isa 59:8
7 [q]Jdg 4:4
8 [r]Dt 32:17; Jdg 2:13; [s]ver 11; Jos 2:5; [t]Nu 25:7
9 [u]ver 2
10 [v]Ge 49:11; Jdg 12:14
11 [w]1Sa 12:7; Da 9:16; Mic 6:5; [x]ver 8
12 [y]Ps 44:23; 57:8; Isa 51:9,17; [z]Jdg 4:4; [a]Jdg 4:6; [b]Ps 68:18; Eph 4:8
14 [c]Ge 41:52; Jdg 1:29; [d]Jdg 3:13; [e]Nu 34:21; [f]Ge 50:23
15 [g]Ge 30:18; [h]Jdg 4:4; [i]Jdg 4:6
16 [j]Ge 49:14; [k]Nu 32:1
17 [l]Jos 12:2; [m]Jos 17:7; [n]Jos 19:29
18 [o]Ge 30:20; [p]Ge 30:8; Ps 68:27; [q]Jdg 4:6
19 [r]Jos 11:5; Jdg 4:13; Rev 16:16; [s]Jos 12:21; [t]ver 30
20 [u]Jos 10:11
21 [v]Jdg 4:7; [w]Jos 1:6
22 [x]Jer 8:16

[a]3 Or *of* [b]3 Or / *with song I will praise*
[c]7 Or *Warriors* [d]7 Or *you*
[e]11 Or *archers*; the meaning of the Hebrew for this word is uncertain. [f]11 Or *villagers*
[g]16 Or *saddlebags*

'Curse its people bitterly,
because they did not come to help the LORD,
to help the LORD against the mighty.'

24"Most blessed of women[y] be Jael,[z]
the wife of Heber the Kenite,[a]
most blessed of tent-dwelling women.
25He asked for water, and she gave him milk;[b]
in a bowl fit for nobles she brought him curdled milk.
26Her hand reached for the tent peg,
her right hand for the workman's hammer.
She struck Sisera, she crushed his head,
she shattered and pierced his temple.[c]
27At her feet he sank,
he fell; there he lay.
At her feet he sank, he fell;
where he sank, there he fell—dead.[d]

28"Through the window[e] peered Sisera's mother;
behind the lattice she cried out,[f]
'Why is his chariot so long in coming?
Why is the clatter of his chariots delayed?'
29The wisest of her ladies answer her;
indeed, she keeps saying to herself,
30'Are they not finding and dividing the spoils:[g]
a girl or two for each man,
colourful garments as plunder for Sisera,
colourful garments embroidered,
highly embroidered garments[h] for my neck—
all this as plunder?'[i]

31"So may all your enemies perish,[j] O LORD!
But may they who love you be like the sun[k]
when it rises in its strength."[l]

Then the land had peace[m] for forty years.

Gideon

6 Again the Israelites did evil in the
eyes of the LORD,[a] and for seven
years he gave them into the hands of
the Midianites.[b] 2Because the power
of Midian was so oppressive,[c] the
Israelites prepared shelters for them-
selves in mountain clefts, caves[d] and
strongholds.[e] 3Whenever the Israelites
planted their crops, the Midianites,
Amalekites[f] and other eastern peoples[g]
invaded the country. 4They camped on
the land and ruined the crops[h] all the
way to Gaza[i] and did not spare a living
thing for Israel, neither sheep nor cattle
nor donkeys. 5They came up with their
livestock and their tents like swarms of
locusts.[j] It was impossible to count the
men and their camels;[k] they invaded the
land to ravage it. 6Midian so impover-
ished the Israelites that they cried out[l] to
the LORD for help.
7When the Israelites cried[m] to the
LORD because of Midian, 8he sent them a
prophet,[n] who said, "This is what the
LORD, the God of Israel, says: I brought
you up out of Egypt,[o] out of the land
of slavery.[p] 9I snatched you from the
power of Egypt and from the hand of all
your oppressors.[q] I drove them from
before you and gave you their land.[r] 10I
said to you, 'I am the LORD your God; do
not worship[s] the gods of the Amorites,[t]
in whose land you live.' But you have
not listened to me."
11The angel of the LORD[u] came and sat
down under the oak in Ophrah[v] that
belonged to Joash[w] the Abiezrite,[x]
where his son Gideon[y] was threshing[z]
wheat in a winepress[a] to keep it from the
Midianites. 12When the angel of the
LORD appeared to Gideon, he said, "The
LORD is with you,[b] mighty warrior.[c]"
13"But sir," Gideon replied, "if the
LORD is with us, why has all this hap-
pened to us? Where are all his wonders[d]
that our fathers told[e] us about when
they said, 'Did not the LORD bring us up
out of Egypt?' But now the LORD has
abandoned[f] us and put us into the hand
of Midian."
14The LORD turned to him and said,
"Go in the strength you have[g] and save[h]
Israel out of Midian's hand. Am I not
sending you?"
15"But Lord,"[a] Gideon asked, "how
can I save Israel? My clan[i] is the weakest
in Manasseh, and I am the least in my
family.[j]"
16The LORD answered, "I will be with
you,[k] and you will strike down all the
Midianites together."
17Gideon replied, "If now I have
found favour in your eyes, give me a
sign[l] that it is really you talking to me.
18Please do not go away until I come

5:24 [y]Lk 1:42; [z]**Jdg 4:17;** [a]**Ge 15:19**
25 [b]**Ge 18:8**
26 [c]Jdg 4:21
27 [d]Jdg 4:22
28 [e]**Jos 2:15;** [f]Pr 7:6
30 [g]Ex 15:9; 1Sa 30:24; Ps 68:12; [h]Ps 45:14; Eze 16:10; [i]ver 19; 2Sa 1:24
31 [j]**Nu 10:35;** [k]2Sa 23:4; Job 37:21; Ps 19:4; 89:36; Isa 18:4; [l]2Sa 18:32; [m]**Jdg 3:11**

Ch. 6

1 [a]**Jdg 2:11;** [b]**Ge 25:2**
2 [c]1Sa 13:6; Isa 5:30; 8:21; 26:16; 37:3; [d]Isa 2:19; Jer 48:28; 49:8,30; [e]Job 24:8; Jer 41:9; Heb 11:38
3 [f]Nu 13:29; [g]**Ge 25:6;** Isa 11:14; Jer 49:28
4 [h]Lev 26:16; Dt 28:30,51; Isa 10:6; 39:6; 42:22; [i]**Ge 10:19**
5 [j]**Dt 28:42;** [k]Jdg 8:10; Isa 21:7; 60:6; Jer 49:32
6 [l]**Jdg 3:9**
7 [m]**Jdg 3:9**
8 [n]Dt 18:15; 1Ki 20:13,22; 2Ki 17:13,23; Ne 9:29; Job 36:10; Jer 25:5; Eze 18:30–31; [o]**Jdg 2:1;** [p]Jos 24:17
9 [q]**Nu 10:9;** Ps 136:24; [r]Ps 44:2
10 [s]**Ex 20:5;** [t]**Jos 24:15**
11 [u]**Ge 16:7;** [v]**Jos 18:23;** [w]ver 29; Jdg 7:14; 8:13, 29; [x]**Nu 26:30;** [y]Jdg 7:1; 8:1; Heb 11:32; [z]Ru 2:17; 3:2; 1Sa 23:1; 1Ch 21:20; [a]Ne 13:15; Isa 16:10; 63:3; La 1:15; Joel 3:13
12 [b]**Jos 1:5;** Ru 2:4; 1Sa 10:7; Ps 129:8; [c]Jdg 11:1
13 [d]**Jos 3:5;** [e]2Sa 7:22; Ps 44:1; 78:3; [f]**Dt 31:17**
14 [g]Heb 11:34; [h]ver 36; Jdg 10:1; 2Ki 14:27
15 [i]Isa 60:22; [j]1Sa 9:21
16 [k]Ex 3:12; **Nu 14:43;** Jos 1:5
17 [l]ver 36–37; **Ge 24:14; Ex 3:12; 4:8**

[a]15 Or *sir*

back and bring my offering and set it
before you."
And the LORD said, "I will wait until
you return."
19Gideon went in, prepared a young
goat,[m] and from an ephah[b][n] of flour he
made bread without yeast. Putting the
meat in a basket and its broth in a pot,
he brought them out and offered them
to him under the oak.[o]
20The angel of God said to him, "Take
the meat and the unleavened bread,
place them on this rock,[p] and pour out
the broth." And Gideon did so. 21With
the tip of the staff[q] that was in his hand,
the angel of the LORD touched the meat
and the unleavened bread.[r] Fire flared
from the rock, consuming the meat and
the bread. And the angel of the LORD
disappeared. 22When Gideon realised[s]
that it was the angel of the LORD, he
exclaimed, "Ah, Sovereign LORD! I have
seen the angel of the LORD face to face!"[t]
23But the LORD said to him, "Peace! Do
not be afraid.[u] You are not going to
die."[v]
24So Gideon built an altar to the LORD
there and called[w] it The LORD is Peace.
To this day it stands in Ophrah[x] of the
Abiezrites.
25That same night the LORD said to
him, "Take the second bull from your
father's herd, the one seven years old.[c]
Tear down your father's altar to Baal
and cut down the Asherah pole[d][y] beside it. 26Then build a proper kind of[e]
altar to the LORD your God on the top of
this height. Using the wood of the
Asherah pole that you cut down, offer
the second[f] bull as a burnt offering.[z]"
27So Gideon took ten of his servants
and did as the LORD told him. But because he was afraid of his family and the
men of the town, he did it at night rather
than in the daytime.
28In the morning when the men of the
town got up, there was Baal's altar,[a]
demolished, with the Asherah pole
beside it cut down and the second bull
sacrificed on the newly-built altar!
29They asked each other, "Who did
this?"
When they carefully investigated,
they were told, "Gideon son of Joash[b]
did it."
30The men of the town demanded of
Joash, "Bring out your son. He must
die, because he has broken down Baal's
altar[c] and cut down the Asherah pole
beside it."
31But Joash replied to the hostile
crowd around him, "Are you going to
plead Baal's cause?[d] Are you trying to
save him? Whoever fights for him shall
be put to death by morning! If Baal
really is a god, he can defend himself
when someone breaks down his altar."
32So that day they called Gideon "Jerub-Baal,[g][e]" saying, "Let Baal contend with
him," because he broke down Baal's
altar.
33Now all the Midianites, Amalekites[f]
and other eastern peoples[g] joined forces
and crossed over the Jordan and
camped in the Valley of Jezreel.[h] 34Then
the Spirit of the LORD came upon[i]
Gideon, and he blew a trumpet,[j] summoning the Abiezrites[k] to follow him.
35He sent messengers throughout Manasseh, calling them to arms, and also
into Asher,[l] Zebulun and Naphtali,[m] so
that they too went up to meet them.[n]
36Gideon said to God, "If you will
save[o] Israel by my hand as you have
promised—37look, I will place a wool
fleece[p] on the threshing-floor.[q] If there is
dew only on the fleece and all the
ground is dry, then I will know[r] that you
will save Israel by my hand, as you
said." 38And that is what happened.
Gideon rose early the next day; he
squeezed the fleece and wrung out the
dew—a bowlful of water.
39Then Gideon said to God, "Do not
be angry with me. Let me make just one
more request.[s] Allow me one more test
with the fleece. This time make the
fleece dry and the ground covered with
dew." 40That night God did so. Only
the fleece was dry; all the ground was
covered with dew.[t]

Gideon Defeats the Midianites

7 Early in the morning, Jerub-Baal[a]
(that is, Gideon[b]) and all his men
camped at the spring of Harod.[c] The
camp of Midian[d] was north of them in
the valley near the hill of Moreh.[e] 2The
LORD said to Gideon, "You have too
many men for me to deliver Midian into
their hands. In order that Israel may not
boast against me that her own strength[f]
has saved her, 3announce now to the
people, 'Anyone who trembles with
fear may turn back and leave Mount
Gilead.[g]'" So twenty-two thousand

19 [m]Jdg 13:15; [n]**Lev 19:36;** [o]Ge 18:7–8
20 [p]Jdg 13:19
21 [q]**Ex 4:2;** [r]**Lev 9:24**
22 [s]Jdg 13:16,21; [t]Ge 32:30; Jdg 13:22
23 [u]Da 10:19; [v]**Ge 16:13; Dt 5:26**
24 [w]**Ge 22:14;** [x]**Jos 18:23**
25 [y]ver 26,28,30; Ex 34:13; **Jdg 2:13**
26 [z]**Ge 8:20**
28 [a]ver 30; 1Ki 16:32; 2Ki 21:3
29 [b]**ver 11**
30 [c]**ver 28**
31 [d]1Sa 24:15; Ps 43:1; Jer 30:13
32 [e]Jdg 7:1; 8:29,35; 9:1; 1Sa 12:11
33 [f]Nu 13:29; [g]**Ge 25:6;** [h]**Jos 15:56;** Eze 25:4; Hos 1:5
34 [i]**Jdg 3:10;** [j]**Jos 6:20; Jdg 3:27;** [k]**Jos 17:2**
35 [l]**Jos 17:7;** [m]**Jdg 4:6;** [n]Jdg 7:23
36 [o]**ver 14**
37 [p]Job 31:20; [q]**Nu 18:27;** 2Sa 6:6; 24:16; [r]**Ge 24:14**
39 [s]Ge 18:32
40 [t]Ex 4:3–7; Isa 38:7

Ch. 7

1 [a]**Jdg 6:32;** [b]**Jdg 6:11;** [c]2Sa 23:25; [d]**Ge 25:2;** [e]**Ge 12:6**
2 [f]**Dt 8:17;** 2Co 4:7
3 [g]Dt 20:8; **Jos 12:2**

b19 That is, probably about 3/5 bushel (about 22 litres)
c25 Or *Take a full-grown, mature bull from your father's herd*
d25 That is, a symbol of the goddess Asherah; here and elsewhere in Judges
e26 Or *build with layers of stone an*
f26 Or *full-grown;* also in verse 28
g32 *Jerub-Baal* means *let Baal contend.*

men left, while ten thousand remained.

4But the LORD said to Gideon, "There are still too many[h] men. Take them down to the water, and I will sift them out for you there. If I say, 'This one shall go with you,' he shall go; but if I say, 'This one shall not go with you,' he shall not go."

5So Gideon took the men down to the water. There the LORD told him, "Separate those who lap the water with their tongues like a dog from those who kneel down to drink." 6Three hundred men[i] lapped with their hands to their mouths. All the rest got down on their knees to drink.

7The LORD said to Gideon, "With the three hundred men that lapped I will save you and give the Midianites into your hands.[j] Let all the other men go, each to his own place."[k] 8So Gideon sent the rest of the Israelites to their tents but kept the three hundred, who took over the provisions and trumpets of the others.

Now the camp of Midian lay below him in the valley. 9During that night the LORD said to Gideon, "Get up, go down against the camp, because I am going to give it into your hands.[l] 10If you are afraid to attack, go down to the camp with your servant Purah 11and listen to what they are saying. Afterwards, you will be encouraged to attack the camp." So he and Purah his servant went down to the outposts of the camp. 12The Midianites, the Amalekites[m] and all the other eastern peoples had settled in the valley, thick as locusts.[n] Their camels[o] could no more be counted than the sand on the seashore.[p]

13Gideon arrived just as a man was telling a friend his dream. "I had a dream," he was saying. "A round loaf of barley bread came tumbling into the Midianite camp. It struck the tent with such force that the tent overturned and collapsed."

14His friend responded, "This can be nothing other than the sword of Gideon son of Joash,[q] the Israelite. God has given the Midianites and the whole camp into his hands."

15When Gideon heard the dream and its interpretation, he worshipped God.[r] He returned to the camp of Israel and called out, "Get up! The LORD has given the Midianite camp into your hands."[s] 16Dividing the three hundred men[t] into three companies,[u] he placed trumpets[v] and empty jars[w] in the hands of all of them, with torches[x] inside.

17"Watch me," he told them. "Follow my lead. When I get to the edge of the camp, do exactly as I do. 18When I and all who are with me blow our trumpets,[y] then from all around the camp blow yours and shout, 'For the LORD and for Gideon.'"

19Gideon and the hundred men with him reached the edge of the camp at the beginning of the middle watch, just after they had changed the guard. They blew their trumpets and broke the jars[z] that were in their hands. 20The three companies blew the trumpets and smashed the jars. Grasping the torches[a] in their left hands and holding in their right hands the trumpets they were to blow, they shouted, "A sword[b] for the LORD and for Gideon!" 21While each man held his position around the camp, all the Midianites ran, crying out as they fled.[c]

22When the three hundred trumpets sounded,[d] the LORD caused the men throughout the camp to turn on each other[e] with their swords.[f] The army fled to Beth Shittah towards Zererah as far as the border of Abel Meholah[g] near Tabbath. 23Israelites from Naphtali, Asher[h] and all Manasseh were called out,[i] and they pursued the Midianites.[j] 24Gideon sent messengers throughout the hill country of Ephraim, saying, "Come down against the Midianites and seize the waters of the Jordan[k] ahead of them as far as Beth Barah."

So all the men of Ephraim were called out and they took the waters of the Jordan as far as Beth Barah. 25They also captured two of the Midianite leaders, Oreb and Zeeb.[l] They killed Oreb at the rock of Oreb,[m] and Zeeb at the winepress of Zeeb. They pursued the Midianites[n] and brought the heads of Oreb and Zeeb to Gideon, who was by the Jordan.[o]

Zebah and Zalmunna

8 Now the Ephraimites asked Gideon,[a] "Why have you treated us like this? Why didn't you call us when you went to fight Midian?[b]"[c] And they criticised him sharply.[d]

2But he answered them, "What have I accomplished compared to you? Aren't the gleanings of Ephraim's grapes better than the full grape harvest of Abiezer?[e] 3God gave Oreb and Zeeb,[f] the Midianite leaders, into your hands. What was I able to do compared to you?" At this, their resentment against him subsided.

4Gideon and his three hundred men,

4 h1Sa 14:6
6 iGe 14:14
7 jJos 8:7; k1Sa 14:6
9 lver 13–15; Jos 2:24; Jdg 1:2
12 mNu 13:29; nDt 28:42; Jer 46:23; oJer 49:29; pJos 11:4
14 qJdg 6:11
15 r1Sa 15:31; sver 9
16 tGe 14:15; uJdg 9:43; 1Sa 11:11; 2Sa 18:2; vLev 25:9; wver 19; Ge 24:14; xGe 15:17
18 yJdg 3:27
19 zver 16
20 aGe 15:17; bDt 32:41
21 c2Ki 7:7
22 dJos 6:20; e1Sa 14:20; 2Ch 20:23; Isa 9:21; 19:2; Eze 38:21; Hag 2:22; Zec 14:13; fHab 3:14; g1Sa 18:19; 1Ki 4:12; 19:16
23 hJos 17:7; iJdg 6:35; jPs 83:9
24 kJos 2:7
25 lJdg 8:3; Ps 83:11; mIsa 10:26; nIsa 9:4; oJdg 8:4; Ps 106:43

Ch. 8

1 aJdg 6:11; bGe 25:2; cJdg 12:1; d2Sa 19:41
2 eNu 26:30
3 fJdg 7:25

exhausted yet keeping up the pursuit,
came to the Jordan[g] and crossed it. 5He
said to the men of Succoth,[h] "Give my
troops some bread; they are worn out,[i]
and I am still pursuing Zebah and
Zalmunna,[j] the kings of Midian."
6But the officials of Succoth[k] said, "Do
you already have the hands of Zebah
and Zalmunna in your possession?
Why should we give bread[l] to your
troops?"[m]
7Then Gideon replied, "Just for that,
when the LORD has given Zebah and
Zalmunna[n] into my hand, I will tear
your flesh with desert thorns and
briers."
8From there he went up to Peniel[a][o]
and made the same request of them, but
they answered as the men of Succoth
had. 9So he said to the men of Peniel,
"When I return in triumph, I will tear
down this tower."[p]
10Now Zebah and Zalmunna were in
Karkor with a force of about fifteen
thousand men, all that were left of the
armies of the eastern peoples; a hun-
dred and twenty thousand swordsmen
had fallen.[q] 11Gideon went up by the
route of the nomads east of Nobah[r] and
Jogbehah[s] and fell upon the unsuspec-
ting army. 12Zebah and Zalmunna, the
two kings of Midian, fled, but he pur-
sued them and captured them, routing
their entire army.
13Gideon son of Joash[t] then returned
from the battle by the Pass of Heres.[u]
14He caught a young man of Succoth
and questioned him, and the young
man wrote down for him the names of
the seventy-seven officials of Succoth,[v]
the elders[w] of the town. 15Then Gideon
came and said to the men of Succoth,
"Here are Zebah and Zalmunna, about
whom you taunted me by saying, 'Do
you already have the hands of Zebah
and Zalmunna in your possession?
Why should we give bread to your ex-
hausted men?[x]'" 16He took the elders of
the town and taught the men of Succoth
a lesson[y] by punishing them with desert
thorns and briers. 17He also pulled
down the tower of Peniel[z] and killed the
men of the town.[a]
18Then he asked Zebah and Zalmun-
na, "What kind of men did you kill at
Tabor?[b]"
"Men like you," they answered,
"each one with the bearing of a prince."
19Gideon replied, "Those were my
brothers, the sons of my own mother.
As surely as the LORD lives,[c] if you had
spared their lives, I would not kill you."
20Turning to Jether, his oldest son, he
said, "Kill them!" But Jether did not
draw his sword, because he was only a
boy and was afraid.
21Zebah and Zalmunna said, "Come,
do it yourself. 'As is the man, so is his
strength.'" So Gideon stepped forward
and killed them, and took the orna-
ments[d] off their camels' necks.

Gideon's Ephod

22The Israelites said to Gideon, "Rule
over us—you, your son and your
grandson—because you have saved us
out of the hand of Midian."
23But Gideon told them, "I will not
rule over you, nor will my son rule over
you. The LORD will rule[e] over you."
24And he said, "I do have one request,
that each of you give me an ear-ring[f]
from your share of the plunder.[g]" (It
was the custom of the Ishmaelites[h] to
wear gold ear-rings.)
25They answered, "We'll be glad to
give them." So they spread out a gar-
ment, and each man threw a ring from
his plunder onto it. 26The weight of the
gold rings he asked for came to seven-
teen hundred shekels,[b] not counting
the ornaments, the pendants and the
purple garments worn by the kings of
Midian or the chains[i] that were on their
camels' necks. 27Gideon made the gold
into an ephod,[j] which he placed in
Ophrah,[k] his town. All Israel prosti-
tuted themselves by worshipping it
there, and it became a snare[l] to Gideon
and his family.[m]

Gideon's Death

28Thus Midian was subdued before
the Israelites and did not raise its head[n]
again. During Gideon's lifetime, the
land enjoyed peace[o] for forty years.
29Jerub-Baal[p] son of Joash[q] went back
home to live. 30He had seventy sons[r] of
his own, for he had many wives. 31His
concubine,[s] who lived in Shechem, also
bore him a son, whom he named
Abimelech.[t] 32Gideon son of Joash died
at a good old age[u] and was buried in the
tomb of his father Joash in Ophrah of
the Abiezrites.
33No sooner had Gideon died than the
Israelites again prostituted themselves
to the Baals.[v] They set up Baal-Berith[w] as
their god[x] and 34did not remember[y] the
LORD their God, who had rescued them

4 [g]Jdg 7:25
5 [h]**Ge 33:17;** [i]Job 16:7; Ps 6:6; Jer 45:3; [j]ver 7,12; Ps 83:11
6 [k]ver 14; [l]1Sa 25:11; [m]ver 15
7 [n]**ver 5**
8 [o]ver 9,17; Ge 32:30; 1Ki 12:25
9 [p]ver 17
10 [q]**Jdg 6:5;** Isa 9:4
11 [r]Nu 32:42; [s]**Nu 32:35**
13 [t]**Jdg 6:11;** [u]Jdg 1:35
14 [v]ver 6; [w]**Ex 3:16**
15 [x]ver 6
16 [y]1Sa 14:12
17 [z]**ver 8;** [a]ver 9
18 [b]**Jos 19:22**
19 [c]**Nu 14:21**
21 [d]ver 26; Isa 3:18
23 [e]**Ex 16:8; Nu 11:20;** 1Sa 12:12
24 [f]**Ge 35:4;** [g]**Ge 49:27;** [h]**Ge 16:11**
26 [i]ver 21
27 [j]Ex 25:7; Jdg 17:5; 18:14; [k]**Jos 18:23;** [l]**Ex 10:7;** [m]**Ex 32:2**
28 [n]Ps 83:2; [o]**Jdg 3:11**
29 [p]**Jdg 6:32;** [q]**Jdg 6:11**
30 [r]Jdg 9:2,5,18, 24; 12:14; 2Ki 10:1
31 [s]**Ge 22:24;** [t]Jdg 9:1; 10:1; 2Sa 11:21
32 [u]**Ge 15:15**
33 [v]**Jdg 2:11,**13, 19; [w]Jdg 9:4; [x]Jdg 9:27,46
34 [y]**Jdg 3:7; Ne 9:17**

[a]8 Hebrew *Penuel*, a variant of *Peniel*; also in verses 9 and 17
[b]26 That is, about 43 pounds (about 19.5 kilograms)

from the hands of all their enemies on every side. 35They also failed to show kindness to the family of Jerub-Baal[z] (that is, Gideon) for all the good things he had done for them.[a]

Abimelech

9 Abimelech[a] son of Jerub-Baal[b] went to his mother's brothers in Shechem and said to them and to all his mother's clan, 2"Ask all the citizens of Shechem, 'Which is better for you: to have all seventy of Jerub-Baal's sons rule over you, or just one man?' Remember, I am your flesh and blood.[c]"

3When the brothers repeated all this to the citizens of Shechem, they were inclined to follow Abimelech, for they said, "He is our brother." 4They gave him seventy shekels**a** of silver from the temple of Baal-Berith,[d] and Abimelech used it to hire reckless adventurers,[e] who became his followers. 5He went to his father's home in Ophrah and on one stone murdered his seventy brothers,[f] the sons of Jerub-Baal. But Jotham,[g] the youngest son of Jerub-Baal, escaped by hiding.[h] 6Then all the citizens of Shechem and Beth Millo[i] gathered beside the great tree[j] at the pillar in Shechem to crown Abimelech king.

7When Jotham[k] was told about this, he climbed up on the top of Mount Gerizim[l] and shouted to them, "Listen to me, citizens of Shechem, so that God may listen to you. 8One day the trees went out to anoint a king for themselves. They said to the olive tree, 'Be our king.'

9"But the olive tree answered, 'Should I give up my oil, by which both gods and men are honoured, to hold sway over the trees?'

10"Next, the trees said to the fig-tree, 'Come and be our king.'

11"But the fig-tree replied, 'Should I give up my fruit, so good and sweet, to hold sway over the trees?'

12"Then the trees said to the vine, 'Come and be our king.'

13"But the vine answered, 'Should I give up my wine,[m] which cheers both gods and men, to hold sway over the trees?'

14"Finally all the trees said to the thornbush, 'Come and be our king.'

15"The thornbush said to the trees, 'If you really want to anoint me king over you, come and take refuge in my shade;[n] but if not, then let fire come out[o] of the thornbush and consume the cedars of Lebanon!'[p]

16"Now if you have acted honourably and in good faith when you made Abimelech king, and if you have been fair to Jerub-Baal and his family, and if you have treated him as he deserves—17and to think that my father fought for you, risked[q] his life to rescue you from the hand of Midian 18(but today you have revolted against my father's family, murdered his seventy sons[r] on a single stone, and made Abimelech, the son of his slave girl, king over the citizens of Shechem because he is your brother)—19if then you have acted honourably and in good faith towards Jerub-Baal and his family today,[s] may Abimelech be your joy, and may you be his, too! 20But if you have not, let fire come out[t] from Abimelech and consume you, citizens of Shechem[u] and Beth Millo,[v] and let fire come out from you, citizens of Shechem and Beth Millo, and consume Abimelech!"

21Then Jotham[w] fled, escaping to Beer,[x] and he lived there because he was afraid of his brother Abimelech.

22After Abimelech had governed Israel for three years, 23God sent an evil spirit[y] between Abimelech and the citizens of Shechem, who acted treacherously against Abimelech. 24God did this in order that the crime against Jerub-Baal's seventy sons,[z] the shedding[a] of their blood, might be avenged[b] on their brother Abimelech and on the citizens of Shechem, who had helped him[c] murder his brothers. 25In opposition to him these citizens of Shechem set men on the hilltops to ambush and rob everyone who passed by, and this was reported to Abimelech.

26Now Gaal son of Ebed[d] moved with his brothers into Shechem, and its citizens put their confidence in him. 27After they had gone out into the fields and gathered the grapes and trodden[e] them, they held a festival in the temple of their god.[f] While they were eating and drinking, they cursed Abimelech. 28Then Gaal son of Ebed[g] said, "Who[h] is Abimelech, and who is Shechem, that we should be subject to him? Isn't he Jerub-Baal's son, and isn't Zebul his deputy? Serve the men of Hamor,[i] Shechem's father! Why should we serve Abimelech? 29If only this people were under my command![j] Then I would get rid of him. I would say to Abimelech, 'Call out your whole army!' "**b**[k]

35 [z]**Jdg 6:32;** [a]Jdg 9:16
Ch. 9
1 [a]**Jdg 8:31;** [b]**Jdg 6:32**
2 [c]**Ge 29:14**
4 [d]**Jdg 8:33;** [e]Jdg 11:3; 1Sa 25:25; 2Ch 13:7; Job 30:8
5 [f]**Jdg 8:30;** [g]ver 7,21,57; [h]2Ki 11:2; 2Ch 22:9
6 [i]ver 20; 2Ki 12:20; [j]**Ge 12:6; Jdg 4:11**
7 [k]**ver 5;** [l]**Dt 11:29;** Jn 4:20
13 [m]**Ge 14:18;** Ecc 2:3; SS 4:10
15 [n]Isa 30:2; [o]ver 20; [p]**Dt 3:25;** 1Ki 5:6; Ps 29:5; 92:12; Isa 2:13
17 [q]Jdg 12:3; 1Sa 19:5; 28:21; Job 13:14; Ps 119:109
18 [r]**Jdg 8:30**
19 [s]ver 16
20 [t]ver 15; [u]ver 45; [v]**ver 6**
21 [w]ver 5; [x]Nu 21:16
23 [y]1Sa 16:14,23; 18:10; 19:9; 1Ki 22:22
24 [z]**Jdg 8:30;** [a]**Ge 9:6;** Nu 35:33; 1Ki 2:32; [b]ver 56–57; [c]Dt 27:25
26 [d]ver 28,31,41
27 [e]Isa 16:10; Am 5:11; 9:13; [f]**Jdg 8:33**
28 [g]**ver 26;** [h]1Sa 25:10; [i]**Ge 33:19**
29 [j]2Sa 15:4; [k]ver 38

a4 That is, about 1¾ pounds (about 0.8 kilogram)
b29 Septuagint; Hebrew *him." Then he said to Abimelech, "Call out your whole army!"*

30When Zebul the governor of the city
heard what Gaal son of Ebed said, he
was very angry. 31Under cover he sent
messengers to Abimelech, saying,
"Gaal son of Ebed and his brothers have
come to Shechem and are stirring up the
city against you. 32Now then, during the
night you and your men should come
and lie in wait[l] in the fields. 33In the
morning at sunrise, advance against the
city. When Gaal and his men come out
against you, do whatever your hand
finds to do.[m]"
34So Abimelech and all his troops set
out by night and took up concealed
positions near Shechem in four com-
panies. 35Now Gaal son of Ebed had
gone out and was standing at the en-
trance to the city gate[n] just as Abimelech
and his soldiers came out from their
hiding-place.[o]
36When Gaal saw them, he said to
Zebul, "Look, people are coming down
from the tops of the mountains!"
Zebul replied, "You mistake the
shadows of the mountains for men."
37But Gaal spoke up again: "Look,
people are coming down from the
centre of the land, and a company is
coming from the direction of the sooth-
sayers' tree."
38Then Zebul said to him, "Where is
your big talk now, you who said, 'Who
is Abimelech that we should be subject
to him?' Aren't these the men you ridi-
culed?[p] Go out and fight them!"
39So Gaal led out[c] the citizens of
Shechem and fought Abimelech.
40Abimelech chased him, and many fell
wounded in the flight—all the way to
the entrance to the gate. 41Abimelech
stayed in Arumah, and Zebul drove
Gaal and his brothers out of Shechem.
42The next day the people of Shechem
went out to the fields, and this was
reported to Abimelech. 43So he took his
men, divided them into three com-
panies[q] and set an ambush[r] in the fields.
When he saw the people coming out
of the city, he rose to attack them.
44Abimelech and the companies with
him rushed forward to a position at the
entrance to the city gate. Then two com-
panies rushed upon those in the fields
and struck them down. 45All that day
Abimelech pressed his attack against
the city until he had captured it and
killed its people. Then he destroyed the
city[s] and scattered salt[t] over it.
46On hearing this, the citizens in
the tower of Shechem went into the
stronghold of the temple[u] of El-Berith.
47When Abimelech heard that they had
assembled there, 48he and all his men
went up Mount Zalmon.[v] He took an
axe and cut off some branches, which he
lifted to his shoulders. He ordered the
men with him, "Quick! Do what you
have seen me do!" 49So all the men
cut branches and followed Abimelech.
They piled them against the strong-
hold and set it on fire over the people
inside. So all the people in the tower of
Shechem, about a thousand men and
women, also died.
50Next Abimelech went to Thebez[w]
and besieged it and captured it. 51Inside
the city, however, was a strong tower,
to which all the men and women—all
the people of the city—fled. They
locked themselves in and climbed up
on the tower roof. 52Abimelech went
to the tower and stormed it. But as
he approached the entrance to the
tower to set it on fire, 53a woman
dropped an upper millstone on his head
and cracked his skull.[x]
54Hurriedly he called to his armour-
bearer, "Draw your sword and kill me,[y]
so that they can't say, 'A woman killed
him.'" So his servant ran him through,
and he died. 55When the Israelites saw
that Abimelech was dead, they went
home.
56Thus God repaid the wickedness
that Abimelech had done to his father
by murdering his seventy brothers.
57God also made the men of Shechem
pay for all their wickedness.[z] The curse
of Jotham[a] son of Jerub-Baal came on
them.

Tola

10 After the time of Abimelech[a] a
man of Issachar,[b] Tola son of
Puah,[c] the son of Dodo, rose to save[d]
Israel. He lived in Shamir,[e] in the hill
country of Ephraim. 2He led[a] Israel for
twenty-three years; then he died, and
was buried in Shamir.

Jair

3He was followed by Jair[f] of Gilead,
who led Israel for twenty-two years.
4He had thirty sons, who rode thirty
donkeys.[g] They controlled thirty towns
in Gilead, which to this day are called
Havvoth Jair.[b][h] 5When Jair[i] died, he was
buried in Kamon.

32 [l]Jos 8:2
33 [m]1Sa 10:7
35 [n]**Jos 2:5**; [o]Ps 32:7; Isa 28:15,17; Jer 49:10
38 [p]ver 28–29
43 [q]**Jdg 7:16**; [r]Jos 8:2
45 [s]ver 20; [t]Jer 48:9
46 [u]**Jdg 8:33**
48 [v]Ps 68:14
50 [w]2Sa 11:21
53 [x]2Sa 11:21
54 [y]1Sa 31:4; 2Sa 1:9
57 [z]ver 24; Ps 94:23; [a]**ver 5**

Ch. 10

1 [a]**Jdg 8:31**; [b]**Ge 30:18**; [c]**Ge 46:13**; [d]**Jdg 6:14**; [e]Jos 15:48
3 [f]**Nu 32:41**
4 [g]**Ge 49:11; 1Ki 1:33**; [h]**Nu 32:41**
5 [i]**Nu 32:41**

[c]39 Or *Gaal went out in the sight of*
[a]2 Traditionally *judged;* also in verse 3
[b]4 Or *called the settlements of Jair*

Jephthah

6Again the Israelites did evil in the eyes of the LORD.[j] They served the Baals and the Ashtoreths,[k] and the gods of Aram,[l] the gods of Sidon,[m] the gods of Moab, the gods of the Ammonites[n,o] and the gods of the Philistines.[p] And because the Israelites forsook the LORD[q] and no longer served him, 7he became angry[r] with them. He sold them[s] into the hands of the Philistines and the Ammonites, 8who that year shattered and crushed them. For eighteen years they oppressed all the Israelites on the east side of the Jordan in Gilead,[t] the land of the Amorites. 9The Ammonites also crossed the Jordan to fight against Judah,[u] Benjamin and the house of Ephraim;[v] and Israel was in great distress. 10Then the Israelites cried[w] out to the LORD, "We have sinned[x] against you, forsaking our God and serving the Baals."[y]

11The LORD replied, "When the Egyptians,[z] the Amorites,[a] the Ammonites,[b] the Philistines,[c] 12the Sidonians, the Amalekites[d] and the Maonites[c,e] oppressed you[f] and you cried to me for help, did I not save you from their hands? 13But you have forsaken[g] me and served other gods,[h] so I will no longer save you. 14Go and cry out to the gods you have chosen. Let them save[i] you when you are in trouble![j]"

15But the Israelites said to the LORD, "We have sinned. Do with us whatever you think best,[k] but please rescue us now." 16Then they got rid of the foreign gods among them and served the LORD.[l] And he could bear Israel's misery[m] no longer.[n]

17When the Ammonites were called to arms and camped in Gilead, the Israelites assembled and camped at Mizpah.[o] 18The leaders of the people of Gilead said to each other, "Whoever will launch the attack against the Ammonites will be the head[p] of all those living in Gilead."

11 Jephthah[a] the Gileadite was a mighty warrior.[b] His father was Gilead;[c] his mother was a prostitute.[d] 2Gilead's wife also bore him sons, and when they were grown up, they drove Jephthah away. "You are not going to get any inheritance in our family," they said, "because you are the son of another woman." 3So Jephthah fled from his brothers and settled in the land of Tob,[e] where a group of adventurers[f] gathered around him and followed him.

4Some time later, when the Ammonites[g] made war on Israel, 5the elders of Gilead went to get Jephthah from the land of Tob. 6"Come," they said, "be our commander, so we can fight the Ammonites."

7Jephthah said to them, "Didn't you hate me and drive me from my father's house?[h] Why do you come to me now, when you're in trouble?"

8The elders of Gilead said to him, "Nevertheless, we are turning to you now; come with us to fight the Ammonites, and you will be our head[i] over all who live in Gilead."

9Jephthah answered, "Suppose you take me back to fight the Ammonites and the LORD gives them to me—will I really be your head?"

10The elders of Gilead replied, "The LORD is our witness;[j] we will certainly do as you say." 11So Jephthah went with the elders[k] of Gilead, and the people made him head and commander over them. And he repeated[l] all his words before the LORD in Mizpah.[m]

12Then Jephthah sent messengers to the Ammonite king with the question: "What do you have against us that you have attacked our country?"

13The king of the Ammonites answered Jephthah's messengers, "When Israel came up out of Egypt, they took away my land from the Arnon[n] to the Jabbok,[o] all the way to the Jordan. Now give it back peaceably."

14Jephthah sent back messengers to the Ammonite king, 15saying:

"This is what Jephthah says: Israel did not take the land of Moab[p] or the land of the Ammonites.[q] 16But when they came up out of Egypt, Israel went through the desert to the Red Sea[a,r] and on to Kadesh.[s] 17Then Israel sent messengers[t] to the king of Edom, saying, 'Give us permission to go through your country,'[u] but the king of Edom would not listen. They sent also to the king of Moab,[v] and he refused.[w] So Israel stayed at Kadesh.

18"Next they travelled through the desert, skirted the lands of Edom[x] and Moab, passed along the eastern side[y] of the country of Moab, and camped on the other side of the Arnon.[z] They did not

6 [j]Jdg 2:11; [k]Jdg 2:13; [l]Eze 27:16; [m]Ge 10:15; [n]Ge 19:38; [o]Nu 21:29; [p]Ge 26:1; Jdg 2:12; [q]Dt 32:15
7 [r]Dt 31:17; [s]Dt 32:30
8 [t]Jos 12:2
9 [u]ver 17; Jdg 11:4; [v]Jdg 1:22
10 [w]Jdg 3:9; [x]Ex 9:27; Ps 32:5; Jer 3:25; 8:14; 14:20; [y]Jer 2:27
11 [z]Ex 14:30; [a]Ge 14:7; [b]Jdg 3:13; [c]Jdg 3:31
12 [d]Ge 14:7; [e]Jos 15:55; [f]Jdg 4:3
13 [g]Dt 32:15; [h]Jer 11:10; 13:10
14 [i]Isa 44:17; 57:13; [j]Dt 32:37; Jer 2:28; 11:12; Hab 2:18
15 [k]1Sa 3:18; 2Sa 10:12; 15:26; Job 1:21; Isa 39:8
16 [l]Jos 24:23; Jer 18:8; [m]Isa 63:9; [n]Dt 32:36
17 [o]Ge 31:49; Jdg 11:29
18 [p]Jdg 11:8–9

Ch. 11

1 [a]Jdg 12:1; 1Sa 12:11; Heb 11:32; [b]Jdg 6:12; [c]Nu 26:29; [d]Ge 38:15
3 [e]ver 5; 2Sa 10:6,8; [f]Jdg 9:4
4 [g]Jdg 10:9
7 [h]Ge 26:16
8 [i]Jdg 10:18
10 [j]Ge 31:50; Isa 1:2
11 [k]1Sa 8:4; 2Sa 3:17; [l]Ex 19:9; 1Sa 8:21; [m]Jos 11:3
13 [n]Nu 21:13; [o]Nu 21:24
15 [p]Dt 2:9; [q]Dt 2:19
16 [r]Nu 14:25; Dt 1:40; [s]Ge 14:7
17 [t]ver 19; Ge 32:3; Nu 20:14; [u]Nu 20:17; [v]Jer 48:1; [w]Jos 24:9
18 [x]Nu 20:21; [y]Dt 2:8; [z]Nu 21:13

[c]12 Hebrew; some Septuagint manuscripts *Midianites*
[a]16 Hebrew *Yam Suph*; that is, Sea of Reeds

enter the territory of Moab, for the Arnon was its border.

19“Then Israel sent messengers[a] to Sihon king of the Amorites, who ruled in Heshbon,[b] and said to him, ‘Let us pass through your country to our own place.’[c] 20Sihon, however, did not trust Israel[b] to pass through his territory. He mustered all his men and encamped at Jahaz and fought with Israel.[d]

21“Then the LORD, the God of Israel, gave Sihon and all his men into Israel’s hands, and they defeated them. Israel took over all the land of the Amorites who lived in that country, 22capturing all of it from the Arnon to the Jabbok and from the desert to the Jordan.[e]

23“Now since the LORD, the God of Israel, has driven the Amorites out before his people Israel, what right have you to take it over? 24Will you not take what your god Chemosh[f] gives you? Likewise, whatever the LORD our God has given us,[g] we will possess. 25Are you better than Balak son of Zippor,[h] king of Moab? Did he ever quarrel with Israel or fight with them?[i] 26For three hundred years Israel occupied[j] Heshbon, Aroer,[k] the surrounding settlements and all the towns along the Arnon. Why didn’t you retake them during that time? 27I have not wronged you, but you are doing me wrong by waging war against me. Let the LORD, the Judge,[c][l] decide[m] the dispute this day between the Israelites and the Ammonites.[n]”

28The king of Ammon, however, paid no attention to the message Jephthah sent him.

29Then the Spirit[o] of the LORD came upon Jephthah. He crossed Gilead and Manasseh, passed through Mizpah[p] of Gilead, and from there he advanced against the Ammonites.[q] 30And Jephthah made a vow[r] to the LORD: “If you give the Ammonites into my hands, 31whatever comes out of the door of my house to meet me when I return in triumph[s] from the Ammonites will be the LORD’s, and I will sacrifice it as a burnt offering.[t]”

32Then Jephthah went over to fight the Ammonites, and the LORD gave them into his hands. 33He devastated twenty towns from Aroer to the vicinity of Minnith,[u] as far as Abel Keramim. Thus Israel subdued Ammon.

34When Jephthah returned to his home in Mizpah, who should come out to meet him but his daughter, dancing[v] to the sound of tambourines![w] She was an only child.[x] Except for her he had neither son nor daughter. 35When he saw her, he tore his clothes[y] and cried, “Oh! My daughter! You have made me miserable and wretched, because I have made a vow to the LORD that I cannot break.[z]”

36“My father,” she replied, “you have given your word to the LORD. Do to me just as you promised,[a] now that the LORD has avenged you[b] of your enemies,[c] the Ammonites. 37But grant me this one request,” she said. “Give me two months to roam the hills and weep with my friends, because I will never marry.”

38“You may go,” he said. And he let her go for two months. She and the girls went into the hills and wept because she would never marry. 39After the two months, she returned to her father and he did to her as he had vowed. And she was a virgin.

From this comes the Israelite custom 40that each year the young women of Israel go out for four days to commemorate the daughter of Jephthah the Gileadite.

Jephthah and Ephraim

12 The men of Ephraim called out their forces, crossed over to Zaphon[a] and said to Jephthah,[b] “Why did you go to fight the Ammonites without calling us to go with you?[c] We’re going to burn down your house over your head.”

2Jephthah answered, “I and my people were engaged in a great struggle with the Ammonites, and although I called, you didn’t save me out of their hands. 3When I saw that you wouldn’t help, I took my life in my hands[d] and crossed over to fight the Ammonites, and the LORD gave me the victory[e] over them. Now why have you come up today to fight me?”

4Jephthah then called together the men of Gilead[f] and fought against Ephraim. The Gileadites struck them down because the Ephraimites had said, “You Gileadites are renegades from Ephraim and Manasseh.[g]” 5The Gileadites captured the fords of the Jordan[h] leading to Ephraim, and whenever

19 [a]ver 17; [b]Jos 12:2; [c]Nu 21:21–22
20 [d]Nu 21:23
22 [e]Nu 21:21–26; Dt 2:26
24 [f]Nu 21:29; Jos 3:10; [g]Dt 2:36
25 [h]Nu 22:2; [i]Jos 24:9
26 [j]Nu 21:25; [k]Nu 32:34; Jos 13:9
27 [l]Ge 18:25; [m]Ge 16:5; [n]2Ch 20:12
29 [o]Jdg 3:10; [p]Ge 31:49; [q]Jdg 10:17
30 [r]Ge 28:20; Nu 30:10; 1Sa 1:11; Pr 31:2
31 [s]Ge 28:21; [t]Ge 8:20; Lev 1:3; Jdg 13:16
33 [u]Eze 27:17
34 [v]Ex 15:20; [w]Ge 31:27; Ex 15:20; [x]Zec 12:10
35 [y]Nu 14:6; [z]Nu 30:2; Dt 23:21; Ecc 5:2,4–5
36 [a]Lk 1:38; [b]Nu 31:3; [c]2Sa 18:19

Ch. 12

1 [a]Jos 13:27; [b]Jdg 11:1; [c]Jdg 8:1
3 [d]Jdg 9:17; [e]Dt 20:4
4 [f]1Ki 17:1; [g]Ge 46:20; Isa 9:21; 19:2
5 [h]Jos 2:7

[b]20 *Or however, would not make an agreement for Israel*
[c]27 *Or Ruler*

a survivor of Ephraim said, "Let me cross over," the men of Gilead asked him, "Are you an Ephraimite?" If he replied, "No," 6they said, "All right, say 'Shibboleth'." If he said, "Sibboleth", because he could not pronounce the word correctly, they seized him and killed him at the fords of the Jordan. Forty-two thousand Ephraimites were killed at that time.

7Jephthah led[a] Israel for six years. Then Jephthah the Gileadite died, and was buried in a town in Gilead.

Ibzan, Elon and Abdon

8After him, Ibzan of Bethlehem[i] led Israel. 9He had thirty sons and thirty daughters. He gave his daughters away in marriage to those outside his clan, and for his sons he brought in thirty young women as wives from outside his clan. Ibzan led Israel for seven years. 10Then Ibzan died, and was buried in Bethlehem.

11After him, Elon the Zebulunite led Israel for ten years. 12Then Elon died, and was buried in Aijalon[j] in the land of Zebulun.

13After him, Abdon son of Hillel, from Pirathon,[k] led Israel. 14He had forty sons and thirty grandsons,[l] who rode on seventy donkeys.[m] He led Israel for eight years. 15Then Abdon son of Hillel died, and was buried at Pirathon in Ephraim, in the hill country of the Amalekites.[n]

The Birth of Samson

13 Again the Israelites did evil in the eyes of the LORD, so the LORD delivered them into the hands of the Philistines[a] for forty years.[b]

2A certain man of Zorah,[c] named Manoah,[d] from the clan of the Danites,[e] had a wife who was sterile and remained childless.[f] 3The angel of the LORD[g] appeared to her[h] and said, "You are sterile and childless, but you are going to conceive and have a son.[i] 4Now see to it that you drink no wine or other fermented drink[j] and that you do not eat anything unclean,[k] 5because you will conceive and give birth to a son.[l] No razor[m] may be used on his head, because the boy is to be a Nazirite,[n] set apart to God from birth, and he will begin[o] the deliverance of Israel from the hands of the Philistines."

6Then the woman went to her husband and told him, "A man of God[p] came to me. He looked like an angel of God,[q] very awesome.[r] I didn't ask him where he came from, and he didn't tell me his name. 7But he said to me, 'You will conceive and give birth to a son. Now then, drink no wine[s] or other fermented drink[t] and do not eat anything unclean, because the boy will be a Nazirite of God from birth until the day of his death.[u]' "

8Then Manoah[v] prayed to the LORD: "O Lord, I beg you, let the man of God[w] you sent to us come again to teach us how to bring up the boy who is to be born."

9God heard Manoah, and the angel of God came again to the woman while she was out in the field; but her husband Manoah was not with her. 10The woman hurried to tell her husband, "He's here! The man who appeared to me[x] the other day!"

11Manoah got up and followed his wife. When he came to the man, he said, "Are you the one who talked to my wife?"

"I am," he said.

12So Manoah asked him, "When your words are fulfilled, what is to be the rule for the boy's life and work?"

13The angel of the LORD answered, "Your wife must do all that I have told her. 14She must not eat anything that comes from the grapevine, nor drink any wine or other fermented drink[y] nor eat anything unclean.[z] She must do everything I have commanded her."

15Manoah said to the angel of the LORD, "We would like you to stay until we prepare a young goat[a] for you."

16The angel of the LORD replied, "Even though you detain me, I will not eat any of your food. But if you prepare a burnt offering,[b] offer it to the LORD." (Manoah did not realise[c] that it was the angel of the LORD.)

17Then Manoah enquired of the angel of the LORD, "What is your name,[d] so that we may honour you when your word comes true?"

18He replied, "Why do you ask my name?[e] It is beyond understanding."[a] 19Then Manoah took a young goat, together with the grain offering, and sacrificed it on a rock[f] to the LORD. And the LORD did an amazing thing while Manoah and his wife watched: 20As the flame[g] blazed up from the altar towards heaven, the angel of the LORD ascended in the flame. Seeing this, Manoah and

8 [i]**Ge 35:19**
12 [j]**Jos 10:12**
13 [k]ver 15; 2Sa 23:30; 1Ch 11:31; 27:14
14 [l]**Jdg 8:30;** [m]**Jdg 5:10**
15 [n]Jdg 5:14

Ch. 13

1 [a]**Jdg 3:31;** [b]Jdg 14:4
2 [c]**Jos 15:33;** [d]ver 8; Jdg 16:31; [e]**Ge 30:6;** [f]**Ge 11:30**
3 [g]**Ge 16:7;** [h]ver 10; [i]Isa 7:14; Lk 1:13
4 [j]**Lev 10:9;** [k]ver 14; Nu 6:2–4; **Lk 1:15**
5 [l]**Ge 3:15;** [m]1Sa 1:11; [n]**Nu 6:2**,13; Am 2:11–12; [o]1Sa 7:13
6 [p]ver 8; 1Sa 2:27; 9:6; 1Ki 13:1; 17:18; [q]**Nu 22:22;** [r]Ps 66:5
7 [s]Jer 35:6; [t]Lev 10:9; [u]1Sa 1:11,28
8 [v]**ver 2;** [w]**ver 6**
10 [x]ver 3
14 [y]Lev 10:9; [z]**ver 4**
15 [a]Jdg 6:19
16 [b]**Jdg 11:31;** [c]**Jdg 6:22**
17 [d]**Ge 32:29**
18 [e]**Ge 32:29**
19 [f]Jdg 6:20
20 [g]**Lev 9:24**

[a]*7* Traditionally *judged;* also in verses 8–14
[a]*18* Or *is wonderful*

his wife fell with their faces to the
ground.[h] 21When the angel of the LORD
did not show himself again to Manoah
and his wife, Manoah realised[i] that it
was the angel of the LORD.
22"We are doomed[j] to die!" he said to
his wife. "We have seen[k] God!"
23But his wife answered, "If the LORD
had meant to kill us, he would not have
accepted a burnt offering and grain
offering from our hands, nor shown us
all these things or now told us this."[l]
24The woman gave birth to a boy and
named him Samson.[m] He grew[n] and the
LORD blessed him,[o] 25and the Spirit of
the LORD began to stir[p] him while he was
in Mahaneh Dan,[q] between Zorah and
Eshtaol.

Samson's Marriage

14 Samson[a] went down to Tim-
nah[b] and saw there a young
Philistine woman. 2When he returned,
he said to his father and mother, "I have
seen a Philistine woman in Timnah;
now get her for me as my wife."[c]
3His father and mother replied, "Isn't
there an acceptable woman among your
relatives or among all our people?[d] Must
you go to the uncircumcised[e] Philistines
to get a wife?[f]"
But Samson said to his father, "Get
her for me. She's the right one for me."
4(His parents did not know that this was
from the LORD,[g] who was seeking an
occasion to confront the Philistines;[h] for
at that time they were ruling over
Israel.)[i] 5Samson went down to Timnah
together with his father and mother. As
they approached the vineyards of Tim-
nah, suddenly a young lion came roar-
ing towards him. 6The Spirit of the LORD
came upon him in power[j] so that he tore
the lion apart[k] with his bare hands as he
might have torn a young goat. But he
told neither his father nor his mother
what he had done. 7Then he went down
and talked with the woman, and he
liked her.
8Some time later, when he went back
to marry her, he turned aside to look at
the lion's carcass. In it was a swarm of
bees and some honey, 9which he
scooped out with his hands and ate as
he went along. When he rejoined his
parents, he gave them some, and they
too ate it. But he did not tell them that he
had taken the honey from the lion's
carcass.
10Now his father went down to see
the woman. And Samson made a feast[l]
there, as was customary for bride-
grooms. 11When he appeared, he was
given thirty companions.
12"Let me tell you a riddle,[m]" Samson
said to them. "If you can give me the
answer within the seven days of the
feast,[n] I will give you thirty linen gar-
ments and thirty sets of clothes.[o] 13If you
can't tell me the answer, you must give
me thirty linen garments and thirty sets
of clothes."
"Tell us your riddle," they said.
"Let's hear it."
14He replied,

"Out of the eater, something to eat;
out of the strong, something
sweet."[p]

For three days they could not give the
answer.
15On the fourth[a] day, they said to
Samson's wife, "Coax[q] your husband
into explaining the riddle for us, or we
will burn you and your father's house-
hold to death.[r] Did you invite us here to
rob us?"
16Then Samson's wife threw herself
on him, sobbing, "You hate me! You
don't really love me.[s] You've given my
people a riddle, but you haven't told me
the answer."
"I haven't even explained it to my
father or mother," he replied, "so why
should I explain it to you?" 17She cried
the whole seven days[t] of the feast. So on
the seventh day he finally told her,
because she continued to press him.
She in turn explained the riddle to her
people.
18Before sunset on the seventh day
the men of the town said to him,

"What is sweeter than honey?
What is stronger than a lion?"[u]

Samson said to them,

"If you had not ploughed with my
heifer,
you would not have solved my
riddle."

19Then the Spirit of the LORD came
upon him in power.[v] He went down to
Ashkelon,[w] struck down thirty of their
men, stripped them of their belongings
and gave their clothes to those who had
explained the riddle. Burning with

20 [h]**Ge 17:3**
21 [i]**Jdg 6:22**
22 [j]**Nu 17:12; Dt 5:26;** [k]**Ge 16:13; Ex 3:6; 24:10; Jdg 6:22**
23 [l]Ps 25:14
24 [m]Jdg 14:1; 15:1; 16:1; Heb 11:32; [n]1Sa 2:21,26; 3:19; [o]Lk 1:80
25 [p]**Jdg 3:10;** [q]Jdg 18:12

Ch. 14

1 [a]**Jdg 13:24;** [b]**Ge 38:12**
2 [c]**Ge 21:21**
3 [d]**Ge 24:4;** [e]**Ge 34:14; 1Sa 14:6;** [f]**Ex 34:16**
4 [g]**Dt 2:30;** [h]**Jos 11:20;** [i]Jdg 13:1; 15:11
6 [j]Jdg 3:10; [k]1Sa 17:35
10 [l]Ge 29:22
12 [m]Nu 12:8; Eze 17:2; 20:49; 24:3; Hos 12:10; [n]Ge 29:27; [o]**Ge 45:22; 2Ki 5:5**
14 [p]ver 18
15 [q]Jdg 16:5; Ecc 7:26; [r]**Lev 20:14;** Jdg 15:6
16 [s]Jdg 16:15
17 [t]Est 1:5
18 [u]ver 14
19 [v]**Jdg 3:10;** [w]**Jos 13:3**

[a]*15* Some Septuagint manuscripts and Syriac; Hebrew *seventh*

anger,[x] he went up to his father's house.
20And Samson's wife was given to the
friend[y] who had attended him at his
wedding.

Samson's Vengeance on the Philistines

15 Later on, at the time of wheat
harvest,[a] Samson[b] took a young
goat[c] and went to visit his wife. He said,
"I'm going to my wife's room."[d] But her
father would not let him go in.
2"I was so sure you thoroughly hated
her," he said, "that I gave her to your
friend.[e] Isn't her younger sister more
attractive? Take her instead."
3Samson said to them, "This time I
have a right to get even with the Philis-
tines; I will really harm them." 4So he
went out and caught three hundred
foxes[f] and tied them tail to tail in pairs.
He then fastened a torch[g] to every pair
of tails, 5lit the torches[h] and let the
foxes loose in the standing corn of the
Philistines. He burned up the shocks[i]
and standing corn, together with the
vineyards and olive groves.
6When the Philistines asked, "Who
did this?" they were told, "Samson, the
Timnite's son-in-law, because his wife
was given to his friend.[j]"
So the Philistines went up and
burned her[k] and her father to death.[l]
7Samson said to them, "Since you've
acted like this, I won't stop until I get my
revenge on you." 8He attacked them
viciously and slaughtered many of
them. Then he went down and stayed
in a cave in the rock[m] of Etam.[n]
9The Philistines went up and camped
in Judah, spreading out near Lehi.[o]
10The men of Judah asked, "Why have
you come to fight us?"
"We have come to take Samson pris-
oner," they answered, "to do to him as
he did to us."
11Then three thousand men from
Judah went down to the cave in the rock
of Etam and said to Samson, "Don't you
realise that the Philistines are rulers
over us?[p] What have you done to us?"
He answered, "I merely did to them
what they did to me."
12They said to him, "We've come to
tie you up and hand you over to the
Philistines."
Samson said, "Swear to me[q] that you
won't kill me yourselves."
13"Agreed," they answered. "We will
only tie you up and hand you over to
them. We will not kill you." So they
bound him with two new ropes[r] and
led him up from the rock. 14As he
approached Lehi,[s] the Philistines came
towards him shouting. The Spirit of the
LORD came upon him in power.[t] The
ropes on his arms became like charred
flax,[u] and the bindings dropped from
his hands. 15Finding a fresh jaw-bone of
a donkey, he grabbed it and struck
down a thousand men.[v]
16Then Samson said,

"With a donkey's jaw-bone
I have made donkeys of them.[a][w]
With a donkey's jaw-bone
I have killed a thousand men."

17When he finished speaking, he threw
away the jaw-bone; and the place was
called Ramath Lehi.[b][x]
18Because he was very thirsty, he
cried out to the LORD,[y] "You have given
your servant this great victory.[z] Must I
now die of thirst and fall into the hands
of the uncircumcised?" 19Then God
opened up the hollow place in Lehi, and
water came out of it. When Samson
drank, his strength returned and he re-
vived.[a] So the spring[b] was called En
Hakkore,[c] and it is still there in Lehi.
20Samson led[d] Israel for twenty years[c]
in the days of the Philistines.

Samson and Delilah

16 One day Samson[a] went to
Gaza,[b] where he saw a prosti-
tute.[c] He went in to spend the night
with her. 2The people of Gaza were told,
"Samson is here!" So they surrounded
the place and lay in wait for him all night
at the city gate.[d] They made no move
during the night, saying, "At dawn[e]
we'll kill him."
3But Samson lay there only until the
middle of the night. Then he got up and
took hold of the doors of the city gate,
together with the two posts, and tore
them loose, bar and all. He lifted them
to his shoulders and carried them to the
top of the hill that faces Hebron.[f]
4Some time later, he fell in love[g] with a
woman in the Valley of Sorek whose
name was Delilah.[h] 5The rulers of the
Philistines[i] went to her and said, "See if
you can lure[j] him into showing you the
secret of his great strength[k] and how we
can overpower him so that we may tie
him up and subdue him. Each one of us

19 [x]1Sa 11:6
20 [y]Jdg 15:2,6; Jn 3:29

Ch. 15

1 [a]**Ge 30:14;** [b]**Jdg 13:24;** [c]**Ge 38:17;** [d]Ge 29:21
2 [e]**Jdg 14:20**
4 [f]SS 2:15; [g]**Ge 15:17**
5 [h]Ge 15:17; [i]Ex 22:6; 2Sa 14:30–31
6 [j]**Jdg 14:20;** [k]**Ge 38:24;** [l]**Jdg 14:15**
8 [m]Isa 2:21; [n]ver 11
9 [o]ver 14,17,19
11 [p]**Jdg 14:4;** Ps 106:40–42
12 [q]**Ge 47:31**
13 [r]Jdg 16:11–12
14 [s]**ver 9;** [t]**Jdg 3:10;** [u]**Jos 2:6**
15 [v]**Lev 26:8**
16 [w]Jer 22:19
17 [x]**ver 9**
18 [y]Jdg 16:28; [z]**Dt 20:4**
19 [a]Ge 45:27; 1Sa 30:12; Isa 40:29; [b]**Ex 17:6**
20 [c]Jdg 16:31

Ch. 16

1 [a]**Jdg 13:24;** [b]Ge 10:19; [c]**Ge 38:15**
2 [d]**Jos 2:5;** [e]1Sa 19:11
3 [f]**Jos 10:36**
4 [g]**Ge 24:67; 34:3;** [h]ver 6
5 [i]**Jos 13:3;** [j]**Ex 10:7; Jdg 14:15;** [k]ver 6, 15

[a]16 Or *made a heap or two*; the Hebrew for *donkey* sounds like the Hebrew for *heap*.
[b]17 *Ramath Lehi* means *jaw-bone hill*.
[c]19 *En Hakkore* means *caller's spring*.
[d]20 Traditionally *judged*

will give you eleven hundred shekels[a] of silver."[l]

6So Delilah[m] said to Samson, "Tell me the secret of your great strength and how you can be tied up and subdued."

7Samson answered her, "If anyone ties me with seven fresh thongs[b] that have not been dried, I'll become as weak as any other man."

8Then the rulers of the Philistines brought her seven fresh thongs that had not been dried, and she tied him with them. 9With men hidden in the room,[n] she called to him, "Samson, the Philistines are upon you!"[o] But he snapped the thongs as easily as a piece of string snaps when it comes close to a flame. So the secret of his strength was not discovered.

10Then Delilah said to Samson, "You have made a fool of me;[p] you lied to me. Come now, tell me how you can be tied."

11He said, "If anyone ties me securely with new ropes[q] that have never been used, I'll become as weak as any other man."

12So Delilah took new ropes and tied him with them. Then, with men hidden in the room, she called to him, "Samson, the Philistines are upon you!"[r] But he snapped the ropes off his arms as if they were threads.

13Delilah then said to Samson, "Until now, you have been making a fool of me and lying to me. Tell me how you can be tied."

He replied, "If you weave the seven braids of my head into the fabric ⌞on the loom⌟ and tighten it with the pin, I'll become as weak as any other man." So while he was sleeping, Delilah took the seven braids of his head, wove them into the fabric 14and[c] tightened it with the pin.

Again she called to him, "Samson, the Philistines are upon you!"[s] He awoke from his sleep and pulled up the pin and the loom, with the fabric.

15Then she said to him, "How can you say, 'I love you,'[t] when you won't confide in me? This is the third time[u] you have made a fool of me and haven't told me the secret of your great strength."[v] 16With such nagging she prodded him day after day until he was tired to death.

17So he told her everything.[w] "No razor has ever been used on my head," he said, "because I have been a Nazirite[x] set apart to God since birth. If my head were shaved, my strength would leave me, and I would become as weak as any other man."

18When Delilah saw that he had told her everything, she sent word to the rulers of the Philistines[y], "Come back once more; he has told me everything." So the rulers of the Philistines returned with the silver in their hands.[z] 19Having put him to sleep on her lap, she called a man to shave off the seven braids of his hair, and so began to subdue him.[d] And his strength left him.[a]

20Then she called, "Samson, the Philistines are upon you!"[b]

He awoke from his sleep and thought, "I'll go out as before and shake myself free." But he did not know that the LORD had left him.[c]

21Then the Philistines[d] seized him, gouged out his eyes[e] and took him down to Gaza.[f] Binding him with bronze shackles, they set him to grinding[g] in the prison. 22But the hair on his head began to grow again after it had been shaved.

The Death of Samson

23Now the rulers of the Philistines assembled to offer a great sacrifice to Dagon[h] their god and to celebrate, saying, "Our god has delivered Samson, our enemy, into our hands."

24When the people saw him, they praised their god,[i] saying,

"Our god has delivered our enemy
  into our hands,[j]
the one who laid waste our land
  and multiplied our slain."

25While they were in high spirits,[k] they shouted, "Bring out Samson to entertain us." So they called Samson out of the prison, and he performed for them.

When they stood him among the pillars, 26Samson said to the servant who held his hand, "Put me where I can feel the pillars that support the temple, so that I may lean against them." 27Now the temple was crowded with men and women; all the rulers of the Philistines were there, and on the roof[l] were about three thousand men and women watching Samson perform. 28Then Samson prayed to the LORD,[m] "O Sovereign

5 [l]ver 18
6 [m]ver 4
9 [n]ver 12; [o]ver 14
10 [p]ver 13
11 [q]**Jdg 15:13**
12 [r]ver 14
14 [s]ver 9,20
15 [t]Jdg 14:16; [u]Nu 24:10; [v]**ver 5**
17 [w]ver 18; Mic 7:5; [x]**Nu 6:2**
18 [y]**Jos 13:3**; 1Sa 5:8; [z]ver 5
19 [a]Pr 7:26–27
20 [b]**ver 14**; [c]Nu 14:42; Jos 7:12; 1Sa 16:14; 18:12; 28:15
21 [d]Jer 47:1; [e]**Nu 16:14**; [f]**Ge 10:19**; [g]Job 31:10; Isa 47:2
23 [h]1Sa 5:2; 1Ch 10:10
24 [i]Da 5:4; [j]1Sa 31:9; 1Ch 10:9
25 [k]Jdg 9:27; 19:6,9,22; Ru 3:7; Est 1:10
27 [l]**Jos 2:8**
28 [m]Jdg 15:18

[a]5 That is, about 28 pounds (about 13 kilograms)
[b]7 Or *bow-strings;* also in verses 8 and 9
[c]13, 14 Some Septuagint manuscripts; Hebrew "⌞I can⌟ *if you weave the seven braids of my head into the fabric* ⌞*on the loom*⌟." [14]*So she*
[d]19 Hebrew; some Septuagint manuscripts *and he began to weaken*

LORD, remember me. O God, please
strengthen me just once more, and let
me with one blow get revenge[n] on the
Philistines for my two eyes." 29Then
Samson reached towards the two cen-
tral pillars on which the temple stood.
Bracing himself against them, his right
hand on the one and his left hand on the
other, 30Samson said, "Let me die with
the Philistines!" Then he pushed with
all his might, and down came the tem-
ple on the rulers and all the people in it.
Thus he killed many more when he died
than while he lived.
31Then his brothers and his father's
whole family went down to get him.
They brought him back and buried him
between Zorah and Eshtaol in the tomb
of Manoah[o] his father. He had led[e][p]
Israel for twenty years.[q]

Micah's Idols

17 Now a man named Micah[a] from
the hill country of Ephraim
2said to his mother, "The eleven hun-
dred shekels[a] of silver that were taken
from you and about which I heard you
utter a curse—I have that silver with
me; I took it."
Then his mother said, "The LORD
bless you,[b] my son!"
3When he returned the eleven hun-
dred shekels of silver to his mother, she
said, "I solemnly consecrate my silver to
the LORD for my son to make a carved
image and a cast idol.[c] I will give it back
to you."
4So he returned the silver to his
mother, and she took two hundred
shekels[b] of silver and gave them to a
silversmith, who made them into the
image and the idol.[d] And they were put
in Micah's house.
5Now this man Micah had a shrine,[e]
and he made an ephod[f] and some idols[g]
and installed[h] one of his sons as his
priest.[i] 6In those days Israel had no
king;[j] everyone did as he saw fit.[k]
7A young Levite[l] from Bethlehem in
Judah,[m] who had been living within the
clan of Judah, 8left that town in search of
some other place to stay. On his way[c]
he came to Micah's house in the hill
country of Ephraim.
9Micah asked him, "Where are you
from?"
"I'm a Levite from Bethlehem in
Judah,[n]" he said, "and I'm looking for a
place to stay."
10Then Micah said to him, "Live with
me and be my father[o] and priest,[p] and
I'll give you ten shekels[d] of silver a year,
your clothes and your food." 11So the
Levite agreed to live with him, and the
young man was to him like one of
his sons. 12Then Micah installed[q] the
Levite, and the young man became his
priest[r] and lived in his house.
13And Micah said, "Now I know that
the LORD will be good to me, since this
Levite has become my priest."[s]

Danites Settle in Laish

18 In those days Israel had no
king.[a]
And in those days the tribe of the
Danites was seeking a place of their own
where they might settle, because they
had not yet come into an inheritance
among the tribes of Israel.[b] 2So the Dan-
ites[c] sent five warriors[d] from Zorah and
Eshtaol to spy out[e] the land and explore
it. These men represented all their
clans. They told them, "Go, explore the
land."[f]
The men entered the hill country of
Ephraim and came to the house of
Micah,[g] where they spent the night.
3When they were near Micah's house,
they recognised the voice of the young
Levite;[h] so they turned in there and
asked him, "Who brought you here?
What are you doing in this place? Why
are you here?"
4He told them what Micah had done
for him, and said, "He has hired me and
I am his priest.[i]"
5Then they said to him, "Please
enquire of God[j] to learn whether our
journey will be successful."
6The priest answered them, "Go in
peace[k]. Your journey has the LORD's
approval."
7So the five men[l] left and came to
Laish,[m] where they saw that the people
were living in safety, like the Sidonians,
unsuspecting and secure.[n] And since
their land lacked nothing, they were
prosperous.[a] Also, they lived a long
way from the Sidonians[o] and had no
relationship with anyone else.[b]
8When they returned to Zorah and
Eshtaol, their brothers asked them,
"How did you find things?"
9They answered, "Come on, let's

28 [n]Jer 15:15
31 [o]**Jdg 13:2**; [p]Ru 1:1; 1Sa 4:18; 7:6; [q]Jdg 15:20

Ch. 17

1 [a]Jdg 18:2,13
2 [b]Ru 2:20; 3:10; 1Sa 15:13; 23:21; 2Sa 2:5
3 [c]**Ex 20:4**
4 [d]**Ex 32:4; Isa 17:8**
5 [e]Isa 44:13; Eze 8:10; [f]**Jdg 8:27**; [g]**Ge 31:19**; [h]**Nu 16:10**; [i]**Ex 29:9**
6 [j]Jdg 18:1; 19:1; 21:25; [k]**Dt 12:8**
7 [l]Jdg 18:3; [m]**Ge 35:19**; Mt 2:1
9 [n]Ru 1:1
10 [o]Ge 45:8; [p]Jdg 18:19
12 [q]**Nu 16:10**; [r]Jdg 18:4
13 [s]Nu 18:7

Ch. 18

1 [a]**Jdg 17:6**; [b]Jos 19:47; Jdg 1:34
2 [c]**Ge 30:6**; [d]ver 17; [e]**Nu 21:32**; [f]**Jos 2:1**; [g]**Jdg 17:1**
3 [h]Jdg 17:7
4 [i]Jdg 17:12
5 [j]**Ge 25:22**; Jdg 20:18,23,27; 1Sa 14:18; 2Sa 5:19; 2Ki 1:2; 8:8
6 [k]1Ki 22:6
7 [l]ver 17; [m]**Jos 19:47**; [n]**Ge 34:25**; [o]ver 28; Jos 11:8

[e]31 Traditionally *judged*
[a]2 That is, about 28 pounds (about 13 kilograms)
[b]4 That is, about 5 pounds (about 2.3 kilograms)
[c]8 Or *To carry on his profession*
[d]10 That is, about 4 ounces (about 115 grams)
[a]7 The meaning of the Hebrew for this clause is uncertain.
[b]7 Hebrew; some Septuagint manuscripts *with the Arameans*

attack them! We have seen that the land
is very good. Aren't you going to do
something? Don't hesitate to go there
and take it over.[p] 10When you get there,
you will find an unsuspecting people
and a spacious land that God has put
into your hands, a land that lacks
nothing[q] whatever.[r]' "
11Then six hundred men[s] from the
clan of the Danites,[t] armed for battle, set
out from Zorah and Eshtaol. 12On their
way they set up camp near Kiriath Jea-
rim[u] in Judah. This is why the place
west of Kiriath Jearim is called Mahaneh
Dan[c][v] to this day. 13From there they
went on to the hill country of Ephraim
and came to Micah's house.[w]
14Then the five men who had spied
out the land of Laish[x] said to their
brothers, "Do you know that one of
these houses has an ephod,[y] other
household gods, a carved image and a
cast idol?[z] Now you know what to do."
15So they turned in there and went to
the house of the young Levite at Micah's
place and greeted him. 16The six hun-
dred Danites,[a] armed for battle, stood at
the entrance to the gate. 17The five men
who had spied out the land went inside
and took the carved image, the ephod,
the other household gods[b] and the cast
idol while the priest and the six hun-
dred armed men[c] stood at the entrance
to the gate.
18When these men went into Micah's
house and took[d] the carved image, the
ephod, the other household gods[e] and
the cast idol, the priest said to them,
"What are you doing?"
19They answered him, "Be quiet![f]
Don't say a word. Come with us, and be
our father and priest.[g] Isn't it better that
you serve a tribe and clan[h] in Israel as
priest rather than just one man's house-
hold?" 20Then the priest was glad. He
took the ephod, the other household
gods and the carved image and went
along with the people. 21Putting their
little children, their livestock and their
possessions in front of them, they
turned away and left.
22When they had gone some distance
from Micah's house, the men who lived
near Micah were called together and
overtook the Danites. 23As they shouted
after them, the Danites turned and said
to Micah, "What's the matter with you
that you called out your men to fight?"
24He replied, "You took[i] the gods I
made, and my priest, and went away.
What else do I have? How can you ask,
'What's the matter with you?' "
25The Danites answered, "Don't
argue with us, or some hot-tempered
men will attack you, and you and your
family will lose your lives." 26So the
Danites went their way, and Micah,
seeing that they were too strong for
him,[j] turned round and went back
home.
27Then they took what Micah had
made, and his priest, and went on
to Laish, against a peaceful and
unsuspecting people.[k] They attacked
them with the sword and burned[l] down
their city.[m] 28There was no-one to rescue
them because they lived a long way
from Sidon[n] and had no relationship
with anyone else. The city was in a
valley near Beth Rehob.[o]
The Danites rebuilt the city and set-
tled there. 29They named it Dan[p] after
their forefather Dan, who was born to
Israel—though the city used to be called
Laish.[q] 30There the Danites set up for
themselves the idols, and Jonathan son
of Gershom,[r] the son of Moses,[d] and his
sons were priests for the tribe of Dan
until the time of the captivity of the
land. 31They continued to use the idols
Micah had made,[s] all the time the house
of God[t] was in Shiloh.[u]

A Levite and His Concubine

19 In those days Israel had no
king.
Now a Levite who lived in a remote
area in the hill country of Ephraim[a] took
a concubine from Bethlehem in Judah.[b]
2But she was unfaithful to him. She left
him and went back to her father's house
in Bethlehem, Judah. After she had
been there for four months, 3her hus-
band went to her to persuade her to
return. He had with him his servant and
two donkeys. She took him into her
father's house, and when her father saw
him, he gladly welcomed him. 4His
father-in-law, the girl's father, pre-
vailed upon him to stay; so he remained
with him three days, eating and drink-
ing,[c] and sleeping there.
5On the fourth day they got up early
and he prepared to leave, but the girl's
father said to his son-in-law, "Refresh
yourself[d] with something to eat; then
you can go." 6So the two of them sat
down to eat and drink together. After-
wards the girl's father said, "Please stay
tonight and enjoy yourself.[e]" 7And

9 [p]Nu 13:30; 1Ki 22:3
10 [q]Dt 8:9; [r]1Ch 4:40
11 [s]ver 16–17; [t]Jdg 13:2
12 [u]**Jos 9:17**; [v]Jdg 13:25
13 [w]**Jdg 17:1**
14 [x]**Jos 19:47**; [y]**Jdg 8:27**; [z]**Ge 31:19**
16 [a]**ver 11**
17 [b]**Ge 31:19**; Mic 5:13; [c]ver 11
18 [d]ver 24; Isa 46:2; Jer 43:11; 48:7; 49:3; Hos 10:5; [e]**Ge 31:19**
19 [f]Job 13:5; 21:5; 29:9; 40:4; Isa 52:15; Mic 7:16; [g]Jdg 17:10; [h]Nu 26:42
24 [i]**ver 17–18**
26 [j]2Sa 3:39; Ps 18:17; 35:10
27 [k]**Ge 34:25**; [l]**Nu 31:10**; [m]Ge 49:17; **Jos 19:47**
28 [n]**ver 7**; **Ge 10:19**; [o]**Nu 13:21**
29 [p]**Ge 14:14**; [q]**Jos 19:47**; 1Ki 15:20
30 [r]Ex 2:22
31 [s]ver 17; [t]Jdg 19:18; 20:18; [u]**Jos 18:1**; Jer 7:14

Ch. 19

1 [a]ver 16,18; [b]Ru 1:1
4 [c]ver 6,8; **Ex 32:6**
5 [d]ver 8; Ge 18:5
6 [e]**Jdg 16:25**

[c]12 *Mahaneh Dan* means *Dan's camp.*
[d]30 An ancient Hebrew scribal tradition, some Septuagint manuscripts and Vulgate; Masoretic Text *Manasseh*

when the man got up to go, his father-
in-law persuaded him, so he stayed
there that night. 8On the morning of the
fifth day, when he rose to go, the girl's
father said, "Refresh yourself. Wait till
afternoon!" So the two of them ate
together.
9Then when the man, with his con-
cubine and his servant, got up to leave,
his father-in-law, the girl's father, said,
"Now look, it's almost evening. Spend
the night here; the day is nearly over.
Stay and enjoy yourself. Early tomor-
row morning you can get up and be on
your way home." 10But, unwilling to
stay another night, the man left and
went towards Jebus[f] (that is, Jeru-
salem), with his two saddled donkeys
and his concubine.
11When they were near Jebus and the
day was almost gone, the servant said to
his master, "Come, let's stop at this city
of the Jebusites[g] and spend the night."
12His master replied, "No. We won't
go into an alien city, whose people are
not Israelites. We will go on to Gibeah."
13He added, "Come, let's try to reach
Gibeah or Ramah[h] and spend the night
in one of those places." 14So they went
on, and the sun set as they neared
Gibeah in Benjamin.[i] 15There they
stopped to spend the night.[j] They went
and sat in the city square,[k] but no-one
took them into his home for the night.
16That evening[l] an old man from the
hill country of Ephraim,[m] who was liv-
ing in Gibeah (the men of the place were
Benjamites), came in from his work in
the fields. 17When he looked and saw
the traveller in the city square, the old
man asked, "Where are you going?
Where did you come from?"[n]
18He answered, "We are on our way
from Bethlehem in Judah to a remote
area in the hill country of Ephraim
where I live. I have been to Bethlehem
in Judah and now I am going to the
house of the LORD.[o] No-one has taken
me into his house. 19We have both straw
and fodder[p] for our donkeys[q] and bread
and wine[r] for ourselves your servants
—me, your maidservant, and the
young man with us. We don't need
anything."
20"You are welcome at my house,"
the old man said. "Let me supply what-
ever you need. Only don't spend the
night in the square." 21So he took him
into his house and fed his donkeys.
After they had washed their feet, they
had something to eat and drink.[s]
22While they were enjoying them-
selves,[t] some of the wicked men[u] of the
city surrounded the house. Pounding
on the door, they shouted to the old
man who owned the house, "Bring out
the man who came to your house so we
can have sex with him."[v]
23The owner of the house went out-
side[w] and said to them, "No, my
friends, don't be so vile. Since this man
is my guest, don't do this disgraceful
thing.[x] 24Look, here is my virgin
daughter,[y] and his concubine. I will
bring them out to you now, and you can
use them and do to them whatever you
wish. But to this man, don't do such a
disgraceful thing."
25But the men would not listen to him.
So the man took his concubine and sent
her outside to them, and they raped
her[z] and abused her[a] throughout the
night, and at dawn they let her go. 26At
daybreak the woman went back to the
house where her master was staying,
fell down at the door and lay there until
daylight.
27When her master got up in the
morning and opened the door of the
house and stepped out to continue on
his way, there lay his concubine, fallen
in the doorway of the house, with her
hands on the threshold. 28He said to
her, "Get up; let's go." But there was no
answer. Then the man put her on his
donkey and set out for home.
29When he reached home, he took a
knife[b] and cut up his concubine, limb by
limb, into twelve parts and sent them
into all the areas of Israel.[c] 30Everyone
who saw it said, "Such a thing has never
been seen or done, not since the day the
Israelites came up out of Egypt.[d] Think
about it! Consider it! Tell us what to
do![e]"

Israelites Fight the Benjamites

20 Then all the Israelites[a] from Dan
to Beersheba[b] and from the land
of Gilead came out as one man[c] and
assembled[d] before the LORD in Mizpah.[e]
2The leaders of all the people of the
tribes of Israel took their places in the
assembly of the people of God, four
hundred thousand soldiers[f] armed with
swords. 3(The Benjamites heard that the
Israelites had gone up to Mizpah.) Then
the Israelites said, "Tell us how this
awful thing happened."
4So the Levite, the husband of the
murdered woman, said, "I and my con-
cubine came to Gibeah[g] in Benjamin to
spend the night.[h] 5During the night the
men of Gibeah came after me and sur-
rounded the house, intending to kill

10 [f]**Ge 10:16; Jos 15:8**
11 [g]**Ge 10:16; Jos 3:10**
13 [h]**Jos 18:25**
14 [i]Jos 15:57; 1Sa 10:26; 11:4; 13:2; 15:34; Isa 10:29
15 [j]**Ge 24:23;** [k]**Ge 19:2**
16 [l]Ps 104:23; [m]**ver 1**
17 [n]**Ge 29:4**
18 [o]**Jdg 18:31**
19 [p]Ge 24:25; [q]**Ge 42:27;** [r]**Ge 14:18**
21 [s]Ge 24:32–33; Lk 7:44
22 [t]**Jdg 16:25;** [u]**Dt 13:13;** [v]Ge 19:4–5; Jdg 20:5; Ro 1:26–27
23 [w]Ge 19:6; [x]**Ge 34:7; Lev 19:29; Jos 7:15; Jdg 20:6;** Ro 1:27
24 [y]Ge 19:8
25 [z]Jdg 20:5; [a]1Sa 31:4
29 [b]**Ge 22:6;** [c]Jdg 20:6; 1Sa 11:7
30 [d]Hos 9:9; [e]Jdg 20:7; Pr 13:10

Ch. 20

1 [a]Jdg 21:5; [b]**Ge 21:14;** 1Sa 3:20; 2Sa 3:10; 17:11; 24:15; 1Ki 4:25; 2Ch 30:5; [c]ver 11; 1Sa 11:7; [d]1Sa 7:5; [e]**Jos 11:3**
2 [f]1Sa 11:8
4 [g]**Jos 15:57;** [h]**Ge 24:23**

me.[i] They raped my concubine, and she
died.[j] 6I took my concubine, cut her into
pieces and sent one piece to each region
of Israel's inheritance,[k] because they
committed this lewd and disgraceful act[l]
in Israel. 7Now, all you Israelites, speak
up and give your verdict."[m]
8All the people rose as one man,
saying, "None of us will go home. No,
not one of us will return to his house.
9But now this is what we'll do to Gibeah:
We'll go up against it as the lot directs.[n]
10We'll take ten men out of every hun-
dred from all the tribes of Israel, and a
hundred from a thousand, and a
thousand from ten thousand, to get pro-
visions for the army. Then, when the
army arrives at Gibeah[a] in Benjamin, it
can give them what they deserve for all
this vileness done in Israel." 11So all the
men of Israel got together and united as
one man[o] against the city.
12The tribes of Israel sent men
throughout the tribe of Benjamin,
saying, "What about this awful crime
that was committed among you?[p]
13Now surrender those wicked men[q] of
Gibeah so that we may put them to
death and purge the evil from Israel."[r]
But the Benjamites would not listen
to their fellow Israelites. 14From their
towns they came together at Gibeah to
fight against the Israelites. 15At once
the Benjamites mobilised twenty-six
thousand swordsmen from their towns,
in addition to seven hundred chosen
men from those living in Gibeah.
16Among all these soldiers there were
seven hundred chosen men who were
left-handed,[s] each of whom could sling
a stone at a hair and not miss.
17Israel, apart from Benjamin, mus-
tered four hundred thousand swords-
men, all of them fighting men.
18The Israelites went up to Bethel[b][t]
and enquired of God.[u] They said, "Who
of us shall go first[v] to fight[w] against the
Benjamites?"
The LORD replied, "Judah[x] shall go
first."
19The next morning the Israelites got
up and pitched camp near Gibeah.
20The men of Israel went out to fight the
Benjamites and took up battle positions
against them at Gibeah. 21The Benja-
mites came out of Gibeah and cut down
twenty-two thousand Israelites[y] on the
battlefield that day. 22But the men of
Israel encouraged one another and
again took up their positions where
they had stationed themselves the first
day. 23The Israelites went up and wept
before the LORD[z] until evening,[a] and
they enquired of the LORD.[b] They said,
"Shall we go up again to battle[c] against
the Benjamites, our brothers?"
The LORD answered, "Go up against
them."
24Then the Israelites drew near to
Benjamin the second day. 25This time,
when the Benjamites came out from
Gibeah to oppose them, they cut down
another eighteen thousand Israelites,[d]
all of them armed with swords.
26Then the Israelites, all the people,
went up to Bethel, and there they sat
weeping before the LORD.[e] They fasted[f]
that day until evening and presented
burnt offerings[g] and fellowship offer-
ings[c][h] to the LORD.[i] 27And the Israelites
enquired of the LORD.[j] (In those days the
ark of the covenant of God[k] was there,
28with Phinehas son of Eleazar,[l] the son
of Aaron, ministering before it.)[m] They
asked, "Shall we go up again to battle
with Benjamin our brother, or not?"
The LORD responded, "Go, for tomor-
row I will give them into your hands."[n]
29Then Israel set an ambush[o] around
Gibeah. 30They went up against the
Benjamites on the third day and took up
positions against Gibeah as they had
done before. 31The Benjamites came out
to meet them and were drawn away[p]
from the city. They began to inflict
casualties on the Israelites as before, so
that about thirty men fell in the open
field and on the roads—the one leading
to Bethel[q] and the other to Gibeah.
32While the Benjamites were saying,
"We are defeating them as before,"[r] the
Israelites were saying, "Let's retreat
and draw them away from the city to the
roads."
33All the men of Israel moved from
their places and took up positions at
Baal Tamar, and the Israelite ambush
charged out of its place[s] on the west[d] of
Gibeah.[e] 34Then ten thousand of Israel's
finest men made a frontal attack on
Gibeah. The fighting was so heavy that
the Benjamites did not realise[t] how near
disaster was.[u] 35The LORD defeated Ben-
jamin[v] before Israel, and on that day the
Israelites struck down 25,100 Benja-
mites, all armed with swords. 36Then
the Benjamites saw that they were
beaten.

5 [i]**Jdg 19:22;** [j]Jdg 19:25–26
6 [k]**Jdg 19:29;** [l]**Jdg 19:23;** 2Sa 13:12
7 [m]**Jdg 19:30**
9 [n]**Lev 16:8**
11 [o]**ver 1**
12 [p]Dt 13:14
13 [q]**Dt 13:13;** [r]**Dt 13:5; 1Co 5:13**
16 [s]**Jdg 3:15**
18 [t]**Jos 12:9; Jdg 18:31;** [u]**Jdg 18:5;** [v]**Jdg 1:1;** [w]ver 23,28; [x]**Ge 49:10**
21 [y]ver 25
23 [z]**Nu 14:1;** [a]Jos 7:6; [b]**Jdg 18:5;** [c]**ver 18**
25 [d]ver 21
26 [e]**Nu 14:1;** [f]2Sa 12:21; [g]Lev 1:3; [h]**Ex 32:6;** [i]Jdg 21:4
27 [j]**Jdg 18:5;** [k]**Nu 10:33**
28 [l]Nu 25:7; [m]Dt 18:5; [n]**Jos 2:24**
29 [o]**Jos 8:2**
31 [p]Jos 8:16; [q]Jos 16:1
32 [r]ver 39
33 [s]Jos 8:19
34 [t]Jos 8:14; [u]ver 41
35 [v]1Sa 9:21

[a]10 One Hebrew manuscript; most Hebrew manuscripts *Geba*, a variant of *Gibeah*
[b]18 Or *to the house of God*; also in verse 26
[c]26 Traditionally *peace offerings*
[d]33 Some Septuagint manuscripts and Vulgate; the meaning of the Hebrew for this word is uncertain.
[e]33 Hebrew *Geba*, a variant of *Gibeah*

Now the men of Israel had given way[w] before Benjamin, because they relied on the ambush[x] they had set near Gibeah. 37The men who had been in ambush made a sudden dash into Gibeah, spread out and put the whole city to the sword.[y] 38The men of Israel had arranged with the ambush that they should send up a great cloud of smoke[z] from the city,[a] 39and then the men of Israel would turn in the battle.

The Benjamites had begun to inflict casualties on the men of Israel (about thirty), and they said, "We are defeating them as in the first battle."[b] 40But when the column of smoke began to rise from the city, the Benjamites turned and saw the smoke of the whole city going up into the sky.[c] 41Then the men of Israel turned on them,[d] and the men of Benjamin were terrified, because they realised that disaster had come[e] upon them. 42So they fled before the Israelites in the direction of the desert, but they could not escape the battle. And the men of Israel who came out of the towns cut them down there. 43They surrounded the Benjamites, chased them and easily[f] overran them in the vicinity of Gibeah on the east. 44Eighteen thousand Benjamites fell, all of them valiant fighters.[f] 45As they turned and fled towards the desert to the rock of Rimmon,[g] the Israelites cut down five thousand men along the roads. They kept pressing after the Benjamites as far as Gidom and struck down two thousand more.

46On that day twenty-five thousand Benjamite[h] swordsmen fell, all of them valiant fighters. 47But six hundred men turned and fled into the desert to the rock of Rimmon, where they stayed for four months. 48The men of Israel went back to Benjamin and put all the towns to the sword, including the animals and everything else they found. All the towns they came across they set on fire.[i]

Wives for the Benjamites

21 The men of Israel had taken an oath[a] at Mizpah:[b] "Not one of us will give[c] his daughter in marriage to a Benjamite."

2The people went to Bethel,[a] where they sat before God until evening, raising their voices and weeping bitterly. 3"O LORD, the God of Israel," they cried, "why has this happened to Israel? Why should one tribe be missing[d] from Israel today?"

4Early the next day the people built an altar and presented burnt offerings and fellowship offerings.[b][e]

5Then the Israelites asked, "Who from all the tribes of Israel[f] has failed to assemble before the LORD?" For they had taken a solemn oath that anyone who failed to assemble before the LORD at Mizpah should certainly be put to death.

6Now the Israelites grieved for their brothers, the Benjamites. "Today one tribe is cut off from Israel," they said. 7"How can we provide wives for those who are left, since we have taken an oath[g] by the LORD not to give them any of our daughters in marriage?" 8Then they asked, "Which one of the tribes of Israel failed to assemble before the LORD at Mizpah?" They discovered that no-one from Jabesh Gilead[h] had come to the camp for the assembly. 9For when they counted the people, they found that none of the people of Jabesh Gilead were there.

10So the assembly sent twelve thousand fighting men with instructions to go to Jabesh Gilead and put to the sword those living there, including the women and children. 11"This is what you are to do," they said. "Kill every male[i] and every woman who is not a virgin.[j]" 12They found among the people living in Jabesh Gilead four hundred young women who had never slept with a man, and they took them to the camp at Shiloh[k] in Canaan.

13Then the whole assembly sent an offer of peace[l] to the Benjamites at the rock of Rimmon.[m] 14So the Benjamites returned at that time and were given the women of Jabesh Gilead who had been spared. But there were not enough for all of them.

15The people grieved for Benjamin,[n] because the LORD had made a gap in the tribes of Israel. 16And the elders of the assembly said, "With the women of Benjamin destroyed, how shall we provide wives for the men who are left? 17The Benjamite survivors must have heirs," they said, "so that a tribe of Israel will not be wiped out.[o] 18We can't give them our daughters as wives, since we Israelites have taken this oath:[p] 'Cursed be anyone who gives[q] a wife to a Benjamite.' 19But look, there is the annual festival of the LORD in Shiloh,[r] to the north of Bethel[s], and east of the road

36 [w]Jos 8:15; [x]Jos 8:2
37 [y]Jos 8:19
38 [z]Jos 8:20; [a]Jos 8:4–8
39 [b]ver 32; Ps 78:9
40 [c]Jos 8:20
41 [d]Jos 8:21; [e]ver 34
44 [f]1Sa 10:26; Ps 76:5
45 [g]**Jos 15:32**
46 [h]1Sa 9:21
48 [i]Jdg 21:23

Ch. 21

1 [a]Jos 9:18; [b]**Jos 11:3**; [c]ver 18,22
3 [d]ver 6,17
4 [e]Jdg 20:26
5 [f]Jdg 20:1
7 [g]**Jos 9:18**
8 [h]1Sa 11:1; 31:11; 2Sa 2:4; 21:12; 1Ch 10:11
11 [i]**Nu 31:7**; [j]Nu 31:17–18
12 [k]**Jos 18:1**
13 [l]**Dt 2:26**; [m]**Jos 15:32**
15 [n]ver 6
17 [o]**ver 3**
18 [p]**Jos 9:18**; [q]**ver 1**
19 [r]**Jos 18:1**; [s]Jos 16:1

f43 The meaning of the Hebrew for this word is uncertain. a2 Or *to the house of God*
b4 Traditionally *peace offerings*

that goes from Bethel to Shechem,[t] and
to the south of Lebonah."
20So they instructed the Benjamites,
saying, "Go and hide in the vineyards
21and watch. When the girls of Shiloh
come out to join in the dancing,[u] then
rush from the vineyards and each of you
seize a wife from the girls of Shiloh and
go to the land of Benjamin. 22When their
fathers or brothers complain to us, we
will say to them, 'Do us a kindness by
helping them, because we did not get
wives for them during the war, and you
are innocent, since you did not give[v]
your daughters to them.'"
23So that is what the Benjamites did.
While the girls were dancing,[w] each
man caught one and carried her off to be
his wife. Then they returned to their
inheritance[x] and rebuilt the towns and
settled in them.[y]
24At that time the Israelites left that
place and went home to their tribes and
clans, each to his own inheritance.
25In those days Israel had no king;
everyone did as he saw fit.[z]

19 [t]**Jos 17:7**
21 [u]**Ex 15:20**
22 [v]**ver 1**
23 [w]ver 21; [x]**Jos 24:28**; [y]Jdg 20:48
25 [z]**Dt 12:8**

Ruth

Naomi and Ruth

1 In the days when the judges ruled,[a][a] there was a famine in the land,[b] and a man from Bethlehem in Judah,[c] together with his wife and two sons, went to live for a while[d] in the country of Moab.[e] 2The man's name was Elimelech,[f] his wife's name Naomi, and the names of his two sons were Mahlon and Kilion.[g] They were Ephrathites[h] from Bethlehem,[i] Judah. And they went to Moab and lived there.

3Now Elimelech, Naomi's husband, died, and she was left with her two sons. 4They married Moabite women,[j] one named Orpah and the other Ruth.[k] After they had lived there about ten years, 5both Mahlon and Kilion[l] also died,[m] and Naomi was left without her two sons and her husband.

6When she heard in Moab[n] that the LORD had come to the aid of his people[o] by providing food[p] for them, Naomi and her daughters-in-law[q] prepared to return home from there. 7With her two daughters-in-law she left the place where she had been living and set out on the road that would take them back to the land of Judah.

8Then Naomi said to her two daughters-in-law, "Go back, each of you, to your mother's home.[r] May the LORD show kindness[s] to you, as you have shown to your dead[t] and to me. 9May the LORD grant that each of you will find rest[u] in the home of another husband."

Then she kissed[v] them and they wept aloud[w] 10and said to her, "We will go back with you to your people."

11But Naomi said, "Return home, my daughters. Why would you come with me? Am I going to have any more sons, who could become your husbands?[x] 12Return home, my daughters; I am too old to have another husband. Even if I thought there was still hope for me—even if I had a husband tonight and then gave birth to sons—13would you wait until they grew up?[y] Would you remain unmarried for them? No, my daughters. It is more bitter[z] for me than for you, because the LORD's hand has gone out against me![a]"

14At this they wept[b] again. Then Orpah kissed her mother-in-law[c] goodbye,[d] but Ruth clung to her.[e]

15"Look," said Naomi, "your sister-in-law[f] is going back to her people and her gods.[g] Go back with her."

16But Ruth replied, "Don't urge me to leave you[h] or to turn back from you. Where you go I will go,[i] and where you stay I will stay. Your people will be my people[j] and your God my God.[k] 17Where you die I will die, and there I will be buried. May the LORD deal with me, be it ever so severely,[l] if anything but death separates you and me."[m] 18When Naomi realised that Ruth was determined to go with her, she stopped urging her.[n]

19So the two women went on until they came to Bethlehem.[o] When they arrived in Bethlehem, the whole town was stirred[p] because of them, and the women exclaimed, "Can this be Naomi?"

20"Don't call me Naomi,"[b] she told them. "Call me Mara,[c] because the Almighty[d][q] has made my life very bitter.[r] 21I went away full, but the LORD has brought me back empty.[s] Why call me Naomi? The LORD has afflicted[e] me;[t] the Almighty has brought misfortune upon me."

22So Naomi returned from Moab accompanied by Ruth the Moabitess,[u] her daughter-in-law,[v] arriving in Bethlehem as the barley harvest[w] was beginning.[x]

Ch. 1
1 [a]Jdg 2:16–18; [b]**Ge 12:10;** 2Ki 6:25; Ps 105:16; Hag 1:11; [c]**Ge 35:19;** [d]Ge 47:4; [e]**Ge 36:35**
2 [f]ver 3; Ru 2:1; 4:3; [g]ver 5; Ru 4:9; [h]**Ge 35:16;** [i]Ge 35:19; 1Sa 16:18
4 [j]1Ki 11:1; 2Ch 24:26; Ezr 9:2; Ne 13:23; [k]ver 14; Ru 4:13; Mt 1:5
5 [l]**ver 2;** [m]ver 8; Ru 2:11
6 [n]**Ge 36:35;** [o]**Ge 50:24;** Ex 4:31; Jer 29:10; Zep 2:7; [p]Ps 132:15; Mt 6:11; [q]**Ge 11:31; 38:16**
8 [r]Ge 38:11; [s]**Ge 19:19;** 2Ti 1:16; [t]**ver 5**
9 [u]Ru 3:1; [v]**Ge 27:27; 29:11;** [w]**Ge 27:38; Nu 25:6**
11 [x]Ge 38:11; Dt 25:5
13 [y]Ge 38:11; [z]ver 20; Ex 1:14; 15:23; 1Sa 30:6; [a]**Jdg 2:15; Job 4:5**
14 [b]ver 9; [c]Ru 2:11; 3:1; Mic 7:6; [d]**Ge 31:28;** [e]**Dt 10:20**
15 [f]Dt 25:7; [g]**Jos 24:14**
16 [h]2Ki 2:2; [i]Ge 24:58; [j]Ps 45:10; [k]**Jos 24:15**
17 [l]1Sa 3:17; 14:44; 20:13; 25:22; 2Sa 3:9, 35; 19:13; 1Ki 2:23; 19:2; 20:10; 2Ki 6:31; [m]2Sa 15:21
18 [n]Ac 21:14
19 [o]**Jdg 17:7;** [p]Mt 21:10
20 [q]**Ge 15:1; 17:1;** Ps 91:1; [r]**ver 13**
21 [s]Job 1:21; [t]Job 30:11; Ps 88:7; Isa 53:4
22 [u]Ru 2:2,6,21; 4:5,10; [v]**Ge 11:31;** [w]**Ex 9:31; Lev 19:9;** [x]2Sa 21:9

[a]1 Traditionally *judged*
[b]20 *Naomi* means *pleasant*; also in verse 21.
[c]20 *Mara* means *bitter*.
[d]20 Hebrew *Shaddai*; also in verse 21
[e]21 Or *has testified against*

Ruth Meets Boaz

2 Now Naomi had a relative[a] on her husband's side from the clan of Elimelech,[b] a man of standing,[c] whose name was Boaz.[d]

2And Ruth the Moabitess[e] said to Naomi, "Let me go to the fields and pick up the leftover grain[f] behind anyone in whose eyes I find favour.[g]"

Naomi said to her, "Go ahead, my daughter." 3So she went out and began to glean in the fields behind the harvesters.[h] As it turned out, she found herself working in a field belonging to Boaz, who was from the clan of Elimelech.[i]

4Just then Boaz arrived from Bethlehem and greeted the harvesters, "The LORD be with you![j]"

"The LORD bless you![k]" they called back.

5Boaz asked the foreman of his harvesters, "Whose young woman is that?"

6The foreman replied, "She is the Moabitess[l] who came back from Moab with Naomi. 7She said, 'Please let me glean and gather among the sheaves[m] behind the harvesters.' She went into the field and has worked steadily from morning till now, except for a short rest[n] in the shelter."

8So Boaz said to Ruth, "My daughter, listen to me. Don't go and glean in another field and don't go away from here. Stay here with my servant girls. 9Watch the field where the men are harvesting, and follow along after the girls. I have told the men not to touch you. And whenever you are thirsty, go and get a drink from the water jars the men have filled."

10At this, she bowed down with her face to the ground.[o] She exclaimed, "Why have I found such favour in your eyes that you notice me[p]—a foreigner?[q]"

11Boaz replied, "I've been told all about what you have done for your mother-in-law[r] since the death of your husband[s]—how you left your father and mother and your homeland and came to live with a people you did not know[t] before.[u] 12May the LORD repay you for what you have done. May you be richly rewarded by the LORD,[v] the God of Israel,[w] under whose wings[x] you have come to take refuge.[y]"

13"May I continue to find favour in your eyes,[z] my lord," she said. "You have given me comfort and have spoken kindly to your servant—though I do not have the standing of one of your servant girls."

14At mealtime Boaz said to her, "Come over here. Have some bread[a] and dip it in the wine vinegar."

When she sat down with the harvesters,[b] he offered her some roasted grain.[c] She ate all she wanted and had some left over.[d] 15As she got up to glean, Boaz gave orders to his men, "Even if she gathers among the sheaves,[e] don't embarrass her. 16Rather, pull out some stalks for her from the bundles and leave them for her to pick up, and don't rebuke[f] her."

17So Ruth gleaned in the field until evening. Then she threshed[g] the barley she had gathered, and it amounted to about an ephah.[a][h] 18She carried it back to town, and her mother-in-law saw how much she had gathered. Ruth also brought out and gave her what she had left over[i] after she had eaten enough.

19Her mother-in-law asked her, "Where did you glean today? Where did you work? Blessed be the man who took notice of you![j]"

Then Ruth told her mother-in-law about the one at whose place she had been working. "The name of the man I worked with today is Boaz," she said.

20"The LORD bless him![k]" Naomi said to her daughter-in-law.[l] "He has not stopped showing his kindness[m] to the living and the dead." She added, "That man is our close relative;[n] he is one of our kinsman-redeemers.[o]"

21Then Ruth the Moabitess[p] said, "He even said to me, 'Stay with my workers until they finish harvesting all my grain.'"

22Naomi said to Ruth her daughter-in-law, "It will be good for you, my daughter, to go with his girls, because in someone else's field you might be harmed."

23So Ruth stayed close to the servant girls of Boaz to glean until the barley[q] and wheat harvests[r] were finished. And she lived with her mother-in-law.

Ruth and Boaz at the Threshing-Floor

3 One day Naomi her mother-in-law[a] said to her, "My daughter, should I not try to find a home[a][b] for you, where you will be well provided for? 2Is not Boaz, with whose servant girls you have been, a kinsman[c] of ours?

Ch. 2

1 [a]Ru 3:2; Pr 7:4; [b]**Ru 1:2;** [c]1Sa 9:1; 1Ki 11:28; [d]Ru 4:21; 1Ch 2:12; Mt 1:5; Lk 3:32
2 [e]**Ru 1:22;** [f]**Lev 19:9; 23:22;** [g]**Ge 6:8; 18:3**
3 [h]ver 14; 2Ki 4:18; Jer 9:22; Am 9:13; [i]ver 1
4 [j]**Jdg 6:12;** Lk 1:28; 2Th 3:16; [k]**Ge 28:3; Nu 6:24**
6 [l]**Ru 1:22**
7 [m]**Ge 37:7; Lev 19:9;** [n]2Sa 4:5
10 [o]**Ge 19:1; 1Sa 20:41;** [p]ver 19; Ps 41:1; [q]**Ge 31:15; Dt 15:3**
11 [r]**Ru 1:14;** [s]**Ru 1:5;** [t]Isa 55:5; [u]Ru 1:16–17
12 [v]1Sa 24:19; 26:23,25; Ps 18:20; Pr 25:22; Jer 31:16; [w]**Jos 24:15;** [x]Ps 17:8; 36:7; 57:1; 61:4; 63:7; 91:4; [y]Ps 71:1
13 [z]**Ge 18:3**
14 [a]**Ge 3:19;** [b]**ver 3;** [c]**Lev 23:14;** [d]ver 18
15 [e]**Ge 37:7; Lev 19:9**
16 [f]**Ge 37:10**
17 [g]**Jdg 6:11;** [h]**Lev 19:36**
18 [i]ver 14
19 [j]**ver 10**
20 [k]**Jdg 17:2; 1Sa 23:21;** [l]**Ge 11:31;** [m]**Ge 19:19;** [n]**Lev 25:25;** [o]Ru 3:9,12; 4:1,14
21 [p]**Ru 1:22**
23 [q]Ex 9:31; [r]**Ge 30:14; 1Sa 6:13**

Ch. 3

1 [a]**Ru 1:14;** [b]**Ru 1:9**
2 [c]**Ru 2:1**

[a]*17* That is, probably about ⅗ bushel (about 22 litres) [a]*1* Hebrew *find rest* (see Ruth 1:9)

Tonight he will be winnowing barley on the threshing-floor.[d] 3Wash[e] and perfume yourself,[f] and put on your best clothes.[g] Then go down to the threshing-floor, but don't let him know you are there until he has finished eating and drinking.[h] 4When he lies down, note the place where he is lying. Then go and uncover his feet and lie down. He will tell you what to do."

5"I will do whatever you say,"[i] Ruth answered. 6So she went down to the threshing-floor[j] and did everything her mother-in-law told her to do.

7When Boaz had finished eating and drinking and was in good spirits,[k] he went over to lie down at the far end of the grain pile.[l] Ruth approached quietly, uncovered his feet and lay down. 8In the middle of the night something startled the man, and he turned and discovered a woman lying at his feet.

9"Who are you?" he asked.

"I am your servant Ruth," she said, "Spread the corner of your garment[m] over me, since you are a kinsman-redeemer.[n]"

10"The LORD bless you,[o] my daughter," he replied. "This kindness is greater than that which you showed earlier:[p] You have not run after the younger men, whether rich or poor. 11And now, my daughter, don't be afraid. I will do for you all you ask. All my fellow townsmen know that you are a woman of noble character.[q] 12Although it is true that I am near of kin, there is a kinsman-redeemer[r] nearer than[s] I. 13Stay here for the night, and in the morning if he wants to redeem,[t] good; let him redeem. But if he is not willing, as surely as the LORD lives[u] I will do it.[v] Lie here until morning."

14So she lay at his feet until morning, but got up before anyone could be recognised; and he said, "Don't let it be known that a woman came to the threshing-floor.[w]"[x]

15He also said, "Bring me the shawl[y] you are wearing and hold it out." When she did so, he poured into it six measures of barley and put it on her. Then he[b] went back to town.

16When Ruth came to her mother-in-law, Naomi asked, "How did it go, my daughter?"

Then she told her everything Boaz had done for her 17and added, "He gave me these six measures of barley, saying, 'Don't go back to your mother-in-law empty-handed.'"

18Then Naomi said, "Wait, my daughter, until you find out what happens. For the man will not rest until the matter is settled today."[z]

Boaz Marries Ruth

4 Meanwhile Boaz went up to the town gate[a] and sat there. When the kinsman-redeemer[b] he had mentioned[c] came along, Boaz said, "Come over here, my friend, and sit down." So he went over and sat down.

2Boaz took ten of the elders[d] of the town and said, "Sit here," and they did so.[e] 3Then he said to the kinsman-redeemer, "Naomi, who has come back from Moab, is selling the piece of land that belonged to our brother Elimelech.[f] 4I thought I should bring the matter to your attention and suggest that you buy it in the presence of these seated here and in the presence of the elders of my people. If you will redeem it, do so. But if you[a] will not, tell me, so that I will know. For no-one has the right to do it except you,[g] and I am next in line."

"I will redeem it," he said.

5Then Boaz said, "On the day you buy the land from Naomi and from Ruth the Moabitess,[h] you acquire[b] the dead man's widow, in order to maintain the name of the dead with his property."[i]

6At this, the kinsman-redeemer said, "Then I cannot redeem[j] it because I might endanger my own estate. You redeem it yourself. I cannot do it."[k]

7(Now in earlier times in Israel, for the redemption[l] and transfer of property to become final, one party took off his sandal[m] and gave it to the other. This was the method of legalising transactions[n] in Israel.)[o]

8So the kinsman-redeemer said to Boaz, "Buy it yourself." And he removed his sandal.[p]

9Then Boaz announced to the elders and all the people, "Today you are witnesses[q] that I have bought from Naomi all the property of Elimelech, Kilion and Mahlon. 10I have also acquired Ruth the Moabitess,[r] Mahlon's widow, as my wife,[s] in order to maintain the name of the dead with his property, so that his name will not disappear from among his family or from the town records.[t] Today you are witnesses![u]"

11Then the elders and all those at the

2 [d]**Lev 2:14; Nu 18:27; Jdg 6:11**
3 [e]2Sa 12:20; 2Ki 5:10; Ps 26:6; 51:2; Isa 1:16; Jer 4:14; Eze 16:9; [f]2Sa 14:2; Isa 61:3; [g]**Ge 41:14**; [h]**Ex 32:6; Ecc 2:3; Jer 15:17**
5 [i]Eph 6:1; Col 3:20
6 [j]**Nu 18:27**
7 [k]Jdg 19:6,22; 1Sa 25:36; 2Sa 13:28; 1Ki 21:7; Est 1:10; [l]2Ch 31:6; SS 7:2; Jer 50:26; Hag 2:16
9 [m]Eze 16:8; [n]**Ru 2:20**
10 [o]**Jdg 17:2**; [p]**Jos 2:12**
11 [q]Pr 12:4; 14:1; 31:10
12 [r]**Ru 2:20**; [s]Ru 4:1
13 [t]Dt 25:5; Ru 4:5; Mt 22:24; [u]**Nu 14:21**; Hos 4:15; [v]Ru 4:6
14 [w]**Nu 18:27**; [x]Ro 14:16; 2Co 8:21
15 [y]Isa 3:22
18 [z]Ps 37:3–5

Ch. 4

1 [a]**Ge 18:1; 23:10**; [b]**Ru 2:20**; [c]Ru 3:12
2 [d]**Ex 3:16**; [e]**Dt 25:7**
3 [f]**Lev 25:25; Ru 1:2**
4 [g]**Lev 25:25**; Jer 32:7–8
5 [h]**Ru 1:22**; [i]**Ge 38:8; Ru 3:13**
6 [j]Lev 25:25; Ru 3:13; [k]**Dt 25:7**
7 [l]**Lev 25:24**; [m]ver 8; [n]Isa 8:1–2,16,20; [o]Dt 25:7–9
8 [p]Dt 25:9
9 [q]Isa 8:2; Jer 32:10,44
10 [r]**Ru 1:22**; [s]**Dt 25:5**; [t]**Dt 25:6**; [u]**Jos 24:22**

b15 Most Hebrew manuscripts; many Hebrew manuscripts, Vulgate and Syriac *she*

a4 Many Hebrew manuscripts, Septuagint, Vulgate and Syriac; most Hebrew manuscripts *he*

b5 Hebrew; Vulgate and Syriac *Naomi, you acquire Ruth the Moabitess,*

gate[v] said, "We are witnesses.[w] May the
LORD make the woman who is coming
into your home like Rachel and Leah,[x]
who together built up the house of
Israel. May you have standing in
Ephrathah[y] and be famous in Beth-
lehem.[z] 12Through the offspring the
LORD gives you by this young woman,
may your family be like that of Perez,[a]
whom Tamar[b] bore to Judah."

The Genealogy of David

4:18–22pp—1Ch 2:5–15; Mt 1:3–6; Lk 3:31–33

13So Boaz took Ruth and she became
his wife. Then he went to her, and the
LORD enabled her to conceive,[c] and she
gave birth to a son.[d] 14The women[e] said
to Naomi: "Praise be to the LORD,[f] who
this day has not left you without a
kinsman-redeemer.[g] May he become
famous throughout Israel! 15He will re-
new your life and sustain you in your
old age. For your daughter-in-law,[h]
who loves you and who is better to you
than seven sons,[i] has given him birth."
16Then Naomi took the child, laid him
in her lap and cared for him. 17The
women living there said, "Naomi has a
son." And they named him Obed. He
was the father of Jesse,[j] the father of
David.[k]
18This, then, is the family line of
Perez[l]:

Perez was the father of Hezron,[m]
19Hezron the father of Ram,
Ram the father of Amminadab,[n]
20Amminadab the father of Nahshon,[o]
Nahshon the father of Salmon,[c]
21Salmon the father of Boaz,[p]
Boaz the father of Obed,
22Obed the father of Jesse,
and Jesse the father of David.

11 [v]Ge 23:10; [w]Dt 25:9; [x]Ge 4:19; 29:16; [y]Ge 35:16; [z]Ru 1:19
12 [a]Ge 38:29; [b]Ge 38:6,24
13 [c]Ge 8:1; 29:31; [d]Ge 29:32; 30:6; Lk 1:57
14 [e]Lk 1:58; [f]Ge 24:27; [g]Ru 2:20
15 [h]Ge 11:31; [i]1Sa 1:8; 2:5; Job 1:2
17 [j]ver 22; 1Sa 16:1,18; 17:12,17,58; 1Ch 2:12–13; Ps 72:20; [k]1Sa 16:13; 1Ch 2:15
18 [l]Ge 38:29; [m]Nu 26:21
19 [n]Ex 6:23
20 [o]Nu 7:12
21 [p]Ru 2:1

[c]20 A few Hebrew manuscripts, some Septuagint manuscripts and Vulgate (see also verse 21 and Septuagint of 1 Chron. 2:11); most Hebrew manuscripts *Salma*

1 Samuel

The Birth of Samuel

1 There was a certain man from
Ramathaim,[a] a Zuphite[a][b] from the
hill country[c] of Ephraim,[d] whose name
was Elkanah[e] son of Jeroham, the son of
Elihu, the son of Tohu, the son of Zuph,
an Ephraimite. 2He had two wives;[f]
one was called Hannah and the other
Peninnah. Peninnah had children, but
Hannah had none.

3Year after year[g] this man went up
from his town to worship[h] and sacrifice
to the LORD Almighty at Shiloh,[i] where
Hophni and Phinehas, the two sons
of Eli,[j] were priests of the LORD.
4Whenever the day came for Elkanah to
sacrifice,[k] he would give portions of the
meat to his wife Peninnah and to all her
sons and daughters.[l] 5But to Hannah
he gave a double portion[m] because he
loved her, and the LORD had closed her
womb.[n] 6And because the LORD had
closed her womb, her rival kept provok-
ing her in order to irritate her.[o] 7This
went on year after year. Whenever
Hannah went up to the house of the
LORD, her rival provoked her till she
wept and would not eat.[p] 8Elkanah her
husband would say to her, "Hannah,
why are you weeping? Why don't you
eat? Why are you downhearted?
Don't I mean more to you than ten
sons?[q]"

9Once when they had finished eating
and drinking in Shiloh, Hannah stood
up. Now Eli the priest was sitting on a
chair by the doorpost of the LORD's tem-
ple.[b][r] 10In bitterness of soul[s] Hannah
wept much and prayed to the LORD.
11And she made a vow,[t] saying, "O
LORD Almighty[u], if you will only look
upon your servant's misery and remem-
ber[v] me, and not forget your servant but
give her a son, then I will give him to the
LORD for all the days of his life,[w] and
no razor[x] will ever be used on his
head."

12As she kept on praying to the LORD,
Eli observed her mouth. 13Hannah was
praying in her heart, and her lips were
moving but her voice was not heard. Eli
thought she was drunk 14and said to
her, "How long will you keep on getting
drunk? Get rid of your wine."

15"Not so, my lord," Hannah replied,
"I am a woman who is deeply troubled.[y]
I have not been drinking wine or beer; I
was pouring[z] out my soul to the LORD.
16Do not take your servant for a wicked
woman; I have been praying here out of
my great anguish and grief."[a]

17Eli answered, "Go in peace,[b] and
may the God of Israel grant you what
you have asked of him.[c]"

18She said, "May your servant find
favour in your eyes.[d]" Then she went
her way and ate something, and her
face was no longer downcast.[e]

19Early the next morning they arose
and worshipped before the LORD and
then went back to their home at Ramah.[f]
Elkanah lay with Hannah his wife, and
the LORD remembered[g] her. 20So in the
course of time Hannah conceived and
gave birth to a son.[h] She named[i] him
Samuel,[c][j] saying, "Because I asked the
LORD for him."

Hannah Dedicates Samuel

21When the man Elkanah went up
with all his family to offer the annual[k]
sacrifice to the LORD and to fulfil his
vow,[l] 22Hannah did not go. She said to
her husband, "After the boy is weaned,
I will take him and present[m] him be-
fore the LORD, and he will live there
always."

23"Do what seems best to you," Elka-
nah her husband told her. "Stay here
until you have weaned him; only may
the LORD make good[n] his[d] word." So the
woman stayed at home and nursed her
son until she had weaned[o] him.

24After he was weaned, she took the
boy with her, young as he was, along

Ch. 1

1 [a]**Jos 18:25**; [b]1Sa 9:5; [c]Jos 17:17–18; [d]Jos 21:20–22; [e]1Ch 6:27,34
2 [f]**Ge 4:19**
3 [g]ver 21; Ex 23:14; 1Sa 2:19; 20:6,29; Lk 2:41; [h]Dt 12:5–7; [i]**Jos 18:1**; [j]1Sa 2:31; 14:3
4 [k]Lev 7:15–18; Dt 12:17–18; [l]**Ge 29:34**
5 [m]**Ge 37:3**; [n]**Ge 11:30; 29:31**
6 [o]**Ge 16:4**
7 [p]2Sa 12:17; Ps 102:4
8 [q]**Ru 4:15**
9 [r]1Sa 3:3
10 [s]Job 3:20; 7:11; 10:1; 21:25; 23:2; 27:2; Isa 38:15; Jer 20:18
11 [t]**Jdg 11:30**; [u]**Ge 17:1**; Ps 24:10; 46:7; Isa 1:9; [v]**Ge 8:1**; [w]**Jdg 13:7**; [x]Nu 6:1–21; Jdg 13:5; Lk 1:15
15 [y]2Ki 4:27; [z]Ps 42:4; 62:8; La 2:19
16 [a]Ps 55:2
17 [b]Nu 6:26; 1Sa 20:42; 2Ki 5:19; **Ac 15:33**; [c]**Ge 25:21**; Ps 20:3–5
18 [d]**Ge 18:3**; Ru 2:13; [e]Ro 15:13
19 [f]**Jos 18:25**; [g]**Ge 8:1; 29:31**
20 [h]**Ge 17:19; 29:32; 30:6**; [i]Ex 2:10; Mt 1:21; [j]1Sa 7:5; 12:23; 1Ch 6:27; Jer 15:1; Heb 11:32
21 [k]**ver 3**; [l]**Ge 28:20**; Nu 30:2; Dt 12:11
22 [m]Ex 13:2; Lk 2:22
23 [n]**Ge 25:21**; [o]Ge 21:8

---

a1 Or *from Ramathaim Zuphim*
b9 That is, tabernacle
c20 *Samuel* sounds like the Hebrew for *heard of God.*
d23 Masoretic Text; Dead Sea Scrolls, Septuagint and Syriac *your*

with a three-year-old bull,[e p] an ephah[f]
of flour and a skin of wine, and brought
him to the house of the LORD at Shiloh.
25When they had slaughtered the bull,
they brought the boy to Eli, 26and she
said to him, "As surely as you live, my
lord, I am the woman who stood here
beside you praying to the LORD. 27I
prayed[q] for this child, and the LORD has
granted me what I asked of him. 28So
now I give him to the LORD. For his
whole life[r] he shall be given over to the
LORD." And he worshipped the LORD
there.

Hannah's Prayer

2 Then Hannah prayed and said:[a]

"My heart rejoices[b] in the LORD;
in the LORD my horn[a c] is lifted high.
My mouth boasts[d] over my enemies,[e]
for I delight in your deliverance.

2"There is no-one holy[b f] like[g] the LORD;
there is no-one besides you;
there is no Rock[h] like our God.

3"Do not keep talking so proudly
or let your mouth speak such
arrogance,[i]
for the LORD is a God who knows,[j]
and by him deeds[k] are weighed.[l]

4"The bows of the warriors are
broken,[m]
but those who stumbled are armed
with strength.[n]
5Those who were full hire themselves
out for food,
but those who were hungry[o] hunger
no more.
She who was barren[p] has borne seven
children,
but she who has had many sons
pines away.

6"The LORD brings death and makes
alive;[q]
he brings down to the grave[c] and
raises up.[r]
7The LORD sends poverty and wealth;[s]
he humbles and he exalts.[t]
8He raises[u] the poor[v] from the dust[w]
and lifts the needy[x] from the ash
heap;
he seats them with princes
and has them inherit a throne of
honour.[y]

"For the foundations[z] of the earth are
the LORD's;
upon them he has set the world.
9He will guard the feet[a] of his saints,[b]
but the wicked will be silenced in
darkness.[c]

"It is not by strength[d] that one
prevails;
10 those who oppose the LORD will be
shattered.[e]
He will thunder[f] against them from
heaven;
the LORD will judge[g] the ends of the
earth.

"He will give strength[h] to his king
and exalt the horn[i] of his anointed."

11Then Elkanah went home to
Ramah,[j] but the boy ministered[k] before
the LORD under Eli the priest.

Eli's Wicked Sons

12Eli's sons were wicked men; they
had no regard[l] for the LORD. 13Now it
was the practice[m] of the priests with the
people that whenever anyone offered a
sacrifice and while the meat[n] was being
boiled, the servant of the priest would
come with a three-pronged fork in his
hand. 14He would plunge it into the pan
or kettle or cauldron or pot, and the
priest would take for himself whatever
the fork brought up. This is how they
treated all the Israelites who came to
Shiloh. 15But even before the fat was
burned, the servant of the priest would
come and say to the man who was sac-
rificing, "Give the priest some meat to
roast; he won't accept boiled meat from
you, but only raw."
16If the man said to him, "Let the fat[o]
be burned up first, and then take what-
ever you want," the servant would then
answer, "No, hand it over now; if you
don't, I'll take it by force."
17This sin of the young men was
very great in the LORD's sight, for they[d]
were treating the LORD's offering with
contempt.[p]

24 [p]Nu 15:8–10
27 [q]1Sa 2:20; Ps 66:19–20
28 [r]**Jdg 13:7**

Ch. 2

1 [a]Lk 1:46–55; [b]Ps 13:5; 33:21; Zec 10:7; [c]Ps 18:2; 89:17,24; 148:14; [d]Ps 6:8; [e]**Nu 10:35**; Ps 6:10
2 [f]**Ex 15:11; Lev 11:44**; [g]**Ex 8:10**; Isa 40:25; 46:5; [h]**Ge 49:24; Ex 33:22**; Dt 32:37; 2Sa 22:2,32; 23:3; Ps 31:3; 71:3
3 [i]Ps 17:10; 31:18; 73:8; 75:4; 94:4; [j]**Jos 22:22**; [k]1Sa 16:7; 1Ki 8:39; 1Ch 28:9; 2Ch 6:30; Pr 15:11; Jer 11:20; 17:10; [l]Pr 16:2; 24:11–12
4 [m]2Sa 1:27; Ps 37:15; 46:9; 76:3; [n]Job 17:9; Isa 40:31; 41:1; 52:1; 57:10
5 [o]Lk 1:53; [p]Ps 113:9; Isa 54:1; Jer 15:9
6 [q]Dt 32:39; [r]Isa 26:19; Eze 37:3,12
7 [s]**Dt 8:18**; [t]Job 5:11; 40:12; Ps 75:7; Isa 2:12; 13:11; 22:19; Da 4:37
8 [u]Ps 113:7–8; [v]Jas 2:5; [w]1Ki 16:2; [x]Ps 72:12; 107:41; 145:14; 146:8; **Mt 23:12**; [y]2Sa 7:8; Job 36:7; Isa 22:23; Eze 21:26; [z]Job 15:7; 38:4; Ps 104:5; Pr 8:29; Isa 40:12; Jer 10:12
9 [a]Ps 91:12; 121:3; Pr 3:26; [b]Pr 2:8; [c]Job 10:22; Isa 5:30; 8:22; 59:9; 60:2; Jer 13:16; Am 5:18,20; Zep 1:14–15; Mt 8:12; [d]1Sa 17:47; Ps 33:16–17; Zec 4:6
10 [e]**Ex 15:6**; [f]**Ex 19:16**; 1Sa 7:10; 12:17; 2Sa 22:14; Job 37:4–5; 38:1; Ps 18:13; 29:3; Isa 66:6; [g]Ps 96:13; 98:9; Mt 25:31–32; [h]Ps 18:1; 21:1; 59:16; [i]**Dt 33:17**; Ps 89:24; **Lk 1:69** *11* [j]**Jos 18:25**; [k]ver 18; **Nu 16:9**; 1Sa 3:1
12 [l]Jer 2:8; 9:6 *13* [m]Dt 18:3; [n]Lev 7:35–36
16 [o]Lev 3:3,14–16; 7:29–34
17 [p]ver 22,29; **Nu 14:11**; Jer 7:21; Eze 22:26; Mal 2:7–9

e24 Dead Sea Scrolls, Septuagint and Syriac; Masoretic Text *with three bulls*
f24 That is, probably about 3/5 bushel (about 22 litres)
a1 *Horn* here symbolises strength; also in verse 10.
b2 Or *no Holy One* c6 Hebrew *Sheol*
d17 Or *men*

18But Samuel was ministering[q] before the LORD—a boy wearing a linen ephod.[r] 19Each year his mother made him a little robe and took it to him when she went up with her husband to offer the annual[s] sacrifice. 20Eli would bless Elkanah and his wife, saying, "May the LORD give you children by this woman to take the place of the one she prayed[t] for and gave to the LORD." Then they would go home. 21And the LORD was gracious to Hannah;[u] she conceived and gave birth to three sons and two daughters. Meanwhile, the boy Samuel grew[v] up in the presence of the LORD.

22Now Eli, who was very old, heard about everything[w] his sons were doing to all Israel and how they slept with the women[x] who served at the entrance to the Tent of Meeting. 23So he said to them, "Why do you do such things? I hear from all the people about these wicked deeds of yours. 24No, my sons; it is not a good report that I hear spreading among the LORD's people. 25If a man sins against another man, God[e] may mediate for him; but if a man sins against the LORD, who will[y] intercede[z] for him?" His sons, however, did not listen to their father's rebuke, for it was the LORD's will to put them to death.

26And the boy Samuel continued to grow[a] in stature and in favour with the LORD and with men.[b]

Prophecy Against the House of Eli

27Now a man of God[c] came to Eli and said to him, "This is what the LORD says: 'Did I not clearly reveal myself to your father's house when they were in Egypt under Pharaoh? 28I chose[d] your father out of all the tribes of Israel to be my priest, to go up to my altar, to burn incense,[e] and to wear an ephod[f] in my presence. I also gave your father's house all the offerings[g] made with fire by the Israelites. 29Why do you[f] scorn my sacrifice and offering[h] that I prescribed for my dwelling?[i] Why do you honour your sons more than me by fattening yourselves on the choice parts of every offering made by my people Israel?'

30"Therefore the LORD, the God of Israel, declares: 'I promised that your house and your father's house would minister before me for ever.[j]' But now the LORD declares: 'Far be it from me! Those who honour me I will honour,[k] but those who despise[l] me will be disdained.[m] 31The time is coming when I will cut short your strength and the strength of your father's house, so that there will not be an old man in your family line[n] 32and you will see distress[o] in my dwelling. Although good will be done to Israel, in your family line there will never be an old man.[p] 33Every one of you that I do not cut off from my altar will be spared only to blind your eyes with tears and to grieve your heart, and all your descendants[q] will die in the prime of life.

34" 'And what happens to your two sons, Hophni and Phinehas, will be a sign[r] to you—they will both die[s] on the same day.[t] 35I will raise up for myself a faithful priest,[u] who will do according to what is in my heart and mind. I will firmly establish his house, and he will minister before my anointed[v] one always. 36Then everyone left in your family line will come and bow down before him for a piece of silver and a crust of bread and plead,[w] "Appoint me to some priestly office so that I can have food to eat.[x]" ' "

The LORD Calls Samuel

3 The boy Samuel ministered[a] before the LORD under Eli. In those days the word of the LORD was rare;[b] there were not many visions.[c]

2One night Eli, whose eyes[d] were becoming so weak that he could barely see,[e] was lying down in his usual place. 3The lamp[f] of God had not yet gone out, and Samuel was lying down in the temple[a][g] of the LORD, where the ark[h] of God was. 4Then the LORD called Samuel.

Samuel answered, "Here I am.[i]" 5And he ran to Eli and said, "Here I am; you called me."

But Eli said, "I did not call; go back and lie down." So he went and lay down.

6Again the LORD called, "Samuel!" And Samuel got up and went to Eli and said, "Here I am; you called me."

"My son," Eli said, "I did not call; go back and lie down."

7Now Samuel did not yet know[j] the LORD: The word[k] of the LORD had not yet been revealed[l] to him.

8The LORD called Samuel a third time, and Samuel got up and went to Eli and said, "Here I am; you called me."

Then Eli realised that the LORD was calling the boy. 9So Eli told Samuel, "Go and lie down, and if he calls you, say,

18 [q]**ver 11**; [r]ver 28; 1Sa 22:18; 23:9; 2Sa 6:14; 1Ch 15:27
19 [s]**1Sa 1:3**
20 [t]**1Sa 1:27**
21 [u]Ge 21:1; [v]**Jdg 13:24**; Lk 1:80; 2:40
22 [w]**ver 17**; [x]**Ex 38:8**
25 [y]Ex 4:21; Jos 11:20; [z]**Ex 32:10; Nu 11:2**; 1Sa 3:14; 1Ki 13:6; Job 9:33; Ps 106:30; Isa 1:18; 22:14; Jer 15:1; Heb 10:26
26 [a]**Jdg 13:24**; Lk 2:52; [b]Pr 3:4
27 [c]**Dt 33:1; Jdg 13:6**
28 [d]**Ex 28:1**; [e]**Ex 30:7**; [f]1Sa 22:18; 23:6,9; 30:7; [g]Lev 7:35–36
29 [h]ver 12–17; [i]**Dt 12:5**
30 [j]**Ex 29:9**; [k]Ps 50:23; 91:15; Pr 8:17; [l]Isa 53:3; Na 3:6; Mal 2:9; [m]Jer 18:10
31 [n]1Sa 4:11–18; 22:16
32 [o]1Sa 4:3; 22:17–20; Jer 7:12,14; [p]1Ki 2:26–27
33 [q]Jer 29:32; Mal 2:12
34 [r]**Dt 13:2**; [s]1Sa 4:11; [t]1Ki 13:3
35 [u]2Sa 8:17; 20:25; 1Ki 1:8,32; 2:35; 4:4; 1Ch 16:39; 29:22; Eze 44:15–16; [v]1Sa 9:16; 10:1; 16:13; 2Sa 2:4; 12:7; 23:1; 1Ki 1:34; Ps 89:20
36 [w]Eze 44:10–14; [x]1Sa 3:12; 1Ki 2:27

Ch. 3

1 [a]**1Sa 2:11**; [b]Ps 74:9; La 2:9; Eze 7:26; [c]Am 8:11
2 [d]1Sa 4:15; [e]**Ge 27:1**
3 [f]Ex 25:31–38; Lev 24:1–4; [g]1Sa 1:9; [h]Dt 10:1–5; 1Ki 6:19; 8:1
4 [i]**Ge 22:1; Ex 3:4**
7 [j]1Sa 2:12; [k]Jer 1:2; [l]**Nu 12:6**; Am 3:7

[e]25 Or *the judges* [f]29 The Hebrew is plural.
[a]3 That is, tabernacle

'Speak, LORD, for your servant is listen-
ing.'" So Samuel went and lay down in
his place.
10The LORD came and stood there,
calling as at the other times, "Samuel!
Samuel![m]"
Then Samuel said, "Speak, for your
servant is listening."
11And the LORD said to Samuel: "See, I
am about to do something in Israel that
will make the ears of everyone who
hears of it tingle.[n] 12At that time I will
carry out against Eli everything[o] I spoke
against his family—from beginning to
end. 13For I told him that I would judge
his family for ever because of the sin he
knew about; his sons made themselves
contemptible,[b] and he failed to restrain[p]
them. 14Therefore, I swore to the house
of Eli, 'The guilt of Eli's house will never
be atoned[q] for by sacrifice or offering.'"
15Samuel lay down until morning and
then opened the doors of the house of
the LORD. He was afraid to tell Eli the
vision, 16but Eli called him and said,
"Samuel, my son."
Samuel answered, "Here I am."
17"What was it he said to you?" Eli
asked. "Do not hide[r] it from me.
May God deal with you, be it ever so
severely,[s] if you hide from me anything
he told you." 18So Samuel told him
everything, hiding nothing from him.
Then Eli said, "He is the LORD; let him
do what is good in his eyes."[t]
19The LORD was with[u] Samuel as he
grew[v] up, and he let none[w] of his words
fall to the ground. 20And all Israel from
Dan to Beersheba[x] recognised that
Samuel was attested as a prophet of the
LORD.[y] 21The LORD continued to appear
at Shiloh, and there he revealed[z] himself
to Samuel through his word.
4 And Samuel's word came to all
Israel.

The Philistines Capture the Ark

Now the Israelites went out to fight
against the Philistines. The Israelites
camped at Ebenezer,[a] and the Philis-
tines at Aphek.[b] 2The Philistines de-
ployed their forces to meet Israel, and as
the battle spread, Israel was defeated by
the Philistines, who killed about four
thousand of them on the battlefield.
3When the soldiers returned to camp,
the elders of Israel asked, "Why[c] did the
LORD bring defeat upon us today before
the Philistines? Let us bring the ark[d] of
the LORD's covenant from Shiloh,[e] so
that it[a] may go with us[f] and save us from
the hand of our enemies."
4So the people sent men to Shiloh,
and they brought back the ark of the
covenant of the LORD Almighty, who is
enthroned between the cherubim.[g] And
Eli's two sons, Hophni and Phinehas,
were there with the ark of the covenant
of God.
5When the ark of the LORD's covenant
came into the camp, all Israel raised
such a great shout[h] that the ground
shook. 6Hearing the uproar, the Philis-
tines asked, "What's all this shouting in
the Hebrew[i] camp?"
When they learned that the ark of the
LORD had come into the camp, 7the Phil-
istines were afraid.[j] "A god has come
into the camp," they said. "We're in
trouble! Nothing like this has happened
before. 8Woe to us! Who will deliver us
from the hand of these mighty gods?
They are the gods who struck[k] the
Egyptians with all kinds of plagues[l]
in the desert. 9Be strong, Philistines!
Be men, or you will be subject to the
Hebrews, as they[m] have been to you. Be
men, and fight!"
10So the Philistines fought, and the
Israelites were defeated[n] and every man
fled to his tent. The slaughter was very
great; Israel lost thirty thousand foot
soldiers. 11The ark of God was captured,
and Eli's two sons, Hophni and
Phinehas, died.[o]

Death of Eli

12That same day a Benjamite[p] ran
from the battle line and went to Shiloh,
his clothes torn and dust[q] on his head.
13When he arrived, there was Eli[r] sitting
on his chair by the side of the road,
watching, because his heart feared for
the ark of God. When the man entered
the town and told what had happened,
the whole town sent up a cry.
14Eli heard the outcry and asked,
"What is the meaning of this uproar?"
The man hurried over to Eli, 15who
was ninety-eight years old and whose
eyes[s] were set so that he could not see.
16He told Eli, "I have just come from the
battle line; I fled from it this very day."
Eli asked, "What happened, my
son?"
17The man who brought the news re-
plied, "Israel fled before the Philistines,
and the army has suffered heavy losses.
Also your two sons, Hophni and

10 [m]Ex 3:4
11 [n]2Ki 21:12; Job 15:21; Jer 19:3
12 [o]**1Sa 2:27–36**
13 [p]1Ki 1:6
14 [q]**1Sa 2:25**
17 [r]1Ki 22:14; Jer 23:28; 38:14; 42:4; [s]**Ru 1:17**
18 [t]**Jdg 10:15**
19 [u]**Ge 21:22; Nu 14:43;** [v]**Jdg 13:24;** [w]1Sa 9:6
20 [x]**Jdg 20:1;** [y]**Dt 18:22;** Eze 33:33
21 [z]**Nu 12:6**

Ch. 4

1 [a]1Sa 5:1; 7:12; [b]Jos 12:18; 1Sa 29:1; 1Ki 20:26
3 [c]Jos 7:7; [d]**Jos 6:7;** [e]**Jos 18:1; 1Sa 2:32;** [f]2Ch 13:8
4 [g]**Ge 3:24;** Ex **25:22**
5 [h]**Jos 6:5,** 10
6 [i]**Ge 14:13**
7 [j]**Ex 15:14**
8 [k]Ex 12:30; 1Sa 5:12; [l]Rev 11:6
9 [m]**Jdg 13:1**
10 [n]**Dt 28:25**
11 [o]Ps 78:64; Jer 7:12
12 [p]Eze 24:26; 33:21; [q]**Jos 7:6; 2Sa 1:2**
13 [r]ver 18
15 [s]**1Sa 3:2**

[b]*13* Masoretic Text; an ancient Hebrew scribal tradition and Septuagint *sons blasphemed God*
[a]3 Or *he*

Phinehas, are dead,[t] and the ark of God
has been captured."[u]
18When he mentioned the ark of God,
Eli fell backwards off his chair by the
side of the gate. His neck was broken
and he died, for he was an old man and
heavy. He had led[b][v] Israel for forty
years.[w]
19His daughter-in-law, the wife of
Phinehas, was pregnant and near the
time of delivery. When she heard the
news that the ark of God had been cap-
tured and that her father-in-law and her
husband were dead, she went into
labour and gave birth, but was over-
come by her labour pains. 20As she was
dying, the women attending her said,
"Don't despair; you have given birth to
a son." But she did not respond or pay
any attention.
21She named the boy Ichabod,[c][x]
saying, "The glory[y] has departed from
Israel"—because of the capture of the
ark of God and the deaths of her father-
in-law and her husband. 22She said,
"The glory[z] has departed from Israel,
for the ark of God has been captured."[a]

The Ark in Ashdod and Ekron

5 After the Philistines had captured
the ark of God, they took it from
Ebenezer[a] to Ashdod.[b] 2Then they car-
ried the ark into Dagon's temple and set
it beside Dagon.[c] 3When the people of
Ashdod rose early the next day, there
was Dagon, fallen[d] on his face on the
ground before the ark of the LORD! They
took Dagon and put him back in his
place. 4But the following morning when
they rose, there was Dagon, fallen on
his face on the ground before the ark of
the LORD! His head and hands had been
broken[e] off and were lying on the
threshold; only his body remained.
5That is why to this day neither the
priests of Dagon nor any others who
enter Dagon's temple at Ashdod step on
the threshold.[f]
6The LORD's hand[g] was heavy upon
the people of Ashdod and its vicinity; he
brought devastation[h] upon them and
afflicted them with tumours.[a][i] 7When
the men of Ashdod saw what was hap-
pening, they said, "The ark of the god of
Israel must not stay here with us, be-
cause his hand is heavy upon us and
upon Dagon our god." 8So they called
together all the rulers[j] of the Philistines
and asked them, "What shall we do
with the ark of the god of Israel?"
They answered, "Have the ark of the
god of Israel moved to Gath.[k]" So they
moved the ark of the God of Israel.
9But after they had moved it, the
LORD's hand was against that city,
throwing it into a great panic.[l] He
afflicted the people of the city, both
young and old, with an outbreak of
tumours.[b] 10So they sent the ark of God
to Ekron.[m]
As the ark of God was entering
Ekron, the people of Ekron cried out,
"They have brought the ark of the god
of Israel round to us to kill us and our
people." 11So they called together all the
rulers[n] of the Philistines and said,
"Send the ark of the god of Israel away;
let it go back to its own place, or it[c] will
kill us and our people." For death had
filled the city with panic; God's hand
was very heavy upon it. 12Those who
did not die[o] were afflicted with
tumours, and the outcry of the city went
up to heaven.

The Ark Returned to Israel

6 When the ark of the LORD had been
in Philistine territory for seven
months, 2the Philistines called for the
priests and the diviners[a] and said,
"What shall we do with the ark of the
LORD? Tell us how we should send it
back to its place."
3They answered, "If you return the
ark of the god of Israel, do not send it
away empty,[b] but by all means send a
guilt offering[c] to him. Then you will be
healed, and you will know why his
hand[d] has not been lifted from you."
4The Philistines asked, "What guilt
offering should we send to him?"
They replied, "Five gold tumours and
five gold rats, according to the number[e]
of the Philistine rulers, because the
same plague[f] has struck both you and
your rulers. 5Make models of the
tumours[g] and of the rats that are de-
stroying the country, and pay honour[h]
to Israel's god. Perhaps he will lift his
hand from you and your gods and your
land. 6Why do you harden[i] your hearts
as the Egyptians and Pharaoh did?
When he[a] treated them harshly,[j] did
they[k] not send the Israelites out so that
they could go on their way?

17 [t]1Sa 22:18; Ps 78:64; [u]Ps 78:61
18 [v]**Jdg 2:16; 16:31**; [w]1Sa 2:31
21 [x]**Ge 35:18**; [y]**Ex 24:16**; Ps 106:20; Jer 2:11; Eze 1:28; 9:3; 10:18
22 [z]**Ex 24:16**; Ps 78:61; [a]Jer 7:12

Ch. 5

1 [a]**1Sa 4:1**; [b]**Jos 11:22; 13:3**
2 [c]**Jdg 16:23**; Isa 2:18; 19:1; 46:1
3 [d]Isa 40:20; 41:7; 46:7; Jer 10:4
4 [e]Eze 6:6; Mic 1:7
5 [f]Zep 1:9
6 [g]**Ex 9:3**; Ac 13:11; [h]2Sa 6:7; Ps 78:66; [i]**Ex 15:26**; 1Sa 6:5
8 [j]**Jdg 16:18**; [k]**Jos 11:22**
9 [l]**Ex 14:24**
10 [m]**Jos 13:3**
11 [n]ver 8
12 [o]**1Sa 4:8**

Ch. 6

2 [a]**Ex 7:11; Isa 44:25**
3 [b]**Ex 22:29; 34:20**; [c]**Lev 5:15**; [d]ver 9
4 [e]**Jos 13:3**; [f]2Sa 24:25
5 [g]**1Sa 5:6**; [h]**Jos 7:19**; Rev 14:7
6 [i]**Ex 4:21**; [j]Ex 10:2; [k]**Ex 12:33**

---

[b]*18* Traditionally *judged*
[c]*21* *Ichabod* means *no glory.*
[a]*6* Hebrew; Septuagint and Vulgate *tumours. And rats appeared in their land, and death and destruction were throughout the city*
[b]*9* Or *with tumours in the groin* (see Septuagint)
[c]*11* Or *he*
[a]*6* That is, God

7"Now then, get a new cart[l] ready,
with two cows that have calved and
have never been yoked.[m] Hitch the
cows to the cart, but take their calves
away and pen them up. 8Take the ark of
the LORD and put it on the cart, and in a
chest beside it put the gold objects you
are sending back to him as a guilt offer-
ing. Send it on its way, 9but keep watch-
ing it. If it goes up to its own territory,
towards Beth Shemesh,[n] then the LORD
has brought this great disaster on us.
But if it does not, then we shall know
that it was not his hand that struck us
and that it happened to us by chance."
10So they did this. They took two such
cows and hitched them to the cart and
penned up their calves. 11They placed
the ark of the LORD on the cart and along
with it the chest containing the gold rats
and the models of the tumours. 12Then
the cows went straight up towards Beth
Shemesh, keeping on the road and low-
ing all the way; they did not turn to the
right or to the left. The rulers of the
Philistines followed them as far as the
border of Beth Shemesh.
13Now the people of Beth Shemesh
were harvesting their wheat[o] in the val-
ley, and when they looked up and saw
the ark, they rejoiced at the sight. 14The
cart came to the field of Joshua of Beth
Shemesh, and there it stopped beside a
large rock. The people chopped up the
wood of the cart and sacrificed the cows
as a burnt offering[p] to the LORD. 15The
Levites[q] took down the ark of the LORD,
together with the chest containing the
gold objects, and placed them on the
large rock.[r] On that day the people of
Beth Shemesh[s] offered burnt offerings
and made sacrifices to the LORD. 16The
five rulers of the Philistines saw all this
and then returned that same day to
Ekron.
17These are the gold tumours the Phil-
istines sent as a guilt offering to the
LORD—one each[t] for Ashdod, Gaza,
Ashkelon, Gath and Ekron. 18And the
number of the gold rats was according
to the number of Philistine towns be-
longing to the five rulers—the fortified
towns with their country villages. The
large rock, on which[b] they set the ark of
the LORD, is a witness to this day in the
field of Joshua of Beth Shemesh.
19But God struck down[u] some of the
men of Beth Shemesh, putting seventy[c]
of them to death because they had
looked[v] into the ark of the LORD. The
people mourned because of the heavy
blow the LORD had dealt them, 20and the
men of Beth Shemesh asked, "Who can
stand[w] in the presence of the LORD, this
holy[x] God? To whom will the ark go up
from here?"
21Then they sent messengers to the
people of Kiriath Jearim,[y] saying, "The
Philistines have returned the ark of the
LORD. Come down and take it up to
7 your place." 1So the men of Kiriath
Jearim came and took up the ark[a] of
the LORD. They took it to Abinadab's[b]
house on the hill and consecrated
Eleazar his son to guard the ark of the
LORD.

Samuel Subdues the Philistines at Mizpah

2It was a long time, twenty years in
all, that the ark remained at Kiriath
Jearim,[c] and all the people of Israel
mourned and sought after the LORD.[d]
3And Samuel said to the whole house of
Israel, "If you are returning[e] to the LORD
with all your hearts, then rid[f]
yourselves of the foreign gods and the
Ashtoreths[g] and commit[h] yourselves to
the LORD and serve him only,[i] and he
will deliver[j] you out of the hand of the
Philistines." 4So the Israelites put away
their Baals and Ashtoreths, and served
the LORD only.
5Then Samuel[k] said, "Assemble all
Israel at Mizpah[l] and I will intercede[m]
with the LORD for you." 6When they had
assembled at Mizpah,[n] they drew water
and poured[o] it out before the LORD. On
that day they fasted and there they con-
fessed, "We have sinned against the
LORD." And Samuel was leader[a][p] of
Israel at Mizpah.
7When the Philistines heard that
Israel had assembled at Mizpah, the
rulers of the Philistines came up to
attack them. And when the Israelites
heard of it, they were afraid[q] because of
the Philistines. 8They said to Samuel,
"Do not stop crying[r] out to the LORD our
God for us, that he may rescue us from
the hand of the Philistines." 9Then
Samuel[s] took a suckling lamb and
offered it up as a whole burnt offering to
the LORD. He cried out to the LORD on
Israel's behalf, and the LORD answered
him.[t]
10While Samuel was sacrificing the
burnt offering, the Philistines drew near
to engage Israel in battle. But that day

7 [l]2Sa 6:3; 1Ch 13:7; [m]**Nu 19:2**
9 [n]**Jos 15:10;** 21:16
13 [o]**Ge 30:14;** Ru 2:23; 1Sa 12:17
14 [p]1Sa 11:7; 2Sa 24:22; 1Ki 19:21
15 [q]Jos 3:3; [r]ver 18; [s]Jos 21:16
17 [t]**Jos 13:3**
19 [u]2Sa 6:7; [v]**Ex 19:21**
20 [w]2Sa 6:9; Ps 130:3; Mal 3:2; Rev 6:17; [x]**Lev 11:45**
21 [y]**Jos 9:17**

Ch. 7

1 [a]**Jos 6:7;** [b]2Sa 6:3; 1Ch 13:7
2 [c]1Ch 13:5; Ps 132:6; [d]1Ch 13:3
3 [e]Dt 30:10; 2Ki 18:5; 23:25; Jer 24:7; [f]**Ge 31:19; Jos 24:14;** [g]**Jdg 2:12–13;** 1Sa 12:10; 31:10; [h]Joel 2:12; [i]**Dt 6:13;** Mt 4:10; Lk 4:8; [j]**Jdg 2:18**
5 [k]**1Sa 1:20;** Ps 99:6; Jer 15:1; [l]**Jos 11:3;** Jdg 21:5; 1Sa 10:17; [m]**ver 8; Ge 20:7; Dt 9:19**
6 [n]**Jos 11:3;** [o]La 2:19; [p]**Jdg 2:16; 16:31**
7 [q]1Sa 17:11
8 [r]ver 5; **Ex 32:30; Nu 21:7;** 1Sa 12:19,23; 1Ki 18:24; Isa 37:4; Jer 15:1; 27:18
9 [s]Ps 99:6; [t]**Ex 32:11; Dt 9:19**

[b]*18* A few Hebrew manuscripts (see also Septuagint); most Hebrew manuscripts *villages as far as Greater Abel, where*
[c]*19* A few Hebrew manuscripts; most Hebrew manuscripts and Septuagint *50,070*
[a]*6* Traditionally *judge*

the LORD thundered[u] with loud thunder
against the Philistines and threw them
into such a panic[v] that they were routed
before the Israelites. 11The men of Israel
rushed out of Mizpah and pursued the
Philistines, slaughtering them along the
way to a point below Beth Car.

12Then Samuel took a stone[w] and set it
up between Mizpah and Shen. He
named it Ebenezer,[b] [x] saying, "Thus far
has the LORD helped us." 13So the Philis-
tines were subdued[y] and did not invade
Israelite territory again.

Throughout Samuel's lifetime, the
hand of the LORD was against the Philis-
tines. 14The towns from Ekron[z] to Gath
that the Philistines had captured from
Israel were restored to her, and Israel
delivered the neighbouring territory
from the power of the Philistines. And
there was peace between Israel and the
Amorites.[a]

15Samuel[b] continued as judge[c] over
Israel all[d] the days of his life. 16From year
to year he went on a circuit from Bethel[e]
to Gilgal[f] to Mizpah, judging[g] Israel in
all those places. 17But he always went
back to Ramah,[h] where his home was,
and there he also judged[i] Israel. And he
built an altar[j] there to the LORD.

Israel Asks for a King

8 When Samuel grew old, he
appointed[a] his sons as judges for
Israel. 2The name of his firstborn was
Joel and the name of his second was
Abijah,[b] and they served at Beersheba.[c]
3But his sons[d] did not walk in his ways.
They turned aside[e] after dishonest gain
and accepted bribes[f] and perverted[g]
justice.

4So all the elders[h] of Israel gathered
together and came to Samuel at Ramah.[i]
5They said to him, "You are old, and
your sons do not walk in your ways;
now appoint a king[j] to lead[a] [k] us, such as
all the other nations[l] have."

6But when they said, "Give us a king[m]
to lead us," this displeased[n] Samuel; so
he prayed to the LORD. 7And the LORD
told him: "Listen[o] to all that the people
are saying to you; it is not you they have
rejected,[p] but they have rejected me as
their king.[q] 8As they have done from the
day I brought them up out of Egypt until
this day, forsaking[r] me and serving
other gods, so they are doing to you.
9Now listen to them; but warn them
solemnly and let them know[s] what the
king who will reign over them will do."

10Samuel told[t] all the words of the
LORD to the people who were asking
him for a king. 11He said, "This is what
the king who will reign over you will do:
He will take[u] your sons and make them
serve[v] with his chariots and horses, and
they will run in front of his chariots.[w]
12Some he will assign to be comman-
ders[x] of thousands and commanders of
fifties, and others to plough his ground
and reap his harvest, and still others to
make weapons of war and equipment
for his chariots. 13He will take your
daughters to be perfumers and cooks
and bakers. 14He will take the best of
your[y] fields and vineyards[z] and olive
groves and give them to his attendants.[a]
15He will take a tenth[b] of your grain and
of your vintage and give it to his officials
and attendants. 16Your menservants
and maidservants and the best of your
cattle[b] and donkeys he will take for his
own use. 17He will take a tenth of your
flocks, and you yourselves will become
his slaves. 18When that day comes, you
will cry out for relief from the king you
have chosen, and the LORD will not
answer[c] you in that day.[d]"

19But the people refused[e] to listen to
Samuel. "No!" they said. "We want[f] a
king[g] over us. 20Then we shall be like all
the other nations,[h] with a king to lead us
and to go out before us and fight our
battles."

21When Samuel heard all that the
people said, he repeated[i] it before the
LORD. 22The LORD answered, "Listen[j] to
them and give them a king."

Then Samuel said to the men of Israel,
"Everyone is to go back to his town."

Samuel Anoints Saul

9 There was a Benjamite,[a] a man of
standing,[b] whose name was Kish[c]
son of Abiel, the son of Zeror, the son of
Becorath, the son of Aphiah of Ben-
jamin. 2He had a son named Saul, an
impressive[d] young man without equal[e]

10 [u]Ex 9:23; 1Sa 2:10; [v]Ge 35:5; Ex 14:24
12 [w]Ge 28:22; Dt 27:2; Jos 4:9; [x]1Sa 4:1
13 [y]Jdg 13:5
14 [z]Jos 13:3; [a]Jdg 1:34
15 [b]ver 6; 1Sa 12:11; [c]Jdg 2:16; [d]Jdg 2:18
16 [e]Ge 12:8; [f]Jos 10:43; 1Sa 10:8; Am 5:5; [g]ver 6; Ac 13:20
17 [h]Jos 18:25; 1Sa 8:4; 15:34; 19:18; 25:1; 28:3; [i]ver 6; [j]1Sa 9:12; 14:35; 20:6; 2Sa 24:25

Ch. 8

1 [a]Dt 16:18–19
2 [b]1Ch 6:28; [c]Ge 22:19; 1Ki 19:3; Am 5:4–5
3 [d]1Sa 2:12; [e]Ne 9:29; Job 34:27; Ps 14:3; 58:3; Isa 53:6; [f]Ex 23:8; 1Sa 12:3; Job 8:22; Pr 17:23; [g]Ex 23:2
4 [h]Jdg 11:11; 1Sa 11:3; [i]1Sa 7:17
5 [j]ver 19; Dt 17:14–20; 1Sa 10:19; 12:12–13; Hos 13:11; [k]1Sa 3:20; 12:2; [l]ver 20
6 [m]Hos 13:10; [n]1Sa 12:17; 15:11; 16:1
7 [o]ver 22; 1Sa 12:1; [p]Nu 11:20; [q]Ex 16:8
8 [r]1Sa 12:10; 2Ki 21:22; Jer 2:17
9 [s]ver 11–18; Dt 17:14–20; 1Sa 10:25
10 [t]Ex 19:7
11 [u]1Sa 14:52; [v]Ge 41:46; [w]Dt 17:16; 2Sa 15:1; 1Ki 1:5; 2Ch 1:14; 9:25; SS 3:7
12 [x]Dt 1:15
14 [y]Eze 46:18; [z]1Ki 21:7,15; Mic 2:2; [a]2Ki 22:12
15 [b]Ge 41:34; 1Sa 17:25
18 [c]1Sa 28:6; Job 27:9; 35:12–13; Ps 18:41; 66:18; Pr 1:28; Isa 1:15; 58:4; 59:2; Jer 14:12; Eze 8:18; Mic 3:4; [d]1Sa 10:25; 1Ki 12:4
19 [e]Pr 1:24; Isa 50:2; 66:4; Jer 7:13; 8:12; 13:10; 44:16; [f]Ac 13:21; [g]ver 5 *20* [h]ver 5 *21* [i]Jdg 11:11
22 [j]ver 7

Ch. 9

1 [a]Jos 18:11–20; [b]Ru 2:1; [c]1Sa 14:51; 1Ch 8:33; 9:39; Est 2:5; Ac 13:21
2 [d]Ge 39:6; [e]1Sa 10:24

[b]*12* *Ebenezer* means *stone of help.*
[a]*5* Traditionally *judge;* also in verses 6 and 20
[b]*16* Septuagint; Hebrew *young men*

among the Israelites—a head taller[f]
than any of the others.
3Now the donkeys[g] belonging to
Saul's father Kish were lost, and Kish
said to his son Saul, "Take one of the
servants with you and go and look for
the donkeys." 4So he passed through
the hill[h] country of Ephraim and
through the area around Shalisha,[i] but
they did not find them. They went on
into the district of Shaalim, but the
donkeys[j] were not there. Then he
passed through the territory of Benja-
min, but they did not find them.
5When they reached the district of
Zuph,[k] Saul said to the servant who was
with him, "Come, let's go back, or my
father will stop thinking about the don-
keys and start worrying[l] about us."
6But the servant replied, "Look, in
this town there is a man of God;[m] he is
highly respected, and everything[n] he
says comes true. Let's go there now.
Perhaps he will tell us what way to
take."
7Saul said to his servant, "If we go,
what can we give the man? The food in
our sacks is gone. We have no gift[o] to
take to the man of God. What do we
have?"
8The servant answered him again.
"Look," he said, "I have a quarter of a
shekel[a] of silver. I will give it to the man
of God so that he will tell us what way to
take." 9(Formerly in Israel, if a man
went to enquire[p] of God, he would say,
"Come, let us go to the seer," because
the prophet of today used to be called a
seer.)[q]
10"Good," Saul said to his servant.
"Come, let's go." So they set out for the
town where the man of God was.
11As they were going up the hill to the
town, they met some girls coming out to
draw[r] water, and they asked them, "Is
the seer here?"
12"He is," they answered. "He's
ahead of you. Hurry now; he has just
come to our town today, for the people
have a sacrifice[s] at the high place.[t] 13As
soon as you enter the town, you will
find him before he goes up to the high
place to eat. The people will not begin
eating until he comes, because he must
bless[u] the sacrifice; afterwards, those
who are invited will eat. Go up now;
you should find him about this time."
14They went up to the town, and as
they were entering it, there was
Samuel, coming towards them on his
way up to the high place.
15Now the day before Saul came, the
LORD had revealed this to Samuel:
16"About this time tomorrow I will send
you a man from the land of Benjamin.
Anoint[v] him leader[w] over my people
Israel; he will deliver[x] my people from
the hand of the Philistines.[y] I have
looked upon my people, for their cry[z]
has reached me."
17When Samuel caught sight of Saul,
the LORD said to him, "This[a] is the man I
spoke to you about; he will govern my
people."
18Saul approached Samuel in the gate-
way and asked, "Would you please tell
me where the seer's house is?"
19"I am the seer," Samuel replied.
"Go up ahead of me to the high place,
for today you are to eat with me, and in
the morning I will let you go and will tell
you all that is in your heart. 20As for the
donkeys[b] you lost three days ago, do not
worry about them; they have been
found. And to whom is all the desire[c] of
Israel turned, if not to you and all your
father's family?"
21Saul answered, "But am I not a
Benjamite, from the smallest tribe[d] of
Israel, and is not my clan the least[e] of all
the clans of the tribe of Benjamin?[f] Why
do you say such a thing to me?"
22Then Samuel brought Saul and his
servant into the hall and seated them at
the head of those who were invited
—about thirty in number. 23Samuel said
to the cook, "Bring the piece of meat I
gave you, the one I told you to lay
aside."
24So the cook took up the leg[g] with
what was on it and set it in front of Saul.
Samuel said, "Here is what has been
kept for you. Eat, because it was set
aside for you for this occasion, from the
time I said, 'I have invited guests.'"
And Saul dined with Samuel that day.
25After they came down from the high
place to the town, Samuel talked with
Saul on the roof[h] of his house. 26They
rose about daybreak and Samuel called
to Saul on the roof, "Get ready, and I
will send you on your way." When Saul
got ready, he and Samuel went outside
together. 27As they were going down to
the edge of the town, Samuel said to
Saul, "Tell the servant to go on ahead of
us"—and the servant did so—"but you
stay here awhile, so that I may give you
a message from God."

10

Then Samuel took a flask[a] of oil
and poured it on Saul's head
and kissed him, saying, "Has not the
LORD anointed[b] you leader over his

2 [f]1Sa 10:23
3 [g]ver 20; 1Sa 10:14,16
4 [h]**Jos 24:33**; [i]2Ki 4:42; [j]1Sa 10:2
5 [k]1Sa 1:1; [l]1Sa 10:2
6 [m]**Dt 33:1; Jdg 13:6**; [n]1Sa 3:19
7 [o]**Ge 32:20**; 1Ki 13:7; 14:3; 2Ki 4:42; 5:5,15; Jer 40:5
9 [p]**Ge 25:22**; [q]2Sa 15:27; 24:11; 2Ki 17:13; 1Ch 9:22; 21:9; 26:28; 29:29; 2Ch 19:2; Isa 29:10; 30:10; Am 7:12
11 [r]**Ge 24:11**,13
12 [s]Nu 28:11–15; **1Sa 7:17**; [t]**Lev 26:30**
13 [u]**Mt 14:19**; 1Co 10:16; 1Ti 4:3–5
16 [v]Ex 30:25; **1Sa 2:35**; 12:3; 15:1; 26:9; 2Ki 11:12; Ps 2:2; [w]2Sa 7:8; 1Ki 8:16; 1Ch 5:2; [x]Ex 3:8; [y]1Sa 23:4; 2Sa 3:18; [z]**Ge 16:11**; Ps 102:1
17 [a]1Sa 16:12
20 [b]**ver 3**; [c]1Sa 12:13; Ezr 6:8; Isa 60:4–9; Da 2:44; Hag 2:7; Mal 3:1
21 [d]Ps 68:27; [e]**Ex 3:11**; Mt 2:6; 1Co 15:9; [f]Jdg 6:15; 20:35,46; 1Sa 18:18
24 [g]**Lev 7:34**
25 [h]**Dt 22:8; Jos 2:8; Mt 24:17**; Lk 5:19

Ch. 10

1 [a]1Sa 16:1; 2Ki 9:1; [b]**Ex 29:7; 1Sa 9:16; 1Ki 1:39**

[a]8 That is, about 1/10 ounce (about 3 grams)

inheritance?[a][c] 2When you leave me today, you will meet two men near Rachel's tomb,[d] at Zelzah on the border of Benjamin. They will say to you, 'The donkeys[e] you set out to look for have been found. And now your father has stopped thinking about them and is worried[f] about you. He is asking, "What shall I do about my son?"'

3"Then you will go on from there until you reach the great tree of Tabor. Three men going up to God at Bethel[g] will meet you there. One will be carrying three young goats, another three loaves of bread, and another a skin of wine. 4They will greet you and offer you two loaves of bread,[h] which you will accept from them.

5"After that you will go to Gibeah[i] of God, where there is a Philistine outpost.[j] As you approach the town, you will meet a procession of prophets[k] coming down from the high place[l] with lyres, tambourines,[m] flutes[n] and harps[o] being played before them, and they will be prophesying.[p] 6The Spirit[q] of the LORD will come upon you in power, and you will prophesy with them; and you will be changed[r] into a different person. 7Once these signs are fulfilled, do whatever[s] your hand[t] finds to do, for God is with[u] you.

8"Go down ahead of me to Gilgal.[v] I will surely come down to you to sacrifice burnt offerings and fellowship offerings,[b] but you must wait seven[w] days until I come to you and tell you what you are to do."

Saul Made King

9As Saul turned to leave Samuel, God changed[x] Saul's heart, and all these signs[y] were fulfilled[z] that day. 10When they arrived at Gibeah, a procession of prophets met him; the Spirit[a] of God came upon him in power, and he joined in their prophesying.[b] 11When all those who had formerly known him saw him prophesying with the prophets, they asked each other, "What is this[c] that has happened to the son of Kish? Is Saul also among the prophets?"[d]

12A man who lived there answered, "And who is their father?" So it became a saying: "Is Saul also among the prophets?"[e] 13After Saul stopped prophesying,[f] he went to the high place.

14Now Saul's uncle[g] asked him and his servant, "Where have you been?"

"Looking for the donkeys,[h]" he said.

1 [c]**Ex 34:9**; 2Sa 20:19; Ps 78:62,71
2 [d]Ge 35:20; [e]1Sa 9:4; [f]1Sa 9:5
3 [g]**Ge 35:8**
4 [h]ver 27; 1Sa 16:20; Pr 18:16
5 [i]ver 26; 1Sa 11:4; 15:34; [j]1Sa 13:3; [k]**Nu 11:29**; 1Ki 20:35; 2Ki 2:3,15; 4:1; 6:1; 9:1; Am 7:14; [l]**Lev 26:30**; [m]**Ge 31:27**; Jer 31:4; [n]1Ki 1:40; Isa 30:29; [o]1Sa 16:16; 18:10; 19:9; 2Ki 3:15; Ps 92:3; [p]ver 10; 1Sa 19:20; 1Ch 25:1; 1Co 14:1
6 [q]**Nu 11:25**; [r]ver 9
7 [s]2Sa 7:3; 1Ki 8:17; 1Ch 22:7; 28:2; 2Ch 6:7; Ecc 9:10; [t]Jdg 9:33; [u]**Jos 1:5**; Lk 1:28; Heb 13:5
8 [v]Jos 4:20; **10:43**; 1Sa 7:16; 11:14; [w]1Sa 13:8
9 [x]ver 6; [y]**Dt 13:2**; [z]ver 7
10 [a]**Nu 11:25**; 1Sa 11:6; [b]**ver 5**
11 [c]Mt 13:54; Jn 7:15; [d]ver 12; 1Sa 19:24; 2Ki 9:11; Jer 29:26; Hos 9:7
12 [e]**ver 11**
13 [f]1Sa 19:23
14 [g]1Sa 14:50; [h]**1Sa 9:3**
16 [i]**1Sa 9:3**
17 [j]**1Sa 7:5**
18 [k]**Ex 1:14; Nu 10:9**
19 [l]**Nu 11:20; Dt 33:5**; [m]Ps 7:10; 18:48; 68:20; 145:19; [n]**1Sa 8:5**; [o]**Dt 17:14**; [p]Jos 7:14
21 [q]Est 3:7; Pr 16:33
22 [r]**Ge 25:22; Jdg 18:5**
23 [s]1Sa 9:2
24 [t]Dt 17:15; 2Sa 21:6; [u]1Sa 9:2; [v]1Ki 1:25,34,39; 2Ki 11:12
25 [w]**1Sa 8:9**; [x]**Dt 17:14-20; 1Sa 8:11-18**; 2Ki 11:12; [y]1Sa 11:14
26 [z]**ver 5; Jdg 19:14**; [a]**Jdg 20:44**

"But when we saw they were not to be found, we went to Samuel."

15Saul's uncle said, "Tell me what Samuel said to you."

16Saul replied, "He assured us that the donkeys[i] had been found." But he did not tell his uncle what Samuel had said about the kingship.

17Samuel summoned the people of Israel to the LORD at Mizpah[j] 18and said to them, "This is what the LORD, the God of Israel, says: 'I brought Israel up out of Egypt, and I delivered you from the power of Egypt and all the kingdoms that oppressed[k] you.' 19But you have now rejected[l] your God, who saves[m] you out of all your calamities and distresses. And you have said, 'No, set a king[n] over us.'[o] So now present[p] yourselves before the LORD by your tribes and clans."

20When Samuel brought all the tribes of Israel near, the tribe of Benjamin was chosen. 21Then he brought forward the tribe of Benjamin, clan by clan, and Matri's clan was chosen.[q] Finally Saul son of Kish was chosen. But when they looked for him, he was not to be found. 22So they enquired[r] further of the LORD, "Has the man come here yet?"

And the LORD said, "Yes, he has hidden himself among the baggage."

23They ran and brought him out, and as he stood among the people he was a head taller[s] than any of the others. 24Samuel said to all the people, "Do you see the man the LORD has chosen?[t] There is no-one like[u] him among all the people."

Then the people shouted, "Long live[v] the king!"

25Samuel explained[w] to the people the regulations[x] of the kingship.[y] He wrote them down on a scroll and deposited it before the LORD. Then Samuel dismissed the people, each to his own home.

26Saul also went to his home in Gibeah,[z] accompanied by valiant men[a] whose hearts God had touched. 27But some troublemakers[b] said, "How can this fellow save us?" They despised him and brought him no gifts.[c] But Saul kept silent.

27 [b]**Dt 13:13; 1Sa 20:7**; [c]**ver 4**; 1Ki 10:25; 2Ch 17:5; 32:23; Ps 68:29

---

[a]1 Hebrew; Septuagint and Vulgate *over his people Israel? You will reign over the LORD's people and save them from the power of their enemies round about. And this will be a sign to you that the LORD has anointed you leader over his inheritance:*

[b]8 Traditionally *peace offerings*

Saul Rescues the City of Jabesh

11 Nahash[a] the Ammonite went up and besieged Jabesh Gilead.[b] And all the men of Jabesh said to him, "Make a treaty[c] with us, and we will be subject to you."

2But Nahash the Ammonite replied, "I will make a treaty with you only on the condition[d] that I gouge[e] out the right eye of every one of you and so bring disgrace[f] on all Israel."

3The elders[g] of Jabesh said to him, "Give us seven days so that we can send messengers throughout Israel; if no-one comes to rescue[h] us, we will surrender[i] to you."

4When the messengers came to Gibeah[j] of Saul and reported these terms to the people, they all wept[k] aloud. 5Just then Saul was returning from the fields, behind his oxen, and he asked, "What is wrong with the people? Why are they weeping?" Then they repeated to him what the men of Jabesh had said.

6When Saul heard their words, the Spirit[l] of God came upon him in power, and he burned with anger. 7He took a pair of oxen,[m] cut them into pieces, and sent the pieces by messengers throughout Israel,[n] proclaiming, "This is what will be done to the oxen of anyone[o] who does not follow Saul and Samuel." Then the terror of the LORD fell on the people, and they turned out as one man.[p] 8When Saul mustered[q] them at Bezek,[r] the men of Israel numbered three hundred thousand and the men of Judah thirty thousand.

9They told the messengers who had come, "Say to the men of Jabesh Gilead, 'By the time the sun is hot tomorrow, you will be delivered.'" When the messengers went and reported this to the men of Jabesh, they were elated. 10They said to the Ammonites, "Tomorrow we will surrender[s] to you, and you can do to us whatever seems good to you."

11The next day Saul separated his men into three divisions;[t] during the last watch of the night they broke into the camp of the Ammonites[u] and slaughtered them until the heat of the day. Those who survived were scattered, so that no two of them were left together.

Saul Confirmed as King

12The people then said to Samuel, "Who[v] was it that asked, 'Shall Saul reign over us?' Bring these men to us and we will put them to death."

13But Saul said, "No-one shall be put to death today,[w] for this day the LORD has rescued[x] Israel."

14Then Samuel said to the people, "Come, let us go to Gilgal[y] and there reaffirm the kingship."[z] 15So all the people went to Gilgal[a] and confirmed Saul as king[b] in the presence of the LORD. There they sacrificed fellowship offerings[a] before the LORD, and Saul and all the Israelites held a great celebration.

Samuel's Farewell Speech

12 Samuel said to all Israel, "I have listened[a] to everything you said to me and have set a king[b] over you. 2Now you have a king as your leader.[c] As for me, I am old and grey, and my sons[d] are here with you. I have been your leader from my youth until this day. 3Here I stand. Testify against me in the presence of the LORD and his anointed.[e] Whose ox have I taken? Whose donkey[f] have I taken? Whom have I cheated? Whom have I oppressed? From whose hand have I accepted a bribe[g] to make me shut my eyes? If I have done[h] any of these, I will make it right."[i]

4"You have not cheated or oppressed us," they replied. "You have not taken anything from anyone's hand."

5Samuel said to them, "The LORD is witness[j] against you, and also his anointed is witness this day, that you have not found anything[k] in my hand."[l]

"He is witness," they said.

6Then Samuel said to the people, "It is the LORD who appointed Moses and Aaron and brought[m] your forefathers up out of Egypt. 7Now then, stand[n] here, because I am going to confront[o] you with evidence before the LORD as to all the righteous acts[p] performed by the LORD for you and your fathers.

8"After Jacob[q] entered Egypt, they cried[r] to the LORD for help, and the LORD sent[s] Moses and Aaron, who brought your forefathers out of Egypt and settled them in this place.

9"But they forgot[t] the LORD their God; so he sold them[u] into the hands of Sisera,[v] the commander of the army of Hazor,[w] and into the hands of the Philistines[x] and the king of Moab,[y] who fought against them. 10They cried[z] out to the LORD and said, 'We have sinned; we have forsaken[a] the LORD and served the Baals and the Ashtoreths.[b] But now

[a]15 Traditionally *peace offerings*

Ch. 11

1 [a]Ge 19:38; 1Sa 12:12; 2Sa 10:2; 17:27; 1Ch 19:1; [b]Jdg 21:8; 1Sa 31:11; 2Sa 2:4–5; 21:12; [c]Ex 23:32; Jer 37:1
2 [d]Ge 34:15; [e]Nu 16:14; [f]1Sa 17:26
3 [g]1Sa 8:4; [h]Jdg 2:16; [i]ver 10
4 [j]1Sa 10:5,26; [k]Ge 27:38; Nu 25:6
6 [l]Jdg 3:10
7 [m]1Sa 6:14; [n]Jdg 19:29; [o]Jdg 21:5; [p]Jdg 20:1
8 [q]Jdg 20:2; [r]Jdg 1:4
10 [s]ver 3
11 [t]Jdg 7:16; [u]Ge 19:38
12 [v]Dt 13:13; Lk 19:27
13 [w]2Sa 19:22; [x]1Sa 19:5; 1Ch 11:14
14 [y]Jos 10:43; 1Sa 10:8; [z]1Sa 10:25
15 [a]Jos 5:9; 2Sa 19:15; [b]1Sa 12:1

Ch. 12

1 [a]1Sa 8:7; [b]1Sa 11:15
2 [c]1Sa 8:5; [d]1Sa 8:3
3 [e]1Sa 9:16; 24:6; 26:9,11; 2Sa 1:14; 19:21; Ps 105:15; [f]Nu 16:15; [g]Ex 18:21; 1Sa 8:3; [h]Ex 20:17; Ac 20:33; [i]Lev 25:14
5 [j]Ge 31:50; [k]Ac 23:9; 24:20; [l]Ex 22:4
6 [m]Ex 3:10; Mic 6:4
7 [n]Jos 24:1; [o]Isa 1:18; 3:14; Jer 2:9; 25:31; Eze 17:20; 20:35; Mic 6:1–5; [p]Jdg 5:11
8 [q]Ge 46:6; [r]Ex 2:23; [s]Ex 3:10; 4:16
9 [t]Dt 32:18; Jdg 3:7; [u]Dt 32:30; [v]Jdg 4:2; [w]Jos 11:1; [x]Jdg 10:7; [y]Jdg 3:12
10 [z]Jdg 3:9; [a]1Sa 8:8; [b]1Sa 7:3

deliver us from the hands of our enemies, and we will serve you.' 11Then the LORD sent Jerub-Baal,[a][c] Barak,[b][d] Jephthah[e] and Samuel,[c][f] and he delivered you from the hands of your enemies on every side, so that you lived securely.

12"But when you saw that Nahash[g] king[h] of the Ammonites was moving against you, you said to me, 'No, we want a king to rule[i] over us'—even though the LORD your God was your king. 13Now here is the king[j] you have chosen, the one you asked[k] for; see, the LORD has set a king over you. 14If you fear[l] the LORD and serve and obey him and do not rebel[m] against his commands, and if both you and the king who reigns over you follow the LORD your God—good! 15But if you do not obey the LORD, and if you rebel against[n] his commands, his hand will be against you, as it was against your fathers.

16"Now then, stand still[o] and see[p] this great thing the LORD is about to do before your eyes! 17Is it not wheat harvest[q] now? I will call[r] upon the LORD to send thunder[s] and rain.[t] And you will realise what an evil[u] thing you did in the eyes of the LORD when you asked for a king."

18Then Samuel called upon the LORD,[v] and that same day the LORD sent thunder and rain. So all the people stood in awe[w] of the LORD and of Samuel.

19The people all said to Samuel, "Pray[x] to the LORD your God for your servants so that we will not die,[y] for we have added to all our other sins the evil of asking for a king."

20"Do not be afraid," Samuel replied. "You have done all this evil;[z] yet do not turn away from the LORD, but serve the LORD with all your heart. 21Do not turn away after useless[a] idols.[b] They can do you no good, nor can they rescue you, because they are useless. 22For the sake[c] of his great name[d] the LORD will not reject[e] his people, because the LORD was pleased to make[f] you his own. 23As for me, far be it from me that I should sin against the LORD by failing to pray[g] for you. And I will teach[h] you the way that is good and right. 24But be sure to fear[i] the LORD and serve him faithfully with all your heart;[j] consider[k] what great[l] things he has done for you. 25Yet if you persist[m] in doing evil, both you and your king[n] will be swept[o] away."

Samuel Rebukes Saul

13 Saul was ⌊thirty⌋[a] years old when he became king, and he reigned over Israel for ⌊forty-⌋[b] two years.

2Saul[c] chose three thousand men from Israel; two thousand[a] were with him at Michmash[b] and in the hill country of Bethel, and a thousand were with Jonathan at Gibeah[c] in Benjamin. The rest of the men he sent back to their homes.

3Jonathan attacked the Philistine outpost[d] at Geba,[e] and the Philistines heard about it. Then Saul had the trumpet[f] blown throughout the land and said, "Let the Hebrews hear!" 4So all Israel heard the news: "Saul has attacked the Philistine outpost, and now Israel has become an offence[g] to the Philistines." And the people were summoned to join Saul at Gilgal.

5The Philistines assembled[h] to fight Israel, with three thousand[d] chariots, six thousand charioteers, and soldiers as numerous as the sand[i] on the seashore. They went up and camped at Michmash,[j] east of Beth Aven.[k] 6When the men of Israel saw that their situation was critical and that their army was hard pressed, they hid[l] in caves and thickets, among the rocks, and in pits and cisterns.[m] 7Some Hebrews even crossed the Jordan to the land of Gad[n] and Gilead.

Saul remained at Gilgal, and all the troops with him were quaking[o] with fear. 8He waited for seven[p] days, the time set by Samuel; but Samuel did not come to Gilgal, and Saul's men began to scatter. 9So he said, "Bring me the burnt offering and the fellowship offerings."[e] And Saul offered[q] up the burnt offering. 10Just as he finished making the offering, Samuel[r] arrived, and Saul went out to greet[s] him.

11"What have you done?" asked Samuel.

Saul replied, "When I saw that the men were scattering, and that you did not come at the set time, and that the

11 [c]Jdg 6:32; [d]**Jdg 4:6**; [e]**Jdg 11:1**; [f]**1Sa 7:15**
12 [g]**1Sa 11:1**; [h]**1Sa 8:5**; [i]1Sa 25:30; 2Sa 5:2; 1Ch 5:2
13 [j]**1Sa 8:5**; [k]**1Sa 9:20**
14 [l]**Jos 24:14**; [m]Jer 4:17; La 1:18
15 [n]Lev 26:16; Jos 24:20; Isa 1:20; Jer 4:17; 26:4
16 [o]**Ex 14:14**; [p]**Ex 14:13**
17 [q]**Ge 30:14**; **1Sa 6:13**; [r]1Ki 18:42; Jas 5:18; [s]**Ex 9:23**; **1Sa 2:10**; [t]Ge 7:12; Ex 9:18; Job 37:13; Pr 26:1; [u]**1Sa 8:6**
18 [v]Ps 99:6; [w]**Ge 3:10**; **Ex 14:31**
19 [x]**Ex 8:8**; **1Sa 7:8**; **Jer 37:3**; Jas 5:18; 1Jn 5:16; [y]**Dt 9:19**
20 [z]**Ex 32:30**
21 [a]Isa 40:20; 41:24,29; 44:9; Jer 2:5,11; 14:22; 16:19; Jnh 2:8; Hab 2:18; Ac 14:15; [b]Dt 11:16
22 [c]Ps 25:11; 106:8; Isa 48:9,11; Jer 14:7; Da 9:19; [d]**Jos 7:9**; 2Sa 7:23; Jn 17:12; [e]**Lev 26:11**; **Dt 31:6**; [f]Dt 7:7; 1Pe 2:9
23 [g]**Nu 11:2**; **1Sa 1:20**; **7:8**; Ro 1:10; [h]1Ki 8:36; Ps 25:4; 34:11; 86:11; 94:12; Pr 4:11
24 [i]Dt 6:2; Ecc 12:13; [j]Dt 6:5; **Jos 24:14**; [k]Job 34:27; Isa 5:12; 22:11; 26:10; [l]**Dt 10:21**
25 [m]1Sa 31:1–5; [n]Dt 28:36; [o]**Jos 24:20**; **1Ki 14:10**

Ch. 13

2 [a]ver 15; [b]ver 5,11,23; Ne 11:31; Isa 10:28; [c]**Jdg 19:14**
3 [d]**1Sa 10:5**; [e]**Jos 18:24**; [f]**Lev 25:9**; **Jdg 3:27**
4 [g]**Ge 34:30**
5 [h]1Sa 17:1; [i]**Jos 11:4**; Rev 20:8; [j]**ver 2**; [k]**Jos 7:2**
6 [l]1Sa 14:11,22; [m]**Jdg 6:2**; Eze 33:27
7 [n]**Nu 32:33**; [o]**Ge 35:5**; **Ex 19:16**
8 [p]1Sa 10:8
9 [q]Dt 12:5–14; 2Sa 24:25; 1Ki 3:4
10 [r]1Sa 15:13; [s]1Sa 25:14

[a]11 Also called *Gideon*
[b]11 Some Septuagint manuscripts and Syriac; Hebrew *Bedan*
[c]11 Hebrew; some Septuagint manuscripts and Syriac *Samson*
[a]1 A few late manuscripts of the Septuagint; Hebrew does not have *thirty.*
[b]1 See the round number in Acts 13:21; Hebrew does not have *forty-.*
[c]1,2 Or *and when he had reigned over Israel for two years,* [2]*he*
[d]5 Some Septuagint manuscripts and Syriac; Hebrew *thirty thousand*
[e]9 Traditionally *peace offerings*

Philistines were assembling at Mich-
mash,[t] 12I thought, 'Now the Philistines
will come down against me at Gilgal,[u]
and I have not sought the LORD's
favour.[v]' So I felt compelled to offer the
burnt offering."
13"You acted foolishly,[w]" Samuel
said. "You have not kept[x] the command
the LORD your God gave you; if you had,
he would have established your king-
dom over Israel for all time.[y] 14But now
your kingdom[z] will not endure; the
LORD has sought out a man after his own
heart[a] and appointed[b] him leader[c] of his
people, because you have not kept[d] the
LORD's command."
15Then Samuel left Gilgal[f] and went
up to Gibeah[e] in Benjamin, and Saul
counted the men who were with him.
They numbered about six hundred.[f]

Israel Without Weapons

16Saul and his son Jonathan and
the men with them were staying in
Gibeah[g][g] of Benjamin, while the
Philistines camped at Michmash.
17Raiding[h] parties went out from the
Philistine camp in three detachments.
One turned towards Ophrah[i] in the
vicinity of Shual, 18another towards
Beth Horon,[j] and the third towards the
borderland overlooking the Valley of
Zeboim[k] facing the desert.
19Not a blacksmith[l] could be found in
the whole land of Israel, because the
Philistines had said, "Otherwise the
Hebrews will make swords or spears![m]"
20So all Israel went down to the Philis-
tines to have their ploughshares, mat-
tocks, axes and sickles[h] sharpened.
21The price was two thirds of a shekel[i]
for sharpening ploughshares and
mattocks, and a third of a shekel[j]
for sharpening forks and axes and for
repointing goads.
22So on the day of the battle not a
soldier with Saul and Jonathan[n] had a
sword or spear[o] in his hand; only Saul
and his son Jonathan had them.

Jonathan Attacks the Philistines

23Now a detachment of Philistines
had gone out to the pass[p] at Michmash.[q]
14 1One day Jonathan son of Saul
said to the young man bearing
his armour, "Come, let's go over to the
Philistine outpost on the other side."
But he did not tell his father.
2Saul was staying[a] on the outskirts of
Gibeah[b] under a pomegranate tree[c] in

11 [t]ver 2
12 [u]**Jos 10:43;** [v]**Dt 4:29;** Ps 119:58; Jer 26:19
13 [w]2Ch 16:9; [x]ver 14; **Jos 22:16;** 1Sa 15:23–24; 2Sa 7:15; 1Ch 10:13; [y]Ps 72:5
14 [z]1Sa 15:28; 18:8; 24:20; 1Ch 10:14; [a]Ac 7:46; 13:22; [b]2Sa 6:21; [c]1Sa 25:30; 2Sa 5:2; Ps 18:43; Isa 16:5; 55:4; Jer 30:9; Eze 34:23–24; 37:24; Da 9:25; Hos 3:5; Mic 5:2; [d]1Sa 15:26; 16:1; 2Sa 12:9; 1Ki 13:21; Hos 13:11
15 [e]1Sa 14:2; [f]ver 2
16 [g]**Jos 18:24**
17 [h]1Sa 14:15; [i]**Jos 18:23**
18 [j]**Jos 10:10;** [k]Ne 11:34
19 [l]**Ge 4:22;** [m]**Nu 25:7**
22 [n]1Ch 9:39; [o]**Nu 25:7;** 1Sa 14:6; 17:47; Zec 4:6
23 [p]1Sa 14:4; [q]**ver 2**

Ch. 14

2 [a]**Jdg 4:5;** [b]1Sa 13:15; [c]**Ex 28:33;** [d]Isa 10:28
3 [e]**Ge 35:18;** [f]1Sa 22:11,20; [g]**1Sa 1:3;** [h]Ps 78:60
4 [i]1Sa 13:23
5 [j]**Jos 18:24**
6 [k]Jdg 14:3; 1Sa 17:26,36; 31:4; Jer 9:26; Eze 28:10; [l]**1Sa 13:22; 1Ki 19:12; Mt 19:26;** Heb 11:34; [m]Jdg 7:4; [n]Ps 33:16
10 [o]**Ge 24:14;** [p]**Jos 2:24**
11 [q]**Ge 14:13;** [r]**1Sa 13:6**
12 [s]Jdg 8:16; [t]1Sa 17:46; 2Sa 5:24

Migron.[d] With him were about six hun-
dred men, 3among whom was Ahijah,
who was wearing an ephod. He was a
son of Ichabod's[e] brother Ahitub[f] son of
Phinehas, the son of Eli,[g] the LORD's
priest in Shiloh.[h] No-one was aware that
Jonathan had left.
4On each side of the pass[i] that Jona-
than intended to cross to reach the
Philistine outpost was a cliff; one was
called Bozez, and the other Seneh. 5One
cliff stood to the north towards Mich-
mash, the other to the south towards
Geba.[j]
6Jonathan said to his young armour-
bearer, "Come, let's go over to the out-
post of those uncircumcised[k] fellows.
Perhaps the LORD will act on our behalf.
Nothing[l] can hinder the LORD from
saving, whether by many[m] or by few.[n]"
7"Do all that you have in mind," his
armour-bearer said. "Go ahead; I am
with you heart and soul."
8Jonathan said, "Come, then; we will
cross over towards the men and let
them see us. 9If they say to us, 'Wait
there until we come to you,' we will stay
where we are and not go up to them.
10But if they say, 'Come up to us,' we
will climb up, because that will be our
sign[o] that the LORD has given them into
our hands.[p]"
11So both of them showed themselves
to the Philistine outpost. "Look!" said
the Philistines. "The Hebrews[q] are
crawling out of the holes they were
hiding[r] in." 12The men of the outpost
shouted to Jonathan and his armour-
bearer, "Come up to us and we'll teach
you a lesson.[s]"
So Jonathan said to his armour-
bearer, "Climb up after me; the LORD
has given them into the hand[t] of Israel."
13Jonathan climbed up, using his
hands and feet, with his armour-bearer
right behind him. The Philistines fell
before Jonathan, and his armour-bearer
followed and killed behind him. 14In
that first attack Jonathan and his
armour-bearer killed some twenty men
in an area of about half an acre.[a]

f15 Hebrew; Septuagint *Gilgal and went his way; the rest of the people went after Saul to meet the army, and they went out of Gilgal*
g16 Two Hebrew manuscripts; most Hebrew manuscripts *Geba*, a variant of *Gibeah*
h20 Septuagint; Hebrew *ploughshares*
i21 Hebrew *pim;* that is, about ¼ ounce (about 8 grams)
j21 That is, about ⅛ ounce (about 4 grams)
a14 Hebrew *half a yoke;* a "yoke" was the land ploughed by a yoke of oxen in one day.

Israel Routs the Philistines

15Then panic[u] struck the whole army
—those in the camp and field, and those
in the outposts and raiding[v] parties—
and the ground shook. It was a panic
sent by God.[b]
16Saul's lookouts[w] at Gibeah of Ben-
jamin saw the army melting away in all
directions. 17Then Saul said to the men
who were with him, "Muster the forces
and see who has left us." When they
did, it was Jonathan and his armour-
bearer who were not there.
18Saul said to Ahijah, "Bring[x] the ark[y]
of God." (At that time it was with the
Israelites.)[c] 19While Saul was talking to
the priest, the tumult in the Philistine
camp increased more and more. So Saul
said to the priest,[z] "Withdraw your
hand."
20Then Saul and all his men assem-
bled and went to the battle. They found
the Philistines in total confusion, strik-
ing[a] each other with their swords.
21Those Hebrews who had previously
been with the Philistines and had gone
up with them to their camp went[b] over
to the Israelites who were with Saul and
Jonathan. 22When all the Israelites who
had hidden[c] in the hill country of
Ephraim heard that the Philistines were
on the run, they joined the battle in hot
pursuit. 23So the LORD rescued[d] Israel
that day, and the battle moved on
beyond Beth Aven.[e]

Jonathan Eats Honey

24Now the men of Israel were in dis-
tress that day, because Saul had bound
the people under an oath,[f] saying,
"Cursed be any man who eats food
before evening comes, before I have
avenged myself on my enemies!" So
none of the troops tasted food.
25The entire army[d] entered the
woods, and there was honey on the
ground. 26When they went into the
woods, they saw the honey oozing out,
yet no-one put his hand to his mouth,
because they feared the oath. 27But
Jonathan had not heard that his father
had bound the people with the oath, so
he reached out the end of the staff that
was in his hand and dipped it into the
honeycomb.[g] He raised his hand to his
mouth, and his eyes brightened.[e]
28Then one of the soldiers told him,
"Your father bound the army under a
strict oath, saying, 'Cursed be any man
who eats food today!' That is why the
men are faint."
29Jonathan said, "My father has made
trouble[h] for the country. See how my
eyes brightened[f] when I tasted a little of
this honey. 30How much better it would
have been if the men had eaten today
some of the plunder they took from
their enemies. Would not the slaughter
of the Philistines have been even
greater?"
31That day, after the Israelites had
struck down the Philistines from Mich-
mash[i] to Aijalon,[j] they were exhausted.
32They pounced on the plunder[k] and,
taking sheep, cattle and calves, they
butchered them on the ground and ate
them, together with the blood.[l] 33Then
someone said to Saul, "Look, the men
are sinning against the LORD by eating
meat that has blood[m] in it."
"You have broken faith," he said.
"Roll a large stone over here at once."
34Then he said, "Go out among the men
and tell them, 'Each of you bring me
your cattle and sheep, and slaughter
them here and eat them. Do not sin
against the LORD by eating meat with
blood still[n] in it.'"
So everyone brought his ox that night
and slaughtered it there. 35Then Saul
built an altar[o] to the LORD; it was the first
time he had done this.
36Saul said, "Let us go down after the
Philistines by night and plunder them
till dawn, and let us not leave one of
them alive."
"Do whatever seems best to you,"
they replied.
But the priest said, "Let us enquire[p] of
God here."
37So Saul asked God, "Shall I go down
after the Philistines? Will you give them
into Israel's hand?" But God did not
answer[q] him that day.
38Saul therefore said, "Come here, all
you who are leaders of the army, and let
us find out what sin has been commit-
ted[r] today. 39As surely as the LORD who
rescues Israel lives,[s] even if it lies with
my son Jonathan,[t] he must die."[u] But
not one of the men said a word.
40Saul then said to all the Israelites,
"You stand over there; I and Jonathan
my son will stand over here."
"Do what seems best to you," the
men replied.
41Then Saul prayed to the LORD, the

15 [u]**Ge 35:5; Ex 14:24; 19:16;** 2Ki 7:5–7; [v]1Sa 13:17
16 [w]2Sa 18:24; 2Ki 9:17; Isa 52:8; Eze 33:2
18 [x]1Sa 30:7; [y]**Jdg 18:5**
19 [z]Nu 27:21
20 [a]**Jdg 7:22**; Eze 38:21; Zec 14:13
21 [b]1Sa 29:4
22 [c]**1Sa 13:6**
23 [d]**Ex 14:30**; [e]**Jos 7:2**
24 [f]Jos 6:26
27 [g]ver 43; Ps 19:10; Pr 16:24; 24:13
29 [h]Jos 7:25; 1Ki 18:18
31 [i]ver 5; [j]**Jos 10:12**
32 [k]1Sa 15:19; Est 9:10; [l]**Ge 9:4**
33 [m]**Ge 9:4**
34 [n]Lev 19:26
35 [o]**1Sa 7:17**
36 [p]**Ge 25:22; Jdg 18:5**
37 [q]1Sa 28:6,15; 2Sa 22:42; Ps 18:41
38 [r]Jos 7:11
39 [s]**Nu 14:21;** 2Sa 12:5; Job 19:25; Ps 18:46; 42:2; [t]ver 44; [u]Jos 7:15

b15 Or *a terrible panic*
c18 Hebrew; Septuagint *"Bring the ephod." (At that time he wore the ephod before the Israelites.)*
d25 Or *Now all the people of the land*
e27 Or *his strength was renewed*
f29 Or *my strength was renewed*

God of Israel, "Give[v] me the right[w] answer."[g] And Jonathan and Saul were taken by lot, and the men were cleared. 42Saul said, "Cast the lot[x] between me and Jonathan my son." And Jonathan was taken.

43Then Saul said to Jonathan, "Tell me what you have done."[y]

So Jonathan told him, "I merely tasted a little honey[z] with the end of my staff. And now must I die?"

44Saul said, "May God deal with me, be it ever so severely,[a] if you do not die, Jonathan.[b]"

45But the men said to Saul, "Should Jonathan die—he who has brought about this great deliverance in Israel? Never! As surely as the LORD lives, not a hair[c] of his head shall fall to the ground, for he did this today with God's help." So the men rescued[d] Jonathan, and he was not put to death.

46Then Saul stopped pursuing the Philistines, and they withdrew to their own land.

47After Saul had assumed rule over Israel, he fought against their enemies on every side: Moab,[e] the Ammonites,[f] Edom,[g] the kings[h] of Zobah,[h] and the Philistines. Wherever he turned, he inflicted punishment on them.[i] 48He fought valiantly and defeated the Amalekites,[i] delivering Israel from the hands of those who had plundered them.

Saul's Family

49Saul's sons were Jonathan, Ishvi and Malki-Shua.[j] The name of his older daughter was Merab, and that of the younger was Michal.[k] 50His wife's name was Ahinoam daughter of Ahimaaz. The name of the commander of Saul's army was Abner[l] son of Ner, and Ner was Saul's uncle.[m] 51Saul's father Kish[n] and Abner's father Ner were sons of Abiel.

52All the days of Saul there was bitter war with the Philistines, and whenever Saul saw a mighty or brave man, he took[o] him into his service.

The LORD Rejects Saul as King

15 Samuel said to Saul, "I am the one the LORD sent to anoint[a] you king over his people Israel; so listen now to the message from the LORD. 2This is what the LORD Almighty says: 'I will punish the Amalekites[b] for what they did to Israel when they waylaid them as they came up from Egypt. 3Now go, attack the Amalekites and totally[c] destroy[a] everything that belongs to them. Do not spare them; put to death men and women, children and infants, cattle and sheep, camels and donkeys.'"

4So Saul summoned the men and mustered them at Telaim—two hundred thousand foot soldiers and ten thousand men from Judah. 5Saul went to the city of Amalek and set an ambush in the ravine. 6Then he said to the Kenites,[d] "Go away, leave the Amalekites so that I do not destroy you along with them; for you showed kindness to all the Israelites when they came up out of Egypt." So the Kenites moved away from the Amalekites.

7Then Saul attacked the Amalekites[e] all the way from Havilah to Shur,[f] to the east of Egypt. 8He took Agag[g] king of the Amalekites alive,[h] and all his people he totally destroyed with the sword. 9But Saul and the army spared[i] Agag and the best of the sheep and cattle, the fat calves[b] and lambs—everything that was good. These they were unwilling to destroy completely, but everything that was despised and weak they totally destroyed.

10Then the word of the LORD came to Samuel: 11"I am grieved[j] that I have made Saul king, because he has turned[k] away from me and has not carried out my instructions."[l] Samuel was troubled,[m] and he cried out to the LORD all that night.

12Early in the morning Samuel got up and went to meet Saul, but he was told, "Saul has gone to Carmel.[n] There he has set up a monument[o] in his own honour and has turned and gone on down to Gilgal."

13When Samuel reached him, Saul said, "The LORD bless you! I have carried out the LORD's instructions."

14But Samuel said, "What then is this bleating of sheep in my ears? What is this lowing of cattle that I hear?"

15Saul answered, "The soldiers

41 [v]Ac 1:24; [w]Pr 16:33
42 [x]Jnh 1:7
43 [y]**Jos 7:19;** [z]**ver 27**
44 [a]**Ru 1:17;** [b]ver 39
45 [c]1Ki 1:52; **Mt 10:30;** [d]2Sa 14:11
47 [e]**Ge 19:37;** [f]**Ge 19:38;** 2Sa 12:31; [g]1Sa 21:7; [h]2Sa 8:3; 10:6; 23:36
48 [i]**Ge 36:12;** Nu 13:29; Jdg 3:13; 1Sa 15:2,7; 27:8; 28:18; 30:13; 2Sa 1:13; 1Ch 4:43
49 [j]1Sa 31:2; 1Ch 8:33; [k]**Ge 29:26**
50 [l]2Sa 2:8; 3:6; 1Ki 2:5; [m]1Sa 10:14
51 [n]**1Sa 9:1**
52 [o]1Sa 8:11

Ch. 15

1 [a]**1Sa 9:16**
2 [b]**Ge 14:7; 1Sa 14:48; 2Sa 1:8**
3 [c]ver 9,19; **Ge 14:23;** Jos 6:17; 1Sa 22:19; 27:9; 28:18; Est 3:13; 9:5
6 [d]**Ge 15:19;** Nu 24:22; Jdg 1:16; 1Sa 30:29
7 [e]**1Sa 14:48;** [f]**Ge 16:7**
8 [g]Ex 17:8–16; **Nu 24:7;** [h]**Jos 8:23**
9 [i]**ver 3**
11 [j]**Ge 6:6; Ex 32:14;** [k]**Jos 22:16;** [l]Job 21:14; 34:27; Ps 28:5; Isa 5:12; 53:6; Jer 48:10; Eze 18:24; [m]**ver 35; 1Sa 8:6**
12 [n]Jos 15:55; [o]**Nu 32:42**

[g]41 Hebrew; Septuagint *"Why have you not answered your servant today? If the fault is in me or my son Jonathan, respond with Urim, but if the men of Israel are at fault, respond with Thummim."*
[h]47 Masoretic Text; Dead Sea Scrolls and Septuagint *king*
[i]47 Hebrew; Septuagint *he was victorious*
[a]3 The Hebrew term refers to the irrevocable giving of things or persons to the LORD, often by totally destroying them; also in verses 8, 9, 15, 18, 20 and 21.
[b]9 Or *the grown bulls;* the meaning of the Hebrew for this phrase is uncertain.

brought them from the Amalekites;
they spared the best of the sheep and
cattle to sacrifice to the LORD your God,
but we totally destroyed the rest."
16"Stop!" Samuel said to Saul. "Let
me tell you what the LORD said to me last
night."
"Tell me," Saul replied.
17Samuel said, "Although you were
once small[p] in your own eyes, did you
not become the head of the tribes of
Israel? The LORD anointed you king over
Israel. 18And he sent you on a mission,
saying, 'Go and completely destroy
those wicked people, the Amalekites;
make war on them until you have wiped
them out.' 19Why did you not obey the
LORD? Why did you pounce on the
plunder[q] and do evil in the eyes of
the LORD?"
20"But I did obey[r] the LORD," Saul
said. "I went on the mission the LORD
assigned me. I completely destroyed
the Amalekites and brought back Agag
their king. 21The soldiers took sheep
and cattle from the plunder, the best of
what was devoted to God, in order to
sacrifice them to the LORD your God at
Gilgal."
22But Samuel replied:

"Does the LORD delight in burnt
offerings and sacrifices
as much as in obeying the voice of
the LORD?
To obey is better than sacrifice,[s]
and to heed is better than the fat of
rams.
23For rebellion is like the sin of
divination,[t]
and arrogance like the evil of
idolatry.
Because you have rejected[u] the word
of the LORD,
he has rejected you as king."

24Then Saul said to Samuel, "I have
sinned.[v] I violated[w] the LORD's com-
mand and your instructions. I was
afraid[x] of the people and so I gave in to
them. 25Now I beg you, forgive[y] my sin
and come back with me, so that I may
worship the LORD."
26But Samuel said to him, "I will not
go back with you. You have rejected[z]
the word of the LORD, and the LORD has
rejected you as king over Israel!"
27As Samuel turned to leave, Saul
caught hold of the hem of his robe,[a] and
it tore.[b] 28Samuel said to him, "The LORD
has torn[c] the kingdom[d] of Israel from
you today and has given it to one of
your neighbours—to one better than
you.[e] 29He who is the Glory of Israel
does not lie[f] or change[g] his mind; for he
is not a man, that he should change his
mind."
30Saul replied, "I have sinned.[h] But
please honour[i] me before the elders of
my people and before Israel; come back
with me, so that I may worship the LORD
your God." 31So Samuel went back with
Saul, and Saul worshipped the LORD.
32Then Samuel said, "Bring me Agag
king of the Amalekites."
Agag came to him confidently,[c] think-
ing, "Surely the bitterness of death is
past."
33But Samuel said,

"As your sword has made women
childless,
so will your mother be childless
among women."[j]

And Samuel put Agag to death before
the LORD at Gilgal.
34Then Samuel left for Ramah,[k] but
Saul went up to his home in Gibeah[l] of
Saul. 35Until the day Samuel[m] died, he
did not go to see Saul again, though
Samuel mourned[n] for him. And the
LORD was grieved[o] that he had made
Saul king over Israel.

Samuel Anoints David

16 The LORD said to Samuel, "How
long will you mourn[a] for Saul,
since I have rejected[b] him as king over
Israel? Fill your horn with oil[c] and be on
your way; I am sending you to Jesse[d] of
Bethlehem. I have chosen[e] one of his
sons to be king."
2But Samuel said, "How can I go?
Saul will hear about it and kill me."
The LORD said, "Take a heifer with
you and say, 'I have come to sacrifice to
the LORD.' 3Invite Jesse to the sacrifice,
and I will show[f] you what to do. You are
to anoint[g] for me the one I indicate."
4Samuel did what the LORD said.
When he arrived at Bethlehem,[h] the
elders of the town trembled[i] when they
met him. They asked, "Do you come in
peace?[j]"
5Samuel replied, "Yes, in peace; I
have come to sacrifice to the LORD. Con-
secrate[k] yourselves and come to the sac-
rifice with me." Then he consecrated
Jesse and his sons and invited them to
the sacrifice.
6When they arrived, Samuel saw
Eliab[l] and thought, "Surely the LORD's

17 [p]**Ex 3:11**
19 [q]**Ge 14:23; 1Sa 14:32**
20 [r]1Sa 28:18
22 [s]Ps 40:6–8; 51:16; Pr 21:3; Isa 1:11–15; Jer 7:22; Hos 6:6; Am 5:25; Mic 6:6–8; **Mk 12:33**
23 [t]Dt 18:10; [u]**1Sa 13:13**
24 [v]**Ex 9:27; Nu 22:34**; Ps 51:4; [w]**1Sa 13:13**; [x]Pr 29:25; Isa 51:12–13; Jer 42:11
25 [y]Ex 10:17
26 [z]**Nu 15:31; 1Sa 13:14; 1Ki 14:10**
27 [a]1Sa 28:14; [b]1Ki 11:11,31; 14:8; 2Ki 17:21
28 [c]1Sa 28:17; [d]**1Sa 13:14**; [e]2Sa 6:21; 7:15
29 [f]Tit 1:2; [g]**Nu 23:19**; Heb 7:21
30 [h]**Nu 22:34**; [i]Isa 29:13; Jn 12:43
33 [j]Est 9:7–10; Jer 18:21
34 [k]**1Sa 7:17**; [l]**Jdg 19:14; 1Sa 10:5**
35 [m]1Sa 19:24; [n]ver 11; 1Sa 16:1; [o]**Ge 6:6**

Ch. 16

1 [a]**1Sa 8:6; 15:35**; [b]**1Sa 13:14**; [c]**1Sa 10:1**; [d]**Ru 4:17**; [e]2Sa 5:2; 7:8; 1Ki 8:16; 1Ch 12:23; Ps 78:70; Ac 13:22
3 [f]Ex 4:15; [g]**Dt 17:15**
4 [h]**Ge 48:7**; Lk 2:4; [i]1Sa 21:1; [j]1Ki 2:13; 2Ki 9:17
5 [k]**Ex 19:10**,22
6 [l]1Sa 17:13; 1Ch 2:13

[c]32 *Or him trembling, yet*

anointed stands here before the LORD."

7But the LORD said to Samuel, 'Do not consider his appearance or his height, for I have rejected him. The LORD does not look at the things man looks at. Man looks at the outward appearance,[m] but the LORD looks at the heart.'"[n]

8Then Jesse called Abinadab[o] and made him pass in front of Samuel. But Samuel said, "The LORD has not chosen this one either." 9Jesse then made Shammah[p] pass by, but Samuel said, "Nor has the LORD chosen this one." 10Jesse made seven of his sons pass before Samuel, but Samuel said to him, "The LORD has not chosen these." 11So he asked Jesse, "Are these all[q] the sons you have?"

"There is still the youngest," Jesse answered, "but he is tending the sheep."[r]

Samuel said, "Send for him; we will not sit down[a] until he arrives."

12So he[s] sent and had him brought in. He was ruddy, with a fine appearance and handsome[t] features.

Then the LORD said, "Rise and anoint him; he is the one."

13So Samuel took the horn of oil and anointed[u] him in the presence of his brothers, and from that day on the Spirit of the LORD[v] came upon David in power.[w] Samuel then went to Ramah.

David in Saul's Service

14Now the Spirit of the LORD had departed[x] from Saul, and an evil[b] spirit[y] from the LORD tormented him.[z]

15Saul's attendants said to him, "See, an evil spirit from God is tormenting you. 16Let our lord command his servants here to search for someone who can play the harp.[a] He will play when the evil spirit from God comes upon you, and you will feel better."

17So Saul said to his attendants, "Find someone who plays well and bring him to me."

18One of the servants answered, "I have seen a son of Jesse[b] of Bethlehem who knows how to play the harp. He is a brave man and a warrior.[c] He speaks well and is a fine-looking man. And the LORD is with[d] him."

19Then Saul sent messengers to Jesse and said, "Send me your son David, who is with the sheep."[e] 20So Jesse took a donkey loaded with bread,[f] a skin of wine and a young goat and sent them with his son David to Saul.

21David came to Saul and entered his service.[g] Saul liked him very much, and David became one of his armour-bearers. 22Then Saul sent word to Jesse, saying, "Allow David to remain in my service, for I am pleased with him."

23Whenever the spirit from God came upon Saul, David would take his harp and play. Then relief would come to Saul; he would feel better, and the evil spirit[h] would leave him.

David and Goliath

17 Now the Philistines gathered their forces for war and assembled[a] at Socoh in Judah. They pitched camp at Ephes Dammim, between Socoh[b] and Azekah.[c] 2Saul and the Israelites assembled and camped in the Valley of Elah[d] and drew up their battle line to meet the Philistines. 3The Philistines occupied one hill and the Israelites another, with the valley between them.

4A champion named Goliath,[e] who was from Gath, came out of the Philistine camp. He was over nine feet[a] tall. 5He had a bronze helmet on his head and wore a coat of scale armour of bronze weighing five thousand shekels;[b] 6on his legs he wore bronze greaves, and a bronze javelin[f] was slung on his back. 7His spear shaft was like a weaver's rod,[g] and its iron point weighed six hundred shekels.[c] His shield-bearer[h] went ahead of him.

8Goliath stood and shouted to the ranks of Israel, "Why do you come out and line up for battle? Am I not a Philistine, and are you not the servants of Saul? Choose[i] a man and have him come down to me. 9If he is able to fight and kill me, we will become your subjects; but if I overcome him and kill him, you will become our subjects and serve us." 10Then the Philistine said, "This day I defy[j] the ranks of Israel! Give me a man and let us fight each other."[k] 11On hearing the Philistine's words, Saul and all the Israelites were dismayed and terrified.

12Now David was the son of an Ephrathite[l] named Jesse,[m] who was from Bethlehem[n] in Judah. Jesse had eight[o] sons, and in Saul's time he was old and well advanced in years. 13Jesse's three oldest sons had followed Saul to the war: The firstborn was Eliab;[p] the

7 [m]Ps 147:10; [n]**1Sa 2:3**; 2Sa 7:20; **Ps 44:21; 139:23; Rev 2:23**
8 [o]1Sa 17:13
9 [p]1Sa 17:13; 2Sa 13:3; 21:21
11 [q]1Sa 17:12; [r]**Ge 37:2**; 2Sa 7:8
12 [s]1Sa 9:17; [t]**Ge 39:6**
13 [u]**1Sa 2:35; 2Sa 22:51**; [v]1Sa 18:12; [w]**1Sa 11:6**
14 [x]**Jdg 16:20**; [y]ver 23; **Jdg 9:23**; 1Sa 18:10; [z]2Sa 7:15
16 [a]ver 23; **1Sa 10:5–6**; 2Ch 29:26–27; Ps 49:4
18 [b]**Ru 4:17**; [c]2Sa 17:8; [d]**Ge 39:2**; 1Sa 17:37; 20:13; 1Ch 22:11; Mt 1:23
19 [e]1Sa 17:15
20 [f]**Ge 32:13; 1Sa 10:4**
21 [g]**Ge 41:46**
23 [h]**ver 14; Jdg 9:23**

Ch. 17

1 [a]1Sa 13:5; [b]Jos 15:35; 2Ch 28:18; [c]**Jos 10:10–11**
2 [d]1Sa 21:9
4 [e]1Sa 21:9; 2Sa 21:19
6 [f]ver 45; 1Sa 18:10
7 [g]2Sa 21:19; 1Ch 11:23; 20:5; [h]ver 41
8 [i]2Sa 2:12–17
10 [j]ver 26,45; 2Sa 21:21; [k]ver 23
12 [l]**Ge 35:16; 48:7**; Ps 132:6; [m]**Ru 4:17**; [n]**Ge 35:19**; [o]1Sa 16:11
13 [p]**1Sa 16:6**

[a]*11* Some Septuagint manuscripts; Hebrew *not gather round*
[b]*14* Or *injurious*; also in verses 15, 16 and 23
[a]*4* Hebrew *was six cubits and a span* (about 3 metres)
[b]*5* That is, about 125 pounds (about 57 kilograms)
[c]*7* That is, about 15 pounds (about 7 kilograms)

second, Abinadab;[q] and the third, Shammah.[r] 14David was the youngest. The three oldest followed Saul, 15but David went back and forth from Saul to tend[s] his father's sheep[t] at Bethlehem.

16For forty days the Philistine came forward every morning and evening and took his stand.

17Now Jesse said to his son David, "Take this ephah[d][u] of roasted grain[v] and these ten loaves of bread for your brothers and hurry to their camp. 18Take along these ten cheeses to the commander of their unit.[e] See how your brothers[w] are and bring back some assurance[f] from them. 19They are with Saul and all the men of Israel in the Valley of Elah, fighting against the Philistines."

20Early in the morning David left the flock with a shepherd, loaded up and set out, as Jesse had directed. He reached the camp as the army was going out to its battle positions, shouting the war cry. 21Israel and the Philistines were drawing up their lines facing each other. 22David left his things with the keeper of supplies,[x] ran to the battle lines and greeted his brothers. 23As he was talking with them, Goliath, the Philistine champion from Gath, stepped out from his lines and shouted his usual[y] defiance, and David heard it. 24When the Israelites saw the man, they all ran from him in great fear.

25Now the Israelites had been saying, "Do you see how this man keeps coming out? He comes out to defy Israel. The king will give great wealth to the man who kills him. He will also give him his daughter[z] in marriage and will exempt his father's family from taxes[a] in Israel."

26David asked the men standing near him, "What will be done for the man who kills this Philistine and removes this disgrace[b] from Israel? Who is this uncircumcised[c] Philistine that he should defy[d] the armies of the living[e] God?"

27They repeated to him what they had been saying and told him, "This is what will be done for the man who kills him."

28When Eliab, David's oldest brother, heard him speaking with the men, he burned with anger[f] at him and asked, "Why have you come down here? And with whom did you leave those few sheep in the desert? I know how conceited you are and how wicked your heart is; you came down only to watch the battle."

29"Now what have I done?" said David. "Can't I even speak?" 30He then turned away to someone else and brought up the same matter, and the men answered him as before. 31What David said was overheard and reported to Saul, and Saul sent for him.

32David said to Saul, "Let no-one lose heart[g] on account of this Philistine; your servant will go and fight him."

33Saul replied,[h] "You are not able to go out against this Philistine and fight him; you are only a boy, and he has been a fighting man from his youth."

34But David said to Saul, "Your servant has been keeping his father's sheep. When a lion[i] or a bear came and carried off a sheep from the flock, 35I went after it, struck it and rescued the sheep from its mouth. When it turned on me, I seized[j] it by its hair, struck it and killed it. 36Your servant has killed both the lion[k] and the bear; this uncircumcised Philistine will be like one of them, because he has defied the armies of the living God. 37The LORD who delivered[l] me from the paw of the lion[m] and the paw of the bear will deliver me from the hand of this Philistine."

Saul said to David, "Go, and the LORD be with[n] you."

38Then Saul dressed David in his own[o] tunic. He put a coat of armour on him and a bronze helmet on his head. 39David fastened on his sword over the tunic and tried walking around, because he was not used to them.

"I cannot go in these," he said to Saul, "because I am not used to them." So he took them off. 40Then he took his staff in his hand, chose five smooth stones from the stream, put them in the pouch of his shepherd's bag and, with his sling in his hand, approached the Philistine.

41Meanwhile, the Philistine, with his shield-bearer[p] in front of him, kept coming closer to David. 42He looked David over and saw that he was only a boy, ruddy and handsome,[q] and he despised[r] him. 43He said to David, "Am I a dog,[s] that you come at me with sticks?" And the Philistine cursed David by his gods. 44"Come here," he said, "and I'll give your flesh to the birds of the air[t] and the beasts of the field!"[u]"

45David said to the Philistine, "You come against me with sword and spear and javelin,[v] but I come against you in the name[w] of the LORD Almighty, the God of the armies of Israel, whom you

13 [q]1Sa 16:8; [r]**1Sa 16:9**
15 [s]**Ge 37:2;** [t]1Sa 16:19
17 [u]**Lev 19:36;** [v]**Lev 23:14;** 1Sa 25:18
18 [w]Ge 37:14
22 [x]**Jos 1:11**
23 [y]ver 8–10
25 [z]1Sa 18:17; [a]**1Sa 8:15**
26 [b]1Sa 11:2; [c]**1Sa 14:6;** [d]**ver 10;** [e]Dt 5:26; **Jos 3:10;** 2Ki 18:35
28 [f]**Ge 27:41;** Pr 18:19
32 [g]**Dt 20:3;** Ps 18:45; Isa 7:4; Jer 4:9; 38:4; Da 11:30
33 [h]Nu 13:31
34 [i]Job 10:16; Isa 31:4; Jer 49:19; Hos 13:8; Am 3:12
35 [j]Jdg 14:6
36 [k]1Ch 11:22
37 [l]2Co 1:10; [m]2Ti 4:17; [n]**1Sa 16:18; 18:12**
38 [o]**Ge 41:42**
41 [p]ver 7
42 [q]1Sa 16:12; [r]Ps 123:3–4; Pr 16:18
43 [s]1Sa 24:14; 2Sa 3:8; 9:8; 2Ki 8:13
44 [t]**Ge 40:19;** Rev 19:17; [u]2Sa 21:10; Jer 34:20
45 [v]**ver 6;** [w]Dt 20:1; 2Ch 13:12; 14:11; 32:8; Ps 20:7–8; 124:8; Heb 11:32–34

[d]17 That is, probably about ⅗ bushel (about 22 litres) [e]18 Hebrew *thousand*
[f]18 Or *some token;* or *some pledge of spoils*

have defied.[x] 46This day the LORD will hand[y] you over to me, and I'll strike you down and cut off your head. Today I will give the carcasses[z] of the Philistine army to the birds of the air and the beasts of the earth, and the whole world[a] will know that there is a God in Israel.[b] 47All those gathered here will know that it is not by sword[c] or spear that the LORD saves;[d] for the battle[e] is the LORD's, and he will give all of you into our hands."

48As the Philistine moved closer to attack him, David ran quickly towards the battle line to meet him. 49Reaching into his bag and taking out a stone, he slung it and struck the Philistine on the forehead. The stone sank into his forehead, and he fell face down on the ground.

50So David triumphed over the Philistine with a sling[f] and a stone; without a sword in his hand he struck down the Philistine and killed him.

51David ran and stood over him. He took hold of the Philistine's sword and drew it from the scabbard. After he killed him, he cut[g] off his head with the sword.[h]

When the Philistines saw that their hero was dead, they turned and ran. 52Then the men of Israel and Judah surged forward with a shout and pursued the Philistines to the entrance of Gath[g] and to the gates of Ekron.[i] Their dead were strewn along the Shaaraim[j] road to Gath and Ekron. 53When the Israelites returned from chasing the Philistines, they plundered their camp. 54David took the Philistine's head and brought it to Jerusalem, and he put the Philistine's weapons in his own tent.

55As Saul watched David[k] going out to meet the Philistine, he said to Abner, commander of the army, "Abner,[l] whose son is that young man?"

Abner replied, "As surely as you live, O king, I don't know."

56The king said, "Find out whose son this young man is."

57As soon as David returned from killing the Philistine, Abner took him and brought him before Saul, with David still holding the Philistine's head.

58"Whose son are you, young man?" Saul asked him.

David said, "I am the son of your servant Jesse[m] of Bethlehem."

Saul's Jealousy of David

18 After David had finished talking with Saul, Jonathan[a] became one in spirit with David, and he loved[b] him as himself.[c] 2From that day Saul kept David with him and did not let him return to his father's house. 3And Jonathan made a covenant[d] with David because he loved him as himself. 4Jonathan took off the robe[e] he was wearing and gave it to David, along with his tunic, and even his sword, his bow and his belt.[f]

5Whatever Saul sent him to do, David did it so successfully[a][g] that Saul gave him a high rank in the army.[h] This pleased all the people, and Saul's officers as well.

6When the men were returning home after David had killed the Philistine, the women came out from all the towns of Israel to meet King Saul with singing and dancing,[i] with joyful songs and with tambourines[j] and lutes. 7As they danced, they sang:[k]

"Saul has slain his thousands,
and David his tens[l] of thousands."

8Saul was very angry; this refrain galled him. "They have credited David with tens of thousands," he thought, "but me with only thousands. What more can he get but the kingdom?[m]" 9And from that time on Saul kept a jealous[n] eye on David.

10The next day an evil[b] spirit[o] from God came forcefully upon Saul. He was prophesying in his house, while David was playing the harp,[p] as he usually[q] did. Saul had a spear[r] in his hand 11and he hurled it, saying to himself,[s] "I'll pin David to the wall." But David eluded[t] him twice.[u]

12Saul was afraid[v] of David, because the LORD[w] was with[x] David but had left[y] Saul. 13So he sent David away from him and gave him command over a thousand men, and David led[z] the troops in their campaigns.[a] 14In everything he did he had great success,[c][b] because the LORD was with[c] him. 15When Saul saw how successful[d] he was, he was afraid of him. 16But all Israel and Judah loved David, because he led them in their campaigns.[d]

17Saul said to David, "Here is my older daughter[e] Merab. I will give her to you in marriage;[f] only serve me bravely and fight the battles[g] of the LORD." For Saul said to himself,[h] "I will not raise a hand against him. Let the Philistines do that!"

45 [x]ver 10
46 [y]**1Sa 14:12;** [z]**Dt 28:26;** [a]**Jos 4:24; Isa 11:9;** [b]1Ki 18:36; 2Ki 5:8; 19:19; Isa 37:20
47 [c]Hos 1:7; [d]1Sa 14:6; 2Ch 14:11; Jer 39:18; [e]**Ex 14:14; Nu 21:14; 1Sa 2:9;** 2Ch 20:15; Ps 44:6–7
50 [f]1Sa 25:29
51 [g]Heb 11:34; [h]1Sa 21:9; 22:10
52 [i]Jos 15:11; [j]**Jos 15:36**
55 [k]1Sa 16:21; [l]1Sa 26:5
58 [m]**Ru 4:17**

Ch. 18

1 [a]1Sa 19:1; 20:16; 31:2; 2Sa 4:4; [b]2Sa 1:26; [c]**Ge 44:30**
3 [d]1Sa 20:8, 16–17,42; 22:8; 23:18; 24:21; 2Sa 21:7
4 [e]**Ge 41:42;** [f]2Sa 18:11
5 [g]ver 30; [h]2Sa 5:2
6 [i]**Ex 15:20;** 2Sa 1:20; [j]Ps 68:25
7 [k]Ex 15:21; [l]1Sa 21:11; 29:5; 2Sa 18:3
8 [m]**1Sa 13:14**
9 [n]1Sa 19:1
10 [o]**Jdg 9:23; 1Sa 16:14;** [p]**1Sa 10:5;** [q]1Sa 16:21; 19:7; [r]**1Sa 17:6**
11 [s]ver 25; 1Sa 20:7,33; [t]1Sa 19:10; [u]Ps 132:1
12 [v]ver 29; [w]1Sa 16:13; [x]Jos 1:5; 1Sa 17:37; 20:13; 1Ch 22:11; [y]**Jdg 16:20**
13 [z]Nu 27:17; [a]2Sa 5:2
14 [b]**Ge 39:3;** [c]**Ge 39:2; Nu 14:43;** 2Sa 7:9
16 [d]2Sa 5:2
17 [e]1Sa 17:25; [f]**Ge 29:26;** [g]**Nu 21:14;** [h]ver 25; 1Sa 20:33

[g]52 Some Septuagint manuscripts; Hebrew *a valley*
[a]5 Or *wisely* [b]10 Or *injurious*
[c]14 Or *he was very wise* [d]15 Or *wise*

18But David said to Saul, "Who am I,[i]
and what is my family or my father's
clan in Israel, that I should become the
king's son-in-law?[j]" 19So[e] when the time
came for Merab,[k] Saul's daughter, to
be given to David, she was given in
marriage to Adriel of Meholah.[l]
20Now Saul's daughter Michal[m] was
in love with David, and when they told
Saul about it, he was pleased.[n] 21"I will
give her to him," he thought, "so that
she may be a snare[o] to him and so that
the hand of the Philistines may be
against him." So Saul said to David,
"Now you have a second opportunity to
become my son-in-law."
22Then Saul ordered his attendants:
"Speak to David privately and say,
'Look, the king is pleased with you, and
his attendants all like you; now become
his son-in-law.'"
23They repeated these words to
David. But David said, "Do you think it
is a small matter to become the king's
son-in-law?[p] I'm only a poor man and
little known."
24When Saul's servants told him what
David had said, 25Saul replied, "Say to
David, 'The king wants no other price[q]
for the bride than a hundred Philistine
foreskins, to take revenge[r] on his ene-
mies.'" Saul's plan[s] was to have David
fall by the hands of the Philistines.
26When the attendants told David
these things, he was pleased to become
the king's son-in-law. So before the
allotted time elapsed, 27David and his
men went out and killed two hundred
Philistines. He brought their foreskins
and presented the full number to the
king so that he might become the king's
son-in-law. Then Saul gave him his
daughter Michal[t] in marriage.
28When Saul realised that the LORD
was with David and that his daughter
Michal[u] loved David, 29Saul became still
more afraid[v] of him, and he remained
his enemy for the rest of his days.
30The Philistine commanders con-
tinued to go out to battle, and as often
as they did, David met with more
success[f][w] than the rest of Saul's officers,
and his name became well known.

Saul Tries to Kill David

19 Saul told his son Jonathan[a] and
all the attendants to kill[b] David.
But Jonathan was very fond of David
2and warned him, "My father Saul is
looking for a chance to kill you. Be on
your guard tomorrow morning; go into
hiding[c] and stay there. 3I will go out and
stand with my father in the field where
you are. I'll speak[d] to him about you and
will tell you what I find out."
4Jonathan spoke[e] well of David to Saul
his father and said to him, "Let not the
king do wrong[f] to his servant David; he
has not wronged you, and what he has
done has benefited you greatly. 5He
took his life[g] in his hands when he killed
the Philistine. The LORD won a great
victory[h] for all Israel, and you saw it and
were glad. Why then would you do
wrong to an innocent[i] man like David by
killing him for no reason?"
6Saul listened to Jonathan and took
this oath: "As surely as the LORD lives,
David will not be put to death."
7So Jonathan called David and told
him the whole conversation. He
brought him to Saul, and David was
with Saul as before.[j]
8Once more war broke out, and David
went out and fought the Philistines. He
struck them with such force that they
fled before him.
9But an evil[a] spirit[k] from the LORD
came upon Saul as he was sitting in his
house with his spear in his hand. While
David was playing the harp,[l] 10Saul
tried to pin him to the wall with his
spear, but David eluded[m] him as Saul
drove the spear into the wall. That night
David made good his escape.
11Saul sent men to David's house to
watch[n] it and to kill him in the morning.[o]
But Michal, David's wife, warned him,
"If you don't run for your life tonight,
tomorrow you'll be killed." 12So Michal
let David down through a window,[p]
and he fled and escaped. 13Then Michal
took an idol[b][q] and laid it on the bed,
covering it with a garment and putting
some goats' hair at the head.
14When Saul sent the men to capture
David, Michal said,[r] "He is ill."
15Then Saul sent the men back to see
David and told them, "Bring him up to
me in his bed so that I may kill him."
16But when the men entered, there was
the idol in the bed, and at the head was
some goats' hair.
17Saul said to Michal, "Why did you
deceive me like this and send my enemy
away so that he escaped?"
Michal told him, "He said to me, 'Let
me get away. Why should I kill you?'"
18When David had fled and made his
escape, he went to Samuel at Ramah[s]
and told him all that Saul had done to

18 [i]**Ex 3:11; 1Sa 9:21**; [j]ver 23
19 [k]2Sa 21:8; [l]**Jdg 7:22**
20 [m]ver 28; **Ge 29:26**; [n]ver 29
21 [o]**Ex 10:7; Dt 7:16**
23 [p]ver 18
25 [q]**Ge 34:12**; [r]Ps 8:2; 44:16; Jer 20:10; [s]**ver 11,17**
27 [t]2Sa 3:14; 6:16
28 [u]**ver 20**
29 [v]ver 12
30 [w]ver 5

Ch. 19

1 [a]**1Sa 18:1**; [b]1Sa 18:9
2 [c]1Sa 20:5,19
3 [d]1Sa 20:12
4 [e]1Sa 20:32; 22:14; Pr 31:8–9; Jer 18:20; [f]1Sa 25:21; Pr 17:13
5 [g]**Jdg 9:17; 12:3**; [h]**1Sa 11:13**; [i]**Ge 31:36**; Dt 19:10–13
7 [j]**1Sa 18:10**
9 [k]**Jdg 9:23**; [l]**1Sa 10:5**
10 [m]1Sa 18:11
11 [n]Ps 59 Title; [o]Jdg 16:2
12 [p]**Jos 2:15**; Ac 9:25; 2Co 11:33
13 [q]**Ge 31:19**
14 [r]**Ex 1:19**; Jos 2:4
18 [s]**1Sa 7:17**

[e]19 Or *However,*
[f]30 Or *David acted more wisely*
[a]9 Or *injurious*
[b]13 Hebrew *teraphim;* also in verse 16

him. Then he and Samuel went to
Naioth and stayed there. 19Word came
to Saul: "David is in Naioth at Ramah";
20so he sent men to capture him. But
when they saw a group of prophets[t]
prophesying, with Samuel standing
there as their leader, the Spirit of God
came upon[u] Saul's men and they also
prophesied.[v] 21Saul was told about it,
and he sent more men, and they
prophesied too. Saul sent men a third
time, and they also prophesied.
22Finally, he himself left for Ramah and
went to the great cistern at Secu. And he
asked, "Where are Samuel and David?"
"Over in Naioth at Ramah," they
said.
23So Saul went to Naioth at Ramah.
But the Spirit of God came even upon
him, and he walked along prophesy-
ing[w] until he came to Naioth. 24He strip-
ped[x] off his robes and also prophesied
in Samuel's[y] presence. He lay that way
all that day and night. This is why
people say, "Is Saul also among the
prophets?"[z]

David and Jonathan

20 Then David fled from Naioth at
Ramah and went to Jonathan
and asked, "What have I done? What is
my crime? How have I wronged[a] your
father, that he is trying to take my life?"[b]
2"Never!" Jonathan replied. "You are
not going to die! Look, my father
doesn't do anything, great or small,
without confiding in me. Why should
he hide this from me? It's not so!"
3But David took an oath[c] and said,
"Your father knows very well that I
have found favour in your eyes, and he
has said to himself, 'Jonathan must not
know this or he will be grieved.' Yet as
surely as the LORD lives and as you live,
there is only a step between me and
death."
4Jonathan said to David, "Whatever
you want me to do, I'll do for you."
5So David said, "Look, tomorrow is
the New Moon festival,[d] and I am sup-
posed to dine with the king; but let me
go and hide[e] in the field until the eve-
ning of the day after tomorrow. 6If your
father misses me at all, tell him, 'David
earnestly asked my permission[f] to hurry
to Bethlehem,[g] his home town, because
an annual[h] sacrifice is being made there
for his whole clan.' 7If he says, 'Very
well,' then your servant is safe. But if he
loses his temper,[i] you can be sure that
he is determined[j] to harm me. 8As for
you, show kindness to your servant, for
you have brought him into a covenant[k]
with you before the LORD. If I am guilty,
then kill[l] me yourself! Why hand me
over to your father?"
9"Never!" Jonathan said. "If I had the
least inkling that my father was deter-
mined to harm you, wouldn't I tell
you?"
10David asked, "Who will tell me if
your father answers you harshly?"
11"Come," Jonathan said, "let's go
out into the field." So they went there
together.
12Then Jonathan said to David: "By
the LORD, the God of Israel, I will surely
sound[m] out my father by this time the
day after tomorrow! If he is favourably
disposed towards you, will I not send
you word and let you know? 13But if my
father is inclined to harm you, may the
LORD deal with me, be it ever so
severely,[n] if I do not let you know and
send you away safely. May the LORD be
with[o] you as he has been with my father.
14But show me unfailing kindness[p] like
that of the LORD as long as I live, so that I
may not be killed, 15and do not ever cut
off your kindness from my family[q]—not
even when the LORD has cut off every
one of David's enemies from the face of
the earth."
16So Jonathan[r] made a covenant[s] with
the house of David, saying, "May the
LORD call David's enemies to account.[t]"
17And Jonathan made David reaffirm
his oath[u] out of love for him, because he
loved him as he loved himself.
18Then Jonathan said to David:
"Tomorrow is the New Moon festival.
You will be missed, because your seat
will be empty.[v] 19The day after tomor-
row, towards evening, go to the place
where you hid[w] when this trouble be-
gan, and wait by the stone Ezel. 20I will
shoot three arrows[x] to the side of it, as
though I were shooting at a target.
21Then I will send a boy and say, 'Go,
find the arrows.' If I say to him, 'Look,
the arrows are on this side of you; bring
them here,' then come, because, as
surely as the LORD lives, you are safe;
there is no danger. 22But if I say to the
boy, 'Look, the arrows are beyond[y]
you,' then you must go, because the
LORD has sent you away. 23And about
the matter you and I discussed—
remember, the LORD is witness[z] be-
tween you and me for ever."
24So David hid in the field, and when
the New Moon festival[a] came, the king
sat down to eat. 25He sat in his cus-
tomary place by the wall, opposite

20 [t]**Nu 11:29;** [u]**Nu 11:25;** [v]**1Sa 10:5**
23 [w]1Sa 10:13
24 [x]2Sa 6:20; Isa 20:2; [y]1Sa 15:35; [z]**1Sa 10:11**

Ch. 20

1 [a]1Sa 24:9; [b]1Sa 22:23; 23:15; 24:11; 25:29; Ps 40:14; 54:3; 63:9; 70:2
3 [c]Dt 6:13
5 [d]**Nu 10:10;** [e]**1Sa 19:2**
6 [f]ver 28; [g]1Sa 17:58; [h]**1Sa 1:3**
7 [i]1Sa 10:27; 25:17; [j]**1Sa 18:11**
8 [k]**1Sa 18:3;** [l]2Sa 14:32
12 [m]1Sa 19:3
13 [n]**Ru 1:17;** [o]**1Sa 16:18; 18:12**
14 [p]**Ge 40:14**
15 [q]1Sa 24:21; 2Sa 9:7
16 [r]**1Sa 18:1;** [s]**1Sa 18:3;** [t]**Jos 22:23**
17 [u]**Jos 9:18; 1Sa 18:3**
18 [v]ver 25
19 [w]**1Sa 19:2**
20 [x]2Ki 13:15
22 [y]ver 37
23 [z]**Ge 31:50**
24 [a]**Nu 10:10**

Jonathan,[a] and Abner sat next to Saul,
but David's place was empty.[b] 26Saul
said nothing that day, for he thought,
"Something must have happened to
David to make him ceremonially un-
clean—surely he is unclean."[c] 27But the
next day, the second day of the month,
David's place was empty again. Then
Saul said to his son Jonathan, "Why
hasn't the son of Jesse come to the meal,
either yesterday or today?"

28Jonathan answered, "David earn-
estly asked me for permission[d] to go
to Bethlehem. 29He said, 'Let me go,
because our family is observing a sac-
rifice[e] in the town and my brother has
ordered me to be there. If I have found
favour in your eyes, let me go to see my
brothers.' That is why he has not come
to the king's table."

30Saul's anger flared up at Jonathan
and he said to him, "You son of a per-
verse and rebellious woman! Don't I
know that you have sided with the son
of Jesse to your own shame and to the
shame of the mother who bore you?
31As long as the son of Jesse lives on this
earth, neither you nor your kingdom[f]
will be established. Now send and bring
him to me, for he must die!"

32"Why[g] should he be put to death?
What[h] has he done?" Jonathan asked
his father. 33But Saul hurled his spear at
him to kill him. Then Jonathan knew
that his father intended[i] to kill David.

34Jonathan got up from the table in
fierce anger; on that second day of the
month he did not eat, because he was
grieved at his father's shameful treat-
ment of David.

35In the morning Jonathan went out to
the field for his meeting with David. He
had a small boy with him, 36and he said
to the boy, "Run and find the arrows I
shoot." As the boy ran, he shot an
arrow beyond him. 37When the boy
came to the place where Jonathan's
arrow had fallen, Jonathan called out
after him, "Isn't the arrow beyond[j]
you?" 38Then he shouted, "Hurry! Go
quickly! Don't stop!" The boy picked up
the arrow and returned to his master.
39(The boy knew nothing of all this; only
Jonathan and David knew.) 40Then
Jonathan gave his weapons to the boy
and said, "Go, carry them back to
town."

41After the boy had gone, David got
up from the south side ⌞of the stone⌟
and bowed down before Jonathan three
times, with his face to the ground.[k]
Then they kissed each other and wept
together—but David wept the most.

25 [b]ver 18
26 [c]Lev 7:20–21
28 [d]ver 6
29 [e]**Ge 8:20**
31 [f]1Sa 23:17; 24:20
32 [g]**1Sa 19:4**; Mt 27:23; [h]**Ge 31:36**
33 [i]**1Sa 18:11**,17
37 [j]ver 22
41 [k]**Ge 33:3**; Ru 2:10; 1Sa 24:8; 25:23; 2Sa 1:2
42 [l]**1Sa 1:17; Ac 15:33**; [m]**Ge 40:14**; 2Sa 1:26; Pr 18:24; [n]Isa 48:1; [o]**Ge 31:50; 1Sa 18:3**; [p]2Sa 9:1

Ch. 21

1 [a]1Sa 22:9,19; Ne 11:32; Isa 10:32; [b]1Sa 16:4
4 [c]Lev 24:8–9; [d]Mt 12:4; [e]**Ex 19:15; Lev 15:18**
5 [f]Dt 23:9–11; Jos 3:5; 2Sa 11:11; [g]1Th 4:4
6 [h]**Ex 25:30**; 1Sa 22:10; Mt 12:3–4; Mk 2:25–28; Lk 6:1–5
7 [i]1Sa 22:9,22; [j]1Sa 14:47; Ps 52 Title
9 [k]**1Sa 17:51**; [l]**1Sa 17:4**; [m]1Sa 17:2

42Jonathan said to David, "Go in
peace,[l] for we have sworn friendship[m]
with each other in the name of the
LORD,[n] saying, 'The LORD is witness[o]
between you and me, and between your
descendants and my descendants for
ever.[p]'" Then David left, and Jonathan
went back to the town.

David at Nob

21 David went to Nob,[a] to Ahi-
melech the priest. Ahimelech
trembled[b] when he met him, and asked,
"Why are you alone? Why is no-one
with you?"

2David answered Ahimelech the
priest, "The king charged me with a
certain matter and said to me, 'No-one
is to know anything about your mission
and your instructions.' As for my men, I
have told them to meet me at a certain
place. 3Now then, what have you to
hand? Give me five loaves of bread, or
whatever you can find."

4But the priest answered David, "I
don't have any ordinary bread[c] to hand;
however, there is some consecrated[d]
bread here—provided the men have
kept[e] themselves from women."

5David replied, "Indeed women have
been kept from us, as usual[f] whenever[a]
I set out. The men's things[b] are holy[g]
even on missions that are not holy. How
much more so today!" 6So the priest
gave him the consecrated bread,[h] since
there was no bread there except the
bread of the Presence that had been
removed from before the LORD and re-
placed by hot bread on the day it was
taken away.

7Now one of Saul's servants was
there that day, detained before the
LORD; he was Doeg[i] the Edomite,[j] Saul's
head shepherd.

8David asked Ahimelech, "Don't you
have a spear or sword here? I haven't
brought my sword or any other
weapon, because the king's business
was urgent."

9The priest replied, "The sword[k] of
Goliath[l] the Philistine, whom you killed
in the Valley of Elah,[m] is here; it is wrap-
ped in a cloth behind the ephod. If you
want it, take it; there is no sword here
but that one."

David said, "There is none like it; give
it to me."

[a]25 Septuagint; Hebrew *wall. Jonathan arose*
[a]5 Or *from us in the past few days since*
[b]5 Or *bodies*

David at Gath

10 That day David fled from Saul and
went[n] to Achish king of Gath. 11 But the
servants of Achish said to him, "Isn't
this David, the king of the land? Isn't he
the one they sing about in their dances:

"'Saul has slain his thousands,
and David his tens of thousands'?"[o]

12 David took these words to heart and
was very much afraid of Achish king of
Gath. 13 So he feigned insanity[p] in their
presence; and while he was in their
hands he acted like a madman, making
marks on the doors of the gate and
letting saliva run down his beard.
14 Achish said to his servants, "Look at
the man! He is insane! Why bring him to
me? 15 Am I so short of madmen that you
have to bring this fellow here to carry on
like this in front of me? Must this man
come into my house?"

David at Adullam and Mizpah

22 David left Gath and escaped to
the cave[a] of Adullam.[b] When
his brothers and his father's household
heard about it, they went down to him
there. 2 All those who were in distress or
in debt or discontented gathered[c] round
him, and he became their leader. About
four hundred men were with him.
3 From there David went to Mizpah in
Moab and said to the king of Moab,
"Would you let my father and mother
come and stay with you until I learn
what God will do for me?" 4 So he left
them with the king of Moab,[d] and they
stayed with him as long as David was in
the stronghold.
5 But the prophet Gad[e] said to David,
"Do not stay in the stronghold. Go into
the land of Judah." So David left and
went to the forest of Hereth.[f]

Saul Kills the Priests of Nob

6 Now Saul heard that David and his
men had been discovered. And Saul,
spear in hand, was seated[g] under the
tamarisk[h] tree on the hill at Gibeah, with
all his officials standing round him.
7 Saul said to them, "Listen, men of Ben-
jamin! Will the son of Jesse give all of
you fields and vineyards? Will he make
all of you commanders[i] of thousands
and commanders of hundreds? 8 Is that
why you have all conspired[j] against me?
No-one tells me when my son makes a
covenant[k] with the son of Jesse.[l] None
of you is concerned[m] about me or tells
me that my son has incited my servant
to lie in wait for me, as he does today."
9 But Doeg[n] the Edomite, who was
standing with Saul's officials, said, "I
saw the son of Jesse come to Ahimelech
son of Ahitub[o] at Nob.[p] 10 Ahimelech
enquired[q] of the LORD for him; he also
gave him provisions[r] and the sword of
Goliath[s] the Philistine."
11 Then the king sent for the priest
Ahimelech son of Ahitub and his
father's whole family, who were the
priests at Nob, and they all came to the
king. 12 Saul said, "Listen now, son of
Ahitub."
"Yes, my lord," he answered.
13 Saul said to him, "Why have you
conspired[t] against me, you and the son
of Jesse, giving him bread and a sword
and enquiring of God for him, so that he
has rebelled against me and lies in wait
for me, as he does today?"
14 Ahimelech answered the king,
"Who[u] of all your servants is as loyal as
David, the king's son-in-law, captain of
your bodyguard and highly respected
in your household? 15 Was that day the
first time I enquired of God for him? Of
course not! Let not the king accuse your
servant or any of his father's family, for
your servant knows nothing at all about
this whole affair."
16 But the king said, "You shall surely
die, Ahimelech, you and your father's
whole family."[v]
17 Then the king ordered the guards at
his side: "Turn and kill the priests of the
LORD, because they too have sided with
David. They knew he was fleeing, yet
they did not tell me."
But the king's officials were not will-
ing[w] to raise a hand to strike the priests
of the LORD.
18 The king then ordered Doeg, "You
turn and strike down the priests."[x] So
Doeg the Edomite turned and struck
them down. That day he killed eighty-
five men who wore the linen ephod.[y]
19 He also put to the sword[z] Nob,[a] the
town of the priests, with its men and
women, its children and infants, and its
cattle, donkeys and sheep.
20 But Abiathar,[b] son of Ahimelech son
of Ahitub,[c] escaped and fled to join
David.[d] 21 He told David that Saul had
killed the priests of the LORD. 22 Then
David said to Abiathar: "That day,
when Doeg[e] the Edomite was there, I
knew he would be sure to tell Saul. I am
responsible for the death of your
father's whole family. 23 Stay with me;
don't be afraid; the man who is seeking

10 [n]1Sa 25:13; 27:2
11 [o]**1Sa 18:7**
13 [p]Ps 34 Title

Ch. 22

1 [a]Ps 57 Title; 142 Title; [b]**Ge 38:1**
2 [c]1Sa 23:13; 25:13; 2Sa 15:20
4 [d]**Ge 19:37**
5 [e]2Sa 24:11; 1Ch 21:9; 29:29; 2Ch 29:25; [f]2Sa 23:14
6 [g]**Jdg 4:5**; [h]**Ge 21:33**
7 [i]**Dt 1:15**
8 [j]ver 13; [k]**1Sa 18:3**; [l]2Sa 20:1; [m]1Sa 23:21
9 [n]**1Sa 21:7**; [o]1Sa 14:3; [p]**1Sa 21:1**
10 [q]**Ge 25:22**; **1Sa 23:2**; [r]**1Sa 21:6**; [s]**1Sa 17:51**
13 [t]ver 8
14 [u]**1Sa 19:4**
16 [v]**1Sa 2:31**
17 [w]**Ex 1:17**
18 [x]**1Sa 4:17**; [y]**1Sa 2:18**
19 [z]**1Sa 15:3**; [a]**1Sa 21:1**
20 [b]1Sa 23:6,9; 30:7; 2Sa 15:24; 20:25; 1Ki 1:7; 2:22,26–27; 4:4; 1Ch 15:11; 27:34; [c]**1Sa 14:3**; [d]**1Sa 2:32**
22 [e]**1Sa 21:7**

your life[f] is seeking mine also. You will be safe with me."

David Saves Keilah

23 When David was told, "Look, the Philistines are fighting against Keilah[a] and are looting the threshing-floors,"[b] 2he enquired[c] of the LORD, saying, "Shall I go and attack these Philistines?"

The LORD answered him, "Go, attack the Philistines and save Keilah."

3But David's men said to him, "Here in Judah we are afraid. How much more, then, if we go to Keilah against the Philistine forces!"

4Once again David enquired[d] of the LORD, and the LORD answered him, "Go down to Keilah, for I am going to give the Philistines[e] into your hand.[f]" 5So David and his men went to Keilah, fought the Philistines and carried off their livestock. He inflicted heavy losses on the Philistines and saved the people of Keilah. 6(Now Abiathar[g] son of Ahimelech had brought the ephod[h] down with him when he fled to David at Keilah.)

Saul Pursues David

7Saul was told that David had gone to Keilah, and he said, "God has handed him over[i] to me, for David has imprisoned himself by entering a town with gates and bars."[j] 8And Saul called up all his forces for battle, to go down to Keilah to besiege David and his men.

9When David learned that Saul was plotting against him, he said to Abiathar[k] the priest, "Bring the ephod.[l]" 10David said, "O LORD, God of Israel, your servant has heard definitely that Saul plans to come to Keilah and destroy the town on account of me. 11Will the citizens of Keilah surrender me to him? Will Saul come down, as your servant has heard? O LORD, God of Israel, tell your servant."

And the LORD said, "He will."

12Again David asked, "Will the citizens of Keilah surrender[m] me and my men to Saul?"

And the LORD said, "They will."

13So David and his men,[n] about six hundred in number, left Keilah and kept moving from place to place. When Saul was told that David had escaped from Keilah, he did not go there.

14David stayed in the desert[o] strongholds and in the hills of the Desert of Ziph.[p] Day after day Saul searched[q] for him, but God did not[r] give David into his hands.

15While David was at Horesh in the Desert of Ziph, he learned that Saul had come out to take his life.[s] 16And Saul's son Jonathan went to David at Horesh and helped him to find strength[t] in God. 17"Don't be afraid," he said. "My father Saul will not lay a hand on you. You shall be king[u] over Israel, and I will be second to you. Even my father Saul knows this." 18The two of them made a covenant[v] before the LORD. Then Jonathan went home, but David remained at Horesh.

19The Ziphites[w] went up to Saul at Gibeah and said, "Is not David hiding among us[x] in the strongholds at Horesh, on the hill of Hakilah,[y] south of Jeshimon? 20Now, O king, come down whenever it pleases you to do so, and we will be responsible for handing[z] him over to the king."

21Saul replied, "The LORD bless[a] you for your concern[b] for me. 22Go and make further preparation. Find out where David usually goes and who has seen him there. They tell me he is very crafty. 23Find out about all the hiding-places he uses and come back to me with definite information.[a] Then I will go with you; if he is in the area, I will track[c] him down among all the clans of Judah."

24So they set out and went to Ziph ahead of Saul. Now David and his men were in the Desert of Maon,[d] in the Arabah south of Jeshimon.[e] 25Saul and his men began the search, and when David was told about it, he went down to the rock and stayed in the Desert of Maon. When Saul heard this, he went into the Desert of Maon in pursuit of David.

26Saul[f] was going along one side of the mountain, and David and his men were on the other side, hurrying to get away from Saul. As Saul and his forces were closing in on David and his men to capture them, 27a messenger came to Saul, saying, "Come quickly! The Philistines are raiding the land." 28Then Saul broke off his pursuit of David and went to meet the Philistines. That is why they call this place Sela Hammahlekoth.[b] 29And David went up from there and lived in the strongholds[g] of En Gedi.[h]

23 [f]1Sa 20:1
Ch. 23
1 [a]Jos 15:44; [b]Nu 18:27; Jdg 6:11
2 [c]ver 4,12; 1Sa 22:10; 30:8; 2Sa 2:1; 5:19; Ps 50:15
4 [d]ver 2; [e]1Sa 9:16; [f]Jos 8:7
6 [g]1Sa 22:20; [h]1Sa 2:28
7 [i]Dt 32:30; [j]Ps 31:21
9 [k]1Sa 22:20; [l]1Sa 2:18
12 [m]ver 20
13 [n]1Sa 22:2
14 [o]Ps 55:7; [p]Jos 15:24; [q]Ps 54:3–4; [r]Ps 32:7
15 [s]1Sa 20:1
16 [t]1Sa 30:6; Ps 18:2; 27:14
17 [u]1Sa 20:31
18 [v]1Sa 18:3; 2Sa 9:1
19 [w]1Sa 26:1; [x]Ps 54 Title; [y]1Sa 26:3
20 [z]ver 12
21 [a]Ru 2:20; 2Sa 2:5; [b]1Sa 22:8
23 [c]Ge 31:36
24 [d]Jos 15:55; [e]1Sa 26:1
26 [f]Ps 17:9
29 [g]1Sa 24:22; [h]Jos 15:62; 2Ch 20:2; SS 1:14

[a]23 Or *me at Nacon*
[b]28 *Sela Hammahlekoth* means *rock of parting*.

David Spares Saul's Life

24 After Saul returned from pursuing the Philistines, he was told, "David is in the Desert of En Gedi.[a]" 2So Saul took three thousand chosen men from all Israel and set out to look[b] for David and his men near the Crags of the Wild Goats.

3He came to the sheep pens along the way; a cave[c] was there, and Saul went in to relieve[d] himself. David and his men were far back in the cave. 4The men said, "This is the day the LORD spoke[e] of when he said[a] to you, 'I will give your enemy into your hands for you to deal with as you wish.'"[f] Then David crept up unnoticed and cut[g] off a corner of Saul's robe.

5Afterwards, David was conscience-stricken[h] for having cut off a corner of his robe. 6He said to his men, "The LORD forbid that I should do such a thing to my master, the LORD's anointed,[i] or lift my hand against him; for he is the anointed of the LORD." 7With these words David rebuked his men and did not allow them to attack Saul. And Saul left the cave and went his way.

8Then David went out of the cave and called out to Saul, "My lord the king!" When Saul looked behind him, David bowed down and prostrated himself with his face to the ground.[j] 9He said to Saul, "Why do you listen[k] when men say, 'David is bent on harming[l] you'? 10This day you have seen with your own eyes how the LORD gave you into my hands in the cave. Some urged me to kill you, but I spared[m] you; I said, 'I will not lift my hand against my master, because he is the LORD's anointed.' 11See, my father, look at this piece of your robe in my hand! I cut[n] off the corner of your robe but did not kill you. Now understand and recognise that I am not guilty[o] of wrongdoing[p] or rebellion. I have not wronged[q] you, but you are hunting[r] me down to take my life.[s] 12May the LORD judge[t] between you and me. And may the LORD avenge[u] the wrongs you have done to me, but my hand will not touch you. 13As the old saying goes, 'From evildoers come evil deeds,'[v] so my hand will not touch you.

14"Against whom has the king of Israel come out? Whom are you pursuing? A dead dog?[w] A flea?[x] 15May the LORD be our judge[y] and decide[z] between us. May he consider my cause and uphold[a] it; may he vindicate[b] me by delivering[c] me from your hand."

16When David finished saying this, Saul asked, "Is that your voice,[d] David my son?" And he wept aloud. 17"You are more righteous than I,"[e] he said. "You have treated me well,[f] but I have treated you badly.[g] 18You have just now told me of the good you did to me; the LORD gave[h] me into your hands, but you did not kill me. 19When a man finds his enemy, does he let him get away unharmed? May the LORD reward[i] you well for the way you treated me today. 20I know that you will surely be king[j] and that the kingdom[k] of Israel will be established in your hands. 21Now swear[l] to me by the LORD that you will not cut off my descendants or wipe out my name from my father's family."[m]

22So David gave his oath to Saul. Then Saul returned home, but David and his men went up to the stronghold.[n]

David, Nabal and Abigail

25 Now Samuel died,[a] and all Israel assembled and mourned[b] for him; and they buried him at his home in Ramah.[c]

Then David moved down into the Desert of Maon.[a] 2A certain man in Maon,[d] who had property there at Carmel, was very wealthy.[e] He had a thousand goats and three thousand sheep, which he was shearing[f] in Carmel. 3His name was Nabal and his wife's name was Abigail.[g] She was an intelligent and beautiful woman, but her husband, a Calebite,[h] was surly and mean in his dealings.

4While David was in the desert, he heard that Nabal was shearing sheep. 5So he sent ten young men and said to them, "Go up to Nabal at Carmel and greet him in my name. 6Say to him: 'Long life to you! Good health[i] to you and your household! And good health to all that is yours![j]

7" 'Now I hear that it is sheep-shearing time. When your shepherds were with us, we did not ill-treat[k] them, and the whole time they were at Carmel nothing of theirs was missing. 8Ask your own servants and they will tell you. Therefore be favourable towards my young men, since we come at a festive time. Please give your servants and your son David whatever[l] you can find for them.' "

9When David's men arrived, they gave Nabal this message in David's name. Then they waited.

Ch. 24

1 [a]**Jos 15:62**
2 [b]1Sa 26:2
3 [c]Ps 57 Title; 142 Title; [d]Jdg 3:24
4 [e]1Sa 25:28–30; [f]2Sa 4:8; [g]ver 10–11
5 [h]1Sa 26:9; 2Sa 24:10
6 [i]**Ge 26:11; 1Sa 12:3**
8 [j]**1Sa 20:41**
9 [k]1Sa 26:19; [l]1Sa 20:1
10 [m]**ver 4**
11 [n]**ver 4**; [o]Ps 7:3; [p]1Sa 25:28; [q]Ps 35:7; [r]**Ge 31:36**; 1Sa 26:20; [s]**1Sa 20:1**
12 [t]**Ge 16:5; 1Sa 25:38; Job 9:15**; [u]**Nu 31:3**
13 [v]Mt 7:20
14 [w]**1Sa 17:43**; [x]1Sa 26:20
15 [y]ver 12; [z]**Ge 16:5**; [a]Ps 35:1,23; Isa 49:25; [b]Ps 26:1; 35:24; 43:1; 50:4; 54:1; 135:14; [c]Ps 119:134, 154
16 [d]1Sa 26:17
17 [e]Ge 38:26; [f]Mt 5:44; [g]**Ex 9:27**
18 [h]1Sa 26:23
19 [i]**Ru 2:12; 2Ch 15:7**
20 [j]**1Sa 20:31**; [k]**1Sa 13:14**
21 [l]Ge 21:23; **47:31; 1Sa 18:3**; 2Sa 21:1–9; [m]**1Sa 20:14–15**
22 [n]1Sa 23:29

Ch. 25

1 [a]1Sa 28:3; [b]**Lev 10:6**; Dt 34:8; [c]**1Sa 7:17**
2 [d]**Jos 15:55**; [e]2Sa 19:32; [f]**Ge 31:19**
3 [g]Pr 31:10; [h]**Jos 14:13; 15:13**
6 [i]Ps 122:7; Mt 10:12; [j]1Ch 12:18
7 [k]ver 15
8 [l]Ne 8:10

[a]4 Or *"Today the LORD is saying*
[a]1 Some Septuagint manuscripts; Hebrew *Paran*

10Nabal answered David's servants, "Who[m] is this David? Who is this son of Jesse? Many servants are breaking away from their masters these days. 11Why should I take my bread[n] and water, and the meat I have slaughtered for my shearers, and give it to men coming from who knows where?"

12David's men turned round and went back. When they arrived, they reported every word. 13David said to his men,[o] "Put on your swords!" So they put on their swords, and David put on his. About four hundred men went[p] up with David, while two hundred stayed with the supplies.[q]

14One of the servants told Nabal's wife Abigail: "David sent messengers from the desert to give our master his greetings,[r] but he hurled insults at them. 15Yet these men were very good to us. They did not ill-treat[s] us, and the whole time we were out in the fields near them nothing was missing.[t] 16Night and day they were a wall[u] around us all the time we were herding our sheep near them. 17Now think it over and see what you can do, because disaster is hanging over our master and his whole household. He is such a wicked[v] man that no-one can talk to him."

18Abigail lost no time. She took two hundred loaves of bread, two skins of wine, five dressed sheep, five seahs[b] of roasted grain,[w] a hundred cakes of raisins[x] and two hundred cakes of pressed figs, and loaded them on donkeys.[y] 19Then she told her servants, "Go on ahead;[z] I'll follow you." But she did not tell[a] her husband Nabal.

20As she came riding her donkey into a mountain ravine, there were David and his men descending towards her, and she met them. 21David had just said, "It's been useless—all my watching over this fellow's property in the desert so that nothing of his was missing.[b] He has paid[c] me back evil[d] for good. 22May God deal with David,[c] be it ever so severely,[e] if by morning I leave alive one male[f] of all who belong to him!"

23When Abigail saw David, she quickly got off her donkey and bowed down before David with her face to the ground.[g] 24She fell at his feet and said: "My lord, let the blame[h] be on me alone. Please let your servant speak to you; hear what your servant has to say. 25May my lord pay no attention to that wicked man Nabal. He is just like his name—his name is Fool[i],[j] and folly goes with him. But as for me, your servant, I did not see the men my master sent.

26"Now since the LORD has kept you, my master, from bloodshed[k] and from avenging[l] yourself with your own hands, as surely as the LORD lives and as you live, may your enemies and all who intend to harm my master be like Nabal.[m] 27And let this gift,[n] which your servant has brought to my master, be given to the men who follow you. 28Please forgive[o] your servant's offence, for the LORD will certainly make a lasting[p] dynasty for my master, because he fights the LORD's battles.[q] Let no wrongdoing[r] be found in you as long as you live. 29Even though someone is pursuing you to take your life,[s] the life of my master will be bound securely in the bundle of the living by the LORD your God. But the lives of your enemies he will hurl[t] away as from the pocket of a sling.[u] 30When the LORD has done for my master every good thing he promised concerning him and has appointed him leader[v] over Israel, 31my master will not have on his conscience the staggering burden of needless bloodshed or of having avenged himself. And when the LORD has brought my master success, remember[w] your servant."[x]

32David said to Abigail, "Praise[y] be to the LORD, the God of Israel, who has sent you today to meet me. 33May you be blessed for your good judgment and for keeping me from bloodshed[z] this day and from avenging myself with my own hands. 34Otherwise, as surely as the LORD, the God of Israel, lives, who has kept me from harming you, if you had not come quickly to meet me, not one male belonging to Nabal[a] would have been left alive by daybreak."

35Then David accepted from her hand what she had brought to him and said, "Go home in peace. I have heard your words and granted[b] your request."

36When Abigail went to Nabal, he was in the house holding a banquet like that of a king. He was in high[c] spirits and very drunk.[d] So she told[e] him nothing until daybreak. 37Then in the morning, when Nabal was sober, his wife told him all these things, and his heart failed him and he became like a stone.[f] 38About ten days later, the LORD struck[g] Nabal and he died.

39When David heard that Nabal was dead, he said, "Praise be to the LORD,

10 [m]Jdg 9:28
11 [n]Jdg 8:6
13 [o]**1Sa 22:2;** [p]**1Sa 21:10;** [q]**Nu 31:27**
14 [r]1Sa 13:10
15 [s]ver 7; [t]ver 21
16 [u]Ex 14:22; Job 1:10; Ps 139:5
17 [v]**Dt 13:13; 1Sa 20:7**
18 [w]**Lev 23:14; 1Sa 17:17;** [x]1Ch 12:40; [y]**Ge 42:26;** 2Sa 16:1; Isa 30:6
19 [z]Ge 32:20; [a]ver 36
21 [b]ver 15; [c]Ps 109:5; [d]**1Sa 19:4**
22 [e]**Ru 1:17;** [f]1Ki 14:10; 21:21; 2Ki 9:8
23 [g]**Ge 19:1; 1Sa 20:41**
24 [h]2Sa 14:9
25 [i]Pr 17:12; [j]Pr 12:16; 14:16; 20:3; Isa 32:5
26 [k]ver 33; [l]Heb 10:30; [m]ver 34; 2Sa 18:32
27 [n]**Ge 33:11**
28 [o]ver 24; 2Sa 14:9; [p]2Sa 7:11,26; [q]1Sa 18:17; [r]1Sa 24:11
29 [s]**1Sa 20:1;** [t]Jer 10:18; 22:26; [u]1Sa 17:50; 2Sa 4:8
30 [v]**1Sa 12:12; 13:14**
31 [w]**Ge 40:14;** [x]2Sa 3:10
32 [y]**Ge 24:27**
33 [z]ver 26
34 [a]**ver 26**
35 [b]**Ge 19:21**
36 [c]**Ru 3:7;** [d]Pr 20:1; Ecc 10:17; Isa 5:11,22; 22:13; 28:7; 56:12; Hos 4:11; [e]ver 19
37 [f]Ex 15:16
38 [g]Dt 32:35; 1Sa 24:12; 26:10; 2Sa 6:7; 12:15

[b]*18* That is, probably about a bushel (about 37 litres)
[c]22 Some Septuagint manuscripts; Hebrew *with David's enemies*

who has upheld my cause against Nabal for treating me with contempt. He has kept his servant from doing wrong and has brought Nabal's wrongdoing down on his own head."

Then David sent word to Abigail, asking her to become his wife. 40His servants went to Carmel and said to Abigail, "David has sent us to you to take you to become his wife."

41She bowed down with her face to the ground and said, "Here is your maidservant, ready to serve you and wash the feet of my master's servants." 42Abigail[h] quickly got on a donkey and, attended by her five maids, went with David's messengers and became his wife. 43David had also married Ahinoam[i] of Jezreel, and they both were his wives.[j] 44But Saul had given his daughter Michal, David's wife, to Paltiel[d][k] son of Laish, who was from Gallim.[l]

David Again Spares Saul's Life

26 The Ziphites[a] went to Saul at Gibeah and said, "Is not David hiding[b] on the hill of Hakilah, which faces Jeshimon?[c]"

2So Saul went down to the Desert of Ziph, with his three thousand chosen men of Israel, to search[d] there for David. 3Saul made his camp beside the road on the hill of Hakilah[e] facing Jeshimon, but David stayed in the desert. When he saw that Saul had followed him there, 4he sent out scouts and learned that Saul had definitely arrived.[a]

5Then David set out and went to the place where Saul had camped. He saw where Saul and Abner[f] son of Ner, the commander of the army, had lain down. Saul was lying inside the camp, with the army encamped around him.

6David then asked Ahimelech the Hittite[g] and Abishai[h] son of Zeruiah,[i] Joab's brother, "Who will go down into the camp with me to Saul?"

"I'll go with you," said Abishai.

7So David and Abishai went to the army by night, and there was Saul, lying asleep inside the camp with his spear stuck in the ground near his head. Abner and the soldiers were lying round him.

8Abishai said to David, "Today God has given your enemy into your hands. Now let me pin him to the ground with one thrust of my spear; I won't strike him twice."

9But David said to Abishai, "Don't destroy him! Who can lay a hand on the LORD's anointed[j] and be guiltless?[k] 10As surely as the LORD lives," he said, "the LORD himself will strike[l] him; either his time[m] will come and he will die,[n] or he will go into battle and perish. 11But the LORD forbid that I should lay a hand on the LORD's anointed. Now get the spear and water jug that are near his head, and let's go."

12So David took the spear and water jug near Saul's head, and they left. No-one saw or knew about it, nor did anyone wake up. They were all sleeping, because the LORD had put them into a deep sleep.[o]

13Then David crossed over to the other side and stood on top of the hill some distance away; there was a wide space between them. 14He called out to the army and to Abner son of Ner, "Aren't you going to answer me, Abner?"

Abner replied, "Who are you who calls to the king?"

15David said, "You're a man, aren't you? And who is like you in Israel? Why didn't you guard your lord the king? Someone came to destroy your lord the king. 16What you have done is not good. As surely as the LORD lives, you and your men deserve to die, because you did not guard your master, the LORD's anointed. Look around you. Where are the king's spear and water jug that were near his head?"

17Saul recognised David's voice and said, "Is that your voice,[p] David my son?"

David replied, "Yes it is, my lord the king." 18And he added, "Why is my lord pursuing his servant? What have I done, and what wrong[q] am I guilty of? 19Now let my lord the king listen[r] to his servant's words. If the LORD has incited you against me, then may he accept an offering.[s] If, however, men have done it, may they be cursed before the LORD! They have now driven me from my share in the LORD's inheritance[t] and have said, 'Go, serve other gods.'[u] 20Now do not let my blood[v] fall to the ground far from the presence of the LORD. The king of Israel has come out to look for a flea[w]—as one hunts a partridge in the mountains.[x]"

21Then Saul said, "I have sinned.[y] Come back, David my son. Because you considered my life precious[z] today, I will not try to harm you again. Surely I have acted like a fool and have erred greatly."

42 [h]2Sa 2:2; 3:3; 1Ch 3:1
43 [i]2Sa 3:2; 1Ch 3:1; [j]1Sa 27:3; 30:5; 2Sa 2:2
44 [k]2Sa 3:15; [l]Isa 10:30

Ch. 26

1 [a]1Sa 23:19; [b]Ps 54 Title; [c]1Sa 23:24
2 [d]1Sa 24:2
3 [e]1Sa 23:19
5 [f]1Sa 17:55
6 [g]**Ge 10:15;** [h]2Sa 2:18; 10:10; 16:9; 18:2; 19:21; 23:18; 1Ch 11:20; 19:11; [i]1Ch 2:16
9 [j]ver 16; **Ge 26:11; 1Sa 9:16;** 2Sa 1:14; 19:21; La 4:20; [k]**1Sa 24:5**
10 [l]**Ge 16:5; 1Sa 25:38; Ro 12:19;** [m]Dt 31:14; Ps 37:13; [n]1Sa 31:6; 2Sa 1:1
12 [o]**Jdg 4:21**
17 [p]1Sa 24:16
18 [q]Job 13:23; Jer 37:18
19 [r]1Sa 24:9; [s]2Sa 16:11; [t]Dt 20:16; 32:9; 2Sa 14:16; 20:19; 21:3; [u]**Dt 4:28; 11:28**
20 [v]**1Sa 24:11;** [w]1Sa 24:14; [x]Jer 4:29; 16:16; Am 9:3
21 [y]**Ex 9:27;** [z]Ps 72:14

d44 Hebrew *Palti*, a variant of *Paltiel*
a4 Or *had come to Nacon*

22"Here is the king's spear," David
answered. "Let one of your young men
come over and get it. 23The LORD re-
wards[a] every man for his righteousness[b]
and faithfulness. The LORD gave[c] you
into my hands today, but I would not
lay a hand on the LORD's anointed. 24As
surely as I valued your life today, so
may the LORD value my life and deliver[d]
me from all trouble."
25Then Saul said to David, "May you
be blessed,[e] my son David; you will do
great things and surely triumph."
So David went on his way, and Saul
returned home.

David Among the Philistines

27 But David thought to himself,
"One of these days I shall be
destroyed by the hand of Saul. The best
thing I can do is to escape to the land of
the Philistines. Then Saul will give up
searching for me anywhere in Israel,
and I will slip out of his hand."
2So David and the six hundred men[a]
with him left and went[b] over to Achish[c]
son of Maoch king of Gath. 3David and
his men settled in Gath with Achish.
Each man had his family with him, and
David had his two wives:[d] Ahinoam of
Jezreel and Abigail of Carmel, the
widow of Nabal. 4When Saul was told
that David had fled to Gath, he no
longer searched for him.
5Then David said to Achish, "If I have
found favour in your eyes, let a place be
assigned to me in one of the country
towns, that I may live there. Why
should your servant live in the royal city
with you?"
6So on that day Achish gave him
Ziklag,[e] and it has belonged to the
kings of Judah ever since. 7David lived[f]
in Philistine territory for a year and
four months.
8Now David and his men went up
and raided the Geshurites,[g] the Girzites
and the Amalekites.[h] (From ancient
times these peoples had lived in the
land extending to Shur[i] and Egypt.)
9Whenever David attacked an area, he
did not leave a man or woman alive,[j] but
took sheep and cattle, donkeys and
camels, and clothes. Then he returned
to Achish.
10When Achish asked, "Where did
you go raiding today?" David would
say, "Against the Negev of Judah" or
"Against the Negev of Jerahmeel[k]" or
"Against the Negev of the Kenites.[l]"
11He did not leave a man or woman alive
to be brought to Gath, for he thought,
"They might inform on us and say,
'This is what David did.'" And such
was his practice as long as he lived in
Philistine territory. 12Achish trusted
David and said to himself, "He has
become so odious[m] to his people, the
Israelites, that he will be my servant for
ever.[n]"

Saul and the Witch of Endor

28 In those days the Philistines
gathered[a] their forces to fight
against Israel. Achish said to David,
"You must understand that you and
your men will accompany me in the
army."
2David said, "Then you will see for
yourself what your servant can do."
Achish replied, "Very well, I will
make you my bodyguard[b] for life."
3Now Samuel was dead,[c] and all
Israel had mourned for him and buried
him in his own town of Ramah.[d] Saul
had expelled[e] the mediums and spirit-
ists[f] from the land.
4The Philistines assembled and came
and set up camp at Shunem,[g] while Saul
gathered all the Israelites and set up
camp at Gilboa.[h] 5When Saul saw the
Philistine army, he was afraid; terror[i]
filled his heart. 6He enquired[j] of the
LORD, but the LORD did not answer him
by dreams[k] or Urim[l] or prophets.[m] 7Saul
then said to his attendants, "Find me a
woman who is a medium,[n] so that I may
go and enquire of her."
"There is one in Endor,[o]" they said.
8So Saul disguised[p] himself, putting
on other clothes, and at night he and
two men went to the woman. "Consult[q]
a spirit for me," he said, "and bring up
for me the one I name."
9But the woman said to him, "Surely
you know what Saul has done. He has
cut off[r] the mediums and spiritists from
the land. Why have you set a trap[s] for
my life to bring about my death?"
10Saul swore to her by the LORD, "As
surely as the LORD lives, you will not be
punished for this."
11Then the woman asked, "Whom
shall I bring up for you?"
"Bring up Samuel," he said.
12When the woman saw Samuel, she
cried out at the top of her voice and said
to Saul, "Why have you deceived me?[t]
You are Saul!"
13The king said to her, "Don't be
afraid. What do you see?"
The woman said, "I see a spirit[a] com-
ing up out of the ground."[u]

23 [a]Ge 16:5; Ru 2:12; Ps 62:12; [b]2Sa 22:21,25; Ps 7:8; 18:20,24; [c]1Sa 24:18
24 [d]Ps 54:7
25 [e]Ru 2:12

Ch. 27

2 [a]1Sa 30:9; 2Sa 2:3; [b]1Sa 21:10; [c]1Ki 2:39
3 [d]1Sa 25:43
6 [e]Jos 15:31; 19:5; 1Sa 30:1; 1Ch 12:20; Ne 11:28
7 [f]1Sa 29:3
8 [g]Jos 12:5; [h]Ex 17:14; 1Sa 14:48; 30:1; 2Sa 1:8; 8:12; [i]Ge 16:7
9 [j]1Sa 15:3
10 [k]1Sa 30:29; [l]Jdg 1:16
12 [m]Ge 34:30; [n]1Sa 29:6

Ch. 28

1 [a]1Sa 29:1
2 [b]1Sa 29:2
3 [c]1Sa 25:1; [d]1Sa 7:17; [e]ver 9; [f]Ex 22:18
4 [g]Jos 19:18; [h]1Sa 31:1,3; 2Sa 1:6,21; 21:12
5 [i]Ex 19:16
6 [j]1Sa 8:18; 14:37; [k]Dt 13:3; [l]Ex 28:30; Lev 8:8; [m]Eze 20:3; Am 8:11; Mic 3:7
7 [n]1Ch 10:13; Ac 16:16; [o]Jos 17:11; Ps 83:10
8 [p]1Ki 22:30; 2Ch 18:29; 35:22; [q]2Ki 1:3; Isa 8:19
9 [r]ver 3; [s]Job 18:10; Ps 31:4; 69:22; Isa 8:14
12 [t]Ge 27:36; 1Ki 14:6
13 [u]ver 15; Lev 19:31; 2Ch 33:6

[a]13 Or *see spirits*; or *see gods*

14"What does he look like?" he asked.

"An old man wearing a robe[v] is coming up," she said.

Then Saul knew it was Samuel, and he bowed down and prostrated himself with his face to the ground.

15Samuel said to Saul, "Why have you disturbed me by bringing me up?"

"I am in great distress," Saul said. "The Philistines are fighting against me, and God has turned[w] away from me. He no longer answers[x] me, either by prophets or by dreams.[y] So I have called on you to tell me what to do."

16Samuel said, "Why do you consult me, now that the LORD has turned away from you and become your enemy? 17The LORD has done what he predicted through me. The LORD has torn[z] the kingdom out of your hands and given it to one of your neighbours—to David. 18Because you did not obey[a] the LORD or carry out his fierce wrath[b] against the Amalekites,[c] the LORD has done this to you today. 19The LORD will hand over both Israel and you to the Philistines, and tomorrow you and your sons[d] will be with me. The LORD will also hand over the army of Israel to the Philistines."

20Immediately Saul fell full length on the ground, filled with fear because of Samuel's words. His strength was gone, for he had eaten nothing all that day and night.

21When the woman came to Saul and saw that he was greatly shaken, she said, "Look, your maidservant has obeyed you. I took my life[e] in my hands and did what you told me to do. 22Now please listen to your servant and let me give you some food so that you may eat and have the strength to go on your way."

23He refused[f] and said, "I will not eat."

But his men joined the woman in urging him, and he listened to them. He got up from the ground and sat on the couch.

24The woman had a fattened calf[g] at the house, which she slaughtered at once. She took some flour, kneaded it and baked bread without yeast. 25Then she set it before Saul and his men, and they ate. That same night they got up and left.

Achish Sends David Back to Ziklag

29 The Philistines gathered[a] all their forces at Aphek,[b] and Israel camped by the spring in Jezreel.[c] 2As the Philistine rulers marched with their units of hundreds and thousands, David and his men were marching at the rear[d] with Achish. 3The commanders of the Philistines asked, "What about these Hebrews?"

Achish replied, "Is this not David,[e] who was an officer of Saul king of Israel? He has already been with me for over a year,[f] and from the day he left Saul until now, I have found no fault in him."

4But the Philistine commanders were angry with him and said, "Send[g] the man back, that he may return to the place you assigned him. He must not go with us into battle, or he will turn[h] against us during the fighting. How better could he regain his master's favour than by taking the heads of our own men? 5Isn't this the David they sang about in their dances:

"'Saul has slain his thousands,
and David his tens of thousands'?"[i]

6So Achish called David and said to him, "As surely as the LORD lives, you have been reliable, and I would be pleased to have you serve with me in the army. From the day[j] you came to me until now, I have found no fault in you, but the rulers[k] don't approve of you. 7Turn back and go in peace; do nothing to displease the Philistine rulers."

8"But what have I done?" asked David. "What have you found against your servant from the day I came to you until now? Why can't I go and fight against the enemies of my lord the king?"

9Achish answered, "I know that you have been as pleasing in my eyes as an angel[l] of God; nevertheless, the Philistine commanders[m] have said, 'He must not go up with us into battle.' 10Now get up early, along with your master's servants who have come with you, and leave[n] in the morning as soon as it is light."

11So David and his men got up early in the morning to go back to the land of the Philistines, and the Philistines went up to Jezreel.

David Destroys the Amalekites

30 David and his men reached Ziklag[a] on the third day. Now the Amalekites[b] had raided the Negev and Ziklag. They had attacked Ziklag and burned[c] it, 2and had taken captive the women and all who were in it, both young and old. They killed none of

14 [v]1Sa 15:27
15 [w]**Jdg 16:20;** [x]**1Sa 14:37;** [y]**Dt 13:3**
17 [z]1Sa 15:28
18 [a]1Sa 15:20; [b]**Dt 9:8; 1Sa 15:3;** [c]**Ge 14:7; 1Sa 14:48**
19 [d]1Sa 31:2; 1Ch 8:33
21 [e]**Jdg 9:17; 12:3**
23 [f]1Ki 21:4
24 [g]**Ge 18:7**

Ch. 29

1 [a]1Sa 28:1; [b]**1Sa 4:1;** [c]Jos 17:16; 1Ki 18:45; 21:1,23; 2Ki 9:30; Jer 50:5; Hos 1:4–5,11; 2:22
2 [d]1Sa 28:2
3 [e]1Ch 12:19; [f]1Sa 27:7
4 [g]1Ch 12:19; [h]1Sa 14:21
5 [i]**1Sa 18:7**
6 [j]1Sa 27:8–12; [k]ver 3
9 [l]2Sa 14:17,20; 19:27; [m]ver 4
10 [n]1Ch 12:19

Ch. 30

1 [a]**1Sa 27:6;** [b]**1Sa 27:8;** [c]ver 14

them, but carried them off as they went on their way.

3When David and his men came to Ziklag, they found it destroyed by fire and their wives and sons and daughters taken captive.[d] 4So David and his men wept[e] aloud until they had no strength left to weep. 5David's two wives[f] had been captured—Ahinoam of Jezreel and Abigail, the widow of Nabal of Carmel. 6David was greatly distressed because the men were talking of stoning[g] him; each one was bitter[h] in spirit because of his sons and daughters. But David found strength[i] in the LORD his God.

7Then David said to Abiathar[j] the priest, the son of Ahimelech, "Bring me the ephod.[k]" Abiathar brought it to him, 8and David enquired[l] of the LORD, "Shall I pursue this raiding party? Will I overtake them?"

"Pursue them," he answered. "You will certainly overtake them and succeed[m] in the rescue.[n]"

9David and the six hundred men[o] with him came to the Besor Ravine, where some stayed behind, 10for two hundred men were too exhausted[p] to cross the ravine. But David and four hundred men continued the pursuit.

11They found an Egyptian in a field and brought him to David. They gave him water to drink and food to eat—12part of a cake of pressed figs and two cakes of raisins. He ate and was revived,[q] for he had not eaten any food or drunk any water for three days and three nights.

13David asked him, "To whom do you belong, and where do you come from?"

He said, "I am an Egyptian, the slave of an Amalekite.[r] My master abandoned me when I became ill three days ago. 14We raided the Negev of the Kerethites[s] and the territory belonging to Judah and the Negev of Caleb.[t] And we burned[u] Ziklag."

15David asked him, "Can you lead me down to this raiding party?"

He answered, "Swear to me before God that you will not kill me or hand me over to my master,[v] and I will take you down to them."

16He led David down, and there they were, scattered over the countryside, eating, drinking and revelling[w] because of the great amount of plunder[x] they had taken from the land of the Philistines and from Judah. 17David fought[y] them from dusk until the evening of the next day, and none of them got away, except four hundred young men who rode off on camels and fled.[z] 18David recovered[a] everything the Amalekites had taken, including his two wives. 19Nothing was missing: young or old, boy or girl, plunder or anything else they had taken. David brought everything back. 20He took all the flocks and herds, and his men drove them ahead of the other livestock, saying, "This is David's plunder."

21Then David came to the two hundred men who had been too exhausted[b] to follow him and who were left behind at the Besor Ravine. They came out to meet David and the people with him. As David and his men approached, he greeted them. 22But all the evil men and troublemakers among David's followers said, "Because they did not go out with us, we will not share with them the plunder we recovered. However, each man may take his wife and children and go."

23David replied, "No, my brothers, you must not do that with what the LORD has given us. He has protected us and handed over to us the forces that came against us. 24Who will listen to what you say? The share of the man who stayed with the supplies is to be the same as that of him who went down to the battle. All shall share alike.[c]" 25David made this a statute and ordinance for Israel from that day to this.

26When David arrived in Ziklag, he sent some of the plunder to the elders of Judah, who were his friends, saying, "Here is a present[d] for you from the plunder of the LORD's enemies."

27He sent it to those who were in Bethel,[e] Ramoth[f] Negev and Jattir;[g] 28to those in Aroer,[h] Siphmoth,[i] Eshtemoa[j] 29and Racal; to those in the towns of the Jerahmeelites[k] and the Kenites;[l] 30to those in Hormah,[m] Bor Ashan,[n] Athach 31and Hebron;[o] and to those in all the other places where David and his men had roamed.

3 [d]Ge 31:26
4 [e]Ge 27:38
5 [f]1Sa 25:43
6 [g]Ex 17:4; Jn 8:59; [h]Ru 1:13; [i]1Sa 23:16; Ro 4:20
7 [j]1Sa 22:20; [k]1Sa 2:28
8 [l]1Sa 23:2; [m]Ge 14:16; [n]Ex 2:17
9 [o]1Sa 27:2
10 [p]ver 21
12 [q]Jdg 15:19
13 [r]1Sa 14:48
14 [s]2Sa 8:18; 15:18; 20:7, 23; 1Ki 1:38,44; 1Ch 18:17; Eze 25:16; Zep 2:5; [t]Jos 14:13; 15:13; [u]ver 1
15 [v]Dt 23:15
16 [w]Lk 12:19; [x]ver 17; Jos 22:8
17 [y]ver 16; 1Sa 11:11; 2Sa 1:1; [z]2Sa 1:8
18 [a]Ge 14:16
21 [b]ver 10
24 [c]Nu 31:27; Jdg 5:30
26 [d]Ge 33:11
27 [e]Jos 7:2; [f]Jos 10:40; [g]Jos 15:48
28 [h]Nu 32:34; Jos 13:16; [i]1Ch 27:27; [j]Jos 15:50
29 [k]1Sa 27:10; [l]1Sa 15:6
30 [m]Nu 14:45; 21:3; [n]Jos 15:42
31 [o]Nu 13:22; Jos 10:36; 2Sa 2:1,4

Ch. 31

1 [a]1Sa 28:4
2 [b]1Sa 28:19; [c]1Sa 18:1; [d]1Sa 14:49
3 [e]1Sa 28:4

Saul Takes His Life

31:1–13pp—2Sa 1:4–12; 1Ch 10:1–12

31 Now the Philistines fought against Israel; the Israelites fled before them, and many fell slain on Mount Gilboa.[a] 2The Philistines pressed hard after Saul and his sons,[b] and they killed his sons Jonathan,[c] Abinadab and Malki-Shua.[d] 3The fighting grew fierce around Saul, and when the archers overtook him, they wounded[e] him critically.

4Saul said to his armour-bearer,
"Draw your sword and run me
through,[f] or these uncircumcised[g]
fellows will come and run me through
and abuse me."
But the armour-bearer was terrified
and would not do it; so Saul took his
own sword and fell on it. 5When the
armour-bearer saw that Saul was dead,
he too fell on his sword and died with
him. 6So Saul and his three sons and his
armour-bearer and all his men died[h]
together that same day.
7When the Israelites along the valley
and those across the Jordan saw that the
Israelite army had fled and that Saul and
his sons had died, they abandoned their
towns and fled. And the Philistines
came and occupied them.
8The next day, when the Philistines[i]
came to strip the dead, they found Saul
and his three sons fallen on Mount Gil-
boa. 9They cut off his head and stripped
off his armour, and they sent messen-
gers throughout the land of the Philis-
tines to proclaim the news[j] in the temple
of their idols and among their people.[k]
10They put his armour in the temple of
the Ashtoreths[l] and fastened his body to
the wall of Beth Shan.[m]
11When the people of Jabesh Gilead[n]
heard of what the Philistines had done
to Saul, 12all their valiant men[o] jour-
neyed through the night to Beth Shan.
They took down the bodies of Saul and
his sons from the wall of Beth Shan and
went to Jabesh, where they burned[p]
them. 13Then they took their bones[q] and
buried them under a tamarisk[r] tree at
Jabesh, and they fasted[s] seven days.[t]

4 [f]Jdg 9:54; [g]Ge 34:14; 1Sa 14:6
6 [h]1Sa 26:10
8 [i]2Sa 1:20
9 [j]2Sa 1:20; 4:4; [k]Jdg 16:24
10 [l]Jdg 2:12–13; 1Sa 7:3; [m]Jos 17:11
11 [n]Jdg 21:8; 1Sa 11:1
12 [o]Ps 76:5; [p]Ge 38:24; Am 6:10
13 [q]2Sa 21:12–14; [r]Ge 21:33; [s]2Sa 3:35; 12:19–23; [t]Ge 50:10

2 Samuel

David Hears of Saul's Death

1:4–12pp—1Sa 31:1–13; 1Ch 10:1–12

1 After the death[a] of Saul, David
returned from defeating[b] the
Amalekites[c] and stayed in Ziklag two
days. 2 On the third day a man[d] arrived
from Saul's camp, with his clothes torn
and with dust on his head.[e] When he
came to David, he fell[f] to the ground to
pay him honour.[g]
3 "Where have you come from?"
David asked him.
He answered, "I have escaped from
the Israelite camp."
4 "What happened?" David asked.
"Tell me."
He said, "The men fled from the bat-
tle. Many of them fell and died. And
Saul and his son Jonathan are dead."
5 Then David said to the young man
who brought him the report, "How do
you know that Saul and his son
Jonathan are dead?"
6 "I happened to be on Mount Gil-
boa,[h]" the young man said, "and there
was Saul, leaning on his spear, with the
chariots and riders almost upon him.
7 When he turned round and saw me, he
called out to me, and I said, 'What can I
do?'
8 "He asked me, 'Who are you?'
"'An Amalekite,[i]' I answered.
9 "Then he said to me, 'Stand over me
and kill me![j] I am in the throes of death,
but I'm still alive.'
10 "So I stood over him and killed him,
because I knew that after he had fallen
he could not survive. And I took the
crown[k] that was on his head and the
band on his arm and have brought them
here to my lord."
11 Then David and all the men with
him took hold of their clothes and tore[l]
them. 12 They mourned and wept and
fasted till evening for Saul and his son
Jonathan, and for the army of the LORD
and the house of Israel, because they
had fallen by the sword.
13 David said to the young man who
brought him the report, "Where are you
from?"

"I am the son of an alien, an Amalek-
ite,[m]" he answered.
14 David asked him, "Why were you
not afraid to lift your hand to destroy
the LORD's anointed?[n]"
15 Then David called one of his men
and said, "Go, strike him down!"[o] So he
struck him down, and he died.[p] 16 For
David had said to him, "Your blood be
on your own head.[q] Your own mouth
testified against you when you said, 'I
killed the LORD's anointed.'"

David's Lament for Saul and Jonathan

17 David took up this lament[r] concern-
ing Saul and his son Jonathan,[s] 18 and
ordered that the men of Judah be taught
this lament of the bow (it is written in
the Book of Jashar):[t]

19 "Your glory, O Israel, lies slain on
your heights.
How the mighty[u] have fallen![v]

20 "Tell it not in Gath,[w]
proclaim it not in the streets of
Ashkelon,[x]
lest the daughters of the Philistines[y] be
glad,
lest the daughters of the
uncircumcised rejoice.[z]

21 "O mountains of Gilboa,[a]
may you have neither dew[b] nor
rain,[c]
nor fields that yield offerings[d] ⌞of
grain⌟.
For there the shield of the mighty was
defiled,
the shield of Saul—no longer
rubbed with oil.[e]

22 From the blood[f] of the slain,
from the flesh of the mighty,
the bow[g] of Jonathan did not turn
back,
the sword of Saul did not return
unsatisfied.

23 "Saul and Jonathan—
in life they were loved and gracious,
and in death they were not parted.

Ch. 1

1 [a]**1Sa 26:10;** 1Ch 10:13; [b]**Jos 22:8; 1Sa 30:17;** [c]**Ge 14:7;** Nu 13:29
2 [d]2Sa 4:10; [e]**1Sa 4:12;** Job 2:12; Eze 27:30; [f]**1Sa 20:41;** [g]**Ge 37:7**
6 [h]ver 21; **1Sa 28:4**
8 [i]ver 13; **1Sa 15:2; 27:8;** 30:13,17
9 [j]**Jdg 9:54**
10 [k]2Ki 11:12
11 [l]**Ge 37:29;** **Nu 14:6**
13 [m]**ver 8;** **1Sa 14:48**
14 [n]**1Sa 12:3;** **26:9**
15 [o]2Sa 4:12; [p]2Sa 4:10
16 [q]**Lev 20:9;** Mt 27:24–25; Ac 18:6
17 [r]**Ge 50:10;** **Eze 32:2;** [s]ver 26
18 [t]Jos 10:13
19 [u]2Sa 23:8; Ps 29:1; 45:3; [v]2Sa 3:38
20 [w]Mic 1:10; [x]**Jos 13:3;** [y]1Sa 31:8; [z]**1Sa 18:6**
21 [a]**ver 6;** [b]**Ge 27:28; Isa 18:4;** [c]Dt 11:17; 1Ki 8:35; 17:1; 18:1; 2Ch 6:26; Job 36:27; 38:28; Ps 65:10; 147:8; Isa 5:6; Jer 5:24; 14:4; Am 1:2; [d]Jer 12:4; Eze 31:15; [e]Isa 21:5
22 [f]Isa 34:3,7; 49:26; [g]Dt 32:42

They were swifter than eagles,[h]
they were stronger than lions.[i]

24"O daughters of Israel,
weep for Saul,
who clothed you in scarlet and finery,
who adorned your garments with
ornaments of gold.[j]

25"How the mighty have fallen in battle!
Jonathan lies slain on your heights.
26I grieve[k] for you, Jonathan[l] my
brother;[m]
you were very dear to me.
Your love for me was wonderful,[n]
more wonderful than that of
women.

27"How the mighty have fallen!
The weapons of war have
perished!"[o]

David Anointed King Over Judah

2 In the course of time, David en-
quired[a] of the LORD. "Shall I go up
to one of the towns of Judah?" he asked.
The LORD said, "Go up."
David asked, "Where shall I go?"
"To Hebron,"[b] the LORD answered.
2So David went up there with his two
wives,[c] Ahinoam of Jezreel and Abi-
gail,[d] the widow of Nabal of Carmel.
3David also took the men who were
with him,[e] each with his family, and
they settled in Hebron[f] and its towns.
4Then the men of Judah came to Heb-
ron[g] and there they anointed[h] David
king over the house of Judah.
When David was told that it was the
men of Jabesh Gilead[i] who had buried
Saul, 5he sent messengers to the men of
Jabesh Gilead to say to them, "The LORD
bless[j] you for showing this kindness to
Saul your master by burying him. 6May
the LORD now show you kindness and
faithfulness,[k] and I too will show you
the same favour because you have done
this. 7Now then, be strong[l] and brave,
for Saul your master is dead, and the
house of Judah has anointed me king
over them."

War Between the Houses of David and Saul

3:2-5—1Ch 3:1-4

8Meanwhile, Abner[m] son of Ner, the
commander of Saul's army, had taken
Ish-Bosheth[n] son of Saul and brought
him over to Mahanaim.[o] 9He made him
king over Gilead,[p] Ashuri[a][q] and Jezreel,
and also over Ephraim, Benjamin and
all Israel.[r]

23 [h]**Dt 28:49**; [i]Jdg 14:18
24 [j]**Jdg 5:30**
26 [k]Jer 22:18; 34:5; [l]ver 17; [m]**1Sa 20:42**; [n]**1Sa 18:1**
27 [o]**1Sa 2:4**

Ch. 2

1 [a]**1Sa 23:2**, 11–12; [b]**Ge 13:18; 23:19**
2 [c]**1Sa 25:43**; [d]**1Sa 25:42**
3 [e]**1Sa 27:2**; 1Ch 12:22; [f]**Ge 13:18**; 23:2; 37:14
4 [g]**1Sa 30:31**; [h]**1Sa 2:35**; 2Sa 5:3–5; 1Ch 12:23–40; [i]**Jdg 21:8; 1Sa 11:1**
5 [j]**Jdg 17:2; 1Sa 23:21**; 2Ti 1:16
6 [k]Ex 34:6
7 [l]**Jos 1:6; Jdg 5:21**
8 [m]**1Sa 14:50; 2Sa 3:27**; [n]2Sa 4:5; 1Ch 8:33; 9:39; [o]**Ge 32:2**
9 [p]**Nu 32:26**; [q]**Jos 19:24–31**; [r]1Ch 12:29
11 [s]2Sa 5:5
12 [t]**Jos 9:3**
13 [u]2Sa 8:16; 19:13; 1Ki 1:7; 1Ch 2:16; 11:6; 27:34
16 [v]**Jdg 3:21**
17 [w]2Sa 3:1; [x]**1Sa 17:8**
18 [y]2Sa 3:39; 16:10; 19:22; [z]2Sa 3:30; 10:7; 11:1; 14:1; 18:14; 20:8; 24:3; 1Ki 1:7; 2:5,34; [a]**1Sa 26:6**; [b]2Sa 23:24; 1Ch 2:16; 11:26; 27:7; [c]1Ch 12:8; Pr 6:5; SS 2:9
22 [d]2Sa 3:27
23 [e]2Sa 3:27; 4:6; [f]2Sa 20:12

10Ish-Bosheth son of Saul was forty
years old when he became king over
Israel, and he reigned two years. The
house of Judah, however, followed
David. 11The length of time David was
king in Hebron over the house of Judah
was seven years and six months.[s]
12Abner son of Ner, together with the
men of Ish-Bosheth son of Saul, left
Mahanaim and went to Gibeon.[t] 13Joab[u]
son of Zeruiah and David's men went
out and met them at the pool of Gibeon.
One group sat down on one side of the
pool and one group on the other side.
14Then Abner said to Joab, "Let's
have some of the young men get up and
fight hand to hand in front of us."
"All right, let them do it," Joab said.
15So they stood up and were counted
off—twelve men for Benjamin and Ish-
Bosheth son of Saul, and twelve for
David. 16Then each man grabbed his
opponent by the head and thrust his
dagger[v] into his opponent's side, and
they fell down together. So that place in
Gibeon was called Helkath Hazzurim.[b]
17The battle that day was very fierce,
and Abner and the men of Israel were
defeated[w] by David's men.[x]
18The three sons of Zeruiah[y] were
there: Joab,[z] Abishai[a] and Asahel.[b] Now
Asahel was as fleet-footed as a wild
gazelle.[c] 19He chased Abner, turning
neither to the right nor to the left as he
pursued him. 20Abner looked behind
him and asked, "Is that you, Asahel?"
"It is," he answered.
21Then Abner said to him, "Turn
aside to the right or to the left; take on
one of the young men and strip him of
his weapons." But Asahel would not
stop chasing him.
22Again Abner warned Asahel, "Stop
chasing me! Why should I strike you
down? How could I look your brother
Joab in the face?"[d]
23But Asahel refused to give up the
pursuit; so Abner thrust the butt of his
spear into Asahel's stomach,[e] and the
spear came out through his back. He fell
there and died on the spot. And every
man stopped when he came to the place
where Asahel had fallen and died.[f]
24But Joab and Abishai pursued
Abner, and as the sun was setting, they
came to the hill of Ammah, near Giah on
the way to the wasteland of Gibeon.
25Then the men of Benjamin rallied be-
hind Abner. They formed themselves

[a]9 Or *Asher*
[b]16 *Helkath Hazzurim* means *field of daggers* or *field of hostilities*.

into a group and took their stand on top of a hill.

26 Abner called out to Joab, "Must the sword devour[g] for ever? Don't you realise that this will end in bitterness? How long before you order your men to stop pursuing their brothers?"

27 Joab answered, "As surely as God lives, if you had not spoken, the men would have continued the pursuit of their brothers until morning."[c]

28 So Joab[h] blew the trumpet,[i] and all the men came to a halt; they no longer pursued Israel, nor did they fight any more.

29 All that night Abner and his men marched through the Arabah.[j] They crossed the Jordan, continued through the whole Bithron[d] and came to Mahanaim.[k]

30 Then Joab returned from pursuing Abner and assembled all his men. Besides Asahel, nineteen of David's men were found missing. 31 But David's men had killed 360 Benjamites who were with Abner. 32 They took Asahel and buried him in his father's tomb[l] at Bethlehem. Then Joab and his men marched all night and arrived at Hebron by daybreak.

3 The war between the house of Saul and the house of David lasted a long time.[a] David grew stronger and stronger,[b] while the house of Saul grew weaker and weaker.[c]

2 Sons were born to David in Hebron:
His firstborn was Amnon[d] the son of Ahinoam[e] of Jezreel;
3 his second, Kileab the son of Abigail[f] the widow of Nabal of Carmel;
the third, Absalom[g] the son of Maacah daughter of Talmai king of Geshur;[h]
4 the fourth, Adonijah[i] the son of Haggith;
the fifth, Shephatiah the son of Abital;
5 and the sixth, Ithream the son of David's wife Eglah.
These were born to David in Hebron.

Abner Goes Over to David

6 During the war between the house of Saul and the house of David, Abner[j] had been strengthening his own position in the house of Saul. 7 Now Saul had had a concubine[k] named Rizpah[l] daughter of Aiah. And Ish-Bosheth said to Abner, "Why did you sleep with my father's concubine?"

8 Abner was very angry because of what Ish-Bosheth said and he answered, "Am I a dog's head[m]—on Judah's side? This very day I am loyal to the house of your father Saul and to his family and friends. I haven't handed you over to David. Yet now you accuse me of an offence involving this woman! 9 May God deal with Abner, be it ever so severely, if I do not do for David what the LORD promised[n] him on oath 10 and transfer the kingdom from the house of Saul and establish David's throne over Israel and Judah from Dan to Beersheba."[o] 11 Ish-Bosheth did not dare to say another word to Abner, because he was afraid of him.

12 Then Abner sent messengers on his behalf to say to David, "Whose land is it? Make an agreement with me, and I will help you bring all Israel over to you."

13 "Good," said David. "I will make an agreement with you. But I demand one thing of you: Do not come into my presence unless you bring Michal daughter of Saul when you come to see me."[p] 14 Then David sent messengers to Ish-Bosheth son of Saul, demanding, "Give me my wife Michal,[q] whom I betrothed to myself for the price of a hundred Philistine foreskins."

15 So Ish-Bosheth gave orders and had her taken away from her husband[r] Paltiel[s] son of Laish. 16 Her husband, however, went with her, weeping behind her all the way to Bahurim.[t] Then Abner said to him, "Go back home!" So he went back.

17 Abner conferred with the elders[u] of Israel and said, "For some time you have wanted to make David your king. 18 Now do it! For the LORD promised David, 'By my servant David I will rescue my people Israel from the hand of the Philistines[v] and from the hand of all their enemies.[w]' "

19 Abner also spoke to the Benjamites in person. Then he went to Hebron to tell David everything that Israel and the whole house of Benjamin[x] wanted to do. 20 When Abner, who had twenty men with him, came to David at Hebron, David prepared a feast[y] for him and his men. 21 Then Abner said to David, "Let me go at once and assemble all

26 [g]**Dt 32:42**; Jer 46:10,14; Na 2:13; 3:15
28 [h]2Sa 18:16; 20:23; [i]**Jdg 3:27**
29 [j]**Dt 3:17**; [k]**Ge 32:2**
32 [l]**Ge 49:29**

Ch. 3

1 [a]1Ki 14:30; [b]2Sa 5:10; [c]2Sa 2:17; 22:44; Est 9:4
2 [d]2Sa 13:1; [e]**1Sa 25:43**
3 [f]**1Sa 25:42**; [g]2Sa 13:1,28; [h]2Sa 13:37; 14:32; 15:8
4 [i]1Ki 1:5,11; 2:13,22
6 [j]**1Sa 14:50**
7 [k]**Ge 22:24**; 2Sa 16:21–22; **1Ki 1:3**; [l]2Sa 21:8–11
8 [m]**1Sa 17:43**; 2Sa 9:8; 16:9; 2Ki 8:13
9 [n]**1Sa 15:28**
10 [o]**Jdg 20:1**; 1Sa 25:28–31; 2Sa 24:2
13 [p]**Ge 43:5**
14 [q]**1Sa 18:27**
15 [r]Dt 24:1–4; [s]1Sa 25:44
16 [t]2Sa 16:5; 17:18
17 [u]**Jdg 11:11**
18 [v]**1Sa 9:16**; [w]2Sa 8:6
19 [x]1Ch 12:2, 16,29
20 [y]1Ch 12:39

[c]27 Or *spoken this morning, the men would not have taken up the pursuit of their brothers;* or *spoken, the men would have given up the pursuit of their brothers by morning*

[d]29 Or *morning;* or *ravine;* the meaning of the Hebrew for this word is uncertain.

Israel for my lord the king, so that they may make a compact[z] with you, and that you may rule over all that your heart desires."[a] So David sent Abner away, and he went in peace.

Joab Murders Abner

22Just then David's men and Joab returned from a raid and brought with them a great deal of plunder. But Abner was no longer with David in Hebron, because David had sent him away, and he had gone in peace. 23When Joab and all the soldiers with him arrived, he was told that Abner son of Ner had come to the king and that the king had sent him away and that he had gone in peace.

24So Joab went to the king and said, "What have you done? Look, Abner came to you. Why did you let him go? Now he is gone! 25You know Abner son of Ner; he came to deceive you and observe your movements and find out everything you are doing."

26Joab then left David and sent messengers after Abner, and they brought him back from the well of Sirah. But David did not know it. 27Now when Abner[b] returned to Hebron, Joab took him aside into the gateway, as though to speak with him privately. And there, to avenge the blood of his brother Asahel, Joab stabbed him[c] in the stomach, and he died.[d]

28Later, when David heard about this, he said, "I and my kingdom are for ever innocent[e] before the LORD concerning the blood of Abner son of Ner. 29May his blood[f] fall upon the head of Joab and upon all his father's house![g] May Joab's house never be without someone who has a running sore[h] or leprosy[a] or who leans on a crutch or who falls by the sword or who lacks food."

30(Joab and his brother Abishai murdered Abner because he had killed their brother Asahel in the battle of Gibeon.)

31Then David said to Joab and all the people with him, "Tear your clothes and put on sackcloth[i] and walk in mourning[j] in front of Abner." King David himself walked behind the bier. 32They buried Abner in Hebron, and the king wept[k] aloud at Abner's tomb. All the people wept also.

33The king sang this lament[l] for Abner:

"Should Abner have died as the
lawless die?
34 Your hands were not bound,
your feet were not fettered.[m]
You fell as one falls before wicked
men."

And all the people wept over him again.

35Then they all came and urged David to eat something while it was still day; but David took an oath, saying, "May God deal with me, be it ever so severely,[n] if I taste bread[o] or anything else before the sun sets!"

36All the people took note and were pleased; indeed, everything the king did pleased them. 37So on that day all the people and all Israel knew that the king had no part[p] in the murder of Abner son of Ner.

38Then the king said to his men, "Do you not realise that a prince and a great man has fallen[q] in Israel this day? 39And today, though I am the anointed king, I am weak, and these sons of Zeruiah[r] are too strong[s] for me.[t] May the LORD repay[u] the evildoer according to his evil deeds!"

Ish-Bosheth Murdered

4 When Ish-Bosheth son of Saul heard that Abner[a] had died in Hebron, he lost courage, and all Israel became alarmed. 2Now Saul's son had two men who were leaders of raiding bands. One was named Baanah and the other Recab; they were sons of Rimmon the Beerothite from the tribe of Benjamin—Beeroth[b] is considered part of Benjamin, 3because the people of Beeroth fled to Gittaim[c] and have lived there as aliens to this day.

4(Jonathan[d] son of Saul had a son who was lame in both feet. He was five years old when the news[e] about Saul and Jonathan came from Jezreel. His nurse picked him up and fled, but as she hurried to leave, he fell and became crippled.[f] His name was Mephibosheth.)[g]

5Now Recab and Baanah, the sons of Rimmon the Beerothite, set out for the house of Ish-Bosheth,[h] and they arrived there in the heat of the day while he was taking his noonday rest.[i] 6They went into the inner part of the house as if to get some wheat, and they stabbed[j] him in the stomach. Then Recab and his brother Baanah slipped away.

7They had gone into the house while he was lying on the bed in his bedroom.

21 [z]2Sa 5:3; [a]1Ki 11:37
27 [b]2Sa 2:8; 4:1; 1Ki 2:5,32; [c]**Ex 21:14; Jdg 3:21; 2Sa 2:23;** [d]2Sa 2:22
28 [e]ver 37; Dt 21:9
29 [f]**Lev 20:9;** [g]1Ki 2:31–33; [h]**Lev 15:2**
31 [i]Ps 30:11; 35:13; 69:11; Isa 20:2; [j]**Ge 37:34**
32 [k]**Nu 14:1;** Pr 24:17
33 [l]**Ge 50:10**
34 [m]Job 36:8; Ps 2:3; 149:8; Isa 45:14; Na 3:10
35 [n]**Ru 1:17;** [o]**1Sa 31:13;** 2Sa 12:17; Jer 16:7
37 [p]**ver 28**
38 [q]2Sa 1:19
39 [r]**2Sa 2:18;** [s]2Sa 16:9; 18:11; [t]**Jdg 18:26;** [u]1Ki 2:32; Ps 41:10; 101:8

Ch. 4

1 [a]**2Sa 3:27**
2 [b]**Jos 9:17**
3 [c]Ne 11:33
4 [d]1Sa 18:1; [e]1Sa 31:9; [f]**Lev 21:18;** [g]2Sa 9:8,12; 16:1–4; 19:24; 21:7–8; 1Ch 8:34; 9:40
5 [h]**2Sa 2:8;** [i]Ru 2:7
6 [j]**2Sa 2:23**

[a]29 The Hebrew word was used for various diseases affecting the skin—not necessarily leprosy.

After they stabbed and killed him, they
cut off his head. Taking it with them,
they travelled all night by way of the
Arabah.[k] 8They brought the head[l] of
Ish-Bosheth to David at Hebron and
said to the king, "Here is the head of
Ish-Bosheth son of Saul,[m] your enemy,
who tried to take your life. This day the
LORD has avenged[n] my lord the king
against Saul and his offspring."
9David answered Recab and his
brother Baanah, the sons of Rimmon
the Beerothite, "As surely as the LORD
lives, who has delivered[o] me out of all
trouble, 10when a man told me, 'Saul is
dead,' and thought he was bringing
good news, I seized him and put him to
death in Ziklag.[p] That was the reward I
gave him for his news! 11How much
more—when wicked men have killed
an innocent man in his own house and
on his own bed—should I not now de-
mand his blood[q] from your hand and rid
the earth of you!"
12So David gave an order to his men,
and they killed them.[r] They cut off their
hands and feet and hung the bodies by
the pool in Hebron. But they took the
head of Ish-Bosheth and buried it in
Abner's tomb at Hebron.

David Becomes King Over Israel

5:1–3pp—1Ch 11:1–3

5 All the tribes of Israel[a] came to
David at Hebron and said, "We are
your own flesh and blood.[b] 2In the past,
while Saul was king over us, you were
the one who led Israel on their military
campaigns.[c] And the LORD said[d] to you,
'You shall shepherd[e] my people Israel,
and you shall become their ruler.[f]'"
3When all the elders of Israel had
come to King David at Hebron, the king
made a compact[g] with them at Hebron
before the LORD, and they anointed[h]
David king over Israel.
4David was thirty years old[i] when he
became king, and he reigned[j] for forty[k]
years. 5In Hebron he reigned over Judah
for seven years and six months,[l] and in
Jerusalem he reigned over all Israel and
Judah for thirty-three years.

David Conquers Jerusalem

5:6–10pp—1Ch 11:4–9
5:11–16pp—1Ch 3:5–9; 14:1–7

6The king and his men marched to
Jerusalem[m] to attack the Jebusites,[n] who
lived there. The Jebusites said to David,
"You will not get in here; even the blind
and the lame can ward you off." They
thought, "David cannot get in here."
7Nevertheless, David captured the
fortress of Zion,[o] the City of David.[p q]
8On that day, David said, "Anyone
who conquers the Jebusites will have to
use the water shaft[a r] to reach those
'lame and blind'[s] who are David's
enemies."[b] That is why they say, "The
'blind and lame' will not enter the
palace."
9David then took up residence in the
fortress and called it the City of David.
He built up the area around it, from the
supporting terraces[c t] inward. 10And he
became more and more powerful,[u]
because the LORD God Almighty[v] was
with him.[w]
11Now Hiram[x] king of Tyre sent mes-
sengers to David, along with cedar logs
and carpenters and stonemasons, and
they built a palace for David. 12And
David knew that the LORD had estab-
lished him as king over Israel and had
exalted his kingdom[y] for the sake of his
people Israel.
13After he left Hebron, David took
more concubines and wives[z] in Jeru-
salem, and more sons and daughters
were born to him. 14These are the names
of the children born to him there:[a]
Shammua, Shobab, Nathan,[b] Solomon,
15Ibhar, Elishua, Nepheg, Japhia,
16Elishama, Eliada and Eliphelet.

David Defeats the Philistines

5:17–25pp—1Ch 14:8–17

17When the Philistines heard that
David had been anointed king over
Israel, they went up in full force to
search for him, but David heard about it
and went down to the stronghold.[c]
18Now the Philistines had come and
spread out in the Valley of Rephaim;[d]
19so David enquired[e] of the LORD, "Shall
I go and attack the Philistines? Will you
hand them over to me?"
The LORD answered him, "Go, for I
will surely hand the Philistines over to
you."
20So David went to Baal Perazim, and
there he defeated them. He said, "As
waters break out, the LORD has broken
out against my enemies before me." So
that place was called Baal Perazim.[d f]
21The Philistines abandoned their idols
there, and David and his men carried
them off.[g]
22Once more the Philistines came up

---

[a]8 Or *use scaling hooks* [b]8 Or *are hated by David*
[c]9 Or *the Millo*
[d]20 *Baal Perazim* means *the lord who breaks out.*

---

7 [k]**Dt 3:17**
8 [l]2Sa 20:21; 2Ki 10:7; [m]1Sa 24:4; 25:29; [n]**Nu 31:3**
9 [o]**Ge 48:16**; 1Ki 1:29
10 [p]2Sa 1:2–16
11 [q]**Ge 4:10**; 9:5; Ps 9:12; 72:14
12 [r]2Sa 1:15

Ch. 5

1 [a]2Sa 19:43; [b]**Ge 29:14**; 35:26
2 [c]1Sa 18:5,13, 16; [d]**1Sa 11:6**; [e]**Ge 48:15**; **1Sa 16:1**; 2Sa 7:7; Mt 2:6; Jn 21:16; [f]**1Sa 12:12; 13:14; 2Sa 6:21**
3 [g]2Sa 3:21; [h]**Dt 17:15**; 2Sa 2:4
4 [i]**Ge 37:2**; Lk 3:23; [j]1Ki 2:11; 1Ch 3:4; [k]1Ch 26:31
5 [l]2Sa 2:11; 1Ki 2:11; 1Ch 3:4
6 [m]**Jdg 1:8**; [n]**Jos 15:8**
7 [o]Ps 76:2; [p]Jer 21:13; [q]2Sa 6:12,16; 1Ki 2:10; 8:1; Isa 29:1; Jer 25:29
8 [r]2Ki 20:20; 2Ch 32:30; [s]Mt 21:14
9 [t]1Ki 9:15,24
10 [u]2Sa 3:1; [v]Ps 24:10; [w]2Sa 7:9
11 [x]1Ki 5:1,18; 2Ch 2:3
12 [y]**Nu 24:7**
13 [z]**Dt 17:17**
14 [a]1Ch 3:5; [b]Lk 3:31
17 [c]2Sa 23:14; 1Ch 11:16
18 [d]**Jos 15:8; 17:15**
19 [e]**Jdg 18:5; 1Sa 23:2**
20 [f]**Ge 38:29**
21 [g]Dt 7:5; Isa 46:2

and spread out in the Valley of
Rephaim; 23so David enquired of the
LORD, and he answered, "Do not go
straight up, but circle round behind
them and attack them in front of the
balsam trees. 24As soon as you hear the
sound[h] of marching in the tops of the
balsam trees, move quickly, because
that will mean the LORD has gone out in
front[i] of you to strike the Philistine
army." 25So David did as the LORD com-
manded him, and he struck down the
Philistines[j] all the way from Gibeon[e][k] to
Gezer.[l]

The Ark Brought to Jerusalem

6:1–11pp—1Ch 13:1–14
6:12–19pp—1Ch 15:25–16:3

6 David again brought together out
of Israel chosen men, thirty
thousand in all. 2He and all his men set
out from Baalah[a] of Judah[a] to bring up
from there the ark[b] of God, which is
called by the Name,[b][c] the name of the
LORD Almighty, who is enthroned[d] be-
tween the cherubim[e] that are on the ark.
3They set the ark of God on a new cart[f]
and brought it from the house of Abina-
dab, which was on the hill.[g] Uzzah and
Ahio, sons of Abinadab, were guiding
the new cart 4with the ark of God on it,[c]
and Ahio was walking in front of it.
5David and the whole house of Israel
were celebrating[h] with all their might
before the LORD, with songs[d] and with
harps, lyres, tambourines, sistrums and
cymbals.[i]
6When they came to the threshing-
floor of Nacon, Uzzah reached out and
took hold of[j] the ark of God, because the
oxen stumbled. 7The LORD's anger
burned against Uzzah because of his
irreverent act;[k] therefore God struck
him down[l] and he died there beside the
ark of God.
8Then David was angry because the
LORD's wrath[m] had broken out against
Uzzah, and to this day that place is
called Perez Uzzah.[e][n]
9David was afraid of the LORD that day
and said, "How[o] can the ark of the LORD
ever come to me?" 10He was not willing
to take the ark of the LORD to be with
him in the City of David. Instead, he
took it aside to the house of Obed-
Edom[p] the Gittite. 11The ark of the LORD
remained in the house of Obed-Edom
the Gittite for three months, and the
LORD blessed him and his entire house-
hold.[q]
12Now King David[r] was told, "The
LORD has blessed the household of
Obed-Edom and everything he has, be-
cause of the ark of God." So David went
down and brought up the ark of God
from the house of Obed-Edom to the
City of David with rejoicing. 13When
those who were carrying the ark of the
LORD had taken six steps, he sacrificed[s] a
bull and a fattened calf. 14David, wear-
ing a linen ephod,[t] danced[u] before the
LORD with all his might, 15while he and
the entire house of Israel brought up the
ark of the LORD with shouts[v] and the
sound of trumpets.[w]
16As the ark of the LORD was entering
the City of David,[x] Michal[y] daughter of
Saul watched from a window. And
when she saw King David leaping and
dancing before the LORD, she despised
him in her heart.
17They brought the ark of the LORD
and set it in its place inside the tent that
David had pitched for it,[z] and David
sacrificed burnt offerings[a] and fel-
lowship offerings[f] before the LORD.
18After he had finished sacrificing[b] the
burnt offerings and fellowship offer-
ings, he blessed[c] the people in the name
of the LORD Almighty. 19Then he gave a
loaf of bread, a cake of dates and a cake
of raisins[d] to each person in the whole
crowd of Israelites, both men and
women.[e] And all the people went to
their homes.
20When David returned home to bless
his household, Michal daughter of Saul
came out to meet him and said, "How
the king of Israel has distinguished him-
self today, disrobing[f] in the sight of the
slave girls of his servants as any vulgar
fellow would."
21David said to Michal, "It was before
the LORD, who chose me rather than
your father or anyone from his house
when he appointed[g] me ruler[h] over the
LORD's people Israel—I will celebrate
before the LORD. 22I will become even
more undignified than this, and I will be
humiliated in my own eyes. But by

24 [h]**Ex 14:24;** [i]Jdg 4:14
25 [j]2Sa 8:12; 21:15; [k]Isa 28:21; [l]**Jos 10:33**

Ch. 6

2 [a]**Jos 15:9;** [b]1Sa 4:4; 7:1; [c]Lev 24:16; Dt 28:10; Isa 63:14; [d]Ps 99:1; 132:14; [e]**Ge 3:24; Ex 25:22**
3 [f]ver 7; Nu 7:4–9; **1Sa 6:7;** [g]2Sa 7:1
5 [h]**Ex 15:20;** [i]Ezr 3:10; Ne 12:27; Ps 150:5
6 [j]**Nu 4:15,** 19–20
7 [k]1Ch 15:13–15; [l]**Ex 19:22; 1Sa 5:6;** 6:19; **25:38**
8 [m]Ps 7:11; [n]**Ge 38:29**
9 [o]**1Sa 6:20**
10 [p]1Ch 15:18; 26:4–5
11 [q]**Ge 30:27;** 39:5
12 [r]1Ki 8:1
13 [s]1Ki 8:5,62; Ezr 6:17
14 [t]Ex 19:6; **1Sa 2:18;** [u]**Ex 15:20**
15 [v]**Jos 6:5;** [w]Ps 47:5; 98:6
16 [x]**2Sa 5:7;** [y]**1Sa 18:27**
17 [z]1Ki 8:6; 1Ch 15:1; 2Ch 1:4; [a]Lev 1:1–17; 1Ki 8:62–64
18 [b]1Ki 8:22; [c]**Ex 39:43**
19 [d]Hos 3:1; [e]Dt 26:13; Ne 8:10
20 [f]**1Sa 19:24**
21 [g]1Sa 13:14; **15:28;** [h]2Sa 5:2; 7:8; 1Ch 5:2; 17:7; Mic 5:2

[e]25 Septuagint (see also 1 Chron. 14:16); Hebrew *Geba*

[a]2 That is, Kiriath Jearim; Hebrew *Baale Judah*, a variant of *Baalah of Judah*

[b]2 Hebrew; Septuagint and Vulgate do not have *the Name*.

[c]3, 4 Dead Sea Scrolls and some Septuagint manuscripts; Masoretic Text *cart* [4]*and they brought it with the ark of God from the house of Abinadab, which was on the hill*

[d]5 See Dead Sea Scrolls, Septuagint and 1 Chron. 13:8; Masoretic Text *celebrating before the LORD with all kinds of instruments made of pine.*

[e]8 *Perez Uzzah* means *the outbreak against Uzzah.*

[f]17 Traditionally *peace offerings;* also in verse 18

these slave girls you spoke of, I will be
held in honour."
23 And Michal daughter of Saul had no
children to the day of her death.

God's Promise to David

7:1–17pp—1Ch 17:1–15

7 After the king was settled in his
palace[a] and the LORD had given
him rest from all his enemies[b] around
him,[c] 2 he said to Nathan[d] the prophet,
"Here I am, living in a palace[e] of cedar,
while the ark of God remains in a tent."[f]
3 Nathan replied to the king, "What-
ever you have in mind,[g] go ahead and
do it, for the LORD is with you."
4 That night the word of the LORD
came to Nathan, saying:

5 "Go and tell my servant David,
'This is what the LORD says: Are
you[h] the one to build me a house to
dwell in?[i] 6 I have not dwelt in a
house from the day I brought the
Israelites up out of Egypt to this
day.[j] I have been moving from
place to place with a tent[k] as my
dwelling.[l] 7 Wherever I have moved
with all the Israelites,[m] did I ever
say to any of their rulers whom I
commanded to shepherd[n] my
people Israel, "Why have you not
built me a house[o] of cedar?[p]" '
8 "Now then, tell my servant
David, 'This is what the LORD
Almighty says: I took you from the
pasture and from following the
flock[q] to be ruler[r] over my people
Israel.[s] 9 I have been with you
wherever you have gone,[t] and I
have cut off all your enemies from
before you.[u] Now I will make your
name great, like the names of the
greatest men of the earth.[v] 10 And I
will provide a place for my people
Israel and will plant[w] them so that
they can have a home of their
own and no longer be disturbed.[x]
Wicked[y] people shall not oppress
them any more,[z] as they did at the
beginning 11 and have done ever
since the time I appointed leaders[a][a]
over my people Israel. I will also
give you rest from all your enemies.[b]
" 'The LORD declares[c] to you that
the LORD himself will establish[d] a
house[e] for you: 12 When your days
are over and you rest[f] with your
fathers, I will raise up your off-
spring to succeed you, who will
come from your own body,[g] and I
will establish his kingdom.[h] 13 He is
the one who will build a house[i] for
my Name,[j] and I will establish the
throne of his kingdom for ever.[k] 14 I
will be his father, and he shall be
my son.[l] When he does wrong, I
will punish him[m] with the rod[n] of
men, with floggings inflicted by
men. 15 But my love will never be
taken away from him,[o] as I took it
away from Saul,[p] whom I removed
from before you. 16 Your house and
your kingdom shall endure for ever
before me;[b] your throne[q] shall be
established[r] for ever.[s]' "

17 Nathan reported to David all the
words of this entire revelation.

David's Prayer

7:18–29pp—1Ch 17:16–27

18 Then King David went in and sat
before the LORD, and he said:

"Who am I,[t] O Sovereign LORD,
and what is my family, that you
have brought me this far? 19 And as
if this were not enough in your
sight, O Sovereign LORD, you have
also spoken about the future of the
house of your servant. Is this your
usual way of dealing with man,[u] O
Sovereign LORD?
20 "What more can David say[v] to
you? For you know[w] your servant,[x]
O Sovereign LORD. 21 For the sake of
your word and according to your
will, you have done this great thing
and made it known to your servant.
22 "How great[y] you are,[z] O
Sovereign LORD! There is no-one
like[a] you, and there is no God[b] but
you, as we have heard with our
own ears.[c] 23 And who is like your
people Israel[d]—the one nation on
earth that God went out to redeem
as a people for himself, and to make
a name[e] for himself, and to perform
great and awesome wonders[f] by
driving out nations and their gods

Ch. 7

1 [a]2Sa 6:3; [b]ver 11; [c]1Ch 22:18
2 [d]2Sa 12:1; 1Ki 1:8,22; 1Ch 29:29; 2Ch 9:29; [e]2Sa 5:11; 1Ki 3:1; 7:1–2,7; 9:1; 2Ch 8:1; Jer 22:14; Hag 1:4; [f]**Ex 26:1**; Ps 132:3; Ac 7:45–46
3 [g]**1Sa 10:7**; Ps 132:1–5
5 [h]1Ki 8:19; 1Ch 22:8; [i]1Ki 5:3–5; 1Ch 28:3
6 [j]Ac 7:45; [k]Ex 40:18,34; Jos 18:1; [l]1Ki 8:16
7 [m]Dt 23:14; [n]**2Sa 5:2**; [o]1Ki 8:27; Isa 66:1; [p]Lev 26:11–12
8 [q]**1Sa 16:11**; 1Ch 21:17; Ps 74:1; Am 7:15; [r]**1Sa 2:7–8**; **9:16**; **16:1**; **2Sa 6:21**; [s]Ps 78:70–72; 2Co 6:18*
9 [t]**1Sa 18:14**; 2Sa 5:10; [u]Ps 18:37–42; [v]**Ex 11:3**
10 [w]**Ex 15:17**; Isa 5:1–7; [x]2Ki 21:8; 2Ch 33:8; [y]Ps 89:22–23; [z]Ps 147:14; Isa 54:14; 60:18
11 [a]**Jdg 2:16**; 1Sa 12:9–11; [b]ver 1; [c]1Ki 2:24; [d]1Sa 25:28; Ps 89:35–37; **Mt 1:1**; Lk 1:32–33; Ac 13:22–23; 2Ti 2:8; [e]**Ex 1:21**; Isa 7:2
12 [f]**Ge 15:15**; 1Ki 2:1; Ac 13:36; [g]1Ki 8:20; Ps 132:11–12; Jer 30:21; 33:15; [h]2Ch 23:3
13 [i]**Dt 12:5**; 1Ki 6:12; [j]Dt 16:11; 1Ki 5:5; 8:19,29; 2Ki 21:4,7; [k]ver 16; **Ge 9:16**; 2Sa 22:51; 1Ki 2:4,45; 1Ch 22:10; 28:6; 2Ch 6:16; 7:18; 13:5; 21:7; Ps 89:3–4,29, 35–37; Pr 25:5; Isa 9:7; 16:5; Jer 17:25; 33:17,21; Da 7:27
14 [l]Ps 2:7; 89:26; Jer 3:19; **Mt 3:17**; Jn 1:49; 2Co 6:18*; Heb 1:5*; Rev 21:7; [m]**Dt 8:5**; 1Ki 11:34; 1Ch 22:10; Heb 12:7; [n]Ps 89:30–33; Pr 13:24
15 [o]ver 25; 1Ki 2:4; 6:12; 8:25; 9:5; 11:13,32; 2Ki 19:34; 2Ch 6:16; 7:18; 21:7; Ps 89:24,33; Jer 33:17; [p]**1Sa 13:13**; **15:28**; 16:14
16 [q]Ps 89:36–37; **Lk 1:33**; [r]Ps 9:7; 93:2; 103:19; [s]**ver 13**
18 [t]**Ex 3:11** *19* [u]Isa 55:8–9
20 [v]Isa 38:15; [w]Jn 21:17; [x]**1Sa 16:7**
22 [y]Ps 48:1; 77:13; 86:10; Jer 10:6; [z]Dt 3:24; [a]**Ex 9:14**; [b]**Ex 8:10**; **20:4**; [c]Ex 10:2; **Jdg 6:13**; Ps 44:1
23 [d]Dt 4:32–38; **33:29**; **1Sa 12:22**; [e]**Nu 6:27**; [f]Dt 10:21

[a]*11* Traditionally *judges*
[b]*16* Some Hebrew manuscripts and Septuagint; most Hebrew manuscripts *you*

from before your people, whom
you redeemed[g] from Egypt?[c] 24You
have established your people Israel
as your very own[h] for ever, and
you, O LORD, have become their
God.[i]
25"And now, LORD God, keep for
ever the promise[j] you have made
concerning your servant and his
house. Do as you promised, 26so
that your name[k] will be great for
ever. Then men will say, 'The LORD
Almighty is God over Israel!' And
the house of your servant David
will be established[l] before you.
27"O LORD Almighty, God of
Israel, you have revealed this to
your servant, saying, 'I will build a
house for you.' So your servant has
found courage to offer you this
prayer. 28O Sovereign LORD, you
are God! Your words are trust-
worthy,[m] and you have promised
these good things to your servant.
29Now be pleased to bless the house
of your servant, that it may con-
tinue for ever in your sight; for you,
O Sovereign LORD, have spoken,
and with your blessing[n] the house
of your servant will be blessed for
ever."

David's Victories

8:1–14pp—1Ch 18:1–13

8 In the course of time, David
defeated the Philistines[a] and
subdued[b] them, and he took Metheg
Ammah from the control of the Philis-
tines.
2David also defeated the Moabites.[c]
He made them lie down on the ground
and measured them off with a length of
cord. Every two lengths of them were
put to death, and the third length was
allowed to live. So the Moabites became
subject to David and brought tribute.[d]
3Moreover, David fought Hadadezer[e]
son of Rehob, king of Zobah,[f] when
he went to restore his control along
the Euphrates[g] River. 4David captured
a thousand of his chariots, seven
thousand charioteers[a] and twenty
thousand foot soldiers. He hamstrung[h]
all but a hundred of the chariot horses.
5When the Arameans of Damascus[i]
came to help Hadadezer king of Zobah,
David struck down twenty-two
thousand of them. 6He put garrisons[j] in
the Aramean kingdom of Damascus,
and the Arameans became subject[k] to
him and brought tribute. The LORD gave
David victory wherever he went.[l]
7David took the gold shields[m] that
belonged to the officers of Hadadezer
and brought them to Jerusalem. 8From
Tebah[b] and Berothai,[n] towns that be-
longed to Hadadezer, King David took a
great quantity of bronze.
9When Tou[c] king of Hamath[o] heard
that David had defeated the entire army
of Hadadezer,[p] 10he sent his son Joram[d]
to King David to greet him and con-
gratulate him on his victory in battle
over Hadadezer, who had been at war
with Tou. Joram brought with him
articles of silver and gold and bronze.
11King David dedicated[q] these articles
to the LORD, as he had done with the
silver and gold from all the nations he
had subdued: 12Edom[e][r] and Moab,[s] the
Ammonites[t] and the Philistines,[u] and
Amalek.[v] He also dedicated the plunder
taken from Hadadezer son of Rehob,
king of Zobah.
13And David became famous[w] after he
returned from striking down eighteen
thousand Edomites[f] in the Valley of
Salt.[x]
14He put garrisons throughout Edom,
and all the Edomites[y] became subject to
David.[z] The LORD gave David victory[a]
wherever he went.[b]

David's Officials

8:15–18pp—1Ch 18:14–17

15David reigned over all Israel, doing
what was just and right[c] for all his
people. 16Joab[d] son of Zeruiah was over
the army; Jehoshaphat[e] son of Ahilud
was recorder;[f] 17Zadok[g] son of Ahitub
and Ahimelech son of Abiathar[h]
were priests; Seraiah was secretary;[i]
18Benaiah[j] son of Jehoiada was over the
Kerethites[k] and Pelethites; and David's
sons were royal advisers.[g]

23 [g]Dt 7:7–8; **9:26**
24 [h]Dt 26:18; [i]Ex 6:6–7; Ps 48:14
25 [j]**ver 15; Nu 23:19**; 2Ch 1:9
26 [k]**Ex 6:3**; Ne 9:5; Ps 72:19; 96:8; Mt 6:9; [l]**1Sa 25:28**
28 [m]Ex 34:6; Jn 17:17
29 [n]Nu 6:23–27

Ch. 8

1 [a]Ps 60:8; 87:4; 108:9; [b]Heb 11:32–33
2 [c]**Ge 19:37; Nu 21:29**; [d]**Jdg 3:15; Isa 45:14**
3 [e]2Sa 10:16,19; 1Ki 11:23; [f]**1Sa 14:47**; [g]**Ge 2:14**
4 [h]**Ge 49:6**; Jos 11:9
5 [i]**Ge 14:15**; 2Sa 10:6; 1Ki 11:24; 2Ki 8:7; 14:28
6 [j]1Ki 20:34; [k]2Sa 10:19; [l]2Sa 3:18
7 [m]1Ki 10:16; 14:26; 2Ki 11:10
8 [n]Eze 47:16
9 [o]1Ki 8:65; 2Ki 14:28; 2Ch 8:4; [p]Lk 14:31–32
11 [q]ver 12; 1Ki 7:51; 15:15; 1Ch 26:26; 2Ch 5:1
12 [r]**Nu 24:18**; [s]ver 2; [t]2Sa 10:14; [u]**2Sa 5:25**; [v]**Nu 24:20; 1Sa 27:8**
13 [w]2Sa 7:9; [x]2Ki 14:7; 1Ch 18:12; Ps 60 Title
14 [y]Nu 24:17–18; Ps 108:9; Isa 34:5; 63:1; Jer 49:7; Eze 25:12; [z]**Ge 27:29**,37–40; [a]Ps 144:10; [b]2Sa 22:44; Ps 18:43
15 [c]**Ge 18:19**; 1Ki 11:38; 14:8; 15:11; 22:43; 2Ki 12:2; Job 29:14; Ps 5:12; 119:121; Heb 11:33
16 [d]**2Sa 2:13**; [e]2Sa 20:24; 1Ki 4:3; [f]Isa 36:3,22
17 [g]**1Sa 2:35**; 2Sa 15:24,29; 20:25; 1Ki 1:8; 4:4; 1Ch 6:8, 53; 16:39; 24:3; 27:17; 2Ch 31:10; Eze 40:46; 43:19; 44:15; 48:11; [h]Mk 2:26; [i]1Ki 4:3; 2Ki 12:10; 19:2; 22:3; Isa 36:3; Jer 36:12
18 [j]2Sa 20:23; 23:20; 1Ki 1:8,38; 2:25,35,46; 4:4; [k]**1Sa 30:14**

[c]23 See Septuagint and 1 Chron. 17:21; Hebrew *wonders for your land and before your people, whom you redeemed from Egypt, from the nations and their gods.*
[a]4 Septuagint (see also Dead Sea Scrolls and 1 Chron. 18:4); Masoretic Text *captured seventeen hundred of his charioteers*
[b]8 See some Septuagint manuscripts (see also 1 Chron. 18:8); Hebrew *Betah.*
[c]9 Hebrew *Toi*, a variant of *Tou*; also in verse 10
[d]10 A variant of *Hadoram*
[e]12 Some Hebrew manuscripts, Septuagint and Syriac (see also 1 Chron. 18:11); most Hebrew manuscripts *Aram*
[f]13 A few Hebrew manuscripts, Septuagint and Syriac (see also 1 Chron. 18:12); most Hebrew manuscripts *Aram* (that is, Arameans)
[g]18 Or *were priests*

David and Mephibosheth

9 David asked, "Is there anyone still left of the house of Saul to whom I can show kindness for Jonathan's sake?"[a]

2Now there was a servant of Saul's household named Ziba.[b] They called him to appear before David, and the king said to him, "Are you Ziba?"

"Your servant," he replied.

3The king asked, "Is there no-one still left of the house of Saul to whom I can show God's kindness?"

Ziba answered the king, "There is still a son of Jonathan;[c] he is crippled[d] in both feet."

4"Where is he?" the king asked.

Ziba answered, "He is at the house of Makir[e] son of Ammiel in Lo Debar."

5So King David had him brought from Lo Debar, from the house of Makir son of Ammiel.

6When Mephibosheth son of Jonathan, the son of Saul, came to David, he bowed down to pay him honour.[f]

David said, "Mephibosheth!"

"Your servant," he replied.

7"Don't be afraid," David said to him, "for I will surely show you kindness for the sake of your father Jonathan.[g] I will restore to you all the land that belonged to your grandfather Saul, and you will always eat at my table.[h]"

8Mephibosheth[i] bowed down and said, "What is your servant, that you should notice a dead dog[j] like me?"

9Then the king summoned Ziba, Saul's servant, and said to him, "I have given your master's grandson everything that belonged to Saul and his family. 10You and your sons and your servants are to farm the land for him and bring in the crops, so that your master's grandson[k] may be provided for. And Mephibosheth, grandson of your master, will always eat at my table." (Now Ziba had fifteen sons and twenty servants.)

11Then Ziba said to the king, "Your servant will do whatever my lord the king commands his servant to do." So Mephibosheth ate at David's[a] table like one of the king's sons.[l]

12Mephibosheth had a young son named Mica, and all the members of Ziba's household were servants of Mephibosheth.[m] 13And Mephibosheth lived in Jerusalem, because he always ate at the king's table, and he was crippled in both feet.

Ch. 9

1 [a]**1Sa 20:14–17,42; 23:18**
2 [b]2Sa 16:1–4; 19:17,26,29
3 [c]1Ch 8:34; [d]**Lev 21:18**
4 [e]2Sa 17:27–29
6 [f]**Ge 37:7**
7 [g]**1Sa 20:14–15;** [h]ver 13; 2Sa 19:28; 21:7; 1Ki 2:7; 2Ki 25:29; Jer 52:33
8 [i]**2Sa 4:4;** [j]**2Sa 3:8**
10 [k]2Sa 16:3
11 [l]Job 36:7; Ps 113:8
12 [m]**2Sa 4:4**

Ch. 10

2 [a]**1Sa 11:1**
3 [b]**Nu 21:32**
4 [c]**Lev 19:27;** Isa 7:20; 15:2; 50:6; 52:14; Jer 48:37; Eze 5:1; [d]Isa 20:4
6 [e]**Ge 34:30;** [f]**2Sa 8:5;** [g]**Nu 13:21;** [h]**1Sa 14:47;** [i]**Dt 3:14;** [j]Jdg 11:3–5
7 [k]**2Sa 2:18**
10 [l]**1Sa 26:6**
12 [m]**Dt 1:21;** 31:6; **Eph 6:10;** [n]**Jdg 10:15;** Ne 4:14

David Defeats the Ammonites

10:1–19pp—1Ch 19:1–19

10 In the course of time, the king of the Ammonites died, and his son Hanun succeeded him as king. 2David thought, "I will show kindness to Hanun son of Nahash,[a] just as his father showed kindness to me." So David sent a delegation to express his sympathy to Hanun concerning his father.

When David's men came to the land of the Ammonites, 3the Ammonite nobles said to Hanun their lord, "Do you think David is honouring your father by sending men to you to express sympathy? Hasn't David sent them to you to explore the city and spy it out[b] and overthrow it?" 4So Hanun seized David's men, shaved off half of each man's beard,[c] cut off their garments in the middle at the buttocks,[d] and sent them away.

5When David was told about this, he sent messengers to meet the men, for they were greatly humiliated. The king said, "Stay at Jericho till your beards have grown, and then come back."

6When the Ammonites realised that they had become an offence[e] to David's nostrils, they hired twenty thousand Aramean[f] foot soldiers from Beth Rehob[g] and Zobah,[h] as well as the king of Maacah[i] with a thousand men, and also twelve thousand men from Tob.[j]

7On hearing this, David sent Joab[k] out with the entire army of fighting men. 8The Ammonites came out and drew up in battle formation at the entrance to their city gate, while the Arameans of Zobah and Rehob and the men of Tob and Maacah were by themselves in the open country.

9Joab saw that there were battle lines in front of him and behind him; so he selected some of the best troops in Israel and deployed them against the Arameans. 10He put the rest of the men under the command of Abishai[l] his brother and deployed them against the Ammonites. 11Joab said, "If the Arameans are too strong for me, then you are to come to my rescue; but if the Ammonites are too strong for you, then I will come to rescue you. 12Be strong[m] and let us fight bravely for our people and the cities of our God. The LORD will do what is good in his sight."[n]

13Then Joab and the troops with him advanced to fight the Arameans, and

[a] *11* Septuagint; Hebrew *my*

they fled before him. 14When the
Ammonites[o] saw that the Arameans
were fleeing, they fled before Abishai
and went inside the city. So Joab re-
turned from fighting the Ammonites
and came to Jerusalem.
15After the Arameans saw that they
had been routed by Israel, they re-
grouped. 16Hadadezer had Arameans
brought from beyond the River;[a] they
went to Helam, with Shobach the com-
mander of Hadadezer's army leading
them.
17When David was told of this, he
gathered all Israel, crossed the Jordan
and went to Helam. The Arameans
formed their battle lines to meet David
and fought against him. 18But they fled
before Israel, and David killed seven
hundred of their charioteers and forty
thousand of their foot soldiers.[b] He also
struck down Shobach the commander
of their army, and he died there.
19When all the kings who were vassals
of Hadadezer saw that they had been
defeated by Israel, they made peace
with the Israelites and became subject[p]
to them.
So the Arameans[q] were afraid to help
the Ammonites any more.

David and Bathsheba

11 In the spring,[a] at the time when
kings go off to war, David sent
Joab[b] out with the king's men and the
whole Israelite army.[c] They destroyed
the Ammonites and besieged Rabbah.[d]
But David remained in Jerusalem.
2One evening David got up from his
bed and walked around on the roof[e] of
the palace. From the roof he saw[f] a
woman bathing. The woman was very
beautiful, 3and David sent someone to
find out about her. The man said, "Isn't
this Bathsheba,[g] the daughter of Eliam[h]
and the wife of Uriah[i] the Hittite?"
4Then David sent messengers to get
her.[j] She came to him, and he slept[k]
with her. (She had purified herself from
her uncleanness.)[l] Then[a] she went back
home. 5The woman conceived and
sent word to David, saying, "I am
pregnant."
6So David sent this word to Joab:
"Send me Uriah[m] the Hittite." And Joab
sent him to David. 7When Uriah came to
him, David asked him how Joab was,
how the soldiers were and how the war
was going. 8Then David said to Uriah,
"Go down to your house and wash your
feet."[n] So Uriah left the palace, and a
gift from the king was sent after him.
9But Uriah slept at the entrance to the
palace with all his master's servants and
did not go down to his house.
10When David was told, "Uriah did
not go home," he asked him, "Haven't
you just come from a distance? Why
didn't you go home?"
11Uriah said to David, "The ark[o] and
Israel and Judah are staying in tents,
and my master Joab and my lord's men
are camped in the open fields. How
could I go to my house to eat and drink
and lie[p] with my wife? As surely as you
live, I will not do such a thing!"
12Then David said to him, "Stay here
one more day, and tomorrow I will send
you back." So Uriah remained in Jeru-
salem that day and the next. 13At
David's invitation, he ate and drank
with him, and David made him drunk.
But in the evening Uriah went out to
sleep on his mat among his master's
servants; he did not go home.
14In the morning David wrote a letter[q]
to Joab and sent it with Uriah. 15In it he
wrote, "Put Uriah in the front line
where the fighting is fiercest. Then
withdraw from him so that he will be
struck down[r] and die.[s]"
16So while Joab had the city under
siege, he put Uriah at a place where he
knew the strongest defenders were.
17When the men of the city came out
and fought against Joab, some of the
men in David's army fell; moreover,
Uriah the Hittite was dead.
18Joab sent David a full account of the
battle. 19He instructed the messenger:
"When you have finished giving the
king this account of the battle, 20the
king's anger may flare up, and he may
ask you, 'Why did you get so close to the
city to fight? Didn't you know they
would shoot arrows from the wall?
21Who killed Abimelech[t] son of Jerub-
Besheth?[b] Didn't a woman throw an
upper millstone on him from the wall,[u]
so that he died in Thebez? Why did you
get so close to the wall?' If he asks you
this, then say to him, 'Also, your ser-
vant Uriah the Hittite is dead.'"
22The messenger set out, and when
he arrived he told David everything
Joab had sent him to say. 23The messen-
ger said to David, "The men over-
powered us and came out against us in

14 o2Sa 8:12
19 p2Sa 8:6; q1Ki 11:25; 22:31; 2Ki 5:1

Ch. 11

1 a1Ki 20:22,26; b**2Sa 2:18;** c1Ch 20:1; d**Dt 3:11**
2 e**Dt 22:8; Jos 2:8;** fMt 5:28
3 g1Ch 3:5; h2Sa 23:34; i2Sa 23:39
4 j**Lev 20:10;** Ps 51 Title; Jas 1:14–15; kDt 22:22; l**Lev 15:25–30**
6 m1Ch 11:41
8 n**Ge 18:4**
11 o2Sa 7:2; p**1Sa 21:5**
14 q1Ki 21:8
15 rver 14–17; 2Sa 12:9; s2Sa 12:12
21 t**Jdg 8:31;** uJdg 9:50–54

a*16* That is, the Euphrates
b*18* Some Septuagint manuscripts (see also 1 Chron. 19:18); Hebrew, *horsemen*
a*4* Or *with her. When she purified herself from her uncleanness,*
b*21* Also known as *Jerub-Baal* (that is, Gideon)

the open, but we drove them back to the entrance to the city gate. 24 Then the archers shot arrows at your servants from the wall, and some of the king's men died. Moreover, your servant Uriah the Hittite is dead."

25 David told the messenger, "Say this to Joab: 'Don't let this upset you; the sword devours one as well as another. Press the attack against the city and destroy it.' Say this to encourage Joab."

26 When Uriah's wife heard that her husband was dead, she mourned for him. 27 After the time of mourning[v] was over, David had her brought to his house, and she became his wife and bore him a son. But the thing David had done displeased[w] the LORD.

Nathan Rebukes David

11:1; 12:29–31pp—1Ch 20:1–3

12 The LORD sent Nathan[a] to David.[b] When he came to him,[c] he said, "There were two men in a certain town, one rich and the other poor. 2 The rich man had a very large number of sheep and cattle, 3 but the poor man had nothing except one little ewe lamb that he had bought. He raised it, and it grew up with him and his children. It shared his food, drank from his cup and even slept in his arms. It was like a daughter to him.

4 "Now a traveller came to the rich man, but the rich man refrained from taking one of his own sheep or cattle to prepare a meal for the traveller who had come to him. Instead, he took the ewe lamb that belonged to the poor man and prepared it for the one who had come to him."

5 David[d] burned with anger[e] against the man[f] and said to Nathan, "As surely as the LORD lives,[g] the man who did this deserves to die! 6 He must pay for that lamb four times over,[h] because he did such a thing and had no pity."

7 Then Nathan said to David, "You are the man![i] This is what the LORD, the God of Israel, says: 'I anointed[j] you[k] king over Israel, and I delivered you from the hand of Saul. 8 I gave your master's house to you,[l] and your master's wives into your arms. I gave you the house of Israel and Judah. And if all this had been too little, I would have given you even more. 9 Why did you despise[m] the word of the LORD by doing what is evil in his eyes? You struck down[n] Uriah[o] the Hittite with the sword and took his wife to be your own. You killed[p] him with the sword of the Ammonites. 10 Now, therefore, the sword[q] shall never depart from your house, because you despised me and took the wife of Uriah the Hittite to be your own.'

11 "This is what the LORD says: 'Out of your own household[r] I am going to bring calamity upon you.[s] Before your very eyes I will take your wives and give them to one who is close to you, and he will lie with your wives in broad daylight.[t] 12 You did it in secret,[u] but I will do this thing in broad daylight[v] before all Israel.' "

13 Then David said to Nathan, "I have sinned[w] against the LORD."

Nathan replied, "The LORD has taken away[x] your sin.[y] You are not going to die.[z] 14 But because by doing this you have made the enemies of the LORD show utter contempt,[a][a] the son born to you will die."

15 After Nathan had gone home, the LORD struck[b] the child that Uriah's wife had borne to David, and he became ill. 16 David pleaded with God for the child. He fasted and went into his house and spent the nights lying[c] on the ground. 17 The elders of his household stood beside him to get him up from the ground, but he refused,[d] and he would not eat any food with them.[e]

18 On the seventh day the child died. David's servants were afraid to tell him that the child was dead, for they thought, "While the child was still living, we spoke to David but he would not listen to us. How can we tell him the child is dead? He may do something desperate."

19 David noticed that his servants were whispering among themselves and he realised that the child was dead. "Is the child dead?" he asked.

"Yes," they replied, "he is dead."

20 Then David got up from the ground. After he had washed,[f] put on lotions and changed his clothes,[g] he went into the house of the LORD and worshipped. Then he went to his own house, and at his request they served him food, and he ate.

21 His servants asked him, "Why are you acting in this way? While the child was alive, you fasted and wept,[h] but now that the child is dead, you get up and eat!"

22 He answered, "While the child was still alive, I fasted and wept. I thought, 'Who knows?[i] The LORD may be

27 [v]Dt 34:8; [w]2Sa 12:9; Ps 51:4–5

Ch. 12

1 [a]**2Sa 7:2;** [b]Ps 51 Title; [c]2Sa 14:4
5 [d]1Ki 20:40; [e]**Ge 34:7;** [f]Ro 2:1; [g]**1Sa 14:39**
6 [h]Ex 22:1
7 [i]2Sa 14:13; Da 4:22; [j]**1Sa 2:35;** [k]1Ki 20:42
8 [l]**2Sa 9:7**
9 [m]**Nu 15:31; 1Sa 13:14;** [n]**2Sa 11:15;** [o]1Ki 15:5; [p]Ps 26:9; 51:14
10 [q]2Sa 13:28; 18:14–15; 1Ki 2:25
11 [r]2Sa 16:11; [s]Dt 28:30; 2Sa 16:21–22; [t]**Dt 17:17**
12 [u]2Sa 11:4–15; [v]2Sa 16:22
13 [w]**Ge 13:13; 20:6; Nu 22:34;** [x]Ps 32:1–5; 51:1,9; 103:12; Isa 43:25; 44:22; Zec 3:4,9; [y]Pr 28:13; Jer 2:35; Mic 7:18–19; [z]Lev 20:10; 24:17
14 [a]Isa 52:5; Ro 2:24
15 [b]**1Sa 25:38**
16 [c]Ps 5:7; 95:6
17 [d]**Ge 37:35; 1Sa 1:7;** [e]**2Sa 3:35;** Da 6:18
20 [f]Mt 6:17; [g]**Ge 41:14**
21 [h]Jdg 20:26
22 [i]Jnh 3:9

[a]*14* Masoretic Text; an ancient Hebrew scribal tradition *this you have shown utter contempt for the LORD*

gracious to me and let the child live.'[j]
23But now that he is dead, why should I
fast? Can I bring him back again? I will
go to him,[k] but he will not return to
me."[l]
24Then David comforted his wife
Bathsheba,[m] and he went to her and lay
with her. She gave birth to a son, and
they named him Solomon.[n] The LORD
loved him; 25and because the LORD
loved him, he sent word through
Nathan the prophet to name him
Jedidiah.[b][o]
26Meanwhile Joab fought against Rab-
bah[p] of the Ammonites and captured
the royal citadel. 27Joab then sent mes-
sengers to David, saying, "I have
fought against Rabbah and taken its
water supply. 28Now muster the rest of
the troops and besiege the city and cap-
ture it. Otherwise I shall take the city,
and it will be named after me."
29So David mustered the entire army
and went to Rabbah, and attacked and
captured it. 30He took the crown[q] from
the head of their king[c]—its weight was
a talent[d] of gold, and it was set with
precious stones—and it was placed on
David's head. He took a great quantity
of plunder from the city 31and brought
out the people who were there, con-
signing them to labour with saws and
with iron picks and axes, and he made
them work at brickmaking.[e] He did
this to all the Ammonite[r] towns. Then
David and his entire army returned to
Jerusalem.

Amnon and Tamar

13 In the course of time, Amnon[a]
son of David fell in love with
Tamar,[b] the beautiful sister of Absalom[c]
son of David.
2Amnon became frustrated to the
point of illness on account of his sister
Tamar, for she was a virgin, and it
seemed impossible for him to do any-
thing to her.
3Now Amnon had a friend named
Jonadab son of Shimeah,[d] David's
brother. Jonadab was a very shrewd
man. 4He asked Amnon, "Why do you,
the king's son, look so haggard morning
after morning? Won't you tell me?"
Amnon said to him, "I'm in love with
Tamar, my brother Absalom's sister."
5"Go to bed and pretend to be ill,"
Jonadab said. "When your father comes
to see you, say to him, 'I would like my
sister Tamar to come and give me some-
thing to eat. Let her prepare the food in
my sight so that I may watch her and
then eat it from her hand.'"
6So Amnon lay down and pretended
to be ill. When the king came to see him,
Amnon said to him, "I would like my
sister Tamar to come and make some
special bread in my sight, so that I may
eat from her hand."
7David sent word to Tamar at the
palace: "Go to the house of your brother
Amnon and prepare some food for
him." 8So Tamar went to the house of
her brother Amnon, who was lying
down. She took some dough, kneaded
it, made the bread in his sight and baked
it. 9Then she took the pan and served
him the bread, but he refused to eat.
"Send everyone out of here,"[e]
Amnon said. So everyone left him.
10Then Amnon said to Tamar, "Bring
the food here into my bedroom so that I
may eat from your hand." And Tamar
took the bread she had prepared and
brought it to her brother Amnon in his
bedroom. 11But when she took it to him
to eat, he grabbed[f] her and said, "Come
to bed with me, my sister."[g]
12"Don't, my brother!" she said to
him. "Don't force me. Such a thing
should not be done in Israel![h] Don't do
this wicked thing.[i] 13What about me?[j]
Where could I get rid of my disgrace?
And what about you? You would be like
one of the wicked fools in Israel. Please
speak to the king; he will not keep me
from being married to you." 14But he
refused to listen to her, and since he was
stronger than she, he raped her.[k]
15Then Amnon hated her with intense
hatred. In fact, he hated her more than
he had loved her. Amnon said to her,
"Get up and get out!"
16"No!" she said to him. "Sending me
away would be a greater wrong than
what you have already done to me."
But he refused to listen to her. 17He
called his personal servant and said,
"Get this woman out of here and bolt
the door after her." 18So his servant put
her out and bolted the door after her.
She was wearing a richly ornamented[a]
robe,[l] for this was the kind of garment
the virgin daughters of the king wore.
19Tamar put ashes[m] on her head and
tore the ornamented robe she was wear-
ing. She put her hand on her head and
went away, weeping aloud as she went.

22 [j]Isa 38:1–5
23 [k]Ge 37:35; [l]**1Sa 31:13;** 2Sa 13:39; Job 7:10; 10:21
24 [m]1Ki 1:11; [n]1Ki 1:10; 1Ch 22:9; 28:5; Mt 1:6
25 [o]Ne 13:26
26 [p]**Dt 3:11**
30 [q]Est 8:15; Ps 21:3; 132:18
31 [r]**1Sa 14:47**

Ch. 13

1 [a]2Sa 3:2; [b]2Sa 14:27; 1Ch 3:9; [c]**2Sa 3:3**
3 [d]**1Sa 16:9**
9 [e]Ge 45:1
11 [f]**Ge 39:12;** [g]**Ge 38:16**
12 [h]Lev 20:17; [i]**Ge 34:7**
13 [j]**Lev 18:9; Dt 22:21,**23–24
14 [k]**Ge 34:2;** Eze 22:11
18 [l]**Ge 37:23**
19 [m]**Jos 7:6;** Est 4:1; Da 9:3

[b]25 *Jedidiah* means *loved by the* LORD.
[c]30 Or *of Milcom* (that is, Molech)
[d]30 That is, about 75 pounds (about 34 kilograms)
[e]31 The meaning of the Hebrew for this clause is uncertain.
[a]18 The meaning of the Hebrew for this phrase is uncertain; also in verse 19.

20Her brother Absalom said to her, "Has that Amnon, your brother, been with you? Be quiet now, my sister; he is your brother. Don't take this thing to heart." And Tamar lived in her brother Absalom's house, a desolate woman.

21When King David heard all this, he was furious.[n] 22Absalom never said a word to Amnon, either good or bad;[o] he hated[p] Amnon because he had disgraced his sister Tamar.

Absalom Kills Amnon

23Two years later, when Absalom's sheep-shearers[q] were at Baal Hazor near the border of Ephraim, he invited all the king's sons to come there. 24Absalom went to the king and said, "Your servant has had shearers come. Will the king and his officials please join me?"

25"No, my son," the king replied. "All of us should not go; we would only be a burden to you." Although Absalom urged him, he still refused to go, but gave him his blessing.

26Then Absalom said, "If not, please let my brother Amnon come with us."

The king asked him, "Why should he go with you?" 27But Absalom urged him, so he sent with him Amnon and the rest of the king's sons.

28Absalom[r] ordered his men, "Listen! When Amnon is in high[s] spirits from drinking wine and I say to you, 'Strike Amnon down,' then kill him. Don't be afraid. Have not I given you this order? Be strong and brave.[t]" 29So Absalom's men did to Amnon what Absalom had ordered. Then all the king's sons got up, mounted their mules and fled.

30While they were on their way, the report came to David: "Absalom has struck down all the king's sons; not one of them is left." 31The king stood up, tore[u] his clothes and lay down on the ground; and all his servants stood by with their clothes torn.

32But Jonadab son of Shimeah, David's brother, said, "My lord should not think that they killed all the princes; only Amnon is dead. This has been Absalom's expressed intention ever since the day that Amnon raped his sister Tamar. 33My lord the king should not be concerned about the report that all the king's sons are dead. Only Amnon is dead."

34Meanwhile, Absalom had fled.

Now the man standing watch looked up and saw many people on the road west of him, coming down the side of the hill. The watchman went and told the king, "I see men in the direction of Horonaim, on the side of the hill."[b]

35Jonadab said to the king, "See, the king's sons are here; it has happened just as your servant said."

36As he finished speaking, the king's sons came in, wailing loudly. The king, too, and all his servants wept very bitterly.

37Absalom fled and went to Talmai[v] son of Ammihud, the king of Geshur. But King David mourned for his son every day.

38After Absalom fled and went to Geshur, he stayed there for three years. 39And the spirit of the king[c] longed to go to Absalom,[w] for he was consoled[x] concerning Amnon's death.

Absalom Returns to Jerusalem

14 Joab[a] son of Zeruiah knew that the king's heart longed for Absalom. 2So Joab sent someone to Tekoa[b] and had a wise woman[c] brought from there. He said to her, "Pretend you are in mourning. Dress in mourning clothes, and don't use any cosmetic lotions.[d] Act like a woman who has spent many days grieving for the dead. 3Then go to the king and speak these words to him." And Joab[e] put the words in her mouth.

4When the woman from Tekoa went[a] to the king, she fell with her face to the ground to pay him honour, and she said, "Help me, O king!"

5The king asked her, "What is troubling you?"

She said, "I am indeed a widow; my husband is dead. 6I your servant had two sons. They got into a fight with each other in the field, and no-one was there to separate them. One struck the other and killed him. 7Now the whole clan has risen up against your servant; they say, 'Hand over the one who struck his brother down, so that we may put him to death[f] for the life of his brother whom he killed; then we will get rid of the heir[g] as well.' They would put out the only burning coal I have left,[h] leaving my husband neither name nor descendant on the face of the earth."

8The king said to the woman, "Go

21 [n]**Ge 34:7**
22 [o]Ge 31:24; [p]Lev 19:17–18; 1Jn 2:9–11
23 [q]1Sa 25:7
28 [r]**2Sa 3:3**; [s]**Ru 3:7**; [t]**2Sa 12:10**
31 [u]**Nu 14:6**
37 [v]**2Sa 3:3**
39 [w]2Sa 14:13; [x]**2Sa 12:19–23**

Ch. 14

1 [a]**2Sa 2:18**
2 [b]Ne 3:5; Jer 6:1; Am 1:1; [c]2Sa 20:16; [d]**Ru 3:3; Isa 1:6**
3 [e]ver 19
7 [f]Nu 35:19; [g]Mt 21:38; [h]Dt 19:10–13

[b]34 Septuagint; Hebrew does not have this sentence.
[c]39 Dead Sea Scrolls and some Septuagint manuscripts; Masoretic Text *But* ⌊*the spirit of*⌋ *David the king*
[a]4 Many Hebrew manuscripts, Septuagint, Vulgate and Syriac; most Hebrew manuscripts *spoke*

home,[i] and I will issue an order on your
behalf."
9But the woman from Tekoa said to
him, "My lord the king, let the blame[j]
rest on me and on my father's family,[k]
and let the king and his throne be with-
out guilt.[l]"
10The king replied, "If anyone says
anything to you, bring him to me, and
he will not bother you again."
11She said, "Then let the king invoke
the LORD his God to prevent the
avenger[m] of blood from adding to the
destruction, so that my son shall not be
destroyed."
"As surely as the LORD lives," he said,
"not one hair[n] of your son's head will
fall to the ground.[o]"
12Then the woman said, "Let your
servant speak a word to my lord the
king."
"Speak," he replied.
13The woman said, "Why then have
you devised a thing like this against the
people of God? When the king says this,
does he not convict himself,[p] for the
king has not brought back his banished
son?[q] 14Like water[r] spilled on the
ground, which cannot be recovered, so
we must die.[s] But God does not take
away life; instead, he devises ways so
that a banished person[t] may not remain
estranged from him.
15"And now I have come to say this to
my lord the king because the people
have made me afraid. Your servant
thought, 'I will speak to the king;
perhaps he will do what his servant
asks. 16Perhaps the king will agree to
deliver his servant from the hand of the
man who is trying to cut off both me and
my son from the inheritance[u] God gave
us.'
17"And now your servant says, 'May
the word of my lord the king bring me
rest, for my lord the king is like an
angel[v] of God in discerning[w] good and
evil. May the LORD your God be with
you.'"
18Then the king said to the woman,
"Do not keep from me the answer to
what I am going to ask you."
"Let my lord the king speak," the
woman said.
19The king asked, "Isn't the hand of
Joab[x] with you in all this?"
The woman answered, "As surely as
you live, my lord the king, no-one can
turn to the right or to the left from
anything my lord the king says. Yes, it
was your servant Joab who instructed
me to do this and who put all these
words into the mouth of your servant.
20Your servant Joab did this to change
the present situation. My lord has wis-
dom[y] like that of an angel of God—he
knows everything that happens in the
land.[z]"
21The king said to Joab, "Very well, I
will do it. Go, bring back the young man
Absalom."
22Joab fell with his face to the ground
to pay him honour, and he blessed the
king.[a] Joab said, "Today your servant
knows that he has found favour in your
eyes, my lord the king, because the king
has granted his servant's request."
23Then Joab went to Geshur and
brought Absalom back to Jerusalem.
24But the king said, "He must go to his
own house; he must not see my face."
So Absalom went to his own house and
did not see the face of the king.
25In all Israel there was not a man so
highly praised for his handsome
appearance as Absalom. From the top of
his head to the sole of his foot there was
no blemish in him. 26Whenever he cut
the hair of his head[b]—he used to cut his
hair from time to time when it became
too heavy for him—he would weigh it,
and its weight was two hundred
shekels[b] by the royal standard.
27Three sons[c] and a daughter were
born to Absalom. The daughter's name
was Tamar,[d] and she became a beautiful
woman.
28Absalom lived for two years in Jeru-
salem without seeing the king's face.
29Then Absalom sent for Joab in order to
send him to the king, but Joab refused to
come to him. So he sent a second time,
but he refused to come. 30Then he said
to his servants, "Look, Joab's field is
next to mine, and he has barley[e] there.
Go and set it on fire." So Absalom's
servants set the field on fire.
31Then Joab did go to Absalom's
house and he said to him, "Why have
your servants set my field on fire?[f]"
32Absalom said to Joab, "Look, I sent
word to you and said, 'Come here so
that I can send you to the king to ask,
"Why have I come from Geshur?[g] It
would be better for me if I were still
there!"' Now then, I want to see the
king's face, and if I am guilty of any-
thing, let him put me to death."[h]
33So Joab went to the king and told
him this. Then the king summoned
Absalom, and he came in and bowed
down with his face to the ground before
the king. And the king kissed[i] Absalom.

8 [i]1Sa 25:35
9 [j]1Sa 25:24; [k]Mt 27:25; [l]1Sa 25:28
11 [m]**Nu 35:12,** 21; [n]**Mt 10:30;** [o]**1Sa 14:45**
13 [p]**2Sa 12:7;** 1Ki 20:40; [q]2Sa 13:38–39
14 [r]Job 14:11; Ps 58:7; Isa 19:5; [s]Job 10:8, 17:13; 30:23; Ps 22:15; Heb 9:27; [t]Nu 35:15,25–28
16 [u]**Ex 34:9; 1Sa 26:19**
17 [v]1Sa 29:9; [w]1Ki 3:9; Da 2:21
19 [x]ver 3
20 [y]1Ki 3:12,28; 10:23–24; Isa 28:6; [z]2Sa 18:13
22 [a]**Ge 47:7**
26 [b]2Sa 18:9
27 [c]2Sa 18:18; [d]**2Sa 13:1**
30 [e]**Ex 9:31**
31 [f]**Jdg 15:5**
32 [g]**2Sa 3:3;** [h]1Sa 20:8
33 [i]Lk 15:20

b26 That is, about 5 pounds (about 2.3 kilograms)

Absalom's Conspiracy

15 In the course of time,[a] Absalom
provided himself with a chariot[b]
and horses and with fifty men to run
ahead of him. 2He would get up early
and stand by the side of the road leading
to the city gate.[c] Whenever anyone
came with a complaint to be placed be-
fore the king for a decision, Absalom
would call out to him, "What town are
you from?" He would answer, "Your
servant is from one of the tribes of
Israel." 3Then Absalom would say to
him, "Look, your claims are valid and
proper, but there is no representative of
the king to hear you."[d] 4And Absalom
would add, "If only I were appointed
judge in the land![e] Then everyone who
has a complaint or case could come to
me and I would see that he receives
justice."
5Also, whenever anyone approached
him to bow down before him, Absalom
would reach out his hand, take hold of
him and kiss him. 6Absalom behaved in
this way towards all the Israelites who
came to the king asking for justice, and
so he stole the hearts[f] of the men of
Israel.
7At the end of four[a] years, Absalom
said to the king, "Let me go to Hebron
and fulfil a vow I made to the LORD.
8While your servant was living at
Geshur[g] in Aram, I made this vow:[h] 'If
the LORD takes me back to Jerusalem, I
will worship the LORD in Hebron.'"[b]
9The king said to him, "Go in peace."
So he went to Hebron.
10Then Absalom sent secret messen-
gers throughout the tribes of Israel to
say, "As soon as you hear the sound of
the trumpets,[i] then say, 'Absalom is
king in Hebron.'" 11Two hundred men
from Jerusalem had accompanied Absa-
lom. They had been invited as guests
and went quite innocently, knowing
nothing about the matter. 12While Absa-
lom was offering sacrifices, he also sent
for Ahithophel[j] the Gilonite, David's
counsellor,[k] to come from Giloh,[l] his
home town. And so the conspiracy
gained strength, and Absalom's follow-
ing kept on increasing.[m]

David Flees

13A messenger came and told David,
"The hearts of the men of Israel are with
Absalom."
14Then David said to all his officials
who were with him in Jerusalem,
"Come! We must flee,[n] or none of us
will escape from Absalom.[o] We must
leave immediately, or he will move
quickly to overtake us and bring ruin
upon us and put the city to the sword."
15The king's officials answered him,
"Your servants are ready to do what-
ever our lord the king chooses."
16The king set out, with his entire
household following him; but he left ten
concubines[p] to take care of the palace.
17So the king set out, with all the people
following him, and they halted at a
place some distance away. 18All his men
marched past him, along with all the
Kerethites[q] and Pelethites; and all the
six hundred Gittites who had ac-
companied him from Gath marched
before the king.
19The king said to Ittai[r] the Gittite,
"Why should you come along with us?
Go back and stay with King Absalom.
You are a foreigner,[s] an exile from your
homeland. 20You came only yesterday.
And today shall I make you wander[t]
about with us, when I do not know
where I am going? Go back, and take
your countrymen. May kindness and
faithfulness[u] be with you."
21But Ittai replied to the king, "As
surely as the LORD lives, and as my lord
the king lives, wherever my lord the
king may be, whether it means life or
death, there will your servant be."[v]
22David said to Ittai, "Go ahead,
march on." So Ittai the Gittite marched
on with all his men and the families that
were with him.
23The whole countryside wept aloud[w]
as all the people passed by. The king
also crossed the Kidron Valley,[x] and all
the people moved on towards the
desert.
24Zadok[y] was there, too, and all the
Levites who were with him were car-
rying the ark[z] of the covenant of God.
They set down the ark of God, and
Abiathar[a] offered sacrifices[c] until all the
people had finished leaving the city.
25Then the king said to Zadok, "Take
the ark of God back into the city. If I find
favour in the LORD's eyes, he will bring
me back and let me see it and his dwell-
ing-place[b] again. 26But if he says, 'I am
not pleased with you,' then I am ready;
let him do to me whatever seems good
to him.[c]"
27The king also said to Zadok the

Ch. 15

1 [a]**2Sa 12:11**; [b]**1Sa 8:11**
2 [c]**Ge 23:10**; 2Sa 19:8
3 [d]Pr 12:2
4 [e]Jdg 9:29
6 [f]Ro 16:18
8 [g]**2Sa 3:3**; [h]**Ge 28:20**
10 [i]1Ki 1:34,39; 2Ki 9:13
12 [j]ver 31,34; 2Sa 16:15,23; 17:14; 23:34; 1Ch 27:33; [k]Job 19:14; Ps 41:9; 55:13; Jer 9:4; [l]Jos 15:51; [m]Ps 3:1
14 [n]1Ki 2:26; Ps 132:1; 3 Title; [o]2Sa 19:9
16 [p]2Sa 16:21–22; 20:3
18 [q]**1Sa 30:14**; 2Sa 20:7,23; 1Ki 1:38,44; 1Ch 18:17
19 [r]2Sa 18:2; [s]**Ge 31:15**
20 [t]**1Sa 22:2**; [u]2Sa 2:6
21 [v]Ru 1:16–17; Pr 17:17
23 [w]1Sa 11:4; Job 2:12; [x]1Ki 2:37; 2Ki 23:12; 2Ch 15:16; 29:16; 30:14; Jer 31:40; Jn 18:1
24 [y]**2Sa 8:17**; 19:11; [z]Nu 4:15; **10:33**; 1Ki 2:26; [a]**1Sa 22:20**
25 [b]Ex 15:13; **Lev 15:31**; Ps 43:3; 46:4; 84:1; 132:7
26 [c]**Jdg 10:15**; 2Sa 22:20

[a]7 Some Septuagint manuscripts, Syriac and Josephus; Hebrew *forty*
[b]8 Some Septuagint manuscripts; Hebrew does not have *in Hebron*.
[c]24 Or *Abiathar went up*

priest, "Aren't you a seer?[d] Go back to the city in peace, with your son Ahimaaz and Jonathan[e] son of Abiathar. You and Abiathar take your two sons with you. 28I will wait at the fords[f] in the desert until word comes from you to inform me." 29So Zadok and Abiathar took the ark of God back to Jerusalem and stayed there.

30But David continued up the Mount of Olives, weeping[g] as he went; his head[h] was covered and he was barefoot. All the people with him covered their heads too and were weeping as they went up. 31Now David had been told, "Ahithophel[i] is among the conspirators with Absalom." So David prayed, "O LORD, turn Ahithophel's counsel into foolishness."

32When David arrived at the summit, where people used to worship God, Hushai[j] the Arkite[k] was there to meet him, his robe torn and dust[l] on his head. 33David said to him, "If you go with me, you will be a burden[m] to me. 34But if you return to the city and say to Absalom, 'I will be your servant, O king; I was your father's servant in the past, but now I will be your servant,'[n] then you can help me by frustrating[o] Ahithophel's advice. 35Won't the priests Zadok and Abiathar be there with you? Tell them anything you hear in the king's palace.[p] 36Their two sons, Ahimaaz[q] son of Zadok and Jonathan[r] son of Abiathar, are there with them. Send them to me with anything you hear."

37So David's friend Hushai[s] arrived at Jerusalem as Absalom[t] was entering the city.

David and Ziba

16 When David had gone a short distance beyond the summit, there was Ziba,[a] the steward of Mephibosheth, waiting to meet him. He had a string of donkeys saddled and loaded with two hundred loaves of bread, a hundred cakes of raisins, a hundred cakes of figs and a skin of wine.[b]

2The king asked Ziba, "Why have you brought these?"

Ziba answered, "The donkeys are for the king's household to ride on, the bread and fruit are for the men to eat, and the wine is to refresh[c] those who become exhausted in the desert."

3The king then asked, "Where is your master's grandson?"[d]

Ziba[e] said to him, "He is staying in Jerusalem, because he thinks, 'Today the house of Israel will give me back my grandfather's kingdom.'"

4Then the king said to Ziba, "All that belonged to Mephibosheth[f] is now yours."

"I humbly bow," Ziba said. "May I find favour in your eyes, my lord the king."

Shimei Curses David

5As King David approached Bahurim,[g] a man from the same clan as Saul's family came out from there. His name was Shimei[h] son of Gera, and he cursed[i] as he came out. 6He pelted David and all the king's officials with stones, though all the troops and the special guard were on David's right and left. 7As he cursed, Shimei said, "Get out, get out, you man of blood, you scoundrel! 8The LORD has repaid you for all the blood you shed in the household of Saul, in whose place you have reigned.[j] The LORD has handed the kingdom over to your son Absalom. You have come to ruin because you are a man of blood!"[k]

9Then Abishai[l] son of Zeruiah said to the king, "Why should this dead dog[m] curse my lord the king? Let me go over and cut off his head."[n]

10But the king said, "What do you and I have in common, you sons of Zeruiah?[o] If he is cursing because the LORD said to him, 'Curse David,' who can ask, 'Why do you do this?'"[p]

11David then said to Abishai and all his officials, "My son,[q] who is of my own flesh, is trying to take my life. How much more, then, this Benjamite! Leave him alone; let him curse, for the LORD has told him to.[r] 12It may be that the LORD will see my distress[s] and repay me with good[t] for the cursing I am receiving today."[u]

13So David and his men continued along the road while Shimei was going along the hillside opposite him, cursing as he went and throwing stones at him and showering him with dirt. 14The king and all the people with him arrived at their destination exhausted.[v] And there he refreshed himself.

The Advice of Hushai and Ahithophel

15Meanwhile, Absalom[w] and all the men of Israel came to Jerusalem, and Ahithophel[x] was with him. 16Then Hushai[y] the Arkite, David's friend, went to Absalom and said to him, "Long live the king! Long live the king!"

17Absalom asked Hushai, "Is this the love you show your friend? Why didn't you go with your friend?"[z]

27 d**1Sa 9:9**; ever 36; 2Sa 17:17; 1Ki 1:42
28 f2Sa 17:16
30 g**Nu 25:6; Ps 30:5**; hEst 6:12
31 i**ver 12**
32 jver 37; 2Sa 16:16; 17:5; 1Ki 4:16; kJos 16:2; l**Jos 7:6**
33 m2Sa 19:35
34 n2Sa 16:19; o2Sa 17:14; Pr 11:14
35 p2Sa 17:15–16
36 q2Sa 18:19; r**ver 27**; 2Sa 17:17; 1Ki 1:42
37 s1Ch 27:33; t2Sa 16:15

Ch. 16

1 a2Sa 9:1–13; b**1Sa 25:18**; 1Ch 12:40
2 c2Sa 17:27–29
3 d2Sa 9:9–10; e**2Sa 9:2**
4 f**2Sa 4:4**
5 g**2Sa 3:16**; h2Sa 19:16–23; 1Ki 2:8–9, 36,44; i**Ex 22:28**
8 j2Sa 19:28; 21:9; k2Sa 19:19; Ps 55:3
9 l**1Sa 26:6**; m**2Sa 3:8**; n**2Sa 3:39**; Lk 9:54
10 o**2Sa 2:18**; 19:22; pRo 9:20
11 q2Sa 12:11; r**Ge 45:5**; 1Sa 26:19
12 sPs 4:1; 25:18; tDt 23:5; Ro 8:28; uPs 109:28
14 v2Sa 17:2
15 w**2Sa 15:37**; x**2Sa 15:12**
16 y**2Sa 15:32**
17 z2Sa 19:25

18Hushai said to Absalom, "No, the one chosen by the LORD, by these people and by all the men of Israel—his I will be, and I will remain with him. 19Furthermore, whom should I serve? Should I not serve the son? Just as I served your father, so I will serve you."[a]

20Absalom said to Ahithophel, "Give us your advice. What should we do?"

21Ahithophel answered, "Lie with your father's concubines whom he left to take care of the palace. Then all Israel will hear that you have made yourself an offence to your father's nostrils, and the hands of everyone with you will be strengthened." 22So they pitched a tent for Absalom on the roof, and he lay with his father's concubines in the sight of all Israel.[b]

23Now in those days the advice[c] Ahithophel gave was like that of one who enquires of God. That was how both David[d] and Absalom regarded all of Ahithophel's advice.

17 Ahithophel said to Absalom, "I would[a] choose twelve thousand men and set out tonight in pursuit of David. 2I would[b] attack him while he is weary and weak.[a] I would[b] strike him with terror, and then all the people with him will flee. I would[b] strike down only the king[b] 3and bring all the people back to you. The death of the man you seek will mean the return of all; all the people will be unharmed." 4This plan seemed good to Absalom and to all the elders of Israel.

5But Absalom said, "Summon also Hushai[c] the Arkite, so that we can hear what he has to say." 6When Hushai came to him, Absalom said, "Ahithophel has given this advice. Should we do what he says? If not, give us your opinion."

7Hushai replied to Absalom, "The advice Ahithophel has given is not good this time. 8You know your father and his men; they are fighters, and as fierce as a wild bear robbed of her cubs.[d] Besides, your father is an experienced fighter;[e] he will not spend the night with the troops. 9Even now, he is hidden in a cave or some other place.[f] If he should attack your troops first,[c] whoever hears about it will say, 'There has been a slaughter among the troops who follow Absalom.' 10Then even the bravest soldier, whose heart is like the heart of a lion,[g] will melt[h] with fear, for all Israel knows that your father is a fighter and that those with him are brave.[i]

11"So I advise you: Let all Israel, from Dan to Beersheba[j]—as numerous as the sand[k] on the seashore—be gathered to you, with you yourself leading them into battle. 12Then we will attack him wherever he may be found, and we will fall on him as dew settles on the ground. Neither he nor any of his men will be left alive. 13If he withdraws into a city, then all Israel will bring ropes to that city, and we will drag it down to the valley[l] until not even a piece of it can be found."

14Absalom and all the men of Israel said, "The advice[m] of Hushai the Arkite is better than that of Ahithophel."[n] For the LORD had determined to frustrate[o] the good advice of Ahithophel in order to bring disaster[p] on Absalom.[q]

15Hushai told Zadok and Abiathar, the priests, "Ahithophel has advised Absalom and the elders of Israel to do such and such, but I have advised them to do so and so. 16Now send a message immediately and tell David, 'Do not spend the night at the fords in the desert;[r] cross over without fail, or the king and all the people with him will be swallowed up.[s]'"

17Jonathan[t] and Ahimaaz were staying at En Rogel.[u] A servant girl was to go and inform them, and they were to go and tell King David, for they could not risk being seen entering the city. 18But a young man saw them and told Absalom. So the two of them left quickly and went to the house of a man in Bahurim.[v] He had a well in his courtyard, and they climbed down into it. 19His wife took a covering and spread it out over the opening of the well and scattered grain over it. No-one knew anything about it.[w]

20When Absalom's men came to the woman[x] at the house, they asked, "Where are Ahimaaz and Jonathan?"

The woman answered them, "They crossed over the brook."[d] The men searched but found no-one, so they returned to Jerusalem.

21After the men had gone, the two climbed out of the well and went to inform King David. They said to him, "Set out and cross the river at once; Ahithophel has advised such and such against you." 22So David and all the people with him set out and crossed the Jordan. By daybreak, no-one was left who had not crossed the Jordan.

23When Ahithophel saw that his

19 [a]2Sa 15:34
22 [b]**2Sa 3:7;** 12:11–12; **15:16**
23 [c]2Sa 17:14,23; [d]**2Sa 15:12**

Ch. 17

2 [a]2Sa 16:14; [b]1Ki 22:31; Zec 13:7
5 [c]**2Sa 15:32**
8 [d]Hos 13:8; [e]1Sa 16:18
9 [f]Jer 41:9
10 [g]1Ch 12:8; [h]Jos 2:9,11; Eze 21:15; [i]2Sa 23:8; 1Ch 11:11
11 [j]**Jdg 20:1**; [k]**Ge 12:2; Jos 11:4**
13 [l]Mic 1:6
14 [m]**2Sa 16:23;** [n]**2Sa 15:12;** [o]**2Sa 15:34;** Ne 4:15; [p]Ps 9:16; [q]2Ch 10:8
16 [r]2Sa 15:28; [s]2Sa 15:35
17 [t]**2Sa 15:27**,36; [u]Jos 15:7; 18:16; 1Ki 1:9
18 [v]**2Sa 3:16**
19 [w]**Jos 2:6**
20 [x]**Ex 1:19**

[a]1 Or *Let me* [b]2 Or *will*
[c]9 Or *When some of the men fall at the first attack*
[d]20 Or *"They passed by the sheep pen towards the water."*

advice[y] had not been followed, he
saddled his donkey and set out for his
house in his home town. He put his
house in order[z] and then hanged him-
self. So he died and was buried in his
father's tomb.
24David went to Mahanaim,[a] and
Absalom crossed the Jordan with all the
men of Israel. 25Absalom had appointed
Amasa[b] over the army in place of Joab.
Amasa was the son of a man named
Jether,[e][c] an Israelite[f] who had married
Abigail,[g] the daughter of Nahash and
sister of Zeruiah the mother of Joab.
26The Israelites and Absalom camped in
the land of Gilead.
27When David came to Mahanaim,
Shobi son of Nahash[d] from Rabbah[e] of
the Ammonites, and Makir[f] son of
Ammiel from Lo Debar, and Barzillai[g]
the Gileadite[h] from Rogelim 28brought
bedding and bowls and articles of pot-
tery. They also brought wheat and bar-
ley, flour and roasted grain, beans and
lentils,[h] 29honey and curds, sheep, and
cheese from cows' milk for David and
his people to eat.[i] For they said, "The
people have become hungry and tired
and thirsty in the desert.[j]"

Absalom's Death

18 David mustered the men who
were with him and appointed
over them commanders of thousands
and commanders of hundreds. 2David
sent the troops out[a]—a third under the
command of Joab, a third under Joab's
brother Abishai[b] son of Zeruiah, and a
third under Ittai[c] the Gittite. The king
told the troops, "I myself will surely
march out with you."
3But the men said, "You must not go
out; if we are forced to flee, they won't
care about us. Even if half of us die, they
won't care; but you are worth ten[d]
thousand of us.[a] It would be better now
for you to give us support from the
city."[e]
4The king answered, "I will do what-
ever seems best to you."
So the king stood beside the gate
while all the men marched out in units
of hundreds and of thousands. 5The
king commanded Joab, Abishai and
Ittai, "Be gentle with the young man
Absalom for my sake." And all the
troops heard the king giving orders
concerning Absalom to each of the
commanders.
6The army marched into the field to
fight Israel, and the battle took place in
the forest[f] of Ephraim. 7There the army
of Israel was defeated by David's men,
and the casualties that day were great
—twenty thousand men. 8The battle
spread out over the whole countryside,
and the forest claimed more lives that
day than the sword.
9Now Absalom happened to meet
David's men. He was riding his mule,
and as the mule went under the thick
branches of a large oak, Absalom's
head[g] got caught in the tree. He was left
hanging in mid-air, while the mule he
was riding kept on going.
10When one of the men saw this, he
told Joab, "I have just seen Absalom
hanging in an oak tree."
11Joab said to the man who had told
him this, "What! You saw him? Why
didn't you strike[h] him to the ground
right there? Then I would have had to
give you ten shekels[b] of silver and a
warrior's belt.[i]"
12But the man replied, "Even if a
thousand shekels[c] were weighed out
into my hands, I would not lift my hand
against the king's son. In our hearing
the king commanded you and Abishai
and Ittai, 'Protect the young man Absa-
lom for my sake.'[d] 13And if I had put my
life in jeopardy[e]—and nothing is hid-
den from the king[j]—you would have
kept your distance from me."
14Joab[k] said, "I am not going to wait
like this for you." So he took three jav-
elins in his hand and plunged them
into Absalom's heart while Absalom
was still alive in the oak tree. 15And ten
of Joab's armour-bearers surrounded
Absalom, struck him and killed him.[l]
16Then Joab[m] sounded the trumpet,
and the troops stopped pursuing Israel,
for Joab halted them. 17They took Absa-
lom, threw him into a big pit in the
forest and piled up[n] a large heap of
rocks[o] over him. Meanwhile, all the
Israelites fled to their homes.
18During his life-time Absalom had

23 [y]**2Sa 16:23;** [z]2Ki 20:1
24 [a]**Ge 32:2**
25 [b]2Sa 19:13; 20:4,9–12; 1Ki 2:5,32; 1Ch 12:18; [c]1Ch 2:13–17
27 [d]**1Sa 11:1;** [e]**Dt 3:11;** [f]2Sa 9:4; [g]2Sa 19:31–39; 1Ki 2:7; [h]2Sa 19:31; Ezr 2:61
29 [i]1Ch 12:40; [j]2Sa 16:2; **Ro 12:13**

Ch. 18

2 [a]**Jdg 7:16;** 1Sa 11:11; [b]**1Sa 26:6;** [c]2Sa 15:19
3 [d]**1Sa 18:7;** [e]2Sa 21:17
6 [f]**Jos 17:15**
9 [g]2Sa 14:26
11 [h]**2Sa 3:39;** [i]1Sa 18:4
13 [j]2Sa 14:19–20
14 [k]**2Sa 2:18**
15 [l]**2Sa 12:10**
16 [m]**2Sa 2:28**
17 [n]Jos 7:26; [o]Jos 8:29

[e]25 Hebrew *Ithra*, a variant of *Jether*
[f]25 Hebrew and some Septuagint manuscripts; other Septuagint manuscripts (see also 1 Chron. 2:17) *Ishmaelite* or *Jezreelite*
[g]25 Hebrew *Abigal*, a variant of *Abigail*
[h]28 Most Septuagint manuscripts and Syriac; Hebrew *lentils, and roasted grain*
[a]3 Two Hebrew manuscripts, some Septuagint manuscripts and Vulgate; most Hebrew manuscripts *care; for now there are ten thousand like us*
[b]11 That is, about 4 ounces (about 115 grams)
[c]12 That is, about 25 pounds (about 11 kilograms)
[d]12 A few Hebrew manuscripts, Septuagint, Vulgate and Syriac; most Hebrew manuscripts may be translated *Absalom, whoever you may be.*
[e]13 Or *Otherwise, if I had acted treacherously towards him*

taken a pillar and erected it in the King's
Valley[p] as a monument[q] to himself, for
he thought, "I have no son[r] to carry on
the memory of my name." He named
the pillar after himself, and it is called
Absalom's Monument to this day.

David Mourns

19 Now Ahimaaz[s] son of Zadok said,
"Let me run and take the news to the
king that the LORD has delivered him
from the hand of his enemies.[t]"
20 "You are not the one to take the
news today," Joab told him. "You may
take the news another time, but you
must not do so today, because the
king's son is dead."
21 Then Joab said to a Cushite, "Go,
tell the king what you have seen." The
Cushite bowed down before Joab and
ran off.
22 Ahimaaz son of Zadok again said to
Joab, "Come what may, please let me
run behind the Cushite."
But Joab replied, "My son, why do
you want to go? You don't have any
news that will bring you a reward."
23 He said, "Come what may, I want to
run."
So Joab said, "Run!" Then Ahimaaz
ran by way of the plain[f] and outran the
Cushite.
24 While David was sitting between
the inner and outer gates, the watch-
man[u] went up to the roof of the gateway
by the wall. As he looked out, he saw a
man running alone. 25 The watchman
called out to the king and reported it.
The king said, "If he is alone, he must
have good news." And the man came
closer and closer.
26 Then the watchman saw another
man running, and he called down to the
gatekeeper, "Look, another man run-
ning alone!"
The king said, "He must be bringing
good news,[v] too."
27 The watchman said, "It seems to me
that the first one runs like[w] Ahimaaz son
of Zadok."
"He's a good man," the king said.
"He comes with good news."
28 Then Ahimaaz called out to the
king, "All is well!" He bowed down
before the king with his face to the
ground and said, "Praise be to the LORD
your God! He has delivered up the men
who lifted their hands against my lord
the king."
29 The king asked, "Is the young man
Absalom safe?"
Ahimaaz answered, "I saw great
confusion just as Joab was about to send
the king's servant and me, your ser-
vant, but I don't know what it was."
30 The king said, "Stand aside and
wait here." So he stepped aside and
stood there.
31 Then the Cushite arrived and said,
"My lord the king, hear the good news!
The LORD has delivered you today from
all who rose up against you."
32 The king asked the Cushite, "Is the
young man Absalom safe?"
The Cushite replied, "May the ene-
mies of my lord the king and all who rise
up to harm you be like that young
man."[x]
33 The king was shaken. He went up to
the room over the gateway and wept.
As he went, he said: "O my son Absa-
lom! My son, my son Absalom! If only I
had died[y] instead of you—O Absalom,
my son, my son!"[z]

19

Joab was told, "The king is
weeping and mourning for
Absalom." 2 And for the whole army the
victory that day was turned into mourn-
ing, because on that day the troops
heard it said, "The king is grieving for
his son." 3 The men stole into the city
that day as men steal in who are
ashamed when they flee from battle.
4 The king covered his face and cried
aloud, "O my son Absalom! O Absa-
lom, my son, my son!"
5 Then Joab went into the house to the
king and said, "Today you have humili-
ated all your men, who have just saved
your life and the lives of your sons and
daughters and the lives of your wives
and concubines. 6 You love those who
hate you and hate those who love you.
You have made it clear today that the
commanders and their men mean no-
thing to you. I see that you would be
pleased if Absalom were alive today and
all of us were dead. 7 Now go out and
encourage your men. I swear by the
LORD that if you don't go out, not a man
will be left with you by nightfall. This
will be worse for you than all the calami-
ties that have come upon you from your
youth till now."[a]
8 So the king got up and took his seat
in the gateway. When the men were
told, "The king is sitting in the gate-
way,[b]" they all came before him.

David Returns to Jerusalem

Meanwhile, the Israelites had fled to
their homes. 9 Throughout the tribes of

18 [p]Ge 14:17; [q]**Ge 50:5; Nu 32:42**; [r]2Sa 14:27
19 [s]**2Sa 15:36**; [t]Jdg 11:36
24 [u]**1Sa 14:16; Jer 51:12**
26 [v]1Ki 1:42; Isa 52:7; 61:1
27 [w]2Ki 9:20
32 [x]Jdg 5:31; **1Sa 25:26**
33 [y]Ex 32:32; [z]**Ge 43:14**; 2Sa 19:4

Ch. 19

7 [a]Pr 14:28
8 [b]**2Sa 15:2**

---

f23 That is, the plain of the Jordan

Israel, the people were all arguing with
each other, saying, "The king delivered
us from the hand of our enemies; he is
the one who rescued us from the hand
of the Philistines.[c] But now he has fled
the country because of Absalom;[d] 10and
Absalom, whom we anointed to rule
over us, has died in battle. So why do
you say nothing about bringing the king
back?"
11King David sent this message to
Zadok[e] and Abiathar, the priests: "Ask
the elders of Judah, 'Why should you be
the last to bring the king back to his
palace, since what is being said
throughout Israel has reached the king
at his quarters? 12You are my brothers,
my own flesh and blood. So why should
you be the last to bring back the king?'
13And say to Amasa,[f] 'Are you not my
own flesh and blood?[g] May God deal
with me, be it ever so severely,[h] if from
now on you are not the commander of
my army in place of Joab.[i]' "
14He won over the hearts of all the
men of Judah as though they were one
man. They sent word to the king, "Re-
turn, you and all your men." 15Then the
king returned and went as far as the
Jordan.
Now the men of Judah had come to
Gilgal[j] to go out and meet the king and
bring him across the Jordan. 16Shimei[k]
son of Gera, the Benjamite from Bahur-
im, hurried down with the men of
Judah to meet King David. 17With him
were a thousand Benjamites, along with
Ziba,[l] the steward of Saul's household,[m]
and his fifteen sons and twenty ser-
vants. They rushed to the Jordan,
where the king was. 18They crossed at
the ford to take the king's household
over and to do whatever he wished.
When Shimei son of Gera crossed the
Jordan, he fell prostrate before the king
19and said to him, "May my lord not
hold me guilty. Do not remember how
your servant did wrong on the day my
lord the king left Jerusalem.[n] May the
king put it out of his mind. 20For I your
servant know that I have sinned, but
today I have come here as the first of the
whole house of Joseph to come down
and meet my lord the king."
21Then Abishai[o] son of Zeruiah said,
"Shouldn't Shimei be put to death for
this? He cursed[p] the LORD's anointed."[q]
22David replied, "What do you and I
have in common, you sons of Zeruiah?[r]
This day you have become my adver-
saries! Should anyone be put to death in
Israel today?[s] Do I not know that today I
am king over Israel?" 23So the king said
to Shimei, "You shall not die." And the
king promised him on oath.[t]
24Mephibosheth,[u] Saul's grandson,
also went down to meet the king. He
had not taken care of his feet or trimmed
his moustache or washed his clothes
from the day the king left until the day
he returned safely. 25When he came
from Jerusalem to meet the king, the
king asked him, "Why didn't you go
with me,[v] Mephibosheth?"
26He said, "My lord the king, since I
your servant am lame,[w] I said, 'I will
have my donkey saddled and will ride
on it, so that I can go with the king.' But
Ziba[x] my servant betrayed me. 27And he
has slandered your servant to my lord
the king. My lord the king is like an
angel[y] of God; so do whatever pleases
you. 28All my grandfather's descend-
ants deserved nothing but death[z] from
my lord the king, but you gave your
servant a place among those who sat at
your table.[a] So what right do I have to
make any more appeals to the king?"
29The king said to him, "Why say
more? I order you and Ziba to divide the
fields."
30Mephibosheth said to the king, "Let
him take everything, now that my lord
the king has arrived home safely."
31Barzillai[b] the Gileadite also came
down from Rogelim to cross the Jordan
with the king and to send him on his
way from there. 32Now Barzillai was a
very old man, eighty years of age. He
had provided for the king during his
stay in Mahanaim, for he was a very
wealthy[c] man. 33The king said to Barzil-
lai, "Cross over with me and stay with
me in Jerusalem, and I will provide for
you."
34But Barzillai answered the king,
"How many more years shall I live, that
I should go up to Jerusalem with the
king? 35I am now eighty[d] years old. Can I
tell the difference between what is good
and what is not? Can your servant taste
what he eats and drinks? Can I still hear
the voices of men and women singers?[e]
Why should your servant be an added[f]
burden to my lord the king? 36Your ser-
vant will cross over the Jordan with the
king for a short distance, but why
should the king reward me in this way?
37Let your servant return, that I may die
in my own town near the tomb of my
father[g] and mother. But here is your
servant Kimham.[h] Let him cross over
with my lord the king. Do for him what-
ever pleases you."
38The king said, "Kimham shall cross
over with me, and I will do for him

9 [c]2Sa 8:1-14; [d]2Sa 15:14
11 [e]**2Sa 15:24**
13 [f]**2Sa 17:25;** [g]**Ge 29:14;** [h]**Ru 1:17;** [i]**2Sa 2:13**
15 [j]**1Sa 11:15**
16 [k]2Sa 16:5-13
17 [l]**2Sa 9:2;** [m]**Ge 43:16**
19 [n]**2Sa 16:6-8**
21 [o]**1Sa 26:6;** [p]**Ex 22:28;** [q]**1Sa 12:3; 26:9**
22 [r]**2Sa 2:18; 16:10;** [s]1Sa 11:13
23 [t]1Ki 2:8,42
24 [u]**2Sa 4:4**
25 [v]2Sa 16:17
26 [w]**Lev 21:18;** [x]**2Sa 9:2**
27 [y]**1Sa 29:9**
28 [z]**2Sa 16:8;** [a]**2Sa 9:7**,13
31 [b]**2Sa 17:27-29;** 1Ki 2:7
32 [c]1Sa 25:2
35 [d]Ps 90:10; [e]2Ch 35:25; Ezr 2:65; Ecc 2:8; 12:1; [f]2Sa 15:33
37 [g]**Ge 49:29;** [h]Jer 41:17

whatever pleases you. And anything
you desire from me I will do for you."
39So all the people crossed the Jordan,
and then the king crossed over. The
king kissed Barzillai and gave him his
blessing,[i] and Barzillai returned to his
home.
40When the king crossed over to Gil-
gal, Kimham crossed with him. All the
troops of Judah and half the troops of
Israel had taken the king over.
41Soon all the men of Israel were com-
ing to the king and saying to him, "Why
did our brothers, the men of Judah,
steal the king away and bring him and
his household across the Jordan,
together with all his men?"[j]
42All the men of Judah answered the
men of Israel, "We did this because the
king is closely related to us. Why are
you angry about it? Have we eaten any
of the king's provisions? Have we taken
anything for ourselves?"
43Then the men of Israel[k] answered
the men of Judah, "We have ten shares
in the king; and besides, we have a
greater claim on David than you have.
So why do you treat us with contempt?
Were we not the first to speak of bring-
ing back our king?"
But the men of Judah responded even
more harshly than the men of Israel.

Sheba Rebels Against David

20 Now a troublemaker named
Sheba son of Bicri, a Benjamite,
happened to be there. He sounded the
trumpet and shouted,

"We have no share[a] in David,[b]
no part in Jesse's son![c]
Every man to his tent, O Israel!"

2So all the men of Israel deserted
David to follow Sheba son of Bicri. But
the men of Judah stayed by their king all
the way from the Jordan to Jerusalem.
3When David returned to his palace in
Jerusalem, he took the ten concubines[d]
he had left to take care of the palace and
put them in a house under guard. He
provided for them, but did not lie with
them. They were kept in confinement
till the day of their death, living as
widows.
4Then the king said to Amasa,[e]
"Summon the men of Judah to come
to me within three days, and be here
yourself." 5But when Amasa went to
summon Judah, he took longer than the
time the king had set for him.
6David said to Abishai,[f] "Now Sheba
son of Bicri will do us more harm than
Absalom did. Take your master's men
and pursue him, or he will find fortified
cities and escape from us." 7So Joab's
men and the Kerethites[g] and Pelethites
and all the mighty warriors went out
under the command of Abishai. They
marched out from Jerusalem to pursue
Sheba son of Bicri.
8While they were at the great rock in
Gibeon,[h] Amasa came to meet them.
Joab[i] was wearing his military tunic,
and strapped over it at his waist was a
belt with a dagger in its sheath. As he
stepped forward, it dropped out of its
sheath.
9Joab said to Amasa, "How are you,
my brother?" Then Joab took Amasa by
the beard with his right hand to kiss
him. 10Amasa was not on his guard
against the dagger[j] in Joab's[k] hand, and
Joab plunged it into his belly, and his
intestines spilled out on the ground.
Without being stabbed again, Amasa
died. Then Joab and his brother Abishai
pursued Sheba son of Bicri.
11One of Joab's men stood beside
Amasa and said, "Whoever favours
Joab, and whoever is for David, let him
follow Joab!" 12Amasa lay wallowing in
his blood in the middle of the road, and
the man saw that all the troops came to a
halt[l] there. When he realised that every-
one who came up to Amasa stopped, he
dragged him from the road into a field
and threw a garment over him. 13After
Amasa had been removed from the
road, all the men went on with Joab to
pursue Sheba son of Bicri.
14Sheba passed through all the tribes
of Israel to Abel Beth Maacah[a] and
through the entire region of the Be-
rites,[m] who gathered together and fol-
lowed him. 15All the troops with Joab
came and besieged Sheba in Abel Beth
Maacah.[n] They built a siege ramp[o] up to
the city, and it stood against the outer
fortifications. While they were battering
the wall to bring it down, 16a wise
woman[p] called from the city, "Listen!
Listen! Tell Joab to come here so that I
can speak to him." 17He went towards
her, and she asked, "Are you Joab?"
"I am," he answered.
She said, "Listen to what your ser-
vant has to say."
"I'm listening," he said.
18She continued, "Long ago they
used to say, 'Get your answer at Abel,'
and that settled it. 19We are the peace-
ful[q] and faithful in Israel. You are trying

39 [i]**Ge 47:7**
41 [j]**Jdg 8:1**; 12:1
43 [k]**2Sa 5:1**

Ch. 20

1 [a]**Ge 31:14**; [b]**Ge 29:14**; 1Ki 12:16; [c]1Sa 22:7–8
3 [d]**2Sa 15:16**
4 [e]**2Sa 17:25**
6 [f]2Sa 21:17
7 [g]**1Sa 30:14; 2Sa 15:18**
8 [h]**Jos 9:3**; [i]**2Sa 2:18**
10 [j]**Jdg 3:21**; [k]1Ki 2:5
12 [l]**2Sa 2:23**
14 [m]Nu 21:16
15 [n]1Ki 15:20; 2Ki 15:29; [o]Isa 37:33; Jer 6:6; 32:24
16 [p]2Sa 14:2
19 [q]**Dt 2:26**

[a]14 Or *Abel, even Beth Maacah*; also in verse 15

to destroy a city that is a mother in
Israel. Why do you want to swallow up
the LORD's inheritance?"[r]
20"Far be it from me!" Joab replied,
"Far be it from me to swallow up or
destroy! 21That is not the case. A man
named Sheba son of Bicri, from the hill
country of Ephraim, has lifted up his
hand against the king, against David.
Hand over this one man, and I'll with-
draw from the city."
The woman said to Joab, "His head[s]
will be thrown to you from the wall."
22Then the woman went to all the
people with her wise advice,[t] and they
cut off the head of Sheba son of Bicri and
threw it to Joab. So he sounded the
trumpet, and his men dispersed from
the city, each returning to his home.
And Joab went back to the king in
Jerusalem.
23Joab[u] was over Israel's entire army;
Benaiah son of Jehoiada was over the
Kerethites and Pelethites; 24Adoniram[b] [v]
was in charge of forced labour; Jehosha-
phat[w] son of Ahilud was recorder;
25Sheva was secretary; Zadok[x] and
Abiathar were priests; 26and Ira the
Jairite was David's priest.

The Gibeonites Avenged

21 During the reign of David,
there was a famine[a] for three
successive years; so David sought[b] the
face of the LORD. The LORD said, "It is on
account of Saul and his blood-stained
house; it is because he put the
Gibeonites to death."
2The king summoned the Gibeonites[c]
and spoke to them. (Now the
Gibeonites were not a part of Israel but
were survivors of the Amorites; the
Israelites had sworn to ⌞spare⌟ them,
but Saul in his zeal for Israel and Judah
had tried to annihilate them.) 3David
asked the Gibeonites, "What shall I do
for you? How shall I make amends
so that you will bless the LORD's
inheritance?"[d]
4The Gibeonites answered him, "We
have no right to demand silver or gold
from Saul or his family, nor do we have
the right to put anyone in Israel to
death."[e]
"What do you want me to do for
you?" David asked.
5They answered the king, "As for the
man who destroyed us and plotted
against us so that we have been deci-
mated and have no place anywhere in
Israel, 6let seven of his male descend-
ants be given to us to be killed and
exposed[f] before the LORD at Gibeah of
Saul—the LORD's chosen[g] one."
So the king said, "I will give them to
you."
7The king spared Mephibosheth[h] son
of Jonathan, the son of Saul, because of
the oath[i] before the LORD between
David and Jonathan son of Saul. 8But
the king took Armoni and Mephib-
osheth, the two sons of Aiah's daughter
Rizpah,[j] whom she had borne to Saul,
together with the five sons of Saul's
daughter Merab,[a] whom she had borne
to Adriel son of Barzillai the Me-
holathite.[k] 9He handed them over to the
Gibeonites, who killed and exposed
them on a hill before the LORD. All seven
of them fell together; they were put to
death[l] during the first days of har-
vest, just as the barley harvest was
beginning.[m]
10Rizpah daughter of Aiah took sack-
cloth and spread it out for herself on a
rock. From the beginning of the harvest
till the rain poured down from the
heavens on the bodies, she did not let
the birds of the air touch them by day or
the wild animals by night.[n] 11When
David was told what Aiah's daughter
Rizpah, Saul's concubine, had done,
12he went and took the bones of Saul[o]
and his son Jonathan from the citizens
of Jabesh Gilead.[p] (They had taken them
secretly from the public square at Beth
Shan,[q] where the Philistines had hung[r]
them after they struck Saul down on
Gilboa.)[s] 13David brought the bones of
Saul and his son Jonathan from there,
and the bones of those who had been
killed and exposed were gathered up.
14They buried the bones of Saul and
his son Jonathan in the tomb of Saul's
father Kish, at Zela[t] in Benjamin, and
did everything the king commanded.
After that,[u] God answered prayer[v] on
behalf of the land.[w]

Wars Against the Philistines

21:15–22pp—1Ch 20:4–8

15Once again there was a battle be-
tween the Philistines[x] and Israel. David
went down with his men to fight against
the Philistines, and he became ex-
hausted. 16And Ishbi-Benob, one of the
descendants of Rapha, whose bronze
spearhead weighed three hundred

19 [r]1Sa 26:19
21 [s]2Sa 4:8
22 [t]Ecc 9:13
23 [u]2Sa 2:28; 8:16–18; 24:2
24 [v]1Ki 4:6; 5:14; 12:18; 2Ch 10:18; [w]2Sa 8:16
25 [x]1Sa 2:35; 2Sa 8:17

Ch. 21

1 [a]Ge 12:10; Dt 32:24; [b]Ex 32:11
2 [c]Jos 9:15
3 [d]1Sa 26:19
4 [e]Nu 35:33–34
6 [f]Nu 25:4; [g]1Sa 10:24
7 [h]2Sa 4:4; [i]1Sa 18:3; 2Sa 9:7
8 [j]2Sa 3:7; [k]1Sa 18:19
9 [l]2Sa 16:8; [m]Ru 1:22
10 [n]Ge 40:19; 1Sa 17:44
12 [o]1Sa 31:11–13; [p]Jdg 21:8; 1Sa 11:1; [q]Jos 17:11; [r]1Sa 31:10; [s]1Sa 28:4
14 [t]Jos 18:28; [u]Jos 7:26; [v]2Sa 24:25; [w]1Ch 8:34
15 [x]2Sa 5:25

[b]24 Some Septuagint manuscripts (see also 1 Kings 4:6 and 5:14); Hebrew *Adoram*

[a]8 Two Hebrew manuscripts, some Septuagint manuscripts and Syriac (see also 1 Samuel 18:19); most Hebrew and Septuagint manuscripts *Michal*

shekels[b] and who was armed with a
new ⌞sword⌟, said he would kill David.
17But Abishai[y] son of Zeruiah came to
David's rescue; he struck the Philistine
down and killed him. Then David's
men swore to him, saying, "Never
again will you go out with us to battle,
so that the lamp[z] of Israel will not be
extinguished.[a]"

18In the course of time, there was
another battle with the Philistines, at
Gob. At that time Sibbecai[b] the
Hushathite killed Saph, one of the
descendants of Rapha.

19In another battle with the Philistines
at Gob, Elhanan son of Jaare-Oregim[c]
the Bethlehemite killed Goliath[d] the
Gittite,[c] who had a spear with a shaft
like a weaver's rod.[d]

20In still another battle, which took
place at Gath, there was a huge man
with six fingers on each hand and six
toes on each foot—twenty-four in all.
He also was descended from Rapha.
21When he taunted[e] Israel, Jonathan son
of Shimeah,[f] David's brother, killed
him.

22These four were descendants of
Rapha in Gath, and they fell at the
hands of David and his men.

David's Song of Praise

22:1–51pp—Ps 18:1–50

22 David sang[a] to the LORD the
words of this song when the
LORD delivered him from the hand of all
his enemies and from the hand of Saul.
2He said:

"The LORD is my rock,[b] my fortress[c]
and my deliverer;[d]
3 my God is my rock, in whom I take
refuge,[e]
my shield[f] and the horn[a][g] of my
salvation.
He is my stronghold,[h] my refuge and
my saviour—
from violent men you save me.
4I call to the LORD, who is worthy[i] of
praise,
and I am saved from my enemies.

5"The waves[j] of death swirled about
me;
the torrents of destruction
overwhelmed me.
6The cords of the grave[b][k] coiled around
me;
the snares of death confronted me.
7In my distress[l] I called[m] to the LORD;
I called out to my God.
From his temple he heard my voice;
my cry came to his ears.

8"The earth[n] trembled and quaked,[o]
the foundations[p] of the heavens[c]
shook;
they trembled because he was
angry.
9Smoke rose from his nostrils;
consuming fire[q] came from his
mouth,
burning coals[r] blazed out of it.
10He parted the heavens and came
down;
dark clouds[s] were under his feet.
11He mounted the cherubim[t] and flew;
he soared[d] on the wings of the
wind.[u]
12He made darkness[v] his canopy around
him—
the dark[e] rain clouds of the sky.
13Out of the brightness of his presence
bolts of lightning[w] blazed forth.
14The LORD thundered[x] from heaven;
the voice of the Most High
resounded.
15He shot arrows[y] and scattered ⌞the
enemies⌟,
bolts of lightning and routed them.
16The valleys of the sea were exposed
and the foundations of the earth laid
bare
at the rebuke[z] of the LORD,
at the blast[a] of breath from his
nostrils.

17"He reached down from on high[b] and
took hold of me;
he drew[c] me out of deep waters.
18He rescued[d] me from my powerful
enemy,
from my foes, who were too strong
for me.
19They confronted me in the day of my
disaster,
but the LORD was my support.[e]
20He brought me out into a spacious[f]
place;
he rescued[g] me because he
delighted[h] in me.[i]

21"The LORD has dealt with me
according to my righteousness;[j]

17 [y]2Sa 20:6; [z]1Ki 11:36; 15:4; 2Ki 8:19; 2Ch 21:7; Ps 132:17; [a]2Sa 18:3
18 [b]1Ch 11:29; 27:11
19 [c]**1Sa 17:4**; [d]**1Sa 17:7**
21 [e]**1Sa 17:10**; [f]**1Sa 16:9**

Ch. 22

1 [a]**Ex 15:1**
2 [b]**1Sa 2:2**; [c]Ps 31:3; 91:2; [d]Ps 144:2
3 [e]**Dt 23:15; 32:37**; Ps 14:6; 31:2; 59:16; 71:7; 91:2; 94:22; Pr 10:29; Isa 25:4; Jer 16:19; Joel 3:16; [f]**Ge 15:1**; [g]**Dt 33:17; Lk 1:69**; [h]Ps 9:9; 52:7
4 [i]Ps 48:1; 96:4; 145:3
5 [j]Ps 69:14–15; Jnh 2:3
6 [k]Ps 116:3; Ac 2:24
7 [l]Ge 35:3; **Jdg 2:15**; 2Ch 15:4; Ps 4:1; 77:2; 120:1; Isa 26:16; [m]Ps 34:6,15; 116:4
8 [n]Jdg 5:4; Ps 97:4; [o]**Ex 19:18; Jdg 5:4**; Ps 68:8; 77:18; Jer 10:10; [p]Job 9:6; 26:11; Ps 75:3
9 [q]Ps 50:3; 97:3; Heb 12:29; **Rev 11:5**; [r]Isa 6:6; Eze 1:13; 10:2
10 [s]**Ex 19:9**; Lev 16:2; **Dt 33:26**; 1Ki 8:12; Job 26:9; Ps 104:3; Isa 19:1; Jer 4:13; Na 1:3
11 [t]**Ge 3:24; Ex 25:22**; [u]Ps 104:3
12 [v]**Ex 19:9**
13 [w]Job 37:3; Ps 77:18
14 [x]**1Sa 2:10**
15 [y]**Dt 32:23**
16 [z]Ps 6:1; 50:8,21; 106:9; Na 1:4; [a]**Ex 14:21**; Isa 30:33; 40:24
17 [b]Ps 144:7; [c]Ex 2:10
18 [d]Lk 1:71
19 [e]Ps 23:4
20 [f]Job 36:16; Ps 31:8; [g]Ps 118:5; [h]Ps 22:8; Isa 42:1; Mt 12:18; [i]**2Sa 15:26**
21 [j]**1Sa 26:23**

[b]*16* That is, about 7½ pounds (about 3.5 kilograms)
[c]*19* Or *son of Jair the weaver*
[d]*19* Hebrew and Septuagint; 1 Chron. 20:5 *son of Jair killed Lahmi the brother of Goliath*
[a]*3* *Horn* here symbolises strength.
[b]*6* Hebrew *Sheol*
[c]*8* Hebrew; Vulgate and Syriac (see also Psalm 18:7) *mountains*
[d]*11* Many Hebrew manuscripts (see also Psalm 18:10); most Hebrew manuscripts *appeared*
[e]*12* Septuagint and Vulgate (see also Psalm 18:11); Hebrew *massed*

according to the cleanness[k] of my hands[l] he has rewarded me.
22For I have kept[m] the ways of the LORD;
I have not done evil by turning from my God.
23All his laws are before me;[n]
I have not turned[o] away from his decrees.
24I have been blameless[p] before him
and have kept myself from sin.
25The LORD has rewarded me according to my righteousness,[q]
according to my cleanness[f] in his sight.

26"To the faithful you show yourself faithful,
to the blameless you show yourself blameless,
27to the pure[r] you show yourself pure,
but to the crooked you show yourself shrewd.[s]
28You save the humble,[t]
but your eyes are on the haughty[u] to bring them low.[v]
29You are my lamp,[w] O LORD;
the LORD turns my darkness into light.
30With your help I can advance against a troop;[g]
with my God I can scale a wall.

31"As for God, his way is perfect;[x]
the word of the LORD is flawless.[y]
He is a shield[z]
for all who take refuge in him.
32For who is God besides the LORD?
And who is the Rock[a] except our God?[b]
33It is God who arms me with strength[h]
and makes my way perfect.
34He makes my feet like the feet of a deer;[c]
he enables me to stand on the heights.[d]
35He trains my hands[e] for battle;
my arms can bend a bow[f] of bronze.
36You give me your shield[g] of victory;
you stoop down to make me great.
37You broaden the path[h] beneath me,
so that my ankles do not turn over.

38"I pursued my enemies and crushed them;
I did not turn back till they were destroyed.
39I crushed[i] them completely, and they could not rise;
they fell beneath my feet.
40You armed me with strength for battle;
you made my adversaries bow at my feet.[j]
41You made my enemies turn their backs[k] in flight,
and I destroyed my foes.
42They cried for help,[l] but there was no-one to save them—[m]
to the LORD, but he did not answer.[n]
43I beat them as fine as the dust[o] of the earth;
I pounded and trampled[p] them like mud[q] in the streets.

44"You have delivered[r] me from the attacks of my people;
you have preserved[s] me as the head of nations.
People[t] I did not know are subject to me,
45 and foreigners come cringing[u] to me;
as soon as they hear me, they obey me.[v]
46They all lose heart;
they come trembling[i] [w] from their strongholds.

47"The LORD lives! Praise be to my Rock!
Exalted[x] be God, the Rock, my Saviour![y]
48He is the God who avenges[z] me,[a]
who puts the nations under me,
49 who sets me free from my enemies.[b]
You exalted me[c] above my foes;
from violent men you rescued me.
50Therefore I will praise you, O LORD,
among the nations;
I will sing praises[d] to your name.[e]
51He gives his king great victories;[f]
he shows unfailing kindness to his anointed,[g]
to David[h] and his descendants for ever."[i]

The Last Words of David

23 These are the last words of David:

"The oracle of David son of Jesse,
the oracle of the man exalted[a] by the Most High,
the man anointed[b] by the God of Jacob,
Israel's singer of songs:[a]

21 [k]Ps 26:6; [l]Job 17:9; 22:30; 42:7–8; Ps 24:4
22 [m]Ge 18:19; Ps 128:1; Pr 8:32
23 [n]Dt 6:4–9; Ps 119:30–32; [o]Ps 119:102
24 [p]**Ge 6:9**; Eph 1:4
25 [q]**1Sa 26:23**
27 [r]Mt 5:8; [s]Lev 26:23–24
28 [t]**Ex 3:8**; 1Sa 2:8–9; Ps 72:12–13; [u]Ps 131:1; Pr 30:13; Da 4:31; Zep 3:11; [v]Isa 2:12,17; 5:15; **Lk 1:51**
29 [w]Ps 27:1; Isa 2:5; Mic 7:8; Rev 21:23; 22:5
31 [x]**Dt 32:4**; Mt 5:48; [y]Ps 12:6; 119:140; Pr 30:5–6; [z]**Ge 15:1**
32 [a]**1Sa 2:2**; [b]**2Sa 7:22**
34 [c]Isa 35:6; Hab 3:19; [d]**Dt 32:13**
35 [e]Ps 144:1; [f]Ps 7:12; 11:2; Zec 9:13
36 [g]Eph 6:16
37 [h]Pr 4:11
39 [i]Ps 44:5; 110:6; Mal 4:3
40 [j]**Jos 10:24**; **1Ki 5:3**
41 [k]**Ex 23:27**
42 [l]Isa 1:15; [m]Ps 50:22; [n]**1Sa 14:37**
43 [o]1Ki 20:10; 2Ki 13:7; Isa 41:2; Am 1:3; [p]Ps 7:5; Isa 41:25; Mic 7:10; Zec 10:5; [q]Isa 5:25; 10:6; 22:5; Mic 7:10
44 [r]**Ex 11:3**; **2Sa 3:1**; [s]Dt 28:13; [t]**2Sa 8:1–14**; Isa 55:3–5
45 [u]Ps 66:3; 81:15; [v]**Dt 33:29**
46 [w]Mic 7:17
47 [x]**Ex 15:2**; [y]Dt 32:15; Ps 18:31; 89:26; 95:1
48 [z]**Nu 31:3**; [a]Ps 144:2
49 [b]Ps 140:1,4; [c]Ps 27:6
50 [d]Ps 9:11; 47:6; 68:4; [e]Ro 15:9*
51 [f]Ps 21:1; 144:9–10; [g]1Sa 16:13; Ps 89:20; Ac 13:23; [h]**2Sa 7:13**; [i]Ps 89:24,29

Ch. 23
1 [a]**Ex 11:3**; Ps 78:70–71; 89:27; [b]1Sa 2:10,35; Ps 18:50; 20:6; 84:9; Isa 45:1; Hab 3:13

f25 Hebrew; Septuagint and Vulgate (see also Psalm 18:24) *to the cleanness of my hands*
g30 Or *can run through a barricade*
h33 Dead Sea Scrolls, some Septuagint manuscripts, Vulgate and Syriac (see also Psalm 18:32); Masoretic Text *who is my strong refuge*
i46 Some Septuagint manuscripts and Vulgate (see also Psalm 18:45); Masoretic Text *they arm themselves.*
a1 Or *Israel's beloved singer*

2"The Spirit[c] of the LORD spoke through
me;
his word was on my tongue.
3The God of Israel spoke,
the Rock[d] of Israel said to me:
'When one rules over men in
righteousness,[e]
when he rules in the fear[f] of God,[g]
4he is like the light[h] of morning[i] at
sunrise[j]
on a cloudless morning,
like the brightness after rain[k]
that brings the grass from the earth.'
5"Is not my house right with God?
Has he not made with me an
everlasting covenant,[l]
arranged and secured in every part?
Will he not bring to fruition my
salvation
and grant me my every desire?
6But evil men are all to be cast aside like
thorns,[m]
which are not gathered with the
hand.
7Whoever touches thorns
uses a tool of iron or the shaft of a
spear;
they are burned up where they lie."

David's Mighty Men

23:8–39pp—1Ch 11:10–41

8These are the names of David's
mighty men:[n]
Josheb-Basshebeth,[b][o] a Tahkemo-
nite,[c] was chief of the Three; he raised
his spear against eight hundred men,
whom he killed[d] in one encounter.
9Next to him was Eleazar son of
Dodai[p] the Ahohite.[q] As one of the three
mighty men, he was with David when
they taunted the Philistines gathered ⌊at
Pas Dammim⌋[e] for battle. Then the men
of Israel retreated, 10but he stood his
ground and struck down the Philistines
till his hand grew tired and froze to the
sword. The LORD brought about a great
victory that day. The troops returned to
Eleazar, but only to strip the dead.
11Next to him was Shammah son of
Agee the Hararite. When the Philistines
banded together at a place where there
was a field full of lentils, Israel's troops
fled from them. 12But Shammah took his
stand in the middle of the field. He
defended it and struck the Philistines
down, and the LORD brought about a
great victory.
13During harvest time, three of the
thirty chief men came down to David at
the cave of Adullam,[r] while a band of
Philistines was encamped in the Valley
of Rephaim.[s] 14At that time David was in
the stronghold,[t] and the Philistine garri-
son was at Bethlehem.[u] 15David longed
for water and said, "Oh, that someone
would get me a drink of water from the
well near the gate of Bethlehem!" 16So
the three mighty men broke through the
Philistine lines, drew water from the
well near the gate of Bethlehem and
carried it back to David. But he refused
to drink it; instead, he poured[v] it out
before the LORD. 17"Far be it from me, O
LORD, to do this!" he said. "Is it not the
blood[w] of men who went at the risk of
their lives?" And David would not
drink it.
Such were the exploits of the three
mighty men.
18Abishai[x] the brother of Joab son of
Zeruiah was chief of the Three.[f] He
raised his spear against three hundred
men, whom he killed, and so he became
as famous as the Three. 19Was he not
held in greater honour than the Three?
He became their commander, even
though he was not included among
them.
20Benaiah[y] son of Jehoiada was a
valiant fighter from Kabzeel,[z] who per-
formed great exploits. He struck down
two of Moab's best men. He also went
down into a pit on a snowy day and
killed a lion. 21And he struck down a
huge Egyptian. Although the Egyptian
had a spear in his hand, Benaiah went
against him with a club. He snatched
the spear from the Egyptian's hand and
killed him with his own spear. 22Such
were the exploits of Benaiah son of
Jehoiada; he too was as famous as the
three mighty men. 23He was held in
greater honour than any of the Thirty,
but he was not included among the
Three. And David put him in charge of
his bodyguard.
24Among the Thirty were:
Asahel[a] the brother of Joab,
Elhanan son of Dodo from
Bethlehem,
25Shammah the Harodite,[b]
Elika the Harodite,
26Helez[c] the Paltite,
Ira[d] son of Ikkesh from Tekoa,

2 [c]Mt 22:43; Mk 12:36; 2Pe 1:21
3 [d]Dt 32:4; **1Sa 2:2**; Ps 18:31; [e]Ps 72:3; [f]**Ge 42:18**; [g]Isa 11:1–5
4 [h]Jn 1:5; [i]Ps 119:147; 130:6; Pr 4:18; [j]**Jdg 5:31**; Mt 13:43; [k]**Dt 32:2**
5 [l]**Ge 9:16**; Ps 89:29
6 [m]Isa 5:6; 9:18; 10:17; 27:4; 33:12; Mic 7:4; Na 1:10; Mt 13:40–41
8 [n]**2Sa 17:10**; [o]1Ch 27:2
9 [p]1Ch 27:4; [q]1Ch 8:4
13 [r]**Ge 38:1; Jos 12:15**; [s]**Jos 17:15**
14 [t]1Sa 22:4–5; **2Sa 5:17**; [u]Ru 1:19
16 [v]**Ge 35:14**
17 [w]Lev 17:10–12
18 [x]**1Sa 26:6**
20 [y]**2Sa 8:18**; 1Ch 27:5; [z]Jos 15:21
24 [a]**2Sa 2:18**
25 [b]Jdg 7:1
26 [c]1Ch 27:10; [d]1Ch 27:9

b8 Hebrew; some Septuagint manuscripts suggest *Ish-Bosheth*, that is, *Esh-Baal* (see also 1 Chron. 11:11 *Jashobeam*).
c8 Probably a variant of *Hacmonite* (see 1 Chron. 11:11)
d8 Some Septuagint manuscripts (see also 1 Chron. 11:11); Hebrew and other Septuagint manuscripts *Three; it was Adino the Eznite who killed eight hundred men*
e9 See 1 Chron. 11:13; Hebrew *gathered there*.
f18 Most Hebrew manuscripts (see also 1 Chron. 11:20); two Hebrew manuscripts and Syriac *Thirty*

27 Abiezer[e] from Anathoth,[f]
Mebunnai[g] the Hushathite,
28 Zalmon the Ahohite,
Maharai[g] the Netophathite,[h]
29 Heled[h] [i] son of Baanah the
Netophathite,
Ithai son of Ribai from Gibeah[j] in
Benjamin,
30 Benaiah the Pirathonite,[k]
Hiddai[i] from the ravines of
Gaash,[l]
31 Abi-Albon the Arbathite,
Azmaveth the Barhumite,[m]
32 Eliahba the Shaalbonite,
the sons of Jashen,
Jonathan 33 son of[j] Shammah the
Hararite,
Ahiam son of Sharar[k] the
Hararite,
34 Eliphelet son of Ahasbai the
Maacathite,[n]
Eliam[o] son of Ahithophel[p] the
Gilonite,
35 Hezro the Carmelite,[q]
Paarai the Arbite,
36 Igal son of Nathan from Zobah,[r]
the son of Hagri,[l]
37 Zelek the Ammonite,
Naharai the Beerothite,[s] the
armour-bearer of Joab son of
Zeruiah,
38 Ira the Ithrite,[t]
Gareb the Ithrite
39 and Uriah[u] the Hittite.
There were thirty-seven in all.

David Counts the Fighting Men

24:1–17pp—1Ch 21:1–17

24 Again[a] the anger of the LORD
burned against Israel,[b] and he
incited David against them, saying, "Go
and take a census of[c] Israel and Judah."
2 So the king said to Joab[d] and the
army commanders[a] with him, "Go
throughout the tribes of Israel from Dan
to Beersheba[e] and enrol[f] the fighting
men, so that I may know how many
there are."
3 But Joab[g] replied to the king, "May
the LORD your God multiply the troops a
hundred times over,[h] and may the eyes
of my lord the king see it. But why does
my lord the king want to do such a
thing?"
4 The king's word, however, over-
ruled Joab and the army commanders;
so they left the presence of the king to
enrol the fighting men of Israel.
5 After crossing the Jordan, they
camped near Aroer,[i] south of the town
in the gorge, and then went through
Gad and on to Jazer.[j] 6 They went to
Gilead and the region of Tahtim Hod-
shi, and on to Dan Jaan and around
towards Sidon.[k] 7 Then they went to-
wards the fortress of Tyre[l] and all the
towns of the Hivites[m] and Canaanites.
Finally, they went on to Beersheba[n] in
the Negev[o] of Judah.
8 After they had gone through the en-
tire land, they came back to Jerusalem at
the end of nine months and twenty
days.
9 Joab reported the number of the
fighting men to the king: In Israel there
were eight hundred thousand able-
bodied men who could handle a sword,
and in Judah five hundred thousand.[p]
10 David was conscience-stricken[q]
after he had counted the fighting men,
and he said to the LORD, "I have sinned[r]
greatly in what I have done. Now, O
LORD, I beg you, take away the guilt of
your servant. I have done a very foolish
thing.[s]"
11 Before David got up the next morn-
ing, the word of the LORD had come to
Gad[t] the prophet, David's seer:[u] 12 "Go
and tell David, 'This is what the LORD
says: I am giving you three options.
Choose one of them for me to carry out
against you.'"
13 So Gad went to David and said to
him, "Shall there come upon you three[b]
years of famine[v] in your land? Or three
months of fleeing from your enemies
while they pursue you? Or three days of
plague[w] in your land? Now then, think
it over and decide how I should answer
the one who sent me."
14 David said to Gad, "I am in deep
distress. Let us fall into the hands of the
LORD, for his mercy[x] is great; but do not
let me fall into the hands of men."
15 So the LORD sent a plague on Israel
from that morning until the end of the
time designated, and seventy thousand
of the people from Dan to Beersheba
died.[y] 16 When the angel stretched out

27 [e]1Ch 27:12; [f]**Jos 21:18**
28 [g]1Ch 27:13; [h]2Ki 25:23; Ezr 2:22; Ne 7:26; Jer 40:8
29 [i]1Ch 27:15; [j]**Jos 15:57**
30 [k]**Jdg 12:13**; [l]Jos 24:30
31 [m]2Sa 3:16
34 [n]**Dt 3:14**; [o]**2Sa 11:3**; [p]**2Sa 15:12**
35 [q]**Jos 12:22**
36 [r]**1Sa 14:47**
37 [s]**Jos 9:17**
38 [t]1Ch 2:53
39 [u]2Sa 11:3

Ch. 24

1 [a]**Jos 9:15**; [b]Job 1:6; Zec 3:1; [c]**Ex 30:12**; 1Ch 27:23
2 [d]**2Sa 20:23**; [e]**2Sa 3:10**; [f]2Ch 2:17; 17:14; 25:5
3 [g]**2Sa 2:18**; [h]**Dt 1:11**
5 [i]**Jos 13:9**; [j]**Nu 21:32**
6 [k]**Ge 10:19**; Jdg 1:31
7 [l]**Jos 19:29**; [m]**Ex 3:8**; [n]Ge 21:31; [o]**Dt 1:7**
9 [p]**Nu 1:44–46**
10 [q]**1Sa 24:5**; [r]**Nu 22:34**; [s]**Nu 12:11**
11 [t]**1Sa 22:5**; [u]1Sa 9:9
13 [v]Dt 28:38–42, 48; **32:24**; Eze 14:21; [w]**Ex 5:3**; **30:12**; **Lev 26:25**; Dt 28:21–22, 27–28,35
14 [x]Ne 9:28; Ps 4:1; 51:1; 86:5; 103:8,13; 119:132; 130:4; Isa 54:7; 55:7; Jer 33:8; 42:12; Da 9:9
15 [y]1Ch 27:24

[g]27 Hebrew; some Septuagint manuscripts (see also 1 Chron. 11:29) *Sibbecai*

[h]29 Some Hebrew manuscripts and Vulgate (see also 1 Chron. 11:30); most Hebrew manuscripts *Heleb*

[i]30 Hebrew; some Septuagint manuscripts (see also 1 Chron. 11:32) *Hurai*

[j]33 Some Septuagint manuscripts (see also 1 Chron. 11:34); Hebrew does not have *son of*.

[k]33 Hebrew; some Septuagint manuscripts (see also 1 Chron. 11:35) *Sacar*

[l]36 Some Septuagint manuscripts (see also 1 Chron. 11:38); Hebrew *Haggadi*

[a]2 Septuagint (see also verse 4 and 1 Chron. 21:2); Hebrew *Joab the army commander*

[b]13 Septuagint (see also 1 Chron. 21:12); Hebrew *seven*

his hand to destroy Jerusalem, the LORD
was grieved[z] because of the calamity
and said to the angel who was afflicting
the people, "Enough! Withdraw your
hand." The angel of the LORD[a] was then
at the threshing-floor of Araunah the
Jebusite.
17 When David saw the angel who was
striking down the people, he said to the
LORD, "I am the one who has sinned and
done wrong. These are but sheep.[b]
What have they done?[c] Let your hand
fall upon me and my family."[d]

David Builds an Altar

24:18–25pp—1Ch 21:18–26

18 On that day Gad went to David and
said to him, "Go up and build an altar to
the LORD on the threshing-floor of
Araunah[e] the Jebusite." 19 So David
went up, as the LORD had commanded
through Gad. 20 When Araunah looked
and saw the king and his men coming
towards him, he went out and bowed
down before the king with his face to
the ground.
21 Araunah said, "Why has my lord
the king come to his servant?"

16 [z]Ge 6:6; [a]Ge 16:7; 19:13; Ex 12:23; Ac 12:23
17 [b]Ps 74:1; 100:3; Jer 49:20; [c]Ge 18:23; [d]Jnh 1:12
18 [e]Ge 22:2; 2Ch 3:1
21 [f]Nu 16:44–50
22 [g]1Sa 6:14
23 [h]Ge 23:11
24 [i]Mal 1:13–14; [j]Ge 23:16
25 [k]1Sa 7:17; [l]2Sa 21:14

"To buy your threshing-floor," David
answered, "so that I can build an altar to
the LORD, that the plague on the people
may be stopped."[f]
22 Araunah said to David, "Let my
lord the king take whatever pleases him
and offer it up. Here are oxen[g] for the
burnt offering, and here are threshing-
sledges and ox yokes for the wood. 23 O
king, Araunah gives[h] all this to the
king." Araunah also said to him, "May
the LORD your God accept you."
24 But the king replied to Araunah,
"No, I insist on paying you for it. I will
not sacrifice to the LORD my God burnt
offerings that cost me nothing."[i]
So David bought the threshing-floor
and the oxen and paid fifty shekels[c][j] of
silver for them. 25 David built an altar[k] to
the LORD there and sacrificed burnt
offerings and fellowship offerings.[d]
Then the LORD answered prayer[l] on
behalf of the land, and the plague on
Israel was stopped.

[c]24 That is, about 1¼ pounds (about 0.6 kilogram)
[d]25 Traditionally *peace offerings*

1 Kings

Adonijah Sets Himself Up as King

1 When King David was old and well
advanced in years, he could not
keep warm even when they put covers
over him. 2So his servants said to him,
"Let us look for a young virgin to attend
the king and take care of him. She can lie
beside him so that our lord the king may
keep warm."
3Then they searched throughout
Israel for a beautiful girl and found
Abishag,[a] a Shunammite,[b] and brought
her to the king. 4The girl was very
beautiful; she took care of the king and
waited on him, but the king had no
intimate relations with her.
5Now Adonijah,[c] whose mother was
Haggith, put himself forward and said,
"I will be king." So he got chariots[d] and
horses[a] ready, with fifty men to run
ahead of him. 6(His father had never
interfered[e] with him by asking, "Why
do you behave as you do?" He was also
very handsome and was born next after
Absalom.)
7Adonijah conferred with Joab[f] son of
Zeruiah and with Abiathar[g] the priest,
and they gave him their support. 8But
Zadok[h] the priest, Benaiah[i] son of
Jehoiada, Nathan[j] the prophet, Shimei[k]
and Rei[b] and David's special guard[l] did
not join Adonijah.
9Adonijah then sacrificed sheep, cattle
and fattened calves at the Stone of
Zoheleth near En Rogel.[m] He invited all
his brothers, the king's sons,[n] and all
the men of Judah who were royal of-
ficials, 10but he did not invite[o] Nathan
the prophet or Benaiah or the special
guard or his brother Solomon.[p]
11Then Nathan asked Bathsheba,[q]
Solomon's mother, "Have you not
heard that Adonijah,[r] the son of Hag-
gith, has become king without our lord
David's knowing it? 12Now then, let me
advise[s] you how you can save your own
life and the life of your son Solomon.
13Go in to King David and say to him,
'My lord the king, did you not swear[t] to
me your servant: "Surely Solomon your
son shall be king after me, and he will sit
on my throne"? Why then has Adonijah
become king?' 14While you are still there
talking to the king, I will come in and
confirm what you have said."
15So Bathsheba went to see the aged
king in his room, where Abishag[u]
the Shunammite was attending him.
16Bathsheba bowed low and knelt
before the king.
"What is it you want?" the king
asked.
17She said to him, "My lord, you
yourself swore[v] to me your servant by
the LORD your God: 'Solomon your son
shall become king after me, and he will
sit on my throne.' 18But now Adonijah
has become king, and you, my lord the
king, do not know about it. 19He has
sacrificed[w] great numbers of cattle, fat-
tened calves, and sheep, and has in-
vited all the king's sons, Abiathar the
priest and Joab the commander of the
army, but he has not invited Solomon
your servant. 20My lord the king, the
eyes of all Israel are on you, to learn
from you who will sit on the throne of
my lord the king after him. 21Otherwise,
as soon as my lord the king is laid to
rest[x] with his fathers, I and my son
Solomon will be treated as criminals."
22While she was still speaking with
the king, Nathan the prophet arrived.
23And they told the king, "Nathan the
prophet is here." So he went before the
king and bowed with his face to the
ground.
24Nathan said, "Have you, my lord
the king, declared that Adonijah shall
be king after you, and that he will sit on
your throne? 25Today he has gone down
and sacrificed great numbers of cattle,
fattened calves, and sheep. He has in-
vited all the king's sons, the comman-
ders of the army and Abiathar the
priest. At this very moment they are
eating and drinking with him and say-
ing, 'Long live King Adonijah!' 26But me
your servant, and Zadok the priest, and
Benaiah son of Jehoiada, and your

Ch. 1
3 [a]ver 15; **2Sa 3:7;** 1Ki 2:17,22; [b]**Jos 19:18**
5 [c]**2Sa 3:4;** [d]**1Sa 8:11**
6 [e]1Sa 3:13
7 [f]**2Sa 2:13,**18; [g]**1Sa 22:20**
8 [h]**1Sa 2:35; 2Sa 8:17;** [i]**2Sa 8:18;** [j]**2Sa 7:2;** [k]1Ki 4:18; [l]2Sa 23:8
9 [m]**2Sa 17:17;** [n]1Ch 29:24
10 [o]ver 26; [p]**2Sa 12:24**
11 [q]2Sa 12:24; [r]**2Sa 3:4**
12 [s]Pr 15:22
13 [t]ver 17,30
15 [u]**ver 3**
17 [v]**ver 13**
19 [w]ver 9
21 [x]**Ge 15:15;** 1Ki 2:10

[a]5 Or *charioteers* [b]8 Or *and his friends*

servant Solomon he did not invite.[y] 27Is
this something my lord the king has
done without letting his servants know
who should sit on the throne of my lord
the king after him?"

David Makes Solomon King

1:28–53pp—1Ch 29:21–25

28Then King David said, "Call in Bath-
sheba." So she came into the king's
presence and stood before him.
29The king then took an oath: "As
surely as the LORD lives, who has deli-
vered me out of every trouble,[z] 30I will
surely carry out today what I swore[a] to
you by the LORD, the God of Israel:
Solomon your son shall be king after
me, and he will sit on my throne in my
place."
31Then Bathsheba bowed low with
her face to the ground and, kneeling
before the king, said, "May my lord
King David live for ever!"
32King David said, "Call in Zadok[b] the
priest, Nathan the prophet and Benaiah
son of Jehoiada." When they came be-
fore the king, 33he said to them: "Take
your lord's servants with you and set
Solomon my son on my own mule[c] and
take him down to Gihon.[d] 34There shall
Zadok the priest and Nathan the
prophet anoint[e] him king over Israel.
Blow the trumpet[f] and shout, 'Long live
King Solomon!' 35Then you are to go up
with him, and he is to come and sit on
my throne and reign in my place. I have
appointed him ruler over Israel and
Judah."
36Benaiah son of Jehoiada answered
the king, "Amen! May the LORD, the
God of my lord the king, so declare it.
37As the LORD was with my lord the
king, so may he be with[g] Solomon to
make his throne even greater[h] than the
throne of my lord King David!"
38So Zadok[i] the priest, Nathan the
prophet, Benaiah son of Jehoiada, the
Kerethites[j] and the Pelethites went
down and put Solomon on King David's
mule and escorted him to Gihon.[k]
39Zadok the priest took the horn of oil[l]
from the sacred tent[m] and anointed
Solomon. Then they sounded the trum-
pet[n] and all the people shouted,[o] "Long
live King Solomon!" 40And all the
people went up after him, playing
flutes[p] and rejoicing greatly, so that the
ground shook with the sound.
41Adonijah and all the guests who
were with him heard it as they were
finishing their feast. On hearing the
sound of the trumpet, Joab asked,
"What's the meaning of all the noise in
the city?"[q]
42Even as he was speaking, Jonathan[r]
son of Abiathar the priest arrived. Ado-
nijah said, "Come in. A worthy man
like you must be bringing good news."[s]
43"Not at all!" Jonathan answered.
"Our lord King David has made Solo-
mon king. 44The king has sent with him
Zadok the priest, Nathan the prophet,
Benaiah son of Jehoiada, the Kerethites
and the Pelethites, and they have put
him on the king's mule, 45and Zadok the
priest and Nathan the prophet have
anointed him king at Gihon. From there
they have gone up cheering, and the
city resounds[t] with it. That's the noise
you hear. 46Moreover, Solomon has
taken his seat[u] on the royal throne.
47Also, the royal officials have come to
congratulate our lord King David,
saying, 'May your God make Solomon's
name more famous than yours and his
throne greater[v] than yours!' And the
king bowed in worship on his bed 48and
said, 'Praise be to the LORD, the God of
Israel, who has allowed my eyes to see a
successor[w] on my throne today.'"
49At this, all Adonijah's guests rose in
alarm and dispersed. 50But Adonijah, in
fear of Solomon, went and took hold of
the horns[x] of the altar. 51Then Solomon
was told, "Adonijah is afraid of King
Solomon and is clinging to the horns of
the altar. He says, 'Let King Solomon
swear to me today that he will not put
his servant to death with the sword.'"
52Solomon replied, "If he shows him-
self to be a worthy man, not a hair[y] of his
head will fall to the ground; but if evil is
found in him, he will die." 53Then King
Solomon sent men, and they brought
him down from the altar. And Adonijah
came and bowed down to King Solo-
mon, and Solomon said, "Go to your
home."

David's Charge to Solomon

2:10–12pp—1Ch 29:26–28

2 When the time drew near for
David to die,[a] he gave a charge to
Solomon his son.
2"I am about to go the way of all the
earth,"[b] he said. "So be strong,[c] show
yourself a man, 3and observe[d] what the
LORD your God requires: Walk in his
ways, and keep his decrees and com-
mands, his laws and requirements, as
written in the Law of Moses, so that you
may prosper[e] in all you do and
wherever you go, 4and that the LORD
may keep his promise[f] to me: 'If your

26 [y]ver 10
29 [z]2Sa 4:9
30 [a]ver 13; 1Ch 23:1
32 [b]1Sa 2:35
33 [c]Jdg 10:4; Zec 9:9; [d]ver 38; 2Ch 32:30; 33:14
34 [e]1Sa 2:35; 10:1; [f]2Sa 15:10
37 [g]Jos 1:5,17; [h]ver 47
38 [i]ver 8; [j]1Sa 30:14; 2Sa 15:18; [k]ver 33
39 [l]Ex 29:7; 1Sa 10:1; 2Ki 11:12; Ps 89:20; [m]Ex 26:1; 27:21; [n]2Sa 15:10; 2Ki 11:14; [o]ver 34; Nu 23:21; Ps 47:5; Zec 9:9
40 [p]1Sa 10:5
41 [q]2Ch 23:12–13
42 [r]2Sa 15:27,36; [s]2Sa 18:26
45 [t]ver 40
46 [u]Dt 17:18
47 [v]ver 37
48 [w]1Ki 3:6
50 [x]Ex 27:2
52 [y]1Sa 14:45

Ch. 2

1 [a]Ge 27:2; Nu 27:13
2 [b]Jos 23:14; [c]Jos 1:6
3 [d]Dt 4:6; 10:12; 17:14–20; Jos 1:7; [e]1Ch 22:13
4 [f]2Sa 7:13,15; 2Ch 23:3

descendants watch how they live, and if they walk faithfully[g] before me with all their heart and soul, you will never fail to have a man on the throne of Israel.'

5"Now you yourself know what Joab[h] son of Zeruiah did to me—what he did to the two commanders of Israel's armies, Abner[i] son of Ner and Amasa[j] son of Jether. He killed them, shedding their blood in peacetime as if in battle, and with that blood stained the belt round his waist and the sandals on his feet. 6Deal with him according to your wisdom,[k] but do not let his grey head go down to the grave[a] in peace.

7"But show kindness[l] to the sons of Barzillai[m] of Gilead and let them be among those who eat at your table.[n] They stood by me when I fled from your brother Absalom.

8"And remember, you have with you Shimei[o] son of Gera, the Benjamite from Bahurim, who called down bitter curses on me the day I went to Mahanaim.[p] When he came down to meet me at the Jordan, I swore[q] to him by the LORD: 'I will not put you to death by the sword.' 9But now, do not consider him innocent. You are a man of wisdom;[r] you will know what to do to him. Bring his grey head down to the grave in blood."

10Then David rested with his fathers and was buried[s] in the City of David.[t] 11He had reigned[u] for forty years over Israel—seven years in Hebron and thirty-three in Jerusalem. 12So Solomon sat on the throne[v] of his father David, and his rule was firmly established.[w]

Solomon's Throne Established

13Now Adonijah,[x] the son of Haggith, went to Bathsheba, Solomon's mother. Bathsheba asked him, "Do you come peacefully?"[y]

He answered, "Yes, peacefully." 14Then he added, "I have something to say to you."

"You may say it," she replied.

15"As you know," he said, "the kingdom was mine. All Israel looked to me as their king. But things changed, and the kingdom has gone to my brother; for it has come to him from the LORD. 16Now I have one request to make of you. Do not refuse me."

"You may make it," she said.

17So he continued, "Please ask King Solomon—he will not refuse you—to give me Abishag[z] the Shunammite as my wife."

18"Very well," Bathsheba replied, "I will speak to the king for you."

19When Bathsheba went to King Solomon to speak to him for Adonijah, the king stood up to meet her, bowed down to her and sat down on his throne. He had a throne brought for the king's mother,[a] and she sat down at his right hand.[b]

20"I have one small request to make of you," she said. "Do not refuse me."

The king replied, "Make it, my mother; I will not refuse you."

21So she said, "Let Abishag[c] the Shunammite be given in marriage to your brother Adonijah."

22King Solomon answered his mother, "Why do you request Abishag[d] the Shunammite for Adonijah? You might as well request the kingdom for him—after all, he is my older brother[e]—yes, for him and for Abiathar[f] the priest and Joab son of Zeruiah!"

23Then King Solomon swore by the LORD: "May God deal with me, be it ever so severely,[g] if Adonijah does not pay with his life for this request! 24And now, as surely as the LORD lives—he who has established me securely on the throne of my father David and has founded a dynasty for me as he promised[h]—Adonijah shall be put to death today!" 25So King Solomon gave orders to Benaiah[i] son of Jehoiada, and he struck down Adonijah and he died.[j]

26To Abiathar[k] the priest the king said, "Go back to your fields in Anathoth.[l] You deserve to die, but I will not put you to death now, because you carried the ark[m] of the Sovereign LORD before my father David and shared all my father's hardships."[n] 27So Solomon removed Abiathar from the priesthood of the LORD, fulfilling[o] the word the LORD had spoken at Shiloh about the house of Eli.

28When the news reached Joab, who had conspired with Adonijah though not with Absalom, he fled to the tent of the LORD and took hold of the horns[p] of the altar. 29King Solomon was told that Joab had fled to the tent of the LORD and was beside the altar.[q] Then Solomon ordered Benaiah[r] son of Jehoiada, "Go, strike him down!"

30So Benaiah entered the tent[s] of the LORD and said to Joab, "The king says, 'Come out!'[t]"

But he answered, "No, I will die here."

Benaiah reported to the king, "This is how Joab answered me."

31Then the king commanded Benaiah,

4 [g]2Ki 18:3–6; 20:3; Ps 26:1–3; 132:12
5 [h]2Sa 2:18; [i]1Sa 14:50; 2Sa 3:27; [j]2Sa 17:25
6 [k]ver 9
7 [l]Ge 40:14; [m]2Sa 17:27; 19:31–39; [n]2Sa 9:7
8 [o]ver 36–46; 2Sa 16:5–13; [p]Ge 32:2; [q]2Sa 19:18–23
9 [r]ver 6
10 [s]Ac 2:29; [t]2Sa 5:7
11 [u]2Sa 5:4–5
12 [v]1Ch 17:14; 29:23; 2Ch 9:8; [w]ver 46; 2Ch 1:1; 12:13; 17:1; 21:4
13 [x]2Sa 3:4; [y]1Sa 16:4
17 [z]1Ki 1:3
19 [a]1Ki 15:13; 2Ki 10:13; 24:15; 2Ch 15:16; Jer 13:18; 22:26; 29:2; [b]Ps 45:9
21 [c]1Ki 1:3
22 [d]Ge 22:24; 1Ki 1:3; [e]1Ch 3:2; [f]1Sa 22:20
23 [g]Ru 1:17
24 [h]2Sa 7:11
25 [i]2Sa 8:18; [j]2Sa 12:10
26 [k]1Sa 22:20; [l]Jos 21:18; [m]2Sa 15:24; [n]2Sa 15:14
27 [o]1Sa 2:27–36
28 [p]Ex 27:2
29 [q]Ex 21:14; [r]ver 25
30 [s]2Ki 11:15; [t]Ex 21:14

[a]6 Hebrew *Sheol*; also in verse 9

"Do as he says. Strike him down and bury him, and so clear me and my father's house of the guilt of the innocent blood[u] that Joab shed. 32The LORD will repay[v] him for the blood he shed,[w] because without the knowledge of my father David he attacked two men and killed them with the sword. Both of them—Abner son of Ner, commander of Israel's army, and Amasa[x] son of Jether, commander of Judah's army—were better[y] men and more upright than he. 33May the guilt of their blood rest on the head of Joab and his descendants for ever. But on David and his descendants, his house and his throne, may there be the LORD's peace for ever."

34So Benaiah[z] son of Jehoiada went up and struck down Joab[a] and killed him, and he was buried on his own land[b] in the desert. 35The king put Benaiah[b] son of Jehoiada over the army in Joab's position and replaced Abiathar with Zadok[c] the priest.

36Then the king sent for Shimei[d] and said to him, "Build yourself a house in Jerusalem and live there, but do not go anywhere else. 37The day you leave and cross the Kidron Valley,[e] you can be sure you will die; your blood will be on your own head."[f]

38Shimei answered the king, "What you say is good. Your servant will do as my lord the king has said." And Shimei stayed in Jerusalem for a long time.

39But three years later, two of Shimei's slaves ran off to Achish[g] son of Maacah, king of Gath, and Shimei was told, "Your slaves are in Gath." 40At this, he saddled his donkey and went to Achish at Gath in search of his slaves. So Shimei went away and brought the slaves back from Gath.

41When Solomon was told that Shimei had gone from Jerusalem to Gath and had returned, 42the king summoned Shimei and said to him, "Did I not make you swear by the LORD and warn[h] you, 'On the day you leave to go anywhere else, you can be sure you will die'? At that time you said to me, 'What you say is good. I will obey.' 43Why then did you not keep your oath to the LORD and obey the command I gave you?"

44The king also said to Shimei, "You know in your heart all the wrong[i] you did to my father David. Now the LORD will repay you for your wrongdoing. 45But King Solomon will be blessed, and David's throne will remain secure[j] before the LORD for ever."

46Then the king gave the order to Benaiah[k] son of Jehoiada, and he went out and struck Shimei[l] down and killed him.

The kingdom was now firmly established[m] in Solomon's hands.

Solomon Asks for Wisdom

3:4–15pp—2Ch 1:2–13

3 Solomon made an alliance with Pharaoh king of Egypt and married[a] his daughter.[b] He brought her to the City of David[c] until he finished building his palace[d] and the temple of the LORD, and the wall around Jerusalem. 2The people, however, were still sacrificing at the high places,[e] because a temple had not yet been built for the Name[f] of the LORD. 3Solomon showed his love[g] for the LORD by walking[h] according to the statutes[i] of his father David, except that he offered sacrifices and burned incense on the high places.[j]

4The king went to Gibeon[k] to offer sacrifices, for that was the most important high place, and Solomon offered a thousand burnt offerings on that altar. 5At Gibeon the LORD appeared[l] to Solomon during the night in a dream,[m] and God said, "Ask[n] for whatever you want me to give you."

6Solomon answered, "You have shown great kindness to your servant, my father David, because he was faithful[o] to you and righteous and upright in heart. You have continued this great kindness to him and have given him a son[p] to sit on his throne this very day.

7"Now, O LORD my God, you have made your servant king in place of my father David. But I am only a little child[q] and do not know how to carry out my duties. 8Your servant is here among the people you have chosen,[r] a great people, too numerous to count or number.[s] 9So give your servant a discerning[t] heart to govern your people and to distinguish[u] between right and wrong. For who is able[v] to govern this great people of yours?"

10The Lord was pleased that Solomon had asked for this. 11So God said to him, "Since you have asked[w] for this and not for long life or wealth for yourself, nor have asked for the death of your enemies but for discernment[x] in administering justice, 12I will do what you have asked.[y] I will give you a wise[z] and discerning heart, so that there will never have been anyone like you, nor will there ever be. 13Moreover, I will

31 [u]**Dt 19:13**
32 [v]Jdg 9:57; [w]**Ge 4:14; Jdg 9:24;** [x]**2Sa 17:25;** [y]2Ch 21:13
34 [z]ver 25; [a]**2Sa 2:18**
35 [b]**2Sa 8:18;** [c]**1Sa 2:35**
36 [d]**2Sa 16:5**
37 [e]**2Sa 15:23;** Jn 18:1; [f]**Lev 20:9**
39 [g]1Sa 27:2
42 [h]**2Sa 19:23**
44 [i]2Sa 16:5–13
45 [j]**2Sa 7:13**
46 [k]**2Sa 8:18;** [l]**ver 8;** [m]**ver 12**

Ch. 3

1 [a]1Ki 7:8; 11:1–13; [b]1Ki 9:24; 2Ch 8:11; [c]2Sa 5:7; 1Ki 2:10; [d]**2Sa 7:2;** 1Ki 9:10
2 [e]Lev 17:3–5; **26:30;** Dt 12:14; 1Ki 15:14; 22:43; [f]**Dt 14:23**
3 [g]Dt 6:5; Ps 31:23; 145:20; [h]**Dt 10:12; Jos 1:7;** [i]**Dt 17:19; 1Ki 14:8;** [j]ver 2; Lev 17:3–5; 2Ki 12:3; 15:4,35; 16:4; 21:3
4 [k]**Jos 9:3**
5 [l]1Ki 9:2; 11:9; [m]**Mt 27:19;** [n]**Mt 7:7**
6 [o]**Ge 17:1;** [p]1Ki 1:48
7 [q]Nu 27:17; 1Ch 22:5; 29:1; Jer 1:6
8 [r]**Dt 7:6;** [s]**Ge 12:2; 1Ch 27:23**
9 [t]**2Sa 14:17;** Jas 1:5; [u]**Dt 1:16;** Heb 5:14; [v]2Co 2:16
11 [w]Jas 4:3; [x]1Ch 22:12
12 [y]1Jn 5:14–15; [z]**2Sa 14:20;** 1Ki 4:29–31; 5:12; 10:23; Ecc 1:16

b34 Or *buried in his tomb*

give you what you have not[a] asked for —both riches and honour[b]—so that in your lifetime you will have no equal[c] among kings. 14And if you walk[d] in my ways and obey my statutes and commands as David your father did, I will give you a long life."[e] 15Then Solomon awoke[f]—and he realised it had been a dream.[g]

He returned to Jerusalem, stood before the ark of the Lord's covenant and sacrificed burnt offerings[h] and fellowship offerings.[a][i] Then he gave a feast[j] for all his court.

A Wise Ruling

16Now two prostitutes came to the king and stood before him. 17One of them said, "My lord, this woman and I live in the same house. I had a baby while she was there with me. 18The third day after my child was born, this woman also had a baby. We were alone; there was no-one in the house but the two of us.

19"During the night this woman's son died because she lay on him. 20So she got up in the middle of the night and took my son from my side while I your servant was asleep. She put him by her breast and put her dead son by my breast. 21The next morning, I got up to nurse my son—and he was dead! But when I looked at him closely in the morning light, I saw that it wasn't the son I had borne."

22The other woman said, "No! The living one is my son; the dead one is yours."

But the first one insisted, "No! The dead one is yours; the living one is mine." And so they argued before the king.

23The king said, "This one says, 'My son is alive and your son is dead,' while that one says, 'No! Your son is dead and mine is alive.'"

24Then the king said, "Bring me a sword." So they brought a sword for the king. 25He then gave an order: "Cut the living child in two and give half to one and half to the other."

26The woman whose son was alive was filled with compassion[k] for her son and said to the king, "Please, my lord, give her the living baby! Don't kill him!"

But the other said, "Neither I nor you shall have him. Cut him in two!"

27Then the king gave his ruling: "Give the living baby to the first woman. Do not kill him; she is his mother."

28When all Israel heard the verdict the king had given, they held the king in awe, because they saw that he had wisdom[l] from God to administer justice.

Solomon's Officials and Governors

4 So King Solomon ruled over all Israel. 2And these were his chief officials:[a]

Azariah[b] son of Zadok—the priest;
3Elihoreph and Ahijah, sons of Shisha—secretaries;[c]
Jehoshaphat[d] son of Ahilud—recorder;
4Benaiah[e] son of Jehoiada—commander-in-chief;
Zadok[f] and Abiathar—priests;
5Azariah son of Nathan—in charge of the district officers;
Zabud son of Nathan—a priest and personal adviser to the king;
6Ahishar—in charge of the palace;[g]
Adoniram[h] son of Abda—in charge of forced labour.[i]

7Solomon also had twelve district governors[j] over all Israel, who supplied provisions for the king and the royal household. Each one had to provide supplies for one month in the year. 8These are their names:

Ben-Hur—in the hill country[k] of Ephraim;
9Ben-Deker—in Makaz, Shaalbim,[l] Beth Shemesh[m] and Elon Bethhanan;
10Ben-Hesed—in Arubboth (Socoh[n] and all the land of Hepher[o] were his);
11Ben-Abinadab—in Naphoth Dor[a][p] (he was married to Taphath daughter of Solomon);
12Baana son of Ahilud—in Taanach and Megiddo, and in all of Beth Shan[q] next to Zarethan[r] below Jezreel, from Beth Shan to Abel Meholah[s] across to Jokmeam;[t]
13Ben-Geber—in Ramoth Gilead (the settlements of Jair[u] son of Manasseh in Gilead[v] were his, as well as the district of Argob in Bashan and its sixty large walled cities[w] with bronze gate bars);
14Ahinadab son of Iddo—in Mahanaim;[x]
15Ahimaaz[y]—in Naphtali (he had married Basemath daughter of Solomon);

13 [a]Mt 6:33; Eph 3:20; [b]Pr 3:1–2,16; 8:18; [c]1Ki 10:23; 2Ch 9:22; Ne 13:26
14 [d]1Ki 9:4; Ps 25:13; 101:2; 128:1; Pr 3:1–2,16; [e]Ps 61:6
15 [f]**Ge 28:16**; [g]ver 5; [h]Lev 6:8–13; [i]Lev 7:11–21; [j]Est 1:3,9; 2:18; 5:8; 6:14; 9:17; Da 5:1
26 [k]Ps 102:13; Isa 49:15; 63:15; Jer 3:12; 31:20; Hos 11:8
28 [l]**2Sa 14:20**; Col 2:3

Ch. 4

2 [a]1Ki 12:6; Job 12:12; [b]1Ch 6:10; 2Ch 26:17
3 [c]**2Sa 8:17**; [d]**2Sa 8:16**
4 [e]**2Sa 8:18**; [f]**2Sa 8:17**
6 [g]**Ge 41:40**; [h]**2Sa 20:24**; [i]**Ge 49:15**
7 [j]ver 27
8 [k]**Jos 24:33**
9 [l]Jdg 1:35; [m]**Jos 15:10**
10 [n]**Jos 15:35**; [o]**Jos 12:17**
11 [p]**Jos 11:2**
12 [q]**Jos 17:11**; [r]**Jos 3:16**; [s]**Jdg 7:22**; [t]1Ch 6:68
13 [u]**Nu 32:41**; [v]Nu 32:40; [w]Dt 3:4
14 [x]Jos 13:26
15 [y]2Sa 15:27

[a]*15* Traditionally *peace offerings*
[a]*11* Or *in the heights of Dor*

16Baana son of Hushai[z]—in Asher and in Aloth;
17Jehoshaphat son of Paruah—in Issachar;
18Shimei[a] son of Ela—in Benjamin;
19Geber son of Uri—in Gilead (the country of Sihon[b] king of the Amorites and the country of Og[c] king of Bashan). He was the only governor over the district.

Solomon's Daily Provisions

20The people of Judah and Israel were as numerous as the sand[d] on the seashore; they ate, they drank and they were happy.[e] 21And Solomon ruled[f] over all the kingdoms from the River[b][g] to the land of the Philistines, as far as the border of Egypt.[h] These countries brought tribute[i] and were Solomon's subjects all his life.

22Solomon's daily provisions[j] were thirty cors[c] of fine flour and sixty cors[d] of meal, 23ten head of stall-fed cattle, twenty of pasture-fed cattle and a hundred sheep and goats, as well as deer, gazelles, roebucks and choice fowl.[k] 24For he ruled over all the kingdoms west of the River, from Tiphsah[l] to Gaza, and had peace[m] on all sides. 25During Solomon's lifetime Judah and Israel, from Dan to Beersheba,[n] lived in safety,[o] each man under his own vine and fig-tree.[p]

26Solomon had four[e] thousand stalls for chariot horses,[q] and twelve thousand horses.[f]

27The district officers,[r] each in his month, supplied provisions for King Solomon and all who came to the king's table. They saw to it that nothing was lacking. 28They also brought to the proper place their quotas of barley and straw for the chariot horses and the other horses.

Solomon's Wisdom

29God gave Solomon wisdom[s] and very great insight, and a breadth of understanding as measureless as the sand[t] on the seashore. 30Solomon's wisdom was greater than the wisdom of all the men of the East,[u] and greater than all the wisdom of Egypt.[v] 31He was wiser[w] than any other man, including Ethan the Ezrahite—wiser than Heman, Calcol and Darda, the sons of Mahol. And his fame spread to all the surrounding nations. 32He spoke three thousand proverbs[x] and his songs[y] numbered a thousand and five. 33He described plant life, from the cedar of Lebanon to the hyssop[z] that grows out of walls. He also taught about animals and birds, reptiles and fish. 34Men of all nations came to listen to Solomon's wisdom, sent by all the kings[a] of the world, who had heard of his wisdom.

16 [z]**2Sa 15:32**
18 [a]1Ki 1:8
19 [b]**Jos 12:2;** [c]Dt 3:8–10; **Jos 12:4**
20 [d]**Ge 12:2; 32:12;** [e]1Ch 22:9
21 [f]2Ch 9:26; Ezr 4:20; Ps 72:11; La 1:1; [g]**Ge 2:14;** Ps 72:8; [h]**Ex 23:31;** [i]**Jdg 3:15;** Eze 16:13
22 [j]1Ki 10:5
23 [k]Ne 5:18
24 [l]2Ki 15:16; [m]**Jos 14:15**
25 [n]**Jdg 20:1;** [o]1Ch 22:9; Jer 23:6; Eze 28:26; 39:26; [p]Dt 8:8; 2Ki 18:31; Ps 105:33; Isa 36:16; Jer 5:17; Joel 2:22; Mic 4:4; Zec 3:10
26 [q]**Dt 17:16**
27 [r]ver 7
29 [s]**1Ki 3:12;** [t]**Ge 32:12**
30 [u]**Ge 25:6; Jdg 6:3;** Da 1:20; Mt 2:1; [v]Isa 19:11; Ac 7:22
31 [w]**1Ki 3:12**
32 [x]Pr 1:1; 10:1; 25:1; Ecc 12:9; [y]Ps 78:63; SS 1:1; Eze 33:32
33 [z]**Lev 14:49**
34 [a]2Ch 9:23

Ch. 5

1 [a]**2Sa 5:11**
3 [b]1Ch 22:8; 28:3; [c]**2Sa 7:5;** [d]2Sa 22:40; Ps 8:6; 110:1; **Mt 22:44;** 1Co 15:25
4 [e]**Jos 14:15;** 1Ch 22:9; Lk 2:14; [f]1Ki 11:14,23
5 [g]**Dt 12:5;** 1Ch 17:12; 1Co 3:16; Rev 21:22; [h]Dt 12:5; 2Sa 7:13
6 [i]1Ch 14:1; 22:4
7 [j]1Ki 10:9; Isa 60:6
9 [k]Ezr 3:7

Preparations for Building the Temple

5:1–16pp—2Ch 2:1–18

5 When Hiram[a] king of Tyre heard that Solomon had been anointed king to succeed his father David, he sent his envoys to Solomon, because he had always been on friendly terms with David. 2Solomon sent back this message to Hiram:

3"You know that because of the wars[b] waged against my father David from all sides, he could not build[c] a temple for the Name of the LORD his God until the LORD put his enemies under his feet.[d] 4But now the LORD my God has given me rest[e] on every side, and there is no adversary[f] or disaster. 5I intend, therefore, to build a temple[g] for the Name of the LORD my God, as the LORD told my father David, when he said, 'Your son whom I will put on the throne in your place will build the temple for my Name.'[h]

6"So give orders that cedars[i] of Lebanon be cut for me. My men will work with yours, and I will pay you for your men whatever wages you set. You know that we have no-one so skilled in felling timber as the Sidonians."

7When Hiram heard Solomon's message, he was greatly pleased and said, "Praise be to the LORD[j] today, for he has given David a wise son to rule over this great nation."

8So Hiram sent word to Solomon:

"I have received the message you sent me and will do all you want in providing the cedar and pine logs. 9My men will haul them down from Lebanon to the sea[k], and I will float them in rafts by sea to the place you

[b]21 That is, the Euphrates; also in verse 24
[c]22 That is, probably about 180 bushels (about 6.6 kilolitres)
[d]22 That is, probably about 365 bushels (about 13.2 kilolitres)
[e]26 Some Septuagint manuscripts (see also 2 Chron. 9:25); Hebrew *forty*
[f]26 Or *charioteers*

specify. There I will separate them and you can take them away. And you are to grant my wish by providing food[l] for my royal household."

10In this way Hiram kept Solomon supplied with all the cedar and pine logs he wanted, 11and Solomon gave Hiram twenty thousand cors[a] of wheat as food[m] for his household, in addition to twenty thousand baths[b,c] of pressed olive oil. Solomon continued to do this for Hiram year after year. 12The LORD gave Solomon wisdom,[n] just as he had promised him. There were peaceful relations between Hiram and Solomon, and the two of them made a treaty.[o]

13King Solomon conscripted labourers[p] from all Israel—thirty thousand men. 14He sent them off to Lebanon in shifts of ten thousand a month, so that they spent one month in Lebanon and two months at home. Adoniram[q] was in charge of the forced labour. 15Solomon had seventy thousand carriers and eighty thousand stonecutters in the hills, 16as well as thirty-three hundred[d] foremen[r] who supervised the project and directed the workmen. 17At the king's command they removed from the quarry[s] large blocks of quality stone[t] to provide a foundation of dressed stone for the temple. 18The craftsmen of Solomon and Hiram[u] and the men of Gebal[e v] cut and prepared the timber and stone for the building of the temple.

Solomon Builds the Temple

6:1–29pp—2Ch 3:1–14

6 In the four hundred and eightieth[a] year after the Israelites had come out of Egypt, in the fourth year of Solomon's reign over Israel, in the month of Ziv, the second month,[a] he began to build the temple of the LORD.[b]

2The temple[c] that King Solomon built for the LORD was sixty cubits long, twenty wide and thirty high.[b] 3The portico[d] at the front of the main hall of the temple extended the width of the temple, that is twenty cubits,[c] and projected ten cubits[d] from the front of the temple. 4He made narrow clerestory windows[e] in the temple. 5Against the walls of the main hall and inner sanctuary he built a structure around the building, in which there were side rooms.[f] 6The lowest floor was five cubits[e] wide, the middle floor six cubits[f] and the third floor seven.[g] He made offset ledges around the outside of the temple so that nothing would be inserted into the temple walls.

7In building the temple, only blocks dressed[g] at the quarry were used, and no hammer, chisel or any other iron tool[h] was heard at the temple site while it was being built.

8The entrance to the lowest[h] floor was on the south side of the temple; a stairway led up to the middle level and from there to the third. 9So he built the temple and completed it, roofing it with beams and cedar[i] planks. 10And he built the side rooms all along the temple. The height of each was five cubits, and they were attached to the temple by beams of cedar.

11The word of the LORD came[j] to Solomon: 12"As for this temple you are building, if you follow my decrees, carry out my regulations and keep all my commands[k] and obey them, I will fulfil through you the promise[l] I gave to David your father. 13And I will live among the Israelites and will not abandon[m] my people Israel."

14So Solomon[n] built the temple and completed[o] it. 15He lined its interior walls with cedar boards, panelling them from the floor of the temple to the ceiling,[p] and covered the floor of the temple with planks of pine.[q] 16He partitioned off twenty cubits[i] at the rear of the temple with cedar boards from floor to ceiling to form within the temple an inner sanctuary, the Most Holy Place.[r] 17The main hall in front of this room was forty cubits[j] long. 18The inside of the temple was cedar,[s] carved with gourds and open flowers. Everything was cedar; no stone was to be seen.

19He prepared the inner sanctuary[t] within the temple to set the ark of the covenant[u] of the LORD there. 20The inner sanctuary[v] was twenty cubits long,

9 [l]ver 11; Eze 27:17; Ac 12:20
11 [m]**ver 9**
12 [n]**1Ki 3:12;** [o]Jos 9:7; 1Ki 15:19; Am 1:9
13 [p]**Ge 49:15; Lev 25:39;** 1Ki 9:15
14 [q]**2Sa 20:24;** 1Ki 4:6; 2Ch 10:18
16 [r]1Ki 9:23
17 [s]1Ki 6:7; [t]1Ch 22:2
18 [u]**2Sa 5:11;** [v]**Jos 13:5**

Ch. 6

1 [a]Ezr 3:8; [b]Ezr 5:11
2 [c]Ex 26:1
3 [d]Eze 40:49
4 [e]Eze 41:16
5 [f]Jer 35:2; Eze 41:5–6
7 [g]**Ex 20:25;** [h]**Dt 27:5**
9 [i]SS 1:17
11 [j]1Ki 12:22; 13:20; 16:1,7; 17:2; 21:17; Jer 40:1
12 [k]1Ki 11:10; [l]2Sa 7:12–16; 1Ki 9:5
13 [m]**Lev 26:11; Dt 31:6;** Jn 14:18; Heb 13:5
14 [n]Ac 7:47; [o]1Ch 28:20; 2Ch 5:1
15 [p]1Ki 7:7; [q]Eze 41:15–16
16 [r]**Ex 26:33**
18 [s]ver 29; Ps 74:6; Eze 41:18
19 [t]1Ki 8:6; [u]**Ex 25:10; 1Sa 3:3**
20 [v]Eze 41:3–4

[a]*11* That is, probably about 121,000 bushels (about 4,400 kilolitres)
[b]*11* Septuagint (see also 2 Chron. 2:10); Hebrew *twenty cors*
[c]*11* That is, about 97,000 gallons (about 440 kilolitres)
[d]*16* Hebrew; some Septuagint manuscripts (see also 2 Chron. 2:2, 18) *thirty-six hundred*
[e]*18* That is, Byblos
[a]*1* Hebrew; Septuagint *four hundred and fortieth*
[b]*2* That is, about 90 feet (about 27 metres) long and 30 feet (about 9 metres) wide and 45 feet (about 13.5 metres) high
[c]*3* That is, about 30 feet (about 9 metres)
[d]*3* That is, about 15 feet (about 4.5 metres)
[e]*6* That is, about 7½ feet (about 2.3 metres); also in verses 10 and 24
[f]*6* That is, about 9 feet (about 2.7 metres)
[g]*6* That is, about 10½ feet (about 3.2 metres)
[h]*8* Septuagint; Hebrew *middle*
[i]*16* That is, about 30 feet (about 9 metres)
[j]*17* That is, about 60 feet (about 18 metres)

twenty wide and twenty high.[k] He
overlaid the inside with pure gold, and
he also overlaid the altar of cedar.[w]
21Solomon covered the inside of the
temple with pure gold, and he extended
gold chains across the front of the inner
sanctuary, which was overlaid with
gold. 22So he overlaid the whole interior
with gold. He also overlaid with gold
the altar that belonged to the inner
sanctuary.

23In the inner sanctuary he made a
pair of cherubim[x] of olive wood, each
ten cubits[l] high. 24One wing of the first
cherub was five cubits long, and the
other wing five cubits—ten cubits from
wing tip to wing tip. 25The second cher-
ub also measured ten cubits, for the two
cherubim were identical in size and
shape. 26The height of each cherub was
ten cubits. 27He placed the cherubim[y]
inside the innermost room of the tem-
ple, with their wings spread out. The
wing of one cherub touched one wall,
while the wing of the other touched the
other wall, and their wings touched
each other in the middle of the room.
28He overlaid the cherubim with gold.

29On the walls[z] all round the temple,
in both the inner and outer rooms, he
carved cherubim,[a] palm trees and open
flowers. 30He also covered the floors of
both the inner and outer rooms of the
temple with gold.

31For the entrance of the inner sanctu-
ary he made doors of olive wood with
five-sided jambs. 32And on the two olive
wood doors[b] he carved cherubim, palm
trees and open flowers, and overlaid the
cherubim and palm trees with beaten
gold. 33In the same way he made four-
sided jambs of olive wood for the en-
trance to the main hall. 34He also made
two pine doors, each having two leaves
that turned in sockets. 35He carved cher-
ubim, palm trees and open flowers on
them and overlaid them with gold
hammered evenly over the carvings.

36And he built the inner courtyard[c] of
three courses[d] of dressed stone and one
course of trimmed cedar beams.

37The foundation of the temple of the
LORD was laid in the fourth year, in the
month of Ziv. 38In the eleventh year in
the month of Bul, the eighth month, the
temple was finished in all its details[e]
according to its specifications.[f] He had
spent seven years building it.

Solomon Builds His Palace

7 It took Solomon thirteen years,
however, to complete the con-
struction of his palace.[a] 2He built the
Palace[b] of the Forest of Lebanon[c] a hun-
dred cubits long, fifty wide and thirty
high,[a] with four rows of cedar columns
supporting trimmed cedar beams. 3It
was roofed with cedar above the beams
that rested on the columns—forty-five
beams, fifteen to a row. 4Its windows
were placed high in sets of three, facing
each other. 5All the doorways had rec-
tangular frames; they were in the front
part in sets of three, facing each other.[b]

6He made a colonnade fifty cubits
long and thirty wide.[c] In front of it was a
portico, and in front of that were pillars
and an overhanging roof.

7He built the throne hall, the Hall of
Justice, where he was to judge,[d] and he
covered it with cedar from floor to
ceiling.[d][e] 8And the palace in which he
was to live, set farther back, was similar
in design. Solomon also made a palace
like this hall for Pharaoh's daughter,
whom he had married.[f]

9All these structures, from the outside
to the great courtyard and from founda-
tion to eaves, were made of blocks of
high-grade stone cut to size and trim-
med with a saw on their inner and outer
faces. 10The foundations were laid with
large stones of good quality, some
measuring ten cubits[e] and some eight.[f]
11Above were high-grade stones, cut
to size, and cedar beams. 12The great
courtyard was surrounded by a wall of
three courses[g] of dressed stone and one
course of trimmed cedar beams, as was
the inner courtyard of the temple of the
LORD with its portico.

The Temple's Furnishings

7:23–26pp—2Ch 4:2–5
7:38–51pp—2Ch 4:6,10–5:1

13King Solomon sent to Tyre and
brought Huram,[g][h] 14whose mother was
a widow from the tribe of Naphtali and
whose father was a man of Tyre and a
craftsman in bronze. Huram was highly
skilled[i] and experienced in all kinds of

20 [w]**Ex 30:1**
23 [x]**Ex 37:7**
27 [y]**Ge 3:24; Ex 25:18**
29 [z]**ver 18**; [a]ver 32,35; Eze 41:18,25
32 [b]Eze 41:23
36 [c]2Ch 4:9; [d]1Ki 7:12; Ezr 6:4
38 [e]1Ch 28:19; [f]Ex 25:9; Heb 8:5

Ch. 7

1 [a]**2Sa 7:2**
2 [b]**2Sa 7:2**; [c]1Ki 10:17; 2Ch 9:16; Isa 22:8; 37:24; Jer 22:6,23
7 [d]1Sa 7:15; Ps 122:5; Pr 20:8; [e]1Ki 6:15
8 [f]**1Ki 3:1**
12 [g]**1Ki 6:36**
13 [h]ver 45; 2Ch 2:13; 4:16
14 [i]Ex 31:2–5; **35:31**

k*20* That is, about 30 feet (about 9 metres) long, wide and high
l*23* That is, about 15 feet (about 4.5 metres)
a*2* That is, about 150 feet (about 46 metres) long, 75 feet (about 23 metres) wide and 45 feet (about 13.5 metres) high
b*5* The meaning of the Hebrew for this verse is uncertain.
c*6* That is, about 75 feet (about 23 metres) long and 45 feet (about 13.5 metres) wide
d*7* Vulgate and Syriac; Hebrew *floor*
e*10* That is, about 15 feet (about 4.5 metres)
f*10* That is, about 12 feet (about 3.7 metres)
g*13* Hebrew *Hiram,* a variant of *Huram;* also in verses 40 and 45

bronze work. He came to King Solomon
and did all[j] the work assigned to him.
15He cast two bronze pillars,[k] each
eighteen cubits high and twelve cubits
round,[h] by line. 16He also made two
capitals[l] of cast bronze to set on the tops
of the pillars; each capital was five cu-
bits[i] high. 17A network of interwoven
chains festooned the capitals on top of
the pillars, seven for each capital. 18He
made pomegranates in two rows[j] en-
circling each network to decorate the
capitals on top of the pillars.[k] He did the
same for each capital. 19The capitals on
top of the pillars in the portico were in
the shape of lilies, four cubits[l] high.
20On the capitals of both pillars, above
the bowl-shaped part next to the net-
work, were the two hundred pome-
granates[m] in rows all around. 21He
erected the pillars at the portico of the
temple. The pillar to the south he
named Jakin[m] and the one to the north
Boaz.[n] [n] 22The capitals on top were in the
shape of lilies. And so the work on the
pillars[o] was completed.
23He made the Sea[p] of cast metal,
circular in shape, measuring ten cubits[o]
from rim to rim and five cubits high. It
took a line[q] of thirty cubits[p] to measure
round it. 24Below the rim, gourds en-
circled it—ten to a cubit. The gourds
were cast in two rows in one piece with
the Sea.
25The Sea stood on twelve bulls,[r]
three facing north, three facing west,
three facing south and three facing east.
The Sea rested on top of them, and their
hindquarters were towards the centre.
26It was a handbreadth[q] in thickness,
and its rim was like the rim of a cup, like
a lily blossom. It held two thousand
baths.[r]
27He also made ten movable stands[s] of
bronze; each was four cubits long, four
wide and three high.[s] 28This is how the
stands were made: They had side
panels attached to uprights. 29On the
panels between the uprights were lions,
bulls and cherubim—and on the up-
rights as well. Above and below the
lions and bulls were wreaths of ham-
mered work. 30Each stand[t] had four
bronze wheels with bronze axles, and
each had a basin resting on four sup-
ports, cast with wreaths on each side.
31On the inside of the stand there was an
opening that had a circular frame one
cubit[t] deep. This opening was round,
and with its basework it measured a
cubit and a half.[u] Around its opening
there was engraving. The panels of the
stands were square, not round. 32The

14 [j]2Ch 4:11
15 [k]2Ki 11:14; 23:3; 25:17; 2Ch 3:15; 23:13; 34:31; Jer 27:19; 52:17,21; Eze 40:49
16 [l]ver 20,42; 2Ki 25:17; Jer 52:22
20 [m]ver 18; 2Ch 3:16; 4:13
21 [n]2Ch 3:17
22 [o]2Ki 25:17
23 [p]ver 47; 2Ki 25:13; 1Ch 18:8; 2Ch 4:18; Jer 52:17; Rev 4:6; [q]Jer 31:39; Zec 2:1
25 [r]Jer 52:20
27 [s]2Ki 16:17
30 [t]2Ki 16:17
38 [u]Ex 30:18
40 [v]Ex 27:3; Jer 52:18

four wheels were under the panels, and
the axles of the wheels were attached to
the stand. The diameter of each wheel
was a cubit and a half. 33The wheels
were made like chariot wheels; the
axles, rims, spokes and hubs were all of
cast metal.
34Each stand had four handles, one on
each corner, projecting from the stand.
35At the top of the stand there was a
circular band half a cubit[v] deep. The
supports and panels were attached to
the top of the stand. 36He engraved
cherubim, lions and palm trees on the
surfaces of the supports and on the
panels, in every available space, with
wreaths all around. 37This is the way he
made the ten stands. They were all cast
in the same moulds and were identical
in size and shape.
38He then made ten bronze basins,[u]
each holding forty baths[w] and measur-
ing four cubits across, one basin to go on
each of the ten stands. 39He placed five
of the stands on the south side of the
temple and five on the north. He placed
the Sea on the south side, at the south-
east corner of the temple. 40He also
made the basins and shovels and
sprinkling bowls.[v]
So Huram finished all the work he
had undertaken for King Solomon in
the temple of the LORD:

41the two pillars;
the two bowl-shaped capitals on
top of the pillars;
the two sets of network decorating
the two bowl-shaped capitals on
top of the pillars;
42the four hundred pomegranates for

[h]*15* That is, about 27 feet (about 8.2 metres) high and 18 feet (about 5.5 metres) round
[i]*16* That is, about 7½ feet (about 2.3 metres); also in verse 23
[j]*18* Two Hebrew manuscripts and Septuagint; most Hebrew manuscripts *made the pillars, and there were two rows*
[k]*18* Many Hebrew manuscripts and Syriac; most Hebrew manuscripts *pomegranates*
[l]*19* That is, about 6 feet (about 1.8 metres); also in verse 38
[m]*21* *Jakin* probably means *he establishes.*
[n]*21* *Boaz* probably means *in him is strength.*
[o]*23* That is, about 15 feet (about 4.5 metres)
[p]*23* That is, about 45 feet (about 13.7 metres)
[q]*26* That is, about 3 inches (about 8 centimetres)
[r]*26* That is, probably about 9,700 gallons (about 44 kilolitres); the Septuagint does not have this sentence.
[s]*27* That is, about 6 feet (about 1.8 metres) long and wide and about 4½ feet (about 1.4 metres) high
[t]*31* That is, about 1½ feet (about 0.5 metre)
[u]*31* That is, about 2¼ feet (about 0.7 metre); also in verse 32
[v]*35* That is about ¾ foot (about 0.2 metre)
[w]*38* That is, about 195 gallons (about 880 litres)

the two sets of network (two rows of pomegranates for each network, decorating the bowl-shaped capitals[w] on top of the pillars);
43the ten stands with their ten basins;
44the Sea and the twelve bulls under it;
45the pots, shovels and sprinkling bowls.[x]

All these objects that Huram[y] made for King Solomon for the temple of the LORD were of burnished bronze. 46The king had them cast in clay moulds in the plain[z] of the Jordan between Succoth[a] and Zarethan.[b] 47Solomon left all these things unweighed,[c] because there were so many;[d] the weight of the bronze[e] was not determined.

48Solomon also made all[f] the furnishings that were in the LORD's temple:

the golden altar;
the golden table[g] on which was the bread of the Presence;[h]
49the lampstands[i] of pure gold (five on the right and five on the left, in front of the inner sanctuary);
the gold floral work and lamps and tongs;
50the pure gold dishes, wick trimmers, sprinkling bowls, dishes[j] and censers;[k]
and the gold sockets for the doors of the innermost room, the Most Holy Place, and also for the doors of the main hall of the temple.

51When all the work King Solomon had done for the temple of the LORD was finished, he brought in the things his father David had dedicated[l]—the silver and gold and the furnishings[m]—and he placed them in the treasuries of the LORD's temple.

The Ark Brought to the Temple

8:1–21pp—2Ch 5:2–6:11

8 Then King Solomon summoned into his presence at Jerusalem the elders of Israel, all the heads of the tribes and the chiefs[a] of the Israelite families, to bring up the ark[b] of the LORD's covenant from Zion, the City of David.[c] 2All the men of Israel came together to King Solomon at the time of the festival[d] in the month of Ethanim, the seventh month.[e]

3When all the elders of Israel had arrived, the priests[f] took up the ark, 4and they brought up the ark of the LORD and the Tent of Meeting[g] and all the sacred furnishings in it. The priests and Levites[h] carried them up, 5and King Solomon and the entire assembly of Israel that had gathered about him were before the ark, sacrificing[i] so many sheep and cattle that they could not be recorded or counted.

6The priests then brought the ark of the LORD's covenant[j] to its place in the inner sanctuary of the temple, the Most Holy Place,[k] and put it beneath the wings of the cherubim.[l] 7The cherubim spread their wings over the place of the ark and overshadowed[m] the ark and its carrying poles. 8These poles were so long that their ends could be seen from the Holy Place in front of the inner sanctuary, but not from outside the Holy Place; and they are still there today.[n] 9There was nothing in the ark except the two stone tablets[o] that Moses had placed in it at Horeb, where the LORD made a covenant with the Israelites after they came out of Egypt.

10When the priests withdrew from the Holy Place, the cloud[p] filled the temple of the LORD. 11And the priests could not perform their service[q] because of the cloud, for the glory[r] of the LORD filled his temple.

12Then Solomon said, "The LORD has said that he would dwell in a dark cloud;[s] 13I have indeed built a magnificent temple for you, a place for you to dwell[t] for ever."

14While the whole assembly of Israel was standing there, the king turned round and blessed[u] them. 15Then he said:

"Praise be to the LORD,[v] the God of Israel, who with his own hand has fulfilled what he promised with his own mouth to my father David. For he said, 16'Since the day I brought my people Israel out of Egypt,[w] I have not chosen a city in any tribe of Israel to have a temple built for my Name[x] to be there, but I have chosen[y] David[z] to rule my people Israel.'

17"My father David had it in his heart[a] to build a temple[b] for the Name of the LORD, the God of Israel. 18But the LORD said to my father David, 'Because it was in your heart to build a temple for my Name, you did well to have this in your heart. 19Nevertheless, you[c] are not the one to build the temple, but your son, who is your own flesh and blood—he is the one who

42 [w]**ver 16**
45 [x]**Ex 27:3**; Jer 52:18; [y]**ver 13**
46 [z]**Ge 13:10**; [a]**Ge 33:17**; [b]Jos 3:16
47 [c]1Ch 22:3; Jer 52:20; [d]Ex 36:5–7; [e]**ver 23**
48 [f]Ex 39:32–33; [g]**Ex 25:23**; [h]**Ex 25:30**
49 [i]**Ex 25:31**
50 [j]**Nu 7:14**; [k]2Ki 25:13; Jer 52:19
51 [l]**2Sa 8:11**; [m]2Ki 12:13; 24:13; Jer 27:19

Ch. 8

1 [a]Nu 7:2; [b]**1Sa 3:3**; Rev 11:19; [c]**2Sa 5:7**
2 [d]ver 65; **Lev 23:36**; Ne 8:17; [e]**Lev 23:34**; **Nu 29:12**
3 [f]**Jos 3:3**
4 [g]**Lev 17:4**; [h]1Ch 15:13
5 [i]**2Sa 6:13**; **2Ch 30:24**
6 [j]**Ex 26:33**; **2Sa 6:17**; Rev 11:19; [k]**Ex 26:33**; [l]**Ge 3:24**; **Ex 25:18**
7 [m]**Ex 25:20**
8 [n]Ex 25:13–15
9 [o]**Ex 16:34**; **25:16**; Heb 9:4
10 [p]**Ex 16:10**; **Lev 16:2**; Rev 15:8
11 [q]2Ch 7:2; Rev 15:8; [r]**Ex 16:7**; **29:43**
12 [s]**Ex 40:34**; **2Sa 22:10**
13 [t]Ex 15:17; Ps 132:13; 135:21; Mt 23:21
14 [u]**Ex 39:43**
15 [v]1Ch 16:36; Lk 1:68
16 [w]**Ex 3:10**; [x]**Dt 12:5**; [y]**1Sa 9:16**; **16:1**; [z]Ps 89:3–4
17 [a]**1Sa 10:7**; Ac 7:46; [b]2Sa 7:27; 1Ch 22:7; Ps 26:8; 132:5
19 [c]**2Sa 7:5**

will build the temple for my
Name.'[d]
20"The LORD has kept the prom-
ise he made: I have succeeded[e]
David my father and now I sit on
the throne of Israel, just as the LORD
promised, and I have built[f] the tem-
ple for the Name of the LORD, the
God of Israel. 21I have provided a
place there for the ark, in which is
the covenant of the LORD that he
made with our fathers when he
brought them out of Egypt."

Solomon's Prayer of Dedication

8:22–53pp—2Ch 6:12–40

22Then Solomon stood before the altar
of the LORD in front of the whole assem-
bly of Israel, spread out his hands[g]
towards heaven 23and said:

"O LORD, God of Israel, there is
no God like[h] you in heaven above
or on earth below—you who keep
your covenant of love[i] with your
servants who continue whole-
heartedly in your way. 24You have
kept your promise to your servant
David my father; with your mouth
you have promised and with your
hand you have fulfilled it—as it is
today.
25"Now LORD, God of Israel, keep
for your servant David my father
the promises[j] you made to him
when you said, 'You shall never fail
to have a man to sit before me on
the throne of Israel, if only your
sons are careful in all they do to
walk before me as you have done.'
26And now, O God of Israel, let
your word that you promised[k] your
servant David my father come true.
27"But will God really dwell[l] on
earth? The heavens, even the high-
est heaven,[m] cannot contain[n] you.
How much less this temple I have
built! 28Yet give attention to your
servant's prayer and his plea for
mercy, O LORD my God. Hear the
cry and the prayer that your ser-
vant is praying in your presence
this day. 29May your eyes be open[o]
towards[p] this temple night and
day, this place of which you said,
'My Name[q] shall be there,' so that
you will hear the prayer your ser-
vant prays towards this place.
30Hear the supplication of your ser-
vant and of your people Israel
when they pray[r] towards this
place. Hear[s] from heaven, your
dwelling-place, and when you
hear, forgive.[t]
31"When a man wrongs his
neighbour and is required to take
an oath and he comes and swears
the oath[u] before your altar in this
temple, 32then hear from heaven
and act. Judge between your ser-
vants, condemning the guilty and
bringing down on his own head
what he has done. Declare the in-
nocent not guilty, and so establish
his innocence.[v]
33"When your people Israel have
been defeated[w] by an enemy be-
cause they have sinned[x] against
you, and when they turn back to
you and confess your name,
praying and making supplication
to you in this temple,[y] 34then hear
from heaven and forgive the sin of
your people Israel and bring them
back to the land you gave to their
fathers.
35"When the heavens are shut up
and there is no rain[z] because your
people have sinned[a] against you,
and when they pray towards this
place and confess your name and
turn from their sin because you
have afflicted them, 36then hear
from heaven and forgive the sin of
your servants, your people Israel.
Teach[b] them the right way[c] to live,
and send rain[d] on the land you gave
your people for an inheritance.
37"When famine[e] or plague[f]
comes to the land, or blight[g] or mil-
dew, locusts or grasshoppers,[h] or
when an enemy besieges them in
any of their cities, whatever disas-
ter or disease may come, 38and
when a prayer or plea is made by
any of your people Israel—each
one aware of the afflictions of his
own heart, and spreading out his
hands[i] towards this temple—
39then hear[j] from heaven, your
dwelling-place. Forgive[k] and act;
deal with each man according to all
he does, since you know[l] his heart
(for you alone know the hearts of all
men), 40so that they will fear[m] you
all the time they live in the land[n]
you gave our fathers.
41"As for the foreigner[o] who does
not belong to your people Israel but
has come from a distant land be-
cause of your name—42for men will
hear[p] of your great name and your
mighty hand[q] and your outstretch-
ed arm—when he comes and prays
towards this temple, 43then hear

19 [d]**2Sa 7:13**
20 [e]**2Sa 7:12;** [f]1Ch 28:6
22 [g]**Ex 9:29**
23 [h]**Ex 9:14;** [i]**Dt 7:9**,12; Ne 1:5; 9:32; Da 9:4
25 [j]**2Sa 7:15**; 1Ch 17:23; 2Ch 1:9
26 [k]**2Sa 7:25**
27 [l]Ac 7:48; 17:24; [m]**Dt 10:14;** [n]2Ch 2:6; Ps 139:7–16; Isa 66:1; Jer 23:24
29 [o]ver 52; 2Ki 19:16; 2Ch 7:15; Ne 1:6; Ps 5:1; 31:2; 102:17; 130:2; Isa 37:17; [p]Ps 28:2; 138:2; Da 6:10; [q]**Dt 11:12**; 12:11; **2Sa 7:13**
30 [r]ver 47; Lev 26:40; Ne 1:6; Jer 29:12; Da 9:4; [s]ver 39; Ps 34:6; [t]**Ex 34:7**,9; Lev 26:40–42; Ps 85:2
31 [u]**Ex 22:11**
32 [v]Dt 25:1; Eze 18:20
33 [w]**Lev 26:17;** [x]Lev 26:39; [y]Isa 37:1, 14,38
35 [z]**Dt 28:24; 2Sa 1:21;** [a]Jer 5:25
36 [b]**Dt 8:3; 1Sa 12:23;** [c]Ps 5:8; 27:11; 107:7; Pr 11:5; Isa 45:13; Jer 6:16; 7:23; 31:21; [d]ver 35; 1Ki 17:1; 18:1,45; Jer 5:24; 10:3; 14:22; Zec 10:1
37 [e]**Lev 26:26;** [f]**Ex 30:12; Lev 26:25;** [g]**Dt 28:22;** [h]**Ex 10:13;** Ps 105:34
38 [i]**Ex 9:29**
39 [j]**ver 30;** [k]Ps 130:4; [l]**Jos 22:22; Ps 44:21**; Jn 2:24; **Rev 2:23**
40 [m]ver 39–40; Dt 6:13; Ps 103:11; 130:4; [n]**Dt 12:1**
41 [o]**Ge 31:15**; Isa 56:3,6; 61:5
42 [p]1Ki 10:1; Isa 60:3; Ac 8:27; [q]Dt 3:24

from heaven, your dwelling-place,
and do whatever the foreigner asks
of you, so that all the peoples of the
earth may know[r] your name and
fear[s] you, as do your own people
Israel, and may know that this
house I have built bears your
Name.[t]
44"When your people go to war
against their enemies, wherever
you send them, and when they
pray[u] to the LORD towards the city
you have chosen and the temple I
have built for your Name, 45then
hear from heaven their prayer and
their plea, and uphold their cause.[v]
46"When they sin against you—
for there is no-one who does not
sin[w]—and you become angry with
them and give them over to the
enemy, who takes them captive[x] to
his own land, far away or near;
47and if they have a change of heart
in the land where they are held
captive, and repent and plead[y] with
you in the land of their conquerors
and say, 'We have sinned, we have
done wrong, we have acted wick-
edly';[z] 48and if they turn back[a] to
you with all their heart[b] and soul in
the land of their enemies who took
them captive, and pray[c] to you
towards the land you gave their
fathers, towards the city you have
chosen and the temple[d] I have built
for your Name;[e] 49then from
heaven, your dwelling-place, hear
their prayer and their plea, and
uphold their cause. 50And forgive
your people, who have sinned
against you; forgive all the offences
they have committed against you,
and cause their conquerors to show
them mercy;[f] 51for they are your
people and your inheritance,[g]
whom you brought out of Egypt,
out of that iron-smelting furnace.[h]
52"May your eyes be open[i] to
your servant's plea and to the plea
of your people Israel, and may you
listen to them whenever they cry
out to you.[j] 53For you singled them
out from all the nations of the world
to be your own inheritance,[k] just as
you declared through your servant
Moses when you, O Sovereign
LORD, brought our fathers out of
Egypt."

54When Solomon had finished all
these prayers and supplications to the
LORD, he rose from before the altar of
the LORD, where he had been kneeling

43 [r]**Jos 4:24; 1Sa 17:46;** [s]Ps 102:15; [t]**Dt 28:10**
44 [u]1Ch 5:20; 2Ch 14:11
45 [v]Ps 9:4; 140:12
46 [w]Ps 130:3; 143:2; Pr 20:9; **Ro 3:9;** [x]Lev 26:33–39; **Dt 4:27; 21:10; 28:64;** 2Ki 25:21
47 [y]**ver 30; Lev 5:5;** Ezr 9:15; Ne 1:6; Jer 14:20; [z]Ezr 9:7; Ps 106:6; Jer 3:25
48 [a]**Dt 4:30;** [b]**Dt 4:29;** [c]1Jn 1:8–10; [d]Ps 5:7; 11:4; Jnh 2:4; [e]Dt 12:11–14; Ne 1:9; Jer 23:3; 31:8
50 [f]2Ki 25:28; 2Ch 30:9; Ps 106:46; Da 1:9
51 [g]**Ex 34:9; Dt 9:29;** [h]**Ex 1:13;** Isa 48:10; Jer 11:4
52 [i]**ver 29;** [j]Job 30:20; Ps 3:4; 22:2; 77:1; 142:1
53 [k]Ex 19:5; **34:9**
55 [l]**Ex 39:43;** Nu 6:23
56 [m]**Ex 33:14;** Dt 12:10; Heb 4:8; [n]**Jos 23:15; Jer 29:10**
57 [o]**Dt 4:31; 31:6; Mt 28:20;** Heb 13:5
58 [p]**Jos 24:23**
60 [q]**Jos 4:24;** [r]**Dt 4:35**
61 [s]Dt 6:5; [t]1Ki 9:4; 11:4; 15:3,14; 22:43; 2Ki 20:3; 1Ch 28:9; 29:19; 2Ch 16:9; 17:6; 25:2; Ps 119:80; Isa 38:3
62 [u]**2Sa 6:13;** 1Ch 29:21; Eze 45:17
63 [v]Ezr 6:16
64 [w]**Ex 29:13;** [x]**Ex 27:1;** 2Ki 16:14; 2Ch 4:1; 8:12; 15:8; Eze 43:13–17; [y]**2Sa 6:17**
65 [z]**ver 2;** [a]**Nu 13:2;** [b]**Ge 15:18**

with his hands spread out towards
heaven. 55He stood and blessed[l] the
whole assembly of Israel in a loud voice,
saying:

56"Praise be to the LORD, who has
given rest[m] to his people Israel just
as he promised. Not one word has
failed of all the good promises[n] he
gave through his servant Moses.
57May the LORD our God be with us
as he was with our fathers; may he
never leave us nor forsake[o] us.
58May he turn our hearts[p] to him, to
walk in all his ways and to keep the
commands, decrees and regula-
tions he gave our fathers. 59And
may these words of mine, which I
have prayed before the LORD, be
near to the LORD our God day and
night, that he may uphold the
cause of his servant and the cause
of his people Israel according to
each day's need, 60so that all the
peoples[q] of the earth may know
that the LORD is God and that there
is no other.[r] 61But your hearts[s] must
be fully committed[t] to the LORD our
God, to live by his decrees and obey
his commands, as at this time."

The Dedication of the Temple

8:62–66pp—2Ch 7:1-10

62Then the king and all Israel with him
offered sacrifices[u] before the LORD.
63Solomon offered a sacrifice of fellow-
ship offerings[a] to the LORD: twenty-two
thousand cattle and a hundred and
twenty thousand sheep and goats. So
the king and all the Israelites dedicated[v]
the temple of the LORD.
64On that same day the king conse-
crated the middle part of the courtyard
in front of the temple of the LORD, and
there he offered burnt offerings, grain
offerings and the fat[w] of the fellowship
offerings, because the bronze altar[x] be-
fore the LORD was too small to hold the
burnt offerings, the grain offerings and
the fat of the fellowship offerings.[y]
65So Solomon observed the festival[z] at
that time, and all Israel with him—a
vast assembly, people from Lebo[b]
Hamath[a] to the Wadi of Egypt.[b] They
celebrated it before the LORD our God
for seven days and seven days more,
fourteen days in all. 66On the following
day he sent the people away. They
blessed the king and then went home,

a63 Traditionally *peace offerings*; also in verse 64
b65 Or *from the entrance to*

joyful and glad in heart for all the good[c] things the LORD had done for his servant David and his people Israel.

The LORD Appears to Solomon

9:1–9pp—2Ch 7:11–22

9 When Solomon had finished[a] building the temple of the LORD and the royal palace, and had achieved all he had desired to do, 2the LORD appeared[b] to him a second time, as he had appeared to him at Gibeon. 3The LORD said to him:

"I have heard[c] the prayer and plea you have made before me; I have consecrated this temple, which you have built, by putting my Name[d] there for ever. My eyes[e] and my heart will always be there.

4"As for you, if you walk before me in integrity of heart[f] and uprightness, as David[g] your father did, and do all I command and observe my decrees and laws,[h] 5I will establish[i] your royal throne over Israel for ever, as I promised David your father when I said, 'You shall never fail[j] to have a man on the throne of Israel.'

6"But if you[a] or your sons turn away[k] from me and do not observe the commands and decrees I have given you[a] and go off to serve other gods[l] and worship them, 7then I will cut off Israel from the land[m] I have given them and will reject this temple I have consecrated for my Name.[n] Israel will then become a byword[o] and an object of ridicule[p] among all peoples. 8And though this temple is now imposing, all who pass by will be appalled[q] and will scoff and say, 'Why has the LORD done such a thing to this land and to this temple?'[r] 9People will answer,[s] 'Because they have forsaken[t] the LORD their God, who brought their fathers out of Egypt, and have embraced other gods, worshipping and serving them—that is why the LORD brought all this disaster[u] on them.'"

Solomon's Other Activities

9:10–28pp—2Ch 8:1–18

10At the end of twenty years, during which Solomon built these two buildings—the temple of the LORD and the royal palace—11King Solomon gave twenty towns in Galilee to Hiram king of Tyre, because Hiram had supplied him with all the cedar and pine and gold[v] he wanted. 12But when Hiram went from Tyre to see the towns that Solomon had given him, he was not pleased with them. 13"What kind of towns are these you have given me, my brother?" he asked. And he called them the Land of Cabul,[b][w] a name they have to this day. 14Now Hiram had sent to the king 120 talents[c] of gold.[x]

15Here is the account of the forced labour King Solomon conscripted[y] to build the LORD's temple, his own palace, the supporting terraces,[d][z] the wall of Jerusalem, and Hazor,[a] Megiddo and Gezer.[b] 16(Pharaoh king of Egypt had attacked and captured Gezer. He had set it on fire. He killed its Canaanite inhabitants, and then gave it as a wedding gift to his daughter,[c] Solomon's wife. 17And Solomon rebuilt Gezer.) He built up Lower Beth Horon,[d] 18Baalath,[e] and Tadmor[e] in the desert, within his land, 19as well as all his store cities[f] and the towns for his chariots[g] and for his horses[f]—whatever he desired to build in Jerusalem, in Lebanon and throughout all the territory he ruled.

20All the people left from the Amorites, Hittites,[h] Perizzites, Hivites and Jebusites[i] (these peoples were not Israelites), 21that is, their descendants[j] remaining in the land, whom the Israelites could not exterminate[g][k]—these Solomon conscripted for his slave labour force,[l] as it is to this day. 22But Solomon did not make slaves[m] of any of the Israelites; they were his fighting men, his government officials, his officers, his captains, and the commanders of his chariots and charioteers. 23They were also the chief officials[n] in charge of Solomon's projects—550 officials supervising the men who did the work.

24After Pharaoh's daughter[o] had come up from the City of David to the palace Solomon had built for her, he constructed the supporting terraces.[p]

25Three[q] times a year Solomon sacrificed burnt offerings and fellowship offerings[h] on the altar he had built for

66 [c]**Ex 18:9**
Ch. 9
1 [a]**2Sa 7:2**
2 [b]**1Ki 3:5**
3 [c]**1Sa 9:16**; 2Ki 19:20; 20:5; Ps 10:17; 34:17; [d]**Ex 20:24**; **Dt 12:5**; [e]**Dt 11:12**
4 [f]Ge 17:1; [g]Dt 17:20; 1Ki 14:8; 15:5; [h]**1Ki 3:14**; 1Ch 28:9; Pr 4:4
5 [i]1Ch 22:10; [j]**2Sa 7:15**
6 [k]Dt 28:15; 2Sa 7:14; 2Ki 18:12; Jer 17:27; 26:4; 32:23; 44:23; [l]1Ki 11:10
7 [m]Lev 18:24–28; Dt 4:26; **Jos 23:13**; 2Ki 17:23; Jer 24:10; [n]Dt 12:5; Jer 7:14; [o]Job 17:6; Ps 44:14; Jer 24:9; Joel 2:17; [p]**Dt 28:37**; Eze 5:15
8 [q]**Lev 26:32**; [r]**Dt 29:24**; Jer 7:4–15; Mt 23:38
9 [s]Dt 29:25; 2Ki 22:17; Jer 5:19; 13:22; 16:11,13; 22:9; [t]**Nu 25:3**; Jer 40:3; 44:23; La 4:12; [u]**Dt 31:29**
11 [v]ver 14
13 [w]Jos 19:27
14 [x]ver 11
15 [y]1Ki 5:13; [z]**2Sa 5:9**; [a]Jos 11:10–11; [b]**Jos 10:33**
16 [c]1Ki 3:1; Ps 45:12; 68:29; 72:10
17 [d]**Jos 10:10**
18 [e]**Jos 19:44**
19 [f]**Ex 1:11**; [g]**Dt 17:16**; 1Ki 4:26; 2Ch 1:14; 9:25
20 [h]**Nu 13:29**; [i]**Jos 11:3**
21 [j]**Ge 9:25–26**; [k]**Jos 15:63**; [l]**Ge 49:15**; **Ex 1:11**; **Dt 20:11**
22 [m]**Lev 25:39**
23 [n]1Ki 5:16
24 [o]**1Ki 3:1**; [p]2Sa 5:9; 1Ki 11:27
25 [q]**Ex 23:14**

[a]6 The Hebrew is plural.
[b]13 *Cabul* sounds like the Hebrew for *good-for-nothing*.
[c]14 That is, about 4 tons (about 4 metric tons)
[d]15 Or *the Millo*; also in verse 24
[e]18 The Hebrew may also be read *Tamar*.
[f]19 Or *charioteers*
[g]21 The Hebrew term refers to the irrevocable giving over of things or persons to the LORD, often by totally destroying them.
[h]25 Traditionally *peace offerings*

the LORD, burning incense before the
LORD along with them, and so fulfilled
the temple obligations.
26King Solomon also built ships[r] at
Ezion Geber,[s] which is near Elath[t] in
Edom, on the shore of the Red Sea.[i]
27And Hiram sent his men—sailors[u]
who knew the sea—to serve in the fleet
with Solomon's men. 28They sailed to
Ophir[v] and brought back 420 talents[j] of
gold,[w] which they delivered to King
Solomon.

The Queen of Sheba Visits Solomon

10:1–13pp—2Ch 9:1–12

10 When the queen of Sheba[a]
heard about the fame[b] of Solo-
mon and his relation to the name of the
LORD, she came to test him with hard
questions.[c] 2Arriving at Jerusalem with
a very great caravan[d]—with camels
carrying spices, large quantities of
gold, and precious stones—she came to
Solomon and talked with him about all
that she had on her mind. 3Solomon
answered all her questions; nothing
was too hard for the king to explain to
her. 4When the queen of Sheba saw all
the wisdom of Solomon and the palace
he had built, 5the food on his table,[e] the
seating of his officials, the attending
servants in their robes, his cupbearers,
and the burnt offerings he made at[a] the
temple of the LORD, she was over-
whelmed.
6She said to the king, "The report I
heard in my own country about your
achievements and your wisdom is true.
7But I did not believe[f] these things until
I came and saw with my own eyes. In-
deed, not even half was told me; in
wisdom and wealth[g] you have far ex-
ceeded the report I heard. 8How happy
your men must be! How happy your
officials, who continually stand before
you and hear[h] your wisdom! 9Praise[i] be
to the LORD your God, who has delight-
ed in you and placed you on the throne
of Israel. Because of the LORD's eternal
love[j] for Israel, he has made you king, to
maintain justice[k] and righteousness."
10And she gave the king 120 talents[b]
of gold,[l] large quantities of spices, and
precious stones. Never again were so
many spices brought in as those the
queen of Sheba gave to King Solomon.
11(Hiram's ships brought gold from
Ophir;[m] and from there they brought
great cargoes of almug-wood[c] and pre-
cious stones. 12The king used the
almug-wood to make supports for the
temple of the LORD and for the royal
palace, and to make harps and lyres for
the musicians. So much almug-wood
has never been imported or seen since
that day.)
13King Solomon gave the queen of
Sheba all she desired and asked for,
besides what he had given her out of his
royal bounty. Then she left and re-
turned with her retinue to her own
country.

Solomon's Splendour

10:14–29pp—2Ch 1:14–17; 9:13–28

14The weight of the gold[n] that Solo-
mon received yearly was 666 talents,[d]
15not including the revenues from mer-
chants and traders and from all the Ara-
bian kings and the governors of the
land.
16King Solomon made two hundred
large shields[o] of hammered gold; six
hundred bekas[e] of gold went into each
shield. 17He also made three hundred
small shields of hammered gold, with
three minas[f] of gold in each shield. The
king put them in the Palace of the Forest
of Lebanon.[p]
18Then the king made a great throne
inlaid with ivory and overlaid with fine
gold. 19The throne had six steps, and its
back had a rounded top. On both sides
of the seat were armrests, with a lion
standing beside each of them. 20Twelve
lions stood on the six steps, one at either
end of each step. Nothing like it had
ever been made for any other kingdom.
21All King Solomon's goblets were gold,
and all the household articles in the
Palace of the Forest of Lebanon were
pure gold.[q] Nothing was made of silver,
because silver was considered of little
value in Solomon's days. 22The king
had a fleet of trading ships[g][r] at sea
along with the ships[s] of Hiram. Once
every three years it returned carrying
gold, silver and ivory, and apes and
baboons.
23King Solomon was greater in riches[t]
and wisdom[u] than all the other kings of
the earth. 24The whole world sought
audience with Solomon to hear the wis-
dom[v] God had put in his heart. 25Year

26 [r]1Ki 10:22; 22:48; 2Ch 20:37; Isa 2:16; [s]**Nu 33:35**; [t]2Ki 14:22; 16:6
27 [u]Eze 27:8
28 [v]**Ge 10:29**; [w]ver 14; 1Ki 10:10–11,14, 21; 2Ch 1:15; Ecc 2:8

Ch. 10

1 [a]**Ge 10:7,28; 25:3**; Mt 12:42; Lk 11:31; [b]Eze 16:14; [c]**Nu 12:8; Jdg 14:12**
2 [d]**Ge 24:10**
5 [e]1Ki 4:22
7 [f]**Ge 45:26**; [g]1Ch 29:25
8 [h]Pr 8:34
9 [i]**1Ki 5:7; Isa 42:10**; [j]**Dt 7:8**; [k]Ps 11:7; 33:5; 72:2; 99:4; 103:6
10 [l]**1Ki 9:28**; Isa 60:6
11 [m]**Ge 10:29**
14 [n]**1Ki 9:28**
16 [o]**2Sa 8:7**
17 [p]**1Ki 7:2**
21 [q]Isa 60:17
22 [r]**1Ki 9:26**; [s]1Ki 9:27; Ps 48:7; Isa 2:16; 23:1, 14; 60:6,9
23 [t]1Ki 3:13; Mt 6:29; [u]**1Ki 3:12**; Mt 12:42
24 [v]**2Sa 14:20**

[i] *26* Hebrew *Yam Suph*; that is, Sea of Reeds
[j] *28* That is, about 14 tons (about 14.5 metric tons)
[a] *5* Or *the ascent by which he went up to*
[b] *10* That is, about 4 tons (about 4 metric tons)
[c] *11* Probably a variant of *algum-wood*; also in verse 12
[d] *14* That is, about 22½ tons (about 23 metric tons)
[e] *16* That is, about 7½ pounds (about 3.5 kilograms)
[f] *17* That is, about 3¾ pounds (about 1.7 kilograms)
[g] *22* Hebrew *of ships of Tarshish*

after year, everyone who came brought
a gift[w]—articles of silver and gold,
robes, weapons and spices, and horses
and mules.
26 Solomon accumulated chariots and
horses;[x] he had fourteen hundred char-
iots and twelve thousand horses,[h]
which he kept in the chariot cities and
also with him in Jerusalem. 27 The king
made silver as common[y] in Jerusalem as
stones,[z] and cedar as plentiful as
sycamore-fig[a] trees in the foothills.
28 Solomon's horses were imported from
Egypt[i] and from Kue[j]—the royal mer-
chants purchased them from Kue.[j]
29 They imported a chariot from Egypt
for six hundred shekels[k] of silver, and a
horse for a hundred and fifty.[l] They also
exported them to all the kings of the
Hittites[b] and of the Arameans.

Solomon's Wives

11 King Solomon, however, loved
many foreign women[a] besides
Pharaoh's daughter—Moabites, Am-
monites,[b] Edomites, Sidonians and
Hittites. 2 They were from nations about
which the LORD had told the Israelites,
"You must not intermarry[c] with them,
because they will surely turn your
hearts after their gods." Nevertheless,
Solomon held fast to them in love. 3 He
had seven hundred wives of royal birth
and three hundred concubines,[d] and his
wives led him astray.[e] 4 As Solomon
grew old, his wives turned his heart
after other gods,[f] and his heart was not
fully devoted[g] to the LORD his God, as
the heart of David his father had been.
5 He followed Ashtoreth[h] the goddess of
the Sidonians, and Molech[a][i] the detest-
able god of the Ammonites. 6 So Solo-
mon did evil[j] in the eyes of the LORD; he
did not follow the LORD completely, as
David his father had done.
7 On a hill east[k] of Jerusalem, Solomon
built a high place for Chemosh[l] the de-
testable god of Moab, and for Molech[m]
the detestable god of the Ammonites.
8 He did the same for all his foreign
wives, who burned incense and offered
sacrifices to their gods.
9 The LORD became angry with Solo-
mon because his heart had turned away
from the LORD, the God of Israel, who
had appeared[n] to him twice. 10 Although
he had forbidden Solomon to follow
other gods,[o] Solomon did not keep the
LORD's command.[p] 11 So the LORD said to
Solomon, "Since this is your attitude
and you have not kept my covenant and
my decrees,[q] which I commanded you, I
will most certainly tear[r] the kingdom
away from you and give it to one of your
subordinates. 12 Nevertheless, for the
sake of David[s] your father, I will not do
it during your lifetime. I will tear it out
of the hand of your son. 13 Yet I will not
tear the whole kingdom from him, but
will give him one tribe[t] for the sake[u] of
David my servant and for the sake of
Jerusalem, which I have chosen."[v]

Solomon's Adversaries

14 Then the LORD raised up against
Solomon an adversary,[w] Hadad the
Edomite, from the royal line of Edom.
15 Earlier when David was fighting with
Edom, Joab the commander of the
army, who had gone up to bury the
dead, had struck down all the men in
Edom.[x] 16 Joab and all the Israelites
stayed there for six months, until they
had destroyed all the men in Edom.
17 But Hadad, still only a boy, fled to
Egypt with some Edomite officials who
had served his father. 18 They set out
from Midian and went to Paran.[y] Then
taking men from Paran with them, they
went to Egypt, to Pharaoh king of
Egypt, who gave Hadad a house and
land and provided him with food.
19 Pharaoh was so pleased with Hadad
that he gave him a sister of his own wife,
Queen Tahpenes, in marriage. 20 The
sister of Tahpenes bore him a son
named Genubath, whom Tahpenes
brought up in the royal palace. There
Genubath lived with Pharaoh's own
children.
21 While he was in Egypt, Hadad
heard that David rested with his fathers
and that Joab the commander of the
army was also dead. Then Hadad said
to Pharaoh, "Let me go, so that I may
return to my own country."
22 "What have you lacked here that
you want to go back to your own
country?" Pharaoh asked.
"Nothing," Hadad replied, "but do
let me go!"
23 And God raised up against Solomon
another adversary,[z] Rezon son of
Eliada, who had fled from his master,
Hadadezer[a] king of Zobah. 24 He
gathered men around him and became
the leader of a band of rebels when

25 w 1Sa 10:27
26 x Dt 17:16
27 y Dt 17:17; z Job 27:16; Isa 60:17; a 1Ch 27:28; Am 7:14
29 b Nu 13:29

Ch. 11

1 a ver 3; Ex 34:16; b 1Ki 14:21,31
2 c Ex 34:16; 1Ki 16:31
3 d Ge 22:24; Est 2:14; e ver 1; Dt 17:17; Ne 13:26; Pr 31:3
4 f Ex 34:16; g 1Ki 8:61; 1Ch 29:19
5 h Jdg 2:13; i ver 7; Lev 18:21; Isa 57:9; Zep 1:5
6 j Dt 4:25
7 k 2Ki 23:13; l Nu 21:29; m Lev 18:21; 20:2–5; Ac 7:43
9 n 1Ki 3:5
10 o 1Ki 9:6; p 1Ki 6:12
11 q Lev 18:4; r ver 31; 1Sa 15:27; 2Ki 17:21; Mt 21:43
12 s Ps 89:33
13 t 1Ki 12:20; u 2Sa 7:15; v Dt 12:11
14 w 1Ki 5:4
15 x 1Ch 18:12
18 y Nu 10:12
23 z 1Ki 5:4; a 2Sa 8:3

h 26 Or *charioteers*
i 28 Or possibly *Muzur*, a region in Cilicia; also in verse 29 j 28 Probably *Cilicia*
k 29 That is, about 15 pounds (about 7 kilograms)
l 29 That is, about 3¾ pounds (about 1.7 kilograms)
a 5 Hebrew *Milcom*; also in verse 33

David destroyed the forces[b] ⌊of Zobah⌋; the rebels went to Damascus,[b] where they settled and took control. 25Rezon was Israel's adversary as long as Solomon lived, adding to the trouble caused by Hadad. So Rezon ruled in Aram[c] and was hostile towards Israel.

Jeroboam Rebels Against Solomon

26Also, Jeroboam son of Nebat rebelled[d] against the king. He was one of Solomon's officials, an Ephraimite from Zeredah, and his mother was a widow named Zeruah.

27Here is the account of how he rebelled against the king: Solomon had built the supporting terraces[c][e] and had filled in the gap in the wall of the city of David his father. 28Now Jeroboam was a man of standing,[f] and when Solomon saw how well[g] the young man did his work, he put him in charge of the whole labour force of the house of Joseph.

29About that time Jeroboam was going out of Jerusalem, and Ahijah[h] the prophet of Shiloh met him on the way, wearing a new cloak. The two of them were alone out in the country, 30and Ahijah took hold of the new cloak he was wearing and tore[i] it into twelve pieces. 31Then he said to Jeroboam, "Take ten pieces for yourself, for this is what the LORD, the God of Israel, says: 'See, I am going to tear[j] the kingdom out of Solomon's hand and give you ten tribes. 32But for the sake[k] of my servant David and the city of Jerusalem, which I have chosen out of all the tribes of Israel, he will have one tribe. 33I will do this because they have[d] forsaken me and worshipped[l] Ashtoreth the goddess of the Sidonians, Chemosh the god of the Moabites, and Molech[e] the god of the Ammonites, and have not walked[m] in my ways, nor done what is right in my eyes, nor kept my statutes[n] and laws as David, Solomon's father, did.

34" 'But I will not take the whole kingdom out of Solomon's hand; I have made him ruler all the days of his life for the sake of David my servant, whom I chose and who observed my commands and statutes. 35I will take the kingdom from his son's hands and give you ten tribes. 36I will give one tribe[o] to his son so that David my servant may always have a lamp[p] before me in Jerusalem, the city where I chose to put my Name. 37However, as for you, I will take you, and you will rule[q] over all that your heart desires;[r] you will be king over Israel. 38If you do whatever I command you and walk in my ways and do what is right[s] in my eyes by keeping my statutes[t] and commands, as David my servant did, I will be with you. I will build you a dynasty[u] as enduring as the one I built for David and will give Israel to you. 39I will humble David's descendants because of this, but not for ever.' "

40Solomon tried to kill Jeroboam, but Jeroboam fled[v] to Egypt, to Shishak[w] the king, and stayed there until Solomon's death.

Solomon's Death

11:41–43pp—2Ch 9:29–31

41As for the other events of Solomon's reign—all he did and the wisdom he displayed—are they not written in the book of the annals of Solomon? 42Solomon reigned in Jerusalem over all Israel for forty years. 43Then he rested with his fathers and was buried in the city of David his father. And Rehoboam[x] his son succeeded him as king.

Israel Rebels Against Rehoboam

12:1–24pp—2Ch 10:1–11:4

12 Rehoboam went to Shechem,[a] for all the Israelites had gone there to make him king. 2When Jeroboam son of Nebat heard this (he was still in Egypt, where he had fled[b] from King Solomon), he returned from[a] Egypt. 3So they sent for Jeroboam, and he and the whole assembly of Israel went to Rehoboam and said to him: 4"Your father put a heavy yoke[c] on us, but now lighten the harsh labour and the heavy yoke he put on us, and we will serve you."

5Rehoboam answered, "Go away for three days and then come back to me." So the people went away.

6Then King Rehoboam consulted the elders[d] who had served his father Solomon during his lifetime. "How would you advise me to answer these people?" he asked.

7They replied, "If today you will be a servant to these people and serve them and give them a favourable answer,[e] they will always be your servants."

8But Rehoboam rejected[f] the advice the elders gave him and consulted the young men who had grown up with him and were serving him. 9He asked

24 [b]2Sa 8:5
25 [c]Ge 10:22; 2Sa 10:19
26 [d]2Ch 13:6
27 [e]1Ki 9:24
28 [f]Ru 2:1; [g]Ge 39:4; Pr 22:29
29 [h]1Ki 12:15; 14:2; 2Ch 9:29; 10:15
30 [i]1Sa 15:27
31 [j]ver 11; 1Sa 15:27
32 [k]2Sa 7:15
33 [l]Jdg 2:13; [m]2Ki 21:22; [n]1Ki 3:3
36 [o]1Ki 12:17; [p]2Sa 21:17
37 [q]1Ki 14:7; [r]2Sa 3:21
38 [s]Dt 12:25; 2Sa 8:15; [t]Dt 17:19; [u]Ex 1:21
40 [v]1Ki 12:2; 2Ch 10:2; [w]2Ch 12:2
43 [x]Mt 1:7

Ch. 12

1 [a]ver 25; Ge 12:6; Jos 24:32
2 [b]1Ki 11:40
4 [c]1Sa 8:11–18; 1Ki 4:20–28
6 [d]1Ki 4:2
7 [e]Pr 15:1
8 [f]Lev 19:32

[b]24 Hebrew *destroyed them* [c]27 Or *the Millo*
[d]33 Hebrew; Septuagint, Vulgate and Syriac *because he has* [e]33 Hebrew *Milcom*
[a]2 Or *he remained in*

them, "What is your advice? How
should we answer these people who say
to me, 'Lighten the yoke your father put
on us'?"
10The young men who had grown up
with him replied, "Tell these people
who have said to you, 'Your father put a
heavy yoke on us, but make our yoke
lighter'—tell them, 'My little finger is
thicker than my father's waist. 11My
father laid on you a heavy yoke; I
will make it even heavier. My father
scourged you with whips; I will scourge
you with scorpions.'"
12Three days later Jeroboam and all
the people returned to Rehoboam, as
the king had said, "Come back to me in
three days." 13The king answered the
people harshly. Rejecting the advice
given him by the elders, 14he followed
the advice of the young men and said,
"My father made your yoke heavy; I
will make it even heavier. My father
scourged[g] you with whips; I will
scourge you with scorpions." 15So the
king did not listen to the people, for this
turn of events was from the LORD,[h] to
fulfil the word the LORD had spoken to
Jeroboam son of Nebat through Ahijah[i]
the Shilonite.
16When all Israel saw that the king
refused to listen to them, they answered
the king:

"What share[j] do we have in David,
what part in Jesse's son?
To your tents, O Israel![k]
Look after your own house, O
David!"

So the Israelites went home.[l] 17But as for
the Israelites who were living in the
towns of Judah,[m] Rehoboam still ruled
over them.
18King Rehoboam sent out Adoniram,[b][n] who was in charge of forced
labour, but all Israel stoned him to
death.[o] King Rehoboam, however,
managed to get into his chariot and
escape to Jerusalem. 19So Israel has been
in rebellion against the house of David[p]
to this day.
20When all the Israelites heard that
Jeroboam had returned, they sent and
called him to the assembly and made
him king over all Israel. Only the tribe of
Judah remained loyal to the house of
David.[q]
21When Rehoboam arrived in Jerusalem, he mustered the whole house of
Judah and the tribe of Benjamin—a
hundred and eighty thousand fighting
men—to make war[r] against the house
of Israel and to regain the kingdom for
Rehoboam son of Solomon.
22But this word of God came to Shemaiah[s] the man of God:[t] 23"Say to Rehoboam son of Solomon king of Judah,
to the whole house of Judah and Benjamin, and to the rest of the people,
24'This is what the LORD says: Do not go
up to fight against your brothers, the
Israelites. Go home, every one of you,
for this is my doing.'" So they obeyed
the word of the LORD and went home
again, as the LORD had ordered.

Golden Calves at Bethel and Dan

25Then Jeroboam fortified Shechem[u]
in the hill country of Ephraim and lived
there. From there he went out and built
up Peniel.[c][v]
26Jeroboam thought to himself, "The
kingdom is now likely to revert to the
house of David. 27If these people go up
to offer sacrifices at the temple of the
LORD in Jerusalem,[w] they will again give
their allegiance to their lord, Rehoboam
king of Judah. They will kill me and
return to King Rehoboam."
28After seeking advice, the king made
two golden calves.[x] He said to the people, "It is too much for you to go up to
Jerusalem. Here are your gods, O Israel,
who brought you up out of Egypt."[y]
29One he set up in Bethel,[z] and the other
in Dan.[a] 30And this thing became a sin;[b]
the people went even as far as Dan to
worship the one there.
31Jeroboam built shrines[c] on high
places and appointed priests[d] from all
sorts of people, even though they were
not Levites. 32He instituted a festival on
the fifteenth day of the eighth[e] month,
like the festival held in Judah, and
offered sacrifices on the altar. This he
did in Bethel,[f] sacrificing to the calves he
had made. And at Bethel he also installed priests at the high places he
had made. 33On the fifteenth day of
the eighth month, a month of his own
choosing, he offered sacrifices on the
altar he had built at Bethel.[g] So he instituted the festival for the Israelites and
went up to the altar to make offerings.

The Man of God From Judah

13 By the word of the LORD a man
of God[a] came from Judah to
Bethel,[b] as Jeroboam was standing by

14 [g]Ex 1:14
15 [h]**Dt 2:30**; 2Ch 25:20; [i]**1Ki 11:29**
16 [j]**Ge 31:14**; [k]**2Sa 20:1**; [l]Isa 7:17
17 [m]1Ki 11:36
18 [n]**2Sa 20:24**; [o]**Jos 7:25**
19 [p]2Ki 17:21
20 [q]1Ki 11:13; Eze 37:16
21 [r]1Ki 14:30; 15:6,16; 2Ch 11:1
22 [s]2Ch 12:5–7; [t]**Dt 33:1**; 2Ki 4:7
25 [u]**ver 1**; [v]**Jdg 8:8**
27 [w]Dt 12:5–6
28 [x]**Ex 32:4; 2Ch 11:15**; [y]**Ex 32:8**
29 [z]**Ge 12:8; Jos 7:2**; [a]Jdg 18:27–31; Am 8:14
30 [b]1Ki 13:34; 14:16; 15:26, 30; 16:2; 2Ki 3:3; 10:29; 13:2; 17:21
31 [c]**Lev 26:30**; 1Ki 13:32; 2Ki 17:29; [d]**Ex 29:9**; 1Ki 13:33; 2Ki 17:32; 2Ch 11:14–15; 13:9
32 [e]**Nu 29:12**; [f]2Ki 10:29
33 [g]2Ki 23:15; Am 7:13

Ch. 13

1 [a]**Dt 33:1; Jdg 13:6**; [b]Am 7:13

[b]18 Some Septuagint manuscripts and Syriac (see also 1 Kings 4:6 and 5:14); Hebrew *Adoram*
[c]25 Hebrew *Penuel*, a variant of *Peniel*

the altar to make an offering. 2He cried out against the altar by the word of the LORD: "O altar, altar! This is what the LORD says: 'A son named Josiah[c] will be born to the house of David. On you he will sacrifice the priests of the high places[d] who now make offerings here, and human bones will be burned on you.'" 3That same day the man of God gave a sign:[e] "This is the sign the LORD has declared: The altar will be split apart and the ashes on it will be poured out."

4When King Jeroboam heard what the man of God cried out against the altar at Bethel, he stretched out his hand from the altar and said, "Seize him!" But the hand he stretched out towards the man shrivelled up, so that he could not pull it back. 5Also, the altar was split apart and its ashes poured out according to the sign given by the man of God by the word of the LORD.

6Then the king said to the man of God, "Intercede[f] with the LORD your God and pray for me that my hand may be restored." So the man of God interceded with the LORD, and the king's hand was restored and became as it was before.

7The king said to the man of God, "Come home with me and have something to eat, and I will give you a gift."[g]

8But the man of God answered the king, "Even if you were to give me half your possessions,[h] I would not go with you, nor would I eat bread[i] or drink water here. 9For I was commanded by the word of the LORD: 'You must not eat bread or drink water or return by the way you came.'" 10So he took another road and did not return by the way he had come to Bethel.

11Now there was a certain old prophet living in Bethel, whose sons came and told him all that the man of God had done there that day. They also told their father what he had said to the king. 12Their father asked them, "Which way did he go?" And his sons showed him which road the man of God from Judah had taken. 13So he said to his sons, "Saddle the donkey for me." And when they had saddled the donkey for him, he mounted it 14and rode after the man of God. He found him sitting under an oak tree and asked, "Are you the man of God who came from Judah?"

"I am," he replied.

15So the prophet said to him, "Come home with me and eat."

16The man of God said, "I cannot turn back and go with you, nor can I eat bread[j] or drink water with you in this place. 17I have been told by the word of the LORD: 'You must not eat bread or drink water there or return by the way you came.'"

18The old prophet answered, "I too am a prophet, as you are. And an angel said to me by the word of the LORD:[k] 'Bring him back with you to your house so that he may eat bread and drink water.'" (But he was lying[l] to him.) 19So the man of God returned with him and ate and drank in his house.

20While they were sitting at the table, the word of the LORD came to the old prophet who had brought him back. 21He cried out to the man of God who had come from Judah, "This is what the LORD says: 'You have defied[m] the word of the LORD and have not kept the command the LORD your God gave you. 22You came back and ate bread and drank water in the place where he told you not to eat or drink. Therefore your body will not be buried in the tomb of your fathers.'"

23When the man of God had finished eating and drinking, the prophet who had brought him back saddled his donkey for him. 24As he went on his way, a lion[n] met him on the road and killed him, and his body was thrown down on the road, with both the donkey and the lion standing beside it. 25Some people who passed by saw the body thrown down there, with the lion standing beside the body, and they went and reported it in the city where the old prophet lived.

26When the prophet who had brought him back from his journey heard of it, he said, "It is the man of God who defied[o] the word of the LORD. The LORD has given him over to the lion, which has mauled him and killed him, as the word of the LORD had warned him."

27The prophet said to his sons, "Saddle the donkey for me," and they did so. 28Then he went out and found the body thrown down on the road, with the donkey and the lion standing beside it. The lion had neither eaten the body nor mauled the donkey. 29So the prophet picked up the body of the man of God, laid it on the donkey, and brought it back to his own city to mourn for him and bury him. 30Then he laid the body in his own tomb,[p] and they mourned over him and said, "Oh, my brother!"[q]

31After burying him, he said to his sons, "When I die, bury me in the grave where the man of God is buried; lay my bones[r] beside his bones. 32For the message he declared by the word of the

2 [c]2Ki 23:15-16, 20; 2Ch 34:5; [d]**Lev 26:30**
3 [e]**Ge 24:14; Ex 4:8; Jn 2:11**
6 [f]**Ge 20:7; Nu 11:2; Jer 37:3;** Ac 8:24
7 [g]**1Sa 9:7**
8 [h]Nu 22:18; [i]ver 16
16 [j]ver 8
18 [k]1Ki 22:6,12; 2Ch 35:21; Isa 36:10; [l]**Ge 19:14; Dt 13:3**
21 [m]ver 26; **1Sa 13:14;** 1Ki 20:35
24 [n]1Ki 20:36
26 [o]**ver 21**
30 [p]2Ki 23:17; [q]Jer 22:18
31 [r]2Ki 23:18

LORD against the altar in Bethel and against all the shrines on the high places[s] in the towns of Samaria[t] will certainly come true."[u]

33Even after this, Jeroboam did not change his evil ways,[v] but once more appointed priests for the high places from all sorts[w] of people. Anyone who wanted to become a priest he consecrated for the high places. 34This was the sin[x] of the house of Jeroboam that led to its downfall and to its destruction[y] from the face of the earth.

Ahijah's Prophecy Against Jeroboam

14 At that time Abijah son of Jeroboam became ill, 2and Jeroboam said to his wife, "Go, disguise yourself, so that you won't be recognised as the wife of Jeroboam. Then go to Shiloh. Ahijah[a] the prophet is there—the one who told me I would be king over this people. 3Take ten loaves of bread[b] with you, some cakes and a jar of honey, and go to him. He will tell you what will happen to the boy." 4So Jeroboam's wife did what he said and went to Ahijah's house in Shiloh.

Now Ahijah could not see; his sight was gone because of his age. 5But the LORD had told Ahijah, "Jeroboam's wife is coming to ask you about her son, for he is ill, and you are to give her such and such an answer. When she arrives, she will pretend to be someone else."

6So when Ahijah heard the sound of her footsteps at the door, he said, "Come in, wife of Jeroboam. Why this pretence?[c] I have been sent to you with bad news. 7Go, tell Jeroboam that this is what the LORD, the God of Israel, says:[d] 'I raised you up from among the people and made you a leader[e] over my people Israel. 8I tore[f] the kingdom away from the house of David and gave it to you, but you have not been like my servant David, who kept my commands and followed me with all his heart, doing only what was right[g] in my eyes. 9You have done more evil[h] than all who lived before you.[i] You have made for yourself other gods, idols[j] made of metal; you have provoked[k] me to anger and thrust me behind your back.[l]

10" 'Because of this, I am going to bring disaster[m] on the house of Jeroboam. I will cut off from Jeroboam every last male in Israel—slave or free.[n] I will burn up the house of Jeroboam as one burns dung, until it is all gone.[o] 11Dogs[p] will eat those belonging to Jeroboam who die in the city, and the birds of the air[q] will feed on those who die in the country. The LORD has spoken!'

12"As for you, go back home. When you set foot in your city, the boy will die. 13All Israel will mourn for him and bury him. He is the only one belonging to Jeroboam who will be buried, because he is the only one in the house of Jeroboam in whom the LORD, the God of Israel, has found anything good.[r]

14"The LORD will raise up for himself a king over Israel who will cut off the family of Jeroboam. This is the day! What? Yes, even now.[a] 15And the LORD will strike Israel, so that it will be like a reed swaying in the water. He will uproot[s] Israel from this good land that he gave to their forefathers and scatter them beyond the River,[b] because they provoked[t] the LORD to anger by making Asherah[u] poles.[c] 16And he will give Israel up because of the sins[v] Jeroboam has committed and has caused Israel to commit."

17Then Jeroboam's wife got up and left and went to Tirzah.[w] As soon as she stepped over the threshold of the house, the boy died. 18They buried him, and all Israel mourned for him, as the LORD had said through his servant the prophet Ahijah.

19The other events of Jeroboam's reign, his wars and how he ruled, are written in the book of the annals of the kings of Israel. 20He reigned for twenty-two years and then rested with his fathers. And Nadab his son succeeded him as king.

Rehoboam King of Judah

14:21,25–31pp—2Ch 12:9–16

21Rehoboam son of Solomon was king in Judah. He was forty-one years old when he became king, and he reigned for seventeen years in Jerusalem, the city the LORD had chosen out of all the tribes of Israel in which to put his Name. His mother's name was Naamah; she was an Ammonite.[x]

22Judah[y] did evil in the eyes of the LORD. By the sins they committed they stirred up his jealous anger[z] more than their fathers had done. 23They also set up for themselves high places, sacred stones[a] and Asherah poles[b] on every high hill and under every spreading tree.[c] 24There were even male shrine-

32 [s]**Lev 26:30; 1Ki 12:31;** [t]1Ki 16:24,28; 20:1; 2Ki 10:1; 15:13; [u]2Ki 23:16
33 [v]1Ki 15:26; [w]**1Ki 12:31**
34 [x]**1Ki 12:30;** [y]1Ki 14:10; 15:29; 2Ki 9:9; Jer 35:17; Am 7:9

Ch. 14

2 [a]**1Ki 11:29**
3 [b]**1Sa 9:7**
6 [c]**1Sa 28:12**
7 [d]1Ki 15:29; [e]1Ki 11:37
8 [f]**1Sa 15:27;** [g]**2Sa 8:15;** 1Ki 3:3; 15:5; 2Ki 14:3; 15:3,34; 16:2; 18:3; 20:3; 22:2
9 [h]1Ki 16:30,33; 21:25; 2Ki 21:9,11; 24:3; [i]1Ki 16:2; [j]**Ex 20:4; 32:4;** 2Ch 11:15; [k]Dt 32:16; 1Ki 16:2; Ps 78:58; Jer 7:18; 8:19; 32:32; 44:3; Eze 8:17; 16:26; [l]Ne 9:26; Ps 50:17; Jer 2:27; 32:33; Eze 23:35
10 [m]**Jos 23:15; 1Ki 13:34;** [n]**Dt 32:36;** 2Ki 9:8–9; [o]1Sa 12:25; 15:26; 1Ki 15:29; Hos 13:11
11 [p]1Ki 16:4; 21:24; [q]**Ge 40:19; Dt 28:26**
13 [r]2Ch 12:12; 19:3
15 [s]**Dt 29:28; 2Ch 7:20;** [t]Jer 44:3; [u]**Dt 12:3**
16 [v]**1Ki 12:30; 15:26**
17 [w]**Jos 12:24; 1Ki 15:33**
21 [x]**1Ki 11:1**
22 [y]2Ki 17:19; 2Ch 12:1; [z]Dt 32:21; Ps 78:58; Jer 44:3; **1Co 10:22**
23 [a]**Ex 23:24;** Dt 16:22; Hos 10:1; [b]**Dt 12:3;** [c]**Dt 12:2;** Eze 6:13

[a]14 The meaning of the Hebrew for this sentence is uncertain. [b]15 That is, the Euphrates
[c]15 That is, symbols of the goddess Asherah; here and elsewhere in 1 Kings

prostitutes[d] in the land; the people en-
gaged in all the detestable[e] practices of
the nations the LORD had driven out
before the Israelites.
25 In the fifth year of King Rehoboam,
Shishak king of Egypt attacked[f] Jeru-
salem. 26 He carried off the treasures of
the temple[g] of the LORD and the trea-
sures of the royal palace. He took every-
thing, including all the gold shields[h]
Solomon had made. 27 So King Re-
hoboam made bronze shields to replace
them and assigned these to the
commanders of the guard on duty at
the entrance to the royal palace.[i]
28 Whenever the king went to the LORD's
temple, the guards bore the shields, and
afterwards they returned them to the
guardroom.
29 As for the other events of Re-
hoboam's reign, and all he did, are they
not written in the book of the annals of
the kings of Judah? 30 There was con-
tinual warfare[j] between Rehoboam and
Jeroboam. 31 And Rehoboam rested with
his fathers and was buried with them in
the City of David. His mother's name
was Naamah; she was an Ammonite.[k]
And Abijah[d] his son succeeded him as
king.

Abijah King of Judah

15:1–2,6–8pp—2Ch 13:1–2,22–14:1

15 In the eighteenth year of the
reign of Jeroboam son of Nebat,
Abijah[a] became king of Judah, 2 and he
reigned in Jerusalem for three years. His
mother's name was Maacah[a] daughter
of Abishalom.[b]
3 He committed all the sins his father
had done before him; his heart was not
fully devoted[b] to the LORD his God, as
the heart of David his forefather had
been. 4 Nevertheless, for David's sake
the LORD his God gave him a lamp[c] in
Jerusalem by raising up a son to succeed
him and by making Jerusalem strong.
5 For David had done what was right in
the eyes of the LORD and had not failed
to keep[d] any of the LORD's commands all
the days of his life—except in the case of
Uriah[e] the Hittite.
6 There was war[f] between Rehoboam[c]
and Jeroboam throughout ⌞Abijah's⌟
lifetime. 7 As for the other events of Abi-
jah's reign, and all he did, are they not
written in the book of the annals of the
kings of Judah? There was war between
Abijah and Jeroboam. 8 And Abijah
rested with his fathers and was buried
in the City of David. And Asa his son
succeeded him as king.

Asa King of Judah

15:9–22pp—2Ch 14:2–3; 15:16–16:6
15:23–24pp—2Ch 16:11–17:1

9 In the twentieth year of Jeroboam
king of Israel, Asa became king of
Judah, 10 and he reigned in Jerusalem for
forty-one years. His grandmother's
name was Maacah[g] daughter of
Abishalom.
11 Asa did what was right in the eyes
of the LORD, as his father David[h] had
done. 12 He expelled the male shrine-
prostitutes[i] from the land and got rid
of all the idols[j] his fathers had made.
13 He even deposed his grandmother
Maacah[k] from her position as queen
mother,[l] because she had made a repul-
sive Asherah pole. Asa cut the pole
down[m] and burned it in the Kidron Val-
ley. 14 Although he did not remove[n] the
high places, Asa's heart was fully com-
mitted[o] to the LORD all his life. 15 He
brought into the temple of the LORD the
silver and gold and the articles that he
and his father had dedicated.[p]
16 There was war[q] between Asa and
Baasha king of Israel throughout their
reigns. 17 Baasha king of Israel went up
against Judah and fortified Ramah[r] to
prevent anyone from leaving or enter-
ing the territory of Asa king of Judah.
18 Asa then took all the silver and gold
that was left in the treasuries of the
LORD's temple[s] and of his own palace.
He entrusted it to his officials and sent[t]
them to Ben-Hadad[u] son of Tabrimmon,
the son of Hezion, the king of Aram,
who was ruling in Damascus. 19 "Let
there be a treaty[v] between me and you,"
he said, "as there was between my
father and your father. See, I am send-
ing you a gift of silver and gold. Now
break your treaty with Baasha king of
Israel so that he will withdraw from
me."
20 Ben-Hadad agreed with King Asa
and sent the commanders of his forces
against the towns of Israel. He con-
quered[w] Ijon, Dan, Abel Beth Maacah
and all Kinnereth in addition to Naph-
tali. 21 When Baasha heard this, he stop-
ped building Ramah[x] and withdrew to
Tirzah.[y] 22 Then King Asa issued an

24 [d] **Dt 23:17;** [e] 1Ki 11:5–7; 2Ki 21:2; Ezr 9:11; Pr 21:27; Isa 1:13; Jer 16:18; 32:35; 44:4
25 [f] 2Ch 12:2
26 [g] 1Ki 15:15,18; [h] **2Sa 8:7**
27 [i] 2Ki 11:5
30 [j] 2Sa 3:1; **1Ki 12:21**
31 [k] **1Ki 11:1**

Ch. 15

2 [a] ver 10,13; 2Ch 11:20
3 [b] **1Ki 8:61**
4 [c] **2Sa 21:17**
5 [d] **Dt 5:32; 1Ki 9:4;** [e] 2Sa 11:2–27; 12:9
6 [f] ver 16,32; **1Ki 12:21;** 2Ch 16:9
10 [g] **ver 2**
11 [h] 1Ki 9:4
12 [i] 1Ki 14:24; [j] 2Ch 15:8
13 [k] **ver 2;** [l] **1Ki 2:19;** [m] **Ex 34:13**
14 [n] 2Ch 14:5; 17:6; [o] **1Ki 8:61**
15 [p] **2Sa 8:11**
16 [q] **ver 6; 1Ki 12:21**
17 [r] **Jos 18:25**
18 [s] **1Ki 14:26;** [t] 2Ki 12:18; 16:8; 18:14–16; Joel 3:5; [u] ver 18–20; 1Ki 20:1; 2Ki 6:24; 13:3; Jer 49:27
19 [v] **Ex 23:32; 1Ki 5:12**
20 [w] 1Ki 20:34
21 [x] **Jos 18:25;** [y] 1Ki 16:15–17

d *31* Some Hebrew manuscripts and Septuagint (see also 2 Chron. 12:16); most Hebrew manuscripts *Abijam*

a *1* Some Hebrew manuscripts and Septuagint (see also 2 Chron. 12:16); most Hebrew manuscripts *Abijam;* also in verses 7 and 8

b *2* A variant of *Absalom;* also in verse 10

c *6* Most Hebrew manuscripts; some Hebrew manuscripts and Syriac *Abijam* (that is, Abijah)

order to all Judah—no-one was exempt
—and they carried away from Ramah[z]
the stones and timber Baasha had been
using there. With them King Asa[a]
built up Geba[b] in Benjamin, and also
Mizpah.[c]
23As for all the other events of Asa's
reign, all his achievements, all he did
and the cities he built, are they not
written in the book of the annals of the
kings of Judah? In his old age, however,
his feet became diseased. 24Then Asa
rested with his fathers and was buried
with them in the city of his father David.
And Jehoshaphat[d] his son succeeded
him as king.

Nadab King of Israel

25Nadab son of Jeroboam became king
of Israel in the second year of Asa king
of Judah, and he reigned over Israel for
two years. 26He did evil[e] in the eyes of
the LORD, walking in the ways of his
father[f] and in his sin, which he had
caused Israel to commit.
27Baasha son of Ahijah of the house of
Issachar plotted against him, and he
struck him down[g] at Gibbethon,[h] a
Philistine town, while Nadab and all
Israel were besieging it. 28Baasha killed
Nadab in the third year of Asa king of
Judah and succeeded him as king.
29As soon as he began to reign, he
killed Jeroboam's whole family.[i] He did
not leave Jeroboam anyone that
breathed, but destroyed them all,
according to the word of the LORD given
through his servant Ahijah the Shilo-
nite—30because of the sins[j] Jeroboam
had committed and had caused[k] Israel
to commit, and because he provoked
the LORD, the God of Israel, to anger.
31As for the other events of Nadab's
reign, and all he did, are they not writ-
ten in the book of the annals[l] of the
kings of Israel? 32There was war[m] be-
tween Asa and Baasha king of Israel
throughout their reigns.

Baasha King of Israel

33In the third year of Asa king of
Judah, Baasha son of Ahijah became
king of all Israel in Tirzah,[n] and he
reigned for twenty-four years. 34He did
evil[o] in the eyes of the LORD, walking in
the ways of Jeroboam and in his sin,
which he had caused Israel to commit.

16 Then the word of the LORD came
to Jehu[a] son of Hanani[b] against
Baasha: 2"I lifted you up from the dust[c]
and made you leader[d] of my people
Israel, but you walked in the ways of
Jeroboam and caused[e] my people Israel
to sin and to provoke me to anger by
their sins. 3So I am about to consume
Baasha[f] and his house,[g] and I will make
your house like that of Jeroboam son of
Nebat. 4Dogs[h] will eat those belonging
to Baasha who die in the city, and the
birds of the air[i] will feed on those who
die in the country."
5As for the other events of Baasha's
reign, what he did and his achieve-
ments, are they not written in the book
of the annals[j] of the kings of Israel?
6Baasha rested with his fathers and
was buried in Tirzah.[k] And Elah his son
succeeded him as king.
7Moreover, the word of the LORD
came[l] through the prophet Jehu[m] son
of Hanani to Baasha and his house,
because of all the evil he had done in
the eyes of the LORD, provoking him
to anger by the things he did, and
becoming like the house of Jeroboam
—and also because he destroyed it.

Elah King of Israel

8In the twenty-sixth year of Asa king
of Judah, Elah son of Baasha became
king of Israel, and he reigned in Tirzah
for two years.
9Zimri, one of his officials, who had
command of half his chariots, plotted
against him. Elah was in Tirzah at the
time, getting drunk[n] in the home of
Arza, the man in charge[o] of the palace at
Tirzah. 10Zimri came in, struck him
down and killed him in the twenty-
seventh year of Asa king of Judah. Then
he succeeded him as king.[p]
11As soon as he began to reign and
was seated on the throne, he killed off
Baasha's whole family.[q] He did not
spare a single male, whether relative or
friend. 12So Zimri destroyed the whole
family of Baasha, in accordance with the
word of the LORD spoken against Baasha
through the prophet Jehu—13because
of all the sins Baasha and his son Elah
had committed and had caused Israel to
commit, so that they provoked the
LORD, the God of Israel, to anger by their
worthless idols.[r]
14As for the other events of Elah's
reign, and all he did, are they not writ-
ten in the book of the annals of the kings
of Israel?

Zimri King of Israel

15In the twenty-seventh year of Asa
king of Judah, Zimri reigned in Tirzah

22 [z]ver 17; [a]ver 9–24; Jer 41:9; [b]**Jos 18:24**; 2Ki 23:8; [c]**Jos 11:3**
24 [d]Mt 1:8
26 [e]**Dt 4:25**; [f]**1Ki 12:30**
27 [g]1Ki 14:14; [h]**Jos 19:44**
29 [i]**1Ki 13:34**
30 [j]**1Ki 12:30**; [k]1Ki 16:26; 2Ki 3:3; 14:24; 15:28; 21:16
31 [l]1Ki 11:41
32 [m]**ver 6**
33 [n]1Ki 14:17; 16:6,23; 2Ki 15:14; SS 6:4
34 [o]ver 26

Ch. 16

1 [a]ver 7; 2Ch 19:2; 20:34; [b]2Ch 16:7
2 [c]1Sa 2:8; [d]**1Ki 14:7–9**; [e]**1Ki 12:30**
3 [f]2Ki 9:9; [g]ver 11; 1Ki 21:22
4 [h]**1Ki 14:11**; [i]**Ge 40:19**
5 [j]1Ki 15:31
6 [k]**1Ki 15:33**
7 [l]**1Ki 6:11**; [m]**ver 1**
9 [n]1Ki 20:12,16; Pr 31:4–5; [o]1Ki 18:3
10 [p]2Ki 9:31
11 [q]**ver 3**
13 [r]**Dt 32:21**

for seven days. The army was encamped near Gibbethon,[s] a Philistine town. 16When the Israelites in the camp heard that Zimri had plotted against the king and murdered him, they proclaimed Omri, the commander of the army, king over Israel that very day there in the camp. 17Then Omri and all the Israelites with him withdrew from Gibbethon and laid siege to Tirzah. 18When Zimri saw that the city was taken, he went into the citadel of the royal palace and set the palace on fire around him. So he died, 19because of the sins he had committed, doing evil in the eyes of the LORD and walking in the ways of Jeroboam and in the sin he had committed and had caused Israel to commit.

20As for the other events of Zimri's reign, and the rebellion he carried out, are they not written in the book of the annals of the kings of Israel?

Omri King of Israel

21Then the people of Israel were split into two factions; half supported Tibni son of Ginath for king, and the other half supported Omri. 22But Omri's followers proved stronger than those of Tibni son of Ginath. So Tibni died and Omri became king.

23In the thirty-first year of Asa king of Judah, Omri became king of Israel, and he reigned for twelve years, six of them in Tirzah.[t] 24He bought the hill of Samaria from Shemer for two talents[a] of silver and built a city on the hill, calling it Samaria,[u] after Shemer, the name of the former owner of the hill.

25But Omri did evil[v] in the eyes of the LORD and sinned more than all those before him. 26He walked in all the ways of Jeroboam son of Nebat and in his sin, which he had caused[w] Israel to commit, so that they provoked the LORD, the God of Israel, to anger by their worthless idols.[x]

27As for the other events of Omri's reign, what he did and the things he achieved, are they not written in the book of the annals of the kings of Israel? 28Omri rested with his fathers and was buried in Samaria.[y] And Ahab his son succeeded him as king.

Ahab Becomes King of Israel

29In the thirty-eighth year of Asa king of Judah, Ahab son of Omri became king of Israel, and he reigned in Samaria over Israel for twenty-two years. 30Ahab son of Omri did more[z] evil in the eyes of the LORD than any of those before him. 31He not only considered it trivial to commit the sins of Jeroboam son of Nebat, but he also married[a] Jezebel daughter[b] of Ethbaal king of the Sidonians, and began to serve Baal[c] and worship him. 32He set up an altar[d] for Baal in the temple[e] of Baal that he built in Samaria. 33Ahab also made an Asherah pole[f] and did more[g] to provoke the LORD, the God of Israel, to anger than did all the kings of Israel before him.

34In Ahab's time, Hiel of Bethel rebuilt Jericho. He laid its foundations at the cost of his firstborn son Abiram, and he set up its gates at the cost of his youngest son Segub, in accordance with the word of the LORD spoken by Joshua son of Nun.[h]

Elijah Fed by Ravens

17 Now Elijah[a] the Tishbite, from Tishbe[a] in Gilead,[b] said to Ahab, "As the LORD, the God of Israel, lives, whom I serve, there will be neither dew nor rain[c] in the next few years except at my word."

2Then the word of the LORD came to Elijah: 3"Leave here, turn eastward and hide[d] in the Kerith Ravine, east of the Jordan. 4You will drink from the brook, and I have ordered the ravens[e] to feed you there."

5So he did what the LORD had told him. He went to the Kerith Ravine, east of the Jordan, and stayed there. 6The ravens brought him bread and meat in the morning[f] and bread and meat in the evening, and he drank from the brook.

The Widow at Zarephath

7Some time later the brook dried up because there had been no rain in the land. 8Then the word of the LORD came to him: 9"Go at once to Zarephath[g] of Sidon and stay there. I have commanded a widow[h] in that place to supply you with food." 10So he went to Zarephath. When he came to the town gate, a widow was there gathering sticks. He called to her and asked, "Would you bring me a little water in a jar so I may have a drink?"[i] 11As she was going to get it, he called, "And bring me, please, a piece of bread."

12"As surely as the LORD your God lives," she replied, "I don't have any

15 [s]**Jos 19:44**
23 [t]**Jos 12:24; 1Ki 15:33**
24 [u]**1Ki 13:32; Mt 10:5**
25 [v]ver 25–26; **Dt 4:25**; Mic 6:16
26 [w]**1Ki 15:30**; [x]**Dt 32:21**
28 [y]**1Ki 13:32**
30 [z]**1Ki 14:9**
31 [a]**1Ki 11:2**; [b]**Jdg 3:6**; 2Ki 9:34; [c]**Jdg 2:11**
32 [d]**Jdg 6:28**; [e]2Ki 10:27; 11:18; Jer 43:12
33 [f]**Jdg 3:7**; 2Ki 13:6; [g]**1Ki 14:9**; 21:25
34 [h]Jos 6:26

Ch. 17

1 [a]Mal 4:5; Mt 11:14; 17:3; [b]Jdg 12:4; [c]**Dt 11:17; 28:24; 2Sa 1:21**; **1Ki 8:36**; Job 12:15; **Lk 4:25**
3 [d]1Ki 18:4,10; Jer 36:19,26
4 [e]**Ge 8:7**
6 [f]Ex 16:8
9 [g]Ob 20; [h]Lk 4:26
10 [i]**Ge 24:17**; Jn 4:7

[a]24 That is, about 150 pounds (about 70 kilograms)
[a]1 Or *Tishbite, of the settlers*

bread—only a handful of flour in a jar and a little oil[j] in a jug. I am gathering a few sticks to take home and make a meal for myself and my son, that we may eat it—and die."

13Elijah said to her, "Don't be afraid. Go home and do as you have said. But first make a small cake of bread for me from what you have and bring it to me, and then make something for yourself and your son. 14For this is what the LORD, the God of Israel, says: 'The jar of flour will not be used up and the jug of oil will not run dry until the day the LORD gives rain[k] on the land.'"

15She went away and did as Elijah had told her. So there was food every day for Elijah and for the woman and her family. 16For the jar of flour was not used up and the jug of oil did not run dry, in keeping with the word of the LORD spoken by Elijah.

17Some time later the son of the woman who owned the house became ill. He grew worse and worse, and finally stopped breathing. 18She said to Elijah, "What do you have against me, man of God? Did you come to remind me of my sin[l] and kill my son?"

19"Give me your son," Elijah replied. He took him from her arms, carried him to the upper room where he was staying, and laid him on his bed. 20Then he cried[m] out to the LORD, "O LORD my God, have you brought tragedy also upon this widow I am staying with, by causing her son to die?" 21Then he stretched[n] himself out on the boy three times and cried to the LORD, "O LORD my God, let this boy's life return to him!"

22The LORD heard Elijah's cry, and the boy's life returned to him, and he lived. 23Elijah picked up the child and carried him down from the room into the house. He gave him to his mother[o] and said, "Look, your son is alive!"

24Then the woman said to Elijah, "Now I know[p] that you are a man of God[q] and that the word of the LORD from your mouth is the truth."[r]

Elijah and Obadiah

18 After a long time, in the third[a] year, the word of the LORD came to Elijah: "Go and present[b] yourself to Ahab, and I will send rain[c] on the land." 2So Elijah went to present himself to Ahab.

Now the famine was severe[d] in Samaria, 3and Ahab had summoned Obadiah, who was in charge[e] of his palace. (Obadiah was a devout believer[f] in the LORD. 4While Jezebel[g] was killing off the LORD's prophets, Obadiah had taken a hundred prophets and hidden[h] them in two caves, fifty in each, and had supplied[i] them with food and water.) 5Ahab had said to Obadiah, "Go through the land to all the springs[j] and valleys. Maybe we can find some grass to keep the horses and mules alive so we will not have to kill any of our animals."[k] 6So they divided the land they were to cover, Ahab going in one direction and Obadiah in another.

7As Obadiah was walking along, Elijah met him. Obadiah recognised[l] him, bowed down to the ground, and said, "Is it really you, my lord Elijah?"

8"Yes," he replied. "Go tell your master, 'Elijah is here.'"

9"What have I done wrong," asked Obadiah, "that you are handing your servant over to Ahab to be put to death? 10As surely as the LORD your God lives, there is not a nation or kingdom where my master has not sent someone to look[m] for you. And whenever a nation or kingdom claimed you were not there, he made them swear they could not find you. 11But now you tell me to go to my master and say, 'Elijah is here.' 12I don't know where the Spirit[n] of the LORD may carry you when I leave you. If I go and tell Ahab and he doesn't find you, he will kill me. Yet I your servant have worshipped the LORD since my youth. 13Haven't you heard, my lord, what I did while Jezebel was killing the prophets of the LORD? I hid a hundred of the LORD's prophets in two caves, fifty in each, and supplied them with food and water. 14And now you tell me to go to my master and say, 'Elijah is here.' He will kill me!"

15Elijah said, "As the LORD Almighty lives, whom I serve, I will surely present[o] myself to Ahab today."

Elijah on Mount Carmel

16So Obadiah went to meet Ahab and told him, and Ahab went to meet Elijah. 17When he saw Elijah, he said to him, "Is that you, you troubler[p] of Israel?"

18"I have not made trouble for Israel," Elijah replied. "But you[q] and your father's family have. You have abandoned[r] the LORD's commands and have followed the Baals. 19Now summon[s] the people from all over Israel to meet me on Mount Carmel.[t] And bring the four hundred and fifty prophets of Baal and the four hundred prophets of Asherah, who eat at Jezebel's table."[u]

12 [j]2Ki 4:2
14 [k]ver 1
18 [l]Lk 5:8
20 [m]2Ki 4:33
21 [n]2Ki 4:34; Ac 20:10
23 [o]Heb 11:35
24 [p]Jn 16:30; [q]ver 18; [r]1Ki 22:16; Ps 119:43; Jn 17:17

Ch. 18

1 [a]1Ki 17:1; Lk 4:25; [b]ver 15; [c]**Dt 28:12**
2 [d]**Lev 26:26**
3 [e]1Ki 16:9; [f]Ne 7:2
4 [g]1Ki 21:23; 2Ki 9:7; [h]**1Ki 17:3**; Isa 16:3; 25:4; 32:2; Ob 14; [i]Jer 26:24
5 [j]Jer 14:3; [k]**Ge 47:4**
7 [l]2Ki 1:8; Zec 13:4
10 [m]**1Ki 17:3**
12 [n]2Ki 2:16; Eze 3:14; Ac 8:39
15 [o]ver 1
17 [p]Jos 7:25; 1Sa 14:29; 1Ki 21:20; Jer 38:4
18 [q]1Ki 16:33; 21:25; [r]**Dt 31:16**
19 [s]2Ki 10:19; [t]**Jos 19:26**; [u]2Ki 9:22

20So Ahab sent word throughout all
Israel and assembled the prophets on
Mount Carmel.[v] 21Elijah went before the
people and said, "How long will you
waver[w] between two opinions? If the
LORD[x] is God, follow him; but if Baal is
God, follow him."

But the people said nothing.

22Then Elijah said to them, "I am the
only one of the LORD's prophets left,[y]
but Baal has four hundred and fifty
prophets.[z] 23Get two bulls for us. Let
them choose one for themselves, and let
them cut it into pieces and put it on the
wood but not set fire to it. I will prepare
the other bull and put it on the wood but
not set fire to it. 24Then you call[a] on the
name of your god, and I will call on the
name of the LORD.[b] The god who
answers by fire[c]—he is God."

Then all the people said, "What you
say is good."

25Elijah said to the prophets of Baal,
"Choose one of the bulls and prepare it
first, since there are so many of you.
Call on the name of your god, but do not
light the fire." 26So they took the bull
given them and prepared it.

Then they called[d] on the name of Baal
from morning till noon. "O Baal,
answer us!" they shouted. But there
was no response;[e] no-one answered.
And they danced around the altar they
had made.

27At noon Elijah began to taunt them.
"Shout louder!" he said. "Surely he is a
god! Perhaps he is deep in thought, or
busy, or travelling. Maybe he is sleep-
ing and must be awakened."[f] 28So they
shouted louder and slashed[g] them-
selves with swords and spears, as was
their custom, until their blood flowed.
29Midday passed, and they continued
their frantic prophesying until the time
for the evening sacrifice.[h] But there was
no response, no-one answered, no-one
paid attention.[i]

30Then Elijah said to all the people,
"Come here to me." They came to him,
and he repaired the altar[j] of the LORD,
which was in ruins. 31Elijah took twelve
stones, one for each of the tribes de-
scended from Jacob, to whom the word
of the LORD had come, saying, "Your
name shall be Israel."[k] 32With the stones
he built an altar in the name[l] of the
LORD, and he dug a trench round it large
enough to hold two seahs[a] of seed. 33He
arranged[m] the wood, cut the bull into
pieces and laid it on the wood. Then he
said to them, "Fill four large jars with
water and pour it on the offering and on
the wood."

34"Do it again," he said, and they did
it again.

"Do it a third time," he ordered, and
they did it the third time. 35The water
ran down around the altar and even
filled the trench.

36At the time[n] of sacrifice, the prophet
Elijah stepped forward and prayed: "O
LORD, God of Abraham,[o] Isaac and
Israel, let it be known[p] today that you
are God in Israel and that I am your
servant and have done all these things
at your command.[q] 37Answer me, O
LORD, answer me, so these people will
know[r] that you, O LORD, are God, and
that you are turning their hearts back
again."

38Then the fire[s] of the LORD fell and
burned up the sacrifice, the wood, the
stones and the soil, and also licked up
the water in the trench.

39When all the people saw this, they
fell prostrate[t] and cried, "The LORD—he
is God! The LORD—he is God!"[u]

40Then Elijah commanded them,
"Seize the prophets of Baal. Don't let
anyone get away!" They seized them,
and Elijah had them brought down to
the Kishon Valley[v] and slaughtered[w]
there.

41And Elijah said to Ahab, "Go, eat
and drink, for there is the sound of a
heavy rain." 42So Ahab went off to eat
and drink, but Elijah climbed to the top
of Carmel, bent down to the ground and
put his face between his knees.[x]

43"Go and look towards the sea," he
told his servant. And he went up and
looked.

"There is nothing there," he said.

Seven times Elijah said, "Go back."

44The seventh time[y] the servant re-
ported, "A cloud[z] as small as a man's
hand is rising from the sea."

So Elijah said, "Go and tell Ahab,
'Hitch up your chariot and go down
before the rain stops you.'"

45Meanwhile, the sky grew black with
clouds, the wind rose, a heavy rain[a]
came on and Ahab rode off to Jezreel.[b]
46The power[c] of the LORD came upon
Elijah and, tucking his cloak into his
belt,[d] he ran ahead of Ahab all the way
to Jezreel.

Elijah Flees to Horeb

19 Now Ahab told Jezebel[a] every-
thing Elijah had done and how
he had killed[b] all the prophets with the
sword. 2So Jezebel sent a messenger to

20 [v]2Ki 2:25; 4:25
21 [w]Jos 24:15; 2Ki 17:41; Ps 119:113; Mt 6:24; [x]ver 39; Ps 100:3; 118:27
22 [y]1Ki 19:10; [z]Jer 2:8; 23:13
24 [a]**1Sa 7:8**; [b]**Ge 4:26**; [c]**ver 38; Ex 19:18; Lev 9:24**
26 [d]Isa 44:17; 45:20; [e]Ps 115:4–5; 135:16; Isa 41:26,28; 46:7; Jer 10:5; 1Co 8:4; 12:2
27 [f]Hab 2:19
28 [g]**Lev 19:28**
29 [h]**Ex 29:41**; [i]2Ki 19:12; Isa 16:12; Jer 10:5
30 [j]1Ki 19:10
31 [k]**Ge 17:5**; 2Ki 17:34
32 [l]**Dt 18:7**; Col 3:17
33 [m]**Ge 22:9**
36 [n]**Ex 29:39,41**; [o]**Ge 24:12**; Ex 4:5; Mt 22:32; [p]**Jos 4:24; 1Sa 17:46; Ps 46:10**; [q]Nu 16:28
37 [r]**Jos 4:24**
38 [s]ver 24; Ex 19:18; Lev 9:24; 2Ki 1:10; 1Ch 21:26; 2Ch 7:1; Job 1:16
39 [t]**Lev 9:24**; [u]**ver 21; Ps 46:10**
40 [v]**Jdg 4:7**; [w]**Ex 22:20; Dt 17:12; 2Ki 11:18**
42 [x]**1Sa 12:17**; Jas 5:18
44 [y]**Jos 6:15**; [z]Lk 12:54
45 [a]**1Ki 8:36**; Job 37:13; [b]**1Sa 29:1; Hos 1:4**
46 [c]**Jdg 3:10; 1Sa 11:6**; Lk 1:35; 4:14; [d]2Ki 4:29; 9:1

Ch. 19

1 [a]1Ki 16:31; [b]**Ex 22:20**

[a]32 That is, probably about 26 pints (about 15 litres)

Elijah to say, "May the gods deal with me, be it ever so severely,[c] if by this time tomorrow I do not make your life like that of one of them."[d]

3Elijah was afraid[a] and ran[e] for his life.[f] When he came to Beersheba[g] in Judah, he left his servant there, 4while he himself went a day's journey into the desert. He came to a broom tree,[h] sat down under it and prayed that he might die. "I have had enough, LORD," he said. "Take my life;[i] I am no better than my ancestors." 5Then he lay down under the tree and fell asleep.[j]

All at once an angel[k] touched him and said, "Get up and eat." 6He looked around, and there by his head was a cake of bread baked over hot coals, and a jar of water. He ate and drank and then lay down again.

7The angel of the LORD came back a second time and touched him and said, "Get up and eat, for the journey is too much for you." 8So he got up and ate and drank. Strengthened by that food, he travelled for forty[l] days and forty nights until he reached Horeb,[m] the mountain of God. 9There he went into a cave[n] and spent the night.

The LORD Appears to Elijah

And the word of the LORD came to him: "What are you doing here, Elijah?"[o]

10He replied, "I have been very zealous[p] for the LORD God Almighty. The Israelites have rejected your covenant,[q] broken down your altars,[r] and put your prophets to death with the sword. I am the only one left,[s] and now they are trying to kill me too."

11The LORD said, "Go out and stand on the mountain[t] in the presence of the LORD, for the LORD is about to pass by."[u]

Then a great and powerful wind[v] tore the mountains apart and shattered[w] the rocks before the LORD, but the LORD was not in the wind. After the wind there was an earthquake, but the LORD was not in the earthquake. 12After the earthquake came a fire,[x] but the LORD was not in the fire. And after the fire came a gentle whisper.[y] 13When Elijah heard it, he pulled his cloak over his face[z] and went out and stood at the mouth of the cave.

Then a voice said to him, "What are you doing here, Elijah?"

14He replied, "I have been very zealous for the LORD God Almighty. The Israelites have rejected your covenant, broken down your altars, and put your prophets to death with the sword. I am the only one left,[a] and now they are trying to kill me too."

15The LORD said to him, "Go back the way you came, and go to the Desert of Damascus. When you get there, anoint Hazael[b] king over Aram. 16Also, anoint[c] Jehu son of Nimshi king over Israel, and anoint Elisha[d] son of Shaphat from Abel Meholah[e] to succeed you as prophet. 17Jehu will put to death any who escape the sword of Hazael,[f] and Elisha will put to death any who escape the sword of Jehu.[g] 18Yet I reserve[h] seven thousand in Israel—all whose knees have not bowed down to Baal and all whose mouths have not kissed[i] him."

The Call of Elisha

19So Elijah went from there and found Elisha son of Shaphat. He was ploughing with twelve yoke of oxen, and he himself was driving the twelfth pair. Elijah went up to him and threw his cloak[j] around him. 20Elisha then left his oxen and ran after Elijah. "Let me kiss my father and mother good-bye,"[k] he said, "and then I will come with you."

"Go back," Elijah replied. "What have I done to you?"

21So Elisha left him and went back. He took his yoke of oxen[l] and slaughtered them. He burned the ploughing equipment to cook the meat and gave it to the people and they ate. Then he set out to follow Elijah and became his attendant.[m]

Ben-Hadad Attacks Samaria

20 Now Ben-Hadad[a] king of Aram mustered his entire army. Accompanied by thirty-two kings with their horses and chariots, he went up and besieged Samaria[b] and attacked it. 2He sent messengers into the city to Ahab king of Israel, saying, "This is what Ben-Hadad says: 3'Your silver and gold are mine, and the best of your wives and children are mine.'"

4The king of Israel answered, "Just as you say, my lord the king. I and all I have are yours."

5The messengers came again and said, "This is what Ben-Hadad says: 'I sent to demand your silver and gold, your wives and your children. 6But about this time tomorrow I am going

2 [c]**Ru 1:17;** [d]Ps 13:4; Jer 20:10; 26:21; 36:26
3 [e]**Ge 31:21;** [f]**Ge 19:17;** [g]**Jos 19:2**
4 [h]Job 30:4; [i]**Nu 11:15;** Job 6:9; 7:16; 10:1; Ps 69:19; Jer 20:18; Jnh 4:8
5 [j]Ge 28:11; [k]**Ge 16:7**
8 [l]Ex 24:18; Mt 4:2; [m]**Ex 3:1**
9 [n]**Ex 33:22;** [o]**Ge 3:9**
10 [p]**Nu 25:13;** Ac 22:3; Gal 4:18; [q]**Dt 31:16;** [r]1Ki 18:30; [s]1Ki 18:22; Jer 5:11; 9:2; Ro 11:3*
11 [t]Ex 34:2; Mt 17:1–3; [u]Ex 33:19; [v]**Ex 14:21; 2Ki 2:1;** [w]Na 1:6
12 [x]**Ex 3:2;** [y]ver 11; **1Sa 14:6;** Job 4:16; Zec 4:6; 2Co 12:9
13 [z]Ex 3:6
14 [a]1Ki 18:22; Ro 11:3*
15 [b]2Ki 8:7–15
16 [c]2Ki 9:6; [d]ver 21; 2Ki 2:1; 3:11; [e]**Jdg 7:22**
17 [f]2Ki 8:12,29; 10:32; 12:17; 13:3,7,22; Am 1:4; [g]Jer 48:44
18 [h]Ro 11:4*; [i]Hos 13:2
19 [j]**Ge 41:42;** 2Ki 2:8,14
20 [k]Lk 9:61
21 [l]**1Sa 6:14;** [m]**ver 16**

Ch. 20

1 [a]**1Ki 15:18;** [b]**1Ki 13:32**

[a]3 Or *Elijah saw*

to send my officials to search your
palace and the houses of your officials.
They will seize everything you value
and carry it away.' "
7The king of Israel summoned all the
elders[c] of the land and said to them,
"See how this man is looking for trou-
ble![d] When he sent for my wives and my
children, my silver and my gold, I did
not refuse him."
8The elders and the people all
answered, "Don't listen to him or agree
to his demands."
9So he replied to Ben-Hadad's mes-
sengers, "Tell my lord the king, 'Your
servant will do all you demanded the
first time, but this demand I cannot
meet.' " They left and took the answer
back to Ben-Hadad.
10Then Ben-Hadad sent another mes-
sage to Ahab: "May the gods deal with
me, be it ever so severely, if enough
dust[e] remains in Samaria to give each of
my men a handful."
11The king of Israel answered, "Tell
him: 'One who puts on his armour
should not boast[f] like one who takes it
off.' "
12Ben-Hadad heard this message
while he and the kings were drinking[g]
in their tents,[a] and he ordered his men:
"Prepare to attack." So they prepared to
attack the city.

Ahab Defeats Ben-Hadad

13Meanwhile a prophet[h] came to Ahab
king of Israel and announced, "This is
what the LORD says: 'Do you see this
vast army? I will give it into your hand
today, and then you will know[i] that I am
the LORD.' "
14"But who will do this?" asked Ahab.
The prophet replied, "This is what
the LORD says: 'The young officers of the
provincial commanders will do it.' "
"And who will start[j] the battle?" he
asked.
The prophet answered, "You will."
15So Ahab summoned the young
officers of the provincial commanders,
232 men. Then he assembled the rest of
the Israelites, 7,000 in all. 16They set out
at noon while Ben-Hadad and the 32
kings allied with him were in their tents
getting drunk.[k] 17The young officers of
the provincial commanders went out
first.
Now Ben-Hadad had dispatched
scouts, who reported, "Men are
advancing from Samaria."
18He said, "If they have come out for
peace, take them alive; if they have
come out for war, take them alive."
19The young officers of the provincial
commanders marched out of the city
with the army behind them 20and each
one struck down his opponent. At that,
the Arameans fled, with the Israelites in
pursuit. But Ben-Hadad king of Aram
escaped on horseback with some of his
horsemen. 21The king of Israel ad-
vanced and overpowered the horses
and chariots and inflicted heavy losses
on the Arameans.
22Afterwards, the prophet[l] came to
the king of Israel and said, "Strengthen
your position and see what must be
done, because next spring[m] the king of
Aram will attack you again."
23Meanwhile, the officials of the king
of Aram advised him, "Their gods are
gods[n] of the hills. That is why they were
too strong for us. But if we fight them on
the plains, surely we will be stronger
than they. 24Do this: Remove all the
kings from their commands and replace
them with other officers. 25You must
also raise an army like the one you lost
—horse for horse and chariot for chariot
—so we can fight Israel on the plains.
Then surely we will be stronger than
they." He agreed with them and acted
accordingly.
26The next spring[o] Ben-Hadad mus-
tered the Arameans and went up to
Aphek[p] to fight against Israel. 27When
the Israelites were also mustered and
given provisions, they marched out to
meet them. The Israelites camped
opposite them like two small flocks of
goats, while the Arameans covered the
countryside.[q]
28The man of God came up and told
the king of Israel, "This is what the LORD
says: 'Because the Arameans think the
LORD is a god of the hills and not a god[r]
of the valleys, I will deliver this vast
army into your hands, and you will
know[s] that I am the LORD.' "
29For seven days they camped oppo-
site each other, and on the seventh day
the battle was joined. The Israelites in-
flicted a hundred thousand casualties
on the Aramean foot soldiers in one
day. 30The rest of them escaped to the
city of Aphek,[t] where the wall col-
lapsed[u] on twenty-seven thousand of
them. And Ben-Hadad fled to the city
and hid[v] in an inner room.
31His officials said to him, "Look, we
have heard that the kings of the house
of Israel are merciful.[w] Let us go to the

7 [c]1Sa 11:3; [d]2Ki 5:7
10 [e]**2Sa 22:43**
11 [f]Pr 27:1; Jer 9:23; Am 2:14
12 [g]**1Ki 16:9**
13 [h]**Jdg 6:8;** [i]**Ex 6:7**
14 [j]**Jdg 1:1**
16 [k]**1Ki 16:9**
22 [l]**Jdg 6:8;** [m]**2Sa 11:1**
23 [n]ver 28; Isa 36:20; Ro 1:21–23
26 [o]**2Sa 11:1;** [p]ver 30; **1Sa 4:1;** 2Ki 13:17
27 [q]Jdg 6:6; **1Sa 13:6**
28 [r]**ver 23;** [s]**Ex 6:7;** Jer 16:19–21
30 [t]**ver 26;** [u]Ps 62:4; Isa 26:21; 30:13; [v]1Ki 22:25
31 [w]Job 41:3

[a]*12* Or *in Succoth;* also in verse 16

king of Israel with sackcloth[x] round our waists and ropes round our heads. Perhaps he will spare your life."

32 Wearing sackcloth round their waists and ropes round their heads, they went to the king of Israel and said, "Your servant Ben-Hadad says: 'Please let me live.'"

The king answered, "Is he still alive? He is my brother."

33 The men took this as a good sign and were quick to pick up his word. "Yes, your brother Ben-Hadad!" they said.

"Go and get him," the king said. When Ben-Hadad came out, Ahab had him come up into his chariot.

34 "I will return the cities[y] my father took from your father," Ben-Hadad[z] offered. "You may set up your own market areas[a] in Damascus,[b] as my father did in Samaria."

⌞Ahab said,⌟ "On the basis of a treaty[c] I will set you free." So he made a treaty with him, and let him go.

A Prophet Condemns Ahab

35 By the word of the LORD one of the sons of the prophets[d] said to his companion, "Strike me with your weapon," but the man refused.[e]

36 So the prophet said, "Because you have not obeyed the LORD, as soon as you leave me a lion[f] will kill you." And after the man went away, a lion found him and killed him.

37 The prophet found another man and said, "Strike me, please." So the man struck him and wounded him. 38 Then the prophet went and stood by the road waiting for the king. He disguised himself with his headband down over his eyes. 39 As the king passed by, the prophet called out to him, "Your servant went into the thick of the battle, and someone came to me with a captive and said, 'Guard this man. If he is missing, it will be your life for his life,[g] or you must pay a talent[b] of silver.' 40 While your servant was busy here and there, the man disappeared."

"That is your sentence,"[h] the king of Israel said. "You have pronounced it yourself."

41 Then the prophet quickly removed the headband from his eyes, and the king of Israel recognised him as one of the prophets. 42 He said to the king, "This is what the LORD says: 'You[i] have set free a man I had determined should die.[c][j] Therefore it is your life for his life,[k] your people for his people.'" 43 Sullen and angry,[l] the king of Israel went to his palace in Samaria.

31 [x]Ge 37:34
34 [y]1Ki 15:20; [z]**Ge 10:22;** [a]2Sa 8:6; [b]**Ge 14:15;** Jer 49:23–27; [c]**Ex 23:32**
35 [d]**1Sa 10:5;** Am 7:14; [e]**1Ki 13:21**
36 [f]1Ki 13:24
39 [g]**Jos 2:14**
40 [h]2Sa 12:5; **14:13**
42 [i]**2Sa 12:7;** [j]Jer 48:10; [k]**Jos 2:14**
43 [l]1Ki 21:4

Ch. 21

1 [a]2Ki 9:21; [b]**1Sa 29:1;** 2Ki 10:1
3 [c]**Lev 25:23**
4 [d]1Ki 20:43; [e]1Sa 28:23
7 [f]**1Sa 8:14**
8 [g]2Sa 11:14; [h]**Ge 38:18**
10 [i]**Dt 13:13;** Ac 6:11; [j]**Ex 22:28;** Lev 24:15–16
12 [k]Isa 58:4

Naboth's Vineyard

21

Some time later there was an incident involving a vineyard belonging to Naboth[a] the Jezreelite. The vineyard was in Jezreel,[b] close to the palace of Ahab king of Samaria. 2 Ahab said to Naboth, "Let me have your vineyard to use for a vegetable garden, since it is close to my palace. In exchange I will give you a better vineyard or, if you prefer, I will pay you whatever it is worth."

3 But Naboth replied, "The LORD forbid that I should give you the inheritance[c] of my fathers."

4 So Ahab went home, sullen and angry[d] because Naboth the Jezreelite had said, "I will not give you the inheritance of my fathers." He lay on his bed sulking and refused[e] to eat.

5 His wife Jezebel came in and asked him, "Why are you so sullen? Why won't you eat?"

6 He answered her, "Because I said to Naboth the Jezreelite, 'Sell me your vineyard; or if you prefer, I will give you another vineyard in its place.' But he said, 'I will not give you my vineyard.'"

7 Jezebel his wife said, "Is this how you act as king over Israel? Get up and eat! Cheer up. I'll get you the vineyard[f] of Naboth the Jezreelite."

8 So she wrote letters[g] in Ahab's name, placed his seal[h] on them, and sent them to the elders and nobles who lived in Naboth's city with him. 9 In those letters she wrote:

> "Proclaim a day of fasting and seat Naboth in a prominent place among the people. 10 But seat two scoundrels[i] opposite him and have them testify that he has cursed[j] both God and the king. Then take him out and stone him to death."

11 So the elders and nobles who lived in Naboth's city did as Jezebel directed in the letters she had written to them. 12 They proclaimed a fast[k] and seated Naboth in a prominent place among the people. 13 Then two scoundrels came and sat opposite him and brought charges against Naboth before the people, saying, "Naboth has cursed

b39 That is, about 75 pounds (about 34 kilograms)
c42 The Hebrew term refers to the irrevocable giving over of things or persons to the LORD, often by totally destroying them.

both God and the king." So they took
him outside the city and stoned him
to death.[l] 14Then they sent word to
Jezebel: "Naboth has been stoned and is
dead."
15As soon as Jezebel heard that
Naboth had been stoned to death, she
said to Ahab, "Get up and take posses-
sion of the vineyard[m] of Naboth the
Jezreelite that he refused to sell you. He
is no longer alive, but dead." 16When
Ahab heard that Naboth was dead, he
got up and went down to take posses-
sion of Naboth's vineyard.
17Then the word of the LORD came to
Elijah the Tishbite: 18"Go down to meet
Ahab king of Israel, who rules in Samar-
ia. He is now in Naboth's vineyard,
where he has gone to take possession of
it. 19Say to him, 'This is what the LORD
says: Have you not murdered a man
and seized his property?'[n] Then say to
him, 'This is what the LORD says: In the
place where dogs licked up Naboth's
blood,[o] dogs[p] will lick up your blood
—yes, yours!' "
20Ahab said to Elijah, "So you have
found me, my enemy!"[q]
"I have found you," he answered,
"because you have sold[r] yourself to do
evil in the eyes of the LORD. 21'I am going
to bring disaster on you. I will consume
your descendants and cut off from Ahab
every last male[s] in Israel—slave or free.[t]
22I will make your house[u] like that of
Jeroboam son of Nebat and that of
Baasha son of Ahijah, because you have
provoked me to anger and have caused
Israel to sin.'[v]
23"And also concerning Jezebel the
LORD says: 'Dogs[w] will devour Jezebel
by the wall of[a] Jezreel.'
24"Dogs[x] will eat those belonging to
Ahab who die in the city, and the birds
of the air[y] will feed on those who die in
the country."
25(There was never[z] a man like Ahab,
who sold himself to do evil in the eyes of
the LORD, urged on by Jezebel his wife.
26He behaved in the vilest manner by
going after idols, like the Amorites[a] the
LORD drove out before Israel.)
27When Ahab heard these words, he
tore his clothes, put on sackcloth[b] and
fasted. He lay in sackcloth and went
around meekly.[c]
28Then the word of the LORD came to
Elijah the Tishbite: 29"Have you noticed
how Ahab has humbled himself before
me? Because he has humbled[d] himself, I
will not bring this disaster in his day,[e]
but I will bring it on his house in the
days of his son."[f]

13 [l]**Lev 24:16**
15 [m]**1Sa 8:14**
19 [n]Job 24:6; 31:39; [o]2Ki 9:26; Ps 9:12; Isa 14:20; [p]1Ki 22:38; Ps 68:23; Jer 15:3
20 [q]**1Ki 18:17**; [r]2Ki 17:17; Ro 7:14
21 [s]Jdg 9:5; 2Ki 10:7; [t]**Dt 32:36**
22 [u]1Ki 16:3; [v]**1Ki 12:30**
23 [w]2Ki 9:10, 34–36
24 [x]1Ki 14:11; [y]**Ge 40:19; Dt 28:26**
25 [z]**1Ki 14:9; 16:33**
26 [a]**Ge 15:16**
27 [b]**Ge 37:34; Jer 4:8**; [c]Isa 38:15
29 [d]**Ex 10:3**; [e]**Ex 32:14**; 2Ki 22:20; [f]Ex 20:5; 2Ki 9:26; 10:6–10

Ch. 22

3 [a]**Dt 4:43**
4 [b]2Ki 3:7
5 [c]Ex 33:7; 2Ki 3:11; Job 38:2; Ps 32:8; 73:24; 107:11
6 [d]**Jdg 18:6**; [e]**1Ki 13:18**
7 [f]Dt 18:15; 2Ki 3:11; 5:8; [g]**Nu 27:21**; 2Ki 3:11
8 [h]Am 5:10; [i]ver 13; Isa 5:20; 30:10; Jer 23:17
10 [j]**Jdg 6:37**
11 [k]ver 24; [l]Dt 33:17; Jer 27:2; 28:10; Zec 1:18–21

Micaiah Prophesies Against Ahab

22:1–28pp—2Ch 18:1–27

22 For three years there was no
war between Aram and Israel.
2But in the third year Jehoshaphat king
of Judah went down to see the king of
Israel. 3The king of Israel had said to his
officials, "Don't you know that Ramoth
Gilead[a] belongs to us and yet we are
doing nothing to retake it from the king
of Aram?"
4So he asked Jehoshaphat, "Will you
go with me to fight[b] against Ramoth
Gilead?"
Jehoshaphat replied to the king of
Israel, "I am as you are, my people as
your people, my horses as your
horses." 5But Jehoshaphat also said to
the king of Israel, "First seek the coun-
sel[c] of the LORD."
6So the king of Israel brought together
the prophets—about four hundred
men—and asked them, "Shall I go to
war against Ramoth Gilead, or shall I
refrain?"
"Go,"[d] they answered, "for the Lord
will give it into the king's hand."[e]
7But Jehoshaphat asked, "Is there not
a prophet[f] of the LORD here whom we
can enquire[g] of?"
8The king of Israel answered
Jehoshaphat, "There is still one man
through whom we can enquire of the
LORD, but I hate[h] him because he never
prophesies anything good[i] about me,
but always bad. He is Micaiah son of
Imlah."
"The king should not say that,"
Jehoshaphat replied.
9So the king of Israel called one of his
officials and said, "Bring Micaiah son of
Imlah at once."
10Dressed in their royal robes, the
king of Israel and Jehoshaphat king of
Judah were sitting on their thrones at
the threshing-floor[j] by the entrance of
the gate of Samaria, with all the
prophets prophesying before them.
11Now Zedekiah[k] son of Kenaanah had
made iron horns[l] and he declared, "This
is what the LORD says: 'With these you
will gore the Arameans until they are
destroyed.' "
12All the other prophets were
prophesying the same thing. "Attack
Ramoth Gilead and be victorious," they
said, "for the LORD will give it into the
king's hand."

[a]23 Most Hebrew manuscripts; a few Hebrew manuscripts, Vulgate and Syriac (see also 2 Kings 9:26) *the plot of ground at*

13The messenger who had gone to
summon Micaiah said to him, "Look, as
one man the other prophets are pre-
dicting success for the king. Let your
word agree with theirs, and speak
favourably."[m]
14But Micaiah said, "As surely as the
LORD lives, I can tell him only what the
LORD tells me."[n]
15When he arrived, the king asked
him, "Micaiah, shall we go to war
against Ramoth Gilead, or shall I
refrain?"
"Attack and be victorious," he
answered, "for the LORD will give it into
the king's hand."
16The king said to him, "How many
times must I make you swear to tell me
nothing but the truth in the name of the
LORD?"
17Then Micaiah answered, "I saw all
Israel scattered[o] on the hills like sheep
without a shepherd,[p] and the LORD said,
'These people have no master. Let each
one go home in peace.'"
18The king of Israel said to
Jehoshaphat, "Didn't I tell you that he
never prophesies anything good about
me, but only bad?"
19Micaiah continued, "Therefore hear
the word of the LORD: I saw the LORD
sitting on his throne[q] with all the host[r] of
heaven standing round him on his right
and on his left. 20And the LORD said,
'Who will entice Ahab into attacking
Ramoth Gilead and going to his death
there?'
"One suggested this, and another
that. 21Finally, a spirit came forward,
stood before the LORD and said, 'I will
entice him.'
22"'By what means?' the LORD asked.
"'I will go out and be a lying[s] spirit in
the mouths of all his prophets,' he said.
"'You will succeed in enticing him,'
said the LORD. 'Go and do it.'
23"So now the LORD has put a lying[t]
spirit in the mouths of all these proph-
ets[u] of yours. The LORD has decreed
disaster[v] for you."
24Then Zedekiah[w] son of Kenaanah
went up and slapped[x] Micaiah in the
face. "Which way did the spirit from[a]
the LORD go when he went from me to
speak[y] to you?" he asked.
25Micaiah replied, "You will find out
on the day you go to hide[z] in an inner
room."
26The king of Israel then ordered,
"Take Micaiah and send him back to
Amon the ruler of the city and to Joash
the king's son 27and say, 'This is what
the king says: Put this fellow in prison[a]
and give him nothing but bread and
water until I return safely.'"
28Micaiah declared, "If you ever re-
turn safely, the LORD has not spoken[b]
through me." Then he added, "Mark
my words, all you people!"

Ahab Killed at Ramoth Gilead

22:29–36pp—2Ch 18:28–34

29So the king of Israel and
Jehoshaphat king of Judah went up to
Ramoth Gilead. 30The king of Israel said
to Jehoshaphat, "I will enter the battle
in disguise,[c] but you wear your royal
robes." So the king of Israel disguised
himself and went into battle.
31Now the king of Aram[d] had ordered
his thirty-two chariot commanders,
"Do not fight with anyone, small or
great, except the king[e] of Israel."
32When the chariot commanders saw
Jehoshaphat, they thought, "Surely this
is the king of Israel." So they turned to
attack him, but when Jehoshaphat cried
out, 33the chariot commanders saw that
he was not the king of Israel and stop-
ped pursuing him.
34But someone drew his bow[f] at ran-
dom and hit the king of Israel between
the sections of his armour. The king told
his chariot driver, "Wheel round and
get me out of the fighting. I've been
wounded." 35All day long the battle
raged, and the king was propped up in
his chariot facing the Arameans. The
blood from his wound ran onto the floor
of the chariot, and that evening he died.
36As the sun was setting, a cry spread
through the army: "Every man to his
town; everyone to his land!"[g]
37So the king died and was brought
to Samaria, and they buried him
there. 38They washed the chariot at a
pool in Samaria (where the prostitutes
bathed),[b] and the dogs[h] licked up his
blood, as the word of the LORD had
declared.
39As for the other events of Ahab's
reign, including all he did, the palace he
built and inlaid with ivory,[i] and the
cities he fortified, are they not written in
the book of the annals of the kings of
Israel? 40Ahab rested with his fathers.
And Ahaziah his son succeeded him as
king.

Jehoshaphat King of Judah

22:41–50pp—2Ch 20:31–21:1

41Jehoshaphat son of Asa became
king of Judah in the fourth year of Ahab

13 [m]**ver 8**
14 [n]**Nu 22:18; 1Sa 3:17**
17 [o]**Ge 11:4**; Na 3:18; [p]Nu 27:17; Isa 13:14; **Mt 9:36**
19 [q]Ps 47:8; Isa 6:1; 63:15; Eze 1:26; Da 7:9; [r]Job 1:6; 15:8; 38:7; Ps 103:20–21; 148:2; Jer 23:18,22; Lk 2:13
22 [s]**Jdg 9:23**; 2Th 2:11
23 [t]**Dt 13:3**; [u]Eze 14:9; [v]**Dt 31:29**
24 [w]ver 11; [x]Ac 23:2; [y]Job 26:4
25 [z]1Ki 20:30
27 [a]2Ch 16:10; Jer 20:2; 26:21; 37:15; Heb 11:36
28 [b]**Dt 18:22**
30 [c]**1Sa 28:8**
31 [d]**Ge 10:22; 2Sa 10:19**; [e]**2Sa 17:2**
34 [f]2Ki 9:24; 2Ch 35:23
36 [g]2Ki 14:12
38 [h]**1Ki 21:19**
39 [i]2Ch 9:17; Ps 45:8; Am 3:15

a24 Or *Spirit of*
b38 Or *Samaria and cleaned the weapons*

king of Israel. 42Jehoshaphat was thirty-
five years old when he became king,
and he reigned in Jerusalem for twenty-
five years. His mother's name was Azu-
bah daughter of Shilhi. 43In everything
he walked in the ways of his father Asa[j]
and did not stray from them; he did
what was right in the eyes of the LORD.
The high places,[k] however, were not
removed, and the people continued to
offer sacrifices and burn incense there.
44Jehoshaphat was also at peace with
the king of Israel.

45As for the other events of Jehosha-
phat's reign, the things he achieved and
his military exploits, are they not writ-
ten in the book of the annals of the kings
of Judah? 46He rid the land of the rest of
the male shrine-prostitutes[l] who re-
mained there even after the reign of his
father Asa. 47There was then no king[m] in
Edom; a deputy ruled.

48Now Jehoshaphat built a fleet of
trading ships[c][n] to go to Ophir for gold,
but they never set sail—they were

43 [j]1Ki 8:61; 2Ch 17:3; [k]1Ki 3:2
46 [l]Dt 23:17
47 [m]1Ki 11:14–18; 2Ki 3:9; 8:20
48 [n]1Ki 9:26; [o]Nu 33:35
52 [p]1Ki 15:26
53 [q]Jdg 2:11; [r]1Ki 21:25

wrecked at Ezion Geber.[o] 49At that time
Ahaziah son of Ahab said to
Jehoshaphat, "Let my men sail with
your men," but Jehoshaphat refused.

50Then Jehoshaphat rested with his
fathers and was buried with them in the
city of David his father. And Jehoram
his son succeeded him.

Ahaziah King of Israel

51Ahaziah son of Ahab became king of
Israel in Samaria in the seventeenth
year of Jehoshaphat king of Judah, and
he reigned over Israel for two years.
52He did evil[p] in the eyes of the LORD,
because he walked in the ways of his
father and mother and in the ways of
Jeroboam son of Nebat, who caused
Israel to sin. 53He served and worship-
ped Baal[q] and provoked the LORD, the
God of Israel, to anger, just as his father[r]
had done.

---

[c]48 Hebrew *of ships of Tarshish*

2 Kings

The LORD's Judgment on Ahaziah

1 After Ahab's death, Moab[a] rebelled against Israel. 2Now Ahaziah had fallen through the lattice of his upper room in Samaria and injured himself. So he sent messengers,[b] saying to them, "Go and consult Baal-Zebub,[c] the god of Ekron,[d] to see if I will recover[e] from this injury."

3But the angel[f] of the LORD said to Elijah[g] the Tishbite, "Go up and meet the messengers of the king of Samaria and ask them, 'Is it because there is no God in Israel[h] that you are going off to consult Baal-Zebub, the god of Ekron?' 4Therefore this is what the LORD says: 'You will not leave[i] the bed you are lying on. You will certainly die!'" So Elijah went.

5When the messengers returned to the king, he asked them, "Why have you come back?"

6"A man came to meet us," they replied. "And he said to us, 'Go back to the king who sent you and tell him, "This is what the LORD says: Is it because there is no God in Israel that you are sending men to consult Baal-Zebub, the god of Ekron? Therefore you will not leave[j] the bed you are lying on. You will certainly die!"'"

7The king asked them, "What kind of man was it who came to meet you and told you this?"

8They replied, "He was a man with a garment of hair[k] and with a leather belt round his waist."

The king said, "That was Elijah the Tishbite."

9Then he sent[l] to Elijah a captain[m] with his company of fifty men. The captain went up to Elijah, who was sitting on the top of a hill, and said to him, "Man of God, the king says, 'Come down!'"

10Elijah answered the captain, "If I am a man of God, may fire come down from heaven and consume you and your fifty men!" Then the fire[n] fell from heaven and consumed the captain and his men.

11At this the king sent to Elijah another captain with his fifty men. The captain said to him, "Man of God, this is what the king says, 'Come down at once!'"

12"If I am a man of God," Elijah replied, "may fire come down from heaven and consume you and your fifty men!" Then the fire of God fell from heaven and consumed him and his fifty men.

13So the king sent a third captain with his fifty men. This third captain went up and fell on his knees before Elijah. "Man of God," he begged, "please have respect for my life[o] and the lives of these fifty men, your servants! 14See, fire has fallen from heaven and consumed the first two captains and all their men. But now have respect for my life!"

15The angel[p] of the LORD said to Elijah, "Go down with him; do not be afraid[q] of him." So Elijah got up and went down with him to the king.

16He told the king, "This is what the LORD says: Is it because there is no God in Israel for you to consult that you have sent messengers[r] to consult Baal-Zebub, the god of Ekron? Because you have done this, you will never leave[s] the bed you are lying on. You will certainly die!" 17So he died,[t] according to the word of the LORD that Elijah had spoken.

Because Ahaziah had no son, Joram[a][u] succeeded him as king in the second year of Jehoram son of Jehoshaphat king of Judah. 18As for all the other events of Ahaziah's reign, and what he did, are they not written in the book of the annals of the kings of Israel?

Elijah Taken Up to Heaven

2 When the LORD was about to take[a] Elijah up to heaven in a whirlwind,[b] Elijah and Elisha[c] were on their way from Gilgal.[d] 2Elijah said to Elisha, "Stay here;[e] the LORD has sent me to Bethel."

Ch. 1

1 [a]**Ge 19:37**; 2Ki 3:5
2 [b]ver 16; [c]**Mk 3:22**; [d]1Sa 6:2; Isa 2:6; 14:29; [e]**Jdg 18:5**
3 [f]ver 15; [g]1Ki 17:1; [h]**1Sa 28:8**
4 [i]ver 6,16; Ps 41:8
6 [j]**ver 4**
8 [k]**1Ki 18:7**; Mt 3:4; Mk 1:6
9 [l]2Ki 6:14; [m]Ex 18:25; Isa 3:3
10 [n]**1Ki 18:38; Rev 11:5; 13:13**
13 [o]Ps 72:14
15 [p]ver 3; [q]Isa 51:12; 57:11; Jer 1:17; Eze 2:6
16 [r]**ver 2**; [s]ver 4
17 [t]2Ki 8:15; Jer 20:6; 28:17; [u]2Ki 3:1; 8:16

Ch. 2

1 [a]**Ge 5:24**; [b]ver 11; 1Ki 19:11; Isa 5:28; 66:15; Jer 4:13; Na 1:3; [c]**1Ki 19:16**; [d]**Dt 11:30**; 2Ki 4:38
2 [e]ver 6

[a]17 Hebrew *Jehoram*, a variant of *Joram*

But Elisha said, "As surely as the LORD lives and as you live, I will not leave you."[f] So they went down to Bethel.

3The company[g] of the prophets at Bethel came out to Elisha and asked, "Do you know that the LORD is going to take your master from you today?"

"Yes, I know," Elisha replied, "but do not speak of it."

4Then Elijah said to him, "Stay here, Elisha; the LORD has sent me to Jericho.[h]"

And he replied, "As surely as the LORD lives and as you live, I will not leave you." So they went to Jericho.

5The company[i] of the prophets at Jericho went up to Elisha and asked him, "Do you know that the LORD is going to take your master from you today?"

"Yes, I know," he replied, "but do not speak of it."

6Then Elijah said to him, "Stay here;[j] the LORD has sent me to the Jordan."[k]

And he replied, "As surely as the LORD lives and as you live, I will not leave you."[l] So the two of them walked on.

7Fifty men of the company of the prophets went and stood at a distance, facing the place where Elijah and Elisha had stopped at the Jordan. 8Elijah took his cloak,[m] rolled it up and struck[n] the water with it. The water divided[o] to the right and to the left, and the two of them crossed over on dry[p] ground.

9When they had crossed, Elijah said to Elisha, "Tell me, what can I do for you before I am taken from you?"

"Let me inherit a double[q] portion of your spirit,"[r] Elisha replied.

10"You have asked a difficult thing," Elijah said, "yet if you see me when I am taken from you, it will be yours—otherwise not."

11As they were walking along and talking together, suddenly a chariot of fire[s] and horses of fire appeared and separated the two of them, and Elijah went up to heaven[t] in a whirlwind.[u] 12Elisha saw this and cried out, "My father! My father! The chariots[v] and horsemen of Israel!" And Elisha saw him no more. Then he took hold of his own clothes and tore[w] them apart.

13He picked up the cloak that had fallen from Elijah and went back and stood on the bank of the Jordan. 14Then he took the cloak[x] that had fallen from him and struck[y] the water with it. "Where now is the LORD, the God of Elijah?" he asked. When he struck the water, it divided to the right and to the left, and he crossed over.

15The company[z] of the prophets from Jericho, who were watching, said, "The spirit[a] of Elijah is resting on Elisha." And they went to meet him and bowed to the ground before him. 16"Look," they said, "we your servants have fifty able men. Let them go and look for your master. Perhaps the Spirit[b] of the LORD has picked him up[c] and set him down on some mountain or in some valley."

"No," Elisha replied, "do not send them."

17But they persisted until he was too ashamed[d] to refuse. So he said, "Send them." And they sent fifty men, who searched for three days but did not find him. 18When they returned to Elisha, who was staying in Jericho, he said to them, "Didn't I tell you not to go?"

Healing of the Water

19The men of the city said to Elisha, "Look, our lord, this town is well situated, as you can see, but the water is bad and the land is unproductive."

20"Bring me a new bowl," he said, "and put salt in it." So they brought it to him.

21Then he went out to the spring and threw[e] the salt into it, saying, "This is what the LORD says: 'I have healed this water. Never again will it cause death or make the land unproductive.'" 22And the water has remained wholesome[f] to this day, according to the word Elisha had spoken.

Elisha Is Jeered

23From there Elisha went up to Bethel. As he was walking along the road, some youths came out of the town and jeered[g] at him. "Go on up, you baldhead!" they said. "Go on up, you baldhead!" 24He turned round, looked at them and called down a curse[h] on them in the name[i] of the LORD. Then two bears came out of the woods and mauled forty-two of the youths. 25And he went on to Mount Carmel[j] and from there returned to Samaria.

Moab Revolts

3 Joram[a] [a] son of Ahab became king of Israel in Samaria in the eighteenth year of Jehoshaphat king of

2 [f]Ru 1:16
3 [g]**1Sa 10:5**
4 [h]Jos 3:16
5 [i]ver 3
6 [j]ver 2; [k]Jos 3:15; [l]Ru 1:16
8 [m]**1Ki 19:19;** [n]ver 14; [o]**Ex 14:21;** [p]Ex 14:22,29
9 [q]**Dt 21:17;** [r]**Nu 11:17**
11 [s]2Ki 6:17; Ps 68:17; 104:3–4; Isa 66:15; Hab 3:8; Zec 6:1; [t]**Ge 5:24;** [u]**ver 1**
12 [v]2Ki 6:17; 13:14; [w]**Ge 37:29**
14 [x]**1Ki 19:19;** [y]ver 8
15 [z]**1Sa 10:5;** [a]**Nu 11:17**
16 [b]**1Ki 18:12;** [c]Ac 8:39
17 [d]**Jdg 3:25**
21 [e]**Ex 15:25;** 2Ki 4:41; 6:6
22 [f]Ex 15:25
23 [g]**Ex 22:28;** 2Ch 30:10; 36:16; Job 19:18; Ps 31:18
24 [h]**Ge 4:11;** [i]**Dt 18:19**
25 [j]**1Ki 18:20**

Ch. 3

1 [a]**2Ki 1:17**

[a]1 Hebrew *Jehoram,* a variant of *Joram;* also in verse 6

Judah, and he reigned for twelve years.
2He did evil[b] in the eyes of the LORD, but
not as his father[c] and mother had done.
He got rid of the sacred stone[d] of Baal
that his father had made. 3Nevertheless
he clung to the sins[e] of Jeroboam son of
Nebat, which he had caused Israel to
commit; he did not turn away from
them.

4Now Mesha king of Moab[f] raised
sheep, and he had to supply the king of
Israel with a hundred thousand lambs[g]
and with the wool of a hundred
thousand rams. 5But after Ahab died,
the king of Moab rebelled[h] against the
king of Israel. 6So at that time King
Joram set out from Samaria and mobil-
ised all Israel. 7He also sent this message
to Jehoshaphat king of Judah: "The king
of Moab has rebelled against me. Will
you go with me to fight[i] against Moab?"

"I will go with you," he replied. "I am
as you are, my people as your people,
my horses as your horses."

8"By what route shall we attack?" he
asked.

"Through the Desert of Edom," he
answered.

9So the king of Israel set out with the
king of Judah and the king of Edom.[j]
After a roundabout march of seven
days, the army had no more water for
themselves or for the animals with
them.

10"What!" exclaimed the king of
Israel. "Has the LORD called us three
kings together only to hand us over to
Moab?"

11But Jehoshaphat asked, "Is there no
prophet of the LORD here, that we may
enquire[k] of the LORD through him?"

An officer of the king of Israel
answered, "Elisha[l] son of Shaphat is
here. He used to pour water on the
hands of Elijah.[b][m]"

12Jehoshaphat said, "The word[n] of the
LORD is with him." So the king of Israel
and Jehoshaphat and the king of Edom
went down to him.

13Elisha said to the king of Israel,
"What do we have to do with each
other? Go to the prophets of your father
and the prophets of your mother."

"No," the king of Israel answered,
"because it was the LORD who called us
three kings together to hand us over to
Moab."

14Elisha said, "As surely as the LORD
Almighty lives, whom I serve, if I did
not have respect for the presence of
Jehoshaphat king of Judah, I would not
look at you or even notice you. 15But
now bring me a harpist."[o]

While the harpist was playing, the
hand[p] of the LORD came upon Elisha
16and he said, "This is what the LORD
says: Make this valley full of ditches.
17For this is what the LORD says: You will
see neither wind nor rain, yet this valley
will be filled with water,[q] and you, your
cattle and your other animals will drink.
18This is an easy[r] thing in the eyes of the
LORD; he will also hand Moab over to
you. 19You will overthrow every forti-
fied city and every major town. You
will cut down every good tree, stop up
all the springs, and ruin every good
field with stones."

20The next morning, about the time[s]
for offering the sacrifice, there it was
—water flowing from the direction of
Edom! And the land was filled with
water.[t]

21Now all the Moabites had heard that
the kings had come to fight against
them; so every man, young and old,
who could bear arms was called up and
stationed on the border. 22When they
got up early in the morning, the sun was
shining on the water. To the Moabites
across the way, the water looked red
—like blood. 23"That's blood!" they
said. "Those kings must have fought
and slaughtered each other. Now to the
plunder, Moab!"

24But when the Moabites came to the
camp of Israel, the Israelites rose up and
fought them until they fled. And the
Israelites invaded the land and slaugh-
tered the Moabites. 25They destroyed
the towns, and each man threw a stone
on every good field until it was covered.
They stopped up all the springs and cut
down every good tree. Only Kir
Hareseth[u] was left with its stones in
place, but men armed with slings sur-
rounded it and attacked it as well.

26When the king of Moab saw that the
battle had gone against him, he took
with him seven hundred swordsmen to
break through to the king of Edom, but
they failed. 27Then he took his firstborn[v]
son, who was to succeed him as king,
and offered him as a sacrifice on the city
wall. The fury against Israel was great;
they withdrew and returned to their
own land.

The Widow's Oil

4 The wife of a man from the com-
pany[a] of the prophets cried out to
Elisha, "Your servant my husband is
dead, and you know that he revered the

---

2 [b]1Ki 15:26; [c]1Ki 16:30; [d]**Ex 23:24**
3 [e]**1Ki 12:30**
4 [f]**Ge 19:37**; 2Ki 1:1; [g]Ezr 7:17; Isa 16:1
5 [h]**2Ki 1:1**
7 [i]1Ki 22:4
9 [j]**1Ki 22:47**
11 [k]**Ge 25:22; 1Ki 22:5;** [l]**Ge 20:7;** [m]**1Ki 19:16**
12 [n]**Nu 11:17**
15 [o]**1Sa 10:5**; [p]Jer 15:17; Eze 1:3
17 [q]Ps 107:35; Isa 12:3; 32:2; 35:6; 41:18; 65:13
18 [r]**Ge 18:14**; 2Ki 20:10; Isa 49:6; Jer 32:17,27; Mk 10:27
20 [s]**Ex 29:41;** [t]**Ex 17:6**
25 [u]Isa 15:1; 16:7; Jer 48:31,36
27 [v]**Dt 12:31**; 2Ki 16:3; 21:6; 2Ch 28:3; Ps 106:38; Jer 19:4–5; Mic 6:7

Ch. 4

1 [a]**1Sa 10:5**

---

b*11* That is, he was Elijah's personal servant.

LORD. But now his creditor[b] is coming to
take my two boys as his slaves."
2Elisha replied to her, "How can I
help you? Tell me, what do you have in
your house?"
"Your servant has nothing there at
all," she said, "except a little oil."[c]
3Elisha said, "Go round and ask all
your neighbours for empty jars. Don't
ask for just a few. 4Then go inside and
shut the door behind you and your
sons. Pour oil into all the jars, and as
each is filled, put it to one side."
5She left him and afterwards shut the
door behind her and her sons. They
brought the jars to her and she kept
pouring. 6When all the jars were full,
she said to her son, "Bring me another
one."
But he replied, "There is not a jar
left." Then the oil stopped flowing.
7She went and told the man of God,[d]
and he said, "Go, sell the oil and pay
your debts. You and your sons can live
on what is left."

The Shunammite's Son Restored to Life

8One day Elisha went to Shunem.[e]
And a well-to-do woman was there,
who urged him to stay for a meal. So
whenever he came by, he stopped there
to eat. 9She said to her husband, "I
know that this man who often comes
our way is a holy man of God. 10Let's
make a small room on the roof and put
in it a bed and a table, a chair and a lamp
for him. Then he can stay[f] there
whenever he comes to us."
11One day when Elisha came, he went
up to his room and lay down there. 12He
said to his servant Gehazi, "Call the
Shunammite."[g] So he called her, and
she stood before him. 13Elisha said to
him, "Tell her, 'You have gone to all this
trouble for us. Now what can be done
for you? Can we speak on your behalf to
the king or the commander of the
army?'"
She replied, "I have a home among
my own people."
14"What can be done for her?" Elisha
asked.
Gehazi said, "Well, she has no son
and her husband is old."
15Then Elisha said, "Call her." So he
called her, and she stood in the door-
way. 16"About this time[h] next year,"
Elisha said, "you will hold a son in your
arms."
"No, my lord," she objected. "Don't
mislead your servant, O man of God!"
17But the woman became pregnant,
and the next year about that same time
she gave birth to a son, just as Elisha
had told her.
18The child grew, and one day he
went out to his father, who was with the
reapers.[i] 19"My head! My head!" he said
to his father.
His father told a servant, "Carry him
to his mother." 20After the servant had
lifted him up and carried him to his
mother, the boy sat on her lap until
noon, and then he died. 21She went up
and laid him on the bed[j] of the man of
God, then shut the door and went out.
22She called her husband and said,
"Please send me one of the servants and
a donkey so I can go to the man of God
quickly and return."
23"Why go to him today?" he asked.
"It's not the New Moon[k] or the
Sabbath."
"It's all right," she said.
24She saddled the donkey and said to
her servant, "Lead on; don't slow down
for me unless I tell you." 25So she set out
and came to the man of God at Mount
Carmel.[l]
When he saw her in the distance, the
man of God said to his servant Gehazi,
"Look! There's the Shunammite! 26Run
to meet her and ask her, 'Are you all
right? Is your husband all right? Is your
child all right?'"
"Everything is all right," she said.
27When she reached the man of God
at the mountain, she took hold of his
feet. Gehazi came over to push her
away, but the man of God said, "Leave
her alone! She is in bitter distress,[m] but
the LORD has hidden it from me and has
not told me why."
28"Did I ask you for a son, my lord?"
she said. "Didn't I tell you, 'Don't raise
my hopes'?"
29Elisha said to Gehazi, "Tuck your
cloak into your belt,[n] take my staff[o] in
your hand and run. If you meet anyone,
do not greet him, and if anyone greets
you, do not answer. Lay my staff on the
boy's face."
30But the child's mother said, "As
surely as the LORD lives and as you live, I
will not leave you." So he got up and
followed her.
31Gehazi went on ahead and laid the
staff on the boy's face, but there was no
sound or response. So Gehazi went
back to meet Elisha and told him, "The
boy has not awakened."
32When Elisha reached the house,
there was the boy lying dead on his
couch.[p] 33He went in, shut the door on
the two of them and prayed[q] to the

1 [b]**Ex 22:26;** Lev 25:39–43; Ne 5:3–5; Job 22:6; 24:9
2 [c]**1Ki 17:12**
7 [d]**1Ki 12:22**
8 [e]**Jos 19:18**
10 [f]Mt 10:41; **Ro 12:13**
12 [g]2Ki 8:1
16 [h]**Ge 18:10**
18 [i]**Ru 2:3**
21 [j]ver 32
23 [k]**Nu 10:10;** 1Ch 23:31; Ps 81:3
25 [l]**1Ki 18:20**
27 [m]1Sa 1:15
29 [n]**1Ki 18:46;** [o]**Ex 4:2**
32 [p]ver 21
33 [q]1Ki 17:20; Mt 6:6

LORD. 34Then he got on the bed and lay upon the boy, mouth to mouth, eyes to eyes, hands to hands. As he stretched[r] himself out upon him, the boy's body grew warm. 35Elisha turned away and walked back and forth in the room and then got onto the bed and stretched out upon him once more. The boy sneezed seven times[s] and opened his eyes.[t]

36Elisha summoned Gehazi and said, "Call the Shunammite." And he did. When she came, he said, "Take your son."[u] 37She came in, fell at his feet and bowed to the ground. Then she took her son and went out.

Death in the Pot

38Elisha returned to Gilgal[v] and there was a famine[w] in that region. While the company of the prophets was meeting with him, he said to his servant, "Put on the large pot and cook some stew for these men."

39One of them went out into the fields to gather herbs and found a wild vine. He gathered some of its gourds and filled the fold of his cloak. When he returned, he cut them up into the pot of stew, though no-one knew what they were. 40The stew was poured out for the men, but as they began to eat it, they cried out, "O man of God, there is death in the pot!" And they could not eat it.

41Elisha said, "Get some flour." He put it into the pot and said, "Serve it to the people to eat." And there was nothing harmful in the pot.[x]

Feeding of a Hundred

42A man came from Baal Shalishah,[y] bringing the man of God twenty loaves[z] of barley bread[a] baked from the first ripe corn, along with some ears of new corn. "Give it to the people to eat," Elisha said.

43"How can I set this before a hundred men?" his servant asked.

But Elisha answered, "Give it to the people to eat.[b] For this is what the LORD says: 'They will eat and have some left over.[c]'" 44Then he set it before them, and they ate and had some left over, according to the word of the LORD.

Naaman Healed of Leprosy

5 Now Naaman was commander of the army of the king of Aram.[a] He was a great man in the sight of his master and highly regarded, because through him the LORD had given victory to Aram. He was a valiant soldier, but he had leprosy.[a][b]

2Now bands[c] from Aram had gone out and had taken captive a young girl from Israel, and she served Naaman's wife. 3She said to her mistress, "If only my master would see the prophet[d] who is in Samaria! He would cure him of his leprosy."

4Naaman went to his master and told him what the girl from Israel had said. 5"By all means, go," the king of Aram replied. "I will send a letter to the king of Israel." So Naaman left, taking with him ten talents[b] of silver, six thousand shekels[c] of gold and ten sets of clothing.[e] 6The letter that he took to the king of Israel read: "With this letter I am sending my servant Naaman to you so that you may cure him of his leprosy."

7As soon as the king of Israel read the letter,[f] he tore his robes and said, "Am I God?[g] Can I kill and bring back to life?[h] Why does this fellow send someone to me to be cured of his leprosy? See how he is trying to pick a quarrel[i] with me!"

8When Elisha the man of God heard that the king of Israel had torn his robes, he sent him this message: "Why have you torn your robes? Make the man come to me and he will know that there is a prophet[j] in Israel." 9So Naaman went with his horses and chariots and stopped at the door of Elisha's house. 10Elisha sent a messenger to say to him, "Go, wash[k] yourself seven times[l] in the Jordan, and your flesh will be restored and you will be cleansed."

11But Naaman went away angry and said, "I thought that he would surely come out to me and stand and call on the name of the LORD his God, wave his hand[m] over the spot and cure me of my leprosy. 12Are not Abana and Pharpar, the rivers of Damascus, better than any of the waters[n] of Israel? Couldn't I wash in them and be cleansed?" So he turned and went off in a rage.[o]

13Naaman's servants went to him and said, "My father,[p] if the prophet had told you to do some great thing, would you not have done it? How much more, then, when he tells you, 'Wash and be cleansed'?" 14So he went down and dipped himself in the Jordan seven times,[q] as the man of God had told him, and his flesh was restored[r] and became clean like that of a young boy.[s]

34 [r]1Ki 17:21; Ac 20:10
35 [s]**Jos 6:15;** [t]2Ki 8:5
36 [u]Heb 11:35
38 [v]**2Ki 2:1;** [w]**Lev 26:26;** 2Ki 8:1
41 [x]**Ex 15:25; 2Ki 2:21**
42 [y]1Sa 9:4; [z]Mt 14:17; 15:36; [a]**1Sa 9:7**
43 [b]Lk 9:13; [c]Mt 14:20; Jn 6:12

Ch. 5

1 [a]**Ge 10:22; 2Sa 10:19;** [b]**Ex 4:6; Nu 12:10;** Lk 4:27
2 [c]2Ki 6:23; 13:20; 24:2
3 [d]**Ge 20:7**
5 [e]ver 22; **Ge 24:53;** Jdg 14:12; **1Sa 9:7**
7 [f]2Ki 19:14; [g]**Ge 30:2;** [h]**Dt 32:39;** [i]1Ki 20:7
8 [j]**1Ki 22:7**
10 [k]Jn 9:7; [l]**Ge 33:3; Lev 14:7**
11 [m]**Ex 7:19**
12 [n]Isa 8:6; [o]Pr 14:17,29; 19:11; 29:11
13 [p]2Ki 6:21; 13:14
14 [q]**Ge 33:3; Lev 14:7; Jos 6:15;** [r]**Ex 4:7;** [s]Job 33:25

[a]*1* The Hebrew word was used for various diseases affecting the skin—not necessarily leprosy; also in verses 3, 6, 7, 11 and 27.
[b]5 That is, about 750 pounds (about 340 kilograms)
[c]5 That is, about 150 pounds (about 70 kilograms)

15Then Naaman and all his attendants went back to the man of God[t]. He stood before him and said, "Now I know[u] that there is no God in all the world except in Israel. Please accept now a gift[v] from your servant."

16The prophet answered, "As surely as the LORD lives, whom I serve, I will not accept a thing." And even though Naaman urged him, he refused.[w]

17"If you will not," said Naaman, "please let me, your servant, be given as much earth[x] as a pair of mules can carry, for your servant will never again make burnt offerings and sacrifices to any other god but the LORD. 18But may the LORD forgive your servant for this one thing: When my master enters the temple of Rimmon to bow down and he is leaning[y] on my arm and I bow there also—when I bow down in the temple of Rimmon, may the LORD forgive your servant for this."

19"Go in peace,"[z] Elisha said.

After Naaman had travelled some distance, 20Gehazi, the servant of Elisha the man of God, said to himself, "My master was too easy on Naaman, this Aramean, by not accepting from him what he brought. As surely as the LORD[a] lives, I will run after him and get something from him."

21So Gehazi hurried after Naaman. When Naaman saw him running towards him, he got down from the chariot to meet him. "Is everything all right?" he asked.

22"Everything is all right," Gehazi answered. "My master sent me to say, 'Two young men from the company of the prophets have just come to me from the hill country of Ephraim. Please give them a talent[d] of silver and two sets of clothing.' "[b]

23"By all means, take two talents," said Naaman. He urged Gehazi to accept them, and then tied up the two talents of silver in two bags, with two sets of clothing. He gave them to two of his servants, and they carried them ahead of Gehazi. 24When Gehazi came to the hill, he took the things from the servants and put them away in the house. He sent the men away and they left. 25Then he went in and stood before his master Elisha.

"Where have you been, Gehazi?" Elisha asked.

"Your servant didn't go anywhere," Gehazi answered.

26But Elisha said to him, "Was not my spirit with you when the man got down from his chariot to meet you? Is this the time[c] to take money, or to accept clothes, olive groves, vineyards, flocks, herds, or menservants and maidservants?[d] 27Naaman's leprosy[e] will cling to you and to your descendants for ever." Then Gehazi[f] went from Elisha's presence and he was leprous, as white as snow.[g]

An Axe-Head Floats

6 The company[a] of the prophets said to Elisha, "Look, the place where we meet with you is too small for us. 2Let us go to the Jordan, where each of us can get a pole; and let us build a place there for us to live."

And he said, "Go."

3Then one of them said, "Won't you please come with your servants?"

"I will," Elisha replied. 4And he went with them.

They went to the Jordan and began to cut down trees. 5As one of them was cutting down a tree, the iron axe-head fell into the water. "Oh, my lord," he cried out, "it was borrowed!"

6The man of God asked, "Where did it fall?" When he showed him the place, Elisha cut a stick and threw[b] it there, and made the iron float. 7"Lift it out," he said. Then the man reached out his hand and took it.

Elisha Traps Blinded Arameans

8Now the king of Aram was at war with Israel. After conferring with his officers, he said, "I will set up my camp in such and such a place."

9The man of God sent word to the king[c] of Israel: "Beware of passing that place, because the Arameans are going down there." 10So the king of Israel checked on the place indicated by the man of God. Time and again Elisha warned[d] the king, so that he was on his guard in such places.

11This enraged the king of Aram. He summoned his officers and demanded of them, "Will you not tell me which of us is on the side of the king of Israel?"

12"None of us, my lord the king[e]," said one of his officers, "but Elisha, the prophet who is in Israel, tells the king of Israel the very words you speak in your bedroom."

13"Go, find out where he is," the king ordered, "so that I can send men and capture him." The report came back: "He is in Dothan."[f] 14Then he sent[g]

15 [t]Jos 2:11; [u]Jos 4:24; 1Sa 17:46; [v]1Sa 9:7
16 [w]ver 20,26; Ge 14:23; Da 5:17
17 [x]Ex 20:24
18 [y]2Ki 7:2
19 [z]1Sa 1:17; Ac 15:33
20 [a]Ex 20:7
22 [b]ver 5; Ge 45:22
26 [c]ver 16; [d]Jer 45:5
27 [e]Nu 12:10; [f]Col 3:5; [g]Ex 4:6

Ch. 6

1 [a]1Sa 10:5
6 [b]Ex 15:25; 2Ki 2:21
9 [c]ver 12
10 [d]Jer 11:18
12 [e]ver 9
13 [f]Ge 37:17
14 [g]2Ki 1:9

d22 That is, about 75 pounds (about 34 kilograms)

horses and chariots and a strong force there. They went by night and surrounded the city.

15When the servant of the man of God got up and went out early the next morning, an army with horses and chariots had surrounded the city. "Oh, my lord, what shall we do?" the servant asked.

16"Don't be afraid,"[h] the prophet answered. "Those who are with us are more[i] than those who are with them."

17And Elisha prayed, "O LORD, open his eyes so that he may see." Then the LORD opened the servant's eyes, and he looked and saw the hills full of horses and chariots[j] of fire all round Elisha.

18As the enemy came down towards him, Elisha prayed to the LORD, "Strike these people with blindness."[k] So he struck them with blindness, as Elisha had asked.

19Elisha told them, "This is not the road and this is not the city. Follow me, and I will lead you to the man you are looking for." And he led them to Samaria.

20After they entered the city, Elisha said, "LORD, open the eyes of these men so that they can see." Then the LORD opened their eyes and they looked, and there they were, inside Samaria.

21When the king of Israel saw them, he asked Elisha, "Shall I kill them, my father?[l] Shall I kill them?"

22"Do not kill them," he answered. "Would you kill men you have captured[m] with your own sword or bow? Set food and water before them so that they may eat and drink and then go back to their master." 23So he prepared a great feast for them, and after they had finished eating and drinking, he sent them away, and they returned to their master. So the bands[n] from Aram stopped raiding Israel's territory.

Famine in Besieged Samaria

24Some time later, Ben-Hadad[o] king of Aram mobilised his entire army and marched up and laid siege[p] to Samaria. 25There was a great famine[q] in the city; the siege lasted so long that a donkey's head sold for eighty shekels[a] of silver, and a fourth of a cab[b] of seed pods[c][r] for five shekels.[d]

26As the king of Israel was passing by on the wall, a woman cried to him, "Help me, my lord the king!"

27The king replied, "If the LORD does not help you, where can I get help for you? From the threshing-floor? From the winepress?" 28Then he asked her, "What's the matter?"

She answered, "This woman said to me, 'Give up your son so that we may eat him today, and tomorrow we'll eat my son.' 29So we cooked my son and ate[s] him. The next day I said to her, 'Give up your son so that we may eat him,' but she had hidden him."

30When the king heard the woman's words, he tore[t] his robes. As he went along the wall, the people looked, and there, underneath, he had sackcloth[u] on his body. 31He said, "May God deal with me, be it ever so severely, if the head of Elisha son of Shaphat remains on his shoulders today!"

32Now Elisha was sitting in his house, and the elders[v] were sitting with him. The king sent a messenger ahead, but before he arrived, Elisha said to the elders, "Don't you see how this murderer[w] is sending someone to cut off my head?[x] Look, when the messenger comes, shut the door and hold it shut against him. Is not the sound of his master's footsteps behind him?"

33While he was still talking to them, the messenger came down to him. And ⌞the king⌟ said, "This disaster is from the LORD. Why should I wait[y] for the LORD any longer?"

7 Elisha said, "Hear the word of the LORD. This is what the LORD says: About this time tomorrow, a seah[a] of flour will sell for a shekel[b] and two seahs[c] of barley for a shekel[a] at the gate of Samaria."

2The officer on whose arm the king was leaning[b] said to the man of God, "Look, even if the LORD should open the floodgates[c] of the heavens, could this happen?"

"You will see it with your own eyes," answered Elisha, "but you will not eat[d] any of it!"

The Siege Lifted

3Now there were four men with leprosy[d][e] at the entrance of the city gate.

16 [h]Ge 15:1; [i]2Ch 32:7; Ps 55:18; Ro 8:31; 1Jn 4:4
17 [j]2Ki 2:11–12
18 [k]Ge 19:11; Ac 13:11
21 [l]2Ki 5:13
22 [m]Dt 20:11; 2Ch 28:8–15
23 [n]2Ki 5:2
24 [o]1Ki 15:18; 2Ki 8:7; [p]Dt 28:52
25 [q]Lev 26:26; Ru 1:1; [r]Isa 36:12
29 [s]Lev 26:29; Dt 28:53–55
30 [t]2Ki 18:37; Isa 22:15; [u]Ge 37:34
32 [v]Eze 8:1; 14:1; 20:1; [w]1Ki 18:4; [x]ver 31
33 [y]Lev 24:11; Job 2:9; 14:14; Isa 40:31

Ch. 7

1 [a]ver 16
2 [b]2Ki 5:18; [c]ver 19; Ge 7:11; Ps 78:23; Mal 3:10; [d]ver 17
3 [e]Lev 13:45–46; Nu 5:1–4

a25 That is, about 2 pounds (about 1 kilogram)
b25 That is, probably about ½ pint (about 0.3 litre)
c25 Or *of dove's dung*
d25 That is, about 2 ounces (about 55 grams)
a1 That is, probably about 13 pints (about 7.3 litres); also in verses 16 and 18
b1 That is, about ⅖ ounce (about 11 grams); also in verses 16 and 18
c1 That is, probably about 13 quarts (about 15 litres); also in verses 16 and 18
d3 The Hebrew word is used for various diseases affecting the skin, not necessarily leprosy; also in verse 8.

They said to each other, "Why stay here until we die? 4If we say, 'We'll go into the city'—the famine is there, and we will die. And if we stay here, we will die. So let's go over to the camp of the Arameans and surrender. If they spare us, we live; if they kill us, then we die."

5At dusk they got up and went to the camp of the Arameans. When they reached the edge of the camp, not a man was there, 6for the LORD had caused the Arameans to hear the sound[f] of chariots and horses and a great army, so that they said to one another, "Look, the king of Israel has hired[g] the Hittite[h] and Egyptian kings to attack us!" 7So they got up and fled[i] in the dusk and abandoned their tents and their horses and donkeys. They left the camp as it was and ran for their lives.

8The men who had leprosy[j] reached the edge of the camp and entered one of the tents. They ate and drank, and carried away silver, gold and clothes, and went off and hid them. They returned and entered another tent and took some things from it and hid them also.

9Then they said to each other, "We're not doing right. This is a day of good news and we are keeping it to ourselves. If we wait until daylight, punishment will overtake us. Let's go at once and report this to the royal palace."

10So they went and called out to the city gatekeepers and told them, "We went into the Aramean camp and not a man was there—not a sound of anyone—only tethered horses and donkeys, and the tents left just as they were." 11The gatekeepers shouted the news, and it was reported within the palace.

12The king got up in the night and said to his officers, "I will tell you what the Arameans have done to us. They know we are starving; so they have left the camp to hide[k] in the countryside, thinking, 'They will surely come out, and then we will take them alive and get into the city.'"

13One of his officers answered, "Make some men take five of the horses that are left in the city. Their plight will be like that of all the Israelites left here—yes, they will only be like all these Israelites who are doomed. So let us send them to find out what happened."

14So they selected two chariots with their horses, and the king sent them after the Aramean army. He commanded the drivers, "Go and find out what has happened." 15They followed them as far as the Jordan, and they found the whole road strewn with the clothing and equipment the Arameans had thrown away in their headlong flight.[l] So the messengers returned and reported to the king. 16Then the people went out and plundered[m] the camp of the Arameans. So a seah of flour sold for a shekel, and two seahs of barley sold for a shekel,[n] as the LORD had said.

17Now the king had put the officer on whose arm he leaned in charge of the gate, and the people trampled him in the gateway, and he died,[o] just as the man of God had foretold when the king came down to his house. 18It happened as the man of God had said to the king: "About this time tomorrow, a seah of flour will sell for a shekel and two seahs of barley for a shekel at the gate of Samaria."

19The officer had said to the man of God, "Look, even if the LORD should open the floodgates[p] of the heavens, could this happen?" The man of God had replied, "You will see it with your own eyes, but you will not eat any of it!" 20And that is exactly what happened to him, for the people trampled him in the gateway, and he died.

The Shunammite's Land Restored

8 Now Elisha had said to the woman[a] whose son he had restored to life, "Go away with your family and stay for a while wherever you can, because the LORD has decreed a famine[b] in the land that will last seven years."[c] 2The woman proceeded to do as the man of God said. She and her family went away and stayed in the land of the Philistines for seven years.

3At the end of the seven years she came back from the land of the Philistines and went to the king to beg for her house and land. 4The king was talking to Gehazi, the servant of the man of God, and had said, "Tell me about all the great things Elisha has done." 5Just as Gehazi was telling the king how Elisha had restored[d] the dead to life, the woman whose son Elisha had brought back to life came to beg the king for her house and land.

Gehazi said, "This is the woman, my lord the king, and this is her son whom Elisha restored to life." 6The king asked the woman about it, and she told him.

Then he assigned an official to her case and said to him, "Give back everything that belonged to her, including all the income from her land from the day she left the country until now."

6 [f]**Ex 14:24**; Eze 1:24; [g]2Sa 10:6; Jer 46:21; [h]**Nu 13:29**
7 [i]Jdg 7:21; Ps 48:4–6; Pr 28:1; Isa 30:17
8 [j]Isa 33:23; 35:6
12 [k]Jos 8:4
15 [l]Job 27:22
16 [m]Isa 33:4,23; [n]ver 1
17 [o]**ver 2**
19 [p]**ver 2**

Ch. 8

1 [a]2Ki 4:8–37; [b]**Lev 26:26; Dt 28:22; Ru 1:1;** [c]**Ge 12:10**
5 [d]2Ki 4:35

Hazael Murders Ben-Hadad

7Elisha went to Damascus,[e] and Ben-
Hadad[f] king of Aram was ill. When the
king was told, "The man of God has
come all the way up here," 8he said to
Hazael,[g] "Take a gift[h] with you and go to
meet the man of God. Consult[i] the LORD
through him; ask him, 'Will I recover
from this illness?' "
9Hazael went to meet Elisha, taking
with him as a gift forty camel-loads of all
the finest wares of Damascus. He went
in and stood before him, and said,
"Your son Ben-Hadad king of Aram has
sent me to ask, 'Will I recover from this
illness?' "
10Elisha answered, "Go and say to
him, 'You will certainly recover';[j] but[a]
the LORD has revealed to me that he will
in fact die." 11He stared at him with a
fixed gaze until Hazael felt ashamed.[k]
Then the man of God began to weep.[l]
12"Why is my lord weeping?" asked
Hazael.
"Because I know the harm[m] you will
do to the Israelites," he answered. "You
will set fire to their fortified places, kill
their young men with the sword, dash[n]
their little children[o] to the ground, and
rip open[p] their pregnant women."
13Hazael said, "How could your ser-
vant, a mere dog,[q] accomplish such a
feat?"
"The LORD has shown me that you
will become king[r] of Aram," answered
Elisha.
14Then Hazael left Elisha and re-
turned to his master. When Ben-Hadad
asked, "What did Elisha say to you?"
Hazael replied, "He told me that you
would certainly recover." 15But the next
day he took a thick cloth, soaked it in
water and spread it over the king's face,
so that he died.[s] Then Hazael succeeded
him as king.

Jehoram King of Judah

8:16–24pp—2Ch 21:5–10,20

16In the fifth year of Joram[t] son of
Ahab king of Israel, when Jehoshaphat
was king of Judah, Jehoram[u] son of
Jehoshaphat began his reign as king of
Judah. 17He was thirty-two years old
when he became king, and he reigned
in Jerusalem for eight years. 18He
walked in the ways of the kings of
Israel, as the house of Ahab had done,
for he married a daughter[v] of Ahab. He
did evil in the eyes of the LORD. 19Never-
theless, for the sake of his servant
David, the LORD was not willing to
destroy[w] Judah. He had promised to
maintain a lamp[x] for David and his
descendants for ever.
20In the time of Jehoram, Edom rebel-
led against Judah and set up its own
king.[y] 21So Jehoram[b] went to Zair with
all his chariots. The Edomites sur-
rounded him and his chariot comman-
ders, but he rose up and broke through
by night; his army, however, fled back
home. 22To this day Edom has been in
rebellion[z] against Judah. Libnah[a] re-
volted at the same time.
23As for the other events of Jehoram's
reign, and all he did, are they not writ-
ten in the book of the annals of the kings
of Judah? 24Jehoram rested with his
fathers and was buried with them in the
City of David. And Ahaziah his son
succeeded him as king.

Ahaziah King of Judah

8:25–29pp—2Ch 22:1–6

25In the twelfth[b] year of Joram son of
Ahab king of Israel, Ahaziah son of
Jehoram king of Judah began to reign.
26Ahaziah was twenty-two years old
when he became king, and he reigned
in Jerusalem for one year. His mother's
name was Athaliah,[c] a granddaughter
of Omri[d] king of Israel. 27He walked in
the ways of the house of Ahab[e] and did
evil[f] in the eyes of the LORD, as the house
of Ahab had done, for he was related by
marriage to Ahab's family.
28Ahaziah went with Joram son of
Ahab to war against Hazael king of
Aram at Ramoth Gilead.[g] The Ara-
means wounded Joram; 29so King Joram
returned to Jezreel[h] to recover from the
wounds the Arameans had inflicted on
him at Ramoth[c] in his battle with
Hazael[i] king of Aram.
Then Ahaziah[j] son of Jehoram king of
Judah went down to Jezreel to see Joram
son of Ahab, because he had been
wounded.

Jehu Anointed King of Israel

9 The prophet Elisha summoned a
man from the company[a] of the
prophets and said to him, "Tuck your
cloak into your belt,[b] take this flask of
oil[c] with you and go to Ramoth Gilead.[d]
2When you get there, look for Jehu son

7 [e]**2Sa 8:5**; [f]**2Ki 6:24**
8 [g]1Ki 19:15; [h]**Ge 32:20; 1Sa 9:7**; [i]**Jdg 18:5**
10 [j]Isa 38:1
11 [k]**Jdg 3:25**; [l]Lk 19:41
12 [m]**1Ki 19:17**; [n]Ps 137:9; Isa 13:16; Hos 13:16; Na 3:10; Lk 19:44; [o]**Ge 34:29**; [p]2Ki 15:16; Am 1:13
13 [q]**1Sa 17:43; 2Sa 3:8**; [r]1Ki 19:15
15 [s]**2Ki 1:17**
16 [t]**2Ki 1:17**; [u]2Ch 21:1–4
18 [v]ver 26; 2Ki 11:1
19 [w]**Ge 6:13**; [x]**2Sa 21:17**; Rev 21:23
20 [y]**1Ki 22:47**
22 [z]Ge 27:40; [a]**Nu 33:20**; Jos 21:13; 2Ki 19:8
25 [b]2Ki 9:29
26 [c]**ver 18**; [d]1Ki 16:23
27 [e]1Ki 16:30; [f]1Ki 15:26
28 [g]**Dt 4:43**; 2Ki 9:1,14
29 [h]1Ki 21:29; 2Ki 9:21; [i]1Ki 19:15,17; [j]2Ki 10:13

Ch. 9

1 [a]**1Sa 10:5**; [b]**1Ki 18:46**; [c]**1Sa 10:1**; [d]**2Ki 8:28**

[a]10 The Hebrew may also be read *Go and say, 'You will certainly not recover,' for.*

[b]21 Hebrew *Joram,* a variant of *Jehoram;* also in verses 23 and 24

[c]29 Hebrew *Ramah,* a variant of *Ramoth*

of Jehoshaphat, the son of Nimshi. Go
to him, get him away from his compan-
ions and take him into an inner room.
3Then take the flask and pour the oil[e] on
his head and declare, 'This is what the
LORD says: I anoint you king over Israel.'
Then open the door and run; don't
delay!"
4So the young man, the prophet,
went to Ramoth Gilead. 5When he ar-
rived, he found the army officers sitting
together. "I have a message for you,
commander," he said.

"For which of us?" asked Jehu.

"For you, commander," he replied.

6Jehu got up and went into the house.
Then the prophet poured the oil[f] on
Jehu's head and declared, "This is what
the LORD, the God of Israel, says: 'I
anoint you king over the LORD's people
Israel. 7You are to destroy the house of
Ahab your master, and I will avenge[g]
the blood of my servants[h] the prophets
and the blood of all the LORD's servants
shed by Jezebel.[i] 8The whole house[j] of
Ahab will perish. I will cut off from
Ahab every last male[k] in Israel—slave or
free. 9I will make the house of Ahab like
the house of Jeroboam[l] son of Nebat and
like the house of Baasha[m] son of Ahijah.
10As for Jezebel, dogs[n] will devour her
on the plot of ground at Jezreel, and
no-one will bury her.' " Then he opened
the door and ran.
11When Jehu went out to his fellow
officers, one of them asked him, "Is
everything all right? Why did this mad-
man[o] come to you?"

"You know the man and the sort of
things he says," Jehu replied.
12"That's not true!" they said. "Tell
us."

Jehu said, "Here is what he told me:
'This is what the LORD says: I anoint you
king over Israel.' "
13They hurried and took their cloaks
and spread[p] them under him on the bare
steps. Then they blew the trumpet[q] and
shouted, "Jehu is king!"

Jehu Kills Joram and Ahaziah

9:21–29pp—2Ch 22:7–9

14So Jehu son of Jehoshaphat, the son
of Nimshi, conspired against Joram.
(Now Joram and all Israel had been de-
fending Ramoth Gilead[r] against Hazael
king of Aram, 15but King Joram[a] had
returned to Jezreel to recover[s] from the
wounds the Arameans had inflicted on
him in the battle with Hazael king of
Aram.) Jehu said, "If this is the way you
feel, don't let anyone slip out of the city
to go and tell the news in Jezreel."
16Then he got into his chariot and rode
to Jezreel, because Joram was resting
there and Ahaziah[t] king of Judah had
gone down to see him.
17When the lookout[u] standing on the
tower in Jezreel saw Jehu's troops
approaching, he called out, "I see some
troops coming."

"Get a horseman," Joram ordered.
"Send him to meet them and ask, 'Do
you come in peace?'[v] "
18The horseman rode off to meet Jehu
and said, "This is what the king says:
'Do you come in peace?' "

"What do you have to do with
peace?" Jehu replied. "Fall in behind
me."

The lookout reported, "The messen-
ger has reached them, but he isn't
coming back."
19So the king sent out a second horse-
man. When he came to them he said,
"This is what the king says: 'Do you
come in peace?' "

Jehu replied, "What do you have to
do with peace? Fall in behind me."
20The lookout reported, "He has
reached them, but he isn't coming
back either. The driving is like[w] that of
Jehu son of Nimshi—he drives like a
madman."
21"Hitch up my chariot," Joram
ordered. And when it was hitched up,
Joram king of Israel and Ahaziah king of
Judah rode out, each in his own chariot,
to meet Jehu. They met him at the plot
of ground that had belonged to Naboth[x]
the Jezreelite. 22When Joram saw Jehu
he asked, "Have you come in peace,
Jehu?"

"How can there be peace," Jehu re-
plied, "as long as all the idolatry and
witchcraft of your mother Jezebel[y]
abound?"
23Joram turned about and fled, calling
out to Ahaziah, "Treachery,[z] Ahaziah!"
24Then Jehu drew his bow[a] and shot
Joram between the shoulders. The
arrow pierced his heart and he slumped
down in his chariot. 25Jehu said to Bid-
kar, his chariot officer, "Pick him up
and throw him on the field that be-
longed to Naboth the Jezreelite. Re-
member how you and I were riding
together in chariots behind Ahab his
father when the LORD made this
prophecy[b] about him: 26'Yesterday I saw
the blood of Naboth[c] and the blood of
his sons, declares the LORD, and I will

3 [e]1Ki 19:16
6 [f]1Ki 19:16
7 [g]Ge 4:24; Rev 6:10; [h]Dt 32:43; [i]1Ki 18:4
8 [j]2Ki 10:17; [k]1Sa 25:22
9 [l]1Ki 13:34; 14:10; [m]1Ki 16:3
10 [n]1Ki 21:23
11 [o]1Sa 10:11; Jn 10:20
13 [p]Mt 21:8; Lk 19:36; [q]2Sa 15:10
14 [r]Dt 4:43; 2Ki 8:28
15 [s]2Ki 8:29
16 [t]2Ch 22:7
17 [u]1Sa 14:16; Isa 21:6; [v]1Sa 16:4
20 [w]2Sa 18:27
21 [x]1Ki 21:1
22 [y]1Ki 18:19; Rev 2:20
23 [z]2Ki 11:14
24 [a]1Ki 22:34
25 [b]1Ki 21:19–22
26 [c]1Ki 21:19

[a]15 Hebrew *Jehoram,* a variant of *Joram;* also in verses 17 and 21–24

surely make you pay for it on this plot of
ground, declares the LORD.'[b] Now then,
pick him up and throw him on that plot,
in accordance with the word of the
LORD."[d]
[27]When Ahaziah king of Judah saw
what had happened, he fled up the road
to Beth Haggan.[c] Jehu chased him,
shouting, "Kill him too!" They wound-
ed him in his chariot on the way up to
Gur near Ibleam,[e] but he escaped to
Megiddo[f] and died there. [28]His servants
took him by chariot[g] to Jerusalem and
buried him with his fathers in his tomb
in the City of David. [29](In the eleventh[h]
year of Joram son of Ahab, Ahaziah had
become king of Judah.)

Jezebel Killed

[30]Then Jehu went to Jezreel. When
Jezebel heard about it, she painted[i] her
eyes, arranged her hair and looked out
of a window. [31]As Jehu entered the gate,
she asked, "Have you come in peace,
Zimri,[j] you murderer of your master?"[d]
[32]He looked up at the window and
called out, "Who is on my side? Who?"
Two or three eunuchs looked down at
him. [33]"Throw her down!" Jehu said. So
they threw her down, and some of her
blood spattered the wall and the horses
as they trampled her underfoot.[k]
[34]Jehu went in and ate and drank.
"Take care of that cursed woman," he
said, "and bury her, for she was a king's
daughter."[l] [35]But when they went out to
bury her, they found nothing except her
skull, her feet and her hands. [36]They
went back and told Jehu, who said,
"This is the word of the LORD that he
spoke through his servant Elijah the
Tishbite: On the plot of ground at Jez-
reel dogs[m] will devour Jezebel's flesh.[e][n]
[37]Jezebel's body will be like refuse[o] on
the ground in the plot at Jezreel, so that
no-one will be able to say, 'This is
Jezebel.'"

Ahab's Family Killed

10 Now there were in Samaria[a]
seventy sons[b] of the house of
Ahab. So Jehu wrote letters and sent
them to Samaria: to the officials of Jez-
reel,[a][c] to the elders and to the guar-
dians[d] of Ahab's children. He said, [2]"As
soon as this letter reaches you, since
your master's sons are with you and
you have chariots and horses, a fortified
city and weapons, [3]choose the best and
most worthy of your master's sons and
set him on his father's throne. Then
fight for your master's house."

[4]But they were terrified and said, "If
two kings could not resist him, how can
we?"
[5]So the palace administrator, the city
governor, the elders and the guardians
sent this message to Jehu: "We are your
servants[e] and we will do anything you
say. We will not appoint anyone as
king; you do whatever you think best."
[6]Then Jehu wrote them a second let-
ter, saying, "If you are on my side and
will obey me, take the heads of your
master's sons and come to me in Jezreel
by this time tomorrow."
Now the royal princes, seventy of
them, were with the leading men of the
city, who were bringing them up.
[7]When the letter arrived, these men
took the princes and slaughtered all
seventy[f] of them. They put their heads[g]
in baskets and sent them to Jehu in
Jezreel. [8]When the messenger arrived,
he told Jehu, "They have brought the
heads of the princes."
Then Jehu ordered, "Put them in two
piles at the entrance of the city gate until
morning."
[9]The next morning Jehu went out. He
stood before all the people and said,
"You are innocent. It was I who con-
spired against my master and killed
him, but who killed all these? [10]Know
then, that not a word the LORD has
spoken against the house of Ahab will
fail. The LORD has done what he prom-
ised[h] through his servant Elijah."[i] [11]So
Jehu[j] killed everyone in Jezreel who re-
mained of the house of Ahab, as well as
all his chief men, his close friends and
his priests, leaving him no survivor.[k]
[12]Jehu then set out and went towards
Samaria. At Beth Eked of the
Shepherds, [13]he met some relatives of
Ahaziah king of Judah and asked,
"Who are you?"
They said, "We are relatives of Aha-
ziah,[l] and we have come down to greet
the families of the king and of the queen
mother."[m]
[14]"Take them alive!" he ordered. So
they took them alive and slaughtered
them by the well of Beth Eked—forty-
two men. He left no survivor.[n]
[15]After he left there, he came upon
Jehonadab[o] son of Recab,[p] who was on
his way to meet him. Jehu greeted him

26 [d]**1Ki 21:29**
27 [e]**Jdg 1:27;** [f]2Ki 23:29
28 [g]2Ki 14:20; 23:30
29 [h]2Ki 8:25
30 [i]Jer 4:30; Eze 23:40
31 [j]1Ki 16:9–10
33 [k]Ps 7:5
34 [l]**1Ki 16:31**
36 [m]Ps 68:23; Jer 15:3; [n]**1Ki 21:23**
37 [o]Ps 83:10; Isa 5:25; Jer 8:2; 9:22; 16:4; 25:33; Zep 1:17

Ch. 10

1 [a]**1Ki 13:32;** [b]**Jdg 8:30;** [c]**1Ki 21:1;** [d]ver 5
5 [e]Jos 9:8
7 [f]**1Ki 21:21;** [g]**2Sa 4:8**
10 [h]2Ki 9:7–10; [i]**1Ki 21:29**
11 [j]Hos 1:4; [k]ver 14; Job 18:19; Mal 4:1
13 [l]2Ki 8:29; 2Ch 22:8; [m]**1Ki 2:19**
14 [n]**ver 11**
15 [o]Jer 35:6, 14–19; [p]1Ch 2:55; Jer 35:2

[b]26 See 1 Kings 21:19.
[c]27 Or *fled by way of the garden house*
[d]31 Or *"Did Zimri have peace, who murdered his master?"* [e]36 See 1 Kings 21:23.
[a]1 Hebrew; some Septuagint manuscripts and Vulgate *of the city*

and said, "Are you in accord with me, as I am with you?"

"I am," Jehonadab answered.

"If so," said Jehu, "give me your hand."[q] So he did, and Jehu helped him up into the chariot. 16Jehu said, "Come with me and see my zeal[r] for the LORD." Then he made him ride in his chariot.

17When Jehu came to Samaria, he killed all who were left there of Ahab's family;[s] he destroyed them, according to the word of the LORD spoken to Elijah.

Ministers of Baal Killed

18Then Jehu brought all the people together and said to them, "Ahab served[t] Baal a little; Jehu will serve him much. 19Now summon[u] all the prophets of Baal, all his ministers and all his priests. See that no-one is missing, because I am going to hold a great sacrifice for Baal. Anyone who fails to come will no longer live." But Jehu was acting deceptively in order to destroy the ministers of Baal.

20Jehu said, "Call an assembly[v] in honour of Baal." So they proclaimed it. 21Then he sent word throughout Israel, and all the ministers of Baal came; not one stayed away. They crowded into the temple of Baal until it was full from one end to the other. 22And Jehu said to the keeper of the wardrobe, "Bring robes for all the ministers of Baal." So he brought out robes for them.

23Then Jehu and Jehonadab son of Recab went into the temple of Baal. Jehu said to the ministers of Baal, "Look around and see that no servants of the LORD are here with you—only ministers of Baal." 24So they went in to make sacrifices and burnt offerings. Now Jehu had posted eighty men outside with this warning: "If one of you lets any of the men I am placing in your hands escape, it will be your life for his life."[w]

25As soon as Jehu had finished making the burnt offering, he ordered the guards and officers: "Go in and kill[x] them; let no-one escape."[y] So they cut them down with the sword. The guards and officers threw the bodies out and then entered the inner shrine of the temple of Baal. 26They brought the sacred stone[z] out of the temple of Baal and burned it. 27They demolished the sacred stone of Baal and tore down the temple[a] of Baal, and people have used it for a latrine to this day.

15 [q]Ezr 10:19; Eze 17:18
16 [r]**Nu 25:13**
17 [s]2Ki 9:8
18 [t]**Jdg 2:11**
19 [u]1Ki 18:19
20 [v]**Ex 32:5**
24 [w]**Jos 2:14**
25 [x]**Ex 22:20; 2Ki 11:18;** [y]**1Ki 18:40**
26 [z]**Ex 23:24**
27 [a]**1Ki 16:32**
28 [b]1Ki 19:17
29 [c]**1Ki 12:30;** [d]**Ex 32:4;** [e]1Ki 12:32
30 [f]2Ki 15:12
31 [g]Dt 4:9; Pr 4:23; [h]1Ki 12:30
32 [i]2Ki 13:25; Ps 107:39; [j]**1Ki 19:17**
33 [k]**Nu 32:34;** Dt 2:36; Jdg 11:26; Isa 17:2; [l]**Nu 21:13**
34 [m]1Ki 15:31

Ch. 11

1 [a]**2Ki 8:18**
2 [b]2Ki 12:1; [c]**Jdg 9:5**
4 [d]ver 19

28So Jehu[b] destroyed Baal worship in Israel. 29However, he did not turn away from the sins[c] of Jeroboam son of Nebat, which he had caused Israel to commit—the worship of the golden calves[d] at Bethel[e] and Dan.

30The LORD said to Jehu, "Because you have done well in accomplishing what is right in my eyes and have done to the house of Ahab all I had in mind to do, your descendants will sit on the throne of Israel to the fourth generation."[f] 31Yet Jehu was not careful[g] to keep the law of the LORD, the God of Israel, with all his heart. He did not turn away from the sins[h] of Jeroboam, which he had caused Israel to commit.

32In those days the LORD began to reduce[i] the size of Israel. Hazael[j] overpowered the Israelites throughout their territory 33east of the Jordan in all the land of Gilead (the region of Gad, Reuben and Manasseh), from Aroer[k] by the Arnon[l] Gorge through Gilead to Bashan.

34As for the other events of Jehu's reign, all he did, and all his achievements, are they not written in the book of the annals[m] of the kings of Israel?

35Jehu rested with his fathers and was buried in Samaria. And Jehoahaz his son succeeded him as king. 36The time that Jehu reigned over Israel in Samaria was twenty-eight years.

Athaliah and Joash

11:1–21pp—2Ch 22:10–23:21

11 When Athaliah[a] the mother of Ahaziah saw that her son was dead, she proceeded to destroy the whole royal family. 2But Jehosheba, the daughter of King Jehoram[a] and sister of Ahaziah, took Joash[b] son of Ahaziah and stole him away from among the royal princes, who were about to be murdered. She put him and his nurse in a bedroom to hide him from Athaliah; so he was not killed.[c] 3He remained hidden with his nurse at the temple of the LORD for six years while Athaliah ruled the land.

4In the seventh year Jehoiada sent for the commanders of units of a hundred, the Carites[d] and the guards and had them brought to him at the temple of the LORD. He made a covenant with them and put them under oath at the temple of the LORD. Then he showed them the

a2 Hebrew *Joram*, a variant of *Jehoram*

king's son. 5He commanded them,
saying, "This is what you are to do: You
who are in the three companies that are
going on duty on the Sabbath[e]—a third
of you guarding the royal palace,[f] 6a
third at the Sur Gate, and a third at the
gate behind the guard, who take turns
guarding the temple—7and you who
are in the other two companies that
normally go off Sabbath duty are all to
guard the temple for the king. 8Station
yourselves round the king, each man
with his weapon in his hand. Anyone
who approaches your ranks[b] must be
put to death. Stay close to the king
wherever he goes."

9The commanders of units of a hun-
dred did just as Jehoiada the priest
ordered. Each one took his men—those
who were going on duty on the Sabbath
and those who were going off duty—
and came to Jehoiada the priest. 10Then
he gave the commanders the spears and
shields[g] that had belonged to King
David and that were in the temple of the
LORD. 11The guards, each with his
weapon in his hand, stationed them-
selves round the king—near the altar
and the temple, from the south side to
the north side of the temple.

12Jehoiada brought out the king's son
and put the crown on him; he presented
him with a copy of the covenant[h] and
proclaimed him king. They anointed[i]
him, and the people clapped their
hands[j] and shouted, "Long live the
king!"[k]

13When Athaliah heard the noise
made by the guards and the people, she
went to the people at the temple of the
LORD. 14She looked and there was the
king, standing by the pillar,[l] as the cus-
tom was. The officers and the trum-
peters were beside the king, and all the
people of the land were rejoicing and
blowing trumpets.[m] Then Athaliah tore[n]
her robes and called out, "Treason!
Treason!"[o]

15Jehoiada the priest ordered the com-
manders of units of a hundred, who
were in charge of the troops: "Bring her
out between the ranks[c] and put to the
sword anyone who follows her." For
the priest had said, "She must not be
put to death in the temple[p] of the LORD."
16So they seized her as she reached the
place where the horses enter[q] the palace
grounds, and there she was put to
death.[r]

17Jehoiada then made a covenant[s] be-
tween the LORD and the king and people
that they would be the LORD's people.[t]
He also made a covenant between the
king and the people. 18All the people of
the land went to the temple[u] of Baal and
tore it down. They smashed[v] the altars
and idols to pieces and killed Mattan the
priest[w] of Baal in front of the altars.

Then Jehoiada the priest posted
guards at the temple of the LORD. 19He
took with him the commanders of hun-
dreds, the Carites,[x] the guards and all
the people of the land, and together
they brought the king down from the
temple of the LORD and went into the
palace, entering by way of the gate of
the guards. The king then took his place
on the royal throne, 20and all the people
of the land rejoiced.[y] And the city was
quiet, because Athaliah had been slain
with the sword at the palace.

21Joash[d] was seven years old when he
began his reign.

5 [e]1Ch 9:25; [f]1Ki 14:27
10 [g]**2Sa 8:7**
12 [h]Ex 25:16; 2Ki 23:3; [i]**1Sa 9:16; 1Ki 1:39;** [j]Ps 47:1; 98:8; Isa 55:12; [k]**1Sa 10:24**
14 [l]**1Ki 7:15;** [m]**1Ki 1:39;** [n]**Ge 37:29;** [o]2Ki 9:23
15 [p]1Ki 2:30
16 [q]Ne 3:28; Jer 31:40; [r]**Ge 4:14**
17 [s]**Ex 24:8;** 2Sa 5:3; 2Ch 15:12; 23:3; 29:10; 34:31; Ezr 10:3; [t]2Ki 23:3; Jer 34:8
18 [u]**1Ki 16:32;** [v]**Dt 12:3;** [w]1Ki 18:40; 2Ki 10:25; 23:20
19 [x]ver 4
20 [y]Pr 11:10; 28:12; 29:2

Joash Repairs the Temple

12:1–21pp—2Ch 24:1–14,23–27

12 In the seventh year of Jehu,
Joash[a][a] became king, and he
reigned in Jerusalem for forty years. His
mother's name was Zibiah; she was
from Beersheba. 2Joash did what was
right[b] in the eyes of the LORD all the
years Jehoiada the priest instructed
him. 3The high places,[c] however, were
not removed; the people continued to
offer sacrifices and burn incense there.

4Joash said to the priests, "Collect[d] all
the money that is brought as sacred
offerings[e] to the temple of the LORD
—the money collected in the census,[f]
the money received from personal vows
and the money brought voluntarily[g] to
the temple. 5Let every priest receive the
money from one of the treasurers, and
let it be used to repair[h] whatever dam-
age is found in the temple."

6But by the twenty-third year of King
Joash the priests still had not repaired
the temple. 7Therefore King Joash sum-
moned Jehoiada the priest and the other
priests and asked them, "Why aren't
you repairing the damage done to the
temple? Take no more money from your
treasurers, but hand it over for repairing
the temple." 8The priests agreed that
they would not collect any more money
from the people and that they would
not repair the temple themselves.

Ch. 12

1 [a]2Ki 11:2
2 [b]**Dt 12:25; 2Sa 8:15**
3 [c]**1Ki 3:3; 2Ki 18:4**
4 [d]2Ki 22:4; [e]Nu 18:19; [f]**Ex 30:12;** [g]**Ex 25:2; 35:29**
5 [h]2Ki 22:5

b8 Or *approaches the precincts*
c15 Or *out from the precincts*
d21 Hebrew *Jehoash*, a variant of *Joash*
a1 Hebrew *Jehoash*, a variant of *Joash*; also in verses 2, 4, 6, 7 and 18

9Jehoiada the priest took a chest and
bored a hole in its lid. He placed it
beside the altar, on the right side as one
enters the temple of the LORD. The
priests who guarded the entrance[i] put
into the chest all the money[j] that was
brought to the temple of the LORD.
10Whenever they saw that there was a
large amount of money in the chest, the
royal secretary[k] and the high priest
came, counted the money that had been
brought into the temple of the LORD and
put it into bags. 11When the amount had
been determined, they gave the money
to the men appointed to supervise the
work on the temple. With it they paid
those who worked on the temple of the
LORD—the carpenters and builders,
12the masons and stonecutters.[l] They
purchased timber and dressed stone for
the repair of the temple of the LORD, and
met all the other expenses of restoring
the temple.
13The money brought into the temple
was not spent for making silver basins,
wick trimmers, sprinkling bowls, trum-
pets or any other articles of gold[m] or
silver for the temple of the LORD; 14it
was paid to the workmen, who used
it to repair the temple. 15They did
not require an accounting from those
to whom they gave the money to
pay the workers, because they acted
with complete honesty.[n] 16The money
from the guilt offerings[o] and sin
offerings[p] was not brought into the
temple of the LORD; it belonged[q] to the
priests.
17About this time Hazael[r] king of
Aram went up and attacked Gath and
captured it. Then he turned to attack
Jerusalem. 18But Joash king of Judah
took all the sacred objects dedicated by
his fathers—Jehoshaphat, Jehoram and
Ahaziah, the kings of Judah—and the
gifts he himself had dedicated and all
the gold found in the treasuries of the
temple of the LORD and of the royal
palace, and he sent[s] them to Hazael king
of Aram, who then withdrew[t] from
Jerusalem.
19As for the other events of the reign
of Joash, and all he did, are they not
written in the book of the annals of the
kings of Judah? 20His officials[u] con-
spired against him and assassinated[v]
him at Beth Millo,[w] on the road down to
Silla. 21The officials who murdered him
were Jozabad son of Shimeath and Jeho-
zabad son of Shomer. He died and was
buried with his fathers in the City of
David. And Amaziah his son succeeded
him as king.

9 [i]2Ki 25:18; Jer 35:4; 52:24; [j]Mk 12:41; Lk 21:1
10 [k]**2Sa 8:17**
12 [l]2Ki 22:5–6
13 [m]**1Ki 7:51**
15 [n]2Ki 22:7; 1Co 4:2
16 [o]Lev 5:14–19; [p]Lev 4:1–35; [q]**Lev 7:7**
17 [r]2Ki 8:12
18 [s]**1Ki 15:18; 2Ch 21:16–17;** [t]1Ki 15:21; 2Ki 15:20; 19:36
20 [u]2Ki 14:5; [v]2Ki 14:19; 15:10,14,25, 30; 21:23; 25:25; [w]Jdg 9:6

Ch. 13

2 [a]1Ki 12:26–33
3 [b]**Dt 31:17;** [c]**1Ki 19:17;** [d]ver 24
4 [e]**Dt 4:29;** [f]**Dt 26:7;** [g]**Nu 10:9;** 2Sa 7:10
5 [h]**Ge 45:7; Dt 28:29; Jdg 2:18**
6 [i]1Ki 12:30; [j]**1Ki 16:33**
7 [k]2Ki 10:32–33; [l]**2Sa 22:43**
12 [m]2Ki 14:15; [n]1Ki 15:31

Jehoahaz King of Israel

13 In the twenty-third year of
Joash son of Ahaziah king of
Judah, Jehoahaz son of Jehu became
king of Israel in Samaria, and he reigned
for seventeen years. 2He did evil[a] in the
eyes of the LORD by following the sins of
Jeroboam son of Nebat, which he had
caused Israel to commit, and he did not
turn away from them. 3So the LORD's
anger[b] burned against Israel, and for a
long time he kept them under the
power[c] of Hazael king of Aram and Ben-
Hadad[d] his son.
4Then Jehoahaz sought[e] the LORD's
favour, and the LORD listened to him,
for he saw[f] how severely the king of
Aram was oppressing[g] Israel. 5The LORD
provided a deliverer[h] for Israel, and
they escaped from the power of Aram.
So the Israelites lived in their own
homes as they had before. 6But they did
not turn away from the sins[i] of the
house of Jeroboam, which he had
caused Israel to commit; they continued
in them. Also, the Asherah pole[a][j]
remained standing in Samaria.
7Nothing had been left[k] of the army of
Jehoahaz except fifty horsemen, ten
chariots and ten thousand foot soldiers,
for the king of Aram had destroyed the
rest and made them like the dust[l] at
threshing time.
8As for the other events of the reign of
Jehoahaz, all he did and his achieve-
ments, are they not written in the book
of the annals of the kings of Israel?
9Jehoahaz rested with his fathers and
was buried in Samaria. And Jehoash[b]
his son succeeded him as king.

Jehoash King of Israel

10In the thirty-seventh year of Joash
king of Judah, Jehoash son of Jehoahaz
became king of Israel in Samaria, and he
reigned for sixteen years. 11He did evil
in the eyes of the LORD and did not turn
away from any of the sins of Jeroboam
son of Nebat, which he had caused
Israel to commit; he continued in them.
12As for the other events of the reign
of Jehoash, all he did and his achieve-
ments, including his war against Ama-
ziah[m] king of Judah, are they not written
in the book of the annals[n] of the kings of
Israel? 13Jehoash rested with his fathers,

---

[a]6 That is, a symbol of the goddess Asherah; here and elsewhere in 2 Kings
[b]9 Hebrew *Joash*, a variant of *Jehoash*; also in verses 12–14 and 25

and Jeroboam[o] succeeded him on the
throne. Jehoash was buried in Samaria
with the kings of Israel.
14Now Elisha was suffering from the
illness from which he died. Jehoash
king of Israel went down to see him and
wept over him. "My father! My father!"
he cried. "The chariots[p] and horsemen
of Israel!"
15Elisha said, "Get a bow and some
arrows,"[q] and he did so. 16"Take the
bow in your hands," he said to the king
of Israel. When he had taken it, Elisha
put his hands on the king's hands.
17"Open the east window," he said,
and he opened it. "Shoot!"[r] Elisha said,
and he shot. "The LORD's arrow of vic-
tory, the arrow of victory over Aram!"
Elisha declared. "You will completely
destroy the Arameans at Aphek."[s]
18Then he said, "Take the arrows,"
and the king took them. Elisha told him,
"Strike the ground." He struck it three
times and stopped. 19The man of God
was angry with him and said, "You
should have struck the ground five or
six times; then you would have defeated
Aram and completely destroyed it. But
now you will defeat it only three
times."[t]
20Elisha died and was buried.
Now Moabite raiders[u] used to enter
the country every spring. 21Once while
some Israelites were burying a man,
suddenly they saw a band of raiders; so
they threw the man's body into Elisha's
tomb. When the body touched Elisha's
bones, the man came to life[v] and stood
up on his feet.
22Hazael king of Aram oppressed[w]
Israel throughout the reign of Jehoahaz.
23But the LORD was gracious to them and
had compassion and showed concern
for them because of his covenant[x] with
Abraham, Isaac and Jacob. To this day
he has been unwilling to destroy[y] them
or banish them from his presence.[z]
24Hazael king of Aram died, and Ben-
Hadad[a] his son succeeded him as king.
25Then Jehoash son of Jehoahaz recap-
tured from Ben-Hadad son of Hazael
the towns he had taken in battle from
his father Jehoahaz. Three times[b]
Jehoash defeated him, and so he re-
covered[c] the Israelite towns.

Amaziah King of Judah

14:1–7pp—2Ch 25:1–4,11–12
14:8–22pp—2Ch 25:17–26:2

14 In the second year of Jehoash[a]
son of Jehoahaz king of Israel,
Amaziah son of Joash king of Judah
began to reign. 2He was twenty-five
years old when he became king, and he
reigned in Jerusalem for twenty-nine
years. His mother's name was Jehoad-
din; she was from Jerusalem. 3He did
what was right in the eyes of the LORD,
but not as his father David had done. In
everything he followed the example of
his father Joash. 4The high places,[a]
however, were not removed; the people
continued to offer sacrifices and burn
incense there.
5After the kingdom was firmly in his
grasp, he executed[b] the officials[c] who
had murdered his father the king. 6Yet
he did not put the sons of the assassins
to death, in accordance with what is
written in the Book of the Law[d] of Moses
where the LORD commanded: "Fathers
shall not be put to death for their
children, nor children put to death for
their fathers; each is to die for his own
sins."[b][e]
7He was the one who defeated ten
thousand Edomites in the Valley of Salt[f]
and captured Sela[g] in battle, calling it
Joktheel, the name it has to this day.
8Then Amaziah sent messengers to
Jehoash son of Jehoahaz, the son of
Jehu, king of Israel, with the challenge:
"Come, meet me face to face."
9But Jehoash king of Israel replied to
Amaziah king of Judah: "A thistle[h] in
Lebanon sent a message to a cedar in
Lebanon, 'Give your daughter to my
son in marriage.' Then a wild beast in
Lebanon came along and trampled the
thistle underfoot. 10You have indeed de-
feated Edom and now you are arrogant.[i]
Glory in your victory, but stay at home!
Why ask for trouble and cause your own
downfall and that of Judah also?"
11Amaziah, however, would not lis-
ten, so Jehoash king of Israel attacked.
He and Amaziah king of Judah faced
each other at Beth Shemesh[j] in Judah.
12Judah was routed by Israel, and every
man fled to his home.[k] 13Jehoash king of
Israel captured Amaziah king of Judah,
the son of Joash, the son of Ahaziah, at
Beth Shemesh. Then Jehoash went to
Jerusalem and broke down the wall[l] of
Jerusalem from the Ephraim Gate[m] to
the Corner Gate[n]—a section about six
hundred feet long.[c] 14He took all the
gold and silver and all the articles found
in the temple of the LORD and in the
treasuries of the royal palace. He also
took hostages and returned to Samaria.

13 [o]2Ki 14:23; Hos 1:1
14 [p]**2Ki 2:12**
15 [q]1Sa 20:20
17 [r]Jos 8:18; [s]**1Ki 20:26**
19 [t]ver 25
20 [u]**2Ki 5:2**
21 [v]Mt 27:52
22 [w]**1Ki 19:17**
23 [x]**Ex 2:24;** [y]**Dt 29:20;** [z]**Ex 33:15;** 2Ki 17:18; 24:3,20
24 [a]ver 3
25 [b]ver 19; [c]**2Ki 10:32**

Ch. 14

4 [a]2Ki 12:3
5 [b]2Ki 21:24; [c]2Ki 12:20
6 [d]**Dt 28:61;** [e]**Nu 26:11;** Job 21:20; Jer 31:30; 44:3; Eze 18:4,20
7 [f]**2Sa 8:13;** [g]**Jdg 1:36**
9 [h]Jdg 9:8–15
10 [i]2Ch 26:16; 32:25
11 [j]**Jos 15:10**
12 [k]1Ki 22:36
13 [l]1Ki 3:1; 2Ch 33:14; 36:19; Jer 39:2; [m]Ne 8:16; 12:39; [n]2Ch 26:9; Jer 31:38; Zec 14:10

a1 Hebrew *Joash*, a variant of *Jehoash*; also in verses 13, 23 and 27 **b**6 Deut. 24:16
c13 Hebrew *four hundred cubits* (about 180 metres)

15As for the other events of the reign
of Jehoash, what he did and his achieve-
ments, including his war[o] against Ama-
ziah king of Judah, are they not written
in the book of the annals of the kings of
Israel? 16Jehoash rested with his fathers
and was buried in Samaria with the
kings of Israel. And Jeroboam his son
succeeded him as king.

17Amaziah son of Joash king of Judah
lived for fifteen years after the death of
Jehoash son of Jehoahaz king of Israel.
18As for the other events of Amaziah's
reign, are they not written in the book of
the annals of the kings of Judah?

19They conspired[p] against him in Jeru-
salem, and he fled to Lachish,[q] but they
sent men after him to Lachish and killed
him there. 20He was brought back by
horse[r] and was buried in Jerusalem with
his fathers, in the City of David.

21Then all the people of Judah took
Azariah,[d][s] who was sixteen years old,
and made him king in place of his father
Amaziah. 22He was the one who rebuilt
Elath[t] and restored it to Judah after
Amaziah rested with his fathers.

Jeroboam II King of Israel

23In the fifteenth year of Amaziah son
of Joash king of Judah, Jeroboam[u] son of
Jehoash king of Israel became king in
Samaria, and he reigned for forty-one
years. 24He did evil in the eyes of the
LORD and did not turn away from any of
the sins of Jeroboam son of Nebat,
which he had caused Israel to commit.[v]
25He was the one who restored the
boundaries of Israel from Lebo[e]
Hamath[w] to the Sea of the Arabah,[f][x] in
accordance with the word of the LORD,
the God of Israel, spoken through his
servant Jonah[y] son of Amittai, the
prophet from Gath Hepher.

26The LORD had seen how bitterly
everyone in Israel, whether slave or
free,[z] was suffering;[a] there was no-one
to help them.[b] 27And since the LORD had
not said he would blot out[c] the name of
Israel from under heaven, he saved[d]
them by the hand of Jeroboam son of
Jehoash.

28As for the other events of Jero-
boam's reign, all he did, and his military
achievements, including how he re-
covered for Israel both Damascus[e] and
Hamath,[f] which had belonged to
Yaudi,[g] are they not written in the book
of the annals[g] of the kings of Israel?
29Jeroboam rested with his fathers, the
kings of Israel. And Zechariah his son
succeeded him as king.

15 [o]2Ki 13:12
19 [p]**2Ki 12:20**; [q]**Jos 10:3**
20 [r]**2Ki 9:28**
21 [s]2Ki 15:1; 2Ch 26:23; Isa 1:1; Hos 1:1; Am 1:1
22 [t]**1Ki 9:26**
23 [u]**2Ki 13:13**; 1Ch 5:17; Am 1:1; 7:10
24 [v]**1Ki 15:30**
25 [w]**Nu 13:21**; [x]Dt 3:17; [y]Jnh 1:1; Mt 12:39
26 [z]Dt 32:36; [a]2Ki 13:4; [b]Ps 18:41; 22:11; 72:12; 107:12; Isa 63:5; La 1:7
27 [c]**Dt 29:20**; [d]**Jdg 6:14**
28 [e]**2Sa 8:5**; [f]**2Sa 8:9**; [g]1Ki 15:31

Ch. 15

1 [a]**ver 32; 2Ki 14:21**
3 [b]**1Ki 14:8**
5 [c]**Ge 12:17**; [d]Lev 13:46; [e]ver 7,32; 2Ch 27:1; Mic 1:1; [f]**Ge 41:40**
7 [g]Isa 6:1; 14:28; [h]**ver 5**
9 [i]1Ki 15:26
10 [j]**2Ki 12:20**
11 [k]1Ki 15:31
12 [l]2Ki 10:30
13 [m]**1Ki 13:32**

Azariah King of Judah

15:1–7pp—2Ch 26:3–4,21–23

15 In the twenty-seventh year of
Jeroboam king of Israel, Azar-
iah[a] son of Amaziah king of Judah began
to reign. 2He was sixteen years old
when he became king, and he reigned
in Jerusalem for fifty-two years. His
mother's name was Jecoliah; she was
from Jerusalem. 3He did what was right[b]
in the eyes of the LORD, just as his father
Amaziah had done. 4The high places,
however, were not removed; the people
continued to offer sacrifices and burn
incense there.

5The LORD afflicted[c] the king with lep-
rosy[a] until the day he died, and he lived
in a separate house.[b][d] Jotham[e] the
king's son had charge of the palace[f] and
governed the people of the land.

6As for the other events of Azariah's
reign, and all he did, are they not writ-
ten in the book of the annals of the kings
of Judah? 7Azariah rested[g] with his
fathers and was buried near them in the
City of David. And Jotham[h] his son suc-
ceeded him as king.

Zechariah King of Israel

8In the thirty-eighth year of Azariah
king of Judah, Zechariah son of Jero-
boam became king of Israel in Samaria,
and he reigned for six months. 9He did
evil[i] in the eyes of the LORD, as his
fathers had done. He did not turn away
from the sins of Jeroboam son of Nebat,
which he had caused Israel to commit.

10Shallum son of Jabesh conspired
against Zechariah. He attacked him in
front of the people,[c] assassinated[j] him
and succeeded him as king. 11The other
events of Zechariah's reign are written
in the book of the annals[k] of the kings of
Israel. 12So the word of the LORD spoken
to Jehu was fulfilled:[l] "Your descen-
dants will sit on the throne of Israel to
the fourth generation."[d]

Shallum King of Israel

13Shallum son of Jabesh became king
in the thirty-ninth year of Uzziah king of
Judah, and he reigned in Samaria[m] for

[d]21 Also called *Uzziah*
[e]25 Or *from the entrance to*
[f]25 That is, the Dead Sea
[g]28 Or *Judah*
[a]5 The Hebrew word was used for various diseases affecting the skin—not necessarily leprosy.
[b]5 Or *in a house where he was relieved of responsibility*
[c]10 Hebrew; some Septuagint manuscripts *in Ibleam*
[d]12 2 Kings 10:30

one month. 14Then Menahem son of
Gadi went from Tirzah[n] up to Samaria.
He attacked Shallum son of Jabesh in
Samaria, assassinated[o] him and suc-
ceeded him as king.
15The other events of Shallum's reign,
and the conspiracy he led, are written in
the book of the annals[p] of the kings of
Israel.
16At that time Menahem, starting out
from Tirzah, attacked Tiphsah[q] and
everyone in the city and its vicinity,
because they refused to open[r] their
gates. He sacked Tiphsah and ripped
open all the pregnant women.

Menahem King of Israel

17In the thirty-ninth year of Azariah
king of Judah, Menahem son of Gadi
became king of Israel, and he reigned in
Samaria for ten years. 18He did evil[s] in
the eyes of the LORD. During his entire
reign he did not turn away from the sins
of Jeroboam son of Nebat, which he had
caused Israel to commit.
19Then Pul[e] [t] king of Assyria invaded
the land, and Menahem gave him a
thousand talents[f] of silver to gain his
support and strengthen his own hold
on the kingdom. 20Menahem exacted
this money from Israel. Every wealthy
man had to contribute fifty shekels[g] of
silver to be given to the king of Assyria.
So the king of Assyria withdrew[u] and
stayed in the land no longer.
21As for the other events of
Menahem's reign, and all he did, are
they not written in the book of the
annals of the kings of Israel?
22Menahem rested with his fathers. And
Pekahiah his son succeeded him as
king.

Pekahiah King of Israel

23In the fiftieth year of Azariah king of
Judah, Pekahiah son of Menahem be-
came king of Israel in Samaria, and he
reigned for two years. 24Pekahiah did
evil[v] in the eyes of the LORD. He did not
turn away from the sins of Jeroboam son
of Nebat, which he had caused Israel to
commit. 25One of his chief officers,
Pekah[w] son of Remaliah, conspired
against him. Taking fifty men of Gilead
with him, he assassinated[x] Pekahiah,
along with Argob and Arieh, in the
citadel of the royal palace at Samaria. So
Pekah killed Pekahiah and succeeded
him as king.
26The other events of Pekahiah's
reign, and all he did, are written in the
book of the annals of the kings of Israel.

14 [n]1Ki 15:33; [o]**2Ki 12:20**
15 [p]1Ki 15:31
16 [q]1Ki 4:24; [r]**2Ki 8:12; Hos 13:16**
18 [s]1Ki 15:26
19 [t]1Ch 5:6,26
20 [u]**2Ki 12:18**
24 [v]1Ki 15:26
25 [w]2Ch 28:6; Isa 7:1; [x]**2Ki 12:20**
27 [y]2Ch 28:6; Isa 7:1; [z]Isa 7:4
29 [a]2Ki 16:7; 17:6; 1Ch 5:26; 2Ch 28:20; Jer 50:17; [b]1Ki 15:20; [c]2Ki 16:9; 17:24; 2Ch 16:4; Isa 7:9; 9:1; 10:9–10; 28:1; 36:19; 37:18; [d]2Ki 24:14–16; 1Ch 5:22; Isa 14:6,17; 36:17; 45:13
30 [e]2Ki 17:1; [f]**2Ki 12:20**
31 [g]1Ki 15:31
32 [h]ver 1,5; 1Ch 5:17; Isa 1:1; Hos 1:1
34 [i]**1Ki 14:8**
35 [j]2Ki 12:3; [k]**Ge 23:10**; 2Ch 23:20
37 [l]2Ki 16:5; Isa 7:1; 8:6; 9:11

Ch. 16

1 [a]Isa 1:1; 7:1; 14:28; Hos 1:1; Mic 1:1

Pekah King of Israel

27In the fifty-second year of Azariah
king of Judah, Pekah[y] son of Remaliah[z]
became king of Israel in Samaria, and he
reigned for twenty years. 28He did evil
in the eyes of the LORD. He did not turn
away from the sins of Jeroboam son of
Nebat, which he had caused Israel to
commit.
29In the time of Pekah king of Israel,
Tiglath-Pileser[a] king of Assyria came
and took Ijon,[b] Abel Beth Maacah,
Janoah, Kedesh and Hazor. He took
Gilead and Galilee, including all the
land of Naphtali,[c] and deported[d] the
people to Assyria. 30Then Hoshea[e] son
of Elah conspired against Pekah son of
Remaliah. He attacked and assassin-
ated[f] him, and then succeeded him as
king in the twentieth year of Jotham son
of Uzziah.
31As for the other events of Pekah's
reign, and all he did, are they not writ-
ten in the book of the annals[g] of the
kings of Israel?

Jotham King of Judah

15:33–38pp—2Ch 27:1–4,7–9

32In the second year of Pekah son of
Remaliah king of Israel, Jotham[h] son of
Uzziah king of Judah began to reign.
33He was twenty-five years old when he
became king, and he reigned in Jeru-
salem for sixteen years. His mother's
name was Jerusha daughter of Zadok.
34He did what was right[i] in the eyes of
the LORD, just as his father Uzziah had
done. 35The high places,[j] however,
were not removed; the people con-
tinued to offer sacrifices and burn in-
cense there. Jotham rebuilt the Upper
Gate[k] of the temple of the LORD.
36As for the other events of Jotham's
reign, and what he did, are they not
written in the book of the annals of the
kings of Judah? 37(In those days the
LORD began to send Rezin[l] king of Aram
and Pekah son of Remaliah against
Judah.) 38Jotham rested with his fathers
and was buried with them in the City of
David, the city of his father. And Ahaz
his son succeeded him as king.

Ahaz King of Judah

16:1–20pp—2Ch 28:1–27

16 In the seventeenth year of
Pekah son of Remaliah, Ahaz[a]
son of Jotham king of Judah began to

[e]19 Also called *Tiglath-Pileser*
[f]19 That is, about 34 tons (about 34 metric tons)
[g]20 That is, about 1¼ pounds (about 0.6 kilogram)

reign. 2Ahaz was twenty years old
when he became king, and he reigned
in Jerusalem for sixteen years. Unlike
David his father, he did not do what
was right[b] in the eyes of the LORD his
God. 3He walked in the ways of the
kings of Israel[c] and even sacrificed his
son[d] in[a] the fire, following the detest-
able[e] ways of the nations the LORD had
driven out before the Israelites. 4He
offered sacrifices and burned incense[f]
at the high places, on the hilltops and
under every spreading tree.[g]
5Then Rezin[h] king of Aram and Pekah
son of Remaliah king of Israel marched
up to fight against Jerusalem and be-
sieged Ahaz, but they could not over-
power him. 6At that time, Rezin[i] king of
Aram recovered Elath[j] for Aram by driv-
ing out the men of Judah. Edomites
then moved into Elath and have lived
there to this day.
7Ahaz sent messengers to say to Tig-
lath-Pileser[k] king of Assyria, "I am your
servant and vassal. Come up and save[l]
me out of the hand of the king of Aram
and of the king of Israel who are attack-
ing me." 8And Ahaz took the silver and
gold found in the temple of the LORD
and in the treasuries of the royal palace
and sent it as a gift[m] to the king of
Assyria. 9The king of Assyria complied
by attacking Damascus[n] and capturing
it. He deported its inhabitants to Kir[o]
and put Rezin to death.
10Then King Ahaz went to Damascus
to meet Tiglath-Pileser king of Assyria.
He saw an altar in Damascus and sent to
Uriah[p] the priest a sketch of the altar,
with detailed plans for its construction.
11So Uriah the priest built an altar in
accordance with all the plans that King
Ahaz had sent from Damascus and
finished it before King Ahaz returned.
12When the king came back from
Damascus and saw the altar, he
approached it and presented offerings[b][q]
on it. 13He offered up his burnt offering[r]
and grain offering,[s] poured out his
drink offering,[t] and sprinkled the blood
of his fellowship offerings[c][u] on the altar.
14The bronze altar[v] that stood before the
LORD he brought from the front of the
temple—from between the new altar
and the temple of the LORD—and put it
on the north side of the new altar.
15King Ahaz then gave these orders to
Uriah the priest: "On the large new
altar, offer the morning[w] burnt offering
and the evening grain offering, the
king's burnt offering and his grain offer-
ing, and the burnt offering of all the
people of the land, and their grain
offering and their drink offering.
Sprinkle on the altar all the blood of the
burnt offerings and sacrifices. But I
will use the bronze altar for seeking
guidance."[x] 16And Uriah the priest did
just as King Ahaz had ordered.
17King Ahaz took away the side
panels and removed the basins from the
movable stands. He removed the Sea
from the bronze bulls that supported it
and set it on a stone base.[y] 18He took
away the Sabbath canopy[d] that had
been built at the temple and removed
the royal entrance outside the temple of
the LORD, in deference to the king of
Assyria.[z]
19As for the other events of the reign
of Ahaz, and what he did, are they not
written in the book of the annals of the
kings of Judah? 20Ahaz rested[a] with his
fathers and was buried with them in the
City of David. And Hezekiah his son
succeeded him as king.

Hoshea Last King of Israel

17:3–7pp—2Ki 18:9–12

17 In the twelfth year of Ahaz king
of Judah, Hoshea[a] son of Elah
became king of Israel in Samaria, and he
reigned for nine years. 2He did evil[b] in
the eyes of the LORD, but not like the
kings of Israel who preceded him.
3Shalmaneser[c] king of Assyria came
up to attack Hoshea, who had been
Shalmaneser's vassal and had paid him
tribute.[d] 4But the king of Assyria dis-
covered that Hoshea was a traitor, for
he had sent envoys to So[a] king of
Egypt,[e] and he no longer paid tribute to
the king of Assyria, as he had done year
by year. Therefore Shalmaneser seized
him and put him in prison.[f] 5The king of
Assyria invaded the entire land, mar-
ched against Samaria and laid siege[g] to it
for three years. 6In the ninth year of
Hoshea, the king of Assyria[h] captured
Samaria[i] and deported[j] the Israelites to
Assyria. He settled them in Halah, in
Gozan[k] on the Habor River and in the
towns of the Medes.

Israel Exiled Because of Sin

7All this took place because the
Israelites had sinned[l] against the LORD

2 [b]1Ki 14:8
3 [c]2Ki 17:19; [d]Lev 18:21; 2Ki 3:27; [e]Lev 18:3; Dt 9:4
4 [f]2Ki 22:17; 23:5; [g]Dt 12:2; Eze 6:13
5 [h]2Ki 15:37
6 [i]Isa 9:12; [j]1Ki 9:26
7 [k]2Ki 15:29; [l]Isa 2:6; 10:20; Jer 2:18; 3:1; Eze 16:28; 23:5; Hos 10:6
8 [m]1Ki 15:18; 2Ki 12:18
9 [n]Ge 14:15; 2Ki 15:29; [o]Isa 22:6; Am 1:5; 9:7
10 [p]ver 11,15–16; Isa 8:2
12 [q]2Ch 26:16
13 [r]Lev 6:8–13; [s]Lev 6:14–23; [t]Ex 29:40; [u]Lev 7:11–21
14 [v]Ex 20:24; 40:6; 1Ki 8:64
15 [w]Ex 29:38–41; [x]1Sa 9:9
17 [y]1Ki 7:27
18 [z]Eze 16:28
20 [a]Isa 14:28

Ch. 17

1 [a]2Ki 15:30
2 [b]Dt 4:25
3 [c]Hos 10:14; [d]Jdg 3:15
4 [e]Ps 146:3; Isa 30:1,7; 36:6; Jer 2:36; Hos 12:1; [f]Hos 13:10
5 [g]Hos 13:16
6 [h]ver 20; 2Ki 15:29; Isa 42:24; [i]Isa 10:9; [j]Dt 4:27; 24:1; 2Ki 15:29; Am 7:17; [k]1Ch 5:26
7 [l]Jos 7:11

[a]3 Or *even made his son pass through*
[b]12 Or *and went up*
[c]13 Traditionally *peace offerings*
[d]18 Or *the dais of his throne* (see Septuagint)
[a]4 Or *to Sais, to the; So* is possibly an abbreviation for *Osorkon.*

their God, who had brought them out of
Egypt[m] from under the power of Phar-
aoh king of Egypt. They worshipped
other gods 8and followed the practices
of the nations[n] the LORD had driven out
before them, as well as the practices that
the kings of Israel had introduced. 9The
Israelites secretly did things against the
LORD their God that were not right.
From watchtower to fortified city[o] they
built themselves high places in all their
towns. 10They set up sacred stones[p] and
Asherah poles[q] on every high hill and
under every spreading tree.[r] 11At every
high place they burned incense, as the
nations whom the LORD had driven out
before them had done. They did wicked
things that provoked the LORD to anger.
12They worshipped idols,[s] though the
LORD had said, "You shall not do this."[b]
13The LORD warned[t] Israel and Judah
through all his prophets and seers:[u]
"Turn from your evil ways.[v] Observe
my commands and decrees, in accord-
ance with the entire Law that I comman-
ded your fathers to obey and that I
delivered to you through my servants
the prophets."[w]
14But they would not listen and were
as stiff-necked[x] as their fathers, who did
not trust in the LORD their God. 15They
rejected his decrees and the covenant[y]
he had made with their fathers and the
warnings he had given them. They fol-
lowed worthless idols[z] and themselves
became worthless.[a] They imitated the
nations[b] around them although the
LORD had ordered them, "Do not do as
they do," and they did the things the
LORD had forbidden them to do.
16They forsook all the commands of
the LORD their God and made for them-
selves two idols cast in the shape of
calves,[c] and an Asherah[d] pole. They
bowed down to all the starry hosts,[e] and
they worshipped Baal.[f] 17They sac-
rificed[g] their sons and daughters in[c] the
fire. They practised divination and sor-
cery[h] and sold[i] themselves to do evil in
the eyes of the LORD, provoking him to
anger.
18So the LORD was very angry with
Israel and removed them from his
presence.[j] Only the tribe of Judah was
left, 19and even Judah did not keep
the commands of the LORD their God.
They followed the practices Israel had
introduced.[k] 20Therefore the LORD
rejected all the people of Israel; he
afflicted them and gave them into the
hands of plunderers,[l] until he thrust
them from his presence.[m]
21When he tore[n] Israel away from the
house of David, they made Jeroboam
son of Nebat their king.[o] Jeroboam en-
ticed Israel away from following the
LORD and caused them to commit a great
sin.[p] 22The Israelites persisted in all the
sins of Jeroboam and did not turn away
from them 23until the LORD removed
them from his presence,[q] as he had
warned[r] through all his servants the
prophets. So the people of Israel were
taken from their homeland[s] into exile in
Assyria, and they are still there.

Samaria Resettled

24The king of Assyria[t] brought people
from Babylon, Cuthah, Avva, Hamath
and Sepharvaim[u] and settled them in
the towns of Samaria to replace the
Israelites. They took over Samaria and
lived in its towns. 25When they first
lived there, they did not worship the
LORD; so he sent lions[v] among them and
they killed some of the people. 26It was
reported to the king of Assyria: "The
people you deported and resettled in
the towns of Samaria do not know what
the god of that country requires. He has
sent lions among them, which are kill-
ing them off, because the people do not
know what he requires."
27Then the king of Assyria gave this
order: "Make one of the priests you took
captive from Samaria go back to live
there and teach the people what the god
of the land requires." 28So one of the
priests who had been exiled from
Samaria came to live in Bethel and
taught them how to worship the LORD.
29Nevertheless, each national group
made its own gods in the several towns[w]
where they settled, and set them up in
the shrines[x] the people of Samaria had
made at the high places.[y] 30The men
from Babylon made Succoth Benoth,
the men from Cuthah made Nergal, and
the men from Hamath made Ashima;
31the Avvites made Nibhaz and Tartak,
and the Sepharvites burned their chil-
dren in the fire as sacrifices to Adram-
melech[z] and Anammelech, the gods of
Sepharvaim.[a] 32They worshipped the
LORD, but they also appointed all sorts[b]
of their own people to officiate for them
as priests in the shrines at the high
places. 33They worshipped the LORD,
but they also served their own gods in
accordance with the customs of the
nations from which they had been
brought.

7 [m]Ex 14:15–31
8 [n]**Ex 34:15; Lev 18:3; Dt 9:4**
9 [o]2Ki 18:8
10 [p]**Ex 23:24;** [q]Ex 34:13; Isa 17:8; Mic 5:14; [r]**Dt 12:2**
12 [s]**Ex 20:4**
13 [t]**Jdg 6:8; 2Ch 7:14; Job 34:33;** Eze 3:17–19; [u]**1Sa 9:9;** [v]Jer 4:1; 18:11; 23:22; 25:5; 35:15; 36:3; Zec 1:4; [w]Mt 23:34
14 [x]**Ex 32:9;** Ac 7:51
15 [y]**Lev 26:11;** Dt 29:25; Jdg 2:20; 1Ki 11:11; 2Ki 18:12; Ps 78:10; Eze 5:6; Mal 2:10; [z]**Dt 32:21;** Hos 11:2; Ro 1:21–23; [a]Jer 2:5; [b]**Dt 12:4**
16 [c]**Ex 32:4;** [d]**Dt 16:21;** [e]**Ge 2:1;** Isa 40:26; Jer 19:13; [f]**Jdg 2:11**
17 [g]**Dt 12:31;** 18:10–12; 2Ki 16:3; Eze 16:21; [h]**Lev 19:26;** [i]**1Ki 21:20;** Ro 7:14
18 [j]**Ge 4:14; Ex 33:15; 2Ki 13:23;** 2Th 1:9
19 [k]2Ki 16:3; Jer 3:6–10; Eze 23:13
20 [l]**ver 6;** [m]Jer 7:15; 15:1
21 [n]**1Sa 15:27; 1Ki 11:11;** [o]1Ki 12:20; [p]**1Ki 12:30**
23 [q]Eze 39:23–24; [r]**Jdg 6:8;** [s]**1Ki 9:7**
24 [t]2Ki 19:37; Ezr 4:2,10; Isa 37:38; [u]ver 31; **2Ki 15:29;** 18:34; Isa 36:19; 37:13; Am 6:2
25 [v]**Ge 37:20;** Isa 5:29; 15:9; Jer 50:17
29 [w]Jer 2:28; 11:13; [x]**Lev 26:30; 1Ki 12:31;** [y]Mic 4:5
31 [z]2Ki 19:37; [a]**ver 24**
32 [b]**1Ki 12:31**

b12 Exodus 20:4, 5
c17 Or *They made their sons and daughters pass through*

34To this day they persist in their for-
mer practices. They neither worship the
LORD nor adhere to the decrees and
ordinances, the laws and commands
that the LORD gave the descendants of
Jacob, whom he named Israel.[c] 35When
the LORD made a covenant with the
Israelites, he commanded them: "Do
not worship[d] any other gods or bow
down to them, serve them or sacrifice to
them.[e] 36But the LORD, who brought you
up out of Egypt with mighty power and
outstretched arm,[f] is the one you must
worship. To him you shall bow down
and to him offer sacrifices. 37You must
always be careful[g] to keep the decrees[h]
and ordinances, the laws and com-
mands he wrote for you. Do not
worship other gods. 38Do not forget[i] the
covenant I have made with you, and do
not worship other gods. 39Rather,
worship the LORD your God; it is he who
will deliver you from the hand of all
your enemies."
40They would not listen, however,
but persisted in their former practices.
41Even while these people were wor-
shipping the LORD,[j] they were serving
their idols. To this day their children
and grandchildren continue to do as
their fathers did.

Hezekiah King of Judah

18:2–4pp—2Ch 29:1–2; 31:1
18:5–7pp—2Ch 31:20–21
18:9–12pp—2Ki 17:3–7

18 In the third year of Hoshea son
of Elah king of Israel, Hezekiah[a]
son of Ahaz king of Judah began to
reign. 2He was twenty-five years old
when he became king, and he reigned
in Jerusalem for twenty-nine years.[b] His
mother's name was Abijah[a] daughter of
Zechariah. 3He did what was right[c] in
the eyes of the LORD, just as his father
David[d] had done. 4He removed[e] the
high places,[f] smashed the sacred
stones[g] and cut down the Asherah
poles. He broke into pieces the bronze
snake[h] Moses had made, for up to
that time the Israelites had been
burning incense to it. (It was called[b]
Nehushtan.[c])
5Hezekiah trusted[i] in the LORD, the
God of Israel. There was no-one like
him among all the kings of Judah, either
before him or after him. 6He held fast[j] to
the LORD and did not cease to follow
him; he kept the commands the LORD
had given Moses. 7And the LORD was
with him; he was successful[k] in what-
ever he undertook. He rebelled[l] against
the king of Assyria and did not serve
him. 8From watchtower to fortified
city,[m] he defeated the Philistines, as far
as Gaza and its territory.
9In King Hezekiah's fourth year,[n]
which was the seventh year of Hoshea
son of Elah king of Israel, Shalmaneser
king of Assyria marched against Sam-
aria and laid siege to it. 10At the end of
three years the Assyrians took it. So
Samaria was captured in Hezekiah's
sixth year, which was the ninth year of
Hoshea king of Israel. 11The king[o] of
Assyria deported Israel to Assyria and
settled them in Halah, in Gozan on the
Habor River, and in towns of the
Medes.[p] 12This happened because they
had not obeyed the LORD their God, but
had violated his covenant[q]—all that
Moses the servant of the LORD com-
manded.[r] They neither listened to the
commands[s] nor carried them out.
13In the fourteenth year[t] of King
Hezekiah's reign, Sennacherib king of
Assyria attacked all the fortified cities of
Judah[u] and captured them. 14So Heze-
kiah king of Judah sent this message to
the king of Assyria at Lachish:[v] "I have
done wrong.[w] Withdraw from me, and I
will pay whatever you demand of me."
The king of Assyria exacted from Heze-
kiah king of Judah three hundred
talents[d] of silver and thirty talents[e] of
gold. 15So Hezekiah gave[x] him all the
silver that was found in the temple of
the LORD and in the treasuries of the
royal palace.
16At this time Hezekiah king of Judah
stripped off the gold with which he had
covered the doors[y] and doorposts of the
temple of the LORD, and gave it to the
king of Assyria.

Sennacherib Threatens Jerusalem

18:13,17–37pp—Isa 36:1–22
18:17–35pp—2Ch 32:9–19

17The king of Assyria sent his sup-
reme commander,[z] his chief officer and
his field commander with a large army,
from Lachish to King Hezekiah at Jeru-
salem. They came up to Jerusalem and
stopped at the aqueduct of the Upper
Pool,[a] on the road to the Washerman's
Field. 18They called for the king; and
Eliakim[b] son of Hilkiah the palace ad-
ministrator, Shebna[c] the secretary, and

34 [c]**Ge 17:5; 1Ki 18:31**
35 [d]**Ex 20:5;** [e]**Ex 20:3**
36 [f]**Ex 3:20;** Ps 136:12
37 [g]Dt 5:32; [h]**Lev 19:37**
38 [i]**Dt 6:12**
41 [j]**1Ki 18:21;** Ezr 4:2; Mt 6:24

Ch. 18

1 [a]Isa 1:1; Hos 1:1; Mic 1:1
2 [b]ver 13; Isa 38:5
3 [c]**1Ki 14:8;** [d]Isa 38:5
4 [e]2Ch 31:1; Isa 36:7; [f]2Ki 12:3; 21:3; [g]**Ex 23:24;** [h]Nu 21:9
5 [i]ver 19; **1Sa 7:3;** 2Ki 19:10; Ps 21:7; 125:1; Pr 3:26
6 [j]**Dt 6:18; 10:20**
7 [k]**Ge 39:3; Job 22:25;** [l]2Ki 24:1; Ezr 4:19; Isa 36:5
8 [m]2Ki 17:9
9 [n]Isa 1:1; 36:1
11 [o]Isa 37:12; [p]Eze 16:39; 23:9
12 [q]**2Ki 17:15;** [r]2Ki 21:8; Da 9:6,10; [s]**1Ki 9:6**
13 [t]**ver 2;** [u]Isa 1:7; Mic 1:9
14 [v]2Ki 19:8; [w]Isa 24:5; 33:8
15 [x]**1Ki 15:18;** Isa 39:2
16 [y]2Ch 29:3
17 [z]Isa 20:1; [a]2Ki 20:20; 2Ch 32:4,30; Ne 2:14; Isa 22:9
18 [b]2Ki 19:2; Isa 22:20; 36:3, 11,22; 37:2; [c]ver 26,37; Isa 22:15

[a]2 Hebrew *Abi*, a variant of *Abijah*
[b]4 Or *He called it*
[c]4 *Nehushtan* sounds like the Hebrew for *bronze* and *snake* and *unclean thing*.
[d]14 That is, about 10 tons (about 10 metric tons)
[e]14 That is, about 1 ton (about 1 metric ton)

Joah son of Asaph the recorder went out
to them.
19The field commander said to them,
"Tell Hezekiah:

"'This is what the great king, the
king of Assyria, says: On what are
you basing this confidence[d] of
yours? 20You say you have strategy
and military strength—but you
speak only empty words. On
whom are you depending, that you
rebel against me? 21Look now, you
are depending on Egypt,[e] that
splintered reed of a staff,[f] which
pierces a man's hand and wounds
him if he leans on it! Such is
Pharaoh king of Egypt to all who
depend on him. 22And if you say to
me, "We are depending on the
LORD our God"—isn't he the one
whose high places and altars Heze-
kiah removed, saying to Judah and
Jerusalem, "You must worship
before this altar in Jerusalem"?

23"'Come now, make a bargain
with my master, the king of Assyr-
ia: I will give you two thousand
horses—if you can put riders on
them! 24How can you repulse one
officer[g] of the least of my master's
officials, even though you are de-
pending on Egypt for chariots and
horsemen?[f] 25Furthermore, have I
come to attack and destroy this
place without word from the
LORD?[h] The LORD himself told me to
march against this country and des-
troy it.'"

26Then Eliakim son of Hilkiah, and
Shebna and Joah said to the field com-
mander, "Please speak to your servants
in Aramaic,[i] since we understand it.
Don't speak to us in Hebrew in the
hearing of the people on the wall."
27But the commander replied, "Was it
only to your master and you that my
master sent me to say these things, and
not to the men sitting on the wall—
who, like you, will have to eat their own
filth and drink their own urine?"
28Then the commander stood and
called out in Hebrew: "Hear the word
of the great king, the king of Assyria!
29This is what the king says: Do not let
Hezekiah deceive[j] you. He cannot deliv-
er you from my hand. 30Do not let Heze-
kiah persuade you to trust in the LORD
when he says, 'The LORD will surely
deliver us; this city will not be given into
the hand of the king of Assyria.'
31"Do not listen to Hezekiah. This is
what the king of Assyria says: Make
peace with me and come out to me.
Then every one of you will eat from his
own vine and fig-tree[k] and drink water
from his own cistern,[l] 32until I come and
take you to a land like your own, a land
of grain and new wine, a land of bread
and vineyards, a land of olive trees and
honey. Choose life[m] and not death!
"Do not listen to Hezekiah, for he is
misleading you when he says, 'The
LORD will deliver us.' 33Has the god[n] of
any nation ever delivered his land from
the hand of the king of Assyria? 34Where
are the gods of Hamath[o] and Arpad?[p]
Where are the gods of Sepharvaim,
Hena and Ivvah? Have they rescued
Samaria from my hand? 35Who of all the
gods of these countries has been able to
save his land from me? How then can
the LORD deliver Jerusalem from my
hand?"[q]
36But the people remained silent and
said nothing in reply, because the king
had commanded, "Do not answer
him."
37Then Eliakim[r] son of Hilkiah the
palace administrator, Shebna the secre-
tary and Joah son of Asaph the recorder
went to Hezekiah, with their clothes
torn,[s] and told him what the field com-
mander had said.

Jerusalem's Deliverance Foretold

19:1–13pp—Isa 37:1–13

19 When King Hezekiah heard
this, he tore[a] his clothes and put
on sackcloth and went into the temple
of the LORD. 2He sent Eliakim[b] the palace
administrator, Shebna the secretary and
the leading priests,[c] all wearing sack-
cloth,[d] to the prophet Isaiah[e] son of
Amoz. 3They told him, "This is what
Hezekiah says: This day is a day of
distress and rebuke and disgrace, as
when children come to the point[f] of
birth and there is no strength to deliver
them. 4It may be that the LORD your God
will hear all the words of the field com-
mander, whom his master, the king of
Assyria, has sent to ridicule[g] the living
God, and that he will rebuke[h] him for
the words the LORD your God has
heard. Therefore pray for the remnant[i]
that still survives."
5When King Hezekiah's officials came
to Isaiah, 6Isaiah said to them, "Tell
your master, 'This is what the LORD
says: Do not be afraid[j] of what you have
heard—those words with which the

19 [d]ver 5; Job 4:6
21 [e]Isa 20:5; 31:1; Eze 29:6; [f]2Ki 24:7; Isa 20:6; 30:5,7; Jer 25:19; 37:7; 46:2
24 [g]Isa 10:8
25 [h]2Ki 19:6,22; 24:3; 2Ch 35:21
26 [i]Ezr 4:7
29 [j]2Ki 19:10
31 [k]Nu 13:23; 1Ki 4:25; [l]Jer 14:3; La 4:4
32 [m]Dt 30:19
33 [n]2Ki 19:12
34 [o]2Ki 17:24; Jer 49:23; [p]Isa 10:9
35 [q]Ps 2:1–2
37 [r]ver 18; Isa 33:7; 36:3,22; [s]2Ki 6:30

Ch. 19

1 [a]Ge 37:34; Nu 14:6
2 [b]2Ki 18:18; [c]Jer 19:1; [d]Ge 37:34; [e]Isa 1:1
3 [f]Hos 13:13
4 [g]1Sa 17:26; [h]2Sa 16:12; [i]Ge 45:7; Jer 37:3
6 [j]Dt 3:2; Jos 1:9

[f]24 Or *charioteers*

underlings of the king of Assyria have
blasphemed[k] me. 7Listen! I am going to
put such a spirit in him that when he
hears a certain report,[l] he will return to
his own country, and there I will have
him cut down with the sword.[m]' "
8When the field commander heard
that the king of Assyria had left Lach-
ish,[n] he withdrew and found the king
fighting against Libnah.[o]
9Now Sennacherib received a report
that Tirhakah, the Cushite[a] king ⌊of
Egypt⌋, was marching out to fight
against him. So he again sent messen-
gers to Hezekiah with this word: 10"Say
to Hezekiah king of Judah: Do not let
the god you depend[p] on deceive[q] you
when he says, 'Jerusalem will not be
handed over to the king of Assyria.'
11Surely you have heard what the kings
of Assyria have done to all the coun-
tries, destroying them completely. And
will you be delivered? 12Did the gods of
the nations that were destroyed by my
forefathers deliver[r] them: the gods of
Gozan,[s] Haran,[t] Rezeph and the people
of Eden who were in Tel Assar? 13Where
is the king of Hamath, the king of
Arpad, the king of the city of Sephar-
vaim, or of Hena or Ivvah?"[u]

Hezekiah's Prayer

19:14–19pp—Isa 37:14–20

14Hezekiah received the letter[v] from
the messengers and read it. Then he
went up to the temple of the LORD and
spread it out before the LORD. 15And
Hezekiah prayed to the LORD: "O LORD,
God of Israel, enthroned between the
cherubim,[w] you alone[x] are God over all
the kingdoms of the earth. You have
made heaven and earth. 16Give ear,[y] O
LORD, and hear;[z] open your eyes,[a] O
LORD, and see; listen to the words
Sennacherib has sent to insult the
living God.
17"It is true, O LORD, that the Assyrian
kings have laid waste these nations and
their lands. 18They have thrown their
gods into the fire and destroyed them,
for they were not gods[b] but only wood
and stone, fashioned by men's hands.[c]
19Now, O LORD our God, deliver[d] us
from his hand, so that all kingdoms[e] on
earth may know[f] that you alone, O
LORD, are God."

Isaiah Prophesies Sennacherib's Fall

19:20–37pp—Isa 37:21–38
19:35–37pp—2Ch 32:20–21

20Then Isaiah son of Amoz sent a mes-
sage to Hezekiah: "This is what the
LORD, the God of Israel, says: I have
heard[g] your prayer concerning Sen-
nacherib king of Assyria. 21This is the
word that the LORD has spoken against[h]
him:

" 'The Virgin Daughter[i] of Zion
despises[j] you and mocks[k] you.
The Daughter of Jerusalem
tosses her head[l] as you flee.
22Who is it you have insulted and
blasphemed?[m]
Against whom have you raised your
voice
and lifted your eyes in pride?
Against the Holy One[n] of Israel!
23By your messengers
you have heaped insults on the
Lord.
And you have said,[o]
"With my many chariots[p]
I have ascended the heights of the
mountains,
the utmost heights of Lebanon.
I have cut down[q] its tallest cedars,
the choicest of its pines.
I have reached its remotest parts,
the finest of its forests.
24I have dug wells in foreign lands
and drunk the water there.
With the soles of my feet
I have dried up all the streams of
Egypt."
25" 'Have you not heard?[r]
Long ago I ordained it.
In days of old I planned[s] it;
now I have brought it to pass,
that you have turned fortified cities
into piles of stone.[t]
26Their people, drained of power,[u]
are dismayed[v] and put to shame.
They are like plants in the field,
like tender green shoots,[w]
like grass sprouting on the roof,
scorched[x] before it grows up.

27" 'But I know[y] where you stay
and when you come and go
and how you rage against me.
28Because you rage against me
and your insolence has reached my
ears,
I will put my hook[z] in your nose
and my bit[a] in your mouth,
and I will make you return[b]
by the way you came.'

29"This will be the sign[c] for you, O
Hezekiah:

6 [k]2Ki 18:25
7 [l]Ex 14:24; Jer 51:46; [m]ver 37; 2Ch 32:21; Isa 10:12
8 [n]2Ki 18:14; [o]Nu 33:20; 2Ki 8:22
10 [p]2Ki 18:5; [q]2Ki 18:29
12 [r]2Ki 18:33; 2Ch 32:17; [s]2Ki 17:6; [t]Ge 11:31
13 [u]Isa 10:9–11; Jer 49:23
14 [v]2Ki 5:7
15 [w]Ge 3:24; Ex 25:22; [x]Ge 1:1; Jos 2:11
16 [y]Ps 31:2; 71:2; 88:2; 102:2; [z]1Ki 8:29; [a]Ex 3:16
18 [b]Isa 44:9–11; Jer 10:3–10; [c]Dt 4:28; Ps 115:4; Ac 17:29
19 [d]1Sa 12:10; Job 6:23; Ps 3:7; 71:4; [e]1Ki 8:43; 1Ch 16:8; [f]Jos 4:24; 1Sa 17:46
20 [g]1Ki 9:3
21 [h]Isa 10:5; 33:1; [i]Isa 47:1; Jer 14:17; 18:13; 31:4; 46:11; La 2:13; Am 5:2; [j]Ps 53:5; [k]Pr 1:26; 3:34; [l]Job 16:4; Ps 44:14; 64:8; 109:25; Jer 18:16
22 [m]2Ki 18:25; [n]Lev 19:2; 1Sa 2:2; Job 6:10; Ps 16:10; 22:3; 71:22; 78:41; 89:18; Isa 1:4; 6:3; 57:15; Hos 11:9
23 [o]Isa 10:18; Jer 21:14; Eze 20:47; [p]Ps 20:7; Jer 50:37; [q]Isa 10:34; 14:8; 33:9; Eze 31:3
25 [r]Isa 40:21,28; [s]Isa 22:11; [t]Mic 1:6
26 [u]Isa 13:7; Eze 7:17; Zep 3:16; [v]Ps 6:10; 71:24; 83:17; Isa 41:23; Jer 8:9; [w]Isa 4:2; 11:1; 53:2; Jer 23:5; [x]Job 8:12; Ps 37:2; 129:6
27 [y]Ps 139:1–4
28 [z]2Ch 33:11; Eze 19:9; 29:4; 38:4; Am 4:2; [a]Isa 30:28; [b]ver 33
29 [c]Ex 7:9; Dt 13:2; Lk 2:12

[a]9 That is, from the upper Nile region

This year you will eat what grows by itself,[d]
and the second year what springs from that.
But in the third year sow and reap,
plant vineyards[e] and eat their fruit.
30Once more a remnant[f] of the house of Judah
will take root[g] below and bear fruit above.
31For out of Jerusalem will come a remnant,[h]
and out of Mount Zion a band of survivors.[i]

The zeal[j] of the LORD Almighty will
accomplish this.

32"Therefore this is what the LORD
says concerning the king of Assyria:

"He will not enter this city
or shoot an arrow here.
He will not come before it with shield
or build a siege ramp against it.
33By the way that he came he will return;[k]
he will not enter this city,
declares the LORD.
34I will defend[l] this city and save it,
for my sake and for the sake of David[m] my servant."

35That night the angel of the LORD[n]
went out and put to death a hundred
and eighty-five thousand men in the
Assyrian camp. When the people got up
the next morning—there were all the
dead bodies![o] 36So Sennacherib king of
Assyria broke camp and withdrew.[p] He
returned to Nineveh[q] and stayed there.
37One day, while he was worshipping
in the temple of his god Nisroch, his
sons Adrammelech[r] and Sharezer cut
him down with the sword,[s] and they
escaped to the land of Ararat.[t] And
Esarhaddon[u] his son succeeded him as
king.

Hezekiah's Illness

20:1–11pp—2Ch 32:24–26; Isa 38:1–8

20 In those days Hezekiah became
ill and was at the point of death.
The prophet Isaiah son of Amoz went to
him and said, "This is what the LORD
says: Put your house in order, because
you are going to die; you will not
recover."
2Hezekiah turned his face to the wall
and prayed to the LORD, 3"Remember,[a]
O LORD, how I have walked[b] before you
faithfully[c] and with wholehearted devotion and have done what is good in your
eyes." And Hezekiah wept bitterly.
4Before Isaiah had left the middle
court, the word of the LORD came to
him: 5"Go back and tell Hezekiah, the
leader of my people, 'This is what the
LORD, the God of your father David,
says: I have heard[d] your prayer and seen
your tears;[e] I will heal you. On the third
day from now you will go up to the
temple of the LORD. 6I will add fifteen
years to your life. And I will deliver you
and this city from the hand of the king of
Assyria. I will defend[f] this city for my
sake and for the sake of my servant
David.'"
7Then Isaiah said, "Prepare a poultice
of figs." They did so and applied it to
the boil,[g] and he recovered.
8Hezekiah had asked Isaiah, "What
will be the sign that the LORD will heal
me and that I will go up to the temple of
the LORD on the third day from now?"
9Isaiah answered, "This is the LORD's
sign[h] to you that the LORD will do what
he has promised: Shall the shadow go
forward ten steps, or shall it go back ten
steps?"
10"It is a simple[i] matter for the
shadow to go forward ten steps,"
said Hezekiah. "Rather, have it go back
ten steps."
11Then the prophet Isaiah called upon
the LORD, and the LORD made the
shadow go back[j] the ten steps it had
gone down on the stairway of Ahaz.

Envoys From Babylon

20:12–19pp—1Sa 39:1–8
20:20–21pp—2Ch 32:32–33

12At that time Merodach-Baladan son
of Baladan king of Babylon sent Hezekiah letters and a gift, because he had
heard of Hezekiah's illness. 13Hezekiah
received the messengers and showed
them all that was in his storehouses
—the silver, the gold, the spices and the
fine oil—his armoury and everything
found among his treasures. There was
nothing in his palace or in all his kingdom that Hezekiah did not show them.
14Then Isaiah the prophet went to
King Hezekiah and asked, "What did
those men say, and where did they
come from?"
"From a distant land," Hezekiah replied. "They came from Babylon."
15The prophet asked, "What did they
see in your palace?"
"They saw everything in my palace,"
Hezekiah said. "There is nothing

29 [d]Lev 25:5; [e]Ps 107:37; Isa 65:21; Am 9:14
30 [f]Ge 45:7; [g]Isa 5:24; 11:1; 27:6; Eze 17:22; Am 2:9
31 [h]Ge 45:7; [i]Isa 66:19; Zep 2:9; Zec 14:16; [j]Isa 9:7
33 [k]ver 28
34 [l]2Ki 20:6; [m]2Sa 7:15
35 [n]Ge 19:13; Ex 12:23; [o]Job 24:24; Isa 17:14; 41:12; Na 3:3
36 [p]2Ki 12:18; [q]Ge 10:11
37 [r]2Ki 17:31; [s]ver 7; [t]Ge 8:4; [u]2Ki 17:24

Ch. 20

3 [a]Ge 8:1; Ne 1:8; 5:19; 13:14; [b]Ge 5:22; [c]1Ki 2:4; 2Ch 31:20
5 [d]1Ki 9:3; [e]Ps 6:6,8; 39:12; 56:8
6 [f]2Ki 19:34; 1Ch 17:19
7 [g]Ex 9:9
9 [h]Dt 13:2; Jer 44:29
10 [i]2Ki 3:18
11 [j]Jos 10:13; 2Ch 32:31

among my treasures that I did not show
them."
16Then Isaiah said to Hezekiah, "Hear
the word of the LORD: 17The time will
surely come when everything in your
palace, and all that your fathers have
stored up until this day, will be carried
off to Babylon.[k] Nothing will be left,
says the LORD. 18And some of your de-
scendants,[l] your own flesh and blood,
that will be born to you, will be taken
away, and they will become eunuchs in
the palace of the king of Babylon."[m]
19"The word of the LORD you have
spoken is good," Hezekiah replied. For
he thought, "Will there not be peace
and security in my lifetime?"
20As for the other events of Heze-
kiah's reign, all his achievements and
how he made the pool[n] and the tunnel[o]
by which he brought water into the city,
are they not written in the book of the
annals of the kings of Judah? 21Hezekiah
rested with his fathers. And Manasseh
his son succeeded him as king.

Manasseh King of Judah

21:1–10pp—2Ch 33:1–10
21:17–18pp—2Ch 33:18–20

21 Manasseh was twelve years old
when he became king, and he
reigned in Jerusalem for fifty-five years.
His mother's name was Hephzibah.[a] 2He
did evil[b] in the eyes of the LORD, follow-
ing the detestable practices[c] of the nations
the LORD had driven out before the
Israelites. 3He rebuilt the high places[d]
his father Hezekiah had destroyed; he
also erected altars to Baal[e] and made
an Asherah pole,[f] as Ahab king of Israel
had done. He bowed down to all the
starry hosts[g] and worshipped them. 4He
built altars[h] in the temple of the LORD, of
which the LORD had said, "In Jerusalem
I will put my Name."[i] 5In both courts[j] of
the temple of the LORD, he built altars to
all the starry hosts. 6He sacrificed his
own son[k] in[a] the fire, practised sorcery
and divination,[l] and consulted
mediums and spiritists.[m] He did much
evil in the eyes of the LORD, provoking[n]
him to anger.
7He took the carved Asherah pole[o] he
had made and put it in the temple,[p] of
which the LORD had said to David and to
his son Solomon, "In this temple and in
Jerusalem, which I have chosen out of
all the tribes of Israel, I will put my
Name[q] for ever. 8I will not again[r] make
the feet of the Israelites wander from the
land I gave their forefathers, if only they
will be careful to do everything I com-
manded them and will keep the whole
Law that my servant Moses[s] gave
them." 9But the people did not listen.
Manasseh led them astray, so that they
did more evil[t] than the nations[u] the
LORD had destroyed before the
Israelites.
10The LORD said through his servants
the prophets: 11"Manasseh king of
Judah has committed these detestable
sins. He has done more evil[v] than the
Amorites[w] who preceded him and has
led Judah into sin with his idols.[x]
12Therefore this is what the LORD, the
God of Israel, says: I am going to bring
such disaster[y] on Jerusalem and Judah
that the ears of everyone who hears of it
will tingle.[z] 13I will stretch out over Jeru-
salem the measuring line used against
Samaria and the plumb-line[a] used
against the house of Ahab. I will wipe[b]
out Jerusalem as one wipes out a dish,
wiping it and turning it upside-down.
14I will forsake[c] the remnant[d] of my
inheritance and hand them over to their
enemies. They will be looted and plun-
dered by all their foes, 15because they
have done evil[e] in my eyes and have
provoked[f] me to anger from the day
their forefathers came out of Egypt until
this day."
16Moreover, Manasseh also shed so
much innocent blood[g] that he filled
Jerusalem from end to end—besides the
sin that he had caused Judah[h] to com-
mit, so that they did evil in the eyes of
the LORD.
17As for the other events of Ma-
nasseh's reign, and all he did, including
the sin he committed, are they not writ-
ten in the book of the annals of the kings
of Judah? 18Manasseh rested with his
fathers and was buried in his palace
garden,[i] the garden of Uzza. And Amon
his son succeeded him as king.

Amon King of Judah

21:19–24pp—2Ch 33:21–25

19Amon was twenty-two years old
when he became king, and he reigned
in Jerusalem for two years. His mother's
name was Meshullemeth daughter of
Haruz; she was from Jotbah. 20He did
evil[j] in the eyes of the LORD, as his father
Manasseh had done. 21He walked in all
the ways of his father; he worshipped
the idols his father had worshipped,

17 [k]2Ki 24:13; 2Ch 36:10; Jer 20:5; 27:22; 52:17–23
18 [l]2Ki 24:15; Da 1:3; [m]Mic 4:10
20 [n]**2Ki 18:17**; [o]**2Sa 5:8**

Ch. 21

1 [a]Isa 62:4
2 [b]ver 16; **Dt 4:25**; Jer 15:4; [c]Dt 9:4; **18:9**; **1Ki 14:24**; 2Ki 16:3
3 [d]**1Ki 3:3**; **2Ki 18:4**; [e]**Jdg 6:28**; [f]**Dt 16:21**; [g]**Ge 2:1**; Dt 17:3; Jer 19:13
4 [h]Isa 66:4; Jer 4:1; 7:30; 23:11; 32:34; Eze 23:39; [i]**Ex 20:24**; **2Sa 7:13**
5 [j]1Ki 7:12; 2Ki 23:12
6 [k]**Lev 18:21**; **Dt 18:10**; **2Ki 3:27**; [l]Dt 18:14; [m]**Lev 19:31**; [n]2Ki 23:26
7 [o]Dt 16:21; 2Ki 23:4; [p]**Lev 15:31**; [q]**Ex 20:24**; **2Sa 7:13**
8 [r]**2Sa 7:10**; [s]**2Ki 18:12**
9 [t]**1Ki 14:9**; Eze 5:7; [u]Dt 9:4
11 [v]**1Ki 14:9**; [w]**Ge 15:16**; [x]Eze 18:12
12 [y]2Ki 23:26; 24:3; Jer 15:4; Eze 7:5; [z]**1Sa 3:11**
13 [a]Isa 28:17; 34:11; La 2:8; Am 7:7–9; [b]2Ki 23:27
14 [c]Ps 78:60; Jer 12:7; 23:33; [d]2Ki 19:4; Ezr 9:8; Ne 1:2; Isa 1:9; 10:21; Jer 6:9; 40:15; 42:2; 44:7,28; 50:20; Mic 2:12
15 [e]**Ex 32:22**; [f]Jer 25:7
16 [g]2Ki 24:4; Job 22:14; Ps 10:11; 94:7; 106:38; Isa 29:15; 47:10; 59:3,7; Jer 2:34; 7:6; 19:4; 22:17; La 4:13; Eze 7:23; 8:12; 9:9; 22:3–4; Hos 4:2; Zep 1:12; [h]**ver 2,11**
18 [i]ver 26; Est 1:5; 7:7
20 [j]1Ki 15:26

[a]6 Or *He made his own son pass through*

and bowed down to them. 22He forsook[k] the LORD, the God of his fathers, and did not walk[l] in the way of the LORD.

23Amon's officials conspired against him and assassinated[m] the king in his palace. 24Then the people of the land killed[n] all who had plotted against King Amon, and they made Josiah[o] his son king in his place.

25As for the other events of Amon's reign, and what he did, are they not written in the book of the annals of the kings of Judah? 26He was buried in his grave in the garden[p] of Uzza. And Josiah his son succeeded him as king.

The Book of the Law Found

22:1-20pp—2Ch 34:1-2,8-28

22 Josiah[a] was eight years old when he became king, and he reigned in Jerusalem for thirty-one years. His mother's name was Jedidah daughter of Adaiah; she was from Bozkath.[b] 2He did what was right[c] in the eyes of the LORD and walked in all the ways of his father David, not turning aside to the right[d] or to the left.

3In the eighteenth year of his reign, King Josiah sent the secretary, Shaphan[e] son of Azaliah, the son of Meshullam, to the temple of the LORD. He said: 4"Go up to Hilkiah[f] the high priest and make him get ready the money that has been brought into the temple of the LORD, which the doorkeepers have collected[g] from the people. 5Make them entrust it to the men appointed to supervise the work on the temple. And make these men pay the workers who repair[h] the temple of the LORD—6the carpenters, the builders and the masons. Also make them purchase timber and dressed stone to repair the temple.[i] 7But they need not account for the money entrusted to them, because they are acting faithfully."[j]

8Hilkiah the high priest said to Shaphan the secretary, "I have found the Book of the Law[k] in the temple of the LORD." He gave it to Shaphan, who read it. 9Then Shaphan the secretary went to the king and reported to him: "Your officials have paid out the money that was in the temple of the LORD and have entrusted it to the workers and supervisors at the temple." 10Then Shaphan the secretary informed the king, "Hilkiah the priest has given me a book." And Shaphan read from it in the presence of the king.[l]

11When the king heard the words of the Book of the Law,[m] he tore his robes. 12He gave these orders to Hilkiah the priest, Ahikam[n] son of Shaphan, Acbor son of Micaiah, Shaphan the secretary and Asaiah the king's attendant:[o] 13"Go and enquire[p] of the LORD for me and for the people and for all Judah about what is written in this book that has been found. Great is the LORD's anger[q] that burns against us because our fathers have not obeyed the words of this book; they have not acted in accordance with all that is written there concerning us."

14Hilkiah the priest, Ahikam, Acbor, Shaphan and Asaiah went to speak to the prophetess[r] Huldah, who was the wife of Shallum son of Tikvah, the son of Harhas, keeper of the wardrobe. She lived in Jerusalem, in the Second District.

15She said to them, "This is what the LORD, the God of Israel, says: Tell the man who sent you to me, 16'This is what the LORD says: I am going to bring disaster[s] on this place and its people, according to everything written in the book[t] the king of Judah has read. 17Because they have forsaken[u] me and burned incense to other gods and provoked me to anger by all the idols their hands have made,[a] my anger will burn against this place and will not be quenched.' 18Tell the king of Judah, who sent you to enquire[v] of the LORD, 'This is what the LORD, the God of Israel, says concerning the words you heard: 19Because your heart was responsive and you humbled[w] yourself before the LORD when you heard what I have spoken against this place and its people, that they would become accursed[x] and laid waste,[y] and because you tore your robes and wept in my presence, I have heard you, declares the LORD. 20Therefore I will gather you to your fathers, and you will be buried in peace.[z] Your eyes[a] will not see all the disaster I am going to bring on this place.'"

So they took her answer back to the king.

Josiah Renews the Covenant

23:1-3pp—2Ch 34:29-32
23:4-20Ref—2Ch 34:3-7,33
23:21-23pp—2Ch 35:1,18-19
23:28-30pp—2Ch 35:20-36:1

23 Then the king called together all the elders of Judah and Jerusalem. 2He went up to the temple of the

---

22 [k]1Sa 8:8; [l]1Ki 11:33
23 [m]2Ki 12:20
24 [n]2Ki 14:5; [o]2Ch 33:21; Zep 1:1
26 [p]ver 18

Ch. 22

1 [a]Jer 1:2; 25:3; [b]Jos 15:39
2 [c]Dt 17:19; 1Ki 14:8; [d]Dt 5:32
3 [e]2Ch 34:20; Jer 39:14
4 [f]Ezr 7:1; [g]2Ki 12:4-5
5 [h]2Ki 12:5
6 [i]2Ki 12:11-12
7 [j]2Ki 12:15
8 [k]Dt 28:61; 31:24; Gal 3:10
10 [l]Jer 36:21
11 [m]ver 8
12 [n]2Ki 25:22; Jer 26:24; 39:14; [o]1Sa 8:14
13 [p]Ge 25:22; 1Sa 9:9; [q]Dt 29:24-28; 31:17; Isa 5:25; 42:25; Am 2:4
14 [r]Ex 15:20
16 [s]Dt 31:29; Jos 23:15; Jer 6:19; 11:11; 18:11; 35:17; [t]Da 9:11
17 [u]1Ki 9:9
18 [v]Jer 21:2; 37:3,7
19 [w]Ex 10:3; Isa 57:15; 61:1; Mic 6:8; [x]Jer 24:9; 25:18; 26:6; [y]Lev 26:31
20 [z]Isa 47:11; 57:1; Jer 18:11; [a]1Ki 21:29

---

[a]17 Or *by everything they have done*

LORD with the men of Judah, the people of Jerusalem, the priests and the prophets—all the people from the least to the greatest. He read[a] in their hearing all the words of the Book of the Covenant,[b] which had been found in the temple of the LORD. 3The king stood by the pillar[c] and renewed the covenant[d] in the presence of the LORD—to follow[e] the LORD and keep his commands, regulations and decrees with all his heart and all his soul, thus confirming the words of the covenant written in this book. Then all the people pledged themselves to the covenant.

4The king ordered Hilkiah the high priest, the priests next in rank and the doorkeepers[f] to remove[g] from the temple of the LORD all the articles made for Baal and Asherah and all the starry hosts. He burned them outside Jerusalem in the fields of the Kidron Valley and took the ashes to Bethel. 5He did away with the pagan priests appointed by the kings of Judah to burn incense on the high places of the towns of Judah and on those around Jerusalem—those who burned incense[h] to Baal, to the sun and moon, to the constellations and to all the starry hosts.[i][j] 6He took the Asherah pole from the temple of the LORD to the Kidron Valley[k] outside Jerusalem and burned it there. He ground it to powder[l] and scattered the dust over the graves[m] of the common people.[n] 7He also tore down the quarters of the male shrine-prostitutes,[o] which were in the temple of the LORD and where women did weaving for Asherah.

8Josiah brought all the priests from the towns of Judah and desecrated the high places, from Geba[p] to Beersheba, where the priests had burned incense. He broke down the shrines[a] at the gates—at the entrance to the Gate of Joshua, the city governor, which is on the left of the city gate. 9Although the priests of the high places did not serve[q] at the altar of the LORD in Jerusalem, they ate unleavened bread with their fellow priests.

10He desecrated Topheth,[r] which was in the Valley of Ben Hinnom,[s] so no-one could use it to sacrifice his son[t] or daughter in[b] the fire to Molech. 11He removed from the entrance to the temple of the LORD the horses that the kings of Judah[u] had dedicated to the sun. They were in the court near the room of an official named Nathan-Melech. Josiah then burned the chariots dedicated to the sun.[v]

12He pulled down[w] the altars the kings of Judah had erected on the roof[x] near the upper room of Ahaz, and the altars Manasseh had built in the two courts[y] of the temple of the LORD. He removed them from there, smashed them to pieces and threw the rubble into the Kidron Valley.[z] 13The king also desecrated the high places that were east of Jerusalem on the south of the Hill of Corruption—the ones Solomon[a] king of Israel had built for Ashtoreth the vile goddess of the Sidonians, for Chemosh the vile god of Moab, and for Molech[c] the detestable[b] god of the people of Ammon.[c] 14Josiah smashed[d] the sacred stones and cut down the Asherah poles and covered the sites with human bones.[e]

15Even the altar[f] at Bethel, the high place made by Jeroboam[g] son of Nebat, who had caused Israel to sin—even that altar and high place he demolished. He burned the high place and ground it to powder, and burned the Asherah pole also. 16Then Josiah[h] looked around, and when he saw the tombs that were there on the hillside, he had the bones removed from them and burned on the altar to defile it, in accordance[i] with the word of the LORD proclaimed by the man of God who foretold these things.

17The king asked, "What is that tombstone I see?"

The men of the city said, "It marks the tomb of the man of God who came from Judah and pronounced against the altar of Bethel the very things you have done to it."

18"Leave it alone," he said. "Don't let anyone disturb his bones[j]." So they spared his bones and those of the prophet[k] who had come from Samaria.

19Just as he had done at Bethel, Josiah removed and defiled all the shrines at the high places that the kings of Israel had built in the towns of Samaria that had provoked the LORD to anger. 20Josiah slaughtered[l] all the priests of those high places on the altars and burned human bones[m] on them. Then he went back to Jerusalem.

21The king gave this order to all the people: "Celebrate the Passover[n] to the LORD your God, as it is written in this Book of the Covenant."[o] 22Not since the days of the judges who led Israel, nor throughout the days of the kings of Israel and the kings of Judah, had any such Passover been observed. 23But in

Ch. 23
2 [a]Dt 31:11; [b]Ex 24:7
3 [c]1Ki 7:15; [d]2Ki 11:12; [e]Dt 13:4
4 [f]2Ki 25:18; Jer 35:4; [g]2Ki 21:7
5 [h]2Ki 16:4; [i]Jer 8:2; [j]Jer 43:13
6 [k]Jer 31:40; [l]Ex 32:20; [m]Nu 19:16; [n]Jer 26:23
7 [o]Ge 38:21; 1Ki 14:24; Eze 16:16
8 [p]Jos 18:24; 1Ki 15:22
9 [q]Eze 44:10–14
10 [r]Isa 30:33; Jer 7:31–32; 19:6; [s]Jos 15:8; [t]Lev 18:21; Dt 18:10
11 [u]ver 5,19; Ne 9:34; Jer 44:9; [v]Dt 4:19
12 [w]2Ch 33:15; [x]Jer 19:13; Zep 1:5; [y]2Ki 21:5; [z]2Sa 15:23
13 [a]1Ki 11:7; [b]Dt 27:15; [c]Jer 11:13
14 [d]Ex 23:24; [e]Nu 19:16; Ps 53:5
15 [f]Jos 7:2; 1Ki 13:1–3; [g]1Ki 12:33
16 [h]1Ki 13:2; [i]1Ki 13:32
18 [j]1Ki 13:31; [k]1Ki 13:29
20 [l]Ex 22:20; 2Ki 11:18; [m]1Ki 13:2
21 [n]Ex 12:11; Dt 16:1–8; [o]Ex 24:7

[a]8 Or *high places*
[b]10 Or *to make his son or daughter pass through*
[c]13 Hebrew *Milcom*

the eighteenth year of King Josiah, this
Passover was celebrated to the LORD in
Jerusalem.[p]
24 Furthermore, Josiah got rid of the
mediums and spiritists,[q] the household
gods,[r] the idols and all the other de-
testable[s] things seen in Judah and
Jerusalem. This he did to fulfil the
requirements of the law written in the
book that Hilkiah the priest had dis-
covered in the temple of the LORD.
25 Neither before nor after Josiah was
there a king like him who turned[t] to the
LORD as he did—with all his heart and
with all his soul and with all his
strength, in accordance with all the Law
of Moses.[u]
26 Nevertheless, the LORD did not turn
away from the heat of his fierce anger,[v]
which burned against Judah because of
all that Manasseh[w] had done to provoke
him to anger. 27 So the LORD said, "I will
remove[x] Judah also from my presence[y]
as I removed Israel, and I will reject[z]
Jerusalem, the city I chose, and this
temple, about which I said, 'There shall
my Name be.'[d]"
28 As for the other events of Josiah's
reign, and all he did, are they not writ-
ten in the book of the annals of the kings
of Judah?
29 While Josiah was king, Pharaoh
Neco[a] king of Egypt went up to the
Euphrates River to help the king of
Assyria. King Josiah marched out to
meet him in battle, but Neco faced him
and killed him at Megiddo.[b] 30 Josiah's
servants brought his body in a chariot[c]
from Megiddo to Jerusalem and buried
him in his own tomb. And the people of
the land took Jehoahaz son of Josiah and
anointed him and made him king in
place of his father.

Jehoahaz King of Judah

23:31–34pp—2Ch 36:2–4

31 Jehoahaz[d] was twenty-three years
old when he became king, and he
reigned in Jerusalem for three months.
His mother's name was Hamutal[e]
daughter of Jeremiah; she was from Lib-
nah. 32 He did evil[f] in the eyes of the
LORD, just as his fathers had done.
33 Pharaoh Neco put him in chains at
Riblah[g] in the land of Hamath[e][h] so that
he might not reign in Jerusalem, and he
imposed on Judah a levy of a hundred
talents[f] of silver and a talent[g] of gold.
34 Pharaoh Neco made Eliakim[i] son of
Josiah king in place of his father Josiah
and changed Eliakim's name to
Jehoiakim. But he took Jehoahaz and
carried him off to Egypt, and there he
died.[j] 35 Jehoiakim paid Pharaoh Neco
the silver and gold he demanded. In
order to do so, he taxed the land and
exacted the silver and gold from the
people of the land according to their
assessments.[k]

Jehoiakim King of Judah

23:36–24:6pp—2Ch 36:5–8

36 Jehoiakim[l] was twenty-five years
old when he became king, and he
reigned in Jerusalem for eleven years.
His mother's name was Zebidah daugh-
ter of Pedaiah; she was from Rumah.
37 And he did evil[m] in the eyes of the
LORD, just as his fathers had done.

24 During Jehoiakim's reign,
Nebuchadnezzar[a] king of Bab-
ylon invaded[b] the land, and Jehoiakim
became his vassal for three years. But
then he changed his mind and rebelled[c]
against Nebuchadnezzar. 2 The LORD
sent Babylonian,[a][d] Aramean,[e] Moabite
and Ammonite raiders[f] against him. He
sent them to destroy[g] Judah, in accord-
ance with the word of the LORD pro-
claimed by his servants the prophets.[h]
3 Surely these things happened to Judah
according to the LORD's command,[i] in
order to remove them from his pres-
ence[j] because of the sins of Manasseh[k]
and all he had done, 4 including the
shedding of innocent blood.[l] For he had
filled Jerusalem with innocent blood,
and the LORD was not willing to
forgive.[m]
5 As for the other events of
Jehoiakim's reign,[n] and all he did, are
they not written in the book of the
annals of the kings of Judah? 6 Jehoiakim
rested[o] with his fathers. And Jehoi-
achin[p] his son succeeded him as king.
7 The king of Egypt[q] did not march out
from his own country again, because
the king of Babylon[r] had taken all his
territory, from the Wadi of Egypt to the
Euphrates River.

Jehoiachin King of Judah

24:8–17pp—2Ch 36:9–10

8 Jehoiachin[s] was eighteen years old
when he became king, and he reigned
in Jerusalem for three months. His

---

23 *p* **Ex 12:11; Nu 28:16**
24 *q* **Lev 19:31; Dt 18:11;** *r* **Ge 31:19;** *s* Dt 7:26; 2Ki 16:3
25 *t* **1Sa 7:3;** *u* **Jer 22:15**
26 *v* 2Ki 21:6; Jer 23:20; 30:24; *w* **2Ki 21:12**
27 *x* 2Ki 21:13; *y* **Ex 33:15;** 2Ki 24:3; *z* Jer 27:10; 32:31
29 *a* ver 33–35; Jer 46:2; *b* 2Ki 9:27
30 *c* **2Ki 9:28**
31 *d* 1Ch 3:15; Jer 22:11; *e* 2Ki 24:18
32 *f* 1Ki 15:26
33 *g* **Nu 34:11;** *h* 1Ki 8:65
34 *i* 2Ki 24:6; 1Ch 3:15; 2Ch 36:5–8; Jer 1:3; *j* Jer 22:12
35 *k* Jer 2:16
36 *l* Jer 26:1
37 *m* 1Ki 15:26

Ch. 24

1 *a* ver 10; 2Ki 25:11; Ezr 5:12; Jer 4:7; 25:1,9; 39:1; 40:1; 50:17; 52:15; Eze 32:2; Da 1:1; 7:4; *b* Jer 35:11; *c* **2Ki 18:7**
2 *d* Jer 5:15; Hab 1:6; *e* Jer 35:11; *f* **2Ki 5:2;** *g* Isa 28:18–19; *h* Jer 12:7–9; 25:1; 26:1; 36:1; Eze 23:23; Da 1:2
3 *i* **2Ki 18:25;** *j* **2Ki 13:23;** *k* **1Ki 14:9; 2Ki 21:12;** Jer 15:4
4 *l* **2Ki 21:16;** Jer 22:3; *m* **Ex 23:21;** La 3:42
5 *n* Jer 22:18–19
6 *o* Jer 22:19; 36:30; *p* 1Ch 3:16; Jer 22:24,28; Eze 19:1
7 *q* **Ge 15:18; 2Ki 18:21; Jer 46:25;** *r* Jer 1:14; 25:9; 46:24
8 *s* 1Ch 3:16; Jer 22:24; 37:1

---

d27 1 Kings 8:29
e33 Hebrew; Septuagint (see also 2 Chron. 36:3) *Neco at Riblah in Hamath removed him*
f33 That is, about 3½ tons (about 3.4 metric tons)
g33 That is, about 75 pounds (about 34 kilograms)
a2 Or *Chaldean*

mother's name was Nehushta[t] daughter of Elnathan; she was from Jerusalem. 9He did evil[u] in the eyes of the LORD, just as his father had done.

10At that time the officers of Nebuchadnezzar[v] king of Babylon advanced on Jerusalem and laid siege to it, 11and Nebuchadnezzar himself came up to the city while his officers were besieging it. 12Jehoiachin king of Judah, his mother, his attendants, his nobles and his officials all surrendered[w] to him.

In the eighth year of the reign of the king of Babylon, he took Jehoiachin prisoner. 13As the LORD had declared,[x] Nebuchadnezzar removed all the treasures[y] from the temple of the LORD and from the royal palace, and took away all the gold articles[z] that Solomon[a] king of Israel had made for the temple of the LORD. 14He carried into exile[b] all Jerusalem: all the officers and fighting men,[c] and all the craftsmen and artisans—a total of ten thousand. Only the poorest[d] people of the land were left.

15Nebuchadnezzar took Jehoiachin[e] captive to Babylon. He also took from Jerusalem to Babylon the king's mother,[f] his wives, his officials and the leading men[g] of the land. 16The king of Babylon also deported to Babylon the entire force of seven thousand fighting men, strong and fit for war, and a thousand craftsmen and artisans.[h] 17He made Mattaniah, Jehoiachin's uncle, king in his place and changed his name to Zedekiah.[i]

Zedekiah King of Judah

24:18–20pp—2Ch 36:11–16; Jer 52:1–3

18Zedekiah[j] was twenty-one years old when he became king, and he reigned in Jerusalem for eleven years. His mother's name was Hamutal[k] daughter of Jeremiah; she was from Libnah. 19He did evil[l] in the eyes of the LORD, just as Jehoiakim had done. 20It was because of the LORD's anger that all this happened to Jerusalem and Judah, and in the end he thrust[m] them from his presence.[n]

The Fall of Jerusalem

25:1–12pp—Jer 39:1–10
25:1–21pp—2Ch 36:17–20; Jer 52:4–27
25:22–26pp—Jer 40:7–9;41:1–3,16–18

Now Zedekiah rebelled against the king of Babylon.

25 So in the ninth[a] year of Zedekiah's reign, on the tenth day of the tenth month, Nebuchadnezzar[b] king of Babylon marched against Jerusalem with his whole army. He encamped outside the city and built siege works[c] all around it. 2The city was kept under siege until the eleventh year of King Zedekiah. 3By the ninth day of the ⌞fourth⌟[a] month the famine[d] in the city had become so severe that there was no food for the people to eat. 4Then the city wall was broken through,[e] and the whole army fled at night through the gate between the two walls near the king's garden, though the Babylonians[b] were surrounding[f] the city. They fled towards the Arabah,[c] 5but the Babylonian[d] army pursued the king and overtook him in the plains of Jericho. All his soldiers were separated from him and scattered,[g] 6and he was captured.[h] He was taken to the king of Babylon at Riblah,[i] where sentence was pronounced on him. 7They killed the sons of Zedekiah before his eyes. Then they put out his eyes, bound him with bronze shackles and took him to Babylon.[j]

8On the seventh day of the fifth month, in the nineteenth year of Nebuchadnezzar king of Babylon, Nebuzaradan commander of the imperial guard, an official of the king of Babylon, came to Jerusalem. 9He set fire[k] to the temple of the LORD, the royal palace and all the houses of Jerusalem. Every important building he burned down.[l] 10The whole Babylonian army, under the commander of the imperial guard, broke down the walls[m] around Jerusalem. 11Nebuzaradan the commander of the guard carried into exile[n] the people who remained in the city, along with the rest of the populace and those who had gone over to the king of Babylon.[o] 12But the commander left behind some of the poorest people[p] of the land to work the vineyards and fields.

13The Babylonians broke[q] up the bronze pillars, the movable stands and the bronze Sea that were at the temple of the LORD and they carried the bronze to Babylon. 14They also took away the pots, shovels, wick trimmers, dishes[r]

8 [t]ver 15; Jer 13:18; 22:26; 29:2
9 [u]1Ki 15:26
10 [v]**ver 1**
12 [w]2Ki 25:27; Jer 13:18; 22:24–30; 24:1; 29:2
13 [x]2Ki 20:17; [y]2Ki 25:15; Isa 39:6; 42:22; [z]2Ki 25:14; Ezr 1:7; Isa 39:6; Jer 15:13; 17:3; 20:5; 27:16; 28:3; Eze 7:21; Da 1:2; 5:2,23; Zep 1:13; [a]**1Ki 7:51**
14 [b]**Dt 28:36; 2Ch 36:20; Mt 1:11**; [c]Isa 3:1–3; [d]Dt 15:11; 2Ki 25:12; Job 5:16; Ps 9:18; Jer 40:7; 52:16
15 [e]**2Ki 20:18**; Eze 19:9; [f]**ver 8; 1Ki 2:19**; [g]Est 2:6; Isa 39:7; La 2:9; Eze 1:2; 17:12–14; Da 1:3
16 [h]Ezr 2:1; Jer 24:1
17 [i]1Ch 3:15; 2Ch 36:11; Jer 1:3; 37:1; 52:1; Eze 17:13
18 [j]1Ch 3:16; Jer 39:1; [k]2Ki 23:31
19 [l]1Ki 15:26; Jer 37:2
20 [m]Dt 4:26; 29:27; [n]**Ex 33:15; 2Ki 13:23**

Ch. 25

1 [a]Jer 32:1; [b]Jer 21:2; 34:1–7; [c]Isa 23:13; 29:3; Jer 4:16–17; 32:2; 33:4; Eze 21:22; 24:2
3 [d]**Lev 26:26**; Isa 22:2; Jer 14:18; 37:21; La 2:20; 4:9
4 [e]Job 30:14; Ps 144:14; Jer 50:15; 51:44, 58; Eze 33:21; [f]Jer 4:17; 6:3
5 [g]**Lev 26:36**; Eze 12:14; 17:21
6 [h]Isa 22:3; Jer 38:23; [i]**Nu 34:11**
7 [j]**Dt 28:36**; Jer 21:7; 32:4–5; 34:3,21; Eze 12:11; 19:9; 40:1

9 [k]Isa 60:7; 63:15,18; 64:11; [l]**Dt 13:16**; Ne 1:3; Ps 74:3–8; 79:1; Jer 2:15; 17:27; 21:10; 26:6,18; La 4:11; Am 2:5; Mic 3:12 *10* [m]Ne 1:3; Jer 50:15
11 [n]**Lev 26:44**; 2Ki 24:14; [o]**Dt 28:36; 2Ki 24:1**
12 [p]**2Ki 24:14** *13* [q]**1Ki 7:50** *14* [r]**Nu 7:14**

a3 See Jer. 52:6.
b4 Or *Chaldeans;* also in verses 13, 25 and 26
c4 Or *the Jordan Valley*
d5 Or *Chaldean;* also in verses 10 and 24

and all the bronze articles[s] used in the
temple service. 15The commander of the
imperial guard took away the censers
and sprinkling bowls—all that were
made of pure gold or silver.[t]

16The bronze from the two pillars, the
Sea and the movable stands, which
Solomon had made for the temple of the
LORD, was more than could be weighed.
17Each pillar[u] was twenty-seven feet[e]
high. The bronze capital on top of one
pillar was four and a half feet[f] high and
was decorated with a network and
pomegranates of bronze all around.
The other pillar, with its network, was
similar.

18The commander of the guard took
as prisoners Seraiah[v] the chief priest,
Zephaniah[w] the priest next in rank and
the three doorkeepers.[x] 19Of those still
in the city, he took the officer in charge
of the fighting men and five royal advis-
ers. He also took the secretary who was
chief officer in charge of conscripting
the people of the land and sixty of his
men who were found in the city.
20Nebuzaradan the commander took
them all and brought them to the king of
Babylon at Riblah. 21There at Riblah,[y] in
the land of Hamath, the king had them
executed.[z]

So Judah went into captivity,[a] away
from her land.[b]

22Nebuchadnezzar king of Babylon
appointed Gedaliah[c] son of Ahikam,[d]
the son of Shaphan, to be over the peo-
ple he had left behind in Judah. 23When
all the army officers and their men
heard that the king of Babylon had
appointed Gedaliah as governor, they
came to Gedaliah at Mizpah—Ishmael
son of Nethaniah, Johanan son of
Kareah, Seraiah son of Tanhumeth the
Netophathite, Jaazaniah the son of the
Maacathite, and their men. 24Gedaliah
took an oath to reassure them and their
men. "Do not be afraid of the Babylo-
nian officials," he said. "Settle down in
the land and serve the king of Babylon,
and it will go well with you."

25In the seventh month, however,
Ishmael son of Nethaniah, the son of
Elishama, who was of royal blood, came
with ten men and assassinated[e] Geda-
liah and also the men of Judah and the
Babylonians who were with him at Miz-
pah.[f] 26At this, all the people from the
least to the greatest, together with the
army officers, fled to Egypt[g] for fear of
the Babylonians.

Jehoiachin Released

25:27–30pp—Jer 52:31–34

27In the thirty-seventh year of the ex-
ile of Jehoiachin king of Judah, in the
year Evil-Merodach[g] became king of
Babylon, he released Jehoiachin[h] from
prison on the twenty-seventh day of the
twelfth month. 28He spoke kindly[i] to
him and gave him a seat of honour[j]
higher than those of the other kings
who were with him in Babylon. 29So
Jehoiachin put aside his prison clothes
and for the rest of his life ate regularly at
the king's table.[k] 30Day by day the king
gave Jehoiachin a regular allowance as
long as he lived.[l]

14 [s]**2Ki 24:13;** Ezr 1:7
15 [t]**2Ki 24:13;** Jer 15:13; 20:5; 27:16–22
17 [u]1Ki 7:15–22
18 [v]ver 18–21; 1Ch 6:14; Ezr 7:1; Ne 11:11; [w]Jer 21:1; 29:25; 37:3; [x]**2Ki 12:9; 23:4**
21 [y]**Nu 34:11;** [z]Jer 34:21; [a]**1Ki 8:46;** [b]**Ge 12:7; Jos 23:13**
22 [c]Jer 39:14; 40:5,7; 41:18; [d]**2Ki 22:12**
25 [e]**2Ki 12:20;** [f]Zec 7:5
26 [g]Isa 30:2; Jer 43:7
27 [h]**2Ki 24:12**
28 [i]**1Ki 8:50;** [j]Ezr 5:5; 7:6,28; 9:9; Ne 2:1; Da 2:48
29 [k]**2Sa 9:7**
30 [l]Ge 43:34; Est 2:9; 9:22; Jer 28:4

e17 Hebrew *eighteen cubits* (about 8.2 metres)
f17 Hebrew *three cubits* (about 1.4 metres)
g27 Also called *Amel-Marduk*

1 Chronicles

Historical Records From Adam to Abraham

To Noah's Sons

1 Adam,[a] Seth, Enosh, 2Kenan,[b]
Mahalalel,[c] Jared,[d] 3Enoch,[e]
Methuselah,[f] Lamech,[g] Noah.[h]

4The sons of Noah:[a][i]
Shem, Ham and Japheth.[j]

The Japhethites

1:5–7pp—Ge 10:2–5

5The sons[b] of Japheth:
Gomer, Magog, Madai, Javan,
Tubal, Meshech and Tiras.
6The sons of Gomer:
Ashkenaz, Riphath[c] and Togar-
mah.
7The sons of Javan:
Elishah, Tarshish, the Kittim and
the Rodanim.

The Hamites

1:8–16pp—Ge 10:6–20

8The sons of Ham:
Cush, Mizraim,[d] Put and Ca-
naan.
9The sons of Cush:
Seba, Havilah, Sabta, Raamah
and Sabteca.
The sons of Raamah:
Sheba and Dedan.
10Cush was the father[e] of
Nimrod, who grew to be a
mighty warrior on earth.
11Mizraim was the father of
the Ludites, Anamites, Leha-
bites, Naphtuhites, 12Pathru-
sites, Casluhites (from whom the
Philistines came) and Caphto-
rites.
13Canaan was the father of
Sidon his firstborn,[f] and of the
Hittites, 14Jebusites, Amorites,
Girgashites, 15Hivites, Arkites,
Sinites, 16Arvadites, Zemarites
and Hamathites.

The Semites

1:17–23pp—Ge 10:21–31; 11:10–27

17The sons of Shem:
Elam, Asshur, Arphaxad, Lud
and Aram.
The sons of Aram:[g]
Uz, Hul, Gether and Meshech.
18Arphaxad was the father of Shelah,
and Shelah the father of Eber.
19Two sons were born to Eber:
One was named Peleg,[h] because
in his time the earth was divided;
his brother was named Joktan.
20Joktan was the father of
Almodad, Sheleph, Hazarma-
veth, Jerah, 21Hadoram, Uzal,
Diklah, 22Obal,[i] Abimael, Sheba,
23Ophir, Havilah and Jobab. All
these were sons of Joktan.

24Shem,[k] Arphaxad,[j] Shelah,
25Eber, Peleg, Reu,
26Serug, Nahor, Terah
27and Abram (that is, Abraham).

The Family of Abraham

28The sons of Abraham:
Isaac and Ishmael.

Descendants of Hagar

1:29–31pp—Ge 25:12–16

29These were their descendants:
Nebaioth the firstborn of
Ishmael, Kedar, Adbeel, Mib-
sam, 30Mishma, Dumah, Massa,
Hadad, Tema, 31Jetur, Naphish
and Kedemah. These were the
sons of Ishmael.

Ch. 1

1 [a]Ge 5:1–32; Lk 3:36–38
2 [b]Ge 5:9; [c]Ge 5:12; [d]Ge 5:15
3 [e]Ge 5:18; Jude 14; [f]Ge 5:21; [g]Ge 5:25; [h]Ge 5:29
4 [i]Ge 6:10; 10:1; [j]Ge 5:32
24 [k]Ge 10:21–25; Lk 3:34–36

[a]4 Septuagint; Hebrew does not have *The sons of Noah:*
[b]5 *Sons* may mean *descendants* or *successors* or *nations;* also in verses 6–10, 17 and 20.
[c]6 Many Hebrew manuscripts and Vulgate (see also Septuagint and Gen. 10:3); most Hebrew manuscripts *Diphath*
[d]8 That is, Egypt; also in verse 11
[e]10 *Father* may mean *ancestor* or *predecessor* or *founder;* also in verses 11, 13, 18 and 20.
[f]13 Or *of the Sidonians, the foremost*
[g]17 One Hebrew manuscript and some Septuagint manuscripts (see also Gen. 10:23); most Hebrew manuscripts do not have this line.
[h]19 *Peleg* means *division.*
[i]22 Some Hebrew manuscripts and Syriac (see also Gen. 10:28); most Hebrew manuscripts *Ebal*
[j]24 Hebrew; some Septuagint manuscripts *Arphaxad, Cainan* (see also note at Gen. 11:10)

Descendants of Keturah

1:32–33pp—Ge 25:1–4

32The sons born to Keturah,
Abraham's concubine:[l]
Zimran, Jokshan, Medan,
Midian, Ishbak and Shuah.
The sons of Jokshan:
Sheba and Dedan.[m]
33The sons of Midian:
Ephah, Epher, Hanoch, Abida
and Eldaah.
All these were descendants of
Keturah.

Descendants of Sarah

1:35–37pp—Ge 36:10–14

34Abraham[n] was the father of Isaac.
The sons of Isaac:[o]
Esau and Israel.[p]

Esau's Sons

35The sons of Esau:[q]
Eliphaz, Reuel,[r] Jeush, Jalam and
Korah.
36The sons of Eliphaz:
Teman, Omar, Zepho,[k] Gatam
and Kenaz;
by Timna: Amalek.[l][s]
37The sons of Reuel:[t]
Nahath, Zerah, Shammah and
Mizzah.

The People of Seir in Edom

1:38–42pp—Ge 36:20–28

38The sons of Seir:
Lotan, Shobal, Zibeon, Anah,
Dishon, Ezer and Dishan.
39The sons of Lotan:
Hori and Homam. Timna was
Lotan's sister.
40The sons of Shobal:
Alvan,[m] Manahath, Ebal,
Shepho and Onam.
The sons of Zibeon:
Aiah and Anah.[u]
41The son of Anah:
Dishon.
The sons of Dishon:
Hemdan,[n] Eshban, Ithran and
Keran.
42The sons of Ezer:
Bilhan, Zaavan and Akan.[o]
The sons of Dishan:[p]
Uz and Aran.

The Rulers of Edom

1:43–54pp—Ge 36:31–43

43These were the kings who reigned
in Edom before any Israelite king
reigned:[q]
Bela son of Beor, whose city was
named Dinhabah.
44When Bela died, Jobab son of Zerah
from Bozrah succeeded him as
king.
45When Jobab died, Husham from
the land of the Temanites[v] succeeded him as king.
46When Husham died, Hadad son of
Bedad, who defeated Midian in
the country of Moab, succeeded
him as king. His city was named
Avith.
47When Hadad died, Samlah from
Masrekah succeeded him as
king.
48When Samlah died, Shaul from Rehoboth on the river[r] succeeded
him as king.
49When Shaul died, Baal-Hanan son
of Acbor succeeded him as king.
50When Baal-Hanan died, Hadad
succeeded him as king. His city
was named Pau,[s] and his wife's
name was Mehetabel daughter of
Matred, the daughter of Me-Zahab. 51Hadad also died.
The chiefs of Edom were:
Timna, Alvah, Jetheth, 52Oholibamah, Elah, Pinon, 53Kenaz,
Teman, Mibzar, 54Magdiel and
Iram. These were the chiefs of
Edom.

Israel's Sons

2:1–2pp—Ge 35:23–26

2 These were the sons of Israel:
Reuben, Simeon, Levi, Judah,
Issachar, Zebulun, 2Dan, Joseph,
Benjamin, Naphtali, Gad and
Asher.

Judah

2:5–15pp—Ru 4:18–22; Mt 1:3–6

To Hezron's Sons

3The sons of Judah:[a]
Er, Onan and Shelah.[b] These
three were born to him by a

---

32 [l]**Ge 22:24;** [m]**Ge 10:7**
34 [n]Lk 3:34; [o]Mt 1:2; Ac 7:8; [p]**Ge 17:5**
35 [q]Ge 36:19; [r]**Ge 36:4**
36 [s]**Ex 17:14**
37 [t]Ge 36:17
40 [u]**Ge 36:2**
45 [v]**Ge 36:11**

Ch. 2

3 [a]**Ge 29:35;** 38:2–10; [b]**Ge 38:5**

---

[k]*36* Many Hebrew manuscripts, some Septuagint manuscripts and Syriac (see also Gen. 36:11); most Hebrew manuscripts *Zephi*
[l]*36* Some Septuagint manuscripts (see also Gen. 36:12); Hebrew *Gatam, Kenaz, Timna and Amalek*
[m]*40* Many Hebrew manuscripts and some Septuagint manuscripts (see also Gen. 36:23); most Hebrew manuscripts *Alian*
[n]*41* Many Hebrew manuscripts and some Septuagint manuscripts (see also Gen. 36:26); most Hebrew manuscripts *Hamran*
[o]*42* Many Hebrew and Septuagint manuscripts (see also Gen. 36:27); most Hebrew manuscripts *Zaavan, Jaakan*
[p]*42* Hebrew *Dishon*, a variant of *Dishan*
[q]*43* Or *before an Israelite king reigned over them*
[r]*48* Possibly the Euphrates
[s]*50* Many Hebrew manuscripts, some Septuagint manuscripts, Vulgate and Syriac (see also Gen. 36:39); most Hebrew manuscripts *Pai*

Canaanite woman, the daughter
of Shua.[c] Er, Judah's firstborn,
was wicked in the LORD's sight;
so the LORD put him to death.[d]
4Tamar,[e] Judah's daughter-in-
law,[f] bore him Perez[g] and Zerah.
Judah had five sons in all.

5The sons of Perez:[h]
Hezron[i] and Hamul.
6The sons of Zerah:
Zimri, Ethan, Heman, Calcol and
Darda[a]—five in all.
7The son of Carmi:
Achar,[b][j] who brought trouble
on Israel by violating the ban on
taking devoted things.[c][k]
8The son of Ethan:
Azariah.
9The sons born to Hezron[l] were:
Jerahmeel, Ram and Caleb.[d]

From Ram Son of Hezron

10Ram[m] was the father of
Amminadab[n], and Amminadab
the father of Nahshon,[o] the
leader of the people of Judah.
11Nahshon was the father of Sal-
mon,[e] Salmon the father of Boaz,
12Boaz[p] the father of Obed and
Obed the father of Jesse.[q]
13Jesse[r] was the father of
Eliab[s] his firstborn; the second
son was Abinadab, the third
Shimea, 14the fourth Nethanel,
the fifth Raddai, 15the sixth Ozem
and the seventh David. 16Their
sisters were Zeruiah[t] and Abi-
gail. Zeruiah's[u] three sons were
Abishai, Joab[v] and Asahel.
17Abigail was the mother of
Amasa,[w] whose father was Jether
the Ishmaelite.

Caleb Son of Hezron

18Caleb son of Hezron had children
by his wife Azubah (and by
Jerioth). These were her sons:
Jesher, Shobab and Ardon.
19When Azubah died, Caleb[x]
married Ephrath, who bore him
Hur. 20Hur was the father of Uri,
and Uri the father of Bezalel.[y]
21Later, Hezron lay with the daugh-
ter of Makir the father of Gilead[z]
(he had married her when he was
sixty years old), and she bore him
Segub. 22Segub was the father of
Jair, who controlled twenty-
three towns in Gilead. 23(But
Geshur and Aram captured Hav-
voth Jair,[f][a] as well as Kenath[b]
with its surrounding settle-
ments—sixty towns.) All these
were descendants of Makir the
father of Gilead.

24After Hezron died in Caleb
Ephrathah, Abijah the wife of
Hezron bore him Ashhur[c] the
father[g] of Tekoa.

Jerahmeel Son of Hezron

25The sons of Jerahmeel the firstborn
of Hezron:
Ram his firstborn, Bunah, Oren,
Ozem and[h] Ahijah. 26Jerahmeel
had another wife, whose name
was Atarah; she was the mother
of Onam.
27The sons of Ram the firstborn of
Jerahmeel:
Maaz, Jamin and Eker.
28The sons of Onam:
Shammai and Jada.
The sons of Shammai:
Nadab and Abishur.
29Abishur's wife was named Abihail,
who bore him Ahban and Molid.
30The sons of Nadab:
Seled and Appaim. Seled died
without children.
31The son of Appaim:
Ishi, who was the father of
Sheshan.
Sheshan was the father of Ahlai.
32The sons of Jada, Shammai's
brother:
Jether and Jonathan. Jether died
without children.
33The sons of Jonathan:
Peleth and Zaza.
These were the descendants of
Jerahmeel.
34Sheshan had no sons—only
daughters.
He had an Egyptian servant
named Jarha. 35Sheshan gave his
daughter in marriage to his ser-
vant Jarha, and she bore him
Attai.
36Attai was the father of Nathan,
Nathan the father of Zabad,[d]

3 [c]Ge 38:2; [d]Nu 26:19
4 [e]Ge 38:11–30; [f]Ge 11:31; [g]Ge 38:29
5 [h]Ge 46:12; [i]Nu 26:21
7 [j]Jos 7:1; [k]Jos 6:18
9 [l]Nu 26:21
10 [m]Lk 3:32–33; [n]Ex 6:23; [o]Nu 1:7
12 [p]Ru 2:1; [q]Ru 4:17
13 [r]Ru 4:17; [s]1Sa 16:6
16 [t]1Sa 26:6; [u]2Sa 2:18; [v]2Sa 2:13
17 [w]2Sa 17:25
19 [x]ver 42,50
20 [y]Ex 31:2
21 [z]Nu 27:1
23 [a]Nu 32:41; Dt 3:14; [b]Nu 32:42
24 [c]1Ch 4:5
36 [d]1Ch 11:41

[a]6 Many Hebrew manuscripts, some Septuagint manuscripts and Syriac (see also 1 Kings 4:31); most Hebrew manuscripts *Dara*
[b]7 *Achar* means *trouble*; *Achar* is called *Achan* in Joshua.
[c]7 The Hebrew term refers to the irrevocable giving over of things or persons to the LORD, often by totally destroying them.
[d]9 Hebrew *Kelubai*, a variant of *Caleb*
[e]11 Septuagint (see also Ruth 4:21); Hebrew *Salma*
[f]23 Or *captured the settlements of Jair*
[g]24 *Father* may mean *civic leader* or *military leader*; also in verses 42, 45, 49–52 and possibly elsewhere.
[h]25 Or *Oren and Ozem, by*

37Zabad the father of Ephlal,
Ephlal the father of Obed,
38Obed the father of Jehu,
Jehu the father of Azariah,
39Azariah the father of Helez,
Helez the father of Eleasah,
40Eleasah the father of Sismai,
Sismai the father of Shallum,
41Shallum the father of Jekamiah,
and Jekamiah the father of Elishama.

The Clans of Caleb

42The sons of Caleb[e] the brother of Jerahmeel:
Mesha his firstborn, who was the father of Ziph, and his son Mareshah,[i] who was the father of Hebron.
43The sons of Hebron:
Korah, Tappuah, Rekem and Shema. 44Shema was the father of Raham, and Raham the father of Jorkeam. Rekem was the father of Shammai. 45The son of Shammai was Maon,[f] and Maon was the father of Beth Zur.[g]
46Caleb's concubine Ephah was the mother of Haran, Moza and Gazez. Haran was the father of Gazez.
47The sons of Jahdai:
Regem, Jotham, Geshan, Pelet, Ephah and Shaaph.
48Caleb's concubine Maacah was the mother of Sheber and Tirhanah.
49She also gave birth to Shaaph the father of Madmannah[h] and to Sheva the father of Macbenah and Gibea. Caleb's daughter was Acsah.[i] 50These were the descendants of Caleb.

The sons of Hur[j] the firstborn of Ephrathah:
Shobal the father of Kiriath Jearim,[k] 51Salma the father of Bethlehem, and Hareph the father of Beth Gader.
52The descendants of Shobal the father of Kiriath Jearim were:
Haroeh, half the Manahathites,
53and the clans of Kiriath Jearim: the Ithrites,[l] Puthites, Shumathites and Mishraites. From these descended the Zorathites and Eshtaolites.
54The descendants of Salma:
Bethlehem, the Netophathites,[m] Atroth Beth Joab, half the Manahathites, the Zorites, 55and the clans of scribes[j] who lived at Jabez: the Tirathites, Shimeathites and Sucathites. These are the Kenites[n] who came from Hammath,[o] the father of the house of Recab.[k][p]

42 [e]**ver 19**
45 [f]**Jos 15:55;** [g]**Jos 15:58**
49 [h]Jos 15:31; [i]Jos 15:16
50 [j]1Ch 4:4; [k]**ver 19**
53 [l]2Sa 23:38
54 [m]Ezr 2:22; Ne 7:26; 12:28
55 [n]**Ge 15:19; Jdg 4:11;** [o]Jos 19:35; [p]2Ki 10:15,23; Jer 35:2–19

Ch. 3

1 [a]1Ch 14:3; 28:5; [b]**1Sa 25:43;** [c]**Jos 15:56;** [d]**1Sa 25:42**
2 [e]1Ki 2:22
4 [f]**2Sa 5:4;** 1Ch 29:27; [g]**2Sa 5:5**
5 [h]2Sa 11:3
9 [i]**2Sa 13:1;** [j]1Ch 14:4
10 [k]1Ki 14:21–31; 2Ch 12:16; [l]1Ki 15:1–8; 2Ch 13:1; [m]1Ki 15:9–24; [n]2Ch 17:1–21:3
11 [o]2Ki 8:16–24; 2Ch 21:1; [p]2Ki 8:25–10:14; 2Ch 22:1–10; [q]2Ki 11:1–12:21; 2Ch 22:11–24:27
12 [r]2Ki 14:1–22; 2Ch 25:1–28; [s]2Ki 15:1–7; 2Ch 26:1–23

The Sons of David

3:1–4pp—2Sa 3:2–5
3:5–8pp—2Sa 5:14–16; 1Ch 14:4–7

3 These were the sons of David[a] born to him in Hebron:
The firstborn was Amnon the son of Ahinoam[b] of Jezreel;[c]
the second, Daniel the son of Abigail[d] of Carmel;
2the third, Absalom the son of Maacah daughter of Talmai king of Geshur;
the fourth, Adonijah[e] the son of Haggith;
3the fifth, Shephatiah the son of Abital;
and the sixth, Ithream, by his wife Eglah.
4These six were born to David in Hebron,[f] where he reigned for seven years and six months.[g]
David reigned in Jerusalem for thirty-three years, 5and these were the children born to him there:
Shammua,[a] Shobab, Nathan and Solomon. These four were by Bathsheba[b][h] daughter of Ammiel. 6There were also Ibhar, Elishua,[c] Eliphelet, 7Nogah, Nepheg, Japhia, 8Elishama, Eliada and Eliphelet—nine in all.
9All these were the sons of David, besides his sons by his concubines. And Tamar[i] was their sister.[j]

The Kings of Judah

10Solomon's son was Rehoboam,[k]
Abijah[l] his son,
Asa[m] his son,
Jehoshaphat[n] his son,
11Jehoram[d][o] his son,
Ahaziah[p] his son,
Joash[q] his son,
12Amaziah[r] his son,
Azariah[s] his son,

i42 The meaning of the Hebrew for this phrase is uncertain. j55 Or *of the Sopherites*
k55 Or *father of Beth Recab*
a5 Hebrew *Shimea*, a variant of *Shammua*
b5 One Hebrew manuscript and Vulgate (see also Septuagint and 2 Sam. 11:3); most Hebrew manuscripts *Bathshua*
c6 Two Hebrew manuscripts (see also 2 Sam. 5:15 and 1 Chron. 14:5); most Hebrew manuscripts *Elishama*
d11 Hebrew *Joram*, a variant of *Jehoram*

Jotham[t] his son,
13 Ahaz[u] his son,
Hezekiah[v] his son,
Manasseh[w] his son,
14 Amon[x] his son,
Josiah[y] his son.
15 The sons of Josiah:
Johanan the firstborn,
Jehoiakim[z] the second son,
Zedekiah[a] the third,
Shallum[b] the fourth.
16 The successors of Jehoiakim:
Jehoiachin[e][c] his son,
and Zedekiah.[d]

The Royal Line After the Exile

17 The descendants of Jehoiachin the captive:
Shealtiel[e] his son, 18 Malkiram,
Pedaiah, Shenazzar,[f] Jekamiah,
Hoshama and Nedabiah.[g]
19 The sons of Pedaiah:
Zerubbabel[h] and Shimei.
The sons of Zerubbabel:
Meshullam and Hananiah.
Shelomith was their sister.
20 There were also five others:
Hashubah, Ohel, Berekiah,
Hasadiah and Jushab-Hesed.
21 The descendants of Hananiah:
Pelatiah and Jeshaiah, and the
sons of Rephaiah, of Arnan, of
Obadiah and of Shecaniah.
22 The descendants of Shecaniah:
Shemaiah and his sons:
Hattush,[i] Igal, Bariah, Neariah
and Shaphat—six in all.
23 The sons of Neariah:
Elioenai, Hizkiah and Azrikam
—three in all.
24 The sons of Elioenai:
Hodaviah, Eliashib, Pelaiah,
Akkub, Johanan, Delaiah and
Anani—seven in all.

Other Clans of Judah

4 The descendants of Judah:[a]
Perez, Hezron,[b] Carmi, Hur and
Shobal.
2 Reaiah son of Shobal was the father
of Jahath, and Jahath the father
of Ahumai and Lahad. These
were the clans of the Zorathites.
3 These were the sons[a] of Etam:
Jezreel, Ishma and Idbash. Their
sister was named Hazzelelponi.
4 Penuel was the father of Gedor,
and Ezer the father of Hushah.
These were the descendants of
Hur,[c] the firstborn of Ephrathah
and father[b] of Bethlehem.[d]
5 Ashhur[e] the father of Tekoa had
two wives, Helah and Naarah.
6 Naarah bore him Ahuzzam,
Hepher, Temeni and Haahashtari. These were the descendants
of Naarah.
7 The sons of Helah:
Zereth, Zohar, Ethnan, 8 and
Koz, who was the father of Anub
and Hazzobebah and of the clans
of Aharhel son of Harum.

9 Jabez was more honourable than his
brothers. His mother had named him
Jabez,[c] saying, "I gave birth to him in
pain." 10 Jabez cried out to the God of
Israel, "Oh, that you would bless me
and enlarge my territory! Let your hand
be with me, and keep me from harm so
that I will be free from pain." And God
granted his request.

11 Kelub, Shuhah's brother, was the
father of Mehir, who was the
father of Eshton. 12 Eshton was
the father of Beth Rapha, Paseah
and Tehinnah the father of Ir
Nahash.[d] These were the men of
Recah.

13 The sons of Kenaz:
Othniel[f] and Seraiah.
The sons of Othniel:
Hathath and Meonothai.[e]
14 Meonothai was the father of
Ophrah.
Seraiah was the father of Joab,
the father of Ge Harashim.[f] It
was called this because its people
were craftsmen.
15 The sons of Caleb son of Jephunneh:
Iru, Elah and Naam.
The son of Elah:
Kenaz.
16 The sons of Jehallelel:
Ziph, Ziphah, Tiria and Asarel.
17 The sons of Ezrah:
Jether, Mered, Epher and Jalon.
One of Mered's wives gave birth
to Miriam,[g] Shammai and Ishbah
the father of Eshtemoa. 18 (His Judean wife gave birth to Jered the
father of Gedor, Heber the father

12 [t]2Ki 15:32–38; 2Ch 27:1; Isa 1:1; Hos 1:1; Mic 1:1
13 [u]2Ki 16:1–20; 2Ch 28:1; Isa 7:1; [v]2Ki 18:1–20:21; 2Ch 29:1; Isa 1:1; Jer 26:19; Hos 1:1; Mic 1:1; [w]2Ki 21:1–18; 2Ch 33:1
14 [x]2Ki 21:19–26; 2Ch 33:21; Zep 1:1; [y]2Ki 22:1; 2Ch 34:1; Jer 1:2; 3:6; 25:3
15 [z]**2Ki 23:34**; [a]Jer 37:1; [b]**2Ki 23:31**
16 [c]**2Ki 24:6**,8; [d]**2Ki 24:18**
17 [e]Ezr 3:2
18 [f]Ezr 1:8; 5:14; [g]Jer 22:30
19 [h]Ezr 2:2; 3:2; 5:2; Ne 7:7; 12:1; Hag 1:1; 2:2; Zec 4:6
22 [i]Ezr 8:2–3

Ch. 4

1 [a]**Ge 29:35; 1Ch 2:3**; [b]Nu 26:21
4 [c]1Ch 2:50; [d]Ru 1:19
5 [e]1Ch 2:24
13 [f]**Jos 15:17**
17 [g]**Ex 15:20**

e16 Hebrew *Jeconiah*, a variant of *Jehoiachin*; also in verse 17
a3 Some Septuagint manuscripts (see also Vulgate); Hebrew *father*
b4 *Father* may mean *civic leader* or *military leader*; also in verses 12, 14, 17, 18 and possibly elsewhere.
c9 *Jabez* sounds like the Hebrew for *pain*.
d12 Or *of the city of Nahash*
e13 Some Septuagint manuscripts and Vulgate; Hebrew does not have *and Meonothai*.
f14 *Ge Harashim* means *valley of craftsmen*.

of Soco, and Jekuthiel the father
of Zanoah.[h]) These were the
children of Pharaoh's daughter
Bithiah, whom Mered had
married.
19The sons of Hodiah's wife, the
sister of Naham:
the father of Keilah[i] the Garmite,
and Eshtemoa the Maacathite.[j]
20The sons of Shimon:
Amnon, Rinnah, Ben-Hanan
and Tilon.
The descendants of Ishi:
Zoheth and Ben-Zoheth.
21The sons of Shelah[k] son of Judah:
Er the father of Lecah, Laadah
the father of Mareshah and the
clans of the linen workers at Beth
Ashbea, 22Jokim, the men of
Cozeba, and Joash and Saraph,
who ruled in Moab and Jashubi
Lehem. (These records are from
ancient times.) 23They were the
potters who lived at Netaim and
Gederah; they stayed there and
worked for the king.

Simeon

4:28–33pp—Jos 19:2–10

24The descendants of Simeon:[l]
Nemuel, Jamin, Jarib,[m] Zerah
and Shaul;
25Shallum was Shaul's son, Mib-
sam his son and Mishma his son.
26The descendants of Mishma:
Hammuel his son, Zaccur his son
and Shimei his son.
27Shimei had sixteen sons and six
daughters, but his brothers did not have
many children; so their entire clan did
not become as numerous as the people
of Judah. 28They lived in Beersheba,[n]
Moladah,[o] Hazar Shual, 29Bilhah,
Ezem,[p] Tolad, 30Bethuel, Hormah,[q] Zik-
lag,[r] 31Beth Marcaboth, Hazar Susim,
Beth Biri and Shaaraim.[s] These were
their towns until the reign of David.
32Their surrounding villages were Etam,
Ain,[t] Rimmon, Token and Ashan[u]—
five towns—33and all the villages
around these towns as far as Baalath.[g]
These were their settlements. And they
kept a genealogical record.

34Meshobab, Jamlech, Joshah son
of Amaziah, 35Joel, Jehu son of
Joshibiah, the son of Seraiah, the
son of Asiel, 36also Elioenai, Jaako-
bah, Jeshohaiah, Asaiah, Adiel,
Jesimiel, Benaiah, 37and Ziza son of
Shiphi, the son of Allon, the son of
Jedaiah, the son of Shimri, the son
of Shemaiah.

38The men listed above by name were
leaders of their clans. Their families in-
creased greatly, 39and they went to the
outskirts of Gedor[v] to the east of the
valley in search of pasture for their
flocks. 40They found rich, good pasture,
and the land was spacious, peaceful and
quiet.[w] Some Hamites had lived there
formerly.
41The men whose names were listed
came in the days of Hezekiah king of
Judah. They attacked the Hamites in
their dwellings and also the Meunites[x]
who were there and completely de-
stroyed[h] them, as is evident to this day.
Then they settled in their place, because
there was pasture for their flocks. 42And
five hundred of these Simeonites, led
by Pelatiah, Neariah, Rephaiah and
Uzziel, the sons of Ishi, invaded the hill
country of Seir.[y] 43They killed the re-
maining Amalekites[z] who had escaped,
and they have lived there to this day.

Reuben

5 The sons of Reuben[a] the firstborn
of Israel (he was the firstborn, but
when he defiled his father's marriage
bed,[b] his rights as firstborn were given
to the sons of Joseph[c] son of Israel;[d] so
he could not be listed in the genealogical
record in accordance with his birth-
right,[e] 2and though Judah[f] was the
strongest of his brothers and a ruler[g]
came from him, the rights of the
firstborn[h] belonged to Joseph)—3the
sons of Reuben[i] the firstborn of Israel:
Hanoch, Pallu,[j] Hezron[k] and
Carmi.
4The descendants of Joel:
Shemaiah his son, Gog his son,
Shimei his son, 5Micah his son,
Reaiah his son, Baal his son,
6and Beerah his son, whom Tig-
lath-Pileser[a][l] king of Assyria took
into exile. Beerah was a leader of
the Reubenites.
7Their relatives by clans,[m] listed
according to their genealogical
records:
Jeiel the chief, Zechariah, 8and

18 [h]Jos 15:34
19 [i]Jos 15:44; [j]Dt 3:14
21 [k]Ge 38:5
24 [l]Ge 29:33; [m]Nu 26:12
28 [n]Ge 21:14; [o]Jos 15:26
29 [p]Jos 15:29
30 [q]Nu 14:45; [r]Jos 15:31
31 [s]Jos 15:36
32 [t]Nu 34:11; [u]Jos 15:42
39 [v]Jos 15:58
40 [w]Jdg 18:7–10
41 [x]2Ch 20:1; 26:7
42 [y]Ge 14:6
43 [z]Ge 14:7; Est 3:1; 9:16

Ch. 5

1 [a]Ge 29:32; [b]Ge 35:22; 49:4; [c]Ge 48:16; 49:26; [d]Ge 48:5; [e]1Ch 26:10
2 [f]Ge 49:10,12; [g]1Sa 9:16; 12:12; 2Sa 6:21; 1Ch 11:2; 2Ch 7:18; Mt 2:6; [h]Ge 25:31
3 [i]Ge 29:32; 46:9; Ex 6:14; Nu 26:5–11; [j]Nu 26:5; [k]Nu 26:6
6 [l]ver 26; 2Ki 15:19; 16:10; 2Ch 28:20
7 [m]Jos 13:15–23

[g]33 Some Septuagint manuscripts (see also Joshua 19:8); Hebrew *Baal*
[h]41 The Hebrew term refers to the irrevocable giving over of things or persons to the LORD, often by totally destroying them.
[a]6 Hebrew *Tilgath-Pilneser,* a variant of *Tiglath-Pileser;* also in verse 26

Bela son of Azaz, the son of She-
ma, the son of Joel. They settled
in the area from Aroer[n] to Nebo[o]
and Baal Meon.[p] 9To the east they
occupied the land up to the edge
of the desert that extends to the
Euphrates[q] River, because their
livestock had increased in
Gilead.[r]

10During Saul's reign they
waged war against the Hagrites,[s]
who were defeated at their
hands; they occupied the dwell-
ings of the Hagrites throughout
the entire region east of Gilead.

Gad

11The Gadites[t] lived next to them in
Bashan, as far as Salecah:[u]
12Joel was the chief, Shapham the
second, then Janai and Shaphat,
in Bashan.
13Their relatives, by families, were:
Michael, Meshullam, Sheba,
Jorai, Jacan, Zia and Eber—
seven in all.
14These were the sons of Abihail
son of Huri, the son of Jaroah,
the son of Gilead, the son of
Michael, the son of Jeshishai,
the son of Jahdo, the son of Buz.
15Ahi son of Abdiel, the son of
Guni, was head of their family.
16The Gadites lived in Gilead, in
Bashan and its outlying villages,
and on all the pasture-lands of
Sharon as far as they extended.
17All these were entered in the
genealogical records during the reigns
of Jotham[v] king of Judah and Jeroboam[w]
king of Israel.

18The Reubenites, the Gadites and the
half-tribe of Manasseh had 44,760 men
ready for military service[x]—able-bodied
men who could handle shield and
sword, who could use a bow, and who
were trained for battle. 19They waged
war against the Hagrites, Jetur,[y] Naph-
ish and Nodab. 20They were helped[z] in
fighting them, and God handed the
Hagrites and all their allies over to
them, because they cried[a] out to him
during the battle. He answered their
prayers, because they trusted[b] in him.
21They seized the livestock of the Hag-
rites—fifty thousand camels, two hun-
dred and fifty thousand sheep and two
thousand donkeys. They also took one
hundred thousand people captive,
22and many others fell slain, because the
battle[c] was God's. And they occupied
the land until the exile.[d]

8 [n]**Nu 32:34**; Jdg 11:26; [o]**Nu 32:3**; [p]**Jos 13:17**
9 [q]**Ge 2:14**; [r]**Nu 32:26**
10 [s]ver 22; 1Ch 27:31
11 [t]**Ge 30:11**; **Nu 1:25**; **Jos 13:24–28**; [u]**Dt 3:10**
17 [v]**2Ki 15:32**; [w]**2Ki 14:23**
18 [x]**Nu 1:3**
19 [y]Ge 25:15
20 [z]Ps 37:40; 46:5; 54:4; [a]1Ki 8:44; 2Ch 6:34; 13:14; 14:11; Ps 20:7–9; 22:5; 107:6; [b]Ps 26:1; Isa 26:3; Da 6:23
22 [c]**Dt 20:4**; 2Ch 32:8; [d]**ver 10**; **2Ki 15:29**
23 [e]1Ch 7:14; [f]**Dt 3:8–9**; SS 4:8
25 [g]Dt 32:15–18; 1Ch 9:1; 10:13; 2Ch 12:2; 26:16; 28:19; 29:6; 30:7; 36:14; [h]**Ex 34:15**; **Lev 18:3**
26 [i]Isa 37:7; [j]**2Ki 15:19**; [k]**ver 6**; **2Ki 15:29**; [l]2Ki 17:6

Ch. 6

1 [a]**Ge 29:34**; **Nu 3:17**
2 [b]**Ex 6:18**
3 [c]**Ex 15:20**; [d]**Lev 10:1**; [e]Lev 10:6; [f]**Ex 6:23**
4 [g]Ezr 7:5
8 [h]**2Sa 8:17**; **1Ch 12:28**; **Ezr 7:2**
10 [i]**1Ki 4:2**
13 [j]2Ki 22:1–20; 2Ch 34:9; 35:8
14 [k]**2Ki 25:18**; **Ezr 2:2**
15 [l]Ne 12:1; Hag 1:1,14; 2:2,4; Zec 6:11

The Half-Tribe of Manasseh

23The people of the half-tribe of Ma-
nasseh[e] were numerous; they settled in
the land from Bashan to Baal Hermon,
that is, to Senir (Mount Hermon).[f]
24These were the heads of their fam-
ilies: Epher, Ishi, Eliel, Azriel, Jeremiah,
Hodaviah and Jahdiel. They were brave
warriors, famous men, and heads of
their families. 25But they were unfaith-
ful[g] to the God of their fathers and pros-
tituted[h] themselves to the gods of the
peoples of the land, whom God had
destroyed before them. 26So the God of
Israel stirred up the spirit[i] of Pul[j] king of
Assyria (that is, Tiglath-Pileser[k] king of
Assyria), who took the Reubenites, the
Gadites and the half-tribe of Manasseh
into exile. He took them to Halah,[l]
Habor, Hara and the river of Gozan,
where they are to this day.

Levi

6 The sons of Levi:[a]
Gershon, Kohath and Merari.
2The sons of Kohath:
Amram, Izhar, Hebron and
Uzziel.[b]
3The children of Amram:
Aaron, Moses and Miriam.[c]
The sons of Aaron:
Nadab, Abihu,[d] Eleazar[e] and
Ithamar.[f]
4Eleazar was the father of Phine-
has,[g]
Phinehas the father of Abishua,
5Abishua the father of Bukki,
Bukki the father of Uzzi,
6Uzzi the father of Zerahiah,
Zerahiah the father of Meraioth,
7Meraioth the father of Amariah,
Amariah the father of Ahitub,
8Ahitub the father of Zadok,[h]
Zadok the father of Ahimaaz,
9Ahimaaz the father of Azariah,
Azariah the father of Johanan,
10Johanan the father of Azariah[i] (it
was he who served as priest in
the temple Solomon built in Jeru-
salem),
11Azariah the father of Amariah,
Amariah the father of Ahitub,
12Ahitub the father of Zadok,
Zadok the father of Shallum,
13Shallum the father of Hilkiah,[j]
Hilkiah the father of Azariah,
14Azariah the father of Seraiah,[k]
and Seraiah the father of Jehoza-
dak.
15Jehozadak[l] was deported when the
LORD sent Judah and Jerusalem into

exile by the hand of Nebuchadnezzar.

16 The sons of Levi:[m]
Gershon,[a] Kohath and Merari.[n]
17 These are the names of the sons of Gershon:
Libni and Shimei.[o]
18 The sons of Kohath:
Amram, Izhar, Hebron and Uzziel.[p]
19 The sons of Merari:[q]
Mahli and Mushi.[r]
These are the clans of the Levites listed according to their fathers:
20 Of Gershon:
Libni his son, Jehath his son,
Zimmah his son, 21 Joah his son,
Iddo his son, Zerah his son
and Jeatherai his son.
22 The descendants of Kohath:
Amminadab his son, Korah[s] his son,
Assir his son, 23 Elkanah his son,
Ebiasaph his son, Assir his son,
24 Tahath his son, Uriel[t] his son,
Uzziah his son and Shaul his son.
25 The descendants of Elkanah:
Amasai, Ahimoth,
26 Elkanah his son,[b] Zophai his son,
Nahath his son, 27 Eliab his son,
Jeroham his son, Elkanah[u] his son
and Samuel[v] his son.[c]
28 The sons of Samuel:
Joel[d][w] the firstborn
and Abijah the second son.
29 The descendants of Merari:
Mahli, Libni his son,
Shimei his son, Uzzah his son,
30 Shimea his son, Haggiah his son
and Asaiah his son.

The Temple Musicians

6:54–80pp—Jos 21:4–39

31 These are the men[x] David put in charge of the music[y] in the house of the LORD after the ark came to rest there.
32 They ministered with music before the tabernacle, the Tent of Meeting, until Solomon built the temple of the LORD in Jerusalem. They performed their duties according to the regulations laid down for them.
33 Here are the men who served, together with their sons:
From the Kohathites:
Heman,[z] the musician,
the son of Joel,[a] the son of Samuel,
34 the son of Elkanah,[b] the son of Jeroham,
the son of Eliel, the son of Toah,
35 the son of Zuph, the son of Elkanah,
the son of Mahath, the son of Amasai,
36 the son of Elkanah, the son of Joel,
the son of Azariah, the son of Zephaniah,
37 the son of Tahath, the son of Assir,
the son of Ebiasaph, the son of Korah,[c]
38 the son of Izhar,[d] the son of Kohath,
the son of Levi, the son of Israel;
39 and Heman's associate Asaph,[e] who served at his right hand:
Asaph son of Berekiah, the son of Shimea,[f]
40 the son of Michael, the son of Baaseiah,[e]
the son of Malkijah, 41 the son of Ethni,
the son of Zerah, the son of Adaiah,
42 the son of Ethan, the son of Zimmah,
the son of Shimei, 43 the son of Jahath,
the son of Gershon, the son of Levi;
44 and from their associates, the Merarites,[g] at his left hand:
Ethan son of Kishi, the son of Abdi,
the son of Malluch, 45 the son of Hashabiah,
the son of Amaziah, the son of Hilkiah,
46 the son of Amzi, the son of Bani,
the son of Shemer, 47 the son of Mahli,
the son of Mushi, the son of Merari,
the son of Levi.

48 Their fellow Levites[h] were assigned to all the other duties of the tabernacle, the house of God. 49 But Aaron and his

16 [m]Ge 29:34; Nu 3:17–20; [n]Nu 26:57
17 [o]Ex 6:17
18 [p]Ex 6:18
19 [q]Ge 46:11; 1Ch 23:21; 24:26; [r]Ex 6:19
22 [s]Ex 6:24
24 [t]1Ch 15:5
27 [u]1Sa 1:1; [v]1Sa 1:20
28 [w]ver 33; 1Sa 8:2
31 [x]1Ch 25:1; 2Ch 29:25–26; Ne 12:45; [y]1Ch 9:33; 15:19; Ezr 3:10; Ps 68:25
33 [z]1Ki 4:31; 1Ch 15:17; 25:1; [a]ver 28
34 [b]1Sa 1:1
37 [c]Ex 6:24
38 [d]Ex 6:21
39 [e]1Ch 25:1,9; 2Ch 29:13; Ne 11:17; [f]1Ch 15:17
44 [g]1Ch 15:17
48 [h]1Ch 23:32

[a] *16* Hebrew *Gershom*, a variant of *Gershon*; also in verses 17, 20, 43, 62 and 71
[b] *26* Some Hebrew manuscripts, Septuagint and Syriac; most Hebrew manuscripts *Ahimoth* [26]*and Elkanah. The sons of Elkanah:*
[c] *27* Some Septuagint manuscripts (see also 1 Sam. 1:19, 20 and 1 Chron. 6:33, 34); Hebrew does not have *and Samuel his son.*
[d] *28* Some Septuagint manuscripts and Syriac (see also 1 Sam. 8:2 and 1 Chron. 6:33); Hebrew does not have *Joel.*
[e] *40* Most Hebrew manuscripts; some Hebrew manuscripts, one Septuagint manuscript and Syriac *Maaseiah*

descendants were the ones who pre-
sented offerings on the altar[i] of burnt
offering and on the altar of incense[j] in
connection with all that was done in the
Most Holy Place, making atonement for
Israel, in accordance with all that Moses
the servant of God had commanded.

50These were the descendants of
Aaron:
Eleazar his son, Phinehas his
son,
Abishua his son, 51Bukki his son,
Uzzi his son, Zerahiah his son,
52Meraioth his son, Amariah his
son,
Ahitub his son, 53Zadok[k] his son
and Ahimaaz his son.

54These were the locations of their
settlements[l] allotted as their territory
(they were assigned to the descendants
of Aaron who were from the Kohathite
clan, because the first lot was for them):
55They were given Hebron in
Judah with its surrounding
pasture-lands. 56But the fields
and villages around the city were
given to Caleb son of Jephunneh.[m]
57So the descendants of Aaron
were given Hebron (a city of
refuge), and Libnah,[f][n] Jattir,[o] Esh-
temoa, 58Hilen, Debir,[p] 59Ashan,[q]
Juttah[g] and Beth Shemesh,
together with their pasture-lands.
60And from the tribe of Benjamin
they were given Gibeon,[h] Geba,
Alemeth and Anathoth,[r] together
with their pasture-lands.
These towns, which were distri-
buted among the Kohathite clans,
were thirteen in all.
61The rest of Kohath's descendants
were allotted ten towns from the clans
of half the tribe of Manasseh.
62The descendants of Gershon, clan
by clan, were allotted thirteen towns
from the tribes of Issachar, Asher and
Naphtali, and from the part of the tribe
of Manasseh that is in Bashan.
63The descendants of Merari, clan by
clan, were allotted twelve towns from
the tribes of Reuben, Gad and Zebulun.
64So the Israelites gave the Levites
these towns[s] and their pasture-lands.
65From the tribes of Judah, Simeon and
Benjamin they allotted the previously
named towns.
66Some of the Kohathite clans were
given as their territory towns from the
tribe of Ephraim.
67In the hill country of Ephraim
they were given Shechem (a city of
refuge), and Gezer,[i][t] 68Jokmeam,[u]
Beth Horon,[v] 69Aijalon[w] and Gath
Rimmon,[x] together with their
pasture-lands.
70And from half the tribe of Ma-
nasseh the Israelites gave Aner
and Bileam, together with their
pasture-lands, to the rest of the
Kohathite clans.

71The Gershonites[y] received the fol-
lowing:
From the clan of the half-tribe of
Manasseh
they received Golan in Bashan[z]
and also Ashtaroth, together
with their pasture-lands:
72from the tribe of Issachar
they received Kedesh, Dab-
erath,[a] 73Ramoth and Anem,
together with their pasture-
lands;
74from the tribe of Asher
they received Mashal, Abdon,[b]
75Hukok[c] and Rehob,[d] together
with their pasture-lands;
76and from the tribe of Naphtali
they received Kedesh in Galilee,
Hammon[e] and Kiriathaim,[f]
together with their pasture-
lands.

77The Merarites (the rest of the
Levites) received the following:
From the tribe of Zebulun
they received Jokneam, Kartah,[j]
Rimmono and Tabor, together
with their pasture-lands;
78from the tribe of Reuben across the
Jordan east of Jericho
they received Bezer[g] in the des-
ert, Jahzah, 79Kedemoth[h] and
Mephaath, together with their
pasture-lands;
80and from the tribe of Gad
they received Ramoth in Gilead,[i]
Mahanaim,[j] 81Heshbon and
Jazer,[k] together with their
pasture-lands.[l]

Issachar

7 The sons of Issachar:[a]
Tola, Puah,[b] Jashub and Shimron
—four in all.

49 [i]Ex 27:1–8; [j]Ex 30:7; 2Ch 26:18
53 [k]2Sa 8:17
54 [l]Nu 31:10
56 [m]Jos 14:13; 15:13
57 [n]Nu 33:20; [o]Jos 15:48
58 [p]Jos 10:3
59 [q]Jos 15:42
60 [r]Jer 1:1
64 [s]Nu 35:1–8
67 [t]Jos 10:33
68 [u]1Ki 4:12; [v]Jos 10:10
69 [w]Jos 10:12; [x]Jos 19:45
71 [y]1Ch 23:7; [z]Jos 20:8
72 [a]Jos 19:12
74 [b]Jos 19:28
75 [c]Jos 19:34; [d]Nu 13:21
76 [e]Jos 19:28; [f]Nu 32:37
78 [g]Jos 20:8
79 [h]Dt 2:26
80 [i]Jos 20:8; [j]Ge 32:2
81 [k]Nu 21:32; [l]2Ch 11:14

Ch. 7

1 [a]Ge 30:18; [b]Ge 46:13

[f]57 See Joshua 21:13; Hebrew *given the cities of refuge: Hebron, Libnah.*
[g]59 Syriac (see also Septuagint and Joshua 21:16); Hebrew does not have *Juttah.*
[h]60 See Joshua 21:17; Hebrew does not have *Gibeon.*
[i]67 See Joshua 21:21; Hebrew *given the cities of refuge: Shechem, Gezer.*
[j]77 See Septuagint and Joshua 21:34; Hebrew does not have *Jokneam, Kartah.*

2 The sons of Tola:
Uzzi, Rephaiah, Jeriel, Jahmai,
Ibsam and Samuel—heads of
their families. During the reign of
David, the descendants of Tola
listed as fighting men in their
genealogy numbered 22,600.
3 The son of Uzzi:
Izrahiah.
The sons of Izrahiah:
Michael, Obadiah, Joel and
Isshiah. All five of them were
chiefs. 4 According to their family
genealogy, they had 36,000 men
ready for battle, for they had
many wives and children.
5 The relatives who were fighting
men belonging to all the clans of
Issachar, as listed in their geneal-
ogy, were 87,000 in all.

Benjamin

6 Three sons of Benjamin:[c]
Bela, Beker and Jediael.
7 The sons of Bela:
Ezbon, Uzzi, Uzziel, Jerimoth
and Iri, heads of families—five in
all. Their genealogical record
listed 22,034 fighting men.
8 The sons of Beker:
Zemirah, Joash, Eliezer, Elio-
enai, Omri, Jeremoth, Abijah,
Anathoth and Alemeth. All
these were the sons of Beker.
9 Their genealogical record listed
the heads of families and 20,200
fighting men.
10 The son of Jediael:
Bilhan.
The sons of Bilhan:
Jeush, Benjamin, Ehud,
Kenaanah, Zethan, Tarshish and
Ahishahar. 11 All these sons of
Jediael were heads of families.
There were 17,200 fighting men
ready to go out to war.
12 The Shuppites and Huppites were
the descendants of Ir, and the
Hushites the descendants of
Aher.

Naphtali

13 The sons of Naphtali:[d]
Jahziel, Guni, Jezer and Shil-
lem[a]—the descendants of
Bilhah.

Manasseh

14 The descendants of Manasseh:[e]
Asriel was his descendant
through his Aramean concubine.

6 [c]Nu 26:38
13 [d]Ge 30:8
14 [e]Ge 41:51; Jos 17:1; 1Ch 5:23; [f]Nu 26:30
15 [g]Nu 26:33; 36:1-12
17 [h]Nu 26:30
18 [i]Jos 17:2
19 [j]Jos 17:2
20 [k]Ge 41:52; Nu 1:33
24 [l]Jos 10:10
28 [m]Jos 10:33

She gave birth to Makir the father of
Gilead.[f] 15 Makir took a wife from
among the Huppites and Shup-
pites. His sister's name was
Maacah.
Another descendant was named
Zelophehad,[g] who had only
daughters.
16 Makir's wife Maacah gave birth
to a son and named him Peresh.
His brother was named Sheresh,
and his sons were Ulam and
Rakem.
17 The son of Ulam:
Bedan.
These were the sons of Gilead[h] son
of Makir, the son of Manasseh.
18 His sister Hammoleketh gave
birth to Ishhod, Abiezer[i] and
Mahlah.
19 The sons of Shemida[j] were:
Ahian, Shechem, Likhi and
Aniam.

Ephraim

20 The descendants of Ephraim:[k]
Shuthelah, Bered his son,
Tahath his son, Eleadah his son,
Tahath his son, 21 Zabad his son
and Shuthelah his son.
Ezer and Elead were killed by the
native-born men of Gath, when
they went down to seize their live-
stock. 22 Their father Ephraim
mourned for them many days, and
his relatives came to comfort him.
23 Then he lay with his wife again,
and she became pregnant and gave
birth to a son. He named him
Beriah,[b] because there had been
misfortune in his family. 24 His
daughter was Sheerah, who built
Lower and Upper Beth Horon[l] as
well as Uzzen Sheerah.
25 Rephah was his son, Resheph his
son,[c]
Telah his son, Tahan his son,
26 Ladan his son, Ammihud his
son,
Elishama his son, 27 Nun his son
and Joshua his son.
28 Their lands and settlements in-
cluded Bethel and its surrounding vil-
lages, Naaran to the east, Gezer[m] and its
villages to the west, and Shechem and

[a] 13 Some Hebrew and Septuagint manuscripts (see also Gen. 46:24 and Num. 26:49); most Hebrew manuscripts *Shallum*
[b] 23 *Beriah* sounds like the Hebrew for *misfortune*.
[c] 25 Some Septuagint manuscripts; Hebrew does not have *his son*.

its villages all the way to Ayyah and its
villages. 29Along the borders of Manasseh
were Beth Shan,[n] Taanach,
Megiddo and Dor,[o] together with their
villages. The descendants of Joseph son
of Israel lived in these towns.

Asher

30The sons of Asher:[p]
Imnah, Ishvah, Ishvi and Beriah.
Their sister was Serah.
31The sons of Beriah:
Heber and Malkiel, who was the
father of Birzaith.
32Heber was the father of Japhlet,
Shomer and Hotham and of their
sister Shua.
33The sons of Japhlet:
Pasach, Bimhal and Ashvath.
These were Japhlet's sons.
34The sons of Shomer:
Ahi, Rohgah,[d] Hubbah and
Aram.
35The sons of his brother Helem:
Zophah, Imna, Shelesh and
Amal.
36The sons of Zophah:
Suah, Harnepher, Shual, Beri,
Imrah, 37Bezer, Hod, Shamma,
Shilshah, Ithran[e] and Beera.
38The sons of Jether:
Jephunneh, Pispah and Ara.
39The sons of Ulla:
Arah, Hanniel and Rizia.
40All these were descendants of
Asher—heads of families, choice men,
brave warriors and outstanding leaders.
The number of men ready for battle, as
listed in their genealogy, was 26,000.

The Genealogy of Saul the Benjamite

8:28–38pp—1Ch 9:34–44

8 Benjamin[a] was the father of Bela his
firstborn,
Ashbel the second son, Aharah
the third,
2Nohah the fourth and Rapha the
fifth.
3The sons of Bela were:
Addar,[b] Gera, Abihud,[a]
4Abishua, Naaman, Ahoah,[c]
5Gera, Shephuphan and Huram.
6These were the descendants of
Ehud,[d] who were heads of families
of those living in Geba and
were deported to Manahath:
7Naaman, Ahijah and Gera, who
deported them and who was the
father of Uzza and Ahihud.
8Sons were born to Shaharaim in
Moab after he had divorced his
wives Hushim and Baara. 9By his
wife Hodesh he had Jobab, Zibia,
Mesha, Malcam, 10Jeuz, Sakia
and Mirmah. These were his
sons, heads of families. 11By
Hushim he had Abitub and
Elpaal.
12The sons of Elpaal:
Eber, Misham, Shemed (who
built Ono[e] and Lod with its surrounding
villages), 13and Beriah
and Shema, who were heads of
families of those living in Aijalon[f]
and who drove out the inhabitants
of Gath.[g]
14Ahio, Shashak, Jeremoth, 15Zebadiah,
Arad, Eder, 16Michael,
Ishpah and Joha were the sons
of Beriah.
17Zebadiah, Meshullam, Hizki, Heber,
18Ishmerai, Izliah and Jobab
were the sons of Elpaal.
19Jakim, Zicri, Zabdi, 20Elienai, Zillethai,
Eliel, 21Adaiah, Beraiah
and Shimrath were the sons of
Shimei.
22Ishpan, Eber, Eliel, 23Abdon, Zicri,
Hanan, 24Hananiah, Elam,
Anthothijah, 25Iphdeiah and
Penuel were the sons of Shashak.
26Shamsherai, Shehariah, Athaliah,
27Jaareshiah, Elijah and Zicri
were the sons of Jeroham.
28All these were heads of families,
chiefs as listed in their genealogy, and
they lived in Jerusalem.

29Jeiel[b] the father[c] of Gibeon lived in
Gibeon.[h]
His wife's name was Maacah,
30and his firstborn son was
Abdon, followed by Zur, Kish,
Baal, Ner,[d] Nadab, 31Gedor,
Ahio, Zeker 32and Mikloth, who
was the father of Shimeah. They
too lived near their relatives in
Jerusalem.
33Ner[i] was the father of Kish,[j] Kish
the father of Saul[k], and Saul the
father of Jonathan, Malki-Shua,
Abinadab and Esh-Baal.[e][l]
34The son of Jonathan:[m]
Merib-Baal,[f][n] who was the father
of Micah.

29 [n]Jos 17:11; [o]Jos 11:2
30 [p]Nu 1:40

Ch. 8

1 [a]Ge 46:21
3 [b]Ge 46:21
4 [c]2Sa 23:9
6 [d]Jdg 3:12–30
12 [e]Ezr 2:33; Ne 6:2; 7:37; 11:35
13 [f]Jos 10:12; [g]Jos 11:22
29 [h]Jos 9:3
33 [i]1Sa 28:19; [j]1Sa 9:1; [k]1Sa 14:49; [l]2Sa 2:8
34 [m]2Sa 9:12; [n]2Sa 4:4; 21:7–14

d34 Or *of his brother Shomer: Rohgah*
e37 Possibly a variant of *Jether*
a3 Or *Gera the father of Ehud*
b29 Some Septuagint manuscripts (see also 1 Chron. 9:35); Hebrew does not have *Jeiel*.
c29 *Father* may mean *civic leader* or *military leader*.
d30 Some Septuagint manuscripts (see also 1 Chron. 9:36); Hebrew does not have *Ner*.
e33 Also known as *Ish-Bosheth*
f34 Also known as *Mephibosheth*

35The sons of Micah:
Pithon, Melech, Tarea and Ahaz.
36Ahaz was the father of Jehoaddah, Jehoaddah was the father of Alemeth, Azmaveth and Zimri, and Zimri was the father of Moza.
37Moza was the father of Binea; Raphah was his son, Eleasah his son and Azel his son.
38Azel had six sons, and these were their names:
Azrikam, Bokeru, Ishmael, Sheariah, Obadiah and Hanan. All these were the sons of Azel.
39The sons of his brother Eshek:
Ulam his firstborn, Jeush the second son and Eliphelet the
third. 40The sons of Ulam were brave warriors who could handle the bow. They had many sons and grandsons—150 in all.
All these were descendants of Benjamin.[o]

9

All Israel[a] was listed in the genealogies in the book of the kings of Israel.

The People in Jerusalem

9:1–17pp—Ne 11:3–19

The people of Judah were taken captive to Babylon[b] because of their unfaithfulness.[c]
2Now the first to resettle on their own property in their own towns[d] were some Israelites, priests, Levites and temple servants.[e]
3Those from Judah, from Benjamin, and from Ephraim and Manasseh who lived in Jerusalem were:
4Uthai son of Ammihud, the son of Omri, the son of Imri, the son of Bani, a descendant of Perez son of Judah.[f]
5Of the Shilonites:
Asaiah the firstborn and his sons.
6Of the Zerahites:
Jeuel.
The people from Judah numbered 690.
7Of the Benjamites:
Sallu son of Meshullam, the son of Hodaviah, the son of Hassenuah;
8Ibneiah son of Jeroham; Elah son of Uzzi, the son of Micri; and Meshullam son of Shephatiah, the son of Reuel, the son of Ibnijah.
9The people from Benjamin, as listed in their genealogy, numbered 956. All these men were heads of their families.

10Of the priests:
Jedaiah; Jehoiarib; Jakin;
11Azariah son of Hilkiah, the son of Meshullam, the son of Zadok, the son of Meraioth, the son of Ahitub, the official in charge of the house of God;
12Adaiah son of Jeroham, the son of Pashhur,[g] the son of Malkijah; and Maasai son of Adiel, the son of Jahzerah, the son of Meshullam, the son of Meshillemith, the son of Immer.
13The priests, who were heads of families, numbered 1,760. They were able men, responsible for ministering in the house of God.
14Of the Levites:
Shemaiah son of Hasshub, the son of Azrikam, the son of
Hashabiah, a Merarite; 15Bakbakkar, Heresh, Galal and Mattaniah[h] son of Mica, the son of Zicri, the son of Asaph;
16Obadiah son of Shemaiah, the son of Galal, the son of Jeduthun; and Berekiah son of Asa, the son of Elkanah, who lived in the villages of the Netophathites.[i]
17The gatekeepers:[j]
Shallum, Akkub, Talmon, Ahiman and their brothers, Shallum
their chief 18being stationed at the King's Gate[k] on the east, up to the present time. These were the gatekeepers belonging to the
camp of the Levites. 19Shallum[l] son of Kore, the son of Ebiasaph, the son of Korah, and his fellow gatekeepers from his family (the Korahites) were responsible for guarding the thresholds of the Tent[a] just as their fathers had been responsible for guarding the entrance to the dwelling of
the LORD. 20In earlier times Phinehas[m] son of Eleazar was in charge of the gatekeepers, and the LORD was with him.
21Zechariah[n] son of Meshelemiah was the gatekeeper at the entrance to the Tent of Meeting.
22Altogether, those chosen to be gatekeepers[o] at the thresholds numbered 212. They were registered by genealogy in their villages. The gatekeepers had been assigned to their positions of trust by David and Samuel
the seer.[p] 23They and their descendants were in charge of guarding the gates of the house of the LORD—the house called

40 [o]**Nu 26:38**
Ch. 9
1 [a]1Ch 11:1,10; 12:38; 14:8; 15:3,28; 18:14; 19:17; 21:5; 28:4,8; 29:21,23; 2Ch 1:2; 5:3; 7:8; 10:3,16; 12:1; 13:4,15; 18:16; 24:5; 28:23; 29:24; 30:1; [b]**Dt 21:10**; [c]**1Ch 5:25**
2 [d]Jos 9:27; Ezr 2:70; [e]Ezr 2:43,58; 8:20; Ne 7:60
4 [f]**Ge 38:29**; 46:12
12 [g]Ezr 2:38; 10:22; Ne 10:3; Jer 21:1; 38:1
15 [h]2Ch 20:14; Ne 11:22
16 [i]Ne 12:28
17 [j]ver 22; 1Ch 26:1; 2Ch 8:14; 31:14; Ezr 2:42; Ne 7:45
18 [k]1Ch 26:14; Eze 43:1; 46:1
19 [l]Jer 35:4
20 [m]Nu 25:11
21 [n]1Ch 26:2,14
22 [o]**ver 17**; [p]**1Sa 9:9**

[a]*19* That is, the temple; also in verses 21 and 23

the Tent. 24The gatekeepers were on the
four sides: east, west, north and south.
25Their brothers in their villages had to
come from time to time and share their
duties for seven-day[q] periods. 26But the
four principal gatekeepers, who were
Levites, were entrusted with the re-
sponsibility for the rooms and treasur-
ies[r] in the house of God. 27They would
spend the night stationed round the
house of God,[s] because they had to
guard it; and they had charge of the key[t]
for opening it each morning.

28Some of them were in charge of the
articles used in the temple service; they
counted them when they were brought
in and when they were taken out.
29Others were assigned to take care of
the furnishings and all the other articles
of the sanctuary,[u] as well as the flour
and wine, and the oil, incense and
spices. 30But some[v] of the priests took
care of mixing the spices. 31A Levite
named Mattithiah, the firstborn son of
Shallum the Korahite, was entrusted
with the responsibility for baking the
offering bread. 32Some of their
Kohathite brothers were in charge of
preparing for every Sabbath the bread
set out on the table.[w]

33Those who were musicians,[x] heads
of Levite families, stayed in the rooms of
the temple and were exempt from other
duties because they were responsible
for the work day and night.[y]

34All these were heads of Levite fam-
ilies, chiefs as listed in their genealogy,
and they lived in Jerusalem.

The Genealogy of Saul

9:34–44pp—1Ch 8:28–38

35Jeiel[z] the father[b] of Gibeon lived in
Gibeon.
His wife's name was Maacah,
36and his firstborn son was
Abdon, followed by Zur, Kish,
Baal, Ner, Nadab, 37Gedor,
Ahio, Zechariah and Mikloth.
38Mikloth was the father of
Shimeam. They too lived near
their relatives in Jerusalem.
39Ner[a] was the father of Kish,[b] Kish
the father of Saul, and Saul the
father of Jonathan,[c] Malki-Shua,
Abinadab and Esh-Baal.[c][d]
40The son of Jonathan:
Merib-Baal,[d][e] who was the father
of Micah.
41The sons of Micah:
Pithon, Melech, Tahrea and
Ahaz.[e]
42Ahaz was the father of Jadah,
Jadah[f] was the father of
Alemeth, Azmaveth and Zimri,
and Zimri was the father of
Moza. 43Moza was the father of
Binea; Rephaiah was his son,
Eleasah his son and Azel his son.
44Azel had six sons, and these were
their names:
Azrikam, Bokeru, Ishmael,
Sheariah, Obadiah and Hanan.
These were the sons of Azel.

Saul Takes His Life

10:1–12pp—1Sa 31:1–13; 2Sa 1:4–12

10 Now the Philistines fought
against Israel; the Israelites fled
before them, and many fell slain on
Mount Gilboa. 2The Philistines pressed
hard after Saul and his sons, and they
killed his sons Jonathan, Abinadab and
Malki-Shua. 3The fighting grew fierce
around Saul, and when the archers
overtook him, they wounded him.

4Saul said to his armour-bearer,
"Draw your sword and run me
through, or these uncircumcised
fellows will come and abuse me."

But his armour-bearer was terrified
and would not do it; so Saul took his
own sword and fell on it. 5When the
armour-bearer saw that Saul was dead,
he too fell on his sword and died. 6So
Saul and his three sons died, and all his
house died together.

7When all the Israelites in the valley
saw that the army had fled and that Saul
and his sons had died, they abandoned
their towns and fled. And the Philis-
tines came and occupied them.

8The next day, when the Philistines
came to strip the dead, they found Saul
and his sons fallen on Mount Gilboa.
9They stripped him and took his head
and his armour, and sent messengers
throughout the land of the Philistines to
proclaim the news among their idols
and their people. 10They put his armour
in the temple of their gods and hung up
his head in the temple of Dagon.[a]

11When all the inhabitants of Jabesh
Gilead[b] heard of everything the Philis-
tines had done to Saul, 12all their valiant
men went and took the bodies of Saul
and his sons and brought them to

25 [q]2Ki 11:5
26 [r]1Ch 26:22
27 [s]**Nu 3:38**; [t]Isa 22:22
29 [u]**Nu 3:28**; 1Ch 23:29
30 [v]**Ex 30:25**
32 [w]Lev 24:5–8; 1Ch 23:29; 2Ch 13:11
33 [x]**1Ch 6:31**; 25:1–31; **2Ch 5:12**; [y]Ps 134:1
35 [z]1Ch 8:29
39 [a]**1Ch 8:33**; [b]**1Sa 9:1**; [c]1Sa 13:22; [d]**2Sa 2:8**
40 [e]**2Sa 4:4**

Ch. 10

10 [a]**Jdg 16:23**
11 [b]**Jdg 21:8**

b35 *Father* may mean *civic leader* or *military leader*.
c39 Also known as *Ish-Bosheth*
d40 Also known as *Mephibosheth*
e41 Vulgate and Syriac (see also Septuagint and 1 Chron. 8:35); Hebrew does not have *and Ahaz*.
f42 Some Hebrew manuscripts and Septuagint (see also 1 Chron. 8:36); most Hebrew manuscripts *Jarah, Jarah*

Jabesh. Then they buried their bones
under the great tree in Jabesh, and they
fasted seven days.
13Saul died[c] because he was unfaith-
ful[d] to the LORD; he did not keep[e] the
word of the LORD, and even consulted a
medium[f] for guidance, 14and did not
enquire of the LORD. So the LORD put
him to death and turned[g] the kingdom[h]
over to David son of Jesse.

David Becomes King Over Israel

11:1–3pp—2Sa 5:1–3

11 All Israel[a] came together to
David at Hebron[b] and said, "We
are your own flesh and blood. 2In the
past, even while Saul was king, you
were the one who led Israel on their
military campaigns.[c] And the LORD your
God said to you, 'You will shepherd[d]
my people Israel, and you will become
their ruler.[e]' "
3When all the elders of Israel had
come to King David at Hebron, he made
a compact with them at Hebron before
the LORD, and they anointed[f] David king
over Israel, as the LORD had promised
through Samuel.

David Conquers Jerusalem

11:4–9pp—2Sa 4:6–10

4David and all the Israelites marched
to Jerusalem, that is, Jebus. The Jebu-
sites[g] who lived there 5said to David,
"You will not get in here." Neverthe-
less, David captured the fortress of
Zion, the City of David.
6David had said, "Whoever leads the
attack on the Jebusites will become com-
mander-in-chief." Joab[h] son of Zeruiah
went up first, and so he received the
command.
7David then took up residence in the
fortress, and so it was called the City of
David. 8He built up the city around it,
from the supporting terraces[a][i] to the
surrounding wall, while Joab restored
the rest of the city. 9And David became
more and more powerful,[j] because the
LORD Almighty was with him.

David's Mighty Men

11:10–41pp—2Sa 23:8–39

10These were the chiefs of David's
mighty men—they, together with all
Israel,[k] gave his kingship strong sup-
port to extend it over the whole land, as
the LORD had promised[l]—11this is the
list of David's mighty men:[m]
Jashobeam,[b] a Hacmonite, was chief
of the officers;[c] he raised his spear
against three hundred men, whom he
killed in one encounter.
12Next to him was Eleazar son of
Dodai the Ahohite, one of the three
mighty men. 13He was with David at Pas
Dammim when the Philistines gathered
there for battle. At a place where there
was a field full of barley, the troops fled
from the Philistines. 14But they took
their stand in the middle of the field.
They defended it and struck the Philis-
tines down, and the LORD brought
about a great victory.[n]
15Three of the thirty chiefs came down
to David to the rock at the cave of Adul-
lam, while a band of Philistines was
encamped in the Valley[o] of Rephaim.
16At that time David was in the strong-
hold,[p] and the Philistine garrison was at
Bethlehem. 17David longed for water
and said, "Oh, that someone would get
me a drink of water from the well near
the gate of Bethlehem!" 18So the Three
broke through the Philistine lines, drew
water from the well near the gate of
Bethlehem and carried it back to David.
But he refused to drink it; instead, he
poured[q] it out before the LORD. 19"God
forbid that I should do this!" he said.
"Should I drink the blood of these men
who went at the risk of their lives?"
Because they risked their lives to bring it
back, David would not drink it.
Such were the exploits of the three
mighty men.
20Abishai[r] the brother of Joab was
chief of the Three. He raised his spear
against three hundred men, whom he
killed, and so he became as famous as
the Three. 21He was doubly honoured
above the Three and became their com-
mander, even though he was not in-
cluded among them.
22Benaiah son of Jehoiada was a
valiant fighter from Kabzeel,[s] who per-
formed great exploits. He struck down
two of Moab's best men. He also went
down into a pit on a snowy day and
killed a lion.[t] 23And he struck down an
Egyptian who was seven and a half feet[d]
tall. Although the Egyptian had a spear
like a weaver's rod[u] in his hand, Be-
naiah went against him with a club. He
snatched the spear from the Egyptian's
hand and killed him with his own spear.
24Such were the exploits of Benaiah son

13 [c]2Sa 1:1; [d]1Ch 5:25; [e]1Sa 13:13; [f]Lev 19:31; 20:6; Dt 18:9–14
14 [g]1Ch 12:23; [h]1Sa 13:14

Ch. 11

1 [a]1Ch 9:1; [b]Ge 13:18; 23:19
2 [c]1Sa 18:5,16; [d]Ps 78:71; Mt 2:6; [e]1Ch 5:2
3 [f]1Sa 16:1–13
4 [g]Ge 10:16; 15:18–21; Jos 3:10; 15:8
6 [h]2Sa 2:13
8 [i]2Sa 5:9; 2Ch 32:5
9 [j]Est 9:4
10 [k]ver 1; [l]1Ch 12:23
11 [m]2Sa 17:10
14 [n]Ex 14:30; 1Sa 11:13
15 [o]1Ch 14:9; Isa 17:5
16 [p]2Sa 5:17
18 [q]Dt 12:16
20 [r]1Sa 26:6
22 [s]Jos 15:21; [t]1Sa 17:36
23 [u]1Sa 17:7

[a]8 Or *the Millo*
[b]11 Possibly a variant of *Jashob-Baal*
[c]11 Or *Thirty*; some Septuagint manuscripts *Three* (see also 2 Sam. 23:8)
[d]23 Hebrew *five cubits* (about 2.3 metres)

of Jehoiada; he too was as famous as the
three mighty men. 25He was held in
greater honour than any of the Thirty,
but he was not included among the
Three. And David put him in charge of
his bodyguard.

26The mighty men were:
Asahel[v] the brother of Joab,
Elhanan son of Dodo from Bethlehem,
27Shammoth[w] the Harorite,
Helez the Pelonite,
28Ira son of Ikkesh from Tekoa,
Abiezer[x] from Anathoth,
29Sibbecai[y] the Hushathite,
Ilai the Ahohite,
30Maharai the Netophathite,
Heled son of Baanah the Netophathite,
31Ithai son of Ribai from Gibeah in Benjamin,
Benaiah[z] the Pirathonite,[a]
32Hurai from the ravines of Gaash,
Abiel the Arbathite,
33Azmaveth the Baharumite,
Eliahba the Shaalbonite,
34the sons of Hashem the Gizonite,
Jonathan son of Shagee the Hararite,
35Ahiam son of Sacar the Hararite,
Eliphal son of Ur,
36Hepher the Mekerathite,
Ahijah the Pelonite,
37Hezro the Carmelite,
Naarai son of Ezbai,
38Joel the brother of Nathan,
Mibhar son of Hagri,
39Zelek the Ammonite,
Naharai the Berothite, the armour-bearer of Joab son of Zeruiah,
40Ira the Ithrite,
Gareb the Ithrite,
41Uriah[b] the Hittite,
Zabad[c] son of Ahlai,
42Adina son of Shiza the Reubenite, who was chief of the Reubenites, and the thirty with him,
43Hanan son of Maacah,
Joshaphat the Mithnite,
44Uzzia the Ashterathite,[d]
Shama and Jeiel the sons of Hotham the Aroerite,
45Jediael son of Shimri,
his brother Joha the Tizite,
46Eliel the Mahavite,
Jeribai and Joshaviah the sons of Elnaam,
Ithmah the Moabite,
47Eliel, Obed and Jaasiel the Mezobaite.

26 [v]2Sa 2:18
27 [w]1Ch 27:8
28 [x]1Ch 27:12
29 [y]2Sa 21:18
31 [z]1Ch 27:14; [a]Jdg 12:13
41 [b]2Sa 11:6; [c]1Ch 2:36
44 [d]Dt 1:4

Ch. 12

1 [a]Jos 15:31
2 [b]Jdg 3:15; [c]2Sa 3:19
4 [d]Jos 15:36
7 [e]Jos 15:58
8 [f]Ge 30:11; [g]2Sa 17:10; [h]2Sa 2:18
14 [i]Lev 26:8; [j]Dt 32:30
15 [k]Jos 3:15
16 [l]2Sa 3:19

Warriors Join David

12 These were the men who came
to David at Ziklag,[a] while he
was banished from the presence of Saul
son of Kish (they were among the warriors who helped him in battle; 2they
were armed with bows and were able to
shoot arrows or to sling stones right-handed or left-handed;[b] they were
kinsmen of Saul[c] from the tribe of
Benjamin):

3Ahiezer their chief and Joash the sons of Shemaah the Gibeathite; Jeziel and Pelet the sons of Azmaveth; Beracah, Jehu the Anathothite,
4and Ishmaiah the Gibeonite, a mighty man among the Thirty, who was a leader of the Thirty; Jeremiah, Jahaziel, Johanan, Jozabad the Gederathite,[d]
5Eluzai, Jerimoth, Bealiah, Shemariah and Shephatiah the Haruphite;
6Elkanah, Isshiah, Azarel, Joezer and Jashobeam the Korahites;
7and Joelah and Zebadiah the sons of Jeroham from Gedor.[e]

8Some Gadites[f] defected to David at
his stronghold in the desert. They were
brave warriors, ready for battle and able
to handle the shield and spear. Their
faces were the faces of lions,[g] and they
were as swift as gazelles[h] in the mountains.

9Ezer was the chief,
Obadiah the second in command,
Eliab the third,
10Mishmannah the fourth, Jeremiah the fifth,
11Attai the sixth, Eliel the seventh,
12Johanan the eighth, Elzabad the ninth,
13Jeremiah the tenth and Macbannai the eleventh.

14These Gadites were army commanders; the least was a match for a
hundred,[i] and the greatest for a
thousand.[j] 15It was they who crossed
the Jordan in the first month when
it was overflowing all its banks,[k] and
they put to flight everyone living in
the valleys, to the east and to the west.

16Other Benjamites[l] and some men
from Judah also came to David in his
stronghold. 17David went out to meet
them and said to them, "If you have
come to me in peace, to help me, I am
ready to have you unite with me. But
if you have come to betray me to my
enemies when my hands are free from
violence, may the God of our fathers
see it and judge you."

18Then the Spirit[m] came upon Ama-
sai,[n] chief of the Thirty, and he said:

"We are yours, O David!
We are with you, O son of Jesse!
Success,[o] success to you,
and success to those who help you,
for your God will help you."

So David received them and made
them leaders of his raiding bands.
19Some of the men of Manasseh de-
fected to David when he went with the
Philistines to fight against Saul. (He and
his men did not help the Philistines
because, after consultation, their rulers
sent him away. They said, "It will cost
us our heads if he deserts to his master
Saul.")[p] 20When David went to Ziklag,[q]
these were the men of Manasseh who
defected to him: Adnah, Jozabad,
Jediael, Michael, Jozabad, Elihu and Zil-
lethai, leaders of units of a thousand in
Manasseh. 21They helped David against
raiding bands, for all of them were
brave warriors, and they were comman-
ders in his army. 22Day after day men
came to help David, until he had a great
army, like the army of God.[a]

Others Join David at Hebron

23These are the numbers of the men
armed for battle who came to David at
Hebron[r] to turn[s] Saul's kingdom over to
him, as the LORD had said:[t]
24men of Judah, carrying shield and
spear—6,800 armed for battle;
25men of Simeon, warriors ready for
battle—7,100;
26men of Levi—4,600, 27including
Jehoiada, leader of the family of
Aaron with 3,700 men, 28and
Zadok,[u] a brave young warrior,
with 22 officers from his family;
29men of Benjamin,[v] Saul's kinsmen
—3,000, most[w] of whom had
remained loyal to Saul's house
until then;
30men of Ephraim, brave warriors,
famous in their own clans—
20,800;
31men of half the tribe of Manasseh,
designated by name to come and
make David king—18,000;
32men of Issachar, who understood
the times and knew what Israel
should do[x]—200 chiefs, with all
their relatives under their com-
mand;
33men of Zebulun, experienced sol-
diers prepared for battle with
every type of weapon, to help

18 [m]**Jdg 3:10;** 1Ch 28:12; 2Ch 15:1; 20:14; 24:20; [n]**2Sa 17:25;** [o]1Sa 25:5-6
19 [p]1Sa 29:2-11
20 [q]**1Sa 27:6**
23 [r]2Sa 2:3-4; [s]1Ch 10:14; [t]**1Sa 16:1;** 1Ch 11:10
28 [u]1Ch 6:8; 15:11; 16:39; 27:17
29 [v]**2Sa 3:19;** [w]2Sa 2:8-9
32 [x]Est 1:13
38 [y]**1Ch 9:1**
39 [z]2Sa 3:20; Isa 25:6-8
40 [a]**2Sa 16:1;** 17:29; [b]1Sa 25:18; [c]1Ch 29:22

Ch. 13

3 [a]1Sa 7:1-2; [b]2Ch 1:5
5 [c]1Ch 11:1; 15:3; [d]**Jos 13:3;** [e]**Nu 13:21;** [f]**1Sa 7:2**
6 [g]**Jos 15:9**

David with undivided loyalty—
50,000;
34men of Naphtali—1,000 officers,
together with 37,000 men carry-
ing shields and spears;
35men of Dan, ready for battle—
28,600;
36men of Asher, experienced soldiers
prepared for battle—40,000;
37and from east of the Jordan, men of
Reuben, Gad, and the half-tribe
of Manasseh, armed with every
type of weapon—120,000.
38All these were fighting men who
volunteered to serve in the ranks. They
came to Hebron fully determined to
make David king over all Israel.[y] All the
rest of the Israelites were also of one
mind to make David king. 39The men
spent three days there with David, eat-
ing and drinking,[z] for their families had
supplied provisions for them. 40Also,
their neighbours from as far away as
Issachar, Zebulun and Naphtali came
bringing food on donkeys, camels,
mules and oxen. There were plentiful
supplies[a] of flour, fig cakes, raisin[b]
cakes, wine, oil, cattle and sheep, for
there was joy[c] in Israel.

Bringing Back the Ark
13:1-14pp—2Sa 6:1-11

13 David conferred with each of
his officers, the commanders of
thousands and commanders of hun-
dreds. 2He then said to the whole
assembly of Israel, "If it seems good to
you and if it is the will of the LORD our
God, let us send word far and wide to
the rest of our brothers throughout the
territories of Israel, and also to the
priests and Levites who are with them
in their towns and pasture-lands, to
come and join us. 3Let us bring the ark
of our God back to us,[a] for we did not
enquire[b] of[a] it[b] during the reign of
Saul." 4The whole assembly agreed to
do this, because it seemed right to all the
people.
5So David assembled all the
Israelites,[c] from the Shihor River[d] in
Egypt to Lebo[c] Hamath,[e] to bring the ark
of God from Kiriath Jearim.[f] 6David and
all the Israelites with him went to
Baalah[g] of Judah (Kiriath Jearim) to
bring up from there the ark of God the
LORD, who is enthroned between the

[a]22 Or *a great and mighty army.*
[a]3 Or *we neglected* [b]3 Or *him*
[c]5 Or *to the entrance to*

cherubim[h]—the ark that is called by the
Name.
7They moved the ark of God from
Abinadab's[i] house on a new cart, with
Uzzah and Ahio guiding it. 8David and
all the Israelites were celebrating with
all their might before God, with songs
and with harps, lyres, tambourines,
cymbals and trumpets.[j]
9When they came to the threshing-
floor of Kidon, Uzzah reached out his
hand to steady the ark, because the
oxen stumbled. 10The LORD's anger[k]
burned against Uzzah, and he struck
him down[l] because he had put his hand
on the ark. So he died there before God.
11Then David was angry because the
LORD's wrath had broken out against
Uzzah, and to this day that place is
called Perez Uzzah.[d][m]
12David was afraid of God that day
and asked, "How can I ever bring the
ark of God to me?" 13He did not take the
ark to be with him in the City of David.
Instead, he took it aside to the house of
Obed-Edom[n] the Gittite. 14The ark of
God remained with the family of Obed-
Edom in his house for three months,
and the LORD blessed his household[o]
and everything he had.

David's House and Family

14:1–7pp—2Sa 5:11–16; 1Ch 3:5–8

14 Now Hiram king of Tyre sent
messengers to David, along
with cedar logs,[a] stonemasons and
carpenters to build a palace for him.
2And David knew that the LORD had
established him as king over Israel and
that his kingdom had been highly ex-
alted[b] for the sake of his people Israel.
3In Jerusalem David took more wives
and became the father of more sons[c] and
daughters. 4These are the names of the
children born to him there:[d] Shammua,
Shobab, Nathan, Solomon, 5Ibhar,
Elishua, Elpelet, 6Nogah, Nepheg,
Japhia, 7Elishama, Beeliada[a] and
Eliphelet.

David Defeats the Philistines

14:8–17pp—2Sa 5:17–25

8When the Philistines heard that
David had been anointed king over all
Israel,[e] they went up in full force to
search for him, but David heard about it
and went out to meet them. 9Now the
Philistines had come and raided the Val-
ley[f] of Rephaim; 10so David enquired of
God: "Shall I go and attack the Philis-
tines? Will you hand them over to me?"
The LORD answered him, "Go, I will
hand them over to you."
11So David and his men went up to
Baal Perazim,[g] and there he defeated
them. He said, "As waters break out,
God has broken out against my enemies
by my hand." So that place was called
Baal Perazim.[b] 12The Philistines had
abandoned their gods there, and David
gave orders to burn[h] them in the fire.[i]
13Once more the Philistines raided the
valley;[j] 14so David enquired of God
again, and God answered him, "Do not
go straight up, but circle round them
and attack them in front of the balsam
trees. 15As soon as you hear the sound
of marching in the tops of the balsam
trees, move out to battle, because that
will mean God has gone out in front of
you to strike the Philistine army." 16So
David did as God commanded him, and
they struck down the Philistine army,
all the way from Gibeon[k] to Gezer.[l]
17So David's fame[m] spread through-
out every land, and the LORD made all
the nations fear[n] him.

The Ark Brought to Jerusalem

15:25–16:3pp—2Sa 6:12–19

15 After David had constructed
buildings for himself in the City
of David, he prepared[a] a place for the
ark of God and pitched[b] a tent for it.
2Then David said, "No-one but the
Levites[c] may carry[d] the ark of God, be-
cause the LORD chose them to carry the
ark of the LORD and to minister[e] before
him for ever."
3David assembled all Israel[f] in Jeru-
salem to bring up the ark of the LORD to
the place he had prepared for it. 4He
called together the descendants of
Aaron and the Levites:[g]
5From the descendants of Kohath,
Uriel[h] the leader and 120 rela-
tives;
6from the descendants of Merari,
Asaiah the leader and 220 rela-
tives;
7from the descendants of Gershon,[a]
Joel the leader and 130 relatives;
8from the descendants of Eliza-
phan,[i]
Shemaiah the leader and 200
relatives;
9from the descendants of Hebron,[j]
Eliel the leader and 80 relatives;

6 [h]Ex 25:22; 2Ki 19:15
7 [i]1Sa 7:1
8 [j]1Ch 15:16, 19,24; 2Ch 5:12; Ps 92:3
10 [k]1Ch 15:13; [l]Lev 10:2
11 [m]1Ch 15:13; Ps 7:11
13 [n]1Ch 15:18, 24; 16:38; 26:4–5,15
14 [o]2Sa 6:11

Ch. 14

1 [a]1Ki 5:6; 1Ch 17:6; 22:4; 2Ch 2:3; Ezr 3:7; Hag 1:8
2 [b]Nu 24:7; Dt 26:19
3 [c]1Ch 3:1
4 [d]1Ch 3:9
8 [e]1Ch 11:1
9 [f]ver 13; Jos 15:8; 1Ch 11:15
11 [g]Ps 94:16; Isa 28:21
12 [h]Ex 32:20; [i]Jos 7:15
13 [j]ver 9
16 [k]Jos 9:3; [l]Jos 10:33
17 [m]Jos 6:27; [n]Ex 15:14–16; Dt 2:25; Ps 2:1–12

Ch. 15

1 [a]Ps 132:1–18; [b]2Sa 6:17; 1Ch 16:1; 17:1
2 [c]Nu 3:6; 4:15; Dt 10:8; 31:25; 2Ch 5:5; [d]Dt 31:9; [e]1Ch 16:4; 23:13; 2Ch 29:11; 31:2; Ps 134:1; 135:2
3 [f]1Ch 13:5
4 [g]Nu 3:17–20
5 [h]1Ch 6:24
8 [i]Ex 6:22
9 [j]Ex 6:18

---

d11 *Perez Uzzah* means *outbreak against Uzzah*.
a7 A variant of *Eliada*
b11 *Baal Perazim* means *the lord who breaks out*.
a7 Hebrew *Gershom*, a variant of *Gershon*

10 from the descendants of Uzziel,
Amminadab the leader and 112
relatives.

11 Then David summoned Zadok[k] and Abiathar[l] the priests, and Uriel, Asaiah, Joel, Shemaiah, Eliel and Amminadab the Levites. 12 He said to them, "You are the heads of the Levitical families; you and your fellow Levites are to consecrate[m] yourselves and bring up the ark of the LORD, the God of Israel, to the place I have prepared for it. 13 It was because you, the Levites,[n] did not bring it up the first time that the LORD our God broke out in anger against us.[o] We did not enquire of him about how to do it in the prescribed way.[p]" 14 So the priests and Levites consecrated themselves in order to bring up the ark of the LORD, the God of Israel. 15 And the Levites carried the ark of God with the poles on their shoulders, as Moses had commanded[q] in accordance with the word of the LORD.[r]

16 David[s] told the leaders of the Levites[t] to appoint their brothers as singers[u] to sing joyful songs, accompanied by musical instruments: lyres, harps and cymbals.[v]

17 So the Levites appointed Heman[w] son of Joel; from his brothers, Asaph[x] son of Berekiah; and from their brothers the Merarites,[y] Ethan son of Kushaiah; 18 and with them their brothers next in rank: Zechariah,[b] Jaaziel, Shemiramoth, Jehiel, Unni, Eliab, Benaiah, Maaseiah, Mattithiah, Eliphelehu, Mikneiah, Obed-Edom[z] and Jeiel,[c] the gatekeepers.

19 The musicians Heman,[a] Asaph and Ethan were to sound the bronze cymbals; 20 Zechariah, Aziel, Shemiramoth, Jehiel, Unni, Eliab, Maaseiah and Benaiah were to play the lyres according to *alamoth*,[d] 21 and Mattithiah, Eliphelehu, Mikneiah, Obed-Edom, Jeiel and Azaziah were to play the harps, directing according to *sheminith*.[e] 22 Kenaniah the head Levite was in charge of the singing; that was his responsibility because he was skilful at it.

23 Berekiah and Elkanah were to be doorkeepers for the ark. 24 Shebaniah, Joshaphat, Nethanel, Amasai, Zechariah, Benaiah and Eliezer the priests were to blow trumpets[b] before the ark of God. Obed-Edom and Jehiah were also to be doorkeepers for the ark.

25 So David and the elders of Israel and the commanders of units of a thousand went to bring up the ark[c] of the covenant of the LORD from the house of Obed-Edom, with rejoicing. 26 Because God had helped the Levites who were carrying the ark of the covenant of the LORD, seven bulls and seven rams[d] were sacrificed. 27 Now David was clothed in a robe of fine linen, as were all the Levites who were carrying the ark, and as were the singers, and Kenaniah, who was in charge of the singing of the choirs. David also wore a linen ephod.[e] 28 So all Israel[f] brought up the ark of the covenant of the LORD with shouts,[g] with the sounding of rams' horns[h] and trumpets, and of cymbals, and the playing of lyres and harps.

29 As the ark of the covenant of the LORD was entering the City of David, Michal daughter of Saul watched from a window. And when she saw King David dancing and celebrating, she despised him in her heart.

16

They brought the ark of God and set it inside the tent that David had pitched[a] for it, and they presented burnt offerings and fellowship offerings[a] before God. 2 After David had finished sacrificing the burnt offerings and fellowship offerings, he blessed[b] the people in the name of the LORD. 3 Then he gave a loaf of bread, a cake of dates and a cake of raisins[c] to each Israelite man and woman.

4 He appointed some of the Levites to minister[d] before the ark of the LORD, to make petition, to give thanks, and to praise the LORD, the God of Israel: 5 Asaph was the chief, Zechariah second, then Jeiel, Shemiramoth, Jehiel, Mattithiah, Eliab, Benaiah, Obed-Edom and Jeiel. They were to play the lyres and harps, Asaph was to sound the cymbals, 6 and Benaiah and Jahaziel the priests were to blow the trumpets regularly before the ark of the covenant of God.

David's Psalm of Thanks

16:8–22pp—Ps 105:1–15
16:23–33pp—Ps 96:1–13
16:34–36pp—Ps 106:1,47–48

7 That day David first committed to Asaph and his associates this psalm[e] of thanks to the LORD:

8 Give thanks[f] to the LORD, call on his
name;

11 [k]1Ch 12:28; [l]1Sa 22:20
12 [m]Ex 29:1; 30:19–21,30; 40:31–32; Lev 11:44
13 [n]1Ki 8:4; [o]1Ch 13:11; [p]Lev 5:10
15 [q]Ex 25:14; [r]2Sa 6:7
16 [s]1Ch 6:31; [t]2Ch 7:6; [u]Ezr 2:41; Ne 11:23; Ps 68:25; [v]1Ch 13:8; 23:5; 2Ch 29:26; Ne 12:27,36; Job 21:12; Ps 150:5; Am 6:5
17 [w]1Ch 6:33; [x]1Ch 6:39; [y]1Ch 6:44
18 [z]2Sa 6:10; 1Ch 26:4–5
19 [a]1Ch 16:41; 25:6
24 [b]2Ch 5:12; 7:6; 29:26
25 [c]2Ch 1:4; 5:2; Jer 3:16
26 [d]Nu 23:1–4,29
27 [e]1Sa 2:18
28 [f]1Ch 9:1; [g]1Ki 1:39; Zec 4:7; [h]Ex 19:13

Ch. 16

1 [a]1Ch 15:1
2 [b]Ex 39:43; Nu 6:23–27
3 [c]Isa 16:7
4 [d]1Ch 15:2
7 [e]Ps 47:7
8 [f]ver 34; Ps 107:1; 118:1; 136:1

[b]18 Three Hebrew manuscripts and most Septuagint manuscripts (see also verse 20 and 1 Chron. 16:5); most Hebrew manuscripts *Zechariah son and* or *Zechariah, Ben and*
[c]18 Hebrew; Septuagint (see also verse 21) *Jeiel and Azaziah* [d]20 Probably a musical term
[e]21 Probably a musical term
[a]1 Traditionally *peace offerings;* also in verse 2

make known among the nations[g]
what he has done.
9Sing to him, sing praise[h] to him;
tell of all his wonderful acts.
10Glory in his holy name;[i]
let the hearts of those who seek the
LORD rejoice.
11Look to the LORD and his strength;
seek[j] his face always.
12Remember[k] the wonders[l] he has done,
his miracles,[m] and the judgments he
pronounced,
13O descendants of Israel his servant,
O sons of Jacob, his chosen ones.

14He is the LORD our God;
his judgments[n] are in all the earth.
15He remembers[b] [o] his covenant for
ever,
the word he commanded, for a
thousand generations,
16the covenant[p] he made with Abraham,
the oath he swore to Isaac.
17He confirmed it to Jacob[q] as a decree,
to Israel as an everlasting covenant:
18"To you I will give the land of Canaan[r]
as the portion you will inherit."

19When they were but few in number,[s]
few indeed, and strangers in it,
20they[c] wandered[t] from nation to
nation,
from one kingdom to another.
21He allowed no man to oppress them;
for their sake he rebuked kings:[u]
22"Do not touch my anointed ones;
do my prophets[v] no harm."

23Sing to the LORD, all the earth;
proclaim his salvation day after day.
24Declare his glory[w] among the nations,
his marvellous deeds among all
peoples.
25For great is the LORD and most worthy
of praise;[x]
he is to be feared[y] above all gods.[z]
26For all the gods of the nations are
idols,
but the LORD made the heavens.[a]
27Splendour and majesty are before
him;
strength and joy in his
dwelling-place.
28Ascribe to the LORD, O families of
nations,
ascribe to the LORD glory and
strength,[b]
29 ascribe to the LORD the glory due to
his name.[c]
Bring an offering and come before
him;
worship the LORD in the splendour
of his[d] holiness.[d]

8 [g]**2Ki 19:19**
9 [h]**Ex 15:1**; Ps 7:17
10 [i]Ps 8:1; 29:2; 66:2
11 [j]ver 10; 1Ch 28:9; 2Ch 7:14; 14:4; 15:2,12; 16:12; 18:4; 20:4; 34:3; Ps 24:6; 27:8; 105:4; 119:2,58; Pr 8:17
12 [k]Ps 77:11; [l]**Dt 4:34**; [m]Ps 78:43
14 [n]Isa 4:4; 26:9
15 [o]**Ge 8:1**; Ps 98:3; 111:5; 115:12; 136:23
16 [p]**Ge 12:7**; **15:18**; 22:16–18
17 [q]Ge 35:9–12
18 [r]Ge 13:14–17
19 [s]Dt 7:7
20 [t]**Ge 20:13**
21 [u]Ge 12:17; **20:3**; Ex 7:15–18; Ps 9:5
22 [v]**Ge 20:7**
24 [w]Isa 42:12; 66:19
25 [x]Ps 18:3; 48:1; [y]Ps 76:7; 89:7; [z]Ex 18:11; Dt 32:39; 2Ch 2:5; Ps 135:5; Isa 40:25
26 [a]Ps 8:3; 102:25
28 [b]Ps 29:1–2
29 [c]Ps 8:1; [d]2Ch 20:21; Ps 29:1–2
30 [e]Ps 2:11; 33:8; 76:8; 99:1; 114:7; [f]Ps 93:1
31 [g]Isa 44:23; 49:13; [h]Ps 9:7; 47:8; 93:1; 97:1; 99:1; 146:10; Isa 52:7; La 5:19
32 [i]Ex 20:11; Isa 42:10
33 [j]Isa 14:8; 55:12; [k]1Sa 2:10; Ps 7:8; 96:10; 98:9; 110:6; Isa 2:4
34 [l]**ver 8**; Ps 105:1; Isa 12:4; [m]Ps 25:7; 34:8; 100:5; 135:3; 145:9; Na 1:7; [n]2Ch 5:13; 7:3; Ezr 3:11; Ps 136:1–26; Jer 33:11
35 [o]Dt 32:15; Ps 18:46; 38:22; Mic 7:7
36 [p]**1Ki 8:15**; Ps 72:18–19
37 [q]2Ch 8:14
38 [r]**1Ch 13:13**; 26:4–5; [s]1Ch 26:10

30Tremble[e] before him, all the earth!
The world is firmly established; it
cannot be moved.[f]
31Let the heavens rejoice, let the earth be
glad;[g]
let them say among the nations,
"The LORD reigns![h]"
32Let the sea resound, and all that is in
it;[i]
let the fields be jubilant, and
everything in them!
33Then the trees[j] of the forest will sing,
they will sing for joy before the
LORD,
for he comes to judge[k] the earth.

34Give thanks[l] to the LORD, for he is
good;[m]
his love endures for ever.[n]
35Cry out, "Save us, O God our
Saviour;[o]
gather us and deliver us from the
nations,
that we may give thanks to your holy
name,
that we may glory in your praise."
36Praise be to the LORD, the God of
Israel,[p]
from everlasting to everlasting.

Then all the people said "Amen" and
"Praise the LORD."

37David left Asaph and his associates
before the ark of the covenant of the
LORD to minister there regularly,
according to each day's requirements.[q]
38He also left Obed-Edom[r] and his sixty-
eight associates to minister with them.
Obed-Edom son of Jeduthun, and also
Hosah,[s] were gatekeepers.
39David left Zadok[t] the priest and his
fellow priests before the tabernacle of
the LORD at the high place in Gibeon[u]
40to present burnt offerings to the LORD
on the altar of burnt offering regularly,
morning and evening, in accordance
with everything written in the Law[v] of
the LORD, which he had given Israel.
41With them were Heman[w] and
Jeduthun and the rest of those chosen
and designated by name to give thanks
to the LORD, "for his love endures for

39 [t]**1Sa 2:35; 2Sa 8:17; 1Ch 12:28**; [u]**Jos 9:3**; 2Ch 1:3
40 [v]**Ex 29:38**; Nu 28:1–8 *41* [w]**1Ch 15:19**

---

b*15* Some Septuagint manuscripts (see also Psalm 105:8); Hebrew *Remember*
c*18–20* One Hebrew manuscript, Septuagint and Vulgate (see also Psalm 105:12); most Hebrew manuscripts *inherit, /*[19] *though you are but few in number, / few indeed, and strangers in it." /*[20] *They*
d*29* Or *LORD with the splendour of*

ever." 42Heman and Jeduthun were re-
sponsible for the sounding of the trum-
pets and cymbals and for the playing of
the other instruments for sacred song.[x]
The sons of Jeduthun[y] were stationed at
the gate.
43Then all the people left, each for his
own home, and David returned home
to bless his family.

God's Promise to David

17:1–15pp—2Sa 7:1–17

17 After David was settled in his
palace, he said to Nathan the
prophet, "Here I am, living in a palace
of cedar, while the ark of the covenant
of the LORD is under a tent.[a]"
2Nathan replied to David, "Whatever
you have in mind,[b] do it, for God is with
you."
3That night the word of God came to
Nathan, saying:
4"Go and tell my servant David,
'This is what the LORD says: You[c]
are not the one to build me a house
to dwell in. 5I have not dwelt in a
house from the day I brought Israel
up out of Egypt to this day. I have
moved from one tent site to
another, from one dwelling-place
to another. 6Wherever I have
moved with all the Israelites, did I
ever say to any of their leaders[a]
whom I commanded to shepherd
my people, "Why have you not
built me a house of cedar?[d]" '
7"Now then, tell my servant
David, 'This is what the LORD
Almighty says: I took you from the
pasture and from following the
flock, to be ruler[e] over my people
Israel. 8I have been with you
wherever you have gone, and I
have cut off all your enemies from
before you. Now I will make your
name like the names of the greatest
men of the earth. 9And I will pro-
vide a place for my people Israel
and will plant them so that they can
have a home of their own and no
longer be disturbed. Wicked peo-
ple will not oppress them any
more, as they did at the beginning
10and have done ever since the time
I appointed leaders[f] over my people
Israel. I will also subdue all your
enemies.
" 'I declare to you that the LORD
will build a house for you: 11When
your days are over and you go to be
with your fathers, I will raise up
your offspring to succeed you, one
of your own sons, and I will estab-
lish his kingdom. 12He is the one
who will build[g] a house for me, and
I will establish his throne for ever.[h]
13I will be his father,[i] and he will be
my son.[j] I will never take my love
away from him, as I took it away
from your predecessor. 14I will set
him over my house and my king-
dom for ever; his throne[k] will be
established for ever.[l]' "
15Nathan reported to David all the
words of this entire revelation.

David's Prayer

17:16–27pp—2Sa 7:18–29

16Then King David went in and sat
before the LORD, and he said:
"Who am I, O LORD God, and
what is my family, that you have
brought me this far? 17And as if this
were not enough in your sight, O
God, you have spoken about the
future of the house of your servant.
You have looked on me as though I
were the most exalted of men, O
LORD God.
18"What more can David say to
you for honouring your servant?
For you know your servant, 19O
LORD. For the sake[m] of your servant
and according to your will, you
have done this great thing and
made known all these great prom-
ises.[n]
20"There is no-one like you, O
LORD, and there is no God but you,[o]
as we have heard with our own
ears. 21And who is like your people
Israel—the one nation on earth
whose God went out to redeem[p] a
people for himself, and to make a
name for yourself, and to perform
great and awesome wonders by
driving out nations from before
your people, whom you redeemed
from Egypt? 22You made your
people Israel your very own for
ever,[q] and you, O LORD, have
become their God.
23"And now, LORD, let the prom-
ise[r] you have made concerning
your servant and his house be
established for ever. Do as you
promised, 24so that it will be estab-
lished and that your name will be
great for ever. Then men will say,

42 [x]2Ch 7:6; [y]1Ch 25:3
Ch. 17
1 [a]**1Ch 15:1**
2 [b]1Ch 22:7; 28:2; 2Ch 6:7
4 [c]1Ch 22:10; 28:3
6 [d]**1Ch 14:1**
7 [e]**2Sa 6:21**
10 [f]**Jdg 2:16**
12 [g]**1Ki 5:5**; [h]1Ch 22:10; 2Ch 7:18; 13:5
13 [i]2Co 6:18; [j]1Ch 28:6; Lk 1:32; Heb 1:5
14 [k]**1Ki 2:12**; 1Ch 28:5; 29:23; 2Ch 9:8; [l]Ps 132:11; Jer 33:17
19 [m]2Sa 7:16–17; 2Ki 20:6; Isa 9:7; 37:35; 55:3; [n]**2Sa 7:25**
20 [o]**Ex 8:10; 9:14; 15:11**; Isa 44:6; 46:9
21 [p]**Ex 6:6**
22 [q]Ex 19:5–6
23 [r]**1Ki 8:25**

[a]6 Traditionally *judges*; also in verse 10

'The LORD Almighty, the God over
Israel, is Israel's God!' And the
house of your servant David will be
established before you.
25"You, my God, have revealed
to your servant that you will build a
house for him. So your servant has
found courage to pray to you. 26O
LORD, you are God! You have
promised these good things to your
servant. 27Now you have been
pleased to bless the house of your
servant, that it may continue for
ever in your sight;[s] for you, O LORD,
have blessed it, and it will be
blessed for ever."

David's Victories

18:1–13pp—2Sa 8:1–14

18 In the course of time, David defeated the Philistines and subdued them, and he took Gath and its
surrounding villages from the control of
the Philistines.
2David also defeated the Moabites,[a]
and they became subject to him and
brought tribute.
3Moreover, David fought Hadadezer
king of Zobah,[b] as far as Hamath, when
he went to establish his control along
the Euphrates River.[c] 4David captured
a thousand of his chariots, seven
thousand charioteers and twenty
thousand foot soldiers. He hamstrung[d]
all but a hundred of the chariot horses.
5When the Arameans of Damascus[e]
came to help Hadadezer king of Zobah,
David struck down twenty-two
thousand of them. 6He put garrisons in
the Aramean kingdom of Damascus,
and the Arameans became subject to
him and brought tribute. The LORD gave
David victory everywhere he went.
7David took the gold shields carried
by the officers of Hadadezer and
brought them to Jerusalem. 8From
Tebah[a] and Cun, towns that belonged
to Hadadezer, David took a great
quantity of bronze, which Solomon
used to make the bronze Sea,[f] the pillars
and various bronze articles.
9When Tou king of Hamath heard
that David had defeated the entire army
of Hadadezer king of Zobah, 10he sent
his son Hadoram to King David to greet
him and congratulate him on his victory
in battle over Hadadezer, who had been
at war with Tou. Hadoram brought all
kinds of articles of gold and silver and
bronze.
11King David dedicated these articles
to the LORD, as he had done with the

27 [s]Ps 16:11; 21:6

Ch. 18

2 [a]**Nu 21:29**
3 [b]1Ch 19:6; [c]**Ge 2:14**
4 [d]**Ge 49:6**
5 [e]2Ki 16:9
8 [f]**1Ki 7:23;** 2Ch 4:2–5
11 [g]**Nu 24:18;** [h]Nu 24:20
12 [i]1Ki 11:15
14 [j]1Ch 29:26; [k]1Ch 11:1
15 [l]2Sa 5:6–8
16 [m]1Ch 6:8; [n]1Ch 24:6
17 [o]**1Sa 30:14; 2Sa 15:18**

Ch. 19

1 [a]**Ge 19:38;** Jdg 10:17–11:33; 2Ch 20:1–2; Zep 2:8–11
3 [b]**Nu 21:32**

silver and gold he had taken from all
these nations: Edom[g] and Moab, the
Ammonites and the Philistines, and
Amalek.[h]
12Abishai son of Zeruiah struck down
eighteen thousand Edomites[i] in the Valley of Salt. 13He put garrisons in Edom,
and all the Edomites became subject to
David. The LORD gave David victory
everywhere he went.

David's Officials

18:14–17pp—2Sa 8:15–18

14David reigned[j] over all Israel,[k] doing
what was just and right for all his people. 15Joab[l] son of Zeruiah was over the
army; Jehoshaphat son of Ahilud was
recorder; 16Zadok[m] son of Ahitub and
Ahimelech[b][n] son of Abiathar were
priests; Shavsha was secretary;
17Benaiah son of Jehoiada was over the
Kerethites and Pelethites;[o] and David's
sons were chief officials at the king's
side.

The Battle Against the Ammonites

19:1–19pp—2Sa 10:1–19

19 In the course of time, Nahash king of the Ammonites[a] died,
and his son succeeded him as king.
2David thought, "I will show kindness
to Hanun son of Nahash, because his
father showed kindness to me." So
David sent a delegation to express his
sympathy to Hanun concerning his
father.
When David's men came to Hanun in
the land of the Ammonites to express
sympathy to him, 3the Ammonite
nobles said to Hanun, "Do you think
David is honouring your father by sending men to you to express sympathy?
Haven't his men come to you to explore
and spy out[b] the country and overthrow
it?" 4So Hanun seized David's men,
shaved them, cut off their garments in
the middle at the buttocks, and sent
them away.
5When someone came and told David
about the men, he sent messengers to
meet them, for they were greatly
humiliated. The king said, "Stay at
Jericho till your beards have grown, and
then come back."
6When the Ammonites realised that

[a]8 Hebrew *Tibhath*, a variant of *Tebah*

[b]16 Some Hebrew manuscripts, Vulgate and Syriac (see also 2 Sam. 8:17); most Hebrew manuscripts *Abimelech*

they had become an offence[c] to David's
nostrils, Hanun and the Ammonites
sent a thousand talents[a] of silver to hire
chariots and charioteers from Aram
Naharaim,[b] Aram Maacah and Zobah.[d]
7They hired thirty-two thousand char-
iots and charioteers, as well as the king
of Maacah with his troops, who came
and camped near Medeba,[e] while the
Ammonites were mustered from their
towns and moved out for battle.
8On hearing this, David sent Joab out
with the entire army of fighting men.
9The Ammonites came out and drew up
in battle formation at the entrance to
their city, while the kings who had
come were by themselves in the open
country.
10Joab saw that there were battle lines
in front of him and behind him; so he
selected some of the best troops in Israel
and deployed them against the Ara-
means. 11He put the rest of the men
under the command of Abishai[f] his
brother, and they were deployed
against the Ammonites. 12Joab said, "If
the Arameans are too strong for me,
then you are to rescue me; but if the
Ammonites are too strong for you, then
I will rescue you. 13Be strong and let us
fight bravely for our people and the
cities of our God. The LORD will do what
is good in his sight."
14Then Joab and the troops with him
advanced to fight the Arameans, and
they fled before him. 15When the
Ammonites saw that the Arameans
were fleeing, they too fled before his
brother Abishai and went inside the
city. So Joab went back to Jerusalem.
16After the Arameans saw that they
had been routed by Israel, they sent
messengers and had Arameans brought
from beyond the River,[c] with Shophach
the commander of Hadadezer's army
leading them.
17When David was told of this, he
gathered all Israel[g] and crossed the Jor-
dan; he advanced against them and
formed his battle lines opposite them.
David formed his lines to meet the Ara-
means in battle, and they fought against
him. 18But they fled before Israel, and
David killed seven thousand of their
charioteers and forty thousand of their
foot soldiers. He also killed Shophach
the commander of their army.
19When the vassals of Hadadezer saw
that they had been defeated by Israel,
they made peace with David and be-
came subject to him.
So the Arameans were not willing to
help the Ammonites any more.

6 [c]Ge 34:30; [d]1Ch 18:3
7 [e]Nu 21:30
11 [f]1Sa 26:6
17 [g]1Ch 9:1

Ch. 20

1 [a]Dt 3:11; [b]Am 1:13–15
3 [c]Dt 29:11
4 [d]Jos 10:33; [e]Ge 14:5
5 [f]1Sa 17:7

Ch. 21

1 [a]2Ch 18:21; Ps 109:6; [b]2Ch 14:8; 25:5
2 [c]1Ch 27:23–24

The Capture of Rabbah

20:1–3pp—2Sa 11:1; 12:29–31

20 In the spring, at the time when
kings go off to war, Joab led out
the armed forces. He laid waste the land
of the Ammonites and went to Rabbah[a]
and besieged it, but David remained in
Jerusalem. Joab attacked Rabbah and
left it in ruins.[b] 2David took the crown
from the head of their king[a]—its weight
was found to be a talent[b] of gold, and it
was set with precious stones—and it
was placed on David's head. He took a
great quantity of plunder from the city
3and brought out the people who were
there, consigning them to labour with
saws and with iron picks and axes.[c]
David did this to all the Ammonite
towns. Then David and his entire army
returned to Jerusalem.

War With the Philistines

2:4–8pp—2Sa 21:15–22

4In the course of time, war broke out
with the Philistines, at Gezer.[d] At that
time Sibbecai the Hushathite killed Sip-
pai, one of the descendants of the
Rephaites,[e] and the Philistines were
subjugated.
5In another battle with the Philistines,
Elhanan son of Jair killed Lahmi the
brother of Goliath the Gittite, who had a
spear with a shaft like a weaver's rod.[f]
6In still another battle, which took
place at Gath, there was a huge man
with six fingers on each hand and six
toes on each foot—twenty-four in all.
He also was descended from Rapha.
7When he taunted Israel, Jonathan son
of Shimea, David's brother, killed him.
8These were descendants of Rapha in
Gath, and they fell at the hands of David
and his men.

David Numbers the Fighting Men

21:1–26pp—2Sa 24:1–25

21 Satan[a] rose up against Israel
and incited David to take a cen-
sus[b] of Israel. 2So David said to Joab and
the commanders of the troops, "Go and
count[c] the Israelites from Beersheba to
Dan. Then report back to me so that I
may know how many there are."
3But Joab replied, "May the LORD

[a]6 That is, about 34 tons (about 34 metric tons)
[b]6 That is, North-west Mesopotamia
[c]16 That is, the Euphrates
[a]2 Or *of Milcom,* that is, Molech
[b]2 That is, about 75 pounds (about 34 kilograms)

multiply his troops a hundred times
over.[d] My lord the king, are they not all
my lord's subjects? Why does my lord
want to do this? Why should he bring
guilt on Israel?"

4The king's word, however, over-
ruled Joab; so Joab left and went
throughout Israel and then came back to
Jerusalem. 5Joab reported the number of
the fighting men to David: In all Israel[e]
there were one million one hundred
thousand men who could handle a
sword, including four hundred and
seventy thousand in Judah.

6But Joab did not include Levi and
Benjamin in the numbering, because
the king's command was repulsive to
him. 7This command was also evil in the
sight of God; so he punished Israel.

8Then David said to God, "I have
sinned greatly by doing this. Now, I beg
you, take away the guilt of your servant.
I have done a very foolish thing."

9The LORD said to Gad,[f] David's seer,[g]
10"Go and tell David, 'This is what
the LORD says: I am giving you three
options. Choose one of them for me
to carry out against you.'"

11So Gad went to David and said to
him, "This is what the LORD says: 'Take
your choice: 12three years of famine,[h]
three months of being swept away[a]
before your enemies, with their swords
overtaking you, or three days of the
sword[i] of the LORD[j]—days of plague in
the land with the angel of the LORD
ravaging every part of Israel.' Now
then, decide how I should answer the
one who sent me."

13David said to Gad, "I am in deep
distress. Let me fall into the hands of the
LORD, for his mercy[k] is very great; but do
not let me fall into the hands of men."

14So the LORD sent a plague on Israel,
and seventy thousand men of Israel fell
dead.[l] 15And God sent an angel[m] to de-
stroy Jerusalem.[n] But as the angel was
doing so, the LORD saw it and was
grieved[o] because of the calamity and
said to the angel who was destroying[p]
the people, "Enough! Withdraw your
hand." The angel of the LORD was then
standing at the threshing-floor of
Araunah[b] the Jebusite.

16David looked up and saw the angel
of the LORD standing between heaven
and earth, with a drawn sword in his
hand extended over Jerusalem. Then
David and the elders, clothed in sack-
cloth, fell face down.[q]

17David said to God, "Was it not I who
ordered the fighting men to be counted?
I am the one who has sinned and done

3 [d]Dt 1:11
5 [e]1Ch 9:1
9 [f]1Sa 22:5; [g]1Sa 9:9
12 [h]Dt 32:24; [i]Eze 30:25; [j]Ge 19:13
13 [k]Ps 6:4; 86:15; 130:4,7
14 [l]1Ch 27:24
15 [m]Ge 32:1; [n]Ps 125:2; [o]Ge 6:6; Ex 32:14; [p]Ge 19:13
16 [q]Nu 14:5; Jos 7:6
17 [r]2Sa 7:8; [s]Jnh 1:12
18 [t]2Ch 3:1
20 [u]Jdg 6:11
26 [v]Ex 19:18; Jdg 6:21
29 [w]Jos 9:3

wrong. These are but sheep.[r] What
have they done? O LORD my God, let
your hand fall upon me and my family,[s]
but do not let this plague remain on
your people."

18Then the angel of the LORD ordered
Gad to tell David to go up and build an
altar to the LORD on the threshing-floor[t]
of Araunah the Jebusite. 19So David
went up in obedience to the word that
Gad had spoken in the name of the
LORD.

20While Araunah was threshing
wheat,[u] he turned and saw the angel;
his four sons who were with him hid
themselves. 21Then David approached,
and when Araunah looked and saw
him, he left the threshing-floor and
bowed down before David with his face
to the ground.

22David said to him, "Let me have the
site of your threshing-floor so that I can
build an altar to the LORD, that the
plague on the people may be stopped.
Sell it to me at the full price."

23Araunah said to David, "Take it! Let
my lord the king do whatever pleases
him. Look, I will give the oxen for the
burnt offerings, the threshing-sledges
for the wood, and the wheat for the
grain offering. I will give all this."

24But King David replied to Araunah,
"No, I insist on paying the full price. I
will not take for the LORD what is yours,
or sacrifice a burnt offering that costs me
nothing."

25So David paid Araunah six hundred
shekels[c] of gold for the site. 26David
built an altar to the LORD there and
sacrificed burnt offerings and fel-
lowship offerings.[d] He called on the
LORD, and the LORD answered him with
fire[v] from heaven on the altar of burnt
offering.

27Then the LORD spoke to the angel,
and he put his sword back into its
sheath. 28At that time, when David saw
that the LORD had answered him on the
threshing-floor of Araunah the Jebusite,
he offered sacrifices there. 29The
tabernacle of the LORD, which Moses
had made in the desert, and the altar of
burnt offering were at that time on the
high place at Gibeon.[w] 30But David
could not go before it to enquire of God,
because he was afraid of the sword of
the angel of the LORD.

[a]*12* Hebrew; Septuagint and Vulgate (see also 2 Sam. 24:13) *of fleeing*
[b]*15* Hebrew *Ornan*, a variant of *Araunah*; also in verses 18–28
[c]*25* That is, about 15 pounds (about 7 kilograms)
[d]*26* Traditionally *peace offerings*

22

Then David said, "The house of
the LORD God[a] is to be here, and
also the altar of burnt offering for
Israel."

Preparations for the Temple

2So David gave orders to assemble the
aliens[b] living in Israel, and from among
them he appointed stonecutters[c] to pre-
pare dressed stone for building the
house of God. 3He provided a large
amount of iron to make nails for the
doors of the gateways and for the
fittings, and more bronze than could be
weighed.[d] 4He also provided more
cedar logs[e] than could be counted, for
the Sidonians and Tyrians had brought
large numbers of them to David.
5David said, "My son Solomon is
young[f] and inexperienced, and the
house to be built for the LORD should be
of great magnificence and fame and
splendour[g] in the sight of all the na-
tions. Therefore I will make prepara-
tions for it." So David made extensive
preparations before his death.
6Then he called for his son Solomon
and charged him to build[h] a house for
the LORD, the God of Israel. 7David said
to Solomon: "My son, I had it in my
heart[i] to build[j] a house for the Name[k] of
the LORD my God. 8But this word of the
LORD came to me: 'You have shed much
blood and have fought many wars.[l] You
are not to build a house for my Name,[m]
because you have shed much blood on
the earth in my sight. 9But you will have
a son who will be a man of peace[n] and
rest,[o] and I will give him rest from all his
enemies on every side. His name will be
Solomon,[a][p] and I will grant Israel peace
and quiet[q] during his reign. 10He is the
one who will build a house for my
Name.[r] He will be my son,[s] and I will
be his father. And I will establish[t] the
throne of his kingdom over Israel for
ever.'"
11"Now, my son, the LORD be with[v]
you, and may you have success and
build the house of the LORD your God,
as he said you would. 12May the LORD
give you discretion and understanding[w]
when he puts you in command over
Israel, so that you may keep the law of
the LORD your God. 13Then you will
have success[x] if you are careful to
observe the decrees and laws[y] that the
LORD gave to Moses for Israel. Be strong
and courageous.[z] Do not be afraid or
discouraged.
14"I have taken great pains to provide
for the temple of the LORD a hundred
thousand talents[b] of gold, a million
talents[c] of silver, quantities of bronze
and iron too great to be weighed, and
wood and stone. And you may add to
them.[a] 15You have many workmen:
stonecutters, masons and carpenters,[b]
as well as men skilled in every kind of
work 16in gold and silver, bronze and
iron—craftsmen[c] beyond number. Now
begin the work, and the LORD be with
you."
17Then David ordered[d] all the leaders
of Israel to help his son Solomon. 18He
said to them, "Is not the LORD your God
with you? And has he not granted you
rest[e] on every side?[f] For he has handed
the inhabitants of the land over to me,
and the land is subject to the LORD and
to his people. 19Now devote your heart
and soul to seeking the LORD your God.[g]
Begin to build the sanctuary of the LORD
God, so that you may bring the ark of
the covenant of the LORD and the sacred
articles belonging to God into the tem-
ple that will be built for the Name of the
LORD."

The Levites

23

When David was old and full
of years, he made his son Sol-
omon[a] king over Israel.[b]
2He also gathered together all the
leaders of Israel, as well as the priests
and Levites. 3The Levites thirty years
old or more[c] were counted,[d] and the
total number of men was thirty-eight
thousand.[e] 4David said, "Of these,
twenty-four thousand are to supervise[f]
the work[g] of the temple of the LORD and
six thousand are to be officials and
judges.[h] 5Four thousand are to be
gatekeepers and four thousand are
to praise the LORD with the musical
instruments[i] I have provided for that
purpose."[j]
6David divided[k] the Levites into
groups corresponding to the sons of
Levi:[l] Gershon, Kohath and Merari.

Gershonites

7Belonging to the Gershonites:[m]
Ladan and Shimei.
8The sons of Ladan:
Jehiel the first, Zetham and Joel
—three in all.

Ch. 22

1 [a]**Ge 28:17**
2 [b]**Ex 1:11**; **Dt 20:11**; 2Ch 8:10; **Isa 56:6**; [c]1Ki 5:17–18; Ezr 3:7
3 [d]**1Ki 7:47**; 1Ch 29:2–5
4 [e]**1Ki 5:6**
5 [f]**1Ki 3:7**; 1Ch 29:1; [g]2Ch 2:5
6 [h]Ac 7:47
7 [i]**1Ch 17:2**; [j]**1Ki 8:17**; [k]Dt 12:5,11
8 [l]**1Ki 5:3**; [m]1Ch 28:3
9 [n]**Jos 14:15**; **1Ki 5:4**; [o]ver 18; 1Ch 23:25; 2Ch 14:6–7; 15:15; 20:30; 36:21; [p]**2Sa 12:24**; **1Ch 23:1**; [q]1Ki 4:20
10 [r]**1Ch 17:12**; [s]**2Sa 7:13**; [t]1Ki 9:5; [u]**2Sa 7:14**; **1Ch 17:4**; 2Ch 6:15
11 [v]**1Sa 16:18**; **18:12**
12 [w]1Ki 3:11
13 [x]1Ki 2:3; [y]1Ch 28:7; [z]**Dt 31:6**
14 [a]1Ch 29:2–5,19
15 [b]Ezr 3:7
16 [c]2Ch 2:7
17 [d]1Ch 28:1
18 [e]**ver 9**; [f]2Sa 7:1
19 [g]2Ch 7:14

Ch. 23

1 [a]1Ch 22:9; 28:5; 2Ch 1:8; [b]**1Ki 1:30**; 1Ch 29:28
3 [c]Nu 8:24; [d]1Ch 21:7; [e]Nu 4:3–49
4 [f]Ezr 3:8; [g]2Ch 34:13; Ne 4:10; [h]1Ch 26:29; 2Ch 19:8; Eze 44:24
5 [i]**1Ch 15:16**; Ps 92:3; [j]Ne 12:45
6 [k]2Ch 8:14; 23:18; 29:25; [l]**Nu 3:17**; 1Ch 24:20
7 [m]1Ch 6:71

[a]9 *Solomon* sounds like and may be derived from the Hebrew for *peace*.
[b]14 That is, about 3,395 tons (about 3,450 metric tons)
[c]14 That is, about 33,950 tons (about 34,500 metric tons)

9The sons of Shimei:
Shelomoth, Haziel and Haran—
three in all.
These were the heads of the
families of Ladan.
10And the sons of Shimei:
Jahath, Ziza,[a] Jeush and Beriah.
These were the sons of Shimei
—four in all.
11Jahath was the first and Ziza the
second, but Jeush and Beriah did
not have many sons; so they
were counted as one family with
one assignment.

Kohathites

12The sons of Kohath:[n]
Amram, Izhar, Hebron and
Uzziel—four in all.
13The sons of Amram:[o]
Aaron and Moses.
Aaron was set apart,[p] he and his
descendants for ever, to conse-
crate the most holy things, to
offer sacrifices before the LORD,
to minister[q] before him and to
pronounce blessings[r] in his name
for ever. 14The sons of Moses the
man[s] of God were counted as
part of the tribe of Levi.
15The sons of Moses:
Gershom and Eliezer.[t]
16The descendants of Gershom:[u]
Shubael was the first.
17The descendants of Eliezer:
Rehabiah[v] was the first.
Eliezer had no other sons, but the
sons of Rehabiah were very
numerous.
18The sons of Izhar:
Shelomith[w] was the first.
19The sons of Hebron:[x]
Jeriah the first, Amariah the
second, Jahaziel the third and
Jekameam the fourth.
20The sons of Uzziel:
Micah the first and Isshiah the
second.

Merarites

21The sons of Merari:[y]
Mahli and Mushi.[z]
The sons of Mahli:
Eleazar and Kish.
22Eleazar died without having
sons: he had only daughters.
Their cousins, the sons of Kish,
married them.[a]
23The sons of Mushi:
Mahli, Eder and Jerimoth—three
in all.

24These were the descendants of Levi
by their families—the heads of families
as they were registered under their
names and counted individually, that
is, the workers twenty years old or
more[b] who served in the temple of the
LORD. 25For David had said, "Since the
LORD, the God of Israel, has granted
rest[c] to his people and has come to dwell
in Jerusalem for ever, 26the Levites no
longer need to carry the tabernacle or
any of the articles used in its service."[d]
27According to the last instructions of
David, the Levites were counted from
those twenty years old or more.
28The duty of the Levites was to help
Aaron's descendants in the service of
the temple of the LORD: to be in charge of
the courtyards, the side rooms, the
purification[e] of all sacred things and the
performance of other duties at the
house of God. 29They were in charge of
the bread set out on the table,[f] the flour
for the grain offerings,[g] the unleavened
wafers, the baking and the mixing, and
all measurements of quantity and size.[h]
30They were also to stand every morn-
ing to thank and praise the LORD. They
were to do the same in the evening[i]
31and whenever burnt offerings were
presented to the LORD on Sabbaths and
at New Moon[j] festivals and at appointed
feasts.[k] They were to serve before the
LORD regularly in the proper number
and in the way prescribed for them.
32And so the Levites[l] carried out
their responsibilities for the Tent of
Meeting,[m] for the Holy Place and, under
their brothers the descendants of
Aaron, for the service of the temple of
the LORD.[n]

The Divisions of Priests

24 These were the divisions[a] of the
sons of Aaron:[b]
The sons of Aaron were Nadab, Abi-
hu, Eleazar and Ithamar.[c] 2But Nadab
and Abihu died before their father did,[d]
and they had no sons; so Eleazar and
Ithamar served as the priests. 3With the
help of Zadok[e] a descendant of Eleazar
and Ahimelech a descendant of Itha-
mar, David separated them into divi-
sions for their appointed order of
ministering. 4A larger number of lead-
ers were found among Eleazar's descend-
ants than among Ithamar's, and they
were divided accordingly: sixteen heads

12 [n]**Ge 46:11; Ex 6:18**
13 [o]Ex 6:20; [p]Ex 30:7–10; [q]**1Ch 15:2;** [r]**Nu 6:23**
14 [s]Dt 33:1
15 [t]Ex 18:4
16 [u]1Ch 26:24–28
17 [v]1Ch 24:21
18 [w]1Ch 26:25
19 [x]1Ch 24:23; 26:31
21 [y]**1Ch 6:19;** [z]**Ex 6:19**
22 [a]Nu 36:8
24 [b]**Nu 4:3**
25 [c]**1Ch 22:9**
26 [d]Nu 4:5,15; 7:9; Dt 10:8
28 [e]2Ch 29:15; Ne 13:9; Mal 3:3
29 [f]**Ex 25:30;** [g]Lev 2:4–7; 6:20–23; [h]Lev 19:35–36; **1Ch 9:29**,32
30 [i]**1Ch 9:33;** Ps 134:1
31 [j]**2Ki 4:23;** [k]Nu 28:9–29:39; Isa 1:13–14; Col 2:16
32 [l]1Ch 6:48; [m]Nu 3:6–8,38; [n]2Ch 23:18; 31:2; Eze 44:14

Ch. 24

1 [a]1Ch 23:6; 28:13; 2Ch 5:11; 8:14; 23:8; 31:2; 35:4–5; Ezr 6:18; [b]Nu 3:2–4; [c]**Ex 6:23**
2 [d]Lev 10:1–2
3 [e]**2Sa 8:17**

a*10* One Hebrew manuscript, Septuagint and Vulgate (see also verse 11); most Hebrew manuscripts *Zina*

of families from Eleazar's descendants
and eight heads of families from Itha-
mar's descendants. 5They divided them
impartially by drawing lots,[f] for there
were officials of the sanctuary and
officials of God among the descendants
of both Eleazar and Ithamar.
6The scribe Shemaiah son of
Nethanel, a Levite, recorded their
names in the presence of the king and
of the officials: Zadok the priest,
Ahimelech[g] son of Abiathar and the
heads of families of the priests and of
the Levites—one family being taken
from Eleazar and then one from
Ithamar.

7The first lot fell to Jehoiarib,
the second to Jedaiah,[h]
8the third to Harim,[i]
the fourth to Seorim,
9the fifth to Malkijah,
the sixth to Mijamin,
10the seventh to Hakkoz,
the eighth to Abijah,[j]
11the ninth to Jeshua,
the tenth to Shecaniah,
12the eleventh to Eliashib,
the twelfth to Jakim,
13the thirteenth to Huppah,
the fourteenth to Jeshebeab,
14the fifteenth to Bilgah,
the sixteenth to Immer,[k]
15the seventeenth to Hezir,[l]
the eighteenth to Happizzez,
16the nineteenth to Pethahiah,
the twentieth to Jehezkel,
17the twenty-first to Jakin,
the twenty-second to Gamul,
18the twenty-third to Delaiah
and the twenty-fourth to Maaziah.

19This was their appointed order of
ministering when they entered the tem-
ple of the LORD, according to the regu-
lations prescribed for them by their
forefather Aaron, as the LORD, the God
of Israel, had commanded him.

The Rest of the Levites

20As for the rest of the descendants of
Levi:[m]
from the sons of Amram: Shubael;
from the sons of Shubael: Jehdeiah.
21As for Rehabiah,[n] from his sons:
Isshiah was the first.
22From the Izharites: Shelomoth;
from the sons of Shelomoth: Jahath.
23The sons of Hebron:[o] Jeriah the
first,[a] Amariah the second, Jahaziel the third and Jekameam the fourth.
24The son of Uzziel: Micah;
from the sons of Micah: Shamir.
25The brother of Micah: Isshiah;
from the sons of Isshiah: Zechariah.
26The sons of Merari:[p] Mahli and Mushi.
The son of Jaaziah: Beno
27The sons of Merari:
from Jaaziah: Beno, Shoham, Zaccur and Ibri.
28From Mahli: Eleazar, who had no sons.
29From Kish: the son of Kish: Jerahmeel.
30And the sons of Mushi: Mahli, Eder and Jerimoth.

These were the Levites, according to
their families. 31They also cast lots,[q] just
as their brothers the descendants of
Aaron did, in the presence of King
David and of Zadok, Ahimelech, and
the heads of families of the priests and
of the Levites. The families of the oldest
brother were treated the same as those
of the youngest.

The Singers

25 David, together with the com-
manders of the army, set apart
some of the sons of Asaph,[a] Heman[b]
and Jeduthun[c] for the ministry of
prophesying,[d] accompanied by harps,
lyres and cymbals.[e] Here is the list of the
men[f] who performed this service:[g]

2From the sons of Asaph:
Zaccur, Joseph, Nethaniah and Asarelah. The sons of Asaph were under the supervision of Asaph, who prophesied under the king's supervision.
3As for Jeduthun, from his sons:[h]
Gedaliah, Zeri, Jeshaiah, Shimei,[a] Hashabiah and Mattithiah, six in all, under the supervision of their father Jeduthun, who prophesied, using the harp[i] in thanking and praising the LORD.
4As for Heman, from his sons:
Bukkiah, Mattaniah, Uzziel, Shubael and Jerimoth; Hananiah,

5 [f]ver 31; 1Ch 25:8; 26:13
6 [g]1Ch 18:16
7 [h]Ezr 2:36; Ne 12:6
8 [i]Ezr 2:39; 10:21; Ne 10:5
10 [j]Ne 12:4,17; Lk 1:5
14 [k]Ezr 2:37; 10:20; Jer 20:1
15 [l]Ne 10:20
20 [m]1Ch 23:6
21 [n]1Ch 23:17
23 [o]1Ch 23:19
26 [p]1Ch 6:19
31 [q]ver 5

Ch. 25

1 [a]1Ch 6:39; [b]1Ch 6:33; [c]1Ch 16:41–42; Ne 11:17; [d]1Sa 10:5; 2Ki 3:15; [e]1Ch 15:16; [f]1Ch 6:31; [g]2Ch 5:12; 8:14; 34:12; 35:15; Ezr 3:10
3 [h]1Ch 16:41–42; [i]Ge 4:21; Ps 33:2

[a]23 Two Hebrew manuscripts and some Septuagint manuscripts (see also 1 Chron. 23:19); most Hebrew manuscripts *The sons of Jeriah:*

[a]3 One Hebrew manuscript and some Septuagint manuscripts (see also verse 17); most Hebrew manuscripts do not have *Shimei.*

Hanani, Eliathah, Giddalti and
Romamti-Ezer; Joshbekashah, Mal-
lothi, Hothir and Mahazioth. 5All
these were sons of Heman the
king's seer. They were given to him
through the promises of God to
exalt him.[b] God gave Heman four-
teen sons and three daughters.

6All these men were under the super-
vision of their fathers[j] for the music of
the temple of the LORD, with cymbals,
lyres and harps, for the ministry at the
house of God. Asaph, Jeduthun and
Heman[k] were under the supervision of
the king.[l] 7Along with their relatives
—all of them trained and skilled in
music for the LORD—they numbered
288. 8Young and old alike, teacher as
well as student, cast lots[m] for their
duties.

9The first lot, which was for Asaph,[n] fell to Joseph,
his sons and relatives,[c] 12[d]
the second to Gedaliah,
he and his relatives and sons, 12
10the third to Zaccur,
his sons and relatives, 12
11the fourth to Izri,[e]
his sons and relatives, 12
12the fifth to Nethaniah,
his sons and relatives, 12
13the sixth to Bukkiah,
his sons and relatives, 12
14the seventh to Jesarelah,[f]
his sons and relatives, 12
15the eighth to Jeshaiah,
his sons and relatives, 12
16the ninth to Mattaniah,
his sons and relatives, 12
17the tenth to Shimei,
his sons and relatives, 12
18the eleventh to Azarel,[g]
his sons and relatives, 12
19the twelfth to Hashabiah,
his sons and relatives, 12
20the thirteenth to Shubael,
his sons and relatives, 12
21the fourteenth to Mattithiah,
his sons and relatives, 12
22the fifteenth to Jerimoth,
his sons and relatives, 12
23the sixteenth to Hananiah,
his sons and relatives, 12
24the seventeenth to Joshbekashah,
his sons and relatives, 12
25the eighteenth to Hanani,
his sons and relatives, 12
26the nineteenth to Mallothi,
his sons and relatives, 12
27the twentieth to Eliathah,
his sons and relatives, 12
28the twenty-first to Hothir,
his sons and relatives, 12
29the twenty-second to Giddalti,
his sons and relatives, 12
30the twenty-third to Mahazioth,
his sons and relatives, 12
31the twenty-fourth to Romamti-Ezer,
his sons and relatives. 12[o]

6 [j]1Ch 15:16; [k]1Ch 15:19; [l]2Ch 23:18; 29:25
8 [m]1Ch 26:13
9 [n]1Ch 6:39
31 [o]1Ch 9:33

Ch. 26

1 [a]1Ch 9:17
2 [b]1Ch 9:21
5 [c]2Sa 6:10; 1Ch 13:13; 16:38

The Gatekeepers

26 The divisions of the gatekeepers:[a]

From the Korahites: Meshelemiah son of Kore, one of the sons of Asaph.
2Meshelemiah had sons:
Zechariah[b] the firstborn,
Jediael the second,
Zebadiah the third,
Jathniel the fourth,
3Elam the fifth,
Jehohanan the sixth
and Eliehoenai the seventh.
4Obed-Edom also had sons:
Shemaiah the firstborn,
Jehozabad the second,
Joah the third,
Sacar the fourth,
Nethanel the fifth,
5Ammiel the sixth,
Issachar the seventh
and Peullethai the eighth.
(For God had blessed Obed-Edom.[c])

6His son Shemaiah also had sons,
who were leaders in their father's
family because they were very
capable men. 7The sons of She-
maiah: Othni, Rephael, Obed
and Elzabad; his relatives Elihu
and Semakiah were also able
men. 8All these were descend-
ants of Obed-Edom; they and
their sons and their relatives
were capable men with the
strength to do the work—
descendants of Obed-Edom, 62
in all.

b5 Hebrew *exalt the horn*
c9 See Septuagint; Hebrew does not have *his sons and relatives.*
d9 See the total in verse 7; Hebrew does not have *twelve.*
e11 A variant of *Zeri*
f14 A variant of *Asarelah*
g18 A variant of *Uzziel*

9Meshelemiah had sons and rela-
tives, who were able men—18 in
all.

10Hosah the Merarite had sons:
Shimri the first (although he was
not the firstborn, his father had
appointed him the first),[d]
11Hilkiah the second, Tabaliah
the third and Zechariah the
fourth. The sons and relatives of
Hosah were 13 in all.

12These divisions of the gatekeepers,
through their chief men, had duties for
ministering[e] in the temple of the LORD,
just as their relatives had. 13Lots[f] were
cast for each gate, according to their
families, young and old alike.
14The lot for the East Gate[g] fell to
Shelemiah.[a] Then lots were cast for his
son Zechariah,[h] a wise counsellor, and
the lot for the North Gate fell to him.
15The lot for the South Gate fell to Obed-
Edom,[i] and the lot for the storehouse
fell to his sons. 16The lots for the West
Gate and the Shalleketh Gate on the
upper road fell to Shuppim and Hosah.
Guard was alongside guard: 17There
were six Levites a day on the east, four a
day on the north, four a day on the
south and two at a time at the store-
house. 18As for the court to the west,
there were four at the road and two at
the court itself.
19These were the divisions of the
gatekeepers who were descendants of
Korah and Merari.[j]

The Treasurers and Other Officials

20Their fellow Levites[k] were[b] in
charge of the treasuries of the house of
God and the treasuries for the dedicated
things.[l]
21The descendants of Ladan, who
were Gershonites through Ladan and
who were heads of families belonging to
Ladan the Gershonite,[m] were Jehieli,
22the sons of Jehieli, Zetham and his
brother Joel. They were in charge of the
treasuries[n] of the temple of the LORD.
23From the Amramites, the Izharites,
the Hebronites and the Uzzielites:[o]

24Shubael,[p] a descendant of Gershom
son of Moses, was the officer in
charge of the treasuries. 25His
relatives through Eliezer: Re-
habiah his son, Jeshaiah his son,
Joram his son, Zicri his son and
Shelomith[q] his son. 26Shelomith
and his relatives were in charge
of all the treasuries for the things
dedicated[r] by King David, by the
heads of families who were the
commanders of thousands and
commanders of hundreds, and
by the other army commanders.
27Some of the plunder taken in
battle they dedicated for the re-
pair of the temple of the LORD.
28And everything dedicated by
Samuel the seer[s] and by Saul son
of Kish, Abner son of Ner and
Joab son of Zeruiah, and all the
other dedicated things were in
the care of Shelomith and his
relatives.

29From the Izharites: Kenaniah and
his sons were assigned duties
away from the temple, as officials
and judges[t] over Israel.

30From the Hebronites: Hashabiah[u]
and his relatives—seventeen
hundred able men—were re-
sponsible in Israel west of the
Jordan for all the work of the
LORD and for the king's service.
31As for the Hebronites,[v] Jeriah
was their chief according to the
genealogical records of their
families. In the fortieth[w] year of
David's reign a search was made
in the records, and capable men
among the Hebronites were
found at Jazer in Gilead. 32Jeriah
had two thousand seven hun-
dred relatives, who were able
men and heads of families, and
King David put them in charge of
the Reubenites, the Gadites and
the half-tribe of Manasseh for
every matter pertaining to God
and for the affairs of the king.

Army Divisions

27 This is the list of the Israelites
—heads of families, comman-
ders of thousands and commanders of
hundreds, and their officers, who
served the king in all that concerned the
army divisions that were on duty month
by month throughout the year. Each
division consisted of 24,000 men.

2In charge of the first division, for the
first month, was Jashobeam[a] son of
Zabdiel. There were 24,000 men in
his division. 3He was a descendant
of Perez and chief of all the army
officers for the first month.
4In charge of the division for the second
month was Dodai[b] the Ahohite;

10 [d]Dt 21:16; 1Ch 5:1
12 [e]1Ch 9:22
13 [f]**1Ch 24:5**
14 [g]**1Ch 9:18;** [h]**1Ch 9:21**
15 [i]**1Ch 13:13;** 2Ch 25:24
19 [j]2Ch 35:15; Ne 7:1; Eze 44:11
20 [k]2Sa 24:5; [l]1Ch 28:12
21 [m]1Ch 23:7; 29:8
22 [n]1Ch 9:26
23 [o]**Nu 3:27**
24 [p]1Ch 23:16
25 [q]**1Ch 23:18**
26 [r]**2Sa 8:11**
28 [s]**1Sa 9:9**
29 [t]Dt 17:8–13; **1Ch 23:4**
30 [u]1Ch 27:17
31 [v]**1Ch 23:19;** [w]**2Sa 5:4**

Ch. 27

2 [a]2Sa 23:8
4 [b]**2Sa 23:9**

[a]14 A variant of *Meshelemiah*
[b]20 Septuagint; Hebrew *As for the Levites, Ahijah was*

Mikloth was the leader of his divi-
sion. There were 24,000 men in his
division.
5The third army commander, for the
third month, was Benaiah[c] son of
Jehoiada the priest. He was chief
and there were 24,000 men in his
division. 6This was the Benaiah
who was a mighty man among the
Thirty and was over the Thirty. His
son Ammizabad was in charge of
his division.
7The fourth, for the fourth month, was
Asahel[d] the brother of Joab; his son
Zebadiah was his successor. There
were 24,000 men in his division.
8The fifth, for the fifth month, was the
commander Shamhuth[e] the Izra-
hite. There were 24,000 men in his
division.
9The sixth, for the sixth month, was Ira[f]
the son of Ikkesh the Tekoite. There
were 24,000 men in his division.
10The seventh, for the seventh month,
was Helez[g] the Pelonite, an
Ephraimite. There were 24,000 men
in his division.
11The eighth, for the eighth month, was
Sibbecai[h] the Hushathite, a Zera-
hite. There were 24,000 men in his
division.
12The ninth, for the ninth month, was
Abiezer[i] the Anathothite, a Benja-
mite. There were 24,000 men in his
division.
13The tenth, for the tenth month, was
Maharai[j] the Netophathite, a Zera-
hite. There were 24,000 men in his
division.
14The eleventh, for the eleventh month,
was Benaiah[k] the Pirathonite, an
Ephraimite. There were 24,000 men
in his division.
15The twelfth, for the twelfth month,
was Heldai[l] the Netophathite, from
the family of Othniel.[m] There were
24,000 men in his division.

Officers of the Tribes

16The officers over the tribes of Israel:

over the Reubenites: Eliezer son of
Zicri;
over the Simeonites: Shephatiah
son of Maacah;
17over Levi: Hashabiah[n] son of
Kemuel;
over Aaron: Zadok;[o]
18over Judah: Elihu, a brother of
David;
over Issachar: Omri son of Michael;
19over Zebulun: Ishmaiah son of
Obadiah;
over Naphtali: Jerimoth son of
Azriel;
20over the Ephraimites: Hoshea son
of Azaziah;
over half the tribe of Manasseh: Joel
son of Pedaiah;
21over the half-tribe of Manasseh in
Gilead: Iddo son of Zechariah;
over Benjamin: Jaasiel son of
Abner;
22over Dan: Azarel son of Jeroham.
These were the officers over the tribes
of Israel.

23David did not take the number of
the men twenty years old or less,[p] be-
cause the LORD had promised to make
Israel as numerous as the stars[q] in the
sky. 24Joab son of Zeruiah began to
count the men but did not finish. Wrath
came on Israel on account of this num-
bering,[r] and the number was not
entered in the book[a] of the annals of
King David.

The King's Overseers

25Azmaveth son of Adiel was in
charge of the royal storehouses.
Jonathan son of Uzziah was in charge
of the storehouses in the outlying dis-
tricts, in the towns, the villages and the
watchtowers.
26Ezri son of Kelub was in charge of
the field workers who farmed the land.
27Shimei the Ramathite was in charge
of the vineyards.
Zabdi the Shiphmite was in charge of
the produce of the vineyards for the
wine vats.
28Baal-Hanan the Gederite was in
charge of the olive and sycamore-fig[s]
trees in the western foothills.
Joash was in charge of the supplies of
olive oil.
29Shitrai the Sharonite was in charge
of the herds grazing in Sharon.[t]
Shaphat son of Adlai was in charge of
the herds in the valleys.
30Obil the Ishmaelite was in charge of
the camels.
Jehdeiah the Meronothite was in
charge of the donkeys.
31Jaziz the Hagrite[u] was in charge of
the flocks.
All these were the officials in charge
of King David's property.

32Jonathan, David's uncle, was a
counsellor, a man of insight and a

5 [c]**2Sa 23:20**
7 [d]**2Sa 2:18**
8 [e]1Ch 11:27
9 [f]2Sa 23:26
10 [g]2Sa 23:26
11 [h]**2Sa 21:18**
12 [i]2Sa 23:27
13 [j]2Sa 23:28
14 [k]**1Ch 11:31**
15 [l]2Sa 23:29; [m]**Jos 15:17**
17 [n]1Ch 26:30; [o]**2Sa 8:17; 1Ch 12:28**
23 [p]**2Sa 24:1;** 1Ch 21:2–5; [q]**Ge 12:2**
24 [r]**2Sa 24:15;** 1Ch 21:14
28 [s]**1Ki 10:27**
29 [t]SS 2:1; Isa 33:9; 35:2; 65:10
31 [u]**1Ch 5:10**

[a]24 Septuagint; Hebrew *number*

scribe. Jehiel son of Hacmoni took care
of the king's sons.
33Ahithophel[v] was the king's counsel-
lor.
Hushai[w] the Arkite was the king's
friend. 34Ahithophel was succeeded
by Jehoiada son of Benaiah and by
Abiathar.[x]
Joab[y] was the commander of the royal
army.

David's Plans for the Temple

28 David summoned[a] all the
officials[b] of Israel to assemble at
Jerusalem: the officers over the tribes,
the commanders of the divisions in the
service of the king, the commanders of
thousands and commanders of hun-
dreds, and the officials in charge of all
the property and livestock belonging to
the king and his sons, together with the
palace officials, the mighty men and all
the brave warriors.
2King David rose to his feet and said:
"Listen to me, my brothers and my peo-
ple. I had it in my heart[c] to build a house
as a place of rest[d] for the ark of the
covenant of the LORD, for the footstool[e]
of our God, and I made plans to build it.[f]
3But God said to me,[g] 'You are not to
build a house for my Name,[h] because
you are a warrior and have shed blood.'[i]
4"Yet the LORD, the God of Israel,
chose me[j] from my whole family[k] to be
king over Israel for ever. He chose
Judah[l] as leader, and from the house of
Judah he chose my family, and from my
father's sons he was pleased to make me
king over all Israel.[m] 5Of all my sons
—and the LORD has given me many[n]
—he has chosen my son Solomon[o] to sit
on the throne[p] of the kingdom of the
LORD over Israel. 6He said to me, 'Solo-
mon your son is the one who will build[q]
my house and my courts, for I have
chosen him to be my son,[r] and I will be
his father. 7I will establish his kingdom
for ever if he is unswerving in carrying
out my commands and laws,[s] as is being
done at this time.'
8"So now I charge you in the sight of
all Israel[t] and of the assembly of the
LORD, and in the hearing of our God: Be
careful to follow all the commands[u] of
the LORD your God, that you may pos-
sess this good land and pass it on as an
inheritance to your descendants for
ever.[v]
9"And you, my son Solomon, ac-
knowledge the God of your father, and
serve him with wholehearted devotion[w]
and with a willing mind, for the LORD
searches every heart[x] and understands
every motive behind the thoughts. If
you seek him,[y] he will be found by you;
but if you forsake[z] him, he will reject[a]
you for ever. 10Consider now, for the
LORD has chosen you to build a temple
as a sanctuary. Be strong and do the
work."
11Then David gave his son Solomon
the plans[b] for the portico of the temple,
its buildings, its storerooms, its upper
parts, its inner rooms and the place of
atonement. 12He gave him the plans of
all that the Spirit[c] had put in his mind for
the courts of the temple of the LORD and
all the surrounding rooms, for the
treasuries of the temple of God and for
the treasuries for the dedicated things.[d]
13He gave him instructions for the div-
isions[e] of the priests and Levites, and
for all the work of serving in the temple
of the LORD, as well as for all the articles
to be used in its service. 14He designated
the weight of gold for all the gold art-
icles to be used in various kinds of ser-
vice, and the weight of silver for all the
silver articles to be used in various kinds
of service: 15the weight of gold for the
gold lampstands[f] and their lamps, with
the weight for each lampstand and its
lamps; and the weight of silver for each
silver lampstand and its lamps, accord-
ing to the use of each lampstand; 16the
weight of gold for each table[g] for conse-
crated bread; the weight of silver for the
silver tables; 17the weight of pure gold
for the forks, sprinkling bowls[h] and
pitchers; the weight of gold for each
gold dish; the weight of silver for each
silver dish; 18and the weight of the re-
fined gold for the altar of incense.[i] He
also gave him the plan for the chariot,[j]
that is, the cherubim of gold that spread
their wings and shelter[k] the ark of the
covenant of the LORD.
19"All this," David said, "I have in
writing from the hand of the LORD upon
me, and he gave me understanding in
all the details[l] of the plan.[m]"
20David also said to Solomon his son,
"Be strong and courageous,[n] and do the
work. Do not be afraid or discouraged,
for the LORD God, my God, is with you.
He will not fail you or forsake[o] you until
all the work for the service of the temple
of the LORD is finished.[p] 21The divisions
of the priests and Levites are ready for
all the work on the temple of God, and
every willing man skilled[q] in any craft
will help you in all the work. The of-
ficials and all the people will obey your
every command."

33 [v]2Sa 15:12; [w]2Sa 15:37
34 [x]1Sa 22:20; [y]2Sa 2:13

Ch. 28

1 [a]1Ch 22:17; [b]1Ch 27:1–31; 29:6
2 [c]1Sa 10:7; 1Ch 17:2; [d]2Ch 6:41; [e]Ps 99:5; 132:7; Isa 60:13; [f]Ps 132:1–5
3 [g]2Sa 7:5; [h]1Ch 22:8; [i]1Ki 5:3; 1Ch 17:4
4 [j]2Ch 6:6; [k]1Sa 16:1–13; [l]Ge 49:10; Nu 24:17–19; [m]1Ch 11:1
5 [n]1Ch 3:1; [o]2Sa 12:24; 1Ch 23:1; [p]1Ch 17:14
6 [q]1Ki 8:20; [r]2Sa 7:13; 1Ch 17:13
7 [s]1Ch 22:13
8 [t]1Ch 9:1; [u]Dt 6:1; [v]Dt 4:1; 17:14–20
9 [w]1Ch 29:19; [x]1Sa 2:3; 2Ch 6:30; Ps 7:9; [y]1Ch 16:11; Ps 40:16; [z]Dt 4:31; Jos 24:20; 2Ch 7:19; 15:2; [a]1Ki 9:7; Ps 44:23; 74:1; 77:7
11 [b]Ex 25:9; Ac 7:44; Heb 8:5
12 [c]1Ch 12:18; [d]1Ch 26:20
13 [e]1Ch 24:1
15 [f]Ex 25:31
16 [g]Ex 25:23
17 [h]Ex 27:3
18 [i]Ex 30:1–10; [j]Ex 25:22; [k]Ex 25:20
19 [l]1Ki 6:38; [m]Ex 25:9
20 [n]Dt 31:6; 1Ch 22:13; 2Ch 19:11; Hag 2:4; [o]Dt 4:31; Jos 24:20; [p]1Ki 6:14; 2Ch 7:11
21 [q]Ex 35:25–36:5

Gifts for Building the Temple

29 Then King David said to the
whole assembly: "My son Solo-
mon, the one whom God has chosen, is
young and inexperienced.[a] The task is
great, because this palatial structure is
not for man but for the LORD God. 2With
all my resources I have provided for the
temple of my God—gold[b] for the gold
work, silver for the silver, bronze for the
bronze, iron for the iron and wood for
the wood, as well as onyx for the set-
tings, turquoise,[a][c] stones of various col-
ours, and all kinds of fine stone and
marble—all of these in large quantities.[d]
3Besides, in my devotion to the temple
of my God I now give my personal
treasures of gold and silver for the tem-
ple of my God, over and above every-
thing I have provided[e] for this holy
temple: 4three thousand talents[b] of gold
(gold of Ophir)[f] and seven thousand
talents[c] of refined silver,[g] for the over-
laying of the walls of the buildings, 5for
the gold work and the silver work, and
for all the work to be done by the crafts-
men. Now, who is willing to consecrate
himself today to the LORD?"
6Then the leaders of families, the
officers of the tribes of Israel, the com-
manders of thousands and commanders
of hundreds, and the officials[h] in charge
of the king's work gave willingly.[i]
7They[j] gave towards the work on the
temple of God five thousand talents[d]
and ten thousand darics[e] of gold, ten
thousand talents[f] of silver, eighteen
thousand talents[g] of bronze and a hun-
dred thousand talents[h] of iron. 8Any
who had precious stones[k] gave them to
the treasury of the temple of the LORD in
the custody of Jehiel the Gershonite.[l]
9The people rejoiced at the willing re-
sponse of their leaders, for they had
given freely and wholeheartedly[m] to the
LORD. David the king also rejoiced
greatly.

David's Prayer

10David praised the LORD in the pres-
ence of the whole assembly, saying,

"Praise be to you, O LORD,
God of our father Israel,
from everlasting to everlasting.
11Yours, O LORD, is the greatness and
the power[n]
and the glory and the majesty and
the splendour,
for everything in heaven and earth
is yours.[o]
Yours, O LORD, is the kingdom;
you are exalted as head over all.[p]
12Wealth and honour[q] come from you;
you are the ruler[r] of all things.
In your hands are strength and power
to exalt and give strength to all.
13Now, our God, we give you thanks,
and praise your glorious name.

14"But who am I, and who are my
people, that we should be able to give as
generously as this?[s] Everything comes
from you, and we have given you only
what comes from your hand.[t] 15We are
aliens and strangers[u] in your sight, as
were all our forefathers. Our days on
earth are like a shadow,[v] without hope.
16O LORD our God, as for all this abund-
ance that we have provided for building
you a temple for your Holy Name, it
comes from your hand, and all of it
belongs to you. 17I know, my God, that
you test the heart[w] and are pleased with
integrity. All these things have I given
willingly and with honest intent. And
now I have seen with joy how willingly
your people who are here have given to
you.[x] 18O LORD, God of our fathers
Abraham, Isaac and Israel, keep this
desire in the hearts of your people for
ever, and keep their hearts loyal to you.
19And give my son Solomon the
wholehearted devotion[y] to keep your
commands, requirements and decrees[z]
and to do everything to build the
palatial structure for which I have
provided."[a]
20Then David said to the whole
assembly, "Praise the LORD your God."
So they all praised the LORD, the God of
their fathers; they bowed low and fell
prostrate before the LORD and the
king.

Solomon Acknowledged as King

21The next day they made sacrifices to
the LORD and presented burnt offerings
to him:[b] a thousand bulls, a thousand
rams and a thousand male lambs,
together with their drink offerings, and

Ch. 29

1 [a]1Ki 3:7; 1Ch 22:5; 2Ch 13:7
2 [b]ver 7,14,16; Ezr 1:4; 6:5; Hag 2:8; [c]Isa 54:11; [d]1Ch 22:2–5
3 [e]2Ch 24:10; 31:3; 35:8
4 [f]**Ge 10:29;** [g]1Ch 22:14
6 [h]1Ch 27:1; **28:1;** [i]ver 9; Ex 25:1–8; 35:20–29; 36:2; 2Ch 24:10; Ezr 7:15
7 [j]**Ex 25:2;** Ne 7:70–71
8 [k]Ex 35:27; [l]**1Ch 26:21**
9 [m]1Ki 8:61
11 [n]Ps 24:8; 59:17; 62:11; [o]Ps 89:11; [p]Rev 5:12–13
12 [q]2Ch 1:12; 32:27; Ezr 7:27; Ecc 5:19; [r]2Ch 20:6
14 [s]Ps 8:4; 144:3; [t]**ver 2**
15 [u]**Ge 17:8; 23:4;** Ps 39:12; **Heb 11:13;** [v]Job 7:6; 8:9; 14:2; 32:7; Ps 102:11; 144:4; Ecc 6:12
17 [w]Ps 139:23; Pr 15:11; 17:3; Jer 11:20; 17:10; [x]1Ch 28:9; Ps 15:1–5; Pr 11:20
19 [y]**1Ki 8:61;** 11:4; 1Ch 28:9; Isa 38:3; [z]Ps 72:1; [a]**1Ch 22:14**
21 [b]**1Ki 8:62**

---

a2 The meaning of the Hebrew for this word is uncertain.
b4 That is, about 100 tons (about 100 metric tons)
c4 That is, about 240 tons (about 240 metric tons)
d7 That is, about 170 tons (about 170 metric tons)
e7 That is, about 185 pounds (about 84 kilograms)
f7 That is, about 340 tons (about 345 metric tons)
g7 That is, about 610 tons (about 620 metric tons)
h7 That is, about 3,400 tons (about 3,450 metric tons)

other sacrifices in abundance for all Israel.[c] 22They ate and drank with great joy[d] in the presence of the LORD that day.

Then they acknowledged Solomon son of David as king a second time, anointing him before the LORD to be ruler and Zadok[e] to be priest. 23So Solomon sat[f] on the throne[g] of the LORD as king in place of his father David. He prospered and all Israel obeyed him. 24All the officers and mighty men, as well as all of King David's sons,[h] pledged their submission to King Solomon.

25The LORD highly exalted[i] Solomon in the sight of all Israel and bestowed on him royal splendour[j] such as no king over Israel ever had before.[k]

21 [c]1Ch 11:1
22 [d]1Ch 12:40; [e]1Sa 2:35
23 [f]Dt 17:18; [g]1Ki 2:12; 1Ch 17:14
24 [h]1Ki 1:9
25 [i]Jos 3:7; [j]1Ki 10:7; 2Ch 1:1,12; [k]Ecc 2:9
26 [l]1Ch 18:14; [m]1Ch 11:1
27 [n]Ge 23:19; [o]2Sa 5:4–5; 1Ch 3:4
28 [p]Ge 15:15; Ac 13:36; [q]1Ch 23:1
29 [r]1Sa 9:9; [s]2Sa 7:2; [t]1Sa 22:5

The Death of David

29:26–28pp—1Ki 2:10–12

26David son of Jesse was king[l] over all Israel.[m] 27He ruled over Israel for forty years—seven in Hebron[n] and thirty-three in Jerusalem.[o] 28He died[p] at a good old age, having enjoyed long life, wealth and honour. His son Solomon succeeded him as king.[q]

29As for the events of King David's reign, from beginning to end, they are written in the records of Samuel the seer,[r] the records of Nathan[s] the prophet and the records of Gad[t] the seer, 30together with the details of his reign and power, and the circumstances that surrounded him and Israel and the kingdoms of all the other lands.

2 Chronicles

Solomon Asks for Wisdom

1:2–15pp—1Ki 3:4–15
1:14–17pp—1Ki 10:26–29; 2Ch 9:25–28

1 Solomon son of David established[a]
himself firmly over his kingdom,
for the LORD his God was with[b] him and
made him exceedingly great.[c]
2Then Solomon spoke to all Israel[d]
—to the commanders of thousands and
commanders of hundreds, to the judges
and to all the leaders in Israel, the heads
of families—3and Solomon and the
whole assembly went to the high place
at Gibeon,[e] for God's Tent of Meeting[f]
was there, which Moses[g] the LORD's ser-
vant had made in the desert. 4Now
David had brought up the ark[h] of God
from Kiriath Jearim to the place he had
prepared for it, because he had pitched
a tent[i] for it in Jerusalem. 5But the
bronze altar[j] that Bezalel[k] son of Uri, the
son of Hur, had made was in Gibeon in
front of the tabernacle of the LORD; so
Solomon and the assembly enquired[l] of
him there. 6Solomon went up to the
bronze altar before the LORD in the Tent
of Meeting and offered a thousand
burnt offerings on it.
7That night God appeared[m] to Sol-
omon and said to him, "Ask for what-
ever you want me to give you."
8Solomon answered God, "You have
shown great kindness to David my
father and have made me[n] king in his
place. 9Now, LORD God, let your prom-
ise[o] to my father David be confirmed, for
you have made me king over a people
who are as numerous as the dust of the
earth.[p] 10Give me wisdom and knowl-
edge, that I may lead[q] this people, for
who is able to govern this great people
of yours?"
11God said to Solomon, "Since this is
your heart's desire and you have not
asked for wealth,[r] riches or honour, nor
for the death of your enemies, and since
you have not asked for a long life but for
wisdom and knowledge to govern my
people over whom I have made you
king, 12therefore wisdom and knowl-
edge will be given you. And I will also
give you wealth, riches and honour,[s]
such as no king who was before you
ever had and none after you will have."[t]
13Then Solomon went to Jerusalem
from the high place at Gibeon, from
before the Tent of Meeting. And he
reigned over Israel.
14Solomon accumulated chariots[u] and
horses; he had fourteen hundred char-
iots and twelve thousand horses,[a]
which he kept in the chariot cities and
also with him in Jerusalem. 15The king
made silver and gold[v] as common in
Jerusalem as stones, and cedar as plenti-
ful as sycamore-fig trees in the foothills.
16Solomon's horses were imported from
Egypt[b] and from Kue[c]—the royal mer-
chants purchased them from Kue.
17They imported a chariot[w] from Egypt
for six hundred shekels[d] of silver, and a
horse for a hundred and fifty.[e] They also
exported them to all the kings of the
Hittites and of the Arameans.

Preparations for Building the Temple

2:1–18pp—1Ki 5:1–16

2 Solomon gave orders to build a
temple[a] for the Name of the LORD
and a royal palace for himself.[b] 2He
conscripted seventy thousand men
as carriers and eighty thousand as
stonecutters in the hills and thirty-six
hundred as foremen over them.[c]
3Solomon sent this message to
Hiram[a][d] king of Tyre:

> "Send me cedar logs[e] as you did
> for my father David when you sent
> him cedar to build a palace to live
> in. 4Now I am about to build a
> temple[f] for the Name of the LORD
> my God and to dedicate it to him for
> burning fragrant incense[g] before

Ch. 1

1 [a]**1Ki 2:12; 2Ch 12:1;** [b]**Ge 21:22; 39:2; Nu 14:43;** [c]**1Ch 29:25**
2 [d]**1Ch 9:1**
3 [e]**Jos 9:3;** [f]**Lev 17:4;** [g]Ex 40:18
4 [h]**1Ch 15:25;** [i]2Sa 6:17
5 [j]Ex 38:2; [k]**Ex 31:2;** [l]1Ch 13:3
7 [m]2Ch 7:12
8 [n]**1Ch 23:1**
9 [o]**2Sa 7:25; 1Ki 8:25;** [p]Ge 12:2
10 [q]Nu 27:17; 2Sa 5:2; Pr 8:15–16
11 [r]**Dt 17:17**
12 [s]**1Ch 29:12;** [t]**1Ch 29:25;** 2Ch 9:22; Ne 13:26
14 [u]**1Sa 8:11; 1Ki 9:19**
15 [v]**1Ki 9:28;** Isa 60:5
17 [w]SS 1:9

Ch. 2

1 [a]**Dt 12:5;** [b]Ecc 2:4
2 [c]2Ch 10:4
3 [d]**2Sa 5:11;** [e]**1Ch 14:1**
4 [f]Dt 12:5; [g]Ex 30:7

---

[a]14 Or *charioteers*
[b]16 Or possibly *Muzur*, a region in Cilicia; also in verse 17 [c]16 Probably Cilicia
[d]17 That is, about 15 pounds (about 7 kilograms)
[e]17 That is, about 3¾ pounds (about 1.7 kilograms)
[a]3 Hebrew *Huram*, a variant of *Hiram*; also in verses 11 and 12

him, for setting out the consecrated bread[h] regularly, and for making burnt offerings[i] every morning and evening and on Sabbaths[j] and New Moons[k] and at the appointed feasts of the LORD our God. This is a lasting ordinance for Israel.

5"The temple I am going to build will be great,[l] because our God is greater than all other gods.[m] 6But who is able to build a temple for him, since the heavens, even the highest heavens, cannot contain him?[n] Who then am I[o] to build a temple for him, except as a place to burn sacrifices before him?

7"Send me, therefore, a man skilled to work in gold and silver, bronze and iron, and in purple, crimson and blue yarn, and experienced in the art of engraving, to work in Judah and Jerusalem with my skilled craftsmen,[p] whom my father David provided.

8"Send me also cedar, pine and algum[b] logs from Lebanon, for I know that your men are skilled in cutting timber there. My men shall work with yours 9to provide me with plenty of timber, because the temple I build must be large and magnificent. 10I will give your servants, the woodsmen who cut the timber, twenty thousand cors[c] of ground wheat, twenty thousand cors of barley, twenty thousand baths[d] of wine and twenty thousand baths of olive oil."[q]

11Hiram king of Tyre replied by letter to Solomon:

"Because the LORD loves[r] his people, he has made you their king."

12And Hiram added:

"Praise be to the LORD, the God of Israel, who made heaven and earth![s] He has given King David a wise son, endowed with intelligence and discernment, who will build a temple for the LORD and a palace for himself.

13"I am sending you Huram-Abi,[t] a man of great skill, 14whose mother was from Dan[u] and whose father was from Tyre. He is trained[v] to work in gold and silver, bronze and iron, stone and wood, and with purple and blue[w] and crimson yarn and fine linen. He is experienced in all kinds of engraving and can execute any design given to him. He will work with your craftsmen and with those of my lord, David your father.

15"Now let my lord send his servants the wheat and barley and the olive oil[x] and wine he promised, 16and we will cut all the logs from Lebanon that you need and will float them in rafts by sea down to Joppa.[y] You can then take them up to Jerusalem."

17Solomon took a census of all the aliens[z] who were in Israel, after the census[a] his father David had taken; and they were found to be 153,600. 18He assigned[b] 70,000 of them to be carriers and 80,000 to be stonecutters in the hills, with 3,600 foremen over them to keep the people working.

Solomon Builds the Temple

3:1–14pp—1Ki 6:1–29

3 Then Solomon began to build[a] the temple of the LORD[b] in Jerusalem on Mount Moriah, where the LORD had appeared to his father David. It was on the threshing-floor of Araunah[a][c] the Jebusite, the place provided by David. 2He began building on the second day of the second month in the fourth year of his reign.[d]

3The foundation Solomon laid for building the temple of God was sixty cubits long and twenty cubits wide[b][e] (using the cubit of the old standard). 4The portico at the front of the temple was twenty cubits[c] long across the width of the building and twenty cubits[d] high.

He overlaid the inside with pure gold. 5He panelled the main hall with pine and covered it with fine gold and decorated it with palm tree[f] and chain designs. 6He adorned the temple with precious stones. And the gold he used was gold of Parvaim. 7He overlaid the ceiling beams, door-frames, walls and doors of the temple with gold, and he carved cherubim[g] on the walls.

4 [h]Ex 25:30; [i]Ex 29:42; 2Ch 13:11; 29:28; [j]**Lev 23:38**; [k]**Nu 28:14**
5 [l]1Ch 22:5; [m]**Ex 12:12; 1Ch 16:25**
6 [n]**1Ki 8:27**; Jer 23:24; [o]**Ex 3:11**
7 [p]**Ex 35:31**; 1Ch 22:16
10 [q]Ezr 3:7
11 [r]1Ki 10:9; 2Ch 9:8
12 [s]Ne 9:6; Ps 8:3; 33:6; 96:5; 102:25; 146:6
13 [t]**1Ki 7:13**
14 [u]**Ex 31:6**; [v]**Ex 35:31**; [w]Ex 35:35
15 [x]Ezr 3:7
16 [y]**Jos 19:46**; Jnh 1:3
17 [z]1Ch 22:2; [a]**2Sa 24:2**
18 [b]1Ch 22:2; 2Ch 8:8

Ch. 3

1 [a]Ac 7:47; [b]**Ge 28:17**; [c]**2Sa 24:18**
2 [d]Ezr 5:11
3 [e]Eze 41:2
5 [f]Eze 40:16
7 [g]Ge 3:24; Eze 41:18

b8 Probably a variant of *almug;* possibly juniper
c10 That is, probably about 120,000 bushels (about 4,400 kilolitres)
d10 That is, probably about 95,000 gallons (about 440 kilolitres)
a1 Hebrew *Ornan,* a variant of *Araunah*
b3 That is, about 90 feet (about 27 metres) long and 30 feet (about 9 metres) wide
c4 That is, about 30 feet (about 9 metres); also in verses 8, 11 and 13
d4 Some Septuagint and Syriac manuscripts; Hebrew *and a hundred and twenty*

8 He built the Most Holy Place,[h] its
length corresponding to the width of
the temple—twenty cubits long and
twenty cubits wide. He overlaid the in-
side with six hundred talents[e] of fine
gold. 9 The gold nails[i] weighed fifty
shekels.[f] He also overlaid the upper
parts with gold.
10 In the Most Holy Place he made a
pair[j] of sculptured cherubim and over-
laid them with gold. 11 The total wing-
span of the cherubim was twenty
cubits. One wing of the first cherub was
five cubits[g] long and touched the
temple wall, while its other wing, also
five cubits long, touched the wing of the
other cherub. 12 Similarly one wing of
the second cherub was five cubits long
and touched the other temple wall, and
its other wing, also five cubits long,
touched the wing of the first cherub.
13 The wings of these cherubim[k] ex-
tended twenty cubits. They stood on
their feet, facing the main hall.[h]
14 He made the curtain[l] of blue, purple
and crimson yarn and fine linen, with
cherubim[m] worked into it.
15 In the front of the temple he made
two pillars,[n] which ⌞together⌟ were
thirty-five cubits[i] long, each with a
capital[o] on top measuring five cubits.
16 He made interwoven chains[j][p] and put
them on top of the pillars. He also made
a hundred pomegranates[q] and attached
them to the chains. 17 He erected the
pillars in the front of the temple, one to
the south and one to the north. The one
to the south he named Jakin[k] and the
one to the north Boaz.[l]

The Temple's Furnishings

4:2–6,10–15:1pp—1Ki 7:23–26, 38–51

4 He made a bronze altar[a] twenty
cubits long, twenty cubits wide
and ten cubits high.[a] 2 He made the Sea[b]
of cast metal, circular in shape, measur-
ing ten cubits from rim to rim and five
cubits[b] high. It took a line of thirty
cubits[c] to measure round it. 3 Below the
rim, figures of bulls encircled it—ten to
a cubit.[d] The bulls were cast in two rows
in one piece with the Sea.
4 The Sea stood on twelve bulls, three
facing north, three facing west, three
facing south and three facing east.[c] The
Sea rested on top of them, and their
hindquarters were towards the centre.
5 It was a handbreadth[e] in thickness, and
its rim was like the rim of a cup, like a
lily blossom. It held three thousand
baths.[f]
6 He then made ten basins[d] for
washing and placed five on the south
side and five on the north. In them the
things to be used for the burnt offerings[e]
were rinsed, but the Sea was to be used
by the priests for washing.
7 He made ten gold lampstands[f]
according to the specifications[g] for them
and placed them in the temple, five on
the south side and five on the north.
8 He made ten tables[h] and placed them
in the temple, five on the south side and
five on the north. He also made a hun-
dred gold sprinkling bowls.[i]
9 He made the courtyard[j] of the
priests, and the large court and the
doors for the court, and overlaid
the doors with bronze. 10 He placed the
Sea on the south side, at the south-east
corner.
11 He also made the pots and shovels
and sprinkling bowls.
So Huram finished[k] the work he had
undertaken for King Solomon in the
temple of God:

12 the two pillars;
the two bowl-shaped capitals on
top of the pillars;
the two sets of network decorating
the two bowl-shaped capitals on
top of the pillars;
13 the four hundred pomegranates for
the two sets of network (two
rows of pomegranates for each
network, decorating the bowl-
shaped capitals on top of the
pillars);
14 the stands[l] with their basins;
15 the Sea and the twelve bulls under
it;
16 the pots, shovels, meat forks and
all related articles.

All the objects that Huram-Abi[m] made
for King Solomon for the temple of the
LORD were of polished bronze. 17 The
king had them cast in clay moulds in the
plain of the Jordan between Succoth[n]

8 [h]**Ex 26:33**
9 [i]Ex 26:32
10 [j]Ex 25:18
13 [k]**Ex 25:18**
14 [l]**Ex 26:31**,33; [m]Ge 3:24
15 [n]**1Ki 7:15**; Rev 3:12; [o]1Ki 7:22
16 [p]1Ki 7:17; [q]**1Ki 7:20**

Ch. 4

1 [a]**Ex 20:24; 40:6; 1Ki 8:64**
2 [b]Rev 4:6; 15:2
4 [c]Nu 2:3–25; Eze 48:30–34; Rev 21:13
6 [d]**Ex 30:18**; [e]Ne 13:5,9; Eze 40:38
7 [f]**Ex 25:31**; [g]Ex 25:40
8 [h]**Ex 25:23**; [i]**Nu 4:14**
9 [j]1Ki 6:36; 2Ch 33:5
11 [k]1Ki 7:14
14 [l]1Ki 7:27–30
16 [m]**1Ki 7:13**
17 [n]**Ge 33:17**

[e]*8* That is, about 20 tons (about 21 metric tons)
[f]*9* That is, about 1¼ pounds (about 0.6 kilogram)
[g]*11* That is, about 7½ feet (about 2.3 metres); also in verse 15
[h]*13* Or *facing inward*
[i]*15* That is, about 52 feet (about 16 metres)
[j]*16* Or possibly *made chains in the inner sanctuary*; the meaning of the Hebrew for this phrase is uncertain.
[k]*17* *Jakin* probably means *he establishes*.
[l]*17* *Boaz* probably means *in him is strength*.
[a]*1* That is, about 30 feet (about 9 metres) long and wide, and about 15 feet (about 4.5 metres) high
[b]*2* That is, about 7½ feet (about 2.3 metres)
[c]*2* That is, about 45 feet (about 13.5 metres)
[d]*3* That is, about 1½ feet (about 0.5 metre)
[e]*5* That is, about 3 inches (about 8 centimetres)
[f]*5* That is, about 14,500 gallons (about 66 kilolitres)

and Zarethan.[g] 18All these things that
Solomon made amounted to so much
that the weight of the bronze[o] was not
determined.

19Solomon also made all the furnishings that were in God's temple:

the golden altar;
the tables[p] on which was the bread of the Presence;
20the lampstands[q] of pure gold with their lamps, to burn in front of the inner sanctuary as prescribed;
21the gold floral work and lamps and tongs (they were solid gold);
22the pure gold wick trimmers, sprinkling bowls, dishes[r] and censers;[s] and the gold doors of the temple: the inner doors to the Most Holy Place and the doors of the main hall.

5 When all the work Solomon had done for the temple of the LORD was finished,[a] he brought in the things his father David had dedicated[b]—the silver and gold and all the furnishings—and he placed them in the treasuries of God's temple.

The Ark Brought to the Temple

5:2–6:11pp—1Ki 8:1–21

2Then Solomon summoned to Jerusalem the elders of Israel, all the heads of the tribes and the chiefs of the Israelite families, to bring up the ark[c] of the LORD's covenant from Zion, the City
of David. 3And all the men of Israel[d]
came together to the king at the time of the festival in the seventh month.

4When all the elders of Israel had ar-
rived, the Levites took up the ark, 5and
they brought up the ark and the Tent of Meeting and all the sacred furnishings in it. The priests, who were Levites,[e]
carried them up; 6and King Solomon
and the entire assembly of Israel that had gathered about him were before the ark, sacrificing so many sheep and cattle that they could not be recorded or counted.

7The priests then brought the ark[f] of the LORD's covenant to its place in the inner sanctuary of the temple, the Most Holy Place, and put it beneath the
wings of the cherubim. 8The cherubim[g]
spread their wings over the place of the ark and covered the ark and its carrying
poles. 9These poles were so long that
their ends, extending from the ark, could be seen from in front of the inner sanctuary, but not from outside the Holy Place; and they are still there to-
day. 10There was nothing in the ark
except[h] the two tablets[i] that Moses had placed in it at Horeb, where the LORD made a covenant with the Israelites after they came out of Egypt.

11The priests then withdrew from the Holy Place. All the priests who were there had consecrated themselves,
regardless of their divisions.[j] 12All the
Levites who were musicians[k]—Asaph, Heman, Jeduthun and their sons and relatives—stood on the east side of the altar, dressed in fine linen and playing cymbals, harps and lyres. They were accompanied by 120 priests sounding
trumpets.[l] 13The trumpeters and singers
joined in unison, as with one voice, to give praise and thanks to the LORD. Accompanied by trumpets, cymbals and other instruments, they raised their voices in praise to the LORD and sang:

"He is good;
his love endures for ever."[m]

Then the temple of the LORD was
filled with a cloud,[n] 14and the priests
could not perform[o] their service because of the cloud,[p] for the glory[q] of the LORD filled the temple of God.

6 Then Solomon said, "The LORD has said that he would dwell in a dark
cloud;[a] 2I have built a magnificent
temple for you, a place for you to dwell for ever.[b]"

3While the whole assembly of Israel was standing there, the king turned
round and blessed them. 4Then he said:

"Praise be to the LORD, the God of Israel, who with his hands has fulfilled what he promised with his mouth to my father David. For he
said, 5'Since the day I brought my
people out of Egypt, I have not chosen a city in any tribe of Israel to have a temple built for my Name to be there, nor have I chosen anyone to be the leader over my people
Israel. 6But now I have chosen Jeru-
salem[c] for my Name[d] to be there, and I have chosen David[e] to rule my people Israel.'

7"My father David had it in his heart[f] to build a temple for the Name of the LORD, the God of
Israel. 8But the LORD said to my
father David, 'Because it was in your heart to build a temple for my

18 [o]1Ki 7:23
19 [p]Ex 25:23
20 [q]Ex 25:31
22 [r]Nu 7:14; [s]Lev 10:1

Ch. 5

1 [a]1Ki 6:14; [b]2Sa 8:11
2 [c]Nu 3:31; 1Ch 15:25
3 [d]1Ch 9:1
5 [e]Nu 3:31; 1Ch 15:2
7 [f]Rev 11:19
8 [g]Ge 3:24
10 [h]Heb 9:4; [i]Ex 16:34; Dt 10:2
11 [j]1Ch 24:1
12 [k]1Ki 10:12; 1Ch 9:33; 25:1; Ps 68:25; [l]1Ch 13:8
13 [m]1Ch 16:34; 2Ch 7:3; 20:21; Ezr 3:11; Ps 100:5; 106:1; 107:1; 118:1; 136:1; Jer 33:11; [n]Ex 40:34
14 [o]Ex 40:35; Rev 15:8; [p]Ex 19:16; [q]Ex 29:43; 40:35

Ch. 6

1 [a]Ex 19:9
2 [b]Ezr 6:12; 7:15; Ps 135:21
6 [c]Dt 12:5; Isa 14:1; [d]Ex 20:24; [e]1Ch 28:4
7 [f]1Sa 10:7; 1Ch 17:2; Ac 7:46

[g]17 Hebrew *Zeredatha*, a variant of *Zarethan*

Name, you did well to have this in
your heart. 9Nevertheless, you are
not the one to build the temple, but
your son, who is your own flesh
and blood—he is the one who will
build the temple for my Name.'

10"The LORD has kept the prom-
ise he made. I have succeeded
David my father and now I sit on
the throne of Israel, just as the LORD
promised, and I have built the
temple for the Name of the LORD,
the God of Israel. 11There I have
placed the ark, in which is the cov-
enant[g] of the LORD that he made
with the people of Israel."

Solomon's Prayer of Dedication

6:12–40pp—1Ki 8:22–53
6:41–42pp—Ps 132:8–10

12Then Solomon stood before the altar
of the LORD in front of the whole as-
sembly of Israel and spread out his
hands. 13Now he had made a bronze
platform,[h] five cubits[a] long, five cubits
wide and three cubits[b] high, and had
placed it in the centre of the outer court.
He stood on the platform and then knelt
down[i] before the whole assembly of
Israel and spread out his hands towards
heaven. 14He said:

"O LORD, God of Israel, there is
no God like you[j] in heaven or on
earth—you who keep your cov-
enant of love[k] with your servants
who continue wholeheartedly in
your way. 15You have kept your
promise to your servant David my
father; with your mouth you have
promised[l] and with your hand you
have fulfilled it—as it is today.

16"Now LORD, God of Israel, keep
for your servant David my father
the promises you made to him
when you said, 'You shall never
fail[m] to have a man to sit before me
on the throne of Israel, if only your
sons are careful in all they do to
walk before me according to my
law,[n] as you have done.' 17And
now, O LORD, God of Israel, let
your word that you promised your
servant David come true.

18"But will God really dwell[o] on
earth with men? The heavens,[p]
even the highest heavens, cannot
contain you. How much less this
temple that I have built! 19Yet give
attention to your servant's prayer
and his plea for mercy, O LORD my
God. Hear the cry and the prayer

11 [g]**Dt 10:2**; Ps 25:10; 50:5
13 [h]Ne 8:4; [i]Ps 95:6
14 [j]**Ex 8:10**; 15:11; [k]**Dt 7:9**
15 [l]**1Ch 22:10**
16 [m]**2Sa 7:13**,15; 2Ch 23:3; [n]Ps 132:12
18 [o]**Rev 21:3**; [p]Ps 11:4; Isa 40:22; 66:1
20 [q]**Ex 3:16**; Ps 34:15; [r]Dt 12:11; [s]2Ch 7:14; 30:20
21 [t]Ps 51:1; Isa 33:24; 40:2; 43:25; 44:22; 55:7; Mic 7:18
22 [u]**Ex 22:11**
23 [v]Isa 3:11; 65:6; **Mt 16:27**
24 [w]**Lev 26:17**
26 [x]Lev 26:19; **Dt 11:17**; 28:24; **2Sa 1:21**
27 [y]ver 30,39; 2Ch 7:14
28 [z]2Ch 20:9

that your servant is praying in your
presence. 20May your eyes[q] be open
towards this temple day and night,
this place of which you said you
would put your Name[r] there. May
you hear[s] the prayer your servant
prays towards this place. 21Hear the
supplications of your servant and
of your people Israel when they
pray towards this place. Hear from
heaven, your dwelling-place; and
when you hear, forgive.[t]

22"When a man wrongs his
neighbour and is required to take
an oath[u] and he comes and swears
the oath before your altar in this
temple, 23then hear from heaven
and act. Judge between your ser-
vants, repaying[v] the guilty by
bringing down on his own head
what he has done. Declare the in-
nocent not guilty and so establish
his innocence.

24"When your people Israel have
been defeated[w] by an enemy be-
cause they have sinned against you
and when they turn back and con-
fess your name, praying and mak-
ing supplication before you in this
temple, 25then hear from heaven
and forgive the sin of your people
Israel and bring them back to the
land you gave to them and their
fathers.

26"When the heavens are shut up
and there is no rain[x] because your
people have sinned against you,
and when they pray towards this
place and confess your name and
turn from their sin because you
have afflicted them, 27then hear
from heaven and forgive[y] the sin of
your servants, your people Israel.
Teach them the right way to live,
and send rain on the land that
you gave your people for an
inheritance.

28"When famine[z] or plague
comes to the land, or blight or
mildew, locusts or grasshoppers, or
when enemies besiege them in any
of their cities, whatever disaster or
disease may come, 29and when a
prayer or plea is made by any of
your people Israel—each one
aware of his afflictions and pains,
and spreading out his hands to-
wards this temple—30then hear
from heaven, your dwelling-place.

[a]*13* That is, about 7½ feet (about 2.3 metres)
[b]*13* That is, about 4½ feet (about 1.4 metres)

Forgive,[a] and deal with each man according to all he does, since you know his heart (for you alone know the hearts of men),[b] 31so that they will fear you[c] and walk in your ways all the time they live in the land that you gave our fathers.

32"As for the foreigner who does not belong to your people Israel but has come[d] from a distant land because of your great name and your mighty hand[e] and your outstretched arm—when he comes and prays towards this temple, 33then hear from heaven, your dwelling-place, and do whatever the foreigner[f] asks of you, so that all the peoples of the earth may know your name and fear you, as do your own people Israel, and may know that this house that I have built bears your Name.

34"When your people go to war against their enemies,[g] wherever you send them, and when they pray[h] to you towards this city you have chosen and the temple I have built for your Name, 35then hear from heaven their prayer and their plea, and uphold their cause.

36"When they sin against you—for there is no-one who does not sin[i]—and you become angry with them and give them over to the enemy, who takes them captive[j] to a land far away or near; 37and if they have a change of heart[k] in the land where they are held captive, and repent and plead with you in the land of their captivity and say, 'We have sinned, we have done wrong and acted wickedly'; 38and if they turn back to you with all their heart and soul in the land of their captivity where they were taken, and pray towards the land that you gave their fathers, towards the city you have chosen and towards the temple that I have built for your Name; 39then from heaven, your dwelling-place, hear their prayer and their pleas, and uphold their cause. And forgive[l] your people, who have sinned against you.

40"Now, my God, may your eyes be open and your ears attentive[m] to the prayers offered in this place.

41"Now arise,[n] O LORD God, and
come to your resting place,[o]
you and the ark of your might.
May your priests,[p] O LORD God,
be clothed with salvation,
may your saints rejoice in your
goodness.[q]
42O LORD God, do not reject your
anointed one.[r]
Remember the great love[s]
promised to David your
servant."

The Dedication of the Temple
7:1–10pp—1Ki 8:62–66

7

When Solomon finished praying, fire[a] came down from heaven and consumed the burnt offering and the sacrifices, and the glory of the LORD filled[b] the temple.[c] 2The priests could not enter[d] the temple of the LORD because the glory[e] of the LORD filled it. 3When all the Israelites saw the fire coming down and the glory of the LORD above the temple, they knelt on the pavement with their faces to the ground, and they worshipped and gave thanks to the LORD, saying,

"He is good;
his love endures for ever."[f]

4Then the king and all the people offered sacrifices before the LORD. 5And King Solomon offered a sacrifice of twenty-two thousand head of cattle and a hundred and twenty thousand sheep and goats. So the king and all the people dedicated the temple of God. 6The priests took their positions, as did the Levites[g] with the LORD's musical instruments,[h] which King David had made for praising the LORD and which were used when he gave thanks, saying, "His love endures for ever." Opposite the Levites, the priests blew their trumpets, and all the Israelites were standing.

7Solomon consecrated the middle part of the courtyard in front of the temple of the LORD, and there he offered burnt offerings and the fat[i] of the fellowship offerings,[a] because the bronze altar he had made could not hold the burnt offerings, the grain offerings and the fat portions.

8So Solomon observed the festival[j] at that time for seven days, and all Israel[k] with him—a vast assembly, people from Lebo[b] Hamath[l] to the Wadi of Egypt.[m] 9On the eighth day they held an assembly, for they had celebrated[n] the dedication of the altar for seven days and the festival[o] for seven days more.

30 [a]**ver 27**; [b]**1Sa 2:3**; Ps 7:9; 44:21; Pr 16:2; 17:3
31 [c]**Dt 6:13**; Ps 34:7,9; 103:11,13; Pr 8:13
32 [d]2Ch 9:6; [e]**Ex 3:19–20**
33 [f]**Ex 12:43**
34 [g]Dt 28:7; [h]**1Ch 5:20**
36 [i]**1Ki 8:46**; Job 11:12; 15:14; Ps 143:2; Ecc 7:20; Jer 9:5; 13:23; 17:9; **Ro 3:9**; Eph 2:3; [j]**Lev 26:44**
37 [k]1Ki 8:48; 2Ch 7:14; 12:6,12; 30:11; 33:12,19,23; 34:27; 36:12; Isa 58:3; Jer 24:7; 29:13
39 [l]**ver 27**; 2Ch 30:9
40 [m]**1Ki 8:29**,52; 2Ch 7:15; Ne 1:6,11; Ps 17:6; 116:1; 130:2; Isa 37:17
41 [n]Ps 3:7; 7:6; 59:4; Isa 33:10; [o]1Ch 28:2; [p]Ps 132:16; [q]Ps 13:6; 27:13; 116:12; 142:7
42 [r]Ps 2:2; [s]Ps 89:24,28

Ch. 7

1 [a]**Ex 19:18**; **Lev 9:24**; **1Ki 18:38**; [b]**Ex 16:10**; [c]Ps 26:8
2 [d]**1Ki 8:11**; [e]**Ex 29:43**; **40:35**
3 [f]**1Ch 16:34**; 2Ch 5:13; Ezr 3:11
6 [g]1Ch 15:16; [h]**1Ch 15:24**
7 [i]**Ex 29:13**
8 [j]2Ch 30:26; Ne 8:17; [k]**1Ch 9:1**; [l]**Nu 13:21**; [m]**Ge 15:18**
9 [n]2Ch 30:23; [o]**Lev 23:36**

[a]7 Traditionally *peace offerings*
[b]8 Or *from the entrance to*

10On the twenty-third day of the
seventh month he sent the people to
their homes, joyful and glad in heart for
the good things the LORD had done for
David and Solomon and for his people
Israel.

The LORD Appears to Solomon
7:11–22pp—1Ki 9:1–9

11When Solomon had finished[p] the
temple of the LORD and the royal palace,
and had succeeded in carrying out all he
had in mind to do in the temple of the
LORD and in his own palace, 12the LORD
appeared[q] to him at night and said:

"I have heard your prayer and
have chosen[r] this place for myself[s]
as a temple for sacrifices.
13"When I shut up the heavens so
that there is no rain,[t] or command
locusts to devour the land or send a
plague among my people, 14if my
people, who are called by my
name,[u] will humble[v] themselves
and pray and seek my face[w] and
turn[x] from their wicked ways, then
will I hear[y] from heaven and will
forgive[z] their sin and will heal[a] their
land. 15Now my eyes will be open
and my ears attentive to the prayers
offered in this place.[b] 16I have
chosen[c] and consecrated this
temple so that my Name may be
there for ever. My eyes and my
heart will always be there.
17"As for you, if you walk before
me[d] as David your father did, and
do all I command, and observe my
decrees[e] and laws, 18I will establish
your royal throne, as I covenanted[f]
with David your father when I said,
'You shall never fail to have a man[g]
to rule over Israel.'[h]
19"But if you[c] turn away[i] and for-
sake[j] the decrees and commands I
have given you[c] and go off to serve
other gods and worship them,
20then I will uproot[k] Israel from my
land,[l] which I have given them, and
will reject this temple which I have
consecrated for my Name. I will
make it a byword and an object of
ridicule[m] among all peoples. 21And
though this temple is now so im-
posing, all who pass by will be
appalled[n] and say,[o] 'Why has the
LORD done such a thing to this land
and to this temple?' 22People will
answer, 'Because they have for-
saken the LORD, the God of their
fathers, who brought them out of
Egypt, and have embraced other
gods, worshipping and serving
them[p]—that is why he brought all
this disaster on them.'"

Solomon's Other Activities
8:1–18pp—1Ki 9:10–28

8 At the end of twenty years, during
which Solomon built the temple of
the LORD and his own palace,[a] 2Solomon
rebuilt the villages that Hiram[a] had
given him, and settled Israelites in
them. 3Solomon then went to Hamath
Zobah and captured it. 4He also built up
Tadmor in the desert and all the store
cities he had built in Hamath.[b] 5He re-
built Upper Beth Horon[c] and Lower
Beth Horon as fortified cities, with walls
and with gates and bars, 6as well as
Baalath[d] and all his store cities, and all
the cities for his chariots and for his
horses[b]—whatever he desired to build
in Jerusalem, in Lebanon and through-
out all the territory that he ruled.
7All the people left from the Hittites,
Amorites, Perizzites, Hivites and Jebu-
sites[e] (these peoples were not Israel-
ites), 8that is, their descendants remain-
ing in the land, whom the Israelites had
not destroyed—these Solomon con-
scripted[f] for his slave labour force, as it
is to this day. 9But Solomon did not
make slaves of the Israelites for his
work; they were his fighting men, com-
manders of his captains, and comman-
ders of his chariots and charioteers.
10They were also King Solomon's chief
officials—two hundred and fifty of-
ficials supervising the men.
11Solomon brought Pharaoh's
daughter[g] up from the City of David to
the palace he had built for her, for he
said, "My wife must not live in the
palace of David king of Israel, because
the places the ark of the LORD has
entered are holy."
12On the altar[h] of the LORD that he had
built in front of the portico, Solomon
sacrificed burnt offerings to the LORD,
13according to the daily requirement[i] for
offerings commanded by Moses for Sab-
baths,[j] New Moons[k] and the three[l]
annual feasts—the Feast of Unleavened
Bread,[m] the Feast of Weeks[n] and the
Feast of Tabernacles.[o] 14In keeping with
the ordinance of his father David, he
appointed the divisions[p] of the priests
for their duties and the Levites[q] to lead

11 [p]**1Ch 28:20**
12 [q]2Ch 1:7; [r]Dt 12:11; [s]**Dt 12:5**
13 [t]**Dt 11:17;** Am 4:7
14 [u]**Nu 6:27;** [v]**Ex 10:3; Lev 26:41; 2Ch 6:37;** [w]**1Ch 16:11;** [x]**2Ki 17:13;** Isa 55:7; Eze 18:32; Zec 1:4; [y]**2Ch 6:20;** [z]**2Ch 6:27;** [a]**Ex 15:26;** 2Ch 30:20; Ps 60:2; Isa 30:26; 53:5; 57:18; Jer 33:6; Mal 4:2
15 [b]**1Ki 8:29; 2Ch 6:40;** Ne 1:6
16 [c]**Dt 12:5;** 2Ch 33:7
17 [d]**1Ki 9:4;** [e]**Lev 19:37**
18 [f]Isa 9:7; Jer 33:17,21; [g]**1Ch 5:2;** Isa 55:4; Mic 5:2; [h]**2Sa 7:13; 1Ch 17:12;** 2Ch 13:5; 23:3
19 [i]**Dt 28:15;** [j]**1Ch 28:9;** 2Ch 12:1; 24:18; Jer 9:13; 11:8
20 [k]**Dt 29:28;** [l]1Ki 14:15; Jer 12:14; 16:13; 50:11; [m]**Dt 28:37**
21 [n]Jer 19:8; [o]Dt 29:24
22 [p]Jer 16:11

Ch. 8

1 [a]**2Sa 7:2**
4 [b]**2Sa 8:9**
5 [c]**Jos 10:10**
6 [d]**Jos 19:44**
7 [e]**Ge 10:16; 15:18–21;** Ezr 9:1
8 [f]**2Ch 2:18**
11 [g]**1Ki 3:1**
12 [h]**1Ki 8:64;** 2Ch 15:8
13 [i]**Ex 29:38;** [j]Nu 28:9; [k]**Nu 10:10;** [l]**Ex 23:14;** [m]**Ex 12:17;** Nu 28:16–25; [n]**Ex 23:16;** [o]Nu 29:12–38; Ne 8:17
14 [p]**1Ch 24:1;** [q]**1Ch 25:1**

[c]*19* The Hebrew is plural.
[a]2 Hebrew *Huram,* a variant of *Hiram;* also in verse 18 [b]6 Or *charioteers*

the praise and to assist the priests
according to each day's requirement.
He also appointed the gatekeepers[r] by
divisions for the various gates, because
this was what David the man of God[s]
had ordered.[t] 15 They did not deviate
from the king's commands to the priests
or to the Levites in any matter, includ-
ing that of the treasuries.
16 All Solomon's work was carried out,
from the day the foundation of the
temple of the LORD was laid until its
completion. So the temple of the LORD
was finished.
17 Then Solomon went to Ezion Geber
and Elath on the coast of Edom. 18 And
Hiram sent him ships commanded by
his own officers, men who knew the
sea. These, with Solomon's men, sailed
to Ophir and brought back four hun-
dred and fifty talents[c] of gold,[u] which
they delivered to King Solomon.

The Queen of Sheba Visits Solomon

9:1–12pp—1Ki 10:1–13

9 When the queen of Sheba[a] heard of
Solomon's fame, she came to Jeru-
salem to test him with hard questions.
Arriving with a very great caravan—
with camels carrying spices, large quan-
tities of gold, and precious stones—she
came to Solomon and talked with him
about all she had on her mind.
2 Solomon answered all her questions;
nothing was too hard for him to explain
to her. 3 When the queen of Sheba saw
the wisdom of Solomon,[b] as well as the
palace he had built, 4 the food on his
table, the seating of his officials, the
attending servants in their robes, the
cupbearers in their robes and the burnt
offerings he made at[a] the temple of the
LORD, she was overwhelmed.
5 She said to the king, "The report I
heard in my own country about your
achievements and your wisdom is true.
6 But I did not believe what they said
until I came[c] and saw with my own
eyes. Indeed, not even half the great-
ness of your wisdom was told me; you
have far exceeded the report I heard.
7 How happy your men must be! How
happy your officials, who continually
stand before you and hear your wis-
dom! 8 Praise be to the LORD your God,
who has delighted in you and placed
you on his throne[d] as king to rule for the
LORD your God. Because of the love of
your God for Israel and his desire to
uphold them for ever, he has made you
king[e] over them, to maintain justice and
righteousness."
9 Then she gave the king 120 talents[b]
of gold,[f] large quantities of spices, and
precious stones. There had never been
such spices as those the queen of Sheba
gave to King Solomon.
10 (The men of Hiram and the men of
Solomon brought gold from Ophir;[g]
they also brought algum-wood[c] and
precious stones. 11 The king used the
algum-wood to make steps for the
temple of the LORD and for the royal
palace, and to make harps and lyres for
the musicians. Nothing like them had
ever been seen in Judah.)
12 King Solomon gave the queen of
Sheba all she desired and asked for; he
gave her more than she had brought to
him. Then she left and returned with
her retinue to her own country.

Solomon's Splendour

9:13–28pp—1Ki 10:14–29; 2Ch 1:14–17

13 The weight of the gold that Solomon
received yearly was 666 talents,[d] 14 not
including the revenues brought in by
merchants and traders. Also all the
kings of Arabia[h] and the governors of
the land brought gold and silver to
Solomon.
15 King Solomon made two hundred
large shields of hammered gold; six
hundred bekas[e] of hammered gold
went into each shield. 16 He also made
three hundred small shields[i] of ham-
mered gold, with three hundred bekas[f]
of gold in each shield. The king put
them in the Palace of the Forest of
Lebanon.[j]
17 Then the king made a great throne
inlaid with ivory[k] and overlaid with
pure gold. 18 The throne had six steps,
and a footstool of gold was attached to
it. On both sides of the seat were
armrests, with a lion standing beside
each of them. 19 Twelve lions stood on
the six steps, one at either end of each
step. Nothing like it had ever been
made for any other kingdom. 20 All King
Solomon's goblets were gold, and all
the household articles in the Palace of
the Forest of Lebanon were pure gold.
Nothing was made of silver, because
silver was considered of little value in
Solomon's day. 21 The king had a fleet of

14 [r]**1Ch 9:17;** [s]Ne 12:24,36; [t]**1Ch 23:6;** Ne 12:45
18 [u]2Ch 9:9

Ch. 9

1 [a]**Ge 10:7;** Eze 23:42; Mt 12:42; Lk 11:31
3 [b]1Ki 5:12
6 [c]2Ch 6:32
8 [d]**1Ki 2:12; 1Ch 17:14;** 2Ch 13:8; [e]2Ch 2:11
9 [f]2Ch 8:18
10 [g]2Ch 8:18
14 [h]2Ch 17:11; Isa 21:13; Jer 25:24; Eze 27:21; 30:5
16 [i]2Ch 12:9; [j]**1Ki 7:2**
17 [k]**1Ki 22:39**

[c] *18* That is, about 17 tons (about 16 metric tons)
[a] *4* Or *the ascent by which he went up to*
[b] *9* That is, about 4 tons (about 4 metric tons)
[c] *10* Probably a variant of *almug-wood*
[d] *13* That is, about 23 tons (about 23 metric tons)
[e] *15* That is, about 7½ pounds (about 3.5 kilograms)
[f] *16* That is, about 3¾ pounds (about 1.7 kilograms)

trading ships[g] manned by Hiram's[h]
men. Once every three years it re-
turned, carrying gold, silver and ivory,
and apes and baboons.
22 King Solomon was greater in riches
and wisdom than all the other kings of
the earth.[l] 23 All the kings[m] of the earth
sought audience with Solomon to hear
the wisdom God had put in his heart.
24 Year after year, everyone who came
brought a gift[n]—articles of silver and
gold, and robes, weapons and spices,
and horses and mules.
25 Solomon had four thousand stalls
for horses and chariots,[o] and twelve
thousand horses,[i] which he kept in the
chariot cities and also with him in Jeru-
salem. 26 He ruled[p] over all the kings
from the River[j][q] to the land of the Philis-
tines, as far as the border of Egypt.[r]
27 The king made silver as common in
Jerusalem as stones, and cedar as plenti-
ful as sycamore-fig trees in the foothills.
28 Solomon's horses were imported from
Egypt[k] and from all other countries.

Solomon's Death

9:29–31pp—1Ki 11:41–43

29 As for the other events of Solomon's
reign, from beginning to end, are they
not written in the records of Nathan[s] the
prophet, in the prophecy of Ahijah[t] the
Shilonite and in the visions of Iddo the
seer concerning Jeroboam[u] son of
Nebat? 30 Solomon reigned in Jerusalem
over all Israel for forty years. 31 Then he
rested with his fathers and was buried
in the city of David[v] his father. And
Rehoboam his son succeeded him as
king.

Israel Rebels Against Rehoboam

10:1–11:4pp—1Ki 12:1–24

10 Rehoboam went to Shechem,
for all the Israelites had gone
there to make him king. 2 When Jero-
boam[a] son of Nebat heard this (he was
in Egypt, where he had fled[b] from King
Solomon), he returned from Egypt. 3 So
they sent for Jeroboam, and he and all
Israel[c] went to Rehoboam and said to
him: 4 "Your father put a heavy yoke on
us,[d] but now lighten the harsh labour
and the heavy yoke he put on us, and
we will serve you."
5 Rehoboam answered, "Come back
to me in three days." So the people
went away.
6 Then King Rehoboam consulted the
elders[e] who had served his father Sol-
omon during his lifetime. "How would
you advise me to answer these people?"
he asked.
7 They replied, "If you will be kind to
these people and please them and give
them a favourable answer,[f] they will
always be your servants."
8 But Rehoboam rejected[g] the advice
the elders[h] gave him and consulted the
young men who had grown up with
him and were serving him. 9 He asked
them, "What is your advice? How
should we answer these people who say
to me, 'Lighten the yoke your father put
on us'?"
10 The young men who had grown up
with him replied, "Tell the people who
have said to you, 'Your father put a
heavy yoke on us, but make our yoke
lighter'—tell them, 'My little finger is
thicker than my father's waist. 11 My
father laid on you a heavy yoke; I will
make it even heavier. My father
scourged you with whips; I will scourge
you with scorpions.'"
12 Three days later Jeroboam and all
the people returned to Rehoboam, as
the king had said, "Come back to me in
three days." 13 The king answered them
harshly. Rejecting the advice of the
elders, 14 he followed the advice of the
young men and said, "My father made
your yoke heavy; I will make it even
heavier. My father scourged you with
whips; I will scourge you with scor-
pions." 15 So the king did not listen to
the people, for this turn of events was
from God,[i] to fulfil the word that the
LORD had spoken to Jeroboam son of
Nebat through Ahijah the Shilonite.[j]
16 When all Israel[k] saw that the king
refused to listen to them, they answered
the king:

"What share do we have in David,[l]
what part in Jesse's son?
To your tents, O Israel!
Look after your own house,
O David!"

So all the Israelites went home. 17 But as
for the Israelites who were living in the
towns of Judah, Rehoboam still ruled
over them.
18 King Rehoboam sent out Adon-
iram,[a][m] who was in charge of forced
labour, but the Israelites stoned him to

22 [l] **1Ki 3:13; 2Ch 1:12**
23 [m] 1Ki 4:34
24 [n] 2Ch 32:23; Ps 45:12; 68:29; 72:10; Isa 18:7
25 [o] **1Sa 8:11**
26 [p] **1Ki 4:21;** [q] Ps 72:8–9; [r] Ge 15:18–21
29 [s] **2Sa 7:2;** [t] **1Ki 11:29;** [u] 2Ch 10:2
31 [v] 1Ki 2:10

Ch. 10

2 [a] **2Ch 9:29;** [b] **1Ki 11:40**
3 [c] **1Ch 9:1**
4 [d] 2Ch 2:2
6 [e] Job 8:8–9; 12:12; 15:10; 32:7
7 [f] Pr 15:1
8 [g] **2Sa 17:14;** [h] Pr 13:20
15 [i] 2Ch 11:4; 25:16–20; [j] **1Ki 11:29**
16 [k] **1Ch 9:1;** [l] **2Sa 20:1**
18 [m] **2Sa 20:24; 1Ki 5:14**

[g] 21 Hebrew *of ships that could go to Tarshish*
[h] 21 Hebrew *Huram*, a variant of *Hiram*
[i] 25 Or *charioteers*
[j] 26 That is, the Euphrates
[k] 28 Or possibly *Muzur*, a region in Cilicia
[a] 18 Hebrew *Hadoram*, a variant of *Adoniram*

death. King Rehoboam, however, man-
aged to get into his chariot and escape to
Jerusalem. 19So Israel has been in re-
bellion against the house of David to
this day.

11 When Rehoboam arrived in
Jerusalem,[a] he mustered the
house of Judah and Benjamin—a hun-
dred and eighty thousand fighting men
—to make war against Israel and to
regain the kingdom for Rehoboam.
2But this word of the LORD came to
Shemaiah[b] the man of God: 3"Say to
Rehoboam son of Solomon king of
Judah and to all the Israelites in Judah
and Benjamin, 4'This is what the LORD
says: Do not go up to fight against your
brothers.[c] Go home, every one of you,
for this is my doing.'" So they obeyed
the words of the LORD and turned back
from marching against Jeroboam.

Rehoboam Fortifies Judah

5Rehoboam lived in Jerusalem and
built up towns for defence in Judah:
6Bethlehem, Etam, Tekoa, 7Beth Zur,
Soco, Adullam, 8Gath, Mareshah, Ziph,
9Adoraim, Lachish, Azekah, 10Zorah,
Aijalon and Hebron. These were for-
tified cities[d] in Judah and Benjamin.
11He strengthened their defences and
put commanders in them, with supplies
of food, olive oil and wine. 12He put
shields and spears in all the cities, and
made them very strong. So Judah and
Benjamin were his.
13The priests and Levites from all their
districts throughout Israel sided with
him. 14The Levites[e] even abandoned
their pasture-lands and property,[f] and
came to Judah and Jerusalem because
Jeroboam and his sons had rejected
them as priests of the LORD. 15And he
appointed[g] his own priests[h] for the high
places and for the goat[i] and calf[j] idols he
had made. 16Those from every tribe of
Israel[k] who set their hearts on seeking
the LORD, the God of Israel, followed the
Levites to Jerusalem to offer sacrifices to
the LORD, the God of their fathers.
17They strengthened[l] the kingdom of
Judah and supported Rehoboam son of
Solomon for three years, walking in the
ways of David and Solomon during this
time.

Rehoboam's Family

18Rehoboam married Mahalath, who
was the daughter of David's son Jeri-
moth and of Abihail, the daughter of
Jesse's son Eliab. 19She bore him sons:
Jeush, Shemariah and Zaham. 20Then
he married Maacah[m] daughter of Absa-
lom, who bore him Abijah,[n] Attai, Ziza
and Shelomith. 21Rehoboam loved
Maacah daughter of Absalom more
than any of his other wives and con-
cubines. In all he had eighteen wives[o]
and sixty concubines, twenty-eight
sons and sixty daughters.
22Rehoboam appointed Abijah[p] son of
Maacah to be the chief prince among his
brothers, in order to make him king.
23He acted wisely, dispersing some of
his sons throughout the districts of
Judah and Benjamin, and to all the for-
tified cities. He gave them abundant
provisions[q] and took many wives for
them.

Shishak Attacks Jerusalem

12:9–16pp—1Ki 14:21,25–31

12 After Rehoboam's position as
king was established[a] and he
had become strong,[b] he and all Israel[a][c]
with him abandoned[d] the law of the
LORD. 2Because they had been unfaith-
ful[e] to the LORD, Shishak[f] king of Egypt
attacked Jerusalem in the fifth year of
King Rehoboam. 3With twelve hundred
chariots and sixty thousand horsemen
and the innumerable troops of
Libyans,[g] Sukkites and Cushites[b][h] that
came with him from Egypt, 4he cap-
tured the fortified cities[i] of Judah and
came as far as Jerusalem.
5Then the prophet Shemaiah[j] came to
Rehoboam and to the leaders of Judah
who had assembled in Jerusalem for
fear of Shishak, and he said to them,
"This is what the LORD says: 'You have
abandoned me; therefore I now aban-
don[k] you to Shishak.'"
6The leaders of Israel and the king
humbled[l] themselves and said, "The
LORD is just."[m]
7When the LORD saw that they hum-
bled themselves, this word of the LORD
came to Shemaiah: "Since they have
humbled themselves, I will not destroy
them but will soon give them deliver-
ance.[n] My wrath[o] will not be poured out
on Jerusalem through Shishak. 8They
will, however, become subject[p] to him,
so that they may learn the difference
between serving me and serving the
kings of other lands."
9When Shishak king of Egypt attack-
ed Jerusalem, he carried off the trea-
sures of the temple of the LORD and the

Ch. 11

1 [a]**1Ki 12:21**
2 [b]**1Ki 12:22**; 2Ch 12:5–7,15
4 [c]2Ch 28:8–11
10 [d]**Jos 10:20**; 2Ch 12:4; 17:2,19; 21:3
14 [e]**Nu 35:2–5**; [f]1Ch 6:81
15 [g]**1Ki 13:33**; [h]**1Ki 12:31**; [i]Lev 17:7; [j]1Ki 12:28; 2Ch 13:8
16 [k]2Ch 15:9
17 [l]2Ch 12:1
20 [m]**1Ki 15:2**; [n]2Ch 12:16; 13:2
21 [o]**Dt 17:17**
22 [p]Dt 21:15–17
23 [q]2Ch 21:3

Ch. 12

1 [a]ver 13; 2Ch 1:1; [b]2Ch 11:17; [c]**1Ch 9:1**; [d]**2Ch 7:19**
2 [e]1Ki 14:22–24; **1Ch 5:25**; [f]1Ki 11:40
3 [g]Da 11:43; [h]**Ge 10:6**; 2Ch 14:9; 16:8; Isa 18:2; Am 9:7; Na 3:9
4 [i]**2Ch 11:10**
5 [j]2Ch 11:2; [k]**Dt 28:15**
6 [l]**Lev 26:41**; **2Ch 6:37**; [m]Ex 9:27; Ezr 9:15; Ps 11:7; 116:5; Da 9:14
7 [n]Ps 78:38; [o]Dt 9:19; Ps 69:24; Jer 7:20; 42:18; Eze 5:13
8 [p]Dt 28:48

[a]1 That is, Judah, as frequently in 2 Chronicles
[b]3 That is, people from the upper Nile region

treasures of the royal palace. He took everything, including the gold shields[q] that Solomon had made. 10So King Rehoboam made bronze shields to replace them and assigned these to the commanders of the guard on duty at the entrance to the royal palace. 11Whenever the king went to the LORD's temple, the guards went with him, bearing the shields, and afterwards they returned them to the guardroom.

12Because Rehoboam humbled[r] himself, the LORD's anger turned from him, and he was not totally destroyed. Indeed, there was some good[s] in Judah.

13King Rehoboam established[t] himself firmly in Jerusalem and continued as king. He was forty-one years old when he became king, and he reigned for seventeen years in Jerusalem, the city the LORD had chosen out of all the tribes of Israel in which to put his Name.[u] His mother's name was Naamah; she was an Ammonite. 14He did evil because he had not set his heart on seeking the LORD.

15As for the events of Rehoboam's reign, from beginning to end, are they not written in the records of Shemaiah[v] the prophet and of Iddo the seer that deal with genealogies? There was continual warfare between Rehoboam and Jeroboam. 16Rehoboam[w] rested with his fathers and was buried in the City of David. And Abijah[x] his son succeeded him as king.

Abijah King of Judah

13:1–2,22–14:1pp—1Ki 15:1–2,6–8

13 In the eighteenth year of the reign of Jeroboam, Abijah became king of Judah, 2and he reigned in Jerusalem for three years. His mother's name was Maacah,[a][a] a daughter[b] of Uriel of Gibeah.

There was war between Abijah[b] and Jeroboam.[c] 3Abijah went into battle with a force of four hundred thousand able fighting men, and Jeroboam drew up a battle line against him with eight hundred thousand able troops.

4Abijah stood on Mount Zemaraim,[d] in the hill country of Ephraim, and said, "Jeroboam and all Israel,[e] listen to me! 5Don't you know that the LORD, the God of Israel, has given the kingship of Israel to David and his descendants for ever[f] by a covenant of salt?[g] 6Yet Jeroboam son of Nebat, an official of Solomon son of David, rebelled[h] against his master. 7Some worthless scoundrels[i] gathered around him and opposed Rehoboam son of Solomon when he was young and indecisive[j] and not strong enough to resist them.

8"And now you plan to resist the kingdom of the LORD, which is in the hands of David's descendants.[k] You are indeed a vast army and have with you[l] the golden calves[m] that Jeroboam made to be your gods. 9But didn't you drive out the priests[n] of the LORD,[o] the sons of Aaron, and the Levites, and make priests of your own as the peoples of other lands do? Whoever comes to consecrate himself with a young bull[p] and seven rams[q] may become a priest of what are not gods.[r]

10"As for us, the LORD is our God, and we have not forsaken him. The priests who serve the LORD are sons of Aaron, and the Levites assist them. 11Every morning and evening[s] they present burnt offerings and fragrant incense[t] to the LORD. They set out the bread on the ceremonially clean table[u] and light the lamps[v] on the gold lampstand every evening. We are observing the requirements of the LORD our God. But you have forsaken him. 12God is with us; he is our leader. His priests with their trumpets will sound the battle cry against you.[w] Men of Israel, do not fight against the LORD,[x] the God of your fathers, for you will not succeed."[y]

13Now Jeroboam had sent troops round to the rear, so that while he was in front of Judah the ambush[z] was behind them. 14Judah turned and saw that they were being attacked at both front and rear. Then they cried out[a] to the LORD. The priests blew their trumpets 15and the men of Judah raised the battle cry. At the sound of their battle cry, God routed Jeroboam and all Israel[b] before Abijah and Judah. 16The Israelites fled before Judah, and God delivered[c] them into their hands. 17Abijah and his men inflicted heavy losses on them, so that there were five hundred thousand casualties among Israel's able men. 18The men of Israel were subdued on that occasion, and the men of Judah were victorious because they relied[d] on the LORD, the God of their fathers.

19Abijah pursued Jeroboam and took from him the towns of Bethel, Jeshanah and Ephron, with their surrounding villages. 20Jeroboam did not regain power during the time of Abijah. And the LORD struck him down and he died.

9 [q]2Ch 9:16
12 [r]**2Ch 6:37;** [s]**1Ki 14:13;** 2Ch 19:3
13 [t]**ver 1; 1Ki 2:12;** [u]**Ex 20:24;** Dt 12:5
15 [v]**2Ch 11:2**
16 [w]**1Ch 3:10;** [x]**2Ch 11:20**

Ch. 13

2 [a]2Ch 15:16; [b]**2Ch 11:20;** [c]1Ki 15:6
4 [d]Jos 18:22; [e]1Ch 11:1
5 [f]**2Sa 7:13; 1Ch 17:12;** [g]**Lev 2:13**
6 [h]1Ki 11:26
7 [i]**Jdg 9:4;** [j]**1Ch 29:1**
8 [k]**2Ch 9:8;** [l]1Sa 4:3; [m]**Ex 32:4; 2Ch 11:15**
9 [n]**1Ki 12:31;** [o]2Ch 11:14–15; [p]Ex 29:35–36; [q]**Ex 29:31;** [r]Jer 2:11; Gal 4:8
11 [s]**Ex 29:39; 2Ch 2:4;** [t]**Ex 25:6;** [u]**1Ch 9:32;** [v]**Ex 25:37**
12 [w]**Nu 10:8–9;** [x]**Jdg 2:15;** Ac 5:39; [y]Job 9:4; Pr 21:30; 29:1
13 [z]Jos 8:9; 2Ch 20:22
14 [a]**1Ch 5:20;** 2Ch 14:11; 18:31
15 [b]**1Ch 9:1**
16 [c]2Ch 16:8
18 [d]2Ch 14:11; 16:7; Ps 22:5

---

[a]2 Most Septuagint manuscripts and Syriac (see also 2 Chron. 11:20 and 1 Kings 15:2); Hebrew *Micaiah* [b]2 Or *granddaughter*

21But Abijah grew in strength. He
married fourteen wives and had twenty-
two sons and sixteen daughters.
22The other events of Abijah's reign,
what he did and what he said, are writ-
ten in the annotations of the prophet
Iddo.
14 And Abijah rested with his
fathers and was buried in the
City of David. Asa his son succeeded
him as king, and in his days the country
was at peace for ten years.

Asa King of Judah

14:2–3pp—1Ki 15:11–12

2Asa did what was good and right in
the eyes of the LORD his God.[a] 3He re-
moved the foreign altars[b] and the high
places, smashed the sacred stones[c] and
cut down the Asherah poles.[a][d] 4He
commanded Judah to seek the LORD,[e]
the God of their fathers, and to obey his
laws and commands. 5He removed the
high places[f] and incense altars[g] in every
town in Judah, and the kingdom was at
peace under him. 6He built up the for-
tified cities of Judah, since the land was
at peace. No-one was at war with him
during those years, for the LORD gave
him rest.[h]
7"Let us build up these towns," he
said to Judah, "and put walls round
them, with towers, gates and bars. The
land is still ours, because we have
sought the LORD our God; we sought
him and he has given us rest[i] on every
side." So they built and prospered.
8Asa had an army of three hundred
thousand[j] men from Judah, equipped
with large shields and with spears, and
two hundred and eighty thousand from
Benjamin, armed with small shields and
with bows. All these were brave
fighting men.
9Zerah the Cushite[k] marched out
against them with a vast army[b] and
three hundred chariots, and came as far
as Mareshah.[l] 10Asa went out to meet
him, and they took up battle positions
in the Valley of Zephathah near
Mareshah.
11Then Asa called[m] to the LORD his
God and said, "LORD, there is no-one
like you to help the powerless against
the mighty. Help us,[n] O LORD our God,
for we rely[o] on you, and in your name[p]
we have come against this vast army. O
LORD, you are our God; do not let man
prevail[q] against you."
12The LORD struck down[r] the Cushites
before Asa and Judah. The Cushites
fled, 13and Asa and his army pursued
them as far as Gerar.[s] Such a great num-
ber of Cushites fell that they could not
recover; they were crushed[t] before the
LORD and his forces. The men of Judah
carried off a large amount of plunder.[u]
14They destroyed all the villages around
Gerar, for the terror[v] of the LORD had
fallen upon them. They plundered all
these villages, since there was much
booty there. 15They also attacked the
camps of the herdsmen and carried off
droves of sheep and goats and camels.
Then they returned to Jerusalem.

Asa's Reform

15:16–19pp—1Ki 15:13–16

15 The Spirit of God came upon[a]
Azariah son of Oded. 2He went
out to meet Asa and said to him, "Listen
to me, Asa and all Judah and Benjamin.
The LORD is with you[b] when you are
with him.[c] If you seek[d] him, he will be
found by you, but if you forsake him, he
will forsake you.[e] 3For a long time Israel
was without the true God, without a
priest to teach[f] and without the law.[g]
4But in their distress they turned to the
LORD, the God of Israel, and sought
him,[h] and he was found by them. 5In
those days it was not safe to travel
about,[i] for all the inhabitants of the
lands were in great turmoil. 6One nation
was being crushed by another and one
city by another,[j] because God was
troubling them with every kind of dis-
tress. 7But as for you, be strong[k] and
do not give up, for your work will be
rewarded."[l]
8When Asa heard these words and
the prophecy of Azariah son of[a] Oded
the prophet, he took courage. He re-
moved the detestable idols[m] from the
whole land of Judah and Benjamin and
from the towns he had captured[n] in the
hills of Ephraim. He repaired the altar[o]
of the LORD that was in front of the
portico of the LORD's temple.
9Then he assembled all Judah and
Benjamin and the people from
Ephraim, Manasseh and Simeon who
had settled among them, for large num-
bers[p] had come over to him from Israel
when they saw that the LORD his God
was with him.
10They assembled at Jerusalem in the

Ch. 14

2 [a]2Ch 21:12
3 [b]Jdg 2:2; [c]Ex 23:24; [d]Ex 34:13
4 [e]1Ch 16:11
5 [f]1Ki 15:14; [g]Isa 27:9; Eze 6:4
6 [h]1Ch 22:9
7 [i]1Ch 22:9
8 [j]1Ch 21:1
9 [k]2Ch 12:3; [l]Ge 10:8–9; 2Ch 11:8; 24:24
11 [m]1Ki 8:44; 2Ch 13:14; 25:8; [n]Ps 60:11–12; 79:9; [o]2Ch 13:18; [p]1Sa 17:45; [q]Ps 9:19
12 [r]1Ki 8:45
13 [s]Ge 10:19; [t]2Sa 22:38; Ne 9:24; Ps 44:2,19; 135:10; [u]2Ch 15:11,18
14 [v]Ge 35:5; Dt 2:25; 11:25

Ch. 15

1 [a]Nu 11:25–26
2 [b]2Ch 20:17; [c]Jas 4:8; [d]2Ch 7:14; Ps 78:34; Isa 45:19; 55:6; Jer 29:13; Hos 3:5; [e]Dt 31:17; 1Ch 28:9
3 [f]Lev 10:11; [g]La 2:9; Am 8:11
4 [h]Dt 4:29
5 [i]Jdg 5:6; 19:20; Zec 8:10
6 [j]Isa 19:2; Mt 24:7; Mk 13:8; Lk 21:10
7 [k]Jos 1:7,9; [l]1Sa 24:19; Ps 18:20; 58:11; Pr 14:14; Jer 31:16
8 [m]1Ki 15:12; [n]2Ch 17:2; [o]1Ki 8:64; 2Ch 8:12
9 [p]2Ch 11:16–17

[a]3 That is, symbols of the goddess Asherah; here and elsewhere in 2 Chronicles
[b]9 Hebrew *with an army of a thousand thousands* or *with an army of thousands upon thousands*
[a]8 Vulgate and Syriac (see also Septuagint and verse 1); Hebrew does not have *Azariah son of*.

third month[q] of the fifteenth year of
Asa's reign. 11At that time they sac-
rificed to the LORD seven hundred head
of cattle and seven thousand sheep and
goats from the plunder[r] they had
brought back. 12They entered into a
covenant[s] to seek the LORD,[t] the God of
their fathers, with all their heart and
soul. 13All who would not seek the
LORD, the God of Israel, were to be put
to death,[u] whether small or great, man
or woman. 14They took an oath to the
LORD with loud acclamation, with
shouting and with trumpets and horns.
15All Judah rejoiced about the oath
because they had sworn it whole-
heartedly. They sought God[v] eagerly,
and he was found by them. So the LORD
gave them rest[w] on every side.
16King Asa also deposed his grand-
mother Maacah[x] from her position as
queen mother,[y] because she had made a
repulsive Asherah pole.[z] Asa cut the
pole down, broke it up and burned it in
the Kidron Valley.[a] 17Although he did
not remove the high places from Israel,
Asa's heart was fully committed ⌞to the
LORD⌟ all his life. 18He brought into the
temple of God the silver and gold and
the articles that he and his father had
dedicated.[b]
19There was no more war until the
thirty-fifth year of Asa's reign.

Asa's Last Years

16:1–6pp—1Ki 15:17–22
16:11–17:1pp—1Ki 15:23–24

16 In the thirty-sixth year of Asa's
reign Baasha[a] king of Israel
went up against Judah and fortified
Ramah to prevent anyone from leaving
or entering the territory of Asa king of
Judah.
2Asa then took the silver and gold out
of the treasuries of the LORD's temple
and of his own palace and sent it to
Ben-Hadad king of Aram, who was rul-
ing in Damascus.[b] 3"Let there be a
treaty[c] between me and you," he said,
"as there was between my father and
your father. See, I am sending you silver
and gold. Now break your treaty with
Baasha king of Israel so that he will
withdraw from me."
4Ben-Hadad agreed with King Asa
and sent the commanders of his forces
against the towns of Israel. They con-
quered Ijon, Dan, Abel Maim[a] and all
the store cities of Naphtali.[d] 5When
Baasha heard this, he stopped building
Ramah and abandoned his work. 6Then
King Asa brought all the men of Judah,
and they carried away from Ramah the
stones and timber Baasha had been
using. With them he built up Geba and
Mizpah.[e]
7At that time Hanani[f] the seer came to
Asa king of Judah and said to him: "Be-
cause you relied[g] on the king of Aram
and not on the LORD your God, the army
of the king of Aram has escaped from
your hand. 8Were not the Cushites[b][h]
and Libyans a mighty army with great
numbers[i] of chariots and horsemen[c]?
Yet when you relied on the LORD, he
delivered[j] them into your hand. 9For the
eyes[k] of the LORD range throughout the
earth to strengthen those whose hearts
are fully committed to him. You have
done a foolish[l] thing, and from now on
you will be at war."[m]
10Asa was angry with the seer because
of this; he was so enraged that he put
him in prison.[n] At the same time Asa
brutally oppressed some of the people.
11The events of Asa's reign, from be-
ginning to end, are written in the book
of the kings of Judah and Israel. 12In the
thirty-ninth year of his reign Asa was
afflicted[o] with a disease in his feet.
Though his disease was severe, even in
his illness he did not seek[p] help from the
LORD,[q] but only from the physicians.
13Then in the forty-first year of his reign
Asa died and rested with his fathers.
14They buried him in the tomb that he
had cut out for himself[r] in the City of
David. They laid him on a bier covered
with spices and various blended per-
fumes,[s] and they made a huge fire[t] in his
honour.

Jehoshaphat King of Judah

17 Jehoshaphat his son succeeded
him as king and strengthened[a]
himself against Israel. 2He stationed
troops in all the fortified cities[b] of Judah
and put garrisons in Judah and in the
towns of Ephraim that his father Asa
had captured.[c]
3The LORD was with Jehoshaphat be-
cause in his early years he walked in the
ways that his father David[d] had fol-
lowed. He did not consult the Baals 4but
sought[e] the God of his father and
followed his commands rather than
the practices of Israel. 5The LORD estab-
lished the kingdom under his control;
and all Judah brought gifts[f] to
Jehoshaphat, so that he had great

10 [q]**Lev 23:15–21**
11 [r]**2Ch 14:13**
12 [s]**2Ki 11:17;** [t]**1Ch 16:11**
13 [u]**Ex 22:20;** Dt 13:9–16
15 [v]Dt 4:29; [w]**1Ch 22:9**
16 [x]2Ch 13:2; [y]**1Ki 2:19;** [z]**Ex 34:13;** [a]**2Sa 15:23**
18 [b]**2Ch 14:13**

Ch. 16

1 [a]2Ki 9:9; Jer 41:9
2 [b]2Ch 19:1–20:37; 22:1–9
3 [c]2Ch 20:35; 25:7
4 [d]**2Ki 15:29**
6 [e]Jer 41:9
7 [f]1Ki 16:1; [g]**2Ch 13:18**
8 [h]**Ge 10:6**,8–9; **2Ch 12:3;** [i]2Ch 24:24; [j]2Ch 13:16
9 [k]Job 24:23; Ps 33:13–15; Pr 15:3; Jer 16:17; Zec 3:9; 4:10; [l]1Sa 13:13; [m]**1Ki 15:6;** 2Ch 19:2; 25:7; 28:16–21
10 [n]**1Ki 22:27**
12 [o]2Ch 21:18; 26:19; Ps 103:3; [p]2Ch 7:14; [q]Jer 17:5–6
14 [r]**Ge 50:5;** [s]**Ge 50:2;** [t]2Ch 21:19; Jer 34:5

Ch. 17

1 [a]**1Ki 2:12**
2 [b]**2Ch 11:10;** [c]2Ch 15:8
3 [d]**1Ki 22:43**
4 [e]2Ch 22:9
5 [f]**1Sa 10:27**

[a]4 Also known as *Abel Beth Maacah*
[b]8 That is, people from the upper Nile region
[c]8 Or *charioteers*

wealth and honour.[g] 6His heart was
devoted[h] to the ways of the LORD;
furthermore, he removed the high
places[i] and the Asherah poles[j] from
Judah.[k]
7In the third year of his reign he sent
his officials Ben-Hail, Obadiah, Zech-
ariah, Nethanel and Micaiah to teach[l] in
the towns of Judah. 8With them were
certain Levites[m]—Shemaiah, Netha-
niah, Zebadiah, Asahel, Shemiramoth,
Jehonathan, Adonijah, Tobijah and
Tob-Adonijah—and the priests Eli-
shama and Jehoram. 9They taught
throughout Judah, taking with them the
Book of the Law[n] of the LORD; they went
round to all the towns of Judah and
taught the people.
10The fear[o] of the LORD fell on all the
kingdoms of the lands surrounding
Judah, so that they did not make war
with Jehoshaphat. 11Some Philistines
brought Jehoshaphat gifts and silver as
tribute, and the Arabs[p] brought him
flocks:[q] seven thousand seven hundred
rams and seven thousand seven hun-
dred goats.
12Jehoshaphat became more and
more powerful; he built forts and store
cities in Judah 13and had large supplies
in the towns of Judah. He also kept
experienced fighting men in Jerusalem.
14Their enrolment[r] by families was as
follows:

From Judah, commanders of units of 1,000:
Adnah the commander, with 300,000 fighting men;
15next, Jehohanan the commander, with 280,000;
16next, Amasiah son of Zicri, who volunteered[s] himself for the service of the LORD, with 200,000.
17From Benjamin:[t]
Eliada, a valiant soldier, with 200,000 men armed with bows and shields;
18next, Jehozabad, with 180,000 men armed for battle.

19These were the men who served the
king, besides those he stationed in the
fortified cities[u] throughout Judah.[v]

Micaiah Prophesies Against Ahab

18:1–27pp—1Ki 22:1–28

18 Now Jehoshaphat had great
wealth and honour,[a] and he
allied[b] himself with Ahab[c] by marriage.
2Some years later he went down to visit
Ahab in Samaria. Ahab slaughtered
many sheep and cattle for him and the
people with him and urged him to
attack Ramoth Gilead. 3Ahab king of
Israel asked Jehoshaphat king of Judah,
"Will you go with me against Ramoth
Gilead?"
Jehoshaphat replied, "I am as you
are, and my people as your people; we
will join you in the war." 4But
Jehoshaphat also said to the king of
Israel, "First seek the counsel of the
LORD."
5So the king of Israel brought together
the prophets—four hundred men—
and asked them, "Shall we go to war
against Ramoth Gilead, or shall I
refrain?"
"Go," they answered, "for God will
give it into the king's hand."
6But Jehoshaphat asked, "Is there not
a prophet of the LORD here whom we
can enquire of?"
7The king of Israel answered
Jehoshaphat, "There is still one man
through whom we can enquire of the
LORD, but I hate him because he never
prophesies anything good about me,
but always bad. He is Micaiah son of
Imlah."
"The king should not say that,"
Jehoshaphat replied.
8So the king of Israel called one of his
officials and said, "Bring Micaiah son of
Imlah at once."
9Dressed in their royal robes, the king
of Israel and Jehoshaphat king of Judah
were sitting on their thrones at the
threshing-floor by the entrance to the
gate of Samaria, with all the prophets
prophesying before them. 10Now Zede-
kiah son of Kenaanah had made iron
horns, and he declared, "This is what
the LORD says: 'With these you will
gore the Arameans until they are
destroyed.'"
11All the other prophets were
prophesying the same thing. "Attack
Ramoth Gilead[d] and be victorious,"
they said, "for the LORD will give it into
the king's hand."
12The messenger who had gone to
summon Micaiah said to him, "Look, as
one man the other prophets are pre-
dicting success for the king. Let your
word agree with theirs, and speak
favourably."
13But Micaiah said, "As surely as the
LORD lives, I can tell him only what my
God says."[e]
14When he arrived, the king asked
him, "Micaiah, shall we go to war
against Ramoth Gilead, or shall I
refrain?"

5 [g]2Ch 18:1
6 [h]**1Ki 8:61;** [i]**1Ki 15:14;** 2Ch 19:3; 20:33; [j]**Ex 34:13;** [k]2Ch 21:12
7 [l]**Lev 10:11;** Dt 6:4–9; 2Ch 19:4–11; 35:3; Ne 8:7; Mal 2:7
8 [m]2Ch 19:8; Ne 8:7–8; Hos 4:6
9 [n]**Dt 28:61**
10 [o]**Ge 35:5; Dt 2:25**
11 [p]**2Ch 9:14;** [q]2Ch 21:16
14 [r]**2Sa 24:2**
16 [s]**Jdg 5:9**
17 [t]**Nu 1:36**
19 [u]**2Ch 11:10;** [v]2Ch 25:5

Ch. 18

1 [a]2Ch 17:5; [b]2Ch 19:1–3; 22:3; [c]2Ch 21:6
11 [d]2Ch 22:5
13 [e]Nu 22:18, 20,35

"Attack and be victorious," he
answered, "for they will be given into
your hand."
15The king said to him, "How many
times must I make you swear to tell me
nothing but the truth in the name of the
LORD?"
16Then Micaiah answered, "I saw all
Israel[f] scattered on the hills like sheep
without a shepherd,[g] and the LORD said,
'These people have no master. Let each
one go home in peace.'"
17The king of Israel said to
Jehoshaphat, "Didn't I tell you that he
never prophesies anything good about
me, but only bad?"
18Micaiah continued, "Therefore hear
the word of the LORD: I saw the LORD
sitting on his throne[h] with all the host of
heaven standing on his right and on his
left. 19And the LORD said, 'Who will lure
Ahab king of Israel into attacking
Ramoth Gilead and going to his death
there?'
"One suggested this, and another
that. 20Finally, a spirit came forward,
stood before the LORD and said, 'I will
lure him.'
"'By what means?' the LORD asked.
21"'I will go and be a lying spirit[i] in the
mouths of all his prophets,' he said.
"'You will succeed in luring him,'
said the LORD. 'Go and do it.'
22"So now the LORD has put a lying
spirit in the mouths of these prophets of
yours.[j] The LORD has decreed disaster
for you."
23Then Zedekiah son of Kenaanah
went up and slapped[k] Micaiah in the
face. "Which way did the spirit from[a]
the LORD go when he went from me to
speak to you?" he asked.
24Micaiah replied, "You will find out
on the day you go to hide in an inner
room."
25The king of Israel then ordered,
"Take Micaiah and send him back to
Amon the ruler of the city and to Joash
the king's son, 26and say, 'This is what
the king says: Put this fellow in prison[l]
and give him nothing but bread and
water until I return safely.'"
27Micaiah declared, "If you ever re-
turn safely, the LORD has not spoken
through me." Then he added, "Mark
my words, all you people!"

Ahab Killed at Ramoth Gilead

18:28–34pp—1Ki 22:29–36

28So the king of Israel and
Jehoshaphat king of Judah went up to
Ramoth Gilead. 29The king of Israel said
to Jehoshaphat, "I will enter the battle
in disguise, but you wear your royal
robes." So the king of Israel disguised[m]
himself and went into battle.
30Now the king of Aram had ordered
his chariot commanders, "Do not fight
with anyone, small or great, except the
king of Israel." 31When the chariot
commanders saw Jehoshaphat, they
thought, "This is the king of Israel."
So they turned to attack him, but
Jehoshaphat cried out,[n] and the LORD
helped him. God drew them away
from him, 32for when the chariot com-
manders saw that he was not the king of
Israel, they stopped pursuing him.
33But someone drew his bow at ran-
dom and hit the king of Israel between
the sections of his armour. The king told
the chariot driver, "Wheel around and
get me out of the fighting. I've been
wounded." 34All day long the battle
raged, and the king of Israel propped
himself up in his chariot facing the
Arameans until evening. Then at sunset
he died.[o]

19 When Jehoshaphat king of
Judah returned safely to his
palace in Jerusalem, 2Jehu[a] the seer, the
son of Hanani, went out to meet him
and said to the king, "Should you help
the wicked[b] and love[a] those who hate
the LORD?[c] Because of this, the wrath[d] of
the LORD is upon you. 3There is, how-
ever, some good[e] in you, for you have
rid the land of the Asherah poles[f] and
have set your heart on seeking God.[g]"

Jehoshaphat Appoints Judges

4Jehoshaphat lived in Jerusalem, and
he went out again among the people
from Beersheba to the hill country of
Ephraim and turned them back to the
LORD, the God of their fathers. 5He
appointed judges[h] in the land, in each of
the fortified cities of Judah. 6He told
them, "Consider carefully what you
do,[i] because you are not judging for
man[j] but for the LORD, who is with you
whenever you give a verdict. 7Now let
the fear of the LORD be upon you. Judge
carefully, for with the LORD our God
there is no injustice[k] or partiality[l] or
bribery."
8In Jerusalem also, Jehoshaphat
appointed some of the Levites,[m] priests[n]
and heads of Israelite families to admin-
ister[o] the law of the LORD and to settle
disputes. And they lived in Jerusalem.

16 [f]**1Ch 9:1;** [g]**Nu 27:17**
18 [h]Da 7:9
21 [i]1Ch 21:1; Job 1:6; Zec 3:1; Jn 8:44
22 [j]Job 12:16; Eze 14:9
23 [k]Ac 23:2
26 [l]Heb 11:36
29 [m]**1Sa 28:8**
31 [n]**2Ch 13:14**
34 [o]2Ch 22:5

Ch. 19

2 [a]**1Ki 16:1;** [b]**2Ch 16:2–9;** [c]Ps 139:21–22; [d]2Ch 24:18; 32:25; Ps 7:11
3 [e]**1Ki 14:13;** [f]**2Ch 17:6;** [g]**2Ch 18:1;** 20:35; 25:7
5 [h]**Ge 47:6;** **Ex 18:26**
6 [i]**Lev 19:15;** [j]Dt 16:18–20; 17:8–13
7 [k]**Ge 18:25;** **Job 8:3;** [l]**Ex 18:16;** Dt 10:17; Job 13:10; 32:21; 34:19
8 [m]**1Ch 23:4;** [n]Eze 44:24; [o]2Ch 17:8–9

[a]23 Or *Spirit of*

[a]2 Or *and make alliances with*

9He gave them these orders: "You must serve faithfully and wholeheartedly in the fear of the LORD. 10In every case that comes before you from your fellow countrymen who live in the cities—whether bloodshed or other concerns of the law, commands, decrees or ordinances—you are to warn them not to sin against the LORD;[p] otherwise his wrath will come on you and your brothers. Do this, and you will not sin.

11"Amariah the chief priest will be over you in any matter concerning the LORD, and Zebadiah son of Ishmael, the leader of the tribe of Judah, will be over you in any matter concerning the king, and the Levites will serve as officials before you. Act with courage,[q] and may the LORD be with those who do well."

Jehoshaphat Defeats Moab and Ammon

20 After this, the Moabites[a] and Ammonites with some of the Meunites[a][b] came to make war on Jehoshaphat.

2Some men came and told Jehoshaphat, "A vast army[c] is coming against you from Edom,[b] from the other side of the Sea.[c] It is already in Hazezon Tamar[d]" (that is, En Gedi).[e] 3Alarmed, Jehoshaphat resolved to enquire of the LORD, and he proclaimed a fast[f] for all Judah. 4The people of Judah[g] came together to seek help from the LORD; indeed, they came from every town in Judah to seek him.

5Then Jehoshaphat stood up in the assembly of Judah and Jerusalem at the temple of the LORD in the front of the new courtyard 6and said:

"O LORD, God of our fathers,[h] are you not the God who is in heaven?[i] You rule over all the kingdoms[j] of the nations. Power and might are in your hand, and no-one can withstand you.[k] 7O our God, did you not drive out the inhabitants of this land[l] before your people Israel and give it for ever to the descendants of Abraham your friend?[m] 8They have lived in it and have built in it a sanctuary[n] for your Name, saying, 9'If calamity comes upon us, whether the sword of judgment, or plague or famine,[o] we will stand in your presence before this temple that bears your Name and will cry out to you in our distress, and you will hear us and save us.'

10"But now here are men from Ammon, Moab and Mount Seir, whose territory you would not allow Israel to invade when they came from Egypt;[p] so they turned away from them and did not destroy them. 11See how they are repaying us by coming to drive us out of the possession[q] you gave us as an inheritance. 12O our God, will you not judge them?[r] For we have no power to face this vast army that is attacking us. We do not know what to do, but our eyes are upon you.[s]"

13All the men of Judah, with their wives and children and little ones, stood there before the LORD.

14Then the Spirit[t] of the LORD came upon Jahaziel son of Zechariah, the son of Benaiah, the son of Jeiel, the son of Mattaniah,[u] a Levite and descendant of Asaph, as he stood in the assembly.

15He said, "Listen, King Jehoshaphat and all who live in Judah and Jerusalem! This is what the LORD says to you: 'Do not be afraid or discouraged[v] because of this vast army. For the battle[w] is not yours, but God's. 16Tomorrow march down against them. They will be climbing up by the Pass of Ziz, and you will find them at the end of the gorge in the Desert of Jeruel. 17You will not have to fight this battle. Take up your positions; stand firm and see[x] the deliverance the LORD will give you, O Judah and Jerusalem. Do not be afraid; do not be discouraged. Go out to face them tomorrow, and the LORD will be with you.'"

18Jehoshaphat bowed[y] with his face to the ground, and all the people of Judah and Jerusalem fell down in worship before the LORD. 19Then some Levites from the Kohathites and Korahites stood up and praised the LORD, the God of Israel, with a very loud voice.

20Early in the morning they left for the Desert of Tekoa. As they set out, Jehoshaphat stood and said, "Listen to me, Judah and people of Jerusalem! Have faith[z] in the LORD your God and you will be upheld; have faith in his prophets and you will be successful.[a]" 21After consulting the people, Jehoshaphat appointed men to sing to the LORD and to praise him for the splendour of his[d] holiness[b] as they went out at the head of the army, saying:

10 [p]Dt 17:8-13
11 [q]1Ch 28:20

Ch. 20

1 [a]Ps 83:6; [b]1Ch 4:41
2 [c]2Ch 24:24; [d]Ge 14:7; [e]1Sa 23:29; SS 1:14
3 [f]1Sa 7:6; Ezr 8:23; Ne 1:4; Est 4:16; Isa 58:6; Jer 36:9; Da 9:3; Joel 1:14; 2:15; Jnh 3:5,7
4 [g]Jer 36:6
6 [h]Mt 6:9; [i]Dt 4:39; [j]1Ch 29:11-12; [k]2Ch 25:8; Job 25:2; 41:10; 42:2; Isa 14:27; Jer 32:27; 49:19
7 [l]Ge 12:7; [m]Isa 41:8; Jas 2:23
8 [n]2Ch 6:20
9 [o]2Ch 6:28
10 [p]Nu 20:14-21; Dt 2:4-6,9, 18-19
11 [q]Ps 83:1-12
12 [r]Jdg 11:27; [s]Ps 25:15; Isa 30:15; 45:22; Mic 7:7
14 [t]1Ch 12:18; [u]1Ch 9:15
15 [v]2Ch 32:7; [w]1Sa 17:47; Ps 91:8
17 [x]Ex 14:13
18 [y]Ge 24:26; 2Ch 29:29
20 [z]Isa 7:9; [a]Ge 39:3; Pr 16:3
21 [b]1Ch 16:29

a1 Some Septuagint manuscripts; Hebrew *Ammonites*

b2 One Hebrew manuscript; most Hebrew manuscripts, Septuagint and Vulgate *Aram*

c2 That is, the Dead Sea

d21 Or *him with the splendour of*

"Give thanks to the LORD,
for his love endures for ever."[c]

22As they began to sing and praise, the LORD set ambushes[d] against the men of Ammon and Moab and Mount Seir who were invading Judah, and they were defeated. 23The men of Ammon[e] and Moab rose up against the men from Mount Seir[f] to destroy and annihilate them. After they finished slaughtering the men from Seir, they helped to destroy one another.[g]

24When the men of Judah came to the place that overlooks the desert and looked towards the vast army, they saw only dead bodies lying on the ground; no-one had escaped. 25So Jehoshaphat and his men went to carry off their plunder, and they found among them a great amount of equipment and clothing[e] and also articles of value—more than they could take away. There was so much plunder that it took three days to collect it. 26On the fourth day they assembled in the Valley of Beracah, where they praised the LORD. This is why it is called the Valley of Beracah[f] to this day.

27Then, led by Jehoshaphat, all the men of Judah and Jerusalem returned joyfully to Jerusalem, for the LORD had given them cause to rejoice over their enemies. 28They entered Jerusalem and went to the temple of the LORD with harps and lutes and trumpets.

29The fear[h] of God came upon all the kingdoms of the countries when they heard how the LORD had fought[i] against the enemies of Israel. 30And the kingdom of Jehoshaphat was at peace, for his God had given him rest[j] on every side.

The End of Jehoshaphat's Reign

20:31–21:1pp—1Ki 22:41–50

31So Jehoshaphat reigned over Judah. He was thirty-five years old when he became king of Judah, and he reigned in Jerusalem for twenty-five years. His mother's name was Azubah daughter of Shilhi. 32He walked in the ways of his father Asa and did not stray from them; he did what was right in the eyes of the LORD. 33The high places,[k] however, were not removed, and the people still had not set their hearts on the God of their fathers.

34The other events of Jehoshaphat's reign, from beginning to end, are written in the annals of Jehu[l] son of Hanani, which are recorded in the book of the kings of Israel.

35Later, Jehoshaphat king of Judah made an alliance[m] with Ahaziah king of Israel, who was guilty of wickedness.[n] 36He agreed with him to construct a fleet of trading ships.[g] After these were built at Ezion Geber, 37Eliezer son of Dodavahu of Mareshah prophesied against Jehoshaphat, saying, "Because you have made an alliance with Ahaziah, the LORD will destroy what you have made." The ships[o] were wrecked and were not able to set sail to trade.[h]

21 Then Jehoshaphat rested with his fathers and was buried with them in the City of David. And Jehoram[a] his son succeeded him as king. 2Jehoram's brothers, the sons of Jehoshaphat, were Azariah, Jehiel, Zechariah, Azariahu, Michael and Shephatiah. All these were sons of Jehoshaphat king of Israel.[a] 3Their father had given them many gifts[b] of silver and gold and articles of value, as well as fortified cities[c] in Judah, but he had given the kingdom to Jehoram because he was his firstborn son.

Jehoram King of Judah

21:5–10,20pp—2Ki 8:16–24

4When Jehoram established[d] himself firmly over his father's kingdom, he put all his brothers[e] to the sword along with some of the princes of Israel. 5Jehoram was thirty-two years old when he became king, and he reigned in Jerusalem for eight years. 6He walked in the ways of the kings of Israel,[f] as the house of Ahab had done, for he married a daughter of Ahab.[g] He did evil in the eyes of the LORD. 7Nevertheless, because of the covenant the LORD had made with David,[h] the LORD was not willing to destroy the house of David.[i] He had promised to maintain a lamp[j] for him and his descendants for ever.

8In the time of Jehoram, Edom[k] rebelled against Judah and set up its own king. 9So Jehoram went there with his officers and all his chariots. The Edomites surrounded him and his chariot commanders, but he rose up and broke through by night. 10To this day Edom has been in rebellion against Judah.

Libnah[l] revolted at the same time, because Jehoram had forsaken the

21 [c]**2Ch 5:13**; Ps 136:1
22 [d]**2Ch 13:13**
23 [e]**Ge 19:38**; [f]2Ch 21:8; [g]**Jdg 7:22**; 1Sa 14:20; Eze 38:21
29 [h]**Ge 35:5**; **Dt 2:25**; [i]**Ex 14:14**
30 [j]**1Ch 22:9**
33 [k]**2Ch 17:6**
34 [l]**1Ki 16:1**
35 [m]**2Ch 16:3**; [n]**2Ch 19:1–3**
37 [o]**1Ki 9:26**

Ch. 21

1 [a]**1Ch 3:11**
3 [b]2Ch 11:23; [c]**2Ch 11:10**
4 [d]**1Ki 2:12**; [e]Jdg 9:5
6 [f]1Ki 12:28–30; [g]2Ch 18:1; 22:3
7 [h]**2Sa 7:13**; [i]**2Sa 7:15**; 2Ch 23:3; [j]**2Sa 21:17**
8 [k]2Ch 20:22–23
10 [l]**Nu 33:20**

e25 Some Hebrew manuscripts and Vulgate; most Hebrew manuscripts *corpses*
f26 *Beracah* means *praise*.
g36 Hebrew *of ships that could go to Tarshish*
h37 Hebrew *sail for Tarshish*
a2 That is, Judah, as frequently in 2 Chronicles

LORD, the God of his fathers. 11He had
also built high places on the hills of
Judah and had caused the people of
Jerusalem to prostitute themselves and
had led Judah astray.
12Jehoram received a letter from
Elijah[m] the prophet, which said:

"This is what the LORD, the God of
your father[n] David, says: 'You have
not walked in the ways of your
father Jehoshaphat or of Asa[o] king
of Judah. 13But you have walked in
the ways of the kings of Israel, and
you have led Judah and the people
of Jerusalem to prostitute them-
selves, just as the house of Ahab
did.[p] You have also murdered your
own brothers, members of your
father's house, men who were bet-
ter[q] than you. 14So now the LORD is
about to strike your people, your
sons, your wives and everything
that is yours, with a heavy blow.
15You yourself will be very ill with a
lingering disease[r] of the bowels,
until the disease causes your
bowels to come out.'"

16The LORD aroused against Jehoram
the hostility of the Philistines and of the
Arabs[s] who lived near the Cushites.
17They attacked Judah, invaded it and
carried off all the goods found in the
king's palace, together with his sons
and wives. Not a son was left to him
except Ahaziah,[b] the youngest.[t]
18After all this, the LORD afflicted
Jehoram with an incurable disease of
the bowels. 19In the course of time, at
the end of the second year, his bowels
came out because of the disease, and he
died in great pain. His people made no
fire in his honour,[u] as they had for his
fathers.
20Jehoram was thirty-two years old
when he became king, and he reigned
in Jerusalem for eight years. He passed
away, to no-one's regret, and was
buried[v] in the City of David, but not in
the tombs of the kings.

Ahaziah King of Judah

22:1–6pp—2Ki 8:25–29
22:7–9pp—2Ki 9:21–29

22 The people[a] of Jerusalem[b] made
Ahaziah, Jehoram's youngest
son, king in his place, since the raiders,[c]
who came with the Arabs into the camp,
had killed all the older sons. So Ahaziah
son of Jehoram king of Judah began to
reign.
2Ahaziah was twenty-two[a] years old
when he became king, and he reigned
in Jerusalem for one year. His mother's
name was Athaliah, a granddaughter of
Omri.
3He too walked[d] in the ways of the
house of Ahab,[e] for his mother encour-
aged him in doing wrong. 4He did evil
in the eyes of the LORD, as the house of
Ahab had done, for after his father's
death they became his advisers, to his
undoing. 5He also followed their coun-
sel when he went with Joram[b] son of
Ahab king of Israel to war against
Hazael king of Aram at Ramoth Gilead.[f]
The Arameans wounded Joram; 6so he
returned to Jezreel to recover from the
wounds they had inflicted on him at
Ramoth[c] in his battle with Hazael[g] king
of Aram.
Then Ahaziah[d] son of Jehoram king of
Judah went down to Jezreel to see Joram
son of Ahab because he had been
wounded.
7Through Ahaziah's[h] visit to Joram,
God brought about Ahaziah's downfall.
When Ahaziah arrived, he went out
with Joram to meet Jehu son of Nimshi,
whom the LORD had anointed to destroy
the house of Ahab. 8While Jehu was
executing judgment on the house of
Ahab,[i] he found the princes of Judah
and the sons of Ahaziah's relatives,
who had been attending Ahaziah, and
he killed them. 9He then went in search
of Ahaziah, and his men captured him
while he was hiding[j] in Samaria. He was
brought to Jehu and put to death. They
buried him, for they said, "He was a son
of Jehoshaphat, who sought[k] the LORD
with all his heart." So there was no-one
in the house of Ahaziah powerful
enough to retain the kingdom.

Athaliah and Joash

22:10–23:21pp—2Ki 11:1–21

10When Athaliah the mother of Aha-
ziah saw that her son was dead, she
proceeded to destroy the whole royal
family of the house of Judah. 11But
Jehosheba,[e] the daughter of King Je-
horam, took Joash son of Ahaziah and

12 [m]2Ki 1:16–17; [n]2Ch 17:3–6; [o]2Ch 14:2
13 [p]1Ki 16:29–33; [q]1Ki 2:32
15 [r]**Nu 12:10**
16 [s]2Ch 17:10–11; 22:1; 26:7
17 [t]2Ki 12:18; 2Ch 22:1; Joel 3:5
19 [u]**2Ch 16:14**
20 [v]2Ch 24:25; 28:27; 33:20

Ch. 22

1 [a]2Ch 33:25; 36:1; [b]2Ch 23:20–21; 26:1; [c]**2Ch 21:16–17**
3 [d]**2Ch 18:1;** [e]**2Ch 21:6**
5 [f]2Ch 18:11,34
6 [g]1Ki 19:15; 2Ki 8:13–15
7 [h]2Ki 9:16
8 [i]**2Ki 10:13**
9 [j]**Jdg 9:5;** [k]2Ch 17:4

b*17* Hebrew *Jehoahaz*, a variant of *Ahaziah*
a*2* Some Septuagint manuscripts and Syriac (see also 2 Kings 8:26); Hebrew *forty-two*
b*5* Hebrew *Jehoram*, a variant of *Joram*; also in verses 6 and 7
c*6* Hebrew *Ramah*, a variant of *Ramoth*
d*6* Some Hebrew manuscripts, Septuagint, Vulgate and Syriac (see also 2 Kings 8:29); most Hebrew manuscripts *Azariah*
e*11* Hebrew *Jehoshabeath*, a variant of *Jehosheba*

stole him away from among the royal
princes who were about to be murdered
and put him and his nurse in a bed-
room. Because Jehosheba,[f] the
daughter of King Jehoram and wife of
the priest Jehoiada, was Ahaziah's sis-
ter, she hid the child from Athaliah so
that she could not kill him. 12He re-
mained hidden with them at the temple
of God for six years while Athaliah ruled
the land.

23 In the seventh year Jehoiada
showed his strength. He made
a covenant with the commanders of
units of a hundred: Azariah son of
Jeroham, Ishmael son of Jehohanan,
Azariah son of Obed, Maaseiah son of
Adaiah, and Elishaphat son of Zicri.
2They went throughout Judah and
gathered the Levites[a] and the heads of
Israelite families from all the towns.
When they came to Jerusalem, 3the
whole assembly made a covenant[b] with
the king at the temple of God.

Jehoiada said to them, "The king's
son shall reign, as the LORD promised
concerning the descendants of David.[c]
4Now this is what you are to do: A third
of you priests and Levites who are going
on duty on the Sabbath are to keep
watch at the doors, 5a third of you at the
royal palace and a third at the Foundation
Gate, and all the other men are to be in
the courtyards of the temple of the
LORD. 6No-one is to enter the temple of
the LORD except the priests and Levites
on duty; they may enter because they
are consecrated, but all the other men
are to guard[d] what the LORD has
assigned to them.[a] 7The Levites are to
station themselves round the king, each
man with his weapons in his hand.
Anyone who enters the temple must be
put to death. Stay close to the king
wherever he goes."

8The Levites and all the men of Judah
did just as Jehoiada the priest ordered.[e]
Each one took his men—those who
were going on duty on the Sabbath and
those who were going off duty—for
Jehoiada the priest had not released any
of the divisions.[f] 9Then he gave the
commanders of units of a hundred the
spears and the large and small shields
that had belonged to King David and
that were in the temple of God. 10He
stationed all the men, each with his
weapon in his hand, round the king
—near the altar and the temple, from
the south side to the north side of the
temple.

11Jehoiada and his sons brought out
the king's son and put the crown on
him; they presented him with a copy[g] of
the covenant and proclaimed him king.
They anointed him and shouted, "Long
live the king!"

12When Athaliah heard the noise of
the people running and cheering the
king, she went to them at the temple of
the LORD. 13She looked, and there was
the king,[h] standing by his pillar[i] at the
entrance. The officers and the trum-
peters were beside the king, and all the
people of the land were rejoicing and
blowing trumpets, and singers with
musical instruments were leading the
praises. Then Athaliah tore her robes
and shouted, "Treason! Treason!"

14Jehoiada the priest sent out the com-
manders of units of a hundred, who
were in charge of the troops, and said to
them: "Bring her out between the
ranks[b] and put to the sword anyone
who follows her." For the priest had
said, "Do not put her to death at the
temple of the LORD." 15So they seized
her as she reached the entrance of the
Horse Gate[j] on the palace grounds, and
there they put her to death.

16Jehoiada then made a covenant[k] that
he and the people and the king[c] would
be the LORD's people. 17All the people
went to the temple of Baal and tore it
down. They smashed the altars and
idols and killed[l] Mattan the priest of
Baal in front of the altars.

18Then Jehoiada placed the oversight
of the temple of the LORD in the hands of
the priests, who were Levites,[m] to
whom David had made assignments in
the temple,[n] to present the burnt offer-
ings of the LORD as written in the Law of
Moses, with rejoicing and singing, as
David had ordered. 19He also stationed
doorkeepers[o] at the gates of the LORD's
temple so that no-one who was in any
way unclean might enter.

20He took with him the commanders
of hundreds, the nobles, the rulers of
the people and all the people of the land
and brought the king down from the
temple of the LORD. They went into the
palace through the Upper Gate[p] and
seated the king on the royal throne,
21and all the people of the land rejoiced.
And the city was quiet, because
Athaliah had been slain with the
sword.[q]

Ch. 23

2 [a]Nu 35:2–5
3 [b]2Ki 11:17; [c]2Sa 7:12; 1Ki 2:4; 2Ch 6:16; 7:18; 21:7
6 [d]Zec 3:7
8 [e]2Ki 11:9; [f]1Ch 24:1
11 [g]Dt 17:18
13 [h]1Ki 1:41; [i]1Ki 7:15
15 [j]Jer 31:40
16 [k]2Ch 29:10; 34:31; Ne 9:38
17 [l]Dt 13:6–9
18 [m]1Ch 23:28–32; [n]1Ch 23:6; 25:6
19 [o]1Ch 9:22
20 [p]2Ki 15:35
21 [q]2Ch 22:1

f11 Hebrew *Jehoshabeath*, a variant of *Jehosheba*
a6 Or *to observe the LORD's command* ⌞*not to enter*⌟
b14 Or *out from the precincts*
c16 Or *covenant between* ⌞*the LORD*⌟ *and the people and the king that they* (see 2 Kings 11:17)

Joash Repairs the Temple

24:1–14pp—2Ki 12:1–16
24:23–27pp—2Ki 12:17–21

24 Joash was seven years old when he became king, and he reigned in Jerusalem for forty years. His mother's name was Zibiah; she was from Beersheba. 2Joash did what was right in the eyes of the LORD[a] all the years of Jehoiada the priest. 3Jehoiada chose two wives for him, and he had sons and daughters.

4Some time later Joash decided to restore the temple of the LORD. 5He called together the priests and Levites and said to them, "Go to the towns of Judah and collect the money[b] due annually from all Israel,[c] to repair the temple of your God. Do it now." But the Levites[d] did not act at once.

6Therefore the king summoned Jehoiada the chief priest and said to him, "Why haven't you required the Levites to bring in from Judah and Jerusalem the tax imposed by Moses the servant of the LORD and by the assembly of Israel for the Tent of the Testimony?"[e]

7Now the sons of that wicked woman Athaliah had broken into the temple of God and had used even its sacred objects for the Baals.

8At the king's command, a chest was made and placed outside, at the gate of the temple of the LORD. 9A proclamation was then issued in Judah and Jerusalem that they should bring to the LORD the tax that Moses the servant of God had required of Israel in the desert. 10All the officials and all the people brought their contributions gladly,[f] dropping them into the chest until it was full. 11Whenever the chest was brought in by the Levites to the king's officials and they saw that there was a large amount of money, the royal secretary and the officer of the chief priest would come and empty the chest and carry it back to its place. They did this regularly and collected a great amount of money. 12The king and Jehoiada gave it to the men who carried out the work required for the temple of the LORD. They hired[g] masons and carpenters to restore the LORD's temple, and also workers in iron and bronze to repair the temple.

13The men in charge of the work were diligent, and the repairs progressed under them. They rebuilt the temple of God according to its original design and reinforced it. 14When they had finished, they brought the rest of the money to the king and Jehoiada, and with it were made articles for the LORD's temple: articles for the service and for the burnt offerings, and also dishes and other objects of gold and silver. As long as Jehoiada lived, burnt offerings were presented continually in the temple of the LORD.

15Now Jehoiada was old and full of years, and he died at the age of a hundred and thirty. 16He was buried with the kings in the City of David, because of the good he had done in Israel for God and his temple.

The Wickedness of Joash

17After the death of Jehoiada, the officials of Judah came and paid homage to the king, and he listened to them. 18They abandoned[h] the temple of the LORD, the God of their fathers, and worshipped Asherah poles and idols.[i] Because of their guilt, God's anger[j] came upon Judah and Jerusalem. 19Although the LORD sent prophets to the people to bring them back to him, and though they testified against them, they would not listen.[k]

20Then the Spirit[l] of God came upon Zechariah[m] son of Jehoiada the priest. He stood before the people and said, "This is what God says: 'Why do you disobey the LORD's commands? You will not prosper.[n] Because you have forsaken the LORD, he has forsaken[o] you.'"

21But they plotted against him, and by order of the king they stoned[p] him to death[q] in the courtyard of the LORD's temple.[r] 22King Joash did not remember the kindness Zechariah's father Jehoiada had shown him but killed his son, who said as he lay dying, "May the LORD see this and call you to account."[s]

23At the turn of the year,[a] the army of Aram marched against Joash; it invaded Judah and Jerusalem and killed all the leaders of the people.[t] They sent all the plunder to their king in Damascus. 24Although the Aramean army had come with only a few men,[u] the LORD delivered into their hands a much larger army.[v] Because Judah had forsaken the LORD, the God of their fathers, judgment was executed on Joash. 25When the Arameans withdrew, they left Joash severely wounded. His officials conspired against him for murdering the son of Jehoiada the priest, and they killed him in his bed. So he died and was buried[w] in the City of David, but not in the tombs of the kings.

Ch. 24

2 [a]2Ch 25:2; 26:5
5 [b]**Ex 30:16**; Ne 10:32–33; Mt 17:24; [c]1Ch 11:1; [d]**1Ch 26:20**
6 [e]**Ex 38:21**
10 [f]**Ex 25:2; 1Ch 29:3,6,9**
12 [g]2Ch 34:11
18 [h]**Jos 24:20; 2Ch 7:19**; [i]**Ex 34:13**; 2Ch 33:3; Jer 17:2; [j]**2Ch 19:2**
19 [k]**Nu 11:29**; Jer 7:25; Zec 1:4
20 [l]**Jdg 3:10; 1Ch 12:18**; [m]Mt 23:35; Lk 11:51; [n]Nu 14:41; [o]**Dt 31:17**
21 [p]**Jos 7:25**; [q]Jer 26:21; [r]Jer 20:2
22 [s]**Ge 9:5**
23 [t]2Ki 12:17–18
24 [u]**2Ch 14:9**; 16:8; 20:2,12; [v]Lev 26:23–25; Dt 28:25
25 [w]**2Ch 21:20**

[a]23 Probably in the spring

26Those who conspired against him were Zabad,[b] son of Shimeath an Ammonite woman, and Jehozabad, son of Shimrith[c][x] a Moabite woman.[y] 27The account of his sons, the many prophecies about him, and the record of the restoration of the temple of God are written in the annotations on the book of the kings. And Amaziah his son succeeded him as king.

Amaziah King of Judah

25:1–4pp—2Ki 14:1–6
25:11–12pp—2Ki 14:7
25:17–28pp—2Ki 14:8–20

25 Amaziah was twenty-five years old when he became king, and he reigned in Jerusalem for twenty-nine years. His mother's name was Jehoaddin;[a] she was from Jerusalem. 2He did what was right in the eyes of the LORD, but not wholeheartedly.[a] 3After the kingdom was firmly in his control, he executed the officials who had murdered his father the king. 4Yet he did not put their sons to death, but acted in accordance with what is written in the Law, in the Book of Moses,[b] where the LORD commanded: "Fathers shall not be put to death for their children, nor children put to death for their fathers; each is to die for his own sins."[b][c]

5Amaziah called the people of Judah together and assigned them according to their families to commanders of thousands and commanders of hundreds for all Judah and Benjamin. He then mustered[d] those twenty years old[e] or more and found that there were three hundred thousand men ready for military service,[f] able to handle the spear and shield. 6He also hired a hundred thousand fighting men from Israel for a hundred talents[c] of silver.

7But a man of God came to him and said, "O king, these troops from Israel[g] must not march with you, for the LORD is not with Israel—not with any of the people of Ephraim. 8Even if you go and fight courageously in battle, God will overthrow you before the enemy, for God has the power to help or to overthrow."[h]

9Amaziah asked the man of God, "But what about the hundred talents I paid for these Israelite troops?"

The man of God replied, "The LORD can give you much more than that."[i]

10So Amaziah dismissed the troops who had come to him from Ephraim and sent them home. They were furious with Judah and left for home in a great rage.[j]

11Amaziah then marshalled his strength and led his army to the Valley of Salt, where he killed ten thousand men of Seir. 12The army of Judah also captured ten thousand men alive, took them to the top of a cliff and threw them down so that all were dashed to pieces.[k]

13Meanwhile the troops that Amaziah had sent back and had not allowed to take part in the war raided Judean towns from Samaria to Beth Horon. They killed three thousand people and carried off great quantities of plunder.

14When Amaziah returned from slaughtering the Edomites, he brought back the gods of the people of Seir. He set them up as his own gods,[l] bowed down to them and burned sacrifices to them. 15The anger of the LORD burned against Amaziah, and he sent a prophet to him, who said, "Why do you consult this people's gods, which could not save[m] their own people from your hand?"

16While he was still speaking, the king said to him, "Have we appointed you an adviser to the king? Stop! Why be struck down?"

So the prophet stopped but said, "I know that God has determined to destroy you, because you have done this and have not listened to my counsel."

17After Amaziah king of Judah consulted his advisers, he sent this challenge to Jehoash[d] son of Jehoahaz, the son of Jehu, king of Israel: "Come, meet me face to face."

18But Jehoash king of Israel replied to Amaziah king of Judah, "A thistle[n] in Lebanon sent a message to a cedar in Lebanon, 'Give your daughter to my son in marriage.' Then a wild beast in Lebanon came along and trampled the thistle underfoot. 19You say to yourself that you have defeated Edom, and now you are arrogant and proud. But stay at home! Why ask for trouble and cause your own downfall and that of Judah also?"

20Amaziah, however, would not listen, for God so worked that he might hand them over to ⌞Jehoash⌟, because they sought the gods of Edom.[o] 21So Jehoash king of Israel attacked. He and

26 [x]2Ki 12:21; [y]**Ru 1:4**

Ch. 25

2 [a]**1Ki 8:61; 2Ch 24:2**
4 [b]**Dt 28:61;** [c]**Nu 26:11**
5 [d]**2Sa 24:2;** [e]**Ex 30:14;** [f]**1Ch 21:1;** 2Ch 17:14–19
7 [g]**2Ch 16:2–9; 19:1–3**
8 [h]**2Ch 14:11; 20:6**
9 [i]Dt 8:18; Pr 10:22
10 [j]ver 13
12 [k]Ps 141:6; Ob 3
14 [l]Ex 20:3; 2Ch 28:23; Isa 44:15
15 [m]Isa 36:20
18 [n]Jdg 9:8–15
20 [o]**2Ch 10:15**

---

[b]26 A variant of *Jozabad*
[c]26 A variant of *Shomer*
[a]1 Hebrew *Jehoaddan*, a variant of *Jehoaddin*
[b]4 Deut. 24:16
[c]6 That is, about 3⅓ tons (about 3.4 metric tons); also in verse 9
[d]17 Hebrew *Joash*, a variant of *Jehoash*; also in verses 18, 21, 23 and 25

Amaziah king of Judah faced each other
at Beth Shemesh in Judah. 22Judah was
routed by Israel, and every man fled to
his home. 23Jehoash king of Israel cap-
tured Amaziah king of Judah, the son of
Joash, the son of Ahaziah,[e] at Beth
Shemesh. Then Jehoash brought him to
Jerusalem and broke down the wall of
Jerusalem from the Ephraim Gate[p] to
the Corner Gate[q]—a section about six
hundred feet[f] long. 24He took all the
gold and silver and all the articles found
in the temple of God that had been in
the care of Obed-Edom,[r] together with
the palace treasures and the hostages,
and returned to Samaria.

25Amaziah son of Joash king of Judah
lived for fifteen years after the death of
Jehoash son of Jehoahaz king of Israel.
26As for the other events of Amaziah's
reign, from beginning to end, are they
not written in the book of the kings of
Judah and Israel? 27From the time that
Amaziah turned away from following
the LORD, they conspired against him in
Jerusalem and he fled to Lachish,[s] but
they sent men after him to Lachish and
killed him there. 28He was brought back
by horse and was buried with his
fathers in the City of Judah.

Uzziah King of Judah

26:1–4pp—2Ki 14:21–22; 15:1–3
26:21–33pp—2Ki 15:5–7

26 Then all the people of Judah[a]
took Uzziah,[a] who was sixteen
years old, and made him king in place of
his father Amaziah. 2He was the one
who rebuilt Elath and restored it to
Judah after Amaziah rested with his
fathers.

3Uzziah was sixteen years old when
he became king, and he reigned in Jeru-
salem for fifty-two years. His mother's
name was Jecoliah; she was from Jeru-
salem. 4He did what was right in the
eyes of the LORD, just as his father Ama-
ziah had done. 5He sought God during
the days of Zechariah, who instructed
him in the fear[b] of God.[b] As long as he
sought the LORD, God gave him suc-
cess.[c]

6He went to war against the Philis-
tines[d] and broke down the walls of
Gath, Jabneh and Ashdod.[e] He then
rebuilt towns near Ashdod and else-
where among the Philistines. 7God
helped him against the Philistines and
against the Arabs[f] who lived in Gur Baal
and against the Meunites.[g] 8The Am-
monites[h] brought tribute to Uzziah, and
his fame spread as far as the border of
Egypt, because he had become very
powerful.

9Uzziah built towers in Jerusalem at
the Corner Gate,[i] at the Valley Gate[j] and
at the angle of the wall, and he fortified
them. 10He also built towers in the des-
ert and dug many cisterns, because he
had much livestock in the foothills and
in the plain. He had people working his
fields and vineyards in the hills and in
the fertile lands, for he loved the soil.

11Uzziah had a well-trained army,
ready to go out by divisions according to
their numbers as mustered by Jeiel the
secretary and Maaseiah the officer
under the direction of Hananiah, one of
the royal officials. 12The total number of
family leaders over the fighting men
was 2,600. 13Under their command was
an army of 307,500 men trained for war,
a powerful force to support the king
against his enemies. 14Uzziah provided
shields, spears, helmets, coats of
armour, bows and slingstones for the
entire army.[k] 15In Jerusalem he made
machines designed by skilful men for
use on the towers and on the corner
defences to shoot arrows and hurl large
stones. His fame spread far and wide,
for he was greatly helped until he be-
came powerful.

16But after Uzziah became powerful,
his pride[l] led to his downfall.[m] He was
unfaithful[n] to the LORD his God, and
entered the temple of the LORD to burn
incense[o] on the altar of incense.
17Azariah[p] the priest with eighty other
courageous priests of the LORD followed
him in. 18They confronted him and said,
"It is not right for you, Uzziah, to burn
incense to the LORD. That is for the
priests,[q] the descendants[r] of Aaron,[s]
who have been consecrated to burn in-
cense.[t] Leave the sanctuary, for you
have been unfaithful; and you will not
be honoured by the LORD God."

19Uzziah, who had a censer in his
hand ready to burn incense, became
angry. While he was raging at the
priests in their presence before the
incense altar in the LORD's temple,
leprosy[c][u] broke out on his forehead.
20When Azariah the chief priest and
all the other priests looked at him,
they saw that he had leprosy on his

23 [p]2Ki 14:13; Ne 8:16; 12:39; [q]2Ch 26:9; Jer 31:38
24 [r]1Ch 26:15
27 [s]Jos 10:3

Ch. 26

1 [a]2Ch 22:1
5 [b]2Ch 24:2; [c]2Ch 27:6
6 [d]Isa 2:6; 11:14; 14:29; Jer 25:20; [e]Am 1:8; 3:9
7 [f]2Ch 21:16; [g]2Ch 20:1
8 [h]Ge 19:38
9 [i]2Ki 14:13; 2Ch 25:23; [j]Ne 2:13; 3:13
14 [k]Jer 46:4
16 [l]2Ki 14:10; [m]Dt 32:15; [n]1Ch 5:25; [o]2Ki 16:12
17 [p]1Ki 4:2
18 [q]Nu 16:39; [r]Nu 18:1–7; [s]Ex 30:7; [t]1Ch 6:49
19 [u]Nu 12:10

[e]23 Hebrew *Jehoahaz*, a variant of *Ahaziah*
[f]23 Hebrew *four hundred cubits* (about 180 metres)
[a]1 Also called *Azariah*
[b]5 Many Hebrew manuscripts, Septuagint and Syriac; other Hebrew manuscripts *vision*
[c]19 The Hebrew word was used for various diseases affecting the skin—not necessarily leprosy; also in verses 20, 21 and 23.

forehead, so they hurried him out.
Indeed, he himself was eager to leave,
because the LORD had afflicted him.
21King Uzziah had leprosy until the
day he died. He lived in a separate
house[d][v]—leprous, and excluded from
the temple of the LORD. Jotham his son
had charge of the palace and governed
the people of the land.
22The other events of Uzziah's reign,
from beginning to end, are recorded by
the prophet Isaiah[w] son of Amoz.
23Uzziah[x] rested with his fathers and
was buried near them in a field for burial
that belonged to the kings, for people
said, "He had leprosy." And Jotham his
son succeeded him as king.[y]

Jotham King of Judah

27:1–4,7–9pp—2Ki 15:33–38

27 Jotham[a] was twenty-five years
old when he became king, and
he reigned in Jerusalem for sixteen
years. His mother's name was Jerusha
daughter of Zadok. 2He did what was
right in the eyes of the LORD, just as his
father Uzziah had done, but unlike him
he did not enter the temple of the LORD.
The people, however, continued their
corrupt practices. 3Jotham rebuilt the
Upper Gate of the temple of the LORD
and did extensive work on the wall at
the hill of Ophel.[b] 4He built towns in the
Judean hills and forts and towers in the
wooded areas.
5Jotham made war on the king of the
Ammonites[c] and conquered them. That
year the Ammonites paid him a hun-
dred talents[a] of silver, ten thousand
cors[b] of wheat and ten thousand cors of
barley. The Ammonites brought him
the same amount also in the second and
third years.
6Jotham grew powerful[d] because he
walked steadfastly before the LORD his
God.
7The other events in Jotham's reign,
including all his wars and the other
things he did, are written in the book of
the kings of Israel and Judah. 8He was
twenty-five years old when he became
king, and he reigned in Jerusalem for
sixteen years. 9Jotham rested with his
fathers and was buried in the City of
David. And Ahaz his son succeeded
him as king.

Ahaz King of Judah

28:1–27pp—2Ki 16:1–20

28 Ahaz[a] was twenty years old
when he became king, and he
reigned in Jerusalem for sixteen years.
Unlike David his father, he did not do
what was right in the eyes of the LORD.
2He walked in the ways of the kings of
Israel and also made cast idols[b] for
worshipping the Baals. 3He burned sac-
rifices in the Valley of Ben Hinnom[c] and
sacrificed his sons[d] in the fire, following
the detestable[e] ways of the nations that
the LORD had driven out before the
Israelites. 4He offered sacrifices and
burned incense at the high places, on
the hilltops and under every spreading
tree.
5Therefore the LORD his God handed
him over to the king of Aram.[f] The Ara-
means defeated him and took many of
his people as prisoners and brought
them to Damascus.
He was also given into the hands of
the king of Israel, who inflicted heavy
casualties on him. 6In one day Pekah[g]
son of Remaliah killed a hundred and
twenty thousand soldiers in Judah[h]—
because Judah had forsaken the LORD,
the God of their fathers. 7Zicri, an
Ephraimite warrior, killed Maaseiah the
king's son, Azrikam the officer in
charge of the palace, and Elkanah,
second to the king. 8The Israelites
took captive from their kinsmen[i] two
hundred thousand wives, sons and
daughters. They also took a great deal
of plunder, which they carried back to
Samaria.[j]
9But a prophet of the LORD named
Oded was there, and he went out to
meet the army when it returned to
Samaria. He said to them, "Because the
LORD, the God of your fathers, was
angry[k] with Judah, he gave them into
your hand. But you have slaughtered
them in a rage that reaches to heaven.[l]
10And now you intend to make the men
and women of Judah and Jerusalem
your slaves.[m] But aren't you also guilty
of sins against the LORD your God?
11Now listen to me! Send back your fel-
low countrymen that you have taken as
prisoners, for the LORD's fierce anger
rests on you."[n]
12Then some of the leaders in
Ephraim—Azariah son of Jehohanan,
Berekiah son of Meshillemoth, Jehiz-
kiah son of Shallum, and Amasa son of
Hadlai—confronted those who were
arriving from the war. 13"You must not
bring those prisoners here," they said,
"or we will be guilty before the LORD.

21 [v]**Ex 4:6**; Lev 13:46; **14:8**; Nu 5:2; **19:12**
22 [w]2Ki 15:1; Isa 1:1; 6:1
23 [x]Isa 1:1; 6:1; [y]**2Ki 14:21**; Am 1:1

Ch. 27

1 [a]**2Ki 15:5**,32; **1Ch 3:12**
3 [b]2Ch 33:14; Ne 3:26
5 [c]**Ge 19:38**
6 [d]2Ch 26:5

Ch. 28

1 [a]**1Ch 3:13**; Isa 1:1
2 [b]Ex 34:17
3 [c]**Jos 15:8**; [d]**Lev 18:21**; **2Ki 3:27**; Eze 20:26; [e]**Dt 18:9**; 2Ch 33:2
5 [f]Isa 7:1
6 [g]**2Ki 15:25**,27; [h]ver 8; Isa 9:21; 11:13
8 [i]Dt 28:25–41; [j]2Ch 29:9
9 [k]Isa 10:6; 47:6; Zec 1:15; [l]Ezr 9:6; Rev 18:5
10 [m]Lev 25:39–46
11 [n]2Ch 11:4

[d]*21* Or *in a house where he was relieved of responsibilities*
[a]5 That is, about 3⅓ tons (about 3.4 metric tons)
[b]5 That is, probably about 60,500 bushels (about 2,200 kilolitres)

Do you intend to add to our sin and
guilt? For our guilt is already great, and
his fierce anger rests on Israel."
14So the soldiers gave up the prison-
ers and plunder in the presence of the
officials and all the assembly. 15The men
designated by name took the prisoners,
and from the plunder they clothed all
who were naked. They provided them
with clothes and sandals, food and
drink,[o] and healing balm. All those who
were weak they put on donkeys. So
they took them back to their fellow
countrymen at Jericho, the City of
Palms,[p] and returned to Samaria.[q]
16At that time King Ahaz sent to the
king[a] of Assyria[r] for help. 17The Edom-
ites[s] had again come and attacked Judah
and carried away prisoners,[t] 18while the
Philistines[u] had raided towns in the
foothills and in the Negev of Judah.
They captured and occupied Beth
Shemesh, Aijalon[v] and Gederoth,[w] as
well as Soco,[x] Timnah[y] and Gimzo, with
their surrounding villages. 19The LORD
had humbled Judah because of Ahaz
king of Israel,[b] for he had promoted
wickedness in Judah and had been most
unfaithful[z] to the LORD. 20Tiglath-
Pileser[c][a] king of Assyria[b] came to him,
but gave him trouble[c] instead of help.[d]
21Ahaz[e] took some of the things from the
temple of the LORD and from the royal
palace and from the princes and pre-
sented them to the king of Assyria, but
that did not help him.[f]
22In his time of trouble King Ahaz
became even more unfaithful[g] to the
LORD. 23He offered sacrifices to the
gods[h] of Damascus, who had defeated
him; for he thought, "Since the gods of
the kings of Aram have helped them, I
will sacrifice to them so that they will
help me."[i] But they were his downfall
and the downfall of all Israel.[j]
24Ahaz gathered together the fur-
nishings[k] from the temple of God[l] and
took them away.[d] He shut the doors[m] of
the LORD's temple and set up altars[n] at
every street corner in Jerusalem. 25In
every town in Judah he built high places
to burn sacrifices to other gods and pro-
voked the LORD, the God of his fathers,
to anger.
26The other events of his reign and all
his ways, from beginning to end, are
written in the book of the kings of Judah
and Israel. 27Ahaz rested[o] with his
fathers and was buried[p] in the city of
Jerusalem, but he was not placed in
the tombs of the kings of Israel. And
Hezekiah his son succeeded him as
king.

15 [o]2Ki 6:22; Pr 25:21–22; [p]Dt 34:3; Jdg 1:16; [q]Lk 10:25–37
16 [r]2Ki 16:7; Eze 23:12
17 [s]Ps 137:7; Isa 34:5; 63:1; Jer 25:21; Eze 16:57; 25:12; Am 1:11; [t]2Ch 29:9
18 [u]Isa 9:12; 11:14; Jer 25:20; Eze 16:27,57; 25:15; [v]Jos 10:12; [w]Jos 15:41; [x]1Sa 17:1; [y]Ge 38:12
19 [z]1Ch 5:25
20 [a]2Ki 15:29; 1Ch 5:6; [b]Isa 7:17; 8:7; 10:5–6; 36:1; [c]Isa 10:20; [d]2Ki 16:7
21 [e]2Ch 16:2–9; [f]Jer 2:36
22 [g]Jer 5:3; 15:7; 17:23
23 [h]2Ch 25:14; [i]Isa 10:20; Jer 44:17–18; [j]1Ch 11:1; Jer 18:15
24 [k]2Ch 29:19; [l]2Ki 16:18; [m]Mal 1:10; [n]2Ch 30:14
27 [o]Isa 14:28–32; [p]2Ch 21:20

Ch. 29

1 [a]1Ch 3:13
2 [b]2Ch 34:2
3 [c]2Ki 18:16
5 [d]Lev 11:44; Ne 13:9
6 [e]Ezr 9:7; Ps 106:6–47; Jer 2:27; 18:17; Eze 23:35; Da 9:5–6; [f]1Ch 5:25
7 [g]Ex 30:7
8 [h]Dt 28:25; [i]Lev 26:32; Jer 18:16; 19:8; 25:9,18
9 [j]2Ch 28:5–8,17
10 [k]2Ki 11:17; 2Ch 23:16; [l]Nu 25:4; 2Ch 30:8; Ezr 10:14
11 [m]Nu 3:6; 8:6,14; [n]1Ch 15:2
12 [o]Nu 3:17–20; [p]2Ch 31:15
13 [q]Ex 6:22

Hezekiah Purifies the Temple

29:1–2pp—2Ki 18:1–3

29 Hezekiah[a] was twenty-five
years old when he became king,
and he reigned in Jerusalem for twenty-
nine years. His mother's name was Abi-
jah daughter of Zechariah. 2He did what
was right in the eyes of the LORD, just as
his father David[b] had done.
3In the first month of the first year of
his reign, he opened the doors of the
temple of the LORD and repaired[c] them.
4He brought in the priests and the Le-
vites, assembled them in the square on
the east side 5and said, "Listen to me,
Levites! Consecrate[d] yourselves now
and consecrate the temple of the LORD,
the God of your fathers. Remove all
defilement from the sanctuary. 6Our
fathers[e] were unfaithful;[f] they did evil in
the eyes of the LORD our God and for-
sook him. They turned their faces away
from the LORD's dwelling-place and
turned their backs on him. 7They also
shut the doors of the portico and put out
the lamps. They did not burn incense[g]
or present any burnt offerings at the
sanctuary to the God of Israel.
8Therefore, the anger of the LORD has
fallen on Judah and Jerusalem; he has
made them an object of dread and hor-
ror[h] and scorn,[i] as you can see with your
own eyes. 9This is why our fathers have
fallen by the sword and why our sons
and daughters and our wives are in
captivity.[j] 10Now I intend to make a
covenant[k] with the LORD, the God of
Israel, so that his fierce anger[l] will turn
away from us. 11My sons, do not be
negligent now, for the LORD has chosen
you to stand before him and serve him,[m]
to minister[n] before him and to burn
incense."
12Then these Levites[o] set to work:
from the Kohathites,
Mahath son of Amasai and Joel
son of Azariah;
from the Merarites,
Kish son of Abdi and Azariah son
of Jehallelel;
from the Gershonites,
Joah son of Zimmah and Eden[p]
son of Joah;
13from the descendants of Elizaphan,[q]
Shimri and Jeiel;

[a]16 One Hebrew manuscript, Septuagint and Vulgate (see also 2 Kings 16:7); most Hebrew manuscripts *kings*
[b]19 That is, Judah, as frequently in 2 Chronicles
[c]20 Hebrew *Tilgath-Pilneser,* a variant of *Tiglath-Pileser*
[d]24 Or *and cut them up*

from the descendants of Asaph,[r]
Zechariah and Mattaniah;
14from the descendants of Heman,
Jehiel and Shimei;
from the descendants of Jeduthun,
Shemaiah and Uzziel.

15When they had assembled their brothers and consecrated themselves, they went in to purify[s] the temple of the LORD, as the king had ordered, following the word of the LORD. 16The priests went into the sanctuary of the LORD to purify it. They brought out to the courtyard of the LORD's temple everything unclean that they found in the temple of the LORD. The Levites took it and carried it out to the Kidron Valley.[t] 17They began the consecration on the first day of the first month, and by the eighth day of the month they reached the portico of the LORD. For eight more days they consecrated the temple of the LORD itself, finishing in the sixteenth day of the first month.

18Then they went in to King Hezekiah and reported: "We have purified the entire temple of the LORD, the altar of burnt offering with all its utensils, and the table for setting out the consecrated bread, with all its articles. 19We have prepared and consecrated all the articles[u] that King Ahaz removed in his unfaithfulness while he was king. They are now in front of the LORD's altar."

20Early the next morning King Hezekiah gathered the city officials together and went up to the temple of the LORD. 21They brought seven bulls, seven rams, seven male lambs and seven male goats[v] as a sin offering[w] for the kingdom, for the sanctuary and for Judah. The king commanded the priests, the descendants of Aaron, to offer these on the altar of the LORD. 22So they slaughtered the bulls, and the priests took the blood and sprinkled it on the altar; next they slaughtered the rams and sprinkled their blood on the altar; then they slaughtered the lambs and sprinkled their blood[x] on the altar. 23The goats[y] for the sin offering were brought before the king and the assembly, and they laid their hands[z] on them. 24The priests then slaughtered the goats and presented their blood on the altar for a sin offering to atone[a] for all Israel, because the king had ordered the burnt offering and the sin offering for all Israel.[b]

25He stationed the Levites in the temple of the LORD with cymbals, harps and lyres in the way prescribed by David[c] and Gad[d] the king's seer and Nathan the prophet; this was commanded by the LORD through his prophets. 26So the Levites stood ready with David's instruments,[e] and the priests with their trumpets.[f]

27Hezekiah gave the order to sacrifice the burnt offering on the altar. As the offering began, singing to the LORD began also, accompanied by trumpets and the instruments[g] of David king of Israel. 28The whole assembly bowed in worship, while the singers sang and the trumpeters played. All this continued until the sacrifice of the burnt offering[h] was completed.

29When the offerings were finished, the king and everyone present with him knelt down and worshipped.[i] 30King Hezekiah and his officials ordered the Levites to praise the LORD with the words of David and of Asaph the seer. So they sang praises with gladness and bowed their heads and worshipped.

31Then Hezekiah said, "You have now dedicated yourselves to the LORD. Come and bring sacrifices[j] and thank-offerings to the temple of the LORD." So the assembly brought sacrifices and thank-offerings, and all whose hearts were willing[k] brought burnt offerings.

32The number of burnt offerings[l] the assembly brought was seventy bulls, a hundred rams and two hundred male lambs—all of them for burnt offerings to the LORD. 33The animals consecrated as sacrifices amounted to six hundred bulls and three thousand sheep and goats. 34The priests, however, were too few to skin all the burnt offerings;[m] so their kinsmen the Levites helped them until the task was finished and until other priests had been consecrated,[n] for the Levites had been more conscientious in consecrating themselves than the priests had been. 35There were burnt offerings in abundance, together with the fat[o] of the fellowship offerings[a][p] and the drink offerings[q] that accompanied the burnt offerings.

So the service of the temple of the LORD was re-established. 36Hezekiah and all the people rejoiced at what God had brought about for his people, because it was done so quickly.[r]

Hezekiah Celebrates the Passover

30 Hezekiah sent word to all Israel[a] and Judah and also wrote letters to Ephraim and Manasseh,[b] inviting them to come to the temple of the LORD

13 [r]1Ch 6:39
15 [s]1Ch 23:28; Isa 1:25
16 [t]2Sa 15:23
19 [u]2Ch 28:24
21 [v]Ezr 6:17; 8:35; [w]Lev 4:13–14
22 [x]Lev 4:18; Nu 18:17
23 [y]Lev 16:5; [z]Lev 4:15
24 [a]Ex 29:36; Lev 4:26; [b]1Ch 11:1; Ezr 8:35
25 [c]1Ch 25:6; 28:19; [d]1Sa 22:5
26 [e]1Ch 15:16; [f]1Ch 15:24
27 [g]1Sa 16:16
28 [h]2Ch 2:4
29 [i]2Ch 20:18
31 [j]Heb 13:15–16; [k]Ex 25:2; 35:22
32 [l]Lev 1:1–17
34 [m]Eze 44:11; [n]2Ch 30:3,15
35 [o]Ge 4:4; Ex 29:13; [p]Lev 7:11–21; [q]Ge 35:14
36 [r]2Ch 35:8

Ch. 30

1 [a]1Ch 9:1; [b]Ge 41:52

[a]35 Traditionally *peace offerings*

in Jerusalem and celebrate the Passover[c]
to the LORD, the God of Israel. 2The king
and his officials and the whole assembly
in Jerusalem decided to celebrate[d] the
Passover in the second month. 3They
had not been able to celebrate it at the
regular time because not enough priests
had consecrated[e] themselves and the
people had not assembled in Jerusalem.
4The plan seemed right both to the king
and to the whole assembly. 5They de-
cided to send a proclamation through-
out Israel, from Beersheba to Dan,[f] call-
ing the people to come to Jerusalem and
celebrate the Passover to the LORD, the
God of Israel. It had not been celebrated
in large numbers according to what was
written.
6At the king's command, couriers
went throughout Israel and Judah with
letters from the king and from his of-
ficials, which read:

"People of Israel, return to the
LORD, the God of Abraham, Isaac
and Israel, that he may return to
you who are left, who have escaped
from the hand of the kings of
Assyria. 7Do not be like your
fathers[g] and brothers, who were
unfaithful[h] to the LORD, the God of
their fathers, so that he made them
an object of horror,[i] as you see. 8Do
not be stiff-necked,[j] as your fathers
were; submit to the LORD. Come to
the sanctuary, which he has conse-
crated for ever. Serve the LORD your
God, so that his fierce anger[k] will
turn away from you. 9If you return[l]
to the LORD, then your brothers and
your children will be shown com-
passion[m] by their captors and will
come back to this land, for the LORD
your God is gracious and com-
passionate.[n] He will not turn his
face from you if you return to him."

10The couriers went from town to
town in Ephraim and Manasseh, as far
as Zebulun, but the people scorned and
ridiculed[o] them. 11Nevertheless, some
men of Asher, Manasseh and Zebulun
humbled[p] themselves and went to Jeru-
salem.[q] 12Also in Judah the hand of God
was on the people to give them unity[r] of
mind to carry out what the king and his
officials had ordered, following the
word of the LORD.
13A very large crowd of people assem-
bled in Jerusalem to celebrate the Feast
of Unleavened Bread[s] in the second
month. 14They removed the altars[t] in
Jerusalem and cleared away the incense
altars and threw them into the Kidron
Valley.[u]
15They slaughtered the Passover lamb
on the fourteenth day of the second
month. The priests and the Levites were
ashamed and consecrated[v] themselves
and brought burnt offerings to the
temple of the LORD. 16Then they took up
their regular positions[w] as prescribed in
the Law of Moses the man of God. The
priests sprinkled the blood handed to
them by the Levites. 17Since many in the
crowd had not consecrated themselves,
the Levites had to kill[x] the Passover
lambs for all those who were not cer-
emonially clean and could not conse-
crate ⌊their lambs⌋ to the LORD.
18Although most of the many people
who came from Ephraim, Manasseh,
Issachar and Zebulun had not purified
themselves,[y] yet they ate the Passover,
contrary to what was written. But Heze-
kiah prayed for them, saying, "May the
LORD, who is good, pardon everyone
19who sets his heart on seeking God
—the LORD, the God of his fathers—
even if he is not clean according to
the rules of the sanctuary." 20And the
LORD heard[z] Hezekiah and healed[a] the
people.[b]
21The Israelites who were present in
Jerusalem celebrated the Feast of Un-
leavened Bread[c] for seven days with
great rejoicing, while the Levites and
priests sang to the LORD every day,
accompanied by the LORD's instruments
of praise.[a]
22Hezekiah spoke encouragingly to all
the Levites, who showed good under-
standing of the service of the LORD. For
the seven days they ate their assigned
portion and offered fellowship offer-
ings[b] and praised the LORD, the God of
their fathers.
23The whole assembly then agreed to
celebrate[d] the festival seven more days;
so for another seven days they cel-
ebrated joyfully. 24Hezekiah king of
Judah provided[e] a thousand bulls and
seven thousand sheep and goats for the
assembly, and the officials provided
them with a thousand bulls and ten
thousand sheep and goats. A great
number of priests consecrated them-
selves. 25The entire assembly of Judah
rejoiced, along with the priests and Le-
vites and all who had assembled from
Israel[f], including the aliens who had
come from Israel and those who lived in

1 [c]Ex 12:11; Nu 28:16
2 [d]Nu 9:10
3 [e]Nu 9:6–13; 2Ch 29:34
5 [f]Jdg 20:1
7 [g]Ps 78:8,57; 106:6; Jer 11:10; Eze 20:18; [h]1Ch 5:25; [i]Dt 28:25
8 [j]Ex 32:9; [k]Nu 25:4; 2Ch 29:10
9 [l]Dt 30:2–5; Isa 1:16; 55:7; Jer 25:5; Eze 33:11; [m]Ex 3:21; 1Ki 8:50; [n]Ex 22:27; Dt 4:31; 2Ch 6:39; Mic 7:18
10 [o]2Ch 36:16
11 [p]2Ch 6:37; [q]ver 25
12 [r]Jer 32:39; Eze 11:19
13 [s]Nu 28:16
14 [t]2Ch 28:24; [u]2Sa 15:23
15 [v]2Ch 29:34
16 [w]2Ch 35:10
17 [x]2Ch 35:11; Ezr 6:20
18 [y]Ex 12:43–49; Nu 9:6–10
20 [z]2Ch 6:20; [a]2Ch 7:14; Mal 4:2; [b]Jas 5:16
21 [c]Ex 12:15,17; 13:6
23 [d]2Ch 7:9
24 [e]1Ki 8:5; 2Ch 35:7; Ezr 6:17; 8:35
25 [f]ver 11

[a]21 Or *priests praised the LORD every day with resounding instruments belonging to the LORD.*
[b]22 Traditionally *peace offerings*

Judah. 26There was great joy in Jerusalem, for since the days of Solomon[g] son of David king of Israel there had been nothing like this in Jerusalem. 27The priests and the Levites stood to bless[h] the people, and God heard them, for their prayer reached heaven, his holy dwelling-place.

31 When all this had ended, the Israelites who were there went out to the towns of Judah, smashed the sacred stones and cut down[a] the Asherah poles. They destroyed the high places and the altars throughout Judah and Benjamin and in Ephraim and Manasseh. After they had destroyed all of them, the Israelites returned to their own towns and to their own property.

Contributions for Worship

31:20–21pp—2Ki 18:5–7

2Hezekiah[b] assigned the priests and Levites to divisions[c]—each of them according to their duties as priests or Levites—to offer burnt offerings and fellowship offerings,[a] to minister,[d] to give thanks and to sing praises[e] at the gates of the LORD's dwelling.[f] 3The king contributed[g] from his own possessions for the morning and evening burnt offerings and for the burnt offerings on the Sabbaths, New Moons and appointed feasts as written in the Law of the LORD.[h] 4He ordered the people living in Jerusalem to give the portion[i] due to the priests and Levites so that they could devote themselves to the Law of the LORD. 5As soon as the order went out, the Israelites generously gave the firstfruits[j] of their grain, new wine,[k] oil and honey and all that the fields produced. They brought a great amount, a tithe of everything. 6The men of Israel and Judah who lived in the towns of Judah also brought a tithe[l] of their herds and flocks and a tithe of the holy things dedicated to the LORD their God, and they piled them in heaps.[m] 7They began doing this in the third month and finished in the seventh month.[n] 8When Hezekiah and his officials came and saw the heaps, they praised the LORD and blessed[o] his people Israel.

9Hezekiah asked the priests and Levites about the heaps; 10and Azariah the chief priest, from the family of Zadok,[p] answered, "Since the people began to bring their contributions to the temple of the LORD, we have had enough to eat and plenty to spare, because the LORD has blessed his people, and this great amount is left over."[q]

11Hezekiah gave orders to prepare storerooms in the temple of the LORD, and this was done. 12Then they faithfully brought in the contributions, tithes and dedicated gifts. Conaniah,[r] a Levite, was in charge of these things, and his brother Shimei was next in rank. 13Jehiel, Azaziah, Nahath, Asahel, Jerimoth, Jozabad,[s] Eliel, Ismakiah, Mahath and Benaiah were supervisors under Conaniah and Shimei his brother, by appointment of King Hezekiah and Azariah the official in charge of the temple of God.

14Kore son of Imnah the Levite, keeper of the East Gate, was in charge of the freewill offerings given to God, distributing the contributions made to the LORD and also the consecrated gifts. 15Eden,[t] Miniamin, Jeshua, Shemaiah, Amariah and Shecaniah assisted him faithfully in the towns[u] of the priests, distributing to their fellow priests according to their divisions, old and young alike.

16In addition, they distributed to the males three years old or more whose names were in the genealogical records[v]—all who would enter the temple of the LORD to perform the daily duties of their various tasks, according to their responsibilities and their divisions. 17And they distributed to the priests enrolled by their families in the genealogical records and likewise to the Levites twenty years old or more, according to their responsibilities and their divisions. 18They included all the little ones, the wives, and the sons and daughters of the whole community listed in these genealogical records. For they were faithful in consecrating themselves.

19As for the priests, the descendants of Aaron, who lived on the farm lands around their towns or in any other towns,[w] men were designated by name to distribute portions to every male among them and to all who were recorded in the genealogies of the Levites.

20This is what Hezekiah did throughout Judah, doing what was good and right and faithful[x] before the LORD his God. 21In everything that he undertook in the service of God's temple and in obedience to the law and the commands, he sought his God and worked wholeheartedly. And so he prospered.[y]

26 [g]2Ch 7:8
27 [h]Ex 39:43

Ch. 31

1 [a]2Ki 18:4; 2Ch 32:12; Isa 36:7
2 [b]2Ch 29:9; [c]1Ch 24:1; [d]1Ch 15:2; [e]Ps 7:17; 9:2; 47:6; 71:22; [f]1Ch 23:28–32
3 [g]1Ch 29:3; 2Ch 35:7; Eze 45:17; [h]Nu 28:1–29:40
4 [i]Nu 18:8; Dt 18:8; Ne 13:10
5 [j]Nu 18:12,24; Ne 13:12; Eze 44:30; [k]Dt 12:17
6 [l]Lev 27:30; Ne 13:10–12; [m]Ru 3:7
7 [n]Ex 23:16
8 [o]Ps 144:13–15
10 [p]2Sa 8:17; [q]Ex 36:5; Eze 44:30; Mal 3:10–12
12 [r]2Ch 35:9
13 [s]2Ch 35:9
15 [t]2Ch 29:12; [u]Jos 21:9–19
16 [v]1Ch 23:23
19 [w]Nu 35:2–5
20 [x]2Ki 20:3
21 [y]Dt 29:9

[a]2 Traditionally *peace offerings*

Sennacherib Threatens Jerusalem

32:9–19pp—2Ki 18:17–35; Isa 36:2–20
32:20–21pp—2Ki 19:35–37; Isa 37:36–38

32 After all that Hezekiah had so
faithfully done, Sennacherib[a]
king of Assyria came and invaded
Judah. He laid siege to the fortified
cities, thinking to conquer them for
himself. 2When Hezekiah saw that Sen-
nacherib had come and that he intended
to make war on Jerusalem,[b] 3he con-
sulted with his officials and military
staff about blocking off the water from
the springs outside the city, and they
helped him. 4A large force of men
assembled, and they blocked all the
springs[c] and the stream that flowed
through the land. "Why should the
kings[a] of Assyria come and find plenty
of water?" they said. 5Then he worked
hard repairing all the broken sections of
the wall[d] and building towers on it. He
built another wall outside that one and
reinforced the supporting terraces[b] [e] of
the City of David. He also made large
numbers of weapons[f] and shields.
6He appointed military officers over
the people and assembled them before
him in the square at the city gate and
encouraged them with these words:
7"Be strong and courageous.[g] Do not be
afraid or discouraged[h] because of the
king of Assyria and the vast army with
him, for there is a greater power with us
than with him.[i] 8With him is only the
arm of flesh,[j] but with us[k] is the LORD
our God to help us and to fight our
battles."[l] And the people gained con-
fidence from what Hezekiah the king of
Judah said.
9Later, when Sennacherib king of
Assyria and all his forces were laying
siege to Lachish,[m] he sent his officers to
Jerusalem with this message for Heze-
kiah king of Judah and for all the people
of Judah who were there:

10"This is what Sennacherib king
of Assyria says: On what are you
basing your confidence,[n] that you
remain in Jerusalem under siege?
11When Hezekiah says, 'The LORD
our God will save us from the hand
of the king of Assyria,' he is mis-
leading[o] you, to let you die of hun-
ger and thirst. 12Did not Hezekiah
himself remove this god's high
places and altars, saying to Judah
and Jerusalem, 'You must worship
before one altar[p] and burn sacrifices
on it'?
13"Do you not know what I and
my fathers have done to all the
peoples of the other lands? Were
the gods of those nations ever able
to deliver their land from my
hand?[q] 14Who of all the gods of
these nations that my fathers des-
troyed has been able to save his
people from me? How then can
your god deliver you from my
hand? 15Now do not let Hezekiah
deceive[r] you and mislead you like
this. Do not believe him, for no god
of any nation or kingdom has been
able to deliver[s] his people from my
hand or the hand of my fathers.[t]
How much less will your god de-
liver you from my hand!"

16Sennacherib's officers spoke further
against the LORD God and against his
servant Hezekiah. 17The king also wrote
letters[u] insulting[v] the LORD, the God of
Israel, and saying this against him: "Just
as the gods[w] of the peoples of the other
lands did not rescue their people from
my hand, so the god of Hezekiah will
not rescue his people from my hand."
18Then they called out in Hebrew to the
people of Jerusalem who were on the
wall, to terrify them and make them
afraid in order to capture the city.
19They spoke about the God of Jeru-
salem as they did about the gods of the
other peoples of the world—the work of
men's hands.[x]
20King Hezekiah and the prophet
Isaiah son of Amoz cried out in prayer[y]
to heaven about this. 21And the LORD
sent an angel,[z] who annihilated all the
fighting men and the leaders and
officers in the camp of the Assyrian
king. So he withdrew to his own land in
disgrace. And when he went into the
temple of his god, some of his sons cut
him down with the sword.[a]
22So the LORD saved Hezekiah and the
people of Jerusalem from the hand of
Sennacherib king of Assyria and from
the hand of all others. He took care of
them[c] on every side. 23Many brought
offerings to Jerusalem for the LORD and
valuable gifts[b] for Hezekiah king of
Judah. From then on he was highly
regarded by all the nations.

Hezekiah's Pride, Success and Death

32:24–33pp—2Ki 20:1–21; Isa 37:21–38; 38:1–8

24In those days Hezekiah became ill
and was at the point of death. He

Ch. 32

1 [a]Isa 36:1; 37:9,17,37
2 [b]Isa 22:7; Jer 1:15
4 [c]**2Ki 18:17**; Isa 22:9,11; Na 3:14
5 [d]Isa 22:10; [e]**1Ch 11:8**; [f]Isa 22:8
7 [g]**Dt 31:6**; [h]2Ch 20:15; [i]**Nu 14:9**; 2Ki 6:16
8 [j]Job 40:9; Isa 52:10; Jer 17:5; 32:21; [k]**Dt 3:22; 1Sa 17:45**; [l]**1Ch 5:22**; Ps 20:7; Isa 28:6
9 [m]**Jos 10:3**,31
10 [n]Eze 29:16
11 [o]Isa 37:10
12 [p]**2Ch 31:1**
13 [q]ver 15
15 [r]Isa 37:10; [s]Da 3:15; [t]Ex 5:2
17 [u]Isa 37:14; [v]Ps 74:22; Isa 37:4,17; [w]**2Ki 19:12**
19 [x]Ps 115:4–8; Isa 2:8; 17:8; 37:19; Jer 1:16
20 [y]Isa 1:15; 37:15
21 [z]**Ge 19:13**; [a]**2Ki 19:7**; Isa 37:7,38; Jer 41:2
23 [b]**1Sa 10:27; 2Ch 9:24**; Ps 68:18,29; 76:11; Isa 16:1; 18:7; 45:14; Zep 3:10; Zec 14:16–17

[a]4 Hebrew; Septuagint and Syriac *king*
[b]5 Or *the Millo*
[c]22 Hebrew; Septuagint and Vulgate *He gave them rest*

prayed to the LORD, who answered him and gave him a miraculous sign.[c] 25But Hezekiah's heart was proud[d] and he did not respond to the kindness shown him; therefore the LORD's wrath[e] was on him and on Judah and Jerusalem. 26Then Hezekiah repented[f] of the pride of his heart, as did the people of Jerusalem; therefore the LORD's wrath did not come upon them during the days of Hezekiah.[g]

27Hezekiah had very great riches and honour,[h] and he made treasuries for his silver and gold and for his precious stones, spices, shields and all kinds of valuables. 28He also made buildings to store the harvest of grain, new wine and oil; and he made stalls for various kinds of cattle, and pens for the flocks. 29He built villages and acquired great numbers of flocks and herds, for God had given him very great riches.[i]

30It was Hezekiah who blocked[j] the upper outlet of the Gihon[k] spring and channelled[l] the water down to the west side of the City of David. He succeeded in everything he undertook. 31But when envoys were sent by the rulers of Babylon[m] to ask him about the miraculous sign[n] that had occurred in the land, God left him to test[o] him and to know everything that was in his heart.

32The other events of Hezekiah's reign and his acts of devotion are written in the vision of the prophet Isaiah son of Amoz in the book of the kings of Judah and Israel. 33Hezekiah rested with his fathers and was buried on the hill where the tombs of David's descendants are. All Judah and the people of Jerusalem honoured him when he died. And Manasseh his son succeeded him as king.

Manasseh King of Judah

33:1–10pp—2Ki 21:1–10
33:18–20pp—2Ki 21:17–18

33 Manasseh[a] was twelve years old when he became king, and he reigned in Jerusalem for fifty-five years. 2He did evil in the eyes of the LORD,[b] following the detestable[c] practices of the nations the LORD had driven out before the Israelites. 3He rebuilt the high places his father Hezekiah had demolished; he also erected altars to the Baals and made Asherah poles.[d] He bowed down[e] to all the starry hosts and worshipped them. 4He built altars in the temple of the LORD, of which the LORD had said, "My Name[f] will remain in Jerusalem for ever." 5In both courts of the temple of the LORD,[g] he built altars to all the starry hosts. 6He sacrificed his sons[h] in[a] the fire in the Valley of Ben Hinnom, practised sorcery, divination and witchcraft, and consulted mediums[i] and spiritists.[j] He did much evil in the eyes of the LORD, provoking him to anger.

7He took the carved image he had made and put it in God's temple,[k] of which God had said to David and to his son Solomon, "In this temple and in Jerusalem, which I have chosen out of all the tribes of Israel, I will put my Name for ever. 8I will not again make the feet of the Israelites leave the land[l] I assigned to your forefathers, if only they will be careful to do everything that I commanded them concerning all the laws, decrees and ordinances given through Moses." 9But Manasseh led Judah and the people of Jerusalem astray, so that they did more evil than the nations the LORD had destroyed before the Israelites.[m]

10The LORD spoke to Manasseh and his people, but they paid no attention. 11So the LORD brought against them the army commanders of the king of Assyria, who took Manasseh prisoner,[n] put a hook[o] in his nose, bound him with bronze shackles[p] and took him to Babylon. 12In his distress he sought the favour of the LORD his God and humbled[q] himself greatly before the God of his fathers. 13And when he prayed to him, the LORD was moved by his entreaty and listened to his plea; so he brought him back to Jerusalem and to his kingdom. Then Manasseh knew that the LORD is God.

14Afterwards he rebuilt the outer wall of the City of David, west of the Gihon[r] spring in the valley, as far as the entrance of the Fish Gate[s] and encircling the hill of Ophel;[t] he also made it much higher. He stationed military commanders in all the fortified cities in Judah.

15He got rid of the foreign gods and removed[u] the image from the temple of the LORD, as well as all the altars he had built on the temple hill and in Jerusalem; and he threw them out of the city. 16Then he restored the altar of the LORD and sacrificed fellowship offerings[b] and thank-offerings[v] on it, and told Judah to serve the LORD, the God of Israel. 17The people, however,

24 [c]ver 31
25 [d]2Ki 14:10; [e]2Ch 19:2
26 [f]Jer 26:18–19; [g]2Ch 34:27–28; Isa 39:8
27 [h]1Ch 29:12; 2Ch 9:24
29 [i]Isa 39:2
30 [j]2Ki 18:17; [k]1Ki 1:33; [l]2Sa 5:8
31 [m]Isa 13:1; 39:1; [n]ver 24; Isa 38:7; [o]Ge 22:1; Dt 8:16

Ch. 33

1 [a]1Ch 3:13
2 [b]Jer 15:4; [c]Dt 18:9
3 [d]Dt 16:21–22; 2Ch 24:18; [e]Dt 17:3
4 [f]2Ch 7:16
5 [g]2Ch 4:9
6 [h]Lev 18:21; Dt 18:10; [i]Ex 22:18; Lev 19:31; [j]1Sa 28:13
7 [k]2Ch 7:16
8 [l]2Sa 7:10
9 [m]Jer 15:4; Eze 5:7
11 [n]Dt 28:36; [o]2Ki 19:28; Isa 37:29; Eze 29:4; 38:4; Am 4:2; [p]Ps 149:8
12 [q]2Ch 6:37
14 [r]1Ki 1:33; [s]Ne 3:3; 12:39; Zep 1:10; [t]2Ch 27:3; Ne 3:26
15 [u]2Ki 23:12
16 [v]Lev 7:11–18

[a]6 Or *He made his sons pass through*
[b]16 Traditionally *peace offerings*

continued to sacrifice at the high places,
but only to the LORD their God.
18The other events of Manasseh's
reign, including his prayer to his God
and the words the seers spoke to him in
the name of the LORD, the God of Israel,
are written in the annals of the kings of
Israel.[c] 19His prayer and how God was
moved by his entreaty, as well as all his
sins and unfaithfulness, and the sites
where he built high places and set up
Asherah poles and idols before he
humbled[w] himself—all are written in
the records of the seers.[d x] 20Manasseh
rested with his fathers and was buried[y]
in his palace. And Amon his son suc-
ceeded him as king.

Amon King of Judah

33:21–25pp—2Ki 21:19–24

21Amon[z] was twenty-two years old
when he became king, and he reigned
in Jerusalem for two years. 22He did evil
in the eyes of the LORD, as his father
Manasseh had done. Amon worship-
ped and offered sacrifices to all the idols
Manasseh had made. 23But unlike his
father Manasseh, he did not humble[a]
himself before the LORD; Amon in-
creased his guilt.
24Amon's officials conspired against
him and assassinated him in his palace.
25Then the people[b] of the land killed all
who had plotted against King Amon,
and they made Josiah his son king in his
place.

Josiah's Reforms

34:1–2pp—2Ki 22:1–2
34:3–7Ref—2Ki 23:4–20
34:8–13pp—2Ki 22:3–7

34 Josiah[a] was eight years old
when he became king,[b] and he
reigned in Jerusalem for thirty-one
years. 2He did what was right in the
eyes of the LORD and walked in the ways
of his father David,[c] not turning aside to
the right or to the left.
3In the eighth year of his reign, while
he was still young, he began to seek the
God[d] of his father David. In his twelfth
year he began to purge Judah and Jeru-
salem of high places, Asherah poles,
carved idols and cast images. 4Under his
direction the altars of the Baals were
torn down; he cut to pieces the incense
altars that were above them, and
smashed the Asherah poles,[e] the idols
and the images. These he broke to
pieces and scattered over the graves of
those who had sacrificed to them.[f] 5He
burned[g] the bones of the priests on their
altars, and so he purged Judah and Jeru-
salem. 6In the towns of Manasseh,
Ephraim and Simeon, as far as Naph-
tali, and in the ruins around them, 7he
tore down the altars and the Asherah
poles and crushed the idols to powder[h]
and cut to pieces all the incense altars
throughout Israel. Then he went back to
Jerusalem.
8In the eighteenth year of Josiah's
reign, to purify the land and the temple,
he sent Shaphan son of Azaliah and
Maaseiah the ruler of the city, with Joah
son of Joahaz, the recorder, to repair the
temple of the LORD his God.
9They went to Hilkiah[i] the high priest
and gave him the money that had been
brought into the temple of God, which
the Levites who were the doorkeepers
had collected from the people of
Manasseh, Ephraim and the entire
remnant of Israel and from all the
people of Judah and Benjamin and the
inhabitants of Jerusalem. 10Then they
entrusted it to the men appointed to
supervise the work on the LORD's
temple. These men paid the workers
who repaired and restored the temple.
11They also gave money[j] to the car-
penters and builders to purchase dressed
stone, and timber for joists and beams
for the buildings that the kings of
Judah had allowed to fall into ruin.[k]
12The men did the work faithfully.[l]
Over them to direct them were Jahath
and Obadiah, Levites descended from
Merari, and Zechariah and Meshullam,
descended from Kohath. The Levites
—all who were skilled in playing
musical instruments[m]—13had charge of
the labourers[n] and supervised all the
workers from job to job. Some of the
Levites were secretaries, scribes and
doorkeepers.

The Book of the Law Found

34:14–28pp—2Ki 22:8–20
34:29–32pp—2Ki 23:1–3

14While they were bringing out the
money that had been taken into the
temple of the LORD, Hilkiah the priest
found the Book of the Law of the LORD
that had been given through Moses.
15Hilkiah said to Shaphan the secretary,
"I have found the Book of the Law[o] in
the temple of the LORD." He gave it to
Shaphan.

19 [w]**2Ch 6:37;** [x]2Ki 21:17
20 [y]2Ki 21:18; **2Ch 21:20**
21 [z]**1Ch 3:14**
23 [a]**Ex 10:3;** 2Ch 7:14; Ps 18:27; 147:6; Pr 3:34
25 [b]**2Ch 22:1**

Ch. 34

1 [a]**1Ch 3:14;** [b]Zep 1:1
2 [c]2Ch 29:2
3 [d]**1Ch 16:11**
4 [e]**Ex 34:13;** [f]Ex 32:20; **Lev 26:30;** 2Ki 23:11; Mic 1:5
5 [g]**1Ki 13:2**
7 [h]**Ex 32:20**
9 [i]**1Ch 6:13**
11 [j]2Ch 24:12; [k]2Ch 33:4–7
12 [l]2Ki 12:15; [m]**1Ch 25:1**
13 [n]**1Ch 23:4**
15 [o]**2Ki 22:8;** Ezr 7:6; Ne 8:1

[c]*18* That is, Judah, as frequently in 2 Chronicles
[d]*19* One Hebrew manuscript and Septuagint; most Hebrew manuscripts *of Hozai*

16Then Shaphan took the book to the
king and reported to him: "Your of-
ficials are doing everything that has
been committed to them. 17They have
paid out the money that was in the
temple of the LORD and have entrusted
it to the supervisors and workers."
18Then Shaphan the secretary informed
the king, "Hilkiah the priest has given
me a book." And Shaphan read from it
in the presence of the king.
19When the king heard the words of
the Law,[p] he tore[q] his robes. 20He gave
these orders to Hilkiah, Ahikam son of
Shaphan,[r] Abdon son of Micah,[a]
Shaphan the secretary and Asaiah the
king's attendant: 21"Go and enquire of
the LORD for me and for the remnant in
Israel and Judah about what is written
in this book that has been found. Great
is the LORD's anger that is poured out[s]
on us because our fathers have not kept
the word of the LORD; they have not
acted in accordance with all that is writ-
ten in this book."
22Hilkiah and those the king had sent
with him[b] went to speak to the
prophetess[t] Huldah, who was the wife
of Shallum son of Tokhath,[c] the son of
Hasrah,[d] keeper of the wardrobe. She
lived in Jerusalem, in the Second
District.
23She said to them, "This is what the
LORD, the God of Israel, says: Tell the
man who sent you to me, 24'This is what
the LORD says: I am going to bring dis-
aster[u] on this place and its people[v]—all
the curses[w] written in the book that has
been read in the presence of the king of
Judah. 25Because they have forsaken
me[x] and burned incense to other gods
and provoked me to anger by all that
their hands have made,[e] my anger will
be poured out on this place and will not
be quenched.' 26Tell the king of Judah,
who sent you to enquire of the LORD,
'This is what the LORD, the God of Israel,
says concerning the words you heard:
27Because your heart was responsive[y]
and you humbled[z] yourself before God
when you heard what he spoke against
this place and its people, and because
you humbled yourself before me and
tore your robes and wept in my pres-
ence, I have heard you, declares the
LORD. 28Now I will gather you to your
fathers,[a] and you will be buried in
peace. Your eyes will not see all the
disaster I am going to bring on this place
and on those who live here.'"[b]
So they took her answer back to the
king.
29Then the king called together all the
elders of Judah and Jerusalem. 30He
went up to the temple of the LORD[c] with
the men of Judah, the people of Jeru-
salem, the priests and the Levites—all
the people from the least to the greatest.
He read in their hearing all the words of
the Book of the Covenant, which had
been found in the temple of the LORD.
31The king stood by his pillar[d] and re-
newed the covenant[e] in the presence of
the LORD—to follow[f] the LORD and keep
his commands, regulations and decrees
with all his heart and all his soul, and to
obey the words of the covenant written
in this book.
32Then he made everyone in Jeru-
salem and Benjamin pledge themselves
to it; the people of Jerusalem did this in
accordance with the covenant of God,
the God of their fathers.
33Josiah removed all the detestable[g]
idols from all the territory belonging to
the Israelites, and he made all who were
present in Israel serve the LORD their
God. As long as he lived, they did not
fail to follow the LORD, the God of their
fathers.

Josiah Celebrates the Passover

35:1,18–19pp—2Ki 23:21–23

35 Josiah celebrated the Passover[a]
to the LORD in Jerusalem, and
the Passover lamb was slaughtered on
the fourteenth day of the first month.
2He appointed the priests to their duties
and encouraged them in the service of
the LORD's temple. 3He said to the Le-
vites, who instructed[b] all Israel and who
had been consecrated to the LORD: "Put
the sacred ark in the temple that Sol-
omon son of David king of Israel built. It
is not to be carried about on your
shoulders. Now serve the LORD your
God and his people Israel. 4Prepare
yourselves by families in your div-
isions,[c] according to the directions
written by David king of Israel and by
his son Solomon.
5"Stand in the holy place with a group
of Levites for each sub-division of the
families of your fellow countrymen, the
lay people. 6Slaughter the Passover
lambs, consecrate yourselves[d] and
prepare ⌞the lambs⌟ for your fellow
countrymen, doing what the LORD com-
manded through Moses."

19 [p]Dt 28:3–68; [q]Isa 36:22; 37:1
20 [r]**2Ki 22:3**
21 [s]La 2:4; 4:11; Eze 36:18
22 [t]**Ex 15:20**; Ne 6:14
24 [u]Pr 16:4; Isa 3:9; Jer 40:2; 42:10; 44:2,11; [v]2Ch 36:14–20; [w]Dt 28:15–68
25 [x]2Ch 33:3–6; Jer 22:9
27 [y]**2Ch 32:26**; [z]**Ex 10:3**; **2Ch 6:37**
28 [a]2Ch 35:20–25; [b]**2Ch 32:26**
30 [c]**2Ki 23:2**
31 [d]**1Ki 7:15**; [e]**2Ki 11:17**; **2Ch 23:16**; [f]**Dt 13:4**
33 [g]**Dt 18:9**

Ch. 35

1 [a]Ex 12:1–30; **Nu 28:16**
3 [b]**2Ch 17:7**
4 [c]ver 10; **1Ch 24:1**; Ezr 6:18
6 [d]**Lev 11:44**

[a]20 Also called *Acbor son of Micaiah*
[b]22 One Hebrew manuscript, Vulgate and Syriac; most Hebrew manuscripts do not have *had sent with him.* [c]22 Also called *Tikvah*
[d]22 Also called *Harhas*
[e]25 Or *by everything they have done*

[7]Josiah provided for all the lay people who were there a total of thirty thousand sheep and goats for the Passover offerings,[e] and also three thousand cattle—all from the king's own possessions.[f]

[8]His officials also contributed[g] voluntarily to the people and the priests and Levites. Hilkiah,[h] Zechariah and Jehiel, the administrators of God's temple, gave the priests two thousand six hundred Passover offerings and three hundred cattle. [9]Also Conaniah[i] along with Shemaiah and Nethanel, his brothers, and Hashabiah, Jeiel and Jozabad,[j] the leaders of the Levites, provided five thousand Passover offerings and five hundred head of cattle for the Levites.

[10]The service was arranged and the priests stood in their places with the Levites in their divisions[k] as the king had ordered.[l] [11]The Passover lambs were slaughtered,[m] and the priests sprinkled the blood handed to them, while the Levites skinned the animals. [12]They set aside the burnt offerings to give them to the sub-divisions of the families of the people to offer to the LORD, as is written in the Book of Moses. They did the same with the cattle. [13]They roasted the Passover animals over the fire as prescribed,[n] and boiled the holy offerings in pots, cauldrons and pans and served them quickly to all the people. [14]After this, they made preparations for themselves and for the priests, because the priests, the descendants of Aaron, were sacrificing the burnt offerings and the fat portions[o] until nightfall. So the Levites made preparations for themselves and for the Aaronic priests.

[15]The musicians,[p] the descendants of Asaph, were in the places prescribed by David, Asaph, Heman and Jeduthun the king's seer. The gatekeepers at each gate did not need to leave their posts, because their fellow Levites made the preparations for them.

[16]So at that time the entire service of the LORD was carried out for the celebration of the Passover and the offering of burnt offerings on the altar of the LORD, as King Josiah had ordered. [17]The Israelites who were present celebrated the Passover at that time and observed the Feast of Unleavened Bread for seven days. [18]The Passover had not been observed like this in Israel since the days of the prophet Samuel; and none of the kings of Israel had ever celebrated such a Passover as did Josiah, with the priests, the Levites and all Judah and Israel who were there with the people of Jerusalem. [19]This Passover was celebrated in the eighteenth year of Josiah's reign.

The Death of Josiah

35:20–36:1pp—2Ki 23:28–30

[20]After all this, when Josiah had set the temple in order, Neco king of Egypt went up to fight at Carchemish[q] on the Euphrates,[r] and Josiah marched out to meet him in battle. [21]But Neco sent messengers to him saying, "What quarrel is there between you and me, O king of Judah? It is not you I am attacking at this time, but the house with which I am at war. God has told[s] me to hurry; so stop opposing God, who is with me, or he will destroy you."

[22]Josiah, however, would not turn away from him, but disguised[t] himself to engage him in battle. He would not listen to what Neco had said at God's command but went to fight him on the plain of Megiddo.

[23]Archers[u] shot King Josiah, and he told his officers, "Take me away; I am badly wounded." [24]So they took him out of his chariot, put him in the other chariot he had and brought him to Jerusalem, where he died. He was buried in the tombs of his fathers, and all Judah and Jerusalem mourned for him.

[25]Jeremiah composed laments for Josiah, and to this day all the men and women singers commemorate Josiah in the laments.[v] These became a tradition in Israel and are written in the Laments.[w]

[26]The other events of Josiah's reign and his acts of devotion, according to what is written in the Law of the LORD —[27]all the events, from beginning to end, are written in the book of the kings of Israel and Judah.

36 [1]And the people[a] of the land took Jehoahaz son of Josiah and made him king in Jerusalem in place of his father.

Jehoahaz King of Judah

36:2–4pp—2Ki 23:31–34

[2]Jehoahaz[a] was twenty-three years old when he became king, and he reigned in Jerusalem for three months. [3]The king of Egypt dethroned him in Jerusalem and imposed on Judah a levy of a hundred talents[b] of silver and a

7 [e]2Ch 30:24; [f]2Ch 31:3
8 [g]1Ch 29:3; 2Ch 29:31–36; [h]1Ch 6:13
9 [i]2Ch 31:12; [j]2Ch 31:13
10 [k]ver 4; [l]2Ch 30:16
11 [m]2Ch 30:17
13 [n]Ex 12:2–11
14 [o]Ex 29:13
15 [p]1Ch 25:1; 26:12–19; 2Ch 29:30; Ne 12:46; Ps 68:25
20 [q]Isa 10:9; Jer 46:2; [r]Ge 2:14
21 [s]1Ki 13:18; 2Ki 18:25
22 [t]1Sa 28:8
23 [u]1Ki 22:34
25 [v]Ge 50:10; Jer 22:10,15–16; [w]2Ch 34:28

Ch. 36
1 [a]2Ch 22:1

[a]2 Hebrew *Joahaz,* a variant of *Jehoahaz;* also in verse 4

[b]3 That is, about 3⅓ tons (about 3.4 metric tons)

talent[c] of gold. 4The king of Egypt made Eliakim, a brother of Jehoahaz, king over Judah and Jerusalem and changed Eliakim's name to Jehoiakim. But Neco[b] took Eliakim's brother Jehoahaz and carried him off to Egypt.[c]

Jehoiakim King of Judah

36:5–8pp—2Ki 23:36–24:6

5Jehoiakim[d] was twenty-five years old when he became king, and he reigned in Jerusalem for eleven years. He did evil in the eyes of the LORD his God. 6Nebuchadnezzar[e] king of Babylon attacked him and bound him with bronze shackles to take him to Babylon.[f] 7Nebuchadnezzar also took to Babylon articles from the temple of the LORD and put them in his temple[d] there.[g]

8The other events of Jehoiakim's reign, the detestable things he did and all that was found against him, are written in the book of the kings of Israel and Judah. And Jehoiachin his son succeeded him as king.

Jehoiachin King of Judah

36:9–10pp—2Ki 24:8–17

9Jehoiachin[h] was eighteen[e] years old when he became king, and he reigned in Jerusalem for three months and ten days. He did evil in the eyes of the LORD. 10In the spring, King Nebuchadnezzar sent for him and brought him to Babylon,[i] together with articles of value from the temple of the LORD, and he made Jehoiachin's uncle,[f] Zedekiah, king over Judah and Jerusalem.

Zedekiah King of Judah

36:11–16pp—2Ki 24:18–20; Jer 52:1–3

11Zedekiah[j] was twenty-one years old when he became king, and he reigned in Jerusalem for eleven years. 12He did evil in the eyes of the LORD[k] his God and did not humble[l] himself before Jeremiah the prophet, who spoke the word of the LORD. 13He also rebelled against King Nebuchadnezzar, who had made him take an oath[m] in God's name. He became stiff-necked[n] and hardened his heart and would not turn to the LORD, the God of Israel. 14Furthermore, all the leaders of the priests and the people became more and more unfaithful,[o] following all the detestable practices of the nations and defiling the temple of the LORD, which he had consecrated in Jerusalem.

The Fall of Jerusalem

36:17–20pp—2Ki 25:1–21; Jer 52:4–27
36:22–23pp—Ezr 1:1–3

15The LORD, the God of their fathers, sent word to them through his messengers[p] again and again,[q] because he had pity on his people and on his dwelling-place. 16But they mocked God's messengers, despised his words and scoffed[r] at his prophets until the wrath[s] of the LORD was aroused against his people and there was no remedy.[t] 17He brought up against them the king of the Babylonians,[g][u] who killed their young men with the sword in the sanctuary, and spared neither young man[v] nor young woman, old man or aged.[w] God handed all of them over to Nebuchadnezzar.[x] 18He carried to Babylon all the articles[y] from the temple of God, both large and small, and the treasures of the LORD's temple and the treasures of the king and his officials. 19They set fire[z] to God's temple[a] and broke down the wall[b] of Jerusalem; they burned all the palaces and destroyed[c] everything of value there.[d]

20He carried into exile[e] to Babylon the remnant who escaped from the sword, and they became servants[f] to him and his sons until the kingdom of Persia came to power. 21The land enjoyed its sabbath rests;[g] all the time of its desolation it rested,[h] until the seventy years[i] were completed in fulfilment of the word of the LORD spoken by Jeremiah.

22In the first year of Cyrus[j] king of Persia, in order to fulfil the word of the LORD spoken by Jeremiah, the LORD moved the heart of Cyrus king of Persia to make a proclamation throughout his realm and to put it in writing:

23"This is what Cyrus king of Persia says:

"'The LORD, the God of heaven, has given me all the kingdoms of the earth and he has appointed[k] me to build a temple for him at Jerusalem in Judah. Anyone of his people among you—may the LORD his God be with him, and let him go up.'"

4 [b]Jer 22:10–12; [c]Eze 19:4
5 [d]Jer 22:18; 25:1; 26:1; 35:1; 36:1; 45:1; 46:2
6 [e]Jer 25:9; 27:6; Eze 29:18; [f]Eze 19:9; Da 1:1
7 [g]ver 18; Ezr 1:7; Jer 27:16; Da 1:2
9 [h]Jer 22:24–28; 24:1; 27:20; 29:21; 52:31
10 [i]ver 18; **2Ki 20:17**; Ezr 1:7; Isa 52:11; Jer 14:18; 21:7; 22:25; 24:1; 27:16,20,22; 29:1; 34:21; 40:1; Eze 17:12; Da 5:2
11 [j]**2Ki 24:17**; Jer 27:1; 28:1; 34:2; 37:1; 39:1
12 [k]Jer 37:1–39:18; [l]**Dt 8:3**; 2Ch 7:14; Jer 44:10
13 [m]Eze 17:13; [n]**Ex 32:9; Dt 9:27**
14 [o]**1Ch 5:25**
15 [p]Isa 5:4; 44:26; Jer 7:25; Hag 1:13; Zec 1:4; Mal 2:7; 3:1; **Mt 5:12**; [q]Jer 7:13,25; 11:7; 25:3–4; 35:14–15; 44:4–6
16 [r]**2Ki 2:23**; Job 8:2; Isa 28:14,22; 29:20; 57:4; Jer 5:13; 43:2; Mic 2:11; [s]Ezr 5:12; Pr 1:30–31; Jer 44:3; [t]Ne 9:30; Pr 29:1; Jer 7:26; 20:8; 25:4; 30:12; Da 9:6; Zec 1:2
17 [u]**Ge 10:10**; [v]Jer 6:11; 9:21; 18:21; 44:7; [w]**Dt 32:25**; Jer 51:22; [x]Ezr 5:12; Jer 32:28; La 2:21; Eze 9:6; 23:47
18 [y]**ver 7,10**; Jer 27:20
19 [z]Jer 11:16; 17:27; 21:10, 14; 22:7; 32:29; 39:8; La 4:11; Eze 20:47; Am 2:5; Zec 11:1; [a]1Ki 9:8–9; [b]**2Ki 14:13**; [c]La 2:6; [d]Ps 79:1–3
20 [e]**Lev 26:44; 2Ki 24:14**; Ezr 2:1; Ne 7:6; [f]Jer 27:7
21 [g]**Lev 25:4**; [h]**1Ch 22:9**; [i]Jer 1:1; 25:11; 27:22; 29:10; 40:1; Da 9:2; Zec 1:12; 7:5
22 [j]Isa 44:28; 45:1,13; Da 1:21; 6:28; 10:1
23 [k]**Jdg 4:10**

---

c3 That is, about 75 pounds (about 34 kilograms)
d7 Or *palace*
e9 One Hebrew manuscript, some Septuagint manuscripts and Syriac (see also 2 Kings 24:8); most Hebrew manuscripts *eight*
f10 Hebrew *brother*, that is, relative (see 2 Kings 24:17) g17 Or *Chaldeans*

Ezra

Cyrus Helps the Exiles to Return
1:1–3pp—2Ch 36:22–23

1 In the first year of Cyrus king of
Persia, in order to fulfil the word of
the LORD spoken by Jeremiah,[a] the LORD
moved the heart[b] of Cyrus king of Persia
to make a proclamation throughout his
realm and to put it in writing:

2“This is what Cyrus king of Persia
says:
“ ‘The LORD, the God of heaven,
has given me all the kingdoms of
the earth and he has appointed[c]
me to build[d] a temple for him at
Jerusalem in Judah. 3Anyone of his
people among you—may his God
be with him, and let him go up to
Jerusalem in Judah and build the
temple of the LORD, the God of
Israel, the God who is in Jerusalem.
4And the people of any place where
survivors[e] may now be living are to
provide him with silver and gold,[f]
with goods and livestock, and with
freewill offerings[g] for the temple of
God[h] in Jerusalem.’ ”[i]

5Then the family heads of Judah and
Benjamin,[j] and the priests and Levites
—everyone whose heart God had
moved[k]—prepared to go up and build
the house[l] of the LORD in Jerusalem. 6All
their neighbours assisted them with
articles of silver and gold,[m] with goods
and livestock, and with valuable gifts,
in addition to all the freewill offerings.
7Moreover, King Cyrus brought out the
articles belonging to the temple of the
LORD, which Nebuchadnezzar had car-
ried away from Jerusalem and had
placed in the temple of his god.[a][n]
8Cyrus king of Persia had them brought
by Mithredath the treasurer, who
counted them out to Sheshbazzar[o] the
prince of Judah.
9This was the inventory:

gold dishes	30
silver dishes	1,000
silver pans[b]	29
10gold bowls	30
matching silver bowls	410
other articles	1,000

11In all, there were 5,400 articles of
gold and of silver. Sheshbazzar brought
all these along when the exiles came up
from Babylon to Jerusalem.

The List of the Exiles Who Returned
2:1–70pp—Ne 7:6–73

2 Now these are the people of the
province who came up from the
captivity of the exiles,[a] whom
Nebuchadnezzar king of Babylon[b] had
taken captive to Babylon (they returned
to Jerusalem and Judah, each to his own
town,[c] 2in company with Zerubbabel,[d]
Jeshua,[e] Nehemiah, Seraiah,[f] Reelaiah,
Mordecai, Bilshan, Mispar, Bigvai,
Rehum and Baanah):

The list of the men of the people of
Israel:

3the descendants of Parosh[g]	2,172
4of Shephatiah	372
5of Arah	775
6of Pahath-Moab (through the line of Jeshua and Joab)	2,812
7of Elam	1,254
8of Zattu	945
9of Zaccai	760
10of Bani	642
11of Bebai	623
12of Azgad	1,222
13of Adonikam[h]	666
14of Bigvai	2,056
15of Adin	454
16of Ater (through Hezekiah)	98
17of Bezai	323
18of Jorah	112
19of Hashum	223
20of Gibbar	95
21the men of Bethlehem[i]	123
22of Netophah	56

Ch. 1

1 [a]Jer 25:11–12; 29:10–14; Zec 1:12–16; [b]Ezr 6:22; 7:27
2 [c]**Jdg 4:10**; Ps 72:11; Isa 41:2,25; 44:28; 45:13; 46:11; 49:7,23; 60:3,10; [d]Hag 1:2
4 [e]Isa 10:20–22; [f]**Ex 3:22**; [g]Nu 15:3; Ps 50:14; 54:6; 116:17; [h]Ps 72:8–11; Rev 21:24; [i]Ezr 3:7; 4:3; 5:13; 6:3,14
5 [j]2Ch 11:1,3, 10,12,23; 15:2, 8–9; 25:5; 31:1; 34:9; Ezr 4:1; 10:9; Ne 11:4; 12:34; [k]ver 1; Ex 35:20–22; 2Ch 36:22; Hag 1:14; **Php 2:13**; [l]Ps 127:1
6 [m]**Ex 3:22**
7 [n]**2Ki 24:13**; **2Ch 36:7**,10; Ezr 5:14; 6:5; Jer 52:17–19
8 [o]**1Ch 3:18**

Ch. 2

1 [a]**2Ch 36:20**; [b]**2Ki 24:16**; 25:12; [c]ver 70; 1Ch 9:2; Ne 7:73; 11:3
2 [d]**1Ch 3:19**; Mt 1:12; Lk 3:27; [e]Ezr 3:2; 5:2; 10:18; Ne 12:1,8; Hag 1:1,12; 2:4; Zec 3:1–10; 6:9–15; [f]1Ch 6:14; Ne 10:2; 11:11; 12:1
3 [g]Ezr 8:3; 10:25; Ne 3:25
13 [h]Ezr 8:13
21 [i]Mic 5:2

[a]7 Or *gods*
[b]9 The meaning of the Hebrew for this word is uncertain.

[23]of Anathoth 128
[24]of Azmaveth 42
[25]of Kiriath Jearim,[a]
Kephirah and Beeroth 743
[26]of Ramah[j] and Geba 621
[27]of Michmash 122
[28]of Bethel and Ai[k] 223
[29]of Nebo 52
[30]of Magbish 156
[31]of the other Elam 1,254
[32]of Harim 320
[33]of Lod, Hadid and Ono 725
[34]of Jericho[l] 345
[35]of Senaah 3,630

[36]The priests:

the descendants of Jedaiah[m]
(through the family of
Jeshua) 973
[37]of Immer[n] 1,052
[38]of Pashhur[o] 1,247
[39]of Harim[p] 1,017

[40]The Levites:[q]

the descendants of Jeshua[r]
and Kadmiel (through
the line of Hodaviah) 74

[41]The singers:[s]

the descendants of Asaph 128

[42]The gatekeepers[t] of the temple:

the descendants of
Shallum, Ater, Talmon,
Akkub, Hatita and Shobai 139

[43]The temple servants:[u]

the descendants of
Ziha, Hasupha, Tabbaoth,
[44]Keros, Siaha, Padon,
[45]Lebanah, Hagabah, Akkub,
[46]Hagab, Shalmai, Hanan,
[47]Giddel, Gahar, Reaiah,
[48]Rezin, Nekoda, Gazzam,
[49]Uzza, Paseah, Besai,
[50]Asnah, Meunim, Nephussim,
[51]Bakbuk, Hakupha, Harhur,
[52]Bazluth, Mehida, Harsha,
[53]Barkos, Sisera, Temah,
[54]Neziah and Hatipha

[55]The descendants of the servants
of Solomon:

the descendants of
Sotai, Hassophereth, Peruda,
[56]Jaala, Darkon, Giddel,
[57]Shephatiah, Hattil,
Pokereth-Hazzebaim and Ami

[58]The temple servants[v] and
the descendants of the
servants of Solomon 392

[59]The following came up from the
towns of Tel Melah, Tel Harsha,
Kerub, Addon and Immer, but they
could not show that their families
were descended[w] from Israel:

[60]The descendants of
Delaiah, Tobiah and
Nekoda 652

[61]And from among the priests:

The descendants of
Hobaiah, Hakkoz and Barzillai (a
man who had married a
daughter of Barzillai the
Gileadite[x] and was called by that
name).
[62]These searched for their family
records, but they could not find
them and so were excluded from
the priesthood[y] as unclean. [63]The
governor ordered them not to eat
any of the most sacred food[z] until
there was a priest ministering with
the Urim and Thummim.[a]

[64]The whole company numbered
42,360, [65]besides their 7,337 men-
servants and maidservants; and
they also had 200 men and women
singers.[b] [66]They had 736 horses,[c]
245 mules, [67]435 camels and 6,720
donkeys.

[68]When they arrived at the house of
the LORD in Jerusalem, some of the
heads of the families[d] gave freewill
offerings towards the rebuilding of the
house of God on its site. [69]According to
their ability they gave to the treasury for
this work 61,000 drachmas[b] of gold,
5,000 minas[c] of silver and 100 priestly
garments.
[70]The priests, the Levites, the singers,
the gatekeepers and the temple ser-
vants settled in their own towns, along
with some of the other people, and the
rest of the Israelites settled in their
towns.[e]

26 [j]Jos 18:25
28 [k]Ge 12:8
34 [l]1Ki 16:34; 2Ch 28:15
36 [m]1Ch 24:7
37 [n]1Ch 24:14
38 [o]1Ch 9:12
39 [p]1Ch 24:8
40 [q]Ge 29:34; Nu 3:9; Dt 18:6–7; 1Ch 16:4; Ezr 7:7; 8:15; Ne 12:24; [r]Ezr 3:9
41 [s]1Ch 15:16
42 [t]1Sa 3:15; 1Ch 9:17
43 [u]1Ch 9:2; Ne 11:21
58 [v]1Ch 9:2
59 [w]Nu 1:18
61 [x]2Sa 17:27
62 [y]Nu 3:10; 16:39–40
63 [z]Lev 2:3,10; [a]Ex 28:30
65 [b]2Sa 19:35
66 [c]Isa 66:20
68 [d]Ex 25:2
70 [e]ver 1; 1Ch 9:2; Ne 11:3–4

[a]25 See Septuagint (see also Neh. 7:29); Hebrew *Kiriath Arim*.
[b]69 That is, about 1,100 pounds (about 500 kilograms)
[c]69 That is, about 2⅘ tons (about 2.9 metric tons)

Rebuilding the Altar

3 When the seventh month came and the Israelites had settled in their towns,[a] the people assembled[b] as one man in Jerusalem. 2Then Jeshua[c] son of Jozadak[d] and his fellow priests and Zerubbabel son of Shealtiel[e] and his associates began to build the altar of the God of Israel to sacrifice burnt offerings on it, in accordance with what is written in the Law of Moses[f] the man of God. 3Despite their fear[g] of the peoples around them, they built the altar on its foundation and sacrificed burnt offerings on it to the LORD, both the morning and evening sacrifices.[h] 4Then in accordance with what is written, they celebrated the Feast of Tabernacles[i] with the required number of burnt offerings prescribed for each day. 5After that, they presented the regular burnt offerings, the New Moon[j] sacrifices and the sacrifices for all the appointed sacred feasts of the LORD,[k] as well as those brought as freewill offerings to the LORD. 6On the first day of the seventh month they began to offer burnt offerings to the LORD, though the foundation of the LORD's temple had not yet been laid.

Rebuilding the Temple

7Then they gave money to the masons and carpenters,[l] and gave food and drink and oil to the people of Sidon and Tyre, so that they would bring cedar logs[m] by sea from Lebanon[n] to Joppa, as authorised by Cyrus[o] king of Persia.

8In the second month[p] of the second year after their arrival at the house of God in Jerusalem, Zerubbabel[q] son of Shealtiel, Jeshua son of Jozadak and the rest of their brothers (the priests and the Levites and all who had returned from the captivity to Jerusalem) began the work, appointing Levites twenty[r] years of age and older to supervise the building of the house of the LORD. 9Jeshua[s] and his sons and brothers and Kadmiel and his sons (descendants of Hodaviah**[a]**) and the sons of Henadad and their sons and brothers—all Levites—joined together in supervising those working on the house of God.

10When the builders laid[t] the foundation of the temple of the LORD, the priests in their vestments and with trumpets,[u] and the Levites (the sons of Asaph) with cymbals, took their places to praise[v] the LORD, as prescribed by David[w] king of Israel.[x] 11With praise and thanksgiving they sang to the LORD:

"He is good;
his love to Israel endures for ever."[y]

And all the people gave a great shout[z] of praise to the LORD, because the foundation[a] of the house of the LORD was laid. 12But many of the older priests and Levites and family heads, who had seen the former temple,[b] wept[c] aloud when they saw the foundation of this temple being laid, while many others shouted for joy. 13No-one could distinguish the sound of the shouts of joy[d] from the sound of weeping, because the people made so much noise. And the sound was heard far away.

Opposition to the Rebuilding

4 When the enemies of Judah and Benjamin heard that the exiles were building[a] a temple for the LORD, the God of Israel, 2they came to Zerubbabel and to the heads of the families and said, "Let us help you build because, like you, we seek your God and have been sacrificing to him since the time of Esarhaddon[b] king of Assyria, who brought us here."[c]

3But Zerubbabel, Jeshua and the rest of the heads of the families of Israel answered, "You have no part with us in building a temple to our God. We alone will build it for the LORD, the God of Israel, as King Cyrus, the king of Persia, commanded us."[d]

4Then the peoples around them set out to discourage the people of Judah and make them afraid to go on building.**[a]**[e] 5They hired counsellors to work against them and frustrate their plans during the entire reign of Cyrus king of Persia and down to the reign of Darius king of Persia.

Later Opposition Under Xerxes and Artaxerxes

6At the beginning of the reign of Xerxes,**[b]**[f] they lodged an accusation against the people of Judah and Jerusalem.[g]

7And in the days of Artaxerxes[h] king of Persia, Bishlam, Mithredath, Tabeel and the rest of his associates wrote a letter to Artaxerxes. The letter was written in Aramaic script and in the Aramaic[i] language.**[c,d]**

Ch. 3

1 [a]Ne 7:73; [b]**Lev 23:24**
2 [c]**Ezr 2:2;** [d]Hag 1:1; Zec 6:11; [e]1Ch 3:17; [f]**Ex 20:24;** Dt 12:5–6
3 [g]Ezr 4:4; Da 9:25; [h]**Ex 29:39;** Nu 28:1–8
4 [i]**Ex 23:16;** Nu 29:12–38; Ne 8:14–18; Zec 14:16–19
5 [j]**Nu 28:14;** Col 2:16; [k]Lev 23:1–44; **Nu 29:39**
7 [l]1Ch 22:15; [m]**1Ch 14:1;** [n]Isa 35:2; 60:13; [o]**Ezr 1:2–4**
8 [p]1Ki 6:1; [q]Zec 4:9; [r]**Nu 4:3**
9 [s]Ezr 2:40
10 [t]Ezr 5:16; 6:3; Hag 2:15; [u]**Nu 10:2; 2Sa 6:5;** 1Ch 16:6; 2Ch 5:13; Ne 12:35; [v]**1Ch 25:1;** [w]**1Ch 6:31;** [x]Zec 6:12
11 [y]1Ch 16:34,41; **2Ch 7:3;** Ps 30:5; 107:1; 118:1; 138:8; [z]**Jos 6:5,**10; [a]Hag 2:18; Zec 4:9; 8:9
12 [b]Hag 2:3,9; [c]Jer 31:9; 50:4
13 [d]Job 8:21; 33:26; Ps 27:6; 42:4; Isa 16:9; Jer 48:33

Ch. 4

1 [a]Ne 2:20
2 [b]**2Ki 17:24;** [c]**2Ki 17:41**
3 [d]Ezr 1:1–4
4 [e]**Ezr 3:3**
6 [f]Est 1:1; Da 9:1; [g]Est 3:13; 9:5
7 [h]Ezr 7:1; Ne 2:1; [i]2Ki 18:26; Isa 36:11; Da 1:4; 2:4

---

a9 Hebrew *Yehudah*, probably a variant of *Hodaviah*
a4 Or *and troubled them as they built*
b6 Hebrew *Ahasuerus*, a variant of Xerxes' name
c7 Or *written in Aramaic and translated*
d7 The text of Ezra 4:8–6:18 is in Aramaic.

8Rehum the commanding officer and
Shimshai the secretary wrote a letter
against Jerusalem to Artaxerxes the king
as follows:

> 9Rehum the commanding officer
> and Shimshai the secretary,
> together with the rest of their as-
> sociates[j]—the judges and officials
> over the men from Tripolis, Persia,[e]
> Erech[k] and Babylon, the Elamites of
> Susa,[l] 10and the other people whom
> the great and honourable Ashur-
> banipal[f] [m] deported and settled in
> the city of Samaria and elsewhere
> in Trans-Euphrates.[n]

11(This is a copy of the letter they sent
him.)

> To King Artaxerxes,
>
> From your servants, the men of
> Trans-Euphrates:
>
> 12The king should know that the
> Jews who came up to us from you
> have gone to Jerusalem and are re-
> building that rebellious and wicked
> city. They are restoring the walls
> and repairing the foundations.[o]
>
> 13Furthermore, the king should
> know that if this city is built and its
> walls are restored, no more taxes,
> tribute or duty[p] will be paid, and
> the royal revenues will suffer.
> 14Now since we are under obli-
> gation to the palace and it is not
> proper for us to see the king dis-
> honoured, we are sending this
> message to inform the king, 15so
> that a search may be made in the
> archives[q] of your predecessors. In
> these records you will find that this
> city is a rebellious city, troublesome
> to kings and provinces, a place of
> rebellion from ancient times. That
> is why this city was destroyed.[r]
> 16We inform the king that if this city
> is built and its walls are restored,
> you will be left with nothing in
> Trans-Euphrates.

17The king sent this reply:

> To Rehum the commanding officer,
> Shimshai the secretary and the
> rest of their associates living in
> Samaria and elsewhere in Trans-
> Euphrates:[s]
>
> Greetings.
>
> 18The letter you sent us has been
> read and translated in my pres-
> ence. 19I issued an order and a
> search was made, and it was found
> that this city has a long history of
> revolt[t] against kings and has been a
> place of rebellion and sedition.
> 20Jerusalem has had powerful kings
> ruling over the whole of Trans-
> Euphrates,[u] and taxes, tribute and
> duty were paid to them. 21Now
> issue an order to these men to stop
> work, so that this city will not be
> rebuilt until I so order. 22Be careful
> not to neglect this matter. Why let
> this threat grow, to the detriment of
> the royal interests?[v]

23As soon as the copy of the letter of
King Artaxerxes was read to Rehum and
Shimshai the secretary and their as-
sociates,[w] they went immediately to the
Jews in Jerusalem and compelled them
by force to stop.

24Thus the work on the house of God
in Jerusalem came to a standstill until
the second year of the reign of Darius[x]
king of Persia.

Tattenai's Letter to Darius

5 Now Haggai[a] the prophet and
Zechariah[b] the prophet, a descend-
ant of Iddo, prophesied[c] to the Jews in
Judah and Jerusalem in the name of the
God of Israel, who was over them.
2Then Zerubbabel[d] son of Shealtiel and
Jeshua[e] son of Jozadak set to work[f] to
rebuild the house of God in Jerusalem.
And the prophets of God were with
them, helping them.

3At that time Tattenai,[g] governor of
Trans-Euphrates, and Shethar-Bozenai[h]
and their associates went to them and
asked, "Who authorised you to rebuild
this temple and restore this structure?"[i]
4They also asked, "What are the names
of the men constructing this building?"[a]
5But the eye of their God[j] was watching
over the elders of the Jews, and they
were not stopped until a report could go
to Darius and his written reply be
received.

6This is a copy of the letter that Tatte-
nai, governor of Trans-Euphrates, and
Shethar-Bozenai and their associates,
the officials of Trans-Euphrates, sent to
King Darius. 7The report they sent him
read as follows:

9 [j]ver 23; Ezr 5:6; 6:6,13; [k]Ge 10:10; [l]Ne 1:1; Est 1:2; Da 8:2
10 [m]**2Ki 17:24**; [n]ver 17; Ne 4:2
12 [o]Ezr 5:3,9
13 [p]Ezr 7:24; Ne 5:4
15 [q]Ezr 5:17; 6:1; [r]Est 3:8
17 [s]**ver 10**
19 [t]**2Ki 18:7**
20 [u]Ge 15:18–21; **Ex 23:31; Jos 1:4; 1Ki 4:21**; 1Ch 18:3; Ps 72:8–11
22 [v]Da 6:2
23 [w]**ver 9**
24 [x]Ne 2:1–8; Da 9:25; Hag 1:1,15; Zec 1:1

Ch. 5

1 [a]Ezr 6:14; Hag 1:1,3,12; 2:1,10,20; [b]Zec 1:1; 7:1; [c]Hag 1:14–2:9; Zec 4:9–10; 8:9
2 [d]**1Ch 3:19**; Hag 1:14; 2:21; Zec 4:6–10; [e]**Ezr 2:2**; [f]ver 8; Hag 2:2–5
3 [g]Ezr 6:6; [h]Ezr 6:6; [i]**Ezr 4:12**
5 [j]**2Ki 25:28**; Ezr 7:6,9,28; 8:18,22,31; Ne 2:8,18; Ps 33:18; Isa 66:14

[e]9 Or *officials, magistrates and governors over the men from*
[f]10 Aramaic *Osnappar*, a variant of *Ashurbanipal*
[a]4 See Septuagint; Aramaic *[4]We told them the names of the men constructing this building.*

To King Darius:

Cordial greetings.

8The king should know that we went to the district of Judah, to the temple of the great God. The people are building it with large stones and placing the timbers in the walls. The work[k] is being carried on with diligence and is making rapid progress under their direction.

9We questioned the elders and asked them, "Who authorised you to rebuild this temple and restore this structure?"[l] 10We also asked them their names, so that we could write down the names of their leaders for your information.

11This is the answer they gave us:

"We are the servants of the God of heaven and earth, and we are rebuilding the temple[m] that was built many years ago, one that a great king of Israel built and finished. 12But because our fathers angered[n] the God of heaven, he handed them over to Nebuchadnezzar the Chaldean, king of Babylon, who destroyed this temple and deported the people to Babylon.[o]

13"However, in the first year of Cyrus king of Babylon, King Cyrus issued a decree[p] to rebuild this house of God. 14He even removed from the temple[b] of Babylon the gold and silver articles of the house of God, which Nebuchadnezzar had taken from the temple in Jerusalem and brought to the temple[b] in Babylon.[q]

"Then King Cyrus gave them to a man named Sheshbazzar,[r] whom he had appointed governor, 15and he told him, 'Take these articles and go and deposit them in the temple in Jerusalem. And rebuild the house of God on its site.' 16So this Sheshbazzar came and laid the foundations of the house of God[s] in Jerusalem. From that day to the present it has been under construction but is not yet finished."

17Now if it pleases the king, let a search be made in the royal archives[t] of Babylon to see if King Cyrus did in fact issue a decree to rebuild this house of God in Jerusalem. Then let the king send us his decision in this matter.

8 [k]ver 2
9 [l]Ezr 4:12
11 [m]1Ki 6:1; 2Ch 3:1–2
12 [n]2Ch 36:16; [o]Dt 21:10; 28:36; 2Ki 24:1; Jer 1:3
13 [p]Ezr 1:2–4
14 [q]Ezr 1:7; [r]1Ch 3:18
16 [s]Ezr 3:10
17 [t]Ezr 4:15

Ch. 6

1 [a]Ezr 4:15
3 [b]Ezr 3:10; Hag 2:3
4 [c]1Ki 6:36; [d]ver 8; Ezr 7:20
5 [e]1Ch 29:2; [f]Ezr 1:7
6 [g]Ezr 5:3; [h]Ezr 5:3
8 [i]ver 4; [j]1Sa 9:20
9 [k]Lev 1:3,10
10 [l]Ezr 7:23; 1Ti 2:1–2

The Decree of Darius

6 King Darius then issued an order, and they searched in the archives[a] stored in the treasury at Babylon. 2A scroll was found in the citadel of Ecbatana in the province of Media, and this was written on it:

Memorandum:

3In the first year of King Cyrus, the king issued a decree concerning the temple of God in Jerusalem:

Let the temple be rebuilt as a place to present sacrifices, and let its foundations be laid.[b] It is to be ninety feet[a] high and ninety feet wide, 4with three courses[c] of large stones and one of timbers. The costs are to be paid by the royal treasury.[d] 5Also, the gold[e] and silver articles of the house of God, which Nebuchadnezzar took from the temple in Jerusalem and brought to Babylon, are to be returned to their places in the temple in Jerusalem; they are to be deposited in the house of God.[f]

6Now then, Tattenai,[g] governor of Trans-Euphrates, and Shethar-Bozenai[h] and you, their fellow officials of that province, stay away from there. 7Do not interfere with the work on this temple of God. Let the governor of the Jews and the Jewish elders rebuild this house of God on its site.

8Moreover, I hereby decree what you are to do for these elders of the Jews in the construction of this house of God:

The expenses of these men are to be fully paid out of the royal treasury,[i] from the revenues[j] of Trans-Euphrates, so that the work will not stop. 9Whatever is needed —young bulls, rams, male lambs for burnt offerings[k] to the God of heaven, and wheat, salt, wine and oil, as requested by the priests in Jerusalem—must be given them daily without fail, 10so that they may offer sacrifices pleasing to the God of heaven and pray for the well-being of the king and his sons.[l]

11Furthermore, I decree that if anyone changes this edict, a beam is to be pulled from his house and

b14 Or *palace*
a3 Aramaic *sixty cubits* (about 27 metres)

he is to be lifted up and impaled[m] on it. And for this crime his house is to be made a pile of rubble.[n] 12May God, who has caused his Name to dwell there,[o] overthrow any king or people who lifts a hand to change this decree or to destroy this temple in Jerusalem.

I Darius[p] have decreed it. Let it be carried out with diligence.

Completion and Dedication of the Temple

13Then, because of the decree King Darius had sent, Tattenai, governor of Trans-Euphrates, and Shethar-Bozenai and their associates[q] carried it out with diligence. 14So the elders of the Jews continued to build and prosper under the preaching[r] of Haggai the prophet and Zechariah, a descendant of Iddo. They finished building the temple according to the command of the God of Israel and the decrees of Cyrus,[s] Darius[t] and Artaxerxes,[u] kings of Persia. 15The temple was completed on the third day of the month Adar, in the sixth year of the reign of King Darius.[v]

16Then the people of Israel—the priests, the Levites and the rest of the exiles—celebrated the dedication[w] of the house of God with joy. 17For the dedication of this house of God they offered[x] a hundred bulls, two hundred rams, four hundred male lambs and, as a sin offering for all Israel, twelve male goats, one for each of the tribes of Israel. 18And they installed the priests in their divisions[y] and the Levites in their groups[z] for the service of God at Jerusalem, according to what is written in the Book of Moses.[a]

The Passover

19On the fourteenth day of the first month, the exiles celebrated the Passover.[b] 20The priests and Levites had purified themselves and were all ceremonially clean. The Levites slaughtered[c] the Passover lamb for all the exiles, for their brothers the priests and for themselves. 21So the Israelites who had returned from the exile ate it, together with all who had separated themselves[d] from the unclean practices[e] of their Gentile neighbours in order to seek the LORD,[f] the God of Israel. 22For seven days they celebrated with joy the Feast of Unleavened Bread,[g] because the LORD had filled them with joy by changing the attitude[h] of the king of Assyria, so that he assisted them in the work on the house of God, the God of Israel.

Ezra Comes to Jerusalem

7 After these things, during the reign of Artaxerxes[a] king of Persia, Ezra son of Seraiah,[b] the son of Azariah, the son of Hilkiah,[c] 2the son of Shallum, the son of Zadok,[d] the son of Ahitub,[e] 3the son of Amariah, the son of Azariah, the son of Meraioth, 4the son of Zerahiah, the son of Uzzi, the son of Bukki, 5the son of Abishua, the son of Phinehas,[f] the son of Eleazar, the son of Aaron the chief priest—6this Ezra[g] came up from Babylon. He was a teacher well versed in the Law of Moses, which the LORD, the God of Israel, had given. The king had granted[h] him everything he asked, for the hand of the LORD his God was on him.[i] 7Some of the Israelites, including priests, Levites, singers, gatekeepers and temple servants, also came up to Jerusalem in the seventh year of King Artaxerxes.[j]

8Ezra arrived in Jerusalem in the fifth month of the seventh year of the king. 9He had begun his journey from Babylon on the first day of the first month, and he arrived in Jerusalem on the first day of the fifth month, for the gracious hand of his God was on him.[k] 10For Ezra had devoted himself to the study and observance of the Law of the LORD, and to teaching[l] its decrees and laws in Israel.

King Artaxerxes' Letter to Ezra

11This is a copy of the letter King Artaxerxes had given to Ezra the priest and teacher, a man learned in matters concerning the commands and decrees of the LORD for Israel:

12[a]Artaxerxes, king of kings,[m]

To Ezra the priest, a teacher of the Law of the God of heaven:

Greetings.

13Now I decree that any of the Israelites in my kingdom, including priests and Levites, who wish to go to Jerusalem with you, may go. 14You are sent by the king and his seven advisers[n] to enquire about Judah and Jerusalem with regard to the Law of your God, which is in

11 [m]**Dt 21:22–23**; Est 2:23; 5:14; 9:14; [n]Ezr 7:26; Da 2:5; 3:29
12 [o]**Ex 20:24; Dt 12:5; 2Ch 6:2;** [p]ver 14
13 [q]**Ezr 4:9**
14 [r]**Ezr 5:1;** [s]**Ezr 1:2–4;** [t]ver 12; [u]Ezr 7:1; Ne 2:1
15 [v]Zec 1:1; 4:9
16 [w]**1Ki 8:63**
17 [x]**2Sa 6:13; 2Ch 29:21; 30:24**
18 [y]**2Ch 35:4;** Lk 1:5; [z]**1Ch 24:1;** [a]Nu 3:6–9; 8:9–11; 18:1–32
19 [b]**Ex 12:11; Nu 28:16**
20 [c]**2Ch 30:17**
21 [d]Ezr 9:1; Ne 9:2; [e]**Dt 18:9;** Eze 36:25; [f]1Ch 22:19; Ps 14:2
22 [g]**Ex 12:17;** [h]**Ezr 1:1**

Ch. 7

1 [a]**Ezr 4:7; 6:14;** [b]**2Ki 25:18;** [c]2Ki 22:4
2 [d]1Ki 1:8; 2:35; 1Ch 6:8; Eze 40:46; 43:19; 44:15; [e]Ne 11:11
5 [f]1Ch 6:4
6 [g]Ne 12:36; [h]**2Ki 25:28;** [i]**Ezr 5:5; Isa 41:20**
7 [j]Ezr 8:1
9 [k]ver 6
10 [l]**Dt 33:10**
12 [m]Eze 26:7; Da 2:37
14 [n]Est 1:14

[a]12 The text of Ezra 7:12–26 is in Aramaic.

your hand. 15Moreover, you are to
take with you the silver and gold
that the king and his advisers have
freely given[o] to the God of Israel,
whose dwelling[p] is in Jerusalem,
16together with all the silver and
gold[q] you may obtain from the
province of Babylon, as well as the
freewill offerings of the people and
priests for the temple of their God
in Jerusalem.[r] 17With this money be
sure to buy bulls, rams and male
lambs,[s] together with their grain
offerings and drink offerings,[t] and
sacrifice[u] them on the altar of the
temple of your God in Jerusalem.
18You and your brother Jews may
then do whatever seems best with
the rest of the silver and gold, in
accordance with the will of your
God. 19Deliver[v] to the God of Jeru-
salem all the articles entrusted to
you for worship in the temple of
your God. 20And anything else
needed for the temple of your God
that you may have occasion to
supply, you may provide from the
royal treasury.[w]
21Now I, King Artaxerxes, order
all the treasurers of Trans-
Euphrates to provide with dili-
gence whatever Ezra the priest, a
teacher of the Law of the God of
heaven, may ask of you—22up to a
hundred talents[b] of silver, a hun-
dred cors[c] of wheat, a hundred
baths[d] of wine, a hundred baths[d] of
olive oil, and salt without limit.
23Whatever the God of heaven has
prescribed, let it be done with dili-
gence for the temple of the God of
heaven. Why should there be
wrath against the realm of the king
and of his sons?[x] 24You are also to
know that you have no authority to
impose taxes, tribute or duty[y] on
any of the priests, Levites, singers,
gatekeepers, temple servants or
other workers at this house of
God.[z]
25And you, Ezra, in accordance
with the wisdom of your God,
which you possess, appoint[a]
magistrates and judges to adminis-
ter justice to all the people of Trans-
Euphrates—all who know the laws
of your God. And you are to teach[b]
any who do not know them.
26Whoever does not obey the law of
your God and the law of the king
must surely be punished by death,
banishment, confiscation of prop-
erty, or imprisonment.[c]

27Praise be to the LORD, the God of our
fathers, who has put it into the king's
heart[d] to bring honour[e] to the house of
the LORD in Jerusalem in this way 28and
who has extended his good favour[f] to
me before the king and his advisers and
all the king's powerful officials. Because
the hand of the LORD my God was on
me,[g] I took courage and gathered lead-
ing men from Israel to go up with me.

List of the Family Heads Returning With Ezra

8 These are the family heads and
those registered with them who
came up with me from Babylon during
the reign of King Artaxerxes:[a]

2of the descendants of Phinehas, Gershom;
of the descendants of Ithamar, Daniel;
of the descendants of David, Hattush 3of the descendants of Shecaniah;[b]

of the descendants of Parosh,[c] Zechariah, and with him were registered 150 men;
4of the descendants of Pahath-Moab,[d] Eliehoenai son of Zerahiah, and with him 200 men;
5of the descendants of Zattu,[a] Shecaniah son of Jahaziel, and with him 300 men;
6of the descendants of Adin,[e] Ebed son of Jonathan, and with him 50 men;
7of the descendants of Elam, Jeshaiah son of Athaliah, and with him 70 men;
8of the descendants of Shephatiah, Zebadiah son of Michael, and with him 80 men;
9of the descendants of Joab, Obadiah son of Jehiel, and with him 218 men;
10of the descendants of Bani,[b] Shelomith son of Josiphiah, and with him 160 men;
11of the descendants of Bebai, Zechariah son of Bebai, and with him 28 men;

15 [o]1Ch 29:6; [p]Dt 12:5; 2Ch 6:2
16 [q]Ex 3:22; [r]Zec 6:10
17 [s]2Ki 3:4; [t]Nu 15:5–12; [u]Dt 12:5–11
19 [v]Ezr 5:14; Jer 27:22
20 [w]Ezr 6:4
23 [x]Ezr 6:10
24 [y]Ezr 4:13; [z]Ezr 8:36
25 [a]Ex 18:21,26; [b]Lev 10:11
26 [c]Ezr 6:11
27 [d]Ezr 1:1; [e]1Ch 29:12
28 [f]2Ki 25:28; [g]Ezr 5:5

Ch. 8

1 [a]Ezr 7:7
3 [b]1Ch 3:22; [c]Ezr 2:3
4 [d]Ezr 2:6
6 [e]Ezr 2:15; Ne 7:20; 10:16

b22 That is, about 3⅓ tons (about 3.4 metric tons)
c22 That is, probably about 600 bushels (about 22 kilolitres)
d22 That is, probably about 500 gallons (about 2.2 kilolitres)
a5 Some Septuagint manuscripts (also 1 Esdras 8:32); Hebrew does not have *Zattu*.
b10 Some Septuagint manuscripts (also 1 Esdras 8:36); Hebrew does not have *Bani*.

12of the descendants of Azgad, Joha-
nan son of Hakkatan, and with
him 110 men;
13of the descendants of Adonikam,[f]
the last ones, whose names were
Eliphelet, Jeuel and Shemaiah,
and with them 60 men;
14of the descendants of Bigvai, Uthai
and Zaccur, and with them 70
men.

The Return to Jerusalem

15I assembled them at the canal that
flows towards Ahava,[g] and we camped
there three days. When I checked
among the people and the priests, I
found no Levites[h] there. 16So I sum-
moned Eliezer, Ariel, Shemaiah,
Elnathan, Jarib, Elnathan, Nathan,
Zechariah and Meshullam, who were
leaders, and Joiarib and Elnathan, who
were men of learning, 17and I sent them
to Iddo, the leader in Casiphia. I told
them what to say to Iddo and his kins-
men, the temple servants[i] in Casiphia,
so that they might bring attendants to
us for the house of our God. 18Because
the gracious hand of our God was on
us,[j] they brought us Sherebiah,[k] a
capable man, from the descendants of
Mahli son of Levi, the son of Israel, and
Sherebiah's sons and brothers, 18 men;
19and Hashabiah, together with
Jeshaiah from the descendants of
Merari, and his brothers and nephews,
20 men. 20They also brought 220 of the
temple servants[l]—a body that David
and the officials had established to
assist the Levites. All were registered by
name.
21There, by the Ahava Canal,[m] I pro-
claimed a fast, so that we might humble
ourselves before our God and ask him
for a safe journey[n] for us and our chil-
dren, with all our possessions. 22I was
ashamed to ask the king for soldiers[o]
and horsemen to protect us from
enemies on the road, because we had
told the king, "The gracious hand of
our God is on everyone[p] who looks to
him, but his great anger is against all
who forsake him.[q]" 23So we fasted[r] and
petitioned our God about this, and
he answered our prayer.
24Then I set apart twelve of the lead-
ing priests, together with Sherebiah,[s]
Hashabiah and ten of their brothers,
25and I weighed out[t] to them the offer-
ing of silver and gold and the articles
that the king, his advisers, his officials
and all Israel present there had donated
for the house of our God. 26I weighed
out to them 650 talents[c] of silver, silver
articles weighing 100 talents,[d] 100
talents[d] of gold, 2720 bowls of gold
valued at 1,000 darics,[e] and two fine
articles of polished bronze, as precious
as gold.
28I said to them, "You as well as these
articles are consecrated to the LORD.[u]
The silver and gold are a freewill offer-
ing to the LORD, the God of your fathers.
29Guard them carefully until you weigh
them out in the chambers of the house
of the LORD in Jerusalem before the lead-
ing priests and the Levites and the fam-
ily heads of Israel." 30Then the priests
and Levites received the silver and gold
and sacred articles that had been
weighed out to be taken to the house of
our God in Jerusalem.
31On the twelfth day of the first
month we set out from the Ahava
Canal[v] to go to Jerusalem. The hand of
our God was on us,[w] and he protected
us from enemies and bandits along the
way. 32So we arrived in Jerusalem,
where we rested three days.[x]
33On the fourth day, in the house of
our God, we weighed out[y] the silver and
gold and the sacred articles into the
hands of Meremoth[z] son of Uriah, the
priest. Eleazar son of Phinehas was with
him, and so were the Levites Jozabad[a]
son of Jeshua and Noadiah son of Bin-
nui.[b] 34Everything was accounted for by
number and weight, and the entire
weight was recorded at that time.
35Then the exiles who had returned
from captivity sacrificed burnt offerings
to the God of Israel: twelve bulls[c] for all
Israel,[d] ninety-six rams, seventy-seven
male lambs and, as a sin offering,
twelve male goats.[e] All this was a burnt
offering to the LORD. 36They also de-
livered the king's orders[f] to the royal
satraps and to the governors of Trans-
Euphrates[g] who then gave assistance to
the people and to the house of God.[h]

Ezra's Prayer About Intermarriage

9 After these things had been done,
the leaders came to me and said,
"The people of Israel, including the
priests and the Levites, have not kept
themselves separate[a] from the neigh-
bouring peoples with their detestable

13 [f]Ezr 2:13
15 [g]ver 21,31; [h]**Ezr 2:40**
17 [i]Ezr 2:43
18 [j]**Ezr 5:5**; [k]ver 24
20 [l]**1Ch 9:2**
21 [m]**ver 15**; [n]Ps 5:8; 27:11; 107:7
22 [o]Ne 2:9; Jer 41:16; [p]**Ezr 5:5**; [q]**Dt 31:17**
23 [r]**2Ch 20:3**; Ac 14:23
24 [s]ver 18
25 [t]ver 33
28 [u]**Lev 21:6**; 22:2–3
31 [v]**ver 15**; [w]**Ezr 5:5**
32 [x]**Ge 40:13**
33 [y]ver 25; [z]Ne 3:4,21; [a]Ne 11:16; [b]Ne 3:24
35 [c]**Lev 1:3**; [d]**2Ch 29:24**; [e]**2Ch 29:21; 30:24**
36 [f]Ezr 7:21–24; [g]Ne 2:7; [h]Est 9:3

Ch. 9

1 [a]**Ezr 6:21**

c26 That is, about 22 tons (about 22 metric tons)
d26 That is, about 3⅓ tons (about 3.4 metric tons)
e27 That is, about 19 pounds (about 8.5 kilograms)

practices, like those of the Canaanites,
Hittites, Perizzites, Jebusites,[b] Ammon-
ites,[c] Moabites,[d] Egyptians and Amor-
ites.[e] 2They have taken some of their
daughters[f] as wives for themselves and
their sons, and have mingled[g] the holy
race[h] with the peoples around them.
And the leaders and officials have led
the way in this unfaithfulness."[i]
3When I heard this, I tore[j] my tunic
and cloak, pulled hair from my head
and beard and sat down appalled.[k]
4Then everyone who trembled[l] at the
words of the God of Israel gathered
round me because of this unfaithfulness
of the exiles. And I sat there appalled[m]
until the evening sacrifice.
5Then, at the evening sacrifice,[n] I rose
from my self-abasement, with my tunic
and cloak torn, and fell on my knees
with my hands[o] spread out to the LORD
my God 6and prayed:

"O my God, I am too ashamed[p]
and disgraced to lift up my face to
you, my God, because our sins are
higher than our heads and our guilt
has reached to the heavens.[q] 7From
the days of our forefathers[r] until
now, our guilt has been great. Be-
cause of our sins, we and our kings
and our priests have been sub-
jected to the sword[s] and captivity,[t]
to pillage and humiliation[u] at the
hand of foreign kings, as it is today.
8"But now, for a brief moment,
the LORD our God has been
gracious[v] in leaving us a remnant[w]
and giving us a firm place[x] in his
sanctuary, and so our God gives
light to our eyes[y] and a little relief in
our bondage. 9Though we are
slaves,[z] our God has not deserted
us in our bondage. He has shown
us kindness[a] in the sight of the
kings of Persia: He has granted us
new life to rebuild the house of our
God and repair its ruins,[b] and he
has given us a wall of protection in
Judah and Jerusalem.
10"But now, O our God, what can
we say after this? For we have
disregarded the commands[c] 11you
gave through your servants the
prophets when you said: 'The land
you are entering[d] to possess is a
land polluted[e] by the corruption of
its peoples. By their detestable
practices[f] they have filled it with
their impurity from one end to the
other. 12Therefore, do not give your
daughters in marriage to their sons
or take their daughters for your
sons. Do not seek a treaty of
friendship with them[g] at any time,
that you may be strong[h] and eat the
good things[i] of the land and leave it
to your children as an everlasting
inheritance.'[j]
13"What has happened to us is a
result of our evil[k] deeds and our
great guilt, and yet, our God, you
have punished us less than our sins
have deserved[l] and have given us a
remnant like this. 14Shall we again
break your commands and inter-
marry[m] with the peoples who com-
mit such detestable practices?
Would you not be angry enough
with us to destroy us,[n] leaving us
no remnant[o] or survivor? 15O LORD,
God of Israel, you are righteous![p]
We are left this day as a remnant.
Here we are before you in our guilt,
though because of it not one of us
can stand[q] in your presence."[r]

The People's Confession of Sin

10 While Ezra was praying and
confessing,[a] weeping[b] and
throwing himself down before the
house of God, a large crowd of Israelites
—men, women and children—
gathered round him. They too wept bit-
terly. 2Then Shecaniah son of Jehiel, one
of the descendants of Elam,[c] said to
Ezra, "We have been unfaithful[d] to our
God by marrying foreign women from
the peoples around us. But in spite of
this, there is still hope for Israel.[e] 3Now
let us make a covenant[f] before our God
to send away[g] all these women and their
children, in accordance with the coun-
sel of my lord and of those who fear the
commands of our God. Let it be done
according to the Law. 4Rise up; this
matter is in your hands. We will support
you, so take courage and do it."
5So Ezra rose up and put the leading
priests and Levites and all Israel under
oath[h] to do what had been suggested.
And they took the oath. 6Then Ezra
withdrew from before the house of God
and went to the room of Jehohanan son
of Eliashib. While he was there, he ate
no food and drank no water,[i] because he

1 [b]**Ge 10:16; Jos 15:8;** [c]Ge 19:38; [d]**Ge 19:37;** [e]Ex 13:5; 23:28; Dt 20:17; **Jos 3:10; Jdg 3:5;** 1Ki 9:20; **2Ch 8:7;** Ne 9:8
2 [f]**Ex 34:16; Ru 1:4;** [g]Ps 106:35; [h]**Ex 22:31; Lev 27:30; Dt 14:2;** [i]Ezr 10:2
3 [j]**Nu 14:6;** [k]**Ex 32:19; 33:4**
4 [l]Ezr 10:3; Ps 119:120; Isa 66:2,5; [m]Ne 1:4; Ps 119:136; Da 10:2
5 [n]**Ex 29:41;** [o]Ne 8:6; Ps 28:2; 134:2
6 [p]Jer 31:19; [q]**2Ch 28:9;** Job 42:6; Ps 38:4; Isa 59:12; Jer 3:25; 14:20; Rev 18:5
7 [r]**2Ch 29:6;** [s]Eze 21:1–32; [t]**Dt 28:64;** [u]**Dt 28:37**
8 [v]Ps 25:16; 67:1; 119:58; Isa 33:2; [w]**Ge 45:7;** [x]Ecc 12:11; Isa 22:23; [y]Ps 13:3; 19:8
9 [z]**Ex 1:14;** Ne 9:36; [a]**2Ki 25:28;** Ps 106:46; [b]Ps 69:35; Isa 43:1; 44:26; 48:20; 52:9; 63:9; Jer 32:44; Zec 1:16–17
10 [c]Dt 11:8; Isa 1:19–20
11 [d]Dt 4:5; [e]**Lev 18:25–28;** [f]**Dt 9:4; 18:9; 1Ki 14:24**
12 [g]**Ex 34:15;** [h]Dt 11:8; [i]**Ge 45:18;** [j]Ps 103:17; Eze 37:25; Joel 3:20
13 [k]**Ex 32:22;** [l]Job 11:6; 15:5; 22:5; 33:27; Ps 103:10
14 [m]Ne 13:27; [n]**Dt 9:8;** [o]Dt 9:14
15 [p]**Ge 18:25; 2Ch 12:6;** Ne 9:8; Ps 51:4; 129:4; 145:17; Isa 24:16; Jer 12:1; 23:6; 33:16; La 1:18; Da 9:7; Zep 3:5; [q]Ps 76:7; 130:3; Mal 3:2; [r]**1Ki 8:47**

Ch. 10
1 [a]2Ch 20:9; Da 9:20; [b]**Nu 25:6**
2 [c]ver 26; [d]**Ezr 9:2;** [e]Dt 30:8–10
3 [f]**2Ki 11:17;** [g]**Ex 34:16** *5* [h]Ne 5:12; 13:25
6 [i]**Ex 34:28;** Dt 9:18; Ps 102:4; Jnh 3:7

continued to mourn over the unfaithfulness of the exiles.

7A proclamation was then issued throughout Judah and Jerusalem for all the exiles to assemble in Jerusalem.
8Anyone who failed to appear within three days would forfeit all his property, in accordance with the decision of the officials and elders, and would himself be expelled from the assembly of the exiles.

9Within the three days, all the men of Judah and Benjamin[j] had gathered in Jerusalem. And on the twentieth day of the ninth month, all the people were sitting in the square before the house of God, greatly distressed by the occasion and because of the rain.
10Then Ezra[k] the priest stood up and said to them, "You have been unfaithful; you have married foreign women, adding to Israel's guilt.[l]
11Now make confession to the LORD, the God of your fathers, and do his will. Separate yourselves from the peoples around you and from your foreign wives."[m]

12The whole assembly responded with a loud voice:[n] "You are right! We must do as you say.
13But there are many people here and it is the rainy season; so we cannot stand outside. Besides, this matter cannot be taken care of in a day or two, because we have sinned greatly in this thing.
14Let our officials act for the whole assembly. Then let everyone in our towns who has married a foreign woman come at a set time, along with the elders and judges[o] of each town, until the fierce anger[p] of our God in this matter is turned away from us."
15Only Jonathan son of Asahel and Jahzeiah son of Tikvah, supported by Meshullam and Shabbethai[q] the Levite, opposed this.

16So the exiles did as was proposed. Ezra the priest selected men who were family heads, one from each family division, and all of them designated by name. On the first day of the tenth month they sat down to investigate the cases,
17and by the first day of the first month they finished dealing with all the men who had married foreign women.

Those Guilty of Intermarriage

18Among the descendants of the priests, the following had married foreign women:[r]

From the descendants of Jeshua[s] son of Jozadak, and his brothers: Maaseiah, Eliezer, Jarib and Gedaliah.
19(They all gave their hands[t] in pledge to put away their wives, and for their guilt they each presented a ram from the flock as a guilt offering.)[u]

20From the descendants of Immer:[v] Hanani and Zebadiah.

21From the descendants of Harim:[w] Maaseiah, Elijah, Shemaiah, Jehiel and Uzziah.

22From the descendants of Pashhur:[x] Elioenai, Maaseiah, Ishmael, Nethanel, Jozabad and Elasah.

23Among the Levites:[y]

Jozabad, Shimei, Kelaiah (that is Kelita), Pethahiah, Judah and Eliezer.

24From the singers: Eliashib.[z]

From the gatekeepers: Shallum, Telem and Uri.

25And among the other Israelites:

From the descendants of Parosh:[a] Ramiah, Izziah, Malkijah, Mijamin, Eleazar, Malkijah and Benaiah.

26From the descendants of Elam:[b] Mattaniah, Zechariah, Jehiel, Abdi, Jeremoth and Elijah.

27From the descendants of Zattu: Elioenai, Eliashib, Mattaniah, Jeremoth, Zabad and Aziza.

28From the descendants of Bebai: Jehohanan, Hananiah, Zabbai and Athlai.

29From the descendants of Bani: Meshullam, Malluch, Adaiah, Jashub, Sheal and Jeremoth.

30From the descendants of Pahath-Moab: Adna, Kelal, Benaiah, Maaseiah, Mattaniah, Bezalel, Binnui and Manasseh.

31From the descendants of Harim: Eliezer, Ishijah, Malkijah, Shemaiah, Shimeon,
32Benjamin, Malluch and Shemariah.

33From the descendants of Hashum: Mattenai, Mattattah, Zabad, Eliphelet, Jeremai, Manasseh and Shimei.

34From the descendants of Bani: Maadai, Amram, Uel,
35Benaiah, Bedeiah, Keluhi,
36Vaniah,

9 [j]Ezr 1:5
10 [k]Ezr 7:21; [l]2Ch 28:13
11 [m]Dt 24:1; Ne 9:2; Mal 2:10–16
12 [n]Jos 6:5
14 [o]Dt 16:18; [p]Nu 25:4; 2Ch 29:10
15 [q]Ne 11:16
18 [r]Jdg 3:6; [s]Ezr 2:2
19 [t]2Ki 10:15; [u]Lev 5:15; 6:6
20 [v]1Ch 24:14
21 [w]1Ch 24:8
22 [x]1Ch 9:12
23 [y]Ne 8:7; 9:4
24 [z]Ne 3:1; 12:10; 13:7,28
25 [a]Ezr 2:3
26 [b]ver 2

Meremoth, Eliashib, 37Mattan-
iah, Mattenai and Jaasu.
38From the descendants of Binnui:[a]
Shimei, 39Shelemiah, Nathan,
Adaiah, 40Macnadebai, Shashai,
Sharai, 41Azarel, Shelemiah,
Shemariah, 42Shallum, Amariah
and Joseph.
43From the descendants of Nebo:
Jeiel, Mattithiah, Zabad, Zebina,
Jaddai, Joel and Benaiah.

44All these had married foreign
women, and some of them had children
by these wives.[b]

[a]37,38 See Septuagint (also 1 Esdras 9:34); Hebrew *Jaasu* 38*and Bani and Binnui,*

[b]44 Or *and they sent them away with their children*

Nehemiah

Nehemiah's Prayer

1 The words of Nehemiah son of Hacaliah:

In the month of Kislev[a] in the twentieth year, while I was in the citadel of Susa,[b] 2Hanani,[c] one of my brothers, came from Judah with some other men, and I questioned them about the Jewish remnant[d] that survived the exile, and also about Jerusalem.

3They said to me, "Those who survived the exile and are back in the province are in great trouble and disgrace. The wall of Jerusalem is broken down, and its gates have been burned with fire.[e]"

4When I heard these things, I sat down and wept.[f] For some days I mourned and fasted[g] and prayed before the God of heaven. 5Then I said:

"O LORD, God of heaven, the great and awesome God,[h] who keeps his covenant of love[i] with those who love him and obey his commands, 6let your ear be attentive and your eyes open to hear[j] the prayer[k] your servant is praying before you day and night for your servants, the people of Israel. I confess[l] the sins we Israelites, including myself and my father's house, have committed against you. 7We have acted very wickedly[m] towards you. We have not obeyed the commands, decrees and laws you gave your servant Moses.

8"Remember[n] the instruction you gave your servant Moses, saying, 'If you are unfaithful, I will scatter[o] you among the nations, 9but if you return to me and obey my commands, then even if your exiled people are at the farthest horizon, I will gather[p] them from there and bring them to the place I have chosen as a dwelling for my Name.'[q]

10"They are your servants and your people, whom you redeemed by your great strength and your mighty hand.[r] 11O Lord, let your ear be attentive[s] to the prayer of this your servant and to the prayer of your servants who delight in revering your name. Give your servant success today by granting him favour[t] in the presence of this man."

I was cupbearer[u] to the king.

Artaxerxes Sends Nehemiah to Jerusalem

2 In the month of Nisan in the twentieth year of King Artaxerxes,[a] when wine was brought for him, I took the wine and gave it to the king. I had not been sad in his presence before; 2so the king asked me, "Why does your face look so sad when you are not ill? This can be nothing but sadness of heart."

I was very much afraid, 3but I said to the king, "May the king live for ever![b] Why should my face not look sad when the city[c] where my fathers are buried lies in ruins, and its gates have been destroyed by fire?[d]"

4The king said to me, "What is it you want?"

Then I prayed to the God of heaven, 5and I answered the king, "If it pleases the king and if your servant has found favour in his sight, let him send me to the city in Judah where my fathers are buried so that I can rebuild it."

6Then the king[e], with the queen sitting beside him, asked me, "How long will your journey take, and when will you get back?" It pleased the king to send me; so I set a time.

7I also said to him, "If it pleases the king, may I have letters to the governors of Trans-Euphrates,[f] so that they will provide me safe-conduct until I arrive in Judah? 8And may I have a letter to Asaph, keeper of the king's forest, so he will give me timber to make beams for the gates of the citadel[g] by the temple and for the city wall and for the residence I will occupy?" And because the gracious hand of my God was upon

Ch. 1

1 [a]Zec 7:1; [b]**Ezr 4:9**; **Est 2:8**
2 [c]Ne 7:2; [d]**2Ki 21:14**; Ne 7:6; Jer 52:28
3 [e]**Lev 26:31**; 2Ki 25:10; Ne 2:3,13,17; Isa 22:9; Jer 39:8; 52:14; La 2:9
4 [f]Ps 137:1; [g]**2Ch 20:3**; **Ezr 9:4**; Da 9:3
5 [h]**Dt 7:21**; Ne 4:14; [i]**Dt 7:9**; **1Ki 8:23**; Da 9:4
6 [j]**1Ki 8:29**; **2Ch 7:15**; [k]**1Ki 8:30**; [l]**1Ki 8:47**
7 [m]Ps 106:6
8 [n]**Ge 8:1**; **2Ki 20:3**; Ne 4:14; 5:19; 6:14; 13:22,29,31; [o]**Lev 26:33**
9 [p]**Dt 30:4**; Ps 106:47; 107:3; Isa 11:12; 56:8; Jer 42:12; Eze 11:17; [q]**1Ki 8:48**; Jer 29:14; Eze 11:17; 20:34–38; 36:24–38; Mic 2:12
10 [r]**Ex 32:11**; Isa 51:9–11
11 [s]**2Ch 6:40**; [t]**Ex 3:21**; [u]**Ge 40:1**

Ch. 2

1 [a]**Ezr 4:7**; **6:14**
3 [b]1Ki 1:31; Da 2:4; 3:9; 5:10; 6:6,21; [c]Ps 137:6; [d]**Ne 1:3**
6 [e]Ne 5:14; 13:6
7 [f]**Ezr 8:36**
8 [g]Ne 7:2

me,[h] the king granted my requests.[i] 9So
I went to the governors of Trans-
Euphrates and gave them the king's
letters. The king had also sent army
officers and cavalry[j] with me.
10When Sanballat[k] the Horonite and
Tobiah[l] the Ammonite official heard
about this, they were very much dis-
turbed that someone had come to pro-
mote the welfare of the Israelites.[m]

Nehemiah Inspects Jerusalem's Walls

11I went to Jerusalem, and after
staying there three days[n] 12I set out dur-
ing the night with a few men. I had not
told anyone what my God had put in
my heart to do for Jerusalem. There
were no mounts with me except the one
I was riding on.
13By night I went out through the
Valley Gate[o] towards the Jackal[a] Well
and the Dung Gate,[p] examining the
walls[q] of Jerusalem, which had been
broken down, and its gates, which had
been destroyed by fire. 14Then I moved
on towards the Fountain Gate[r] and the
King's Pool,[s] but there was not enough
room for my mount to get through; 15so I
went up the valley by night, examining
the wall. Finally, I turned back and re-
entered through the Valley Gate. 16The
officials did not know where I had gone
or what I was doing, because as yet I
had said nothing to the Jews or the
priests or nobles or officials or any
others who would be doing the work.
17Then I said to them, "You see the
trouble we are in: Jerusalem lies in
ruins, and its gates have been burned
with fire.[t] Come, let us rebuild the wall[u]
of Jerusalem, and we will no longer be
in disgrace."[v] 18I also told them about
the gracious hand of my God upon me[w]
and what the king had said to me.
They replied, "Let us start rebuild-
ing." So they began this good work.
19But when Sanballat[x] the Horonite,
Tobiah the Ammonite official and
Geshem[y] the Arab heard about it, they
mocked and ridiculed us.[z] "What is this
you are doing?" they asked. "Are you
rebelling against the king?"
20I answered them by saying, "The
God of heaven will give us success. We
his servants will start rebuilding,[a] but as
for you, you have no share[b] in Jerusalem
or any claim or historic right to it."

Builders of the Wall

3 Eliashib[a] the high priest and his
fellow priests went to work and
rebuilt[b] the Sheep Gate.[c] They dedicated
it and set its doors in place, building as
far as the Tower of the Hundred, which
they dedicated, and as far as the Tower
of Hananel.[d] 2The men of Jericho[e] built
the adjoining section, and Zaccur son of
Imri built next to them.

3The Fish Gate[f] was rebuilt by the
sons of Hassenaah. They laid its beams
and put its doors and bolts and bars in
place. 4Meremoth[g] son of Uriah, the son
of Hakkoz, repaired the next section.
Next to him Meshullam son of Berekiah,
the son of Meshezabel, made repairs,
and next to him Zadok son of Baana also
made repairs. 5The next section was re-
paired by the men of Tekoa,[h] but their
nobles would not put their shoulders to
the work under their supervisors.[a]

6The Jeshanah[b] Gate[i] was repaired by
Joiada son of Paseah and Meshullam
son of Besodeiah. They laid its beams
and put its doors and bolts and bars in
place. 7Next to them, repairs were made
by men from Gibeon[j] and Mizpah—
Melatiah of Gibeon and Jadon of Mero-
noth—places under the authority of the
governor of Trans-Euphrates. 8Uzziel
son of Harhaiah, one of the goldsmiths,
repaired the next section; and Hana-
niah, one of the perfume-makers, made
repairs next to that. They restored[c]
Jerusalem as far as the Broad Wall.[k]
9Rephaiah son of Hur, ruler of a half-
district of Jerusalem, repaired the next
section. 10Adjoining this, Jedaiah son of
Harumaph made repairs opposite his
house, and Hattush son of Hashab-
neiah made repairs next to him.
11Malkijah son of Harim and Hasshub
son of Pahath-Moab repaired another
section and the Tower of the Ovens.[l]
12Shallum son of Hallohesh, ruler of
a half-district of Jerusalem, repaired
the next section with the help of his
daughters.

13The Valley Gate[m] was repaired by
Hanun and the residents of Zanoah.[n]
They rebuilt it and put its doors and
bolts and bars in place. They also re-
paired five hundred yards[d] of the wall
as far as the Dung Gate.[o]

14The Dung Gate was repaired by
Malkijah son of Recab, ruler of the dis-
trict of Beth Hakkerem.[p] He rebuilt it

8 [h]Ezr 5:5; [i]**Ezr 4:24**
9 [j]**Ezr 8:22**
10 [k]ver 19; Ne 4:1,7; 6:1–2, 5,12,14; 13:28; [l]Ne 4:3; 13:4–7; [m]Est 10:3
11 [n]**Ge 40:13**
13 [o]**2Ch 26:9**; [p]Ne 3:13; 12:31; [q]**Ne 1:3**
14 [r]Ne 3:15; 12:37; [s]**2Ki 18:17**
17 [t]**Ne 1:3**; [u]Ps 102:16; Isa 30:13; 58:12; [v]Eze 5:14
18 [w]**Ezr 5:5**
19 [x]**ver 10**; [y]Ne 6:1–2,6; [z]Ps 44:13–16
20 [a]Ezr 4:1; [b]Ezr 4:3; Ac 8:21

Ch. 3

1 [a]**Ezr 10:24**; [b]Isa 58:12; [c]ver 32; Ne 12:39; Jn 5:2; [d]Ne 12:39; Ps 48:12; Jer 31:38; Zec 14:10
2 [e]Ne 7:36
3 [f]**2Ch 33:14**
4 [g]**Ezr 8:33**
5 [h]ver 27; **2Sa 14:2**
6 [i]Ne 12:39
7 [j]**Jos 9:3**
8 [k]Ne 12:38
11 [l]Ne 12:38
13 [m]**2Ch 26:9**; [n]**Jos 15:34**; [o]**Ne 2:13**
14 [p]Jer 6:1

[a]13 Or *Serpent* or *Fig*
[a]5 Or *their Lord* or *the governor*
[b]6 Or *Old*
[c]8 Or *They left out part of*
[d]13 Hebrew *a thousand cubits* (about 450 metres)

and put its doors and bolts and bars in
place.

15The Fountain Gate was repaired by
Shallun son of Col-Hozeh, ruler of the
district of Mizpah. He rebuilt it, roofing
it over and putting its doors and bolts
and bars in place. He also repaired the
wall of the Pool of Siloam,[e][q] by the
King's Garden, as far as the steps going
down from the City of David. 16Beyond
him, Nehemiah son of Azbuk, ruler of a
half-district of Beth Zur,[r] made repairs
up to a point opposite the tombs[f][s] of
David, as far as the artificial pool and
the House of the Heroes.

17Next to him, the repairs were made
by the Levites under Rehum son of
Bani. Beside him, Hashabiah, ruler of
half the district of Keilah,[t] carried out
repairs for his district. 18Next to him, the
repairs were made by their countrymen
under Binnui[g] son of Henadad, ruler of
the other half-district of Keilah. 19Next
to him, Ezer son of Jeshua, ruler of
Mizpah, repaired another section, from
a point facing the ascent to the armoury
as far as the angle. 20Next to him, Baruch
son of Zabbai zealously repaired
another section, from the angle to the
entrance of the house of Eliashib the
high priest. 21Next to him, Meremoth[u]
son of Uriah, the son of Hakkoz, re-
paired another section, from the entr-
ance of Eliashib's house to the end of it.

22The repairs next to him were made
by the priests from the surrounding re-
gion. 23Beyond them, Benjamin and
Hasshub made repairs in front of their
house; and next to them, Azariah son of
Maaseiah, the son of Ananiah, made
repairs beside his house. 24Next to him,
Binnui[v] son of Henadad repaired
another section, from Azariah's house
to the angle and the corner, 25and Palal
son of Uzai worked opposite the angle
and the tower projecting from the upper
palace near the court of the guard.[w]
Next to him, Pedaiah son of Parosh[x]
26and the temple servants[y] living on the
hill of Ophel[z] made repairs up to a point
opposite the Water Gate[a] towards the
east and the projecting tower. 27Next
to them, the men of Tekoa[b] repaired
another section, from the great project-
ing tower[c] to the wall of Ophel.

28Above the Horse Gate,[d] the priests
made repairs, each in front of his own
house. 29Next to them, Zadok son of
Immer made repairs opposite his
house. Next to him, Shemaiah son of
Shecaniah, the guard at the East Gate,
made repairs. 30Next to him, Hananiah
son of Shelemiah, and Hanun, the sixth
son of Zalaph, repaired another section.
Next to them, Meshullam son of Bere-
kiah made repairs opposite his living
quarters. 31Next to him, Malkijah, one
of the goldsmiths, made repairs as far as
the house of the temple servants and
the merchants, opposite the Inspection
Gate, and as far as the room above the
corner; 32and between the room above
the corner and the Sheep Gate[e] the gold-
smiths and merchants made repairs.

Opposition to the Rebuilding

4 When Sanballat[a] heard that we
were rebuilding the wall, he be-
came angry and was greatly incensed.
He ridiculed the Jews, 2and in the pres-
ence of his associates[b] and the army of
Samaria, he said, "What are those
feeble Jews doing? Will they restore
their wall? Will they offer sacrifices?
Will they finish in a day? Can they bring
the stones back to life from those heaps
of rubble[c]—burned as they are?"

3Tobiah[d] the Ammonite, who was at
his side, said, "What they are building
—if even a fox climbed up on it, he
would break down their wall of
stones!"[e]

4Hear us, O our God, for we are des-
pised.[f] Turn their insults back on their
own heads. Give them over as plunder
in a land of captivity. 5Do not cover up
their guilt[g] or blot out their sins from
your sight,[h] for they have thrown in-
sults in the face of[a] the builders.

6So we rebuilt the wall till all of it
reached half its height, for the people
worked with all their heart.

7But when Sanballat, Tobiah,[i] the
Arabs, the Ammonites and the men of
Ashdod heard that the repairs to Jeru-
salem's walls had gone ahead and that
the gaps were being closed, they were
very angry. 8They all plotted together[j] to
come and fight against Jerusalem and
stir up trouble against it. 9But we prayed
to our God and posted a guard day and
night to meet this threat.

10Meanwhile, the people in Judah
said, "The strength of the labourers[k] is

15 [q]Isa 8:6; Jn 9:7
16 [r]**Jos 15:58**; [s]Ac 2:29
17 [t]**Jos 15:44**
21 [u]**Ezr 8:33**
24 [v]**Ezr 8:33**
25 [w]Jer 32:2; 37:21; 39:14; [x]**Ezr 2:3**
26 [y]Ne 7:46; 11:21; [z]**2Ch 33:14**; [a]Ne 8:1,3,16; 12:37
27 [b]**ver 5**; [c]Ps 48:12
28 [d]**2Ki 11:16**
32 [e]**ver 1**; Jn 5:2

Ch. 4

1 [a]**Ne 2:10**
2 [b]**Ezr 4:9–10**; [c]Ps 79:1; Jer 26:18
3 [d]**Ne 2:10**; [e]Job 13:12; 15:3
4 [f]Ps 44:13; 123:3–4; Jer 33:24
5 [g]Isa 2:9; La 1:22; [h]2Ki 14:27; Ps 51:1; 69:27–28; 109:14; Jer 18:23
7 [i]**Ne 2:10**
8 [j]Ps 2:2; 83:1–18
10 [k]**1Ch 23:4**

[e]*15* Hebrew *Shelah,* a variant of *Shiloah,* that is, *Siloam*
[f]*16* Hebrew; Septuagint, some Vulgate manuscripts and Syriac *tomb*
[g]*18* Two Hebrew manuscripts and Syriac (see also Septuagint and verse 24); most Hebrew manuscripts *Bavvai*
[a]*5* Or *have provoked you to anger before*

giving out, and there is so much rubble that we cannot rebuild the wall."

11 Also our enemies said, "Before they know it or see us, we will be right there among them and will kill them and put an end to the work."

12 Then the Jews who lived near them came and told us ten times over, "Wherever you turn, they will attack us."

13 Therefore I stationed some of the people behind the lowest points of the wall at the exposed places, posting them by families, with their swords, spears and bows. 14 After I looked things over, I stood up and said to the nobles, the officials and the rest of the people, "Don't be afraid[l] of them. Remember[m] the Lord, who is great and awesome,[n] and fight[o] for your brothers, your sons and your daughters, your wives and your homes."

15 When our enemies heard that we were aware of their plot and that God had frustrated it,[p] we all returned to the wall, each to his own work.

16 From that day on, half of my men did the work, while the other half were equipped with spears, shields, bows and armour. The officers posted themselves behind all the people of Judah 17 who were building the wall. Those who carried materials did their work with one hand and held a weapon[q] in the other, 18 and each of the builders wore his sword at his side as he worked. But the man who sounded the trumpet[r] stayed with me.

19 Then I said to the nobles, the officials and the rest of the people, "The work is extensive and spread out, and we are widely separated from each other along the wall. 20 Wherever you hear the sound of the trumpet,[s] join us there. Our God will fight[t] for us!"

21 So we continued the work with half the men holding spears, from the first light of dawn till the stars came out. 22 At that time I also said to the people, "Have every man and his helper stay inside Jerusalem at night, so that they can serve us as guards by night and workmen by day." 23 Neither I nor my brothers nor my men nor the guards with me took off our clothes; each had his weapon, even when he went for water.[b]

Nehemiah Helps the Poor

5 Now the men and their wives raised a great outcry against their Jewish brothers. 2 Some were saying, "We and our sons and daughters are numerous; in order for us to eat and stay alive, we must get grain."

3 Others were saying, "We are mortgaging our fields,[a] our vineyards and our homes to get grain during the famine."[b]

4 Still others were saying, "We have had to borrow money to pay the king's tax[c] on our fields and vineyards. 5 Although we are of the same flesh and blood[d] as our countrymen and though our sons are as good as theirs, yet we have to subject our sons and daughters to slavery.[e] Some of our daughters have already been enslaved, but we are powerless, because our fields and our vineyards belong to others."[f]

6 When I heard their outcry and these charges, I was very angry. 7 I pondered them in my mind and then accused the nobles and officials. I told them, "You are exacting usury[g] from your own countrymen!" So I called together a large meeting to deal with them 8 and said: "As far as possible, we have bought[h] back our Jewish brothers who were sold to the Gentiles. Now you are selling your brothers, only for them to be sold back to us!" They kept quiet, because they could find nothing to say.[i]

9 So I continued, "What you are doing is not right. Shouldn't you walk in the fear of our God to avoid the reproach[j] of our Gentile enemies? 10 I and my brothers and my men are also lending the people money and grain. But let the exacting of usury stop![k] 11 Give back to them immediately their fields, vineyards, olive groves and houses, and also the usury[l] you are charging them—the hundredth part of the money, grain, new wine and oil."

12 "We will give it back," they said. "And we will not demand anything more from them. We will do as you say."

Then I summoned the priests and made the nobles and officials take an oath[m] to do what they had promised. 13 I also shook[n] out the folds of my robe and said, "In this way may God shake out of his house and possessions every man who does not keep this promise. So may such a man be shaken out and emptied!"

At this the whole assembly said, "Amen,"[o] and praised the LORD. And the people did as they had promised.

14 [l]**Ge 28:15; Dt 1:29;** [m]**Ne 1:8;** [n]**Ne 1:5;** [o]**2Sa 10:12**
15 [p]**2Sa 17:14;** Job 5:12
17 [q]Ps 149:6
18 [r]**Nu 10:2**
20 [s]Eze 33:3; [t]**Ex 14:14; Dt 20:4;** Jos 10:14

Ch. 5

3 [a]Ps 109:11; [b]Ge 47:23
4 [c]**Ezr 4:13**
5 [d]**Ge 29:14;** [e]Lev 25:39–43,47; **2Ki 4:1;** Isa 50:1; [f]Dt 15:7–11; **2Ki 4:1**
7 [g]Ex 22:25–27; **Lev 25:35–37;** Dt 23:19–20; 24:10–13
8 [h]Lev 25:47; [i]Jer 34:8
9 [j]Isa 52:5
10 [k]**Ex 22:25**
11 [l]Isa 58:6
12 [m]**Ezr 10:5**
13 [n]**Mt 10:14;** [o]Dt 27:15–26

b23 The meaning of the Hebrew for this clause is uncertain.

14Moreover, from the twentieth year of King Artaxerxes,[p] when I was appointed to be their governor[q] in the land of Judah, until his thirty-second year—twelve years—neither I nor my brothers ate the food allotted to the governor. 15But the earlier governors—those preceding me—placed a heavy burden on the people and took forty shekels[a] of silver from them in addition to food and wine. Their assistants also lorded it over the people. But out of reverence for God[r] I did not act like that. 16Instead,[s] I devoted myself to the work on this wall. All my men were assembled there for the work; we[b] did not acquire any land.

17Furthermore, a hundred and fifty Jews and officials ate at my table, as well as those who came to us from the surrounding nations. 18Each day one ox, six choice sheep and some poultry[t] were prepared for me, and every ten days an abundant supply of wine of all kinds. In spite of all this, I never demanded the food allotted to the governor, because the demands were heavy on these people.

19Remember[u] me with favour, O my God, for all I have done for these people.

Further Opposition to the Rebuilding

6 When word came to Sanballat, Tobiah,[a] Geshem[b] the Arab and the rest of our enemies that I had rebuilt the wall and not a gap was left in it—though up to that time I had not set the doors in the gates—2Sanballat and Geshem sent me this message: "Come, let us meet together in one of the villages[a] on the plain of Ono.[c]"

But they were scheming to harm me; 3so I sent messengers to them with this reply: "I am carrying on a great project and cannot go down. Why should the work stop while I leave it and go down to you?" 4Four times they sent me the same message, and each time I gave them the same answer.

5Then, the fifth time, Sanballat[d] sent his assistant to me with the same message, and in his hand was an unsealed letter 6in which was written:

"It is reported among the nations—and Geshem[b][e] says it is true—that you and the Jews are plotting to revolt, and therefore you are building the wall. Moreover, according to these reports you are about to become their king 7and have even appointed prophets to make this proclamation about you in Jerusalem: 'There is a king in Judah!' Now this report will get back to the king; so come, let us confer together."

8I sent him this reply: "Nothing like what you are saying is happening; you are just making it up out of your head."

9They were all trying to frighten us, thinking, "Their hands will get too weak for the work, and it will not be completed."

⌊But I prayed,⌋ "Now strengthen my hands."

10One day I went to the house of Shemaiah son of Delaiah, the son of Mehetabel, who was shut in at his home. He said, "Let us meet in the house of God, inside the temple[f], and let us close the temple doors, because men are coming to kill you—by night they are coming to kill you."

11But I said, "Should a man like me run away? Or should one like me go into the temple to save his life? I will not go!" 12I realised that God had not sent him, but that he had prophesied against me[g] because Tobiah and Sanballat[h] had hired him. 13He had been hired to intimidate me so that I would commit a sin by doing this, and then they would give me a bad name to discredit me.[i]

14Remember[j] Tobiah and Sanballat,[k] O my God, because of what they have done; remember also the prophetess[l] Noadiah and the rest of the prophets[m] who have been trying to intimidate me.

The Completion of the Wall

15So the wall was completed on the twenty-fifth of Elul, in fifty-two days. 16When all our enemies heard about this, all the surrounding nations were afraid and lost their self-confidence, because they realised that this work had been done with the help of our God.

17Also, in those days the nobles of Judah were sending many letters to Tobiah, and replies from Tobiah kept coming to them. 18For many in Judah were under oath to him, since he was son-in-law to Shecaniah son of Arah, and his son Jehohanan had married the

14 [p]Ne 2:6; [q]Ge 42:6; Ezr 6:7; Jer 40:7; Hag 1:1
15 [r]Ge 20:11
16 [s]2Th 3:7–10
18 [t]1Ki 4:23
19 [u]Ge 8:1; 2Ki 20:3; Ne 1:8

Ch. 6

1 [a]Ne 2:10; [b]Ne 2:19
2 [c]1Ch 8:12
5 [d]Ne 2:10
6 [e]Ne 2:19
10 [f]Nu 18:7
12 [g]Eze 13:22–23; [h]Ne 2:10
13 [i]Jer 20:10
14 [j]Ne 1:8; [k]Ne 2:10; [l]Ex 15:20; Eze 13:17–23; Ac 21:9; Rev 2:20; [m]Jer 23:9–40; Zec 13:2–3

[a]15 That is, about 1 pound (about 0.5 kilogram)
[b]16 Most Hebrew manuscripts; some Hebrew manuscripts, Septuagint, Vulgate and Syriac *I*
[a]2 Or *in Kephirim*
[b]6 Hebrew *Gashmu*, a variant of *Geshem*

daughter of Meshullam son of Berekiah.
19 Moreover, they kept reporting to me
his good deeds and then telling him
what I said. And Tobiah sent letters to
intimidate me.

7 After the wall had been rebuilt and
I had set the doors in place, the
gatekeepers[a] and the singers[b] and the
Levites[c] were appointed. 2 I put in
charge of Jerusalem my brother Hana-
ni,[d] along with[a] Hananiah[e] the comman-
der of the citadel,[f] because he was a man
of integrity and feared[g] God more than
most men do. 3 I said to them, "The
gates of Jerusalem are not to be opened
until the sun is hot. While the gatekeep-
ers are still on duty, make them shut the
doors and bar them. Also appoint resi-
dents of Jerusalem as guards, some at
their posts and some near their own
houses."

The List of the Exiles Who Returned

7:6–73pp—Ezr 2:1–70

4 Now the city was large and spacious,
but there were few people in it,[h] and the
houses had not yet been rebuilt. 5 So my
God put it into my heart to assemble the
nobles, the officials and the common
people for registration by families. I
found the genealogical record of those
who had been the first to return. This is
what I found written there:

6 These are the people of the pro-
vince who came up from the captiv-
ity of the exiles[i] whom Nebuchad-
nezzar king of Babylon had taken
captive (they returned to Jerusalem
and Judah, each to his own town,
7 in company with Zerubbabel,[j]
Jeshua, Nehemiah, Azariah,
Raamiah, Nahamani, Mordecai,
Bilshan, Mispereth, Bigvai, Nehum
and Baanah):

The list of the men of Israel:

8 the descendants of Parosh	2,172
9 of Shephatiah	372
10 of Arah	652
11 of Pahath-Moab (through the line of Jeshua and Joab)	2,818
12 of Elam	1,254
13 of Zattu	845
14 of Zaccai	760
15 of Binnui	648
16 of Bebai	628
17 of Azgad	2,322
18 of Adonikam	667
19 of Bigvai	2,067
20 of Adin[k]	655
21 of Ater (through Hezekiah)	98
22 of Hashum	328
23 of Bezai	324
24 of Hariph	112
25 of Gibeon	95
26 the men of Bethlehem and Netophah[l]	188
27 of Anathoth[m]	128
28 of Beth Azmaveth	42
29 of Kiriath Jearim, Kephirah[n] and Beeroth[o]	743
30 of Ramah and Geba	621
31 of Michmash	122
32 of Bethel and Ai[p]	123
33 of the other Nebo	52
34 of the other Elam	1,254
35 of Harim	320
36 of Jericho[q]	345
37 of Lod, Hadid and Ono[r]	721
38 of Senaah	3,930

39 The priests:

the descendants of Jedaiah (through the family of Jeshua)	973
40 of Immer	1,052
41 of Pashhur	1,247
42 of Harim	1,017

43 The Levites:

the descendants of Jeshua (through Kadmiel through the line of Hodaviah)	74

44 The singers:[s]

the descendants of Asaph	148

45 The gatekeepers:[t]

the descendants of Shallum, Ater, Talmon, Akkub, Hatita and Shobai	138

46 The temple servants:[u]

the descendants of
Ziha, Hasupha, Tabbaoth,
47 Keros, Sia, Padon,
48 Lebana, Hagaba, Shalmai,
49 Hanan, Giddel, Gahar,
50 Reaiah, Rezin, Nekoda,
51 Gazzam, Uzza, Paseah,
52 Besai, Meunim, Nephussim,
53 Bakbuk, Hakupha, Harhur,
54 Bazluth, Mehida, Harsha,

Ch. 7
1 [a]1Ch 9:27; 26:12–19; [b]Ps 68:25; [c]Ne 8:9
2 [d]Ne 1:2; [e]Ne 10:23; [f]Ne 2:8; [g]1Ki 18:3
4 [h]Ne 11:1
6 [i]2Ch 36:20; Ne 1:2
7 [j]1Ch 3:19
20 [k]Ezr 8:6
26 [l]2Sa 23:28; 1Ch 2:54
27 [m]Jos 21:18
29 [n]Jos 18:26; [o]Jos 18:25
32 [p]Ge 12:8
36 [q]Ne 3:2
37 [r]1Ch 8:12
44 [s]Ne 11:23
45 [t]1Ch 9:17
46 [u]Ne 3:26

[a]2 Or *Hanani, that is,*

55 Barkos, Sisera, Temah,
56 Neziah and Hatipha

57 The descendants of the servants
of Solomon:

the descendants of
Sotai, Sophereth, Perida,
58 Jaala, Darkon, Giddel,
59 Shephatiah, Hattil, Pokereth-
Hazzebaim and Amon

60 The temple servants and
the descendants of the
servants of Solomon[v] 392

61 The following came up from the
towns of Tel Melah, Tel Harsha,
Kerub, Addon and Immer, but they
could not show that their families
were descended from Israel:

62 the descendants of
Delaiah, Tobiah and
Nekoda 642

63 And from among the priests:

the descendants of
Hobaiah, Hakkoz and Barzillai (a
man who had married a daugh-
ter of Barzillai the Gileadite and
was called by that name).
64 These searched for their family
records, but they could not find
them and so were excluded from
the priesthood as unclean. 65 The
governor, therefore, ordered them
not to eat any of the most sacred
food until there should be a priest
ministering with the Urim and
Thummim.[w]

66 The whole company numbered
42,360, 67 besides their 7,337 men-
servants and maidservants; and
they also had 245 men and women
singers. 68 There were 736 horses,
245 mules,[b] 69 435 camels and 6,720
donkeys.

70 Some of the heads of the fam-
ilies contributed to the work. The
governor gave to the treasury 1,000
drachmas[c] of gold, 50 bowls and
530 garments for priests. 71 Some of
the heads of the families[x] gave to
the treasury for the work 20,000
drachmas[d] of gold and 2,200 minas[e]
of silver. 72 The total given by the
rest of the people was 20,000 drach-
mas of gold, 2,000 minas[f] of silver
and 67 garments for priests.[y]

60 [v]**1Ch 9:2**
65 [w]**Ex 28:30**
71 [x]**1Ch 29:7**
72 [y]**Ex 25:2**
73 [z]Ne 1:10; Ps 34:22; 103:21; 113:1; 135:1; [a]**Ezr 3:1**; Ne 11:1; [b]Ezr 3:1

Ch. 8

1 [a]**Ne 3:26**; [b]**Dt 28:61; 2Ch 34:15**
2 [c]Lev 23:23–25; Nu 29:1–6; [d]**Dt 31:11**
3 [e]**Ne 3:26**
4 [f]2Ch 6:13
5 [g]Jdg 3:20
6 [h]**Ezr 9:5**; 1Ti 2:8
7 [i]**Ezr 10:23**; [j]**Lev 10:11; 2Ch 17:7**

73 The priests, the Levites, the
gatekeepers, the singers and the
temple servants,[z] along with cer-
tain of the people and the rest of the
Israelites, settled in their own
towns.[a]

Ezra Reads the Law

When the seventh month came and
the Israelites had settled in their
8 towns,[b] 1 all the people assembled
as one man in the square before the
Water Gate.[a] They told Ezra the scribe to
bring out the Book of the Law of Moses,[b]
which the LORD had commanded for
Israel.
2 So on the first day of the seventh
month,[c] Ezra the priest brought the
Law[d] before the assembly, which was
made up of men and women and all
who were able to understand. 3 He read
it aloud from daybreak till noon as he
faced the square before the Water Gate[e]
in the presence of the men, women and
others who could understand. And all
the people listened attentively to the
Book of the Law.
4 Ezra the scribe stood on a high
wooden platform[f] built for the occasion.
Beside him on his right stood Mat-
tithiah, Shema, Anaiah, Uriah, Hil-
kiah and Maaseiah; and on his left
were Pedaiah, Mishael, Malkijah, Ha-
shum, Hashbaddanah, Zechariah and
Meshullam.
5 Ezra opened the book. All the people
could see him because he was standing[g]
above them; and as he opened it, the
people all stood up. 6 Ezra praised the
LORD, the great God; and all the people
lifted their hands[h] and responded,
"Amen! Amen!" Then they bowed
down and worshipped the LORD with
their faces to the ground.
7 The Levites[i]—Jeshua, Bani, Shere-
biah, Jamin, Akkub, Shabbethai,
Hodiah, Maaseiah, Kelita, Azariah,
Jozabad, Hanan and Pelaiah—
instructed[j] the people in the Law while
the people were standing there. 8 They
read from the Book of the Law of God,
making it clear[a] and giving the meaning
so that the people could understand
what was being read.

---

b*68* Some Hebrew manuscripts (see also Ezra 2:66); most Hebrew manuscripts do not have this verse.
c*70* That is, about 19 pounds (about 8.5 kilograms)
d*71* That is, about 375 pounds (about 170 kilograms); also in verse 72
e*71* That is, about 1¼ tons (about 1.3 metric tons)
f*72* That is, about 1 ton (about 1.1 metric tons)
a*8* Or *God, translating it*

9Then Nehemiah the governor, Ezra
the priest and scribe, and the Levites[k]
who were instructing the people said to
them all, "This day is sacred to the LORD
your God. Do not mourn or weep."[l] For
all the people had been weeping as they
listened to the words of the Law.
10Nehemiah said, "Go and enjoy
choice food and sweet drinks, and send
some to those who have nothing[m] pre-
pared. This day is sacred to our Lord.
Do not grieve, for the joy[n] of the LORD is
your strength."
11The Levites calmed all the people
saying, "Be still, for this is a sacred day.
Do not grieve."
12Then all the people went away to eat
and drink, to send portions of food and
to celebrate with great joy,[o] because
they now understood the words that
had been made known to them.
13On the second day of the month, the
heads of all the families, along with the
priests and the Levites, gathered round
Ezra the scribe to give attention to the
words of the Law. 14They found written
in the Law, which the LORD had com-
manded through Moses, that the
Israelites were to live in booths[p] during
the feast of the seventh month 15and
that they should proclaim this word and
spread it throughout their towns and in
Jerusalem: "Go out into the hill country
and bring back branches from olive and
wild olive trees, and from myrtles,
palms and shade trees, to make booths"
—as it is written.[b]
16So the people went out and brought
back branches and built themselves
booths on their own roofs, in their
courtyards, in the courts of the house of
God and in the square by the Water
Gate[q] and the one by the Gate of
Ephraim.[r] 17The whole company that
had returned from exile built booths
and lived in them.[s] From the days of
Joshua son of Nun until that day, the
Israelites had not celebrated[t] it like this.
And their joy was very great.
18Day after day, from the first day to
the last, Ezra read[u] from the Book of the
Law[v] of God. They celebrated the feast
for seven days, and on the eighth day,
in accordance with the regulation,[w]
there was an assembly.[x]

The Israelites Confess Their Sins

9 On the twenty-fourth day of
the same month, the Israelites
gathered together, fasting and wearing
sackcloth and having dust on their
heads.[a] 2Those of Israelite descent had
separated themselves from all foreign-
ers.[b] They stood in their places and con-
fessed their sins and the wickedness of
their fathers.[c] 3They stood where they
were and read from the Book of the Law
of the LORD their God for a quarter of the
day, and spent another quarter in con-
fession and in worshipping the LORD
their God. 4Standing on the stairs were
the Levites[d]—Jeshua, Bani, Kadmiel,
Shebaniah, Bunni, Sherebiah, Bani and
Kenani—who called with loud voices to
the LORD their God. 5And the Levites
—Jeshua, Kadmiel, Bani, Hashabneiah,
Sherebiah, Hodiah, Shebaniah and
Pethahiah—said: "Stand up and praise
the LORD your God,[e] who is from ever-
lasting to everlasting."[a]

"Blessed be your glorious name,[f]
and may it be exalted above all bless-
ing and praise. 6You alone are the
LORD.[g] You made the heavens,[h]
even the highest heavens, and all
their starry host,[i] the earth[j] and all
that is on it, the seas[k] and all that is
in them.[l] You give life to every-
thing, and the multitudes of
heaven[m] worship you.
7"You are the LORD God, who
chose Abram[n] and brought him out
of Ur of the Chaldeans[o] and named
him Abraham.[p] 8You found his
heart faithful to you, and you
made a covenant with him to give
to his descendants the land of
the Canaanites, Hittites, Amor-
ites, Perizzites, Jebusites and
Girgashites.[q] You have kept
your promise[r] because you are
righteous.[s]
9"You saw the suffering of our
forefathers in Egypt;[t] you heard
their cry at the Red Sea.[b][u] 10You
sent miraculous signs[v] and won-
ders[w] against Pharaoh, against all
his officials and all the people of his
land, for you knew how arrogantly
the Egyptians treated them. You
made a name[x] for yourself,[y] which
remains to this day. 11You divided
the sea before them,[z] so that they
passed through it on dry ground,
but you hurled their pursuers into
the depths,[a] like a stone into
mighty waters.[b] 12By day[c] you led[d]
them with a pillar of cloud,[e] and by
night with a pillar of fire to give

9 [k]Ne 7:1; [l]Dt 12:7,12; 16:14–15
10 [m]1Sa 25:8; **2Sa 6:19**; Est 9:22; Lk 14:12–14; [n]**Lev 23:40; Dt 12:18**; 16:11,14–15
12 [o]Est 9:22
14 [p]**Ex 23:16**
16 [q]**Ne 3:26**; [r]**2Ch 25:23**
17 [s]Hos 12:9; [t]**1Ki 8:2; 2Ch 7:8; 8:13**
18 [u]Dt 31:11; **33:10**; [v]**Dt 28:61**; [w]**Lev 23:40; Ezr 3:4**; [x]**Lev 23:36**

Ch. 9

1 [a]Lev 26:40–45; **Jos 7:6**; 2Ch 7:14–16
2 [b]**Ezr 6:21**; Ne 10:28; 13:3,30; [c]**Lev 26:40; Ezr 10:11**; Ps 106:6
4 [d]**Ezr 10:23**
5 [e]Ps 78:4; [f]**2Sa 7:26**
6 [g]**Dt 6:4**; [h]**Ex 8:19**; [i]Isa 40:26; 45:12; [j]**Ge 1:1**; Isa 37:16; [k]Ps 95:5; 146:6; Jnh 1:9; [l]Dt 10:14; Ac 4:24; Rev 10:6; [m]Ps 103:20; 148:2
7 [n]**Ge 16:11**; [o]**Ge 11:28**; [p]**Ge 17:5**
8 [q]**Ge 15:18–21; Ezr 9:1**; [r]**Jos 21:45**; [s]**Ge 15:6; Ezr 9:15**
9 [t]Ex 2:23–25; 3:7; [u]Ex 14:10–30
10 [v]**Ex 10:1**; Ps 74:9; [w]**Ex 3:20; 6:6**; [x]Jer 32:20; Da 9:15; [y]**Nu 6:27**
11 [z]Ps 78:13; [a]**Ex 14:28**; [b]Ex 15:4–5,10; Heb 11:29
12 [c]**Dt 1:33**; [d]**Ex 15:13**; [e]**Ex 13:21**

b15 See Lev. 23:37–40.
a5 Or *God for ever and ever*
b9 Hebrew *Yam Suph*; that is, Sea of Reeds

them light on the way they were to
take.
13"You came down on Mount
Sinai;[f] you spoke[g] to them from
heaven.[h] You gave them regula-
tions and laws that are just[i] and
right, and decrees and commands
that are good.[j] 14You made known
to them your holy Sabbath[k] and
gave them commands, decrees and
laws through your servant Moses.
15In their hunger you gave them
bread from heaven[l] and in their
thirst you brought them water from
the rock;[m] you told them to go in
and take possession of the land you
had sworn with uplifted hand[n] to
give them.[o]
16"But they, our forefathers, be-
came arrogant and stiff-necked,[p]
and did not obey your commands.[q]
17They refused to listen and failed
to remember[r] the miracles[s] you per-
formed among them. They became
stiff-necked[t] and in their rebellion
appointed a leader in order to re-
turn to their slavery.[u] But you are a
forgiving God,[v] gracious and com-
passionate,[w] slow to anger[x] and
abounding in love.[y] Therefore you
did not desert them,[z] 18even when
they cast for themselves an image
of a calf[a] and said, 'This is your god,
who brought you up out of Egypt,'
or when they committed awful
blasphemies.[b]
19"Because of your great compas-
sion you did not abandon[c] them in
the desert. By day the pillar of
cloud[d] did not cease to guide them
on their path, nor the pillar of fire
by night to shine on the way they
were to take. 20You gave your good
Spirit[e] to instruct[f] them. You did
not withhold your manna[g] from
their mouths, and you gave them
water[h] for their thirst. 21For forty
years[i] you sustained them in the
desert; they lacked nothing,[j] their
clothes did not wear out nor did
their feet become swollen.[k]
22"You gave them kingdoms and
nations, allotting to them even the
remotest frontiers. They took over
the country of Sihon[c][l] king of Hesh-
bon and the country of Og king of
Bashan.[m] 23You made their sons as
numerous as the stars in the sky,[n]
and you brought them into the land
that you told their fathers to enter
and possess. 24Their sons went in
and took possession of the land.[o]
You subdued[p] before them the

13 [f]**Ex 19:11**; [g]**Ex 19:19**; [h]**Ex 20:22**; [i]Ps 119:137; [j]**Ex 20:1**; Dt 4:7–8
14 [k]**Ge 2:3**; Ex 20:8–11
15 [l]**Ex 16:4**; Ps 78:24–25; Jn 6:31; [m]Ex 17:6; Nu 20:7–13; [n]**Ge 14:22**; [o]Dt 1:8,21
16 [p]**Ex 32:9**; Jer 7:26; 17:23; 19:15; [q]Dt 1:26–33; 31:29
17 [r]Jdg 8:34; Ps 78:42; [s]Ps 77:11; 78:12; 105:5; 106:7; [t]Jer 7:26; 19:15; [u]Nu 14:1–4; [v]Ps 130:4; Da 9:9; [w]**Dt 4:31**; [x]**Ex 34:6**; Ps 103:8; Na 1:3; [y]**Ex 22:27**; Nu 14:17–19; Ps 86:15; [z]Ps 78:11; Eze 5:6
18 [a]**Ex 32:4**; [b]**Ex 20:23**
19 [c]Ex 13:22; [d]**Ex 13:21**
20 [e]Nu 9:17; 11:17; Isa 63:11,14; Hag 2:5; Zec 4:6; [f]Ps 23:3; 143:10; [g]**Ex 16:15**; [h]Ex 17:6
21 [i]**Ex 16:35**; [j]**Dt 2:7**; [k]**Dt 8:4**
22 [l]**Nu 21:21**; [m]**Nu 21:33**; Dt 2:26–3:11
23 [n]**Ge 12:2**; **Lev 26:9**; **Nu 10:36**
24 [o]**Jos 11:23**; [p]**Jdg 4:23**; **2Ch 14:13**
25 [q]**Dt 11:11**; [r]**Ex 18:9**; [s]Dt 6:10–12; [t]Dt 8:8–11; 32:12–15; Ps 23:6; 25:7; 69:16
26 [u]**1Ki 14:9**; Jer 44:10; [v]**Jos 7:25**; [w]Jer 2:30; 26:8; Mt 21:35–36; 23:29–36; Ac 7:52; [x]**Jdg 2:12–13**
27 [y]**Nu 25:17**; **Jdg 2:14**; [z]Ps 51:1; 103:8; 106:45; 119:156; [a]**Jdg 3:9**
28 [b]**Ex 32:22**; **Jdg 2:17**; [c]**2Sa 24:14**; [d]Ps 22:4; 106:43; 136:24

Canaanites, who lived in the land;
you handed the Canaanites over to
them, along with their kings and
the peoples of the land, to deal with
them as they pleased. 25They cap-
tured fortified cities and fertile
land;[q] they took possession of
houses filled with all kinds of good
things,[r] wells already dug, vine-
yards, olive groves and fruit trees
in abundance. They ate to the full
and were well-nourished;[s] they
revelled in your great goodness.[t]
26"But they were disobedient and
rebelled against you; they put your
law behind their backs.[u] They
killed[v] your prophets,[w] who had
admonished them in order to turn
them back to you; they committed
awful blasphemies.[x] 27So you hand-
ed them over to their enemies,[y]
who oppressed them. But when
they were oppressed they cried out
to you. From heaven you heard
them, and in your great compas-
sion[z] you gave them deliverers,[a]
who rescued them from the hand of
their enemies.
28"But as soon as they were at
rest, they again did what was evil in
your sight.[b] Then you abandoned
them to the hand of their enemies
so that they ruled over them. And
when they cried out to you again,
you heard from heaven, and in
your compassion[c] you delivered
them[d] time after time.
29"You warned[e] them to return to
your law, but they became arro-
gant[f] and disobeyed your com-
mands. They sinned against your
ordinances, by which a man will
live if he obeys them.[g] Stubbornly
they turned their backs[h] on you,
became stiff-necked[i] and refused to
listen.[j] 30For many years you were
patient with them. By your Spirit
you admonished them through
your prophets.[k] Yet they paid no
attention, so you handed them
over to the neighbouring peoples.[l]
31But in your great mercy you did
not put an end[m] to them or abandon
them, for you are a gracious and
merciful[n] God.

29 [e]**Jdg 6:8**; [f]ver 16–17; Ps 5:5; Isa 2:11; Jer 43:2; [g]**Dt 30:16**; [h]**1Sa 8:3**; [i]Jer 19:15; [j]Zec 7:11–12
30 [k]2Ki 17:13–18; **2Ch 36:16**; [l]Jer 16:11; Zec 7:12
31 [m]Isa 48:9; 65:9; [n]**Dt 4:31**

---

[c]22 One Hebrew manuscript and Septuagint; most Hebrew manuscripts *Sihon, that is, the country of the*

[32]"Now therefore, O our God,
the great, mighty[o] and awesome
God,[p] who keeps his covenant of
love,[q] do not let all this hardship
seem trifling in your eyes—the
hardship[r] that has come upon us,
upon our kings and leaders, upon
our priests and prophets, upon our
fathers and all your people, from
the days of the kings of Assyria
until today. [33]In all that has hap-
pened to us, you have been just;[s]
you have acted faithfully, while we
did wrong.[t] [34]Our kings,[u] our lead-
ers, our priests and our fathers[v] did
not follow your law; they did not
pay attention to your commands or
the warnings you gave them.
[35]Even while they were in their
kingdom, enjoying your great
goodness[w] to them in the spacious
and fertile land you gave them,
they did not serve you[x] or turn from
their evil ways.

[36]"But see, we are slaves[y] today,
slaves in the land you gave our
forefathers so that they could eat its
fruit and the other good things it
produces. [37]Because of our sins, its
abundant harvest goes to the kings
you have placed over us. They rule
over our bodies and our cattle as
they please. We are in great
distress.[z]

The Agreement of the People

[38]"In view of all this, we are making a
binding agreement,[a] putting it in wri-
ting,[b] and our leaders, our Levites and
our priests are affixing their seals to it."

10 Those who sealed it were:

Nehemiah the governor, the son of Hacaliah.

Zedekiah, [2]Seraiah,[a] Azariah, Jeremiah,
[3]Pashhur,[b] Amariah, Malkijah,
[4]Hattush, Shebaniah, Malluch,
[5]Harim,[c] Meremoth, Obadiah,
[6]Daniel, Ginnethon, Baruch,
[7]Meshullam, Abijah, Mijamin,
[8]Maaziah, Bilgai and Shemaiah.
These were the priests.[d]

[9]The Levites:[e]

Jeshua son of Azaniah,
Binnui of the sons of Henadad,
Kadmiel,
[10]and their associates:
Shebaniah, Hodiah, Kelita,
Pelaiah, Hanan,
[11]Mica, Rehob, Hashabiah,
[12]Zaccur, Sherebiah, Shebaniah,
[13]Hodiah, Bani and Beninu.

[14]The leaders of the people:

Parosh, Pahath-Moab, Elam,
Zattu, Bani,
[15]Bunni, Azgad, Bebai,
[16]Adonijah, Bigvai, Adin,[f]
[17]Ater, Hezekiah, Azzur,
[18]Hodiah, Hashum, Bezai,
[19]Hariph, Anathoth, Nebai,
[20]Magpiash, Meshullam, Hezir,[g]
[21]Meshezabel, Zadok, Jaddua,
[22]Pelatiah, Hanan, Anaiah,
[23]Hoshea, Hananiah,[h] Hasshub,
[24]Hallohesh, Pilha, Shobek,
[25]Rehum, Hashabnah, Maaseiah,
[26]Ahiah, Hanan, Anan,
[27]Malluch, Harim and Baanah.

[28]"The rest of the people—
priests, Levites, gatekeepers, sing-
ers, temple servants[i] and all who
separated themselves from the
neighbouring peoples[j] for the sake
of the Law of God, together with
their wives and all their sons and
daughters who are able to under-
stand—[29]all these now join their
brothers the nobles, and bind
themselves with a curse and an
oath[k] to follow the Law of God
given through Moses the servant of
God and to obey carefully all the
commands, regulations and de-
crees of the LORD our Lord.

[30]"We promise not to give our
daughters in marriage to the
peoples around us or take their
daughters for our sons.[l]

[31]"When the neighbouring
peoples bring merchandise or grain
to sell on the Sabbath,[m] we will not
buy from them on the Sabbath or
on any holy day. Every seventh
year we will forgo working the
land[n] and will cancel all debts.[o]

[32]"We assume the responsibility
for carrying out the commands to
give a third of a shekel[a] each year
for the service of the house of our
God: [33]for the bread set out on the
table;[p] for the regular grain offer-
ings and burnt offerings; for the
offerings on the Sabbaths, New
Moon[q] festivals and appointed
feasts; for the holy offerings; for sin

32 [o]Job 9:19; Ps 24:8; 89:8; 93:4; [p]**Dt 7:21;** [q]**Dt 7:9; 1Ki 8:23;** Da 9:4; [r]**Ex 18:8**
33 [s]**Ge 18:25;** [t]Jer 44:3; Da 9:7–8,14
34 [u]**2Ki 23:11;** [v]Jer 44:17
35 [w]Isa 63:7; [x]Dt 28:45–48
36 [y]**Ezr 9:9**
37 [z]Dt 28:33; La 5:5
38 [a]**2Ch 23:16;** [b]Isa 44:5

Ch. 10

2 [a]**Ezr 2:2**
3 [b]**1Ch 9:12**
5 [c]**1Ch 24:8**
8 [d]Ne 12:1
9 [e]Ne 12:1
16 [f]**Ezr 8:6**
20 [g]1Ch 24:15
23 [h]**Ne 7:2**
28 [i]Ps 135:1; [j]2Ch 6:26; **Ne 9:2**
29 [k]**Nu 5:21;** Ps 119:106
30 [l]**Ex 34:16;** Ne 13:23
31 [m]Ne 13:16,18; Jer 17:27; Eze 23:38; Am 8:5; [n]**Ex 23:11;** Lev 25:1–7; [o]**Dt 15:1**
33 [p]Lev 24:6; [q]Nu 10:10; Ps 81:3; Isa 1:14

[a]32 That is, about ⅛ ounce (about 4 grams)

offerings to make atonement for
Israel; and for all the duties of the
house of our God.[r]
34"We—the priests, the Levites
and the people—have cast lots[s] to
determine when each of our fam-
ilies is to bring to the house of our
God at set times each year a con-
tribution of wood[t] to burn on the
altar of the LORD our God, as it is
written in the Law.
35"We also assume responsibility
for bringing to the house of the
LORD each year the firstfruits[u] of
our crops and of every fruit tree.[v]
36"As it is also written in the Law,
we will bring the firstborn[w] of our
sons and of our cattle, of our herds
and of our flocks to the house of our
God, to the priests ministering
there.[x]
37"Moreover, we will bring to the
storerooms of the house of our
God, to the priests, the first of our
ground meal, of our ⌞grain⌟ offer-
ings, of the fruit of all our trees and
of our new wine and oil.[y] And we
will bring a tithe[z] of our crops to the
Levites,[a] for it is the Levites who
collect the tithes in all the towns
where we work.[b] 38A priest de-
scended from Aaron is to accom-
pany the Levites when they receive
the tithes, and the Levites are to
bring a tenth of the tithes[c] up to
the house of our God, to the
storerooms of the treasury. 39The
people of Israel, including the Le-
vites, are to bring their contribu-
tions of grain, new wine and oil to
the storerooms where the articles
for the sanctuary are kept and
where the ministering priests, the
gatekeepers and the singers stay.
"We will not neglect the house of
our God."[d]

The New Residents of Jerusalem

11:3–19pp—1Ch 9:1–17

11 Now the leaders of the people
settled in Jerusalem, and the
rest of the people cast lots to bring one
out of every ten to live in Jerusalem,[a] the
holy city,[b] while the remaining nine
were to stay in their own towns.[c] 2The
people commended all the men who
volunteered to live in Jerusalem.
3These are the provincial leaders who
settled in Jerusalem (now some
Israelites, priests, Levites, temple ser-
vants and descendants of Solomon's
servants lived in the towns of Judah,

33 [r]2Ch 24:5
34 [s]Lev 16:8; [t]Ne 13:31
35 [u]Ex 22:29; Nu 18:12; [v]Dt 26:1–11
36 [w]Ex 13:2; Nu 18:14–16; [x]Ne 13:31
37 [y]Nu 18:12; [z]Lev 27:30; Nu 18:21; [a]Dt 14:22–29; [b]Eze 44:30
38 [c]Nu 18:26
39 [d]Ne 13:11–12

Ch. 11

1 [a]Ne 7:4; [b]Isa 48:2; 52:1; 64:10; Zec 14:20–21; [c]Ne 7:73
3 [d]Ezr 2:1
4 [e]Ezr 1:5; [f]Ezr 2:70
11 [g]2Ki 25:18; Ezr 2:2; [h]Ezr 7:2
16 [i]Ezr 10:15; [j]Ezr 8:33

each on his own property in the vari-
ous towns,[d] 4while other people from
both Judah and Benjamin[e] lived in
Jerusalem):[f]

From the descendants of Judah:

Athaiah son of Uzziah, the son of
Zechariah, the son of Amariah, the
son of Shephatiah, the son of
Mahalalel, a descendant of Perez;
5and Maaseiah son of Baruch, the
son of Col-Hozeh, the son of
Hazaiah, the son of Adaiah, the son
of Joiarib, the son of Zechariah, a
descendant of Shelah. 6The descen-
dants of Perez who lived in Jeru-
salem totalled 468 able men.

7From the descendants of Benjamin:

Sallu son of Meshullam, the son of
Joed, the son of Pedaiah, the son of
Kolaiah, the son of Maaseiah, the
son of Ithiel, the son of Jeshaiah,
8and his followers, Gabbai and Sal-
lai—928 men. 9Joel son of Zicri was
their chief officer, and Judah son of
Hassenuah was over the Second
District of the city.

10From the priests:

Jedaiah; the son of Joiarib; Jakin;
11Seraiah[g] son of Hilkiah, the son of
Meshullam, the son of Zadok, the
son of Meraioth, the son of Ahi-
tub,[h] supervisor in the house of
God, 12and their associates, who
carried on work for the temple—
822 men; Adaiah son of Jeroham,
the son of Pelaliah, the son of
Amzi, the son of Zechariah, the son
of Pashhur, the son of Malkijah,
13and his associates, who were
heads of families—242 men;
Amashsai son of Azarel, the son of
Ahzai, the son of Meshillemoth,
the son of Immer, 14and his[a] associ-
ates, who were able men—128
men. Their chief officer was Zab-
diel son of Haggedolim.

15From the Levites:

Shemaiah son of Hasshub, the son
of Azrikam, the son of Hashabiah,
the son of Bunni; 16Shabbethai[i] and
Jozabad,[j] two of the heads of the
Levites, who had charge of the out-
side work of the house of God;

[a]14 Most Septuagint manuscripts; Hebrew *their*

17Mattaniah[k] son of Mica, the son of
Zabdi, the son of Asaph,[l] the direc-
tor who led in thanksgiving and
prayer; Bakbukiah, second among
his associates; and Abda son of
Shammua, the son of Galal, the son
of Jeduthun.[m] 18The Levites in the
holy city[n] totalled 284.

19The gatekeepers:

Akkub, Talmon and their associ-
ates, who kept watch at the gates
—172 men.

20The rest of the Israelites, with the
priests and Levites, were in all the
towns of Judah, each on his ancestral
property.
21The temple servants[o] lived on the
hill of Ophel, and Ziha and Gishpa were
in charge of them.
22The chief officer of the Levites in
Jerusalem was Uzzi son of Bani, the son
of Hashabiah, the son of Mattaniah,[p]
the son of Mica. Uzzi was one of
Asaph's descendants, who were the
singers responsible for the service of the
house of God. 23The singers[q] were
under the king's orders, which reg-
ulated their daily activity.
24Pethahiah son of Meshezabel, one
of the descendants of Zerah[r] son of
Judah, was the king's agent in all affairs
relating to the people.
25As for the villages with their fields,
some of the people of Judah lived in
Kiriath Arba[s] and its surrounding settle-
ments, in Dibon[t] and its settlements, in
Jekabzeel and its villages, 26in Jeshua, in
Moladah,[u] in Beth Pelet,[v] 27in Hazar
Shual,[w] in Beersheba[x] and its settle-
ments, 28in Ziklag,[y] in Meconah and its
settlements, 29in En Rimmon, in Zorah,[z]
in Jarmuth,[a] 30Zanoah,[b] Adullam[c] and
their villages, in Lachish[d] and its fields,
and in Azekah[e] and its settlements. So
they were living all the way from Beer-
sheba[f] to the Valley of Hinnom.
31The descendants of the Benjamites
from Geba[g] lived in Michmash,[h] Aija,
Bethel[i] and its settlements, 32in Ana-
thoth,[j] Nob[k] and Ananiah, 33in Hazor,[l]
Ramah[m] and Gittaim,[n] 34in Hadid, Ze-
boim[o] and Neballat, 35in Lod and Ono,[p]
and in the Valley of the Craftsmen.
36Some of the divisions of the Levites
of Judah settled in Benjamin.

Priests and Levites

12 These were the priests[a] and
Levites[b] who returned with
Zerubbabel[c] son of Shealtiel[d] and with
Jeshua:[e]

Seraiah,[f] Jeremiah, Ezra,
2Amariah, Malluch, Hattush,
3Shecaniah, Rehum, Meremoth,
4Iddo,[g] Ginnethon,[a] Abijah,[h]
5Mijamin,[b] Moadiah, Bilgah,
6Shemaiah, Joiarib, Jedaiah,[i]
7Sallu, Amok, Hilkiah and Jedaiah.

These were the leaders of the priests
and their associates in the days of
Jeshua.
8The Levites were Jeshua,[j] Binnui,
Kadmiel, Sherebiah, Judah, and also
Mattaniah,[k] who, together with his
associates, was in charge of the songs of
thanksgiving. 9Bakbukiah and Unni,
their associates, stood opposite them in
the services.
10Jeshua was the father of Joiakim,
Joiakim the father of Eliashib,[l] Eliashib
the father of Joiada, 11Joiada the father
of Jonathan, and Jonathan the father of
Jaddua.
12In the days of Joiakim, these were
the heads of the priestly families:

of Seraiah's family, Meraiah;
of Jeremiah's, Hananiah;
13of Ezra's, Meshullam;
of Amariah's, Jehohanan;
14of Malluch's, Jonathan;
of Shecaniah's,[c] Joseph;
15of Harim's, Adna;
of Meremoth's,[d] Helkai;
16of Iddo's,[m] Zechariah;
of Ginnethon's, Meshullam;
17of Abijah's,[n] Zicri;
of Miniamin's and of Moadiah's,
Piltai;
18of Bilgah's, Shammua;
of Shemaiah's, Jehonathan;
19of Joiarib's, Mattenai;
of Jedaiah's, Uzzi;
20of Sallu's, Kallai;
of Amok's, Eber;
21of Hilkiah's, Hashabiah;
of Jedaiah's, Nethanel.

22The family heads of the Levites in
the days of Eliashib, Joiada, Johanan
and Jaddua, as well as those of the
priests, were recorded in the reign of
Darius the Persian. 23The family heads
among the descendants of Levi up to
the time of Johanan son of Eliashib were
recorded in the book of the annals.
24And the leaders of the Levites[o] were
Hashabiah, Sherebiah, Jeshua son of

17 [k]1Ch 9:15; Ne 12:8; [l]2Ch 5:12; [m]1Ch 25:1
18 [n]Rev 21:2
21 [o]Ezr 2:43; Ne 3:26
22 [p]1Ch 9:15
23 [q]1Ch 15:16; Ne 7:44
24 [r]Ge 38:30
25 [s]Ge 35:27; [t]Nu 21:30
26 [u]Jos 15:26; [v]Jos 15:27
27 [w]Jos 15:28; [x]Ge 21:14
28 [y]1Sa 27:6
29 [z]Jos 15:33; [a]Jos 10:3; 15:35
30 [b]Jos 15:34; [c]Jos 15:35; [d]Jos 10:3; 15:39; [e]Jos 10:10; [f]Jos 15:28
31 [g]Jos 21:17; Isa 10:29; [h]1Sa 13:2; [i]Jos 12:9
32 [j]Jos 21:18; Isa 10:30; Jer 1:1; [k]1Sa 21:1
33 [l]Jos 11:1; [m]Jos 18:25; [n]2Sa 4:3
34 [o]1Sa 13:18
35 [p]1Ch 8:12

Ch. 12

1 [a]Ne 10:1-8; [b]Ne 10:9; [c]1Ch 3:19; Ezr 3:2; Zec 4:6-10; [d]Ezr 3:2; [e]Ezr 2:2; [f]Ezr 2:2
4 [g]ver 16; Zec 1:1; [h]1Ch 24:10; Lk 1:5
6 [i]1Ch 24:7
8 [j]Ezr 2:2; [k]Ne 11:17
10 [l]Ezr 10:24; Ne 3:20
16 [m]ver 4
17 [n]1Ch 24:10
24 [o]Ezr 2:40

[a]4 Many Hebrew manuscripts and Vulgate (see also Neh. 12:16); most Hebrew manuscripts *Ginnethoi*
[b]5 A variant of *Miniamin*
[c]14 Very many Hebrew manuscripts, some Septuagint manuscripts and Syriac (see also Neh. 12:3); most Hebrew manuscripts *Shebaniah's*
[d]15 Some Septuagint manuscripts (see also Neh. 12:3); Hebrew *Meraioth's*

Kadmiel, and their associates, who stood opposite them to give praise and thanksgiving, one section responding to the other, as prescribed by David the man of God.[p]

25 Mattaniah, Bakbukiah, Obadiah, Meshullam, Talmon and Akkub were gatekeepers who guarded the storerooms at the gates. 26 They served in the days of Joiakim son of Jeshua, the son of Jozadak, and in the days of Nehemiah the governor and of Ezra the priest and scribe.

Dedication of the Wall of Jerusalem

27 At the dedication[q] of the wall of Jerusalem, the Levites were sought out from where they lived and were brought to Jerusalem to celebrate joyfully the dedication with songs of thanksgiving and with the music of cymbals,[r] harps and lyres.[s] 28 The singers also were brought together from the region around Jerusalem—from the villages of the Netophathites,[t] 29 from Beth Gilgal, and from the area of Geba and Azmaveth, for the singers had built villages for themselves around Jerusalem. 30 When the priests and Levites had purified themselves ceremonially, they purified the people,[u] the gates and the wall.

31 I had the leaders of Judah go up on top[e] of the wall. I also assigned two large choirs to give thanks. One was to proceed on top[f] of the wall to the right, towards the Dung Gate.[v] 32 Hoshaiah and half the leaders of Judah followed them, 33 along with Azariah, Ezra, Meshullam, 34 Judah, Benjamin,[w] Shemaiah, Jeremiah, 35 as well as some priests with trumpets,[x] and also Zechariah son of Jonathan, the son of Shemaiah, the son of Mattaniah, the son of Micaiah, the son of Zaccur, the son of Asaph, 36 and his associates—Shemaiah, Azarel, Milalai, Gilalai, Maai, Nethanel, Judah and Hanani—with musical instruments[y] ⌊prescribed by⌋ David the man of God.[z] Ezra[a] the scribe led the procession. 37 At the Fountain Gate[b] they continued directly up the steps of the City of David on the ascent to the wall and passed above the house of David to the Water Gate[c] on the east.

38 The second choir proceeded in the opposite direction. I followed them on top[g] of the wall, together with half the people—past the Tower of the Ovens[d] to the Broad Wall,[e] 39 over the Gate of Ephraim,[f] the Jeshanah[h] Gate,[g] the Fish Gate,[h] the Tower of Hananel[i] and the Tower of the Hundred,[j] as far as the Sheep Gate.[k] At the Gate of the Guard they stopped.

40 The two choirs that gave thanks then took their places in the house of God; so did I, together with half the officials, 41 as well as the priests—Eliakim, Maaseiah, Miniamin, Micaiah, Elioenai, Zechariah and Hananiah with their trumpets—42 and also Maaseiah, Shemaiah, Eleazar, Uzzi, Jehohanan, Malkijah, Elam and Ezer. The choirs sang under the direction of Jezrahiah. 43 And on that day they offered great sacrifices, rejoicing because God had given them great joy. The women and children also rejoiced. The sound of rejoicing in Jerusalem could be heard far away.

44 At that time men were appointed to be in charge of the storerooms[l] for the contributions, firstfruits and tithes.[m] From the fields around the towns they were to bring into the storerooms the portions required by the Law for the priests and the Levites, for Judah was pleased with the ministering priests and Levites.[n] 45 They performed the service of their God and the service of purification, as did also the singers and gatekeepers, according to the commands of David[o] and his son Solomon.[p] 46 For long ago, in the days of David and Asaph,[q] there had been directors for the singers and for the songs of praise[r] and thanksgiving to God. 47 So in the days of Zerubbabel and of Nehemiah, all Israel contributed the daily portions for the singers and gatekeepers. They also set aside the portion for the other Levites, and the Levites set aside the portion for the descendants of Aaron.[s]

Nehemiah's Final Reforms

13 On that day the Book of Moses was read aloud in the hearing of the people and there it was found written that no Ammonite or Moabite should ever be admitted into the assembly of God,[a] 2 because they had not met the Israelites with food and water but had hired Balaam[b] to call a curse down on them.[c] (Our God, however, turned the curse into a blessing.)[d] 3 When the people heard this law, they excluded from Israel all who were of foreign descent.[e]

24 [p]**2Ch 8:14**
27 [q]Dt 20:5; [r]**2Sa 6:5**; [s]**1Ch 15:16**,28; 25:6; Ps 92:3
28 [t]**1Ch 2:54**; 9:16
30 [u]Ex 19:10; Job 1:5
31 [v]Ne 2:13
34 [w]**Ezr 1:5**
35 [x]**Ezr 3:10**
36 [y]**1Ch 15:16**; [z]**2Ch 8:14**; [a]Ezr 7:6
37 [b]**Ne 2:14**; [c]**Ne 3:26**
38 [d]Ne 3:11; [e]Ne 3:8
39 [f]**2Ki 14:13**; [g]Ne 3:6; [h]**2Ch 33:14**; [i]**Ne 3:1**; [j]Ne 3:1; [k]**Ne 3:1**
44 [l]Ne 13:4,13; [m]**Lev 27:30**; [n]**Dt 18:8**
45 [o]**2Ch 8:14**; [p]**1Ch 6:31**; 23:5
46 [q]**2Ch 35:15**; [r]2Ch 29:27; Ps 137:4
47 [s]**Dt 18:8**

Ch. 13

1 [a]ver 23; Dt 23:3
2 [b]Nu 22:3–11; [c]**Nu 23:7**; **Dt 23:3**; [d]**Nu 23:11**; Dt 23:4–5
3 [e]ver 23; **Ne 9:2**

[e]31 Or *go alongside* [f]31 Or *proceed alongside*
[g]38 Or *them alongside* [h]39 Or *Old*

4Before this, Eliashib the priest had been put in charge of the storerooms[f] of the house of our God. He was closely associated with Tobiah,[g] 5and he had provided him with a large room formerly used to store the grain offerings and incense and temple articles, and also the tithes[h] of grain, new wine and oil prescribed for the Levites, singers and gatekeepers, as well as the contributions for the priests.

6But while all this was going on, I was not in Jerusalem, for in the thirty-second year of Artaxerxes[i] king of Babylon I had returned to the king. Some time later I asked his permission 7and came back to Jerusalem. Here I learned about the evil thing Eliashib[j] had done in providing Tobiah[k] a room in the courts of the house of God. 8I was greatly displeased and threw all Tobiah's household goods out of the room.[l] 9I gave orders to purify the rooms,[m] and then I put back into them the equipment of the house of God, with the grain offerings and the incense.[n]

10I also learned that the portions assigned to the Levites had not been given to them,[o] and that all the Levites and singers responsible for the service had gone back to their own fields.[p] 11So I rebuked the officials and asked them, "Why is the house of God neglected?"[q] Then I called them together and stationed them at their posts.

12All Judah brought the tithes[r] of grain, new wine and oil into the storerooms.[s] 13I put Shelemiah the priest, Zadok the scribe, and a Levite named Pedaiah in charge of the storerooms and made Hanan son of Zaccur, the son of Mattaniah, their assistant, because these men were considered trustworthy. They were made responsible for distributing the supplies to their brothers.[t]

14Remember[u] me for this, O my God, and do not blot out what I have so faithfully done for the house of my God and its services.

15In those days I saw men in Judah treading winepresses on the Sabbath and bringing in grain and loading it on donkeys, together with wine, grapes, figs and all other kinds of loads. And they were bringing all this into Jerusalem on the Sabbath.[v] Therefore I warned them against selling food on that day. 16Men from Tyre who lived in Jerusalem were bringing in fish and all kinds of merchandise and selling them in Jerusalem on the Sabbath[w] to the people of Judah. 17I rebuked the nobles of Judah and said to them, "What is this wicked thing you are doing—desecrating the Sabbath day? 18Didn't your forefathers do the same things, so that our God brought all this calamity upon us and upon this city?[x] Now you are stirring up more wrath against Israel by desecrating the Sabbath."[y]

19When evening shadows fell on the gates of Jerusalem before the Sabbath,[z] I ordered the doors to be shut and not opened until the Sabbath was over. I stationed some of my own men at the gates so that no load could be brought in on the Sabbath day. 20Once or twice the merchants and sellers of all kinds of goods spent the night outside Jerusalem. 21But I warned them and said, "Why do you spend the night by the wall? If you do this again, I will lay hands on you." From that time on they no longer came on the Sabbath. 22Then I commanded the Levites to purify themselves and go and guard the gates in order to keep the Sabbath day holy.

Remember[a] me for this also, O my God, and show mercy to me according to your great love.

23Moreover, in those days I saw men of Judah who had married[b] women from Ashdod, Ammon and Moab.[c] 24Half of their children spoke the language of Ashdod or the language of one of the other peoples, and did not know how to speak the language[d] of Judah. 25I rebuked them and called curses down on them. I beat some of the men and pulled out their hair. I made them take an oath[e] in God's name and said: "You are not to give your daughters in marriage to their sons, nor are you to take their daughters in marriage for your sons or for yourselves.[f] 26Was it not because of marriages like these that Solomon king of Israel sinned? Among the many nations there was no king like him.[g] He was loved by his God,[h] and God made him king over all Israel, but even he was led into sin by foreign women.[i] 27Must we hear now that you too are doing all this terrible wickedness and are being unfaithful to our God by marrying[j] foreign women?"

28One of the sons of Joiada son of Eliashib[k] the high priest was son-in-law to Sanballat[l] the Horonite. And I drove him away from me.

29Remember[m] them, O my God, because they defiled the priestly office and

4 [f]**Ne 12:44;** [g]Ne 2:10
5 [h]**Lev 27:30; Nu 18:21**
6 [i]**Ne 2:6**
7 [j]**Ezr 10:24;** [k]**Ne 2:10**
8 [l]Mt 21:12–13; Mk 11:15–17; Lk 19:45–46; Jn 2:13–16
9 [m]**1Ch 23:28; 2Ch 29:5;** [n]**Lev 2:1**
10 [o]**Dt 12:19;** [p]**2Ch 31:4**
11 [q]**Ne 10:37–39;** Hag 1:1–9; Mal 3:8–9
12 [r]**2Sa 31:6;** [s]**Dt 18:8;** 1Ki 7:51; **2Ch 31:5; Ne 10:37–39;** Mal 3:10
13 [t]**Ne 12:44;** Ac 6:1–5
14 [u]**Ge 8:1; 2Ki 20:3**
15 [v]Ex 20:8–11; **34:21;** Dt 5:12–15
16 [w]**Ne 10:31**
18 [x]Jer 44:23; [y]**Ne 10:31**
19 [z]Lev 23:32
22 [a]**Ge 8:1; Ne 1:8**
23 [b]Ezr 9:1–2; Mal 2:11; [c]**ver** 1,3; Ex 34:16; **Ru 1:4; Ne 10:30**
24 [d]Est 1:22; 3:12; 8:9
25 [e]**Ezr 10:5;** [f]**Ex 34:16**
26 [g]**1Ki 3:13; 2Ch 1:12;** [h]2Sa 12:25; [i]**Ex 34:16; 1Ki 11:3**
27 [j]Ezr 9:14
28 [k]**Ezr 10:24;** [l]**Ne 2:10**
29 [m]**Ne 1:8**

the covenant of the priesthood and of
the Levites.[n]

30So I purified the priests and the
Levites of everything foreign,[o] and
assigned them duties, each to his own
task. 31I also made provision for con-
tributions of wood[p] at designated times,
and for the firstfruits.[q]

Remember[r] me with favour, O my
God.

29 [n]Nu 3:12
30 [o]Ne 9:2
31 [p]Ne 10:34; [q]Ne 10:35–36; [r]Ge 8:1; Ne 1:8

Esther

Queen Vashti Deposed

1 This is what happened during the
time of Xerxes,[a][a] the Xerxes who
ruled over 127 provinces[b] stretching
from India to Cush:[b][c] 2At that time King
Xerxes reigned from his royal throne in
the citadel of Susa,[d] 3and in the third
year of his reign he gave a banquet[e] for
all his nobles and officials. The military
leaders of Persia and Media, the
princes, and the nobles of the provinces
were present.
4For a full 180 days he displayed the
vast wealth of his kingdom and the
splendour and glory of his majesty.
5When these days were over, the king
gave a banquet, lasting seven days,[f] in
the enclosed garden[g] of the king's
palace, for all the people from the least
to the greatest, who were in the citadel
of Susa. 6The garden had hangings of
white and blue linen, fastened with
cords of white linen and purple material
to silver rings on marble pillars. There
were couches[h] of gold and silver on a
mosaic pavement of porphyry, marble,
mother-of-pearl and other costly
stones. 7Wine was served in goblets of
gold, each one different from the other,
and the royal wine was abundant, in
keeping with the king's liberality.[i]
8By the king's command each guest
was allowed to drink in his own way,
for the king instructed all the wine
stewards to serve each man what he
wished.
9Queen Vashti also gave a banquet[j]
for the women in the royal palace of
King Xerxes.
10On the seventh day, when King
Xerxes was in high spirits[k] from wine,[l]
he commanded the seven eunuchs who
served him—Mehuman, Biztha, Har-
bona,[m] Bigtha, Abagtha, Zethar and
Carcas— 11to bring[n] before him Queen
Vashti, wearing her royal crown, in
order to display her beauty[o] to the
people and nobles, for she was lovely
to look at. 12But when the attendants
delivered the king's command, Queen
Vashti refused to come. Then the king
became furious and burned with
anger.[p]
13Since it was customary for the king
to consult experts in matters of law and
justice, he spoke with the wise men
who understood the times[q] 14and were
closest to the king—Carshena, Shethar,
Admatha, Tarshish, Meres, Marsena
and Memucan, the seven nobles[r] of
Persia and Media who had special
access to the king and were highest in
the kingdom.
15"According to law, what must be
done to Queen Vashti?" he asked. "She
has not obeyed the command of King
Xerxes that the eunuchs have taken to
her."
16Then Memucan replied in the pres-
ence of the king and the nobles, "Queen
Vashti has done wrong, not only
against the king but also against all the
nobles and the peoples of all the pro-
vinces of King Xerxes. 17For the queen's
conduct will become known to all the
women, and so they will despise their
husbands and say, 'King Xerxes com-
manded Queen Vashti to be brought
before him, but she would not come.'
18This very day the Persian and Median
women of the nobility who have heard
about the queen's conduct will respond
to all the king's nobles in the same way.
There will be no end of disrespect and
discord.[s]
19"Therefore, if it pleases the king,[t] let
him issue a royal decree and let it be
written in the laws of Persia and Media,
which cannot be repealed,[u] that Vashti
is never again to enter the presence of
King Xerxes. Also let the king give her
royal position to someone else who is
better than she. 20Then when the king's
edict is proclaimed throughout all his
vast realm, all the women will respect
their husbands, from the least to the
greatest."
21The king and his nobles were
pleased with this advice, so the king did

Ch. 1

1 [a]**Ezr 4:6;** [b]Est 9:30; Da 3:2; 6:1; [c]Est 8:9
2 [d]**Ezr 4:9; Est 2:8**
3 [e]**1Ki 3:15**
5 [f]Jdg 14:17; [g]**2Ki 21:18**
6 [h]Est 7:8; Eze 23:41; Am 3:12; 6:4
7 [i]Est 2:18; Da 5:2
9 [j]**1Ki 3:15**
10 [k]**Jdg 16:25; Ru 3:7;** [l]**Ge 14:18;** Est 3:15; 5:6; 7:2; Pr 31:4–7; Da 5:1–4; [m]Est 7:9
11 [n]SS 2:4; [o]Ps 45:11; Eze 16:14
12 [p]Ge 39:19; Est 2:21; 7:7; Pr 19:12
13 [q]1Ch 12:32
14 [r]Ezr 7:14
18 [s]Pr 19:13; 27:15
19 [t]Ecc 8:4; [u]Est 8:8; Da 6:8,12

[a]*1* Hebrew *Ahasuerus*, a variant of Xerxes' name; here and throughout Esther
[b]*1* That is, the upper Nile region

as Memucan proposed. 22He sent dispatches to all parts of the kingdom, to each province in its own script and to each people in its own language,[v] proclaiming in each people's tongue that every man should be ruler over his own household.

Esther Made Queen

2 Later when the anger of King Xerxes had subsided,[a] he remembered Vashti and what she had done and what he had decreed about her. 2Then the king's personal attendants proposed, "Let a search be made for beautiful young virgins for the king. 3Let the king appoint commissioners in every province of his realm to bring all these beautiful girls into the harem at the citadel of Susa. Let them be placed under the care of Hegai, the king's eunuch, who is in charge of the women; and let beauty treatments be given to them. 4Then let the girl who pleases the king be queen instead of Vashti." This advice appealed to the king, and he followed it.

5Now there was in the citadel of Susa a Jew of the tribe of Benjamin, named Mordecai son of Jair, the son of Shimei, the son of Kish,[b] 6who had been carried into exile from Jerusalem by Nebuchadnezzar king of Babylon, among those taken captive with Jehoiachin[a][c] king of Judah.[d] 7Mordecai had a cousin named Hadassah, whom he had brought up because she had neither father nor mother. This girl, who was also known as Esther,[e] was lovely[f] in form and features, and Mordecai had taken her as his own daughter when her father and mother died.

8When the king's order and edict had been proclaimed, many girls were brought to the citadel of Susa[g] and put under the care of Hegai. Esther also was taken to the king's palace and entrusted to Hegai, who had charge of the harem. 9The girl pleased him and won his favour.[h] Immediately he provided her with her beauty treatments and special food.[i] He assigned to her seven maids selected from the king's palace and moved her and her maids into the best place in the harem.

10Esther had not revealed her nationality and family background, because Mordecai had forbidden her to do so.[j] 11Every day he walked to and fro near the courtyard of the harem to find out how Esther was and what was happening to her.

12Before a girl's turn came to go in to King Xerxes, she had to complete twelve months of beauty treatments prescribed for the women, six months with oil of myrrh and six with perfumes[k] and cosmetics. 13And this is how she would go to the king: Anything she wanted was given to her to take with her from the harem to the king's palace. 14In the evening she would go there and in the morning return to another part of the harem to the care of Shaashgaz, the king's eunuch who was in charge of the concubines.[l] She would not return to the king unless he was pleased with her and summoned her by name.[m]

15When the turn came for Esther (the girl Mordecai had adopted, the daughter of his uncle Abihail[n]) to go to the king,[o] she asked for nothing other than what Hegai, the king's eunuch who was in charge of the harem, suggested. And Esther won the favour[p] of everyone who saw her. 16She was taken to King Xerxes in the royal residence in the tenth month, the month of Tebeth, in the seventh year of his reign.

17Now the king was attracted to Esther more than to any of the other women, and she won his favour and approval more than any of the other virgins. So he set a royal crown on her head and made her queen[q] instead of Vashti. 18And the king gave a great banquet,[r] Esther's banquet, for all his nobles and officials.[s] He proclaimed a holiday throughout the provinces and distributed gifts with royal liberality.[t]

Mordecai Uncovers a Conspiracy

19When the virgins were assembled a second time, Mordecai was sitting at the king's gate.[u] 20But Esther had kept secret her family background and nationality just as Mordecai had told her to do, for she continued to follow Mordecai's instructions as she had done when he was bringing her up.[v]

21During the time Mordecai was sitting at the king's gate, Bigthana[b] and Teresh, two of the king's officers[w] who guarded the doorway, became angry[x] and conspired to assassinate King Xerxes. 22But Mordecai found out about the plot and told Queen Esther, who in turn reported it to the king, giving credit to Mordecai. 23And when the report was investigated and found to be true, the

22 [v]**Ne 13:24**

Ch. 2

1 [a]Est 7:10
5 [b]**1Sa 9:1**
6 [c]**2Ki 24:15**; [d]Da 1:1–5; 5:13
7 [e]Ge 41:45; [f]**Ge 39:6**
8 [g]Ne 1:1; Est 1:2; Da 8:2
9 [h]**Ge 39:21**; [i]**Ge 37:3**; 1Sa 9:22–24; **2Ki 25:30**; Est 9:19; Eze 16:9–13; Da 1:5
10 [j]ver 20
12 [k]Pr 27:9; SS 1:3; Isa 3:24
14 [l]1Ki 11:3; SS 6:8; Da 5:2; [m]Est 4:11
15 [n]Est 9:29; [o]Ps 45:14; [p]**Ge 18:3**; **30:27**; Est 5:8; 7:3; 8:5
17 [q]Eze 16:9–13
18 [r]**1Ki 3:15**; [s]**Ge 40:20**; [t]**Est 1:7**
19 [u]Est 4:2; 5:13
20 [v]ver 10
21 [w]**Ge 40:2**; [x]**Est 1:12**; 3:5; 5:9; 7:7

[a]6 Hebrew *Jeconiah*, a variant of *Jehoiachin*
[b]21 Hebrew *Bigthan*, a variant of *Bigthana*

two officials were hanged[y] on a gal-
lows.[c] All this was recorded in the book
of the annals[z] in the presence of the
king.[a]

Haman's Plot to Destroy the Jews

3 After these events, King Xerxes
honoured Haman son of Hamme-
datha, the Agagite,[a] elevating him and
giving him a seat of honour higher than
that of all the other nobles. 2All the royal
officials at the king's gate knelt down
and paid honour to Haman, for the king
had commanded this concerning him.
But Mordecai would not kneel down or
pay him honour.
3Then the royal officials at the king's
gate asked Mordecai, "Why do you dis-
obey the king's command?"[b] 4Day after
day they spoke to him but he refused to
comply.[c] Therefore they told Haman
about it to see whether Mordecai's
behaviour would be tolerated, for he
had told them he was a Jew.
5When Haman saw that Mordecai
would not kneel down or pay him
honour, he was enraged.[d] 6Yet having
learned who Mordecai's people were,
he scorned the idea of killing only Mor-
decai. Instead Haman looked for a way[e]
to destroy[f] all Mordecai's people, the
Jews,[g] throughout the whole kingdom
of Xerxes.
7In the twelfth year of King Xerxes, in
the first month, the month of Nisan,
they cast the *pur*[h] (that is, the lot[i]) in the
presence of Haman to select a day and
month. And the lot fell on [a] the twelfth
month, the month of Adar.[j]
8Then Haman said to King Xerxes,
"There is a certain people dispersed and
scattered among the peoples in all the
provinces of your kingdom whose
customs[k] are different from those of all
other people and who do not obey[l] the
king's laws; it is not in the king's best
interest to tolerate them.[m] 9If it pleases
the king, let a decree be issued to de-
stroy them, and I will put ten thousand
talents[b] of silver into the royal treasury
for the men who carry out this
business."[n]
10So the king took his signet ring[o]
from his finger and gave it to Haman
son of Hammedatha, the Agagite, the
enemy of the Jews. 11"Keep the
money," the king said to Haman, "and
do with the people as you please."
12Then on the thirteenth day of the
first month the royal secretaries were
summoned. They wrote out in the script
of each province and in the language[p] of
each people all Haman's orders to the
king's satraps, the governors of the
various provinces and the nobles of the
various peoples. These were written in
the name of King Xerxes himself and
sealed[q] with his own ring. 13Dispatches
were sent by couriers to all the king's
provinces with the order to destroy, kill
and annihilate all the Jews[r]—young and
old, women and little children—on a
single day, the thirteenth day of the
twelfth month, the month of Adar,[s] and
to plunder[t] their goods. 14A copy of the
text of the edict was to be issued as law
in every province and made known to
the people of every nationality so that
they would be ready for that day.[u]
15Spurred on by the king's command,
the couriers went out, and the edict was
issued in the citadel of Susa.[v] The king
and Haman sat down to drink,[w] but the
city of Susa was bewildered.[x]

Mordecai Persuades Esther to Help

4 When Mordecai learned of all
that had been done, he tore his
clothes,[a] put on sackcloth and ashes,[b]
and went out into the city, wailing[c]
loudly and bitterly. 2But he went only
as far as the king's gate,[d] because no-
one clothed in sackcloth was allowed to
enter it. 3In every province to which the
edict and order of the king came, there
was great mourning among the Jews,
with fasting, weeping and wailing.
Many lay in sackcloth and ashes.
4When Esther's maids and eunuchs
came and told her about Mordecai, she
was in great distress. She sent clothes
for him to put on instead of his sack-
cloth, but he would not accept them.
5Then Esther summoned Hathach, one
of the king's eunuchs assigned to attend
her, and ordered him to find out what
was troubling Mordecai and why.
6So Hathach went out to Mordecai in
the open square of the city in front of the
king's gate. 7Mordecai told him every-
thing that had happened to him, includ-
ing the exact amount of money Haman
had promised to pay into the royal
treasury for the destruction of the Jews.[e]
8He also gave him a copy of the text of
the edict for their annihilation, which
had been published in Susa, to show to
Esther and explain it to her, and he told
him to urge her to go into the king's

2:23 [y]**Ge 40:19; Dt 21:22–23;** Ps 7:14–16; Pr 26:27; Ecc 10:8; [z]Est 6:1; 10:2; [a]Est 6:2

Ch. 3

1 [a]**Ex 17:8–16; Nu 24:7;** Dt 25:17–19; 1Sa 14:48
3 [b]Est 5:9; Da 3:12
4 [c]Ge 39:10
5 [d]**Est 2:21**
6 [e]Pr 16:25; [f]Ps 74:8; 83:4; [g]Est 9:24
7 [h]Est 9:24,26; [i]**Lev 16:8; 1Sa 10:21;** [j]ver 13; Est 9:19
8 [k]Ac 16:20–21; [l]Jer 29:7; Da 6:13; [m]Ezr 4:15
9 [n]Est 7:4
10 [o]**Ge 41:42**
12 [p]**Ne 13:24;** [q]**Ge 38:18**
13 [r]**1Sa 15:3; Ezr 4:6;** [s]**ver 7;** [t]Est 8:11; 9:10
14 [u]Est 8:8; 9:1
15 [v]Est 8:14; [w]**Est 1:10;** [x]Est 8:15

Ch. 4

1 [a]**Nu 14:6;** [b]**2Sa 13:19;** Eze 27:30–31; [c]**Ex 11:6;** Ps 30:11
2 [d]**Est 2:19**
7 [e]Est 7:4

[c]23 Or *were hung* (or *impaled*) *on poles;* similarly elsewhere in Esther
[a]7 Septuagint; Hebrew does not have *And the lot fell on.*
[b]9 That is, about 340 tons (about 345 metric tons)

presence to beg for mercy and plead with him for her people.

9Hathach went back and reported to Esther what Mordecai had said. 10Then she instructed him to say to Mordecai, 11"All the king's officials and the people of the royal provinces know that for any man or woman who approaches the king in the inner court without being summoned[f] the king has but one law:[g] that he be put to death. The only exception to this is for the king to extend the gold sceptre[h] to him and spare his life. But thirty days have passed since I was called to go to the king."

12When Esther's words were reported to Mordecai, 13he sent back this answer: "Do not think that because you are in the king's house you alone of all the Jews will escape. 14For if you remain silent[i] at this time, relief[j] and deliverance[k] for the Jews will arise from another place, but you and your father's family will perish. And who knows but that you have come to royal position for such a time as this?"[l]

15Then Esther sent this reply to Mordecai: 16"Go, gather together all the Jews who are in Susa, and fast[m] for me. Do not eat or drink for three days, night or day. I and my maids will fast as you do. When this is done, I will go to the king, even though it is against the law. And if I perish, I perish."[n]

17So Mordecai went away and carried out all of Esther's instructions.

Esther's Request to the King

5 On the third day Esther put on her royal robes[a] and stood in the inner court of the palace, in front of the king's[b] hall. The king was sitting on his royal throne in the hall, facing the entrance. 2When he saw Queen Esther standing in the court, he was pleased with her and held out to her the gold sceptre that was in his hand. So Esther approached and touched the tip of the sceptre.[c]

3Then the king asked, "What is it, Queen Esther? What is your request? Even up to half the kingdom,[d] it will be given you."

4"If it pleases the king," replied Esther, "let the king, together with Haman, come today to a banquet I have prepared for him."

5"Bring Haman at once," the king said, "so that we may do what Esther asks."

So the king and Haman went to the banquet Esther had prepared. 6As they were drinking wine,[e] the king again asked Esther, "Now what is your petition? It will be given you. And what is your request? Even up to half the kingdom,[f] it will be granted."[g]

7Esther replied, "My petition and my request is this: 8If the king regards me with favour[h] and if it pleases the king to grant my petition and fulfil my request, let the king and Haman come tomorrow to the banquet[i] I will prepare for them. Then I will answer the king's question."

Haman's Rage Against Mordecai

9Haman went out that day happy and in high spirits. But when he saw Mordecai at the king's gate and observed that he neither rose nor showed fear in his presence, he was filled with rage[j] against Mordecai.[k] 10Nevertheless, Haman restrained himself and went home.

Calling together his friends and Zeresh,[l] his wife, 11Haman boasted[m] to them about his vast wealth, his many sons,[n] and all the ways the king had honoured him and how he had elevated him above the other nobles and officials. 12"And that's not all," Haman added. "I'm the only person[o] Queen Esther invited to accompany the king to the banquet she gave. And she has invited me along with the king tomorrow. 13But all this gives me no satisfaction as long as I see that Jew Mordecai sitting at the king's gate.[p]"

14His wife Zeresh and all his friends said to him, "Have a gallows built, seventy-five feet[a] high,[q] and ask the king in the morning to have Mordecai hanged[r] on it. Then go with the king to the dinner and be happy." This suggestion delighted Haman, and he had the gallows built.

Mordecai Honoured

6 That night the king could not sleep;[a] so he ordered the book of the chronicles,[b] the record of his reign, to be brought in and read to him. 2It was found recorded there that Mordecai had exposed Bigthana and Teresh, two of the king's officers who guarded the doorway, who had conspired to assassinate King Xerxes.[c]

3"What honour and recognition has Mordecai received for this?" the king asked.

"Nothing has been done for him,"[d] his attendants answered.

11 [f]Est 2:14; [g]Da 2:9; [h]Est 5:2; 8:4; Ps 125:3
14 [i]Job 34:29; Ps 28:1; 35:22; Ecc 3:7; Isa 42:14; 57:11; 62:1; 64:12; Am 5:13; [j]Est 9:16,22; [k]**Ge 45:7**; **Dt 28:29**; [l]**Ge 50:20**
16 [m]**2Ch 20:3**; Est 9:31; [n]**Ge 43:14**

Ch. 5

1 [a]Eze 16:13; [b]Pr 21:1
2 [c]**Est 4:11**
3 [d]Est 7:2; Da 5:16; Mk 6:23
6 [e]**Est 1:10**; [f]Da 5:16; Mk 6:23; [g]Est 9:12
8 [h]**Est 2:15**; [i]**1Ki 3:15**
9 [j]**Est 2:21**; Pr 14:17; [k]**Est 3:3**
10 [l]Est 6:13
11 [m]Pr 13:16; [n]Est 9:10,13
12 [o]Job 22:29; Pr 16:18; 29:23
13 [p]**Est 2:19**
14 [q]Est 7:9; [r]**Ezr 6:11**

Ch. 6

1 [a]Da 2:1; 6:18; [b]**Est 2:23**
2 [c]Est 2:21–23
3 [d]Ecc 9:13–16

[a]14 Hebrew *fifty cubits* (about 23 metres)

4The king said, "Who is in the court?"
Now Haman had just entered the outer
court of the palace to speak to the king
about hanging Mordecai on the gallows
he had erected for him.
5His attendants answered, "Haman is
standing in the court."
"Bring him in," the king ordered.
6When Haman entered, the king
asked him, "What should be done for
the man the king delights to honour?"
Now Haman thought to himself,
"Who is there that the king would
rather honour than me?" 7So he
answered the king, "For the man the
king delights to honour, 8have them
bring a royal robe[e] the king has worn
and a horse[f] the king has ridden, one
with a royal crest placed on its head.
9Then let the robe and horse be en-
trusted to one of the king's most noble
princes. Let them robe the man the king
delights to honour, and lead him on the
horse through the city streets, proclaim-
ing before him, 'This is what is done for
the man the king delights to honour![g]' "
10"Go at once," the king commanded
Haman. "Get the robe and the horse
and do just as you have suggested for
Mordecai the Jew, who sits at the king's
gate. Do not neglect anything you have
recommended."
11So Haman got[h] the robe and the
horse. He robed Mordecai, and led him
on horseback through the city streets,
proclaiming before him, "This is what is
done for the man the king delights to
honour!"
12Afterwards Mordecai returned to
the king's gate. But Haman rushed
home, with his head covered,[i] in grief,
13and told Zeresh[j] his wife and all his
friends everything that had happened
to him.
His advisers and his wife Zeresh said
to him, "Since Mordecai, before whom
your downfall[k] has started, is of Jewish
origin, you cannot stand against him
—you will surely come to ruin!"[l]
14While they were still talking with him,
the king's eunuchs arrived and hurried
Haman away to the banquet[m] Esther
had prepared.

Haman Hanged

7 So the king and Haman went to
dine[a] with Queen Esther, 2and as
they were drinking wine[b] on that
second day, the king again asked,
"Queen Esther, what is your petition? It
will be given you. What is your request?
Even up to half the kingdom,[c] it will be
granted.[d]"
3Then Queen Esther answered, "If I
have found favour[e] with you, O king,
and if it pleases your majesty, grant me
my life—this is my petition. And spare
my people—this is my request. 4For I
and my people have been sold for de-
struction and slaughter and annihil-
ation.[f] If we had merely been sold as
male and female slaves, I would have
kept quiet, because no such distress
would justify disturbing the king."[a]
5King Xerxes asked Queen Esther,
"Who is he? Where is the man who has
dared to do such a thing?"
6Esther said, "The adversary and
enemy is this vile Haman."
Then Haman was terrified before the
king and queen. 7The king got up in a
rage,[g] left his wine and went out into the
palace garden.[h] But Haman, realising
that the king had already decided his
fate,[i] stayed behind to beg Queen
Esther for his life.
8Just as the king returned from the
palace garden to the banquet hall,
Haman was falling on the couch[j]
where Esther was reclining.[k]
The king exclaimed, "Will he even
molest the queen while she is with me in
the house?"[l]
As soon as the word left the king's
mouth, they covered Haman's face.[m]
9Then Harbona,[n] one of the eunuchs
attending the king, said, "A gallows
seventy-five feet[b] high[o] stands by
Haman's house. He had it made for
Mordecai, who spoke up to help the
king."
The king said, "Hang him on it!"[p] 10So
they hanged[q] Haman[r] on the gallows[s]
he had prepared for Mordecai.[t] Then
the king's fury subsided.[u]

The King's Edict on Behalf of the Jews

8 That same day King Xerxes
gave Queen Esther the estate of
Haman,[a] the enemy of the Jews. And
Mordecai came into the presence of the
king, for Esther had told how he was
related to her. 2The king took off his
signet ring,[b] which he had reclaimed
from Haman, and presented it to Mor-
decai. And Esther appointed him over
Haman's estate.[c]
3Esther again pleaded with the king,
falling at his feet and weeping. She beg-
ged him to put an end to the evil plan of

6:8 [e]**Ge 41:42; Isa 52:1;** [f]1Ki 1:33
6:9 [g]Ge 41:43
6:11 [h]**Ge 41:42**
6:12 [i]2Sa 15:30; Est 7:8; Jer 14:3–4; Mic 3:7
6:13 [j]Est 5:10; [k]Ps 57:6; Pr 26:27; 28:18; [l]Est 7:7
6:14 [m]**1Ki 3:15**

Ch. 7

7:1 [a]Ge 40:20–22; Mt 22:1–14
7:2 [b]**Est 1:10;** [c]**Est 5:3;** [d]Est 9:12
7:3 [e]**Est 2:15**
7:4 [f]Est 3:9; **4:7**
7:7 [g]**Ge 34:7; Est 1:12;** Pr 19:12; 20:1–2; [h]**2Ki 21:18;** [i]Est 6:13
7:8 [j]**Est 1:6;** [k]Ge 39:14; Jn 13:23; [l]**Ge 34:7;** [m]**Est 6:12**
7:9 [n]Est 1:10; [o]Est 5:14; [p]**Dt 21:22–23;** Ps 7:14–16; 9:16; Pr 11:5–6; **26:27; Mt 7:2**
7:10 [q]Ge 40:22; [r]Pr 10:28; [s]Est 9:25; [t]Da 6:24; [u]Est 2:1

Ch. 8

8:1 [a]Pr 22:22–23
8:2 [b]**Ge 24:22; 41:42;** [c]**Ge 41:41;** Pr 13:22; 14:35; Da 2:48

[a]4 Or *quiet, but the compensation our adversary offers cannot be compared with the loss the king would suffer*
[b]9 Hebrew *fifty cubits* (about 23 metres)

Haman the Agagite,[d] which he had devised against the Jews. 4Then the king extended the gold sceptre[e] to Esther and she arose and stood before him.

5"If it pleases the king," she said, "and if he regards me with favour[f] and thinks it the right thing to do, and if he is pleased with me, let an order be written overruling the dispatches that Haman son of Hammedatha, the Agagite, devised and wrote to destroy the Jews in all the king's provinces. 6For how can I bear to see disaster fall on my people? How can I bear to see the destruction of my family?"[g]

7King Xerxes replied to Queen Esther and to Mordecai the Jew, "Because Haman attacked the Jews, I have given his estate to Esther, and they have hanged[h] him on the gallows. 8Now write another decree[i] in the king's name on behalf of the Jews as seems best to you, and seal[j] it with the king's signet ring[k]—for no document written in the king's name and sealed with his ring can be revoked."[l]

9At once the royal secretaries were summoned—on the twenty-third day of the third month, the month of Sivan. They wrote out all Mordecai's orders to the Jews, and to the satraps, governors and nobles of the 127 provinces stretching from India to Cush.[a][m] These orders were written in the script of each province and the language of each people and also to the Jews in their own script and language.[n] 10Mordecai wrote in the name of King Xerxes, sealed the dispatches with the king's signet ring, and sent them by mounted couriers, who rode fast horses especially bred for the king.

11The king's edict granted the Jews in every city the right to assemble and protect themselves; to destroy, kill and annihilate any armed force of any nationality or province that might attack them and their women and children; and to plunder[o] the property of their enemies. 12The day appointed for the Jews to do this in all the provinces of King Xerxes was the thirteenth day of the twelfth month, the month of Adar.[p] 13A copy of the text of the edict was to be issued as law in every province and made known to the people of every nationality so that the Jews would be ready on that day[q] to avenge themselves on their enemies.

14The couriers, riding the royal horses, raced out, spurred on by the king's command. And the edict was also issued in the citadel of Susa.[r]

15Mordecai[s] left the king's presence wearing royal garments of blue and white, a large crown of gold[t] and a purple robe of fine linen.[u] And the city of Susa held a joyous celebration.[v] 16For the Jews it was a time of happiness and joy,[w] gladness and honour.[x] 17In every province and in every city, wherever the edict of the king went, there was joy[y] and gladness among the Jews, with feasting and celebrating. And many people of other nationalities became Jews because fear[z] of the Jews had seized them.[a]

Triumph of the Jews

9 On the thirteenth day of the twelfth month, the month of Adar,[a] the edict commanded by the king was to be carried out. On this day the enemies of the Jews had hoped to overpower them, but now the tables were turned and the Jews got the upper hand[b] over those who hated them.[c] 2The Jews assembled in their cities[d] in all the provinces of King Xerxes to attack those seeking their destruction. No-one could stand against them,[e] because the people of all the other nationalities were afraid of them. 3And all the nobles of the provinces, the satraps, the governors and the king's administrators helped the Jews,[f] because fear of Mordecai had seized them.[g] 4Mordecai[h] was prominent[i] in the palace; his reputation spread throughout the provinces, and he became more and more powerful.[j]

5The Jews struck down all their enemies with the sword, killing and destroying them,[k] and they did what they pleased to those who hated them. 6In the citadel of Susa, the Jews killed and destroyed five hundred men. 7They also killed Parshandatha, Dalphon, Aspatha, 8Poratha, Adalia, Aridatha, 9Parmashta, Arisai, Aridai and Vaizatha, 10the ten sons[l] of Haman son of Hammedatha, the enemy of the Jews.[m] But they did not lay their hands on the plunder.[n]

11The number of those slain in the citadel of Susa was reported to the king that same day. 12The king said to Queen Esther, "The Jews have killed and destroyed five hundred men and the ten sons of Haman in the citadel of Susa. What have they done in the rest of the king's provinces? Now what is your petition? It will be given you. What is your request? It will also be granted."[o]

3 [d]Ex 17:8–16
4 [e]Est 4:11
5 [f]Est 2:15
6 [g]Ge 44:34
7 [h]Dt 21:22–23
8 [i]Est 3:12–14; [j]Ge 38:18; [k]Ge 41:42; [l]Est 1:19; Da 6:15
9 [m]Est 1:1; [n]Ne 13:24
11 [o]Ge 14:23; Est 3:13; 9:15–16
12 [p]Est 3:13; 9:1
13 [q]Est 3:14
14 [r]Est 3:15
15 [s]Est 9:4; 10:2; [t]2Sa 12:30; [u]Ge 41:42; [v]Est 3:15
16 [w]Ps 97:10–12; [x]Est 4:1–3; Ps 112:4; Jer 29:4–7
17 [y]Ps 35:27; 45:15; 51:8; Pr 11:10; [z]Ex 15:14,16; Dt 11:25; Da 6:26; [a]Est 9:3

Ch. 9

1 [a]Est 8:12; [b]Jer 29:4–7; [c]Est 3:12–14; Pr 22:22–23
2 [d]Ge 22:17; [e]Ps 35:26; 40:14; 70:2; 71:13,24
3 [f]Ezr 8:36; [g]Est 8:17
4 [h]Est 8:15; [i]Ex 11:3; [j]2Sa 3:1; 1Ch 11:9
5 [k]Dt 25:17–19; 1Sa 15:3; Ezr 4:6
10 [l]Est 5:11; Ps 127:3–5; [m]1Sa 15:33; [n]Ge 14:23; 1Sa 14:32; Est 3:13
12 [o]Est 5:6; 7:2

[a]9 That is, the upper Nile region

13"If it pleases the king," Esther
answered, "give the Jews in Susa per-
mission to carry out this day's edict
tomorrow also, and let Haman's ten
sons[p] be hanged[q] on gallows."
14So the king commanded that this be
done. An edict was issued in Susa, and
they hanged[r] the ten sons of Haman.
15The Jews in Susa came together on the
fourteenth day of the month of Adar,
and they put to death in Susa three
hundred men, but they did not lay their
hands on the plunder.[s]
16Meanwhile, the remainder of the
Jews who were in the king's provinces
also assembled to protect themselves
and get relief[t] from their enemies.[u] They
killed seventy-five thousand of them[v]
but did not lay their hands on the plun-
der.[w] 17This happened on the thirteenth
day of the month of Adar, and on the
fourteenth they rested and made it a
day of feasting[x] and joy.

Purim Celebrated

18The Jews in Susa, however, had
assembled on the thirteenth and four-
teenth, and then on the fifteenth they
rested and made it a day of feasting and
joy.
19That is why rural Jews—those living
in villages—observe the fourteenth of
the month of Adar[y] as a day of joy and
feasting, a day for giving presents to
each other.[z]
20Mordecai recorded these events,
and he sent letters to all the Jews
throughout the provinces of King
Xerxes, near and far, 21to have them
celebrate annually the fourteenth and
fifteenth days of the month of Adar 22as
the time when the Jews got relief[a] from
their enemies, and as the month when
their sorrow was turned into joy and
their mourning into a day of celebra-
tion.[b] He wrote to them to observe the
days as days of feasting and joy and
giving presents of food[c] to one another
and gifts to the poor.[d]
23So the Jews agreed to continue the
celebration they had begun, doing what
Mordecai had written to them. 24For
Haman son of Hammedatha, the Agag-
ite,[e] the enemy of all the Jews, had
plotted against the Jews to destroy them
and had cast the *pur*[f] (that is, the lot[g]) for
their ruin and destruction.[h] 25But when
the plot came to the king's attention,[a] he
issued written orders that the evil
scheme Haman had devised against the
Jews should come back on to his own
head,[i] and that he and his sons should
be hanged[j] on the gallows.[k] 26(Therefore
these days were called Purim, from the
word *pur*.[l]) Because of everything writ-
ten in this letter and because of what
they had seen and what had happened
to them, 27the Jews took it upon them-
selves to establish the custom that they
and their descendants and all who join
them should without fail observe these
two days every year, in the way pre-
scribed and at the time appointed.
28These days should be remembered
and observed in every generation by
every family, and in every province and
in every city. And these days of Purim
should never cease to be celebrated by
the Jews, nor should the memory of
them die out among their descendants.
29So Queen Esther, daughter of Abi-
hail,[m] along with Mordecai the Jew,
wrote with full authority to confirm this
second letter concerning Purim. 30And
Mordecai sent letters to all the Jews in
the 127 provinces[n] of the kingdom of
Xerxes—words of good will and assur-
ance—31to establish these days of
Purim at their designated times, as Mor-
decai the Jew and Queen Esther had
decreed for them, and as they had
established for themselves and their
descendants in regard to their times of
fasting[o] and lamentation.[p] 32Esther's de-
cree confirmed these regulations about
Purim, and it was written down in the
records.

The Greatness of Mordecai

10 King Xerxes imposed tribute
throughout the empire, to its
distant shores.[a] 2And all his acts of
power and might, together with a full
account of the greatness of Mordecai[b] to
which the king had raised him,[c] are they
not written in the book of the annals[d]
of the kings of Media and Persia?
3Mordecai the Jew was second[e] in rank[f]
to King Xerxes,[g] pre-eminent among the
Jews, and held in high esteem by his
many fellow Jews, because he worked
for the good of his people and spoke up
for the welfare of all the Jews.[h]

13 [p]Est 5:11; [q]Dt 21:22–23
14 [r]Ezr 6:11
15 [s]Ge 14:23; Est 8:11
16 [t]Est 4:14; [u]Dt 25:19; [v]1Ch 4:43; [w]Est 8:11
17 [x]1Ki 3:15
19 [y]Est 3:7; [z]Est 2:9; Rev 11:10
22 [a]Est 4:14; [b]Ne 8:12; Ps 30:11–12; [c]2Ki 25:30; [d]Ne 8:10
24 [e]Ex 17:8–16; [f]Est 3:7; [g]Lev 16:8; [h]Est 3:6
25 [i]Ps 7:16; [j]Dt 21:22–23; [k]Est 7:10
26 [l]Est 3:7
29 [m]Est 2:15
30 [n]Est 1:1
31 [o]Est 4:16; [p]Est 4:1–3

Ch. 10

1 [a]Ps 72:10; 97:1
2 [b]Est 8:15; [c]Ge 41:44; [d]Est 2:23
3 [e]Da 5:7; [f]Ge 41:43; [g]Ge 41:40; [h]Ne 2:10; Jer 29:4–7; Da 6:3

[a]25 Or *when Esther came before the king*

Job

Prologue

1 In the land of Uz[a] there lived a man whose name was Job.[b] This man was blameless[c] and upright;[d] he feared God[e] and shunned evil.[f] 2He had seven sons[g] and three daughters,[h] 3and he owned seven thousand sheep, three thousand camels, five hundred yoke of oxen and five hundred donkeys,[i] and had a large number of servants.[j] He was the greatest man[k] among all the people of the East.[l]

4His sons used to take turns holding feasts[m] in their homes, and they would invite their three sisters to eat and drink with them. 5When a period of feasting had run its course, Job would send and have them purified.[n] Early in the morning he would sacrifice a burnt offering[o] for each of them, thinking, "Perhaps my children have sinned[p] and cursed God[q] in their hearts." This was Job's regular custom.

Job's First Test

6One day the angels[a][r] came to present themselves before the LORD, and Satan[b][s] also came with them.[t] 7The LORD said to Satan, "Where have you come from?"

Satan answered the LORD, "From roaming through the earth and going to and fro in it."[u]

8Then the LORD said to Satan, "Have you considered my servant Job?[v] There is no-one on earth like him; he is blameless and upright, a man who fears God[w] and shuns evil."[x]

9"Does Job fear God for nothing?"[y] Satan replied. 10"Have you not put a hedge[z] around him and his household and everything he has?[a] You have blessed the work of his hands, so that his flocks and herds are spread throughout the land.[b] 11But stretch out your hand and strike everything he has,[c] and he will surely curse you to your face."[d]

12The LORD said to Satan, "Very well, then, everything he has[e] is in your hands, but on the man himself do not lay a finger."[f]

Then Satan went out from the presence of the LORD.

13One day when Job's sons and daughters[g] were feasting[h] and drinking wine at the oldest brother's house, 14a messenger came to Job and said, "The oxen were ploughing and the donkeys were grazing[i] nearby, 15and the Sabeans[j] attacked and carried them off. They put the servants to the sword, and I am the only one who has escaped to tell you!"

16While he was still speaking, another messenger came and said, "The fire of God fell from the sky[k] and burned up the sheep and the servants,[l] and I am the only one who has escaped to tell you!"

17While he was still speaking, another messenger came and said, "The Chaldeans[m] formed three raiding parties and swept down on your camels and carried them off. They put the servants to the sword, and I am the only one who has escaped to tell you!"

18While he was still speaking, yet another messenger came and said, "Your sons and daughters[n] were feasting[o] and drinking wine at the oldest brother's house, 19when suddenly a mighty wind[p] swept in from the desert and struck the four corners of the house. It collapsed on them and they are dead,[q] and I am the only one who has escaped to tell you!"[r]

20At this, Job got up and tore his robe[s] and shaved his head.[t] Then he fell to the ground in worship[u] 21and said:

"Naked I came from my mother's
    womb,
  and naked I shall depart.[c][v]

Ch. 1

1 [a]**Ge 10:23;** [b]Eze 14:14,20; Jas 5:11; [c]**Ge 6:9; Job 23:10;** [d]Job 23:7; Ps 11:7; 107:42; Pr 21:29; Mic 7:2; [e]**Ge 22:12;** [f]ver 8; **Dt 4:6;** Job 2:3; 1Th 5:22
2 [g]**Ru 4:15;** [h]ver 13,18; Job 42:13; Ps 127:3; 144:12
3 [i]**Ge 13:2;** [j]**Ge 12:16;** [k]ver 8; Job 29:25; [l]**Ge 25:6;** Job 42:10; Ps 103:10
4 [m]ver 13,18
5 [n]**Ne 12:30;** [o]**Ge 8:20;** [p]Job 8:4; [q]1Ki 21:10,13; Ps 10:3; 74:10
6 [r]**1Ki 22:19;** *fn* Ge 6:2; [s]**2Sa 24:1; 2Ch 18:21; Ps 109:6;** Lk 22:31; [t]Job 2:1
7 [u]**Ge 3:1;** 1Pe 5:8
8 [v]**Jos 1:7;** [w]Ps 25:12; 112:1; 128:4; [x]**ver 1; Ex 20:20**
9 [y]1Ti 6:5
10 [z]**1Sa 25:16;** [a]ver 12; Job 2:4; Ps 34:7; [b]ver 3; Job 8:7; 29:6; 42:12,17
11 [c]Job 19:21; Lk 22:31; [d]Lev 24:11; Job 2:5; Isa 3:8; 65:3; Rev 12:9–10
12 [e]**ver 10;** [f]Job 2:6; 1Co 10:13
13 [g]**ver 2;** [h]**ver 4**
14 [i]Ge 36:24
15 [j]**Ge 10:7; Job 9:24**
16 [k]**1Ki 18:38;** 2Ki 1:12; Job 20:26; [l]**Ge 18:17; Lev 10:2; Nu 11:1–3**
17 [m]**Ge 11:28; Job 9:24**
18 [n]**ver 2;** [o]**ver 4**
19 [p]Ps 11:6; Isa 5:28; 21:1; Jer 4:11; 13:24; 18:17; Eze 17:10; Hos 13:15; Mt 7:25; [q]Job 16:7; 19:13–15; [r]Eze 24:26
20 [s]**Ge 37:29; Mk 14:63;** [t]Isa 3:24; 15:2; 22:12; Jer 7:29; 16:6; Eze 27:31; 29:18; Mic 1:16; [u]1Pe 5:6
21 [v]Ecc 5:15; 1Ti 6:7

[a]6 Hebrew *the sons of God*
[b]6 *Satan* means *accuser.*
[c]21 Or *shall return there*

The LORD gave and the LORD has taken
away;[w]
may the name of the LORD be
praised."[x]

22In all this, Job did not sin by
charging God with wrongdoing.[y]

Job's Second Test

2 On another day the angels[a][a] came
to present themselves before the
LORD, and Satan also came with them[b] to
present himself before him. 2And the
LORD said to Satan, "Where have you
come from?"

Satan answered the LORD, "From
roaming through the earth and going to
and fro in it."[c]

3Then the LORD said to Satan, "Have
you considered my servant Job? There is
no-one on earth like him; he is blame-
less and upright, a man who fears God
and shuns evil.[d] And he still maintains
his integrity,[e] though you incited me
against him to ruin him without any
reason."[f]

4"Skin for skin!" Satan replied. "A
man will give all he has[g] for his own life.
5But stretch out your hand and strike his
flesh and bones,[h] and he will surely
curse you to your face."[i]

6The LORD said to Satan, "Very well,
then, he is in your hands;[j] but you must
spare his life."[k]

7So Satan went out from the presence
of the LORD and afflicted Job with pain-
ful sores from the soles of his feet to the
top of his head.[l] 8Then Job took a piece
of broken pottery and scraped himself
with it as he sat among the ashes.[m]

9His wife said to him, "Are you still
holding on to your integrity?[n] Curse
God and die!"[o]

10He replied, "You are talking like a
foolish[b] woman. Shall we accept good
from God, and not trouble?"[p]

In all this, Job did not sin in what he
said.[q]

Job's Three Friends

11When Job's three friends, Eliphaz
the Temanite,[r] Bildad the Shuhite[s] and
Zophar the Naamathite,[t] heard about all
the troubles that had come upon him,
they set out from their homes and met
together by agreement to go and sym-
pathise with him and comfort him.[u]
12When they saw him from a distance,
they could hardly recognise him;[v] they
began to weep aloud,[w] and they tore
their robes[x] and sprinkled dust on their
heads.[y] 13Then they sat on the ground[z]
with him for seven days and seven
nights.[a] No-one said a word to him,[b]
because they saw how great his suffer-
ing was.

Job Speaks

3 After this, Job opened his mouth
and cursed the day of his birth.[a]
2He said:

3"May the day of my birth perish,
and the night it was said, 'A boy is
born!'[b]
4That day—may it turn to darkness;
may God above not care about it;
may no light shine upon it.
5May darkness and deep shadow[a][c]
claim it once more;
may a cloud settle over it;
may blackness overwhelm its light.
6That night—may thick darkness[d]
seize it;
may it not be included among the
days of the year
nor be entered in any of the months.
7May that night be barren;
may no shout of joy[e] be heard in it.
8May those who curse days[b] curse that
day,[f]
those who are ready to rouse
Leviathan.[g]
9May its morning stars become dark;
may it wait for daylight in vain
and not see the first rays of dawn,[h]
10for it did not shut the doors of the
womb on me
to hide trouble from my eyes.

11"Why did I not perish at birth,
and die as I came from the womb?[i]
12Why were there knees to receive me[j]
and breasts that I might be nursed?
13For now I would be lying down[k] in
peace;
I would be asleep and at rest[l]
14with kings and counsellors of the
earth,[m]
who built for themselves places now
lying in ruins,[n]

21 [w]Ru 1:21; 1Sa 2:7; [x]**Jdg 10:15**; Job 2:10; Ecc 7:14; Jer 40:2; **Eph 5:20**; 1Th 5:18; Jas 5:11
22 [y]Job 2:10; Ps 39:1; Pr 10:19; 13:3; Isa 53:7; Ro 9:20

Ch. 2

1 [a]*fn* Ge 6:2; [b]**Job 1:6**
2 [c]**Ge 3:1**
3 [d]**Ex 20:20; Job 1:1**; [e]Job 6:29; 13:18; 27:6; 31:6; 32:1; 40:8; [f]Job 9:17; Ps 44:17
4 [g]**Job 1:10**
5 [h]Job 16:8; 19:20; 33:21; Ps 102:5; La 4:8; [i]**Ex 20:7; Job 1:11**
6 [j]2Co 12:7; [k]**Job 1:12**
7 [l]**Dt 28:35; Job 16:16**
8 [m]Ge 18:27; Est 4:3; Job 16:15; 19:9; 30:19; 42:6; Ps 7:5; Isa 58:5; 61:3; Jer 6:26; La 3:29; Eze 26:16; Jnh 3:5–8; Mt 11:21
9 [n]Job 6:29; 13:15; 27:5; 33:9; 35:2; 1Th 5:8; [o]**Ex 20:7; 2Ki 6:33**
10 [p]**Job 1:21; Ecc 2:24**; La 3:38; [q]**Job 1:22; 6:24**; Jas 1:12; 5:11
11 [r]**Ge 36:11**; [s]**Ge 25:2**; [t]Job 11:1; 20:1; [u]**Ge 37:35; Job 6:10**; Jn 11:19
12 [v]Job 17:7; Isa 52:14; [w]**2Sa 15:23**; [x]**Ge 37:29; Mk 14:63**; [y]**Jos 7:6; 2Sa 1:2**
13 [z]Isa 3:26; 47:1; Jer 48:18; La 2:10; Eze 26:16; Jnh 3:6; Hag 2:22; [a]**Ge 50:10**; [b]Pr 17:28; Isa 23:2; 47:5

Ch. 3

1 [a]Jer 15:10; 20:14
3 [b]ver 11,16; Job 10:18–19; Ecc 4:2; 6:3; Jer 20:14–18; Mt 26:24
5 [c]Job 10:21–22; 34:22; 38:17; Ps 23:4; 44:19; 88:12; Jer 2:6; 13:16 **6** [d]Job 23:17; 30:26
7 [e]Ps 20:5; 33:3; 65:13; Isa 26:19; Jer 51:48
8 [f]Job 10:18; Jer 20:14; [g]**Ge 1:21**; Job 41:1,8,10,25; Ps 74:14; 104:26 **9** [h]Job 41:18; Hab 3:4
11 [i]ver 3 **12** [j]**Ge 48:12**; Isa 66:12
13 [k]Job 17:13; 30:23; [l]ver 17; Job 7:8–10,21; 10:22; 13:19; 14:10–12; 19:27; 21:13,23; 27:19; Ps 139:11; Isa 8:22
14 [m]Job 9:24; 12:17; Isa 14:9; Eze 32:28–32; [n]Job 15:28; Jer 51:37; Na 3:7

[a]1 Hebrew *the sons of God*
[b]10 The Hebrew word rendered *foolish* denotes moral deficiency. [a]5 Or *and the shadow of death*
[b]8 Or *the sea*

15with rulers[o] who had gold,
who filled their houses with silver.[p]
16Or why was I not hidden in the
ground like a stillborn child,[q]
like an infant who never saw the
light of day?[r]
17There the wicked cease from turmoil,[s]
and there the weary are at rest.[t]
18Captives[u] also enjoy their ease;
they no longer hear the slave
driver's[v] shout.[w]
19The small and the great are there,[x]
and the slave is freed from his
master.

20"Why is light given to those in misery,
and life to the bitter of soul,[y]
21to those who long for death that does
not come,[z]
who search for it more than for
hidden treasure,[a]
22who are filled with gladness
and rejoice when they reach the
grave?[b]
23Why is life given to a man
whose way is hidden,[c]
whom God has hedged in?[d]
24For sighing[e] comes to me instead of
food;[f]
my groans[g] pour out like water.[h]
25What I feared has come upon me;
what I dreaded[i] has happened to
me.[j]
26I have no peace,[k] no quietness;
I have no rest,[l] but only turmoil."[m]

Eliphaz

4 Then Eliphaz the Temanite[a] replied:

2"If someone ventures a word with
you, will you be impatient?
But who can keep from speaking?[b]
3Think how you have instructed
many,[c]
how you have strengthened feeble
hands.[d]
4Your words have supported those
who stumbled;[e]
you have strengthened faltering
knees.[f]
5But now trouble comes to you, and
you are discouraged;[g]
it strikes[h] you, and you are
dismayed.[i]
6Should not your piety be your
confidence[j]
and your blameless[k] ways your
hope?

7"Consider now: Who, being innocent,
has ever perished?[l]
Where were the upright ever
destroyed?[m]
8As I have observed,[n] those who
plough evil[o]
and those who sow trouble reap it.[p]
9At the breath of God[q] they are
destroyed;
at the blast of his anger they perish.[r]
10The lions may roar[s] and growl,
yet the teeth of the great lions[t] are
broken.[u]
11The lion perishes for lack of prey,[v]
and the cubs of the lioness are
scattered.[w]

12"A word[x] was secretly brought to me,
my ears caught a whisper[y] of it.[z]
13Amid disquieting dreams in the night,
when deep sleep falls on men,[a]
14fear and trembling[b] seized me
and made all my bones shake.[c]
15A spirit glided past my face,
and the hair on my body stood on
end.[d]
16It stopped,
but I could not tell what it was.
A form stood before my eyes,
and I heard a hushed voice:[e]
17'Can a mortal be more righteous than
God?[f]
Can a man be more pure than his
Maker?[g]
18If God places no trust in his servants,[h]
if he charges his angels with error,[i]
19how much more those who live in
houses of clay,[j]
whose foundations[k] are in the dust,[l]
who are crushed[m] more readily than
a moth![n]
20Between dawn and dusk they are
broken to pieces;
unnoticed, they perish for ever.[o]

15 [o]Job 12:21; Isa 45:1; [p]Job 15:29; 20:10; 27:17; Ps 49:16–17; Pr 13:22; 28:8; Ecc 2:26; Isa 2:7; Zep 1:11
16 [q]Ps 58:8; Ecc 4:3; 6:3; [r]**ver 3**; Ps 71:6
17 [s]ver 26; Job 30:26; Ecc 4:2; Isa 14:3; [t]**ver 13**
18 [u]Isa 51:14; [v]**Ge 15:13**; [w]Job 39:7
19 [x]Job 9:22; 17:16; 21:33; 24:24; 30:23; Ecc 12:5
20 [y]**1Sa 1:10**; Eze 27:30–31
21 [z]Rev 9:6; [a]Ps 119:127; Pr 2:4
22 [b]Job 7:16; Ecc 4:3; Jer 8:3
23 [c]Pr 4:19; Isa 59:10; Jer 13:16; 23:12; [d]Job 6:4; 16:13; 19:12; Ps 88:8; La 2:4; 3:7; Hos 2:6
24 [e]Ps 5:1; 38:9; Isa 35:10; [f]Job 6:7; 33:20; Ps 107:18; [g]Ps 22:1; 32:3; 38:8; [h]1Sa 1:15; Job 30:16; Ps 6:6; 22:14; 42:3–4; 80:5; Isa 53:12; La 2:12
25 [i]Job 7:9; 9:28; 30:15; Hos 13:3; [j]**Ge 42:36**
26 [k]Isa 48:22; Jn 14:27; [l]Job 7:4,14; Ps 6:6; Da 4:5; Mt 11:28; [m]**ver 17; Job 10:18; 19:8**

Ch. 4

1 [a]**Ge 36:11**; Job 15:1; 22:1
2 [b]Job 32:20; Jer 4:19; 20:9
3 [c]Dt 32:2; Job 29:23; Hos 6:3; [d]Job 26:2; Ps 71:9; Isa 13:7; 35:3; Zep 3:16; Heb 12:12
4 [e]Job 16:5; 29:16,25; Isa 1:17; [f]Job 29:11,15; Isa 35:3; Jer 31:8; Heb 12:12
5 [g]**Jos 1:9**; [h]Ru 1:13; Job 1:11; 19:21; 30:21; Ps 38:2; Isa 53:4; [i]Job 6:14; Pr 24:10
6 [j]2Ki 18:19; Ps 27:3; 71:5; Pr 3:26; [k]**Ge 6:9**
7 [l]Job 5:11; 36:7; Ps 41:12; 2Pe 2:9; [m]Job 8:20; Ps 37:25; 91:9–10; Pr 12:21; 19:23
8 [n]Job 5:3; 15:17; [o]Jdg 14:18; Job 5:6; 15:35; Ps 7:14; Isa 59:4; [p]Ps 7:15; 9:15; Pr 11:18; 22:8; Isa 17:11; Hos 8:7; 10:13; Gal 6:7–8
9 [q]**Ex 15:10; Job 41:21**; 2Th 2:8; [r]**Lev 26:38**; Job 40:13; Isa 25:7
10 [s]Ps 22:13; [t]Ps 17:12; 22:21; Pr 28:15; [u]Job 5:15; 29:17; 36:6; 38:15; Ps 35:10; 58:6
11 [v]Dt 28:41; Job 27:14; 29:17; Ps 34:10; 58:6; Pr 30:14; [w]Job 5:4
12 [x]ver 17–21; Job 32:13; Jer 9:23; [y]Job 26:14; [z]Job 33:14
13 [a]Job 33:15
14 [b]Job 21:6; Ps 48:6; 55:5; 119:120,161; Jer 5:22; Hab 3:16; **2Co 7:15**; [c]Jer 23:9; Da 10:8
15 [d]Da 5:6; 7:15,28; 10:8; Mt 14:26
16 [e]**1Ki 19:12**
17 [f]Job 9:2; 13:18; Ps 143:2; [g]Job 8:3; 10:3; 14:4; 15:14; 21:14; 25:4; 31:15; 32:22; 35:10; 36:3,13; 37:23; 40:19; Ps 18:26; 51:5; 119:73; Pr 20:9; Ecc 7:20; Isa 51:13; Mal 2:10; Ac 17:24
18 [h]Heb 1:14; [i]Job 15:15; 21:22; 25:5
19 [j]Job 10:9; 33:6; Isa 64:8; Ro 9:21; 2Co 4:7; 5:1; [k]Job 22:16; [l]**Ge 2:7**; [m]Job 5:4; [n]Job 7:17; 15:16; 17:14; 25:6; Ps 22:6; Isa 41:14
20 [o]Job 14:2,20; 15:33; 20:7; 24:24; Ps 89:47; 90:5–6; Jas 4:14

21 Are not the cords of their tent pulled
up,[p]
so that they die[q] without wisdom?’[a][r]

5 “Call if you will, but who will
answer you?[a]
To which of the holy ones[b] will you
turn?
2 Resentment[c] kills a fool,
and envy slays the simple.[d]
3 I myself have seen[e] a fool taking root,[f]
but suddenly[g] his house was
cursed.[h]
4 His children[i] are far from safety,[j]
crushed in court[k] without a
defender.[l]
5 The hungry consume his harvest,[m]
taking it even from among thorns,
and the thirsty pant after his wealth.
6 For hardship does not spring from the
soil,
nor does trouble sprout from the
ground.[n]
7 Yet man is born to trouble[o]
as surely as sparks fly upward.

8 “But if it were I, I would appeal to
God;
I would lay my cause before him.[p]
9 He performs wonders[q] that cannot be
fathomed,[r]
miracles that cannot be counted.[s]
10 He bestows rain on the earth;[t]
he sends water upon the
countryside.[u]
11 The lowly he sets on high,[v]
and those who mourn[w] are lifted[x] to
safety.
12 He thwarts the plans[y] of the crafty,
so that their hands achieve no
success.[z]
13 He catches the wise[a] in their
craftiness,[b]
and the schemes of the wily are
swept away.[c]
14 Darkness[d] comes upon them in the
daytime;
at noon they grope as in the night.[e]
15 He saves the needy[f] from the sword in
their mouth;
he saves them from the clutches of
the powerful.[g]
16 So the poor[h] have hope,
and injustice shuts its mouth.[i]

17 “Blessed is the man whom God
corrects;[j]
so do not despise the discipline[k] of
the Almighty.[a][l]
18 For he wounds, but he also binds up;[m]
he injures, but his hands also heal.[n]
19 From six calamities he will rescue[o]
you;
in seven no harm will befall you.[p]
20 In famine[q] he will ransom you from
death,
and in battle from the stroke of the
sword.[r]
21 You will be protected from the lash of
the tongue,[s]
and need not fear[t] when destruction
comes.[u]
22 You will laugh[v] at destruction and
famine,[w]
and need not fear the beasts of the
earth.[x]
23 For you will have a covenant[y] with the
stones[z] of the field,
and the wild animals will be at peace
with you.[a]
24 You will know that your tent is
secure;[b]
you will take stock of your property
and find nothing missing.[c]
25 You will know that your children will
be many,[d]
and your descendants like the grass
of the earth.[e]
26 You will come to the grave in full
vigour,[f]
like sheaves gathered in season.[g]

27 “We have examined this, and it is true.
So hear it[h] and apply it to yourself.”[i]

Job

6 Then Job replied:

2 “If only my anguish could be weighed
and all my misery be placed on the
scales![a]

4:21 *p* Job 8:22; Isa 38:12; *q* Jn 8:24; *r* Job 18:21; 36:12; Pr 5:23; Jer 9:3

Ch. 5

1 *a* Hab 1:2; *b* Job 15:15; Ps 89:5,7
2 *c* Job 21:15; 36:13; *d* Pr 12:16; Gal 5:26
3 *e* **Job 4:8**; *f* Ps 37:35; Isa 40:24; Jer 12:2; Eze 17:6; *g* Pr 6:15; *h* Job 24:18; Ps 37:22,35–36; 109:9–10; Pr 3:33
4 *i* Job 20:10; 27:14; *j* **Job 4:11**; *k* Job 4:19; Am 5:12; *l* Ps 109:12; Isa 9:17; 1Jn 2:1
5 *m* Lev 26:16; **Jdg 2:15**; Job 20:18; 31:8; Mic 6:15
6 *n* **Job 4:8**
7 *o* **Ge 3:17**; Job 10:17; 15:35; Ps 51:5; 58:3; 90:10; Pr 22:8
8 *p* Job 8:5; 11:13; 13:3,15; 23:4; 40:1; Ps 35:23; 50:15; Jer 12:1; 1Co 4:4
9 *q* Ps 78:4; 111:2; *r* Dt 29:29; Job 9:4,10; 11:7; 25:2; 26:14; 33:12; 36:5,22,26; 37:5,14,16, 23; 42:3; Ps 40:5; 71:17; 72:18; 86:10; 131:1; 139:6, 17; 145:3; Isa 40:28; Ro 11:33; *s* Ps 71:15
10 *t* Mt 5:45; *u* **Lev 26:4**; Job 36:28; 37:6,13; 38:28,34; Ps 135:7; Jer 14:22
11 *v* **1Sa 2:7–8**; **Job 4:7**; Ps 75:7; 113:7–8; *w* Isa 61:2; Mt 5:4; Ro 12:15; *x* **Mt 23:12**; Jas 4:10
12 *y* Ne 4:15; Ps 33:10; Isa 8:10; 19:3; Jer 19:7; *z* Job 12:23; Ps 78:59; 140:8
13 *a* Job 37:24; Isa 29:14; 44:25; Jer 8:8; 18:18; 51:57; *b* Job 15:5; Ps 36:3; Lk 20:23; 1Co 3:19*; 2Co 11:3; Eph 4:14; *c* Job 9:4; 18:7; Pr 21:30; 29:6; Jer 8:9
14 *d* Job 15:22,30; 18:6,18; 20:26; 22:11; 27:20; Isa 8:22; Jn 12:35; *e* **Dt 28:29**; **Job 18:5**; Am 8:9
15 *f* **Ex 22:23**; Job 8:6; 22:27; 33:26; 36:15; *g* **Job 4:10**; **31:22**
16 *h* Job 20:19; 31:16; Pr 17:5; 22:22; Isa 11:4; 41:17; 61:1; *i* Ps 63:11; 107:42; Ro 3:19
17 *j* Dt 8:5; Job 33:19; 36:10; Zep 3:7; Jas 1:12; *k* Ps 94:12; Pr 3:11; Jer 31:18; *l* **Ge 17:1**; **Job 15:11**; Heb 12:5–11
18 *m* Ps 147:3; Isa 57:15; 61:1; Hos 6:1; *n* **Dt 32:39**
19 *o* Da 3:17; 6:16; *p* Ps 34:19; 91:10; Pr 3:25–26; 24:15–16
20 *q* ver 22; Ps 33:19; 37:19; *r* Ps 22:20; 91:7; 140:7; 144:10; Jer 39:18
21 *s* Ps 12:2–4; 31:20; *t* Ps 23:4; 27:1; 91:5; *u* ver 15
22 *v* Job 8:21; 39:7,18,22; 41:29; *w* **ver 20**; *x* **Lev 25:18**; Ps 91:13; Hos 2:18; Mk 1:13
23 *y* Isa 28:15; Hos 2:18; *z* 2Ki 3:19,25; Ps 91:12; Mt 13:8; *a* Job 40:20; Isa 11:6–9; 65:25; Eze 34:25
24 *b* Job 12:6; 21:9; *c* Job 8:6; 22:23
25 *d* Dt 28:4; Ps 112:2; *e* Ps 72:16; Isa 44:3–4; 48:19
26 *f* **Ge 15:15**; **Dt 11:21**; **Ecc 8:13**; *g* Pr 3:21–26
27 *h* Job 32:10,17; *i* Job 8:5; 11:13; 22:27

Ch. 6

2 *a* Job 31:6; Pr 11:1; Da 5:27

[a] *21* Some interpreters end the quotation after verse 17.
[a] *17* Hebrew *Shaddai*; here and throughout Job

3It would surely outweigh the sand[b] of the seas—
no wonder my words have been impetuous.[c]
4The arrows[d] of the Almighty[e] are in me,[f]
my spirit drinks[g] in their poison;[h]
God's terrors[i] are marshalled against me.[j]
5Does a wild donkey[k] bray[l] when it has grass,
or an ox bellow when it has fodder?[m]
6Is tasteless food eaten without salt,
or is there flavour in the white of an egg?[a] [n]
7I refuse to touch it;
such food makes me ill.[o]

8"Oh, that I might have my request,
that God would grant what I hope for,[p]
9that God would be willing to crush[q] me,
to let loose his hand and cut me off![r]
10Then I would still have this consolation[s]—
my joy in unrelenting pain[t]—
that I had not denied the words[u] of the Holy One.[v]

11"What strength do I have, that I should still hope?
What prospects, that I should be patient?[w]
12Do I have the strength of stone?
Is my flesh bronze?[x]
13Do I have any power to help myself,[y]
now that success has been driven from me?

14"A despairing man[z] should have the devotion[a] of his friends,[b]
even though he forsakes the fear of the Almighty.[c]
15But my brothers are as undependable as intermittent streams,[d]
as the streams that overflow
16when darkened by thawing ice
and swollen with melting snow,[e]
17but that cease to flow in the dry season,
and in the heat[f] vanish from their channels.
18Caravans turn aside from their routes;
they go up into the wasteland and perish.
19The caravans of Tema[g] look for water,
the travelling merchants of Sheba[h] look in hope.
20They are distressed, because they had been confident;
they arrive there, only to be disappointed.[i]
21Now you too have proved to be of no help;
you see something dreadful and are afraid.[j]
22Have I ever said, 'Give something on my behalf,
pay a ransom[k] for me from your wealth,[l]
23deliver me from the hand of the enemy,
ransom me from the clutches of the ruthless'?[m]

24"Teach me, and I will be quiet;[n]
show me where I have been wrong.[o]
25How painful are honest words![p]
But what do your arguments prove?
26Do you mean to correct what I say,
and treat the words of a despairing man as wind?[q]
27You would even cast lots[r] for the fatherless[s]
and barter away your friend.

28"But now be so kind as to look at me.
Would I lie to your face?[t]
29Relent, do not be unjust;[u]
reconsider, for my integrity[v] is at stake.[b] [w]
30Is there any wickedness on my lips?[x]
Can my mouth not discern[y] malice?

7 "Does not man have hard service[a] on earth?[b]
Are not his days like those of a hired man?[c]
2Like a slave longing for the evening shadows,[d]
or a hired man waiting eagerly for his wages,[e]
3so I have been allotted months of futility,
and nights of misery have been assigned to me.[f]
4When I lie down I think, 'How long before I get up?'[g]
The night drags on, and I toss till dawn.[h]

3 [b]1Ki 4:29; Pr 27:3; [c]ver 11, 26; Job 7:11; 16:6; 21:4; 23:2 **4** [d]**Dt 32:23;** Ps 38:2; [e]**Ge 17:1;** [f]Job 7:20; 16:12–13; 19:12; La 3:12; [g]Job 21:20; [h]**Dt 32:32;** Job 30:21; 34:6; Jer 15:18; 30:12; [i]Job 9:34; 13:21; 18:11; 23:6; 27:20; 30:15; 33:16; [j]**Job 3:23;** Ps 88:15–18 **5** [k]**Ge 16:12;** [l]Job 30:7; [m]Job 24:6; Isa 30:24 **6** [n]Job 33:20; Ps 107:18 **7** [o]**Job 3:24** **8** [p]Job 14:13 **9** [q]Job 19:2; [r]**Nu 11:15; Ps 31:22** **10** [s]**Job 2:11;** 15:11; Ps 94:19; [t]Ps 38:17; Jer 4:19; 45:3; [u]Job 22:22; 23:12; Ps 119:102; Mk 8:38; [v]**Lev 11:44; 2Ki 19:22; Isa 31:1** **11** [w]**ver 3** **12** [x]Job 26:2 **13** [y]Job 26:2 **14** [z]**Job 4:5;** [a]1Sa 20:42; Job 15:4; [b]Job 12:4; 17:2,6; 19:19,21; 21:3; 30:1,10; Ps 38:11; 69:20; 1Jn 3:17; [c]**Ge 17:1** **15** [d]Job 13:4; 16:2; 21:34; Ps 22:1; 38:11; Jer 15:18 **16** [e]Ps 147:18 **17** [f]Job 24:19 **19** [g]**Ge 25:15;** [h]**Ge 10:7**,28 **20** [i]Jer 14:3; Joel 1:11 **21** [j]Ps 38:11 **22** [k]**Nu 35:31;** Job 33:24; Ps 49:7; [l]Jer 15:10 **23** [m]**2Ki 19:19** **24** [n]**Job 2:10;** 33:33; Ps 39:1; 141:3; Pr 10:19; 11:12; 17:27; Ecc 5:2; [o]Job 19:4 **25** [p]Ecc 12:11; Isa 22:23 **26** [q]**ver 3; Ge 41:6;** Job 8:2; 15:3; 16:3; Jer 5:13

27 [r]Eze 24:6; Joel 3:3; Ob 11; Na 3:10; [s]**Ex 22:22**,24; Job 31:17,21; Isa 10:2 **28** [t]Job 9:15; 24:25; 27:4; 32:10; 33:1,3; 34:6; 36:3,4 **29** [u]Job 19:6; 27:2; 40:8; Isa 40:27; [v]**Job 2:3;** [w]Job 9:21; 10:7; 11:2; 12:4; 23:7,10; 33:9,32; 34:5,36; 35:2; 42:6; Ps 66:10; Zec 13:9 **30** [x]Job 27:4; [y]Job 12:11

Ch. 7

1 [a]Job 14:14; Isa 40:2; [b]**Job 5:7;** [c]**Lev 25:50** **2** [d]Job 14:1; Ecc 2:23; [e]**Lev 19:13; Job 14:6** **3** [f]Job 16:7; Ps 6:6; 42:3; 56:8; Ecc 4:1; Isa 16:9; Jer 9:1; La 1:2,16 **4** [g]Dt 28:67; [h]ver 13–14

[a]6 The meaning of the Hebrew for this phrase is uncertain.
[b]29 Or *my righteousness still stands*

5My body is clothed with worms[i] and
scabs,
my skin is broken and festering.[j]

6"My days are swifter than a weaver's
shuttle,[k]
and they come to an end without
hope.[l]
7Remember, O God, that my life is but
a breath;[m]
my eyes will never see happiness
again.[n]
8The eye that now sees me will see me
no longer;
you will look for me, but I will be no
more.[o]
9As a cloud vanishes[p] and is gone,
so he who goes down to the grave[a][q]
does not return.[r]
10He will never come to his house again;
his place[s] will know him no more.[t]

11"Therefore I will not keep silent;[u]
I will speak out in the anguish[v] of
my spirit,
I will complain[w] in the bitterness of
my soul.[x]
12Am I the sea,[y] or the monster of the
deep,[z]
that you put me under guard?[a]
13When I think my bed will comfort me
and my couch will ease my
complaint,[b]
14even then you frighten me with
dreams
and terrify[c] me with visions,[d]
15so that I prefer strangling and death,[e]
rather than this body of mine.[f]
16I despise my life;[g] I would not live for
ever.[h]
Let me alone;[i] my days have no
meaning.[j]

17"What is man that you make so much
of him,
that you give him so much
attention,[k]
18that you examine him every morning[l]
and test him[m] every moment?[n]
19Will you never look away from me,[o]
or let me alone even for an instant?[p]
20If I have sinned, what have I done to
you,[q]
O watcher of men?
Why have you made me your target?[r]
Have I become a burden to you?[b][s]
21Why do you not pardon my offences
and forgive my sins?[t]
For I shall soon lie down in the dust;[u]
you will search for me, but I shall be
no more."[v]

5 [i]Job 17:14; 21:26; 24:20; 25:6; Isa 14:11; [j]**Dt 28:35**
6 [k]Job 9:25; Ps 39:5; Isa 38:12; [l]Job 13:15; 14:19; 17:11, 15; 19:10; Ps 37:4; 52:9
7 [m]ver 16; Ge 27:46; Ps 39:4–5,11; 62:9; 78:39; 89:47; 144:4; Ecc 7:15; **Jas 4:14**; [n]Job 10:20
8 [o]**Job 3:13**; 8:18; 15:29; 20:7,9,21; 27:17; Ps 37:36; 103:16; Isa 41:12; Jn 16:16; Ac 20:25
9 [p]**Job 3:25**; [q]**Job 3:13**; 11:8; 14:13; 17:16; 26:6; 38:17; Am 9:2; [r]2Sa 12:23
10 [s]Job 18:21; 21:18; 27:21,23; Ps 58:9; Jer 18:17; 19:8; [t]**ver 8**; Ps 37:10; 104:35
11 [u]Job 9:35; 13:13; Ps 22:2; 40:9; [v]Job 10:1; Ps 6:3; Isa 38:15,17; [w]ver 13; Job 9:27; 21:4; 23:2; [x]**1Sa 1:10; Job 6:3**
12 [y]Job 38:8–11; [z]**Ge 1:21**; [a]ver 20; Isa 1:14
13 [b]**ver 11**
14 [c]Job 9:34; [d]**Ge 41:8; Job 3:26**
15 [e]1Ki 19:4; Jnh 4:3; [f]Job 6:9; Rev 9:6
16 [g]**1Ki 19:4**; Job 9:21; [h]**Job 3:22**; [i]ver 19; Job 10:20; Ps 39:13; [j]**ver 7**
17 [k]**Job 4:19**; 22:2; Ps 8:4; 144:3; Heb 2:6
18 [l]Ps 73:14; [m]Job 23:10; Ps 139:23; [n]Job 14:3; Ps 17:3; 26:2; 66:10; 139:1–6; 143:2
19 [o]**ver 16**; [p]Job 9:18; 13:26; 14:6; 27:2; Ps 139:7
20 [q]Job 35:6; Jer 7:19; [r]**Job 6:4**; [s]**ver 12**

Bildad

8 Then Bildad the Shuhite[a] replied:

2"How long will you say such things?[b]
Your words are a blustering wind.[c]
3Does God pervert justice?[d]
Does the Almighty pervert what is
right?[e]
4When your children sinned against
him,
he gave them over to the penalty of
their sin.[f]
5But if you will look to God
and plead[g] with the Almighty,[h]
6if you are pure and upright,
even now he will rouse himself on
your behalf[i]
and restore you to your rightful
place.[j]
7Your beginnings will seem humble,
so prosperous[k] will your future be.[l]

8"Ask the former generations[m]
and find out what their fathers
learned,
9for we were born only yesterday and
know nothing,[n]
and our days on earth are but a
shadow.[o]
10Will they not instruct[p] you and tell
you?
Will they not bring forth words from
their understanding?[q]
11Can papyrus grow tall where there is
no marsh?[r]
Can reeds[s] thrive without water?
12While still growing and uncut,
they wither more quickly than
grass.[t]
13Such is the destiny[u] of all who forget
God;[v]

21 [t]Job 9:28; 10:14; 16:6; Ps 119:120; Isa 43:25; Jer 31:34; Heb 1:3; [u]**Ge 3:19**; Job 10:9; 34:15; Ps 7:5; 22:15; 90:3; 104:29; [v]**ver 8; Job 3:13**

Ch. 8

1 [a]**Ge 25:2**; Job 18:1; 25:1
2 [b]Job 11:2; 18:2; [c]**2Ch 36:16; Job 6:26**
3 [d]**Job 4:17**; 34:12; Isa 29:15; Ro 3:5; [e]**Ge 18:25; Jer 12:1**
4 [f]Job 1:19 *5* [g]Job 9:15; [h]**Job 5:8**,27
6 [i]**Job 5:15**; 22:27; 33:26; 34:28; Isa 58:9; 65:24; [j]**Job 5:24**
7 [k]Job 21:13; 22:21; 36:11; Ps 25:13; [l]**Job 1:10**; Jer 29:11; 31:17 *8* [m]**Dt 32:7; Ps 71:18**
9 [n]**Ge 47:9**; [o]**1Ch 29:15; 2Ch 10:6; Ps 39:6**
10 [p]Pr 1:8; [q]Pr 2:1–2; 4:1
11 [r]Job 40:21; [s]**Ex 2:3**; Isa 19:6; 35:7
12 [t]ver 19; **2Ki 19:26**; Job 18:16; 20:5; Ps 90:5–6; 102:11; Isa 34:4; 40:7,24
13 [u]Ps 37:38; 73:17; [v]Ps 9:17; 50:22; Isa 51:13; Jer 17:6

[a]9 Hebrew *Sheol*
[b]20 A few manuscripts of the Masoretic Text, an ancient Hebrew scribal tradition and Septuagint; most manuscripts of the Masoretic Text *I have become a burden to myself.*

so perishes the hope of the
godless.[w]
14What he trusts in is fragile;[a]
what he relies on is a spider's web.[x]
15He leans on his web,[y] but it gives way;
he clings to it, but it does not hold.[z]
16He is like a well-watered plant in the
sunshine,
spreading its shoots[a] over the
garden;[b]
17it entwines its roots around a pile of
rocks
and looks for a place among the
stones.
18But when it is torn from its spot,
that place disowns[c] it and says, 'I
never saw you.'[d]
19Surely its life withers[e] away,
and[b] from the soil other plants
grow.[f]

20"Surely God does not reject a
blameless[g] man
or strengthen the hands of
evildoers.[h]
21He will yet fill your mouth with
laughter[i]
and your lips with shouts of joy.[j]
22Your enemies will be clothed in
shame,[k]
and the tents[l] of the wicked will be
no more."[m]

Job

9 Then Job replied:

2"Indeed, I know that this is true.
But how can a mortal be righteous
before God?[a]
3Though one wished to dispute with
him,[b]
he could not answer him one time
out of a thousand.[c]
4His wisdom[d] is profound, his power is
vast.[e]
Who has resisted[f] him and come
out unscathed?[g]
5He moves mountains[h] without their
knowing it
and overturns them in his anger.[i]
6He shakes the earth[j] from its place
and makes its pillars tremble.[k]
7He speaks to the sun and it does not
shine;[l]
he seals off the light of the stars.[m]
8He alone stretches out the heavens[n]
and treads on the waves of the sea.[o]
9He is the Maker[p] of the Bear and
Orion,
the Pleiades and the constellations
of the south.[q]
10He performs wonders[r] that cannot be
fathomed,
miracles that cannot be counted.[s]
11When he passes me, I cannot see him;
when he goes by, I cannot perceive
him.[t]
12If he snatches away, who can stop
him?[u]
Who can say to him, 'What are you
doing?'[v]
13God does not restrain his anger;[w]
even the cohorts of Rahab[x] cowered
at his feet.

14"How then can I dispute with him?
How can I find words to argue with
him?[y]
15Though I were innocent, I could not
answer him;[z]
I could only plead[a] with my Judge[b]
for mercy.[c]
16Even if I summoned him and he
responded,
I do not believe he would give me a
hearing.[d]
17He would crush[e] me with a storm[f]
and multiply[g] my wounds for no
reason.[h]
18He would not let me regain my breath
but would overwhelm me with
misery.[i]
19If it is a matter of strength, he is
mighty![j]
And if it is a matter of justice, who
will summon him[a]?[k]
20Even if I were innocent, my mouth
would condemn me;
if I were blameless, it would
pronounce me guilty.[l]

21"Although I am blameless,[m]
I have no concern for myself;[n]
I despise my own life.[o]

13 [w]Job 6:9; 11:20; 13:16; 15:34; 20:5; 27:8; 34:30; Ps 37:1–2; 112:10; Pr 10:28; 11:7; Jer 15:9
14 [x]ver 15; Job 27:18; Isa 59:5
15 [y]**ver 14**; [z]Ps 49:11; Mt 7:26–27
16 [a]Ps 80:11; Isa 16:8; [b]Ps 37:35; Jer 11:16
18 [c]Job 20:9; Ps 103:16; [d]**Job 7:8; 14:20**
19 [e]**ver 12; Job 15:30**; [f]Ps 119:90; Ecc 1:4
20 [g]Job 1:1; [h]**Ge 18:25**
21 [i]**Job 5:22**; [j]**Ezr 3:13**; Job 35:10; Ps 47:5; 107:22; 118:15; 126:2; 132:16; Isa 35:6
22 [k]Job 27:7; Ps 6:10; 35:26; 44:7; 53:5; 71:13; 86:17; 109:29; 132:18; Eze 7:27; 26:16; [l]**Job 4:21**; [m]**1Sa 8:3**; Job 18:6,14,21; 21:28; 27:8,18; 34:26; 36:6; 38:13; Ps 52:5; Pr 14:11

Ch. 9

2 [a]**Job 4:17**; Ro 3:20
3 [b]ver 32; Job 40:5; [c]ver 12,14,29,32; Job 10:2; 12:14; 13:9,14; 22:4; 23:7,13; 37:19; 40:2; Ps 44:21; Isa 14:24
4 [d]Job 11:6; 28:12,20,23; 38:36; Ps 51:6; Pr 2:6; Ecc 2:26; [e]ver 19: **Job 5:9**; 12:13,16; 23:6; 24:22; 26:12; 30:18; Ps 93:4; 95:3; Pr 8:14; Isa 40:26; 63:1; Da 2:20; 4:35; [f]Jer 50:24; [g]**2Ch 13:12; Job 5:13**
5 [h]Mt 17:20; [i]Ps 18:7; 46:2–3; Isa 13:13; Mic 1:4
6 [j]**Ex 19:18**; Isa 2:21; 13:13; 24:18–20; Am 8:8; Heb 12:26; [k]**2Sa 22:8**; Job 26:14; 36:29; 37:4–5; Ps 75:3; Hab 3:4
7 [l]Isa 34:4; Jer 4:28; Joel 2:2,10,31; 3:15; Zep 1:15; Zec 14:6; [m]Isa 13:10; Jer 4:23; Eze 32:8
8 [n]**Ge 1:1**,8; **Isa 48:13**; [o]Job 38:16; Ps 77:19; Pr 8:28; Hab 3:15; Mt 14:25; Mk 6:48; Jn 6:19
9 [p]Job 32:22; 40:15,19; [q]**Ge 1:16**
10 [r]Dt 6:22; Ps 72:18; 136:4; Jer 32:20; [s]**Job 5:9**
11 [t]Job 23:8–9; 35:14
12 [u]Nu 23:20; Job 11:10; Isa 14:27; 43:13; [v]**ver 3**; **Dt 32:39**; Isa 29:16; 45:9; Da 2:21; 4:32; Ro 9:20
13 [w]Nu 14:18; Job 10:15; Ps 78:38; Isa 3:11; 6:5; 48:9; [x]Job 26:12; Ps 87:4; 89:10; Isa 30:7; 51:9
14 [y]**ver 3**
15 [z]Job 10:15; 13:19; 34:5–6; 40:5; 42:7; [a]Job 8:5; [b]**Ge 18:25**; 1Sa 24:12; Ps 50:6; 96:13; [c]ver 20,29; Job 15:6; 23:4; 40:2
16 [d]Job 13:22; Ro 9:20–21
17 [e]Job 16:12; 30:16; Ps 10:10; Isa 38:13; [f]Job 30:22; Ps 83:15; Jnh 1:4; [g]Job 16:14; [h]**Job 2:3**
18 [i]**Job 7:19; 10:1**
19 [j]**ver 4; Ne 9:32**; [k]ver 33; Jer 49:19
20 [l]**ver 15**
21 [m]**Ge 6:9**; Job 34:6–7; [n]ver 14; **Job 6:29**; 10:1; 13:13; [o]**Nu 11:15; Job 7:16**

[a]14 The meaning of the Hebrew for this word is uncertain. [b]19 Or *Surely all the joy it has / is that*
[a]19 See Septuagint; Hebrew *me.*

22It is all the same; that is why I say,
'He destroys both the blameless and
the wicked.'[p]
23When a scourge[q] brings sudden death,
he mocks the despair of the
innocent.[r]
24When a land falls into the hands of the
wicked,[s]
he blindfolds its judges.[t]
If it is not he, then who is it?[u]

25"My days are swifter than a runner;[v]
they fly away without a glimpse of
joy.[w]
26They skim past[x] like boats of
papyrus,[y]
like eagles swooping down on their
prey.[z]
27If I say, 'I will forget my complaint,[a]
I will change my expression, and
smile,'
28I still dread[b] all my sufferings,
for I know you will not hold me
innocent.[c]
29Since I am already found guilty,
why should I struggle in vain?[d]
30Even if I washed myself with soap[b][e]
and my hands[f] with washing soda,[g]
31you would plunge me into a slime pit[h]
so that even my clothes would
detest me.[i]

32"He is not a man[j] like me that I might
answer him,[k]
that we might confront each other in
court.[l]
33If only there were someone to arbitrate
between us,[m]
to lay his hand upon us both,[n]
34someone to remove God's rod from
me,[o]
so that his terror would frighten me
no more.[p]
35Then I would speak up without fear of
him,[q]
but as it now stands with me, I
cannot.[r]

10 "I loathe my very life;[a]
therefore I will give free rein to
my complaint
and speak out in the bitterness of
my soul.[b]
2I will say to God:[c] Do not condemn
me,
but tell me what charges[d] you have
against me.[e]
3Does it please you to oppress me,[f]
to spurn the work of your hands,[g]
while you smile on the schemes of
the wicked?[h]
4Do you have eyes of flesh?
Do you see as a mortal sees?[i]
5Are your days like those of a mortal
or your years like those of a man,[j]
6that you must search out my faults
and probe after my sin[k]—
7though you know that I am not guilty[l]
and that no-one can rescue me from
your hand?[m]

8"Your hands shaped[n] me and made
me.
Will you now turn and destroy me?[o]
9Remember that you moulded me like
clay.[p]
Will you now turn me to dust
again?[q]
10Did you not pour me out like milk
and curdle me like cheese,
11clothe me with skin and flesh
and knit me together[r] with bones
and sinews?
12You gave me life[s] and showed me
kindness,[t]
and in your providence[u] watched
over[v] my spirit.

13"But this is what you concealed in
your heart,
and I know that this was in your
mind:[w]
14If I sinned, you would be watching
me[x]
and would not let my offence go
unpunished.[y]
15If I am guilty[z]—woe to me![a]
Even if I am innocent, I cannot lift
my head,[b]
for I am full of shame
and drowned in[a] my affliction.[c]
16If I hold my head high, you stalk me
like a lion[d]
and again display your awesome
power against me.[e]
17You bring new witnesses against me[f]
and increase your anger towards
me;[g]
your forces come against me wave
upon wave.[h]

22 [p]Job 3:19; 10:8; Ecc 9:2–3; Eze 21:3
23 [q]Heb 11:36; [r]Job 24:1,12; Ps 64:4; Hab 1:3; 1Pe 1:7
24 [s]Job 1:15,17; 10:3; 16:11; 21:16; 22:18; 27:2; 40:8; Ps 73:3; [t]Job 3:14; 12:6; 19:7; 21:7; 24:23; 31:35; 35:15; Ps 73:12; Ecc 8:11; Jer 12:1; La 3:9; [u]Job 12:9; 13:1; 24:12; Isa 41:20
25 [v]Job 7:6; [w]Job 7:7; 10:20
26 [x]Job 24:18; Ps 46:3; [y]Isa 18:2; [z]Job 39:29; Hab 1:8
27 [a]Job 7:11
28 [b]Job 3:25; [c]Ex 34:7; Job 7:21
29 [d]ver 3,15; Ps 37:33
30 [e]Mal 3:2; [f]Job 17:9; 31:7; Isa 1:15; [g]Job 14:4,17; 33:9; Isa 1:18; Jer 2:22; Hos 13:12
31 [h]Ps 35:7; 40:2; 51:9; Jer 2:22; Na 3:6; Mal 2:3; [i]Job 7:20; 34:9; 35:3; Ps 73:13
32 [j]Nu 23:19; [k]ver 3; Ro 9:20; [l]Ps 143:2; Ecc 6:10
33 [m]1Sa 2:25; [n]ver 19
34 [o]Job 21:9; Ps 39:10; 73:5; [p]Job 6:4; 7:14; 33:7; Ps 32:4
35 [q]Job 7:11; [r]Job 7:15; 13:21

Ch. 10

1 [a]Nu 11:15; 1Ki 19:4; [b]1Sa 1:10; Job 7:11; 9:18,21
2 [c]Job 13:3; 40:1; [d]Isa 3:13; Hos 4:1; 5:1; 12:2; Mic 6:2; Ro 8:33; [e]Job 9:3
3 [f]Job 9:22; 16:9,14; 19:6,21; 22:10; 30:13,21; 31:23; 34:6; [g]ver 8; Ge 1:26; Job 4:17; 14:15; 34:19; Ps 8:6; 95:6; 100:3; 138:8; 149:2; Isa 60:21; 64:8; [h]Job 9:24
4 [i]1Sa 16:7; Job 11:11; 14:16; 24:23; 28:24; 31:4; 34:21; 41:11; Ps 11:4; 33:15; 119:168; 139:12; Pr 5:21; 15:3; Jer 11:20–23; 16:17
5 [j]Job 36:26; Ps 39:5; 90:2,4; 102:24; 2Pe 3:8
6 [k]Job 14:16
7 [l]ver 15; Job 6:29; 11:4; 16:17; 27:5–6; 31:6; 32:1; [m]Dt 32:39
8 [n]Ge 2:7; [o]ver 3; 2Sa 14:14; Job 30:15
9 [p]Job 4:19; Isa 29:16; [q]Ge 2:7; Job 7:21
11 [r]Ps 139:13,15
12 [s]Ge 2:7; [t]Ge 24:12; [u]Ge 45:5; [v]1Pe 2:25
13 [w]Job 23:13; Ps 115:3
14 [x]Job 13:27; [y]Ex 34:7; Job 7:21
15 [z]ver 7; [a]Job 9:13; [b]Job 9:15; [c]Ps 25:16
16 [d]1Sa 17:34; Ps 7:2; Isa 38:13; Jer 5:6; 25:38; La 3:10; Hos 5:14; 13:7; [e]Job 5:9; Isa 28:21; 29:14; 65:7
17 [f]1Ki 21:10; Job 16:8; [g]Ru 1:21; [h]Job 5:7

b30 Or *snow* a15 Or *and aware of*

18"Why then did you bring me out of the
womb?[i]
I wish I had died before any eye saw
me.[j]
19If only I had never come into being,
or had been carried straight from the
womb to the grave![k]
20Are not my few days[l] almost over?[m]
Turn away from me[n] so that I can
have a moment's joy[o]
21before I go to the place of no return,[p]
to the land of gloom and deep
shadow,[b q]
22to the land of deepest night,
of deep shadow[r] and disorder,
where even the light is like
darkness."[s]

Zophar

11 Then Zophar the Naamathite[a]
replied:

2"Are all these words to go
unanswered?[b]
Is this talker to be vindicated?[c]
3Will your idle talk[d] reduce men to
silence?
Will no-one rebuke you when you
mock?[e]
4You say to God, 'My beliefs are
flawless[f]
and I am pure[g] in your sight.'
5Oh, how I wish that God would
speak,[h]
that he would open his lips against
you
6and disclose to you the secrets of
wisdom,[i]
for true wisdom has two sides.
Know this: God has even forgotten
some of your sin.[j]

7"Can you fathom[k] the mysteries of
God?
Can you probe the limits of the
Almighty?
8They are higher[l] than the
heavens[m]—what can you do?
They are deeper than the depths of
the grave[a n]—what can you
know?[o]
9Their measure[p] is longer than the
earth
and wider than the sea.[q]

10"If he comes along and confines you in
prison
and convenes a court, who can
oppose him?[r]
11Surely he recognises deceitful men;
and when he sees evil, does he not
take note?[s]

18 [i]Job 3:8; Ps 22:9; [j]Job 3:26; Ecc 4:2; 7:1
19 [k]Job 3:3; Jer 15:10
20 [l]Job 14:1; Ecc 6:12; [m]Job 7:7; [n]Job 7:16; [o]Job 9:25
21 [p]2Sa 12:23; Job 3:13; 16:22; Ps 39:13; Ecc 12:5; [q]Job 3:5
22 [r]Job 3:5; [s]1Sa 2:9; Job 3:13

Ch. 11

1 [a]Job 2:11
2 [b]Job 8:2; 16:3; [c]Ge 41:6; Job 6:29
3 [d]Eph 4:29; 5:4; [e]Job 12:4; 16:10; 17:2; 21:3; 30:1; Ps 1:1
4 [f]Job 9:21; [g]Job 10:7
5 [h]Ex 20:19; Job 23:5; 32:13; 38:1
6 [i]Job 9:4; 1Co 2:10; [j]Ezr 9:13; Job 15:5
7 [k]Job 5:9; Ecc 3:11
8 [l]Eph 3:18; [m]Ge 15:5; Job 22:12; 25:2; Ps 57:10; Isa 55:9; [n]Job 7:9; [o]Job 15:13,25; 33:13; 40:2; Ps 139:8
9 [p]Eph 3:19–20; [q]Job 22:12; 35:5; 36:26; 37:5,23; Isa 40:26
10 [r]Job 9:12; Rev 3:7
11 [s]Job 10:4; 31:37; 34:11, 25; 36:7; Ps 10:14
12 [t]Ge 16:12; [u]2Ch 6:36
13 [v]1Sa 7:3; Ps 78:8; [w]Ex 9:29; [x]Job 5:8,27
14 [y]Jos 24:14; [z]Ps 101:4; [a]Job 22:23
15 [b]Job 22:26; [c]1Sa 2:9; Ps 20:8; 37:23; 40:2; 119:5; Eph 6:14; [d]Ge 4:7; Ps 3:6
16 [e]Isa 26:16; 37:3; 65:16; [f]Jos 7:5; Job 22:11; Ps 58:7; 112:10; Eze 21:7

12But a witless man can no more become
wise
than a wild donkey's colt[t] can be
born a man.[b u]

13"Yet if you devote your heart[v] to him
and stretch out your hands[w] to him,[x]
14if you put away[y] the sin that is in your
hand
and allow no evil[z] to dwell in your
tent,[a]
15then you will lift up your face[b] without
shame;
you will stand firm[c] and without
fear.[d]
16You will surely forget your trouble,[e]
recalling it only as waters gone by.[f]
17Life will be brighter than noonday,[g]
and darkness will become like
morning.[h]
18You will be secure, because there is
hope;
you will look about you and take
your rest[i] in safety.[j]
19You will lie down, with no-one to
make you afraid,[k]
and many will court your favour.[l]
20But the eyes of the wicked will fail,[m]
and escape will elude them;[n]
their hope will become a dying
gasp."[o]

Job

12 Then Job replied:

2"Doubtless you are the people,
and wisdom will die with you![a]
3But I have a mind as well as you;
I am not inferior to you.
Who does not know all these
things?[b]

4"I have become a laughing-stock[c] to
my friends,[d]
though I called upon God and he
answered[e]—
a mere laughing-stock, though
righteous and blameless![f]

17 [g]Job 22:28; Ps 37:6; Isa 58:8,10; 62:1; [h]Job 17:12; 18:6; 29:3; Ps 18:28; 112:4; 119:105; Isa 5:20; Jn 8:12
18 [i]Ps 3:5; 4:8; 127:2; Ecc 5:12; [j]Lev 26:6; Pr 3:24; Isa 11:10; 14:3; 28:12; 30:15; 32:18; Zec 3:10
19 [k]Lev 26:6; [l]Isa 45:14
20 [m]Dt 28:65; Job 17:5; [n]Job 12:10; 18:18; 27:22; 34:22; 36:6; Ps 139:11–12; Jer 11:11; 23:24; 25:35; Am 2:14; 9:2–3; [o]Job 8:13

Ch. 12

2 [a]Job 15:8; 17:10 3 [b]Job 13:2; 15:9
4 [c]Ge 38:23; [d]Job 6:14; 11:3; 16:10; 19:14; [e]Ps 91:15; [f]Ge 6:9; Job 6:29; 15:16

[b]21 Or *and the shadow of death;* also in verse 22
[a]8 Hebrew *than Sheol*
[b]12 Or *wild donkey can be born tame*

5Men at ease have contempt[g] for
misfortune
as the fate of those whose feet are
slipping.[h]
6The tents of marauders are
undisturbed,[i]
and those who provoke God are
secure[j]—
those who carry their god in their
hands.[a]

7"But ask the animals, and they will
teach you,[k]
or the birds of the air,[l] and they will
tell you;[m]
8or speak to the earth, and it will teach
you,
or let the fish of the sea inform you.
9Which of all these does not know[n]
that the hand of the LORD has done
this?[o]
10In his hand is the life[p] of every creature
and the breath of all mankind.[q]
11Does not the ear test words
as the tongue tastes food?[r]
12Is not wisdom found among the
aged?[s]
Does not long life bring
understanding?[t]

13"To God belong wisdom[u] and power;[v]
counsel and understanding are
his.[w]
14What he tears down[x] cannot be
rebuilt;[y]
the man he imprisons cannot be
released.[z]
15If he holds back the waters,[a] there is
drought;[b]
if he lets them loose, they devastate
the land.[c]
16To him belong strength and victory;[d]
both deceived and deceiver are his.[e]
17He leads counsellors away stripped[f]
and makes fools of judges.[g]
18He takes off the shackles[h] put on by
kings
and ties a loincloth[b] round their
waist.[i]
19He leads priests away stripped[j]
and overthrows men long
established.[k]
20He silences the lips of trusted advisers
and takes away the discernment of
elders.[l]
21He pours contempt on nobles[m]
and disarms the mighty.[n]
22He reveals the deep things of
darkness[o]
and brings deep shadows[p] into the
light.[q]
23He makes nations great, and destroys
them;[r]
he enlarges nations,[s] and disperses
them.[t]
24He deprives the leaders of the earth of
their reason;[u]
he sends them wandering through a
trackless waste.[v]
25They grope in darkness with no light;[w]
he makes them stagger like
drunkards.[x]

13 "My eyes have seen all this,[a]
my ears have heard and
understood it.
2What you know, I also know;
I am not inferior to you.[b]
3But I desire to speak to the Almighty[c]
and to argue my case with God.[d]
4You, however, smear me with lies;[e]
you are worthless physicians,[f] all of
you![g]
5If only you would be altogether silent![h]
For you, that would be wisdom.[i]
6Hear now my argument;
listen to the plea of my lips.[j]
7Will you speak wickedly on God's
behalf?
Will you speak deceitfully for him?[k]
8Will you show him partiality?[l]
Will you argue the case for God?
9Would it turn out well if he examined
you?[m]
Could you deceive him as you
might deceive men?[n]
10He would surely rebuke you
if you secretly showed partiality.[o]
11Would not his splendour[p] terrify you?
Would not the dread of him fall on
you?[q]
12Your maxims are proverbs of ashes;
your defences are defences of clay.[r]

13"Keep silent[s] and let me speak;[t]
then let come to me what may.[u]
14Why do I put myself in jeopardy
and take my life in my hands?[v]
15Though he slay me, yet will I hope[w] in
him;[x]

5 [g]Ps 123:4; [h]Ps 17:5; 37:31; 38:16; 66:9; 73:2; 94:18
6 [i]**Job 5:24;** [j]**Job 9:24**
7 [k]Job 35:11 *fn*[c]; [l]Mt 6:26; [m]Job 18:3; Ro 1:20
9 [n]Isa 1:3; [o]**Job 9:24**
10 [p]Da 5:23; [q]**Ge 2:7; Nu 16:22; Job 11:20;** Ac 17:28
11 [r]Job 34:3
12 [s]**1Ki 4:2;** Job 15:10; [t]ver 20; Job 17:4; 32:7,9; 34:4,10
13 [u]Pr 21:30; Isa 45:9; [v]**Job 9:4; Jer 32:19;** 1Co 1:24; [w]**Nu 23:19;** 1Ki 3:12; Job 32:8; 38:36; Pr 2:6; Isa 40:13–14; Da 1:17
14 [x]Job 16:9; 19:10; [y]Dt 13:16; Ps 127:1; Isa 24:20; 25:2; Eze 26:14; [z]**Job 9:3;** Isa 22:22; Rev 3:7
15 [a]Job 28:25; Isa 40:12; [b]**Dt 28:22; 1Ki 17:1;** [c]**Ge 7:24**
16 [d]**Job 9:4;** [e]2Ch 18:22; Job 13:7,9; 27:4; Ro 2:11
17 [f]ver 19; Job 19:9; Isa 20:4; [g]**Job 3:14;** 1Co 1:20
18 [h]Ps 107:14; 116:16; Na 1:13; [i]ver 21; Job 34:18; Ps 107:40; Isa 5:27; 40:23
19 [j]**ver 17;** [k]**Dt 24:15; Job 9:24;** 14:20; 22:8; 24:12,22; 34:20,28; 35:9; Isa 2:22; 31:8; 40:17,23; Jer 25:18; Da 2:21,34; Lk 1:52
20 [l]**ver 12,**24; Da 4:33–34
21 [m]**ver 18; Isa 34:12;** [n]**Job 3:15**
22 [o]1Co 4:5; [p]Job 3:5; [q]Ps 139:12; Da 2:22
23 [r]Ps 2:1; 46:6; Isa 13:4; Jer 25:9; [s]**Ex 34:24;** Ps 107:38; Isa 9:3; 26:15; 54:3; [t]**Job 5:12;** Ac 17:26
24 [u]**ver 20;** [v]Ps 107:40
25 [w]**Dt 28:29;** Job 18:6; 21:17; 29:3; [x]Ps 107:27; Isa 24:20

Ch. 13
1 [a]**Job 9:24** *2* [b]**Job 12:3**
3 [c]Job 5:17; 40:2; [d]**Job 5:8;** 9:14–20; **10:2**
4 [e]Ps 119:69; Isa 9:15; Jer 23:32; [f]Jer 8:22; [g]**Job 6:15**
5 [h]ver 13; **Jdg 18:19;** [i]Pr 17:28 *6* [j]Job 33:1; 36:4
7 [k]**Job 12:16; 16:17** *8* [l]**Lev 19:15**
9 [m]**Job 9:3;** [n]**Job 12:16;** Gal 6:7
10 [o]**Lev 19:15; 2Ch 19:7** *11* [p]Job 31:23; [q]**Ex 3:6**
12 [r]**Ne 4:2–3** *13* [s]**ver 5;** [t]**Job 7:11;** [u]**Job 9:21**
14 [v]**Jdg 9:17**
15 [w]**Job 7:6;** [x]Ps 23:4; 27:1; Pr 14:32; Isa 12:2; Da 3:28

[a]6 Or *secure / in what God's hand brings them*
[b]18 Or *shackles of kings / and ties a belt*

I will surely[a] defend my ways to his face.[y]
16Indeed, this will turn out for my deliverance,[z]
for no godless[a] man would dare come before him![b]
17Listen carefully to my words;[c]
let your ears take in what I say.
18Now that I have prepared my case,[d]
I know I will be vindicated.[e]
19Can anyone bring charges against me?[f]
If so, I will be silent[g] and die.[h]

20"Only grant me these two things, O God,
and then I will not hide from you:
21Withdraw your hand[i] far from me,
and stop frightening me with your terrors.[j]
22Then summon me and I will answer,[k]
or let me speak, and you reply.[l]
23How many wrongs and sins have I committed?[m]
Show me my offence and my sin.[n]
24Why do you hide your face[o]
and consider me your enemy?[p]
25Will you torment[q] a wind-blown leaf?[r]
Will you chase[s] after dry chaff?[t]
26For you write down bitter things against me
and make me inherit the sins of my youth.[u]
27You fasten my feet in shackles;[v]
you keep close watch on all my paths[w]
by putting marks on the soles of my feet.

28"So man wastes away like something rotten,
like a garment[x] eaten by moths.[y]

14

"Man born of woman[a]
is of few days[b] and full of trouble.[c]
2He springs up like a flower[d] and withers away;[e]
like a fleeting shadow,[f] he does not endure.[g]
3Do you fix your eye on such a one?[h]
Will you bring him[a] before you for judgment?[i]
4Who can bring what is pure[j] from the impure?[k]
No-one![l]
5Man's days are determined;[m]
you have decreed the number of his months[n]
and have set limits he cannot exceed.[o]
6So look away from him and let him alone,[p]
till he has put in his time like a hired man.[q]

7"At least there is hope for a tree:[r]
If it is cut down, it will sprout again,
and its new shoots[s] will not fail.[t]
8Its roots may grow old in the ground
and its stump[u] die in the soil,
9yet at the scent of water[v] it will bud
and put forth shoots like a plant.[w]
10But man dies and is laid low;[x]
he breathes his last and is no more.[y]
11As water disappears from the sea
or a river bed becomes parched and dry,[z]
12so man lies down and does not rise;[a]
till the heavens are no more,[b] men will not awake
or be roused from their sleep.[c]

13"If only you would hide me in the grave[b][d]
and conceal me till your anger has passed![e]
If only you would set me a time
and then remember[f] me![g]
14If a man dies, will he live again?
All the days of my hard service[h]
I will wait for my renewal[c][i] to come.
15You will call and I will answer you;[j]
you will long for the creature your hands have made.[k]
16Surely then you will count my steps[l]
but not keep track of my sin.[m]
17My offences will be sealed[n] up in a bag;[o]
you will cover over my sin.[p]

18"But as a mountain erodes and crumbles[q]
and as a rock is moved from its place,[r]
19as water wears away stones
and torrents[s] wash away the soil,[t]
so you destroy man's hope.[u]

15 [y]**Job 5:8**; 27:5
16 [z]Ps 30:5; Isa 12:1; 54:7–8; Hos 14:4; Php 1:19; [a]**Job 8:13**; [b]**Ge 3:8**
17 [c]Job 21:2
18 [d]**ver 3**; Job 23:4; 37:19; [e]**Job 2:3**; **9:21**
19 [f]Job 40:4; Isa 50:8; Ro 8:33; [g]**Job 9:15**; [h]**Job 3:13**; 10:8
21 [i]**Ex 9:3**; Heb 10:31; [j]**Job 6:4**
22 [k]Job 9:35; 14:15; [l]**Job 9:16**
23 [m]**1Sa 26:18**; [n]Job 7:21; 9:21; 14:17; 33:9
24 [o]**Dt 32:20**; [p]Job 16:9; 19:11; 33:10; Ps 88:14–15; Jer 30:14; La 2:5
25 [q]Job 19:2; [r]Lev 26:36; [s]Job 19:22,28; [t]Job 21:18; Ps 1:4; 35:5; 83:13; Isa 17:13; 42:3; 43:17; Hos 13:3
26 [u]Job 18:7; 20:11; 21:23; Ps 25:7
27 [v]**Ge 40:15**; Job 33:11; Jer 20:2; Ac 16:24; [w]Job 10:14
28 [x]Ps 102:26; Mk 2:21; [y]**Dt 28:35**; Ps 39:11; Isa 50:9; 51:8; Hos 5:12; Jas 5:2

Ch. 14

1 [a]Job 15:14; Mt 11:11; [b]**Job 10:20**; [c]**Ge 3:17**; **Job 7:2**
2 [d]Ps 103:15; **Jas 1:10**; [e]Ps 37:2; 90:5–6; Isa 40:6–8; [f]Job 8:9; Ps 39:4; 102:11; 109:23; 144:4; Ecc 6:12; [g]**Job 4:20**; Ps 49:12
3 [h]Ps 8:4; 144:3; [i]**Job 7:18**
4 [j]Ps 51:10; [k]**Job 4:17**; Eph 2:1–3; [l]**Job 9:30**; Jn 3:6; Ro 5:12; 7:14
5 [m]Job 24:1; Ps 31:15; 139:16; [n]Job 21:21; Ps 39:4; 90:12; [o]Ac 17:26
6 [p]**Job 7:19**; [q]Job 7:1–2; Ps 39:13; Isa 16:14; 21:16
7 [r]Job 19:10; 24:20; Ps 52:5; [s]Isa 11:1; 53:2; 60:21; [t]Isa 6:13 *8* [u]Isa 6:13; 11:1; 53:2
9 [v]Job 29:19; Ps 1:3; Jer 17:8; Eze 31:7; [w]Lev 26:4; Eze 34:27; Zec 10:1 *10* [x]ver 12; [y]**Job 10:21**; 13:19
11 [z]**2Sa 14:14**
12 [a]ver 10; [b]Ps 102:26; Rev 20:11; 21:1; [c]Ac 3:21
13 [d]**Job 7:9**; [e]Ps 30:5; Isa 26:20; 54:7; [f]**Ge 8:1**; [g]Job 6:8
14 [h]**Job 7:1**; [i]**2Ki 6:33** *15* [j]**Job 13:22**; [k]**Job 10:3**
16 [l]**Job 10:4**; Ps 139:1–3; Pr 5:21; Jer 16:17; 32:19; [m]Job 10:6; 1Co 13:5
17 [n]Jer 32:10; [o]**Dt 32:34**; [p]**Job 9:30**; **13:23**
18 [q]Eze 38:20; [r]Job 18:4
19 [s]Eze 13:13; [t]**Ge 7:23**; [u]**Job 7:6**

[a]*15* Or *He will surely slay me; I have no hope— / yet I will*
[a]*3* Septuagint, Vulgate and Syriac; Hebrew *me*
[b]*13* Hebrew *Sheol* [c]*14* Or *release*

20You overpower him once for all, and
he is gone;[v]
you change his countenance and
send him away.[w]
21If his sons are honoured, he does not
know it;
if they are brought low, he does not
see it.[x]
22He feels but the pain of his own body[y]
and mourns only for himself.[z]"

Eliphaz

15 Then Eliphaz the Temanite[a]
replied:

2"Would a wise man answer with
empty notions
or fill his belly with the hot east
wind?[b]
3Would he argue with useless words,
with speeches that have no value?[c]
4But you even undermine piety
and hinder devotion to God.[d]
5Your sin[e] prompts your mouth;[f]
you adopt the tongue of the crafty.[g]
6Your own mouth condemns you, not
mine;
your own lips testify against you.[h]

7"Are you the first man ever born?[i]
Were you brought forth before the
hills?[j]
8Do you listen in on God's council?[k]
Do you limit wisdom to yourself?[l]
9What do you know that we do not
know?
What insights do you have that we
do not have?[m]
10The grey-haired and the aged[n] are on
our side,
men even older than your father.[o]
11Are God's consolations[p] not enough
for you,
words[q] spoken gently to you?[r]
12Why has your heart[s] carried you
away,
and why do your eyes flash,
13so that you vent your rage[t] against
God
and pour out such words[u] from your
mouth?[v]

14"What is man, that he could be pure,
or one born of woman,[w] that he
could be righteous?[x]
15If God places no trust in his holy ones,[y]
if even the heavens are not pure in
his eyes,[z]
16how much less man, who is vile and
corrupt,[a]
who drinks up evil[b] like water![c]

17"Listen to me and I will explain to you;
let me tell you what I have seen,[d]
18what wise men have declared,
hiding nothing received from their
fathers[e]
19(to whom alone the land[f] was given
when no alien passed among them):
20All his days the wicked man suffers
torment,[g]
the ruthless through all the years
stored up for him.[h]
21Terrifying sounds fill his ears;[i]
when all seems well, marauders
attack him.[j]
22He despairs of escaping the darkness;[k]
he is marked for the sword.[l]
23He wanders about[m]—food for
vultures;[a][n]
he knows the day of darkness[o] is at
hand.[p]
24Distress and anguish[q] fill him with
terror;[r]
they overwhelm him, like a king[s]
poised to attack,
25because he shakes his fist[t] at God
and vaunts himself against the
Almighty,[u]
26defiantly charging against him
with a thick, strong shield.[v]

27"Though his face is covered with fat
and his waist bulges with flesh,[w]
28he will inhabit ruined towns
and houses where no-one lives,[x]
houses crumbling to rubble.[y]
29He will no longer be rich and his
wealth will not endure,[z]
nor will his possessions spread over
the land.[a]
30He will not escape the darkness;[b]
a flame[c] will wither his shoots,[d]
and the breath of God's mouth[e] will
carry him away.[f]
31Let him not deceive[g] himself by
trusting what is worthless,[h]
for he will get nothing in return.[i]

14:20 [v]Job 4:20; [w]Job 7:10; 8:18; 12:19; 27:19; Jas 1:10
14:21 [x]Job 21:21; Ecc 9:5; Isa 63:16
14:22 [y]Ps 38:7; Isa 21:3; Jer 4:19; [z]Job 21:21

Ch. 15

1 [a]Job 4:1
2 [b]Ge 41:6
3 [c]Ne 4:2–3; Job 6:26
4 [d]Job 25:6
5 [e]Job 11:6; 22:5; [f]Pr 16:23; [g]Job 5:13
6 [h]Job 9:15; 18:7; Ps 10:2; Mt 12:37; Lk 19:22
7 [i]Job 38:21; [j]1Sa 2:8; Ps 90:2; Pr 8:25
8 [k]Job 29:4; Isa 9:6; 40:13; 41:28; Jer 23:18; Ro 11:34; 1Co 2:11; [l]Job 12:2
9 [m]Job 12:3
10 [n]Job 12:12; [o]2Ch 10:6
11 [p]Ge 37:35; Job 6:10; 2Co 1:3–4; [q]Zec 1:13; [r]Dt 8:3; 32:39; Job 5:17; 22:22; 23:12; 36:16; Ps 119:11,72; Jer 15:16
12 [s]Job 11:13; 36:13
13 [t]Pr 29:11; Da 11:30; [u]Ps 94:4; [v]Job 11:8; 22:5; 32:3
14 [w]Job 14:1; [x]2Ch 6:36; Job 4:17
15 [y]Job 5:1; [z]Job 4:18
16 [a]Lev 5:2; Job 4:19; Ps 14:1; [b]Job 20:12; [c]Job 12:4; 34:7; Pr 19:28
17 [d]Job 4:8
18 [e]Dt 32:7
19 [f]Ge 12:1; Job 22:8
20 [g]ver 24; Isa 8:22; 50:11; 66:24; [h]Job 24:1; 27:13–23; Isa 2:12; Jer 46:10 Ob 15; Zep 1:7
21 [i]ver 24; 1Sa 3:11; Job 18:11; 20:25; Jer 6:25; 20:3; [j]Job 22:10; 27:20; Isa 13:3; Jer 51:25,53,56; 1Th 5:3
22 [k]ver 23; Job 5:14; 24:17; 38:15; Ps 91:5; SS 3:8; [l]Job 16:13; 18:19; 19:29; 20:24; 27:14; 33:18; 36:12; Pr 7:23; Isa 1:20; Jer 44:27; Hos 9:13; Am 5:19
23 [m]Ps 109:10; [n]Pr 30:17; Eze 39:17; Mt 24:28; Lk 17:37; [o]ver 22; [p]Job 18:12
24 [q]Isa 8:22; 9:1; [r]ver 20; [s]Job 18:14
25 [t]Ps 44:16; Isa 10:32; 37:23; [u]Job 11:8; 35:12; 36:9; 40:8; Ps 2:2–3; 73:9; 75:5; Pr 21:30; Isa 3:16; 45:9
26 [v]Jer 44:16 **27** [w]Jdg 3:17
28 [x]Isa 5:9; [y]Job 3:14 **29** [z]Job 3:15; 7:8; [a]Isa 5:8
30 [b]Job 5:14; [c]ver 34; Job 16:7; 20:26; 22:20; 31:12; [d]ver 32; Job 8:19; 18:16; 29:19; Hos 9:1–16; Mal 4:1; [e]Ex 15:10; [f]Isa 40:23–24
31 [g]Job 31:5; Pr 1:16; 6:18; Isa 44:20; 59:7; Mic 2:11; Mk 13:5; Jas 1:16; [h]Isa 30:12; 47:10; 59:4; Jer 7:4,8; Mt 6:19; [i]Job 20:7; 22:13; 27:9; 35:13; Pr 15:29; Isa 1:15; Jer 11:11; Mic 3:4

[a]23 Or *about, looking for food*

32Before his time[j] he will be paid in full,[k]
and his branches will not flourish.[l]
33He will be like a vine stripped of its
unripe grapes,[m]
like an olive tree shedding its
blossoms.[n]
34For the company of the godless[o] will
be barren,
and fire will consume[p] the tents of
those who love bribes.[q]
35They conceive trouble[r] and give birth
to evil;[s]
their womb fashions deceit."

Job

16 Then Job replied:

2"I have heard many things like these;
miserable comforters[a] are you all![b]
3Will your long-winded speeches
never end?[c]
What ails you that you keep on
arguing?[d]
4I also could speak like you,
if you were in my place;
I could make fine speeches against
you
and shake my head[e] at you.
5But my mouth would encourage you;
comfort[f] from my lips would bring
you relief.[g]

6"Yet if I speak, my pain is not relieved;
and if I refrain, it does not go away.[h]
7Surely, O God, you have worn me
out;[i]
you have devastated my entire
household.[j]
8You have bound me—and it has
become a witness;
my gauntness[k] rises up and testifies
against me.[l]
9God assails me and tears[m] me in his
anger[n]
and gnashes his teeth at me;[o]
my opponent fastens on me his
piercing eyes.[p]
10Men open their mouths[q] to jeer at me;[r]
they strike my cheek[s] in scorn
and unite together against me.[t]
11God has turned me over to evil men
and thrown me into the clutches of
the wicked.[u]
12All was well with me, but he shattered
me;
he seized me by the neck and
crushed me.[v]
He has made me his target;[w]
13 his archers surround me.[x]
Without pity, he pierces[y] my kidneys
and spills my gall on the ground.
14Again and again[z] he bursts upon me;
he rushes at me like a warrior.[a]

15"I have sewed sackcloth[b] over my skin
and buried my brow in the dust.[c]
16My face is red with weeping,[d]
deep shadows ring my eyes;[e]
17yet my hands have been free of
violence[f]
and my prayer is pure.[g]

18"O earth, do not cover my blood;[h]
may my cry[i] never be laid to rest![j]
19Even now my witness[k] is in heaven;[l]
my advocate is on high.[m]
20My intercessor[n] is my friend[a][o]
as my eyes pour out[p] tears[q] to God;
21on behalf of a man he pleads[r] with God
as a man pleads for his friend.

22"Only a few years will pass
before I go on the journey of no
return.[s]

17 1My spirit[a] is broken,
my days are cut short,[b]
the grave awaits me.[c]
2Surely mockers[d] surround me;[e]
my eyes must dwell on their
hostility.

3"Give me, O God, the pledge you
demand.[f]
Who else will put up security[g] for
me?[h]
4You have closed their minds to
understanding;[i]
therefore you will not let them
triumph.
5If a man denounces his friends for
reward,[j]
the eyes of his children will fail.[k]

6"God has made me a byword[l] to
everyone,[m]
a man in whose face people spit.[n]
7My eyes have grown dim with grief[o];
my whole frame is but a shadow.[p]
8Upright men are appalled at this;
the innocent are aroused[q] against
the ungodly.

15:32 [j]Ecc 7:17; [k]Job 22:16; 36:14; Ps 55:23; 109:8; Pr 10:27; [l]ver 30
33 [m]Hab 3:17; [n]**Job 4:20**
34 [o]**Job 8:13**; [p]**ver 30**; Heb 10:27; [q]**Ex 23:8; 1Sa 8:3**
35 [r]**Job 5:7**; [s]**Job 4:8; Isa 29:20**; Gal 6:7; Jas 1:15

Ch. 16

2 [a]Ps 69:20; [b]**Job 6:15**
3 [c]Job 11:2; 18:2; [d]**Job 6:26**
4 [e]**2Ki 19:21**; Ps 22:7; Isa 37:22; Jer 48:27; La 2:15; Zep 2:15; **Mt 27:39**
5 [f]Job 29:25; [g]**Ge 37:35**
6 [h]**Job 6:3; 7:21**
7 [i]**Jdg 8:5; Job 7:3**; [j]**Job 1:19**
8 [k]Job 17:7; 19:20; 33:21; Ps 6:7; 22:17; 88:9; 102:5; 109:24; La 5:17; [l]**Job 10:17**
9 [m]**Job 12:14**; Hos 6:1; [n]**Job 9:5**; 18:4; 19:11; [o]Job 30:21; Ps 35:16; 37:12; 112:10; La 2:16; Ac 7:54; [p]**Job 13:24**
10 [q]Ps 22:13; 35:21; [r]Job 12:4; 19:18; 21:3; 30:1,9; Ps 22:13; 69:12; 119:51; [s]Isa 50:6; La 3:30; Mic 5:1; Ac 23:2; [t]ver 7; **Job 11:3**; 19:12; 30:12; Ps 27:3; 35:15; Ac 7:57
11 [u]**Job 9:24**
12 [v]**Job 9:17**; [w]**Job 6:4**; La 3:12
13 [x]**Job 3:23**; [y]Job 20:24; Pr 7:23; La 3:13
14 [z]Job 9:17; [a]**Job 10:3**; Joel 2:7
15 [b]**Ge 37:34**; [c]**Job 2:8**
16 [d]ver 20; Ps 6:6; [e]Job 2:7; 17:7; 30:17,30; 33:19; Isa 52:14
17 [f]Isa 55:7; 59:6; Jer 18:11; Jnh 3:8; [g]**Job 6:28; 10:7**; 13:7; Isa 53:9; Zep 3:13
18 [h]**Ge 4:10**; Isa 26:21; [i]Ps 5:2; 18:6; 102:1; 119:169; [j]Job 19:24; Ps 66:18–19; Heb 11:4
19 [k]**Ge 31:50; Ro 1:9**; 1Th 2:5; [l]Job 22:12; 42:2; [m]Job 19:27; 21:17; 25:2; 27:13; 31:2; Ps 113:5; Isa 33:5; 57:15; 58:4; 66:1; Mk 11:10
20 [n]**Ro 8:34**; [o]Jn 15:15; [p]La 2:19; [q]**ver 16**
21 [r]1Ki 8:45; Ps 9:4; 140:12
22 [s]**Job 10:21**

Ch. 17

1 [a]Ps 143:4; [b]Isa 38:12; [c]Ps 88:3–4; Ecc 12:1–7
2 [d]**Job 11:3**; [e]**Job 6:14**; Ps 22:7; 119:51; Jer 20:7; La 3:14
3 [f]Ps 35:27; 119:122; [g]Pr 6:1; [h]Ps 35:2; 40:17; Isa 38:14
4 [i]**Job 12:12** *5* [j]**Ex 22:15**; [k]**Job 11:20**
6 [l]**1Ki 9:7**; Job 30:9; Jer 15:4; [m]**ver 2**; [n]**Nu 12:14**
7 [o]**Job 16:8**; [p]**Job 2:12; 16:16** *8* [q]**Ex 4:14**

[a]20 Or *My friends treat me with scorn*

9Nevertheless, the righteous[r] will hold
to their ways,
and those with clean hands[s] will
grow stronger.[t]

10"But come on, all of you, try again!
I will not find a wise man among
you.[u]
11My days have passed,[v] my plans are
shattered,
and so are the desires of my heart.[w]
12These men turn night into day;[x]
in the face of darkness they say,
'Light is near.'[y]
13If the only home I hope for is the
grave,[a][z]
if I spread out my bed[a] in darkness,[b]
14if I say to corruption,[c] 'You are my
father,'
and to the worm,[d] 'My mother' or
'My sister',
15where then is my hope?[e]
Who can see any hope for me?[f]
16Will it go down to the gates of death[b]?[g]
Will we descend together into the
dust?"[h]

Bildad

18

Then Bildad the Shuhite[a] replied:

2"When will you end these speeches?[b]
Be sensible, and then we can talk.
3Why are we regarded as cattle[c]
and considered stupid in your
sight?[d]
4You who tear yourself[e] to pieces in
your anger,[f]
is the earth to be abandoned for
your sake?
Or must the rocks be moved from
their place?[g]

5"The lamp of the wicked is snuffed
out;[h]
the flame of his fire stops burning.[i]
6The light in his tent[j] becomes dark;[k]
the lamp beside him goes out.[l]
7The vigour[m] of his step is weakened;[n]
his own schemes[o] throw him
down.[p]
8His feet thrust him into a net[q]
and he wanders into its mesh.
9A trap seizes him by the heel;
a snare[r] holds him fast.[s]
10A noose[t] is hidden for him on the
ground;
a trap[u] lies in his path.[v]
11Terrors[w] startle him on every side[x]
and dog[y] his every step.
12Calamity[z] is hungry[a] for him;
disaster[b] is ready for him when he
falls.[c]

9 [r]Pr 4:18; [s]**2Sa 22:21; Job 9:30;** [t]**1Sa 2:4;** Ps 84:7
10 [u]**Job 12:2**
11 [v]ver 15; Isa 38:10; [w]**Job 7:6**
12 [x]Isa 50:11; [y]Job 5:17–26; **11:17**
13 [z]**2Sa 14:14; Job 3:13;** [a]Ps 139:8; [b]Ps 88:18
14 [c]Job 13:28; 30:28,30; Ps 16:10; 49:9; [d]**Job 4:19; 7:5**
15 [e]**Job 7:6;** [f]Ps 31:22; La 3:18; Eze 37:11
16 [g]**Job 7:9;** 33:28; Ps 9:13; 30:3; 107:18; Isa 38:10,17; Jnh 2:6; [h]**Ge 2:7; Job 3:19;** 20:11; 21:26

Ch. 18

1 [a]**Job 8:1**
2 [b]**Job 8:2; 16:3**
3 [c]**Job 12:7;** [d]Ps 73:22
4 [e]Job 13:14; [f]**Job 16:9;** [g]Job 14:18
5 [h]Job 21:17; 35:15; Pr 13:9; 20:20; 24:20; Jer 25:10; Mt 25:8; Jn 8:12; [i]**Job 5:14;** 12:25; 24:17; 38:15
6 [j]**Job 8:22;** [k]**Job 5:14;** [l]**Job 11:17; 12:25**
7 [m]**Job 13:26;** [n]Ps 18:36; Pr 4:12; [o]**Job 5:13;** [p]**Job 15:6**
8 [q]Job 19:6; Ps 9:15; 10:9; 35:7; 57:6; 66:11; 140:5; La 1:13; Mic 7:2; Hab 1:15
9 [r]Job 22:10; 30:12; Isa 24:18; Jer 48:44; Am 5:19; [s]Pr 5:22
10 [t]Pr 7:22; Isa 51:20; [u]**1Sa 28:9;** [v]Ps 140:5
11 [w]ver 14; **Job 6:4;** 20:25; 24:17; Ps 55:4; 88:15; Isa 28:19; Jer 15:8; La 2:22; [x]**Job 15:21;** Ps 31:13; [y]ver 18; Job 20:8; Isa 22:18

13It eats away parts of his skin;[d]
death's firstborn devours his limbs.[e]
14He is torn from the security of his tent[f]
and marched off to the king[g] of
terrors.[h]
15Fire resides[a] in his tent;[i]
burning sulphur[j] is scattered over
his dwelling.
16His roots dry up below[k]
and his branches wither above.[l]
17The memory of him perishes from the
earth;[m]
he has no name[n] in the land.[o]
18He is driven from light into darkness[p]
and is banished[q] from the world.[r]
19He has no offspring[s] or descendants[t]
among his people,
no survivor[u] where once he lived.[v]
20Men of the west are appalled[w] at his
fate;[x]
men of the east are seized with
horror.
21Surely such is the dwelling[y] of an evil
man;[z]
such is the place[a] of one who knows
not God."[b]

Job

19

Then Job replied:

2"How long will you torment[a] me
and crush[b] me with words?
3Ten times[c] now you have reproached[d]
me;
shamelessly you attack me.
4If it is true that I have gone astray,
my error[e] remains my concern
alone.
5If indeed you would exalt yourselves
above me[f]
and use my humiliation against me,
6then know that God has wronged me[g]
and drawn his net[h] around me.[i]

12 [z]Job 21:17; [a]Isa 8:21; 9:20; 65:13; [b]Job 31:3; [c]Job 15:23
13 [d]Nu 12:12; [e]Zec 14:12
14 [f]**Job 8:22;** [g]Job 15:24; [h]**ver 11**
15 [i]ver 18; Job 20:26; [j]**Ge 19:24**
16 [k]Isa 5:24; Hos 5:12; Am 2:9; [l]**Ge 27:28; Job 8:12; 15:30**
17 [m]**Dt 32:26;** [n]Dt 9:14; Ps 9:5; 69:28; Pr 10:7; Isa 14:22; [o]Job 24:20; Ps 34:16; Pr 2:22; 10:7; Isa **49:15**
18 [p]**Job 5:14;** [q]**ver 11;** [r]**Job 11:20;** 30:8
19 [s]Ps 37:28; Isa 1:4; 14:20; Jer 22:30; [t]Ps 21:10; 109:13; Isa 14:22; [u]**2Ki 10:11; Eze 17:8;** [v]Job 27:14–15
20 [w]Ps 22:6–7; Isa 52:14; 53:2–3; Eze 27:35; [x]Ps 37:13; Jer 46:21; 50:27,31; Eze 7:7
21 [y]Job 21:28; [z]Isa 57:20; [a]**Job 7:10;** [b]**Job 4:21;** 1Th 4:5

Ch. 19

2 [a]Job 13:25; [b]Job 6:9 *3* [c]**Ge 31:7;** [d]Job 20:3
4 [e]Job 6:24 *5* [f]Ps 35:26; 38:16; 55:12
6 [g]**Job 6:29;** [h]**Job 18:8;** [i]**Job 10:3**

[a]13 Hebrew *Sheol* [b]16 Hebrew *to Sheol*
[a]15 Or *Nothing he had remains*

7"Though I cry, 'I've been wronged!' I
get no response;[j]
though I call for help,[k] there is no
justice.[l]
8He has blocked my way so that I
cannot pass;[m]
he has shrouded my paths in
darkness.[n]
9He has stripped[o] me of my honour[p]
and removed the crown from my
head.[q]
10He tears me down[r] on every side till I
am gone;
he uproots my hope[s] like a tree.[t]
11His anger[u] burns against me;
he counts me among his enemies.[v]
12His troops advance in force;[w]
they build a siege ramp[x] against me
and encamp around my tent.[y]

13"He has alienated my brothers[z] from
me;
my acquaintances are completely
estranged from me.[a]
14My kinsmen have gone away;
my friends[b] have forgotten me.
15My guests[c] and my maidservants[d]
count me a stranger;
they look upon me as an alien.
16I summon my servant, but he does not
answer,
though I beg him with my own
mouth.
17My breath is offensive to my wife;
I am loathsome[e] to my own
brothers.
18Even the little boys[f] scorn me;
when I appear, they ridicule me.[g]
19All my intimate friends[h] detest me;[i]
those I love have turned against
me.[j]
20I am nothing but skin and bones;[k]
I have escaped by only the skin of
my teeth.[a]

21"Have pity on me, my friends,[l] have
pity,
for the hand of God has struck[m] me.
22Why do you pursue[n] me as God does?[o]
Will you never get enough of my
flesh?[p]

23"Oh, that my words were recorded,
that they were written on a scroll,[q]
24that they were inscribed with an iron
tool[r] on[b] lead,
or engraved in rock for ever![s]
25I know that my Redeemer[c] [t] lives,[u]
and that in the end he will stand
upon the earth.[d]
26And after my skin has been destroyed,
yet[e] in[f] my flesh I will see God;[v]
27I myself will see him
with my own eyes[w]—I, and not
another.
How my heart yearns[x] within me!
28"If you say, 'How we will hound[y] him,
since the root of the trouble lies in
him,'[g]
29you should fear the sword yourselves;
for wrath will bring punishment by
the sword,[z]
and then you will know that there is
judgment."[h] [a]

Zophar

20 Then Zophar the Naamathite[a]
replied:

2"My troubled thoughts prompt me to
answer
because I am greatly disturbed.[b]
3I hear a rebuke[c] that dishonours me,
and my understanding inspires me
to reply.
4"Surely you know how it has been
from of old,[d]
ever since man[a] was placed on the
earth,
5that the mirth of the wicked[e] is brief,
the joy of the godless[f] lasts but a
moment.[g]
6Though his pride[h] reaches to the
heavens[i]
and his head touches the clouds,[j]
7he will perish for ever,[k] like his own
dung;
those who have seen him will say,
'Where is he?'[l]
8Like a dream[m] he flies away,[n] no more
to be found,
banished[o] like a vision of the night.[p]
9The eye that saw him will not see him
again;
his place will look on him no more.[q]

7 [j]Job 30:20; Ps 22:2; [k]Job 30:24,28; 31:35; Ps 5:2; [l]**Job 9:24**; Hab 1:2–4
8 [m]La 3:7; Hos 2:6; [n]Job 3:26; 23:17; 30:26; Ecc 6:4; Isa 59:9; Jer 8:15; 14:19; La 3:2
9 [o]**Job 12:17**; [p]Ge 43:28; Ex 12:42; Ps 15:4; 50:23; Pr 14:31; [q]**Job 2:8**; 29:14; Ps 89:39,44; La 5:16
10 [r]**Job 12:14**; [s]**Job 7:6**; [t]**Job 14:7**
11 [u]Job 16:9; [v]**Job 13:24**
12 [w]**Job 16:13**; [x]**Job 16:10**; [y]**Job 3:23**
13 [z]Ps 69:8; [a]ver 19; Job 16:7; 42:11; Ps 31:11; 38:11; 88:8
14 [b]ver 19; **2Sa 15:12**; Job 12:4; 16:20; Ps 88:18; Jer 20:10; 38:22
15 [c]Ge 14:14; [d]Ecc 2:7
17 [e]Ps 38:5
18 [f]**2Ki 2:23**; [g]**Job 16:10**
19 [h]**ver 14**; **Job 6:14**; Ps 55:12–13; [i]Job 30:10; [j]**ver 13**; Jn 13:18
20 [k]**Job 2:5**
21 [l]**Job 6:14**; [m]**Jdg 2:15**; **Job 4:5**; **10:3**; La 3:1
22 [n]**Job 13:25**; [o]ver 6; [p]**2Ch 28:9**; Ps 14:4; 27:2; 69:26; Pr 30:14; Isa 53:4
23 [q]**Ex 17:14**; **Ps 40:7**; **Isa 8:1**
24 [r]Jer 17:1; [s]**Job 16:18**
25 [t]**Ex 6:6**; **Lev 25:25**; Ps 68:5; 78:35; Pr 23:11; Isa 41:14; 43:14; 44:6,24; 47:4; 48:17; 49:26; 54:5; 59:20; 60:16; [u]**1Sa 14:39**; Job 16:19
26 [v]**Nu 12:8**; **Mt 5:8**; 1Co 13:12; 1Jn 3:2
27 [w]Lk 2:30; [x]Ps 42:1; 63:1; 84:2
28 [y]**Job 13:25**
29 [z]Job 15:22; [a]Job 27:13–23; Ps 1:5; 9:7; 58:11; Ecc 3:17; 11:9; 12:14

Ch. 20
1 [a]**Job 2:11** **2** [b]Ps 42:5; La 1:20
3 [c]Job 19:3 **4** [d]Dt 4:32; **32:7**
5 [e]Ps 94:3; [f]**Job 8:13**; [g]**Job 8:12**; Ps 37:35–36; 73:19
6 [h]Job 33:17; Isa 16:6; [i]**Ge 11:4**; [j]Isa 14:13–14; Ob 3–4
7 [k]**Job 4:20**; [l]**Job 7:8**; **14:20**
8 [m]Ps 73:20; Ecc 5:3; [n]Ps 90:10; Ecc 6:12; 12:7; [o]**Job 18:11**; [p]Job 27:20; 34:20; Ps 90:5; Isa 17:14; 29:7
9 [q]**Job 7:8**

[a]20 Or *only my gums* [b]24 Or *and*
[c]25 Or *defender* [d]25 Or *upon my grave*
[e]26 Or *And after I awake, / though this* ⌊*body*⌋ *has been destroyed, / then* [f]26 Or */ apart from*
[g]28 Many Hebrew manuscripts, Septuagint and Vulgate; most Hebrew manuscripts *me*
[h]29 Or */ that you may come to know the Almighty*
[a]4 Or *Adam*

10His children[r] must make amends to
the poor;
his own hands must give back his
wealth.[s]
11The youthful vigour[t] that fills his
bones[u]
will lie with him in the dust.[v]

12"Though evil[w] is sweet in his mouth
and he hides it under his tongue,[x]
13though he cannot bear to let it go
and keeps it in his mouth,[y]
14yet his food will turn sour in his
stomach;[z]
it will become the venom of
serpents[a] within him.
15He will spit out the riches[b] he
swallowed;
God will make his stomach vomit[c]
them up.
16He will suck the poison[d] of serpents;
the fangs of an adder will kill him.[e]
17He will not enjoy the streams,
the rivers[f] flowing with honey[g] and
cream.[h]
18What he toiled for he must give back
uneaten;[i]
he will not enjoy the profit from his
trading.[j]
19For he has oppressed the poor[k] and
left them destitute;[l]
he has seized houses[m] he did not
build.

20"Surely he will have no respite from
his craving;[n]
he cannot save himself by his
treasure.[o]
21Nothing is left for him to devour;
his prosperity will not endure.[p]
22In the midst of his plenty, distress will
overtake him;[q]
the full force of misery will come
upon him.[r]
23When he has filled his belly,[s]
God will vent his burning anger[t]
against him
and rain down his blows upon him.[u]
24Though he flees[v] from an iron
weapon,
a bronze-tipped arrow pierces him.[w]
25He pulls it out of his back,
the gleaming point out of his liver.
Terrors[x] will come over him;[y]
26 total darkness[z] lies in wait for his
treasures.
A fire[a] unfanned will consume him[b]
and devour what is left in his tent.[c]
27The heavens will expose his guilt;
the earth will rise up against him.[d]
28A flood will carry off his house,[e]
rushing waters[b] on the day of God's
wrath.[f]
29Such is the fate God allots the wicked,
the heritage appointed for them by
God."[g]

Job

21

Then Job replied:

2"Listen carefully to my words;[a]
let this be the consolation you give
me.[b]
3Bear with me while I speak,
and after I have spoken, mock on.[c]

4"Is my complaint[d] directed to man?
Why should I not be impatient?[e]
5Look at me and be astonished;
clap your hand over your mouth.[f]
6When I think about this, I am
terrified;[g]
trembling seizes my body.[h]
7Why do the wicked live on,
growing old and increasing in
power?[i]
8They see their children established
around them,
their offspring before their eyes.[j]
9Their homes are safe and free from
fear;[k]
the rod of God is not upon them.[l]
10Their bulls never fail to breed;
their cows calve and do not
miscarry.[m]
11They send forth their children as a
flock;[n]
their little ones dance about.
12They sing to the music of tambourine
and harp;[o]
they make merry to the sound of the
flute.[p]
13They spend their years in prosperity[q]
and go down to the grave[a][r] in
peace.[b][s]
14Yet they say to God, 'Leave us alone![t]
We have no desire to know your
ways.[u]
15Who is the Almighty, that we should
serve him?

10 [r]**Job 5:4**; [s]ver 15,18,20; **Job 3:15**; 31:8
11 [t]**Job 13:26**; [u]Job 21:24; [v]**Job 17:16**
12 [w]**Job 15:16**; [x]Ps 10:7; 140:3
13 [y]**Nu 11:18–20**
14 [z]Pr 20:17; Jer 2:19; 4:18; Rev 10:9; [a]**Nu 21:6**
15 [b]**ver 10**; [c]**Lev 18:25**
16 [d]**Dt 32:32**; [e]Dt 32:24
17 [f]Ps 36:8; [g]Dt 32:13; [h]Dt 32:14; Job 29:6
18 [i]**ver 10**; **Job 5:5**; [j]Ps 109:11
19 [k]**Job 5:16**; Ps 10:2; 94:6; 109:16; [l]**Dt 15:11**; 24:14; Job 24:4,14; 35:9; Pr 14:31; 28:28; Am 8:4; [m]Isa 5:8
20 [n]Ecc 5:12; [o]**ver 10**; Pr 11:4; Zep 1:18; Lk 12:15
21 [p]**Job 7:8**
22 [q]**Jdg 2:15**; Lk 12:16–20; [r]ver 29; Job 21:17,30; 31:2–3
23 [s]**Nu 11:18–20**; [t]La 4:11; Eze 5:13; 6:12; [u]ver 14; Ps 78:30–31
24 [v]Isa 24:18; Jer 46:21; 48:44; [w]**Job 15:22**
25 [x]**Job 18:11**; [y]**Job 15:21**; Ps 88:15–16
26 [z]**Job 5:14**; [a]**Job 1:16**; [b]Job 15:34; 26:6; 28:22; 31:12; Ps 21:9; [c]**Job 18:15**
27 [d]**Dt 31:28**
28 [e]Dt 28:31; Mt 7:26–27; [f]ver 29; Nu 14:28–32; Job 21:17,20,30; 40:11; Ps 60:3; 75:8; Pr 16:4; Isa 24:18; 51:17; Am 5:18; Jn 3:36; Ro 1:18; Eph 5:6
29 [g]**ver 22**; **Job 15:20**; 22:5; 31:2; 36:17; Jer 13:25; Rev 21:8

Ch. 21

2 [a]**Job 13:17**; [b]ver 34
3 [c]**Job 6:14**; **11:3**; **16:10** *4* [d]**Job 7:11**; [e]**Job 6:3**
5 [f]**Jdg 18:19** *6* [g]**Ge 45:3**; [h]**Job 4:14**
7 [i]ver 13; **Job 9:24**; 12:19; Ps 37:1; 73:3; Ecc 7:15; 8:14; Hab 1:13; Mal 3:15 *8* [j]Ps 17:14; Mal 3:15
9 [k]**Job 5:24**; [l]**Job 9:34** *10* [m]Ex 23:26
11 [n]Ps 78:52; 107:41
12 [o]Ps 33:2; [p]**Ge 4:21**; **1Ch 15:16**; Ps 71:22; 81:2; 108:2; Isa 5:12; Mt 11:17
13 [q]**ver 7**; **Job 8:7**; Ps 10:1–12; 94:3; [r]Job 24:19; Ps 49:14; Isa 14:15; [s]**Job 3:13**
14 [t]**Job 4:17**; 22:17; Isa 30:11; [u]**Dt 32:15**; **1Sa 15:11**; Ps 95:10; Pr 1:29; Jer 2:20,31

b28 Or *The possessions in his house will be carried off, / washed away* a13 Hebrew *Sheol*
b13 Or *in an instant*

What would we gain by praying to
him?'[v]
16But their prosperity is not in their own
hands,
so I stand aloof from the counsel of
the wicked.[w]
17"Yet how often is the lamp of the
wicked snuffed out?[x]
How often does calamity[y] come
upon them,
the fate God allots in his anger?[z]
18How often are they like straw before
the wind,
like chaff[a] swept away[b][c] by a gale?[d]
19⌞It is said,⌟ 'God stores up a man's
punishment for his sons.'[e]
Let him repay the man himself, so
that he will know it![f]
20Let his own eyes see his destruction;[g]
let him drink[h] of the wrath of the
Almighty.[c][i]
21For what does he care about the family
he leaves behind[j]
when his allotted months[k] come to
an end?[l]

22"Can anyone teach knowledge to
God,[m]
since he judges even the highest?[n]
23One man dies in full vigour,[o]
completely secure and at ease,[p]
24his body[d] well nourished,[q]
his bones[r] rich with marrow.[s]
25Another man dies in bitterness of
soul,[t]
never having enjoyed anything
good.
26Side by side they lie in the dust,[u]
and worms[v] cover them both.[w]

27"I know full well what you are
thinking,
the schemes by which you would
wrong me.
28You say, 'Where now is the great
man's[x] house,
the tents where wicked men lived?'[y]
29Have you never questioned those who
travel?
Have you paid no regard to their
accounts—
30that the evil man is spared from the
day of calamity,[z]
that he is delivered from[e] the day of
wrath?[a]
31Who denounces his conduct to his
face?
Who repays him for what he has
done?[b]
32He is carried to the grave,
and watch is kept over his tomb.[c]
33The soil in the valley is sweet to him;[d]
all men follow after him,
and a countless throng goes[f] before
him.[e]

34"So how can you console me[f] with
your nonsense?
Nothing is left of your answers but
falsehood!"[g]

Eliphaz

22 Then Eliphaz the Temanite[a]
replied:

2"Can a man be of benefit to God?[b]
Can even a wise man benefit him?[c]
3What pleasure[d] would it give the
Almighty if you were righteous?[e]
What would he gain if your ways
were blameless?[f]

4"Is it for your piety that he rebukes
you
and brings charges against you?[g]
5Is not your wickedness great?
Are not your sins[h] endless?[i]
6You demanded security[j] from your
brothers for no reason;[k]
you stripped men of their clothing,
leaving them naked.[l]
7You gave no water[m] to the weary
and you withheld food from the
hungry,[n]
8though you were a powerful man,
owning land[o]—
an honoured man,[p] living on it.[q]
9And you sent widows[r] away
empty-handed[s]
and broke the strength of the
fatherless.[t]
10That is why snares[u] are all around
you,[v]
why sudden peril terrifies you,[w]
11why it is so dark[x] that you cannot see,
and why a flood of water covers
you.[y]

12"Is not God in the heights of heaven?[z]
And see how lofty are the highest
stars!

15 [v]Job 5:2; 34:9; 35:3; Ps 73:13; 139:20; Isa 48:5; Jer 9:6; 44:17
16 [w]Job 22:18; Ps 1:1; 26:5; 36:1
17 [x]**Job 18:5**; [y]Job 18:12; [z]**Job 20:22**,28
18 [a]**Job 13:25**; [b]**Ge 19:15**; [c]**Job 7:10**; Pr 10:25; [d]**Ge 7:23**
19 [e]Ex 20:5; Jer 31:29; Eze 18:2; Jn 9:2; [f]Jer 25:14; 50:29; 51:6,24,56
20 [g]**Ex 32:33**; Nu 16:22; **2Ki 14:6**; Jer 42:16; [h]Job 6:4; [i]**Job 20:28**; Jer 25:15; Rev 14:10
21 [j]Job 14:22; [k]**Job 14:5**; [l]**Job 14:21**; Ecc 9:5–6
22 [m]Job 35:11; 36:22; 39:17; Ps 94:12; Isa 40:13–14; Jer 32:33; Ro 11:34; [n]**Job 4:18**; Ps 82:1; 86:8; 135:5
23 [o]**Ge 15:15**; **Job 13:26**; [p]**Job 3:13**
24 [q]Ps 73:4; [r]Job 20:11; [s]Pr 3:8
25 [t]**Job 10:1**
26 [u]**Job 17:16**; [v]**Job 7:5**; [w]Job 24:20; Ecc 9:2–3; Isa 14:11
28 [x]Job 1:3; 12:21; 29:25; 31:37; [y]**Job 8:22**
30 [z]Job 31:3; [a]**Job 20:22**,28; **Isa 5:30**; Ro 2:5; 2Pe 2:9
31 [b]Job 34:11; Ps 62:12; Pr 24:11–12; Isa 59:18
32 [c]Isa 14:18
33 [d]Job 3:22; [e]**Job 3:19**
34 [f]ver 2; [g]**Job 6:15**; 8:20

Ch. 22

1 [a]**Job 4:1**
2 [b]Lk 17:10; [c]**Job 7:17**
3 [d]Isa 1:11; Hag 1:8; [e]Ps 143:2; [f]Job 35:7; Pr 9:12
4 [g]**Job 9:3**; 19:29; Ps 143:2; Isa 3:14; Eze 20:35
5 [h]**Ezr 9:13**; **Job 15:5**; [i]**Job 15:13**; **20:29**; 29:17
6 [j]**Ex 22:26**; [k]**2Ki 4:1**; [l]**Ex 22:27**; Dt 24:12–13
7 [m]Mt 10:42; [n]ver 9; Job 29:12; 31:17,21,31; Isa 58:7, 10; Eze 18:7; Mt 25:42
8 [o]**Job 15:19**; [p]Isa 3:3; 5:13; 9:15; [q]**Job 12:19**
9 [r]Job 29:13; 31:16; Ps 146:9; [s]Job 24:3,21; Isa 10:2; Lk 1:53; [t]**ver 7**; **Job 6:27**; **Isa 1:17**
10 [u]**Job 18:9**; [v]**Job 10:3**; [w]**Job 15:21**
11 [x]**Job 5:14**; [y]**Ge 7:23**; Job 36:28; 38:34,37; Ps 69:1–2; 124:4–5; Isa 58:10–11; La 3:54
12 [z]**Job 11:8**; **16:19**

c17–20 Verses 17 and 18 may be taken as exclamations and 19 and 20 as declarations.
d24 The meaning of the Hebrew for this word is uncertain.
e30 Or *man is reserved for the day of calamity, / that he is brought forth to*
f33 Or / *as a countless throng went*

13Yet you say, 'What does God know?[a]
Does he judge through such
darkness?[b]
14Thick clouds[c] veil him, so he does not
see us[d]
as he goes about in the vaulted
heavens.'[e]
15Will you keep to the old path
that evil men[f] have trod?[g]
16They were carried off before their
time,[h]
their foundations[i] washed away by
a flood.[j]
17They said to God, 'Leave us alone!
What can the Almighty do to us?'[k]
18Yet it was he who filled their houses
with good things,[l]
so I stand aloof from the counsel of
the wicked.[m]

19"The righteous see their ruin and
rejoice;[n]
the innocent mock[o] them, saying,
20'Surely our foes are destroyed,[p]
and fire[q] devours their wealth.'

21"Submit to God and be at peace[r] with
him;[s]
in this way prosperity will come to
you.[t]
22Accept instruction from his mouth[u]
and lay up his words[v] in your
heart.[w]
23If you return[x] to the Almighty, you
will be restored:[y]
If you remove wickedness far from
your tent[z]
24and assign your nuggets[a] to the dust,
your gold[b] of Ophir[c] to the rocks in
the ravines,[d]
25then the Almighty will be your gold,[e]
the choicest silver for you.[f]
26Surely then you will find delight in the
Almighty[g]
and will lift up your face[h] to God.[i]
27You will pray to him,[j] and he will hear
you,[k]
and you will fulfil your vows.[l]
28What you decide on will be done,[m]
and light[n] will shine on your ways.[o]
29When men are brought low[p] and you
say, 'Lift them up!'
then he will save the downcast.[q]
30He will deliver even one who is not
innocent,[r]
who will be delivered through the
cleanness of your hands."[s]

Job

23 Then Job replied:

2"Even today my complaint[a] is bitter;[b]
his hand[a] is heavy in spite of[b] my
groaning.[c]
3If only I knew where to find him;
if only I could go to his dwelling![d]
4I would state my case[e] before him
and fill my mouth with arguments.[f]
5I would find out what he would
answer me,[g]
and consider what he would say.
6Would he oppose me with great
power?[h]
No, he would not press charges
against me.[i]
7There an upright man[j] could present
his case before him,[k]
and I would be delivered for ever
from my judge.[l]

8"But if I go to the east, he is not there;
if I go to the west, I do not find him.
9When he is at work in the north, I do
not see him;
when he turns to the south, I catch
no glimpse of him.[m]
10But he knows the way that I take;[n]
when he has tested me,[o] I shall come
forth as gold.[p]
11My feet have closely followed his
steps;[q]
I have kept to his way without
turning aside.[r]
12I have not departed from the
commands of his lips;[s]
I have treasured the words of his
mouth more than my daily
bread.[t]

13"But he stands alone, and who can
oppose him?[u]
He does whatever he pleases.[v]
14He carries out his decree against me,
and many such plans he still has in
store.[w]
15That is why I am terrified before him;[x]
when I think of all this, I fear him.[y]

13 [a]ver 14; Ps 10:11; 59:7; 64:5; 73:11; 94:7; Isa 29:15; Eze 9:9; Zep 1:12; [b]Ps 139:11; Eze 8:12; Eph 6:12
14 [c]Job 26:9; Ps 97:2; 105:39; [d]**ver 13; 2Ki 21:16;** [e]Job 37:18; Ps 18:11; Pr 8:27; Isa 40:22; Jer 23:23–24
15 [f]Job 23:10; 34:36; [g]Job 34:8; Ps 1:1; 50:18
16 [h]**Job 15:32;** [i]**Job 4:19;** [j]**Ge 7:23;** Mt 7:26–27
17 [k]Job 21:15
18 [l]**Job 12:6;** [m]**Job 21:16**
19 [n]Ps 5:11; 9:2; 32:11; 58:10; 64:10; 97:12; 107:42; [o]Job 21:3; Ps 52:6
20 [p]Ps 18:39; [q]**Job 15:30**
21 [r]Isa 26:3,12; 27:5; Ro 5:1; [s]**Ge 17:1**; Jer 9:24; [t]**Job 8:7**; Ps 34:8–10; Pr 3:10; 1Pe 5:6
22 [u]**Dt 8:3;** [v]**Job 6:10;** [w]**Job 15:11**; 28:23; Ps 37:31; 40:8; Pr 2:6; Eze 3:10
23 [x]Isa 31:6; 44:22; 55:7; 59:20; Jer 3:14,22; Eze 18:32; Zec 1:3; Mal 3:7; [y]**Job 5:24**; Isa 19:22; Ac 20:32; [z]Job 11:14
24 [a]Job 28:6; [b]Ps 19:10; [c]**Ge 10:29;** [d]**Job 1:10**; 31:25; Isa 2:20; 30:22; 31:7; 40:19–20; Mt 6:19
25 [e]Job 31:24; Ps 49:6; 52:7; Pr 11:28; [f]2Ki 18:7; Isa 33:6; Mt 6:20–21
26 [g]Job 27:10; Ps 2:8; 16:6; 37:4; Isa 58:14; 61:10; [h]Job 11:15; [i]Job 11:17; 33:26; Ps 27:6; 100:1
27 [j]**Job 5:27;** [k]**Job 5:15; Ps 86:7; Isa 30:19;** [l]**Nu 30:2**
28 [m]Ps 103:11; 145:19; [n]Job 33:28; Ps 97:11; Pr 4:18; [o]**Job 11:17** *29* [p]**Est 5:12;** [q]Ps 18:27; **Mt 23:12**
30 [r]Isa 1:18; Ro 4:5; [s]**2Sa 22:21**

Ch. 23
2 [a]**Job 7:11;** [b]**1Sa 1:10; Job 6:3;** [c]Ps 6:6; 32:4; Jer 45:3; Eze 21:7 *3* [d]Dt 4:29
4 [e]**Job 13:18;** [f]**Job 9:15** *5* [g]**Job 11:5**
6 [h]**Job 9:4;** [i]**Job 6:4**
7 [j]**Job 1:1;** [k]**Ge 3:8; Job 9:3**; 13:3; [l]**Job 6:29**
9 [m]**Job 9:11**
10 [n]Job 1:1; 27:6; 31:6; 36:7; Ps 7:9; 11:5; 34:15; 37:18; 94:11; 119:168; 146:8; [o]**Job 7:18**; Ps 139:1–3; [p]**Job 6:29; 22:15; Ps 12:6**; 1Pe 1:7
11 [q]Ps 17:5; [r]Job 31:7; Ps 40:4; 44:18; 119:51,59,157; 125:5; Jer 11:20
12 [s]**Job 6:10;** [t]**Job 15:11**; Mt 4:4; Jn 4:32,34
13 [u]**Job 9:3;** [v]**Job 10:13**; Isa 55:11
14 [w]1Th 3:3; 1Pe 4:12
15 [x]**Ge 45:3;** [y]**Jos 24:14**; Ps 34:9; 36:1; 111:10; Pr 1:7; Ecc 3:14; 12:13; 2Co 5:11

[a]2 Septuagint and Syriac; Hebrew / *the hand on me*
[b]2 Or *heavy on me in*

16God has made my heart faint;[z]
the Almighty[a] has terrified me.[b]
17Yet I am not silenced by the darkness,[c]
by the thick darkness that covers my face.

24 "Why does the Almighty not set times[a] for judgment?[b]
Why must those who know him look in vain for such days?[c]
2Men move boundary stones;[d]
they pasture flocks they have stolen.[e]
3They drive away the orphan's donkey
and take the widow's ox in pledge.[f]
4They thrust the needy[g] from the path
and force all the poor[h] of the land into hiding.[i]
5Like wild donkeys[j] in the desert,
the poor go about their labour[k] of foraging food;
the wasteland[l] provides food for their children.
6They gather fodder[m] in the fields
and glean in the vineyards[n] of the wicked.[o]
7Lacking clothes, they spend the night naked;
they have nothing to cover themselves in the cold.[p]
8They are drenched[q] by mountain rains
and hug[r] the rocks for lack of shelter.[s]
9The fatherless[t] child is snatched[u] from the breast;
the infant of the poor is seized[v] for a debt.[w]
10Lacking clothes, they go about naked;[x]
they carry the sheaves,[y] but still go hungry.
11They crush olives among the terraces;[a]
they tread the winepresses,[z] yet suffer thirst.[a]
12The groans of the dying rise from the city,
and the souls of the wounded cry out for help.[b]
But God charges no-one with wrongdoing.[c]

13"There are those who rebel against the light,[d]
who do not know its ways
or stay in its paths.[e]
14When daylight is gone, the murderer rises up
and kills[f] the poor and needy;[g]
in the night he steals forth like a thief.[h]
15The eye of the adulterer[i] watches for dusk;[j]
he thinks, 'No eye will see me,'[k]
and he keeps his face concealed.
16In the dark, men break into houses,[l]
but by day they shut themselves in;
they want nothing to do with the light.[m]
17For all of them, deep darkness is their morning;[b]
they make friends with the terrors[n] of darkness.[c][o]

18"Yet they are foam[p] on the surface of the water;[q]
their portion of the land is cursed,[r]
so that no-one goes to the vineyards.[s]
19As heat and drought snatch away the melted snow,[t]
so the grave[d][u] snatches away those who have sinned.
20The womb forgets them,
the worm[v] feasts on them;[w]
evil men are no longer remembered[x]
but are broken like a tree.[y]
21They prey on the barren and childless woman,
and to the widow show no kindness.[z]
22But God drags away the mighty by his power;[a]
though they become established,[b]
they have no assurance of life.[c]
23He may let them rest in a feeling of security,[d]
but his eyes[e] are on their ways.[f]
24For a little while they are exalted, and then they are gone;[g]
they are brought low and gathered up like all others;[h]
they are cut off like ears of corn.[i]

25"If this is not so, who can prove me false
and reduce my words to nothing?"[j]

Bildad

25 Then Bildad the Shuhite[a] replied:

2"Dominion and awe belong to God;[b]
he establishes order in the heights of heaven.[c]

16 [z]Dt 20:3; [a]Job 27:2; [b]**Ex 3:6;** Rev 6:16
17 [c]**Job 3:6; 19:8**

Ch. 24

1 [a]**Job 14:5;** [b]**Job 9:23;** 2Pe 3:7; [c]**Job 15:20;** Ac 1:7
2 [d]**Dt 19:14;** [e]Ex 20:15; Dt 28:31
3 [f]**Job 6:27; 22:9**
4 [g]Job 29:16; 31:19; [h]Job 29:12; 30:25; Ps 12:5; 41:1; 82:3–4; Isa 11:4; [i]**Job 20:19; Pr 28:12**
5 [j]**Ge 16:12;** [k]Ps 104:23; [l]Job 30:3
6 [m]**Job 6:5;** [n]ver 18; [o]Ru 2:22; **1Ki 21:19**
7 [p]**Ex 22:27**
8 [q]Da 4:25,33; [r]La 4:5; [s]**Jdg 6:2**
9 [t]**Dt 24:17;** [u]Job 29:17; [v]Ps 14:4; Pr 30:14; Isa 3:14; 10:1–2; Eze 18:12; [w]**Lev 25:47; 2Ki 4:1**
10 [x]Dt 24:12–13; [y]**Lev 19:9**
11 [z]Isa 5:2; 16:10; Hag 2:16; [a]Mic 6:15
12 [b]**Job 12:19;** 30:28; Ps 5:2; 22:24; 39:12; 119:147; Isa 30:19; Jer 50:46; 51:52, 54; Eze 26:15; Rev 6:10; [c]**Job 9:23**
13 [d]ver 16; Job 38:15; Jn 3:19–20; 1Th 5:4–5; [e]Job 17:12; 38:20; Ps 18:28; Isa 5:20; Eph 5:8–14
14 [f]Isa 3:15; Mic 3:3; [g]**Job 20:19;** Ps 37:32; [h]Ps 10:9
15 [i]Job 31:9,27; Pr 1:10; [j]Pr 7:8–9; [k]Ps 10:11
16 [l]**Ex 22:2;** Mt 6:19; [m]**ver 13**
17 [n]**Job 18:11;** [o]**Job 15:22;** 18:5
18 [p]**Job 9:26;** Jude 13; [q]Job 22:16; Isa 57:20; [r]**Job 5:3;** [s]ver 6
19 [t]Job 6:17; [u]**Job 21:13**
20 [v]**Job 7:5;** [w]**Job 21:26;** [x]**Job 18:17;** [y]**Job 14:7;** Ps 31:12; Da 4:14 21 [z]**Job 22:9**
22 [a]**Job 9:4;** [b]**Job 12:19;** [c]Dt 28:66; Mt 6:27; Jas 4:14
23 [d]**Job 9:24;** Am 6:1; [e]**2Ch 16:9;** [f]**Job 10:4**
24 [g]**2Ki 19:35; Job 4:20;** Ps 37:10; 83:13; Isa 5:24; 17:13; 40:24; 41:2,15; [h]**Job 3:19;** [i]Isa 17:5
25 [j]**Job 6:28; 16:17**

Ch. 25

1 [a]**Job 8:1**
2 [b]**Job 9:4;** Ps 47:9; 89:18; Zec 9:7; Rev 1:6; [c]**2Ch 20:6; Job 11:8; 16:19**

[a]11 Or *olives between the millstones*; the meaning of the Hebrew for this word is uncertain.
[b]17 Or *them, their morning is like the shadow of death*
[c]17 Or *of the shadow of death*
[d]19 Hebrew *Sheol*

3Can his forces be numbered?
Upon whom does his light not rise?[d]
4How then can a man be righteous
before God?
How can one born of woman be
pure?[e]
5If even the moon[f] is not bright
and the stars are not pure in his
eyes,[g]
6how much less man, who is but a
maggot—
a son of man,[h] who is only a worm!"[i]

Job

26 Then Job replied:

2"How you have helped the
powerless![a]
How you have saved the arm that is
feeble![b]
3What advice you have offered to one
without wisdom!
And what great insight[c] you have
displayed!
4Who has helped you utter these
words?
And whose spirit spoke from your
mouth?[d]

5"The dead are in deep anguish,[e]
those beneath the waters and all
that live in them.
6Death[a][f] is naked before God;
Destruction[b][g] lies uncovered.[h]
7He spreads out the northern ⌊skies⌋[i]
over empty space;
he suspends the earth over
nothing.[j]
8He wraps up the waters[k] in his clouds,[l]
yet the clouds do not burst under
their weight.
9He covers the face of the full moon,
spreading his clouds[m] over it.
10He marks out the horizon on the face
of the waters[n]
for a boundary between light and
darkness.[o]
11The pillars of the heavens quake,[p]
aghast at his rebuke.
12By his power he churned up the sea;[q]
by his wisdom[r] he cut Rahab[s] to
pieces.
13By his breath the skies[t] became fair;
his hand pierced the gliding
serpent.[u]
14And these are but the outer fringe of
his works;
how faint the whisper[v] we hear of
him![w]
Who then can understand the
thunder of his power?"[x]

27 And Job continued his discourse:[a]

2"As surely as God lives, who has
denied me justice,[b]
the Almighty,[c] who has made me
taste bitterness of soul,[d]
3as long as I have life within me,
the breath of God[e] in my nostrils,
4my lips will not speak wickedness,
and my tongue will utter no deceit.[f]
5I will never admit you are in the right;
till I die, I will not deny my
integrity.[g]
6I will maintain my righteousness[h] and
never let go of it;
my conscience[i] will not reproach me
as long as I live.[j]

7"May my enemies be like the wicked,[k]
my adversaries[l] like the unjust!
8For what hope has the godless[m] when
he is cut off,
when God takes away his life?[n]
9Does God listen to his cry
when distress comes upon him?[o]
10Will he find delight in the Almighty?[p]
Will he call upon God at all times?

11"I will teach you about the power of
God;
the ways[q] of the Almighty I will not
conceal.[r]
12You have all seen this yourselves.
Why then this meaningless talk?

13"Here is the fate God allots to the
wicked,
the heritage a ruthless man receives
from the Almighty:[s]
14However many his children,[t] their fate
is the sword;[u]
his offspring will never have
enough to eat.[v]
15The plague will bury those who
survive him,
and their widows will not weep for
them.[w]
16Though he heaps up silver like dust[x]
and clothes like piles of clay,[y]
17what he lays up[z] the righteous will
wear,[a]
and the innocent will divide his
silver.[b]

3 [d]Mt 5:45; Jas 1:17
4 [e]**Job 4:17**
5 [f]Job 31:26; [g]**Job 4:18**
6 [h]Ps 80:17; 144:3; Eze 2:1; [i]**Job 4:19; 7:5**

Ch. 26

2 [a]Job 6:12; [b]**Job 4:3**
3 [c]Job 34:35
4 [d]1Ki 22:24
5 [e]Ps 88:10; Isa 14:9; 26:14
6 [f]Ps 139:8; [g]**Job 20:26; Rev 9:11**; [h]Job 10:22; 11:8; 38:17; 41:11; Ps 139:11–12; Pr 15:11; **Heb 4:13**
7 [i]Job 9:8; [j]Job 38:6; Ps 104:5; Pr 3:19–20; 8:27; Isa 40:22
8 [k]Pr 30:4; [l]**Ge 1:2**; Job 36:27; 37:11; Ps 147:8
9 [m]**2Sa 22:10; Job 22:14**
10 [n]Pr 8:27; Isa 40:22; [o]**Ge 1:4; Job 28:3**; 38:8–11
11 [p]**2Sa 22:8**
12 [q]**Ex 14:21**; [r]Job 12:13; [s]**Job 9:13**
13 [t]Job 9:8; [u]Isa 27:1
14 [v]Job 4:12; [w]Job 42:5; Hab 3:2; 1Co 13:12; [x]**Job 9:6**

Ch. 27

1 [a]Job 29:1
2 [b]**Job 6:29; 9:24**; Isa 45:9; 49:4,14; [c]Job 23:16; [d]**1Sa 1:10; Job 7:19; 10:1**
3 [e]**Ge 2:7**; Job 32:8; 33:4; 34:14; **Ps 144:4**
4 [f]**Job 6:28; 12:16; 16:17**
5 [g]**Job 2:9; 10:7; 32:2**
6 [h]Job 29:14; Ps 119:121; 132:9; Isa 59:17; 61:10; [i]**Ac 23:1**; Ro 2:15; [j]**Job 2:3; 10:7; 23:10; 34:17**
7 [k]**Job 8:22**; [l]Job 31:35
8 [m]**Job 8:13**; [n]**Nu 16:22; Job 8:22; 11:20**; Lk 12:20
9 [o]**Dt 1:45; 1Sa 8:18; Job 15:31** 10 [p]**Job 22:26**
11 [q]Job 36:23; [r]ver 13 13 [s]**Job 16:19; 20:29**
14 [t]**Job 5:4**; [u]**Job 15:22; La 2:22**; [v]**Job 4:11**
15 [w]Ps 78:64 16 [x]**1Ki 10:27**; [y]Zec 9:3
17 [z]Ps 39:6; 49:10; Ecc 2:26; [a]**Job 7:8**; Pr 13:22; 28:8; [b]Ex 3:22; **Job 3:15**

[a]6 Hebrew *Sheol*
[b]6 Hebrew *Abaddon*

18The house[c] he builds is like a moth's
cocoon,[d]
like a hut[e] made by a watchman.
19He lies down wealthy, but will do so
no more;[f]
when he opens his eyes, all is gone.[g]
20Terrors[h] overtake him like a flood;[i]
a tempest snatches him away in the
night.[j]
21The east wind[k] carries him off, and he
is gone;[l]
it sweeps him out of his place.[m]
22It hurls itself against him without
mercy[n]
as he flees headlong[o] from its
power.[p]
23It claps its hands[q] in derision
and hisses him out of his place.[r]

28 "There is a mine for silver
and a place where gold is
refined.[a]
2Iron is taken from the earth,
and copper is smelted from ore.[b]
3Man puts an end to the darkness;[c]
he searches the farthest recesses
for ore in the blackest darkness.[d]
4Far from where people dwell he cuts a
shaft,[e]
in places forgotten by the foot of
man;
far from men he dangles and sways.
5The earth, from which food comes,[f]
is transformed below as by fire;
6sapphires[a][g] come from its rocks,
and its dust contains nuggets of
gold.[h]
7No bird of prey knows that hidden
path,
no falcon's eye has seen it.[i]
8Proud beasts[j] do not set foot on it,
and no lion prowls there.[k]
9Man's hand assaults the flinty rock[l]
and lays bare the roots of the
mountains.[m]
10He tunnels through the rock;[n]
his eyes see all its treasures.[o]
11He searches[b] the sources of the rivers[p]
and brings hidden things[q] to light.

12"But where can wisdom be found?[r]
Where does understanding dwell?[s]
13Man does not comprehend its worth;[t]
it cannot be found in the land of the
living.[u]
14The deep[v] says, 'It is not in me';
the sea[w] says, 'It is not with me.'
15It cannot be bought with the finest
gold,
nor can its price be weighed in
silver.[x]
16It cannot be bought with the gold of
Ophir,[y]
with precious onyx or sapphires.[z]

18 [c]**Job 8:22;** [d]**Job 8:14;** [e]Isa 1:8; 24:20
19 [f]**Job 3:13**; 7:8; [g]**Job 14:20**
20 [h]**Job 6:4;** [i]**Job 15:21;** [j]**Job 20:8**
21 [k]Job 38:24; Jer 13:24; 22:22; [l]Job 30:22; [m]**Job 7:10**
22 [n]Jer 13:14; Eze 5:11; 24:14; [o]2Ki 7:15; [p]**Job 11:20**
23 [q]**Nu 24:10;** Na 3:19; [r]**Job 7:10**

Ch. 28

1 [a]Ps 12:6; 66:10; Jer 9:7; Da 11:35; Mal 3:3
2 [b]Dt 8:9
3 [c]Ecc 1:13; 7:25; 8:17; [d]**Job 26:10**; 38:19
4 [e]ver 10; 2Sa 5:8
5 [f]Ge 1:29; Ps 104:14; 145:15
6 [g]ver 16; SS 5:14; Isa 54:11; [h]**Job 22:24**
7 [i]ver 21
8 [j]Job 41:34; [k]Isa 35:9
9 [l]**Dt 8:15**; [m]Jnh 2:6
10 [n]**ver 4**; [o]Pr 2:4
11 [p]**Ge 7:11**; [q]Isa 48:6; Jer 33:3
12 [r]ver 28; Pr 1:20; 3:13–20; 8:1; 9:1–3; Ecc 7:24; [s]ver 20,23
13 [t]Pr 3:15; Mt 13:44–46; [u]Dt 29:29; Ps 27:13; 52:5; 116:9; 142:5; Isa 38:11; Jer 11:19; Eze 26:20; 32:24
14 [v]Ps 42:7; Ro 10:7; [w]Dt 30:13
15 [x]ver 17; Pr 3:13–14; 8:10–11; 16:16; Ac 8:20
16 [y]**Ge 10:29**; [z]**ver 6; Ex 24:10**
17 [a]Ps 119:72; Pr 8:10; [b]**ver 15**
18 [c]Eze 27:16; [d]Rev 21:11; [e]Pr 3:15; 8:11
19 [f]Ex 28:17; [g]Isa 11:11; [h]Pr 3:14–15; 8:10–11,19
20 [i]**Job 9:4**
21 [j]ver 7

17Neither gold nor crystal can compare
with it,[a]
nor can it be had for jewels of gold.[b]
18Coral[c] and jasper[d] are not worthy of
mention;
the price of wisdom is beyond
rubies.[e]
19The topaz[f] of Cush[g] cannot compare
with it;
it cannot be bought with pure gold.[h]

20"Where then does wisdom come
from?
Where does understanding dwell?[i]
21It is hidden from the eyes of every
living thing,
concealed even from the birds of the
air.[j]
22Destruction[c][k] and Death[l] say,
'Only a rumour of it has reached our
ears.'
23God understands the way to it
and he alone[m] knows where it
dwells,[n]
24for he views the ends of the earth[o]
and sees everything under the
heavens.[p]
25When he established the force of the
wind
and measured out the waters,[q]
26when he made a decree for the rain[r]
and a path for the thunderstorm,[s]
27then he looked at wisdom and
appraised it;
he confirmed it and tested it.[t]
28And he said to man,
'The fear of the Lord—that is
wisdom,
and to shun evil[u] is
understanding.[v]'"

29 Job continued his discourse:[a]
2"How I long for the months gone by,[b]
for the days when God watched
over me,[c]
3when his lamp shone upon my head

22 [k]**Job 20:26; Rev 9:11;** [l]Pr 8:32–36
23 [m]Ecc 3:11; 8:17; [n]**Job 9:4; 22:22;** Pr 8:22–31
24 [o]Job 36:32; 37:3; 38:18,24,35; Ps 33:13–14; 66:7; Isa 11:12; [p]**Jos 3:11; Job 10:4; Heb 4:13**
25 [q]**Job 12:15**; 38:8–11
26 [r]Job 36:28; 37:6; Jer 51:16; [s]Job 36:33; 37:3,8,11; 38:27; Ps 65:12; 104:14; 147:8; Isa 35:7
27 [t]Pr 3:19; 8:22–31
28 [u]Ps 11:5; 97:10; Pr 3:7; 8:13; [v]**Ex 20:20; Dt 4:6; Job 37:24**

Ch. 29

1 [a]Job 27:1 2 [b]**Ge 31:30**; [c]Jer 1:12; 31:28; 44:27

[a]6 Or *lapis lazuli;* also in verse 16
[b]11 Septuagint, Aquila and Vulgate; Hebrew *He dams up*
[c]22 Hebrew *Abaddon*

and by his light I walked through
darkness![d]
4 Oh, for the days when I was in my
prime,
when God's intimate friendship[e]
blessed my house,[f]
5 when the Almighty was still with me
and my children[g] were around me,[h]
6 when my path was drenched with
cream[i]
and the rock[j] poured out for me
streams of olive oil.[k]

7 "When I went to the gate[l] of the city
and took my seat in the public
square,
8 the young men saw me and stepped
aside[m]
and the old men rose to their feet;[n]
9 the chief men refrained from
speaking[o]
and covered their mouths with their
hands;[p]
10 the voices of the nobles were hushed,[q]
and their tongues stuck to the roof
of their mouths.[r]
11 Whoever heard me spoke well of me,
and those who saw me commended
me,[s]
12 because I rescued the poor[t] who cried
for help,
and the fatherless[u] who had none to
assist him.[v]
13 The man who was dying blessed me;[w]
I made the widow's[x] heart sing.
14 I put on righteousness[y] as my clothing;
justice was my robe and my turban.[z]
15 I was eyes[a] to the blind
and feet to the lame.[b]
16 I was a father to the needy;[c]
I took up the case[d] of the stranger.[e]
17 I broke the fangs of the wicked
and snatched the victims[f] from their
teeth.[g]

18 "I thought, 'I shall die in my own
house,
my days as numerous as the grains
of sand.[h]
19 My roots will reach to the water,[i]
and the dew will lie all night on my
branches.[j]
20 My glory will remain fresh[k] in me,
the bow[l] ever new in my hand.'[m]

21 "Men listened to me expectantly,
waiting in silence for my counsel.[n]
22 After I had spoken, they spoke no
more;[o]
my words fell gently on their ears.[p]
23 They waited for me as for showers
and drank in my words as the spring
rain.[q]

3 [d]**Job 11:17; 12:25**
4 [e]**Job 15:8;** [f]Ps 25:14; Pr 3:32
5 [g]Ps 127:3–5; 128:3; [h]Ru 4:1
6 [i]**Job 20:17;** [j]Ps 81:16; [k]Ge 49:20; **Dt 32:13**
7 [l]ver 21; Job 5:4; 31:21; Jer 20:2; 38:7
8 [m]1Ti 5:1; [n]**Lev 19:32**
9 [o]ver 21; Job 31:21; [p]**Jdg 18:19;** Job 40:4; Pr 30:32
10 [q]ver 22; [r]Ps 137:6
11 [s]**Job 4:4;** Heb 11:4
12 [t]**Job 24:4;** [u]**Dt 24:17;** Job 31:17,21; [v]Ps 72:12; Pr 21:13
13 [w]Job 31:20; [x]**Dt 10:18; Job 22:9**
14 [y]**2Sa 8:15; Job 27:6;** Eph 4:24; 6:14; [z]**Job 19:9**
15 [a]Nu 10:31; [b]**Job 4:4**
16 [c]**Job 24:4;** [d]Ex 18:26; [e]**Job 4:4;** Pr 22:22–23
17 [f]Job 24:9; [g]**Job 4:10,11; Ps 3:7**
18 [h]Ps 1:1–3; 15:5; 16:8; 30:6; 62:2; 139:18; Pr 3:1–2
19 [i]**Nu 24:6; Job 14:9;** [j]**Ge 27:28; Job 15:30; Ps 133:3**
20 [k]Ps 92:14; [l]Job 30:11; Ps 18:34; Isa 38:12; [m]Ge 49:24
21 [n]**ver 7,9**
22 [o]ver 10; [p]Dt 32:2
23 [q]**Job 4:3**
24 [r]**Nu 6:25;** [s]Pr 16:14–15
25 [t]**Job 21:28;** [u]**Job 1:3;** [v]**Job 4:4**

Ch. 30

1 [a]**Job 6:14; 11:3; Ps 119:21;** [b]Isa 56:10
3 [c]Isa 8:21; [d]Job 24:5; [e]Jer 17:6
4 [f]Job 39:6; [g]**1Ki 19:4**
6 [h]Isa 2:19; Hos 10:8
7 [i]Job 6:5; [j]Job 39:5–6
8 [k]**Jdg 9:4;** [l]**Job 18:18**

24 When I smiled at them, they scarcely
believed it;
the light of my face[r] was precious to
them.[a][s]
25 I chose the way for them and sat as
their chief;[t]
I dwelt as a king[u] among his troops;
I was like one who comforts
mourners.[v]

30

"But now they mock me,[a]
men younger than I,
whose fathers I would have disdained
to put with my sheep dogs.[b]
2 Of what use was the strength of their
hands to me,
since their vigour had gone from
them?
3 Haggard from want and hunger,
they roamed[a] the parched land[c]
in desolate wastelands[d] at night.[e]
4 In the brush they gathered salt herbs,[f]
and their food[b] was the root of the
broom tree.[g]
5 They were banished from their
fellow-men,
shouted at as if they were thieves.
6 They were forced to live in the dry
stream beds,
among the rocks and in holes in the
ground.[h]
7 They brayed[i] among the bushes[j]
and huddled in the undergrowth.
8 A base and nameless brood,[k]
they were driven out of the land.[l]

9 "And now their sons mock me[m] in
song;[n]
I have become a byword[o] among
them.
10 They detest me[p] and keep their
distance;
they do not hesitate to spit in my
face.[q]
11 Now that God has unstrung my bow[r]
and afflicted me,[s]
they throw off restraint[t] in my
presence.
12 On my right[u] the tribe[c] attacks;
they lay snares[v] for my feet,[w]
they build their siege ramps against
me.[x]

9 [m]**Job 16:10;** Ps 69:11; [n]Job 12:4; La 3:14,63; [o]**Job 17:6**
10 [p]Job 19:19; [q]**Dt 25:9;** Mt 26:67
11 [r]**Job 29:20;** [s]**Ge 12:17; Ru 1:21;** [t]Job 41:13; Ps 32:9
12 [u]Ps 109:6; Zec 3:1; [v]**Job 18:9;** [w]Ps 140:4–5; [x]**Job 16:10**

[a]24 The meaning of the Hebrew for this clause is uncertain. [a]3 Or *gnawed*
[b]4 Or *fuel*
[c]12 The meaning of the Hebrew for this word is uncertain.

[13]They break up my road;[y]
they succeed in destroying me[z]—
without anyone's helping them.[d]
[14]They advance as through a gaping
breach;[a]
amid the ruins they come rolling in.
[15]Terrors[b] overwhelm me;[c]
my dignity is driven away as by the
wind,
my safety vanishes like a cloud.[d]

[16]"And now my life ebbs away;[e]
days of suffering grip me.[f]
[17]Night pierces my bones;
my gnawing pains never rest.[g]
[18]In his great power[h] ⌞God⌟ becomes like
clothing to me;[e]
he binds me like the neck of my
garment.
[19]He throws me into the mud,[i]
and I am reduced to dust and ashes.[j]

[20]"I cry out to you,[k] O God, but you do
not answer;[l]
I stand up, but you merely look at
me.
[21]You turn on me ruthlessly;[m]
with the might of your hand[n] you
attack me.[o]
[22]You snatch me up and drive me before
the wind;[p]
you toss me about in the storm.[q]
[23]I know you will bring me down to
death,[r]
to the place appointed for all the
living.[s]

[24]"Surely no-one lays a hand on a
broken man[t]
when he cries for help in his
distress.[u]
[25]Have I not wept for those in trouble?[v]
Has not my soul grieved for the
poor?[w]
[26]Yet when I hoped for good, evil came;
when I looked for light, then came
darkness.[x]
[27]The churning inside me never stops;[y]
days of suffering confront me.[z]
[28]I go about blackened,[a] but not by the
sun;
I stand up in the assembly and cry
for help.[b]
[29]I have become a brother of jackals,[c]
a companion of owls.[d]
[30]My skin grows black[e] and peels;[f]
my body burns with fever.[g]
[31]My harp is tuned to mourning,[h]
and my flute[i] to the sound of
wailing.

31 "I made a covenant with my
eyes[a]
not to look lustfully at a girl.[b]

13 [y]Isa 3:12; [z]**Job 10:3**
14 [a]**2Ki 25:4**
15 [b]**Job 6:4**; [c]**Ex 3:6**; Job 10:8; 31:2–3,23; Ps 55:4–5; [d]**Job 3:25**
16 [e]**Job 3:24**; [f]ver 27; **Job 9:17**
17 [g]**Dt 28:35; Job 16:16**
18 [h]**Job 9:4**
19 [i]Ps 40:2; 69:2,14; 130:1; Jer 38:6,22; [j]**Ge 3:19; Job 2:8**
20 [k]**1Ki 8:52**; Ps 34:17; Pr 2:3; Mic 4:9; [l]**Job 19:7**; La 3:8
21 [m]Jer 6:23; 30:14; 50:42; [n]Isa 9:12; 14:26; 31:3; Eze 6:14; [o]**Job 4:5; 6:4; 10:3**
22 [p]Job 27:21; Jude 12; [q]**Job 9:17**
23 [r]**2Sa 14:14; Job 3:13; 10:3**; [s]**Job 3:19**
24 [t]Ps 145:14; Isa 42:3; 57:15; [u]**Job 19:7**
25 [v]Lk 19:41; Php 3:18; [w]**Job 24:4**; Ps 35:13–14; Ro 12:15
26 [x]**Job 3:6**,17; **19:8; Ps 82:5; Jer 4:23**
27 [y]Ps 38:8; La 2:11; [z]**ver 16**
28 [a]**Job 17:14**; La 4:8; [b]**Job 19:7; 24:12**
29 [c]Ps 44:19; Isa 34:13; Jer 9:11; [d]Ps 102:6; Mic 1:8
30 [e]**Job 17:14**; [f]La 3:4; 4:8; [g]**Dt 28:35; Job 16:16**; Ps 102:3; La 1:13; 5:10
31 [h]**Ge 8:8**; Ps 137:2; Isa 16:11; 24:8; Eze 26:13; [i]**Ge 4:21**

Ch. 31

1 [a]Pr 4:25; 17:24; 2Pe 2:14; [b]Ex 20:14,17; Dt 5:18; Mt 5:28
2 [c]Nu 26:55; Ps 11:6; 16:5; 50:18; Ecc 3:22; 5:19; 9:9; [d]**Job 16:19; 20:29**
3 [e]**Job 21:30**; [f]Job 18:12; [g]Job 34:22; Ro 2:9

[2]For what is man's lot[c] from God above,
his heritage from the Almighty on
high?[d]
[3]Is it not ruin[e] for the wicked,
disaster[f] for those who do wrong?[g]
[4]Does he not see my ways[h]
and count my every step?[i]

[5]"If I have walked in falsehood
or my foot has hurried after
deceit[j]—
[6]let God weigh me[k] in honest scales[l]
and he will know that I am
blameless[m]—
[7]if my steps have turned from the
path,[n]
if my heart has been led by my eyes,
or if my hands[o] have been defiled,[p]
[8]then may others eat what I have
sown,[q]
and may my crops be uprooted.[r]

[9]"If my heart has been enticed[s] by a
woman,[t]
or if I have lurked at my neighbour's
door,
[10]then may my wife grind[u] another
man's grain,
and may other men sleep with her.[v]
[11]For that would have been shameful,[w]
a sin to be judged.[x]
[12]It is a fire[y] that burns to Destruction[a];[z]
it would have uprooted my
harvest.[a]

[13]"If I have denied justice to my
menservants and maidservants[b]
when they had a grievance against
me,[c]
[14]what will I do when God confronts
me?[d]
What will I answer when called to
account?[e]
[15]Did not he who made me in the womb
make them?[f]
Did not the same one form us both
within our mothers?[g]

4 [h]2Ch 16:9; Ps 139:3; Da 4:37; 5:23; [i]**ver 14; Job 10:4**
5 [j]**Job 15:31**
6 [k]Ps 139:23; [l]**Lev 19:36; Job 6:2**; [m]**Ge 6:9; Job 2:3; 23:10**
7 [n]**Job 23:11**; [o]**Job 9:30**; [p]Ps 7:3
8 [q]**Job 5:5; 20:10**; Jn 4:37; [r]ver 12; Mic 6:15
9 [s]**Dt 11:16; Job 24:15**; Jas 1:14; [t]Pr 5:3; 7:5
10 [u]**Jdg 16:21**; [v]Dt 28:30
11 [w]Pr 6:32–33; [x]**Ge 38:24; Ex 21:12**; Jn 8:4–5
12 [y]**Job 15:30**; [z]**Job 26:6**; [a]**ver 8**
13 [b]**Dt 5:14**; [c]Ex 21:2–11; Lev 25:39–46; Dt 24:14–15
14 [d]Job 33:5; [e]ver 4,37; Ps 10:13,15; 94:7; Isa 10:3; Jer 5:31; Hos 9:7; Mic 7:4; Col 4:1
15 [f]**Job 4:17**; Pr 22:2; [g]**Job 10:3**; Eph 6:9

[d]13 Or *me. / 'No-one can help him,' ⌞they say⌟*
[e]18 Hebrew; Septuagint *⌞God⌟ grasps my clothing*
[a]12 Hebrew *Abaddon*

16"If I have denied the desires of the
poor[h]
or let the eyes of the widow[i] grow
weary,[j]
17if I have kept my bread to myself,
not sharing it with the fatherless[k]—
18but from my youth I reared him as
would a father,
and from my birth I guided the
widow[l]—
19if I have seen anyone perishing for lack
of clothing,[m]
or a needy[n] man without a garment,
20and his heart did not bless me[o]
for warming him with the fleece[p]
from my sheep,
21if I have raised my hand against the
fatherless,[q]
knowing that I had influence in
court,[r]
22then let my arm fall from the shoulder,
let it be broken off at the joint.[s]
23For I dreaded destruction from God,[t]
and for fear of his splendour[u] I could
not do such things.[v]

24"If I have put my trust in gold[w]
or said to pure gold, 'You are my
security,'[x]
25if I have rejoiced over my great
wealth,[y]
the fortune my hands had gained,[z]
26if I have regarded the sun[a] in its
radiance
or the moon[b] moving in splendour,
27so that my heart was secretly enticed[c]
and my hand offered them a kiss of
homage,[d]
28then these also would be sins to be
judged,[e]
for I would have been unfaithful to
God on high.[f]

29"If I have rejoiced at my enemy's
misfortune[g]
or gloated over the trouble that
came to him[h]—
30I have not allowed my mouth to sin
by invoking a curse against his
life[i]—
31if the men of my household have
never said,
'Who has not had his fill of Job's
meat?'[j]—
32but no stranger had to spend the night
in the street,
for my door was always open to the
traveller[k]—
33if I have concealed[l] my sin as men do,[b]
by hiding[m] my guilt in my heart
34because I so feared the crowd[n]
and so dreaded the contempt of the
clans
that I kept silent[o] and would not go
outside—
35("Oh, that I had someone to hear me![p]
I sign now my defence—let the
Almighty answer me;
let my accuser[q] put his indictment in
writing.
36Surely I would wear it on my
shoulder,[r]
I would put it on like a crown.[s]
37I would give him an account of my
every step;[t]
like a prince[u] I would approach
him.)—
38"if my land cries out against me[v]
and all its furrows are wet[w] with
tears,
39if I have devoured its yield without
payment[x]
or broken the spirit of its tenants,[y]
40then let briers[z] come up instead of
wheat
and weeds[a] instead of barley."

The words of Job are ended.[b]

Elihu

32 So these three men stopped
answering Job,[a] because he was
righteous in his own eyes.[b] 2But Elihu
son of Barakel the Buzite,[c] of the family
of Ram, became very angry with Job for
justifying himself[d] rather than God.[e]
3He was also angry with the three
friends,[f] because they had found no
way to refute Job,[g] and yet had con-
demned him.[a][h] 4Now Elihu had waited
before speaking to Job because they
were older than he.[i] 5But when he saw
that the three men had nothing more to
say, his anger was aroused.
6So Elihu son of Barakel the Buzite
said:

"I am young in years,
and you are old;[j]
that is why I was fearful,
not daring to tell you what I know.
7I thought, 'Age should speak;
advanced years should teach
wisdom.'[k]

16 hLev 25:17; Job 5:16; iJob 22:9; Jas 1:27; jJob 22:7
17 kJob 6:27; 22:7
18 lIsa 51:18
19 mJob 22:6; Isa 58:7; nJob 24:4
20 oJob 29:13; pJdg 6:37
21 qJob 22:7; Jas 1:27; rJob 29:7,9
22 sNu 15:30; Job 5:15; 38:15; Ps 10:15; 37:17; 137:5
23 tJob 10:3; 30:15; uJob 13:11; vGe 20:11
24 wJob 22:25; xMt 6:24; Lk 12:15
25 yGe 12:16; Ps 49:6; 52:7; 62:10; Isa 10:14; zJob 22:24; Eze 28:5; Lk 12:20–21
26 aGe 1:16; bJob 25:5
27 cDt 11:16; Job 24:15; Jas 1:14; dJer 8:2; 16:11
28 eGe 38:24; Dt 17:2–7; fNu 11:20; Eze 8:16
29 gNu 14:1; Ps 35:15; Ob 12; Mt 5:44; hPr 17:5; 24:17–18
30 iJob 5:3; Ro 12:14
31 jJob 22:7
32 kGe 19:2–3; Jdg 19:20; Mt 25:35; Ro 12:13
33 lPs 32:5; Pr 28:13; mGe 3:8
34 nEx 23:2; oPs 32:3; 39:2
35 pJob 9:24; 30:28; qJob 27:7
36 rEx 28:12; sJob 29:14
37 tver 14; Job 11:11; uJob 21:28
38 vGe 4:10; wPs 65:10
39 x1Ki 21:19; yLev 19:13; Jas 5:4
40 zGe 3:18; Mt 13:7; aZep 2:9; Mt 13:26; bPs 72:20; Jer 51:64

Ch. 32

1 aver 15; bJob 2:3; 10:7
2 cGe 22:21; dver 1; eJob 13:19; 27:5; 30:21; 35:2
3 fJob 42:7; gver 12–13; hJob 15:13 4 iLev 19:32
6 jJob 15:10 7 k1Ch 29:15; 2Ch 10:6

b33 Or *as Adam did*
a3 Masoretic Text; an ancient Hebrew scribal tradition *Job, and so had condemned God*

8But it is the spirit[b] [l] in a man,
the breath of the Almighty,[m] that
gives him understanding.[n]
9It is not only the old[c] who are wise,[o]
not only the aged[p] who understand
what is right.[q]

10"Therefore I say: Listen to me;[r]
I too will tell you what I know.[s]
11I waited while you spoke,
I listened to your reasoning;
while you were searching for words,
12 I gave you my full attention.
But not one of you has proved Job
wrong;
none of you has answered his
arguments.[t]
13Do not say, 'We have found wisdom;[u]
let God refute[v] him, not man.'
14But Job has not marshalled his words
against me,[w]
and I will not answer him with your
arguments.

15"They are dismayed and have no more
to say;
words have failed them.[x]
16Must I wait, now that they are silent,
now that they stand there with no
reply?
17I too will have my say;
I too will tell what I know.[y]
18For I am full of words,
and the spirit[z] within me compels
me;[a]
19inside I am like bottled-up wine,
like new wineskins ready to burst.[b]
20I must speak and find relief;
I must open my lips and reply.[c]
21I will show partiality[d] to no-one,[e]
nor will I flatter any man;[f]
22for if I were skilled in flattery,
my Maker[g] would soon take me
away.[h]

33

"But now, Job, listen[a] to my
words;
pay attention to everything I say.[b]
2I am about to open my mouth;
my words are on the tip of my
tongue.
3My words come from an upright
heart;[c]
my lips sincerely speak what I
know.[d]
4The Spirit[e] of God has made me;[f]
the breath of the Almighty[g] gives
me life.[h]
5Answer me[i] then, if you can;
prepare[j] yourself and confront me.[k]
6I am just like you before God;[l]
I too have been taken from clay.[m]
7No fear of me should alarm you,
nor should my hand be heavy upon
you.[n]

8"But you have said in my hearing—
I heard the very words—
9'I am pure[o] and without sin;[p]
I am clean and free from guilt.[q]
10Yet God has found fault with me;
he considers me his enemy.[r]
11He fastens my feet in shackles;[s]
he keeps close watch on all my
paths.'[t]

12"But I tell you, in this you are not
right,
for God is greater than man.[u]
13Why do you complain to him[v]
that he answers none of man's
words?[a] [w]
14For God does speak[x]—now one way,
now another[y]—
though man may not perceive it.[z]
15In a dream,[a] in a vision[b] of the night,[c]
when deep sleep[d] falls on men
as they slumber in their beds,
16he may speak[e] in their ears
and terrify them[f] with warnings,[g]
17to turn man from wrongdoing
and keep him from pride,[h]
18to preserve his soul from the pit,[b] [i]
his life from perishing by the
sword.[c] [j]
19Or a man may be chastened[k] on a bed
of pain[l]
with constant distress in his bones,[m]
20so that his very being finds food[n]
repulsive
and his soul loathes the choicest
meal.[o]
21His flesh wastes away to nothing,
and his bones,[p] once hidden, now
stick out.[q]
22His soul draws near to the pit,[d] [r]
and his life to the messengers of
death.[e] [s]

8 [l]ver 18; [m]**Job 27:3;** [n]**Job 12:13; Ps 119:34;** Jas 1:5
9 [o]1Co 1:26; [p]Ps 119:100; [q]**Job 12:12,**20; Lk 2:47; 1Ti 4:12
10 [r]Job 33:1,31, 33; 34:2,16; 37:2,14; Ps 34:11; [s]**Job 5:27**
12 [t]ver 3
13 [u]**Job 4:12; Ecc 9:11;** [v]**Job 11:5**
14 [w]Job 23:4
15 [x]ver 1
17 [y]**Job 5:27;** 33:3; 36:4
18 [z]ver 8; [a]Ac 4:20; 1Co 9:16; 2Co 5:14
19 [b]Jer 20:9; Am 3:8; Mt 9:17
20 [c]**Job 4:2; Jer 6:11**
21 [d]**Lev 19:15; 2Ch 19:7; Job 13:10;** [e]Mt 22:16; [f]Pr 29:5; 1Th 2:5
22 [g]**Job 4:17; 9:9;** [h]Ps 12:2–4

Ch. 33

1 [a]Job 32:10; [b]**Job 6:28; 13:6**
3 [c]1Ki 3:6; Ps 7:10; 11:2; 64:10; [d]**Job 6:28**
4 [e]**Ge 1:2;** [f]Job 10:3; [g]**Job 27:3;** [h]Nu 16:22; **Job 12:10**
5 [i]ver 32; [j]Job 13:18; [k]**Job 31:14**
6 [l]Ac 14:15; Jas 5:17; [m]**Job 4:19**
7 [n]**Job 9:34;** 2Co 2:4
9 [o]**Job 10:7;** [p]**Job 9:30; 13:23;** [q]**Job 2:9**
10 [r]**Job 13:24**
11 [s]**Job 13:27;** [t]Job 14:16; Pr 3:6; Isa 30:21
12 [u]**Job 5:9;** Ps 8:4; 50:21; Ecc 7:20; Isa 55:8–9
13 [v]Job 40:2; Isa 45:9; [w]**Job 11:8**
14 [x]Ps 62:11; [y]ver 29; [z]Job 4:12
15 [a]**Ge 20:3;** Job 4:13; **Mt 27:19;** [b]Ac 16:9; [c]**Ge 15:1;** Da 2:19; [d]**Ge 2:21**
16 [e]Job 36:10,15; [f]**Job 6:4;** [g]Ps 88:15–16
17 [h]**Job 20:6**
18 [i]ver 22,24,28,30; Ps 28:1; 30:9; 69:15; 88:6; 103:4; Pr 1:12; Isa 14:15; 38:17; Jnh 2:6; Zec 9:11; [j]**Job 15:22;** Mt 26:52
19 [k]**Job 5:17;** [l]**Ge 17:1; Dt 8:5;** 2Co 12:7–10; Jas 1:3; [m]**Job 16:16;** Ps 6:2; 38:3; Isa 38:13
20 [n]Ps 102:4; 107:18; [o]**Job 3:24; 6:6**
21 [p]**Job 2:5;** [q]**Job 16:8**
22 [r]**ver 18;** [s]Job 38:17; Ps 9:13; 88:3; 107:18; 116:3

[b]8 Or *Spirit;* also in verse 18
[c]9 Or *many;* or *great*
[a]13 Or *that he does not answer for any of his actions*
[b]18 Or *preserve him from the grave*
[c]18 Or *from crossing the River*
[d]22 Or *He draws near to the grave*
[e]22 Or *to the dead*

23"Yet if there is an angel on his side
as a mediator,[t] one out of a
thousand,
to tell a man what is right for him,[u]
24to be gracious to him and say,
'Spare him from going down to the
pit[f];[v]
I have found a ransom for him'[w]—
25then his flesh is renewed[x] like a
child's;
it is restored as in the days of his
youth.[y]
26He prays to God and finds favour with
him,[z]
he sees God's face and shouts for
joy;[a]
he is restored by God to his
righteous state.[b]
27Then he comes to men and says,
'I have sinned,[c] and perverted what
was right,[d]
but I did not get what I deserved.[e]
28He redeemed[f] my soul from going
down to the pit,[g][g]
and I shall live to enjoy the light.'[h]

29"God does all these things to a man[i]—
twice, even three times[j]—
30to turn back[k] his soul from the pit,[h][l]
that the light of life[m] may shine on
him.[n]

31"Pay attention, Job, and listen[o] to me;[p]
be silent,[q] and I will speak.
32If you have anything to say, answer
me;[r]
speak up, for I want you to be
cleared.[s]
33But if not, then listen to me;[t]
be silent,[u] and I will teach you
wisdom.[v]"

34

Then Elihu said:

2"Hear my words, you wise men;
listen to me,[a] you men of learning.
3For the ear tests words
as the tongue tastes food.[b]
4Let us discern for ourselves what is
right;[c]
let us learn together what is good.[d]

5"Job says, 'I am innocent,[e]
but God denies me justice.[f]
6Although I am right,
I am considered a liar;[g]
although I am guiltless,[h]
his arrow inflicts an incurable
wound.'[i]
7What man is like Job,
who drinks scorn like water?[j]
8He keeps company with evildoers;
he associates with wicked men.[k]
9For he says, 'It profits a man nothing
when he tries to please God.'[l]

10"So listen to me,[m] you men of
understanding.[n]
Far be it from God to do evil,[o]
from the Almighty to do wrong.[p]
11He repays a man for what he has
done;[q]
he brings upon him what his
conduct deserves.[r]
12It is unthinkable that God would do
wrong,[s]
that the Almighty would pervert
justice.[t]
13Who appointed[u] him over the earth?
Who put him in charge of the whole
world?[v]
14If it were his intention
and he withdrew his spirit[a][w] and
breath,[x]
15all mankind would perish[y] together
and man would return to the dust.[z]

16"If you have understanding,[a] hear
this;
listen to what I say.[b]
17Can he who hates justice govern?[c]
Will you condemn the just and
mighty One?[d]
18Is he not the One who says to kings,
'You are worthless,'
and to nobles,[e] 'You are wicked,'[f]
19who shows no partiality[g] to princes
and does not favour the rich over
the poor,[h]
for they are all the work of his
hands?[i]
20They die in an instant, in the middle of
the night;[j]
the people are shaken and they pass
away;
the mighty are removed without
human hand.[k]

21"His eyes are on the ways of men;[l]
he sees their every step.[m]
22There is no dark place,[n] no deep
shadow,[o]
where evildoers can hide.[p]

23 [t]Gal 3:19; Heb 8:6; 9:15; [u]Job 36:9–10; Mic 6:8
24 [v]ver 18; [w]Job 6:22
25 [x]Ps 103:5; [y]2Ki 5:14
26 [z]Job 5:15; Pr 8:35; 12:2; 18:22; Lk 2:52; [a]Ezr 3:13; Job 22:26; [b]Ps 13:5; 50:15; 51:12; 1Jn 1:9
27 [c]Nu 22:34; [d]Lk 15:21; [e]Ezr 9:13; Ps 22:27; 51:13; Ro 6:21; Jas 2:13
28 [f]Ex 15:13; Ps 34:22; 107:20; [g]ver 18; Job 17:16; [h]Job 22:28
29 [i]Ps 139:16; Pr 16:9; 20:24; Jer 10:23; 1Co 12:6; Eph 1:11; Php 2:13; [j]ver 14
30 [k]Jas 5:19; [l]ver 18; [m]Ps 49:19; 56:13; 116:9; Isa 53:11; [n]Isa 60:1; Eph 5:14
31 [o]Jer 23:18; [p]Job 32:10; [q]ver 33
32 [r]ver 5; [s]Job 6:29; 35:2
33 [t]Job 32:10; [u]ver 31; [v]Job 6:24; Pr 10:8,10,19

Ch. 34

2 [a]Job 32:10
3 [b]Job 12:11
4 [c]Job 12:12; Heb 5:14; [d]1Th 5:21
5 [e]Job 10:7; [f]Job 6:29
6 [g]Job 6:28; [h]Job 9:21; [i]Job 6:4; 10:3; Jer 10:19
7 [j]Job 9:21; 15:16
8 [k]Job 22:15
9 [l]Job 9:29–31; 21:15
10 [m]Job 32:10; [n]ver 16; Job 12:12; [o]Ge 18:25; [p]ver 12; Dt 32:4; Job 8:3; 36:23; Ps 92:15; Ro 3:5; 9:14
11 [q]Job 21:31; Mt 16:27; [r]Jer 17:10; 32:19; Eze 33:20
12 [s]ver 10; Tit 1:2; Heb 6:18; [t]Job 8:3; Ps 9:16; Col 3:25; 2Th 1:6
13 [u]Heb 1:2; [v]Job 36:23; 38:4,6; Isa 40:14
14 [w]Ge 6:3; [x]Nu 16:22; Job 27:3
15 [y]Ge 6:13; La 3:22; Mal 3:6; Jn 3:16; [z]Ge 2:7; Job 7:21; 9:22; Ps 90:10
16 [a]ver 10; [b]Job 32:10
17 [c]ver 30; 2Sa 23:3–4; Pr 20:8,26; 24:23–25; 28:28; [d]ver 29; Job 10:7; 40:8; Ro 3:5–6
18 [e]Job 12:18; [f]Ex 22:28; Isa 40:24
19 [g]Job 13:10; Ac 10:34; [h]Lev 19:15; Jas 2:5; [i]Job 10:3
20 [j]ver 25; Ex 11:4; Job 20:8; [k]Job 12:19
21 [l]Jer 32:19; [m]Job 14:16; Pr 15:3; Heb 4:13
22 [n]Ps 74:20; [o]Job 3:5; [p]Ge 3:8; Job 11:20

[f]24 Or *grave*
[g]28 Or *redeemed me from going down to the grave*
[h]30 Or *turn him back from the grave*
[a]14 Or *Spirit*

23 God has no need to examine men further,[q]
that they should come before him for judgment.[r]
24 Without enquiry he shatters[s] the mighty[t]
and sets up others in their place.[u]
25 Because he takes note of their deeds,[v]
he overthrows them in the night[w] and they are crushed.[x]
26 He punishes them for their wickedness[y]
where everyone can see them,
27 because they turned from following him[z]
and had no regard for any of his ways.[a]
28 They caused the cry of the poor to come before him,
so that he heard the cry of the needy.[b]
29 But if he remains silent,[c] who can condemn him?[d]
If he hides his face,[e] who can see him?
Yet he is over man and nation alike,[f]
30 to keep a godless[g] man from ruling,[h]
from laying snares for the people.[i]

31 "Suppose a man says to God,
'I am guilty[j] but will offend no more.
32 Teach me what I cannot see;[k]
if I have done wrong, I will not do so again.'[l]
33 Should God then reward you on your terms,
when you refuse to repent?[m]
You must decide, not I;
so tell me what you know.

34 "Men of understanding declare,
wise men who hear me say to me,
35 'Job speaks without knowledge;[n]
his words lack insight.'[o]
36 Oh, that Job might be tested to the utmost
for answering like a wicked man![p]
37 To his sin he adds rebellion;
scornfully he claps his hands[q] among us
and multiplies his words[r] against God."[s]

35

Then Elihu said:

2 "Do you think this is just?
You say, 'I shall be cleared[a] by God.'[a][b]
3 Yet you ask him, 'What profit is it to me,[b]
and what do I gain by not sinning?'[c]

4 "I would like to reply to you
and to your friends with you.
5 Look up at the heavens[d] and see;
gaze at the clouds so high above you.[e]
6 If you sin, how does that affect him?
If your sins are many, what does that do to him?[f]
7 If you are righteous, what do you give to him,[g]
or what does he receive[h] from your hand?[i]
8 Your wickedness affects only a man like yourself,[j]
and your righteousness only the sons of men.[k]

9 "Men cry out[l] under a load of oppression;[m]
they plead for relief from the arm of the powerful.[n]
10 But no-one says, 'Where is God my Maker,[o]
who gives songs[p] in the night,[q]
11 who teaches[r] more to[s] us than to[c] the beasts of the earth
and makes us wiser than[d] the birds of the air?'
12 He does not answer[t] when men cry out
because of the arrogance[u] of the wicked.[v]
13 Indeed, God does not listen to their empty plea;
the Almighty pays no attention to it.[w]
14 How much less, then, will he listen
when you say that you do not see him,[x]
that your case[y] is before him
and you must wait for him,[z]
15 and further, that his anger never punishes[a]
and he does not take the least notice of wickedness.[e][b]
16 So Job opens his mouth with empty talk;[c]
without knowledge he multiplies words."[d]

36

Elihu continued:

2 "Bear with me a little longer and I will show you

23 [q]Ps 11:4; [r]Job 11:11
24 [s]Isa 8:9; 9:4; Jer 51:20; Da 2:34; [t]Job 12:19; [u]Da 2:21
25 [v]Job 11:11; [w]ver 20; [x]Pr 5:21–23
26 [y]Ge 6:5; Job 8:22; 28:24; Ps 9:5; Jer 44:5
27 [z]Ps 14:3; [a]1Sa 15:11
28 [b]Ex 22:23; Job 5:15; 12:19
29 [c]Ps 28:1; 83:1; 109:1; [d]ver 17; Ro 8:34; [e]Ps 13:1; [f]Ps 83:18; 97:9
30 [g]Job 8:13; [h]ver 17; [i]Ps 25:15; 31:4; 91:3; 124:7; 140:5; Pr 29:2–12
31 [j]Ps 51:5; Lk 15:21; Ro 7:24; 1Jn 1:8,10
32 [k]Ex 33:13; Job 35:11; 38:36; Ps 15:2; 25:4; 27:11; 51:6; 86:11; 139:23–24; 143:8; [l]Job 33:27; Lk 19:8
33 [m]2Ki 17:13; Job 33:23; 36:10,15,18,21; 41:11; 42:6; Pr 17:23; Jnh 3:8
35 [n]Job 35:16; 38:2; 42:3; [o]Job 26:3
36 [p]Job 6:29; 22:15
37 [q]Job 27:23; [r]Job 35:16; [s]Job 23:2

Ch. 35

2 [a]Job 33:32; [b]Job 2:9; 32:2
3 [c]Job 9:29–31; 21:15
5 [d]Ge 15:5; Dt 10:14; [e]Job 11:7–9; Ps 19:1–4
6 [f]Job 7:20
7 [g]Ro 11:35; [h]1Co 4:7; [i]Job 22:2–3; Lk 17:10
8 [j]Eze 18:24; [k]Eze 18:5–9; Zec 7:9–10
9 [l]Ex 2:23; [m]Job 20:19; [n]Job 5:15; 12:19
10 [o]Job 4:17; [p]Job 8:21; [q]Ps 42:8; 77:6; 119:62; 149:5; Ac 16:25
11 [r]Job 21:22; Lk 12:24; [s]Job 12:7
12 [t]1Sa 8:18; [u]Job 15:25; [v]Ps 66:18
13 [w]Dt 1:45; 1Sa 8:18; Job 15:31; Pr 15:8
14 [x]Job 9:11; [y]Ps 37:6; [z]Job 31:35
15 [a]Job 9:24; [b]Job 18:5; Ps 10:11; Hos 7:2; Am 8:7
16 [c]Tit 1:10; [d]Job 34:35,37; 1Co 4:20; Jude 10

[a]2 Or *My righteousness is more than God's*
[b]3 Or *you*
[c]11 Or *teaches us by*
[d]11 Or *us wise by*
[e]15 Symmachus, Theodotion and Vulgate; the meaning of the Hebrew for this word is uncertain.

that there is more to be said on
God's behalf.
3I get my knowledge from afar;[a]
I will ascribe justice to my Maker.[b]
4Be assured that my words are not
false;[c]
one perfect in knowledge[d] is with
you.[e]

5"God is mighty,[f] but does not despise
men;[g]
he is mighty, and firm in his
purpose.[h]
6He does not keep the wicked alive[i]
but gives the afflicted their rights.[j]
7He does not take his eyes off the
righteous;[k]
he enthrones them with kings[l]
and exalts them for ever.[m]
8But if men are bound in chains,[n]
held fast by cords of affliction,[o]
9he tells them what they have done—
that they have sinned arrogantly.[p]
10He makes them listen[q] to correction[r]
and commands them to repent of
their evil.[s]
11If they obey and serve him,[t]
they will spend the rest of their days
in prosperity[u]
and their years in contentment.[v]
12But if they do not listen,
they will perish by the sword[a][w]
and die without knowledge.[x]

13"The godless in heart[y] harbour
resentment;[z]
even when he fetters them, they do
not cry for help.[a]
14They die in their youth,[b]
among male prostitutes of the
shrines.[c]
15But those who suffer[d] he delivers in
their suffering;[e]
he speaks[f] to them in their
affliction.[g]

16"He is wooing[h] you from the jaws of
distress
to a spacious place[i] free from
restriction,[j]
to the comfort of your table[k] laden
with choice food.[l]
17But now you are laden with the
judgment due to the wicked;[m]
judgment and justice have taken
hold of you.[n]
18Be careful that no-one entices you by
riches;
do not let a large bribe[o] turn you
aside.[p]
19Would your wealth[q]
or even all your mighty efforts
sustain you so you would not be in
distress?

20Do not long for the night,[r]
to drag people away from their
homes.[b]
21Beware of turning to evil,[s]
which you seem to prefer to
affliction.[t]

22"God is exalted in his power.[u]
Who is a teacher like him?[v]
23Who has prescribed his ways[w] for
him,[x]
or said to him, 'You have done
wrong'?[y]
24Remember to extol his work,[z]
which men have praised in song.[a]
25All mankind has seen it;[b]
men gaze on it from afar.
26How great is God—beyond our
understanding![c]
The number of his years is past
finding out.[d]

27"He draws up the drops of water,[e]
which distil as rain to the streams;[c][f]
28the clouds pour down their moisture
and abundant showers[g] fall on
mankind.[h]
29Who can understand how he spreads
out the clouds,
how he thunders[i] from his
pavilion?[j]
30See how he scatters his lightning[k]
about him,
bathing the depths of the sea.[l]
31This is the way he governs[d] the
nations[m]
and provides food[n] in abundance.[o]
32He fills his hands with lightning
and commands it to strike its mark.[p]
33His thunder announces the coming
storm;[q]
even the cattle make known its
approach.[e][r]

Ch. 36

3 [a]**Job 6:28**; [b]**Job 4:17**
4 [c]**Job 6:28; 13:6**; [d]Job 37:5,16,23; [e]**Job 32:17**
5 [f]**Job 9:4**; [g]Ps 5:2; 22:24; 31:22; 69:33; 102:17; 103:10; [h]**Nu 23:19**; Ro 11:29
6 [i]**Job 34:26**; [j]**Job 4:10**
7 [k]**Job 11:11**; Ps 11:5; 33:18; 34:15; Mt 6:18; [l]Ps 113:8; Isa 22:23; [m]**1Sa 2:7–8; Job 4:7**
8 [n]**2Sa 3:34**; 2Ki 23:33; Ps 107:10,14; [o]ver 10,15,21; Ps 119:67,71
9 [p]**Job 15:25**
10 [q]**Job 33:16**; [r]**Job 5:17**; [s]**ver 8; Jdg 6:8; Job 34:33**; 1Th 5:22
11 [t]**Lev 26:33**; Dt 28:1; Isa 1:19; Hag 1:12; [u]**Dt 30:15; Job 8:7**; [v]**Ex 8:22; Dt 8:1**; Jn 14:21; 1Ti 4:8
12 [w]**Lev 26:38; Job 15:22**; [x]**Job 4:21**; Eph 4:18
13 [y]**Job 15:12**; Ro 2:5; [z]**Job 5:2**; [a]**Job 4:17**; Am 4:11
14 [b]**Job 15:32**; [c]**Dt 23:17**
15 [d]**Job 5:15**; [e]2Co 12:10; [f]**Job 33:16**; [g]**ver 8; Job 34:33**
16 [h]Hos 2:14; [i]**2Sa 22:20**; Ps 18:19; [j]Ps 118:5; [k]Ps 23:5; 78:19; [l]**Ge 17:1; Job 15:11**
17 [m]**Job 20:29**; [n]Job 22:11
18 [o]**Ex 23:8**; Am 5:12; [p]**Job 34:33**
19 [q]Ps 49:6; Jer 9:23
20 [r]Job 34:20,25
21 [s]**Job 34:33**; Ps 66:18; [t]**ver 8**; Heb 11:25
22 [u]**Job 5:9; 9:4**; [v]**Job 21:22; Ro 11:34**

23 [w]Job 27:11; [x]**Job 34:13**; Ro 11:33; [y]**Ge 18:25; Job 34:10**
24 [z]1Ch 16:24; Ps 35:27; 92:5; 111:2; 138:5; 145:10; [a]**Ex 15:1**; Rev 15:3 *25* [b]Ro 1:20
26 [c]**Job 5:9**; 1Co 13:12; [d]**Ge 21:33; Job 10:5**; Heb 1:12
27 [e]**Job 26:8**; [f]**2Sa 1:21**; Job 28:26; 38:28; Isa 55:10
28 [g]Ps 65:10; 72:6; Joel 2:23; [h]**Job 5:10; 22:11; 28:26**; Mt 5:45
29 [i]Ps 29:3; Jer 10:13; [j]**Job 9:6**; 37:16; Ps 18:7–15; 19:4–5; 104:2; Pr 8:28; Isa 40:22
30 [k]Ex 19:16; Job 37:11,15; Ps 18:12,14; 97:4; Jer 10:13; Hab 3:11; [l]Ps 68:22; Isa 51:10
31 [m]Dt 28:23–24; 1Ki 17:1; Job 37:13; Am 4:7–8; [n]Ps 145:15; [o]Ps 104:14–15,27–28; Isa 30:23; Ac 14:17
32 [p]**Job 28:24**; 37:12,15; Ps 18:14; 29:7–9
33 [q]Job 37:5; 40:9; [r]**Job 28:26**

[a]*12* Or *will cross the River*
[b]*20* The meaning of the Hebrew for verses 18–20 is uncertain. [c]*27* Or *distil from the mist as rain*
[d]*31* Or *nourishes*
[e]*33* Or *announces his coming—/ the One zealous against evil*

37

"At this my heart pounds[a]
and leaps from its place.
2Listen![b] Listen to the roar of his voice,[c]
to the rumbling that comes from his
mouth.[d]
3He unleashes his lightning[e] beneath
the whole heaven
and sends it to the ends of the earth.[f]
4After that comes the sound of his roar;
he thunders[g] with his majestic
voice.[h]
When his voice resounds,
he holds nothing back.
5God's voice thunders[i] in marvellous
ways;[j]
he does great things beyond our
understanding.[k]
6He says to the snow,[l] 'Fall on the
earth,'
and to the rain shower, 'Be a mighty
downpour.'[m]
7So that all men he has made may know
his work,[n]
he stops every man from his
labour.[a] [o]
8The animals take cover;[p]
they remain in their dens.[q]
9The tempest comes out from its
chamber,[r]
the cold from the driving winds.[s]
10The breath of God produces ice,
and the broad waters become
frozen.[t]
11He loads the clouds with moisture;[u]
he scatters his lightning[v] through
them.[w]
12At his direction they swirl around
over the face of the whole earth
to do whatever he commands
them.[x]
13He brings the clouds to punish men,[y]
or to water his earth[b] and show his
love.[z]

14"Listen[a] to this, Job;
stop and consider God's wonders.[b]
15Do you know how God controls the
clouds
and makes his lightning[c] flash?[d]
16Do you know how the clouds hang
poised,[e]
those wonders of him who is perfect
in knowledge?[f]
17You who swelter in your clothes
when the land lies hushed under
the south wind,[g]
18can you join him in spreading out the
skies,[h]
hard as a mirror of cast bronze?[i]

19"Tell us what we should say to him;[j]
we cannot draw up our case[k]
because of our darkness.[l]
20Should he be told that I want to speak?
Would any man ask to be swallowed
up?
21Now no-one can look at the sun,[m]
bright as it is in the skies
after the wind has swept them
clean.
22Out of the north he comes in golden
splendour;[n]
God comes in awesome majesty.[o]
23The Almighty is beyond our reach and
exalted in power;[p]
in his justice[q] and great
righteousness, he does not
oppress.[r]
24Therefore, men revere him,[s]
for does he not have regard for all
the wise[t] in heart?"[c]

The LORD Speaks

38

Then the LORD answered Job[a]
out of the storm.[b] He said:

2"Who is this that darkens my counsel[c]
with words without knowledge?[d]
3Brace yourself like a man;
I will question you,
and you shall answer me.[e]

4"Where were you when I laid the
earth's foundation?[f]
Tell me, if you understand.[g]
5Who marked off its dimensions?[h]
Surely you know!
Who stretched a measuring line[i]
across it?
6On what were its footings set,[j]
or who laid its cornerstone[k]—
7while the morning stars[l] sang
together[m]
and all the angels[a] [n] shouted for
joy?[o]

8"Who shut up the sea behind doors[p]
when it burst forth from the womb,[q]
9when I made the clouds its garment
and wrapped it in thick darkness,[r]
10when I fixed limits for it[s]
and set its doors and bars in place,[t]

Ch. 37

1 [a]Ps 38:10; Isa 15:5; Jer 4:19; Hab 3:16
2 [b]Job 32:10; [c]ver 5; [d]Ps 18:13; 29:3–9
3 [e]2Sa 22:13; Ps 18:14; [f]Job 36:32; Mt 24:27; Lk 17:24
4 [g]1Sa 2:10; [h]Ex 20:19
5 [i]1Sa 2:10; Jn 12:29; [j]Job 36:33; [k]Job 5:9; 11:7–9; 36:4
6 [l]Dt 28:12; Job 38:22; [m]Ge 7:4; Job 5:10; 28:26
7 [n]Ps 109:27; [o]Ps 104:19–23; 111:2
8 [p]Job 28:26; [q]Job 38:40; Ps 104:22
9 [r]Ps 50:3; [s]Ps 147:17
10 [t]Job 38:29–30; Ps 147:17
11 [u]Job 26:8; [v]Job 36:30; [w]Job 28:26
12 [x]ver 3; Ps 147:16; 148:8
13 [y]Ge 7:4; Ex 9:22–23; 1Sa 12:17; [z]1Ki 18:45; Job 5:10; 36:31; 38:27
14 [a]Job 32:10; [b]Job 5:9
15 [c]Job 36:30; [d]Job 36:32
16 [e]Job 36:29; [f]Job 5:9; 36:4
17 [g]Ac 27:13
18 [h]Ge 1:1,8; Job 22:14; [i]Dt 28:23
19 [j]Ro 8:26; [k]Job 13:18; [l]Job 9:3
21 [m]Jdg 5:31; Ac 22:11; 26:13
22 [n]Ps 19:5; [o]Ex 24:17
23 [p]Job 5:9; 36:4; Ro 11:33; 1Ti 6:16; [q]Job 8:3; [r]Job 4:17; Ps 44:1; Isa 63:9; Jer 25:5; La 3:33; Eze 18:23,32
24 [s]Ge 22:12; Job 28:28; Ecc 12:13; Mic 6:8; Mt 10:28; [t]Job 5:13; Eph 5:15

Ch. 38

1 [a]Job 11:5; [b]Ex 14:21; 1Sa 2:10; Job 40:6; Isa 21:1; Eze 1:4
2 [c]1Ki 22:5; Isa 40:13; [d]Job 34:35; Mk 10:38; 1Ti 1:7
3 [e]Job 40:7; 42:4; Mk 11:29
4 [f]ver 5; Ge 1:1; 1Sa 2:8; [g]ver 18; Job 34:13; Pr 30:4
5 [h]ver 4; Ps 102:25; Pr 8:29; Isa 40:12; 48:13; Jer 31:37; [i]Jer 31:39; Zec 1:16; 4:9–10
6 [j]Pr 8:25; [k]Job 26:7
7 [l]Ge 1:16; [m]Ps 19:1–4; 148:2–3; [n]1Ki 22:19; [o]Dt 16:15
8 [p]ver 11; Ps 33:7; Pr 8:29; Jer 5:22; [q]Ge 1:9–10
9 [r]Ge 1:2
10 [s]Job 28:25; Ps 33:7; 104:9; Isa 40:12; [t]Ne 3:3; Job 7:12; 26:10

[a]7 Or / *he fills all men with fear by his power*
[b]13 Or *to favour them*
[c]24 Or *for he does not have regard for any who think they are wise.*
[a]7 Hebrew *the sons of God*

11when I said, 'This far you may come
and no farther;[u]
here is where your proud waves
halt'?[v]

12"Have you ever given orders to the
morning,[w]
or shown the dawn its place,[x]
13that it might take the earth by the
edges
and shake the wicked[y] out of it?[z]
14The earth takes shape like clay under a
seal;[a]
its features stand out like those of a
garment.
15The wicked are denied their light,[b]
and their upraised arm is broken.[c]

16"Have you journeyed to the springs of
the sea
or walked in the recesses of the
deep?[d]
17Have the gates of death[e] been shown
to you?
Have you seen the gates of the
shadow of death[b]?[f]
18Have you comprehended the vast
expanses of the earth?[g]
Tell me, if you know all this.[h]

19"What is the way to the abode of light?
And where does darkness reside?[i]
20Can you take them to their places?
Do you know the paths[j] to their
dwellings?
21Surely you know, for you were
already born![k]
You have lived so many years!

22"Have you entered the storehouses of
the snow[l]
or seen the storehouses[m] of the
hail,[n]
23which I reserve for times of trouble,[o]
for days of war and battle?[p]
24What is the way to the place where the
lightning is dispersed,[q]
or the place where the east winds[r]
are scattered over the earth?[s]
25Who cuts a channel for the torrents of
rain,
and a path for the thunderstorm,[t]
26to water[u] a land where no man lives,
a desert with no-one in it,[v]
27to satisfy a desolate wasteland
and make it sprout with grass?[w]
28Does the rain have a father?[x]
Who fathers the drops of dew?
29From whose womb comes the ice?
Who gives birth to the frost from the
heavens[y]
30when the waters become hard as
stone,
when the surface of the deep is
frozen?[z]

31"Can you bind the beautiful[c] Pleiades?
Can you loose the cords of Orion?[a]
32Can you bring forth the constellations[b]
in their seasons[d]
or lead out the Bear[e] with its cubs?[c]
33Do you know the laws[d] of the
heavens?[e]
Can you set up ⌞God's[f]⌟ dominion
over the earth?

34"Can you raise your voice to the
clouds
and cover yourself with a flood of
water?[f]
35Do you send the lightning bolts on
their way?[g]
Do they report to you, 'Here we
are'?
36Who endowed the heart[g] with
wisdom[h]
or gave understanding[i] to the
mind?[h]
37Who has the wisdom to count the
clouds?
Who can tip over the water jars[j] of
the heavens[k]
38when the dust becomes hard[l]
and the clods of earth stick
together?[m]

39"Do you hunt the prey for the lioness
and satisfy the hunger of the lions[n]
40when they crouch in their dens[o]
or lie in wait in a thicket?[p]
41Who provides food[q] for the raven[r]
when its young cry out to God
and wander about for lack of food?[s]

39

"Do you know when the
mountain goats[a] give birth?
Do you watch when the doe bears
her fawn?[b]
2Do you count the months till they
bear?
Do you know the time they give
birth?[c]
3They crouch down and bring forth
their young;
their labour pains are ended.
4Their young thrive and grow strong in
the wilds;
they leave and do not return.

11 [u]ver 8; [v]Ps 65:7; 89:9; 104:6–9
12 [w]Ps 57:8; [x]Ps 74:16; Am 5:8
13 [y]Ps 104:35; [z]Job 8:22
14 [a]Ex 28:11
15 [b]Dt 28:29; Job 15:22; 18:5; [c]Ge 17:14; Job 4:10; 31:22
16 [d]Ge 1:7; Job 9:8
17 [e]Job 33:22; Mt 16:18; Rev 1:18; [f]Job 7:9
18 [g]Job 28:24; Isa 40:12; [h]ver 4
19 [i]Ge 1:4; Job 28:3; Ps 139:11–12
20 [j]Job 24:13
21 [k]Job 15:7
22 [l]Job 37:6; [m]Dt 28:12; [n]Ps 105:32; 147:17
23 [o]Ps 27:5; Isa 28:17; 30:30; Eze 13:11; [p]Ex 9:26; Jos 10:11; Eze 13:13; Rev 16:21
24 [q]Job 28:24; [r]Job 27:21; [s]Jer 10:13; 51:16
25 [t]Job 28:26
26 [u]Job 36:27; [v]Ps 84:6; 107:35; Isa 41:18
27 [w]Job 28:26; 37:13; Ps 104:14
28 [x]2Sa 1:21; Job 5:10
29 [y]Ps 147:16–17
30 [z]Job 37:10
31 [a]Job 9:9; Am 5:8
32 [b]2Ki 23:5; Isa 13:10; 40:26; 45:12; Jer 19:13; [c]Ge 1:16
33 [d]Ps 148:6; Jer 31:36; [e]Ge 1:16
34 [f]Job 5:10; 22:11
35 [g]Job 36:32
36 [h]Job 9:4; 34:32; Jas 1:5; [i]Job 12:13
37 [j]Jos 3:16; [k]Job 22:11
38 [l]Lev 26:19; [m]1Ki 18:45
39 [n]Ge 49:9
40 [o]Job 37:8; [p]Ge 49:9
41 [q]Ge 1:30; [r]Ge 8:7; Lk 12:24; [s]Ps 147:9; Mt 6:26

Ch. 39

1 [a]Dt 14:5; [b]Ge 49:21
2 [c]Ge 31:7–9

b17 Or *gates of deep shadows*
c31 Or *the twinkling; or the chains of the*
d32 Or *the morning star in its season*
e32 Or *out Leo*
f33 Or *his; or their*
g36 The meaning of the Hebrew for this word is uncertain.
h36 The meaning of the Hebrew for this word is uncertain.

5"Who let the wild donkey[d] go free?
Who untied his ropes?
6I gave him the wasteland[e] as his home,
the salt flats[f] as his habitat.[g]
7He laughs[h] at the commotion in the town;
he does not hear a driver's shout.[i]
8He ranges the hills[j] for his pasture
and searches for any green thing.

9"Will the wild ox[k] consent to serve you?[l]
Will he stay by your manger[m] at night?
10Can you hold him to the furrow with a harness?[n]
Will he till the valleys behind you?
11Will you rely on him for his great strength?[o]
Will you leave your heavy work to him?
12Can you trust him to bring in your grain
and gather it to your threshing-floor?

13"The wings of the ostrich flap joyfully,
but they cannot compare with the pinions and feathers of the stork.[p]
14She lays her eggs on the ground
and lets them warm in the sand,
15unmindful that a foot may crush them,
that some wild animal may trample them.[q]
16She treats her young harshly,[r] as if they were not hers;
she cares not that her labour was in vain,
17for God did not endow her with wisdom
or give her a share of good sense.[s]
18Yet when she spreads her feathers to run,
she laughs[t] at horse and rider.

19"Do you give the horse his strength[u]
or clothe his neck with a flowing mane?
20Do you make him leap like a locust,[v]
striking terror[w] with his proud snorting?[x]
21He paws fiercely, rejoicing in his strength,[y]
and charges into the fray.[z]
22He laughs[a] at fear, afraid of nothing;
he does not shy away from the sword.
23The quiver[b] rattles against his side,
along with the flashing spear[c] and lance.
24In frenzied excitement he eats up the ground;
he cannot stand still when the trumpet sounds.[d]
25At the blast of the trumpet[e] he snorts, 'Aha!'
He catches the scent of battle from afar,
the shout of commanders and the battle cry.[f]

26"Does the hawk take flight by your wisdom
and spread his wings towards the south?[g]
27Does the eagle soar at your command
and build his nest on high?[h]
28He dwells on a cliff and stays there at night;
a rocky crag[i] is his stronghold.
29From there he seeks out his food;[j]
his eyes detect it from afar.
30His young ones feast on blood,
and where the slain are, there is he."[k]

40

The LORD said to Job:[a]

2"Will the one who contends with the Almighty[b] correct him?[c]
Let him who accuses God answer him!"[d]

3Then Job answered the LORD:

4"I am unworthy[e]—how can I reply to you?
I put my hand over my mouth.[f]
5I spoke once, but I have no answer[g]—
twice, but I will say no more."[h]

6Then the LORD spoke to Job out of the storm:[i]

7"Brace yourself like a man;
I will question you,
and you shall answer me.[j]

8"Would you discredit my justice?[k]
Would you condemn me to justify yourself?[l]
9Do you have an arm like God's,[m]
and can your voice[n] thunder like his?[o]
10Then adorn yourself with glory and splendour,
and clothe yourself in honour and majesty.[p]
11Unleash the fury of your wrath,[q]
look at every proud man and bring him low,[r]

5 [d]**Ge 16:12**
6 [e]Job 24:5; Ps 107:34; Jer 2:24; [f]Job 30:4; [g]Job 30:7; Jer 14:6; 17:6
7 [h]**Job 5:22**; [i]Job 3:18
8 [j]Isa 32:20
9 [k]**Nu 23:22**; [l]**Ex 21:6**; [m]**Ge 42:27**
10 [n]Job 41:13; Ps 32:9
11 [o]ver 19; Job 40:16; 41:12, 22; Ps 147:10
13 [p]Zec 5:9
15 [q]2Ki 14:9
16 [r]ver 17; La 4:3
17 [s]**ver 16**; **Job 21:22**
18 [t]**Job 5:22**
19 [u]**ver 11**
20 [v]Joel 2:4–5; Rev 9:7; [w]Job 41:25; [x]Jer 8:16
21 [y]ver 11; [z]Jer 8:6
22 [a]**Job 5:22**
23 [b]Isa 5:28; Jer 5:16; [c]Na 3:3
24 [d]Nu 10:9; Jer 4:5,19; Eze 7:14; Am 3:6
25 [e]Jos 6:5; [f]Jer 8:6; Am 1:14; 2:2
26 [g]Jer 8:7
27 [h]Jer 49:16; Ob 4; Hab 2:9
28 [i]Jer 49:16; Ob 3
29 [j]**Job 9:26**
30 [k]Mt 24:28; Lk 17:37

Ch. 40

1 [a]**Job 5:8; 10:2**
2 [b]**Job 13:3**; [c]**Job 9:15; 11:8; 33:13**; Ro 9:20; [d]**Job 9:3**
4 [e]Job 42:6; [f]**Jdg 18:19; Job 29:9**
5 [g]**Job 9:3**; [h]**Job 9:15**
6 [i]**Ex 14:21; Job 38:1**
7 [j]**Job 38:3**
8 [k]**Job 15:25; 27:2**; Ro 3:3; [l]**Job 2:3; 34:17**
9 [m]**2Ch 32:8; Ps 98:1**; [n]Isa 6:8; Eze 10:5; [o]**Ex 20:19; Job 36:33**
10 [p]Ps 29:1–2; 45:3; 93:1; 96:6; 104:1; 145:5

11 [q]**Job 20:28**; Ps 7:11; Isa 5:25; 9:12,19; 10:5; 13:3,5; 30:27; 42:25; 51:20; Jer 7:20; Na 1:6; Zep 1:18; [r]Ps 18:27; Isa 2:11–12,17; 23:9; 24:10; 25:12; 26:5; 32:19

[12]look at every proud[s] man and humble
him,[t]
crush[u] the wicked where they
stand.
[13]Bury them all in the dust together;[v]
shroud their faces in the grave.[w]
[14]Then I myself will admit to you
that your own right hand can save
you.[x]

[15]"Look at the behemoth,[a]
which I made[y] along with you
and which feeds on grass like an ox.[z]
[16]What strength[a] he has in his loins,
what power in the muscles of his
belly![b]
[17]His tail[b] sways like a cedar;
the sinews of his thighs are
close-knit.[c]
[18]His bones are tubes of bronze,
his limbs[d] like rods of iron.[e]
[19]He ranks first among the works of
God,[f]
yet his Maker[g] can approach him
with his sword.[h]
[20]The hills bring him their produce,[i]
and all the wild animals play[j]
nearby.[k]
[21]Under the lotus plant he lies,
hidden among the reeds[l] in the
marsh.[m]
[22]The lotuses conceal him in their
shadow;
the poplars by the stream[n] surround
him.
[23]When the river rages,[o] he is not
alarmed;
he is secure, though the Jordan[p]
should surge against his mouth.
[24]Can anyone capture him by the eyes,[c]
or trap him and pierce his nose?[q]

41

"Can you pull in the leviathan[a][a]
with a fishhook[b]
or tie down his tongue with a rope?
[2]Can you put a cord through his nose[c]
or pierce his jaw with a hook?[d]
[3]Will he keep begging you for mercy?[e]
Will he speak to you with gentle
words?
[4]Will he make an agreement with you
for you to take him as your slave for
life?[f]
[5]Can you make a pet of him like a bird
or put him on a leash for your girls?
[6]Will traders barter for him?
Will they divide him up among the
merchants?
[7]Can you fill his hide with harpoons
or his head with fishing spears?[g]
[8]If you lay a hand on him,
you will remember the struggle and
never do it again![h]
[9]Any hope of subduing him is false;
the mere sight of him is
overpowering.[i]
[10]No-one is fierce enough to rouse him.[j]
Who then is able to stand against
me?[k]
[11]Who has a claim against me that I must
pay?[l]
Everything under heaven belongs
to me.[m]

[12]"I will not fail to speak of his limbs,[n]
his strength[o] and his graceful form.
[13]Who can strip off his outer coat?
Who would approach him with a
bridle?[p]
[14]Who dares open the doors of his
mouth,[q]
ringed about with his fearsome
teeth?
[15]His back has[b] rows of shields
tightly sealed together;[r]
[16]each is so close to the next
that no air can pass between.
[17]They are joined fast to one another;
they cling together and cannot be
parted.
[18]His snorting throws out flashes of
light;
his eyes are like the rays of dawn.[s]
[19]Firebrands[t] stream from his mouth;
sparks of fire shoot out.
[20]Smoke pours from his nostrils[u]
as from a boiling pot over a fire of
reeds.
[21]His breath[v] sets coals ablaze,
and flames dart from his mouth.[w]
[22]Strength[x] resides in his neck;
dismay goes before him.
[23]The folds of his flesh are tightly joined;
they are firm and immovable.
[24]His chest is hard as rock,
hard as a lower millstone.[y]
[25]When he rises up, the mighty are
terrified;[z]
they retreat before his thrashing.[a]
[26]The sword that reaches him has no
effect,
nor does the spear or the dart or the
javelin.[b][c]
[27]Iron he treats like straw[d]
and bronze like rotten wood.
[28]Arrows do not make him flee;[e]
slingstones are like chaff to him.

12 [s]Ps 10:4; Isa 25:11; Jer 48:29; 49:16; Zep 2:10; [t]**1Sa 2:7; Ps 52:5;** 1Pe 5:5; [u]Ps 60:12; Isa 22:5; 28:3; 63:2–3,6; Da 5:20; Mic 5:8; 7:10; Zec 10:5; Mal 4:3
13 [v]Nu 16:31–34; [w]**Job 4:9**
14 [x]Ex 15:6,12; Ps 18:35; 20:6; 48:10; 60:5; 108:6; Isa 41:10; 63:5
15 [y]**Job 9:9;** [z]Isa 11:7; 65:25
16 [a]**Job 39:11;** [b]Job 41:9
17 [c]Job 41:15
18 [d]Job 41:12; [e]Isa 11:4; 49:2
19 [f]Job 41:33; Ps 40:5; 139:14; Isa 27:1; [g]**Job 4:17; 9:9;** [h]**Ge 3:24**
20 [i]Ps 104:14; [j]Ps 104:26; [k]**Job 5:23**
21 [l]**Ge 41:2;** Ps 68:30; Isa 35:7; [m]Job 8:11
22 [n]Ps 1:3; Isa 44:4
23 [o]Isa 8:7; 11:15; [p]**Jos 3:1**
24 [q]2Ki 19:28; Job 41:2,7,26; Isa 37:29

Ch. 41

1 [a]Job 3:8; [b]Am 4:2
2 [c]**Job 40:24;** [d]Eze 19:4
3 [e]1Ki 20:31
4 [f]**Ex 21:6**
7 [g]**Job 40:24**
8 [h]**Job 3:8**
9 [i]Job 40:16
10 [j]**Job 3:8;** [k]**2Ch 20:6; Isa 46:5;** Jer 50:44; Rev 6:17
11 [l]**Job 34:33;** Ro 11:35; [m]**Jos 3:11; Job 10:4;** Ac 4:24; 1Co 10:26
12 [n]Job 40:18; [o]**Job 39:11**
13 [p]**Job 30:11; 39:10**
14 [q]Ps 22:13
15 [r]Job 40:17
18 [s]**Job 3:9**
19 [t]Da 10:6
20 [u]Ps 18:8
21 [v]**Job 4:9;** Isa 11:4; 40:7; [w]Ps 18:8; Isa 10:17; 30:27; 33:14; 66:14–16; Jer 4:4
22 [x]**Job 39:11**
24 [y]Mt 18:6
25 [z]Job 39:20; [a]**Job 3:8** *26* [b]**Jos 8:18;** [c]**Job 40:24**
27 [d]ver 29 *28* [e]Ps 91:5

[a]*15* Possibly the hippopotamus or the elephant
[b]*17* Possibly trunk [c]*24* Or *by a water hole*
[a]*1* Possibly the crocodile [b]*15* Or *His pride is his*

29A club seems to him but a piece of straw;[f]
he laughs[g] at the rattling of the lance.
30His undersides are jagged potsherds,
leaving a trail in the mud like a threshing-sledge.[h]
31He makes the depths churn like a boiling cauldron[i]
and stirs up the sea like a pot of ointment.[j]
32Behind him he leaves a glistening wake;
one would think the deep had white hair.
33Nothing on earth is his equal[k]—
a creature without fear.
34He looks down on all that are haughty;[l]
he is king over all that are proud."[m]

Job

42

Then Job replied to the LORD:

2"I know that you can do all things;[a]
no plan of yours can be thwarted.[b]
3⌞You asked,⌟ 'Who is this that obscures my counsel without knowledge?'[c]
Surely I spoke of things I did not understand,
things too wonderful for me to know.[d]

4⌞"You said,⌟ 'Listen now, and I will speak;
I will question you,
and you shall answer me.'[e]
5My ears had heard of you[f]
but now my eyes have seen you.[g]
6Therefore I despise myself[h]
and repent[i] in dust and ashes."[j]

Epilogue

7After the LORD had said these things
to Job[k], he said to Eliphaz the Temanite,
"I am angry with you and your two
friends,[l] because you have not spoken
of me what is right, as my servant Job
has.[m] 8So now take seven bulls and
seven rams[n] and go to my servant Job[o]
and sacrifice a burnt offering[p] for
yourselves. My servant Job will pray for
you, and I will accept his prayer[q] and
not deal with you according to your
folly.[r] You have not spoken of me what
is right, as my servant Job has."[s] 9So
Eliphaz the Temanite, Bildad the Shu-
hite and Zophar the Naamathite[t] did
what the LORD told them; and the LORD
accepted Job's prayer.[u]
10After Job had prayed for his friends,
the LORD made him prosperous again[v]
and gave him twice as much as he had
before.[w] 11All his brothers and sisters
and everyone who had known him
before[x] came and ate with him in his
house. They comforted and consoled
him over all the trouble the LORD had
brought upon him,[y] and each one gave
him a piece of silver[a] and a gold ring.
12The LORD blessed the latter part of
Job's life more than the first. He had
fourteen thousand sheep, six thousand
camels, a thousand yoke of oxen and a
thousand donkeys. 13And he also had
seven sons and three daughters. 14The
first daughter he named Jemimah, the
second Keziah and the third Keren-
Happuch. 15Nowhere in all the land
were there found women as beautiful
as Job's daughters, and their father
granted them an inheritance along with
their brothers.
16After this, Job lived a hundred and
forty years; he saw his children and
their children to the fourth generation.
17And so he died, old and full of years.[z]

---

29 [f]ver 27; [g]**Job 5:22**
30 [h]Isa 28:27; 41:15; Am 1:3
31 [i]1Sa 2:14; [j]Eze 32:2
33 [k]**Job 40:19**
34 [l]Ps 18:27; 101:5; 131:1; Pr 6:17; 21:4; 30:13; [m]Job 28:8

Ch. 42

2 [a]**Ge 18:14; Mt 19:26;** [b]**2Ch 20:6; Job 16:19;** Ac 4:28; Eph 1:11
3 [c]**Job 34:35;** [d]**Job 5:9**
4 [e]**Job 38:3**
5 [f]**Job 26:14;** Ro 10:17; [g]Jdg 13:22; Isa 6:5; **Mt 5:8;** Lk 2:30; Eph 1:17–18
6 [h]Job 40:4; Eze 6:9; Ro 12:3; [i]**Job 34:33;** [j]**Ex 10:3; Ezr 9:6; Job 2:8; 6:29**
7 [k]**Jos 1:7;** [l]Job 32:3; [m]ver 8; **Job 9:15**
8 [n]Nu 23:1,29; Eze 45:23; [o]Job 1:8; [p]**Ge 8:20;** [q]Jas 5:15–16; 1Jn 5:16; [r]Ge 20:7; Job 22:30; [s]**ver 7**
9 [t]Job 2:11; [u]**Ge 19:21; 20:17;** Eze 14:14
10 [v]Dt 30:3; Ps 14:7; [w]**Job 1:3;** Ps 85:1–3; 126:5–6; Php 2:8–9; Jas 5:11
11 [x]**Job 19:13;** [y]**Ge 37:35**
17 [z]**Ge 15:15**

---

[a]*11* Hebrew *him a kesitah;* a kesitah was a unit of money of unknown weight and value.

Psalms

BOOK I

Psalms 1–41

Psalm 1

1Blessed is the man[a]
who does not walk[b] in the counsel of the wicked[c]
or stand in the way[d] of sinners[e]
or sit[f] in the seat of mockers.[g]
2But his delight[h] is in the law of the LORD,[i]
and on his law he meditates[j] day and night.
3He is like a tree[k] planted by streams[l] of water,[m]
which yields its fruit[n] in season
and whose leaf[o] does not wither.
Whatever he does prospers.[p]

4Not so the wicked!
They are like chaff[q]
that the wind blows away.
5Therefore the wicked will not stand[r] in the judgment,[s]
nor sinners in the assembly[t] of the righteous.

6For the LORD watches over[u] the way of the righteous,
but the way of the wicked will perish.[v]

Psalm 2

1Why do the nations conspire[a]
and the peoples plot[a] in vain?
2The kings[b] of the earth take their stand
and the rulers gather together
against the LORD
and against his Anointed[c] One.[b][d]
3"Let us break their chains,[e]" they say,
"and throw off their fetters."[f]

4The One enthroned[g] in heaven laughs;[h]
the LORD scoffs at them.
5Then he rebukes them in his anger[i]
and terrifies them in his wrath,[j] saying,
6"I have installed my King[c][k]
on Zion,[l] my holy hill.[m]"

7I will proclaim the decree of the LORD:

He said to me, "You are my Son[d];[n]
today I have become your Father.[e][o]
8Ask of me,
and I will make the nations[p] your inheritance,[q]
the ends of the earth[r] your possession.
9You will rule them with an iron sceptre;[f][s]
you will dash them to pieces[t] like pottery.[u]"

10Therefore, you kings, be wise;[v]
be warned, you rulers[w] of the earth.
11Serve the LORD with fear[x]
and rejoice[y] with trembling.[z]
12Kiss the Son,[a] lest he be angry
and you be destroyed in your way,
for his wrath[b] can flare up in a moment.
Blessed[c] are all who take refuge[d] in him.

Psalm 3

A psalm of David. When he fled from his son Absalom.[a]

1O LORD, how many are my foes!
How many rise up against me!
2Many are saying of me,
"God will not deliver him.[b]" *Selah*[a]

Ps. 1

1 [a]**Dt 33:29**; Ps 40:4; 128:4; [b]Ps 89:15; [c]**Job 21:16**; Ps 10:2–11; [d]**Ge 49:6**; [e]Ps 26:9; 37:38; 51:13; 104:35; [f]Ps 26:4; [g]**Job 11:3**; Pr 1:22; Isa 28:14; Hos 7:5
2 [h]Ps 112:1; 119:16,35; Ro 7:22; [i]Ps 19:7; 119:1; Eze 11:20; 18:17; [j]**Ge 24:63**
3 [k]Ps 52:8; 92:12; 128:3; Jer 11:16; Zec 4:3; [l]Ps 46:4; 65:9; Isa 33:21; Jer 31:9; [m]**Nu 24:6**; **Job 14:9**; **Eze 17:5**; [n]Ps 92:14; Eze 47:12; [o]Isa 1:30; 64:6; [p]**Ge 39:3**
4 [q]**Job 13:25**; Isa 40:24; Jer 13:24
5 [r]Ps 5:5; [s]**Job 19:29**; [t]Ps 26:12; 35:18; 82:1; 89:5; 107:32; 111:1; 149:1
6 [u]Ps 37:18; 121:5; 145:20; Na 1:7; [v]**Lev 26:38**; Ps 9:6

Ps. 2

1 [a]Ps 21:11; 83:5; Pr 24:2
2 [b]Ps 48:4; [c]**1Sa 9:16**; Jn 1:41; [d]Ac 4:25–26*
3 [e]**Job 36:8**; [f]**2Sa 3:34**
4 [g]Isa 37:16; 40:22; 66:1; [h]Ps 37:13; Pr 1:26
5 [i]Ps 6:1; 27:9; 38:1; [j]Ps 21:9; 79:6; 90:7; 110:5
6 [k]Ps 10:16; 24:10; [l]2Ki 19:31; Ps 9:11; 48:2,11; 78:68; 110:2; 133:3; [m]**Ex 15:17**
7 [n]**Mt 3:17**; **4:3**; [o]**2Sa 7:14**; Ac 13:33*; Heb 1:5*; 6:5
8 [p]Rev 2:26; [q]**Job 22:26**; Mt 21:38; [r]Ps 22:27; 67:7
9 [s]**Ge 49:10**; Rev 12:5; [t]**Ex 15:6**; [u]Isa 30:14; Jer 19:10; Rev 2:27*; 19:15
10 [v]Pr 27:11; [w]Ps 141:6; Pr 8:15; Am 2:3
11 [x]Ps 103:11; [y]Ps 9:2; 35:9; 104:34; Isa 61:10; [z]**1Ch 16:30**
12 [a]ver 7; [b]**Dt 9:8**; Rev 6:16; [c]Ps 84:12; [d]Ps 5:11; 34:8; 64:10

Ps. 3

Title [a]2Sa 15:14 *2* [b]Ps 22:8; 71:11; Isa 36:15; 37:20

---

[a]*1* Hebrew; Septuagint *rage* [b]2 Or *anointed one*
[c]6 Or *king* [d]7 Or *son*; also in verse 12
[e]7 Or *have begotten you*
[f]9 Or *will break them with a rod of iron*
[a]2 A word of uncertain meaning, occurring frequently in the Psalms; possibly a musical term

3But you are a shield[c] around me, O LORD;
you bestow glory on me and lift[b] up my head.[d]
4To the LORD I cry aloud,[e]
and he answers me from his holy hill.[f] *Selah*

5I lie down and sleep;[g]
I wake again,[h] because the LORD sustains me.
6I will not fear[i] the tens of thousands
drawn up against me on every side.[j]

7Arise,[k] O LORD!
Deliver me,[l] O my God!
Strike[m] all my enemies on the jaw;
break the teeth[n] of the wicked.

8From the LORD comes deliverance.[o]
May your blessing[p] be on your people. *Selah*

Psalm 4

For the director of music. With stringed instruments. A psalm of David.

1Answer me[a] when I call to you,
O my righteous God.
Give me relief from my distress;[b]
be merciful[c] to me and hear my prayer.[d]

2How long, O men, will you turn my glory[e] into shame[a]?[f]
How long will you love delusions
and seek false gods[b]?[g] *Selah*
3Know that the LORD has set apart the godly[h] for himself;
the LORD will hear[i] when I call to him.

4In your anger do not sin;[j]
when you are on your beds,[k]
search your hearts and be silent. *Selah*
5Offer right sacrifices
and trust in the LORD.[l]

6Many are asking, "Who can show us any good?"
Let the light of your face shine upon us,[m] O LORD.
7You have filled my heart[n] with greater joy[o]
than when their grain and new wine[p] abound.
8I will lie down and sleep[q] in peace,[r]
for you alone, O LORD,
make me dwell in safety.[s]

3 [c]Ge 15:1; [d]Ps 27:6
4 [e]Job 30:20; [f]Ps 2:6
5 [g]Lev 26:6; [h]Ps 17:15; 139:18
6 [i]Job 11:15; Ps 23:4; 27:3; [j]Ps 118:11
7 [k]2Ch 6:41; [l]Ps 6:4; 7:1; 59:1; 109:21; 119:153; Isa 25:9; 33:22; 35:4; 36:15; 37:20; Jer 42:11; Mt 6:13; [m]Job 16:10; [n]Job 29:17; Ps 57:4; Pr 30:14; La 3:16
8 [o]Ps 27:1; 37:39; 62:1; Isa 43:3,11; 44:6, 8; 45:21; Hos 13:4; Jnh 2:9; Rev 7:10; [p]Nu 6:23; Ps 29:11; 129:8

Ps. 4

1 [a]Ps 13:3; 27:7; 69:16; 86:7; 102:2; [b]Ge 32:7; Jdg 2:15; [c]Ps 30:10; [d]Ps 17:6; 54:2; 84:8; 88:2
2 [e]Ex 16:7; 1Sa 4:21; [f]2Ki 19:26; Job 8:22; Ps 35:26; [g]Jdg 2:17; Ps 31:6; 40:4; Jer 13:25; 16:19; Am 2:4
3 [h]Ps 12:1; 30:4; 31:23; 79:2; Mic 7:2; 1Ti 4:7; 2Pe 3:11; [i]Ps 6:8; Mic 7:7
4 [j]Eph 4:26*; [k]Ps 63:6; Da 2:28
5 [l]Ps 31:6; 115:9; Pr 3:5; 28:26; Isa 26:4; Jn 14:1
6 [m]Nu 6:25
7 [n]Ac 14:17; [o]Isa 9:3; 35:10; 65:14, 18; [p]Ge 27:28; Dt 28:51
8 [q]Lev 26:6; [r]Nu 6:26; Job 11:18; [s]Dt 33:28; Jer 32:37

Ps. 5

1 [a]1Ki 8:29; Ps 17:1; 40:1; 116:2; Da 9:18; [b]Ps 38:9; Isa 35:10; 51:11

Psalm 5

For the director of music. For flutes. A psalm of David.

1Give ear[a] to my words, O LORD.
consider my sighing.[b]
2Listen to my cry for help,[c]
my King and my God,[d]
for to you I pray.
3In the morning,[e] O LORD, you hear my voice;
in the morning I lay my requests before you
and wait in expectation.[f]

4You are not a God who takes pleasure in evil;
with you the wicked[g] cannot dwell.
5The arrogant[h] cannot stand[i] in your presence;
you hate[j] all who do wrong.
6You destroy those who tell lies;[k]
bloodthirsty and deceitful men
the LORD abhors.

7But I, by your great mercy,
will come into your house;
in reverence[l] will I bow down[m]
towards your holy temple.[n]
8Lead me, O LORD, in your righteousness[o]
because of my enemies—
make straight your way[p] before me.

9Not a word from their mouth can be trusted;
their heart is filled with destruction.
Their throat is an open grave;[q]
with their tongue they speak deceit.[r]
10Declare them guilty, O God!
Let their intrigues be their downfall.
Banish them for their many sins,[s]
for they have rebelled[t] against you.

11But let all who take refuge in you be glad;

2 [c]Job 19:7; 24:12; 36:5; [d]Ps 44:4; 68:24; 84:3
3 [e]Isa 28:19; 50:4; Jer 21:12; Eze 46:13; Zep 3:5; [f]Ps 62:1; 119:81; 130:5; Hab 2:1; Ro 8:19
4 [g]Ps 1:5; 11:5; 104:35; Pr 2:22
5 [h]2Ki 19:32; Ps 73:3; 75:4; Isa 33:19; 37:33; [i]Ps 1:5; [j]Ps 45:7; 101:3; 119:104; Pr 8:13
6 [k]Pr 19:22; Jn 8:44; Ac 5:3; Rev 21:8
7 [l]Dt 13:4; Jer 44:10; Da 6:26; [m]2Sa 12:16; Ps 138:2; [n]1Ki 8:48
8 [o]Ps 23:3; 31:1; 71:2; 85:13; 89:16; Pr 8:20; [p]1Ki 8:36; Jn 1:23
9 [q]Jer 5:16; Lk 11:44; [r]Ps 12:2; 28:3; 36:3; Pr 15:4; Jer 9:8; Ro 3:13*
10 [s]La 1:5; [t]Ps 78:40; 106:7; 107:11; La 3:42

---

[b]3 Or *LORD, / my Glorious One, who lifts*
[a]2 Or *you dishonour my Glorious One*
[b]2 Or *seek lies*

let them ever sing for joy.[u]
Spread your protection over them,
that those who love your name[v] may
rejoice in you.[w]
12For surely, O LORD, you bless the
righteous;[x]
you surround them[y] with your
favour as with a shield.[z]

Psalm 6

For the director of music. With stringed instruments. According to *sheminith*.[a] A psalm of David.

1O LORD, do not rebuke me in your
anger[a]
or discipline me in your wrath.
2Be merciful to me,[b] LORD, for I am
faint;[c]
O LORD, heal me,[d] for my bones are
in agony.[e]
3My soul is in anguish.[f]
How long,[g] O LORD, how long?

4Turn,[h] O LORD, and deliver me;
save me because of your unfailing
love.[i]
5No-one remembers you when he is
dead.
Who praises you from his grave[b]?[j]

6I am worn out[k] from groaning;[l]
all night long I flood my bed with
weeping[m]
and drench my couch with tears.[n]
7My eyes grow weak[o] with sorrow;
they fail because of all my foes.

8Away from me,[p] all you who do evil,[q]
for the LORD has heard my weeping.
9The LORD has heard my cry for mercy;[r]
the LORD accepts my prayer.
10All my enemies will be ashamed and
dismayed;[s]
they will turn back in sudden
disgrace.[t]

Psalm 7

A *shiggaion*[a][a] of David, which he sang to the LORD concerning Cush, a Benjamite.

1O LORD my God, I take refuge[b] in you;
save and deliver me[c] from all who
pursue me,[d]
2or they will tear me like a lion[e]
and rip me to pieces with no-one to
rescue[f] me.

3O LORD my God, if I have done this
and there is guilt on my hands[g]—
4if I have done evil to him who is at
peace with me
or without cause[h] have robbed my
foe—
5then let my enemy pursue and
overtake[i] me;
let him trample my life to the
ground[j]
and make me sleep in the dust.[k]
Selah

6Arise,[l] O LORD, in your anger;
rise up against the rage of my
enemies.[m]
Awake,[n] my God; decree justice.
7Let the assembled peoples gather
round you.
Rule over them from on high;[o]
8 let the LORD judge[p] the peoples.
Judge me, O LORD, according to my
righteousness,[q]
according to my integrity,[r] O Most
High.[s]
9O righteous God,[t]
who searches minds and hearts,[u]
bring to an end the violence of the
wicked
and make the righteous secure.[v]

10My shield[b][w] is God Most High,
who saves the upright in heart.[x]
11God is a righteous judge,[y]
a God who expresses his wrath[z]
every day.
12If he does not relent,[a]
he[c] will sharpen his sword;[b]
he will bend and string his bow.[c]
13He has prepared his deadly weapons;
he makes ready his flaming arrows.[d]

14He who is pregnant with evil
and conceives trouble gives birth[e] to
disillusionment.
15He who digs a hole and scoops it out
falls into the pit[f] he has made.[g]
16The trouble he causes recoils on
himself;
his violence comes down on his own
head.

11 [u]Ps 33:1; 81:1; 90:14; 92:4; 95:1; 145:7; [v]Ps 69:36; 119:132; [w]**Job 22:19**
12 [x]Ps 112:2; [y]Ps 32:7; [z]**Ge 15:1**

Ps. 6

1 [a]**Ps 2:5**
2 [b]Ps 4:1; 26:11; Jer 3:12; 12:15; 31:20; [c]Ps 61:2; 77:3; 142:3; Isa 40:31; Jer 8:18; Eze 21:7; [d]**Nu 12:13**; [e]Ps 22:14; 31:10; 32:3; 38:3; 42:10; 102:3
3 [f]**Job 7:11**; Ps 31:7; 38:8; 55:4; **Jn 12:27**; Ro 9:2; 2Co 2:4; [g]1Sa 1:14; 1Ki 18:21; Ps 4:2; 89:46; Isa 6:11; Jer 4:14; Hab 1:2; Zec 1:12
4 [h]Ps 25:16; 31:2; 69:16; 71:2; 86:16; 88:2; 102:2; 119:132; [i]Ps 13:5; 31:16; 77:8; 85:7; 119:41; Isa 54:8,10
5 [j]Ps 30:9; 88:10–12; 115:17; Ecc 9:10; Isa 38:18
6 [k]**Jdg 8:5**; [l]**Job 3:24**; **23:2**; Ps 12:5; 77:3; 102:5; La 1:8, 11,21–22; [m]**Job 16:16**; [n]**Job 7:3**; Lk 7:38; Ac 20:19
7 [o]**Job 16:8**; Ps 31:9; 69:3; 119:82; Isa 38:14
8 [p]Ps 119:115; 139:19; [q]Ps 5:5; **Mt 7:23**
9 [r]Ps 28:6; 116:1
10 [s]**2Ki 19:26**; [t]Ps 40:14

Ps. 7

Title [a]Hab 3:1
1 [b]Ps 2:12; 11:1; 31:1; [c]**Ps 3:7**; [d]Ps 31:15; 119:86,157,161
2 [e]**Ge 49:9**; Rev 4:7; [f]Ps 3:2; 71:11
3 [g]Isa 59:3
4 [h]Ps 35:7,19; Pr 24:28
5 [i]**Ex 15:9**; [j]**2Sa 22:43**; 2Ki 9:33; Isa 10:6; La 3:16; [k]**Job 7:21**
6 [l]**2Ch 6:41**; [m]Ps 138:7; [n]Ps 35:23; 44:23
7 [o]Ps 68:18
8 [p]**1Ch 16:33**; [q]**1Sa 26:23**; Ps 18:20; [r]**Ge 20:5**; [s]**Ge 3:5**; **Nu 24:16**; **Mk 5:7**
9 [t]Jer 11:20; [u]**1Ch 28:9**; Ps 26:2; Rev 2:23; [v]Ps 37:23; 40:2
10 [w]Ps 3:3; [x]**Job 33:3**
11 [y]**Ge 18:25**; Ps 9:8; 67:4; 75:2; 96:13; 98:9; Isa 11:4; Jer 11:20; [z]**Dt 9:8**
12 [a]Eze 3:19; 33:9; [b]**Dt 32:41**; [c]**2Sa 22:35**; Ps 21:12; Isa 5:28; 13:18
13 [d]Ps 11:2; 18:14; 64:3
14 [e]Isa 59:4; Jas 1:15
15 [f]Ps 35:7–8; 40:2; 94:13; Pr 26:27; [g]**Job 4:8**

[a]Title: Probably a musical term
[b]5 Hebrew *Sheol*
[a]Title: Probably a literary or musical term
[b]10 Or *sovereign*
[c]12 Or *If a man does not repent, / God*

17I will give thanks to the LORD because
of his righteousness[h]
and will sing praise[i] to the name of
the LORD Most High.[j]

Psalm 8

For the director of music. According to *gittith*.[a] A psalm of David.

1O LORD, our Lord,
how majestic is your name[a] in all the
earth!

You have set your glory[b]
above the heavens.[c]
2From the lips of children and infants
you have ordained praise[b d]
because of your enemies,
to silence the foe[e] and the avenger.

3When I consider your heavens,[f]
the work of your fingers,[g]
the moon and the stars,[h]
which you have set in place,
4what is man that you are mindful of
him,
the son of man that you care for
him?[i]
5You made him a little lower than the
heavenly beings[c j]
and crowned him with glory and
honour.[k]

6You made him ruler[l] over the works of
your hands;[m]
you put everything under his feet:[n o]
7all flocks and herds,[p]
and the beasts of the field,[q]
8the birds of the air,
and the fish of the sea,[r]
all that swim the paths of the seas.

9O LORD, our Lord,
how majestic is your name in all the
earth![s]

Psalm 9[a]

For the director of music. To ⌞the tune of⌟ "The Death of the Son". A psalm of David.

1I will praise you, O LORD, with all my
heart;[a]
I will tell of all your wonders.[b]
2I will be glad and rejoice[c] in you;
I will sing praise[d] to your name,[e] O
Most High.

3My enemies turn back;
they stumble and perish before you.
4For you have upheld my right[f] and my
cause;[g]
you have sat on your throne,[h]
judging righteously.[i]
5You have rebuked the nations[j] and
destroyed the wicked;
you have blotted out their name[k] for
ever and ever.
6Endless ruin has overtaken the
enemy,
you have uprooted their cities;[l]
even the memory of them[m] has
perished.

7The LORD reigns for ever;[n]
he has established his throne[o] for
judgment.
8He will judge the world in
righteousness;[p]
he will govern the peoples with
justice.[q]
9The LORD is a refuge[r] for the
oppressed,[s]
a stronghold in times of trouble.[t]
10Those who know your name[u] will
trust in you,
for you, LORD, have never forsaken[v]
those who seek you.[w]

11Sing praises[x] to the LORD, enthroned
in Zion;[y]
proclaim among the nations[z] what
he has done.[a]
12For he who avenges blood[b]
remembers;
he does not ignore the cry of the
afflicted.[c]

13O LORD, see how my enemies[d]
persecute me!
Have mercy[e] and lift me up from the
gates of death,[f]
14that I may declare your praises[g]
in the gates of the Daughter of Zion[h]
and there rejoice in your salvation.[i]
15The nations have fallen into the pit
they have dug;[j]

17 [h]Ps 5:8; [i]**2Ch 31:2**; Ro 15:11; Heb 2:12; [j]**Ge 14:18**

Ps. 8

1 [a]**1Ch 16:10**; [b]**Ex 15:11**; Lk 2:9; [c]Ps 57:5; 108:5; 113:4; 148:13; Hab 3:3
2 [d]Mt 21:16*; [e]Ps 143:12
3 [f]**Ge 15:5**; **Dt 10:14**; [g]**Ex 8:19**; **1Ch 16:26**; **2Ch 2:12**; Ps 102:25; [h]**Ge 1:16**; 1Co 15:41
4 [i]**1Ch 29:14**
5 [j]**Ge 1:26**; [k]Ps 21:5; 103:4
6 [l]**Ge 1:28**; [m]**Job 10:3**; Ps 19:1; 102:25; 145:10; Isa 26:12; 29:23; 45:11; Heb 1:10; [n]Heb 2:6–8*; [o]**1Ki 5:3**; 1Co 15:25,27; Eph 1:22
7 [p]Ge 13:5; 26:14; [q]**Ge 2:19**
8 [r]Ge 1:26
9 [s]ver 1

Ps. 9

1 [a]Ps 86:12; 111:1; 119:2, 10,145; 138:1; [b]**Dt 4:34**
2 [c]**Job 22:19**; Ps 14:7; 31:7; 70:4; 97:8; 126:3; Pr 23:15; Isa 25:9; Jer 30:19; Joel 2:21; Zep 3:14; **Mt 5:12**; Rev 19:7; [d]**2Ch 31:2**; [e]Ps 92:1
4 [f]**1Ki 8:45**; [g]**Job 16:21**; [h]Ps 11:4; 47:8; Isa 6:1; [i]Ps 7:11; 67:4; 98:9; 1Pe 2:23
5 [j]Ge 20:7; **37:10**; **1Ch 16:21**; Ps 59:5; 105:14; Isa 26:14; 66:15; [k]**Job 18:17**
6 [l]**Dt 29:28**; Jer 2:3; 46:1–51:58; Zep 2:8–10; [m]Ps 34:16; 109:15; Ecc 9:5; Isa 14:22; 26:14
7 [n]**1Ch 16:31**; Rev 19:6; [o]Ps 11:4; 47:8; 93:2; Isa 6:1; 66:1
8 [p]**ver 4**; Ps 7:11; [q]Ps 11:7; 45:6; 72:2
9 [r]**Dt 33:27**; **2Sa 22:3**; [s]Ps 10:18; 74:21; [t]Ps 32:7; 121:7
10 [u]Ps 91:14; [v]**Ge 28:15**; **Dt 4:31**; Ps 22:1; 37:25; 71:11; Isa 49:14; Jer 15:18; Heb 13:5; [w]Ps 70:4
11 [x]Ps 7:17; [y]**Ps 2:6**; [z]Ps 18:49; 44:11; 57:9; 106:27; Isa 24:13; Eze 20:23; 1Ti 3:16; [a]Ps 105:1
12 [b]**2Sa 4:11**; [c]ver 18; Ps 10:17; 22:24; 72:4; Isa 49:13
13 [d]Nu 10:9; Ps 3:7; 18:3; [e]Ps 6:2; 41:4; 51:1; 86:3,16; 119:132; [f]**Job 17:16**; Mt 16:18
14 [g]Ps 51:15; 1Pe 2:9; [h]2Ki 19:21; Isa 1:8; 10:32; 37:22; 62:11; Jer 4:31; 6:2; La 1:6; Mic 1:13; Zep 3:14; Zec 2:10; Mt 21:5; Jn 12:15; [i]Ps 13:5; 35:9; 50:23; 51:12
15 [j]**Job 4:8**; Ps 35:7

[a]Title: Probably a musical term
[b]2 Or *strength* [c]5 Or *than God*
[a]Psalms 9 and 10 may have been originally a single acrostic poem, the stanzas of which begin with the successive letters of the Hebrew alphabet. In the Septuagint they constitute one psalm.

their feet are caught in the net they
have hidden.[k]
16The LORD is known by his justice;
the wicked are ensnared by the
work of their hands.[l]
Higgaion.[b] *Selah*

17The wicked return to the grave,[c m]
all the nations that forget God.[n]
18But the needy will not always be
forgotten,
nor the hope[o] of the afflicted[p] ever
perish.
19Arise,[q] O LORD, let not man triumph;[r]
let the nations be judged[s] in your
presence.
20Strike them with terror,[t] O LORD;
let the nations know they are but
men.[u]
Selah

Psalm 10[a]

1Why, O LORD, do you stand far off?[a]
Why do you hide yourself[b] in times
of trouble?

2In his arrogance the wicked man
hunts down the weak,[c]
who are caught in the schemes he
devises.
3He boasts[d] of the cravings of his heart;
he blesses the greedy and reviles the
LORD.[e]
4In his pride the wicked does not seek
him;
in all his thoughts there is no room
for God.[f]
5His ways are always prosperous;
he is haughty[g] and your laws are far
from him;
he sneers at all his enemies.
6He says to himself, "Nothing will
shake me;
I'll always be happy[h] and never
have trouble."
7His mouth is full of curses[i] and lies
and threats;[j]
trouble and evil are under his
tongue.[k]
8He lies in wait[l] near the villages;
from ambush he murders the
innocent,[m]
watching in secret for his victims.
9He lies in wait like a lion in cover;
he lies in wait to catch the helpless;[n]
he catches the helpless and drags
them off in his net.[o]
10His victims are crushed,[p] they
collapse;
they fall under his strength.
11He says to himself, "God has
forgotten;[q]
he covers his face and never sees."[r]

12Arise,[s] LORD! Lift up your hand,[t] O
God.
Do not forget the helpless.[u]
13Why does the wicked man revile
God?[v]
Why does he say to himself,
"He won't call me to account"?[w]
14But you, O God, do see trouble[x] and
grief;
you consider it to take it in hand.
The victim commits himself to you;[y]
you are the helper[z] of the fatherless.
15Break the arm of the wicked and evil
man;[a]
call him to account for his
wickedness
that would not be found out.

16The LORD is King for ever and ever;[b]
the nations[c] will perish from his
land.
17You hear, O LORD, the desire of the
afflicted;[d]
you encourage them, and you listen
to their cry,[e]
18defending the fatherless[f] and the
oppressed,[g]
in order that man, who is of the
earth, may terrify no more.

Psalm 11

For the director of music. Of David.

1In the LORD I take refuge.[a]
How then can you say to me:
"Flee[b] like a bird to your mountain.[c]
2For look, the wicked bend their bows;[d]
they set their arrows[e] against the
strings
to shoot from the shadows[f]
at the upright in heart.[g]
3When the foundations[h] are being
destroyed,
what can the righteous do?"[a]

4The LORD is in his holy temple;[i]
the LORD is on his heavenly throne.[j]
He observes the sons of men;[k]
his eyes examine[l] them.
5The LORD examines the righteous,[m]

15 [k]Ps 35:8; 57:6
16 [l]Pr 5:22
17 [m]**Nu 16:30**; Pr 5:5; [n]**Job 8:13**
18 [o]Ps 25:3; 39:7; 71:5; Pr 23:18; Jer 14:8; [p]ver 12; Ps 74:19
19 [q]Ps 3:7; [r]2Ch 14:11; [s]Ps 110:6; Isa 2:4; Joel 3:12
20 [t]**Ge 35:5**; Ps 31:13; Isa 13:8; Lk 21:26; [u]Ps 62:9; Isa 31:3; Eze 28:2

Ps. 10

1 [a]Ps 22:1,11; 35:22; 38:21; 71:12; [b]Ps 13:1
2 [c]ver 9; **Job 20:19**
3 [d]Ps 49:6; 94:4; Jer 48:30; [e]**Job 1:5**
4 [f]Ps 36:1
5 [g]Ps 18:27; 101:5; Pr 6:17; Isa 13:11; Jer 48:29
6 [h]Rev 18:7
7 [i]Ro 3:14*; [j]Ps 73:8; 119:134; Ecc 4:1; Isa 30:12; [k]**Job 20:12**
8 [l]Ps 37:32; 59:3; 71:10; Pr 1:11; Jer 5:26; Mic 7:2; [m]Hos 6:9
9 [n]**ver 2**; [o]**Job 18:8**
10 [p]**Job 9:17**
11 [q]Job 22:13; Ps 42:9; 77:9; [r]**Job 22:14**
12 [s]Ps 3:7; [t]Ps 17:7; 20:6; 106:26; Isa 26:11; Mic 5:9; [u]Ps 9:12
13 [v]ver 3; [w]**Job 31:14**
14 [x]ver 7; Ps 22:11; [y]Ps 37:5; [z]**Dt 33:29**
15 [a]**Job 31:22**
16 [b]**Ex 15:18**; [c]**Dt 8:20**
17 [d]Ps 9:12; [e]**Ex 22:23**
18 [f]Dt 24:17; Ps 146:9; [g]**Ps 9:9**

Ps. 11

1 [a]Ps 7:1; [b]**Ge 14:10**; [c]Ps 50:11
2 [d]2Sa 22:35; [e]**Ps 7:13; 58:7**; [f]Ps 10:8; [g]**Job 33:3**; Ps 7:10
3 [h]Ps 18:15; 82:5; Isa 24:18

4 [i]**1Ki 8:48**; Ps 18:6; 27:4; Jnh 2:7; Mic 1:2; Hab 2:20; [j]**2Ch 6:18**; **Ps 9:7**; Mt 5:34; 23:22; **Rev 4:2**; [k]Pr 15:3; [l]Ps 33:18; 66:7 *5* [m]**Dt 7:13; Job 23:10**

b*16* Or *Meditation*; possibly a musical notation
c*17* Hebrew *Sheol*
aPsalms 9 and 10 may have been originally a single acrostic poem, the stanzas of which begin with the successive letters of the Hebrew alphabet. In the Septuagint they constitute one psalm.
a*3* Or *what is the Righteous One doing*

but the wicked[b] and those who love violence
his soul hates.[n]
6On the wicked he will rain
fiery coals and burning sulphur;[o]
a scorching wind[p] will be their lot.

7For the LORD is righteous,[q]
he loves justice;[r]
upright men[s] will see his face.[t]

Psalm 12

For the director of music. According to *sheminith*.[a] A psalm of David.

1Help, LORD, for the godly are no more;[a]
the faithful have vanished from among men.
2Everyone lies[b] to his neighbour;
their flattering lips speak with deception.[c]

3May the LORD cut off all flattering lips[d]
and every boastful tongue[e]
4that says, "We will triumph with our tongues;[f]
we own our lips[b]—who is our master?"

5"Because of the oppression[g] of the weak
and the groaning[h] of the needy,
I will now arise,[i]" says the LORD.
"I will protect them[j] from those who malign them."
6And the words of the LORD are flawless,[k]
like silver refined[l] in a furnace[m] of clay,
purified seven times.

7O LORD, you will keep us safe[n]
and protect us from such people for ever.[o]
8The wicked freely strut[p] about
when what is vile is honoured among men.

Psalm 13

For the director of music. A psalm of David.

1How long,[a] O LORD? Will you forget me[b] for ever?
How long will you hide your face[c] from me?
2How long must I wrestle with my thoughts[d]
and every day have sorrow in my heart?
How long will my enemy triumph over me?[e]

5 [n]**Job 28:28**; Ps 5:5; 45:7; Isa 1:14
6 [o]**Ge 19:24; Rev 9:17**; [p]**Ge 41:6; Job 1:19**
7 [q]**2Ch 12:6; Ezr 9:15**; 2Ti 4:8; [r]**Ps 9:8**; 33:5; 99:4; Isa 28:17; 30:18; 56:1; 61:8; Jer 9:24; [s]**Job 1:1**; Lk 23:50; [t]Ps 17:15; 140:13

Ps. 12

1 [a]Isa 57:1; Mic 7:2
2 [b]Ps 5:6; 34:13; 141:3; Pr 6:19; 12:17; 13:3; Isa 32:7; [c]**Ps 5:9**; Ro 16:18
3 [d]Pr 26:28; 28:23; [e]Ps 73:9; Da 7:8; Jas 3:5; Rev 13:5
4 [f]Pr 18:21; Jas 3:6
5 [g]Ps 44:24; 62:10; 72:14; 73:8; Ecc 4:1; 5:8; Isa 3:15; 5:7; 30:12; 59:13; Ac 7:34; [h]**Ps 6:6**; [i]Ps 3:7; [j]Ps 34:6; 35:10
6 [k]**2Sa 22:31**; Ps 18:30; [l]**Job 23:10; 28:1**; Isa 48:10; Zec 13:9; [m]Ps 119:140
7 [n]Ps 16:1; 27:5; [o]Ps 37:28; Jn 17:12
8 [p]Ps 55:10–11

Ps. 13

1 [a]Ps 6:3; [b]Ps 42:9; La 5:20; [c]**Dt 31:17; Ps 22:24; Isa 8:17; 54:9**
2 [d]Ps 42:4; 55:2; 139:23; Isa 33:18; Da 7:28; [e]Ps 94:3
3 [f]Ps 9:12; 25:18; 31:7; 35:23; 59:4; 80:14; 107:41; 119:50,153; [g]**Ps 4:1**; [h]**Ezr 9:8**; [i]Ps 76:5; 90:5; Jer 51:39
4 [j]**1Ki 19:2**; Ps 25:2; [k]Ps 38:16; 118:13
5 [l]**Ps 6:4**; [m]**Job 33:26**; Ps 9:14; Isa 25:9; 33:2
6 [n]**Ex 15:1**; Ps 7:17

Ps. 14

1 [a]Ps 10:4

3Look on me[f] and answer,[g] O LORD my God.
Give light to my eyes,[h] or I will sleep in death;[i]
4my enemy will say, "I have overcome him,[j]"
and my foes will rejoice when I fall.[k]

5But I trust in your unfailing love;[l]
my heart rejoices in your salvation.[m]
6I will sing[n] to the LORD,
for he has been good to me.

Psalm 14

14:1–7pp—Ps 53:1–6

For the director of music. Of David.

1The fool[a] says in his heart,
"There is no God."[a]
They are corrupt, their deeds are vile;
there is no-one who does good.

2The LORD looks down from heaven[b]
on the sons of men
to see if there are any who understand,[c]
any who seek God.[d]
3All have turned aside,[e]
they have together become corrupt;[f]
there is no-one who does good,[g]
not even one.[h]

4Will evildoers never learn—[i]
those who devour my people[j] as men eat bread
and who do not call on the LORD?[k]
5There they are, overwhelmed with dread,
for God is present in the company of the righteous.
6You evildoers frustrate the plans of the poor,
but the LORD is their refuge.[l]

7Oh, that salvation for Israel would come out of Zion![m]
When the LORD restores the fortunes[n] of his people,
let Jacob rejoice and Israel be glad!

2 [b]Job 41:34; Ps 85:11; 102:19; La 3:50; [c]Ps 92:6; [d]**Ezr 6:21**
3 [e]**1Sa 8:3**; 1Ti 5:15; [f]2Pe 2:7; [g]1Ki 8:46; Ps 143:2; Ecc 7:20; [h]Ro 3:10–12*
4 [i]Ps 82:5; Jer 4:22; [j]Ps 27:2; Mic 3:3; [k]Ps 79:6; Isa 64:7; 65:1; Jer 10:25; Hos 7:7
6 [l]**2Sa 22:3**
7 [m]Ps 2:6; [n]**Dt 30:3; Jer 48:47**

---

b5 Or *The LORD, the Righteous One, examines the wicked, /*
aTitle: Probably a musical term
b4 Or / *our lips are our ploughshares*
a1 The Hebrew words rendered *fool* in Psalms denote one who is morally deficient.

Psalm 15

A psalm of David.

1LORD, who may dwell[a] in your
sanctuary?[b]
Who may live on your holy hill?[c]

2He whose walk is blameless[d]
and who does what is righteous,
who speaks the truth[e] from his heart
3 and has no slander[f] on his tongue,
who does his neighbour no wrong
and casts no slur on his fellow-man,
4who despises a vile man
but honours[g] those who fear the
LORD,
who keeps his oath[h]
even when it hurts,
5who lends his money without usury[i]
and does not accept a bribe[j] against
the innocent.

He who does these things
will never be shaken.[k]

Psalm 16

A *miktam*[a] of David.

1Keep me safe,[a] O God,
for in you I take refuge.[b]

2I said to the LORD, "You are my Lord;[c]
apart from you I have no good
thing."[d]
3As for the saints[e] who are in the land,[f]
they are the glorious ones in whom
is all my delight.[b]
4The sorrows[g] of those will increase
who run after other gods.[h]
I will not pour out their libations of
blood
or take up their names[i] on my lips.

5LORD, you have assigned me my
portion[j] and my cup;[k]
you have made my lot[l] secure.
6The boundary lines[m] have fallen for
me in pleasant places;
surely I have a delightful
inheritance.[n]

7I will praise the LORD, who counsels
me;[o]
even at night[p] my heart instructs
me.
8I have set the LORD always before me.
Because he is at my right hand,[q]
I shall not be shaken.[r]

9Therefore my heart is glad[s] and my
tongue rejoices;
my body also will rest secure,[t]

Ps. 15

1 [a]Ex 29:46; Ps 23:6; 27:4; 61:4; [b]Ex 25:8; 1Ch 22:19; Ps 20:2; 78:69; 150:1; [c]**Ex 15:17**
2 [d]**Ge 6:9**; **Ps 18:32**; Eph 1:4; **1Th 3:13**; Tit 1:6; [e]Pr 16:13; Isa 45:19; Jer 7:28; 9:5; Zec 8:3,16; Ro 9:1; **Eph 4:25**
3 [f]**Lev 19:16**
4 [g]**Job 19:9**; Ac 28:10; [h]**Dt 23:21**; **Jos 9:18**; Mt 5:33
5 [i]**Ex 22:25**; [j]**Ex 18:21**; **1Sa 8:3**; Ac 24:26; [k]**Job 29:18**; Ps 21:7; 112:6; Ac 2:25; Heb 12:28; 2Pe 1:10

Ps. 16

1 [a]**Ps 12:7**; [b]Ps 2:12
2 [c]Ps 31:14; 118:28; 140:6; [d]Ps 73:25
3 [e]Dt 33:3; Ps 30:4; 85:8; Da 7:18; Ac 9:13; Ro 1:7; [f]Ps 101:6
4 [g]Ps 32:10; Pr 23:29; [h]Ex 18:11; 20:3; **Dt 8:19**; **31:20**; [i]**Ex 23:13**
5 [j]**Lev 2:2**; [k]Ps 23:5; 75:8; 116:13; Isa 51:17; La 4:21; Eze 23:32–34; Hab 2:16; [l]**Job 31:2**
6 [m]**Dt 19:14**; Ps 104:9; Pr 8:29; Jer 5:22; [n]**Job 22:26**
7 [o]Ps 73:24; Pr 15:22; Isa 11:2; [p]Job 35:10; Ps 42:8; 77:6
8 [q]1Ki 2:19; 1Ch 6:39; Ps 73:23; [r]Ps 15:5
9 [s]Ps 4:7; 13:5; 28:7; 30:11; [t]**Dt 33:28**
10 [u]**Nu 16:30**; Ps 30:3; 31:17; 86:13; Hos 13:14; [v]**2Ki 19:22**; [w]**Job 17:14**; Ac 2:31; 13:35*
11 [x]Ps 139:24; Mt 7:14; [y]Ac 2:25–28*; [z]Ps 21:6; [a]Ps 80:17

10because you will not abandon me to
the grave,[c u]
nor will you let your Holy One[d v] see
decay.[w]
11You have made known[e] to me the path
of life;[x]
you will fill me with joy in your
presence,[y]
with eternal pleasures[z] at your right
hand.[a]

Psalm 17

A prayer of David.

1Hear,[a] O LORD, my righteous plea;
listen to my cry.[b]
Give ear[c] to my prayer—
it does not rise from deceitful lips.[d]
2May my vindication[e] come from you;
may your eyes see what is right.[f]

3Though you probe my heart[g] and
examine me at night,
though you test me,[h] you will find
nothing;[i]
I have resolved that my mouth will
not sin.[j]
4As for the deeds of men—
by the word of your lips
I have kept myself
from the ways of the violent.
5My steps have held to your paths;[k]
my feet have not slipped.[l]

6I call on you, O God, for you will
answer me;[m]
give ear to me[n] and hear my prayer.[o]
7Show the wonder of your great love,[p]
you who save by your right hand[q]
those who take refuge[r] in you from
their foes.
8Keep me[s] as the apple of your eye;[t]
hide me[u] in the shadow of your
wings[v]
9from the wicked who assail me,
from my mortal enemies who
surround me.[w]

Ps. 17

1 [a]Ps 30:10; 64:1; 80:1; 140:6; [b]Ps 5:2; 39:12; 142:6; 143:1; [c]**Ps 5:1**; [d]Isa 29:13
2 [e]Ps 24:5; 26:1; Isa 46:13; 50:8–9; 54:17; [f]Ps 99:4
3 [g]Ps 139:1; Jer 12:3; [h]**Job 7:18**; [i]Job 23:10; Jer 50:20; [j]Ps 39:1
5 [k]Job 23:11; Ps 44:18; 119:133; [l]Dt 32:35; Ps 73:2; 121:3
6 [m]Ps 86:7; [n]Ps 116:2; [o]**Ps 4:1**
7 [p]Ps 31:21; 69:13; 106:45; 107:43; 117:2; [q]**Ps 10:12**; [r]Ps 2:12
8 [s]**Nu 6:24**; [t]**Dt 32:10**; Pr 7:2; [u]Ps 27:5; 31:20; 32:7; [v]Ru 2:12; Ps 36:7; 63:7; Isa 34:15 *9* [w]Ps 109:3

[a]Title: Probably a literary or musical term
[b]3 Or *As for the pagan priests who are in the land / and the nobles in whom all delight, I said:*
[c]10 Hebrew *Sheol* [d]10 Or *your faithful one*
[e]11 Or *You will make known*

10They close up their callous hearts,[x]
and their mouths speak with
arrogance.[y]
11They have tracked me down, they
now surround me,[z]
with eyes alert, to throw me to the
ground.
12They are like a lion[a] hungry for prey,[b]
like a great lion crouching in cover.

13Rise up,[c] O LORD, confront them,
bring them down;[d]
rescue me from the wicked by your
sword.
14O LORD, by your hand save me from
such men,
from men of this world[e] whose
reward is in this life.[f]

You still the hunger of those you
cherish;
their sons have plenty,
and they store up wealth[g] for their
children.
15And I—in righteousness I shall see
your face;
when I awake,[h] I shall be satisfied
with seeing your likeness.[i]

Psalm 18

18:Title–50pp—2Sa 22:1–51

For the director of music. Of David the servant of the LORD. He sang to the LORD the words of this song when the LORD delivered him from the hand of all his enemies and from the hand of Saul. He said:

1I love you, O LORD, my strength.[a]

2The LORD is my rock,[b] my fortress[c] and
my deliverer;[d]
my God is my rock, in whom I take
refuge.[e]
He is my shield[f] and the horn[a] of my
salvation,[g] my stronghold.
3I call to the LORD, who is worthy of
praise,[h]
and I am saved from my enemies.[i]

4The cords of death[j] entangled me;
the torrents[k] of destruction
overwhelmed me.
5The cords of the grave[b] coiled around
me;
the snares of death[l] confronted me.
6In my distress[m] I called to the LORD;[n]
I cried to my God for help.
From his temple he heard my voice;[o]
my cry came[p] before him, into his
ears.

10 [x]Ps 73:7; 119:70; Isa 6:10; [y]**1Sa 2:3**
11 [z]Ps 88:17
12 [a]Ps 7:2; Jer 5:6; 12:8; La 3:10; [b]**Ge 49:9**
13 [c]**Nu 10:35;** [d]Ps 35:8; 55:23; 73:18
14 [e]Lk 16:8; [f]Ps 49:17; Lk 16:25; [g]Isa 2:7; 57:17
15 [h]**Ps 3:5;** [i]**Nu 12:8; Mt 5:8;** 1Jn 3:2

Ps. 18

1 [a]**Ex 15:2; Dt 33:29; 1Sa 2:10;** Ps 22:19; 28:7; 59:9; 81:1; Isa 12:2; 49:5; Jer 16:19
2 [b]**Ex 33:22;** [c]Ps 28:8; 31:2–3; Isa 17:10; Jer 16:19; [d]Ps 40:17; [e]Ps 2:12; 9:9; 94:22; [f]**Ge 15:1;** Ps 28:7; 84:9; 119:114; 144:2; [g]**1Sa 2:1; Lk 1:69**
3 [h]**1Ch 16:25;** [i]**Ps 9:13**
4 [j]Ps 116:3; [k]Ps 93:4; 124:4; Isa 5:30; 17:12; Jer 6:23; 51:42, 55; Eze 43:2
5 [l]Pr 13:14
6 [m]**Dt 4:30;** [n]Ps 30:2; 99:6; 102:2; 120:1; [o]Ps 66:19; 116:1; [p]**Job 16:18**
7 [q]Ps 97:4; Isa 5:25; 64:3; [r]**Jdg 5:4;** [s]**Jdg 5:5;** [t]**Job 9:5;** Jer 10:10
8 [u]**Job 41:20;** [v]**Ex 15:7; 19:18; Job 41:21;** Ps 50:3; 97:3; Da 7:10; [w]Pr 25:22; Ro 12:20
9 [x]**Ge 11:5; Ps 57:3;** [y]**Ex 20:21; Dt 33:26; Ps 104:3**
10 [z]**Ge 3:24;** Eze 10:18; [a]**Dt 33:26;** [b]Ps 104:3
11 [c]**Ex 19:9; Dt 4:11;** [d]**Job 22:14;** Isa 4:5; Jer 43:10
12 [e]Ps 104:2; [f]**Jos 10:11;** [g]**Job 36:30**
13 [h]**Ex 9:23; 1Sa 2:10**

7The earth trembled[q] and quaked,[r]
and the foundations of the
mountains shook;[s]
they trembled because he was
angry.[t]
8Smoke rose from his nostrils;[u]
consuming fire[v] came from his
mouth,
burning coals[w] blazed out of it.
9He parted the heavens and came
down;[x]
dark clouds[y] were under his feet.
10He mounted the cherubim[z] and flew;
he soared[a] on the wings of the
wind.[b]
11He made darkness his covering,[c] his
canopy[d] around him—
the dark rain clouds of the sky.
12Out of the brightness of his presence[e]
clouds advanced,
with hailstones[f] and bolts of
lightning.[g]
13The LORD thundered[h] from heaven;
the voice of the Most High
resounded.[c]
14He shot his arrows[i] and scattered ⌊the
enemies⌋,
great bolts of lightning[j] and routed
them.[k]
15The valleys of the sea were exposed
and the foundations[l] of the earth
laid bare
at your rebuke,[m] O LORD,
at the blast of breath from your
nostrils.[n]

16He reached down from on high and
took hold of me;
he drew me out of deep waters.[o]
17He rescued me from my powerful
enemy,[p]
from my foes, who were too strong
for me.[q]
18They confronted me in the day of my
disaster,[r]
but the LORD was my support.[s]
19He brought me out into a spacious
place;[t]
he rescued me because he delighted
in me.[u]

14 [i]**Dt 32:23;** [j]**Job 36:30;** Rev 4:5; [k]**Jdg 4:15**
15 [l]**Ps 11:3;** [m]Ps 76:6; 104:7; 106:9; Isa 50:2; [n]**Ex 15:8**
16 [o]Ex 15:5; Ps 69:2; Pr 18:4; 20:5
17 [p]ver 48; Ps 38:19; 59:1; 143:9; [q]**Jdg 18:26**
18 [r]Pr 1:27; 16:4; Jer 17:17; 40:2; Ob 13; [s]Ps 20:2; Isa 3:1
19 [t]Ps 31:8; [u]**Nu 14:8**

a2 *Horn* here symbolises strength.
b5 Hebrew *Sheol*
c13 Some Hebrew manuscripts and Septuagint (see also 2 Samuel 22:14); most Hebrew manuscripts *resounded, / amid hailstones and bolts of lightning*

20The LORD has dealt with me according
to my righteousness;[v]
according to the cleanness of my
hands[w] he has rewarded me.[x]
21For I have kept the ways of the LORD;[y]
I have not done evil by turning[z]
from my God.
22All his laws are before me;[a]
I have not turned away from his
decrees.
23I have been blameless[b] before him
and have kept myself from sin.
24The LORD has rewarded me according
to my righteousness,[c]
according to the cleanness of my
hands in his sight.

25To the faithful[d] you show yourself
faithful,[e]
to the blameless you show yourself
blameless,
26to the pure[f] you show yourself pure,
but to the crooked you show
yourself shrewd.[g]
27You save the humble[h]
but bring low those whose eyes are
haughty.[i]
28You, O LORD, keep my lamp[j] burning;
my God turns my darkness into
light.[k]
29With your help[l] I can advance against
a troop;[d]
with my God I can scale a wall.

30As for God, his way is perfect;[m]
the word of the LORD is flawless.[n]
He is a shield[o]
for all who take refuge[p] in him.
31For who is God besides the LORD?[q]
And who is the Rock[r] except our
God?
32It is God who arms me with strength[s]
and makes my way perfect.[t]
33He makes my feet like the feet of a
deer;[u]
he enables me to stand on the
heights.[v]
34He trains my hands for battle;[w]
my arms can bend a bow of bronze.
35You give me your shield of victory,
and your right hand sustains[x] me;
you stoop down to make me great.
36You broaden the path[y] beneath me,
so that my ankles do not turn over.[z]

37I pursued my enemies[a] and overtook
them;
I did not turn back till they were
destroyed.
38I crushed them[b] so that they could not
rise;[c]
they fell beneath my feet.[d]
39You armed me with strength[e] for
battle;
you made my adversaries bow[f] at
my feet.
40You made my enemies turn their
backs[g] in flight,
and I destroyed[h] my foes.
41They cried for help, but there was
no-one to save them[i]—
to the LORD, but he did not answer.[j]
42I beat them as fine as dust[k] borne on
the wind;
I poured them out like mud in the
streets.

43You have delivered me from the
attacks of the people;
you have made me the head of
nations;[l]
people I did not know[m] are subject
to me.
44As soon as they hear me, they obey
me;
foreigners[n] cringe before me.
45They all lose heart;[o]
they come trembling[p] from their
strongholds.[q]

46The LORD lives![r] Praise be to my Rock![s]
Exalted be God[t] my Saviour![u]
47He is the God who avenges[v] me,
who subdues nations[w] under me,
48 who saves[x] me from my enemies.[y]
You exalted me above my foes;
from violent men[z] you rescued me.
49Therefore I will praise you among the
nations,[a] O LORD;
I will sing[b] praises to your name.[c]
50He gives his king great victories;
he shows unfailing kindness to his
anointed,[d]
to David[e] and his descendants for
ever.[f]

Psalm 19

For the director of music. A psalm of David.

1The heavens[a] declare[b] the glory of
God;[c]
the skies[d] proclaim the work of his
hands.[e]

20 [v]**1Sa 26:23**; [w]Job 22:30; Ps 24:4; [x]**Ru 2:12; 2Ch 15:7**; 1Co 3:8
21 [y]2Ch 34:33; Ps 37:34; 119:2; Pr 8:32; 23:26; [z]Ps 119:102
22 [a]Ps 119:30
23 [b]**Ge 6:9**
24 [c]**1Sa 26:23**
25 [d]Ps 31:23; 37:28; 50:5; Pr 2:8; [e]Ps 25:10; 40:11; 89:24; 146:6
26 [f]Pr 15:26; Mt 5:8; Php 1:10; 1Ti 5:22; Tit 1:15; 1Jn 3:3; [g]Pr 3:34; Mt 10:16; Lk 16:8
27 [h]**2Ch 33:23; Mt 23:12**; [i]**Job 41:34; Ps 10:5**; Pr 3:33–34
28 [j]1Ki 11:36; Ps 132:17; [k]Job 29:3; Ps 97:11; 112:4; Jn 1:5; **Ac 26:18**; 2Co 4:6; 2Pe 1:19
29 [l]ver 32,39; Isa 45:5; Heb 11:34
30 [m]**Dt 32:4**; [n]**Ps 12:6**; Pr 30:5; [o]Ps 3:3; [p]Ps 2:12
31 [q]**Dt 4:35**; 32:39; Ps 35:10; 86:8; 89:6; Isa 44:6, 8; 45:5–6,14, 18,21; 46:9; [r]**Ge 49:24**
32 [s]**ver 29**; 1Pe 5:10; [t]**Ps 15:2**; 19:13; Heb 10:14; Jas 3:2
33 [u]Ps 42:1; Pr 5:19; Isa 35:6; Hab 3:19; [v]**Dt 32:13**
34 [w]Ps 144:1
35 [x]Ps 3:5; 37:5,17; 41:3; 51:12; 54:4; 55:22; 119:116; Isa 41:4,10,13; 43:2; 46:4
36 [y]Ps 31:8; [z]**Job 18:7**; Ps 66:9
37 [a]**Lev 26:7**
38 [b]Ps 68:21; 110:6; [c]Ps 36:12; 140:10; Isa 26:14; [d]Ps 47:3
39 [e]ver 32; Isa 45:5,24; [f]ver 47; Ps 47:3; 144:2
40 [g]**Jos 7:12**; [h]ver 37
41 [i]**2Ki 14:26**; Ps 50:22; [j]**1Sa 8:18; 14:37**; Jer 11:11
42 [k]**Dt 9:21; Isa 2:22**
43 [l]2Sa 8:1–14; [m]Isa 55:5
44 [n]Ps 54:3; 144:7,11; Isa 25:5
45 [o]**1Sa 17:32**; 2Co 4:1; Heb 12:3; [p]Isa 66:2; Hos 3:5; 11:10; [q]Ps 9:9; Mic 7:17
46 [r]**Jos 3:10; 1Sa 14:39**; 2Co 13:4; [s]ver 31; Ex 33:22; [t]Ps 21:13; 35:27; 40:16; 108:5; [u]**1Ch 16:35; Lk 1:47**
47 [v]**Ge 4:24**; [w]**ver 39; Jdg 4:23**
48 [x]Ps 7:10; 37:40; Da 3:17; [y]**ver 17**; [z]Ps 140:1
49 [a]**Ps 9:11**; [b]Ps 7:17; 9:2; 101:1; 108:1; 146:2; [c]Ro 15:9*
50 [d]**2Sa 23:1**; [e]Ps 144:10; [f]Ps 89:4

Ps. 19

1 [a]Ps 89:5; Isa 40:22; [b]Ps 50:6; 148:3; Ro 1:19; [c]Ps 4:2; 8:1; 97:6; Isa 6:3; [d]**Ge 1:8**; [e]**Ps 8:6; 103:22**

d29 Or *can run through a barricade*

[2]Day after day they pour forth speech;
night after night they display knowledge.[f]
[3]There is no speech or language
where their voice is not heard.[a]
[4]Their voice[b] goes out into all the earth,
their words to the ends of the world.[g]

In the heavens he has pitched a tent[h]
for the sun,[i]
5 which is like a bridegroom[j] coming forth from his pavilion,[k]
like a champion[l] rejoicing to run his course.
[6]It rises at one end of the heavens[m]
and makes its circuit to the other;[n]
nothing is hidden from its heat.

[7]The law of the LORD[o] is perfect,[p]
reviving the soul.[q]
The statutes of the LORD are trustworthy,[r]
making wise the simple.[s]
[8]The precepts of the LORD are right,[t]
giving joy[u] to the heart.
The commands of the LORD are radiant,
giving light to the eyes.[v]
[9]The fear of the LORD[w] is pure,
enduring for ever.
The ordinances of the LORD are sure
and altogether righteous.[x]
[10]They are more precious than gold,[y]
than much pure gold;
they are sweeter than honey,[z]
than honey from the comb.[a]
[11]By them is your servant warned;
in keeping them there is great reward.

[12]Who can discern his errors?
Forgive my hidden faults.[b]
[13]Keep your servant also from wilful sins;[c]
may they not rule over me.[d]
Then will I be blameless,[e]
innocent of great transgression.

[14]May the words of my mouth and the meditation of my heart
be pleasing[f] in your sight,
O LORD, my Rock[g] and my Redeemer.[h]

Psalm 20

For the director of music. A psalm of David.

[1]May the LORD answer you when you are in distress;[a]
may the name of the God of Jacob[b] protect you.[c]

2 [f]Ps 74:16
4 [g]Ro 10:18*; [h]**Job 36:29;** Ps 104:2; [i]**Jdg 5:31**
5 [j]Joel 2:16; [k]**Job 36:29;** [l]1Sa 17:4
6 [m]Dt 30:4; [n]Ps 113:3; Ecc 1:5
7 [o]**Ps 1:2;** [p]Ps 119:142; Jas 1:25; [q]Ps 23:3; [r]Ps 93:5; 111:7; 119:138,144; [s]**Dt 4:6;** Ps 119:130
8 [t]Ps 33:4; 119:128; [u]Ps 119:14; [v]**Ezr 9:8;** Ps 38:10
9 [w]Ps 34:11; 111:10; Pr 1:7; Ecc 12:13; Isa 33:6; [x]Ps 119:138
10 [y]**Job 22:24;** Ps 119:72; Pr 8:10; [z]Ps 119:103; SS 4:11; Eze 3:3; [a]**1Sa 14:27**
12 [b]Ps 51:2; 90:8; Ecc 12:14
13 [c]**Nu 15:30;** [d]Ps 119:133; [e]**Ge 6:9; Ps 18:32**
14 [f]Ps 104:34; [g]Ps 18:31; [h]**Ex 6:6; Job 19:25**

Ps. 20

1 [a]Ps 4:1; [b]Ex 3:6; Ps 46:7, 11; [c]Ps 59:1; 69:29; 91:14
2 [d]Ps 30:10; 33:20; 37:40; 40:17; 54:4; 118:7; [e]**Nu 3:28;** [f]**Ps 18:18;** [g]Ps 2:6; 128:5; 134:3; 135:21
3 [h]Ac 10:4; [i]**Dt 33:11**
4 [j]Ps 21:2; 37:4; 145:16,19; Isa 26:8; Eze 24:25; Ro 10:1; [k]Ps 140:8; Pr 16:3; Da 11:17
5 [l]**Job 3:7;** [m]**Nu 1:52;** Ps 60:4; Isa 5:26; 11:10,12; 13:2; 30:17; 49:22; 62:10; Jer 50:2; 51:12,27; [n]1Sa 1:17
6 [o]**2Sa 23:1;** Ps 28:8; [p]**Job 40:14;** Hab 3:13
7 [q]**2Ki 19:23;** [r]**Dt 17:16;** Ps 33:17; 147:10; Pr 21:31; Isa 31:1; 36:8–9; [s]**2Ch 32:8**

[2]May he send you help[d] from the sanctuary[e]
and grant you support[f] from Zion.[g]
[3]May he remember[h] all your sacrifices
and accept your burnt offerings.[i]
Selah
[4]May he give you the desire of your heart[j]
and make all your plans succeed.[k]
[5]We will shout for joy[l] when you are victorious
and will lift up our banners[m] in the name of our God.
May the LORD grant all your requests.[n]

[6]Now I know that the LORD saves his anointed;[o]
he answers him from his holy heaven
with the saving power of his right hand.[p]
[7]Some trust in chariots[q] and some in horses,[r]
but we trust in the name of the LORD our God.[s]
[8]They are brought to their knees and fall,[t]
but we rise up[u] and stand firm.[v]

[9]O LORD, save the king!
Answer[a] us[w] when we call!

Psalm 21

For the director of music. A psalm of David.

[1]O LORD, the king rejoices in your strength.[a]
How great is his joy in the victories you give![b]
[2]You have granted him the desire of his heart[c]
and have not withheld the request of his lips.
Selah
[3]You welcomed him with rich blessings
and placed a crown of pure gold[d] on his head.[e]
[4]He asked you for life, and you gave it to him—
length of days, for ever and ever.[f]

8 [t]Ps 27:2; Isa 40:30; Jer 46:6; 50:32; [u]Mic 7:8; [v]**Job 11:15;** Ps 37:23; Pr 10:25; Isa 7:9 *9* [w]Ps 17:6

Ps. 21

1 [a]**1Sa 2:10;** [b]**2Sa 22:51** *2* [c]**Ps 20:4**
3 [d]**2Sa 12:30;** Rev 14:14; [e]Zec 6:11
4 [f]Ps 10:16; 45:17; 48:14; 133:3

[a]3 Or *They have no speech, there are no words; / no sound is heard from them*
[b]4 Septuagint, Jerome and Syriac; Hebrew *line*
[a]9 Or *save! / O King, answer*

5 Through the victories[g] you gave, his
glory is great;
you have bestowed on him
splendour and majesty.[h]
6 Surely you have granted him eternal
blessings
and made him glad with the joy[i] of
your presence.[j]
7 For the king trusts in the LORD;[k]
through the unfailing love[l] of the
Most High[m]
he will not be shaken.[n]

8 Your hand will lay hold[o] on all your
enemies;
your right hand will seize your foes.
9 At the time of your appearing
you will make them like a fiery
furnace.
In his wrath the LORD will swallow
them up,
and his fire will consume them.[p]
10 You will destroy their descendants
from the earth,
their posterity from mankind.[q]
11 Though they plot evil[r] against you
and devise wicked schemes,[s] they
cannot succeed;
12 for you will make them turn their
backs[t]
when you aim at them with drawn
bow.

13 Be exalted,[u] O LORD, in your strength;[v]
we will sing and praise your might.

Psalm 22

For the director of music. To ⌞the tune of⌟ "The Doe of the Morning". A psalm of David.

1 My God, my God, why have you
forsaken me?[a]
Why are you so far[b] from saving me,
so far from the words of my
groaning?[c]
2 O my God, I cry out by day, but you do
not answer,[d]
by night,[e] and am not silent.

3 Yet you are enthroned as the Holy
One;[f]
you are the praise[g] of Israel.[a]
4 In you our fathers put their trust;
they trusted and you delivered
them.[h]
5 They cried to you[i] and were saved;
in you they trusted[j] and were not
disappointed.[k]

6 But I am a worm[l] and not a man,
scorned by men[m] and despised[n] by
the people.
7 All who see me mock me;[o]
they hurl insults,[p] shaking their
heads:[q]
8 "He trusts in the LORD;
let the LORD rescue him.[r]
Let him deliver him,[s]
since he delights[t] in him."

9 Yet you brought me out of the womb;[u]
you made me trust[v] in you
even at my mother's breast.
10 From birth[w] I was cast upon you;
from my mother's womb you have
been my God.
11 Do not be far from me,[x]
for trouble is near[y]
and there is no-one to help.[z]

12 Many bulls[a] surround me;[b]
strong bulls of Bashan[c] encircle me.
13 Roaring lions[d] tearing their prey[e]
open their mouths wide[f] against
me.
14 I am poured out like water,
and all my bones are out of joint.[g]
My heart has turned to wax;[h]
it has melted away[i] within me.
15 My strength is dried up like a
potsherd,[j]
and my tongue sticks to the roof of
my mouth;[k]
you lay me[b] in the dust[l] of death.
16 Dogs[m] have surrounded me;
a band of evil men has encircled me,
they have pierced[c] [n] my hands and
my feet.
17 I can count all my bones;
people stare[o] and gloat over me.[p]
18 They divide my garments among
them
and cast lots[q] for my clothing.[r]

19 But you, O LORD, be not far off;[s]
O my Strength,[t] come quickly[u] to
help me.[v]
20 Deliver my life from the sword,[w]
my precious life[x] from the power of
the dogs.[y]

5 [g]ver 1; Ps 18:50; 44:4; [h]**Ps 8:5;** 45:3; 93:1; 96:6; 104:1
6 [i]Ps 43:4; 126:3; [j]**1Ch 17:27**
7 [k]**2Ki 18:5;** [l]Ps 6:4; [m]Ge 14:18; [n]**Ps 15:5; 55:22**
8 [o]Isa 10:10
9 [p]**Dt 32:22;** Ps 50:3; Jer 15:14
10 [q]Dt 28:18
11 [r]Ps 2:1; [s]Job 10:3; Ps 10:2; 26:10; 37:7
12 [t]**Ex 23:27**
13 [u]**Ps 18:46;** [v]Ps 18:1

Ps. 22

1 [a]**Job 6:15; Ps 9:10;** Mt 27:46*; Mk 15:34*; [b]Ps 10:1; [c]**Job 3:24**
2 [d]**Job 19:7;** [e]Ps 42:3; 88:1
3 [f]**2Ki 19:22;** Ps 71:22; **Mk 1:24;** [g]**Ex 15:2;** Ps 148:14
4 [h]Ps 78:53; 107:6
5 [i]**1Ch 5:20;** [j]Isa 8:17; 25:9; 26:3; 30:18; [k]**2Ch 13:18;** Ps 25:3; 31:17; 71:1; Isa 49:23; Ro 9:33
6 [l]**Job 4:19;** [m]**2Sa 12:14;** Ps 31:11; 64:8; 69:19; 109:25; [n]Ps 119:141; Isa 49:7; 53:3; 60:14; Mal 2:9; Mt 16:21
7 [o]**Job 17:2;** Ps 35:16; 69:12; 74:18; Mt 27:41; Mk 15:31; Lk 23:36; [p]Mt 27:39,44; Mk 15:32; Lk 23:39; [q]Mk 15:29
8 [r]Ps 91:14; [s]**Ps 3:2;** [t]**2Sa 22:20; Mt 3:17;** 27:43
9 [u]Job 10:18; Ps 71:6; [v]Ps 78:7; Na 1:7
10 [w]Ps 71:6; Isa 46:3; 49:1
11 [x]ver 19; **Ps 10:1;** [y]**Ps 10:14;** [z]**2Ki 14:26; Isa 41:28**
12 [a]Ps 68:30; [b]Ps 17:9; 27:6; 49:5; 109:3; 140:9; [c]Dt 32:14; Isa 2:13; Eze 27:6; 39:18; Am 4:1
13 [d]ver 21; Eze 22:25; Zep 3:3; [e]**Ge 49:9;** [f]La 3:46
14 [g]**Ps 6:2;** [h]Job 23:16; Ps 68:2; 97:5; Mic 1:4; [i]Jos 7:5; Ps 107:26; Da 5:6
15 [j]Isa 45:9; [k]Ps 137:6; La 4:4; Eze 3:26; Jn 19:28; [l]**Job 7:21;** Ps 104:29
16 [m]Php 3:2; [n]Isa 51:9; 53:5; Zec 12:10; Jn 20:25
17 [o]Lk 23:35; [p]Ps 25:2; 30:1; 35:19; 38:16; La 2:17; Mic 7:8
18 [q]**Lev 16:8;** Mt 27:35*; Mk 15:24; Lk 23:34; Jn 19:24*; [r]Mk 9:12
19 [s]**ver 11;** [t]**Ps 18:1;** [u]Ps 38:22; 70:5; 141:1; [v]Ps 40:13
20 [w]**Job 5:20;** Ps 37:14; [x]Ps 35:17; [y]Php 3:2

---

a3 Or *Yet you are holy, / enthroned on the praises of Israel*
b15 Or / *I am laid*
c16 Some Hebrew manuscripts, Septuagint and Syriac; most Hebrew manuscripts / *like the lion,*

21Rescue me from the mouth of the lions;[z]
saved[d] me from the horns of the wild oxen.[a]

22I will declare your name to my brothers;
in the congregation[b] I will praise you.[c]
23You who fear the LORD, praise him![d]
All you descendants of Jacob, honour him![e]
Revere him,[f] all you descendants of Israel!
24For he has not despised[g] or disdained
the suffering of the afflicted one;[h]
he has not hidden his face[i] from him
but has listened to his cry for help.[j]

25From you comes the theme of my praise in the great assembly;[k]
before those who fear you[e] will I fulfil my vows.[l]
26The poor will eat[m] and be satisfied;
they who seek the LORD will praise him—[n]
may your hearts live for ever!
27All the ends of the earth[o]
will remember and turn to the LORD,
and all the families of the nations
will bow down before him,[p]
28for dominion belongs to the LORD[q]
and he rules over the nations.

29All the rich[r] of the earth will feast and worship;[s]
all who go down to the dust[t] will kneel before him—
those who cannot keep themselves alive.[u]
30Posterity[v] will serve him;
future generations[w] will be told about the LORD.
31They will proclaim his righteousness[x]
to a people yet unborn[y]—
for he has done it.[z]

Psalm 23

A psalm of David.

1The LORD is my shepherd,[a] I shall not be in want.[b]
2 He makes me lie down in green pastures,
he leads me beside quiet waters,[c]
3 he restores my soul.[d]
He guides me[e] in paths of righteousness[f]
for his name's sake.[g]
4Even though I walk
through the valley of the shadow of death,[a] [h]
I will fear no evil,[i]
for you are with me;[j]
your rod and your staff,
they comfort me.

5You prepare a table[k] before me
in the presence of my enemies.
You anoint my head with oil;[l]
my cup[m] overflows.
6Surely goodness and love[n] will follow me
all the days of my life,
and I will dwell in the house of the LORD
for ever.

Psalm 24

Of David. A psalm.

1The earth is the LORD's,[a] and everything in it,
the world, and all who live in it;[b]
2for he founded it upon the seas
and established it upon the waters.[c]

3Who may ascend the hill[d] of the LORD?
Who may stand in his holy place?[e]
4He who has clean hands[f] and a pure heart,[g]
who does not lift up his soul to an idol[h]
or swear by what is false.[a]
5He will receive blessing[i] from the LORD
and vindication[j] from God his Saviour.
6Such is the generation of those who seek him,
who seek your face,[k] O God of Jacob.[b] *Selah*

7Lift up your heads, O you gates;[l]
be lifted up, you ancient doors,
that the King[m] of glory[n] may come in.[o]
8Who is this King of glory?
The LORD strong and mighty,[p]
the LORD mighty in battle.[q]
9Lift up your heads, O you gates;
lift them up, you ancient doors,
that the King of glory may come in.

21 [z]**ver 13; Job 4:10;** [a]ver 12; **Nu 23:22**
22 [b]Ps 26:12; 40:9–10; 68:26; [c]Ps 35:18; Heb 2:12*
23 [d]Ps 33:2; 66:8; 86:12; 103:1; 106:1; 113:1; 117:1; 135:19; [e]Ps 50:15; Isa 24:15; 25:3; 49:23; 60:9; Jer 3:17; [f]**Dt 14:23;** Ps 33:8
24 [g]Ps 102:17; [h]**Ps 9:12;** [i]Ps 13:1; 27:9; 69:17; 102:2; 143:7; [j]**Job 24:12; 36:5;** Heb 5:7
25 [k]Ps 26:12; 35:18; 40:9; 82:1; [l]**Nu 30:2**
26 [m]Ps 107:9; [n]Ps 40:16
27 [o]**Ps 2:8;** [p]Ps 86:9; 102:22; Da 7:27; Mic 4:1
28 [q]Ps 47:7; Zec 14:9
29 [r]Ps 45:12; [s]Ps 95:6; 96:9; 99:5; Isa 27:13; 49:7; 66:23; Zec 14:16; [t]Isa 26:19; [u]Ps 89:48
30 [v]Isa 53:10; 54:3; 61:9; 66:22; [w]Ps 102:18
31 [x]**Ps 5:8;** 40:9; [y]Ps 71:18; 78:6; 102:18; [z]Lk 18:31; 24:44

Ps. 23

1 [a]**Ge 48:15; Ps 28:9; Jn 10:11;** [b]Ps 34:9–10; 84:11; 107:9; Php 4:19
2 [c]Ps 36:8; 46:4; Rev 7:17
3 [d]**Ps 19:7;** [e]Ps 25:9; 73:24; Isa 42:16; [f]**Ps 5:8;** [g]Ps 25:11; 31:3; 79:9; 106:8; 109:21; 143:11
4 [h]**Job 3:5;** Ps 107:14; [i]Ps 3:6; 27:1; [j]Ps 16:8; Isa 43:2
5 [k]**Job 36:16;** [l]Ps 45:7; 92:10; Lk 7:46; [m]**Ps 16:5**
6 [n]**Ne 9:25**

Ps. 24

1 [a]**Ex 9:29;** Job 41:11; [b]1Co 10:26*
2 [c]**Ge 1:6;** Ps 104:3; 2Pe 3:5
3 [d]Ps 2:6; [e]Ps 15:1; 65:4
4 [f]**2Sa 22:21;** [g]Ps 51:10; 73:1; Mt 5:8; [h]Eze 18:15
5 [i]Dt 11:26; [j]Ps 17:2
6 [k]Ps 27:8; 105:4; 119:58; Hos 5:15
7 [l]Ps 118:19–20; Isa 26:2; 60:11,18; 62:10; [m]Ps 44:4; 74:12; [n]Ps 29:3; Ac 7:2; 1Co 2:8; [o]Zec 9:9; Mt 21:5
8 [p]**1Ch 29:11;** Ps 89:13; Jer 50:34; Eph 6:10; [q]Ex 15:3, 6; Dt 4:34

d21 Or / *you have heard* e25 Hebrew *him*
a4 Or *through the darkest valley*
a4 Or *swear falsely*
b6 Two Hebrew manuscripts and Syriac (see also Septuagint); most Hebrew manuscripts *face, Jacob*

[10]Who is he, this King of glory?
The LORD Almighty[r]—
he is the King of glory. *Selah*

Psalm 25[a]

Of David.

[1]To you, O LORD, I lift up my soul;[a]
2 in you I trust,[b] O my God.
Do not let me be put to shame,
nor let my enemies triumph over me.
[3]No-one whose hope is in you
will ever be put to shame,[c]
but they will be put to shame
who are treacherous[d] without excuse.

[4]Show me your ways, O LORD,
teach me your paths;[e]
[5]guide me in your truth[f] and teach me,
for you are God my Saviour,[g]
and my hope is in you[h] all day long.
[6]Remember, O LORD, your great mercy and love,[i]
for they are from of old.
[7]Remember not the sins of my youth[j]
and my rebellious ways;[k]
according to your love[l] remember me,
for you are good,[m] O LORD.

[8]Good and upright[n] is the LORD;
therefore he instructs[o] sinners in his ways.
[9]He guides[p] the humble in what is right
and teaches them[q] his way.
[10]All the ways of the LORD are loving and faithful[r]
for those who keep the demands of his covenant.[s]
[11]For the sake of your name,[t] O LORD,
forgive[u] my iniquity,[v] though it is great.
[12]Who, then, is the man that fears the LORD?[w]
He will instruct him in the way[x] chosen for him.
[13]He will spend his days in prosperity,[y]
and his descendants will inherit the land.[z]
[14]The LORD confides[a] in those who fear him;
he makes his covenant known[b] to them.
[15]My eyes are ever on the LORD,[c]
for only he will release my feet from the snare.[d]

[16]Turn to me[e] and be gracious to me,[f]
for I am lonely[g] and afflicted.
[17]The troubles[h] of my heart have multiplied;
free me from my anguish.[i]
[18]Look upon my affliction[j] and my distress[k]
and take away all my sins.[l]
[19]See how my enemies[m] have increased
and how fiercely they hate me![n]
[20]Guard my life[o] and rescue me;[p]
let me not be put to shame,[q]
for I take refuge[r] in you.
[21]May integrity[s] and uprightness[t] protect me,
because my hope is in you.[u]

[22]Redeem Israel,[v] O God,
from all their troubles!

Psalm 26

Of David.

[1]Vindicate me,[a] O LORD,
for I have led a blameless life;[b]
I have trusted[c] in the LORD
without wavering.[d]
[2]Test me,[e] O LORD, and try me,
examine my heart and my mind;[f]
[3]for your love[g] is ever before me,
and I walk continually[h] in your truth.[i]
[4]I do not sit[j] with deceitful men,
nor do I consort with hypocrites;[k]
[5]I abhor[l] the assembly of evildoers
and refuse to sit with the wicked.
[6]I wash my hands in innocence,[m]
and go about your altar, O LORD,
[7]proclaiming aloud your praise[n]
and telling of all your wonderful deeds.[o]
[8]I love[p] the house where you live, O LORD,
the place where your glory dwells.[q]

[9]Do not take away my soul along with sinners,
my life with bloodthirsty men,[r]
[10]in whose hands are wicked schemes,[s]
whose right hands are full of bribes.[t]
[11]But I lead a blameless life;
redeem me[u] and be merciful to me.

10 [r]**1Sa 1:11**

Ps. 25

1 [a]Ps 86:4; 143:8
2 [b]Ps 31:6; 143:8
3 [c]**Ps 22:5; Isa 29:22**; [d]Isa 24:16; Hab 1:13; Zep 3:4; 2Ti 3:4
4 [e]**Job 34:32**
5 [f]Ps 31:3; 43:3; Jn 16:13; [g]Ps 24:5; [h]ver 3; Ps 33:20; 39:7; 42:5; 71:5; 130:7; 131:3
6 [i]Ps 5:7; 98:3; Isa 63:7,15; Jer 31:20; Hos 11:8
7 [j]Job 13:26; Isa 54:4; Jer 3:25; 31:19; 32:30; Eze 16:22,60; 23:3; 2Ti 2:22; [k]**Ex 23:21**; Ps 107:17; [l]Ps 6:4; 51:1; 69:16; 109:26; 119:124; [m]**1Ch 16:34**; Ps 34:8; 73:1
8 [n]Ps 92:15; Isa 26:7; [o]Ps 32:8; Isa 28:26
9 [p]**Ps 23:3**; [q]ver 4; Ps 27:11
10 [r]**Ps 18:25**; [s]Ps 103:18; 132:12
11 [t]**Ex 9:16**; Ps 31:3; 79:9; Jer 14:7; [u]**Ex 34:9**; [v]**Ex 32:30; Ps 78:38**
12 [w]**Job 1:8**; [x]ver 8
13 [y]**Dt 30:15; 1Ki 3:14; Job 8:7**; [z]**Nu 14:24**; Mt 5:5
14 [a]Pr 3:32; [b]Ge 17:2; Jn 7:17
15 [c]**2Ch 20:12**; Ps 123:2; Heb 12:2; [d]**Job 34:30; Ps 119:110**
16 [e]**Ps 6:4**; [f]**Nu 6:25**; [g]Ps 68:6
17 [h]1Ki 1:29; Ps 34:6,17; 40:12; 54:7; 116:3; [i]Ps 6:3; 39:2
18 [j]**Ps 13:3**; Ro 12:12; [k]**2Sa 16:12**; [l]Ps 103:3
19 [m]Ps 3:1; 9:13; [n]Ps 35:19; 38:19; 69:4
20 [o]Ps 86:2; [p]Ps 17:13; 22:21; 43:1; 71:2; 116:4; 140:1; 142:6; 144:11; [q]ver 3; [r]Ps 2:12
21 [s]**Ge 20:5**; Pr 10:9; [t]1Ki 9:4; Ps 85:10; 111:8; Isa 60:17; Mal 2:6; [u]ver 3 **22** [v]Ps 130:8; Lk 24:21

Ps. 26

1 [a]**1Sa 24:15**; [b]Ps 15:2; Pr 20:7; [c]Ps 22:4; 40:4; Isa 12:2; 25:9; Jer 17:7; Da 3:28; [d]2Ki 20:3; Heb 10:23
2 [e]Ps 66:10; [f]**Dt 6:6; Ps 7:9**; Jer 11:20; 20:12; Eze 11:5
3 [g]Ps 6:4; [h]**1Ki 2:4**; [i]Ps 40:11; 43:3; 86:11; 119:30
4 [j]Ps 1:1; [k]Ps 28:3; Mt 6:2
5 [l]Ps 139:21 **6** [m]Ps 73:13; Mt 27:24
7 [n]Isa 42:12; 60:6; [o]**Jos 3:5**; Ps 9:1
8 [p]Ps 122:6; Isa 66:10; [q]**Ex 29:43**; 2Ch 7:1; Ps 96:6
9 [r]Ps 5:6; 28:3; 55:23; 139:19; Pr 29:10
10 [s]**Ps 21:11**; [t]**Job 36:18; Isa 1:23; Eze 22:12**
11 [u]Ps 31:5; 69:18; 119:134; Tit 2:14

[a]This psalm is an acrostic poem, the verses of which begin with the successive letters of the Hebrew alphabet.

12My feet stand on level ground;[v]
in the great assembly[w] I will praise
the LORD.

Psalm 27

Of David.

1The LORD is my light[a] and my
salvation[b]—
whom shall I fear?
The LORD is the stronghold[c] of my
life—
of whom shall I be afraid?[d]
2When evil men advance against me
to devour my flesh,[a]
when my enemies and my foes attack
me,
they will stumble and fall.[e]
3Though an army besiege me,
my heart will not fear;[f]
though war break out against me,
even then will I be confident.[g]

4One thing[h] I ask of the LORD,
this is what I seek:
that I may dwell in the house of the
LORD
all the days of my life,[i]
to gaze upon the beauty of the LORD
and to seek him in his temple.
5For in the day of trouble[j]
he will keep me safe[k] in his
dwelling;
he will hide me[l] in the shelter of his
tabernacle
and set me high upon a rock.[m]
6Then my head will be exalted[n]
above the enemies who surround
me;[o]
at his tabernacle will I sacrifice[p] with
shouts of joy;[q]
I will sing[r] and make music[s] to the
LORD.

7Hear my voice[t] when I call, O LORD;
be merciful to me and answer me.[u]
8My heart says of you, "Seek his[b]
face!"[v]
Your face, LORD, I will seek.
9Do not hide your face[w] from me,
do not turn your servant away in
anger;[x]
you have been my helper.[y]
Do not reject me or forsake[z] me,
O God my Saviour.[a]
10Though my father and mother forsake
me,
the LORD will receive me.
11Teach me your way,[b] O LORD;
lead me in a straight path[c]
because of my oppressors.[d]
12Do not hand me over to the desire of
my foes,

12 [v]Ps 27:11; 40:2; 143:10; Isa 26:7; 40:3–4; 45:13; Zec 4:7; Lk 6:17; [w]Ps 22:25

Ps. 27

1 [a]2Sa 22:29; [b]Ex 15:2; Ps 3:8; [c]Ps 9:9; [d]Job 13:15; Ps 56:4,11; 118:6
2 [e]Ps 9:3; 20:8; 37:24; Da 11:19; Ro 11:11
3 [f]Ge 4:7; Ps 3:6; [g]Job 4:6
4 [h]Lk 10:42; [i]Ps 23:6; 61:4
5 [j]Job 38:23; [k]Ps 12:7; [l]Ps 17:8; [m]Ps 40:2
6 [n]2Sa 22:49; Ps 3:3; 18:48; [o]Ps 22:12; [p]Ps 50:14; 54:6; 107:22; 116:17; [q]Ezr 3:13; Job 22:26; [r]Ex 15:1; [s]Ps 33:2; 92:1; 147:7; Eph 5:19
7 [t]Ps 5:3; 18:6; 55:17; 119:149; 130:2; Isa 28:23; [u]Ps 4:1
8 [v]1Ch 16:11
9 [w]Dt 31:17; Ps 22:24; [x]Ps 2:5; [y]Ge 49:25; Dt 33:29; [z]Dt 4:31; Ps 37:28; 119:8; Isa 41:17; 62:12; Jer 14:9; [a]Ps 18:46
11 [b]Ex 33:13; [c]Ezr 8:21; Ps 5:8; [d]Ps 72:4; 78:42; 106:10; Jer 21:12
12 [e]Dt 19:16; Mt 26:60; Ac 6:13; 1Co 15:15
13 [f]Ex 33:19; 2Ch 6:41; Ps 23:6; 31:19; 145:7; [g]Job 28:13
14 [h]Ps 33:20; 130:5–6; Isa 8:17; 30:18; Hab 2:3; Zep 3:8; Ac 1:4; [i]Dt 1:21; Jdg 5:21; Eph 6:10

Ps. 28

1 [a]Dt 1:45; [b]Est 4:14; [c]Job 33:18
2 [d]Ps 17:1; 61:1; 116:1; 130:2; 142:1; 143:1; [e]Ezr 9:5; Ps 63:4; 141:2; La 2:19; 1Ti 2:8; [f]Ps 5:7; 11:4
3 [g]Ps 12:2; 26:4; 55:21; Jer 9:8

for false witnesses[e] rise up against
me,
breathing out violence.

13I am still confident of this:
I will see the goodness of the LORD[f]
in the land of the living.[g]
14Wait[h] for the LORD;
be strong[i] and take heart
and wait for the LORD.

Psalm 28

Of David.

1To you I call, O LORD my Rock;
do not turn a deaf ear[a] to me.
For if you remain silent,[b]
I shall be like those who have gone
down to the pit.[c]
2Hear my cry for mercy[d]
as I call to you for help,
as I lift up my hands[e]
towards your Most Holy Place.[f]

3Do not drag me away with the wicked,
with those who do evil,
who speak cordially with their
neighbours
but harbour malice in their hearts.[g]
4Repay them for their deeds
and for their evil work;
repay them for what their hands have
done[h]
and bring back upon them what
they deserve.[i]
5Since they show no regard for the
works of the LORD
and what his hands have done,[j]
he will tear them down
and never build them up again.

6Praise be to the LORD,[k]
for he has heard my cry for mercy.[l]
7The LORD is my strength[m] and my
shield;
my heart trusts[n] in him, and I am
helped.
My heart leaps for joy[o]
and I will give thanks to him in
song.[p]

8The LORD is the strength[q] of his
people,
a fortress of salvation[r] for his
anointed one.[s]

4 [h]Ps 62:12; 2Ti 4:14; Rev 22:12; [i]La 3:64; Rev 18:6
5 [j]Isa 5:12
6 [k]Ge 24:27; 2Co 1:3; Eph 1:3; 1Pe 1:3; [l]ver 2
7 [m]Ps 18:1; [n]Ps 13:5; 112:7; Isa 26:3; [o]Dt 16:15; Ps 16:9; [p]Ps 33:3; 40:3; 69:30; 144:9; 149:1
8 [q]Ps 18:1; [r]Ex 15:2; Ps 27:1; Hab 3:13; [s]Ps 20:6

[a]2 Or *to slander me*
[b]8 Or *To you, O my heart, he has said, "Seek my*

9Save your people[t] and bless your
inheritance;[u]
be their shepherd[v] and carry them[w]
for ever.

Psalm 29

A psalm of David.

1Ascribe to the LORD,[a] O mighty ones,[b]
ascribe to the LORD glory[c] and
strength.
2Ascribe to the LORD the glory due to
his name;
worship the LORD in the splendour
of his[a] holiness.[d]

3The voice[e] of the LORD is over the
waters;
the God of glory[f] thunders,[g]
the LORD thunders over the mighty
waters.[h]
4The voice of the LORD is powerful;[i]
the voice of the LORD is majestic.
5The voice of the LORD breaks the
cedars;
the LORD breaks in pieces the cedars
of Lebanon.[j]
6He makes Lebanon skip[k] like a calf,
Sirion[b][l] like a young wild ox.[m]
7The voice of the LORD strikes
with flashes of lightning.[n]
8The voice of the LORD shakes the
desert;
the LORD shakes the Desert of
Kadesh.[o]
9The voice of the LORD twists the oaks[c][p]
and strips the forests bare.
And in his temple all cry, "Glory!"[q]

10The LORD sits[d] enthroned over the
flood;[r]
the LORD is enthroned as King for
ever.[s]
11The LORD gives strength to his people;[t]
the LORD blesses his people with
peace.[u]

Psalm 30

A psalm. A song. For the dedication of the temple.[a] Of David.

1I will exalt[a] you, O LORD,
for you lifted me out of the depths[b]
and did not let my enemies gloat
over me.[c]
2O LORD my God, I called to you for
help[d]
and you healed me.[e]
3O LORD, you brought me up from the
grave;[b][f]
you spared me from going down
into the pit.[g]

9 [t]1Ch 16:35; Ps 106:47; 118:25; [u]Ex 34:9; [v]1Ch 11:2; Ps 23:1; 78:52,71; 80:1; Isa 40:11; Jer 31:10; Eze 34:12-16,23, 31; Mic 7:14; [w]Dt 1:31; 32:11; Isa 46:3; 63:9

Ps. 29

1 [a]ver 2; 1Ch 16:28; [b]2Sa 1:19; Ps 103:20; Isa 10:13; [c]Ps 8:1
2 [d]1Ch 16:29; Ps 96:7-9
3 [e]Job 37:5; [f]Ps 24:7; Ac 7:2; [g]1Sa 2:10; Ps 18:13; 46:6; 68:33; 77:17; Jer 10:13; 25:30; Joel 2:11; Am 1:2; [h]Ex 15:10
4 [i]Ps 68:33
5 [j]Jdg 9:15
6 [k]Ps 114:4; [l]Dt 3:9; [m]Nu 23:22; Job 39:9; Ps 92:10
7 [n]Eze 1:14; Rev 8:5
8 [o]Nu 13:26; 20:1
9 [p]Nu 13:32; Isa 2:13; Eze 27:6; Am 2:9; [q]Ps 26:8
10 [r]Ge 6:17; [s]Ex 15:18
11 [t]Ps 18:1; 28:8; 68:35; [u]Lev 26:6; Nu 6:26

Ps. 30

1 [a]Ex 15:2; [b]Job 11:8; Ps 63:9; 107:26; Pr 9:18; Isa 14:15; [c]Ps 22:17
2 [d]Ps 5:2; 88:13; [e]Nu 12:13
3 [f]Ps 16:10; 56:13; [g]Ps 28:1; 55:23; 69:15; 86:13; 143:7; Pr 1:12; Isa 38:17; Jnh 2:6
4 [h]Ps 33:1; 47:7; 68:4; [i]Ps 16:3; [j]Ex 3:15; Ps 33:21; 103:1; 145:21
5 [k]Ps 103:9; [l]Job 14:13; [m]Ezr 3:11; [n]2Sa 15:30; Ps 6:6; 126:6; Jer 31:16; [o]2Co 4:17
6 [p]Job 29:18
7 [q]Dt 31:17

4Sing[h] to the LORD, you saints[i] of his;
praise his holy name.[j]
5For his anger[k] lasts only a moment,[l]
but his favour lasts a lifetime;[m]
weeping[n] may remain for a night,
but rejoicing comes in the morning.[o]

6When I felt secure, I said,
"I shall never be shaken."[p]
7O LORD, when you favoured me,
you made my mountain[c] stand firm;
but when you hid your face,[q]
I was dismayed.

8To you, O LORD, I called;
to the Lord I cried for mercy:
9"What gain is there in my
destruction,[d]
in my going down into the pit?[r]
Will the dust praise you?
Will it proclaim your faithfulness?[s]
10Hear,[t] O LORD, and be merciful to me;[u]
O LORD, be my help."[v]

11You turned my wailing[w] into
dancing;[x]
you removed my sackcloth[y] and
clothed me with joy,[z]
12that my heart may sing to you and not
be silent.
O LORD my God, I will give you
thanks[a] for ever.[b]

Psalm 31

31:1-4pp—Ps 71:1-3

For the director of music. A psalm of David.

1In you, O LORD, I have taken refuge;[a]
let me never be put to shame;
deliver me in your righteousness.[b]
2Turn your ear to me,[c]
come quickly to my rescue;[d]
be my rock of refuge,[e]
a strong fortress to save me.
3Since you are my rock and my
fortress,[f]
for the sake of your name[g] lead and
guide me.

9 [r]Job 33:18; Isa 38:18; [s]Ps 6:5; 88:11
10 [t]Ps 17:1; [u]Ps 4:1; [v]Ps 20:2
11 [w]Est 4:1; [x]Ex 15:20; [y]2Sa 3:31; Ps 35:13; [z]Dt 16:15; Ps 16:9
12 [a]Ps 35:18; 75:1; 118:21; Rev 11:17; [b]Ps 44:8; 52:9

Ps. 31

1 [a]Ps 7:1; [b]Ps 5:8
2 [c]Ps 6:4; [d]Ex 2:17; [e]2Sa 22:3; Ps 18:2
3 [f]Ps 18:2; [g]Ps 23:3

[a]2 Or *LORD with the splendour of*
[b]6 That is, Mount Hermon
[c]9 Or *LORD makes the deer give birth*
[d]10 Or *sat*
[a]Title: Or *palace*
[b]3 Hebrew *Sheol*
[c]7 Or *hill country*
[d]9 Or *there if I am silenced*

4Free me from the trap[h] that is set for
me,
for you are my refuge.[i]
5Into your hands I commit my spirit;[j]
redeem me, O LORD, the God of
truth.[k]

6I hate those who cling to worthless
idols;[l]
I trust in the LORD.[m]
7I will be glad and rejoice in your love,
for you saw my affliction[n]
and knew the anguish[o] of my soul.
8You have not handed me over[p] to the
enemy
but have set my feet in a spacious
place.[q]

9Be merciful to me, O LORD, for I am in
distress;[r]
my eyes grow weak with sorrow,[s]
my soul and my body[t] with grief.
10My life is consumed by anguish[u]
and my years by groaning;[v]
my strength fails[w] because of my
affliction,[a x]
and my bones grow weak.[y]
11Because of all my enemies,[z]
I am the utter contempt[a] of my
neighbours;[b]
I am a dread to my friends—
those who see me on the street flee
from me.
12I am forgotten by them as though I
were dead;[c]
I have become like broken pottery.
13For I hear the slander[d] of many;
there is terror on every side;[e]
they conspire against me[f]
and plot to take my life.[g]

14But I trust[h] in you, O LORD;
I say, "You are my God."
15My times[i] are in your hands;
deliver me from my enemies
and from those who pursue me.
16Let your face shine[j] on your servant;
save me in your unfailing love.[k]
17Let me not be put to shame,[l] O LORD,
for I have cried out to you;
but let the wicked be put to shame
and lie silent[m] in the grave.[b]
18Let their lying lips[n] be silenced,
for with pride and contempt
they speak arrogantly[o] against the
righteous.

19How great is your goodness,[p]
which you have stored up for those
who fear you,
which you bestow in the sight of men[q]
on those who take refuge[r] in you.
20In the shelter[s] of your presence you
hide[t] them
from the intrigues of men;[u]
in your dwelling you keep them safe
from accusing tongues.

21Praise be to the LORD,[v]
for he showed his wonderful love[w]
to me
when I was in a besieged city.[x]
22In my alarm[y] I said,
"I am cut off[z] from your sight!"
Yet you heard my cry[a] for mercy
when I called to you for help.

23Love the LORD, all his saints![b]
The LORD preserves the faithful,[c]
but the proud he pays back[d] in full.
24Be strong and take heart,[e]
all you who hope in the LORD.

Psalm 32

Of David. A *maskil*.[a]

1Blessed is he
whose transgressions are forgiven,
whose sins are covered.[a]
2Blessed is the man
whose sin the LORD does not count
against him[b]
and in whose spirit is no deceit.[c]

3When I kept silent,[d]
my bones wasted away[e]
through my groaning[f] all day long.
4For day and night
your hand was heavy[g] upon me;
my strength was sapped[h]
as in the heat of summer. *Selah*
5Then I acknowledged my sin to you
and did not cover up my iniquity.[i]
I said, "I will confess[j]
my transgressions[k] to the LORD"—
and you forgave
the guilt of my sin.[l] *Selah*
6Therefore let everyone who is godly
pray to you
while you may be found;[m]
surely when the mighty waters[n] rise,[o]
they will not reach him.[p]
7You are my hiding-place;[q]
you will protect me from trouble[r]
and surround me with songs of
deliverance.[s] *Selah*

4 [h]**1Sa 28:9; Job 18:10;** [i]Ps 9:9
5 [j]Lk 23:46; Ac 7:59; [k]Isa 45:19; 65:16
6 [l]**Dt 32:21;** [m]**Ps 4:5**
7 [n]**Ps 13:3;** [o]**Ps 25:17;** Lk 22:44
8 [p]**Dt 32:30;** [q]**2Sa 22:20**
9 [r]Ps 4:1; [s]Ps 6:7; [t]Ps 63:1
10 [u]ver 7; [v]Ps 6:6; [w]Ps 22:15; 32:4; 38:10; 73:26; [x]Ps 25:18; [y]**Ps 6:2**
11 [z]Dt 30:7; Ps 3:7; 25:19; 102:8; [a]**Ps 22:6;** [b]Ps 38:11
12 [c]Ps 28:1; 88:4
13 [d]**Lev 19:16;** Ps 50:20; [e]**Job 18:11;** Isa 13:8; Jer 6:25; 20:3,10; 46:5; 49:5; La 2:22; [f]Ps 41:7; 56:6; 71:10; 83:3; [g]**Ge 37:18; Mt 12:14**
14 [h]Ps 4:5
15 [i]**Job 14:5**
16 [j]**Nu 6:25;** [k]**Ps 6:4**
17 [l]**Ps 22:5;** [m]1Sa 2:9; Ps 94:17; 115:17
18 [n]Ps 120:2; Pr 10:18; 26:24; [o]**1Sa 2:3;** Jude 15
19 [p]**Ps 27:13;** Ro 11:22; [q]Ps 23:5; [r]Ps 2:12
20 [s]Ps 55:8; [t]**Ps 17:8;** [u]**Ge 37:18**
21 [v]Ps 28:6; [w]**Ps 17:7;** [x]1Sa 23:7
22 [y]Ps 116:11; [z]Job 6:9; 17:1; Ps 37:9; 88:5; Isa 38:12; [a]Ps 6:9; 66:19; 116:1; 145:19
23 [b]**Ps 4:3;** [c]**Ps 18:25;** Rev 2:10; [d]Dt 32:41; Ps 94:2
24 [e]Ps 27:14

Ps. 32

1 [a]Ps 85:2; 103:3
2 [b]**Ro 4:7–8*;** [c]Jn 1:47; Rev 14:5
3 [d]**Job 31:34;** [e]Ps 31:10; [f]**Job 3:24;** Ps 6:6
4 [g]1Sa 5:6; **Job 9:34;** Ps 38:2; 39:10; [h]Ps 22:15
5 [i]Job 31:33; [j]Pr 28:13; [k]Ps 103:12; [l]**Lev 26:40;** 1Jn 1:9
6 [m]Ps 69:13; Isa 55:6; [n]**Ex 15:10;** [o]Ps 69:1; [p]Isa 43:2
7 [q]**Jdg 9:35;** [r]**Ps 9:9;** [s]**Jdg 5:1**

[a]*10* Or *guilt* [b]*17* Hebrew *Sheol*
[a]Title: Probably a literary or musical term

8I will instruct[t] you and teach you[u] in
the way you should go;
I will counsel you and watch over[v]
you.
9Do not be like the horse or the mule,
which have no understanding
but must be controlled by bit and
bridle[w]
or they will not come to you.
10Many are the woes of the wicked,[x]
but the LORD's unfailing love
surrounds the man who trusts[y] in
him.

11Rejoice in the LORD[z] and be glad, you
righteous;
sing, all you who are upright in
heart!

Psalm 33

1Sing joyfully[a] to the LORD, you
righteous;
it is fitting[b] for the upright[c] to praise
him.
2Praise the LORD with the harp;[d]
make music to him on the
ten-stringed lyre.[e]
3Sing to him a new song;[f]
play skilfully, and shout for joy.[g]

4For the word of the LORD is right[h] and
true;[i]
he is faithful[j] in all he does.
5The LORD loves righteousness and
justice;[k]
the earth is full of his unfailing love.[l]

6By the word[m] of the LORD were the
heavens made,[n]
their starry host[o] by the breath of his
mouth.
7He gathers the waters[p] of the sea into
jars;[a q]
he puts the deep into storehouses.
8Let all the earth fear the LORD;[r]
let all the people of the world[s] revere
him.[t]
9For he spoke, and it came to be;
he commanded,[u] and it stood firm.
10The LORD foils[v] the plans[w] of the
nations;[x]
he thwarts the purposes of the
peoples.
11But the plans of the LORD stand firm[y]
for ever,
the purposes[z] of his heart through
all generations.

12Blessed is the nation whose God is the
LORD,[a]
the people he chose[b] for his
inheritance.[c]
13From heaven the LORD looks down[d]
and sees all mankind;[e]
14from his dwelling-place[f] he watches
all who live on earth—
15he who forms[g] the hearts of all,
who considers everything they do.[h]
16No king is saved by the size of his
army;[i]
no warrior escapes by his great
strength.
17A horse[j] is a vain hope for deliverance;
despite all its great strength it
cannot save.
18But the eyes[k] of the LORD are on those
who fear him,
on those whose hope is in his
unfailing love,[l]
19to deliver them from death[m]
and keep them alive in famine.[n]

20We wait[o] in hope for the LORD;
he is our help and our shield.
21In him our hearts rejoice,[p]
for we trust in his holy name.[q]
22May your unfailing love[r] rest upon us,
O LORD,
even as we put our hope in you.

Psalm 34[a]

Of David. When he pretended to be insane[a] before Abimelech, who drove him away, and he left.

1I will extol the LORD at all times;[b]
his praise will always be on my lips.
2My soul will boast[c] in the LORD;
let the afflicted hear and rejoice.[d]
3Glorify the LORD[e] with me;
let us exalt[f] his name together.

4I sought the LORD,[g] and he answered
me;
he delivered[h] me from all my fears.
5Those who look to him are radiant;[i]
their faces are never covered with
shame.[j]
6This poor man called, and the LORD
heard him;
he saved him out of all his troubles.[k]
7The angel of the LORD[l] encamps
around those who fear him,
and he delivers[m] them.

8 [t]Ps 25:8; [u]Ps 34:11; [v]Ps 33:18
9 [w]Job 30:11; 39:10; Jas 3:3
10 [x]Ro 2:9; [y]Ps 4:5; Pr 16:20
11 [z]Ps 64:10

Ps. 33

1 [a]Ps 5:11; 101:1; [b]Ps 147:1; [c]Ps 11:7
2 [d]Ge 4:21; 1Co 14:7; Rev 5:8; [e]Ps 92:3; 144:9
3 [f]Ps 40:3; Isa 42:10; Rev 5:9; [g]Job 3:7; Ps 35:27; 47:1
4 [h]Ps 19:8; [i]Ps 119:142; Rev 19:9; 22:6; [j]Ps 18:25; 25:10
5 [k]Ps 11:7; [l]Ps 6:4
6 [m]Ge 1:3; Heb 11:3; [n]Ex 8:19; 2Ch 2:12; [o]Ge 1:16
7 [p]Ge 1:10; [q]Jos 3:16
8 [r]Dt 6:13; Ps 2:11; [s]Ps 49:1; Isa 18:3; Mic 1:2; [t]Dt 14:23
9 [u]Ps 148:5
10 [v]Isa 44:25; [w]Job 5:12; [x]Ps 2:1
11 [y]Nu 23:19; [z]Jer 51:12,29
12 [a]Ps 144:15; [b]Ex 8:22; Dt 7:6; Ps 4:3; 65:4; 84:4; [c]Ex 34:9
13 [d]Ps 53:2; 102:19; [e]Job 28:24; Ps 11:4; 14:2; Heb 4:13
14 [f]Lev 15:31; 1Ki 8:39
15 [g]Job 10:8; Ps 119:73; [h]Job 10:4; Jer 32:19
16 [i]1Sa 14:6
17 [j]Ps 20:7
18 [k]Ex 3:16; Ps 11:4; 1Pe 3:12; [l]Ps 6:4
19 [m]Ps 56:13; Ac 12:11; [n]Job 5:20
20 [o]Ps 27:14
21 [p]1Sa 2:1; Joel 2:23; [q]Ps 30:4; 99:3
22 [r]Ps 6:4

Ps. 34

Title [a]1Sa 21:13
1 [b]Ps 71:6; Eph 5:20; 1Th 5:18
2 [c]Ps 44:8; Jer 9:24; 1Co 1:31; [d]Ps 69:32; 107:42; 119:74
3 [e]Ps 63:3; 86:12; Da 4:37; Jn 17:1; Ro 15:6; [f]Ex 15:2
4 [g]Ex 32:11; Ps 77:2; [h]ver 17; Ps 18:43; 22:4; 56:13; 86:13
5 [i]Ex 34:29; [j]Ps 25:3; 44:15; 69:7; 83:16
6 [k]Ps 25:17
7 [l]Ge 32:1; Da 3:28; Mt 18:10; [m]Ps 22:4; 37:40; 41:1; 97:10; Isa 31:5; Ac 12:11

[a]7 Or *sea as into a heap*

[a]This psalm is an acrostic poem, the verses of which begin with the successive letters of the Hebrew alphabet.

8Taste and see that the LORD is good;[n]
blessed is the man who takes
refuge[o] in him.
9Fear the LORD,[p] you his saints,
for those who fear him lack
nothing.[q]
10The lions may grow weak and hungry,
but those who seek the LORD lack no
good thing.[r]

11Come, my children, listen[s] to me;
I will teach you[t] the fear of the
LORD.[u]
12Whoever of you loves life[v]
and desires to see many good days,
13keep your tongue[w] from evil
and your lips from speaking lies.[x]
14Turn from evil and do good;[y]
seek peace[z] and pursue it.

15The eyes of the LORD[a] are on the
righteous[b]
and his ears are attentive[c] to their
cry;
16the face of the LORD is against[d] those
who do evil,[e]
to cut off the memory[f] of them from
the earth.

17The righteous cry out, and the LORD
hears[g] them;
he delivers them from all their
troubles.
18The LORD is close[h] to the
broken-hearted[i]
and saves those who are crushed in
spirit.

19A righteous man may have many
troubles,[j]
but the LORD delivers him from
them all;[k]
20he protects all his bones,
not one of them will be broken.[l]

21Evil will slay the wicked;[m]
the foes of the righteous will be
condemned.
22The LORD redeems[n] his servants;
no-one will be condemned who
takes refuge[o] in him.

Psalm 35

Of David.

1Contend,[a] O LORD, with those who
contend with me;
fight[b] against those who fight
against me.
2Take up shield[c] and buckler;
arise[d] and come to my aid.[e]
3Brandish spear[f] and javelin[a][g]
against those who pursue me.
Say to my soul,
"I am your salvation.[h]"

4May those who seek my life[i]
be disgraced[j] and put to shame;[k]
may those who plot my ruin
be turned back[l] in dismay.
5May they be like chaff[m] before the
wind,
with the angel of the LORD[n] driving
them away;
6may their path be dark and slippery,
with the angel of the LORD pursuing
them.
7Since they hid their net[o] for me
without cause[p]
and without cause dug a pit[q] for me,
8may ruin overtake them by
surprise—[r]
may the net they hid entangle them,
may they fall into the pit,[s] to their
ruin.
9Then my soul will rejoice[t] in the LORD
and delight in his salvation.[u]
10My whole being will exclaim,
"Who is like you,[v] O LORD?
You rescue the poor from those too
strong[w] for them,
the poor and needy[x] from those who
rob them."

11Ruthless witnesses[y] come forward;
they question me on things I know
nothing about.
12They repay me evil for good[z]
and leave my soul forlorn.
13Yet when they were ill, I put on
sackcloth[a]
and humbled myself with fasting.[b]
When my prayers returned to me
unanswered,
14 I went about mourning[c]
as though for my friend or brother.
I bowed my head in grief
as though weeping for my mother.
15But when I stumbled, they gathered in
glee;[d]
attackers gathered against me when
I was unaware.
They slandered[e] me without
ceasing.
16Like the ungodly they maliciously
mocked;[b][f]
they gnashed their teeth[g] at me.

8 [n]Heb 6:5; 1Pe 2:3; [o]**Ps 2:12**
9 [p]**Dt 6:13**; Rev 14:7; [q]**Ps 23:1**
10 [r]**Ps 23:1**
11 [s]Ps 66:16; [t]**Ps 32:8**; [u]**Ps 19:9**
12 [v]Ecc 3:13
13 [w]Ps 39:1; 141:3; Pr 13:3; 21:23; Jas 1:26; [x]**Ps 12:2**; 1Pe 2:22
14 [y]Ps 37:27; Isa 1:17; 3Jn 11; [z]**Ro 14:19**
15 [a]Ps 33:18; [b]**Job 23:10; 36:7**; [c]Mal 3:16; **Jn 9:31**
16 [d]Lev 17:10; Jer 23:30; [e]1Pe 3:10–12*; [f]**Ex 17:14**; Ps 9:6
17 [g]Ps 145:19
18 [h]Dt 4:7; Ps 119:151; 145:18; Isa 50:8; [i]Ps 51:17; 109:16; 147:3; Isa 61:1
19 [j]ver 17; Ps 25:17; [k]**Job 5:19**; 2Ti 3:11
20 [l]Jn 19:36*
21 [m]Ps 7:9; 9:16; 11:5; 37:20; 73:27; 94:23; 106:43; 112:10; 140:11; Pr 14:32; 24:16
22 [n]**Ex 6:6; 15:13**; Lk 1:68; Rev 14:3; [o]Ps 2:12

Ps. 35

1 [a]**1Sa 24:15**; [b]**Ex 14:14**
2 [c]Ps 3:3; [d]Ps 3:7; [e]**Ge 50:24; Job 17:3**
3 [f]**Nu 25:7**; [g]**Jos 8:18**; [h]Ps 27:1
4 [i]Ps 38:12; 40:14; Jer 4:30; [j]Ps 69:6, 19; 70:2; 83:17; Isa 45:16; Mal 2:9; [k]Ps 25:3; [l]Ps 129:5
5 [m]**Job 13:25**; Ps 1:4; [n]Ps 34:7
7 [o]**Job 18:8**; [p]**Ps 7:4**; [q]**Job 9:31; Ps 7:15; 55:23**
8 [r]Isa 47:11; 1Th 5:3; [s]**Ps 7:15**
9 [t]**Ps 2:11; Lk 1:47**; [u]Ps 9:14; 13:5; 27:1
10 [v]**Ex 9:14; Ps 18:31**; 113:5; [w]Ps 18:17; [x]Ps 12:5; 37:14; 74:21; 86:1; 109:16; 140:12; Isa 41:17

11 [y]**Ex 23:1; Mt 26:60**
12 [z]Ps 38:20; 109:5; Pr 17:13; Jer 18:20
13 [a]**2Sa 3:31**; 1Ki 20:31; Ps 30:11; 69:11; [b]Job 30:25; Ps 69:10; 109:24 *14* [c]Ps 38:6; 42:9; 43:2
15 [d]**Job 31:29**; [e]**Job 16:10**
16 [f]**Ps 22:7**; Mk 10:34; [g]**Job 16:9**; Mk 9:18; Ac 7:54

a3 Or *and block the way*
b16 Septuagint; Hebrew may mean *ungodly circle of mockers.*

17O Lord, how long[h] will you look on?
Rescue my life from their ravages,
my precious life[i] from these lions.[j]
18I will give you thanks in the great
assembly;[k]
among throngs[l] of people I will
praise you.[m]

19Let not those gloat over me
who are my enemies[n] without
cause;
let not those who hate me without
reason[o]
maliciously wink the eye.[p]
20They do not speak peaceably,
but devise false accusations[q]
against those who live quietly in the
land.
21They gape[r] at me and say, "Aha! Aha![s]
With our own eyes we have seen it."

22O LORD, you have seen[t] this; be not
silent.
Do not be far[u] from me, O LORD.
23Awake,[v] and rise[w] to my defence!
Contend[x] for me, my God and LORD.
24Vindicate me in your righteousness, O
LORD my God;
do not let them gloat[y] over me.
25Do not let them think, "Aha,[z] just
what we wanted!"
or say, "We have swallowed him
up."[a]

26May all who gloat[b] over my distress[c]
be put to shame[d] and confusion;
may all who exalt themselves over me[e]
be clothed with shame and disgrace.
27May those who delight in my
vindication[f]
shout for joy[g] and gladness;
may they always say, "The LORD be
exalted,
who delights[h] in the well-being of
his servant."[i]
28My tongue will speak of your
righteousness[j]
and of your praises all day long.[k]

Psalm 36

For the director of music. Of David the servant of the LORD.

1An oracle is within my heart
concerning the sinfulness of the
wicked:[a] [a]
There is no fear[b] of God
before his eyes.[c]
2For in his own eyes he flatters himself
too much to detect or hate his sin.[d]
3The words of his mouth[e] are wicked
and deceitful;[f]
he has ceased to be wise[g] and to do
good.[h]
4Even on his bed he plots evil;[i]
he commits himself to a sinful
course[j]
and does not reject what is wrong.[k]

5Your love, O LORD, reaches to the
heavens,
your faithfulness[l] to the skies.[m]
6Your righteousness[n] is like the mighty
mountains,[o]
your justice like the great deep.[p]
O LORD, you preserve both man and
beast.[q]
7 How priceless is your unfailing
love![r]
Both high and low among men
find[b] refuge in the shadow of your
wings.[s]
8They feast in the abundance of your
house;[t]
you give them drink from your
river[u] of delights.[v]
9For with you is the fountain of life;[w]
in your light[x] we see light.

10Continue your love[y] to those who
know you,[z]
your righteousness to the upright in
heart.[a]
11May the foot of the proud not come
against me,
nor the hand of the wicked[b] drive
me away.
12See how the evildoers lie fallen—
thrown down, not able to rise![c]

Psalm 37[a]

Of David.

1Do not fret because of evil men
or be envious[a] of those who do
wrong;[b]
2for like the grass they will soon
wither,[c]
like green plants they will soon die
away.[d]

17 [h]Ps 6:3; [i]Ps 22:20; [j]Ps 22:21; 57:4; 58:6
18 [k]**Ps 22:25**; [l]Ps 42:4; 109:30; [m]**Ps 22:22**
19 [n]Ps 9:13; [o]ver 7; Ps 38:19; 69:4; Jn 15:25*; [p]Pr 6:13; 10:10
20 [q]Ps 38:12; 55:21; Jer 9:8; Mic 6:12
21 [r]**Job 16:10**; [s]Ps 40:15; 70:3; Eze 25:3
22 [t]Ex 3:7; Ps 10:14; [u]**Ps 10:1**
23 [v]**Ps 7:6**; 80:2; [w]Ps 17:13; [x]**1Sa 24:15**
24 [y]Ps 22:17
25 [z]ver 21; [a]Ps 124:3; Pr 1:12; La 2:16
26 [b]Ps 22:17; [c]Ps 4:1; [d]**Job 8:22**; Ps 109:29; Mic 7:10; [e]Job 19:5; Ps 38:16
27 [f]Ps 9:4; [g]Ps 20:5; **33:3**; [h]Ps 147:11; 149:4; [i]**Job 17:3**
28 [j]Ps 5:8; 51:14; [k]Ps 71:15,24; 72:15

Ps. 36

1 [a]**Job 21:16**; [b]Jer 2:19; 36:16,24; [c]**Job 23:15**; Ro 3:18*
2 [d]Dt 29:19
3 [e]Ps 10:7; [f]**Job 5:13**; Ps 5:6,9; 43:1; 144:8,11; Isa 44:20; [g]Ps 94:8; [h]Jer 4:22; 13:23; Am 3:10
4 [i]Pr 4:16; [j]Isa 65:2; [k]Ps 52:3; Ro 12:9
5 [l]Ps 89:1; 119:90; [m]Ps 57:10; 71:19; 89:2; 103:11; 108:4
6 [n]Ps 5:8; [o]Ps 68:15; [p]**Ge 1:2; 7:11**; [q]Ne 9:6; Ps 104:14; 145:16
7 [r]Ps 6:4; [s]**Ru 2:12; Ps 17:8**; 57:1; 91:4
8 [t]Ps 65:4; Isa 25:6; Jer 31:12, 14; [u]Job 20:17; Rev 22:1; [v]**Ps 23:2**; 63:5
9 [w]Ps 87:7; Pr 10:11; 16:22; Jer 2:13; [x]Ps 4:6; 27:1; 76:4; 104:2; Isa 2:5; 9:2; 60:1,19; Jn 1:4; 1Pe 2:9
10 [y]Jer 31:3; [z]Jer 9:24; 22:16; [a]Ps 7:10; 11:2; 94:15; 125:4
11 [b]Ps 71:4; 140:4 *12* [c]**Ps 18:38**

Ps. 37

1 [a]Pr 3:31; 23:17–18; [b]Ps 73:3; Pr 19:24
2 [c]**2Ki 19:26**; Job 14:2; Ps 102:4; Isa 40:7; [d]ver 38; Ps 90:6; 92:7; Jas 1:10

[a]*1* Or *heart: / Sin proceeds from the wicked.*
[b]*7* Or *love, O God! / Men find*; or *love! / Both heavenly beings and men / find*
[a]This psalm is an acrostic poem, the stanzas of which begin with the successive letters of the Hebrew alphabet.

3Trust in the LORD and do good;
dwell in the land[e] and enjoy safe pasture.[f]
4Delight[g] yourself in the LORD
and he will give you the desires of your heart.[h]

5Commit your way to the LORD;
trust in him[i] and he will do this:
6He will make your righteousness[j] shine like the dawn,[k]
the justice of your cause like the noonday sun.

7Be still[l] before the LORD and wait patiently[m] for him;
do not fret[n] when men succeed in their ways,[o]
when they carry out their wicked schemes.[p]

8Refrain from anger[q] and turn from wrath;
do not fret[r]—it leads only to evil.
9For evil men will be cut off,[s]
but those who hope[t] in the LORD will inherit the land.[u]

10A little while, and the wicked will be no more;[v]
though you look for them, they will not be found.
11But the meek will inherit the land[w]
and enjoy great peace.[x]

12The wicked plot[y] against the righteous
and gnash their teeth[z] at them;
13but the Lord laughs at the wicked,
for he knows their day is coming.[a]

14The wicked draw the sword[b]
and bend the bow[c]
to bring down the poor and needy,[d]
to slay those whose ways are upright.
15But their swords will pierce their own hearts,[e]
and their bows will be broken.[f]

16Better the little that the righteous have
than the wealth[g] of many wicked;
17for the power of the wicked will be broken,[h]
but the LORD upholds[i] the righteous.

18The days of the blameless are known to the LORD,[j]
and their inheritance will endure for ever.[k]
19In times of disaster they will not wither;
in days of famine they will enjoy plenty.

20But the wicked will perish:[l]
The LORD's enemies will be like the beauty of the fields,
they will vanish—vanish like smoke.[m]

21The wicked borrow and do not repay,
but the righteous give generously;[n]
22those the LORD blesses will inherit the land,
but those he curses[o] will be cut off.[p]

23If the LORD delights[q] in a man's way,
he makes his steps firm;[r]
24though he stumble, he will not fall,[s]
for the LORD upholds[t] him with his hand.

25I was young and now I am old,
yet I have never seen the righteous forsaken[u]
or their children begging[v] bread.
26They are always generous and lend freely;[w]
their children will be blessed.[x]

27Turn from evil and do good;[y]
then you will dwell in the land for ever.[z]
28For the LORD loves the just
and will not forsake his faithful ones.[a]

They will be protected for ever,
but the offspring of the wicked will be cut off;[b]
29the righteous will inherit the land[c]
and dwell in it for ever.[d]

30The mouth of the righteous man utters wisdom,[e]
and his tongue speaks what is just.
31The law of his God is in his heart;[f]
his feet do not slip.[g]

32The wicked lie in wait[h] for the righteous,[i]
seeking their very lives;
33but the LORD will not leave them in their power
or let them be condemned[j] when brought to trial.[k]

34Wait for the LORD[l]
and keep his way.[m]
He will exalt you to inherit the land;
when the wicked are cut off,[n] you will see[o] it.

3 [e]Dt 30:20; [f]Eze 34:14; Jn 10:9
4 [g]**Job 27:10;** [h]**Job 7:6;** Ps 21:2; 145:19; Mt 6:33
5 [i]Ps 4:5
6 [j]Ps 18:24; 103:17; 112:3; [k]**Job 11:17**
7 [l]**Ex 14:14; Isa 41:1;** [m]**Ps 27:14;** 40:1; 130:5; Isa 38:13; Hab 3:16; Ro 8:25; [n]ver 1; [o]Jer 12:1; [p]Ps 21:11; 26:10; 119:150
8 [q]Eph 4:31; Col 3:8; [r]ver 1
9 [s]**Ps 31:22;** 101:8; 118:10; Pr 2:22; [t]Isa 25:9; 26:8; 40:31; 49:23; 51:5; [u]ver 22; Ps 25:13; Isa 49:8; 57:13; Mt 5:5
10 [v]**Job 7:10;** Eze 27:36
11 [w]**Nu 14:24;** Mt 5:5; [x]**Lev 26:6; Nu 6:26**
12 [y]Ps 2:1; 31:13; [z]**Job 16:9;** Ps 35:16; 112:10
13 [a]1Sa 26:10; Eze 12:23
14 [b]**Ps 22:20;** [c]Ps 11:2; [d]**Ps 35:10**
15 [e]**Ps 9:16;** [f]**1Sa 2:4;** Ps 46:9; Jer 49:35
16 [g]Pr 15:16; 16:8
17 [h]Job 38:15; Ps 10:15; [i]Ps 41:12; 140:12; 145:14; 146:7
18 [j]**Job 23:10;** Ps 44:21; [k]ver 27,29
20 [l]**Ps 34:21;** [m]Ps 68:2; 102:3; Isa 51:6
21 [n]**Lev 25:35;** Ps 112:5
22 [o]**Job 5:3;** [p]ver 9
23 [q]**Nu 14:8;** Ps 147:11; [r]**Job 11:15; Ps 7:9;** 66:9
24 [s]**Ps 13:4;** 27:2; 38:17; 55:22; 119:165; Pr 3:23; 10:9; [t]2Ch 9:8; Ps 41:12; 145:14
25 [u]ver 28; **Ge 15:1;** Heb 13:5; [v]Ps 111:5; 145:15; Mk 10:46
26 [w]**Lev 25:35;** [x]Dt 28:4; Ps 112:2
27 [y]Ps 34:14; 3Jn 11; [z]**Nu 24:21**
28 [a]**Dt 7:6; Ps 18:25; 97:10;** [b]**Ge 17:14; Dt 32:26;** Pr 2:22
29 [c]ver 9; Pr 2:21; [d]Isa 34:17
30 [e]Ps 49:3; Pr 10:13
31 [f]**Dt 6:6; Job 22:22;** [g]**Dt 32:35**
32 [h]**Ps 10:8;** [i]Ps 11:5
33 [j]Job 32:3; Ps 34:22; 79:11; [k]2Pe 2:9
34 [l]Ps 27:14; [m]**Ps 18:21;** [n]ver 9; [o]Ps 52:6

35I have seen a wicked and ruthless man
flourishing[p] like a green tree in its
native soil,
36but he soon passed away and was no
more;
though I looked for him, he could
not be found.[q]

37Consider the blameless,[r] observe the
upright;[s]
there is a future[b] for the man of
peace.[t]
38But all sinners[u] will be destroyed;[v]
the future[c] of the wicked will be cut
off.[w]

39The salvation[x] of the righteous comes
from the LORD;
he is their stronghold in time of
trouble.[y]
40The LORD helps[z] them and delivers[a]
them;
he delivers them from the wicked
and saves[b] them,
because they take refuge[c] in him.

35 [p]Job 5:3
36 [q]ver 10; Pr 12:7; Isa 41:12; Da 11:19
37 [r]ver 18; Ge 6:9; Ps 18:25; [s]Ps 11:7; [t]Isa 57:1–2
38 [u]Ps 1:1; [v]ver 2; Ps 73:19; [w]ver 9
39 [x]Ps 3:8; [y]Ps 9:9
40 [z]1Ch 5:20; Ps 20:2; [a]Ps 34:7; [b]Ps 18:48; [c]Ps 2:12

Psalm 38

A psalm of David. A petition.

1O LORD, do not rebuke me in your
anger
or discipline me in your wrath.[a]
2For your arrows[b] have pierced me,
and your hand has come down
upon me.
3Because of your wrath there is no
health[c] in my body;
my bones[d] have no soundness
because of my sin.
4My guilt has overwhelmed[e] me
like a burden too heavy to bear.[f]

5My wounds[g] fester and are
loathsome[h]
because of my sinful folly.[i]
6I am bowed down[j] and brought very
low;
all day long I go about mourning.[k]
7My back is filled with searing pain;[l]
there is no health[m] in my body.
8I am feeble and utterly crushed;[n]
I groan[o] in anguish of heart.[p]

9All my longings[q] lie open before you,
O LORD;
my sighing[r] is not hidden from you.
10My heart pounds,[s] my strength fails[t]
me;
even the light has gone from my
eyes.[u]
11My friends and companions avoid me
because of my wounds;[v]
my neighbours stay far away.
12Those who seek my life set their
traps,[w]
those who would harm me talk of
my ruin;[x]
all day long they plot deception.[y]

13I am like a deaf man, who cannot
hear,[z]
like a mute, who cannot open his
mouth;
14I have become like a man who does not
hear,
whose mouth can offer no reply.
15I wait[a] for you, O LORD;
you will answer,[b] O Lord my God.
16For I said, "Do not let them gloat[c]
or exalt themselves over me when
my foot slips."[d]

17For I am about to fall,[e]
and my pain[f] is ever with me.
18I confess my iniquity;[g]
I am troubled by my sin.
19Many are those who are my vigorous
enemies;[h]
those who hate me[i] without reason[j]
are numerous.
20Those who repay my good with evil[k]
slander[l] me when I pursue what is
good.

21O LORD, do not forsake me;[m]
be not far[n] from me, O my God.
22Come quickly[o] to help me,[p]
O LORD my Saviour.[q]

Ps. 38
1 [a]Ps 6:1
2 [b]Job 6:4
3 [c]Pr 3:8; 4:22; Isa 66:14; [d]Job 33:19
4 [e]Ps 40:12; 65:3; [f]Nu 11:14; Ezr 9:6; Lk 11:46
5 [g]ver 11; Ps 147:3; [h]Job 19:17; [i]Ps 69:5; Pr 5:23; 12:23; 13:16; Ecc 10:3
6 [j]Ps 57:6; 145:14; 146:8; [k]Ps 35:14
7 [l]Job 14:22; [m]ver 3
8 [n]Ps 34:18; Pr 17:22; [o]Ps 6:6; 22:1; Pr 5:11; [p]Ps 6:3
9 [q]Ps 119:20; 143:7; [r]Job 3:24
10 [s]Job 37:1; [t]Ps 31:10; [u]Ps 6:7; 19:8; 88:9
11 [v]ver 5
12 [w]Ps 31:4; 140:5; 141:9; [x]Ps 35:4; 41:5; [y]Ps 35:20
13 [z]Ps 115:6; 135:17; Isa 43:8; Mk 7:37
15 [a]Ps 27:14; [b]Ps 17:6
16 [c]Ps 22:17; [d]Dt 32:35
17 [e]Ps 37:24; [f]ver 7; Job 6:10
18 [g]Lev 26:40
19 [h]Ps 18:17; [i]Ps 25:19; [j]Ps 35:19
20 [k]Ge 44:4; 1Jn 3:12; [l]Ps 54:5; 59:10; 119:23
21 [m]Ps 27:9; 71:18; 119:8; [n]Ps 10:1; 22:11; 35:22; 71:12
22 [o]Ps 22:19; [p]Ps 40:13; [q]1Ch 16:35

Psalm 39

For the director of music. For Jeduthun. A psalm of David.

1I said, "I will watch my ways[a]
and keep my tongue from sin;[b]
I will put a muzzle on my mouth[c]
as long as the wicked are in my
presence."
2But when I was silent[d] and still,
not even saying anything good,
my anguish[e] increased.
3My heart grew hot[f] within me,
and as I meditated,[g] the fire[h]
burned;
then I spoke with my tongue:

Ps. 39
1 [a]1Ki 2:4; Ps 119:9,59; Pr 20:11; [b]Job 1:22; Ps 34:13; Jas 3:2; [c]Job 6:24; Jas 1:26
2 [d]ver 9; Job 31:34; Ps 77:4; [e]Ps 6:3; 25:17; 31:10
3 [f]Lk 24:32; [g]Ps 1:2; 48:9; 77:12; 119:15; [h]Jer 5:14; 20:9; 23:29

b37 Or *there will be posterity*
c38 Or *posterity*

4"Show me, O LORD, my life's end
and the number of my days;[i]
let me know how fleeting[j] is my
life.[k]
5You have made my days[l] a mere
handbreadth;
the span of my years is as nothing
before you.
Each man's life is but a breath.[m] *Selah*
6Man is a mere phantom[n] as he goes to
and fro:[o]
He bustles about, but only in vain;[p]
he heaps up wealth,[q] not knowing
who will get it.[r]

7"But now, Lord, what do I look for?
My hope is in you.[s]
8Save me[t] from all my transgressions;[u]
do not make me the scorn[v] of fools.
9I was silent;[w] I would not open my
mouth,[x]
for you are the one who has done
this.[y]
10Remove your scourge from me;
I am overcome by the blow[z] of your
hand.[a]
11You rebuke[b] and discipline[c] men for
their sin;
you consume[d] their wealth like a
moth[e]—
each man is but a breath.[f] *Selah*

12"Hear my prayer, O LORD,
listen to my cry for help;[g]
be not deaf[h] to my weeping.[i]
For I dwell with you as an alien,[j]
a stranger,[k] as all my fathers were.[l]
13Look away from me, that I may rejoice
again
before I depart and am no more."[m]

Psalm 40

40:13–17pp—Ps 70:1–5

For the director of music. Of David.
A psalm.

1I waited patiently[a] for the LORD;
he turned to me and heard my cry.[b]
2He lifted me out of the slimy pit,[c]
out of the mud[d] and mire;[e]
he set my feet[f] on a rock[g]
and gave me a firm place to stand.
3He put a new song[h] in my mouth,
a hymn of praise to our God.
Many will see and fear[i]
and put their trust[j] in the LORD.

4Blessed is the man[k]
who makes the LORD his trust,[l]
who does not look to the proud,[m]
to those who turn aside to false
gods.[a][n]

4 [i]**Job 14:5;** [j]**Job 14:2;** [k]**Ge 47:9; Job 7:7**
5 [l]**Job 10:20;** Ps 89:45; 102:23; [m]**Job 7:7;** Ps 62:9
6 [n]Job 8:9; Ps 102:11; Ecc 6:12; **Jas 4:14;** [o]Jas 1:11; [p]Ps 127:2; [q]**Job 27:17;** [r]Lk 12:20
7 [s]**Ps 9:18; 25:5**
8 [t]Ps 6:4; 51:14; [u]Ps 32:1; 51:1; Isa 53:5,8,10; [v]**Dt 28:37;** Ps 69:7; 79:4; Isa 43:28; Da 9:16
9 [w]**ver 2;** [x]Ps 38:13; [y]Isa 38:15
10 [z]2Ch 21:14; Eze 7:9; 24:16; [a]**Ex 9:3**
11 [b]**Dt 28:20;** Isa 66:15; Eze 5:15; 2Pe 2:16; [c]Ps 94:10; Isa 26:16; [d]Ps 90:7; [e]**Job 13:28; Isa 51:8;** Lk 12:33; **Jas 5:2;** [f]**Job 7:7**
12 [g]**Ps 17:1;** [h]**Dt 1:45;** [i]**2Ki 20:5;** [j]**Lev 25:23;** [k]**Ge 23:4; Heb 11:13;** [l]**Ge 47:9; 1Ch 29:15**
13 [m]**Job 10:21**

Ps. 40

1 [a]**Ps 37:7;** [b]Ps 6:9; **31:22;** 34:15; 116:1; 145:19
2 [c]**Job 9:31; Ps 7:15;** [d]**Job 30:19;** [e]Ps 69:14; [f]Ps 31:8; [g]Ps 27:5
3 [h]**Ps 28:7; 96:1;** Rev 5:9; [i]Ps 52:6; 64:9; [j]**Ex 14:31**
4 [k]Ps 34:8; [l]Ps 84:12; [m]Ps 101:5; 138:6; Pr 3:34; 16:5; Isa 65:5; 1Pe 5:5; [n]**Dt 31:20; Ps 4:2; 26:1**
5 [o]**Dt 4:34;** Ps 75:1; 105:5; 136:4; [p]Ps 139:18; [q]Ps 71:15; 139:17
6 [r]**1Sa 15:22;** Jer 6:20; Am 5:22; [s]Ex 21:6; [t]Ps 50:8; 51:16; Isa 1:11; Hos 6:6
7 [u]Job 19:23; Jer 36:2; 45:1; Eze 2:9; Zec 5:1

5Many, O LORD my God,
are the wonders[o] you have done.
The things you planned for us
no-one can recount[p] to you;
were I to speak and tell of them,
they would be too many[q] to declare.

6Sacrifice and offering you did not
desire,[r]
but my ears you have pierced[b,c];[s]
burnt offerings[t] and sin offerings
you did not require.
7Then I said, "Here I am, I have come—
it is written about me in the scroll.[d][u]
8I desire to do your will,[v] O my God;[w]
your law is within my heart."[x]

9I proclaim righteousness[y] in the great
assembly;[z]
I do not seal my lips,
as you know,[a] O LORD.
10I do not hide your righteousness in my
heart;
I speak of your faithfulness[b] and
salvation.
I do not conceal your love and your
truth
from the great assembly.[c]

11Do not withhold your mercy[d] from
me, O LORD;
may your love[e] and your truth[f]
always protect[g] me.
12For troubles[h] without number
surround me;
my sins have overtaken me, and I
cannot see.[i]
They are more than the hairs of my
head,[j]
and my heart fails[k] within me.

13Be pleased, O LORD, to save me;
O LORD, come quickly to help me.[l]
14May all who seek to take my life[m]
be put to shame and confusion;[n]
may all who desire my ruin[o]
be turned back in disgrace.
15May those who say to me, "Aha!
Aha!"[p]
be appalled at their own shame.

8 [v]**Mt 26:39;** [w]Heb 10:5–7*; [x]**Dt 6:6; Job 22:22;** Ro 7:22
9 [y]**Ps 22:31;** [z]**Ps 22:25;** [a]**Jos 22:22**
10 [b]Ps 89:1; [c]**Ps 22:22**
11 [d]Zec 1:12; [e]Pr 20:28; [f]**Ps 26:3;** [g]Ps 61:7
12 [h]**Ps 25:17;** [i]Ps 38:4; 65:3; [j]Ps 69:4; [k]Ps 73:26
13 [l]Ps 22:19; 38:22
14 [m]**1Sa 20:1;** [n]**Est 9:2;** Ps 35:26; [o]**Ps 35:4**
15 [p]**Ps 35:21**

---

[a]4 Or *to falsehood*
[b]6 Hebrew; Septuagint *but a body you have prepared for me* (see also Symmachus and Theodotion)
[c]6 Or *opened*
[d]7 Or *come / with the scroll written for me*

16But may all who seek you[q]
rejoice and be glad[r] in you;
may those who love your salvation
always say,
"The LORD be exalted!"[s]

17Yet I am poor and needy;[t]
may the Lord think[u] of me.
You are my help[v] and my deliverer;[w]
O my God, do not delay.[x]

Psalm 41

For the director of music. A psalm of David.

1Blessed[a] is he who has regard for the
weak;[b]
the LORD delivers him in times of
trouble.[c]
2The LORD will protect[d] him and
preserve his life;[e]
he will bless him in the land[f]
and not surrender him to the desire
of his foes.[g]
3The LORD will sustain him on his
sick-bed[h]
and restore him from his bed of
illness.[i]

4I said, "O LORD, have mercy[j] on me;
heal[k] me, for I have sinned[l] against
you."
5My enemies say of me in malice,
"When will he die and his name
perish?[m]"
6Whenever one comes to see me,
he speaks falsely,[n] while his heart
gathers slander;[o]
then he goes out and spreads[p] it
abroad.

7All my enemies whisper together[q]
against me;
they imagine the worst for me,
saying,
8"A vile disease has beset him;
he will never get up[r] from the place
where he lies."
9Even my close friend,[s] whom I
trusted,
he who shared my bread,
has lifted up his heel against me.[t]

10But you, O LORD, have mercy[u] on me;
raise me up,[v] that I may repay[w]
them.
11I know that you are pleased with me,[x]
for my enemy does not triumph
over me.[y]
12In my integrity[z] you uphold me[a]
and set me in your presence for
ever.[b]

16 [q]Dt 4:29; 1Ch 28:9; Ps 9:10; 119:2; [r]Ps 9:2; [s]Ps 35:27
17 [t]Ps 86:1; 109:22; [u]Ps 144:3; [v]**Ps 20:2**; [w]**Ps 18:2**; [x]Ps 119:60

Ps. 41

1 [a]**Dt 14:29**; [b]**Job 24:4**; [c]Ps 25:17
2 [d]Ps 12:5; 32:7; [e]Ezr 9:9; Ps 71:20; 119:88,159; 138:7; 143:11; [f]Ps 37:22; [g]**Dt 6:24**
3 [h]Ps 6:6; [i]2Sa 13:5; 2Ki 1:4
4 [j]Ps 6:2; **9:13**; [k]**Dt 32:39**; [l]Ps 51:4
5 [m]**Ps 38:12**
6 [n]Ps 12:2; 101:7; Mt 5:11; [o]Pr 26:24; [p]**Lev 19:16**
7 [q]Ps 71:10
8 [r]**2Ki 1:4**
9 [s]**2Sa 15:12**; **Job 19:14**; [t]Nu 30:2; Job 19:19; Ps 55:20; 89:34; Mt 26:23; Lk 22:21; Jn 13:18*
10 [u]ver 4; [v]Ps 3:3; 9:13; [w]**2Sa 3:39**
11 [x]**Nu 14:8**; [y]Ps 25:2
12 [z]**Ps 25:21**; [a]Ps 18:35; **37:17**; 63:8; [b]**Job 4:7**; Ps 21:6; 61:7
13 [c]**Ge 24:27**; [d]Ps 72:18; [e]Ps 72:19; 89:52; 106:48

Ps. 42

1 [a]**Ps 18:33**; [b]**Dt 10:7**; [c]**Job 19:27**; Ps 119:131; Joel 1:20
2 [d]Ps 63:1; 143:6; [e]**Jos 3:10**; **1Sa 14:39**; **Mt 16:16**; Ro 9:26; [f]Ps 43:4; 84:7
3 [g]**Job 3:24**; [h]ver 10; Ps 79:10; 115:2; Joel 2:17; Mic 7:10
4 [i]**1Sa 1:15**; [j]Ps 55:14; 122:1; Isa 2:2; 30:29; [k]**Ezr 3:13**; [l]**Jos 6:5**; Ps 95:2; 100:4; 147:7; Jnh 2:9; [m]Ps 35:18; 109:30

13Praise[c] be to the LORD, the God of
Israel,[d]
from everlasting to everlasting.
Amen and Amen.[e]

BOOK II

Psalms 42–72

Psalm 42[a]

For the director of music. A *maskil*[b] of the Sons of Korah.

1As the deer[a] pants for streams of
water,[b]
so my soul pants[c] for you, O God.
2My soul thirsts[d] for God, for the living
God.[e]
When can I go[f] and meet with God?
3My tears[g] have been my food
day and night,
while men say to me all day long,
"Where is your God?"[h]
4These things I remember
as I pour out my soul:[i]
how I used to go with the multitude,
leading the procession to the house
of God,[j]
with shouts of joy[k] and thanksgiving[l]
among the festive throng.[m]

5Why are you downcast,[n] O my soul?
Why so disturbed[o] within me?
Put your hope in God,[p]
for I will yet praise[q] him,
my Saviour[r] and 6my God.[s]

My[c] soul is downcast within me;
therefore I will remember[t] you
from the land of the Jordan,[u]
the heights of Hermon[v]—from
Mount Mizar.
7Deep calls to deep[w]
in the roar of your waterfalls;
all your waves and breakers
have swept over me.[x]

8By day the LORD directs his love,[y]
at night[z] his song[a] is with me—
a prayer to the God of my life.[b]

5 [n]Ps 38:6; 77:3; La 3:20; Mt 26:38; [o]**Job 20:2**; [p]**Ps 25:5**; **71:14**; [q]Ps 9:1; [r]Ps 18:46
6 [s]ver 11; Ps 43:5; [t]Ps 63:6; 77:11; [u]**Ge 13:10**; **Nu 13:29**; [v]**Dt 3:8**; **4:48** 7 [w]**Ge 1:2**; **7:11**; [x]Ps 69:2; Jnh 2:3
8 [y]Ps 57:3; [z]**Ps 16:7**; [a]Ps 77:6; [b]Ps 133:3; Ecc 5:18; 8:15

[a]In many Hebrew manuscripts Psalms 42 and 43 constitute one psalm.
[b]Title: Probably a literary or musical term
[c]5,6 A few Hebrew manuscripts, Septuagint and Syriac; most Hebrew manuscripts *praise him for his saving help. / 6O my God, my*

[9]I say to God my Rock,[c]
"Why have you forgotten[d] me?
Why must I go about mourning,[e]
oppressed[f] by the enemy?"[g]
[10]My bones suffer mortal agony[h]
as my foes taunt[i] me,
saying to me all day long,
"Where is your God?"[j]

[11]Why are you downcast, O my soul?
Why so disturbed within me?
Put your hope in God,
for I will yet praise him,
my Saviour and my God.[k]

Psalm 43[a]

[1]Vindicate me, O God,
and plead my cause[a] against an
ungodly nation;
rescue me[b] from deceitful and
wicked men.[c]
[2]You are God my stronghold.
Why have you rejected[d] me?
Why must I go about mourning,[e]
oppressed by the enemy?[f]
[3]Send forth your light[g] and your truth,[h]
let them guide me;[i]
let them bring me to your holy
mountain,[j]
to the place where you dwell.[k]
[4]Then will I go[l] to the altar[m] of God,
to God, my joy[n] and my delight.[o]
I will praise you with the harp,[p]
O God, my God.

[5]Why are you downcast, O my soul?
Why so disturbed within me?
Put your hope in God,
for I will yet praise him,
my Saviour and my God.[q]

Psalm 44

For the director of music. Of the Sons of Korah. A *maskil*.[a]

[1]We have heard with our ears,[a] O God;
our fathers have told us[b]
what you did in their days,
in days long ago.[c]
[2]With your hand you drove out[d] the
nations
and planted[e] our fathers;
you crushed[f] the peoples
and made our fathers flourish.[g]
[3]It was not by their sword[h] that they
won the land,
nor did their arm bring them
victory;
it was your right hand,[i] your arm,[j]
and the light[k] of your face, for you
loved[l] them.

[4]You are my King[m] and my God,[n]
who decrees[b] victories[o] for Jacob.
[5]Through you we push back[p] our
enemies;
through your name we trample[q] our
foes.
[6]I do not trust in my bow,[r]
my sword does not bring me
victory;
[7]but you give us victory[s] over our
enemies,
you put our adversaries to shame.[t]
[8]In God we make our boast[u] all day
long,[v]
and we will praise your name for
ever.[w] *Selah*

[9]But now you have rejected[x] and
humbled us;[y]
you no longer go out with our
armies.[z]
[10]You made us retreat[a] before the
enemy,
and our adversaries have
plundered[b] us.
[11]You gave us up to be devoured like
sheep[c]
and have scattered us among the
nations.[d]
[12]You sold your people for a pittance,[e]
gaining nothing from their sale.

[13]You have made us a reproach[f] to our
neighbours,[g]
the scorn[h] and derision[i] of those
around us.
[14]You have made us a byword[j] among
the nations;
the peoples shake their heads[k] at us.
[15]My disgrace[l] is before me all day long,
and my face is covered with shame[m]
[16]at the taunts[n] of those who reproach
and revile[o] me,
because of the enemy,[p] who is bent
on revenge.

[17]All this happened to us,
though we had not forgotten[q] you
or been false to your covenant.
[18]Our hearts had not turned[r] back;

9 [c]Ps 18:31; [d]**Ps 10:11**; [e]**Ps 35:14**; [f]Job 20:19; Ps 43:2; 106:42; [g]Ps 9:13; 43:2
10 [h]**Ps 6:2**; [i]Dt 32:27; Ps 44:16; 89:51; 102:8; 119:42; [j]**ver 3**
11 [k]ver 5; Ps 43:5

Ps. 43

1 [a]**Jdg 6:31**; [b]**Ps 25:20**; [c]**Ps 36:3**; 109:2
2 [d]Ps 44:9; 74:1; 88:14; 89:38; [e]**Ps 35:14**; [f]**Ps 42:9**
3 [g]Ps 27:1; [h]**Ps 26:3**; [i]**Ps 25:5**; [j]Ps 2:6; [k]**2Sa 15:25**
4 [l]**Ps 42:2**; [m]Ps 26:6; 84:3; [n]**Ps 21:6**; [o]Ps 16:3; [p]**Ge 4:21**
5 [q]**Ps 42:6**

Ps. 44

1 [a]2Sa 7:22; 1Ch 17:20; Jer 26:11; [b]**Jdg 6:13**; [c]**Dt 32:7**; **Job 37:23**
2 [d]**Jos 3:10**; Ac 7:45; [e]**Ex 15:17**; **Isa 60:21**; [f]**Jdg 4:23**; **2Ch 14:13**; [g]Ps 80:9; Jer 32:23
3 [h]Jos 24:12; [i]Ps 78:54; [j]Ex 15:16; Ps 77:15; 79:11; 89:10; 98:1; Isa 40:10; 52:10; 63:5; [k]Ps 89:15; [l]**Dt 4:37**
4 [m]**Ps 24:7**; [n]Ps 5:2; [o]**Ps 21:5**
5 [p]**Jos 23:5**; [q]Ps 60:12; 108:13
6 [r]Ge 48:22; Hos 1:7
7 [s]**Dt 20:4**; [t]**Job 8:22**
8 [u]**Ps 34:2**; 1Co 1:31; 2Co 10:17; [v]Ps 52:1; [w]**Ps 30:12**
9 [x]**Ps 43:2**; [y]**Dt 8:3**; **31:17**; Ps 107:39; Isa 5:15; [z]**Jos 7:12**; Ps 108:11
10 [a]**Lev 26:17**; [b]**Jdg 2:14**
11 [c]ver 22; Jer 12:3; [d]**Lev 26:33**; **Ps 9:11**; Eze 6:8; Zec 2:6
12 [e]**Dt 32:30**; Isa 50:1; 52:3; Jer 15:13
13 [f]**2Ch 29:8**; Isa 30:3; Jer 25:9; 42:18; 44:8; [g]Ps 79:4; 80:6; 89:41; [h]**Dt 28:37**; **Mic 2:6**; [i]Eze 23:32
14 [j]**1Ki 9:7**; [k]**2Ki 19:21**
15 [l]Ge 30:23; 2Ch 32:21; Ps 35:26; [m]**Ps 34:5**
16 [n]**Ps 42:10**; [o]Ps 10:13; 55:3; 74:10; [p]**1Sa 18:25**; **Jer 11:19**; Ro 12:19
17 [q]**Dt 6:12**; **32:18**; Ps 119:16,61,153,176; Pr 3:1
18 [r]Ps 119:51,157

[a]In many Hebrew manuscripts Psalms 42 and 43 constitute one psalm.
[a]Title: Probably a literary or musical term
[b]4 Septuagint, Aquila and Syriac; Hebrew *King, O God; / command*

our feet had not strayed from your
path.
19But you crushed[s] us and made us a
haunt for jackals[t]
and covered us over with deep
darkness.[u]

20If we had forgotten[v] the name of our
God
or spread out our hands to a foreign
god,[w]
21would not God have discovered it,
since he knows the secrets of the
heart?[x]
22Yet for your sake we face death all day
long;
we are considered as sheep[y] to be
slaughtered.[z]

23Awake,[a] O Lord! Why do you sleep?[b]
Rouse yourself![c] Do not reject us for
ever.[d]
24Why do you hide your face[e]
and forget[f] our misery and
oppression?[g]

25We are brought down to the dust;[h]
our bodies cling to the ground.
26Rise up[i] and help us;
redeem[j] us because of your
unfailing love.[k]

Psalm 45

For the director of music. To ⌞the tune of⌟ "Lilies". Of the Sons of Korah. A *maskil*.[a] A wedding song.[a]

1My heart is stirred by a noble theme
as I recite my verses for the king;
my tongue is the pen of a skilful
writer.

2You are the most excellent of men
and your lips have been anointed
with grace,[b]
since God has blessed you for ever.[c]
3Gird your sword[d] upon your side, O
mighty one;[e]
clothe yourself with splendour and
majesty.[f]
4In your majesty ride forth
victoriously[g]
on behalf of truth, humility and
righteousness;[h]
let your right hand[i] display
awesome deeds.[j]
5Let your sharp arrows[k] pierce the
hearts[l] of the king's enemies;[m]
let the nations fall beneath your
feet.
6Your throne, O God, will last for ever
and ever;[n]
a sceptre of justice will be the
sceptre of your kingdom.
7You love righteousness[o] and hate
wickedness;[p]
therefore God, your God, has set
you above your companions
by anointing[q] you with the oil of
joy.[r]
8All your robes are fragrant[s] with
myrrh[t] and aloes[u] and cassia;[v]
from palaces adorned with ivory[w]
the music of the strings[x] makes you
glad.
9Daughters of kings[y] are among your
honoured women;
at your right hand[z] is the royal
bride[a] in gold of Ophir.[b]

10Listen, O daughter,[c] consider[d] and
give ear:
Forget your people[e] and your
father's house.
11The king is enthralled by your beauty;[f]
honour[g] him, for he is your lord.[h]
12The Daughter of Tyre[i] will come with a
gift,[b j]
men of wealth will seek your favour.

13All glorious[k] is the princess within ⌞her
chamber⌟;
her gown is interwoven with gold.[l]
14In embroidered garments[m] she is led
to the king;[n]
her virgin companions[o] follow her
and are brought to you.
15They are led in with joy and gladness;[p]
they enter the palace of the king.

16Your sons will take the place of your
fathers;
you will make them princes[q]
throughout the land.
17I will perpetuate your memory
through all generations;[r]
therefore the nations will praise
you[s] for ever and ever.[t]

Psalm 46

For the director of music. Of the Sons of Korah. According to *alamoth*.[a] A song.

1God is our refuge[a] and strength,[b]
an ever-present[c] help[d] in trouble.[e]

19 [s]**2Ch 14:13;** Ps 51:8; [t]**Job 30:29; Isa 34:13;** [u]**Job 3:5**
20 [v]**Dt 32:18; Jdg 3:7;** [w]**Ex 20:3;** Isa 43:12; Jer 5:19
21 [x]**1Sa 16:7;** 1Ki 8:39; Pr 15:11; Jer 12:3; 17:10
22 [y]**ver 11;** [z]Isa 53:7; Jer 11:19; 12:3; Ro 8:36*
23 [a]**Ps 7:6;** [b]Ps 78:65; [c]Ps 59:5; [d]Ps 74:1; 77:7
24 [e]**Dt 32:20;** Ps 13:1; [f]La 5:20; [g]**Dt 26:7**
25 [h]Ps 119:25
26 [i]**Nu 10:35; Ps 12:5;** 102:13; [j]Ps 26:11; [k]Ps 6:4

Ps. 45

Title [a]SS 1:1
2 [b]Lk 4:22; [c]Ps 21:6
3 [d]Dt 32:41; Ps 149:6; Rev 1:16; [e]**2Sa 1:19;** [f]**Job 40:10; Ps 21:5**
4 [g]Rev 6:2; [h]Zep 2:3; [i]Ps 21:8; [j]**Dt 4:34;** Ps 65:5; 66:3
5 [k]Dt 32:23; [l]**Nu 24:8;** [m]Ps 9:13; 92:9
6 [n]**Ge 21:33;** La 5:19
7 [o]Ps 33:5; [p]**Ps 11:5;** [q]Ps 2:2; Isa 45:1; 61:1; Zec 4:14; [r]**Ps 23:5;** Heb 1:8–9*
8 [s]Pr 27:9; SS 1:3; 4:10; [t]**Ge 37:25;** [u]**Nu 24:6;** Jn 19:39; [v]**Ex 30:24;** [w]**1Ki 22:39;** [x]Ps 144:9; 150:4; Isa 38:20
9 [y]SS 6:8; [z]1Ki 2:19; [a]Isa 62:5; [b]**Ge 10:29**
10 [c]Ru 1:11; [d]Jer 5:1; [e]Ru 1:16
11 [f]**Est 1:11;** La 2:15; [g]Eph 5:33; [h]1Pe 3:6
12 [i]**Jos 19:29;** [j]**1Ki 9:16; 2Ch 9:24**
13 [k]Isa 61:10; [l]Ex 39:3
14 [m]**Jdg 5:30;** [n]Est 2:15; [o]SS 1:3
15 [p]**Est 8:17**
16 [q]1Sa 2:8; Ps 68:27; 113:8
17 [r]**Ex 3:15;** Ps 33:11; 119:90; 135:13; [s]Ps 138:4; [t]**Ps 21:4;** Rev 22:5

Ps. 46

1 [a]Ps 9:9; 37:39; 61:3; 73:26; 91:2,9; 142:5; Isa 33:16; Jer 16:19; 17:17; Joel 3:16; Na 1:7; [b]Ps 18:1; [c]Ps 34:18; La 3:57; [d]Ps 18:6; Lk 1:54; [e]**Dt 4:30;** Ps 25:17

[a]Title: Probably a literary or musical term
[b]*12* Or *A Tyrian robe is among the gifts*
[a]Title: Probably a musical term

2 Therefore we will not fear,[f] though the
earth give way[g]
and the mountains fall[h] into the
heart of the sea,[i]
3 though its waters roar[j] and foam[k]
and the mountains quake[l] with their
surging. *Selah*

4 There is a river[m] whose streams[n] make
glad the city of God,[o]
the holy place where the Most High[p]
dwells.[q]
5 God is within her,[r] she will not fall;[s]
God will help[t] her at break of day.
6 Nations[u] are in uproar,[v] kingdoms[w]
fall;
he lifts his voice,[x] the earth melts.[y]

7 The LORD Almighty[z] is with us;[a]
the God of Jacob[b] is our fortress.[c]
Selah

8 Come and see the works of the LORD,[d]
the desolations[e] he has brought on
the earth.
9 He makes wars[f] cease to the ends of
the earth;
he breaks the bow[g] and shatters the
spear,
he burns the shields**[b]** with fire.[h]
10 "Be still, and know that I am God;[i]
I will be exalted[j] among the nations,
I will be exalted in the earth."

11 The LORD Almighty is with us;
the God of Jacob[k] is our fortress.[l]
Selah

Psalm 47

For the director of music. Of the Sons of Korah. A psalm.

1 Clap your hands,[a] all you nations;
shout to God with cries of joy.[b]
2 How awesome[c] is the LORD Most
High,[d]
the great King[e] over all the earth!
3 He subdued[f] nations under us,
peoples under our feet.
4 He chose our inheritance[g] for us,
the pride of Jacob,[h] whom he loved.
Selah

5 God has ascended[i] amid shouts of
joy,[j]
the LORD amid the sounding of
trumpets.[k]
6 Sing praises[l] to God, sing praises;
sing praises to our King, sing
praises.

7 For God is the King of all the earth;[m]
sing to him a psalm**[a]**[n] of praise.

2 [f]**Ge 4:7**; Ps 3:6; [g]Ps 82:5; Isa 13:13; 24:1,19–20; Jer 4:23; Da 11:19; Am 8:14; **Rev 6:14**; [h]ver 6; Ps 18:7; 97:5; Isa 54:10; Am 9:5; Mic 1:4; Na 1:5; Hab 3:6; [i]Ex 15:8
3 [j]Ps 93:3; Isa 17:13; Jer 5:22; Eze 1:24; Rev 19:6; [k]**Job 9:26**; [l]**Jdg 5:5**
4 [m]**Ge 2:10**; Rev 22:1; [n]**Ps 1:3**; [o]Ps 48:1, 8; 87:3; 101:8; Rev 3:12; [p]Ge 14:18; [q]**2Sa 15:25**
5 [r]Dt 23:14; **Ps 26:8**; Isa 12:6; Zec 2:5; [s]Ps 125:1; [t]**1Ch 5:20**
6 [u]**Job 12:23**; [v]Ps 74:23; Isa 5:30; 17:12; [w]Ps 68:32; 102:22; Isa 13:4,13; 23:11; Eze 26:18; Mt 4:8; [x]**Ps 29:3**; Isa 33:3; [y]**ver 2**
7 [z]**1Sa 1:11**; [a]**Ge 21:22**; [b]**Ps 20:1**; [c]ver 11; Ps 18:2
8 [d]Ps 66:5; [e]Isa 17:9; 64:10; Da 9:26; Lk 21:20
9 [f]Isa 2:4; [g]**Ps 37:15; Isa 22:6**; [h]Isa 9:5; Eze 39:9; Hos 2:18
10 [i]Dt 4:35; 1Ki 18:36,39; Ps 100:3; Isa 37:16,20; 43:11; 45:21; Eze 36:23; [j]Ps 18:46; Isa 2:11
11 [k]**Ps 20:1**; [l]**ver 7**

Ps. 47

1 [a]**2Ki 11:12**; [b]**Ps 33:3**
2 [c]**Dt 7:21**; [d]Ge 14:18; [e]Ps 2:6; 48:2; 95:3; Mt 5:35
3 [f]Ps 18:39,47; Isa 14:6
4 [g]Ps 2:8; 16:6; 78:55; 1Pe 1:4; [h]Am 6:8; 8:7
5 [i]Ps 68:18; Eph 4:8; [j]**Job 8:21; Ps 106:5**; [k]**Nu 10:2; 2Sa 6:15**
6 [l]**2Sa 22:50**
7 [m]Zec 14:9; [n]1Ch 16:7; Col 3:16

8 God reigns[o] over the nations;
God is seated on his holy throne.[p]
9 The nobles of the nations assemble
as the people of the God of
Abraham,
for the kings**[b]** of the earth belong to
God;[q]
he is greatly exalted.[r]

Psalm 48

A song. A psalm of the Sons of Korah.

1 Great is the LORD,[a] and most worthy of
praise,[b]
in the city of our God,[c] his holy
mountain.[d]
2 It is beautiful[e] in its loftiness,
the joy of the whole earth.
Like the utmost heights of Zaphon**[a]**[f] is
Mount Zion,[g]
the**[b]** city of the Great King.[h]
3 God is in her citadels;[i]
he has shown himself to be her
fortress.[j]

4 When the kings joined forces,
when they advanced together,[k]
5 they saw ⌞her⌟ and were astounded;
they fled in terror.[l]
6 Trembling seized[m] them there,
pain like that of a woman in labour.[n]
7 You destroyed them like ships of
Tarshish[o]
shattered by an east wind.[p]

8 As we have heard,
so have we seen
in the city of the LORD Almighty,
in the city of our God:
God makes her secure for ever.[q]
Selah

9 Within your temple, O God,
we meditate[r] on your unfailing
love.[s]

8 [o]**1Ch 16:31**; [p]**1Ki 22:19; Ps 9:4**; Rev 4:9
9 [q]**Job 25:2**; [r]Ps 46:10; 97:9

Ps. 48

1 [a]Ps 86:10; 96:4; 99:2; 135:5; 147:5; Jer 10:6; [b]**2Sa 22:4; 1Ch 16:25**; Ps 18:3; [c]**Ps 46:4**; [d]**Dt 33:19**; Ps 2:6; 87:1; Isa 11:9; 32:16; Jer 31:23; Da 9:16; Mic 4:1; Zec 8:3
2 [e]Ps 50:2; La 2:15; Eze 16:14; [f]**Jos 13:27**; [g]**Ps 2:6**; [h]Mt 5:35 **3** [i]ver 13; Ps 122:7; [j]Ps 18:2
4 [k]2Sa 10:1–19
5 [l]Ex 15:16; Isa 13:8; Jer 46:5; Da 5:9
6 [m]**Job 4:14**; [n]**Ge 3:16**
7 [o]**Ge 10:4; 1Ki 10:22**; 22:48; [p]**Ge 41:6**
8 [q]Jer 23:6; Zec 8:13; 14:11 **9** [r]**Ps 39:3**; [s]Ps 6:4

b9 Or *chariots*
a7 Or *a maskil* (probably a literary or musical term)
b9 Or *shields*
a2 *Zaphon* can refer to a sacred mountain or the direction north.
b2 Or *earth, / Mount Zion, on the northern side / of the*

10Like your name,[t] O God,
your praise reaches to the ends of the earth;[u]
your right hand is filled with righteousness.
11Mount Zion rejoices,
the villages of Judah are glad
because of your judgments.[v]

12Walk about Zion, go round her,
count her towers,[w]
13consider well her ramparts,[x]
view her citadels,[y]
that you may tell of them to the next generation.[z]
14For this God is our God for ever and ever;
he will be our guide[a] even to the end.

Psalm 49

For the director of music. Of the Sons of Korah. A psalm.

1Hear[a] this, all you peoples;[b]
listen, all who live in this world,[c]
2both low and high,[d]
rich and poor alike:
3My mouth will speak words of wisdom;[e]
the utterance from my heart will give understanding.[f]
4I will turn my ear to a proverb;[g]
with the harp[h] I will expound my riddle:[i]

5Why should I fear[j] when evil days come,
when wicked deceivers surround me—
6those who trust in their wealth[k]
and boast[l] of their great riches?[m]
7No man can redeem the life of another
or give to God a ransom for him—
8the ransom[n] for a life is costly,
no payment is ever enough—[o]
9that he should live on[p] for ever
and not see decay.[q]

10For all can see that wise men die;[r]
the foolish and the senseless[s] alike perish
and leave their wealth[t] to others.[u]
11Their tombs[v] will remain their houses[a]
for ever,
their dwellings for endless generations,[w]
though they had[b] named[x] lands after themselves.

12But man, despite his riches, does not endure;[y]
he is[c] like the beasts that perish.[z]

13This is the fate of those who trust in themselves,[a]
and of their followers, who approve their sayings. *Selah*
14Like sheep they are destined[b] for the grave,[d][c]
and death will feed on them.
The upright will rule[d] over them in the morning;
their forms will decay in the grave,[d]
far from their princely mansions.
15But God will redeem my life[e] from the grave;[e]
he will surely take me to himself.[f] *Selah*

16Do not be overawed when a man grows rich,
when the splendour of his house increases;
17for he will take nothing[g] with him when he dies,
his splendour will not descend with him.[h]
18Though while he lived he counted himself blessed—[i]
and men praise you when you prosper—
19he will join the generation of his fathers,[j]
who will never see the light[k] ⌞of life⌟.

20A man who has riches without understanding[l]
is like the beasts that perish.[m]

Psalm 50

A psalm of Asaph.

1The Mighty One, God, the LORD,[a]
speaks and summons the earth
from the rising of the sun to the place where it sets.[b]
2From Zion,[c] perfect in beauty,[d]
God shines forth.[e]
3Our God comes[f] and will not be silent;[g]
a fire devours[h] before him,[i]
and around him a tempest[j] rages.
4He summons the heavens above,
and the earth,[k] that he may judge his people:[l]

10 [t]**Ex 6:3; Jos 7:9;** [u]1Sa 2:10; Ps 22:27; 65:5; 98:3; 100:1; Isa 11:12; 24:16; 42:10; 49:6
11 [v]Ps 97:8
12 [w]**Ne 3:1**
13 [x]2Sa 20:15; Isa 26:1; La 2:8; Hab 2:1; [y]**ver 3;** [z]Ps 71:18; 78:6; 109:13
14 [a]Ps 25:5; 73:24; Pr 6:22; Isa 49:10; 57:18; 58:11

Ps. 49

1 [a]Isa 1:2; [b]Ps 78:1; [c]**Ps 33:8**
2 [d]Ps 62:9
3 [e]**Ps 37:30;** [f]Ps 119:130
4 [g]Ps 78:2; Pr 1:6; Eze 12:22; 16:44; 18:2–3; Lk 4:23; [h]**1Sa 16:16;** Ps 33:2; [i]**Nu 12:8**
5 [j]Ps 23:4; 27:1
6 [k]**Job 22:25;** Ps 73:12; Jer 48:7; [l]**Ps 10:3;** [m]**Job 36:19**
8 [n]**Nu 35:31;** [o]Mt 16:26
9 [p]Ps 22:29; 89:48; [q]Ps 16:10
10 [r]Ecc 2:16; [s]Ps 92:6; 94:8; [t]**Job 27:17;** [u]Ecc 2:18,21; Lk 12:20
11 [v]Mk 5:3; Lk 8:27; [w]Ps 106:31; [x]**Dt 3:14**
12 [y]**Job 14:2;** [z]ver 20; 2Pe 2:12
13 [a]Lk 12:20
14 [b]Jer 43:11; Eze 31:14; [c]Nu 16:30; **Job 21:13;** Ps 9:17; 55:15; [d]Isa 14:2; Da 7:18; 1Co 6:2
15 [e]Ps 56:13; Hos 13:14; [f]**Ge 5:24**
17 [g]1Ti 6:7; [h]**Ps 17:14**
18 [i]Ps 10:6; Lk 12:19
19 [j]**Ge 15:15;** [k]**Job 33:30**
20 [l]Pr 16:16; [m]**ver 12**

Ps. 50

1 [a]Jos 22:22; [b]Ps 113:3
2 [c]Ps 2:6; [d]**Ps 48:2; La 2:15;** [e]**Dt 33:2**
3 [f]Ps 96:13; [g]ver 21; Isa 42:14; 64:12; 65:6; [h]**Lev 10:2;** [i]**Ps 18:8;** [j]Job 37:9; Ps 83:15; 107:25; 147:18; Isa 29:6; 30:28; Jnh 1:4; Na 1:3
4 [k]Dt 4:26; 31:28; Isa 1:2; [l]Heb 10:30

[a]*11* Septuagint and Syriac; Hebrew *In their thoughts their houses will remain* [b]*11* Or / *for they have* [c]*12* Hebrew; Septuagint and Syriac read verse 12 the same as verse 20. [d]*14* Hebrew *Sheol*; also in verse 15 [e]*15* Or *soul*

5"Gather to me my consecrated ones,[m]
who made a covenant[n] with me by
sacrifice."
6And the heavens proclaim[o] his
righteousness,
for God himself is judge.[p] *Selah*

7"Hear, O my people, and I will speak,
O Israel, and I will testify[q] against
you:
I am God, your God.[r]
8I do not rebuke[s] you for your sacrifices
or your burnt offerings,[t] which are
ever before me.
9I have no need of a bull[u] from your
stall
or of goats[v] from your pens,[w]
10for every animal of the forest[x] is mine,
and the cattle on a thousand hills.[y]
11I know every bird[z] in the mountains,
and the creatures of the field[a] are
mine.
12If I were hungry I would not tell you,
for the world[b] is mine, and all that is
in it.[c]
13Do I eat the flesh of bulls
or drink the blood of goats?
14Sacrifice thank-offerings[d] to God,
fulfil your vows[e] to the Most High,[f]
15and call[g] upon me in the day of
trouble;[h]
I will deliver[i] you, and you will
honour[j] me."

16But to the wicked, God says:

"What right have you to recite my laws
or take my covenant[k] on your lips?[l]
17You hate[m] my instruction
and cast my words behind[n] you.
18When you see a thief, you join[o] with
him;
you throw in your lot with
adulterers.[p]
19You use your mouth for evil
and harness your tongue to deceit.[q]
20You speak continually against your
brother[r]
and slander your own mother's son.
21These things you have done and I kept
silent;[s]
you thought I was altogether[a] like
you.
But I will rebuke[t] you
and accuse[u] you to your face.

22"Consider this, you who forget God,[v]
or I will tear you to pieces, with
none to rescue:[w]
23He who sacrifices thank-offerings
honours me,
and he prepares the way[x]
so that I may show him[b] the
salvation of God.[y]"

5 [m]Dt 7:6; **Ps 18:25**; [n]Ex 24:7; **2Ch 6:11**
6 [o]**Ps 19:1**; [p]**Ge 16:5; Job 9:15**
7 [q]Heb 2:4; [r]Ex 20:2; Ps 48:14
8 [s]**2Sa 22:16**; [t]**Ps 40:6**
9 [u]**Lev 1:5**; [v]**Lev 16:5**; [w]**Nu 32:16**
10 [x]Ps 104:20; Isa 56:9; Mic 5:8; [y]Ps 104:24
11 [z]Mt 6:26; [a]Ps 8:7; 80:13
12 [b]Ex 19:5; [c]Dt 10:14; **Jos 3:11**; Ps 24:1; 1Co 10:26
14 [d]**Ezr 1:4; Ps 27:6**; [e]**Nu 30:2; Ps 66:13**; 76:11; [f]Ps 7:8
15 [g]Ps 4:1; 81:7; Isa 55:6; 58:9; Zec 13:9; [h]Ps 69:17; 86:7; 107:6; 142:2; Jas 5:13; [i]Ps 3:7; [j]**Ps 22:23**
16 [k]Ps 25:10; [l]Isa 29:13
17 [m]Pr 1:22; [n]**1Ki 14:9**
18 [o]Ro 1:32; 1Ti 5:22; [p]**Job 22:15**
19 [q]Ps 10:7; 36:3; 52:2; 101:7
20 [r]Mt 10:21
21 [s]Isa 42:14; 57:11; 62:1; 64:12; [t]Ps 6:1; **18:15**; 76:6; 104:7; Isa 50:2; [u]Ps 85:5; Isa 57:16
22 [v]**Job 8:13; Isa 17:10**; [w]**Dt 32:39**; Mic 5:8
23 [x]Ps 85:13; [y]**Ps 9:14**; 91:16; 98:3; Isa 52:10

Ps. 51

Title [a]2Sa 11:4; 12:1
1 [b]**2Sa 24:14; Ps 9:13**; [c]**Ps 25:7; 119:88**; [d]**Ne 9:27**; Ps 86:15; Isa 63:7; [e]**2Sa 12:13; 2Ch 6:21; Ne 4:5**; Ac 3:19; [f]**Ps 39:8**
2 [g]**Ru 3:3**; Jer 2:22; 13:27; Ac 22:16; 1Jn 1:9; [h]Pr 20:30; Isa 4:4; Eze 36:25; Zec 13:1; Mt 23:25–26; Heb 9:14
3 [i]Isa 59:12
4 [j]**1Sa 15:24**; [k]**Ge 20:6**; Lk 15:21; [l]Ro 3:4*
5 [m]**Lev 5:2**; [n]**Job 5:7**

Psalm 51

For the director of music. A psalm of David. When the prophet Nathan came to him after David had committed adultery with Bathsheba.[a]

1Have mercy[b] on me, O God,
according to your unfailing love;[c]
according to your great compassion[d]
blot out[e] my transgressions.[f]
2Wash away[g] all my iniquity
and cleanse[h] me from my sin.

3For I know my transgressions,
and my sin is always before me.[i]
4Against you, you only, have I sinned[j]
and done what is evil in your sight,[k]
so that you are proved right when you
speak
and justified when you judge.[l]
5Surely I was sinful[m] at birth,[n]
sinful from the time my mother
conceived me.
6Surely you desire truth in the inner
parts;[a]
you teach[b] me wisdom[o] in the
inmost place.[p]

7Cleanse[q] me with hyssop,[r] and I shall
be clean;
wash me, and I shall be whiter than
snow.[s]
8Let me hear joy and gladness;[t]
let the bones[u] you have crushed
rejoice.
9Hide your face from my sins[v]
and blot out[w] all my iniquity.

10Create in me a pure heart,[x] O God,
and renew a steadfast spirit within
me.[y]
11Do not cast me[z] from your presence[a]
or take your Holy Spirit[b] from me.
12Restore to me the joy of your salvation[c]
and grant me a willing spirit,[d] to
sustain me.[e]

13Then I will teach transgressors your
ways,[f]
and sinners[g] will turn back to you.[h]

6 [o]Ps 119:66; 143:10; [p]**Job 9:4; 34:32**
7 [q]Isa 4:4; Eze 36:25; Zec 13:1; [r]**Ex 12:22; Nu 19:6**; Heb 9:19; [s]Isa 1:18; 43:25; 44:22
8 [t]Isa 35:10; Jer 33:11; Joel 1:16; [u]**Ex 12:46**
9 [v]Jer 16:17; Zec 4:10; [w]**2Sa 12:13**
10 [x]**Ps 24:4**; 78:37; Mt 5:8; Ac 15:9; [y]Eze 18:31; 36:26
11 [z]Ps 27:9; 71:9; 138:8; [a]**Ge 4:14; Ex 33:15**; [b]Ps 106:33; Isa 63:10; Eph 4:30
12 [c]**Job 33:26**; [d]Ps 110:3; [e]**Ps 18:35**
13 [f]**Ex 33:13**; Ac 9:21–22; [g]**Ps 1:1**; [h]**Job 33:27**

[a]21 Or *thought the 'I AM' was*
[b]23 Or *and to him who considers his way / I will show*
[a]6 The meaning of the Hebrew for this phrase is uncertain. [b]6 Or *you desired . . . ; / you taught*

14Save me[i] from bloodguilt,[j] O God,
the God who saves me,[k]
and my tongue will sing of your
righteousness.[l]
15O Lord, open my lips,[m]
and my mouth will declare your
praise.
16You do not delight in sacrifice,[n] or I
would bring it;
you do not take pleasure in burnt
offerings.
17The sacrifices[o] of God are[c] a broken
spirit;
a broken and contrite heart,[p]
O God, you will not despise.

18In your good pleasure make Zion[q]
prosper;
build up the walls of Jerusalem.[r]
19Then there will be righteous
sacrifices,[s]
whole burnt offerings[t] to delight
you;
then bulls[u] will be offered on your
altar.

Psalm 52

For the director of music. A *maskil*[a] of David. When Doeg the Edomite[a] had gone to Saul and told him: "David has gone to the house of Ahimelech."

1Why do you boast of evil, you mighty
man?
Why do you boast[b] all day long,[c]
you who are a disgrace in the eyes of
God?
2Your tongue plots destruction;[d]
it is like a sharpened razor,[e]
you who practise deceit.[f]
3You love evil[g] rather than good,
falsehood[h] rather than speaking the
truth. *Selah*
4You love every harmful word,
O you deceitful tongue![i]

5Surely God will bring you down to
everlasting ruin:
He will snatch you up and tear[j] you
from your tent;
he will uproot[k] you from the land of
the living.[l] *Selah*
6The righteous will see and fear;
they will laugh[m] at him, saying,
7"Here now is the man
who did not make God his
stronghold[n]
but trusted in his great wealth[o]
and grew strong by destroying
others!"

8But I am like an olive tree[p]
flourishing in the house of God;
I trust[q] in God's unfailing love
for ever and ever.
9I will praise you for ever[r] for what you
have done;
in your name I will hope,[s] for your
name is good.[t]
I will praise you in the presence of
your saints.[u]

Psalm 53

53:1–6pp—Ps 14:1–7

For the director of music. According to *mahalath*.[a] A *maskil*[b] of David.

1The fool[a] says in his heart,
"There is no God."[b]
They are corrupt, and their ways are
vile;
there is no-one who does good.

2God looks down from heaven[c]
on the sons of men
to see if there are any who
understand,[d]
any who seek God.[e]
3Everyone has turned away,
they have together become corrupt;
there is no-one who does good,
not even one.[f]

4Will the evildoers never learn—
those who devour my people as
men eat bread
and who do not call on God?
5There they were, overwhelmed with
dread,
where there was nothing to dread.[g]
God scattered the bones[h] of those who
attacked you;[i]
you put them to shame,[j] for God
despised them.[k]

6Oh, that salvation for Israel would
come out of Zion!
When God restores the fortunes of
his people,
let Jacob rejoice and Israel be glad!

Psalm 54

For the director of music. With stringed instruments. A *maskil*[a] of David. When the Ziphites[a] had gone to Saul and said, "Is not David hiding among us?"

1Save me,[b] O God, by your name;[c]
vindicate me by your might.[d]

---

14 [i]Ps 39:8; [j]2Sa 12:9; [k]Ps 25:5; 68:20; 88:1; [l]Ps 5:8; 35:28; 71:15
15 [m]Ex 4:15
16 [n]1Sa 15:22
17 [o]Pr 15:8; Hag 2:14; [p]Mt 11:29
18 [q]Ps 102:16; 147:2; Isa 14:32; 51:3; Zec 1:16–17; [r]Ps 69:35; Isa 44:26
19 [s]Dt 33:19; [t]Ps 66:13; 96:8; Jer 17:26; [u]Ps 66:15

Ps. 52

Title [a]1Sa 21:7; 22:9
1 [b]Ps 10:3; 94:4; [c]Ps 44:8
2 [d]Ps 5:9; [e]Nu 6:5; [f]Ps 50:19
3 [g]Ex 10:10; 1Sa 12:25; Am 5:14–15; Jn 3:20; [h]Ps 58:3; Jer 9:5; Rev 21:8
4 [i]Ps 5:9; 10:7; 109:2; 120:2–3; Pr 10:31; 12:19
5 [j]Dt 29:28; Job 40:12; Isa 22:19; Eze 17:24; [k]Dt 28:63; [l]Job 28:13
6 [m]Job 22:19
7 [n]2Sa 22:3; [o]Ps 49:6; Pr 11:28; Mk 10:23
8 [p]Ps 1:3; Rev 11:4; [q]Ps 6:4; 13:5
9 [r]Ps 30:12; [s]Job 7:6; Ps 25:3; [t]Ps 54:6; [u]Dt 7:6; Ps 16:3

Ps. 53

1 [a]Ps 74:22; 107:17; Pr 10:23; [b]Ps 10:4
2 [c]Ps 33:13; [d]Ps 82:5; Jer 4:22; 8:8; [e]2Ch 15:2
3 [f]Ro 3:10–12*
5 [g]Lev 26:17; [h]2Ki 23:14; Ps 141:7; Jer 8:1; Eze 6:5; [i]2Ki 17:20; [j]Job 8:22; [k]Jer 6:30; 14:19; La 5:22

Ps. 54

Title [a]1Sa 23:19; 26:1
1 [b]1Sa 24:15; [c]Ps 20:1; [d]2Ch 20:6

---

[c]17 Or *My sacrifice, O God, is*
[a]Title: Probably a literary or musical term
[a]Title: Probably a musical term
[b]Title: Probably a literary or musical term
[a]Title: Probably a literary or musical term

[2]Hear my prayer, O God;[e]
listen to the words of my mouth.

[3]Strangers are attacking me;[f]
ruthless men[g] seek my life[h]—
men without regard for God.[i] *Selah*

[4]Surely God is my help;[j]
the Lord is the one who sustains
me.[k]

[5]Let evil recoil[l] on those who slander
me;
in your faithfulness[m] destroy them.

[6]I will sacrifice a freewill offering[n] to
you;
I will praise[o] your name, O LORD,
for it is good.[p]
[7]For he has delivered me[q] from all my
troubles,
and my eyes have looked in
triumph on my foes.[r]

Psalm 55

For the director of music. With stringed instruments. A *maskil*[a] of David.

[1]Listen to my prayer, O God,
do not ignore my plea;[a]
[2] hear me and answer me.[b]
My thoughts trouble me and I am
distraught[c]
[3] at the voice of the enemy,
at the stares of the wicked;
for they bring down suffering upon
me[d]
and revile[e] me in their anger.[f]

[4]My heart is in anguish[g] within me;
the terrors[h] of death assail me.
[5]Fear and trembling[i] have beset me;
horror[j] has overwhelmed me.
[6]I said, "Oh, that I had the wings of a
dove!
I would fly away and be at rest—
[7]I would flee far away
and stay in the desert;[k] *Selah*
[8]I would hurry to my place of shelter,[l]
far from the tempest and storm."[m]

[9]Confuse the wicked, O Lord,
confound their speech,[n]
for I see violence and strife[o] in the
city.[p]
[10]Day and night they prowl[q] about on its
walls;
malice and abuse are within it.
[11]Destructive forces[r] are at work in the
city;
threats and lies[s] never leave its
streets.

[12]If an enemy were insulting me,
I could endure it;
if a foe were raising himself against
me,
I could hide from him.
[13]But it is you, a man like myself,
my companion, my close friend,[t]
[14]with whom I once enjoyed sweet
fellowship[u]
as we walked with the throng at the
house of God.[v]

[15]Let death take my enemies by
surprise;[w]
let them go down alive to the
grave,[b x]
for evil finds lodging among them.

[16]But I call to God,
and the LORD saves me.
[17]Evening,[y] morning[z] and noon[a]
I cry out in distress,
and he hears my voice.
[18]He ransoms me unharmed
from the battle waged against me,
even though many oppose me.
[19]God, who is enthroned for ever,[b]
will hear[c] them and afflict
them— *Selah*
men who never change their ways
and have no fear of God.[d]

[20]My companion attacks his friends;[e]
he violates his covenant.[f]
[21]His speech is smooth as butter,[g]
yet war is in his heart;
his words are more soothing than oil,[h]
yet they are drawn swords.[i]

[22]Cast your cares on the LORD
and he will sustain you;[j]
he will never let the righteous fall.[k]
[23]But you, O God, will bring down the
wicked
into the pit[l] of corruption;
bloodthirsty and deceitful men[m]
will not live out half their days.[n]

But as for me, I trust in you.[o]

Psalm 56

For the director of music. To ⌊the tune of⌋ "A Dove on Distant Oaks". Of David. A *miktam*.[a] When the Philistines had seized him in Gath.

[1]Be merciful to me,[a] O God, for men
hotly pursue me;[b]
all day long they press their attack.[c]

2 [e]**Ps 4:1**; 5:1; 55:1 *3* [f]Ps 86:14; [g]Ps 18:48; 140:1,4,11; [h]**1Sa 20:1**; [i]Ps 36:1 *4* [j]**1Ch 5:20; Ps 20:2**; [k]**Ps 18:35** *5* [l]**Dt 32:35**; Ps 94:23; Pr 24:12; [m]Ps 89:49; Isa 42:3 *6* [n]**Lev 7:12**,16; **Ezr 1:4; Ps 27:6**; [o]Ps 44:8; 69:30; 138:2; 142:7; 145:1; [p]Ps 52:9 *7* [q]Ps 34:6; [r]Ps 59:10; 92:11; 112:8; 118:7

Ps. 55
1 [a]Ps 27:9; La 3:56 *2* [b]Ps 4:1; [c]1Sa 1:15–16; Ps 77:3; 86:6–7; 142:2 *3* [d]**2Sa 16:6–8**; Ps 17:9; 143:3; [e]**Ps 44:16**; [f]Ps 71:11 *4* [g]**Ps 6:3**; [h]**Job 18:11** *5* [i]**Job 4:14; 2Co 7:15**; [j]Dt 28:67; Isa 21:4; Jer 46:5; 49:5; Eze 7:18 *7* [k]1Sa 23:14 *8* [l]Ps 31:20; [m]Ps 77:18; Isa 4:6; 25:4; 28:2; 29:6; 32:2 *9* [n]Ge 11:9; Ac 2:4; [o]Ps 11:5; Isa 59:6; Jer 6:7; Eze 7:11; Hab 1:3; [p]Ge 4:17 *10* [q]1Pe 5:8 *11* [r]Ps 5:9; [s]Ps 10:7 *13* [t]**2Sa 15:12** *14* [u]Ac 1:16–17; [v]Ps 42:4 *15* [w]Ps 64:7; Pr 6:15; Isa 29:5; 47:9,11; 1Th 5:3; [x]**Ps 49:14** *17* [y]Ps 141:2; Ac 3:1; 10:3,30; [z]Ps 5:3; 88:13; 92:2; [a]Ac 10:9 *19* [b]**Ex 15:18**; Dt 33:27; Ps 29:10; [c]Ps 78:59; [d]Ps 36:1; 64:4 *20* [e]Ps 7:4; [f]**Ps 41:9** *21* [g]Ps 12:2; [h]Pr 5:3; 6:24; [i]Ps 57:4; 59:7; 64:3; Pr 12:18; Rev 1:16 *22* [j]**Ps 18:35**; Mt 6:25–34; 1Pe 5:7; [k]Ps 15:5; 21:7; 37:24; 112:6 *23* [l]Ps 9:15; **30:3**; 73:18; 94:13; Isa 14:15; Eze 28:8; **Lk 8:31**; [m]Ps 5:6; [n]**Job 15:32**; [o]Ps 11:1; 25:2; 56:3

Ps. 56
1 [a]Ps 6:2; [b]Ps 57:1–3; [c]Ps 17:9

[a]Title: Probably a literary or musical term
[b]*15* Hebrew *Sheol*
[a]Title: Probably a literary or musical term

2My slanderers pursue me all day
long;[d]
many are attacking me in their
pride.[e]

3When I am afraid,[f]
I will trust in you.[g]
4In God, whose word I praise,[h]
in God I trust; I will not be afraid.[i]
What can mortal man do to me?[j]

5All day long they twist my words;[k]
they are always plotting to harm
me.
6They conspire,[l] they lurk,
they watch my steps,[m]
eager to take my life.[n]

7On no account let them escape;[o]
in your anger, O God, bring down
the nations.[p]
8Record my lament;
list my tears on your scroll[b] [q]—
are they not in your record?[r]

9Then my enemies will turn back[s]
when I call for help.[t]
By this I will know that God is for
me.[u]
10In God, whose word I praise,
in the LORD, whose word I praise—
11in God I trust; I will not be afraid.
What can man do to me?

12I am under vows[v] to you, O God;
I will present my thank-offerings to
you.
13For you have delivered me[c] from
death[w]
and my feet from stumbling,
that I may walk before God
in the light of life.[d] [x]

Psalm 57

57:7–11pp—Ps 108:1–5

For the director of music. ⌞To the tune of⌟ "Do Not Destroy". Of David. A *miktam*.[a] When he had fled from Saul into the cave.[a]

1Have mercy on me, O God, have
mercy on me,
for in you my soul takes refuge.[b]
I will take refuge in the shadow of
your wings[c]
until the disaster has passed.[d]

2I cry out to God Most High,
to God, who fulfils ⌞his purpose⌟ for
me.[e]
3He sends from heaven and saves me,[f]
rebuking those who hotly pursue
me;[g] *Selah*

2 [d]Ps 35:25; 124:3; [e]Ps 35:1
3 [f]Ps 55:4–5; [g]**Ps 55:23**
4 [h]ver 10; [i]**Ps 27:1;** [j]Ps 118:6; Mt 10:28; Heb 13:6
5 [k]Ps 41:7; 2Pe 3:16
6 [l]Ps 59:3; 94:21; Mk 3:6; [m]Ps 17:11; [n]Ps 71:10
7 [o]Pr 19:5; Eze 17:15; Ro 2:3; Heb 12:25; [p]Ps 36:12; 55:23
8 [q]**2Ki 20:5;** [r]Isa 4:3; Da 7:10; 12:1; Mal 3:16
9 [s]Ps 9:3; [t]Ps 102:2; [u]**Nu 14:8; Dt 31:6;** Ro 8:31
12 [v]Ps 50:14
13 [w]Ps 30:3; 33:19; 49:15; 86:13; 107:20; 116:8; [x]**Job 33:30**

Ps. 57

Title [a]1Sa 22:1; 24:3; Ps 142 Title
1 [b]Ps 2:12; 9:9; 34:22; [c]**Ru 2:12; Mt 23:37;** [d]Isa 26:20
2 [e]Ps 138:8
3 [f]Ps 18:9,16; 69:14; 142:6; 144:5,7; [g]Ps 56:1; [h]Ps 25:10; 40:11; 115:1
4 [i]**Ps 35:17;** [j]**Ps 55:21;** Pr 30:14
5 [k]ver 11; Ps 108:5
6 [l]Ps 10:9; 31:4; 140:5; [m]**Ps 38:6;** 145:14; [n]**Ps 9:15;** [o]**Est 6:13;** Ps 7:15; Pr 28:10; Ecc 10:8
7 [p]Ps 112:7
8 [q]Ps 33:2; 149:3; 150:3
10 [r]**Ps 36:5**
11 [s]**Ps 8:1;** 113:4; [t]**ver 5**

Ps. 58

1 [a]Ps 82:2
2 [b]Mt 15:19; [c]Ps 94:20; Isa 10:1; Lk 6:38
4 [d]**Nu 21:6**

God sends his love and his
faithfulness.[h]

4I am in the midst of lions;[i]
I lie among ravenous beasts—
men whose teeth are spears and
arrows,
whose tongues are sharp swords.[j]

5Be exalted, O God, above the heavens;
let your glory be over all the earth.[k]

6They spread a net for my feet[l]—
I was bowed down[m] in distress.
They dug a pit[n] in my path—
but they have fallen into it
themselves.[o] *Selah*

7My heart is steadfast, O God,
my heart is steadfast;[p]
I will sing and make music.
8Awake, my soul!
Awake, harp and lyre![q]
I will awaken the dawn.

9I will praise you, O Lord, among the
nations;
I will sing of you among the
peoples.
10For great is your love, reaching to the
heavens;
your faithfulness reaches to the
skies.[r]

11Be exalted, O God, above the
heavens;[s]
let your glory be over all the earth.[t]

Psalm 58

For the director of music. ⌞To the tune of⌟ "Do Not Destroy". Of David. A *miktam*.[a]

1Do you rulers indeed speak justly?[a]
Do you judge uprightly among
men?
2No, in your heart you devise
injustice,[b]
and your hands mete out violence
on the earth.[c]
3Even from birth the wicked go astray;
from the womb they are wayward
and speak lies.
4Their venom is like the venom of a
snake,[d]
like that of a cobra that has stopped
its ears,

[b]8 Or / *put my tears in your wineskin*
[c]13 Or *my soul*
[d]13 Or *the land of the living*
[a]Title: Probably a literary or musical term
[a]Title: Probably a literary or musical term

5that will not heed[e] the tune of the
charmer,[f]
however skilful the enchanter may
be.

6Break the teeth in their mouths, O
God;[g]
tear out, O LORD, the fangs of the
lions![h]
7Let them vanish like water that flows
away;[i]
when they draw the bow, let their
arrows be blunted.[j]
8Like a slug melting away as it moves
along,[k]
like a stillborn child,[l] may they not
see the sun.

9Before your pots can feel ⌞the heat of⌟
the thorns[m]—
whether they be green or dry—the
wicked will be swept away.[b] [n]
10The righteous will be glad[o] when they
are avenged,[p]
when they bathe their feet in the
blood of the wicked.[q]
11Then men will say,
"Surely the righteous still are
rewarded;[r]
surely there is a God who judges the
earth."[s]

Psalm 59

For the director of music. ⌞To the tune of⌟ "Do Not Destroy". Of David. A *miktam*.[a] When Saul had sent men to watch David's house[a] in order to kill him.

1Deliver me from my enemies, O God;[b]
protect me from those who rise up
against me.[c]
2Deliver me from evildoers[d]
and save me from bloodthirsty
men.[e]

3See how they lie in wait for me!
Fierce men conspire[f] against me
for no offence or sin of mine, O
LORD.
4I have done no wrong,[g] yet they are
ready to attack me.[h]
Arise to help me; look on my plight![i]
5O LORD God Almighty, the God of
Israel,[j]
rouse yourself[k] to punish all the
nations;[l]
show no mercy to wicked traitors.[m]
Selah
6They return at evening,
snarling like dogs,[n]
and prowl about the city.
7See what they spew from their
mouths[o]—

5 [e]Ps 81:11; [f]Ecc 10:11; Jer 8:17
6 [g]Ps 3:7; [h]**Job 4:10**
7 [i]**Lev 26:36; Job 11:16;** [j]Ps 11:2; 57:4; 64:3
8 [k]Isa 13:7; [l]**Job 3:16**
9 [m]Ps 118:12; Ecc 7:6; [n]**Job 7:10; 21:18**
10 [o]**Job 22:19;** [p]Dt 32:35; Ps 7:9; 91:8; Jer 11:20; Ro 12:17–21; [q]Ps 68:23
11 [r]**Ge 15:1; Ps 128:2;** Lk 6:23; [s]**Ge 18:25**

Ps. 59

Title [a]1Sa 19:11
1 [b]Ps 143:9; [c]**Ps 20:1**
2 [d]Ps 14:4; 36:12; 53:4; 92:7; 94:16; [e]**Ps 26:9;** 139:19; Pr 29:10
3 [f]**Ps 56:6**
4 [g]Ps 119:3; [h]Mt 5:11; [i]**Ps 13:3**
5 [j]Ps 69:6; 80:4; 84:8; [k]**Ps 44:23;** [l]**Ps 9:5; Isa 10:3;** [m]Jer 18:23
6 [n]ver 14; Ps 22:16
7 [o]Ps 94:4; Pr 10:32; 12:23; 15:2,28; [p]**Ps 55:21;** [q]**Job 22:13**
8 [r]Ps 37:13; Pr 1:26; [s]Ps 2:4
9 [t]**Ps 18:1;** [u]Ps 9:9; 18:2; 62:2; 71:3
11 [v]Ps 3:3; 84:9; [w]Dt 4:9; 6:12; [x]Ps 89:10; 106:27; 144:6; Isa 33:3
12 [y]Ps 10:7; [z]Ps 64:8; Pr 10:14; 12:13; [a]Isa 2:12; 5:15; Zep 3:11
13 [b]Ps 104:35; [c]Ps 83:18
15 [d]Job 15:23
16 [e]Ps 108:1; [f]**1Sa 2:10;** [g]Ps 5:3; 88:13; [h]Ps 101:1; [i]**2Sa 22:3;** [j]**Dt 4:30**
17 [k]ver 10

Ps. 60

Title [a]2Sa 8:13
1 [b]2Sa 5:20; Ps 44:9; [c]Ps 79:5; [d]Ps 80:3

they spew out swords[p] from their
lips,
and they say, "Who can hear us?"[q]
8But you, O LORD, laugh at them;[r]
you scoff at all those nations.[s]

9O my Strength,[t] I watch for you;
you, O God, are my fortress,[u] 10my
loving God.

God will go before me
and will let me gloat over those who
slander me.
11But do not kill them, O Lord our
shield,[b] [v]
or my people will forget.[w]
In your might make them wander
about,
and bring them down.[x]
12For the sins of their mouths,[y]
for the words of their lips,[z]
let them be caught in their pride.[a]
For the curses and lies they utter,
13 consume them in wrath,
consume them till they are no more.[b]
Then it will be known to the ends of
the earth
that God rules over Jacob.[c] *Selah*

14They return at evening,
snarling like dogs,
and prowl about the city.
15They wander about for food[d]
and howl if not satisfied.
16But I will sing[e] of your strength,[f]
in the morning[g] I will sing of your
love;[h]
for you are my fortress,[i]
my refuge in times of trouble.[j]

17O my Strength, I sing praise to you;
you, O God, are my fortress, my
loving God.[k]

Psalm 60

60:5–12pp—Ps 108:6–13

For the director of music. To ⌞the tune of⌟ "The Lily of the Covenant". A *miktam*[a] of David. For teaching. When he fought Aram Naharaim[b] and Aram Zobah,[c] and when Joab returned and struck down twelve thousand Edomites in the Valley of Salt.[a]

1You have rejected us,[b] O God, and
burst forth upon us;
you have been angry[c]—now restore
us![d]

b9 The meaning of the Hebrew for this verse is uncertain. aTitle: Probably a literary or musical term b11 Or *sovereign*
aTitle: Probably a literary or musical term
bTitle: That is, Arameans of North-west Mesopotamia cTitle: That is, Arameans of central Syria

2 You have shaken the land[e] and torn it
open;
mend its fractures,[f] for it is quaking.
3 You have shown your people
desperate times;[g]
you have given us wine that makes
us stagger.[h]

4 But for those who fear you, you have
raised a banner[i]
to be unfurled against the bow.
Selah

5 Save us and help us with your right
hand,[j]
that those you love[k] may be
delivered.
6 God has spoken from his sanctuary:
"In triumph I will parcel out
Shechem[l]
and measure off the Valley of
Succoth.[m]
7 Gilead[n] is mine, and Manasseh is
mine;
Ephraim[o] is my helmet,
Judah[p] my sceptre.[q]
8 Moab is my washbasin,
upon Edom I toss my sandal;
over Philistia I shout in triumph."[r]

9 Who will bring me to the fortified city?
Who will lead me to Edom?
10 Is it not you, O God, you who have
rejected us
and no longer go out with our
armies?[s]
11 Give us aid against the enemy,
for the help of man is worthless.[t]
12 With God we shall gain the victory,
and he will trample down our
enemies.[u]

Psalm 61

For the director of music. With stringed instruments. Of David.

1 Hear my cry, O God;[a]
listen to my prayer.[b]

2 From the ends of the earth I call to you,
I call as my heart grows faint;[c]
lead me to the rock[d] that is higher
than I.
3 For you have been my refuge,[e]
a strong tower against the foe.[f]

4 I long to dwell[g] in your tent for ever
and take refuge in the shelter of
your wings.[h] *Selah*
5 For you have heard my vows,[i] O God;
you have given me the heritage of
those who fear your name.[j]

6 Increase the days of the king's life,[k]
his years for many generations.[l]
7 May he be enthroned in God's
presence for ever;[m]
appoint your love and faithfulness
to protect him.[n]

8 Then will I ever sing praise to your
name[o]
and fulfil my vows day after day.[p]

Psalm 62

For the director of music. For Jeduthun. A psalm of David.

1 My soul finds rest[a] in God alone;[b]
my salvation comes from him.
2 He alone is my rock[c] and my
salvation;[d]
he is my fortress,[e] I shall never be
shaken.[f]

3 How long will you assault a man?
Would all of you throw him down—
this leaning wall,[g] this tottering
fence?
4 They fully intend to topple him
from his lofty place;
they take delight in lies.
With their mouths they bless,
but in their hearts they curse.[h] *Selah*

5 Find rest, O my soul, in God alone;[i]
my hope comes from him.
6 He alone is my rock and my salvation;
he is my fortress, I shall not be
shaken.
7 My salvation and my honour depend
on God;[a]
he is my mighty rock, my refuge.[j]
8 Trust in him at all times, O people;[k]
pour out your hearts to him,[l]
for God is our refuge. *Selah*

9 Lowborn men[m] are but a breath,[n]
the highborn are but a lie;
if weighed on a balance,[o] they are
nothing;
together they are only a breath.
10 Do not trust in extortion[p]
or take pride in stolen goods;[q]
though your riches increase,
do not set your heart on them.[r]

11 One thing God has spoken,
two things have I heard:
that you, O God, are strong,[s]
12 and that you, O Lord, are loving.[t]
Surely you will reward each person
according to what he has done.[u]

2 [e]Ps 18:7; [f]2Ch 7:14
3 [g]Ps 71:20; [h]Ps 75:8; Isa 29:9; 51:17; 63:6; Jer 25:16; Zec 12:2; Rev 14:10
4 [i]Isa 5:26; 11:10,12; 18:3
5 [j]Job 40:14; [k]Dt 33:12
6 [l]Ge 12:6; [m]Ge 33:17
7 [n]Jos 13:31; [o]Ge 41:52; [p]Nu 34:19; [q]Ge 49:10
8 [r]2Sa 8:1
10 [s]Jos 7:12
11 [t]Ps 146:3; Pr 3:5
12 [u]Job 40:12; Ps 44:5

Ps. 61

1 [a]Ps 64:1; [b]Ps 4:1; 86:6
2 [c]Ps 6:2; [d]Ps 18:2; 31:2; 94:22
3 [e]Ps 9:9; 46:1; 62:7; [f]Ps 59:9; Pr 18:10
4 [g]Ps 15:1; [h]Dt 32:11; Mt 23:37
5 [i]Nu 30:2; Ps 56:12; [j]Ex 6:3; Dt 33:9; Ne 1:11; Ps 102:15; Isa 59:19; Mt 6:9
6 [k]1Ki 3:14; [l]Ps 21:4
7 [m]Ps 41:12; Lk 22:69; Eph 1:20; Col 3:1; [n]Ps 40:11
8 [o]Ex 15:1; Ps 7:17; 30:4; [p]Nu 30:2; Dt 23:21

Ps. 62

1 [a]Ps 5:3; [b]ver 5
2 [c]Ps 18:31; 89:26; [d]Ex 15:2; [e]Ps 59:9; [f]Job 29:18
3 [g]Isa 30:13
4 [h]Ps 28:3; 55:21
5 [i]ver 1
7 [j]Ps 61:3
8 [k]Ps 37:5; Isa 26:4; [l]1Sa 1:15; Ps 42:4; Mt 26:36–46
9 [m]Ps 49:2; [n]Job 7:7; [o]Isa 40:15
10 [p]Ps 12:5; 1Ti 6:17; [q]Isa 61:8; Eze 22:29; Na 3:1; [r]Job 31:25; Mt 19:23–24; 1Ti 6:6–10
11 [s]1Ch 29:11; Rev 19:1
12 [t]Ps 86:5; 103:8; 130:7; [u]Job 21:31; Ps 28:4; Mt 16:27; Ro 2:6*; 1Co 3:8; Col 3:25

[a]7 Or / *God Most High is my salvation and my honour*

Psalm 63

A psalm of David. When he was in the Desert of Judah.

1O God, you are my God,
earnestly I seek you;
my soul thirsts for you,[a]
my body longs for you,
in a dry and weary land
where there is no water.[b]

2I have seen you in the sanctuary[c]
and beheld your power and your glory.[d]
3Because your love is better than life,[e]
my lips will glorify you.
4I will praise you as long as I live,[f]
and in your name I will lift up my hands.[g]
5My soul will be satisfied as with the richest of foods;[h]
with singing lips my mouth will praise you.

6On my bed I remember you;
I think of you through the watches of the night.[i]
7Because you are my help,[j]
I sing in the shadow of your wings.[k]
8My soul clings to you;[l]
your right hand upholds me.[m]

9They who seek my life will be destroyed;[n]
they will go down to the depths of the earth.[o]
10They will be given over to the sword[p]
and become food for jackals.[q]

11But the king will rejoice in God;
all who swear by God's name will praise him,[r]
while the mouths of liars will be silenced.[s]

Psalm 64

For the director of music. A psalm of David.

1Hear me, O God, as I voice my complaint;[a]
protect my life from the threat of the enemy.[b]
2Hide me from the conspiracy[c] of the wicked,[d]
from that noisy crowd of evildoers.

3They sharpen their tongues like swords[e]
and aim their words like deadly arrows.[f]

Ps. 63

1 [a]Ps 42:2; 84:2; [b]Ps 143:6
2 [c]**Ps 15:1**; 27:4; 68:24; [d]**Ex 16:7**
3 [e]Ps 36:7; 69:16; 106:45; 109:21
4 [f]Ps 104:33; 146:2; Isa 38:20; [g]**Ps 28:2**; 1Ti 2:8
5 [h]**Ps 36:8**; Mt 5:6
6 [i]Dt 6:4–9; Ps 16:7; 119:148; Mt 14:25
7 [j]Ps 27:9; 118:7; [k]**Ru 2:12**
8 [l]**Nu 32:12**; Hos 6:3; [m]**Ps 41:12**
9 [n]Ps 40:14; [o]Ps 55:15; 71:20; 95:4; 139:15
10 [p]Jer 18:21; Eze 35:5; Am 1:11; [q]La 5:18
11 [r]Isa 19:18; 45:23; 65:16; [s]**Job 5:16**; Ro 3:19

Ps. 64

1 [a]Ps 142:2; [b]Ps 140:1
2 [c]**Ex 1:10**; [d]Ps 56:6; 59:2
3 [e]**Ps 55:21**; Isa 49:2; [f]**Ps 7:13; 58:7**
4 [g]**Job 9:23**; Ps 10:8; 11:2; [h]**Ps 55:19**
5 [i]Ps 91:3; 119:110; 140:5; 141:9; [j]**Job 22:13**
8 [k]**Ps 59:12**; Pr 18:7; [l]**2Ki 19:21**; Ps 109:25; [m]**Dt 28:37**
9 [n]**Ps 40:3**; [o]Jer 51:10
10 [p]**Job 22:19**; [q]Ps 11:1; 25:20; 31:2; [r]Ps 32:11

Ps. 65

1 [a]Ps 2:6; [b]**Dt 23:21**; Ps 116:18
2 [c]Ps 86:9; Isa 66:23
3 [d]**Ps 40:12**; [e]Ps 79:9; Ro 3:25; Heb 9:14
4 [f]**Ps 33:12**; [g]**Nu 16:5**; [h]**Ps 36:8**
5 [i]**Dt 4:34; Ps 45:4**; 106:22; Isa 64:3; [j]Ps 18:46; 68:19; 85:4; [k]**Ps 48:10**; [l]Ps 107:23

4They shoot from ambush at the innocent man;[g]
they shoot at him suddenly,
without fear.[h]

5They encourage each other in evil plans,
they talk about hiding their snares;[i]
they say, "Who will see them?"[a][j]
6They plot injustice and say,
"We have devised a perfect plan!"
Surely the mind and heart of man are cunning.

7But God will shoot them with arrows;
suddenly they will be struck down.
8He will turn their own tongues against them[k]
and bring them to ruin;
all who see them will shake their heads[l] in scorn.[m]

9All mankind will fear;[n]
they will proclaim the works of God
and ponder what he has done.[o]
10Let the righteous rejoice in the LORD[p]
and take refuge in him;[q]
let all the upright in heart praise him![r]

Psalm 65

For the director of music. A psalm of David. A song.

1Praise awaits[a] you, O God, in Zion;[a]
to you our vows will be fulfilled.[b]
2O you who hear prayer,
to you all men will come.[c]
3When we were overwhelmed by sins,[d]
you forgave[b] our transgressions.[e]
4Blessed are those you choose[f]
and bring near[g] to live in your courts!
We are filled with the good things of your house,[h]
of your holy temple.

5You answer us with awesome deeds of righteousness,[i]
O God our Saviour,[j]
the hope of all the ends of the earth[k]
and of the farthest seas,[l]
6who formed the mountains[m] by your power,
having armed yourself with strength,[n]

6 [m]Am 4:13; [n]**Ps 18:1**; 93:1; Isa 51:9

[a]*5* Or *us*

[a]*1* Or *befits*; the meaning of the Hebrew for this word is uncertain. [b]*3* Or *made atonement for*

7who stilled the roaring of the seas,[o]
the roaring of their waves,
and the turmoil of the nations.[p]
8Those living far away fear your
wonders;
where morning dawns and evening
fades
you call forth songs of joy.[q]

9You care for the land and water it;[r]
you enrich it abundantly.[s]
The streams of God are filled with
water
to provide the people with corn,[t]
for so you have ordained it.[c]
10You drench its furrows
and level its ridges;
you soften it with showers[u]
and bless its crops.
11You crown the year with your
bounty,[v]
and your carts overflow with
abundance.[w]
12The grasslands of the desert
overflow;[x]
the hills are clothed with gladness.[y]
13The meadows are covered with flocks[z]
and the valleys are mantled with
corn;[a]
they shout for joy and sing.[b]

Psalm 66

For the director of music.
A song. A psalm.

1Shout with joy to God, all the earth![a]
2 Sing the glory of his name;[b]
make his praise glorious![c]
3Say to God, "How awesome are your
deeds![d]
So great is your power
that your enemies cringe[e] before
you.
4All the earth bows down[f] to you;
they sing praise[g] to you,
they sing praise to your name."
Selah

5Come and see what God has done,
how awesome his works[h] on man's
behalf!
6He turned the sea into dry land,[i]
they passed through[j] the waters on
foot—
come, let us rejoice[k] in him.
7He rules for ever[l] by his power,
his eyes watch[m] the nations—
let not the rebellious[n] rise up against
him. *Selah*

8Praise[o] our God, O peoples,
let the sound of his praise be heard;
9he has preserved our lives[p]
and kept our feet from slipping.[q]
10For you, O God, tested[r] us;
you refined us like silver.[s]
11You brought us into prison[t]
and laid burdens[u] on our backs.
12You let men ride over our heads;[v]
we went through fire and water,
but you brought us to a place of
abundance.[w]

13I will come to your temple with burnt
offerings[x]
and fulfil my vows[y] to you—
14vows my lips promised and my mouth
spoke
when I was in trouble.
15I will sacrifice fat animals to you
and an offering of rams;
I will offer bulls and goats.[z] *Selah*

16Come and listen,[a] all you who fear
God;
let me tell[b] you what he has done for
me.
17I cried out to him with my mouth;
his praise was on my tongue.
18If I had cherished sin in my heart,
the Lord would not have listened;[c]
19but God has surely listened
and heard my voice[d] in prayer.
20Praise be to God,
who has not rejected[e] my prayer
or withheld his love from me!

Psalm 67

For the director of music. With stringed
instruments. A psalm. A song.

1May God be gracious to us and bless
us
and make his face shine upon us,[a]
Selah
2that your ways may be known on
earth,
your salvation[b] among all nations.[c]

3May the peoples praise you, O God;
may all the peoples praise you.[d]
4May the nations be glad and sing for
joy,[e]
for you rule the peoples justly[f]
and guide the nations of the earth.[g]
Selah

7 [o]Ps 89:9; 93:3–4; 107:29; Mt 8:26; [p]Dt 32:41; Ps 2:1; 74:23; 139:20; Isa 17:12–13
8 [q]Ps 100:2; 107:22; 126:2; Isa 24:16; 52:9
9 [r]Lev 26:4; Ps 68:9–10; [s]Ps 104:24; [t]Ge 27:28; Dt 32:14; Ps 104:14
10 [u]Dt 32:2; 2Sa 1:21; Job 36:28; Ac 14:17
11 [v]Dt 28:12; Ps 104:28; Jn 10:10; [w]Job 36:28; Ps 147:14; Lk 6:38
12 [x]Job 28:26; Joel 2:22; [y]Ps 98:8
13 [z]Ps 144:13; Isa 30:23; Zec 8:12; [a]Ps 72:16; [b]Ps 98:8; Isa 14:8; 44:23; 49:13; 55:12

Ps. 66

1 [a]Ps 81:1; 84:8; 95:1; 98:4; 100:1
2 [b]Ps 79:9; 86:9; [c]Isa 42:8,12; 43:21
3 [d]Dt 7:21; 10:21; Ps 65:5; 106:22; 111:6; 145:6; [e]2Sa 22:45
4 [f]Ps 22:27; [g]Ps 7:17; 67:3
5 [h]ver 3; Ps 106:22
6 [i]Ge 8:1; Ex 14:22; [j]1Co 10:1; [k]Lev 23:40
7 [l]Ex 15:18; Ps 145:13; [m]Ex 3:16; Ps 11:4; [n]Nu 17:10; Ps 112:10; 140:8
8 [o]Ps 22:23
9 [p]Ps 30:3; [q]Dt 32:35; Job 12:5
10 [r]Ex 15:25; [s]Job 6:29; 28:1; Ps 12:6
11 [t]Ps 142:7; 146:7; Isa 42:7,22; 61:1; [u]Ge 3:17; Ex 1:14; Ps 38:4; Isa 10:27
12 [v]Isa 51:23; [w]Ps 18:19
13 [x]Ps 51:19; [y]Ps 22:25; 50:14; 116:14; Ecc 5:4; Jnh 2:9
15 [z]Lev 16:5; Ps 51:19
16 [a]Ps 34:11; [b]Ps 71:15,24
18 [c]Dt 1:45; 1Sa 8:18; Jas 4:3 19 [d]Ps 18:6
20 [e]Ps 22:24

Ps. 67

1 [a]Nu 6:24–26
2 [b]Isa 40:5; 52:10; 62:1; [c]Ps 98:2; Isa 62:2; Ac 10:35; Tit 2:11 3 [d]ver 5
4 [e]Ps 100:1–2; [f]Ps 9:4; 96:10–13; [g]Ps 68:32

[c]9 Or *for that is how you prepare the land*

5 May the peoples praise you, O God;
may all the peoples praise you.

6 Then the land will yield its harvest,[h]
and God, our God, will bless us.[i]
7 God will bless us,
and all the ends of the earth[j] will fear
him.[k]

Psalm 68

For the director of music. Of David.
A psalm. A song.

1 May God arise,[a] may his enemies be
scattered;[b]
may his foes flee[c] before him.
2 As smoke[d] is blown away by the wind,
may you blow them away;
as wax melts[e] before the fire,
may the wicked perish[f] before God.
3 But may the righteous be glad
and rejoice[g] before God;
may they be happy and joyful.

4 Sing to God, sing praise to his name,[h]
extol him who rides on the
clouds[a][i]—
his name is the LORD[j]—
and rejoice before him.
5 A father to the fatherless,[k] a defender
of widows,[l]
is God in his holy dwelling.[m]
6 God sets the lonely[n] in families,[b][o]
he leads forth the prisoners[p] with
singing;
but the rebellious live in a
sun-scorched land.[q]

7 When you went out[r] before your
people, O God,
when you marched through the
wasteland,[s] *Selah*
8 the earth shook,[t]
the heavens poured down rain,[u]
before God, the One of Sinai,[v]
before God, the God of Israel.[w]
9 You gave abundant showers,[x] O God;
you refreshed your weary
inheritance.
10 Your people settled in it,
and from your bounty,[y] O God, you
provided[z] for the poor.

11 The Lord announced the word,
and great was the company[a] of
those who proclaimed it:
12 "Kings and armies flee[b] in haste;
in the camps men divide the
plunder.[c]
13 Even while you sleep among the
campfires,[c][d]

the wings of ⌞my⌟ dove are sheathed
with silver,
its feathers with shining gold."
14 When the Almighty[d] scattered[e] the
kings in the land,
it was like snow fallen on Zalmon.[f]

15 The mountains of Bashan[g] are majestic
mountains;[h]
rugged are the mountains of
Bashan.
16 Why gaze in envy, O rugged
mountains,
at the mountain where God
chooses[i] to reign,
where the LORD himself will dwell
for ever?[j]
17 The chariots[k] of God are tens of
thousands
and thousands of thousands;[l]
the Lord ⌞has come⌟ from Sinai into
his sanctuary.
18 When you ascended[m] on high,[n]
you led captives[o] in your train;
you received gifts from men,[p]
even from[e] the rebellious[q]—
that you,[f] O LORD God, might dwell
there.

19 Praise be to the Lord, to God our
Saviour,[r]
who daily bears our burdens.[s] *Selah*
20 Our God is a God who saves;[t]
from the Sovereign LORD comes
escape from death.[u]

21 Surely God will crush the heads[v] of his
enemies,
the hairy crowns of those who go on
in their sins.
22 The Lord says, "I will bring them from
Bashan;
I will bring them from the depths of
the sea,[w]
23 that you may plunge your feet in the
blood of your foes,[x]
while the tongues of your dogs[y]
have their share."

24 Your procession has come into view,
O God,
the procession of my God and King
into the sanctuary.[z]
25 In front are the singers,[a] after them the
musicians;[b]

6 *h*Ge 8:22; Lev 26:4; Ps 85:12; Isa 55:10; Eze 34:27; Zec 8:12; *i*Ge 12:2
7 *j*Ps 2:8; *k*Ps 33:8
Ps. 68
1 *a*Ps 12:5; 132:8; *b*Ps 18:14; 89:10; 92:9; 144:6; *c*Nu 10:35; Isa 17:13; 21:15; 33:3
2 *d*Ps 37:20; *e*Ps 22:14; *f*Nu 10:35; Ps 9:3; 80:16
3 *g*Ps 64:10; 97:12
4 *h*2Sa 22:50; Ps 7:17; 30:4; 66:2; 96:2; 100:4; 135:3; *i*ver 33; Ex 20:21; Dt 33:26; *j*Ex 6:3; Ps 83:18
5 *k*Ps 10:14; *l*Ex 22:22; Dt 10:18; *m*Dt 26:15; Jer 25:30
6 *n*Ps 25:16; *o*Ps 113:9; *p*Ps 79:11; 102:20; 146:7; Isa 61:1; Lk 4:18; *q*Isa 35:7; 49:10; 58:11
7 *r*Ex 13:21; *s*Ps 78:40; 106:14
8 *t*2Sa 22:8; *u*Jdg 5:4; 2Sa 21:10; Ecc 11:3; *v*Dt 33:2; *w*Jdg 5:5
9 *x*Dt 32:2; Job 36:28; Eze 34:26
10 *y*Dt 28:12; *z*Ps 65:9
11 *a*Lk 2:13
12 *b*Jos 10:16; *c*Jdg 5:30
13 *d*Ge 49:14
14 *e*2Sa 22:15; *f*Jdg 9:48
15 *g*ver 22; Nu 21:33; Jer 22:20; *h*Ps 36:6
16 *i*Dt 12:5; Ps 2:6; 132:13; *j*Ps 132:14
17 *k*2Ki 2:11; Isa 66:15; Hab 3:8; *l*Da 7:10
18 *m*Ps 47:5; *n*Ps 7:7; *o*Jdg 5:12; *p*Eph 4:8*; *q*Nu 17:10
19 *r*Ps 65:5; *s*Ps 81:6
20 *t*1Sa 10:19; *u*Ps 56:13; Jer 45:5; Eze 6:8
21 *v*Ps 74:14; 110:5; Hab 3:13
22 *w*Job 36:30; Mt 18:6
23 *x*Ps 58:10; *y*1Ki 21:19; 2Ki 9:36 *24* *z*Ps 63:2
25 *a*1Ch 15:16; *b*1Ch 6:31; 2Ch 5:12; Rev 18:22

a4 Or / *prepare the way for him who rides through the deserts* **b**6 Or *the desolate in a homeland*
c13 Or *saddlebags* **d**14 Hebrew *Shaddai*
e18 Or *gifts for men, / even* **f**18 Or *they*

with them are the maidens playing
tambourines.[c]
26 Praise God in the great congregation;[d]
praise the LORD in the assembly of
Israel.[e]
27 There is the little tribe[f] of Benjamin,[g]
leading them,
there the great throng of Judah's
princes,
and there the princes of Zebulun
and of Naphtali.[h]

28 Summon your power,[i] O God;[g]
show us your strength,[j] O God, as
you have done[k] before.
29 Because of your temple at Jerusalem
kings will bring you gifts.[l]
30 Rebuke the beast[m] among the reeds,[n]
the herd of bulls[o] among the calves
of the nations.
Humbled, may it bring bars of silver.
Scatter the nations[p] who delight in
war.[q]
31 Envoys will come from Egypt;[r]
Cush[h][s] will submit herself to God.

32 Sing to God, O kingdoms of the earth,[t]
sing praise[u] to the Lord, *Selah*
33 to him who rides[v] the ancient skies
above,
who thunders[w] with mighty voice.[x]
34 Proclaim the power[y] of God,
whose majesty[z] is over Israel,
whose power is in the skies.
35 You are awesome,[a] O God, in your
sanctuary;[b]
the God of Israel gives power and
strength[c] to his people.[d]

Praise be to God![e]

Psalm 69

For the director of music. To ⌞the tune of⌟ "Lilies". Of David.

1 Save me, O God,
for the waters[a] have come up to my
neck.[b]
2 I sink in the miry depths,[c]
where there is no foothold.
I have come into the deep waters;
the floods engulf me.
3 I am worn out calling for help;[d]
my throat is parched.
My eyes fail,[e]
looking for my God.
4 Those who hate me[f] without reason[g]
outnumber the hairs of my head;
many are my enemies without cause,[h]
those who seek to destroy me.[i]
I am forced to restore
what I did not steal.

5 You know my folly,[j] O God;
my guilt is not hidden from you.[k]

6 May those who hope in you
not be disgraced because of me,
O Lord, the LORD Almighty;
may those who seek you
not be put to shame because of me,
O God of Israel.
7 For I endure scorn[l] for your sake,[m]
and shame covers my face.[n]
8 I am a stranger to my brothers,
an alien to my own mother's sons;[o]
9 for zeal for your house consumes me,[p]
and the insults of those who insult
you fall on me.[q]
10 When I weep and fast,[r]
I must endure scorn;
11 when I put on sackcloth,[s]
people make sport of me.
12 Those who sit at the gate[t] mock me,
and I am the song of the drunkards.[u]

13 But I pray to you, O LORD,
in the time of your favour;[v]
in your great love,[w] O God,
answer me with your sure salvation.
14 Rescue me from the mire,
do not let me sink;
deliver me from those who hate me,
from the deep waters.[x]
15 Do not let the floodwaters[y] engulf me
or the depths swallow me up[z]
or the pit close its mouth over me.[a]
16 Answer me, O LORD, out of the
goodness of your love;[b]
in your great mercy turn to me.
17 Do not hide your face[c] from your
servant;
answer me quickly,[d] for I am in
trouble.[e]
18 Come near and rescue me;
redeem[f] me because of my foes.

19 You know how I am scorned,[g]
disgraced and shamed;
all my enemies are before you.
20 Scorn has broken my heart
and has left me helpless;
I looked for sympathy, but there was
none,
for comforters,[h] but I found none.[i]
21 They put gall in my food
and gave me vinegar[j] for my thirst.[k]

25 [c]**Ge 31:27; Isa 5:12**
26 [d]**Ps 22:22;** Heb 2:12; [e]**Lev 19:2**
27 [f]**1Sa 9:21;** [g]**Nu 34:21;** [h]**Jdg 5:18**
28 [i]**Ex 9:16;** [j]Ps 29:11; [k]Isa 26:12; 29:23; 45:11; 60:21; 64:8
29 [l]**2Ch 9:24; 32:23**
30 [m]Isa 27:1; 51:9; Eze 29:3; [n]**Job 40:21;** [o]Ps 22:12; Isa 34:7; Jer 50:27; [p]Ps 18:14; 89:10; [q]Ps 120:7; 140:2
31 [r]Isa 19:19; 43:3; 45:14; [s]Isa 11:11; 18:1; Zep 3:10
32 [t]**Ps 46:6;** 67:4; [u]Ps 7:17
33 [v]**Dt 33:26;** [w]**Ex 9:23; Ps 29:3;** [x]Ps 29:4; Isa 30:30; 33:3; 66:6
34 [y]ver 28; [z]Ps 45:3
35 [a]**Dt 7:21;** [b]**Ge 28:17;** [c]Ps 18:1; Isa 40:29; 41:10; 50:2; [d]**Ps 29:11;** [e]Ps 28:6; 66:20; 2Co 1:3

Ps. 69

1 [a]**Ps 42:7;** [b]Ps 32:6; Jnh 2:5
2 [c]**Job 30:19**
3 [d]Ps 6:6; [e]Ps 119:82
4 [f]**Ps 25:19;** [g]Jn 15:25*; [h]**Ps 35:19;** 38:19; [i]Ps 40:14; 119:95; Isa 32:7
5 [j]Ps 38:5; [k]**Ps 44:21**
7 [l]**Ps 39:8;** [m]Jer 15:15; [n]Ps 44:15
8 [o]Job 19:13–15; Ps 31:11; 38:11; Isa 53:3; Jn 7:5
9 [p]Jn 2:17*; [q]Ps 89:50–51; Ro 15:3
10 [r]**Ps 35:13**
11 [s]**2Sa 3:31; Ps 35:13**
12 [t]**Ge 18:1; 23:10;** [u]Job 30:9
13 [v]Isa 49:8; 2Co 6:2; [w]**Ps 17:7;** 51:1
14 [x]ver 2; Ps 144:7
15 [y]Ps 124:4–5; [z]Nu 16:33; [a]Ps 28:1 *16* [b]**Ps 63:3**
17 [c]**Ps 22:24;** [d]Ps 143:7; [e]**Ps 50:15;** 66:14
18 [f]Ps 49:15 *19* [g]**Ps 22:6**
20 [h]Job 16:2; [i]Ps 142:4; Isa 63:5
21 [j]**Nu 6:3;** Mt 27:48; Mk 15:36; Lk 23:36; [k]Mt 27:34; Mk 15:23; Jn 19:28–30

[g]*28* Many Hebrew manuscripts, Septuagint and Syriac; most Hebrew manuscripts *Your God has summoned power for you*
[h]*31* That is, the upper Nile region

22May the table set before them become
a snare;
may it become retribution and[a] a
trap.[l]
23May their eyes be darkened so that
they cannot see,
and their backs be bent for ever.[m]
24Pour out your wrath[n] on them;
let your fierce anger overtake them.
25May their place be deserted;[o]
let there be no-one to dwell in their
tents.[p]
26For they persecute those you wound
and talk about the pain of those you
hurt.[q]
27Charge them with crime upon crime;[r]
do not let them share in your
salvation.[s]
28May they be blotted out of the book of
life[t]
and not be listed with the
righteous.[u]

29I am in pain and distress;
may your salvation, O God, protect
me.[v]

30I will praise God's name in song[w]
and glorify him[x] with thanksgiving.
31This will please the LORD more than an
ox,
more than a bull with its horns and
hoofs.[y]
32The poor will see and be glad[z]—
you who seek God, may your hearts
live![a]
33The LORD hears the needy[b]
and does not despise his captive
people.

34Let heaven and earth praise him,
the seas and all that move in them,[c]
35for God will save Zion[d]
and rebuild the cities of Judah.[e]
Then people will settle there and
possess it;
36 the children of his servants will
inherit it,[f]
and those who love his name will
dwell there.[g]

Psalm 70

70:1–5pp—Ps 40:13–17

For the director of music. Of David.
A petition.

1Hasten, O God, to save me;
O LORD, come quickly to help me.[a]
2May those who seek my life[b]
be put to shame and confusion;
may all who desire my ruin
be turned back in disgrace.[c]

22 [l]1Sa 28:9; **Job 18:10**
23 [m]Ro 11:9–10*
24 [n]Ps 79:6; Jer 10:25
25 [o]**Lev 26:43**; Mt 23:38; [p]Ac 1:20*
26 [q]**Job 19:22**; Zec 1:15
27 [r]Ne 4:5; [s]Ps 109:14
28 [t]Ex 32:32–33; **Lk 10:20**; [u]Eze 13:9
29 [v]**Ps 20:1**
30 [w]Ps 28:7; [x]Ps 34:3
31 [y]Ps 50:9–13; 51:16
32 [z]**Ps 34:2**; [a]Ps 22:26
33 [b]Ps 12:5
34 [c]Ps 96:11; 98:7; Isa 44:23
35 [d]Ob 17; [e]**Ezr 9:9; Ps 51:18**
36 [f]Ps 25:13; [g]**Ps 37:29**

Ps. 70

1 [a]Ps 22:19; 71:12
2 [b]Ps 35:4; [c]Ps 6:10; 35:26; 71:13; 109:29; 129:5
3 [d]**Ps 35:21**
4 [e]Ps 9:10; [f]Ps 31:6–7; 32:11; 118:24; [g]Ps 35:27
5 [h]Ps 86:1; 109:22; [i]Ps 141:1; [j]Ps 30:10; 33:20; [k]Ps 18:2; [l]Ps 119:60

Ps. 71

1 [a]**Dt 23:15**; Ru 2:12; [b]**Ps 22:5**
2 [c]**2Ki 19:16**
3 [d]Ps 18:2
4 [e]**2Ki 19:19**; [f]Ps 140:4; [g]**Ge 48:16**
5 [h]**Ps 9:18; 25:5**; [i]**Job 4:6**; Jer 17:7
6 [j]**Ps 22:10**; [k]**Job 3:16; Ps 22:9**; [l]Ps 9:1; 34:1; 52:9; 119:164; 145:2
7 [m]**Dt 28:46**; Isa 8:18; 1Co 4:9; [n]**2Sa 22:3**; Ps 61:3
8 [o]ver 15; Ps 51:15; 63:5; [p]Ps 96:6; 104:1
9 [q]**Ps 51:11**; [r]Ps 92:14; Isa 46:4; [s]**Dt 4:31; 31:6**
10 [t]Ps 3:7; [u]**Ps 10:8**; 59:3; Pr 1:18; [v]**Ex 1:10; Ps 31:13; Mt 12:14**

3May those who say to me, "Aha!
Aha!"[d]
turn back because of their shame.
4But may all who seek you[e]
rejoice and be glad[f] in you;
may those who love your salvation
always say,
"Let God be exalted!"[g]

5Yet I am poor and needy;[h]
come quickly to me,[i] O God.
You are my help[j] and my deliverer;[k]
O LORD, do not delay.[l]

Psalm 71

71:1–3pp—Ps 31:1–4

1In you, O LORD, I have taken refuge;[a]
let me never be put to shame.[b]
2Rescue me and deliver me in your
righteousness;
turn your ear[c] to me and save me.
3Be my rock of refuge,
to which I can always go;
give the command to save me,
for you are my rock and my
fortress.[d]
4Deliver[e] me, O my God, from the hand
of the wicked,[f]
from the grasp of evil and cruel
men.[g]

5For you have been my hope,[h] O
Sovereign LORD,
my confidence[i] since my youth.
6From my birth[j] I have relied on you;
you brought me forth from my
mother's womb.[k]
I will ever praise[l] you.
7I have become like a portent[m] to many,
but you are my strong refuge.[n]
8My mouth[o] is filled with your praise,
declaring your splendour[p] all day
long.

9Do not cast[q] me away when I am old;[r]
do not forsake[s] me when my
strength is gone.
10For my enemies[t] speak against me;
those who wait to kill[u] me conspire[v]
together.
11They say, "God has forsaken[w] him;
pursue him and seize him,
for no-one will rescue[x] him."
12Be not far[y] from me, O God;
come quickly, O my God, to help[z]
me.

11 [w]**Ps 9:10**; Isa 40:27; 54:7; La 5:20; Mt 27:46; [x]**Ps 7:2**
12 [y]**Ps 38:21**; [z]Ps 22:19; 38:22

[a]22 Or *snare / and their fellowship become*

13May my accusers[a] perish in shame;[b]
may those who want to harm me
be covered with scorn and disgrace.[c]

14But as for me, I shall always have
hope;[d]
I will praise you more and more.
15My mouth will tell[e] of your
righteousness,[f]
of your salvation all day long,
though I know not its measure.
16I will come and proclaim your mighty
acts,[g] O Sovereign LORD;
I will proclaim your righteousness,
yours alone.
17Since my youth, O God, you have
taught[h] me,
and to this day I declare your
marvellous deeds.[i]
18Even when I am old and grey,[j]
do not forsake me, O God,
till I declare your power[k] to the next
generation,
your might to all who are to come.[l]

19Your righteousness reaches to the
skies,[m] O God,
you who have done great things.[n]
Who, O God, is like you?[o]
20Though you have made me see
troubles,[p] many and bitter,
you will restore[q] my life again;
from the depths of the earth[r]
you will again bring me up.
21You will increase my honour[s]
and comfort[t] me once again.

22I will praise you with the harp[u]
for your faithfulness, O my God;
I will sing praise to you with the lyre,[v]
O Holy One of Israel.[w]
23My lips will shout for joy[x]
when I sing praise to you—
I, whom you have redeemed.[y]
24My tongue will tell of your righteous
acts
all day long,[z]
for those who wanted to harm me[a]
have been put to shame and
confusion.[b]

Psalm 72

Of Solomon.

1Endow the king with your justice,[a] O
God,
the royal son with your
righteousness.
2He will[a] judge your people in
righteousness,[b]
your afflicted ones with justice.
3The mountains will bring prosperity
to the people,
the hills the fruit of righteousness.
4He will defend the afflicted[c] among
the people
and save the children of the needy;[d]
he will crush the oppressor.[e]

5He will endure[b][f] as long as the sun,
as long as the moon, through all
generations.[g]
6He will be like rain[h] falling on a mown
field,
like showers watering the earth.
7In his days the righteous will flourish;[i]
prosperity will abound till the moon
is no more.

8He will rule from sea to sea
and from the River[c][j] to the ends of
the earth.[d][k]
9The desert tribes will bow before him
and his enemies will lick the dust.
10The kings of Tarshish[l] and of distant
shores[m]
will bring tribute to him;
the kings of Sheba[n] and Seba
will present him gifts.[o]
11All kings will bow down[p] to him
and all nations will serve[q] him.

12For he will deliver the needy who cry
out,
the afflicted who have no-one to
help.
13He will take pity[r] on the weak and the
needy
and save the needy from death.
14He will rescue[s] them from oppression
and violence,
for precious[t] is their blood in his
sight.

15Long may he live!
May gold from Sheba[u] be given to
him.
May people ever pray for him
and bless him all day long.[v]
16Let corn[w] abound throughout the
land;
on the tops of the hills may it sway.
Let its fruit[x] flourish like Lebanon;[y]
let it thrive like the grass of the
field.[z]

71:13 [a]Jer 18:19; [b]**Job 8:22**; Ps 25:3; [c]**Ps 70:2**
14 [d]Ps 25:3; 42:5; 130:7; 131:3
15 [e]**ver 8**; **Ps 66:16**; [f]**Ps 51:14**
16 [g]Ps 9:1; 77:12; 106:2; 118:15; 145:4
17 [h]**Dt 4:5**; **Jer 7:13**; [i]**Job 5:9**; Ps 26:7; 86:10; 96:3
18 [j]Isa 46:4; [k]**Ex 9:16**; [l]Job 8:8; Ps 22:30–31; 78:4; 145:4; Joel 1:3
19 [m]**Ps 36:5**; [n]Ps 126:2; Lk 1:49; [o]Ps 35:10; 77:13; 89:8
20 [p]Ps 25:17; [q]Ps 80:3,19; 85:4; Hos 6:2; [r]**Ps 63:9**
21 [s]Ps 18:35; [t]Ps 23:4; 86:17; Isa 12:1; 40:1–2; 49:13; 54:10
22 [u]Ps 33:2; [v]**Job 21:12**; Ps 92:3; 144:9; [w]**2Ki 19:22**
23 [x]Ps 20:5; [y]**Ex 15:13**
24 [z]**Ps 35:28**; [a]ver 13; [b]**Est 9:2**

Ps. 72

1 [a]**Dt 1:16**; **Ps 9:8**
2 [b]Isa 9:7; 11:4–5; 16:5; 32:1; 59:17; 63:1; Jer 23:5; 33:15
4 [c]**Ps 9:12**; 76:9; Isa 49:13; [d]ver 13; Isa 11:4; 29:19; 32:7; [e]**Ps 27:11**
5 [f]1Sa 13:13; [g]Ps 33:11
6 [h]**Dt 32:2**
7 [i]Ps 92:12; Pr 14:11
8 [j]**Ex 23:31**; **1Ki 4:21**; [k]Zec 9:10
10 [l]**Ge 10:4**; [m]**Est 10:1**; [n]**Ge 10:7**; [o]**1Ki 9:16**; **2Ch 9:24**
11 [p]**Ge 27:29**; [q]**Ezr 1:2**
13 [r]Isa 60:10; Joel 2:18; Lk 10:33
14 [s]Ps 69:18; Eze 13:23; 34:10; [t]1Sa 26:21
15 [u]**Ge 10:7**; [v]**Ps 35:28**
16 [w]**Ge 27:28**; Ps 4:7; [x]Isa 4:2; 27:6; Eze 34:27; [y]Ps 92:12; 104:16; [z]**Nu 22:4**; Isa 44:4; 58:11; 66:14

[a]2 Or *May he;* similarly in verses 3–11 and 17
[b]5 Septuagint; Hebrew *You will be feared*
[c]8 That is, the Euphrates
[d]8 Or *the end of the land*

17May his name endure for ever;[a]
may it continue as long as the sun.[b]

All nations will be blessed through him,
and they will call him blessed.[c]

18Praise be to the LORD God, the God of Israel,[d]
who alone does marvellous deeds.[e]
19Praise be to his glorious name[f] for ever;
may the whole earth be filled with his glory.[g]
Amen and Amen.[h]

20This concludes the prayers of David son of Jesse.[i]

BOOK III

Psalms 73–89

Psalm 73

A psalm of Asaph.

1Surely God is good to Israel,
to those who are pure in heart.[a]

2But as for me, my feet had almost slipped;[b]
I had nearly lost my foothold.[c]
3For I envied[d] the arrogant
when I saw the prosperity of the wicked.[e]

4They have no struggles;
their bodies are healthy and strong.[a]
5They are free[f] from the burdens common to man;
they are not plagued by human ills.
6Therefore pride[g] is their necklace;[h]
they clothe themselves with violence.[i]
7From their callous hearts[j] comes iniquity;[b]
the evil conceits of their minds know no limits.
8They scoff, and speak with malice;[k]
in their arrogance[l] they threaten oppression.[m]
9Their mouths lay claim to heaven,
and their tongues take possession of the earth.
10Therefore their people turn to them
and drink up waters in abundance.[c]
11They say, "How can God know?
Does the Most High have knowledge?"

17 [a]Ex 3:15; [b]Ps 89:36; [c]Ge 12:3; Lk 1:48
18 [d]1Ch 29:10; Ps 41:13; 106:48; Lk 1:68; [e]Job 5:9
19 [f]2Sa 7:26; [g]Nu 14:21; [h]Ps 41:13
20 [i]Ru 4:17

Ps. 73

1 [a]Ps 24:4; Mt 5:8
2 [b]Dt 32:35; [c]Ps 69:2; Eph 4:27
3 [d]Pr 3:31; 23:17; 24:1–2; [e]Job 9:24; 21:7; Jer 12:1; Mal 3:15
5 [f]ver 12; Eze 23:42
6 [g]Lev 26:19; [h]Ge 41:42; SS 4:9; Eze 16:11; [i]Ge 6:11; Pr 4:17
7 [j]Ps 17:10
8 [k]Ps 41:5; Eze 25:15; Col 3:8; [l]Ps 17:10; [m]Ps 10:7; 12:5
12 [n]ver 5; [o]Ps 49:6
13 [p]Job 9:29–31; 21:15; [q]Ge 44:16
14 [r]ver 5
16 [s]Ecc 8:17
17 [t]Ex 15:17; Ps 15:1; [u]Job 8:13; Php 3:19
18 [v]Dt 32:35; Ps 35:6; [w]Ps 17:13
19 [x]Dt 28:20; Pr 24:22; Isa 47:11; [y]Ge 19:15
20 [z]Job 20:8; [a]Ps 78:65; Isa 29:8; [b]Pr 12:11; 28:19
22 [c]Ps 49:10; 92:6; 94:8; [d]Ps 49:12,20; Ecc 3:18; 9:12
23 [e]Ge 48:13
24 [f]Ps 48:14; [g]1Ki 22:5
25 [h]Ps 16:2; [i]Php 3:8
26 [j]Ps 84:2; [k]Ps 31:10; 40:12; [l]Ps 18:1; [m]Dt 32:9
27 [n]Ps 34:21; [o]Lev 6:2; Jer 5:11; Hos 4:12; 9:1
28 [p]Zep 3:2; Heb 10:22; Jas 4:8; [q]Ps 9:9; [r]Ps 26:7; 40:5

12This is what the wicked are like—
always carefree,[n] they increase in wealth.[o]

13Surely in vain[p] have I kept my heart pure;
in vain have I washed my hands in innocence.[q]
14All day long I have been plagued;[r]
I have been punished every morning.

15If I had said, "I will speak thus,"
I would have betrayed your children.
16When I tried to understand[s] all this,
it was oppressive to me
17till I entered the sanctuary[t] of God;
then I understood their final destiny.[u]

18Surely you place them on slippery ground;[v]
you cast them down to ruin.[w]
19How suddenly[x] are they destroyed,
completely swept away[y] by terrors!
20As a dream[z] when one awakes,[a]
so when you arise, O Lord,
you will despise them as fantasies.[b]

21When my heart was grieved
and my spirit embittered,
22I was senseless[c] and ignorant;
I was a brute beast[d] before you.

23Yet I am always with you;
you hold me by my right hand.[e]
24You guide[f] me with your counsel,[g]
and afterwards you will take me into glory.
25Whom have I in heaven but you?[h]
And earth has nothing I desire besides you.[i]
26My flesh and my heart[j] may fail,[k]
but God is the strength[l] of my heart
and my portion[m] for ever.

27Those who are far from you will perish;[n]
you destroy all who are unfaithful[o] to you.
28But as for me, it is good to be near God.[p]
I have made the Sovereign LORD my refuge;[q]
I will tell of all your deeds.[r]

---

[a]4 With a different word division of the Hebrew; Masoretic Text *struggles at their death; / their bodies are healthy*
[b]7 Syriac (see also Septuagint); Hebrew *Their eyes bulge with fat*
[c]10 The meaning of the Hebrew for this verse is uncertain.

Psalm 74

A *maskil*[a] of Asaph.

1Why have you rejected[a] us for ever,[b] O
God?
Why does your anger smoulder
against the sheep of your
pasture?[c]
2Remember the people you purchased[d]
of old,[e]
the tribe of your inheritance,[f] whom
you redeemed[g]—
Mount Zion,[h] where you dwelt.[i]
3Turn your steps towards these
everlasting ruins,[j]
all this destruction the enemy has
brought on the sanctuary.

4Your foes roared[k] in the place where
you met with us;
they set up their standards[l] as signs.
5They behaved like men wielding axes
to cut through a thicket of trees.[m]
6They smashed all the carved[n]
panelling
with their axes and hatchets.
7They burned your sanctuary to the
ground;
they defiled[o] the dwelling-place[p] of
your Name.[q]
8They said in their hearts, "We will
crush[r] them completely!"
They burned[s] every place where
God was worshipped in the
land.
9We are given no miraculous signs;[t]
no prophets[u] are left,
and none of us knows how long this
will be.

10How long[v] will the enemy mock[w] you,
O God?
Will the foe revile[x] your name for
ever?
11Why do you hold back your hand,
your right hand?[y]
Take it from the folds of your
garment[z] and destroy them!

12But you, O God, are my king[a] from of
old;
you bring salvation[b] upon the earth.
13It was you who split open the sea[c] by
your power;
you broke the heads of the monster[d]
in the waters.
14It was you who crushed the heads of
Leviathan[e]
and gave him as food to the
creatures of the desert.[f]
15It was you who opened up springs[g]
and streams;
you dried up[h] the ever-flowing
rivers.
16The day is yours, and yours also the
night;
you established the sun and moon.[i]
17It was you who set all the boundaries[j]
of the earth;
you made both summer and
winter.[k]

18Remember how the enemy has
mocked you, O LORD,
how foolish people[l] have reviled
your name.
19Do not hand over the life of your
dove[m] to wild beasts;
do not forget the lives of your
afflicted[n] people for ever.
20Have regard for your covenant,[o]
because haunts of violence fill the
dark places[p] of the land.
21Do not let the oppressed[q] retreat in
disgrace;
may the poor and needy[r] praise
your name.

22Rise up,[s] O God, and defend your
cause;
remember how fools[t] mock you all
day long.
23Do not ignore the clamour[u] of your
adversaries,[v]
the uproar[w] of your enemies,[x] which
rises continually.

Ps. 74

1 [a]Ps 43:2; [b]Ps 44:23; [c]Ps 79:13; 95:7; 100:3
2 [d]Ex 15:16; 1Co 6:20; [e]Dt 32:7; [f]Ex 34:9; [g]Ex 15:13; Isa 48:20; [h]Ps 2:6; [i]Ps 43:3; 68:16; Isa 46:13; Joel 3:17,21; Ob 17
3 [j]Isa 44:26; 52:9
4 [k]La 2:7; [l]Nu 2:2; Jer 4:6
5 [m]Jer 46:22
6 [n]1Ki 6:18
7 [o]Lev 20:3; Ac 21:28; [p]Lev 15:31; [q]Ps 75:1
8 [r]Ps 94:5; [s]2Ki 25:9; 2Ch 36:19; Jer 21:10; 34:22; 52:13
9 [t]Ex 4:17; 10:1; [u]1Sa 3:1
10 [v]Ps 6:3; 79:5; 80:4; [w]ver 22; [x]Ps 44:16
11 [y]Ex 15:6; [z]Ne 5:13; Eze 5:3
12 [a]Ps 2:6; 24:7; 68:24; [b]Ps 27:1
13 [c]Ex 14:21; [d]Isa 27:1; 51:9; Eze 29:3; 32:2
14 [e]Job 3:8; [f]Isa 13:21; 23:13; 34:14; Jer 50:39
15 [g]Ex 17:6; Nu 20:11; [h]Ex 14:29; Jos 2:10
16 [i]Ge 1:16; Ps 136:7–9
17 [j]Dt 32:8; Ac 17:26; [k]Ge 8:22
18 [l]Dt 32:6
19 [m]Ge 8:8; Isa 59:11; [n]Ps 9:18
20 [o]Ge 6:18; [p]Job 34:22
21 [q]Ps 9:9; 10:18; 103:6; Isa 58:10; [r]Ps 35:10
22 [s]Ps 17:13; [t]Ps 53:1
23 [u]Isa 31:4; [v]Ps 65:7; [w]Ps 46:6; [x]Nu 25:17

Psalm 75

For the director of music. ⌞To the tune of⌟ "Do Not Destroy". A psalm of Asaph. A song.

1We give thanks to you, O God,
we give thanks, for your Name is
near;[a]
men tell of your wonderful deeds.[b]

2You say, "I choose the appointed
time;[c]
it is I who judge uprightly.[d]
3When the earth and all its people
quake,[e]
it is I who hold its pillars[f] firm. *Selah*
4To the arrogant[g] I say, 'Boast no
more,'[h]
and to the wicked, 'Do not lift up
your horns.[i]
5Do not lift your horns against heaven;
do not speak with outstretched
neck.[j]'"

Ps. 75

1 [a]Ps 145:18; [b]Jos 3:5; Ps 44:1; 71:16; 77:12; 105:2; 107:8,15; 145:5,12
2 [c]Ex 13:10; [d]Ps 7:11
3 [e]Isa 24:19; [f]1Sa 2:8; 2Sa 22:8
4 [g]Ps 5:5; [h]1Sa 2:3; [i]Zec 1:21
5 [j]Job 15:25

[a]Title: Probably a literary or musical term

6No-one from the east or the west
or from the desert can exalt a man.
7But it is God who judges:[k]
He brings one down, he exalts
another.[l]
8In the hand of the LORD is a cup
full of foaming wine mixed[m] with
spices;
he pours it out, and all the wicked of
the earth
drink it down to its very dregs.[n]

9As for me, I will declare[o] this for ever;
I will sing[p] praise to the God of
Jacob.[q]
10I will cut off the horns of all the
wicked,
but the horns of the righteous shall
be lifted up.[r]

Psalm 76

For the director of music. With stringed instruments. A psalm of Asaph. A song.

1In Judah God is known;
his name is great[a] in Israel.
2His tent is in Salem,[b]
his dwelling-place in Zion.[c]
3There he broke the flashing arrows,[d]
the shields and the swords, the
weapons of war.[e] *Selah*

4You are resplendent with light,[f]
more majestic than mountains rich
with game.
5Valiant men[g] lie plundered,
they sleep their last sleep;[h]
not one of the warriors
can lift his hands.
6At your rebuke,[i] O God of Jacob,
both horse and chariot[j] lie still.
7You alone are to be feared.[k]
Who can stand[l] before you when
you are angry?[m]
8From heaven you pronounced
judgment,
and the land feared[n] and was
quiet—
9when you, O God, rose up to judge,[o]
to save all the afflicted[p] of the land.
Selah
10Surely your wrath against men brings
you praise,[q]
and the survivors of your wrath are
restrained.[a]

11Make vows to the LORD your God and
fulfil them;[r]
let all the neighbouring lands
bring gifts[s] to the One to be feared.
12He breaks the spirit of rulers;
he is feared by the kings of the earth.

7 [k]Ge 16:5; Ps 50:6; 58:11; Rev 18:8; [l]1Sa 2:7; **Job 5:11**; Ps 147:6; Eze 21:26; Da 2:21
8 [m]Pr 23:30; [n]Isa 51:17; Jer 25:15; Zec 12:2
9 [o]Ps 40:10; [p]Ps 108:1; [q]**Ge 24:12**; Ps 76:6
10 [r]Ps 89:17; 92:10; 112:9; 148:14

Ps. 76

1 [a]Ps 99:3
2 [b]**Ge 14:18**; Heb 7:1; [c]**2Sa 5:7**; Ps 2:6
3 [d]Eze 39:9; [e]Ps 46:9
4 [f]**Ps 36:9**
5 [g]**Jdg 20:44**; [h]**Ps 13:3**; **Mt 9:24**
6 [i]**Ps 50:21**; [j]**Ex 15:1**
7 [k]**1Ch 16:25**; [l]**Ezr 9:15**; Rev 6:17; [m]Ps 2:5; Na 1:6
8 [n]**1Ch 16:30**; Eze 38:20
9 [o]**Ps 9:8**; 58:11; 74:22; 82:8; 96:13; [p]**Ps 72:4**
10 [q]**Ex 9:16**; Ro 9:17
11 [r]**Lev 22:18**; **Ps 50:14**; Ecc 5:4–5; [s]**2Ch 32:23**

Ps. 77

1 [a]**1Ki 8:52**
2 [b]**Ge 32:7**; **2Sa 22:7**; **Ps 118:5**; [c]Ps 6:6; 22:2; 88:1; [d]**Ex 9:29**; **Job 11:13**; [e]**Ge 37:35**; Mt 2:18
3 [f]Ps 78:35; [g]Ex 2:23; **Ps 6:6**; Jer 45:3; [h]**Ps 6:2**
4 [i]**Ps 39:2**
5 [j]Dt 32:7; Ps 44:1; 143:5; Ecc 7:10
7 [k]**1Ch 28:9**; [l]Ps 85:1; 102:13; 106:4
8 [m]**Ps 6:4**; 90:14; [n]2Pe 3:9
9 [o]Ps 25:6; 40:11; 51:1; [p]Isa 49:15
10 [q]**Ex 15:6**
11 [r]**Ne 9:17**
12 [s]**Ge 24:63**; [t]Ps 143:5
13 [u]**Ex 15:11**; **Ps 71:19**; 86:8
14 [v]**Ex 3:20**; **34:10**
15 [w]**Ex 6:6**
16 [x]Ex 14:21,28; Isa 50:2; Hab 3:8; [y]Ps 114:4; Hab 3:10

Psalm 77

For the director of music. For Jeduthun. Of Asaph. A psalm.

1I cried out to God[a] for help;
I cried out to God to hear me.
2When I was in distress,[b] I sought the
Lord;
at night[c] I stretched out untiring
hands[d]
and my soul refused to be
comforted.[e]

3I remembered[f] you, O God, and I
groaned;[g]
I mused, and my spirit grew faint.[h]
Selah
4You kept my eyes from closing;
I was too troubled to speak.[i]
5I thought about the former days,[j]
the years of long ago;
6I remembered my songs in the night.
My heart mused and my spirit
enquired:

7"Will the LORD reject for ever?[k]
Will he never show his favour[l]
again?
8Has his unfailing love[m] vanished for
ever?
Has his promise[n] failed for all time?
9Has God forgotten to be merciful?[o]
Has he in anger withheld his
compassion?[p]" *Selah*
10Then I thought, "To this I will appeal:
the years of the right hand[q] of the
Most High."
11I will remember the deeds of the LORD;
yes, I will remember your miracles[r]
of long ago.
12I will meditate[s] on all your works
and consider all your mighty deeds.[t]

13Your ways, O God, are holy.
What god is so great as our God?[u]
14You are the God who performs
miracles;[v]
you display your power among the
peoples.
15With your mighty arm you redeemed
your people,[w]
the descendants of Jacob and
Joseph. *Selah*

16The waters[x] saw you, O God,
the waters saw you and writhed;[y]
the very depths were convulsed.

[a]10 Or *Surely the wrath of men brings you praise, / and with the remainder of wrath you arm yourself*

17The clouds poured down water,[z]
the skies resounded with thunder;[a]
your arrows[b] flashed back and forth.
18Your thunder was heard in the whirlwind,[c]
your lightning[d] lit up the world;
the earth trembled and quaked.[e]
19Your path[f] led through the sea,[g]
your way through the mighty waters,
though your footprints were not seen.

20You led your people[h] like a flock[i]
by the hand of Moses and Aaron.[j]

Psalm 78

A *maskil*[a] of Asaph.

1O my people, hear my teaching;[a]
listen to the words of my mouth.
2I will open my mouth in parables,[b]
I will utter hidden things, things from of old—
3what we have heard and known,
what our fathers have told us.[c]
4We will not hide them from their children;[d]
we will tell the next generation[e]
the praiseworthy deeds[f] of the LORD,
his power, and the wonders[g] he has done.
5He decreed statutes[h] for Jacob[i]
and established the law in Israel,
which he commanded our forefathers
to teach their children,
6so that the next generation would know them,
even the children yet to be born,[j]
and they in turn would tell their children.
7Then they would put their trust in God
and would not forget[k] his deeds
but would keep his commands.[l]
8They would not be like their forefathers[m]—
a stubborn[n] and rebellious[o] generation,
whose hearts were not loyal to God,
whose spirits were not faithful to him.

9The men of Ephraim, though armed with bows,[p]
turned back on the day of battle;[q]
10they did not keep God's covenant[r]
and refused to live by his law.[s]
11They forgot what he had done,[t]
the wonders he had shown them.
12He did miracles[u] in the sight of their fathers
in the land of Egypt,[v] in the region of Zoan.[w]
13He divided the sea[x] and led them through;
he made the water stand firm like a wall.[y]
14He guided them with the cloud by day
and with light from the fire all night.[z]
15He split the rocks[a] in the desert
and gave them water as abundant as the seas;
16he brought streams out of a rocky crag
and made water flow down like rivers.

17But they continued to sin[b] against him,
rebelling in the desert against the Most High.
18They wilfully put God to the test[c]
by demanding the food they craved.[d]
19They spoke against God,[e] saying,
"Can God spread a table in the desert?
20When he struck the rock, water gushed out,[f]
and streams flowed abundantly.
But can he also give us food?
Can he supply meat[g] for his people?"
21When the LORD heard them, he was very angry;
his fire broke out[h] against Jacob,
and his wrath rose against Israel,
22for they did not believe in God
or trust[i] in his deliverance.
23Yet he gave a command to the skies above
and opened the doors of the heavens;[j]
24he rained down manna[k] for the people to eat,
he gave them the grain of heaven.
25Men ate the bread of angels;
he sent them all the food they could eat.
26He let loose the east wind[l] from the heavens
and led forth the south wind by his power.
27He rained meat down on them like dust,
flying birds[m] like sand on the seashore.
28He made them come down inside their camp,
all around their tents.
29They ate till they had more than enough,[n]

17 [z]Jdg 5:4; [a]Ex 9:23; Ps 29:3; [b]Dt 32:23
18 [c]Ps 55:8; [d]2Sa 22:13; [e]Jdg 5:4
19 [f]Ex 14:22; [g]Job 9:8
20 [h]Ex 13:21; [i]Ps 78:52; Isa 63:11; [j]Ex 4:16; Nu 33:1

Ps. 78

1 [a]Isa 51:4; 55:3
2 [b]Ps 49:4; Mt 13:35*
3 [c]Jdg 6:13
4 [d]Dt 11:19; [e]Dt 32:7; Ps 71:18; [f]Ps 26:7; 71:17; [g]Job 5:9
5 [h]Ps 19:7; 81:5; [i]Ps 147:19
6 [j]Ps 22:31
7 [k]Dt 6:12; [l]Dt 5:29
8 [m]2Ch 30:7; [n]Ex 32:9; [o]Ex 23:21; Dt 21:18; Isa 30:9; 65:2
9 [p]ver 57; 1Ch 12:2; Hos 7:16; [q]Jdg 20:39
10 [r]Jos 7:11; 2Ki 17:15; [s]Ex 16:28; Jer 11:8
11 [t]Ps 106:13
12 [u]Ne 9:17; Ps 106:22; [v]Ex 11:9; [w]Nu 13:22
13 [x]Ex 14:21; Ps 66:6; 136:13; [y]Ex 14:22; 15:8
14 [z]Ex 13:21; Ps 105:39
15 [a]Nu 20:11; 1Co 10:4
17 [b]ver 32,40; Dt 9:22; Isa 30:1; 63:10; Heb 3:16
18 [c]Ex 17:2; 1Co 10:9; [d]Ex 15:24; Nu 11:4
19 [e]Nu 21:5
20 [f]Nu 20:11; Isa 35:6; [g]Nu 11:18
21 [h]Nu 11:1
22 [i]Dt 1:32; Heb 3:19
23 [j]Ge 7:11; 2Ki 7:2
24 [k]Ex 16:4; Jn 6:31*
26 [l]Nu 11:31
27 [m]Ex 16:13; Nu 11:31
29 [n]Nu 11:20

[a]Title: Probably a literary or musical term

for he had given them what they
craved.
30But before they turned from the food
they craved,
even while it was still in their
mouths,[o]
31God's anger rose against them;
he put to death the sturdiest[p] among
them,
cutting down the young men of
Israel.

32In spite of all this, they kept on
sinning;[q]
in spite of his wonders,[r] they did not
believe.[s]
33So he ended their days in futility[t]
and their years in terror.
34Whenever God slew them, they
would seek[u] him;
they eagerly turned to him again.
35They remembered that God was their
Rock,[v]
that God Most High was their
Redeemer.[w]
36But then they would flatter him with
their mouths,[x]
lying to him with their tongues;
37their hearts were not loyal[y] to him,
they were not faithful to his
covenant.
38Yet he was merciful;[z]
he forgave[a] their iniquities[b]
and did not destroy them.
Time after time he restrained his
anger[c]
and did not stir up his full wrath.
39He remembered that they were but
flesh,[d]
a passing breeze[e] that does not
return.

40How often they rebelled[f] against him
in the desert[g]
and grieved him[h] in the wasteland!
41Again and again they put God to the
test;[i]
they vexed the Holy One of Israel.[j]
42They did not remember[k] his power—
the day he redeemed them from the
oppressor,[l]
43the day he displayed his miraculous
signs[m] in Egypt,
his wonders[n] in the region of Zoan.
44He turned their rivers to blood;[o]
they could not drink from their
streams.
45He sent swarms of flies[p] that devoured
them,
and frogs[q] that devastated them.
46He gave their crops to the
grasshopper,[r]
their produce to the locust.[s]
47He destroyed their vines with hail[t]
and their sycamore-figs with sleet.
48He gave over their cattle to the hail,
their livestock[u] to bolts of lightning.
49He unleashed against them his hot
anger,[v]
his wrath, indignation and
hostility—
a band of destroying angels.[w]
50He prepared a path for his anger;
he did not spare them from death
but gave them over to the plague.
51He struck down all the firstborn of
Egypt,[x]
the firstfruits of manhood in the
tents of Ham.[y]
52But he brought his people out like a
flock;[z]
he led them like sheep through the
desert.
53He guided them safely, so they were
unafraid;
but the sea engulfed[a] their enemies.[b]
54Thus he brought them to the border of
his holy land,
to the hill country his right hand[c]
had taken.
55He drove out nations[d] before them
and allotted their lands to them as
an inheritance;[e]
he settled the tribes of Israel in their
homes.

56But they put God to the test
and rebelled against the Most High;
they did not keep his statutes.
57Like their fathers[f] they were disloyal
and faithless,
as unreliable as a faulty bow.[g]
58They angered him[h] with their high
places;[i]
they aroused his jealousy with their
idols.[j]
59When God heard[k] them, he was very
angry;[l]
he rejected Israel[m] completely.
60He abandoned the tabernacle of
Shiloh,[n]
the tent he had set up among men.[o]
61He sent ⌊the ark of⌋ his might[p] into
captivity,[q]
his splendour into the hands of the
enemy.
62He gave his people over to the sword;[r]
he was very angry with his
inheritance.[s]
63Fire consumed[t] their young men,
and their maidens had no wedding
songs;[u]
64their priests were put to the sword,[v]
and their widows could not weep.

65Then the Lord awoke as from sleep,[w]

30 [o]**Nu 11:33**
31 [p]Isa 10:16
32 [q]**ver 17**; [r]ver 11; [s]ver 22
33 [t]Nu 14:29,35
34 [u]**Dt 4:29**; Hos 5:15
35 [v]**Ge 49:24**; [w]**Dt 9:26**
36 [x]Eze 33:31
37 [y]ver 8; Ac 8:21
38 [z]**Ex 34:6**; [a]Isa 1:25; 27:9; 48:10; Da 11:35; [b]Ps 25:11; 85:2; [c]**Job 9:13**; **Isa 30:18**
39 [d]**Ge 6:3**; **Isa 29:5**; [e]**Job 7:7**; Jas 4:14
40 [f]**Ex 23:21**; [g]Ps 95:8; 106:14; [h]Eph 4:30
41 [i]Ex 17:2; [j]**2Ki 19:22**; Ps 71:22; 89:18
42 [k]**Jdg 3:7**; **Ne 9:17**; [l]**Ps 27:11**
43 [m]Ex 10:1; [n]**Ex 3:20**
44 [o]Ex 7:20–21; Ps 105:29
45 [p]Ex 8:24; Ps 105:31; [q]**Ex 8:2,6**
46 [r]Na 3:15; [s]**Ex 10:13**
47 [t]Ex 9:23; Ps 105:32; 147:17
48 [u]Ex 9:25
49 [v]Ex 15:7; [w]**Ge 19:13**; 1Co 10:10
51 [x]**Ex 12:12**; Ps 135:8; [y]Ps 105:23; 106:22
52 [z]**Job 21:11**; **Ps 28:9**; 77:20
53 [a]**Ex 14:28**; [b]Ex 15:7; Ps 106:10
54 [c]Ps 44:3
55 [d]Ps 44:2; [e]**Dt 1:38**; **Jos 13:7**; Ac 13:19
57 [f]**2Ch 30:7**; Eze 20:27; [g]**ver 9**
58 [h]**Jdg 2:12**; [i]**Lev 26:30**; [j]Ex 20:4; **Dt 5:8**; 32:21
59 [k]Ps 55:19; [l]**Lev 26:28**; **Nu 32:14**; [m]**Dt 32:19**
60 [n]**Jos 18:1**; [o]Eze 8:6
61 [p]Ps 132:8; [q]**1Sa 4:17**
62 [r]**Dt 28:25**; [s]**1Sa 10:1**
63 [t]**Nu 11:1**; [u]**1Ki 4:32**; Jer 7:34; 16:9; 25:10
64 [v]1Sa 4:17
65 [w]Ps 44:23

as a man wakes from the stupor of
wine.
66He beat back his enemies;
he put them to everlasting shame.[x]
67Then he rejected the tents of Joseph,
he did not choose the tribe of
Ephraim;[y]
68but he chose the tribe of Judah,[z]
Mount Zion,[a] which he loved.
69He built his sanctuary[b] like the
heights,
like the earth that he established for
ever.
70He chose David[c] his servant
and took him from the sheep pens;
71from tending the sheep[d] he brought
him
to be the shepherd[e] of his people
Jacob,
of Israel his inheritance.
72And David shepherded them with
integrity of heart;[f]
with skilful hands he led them.

Psalm 79

A psalm of Asaph.

1O God, the nations have invaded your
inheritance;[a]
they have defiled[b] your holy
temple,
they have reduced Jerusalem to
rubble.[c]
2They have given the dead bodies of
your servants
as food to the birds of the air,[d]
the flesh of your saints to the beasts
of the earth.[e]
3They have poured out blood like water
all around Jerusalem,
and there is no-one to bury[f] the
dead.[g]
4We are objects of reproach to our
neighbours,
of scorn[h] and derision to those
around us.[i]

5How long,[j] O LORD? Will you be
angry[k] for ever?
How long will your jealousy burn
like fire?[l]
6Pour out your wrath[m] on the nations
that do not acknowledge[n] you,
on the kingdoms
that do not call on your name;[o]
7for they have devoured[p] Jacob
and destroyed his homeland.
8Do not hold against us the sins of the
fathers;[q]
may your mercy come quickly to
meet us,
for we are in desperate need.[r]

9Help us,[s] O God our Saviour,
for the glory of your name;
deliver us and forgive our sins
for your name's sake.[t]
10Why should the nations say,
"Where is their God?"[u]
Before our eyes, make known among
the nations
that you avenge[v] the outpoured
blood[w] of your servants.
11May the groans of the prisoners come
before you;
by the strength of your arm
preserve those condemned to die.

12Pay back into the laps[x] of our
neighbours seven times[y]
the reproach they have hurled at
you, O Lord.
13Then we your people, the sheep of
your pasture,[z]
will praise you for ever;[a]
from generation to generation
we will recount your praise.

Psalm 80

For the director of music. To ⌊the tune of⌋ "The Lilies of the Covenant". Of Asaph. A psalm.

1Hear us, O Shepherd of Israel,
you who lead Joseph like a flock;[a]
you who sit enthroned between the
cherubim,[b] shine forth
2 before Ephraim, Benjamin and
Manasseh.[c]
Awaken[d] your might;
come and save us.[e]

3Restore[f] us,[g] O God;
make your face shine upon us,
that we may be saved.[h]

4O LORD God Almighty,
how long[i] will your anger smoulder[j]
against the prayers of your people?
5You have fed them with the bread of
tears;[k]
you have made them drink tears by
the bowlful.[l]
6You have made us a source of
contention to our neighbours,
and our enemies mock us.[m]

7Restore us, O God Almighty;
make your face shine upon us,
that we may be saved.[n]

8You brought a vine[o] out of Egypt;
you drove out[p] the nations and
planted[q] it.

---

66 [x]1Sa 5:6
67 [y]Jer 7:15; Hos 9:13; 12:1
68 [z]Nu 1:7; Ps 108:8; [a]**Ex 15:17; Ps 68:16**
69 [b]**Ps 15:1**
70 [c]**1Sa 16:1**
71 [d]**Ge 37:2**; [e]**Ps 28:9**
72 [f]**Ge 17:1**

Ps. 79

1 [a]**Ex 34:9**; [b]**Lev 20:3**; [c]**2Ki 25:9; Ne 4:2; Isa 6:11**
2 [d]Rev 19:17–18; [e]**Dt 28:26**; Jer 7:33
3 [f]Jer 25:33; Rev 11:9; [g]Jer 16:4
4 [h]**Ps 39:8; Eze 5:14**; [i]Ps 44:13; 80:6
5 [j]**Ps 74:10**; [k]Ps 74:1; 85:5; [l]**Dt 29:20**; Ps 89:46; Zep 3:8
6 [m]**Ps 2:5**; 69:24; 110:5; Rev 16:1; [n]Ps 147:20; Jer 10:25; [o]**Ps 14:4**
7 [p]Isa 9:12; Jer 10:25
8 [q]**Ge 9:25**; Jer 44:21; [r]Ps 116:6; 142:6
9 [s]**2Ch 14:11**; [t]Ps 25:11; 31:3; Jer 14:7
10 [u]**Ps 42:3**; [v]Ps 94:1; **Rev 6:10**; [w]ver 3
12 [x]Isa 65:6; Jer 32:18; [y]**Ge 4:15**
13 [z]**Ps 74:1**; [a]Ps 44:8

Ps. 80

1 [a]Ps 77:20; [b]**Ex 25:22**
2 [c]Nu 2:18–24; [d]**Ps 35:23**; [e]Ps 54:1; 69:1; 71:2; 109:26; 116:4; 119:94
3 [f]**Ps 71:20**; 85:4; Jer 31:18; La 5:21; [g]**Nu 6:25**; [h]ver 7,19
4 [i]**Ps 74:10**; [j]**Dt 29:20**
5 [k]**Job 3:24**; [l]Isa 30:20
6 [m]**Ps 79:4**
7 [n]ver 3
8 [o]Isa 5:1–2; Jer 2:21; Mt 21:33–41; [p]Ex 23:28–30; **Jos 13:6**; Ac 7:45; [q]**Ex 15:17**

[9]You cleared the ground for it,
and it took root and filled the land.
[10]The mountains were covered with its shade,
the mighty cedars with its branches.
[11]It sent out its boughs to the Sea,[a]
its shoots as far as the River.[b] [r]

[12]Why have you broken down its walls[s]
so that all who pass by pick its grapes?
[13]Boars from the forest ravage[t] it
and the creatures of the field feed on it.
[14]Return to us, O God Almighty!
Look down from heaven and see![u]
Watch over this vine,
15 the root your right hand has planted,
the son[c] you have raised up for yourself.

[16]Your vine is cut down, it is burned with fire;[v]
at your rebuke[w] your people perish.
[17]Let your hand rest on the man at your right hand,
the son of man[x] you have raised up for yourself.
[18]Then we will not turn away from you;
revive[y] us, and we will call on your name.

[19]Restore us, O LORD God Almighty;
make your face shine upon us,
that we may be saved.

Psalm 81

For the director of music. According to *gittith*.[a] Of Asaph.

[1]Sing for joy to God our strength;
shout aloud to the God of Jacob![a]
[2]Begin the music, strike the tambourine,[b]
play the melodious harp[c] and lyre.[d]
[3]Sound the ram's horn[e] at the New Moon,[f]
and when the moon is full, on the day of our Feast;
[4]this is a decree for Israel,
an ordinance of the God of Jacob.[g]
[5]He established it as a statute for Joseph
when he went out against Egypt,[h]
where we heard a language we did not understand.[b] [i]

[6]He says, "I removed the burden[j] from their shoulders;[k]
their hands were set free from the basket.

11 [r]Ps 72:8
12 [s]Ps 89:40; Isa 5:5; 30:13; Jer 39:8
13 [t]Jer 5:6
14 [u]**Dt 26:15**
16 [v]Ps 79:1; [w]**Dt 28:20**
17 [x]**Job 25:6**
18 [y]Ps 85:6; Isa 57:15; Hos 6:2

Ps. 81

1 [a]**Ps 66:1**
2 [b]**Ex 15:20**; [c]Ps 92:3; [d]**Job 21:12**
3 [e]**Ex 19:13**; [f]**Ne 10:33**
4 [g]ver 1
5 [h]**Ex 11:4**; [i]Ps 114:1
6 [j]**Ex 1:14**; [k]Isa 9:4; 52:2
7 [l]**Ex 2:23**; [m]Ex 19:19; [n]**Ex 17:7; Dt 33:8**
8 [o]Ps 50:7; 78:1
9 [p]**Ex 20:3**
10 [q]**Ex 6:6; 13:3; 29:46**; [r]Eze 2:8; [s]Ps 107:9
11 [t]Ex 32:1–6
12 [u]Eze 20:25; Ac 7:42; Ro 1:24
13 [v]**Dt 5:29**
14 [w]Ps 47:3; [x]Am 1:8
15 [y]**2Sa 22:45**
16 [z]**Dt 32:14**

Ps. 82

1 [a]Ps 7:8; 58:11; Isa 3:13; 66:16; Joel 3:12; [b]**Job 21:22**
2 [c]Dt 1:17; [d]Ps 58:1–2; Pr 18:5
3 [e]**Dt 24:17**; [f]Ps 140:12; Jer 5:28; 22:16

[7]In your distress you called[l] and I rescued you,
I answered[m] you out of a thundercloud;
I tested you at the waters of Meribah.[n] *Selah*

[8]"Hear, O my people,[o] and I will warn you—
if you would but listen to me, O Israel!
[9]You shall have no foreign god[p] among you;
you shall not bow down to an alien god.
[10]I am the LORD your God,
who brought you up out of Egypt.[q]
Open[r] wide your mouth and I will fill[s] it.

[11]"But my people would not listen to me;
Israel would not submit to me.[t]
[12]So I gave them over[u] to their stubborn hearts
to follow their own devices.

[13]"If my people would but listen to me,[v]
if Israel would follow my ways,
[14]how quickly would I subdue[w] their enemies
and turn my hand against[x] their foes!
[15]Those who hate the LORD would cringe[y] before him,
and their punishment would last for ever.
[16]But you would be fed with the finest of wheat;[z]
with honey from the rock I would satisfy you."

Psalm 82

A psalm of Asaph.

[1]God presides in the great assembly;
he gives judgment[a] among the "gods":[b]

[2]"How long will you[a] defend the unjust
and show partiality[c] to the wicked?[d] *Selah*
[3]Defend the cause of the weak and fatherless;[e]
maintain the rights of the poor[f] and oppressed.

---

[a]*11* Probably the Mediterranean
[b]*11* That is, the Euphrates [c]*15* Or *branch*
[a]Title: Probably a musical term
[b]*5* Or / *and we heard a voice we had not known*
[a]*2* The Hebrew is plural.

4Rescue the weak and needy;
deliver them from the hand of the wicked.

5"They know nothing, they understand nothing.[g]
They walk about in darkness;[h]
all the foundations[i] of the earth are shaken.

6"I said, 'You are "gods";[j]
you are all sons of the Most High.'
7But you will die[k] like mere men;
you will fall like every other ruler."

8Rise up,[l] O God, judge[m] the earth,
for all the nations are your inheritance.[n]

Psalm 83

A song. A psalm of Asaph.

1O God, do not keep silent;[a]
be not quiet, O God, be not still.
2See how your enemies are astir,[b]
how your foes rear their heads.[c]
3With cunning they conspire[d] against your people;
they plot against those you cherish.[e]
4"Come," they say, "let us destroy[f] them as a nation,[g]
that the name of Israel be remembered[h] no more."

5With one mind they plot together;[i]
they form an alliance against you—
6the tents of Edom[j] and the Ishmaelites,
of Moab[k] and the Hagrites,[l]
7Gebal,[a][m] Ammon[n] and Amalek,[o]
Philistia,[p] with the people of Tyre.[q]
8Even Assyria[r] has joined them
to lend strength to the descendants of Lot.[s] *Selah*

9Do to them as you did to Midian,[t]
as you did to Sisera[u] and Jabin[v] at the river Kishon,[w]
10who perished at Endor[x]
and became like refuse[y] on the ground.
11Make their nobles like Oreb and Zeeb,[z]
all their princes like Zebah and Zalmunna,[a]
12who said, "Let us take possession[b]
of the pasture-lands of God."

13Make them like tumble-weed, O my God,
like chaff[c] before the wind.

5 [g]**Ps 14:4; 53:2;** [h]Job 30:26; Isa 5:30; 8:21–22; 9:2; 59:9; 60:2; Jer 13:16; 23:12; La 3:2; [i]**Jdg 5:4; Ps 11:3**
6 [j]Jn 10:34*
7 [k]Ps 49:12; Eze 31:14
8 [l]Ps 12:5; [m]**Ps 76:9;** [n]Ps 2:8

Ps. 83

1 [a]Ps 28:1; 35:22; Isa 42:14; 57:11; 62:1; 64:12
2 [b]Ps 2:1; Isa 17:12; [c]Jdg 8:28
3 [d]**Ex 1:10; Ps 31:13;** [e]Ps 17:14
4 [f]**Est 3:6;** [g]Jer 33:24; [h]Jer 11:19
5 [i]Ps 2:2
6 [j]Ps 137:7; Isa 34:5; Jer 49:7; Am 1:11; [k]2Ch 20:1; [l]**Ge 25:16**
7 [m]**Jos 13:5;** [n]Ge 19:38; [o]**Ge 14:7; Ex 17:14;** [p]Ex 15:14; [q]Isa 23:3; Eze 27:3
8 [r]**Ge 10:11;** [s]**Dt 2:9**
9 [t]**Ge 25:2;** Jdg 7:1–23; [u]**Jdg 4:2;** [v]**Jos 11:1;** [w]**Jdg 4:23–24**
10 [x]**1Sa 28:7;** [y]**2Ki 9:37;** Isa 5:25; Jer 8:2; 9:22; 16:4; 25:33; Zep 1:17
11 [z]Jdg 7:25; [a]**Jdg 8:5**
12 [b]2Ch 20:11; Eze 35:10
13 [c]**Job 13:25**
14 [d]Dt 32:22; Isa 9:18
15 [e]**Ps 50:3;** [f]**Job 9:17**
16 [g]**Ps 34:5;** 109:29; 132:18
17 [h]**2Ki 19:26;** [i]**Ps 35:4**
18 [j]**Ps 68:4;** [k]Ps 7:8; 18:13; [l]**Job 34:29**

Ps. 84

1 [a]**Dt 33:27;** Ps 27:4; 43:3; 90:1; 132:5
2 [b]**Job 19:27;** [c]**Jos 3:10**
3 [d]**Ps 43:4;** [e]Jer 44:11; [f]Ps 2:6; [g]Ps 5:2
5 [h]Ps 81:1; [i]Jer 31:6
6 [j]**Job 38:26;** [k]Joel 2:23

14As fire consumes the forest
or a flame sets the mountains ablaze,[d]
15so pursue them with your tempest[e]
and terrify them with your storm.[f]
16Cover their faces with shame[g]
so that men will seek your name, O LORD.

17May they ever be ashamed and dismayed;[h]
may they perish in disgrace.[i]
18Let them know that you, whose name is the LORD[j]—
that you alone are the Most High[k]
over all the earth.[l]

Psalm 84

For the director of music. According to *gittith*.[a] Of the Sons of Korah. A psalm.

1How lovely is your dwelling-place,[a]
O LORD Almighty!
2My soul yearns,[b] even faints,
for the courts of the LORD;
my heart and my flesh cry out
for the living God.[c]

3Even the sparrow has found a home,
and the swallow a nest for herself,
where she may have her young—
a place near your altar,[d]
O LORD Almighty,[e] my King[f] and my God.[g]
4Blessed are those who dwell in your house;
they are ever praising you. *Selah*

5Blessed are those whose strength[h] is in you,
who have set their hearts on pilgrimage.[i]
6As they pass through the Valley of Baca,
they make it a place of springs;[j]
the autumn[k] rains also cover it with pools.[b]
7They go from strength to strength,[l]
till each appears[m] before God in Zion.[n]

8Hear my prayer,[o] O LORD God Almighty;
listen to me, O God of Jacob. *Selah*
9Look upon our shield,[c][p] O God;
look with favour on your anointed one.[q]

7 [l]**Job 17:9;** [m]**Dt 16:16;** [n]1Ki 8:1 8 [o]Ps 4:1
9 [p]**Ps 59:11;** [q]1Sa 16:6; Ps 2:2; 18:50; 132:17

[a]7 That is, Byblos [a]Title: Probably a musical term
[b]6 Or *blessings* [c]9 Or *sovereign*

10Better is one day in your courts
than a thousand elsewhere;
I would rather be a doorkeeper[r] in the
house of my God
than dwell in the tents of the
wicked.
11For the LORD God is a sun[s] and shield;[t]
the LORD bestows favour and
honour;
no good thing does he withhold[u]
from those whose walk is blameless.

12O LORD Almighty,
blessed[v] is the man who trusts in
you.

Psalm 85

For the director of music. Of the Sons of Korah. A psalm.

1You showed favour to your land, O
LORD;
you restored the fortunes[a] of Jacob.
2You forgave[b] the iniquity[c] of your
people
and covered all their sins. *Selah*
3You set aside all your wrath[d]
and turned from your fierce anger.[e]

4Restore[f] us again, O God our Saviour,[g]
and put away your displeasure
towards us.
5Will you be angry with us for ever?[h]
Will you prolong your anger
through all generations?
6Will you not revive[i] us again,
that your people may rejoice[j] in
you?
7Show us your unfailing love,[k] O LORD,
and grant us your salvation.[l]

8I will listen to what God the LORD will
say;
he promises peace[m] to his people,
his saints—
but let them not return to folly.[n]
9Surely his salvation[o] is near those who
fear him,
that his glory[p] may dwell in our
land.

10Love and faithfulness[q] meet together;
righteousness[r] and peace kiss each
other.
11Faithfulness springs forth from the
earth,
and righteousness[s] looks down
from heaven.
12The LORD will indeed give what is
good,[t]
and our land will yield[u] its harvest.
13Righteousness goes before him
and prepares the way for his steps.

10 [r]1Ch 23:5
11 [s]Isa 60:19; Jer 43:13; Rev 21:23; [t]Ge 15:1; [u]Ps 34:10
12 [v]Ps 2:12

Ps. 85

1 [a]Dt 30:3; Ps 14:7
2 [b]Nu 14:19; [c]Ex 32:30; Ps 78:38
3 [d]Ps 106:23; Da 9:16; [e]Ex 32:12; Dt 13:17; Ps 78:38; Jnh 3:9
4 [f]Ps 71:20; [g]Ps 65:5
5 [h]Ps 50:21
6 [i]Ps 80:18; [j]Php 3:1
7 [k]Ps 6:4; [l]Ps 27:1
8 [m]Lev 26:6; Isa 60:17; Jn 14:27; 2Th 3:16; [n]Pr 26:11; 27:22
9 [o]Ps 27:1; Isa 43:3; 45:8; 46:13; 51:5; 56:1; 62:11; [p]Ex 29:43; Isa 60:19; Hag 2:9; Zec 2:5
10 [q]Ps 89:14; 115:1; Pr 3:3; [r]Ps 72:2–3; Isa 32:17
11 [s]Isa 45:8
12 [t]Ps 84:11; Jas 1:17; [u]Lev 26:4; Ps 67:6; Zec 8:12

Ps. 86

1 [a]Ps 17:6
2 [b]Ps 25:2; 31:14
3 [c]Ps 4:1; 9:13; 57:1; [d]Ps 88:9
4 [e]Ps 46:5; 143:8
5 [f]Ex 34:6; Ne 9:17; Ps 103:8; 145:8; Joel 2:13; Jnh 4:2
6 [g]Ps 5:2; 17:1
7 [h]Ps 27:5; 50:15; 94:13; Hab 3:16; [i]Job 22:27; Ps 4:3; 80:18; 91:15; Isa 30:19; 58:9; 65:24; Zec 13:9; [j]Ps 3:4
8 [k]Ex 8:10; Job 21:22; [l]Ps 18:31
9 [m]Ps 65:2; [n]Ps 66:4; Isa 19:21; 27:13; 49:7; Zec 8:20–22; 14:16; Rev 15:4; [o]Isa 43:7; 44:23

Psalm 86

A prayer of David.

1Hear, O LORD, and answer[a] me,
for I am poor and needy.
2Guard my life, for I am devoted to
you.
You are my God; save your servant
who trusts in you.[b]
3Have mercy[c] on me, O Lord,
for I call[d] to you all day long.
4Bring joy to your servant,
for to you, O Lord,
I lift[e] up my soul.

5You are forgiving and good, O Lord,
abounding in love[f] to all who call to
you.
6Hear my prayer, O LORD;
listen to my cry[g] for mercy.
7In the day of my trouble[h] I will call[i] to
you,
for you will answer[j] me.

8Among the gods[k] there is none like
you,[l] O Lord;
no deeds can compare with yours.
9All the nations you have made
will come[m] and worship[n] before
you, O Lord;
they will bring glory[o] to your name.
10For you are great[p] and do marvellous
deeds;[q]
you alone[r] are God.

11Teach me your way,[s] O LORD,
and I will walk in your truth;[t]
give me an undivided[u] heart,
that I may fear[v] your name.
12I will praise you, O Lord my God, with
all my heart;[w]
I will glorify your name for ever.
13For great is your love towards me;
you have delivered me[x] from the
depths of the grave.[a][y]

14The arrogant are attacking me, O God;
a band of ruthless men seeks my
life—
men without regard for you.[z]
15But you, O Lord, are a compassionate
and gracious[a] God,
slow to anger,[b] abounding[c] in love
and faithfulness.[d]

10 [p]2Sa 7:22; Ps 48:1; [q]Ex 3:20; Ps 71:17; 72:18; [r]Dt 6:4; Isa 43:10; Mk 12:29; 1Co 8:4
11 [s]Ex 33:13; 1Sa 12:23; Ps 25:5; [t]Ps 26:3; [u]Jer 24:7; 32:39; Eze 11:19; 1Co 7:35; [v]Dt 6:24 *12* [w]Ps 9:1
13 [x]Ps 34:4; 49:15; 116:8; [y]Ps 16:10; 56:13
14 [z]Ps 54:3
15 [a]Ps 51:1; 103:8; 111:4; 116:5; 145:8; [b]Nu 14:18; [c]ver 5; [d]Ex 34:6; Ne 9:17; Joel 2:13

[a]*13* Hebrew *Sheol*

16Turn to me[e] and have mercy[f] on me;
grant your strength[g] to your servant
and save the son of your
maidservant.[b][h]
17Give me a sign[i] of your goodness,
that my enemies may see it and be
put to shame,
for you, O LORD, have helped me
and comforted me.

Psalm 87

Of the Sons of Korah. A psalm. A song.

1He has set his foundation on the holy
mountain;[a]
2 the LORD loves the gates of Zion[b]
more than all the dwellings of Jacob.
3Glorious things are said of you,
O city of God:[c] *Selah*
4"I will record Rahab[a][d] and Babylon
among those who acknowledge
me—
Philistia[e] too, and Tyre,[f] along with
Cush[b]—
and will say, 'This[c] one was born in
Zion.[g]' "

5Indeed, of Zion it will be said,
"This one and that one were born in
her,
and the Most High himself will
establish her."
6The LORD will write in the register[h] of
the peoples:
"This one was born in Zion." *Selah*
7As they make music[i] they will sing,
"All my fountains[j] are in you."

Psalm 88

A song. A psalm of the Sons of Korah. For the director of music. According to *mahalath leannoth*.[a] A *maskil*[b] of Heman the Ezrahite.

1O LORD, the God who saves me,[a]
day and night I cry out[b] before you.
2May my prayer come before you;
turn your ear to my cry.

3For my soul is full of trouble[c]
and my life draws near the grave.[c][d]
4I am counted among those who go
down to the pit;[e]
I am like a man without strength.[f]
5I am set apart with the dead,
like the slain who lie in the grave,
whom you remember no more,
who are cut off[g] from your care.

6You have put me in the lowest pit,
in the darkest depths.[h]

16 [e]**Ps 6:4**; [f]**Ps 9:13**; [g]Ps 18:1; [h]Ps 116:16
17 [i]**Ex 3:12**; Mt 24:3; **Jn 2:11**

Ps. 87

1 [a]**Ps 48:1**
2 [b]Ps 2:6
3 [c]**Ps 46:4**
4 [d]**Job 9:13**; [e]**2Sa 8:1**; Ps 83:7; [f]Ps 45:12; Joel 3:4; [g]Isa 19:25
6 [h]Ex 32:32; Ps 69:28; Isa 4:3; Mal 3:16
7 [i]Ps 149:3; [j]**Ps 36:9**

Ps. 88

1 [a]**Ps 51:14**; [b]Ps 3:4; 22:2; Lk 18:7
3 [c]Ps 6:3; 25:17; [d]**Job 33:22**
4 [e]**Ps 31:12**; [f]Ps 18:1
5 [g]**Ps 31:22**
6 [h]Ps 30:1; **69:15**; La 3:55; Jnh 2:3
7 [i]Ps 7:11; [j]**Ps 42:7**
8 [k]**Job 19:13**; Ps 31:11; [l]Jer 32:2; 33:1; [m]**Job 3:23**
9 [n]**Ps 38:10**; [o]Ps 5:2; [p]Job 11:13; Ps 143:6
10 [q]**Ps 6:5**
11 [r]**Ps 30:9**
13 [s]**Ps 30:2**; [t]Ps 5:3; **55:17**; [u]Ps 119:147
14 [v]**Ps 43:2**; [w]Ps 13:1
15 [x]Ps 129:1; Jer 22:21; Eze 16:22; Hos 2:15; [y]Ps 9:12; [z]Job 6:4; **18:11**; [a]2Co 4:8
16 [b]Ps 7:11; [c]Job 6:4
17 [d]Ps 124:4
18 [e]ver 8; Ps 38:11

Ps. 89

1 [a]Ps 59:16; [b]**Ps 36:5**; 40:10

7Your wrath[i] lies heavily upon me;
you have overwhelmed me with all
your waves.[j] *Selah*
8You have taken from me my closest
friends[k]
and have made me repulsive to
them.
I am confined[l] and cannot escape;[m]
9 my eyes[n] are dim with grief.

I call[o] to you, O LORD, every day;
I spread out my hands[p] to you.
10Do you show your wonders to the
dead?
Do those who are dead rise up and
praise you?[q] *Selah*
11Is your love declared in the grave,
your faithfulness[r] in Destruction?[d]
12Are your wonders known in the place
of darkness,
or your righteous deeds in the land
of oblivion?

13But I cry to you for help,[s] O LORD;
in the morning[t] my prayer comes
before you.[u]
14Why, O LORD, do you reject[v] me
and hide your face[w] from me?

15From my youth[x] I have been afflicted[y]
and close to death;
I have suffered your terrors[z] and am
in despair.[a]
16Your wrath[b] has swept over me;
your terrors[c] have destroyed me.
17All day long they surround me like a
flood;[d]
they have completely engulfed me.
18You have taken my companions[e] and
loved ones from me;
the darkness is my closest friend.

Psalm 89

A *maskil*[a] of Ethan the Ezrahite.

1I will sing[a] of the LORD's great love for
ever;
with my mouth I will make your
faithfulness known[b] through all
generations.
2I will declare that your love stands
firm for ever,

[b]16 Or *save your faithful son*
[a]4 A poetic name for Egypt
[b]4 That is, the upper Nile region
[c]4 Or *"O Rahab and Babylon, / Philistia, Tyre and Cush, / I will record concerning those who acknowledge me: / 'This*
[a]Title: Possibly a tune, "The Suffering of Affliction"
[b]Title: Probably a literary or musical term
[c]3 Hebrew *Sheol* [d]11 Hebrew *Abaddon*
[a]Title: Probably a literary or musical term

that you established your
faithfulness in heaven itself.[c]

3You said, "I have made a covenant
with my chosen one,
I have sworn to David my servant,
4'I will establish your line for ever
and make your throne firm through
all generations.' "[d] *Selah*

5The heavens[e] praise your wonders, O
LORD,
your faithfulness too, in the
assembly[f] of the holy ones.
6For who in the skies above can
compare with the LORD?
Who is like the LORD among the
heavenly beings?[g]
7In the council[h] of the holy ones[i] God is
greatly feared;
he is more awesome than all who
surround him.[j]
8O LORD God Almighty,[k] who is like
you?[l]
You are mighty, O LORD, and your
faithfulness surrounds you.

9You rule over the surging sea;
when its waves mount up, you still
them.[m]
10You crushed Rahab[n] like one of the
slain;
with your strong arm you scattered[o]
your enemies.
11The heavens are yours,[p] and yours
also the earth;[q]
you founded the world and all that
is in it.[r]
12You created the north and the south;
Tabor[s] and Hermon[t] sing for joy[u] at
your name.
13Your arm is endued with power;
your hand is strong, your right hand
exalted.[v]

14Righteousness and justice are the
foundation of your throne;[w]
love and faithfulness go before
you.[x]
15Blessed are those who have learned to
acclaim you,
who walk[y] in the light[z] of your
presence, O LORD.
16They rejoice in your name[a] all day
long;
they exult in your righteousness.
17For you are their glory and strength,[b]
and by your favour you exalt our
horn.[b][c]
18Indeed, our shield[c][d] belongs to the
LORD,
our king[e] to the Holy One of Israel.

19Once you spoke in a vision,
to your faithful people you said:
"I have bestowed strength on a
warrior;
I have exalted a young man from
among the people.
20I have found David[f] my servant;[g]
with my sacred oil[h] I have anointed[i]
him.
21My hand will sustain him;
surely my arm will strengthen him.[j]
22No enemy will subject him to tribute;[k]
no wicked man will oppress[l] him.
23I will crush his foes before him[m]
and strike down his adversaries.[n]
24My faithful love will be with him,[o]
and through my name his horn[d] will
be exalted.
25I will set his hand over the sea,
his right hand over the rivers.[p]
26He will call out to me, 'You are my
Father,[q]
my God, the Rock[r] my Saviour.'[s]
27I will also appoint him my firstborn,[t]
the most exalted[u] of the kings[v] of the
earth.
28I will maintain my love to him for ever,
and my covenant with him will
never fail.[w]
29I will establish his line for ever,
his throne as long as the heavens
endure.[x]

30"If his sons forsake my law
and do not follow my statutes,
31if they violate my decrees
and fail to keep my commands,
32I will punish their sin with the rod,
their iniquity with flogging;[y]
33but I will not take my love from him,[z]
nor will I ever betray my
faithfulness.
34I will not violate my covenant
or alter what my lips have uttered.[a]
35Once for all, I have sworn by my
holiness—
and I will not lie to David—
36that his line will continue for ever
and his throne endure before me
like the sun;[b]
37it will be established for ever like the
moon,
the faithful witness in the sky."[c]
Selah

38But you have rejected,[d] you have
spurned,
you have been very angry with your
anointed one.

2 [c]Ps 36:5
4 [d]2Sa 7:12–16; 1Ki 8:16; Ps 132:11–12; Isa 9:7; Eze 37:24–25; **Mt 1:1; Lk 1:33**
5 [e]**Ps 19:1;** [f]**Ps 1:5**
6 [g]**Ge 1:26; Ex 9:14; Ps 18:31;** 113:5
7 [h]Ps 111:1; [i]**Job 5:1;** [j]Ps 47:2
8 [k]Isa 6:3; [l]**Ps 71:19**
9 [m]**Ps 65:7**
10 [n]**Job 9:13;** [o]**Ps 59:11; 68:1;** 92:9
11 [p]**Dt 10:14;** Ps 115:16; [q]1Ch 29:11; **Ps 24:1;** [r]**Ge 1:1**
12 [s]**Jos 19:22;** [t]**Dt 3:8; 4:48;** [u]Ps 98:8
13 [v]**Jos 4:24**
14 [w]Ps 97:2; [x]Ps 85:10–11
15 [y]Ps 1:1; [z]Ps 44:3
16 [a]Ps 30:4; 105:3
17 [b]Ps 18:1; [c]ver 24; Ps 75:10; 92:10; 112:9; 148:14
18 [d]Ps 18:2; [e]Ps 47:9; Isa 16:5; 33:17,22
20 [f]Ac 13:22; [g]Ps 78:70; [h]**Ex 29:7; 1Ki 1:39;** [i]**1Sa 2:35; 2Sa 22:51**
21 [j]ver 13; Ps 18:35
22 [k]**Jdg 3:15;** [l]2Sa 7:10
23 [m]Ps 18:40; [n]2Sa 7:9
24 [o]**2Sa 7:15**
25 [p]Ps 72:8
26 [q]**2Sa 7:14; Jer 3:4;** Heb 1:5; [r]**Ps 62:2;** [s]**2Sa 22:47**
27 [t]**Col 1:18;** [u]**Nu 24:7;** [v]Ps 2:6; Rev 1:5; 19:16
28 [w]ver 33–34; Isa 55:3
29 [x]ver 4,36
32 [y]2Sa 7:14
33 [z]**2Sa 7:15**
34 [a]**Nu 23:19**
36 [b]ver 4
37 [c]Jer 33:20–21
38 [d]1Ch 28:9; Ps 44:9; 78:59

b17 *Horn* here symbolises strong one.
c18 Or *sovereign*
d24 *Horn* here symbolises strength.

39You have renounced the covenant with your servant
and have defiled his crown in the dust.[e]
40You have broken through all his walls[f]
and reduced his strongholds[g] to ruins.
41All who pass by have plundered[h] him;
he has become the scorn of his neighbours.[i]
42You have exalted the right hand of his foes;
you have made all his enemies rejoice.[j]
43You have turned back the edge of his sword
and have not supported him in battle.[k]
44You have put an end to his splendour
and cast his throne to the ground.
45You have cut short[l] the days of his youth;
you have covered him with a mantle of shame.[m] *Selah*

46How long, O LORD? Will you hide yourself for ever?
How long will your wrath burn like fire?[n]
47Remember how fleeting is my life.[o]
For what futility you have created all men!
48What man can live and not see death,
or save himself from the power of the grave?[e][p] *Selah*
49O Lord, where is your former great love,
which in your faithfulness you swore to David?
50Remember, Lord, how your servant has[f] been mocked,[q]
how I bear in my heart the taunts of all the nations,
51the taunts with which your enemies have mocked, O LORD,
with which they have mocked every step of your anointed one.[r]

52Praise be to the LORD for ever!
Amen and Amen.[s]

BOOK IV

Psalms 90–106

Psalm 90

A prayer of Moses the man of God.

1Lord, you have been our dwelling-place[a]
throughout all generations.
2Before the mountains were born[b]
or you brought forth the earth and the world,
from everlasting to everlasting[c] you are God.[d]

3You turn men back to dust,
saying, "Return to dust, O sons of men."[e]
4For a thousand years in your sight
are like a day that has just gone by,
or like a watch in the night.[f]
5You sweep men away[g] in the sleep of death;
they are like the new grass of the morning—
6though in the morning it springs up new,
by evening it is dry and withered.[h]

7We are consumed by your anger
and terrified by your indignation.
8You have set our iniquities before you,
our secret sins[i] in the light of your presence.[j]
9All our days pass away under your wrath;
we finish our years with a moan.[k]
10The length of our days is seventy years[l]—
or eighty,[m] if we have the strength;
yet their span[a] is but trouble and sorrow,[n]
for they quickly pass, and we fly away.[o]

11Who knows the power of your anger?
For your wrath[p] is as great as the fear that is due to you.[q]
12Teach us to number our days[r] aright,
that we may gain a heart of wisdom.[s]

13Relent, O LORD! How long[t] will it be?
Have compassion on your servants.[u]
14Satisfy[v] us in the morning with your unfailing love,[w]
that we may sing for joy[x] and be glad all our days.[y]
15Make us glad for as many days as you have afflicted us,
for as many years as we have seen trouble.
16May your deeds be shown to your servants,
your splendour to their children.[z]

17May the favour[b] of the Lord our God rest upon us;

39 [e]La 5:16
40 [f]**Ps 80:12;** [g]Isa 22:5; La 2:2
41 [h]**Jdg 2:14;** [i]**Ps 44:13**
42 [j]Ps 13:2; 80:6
43 [k]Ps 44:10
45 [l]**Ps 39:5;** [m]Ps 44:15; 109:29
46 [n]Ps 79:5
47 [o]**Ge 47:9; Job 7:7;** Ps 39:5; 1Pe 1:24
48 [p]**Ge 5:24;** Ps 22:29
50 [q]Ps 69:19
51 [r]Ps 74:10
52 [s]**Ps 41:13; 72:19**

Ps. 90

1 [a]**Dt 33:27;** Eph 2:22; Rev 21:3
2 [b]**Job 15:7;** [c]Isa 9:6; 57:15; [d]**Ge 21:33; Job 10:5;** Ps 102:24–27; Pr 8:23–26
3 [e]**Ge 2:7; Job 7:21;** 34:15; 1Co 15:47
4 [f]**Job 10:5;** 2Pe 3:8
5 [g]**Ge 19:15**
6 [h]Isa 40:6–8; Mt 6:30; Jas 1:10
8 [i]**Ps 19:12;** 2Co 4:2; Eph 5:12; [j]**Heb 4:13**
9 [k]Ps 78:33
10 [l]Isa 23:15,17; Jer 25:11; [m]2Sa 19:35; [n]**Job 5:7;** [o]**Job 20:8; 34:15**
11 [p]Ps 7:11; [q]Ps 76:7
12 [r]Ps 39:4; 139:16; Pr 16:9; 20:24; [s]Dt 32:29
13 [t]Ps 6:3; [u]**Dt 32:36**
14 [v]Ps 103:5; 107:9; 145:16, 19; [w]**Ps 77:8;** 143:8; [x]**Ps 5:11;** [y]Ps 31:7
16 [z]Ps 44:1; Hab 3:2

[e]*48* Hebrew *Sheol* [f]*50* Or *your servants have*
[a]*10* Or *yet the best of them* [b]*17* Or *beauty*

establish the work of our hands for
us—
yes, establish the work of our
hands.[a]

Psalm 91

1 He who dwells in the shelter[a] of the
Most High
will rest in the shadow[b] of the
Almighty.[a]
2 I will say[b] of the LORD, "He is my
refuge[c] and my fortress,[d]
my God, in whom I trust."

3 Surely he will save you from the
fowler's snare[e]
and from the deadly pestilence.[f]
4 He will cover you with his feathers,
and under his wings you will find
refuge;[g]
his faithfulness will be your shield[h]
and rampart.
5 You will not fear[i] the terror of night,
nor the arrow that flies by day,
6 nor the pestilence that stalks in the
darkness,
nor the plague that destroys at
midday.
7 A thousand may fall at your side,
ten thousand at your right hand,
but it will not come near you.
8 You will only observe with your eyes
and see the punishment of the
wicked.[j]

9 If you make the Most High your
dwelling—
even the LORD, who is my refuge—
10 then no harm[k] will befall you,
no disaster will come near your tent.
11 For he will command his angels[l]
concerning you
to guard you in all your ways;[m]
12 they will lift you up in their hands,
so that you will not strike your foot
against a stone.[n]
13 You will tread upon the lion and the
cobra;
you will trample the great lion and
the serpent.[o]

14 "Because he loves me," says the LORD,
"I will rescue him;
I will protect him, for he
acknowledges my name.
15 He will call upon me, and I will answer
him;
I will be with him in trouble,
I will deliver him and honour him.[p]
16 With long life[q] will I satisfy him
and show him my salvation."[r]

17 [a]Isa 26:12

Ps. 91

1 [a]Ex 33:22; [b]Ps 63:7; Isa 49:2; La 4:20
2 [c]ver 9; 2Sa 22:3; Ps 9:9; [d]2Sa 22:2
3 [e]Ps 124:7; Pr 6:5; [f]1Ki 8:37
4 [g]Ru 2:12; Ps 17:8; [h]Dt 32:10; Ps 35:2; Isa 27:3; 31:5; Zec 12:8
5 [i]Job 5:21
8 [j]Ps 37:34; 58:10
10 [k]Pr 12:21
11 [l]Ge 32:1; Heb 1:14; [m]Ps 34:7
12 [n]Mt 4:6*; Lk 4:10–11*
13 [o]Da 6:22; Lk 10:19
15 [p]1Sa 2:30; Jn 12:26
16 [q]Dt 6:2; Ps 21:4; [r]Ps 50:23

Ps. 92

1 [a]Ps 27:6; [b]Ps 9:2; 147:1; [c]Ps 135:3
2 [d]Ps 55:17
3 [e]Ps 71:22; [f]1Sa 10:5; Ne 12:27; Ps 33:2; 81:2
4 [g]Ps 5:11; 27:6; [h]Ps 8:6; 111:7; 143:5
5 [i]Job 36:24; Rev 15:3; [j]Ps 40:5; 139:17; Isa 28:29; 31:2; Ro 11:33
6 [k]Ps 73:22
7 [l]Ps 37:2
9 [m]Ps 45:5; [n]Ps 68:1; 89:10
10 [o]Ps 89:17; [p]Ps 29:6; [q]Ps 23:5
11 [r]Ps 54:7; 91:8
12 [s]Ps 72:7; [t]Ps 1:3; 52:8; Jer 17:8; Hos 14:6
13 [u]Ps 135:2
14 [v]Ps 1:3; Jn 15:2
15 [w]Job 34:10

Ps. 93

1 [a]1Ch 16:31; Ps 97:1; [b]Job 40:10; Ps 21:5; [c]Ps 65:6; [d]Ps 24:2; 78:69; 119:90; [e]1Ch 16:30; Ps 96:10

Psalm 92

A psalm. A song. For the Sabbath day.

1 It is good to praise the LORD
and make music[a] to your name,[b] O
Most High,[c]
2 to proclaim your love in the morning[d]
and your faithfulness at night,
3 to the music of the ten-stringed lyre[e]
and the melody of the harp.[f]

4 For you make me glad by your deeds,
O LORD;
I sing for joy[g] at the work of your
hands.[h]
5 How great are your works,[i] O LORD,
how profound your thoughts![j]
6 The senseless man[k] does not know,
fools do not understand,
7 that though the wicked spring up like
grass
and all evildoers flourish,
they will be for ever destroyed.[l]

8 But you, O LORD, are exalted for ever.

9 For surely your enemies,[m] O LORD,
surely your enemies will perish;
all evildoers will be scattered.[n]
10 You have exalted my horn[a][o] like that
of a wild ox;[p]
fine oils[q] have been poured upon
me.
11 My eyes have seen the defeat of my
adversaries;
my ears have heard the rout of my
wicked foes.[r]

12 The righteous will flourish[s] like a palm
tree,
they will grow like a cedar of
Lebanon;[t]
13 planted in the house of the LORD,
they will flourish in the courts of our
God.[u]
14 They will still bear fruit[v] in old age,
they will stay fresh and green,
15 proclaiming, "The LORD is upright;
he is my Rock, and there is no
wickedness in him."[w]

Psalm 93

1 The LORD reigns,[a] he is robed in
majesty;[b]
the LORD is robed in majesty
and is armed with strength.[c]
The world is firmly established;[d]
it cannot be moved.[e]

---

[a]1 Hebrew *Shaddai*
[b]2 Or *He says*
[a]10 *Horn* here symbolises strength.

2Your throne was established[f] long
ago;
you are from all eternity.[g]

3The seas[h] have lifted up, O LORD,
the seas have lifted up their voice;[i]
the seas have lifted up their
pounding waves.[j]
4Mightier than the thunder[k] of the
great waters,
mightier than the breakers[l] of the
sea—
the LORD on high is mighty.[m]

5Your statutes stand firm;
holiness[n] adorns your house[o]
for endless days, O LORD.

Psalm 94

1O LORD, the God who avenges,[a]
O God who avenges, shine forth.[b]
2Rise up,[c] O Judge[d] of the earth;
pay back[e] to the proud what they
deserve.
3How long will the wicked, O LORD,
how long will the wicked be
jubilant?[f]

4They pour out arrogant[g] words;
all the evildoers are full of boasting.[h]
5They crush your people,[i] O LORD;
they oppress your inheritance.[j]
6They slay the widow[k] and the alien;
they murder the fatherless.[l]
7They say, "The LORD does not see;[m]
the God of Jacob[n] pays no heed."

8Take heed, you senseless ones[o]
among the people;
you fools, when will you become
wise?
9Does he who implanted the ear not
hear?
Does he who formed the eye not
see?[p]
10Does he who disciplines[q] nations not
punish?
Does he who teaches[r] man lack
knowledge?
11The LORD knows the thoughts[s] of man;
he knows that they are futile.[t]

12Blessed is the man you discipline,[u] O
LORD,
the man you teach[v] from your law;
13you grant him relief from days of
trouble,[w]
till a pit[x] is dug for the wicked.
14For the LORD will not reject his people;[y]
he will never forsake his
inheritance.

15Judgment will again be founded on
righteousness,[z]
and all the upright in heart[a] will
follow it.

16Who will rise up[b] for me against the
wicked?
Who will take a stand for me against
evildoers?[c]
17Unless the LORD had given me help,[d]
I would soon have dwelt in the
silence of death.[e]
18When I said, "My foot is slipping,[f]"
your love, O LORD, supported me.
19When anxiety[g] was great within me,
your consolation[h] brought joy to my
soul.

20Can a corrupt throne[i] be allied with
you—
one that brings on misery by its
decrees?[j]
21They band together[k] against the
righteous
and condemn the innocent[l] to
death.[m]
22But the LORD has become my fortress,
and my God the rock[n] in whom I
take refuge.[o]
23He will repay[p] them for their sins
and destroy[q] them for their
wickedness;
the LORD our God will destroy them.

Psalm 95

1Come,[a] let us sing for joy[b] to the LORD;
let us shout aloud[c] to the Rock[d] of
our salvation.
2Let us come before him[e] with
thanksgiving[f]
and extol him with music[g] and song.

3For the LORD is the great God,[h]
the great King[i] above all gods.[j]
4In his hand are the depths of the
earth,[k]
and the mountain peaks belong to
him.
5The sea is his, for he made it,
and his hands formed the dry land.[l]

6Come, let us bow down[m] in worship,[n]
let us kneel[o] before the LORD our
Maker;[p]

2 [f]2Sa 7:16; [g]Ge 21:33
3 [h]Ps 96:11; 98:7; Isa 5:30; 17:12–13; Jer 6:23; [i]Ps 46:3; [j]Job 9:8; Ps 107:25,29; Isa 51:15; Jer 31:35; Hab 3:10
4 [k]Ps 65:7; Jer 6:23; [l]Ps 18:4; Jnh 1:15; [m]Ne 9:32; Job 9:4
5 [n]Ps 29:2; 96:9; [o]Ps 5:7; 23:6

Ps. 94

1 [a]Ge 4:24; Ro 12:19; [b]Dt 33:2; Ps 80:1
2 [c]Nu 10:35; [d]Ge 18:25; Heb 12:23; Jas 5:9; [e]Ps 31:23
3 [f]Ps 13:2
4 [g]Jer 43:2; [h]Ps 52:1
5 [i]Ps 44:2; 74:8; Isa 3:15; Jer 8:21; [j]Ps 28:9
6 [k]Dt 10:18; Isa 1:17; [l]Dt 24:19
7 [m]Job 22:14; [n]Ge 24:12
8 [o]Dt 32:6; Ps 73:22
9 [p]Ex 4:11; Pr 20:12
10 [q]Ps 39:11; [r]Ex 35:34; Job 35:11; Isa 28:26
11 [s]Ps 139:2; Pr 15:26; Mt 9:4; [t]1Co 3:20*
12 [u]Job 5:17; 1Co 11:32; Heb 12:5; [v]Dt 8:3; 1Sa 12:23
13 [w]Ps 86:7; [x]Ps 7:15; 55:23
14 [y]Dt 31:6; Ps 37:28; Ro 11:2
15 [z]Ps 97:2; [a]Ps 7:10; 11:2; 36:10
16 [b]Nu 10:35; Ps 17:13; Isa 14:22; [c]Ps 59:2
17 [d]Ps 124:2; [e]Ps 31:17
18 [f]Dt 32:35; Job 12:5
19 [g]Ecc 11:10; [h]Job 6:10
20 [i]Jer 22:30; 36:30; [j]Ps 58:2
21 [k]Ps 56:6; [l]Ps 106:38; Pr 17:15,26; 28:21; Isa 5:20,23; Mt 27:4; [m]Ge 18:23
22 [n]Ps 61:2; [o]2Sa 22:3; Ps 18:2
23 [p]Ex 32:34; Ps 54:5; [q]Ps 9:5; 37:38; 145:20

Ps. 95

1 [a]Ps 34:11; 80:2; [b]Ps 5:11; [c]Ps 81:1; Isa 44:23; Zep 3:14; [d]2Sa 22:47
2 [e]Ps 100:2; Mic 6:6; [f]Ps 42:4; [g]Ps 81:2; Eph 5:19
3 [h]Ps 48:1; 86:10; 145:3; 147:5; [i]Ps 47:2; [j]Ps 96:4; 97:9
4 [k]Ps 63:9
5 [l]Ge 1:9; Ps 146:6
6 [m]2Sa 12:16; Php 2:10; [n]Ps 22:29; [o]2Ch 6:13; [p]Ps 100:3; 149:2; Isa 17:7; 54:5; Da 6:10–11; Hos 8:14

[7]for he is our God
and we are the people of his
pasture,[q]
the flock under his care.

Today, if you hear his voice,
8 do not harden your hearts[r] as you
did at Meribah,[a s]
as you did that day at Massah[b] in
the desert,[t]
[9]where your fathers tested[u] and tried
me,
though they had seen what I did.
[10]For forty years[v] I was angry with that
generation;
I said, "They are a people whose
hearts go astray,[w]
and they have not known my
ways."[x]
[11]So I declared on oath[y] in my anger,
"They shall never enter my rest."[z]

Psalm 96

96:1–13pp—1Ch 16:23–33

[1]Sing to the LORD[a] a new song;[b]
sing to the LORD, all the earth.
[2]Sing to the LORD, praise his name;[c]
proclaim his salvation[d] day after
day.
[3]Declare his glory[e] among the nations,
his marvellous deeds[f] among all
peoples.

[4]For great is the LORD and most worthy
of praise;[g]
he is to be feared[h] above all gods.[i]
[5]For all the gods of the nations are
idols,[j]
but the LORD made the heavens.[k]
[6]Splendour and majesty[l] are before
him;
strength and glory[m] are in his
sanctuary.

[7]Ascribe to the LORD,[n] O families of
nations,[o]
ascribe to the LORD glory and
strength.
[8]Ascribe to the LORD the glory due to
his name;
bring an offering[p] and come into his
courts.[q]
[9]Worship the LORD[r] in the splendour of
his[a] holiness;[s]
tremble[t] before him, all the earth.[u]

[10]Say among the nations, "The LORD
reigns.[v]"
The world is firmly established,[w] it
cannot be moved;[x]
he will judge[y] the peoples with
equity.[z]

7 [q]**Ps 74:1**
8 [r]Mk 10:5; Heb 3:8; [s]**Ex 17:7; Dt 33:8**; Heb 3:15*; 4:7; [t]**Ps 78:40**
9 [u]**Nu 14:22**; 1Co 10:9
10 [v]**Ex 16:35; Nu 14:34**; Ac 7:36; Heb 3:17; [w]Ps 58:3; 119:67, 176; Pr 12:26; 16:29; Isa 53:6; Jer 31:19; 50:6; Eze 34:6; [x]**Dt 8:6**
11 [y]**Nu 14:23**; [z]Dt 1:35; Heb 3:7–11*; 4:3*

Ps. 96

1 [a]Ps 30:4; [b]Ps 33:3; **40:3**; 98:1; 144:9; 149:1; Isa 42:10; **Rev 5:9**
2 [c]**Ps 68:4**; [d]Ps 27:1; 71:15
3 [e]Ps 8:1; [f]**Ps 71:17**; Rev 15:3
4 [g]**Ps 48:1**; [h]**Dt 28:58; 1Ch 16:25**; Ps 89:7; [i]**Ps 95:3**
5 [j]**Lev 19:4**; [k]**Ge 1:1; 2Ch 2:12**
6 [l]**Ps 21:5**; [m]Ps 29:1; 89:17
7 [n]Ps 29:1; [o]Ps 22:27
8 [p]Ps 45:12; **51:19**; 72:10; [q]Ps 65:4; 84:10; 92:13; 100:4
9 [r]Ex 23:25; Jnh 1:9; [s]**Ps 93:5**; [t]**Ex 15:14**; Ps 114:7; [u]Ps 33:8
10 [v]Ps 97:1; [w]Ps 24:2; 78:69; 119:90; [x]**Ps 93:1**; [y]Ps 58:11; [z]Ps 67:4; 98:9
11 [a]**Rev 12:12**; [b]Ps 97:1; Isa 49:13
12 [c]Isa 44:23; 55:12; Eze 17:24; [d]Ps 65:13
13 [e]Rev 19:11; [f]**Ps 7:11**; Ac 17:31; [g]Ps 86:11

Ps. 97

1 [a]Ex 15:18; Ps 93:1; 96:10; 99:1; Isa 24:23; 52:7; [b]**Ps 96:11**; [c]**Est 10:1**
2 [d]**Job 22:14**; [e]**Ex 19:9**; [f]Ps 89:14
3 [g]Isa 9:19; Da 7:10; Joel 1:19; 2:3; [h]Hab 3:5; [i]**2Sa 22:9**

[11]Let the heavens rejoice,[a] let the earth
be glad;[b]
let the sea resound, and all that is in
it;
12 let the fields be jubilant, and
everything in them.
Then all the trees of the forest[c] will
sing for joy;[d]
13 they will sing before the LORD, for he
comes,
he comes to judge[e] the earth.
He will judge the world in
righteousness[f]
and the peoples in his truth.[g]

Psalm 97

[1]The LORD reigns,[a] let the earth be
glad;[b]
let the distant shores[c] rejoice.

[2]Clouds[d] and thick darkness[e] surround
him;
righteousness and justice are the
foundation of his throne.[f]
[3]Fire[g] goes before[h] him
and consumes[i] his foes on every
side.
[4]His lightning[j] lights up the world;
the earth[k] sees and trembles.[l]
[5]The mountains melt[m] like wax[n] before
the LORD,
before the Lord of all the earth.[o]
[6]The heavens proclaim his
righteousness,[p]
and all the peoples see his glory.[q]

[7]All who worship images[r] are put to
shame,[s]
those who boast in idols[t]—
worship him,[u] all you gods![v]

[8]Zion hears and rejoices
and the villages of Judah are glad[w]
because of your judgments,[x] O
LORD.
[9]For you, O LORD, are the Most High[y]
over all the earth;[z]
you are exalted[a] far above all gods.

[10]Let those who love the LORD hate evil,[b]
for he guards[c] the lives of his faithful
ones[d]

4 [j]**Job 36:30**; [k]**2Sa 22:8**; [l]**Ps 18:7**; 104:32; **Rev 6:12**
5 [m]**Ps 46:2**, 6; [n]**Ps 22:14**; [o]**Jos 3:11**
6 [p]Ps 50:6; 98:2; [q]**Ps 19:1**
7 [r]**Lev 26:1**; [s]Isa 42:17; Jer 10:14; [t]**Dt 5:8**; [u]Heb 1:6; [v]Ex 12:12; Ps 16:4 *8* [w]**Ps 9:2**; [x]Ps 48:11
9 [y]Ps 7:8; [z]**Job 34:29**; [a]**Ps 47:9**
10 [b]**Job 28:28**; Am 5:15; Ro 12:9; [c]Ps 145:20; [d]Ps 31:23; 37:28; Pr 2:8

[a]8 *Meribah* means *quarrelling*.
[b]8 *Massah* means *testing*.
[a]9 Or *LORD with the splendour of*

and delivers[e] them from the hand of
the wicked.[f]
11Light is shed[g] upon the righteous[h]
and joy on the upright in heart.[i]
12Rejoice in the LORD,[j] you who are
righteous,
and praise his holy name.[k]

Psalm 98

A psalm.

1Sing to the LORD[a] a new song,[b]
for he has done marvellous things;[c]
his right hand[d] and his holy arm[e]
have worked salvation[f] for him.
2The LORD has made his salvation
known[g]
and revealed his righteousness[h] to
the nations.[i]
3He has remembered[j] his love
and his faithfulness to the house of
Israel;
all the ends of the earth[k] have seen
the salvation of our God.[l]

4Shout for joy[m] to the LORD, all the
earth,
burst into jubilant song with music;
5make music to the LORD with the
harp,[n]
with the harp and the sound of
singing,[o]
6with trumpets[p] and the blast of the
ram's horn[q]—
shout for joy[r] before the LORD, the
King.[s]

7Let the sea[t] resound, and everything
in it,
the world, and all who live in it.[u]
8Let the rivers clap their hands,[v]
let the mountains[w] sing together for
joy;
9let them sing before the LORD,
for he comes to judge the earth.
He will judge the world in
righteousness
and the peoples with equity.[x]

Psalm 99

1The LORD reigns,[a]
let the nations tremble;[b]
he sits enthroned[c] between the
cherubim,[d]
let the earth shake.
2Great is the LORD[e] in Zion;[f]
he is exalted[g] over all the nations.
3Let them praise[h] your great and
awesome name[i]—
he is holy.[j]

4The King[k] is mighty, he loves
justice[l]—
you have established equity;[m]
in Jacob you have done
what is just and right.[n]
5Exalt[o] the LORD our God
and worship at his footstool;
he is holy.

6Moses[p] and Aaron[q] were among his
priests,
Samuel[r] was among those who
called on his name;
they called on the LORD
and he answered[s] them.
7He spoke to them from the pillar of
cloud;[t]
they kept his statutes and the
decrees he gave them.

8O LORD our God,
you answered them;
you were to Israel[a] a forgiving God,[u]
though you punished[v] their
misdeeds.[b]
9Exalt the LORD our God
and worship at his holy mountain,
for the LORD our God is holy.

Psalm 100

A psalm. For giving thanks.

1Shout for joy[a] to the LORD, all the
earth.
2 Worship the LORD[b] with gladness;
come before him[c] with joyful songs.
3Know that the LORD is God.[d]
It is he who made us,[e] and we are
his;[a]
we are his people,[f] the sheep of his
pasture.[g]

4Enter his gates with thanksgiving[h]
and his courts[i] with praise;
give thanks to him and praise his
name.[j]
5For the LORD is good[k] and his love
endures for ever;[l]
his faithfulness[m] continues through
all generations.

10 [e]Ps 34:7; Da 3:28; 6:16; [f]Ps 37:40; Jer 15:21; 20:13
11 [g]**Job 22:28;** [h]Ps 11:5; [i]Ps 7:10
12 [j]**Job 22:19;** Ps 104:34; Isa 41:16; Php 4:4; [k]**Ex 3:15; Ps 99:3**

Ps. 98

1 [a]Ps 30:4; [b]**Ps 96:1;** [c]Ex 15:1; Ps 96:3; Isa 12:5; Lk 1:51; [d]**Ex 15:6;** [e]**Jos 4:24;** Job 40:9; Isa 51:9; 52:10; 53:1; 63:5; [f]**Ps 44:3;** Isa 59:16
2 [g]Isa 52:10; Lk 3:6; [h]**Ps 97:6;** [i]**Ps 67:2**
3 [j]**1Ch 16:15;** [k]**Ge 49:10; Ps 48:10;** [l]**Ps 50:23**
4 [m]Ps 20:5; Isa 12:6; 44:23; 52:9; 54:1; 55:12
5 [n]Ps 33:2; 92:3; 147:7; [o]Isa 51:3
6 [p]**Nu 10:2; 2Sa 6:15;** [q]**Ex 19:13;** [r]Ps 20:5; 100:1; Isa 12:6; [s]Ps 2:6; 47:7
7 [t]**Ps 93:3;** [u]**Ps 24:1**
8 [v]**2Ki 11:12;** [w]Ps 148:9; Isa 44:23; 55:12
9 [x]**Ps 96:10**

Ps. 99

1 [a]**1Ch 16:31; Ps 97:1;** [b]**Ex 15:14; 1Ch 16:30;** [c]**2Sa 6:2;** [d]**Ex 25:22**
2 [e]**Ps 48:1;** [f]Ps 2:6; [g]Ex 15:1; Ps 46:10; 97:9; 113:4; 148:13
3 [h]Ps 30:4; 33:21; 97:12; 103:1; 106:47; 111:9; 145:21; 148:5; [i]Ps 76:1; [j]**Ex 15:11; Lev 11:44;** Rev 4:8
4 [k]Ps 2:6; [l]**1Ki 10:9;** [m]Ps 98:9; [n]**Ge 18:19;** Rev 15:3
5 [o]**Ex 15:2**
6 [p]**Ex 24:6;** [q]**Ex 28:1;** [r]1Sa 7:5; [s]Ps 4:3; 91:15
7 [t]**Ex 13:21; 19:9; Nu 11:25**
8 [u]**Ex 22:27; Nu 14:20;** [v]**Lev 26:18**

Ps. 100

1 [a]**Ps 98:6** *2* [b]**Dt 10:12;** [c]**Ps 95:2**
3 [d]**1Ki 18:21; Ps 46:10;** [e]**Job 10:3;** [f]Ps 79:13; Isa 19:25; 63:8,17–19; 64:9; [g]**2Sa 24:17; Ps 74:1**
4 [h]**Ps 42:4;** [i]**Ps 96:8;** [j]Ps 116:17
5 [k]**1Ch 16:34;** [l]**Ezr 3:11;** Ps 106:1; [m]Ps 108:4; 119:90

---

[a]8 Hebrew *them*
[b]8 Or / *an avenger of the wrongs done to them*
[a]3 Or *and not we ourselves*

Psalm 101

Of David. A psalm.

[1]I will sing of your love[a] and justice;
to you, O LORD, I will sing praise.
[2]I will be careful to lead a blameless life[b]—
when will you come to me?

I will walk[c] in my house
with blameless heart.
[3]I will set before my eyes
no vile thing.[d]

The deeds of faithless men I hate;[e]
they shall not cling to me.
[4]Men of perverse heart[f] shall be far from me;
I will have nothing to do with evil.

[5]Whoever slanders his neighbour[g] in secret,
him will I put to silence;
whoever has haughty eyes[h] and a proud heart,
him will I not endure.

[6]My eyes will be on the faithful in the land,
that they may dwell with me;
he whose walk is blameless[i]
will minister to me.

[7]No-one who practises deceit
will dwell in my house;
no-one who speaks falsely
will stand in my presence.

[8]Every morning[j] I will put to silence
all the wicked[k] in the land;
I will cut off every evildoer[l]
from the city of the LORD.[m]

Psalm 102

A prayer of an afflicted man. When he is faint and pours out his lament before the LORD.

[1]Hear my prayer,[a] O LORD;
let my cry for help[b] come to you.
[2]Do not hide your face[c] from me
when I am in distress.
Turn your ear[d] to me;
when I call, answer me quickly.

[3]For my days vanish like smoke;[e]
my bones[f] burn like glowing embers.
[4]My heart is blighted and withered like grass;[g]
I forget to eat my food.[h]
[5]Because of my loud groaning[i]
I am reduced to skin and bones.
[6]I am like a desert owl,[j]
like an owl among the ruins.
[7]I lie awake;[k] I have become
like a bird alone[l] on a roof.
[8]All day long my enemies[m] taunt me;[n]
those who rail against me use my name as a curse.[o]
[9]For I eat ashes[p] as my food
and mingle my drink with tears[q]
[10]because of your great wrath,[r]
for you have taken me up and thrown me aside.
[11]My days are like the evening shadow;[s]
I wither[t] away like grass.

[12]But you, O LORD, sit enthroned for ever;[u]
your renown endures[v] through all generations.[w]
[13]You will arise[x] and have compassion[y] on Zion,
for it is time[z] to show favour[a] to her;
the appointed time[b] has come.
[14]For her stones are dear to your servants;
her very dust moves them to pity.
[15]The nations will fear[c] the name of the LORD,
all the kings[d] of the earth will revere your glory.
[16]For the LORD will rebuild Zion[e]
and appear in his glory.[f]
[17]He will respond to the prayer[g] of the destitute;
he will not despise their plea.

[18]Let this be written[h] for a future generation,
that a people not yet created[i] may praise the LORD:
[19]"The LORD looked down[j] from his sanctuary on high,
from heaven he viewed the earth,
[20]to hear the groans of the prisoners[k]
and release those condemned to death."
[21]So the name of the LORD will be declared[l] in Zion
and his praise[m] in Jerusalem
[22]when the peoples and the kingdoms
assemble to worship[n] the LORD.

Ps. 101

1 [a]Ps 33:1; 51:14; 89:1; 145:7
2 [b]**Ge 17:1**; Php 1:10; [c]**1Ki 3:14**
3 [d]Jer 16:18; Eze 11:21; Hos 9:10; [e]**Ps 5:5**
4 [f]Pr 3:32; 6:16–19; 11:20
5 [g]**Ex 20:16; Lev 19:16**; [h]**Ps 10:5**
6 [i]ver 2; Ps 119:1
8 [j]Ps 5:3; Jer 21:12; [k]Ps 75:10; [l]**2Sa 3:39**; Ps 118:10–12; [m]**Ps 46:4**

Ps. 102

1 [a]Ps 4:1; [b]**Ex 2:23**
2 [c]**Ps 22:24**; [d]**2Ki 19:16**; Ps 31:2; 88:2
3 [e]**Ps 37:20; Jas 4:14**; [f]La 1:13
4 [g]**Ps 37:2**; 90:5–6; [h]**1Sa 1:7; Ezr 10:6; Job 33:20**
5 [i]**Ps 6:6**
6 [j]**Dt 14:15–17**; Job 30:29; Isa 34:11; Zep 2:14
7 [k]Ps 77:4; [l]Ps 38:11
8 [m]**Ps 31:11**; [n]**Ps 42:10**; Lk 22:63–65; 23:35–37; [o]**Ex 22:28**; Isa 65:15; Jer 24:9; 25:18; 42:18; 44:12; Eze 14:8; Zec 8:13
9 [p]Isa 44:20; [q]Ps 6:6; 42:3; 80:5
10 [r]Ps 7:11; 38:3
11 [s]**1Ch 29:15; Job 14:2; Ps 39:6**; [t]**Job 8:12**; Jas 1:10
12 [u]**Ex 15:18**; [v]Ps 135:13; Isa 55:13; 63:12; [w]**Ex 3:15**
13 [x]**Ps 44:26**; [y]**Dt 32:36; 1Ki 3:26**; Isa 54:8; 60:10; Zec 10:6; [z]Ps 119:126; [a]**Ps 77:7**; [b]**Ex 13:10**; Da 8:19; Ac 1:7
15 [c]1Ki 8:43; Ps 67:7; Isa 2:2; [d]Ps 76:12; 138:4; 148:11
16 [e]**Ps 51:18**; [f]Ps 8:1; Isa 60:1–2

17 [g]**1Ki 8:29**; Ps 4:1; 6:9 *18* [h]**Ro 4:24**; [i]**Ps 22:31**
19 [j]Ps 53:2 *20* [k]**Ps 68:6; Lk 4:19**
21 [l]Ps 22:22; [m]Ps 9:14
22 [n]**Ps 22:27**; Isa 49:22–23; Zec 8:20–23

23In the course of my life[a] he broke my
strength;
he cut short my days.[o]
24So I said:
"Do not take me away, O my God,
in the midst of my days;
your years go on[p] through all
generations.
25In the beginning[q] you laid the
foundations of the earth,
and the heavens[r] are the work of
your hands.[s]
26They will perish,[t] but you remain;
they will all wear out like a garment.
Like clothing you will change them
and they will be discarded.
27But you remain the same,[u]
and your years will never end.[v]
28The children of your servants[w] will live
in your presence;
their descendants[x] will be
established before you."

Psalm 103

Of David.

1Praise the LORD,[a] O my soul;[b]
all my inmost being, praise his holy
name.[c]
2Praise the LORD,[d] O my soul,
and forget not[e] all his benefits—
3who forgives all your sins[f]
and heals[g] all your diseases,
4who redeems your life[h] from the pit
and crowns you with love and
compassion,[i]
5who satisfies[j] your desires with good
things
so that your youth is renewed[k] like
the eagle's.[l]

6The LORD works righteousness[m]
and justice for all the oppressed.[n]

7He made known[o] his ways[p] to Moses,
his deeds[q] to the people of Israel:
8The LORD is compassionate and
gracious,[r]
slow to anger, abounding in love.
9He will not always accuse,
nor will he harbour his anger for
ever;[s]
10he does not treat us as our sins
deserve[t]
or repay us according to our
iniquities.
11For as high as the heavens are above
the earth,
so great is his love[u] for those who
fear him;[v]
12as far as the east is from the west,
so far has he removed our
transgressions[w] from us.
13As a father has compassion[x] on his
children,
so the LORD has compassion on
those who fear him;
14for he knows how we are formed,[y]
he remembers that we are dust.[z]
15As for man, his days are like grass,[a]
he flourishes like a flower[b] of the
field;
16the wind blows[c] over it and it is gone,
and its place[d] remembers it no more.
17But from everlasting to everlasting
the LORD's love is with those who
fear him,
and his righteousness with their
children's children[e]—
18with those who keep his covenant[f]
and remember[g] to obey his
precepts.[h]

19The LORD has established his throne[i]
in heaven,
and his kingdom rules[j] over all.

20Praise the LORD,[k] you his angels,[l]
you mighty ones[m] who do his
bidding,[n]
who obey his word.
21Praise the LORD, all his heavenly
hosts,[o]
you his servants[p] who do his will.
22Praise the LORD, all his works[q]
everywhere in his dominion.

Praise the LORD, O my soul.[r]

Psalm 104

1Praise the LORD, O my soul.[a]

O LORD my God, you are very great;
you are clothed with splendour and
majesty.[b]
2He wraps[c] himself in light[d] as with a
garment;
he stretches[e] out the heavens[f] like a
tent[g]
3 and lays the beams[h] of his upper
chambers on their waters.[i]
He makes the clouds[j] his chariot[k]
and rides on the wings of the wind.[l]

23 [o]Ps 39:5 **24** [p]**Ge 21:33**; Job 36:26; Ps 90:2 **25** [q]**Ge 1:1**; Heb 1:10–12*; [r]**2Ch 2:12**; [s]**Ps 8:3** **26** [t]Isa 13:10,13; 34:4; 51:6; Eze 32:8; Joel 2:10; Mt 24:35; 2Pe 3:7–10; Rev 20:11 **27** [u]**Nu 23:19**; Heb 13:8; Jas 1:17; [v]Ps 9:7 **28** [w]Ps 69:36; [x]Ps 25:13; 89:4

Ps. 103

1 [a]Ps 28:6; [b]Ps 104:1; [c]**Ps 30:4** **2** [d]Ps 106:1; 117:1; [e]**Dt 6:12**; Ps 77:11 **3** [f]**Ex 34:7**; [g]**Ex 15:26**; Col 3:13; 1Pe 2:24; 1Jn 1:9 **4** [h]Ps 34:22; 56:13; Isa 43:1; [i]**Ps 8:5**; 23:6 **5** [j]**Ps 90:14; 104:28**; [k]Job 33:25; Ps 119:25,93; 2Co 4:16; [l]**Ex 19:4** **6** [m]Ps 9:8; 65:5; Isa 9:7; [n]**Ps 74:21; Lk 4:19** **7** [o]Ps 99:7; 147:19; [p]**Ex 33:13**; [q]Ps 106:22 **8** [r]**Ex 22:27; Ps 86:15**; Mic 7:18–19; Jas 5:11 **9** [s]Ps 30:5; 79:5; Isa 57:16; Jer 3:5,12; Mic 7:18 **10** [t]**Ezr 9:13**; Ro 6:23 **11** [u]Ps 13:5; 57:10; 100:5; 106:45; 117:2; La 3:22; Eph 3:18; [v]**2Ch 6:31** **12** [w]**2Sa 12:13**; Ro 4:7; Eph 2:5 **13** [x]Mal 3:17; 1Jn 3:1 **14** [y]Ps 119:73; 139:13–15; Isa 29:16; [z]**Ge 2:7; Ps 146:4** **15** [a]Ps 37:2; 90:5; 102:11; Isa 40:6; [b]**Job 14:2**; Jas 1:10 **16** [c]Isa 40:7; Hag 1:9; [d]**Job 7:8** **17** [e]**Ge 48:11; Ezr 9:12** **18** [f]**Dt 29:9**; [g]Ps 119:52; [h]**Nu 15:40**; Jn 14:15 **19** [i]Ps 47:8; 80:1; 113:5; [j]Ps 22:28; 66:7; Da 4:17 **20** [k]Ps 28:6; [l]**Ne 9:6**; Lk 2:13; Heb 1:14; [m]**Ps 29:1**; [n]Ps 107:25; 135:7; 148:8 **21** [o]**1Ki 22:19**; [p]**Ne 7:73** **22** [q]Ps 19:1; 67:3; 145:10; 150:6; [r]ver 1; Ps 104:1

Ps. 104

1 [a]**Ps 103:22**; [b]**Job 40:10** **2** [c]Isa 49:18; Jer 43:12; [d]Ps 18:12; 1Ti 6:16; [e]Job 9:8; Jer 51:15; [f]Job 37:18; Isa 40:22; 42:5; 44:24; Zec 12:1; [g]**Ps 19:4** **3** [h]Am 9:6; [i]**Ps 24:2**; [j]**Dt 33:26**; Isa 19:1; Na 1:3; [k]**2Ki 2:11**; [l]Ps 18:10

[a]23 Or *By his power*

[4]He makes winds his messengers,[a m]
flames of fire[n] his servants.
[5]He set the earth[o] on its foundations;[p]
it can never be moved.
[6]You covered it[q] with the deep[r] as with
a garment;
the waters stood[s] above the
mountains.
[7]But at your rebuke[t] the waters fled,
at the sound of your thunder[u] they
took to flight;
[8]they flowed over the mountains,
they went down into the valleys,
to the place you assigned[v] for them.
[9]You set a boundary[w] they cannot
cross;
never again will they cover the
earth.

[10]He makes springs[x] pour water into the
ravines;
it flows between the mountains.
[11]They give water[y] to all the beasts of the
field;
the wild donkeys[z] quench their
thirst.
[12]The birds of the air[a] nest by the waters;
they sing among the branches.[b]
[13]He waters the mountains[c] from his
upper chambers;[d]
the earth is satisfied by the fruit of
his work.[e]
[14]He makes grass grow[f] for the cattle,
and plants for man to cultivate—
bringing forth food[g] from the earth:
[15]wine[h] that gladdens the heart of man,
oil[i] to make his face shine,
and bread that sustains[j] his heart.
[16]The trees of the LORD[k] are well
watered,
the cedars of Lebanon[l] that he
planted.
[17]There the birds[m] make their nests;
the stork has its home in the pine
trees.
[18]The high mountains belong to the wild
goats;[n]
the crags are a refuge for the
conies.[b o]

[19]The moon marks off the seasons,[p]
and the sun[q] knows when to go
down.
[20]You bring darkness,[r] it becomes night,[s]
and all the beasts of the forest[t] prowl.
[21]The lions roar for their prey[u]
and seek their food from God.[v]
[22]The sun rises, and they steal away;
they return and lie down in their
dens.[w]
[23]Then man goes out to his work,[x]
to his labour until evening.[y]

4 [m]Ps 148:8; Heb 1:7*; [n]Ge 3:24; 2Ki 2:11
5 [o]Ex 31:17; Job 26:7; Ps 24:1–2; 102:25; 121:2; [p]**1Sa 2:8**
6 [q]Ge 7:19; [r]**Ge 1:2**; [s]2Pe 3:6
7 [t]**Ps 18:15**; [u]**Ex 9:23**; Ps 29:3
8 [v]Ps 33:7
9 [w]**Ge 1:9**; **Ps 16:6**
10 [x]Ps 107:33; Isa 41:18
11 [y]ver 13; [z]**Ge 16:12**; Isa 32:14; Jer 14:6
12 [a]ver 17; Mt 8:20; [b]Mt 13:32
13 [c]Ps 135:7; 147:8; Jer 10:13; Zec 10:1; [d]**Lev 26:4**; [e]Am 9:6
14 [f]**Job 38:27**; Ps 147:8; [g]**Ge 1:30**; **Job 28:5**
15 [h]**Ge 14:18**; **Jdg 9:13**; [i]Ps 23:5; 92:10; Lk 7:46; [j]**Dt 8:3**; Mt 6:11
16 [k]Ge 1:11; [l]**Ps 72:16**
17 [m]ver 12
18 [n]**Dt 14:5**; [o]Pr 30:26
19 [p]**Ge 1:14**; [q]Ps 19:6
20 [r]Isa 45:7; Am 5:8; [s]Ps 74:16; [t]**Ps 50:10**
21 [u]Am 3:4; [v]Ps 145:15; Joel 1:20; **Mt 6:26**
22 [w]**Job 37:8**
23 [x]**Ge 3:19**; [y]Jdg 19:16
24 [z]Ps 40:5; [a]**Ge 1:31**; [b]Ps 24:1; 50:10–11
25 [c]Ps 69:34; [d]Eze 47:10
26 [e]Ps 107:23; Eze 27:9; Jnh 1:3; [f]**Job 3:8**; 41:1; [g]Job 40:20; [h]**Ge 1:21**
27 [i]Job 36:31; Ps 145:15; 147:9
28 [j]Ps 103:5; 145:16; Isa 58:11
29 [k]**Dt 31:17**; [l]**Job 7:21**
30 [m]**Ge 1:2**
31 [n]Ex 40:35; Ps 8:1; **Ro 11:36**; [o]**Ge 1:4**
32 [p]**Ps 97:4**; [q]Ex 19:18; [r]Ps 144:5
33 [s]**Ex 15:1**; Ps 108:1
34 [t]**Ps 2:11**; 9:2; 32:11

[24]How many are your works,[z] O LORD!
In wisdom you made[a] them all;
the earth is full of your creatures.[b]
[25]There is the sea,[c] vast and spacious,
teeming with creatures beyond
number—
living things both large and small.[d]
[26]There the ships[e] go to and fro,
and the leviathan,[f] which you
formed to frolic[g] there.[h]

[27]These all look to you
to give them their food[i] at the proper
time.
[28]When you give it to them,
they gather it up;
when you open your hand,
they are satisfied[j] with good things.
[29]When you hide your face,[k]
they are terrified;
when you take away their breath,
they die and return to the dust.[l]
[30]When you send your Spirit,[m]
they are created,
and you renew the face of the earth.

[31]May the glory of the LORD[n] endure for
ever;
may the LORD rejoice in his works[o]—
[32]he who looks at the earth, and it
trembles,[p]
who touches the mountains,[q] and
they smoke.[r]

[33]I will sing[s] to the LORD all my life;
I will sing praise to my God as long
as I live.
[34]May my meditation be pleasing to
him,
as I rejoice[t] in the LORD.
[35]But may sinners vanish[u] from the
earth
and the wicked be no more.[v]

Praise the LORD, O my soul.

Praise the LORD.[c w]

Psalm 105

105:1–15pp—1Ch 16:8–22

[1]Give thanks to the LORD,[a] call on his
name;[b]
make known among the nations
what he has done.

35 [u]Ps 37:38; [v]**Job 7:10**; [w]Ps 28:6; 105:45; 106:48

Ps. 105

1 [a]**1Ch 16:34**; [b]Ps 80:18; 99:6; 116:13; Joel 2:32; Ac 2:21

[a]4 Or *angels*
[b]18 That is, the hyrax or rock badger
[c]35 Hebrew *Hallelu Yah*; in the Septuagint this line stands at the beginning of Psalm 105.

2Sing to him,[c] sing praise[d] to him;
tell of all his wonderful acts.[e]
3Glory in his holy name;[f]
let the hearts of those who seek the LORD rejoice.
4Look to the LORD and his strength;
seek his face[g] always.

5Remember the wonders[h] he has done,
his miracles, and the judgments he pronounced,[i]
6O descendants of Abraham his servant,[j]
O sons of Jacob, his chosen[k] ones.
7He is the LORD our God;
his judgments are in all the earth.

8He remembers his covenant[l] for ever,
the word he commanded, for a thousand generations,
9the covenant he made with Abraham,[m]
the oath he swore to Isaac.
10He confirmed it[n] to Jacob as a decree,
to Israel as an everlasting covenant:[o]
11"To you I will give the land of Canaan[p]
as the portion you will inherit."[q]

12When they were but few in number,[r]
few indeed, and strangers in it,[s]
13they wandered from nation to nation,[t]
from one kingdom to another.
14He allowed no-one to oppress[u] them;
for their sake he rebuked kings:[v]
15"Do not touch[w] my anointed ones;
do my prophets[x] no harm."

16He called down famine[y] on the land
and destroyed all their supplies of food;
17and he sent a man before them—
Joseph, sold as a slave.[z]
18They bruised his feet with shackles,[a]
his neck was put in irons,
19till what he foretold[b] came to pass,
till the word[c] of the LORD proved him true.
20The king sent and released him,
the ruler of peoples set him free.[d]
21He made him master of his household,
ruler over all he possessed,
22to instruct his princes[e] as he pleased
and teach his elders wisdom.[f]

23Then Israel entered Egypt;[g]
Jacob lived[h] as an alien in the land of Ham.[i]
24The LORD made his people very fruitful;
he made them too numerous[j] for their foes,
25whose hearts he turned[k] to hate his people,
to conspire[l] against his servants.
26He sent Moses[m] his servant,
and Aaron,[n] whom he had chosen.[o]
27They performed[p] his miraculous signs[q] among them,
his wonders[r] in the land of Ham.
28He sent darkness[s] and made the land dark—
for had they not rebelled against[t] his words?
29He turned their waters into blood,[u]
causing their fish to die.[v]
30Their land teemed with frogs,[w]
which went up into the bedrooms of their rulers.
31He spoke,[x] and there came swarms of flies,[y]
and gnats[z] throughout their country.
32He turned their rain into hail,[a]
with lightning throughout their land;
33he struck down their vines[b] and fig-trees[c]
and shattered the trees of their country.
34He spoke,[d] and the locusts came,[e]
grasshoppers[f] without number;[g]
35they ate up every green thing in their land,
ate up the produce of their soil.
36Then he struck down all the firstborn[h] in their land,
the firstfruits of all their manhood.

37He brought out Israel, laden with silver and gold,[i]
and from among their tribes no-one faltered.
38Egypt was glad when they left,
because dread of Israel[j] had fallen on them.
39He spread out a cloud[k] as a covering,
and a fire to give light at night.[l]
40They asked,[m] and he brought them quail[n]
and satisfied them with the bread of heaven.[o]
41He opened the rock[p] and water gushed out;
like a river it flowed in the desert.

42For he remembered his holy promise[q]
given to his servant Abraham.
43He brought out his people with rejoicing,[r]
his chosen ones with shouts of joy;

2 [c]Ps 30:4; 33:3; 96:1; [d]Ps 7:17; 18:49; 27:6; 59:17; 71:22; 146:2; [e]**Ps 75:1**
3 [f]**Ps 89:16**
4 [g]**Ps 24:6**
5 [h]**Ps 40:5;** [i]**Dt 7:18**
6 [j]ver 42; [k]**Dt 10:15;** Ps 106:5
8 [l]**Ge 9:15;** Ps 106:45; 111:5; Eze 16:60; **Lk 1:72**
9 [m]Ge 12:7; **15:18; 22:16–18;** Lk 1:73; Gal 3:15–18
10 [n]Ge 28:13–15; [o]Isa 55:3
11 [p]**Ge 12:7;** [q]**Nu 34:2**
12 [r]Dt 7:7; [s]Ge 23:4; Heb 11:9
13 [t]Ge 15:13–16; Nu 32:13; 33:3–49
14 [u]Ge 35:5; [v]Ge 12:17–20; **20:3; Ps 9:5**
15 [w]**Ge 26:11; 1Sa 12:3;** [x]**Ge 20:7**
16 [y]**Ge 12:10; Lev 26:26;** Isa 3:1; Eze 4:16
17 [z]**Ge 37:28;** Ac 7:9
18 [a]**Ge 40:15**
19 [b]**Ge 12:10;** 40:20–22; [c]Ge 41:40
20 [d]Ge 41:14
22 [e]Ge 41:43–44; [f]**Ge 41:40**
23 [g]Ge 46:6; Ac 7:15; 13:17; [h]Ge 47:28; [i]**Ps 78:51**
24 [j]Ex 1:7,9; Ac 7:17
25 [k]**Ex 4:21;** [l]Ex 1:6–10; Ac 7:19
26 [m]**Ex 3:10;** [n]**Ex 4:16; Nu 33:1;** [o]**Nu 16:5;** 17:5–8
27 [p]ver 28–37; Ex 7:8–12:51; [q]**Ex 4:17; 10:1;** [r]**Ex 3:20;** Da 4:3
28 [s]**Ge 1:4; Ex 10:22;** [t]**Ex 7:22**
29 [u]**Ps 78:44;** [v]Ex 7:21
30 [w]**Ex 8:2,6**
31 [x]Ps 107:25; 148:8; [y]Ex 8:21–24; **Ps 78:45;** [z]Ex 8:16–18
32 [a]Ex 9:22–25; **Job 38:22; Ps 78:47**
33 [b]Ps 78:47; [c]Ex 10:5,12

34 [d]Ps 107:25; [e]**Ex 10:4,**12–15; [f]**1Ki 8:37;** [g]Joel 1:6
36 [h]**Ex 4:23; 12:12** *37* [i]**Ex 3:21–22**
38 [j]Ex 15:16 *39* [k]**Ex 13:21;** 1Co 10:1; [l]**Ps 78:14**
40 [m]Ps 78:18; [n]**Ex 16:13;** [o]**Ex 16:4;** Jn 6:31
41 [p]**Nu 20:11;** 1Co 10:4
42 [q]Ge 12:1–3; 13:14–17; 15:13–16
43 [r]Ex 15:1–18; Ps 106:12

44he gave them the lands of the nations,[s]
and they fell heir to what others had
toiled[t] for—
45that they might keep his precepts
and observe his laws.[u]

Praise the LORD.[a][v]

Psalm 106

106:1,47–48pp—1Ch 16:34–36

1Praise the LORD.[a][a]

Give thanks to the LORD, for he is
good;[b]
his love endures for ever.[c]
2Who can proclaim the mighty acts[d] of
the LORD
or fully declare his praise?
3Blessed are they who maintain
justice,[e]
who constantly do what is right.[f]
4Remember me,[g] O LORD, when you
show favour[h] to your people,
come to my aid[i] when you save
them,
5that I may enjoy the prosperity[j] of
your chosen ones,[k]
that I may share in the joy[l] of your
nation
and join your inheritance[m] in giving
praise.

6We have sinned,[n] even as our fathers[o]
did;
we have done wrong and acted
wickedly.[p]
7When our fathers were in Egypt,
they gave no thought[q] to your
miracles;
they did not remember[r] your many
kindnesses,
and they rebelled by the sea,[s] the
Red Sea.[b]
8Yet he saved them[t] for his name's
sake,[u]
to make his mighty power[v] known.
9He rebuked[w] the Red Sea, and it dried
up;[x]
he led them through[y] the depths as
through a desert.
10He saved them[z] from the hand of the
foe;[a]
from the hand of the enemy he
redeemed them.[b]
11The waters covered[c] their adversaries;
not one of them survived.
12Then they believed his promises
and sang his praise.[d]

13But they soon forgot[e] what he had
done
and did not wait for his counsel.[f]

44 [s]Ex 32:13; Jos 11:16–23; 12:8; 13:6–7; Ps 111:6; [t]Dt 6:10–11; Ps 78:55
45 [u]**Dt 4:40;** 6:21–24; Ps 78:5–7; [v]**Ps 104:35**

Ps. 106

1 [a]**Ps 22:23; 103:2;** [b]**Ps 119:68;** [c]**Ezr 3:11;** Ps 136:1–26; Jer 33:11
2 [d]**Ps 71:16**
3 [e]Ps 112:5; Hos 12:6; [f]Ps 15:2
4 [g]Ps 25:6–7; [h]**Ps 77:7;** [i]**Ge 50:24**
5 [j]**Dt 30:15;** Ps 1:3; [k]**Ps 105:6;** [l]Ps 20:5; 27:6; 47:5; 118:15; [m]**Ex 34:9**
6 [n]**1Ki 8:47; Ro 3:9;** [o]**2Ch 30:7;** [p]Ne 1:7
7 [q]**Jdg 3:7;** [r]Ps 78:42; [s]Ex 14:11–12
8 [t]Ex 14:30; **Ps 80:3;** 107:13; Isa 25:9; Joel 2:32; [u]**Ex 9:16; Ps 23:3;** [v]**Ex 14:31**
9 [w]Ps 18:15; Isa 50:2; [x]**Ex 14:21;** Na 1:4; [y]Ps 78:13; Isa 63:11–14
10 [z]Ex 14:30; Ps 107:13; [a]**Ps 78:53;** [b]Ps 78:42; 107:2; Isa 35:9; 62:12
11 [c]Ex 14:28
12 [d]Ex 15:1–21; **Ps 105:43**
13 [e]**Ex 15:24;** [f]**Ex 16:28; Nu 27:21**
14 [g]**Ps 78:40;** [h]**Ps 68:7;** [i]**Ex 17:2;** 1Co 10:9
15 [j]**Ex 16:13;** Ps 78:29; [k]**Nu 11:33**
16 [l]Nu 16:1–3
17 [m]Dt 11:6; [n]**Ex 15:12;** [o]**Nu 16:1**
18 [p]**Lev 10:2**
19 [q]**Ex 32:4;** Ac 7:41
20 [r]Jer 2:11; Ro 1:23
21 [s]Ps 78:11; [t]Dt 10:21; Ps 75:1
22 [u]**Ps 78:51;** [v]**Ex 3:20; Dt 4:34**
23 [w]**Ex 32:10;** [x]Ex 32:11–14; **Nu 11:2; Dt 9:19**

14In the desert[g] they gave in to their
craving;
in the wasteland[h] they put God to
the test.[i]
15So he gave them[j] what they asked for,
but sent a wasting disease[k] upon
them.

16In the camp they grew envious[l] of
Moses
and of Aaron, who was consecrated
to the LORD.
17The earth opened[m] up and swallowed
Dathan;[n]
it buried the company of Abiram.[o]
18Fire blazed[p] among their followers;
a flame consumed the wicked.

19At Horeb they made a calf[q]
and worshipped an idol cast from
metal.
20They exchanged their Glory[r]
for an image of a bull, which eats
grass.
21They forgot the God[s] who saved them,
who had done great things[t] in
Egypt,
22miracles in the land of Ham[u]
and awesome deeds[v] by the Red
Sea.
23So he said he would destroy[w] them—
had not Moses, his chosen one,
stood in the breach[x] before him
to keep his wrath from destroying
them.

24Then they despised[y] the pleasant
land;[z]
they did not believe[a] his promise.
25They grumbled[b] in their tents
and did not obey the LORD.
26So he swore[c] to them with uplifted
hand
that he would make them fall in the
desert,[d]
27make their descendants fall among the
nations
and scatter[e] them throughout the
lands.

28They yoked themselves to the Baal of
Peor[f]
and ate sacrifices offered to lifeless
gods;

24 [y]Nu 14:30–31; [z]**Dt 8:7; Jer 3:19;** [a]**Nu 14:11;** Heb 3:18–19 *25* [b]**Ex 15:24;** Dt 1:27; 1Co 10:10
26 [c]**Nu 14:23;** Heb 4:3; [d]**Dt 2:14;** Heb 3:17
27 [e]**Lev 26:33** *28* [f]**Nu 23:28**

[a]45 Hebrew *Hallelu Yah*
[a]1 Hebrew *Hallelu Yah;* also in verse 48
[b]7 Hebrew *Yam Suph;* that is, Sea of Reeds; also in verses 9 and 22

29they provoked the LORD to anger[g] by
their wicked deeds,[h]
and a plague[i] broke out among
them.
30But Phinehas[j] stood up and
intervened,
and the plague was checked.[k]
31This was credited to him[l] as
righteousness
for endless generations[m] to come.

32By the waters of Meribah[n] they
angered the LORD,
and trouble came to Moses because
of them;
33for they rebelled[o] against the Spirit[p] of
God,
and rash words came from Moses'
lips.[c][q]

34They did not destroy[r] the peoples
as the LORD had commanded[s] them,
35but they mingled[t] with the nations
and adopted their customs.
36They worshipped their idols,[u]
which became a snare[v] to them.
37They sacrificed their sons[w]
and their daughters to demons.[x]
38They shed innocent blood,
the blood of their sons[y] and
daughters,
whom they sacrificed to the idols of
Canaan,
and the land was desecrated by their
blood.
39They defiled themselves[z] by what they
did;
by their deeds they prostituted[a]
themselves.

40Therefore the LORD was angry[b] with
his people
and abhorred his inheritance.[c]
41He handed them over[d] to the nations,
and their foes ruled over them.
42Their enemies oppressed[e] them
and subjected them to their power.
43Many times he delivered them,[f]
but they were bent on rebellion[g]
and they wasted away in their sin.

44But he took note of their distress
when he heard their cry;[h]
45for their sake he remembered his
covenant[i]
and out of his great love[j] he
relented.[k]
46He caused them to be pitied[l]
by all who held them captive.

47Save us,[m] O LORD our God,
and gather us[n] from the nations,
that we may give thanks[o] to your holy
name[p]
and glory in your praise.

48Praise be to the LORD, the God of
Israel,
from everlasting to everlasting.
Let all the people say, "Amen!"[q]

Praise the LORD.

BOOK V

Psalms 107–150

Psalm 107

1Give thanks to the LORD,[a] for he is
good;[b]
his love endures for ever.
2Let the redeemed[c] of the LORD say
this—
those he redeemed from the hand of
the foe,
3those he gathered[d] from the lands,
from east and west, from north and
south.[a]

4Some wandered in desert[e] wastelands,
finding no way to a city[f] where they
could settle.
5They were hungry[g] and thirsty,[h]
and their lives ebbed away.
6Then they cried out[i] to the LORD in
their trouble,
and he delivered them from their
distress.
7He led them by a straight way[j]
to a city[k] where they could settle.
8Let them give thanks[l] to the LORD for
his unfailing love[m]
and his wonderful deeds[n] for men,
9for he satisfies[o] the thirsty
and fills the hungry with good
things.[p]

10Some sat in darkness[q] and the deepest
gloom,
prisoners suffering[r] in iron chains,[s]
11for they had rebelled[t] against the
words of God
and despised[u] the counsel[v] of the
Most High.

29 [g]Nu 25:3; [h]**Ps 64:2**; 141:4; [i]**Nu 16:46**; 25:8
30 [j]**Ex 6:25**; [k]Nu 25:8
31 [l]**Ge 15:6**; **Nu 25:11–13**; [m]Ps 49:11
32 [n]**Ex 17:7**; Nu 20:2–13
33 [o]**Ex 23:21**; Ps 107:11; [p]**Ps 51:11**; Isa 63:10; [q]Ex 17:4–7; Nu 20:8–12
34 [r]**Jos 9:15**; Jdg 1:27–36; [s]Ex 23:24; **Dt 2:34**; 7:16; 20:17
35 [t]Jdg 3:5–6; Ezr 9:1–2
36 [u]**Dt 7:16**; [v]**Ex 10:7**
37 [w]**Lev 18:21**; **Dt 12:31**; Eze 16:20–21; [x]**Ex 22:20**; **Dt 32:17**; 1Co 10:20
38 [y]**Lev 18:21**; **Dt 18:10**; **2Ki 3:27**
39 [z]**Ge 3:17**; Lev 18:24; Eze 20:18; [a]**Nu 15:39**
40 [b]**Lev 26:28**; [c]**Ex 34:9**; **Dt 9:29**
41 [d]**Jdg 2:14**
42 [e]**Jdg 4:3**
43 [f]**Jos 10:14**; Jdg 7:1–25; **Ne 9:28**; Ps 81:13–14; [g]**Jdg 2:16–19**; 6:1–7
44 [h]**Jdg 3:9**
45 [i]**Ge 9:15**; Ps 105:8; **Lk 1:72**; [j]**Ps 17:7**; **103:11**; [k]**Ex 32:14**
46 [l]**Ex 3:21**; **1Ki 8:50**
47 [m]**Ps 28:9**; [n]Ps 107:3; 147:2; Isa 11:12; 27:13; 56:8; 66:20; Jer 31:8; Eze 20:34; Mic 4:6; [o]Ps 105:1; [p]Ps 30:4; **99:3**
48 [q]**Ps 41:13**; **72:19**

Ps. 107

1 [a]**1Ch 16:8**; **2Ch 5:13**; [b]**2Ch 7:3**
2 [c]**Ps 106:10**; **Isa 35:9**
3 [d]**Ne 1:9**
4 [e]**Jos 5:6**; [f]ver 36
5 [g]Ex 16:3; [h]**Ex 15:22**; **17:2**
6 [i]**Ex 14:10**
7 [j]**Ezr 8:21**; [k]ver 36
8 [l]Ps 105:1; [m]Ps 6:4; [n]**Ps 75:1**
9 [o]Ps 22:26; 63:5; Isa 58:11; Mt 5:6; Lk 1:53; [p]**Ps 23:1**; Jer 31:25
10 [q]ver 14; Ps 88:6; 143:3; Isa 9:2; 42:7,16; 49:9; Mic 7:9; [r]Ps 102:20; Isa 61:1; [s]**Job 36:8**
11 [t]**Ps 5:10**; [u]**Nu 14:11**; [v]**1Ki 22:5**; 2Ch 36:16

[c]33 Or *against his spirit, / and rash words came from his lips*   [a]3 Hebrew *north and the sea*

12So he subjected them to bitter labour;
they stumbled, and there was
no-one to help.[w]
13Then they cried to the LORD in their
trouble,
and he saved them[x] from their
distress.
14He brought them out of darkness[y] and
the deepest gloom[z]
and broke away their chains.[a]
15Let them give thanks[b] to the LORD for
his unfailing love[c]
and his wonderful deeds[d] for men,
16for he breaks down gates of bronze
and cuts through bars of iron.

17Some became fools[e] through their
rebellious ways[f]
and suffered affliction[g] because of
their iniquities.
18They loathed all food[h]
and drew near the gates of death.[i]
19Then they cried[j] to the LORD in their
trouble,
and he saved them[k] from their
distress.
20He sent forth his word[l] and healed
them;[m]
he rescued[n] them from the grave.[o]
21Let them give thanks[p] to the LORD for
his unfailing love[q]
and his wonderful deeds[r] for men.
22Let them sacrifice thank-offerings[s]
and tell of his works[t] with songs of
joy.[u]

23Others went out on the sea[v] in ships;[w]
they were merchants on the mighty
waters.
24They saw the works of the LORD,[x]
his wonderful deeds in the deep.
25For he spoke[y] and stirred up a
tempest[z]
that lifted high the waves.[a]
26They mounted up to the heavens and
went down to the depths;
in their peril[b] their courage melted[c]
away.
27They reeled[d] and staggered like
drunken men;
they were at their wits' end.
28Then they cried[e] out to the LORD in
their trouble,
and he brought them out of their
distress.[f]
29He stilled the storm[g] to a whisper;
the waves[h] of the sea were hushed.[i]
30They were glad when it grew calm,
and he guided them[j] to their desired
haven.
31Let them give thanks[k] to the LORD for
his unfailing love[l]
and his wonderful deeds[m] for men.

32Let them exalt[n] him in the assembly[o] of
the people
and praise him in the council of the
elders.

33He turned rivers into a desert,[p]
flowing springs[q] into thirsty
ground,
34and fruitful land into a salt waste,[r]
because of the wickedness of those
who lived there.
35He turned the desert into pools of
water[s]
and the parched ground into
flowing springs;[t]
36there he brought the hungry to live,
and they founded a city where they
could settle.
37They sowed fields and planted
vineyards[u]
that yielded a fruitful harvest;
38he blessed them, and their numbers
greatly increased,[v]
and he did not let their herds
diminish.[w]

39Then their numbers decreased,[x] and
they were humbled[y]
by oppression, calamity and
sorrow;
40he who pours contempt on nobles[z]
made them wander in a trackless
waste.[a]
41But he lifted the needy[b] out of their
affliction
and increased their families like
flocks.[c]
42The upright see and rejoice,[d]
but all the wicked shut their
mouths.[e]

43Whoever is wise,[f] let him heed these
things
and consider the great love[g] of the
LORD.

Psalm 108

108:1–5pp—Ps 57:7–11
108:6–13pp—Ps 60:5–12

A song. A psalm of David.

1My heart is steadfast,[a] O God;
I will sing[b] and make music with all
my soul.
2Awake, harp and lyre![c]
I will awaken the dawn.

12 [w]**2Ki 14:26**; Ps 72:12
13 [x]**Ps 106:8**
14 [y]**ver 10**; Isa 9:2; 42:7; 50:10; 59:9; 60:2; **Lk 1:79**; [z]Ps 86:13; Isa 29:18; [a]**Job 36:8**; Ps 116:16; Ac 12:7
15 [b]ver 8,21,31; Ps 105:1; [c]Ps 6:4; [d]**Ps 75:1**
17 [e]**Ps 53:1**; [f]**Ps 25:7**; [g]**Lev 26:16**; Isa 65:6–7; Jer 30:14–15; Gal 6:7–8
18 [h]**Job 3:24; 6:6**; [i]**Job 17:16; 33:22**
19 [j]ver 28; Ps 5:2; [k]ver 13; Ps 34:4
20 [l]**Dt 32:2**; Ps 147:15; Mt 8:8; Lk 7:7; [m]**Ex 15:26**; [n]**Job 33:28**; [o]Ps 16:10; 30:3; **56:13**
21 [p]ver 15; [q]Ps 6:4; [r]Ps 75:1
22 [s]**Lev 7:12**; [t]Ps 9:11; 73:28; 118:17; [u]**Job 8:21; Ps 65:8**
23 [v]Isa 42:10; [w]**Ps 104:26**
24 [x]Ps 64:9; 111:2; 143:5
25 [y]**Ps 105:31**; [z]**Ps 50:3**; [a]**Ps 93:3**
26 [b]Lk 8:23; [c]**Jos 2:11**
27 [d]Isa 19:14; 24:20; 28:7
28 [e]**ver 19**; [f]Ps 4:1; Jnh 1:6
29 [g]Lk 8:24; [h]**Ps 93:3**; [i]**Ps 65:7**; Jnh 1:15
30 [j]ver 7
31 [k]**ver 15**; [l]Ps 6:4; [m]Ps 75:1; 106:2
32 [n]Ps 30:1; 34:3; 99:5; [o]**Ps 1:5**; 22:22; 26:12; 35:18
33 [p]1Ki 17:1; Ps 74:15; Isa 41:15; 42:15; 50:2; [q]**Ps 104:10**
34 [r]**Ge 13:10**
35 [s]**2Ki 3:17**; Ps 105:41; 126:4; Isa 43:19; 51:3; [t]**Job 38:26; Isa 35:7**
37 [u]**2Ki 19:29; Isa 37:30**
38 [v]**Ge 12:2; Dt 7:13**; [w]**Ge 49:25**
39 [x]**2Ki 10:32**; Eze 5:12; [y]**Ps 44:9**

40 [z]**Job 12:18**; [a]**Dt 32:10**
41 [b]**1Sa 2:8**; Ps 113:7–9; [c]**Job 21:11**
42 [d]**Job 22:19**; Ps 97:10–12; [e]**Job 5:16**; Ro 3:19
43 [f]Jer 9:12; Hos 14:9; [g]Ps 103:11

Ps. 108
1 [a]Ps 112:7; 119:30,112; [b]**Ps 18:49** *2* [c]**Job 21:12**

3 I will praise you, O LORD, among the nations;
I will sing of you among the peoples.
4 For great is your love,[d] higher than the heavens;
your faithfulness[e] reaches to the skies.[f]
5 Be exalted, O God, above the heavens,[g]
and let your glory be over all the earth.[h]

6 Save us and help us with your right hand,[i]
that those you love may be delivered.
7 God has spoken[j] from his sanctuary:[k]
"In triumph I will parcel out Shechem[l]
and measure off the Valley of Succoth.[m]
8 Gilead is mine, Manasseh is mine;
Ephraim is my helmet,
Judah[n] my sceptre.
9 Moab[o] is my washbasin,
upon Edom[p] I toss my sandal;
over Philistia[q] I shout in triumph."

10 Who will bring me to the fortified city?
Who will lead me to Edom?
11 Is it not you, O God, you who have rejected us
and no longer go out with our armies?[r]
12 Give us aid against the enemy,
for the help of man is worthless.[s]
13 With God we shall gain the victory,
and he will trample down[t] our enemies.

Psalm 109

For the director of music. Of David. A psalm.

1 O God, whom I praise,[a]
do not remain silent,[b]
2 for wicked and deceitful men[c]
have opened their mouths against me;
they have spoken against me with lying tongues.[d]
3 With words of hatred[e] they surround me;
they attack me without cause.[f]
4 In return for my friendship they accuse me,
but I am a man of prayer.[g]
5 They repay me evil for good,[h]
and hatred for my friendship.

4 [d]Nu 14:18; Ps 106:45; [e]Ex **34:6**; [f]**Ps 36:5**
5 [g]**Ps 8:1**; [h]**Ps 57:5**
6 [i]**Job 40:14**
7 [j]Ps 89:35; [k]Ps 68:35; 102:19; [l]**Ge 12:6**; [m]**Ge 33:17**
8 [n]**Ps 78:68**
9 [o]**Ge 19:37**; [p]**2Sa 8:13–14**; [q]**2Sa 8:1**
11 [r]**Ps 44:9**
12 [s]Ps 118:8; 146:3; Isa 10:3; 30:5; 31:3; Jer 2:36; 17:5
13 [t]Ps 44:5; Isa 22:5; 63:3,6

Ps. 109

1 [a]**Ex 15:2**; Jer 17:14; [b]**Job 34:29**
2 [c]**Ps 43:1**; [d]**Ps 52:4**
3 [e]Ps 69:4; [f]Ps 35:7; Jn 15:25
4 [g]Ps 69:13; 141:5
5 [h]**Ge 44:4**
6 [i]1Ch 21:1; Job 1:6; Zec 3:1
7 [j]Ps 1:5; [k]Pr 28:9; Isa 41:24
8 [l]**Job 15:32**; [m]Ac 1:20*
9 [n]Ex 22:24; Jer 18:21
10 [o]**Ge 4:12**
11 [p]Ne 5:3; [q]**Nu 14:3**; Isa 1:7; 6:11; 36:1; La 5:2; [r]Job 20:18
12 [s]**Job 5:4**
13 [t]Job 18:19; Ps 21:10; [u]**Nu 14:12**; Ps 9:5; Pr 10:7
14 [v]Ex 20:5; Nu 14:18; Isa 65:6–7; Jer 32:18
15 [w]Ps 90:8; [x]**Ex 17:14; Dt 32:26**
16 [y]**Job 20:19; Ps 35:10**; [z]**Ps 34:18**
17 [a]Pr 28:27; **Mt 7:2**
18 [b]Ps 10:7; [c]Nu 5:22
19 [d]ver 29; Ps 73:6; Eze 7:27
20 [e]**Ex 32:34**; Ps 54:5; 94:23; Isa 3:11; 2Ti 4:14; [f]Ps 71:10
21 [g]**Ex 9:16; Ps 23:3**; [h]Ps 69:16; [i]**Ps 3:7**

6 Appoint[a] an evil man[b] to oppose him;
let an accuser[c][i] stand at his right hand.
7 When he is tried, let him be found guilty,[j]
and may his prayers condemn[k] him.
8 May his days be few;[l]
may another take his place[m] of leadership.
9 May his children be fatherless
and his wife a widow.[n]
10 May his children be wandering beggars;[o]
may they be driven[d] from their ruined homes.
11 May a creditor[p] seize all he has;
may strangers plunder[q] the fruits of his labour.[r]
12 May no-one extend kindness to him
or take pity[s] on his fatherless children.
13 May his descendants be cut off,[t]
their names blotted out[u] from the next generation.
14 May the iniquity of his fathers[v] be remembered before the LORD;
may the sin of his mother never be blotted out.
15 May their sins always remain before[w] the LORD,
that he may cut off the memory[x] of them from the earth.

16 For he never thought of doing a kindness,
but hounded to death the poor
and the needy[y] and the broken-hearted.[z]
17 He loved to pronounce a curse—
may it[e] come on him;[a]
he found no pleasure in blessing—
may it be[f] far from him.
18 He wore cursing[b] as his garment;
it entered into his body like water,[c]
into his bones like oil.
19 May it be like a cloak wrapped[d] about him,
like a belt tied for ever round him.
20 May this be the LORD's payment[e] to my accusers,
to those who speak evil[f] of me.

21 But you, O Sovereign LORD,
deal well with me for your name's sake;[g]
out of the goodness of your love,[h]
deliver me.[i]

---

[a]6 Or ⌊*They say:*⌋ "*Appoint* (with quotation marks at the end of verse 19) [b]6 Or *the Evil One*
[c]6 Or *let Satan* [d]10 Septuagint; Hebrew *sought*
[e]17 Or *curse, / and it has* [f]17 Or *blessing, / and it is*

22For I am poor and needy,
and my heart is wounded within me.
23I fade away like an evening shadow;[j]
I am shaken off like a locust.
24My knees give[k] way from fasting;[l]
my body is thin and gaunt.[m]
25I am an object of scorn[n] to my accusers;
when they see me, they shake their heads.[o]

26Help me,[p] O LORD my God;
save me in accordance with your love.
27Let them know[q] that it is your hand,
that you, O LORD, have done it.
28They may curse,[r] but you will bless;
when they attack they will be put to shame,
but your servant will rejoice.[s]
29My accusers will be clothed with disgrace
and wrapped in shame[t] as in a cloak.

30With my mouth I will greatly extol the LORD;
in the great throng[u] I will praise him.
31For he stands at the right hand[v] of the needy one,
to save his life from those who condemn him.

Psalm 110

Of David. A psalm.

1The LORD says[a] to my Lord:
"Sit at my right hand[b]
until I make your enemies
a footstool for your feet."[c]

2The LORD will extend your mighty sceptre[d] from Zion;[e]
you will rule[f] in the midst of your enemies.
3Your troops will be willing
on your day of battle.
Arrayed in holy majesty,[g]
from the womb of the dawn
you will receive the dew of your youth.[a][h]

4The LORD has sworn
and will not change his mind:[i]
"You are a priest for ever,[j]
in the order of Melchizedek.[k]"

5The Lord is at your right hand;[l]
he will crush kings[m] on the day of his wrath.[n]
6He will judge nations,[o] heaping up the dead[p]
and crushing the rulers[q] of the whole earth.
7He will drink from a brook beside the way;[b]
therefore he will lift up his head.[r]

Psalm 111[a]

1Praise the LORD.[b]

I will extol the LORD[a] with all my heart[b]
in the council[c] of the upright and in the assembly.[d]

2Great are the works[e] of the LORD;
they are pondered by all[f] who delight in them.
3Glorious and majestic are his deeds,
and his righteousness endures[g] for ever.
4He has caused his wonders to be remembered;
the LORD is gracious and compassionate.[h]
5He provides food[i] for those who fear him;[j]
he remembers his covenant[k] for ever.
6He has shown his people the power of his works,[l]
giving them the lands of other nations.[m]
7The works of his hands[n] are faithful and just;
all his precepts are trustworthy.[o]
8They are steadfast for ever[p] and ever,
done in faithfulness and uprightness.
9He provided redemption[q] for his people;
he ordained his covenant for ever—
holy and awesome[r] is his name.

10The fear of the LORD[s] is the beginning of wisdom;[t]
all who follow his precepts have good understanding.[u]
To him belongs eternal praise.[v]

23 [j]**Job 14:2**
24 [k]Heb 12:12; [l]**Ps 35:13;** [m]**Job 16:8**
25 [n]**Ps 22:6;** [o]**Job 16:4; Mt 27:39;** Mk 15:29
26 [p]Ps 12:1; 119:86
27 [q]**Job 37:7**
28 [r]**2Sa 16:12;** [s]Ps 66:4; Isa 35:10; 51:11; 54:1; 65:14
29 [t]**Ps 35:26**
30 [u]**Ps 35:18**
31 [v]Ps 16:8; 108:6

Ps. 110

1 [a]Mt 22:44*; Mk 12:36*; Lk 20:42*; Ac 2:34*; [b]**Mk 16:19;** Heb 1:13*; 12:2; [c]**Jos 10:24; 1Ki 5:3;** 1Co 15:25
2 [d]**Ge 49:10;** Ps 45:6; Isa 14:5; Jer 48:17; [e]**Ps 2:6;** [f]Ps 72:8
3 [g]**Ex 15:11;** [h]Mic 5:7
4 [i]**Nu 23:19;** [j]Zec 6:13; Heb 5:6*; 7:21*; [k]**Ge 14:18;** Heb 5:10; 7:15–17*
5 [l]Ps 16:8; [m]**Dt 7:24;** Ps 2:12; 68:21; 76:12; Isa 60:12; Da 2:44; [n]**Ps 2:5;** Ro 2:5; Rev 6:17; 11:18
6 [o]**Ps 9:19;** [p]Isa 5:25; 34:3; 66:24; [q]**Ps 18:38**
7 [r]Ps 3:3; 27:6

Ps. 111

1 [a]Ps 34:1; 109:30; 115:18; 145:10; [b]**Ps 9:1;** [c]Ps 89:7; [d]**Ps 1:5**
2 [e]**Job 36:24;** Ps 143:5; Rev 15:3; [f]Ps 64:9
3 [g]Ps 112:3,9; 119:142
4 [h]**Dt 4:31; Ps 86:15**
5 [i]**Ge 1:30; Ps 37:25;** Mt 6:31–33; [j]Ps 103:11; [k]**1Ch 16:15; Ps 105:8**
6 [l]Ps 64:9; **66:3,** 5; [m]**Ps 105:44**
7 [n]**Ps 92:4;** [o]Ps 19:7; 119:128
8 [p]Ps 119:89, 152,160; Isa 40:8; **Mt 5:18**
9 [q]Ps 34:22; **103:4;** 130:7; Lk 1:68; [r]Ps 30:4; 99:3; Lk 1:49
10 [s]**Job 23:15; Ps 19:9;** [t]Dt 4:6; [u]**Dt 4:6;** Ps 119:98,104, 130; [v]Ps 28:6; 89:52

[a]3 Or / *your young men will come to you like the dew*
[b]7 Or / *The One who grants succession will set him in authority*
[a]This psalm is an acrostic poem, the lines of which begin with the successive letters of the Hebrew alphabet. [b]1 Hebrew *Hallelu Yah*

Psalm 112[a]

[1]Praise the LORD.[b][a]

Blessed is the man[b] who fears the
LORD,[c]
who finds great delight[d] in his
commands.

[2]His children[e] will be mighty in the
land;
the generation of the upright will be
blessed.
[3]Wealth and riches[f] are in his house,
and his righteousness endures[g] for
ever.
[4]Even in darkness light dawns[h] for the
upright,
for the gracious and compassionate
and righteous[i] man.[c]
[5]Good will come to him who is
generous and lends freely,[j]
who conducts his affairs with
justice.
[6]Surely he will never be shaken;[k]
a righteous man will be
remembered[l] for ever.
[7]He will have no fear of bad news;
his heart is steadfast,[m] trusting in
the LORD.[n]
[8]His heart is secure, he will have no
fear;[o]
in the end he will look in triumph on
his foes.[p]
[9]He has scattered abroad his gifts to the
poor,[q]
his righteousness endures[r] for ever;
his horn[d] will be lifted[s] high in
honour.

[10]The wicked man will see[t] and be
vexed,
he will gnash his teeth[u] and waste
away;[v]
the longings of the wicked will come
to nothing.[w]

Psalm 113

[1]Praise the LORD.[a][a]

Praise, O servants of the LORD,[b]
praise the name of the LORD.
[2]Let the name of the LORD be praised,[c]
both now and for evermore.[d]
[3]From the rising of the sun[e] to the place
where it sets,
the name of the LORD is to be
praised.

[4]The LORD is exalted[f] over all the
nations,
his glory above the heavens.[g]
[5]Who is like the LORD our God,[h]
the One who sits enthroned[i] on
high,[j]
[6]who stoops down to look[k]
on the heavens and the earth?

[7]He raises the poor[l] from the dust
and lifts the needy[m] from the ash
heap;
[8]he seats them[n] with princes,
with the princes of their people.
[9]He settles the barren[o] woman in her
home
as a happy mother of children.

Praise the LORD.

Psalm 114

[1]When Israel came out of Egypt,[a]
the house of Jacob from a people of
foreign tongue,
[2]Judah[b] became God's sanctuary,[c]
Israel his dominion.

[3]The sea looked and fled,[d]
the Jordan turned back;[e]
[4]the mountains skipped[f] like rams,
the hills like lambs.

[5]Why was it, O sea, that you fled,[g]
O Jordan, that you turned back,
[6]you mountains, that you skipped like
rams,
you hills, like lambs?

[7]Tremble, O earth,[h] at the presence of
the Lord,
at the presence of the God of Jacob,
[8]who turned the rock into a pool,
the hard rock into springs of water.[i]

Psalm 115

115:4–11pp—Ps 135:15–20

[1]Not to us, O LORD, not to us
but to your name be the glory,[a]
because of your love and
faithfulness.[b]

[2]Why do the nations say,
"Where is their God?"[c]

Ps. 112

1 [a]Ps 33:2; 103:1; 150:1; [b]Ps 1:1–2; [c]**Job 1:8**; Ps 103:11; 115:13; 128:1; [d]**Ps 1:2**; 119:14, 16,47,92
2 [e]Ps 25:13; 37:26; 128:2–4
3 [f]**Dt 8:18**; [g]**Ps 37:6; 111:3**
4 [h]**Ps 18:28**; [i]Ps 5:12
5 [j]**Ps 37:21**,26; Lk 6:35
6 [k]**Ps 15:5; 55:22**; [l]Pr 10:7; Ecc 2:16
7 [m]Ps 57:7; 108:1; [n]**Ps 28:7**; 56:3–4; **Isa 12:2**
8 [o]Ps 3:6; 27:1; 56:11; Pr 1:33; Isa 12:2; [p]**Ps 54:7**
9 [q]Lk 19:8; Ac 9:36; 2Co 9:9*; [r]**Ps 111:3**; [s]**Ps 75:10**
10 [t]Ps 86:17; [u]**Ps 37:12; Mt 8:12**; [v]**Ps 34:21**; [w]**Job 8:13**

Ps. 113

1 [a]**Ps 22:23**; [b]Ps 34:22; **103:21**; 134:1
2 [c]**Ps 30:4**; 48:10; 145:21; 148:13; 149:3; Isa 12:4; [d]Ps 115:18; 131:3; Da 2:20
3 [e]Isa 24:15; 45:6; 59:19; Mal 1:11
4 [f]**Ps 99:2**; [g]**Ps 8:1; 57:11**
5 [h]**Ex 8:10; Ps 35:10**; [i]**Ps 103:19**; [j]**Job 16:19**
6 [k]Ps 11:4; 138:6; Isa 57:15
7 [l]1Sa 2:8; Ps 35:10; 68:10; 140:12; [m]Ps 107:41
8 [n]**2Sa 9:11**
9 [o]**1Sa 2:5**

Ps. 114

1 [a]**Ex 13:3; 29:46**
2 [b]Ps 76:1; [c]**Ex 15:17**; Ps 78:68–69
3 [d]Ex 14:21; Ps 77:16; [e]**Ex 15:8; Jos 3:16**
4 [f]**Jdg 5:5**
5 [g]**Ex 14:21**
7 [h]**Ex 15:14; 1Ch 16:30**
8 [i]**Ex 17:6; Nu 20:11**

Ps. 115

1 [a]Ps 29:2; 66:2; 96:8; [b]**Ex 34:6** 2 [c]**Ps 42:3**

[a]This psalm is an acrostic poem, the lines of which begin with the successive letters of the Hebrew alphabet. [b]*1* Hebrew *Hallelu Yah*
[c]*4* Or / *for ⌞the LORD⌟ is gracious and compassionate and righteous* [d]*9* *Horn* here symbolises dignity.
[a]*1* Hebrew *Hallelu Yah*; also in verse 9

3Our God is in heaven;[d]
he does whatever pleases him.[e]
4But their idols are silver and gold,[f]
made by the hands of men.[g]
5They have mouths, but cannot speak,[h]
eyes, but they cannot see;
6they have ears, but cannot hear,
noses, but they cannot smell;
7they have hands, but cannot feel,
feet, but they cannot walk;
nor can they utter a sound with their throats.
8Those who make them will be like them,
and so will all who trust in them.

9O house of Israel, trust[i] in the LORD—
he is their help and shield.
10O house of Aaron,[j] trust in the LORD—
he is their help and shield.
11You who fear him,[k] trust in the LORD—
he is their help and shield.

12The LORD remembers[l] us and will bless us:[m]
He will bless the house of Israel,
he will bless the house of Aaron,
13he will bless those who fear[n] the LORD—
small and great alike.

14May the LORD make you increase,[o]
both you and your children.
15May you be blessed by the LORD,
the Maker of heaven[p] and earth.

16The highest heavens belong to the LORD,[q]
but the earth he has given[r] to man.
17It is not the dead[s] who praise the LORD,
those who go down to silence;
18it is we who extol the LORD,[t]
both now and for evermore.[u]

Praise the LORD.[a][v]

Psalm 116

1I love the LORD,[a] for he heard my voice;
he heard my cry[b] for mercy.[c]
2Because he turned his ear[d] to me,
I will call on him as long as I live.

3The cords of death[e] entangled me,
the anguish of the grave[a] came upon me;
I was overcome by trouble and sorrow.
4Then I called on the name[f] of the LORD:
"O LORD, save me![g]"

5The LORD is gracious and righteous;[h]
our God is full of compassion.[i]
6The LORD protects the simple-hearted;
when I was in great need,[j] he saved me.[k]

7Be at rest[l] once more, O my soul,
for the LORD has been good[m] to you.

8For you, O LORD, have delivered my soul[n] from death,
my eyes from tears,
my feet from stumbling,
9that I may walk before the LORD[o]
in the land of the living.[p]
10I believed;[q] therefore[b] I said,
"I am greatly afflicted."[r]
11And in my dismay I said,
"All men are liars."[s]

12How can I repay the LORD
for all his goodness[t] to me?
13I will lift up the cup of salvation
and call on the name[u] of the LORD.
14I will fulfil my vows[v] to the LORD
in the presence of all his people.

15Precious in the sight[w] of the LORD
is the death of his saints.[x]
16O LORD, truly I am your servant;[y]
I am your servant, the son of your maidservant;[c][z]
you have freed me from my chains.[a]

17I will sacrifice a thank-offering[b] to you
and call on the name of the LORD.
18I will fulfil my vows[c] to the LORD
in the presence of all his people,
19in the courts[d] of the house of the LORD—
in your midst, O Jerusalem.[e]

Praise the LORD.[d]

Psalm 117

1Praise the LORD,[a] all you nations;[b]
extol him, all you peoples.
2For great is his love[c] towards us,
and the faithfulness of the LORD[d]
endures for ever.

Praise the LORD.[d]

3 [d]Ezr 5:11; Ne 1:4; Ps 103:19; 136:26; Mt 6:9; [e]Ps 135:6
4 [f]Rev 9:20; [g]**2Ki 19:18; 2Ch 32:19;** Jer 10:3–5; Ac 19:26
5 [h]Jer 10:5
9 [i]Ps 37:3; 62:8
10 [j]Ex 30:30; Ps 118:3
11 [k]Ps 22:23; 103:11; 118:4
12 [l]**1Ch 16:15;** [m]**Ge 12:2**
13 [n]**Ps 112:1**
14 [o]Dt 1:11
15 [p]**Ge 1:1;** Ac 14:15; **Rev 10:6**
16 [q]**Ps 89:11;** [r]**Ge 1:28;** Ps 8:6–8
17 [s]Ps 88:10–12
18 [t]**Ps 111:1;** [u]**Ps 113:2;** [v]Ps 28:6; 33:2; 103:1

Ps. 116

1 [a]Ps 18:1; [b]**Ps 31:22; 40:1;** [c]**Ps 6:9; 28:2**
2 [d]**Ps 5:1**
3 [e]**2Sa 22:6;** Ps 18:4–5
4 [f]Ps 80:18; 118:5; [g]**Ps 80:2**
5 [h]**Ex 9:27; 2Ch 12:6; Ezr 9:15;** [i]**Ex 22:27; Ps 86:15**
6 [j]**Ps 79:8;** [k]Ps 18:3; 22:5; 107:13
7 [l]Ps 46:10; 62:1; 131:2; Mt 11:29; [m]Ps 13:6; 106:1; 142:7
8 [n]**Ps 86:13**
9 [o]**Ge 5:22;** Ps 56:13; 89:15; [p]**Job 28:13;** Ps 27:13; Isa 38:11; Jer 11:19
10 [q]2Co 4:13*; [r]Ps 9:18; 72:2; **107:17;** 119:67,71,75
11 [s]Jer 9:3–5; Hos 7:13; Mic 6:12; Ro 3:4
12 [t]Ps 103:2; 106:1
13 [u]**Ps 105:1**
14 [v]**Nu 30:2; Ps 66:13**
15 [w]Ps 72:14; [x]**Nu 23:10**
16 [y]Ps 119:125; 143:12; [z]**Ps 86:16;** [a]**Job 12:18**
17 [b]**Lev 7:12; Ezr 1:4**
18 [c]ver 14; **Lev 22:18**
19 [d]Ps 92:13; 96:8; 100:4; 135:2; [e]Ps 102:21

Ps. 117

1 [a]**Ps 22:23; 103:2;** [b]**Ro 15:11***
2 [c]**Ps 17:7; 103:11;** [d]**Ps 119:90; 146:6**

[a]*18* Hebrew *Hallelu Yah*
[a]*3* Hebrew *Sheol*
[b]*10* Or *believed even when*
[c]*16* Or *servant, your faithful son*
[d]*19, 2* Hebrew *Hallelu Yah*

Psalm 118

[1]Give thanks to the LORD,[a] for he is
good;[b]
his love endures for ever.[c]

[2]Let Israel say:[d]
"His love endures for ever."[e]
[3]Let the house of Aaron say:[f]
"His love endures for ever."
[4]Let those who fear the LORD[g] say:
"His love endures for ever."

[5]In my anguish[h] I cried to the LORD,
and he answered[i] by setting me
free.
[6]The LORD is with me;[j] I will not be
afraid.
What can man do to me?[k]
[7]The LORD is with me; he is my helper.[l]
I will look in triumph on my
enemies.[m]

[8]It is better to take refuge in the LORD[n]
than to trust in man.[o]
[9]It is better to take refuge in the LORD
than to trust in princes.[p]

[10]All the nations surrounded me,
but in the name of the LORD I cut
them off.[q]
[11]They surrounded me[r] on every side,[s]
but in the name of the LORD I cut
them off.
[12]They swarmed around me like bees,[t]
but they died out as quickly as
burning thorns;[u]
in the name of the LORD I cut them
off.[v]

[13]I was pushed back and about to fall,
but the LORD helped me.[w]
[14]The LORD is my strength[x] and my
song;
he has become my salvation.[y]

[15]Shouts of joy[z] and victory
resound in the tents of the
righteous:
"The LORD's right hand[a] has done
mighty things![b]
16 The LORD's right hand is lifted high;
the LORD's right hand has done
mighty things!"

[17]I will not die[c] but live,
and will proclaim[d] what the LORD
has done.
[18]The LORD has chastened[e] me severely,
but he has not given me over to
death.[f]

[19]Open for me the gates[g] of
righteousness;
I will enter[h] and give thanks to the
LORD.
[20]This is the gate of the LORD[i]
through which the righteous may
enter.[j]
[21]I will give you thanks, for you
answered me;[k]
you have become my salvation.[l]

[22]The stone[m] the builders rejected
has become the capstone;[n]
[23]the LORD has done this,
and it is marvellous[o] in our eyes.
[24]This is the day the LORD has made;
let us rejoice and be glad[p] in it.

[25]O LORD, save us;[q]
O LORD, grant us success.
[26]Blessed is he who comes[r] in the name
of the LORD.
From the house of the LORD we bless
you.[a][s]
[27]The LORD is God,[t]
and he has made his light shine[u]
upon us.
With boughs in hand,[v] join in the
festal procession
up[b] to the horns of the altar.[w]

[28]You are my God, and I will give
thanks;
you are my God,[x] and I will exalt[y]
you.

[29]Give thanks to the LORD, for he is
good;
his love endures for ever.

Psalm 119[a]

א Aleph

[1]Blessed are they whose ways are
blameless,[a]
who walk[b] according to the law of
the LORD.[c]
[2]Blessed[d] are they who keep his
statutes[e]
and seek him[f] with all their heart.[g]
[3]They do nothing wrong;[h]
they walk in his ways.[i]

Ps. 118

1 [a]**1Ch 16:8;** [b]**2Ch 5:13;** 7:3; [c]**Ezr 3:11**
2 [d]Ps 115:9; [e]Ps 106:1; 136:1–26
3 [f]Ex 30:30; Ps 115:10
4 [g]**Ps 115:11**
5 [h]Ps 18:6; 31:7; 77:2; 120:1; [i]ver 21; Ps 34:4; 86:7; 116:1; 138:3
6 [j]**Dt 31:6;** Heb 13:5; [k]**Ps 56:4**
7 [l]**Dt 33:29;** Heb 13:6*; [m]**Ps 54:7**
8 [n]Ps 2:12; 5:11; 9:9; 37:3; 40:4; Isa 25:4; 57:13; [o]2Ch 32:7–8; **Ps 108:12; Isa 2:22**
9 [p]Ps 146:3
10 [q]**Ps 37:9**
11 [r]Ps 88:17; [s]Ps 3:6
12 [t]Dt 1:44; [u]**Ps 58:9;** [v]Ps 37:9
13 [w]ver 7; 2Ch 18:31; Ps 86:17
14 [x]**Ex 15:2;** [y]**Ps 62:2**
15 [z]**Job 8:21; Ps 106:5;** [a]**Ex 15:6;** Ps 89:13; 108:6; [b]Lk 1:51
17 [c]Hab 1:12; [d]**Dt 32:3;** Ps 64:9; 71:16; 73:28
18 [e]Jer 31:18; 1Co 11:32; Heb 12:5; [f]Ps 86:13
19 [g]**Ps 24:7;** [h]Ps 100:4
20 [i]Ps 122:1–2; [j]Ps 15:1–2; 24:3–4; Rev 22:14
21 [k]**ver 5;** [l]Ps 27:1
22 [m]Isa 8:14; [n]Isa 17:10; 19:13; 28:16; Zec 4:7; 10:4; Mt 21:42; Mk 12:10; Lk 20:17*; **Ac 4:11***; 1Pe 2:7
23 [o]Mt 21:42*; Mk 12:11*
24 [p]**Ps 70:4**
25 [q]**Ps 28:9;** 116:4
26 [r]**Mt 11:3;** 21:9*; 23:39; Mk 11:9*; Lk 13:35*; 19:38; Jn 12:13*; [s]Ps 129:8
27 [t]**1Ki 18:21;** [u]Ps 27:1; Isa 58:10; 60:1, 19–20; Mal 4:2; 1Pe 2:9; [v]**Lev 23:40;** [w]Ex 27:2
28 [x]**Ge 28:21; Ps 16:2;** 63:1; Isa 25:1; [y]**Ex 15:2**

Ps. 119

1 [a]**Ge 17:1; Dt 18:13;** Pr 11:20; [b]Ps 128:1; [c]**Ps 1:2**
2 [d]Ps 112:1; Isa 56:2; [e]ver 146; Ps 99:7; [f]**1Ch 16:11; Ps 40:16;** [g]**Dt 10:12**
3 [h]**Ps 59:4;** 1Jn 3:9; 5:18; [i]Ps 128:1; Jer 6:16; 7:23

---

[a]26 The Hebrew is plural.
[b]27 Or *Bind the festal sacrifice with ropes / and take it*
[a]This psalm is an acrostic poem; the verses of each stanza begin with the same letter of the Hebrew alphabet.

4 You have laid down precepts[j]
that are to be fully obeyed.[k]
5 Oh, that my ways were steadfast
in obeying your decrees![l]
6 Then I would not be put to shame[m]
when I consider all your
commands.[n]
7 I will praise you with an upright heart
as I learn your righteous laws.[o]
8 I will obey your decrees;
do not utterly forsake me.[p]

ב Beth

9 How can a young man keep his way
pure?[q]
By living according to your word.[r]
10 I seek you with all my heart;[s]
do not let me stray from your
commands.[t]
11 I have hidden your word in my heart[u]
that I might not sin[v] against you.
12 Praise be[w] to you, O LORD;
teach me[x] your decrees.[y]
13 With my lips I recount
all the laws that come from your
mouth.[z]
14 I rejoice in following your statutes[a]
as one rejoices in great riches.
15 I meditate on your precepts[b]
and consider your ways.
16 I delight[c] in your decrees;
I will not neglect your word.

ג Gimel

17 Do good to your servant,[d] and I will
live;
I will obey your word.[e]
18 Open my eyes that I may see
wonderful things in your law.
19 I am a stranger on earth;[f]
do not hide your commands from
me.
20 My soul is consumed[g] with longing
for your laws[h] at all times.
21 You rebuke the arrogant,[i] who are
cursed[j]
and who stray[k] from your
commands.
22 Remove from me scorn[l] and
contempt,
for I keep your statutes.[m]
23 Though rulers sit together and slander
me,
your servant will meditate on your
decrees.
24 Your statutes are my delight;
they are my counsellors.

ד Daleth

25 I am laid low in the dust;[n]
preserve my life[o] according to your
word.[p]
26 I recounted my ways and you
answered me;
teach me your decrees.[q]
27 Let me understand the teaching of
your precepts;
then I will meditate on your
wonders.[r]
28 My soul is weary with sorrow;[s]
strengthen me[t] according to your
word.[u]
29 Keep me from deceitful ways;[v]
be gracious to me[w] through your
law.
30 I have chosen[x] the way of truth;[y]
I have set my heart[z] on your laws.
31 I hold fast[a] to your statutes, O LORD;
do not let me be put to shame.
32 I run in the path of your commands,
for you have set my heart free.

ה He

33 Teach me,[b] O LORD, to follow your
decrees;
then I will keep them to the end.
34 Give me understanding,[c] and I will
keep your law[d]
and obey it with all my heart.[e]
35 Direct me[f] in the path of your
commands,[g]
for there I find delight.[h]
36 Turn my heart[i] towards your statutes
and not towards selfish gain.[j]
37 Turn my eyes away from worthless
things;
preserve my life[k] according to your
word.[b] [l]
38 Fulfil your promise[m] to your servant,
so that you may be feared.
39 Take away the disgrace[n] I dread,
for your laws are good.
40 How I long[o] for your precepts!
Preserve my life[p] in your
righteousness.

ו Waw

41 May your unfailing love[q] come to me,
O LORD,
your salvation according to your
promise;[r]
42 then I will answer[s] the one who taunts
me,[t]
for I trust in your word.
43 Do not snatch the word of truth from
my mouth,[u]

4 [j]Ps 103:18; [k]**ver 56; Dt 6:17**
5 [l]**Lev 19:37**
6 [m]ver 46,80; [n]ver 117
7 [o]**Dt 4:8**
8 [p]**Ps 38:21**
9 [q]**Ps 39:1**; [r]ver 65,169
10 [s]**Ps 9:1**; [t]ver 21,118
11 [u]**Dt 6:6; Job 22:22**; [v]ver 133,165; Ps 18:22–23; 19:13; Pr 3:23; Isa 63:13
12 [w]Ps 28:6; [x]Ps 143:8,10; [y]**Ex 18:20**
13 [z]ver 72
14 [a]ver 111
15 [b]ver 97,148; Ps 1:2
16 [c]**Ps 112:1**
17 [d]Ps 13:6; 116:7; [e]ver 67; Ps 103:20
19 [f]**Ge 23:4**; Heb 11:13
20 [g]Ps 42:2; 84:2; [h]ver 131; **Ps 63:1**; Isa 26:9
21 [i]ver 51; Job 30:1; Ps 5:5; Jer 20:7; 50:32; Da 4:37; Mal 3:15; [j]Dt 27:26; [k]**ver 10**
22 [l]Ps 39:8; [m]ver 2
25 [n]Ps 44:25; [o]ver 50,107; Ps 143:11; [p]ver 9
26 [q]Ps 25:4; 27:11; 86:11
27 [r]Ps 105:2; 145:5
28 [s]Ps 6:7; 116:3; Isa 51:11; Jer 45:3; [t]Ps 18:1; Isa 40:29; 41:10; [u]ver 9
29 [v]Ps 26:4; [w]**Nu 6:25**
30 [x]**Jos 24:22**; [y]**Ps 26:3**; [z]**Ps 108:1**
31 [a]**Dt 10:20**
33 [b]ver 12
34 [c]ver 27,73, 144,169; **Job 32:8**; Pr 2:6; Da 2:21; Jas 1:5; [d]**Dt 6:25**; [e]ver 69
35 [f]Ps 25:4–5; [g]ver 32; [h]**Ps 1:2**
36 [i]**Jos 24:23**; [j]Eze 33:31
37 [k]ver 25; Ps 71:20; [l]ver 9
38 [m]**Nu 23:19**
39 [n]ver 22; Ps 69:9; 89:51; Isa 25:8; 51:7; 54:4
40 [o]ver 20; [p]ver 25,149,154
41 [q]**Ps 6:4**; [r]ver 76,116,154,170
42 [s]Pr 27:11; [t]**Ps 42:10**
43 [u]**1Ki 17:24**

b37 Two manuscripts of the Masoretic Text and Dead Sea Scrolls; most manuscripts of the Masoretic Text *life in your way*

for I have put my hope[v] in your
laws.
44 I will always obey your law,[w]
for ever and ever.
45 I will walk about in freedom,
for I have sought out your precepts.[x]
46 I will speak of your statutes before
kings[y]
and will not be put to shame,[z]
47 for I delight[a] in your commands
because I love them.[b]
48 I lift up my hands to[c] your commands,
which I love,
and I meditate[c] on your decrees.

ז Zayin

49 Remember your word[d] to your
servant,
for you have given me hope.[e]
50 My comfort in my suffering is this:
Your promise preserves my life.[f]
51 The arrogant mock me[g] without
restraint,
but I do not turn[h] from your law.
52 I remember[i] your ancient laws, O
LORD,
and I find comfort in them.
53 Indignation grips me[j] because of the
wicked,
who have forsaken your law.[k]
54 Your decrees are the theme of my
song[l]
wherever I lodge.
55 In the night I remember[m] your name,
O LORD,
and I will keep your law.[n]
56 This has been my practice:
I obey your precepts.[o]

ח Heth

57 You are my portion,[p] O LORD;
I have promised to obey your
words.[q]
58 I have sought[r] your face with all my
heart;
be gracious to me[s] according to your
promise.[t]
59 I have considered my ways[u]
and have turned my steps to your
statutes.
60 I will hasten and not delay
to obey your commands.[v]
61 Though the wicked bind me with
ropes,
I will not forget[w] your law.
62 At midnight[x] I rise to give you thanks
for your righteous laws.[y]
63 I am a friend to all who fear you,[z]
to all who follow your precepts.[a]
64 The earth is filled with your love,[b] O
LORD;
teach me your decrees.[c]

ט Teth

65 Do good[d] to your servant
according to your word,[e] O LORD.
66 Teach me knowledge[f] and good
judgment,
for I believe in your commands.
67 Before I was afflicted[g] I went astray,[h]
but now I obey your word.[i]
68 You are good,[j] and what you do is
good;
teach me your decrees.[k]
69 Though the arrogant have smeared
me with lies,[l]
I keep your precepts with all my
heart.
70 Their hearts are callous[m] and
unfeeling,
but I delight in your law.
71 It was good for me to be afflicted[n]
so that I might learn your decrees.
72 The law from your mouth is more
precious to me
than thousands of pieces of silver
and gold.[o]

י Yodh

73 Your hands made me[p] and formed me;
give me understanding to learn
your commands.
74 May those who fear you rejoice[q] when
they see me,
for I have put my hope in your
word.[r]
75 I know, O LORD, that your laws are
righteous,[s]
and in faithfulness[t] you have
afflicted me.
76 May your unfailing love[u] be my
comfort,
according to your promise[v] to your
servant.
77 Let your compassion[w] come to me that
I may live,
for your law is my delight.[x]
78 May the arrogant[y] be put to shame for
wronging me without cause;[z]
but I will meditate on your precepts.
79 May those who fear you turn to me,
those who understand your
statutes.[a]
80 May my heart be blameless[b] towards
your decrees,[c]
that I may not be put to shame.[d]

43 [v]ver 74,81, 114,147
44 [w]ver 33–34, 55; **Dt 6:25**
45 [x]ver 94,155
46 [y]Mt 10:18; Ac 26:1–2; [z]**ver 6**
47 [a]ver 77,143; **Ps 112:1**; [b]ver 97,127, 159,163,165
48 [c]**Ge 24:63**
49 [d]ver 9; [e]ver 43
50 [f]**ver 25**
51 [g]**ver 21; Job 16:10; 17:2**; [h]**Job 23:11**
52 [i]Ps 103:18
53 [j]**Ex 32:19; 33:4**; [k]Ps 89:30
54 [l]ver 172; Ps 101:1; 138:5
55 [m]ver 62,72; Ps 1:2; 42:8; **63:6**; 77:2; Isa 26:9; Ac 16:25; [n]**ver 44**
56 [o]ver 4,100, 134,168; **Nu 15:40**
57 [p]**Dt 32:9**; Jer 51:19; La 3:24; [q]ver 17, 67,101
58 [r]**Dt 4:29; 1Ch 16:11**; Ps 34:4; [s]**Ge 43:29; Ezr 9:8**; [t]ver 41
59 [u]Jos 24:14–15; **Ps 39:1**
60 [v]ver 115
61 [w]ver 83,109, 153,176
62 [x]**ver 55**; Ac 16:25; [y]ver 7
63 [z]Ps 15:4; 101:6–7; 103:11; [a]ver 56; Ps 111:10
64 [b]Ps 33:5; [c]ver 12,108
65 [d]ver 17; Ps 125:4; Isa 50:2; 59:1; Mic 2:7; [e]**ver 9**
66 [f]**Ps 51:6**
67 [g]**Ps 116:10**; [h]**Ps 95:10; Jer 8:4**; [i]**ver 17**
68 [j]Ps 100:5; 106:1; 107:1; 135:3; [k]**Ex 18:20**
69 [l]Job 13:4; Ps 109:2
70 [m]**Ps 17:10**; Isa 29:13; Ac 28:27
71 [n]ver 67,75
72 [o]**Job 28:17; Ps 19:10**
73 [p]**Ge 1:27; Job 4:17**; 10:8; Ps 138:8; 139:13–16
74 [q]**Ps 34:2**; [r]ver 9; Ps 130:5
75 [s]ver 7,138,172; [t]Heb 12:5–11
76 [u]Ps 6:4; [v]**ver 41**
77 [w]Ps 90:13; 103:13; [x]**ver 47**
78 [y]ver 51; Jer 50:32; [z]ver 86,161; Ps 35:19
79 [a]ver 27,125
80 [b]ver 1; **1Ki 8:61**; [c]**Ge 26:5**; [d]**ver 6**

[c]48 Or *for*

כ Kaph

81My soul faints[e] with longing for your
salvation,[f]
but I have put my hope[g] in your
word.
82My eyes fail,[h] looking for your
promise;[i]
I say, "When will you comfort me?"
83Though I am like a wineskin in the
smoke,
I do not forget[j] your decrees.
84How long[k] must your servant wait?
When will you punish my
persecutors?[l]
85The arrogant[m] dig pitfalls[n] for me,
contrary to your law.
86All your commands are trustworthy;[o]
help me,[p] for men persecute me[q]
without cause.[r]
87They almost wiped me from the earth,
but I have not forsaken[s] your
precepts.
88Preserve my life[t] according to your
love,[u]
and I will obey the statutes[v] of your
mouth.

ל Lamedh

89Your word, O LORD, is eternal;[w]
it stands firm in the heavens.
90Your faithfulness[x] continues through
all generations;[y]
you established the earth, and it
endures.[z]
91Your laws endure[a] to this day,
for all things serve you.[b]
92If your law had not been my delight,[c]
I would have perished in my
affliction.[d]
93I will never forget[e] your precepts,
for by them you have preserved my
life.[f]
94Save me,[g] for I am yours;
I have sought out your precepts.[h]
95The wicked are waiting to destroy me,[i]
but I will ponder your statutes.[j]
96To all perfection I see a limit;
but your commands are boundless.[k]

מ Mem

97Oh, how I love your law![l]
I meditate[m] on it all day long.
98Your commands make me wiser[n] than
my enemies,
for they are ever with me.
99I have more insight than all my
teachers,
for I meditate on your statutes.[o]
100I have more understanding than the
elders,
for I obey your precepts.[p]
101I have kept my feet[q] from every evil
path
so that I might obey your word.[r]
102I have not departed from your laws,[s]
for you yourself have taught[t] me.
103How sweet are your words to my
taste,
sweeter than honey[u] to my mouth![v]
104I gain understanding[w] from your
precepts;
therefore I hate every wrong path.[x]

נ Nun

105Your word is a lamp[y] to my feet
and a light[z] for my path.
106I have taken an oath[a] and confirmed
it,
that I will follow your righteous
laws.[b]
107I have suffered much;
preserve my life,[c] O LORD, according
to your word.
108Accept, O LORD, the willing praise of
my mouth,[d]
and teach me your laws.[e]
109Though I constantly take my life in
my hands,[f]
I will not forget[g] your law.
110The wicked have set a snare[h] for me,
but I have not strayed[i] from your
precepts.
111Your statutes are my heritage for
ever;
they are the joy of my heart.[j]
112My heart is set[k] on keeping your
decrees
to the very end.[l]

ס Samekh

113I hate double-minded men,[m]
but I love your law.[n]
114You are my refuge and my shield;[o]
I have put my hope[p] in your word.
115Away from me,[q] you evildoers,
that I may keep the commands of
my God!
116Sustain me[r] according to your
promise,[s] and I shall live;
do not let my hopes be dashed.[t]
117Uphold me,[u] and I shall be delivered;[v]
I shall always have regard for your
decrees.[w]
118You reject all who stray[x] from your
decrees,
for their deceitfulness is in vain.

81 [e]ver 20; Ps 84:2; [f]ver 123; [g]**ver 43**
82 [h]**Ps 6:7**; 69:3; La 2:11; [i]ver 41,123
83 [j]**ver 61**
84 [k]Ps 6:3; Rev 6:10; [l]ver 51; Jer 12:3; 15:15; 20:11
85 [m]ver 51; [n]Ps 35:7; 57:6; Jer 18:20,22
86 [o]ver 138; [p]**Ps 109:26**; [q]**Ps 7:1**; [r]**ver 78**
87 [s]ver 150; Isa 1:4,28; 58:2; 59:13
88 [t]**Ps 41:2**; [u]ver 124; Ps 51:1; 109:26; [v]ver 2,100, 129,134,168
89 [w]ver 111,144; **Ps 111:8**; Isa 51:6; **Mt 5:18**; 1Pe 1:25
90 [x]**Ps 36:5**; [y]**Ps 45:17**; [z]**Job 8:19**; Ps 148:6
91 [a]Jer 33:25; [b]Ps 104:2–4; Jer 31:35
92 [c]Ps 37:4; **112:1**; [d]ver 50,67
93 [e]ver 83; [f]**Ps 103:5**
94 [g]ver 146; Ps 54:1; 116:4; Jer 17:14; 31:18; 42:11; [h]**ver 45**
95 [i]**Ps 69:4**; [j]ver 99
96 [k]Ps 19:7
97 [l]**ver 47**; [m]**ver 15**
98 [n]ver 130; **Dt 4:6**; Ps 19:7; 2Ti 3:15
99 [o]ver 15
100 [p]**ver 56**; **Dt 6:17**
101 [q]Pr 1:15; [r]**ver 57**
102 [s]**Dt 17:20**; [t]**Dt 4:5**
103 [u]**Ps 19:10**; [v]Pr 24:13–14
104 [w]**Ps 111:10**; [x]ver 128
105 [y]Pr 20:27; 2Pe 1:19; [z]ver 130; Pr 6:23
106 [a]**Ne 10:29**; [b]ver 7
107 [c]**ver 25**
108 [d]Ps 51:15; 63:5; 71:8; 109:30; [e]**ver 64**
109 [f]**Jdg 12:3**; [g]**ver 61**
110 [h]Ps 25:15; **64:5**; Isa 8:14; Am 3:5; [i]ver 10

111 [j]ver 14,162 *112* [k]**Ps 108:1**; [l]ver 33
113 [m]**1Ki 18:21**; Jas 1:8; 4:8; [n]ver 47
114 [o]**Ge 15:1**; **Ps 18:2**; [p]**ver 43** *115* [q]**Ps 6:8**
116 [r]**Ps 18:35**; 41:3; 55:22; Isa 46:4; [s]**ver 41**; [t]Ro 5:5
117 [u]Isa 41:10; 46:4; [v]Ps 34:4; [w]ver 6 *118* [x]**ver 10**

119All the wicked of the earth you
discard like dross;[y]
therefore I love your statutes.[z]
120My flesh trembles[a] in fear of you;[b]
I stand in awe[c] of your laws.

ע Ayin

121I have done what is righteous and
just;[d]
do not leave me to my oppressors.
122Ensure your servant's well-being;[e]
let not the arrogant oppress me.[f]
123My eyes fail,[g] looking for your
salvation,[h]
looking for your righteous promise.[i]
124Deal with your servant according to
your love[j]
and teach me your decrees.[k]
125I am your servant;[l] give me
discernment
that I may understand your
statutes.[m]
126It is time for you to act, O LORD;
your law is being broken.[n]
127Because I love your commands[o]
more than gold,[p] more than pure
gold,[q]
128and because I consider all your
precepts right,[r]
I hate every wrong path.[s]

פ Pe

129Your statutes are wonderful;[t]
therefore I obey them.[u]
130The unfolding of your words gives
light;[v]
it gives understanding to the
simple.[w]
131I open my mouth and pant,[x]
longing for your commands.[y]
132Turn to me[z] and have mercy[a] on me,
as you always do to those who love
your name.[b]
133Direct my footsteps according to your
word;[c]
let no sin rule[d] over me.
134Redeem me from the oppression of
men,[e]
that I may obey your precepts.[f]
135Make your face shine[g] upon your
servant
and teach me your decrees.[h]
136Streams of tears[i] flow from my eyes,
for your law is not obeyed.[j]

צ Tsadhe

137Righteous are you,[k] O LORD,
and your laws are right.[l]
138The statutes you have laid down are
righteous;[m]
they are fully trustworthy.[n]

119 [y]Isa 1:22,25; Eze 22:18-19; [z]ver 47
120 [a]**Job 4:14; Isa 64:2;** [b]**Jos 24:14;** [c]Jer 10:7; Hab 3:2
121 [d]2Sa 8:15; **Job 27:6**
122 [e]**Job 17:3;** [f]ver 21,121, 134; Ps 106:42
123 [g]Isa 38:14; [h]ver 81; [i]**ver 82**
124 [j]**ver 88; Ps 25:7;** [k]ver 12
125 [l]**Ps 116:16;** [m]**ver 79**
126 [n]**Nu 15:31**
127 [o]**ver 47;** [p]Ps 19:10; [q]**Job 3:21**
128 [r]**Ps 19:8;** [s]ver 104,163; Ps 31:6; Pr 13:5
129 [t]ver 18; [u]ver 22,88
130 [v]**ver 105;** [w]**Ps 19:7**
131 [x]Ps 42:1; [y]**ver 20**
132 [z]**Ps 6:4;** [a]**2Sa 24:14; Ps 9:13;** [b]**Ps 5:11**
133 [c]ver 9; [d]**ver 11; Ro 6:16**
134 [e]**ver 122;** [f]**ver 56,88**
135 [g]**Nu 6:25;** Ps 4:6; 67:1; 80:3; [h]ver 12
136 [i]Ps 6:6; Isa 22:4; Jer 9:1,18; 13:17; 14:17; La 1:16; 3:48; [j]ver 158; Ps 106:25; Isa 42:24; Eze 9:4
137 [k]**Ex 9:27; Ezr 9:15;** [l]**Ne 9:13**
138 [m]**ver 75; Ps 19:7;** [n]ver 86
139 [o]Ps 69:9; Jn 2:17
140 [p]**Jos 23:14;** [q]Ps 12:6; [r]ver 47
141 [s]**Ps 22:6;** [t]ver 61,134
142 [u]ver 151,160; Ps 19:7
143 [v]**ver 24,47**
144 [w]**ver 34**
145 [x]ver 10; [y]ver 22,55
146 [z]**ver 94**
147 [a]Ps 5:3; 57:8; 108:2
148 [b]Ps 63:6
149 [c]Ps 27:7; [d]ver 124; [e]**ver 40**
150 [f]**Ps 37:7**
151 [g]**Ps 34:18;** Php 4:5; [h]**ver 142**

139My zeal wears me out,[o]
for my enemies ignore your words.
140Your promises[p] have been
thoroughly tested,[q]
and your servant loves them.[r]
141Though I am lowly and despised,[s]
I do not forget your precepts.[t]
142Your righteousness is everlasting
and your law is true.[u]
143Trouble and distress have come upon
me,
but your commands are my
delight.[v]
144Your statutes are for ever right;
give me understanding[w] that I may
live.

ק Qoph

145I call with all my heart;[x] answer me, O
LORD,
and I will obey your decrees.[y]
146I call out to you; save me[z]
and I will keep your statutes.
147I rise before dawn[a] and cry for help;
I have put my hope in your word.
148My eyes stay open through the
watches of the night,[b]
that I may meditate on your
promises.
149Hear my voice[c] in accordance with
your love;[d]
preserve my life,[e] O LORD, according
to your laws.
150Those who devise wicked schemes[f]
are near,
but they are far from your law.
151Yet you are near,[g] O LORD,
and all your commands are true.[h]
152Long ago I learned from your statutes[i]
that you established them to last for
ever.[j]

ר Resh

153Look upon my suffering[k] and deliver
me,[l]
for I have not forgotten[m] your law.
154Defend my cause[n] and redeem me;[o]
preserve my life[p] according to your
promise.[q]
155Salvation is far from the wicked,
for they do not seek out[r] your
decrees.
156Your compassion is great,[s] O LORD;
preserve my life[t] according to your
laws.[u]

152 [i]ver 7,73; [j]**ver 89; Ps 111:8;** Lk 21:33
153 [k]**Ps 13:3;** [l]**Ps 3:7;** [m]**Ps 44:17**
154 [n]Ps 35:1; Jer 50:34; Mic 7:9; [o]**1Sa 24:15;** [p]ver 25; [q]**ver 41**
155 [r]ver 94,118
156 [s]**Ne 9:27;** Jas 5:11; [t]ver 25; [u]ver 149

157Many are the foes who persecute me,[v]
but I have not turned[w] from your statutes.
158I look on the faithless with loathing,[x]
for they do not obey your word.[y]
159See how I love your precepts;
preserve my life,[z] O LORD,
according to your love.
160All your words are true;
all your righteous laws are eternal.[a]

ש Sin and Shin

161Rulers persecute me[b] without cause,
but my heart trembles[c] at your word.
162I rejoice[d] in your promise
like one who finds great spoil.[e]
163I hate and abhor[f] falsehood
but I love your law.[g]
164Seven times a day I praise you
for your righteous laws.[h]
165Great peace[i] have they who love your law,
and nothing can make them stumble.[j]
166I wait for your salvation,[k] O LORD,
and I follow your commands.
167I obey your statutes,
for I love them[l] greatly.
168I obey your precepts[m] and your statutes,[n]
for all my ways are known[o] to you.

ת Taw

169May my cry come[p] before you, O LORD;
give me understanding[q] according to your word.[r]
170May my supplication come[s] before you;
deliver me[t] according to your promise.[u]
171May my lips overflow with praise,[v]
for you teach me[w] your decrees.
172May my tongue sing[x] of your word,
for all your commands are righteous.[y]
173May your hand be ready to help[z] me,
for I have chosen[a] your precepts.
174I long for your salvation,[b] O LORD,
and your law is my delight.[c]
175Let me live[d] that I may praise you,
and may your laws sustain me.
176I have strayed like a lost sheep.[e]
Seek your servant,
for I have not forgotten[f] your commands.

157 [v]Ps 7:1; [w]**Ps 44:18**
158 [x]ver 104; **Ex 32:19;** [y]**ver 136**
159 [z]ver 25; **Ps 41:2**
160 [a]**ver 89; Ps 111:8**
161 [b]ver 23,122, 157; 1Sa 24:14–15; [c]ver 120
162 [d]**ver 111;** [e]1Sa 30:16; Isa 9:3; 53:12
163 [f]**ver 128;** [g]ver 47
164 [h]ver 7,160
165 [i]Ps 37:11; Isa 26:3,12; 27:5; 32:17; 57:19; 66:12; [j]**ver 11; Ps 37:24;** 1Jn 2:10
166 [k]ver 81
167 [l]ver 47
168 [m]**ver 56,88;** [n]ver 2,22; [o]**Job 10:4; 23:10;** Ps 139:3; Pr 5:21
169 [p]**Job 16:18;** [q]**ver 34;** [r]**ver 9**
170 [s]1Ki 8:30; 2Ch 6:24; Ps 28:2; 140:6; 143:1; [t]Ps 3:7; 22:20; 59:1; [u]**ver 41**
171 [v]Ps 51:15; 63:3; [w]Ps 94:12; Isa 2:3; Mic 4:2
172 [x]Ps 51:14; [y]**ver 7,75**
173 [z]Ps 37:24; 73:23; Isa 41:10; [a]**Jos 24:22**
174 [b]ver 166; [c]ver 16,24
175 [d]ver 116,159; Isa 55:3
176 [e]ver 10; **Ps 95:10;** Jer 50:17; Eze 34:11; **Lk 15:4;** [f]**Ps 44:17**

Ps. 120

1 [a]**Ps 18:6;** [b]**2Sa 22:7; Ps 118:5**
2 [c]**Ps 31:18;** [d]**Ps 52:4**
4 [e]**Dt 32:23**
5 [f]Ge 25:13; Jer 2:10

Ps. 121

2 [a]**Ge 1:1;** [b]**Ps 104:5**
4 [c]Ps 127:1
5 [d]**Ps 1:6**
6 [e]Isa 49:10
7 [f]**Ps 9:9**
8 [g]Dt 28:6

Psalm 120

A song of ascents.

1I call on the LORD[a] in my distress,[b]
and he answers me.
2Save me, O LORD, from lying lips[c]
and from deceitful tongues.[d]

3What will he do to you,
and what more besides, O deceitful tongue?
4He will punish you with a warrior's sharp arrows,[e]
with burning coals of the broom tree.

5Woe to me that I dwell in Meshech,
that I live among the tents of Kedar![f]
6Too long have I lived
among those who hate peace.
7I am a man of peace;
but when I speak, they are for war.

Psalm 121

A song of ascents.

1I lift up my eyes to the hills—
where does my help come from?
2My help comes from the LORD,
the Maker of heaven[a] and earth.[b]

3He will not let your foot slip—
he who watches over you will not slumber;
4indeed, he who watches[c] over Israel
will neither slumber nor sleep.

5The LORD watches over[d] you—
the LORD is your shade at your right hand;
6the sun[e] will not harm you by day,
nor the moon by night.

7The LORD will keep you from all harm[f]—
he will watch over your life;
8the LORD will watch over your coming and going
both now and for evermore.[g]

Psalm 122

A song of ascents. Of David.

1I rejoiced with those who said to me,
"Let us go to the house of the LORD."
2Our feet are standing
in your gates, O Jerusalem.

3Jerusalem is built like a city
that is closely compacted together.

4That is where the tribes go up,
the tribes of the LORD,
to praise the name of the LORD
according to the statute given to
Israel.
5There the thrones for judgment stand,
the thrones of the house of David.

6Pray for the peace of Jerusalem:
"May those who love[a] you be
secure.
7May there be peace[b] within your walls
and security within your citadels.[c]"
8For the sake of my brothers and
friends,
I will say, "Peace be within you."
9For the sake of the house of the LORD
our God,
I will seek your prosperity.[d]

Psalm 123

A song of ascents.

1I lift up my eyes to you,
to you whose throne[a] is in heaven.
2As the eyes of slaves look to the hand
of their master,
as the eyes of a maid look to the
hand of her mistress,
so our eyes look to the LORD[b] our God,
till he shows us his mercy.

3Have mercy on us, O LORD, have
mercy on us,
for we have endured much
contempt.
4We have endured much ridicule from
the proud,
much contempt from the arrogant.

Psalm 124

A song of ascents. Of David.

1If the LORD had not been on our side—
let Israel say[a]—
2if the LORD had not been on our side
when men attacked us,
3when their anger flared against us,
they would have swallowed us
alive;
4the flood[b] would have engulfed us,
the torrent[c] would have swept over
us,
5 the raging waters would have swept
us away.

6Praise be to the LORD,
who has not let us be torn by their
teeth.
7We have escaped like a bird
out of the fowler's snare;[d]
the snare has been broken,[e]
and we have escaped.
8Our help is in the name[f] of the LORD,
the Maker of heaven[g] and earth.

Psalm 125

A song of ascents.

1Those who trust in the LORD are like
Mount Zion,[a]
which cannot be shaken[b] but
endures for ever.
2As the mountains surround
Jerusalem,[c]
so the LORD surrounds[d] his people
both now and for evermore.

3The sceptre[e] of the wicked will not
remain[f]
over the land allotted to the
righteous,
for then the righteous might use
their hands to do evil.[g]

4Do good, O LORD,[h] to those who are
good,
to those who are upright in heart.[i]
5But those who turn[j] to crooked ways[k]
the LORD will banish[l] with the
evildoers.

Peace be upon Israel.[m]

Psalm 126

A song of ascents.

1When the LORD brought back[a] the
captives to[a] Zion,
we were like men who dreamed.[b]
2Our mouths were filled with
laughter,[b]
our tongues with songs of joy.[c]
Then it was said among the nations,
"The LORD has done great things[d]
for them."
3The LORD has done great things[e] for
us,
and we are filled with joy.[f]

4Restore our fortunes,[c][g] O LORD,
like streams in the Negev.[h]
5Those who sow in tears[i]
will reap[j] with songs of joy.[k]
6He who goes out weeping,[l]
carrying seed to sow,
will return with songs of joy,
carrying sheaves with him.

a1 Or *LORD restored the fortunes of*
b1 Or *men restored to health*
c4 Or *Bring back our captives*

Ps. 122
6 [a]**Ps 26:8**
7 [b]**1Sa 25:6;** [c]**Ps 48:3**
9 [d]Ps 128:5

Ps. 123
1 [a]**Ps 68:5;** Isa 6:1; 63:15
2 [b]**Ps 25:15**

Ps. 124
1 [a]Ps 129:1
4 [b]**Ps 88:17;** [c]**Ps 18:4**
7 [d]**Ps 91:3;** [e]Ps 25:15
8 [f]**1Sa 17:45;** [g]Ge 1:1; Ps 115:15; 121:2; 134:3

Ps. 125
1 [a]Ps 48:12; Isa 33:20; [b]Ps 46:5; 48:2–5
2 [c]**1Ch 21:15;** [d]Ps 32:10; Zec 2:4–5
3 [e]**Est 4:11;** [f]Ps 89:22; Pr 22:8; Isa 13:11; 14:5; [g]1Sa 24:10
4 [h]**Ps 119:65;** [i]**Ps 36:10**
5 [j]**Job 23:11;** [k]Pr 2:15; Isa 59:8; [l]Ps 92:7; [m]Ps 128:6; Pr 17:6; Gal 6:16

Ps. 126
1 [a]Ezr 1:1–3; Ps 85:1; Hos 6:11
2 [b]**Ge 21:6;** [c]**Job 8:21; Ps 65:8;** [d]**Dt 10:21;** Ps 71:19; Lk 1:49
3 [e]Ps 106:21; Joel 2:21,26; [f]**Ps 9:2;** 16:11
4 [g]**Dt 30:3;** [h]**Ps 107:35;** Isa 43:19; 51:3
5 [i]Ps 6:6; 80:5; Jer 50:4; [j]Gal 6:9; [k]Ps 16:11; 20:5; 23:6; Isa 35:10; 51:11; 60:15; 61:7; Jer 31:6–7,12
6 [l]**Nu 25:6;** **Ps 30:5**

Psalm 127

A song of ascents. Of Solomon.

[1]Unless the LORD builds[a] the house,
its builders labour in vain.
Unless the LORD watches[b] over the city,
the watchmen stand guard in vain.
[2]In vain you rise early
and stay up late,
toiling for food[c] to eat—
for he grants sleep[d] to[a] those he loves.[e]

[3]Sons are a heritage from the LORD,
children a reward[f] from him.
[4]Like arrows[g] in the hands of a warrior
are sons born in one's youth.
[5]Blessed is the man
whose quiver is full of them.[h]
They will not be put to shame
when they contend with their enemies[i] in the gate.[j]

Psalm 128

A song of ascents.

[1]Blessed are all who fear the LORD,[a]
who walk in his ways.[b]
[2]You will eat the fruit of your labour;[c]
blessings and prosperity[d] will be yours.
[3]Your wife will be like a fruitful vine[e]
within your house;
your sons[f] will be like olive shoots[g]
round your table.
[4]Thus is the man blessed[h]
who fears the LORD.[i]

[5]May the LORD bless you from Zion[j]
all the days of your life;
may you see the prosperity of Jerusalem,[k]
6 and may you live to see your children's children.[l]

Peace be upon Israel.[m]

Psalm 129

A song of ascents.

[1]They have greatly oppressed[a] me from my youth[b]—
let Israel say[c]—
[2]they have greatly oppressed me from my youth,
but they have not gained the victory[d] over me.
[3]Ploughmen have ploughed my back
and made their furrows long.
[4]But the LORD is righteous;[e]
he has cut me free[f] from the cords of the wicked.[g]

[5]May all who hate Zion[h]
be turned back in shame.[i]
[6]May they be like grass on the roof,[j]
which withers[k] before it can grow;
[7]with it the reaper cannot fill his hands,[l]
nor the one who gathers fill his arms.
[8]May those who pass by not say,
"The blessing of the LORD be upon you;
we bless you[m] in the name of the LORD."

Psalm 130

A song of ascents.

[1]Out of the depths[a] I cry to you,[b] O LORD;
2 O Lord, hear my voice.[c]
Let your ears be attentive[d]
to my cry for mercy.[e]

[3]If you, O LORD, kept a record of sins,
O Lord, who could stand?[f]
[4]But with you there is forgiveness;[g]
therefore you are feared.[h]

[5]I wait for the LORD,[i] my soul waits,[j]
and in his word[k] I put my hope.
[6]My soul waits for the Lord
more than watchmen[l] wait for the morning,
more than watchmen wait for the morning.[m]

[7]O Israel, put your hope[n] in the LORD,
for with the LORD is unfailing love[o]
and with him is full redemption.[p]
[8]He himself will redeem[q] Israel
from all their sins.[r]

Psalm 131

A song of ascents. Of David.

[1]My heart is not proud,[a] O LORD,
my eyes are not haughty;[b]
I do not concern myself with great matters[c]
or things too wonderful for me.[d]
[2]But I have stilled and quietened my soul;[e]

Ps. 127
1 [a]Ps 78:69; [b]Ps 121:4
2 [c]**Ge 3:17**; [d]**Nu 6:26**; **Job 11:18**; [e]**Dt 33:12**; Ecc 2:25
3 [f]**Ge 1:28**
4 [g]Ps 112:2
5 [h]Ps 128:2–3; [i]**Ge 24:60**; [j]**Ge 23:10**

Ps. 128
1 [a]Ps 103:11; **112:1**; [b]Ps 119:1–3
2 [c]**Ps 58:11**; 109:11; Isa 3:10; [d]**Ge 39:3**; Pr 10:22
3 [e]**Ge 49:22**; [f]**Job 29:5**; [g]Ps 52:8; 144:12
4 [h]**Ps 1:1**; [i]Ps 112:1
5 [j]**Ps 20:2**; [k]Ps 122:9
6 [l]**Ge 48:11**; [m]**Ps 125:5**

Ps. 129
1 [a]**Ex 1:13**; [b]**Ps 88:15**; [c]Ps 124:1
2 [d]Jer 1:19; 15:20; 20:11; Mt 16:18
4 [e]**Ex 9:27**; [f]Ps 37:9; [g]Ps 140:5
5 [h]Mic 4:11; [i]**Ps 70:2**
6 [j]Isa 37:27; [k]**2Ki 19:26**; Ps 102:11
7 [l]**Dt 28:38**; Ps 79:12
8 [m]Ps 118:26

Ps. 130
1 [a]**Job 30:19**; Ps 42:7; La 3:55; [b]Ps 22:2; 55:17; 142:5
2 [c]**Ps 27:7**; 28:2; [d]**2Ch 6:40**; [e]**Ps 28:6**; 31:22; 86:6; 140:6
3 [f]**1Sa 6:20**; **Ezr 9:15**; Ps 143:2; Na 1:6; Rev 6:17
4 [g]**Ex 34:7**; **2Sa 24:14**; **Jer 31:34**; [h]**1Ki 8:40**
5 [i]**Ps 27:14**; Isa 8:17; 26:8; 30:18; 49:23; [j]**Ps 5:3**; [k]**Ps 119:74**
6 [l]Ps 63:6; [m]**2Sa 23:4**
7 [n]**Ps 25:5**; **71:14**; [o]**1Ch 21:13**; [p]**Ps 111:9**; **Ro 3:24**
8 [q]Lk 1:68; [r]**Ex 34:7**; **Mt 1:21**

Ps. 131
1 [a]Ps 101:5; Isa 2:12; Ro 12:16; [b]**2Sa 22:28**; **Job 41:34**; [c]Jer 45:5; [d]**Job 5:9**; Ps 139:6 *2* [e]**Ps 116:7**

[a]2 Or *eat— / for while they sleep he provides for*

like a weaned child with its mother,
like a weaned child is my soul[f]
within me.

3 O Israel, put your hope[g] in the LORD
both now and for evermore.[h]

Psalm 132

132:8–10pp—2Ch 6:41–42

A song of ascents.

1 O LORD, remember David
and all the hardships he endured.[a]

2 He swore an oath to the LORD
and made a vow to the Mighty One
of Jacob:[b]
3 "I will not enter my house[c]
or go to my bed—
4 I will allow no sleep to my eyes,
no slumber to my eyelids,
5 till I find a place[d] for the LORD,
a dwelling for the Mighty One of
Jacob."

6 We heard it in Ephrathah,[e]
we came upon it in the fields of
Jaar[a]:[b][f]
7 "Let us go to his dwelling-place;[g]
let us worship at his footstool[h]—
8 arise, O LORD,[i] and come to your
resting place,
you and the ark of your might.
9 May your priests be clothed with
righteousness;[j]
may your saints[k] sing for joy."

10 For the sake of David your servant,
do not reject your anointed one.

11 The LORD swore an oath to David,[l]
a sure oath that he will not revoke:
"One of your own descendants[m]
I will place on your throne—
12 if your sons keep my covenant[n]
and the statutes I teach them,
then their sons shall sit
on your throne[o] for ever and ever."

13 For the LORD has chosen Zion,[p]
he has desired it for his dwelling:[q]
14 "This is my resting place for ever and
ever;[r]
here I will sit enthroned,[s] for I have
desired it—
15 I will bless her with abundant
provisions;
her poor will I satisfy with food.[t]
16 I will clothe her priests[u] with
salvation,
and her saints shall ever sing for
joy.[v]

2 [f]Mt 18:3; 1Co 13:11; 14:20
3 [g]Ps 25:5; 119:43; 130:7; [h]Ps 113:2

Ps. 132

1 [a]1Sa 18:11; 2Sa 15:14
2 [b]Ge 49:24; Isa 49:26; 60:16
3 [c]2Sa 7:2,27
5 [d]1Ki 8:17; Ac 7:46
6 [e]1Sa 17:12; [f]Jos 9:17; 1Sa 7:2
7 [g]2Sa 15:25; Ps 5:7; 122:1; [h]1Ch 28:2
8 [i]Nu 10:35
9 [j]Job 27:6; Isa 61:3,10; Zec 3:4; Mal 3:3; Eph 6:14; [k]Ps 16:3; 30:4; 149:5
11 [l]Ps 89:3–4,35; [m]1Ch 17:11–14; Mt 1:1; Lk 3:31
12 [n]2Ch 6:16; Ps 25:10; [o]Lk 1:32; Ac 2:30
13 [p]Ex 15:17; Ps 48:1–2; 68:16; [q]1Ki 8:13
14 [r]ver 8; Ps 68:16; [s]2Sa 6:2; Ps 80:1
15 [t]Ps 107:9; 147:14
16 [u]2Ch 6:41; [v]Job 8:21; Ps 149:5
17 [w]1Sa 2:10; Ps 92:10; Eze 29:21; Lk 1:69; [x]1Ki 11:36; 2Ki 8:19; 2Ch 21:7; Ps 18:28; [y]Ps 84:9
18 [z]Job 8:22; [a]2Sa 12:30

Ps. 133

1 [a]Ge 13:8; Ro 12:10; [b]Jn 17:11
2 [c]Ex 29:7
3 [d]Job 29:19; Pr 19:12; Isa 18:4; 26:19; 45:8; Hos 14:5; Mic 5:7; [e]Dt 3:8; 4:48; [f]Ex 15:17; Ps 2:6; 74:2; [g]Lev 25:21; [h]Ps 21:4

Ps. 134

1 [a]Ps 113:1; 135:1–2; Rev 19:5; [b]Nu 16:9; 1Ch 15:2; [c]1Ch 23:30
2 [d]Ps 28:2; 1Ti 2:8; [e]Ps 15:1; [f]Ps 33:2; 103:1
3 [g]Ps 124:8; [h]Lev 25:21; Ps 20:2

17 "Here I will make a horn[c] grow[w] for
David
and set up a lamp[x] for my anointed
one.[y]
18 I will clothe his enemies with shame,[z]
but the crown on his head[a] shall be
resplendent."

Psalm 133

A song of ascents. Of David.

1 How good and pleasant it is
when brothers live together[a] in
unity![b]
2 It is like precious oil poured on the
head,[c]
running down on the beard,
running down on Aaron's beard,
down upon the collar of his robes.
3 It is as if the dew[d] of Hermon[e]
were falling on Mount Zion.[f]
For there the LORD bestows his
blessing,[g]
even life for evermore.[h]

Psalm 134

A song of ascents.

1 Praise the LORD, all you servants[a] of
the LORD
who minister[b] by night[c] in the house
of the LORD.
2 Lift up your hands[d] in the sanctuary[e]
and praise the LORD.[f]

3 May the LORD, the Maker of heaven[g]
and earth,
bless you from Zion.[h]

Psalm 135

135:15–20pp—Ps 115:4–11

1 Praise the LORD.[a]

Praise the name of the LORD;
praise him, you servants[a] of the
LORD,
2 you who minister in the house[b] of the
LORD,
in the courts[c] of the house of our
God.

3 Praise the LORD, for the LORD is good;[d]
sing praise to his name,[e] for that is
pleasant.[f]

Ps. 135

1 [a]Ne 7:73
2 [b]1Ch 15:2; Lk 2:37; [c]Ps 116:19
3 [d]1Ch 16:34; Ps 119:68; [e]Ps 68:4; [f]Ps 92:1; 147:1

---

[a]6 That is, Kiriath Jearim
[b]6 Or *heard of it in Ephrathah, / we found it in the fields of Jaar.* (and no quotation marks around verses 7–9)
[c]17 *Horn* here symbolises strong one, that is, king.
[a]1 Hebrew *Hallelu Yah;* also in verses 3 and 21

4For the LORD has chosen Jacob[g] to be
his own,
Israel to be his treasured
possession.[h]

5I know that the LORD is great,[i]
that our Lord is greater than all
gods.[j]
6The LORD does whatever pleases him,[k]
in the heavens and on the earth,[l]
in the seas and all their depths.
7He makes clouds rise from the ends of
the earth;
he sends lightning with the rain[m]
and brings out the wind[n] from his
storehouses.[o]

8He struck down the firstborn[p] of
Egypt,
the firstborn of men and animals.
9He sent his signs[q] and wonders into
your midst, O Egypt,
against Pharaoh and all his
servants.[r]
10He struck down many[s] nations
and killed mighty kings—
11Sihon[t] king of the Amorites,[u]
Og king of Bashan[v]
and all the kings of Canaan[w]—
12and he gave their land as an
inheritance,[x]
an inheritance to his people Israel.

13Your name, O LORD, endures for
ever,[y]
your renown,[z] O LORD, through all
generations.
14For the LORD will vindicate his people[a]
and have compassion on his
servants.[b]
15The idols of the nations[c] are silver and
gold,
made by the hands of men.[d]
16They have mouths, but cannot speak,[e]
eyes, but they cannot see;
17they have ears, but cannot hear,
nor is there breath[f] in their mouths.
18Those who make them will be like
them,
and so will all who trust in them.

19O house of Israel, praise the LORD;[g]
O house of Aaron, praise the LORD;
20O house of Levi, praise the LORD;
you who fear him, praise the LORD.
21Praise be to the LORD from Zion,[h]
to him who dwells in Jerusalem.[i]

Praise the LORD.

Psalm 136

1Give thanks[a] to the LORD, for he is
good.[b]
His love endures for ever.[c]

4 [g]**Dt 10:15**; [h]Ex 19:5; Dt 7:6; Mal 3:17; **Tit 2:14**
5 [i]Ps 48:1; 145:3; [j]**Ex 12:12; 1Ch 16:25; Job 21:22**
6 [k]Ps 115:3; Da 4:35; [l]Mt 6:10
7 [m]**Job 5:10;** Ps 68:9; Isa 30:23; Jer 10:13; 51:16; Joel 2:23; Zec 10:1; [n]Am 4:13; [o]**Dt 28:12**
8 [p]Ex 4:23; **12:12**
9 [q]Ex 7:9; [r]Ps 136:10–15
10 [s]Nu 21:21–25; Jos 24:8–11; Ps 44:2; 78:55; 136:17–21
11 [t]**Nu 21:21;** [u]**Nu 21:26;** [v]**Nu 21:33;** [w]**Jos 12:7–24;** 24:12
12 [x]**Dt 29:8**
13 [y]Ex 3:15; [z]**Ps 102:12**
14 [a]**1Sa 24:15;** Heb 10:30*; [b]**Dt 32:36**
15 [c]Ps 96:5; Rev 9:20; [d]Isa 2:8; 31:7; 37:19; 40:19; Jer 1:16; 10:5
16 [e]**1Ki 18:26**
17 [f]Jer 10:14; Hab 2:19
19 [g]**Ps 22:23**
21 [h]Ps 128:5; 134:3; [i]**1Ki 8:13; 2Ch 6:2**

Ps. 136

1 [a]Ps 105:1; [b]Ps 100:5; 106:1; 145:9; Jer 33:11; Na 1:7; [c]ver 2–26; **2Ch 5:13; Ezr 3:11;** Ps 118:1–4
2 [d]Ps 105:1; [e]**Dt 10:17**
3 [f]Ps 105:1; [g]**Dt 10:17; 1Ti 6:15**
4 [h]**Ex 3:20; Job 9:10**
5 [i]Pr 3:19; Jer 51:15; [j]**Ge 1:1**
6 [k]**Ge 1:1;** Isa 42:5; Jer 10:12; 33:2; [l]**Ge 1:6**
7 [m]Ge 1:14,16; Ps 74:16; Jas 1:17
8 [n]**Ge 1:16**
10 [o]**Ex 4:23; 12:12**
11 [p]Ex 6:6; 13:3; Ps 105:43
12 [q]**Ex 3:20; Dt 5:15;** [r]**Dt 9:29**
13 [s]**Ps 78:13**

2Give thanks[d] to the God of gods.[e]
His love endures for ever.
3Give thanks[f] to the Lord of lords:[g]
His love endures for ever.

4to him who alone does great
wonders,[h]
His love endures for ever.
5who by his understanding[i] made the
heavens,[j]
His love endures for ever.
6who spread out the earth[k] upon the
waters,[l]
His love endures for ever.
7who made the great lights[m]—
His love endures for ever.
8the sun to govern[n] the day,
His love endures for ever.
9the moon and stars to govern the
night;
His love endures for ever.

10to him who struck down the firstborn[o]
of Egypt
His love endures for ever.
11and brought Israel out[p] from among
them
His love endures for ever.
12with a mighty hand[q] and outstretched
arm;[r]
His love endures for ever.

13to him who divided the Red Sea[a] [s]
asunder
His love endures for ever.
14and brought Israel through[t] the midst
of it,
His love endures for ever.
15but swept Pharaoh and his army into
the Red Sea;[u]
His love endures for ever.

16to him who led his people through the
desert,[v]
His love endures for ever.
17who struck down great kings,[w]
His love endures for ever.
18and killed mighty kings[x]—
His love endures for ever.
19Sihon king of the Amorites[y]
His love endures for ever.
20and Og king of Bashan[z]—
His love endures for ever.
21and gave their land[a] as an inheritance,[b]
His love endures for ever.

14 [t]Ex 14:22; Ps 106:9 15 [u]**Ex 14:27**
16 [v]**Ex 13:18;** Ps 78:52
17 [w]Nu 21:23–25; Jos 24:8–11; Ps 78:55; 135:9–12
18 [x]Dt 29:7; **Jos 12:7–24** 19 [y]Nu 21:21–25
20 [z]Nu 21:33–35 21 [a]Jos 12:1; [b]**Dt 1:38; Jos 14:1**

[a]13 Hebrew *Yam Suph;* that is, Sea of Reeds; also in verse 15

22 an inheritance[c] to his servant Israel;[d]
His love endures for ever.

23 to the One who remembered us[e] in our
low estate
His love endures for ever.
24 and freed us[f] from our enemies,[g]
His love endures for ever.
25 and who gives food[h] to every creature.
His love endures for ever.

26 Give thanks[i] to the God of heaven.[j]
His love endures for ever.[k]

Psalm 137

1 By the rivers of Babylon[a] we sat and
wept[b]
when we remembered Zion.[c]
2 There on the poplars[d]
we hung our harps,[e]
3 for there our captors[f] asked us for
songs,
our tormentors demanded[g] songs of
joy;
they said, "Sing us one of the songs
of Zion!"[h]

4 How can we sing the songs of the
LORD[i]
while in a foreign land?
5 If I forget you,[j] O Jerusalem,
may my right hand forget ⌞its skill⌟.
6 May my tongue cling to the roof[k] of my
mouth
if I do not remember[l] you,
if I do not consider Jerusalem[m]
my highest joy.

7 Remember, O LORD, what the
Edomites[n] did
on the day Jerusalem fell.[o]
"Tear it down," they cried,
"tear it down to its foundations!"[p]

8 O Daughter of Babylon, doomed to
destruction,[q]
happy is he who repays you
for what you have done to us—
9 he who seizes your infants
and dashes them[r] against the rocks.

Psalm 138

Of David.

1 I will praise you, O LORD, with all my
heart;
before the "gods"[a] I will sing[b] your
praise.
2 I will bow down towards your holy
temple[c]
and will praise your name[d]
for your love and your faithfulness,[e]
for you have exalted above all things
your name and your word.[f]
3 When I called,[g] you answered me;[h]
you made me bold[i] and
stout-hearted.[j]

4 May all the kings of the earth[k] praise
you, O LORD,
when they hear the words of your
mouth.
5 May they sing[l] of the ways of the
LORD,
for the glory of the LORD[m] is great.

6 Though the LORD is on high, he looks
upon the lowly,[n]
but the proud[o] he knows from afar.
7 Though I walk[p] in the midst of trouble,
you preserve my life;[q]
you stretch out your hand[r] against the
anger of my foes,[s]
with your right hand[t] you save me.[u]
8 The LORD will fulfil ⌞his purpose⌟[v] for
me;
your love, O LORD, endures for
ever[w]—
do not abandon[x] the works of your
hands.[y]

Psalm 139

For the director of music. Of David.
A psalm.

1 O LORD, you have searched me[a]
and you know[b] me.
2 You know when I sit and when I rise;[c]
you perceive my thoughts[d] from
afar.
3 You discern my going out[e] and my
lying down;
you are familiar with all my ways.[f]
4 Before a word is on my tongue
you know it completely,[g] O LORD.

5 You hem me in[h]—behind and before;
you have laid your hand upon me.
6 Such knowledge is too wonderful for
me,[i]
too lofty[j] for me to attain.

7 Where can I go from your Spirit?
Where can I flee[k] from your
presence?

22 [c]**Dt 29:8**; Ps 78:55; [d]Isa 20:3; 41:8; 42:19; 43:10; 44:1,21; 45:4; 49:5–7
23 [e]Ps 78:39; 103:14; 115:12
24 [f]**Jos 10:14; Ne 9:28**; [g]**Dt 6:19**
25 [h]**Ge 1:30; Mt 6:26**
26 [i]Ps 105:1; [j]**Ps 115:3**; [k]**Ezr 3:11**

Ps. 137

1 [a]Eze 1:1,3; 3:15; 10:15; [b]Ne 1:4; [c]Isa 3:26; La 1:4
2 [d]**Lev 23:40**; [e]Job 30:31; Isa 24:8; Eze 26:13; Am 6:5
3 [f]Ps 79:1–4; La 1:5; [g]**Job 30:9**; Ps 80:6; [h]Eze 16:57; 22:4; 34:29
4 [i]**Ne 12:46**
5 [j]Isa 2:3; 56:7; 65:11; 66:20
6 [k]**Ps 22:15**; [l]Ne 2:3; [m]**Dt 4:29**; Jer 51:50; Eze 6:9
7 [n]**Ge 25:30; 2Ch 28:17; Ps 83:6**; La 4:21–22; [o]2Ki 25:1–10; Ob 11; [p]Ps 74:8
8 [q]Isa 13:1,19; 47:1–15; Jer 25:12,26; 50:1–51:58
9 [r]**2Ki 8:12; Isa 13:16**; Lk 19:44

Ps. 138

1 [a]Ps 95:3; 96:4; [b]Ps 27:6; 108:1
2 [c]**1Ki 8:29; Ps 5:7**; [d]Ps 74:21; 97:12; 140:13; [e]Ps 108:4; 115:1; [f]Ps 119:9
3 [g]Ps 18:6; 30:2; 99:6; 116:4; [h]**Ps 118;5**; [i]Pr 28:1; **Ac 4:29**; [j]Ps 28:7
4 [k]Ps 72:11; 102:15
5 [l]**Ps 51:14**; 71:16; 145:7; [m]Ps 21:5
6 [n]**Ps 113:6**; [o]**Ps 40:4; Mt 23:12**
7 [p]Ps 23:4; [q]**Ps 41:2**; [r]**Ex 7:5**; [s]Ps 7:6; [t]Ps 20:6; 60:5; 108:6; [u]Ps 17:7,14
8 [v]Php 1:6; [w]**Ezr 3:11**; Ps 100:5; [x]**Ps 51:11**; [y]**Job 10:3**,8

Ps. 139

1 [a]**Ps 17:3**; Ro 8:27; [b]Ps 44:21
2 [c]2Ki 19:27; [d]Ps 94:11; Pr 24:12; Jer 12:3
3 [e]2Ki 19:27; [f]**Job 31:4** *4* [g]**Heb 4:13**
5 [h]**1Sa 25:16**; Ps 32:10; 34:7; 125:2
6 [i]**Ps 131:1**; [j]Ro 11:33 *7* [k]Jer 23:24; Jnh 1:3

8 If I go up to the heavens,[l] you are there;
if I make my bed[m] in the depths,[a]
you are there.
9 If I rise on the wings of the dawn,
if I settle on the far side of the sea,
10 even there your hand will guide me,[n]
your right hand[o] will hold me fast.

11 If I say, "Surely the darkness will hide me
and the light become night around me,"
12 even the darkness will not be dark[p] to you;
the night will shine like the day,
for darkness is as light to you.

13 For you created my inmost being;[q]
you knit me together[r] in my mother's womb.[s]
14 I praise you[t] because I am fearfully and wonderfully made;
your works are wonderful,[u]
I know that full well.
15 My frame was not hidden from you
when I was made[v] in the secret place.
When I was woven together[w] in the depths of the earth,[x]
16 your eyes saw my unformed body.
All the days ordained[y] for me
were written in your book
before one of them came to be.

17 How precious to[b] me are your thoughts,[z] O God![a]
How vast is the sum of them!
18 Were I to count them,[b]
they would outnumber the grains of sand.[c]
When I awake,[d]
I am still with you.

19 If only you would slay the wicked,[e] O God!
Away from me,[f] you bloodthirsty men![g]
20 They speak of you with evil intent;
your adversaries[h] misuse your name.[i]
21 Do I not hate those[j] who hate you, O LORD,
and abhor[k] those who rise up against you?
22 I have nothing but hatred for them;
I count them my enemies.[l]

23 Search me,[m] O God, and know my heart;[n]
test me and know my anxious thoughts.
24 See if there is any offensive way[o] in me,
and lead me[p] in the way everlasting.

8 [l]Dt 30:12–15; Am 9:2–3; [m]Job 17:13
10 [n]Ps 23:3; [o]Ps 108:6; Isa 41:10
12 [p]Job 34:22; Da 2:22
13 [q]Ps 119:73; [r]**Job 10:11**; [s]Isa 44:2,24; 46:3; 49:5; Jer 1:5
14 [t]Ps 119:164; 145:10; [u]**Job 40:19**
15 [v]Ecc 11:5; [w]**Job 10:11**; [x]**Ps 63:9**
16 [y]**Job 33:29; Ps 90:12**
17 [z]**Ps 92:5**; [a]**Job 5:9**
18 [b]Ps 40:5; [c]**Job 29:18**; [d]**Ps 3:5**
19 [e]Ps 5:6; Isa 11:4; [f]**Ps 6:8**; [g]**Ps 59:2**
20 [h]**Ps 65:7**; [i]**Dt 5:11**
21 [j]2Ch 19:2; Ps 31:6; 119:113; [k]**Ps 26:5**
22 [l]Mt 5:43
23 [m]Job 31:6; [n]**1Sa 16:7; 1Ch 29:17; Ps 7:9**; Pr 17:3; Jer 11:20; **Rev 2:23**
24 [o]Jer 25:5; 36:3; [p]Ps 5:8; 23:2; 143:10

Ps. 140

1 [a]Ps 17:13; **25:20**; 59:2; 71:4; 142:6; 143:9; [b]ver 11; Ps 86:14
2 [c]Ps 36:4; 52:2; Pr 6:14; 16:27; Isa 59:4; Hos 7:15; [d]**Ps 68:30**
3 [e]Ps 57:4; [f]Ps 58:4; Ro 3:13*; Jas 3:8
4 [g]Ps 141:9; [h]**Ps 36:11**
5 [i]**Job 34:30; Ps 119:110**; [j]**Job 18:8**; [k]Job 18:9; Ps 31:4; **38:12**
6 [l]**Ps 16:2**; [m]**Ps 28:2**,6
7 [n]Ps 68:20
8 [o]Ps 10:2–3; **66:7**
9 [p]Pr 18:7
10 [q]Ps 11:6; 21:9; **Mt 3:10**; Lk 12:49; Rev 20:15
11 [r]**Ps 34:21**
12 [s]**Ps 82:3**; [t]**1Ki 8:45**; [u]**Ps 35:10**
13 [v]**Ps 138:2**; [w]**Ps 11:7**; [x]Ps 16:11

Psalm 140

For the director of music. A psalm of David.

1 Rescue me,[a] O LORD, from evil men;
protect me from men of violence,[b]
2 who devise evil plans[c] in their hearts
and stir up war[d] every day.
3 They make their tongues as sharp as[e] a serpent's;
the poison of vipers[f] is on their lips.
Selah

4 Keep me,[g] O LORD, from the hands of the wicked;[h]
protect me from men of violence
who plan to trip my feet.
5 Proud men have hidden a snare[i] for me;
they have spread out the cords of their net[j]
and have set traps[k] for me along my path. *Selah*

6 O LORD, I say to you, "You are my God."[l]
Hear, O LORD, my cry for mercy.[m]
7 O Sovereign LORD,[n] my strong deliverer,
who shields my head in the day of battle—
8 do not grant the wicked[o] their desires, O LORD;
do not let their plans succeed,
or they will become proud. *Selah*

9 Let the heads of those who surround me
be covered with the trouble their lips have caused.[p]
10 Let burning coals fall upon them;
may they be thrown into the fire,[q]
into miry pits, never to rise.
11 Let slanderers not be established in the land;
may disaster hunt down men of violence.[r]

12 I know that the LORD secures justice for the poor[s]
and upholds the cause[t] of the needy.[u]
13 Surely the righteous will praise your name[v]
and the upright will live[w] before you.[x]

[a]8 Hebrew *Sheol* [b]17 Or *concerning*

Psalm 141

A psalm of David.

1 O LORD, I call to you; come quickly[a] to
me.
Hear my voice[b] when I call to you.
2 May my prayer be set before you like
incense;[c]
may the lifting up of my hands[d] be
like the evening sacrifice.[e]

3 Set a guard over my mouth,[f] O LORD;
keep watch over the door of my
lips.[g]
4 Let not my heart[h] be drawn to what is
evil,
to take part in wicked deeds[i]
with men who are evildoers;
let me not eat of their delicacies.[j]

5 Let a righteous man[a] strike me—it is a
kindness;
let him rebuke me[k]—it is oil on my
head.[l]
My head will not refuse it.

Yet my prayer is ever against the
deeds of evildoers;
6 their rulers will be thrown down
from the cliffs,[m]
and the wicked will learn that my
words were well spoken.
7 ⌞They will say,⌟ "As one ploughs[n] and
breaks up the earth,[o]
so our bones have been scattered at
the mouth[p] of the grave."[b]
8 But my eyes are fixed[q] on you, O
Sovereign LORD;
in you I take refuge[r]—do not give
me over to death.
9 Keep me[s] from the snares they have
laid[t] for me,
from the traps set[u] by evildoers.
10 Let the wicked fall[v] into their own
nets,
while I pass by in safety.[w]

Psalm 142

A *maskil*[a] of David. When he was in the
cave.[a] A prayer.

1 I cry aloud[b] to the LORD;
I lift up my voice to the LORD for
mercy.[c]
2 I pour out my complaint[d] before him;
before him I tell my trouble.[e]

3 When my spirit grows faint[f] within
me,
it is you who know my way.
In the path where I walk
men have hidden a snare for me.
4 Look to my right and see;
no-one is concerned for me.
I have no refuge;[g]
no-one cares[h] for my life.

5 I cry to you, O LORD;
I say, "You are my refuge,[i]
my portion[j] in the land of the
living."[k]
6 Listen to my cry,[l]
for I am in desperate need;[m]
rescue me[n] from those who pursue
me,
for they are too strong[o] for me.
7 Set me free from my prison,[p]
that I may praise your name.[q]

Then the righteous will gather about
me
because of your goodness to me.[r]

Psalm 143

A psalm of David.

1 O LORD, hear my prayer,[a]
listen to my cry for mercy;[b]
in your faithfulness[c] and
righteousness[d]
come to my relief.
2 Do not bring your servant into
judgment,
for no-one living is righteous[e] before
you.

3 The enemy pursues me,
he crushes me to the ground;
he makes me dwell in darkness[f]
like those long dead.[g]
4 So my spirit grows faint within me;
my heart within me is dismayed.[h]

5 I remember[i] the days of long ago;
I meditate[j] on all your works
and consider what your hands have
done.
6 I spread out my hands[k] to you;
my soul thirsts for you like a
parched land. *Selah*

7 Answer me quickly,[l] O LORD;
my spirit faints[m] with longing.
Do not hide your face[n] from me
or I will be like those who go down
to the pit.
8 Let the morning bring me word of
your unfailing love,[o]
for I have put my trust in you.
Show me the way[p] I should go,
for to you I lift up my soul.[q]

Ps. 141

1 [a]**Ps 22:19**; [b]**Ps 4:1**; 5:1–2; 27:7; 143:1
2 [c]**Lk 1:9**; Rev 5:8; 8:3; [d]Ps 28:2; 63:4; 1Ti 2:8; [e]**Ex 29:39**,41; 30:8
3 [f]**Ps 34:13**; Jas 1:26; 3:8; [g]**Ps 12:2**
4 [h]**Jos 24:23**; [i]**Ps 106:29**; [j]Pr 23:1–3
5 [k]Pr 9:8; 19:25; 25:12; Ecc 7:5; [l]**Ex 29:7**; Ps 23:5
6 [m]**2Ch 25:12**
7 [n]Ps 129:3; [o]Nu 16:32–33; [p]**Nu 16:30**
8 [q]Ps 123:2; [r]Ps 2:12; 11:1
9 [s]Ps 140:4; [t]**Ps 64:5**; [u]**Ps 38:12**
10 [v]Ps 7:15; 35:8; 57:6; [w]Ps 124:7

Ps. 142

Title [a]1Sa 22:1; 24:3; Ps 57 Title
1 [b]**1Ki 8:52**; Ps 3:4; [c]Ps 30:8
2 [d]Ps 64:1; [e]**Ps 50:15**
3 [f]Ps 6:2; 77:3; 84:2; 88:4; 143:4,7; Jer 8:18; La 1:22
4 [g]Jer 25:35; [h]Jer 30:17
5 [i]**Ps 46:1**; [j]**Dt 32:9**; Ps 16:5; [k]**Job 28:13**; Ps 27:13
6 [l]**Ps 17:1**; [m]**Ps 79:8**; [n]**Ps 25:20**; [o]Jer 31:11
7 [p]**Ps 66:11**; [q]Ps 7:17; 9:2; [r]**2Ch 6:41**

Ps. 143

1 [a]**Ps 141:1**; [b]**Ps 28:2**; 130:2; [c]**Ex 34:6**; Ps 89:1–2; [d]Ps 71:2
2 [e]**Ps 14:3**; Ro 3:10
3 [f]**Ps 107:10**; [g]La 3:6
4 [h]Ps 30:7
5 [i]Ps 77:6; [j]**Ge 24:63**
6 [k]**Ex 9:29**; **Job 11:13**
7 [l]**Ps 69:17**; [m]**Ps 142:3**; [n]**Ps 22:24**; 27:9; 30:7
8 [o]Ps 6:4; 90:14; [p]**Ex 33:13**; **Job 34:32**; Ps 27:11; 32:8; [q]Ps 25:1–2; **86:4**

---

[a]5 Or *Let the Righteous One* [b]7 Hebrew *Sheol*
[a]Title: Probably a literary or musical term

9Rescue me[r] from my enemies,[s] O
LORD,
for I hide myself in you.
10Teach me[t] to do your will,
for you are my God;[u]
may your good Spirit
lead[v] me on level ground.[w]

11For your name's sake,[x] O LORD,
preserve my life;[y]
in your righteousness,[z] bring me
out of trouble.
12In your unfailing love, silence my
enemies;[a]
destroy all my foes,[b]
for I am your servant.[c]

Psalm 144

Of David.

1Praise be to the LORD my Rock,[a]
who trains my hands for war,
my fingers for battle.
2He is my loving God and my fortress,[b]
my stronghold[c] and my deliverer,
my shield,[d] in whom I take refuge,
who subdues peoples[a] [e] under me.

3O LORD, what is man[f] that you care for
him,
the son of man that you think of
him?
4Man is like a breath;[g]
his days are like a fleeting shadow.[h]

5Part your heavens,[i] O LORD, and come
down;[j]
touch the mountains, so that they
smoke.[k]
6Send forth lightning[l] and scatter[m] ⌊the
enemies⌋;
shoot your arrows[n] and rout them.
7Reach down your hand from on high;[o]
deliver me and rescue me[p]
from the mighty waters,[q]
from the hands of foreigners[r]
8whose mouths are full of lies,[s]
whose right hands[t] are deceitful.[u]

9I will sing a new song[v] to you, O God;
on the ten-stringed lyre[w] I will make
music to you,
10to the One who gives victory to kings,[x]
who delivers his servant David[y]
from the deadly sword.[z]

11Deliver me and rescue me[a]
from the hands of foreigners[b]
whose mouths are full of lies,[c]
whose right hands are deceitful.[d]

12Then our sons in their youth
will be like well-nurtured plants,[e]
and our daughters will be like pillars[f]
carved to adorn a palace.
13Our barns will be filled[g]
with every kind of provision.
Our sheep will increase by thousands,
by tens of thousands in our fields;
14 our oxen[h] will draw heavy loads.[b]
There will be no breaching of walls,[i]
no going into captivity,
no cry of distress in our streets.[j]

15Blessed are the people[k] of whom this is
true;
blessed are the people whose God is
the LORD.

Psalm 145[a]

A psalm of praise. Of David.

1I will exalt you,[a] my God the King;[b]
I will praise your name[c] for ever and
ever.
2Every day I will praise[d] you
and extol your name[e] for ever and
ever.

3Great is the LORD[f] and most worthy of
praise;[g]
his greatness no-one can fathom.[h]
4One generation[i] will commend your
works to another;
they will tell[j] of your mighty acts.[k]
5They will speak of the glorious
splendour[l] of your majesty,
and I will meditate on your
wonderful works.[b] [m]
6They will tell[n] of the power of your
awesome works,[o]
and I will proclaim[p] your great
deeds.[q]
7They will celebrate your abundant
goodness[r]
and joyfully sing[s] of your
righteousness.[t]

8The LORD is gracious and
compassionate,[u]
slow to anger and rich in love.[v]

9 [r]Ps 140:1; [s]Ps 18:17; 31:15
10 [t]Ps 119:12; [u]Ps 31:14; [v]Ne 9:20; Ps 25:4–5; [w]Ps 26:12
11 [x]Ps 25:11; [y]Ps 41:2; [z]Ps 31:1; 71:2
12 [a]Ps 8:2; [b]Ps 54:5; [c]Ps 116:16

Ps. 144
1 [a]Ge 49:24
2 [b]Ps 59:9; 91:2; [c]Ps 27:1; 37:39; 43:2; [d]Ge 15:1; Ps 18:2; [e]Jdg 4:23; Ps 18:39
3 [f]Heb 2:6
4 [g]Job 7:7; 27:3; Isa 2:22; [h]1Ch 29:15; Job 14:2; Jas 4:14
5 [i]Ps 18:9; Isa 64:1; [j]Ge 11:5; Ps 57:3; [k]Ps 104:32
6 [l]Hab 3:11; Zec 9:14; [m]Ps 59:11; 68:1; [n]Ps 7:12–13; 18:14
7 [o]2Sa 22:17; [p]Ps 3:7; 57:3; [q]Ps 69:2; [r]Ps 18:44
8 [s]Ps 12:2; 41:6; [t]Ge 14:22; Dt 32:40; [u]Ps 36:3
9 [v]Ps 28:7; 96:1; [w]Ps 33:2–3; 71:22
10 [x]2Sa 8:14; [y]Ps 18:50; [z]Job 5:20
11 [a]Ps 3:7; 25:20; [b]Ps 18:44; [c]Ps 41:6–7; [d]Ps 12:2; 36:3; 106:26; Isa 44:20
12 [e]Ps 92:12–14; 128:3; [f]SS 4:4; 7:4
13 [g]Pr 3:10
14 [h]Pr 14:4; [i]2Ki 25:11; [j]Isa 24:11; Jer 14:2–3
15 [k]Dt 28:3

Ps. 145
1 [a]Ps 30:1; 34:1; [b]Ps 2:6; 5:2; [c]Ps 54:6
2 [d]Ps 71:6; [e]Ps 34:1; Isa 25:1; 26:8
3 [f]Ps 95:3; [g]2Sa 22:4; Ps 96:4; [h]Job 5:9
4 [i]Ps 22:30; [j]Dt 11:19; [k]Ps 71:16
5 [l]Ps 96:6; 148:13; [m]Ps 75:1
6 [n]Ps 78:4; [o]Ps 66:3; [p]Dt 32:3; [q]Ps 75:1; 106:22
7 [r]Ex 18:9; Ps 27:13; [s]Ps 5:11; 101:1; [t]Ps 138:5
8 [u]Ps 86:15; 103:8; [v]Ps 86:5

a2 Many manuscripts of the Masoretic Text, Dead Sea Scrolls, Aquila, Jerome and Syriac; most manuscripts of the Masoretic Text *subdues my people*
b14 Or *our chieftains will be firmly established*
aThis psalm is an acrostic poem, the verses of which (including verse 13b) begin with the successive letters of the Hebrew alphabet.
b5 Dead Sea Scrolls and Syriac (see also Septuagint); Masoretic Text *On the glorious splendour of your majesty / and on your wonderful works I will meditate*

9The LORD is good[w] to all;
he has compassion[x] on all he has made.
10All you have made will praise you,[y] O LORD;
your saints will extol[z] you.[a]
11They will tell of the glory of your kingdom[b]
and speak of your might,[c]
12so that all men may know of your mighty acts[d]
and the glorious splendour of your kingdom.[e]
13Your kingdom is an everlasting kingdom,[f]
and your dominion endures through all generations.

The LORD is faithful[g] to all his promises[h]
and loving towards all he has made.[c]
14The LORD upholds[i] all those who fall
and lifts up all[j] who are bowed down.[k]
15The eyes of all look to you,
and you give them their food[l] at the proper time.
16You open your hand
and satisfy the desires[m] of every living thing.

17The LORD is righteous[n] in all his ways
and loving towards all he has made.[o]
18The LORD is near[p] to all who call on him,[q]
to all who call on him in truth.
19He fulfils the desires[r] of those who fear him;[s]
he hears their cry[t] and saves them.[u]
20The LORD watches over[v] all who love him,[w]
but all the wicked he will destroy.[x]

21My mouth will speak[y] in praise of the LORD.
Let every creature[z] praise his holy name[a]
for ever and ever.

Psalm 146

1Praise the LORD.[a]

Praise the LORD,[a] O my soul.
2 I will praise the LORD all my life;[b]
I will sing praise[c] to my God as long as I live.[d]

3Do not put your trust in princes,[e]
in mortal men,[f] who cannot save.
4When their spirit departs, they return to the ground;[g]
on that very day their plans come to nothing.[h]

5Blessed is he[i] whose help[j] is the God of Jacob,
whose hope is in the LORD his God,
6the Maker of heaven[k] and earth,
the sea, and everything in them—
the LORD, who remains faithful[l] for ever.
7He upholds[m] the cause of the oppressed[n]
and gives food to the hungry.[o]
The LORD sets prisoners free,[p]
8 the LORD gives sight[q] to the blind,[r]
the LORD lifts up those who are bowed down,[s]
the LORD loves the righteous.[t]
9The LORD watches over the alien[u]
and sustains the fatherless[v] and the widow,[w]
but he frustrates the ways of the wicked.

10The LORD reigns[x] for ever,
your God, O Zion, for all generations.

Praise the LORD.

Psalm 147

1Praise the LORD.[a]

How good it is to sing praises to our God,
how pleasant[a] and fitting to praise him![b]

2The LORD builds up Jerusalem;[c]
he gathers the exiles[d] of Israel.
3He heals the broken-hearted[e]
and binds up their wounds.[f]

4He determines the number of the stars[g]
and calls them each by name.

9 [w]**1Ch 16:34; Ps 136:1;** Mt 19:17; Mk 10:18; [x]Ps 103:13–14
10 [y]**Ps 8:6; 103:22; 139:14;** [z]Ps 30:4; 148:14; 149:9; [a]Ps 115:17–18
11 [b]ver 12–13; Ex 15:2; Mt 6:33; [c]Ps 21:13
12 [d]**Ps 75:1;** 105:1; [e]ver 11; Ps 103:19; Isa 2:10,19,21
13 [f]**Ex 15:18;** 1Ti 1:17; 2Pe 1:11; Rev 11:15; [g]**Dt 7:9; 1Co 1:9;** [h]**Jos 23:14**
14 [i]**Ps 37:17;** [j]**1Sa 2:8;** Ps 146:8; [k]**Ps 38:6**
15 [l]**Ge 1:30; Job 28:5; Ps 37:25; Mt 6:26**
16 [m]**Ps 90:14; 104:28**
17 [n]**Ex 9:27; Ezr 9:15;** [o]ver 13
18 [p]**Nu 23:21; Ps 46:1;** Php 4:5; [q]Ps 18:6; 80:18
19 [r]**Ps 20:4;** [s]**Job 22:28;** [t]**Ps 31:22; 40:1;** [u]**1Sa 10:19;** Ps 7:10; 34:18
20 [v]**Ps 1:6;** [w]Ps 31:23; 91:14; 97:10; [x]**Ps 94:23**
21 [y]Ps 71:8; [z]Ps 65:2; 150:6; [a]**Ex 3:15; Ps 30:4; 99:3**

Ps. 146

1 [a]Ps 103:1; 104:1
2 [b]Ps 104:33; [c]**Ps 105:2;** [d]**Ps 63:4**
3 [e]Ps 118:9; [f]Ps 60:11; **108:12;** Isa 2:22
4 [g]**Ge 3:19; Job 7:21;** Ps 103:14; Ecc 12:7; [h]Ps 33:10; 1Co 2:6
5 [i]Ps 33:18; 37:9; 119:43; 144:15; Jer 17:7; [j]Ps 70:5; 71:5; 121:2
6 [k]2Ch 2:12; Ps 115:15; Ac 14:15; **Rev 10:6;** [l]**Dt 7:9; Ps 18:25;** 108:4; 117:2
7 [m]**Ps 37:17;** [n]Ps 103:6; [o]Ps 107:9; 145:15; [p]**Ps 66:11; 68:6**
8 [q]Pr 20:12; Isa 29:18; 32:3; 35:5; 42:7,18–19; 43:8; Mt 11:5; [r]**Ex 4:11;** [s]**Ps 38:6;** [t]**Dt 7:13; Job 23:10**
9 [u]**Lev 19:34;** [v]**Ps 10:18;** [w]**Ex 22:22;** Jas 1:27
10 [x]**Ge 21:33; 1Ch 16:31;** Ps 93:1; 99:1; Rev 11:15

Ps. 147

1 [a]**Ps 135:3;** [b]Ps 33:1 *2* [c]**Ps 51:18;** [d]**Ps 106:47**
3 [e]**Ps 34:18;** [f]**Nu 12:13; Job 5:18;** Isa 1:6; Eze 34:16
4 [g]**Ge 15:5**

---

c*13* One manuscript of the Masoretic Text, Dead Sea Scrolls and Syriac (see also Septuagint); most manuscripts of the Masoretic Text do not have the last two lines of verse 13.
a*1* Hebrew *Hallelu Yah;* also in verse 10
a*1* Hebrew *Hallelu Yah;* also in verse 20

5Great is our Lord[h] and mighty in power;[i]
his understanding has no limit.[j]
6The LORD sustains the humble[k]
but casts the wicked[l] to the ground.

7Sing to the LORD[m] with thanksgiving;[n]
make music[o] to our God on the harp.[p]
8He covers the sky with clouds;[q]
he supplies the earth with rain[r]
and makes grass grow[s] on the hills.
9He provides food[t] for the cattle
and for the young ravens[u] when they call.

10His pleasure is not in the strength[v] of the horse,[w]
nor his delight in the legs of a man;
11the LORD delights[x] in those who fear him,[y]
who put their hope[z] in his unfailing love.[a]

12Extol the LORD, O Jerusalem;[b]
praise your God, O Zion,
13for he strengthens the bars of your gates[c]
and blesses your people[d] within you.
14He grants peace[e] to your borders
and satisfies you[f] with the finest of wheat.[g]

15He sends his command[h] to the earth;
his word runs[i] swiftly.
16He spreads the snow[j] like wool
and scatters the frost[k] like ashes.
17He hurls down hail[l] like pebbles.
Who can withstand his icy blast?
18He sends his word[m] and melts them;
he stirs up his breezes,[n] and the waters flow.

19He has revealed his word[o] to Jacob,[p]
his laws and decrees[q] to Israel.
20He has done this for no other nation;[r]
they do not know[s] his laws.

Praise the LORD.[t]

Psalm 148

1Praise the LORD.[a][a]

Praise the LORD from the heavens,[b]
praise him in the heights above.
2Praise him, all his angels,[c]
praise him, all his heavenly hosts.[d]
3Praise him, sun[e] and moon,
praise him, all you shining stars.
4Praise him, you highest heavens[f]
and you waters above the skies.[g]
5Let them praise the name[h] of the LORD,
for he commanded[i] and they were created.
6He set them in place for ever and ever;
he gave a decree[j] that will never pass away.

7Praise the LORD[k] from the earth,
you great sea creatures[l] and all ocean depths,[m]
8lightning and hail,[n] snow and clouds,
stormy winds that do his bidding,[o]
9you mountains and all hills,[p]
fruit trees and all cedars,
10wild animals[q] and all cattle,
small creatures and flying birds,
11kings[r] of the earth and all nations,
you princes and all rulers on earth,
12young men and maidens,
old men and children.

13Let them praise the name of the LORD,[s]
for his name alone is exalted;
his splendour[t] is above the earth and the heavens.[u]
14He has raised up for his people a horn,[b][v]
the praise[w] of all his saints,[x]
of Israel, the people close to his heart.[y]

Praise the LORD.

Psalm 149

1Praise the LORD.[a][a]

Sing to the LORD a new song,[b]
his praise in the assembly[c] of the saints.

2Let Israel rejoice[d] in their Maker;[e]
let the people of Zion be glad in their King.[f]
3Let them praise his name with dancing[g]
and make music to him with tambourine and harp.[h]
4For the LORD takes delight[i] in his people;
he crowns the humble with salvation.[j]

5 [h]Ps 48:1; [i]Ex 14:31; [j]Ps 145:3; Isa 40:28
6 [k]2Ch 33:23; Ps 146:8–9; [l]Ps 37:9–10; 145:20
7 [m]Ps 30:4; 33:3; [n]Ps 42:4; [o]Ps 27:6; [p]Ps 98:5
8 [q]Job 26:8; [r]Dt 11:14; 32:2; 2Sa 1:21; Job 5:10; [s]Job 28:26; Ps 104:14
9 [t]Ge 1:30; Ps 104:27–28; Mt 6:26; [u]Ge 8:7
10 [v]1Sa 16:7; [w]Job 39:11; Ps 33:16–17
11 [x]Ps 35:27; [y]Ps 33:18; 103:11; [z]Ps 119:43; [a]Ps 6:4
12 [b]Ps 48:1
13 [c]Dt 33:25; [d]Lev 25:21; Ps 128:5; 134:3
14 [e]Lev 26:6; 2Sa 7:10; Isa 48:18; [f]Ps 132:15; [g]Dt 32:14
15 [h]Job 37:12; Ps 33:9; 148:5; [i]Isa 55:11
16 [j]Ps 148:8; [k]Job 37:12; 38:29
17 [l]Ex 9:22–23; Job 38:22; Ps 78:47
18 [m]ver 15; Ps 33:9; 107:20; [n]Ps 50:3
19 [o]Ex 20:1; Ro 3:2; [p]Ps 78:5; [q]Dt 33:4; Jos 1:8; 2Ki 22:8; Mal 4:4; Ro 9:4
20 [r]Dt 4:7–8, 32–34; [s]Ps 79:6; [t]Ps 33:2; 103:1

Ps. 148

1 [a]Ps 33:2; 103:1; [b]Ps 19:1; 69:34; 150:1
2 [c]Ps 103:20; [d]1Ki 22:19
3 [e]Ps 19:1
4 [f]Dt 10:14; [g]Ge 1:7
5 [h]Ps 145:21; [i]Ps 147:15
6 [j]Jer 31:35–36; 33:25
7 [k]Ps 33:2; [l]Ge 1:21; Ps 74:13–14; [m]Dt 33:13
8 [n]Ex 9:18; Jos 10:11; [o]Job 37:11–12; Ps 103:20; 147:15–18
9 [p]Isa 44:23; 49:13; 55:12
10 [q]Isa 43:20; Hos 2:18
11 [r]Ps 102:15
13 [s]Ps 113:2; 138:4; [t]Ps 145:5; [u]Ps 8:1
14 [v]1Sa 2:1; [w]Ex 15:2; Ps 22:3; [x]Ps 145:10; [y]Dt 26:19

Ps. 149

1 [a]Ps 33:2; 103:1; [b]Ps 28:7; 96:1; Rev 5:9; [c]Ps 1:5
2 [d]Isa 13:3; Jer 51:48; [e]Job 10:3; Ps 95:6; Isa 44:2; 45:11; 54:5; [f]Ps 10:16; 47:6; Isa 32:1; Zec 9:9
3 [g]Ex 15:20; [h]Ps 57:8
4 [i]Ps 35:27; 147:11; [j]Ps 132:16

[a]*1* Hebrew *Hallelu Yah*; also in verse 14
[b]*14* *Horn* here symbolises strong one, that is, king.
[a]*1* Hebrew *Hallelu Yah*; also in verse 9

5Let the saints rejoice[k] in this honour
and sing for joy on their beds.[l]

6May the praise of God be in their
mouths[m]
and a double-edged[n] sword in their
hands,[o]
7to inflict vengeance[p] on the nations
and punishment[q] on the peoples,
8to bind their kings with fetters,[r]
their nobles with shackles of iron,[s]
9to carry out the sentence written
against them.[t]
This is the glory of all his saints.[u]

Praise the LORD.

Psalm 150

1Praise the LORD.[a a]

Praise God in his sanctuary;[b]
praise him in his mighty heavens.[c]
2Praise him for his acts of power;[d]
praise him for his surpassing
greatness.[e]
3Praise him with the sounding of the
trumpet,[f]
praise him with the harp and lyre,[g]
4praise him with tambourine and
dancing,[h]
praise him with the strings[i] and
flute,[j]
5praise him with the clash of cymbals,[k]
praise him with resounding
cymbals.

6Let everything[l] that has breath praise
the LORD.

Praise the LORD.

5 [k]Ps 132:16; [l]Job 35:10; Ps 42:8
6 [m]Ps 66:17; [n]Heb 4:12; Rev 1:16; [o]Ne 4:17
7 [p]Nu 31:3; Dt 32:41; [q]Ps 81:15
8 [r]2Sa 3:34; Isa 14:1–2; [s]2Ch 33:11
9 [t]Dt 7:1; Eze 28:26; [u]Ps 145:10

Ps. 150

1 [a]Ps 112:1; [b]Ps 68:24–26; 73:17; 102:19; [c]Ps 148:1
2 [d]Dt 3:24; [e]Ex 15:7
3 [f]Nu 10:2; [g]Ps 57:8
4 [h]Ex 15:20; [i]Ps 45:8; [j]Ge 4:21
5 [k]2Sa 6:5
6 [l]Ps 103:22

[a]1 Hebrew *Hallelu Yah*; also in verse 6

Proverbs

Prologue: Purpose and Theme

1 The proverbs[a] of Solomon[b] son of David, king of Israel:[c]

[2]for attaining wisdom and discipline;
for understanding words of insight;
[3]for acquiring a disciplined and
prudent life,
doing what is right and just and fair;
[4]for giving prudence to the simple,[d]
knowledge and discretion[e] to the
young—
[5]let the wise listen and add to their
learning,[f]
and let the discerning get
guidance—
[6]for understanding proverbs and
parables,[g]
the sayings and riddles[h] of the wise.[i]

[7]The fear of the LORD[j] is the beginning
of knowledge,
but fools[a] despise wisdom[k] and
discipline.[l]

Exhortations to Embrace Wisdom

Warning Against Enticement

[8]Listen, my son,[m] to your father's[n]
instruction
and do not forsake your mother's
teaching.[o]
[9]They will be a garland to grace your
head
and a chain to adorn your neck.[p]

[10]My son, if sinners entice[q] you,
do not give in[r] to them.[s]
[11]If they say, "Come along with us;
let's lie in wait[t] for someone's blood,
let's waylay some harmless soul;
[12]let's swallow[u] them alive, like the
grave,[b]
and whole, like those who go down
to the pit;[v]
[13]we will get all sorts of valuable things
and fill our houses with plunder;
[14]throw in your lot with us,
and we will share a common
purse[w]"—

[15]my son, do not go along with them,
do not set foot[x] on their paths;[y]
[16]for their feet rush into sin,[z]
they are swift to shed blood.[a]
[17]How useless to spread a net
in full view of all the birds!
[18]These men lie in wait[b] for their own
blood;
they waylay only themselves![c]
[19]Such is the end of all who go after
ill-gotten gain;
it takes away the lives of those who
get it.[d]

Warning Against Rejecting Wisdom

[20]Wisdom calls aloud[e] in the street,
she raises her voice in the public
squares;
[21]at the head of the noisy streets[c] she
cries out,
in the gateways of the city she
makes her speech:

[22]"How long will you simple ones[d][f] love
your simple ways?
How long will mockers delight in
mockery
and fools hate[g] knowledge?
[23]If you had responded to my rebuke,
I would have poured out my heart to
you
and made my thoughts known to
you.
[24]But since you rejected[h] me when I
called[i]
and no-one gave heed[j] when I
stretched out my hand,
[25]since you ignored all my advice
and would not accept my rebuke,
[26]I in turn will laugh[k] at your disaster;[l]
I will mock[m] when calamity
overtakes you[n]—

Ch. 1
1 [a]Mt 13:3; [b]1Ki 4:29–34; [c]Pr 10:1; 25:1; Ecc 1:1
4 [d]Pr 8:5; [e]Pr 8:12
5 [f]Pr 9:9
6 [g]**Ps 49:4;** Mt 13:10–17; [h]**Nu 12:8; Jdg 14:12;** [i]Pr 22:17; 24:23
7 [j]**Ex 20:20; Job 23:15;** Ps 34:4–22; **112:1;** Pr 9:10; 15:33; Isa 33:6; 50:10; 59:19; [k]**Dt 4:6;** Jer 8:9; [l]Pr 8:33–36; 9:7–9; 12:1; 13:18; 15:32
8 [m]ver 8–9; Pr 2:1; 3:1; 4:1; 5:1; 6:1; 7:1; 19:27; 22:17; 23:26–28; [n]Jer 35:8; [o]**Dt 21:18;** Pr 6:20
9 [p]Pr 3:21–22; 4:1–9
10 [q]**Job 24:15;** [r]Dt 13:8; [s]ver 15; Ps 1:1; Pr 16:29
11 [t]**Ps 10:8**
12 [u]**Ps 35:25;** [v]ver 16–18; **Job 33:18; Ps 30:3**
14 [w]ver 19
15 [x]**Ps 119:101;** [y]**Ge 49:6;** Pr 4:14
16 [z]**Job 15:31;** [a]Pr 6:18; Isa 59:7
18 [b]Ps 71:10; [c]**ver 11–12**
19 [d]**ver 13–14;** Pr 4:14–17; 11:19
20 [e]**Job 28:12;** Pr 7:10–13; 9:1–3, 13–15
22 [f]Pr 6:32; 7:7; 8:5; 9:4, 16; [g]Ps 50:17
24 [h]Jer 26:5; 35:17; 36:31; [i]Isa 65:12; 66:4; Jer 7:13; [j]**1Sa 8:19**
26 [k]**Ps 2:4;** [l]ver 33; **Ps 59:8;** [m]**2Ki 19:21;** [n]Dt 28:63

[a]7 The Hebrew words rendered *fool* in Proverbs, and often elsewhere in the Old Testament, denote one who is morally deficient.
[b]12 Hebrew *Sheol*
[c]21 Hebrew; Septuagint / *on the tops of the walls*
[d]22 The Hebrew word rendered *simple* in Proverbs generally denotes one without moral direction and inclined to evil.

27when calamity overtakes you like a storm,
when disaster[o] sweeps over you like a whirlwind,
when distress and trouble overwhelm you.

28"Then they will call to me but I will not answer;[p]
they will look for me but will not find me.[q]
29Since they hated knowledge
and did not choose to fear the LORD,[r]
30since they would not accept my advice
and spurned my rebuke,[s]
31they will eat the fruit of their ways
and be filled with the fruit of their schemes.[t]
32For the waywardness of the simple will kill them,
and the complacency of fools will destroy them;[u]
33but whoever listens to me will live in safety[v]
and be at ease, without fear of harm."[w]

Moral Benefits of Wisdom

2 My son,[a] if you accept my words
and store up my commands within you,
2turning your ear to wisdom
and applying your heart to understanding,[b]
3and if you call out for insight[c]
and cry aloud for understanding,
4and if you look for it as for silver
and search for it as for hidden treasure,[d]
5then you will understand the fear of the LORD
and find the knowledge of God.[e]
6For the LORD gives wisdom,[f]
and from his mouth come knowledge and understanding.[g]
7He holds victory in store for the upright,
he is a shield[h] to those whose walk is blameless,[i]
8for he guards the course of the just
and protects the way of his faithful ones.[j]

9Then you will understand[k] what is right and just
and fair—every good path.
10For wisdom will enter your heart,[l]
and knowledge will be pleasant to your soul.
11Discretion will protect you,
and understanding will guard you.[m]
12Wisdom will save[n] you from the ways of wicked men,
from men whose words are perverse,
13who leave the straight paths
to walk in dark ways,[o]
14who delight in doing wrong
and rejoice in the perverseness of evil,[p]
15whose paths are crooked[q]
and who are devious in their ways.[r]

16It will save you also from the adulteress,[s]
from the wayward wife with her seductive words,
17who has left the partner of her youth
and ignored the covenant she made before God.[a][t]
18For her house leads down to death
and her paths to the spirits of the dead.[u]
19None who go to her return
or attain the paths of life.[v]

20Thus you will walk in the ways of good men
and keep to the paths of the righteous.
21For the upright will live in the land,[w]
and the blameless will remain in it;
22but the wicked[x] will be cut off from the land,[y]
and the unfaithful will be torn from it.[z]

Further Benefits of Wisdom

3 My son,[a] do not forget my teaching,[b]
but keep my commands in your heart,
2for they will prolong your life many years[c]
and bring you prosperity.[d]

3Let love and faithfulness[e] never leave you;
bind them around your neck,
write them on the tablet of your heart.[f]
4Then you will win favour and a good name
in the sight of God and man.[g]

5Trust in the LORD[h] with all your heart
and lean not on your own understanding;
6in all your ways acknowledge him,
and he will make your paths[i] straight.[a][j]

27 [o]**Ps 18:18**; Pr 5:12–14
28 [p]**Dt 1:45; 1Sa 8:18; Jer 11:11**; [q]**Job 27:9**; Pr 8:17; Eze 8:18; Hos 5:6; Zec 7:13
29 [r]**Job 21:14**
30 [s]ver 25
31 [t]**2Ch 36:16**; Pr 14:14; Jer 6:19; 14:16; 21:14; 30:15
32 [u]Pr 5:22; 15:10; Isa 66:4
33 [v]**Nu 24:21; Dt 33:28**; Pr 3:23; [w]**ver 21–26; Ps 112:8**

Ch. 2

1 [a]**Pr 1:8**
2 [b]Pr 22:17; 23:12
3 [c]Jas 1:5
4 [d]**Job 3:21**; Mt 13:44
5 [e]**Dt 4:6**
6 [f]**Job 12:13; Ps 119:34**; [g]**Job 9:4; 22:22**
7 [h]**Ge 15:1**; Pr 30:5–6; [i]**Ge 6:9**; Ps 84:11
8 [j]1Sa 2:9; **Ps 18:25; 97:10**
9 [k]**Dt 1:16**
10 [l]Pr 14:33
11 [m]Pr 4:6
12 [n]ver 16; Pr 3:13–18; 4:5
13 [o]Pr 4:19
14 [p]Pr 10:23; 15:21
15 [q]**Ps 125:5**; [r]Pr 21:8
16 [s]Pr 5:1–6; 6:20–29; 7:5–27
17 [t]Mal 2:14
18 [u]Pr 5:5; 7:27; 9:18
19 [v]Pr 3:16–18; 5:8; Ecc 7:26
21 [w]**Ps 37:29**
22 [x]**Ps 5:4**; [y]**Job 18:17**; [z]Dt 28:63; **29:28**; Ps 37:9, 28–29; Pr 10:30

Ch. 3

1 [a]**Pr 1:8**; [b]**Ps 44:17**
2 [c]**Dt 11:21**; [d]**Dt 5:16; 30:15, 16; 1Ki 3:13, 14**; Pr 9:6, 10–11
3 [e]**Ps 85:10**; [f]**Ex 13:9; Dt 6:6**; Pr 6:21; 7:3; **2Co 3:3**
4 [g]**1Sa 2:26**; Lk 2:52
5 [h]**Ps 4:5**
6 [i]**Job 33:11; Isa 30:11**; [j]Ps 5:8; Pr 16:3; Isa 40:3; Jer 42:3

[a]17 Or *covenant of her God*
[a]6 Or *will direct your paths*

7Do not be wise in your own eyes;[k]
fear the LORD[l] and shun evil.[m]
8This will bring health to your body[n]
and nourishment to your bones.[o]

9Honour the LORD with your wealth,
with the firstfruits[p] of all your crops;
10then your barns will be filled[q] to
overflowing,
and your vats will brim over with
new wine.[r]

11My son,[s] do not despise the LORD's
discipline[t]
and do not resent his rebuke,
12because the LORD disciplines those he
loves,[u]
as a father[b] the son he delights in.[v]

13Blessed is the man who finds wisdom,
the man who gains understanding,
14for she is more profitable than silver
and yields better returns than gold.[w]
15She is more precious than rubies;[x]
nothing you desire can compare
with her.[y]
16Long life is in her right hand;[z]
in her left hand are riches and
honour.[a]
17Her ways are pleasant ways,
and all her paths are peace.[b]
18She is a tree of life[c] to those who
embrace her;
those who lay hold of her will be
blessed.[d]

19By wisdom[e] the LORD laid the earth's
foundations,[f]
by understanding he set the
heavens[g] in place;
20by his knowledge the deeps were
divided,
and the clouds let drop the dew.

21My son,[h] preserve sound judgment
and discernment,
do not let them out of your sight;[i]
22they will be life for you,[j]
an ornament to grace your neck.[k]
23Then you will go on your way in
safety,[l]
and your foot will not stumble;[m]
24when you lie down,[n] you will not be
afraid;[o]
when you lie down, your sleep[p] will
be sweet.
25Have no fear of sudden disaster
or of the ruin that overtakes the
wicked,
26for the LORD will be your confidence[q]
and will keep your foot[r] from being
snared.[s]

7 [k]Pr 26:5,12; Isa 5:21; [l]Ps 111:10; [m]Ex 20:20; Dt 4:6; Job 1:1
8 [n]Ps 38:3; Pr 4:22; [o]Job 21:24
9 [p]Ex 22:29; Dt 26:1–15
10 [q]Ps 144:13; [r]Job 22:21; Joel 2:24; Mal 3:10–12
11 [s]Pr 1:8–9; [t]Job 5:17
12 [u]Pr 13:24; Rev 3:19; [v]Dt 8:5; Job 5:17; Heb 12:5–6*
14 [w]Job 28:15; Pr 8:19; 16:16
15 [x]Job 28:18; [y]Job 28:17–19
16 [z]Ge 15:15; [a]1Ki 3:13,14
17 [b]Mt 11:28–30
18 [c]Ge 2:9; Pr 10:11; Rev 2:7; [d]Pr 2:12; 4:3–9; 8:17–21
19 [e]Ge 1:31; Ps 136:5–9; [f]Job 28:25–27; [g]Pr 8:27–29
21 [h]Pr 1:8–9; 6:20; [i]Pr 4:20–22
22 [j]Dt 30:20; Pr 4:13; [k]Pr 1:8–9
23 [l]Pr 1:33; [m]Ps 37:24; 119:11; Pr 4:12
24 [n]Lev 26:6; [o]Ps 91:5; 112:8; [p]Job 11:18; Jer 31:26
26 [q]2Ki 18:5; Job 4:6; [r]1Sa 2:9; [s]Job 5:19
28 [t]Lev 19:13; Dt 24:15; Lk 10:25–37
29 [u]Zec 8:17
31 [v]Ps 37:1; Pr 24:1–2
32 [w]Ps 101:4; [x]Job 29:4
33 [y]Job 5:3; [z]Zec 5:4; [a]Ps 37:22; Pr 14:11
34 [b]2Ki 19:21; [c]Ps 40:4; [d]Ps 18:25–27; Mt 23:12; Jas 4:6*; 1Pe 5:5*

Ch. 4

1 [a]Pr 1:8; [b]Pr 19:20; [c]Job 8:10
4 [d]1Ki 9:4; [e]Pr 7:2
5 [f]Pr 2:12; 3:13–18
6 [g]2Th 2:10; [h]Pr 2:11
7 [i]Mt 13:44–46; [j]Pr 23:23
8 [k]Pr 3:18

27Do not withhold good from those who
deserve it,
when it is in your power to act.
28Do not say to your neighbour,
"Come back later; I'll give it
tomorrow" —
when you now have it with you.[t]

29Do not plot harm against your
neighbour,
who lives trustfully near you.[u]
30Do not accuse a man for no reason—
when he has done you no harm.

31Do not envy[v] a violent man
or choose any of his ways,
32for the LORD detests a perverse man[w]
but takes the upright into his
confidence.[x]

33The LORD's curse[y] is on the house of
the wicked,[z]
but he blesses the home of the
righteous.[a]
34He mocks[b] proud mockers[c]
but gives grace to the humble.[d]
35The wise inherit honour,
but fools he holds up to shame.

Wisdom Is Supreme

4 Listen, my sons,[a] to a father's
instruction;[b]
pay attention and gain
understanding.[c]
2I give you sound learning,
so do not forsake my teaching.
3When I was a boy in my father's
house,
still tender, and an only child of my
mother,
4he taught me and said,
"Lay hold[d] of my words with all
your heart;
keep my commands and you will
live.[e]
5Get wisdom,[f] get understanding;
do not forget my words or swerve
from them.
6Do not forsake wisdom, and she will
protect you;[g]
love her, and she will watch over
you.[h]
7Wisdom is supreme; therefore get
wisdom.
Though it cost all[i] you have,[a] get
understanding.[j]
8Esteem her, and she will exalt you;
embrace her, and she will honour
you.[k]

[b]12 Hebrew; Septuagint / *and he punishes*
[a]7 Or *Whatever else you get*

9She will set a garland of grace on your
head
and present you with a crown of
splendour.[l]"
10Listen, my son,[m] accept what I say,
and the years of your life will be
many.[n]
11I guide[o] you in the way of wisdom
and lead you along straight paths.[p]
12When you walk, your steps will not be
hampered;
when you run, you will not
stumble.[q]
13Hold on to instruction, do not let it go;
guard it well, for it is your life.[r]
14Do not set foot on the path of the
wicked
or walk in the way of evil men.[s]
15Avoid it, do not travel on it;
turn from it and go on your way.
16For they cannot sleep till they do evil;[t]
they are robbed of slumber till they
make someone fall.
17They eat the bread of wickedness
and drink the wine of violence.[u]

18The path of the righteous[v] is like the
first gleam of dawn,[w]
shining ever brighter till the full
light of day.[x]
19But the way of the wicked is like deep
darkness;[y]
they do not know what makes them
stumble.[z]

20My son,[a] pay attention to what I say;
listen closely to my words.[b]
21Do not let them out of your sight,[c]
keep them within your heart;
22for they are life to those who find them
and health to a man's whole body.[d]
23Above all else, guard[e] your heart,
for it is the wellspring of life.[f]
24Put away perversity from your mouth;
keep corrupt talk far from your lips.
25Let your eyes[g] look straight ahead,
fix your gaze directly before you.
26Make level[b] paths for your feet[h]
and take only ways that are firm.
27Do not swerve to the right or the left;[i]
keep your foot from evil.

Warning Against Adultery

5 My son,[a] pay attention to my
wisdom,
listen well to my words[b] of insight,
2that you may maintain discretion
and your lips may preserve
knowledge.
3For the lips of an adulteress drip
honey,
and her speech is smoother than
oil;[c]
4but in the end she is bitter as gall,[d]
sharp as a double-edged sword.
5Her feet go down to death;
her steps lead straight to the
grave.[a][e]
6She gives no thought to the way of life;
her paths are crooked, but she
knows it not.[f]

7Now then, my sons, listen[g] to me;
do not turn aside from what I say.
8Keep to a path far from her,[h]
do not go near the door of her
house,
9lest you give your best strength to
others
and your years to one who is cruel,
10lest strangers feast on your wealth
and your toil enrich another man's
house.[i]
11At the end of your life you will groan,
when your flesh and body are
spent.
12You will say, "How I hated discipline!
How my heart spurned correction![j]
13I would not obey my teachers
or listen to my instructors.
14I have come to the brink of utter ruin[k]
in the midst of the whole
assembly."[l]

15Drink water from your own cistern,
running water from your own well.
16Should your springs overflow in the
streets,
your streams of water in the public
squares?
17Let them be yours alone,
never to be shared with strangers.
18May your fountain[m] be blessed,
and may you rejoice in the wife of
your youth.[n]
19A loving doe, a graceful deer[o]—
may her breasts satisfy you always,
may you ever be captivated by her
love.
20Why be captivated, my son, by an
adulteress?
Why embrace the bosom of another
man's wife?

21For a man's ways are in full view[p] of
the LORD,
and he examines[q] all his paths.[r]
22The evil deeds of a wicked man
ensnare him;[s]
the cords of his sin hold him fast.[t]
23He will die for lack of discipline,[u]
led astray by his own great folly.[v]

4:9 [l]Pr 1:8–9
10 [m]Ps 34:11–16; Pr 1:8–9; [n]Dt 11:21
11 [o]1Sa 12:23; [p]2Sa 22:37; Ps 5:8
12 [q]Job 18:7; Pr 3:23
13 [r]Pr 3:22
14 [s]Ps 1:1; Pr 1:15
16 [t]Ps 36:4; Mic 7:3
17 [u]Ge 49:5; Ps 73:6; Pr 1:10–19; 14:22; Isa 59:6; Jer 22:3; Hab 1:2; Mal 2:16
18 [v]Job 17:9; [w]Job 22:28; [x]2Sa 23:4; Da 12:3; Mt 5:14; Jn 8:12; Php 2:15
19 [y]Pr 2:13; [z]Dt 32:35; Job 3:23; Pr 13:9; Isa 8:15
20 [a]Ps 34:11–16; Pr 1:8–9; [b]Pr 5:1
21 [c]Pr 3:21
22 [d]Pr 3:8
23 [e]2Ki 10:31; [f]Pr 10:11; Lk 6:45
25 [g]Job 31:1
26 [h]Heb 12:13*
27 [i]Lev 10:11; Dt 5:32

Ch. 5
1 [a]Pr 1:8; [b]Pr 4:20
3 [c]Ps 55:21; Pr 7:5
4 [d]Ecc 7:26
5 [e]Ps 9:17; Pr 2:18; 7:26–27
6 [f]Pr 9:13; 30:20
7 [g]Pr 1:8–9
8 [h]Pr 2:16–19; 6:20–29; 7:1–27
10 [i]Pr 29:3
12 [j]Pr 12:1
14 [k]Pr 1:24–27; 6:33; [l]Pr 31:3
18 [m]SS 4:12–15; [n]Dt 20:7; Pr 2:17; Ecc 9:9; Mal 2:14
19 [o]SS 4:5; 8:14
21 [p]Ps 119:168; [q]Jer 29:23; [r]Job 10:4; 14:16; Pr 15:3; Jer 32:19; Heb 4:13
22 [s]Ps 9:16; [t]Nu 32:23; Job 18:9; Ps 7:15–16; Pr 1:31–32
23 [u]Job 4:21; Pr 10:21; [v]Job 34:21–25; Pr 11:5

[b]26 Or *Consider the*
[a]5 Hebrew *Sheol*

Warnings Against Folly

6 My son,[a] if you have put up
security[b] for your neighbour,[c]
if you have struck hands in pledge[d]
for another,
2if you have been trapped by what you
said,
ensnared by the words of your
mouth,
3then do this, my son, to free yourself,
since you have fallen into your
neighbour's hands:
Go and humble yourself;
press your plea with your
neighbour!
4Allow no sleep to your eyes,
no slumber to your eyelids.[e]
5Free yourself, like a gazelle[f] from the
hand of the hunter,[g]
like a bird from the snare of the
fowler.[h]

6Go to the ant, you sluggard;[i]
consider its ways and be wise!
7It has no commander,
no overseer or ruler,
8yet it stores its provisions in summer[j]
and gathers its food at harvest.[k]
9How long will you lie there, you
sluggard?[l]
When will you get up from your
sleep?
10A little sleep, a little slumber,
a little folding of the hands to
rest[m]—
11and poverty[n] will come on you like a
bandit
and scarcity like an armed man.[a]

12A scoundrel and villain,
who goes about with a corrupt
mouth,
13 who winks with his eye,[o]
signals with his feet
and motions with his fingers,[p]
14 who plots evil[q] with deceit in his
heart—
he always stirs up dissension.[r]
15Therefore disaster will overtake him in
an instant;[s]
he will suddenly[t] be destroyed—
without remedy.[u]

16There are six things the LORD hates,[v]
seven that are detestable to him:
17 haughty eyes,[w]
a lying tongue,[x]
hands that shed innocent blood,[y]
18 a heart that devises wicked
schemes,
feet that are quick to rush into
evil,[z]
19 a false witness[a] who pours out
lies[b]
and a man who stirs up
dissension among brothers.[c]

Warning Against Adultery

20My son,[d] keep your father's
commands
and do not forsake your mother's
teaching.[e]
21Bind them upon your heart for ever;
fasten them around your neck.[f]
22When you walk, they will guide you;
when you sleep, they will watch
over you;
when you awake, they will speak to
you.
23For these commands are a lamp,
this teaching is a light,[g]
and the corrections of discipline
are the way to life,[h]
24keeping you from the immoral
woman,
from the smooth tongue of the
wayward wife.[i]
25Do not lust in your heart after her
beauty
or let her captivate you with her
eyes,
26for the prostitute reduces you to a loaf
of bread,
and the adulteress preys upon your
very life.[j]
27Can a man scoop fire into his lap
without his clothes being burned?
28Can a man walk on hot coals
without his feet being scorched?
29So is he who sleeps[k] with another
man's wife;[l]
no-one who touches her will go
unpunished.

30Men do not despise a thief if he steals
to satisfy his hunger when he is
starving.
31Yet if he is caught, he must pay
sevenfold,[m]
though it costs him all the wealth of
his house.
32But a man who commits adultery[n]
lacks judgment;[o]
whoever does so destroys himself.
33Blows and disgrace are his lot,
and his shame will never[p] be wiped
away;
34for jealousy[q] arouses a husband's
fury,[r]
and he will show no mercy when he
takes revenge.

Ch. 6
1 [a]**Pr 1:8;** [b]Job 17:3; [c]Pr 17:18; [d]Pr 11:15; 22:26–27
4 [e]Ps 132:4
5 [f]**2Sa 2:18;** [g]Isa 13:14; [h]**Ps 91:3**
6 [i]ver 6–11; Pr 20:4
8 [j]Pr 30:24–25; [k]Pr 10:4
9 [l]Pr 24:30–34; 26:13–16
10 [m]Pr 24:33; Ecc 4:5
11 [n]ver 10–11; Pr 20:13; 24:30–34
13 [o]**Ps 35:19;** Pr 16:30; [p]Isa 58:9
14 [q]**Ps 140:2;** [r]ver 16–19
15 [s]**Ps 55:15;** [t]Job 5:3; [u]Pr 14:32; 29:1
16 [v]ver 16–19; Pr 3:32; 8:13; 15:8–9,26; 16:5
17 [w]**Job 41:34; Ps 10:5;** [x]Pr 12:22; [y]**Dt 19:10;** Pr 1:16; Isa 1:21; 59:7; Jer 2:34; Mic 7:2
18 [z]**Job 15:31**
19 [a]**Dt 19:16;** [b]**Ps 12:2;** [c]ver 12–15; Pr 15:18; Zec 8:17
20 [d]**Pr 3:21;** [e]Pr 1:8
21 [f]Dt 6:8; **Pr 3:3;** 7:1–3
23 [g]**Ps 119:105;** [h]Pr 10:17
24 [i]Ge 39:8; **Ps 55:21;** Pr 2:16; 7:5
26 [j]Pr 7:22–23
29 [k]**Ex 20:14;** [l]Pr 2:16–19; **5:8**
31 [m]Ex 22:1–14
32 [n]**Ex 20:14;** [o]Pr 7:7; 9:4,16
33 [p]Pr 5:9–14
34 [q]**Nu 5:14;** [r]**Ge 34:7**

[a]*11* Or *like a vagrant / and scarcity like a beggar*

35He will not accept any compensation;
he will refuse the bribe, however
great it is.[s]

Warning Against the Adulteress

7 My son,[a] keep my words
and store up my commands
within you.
2Keep my commands and you will
live;[b]
guard my teachings as the apple of
your eye.
3Bind them on your fingers;
write them on the tablet of your
heart.[c]
4Say to wisdom, "You are my sister,"
and call understanding your
kinsman;
5they will keep you from the
adulteress,
from the wayward wife with her
seductive words.[d]

6At the window of my house
I looked out through the lattice.
7I saw among the simple,
I noticed among the young men,
a youth who lacked judgment.[e]
8He was going down the street near her
corner,
walking along in the direction of her
house
9at twilight,[f] as the day was fading,
as the dark of night set in.

10Then out came a woman to meet him,
dressed like a prostitute and with
crafty intent.
11(She is loud[g] and defiant,
her feet never stay at home;
12now in the street, now in the squares,
at every corner she lurks.)[h]
13She took hold of him[i] and kissed him
and with a brazen face she said:[j]

14"I have fellowship offerings[a][k] at
home;
today I fulfilled my vows.
15So I came out to meet you;
I looked for you and have found
you!
16I have covered my bed
with coloured linens from Egypt.
17I have perfumed my bed[l]
with myrrh,[m] aloes and cinnamon.
18Come, let's drink deep of love till
morning;
let's enjoy ourselves with love![n]
19My husband is not at home;
he has gone on a long journey.
20He took his purse filled with money
and will not be home till full moon."

35 [s]Job 31:9–11; SS 8:7

Ch. 7

1 [a]Pr 1:8
2 [b]Pr 4:4
3 [c]Pr 3:3
5 [d]ver 21; Job 31:9; Pr 2:16; 6:24
7 [e]Pr 1:22; 6:32
9 [f]Job 24:15
11 [g]Pr 9:13
12 [h]Pr 8:1–36; 23:26–28
13 [i]Ge 39:12; [j]Pr 1:20
14 [k]Lev 7:11–18
17 [l]Est 1:6; Isa 57:7; Eze 23:41; Am 6:4; [m]Ge 37:25
18 [n]Ge 39:7
21 [o]ver 5
22 [p]Job 18:10
23 [q]Job 15:22; 16:13; [r]Pr 6:26; Ecc 7:26
24 [s]Pr 1:8–9; 8:32
25 [t]Pr 5:7–8
27 [u]Jdg 16:19; Pr 2:18; Rev 22:15

Ch. 8

1 [a]Job 28:12
3 [b]Pr 7:6–13
4 [c]Isa 42:2
5 [d]Pr 1:22; [e]Pr 1:4
7 [f]Jn 8:14
10 [g]Job 28:17; Ps 19:10
11 [h]ver 19; Job 28:17–19; [i]Pr 3:13–15

21With persuasive words she led him
astray;
she seduced him with her smooth
talk.[o]
22All at once he followed her
like an ox going to the slaughter,
like a deer[b] stepping into a noose[c][p]
23 till an arrow pierces[q] his liver,
like a bird darting into a snare,
little knowing it will cost him his
life.[r]

24Now then, my sons, listen[s] to me;
pay attention to what I say.
25Do not let your heart turn to her ways
or stray into her paths.[t]
26Many are the victims she has brought
down;
her slain are a mighty throng.
27Her house is a highway to the grave,[d]
leading down to the chambers of
death.[u]

Wisdom's Call

8 Does not wisdom call out?[a]
Does not understanding raise her
voice?
2On the heights along the way,
where the paths meet, she takes her
stand;
3beside the gates leading into the city,
at the entrances, she cries aloud:[b]
4"To you, O men, I call out;[c]
I raise my voice to all mankind.
5You who are simple,[d] gain prudence;[e]
you who are foolish, gain
understanding.
6Listen, for I have worthy things to say;
I open my lips to speak what is
right.
7My mouth speaks what is true,[f]
for my lips detest wickedness.
8All the words of my mouth are just;
none of them is crooked or
perverse.
9To the discerning all of them are right;
they are faultless to those who have
knowledge.
10Choose my instruction instead of
silver,
knowledge rather than choice gold,[g]
11for wisdom is more precious[h] than
rubies,
and nothing you desire can compare
with her.[i]

12"I, wisdom, dwell together with
prudence;

[a]14 Traditionally *peace offerings*
[b]22 Syriac (see also Septuagint); Hebrew *fool*
[c]22 The meaning of the Hebrew for this line is uncertain. [d]27 Hebrew *Sheol*

I possess knowledge and
discretion.[j]
13To fear the LORD[k] is to hate evil;[l]
I hate[m] pride and arrogance,
evil behaviour and perverse speech.
14Counsel and sound judgment are
mine;
I have understanding and power.[n]
15By me kings reign
and rulers[o] make laws that are just;
16by me princes govern,[p]
and all nobles who rule on earth.[a]
17I love those who love me,[q]
and those who seek me find me.[r]
18With me are riches and honour,[s]
enduring wealth and prosperity.[t]
19My fruit is better than fine gold;[u]
what I yield surpasses choice silver.[v]
20I walk in the way of righteousness,[w]
along the paths of justice,
21bestowing wealth on those who
love me
and making their treasuries full.[x]

22"The LORD brought me forth[b] as the
first of his works,[c]
before his deeds of old;
23I was appointed[d] from eternity,
from the beginning, before the
world began.
24When there were no oceans, I was
given birth,
when there were no springs
abounding with water;[y]
25before the mountains were settled in
place,[z]
before the hills, I was given birth,[a]
26before he made the earth or its fields
or any of the dust of the world.[b]
27I was there when he set the heavens in
place,[c]
when he marked out the horizon[d]
on the face of the deep,
28when he established the clouds above[e]
and fixed securely the fountains of
the deep,[f]
29when he gave the sea its boundary[g]
so that the waters would not
overstep his command,[h]
and when he marked out the
foundations of the earth.[i]
30 Then I was the craftsman at his
side.[j]
I was filled with delight day after day,
rejoicing always in his presence,
31rejoicing in his whole world
and delighting in mankind.[k]

32"Now then, my sons, listen[l] to me;
blessed are[m] those who keep my
ways.[n]
33Listen to my instruction and be wise;
do not ignore it.
34Blessed is the man who listens[o] to me,
watching daily at my doors,
waiting at my doorway.
35For whoever finds me[p] finds life[q]
and receives favour from the LORD.[r]
36But whoever fails to find me harms
himself;[s]
all who hate me love death."[t]

Invitations of Wisdom and of Folly

9 Wisdom has built[a] her house;
she has hewn out its seven pillars.
2She has prepared her meat and mixed
her wine;[b]
she has also set her table.[c]
3She has sent out her maids, and she
calls[d]
from the highest point of the city.[e]
4"Let all who are simple[f] come in
here!"
she says to those who lack
judgment.[g]
5"Come,[h] eat my food
and drink the wine I have mixed.[i]
6Leave your simple ways and you will
live;[j]
walk in the way of understanding.[k]

7"Whoever corrects a mocker invites
insult;
whoever rebukes a wicked man
incurs abuse.[l]
8Do not rebuke a mocker[m] or he will
hate you;
rebuke a wise man and he will love
you.[n]
9Instruct a wise man and he will be
wiser still;
teach a righteous man and he will
add to his learning.[o]

10"The fear of the LORD[p] is the beginning
of wisdom,
and knowledge of the Holy One[q] is
understanding.[r]
11For through me your days will be
many,
and years will be added to your life.[s]
12If you are wise, your wisdom will
reward you;
if you are a mocker, you alone will
suffer."

13The woman Folly is loud;[t]
she is undisciplined and without
knowledge.[u]

12 [j]Pr 1:4
13 [k]**Ge 22:12;** [l]**Ex 20:20; Job 28:28;** [m]Jer 44:4
14 [n]**Job 9:4;** Pr 21:22; Ecc 7:19
15 [o]**Ps 2:10**
16 [p]**2Ch 1:10;** Pr 29:4
17 [q]**1Sa 2:30;** Jn 14:21–24; [r]**1Ch 16:11; Pr 1:28;** 3:13–18; Mt 7:7–11
18 [s]**1Ki 3:13;** [t]**Dt 8:18**
19 [u]**Job 28:17–19;** [v]**Pr 3:13–14**
20 [w]**Ps 5:8**
21 [x]Pr 15:6; 24:4
24 [y]**Ge 7:11**
25 [z]**Job 38:6;** [a]**Job 15:7**
26 [b]**Ps 90:2**
27 [c]**Job 26:7;** [d]**Job 22:14**
28 [e]**Job 36:29;** [f]**Ge 1:7; Job 9:8; 26:10**
29 [g]**Ge 1:9; Ps 16:6;** [h]**Job 38:8;** [i]**1Sa 2:8; Job 38:5**
30 [j]Pr 3:19–20; Rev 3:14
31 [k]**Job 28:25–27;** 38:4–38; Ps 104:1–30; Pr 30:4; Jn 1:1–4; Col 1:15–20
32 [l]**Pr 7:24;** [m]Lk 11:28; [n]**2Sa 22:22; Ps 18:21**
34 [o]1Ki 10:8
35 [p]Pr 3:13–18; [q]Pr 9:6; Jn 5:39–40; [r]**Job 33:26**
36 [s]Pr 15:32; Isa 3:9; Jer 40:2; [t]**Job 28:22**

Ch. 9

1 [a]Eph 2:20–22; 1Pe 2:5
2 [b]Isa 25:6; 62:8; [c]Lk 14:16–23
3 [d]**Pr 1:20;** 8:1–3; [e]ver 14
4 [f]**Pr 1:22;** [g]ver 16; **Pr 6:32**
5 [h]Jn 7:37–38; [i]**Ps 42:2;** 63:1; 143:6; Isa 44:3; 55:1
6 [j]**Pr 8:35;** [k]**Pr 3:1–2**
7 [l]Pr 23:9; Mt 7:6
8 [m]Pr 15:12; [n]Ps 141:5
9 [o]Pr 1:5,7; 12:15; 13:10; 14:6; 15:31; 19:25
10 [p]**Pr 1:7;** [q]Ps 22:3; Pr 30:3; [r]**Dt 4:6**
11 [s]**Ge 15:15; Dt 11:21; Pr 3:1–2;** 10:27
13 [t]Pr 7:11; [u]**Pr 5:6**

[a]16 Many Hebrew manuscripts and Septuagint; most Hebrew manuscripts *all righteous rulers*
[b]22 Or *The LORD possessed me*
[c]22 Or *way;* or *dominion*
[d]23 Or *fashioned*

14She sits at the door of her house,
on a seat at the highest point of the city,[v]
15calling out[w] to those who pass by,
who go straight on their way.
16"Let all who are simple come in here!"
she says to those who lack judgment.[x]
17"Stolen water is sweet;
food eaten in secret is delicious![y]"
18But little do they know that the dead are there,
that her guests are in the depths of the grave.[a][z]

Proverbs of Solomon

10

The proverbs[a] of Solomon:[b]

A wise son brings joy to his father,[c]
but a foolish son grief to his mother.

2Ill-gotten treasures are of no value,[d]
but righteousness delivers from death.[e]

3The LORD does not let the righteous go hungry[f]
but he thwarts the craving of the wicked.[g]

4Lazy hands make a man poor,[h]
but diligent hands bring wealth.[i]

5He who gathers crops in summer is a wise son,
but he who sleeps during harvest is a disgraceful son.[j]

6Blessings crown the head of the righteous,
but violence overwhelms the mouth of the wicked.[a][k]

7The memory of the righteous[l] will be a blessing,
but the name of the wicked[m] will rot.[n]

8The wise in heart accept commands,
but a chattering fool comes to ruin.[o]

9The man of integrity[p] walks securely,[q]
but he who takes crooked paths will be found out.[r]

10He who winks maliciously[s] causes grief,
and a chattering fool comes to ruin.

11The mouth of the righteous is a fountain of life,[t]
but violence overwhelms the mouth of the wicked.[u]

12Hatred stirs up dissension,
but love covers over all wrongs.[v]

13Wisdom is found on the lips of the discerning,[w]
but a rod is for the back of him who lacks judgment.[x]

14Wise men store up knowledge,[y]
but the mouth of a fool invites ruin.[z]

15The wealth of the rich is their fortified city,[a]
but poverty is the ruin of the poor.[b]

16The wages of the righteous bring them life,[c]
but the income of the wicked brings them punishment.[d]

17He who heeds discipline shows the way to life,[e]
but whoever ignores correction leads others astray.

18He who conceals his hatred has lying lips,[f]
and whoever spreads slander is a fool.

19When words are many, sin is not absent,
but he who holds his tongue is wise.[g]

20The tongue of the righteous is choice silver,
but the heart of the wicked is of little value.

21The lips of the righteous nourish many,
but fools die for lack of judgment.[h]

22The blessing of the LORD[i] brings wealth,[j]
and he adds no trouble to it.[k]

23A fool finds pleasure in evil conduct,[l]
but a man of understanding delights in wisdom.

24What the wicked dreads[m] will overtake him;[n]
what the righteous desire will be granted.[o]

25When the storm has swept by, the wicked are gone,

14 [v]ver 3; Eze 16:25
15 [w]**Pr 1:20**
16 [x]**Pr 1:22**
17 [y]Pr 20:17
18 [z]**Pr 2:18;** 7:26–27

Ch. 10

1 [a]**1Ki 4:32;** [b]**Pr 1:1;** [c]Pr 15:20; 17:21; 19:13; 23:22–25; 27:11; 29:3
2 [d]Pr 13:11; 21:6; [e]ver 16; Pr 11:4,19; 12:28
3 [f]Mt 6:25–34; [g]Pr 13:25
4 [h]Pr 6:6–8; 19:15; 24:30–34; [i]Pr 12:24; 21:5
5 [j]Pr 24:30–34
6 [k]ver 8,11,14; Pr 12:13; 13:3; Ecc 10:12
7 [l]**Ps 112:6;** [m]**Job 18:17; Ps 109:13;** [n]**Job 18:17;** Ps 9:6
8 [o]ver 14; **Job 33:33;** Mt 7:24–27
9 [p]**Ps 25:21;** [q]**Ps 37:24;** [r]Pr 28:18
10 [s]**Ps 35:19**
11 [t]ver 27; **Pr 3:18; 4:23;** 11:30; 13:12, 14,19; 14:27; 15:4; 16:22; [u]**ver 6**
12 [v]Pr 17:9; 1Co 13:4–7; 1Pe 4:8
13 [w]ver 31; **Ps 37:30;** Pr 15:7; [x]Dt 25:2; Pr 14:3; 26:3
14 [y]Pr 11:13; 12:23; [z]**ver 6; Ps 59:12; Pr 14:3;** 18:6–7; **Mt 12:37**
15 [a]Pr 18:11; [b]Pr 19:7
16 [c]**Dt 30:15;** [d]Pr 11:18–19; 15:6; **Ro 6:23**
17 [e]Pr 6:23; 15:5
18 [f]**Ps 31:18**
19 [g]**Job 1:22; 6:24;** Pr 17:28; **20:25;** 21:23; Jas 1:19; 3:2–12
21 [h]Pr 5:22–23; Isa 5:13; Jer 5:4; Hos 4:1, 6,14
22 [i]**Ps 128:2;** [j]**Ge 13:2; 49:25; Dt 8:18;** [k]**2Ch 25:9**
23 [l]**Pr 2:14**
24 [m]Isa 65:7; 66:4; [n]**Ge 42:36;** [o]**Ps 37:4;** 145:17–19; Eze 11:8

[a]*18* Hebrew *Sheol*
[a]*6* Or *but the mouth of the wicked conceals violence;* also in verse 11

but the righteous stand firm[p] for
ever.[q]

26As vinegar to the teeth and smoke[r] to
the eyes,
so is a sluggard to those who send
him.[s]

27The fear of the LORD adds length to
life,[t]
but the years of the wicked are cut
short.[u]

28The prospect of the righteous is joy,
but the hopes of the wicked come to
nothing.[v]

29The way of the LORD is a refuge for the
righteous,
but it is the ruin of those who do
evil.[w]

30The righteous will never be uprooted,
but the wicked will not remain in the
land.[x]

31The mouth of the righteous brings
forth wisdom,[y]
but a perverse tongue[z] will be cut
out.

32The lips of the righteous know what is
fitting,[a]
but the mouth of the wicked only
what is perverse.[b]

11

1The LORD abhors dishonest
scales,[a]
but accurate weights are his
delight.[b]

2When pride comes, then comes
disgrace,[c]
but with humility comes wisdom.[d]

3The integrity of the upright guides
them,
but the unfaithful are destroyed by
their duplicity.[e]

4Wealth[f] is worthless in the day of
wrath,[g]
but righteousness delivers from
death.[h]

5The righteousness of the blameless
makes a straight way[i] for them,
but the wicked are brought down by
their own wickedness.[j]

6The righteousness of the upright
delivers them,
but the unfaithful are trapped by
evil desires.[k]

25 [p]**Ps 20:8**; [q]Pr 12:3,7; Mt 7:24–27
26 [r]Isa 65:5; [s]Pr 13:17; 25:13; 26:6
27 [t]**ver 11**; Dt 11:9; Pr 9:10–11; 19:23; 22:4; [u]**Job 15:32**
28 [v]Est 7:10; **Job 8:13**; Ps 112:10; Pr 11:7
29 [w]Pr 21:15; Hos 14:9
30 [x]Ps 37:9, 28–29; **Pr 2:20–22**
31 [y]**ver 13**; **Pr 15:2**; 31:26; [z]**Ps 52:4**
32 [a]Ecc 10:12; [b]Ps 59:7

Ch. 11

1 [a]**Lev 19:36**; Dt 25:13–16; **Job 6:2**; Pr 20:10,23; [b]Pr 16:11; Eze 45:10
2 [c]Pr 16:18; [d]Pr 18:12; 29:23
3 [e]ver 5; Pr 13:6
4 [f]Eze 27:27; [g]**Job 20:20**; **Eze 7:19**; [h]**Pr 10:2**
5 [i]1Ki 8:36; [j]ver 3; Pr 5:21–23; 13:6; 21:7
6 [k]**Est 7:9**
7 [l]**Job 8:13**; [m]**Pr 10:28**
8 [n]Pr 21:18
9 [o]Pr 12:6; Jer 45:5
10 [p]**2Ki 11:20**; [q]**Est 8:17**
11 [r]Pr 14:34; [s]Pr 29:8
12 [t]Pr 14:21; [u]**Job 6:24**
13 [v]Pr 20:19; [w]**Pr 10:14**
14 [x]Pr 20:18; [y]**2Sa 15:34**; Pr 15:22; 24:6
15 [z]**Pr 6:1**; [a]Pr 17:18; 22:26–27
16 [b]Pr 31:31
18 [c]**Ex 1:20**; **Job 4:8**; Hos 10:12–13
19 [d]**Dt 30:15**; **Pr 10:2**; [e]1Sa 2:6; Ps 89:48; Pr 1:18–19; Ecc 7:2; Jer 43:11
20 [f]Pr 3:32; [g]**Nu 14:8**; [h]**1Ch 29:17**; **Ps 15:2**; 101:1–4; **119:1**; Pr 12:2,22; 15:9

7When a wicked man dies, his hope
perishes;[l]
all he expected from his power
comes to nothing.[m]

8The righteous man is rescued from
trouble,
and it comes on the wicked
instead.[n]

9With his mouth the godless destroys
his neighbour,
but through knowledge the
righteous escape.[o]

10When the righteous prosper, the city
rejoices;[p]
when the wicked perish, there are
shouts of joy.[q]

11Through the blessing of the upright a
city is exalted,[r]
but by the mouth of the wicked it is
destroyed.[s]

12A man who lacks judgment derides
his neighbour,[t]
but a man of understanding holds
his tongue.[u]

13A gossip betrays a confidence,[v]
but a trustworthy man keeps a
secret.[w]

14For lack of guidance a nation falls,[x]
but many advisers make victory
sure.[y]

15He who puts up security[z] for another
will surely suffer,
but whoever refuses to strike hands
in pledge is safe.[a]

16A kind-hearted woman gains respect,[b]
but ruthless men gain only wealth.

17A kind man benefits himself,
but a cruel man brings trouble on
himself.

18The wicked man earns deceptive
wages,
but he who sows righteousness
reaps a sure reward.[c]

19The truly righteous man attains life,[d]
but he who pursues evil goes to his
death.[e]

20The LORD detests men of perverse
heart[f]
but he delights[g] in those whose
ways are blameless.[h]

21Be sure of this: The wicked will not go
unpunished,
but those who are righteous will go
free.[i]

22Like a gold ring in a pig's snout
is a beautiful woman who shows no
discretion.

23The desire of the righteous ends only
in good,
but the hope of the wicked only in
wrath.

24One man gives freely, yet gains even
more;
another withholds unduly, but
comes to poverty.

25A generous[j] man will prosper;
he who refreshes others will himself
be refreshed.[k]

26People curse the man who hoards
grain,
but blessing crowns him who is
willing to sell.

27He who seeks good finds goodwill,
but evil comes to him who searches
for it.[l]

28Whoever trusts in his riches will fall,[m]
but the righteous will thrive like a
green leaf.[n]

29He who brings trouble on his family
will inherit only wind,
and the fool will be servant to the
wise.[o]

30The fruit of the righteous is a tree of
life,[p]
and he who wins souls is wise.

31If the righteous receive their due[q] on
earth,
how much more the ungodly and
the sinner!

12

Whoever loves discipline loves
knowledge,
but he who hates correction is
stupid.[a]

2A good man obtains favour from the
LORD,[b]
but the LORD condemns a crafty
man.[c]

3A man cannot be established through
wickedness,
but the righteous cannot be
uprooted.[d]

4A wife of noble character[e] is her
husband's crown,
but a disgraceful wife is like decay in
his bones.[f]

5The plans of the righteous are just,
but the advice of the wicked is
deceitful.

6The words of the wicked lie in wait for
blood,
but the speech of the upright
rescues them.[g]

7Wicked men are overthrown and are
no more,[h]
but the house of the righteous
stands firm.[i]

8A man is praised according to his
wisdom,
but men with warped[j] minds are
despised.

9Better to be a nobody and yet have a
servant
than pretend to be somebody and
have no food.

10A righteous man cares for the needs of
his animal,[k]
but the kindest acts of the wicked
are cruel.

11He who works his land will have
abundant food,
but he who chases fantasies lacks
judgment.[l]

12The wicked desire the plunder of evil
men,
but the root of the righteous
flourishes.

13An evil man is trapped by his sinful
talk,[m]
but a righteous man escapes
trouble.[n]

14From the fruit of his lips a man is filled
with good things[o]
as surely as the work of his hands
rewards him.[p]

15The way of a fool seems right to him,[q]
but a wise man listens to advice.[r]

16A fool[s] shows his annoyance at once,[t]
but a prudent man overlooks an
insult.[u]

17A truthful witness gives honest
testimony,
but a false witness tells lies.[v]

---

21 [i]Pr 16:5
25 [j]1Ch 29:17; Isa 32:8; [k]Pr 22:9; 2Co 9:6–9
27 [l]Ps 7:15–16
28 [m]Job 31:24–28; **Ps 49:6;** 52:7; 62:10; Jer 9:23; 48:7; [n]Ps 52:8; 92:12–14
29 [o]Pr 14:19
30 [p]**Ge 2:9; Pr 10:11**
31 [q]Jer 25:29; 49:12; 1Pe 4:18

Ch. 12

1 [a]Pr 5:11–14; **9:7–9**; 13:1,18; 15:5,10,12,32
2 [b]**Job 33:26**; Ps 84:11; [c]2Sa 15:3; **Pr 11:20**
3 [d]**Pr 10:25**
4 [e]**Ru 3:11**; Pr 31:10–11; [f]Pr 18:22
6 [g]**Pr 11:9**; 14:3
7 [h]**Ps 37:36**; [i]**Pr 10:25**; 14:11; 15:25
8 [j]Isa 19:14; 29:24
10 [k]**Nu 22:29**
11 [l]Pr 28:19
13 [m]**Ps 59:12; Pr 10:6**; 18:7; [n]Pr 21:23
14 [o]Pr 13:2; 15:23; 18:20; [p]Pr 14:14
15 [q]Pr 14:12; 16:2,25; [r]**Pr 9:7–9**; 19:20
16 [s]**1Sa 25:25**; [t]**Job 5:2**; [u]Pr 29:11
17 [v]**Ps 12:2**; Pr 14:5,25

[18]Reckless words pierce like a sword,[w]
but the tongue of the wise brings
healing.[x]

[19]Truthful lips endure for ever,
but a lying tongue lasts only a
moment.

[20]There is deceit in the hearts of those
who plot evil,
but joy for those who promote
peace.[y]

[21]No harm befalls the righteous,[z]
but the wicked have their fill of
trouble.

[22]The LORD detests lying lips,[a]
but he delights[b] in men who are
truthful.[c]

[23]A prudent man keeps his knowledge
to himself,[d]
but the heart of fools blurts out
folly.[e]

[24]Diligent hands will rule,
but laziness ends in slave labour.[f]

[25]An anxious heart weighs a man
down,[g]
but a kind word cheers him up.

[26]A righteous man is cautious in
friendship,[a]
but the way of the wicked leads
them astray.[h]

[27]The lazy man does not roast[b] his
game,
but the diligent man prizes his
possessions.

[28]In the way of righteousness there is
life;[i]
along that path is immortality.

13 A wise son heeds his father's
instruction,
but a mocker does not listen to
rebuke.[a]

[2]From the fruit of his lips a man enjoys
good things,[b]
but the unfaithful have a craving for
violence.

[3]He who guards his lips[c] guards his
life,[d]
but he who speaks rashly will come
to ruin.[e]

[4]The sluggard craves and gets
nothing,[f]
but the desires of the diligent are
fully satisfied.

[5]The righteous hate what is false,[g]
but the wicked bring shame and
disgrace.

[6]Righteousness guards the man of
integrity,
but wickedness overthrows the
sinner.[h]

[7]One man pretends to be rich, yet has
nothing;[i]
another pretends to be poor, yet has
great wealth.[j]

[8]A man's riches may ransom his life,
but a poor man hears no threat.[k]

[9]The light of the righteous shines
brightly,
but the lamp of the wicked is
snuffed out.[l]

[10]Pride only breeds quarrels,
but wisdom is found in those who
take advice.[m]

[11]Dishonest money dwindles away,[n]
but he who gathers money little by
little makes it grow.

[12]Hope deferred makes the heart sick,
but a longing fulfilled is a tree of
life.[o]

[13]He who scorns instruction will pay
for it,[p]
but he who respects[q] a command is
rewarded.[r]

[14]The teaching of the wise is a fountain
of life,[s]
turning a man from the snares of
death.[t]

[15]Good understanding wins favour,
but the way of the unfaithful is
hard.[a]

[16]Every prudent man acts out of
knowledge,
but a fool exposes[u] his folly.[v]

[17]A wicked messenger falls into
trouble,[w]
but a trustworthy envoy brings
healing.[x]

18 [w]Ps 55:21; Pr 25:18; [x]Pr 15:4
20 [y]Ro 14:19
21 [z]Job 4:7
22 [a]1Ki 13:18; Pr 6:17; [b]Ps 18:19; [c]Pr 11:20
23 [d]Pr 10:14; [e]Ps 38:5; 59:7; Pr 18:2
24 [f]Pr 10:4
25 [g]Pr 15:13
26 [h]Ps 95:10
28 [i]Dt 30:15; Pr 10:2

Ch. 13

1 [a]Pr 12:1; 15:5
2 [b]Pr 12:14
3 [c]Ps 12:2; 34:13; [d]Pr 10:6; 21:23; [e]Job 1:22; Pr 18:7,20–21
4 [f]Pr 21:25–26
5 [g]Ps 119:128
6 [h]Pr 11:3,5; Jer 44:5
7 [i]Rev 3:17; [j]2Co 6:10
8 [k]Pr 15:16
9 [l]Job 18:5; Pr 4:18–19
10 [m]Jdg 19:30; Pr 9:9
11 [n]Pr 10:2
12 [o]Pr 10:11
13 [p]Nu 15:31; [q]Ex 9:20; [r]Pr 16:20
14 [s]Pr 10:11; [t]Pr 14:27
16 [u]Ecc 10:3; [v]Est 5:11; Ps 38:5
17 [w]Pr 10:26; [x]Pr 25:13

[a]26 Or *man is a guide to his neighbour*
[b]27 The meaning of the Hebrew for this word is uncertain. [a]15 Or *unfaithful does not endure*

18He who ignores discipline comes to
poverty and shame,[y]
but whoever heeds correction is
honoured.[z]

19A longing fulfilled is sweet to the
soul,[a]
but fools detest turning from evil.

20He who walks with the wise grows
wise,
but a companion of fools suffers
harm.[b]

21Misfortune pursues the sinner,[c]
but prosperity[d] is the reward of the
righteous.[e]

22A good man leaves an inheritance for
his children's children,
but a sinner's wealth is stored up for
the righteous.[f]

23A poor man's field may produce
abundant food,
but injustice sweeps it away.

24He who spares the rod[g] hates his son,
but he who loves him is careful to
discipline[h] him.[i]

25The righteous eat to their hearts'
content,
but the stomach of the wicked goes
hungry.[j]

14

The wise woman builds her
house,[a]
but with her own hands the foolish
one tears hers down.

2He whose walk is upright fears the
LORD,
but he whose ways are devious
despises him.

3A fool's talk brings a rod to his back,[b]
but the lips of the wise protect
them.[c]

4Where there are no oxen, the manger
is empty,
but from the strength of an ox[d]
comes an abundant harvest.

5A truthful witness does not deceive,
but a false witness pours out lies.[e]

6The mocker seeks wisdom and finds
none,
but knowledge comes easily to the
discerning.[f]

7Stay away from a foolish man,
for you will not find knowledge on
his lips.

8The wisdom of the prudent is to give
thought to their ways,[g]
but the folly of fools is deception.[h]

9Fools mock at making amends for sin,
but goodwill is found among the
upright.

10Each heart knows its own bitterness,
and no-one else can share its joy.

11The house of the wicked will be
destroyed,[i]
but the tent of the upright will
flourish.[j]

12There is a way that seems right to a
man,[k]
but in the end it leads to death.[l]

13Even in laughter[m] the heart may ache,
and joy may end in grief.

14The faithless will be fully repaid for
their ways,[n]
and the good man rewarded for
his.[o]

15A simple man believes anything,
but a prudent man gives thought to
his steps.[p]

16A wise man fears the LORD and shuns
evil,[q]
but a fool[r] is hotheaded and
reckless.

17A quick-tempered[s] man does foolish
things,[t]
and a crafty man is hated.[u]

18The simple inherit folly,
but the prudent are crowned with
knowledge.

19Evil men will bow down in the
presence of the good,
and the wicked at the gates of the
righteous.[v]

20The poor are shunned even by their
neighbours,
but the rich have many friends.[w]

21He who despises his neighbour sins,[x]
but blessed is he who is kind to the
needy.[y]

18 [y]**Pr 1:7; 12:1;** [z]Ps 141:5; Pr 25:12; Ecc 7:5
19 [a]**Pr 10:11**
20 [b]2Ch 10:8
21 [c]2Sa 3:39; Jer 40:3; 50:7; Eze 14:13; 18:4; [d]Ps 25:13; [e]Ps 32:10
22 [f]**Est 8:2; Job 27:17**; Ecc 2:26
24 [g]**2Sa 7:14**; [h]**Pr 3:12**; [i]Pr 19:18; 22:15; 23:13–14; 29:15,17; Eph 6:4; Heb 12:7
25 [j]Pr 10:3

Ch. 14

1 [a]**Ru 3:11;** Pr 24:3
3 [b]**Pr 10:14**; Ecc 10:12; [c]**Pr 10:13; 12:6**
4 [d]Ps 144:14
5 [e]**Ps 12:2; Pr 12:17**
6 [f]**Pr 9:9**
8 [g]ver 15; Pr 15:28; 21:29; [h]ver 24
11 [i]**Job 8:22**; Pr 21:12; [j]**Ps 72:7; Pr 3:33; 12:7**
12 [k]**Pr 12:15;** [l]Pr 16:25
13 [m]Ecc 2:2; 7:3,6
14 [n]**Pr 1:31;** [o]**2Ch 15:7;** Pr 12:14
15 [p]**ver 8**
16 [q]**Ex 20:20;** Pr 22:3; [r]**1Sa 25:25**
17 [s]**2Ki 5:12;** [t]ver 29; Pr 15:18; 16:28; 26:21; 28:25; 29:22; [u]**Est 5:9**
19 [v]Pr 11:29
20 [w]Pr 19:4,7
21 [x]Pr 11:12; [y]Pr 19:17

[22]Do not those who plot evil go astray?[z]
But those who plan what is good
find[a] love and faithfulness.

[23]All hard work brings a profit,
but mere talk leads only to poverty.

[24]The wealth of the wise is their crown,
but the folly of fools yields folly.[a]

[25]A truthful witness saves lives,
but a false witness is deceitful.[b]

[26]He who fears the LORD has a secure
fortress,[c]
and for his children it will be a
refuge.[d]

[27]The fear of the LORD is a fountain of
life,[e]
turning a man from the snares of
death.[f]

[28]A large population is a king's glory,
but without subjects a prince is
ruined.[g]

[29]A patient man has great
understanding,[h]
but a quick-tempered man displays
folly.[i]

[30]A heart at peace gives life to the body,
but envy rots the bones.[j]

[31]He who oppresses the poor shows
contempt for their Maker,[k]
but whoever is kind to the needy
honours God.[l]

[32]When calamity comes, the wicked are
brought down,[m]
but even in death the righteous have
a refuge.[n]

[33]Wisdom reposes in the heart of the
discerning[o]
and even among fools she lets
herself be known.[b]

[34]Righteousness exalts a nation,[p]
but sin is a disgrace to any people.

[35]A king delights in a wise servant,
but a shameful servant incurs his
wrath.[q]

15

A gentle answer[a] turns away
wrath,[b]
but a harsh word stirs up anger.

[2]The tongue of the wise commends
knowledge,[c]
but the mouth of the fool gushes
folly.[d]

[3]The eyes[e] of the LORD are everywhere,[f]
keeping watch on the wicked and
the good.[g]

[4]The tongue[h] that brings healing is a
tree of life,[i]
but a deceitful tongue crushes the
spirit.[j]

[5]A fool spurns his father's discipline,
but whoever heeds correction
shows prudence.[k]

[6]The house of the righteous contains
great treasure,[l]
but the income of the wicked brings
them trouble.[m]

[7]The lips of the wise spread
knowledge;[n]
not so the hearts of fools.

[8]The LORD detests the sacrifice[o] of the
wicked,[p]
but the prayer of the upright pleases
him.[q]

[9]The LORD detests the way of the
wicked[r]
but he loves those who pursue
righteousness.[s]

[10]Stern discipline awaits him who leaves
the path;
he who hates correction will die.[t]

[11]Death and Destruction[a] lie open
before the LORD[u]—
how much more the hearts of men![v]

[12]A mocker resents correction;[w]
he will not consult the wise.

[13]A happy heart makes the face
cheerful,[x]
but heartache crushes the spirit.[y]

[14]The discerning heart seeks
knowledge,[z]
but the mouth of a fool feeds on
folly.

[15]All the days of the oppressed are
wretched,
but the cheerful heart has a
continual feast.[a]

22 [z]Pr 4:16–17
24 [a]ver 8
25 [b]**Pr 12:17**
26 [c]Pr 18:10; [d]Ps 9:9
27 [e]**Pr 10:11**; [f]Ps 18:5; Pr 13:14
28 [g]**2Sa 19:7**
29 [h]**2Ki 5:12**; Pr 17:27; [i]**ver 17**; Ecc 7:8–9
30 [j]Pr 17:22
31 [k]Pr 17:5; [l]**Dt 24:14; Job 20:19; Mt 10:42**
32 [m]**Ps 34:21; Pr 6:15**; [n]**Job 13:15**
33 [o]Pr 2:6–10
34 [p]Pr 11:11
35 [q]**Est 8:2**; Mt 24:45–51; 25:14–30

Ch. 15

1 [a]1Ki 12:7; 2Ch 10:7; [b]Pr 25:15
2 [c]ver 7; **Pr 10:31**; [d]**Ps 59:7**; Ecc 10:12
3 [e]**2Ch 16:9**; [f]**Job 10:4; 31:4; Heb 4:13**; [g]**Job 34:21**; Pr 5:21; Jer 16:17
4 [h]**Ps 5:9**; [i]**Pr 10:11**; [j]Pr 12:18
5 [k]**Pr 10:17; 12:1; 13:1**
6 [l]**Pr 8:21**; [m]**Pr 10:16**
7 [n]**ver 2; Pr 10:13**
8 [o]**Ps 51:17; Isa 1:13**; [p]**Pr 6:16; 21:27**; [q]ver 29; Job 35:13; Pr 28:9; **Jn 9:31**
9 [r]**Pr 6:16**; [s]**Dt 7:13; Pr 11:20**
10 [t]**Pr 1:31–32; 12:1**
11 [u]**Job 26:6**; [v]**1Sa 2:3; 2Ch 6:30; Ps 44:21; Rev 2:23**
12 [w]**Pr 9:8; 12:1**
13 [x]ver 15; [y]Pr 12:25; 17:22; 18:14
14 [z]Pr 18:15
15 [a]ver 13

[a]22 Or *show*
[b]33 Hebrew; Septuagint and Syriac / *but in the heart of fools she is not known*
[a]11 Hebrew *Sheol and Abaddon*

16Better a little with the fear of the LORD
than great wealth with turmoil.[b]

17Better a meal of vegetables where
there is love
than a fattened calf with hatred.[c]

18A hot-tempered man stirs up
dissension,[d]
but a patient man calms a quarrel.[e]

19The way of the sluggard is blocked
with thorns,[f]
but the path of the upright is a
highway.

20A wise son brings joy to his father,[g]
but a foolish man despises his
mother.

21Folly delights a man who lacks
judgment,[h]
but a man of understanding keeps a
straight course.

22Plans fail for lack of counsel,[i]
but with many advisers[j] they
succeed.[k]

23A man finds joy in giving an apt
reply[l]—
and how good is a timely word![m]

24The path of life leads upward for the
wise
to keep him from going down to the
grave.[b]

25The LORD tears down the proud man's
house[n]
but he keeps the widow's
boundaries intact.[o]

26The LORD detests the thoughts[p] of the
wicked,[q]
but those of the pure[r] are pleasing to
him.

27A greedy man brings trouble to his
family,
but he who hates bribes will live.[s]

28The heart of the righteous weighs its
answers,[t]
but the mouth of the wicked gushes
evil.[u]

29The LORD is far from the wicked
but he hears the prayer of the
righteous.[v]

30A cheerful look brings joy to the heart,
and good news gives health to the
bones.[w]

31He who listens to a life-giving rebuke
will be at home among the wise.[x]

32He who ignores discipline despises
himself,[y]
but whoever heeds correction gains
understanding.[z]

33The fear of the LORD[a] teaches a man
wisdom,[c]
and humility comes before honour.[b]

16

1To man belong the plans of the
heart,
but from the LORD comes the reply
of the tongue.[a]

2All a man's ways seem innocent to
him,[b]
but motives are weighed[c] by the
LORD.[d]

3Commit to the LORD whatever you do,
and your plans will succeed.[e]

4The LORD works out everything for his
own ends[f]—
even the wicked for a day of
disaster.[g]

5The LORD detests all the proud of
heart.[h]
Be sure of this: They will not go
unpunished.[i]

6Through love and faithfulness sin is
atoned for;
through the fear of the LORD[j] a man
avoids evil.[k]

7When a man's ways are pleasing to the
LORD,
he makes even his enemies live at
peace[l] with him.[m]

8Better a little with righteousness
than much gain[n] with injustice.[o]

9In his heart a man plans his course,
but the LORD determines his steps.[p]

10The lips of a king speak as an oracle,
and his mouth should not betray
justice.[q]

11Honest scales and balances are from
the LORD;
all the weights in the bag are of his
making.[r]

16 [b]ver 17; Ps 37:16–17; Pr 13:8; 16:8; 17:1
17 [c]ver 16; Pr 17:1; Ecc 4:6
18 [d]Pr 6:16–19; 14:17; [e]Ge 13:8
19 [f]Pr 22:5
20 [g]Pr 10:1
21 [h]Pr 2:14
22 [i]Ps 16:7; [j]1Ki 1:12; Pr 24:6; [k]Pr 11:14
23 [l]Pr 12:14; [m]Pr 25:11
25 [n]Pr 12:7; [o]Dt 19:14; Pr 23:10–11
26 [p]Ps 94:11; [q]Pr 6:16; [r]Ps 18:26
27 [s]Ex 23:8; Ps 15:5; Isa 1:23; 33:15
28 [t]Pr 14:8; [u]Ps 59:7
29 [v]ver 8; Job 15:31; Ps 145:18–19; Isa 59:2; Jn 9:31
30 [w]Pr 25:25
31 [x]Pr 9:7–9; 12:1
32 [y]Pr 1:7; 12:1; [z]Pr 9:7–9; 12:1; Ecc 7:5
33 [a]Pr 1:7; [b]Pr 16:18; 18:12; 22:4; 29:23; Isa 66:2

Ch. 16

1 [a]ver 9; Pr 19:21
2 [b]Pr 12:15; 30:12; [c]1Sa 2:3; [d]2Ch 6:30; Pr 20:27; 21:2; Lk 16:15
3 [e]2Ch 20:20; Ps 20:4; 37:5–6; Pr 3:5–6
4 [f]Ex 9:16; [g]2Ch 34:24; Ps 18:18; Ro 9:22
5 [h]Ps 40:4; Pr 6:16; [i]Pr 11:20–21
6 [j]Ge 20:11; Ex 1:17; [k]Ex 20:20
7 [l]Ge 39:21; [m]Ps 105:15; Jer 39:12; 40:1; 42:12; Da 1:9
8 [n]Ps 37:16; [o]Pr 15:16; 17:1; Ecc 4:6
9 [p]ver 1; Job 33:29; Ps 90:12
10 [q]Pr 17:7
11 [r]Pr 11:1; Eze 45:10

b24 Hebrew *Sheol*
c33 Or *Wisdom teaches the fear of the LORD*

12 Kings detest wrongdoing,
for a throne is established through righteousness.[s]

13 Kings take pleasure in honest lips;
they value a man who speaks the truth.[t]

14 A king's wrath is a messenger of death,[u]
but a wise man will appease it.[v]

15 When a king's face brightens, it means life;[w]
his favour is like a rain cloud in spring.[x]

16 How much better to get wisdom than gold,
to choose understanding[y] rather than silver![z]

17 The highway of the upright avoids evil;
he who guards his way guards his life.[a]

18 Pride[b] goes before destruction,
a haughty spirit[c] before a fall.[d]

19 Better to be lowly in spirit and among the oppressed
than to share plunder with the proud.

20 Whoever gives heed to instruction prospers,[e]
and blessed is he who trusts in the LORD.[f]

21 The wise in heart are called discerning,
and pleasant words promote instruction.[a][g]

22 Understanding is a fountain of life to those who have it,[h]
but folly brings punishment to fools.

23 A wise man's heart guides his mouth,[i]
and his lips promote instruction.[b][j]

24 Pleasant words are a honeycomb,[k]
sweet to the soul and healing to the bones.[l]

25 There is a way that seems right to a man,[m]
but in the end it leads to death.[n]

26 The labourer's appetite works for him;
his hunger drives him on.

12 [s]Pr 20:28; 25:5; 29:14; 31:5
13 [t]Pr 22:11
14 [u]**Ge 40:2; Job 29:24;** Pr 20:2; [v]Pr 25:15; 29:8; Ecc 10:4
15 [w]**Ge 40:2; Job 29:24;** [x]Pr 19:12; 25:2–7
16 [y]Ps 49:20; [z]**Job 28:15; Pr 3:13–14**
17 [a]Pr 19:16
18 [b]**1Sa 17:42;** [c]Ps 18:27; Isa 13:11; Jer 48:29; [d]**Est 5:12;** Pr 11:2; **15:33;** 18:12; 29:23
20 [e]Pr 13:13; [f]**Ps 32:10;** 40:4; Pr 19:8; 29:25; Jer 17:7
21 [g]ver 23
22 [h]**Pr 10:11**
23 [i]Job 15:5; [j]ver 21
24 [k]**1Sa 14:27;** [l]Pr 24:13–14
25 [m]**Pr 12:15;** [n]Est 3:6; Pr 14:12
27 [o]**Ps 140:2;** [p]Jas 3:6
28 [q]**Pr 14:17;** [r]Pr 17:9
29 [s]**Pr 1:10;** 12:26
30 [t]**Pr 6:13**
31 [u]Pr 20:29
33 [v]**Lev 16:8; 1Sa 10:21;** Eze 21:21; [w]1Sa 14:41; [x]Jos 7:14; Pr 18:18; 29:26; Jnh 1:7

Ch. 17

1 [a]**Pr 15:16–17; 16:8**
3 [b]Pr 27:21; [c]**1Ch 29:17;** Ps 26:2; **139:23;** 1Pe 1:7
5 [d]**Job 5:16;** [e]Pr 14:31; [f]**Job 31:29;** [g]Eze 25:3; Ob 12
6 [h]**Ps 125:5**
7 [i]Pr 16:10

27 A scoundrel[o] plots evil,
and his speech is like a scorching fire.[p]

28 A perverse man stirs up dissension,[q]
and a gossip separates close friends.[r]

29 A violent man entices his neighbour
and leads him down a path that is not good.[s]

30 He who winks[t] with his eye is plotting perversity;
he who purses his lips is bent on evil.

31 Grey hair is a crown of splendour;[u]
it is attained by a righteous life.

32 Better a patient man than a warrior,
a man who controls his temper than one who takes a city.

33 The lot is cast[v] into the lap,
but its every decision[w] is from the LORD.[x]

17

1 Better a dry crust with peace and quiet
than a house full of feasting,[a] with strife.[a]

2 A wise servant will rule over a disgraceful son,
and will share the inheritance as one of the brothers.

3 The crucible for silver and the furnace for gold,[b]
but the LORD tests the heart.[c]

4 A wicked man listens to evil lips;
a liar pays attention to a malicious tongue.

5 He who mocks the poor[d] shows contempt for their Maker;[e]
whoever gloats over disaster[f] will not go unpunished.[g]

6 Children's children[h] are a crown to the aged,
and parents are the pride of their children.

7 Arrogant[b] lips are unsuited to a fool—
how much worse lying lips to a ruler![i]

---

[a]21 Or *words make a man persuasive*
[b]23 Or *mouth / and makes his lips persuasive*
[a]1 Hebrew *sacrifices* [b]7 Or *Eloquent*

8A bribe is a charm to the one who
gives it;
wherever he turns, he succeeds.[j]

9He who covers over an offence
promotes love,[k]
but whoever repeats the matter
separates close friends.[l]

10A rebuke impresses a man of
discernment
more than a hundred lashes a fool.

11An evil man is bent only on rebellion;
a merciless official will be sent
against him.

12Better to meet a bear robbed of her
cubs
than a fool in his folly.[m]

13If a man pays back evil[n] for good,[o]
evil will never leave his house.

14Starting a quarrel is like breaching a
dam;
so drop the matter before a dispute
breaks out.[p]

15Acquitting the guilty and condemning
the innocent[q]—
the LORD detests them both.[r]

16Of what use is money in the hand of a
fool,
since he has no desire to get
wisdom?[s]

17A friend loves at all times,
and a brother is born for adversity.[t]

18A man lacking in judgment strikes
hands in pledge
and puts up security for his
neighbour.[u]

19He who loves a quarrel loves sin;
he who builds a high gate invites
destruction.

20A man of perverse heart does not
prosper;
he whose tongue is deceitful falls
into trouble.

21To have a fool for a son brings grief;
there is no joy for the father of a
fool.[v]

22A cheerful heart is good medicine,
but a crushed[w] spirit dries up the
bones.[x]

23A wicked man accepts a bribe[y] in
secret
to pervert the course of justice.[z]

24A discerning man keeps wisdom in
view,
but a fool's eyes[a] wander to the ends
of the earth.

25A foolish son brings grief to his father
and bitterness to the one who bore
him.[b]

26It is not good to punish an innocent
man,[c]
or to flog officials for their integrity.

27A man of knowledge uses words with
restraint,[d]
and a man of understanding is
even-tempered.[e]

28Even a fool is thought wise if he keeps
silent,
and discerning if he holds his
tongue.[f]

18 An unfriendly man pursues
selfish ends;
he defies all sound judgment.

2A fool finds no pleasure in
understanding
but delights in airing his own
opinions.[a]

3When wickedness comes, so does
contempt,
and with shame comes disgrace.

4The words of a man's mouth are deep
waters,[b]
but the fountain of wisdom is a
bubbling brook.

5It is not good to be partial to the
wicked[c]
or to deprive the innocent of
justice.[d]

6A fool's lips bring him strife,
and his mouth invites a beating.[e]

7A fool's mouth is his undoing,
and his lips are a snare[f] to his soul.[g]

8The words of a gossip are like choice
morsels;
they go down to a man's inmost
parts.[h]

9One who is slack in his work
is brother to one who destroys.[i]

8 [j]Ex 23:8; Pr 19:6
9 [k]Pr 10:12; [l]Pr 16:28
12 [m]1Sa 25:25
13 [n]1Sa 19:4; [o]Ge 44:4; Ps 35:12
14 [p]Mt 5:25–26
15 [q]Ps 94:21; Pr 18:5; [r]Ex 23:6–7; Isa 5:23; La 3:34–36
16 [s]Pr 23:23
17 [t]2Sa 15:21; Pr 27:10
18 [u]Pr 6:1–5; 11:15; 22:26–27
21 [v]Pr 10:1
22 [w]Ps 38:8; [x]Ex 12:46; Pr 14:30; 15:13; 18:14
23 [y]Ex 18:21; 23:8; 1Sa 8:3; [z]Job 34:33
24 [a]Job 31:1
25 [b]Pr 10:1
26 [c]Ps 94:21
27 [d]Job 6:24; [e]Pr 14:29
28 [f]Job 2:13; 13:5; Pr 10:19

Ch. 18

2 [a]Pr 12:23
4 [b]Ps 18:16
5 [c]Pr 24:23–25; 28:21; [d]Ps 82:2; Pr 17:15
6 [e]Pr 10:14
7 [f]Ps 140:9; [g]Ps 64:8; Pr 10:14; 12:13; 13:3; Ecc 10:12
8 [h]Pr 26:22
9 [i]Pr 28:24

[10]The name of the LORD is a strong
tower;[j]
the righteous run to it and are safe.[k]

[11]The wealth of the rich is their fortified
city;[l]
they imagine it an unscalable wall.

[12]Before his downfall a man's heart is
proud,
but humility comes before
honour.[m]

[13]He who answers before listening—
that is his folly and his shame.[n]

[14]A man's spirit sustains him in
sickness,
but a crushed spirit who can bear?[o]

[15]The heart of the discerning acquires
knowledge;[p]
the ears of the wise seek it out.

[16]A gift[q] opens the way for the giver
and ushers him into the presence of
the great.

[17]The first to present his case seems
right,
till another comes forward and
questions him.

[18]Casting the lot settles disputes[r]
and keeps strong opponents apart.

[19]An offended[s] brother is more
unyielding than a fortified city,
and disputes are like the barred
gates of a citadel.

[20]From the fruit of his mouth a man's
stomach is filled;
with the harvest from his lips he is
satisfied.[t]

[21]The tongue has the power of life and
death,[u]
and those who love it will eat its
fruit.[v]

[22]He who finds a wife finds what is
good[w]
and receives favour from the
LORD.[x]

[23]A poor man pleads for mercy,
but a rich man answers harshly.

[24]A man of many companions may
come to ruin,
but there is a friend who sticks
closer than a brother.[y]

10 [j]Ps 61:3; [k]Ps 20:1; Pr 14:26
11 [l]Pr 10:15
12 [m]Pr 11:2; 15:33; **16:18**
13 [n]Pr 20:25
14 [o]Pr 15:13; **17:22**
15 [p]Pr 15:14
16 [q]Ge 32:13; 1Sa 10:4; Pr 19:6
18 [r]Pr 16:33
19 [s]1Sa 17:28
20 [t]Pr 12:14
21 [u]Ps 12:4; [v]Pr 13:2–3; **Mt 12:37**
22 [w]Pr 12:4; [x]**Job 33:26**; Pr 19:14; 31:10
24 [y]1Sa 20:42; Jn 15:13–15

Ch. 19

1 [a]Pr 28:6
2 [b]Pr 29:20
3 [c]Ps 14:1; Pr 9:13; 24:9; Isa 32:6; [d]Jas 1:13–15
4 [e]ver 7; Pr 14:20
5 [f]Ex 23:1; [g]Ps 56:7; [h]ver 9; **Dt 19:19**; Pr 21:28
6 [i]Pr 29:26; [j]Pr **17:8; 18:16**
7 [k]Pr 10:15; [l]**ver 4**
8 [m]**Pr 16:20**
9 [n]**ver 5; Dt 19:19**
10 [o]Pr 26:1; [p]Pr 30:21–23; Ecc 10:5–7
11 [q]**2Ki 5:12**
12 [r]Pr 20:2; [s]**Ps 133:3**; [t]**Est 1:12; 7:7**; Ps 72:5–6; Pr 16:14–15
13 [u]**Pr 10:1**; [v]**Est 1:18**; Pr 21:9

19

[1]Better a poor man whose walk
is blameless
than a fool whose lips are perverse.[a]

[2]It is not good to have zeal without
knowledge,
nor to be hasty and miss the way.[b]

[3]A man's own folly[c] ruins his life,
yet his heart rages against the
LORD.[d]

[4]Wealth brings many friends,
but a poor man's friend deserts
him.[e]

[5]A false witness[f] will not go
unpunished,[g]
and he who pours out lies will not
go free.[h]

[6]Many curry favour with a ruler,[i]
and everyone is the friend of a man
who gives gifts.[j]

[7]A poor man is shunned by all his
relatives—
how much more do his friends
avoid him![k]
Though he pursues them with
pleading,
they are nowhere to be found.[a][l]

[8]He who gets wisdom loves his own
soul;
he who cherishes understanding
prospers.[m]

[9]A false witness will not go
unpunished,
and he who pours out lies will
perish.[n]

[10]It is not fitting for a fool[o] to live in
luxury—
how much worse for a slave to rule
over princes![p]

[11]A man's wisdom gives him patience;[q]
it is to his glory to overlook an
offence.

[12]A king's rage is like the roar of a lion,[r]
but his favour is like dew[s] on the
grass.[t]

[13]A foolish son is his father's ruin,[u]
and a quarrelsome wife is like a
constant dripping.[v]

[a]7 The meaning of the Hebrew for this sentence is uncertain.

14Houses and wealth are inherited from parents,[w]
but a prudent wife is from the LORD.[x]

15Laziness brings on deep sleep,
and the shiftless man goes hungry.[y]

16He who obeys instructions guards his life,
but he who is contemptuous of his ways will die.[z]

17He who is kind to the poor lends to the LORD,[a]
and he will reward him for what he has done.[b]

18Discipline your son, for in that there is hope;
do not be a willing party to his death.[c]

19A hot-tempered man must pay the penalty;
if you rescue him, you will have to do it again.

20Listen to advice and accept instruction,[d]
and in the end you will be wise.[e]

21Many are the plans in a man's heart,
but it is the LORD's purpose that prevails.[f]

22What a man desires is unfailing love;[b]
better to be poor than a liar.

23The fear of the LORD leads to life:
Then one rests content, untouched by trouble.[g]

24The sluggard buries his hand in the dish;
he will not even bring it back to his mouth![h]

25Flog a mocker, and the simple will learn prudence;
rebuke a discerning man,[i] and he will gain knowledge.[j]

26He who robs his father and drives out his mother[k]
is a son who brings shame and disgrace.

27Stop listening to instruction, my son,[l]
and you will stray from the words of knowledge.

28A corrupt witness mocks at justice,
and the mouth of the wicked gulps down evil.[m]

29Penalties are prepared for mockers,
and beatings for the backs of fools.[n]

20

Wine[a] is a mocker[b] and beer a brawler;
whoever is led astray[c] by them is not wise.[d]

2A king's wrath is like the roar of a lion;[e]
he who angers him forfeits his life.[f]

3It is to a man's honour to avoid strife,
but every fool[g] is quick to quarrel.[h]

4A sluggard[i] does not plough in season;
so at harvest time he looks but finds nothing.[j]

5The purposes of a man's heart are deep waters,[k]
but a man of understanding draws them out.

6Many a man claims to have unfailing love,
but a faithful man who can find?[l]

7The righteous man leads a blameless life;[m]
blessed are his children after him.[n]

8When a king sits on his throne to judge,[o]
he winnows out all evil with his eyes.[p]

9Who can say, "I have kept my heart pure;[q]
I am clean and without sin"?[r]

10Differing weights and differing measures—
the LORD detests them both.[s]

11Even a child is known by his actions,
by whether his conduct is pure[t] and right.

12Ears that hear and eyes that see—
the LORD has made them both.[u]

13Do not love sleep or you will grow poor;[v]
stay awake and you will have food to spare.

b22 Or *A man's greed is his shame*

14 [w]2Co 12:14; [x]Pr 18:22
15 [y]Pr 10:4; 20:13
16 [z]Pr 16:17; Ro 10:5
17 [a]Dt 24:14; [b]Dt 24:19; Pr 14:21; 22:9; Mt 10:42
18 [c]Pr 13:24; 23:13–14
20 [d]Pr 4:1; [e]Pr 12:15
21 [f]Ps 33:11; Pr 16:9; 20:24; Isa 8:10; 14:24,27; 31:2; 40:8; 46:10; 48:14; 55:11; Jer 44:29; La 3:37
23 [g]Job 4:7; Pr 10:27
24 [h]Pr 26:15
25 [i]Ps 141:5; [j]Pr 9:9; 21:11
26 [k]Pr 28:24
27 [l]Pr 1:8
28 [m]Job 15:16
29 [n]Dt 25:2

Ch. 20

1 [a]Lev 10:9; Hab 2:5; [b]1Sa 25:36; [c]1Ki 20:16; [d]Pr 31:4
2 [e]Pr 19:12; [f]Est 7:7; Pr 16:14
3 [g]1Sa 25:25; [h]Ge 13:8
4 [i]Pr 6:6; [j]Ecc 10:18
5 [k]Ps 18:16
6 [l]Ps 12:1
7 [m]Ps 26:1; [n]Ps 37:25–26; 112:2
8 [o]1Ki 7:7; [p]ver 26; Pr 25:4–5
9 [q]Job 15:14; [r]1Ki 8:46; Ecc 7:20; 1Jn 1:8
10 [s]ver 23; Pr 11:1
11 [t]Ps 39:1
12 [u]Ps 94:9
13 [v]Pr 6:11; 19:15

14"It's no good, it's no good!" says the
buyer;
then off he goes and boasts about
his purchase.

15Gold there is, and rubies in
abundance,
but lips that speak knowledge are a
rare jewel.

16Take the garment of one who puts up
security for a stranger;
hold it in pledge[w] if he does it for a
wayward woman.[x]

17Food gained by fraud tastes sweet to a
man,[y]
but he ends up with a mouth full of
gravel.[z]

18Make plans by seeking advice;
if you wage war, obtain guidance.[a]

19A gossip betrays a confidence;[b]
so avoid a man who talks too much.

20If a man curses his father or mother,[c]
his lamp will be snuffed out in pitch
darkness.[d]

21An inheritance quickly gained at the
beginning
will not be blessed at the end.

22Do not say, "I'll pay you back for this
wrong!"[e]
Wait for the LORD, and he will
deliver you.[f]

23The LORD detests differing weights,
and dishonest scales do not please
him.[g]

24A man's steps are directed[h] by the
LORD.[i]
How then can anyone understand
his own way?[j]

25It is a trap for a man to dedicate
something rashly
and only later to consider his vows.[k]

26A wise king winnows out the wicked;
he drives the threshing wheel over
them.[l]

27The lamp of the LORD[m] searches the
spirit of a man;[a]
it searches out his inmost being.[n]

28Love and faithfulness keep a king safe;
through love[o] his throne is made
secure.[p]

16 [w]Ex 22:26; [x]Pr 27:13
17 [y]Pr 9:17; [z]Job 20:14; La 3:16
18 [a]Pr 11:14; 24:6
19 [b]Pr 11:13
20 [c]Pr 30:11; [d]Ex 21:17; Job 18:5
22 [e]Pr 24:29; [f]Isa 37:20; Jer 1:19; 42:11; Ro 12:19
23 [g]ver 10; Dt 25:13
24 [h]Ps 90:12; [i]Job 33:29; [j]Pr 19:21; Jer 10:23
25 [k]Pr 10:19; 18:13; Ecc 5:2, 4–5; Jer 44:25
26 [l]ver 8
27 [m]Ps 119:105; [n]Pr 16:2
28 [o]Ps 40:11; [p]Pr 16:12; Isa 16:5
29 [q]Pr 16:31
30 [r]Ps 51:2; Pr 22:15; [s]Isa 1:5

Ch. 21

1 [a]Est 5:1; Jer 39:11–12
2 [b]Pr 16:2
3 [c]1Sa 15:22; Isa 1:11; Mic 6:6–8
4 [d]Job 41:34
5 [e]Pr 10:4
6 [f]Pr 10:2
7 [g]Pr 11:5
8 [h]Pr 2:15
9 [i]ver 19; Pr 19:13; 25:24
11 [j]Pr 19:25
12 [k]Pr 14:11

29The glory of young men is their
strength,
grey hair the splendour of the old.[q]

30Blows and wounds cleanse[r] away evil,
and beatings[s] purge the inmost
being.

21

The king's heart is in the hand
of the LORD;
he directs it like a watercourse
wherever he pleases.[a]

2All a man's ways seem right to him,
but the LORD weighs the heart.[b]

3To do what is right and just
is more acceptable to the LORD than
sacrifice.[c]

4Haughty eyes[d] and a proud heart,
the lamp of the wicked, are sin!

5The plans of the diligent lead to profit[e]
as surely as haste leads to poverty.

6A fortune made by a lying tongue
is a fleeting vapour and a deadly
snare.[a][f]

7The violence of the wicked will drag
them away,[g]
for they refuse to do what is right.

8The way of the guilty is devious,[h]
but the conduct of the innocent is
upright.

9Better to live on a corner of the roof
than share a house with a
quarrelsome wife.[i]

10The wicked man craves evil;
his neighbour gets no mercy from
him.

11When a mocker is punished, the
simple gain wisdom;
when a wise man is instructed, he
gets knowledge.[j]

12The Righteous One[b] takes note of the
house of the wicked
and brings the wicked to ruin.[k]

13If a man shuts his ears to the cry of the
poor,

---

[a]27 Or *The spirit of man is the LORD's lamp*
[a]6 Some Hebrew manuscripts, Septuagint and Vulgate; most Hebrew manuscripts *vapour for those who seek death* [b]12 Or *The righteous man*

he too will cry out[l] and not be answered.[m]

14A gift given in secret soothes anger,
and a bribe concealed in the cloak pacifies great wrath.[n]

15When justice is done, it brings joy to the righteous
but terror to evildoers.[o]

16A man who strays from the path of understanding
comes to rest in the company of the dead.[p]

17He who loves pleasure will become poor;
whoever loves wine and oil will never be rich.[q]

18The wicked become a ransom[r] for the righteous,
and the unfaithful for the upright.

19Better to live in a desert
than with a quarrelsome and ill-tempered wife.[s]

20In the house of the wise are stores of choice food and oil,
but a foolish man devours all he has.

21He who pursues righteousness and love
finds life, prosperity[c][t] and honour.[u]

22A wise man attacks the city of the mighty[v]
and pulls down the stronghold in which they trust.

23He who guards his mouth[w] and his tongue
keeps himself from calamity.[x]

24The proud and arrogant[y] man—
"Mocker" is his name;
he behaves with overweening pride.

25The sluggard's craving will be the death of him,[z]
because his hands refuse to work.
26All day long he craves for more,
but the righteous[a] give without sparing.[b]

27The sacrifice of the wicked is detestable[c]—
how much more so when brought with evil intent![d]

13 [l]Ex 11:6; [m]Job 29:12
14 [n]Ge 32:20
15 [o]Pr 10:29
16 [p]Eze 18:24
17 [q]Pr 23:20–21, 29–35
18 [r]Pr 11:8; Isa 43:3
19 [s]ver 9
21 [t]Ps 25:13; [u]Mt 5:6
22 [v]Pr 8:14
23 [w]Ps 34:13; [x]Pr 10:19; 12:13; 13:3
24 [y]Jer 43:2
25 [z]Pr 13:4
26 [a]2Sa 17:27; [b]Lev 25:35
27 [c]1Ki 14:24; [d]Pr 15:8
28 [e]Isa 29:21; [f]Pr 19:5
29 [g]Pr 14:8
30 [h]Job 12:13; 15:25; [i]2Ch 13:12; Job 5:13; Isa 8:10
31 [j]Ps 33:12–19; Isa 31:1

Ch. 22

1 [a]Ecc 7:1
2 [b]Job 31:15; Pr 29:13; Mt 5:45
3 [c]Pr 14:16; [d]Pr 27:12
4 [e]Pr 15:33; [f]Pr 10:27; Da 4:36
5 [g]Pr 15:19
6 [h]Ge 14:14; [i]Eph 6:4; [j]Dt 6:7
8 [k]Ex 1:20; Job 4:8; Gal 6:7–8; [l]Hos 8:7
9 [m]Dt 14:29; [n]Pr 11:25; 19:17; 28:27
10 [o]Pr 26:20

28A false witness[e] will perish,[f]
and whoever listens to him will be destroyed for ever.[d]

29A wicked man puts up a bold front,
but an upright man gives thought to his ways.[g]

30There is no wisdom,[h] no insight, no plan
that can succeed against the LORD.[i]

31The horse is made ready for the day of battle,
but victory rests with the LORD.[j]

22 A good name is more desirable than great riches;
to be esteemed is better than silver or gold.[a]

2Rich and poor have this in common:
The LORD is the Maker of them all.[b]

3A prudent man sees danger and takes refuge,[c]
but the simple keep going and suffer for it.[d]

4Humility and the fear of the LORD
bring wealth and honour[e] and life.[f]

5In the paths of the wicked lie thorns and snares,[g]
but he who guards his soul stays far from them.

6Train[a][h] a child in the way he should go,[i]
and when he is old he will not turn from it.[j]

7The rich rule over the poor,
and the borrower is servant to the lender.

8He who sows wickedness reaps trouble,[k]
and the rod of his fury will be destroyed.[l]

9A generous man will himself be blessed,[m]
for he shares his food with the poor.[n]

10Drive out the mocker, and out goes strife;
quarrels and insults are ended.[o]

[c]21 Or *righteousness*
[d]28 Or / *but the words of an obedient man will live on*
[a]6 Or *Start*

11He who loves a pure heart and whose
speech is gracious
will have the king for his friend.[p]

12The eyes of the LORD keep watch over
knowledge,
but he frustrates the words of the
unfaithful.

13The sluggard says, "There is a lion
outside!"[q]
or, "I will be murdered in the
streets!"

14The mouth of an adulteress is a deep
pit;[r]
he who is under the LORD's wrath
will fall into it.[s]

15Folly is bound up in the heart of a
child,
but the rod of discipline will drive it
far from him.[t]

16He who oppresses the poor to increase
his wealth
and he who gives gifts to the
rich—both come to poverty.

Sayings of the Wise

17Pay attention[u] and listen to the sayings
of the wise;[v]
apply your heart to what I teach,[w]
18for it is pleasing when you keep them
in your heart
and have all of them ready on your
lips.
19So that your trust may be in the LORD,
I teach you today, even you.
20Have I not written thirty[b] sayings for
you,
sayings of counsel and knowledge,
21teaching you true and reliable words,[x]
so that you can give sound answers
to him who sent you?

22Do not exploit the poor[y] because they
are poor
and do not crush the needy in
court,[z]
23for the LORD will take up their case[a]
and will plunder those who plunder
them.[b]

24Do not make friends with a
hot-tempered man,
do not associate with one easily
angered,
25or you may learn his ways
and get yourself ensnared.[c]

26Do not be a man who strikes hands in
pledge[d]
or puts up security for debts;
27if you lack the means to pay,
your very bed will be snatched from
under you.[e]

28Do not move an ancient boundary
stone[f]
set up by your forefathers.

29Do you see a man skilled[g] in his work?
He will serve[h] before kings;[i]
he will not serve before obscure
men.

23 When you sit to dine with a
ruler,
note well what[a] is before you,
2and put a knife to your throat
if you are given to gluttony.
3Do not crave his delicacies,[a]
for that food is deceptive.

4Do not wear yourself out to get rich;
have the wisdom to show restraint.
5Cast but a glance at riches, and they
are gone,[b]
for they will surely sprout wings
and fly off to the sky like an eagle.[c]

6Do not eat the food of a stingy man,
do not crave his delicacies;[d]
7for he is the kind of man
who is always thinking about the
cost.[b]
"Eat and drink," he says to you,
but his heart is not with you.
8You will vomit up the little you have
eaten
and will have wasted your
compliments.

9Do not speak to a fool,
for he will scorn the wisdom of your
words.[e]

10Do not move an ancient boundary
stone[f]
or encroach on the fields of the
fatherless,
11for their Defender[g] is strong;[h]
he will take up their case against
you.[i]

12Apply your heart to instruction[j]
and your ears to words of
knowledge.

11 [p]Pr 16:13; Mt 5:8
13 [q]Pr 26:13
14 [r]Pr 5:3–5; 23:27; [s]Ecc 7:26
15 [t]Pr 13:24; 20:30
17 [u]Pr 1:8; [v]Pr 1:6; 30:1; 31:1; [w]Pr 2:2
21 [x]Ecc 12:10
22 [y]Lev 25:17; Job 5:16; [z]Ex 23:6
23 [a]Job 29:16; Ps 140:12; [b]Est 8:1; 9:1; Pr 23:10–11
25 [c]1Co 15:33
26 [d]Pr 6:1–5
27 [e]Pr 11:15; 17:18
28 [f]Dt 19:14
29 [g]1Ki 11:28; [h]Ge 41:46; [i]Ge 39:4

Ch. 23

3 [a]ver 6–8; Ps 141:4
5 [b]Mt 6:19; [c]Pr 27:24
6 [d]ver 1–3; Ps 141:4
9 [e]Pr 9:7
10 [f]Dt 19:14
11 [g]Job 19:25; [h]Ps 24:8; [i]Ex 22:22–24; Pr 15:25; 22:22–23
12 [j]Pr 2:2

b20 Or *not formerly written;* or *not written excellent*
a1 Or *who*
b7 Or *for as he thinks within himself, / so he is;* or *for as he puts on a feast, / so he is*

13Do not withhold discipline from a
child;
if you punish him with the rod, he
will not die.
14Punish him with the rod
and save his soul from death.[c][k]

15My son, if your heart is wise,
then my heart will be glad;
16my inmost being will rejoice
when your lips speak what is right.[l]

17Do not let your heart envy[m] sinners,
but always be zealous for the fear of
the LORD.
18There is surely a future hope for you,
and your hope will not be cut off.[n]

19Listen, my son,[o] and be wise,
and keep your heart on the right
path.
20Do not join those who drink too much
wine[p]
or gorge themselves on meat,
21for drunkards and gluttons become
poor,[q]
and drowsiness clothes them in
rags.

22Listen to your father, who gave you
life,
and do not despise your mother
when she is old.[r]
23Buy the truth and do not sell it;
get wisdom, discipline and
understanding.[s]
24The father of a righteous man has
great joy;
he who has a wise son delights in
him.[t]
25May your father and mother be glad;
may she who gave you birth
rejoice![u]

26My son,[v] give me your heart
and let your eyes keep to my ways,[w]
27for a prostitute is a deep pit[x]
and a wayward wife is a narrow
well.
28Like a bandit she lies in wait,[y]
and multiplies the unfaithful among
men.

29Who has woe? Who has sorrow?
Who has strife? Who has
complaints?
Who has needless bruises? Who has
bloodshot eyes?
30Those who linger over wine,[z]
who go to sample bowls of mixed
wine.
31Do not gaze at wine when it is red,
when it sparkles in the cup,
when it goes down smoothly!
32In the end it bites like a snake
and poisons like a viper.
33Your eyes will see strange sights
and your mind imagine confusing
things.
34You will be like one sleeping on the
high seas,
lying on top of the rigging.
35"They hit me," you will say, "but I'm
not hurt!
They beat me, but I don't feel it!
When will I wake up
so I can find another drink?"[a]

24

Do not envy[a] wicked men,
do not desire their company;
2for their hearts plot violence,[b]
and their lips talk about making
trouble.[c]

3By wisdom a house is built,[d]
and through understanding it is
established;
4through knowledge its rooms are
filled
with rare and beautiful treasures.[e]

5A wise man has great power,
and a man of knowledge increases
strength;
6for waging war you need guidance,
and for victory many advisers.[f]

7Wisdom is too high for a fool;
in the assembly at the gate he has
nothing to say.

8He who plots evil
will be known as a schemer.
9The schemes of folly are sin,
and men detest a mocker.

10If you falter in times of trouble,
how small is your strength![g]

11Rescue those being led away to death;
hold back those staggering towards
slaughter.[h]
12If you say, "But we knew nothing
about this,"
does not he who weighs[i][j] the heart
perceive it?
Does not he who guards your life
know it?
Will he not repay[k] each person
according to what he has done?[l]

13Eat honey, my son, for it is good;
honey from the comb is sweet to
your taste.

14 [k]**Pr 13:24; 19:18**
16 [l]ver 24; Pr 27:11; 29:3
17 [m]**Ps 37:1; 73:3**
18 [n]**Ps 9:18;** 37:1–4; Pr 24:14,19–20
19 [o]Dt 4:9; Pr 28:7
20 [p]Isa 5:11,22; 56:12; Hab 2:15
21 [q]**Pr 21:17**
22 [r]**Lev 19:32**
23 [s]Pr 4:7; 17:16
24 [t]**ver 15–16**
25 [u]**Pr 10:1**
26 [v]Pr 5:1–6; [w]**Ps 18:21**
27 [x]**Pr 22:14**
28 [y]Pr 7:11–12
30 [z]ver 20–21; Isa 5:11
35 [a]Pr 20:1

Ch. 24

1 [a]Pr 3:31–32; 23:17–18
2 [b]**Ps 2:1;** Isa 32:6; 55:7–8; 59:7; 65:2; 66:18; Hos 4:1; [c]Ps 10:7
3 [d]**Pr 14:1**
4 [e]**Pr 8:21**
6 [f]**Pr 11:14; 20:18;** Lk 14:31
10 [g]**Job 4:5**
11 [h]Ps 82:4
12 [i]**Ps 139:2;** [j]**1Sa 2:3;** [k]**Ps 54:5;** [l]Job 34:11; Ps 62:12; **Mt 16:27;** Ro 2:6*

[c]14 Hebrew *Sheol*

14Know also that wisdom is sweet to
your soul;
if you find it, there is a future hope
for you,
and your hope will not be cut off.[m n]

15Do not lie in wait like an outlaw
against a righteous man's house,
do not raid his dwelling-place;
16for though a righteous man falls seven
times, he rises again,
but the wicked are brought down by
calamity.[o]

17Do not gloat[p] when your enemy falls;
when he stumbles, do not let your
heart rejoice,[q]
18or the LORD will see and disapprove
and turn his wrath away from him.[r]

19Do not fret[s] because of evil men
or be envious of the wicked,
20for the evil man has no future hope,
and the lamp of the wicked will be
snuffed out.[t]

21Fear the LORD and the king,[u] my son,
and do not join with the rebellious,
22for those two will send sudden
destruction[v] upon them,
and who knows what calamities
they can bring?

Further Sayings of the Wise

23These also are sayings of the wise:[w]

To show partiality[x] in judging is not
good:[y]
24Whoever says to the guilty, "You are
innocent"[z]—
peoples will curse him and nations
denounce him.
25But it will go well with those who
convict the guilty,
and rich blessing will come upon
them.

26An honest answer
is like a kiss on the lips.

27Finish your outdoor work
and get your fields ready;
after that, build your house.

28Do not testify against your neighbour
without cause,[a]
or use your lips to deceive.
29Do not say, "I'll do to him as he has
done to me;
I'll pay that man back for what he
did."[b]

14 [m]Ps 119:103; Pr 16:24; [n]Pr 23:18
16 [o]**Job 5:19; Ps 34:21**
17 [p]Ob 12; [q]**2Sa 3:32;** Mic 7:8
18 [r]**Job 31:29**
19 [s]Ps 37:1
20 [t]**Job 18:5; Pr 23:17–18**
21 [u]Ro 13:1–5
22 [v]**Ps 73:19**
23 [w]**Pr 1:6;** [x]**Ex 18:16; Lev 19:15;** [y]Ps 72:2; Pr 28:21; 31:8–9; Jer 22:16
24 [z]**Pr 17:15**
28 [a]**Ps 7:4**
29 [b]Pr 20:22; Mt 5:38–41
30 [c]Pr 6:6–11; 26:13–16
33 [d]**Pr 6:10**
34 [e]**Pr 10:4;** Ecc 10:18

Ch. 25

1 [a]**1Ki 4:32;** [b]**Pr 1:1**
2 [c]Pr 16:10–15
5 [d]**Pr 20:8;** [e]**2Sa 7:13;** [f]**Pr 16:12;** 29:14
7 [g]Lk 14:7–10
8 [h]Mt 5:25–26

30I went past the field of the sluggard,[c]
past the vineyard of the man who
lacks judgment;
31thorns had come up everywhere,
the ground was covered with
weeds,
and the stone wall was in ruins.
32I applied my heart to what I observed
and learned a lesson from what I
saw:
33A little sleep, a little slumber,
a little folding of the hands to
rest[d]—
34and poverty will come on you like a
bandit
and scarcity like an armed man.[a e]

More Proverbs of Solomon

25 These are more proverbs[a] of Solomon, copied by the men of Hezekiah king of Judah:[b]

2It is the glory of God to conceal a
matter;
to search out a matter is the glory of
kings.[c]

3As the heavens are high and the earth
is deep,
so the hearts of kings are
unsearchable.

4Remove the dross from the silver,
and out comes material for[a] the
silversmith;
5remove the wicked from the king's
presence,[d]
and his throne will be established[e]
through righteousness.[f]

6Do not exalt yourself in the king's
presence,
and do not claim a place among
great men;
7it is better for him to say to you,
"Come up here,"[g]
than for him to humiliate you before
a nobleman.

What you have seen with your eyes
8 do not bring[b] hastily to court,
for what will you do in the end
if your neighbour puts you to
shame?[h]

9If you argue your case with a
neighbour,

[a]34 Or *like a vagrant / and scarcity like a beggar*
[a]4 Or *comes a vessel from*
[b]7, 8 Or *nobleman / on whom you had set your eyes. /* [8]*Do not go*

do not betray another man's
confidence,
10or he who hears it may shame you
and you will never lose your bad
reputation.

11A word aptly spoken
is like apples of gold in settings of
silver.[i]

12Like an ear-ring of gold or an
ornament of fine gold
is a wise man's rebuke to a listening
ear.[j]

13Like the coolness of snow at harvest
time
is a trustworthy messenger to those
who send him;
he refreshes the spirit of his
masters.[k]

14Like clouds and wind without rain
is a man who boasts of gifts he does
not give.

15Through patience a ruler can be
persuaded,[l]
and a gentle tongue can break a
bone.[m]

16If you find honey, eat just enough—
too much of it, and you will vomit.[n]
17Seldom set foot in your neighbour's
house—
too much of you, and he will hate
you.

18Like a club or a sword or a sharp arrow
is the man who gives false
testimony against his
neighbour.[o]

19Like a bad tooth or a lame foot
is reliance on the unfaithful in times
of trouble.

20Like one who takes away a garment on
a cold day,
or like vinegar poured on soda,
is one who sings songs to a heavy
heart.

21If your enemy is hungry, give him
food to eat;
if he is thirsty, give him water to
drink.
22In doing this, you will heap burning
coals[p] on his head,
and the LORD will reward you.[q]

23As a north wind brings rain,
so a sly tongue brings angry looks.

11 [i]ver 12; Pr 15:23
12 [j]ver 11; Ps 141:5; Pr 13:18
13 [k]Pr 10:26; 13:17
15 [l]Ecc 10:4; [m]Pr 15:1
16 [n]ver 27
18 [o]Pr 12:18
22 [p]Ps 18:8; [q]2Ch 28:15; Mt 5:44; Ro 12:20*
24 [r]Pr 21:9
25 [s]Pr 15:30
27 [t]ver 16; [u]Pr 27:2; Mt 23:12

Ch. 26

1 [a]1Sa 12:17; [b]ver 8; Pr 19:10
2 [c]Dt 23:5
3 [d]Ps 32:9; [e]Pr 10:13
4 [f]ver 5; Isa 36:21
5 [g]ver 4; Pr 3:7
6 [h]Pr 10:26
7 [i]ver 9
8 [j]ver 1
9 [k]ver 7
11 [l]2Pe 2:22*; [m]Ps 85:8
12 [n]Pr 3:7

24Better to live on a corner of the roof
than share a house with a
quarrelsome wife.[r]

25Like cold water to a weary soul
is good news from a distant land.[s]

26Like a muddied spring or a polluted
well
is a righteous man who gives way to
the wicked.

27It is not good to eat too much honey,[t]
nor is it honourable to seek one's
own honour.[u]

28Like a city whose walls are broken
down
is a man who lacks self-control.

26

Like snow in summer or rain[a] in
harvest,
honour is not fitting for a fool.[b]

2Like a fluttering sparrow or a darting
swallow,
an undeserved curse does not come
to rest.[c]

3A whip for the horse, a halter for the
donkey,[d]
and a rod for the backs of fools![e]

4Do not answer a fool according to his
folly,
or you will be like him yourself.[f]

5Answer a fool according to his folly,
or he will be wise in his own eyes.[g]

6Like cutting off one's feet or drinking
violence
is the sending of a message by the
hand of a fool.[h]

7Like a lame man's legs that hang limp
is a proverb in the mouth of a fool.[i]

8Like tying a stone in a sling
is the giving of honour to a fool.[j]

9Like a thornbush in a drunkard's hand
is a proverb in the mouth of a fool.[k]

10Like an archer who wounds at random
is he who hires a fool or any
passer-by.

11As a dog returns to its vomit,[l]
so a fool repeats his folly.[m]

12Do you see a man wise in his own
eyes?[n]

There is more hope for a fool than
for him.[o]

13The sluggard says,[p] "There is a lion in
the road,
a fierce lion roaming the streets!"[q]

14As a door turns on its hinges,
so a sluggard turns on his bed.[r]

15The sluggard buries his hand in the
dish;
he is too lazy to bring it back to his
mouth.[s]

16The sluggard is wiser in his own eyes
than seven men who answer
discreetly.

17Like one who seizes a dog by the ears
is a passer-by who meddles in a
quarrel not his own.

18Like a madman shooting
firebrands or deadly arrows
19is a man who deceives his neighbour
and says, "I was only joking!"

20Without wood a fire goes out;
without gossip a quarrel dies down.[t]

21As charcoal to embers and as wood to
fire,
so is a quarrelsome man for kindling
strife.[u]

22The words of a gossip are like choice
morsels;
they go down to a man's inmost
parts.[v]

23Like a coating of glaze[a] over
earthenware
are fervent lips with an evil heart.

24A malicious man disguises himself
with his lips,[w]
but in his heart he harbours deceit.[x]
25Though his speech is charming,[y] do
not believe him,
for seven abominations fill his
heart.[z]
26His malice may be concealed by
deception,
but his wickedness will be exposed
in the assembly.

27If a man digs a pit,[a] he will fall into it;[b]
if a man rolls a stone, it will roll back
on him.[c]

28A lying tongue hates those it hurts,
and a flattering mouth[d] works ruin.

12 [o]Pr 29:20
13 [p]Pr 6:6–11; 24:30–34; [q]Pr 22:13
14 [r]**Pr 6:9**
15 [s]Pr 19:24
20 [t]Pr 22:10
21 [u]**Pr 14:17**
22 [v]Pr 18:8
24 [w]**Ps 31:18;** [x]Ps 41:6
25 [y]Ps 28:3; [z]Jer 9:4
27 [a]**Ps 7:15;** [b]**Est 6:13;** [c]**Est 2:23;** 7:9; Ps 35:8; 141:10; Pr 28:10; 29:6; Isa 50:11
28 [d]**Ps 12:3;** Pr 29:5

Ch. 27

1 [a]**1Ki 20:11;** [b]Mt 6:34; Jas 4:13–16
2 [c]Pr 25:27
3 [d]**Job 6:3**
4 [e]**Nu 5:14**
6 [f]Ps 141:5; Pr 28:23
8 [g]Isa 16:2
9 [h]**Est 2:12; Ps 45:8**
10 [i]**Pr 17:17**
11 [j]**Pr 10:1; 23:15–16;** [k]**Ge 24:60**
12 [l]Pr 22:3
13 [m]Pr 20:16

27 Do not boast[a] about tomorrow,
for you do not know what a day
may bring forth.[b]

2Let another praise you, and not your
own mouth;
someone else, and not your own
lips.[c]

3Stone is heavy and sand[d] a burden,
but provocation by a fool is heavier
than both.

4Anger is cruel and fury
overwhelming,
but who can stand before
jealousy?[e]

5Better is open rebuke
than hidden love.

6Wounds from a friend can be trusted,
but an enemy multiplies kisses.[f]

7He who is full loathes honey,
but to the hungry even what is bitter
tastes sweet.

8Like a bird that strays from its nest[g]
is a man who strays from his home.

9Perfume[h] and incense bring joy to the
heart,
and the pleasantness of one's friend
springs from his earnest
counsel.

10Do not forsake your friend and the
friend of your father,
and do not go to your brother's
house when disaster[i] strikes
you—
better a neighbour nearby than a
brother far away.

11Be wise, my son, and bring joy to my
heart;[j]
then I can answer anyone who
treats me with contempt.[k]

12The prudent see danger and take
refuge,
but the simple keep going and suffer
for it.[l]

13Take the garment of one who puts up
security for a stranger;
hold it in pledge if he does it for a
wayward woman.[m]

---

[a]23 With a different word division of the Hebrew; Masoretic Text *of silver dross*

[14]If a man loudly blesses his neighbour
early in the morning,
it will be taken as a curse.

[15]A quarrelsome wife is like
a constant dripping[n] on a rainy day;
[16]restraining her is like restraining the
wind
or grasping oil with the hand.

[17]As iron sharpens iron,
so one man sharpens another.

[18]He who tends a fig-tree will eat its
fruit,[o]
and he who looks after his master
will be honoured.[p]

[19]As water reflects a face,
so a man's heart reflects the man.

[20]Death and Destruction[a] are never
satisfied,[q]
and neither are the eyes of man.[r]

[21]The crucible for silver and the furnace
for gold,[s]
but man is tested by the praise he
receives.

[22]Though you grind a fool in a mortar,
grinding him like grain with a
pestle,
you will not remove his folly from
him.

[23]Be sure you know the condition of
your flocks,[t]
give careful attention to your herds;
[24]for riches do not endure for ever,[u]
and a crown is not secure for all
generations.
[25]When the hay is removed and new
growth appears
and the grass from the hills is
gathered in,
[26]the lambs will provide you with
clothing,
and the goats with the price of a
field.
[27]You will have plenty of goats' milk
to feed you and your family
and to nourish your servant girls.

28 The wicked man flees[a]
though no-one pursues,[b]
but the righteous are as bold as a
lion.[c]

[2]When a country is rebellious, it has
many rulers,
but a man of understanding and
knowledge maintains order.

[3]A ruler[a] who oppresses the poor
is like a driving rain that leaves no
crops.

[4]Those who forsake the law praise the
wicked,
but those who keep the law resist
them.

[5]Evil men do not understand justice,
but those who seek the LORD
understand it fully.

[6]Better a poor man whose walk is
blameless
than a rich man whose ways are
perverse.[d]

[7]He who keeps the law is a discerning
son,
but a companion of gluttons
disgraces his father.[e]

[8]He who increases his wealth by
exorbitant interest[f]
amasses it for another,[g] who will be
kind to the poor.[h]

[9]If anyone turns a deaf ear to the law,
even his prayers are detestable.[i]

[10]He who leads the upright along an evil
path
will fall into his own trap,[j]
but the blameless will receive a good
inheritance.

[11]A rich man may be wise in his own
eyes,
but a poor man who has
discernment sees through him.

[12]When the righteous triumph, there is
great elation;[k]
but when the wicked rise to power,
men go into hiding.[l]

[13]He who conceals his sins[m] does not
prosper,
but whoever confesses[n] and
renounces them finds mercy.[o]

[14]Blessed is the man who always fears
the LORD,
but he who hardens his heart falls
into trouble.

[15]Like a roaring lion or a charging bear
is a wicked man ruling over a
helpless people.

15 [n]**Est 1:18**
18 [o]1Co 9:7; [p]Lk 19:12–27
20 [q]Pr 30:15–16; Hab 2:5; [r]Ecc 1:8; 6:7
21 [s]**Pr 17:3**
23 [t]Pr 12:10
24 [u]Pr 23:5

Ch. 28

1 [a]**2Ki 7:7;** [b]**Lev 26:17;** [c]**Ps 138:3**
6 [d]Pr 19:1
7 [e]Pr 23:19–21
8 [f]**Ex 18:21;** Eze 18:8; [g]**Job 27:17;** [h]**Job 3:15;** Ps 112:9; Lk 14:12–14
9 [i]**Ps 109:7; Pr 15:8; Isa 1:13**
10 [j]**Ps 57:6; Pr 26:27**
12 [k]**2Ki 11:20;** [l]ver 28; Job 24:4; Pr 29:2
13 [m]**2Sa 12:13; Job 31:33;** [n]**Lev 5:5;** [o]Ps 32:1–5; Da 4:27; 1Jn 1:9

[a]20 Hebrew *Sheol and Abaddon*
[a]3 Or *A poor man*

16A tyrannical ruler lacks judgment,
but he who hates ill-gotten gain will enjoy a long life.

17A man tormented by the guilt of murder
will be a fugitive[p] till death;
let no-one support him.

18He whose walk is blameless is kept safe,[q]
but he whose ways are perverse will suddenly fall.[r]

19He who works his land will have abundant food,
but the one who chases fantasies will have his fill of poverty.[s]

20A faithful man will be richly blessed,
but one eager to get rich will not go unpunished.[t]

21To show partiality[u] is not good[v]—
yet a man will do wrong for a piece of bread.[w]

22A stingy man is eager to get rich
and is unaware that poverty awaits him.[x]

23He who rebukes a man will in the end gain more favour
than he who has a flattering tongue.[y]

24He who robs his father or mother[z]
and says, "It's not wrong"—
he is partner to him who destroys.[a]

25A greedy man stirs up dissension,[b]
but he who trusts in the LORD[c] will prosper.

26He who trusts in himself is a fool,[d]
but he who walks in wisdom is kept safe.[e]

27He who gives to the poor will lack nothing,[f]
but he who closes his eyes to them receives many curses.[g]

28When the wicked rise to power, people go into hiding;[h]
but when the wicked perish, the righteous thrive.

29

A man who remains stiff-necked[a] after many rebukes
will suddenly be destroyed[b]—
without remedy.[c]

17 [p]1Sa 30:17; 1Ki 20:20; Jer 41:15; 44:14
18 [q]Jer 39:18; [r]**Est 6:13**; Pr 10:9
19 [s]Pr 12:11
20 [t]ver 22
21 [u]**Lev 19:15**; [v]**Ps 94:21**; Pr 18:5; [w]Eze 13:19
22 [x]ver 20
23 [y]**Pr 27:5–6**
24 [z]Pr 19:26; [a]**Pr 18:9**
25 [b]**Pr 14:17**; [c]Pr 29:25
26 [d]**Ps 4:5**; [e]1Co 3:18
27 [f]**Dt 24:19**; **Pr 22:9**; [g]**Ps 109:17**
28 [h]**ver 12**; **Job 20:19**

Ch. 29

1 [a]**Ex 32:9**; **Dt 9:27**; [b]Jer 19:15; 36:31; Hab 2:7; [c]**2Ch 36:16**; Pr 6:15
2 [d]**2Ki 11:20**; [e]Pr 30:22; Ecc 10:6; [f]**Pr 28:12**
3 [g]**Pr 10:1**; **23:15–16**; [h]Pr 5:8–10; Lk 15:11–32
4 [i]ver 14; **Pr 8:15–16**
5 [j]**Job 32:21**; **Pr 26:28**
6 [k]**Job 5:13**; **Pr 26:27**; Ecc 9:12
7 [l]Pr 31:8–9
8 [m]Pr 11:11; **16:14**
10 [n]ver 27; 1Jn 3:12
11 [o]**Job 15:13**; [p]Pr 12:16
12 [q]2Ki 21:9; [r]**Job 34:30**
13 [s]**Pr 22:2**; Mt 5:45
14 [t]**ver 4**; Ps 72:1–5; **Pr 16:12**
15 [u]ver 17; Pr 13:24
16 [v]**Ps 91:8**; **92:11**
17 [w]**ver 15**

2When the righteous thrive, the people rejoice;[d]
when the wicked rule,[e] the people groan.[f]

3A man who loves wisdom brings joy to his father,[g]
but a companion of prostitutes squanders his wealth.[h]

4By justice a king gives a country stability,[i]
but one who is greedy for bribes tears it down.

5Whoever flatters his neighbour
is spreading a net for his feet.[j]

6An evil man is snared by his own sin,[k]
but a righteous one can sing and be glad.

7The righteous care about justice for the poor,[l]
but the wicked have no such concern.

8Mockers stir up a city,
but wise men turn away anger.[m]

9If a wise man goes to court with a fool,
the fool rages and scoffs, and there is no peace.

10Bloodthirsty men hate a man of integrity
and seek to kill the upright.[n]

11A fool gives full vent to his anger,[o]
but a wise man keeps himself under control.[p]

12If a ruler[q] listens to lies,
all his officials become wicked.[r]

13The poor man and the oppressor have this in common:
The LORD gives sight to the eyes of both.[s]

14If a king judges the poor with fairness,
his throne will always be secure.[t]

15The rod of correction imparts wisdom,
but a child left to himself disgraces his mother.[u]

16When the wicked thrive, so does sin,
but the righteous will see their downfall.[v]

17Discipline your son, and he will give you peace;
he will bring delight to your soul.[w]

18Where there is no revelation, the
people cast off restraint;
but blessed is he who keeps the
law.[x]

19A servant cannot be corrected by mere
words;
though he understands, he will not
respond.

20Do you see a man who speaks in
haste?
There is more hope for a fool than
for him.[y]

21If a man pampers his servant from
youth,
he will bring grief[a] in the end.

22An angry man stirs up dissension,
and a hot-tempered one commits
many sins.[z]

23A man's pride brings him low,[a]
but a man of lowly spirit gains
honour.[b]

24The accomplice of a thief is his own
enemy;
he is put under oath and dare not
testify.[c]

25Fear[d] of man will prove to be a snare,
but whoever trusts in the LORD[e] is
kept safe.[f]

26Many seek an audience with a ruler,[g]
but it is from the LORD that man gets
justice.[h]

27The righteous detest the dishonest;
the wicked detest the upright.[i]

Sayings of Agur

30 The sayings[a] of Agur son of
Jakeh—an oracle:[a]

This man declared to Ithiel,
to Ithiel and to Ucal:[b]

2"I am the most ignorant of men;
I do not have a man's
understanding.
3I have not learned wisdom,
nor have I knowledge of the Holy
One.[b]
4Who has gone up[c] to heaven and come
down?
Who has gathered up the wind in
the hollow[d] of his hands?
Who has wrapped up the waters[e] in
his cloak?[f]
Who has established all the ends of
the earth?
What is his name,[g] and the name of his
son?
Tell me if you know!

5"Every word of God is flawless;[h]
he is a shield[i] to those who take
refuge in him.
6Do not add[j] to his words,
or he will rebuke you and prove you
a liar.

7"Two things I ask of you, O LORD;
do not refuse me before I die:
8Keep falsehood and lies far from me;
give me neither poverty nor riches,
but give me only my daily bread.[k]
9Otherwise, I may have too much and
disown[l] you
and say, 'Who is the LORD?'[m]
Or I may become poor and steal,
and so dishonour the name of my
God.[n]

10"Do not slander a servant to his
master,
or he will curse you, and you will
pay for it.

11"There are those who curse their
fathers
and do not bless their mothers;[o]
12those who are pure in their own eyes[p]
and yet are not cleansed of their
filth;[q]
13those whose eyes are ever so
haughty,[r]
whose glances are so disdainful;
14those whose teeth[s] are swords
and whose jaws are set with knives[t]
to devour[u] the poor[v] from the earth,
the needy from among mankind.[w]

15"The leech has two daughters.
'Give! Give!' they cry.

"There are three things that are never
satisfied,[x]
four that never say, 'Enough!':
16the grave,[c][y] the barren womb,
land, which is never satisfied with
water,
and fire, which never says,
'Enough!'

18 [x]Ps 1:1–2; 19:11; 119:1–2
20 [y]Pr 19:2; 26:12
22 [z]**Pr 14:17**
23 [a]**Est 5:12;** [b]**Pr 11:2; 15:33; 16:18**
24 [c]**Lev 5:1**
25 [d]**1Sa 15:24;** [e]Pr 28:25; [f]**Pr 16:20**
26 [g]Pr 19:6; [h]**Pr 16:33**
27 [i]**ver 10**

Ch. 30

1 [a]**Pr 22:17**
3 [b]**Pr 9:10**
4 [c]Dt 30:12; Ps 24:1–2; **Pr 8:22–31;** Jn 3:13; Eph 4:7–10; [d]Isa 40:12; [e]Job 26:8; [f]**Ge 1:2;** [g]Rev 19:12
5 [h]**Ps 12:6; 18:30;** [i]**Ge 15:1**
6 [j]**Dt 4:2**
8 [k]Mt 6:11
9 [l]Jos 24:27; Isa 1:4; 59:13; [m]Dt 6:12; 8:10–14; Hos 13:6; [n]**Dt 8:12**
11 [o]**Pr 20:20**
12 [p]**Pr 16:2;** [q]Jer 2:23,35
13 [r]**2Sa 22:28; Job 41:34**
14 [s]**Job 4:11; Ps 3:7;** [t]Ps 57:4; [u]**Job 24:9;** [v]Am 8:4; Mic 2:2; [w]**Job 19:22**
15 [x]Pr 27:20
16 [y]Isa 5:14; 14:9,11; Hab 2:5

a*21* The meaning of the Hebrew for this word is uncertain. **a***1* Or *Jakeh of Massa*
b*1* Masoretic Text; with a different word division of the Hebrew *declared, "I am weary, O God; / I am weary, O God, and faint.* **c***16* Hebrew *Sheol*

17"The eye that mocks[z] a father,
that scorns obedience to a mother,
will be pecked out by the ravens of the valley,
will be eaten by the vultures.[a]

18"There are three things that are too amazing for me,
four that I do not understand:
19the way of an eagle in the sky,
the way of a snake on a rock,
the way of a ship on the high seas,
and the way of a man with a maiden.

20"This is the way of an adulteress:
She eats and wipes her mouth
and says, 'I've done nothing wrong.'[b]

21"Under three things the earth trembles,
under four it cannot bear up:
22a servant who becomes king,[c]
a fool who is full of food,
23an unloved woman who is married,
and a maidservant who displaces her mistress.

24"Four things on earth are small,
yet they are extremely wise:
25Ants are creatures of little strength,
yet they store up their food in the summer;[d]
26conies[d] [e] are creatures of little power,
yet they make their home in the crags;
27locusts[f] have no king,
yet they advance together in ranks;
28a lizard can be caught with the hand,
yet it is found in kings' palaces.

29"There are three things that are stately in their stride,
four that move with stately bearing:
30a lion, mighty among beasts,
who retreats before nothing;
31a strutting cock, a he-goat,
and a king with his army around him.[e]

32"If you have played the fool and exalted yourself,
or if you have planned evil,
clap your hand over your mouth![g]
33For as churning the milk produces butter,
and as twisting the nose produces blood,
so stirring up anger produces strife."

17 [z]Dt 21:18–21; [a]Job 15:23
20 [b]Pr 5:6
22 [c]Pr 19:10; 29:2
25 [d]Pr 6:6–8
26 [e]Ps 104:18
27 [f]Ex 10:4
32 [g]Job 29:9

Ch. 31

1 [a]Pr 22:17
2 [b]Jdg 11:30
3 [c]Dt 17:17; 1Ki 11:3; Pr 5:1–14
4 [d]Pr 20:1; Ecc 10:16–17; Isa 5:22
5 [e]1Ki 16:9; [f]Pr 16:12
6 [g]Ge 14:18
7 [h]Est 1:10
8 [i]1Sa 19:4
9 [j]Pr 24:23; 29:7
10 [k]Ru 3:11; Pr 18:22; [l]Pr 8:35
11 [m]Ge 2:18; [n]Pr 12:4
13 [o]1Ti 2:9–10

Sayings of King Lemuel

31 The sayings[a] of King Lemuel—an oracle[a] his mother taught him:

2"O my son, O son of my womb,
O son of my vows,[b] [b]
3do not spend your strength on women,
your vigour on those who ruin kings.[c]

4"It is not for kings, O Lemuel—
not for kings to drink wine,[d]
not for rulers to crave beer,
5lest they drink[e] and forget what the law decrees,[f]
and deprive all the oppressed of their rights.
6Give beer to those who are perishing,
wine[g] to those who are in anguish;
7let them drink[h] and forget their poverty
and remember their misery no more.

8"Speak[i] up for those who cannot speak for themselves,
for the rights of all who are destitute.
9Speak up and judge fairly;
defend the rights of the poor and needy."[j]

Epilogue: The Wife of Noble Character

10[c]A wife of noble character[k] who can find?[l]
She is worth far more than rubies.
11Her husband[m] has full confidence in her
and lacks nothing of value.[n]
12She brings him good, not harm,
all the days of her life.
13She selects wool and flax
and works with eager hands.[o]
14She is like the merchant ships,
bringing her food from afar.
15She gets up while it is still dark;
she provides food for her family
and portions for her servant girls.
16She considers a field and buys it;
out of her earnings she plants a vineyard.

[d]26 That is, the hyrax or rock badger
[e]31 Or *king secure against revolt*
[a]1 Or *of Lemuel king of Massa, which*
[b]2 Or / *the answer to my prayers*
[c]10 Verses 10–31 are an acrostic, each verse beginning with a successive letter of the Hebrew alphabet.

17She sets about her work vigorously;
her arms are strong for her tasks.
18She sees that her trading is profitable,
and her lamp does not go out at night.
19In her hand she holds the distaff
and grasps the spindle with her fingers.
20She opens her arms to the poor
and extends her hands to the needy.[p]
21When it snows, she has no fear for her household;
for all of them are clothed in scarlet.
22She makes coverings for her bed;
she is clothed in fine linen and purple.
23Her husband is respected at the city gate,
where he takes his seat among the elders[q] of the land.
24She makes linen garments and sells them,
and supplies the merchants with sashes.
25She is clothed with strength and dignity;
she can laugh at the days to come.
26She speaks with wisdom,
and faithful instruction is on her tongue.[r]
27She watches over the affairs of her household
and does not eat the bread of idleness.
28Her children arise and call her blessed;
her husband also, and he praises her:
29"Many women do noble things,
but you surpass them all."
30Charm is deceptive, and beauty is fleeting;
but a woman who fears the LORD is to be praised.
31Give her the reward she has earned,
and let her works bring her praise[s] at the city gate.

20 [p]Dt 15:11
23 [q]Ex 3:16
26 [r]Pr 10:31
31 [s]Pr 11:16

Ecclesiastes

Everything Is Meaningless

1 The words of the Teacher,[a][a] son of
David, king of Jerusalem:[b]

2“Meaningless! Meaningless!”
says the Teacher.
“Utterly meaningless!
Everything is meaningless.”[c]

3What does man gain from all his
labour
at which he toils under the sun?[d]
4Generations come and generations
go,
but the earth remains for ever.[e]
5The sun rises and the sun sets,
and hurries back to where it rises.[f]
6The wind blows to the south
and turns to the north;
round and round it goes,
ever returning on its course.
7All streams flow into the sea,
yet the sea is never full.
To the place the streams come from,
there they return again.[g]
8All things are wearisome,
more than one can say.
The eye never has enough of seeing,[h]
nor the ear its fill of hearing.
9What has been will be again,
what has been done will be done
again;[i]
there is nothing new under the sun.
10Is there anything of which one can
say,
“Look! This is something new”?
It was here already, long ago;
it was here before our time.
11There is no remembrance of men of
old,[j]
and even those who are yet to come
will not be remembered
by those who follow.[k]

Wisdom Is Meaningless

12I, the Teacher,[l] was king over Israel
in Jerusalem.[m] 13I devoted myself to
study and to explore by wisdom all that
is done under heaven.[n] What a heavy
burden God has laid on men![o] 14I have
seen all the things that are done under
the sun; all of them are meaningless, a
chasing after the wind.[p]

15What is twisted cannot be
straightened;[q]
what is lacking cannot be counted.

16I thought to myself, “Look, I have
grown and increased in wisdom more
than anyone who has ruled over Jeru-
salem before me;[r] I have experienced
much of wisdom and knowledge.”
17Then I applied myself to the under-
standing of wisdom,[s] and also of
madness and folly,[t] but I learned that
this, too, is a chasing after the wind.

18For with much wisdom comes much
sorrow;[u]
the more knowledge, the more
grief.[v]

Pleasures Are Meaningless

2 I thought in my heart, “Come
now, I will test you with pleasure[a]
to find out what is good.” But that
also proved to be meaningless.
2“Laughter,”[b] I said, “is foolish. And
what does pleasure accomplish?” 3I
tried cheering myself with wine,[c] and
embracing folly[d]—my mind still guid-
ing me with wisdom. I wanted to see
what was worth while for men to do
under heaven during the few days of
their lives.

4I undertook great projects: I built
houses for myself[e] and planted
vineyards.[f] 5I made gardens and parks
and planted all kinds of fruit trees in
them. 6I made reservoirs to water
groves of flourishing trees. 7I bought
male and female slaves and had other
slaves[g] who were born in my house. I
also owned more herds and flocks than
anyone in Jerusalem before me. 8I
amassed silver and gold[h] for myself,
and the treasure of kings and prov-
inces.[i] I acquired men and women

Ch. 1

1 [a]ver 12; Ecc 7:27; 12:10; [b]**Pr 1:1**
2 [c]Ps 39:5–6; 62:9; Ecc 12:8; Ro 8:20–21
3 [d]Ecc 2:11,22; 3:9; 5:15–16
4 [e]**Job 8:19**
5 [f]Ps 19:5–6
7 [g]Job 36:28
8 [h]Pr 27:20
9 [i]Ecc 2:12; 3:15
11 [j]Ge 40:23; Ecc 9:15; [k]Ps 88:12; Ecc 2:16; 8:10; 9:5
12 [l]**ver 1**; [m]Ecc 2:9
13 [n]**Job 28:3**; [o]**Ge 3:17**; Ecc 3:10
14 [p]Ecc 2:11,17; 4:4; 6:9
15 [q]Ecc 7:13
16 [r]**1Ki 3:12**
17 [s]Ecc 7:23; 8:16; [t]Ecc 2:3, 12; 7:25
18 [u]Jer 45:3; [v]Ecc 2:23; 12:12

Ch. 2

1 [a]ver 24; Ecc 7:4; 8:15
2 [b]**Pr 14:13**
3 [c]ver 24–25; **Jdg 9:13**; Ru 3:3; Ecc 3:12–13; 5:18; 8:15; [d]**Ecc 1:17**
4 [e]2Ch 2:1; 8:1–6; [f]SS 8:11
7 [g]2Ch 8:7–8
8 [h]**1Ki 9:28**; [i]**Jdg 3:15**

[a]1 Or *leader of the assembly*; also in verses 2 and 12

singers,[j] and a harem[a] as well—the
delights of the heart of man. 9I became
greater by far than anyone in Jerusa-
lem[k] before me.[l] In all this my wisdom
stayed with me.

10I denied myself nothing my eyes
desired;
I refused my heart no pleasure.
My heart took delight in all my work,
and this was the reward for all my
labour.
11Yet when I surveyed all that my hands
had done
and what I had toiled to achieve,
everything was meaningless, a
chasing after the wind;[m]
nothing was gained under the sun.[n]

Wisdom and Folly Are Meaningless

12Then I turned my thoughts to consider
wisdom,
and also madness and folly.[o]
What more can the king's successor do
than what has already been done?[p]
13I saw that wisdom[q] is better than folly,[r]
just as light is better than darkness.
14The wise man has eyes in his head,
while the fool walks in the darkness;
but I came to realise
that the same fate overtakes them
both.[s]

15Then I thought in my heart,

"The fate of the fool will overtake me
also.
What then do I gain by being
wise?"[t]
I said in my heart,
"This too is meaningless."
16For the wise man, like the fool, will not
be long remembered;[u]
in days to come both will be
forgotten.[v]
Like the fool, the wise man too must
die![w]

Toil Is Meaningless

17So I hated life, because the work that
is done under the sun was grievous to
me. All of it is meaningless, a chasing
after the wind.[x] 18I hated all the things I
had toiled for under the sun, because I
must leave them to the one who comes
after me.[y] 19And who knows whether he
will be a wise man or a fool?[z] Yet he will
have control over all the work into
which I have poured my effort and skill
under the sun. This too is meaningless.
20So my heart began to despair over all
my toilsome labour under the sun. 21For
a man may do his work with wisdom,
knowledge and skill, and then he must
leave all he owns to someone who has
not worked for it. This too is meaning-
less and a great misfortune. 22What does
a man get for all the toil and anxious
striving with which he labours under
the sun?[a] 23All his days his work is pain
and grief;[b] even at night his mind does
not rest.[c] This too is meaningless.
24A man can do nothing better than to
eat and drink[d] and find satisfaction in
his work.[e] This too, I see, is from the
hand of God,[f] 25for without him, who
can eat or find enjoyment?[g] 26To the
man who pleases him, God gives wis-
dom,[h] knowledge and happiness, but to
the sinner he gives the task of gathering
and storing up wealth[i] to hand it over to
the one who pleases God.[j] This too is
meaningless, a chasing after the wind.

A Time for Everything

3 There is a time[a] for everything,
and a season for every activity
under heaven:

2 a time to be born and a time to die,
a time to plant and a time to uproot,[b]
3 a time to kill[c] and a time to heal,
a time to tear down and a time to
build,
4 a time to weep and a time to laugh,
a time to mourn and a time to dance,
5 a time to scatter stones and a time to
gather them,
a time to embrace and a time to
refrain,
6 a time to search and a time to give
up,
a time to keep and a time to throw
away,
7 a time to tear and a time to mend,
a time to be silent[d] and a time to
speak,
8 a time to love and a time to hate,
a time for war and a time for peace.

9What does the worker gain from his
toil?[e] 10I have seen the burden God has
laid on men.[f] 11He has made everything
beautiful in its time.[g] He has also set
eternity in the hearts of men; yet they
cannot fathom[h] what God has done
from beginning to end.[i] 12I know that
there is nothing better for men than to
be happy and do good while they live.
13That everyone may eat and drink,[j] and

8 [j]2Sa 19:35
9 [k]Ecc 1:12; [l]1Ch 29:25
11 [m]Ecc 1:14; [n]Ecc 1:3
12 [o]Ecc 1:17; [p]Ecc 1:9
13 [q]Ecc 7:19; 9:18; [r]Ecc 7:11–12
14 [s]Ps 49:10; Ecc 3:19; 6:6; 7:2; 9:3,11–12
15 [t]ver 19; Ecc 6:8
16 [u]Ps 112:6; [v]Ecc 1:11; [w]Ps 49:10
17 [x]Ecc 1:14
18 [y]Ps 39:6; 49:10
19 [z]ver 15
22 [a]Ecc 1:3
23 [b]Ecc 1:18; [c]Ge 3:17; Job 7:2
24 [d]ver 3; 1Co 15:32; [e]ver 1; Ecc 3:22; [f]Job 2:10; Ecc 3:12–13; 5:17–19; 7:14; 9:7–10; 11:7–10
25 [g]Ps 127:2
26 [h]Job 9:4; [i]Job 27:17; [j]Pr 13:22

Ch. 3

1 [a]ver 11,17; Ecc 8:6
2 [b]Isa 28:24
3 [c]Dt 5:17
7 [d]Est 4:14
9 [e]Ecc 1:3
10 [f]Ecc 1:13
11 [g]ver 1; [h]Job 11:7; [i]Job 28:23; Ro 11:33
13 [j]Ecc 2:3

[a]8 The meaning of the Hebrew for this phrase is uncertain.

find satisfaction[k] in all his toil—this is
the gift of God.[l] 14I know that every-
thing God does will endure for ever;
nothing can be added to it and nothing
taken from it. God does it so that men
will revere him.[m]

15Whatever is has already been,[n]
and what will be has been before;[o]
and God will call the past to
account.[a]

16And I saw something else under the
sun:

In the place of judgment—
wickedness was there,
in the place of justice—wickedness
was there.

17I thought in my heart,

"God will bring to judgment[p]
both the righteous and the wicked,
for there will be a time for every
activity,
a time for every deed."[q]

18I also thought, "As for men, God
tests them so that they may see that they
are like the animals.[r] 19Man's fate[s] is like
that of the animals; the same fate awaits
them both: As one dies, so dies the
other. All have the same breath;[b] man
has no advantage over the animal.
Everything is meaningless. 20All go
to the same place; all come from dust,
and to dust all return.[t] 21Who knows if
the spirit of man rises upward[u] and
if the spirit of the animal[c] goes down
into the earth?"
22So I saw that there is nothing better
for a man than to enjoy his work,[v] be-
cause that is his lot.[w] For who can bring
him to see what will happen after him?

Oppression, Toil, Friendlessness

4 Again I looked and saw all the
oppression[a] that was taking place
under the sun:

I saw the tears of the oppressed—
and they have no comforter;
power was on the side of their
oppressors—
and they have no comforter.[b]
2And I declared that the dead,[c]
who had already died,
are happier than the living,
who are still alive.[d]
3But better than both
is he who has not yet been,[e]
who has not seen the evil
that is done under the sun.[f]

4And I saw that all labour and all
achievement spring from man's envy of
his neighbour. This too is meaningless,
a chasing after the wind.[g]

5The fool folds his hands[h]
and ruins himself.
6Better one handful with tranquillity
than two handfuls with toil[i]
and chasing after the wind.

7Again I saw something meaningless
under the sun:

8There was a man all alone;
he had neither son nor brother.
There was no end to his toil,
yet his eyes were not content[j] with
his wealth.
"For whom am I toiling," he asked,
"and why am I depriving myself of
enjoyment?"
This too is meaningless—
a miserable business!

9Two are better than one,
because they have a good return for
their work:
10If one falls down,
his friend can help him up.
But pity the man who falls
and has no-one to help him up!
11Also, if two lie down together, they
will keep warm.
But how can one keep warm alone?
12Though one may be overpowered,
two can defend themselves.
A cord of three strands is not quickly
broken.

Advancement Is Meaningless

13Better a poor but wise youth than an
old but foolish king who no longer
knows how to take warning. 14The
youth may have come from prison to
the kingship, or he may have been born
in poverty within his kingdom. 15I saw
that all who lived and walked under the
sun followed the youth, the king's suc-
cessor. 16There was no end to all the
people who were before them. But
those who came later were not pleased
with the successor. This too is meaning-
less, a chasing after the wind.

13 [k]Ps 34:12; [l]Dt 12:7,18; Ecc 2:24
14 [m]Job 23:15; Ecc 5:7; 7:18; 8:12–13
15 [n]Ecc 6:10; [o]Ecc 1:9
17 [p]Job 19:29; Ecc 11:9; 12:14; [q]ver 1
18 [r]Ps 73:22
19 [s]Ecc 2:14
20 [t]Ge 2:7; Job 34:15
21 [u]Ecc 12:7
22 [v]Ecc 2:24; [w]Job 31:2

Ch. 4

1 [a]Ps 12:5; [b]La 1:16
2 [c]Jer 20:17–18; 22:10; [d]Job 3:17; 10:18
3 [e]Job 3:16; [f]Job 3:22
4 [g]Ecc 1:14
5 [h]Pr 6:10
6 [i]Pr 15:16–17; 16:8
8 [j]Pr 27:20

[a]15 Or *God calls back the past* [b]19 Or *spirit*
[c]21 Or *Who knows the spirit of man, which rises upward, or the spirit of the animal, which*

Stand in Awe of God

5 Guard your steps when you go to
the house of God. Go near to listen
rather than to offer the sacrifice of fools,
who do not know that they do wrong.

2Do not be quick with your mouth,
do not be hasty in your heart
to utter anything before God.[a]
God is in heaven
and you are on earth,
so let your words be few.[b]
3As a dream[c] comes when there are
many cares,
so the speech of a fool when there
are many words.[d]

4When you make a vow to God, do
not delay in fulfilling it.[e] He has no
pleasure in fools; fulfil your vow.[f] 5It is
better not to vow than to make a vow
and not fulfil it.[g] 6Do not let your mouth
lead you into sin. And do not protest to
the ⌞temple⌟ messenger, "My vow was
a mistake." Why should God be angry
at what you say and destroy the work of
your hands? 7Much dreaming and
many words are meaningless. There-
fore stand in awe of God.[h]

Riches Are Meaningless

8If you see the poor oppressed[i] in a
district, and justice and rights denied,
do not be surprised at such things; for
one official is eyed by a higher one, and
over them both are others higher still.
9The increase from the land is taken by
all; the king himself profits from the
fields.

10Whoever loves money never has
money enough;
whoever loves wealth is never
satisfied with his income.
This too is meaningless.

11As goods increase,
so do those who consume them.
And what benefit are they to the
owner
except to feast his eyes on them?

12The sleep of a labourer is sweet,
whether he eats little or much,
but the abundance of a rich man
permits him no sleep.[j]

13I have seen a grievous evil under the
sun:[k]

wealth hoarded to the harm of its
owner,
14 or wealth lost through some
misfortune,
so that when he has a son
there is nothing left for him.
15Naked a man comes from his mother's
womb,
and as he comes, so he departs.[l]
He takes nothing from his labour[m]
that he can carry in his hand.[n]

16This too is a grievous evil:

As a man comes, so he departs,
and what does he gain,
since he toils for the wind?[o]
17All his days he eats in darkness,
with great frustration, affliction and
anger.

18Then I realised that it is good and
proper for a man to eat and drink,[p] and
to find satisfaction in his toilsome
labour[q] under the sun during the few
days of life God has given him—for this
is his lot. 19Moreover, when God gives
any man wealth and possessions,[r] and
enables him to enjoy them,[s] to accept
his lot[t] and be happy in his work—this
is a gift of God.[u] 20He seldom reflects on
the days of his life, because God keeps
him occupied with gladness of heart.[v]

6 I have seen another evil under the
sun, and it weighs heavily on men:
2God gives a man wealth, possessions
and honour, so that he lacks nothing his
heart desires, but God does not enable
him to enjoy them,[a] and a stranger en-
joys them instead. This is meaningless,
a grievous evil.[b]
3A man may have a hundred children
and live many years; yet no matter how
long he lives, if he cannot enjoy his
prosperity and does not receive proper
burial, I say that a stillborn[c] child is
better off than he.[d] 4It comes without
meaning, it departs in darkness, and
in darkness its name is shrouded.
5Though it never saw the sun or knew
anything, it has more rest than does that
man—6even if he lives a thousand years
twice over but fails to enjoy his prosper-
ity. Do not all go to the same place?[e]

7All man's efforts are for his mouth,
yet his appetite is never satisfied.[f]
8What advantage has a wise man
over a fool?[g]
What does a poor man gain
by knowing how to conduct himself
before others?
9Better what the eye sees
than the roving of the appetite.
This too is meaningless,
a chasing after the wind.[h]

Ch. 5

2 [a]**Jdg 11:35;** [b]**Job 6:24; Pr** 20:25
3 [c]**Job 20:8;** [d]Ecc 10:14
4 [e]**Dt 23:21; Jdg 11:35;** Ps 119:60; [f]**Nu 30:2;** Ps 66:13–14
5 [g]Nu 30:2–4; Jnh 2:9
7 [h]Ecc 3:14
8 [i]**Ps 12:5**
12 [j]Job 20:20
13 [k]Ecc 6:1–2
15 [l]**Job 1:21;** [m]Ps 49:17; 1Ti 6:7; [n]Ecc 1:3
16 [o]**Ecc 1:3**
18 [p]**Ecc 2:3;** [q]Ecc 2:24
19 [r]**1Ch 29:12;** [s]Ecc 6:2; [t]**Job 31:2;** [u]**Ecc 2:24**
20 [v]**Dt 12:7,18**

Ch. 6

2 [a]Ecc 5:19; [b]Ecc 5:13
3 [c]**Job 3:16;** [d]**Job 3:3**
6 [e]Ecc 2:14
7 [f]**Pr 27:20**
8 [g]**Ecc 2:15**
9 [h]**Ecc 1:14**

[10]Whatever exists has already been
named,[i]
and what man is has been known;
no man can contend
with one who is stronger than he.
[11]The more the words,
the less the meaning,
and how does that profit anyone?

[12]For who knows what is good for a
man in life, during the few and
meaningless days[j] he passes through
like a shadow?[k] Who can tell him what
will happen under the sun after he is
gone?

Wisdom

7 A good name is better than fine
perfume,[a]
and the day of death better than the
day of birth.[b]
[2]It is better to go to a house of
mourning
than to go to a house of feasting,
for death[c] is the destiny[d] of every man;
the living should take this to heart.
[3]Sorrow is better than laughter,[e]
because a sad face is good for the
heart.
[4]The heart of the wise is in the house of
mourning,
but the heart of fools is in the house
of pleasure.[f]
[5]It is better to heed a wise man's
rebuke[g]
than to listen to the song of fools.
[6]Like the crackling of thorns[h] under the
pot,
so is the laughter[i] of fools.
This too is meaningless.

[7]Extortion turns a wise man into a fool,
and a bribe[j] corrupts the heart.

[8]The end of a matter is better than its
beginning,
and patience[k] is better than pride.
[9]Do not be quickly provoked[l] in your
spirit,
for anger resides in the lap of fools.[m]
[10]Do not say, "Why were the old days[n]
better than these?"
For it is not wise to ask such
questions.

[11]Wisdom, like an inheritance, is a good
thing[o]
and benefits those who see the sun.[p]
[12]Wisdom is a shelter
as money is a shelter,
but the advantage of knowledge is
this:
that wisdom preserves the life of its
possessor.

[13]Consider what God has done:[q]

Who can straighten
what he has made crooked?[r]
[14]When times are good, be happy;
but when times are bad, consider:
God has made the one
as well as the other.[s]
Therefore, a man cannot discover
anything about his future.

[15]In this meaningless life[t] of mine I
have seen both of these:

a righteous man perishing in his
righteousness,
and a wicked man living long in his
wickedness.[u]
[16]Do not be over-righteous,
neither be overwise—
why destroy yourself?
[17]Do not be overwicked,
and do not be a fool—
why die before your time?[v]
[18]It is good to grasp the one
and not let go of the other.
The man who fears God[w] will avoid
all ⌞extremes⌟.[a]
[19]Wisdom[x] makes one wise man more
powerful[y]
than ten rulers in a city.

[20]There is not a righteous man[z] on earth
who does what is right and never
sins.[a]
[21]Do not pay attention to every word
people say,
or you[b] may hear your servant
cursing you—
[22]for you know in your heart
that many times you yourself have
cursed others.

[23]All this I tested by wisdom and I
said,

"I am determined to be wise"[c]—
but this was beyond me.
[24]Whatever wisdom may be,
it is far off and most profound—
who can discover it?[d]
[25]So I turned my mind to understand,
to investigate and to search out
wisdom and the scheme of
things[e]

10 [i]Ecc 3:15
12 [j]**Job 10:20; 20:8;** [k]**1Ch 29:15; Job 14:2; Ps 39:6**

Ch. 7

1 [a]Pr 22:1; SS 1:3; [b]Job 10:18
2 [c]Pr 11:19; [d]Ecc 2:14
3 [e]**Pr 14:13**
4 [f]Ecc 2:1; Jer 16:8
5 [g]Pr 13:18; 15:31–32
6 [h]Ps 58:9; [i]Pr 14:13
7 [j]Ex 18:21; 23:8
8 [k]Pr 14:29
9 [l]Mt 5:22; [m]Pr 14:29
10 [n]Ps 77:5
11 [o]Ecc 2:13; [p]Ecc 11:7
13 [q]Ecc 2:24; [r]Ecc 1:15
14 [s]**Job 1:21; Ecc 2:24**
15 [t]Job 7:7; [u]Job 21:7; Ecc 8:12–14; Jer 12:1
17 [v]Job 15:32
18 [w]Ecc 3:14
19 [x]Ecc 2:13; [y]Pr 8:14
20 [z]Ps 14:3; [a]2Ch 6:36; Ro 3:12; **Job 4:17; Pr 20:9**
21 [b]Pr 30:10
23 [c]Ecc 1:17
24 [d]Job 28:12
25 [e]Job 28:3

[a]18 Or *will follow them both*

and to understand the stupidity of
wickedness
and the madness of folly.[f]

26I find more bitter than death
the woman who is a snare,[g]
whose heart is a trap
and whose hands are chains.
The man who pleases God will escape
her,
but the sinner she will ensnare.[h]

27"Look," says the Teacher,[b] [i] "this is
what I have discovered:

"Adding one thing to another to
discover the scheme of things—
28 while I was still searching
but not finding—
I found one ⌞upright⌟ man among a
thousand,
but not one ⌞upright⌟ woman[j]
among them all.
29This only have I found:
God made mankind upright,
but men have gone in search of
many schemes."

8

Who is like the wise man?
Who knows the explanation of
things?
Wisdom brightens a man's face
and changes its hard appearance.

Obey the King

2Obey the king's command, I say,
because you took an oath before God.
3Do not be in a hurry to leave the king's
presence.[a] Do not stand up for a bad
cause, for he will do whatever he
pleases. 4Since a king's word is su-
preme, who can say to him, "What are
you doing?[b]"

5Whoever obeys his command will
come to no harm,
and the wise heart will know the
proper time and procedure.
6For there is a proper time and
procedure for every matter,[c]
though a man's misery weighs
heavily upon him.

7Since no man knows the future,
who can tell him what is to come?
8No man has power over the wind to
contain it;[a]
so no-one has power over the day of
his death.
As no-one is discharged in time of
war,
so wickedness will not release those
who practise it.

25 [f]Ecc 1:17
26 [g]Ex 10:7; Jdg 14:15; [h]Pr 2:16–19; 5:3–5; 7:23; 22:14
27 [i]Ecc 1:1
28 [j]1Ki 11:3

Ch. 8

3 [a]Ecc 10:4
4 [b]Est 1:19
6 [c]Ecc 3:1
10 [d]Ecc 1:11
12 [e]Dt 12:28; [f]Ex 1:20; [g]Ecc 3:14
13 [h]Ecc 3:14; [i]Dt 4:40; Job 5:26; Ps 34:12; Isa 65:20
14 [j]Job 21:7; [k]Ecc 7:15
15 [l]Ps 42:8; [m]Ex 32:6; Ecc 2:3; [n]Ecc 2:1
16 [o]Ecc 1:17; [p]Ecc 1:13
17 [q]Job 28:3; [r]Job 28:23; Ro 11:33

Ch. 9

1 [a]Ecc 10:14

9All this I saw, as I applied my mind to
everything done under the sun. There is
a time when a man lords it over others to
his own[b] hurt. 10Then too, I saw the
wicked buried[d]—those who used to
come and go from the holy place and
receive praise[c] in the city where they did
this. This too is meaningless.
11When the sentence for a crime is not
quickly carried out, the hearts of the
people are filled with schemes to do
wrong. 12Although a wicked man com-
mits a hundred crimes and still lives a
long time, I know that it will go better[e]
with God-fearing men,[f] who are rever-
ent before God.[g] 13Yet because the
wicked do not fear God,[h] it will not go
well with them, and their days[i] will not
lengthen like a shadow.
14There is something else meaning-
less that occurs on earth: righteous men
who get what the wicked deserve, and
wicked men who get what the righteous
deserve.[j] This too, I say, is meaning-
less.[k] 15So I commend the enjoyment of
life,[l] because nothing is better for a man
under the sun than to eat and drink[m]
and be glad.[n] Then joy will accompany
him in his work all the days of the life
God has given him under the sun.
16When I applied my mind to know
wisdom[o] and to observe man's labour
on earth[p]—his eyes not seeing sleep day
or night—17then I saw all that God has
done.[q] No-one can comprehend what
goes on under the sun. Despite all his
efforts to search it out, man cannot dis-
cover its meaning. Even if a wise man
claims he knows, he cannot really com-
prehend it.[r]

A Common Destiny for All

9

So I reflected on all this and con-
cluded that the righteous and the
wise and what they do are in God's
hands, but no man knows whether love
or hate awaits him.[a] 2All share a com-
mon destiny—the righteous and the
wicked, the good and the bad,[a] the
clean and the unclean, those who offer
sacrifices and those who do not.

As it is with the good man,
so with the sinner;
as it is with those who take oaths,

[b]27 Or *leader of the assembly*
[a]8 Or *over his spirit to retain it* [b]9 Or *to their*
[c]10 Some Hebrew manuscripts and Septuagint (Aquila); most Hebrew manuscripts *and are forgotten*
[a]2 Septuagint (Aquila), Vulgate and Syriac; Hebrew does not have *and the bad*.

so with those who are afraid to take
them.[b]

3This is the evil in everything that
happens under the sun: The same des-
tiny overtakes all.[c] The hearts of men,
moreover, are full of evil and there is
madness in their hearts while they live,[d]
and afterwards they join the dead.[e]
4Anyone who is among the living has
hope[b]—even a live dog is better off than
a dead lion!

5For the living know that they will die,
but the dead know nothing;[f]
they have no further reward,
and even the memory of them[g] is
forgotten.[h]
6Their love, their hate
and their jealousy have long since
vanished;
never again will they have a part
in anything that happens under the
sun.[i]

7Go, eat your food with gladness, and
drink your wine[j] with a joyful heart,[k] for
it is now that God favours what you do.
8Always be clothed in white,[l] and al-
ways anoint your head with oil. 9Enjoy
life with your wife,[m] whom you love, all
the days of this meaningless life that
God has given you under the sun—all
your meaningless days. For this is your
lot[n] in life and in your toilsome labour
under the sun. 10Whatever[o] your hand
finds to do, do it with all your might,[p]
for in the grave,[c][q] where you are going,
there is neither working nor planning
nor knowledge nor wisdom.[r]

11I have seen something else under
the sun:

The race is not to the swift
or the battle to the strong,[s]
nor does food come to the wise[t]
or wealth to the brilliant
or favour to the learned;
but time and chance[u] happen to them
all.[v]

12Moreover, no man knows when his
hour will come:

As fish are caught in a cruel net,
or birds are taken in a snare,
so men are trapped by evil times[w]
that fall unexpectedly upon them.[x]

Wisdom Better Than Folly

13I also saw under the sun this exam-
ple of wisdom[y] that greatly impressed
me: 14There was once a small city with
only a few people in it. And a powerful
king came against it, surrounded it and
built huge siegeworks against it. 15Now
there lived in that city a man poor but
wise, and he saved the city by his wis-
dom. But nobody remembered that
poor man.[z] 16So I said, "Wisdom is bet-
ter than strength." But the poor man's
wisdom is despised, and his words are
no longer heeded.[a]

17The quiet words of the wise are more
to be heeded
than the shouts of a ruler of fools.
18Wisdom[b] is better than weapons of
war,
but one sinner destroys much good.

10 As dead flies give perfume a
bad smell,
so a little folly[a] outweighs wisdom
and honour.
2The heart of the wise inclines to the
right,
but the heart of the fool to the left.
3Even as he walks along the road,
the fool lacks sense
and shows everyone[b] how stupid
he is.
4If a ruler's anger rises against you,
do not leave your post;[c]
calmness can lay great errors to
rest.[d]

5There is an evil I have seen under the
sun,
the sort of error that arises from a
ruler:
6Fools are put in many high positions,[e]
while the rich occupy the low ones.
7I have seen slaves on horseback,
while princes go on foot like slaves.[f]

8Whoever digs a pit may fall into it;[g]
whoever breaks through a wall may
be bitten by a snake.[h]
9Whoever quarries stones may be
injured by them;
whoever splits logs may be
endangered by them.[i]

10If the axe is dull
and its edge unsharpened,
more strength is needed
but skill will bring success.

11If a snake bites before it is charmed,
there is no profit for the charmer.[j]

2 [b]Job 9:22; Ecc 2:14
3 [c]Job 9:22; Ecc 2:14; [d]Jer 11:8; 13:10; 16:12; 17:9; [e]Job 21:26
5 [f]Job 14:21; [g]Ps 9:6; [h]Ecc 1:11
6 [i]Job 21:21
7 [j]Nu 6:20; [k]Ecc 2:24
8 [l]Rev 3:4
9 [m]Pr 5:18; [n]Job 31:2
10 [o]1Sa 10:7; [p]Ecc 11:6; [q]Nu 16:33; Ps 6:5; Isa 38:18; [r]Ecc 2:24
11 [s]Am 2:14–15; [t]Job 32:13; Isa 47:10; Jer 9:23; [u]Ecc 2:14; [v]Dt 8:18
12 [w]Pr 29:6; [x]Ps 73:22; Ecc 2:14
13 [y]2Sa 20:22
15 [z]Ge 40:14; Ecc 1:11
16 [a]Est 6:3
18 [b]Ecc 2:13

Ch. 10

1 [a]Pr 13:16; 18:2
3 [b]Pr 13:16
4 [c]Ecc 8:3; [d]Pr 16:14
6 [e]Pr 29:2
7 [f]Pr 19:10
8 [g]Ps 57:6; [h]Est 2:23; Ps 9:16; Am 5:19
9 [i]Pr 26:27
11 [j]Ps 58:5; Isa 3:3

b4 Or *What then is to be chosen? With all who live, there is hope* c10 Hebrew *Sheol*

[12]Words from a wise man's mouth are
gracious,[k]
but a fool is consumed by his own
lips.[l]
[13]At the beginning his words are folly;
at the end they are wicked
madness—
[14] and the fool multiplies words.[m]

No-one knows what is coming—
who can tell him what will happen
after him?[n]

[15]A fool's work wearies him;
he does not know the way to town.

[16]Woe to you, O land whose king was a
servant[a] [o]
and whose princes feast in the
morning.
[17]Blessed are you, O land whose king is
of noble birth
and whose princes eat at a proper
time—
for strength and not for
drunkenness.[p]

[18]If a man is lazy, the rafters sag;
if his hands are idle, the house
leaks.[q]

[19]A feast is made for laughter,
and wine[r] makes life merry,
but money is the answer for
everything.

[20]Do not revile the king[s] even in your
thoughts,
or curse the rich in your bedroom,
because a bird of the air may carry
your words,
and a bird on the wing may report
what you say.

Bread Upon the Waters

11 Cast[a] your bread upon the
waters,
for after many days you will find it
again.[b]
[2]Give portions to seven, yes to eight,
for you do not know what disaster
may come upon the land.

[3]If clouds are full of water,
they pour rain upon the earth.
Whether a tree falls to the south or to
the north,
in the place where it falls, there will
it lie.
[4]Whoever watches the wind will not
plant;
whoever looks at the clouds will not
reap.

[5]As you do not know the path of the
wind,[c]
or how the body is formed[a] in a
mother's womb,[d]
so you cannot understand the work of
God,
the Maker of all things.

[6]Sow your seed in the morning,
and at evening let not your hands be
idle,[e]
for you do not know which will
succeed,
whether this or that,
or whether both will do equally
well.

Remember Your Creator While Young

[7]Light is sweet,
and it pleases the eyes to see the
sun.[f]
[8]However many years a man may live,
let him enjoy them all.
But let him remember[g] the days of
darkness,
for they will be many.
Everything to come is meaningless.

[9]Be happy, young man, while you are
young,
and let your heart give you joy in the
days of your youth.
Follow the ways of your heart
and whatever your eyes see,
but know that for all these things
God will bring you to judgment.[h]
[10]So then, banish anxiety[i] from your
heart
and cast off the troubles of your
body,
for youth and vigour are
meaningless.[j]

12 Remember[a] your Creator
in the days of your youth,
before the days of trouble[b] come
and the years approach when you
will say,
"I find no pleasure in them"—
[2]before the sun and the light
and the moon and the stars grow
dark,
and the clouds return after the rain;
[3]when the keepers of the house
tremble,
and the strong men stoop,
when the grinders cease because they
are few,

12 [k]Pr 10:32; [l]Pr 10:6; 14:3; 15:2; 18:7
14 [m]Ecc 5:3; [n]Ecc 9:1
16 [o]Isa 3:4–5,12
17 [p]Dt 14:26; 1Sa 25:36; Pr 31:4
18 [q]Pr 20:4; 24:30–34
19 [r]Ge 14:18; Jdg 9:13
20 [s]Ex 22:28

Ch. 11
1 [a]ver 6; Isa 32:20; Hos 10:12; [b]Dt 24:19
5 [c]Jn 3:8–10; [d]Ps 139:14–16
6 [e]Ecc 9:10
7 [f]Ecc 7:11
8 [g]Ecc 12:1
9 [h]Job 19:29; Ecc 2:24; 3:17
10 [i]Ps 94:19; [j]Ecc 2:24

Ch. 12
1 [a]Ecc 11:8; [b]2Sa 19:35

[a]16 Or *king is a child*
[a]5 Or *know how life* (or *the spirit*) */ enters the body being formed*

and those looking through the
windows grow dim;
4when the doors to the street are closed
and the sound of grinding fades;
when men rise up at the sound of
birds,
but all their songs grow faint;[c]
5when men are afraid of heights
and of dangers in the streets;
when the almond tree blossoms
and the grasshopper drags himself
along
and desire no longer is stirred.
Then man goes to his eternal home[d]
and mourners[e] go about the streets.

6Remember him—before the silver
cord is severed,
or the golden bowl is broken;
before the pitcher is shattered at the
spring,
or the wheel broken at the well,
7and the dust returns[f] to the ground it
came from,
and the spirit returns to God[g] who
gave it.[h]

8"Meaningless! Meaningless!" says the
Teacher.[a] [i]
"Everything is meaningless!"[j]

4 [c]Jer 25:10
5 [d]**Job 10:21;** [e]Jer 9:17; Am 5:16
7 [f]**Ge 2:7; Ps 146:4;** [g]Ecc 3:21; [h]**Job 20:8**
8 [i]Ecc 1:1; [j]**Ecc 1:2**
9 [k]1Ki 4:32
10 [l]**Ecc 1:1;** [m]Pr 22:20–21
11 [n]**Ezr 9:8; Job 6:25**
12 [o]**Ecc 1:18**
13 [p]**Ex 20:20; 1Sa 12:24; Job 23:15; Ps 19:9;** [q]**Dt 4:2;** [r]**Dt 4:6; Job 37:24**
14 [s]**Job 19:29; Ecc 3:17;** [t]**Job 34:21; Ps 19:12; Jer 16:17; 23:24**

The Conclusion of the Matter

9Not only was the Teacher wise, but
also he imparted knowledge to the
people. He pondered and searched
out and set in order many proverbs.[k]
10The Teacher[l] searched to find just the
right words, and what he wrote was
upright and true.[m]
11The words of the wise are like
goads, their collected sayings like
firmly embedded nails[n]—given by one
Shepherd. 12Be warned, my son, of
anything in addition to them.
Of making many books there is no
end, and much study wearies the body.[o]

13Now all has been heard;
here is the conclusion of the matter:
Fear God[p] and keep his
commandments,[q]
for this is the whole ⌞duty⌟ of man.[r]
14For God will bring every deed into
judgment,[s]
including every hidden thing,[t]
whether it is good or evil.

[a]8 Or *the leader of the assembly;* also in verses 9 and 10

Song of Songs

1 Solomon's Song of Songs.[a]

Beloved[a]

[2]Let him kiss me with the kisses of his
mouth—
for your love[b] is more delightful
than wine.[c]
[3]Pleasing is the fragrance of your
perfumes;[d]
your name[e] is like perfume poured
out.
No wonder the maidens[f] love you!
[4]Take me away with you—let us hurry!
Let the king bring me into his
chambers.[g]

Friends

We rejoice and delight[h] in you;[b]
we will praise your love[i] more than
wine.

Beloved

How right they are to adore you!

[5]Dark am I, yet lovely,[j]
O daughters of Jerusalem,[k]
dark like the tents of Kedar,[l]
like the tent curtains of Solomon.[c]
[6]Do not stare at me because I am dark,
because I am darkened by the sun.
My mother's sons were angry with me
and made me take care of the
vineyards;[m]
my own vineyard I have neglected.
[7]Tell me, you whom I love, where you
graze your flock
and where you rest your sheep[n] at
midday.
Why should I be like a veiled[o] woman
beside the flocks of your friends?

Friends

[8]If you do not know, most beautiful of
women,[p]
follow the tracks of the sheep
and graze your young goats
by the tents of the shepherds.

Lover

[9]I liken you, my darling, to a mare
harnessed to one of the chariots[q] of
Pharaoh.
[10]Your cheeks[r] are beautiful with
ear-rings,
your neck with strings of jewels.[s]
[11]We will make you ear-rings of gold,
studded with silver.

Beloved

[12]While the king was at his table,
my perfume spread its fragrance.[t]
[13]My lover is to me a sachet of myrrh[u]
resting between my breasts.
[14]My lover[v] is to me a cluster of henna[w]
blossoms
from the vineyards of En Gedi.[x]

Lover

[15]How beautiful[y] you are, my darling!
Oh, how beautiful!
Your eyes are doves.[z]

Beloved

[16]How handsome you are, my lover![a]
Oh, how charming!
And our bed is verdant.

Lover

[17]The beams of our house are cedars;[b]
our rafters are firs.

Beloved[a]

2 I am a rose[b][a] of Sharon,[b]
a lily[c] of the valleys.

Ch. 1

1 [a]**1Ki 4:32**; Ps 45 Title
2 [b]ver 4; SS 4:10; 8:6; [c]**Ge 14:18; Jdg 9:13**
3 [d]**Est 2:12; Ps 45:8;** [e]**Ecc 7:1;** [f]Ps 45:14
4 [g]Ps 45:15; [h]SS 2:3; [i]ver 2
5 [j]SS 2:14; 4:3; [k]SS 5:16; [l]**Ge 25:13**
6 [m]SS 2:15; 7:12; 8:12
7 [n]Isa 13:20; [o]**Ge 24:65**
8 [p]SS 5:9; 6:1
9 [q]2Ch 1:17
10 [r]SS 5:13; [s]Isa 61:10
12 [t]SS 4:11–14
13 [u]**Ge 37:25**
14 [v]ver 16; SS 2:3,17; 5:8; [w]SS 4:13; [x]**1Sa 23:29; 2Ch 20:2**
15 [y]SS 4:7; 7:6; [z]Ps 74:19; SS 2:14; 4:1; 5:2, 12; 6:9; Jer 48:28
16 [a]**ver 14**
17 [b]1Ki 6:9

Ch. 2

1 [a]Isa 35:1; [b]**1Ch 27:29;** [c]SS 5:13; Hos 14:5

---

[a]2 Primarily on the basis of the gender of the Hebrew pronouns used, male and female speakers are indicated in the margins by the captions *Lover* and *Beloved* respectively. The words of others are marked *Friends*. In some instances the divisions and their captions are debatable.
[b]4 The Hebrew is masculine singular.
[c]5 Or *Salma*
[a]*1* Or *Lover*
[b]*1* Possibly a member of the crocus family

Lover

[2]Like a lily among thorns
is my darling among the maidens.

Beloved

[3]Like an apple tree among the trees of the forest
is my lover[d] among the young men.
I delight[e] to sit in his shade,
and his fruit is sweet to my taste.[f]
[4]He has taken me to the banquet hall,[g]
and his banner[h] over me is love.
[5]Strengthen me with raisins,
refresh me with apples,[i]
for I am faint with love.[j]
[6]His left arm is under my head,
and his right arm embraces me.[k]
[7]Daughters of Jerusalem, I charge you[l]
by the gazelles and by the does of the field:
Do not arouse or awaken love
until it so desires.[m]

[8]Listen! My lover!
Look! Here he comes,
leaping across the mountains,
bounding over the hills.[n]
[9]My lover is like a gazelle[o] or a young stag.[p]
Look! There he stands behind our wall,
gazing through the windows,
peering through the lattice.
[10]My lover spoke and said to me,
"Arise, my darling,
my beautiful one, and come with me.
[11]See! The winter is past;
the rains are over and gone.
[12]Flowers appear on the earth;
the season of singing has come,
the cooing of doves
is heard in our land.
[13]The fig-tree forms its early fruit;[q]
the blossoming[r] vines spread their fragrance.
Arise, come, my darling;
my beautiful one, come with me."

Lover

[14]My dove[s] in the clefts of the rock,
in the hiding-places on the mountainside,
show me your face,
let me hear your voice;
for your voice is sweet,
and your face is lovely.[t]
[15]Catch for us the foxes,[u]
the little foxes
that ruin the vineyards,[v]
our vineyards that are in bloom.[w]

3 [d]SS 1:14; [e]SS 1:4; [f]SS 4:16
4 [g]Est 1:11; [h]**Nu 1:52**
5 [i]SS 7:8; [j]SS 5:8
6 [k]SS 8:3
7 [l]SS 5:8; [m]SS 3:5; 8:4
8 [n]ver 17; SS 8:14
9 [o]**2Sa 2:18**; [p]ver 17; SS 8:14
13 [q]Isa 28:4; Jer 24:2; Hos 9:10; Mic 7:1; Na 3:12; [r]SS 7:12
14 [s]**Ge 8:8; SS 1:15**; [t]**SS 1:5**
15 [u]**Jdg 15:4**; [v]**SS 1:6**; [w]SS 7:12
16 [x]SS 7:10; [y]SS 4:5; 6:3
17 [z]SS 4:6; [a]**SS 1:14**; [b]**ver 9**; [c]**ver 8**

Ch. 3

1 [a]SS 5:6
3 [b]SS 5:7
4 [c]SS 8:2; [d]SS 6:9; 8:5
5 [e]**SS 2:7**; [f]SS 8:4
6 [g]SS 8:5; [h]SS 4:6,14; [i]Ex 30:34
7 [j]**1Sa 8:11**
8 [k]**Job 15:22**; Ps 91:5

Beloved

[16]My lover is mine and I am his;[x]
he browses among the lilies.[y]
[17]Until the day breaks
and the shadows flee,[z]
turn, my lover,[a]
and be like a gazelle
or like a young stag[b]
on the rugged hills.[c][c]

3

All night long on my bed
I looked[a] for the one my heart loves;
I looked for him but did not find him.
[2]I will get up now and go about the city,
through its streets and squares;
I will search for the one my heart loves.
So I looked for him but did not find him.
[3]The watchmen found me
as they made their rounds in the city.[b]
"Have you seen the one my heart loves?"
[4]Scarcely had I passed them
when I found the one my heart loves.
I held him and would not let him go
till I had brought him to my mother's house,[c]
to the room of the one who conceived me.[d]
[5]Daughters of Jerusalem, I charge you[e]
by the gazelles and by the does of the field:
Do not arouse or awaken love
until it so desires.[f]

[6]Who is this coming up from the desert[g]
like a column of smoke,
perfumed with myrrh[h] and incense
made from all the spices[i] of the merchant?
[7]Look! It is Solomon's carriage,
escorted by sixty warriors,[j]
the noblest of Israel,
[8]all of them wearing the sword,
all experienced in battle,
each with his sword at his side,
prepared for the terrors of the night.[k]
[9]King Solomon made for himself the carriage;
he made it of wood from Lebanon.
[10]Its posts he made of silver,
its base of gold.

[c]17 Or *the hills of Bether*

Its seat was upholstered with purple,
its interior lovingly inlaid
by[a] the daughters of Jerusalem.
11Come out, you daughters of Zion,[l]
and look at King Solomon wearing the crown,
the crown with which his mother crowned him
on the day of his wedding,
the day his heart rejoiced.[m]

Lover

4 How beautiful you are, my darling!
Oh, how beautiful!
Your eyes behind your veil[a] are doves.[b]
Your hair is like a flock of goats
descending from Mount Gilead.[c]
2Your teeth are like a flock of sheep just shorn,
coming up from the washing.
Each has its twin;
not one of them is alone.[d]
3Your lips are like a scarlet ribbon;
your mouth[e] is lovely.[f]
Your temples behind your veil
are like the halves of a pomegranate.[g]
4Your neck is like the tower[h] of David,
built with elegance;[a]
on it hang a thousand shields,[i]
all of them shields of warriors.
5Your two breasts[j] are like two fawns,
like twin fawns of a gazelle[k]
that browse among the lilies.[l]
6Until the day breaks
and the shadows flee,[m]
I will go to the mountain of myrrh[n]
and to the hill of incense.
7All beautiful[o] you are, my darling;
there is no flaw[p] in you.

8Come with me from Lebanon, my bride,[q]
come with me from Lebanon.
Descend from the crest of Amana,
from the top of Senir,[r] the summit of Hermon,[s]
from the lions' dens
and the mountain haunts of the leopards.
9You have stolen my heart, my sister, my bride;[t]
you have stolen my heart
with one glance of your eyes,
with one jewel of your necklace.[u]
10How delightful[v] is your love,[w] my sister, my bride!
How much more pleasing is your love than wine,[x]
and the fragrance of your perfume[y]
than any spice!
11Your lips drop sweetness as the honeycomb, my bride;
milk and honey are under your tongue.[z]
The fragrance of your garments is like that of Lebanon.[a]
12You are a garden[b] locked up, my sister, my bride;[c]
you are a spring enclosed, a sealed fountain.[d]
13Your plants are an orchard of pomegranates[e]
with choice fruits,
with henna[f] and nard,
14 nard and saffron,
calamus and cinnamon,[g]
with every kind of incense tree,
with myrrh[h] and aloes[i]
and all the finest spices.[j]
15You are[b] a garden[k] fountain,[l]
a well of flowing water
streaming down from Lebanon.

Beloved

16Awake, north wind,
and come, south wind!
Blow on my garden,[m]
that its fragrance[n] may spread abroad.
Let my lover[o] come into his garden
and taste its choice fruits.[p]

Lover

5 I have come into my garden,[a] my sister, my bride;[b]
I have gathered my myrrh with my spice.
I have eaten my honeycomb and my honey;
I have drunk my wine and my milk.[c]

Friends

Eat, O friends, and drink;
drink your fill, O lovers.

Beloved

2I slept but my heart was awake.
Listen! My lover is knocking:
"Open to me, my sister, my darling,
my dove,[d] my flawless[e] one.[f]
My head is drenched with dew,
my hair with the dampness of the night."

11 [l]Isa 3:16; 4:4; 32:9–13; [m]Isa 54:5; 62:5; Jer 3:14

Ch. 4

1 [a]**Ge 24:65;** [b]**SS 1:15;** [c]Ge 37:25; Nu 32:1; SS 6:5; Jer 22:6; Mic 7:14
2 [d]SS 6:6
3 [e]SS 5:16; [f]**SS 1:5;** [g]SS 6:7
4 [h]**Ps 144:12;** [i]Eze 27:10
5 [j]SS 7:3; [k]**Pr 5:19;** [l]**SS 2:16**
6 [m]SS 2:17; [n]**SS 3:6**
7 [o]**SS 1:15;** [p]SS 5:2
8 [q]ver 9,12; SS 5:1; [r]**Dt 3:9;** [s]**1Ch 5:23**
9 [t]**ver 8;** [u]**Ge 41:42; Ps 73:6**
10 [v]SS 7:6; [w]**SS 1:2;** [x]**Jdg 9:13;** [y]ver 16; **Ps 45:8;** Isa 57:9
11 [z]**Ps 19:10;** SS 5:1; [a]Hos 14:6
12 [b]ver 16; SS 5:1; 6:2; Isa 5:7; [c]**ver 8;** [d]Pr 5:15–18
13 [e]SS 7:12; [f]SS 1:14
14 [g]**Ex 30:23;** [h]**SS 3:6;** [i]**Nu 24:6;** [j]SS 1:12
15 [k]Isa 27:2; 58:11; Jer 31:12; [l]Pr 5:18
16 [m]**ver 12;** [n]**ver 10;** [o]SS 7:13; [p]SS 2:3

Ch. 5

1 [a]**SS 4:12;** [b]**SS 4:8;** [c]**SS 4:11;** Isa 55:1; Joel 3:18
2 [d]**SS 1:15;** [e]SS 4:7; [f]SS 6:9

---

[a]10 Or *its inlaid interior a gift of love / from*
[a]4 The meaning of the Hebrew for this word is uncertain. [b]15 Or *I am* (spoken by the *Beloved*)

3I have taken off my robe—
must I put it on again?
I have washed my feet—
must I soil them again?
4My lover thrust his hand through the latch-opening;
my heart began to pound for him.
5I arose to open for my lover,
and my hands dripped with myrrh,[g]
my fingers with flowing myrrh,
on the handles of the lock.
6I opened for my lover,[h]
but my lover had left; he was gone.[i]
My heart sank at his departure.[a]
I looked[j] for him but did not find him.
I called him but he did not answer.
7The watchmen found me
as they made their rounds in the city.[k]
They beat me, they bruised me;
they took away my cloak,
those watchmen of the walls!
8O daughters of Jerusalem, I charge you[l]—
if you find my lover,[m]
what will you tell him?
Tell him I am faint with love.[n]

Friends

9How is your beloved better than others,
most beautiful of women?[o]
How is your beloved better than others,
that you charge us so?

Beloved

10My lover is radiant and ruddy,
outstanding among ten thousand.[p]
11His head is purest gold;
his hair is wavy
and black as a raven.
12His eyes are like doves[q]
by the water streams,
washed in milk,[r]
mounted like jewels.
13His cheeks[s] are like beds of spice[t]
yielding perfume.
His lips are like lilies[u]
dripping with myrrh.[v]
14His arms are rods of gold
set with chrysolite.
His body is like polished ivory
decorated with sapphires.[b][w]
15His legs are pillars of marble
set on bases of pure gold.
His appearance is like Lebanon,[x]
choice as its cedars.
16His mouth[y] is sweetness itself;
he is altogether lovely.
This is my lover,[z] this my friend,
O daughters of Jerusalem.[a]

5 [g]ver 13
6 [h]SS 6:1; [i]SS 6:2; [j]SS 3:1
7 [k]SS 3:3
8 [l]SS 2:7; [m]**SS 1:14**; [n]SS 2:5
9 [o]**SS 1:8**
10 [p]Ps 45:2
12 [q]**SS 1:15**; [r]Ge 49:12
13 [s]SS 1:10; [t]SS 6:2; [u]**SS 2:1**; [v]ver 5
14 [w]**Job 28:6**
15 [x]1Ki 4:33; SS 7:4
16 [y]SS 4:3; [z]SS 7:9; [a]SS 1:5

Ch. 6

1 [a]SS 5:6; [b]**SS 1:8**
2 [c]SS 5:6; [d]**SS 4:12**; [e]SS 5:13
3 [f]SS 7:10; [g]**SS 2:16**
4 [h]**Jos 12:24; 1Ki 15:33**; [i]Ps 48:2; 50:2; [j]**Nu 1:52**
5 [k]**SS 4:1**
6 [l]SS 4:2
7 [m]**Ge 24:65**; [n]SS 4:3
8 [o]Ps 45:9; [p]**Ge 22:24; Est 2:14**
9 [q]**SS 1:15**; [r]SS 5:2; [s]**SS 3:4**

Friends

6 Where has your lover[a] gone,
most beautiful of women?[b]
Which way did your lover turn,
that we may look for him with you?

Beloved

2My lover has gone[c] down to his garden,[d]
to the beds of spices,[e]
to browse in the gardens
and to gather lilies.
3I am my lover's and my lover is mine;[f]
he browses among the lilies.[g]

Lover

4You are beautiful, my darling, as Tirzah,[h]
lovely as Jerusalem,[i]
majestic as troops with banners.[j]
5Turn your eyes from me;
they overwhelm me.
Your hair is like a flock of goats
descending from Gilead.[k]
6Your teeth are like a flock of sheep
coming up from the washing.
Each has its twin,
not one of them is alone.[l]
7Your temples behind your veil[m]
are like the halves of a pomegranate.[n]
8Sixty queens[o] there may be,
and eighty concubines,[p]
and virgins beyond number;
9but my dove,[q] my perfect one,[r] is unique,
the only daughter of her mother,
the favourite of the one who bore her.[s]
The maidens saw her and called her blessed;
the queens and concubines praised her.

Friends

10Who is this that appears like the dawn,
fair as the moon, bright as the sun,
majestic as the stars in procession?

Lover

11I went down to the grove of nut trees
to look at the new growth in the valley,

---

[a]6 Or *heart had gone out to him when he spoke*
[b]14 Or *lapis lazuli*

to see if the vines had budded
or the pomegranates were in
bloom.[t]
12Before I realised it,
my desire set me among the royal
chariots of my people.[a]

Friends

13Come back, come back, O
Shulammite;
come back, come back, that we may
gaze on you!

Lover

Why would you gaze on the
Shulammite
as on the dance[u] of Mahanaim?

7 How beautiful your sandalled feet,
O prince's[a] daughter!
Your graceful legs are like jewels,
the work of a craftsman's hands.
2Your navel is a rounded goblet
that never lacks blended wine.
Your waist is a mound of wheat
encircled by lilies.
3Your breasts[b] are like two fawns,
twins of a gazelle.
4Your neck is like an ivory tower.[c]
Your eyes are the pools of Heshbon[d]
by the gate of Bath Rabbim.
Your nose is like the tower of
Lebanon[e]
looking towards Damascus.
5Your head crowns you like Mount
Carmel.[f]
Your hair is like royal tapestry;
the king is held captive by its
tresses.
6How beautiful[g] you are and how
pleasing,
O love, with your delights![h]
7Your stature is like that of the palm,
and your breasts[i] like clusters of
fruit.
8I said, "I will climb the palm tree;
I will take hold of its fruit."
May your breasts be like the clusters of
the vine,
the fragrance of your breath like
apples,[j]
9 and your mouth like the best wine.

Beloved

May the wine go straight to my lover,[k]
flowing gently over lips and teeth.[a]
10I belong to my lover,
and his desire[l] is for me.[m]
11Come, my lover, let us go to the
countryside,

11 [t]SS 7:12
13 [u]**Ex 15:20**

Ch. 7

1 [a]Ps 45:13
3 [b]SS 4:5
4 [c]**Ps 144:12**; [d]Nu 21:26; [e]**SS 5:15**
5 [f]Isa 35:2
6 [g]**SS 1:15**; [h]SS 4:10
7 [i]SS 4:5
8 [j]SS 2:5
9 [k]SS 5:16
10 [l]Ps 45:11; [m]SS 2:16; 6:3
12 [n]**SS 1:6**; [o]SS 2:15; [p]SS 2:13; [q]**SS 4:13**; [r]SS 6:11
13 [s]**Ge 30:14**; [t]SS 4:16

Ch. 8

2 [a]SS 3:4
3 [b]SS 2:6
4 [c]SS 2:7; **3:5**
5 [d]SS 3:6; [e]**SS 3:4**
6 [f]**SS 1:2**; [g]**Nu 5:14**

let us spend the night in the
villages.[b]
12Let us go early to the vineyards[n]
to see if the vines have budded,[o]
if their blossoms[p] have opened,
and if the pomegranates[q] are in
bloom[r]—
there I will give you my love.
13The mandrakes[s] send out their
fragrance,
and at our door is every delicacy,
both new and old,
that I have stored up for you, my
lover.[t]

8 If only you were to me like a
brother,
who was nursed at my mother's
breasts!
Then, if I found you outside,
I would kiss you,
and no-one would despise me.
2I would lead you
and bring you to my mother's
house[a]—
she who has taught me.
I would give you spiced wine to drink,
the nectar of my pomegranates.
3His left arm is under my head
and his right arm embraces me.[b]
4Daughters of Jerusalem, I charge you:
Do not arouse or awaken love
until it so desires.[c]

Friends

5Who is this coming up from the
desert[d]
leaning on her lover?

Beloved

Under the apple tree I roused you;
there your mother conceived[e] you,
there she who was in labour gave
you birth.
6Place me like a seal over your heart,
like a seal on your arm;
for love[f] is as strong as death,
its jealousy[a][g] unyielding as the
grave.[b]
It burns like blazing fire,
like a mighty flame.[c]
7Many waters cannot quench love;
rivers cannot wash it away.

---

[a]*12* Or *among the chariots of Amminadab;* or *among the chariots of the people of the prince*
[a]*9* Septuagint, Aquila, Vulgate and Syriac; Hebrew *lips of sleepers*
[b]*11* Or *henna bushes*
[a]*6* Or *ardour*
[b]*6* Hebrew *Sheol*
[c]*6* Or / *like the very flame of the* LORD

If one were to give
all the wealth of his house for love,
it[d] would be utterly scorned.[h]

Friends

8We have a young sister,
and her breasts are not yet grown.
What shall we do for our sister
for the day she is spoken for?
9If she is a wall,
we will build towers of silver on her.
If she is a door,
we will enclose her with panels of cedar.

Beloved

10I am a wall,
and my breasts are like towers.
Thus I have become in his eyes
like one bringing contentment.
11Solomon had a vineyard[i] in Baal Hamon;
he let out his vineyard to tenants.
Each was to bring for its fruit
a thousand shekels[e][j] of silver.
12But my own vineyard[k] is mine to give;
the thousand shekels are for you, O Solomon,
and two hundred[f] are for those who tend its fruit.

Lover

13You who dwell in the gardens
with friends in attendance,
let me hear your voice!

Beloved

14Come away, my lover,
and be like a gazelle[l]
or like a young stag[m]
on the spice-laden mountains.[n]

7 [h]Pr 6:35
11 [i]Ecc 2:4; [j]Isa 7:23
12 [k]SS 1:6
14 [l]Pr 5:19; [m]SS 2:9; [n]SS 2:8

d7 Or *he*
e*11* That is, about 25 pounds (about 11.5 kilograms); also in verse 12
f*12* That is, about 5 pounds (about 2.3 kilograms)

Isaiah

1 The vision[a] concerning Judah and
Jerusalem[b] that Isaiah son of Amoz
saw[c] during the reigns of Uzziah,[d]
Jotham,[e] Ahaz[f] and Hezekiah,[g] kings of
Judah.

A Rebellious Nation

2 Hear, O heavens! Listen, O earth![h]
For the LORD has spoken:[i]
"I reared children[j] and brought them up,
but they have rebelled[k] against me.
3 The ox knows[l] his master,
the donkey his owner's manger,[m]
but Israel does not know,[n]
my people do not understand.[o]"

4 Ah, sinful nation,
a people loaded with guilt,[p]
a brood of evildoers,[q]
children given to corruption![r]
They have forsaken[s] the LORD;
they have spurned the Holy One[t] of Israel
and turned their backs[u] on him.

5 Why should you be beaten[v] any more?
Why do you persist[w] in rebellion?[x]
Your whole head is injured,
your whole heart[y] afflicted.[z]
6 From the sole of your foot to the top of your head[a]
there is no soundness[b]—
only wounds and bruises[c]
and open sores,
not cleansed or bandaged[d]
or soothed with oil.[e]

7 Your country is desolate,[f]
your cities burned with fire;[g]
your fields are being stripped by foreigners[h]
right before you,
laid waste as when overthrown by strangers.[i]
8 The Daughter of Zion[j] is left[k]
like a shelter in a vineyard,
like a hut[l] in a field of melons,
like a city under siege.
9 Unless the LORD Almighty
had left us some survivors,[m]
we would have become like Sodom,
we would have been like Gomorrah.[n]

10 Hear the word of the LORD,[o]
you rulers of Sodom;[p]
listen to the law[q] of our God,
you people of Gomorrah![r]
11 "The multitude of your sacrifices—
what are they to me?" says the LORD.
"I have more than enough of burnt offerings,
of rams and the fat of fattened animals;[s]
I have no pleasure[t]
in the blood of bulls[u] and lambs and goats.[v]
12 When you come to appear before me,
who has asked this of you,[w]
this trampling of my courts?
13 Stop bringing meaningless offerings![x]
Your incense[y] is detestable[z] to me.
New Moons,[a] Sabbaths and convocations[b]—
I cannot bear your evil assemblies.
14 Your New Moon[c] festivals and your appointed feasts[d]
my soul hates.[e]
They have become a burden to me;[f]
I am weary[g] of bearing them.
15 When you spread out your hands[h] in prayer,
I will hide[i] my eyes from you;
even if you offer many prayers,
I will not listen.[j]
Your hands[k] are full of blood;[l]

Ch. 1

1 [a]1Sa 3:1; Isa 22:1,5; Ob 1; Na 1:1; [b]Isa 40:9; 44:26; [c]Isa 2:1; 13:1; [d]**2Ki 14:21; 2Ch 26:22;** [e]**1Ch 3:12;** [f]**2Ki 16:1;** [g]**1Ch 3:13**
2 [h]**Dt 4:26**; [i]Jdg 11:10; Jer 42:5; Mic 1:2; [j]Isa 23:4; 63:16; [k]ver 4, 23; Isa 24:5,20; 30:1,9; 46:8; 48:8; 57:4; 65:2; 66:24; Eze 24:3; Hag 1:12; Mal 1:6; 3:5
3 [l]Job 12:9; [m]**Ge 42:27**; [n]Jer 4:22; 5:4; 9:3,6; Hos 2:8; 4:1; [o]**Dt 32:28**; Isa 42:25; 48:8; Hos 4:6; 7:9
4 [p]Isa 5:18; [q]**ver 2**; Isa 9:17; 14:20; 31:2; Jer 23:14; [r]Ps 14:3; [s]**Dt 32:15; Ps 119:87**; [t]**2Ki 19:22**; Isa 5:19,24; 31:1; 37:23; 41:14; 43:14; 45:11; 47:4; Eze 39:7; [u]**Pr 30:9**; Isa 59:13
5 [v]Pr 20:30; [w]Jer 2:30; 5:3; 8:5; [x]**ver 2**; Isa 31:6; Jer 44:16–17; Heb 3:16; [y]La 2:11; 5:17; [z]Isa 30:26; 33:6,24; 58:8; Jer 30:17
6 [a]**Dt 28:35**; [b]Ps 38:3; [c]Isa 53:5; [d]**Ps 147:3**; Isa 30:26; Jer 8:22; 14:19; 30:17; La 2:13; Eze 34:4; [e]2Sa 14:2; Ps 23:5; 45:7; 104:15; Isa 61:3; Lk 10:34

7 [f]**Lev 26:34**; [g]**Lev 26:31**; **Dt 29:23**; [h]Lev 26:16; Jdg 6:3–6; Isa 62:8; Jer 5:17; [i]**2Ki 18:13**; **Ps 109:11**
8 [j]**Ps 9:14**; **Isa 10:32**; [k]Isa 30:17; 49:21; [l]**Job 27:18**
9 [m]**Ge 45:7**; **2Ki 21:14**; Isa 4:2; 6:13; 27:12; 28:5; 37:4, 31–32; 45:25; 56:8; Jer 23:3; Joel 2:32; [n]**Ge 19:24**; Ro 9:29*
10 [o]Isa 28:14; [p]**Ge 13:13**; **18:20**; Eze 16:49; Ro 9:29; Rev 11:8; [q]Isa 5:24; 8:20; 30:9; [r]Isa 13:19
11 [s]Ps 50:8; Am 6:4; [t]**Job 22:3**; [u]Isa 66:3; Jer 6:20; [v]1Sa 15:22; **Ps 40:6**; Mal 1:10; Heb 10:4
12 [w]Ex 23:17; Dt 31:11
13 [x]Pr 15:8; Isa 66:3; Hag 2:14; [y]Jer 7:9; 18:15; 44:8; [z]**1Ki 14:24**; Ps 115:8; Pr 28:9; Isa 41:24; Mal 2:11; [a]**Nu 10:10**; [b]1Ch 23:31
14 [c]**Ne 10:33**; [d]Ex 12:16; Lev 23:1–44; Nu 28:11–29:39; Dt 16:1–17; Isa 5:12; 29:1; Hos 2:11; [e]**Ps 11:5**; [f]**Job 7:12**; [g]Ps 69:3; Isa 7:13; 43:22,24; Jer 44:22; Mal 2:17; 3:14
15 [h]**Ex 9:29**; [i]**Dt 31:17**; Isa 57:17; 59:2; [j]**Dt 1:45**; **1Sa 8:18**; **Job 15:31**; **Jn 9:31**; [k]**Job 9:30**; [l]Isa 4:4; 59:3; Jer 2:34; Eze 7:23; Hos 4:2; Joel 3:21

16 wash[m] and make yourselves clean.
Take your evil deeds
out of my sight![n]
Stop doing wrong,[o]
17 learn to do right![p]
Seek justice,[q]
encourage the oppressed.[a r]
Defend the cause of the fatherless,[s]
plead the case of the widow.[t]

18"Come now, let us reason together,"[u]
says the LORD.
"Though your sins are like scarlet,
they shall be as white as snow;[v]
though they are red as crimson,
they shall be like wool.[w]
19If you are willing and obedient,[x]
you will eat the best from the land;[y]
20but if you resist and rebel,[z]
you will be devoured by the
sword."[a]
For the mouth of the LORD has
spoken.[b]

21See how the faithful city
has become a harlot![c]
She once was full of justice;
righteousness[d] used to dwell in
her—
but now murderers![e]
22Your silver has become dross,[f]
your choice wine is diluted with
water.
23Your rulers are rebels,[g]
companions of thieves;[h]
they all love bribes[i]
and chase after gifts.
They do not defend the cause of the
fatherless;
the widow's case does not come
before them.[j]
24Therefore the Lord, the LORD
Almighty,
the Mighty One[k] of Israel, declares:
"Ah, I will get relief from my foes
and avenge[l] myself on my
enemies.[m]
25I will turn my hand against you;[n]
I will thoroughly purge[o] away your
dross[p]
and remove all your impurities.[q]
26I will restore your judges as in days of
old,[r]
your counsellors as at the
beginning.
Afterwards you will be called[s]
the City of Righteousness,[t]
the Faithful City."[u]

27Zion will be redeemed with justice,
her penitent[v] ones with
righteousness.[w]

16 [m]**Ru 3:3**; Mt 27:24; Jas 4:8; [n]Nu 19:11,16; Isa 52:11; [o]Isa 55:7; Jer 25:5
17 [p]**Ps 34:14**; [q]**Ps 72:1**; Isa 11:4; 33:5; 56:1; 61:8; Am 5:14–15; Mic 6:8; Zep 2:3; [r]**Dt 14:29**; [s]ver 23; Job 22:9; Ps 82:3; 94:6; Isa 10:2; [t]**Ex 22:22**; Eze 18:31; 22:7; Lk 18:3; Jas 1:27
18 [u]**1Sa 2:25**; Isa 41:1; 43:9,26; [v]**Ps 51:7**; Rev 7:14; [w]Isa 55:7
19 [x]**Job 36:11**; **Isa 50:10**; [y]Dt 30:15–16; Ezr 9:12; Ps 34:10; Isa 30:23; 55:2; 58:14; 62:9; 65:13,21–22
20 [z]**1Sa 12:15**; [a]**Job 15:22**; Isa 3:25; 27:1; 65:12; 66:16; Jer 17:27; [b]Nu 23:19; Isa 21:17; 34:16; 40:5; 58:14; Jer 49:13; Mic 4:4; Zec 1:6; Rev 1:16
21 [c]Isa 57:3–9; Jer 2:20; 3:2,9; 13:27; Eze 23:3; Hos 2:1–13; [d]Isa 5:7; 46:13; 59:14; Am 6:12; [e]**Pr 6:17**
22 [f]**Ps 119:119**
23 [g]**ver 2**; [h]**Dt 19:14**; Mic 2:1–2; 6:12; [i]**Ex 23:8**; Am 5:12; [j]Isa 10:2; Jer 5:28; Eze 22:6–7; Mic 3:9; Hab 1:4
24 [k]**Ge 49:24**; [l]Isa 34:2,8; 35:4; 47:3; 59:17; 61:2; 63:4; Jer 51:6; Eze 5:13; [m]**Dt 32:43**; **Isa 10:3**
25 [n]Dt 28:63; [o]**Ps 78:38**; [p]**Ps 119:119**; [q]2Ch 29:15; Isa 48:10; Jer 6:29; 9:7; Eze 22:22; Mal 3:3
26 [r]Jer 33:7,11; Mic 4:8; [s]**Ge 32:28**; [t]Isa 32:16; 33:5; 46:13; 48:18; 61:11; 62:1; Jer 31:23; Zec 8:3; [u]Isa 4:3; 48:2; 52:1; 60:14; 62:2; 64:10; Da 9:24

28But rebels and sinners[x] will both be
broken,
and those who forsake[y] the LORD
will perish.[z]

29"You will be ashamed[a] because of the
sacred oaks[b]
in which you have delighted;
you will be disgraced because of the
gardens[c]
that you have chosen.
30You will be like an oak with fading
leaves,[d]
like a garden without water.
31The mighty man will become tinder
and his work a spark;
both will burn together,
with no-one to quench the fire."[e]

The Mountain of the LORD

2:1–4pp—Mic 4:1–3

2 This is what Isaiah son of Amoz
saw concerning Judah and Jeru-
salem:[a]

2In the last days[b]

the mountain[c] of the LORD's temple
will be established
as chief among the mountains;[d]
it will be raised[e] above the hills,
and all nations will stream to it.[f]

3Many peoples[g] will come and say,

"Come, let us go[h] up to the mountain[i]
of the LORD,
to the house of the God of Jacob.
He will teach us his ways,
so that we may walk in his paths."
The law[j] will go out from Zion,
the word of the LORD from
Jerusalem.[k]

27 [v]Isa 30:15; 31:6; 59:20; Eze 18:30; [w]Isa 35:10; 41:14; 43:1; 52:3; 62:12; 63:4; Hos 2:19
28 [x]Isa 33:14; 43:27; 48:8; 50:1; 59:2; Jer 4:18; [y]**Dt 32:15**; [z]Ps 9:5; Isa 24:20; 66:24; Jer 16:4; 42:22; 44:12; 2Th 1:8–9
29 [a]Ps 97:7; Isa 42:17; 44:9,11; 45:16; Jer 10:14; [b]Isa 57:5; Eze 6:13; Hos 4:13; [c]Isa 65:3; 66:17 *30* [d]**Ps 1:3**
31 [e]Isa 4:4; 5:24; 9:18–19; 10:17; 24:6; 26:11; 30:27,33; 33:14; 34:10; 66:15–16,24; Jer 5:14; 7:20; 21:12; Ob 18; Mal 3:2; 4:1; **Mt 25:41**

Ch. 2

1 [a]Isa 1:1
2 [b]Ac 2:17; Heb 1:2; [c]Isa 11:9; 24:23; 25:6,10; 27:13; 56:7; 57:13; 65:25; 66:20; Jer 31:23; Da 11:45; Joel 3:17; Mic 4:7; [d]Isa 65:9; [e]Zec 14:10; [f]**Ps 102:15**; Jer 16:19
3 [g]Isa 45:23; 49:1; 60:3–6,14; 66:18; Jer 3:17; Joel 3:2; Zep 3:8; Zec 14:2; [h]Isa 45:14; 49:12,23; 55:5; [i]**Dt 33:19**; **Ps 137:5**; [j]**Isa 1:10**; 33:22; 51:4,7; [k]Lk 24:47; **Jn 4:22**

[a]*17* Or / *rebuke the oppressor*

4He will judge[l] between the nations
and will settle disputes[m] for many peoples.
They will beat their swords into ploughshares
and their spears into pruning hooks.[n]
Nation will not take up sword against nation,[o]
nor will they train for war any more.

5Come, O house of Jacob,[p]
let us walk in the light[q] of the LORD.

The Day of the LORD

6You have abandoned[r] your people,
the house of Jacob.[s]
They are full of superstitions from the East;
they practise divination[t] like the Philistines[u]
and clasp hands[v] with pagans.[w]
7Their land is full of silver and gold;[x]
there is no end to their treasures.[y]
Their land is full of horses;[z]
there is no end to the chariots.[a]
8Their land is full of idols;[b]
they bow down[c] to the work of their hands,[d]
to what their fingers[e] have made.
9So man will be brought low[f]
and mankind humbled[g]—
do not forgive them.[a][h]

10Go into the rocks,
hide[i] in the ground
from dread of the LORD
and the splendour of his majesty![j]
11The eyes of the arrogant[k] man will be humbled[l]
and the pride[m] of men brought low;[n]
the LORD alone will be exalted[o] in that day.[p]

12The LORD Almighty has a day[q] in store
for all the proud[r] and lofty,[s]
for all that is exalted[t]
(and they will be humbled),[u]
13for all the cedars of Lebanon,[v] tall and lofty,[w]
and all the oaks of Bashan,[x]
14for all the towering mountains
and all the high hills,[y]
15for every lofty tower[z]
and every fortified wall,[a]
16for every trading ship[b][b]
and every stately vessel.
17The arrogance of man will be brought low[c]
and the pride of men humbled;[d]
the LORD alone will be exalted in that day,[e]
18and the idols[f] will totally disappear.[g]

19Men will flee to caves[h] in the rocks
and to holes in the ground[i]
from the dread[j] of the LORD
and the splendour of his majesty,[k]
when he rises to shake the earth.[l]
20In that day[m] men will throw away
to the rodents and bats[n]
their idols of silver and idols of gold,[o]
which they made to worship.[p]
21They will flee to caverns in the rocks[q]
and to the overhanging crags
from dread of the LORD
and the splendour of his majesty,[r]
when he rises[s] to shake the earth.[t]

22Stop trusting in man,[u]
who has but a breath[v] in his nostrils.
Of what account is he?[w]

Judgment on Jerusalem and Judah

3 See now, the Lord,
the LORD Almighty,
is about to take from Jerusalem and Judah
both supply and support:[a]
all supplies of food[b] and all supplies of water,[c]
2 the hero and warrior,[d]
the judge and prophet,
the soothsayer[e] and elder,[f]
3the captain of fifty[g] and man of rank,[h]
the counsellor, skilled craftsman[i]
and clever enchanter.[j]

4I will make boys their officials;
mere children will govern them.[k]
5People will oppress each other—
man against man, neighbour against neighbour.[l]
The young will rise up against the old,
the base against the honourable.

4 [l]Ps 7:6; 9:19; 96:13; 98:9; Isa 1:27; 3:13; 9:7; 42:4; 51:4; Joel 3:14; [m]Ge 49:10; [n]Joel 3:10; [o]Ps 46:9; Isa 9:5; 11:6–9; 32:18; 57:19; 65:25; Jer 30:10; Da 11:45; Hos 2:18; Mic 4:3; Zec 9:10
5 [p]Isa 58:1; [q]Isa 60:1,19–20; 1Jn 1:5,7
6 [r]Dt 31:17; [s]Jer 12:7; [t]Dt 18:10; Isa 44:25; [u]2Ki 1:2; 2Ch 26:6; [v]Pr 6:1; [w]2Ki 16:7; Mic 5:12
7 [x]Dt 17:17; [y]Ps 17:14; [z]Dt 17:16; [a]Ge 41:43; Isa 31:1; Mic 5:10
8 [b]Isa 10:9–11; Rev 9:20; [c]Isa 44:17; [d]2Ch 32:19; Ps 135:15; Mic 5:13; [e]Isa 17:8
9 [f]Ps 62:9; [g]ver 11,17; Isa 5:15; 13:11; [h]Ne 4:5
10 [i]ver 19; Na 3:11; [j]Ps 145:12; 2Th 1:9; Rev 6:15–16
11 [k]Ne 9:29; Hab 2:5; [l]ver 9; [m]Isa 5:15; 10:12; 37:23; Eze 31:10; [n]Job 40:11; [o]Ps 46:10; [p]ver 17,20; Isa 3:7,18; 4:1–2; 5:30; 7:18; 17:4,7; 24:21; 25:9; 26:1; 27:1
12 [q]Isa 13:6,9; 22:5,8,12; 34:8; 61:2; Jer 30:7; La 1:12; Eze 7:7; 30:3; Joel 1:15; 2:11; Am 5:18; Zep 1:14; [r]Ps 59:12; [s]2Sa 22:28; [t]Ps 76:12; Isa 24:4,21; 60:11; Mal 4:1; [u]Job 40:11
13 [v]Jdg 9:15; Isa 10:34; 29:17; Eze 27:5; [w]Isa 10:33; [x]Ps 22:12; Zec 11:2
14 [y]Isa 30:25; 40:4
15 [z]Isa 30:25; 32:14; 33:18; [a]Isa 25:2,12; Zep 1:16
16 [b]*fn* Ge 10:4; 1Ki 9:26
17 [c]2Sa 22:28; Job 40:11; [d]ver 9; [e]ver 11
18 [f]1Sa 5:2; Eze 36:25; [g]Dt 9:21; Isa 21:9; Jer 10:11; Mic 5:13
19 [h]Jdg 6:2; Isa 7:19; [i]Jdg 6:2; Job 30:6; Lk 23:30; Rev 6:15; [j]Dt 2:25; [k]Ps 145:12; [l]ver 21; Job 9:6; Isa 14:16; Heb 12:26
20 [m]ver 11; [n]Lev 11:19; [o]Job 22:24; Eze 36:25; Rev 9:20; [p]Eze 7:19–20; 14:6
21 [q]Ex 33:22; [r]Ps 145:12; [s]Isa 33:10; [t]ver 19
22 [u]Ps 118:6,8; 146:3; Isa 51:12; Jer 17:5; [v]Ge 2:7; Ps 144:4; [w]Job 12:19; Ps 8:4; 18:42; 144:3; Isa 17:13; 29:5; 40:15; Jas 4:14

Ch. 3
1 [a]Ps 18:18; [b]Lev 26:26; Am 4:6; [c]Isa 5:13; 65:13; Eze 4:16 2 [d]Eze 17:13; [e]Dt 18:10; [f]Isa 9:14–15
3 [g]2Ki 1:9; [h]Job 22:8; [i]2Ki 24:14; [j]Ecc 10:11; Jer 8:17
4 [k]ver 12; Ecc 10:16 *fn*
5 [l]Ps 28:3; Isa 9:19; Jer 9:8; Mic 7:2,6

[a]9 Or *not raise them up*
[b]16 Hebrew *every ship of Tarshish*

6 A man will seize one of his brothers
at his father's home, and say,
"You have a cloak, you be our leader;
take charge of this heap of ruins!"
7 But in that day[m] he will cry out,
"I have no remedy.[n]
I have no food[o] or clothing in my
house;
do not make me the leader of the
people."[p]

8 Jerusalem staggers,
Judah is falling;[q]
their words[r] and deeds[s] are against the
LORD,
defying[t] his glorious presence.
9 The look on their faces testifies[u]
against them;
they parade their sin like Sodom;[v]
they do not hide it.
Woe to them!
They have brought disaster[w] upon
themselves.

10 Tell the righteous it will be well[x] with
them,
for they will enjoy the fruit of their
deeds.[y]
11 Woe to the wicked![z] Disaster[a] is upon
them!
They will be paid back[b] for what
their hands have done.[c]

12 Youths[d] oppress my people,
women rule over them.
O my people, your guides lead you
astray;[e]
they turn you from the path.

13 The LORD takes his place in court;[f]
he rises to judge[g] the people.
14 The LORD enters into judgment[h]
against the elders and leaders of his
people:
"It is you who have ruined my
vineyard;
the plunder[i] from the poor[j] is in
your houses.
15 What do you mean by crushing my
people[k]
and grinding[l] the faces of the
poor?"[m]
declares the Lord, the LORD
Almighty.[n]

16 The LORD says,
"The women of Zion[o] are haughty,
walking along with outstretched
necks,[p]
flirting with their eyes,
tripping along with mincing steps,
with ornaments jingling on their
ankles.
17 Therefore the LORD will bring sores on
the heads of the women of Zion;
the LORD will make their scalps
bald."[q]

18 In that day[r] the Lord will snatch
away their finery: the bangles and head-
bands and crescent necklaces,[s] 19 the ear-
rings and bracelets[t] and veils,[u] 20 the
head-dresses[v] and ankle chains and
sashes, the perfume bottles and
charms, 21 the signet rings and nose
rings,[w] 22 the fine robes and the capes
and cloaks,[x] the purses 23 and mirrors,
and the linen garments[y] and tiaras[z] and
shawls.

24 Instead of fragrance[a] there will be a
stench;[b]
instead of a sash,[c] a rope;
instead of well-dressed hair,
baldness;[d]
instead of fine clothing, sackcloth;[e]
instead of beauty,[f] branding.[g]
25 Your men will fall by the sword,[h]
your warriors in battle.[i]
26 The gates[j] of Zion will lament and
mourn;[k]
destitute,[l] she will sit on the
ground.[m]

4

In that day[a] seven women
will take hold of one man[b]
and say, "We will eat our own food[c]
and provide our own clothes;
only let us be called by your name.
Take away our disgrace!"[d]

The Branch of the LORD

2 In that day[e] the Branch of the LORD[f]
will be beautiful[g] and glorious, and the
fruit[h] of the land will be the pride and
glory[i] of the survivors[j] in Israel. 3 Those
who are left in Zion,[k] who remain[l] in
Jerusalem, will be called holy,[m] all who
are recorded[n] among the living in Jeru-
salem. 4 The Lord will wash away the
filth[o] of the women of Zion;[p] he will
cleanse[q] the bloodstains[r] from Jeru-
salem by a spirit[a] of judgment[s] and a
spirit[a] of fire.[t] 5 Then the LORD will

7 [m]Isa 2:11; [n]Jer 30:12; Eze 34:4; Hos 5:13; [o]Joel 1:16; [p]Isa 24:2
8 [q]Isa 1:7; [r]Isa 9:15,17; 28:15; 30:9; 59:3,13; [s]2Ch 33:6; [t]Job 1:11; Ps 73:9,11; Isa 65:7
9 [u]Nu 32:23; Isa 59:12; Jer 14:7; Hos 5:5; [v]Ge 13:13; [w]2Ch 34:24; Pr 8:36; Ro 6:23
10 [x]Dt 5:33; 12:28; 28:1–14; Ps 37:17; Jer 22:15; [y]Ge 15:1; Ps 128:2
11 [z]Job 9:13; Isa 57:20; [a]Dt 28:15–68; [b]2Ch 6:23; [c]Jer 21:14; La 5:16; Eze 24:14
12 [d]ver 4; [e]Isa 9:16; 19:14; 28:7; 29:9; Jer 23:13; 25:16; Mic 3:5
13 [f]Job 10:2; [g]Ps 82:1; Isa 2:4
14 [h]1Sa 12:7; Job 22:4; [i]Job 24:9; Jas 2:6; [j]Isa 11:4; 25:4
15 [k]Ps 94:5; [l]Job 24:14; [m]Isa 10:6; 11:4; 26:6; 29:19; 32:6; 51:23; [n]Isa 5:7
16 [o]SS 3:11; [p]Job 15:25
17 [q]ver 24; Eze 27:31; Am 8:10
18 [r]Isa 2:11; [s]Ge 41:42; Jdg 8:21
19 [t]Ge 24:47; [u]Eze 16:11–12
20 [v]Ex 39:28; Eze 24:17,23; 44:18
21 [w]Ge 24:22
22 [x]Ru 3:15
23 [y]Eze 16:10; 23:26; [z]Ex 29:6; SS 3:11; Isa 61:3; 62:3
24 [a]Est 2:12; [b]Isa 4:4; [c]Pr 31:24; [d]ver 17; Lev 13:40; Job 1:20; [e]Ge 37:34; Job 16:15; Isa 20:2; Jer 4:8; La 2:10; Eze 27:30–31; Jnh 3:5–8; [f]1Pe 3:3; [g]2Sa 10:4; Isa 20:4
25 [h]Isa 1:20; [i]Jer 15:8
26 [j]Isa 14:31; 24:12; 45:2; [k]Ps 137:1; Isa 24:4,7; 29:2; 33:9; Jer 4:28; 14:2; [l]Lev 26:31; [m]Job 2:13; La 4:5

Ch. 4
1 [a]Isa 2:11; [b]Isa 13:12; 32:9; [c]2Th 3:12; [d]Ge 30:23
2 [e]Isa 2:11; [f]Isa 11:1–5; 52:13; 53:2; Jer 23:5–6; 33:15–16; Eze 17:22; Zec 3:8; 6:12; [g]Isa 33:17; 53:2; [h]Ps 72:16; Eze 36:8; [i]Isa 60:15; Eze 34:29; [j]Isa 1:9
3 [k]Isa 1:26; [l]Isa 1:9; Ro 11:5; [m]Ex 19:6; Isa 26:2; 45:25; 52:1; 60:21; Joel 3:17; Ob 17; Zep 3:13; [n]Ps 56:8; 87:6; Lk 10:20
4 [o]Isa 3:24; [p]SS 3:11; [q]Ps 51:2; [r]Isa 1:15; [s]Isa 28:6; [t]Isa 1:31; 30:30; Zec 13:9; Mt 3:11; Lk 3:17

[a]4 Or *the Spirit*

create[u] over all of Mount Zion[v] and over
those who assemble there a cloud of
smoke by day and a glow of flaming fire
by night;[w] over all the glory[x] will be a
canopy.[y] 6It will be a shelter[z] and shade
from the heat of the day, and a refuge[a]
and hiding-place from the storm[b] and
rain.

The Song of the Vineyard

5 I will sing for the one I love
a song about his vineyard:[a]
My loved one had a vineyard
on a fertile hillside.
2He dug it up and cleared it of stones
and planted it with the choicest
vines.[b]
He built a watchtower[c] in it
and cut out a winepress[d] as well.
Then he looked for a crop of good
grapes,
but it yielded only bad fruit.[e]

3"Now you dwellers in Jerusalem and
men of Judah,
judge between me and my
vineyard.[f]
4What more could have been done for
my vineyard
than I have done for it?[g]
When I looked for good grapes,
why did it yield only bad?[h]
5Now I will tell you
what I am going to do to my
vineyard:
I will take away its hedge,
and it will be destroyed;[i]
I will break down its wall,[j]
and it will be trampled.[k]
6I will make it a wasteland,[l]
neither pruned nor cultivated,
and briers and thorns[m] will grow
there.
I will command the clouds
not to rain[n] on it."

7The vineyard[o] of the LORD Almighty
is the house of Israel,
and the men of Judah
are the garden of his delight.
And he looked for justice,[p] but saw
bloodshed;
for righteousness,[q] but heard cries
of distress.[r]

Woes and Judgments

8Woe[s] to you who add house to house
and join field to field[t]
till no space is left
and you live alone in the land.

5 [u]Isa 41:20; 65:18; [v]Rev 14:1; [w]**Ex 13:21**; [x]Isa 35:2; 58:8; 60:1; [y]**Ps 18:11**; Rev 7:15
6 [z]Lev 23:34–43; Ps 27:5; Isa 8:14; 25:4; Eze 11:16; [a]Isa 14:32; 25:4; 30:2; 57:13; [b]**Ps 55:8**

Ch. 5

1 [a]Ps 80:8–9; Isa 27:2; Jn 15:1
2 [b]**Ex 15:17**; Isa 16:8; [c]1Sa 2:9; Isa 27:3; 31:5; 49:8; Mt 21:33; [d]**Job 24:11**; [e]Mt 21:19; Mk 11:13; Lk 13:6
3 [f]Mt 21:40
4 [g]**2Ch 36:15**; Jer 2:5–7; Mic 6:3–4; Mt 23:37; [h]Jer 2:21; 24:2; 29:17
5 [i]2Ch 36:21; Isa 6:12; 27:10; [j]**Ps 80:12; Isa 22:5**; [k]Isa 10:6; 26:6; 28:3,18; 41:25; 63:3; Jer 12:10; 34:22; La 1:15; Hos 2:12; Mic 7:10; Mal 4:3; **Lk 21:24**
6 [l]**Ge 6:13; Lev 26:32**; Isa 6:13; 49:17,19; 51:3; Joel 1:10; [m]ver 10,17; **2Sa 23:6**; Isa 7:23–24; 32:13; 34:13; 55:13; Eze 28:24; Hos 2:12; Heb 6:8; [n]**Dt 28:24; 2Sa 1:21**; Am 4:7
7 [o]Ps 80:8; Isa 17:10; 18:5; 37:30; [p]Isa 10:2; 29:21; 32:7; 59:15; 61:8; Eze 9:9; 22:29; [q]**Isa 1:21**; [r]**Ps 12:5**
8 [s]ver 11,18,20; Isa 6:5; 10:1; 24:16; Jer 22:13; [t]Job 20:19; Mic 2:2; Hab 2:9–12
9 [u]Jer 44:11; [v]Isa 22:14; [w]Isa 6:11–12; Mt 23:38
10 [x]**ver 6**; Lev 26:26; **Dt 28:38**; Zec 8:10

9The LORD Almighty[u] has declared in
my hearing:[v]

"Surely the great houses will become
desolate,[w]
the fine mansions left without
occupants.
10A ten-acre[a] vineyard will produce only
a bath[b] of wine,
a homer[c] of seed only an ephah[d] of
grain."[x]

11Woe[y] to those who rise early in the
morning
to run after their drinks,
who stay up late at night
till they are inflamed with wine.[z]
12They have harps and lyres at their
banquets,
tambourines[a] and flutes[b] and wine,
but they have no regard[c] for the deeds
of the LORD,
no respect for the work of his
hands.[d]
13Therefore my people will go into exile[e]
for lack of understanding;[f]
their men of rank[g] will die of hunger
and their masses will be parched
with thirst.[h]
14Therefore the grave[e] [i] enlarges its
appetite
and opens its mouth[j] without limit;
into it will descend their nobles and
masses
with all their brawlers and
revellers.[k]
15So man will be brought low[l]
and mankind humbled,[m]
the eyes of the arrogant[n] humbled.
16But the LORD Almighty will be exalted[o]
by his justice,[p]
and the holy God will show himself
holy[q] by his righteousness.
17Then sheep will graze as in their own
pasture;[r]
lambs will feed[f] among the ruins of
the rich.

11 [y]**ver 8**; [z]**1Sa 25:36**; **Pr 23:29–30**
12 [a]Ps 68:25; Isa 24:8; [b]**Job 21:12**; [c]**1Sa 12:24**; [d]Ps 28:5; Eze 26:13
13 [e]Isa 49:21; [f]**Pr 10:21**; **Isa 1:3**; [g]**Job 22:8**; [h]**Isa 3:1**
14 [i]**Pr 30:16**; [j]**Nu 16:30**; [k]Isa 22:2,13; 23:7; 24:8
15 [l]Isa 10:33; [m]**Isa 2:9**; [n]**Isa 2:11**
16 [o]Ps 97:9; Isa 33:10; [p]Isa 28:17; 30:18; 33:5; 61:8; [q]**Lev 10:3**; Isa 29:23; Eze 36:23
17 [r]Isa 7:25; 17:2; 32:14; Zep 2:6,14

[a]*10* Hebrew *ten-yoke*, that is, the land ploughed by 10 yoke of oxen in one day
[b]*10* That is, probably about 5 gallons (about 22 litres)
[c]*10* That is, probably about 6 bushels (about 220 litres)
[d]*10* That is, probably about 3/5 bushel (about 22 litres) [e]*14* Hebrew *Sheol*
[f]*17* Septuagint; Hebrew / *strangers will eat*

18Woe[s] to those who draw sin along
with cords[t] of deceit,
and wickedness[u] as with cart ropes,
19to those who say, "Let God hurry,
let him hasten[v] his work
so that we may see it.
Let it approach,
let the plan of the Holy One[w] of
Israel come,
so that we may know it."[x]

20Woe[y] to those who call evil good[z]
and good evil,[a]
who put darkness for light
and light for darkness,[b]
who put bitter for sweet
and sweet for bitter.[c]

21Woe to those who are wise in their
own eyes[d]
and clever in their own sight.

22Woe to those who are heroes at
drinking wine[e]
and champions at mixing drinks,[f]
23who acquit the guilty for a bribe,[g]
but deny justice[h] to the innocent.[i]
24Therefore, as tongues of fire[j] lick up
straw[k]
and as dry grass sinks down in the
flames,
so their roots will decay[l]
and their flowers blow away like
dust;[m]
for they have rejected the law of the
LORD Almighty
and spurned the word[n] of the Holy
One[o] of Israel.
25Therefore the LORD's anger[p] burns
against his people;
his hand is raised and he strikes
them down.
The mountains shake,[q]
and the dead bodies[r] are like refuse[s]
in the streets.[t]

Yet for all this, his anger is not turned
away,[u]
his hand is still upraised.[v]

26He lifts up a banner[w] for the distant
nations,
he whistles[x] for those at the ends of
the earth.[y]
Here they come,
swiftly and speedily!
27Not one of them grows tired[z] or
stumbles,
not one slumbers or sleeps;
not a belt[a] is loosened at the waist,[b]
not a sandal thong is broken.[c]
28Their arrows are sharp,[d]

18 [s]**ver 8**; [t]Hos 11:4; [u]Isa 59:4–8; Jer 23:14
19 [v]Isa 60:22; [w]**Isa 1:4**; 29:23; 30:11–12; [x]Jer 17:15; Eze 12:22; 2Pe 3:4
20 [y]**ver 8**; [z]**Ge 18:25**; **1Ki 22:8**; [a]**Ps 94:21**; [b]**Job 24:13**; Mt 6:22–23; Lk 11:34–35; [c]Am 5:7
21 [d]**Pr 3:7**; Isa 47:10; Ro 12:16; 1Co 3:18–20
22 [e]**1Sa 25:36**; **Pr 23:20**; **Isa 22:13**; [f]Pr 31:4; Isa 65:11; Jer 7:18
23 [g]**Ex 23:8**; **Eze 22:12**; [h]ver 7; **Isa 1:17**; 10:2; 29:21; 59:4, 13–15; [i]**Ps 94:21**; Am 5:12; Jas 5:6
24 [j]**Isa 1:31**; [k]Isa 47:14; Na 1:10; [l]**2Ki 19:30**; **Job 18:16**; [m]**Job 24:24**; Isa 40:8; [n]Ps 107:11; Isa 8:6; 30:9,12; [o]Job 6:10; Isa 1:4; 10:20; 12:6
25 [p]**2Ki 22:13**; **Job 40:11**; Isa 10:17; 26:11; 31:9; 66:15; **Jer 6:12**; [q]**Ex 19:18**; [r]**Ps 110:6**; [s]**2Ki 9:37**; [t]**2Sa 22:43**; [u]Jer 4:8; Da 9:16; [v]Isa 9:12,17, 21; 10:4
26 [w]**Ps 20:5**; [x]Isa 7:18; Zec 10:8; [y]Dt 28:49; Isa 13:5; 18:3
27 [z]Isa 14:31; 40:29–31; [a]Isa 22:21; Eze 23:15; [b]**Job 12:18**; [c]Joel 2:7–8
28 [d]**Job 39:23**; Ps 45:5; [e]**Ps 7:12**; [f]Eze 26:11; [g]**2Ki 2:1**; **Job 1:19**
29 [h]2Ki 17:25; Jer 51:38; Zep 3:3; Zec 11:3; [i]Isa 10:6; 49:24–25; [j]Isa 42:22; Mic 5:8

all their bows[e] are strung;
their horses' hoofs[f] seem like flint,
their chariot wheels like a
whirlwind.[g]
29Their roar is like that of the lion,[h]
they roar like young lions;
they growl as they seize[i] their prey
and carry it off with no-one to
rescue.[j]
30In that day[k] they will roar over it
like the roaring of the sea.[l]
And if one looks at the land,
he will see darkness[m] and distress;[n]
even the light will be darkened[o] by
the clouds.

Isaiah's Commission

6 In the year that King Uzziah[a] died,[b]
I saw the Lord[c] seated on a throne,[d]
high and exalted,[e] and the train of his
robe[f] filled the temple. 2Above him were
seraphs,[g] each with six wings: With two
wings they covered their faces, with
two they covered their feet,[h] and with
two they were flying. 3And they were
calling to one another:

"Holy, holy,[i] holy is the LORD
Almighty;[j]
the whole earth[k] is full of his glory."[l]

4At the sound of their voices the door-
posts and thresholds shook and the
temple was filled with smoke.[m]
5"Woe[n] to me!" I cried. "I am ruined![o]
For I am a man of unclean lips,[p q] and I
live among a people of unclean lips,[r]
and my eyes have seen[s] the King,[t] the
LORD Almighty."[u]
6Then one of the seraphs flew to me
with a live coal[v] in his hand, which he
had taken with tongs from the altar.
7With it he touched my mouth and said,
"See, this has touched your lips;[w] your
guilt is taken away and your sin atoned
for.[x]"

30 [k]**Isa 2:11**; [l]**Ps 93:3**; Jer 50:42; Lk 21:25; [m]**1Sa 2:9**; **Job 21:30**; Ps 18:28; 44:19; **82:5**; [n]**Jdg 6:2**; Isa 22:5; 33:2; Jer 4:23–28; [o]Isa 13:10; 50:3; Joel 2:10

Ch. 6

1 [a]**2Ch 26:22–23**; [b]**2Ki 15:7**; [c]**Ex 24:10**; **Nu 12:8**; Jn 12:41; [d]**1Ki 22:19**; **Ps 9:4**; **123:1**; **Rev 4:2**; [e]Isa 52:13; 53:12; [f]Rev 1:13
2 [g]Eze 1:5; 10:15; Rev 4:8; [h]Eze 1:11
3 [i]**Ex 15:11**; [j]Ps 89:8; [k]Isa 11:9; 54:5; Mal 1:11; [l]**Ex 16:7**; Nu 14:21; Ps 72:19; Rev 4:8
4 [m]**Ex 19:18**; **40:34**; Eze 43:5; 44:4; Rev 15:8
5 [n]**Isa 5:8**; [o]**Nu 17:12**; **Dt 5:26**; [p]Lk 5:8; [q]Ex 6:12; [r]Isa 59:3; Jer 9:3–8; [s]**Ex 24:10**; [t]Ps 45:3; Isa 24:23; 32:1; 33:17; Jer 51:57; [u]**Job 42:5**
6 [v]**Lev 10:1**; Eze 10:2
7 [w]Jer 1:9; Da 10:16; [x]**Lev 26:41**; Isa 45:25; Da 12:3; 1Jn 1:7

8Then I heard the voice[y] of the Lord
saying, "Whom shall I send?[z] And who
will go for us?[a]"
And I said, "Here am I.[b] Send me!"
9He said, "Go[c] and tell this people:

"'Be ever hearing, but never
understanding;
be ever seeing, but never
perceiving.'[d]
10Make the heart of this people
calloused;[e]
make their ears dull
and close their eyes.[a][f]
Otherwise they might see with their
eyes,
hear with their ears,[g]
understand with their hearts,
and turn and be healed."[h]

11Then I said, "For how long, O
Lord?"[i]
And he answered:

"Until the cities lie ruined[j]
and without inhabitant,
until the houses are left deserted[k]
and the fields ruined and ravaged,[l]
12until the LORD has sent everyone far
away[m]
and the land is utterly forsaken.[n]
13And though a tenth remains[o] in the
land,
it will again be laid waste.[p]
But as the terebinth and oak
leave stumps[q] when they are cut
down,
so the holy[r] seed will be the stump
in the land."[s]

The Sign of Immanuel

7 When Ahaz[a] son of Jotham, the
son of Uzziah, was king of Judah,
King Rezin[b] of Aram[c] and Pekah[d] son of
Remaliah[e] king of Israel marched up to
fight against Jerusalem, but they could
not overpower it.
2Now the house of David[f] was told,
"Aram has allied itself with[a] Ephraim[g]";
so the hearts of Ahaz and his people
were shaken,[h] as the trees of the forest
are shaken by the wind.
3Then the LORD said to Isaiah, "Go
out, you and your son Shear-Jashub,[b][i]
to meet Ahaz at the end of the aqueduct
of the Upper Pool, on the road to the
Washerman's Field.[j] 4Say to him, 'Be
careful, keep calm[k] and don't be afraid.[l]
Do not lose heart[m] because of these
two smouldering stubs[n] of firewood—
because of the fierce anger[o] of Rezin and
Aram and of the son of Remaliah.[p]
5Aram, Ephraim and Remaliah's[q] son
have plotted[r] your ruin, saying, 6"Let us
invade Judah; let us tear it apart and
divide it among ourselves, and make
the son of Tabeel king over it." 7Yet this
is what the Sovereign LORD says:[s]

"'It will not take place,
it will not happen,[t]
8for the head of Aram is Damascus,[u]
and the head of Damascus is only
Rezin.[v]
Within sixty-five years
Ephraim will be too shattered[w] to be
a people.
9The head of Ephraim is Samaria,[x]
and the head of Samaria is only
Remaliah's son.
If you do not stand[y] firm in your faith,[z]
you will not stand at all.'"[a]

10Again the LORD spoke to Ahaz,
11"Ask the LORD your God for a sign,[b]
whether in the deepest depths or in the
highest heights."[c]
12But Ahaz said, "I will not ask; I will
not put the LORD to the test."[d]
13Then Isaiah said, "Hear now, you
house of David![e] Is it not enough[f] to try
the patience of men? Will you try the
patience[g] of my God[h] also? 14Therefore
the LORD himself will give you[c] a sign:[i]
The virgin[j] will be with child and will
give birth to a son,[k] and[d] will call him
Immanuel.[e][l] 15He will eat curds[m] and
honey[n] when he knows enough to reject
the wrong and choose the right. 16But
before the boy knows[o] enough to reject
the wrong and choose the right,[p] the
land of the two kings you dread will be
laid waste.[q] 17The LORD will bring on
you and on your people and on the
house of your father a time unlike any
since Ephraim broke away[r] from
Judah—he will bring the king of
Assyria.[s]"

8 [y]**Job 40:9;** Ac 9:4; [z]Jer 26:12,15; [a]**Ge 1:26;** [b]**Ge 22:1; Ex 3:4**
9 [c]Eze 3:11; Am 7:15; Mt 28:19; [d]Jer 5:21; **Mt 13:15***; Lk 8:10*
10 [e]**Ex 4:21;** Dt 32:15; Ps 119:70; [f]Isa 29:9; 42:18–20; 43:8; 44:18; [g]**Dt 29:4;** Eze 12:2; Mk 8:18; [h]**Dt 32:39;** Mt 13:13–15; Mk 4:12*; Jn 12:40*; Ac 28:26–27*
11 [i]Ps 79:5; [j]**Lev 26:31; Jer 4:13;** [k]**Lev 26:43;** Isa 24:10; [l]Ps 79:1; **109:11;** Jer 35:17
12 [m]**Dt 28:64;** [n]**Isa 5:5,9;** 60:15; 62:4; Jer 4:29; 30:17
13 [o]**Isa 1:9;** 10:22; [p]**Isa 5:6;** [q]**Job 14:8;** [r]**Lev 27:30; Dt 14:2;** [s]**Job 14:7**

Ch. 7

1 [a]**1Ch 3:13;** [b]**ver 8; 2Ki 15:37;** [c]2Ch 28:5; [d]**2Ki 15:25;** [e]ver 5, 9; Isa 8:6
2 [f]ver 13; **2Sa 7:11;** Isa 16:5; 22:22; Jer 21:12; Am 9:11; [g]Isa 9:9; Hos 5:3; [h]Isa 6:4; Da 5:6
3 [i]Isa 10:21–22; [j]2Ki 18:17; Isa 36:2
4 [k]Isa 30:15; La 3:26; [l]**Ge 15:1; Dt 3:2;** Isa 8:12; 12:2; 35:4; 37:6; Mt 24:6; [m]**Dt 20:3; Isa 21:4;** [n]Am 4:11; Zec 3:2; [o]Isa 10:24; 51:13; 54:14; [p]**2Ki 15:27**
5 [q]**ver 1;** [r]ver 2
7 [s]Isa 24:3; 25:8; 28:16; [t]Ps 2:1; Isa 8:10; 14:24; 28:18; 40:8; 46:10; Ac 4:25
8 [u]**Ge 14:15;** [v]ver 1; Isa 9:11; [w]2Ki 17:24; Isa 8:4; 17:1–3
9 [x]**2Ki 15:29;** Isa 9:9; 28:1,3; [y]**Ps 20:8;** Isa 8:10; 40:8; [z]2Ch 20:20; [a]Isa 8:6–8; 30:12–14
11 [b]**Ex 7:9; Dt 13:2;** [c]Ps 139:8 12 [d]Dt 4:34
13 [e]**ver 2;** [f]**Ge 30:15;** [g]**Isa 1:14;** [h]Ps 63:1; 118:28; Isa 25:1; 49:4; 61:10
14 [i]**Ex 3:12; Lk 2:12;** [j]**Ge 24:43;** [k]**Ge 3:15;** Lk 1:31; [l]**Ge 21:22;** Isa 8:8,10; Mt 1:23*
15 [m]**Ge 18:8;** [n]ver 22
16 [o]Isa 8:4; [p]Dt 1:39; [q]**Dt 13:16;** Isa 17:3; Jer 7:15; Hos 5:9,13; Am 1:3–5
17 [r]1Ki 12:16; [s]**ver 20; 2Ch 28:20**

[a]*9, 10* Hebrew; Septuagint *'You will be ever hearing, but never understanding; / you will be ever seeing, but never perceiving.' / [10]This people's heart has become calloused; / they hardly hear with their ears, / and they have closed their eyes* [a]2 Or *has set up camp in*
[b]3 *Shear-Jashub* means *a remnant will return.*
[c]14 The Hebrew is plural.
[d]14 Masoretic Text; Dead Sea Scrolls *and he* or *and they* [e]14 *Immanuel* means *God with us.*

18In that day[t] the LORD will whistle[u]
for flies from the distant streams of
Egypt and for bees from the land of
Assyria.[v] 19They will all come and settle
in the steep ravines and in the crevices[w]
in the rocks, on all the thornbushes[x] and
at all the water holes. 20In that day[y] the
Lord will use[z] a razor hired from beyond
the River[f] [a]—the king of Assyria[b]—to
shave your head and the hair of your
legs, and to take off your beards[c] also.[d]
21In that day,[e] a man will keep alive a
young cow and two goats.[f] 22And be-
cause of the abundance of the milk they
give, he will have curds to eat. All who
remain in the land will eat curds[g] and
honey.[h] 23In that day,[i] in every place
where there were a thousand vines
worth a thousand silver shekels,[g] [j] there
will be only briers and thorns.[k] 24Men
will go there with bow and arrow, for
the land will be covered with briers[l] and
thorns. 25As for all the hills[m] once culti-
vated by the hoe, you will no longer go
there for fear of the briers and thorns;[n]
they will become places where cattle are
turned loose and where sheep run.[o]

Assyria, the LORD's Instrument

8 The LORD said to me, "Take a large
scroll[a] and write on it with an
ordinary pen: Maher-Shalal-Hash-
Baz.[a] [b] 2And I will call in Uriah[c] the
priest and Zechariah son of Jeberekiah
as reliable witnesses[d] for me."

3Then I went to the prophetess,[e] and
she conceived and gave birth to a son.[f]
And the LORD said to me, "Name him
Maher-Shalal-Hash-Baz.[g] 4Before the
boy knows[h] how to say 'My father' or
'My mother', the wealth of Damascus[i]
and the plunder of Samaria will be
carried off by the king of Assyria.[j]"

5The LORD spoke to me again:

6"Because this people has rejected[k]
the gently flowing waters of
Shiloah[l]
and rejoices over Rezin
and the son of Remaliah,[m]
7therefore the Lord is about to bring
against them
the mighty floodwaters[n] of the
River[b]—
the king of Assyria[o] with all his
pomp.[p]
It will overflow all its channels,
run over all its banks[q]
8and sweep on into Judah, swirling
over it,[r]
passing through it and reaching up
to the neck.
Its outspread wings[s] will cover the
breadth of your land,
O Immanuel!"[c] [t]

9Raise the war cry,[d] [u] you nations, and
be shattered![v]
Listen, all you distant lands.
Prepare[w] for battle, and be shattered!
Prepare for battle, and be shattered!
10Devise your strategy, but it will be
thwarted;[x]
propose your plan, but it will not
stand,[y]
for God is with us.[e] [z]

Fear God

11The LORD spoke to me with his
strong hand upon me,[a] warning me not
to follow[b] the way of this people. He
said:

12"Do not call conspiracy[c]
everything that these people call
conspiracy;[f]
do not fear what they fear,[d]
and do not dread it.[e]
13The LORD Almighty is the one you are
to regard as holy,[f]
he is the one you are to fear,[g]
he is the one you are to dread,[h]
14and he will be a sanctuary;[i]
but for both houses of Israel he
will be
a stone[j] that causes men to stumble[k]
and a rock that makes them fall.[l]
And for the people of Jerusalem he
will be
a trap and a snare.[m]
15Many of them will stumble;[n]
they will fall and be broken,
they will be snared and captured."

16Bind up the testimony[o]
and seal[p] up the law among my
disciples.
17I will wait[q] for the LORD,
who is hiding[r] his face from the
house of Jacob.
I will put my trust in him.[s]

18 [t]ver 20–21; **Isa 2:11**; [u]**Isa 5:26**; [v]Isa 13:5
19 [w]**Isa 2:19**; [x]ver 25; Isa 17:9; 34:13; 55:13
20 [y]**ver 18**; [z]Isa 10:15; 29:16; [a]Isa 11:15; Jer 2:18; [b]ver 17; 2Ki 18:16; Isa 8:7; 10:5; [c]**2Sa 10:4**; [d]**Dt 28:49**
21 [e]ver 23; Isa 2:17; [f]Jer 39:10
22 [g]**Ge 18:8**; [h]ver 15; Isa 14:30
23 [i]ver 21; [j]SS 8:11; [k]**Isa 5:6**; Hos 2:12
24 [l]**Isa 5:6**
25 [m]Hag 1:11; [n]**ver 19**; [o]**Isa 5:17**

Ch. 8

1 [a]**Dt 27:8**; Job 19:23; Isa 30:8; Jer 51:60; [b]ver 3; Jer 20:3; Hos 1:4
2 [c]**2Ki 16:10**; [d]ver 16; **Jos 24:22**; **Ru 4:9**; Jer 32:10,12, 25,44
3 [e]**Ex 15:20**; [f]**Ge 3:15**; [g]**ver 1**
4 [h]Isa 7:16; [i]**Ge 14:15**; [j]**Isa 7:8**
6 [k]**Isa 5:24**; [l]**Ne 3:15**; Jn 9:7; [m]**Isa 7:1**
7 [n]Isa 17:12–13; 28:2,17; 30:28; 43:2; Da 11:40; Na 1:8; [o]**2Ch 28:20**; **Isa 7:20**; [p]Isa 10:16; [q]**Jos 3:15**
8 [r]Isa 28:15; [s]Isa 18:6; 46:11; Jer 4:13; 48:40; [t]**Isa 7:14**
9 [u]**Jos 6:5**; Isa 17:12–13; [v]**Job 34:24**; [w]Jer 6:4; 46:3; 51:12,27–28; Eze 38:7; Joel 3:9; Zec 14:2–3
10 [x]**Job 5:12**; [y]**Pr 19:21**; **21:30**; **Isa 7:7**; [z]**Isa 7:14**; Mt 1:23; Ro 8:31
11 [a]Eze 1:3; 3:14; [b]Eze 2:8
12 [c]Isa 7:2; 20:5; 30:1; 36:6; [d]**Isa 7:4**; Mt 10:28; [e]1Pe 3:14*
13 [f]**Nu 20:12**; [g]**Ex 20:20**; [h]Isa 29:23
14 [i]**Isa 4:6**; [j]**Ps 118:22**; [k]Jer 6:21; Eze 3:20; 14:3,7; Lk 20:18; [l]**Lk 2:34**; Ro 9:33*; 1Pe 2:8*; [m]**Ps 119:110**; Isa 24:17–18
15 [n]Pr 4:19; Isa 28:13; 59:10; Ro 9:32
16 [o]**Ru 4:7**; [p]Isa 29:11–12; Jer 32:14; Da 8:26; 12:4
17 [q]**Ps 27:14**; [r]**Dt 31:17**; [s]**Ps 22:5**; Heb 2:13*

f20 That is, the Euphrates
g23 That is, about 25 pounds (about 11.5 kilograms)
a1 *Maher-Shalal-Hash-Baz* means *quick to the plunder, swift to the spoil*; also in verse 3.
b7 That is, the Euphrates
c8 *Immanuel* means *God with us*.
d9 Or *Do your worst*
e10 Hebrew *Immanuel*
f12 Or *Do not call for a treaty / every time these people call for a treaty*

18Here am I, and the children the
LORD has given me.[t] We are signs[u] and
symbols[v] in Israel from the LORD
Almighty, who dwells on Mount Zion.[w]
19When men tell you to consult[x]
mediums and spiritists,[y] who whisper
and mutter,[z] should not a people en-
quire[a] of their God? Why consult the
dead on behalf of the living? 20To the
law[b] and to the testimony![c] If they do not
speak according to this word, they have
no light[d] of dawn. 21Distressed and hun-
gry,[e] they will roam through the land;[f]
when they are famished, they will
become enraged and, looking upward,
will curse[g] their king and their God.
22Then they will look towards the earth
and see only distress and darkness and
fearful gloom,[h] and they will be thrust
into utter darkness.[i]

To Us a Child Is Born

9 Nevertheless, there will be no
more gloom[a] for those who were in
distress. In the past he humbled the
land of Zebulun and the land of Naph-
tali,[b] but in the future he will honour
Galilee of the Gentiles, by the way of the
sea, along the Jordan—

2The people walking in darkness[c]
have seen a great light;[d]
on those living in the land of the
shadow of death[a][e]
a light has dawned.[f]
3You have enlarged the nation[g]
and increased their joy;[h]
they rejoice before you
as people rejoice at the harvest,
as men rejoice
when dividing the plunder.[i]
4For as in the day of Midian's defeat,[j]
you have shattered[k]
the yoke[l] that burdens them,
the bar across their shoulders,[m]
the rod of their oppressor.[n]
5Every warrior's boot used in battle
and every garment rolled in blood
will be destined for burning,[o]
will be fuel for the fire.
6For to us a child is born,[p]
to us a son is given,[q]
and the government[r] will be on his
shoulders.[s]
And he will be called
Wonderful Counsellor,[b][t] Mighty
God,[u]
Everlasting[v] Father,[w] Prince of
Peace.[x]
7Of the increase of his government[y]
and peace[z]
there will be no end.[a]

18 [t]Ge 33:5; Heb 2:13*; [u]Ex 3:12; Eze 4:3; 12:6; 24:24; Lk 2:34; [v]Dt 28:46; Eze 12:11; [w]Ps 9:11
19 [x]1Sa 28:8; [y]Lev 19:31; [z]Isa 29:4; [a]Nu 27:21
20 [b]Isa 1:10; Lk 16:29; [c]Ru 4:7; [d]ver 22; Isa 9:2; 59:9; 60:2; Mic 3:6
21 [e]Job 18:12; [f]Job 30:3; [g]Ex 22:28; Rev 16:11
22 [h]Job 15:24; [i]ver 20; Job 3:13; Isa 5:30; Joel 2:2; Mt 25:30; Rev 16:10

Ch. 9

1 [a]Job 15:24; [b]2Ki 15:29
2 [c]Ps 82:5; 107:10,14; Isa 8:20; [d]Ps 36:9; Isa 42:6; 49:6; 60:19; Mal 4:2; Eph 5:8; [e]Lk 1:79; [f]Isa 58:8; Mt 4:15–16*
3 [g]Job 12:23; [h]Ps 4:7; Isa 25:9; [i]Ex 15:9; Jos 22:8; Ps 119:162
4 [j]Jdg 7:25; [k]Job 34:24; Isa 37:36–38; [l]Isa 14:25; 58:6,9; Jer 2:20; 30:8; Eze 30:18; Na 1:13; Mt 11:30; [m]Ps 81:6; Isa 10:27; [n]Isa 14:4; 16:4; 29:5,20; 49:26; 51:13; 54:14; 60:18
5 [o]Isa 2:4
6 [p]Ge 3:15; Isa 53:2; Lk 2:11; [q]Jn 3:16; [r]Mt 28:18; [s]Isa 22:22; [t]Job 15:8; Isa 28:29; [u]Dt 7:21; Ps 24:8; Isa 10:21; 11:2; 42:13; [v]Ps 90:2; [w]Ex 4:22; Isa 64:8; Jn 14:9–10; [x]Isa 26:3,12; 53:5; 66:12; Jer 33:6; Mic 5:5; Lk 2:14

He will reign[b] on David's throne
and over his kingdom,
establishing and upholding it
with justice[c] and righteousness[d]
from that time on and for ever.[e]
The zeal[f] of the LORD Almighty
will accomplish this.

The LORD's Anger Against Israel

8The LORD has sent a message[g] against
Jacob;
it will fall on Israel.
9All the people will know it—
Ephraim[h] and the inhabitants of
Samaria[i]—
who say with pride
and arrogance[j] of heart,
10"The bricks have fallen down,
but we will rebuild with dressed
stone;[k]
the fig[l]-trees have been felled,
but we will replace them with
cedars.[m]"
11But the LORD has strengthened
Rezin's[n] foes against them
and has spurred their enemies on.
12Arameans[o] from the east and
Philistines[p] from the west
have devoured[q] Israel with open
mouth.

Yet for all this, his anger[r] is not turned
away,
his hand is still upraised.[s]

13But the people have not returned[t] to
him who struck[u] them,
nor have they sought[v] the LORD
Almighty.
14So the LORD will cut off from Israel
both head and tail,
both palm branch and reed[w] in a
single day;[x]
15the elders[y] and prominent men[z] are
the head,
the prophets[a] who teach lies[b] are the
tail.

7 [y]Isa 2:4; [z]Ps 85:8; 119:165; Isa 11:9; 26:3,12; 32:17; 48:18; [a]Da 2:44; 4:3; Lk 1:33; Jn 12:34; [b]Isa 1:26; 32:1; 60:17; 1Co 15:25; [c]Isa 11:4; 16:5; 32:1,16; 33:5; 42:1; Jer 23:5; 33:14; [d]Ps 72:2; [e]2Sa 7:13; [f]2Ki 19:31; Isa 26:11; 37:32; 42:13; 59:17; 63:15 8 [g]Dt 32:2
9 [h]Isa 7:2; [i]Isa 7:9; [j]Isa 46:12; 48:4; Eze 2:4; Zec 7:11
10 [k]Ge 11:3; [l]Am 7:14; Lk 19:4; [m]1Ki 7:2–3
11 [n]Isa 7:8
12 [o]2Ki 16:6; [p]2Ch 28:18; [q]Ps 79:7; [r]Job 40:11; [s]Isa 5:25
13 [t]2Ch 28:22; Am 4:9; Zep 3:7; Hag 2:17; [u]Jer 5:3; Eze 7:9; [v]Isa 2:3; 17:7; 31:1; 55:6; Jer 50:4; Da 9:13; Hos 3:5; 7:7,10; Am 4:6,10; Zep 1:6
14 [w]ver 14–15; Isa 19:15; [x]Rev 18:8
15 [y]Isa 3:2–3; [z]Isa 5:13; [a]Isa 28:7; Eze 13:2; [b]Job 13:4; Isa 3:8; 44:20; Eze 13:22; Mt 24:24

a2 Or *land of darkness*
b6 Or *Wonderful, Counsellor*

16Those who guide[c] this people mislead
them,
and those who are guided are led
astray.[d]
17Therefore the Lord will take no
pleasure in the young men,[e]
nor will he pity[f] the fatherless and
widows,
for everyone is ungodly[g] and wicked,[h]
every mouth speaks vileness.[i]

Yet for all this, his anger is not turned
away,
his hand is still upraised.[j]

18Surely wickedness burns like a fire;[k]
it consumes briers and thorns,[l]
it sets the forest thickets ablaze,[m]
so that it rolls upward in a column of
smoke.
19By the wrath[n] of the LORD Almighty
the land will be scorched[o]
and the people will be fuel for the fire;[p]
no-one will spare his brother.[q]
20On the right they will devour,
but still be hungry;[r]
on the left they will eat,[s]
but not be satisfied.
Each will feed on the flesh of his own
offspring:[c]
21 Manasseh will feed on Ephraim,
and Ephraim on Manasseh;[t]
together they will turn against
Judah.[u]

Yet for all this, his anger is not turned
away,
his hand is still upraised.[v]

10 Woe[a] to those who make unjust
laws,
to those who issue oppressive
decrees,[b]
2to deprive[c] the poor of their rights
and withhold justice from the
oppressed of my people,[d]
making widows their prey
and robbing the fatherless.[e]
3What will you do on the day of
reckoning,[f]
when disaster[g] comes from afar?
To whom will you run for help?[h]
Where will you leave your riches?
4Nothing will remain but to cringe
among the captives[i]
or fall among the slain.[j]

Yet for all this, his anger is not turned
away,[k]
his hand is still upraised.

God's Judgment on Assyria

5"Woe[l] to the Assyrian,[m] the rod[n] of my
anger,
in whose hand is the club[o] of my
wrath![p]
6I send him against a godless[q] nation,
I dispatch[r] him against a people
who anger me,[s]
to seize loot and snatch plunder,[t]
and to trample[u] them down like
mud in the streets.
7But this is not what he intends,[v]
this is not what he has in mind;
his purpose is to destroy,
to put an end to many nations.
8'Are not my commanders[w] all kings?'
he says.
9 'Has not Calno[x] fared like
Carchemish?[y]
Is not Hamath[z] like Arpad,[a]
and Samaria[b] like Damascus?[c]
10As my hand seized the kingdoms of
the idols,[d]
kingdoms whose images excelled
those of Jerusalem and
Samaria—
11shall I not deal with Jerusalem and her
images
as I dealt with Samaria and her
idols?[e]' "

12When the Lord has finished all his
work[f] against Mount Zion[g] and Jeru-
salem, he will say, "I will punish the
king of Assyria[h] for the wilful pride[i] of
his heart and the haughty look[j] in his
eyes. 13For he says:

" 'By the strength of my hand[k] I have
done this,[l]
and by my wisdom, because I have
understanding.
I removed the boundaries of nations,
I plundered their treasures;[m]
like a mighty one I subdued[a] their
kings.[n]
14As one reaches into a nest,[o]
so my hand reached for the wealth[p]
of the nations;
as men gather abandoned eggs,
so I gathered all the countries;[q]
not one flapped a wing,
or opened its mouth to chirp.' "[r]

15Does the axe raise itself above him
who swings it,

16 [c]Mt 15:14; 23:16,24; [d]**Isa 3:12**
17 [e]Jer 9:21; 11:22; 18:21; 48:15; 49:26; Am 4:10; 8:13; [f]**Job 5:4**; Isa 27:11; Jer 13:14; [g]Isa 10:6; 32:6; Mic 7:2; [h]**Isa 1:4**; [i]**Isa 3:8**; Mt 12:34; Ro 3:13–14; [j]**Isa 5:25**
18 [k]**Dt 29:23; Isa 1:31**; [l]**Isa 5:6**; [m]**Ps 83:14**
19 [n]**Job 40:11**; Isa 13:9,13; [o]Jer 17:27; [p]**Ps 97:3; Isa 1:31**; [q]**Isa 3:5**
20 [r]**Lev 26:26; Job 18:12**; [s]Isa 49:26; Zec 11:9
21 [t]**Jdg 7:22; 12:4**; [u]**2Ch 28:6**; [v]**Isa 5:25**
Ch. 10
1 [a]**Isa 5:8**; [b]**Ps 58:2**
2 [c]Isa 3:14; [d]**Isa 5:23**; [e]**Dt 10:18; Job 6:27; Isa 1:17**
3 [f]**Job 31:14**; [g]ver 25; Ps 59:5; Isa 1:24; 13:6; 14:23; 24:6; 26:14; 47:11; Jer 5:9; 9:9; 50:15; Lk 19:44; [h]**Ps 108:12**; Isa 20:6; 30:7; 31:3
4 [i]Isa 24:22; Zec 9:11; [j]Isa 22:2; 34:3; 66:16; Jer 39:6; Na 3:3; [k]**Isa 5:25**; 12:1; 63:10; 64:5; Jer 4:8; 30:24; La 1:12
5 [l]**2Ki 19:21; Isa 28:1**; [m]ver 12, 18; **Isa 7:20**; 14:25; 31:8; 37:7; Zep 2:13; [n]Isa 14:5; 54:16; [o]ver 15, 24; Isa 30:31; 41:15; 45:1; Jer 50:23; 51:20; [p]Isa 9:4; 13:3, 5,13; 26:20; 30:30; 34:2; 63:6; 66:14; Eze 30:24–25
6 [q]**Isa 9:17**; [r]Hab 1:12; [s]**2Ch 28:9**; Isa 9:19; [t]**Jdg 6:4; Isa 5:29**; 8:1; [u]**2Sa 22:43; Ps 7:5; Isa 5:5**; 37:26–27
7 [v]**Ge 50:20**; Ac 4:23–28
8 [w]2Ki 18:24
9 [x]**Ge 10:10**; [y]**2Ch 35:20**; [z]Nu 34:8; 2Ch 8:4; Isa 11:11; [a]2Ki 18:34; [b]2Ki 17:6; [c]**Ge 14:15**; 2Ki 16:9; Jer 49:24
10 [d]2Ki 19:18
11 [e]**2Ki 19:13; Isa 2:8**; 36:18–20; 37:10–13
12 [f]Isa 28:21–22; 65:7; 66:4; Jer 5:29; [g]2Ki 19:31; [h]**ver 5; 2Ki 19:7**; Isa 30:31–33; 37:36–38; Jer 50:18; [i]**Isa 2:11; Eze 28:17**; [j]Ps 18:27
13 [k]**Dt 8:17**; [l]**Dt 32:26–27**; Isa 47:7; Da 4:30; [m]Eze 28:4; [n]Isa 14:13–14
14 [o]Jer 49:16; Ob 4; Hab 2:6–11; [p]**Job 31:25**; [q]Isa 14:6; [r]2Ki 19:22–24; Isa 37:24–25

[c]20 Or *arm*   [a]13 Or / *I subdued the mighty,*

or the saw boast against him who
uses it?[s]
As if a rod were to wield him who lifts
it up,
or a club[t] brandish him who is not
wood!
16Therefore, the Lord, the LORD
Almighty,
will send a wasting disease[u] upon
his sturdy warriors;[v]
under his pomp[w] a fire[x] will be kindled
like a blazing flame.
17The Light of Israel will become a fire,[y]
their Holy One[z] a flame;
in a single day it will burn and
consume
his thorns[a] and his briers.[b]
18The splendour of his forests[c] and
fertile fields
it will completely destroy,[d]
as when a sick man wastes away.
19And the remaining trees of his forests[e]
will be so few[f]
that a child could write them down.

The Remnant of Israel

20In that day[g] the remnant of Israel,
the survivors[h] of the house of Jacob,
will no longer rely[i] on him
who struck them down[j]
but will truly rely[k] on the LORD,
the Holy One of Israel.[l]
21A remnant[m] will return,[b][n] a remnant
of Jacob
will return to the Mighty God.[o]
22Though your people, O Israel, be like
the sand[p] by the sea,
only a remnant will return.[q]
Destruction has been decreed,[r]
overwhelming and righteous.
23The Lord, the LORD Almighty, will
carry out
the destruction decreed[s] upon the
whole land.[t]

24Therefore, this is what the Lord, the LORD Almighty, says:

"O my people who live in Zion,[u]
do not be afraid[v] of the Assyrians,
who beat[w] you with a rod[x]
and lift up a club against you, as
Egypt did.
25Very soon[y] my anger against you will
end
and my wrath[z] will be directed to
their destruction.[a]"

26The LORD Almighty will lash[b] them
with a whip,
as when he struck down Midian[c] at
the rock of Oreb;
and he will raise his staff[d] over the
waters,[e]
as he did in Egypt.
27In that day[f] their burden[g] will be lifted
from your shoulders,
their yoke[h] from your neck;[i]
the yoke[j] will be broken
because you have grown so fat.[c]
28They enter Aiath;
they pass through Migron;[k]
they store supplies[l] at Michmash.[m]
29They go over the pass, and say,
"We will camp overnight at Geba.[n]"
Ramah[o] trembles;
Gibeah[p] of Saul flees.[q]
30Cry out, O Daughter of Gallim![r]
Listen, O Laishah!
Poor Anathoth![s]
31Madmenah is in flight;
the people of Gebim take cover.
32This day they will halt at Nob;[t]
they will shake their fist[u]
at the mount of the Daughter of Zion,[v]
at the hill of Jerusalem.

33See, the Lord, the LORD Almighty,
will lop off[w] the boughs with great
power.
The lofty trees will be felled,[x]
the tall[y] ones will be brought low.[z]
34He will cut down[a] the forest thickets
with an axe;
Lebanon[b] will fall before the Mighty
One.[c]

The Branch From Jesse

11 A shoot[a] will come up from the
stump[b] of Jesse;[c]
from his roots a Branch[d] will bear
fruit.[e]
2The Spirit[f] of the LORD will rest on
him—
the Spirit of wisdom[g] and of
understanding,
the Spirit of counsel and of power,[h]
the Spirit of knowledge and of the
fear of the LORD—

15 [s]Isa 7:20; 45:9; Ro 9:20–21; [t]ver 5
16 [u]ver 18; Nu 11:33; Isa 17:4; [v]Ps 78:31; [w]Isa 8:7; [x]Jer 21:14
17 [y]Job 41:21; Isa 1:31; 31:9; Zec 2:5; [z]Isa 37:23; [a]Nu 11:1–3; 2Sa 23:6; [b]Isa 9:18
18 [c]2Ki 19:23; [d]ver 5
19 [e]ver 33–34; Isa 32:19; [f]Isa 17:6; 21:17; 27:13; Jer 44:28
20 [g]ver 27; Isa 11:10–11; 12:1,4; 19:18–19; 24:21; 28:5; 52:6; Zec 9:16; [h]Isa 1:9; Eze 7:16; [i]2Ki 16:7; [j]2Ch 28:20; [k]2Ch 14:11; Isa 17:7; 48:2; 50:10; Jer 21:2; Hos 3:5; 6:1; Mic 3:11; 7:7; [l]Isa 5:24
21 [m]Ge 45:7; Isa 6:13; Zep 3:13; [n]Isa 7:3; [o]Isa 9:6
22 [p]Ge 12:2; Isa 48:19; Jer 33:22; [q]Ezr 1:4; Isa 11:11; 46:3; [r]ver 23; Isa 28:22; Jer 40:2; Da 9:27
23 [s]ver 22; [t]Isa 6:12; 28:22; Ro 9:27–28*
24 [u]Ps 87:5–6; [v]Isa 7:4; [w]Ex 5:14; [x]ver 5
25 [y]Isa 17:14; 29:17; Hag 2:6; [z]ver 5; Ps 30:5; Isa 13:5; 24:21; 26:20; 30:30; 34:2; 66:14; Da 8:19; 11:36; [a]ver 3; Mic 5:6
26 [b]Isa 37:36–38; [c]Isa 9:4; [d]Isa 30:32; [e]Ex 14:16
27 [f]ver 20; [g]Ps 66:11; [h]Lev 26:13; Isa 9:4; [i]Isa 14:25; 47:6; 52:2; [j]Jer 30:8
28 [k]1Sa 14:2; [l]Jos 1:11; [m]1Sa 13:2
29 [n]Jos 18:24; Ne 11:31; [o]Jos 18:25; [p]Jdg 19:14; [q]Isa 15:5
30 [r]1Sa 25:44; [s]Ne 11:32
32 [t]1Sa 21:1; [u]Job 15:25; [v]Ps 9:14; Isa 16:1; Jer 6:23
33 [w]Isa 18:5; 27:11; Eze 17:4; [x]Ex 12:12; [y]Isa 2:13; Am 2:9; [z]Isa 5:15
34 [a]Na 1:12; Zec 11:2; [b]2Ki 19:23; [c]Ge 49:24; Ps 93:4; Isa 33:21

Ch. 11
1 [a]2Ki 19:26; Job 14:7; [b]Job 14:8; [c]ver 10; Isa 9:7; Mt 1:1; Rev 5:5; [d]Isa 4:2; [e]2Ki 19:30; Isa 27:6
2 [f]Jdg 3:10; Isa 32:15; 42:1; 44:3; 48:16; 59:21; 61:1; Eze 37:14; 39:29; Joel 2:28; Mt 3:16; Jn 1:32–33; 16:13; [g]Ex 28:3; Eph 1:17; Col 2:3; [h]Isa 9:6; 2Ti 1:7

b21 Hebrew *shear-jashub;* also in verse 22
c27 Hebrew; Septuagint *broken / from your shoulders*

3and he will delight in the fear[i] of the
LORD.

He will not judge by what he sees with
his eyes,[j]
or decide by what he hears with his
ears;[k]
4but with righteousness[l] he will judge
the needy,[m]
with justice[n] he will give decisions
for the poor[o] of the earth.
He will strike[p] the earth with the rod of
his mouth;[q]
with the breath[r] of his lips he will
slay the wicked.[s]
5Righteousness will be his belt[t]
and faithfulness[u] the sash round his
waist.[v]

6The wolf will live with the lamb,[w]
the leopard will lie down with the
goat,
the calf and the lion and the yearling[a]
together;
and a little child will lead them.
7The cow will feed with the bear,
their young will lie down together,
and the lion will eat straw like
the ox.[x]
8The infant[y] will play near the hole of
the cobra,
and the young child put his hand
into the viper's[z] nest.
9They will neither harm nor destroy[a]
on all my holy mountain,[b]
for the earth[c] will be full of the
knowledge[d] of the LORD
as the waters cover the sea.

10In that day[e] the Root of Jesse[f] will
stand as a banner[g] for the peoples; the
nations[h] will rally to him,[i] and his place
of rest[j] will be glorious.[k] 11In that day[l]
the Lord will reach out his hand a
second time to reclaim the remnant[m]
that is left of his people from Assyria,[n]
from Lower Egypt, from Upper
Egypt,[b][o] from Cush,[c][p] from Elam,[q] from
Babylonia,[d] from Hamath[r] and from the
islands[s] of the sea.[t]

12He will raise a banner[u] for the nations
and gather[v] the exiles of Israel;[w]
he will assemble the scattered people[x]
of Judah
from the four quarters of the earth.[y]
13Ephraim's jealousy will vanish,
and Judah's enemies[e] will be cut off;
Ephraim will not be jealous of Judah,
nor Judah hostile towards
Ephraim.[z]
14They will swoop down on the slopes
of Philistia[a] to the west;

3 [i]Isa 33:6; [j]Jn 7:24; [k]Jn 2:25
4 [l]**Ps 72:2**; [m]**Ps 72:4; Isa 14:30**; [n]**Isa 9:7**; Rev 19:11; [o]**Job 5:16; Isa 3:14**; [p]Isa 27:7; 30:31; Zec 14:12; Mal 4:6; [q]**Job 40:18**; Ps 2:9; Rev 19:15; [r]**Job 4:9**; Ps 18:8; Isa 30:28,33; 40:24; 59:19; Eze 21:31; 2Th 2:8; [s]**Ps 139:19**
5 [t]Ex 12:11; 1Ki 18:46; [u]Isa 25:1; [v]Eph 6:14
6 [w]Isa 65:25
7 [x]**Job 40:15**
8 [y]Isa 65:20; [z]Isa 14:29; 30:6; 59:5
9 [a]**Nu 25:12; Isa 2:4; 9:7**; [b]**Ps 48:1; Isa 2:2**; [c]1Sa 17:46; Ps 98:2–3; Isa 45:22; 48:20; 52:10; [d]Ex 7:5; Isa 19:21; 45:6,14; 49:26; Jer 24:7; 31:34; Hab 2:14
10 [e]**Isa 10:20**; [f]**ver 1**; [g]**Ps 20:5**; Isa 18:3; Jer 4:6; Jn 12:32; [h]Isa 2:4; 14:1; 49:23; 56:3,6; 60:5,10; Lk 2:32; Ac 11:18; [i]Ro 15:12*; [j]**Ps 116:7**; Isa 14:3; 28:12; 32:17–18; 40:2; Jer 6:16; 30:10; 46:27; [k]Hag 2:9; Zec 2:5
11 [l]**Isa 10:20**; [m]**Dt 30:4**; **Isa 1:9**; [n]Isa 19:24; Hos 11:11; Mic 7:12; Zec 10:10; [o]Jer 44:1,15; Eze 29:14; 30:14; [p]**Ge 10:6**; Ac 8:27; [q]**Ge 10:22**; [r]**Isa 10:9**; [s]Isa 24:15; 41:1,5; 42:4,10,12; 49:1; 51:5; 59:18; 60:9; 66:19; [t]Isa 49:12; Jer 16:15; 46:27; Eze 38:8; Zec 8:7

together they will plunder the
people to the east.[b]
They will lay hands on Edom[c] and
Moab,[d]
and the Ammonites[e] will be subject
to them.[f]
15The LORD will dry up[g]
the gulf of the Egyptian sea;
with a scorching wind[h] he will sweep
his hand[i]
over the Euphrates River.[f][j]
He will break it up into seven streams
so that men can cross over in
sandals.[k]
16There will be a highway[l] for the
remnant[m] of his people
that is left from Assyria,[n]
as there was for Israel
when they came up from Egypt.[o]

Songs of Praise

12

In that day[a] you will say:

"I will praise[b] you, O LORD.
Although you were angry with me,
your anger has turned away[c]
and you have comforted[d] me.
2Surely God is my salvation;[e]
I will trust[f] and not be afraid.
The LORD, the LORD,[g] is my strength[h]
and my song;
he has become my salvation.[i]"
3With joy you will draw water[j]
from the wells[k] of salvation.

4In that day[l] you will say:

"Give thanks to the LORD, call on his
name;[m]

12 [u]**Ps 20:5**; [v]Isa 14:2; 43:5; 49:22; 54:7; Jer 16:15; 31:10; 32:37; [w]**Ne 1:9; Ps 106:47**; Isa 14:1; 41:14; 49:5; [x]Eze 28:25; Zep 3:10; [y]**Ps 48:10**; 67:7; Isa 41:5; Rev 7:1
13 [z]**2Ch 28:6**; Jer 3:18; Eze 37:16–17,22; Hos 1:11
14 [a]**2Ch 26:6; 28:18**; [b]**Jdg 6:3**; [c]**Nu 24:18; Ps 137:7**; Isa 34:5–6; 63:1; Jer 49:22; Eze 25:12; Da 11:41; Joel 3:19; Ob 1; Mal 1:4; [d]Isa 15:1; 16:14; 25:10; Jer 48:40; Zep 2:8–11; [e]Jdg 11:14–18; [f]Isa 25:3; 60:12
15 [g]**Ex 14:22; Dt 11:10**; Isa 37:25; 42:15; Jer 50:38; 51:36; [h]**Ge 41:6**; [i]Isa 19:16; 30:32; [j]**Isa 7:20**; [k]**Ex 14:29**
16 [l]Isa 19:23; 35:8; 40:3; 49:11; 51:10; 57:14; 62:10; Jer 50:5; [m]**Ge 45:7**; [n]**ver 11**; [o]Ex 14:26–31

Ch. 12

1 [a]**Isa 10:20**; [b]Ps 9:1; Isa 25:1; [c]**Job 13:16**; [d]**Ps 71:21**
2 [e]Isa 17:10; 25:9; 33:6; 45:17; 51:5–6; 54:8; 59:16; 61:10; 62:11; [f]**Job 13:15; Ps 26:1; 112:7**; Isa 26:3; Da 6:23; [g]Isa 26:4; 38:11; [h]**Ps 18:1**; [i]**Ex 15:2**
3 [j]**2Ki 3:17**; Ps 36:9; Jer 2:13; 17:13; Jn 4:10,14; [k]Ex 15:25
4 [l]**Isa 10:20**; [m]Ex 3:15; Ps 80:18; 105:1; Isa 24:15; 25:1; 26:8,13; Hos 12:5

---

[a]*6* Hebrew; Septuagint *lion will feed*
[b]*11* Hebrew *from Pathros*
[c]*11* That is, the upper Nile region
[d]*11* Hebrew *Shinar* [e]*13* Or *hostility*
[f]*15* Hebrew *the River*

make known among the nations[n]
what he has done,
and proclaim that his name is
exalted.[o]
5Sing[p] to the LORD, for he has done
glorious things;[q]
let this be known to all the world.
6Shout aloud and sing for joy,[r] people
of Zion,
for great[s] is the Holy One of Israel[t]
among you.[u]"

A Prophecy Against Babylon

13 An oracle[a] concerning Babylon[b]
that Isaiah son of Amoz[c] saw:[d]

2Raise a banner[e] on a bare hilltop,
shout to them;
beckon to them
to enter the gates[f] of the nobles.
3I have commanded my holy ones;
I have summoned my warriors[g] to
carry out my wrath[h]—
those who rejoice[i] in my triumph.

4Listen, a noise on the mountains,
like that of a great multitude![j]
Listen, an uproar[k] among the
kingdoms,
like nations massing together!
The LORD Almighty[l] is mustering[m]
an army for war.
5They come from faraway lands,
from the ends of the heavens[n]—
the LORD and the weapons[o] of his
wrath[p]—
to destroy[q] the whole country.

6Wail,[r] for the day[s] of the LORD is near;
it will come like destruction[t] from
the Almighty.[a][u]
7Because of this, all hands will go
limp,[v]
every man's heart will melt.[w]
8Terror[x] will seize them,
pain and anguish will grip[y] them;
they will writhe like a woman in
labour.[z]
They will look aghast at each other,
their faces aflame.[a]

9See, the day[b] of the LORD is coming
—a cruel[c] day, with wrath[d] and
fierce anger[e]—
to make the land desolate
and destroy the sinners within it.
10The stars of heaven and their
constellations
will not show their light.[f]
The rising sun[g] will be darkened[h]
and the moon will not give its light.[i]
11I will punish[j] the world for its evil,
the wicked[k] for their sins.
I will put an end to the arrogance of the
haughty[l]
and will humble[m] the pride of the
ruthless.[n]
12I will make man[o] scarcer than pure
gold,
more rare than the gold of Ophir.[p]
13Therefore I will make the heavens
tremble;[q]
and the earth will shake[r] from its
place
at the wrath[s] of the LORD Almighty,
in the day of his burning anger.[t]

14Like a hunted[u] gazelle,
like sheep without a shepherd,[v]
each will return to his own people,
each will flee[w] to his native land.[x]
15Whoever is captured will be thrust
through;
all who are caught will fall[y] by the
sword.[z]
16Their infants[a] will be dashed to pieces
before their eyes;
their houses will be looted and their
wives ravished.[b]
17See, I will stir up[c] against them the
Medes,[d]
who do not care for silver
and have no delight in gold.[e]
18Their bows[f] will strike down the
young men;[g]
they will have no mercy[h] on infants
nor will they look with compassion
on children.[i]
19Babylon,[j] the jewel of kingdoms,[k]
the glory[l] of the Babylonians'[b]
pride,
will be overthrown[m] by God
like Sodom and Gomorrah.[n]
20She will never be inhabited[o]
or lived in through all generations;
no Arab[p] will pitch his tent there,
no shepherd will rest his flocks
there.

4 [n]Isa 54:5; 60:3; Jer 10:7; Zep 2:11; Mal 1:11; [o]**Ps 113:2**
5 [p]**Ex 15:1;** [q]**Ps 98:1**
6 [r]**Ge 21:6; Ps 98:4;** Isa 24:14; 48:20; 52:8; Jer 20:13; 31:7; Zec 2:10; [s]Ps 48:1; [t]**Ps 78:41;** 99:2; Isa 1:24; 10:20; 17:7; 29:19; 37:23; 43:3,14; 45:11; 49:26; 55:5; Eze 39:7; [u]**Ps 46:5;** Zep 3:14–17

Ch. 13

1 [a]Isa 14:28; 15:1; 21:1; Na 1:1; Hab 1:1; Zec 9:1; 12:1; Mal 1:1; [b]ver 19; **Ge 10:10;** Isa 14:4; 21:9; 46:1–2; 48:14; Jer 24:1; 25:12; Rev 14:8; [c]Isa 20:2; 37:2; [d]**Isa 1:1**
2 [e]**Ps 20:5;** Jer 50:2; 51:27; [f]Isa 24:12; 45:2; Jer 51:58
3 [g]ver 17; Isa 21:2; Jer 51:11; Da 5:28,31; Joel 3:11; [h]**Job 40:11; Isa 10:5;** [i]**Ps 149:2**
4 [j]Joel 3:14; [k]**Ps 46:6;** [l]Isa 47:4; 51:15; [m]Isa 42:13; Jer 50:41
5 [n]**Isa 5:26;** [o]Isa 45:1; 54:16; Jer 50:25; [p]**Isa 10:25;** [q]**Jos 6:17;** Isa 24:1; 30:25; 34:2
6 [r]Isa 14:31; 15:2; 16:7; 23:1; Eze 30:2; Jas 5:1; [s]**Isa 2:12;** [t]**Isa 10:3; 14:15;** [u]**Ge 17:1**
7 [v]**2Ki 19:26; Job 4:3; Jer 47:3;** [w]**Jos 2:11;** Eze 21:7
8 [x]**Ps 31:13; 48:5; Isa 21:4;** [y]Ex 15:14; [z]**Ge 3:16; Jn 16:21;** [a]Joel 2:6; Na 2:10
9 [b]**Isa 2:12;** Jer 51:2; [c]Jer 6:23; [d]**Isa 9:19;** [e]Isa 26:21; 66:16; Jer 25:31; Joel 3:2
10 [f]**Job 9:7;** [g]Isa 24:23; Zec 14:7; [h]**Ex 10:22; Isa 5:30;** Rev 8:12; [i]Eze 32:7; Am 5:20; 8:9; **Mt 24:29***; Mk 13:24*
11 [j]Isa 3:11; 11:4; 26:21; 65:6–7; 66:16; [k]**Ps 125:3;** [l]**Ps 10:5; Pr 16:18;** Da 5:23; [m]**Isa 2:9;** 23:9; Eze 28:2; Da 4:37; [n]Isa 25:3,5; 29:5,20; 49:25–26
12 [o]**Isa 4:1;** [p]**Ge 10:29**
13 [q]**Ps 102:26;** Isa 34:4; 51:6; [r]**Job 9:6; Isa 14:16;** Mt 24:7; Mk 13:8; [s]**Isa 9:19;** [t]**Job 9:5**
14 [u]Pr 6:5; [v]**1Ki 22:17; Mt 9:36; Jn 10:11;** [w]**Ge 11:9;** Isa 17:13; 21:15; 22:3; 33:3; Jer 4:9; [x]Jer 46:16; 50:16; 51:9; Na 3:7
15 [y]Jer 51:4; [z]Isa 14:19; Jer 50:25
16 [a]ver 18; **Nu 16:27; 2Ki 8:12;** [b]**Ge 34:29; Hos 13:16**
17 [c]Jer 50:9,41; 51:1; [d]**ver 3;** [e]2Ki 18:14–16; Pr 6:34–35
18 [f]**Ps 7:12;** Isa 41:2; Jer 50:9,14,29; [g]**Dt 32:25;** Jer 49:26; 50:30; 51:4; [h]Isa 47:6; Jer 6:23; 50:42; [i]**ver 16;** Isa 14:22; 47:9
19 [j]**ver 1;** [k]Isa 47:5; Da 2:37–38; [l]Da 4:30; [m]**Ps 137:8; Rev 14:8;** [n]**Ge 19:25;** Isa 1:9–10; Ro 9:29
20 [o]Isa 14:23; 34:10–15; Jer 51:29,37–43,62; [p]2Ch 17:11

[a]6 Hebrew *Shaddai* [b]19 Or *Chaldeans'*

21But desert creatures[q] will lie there,
jackals[r] will fill her houses;
there the owls[s] will dwell,
and there the wild goats[t] will leap about.
22Hyenas[u] will howl in her strongholds,[v]
jackals[w] in her luxurious palaces.
Her time is at hand,[x]
and her days will not be prolonged.[y]

14

The LORD will have compassion[a] on Jacob;
once again he will choose[b] Israel
and will settle them in their own land.[c]
Aliens[d] will join them
and unite with the house of Jacob.
2Nations will take them
and bring[e] them to their own place.
And the house of Israel will possess the nations[f]
as menservants and maidservants
in the LORD's land.
They will make captives[g] of their captors
and rule over their oppressors.[h]

3On the day the LORD gives you relief[i]
from suffering and turmoil[j] and cruel
bondage,[k] 4you will take up this taunt[l]
against the king of Babylon:[m]

How the oppressor[n] has come to an end!
How his fury[a] has ended!
5The LORD has broken the rod[o] of the wicked,[p]
the sceptre[q] of the rulers,
6which in anger struck down peoples[r]
with unceasing blows,
and in fury subdued[s] nations
with relentless aggression.[t]
7All the lands are at rest and at peace;[u]
they break into singing.[v]
8Even the pine trees[w] and the cedars of Lebanon
exult over you and say,
"Now that you have been laid low,
no woodsman comes to cut us down."[x]

9The grave[b] [y] below is all astir
to meet you at your coming;
it rouses the spirits of the departed[z] to greet you—
all those who were leaders[a] in the world;
it makes them rise from their thrones—
all those who were kings over the nations.[b]

21 [q]**Ps 74:14;** Rev 18:2; [r]Jer 14:6; [s]**Lev 11:16–18; Dt 14:15–17;** [t]Lev 17:7; 2Ch 11:15
22 [u]Isa 34:14; [v]Isa 25:2; 32:14; [w]Isa 34:13; 35:7; 43:20; Jer 9:11; 49:33; 51:37; Mal 1:3; [x]Dt 32:35; Jer 48:16; 51:33; [y]Jer 50:39

Ch. 14

1 [a]Ps 102:13; Isa 49:10,13; 54:7–8,10; Jer 33:26; Zec 10:6; [b]Ge 18:19; 2Ch 6:6; Isa 41:8; 42:1; 44:1; 45:4; 49:7; 65:9,22; Zec 1:17; 2:12; 3:2; [c]Jer 3:18; 16:15; 23:8; [d]**Ex 12:43; Isa 11:10;** Eze 47:22; Zec 8:22–23; Eph 2:12–19
2 [e]**Isa 11:12;** 60:9; [f]**Ps 49:14;** Isa 26:15; 43:14; 49:7,23; 54:3; [g]Ps 149:8; Isa 45:14; 49:25; 60:12; Jer 40:1; [h]Isa 60:14; 61:5; Jer 30:16; 49:2; Eze 39:10; Zep 3:19; Zec 2:9
3 [i]**Isa 11:10;** [j]**Job 3:17;** [k]**Ex 1:14**
4 [l]Mic 2:4; Hab 2:6; [m]**Isa 13:1;** [n]**Isa 9:4**
5 [o]**Isa 10:15;** [p]**Ps 125:3;** [q]**Ps 110:2**
6 [r]Isa 10:14; [s]**Ps 47:3;** [t]**2Ki 15:29;** Isa 47:6; Hab 1:17
7 [u]**Nu 6:26;** Jer 50:34; Zec 1:11; [v]Ps 98:1; 126:1–3; Isa 12:6
8 [w]**1Ch 16:33; Ps 65:13;** Eze 31:16; [x]**2Ki 19:23;** Isa 37:24
9 [y]**Pr 30:16;** Eze 32:21; [z]**Job 26:5;** [a]Zec 10:3; [b]**Job 3:14**
10 [c]Eze 26:20; 32:21

10They will all respond,
they will say to you,
"You also have become weak, as we are;
you have become like us."[c]
11All your pomp has been brought
down to the grave,[d]
along with the noise of your harps;[e]
maggots are spread out beneath you
and worms[f] cover you.[g]

12How you have fallen[h] from heaven,
O morning star,[i] son of the dawn!
You have been cast down to the earth,
you who once laid low the nations![j]
13You said in your heart,
"I will ascend[k] to heaven;
I will raise my throne[l]
above the stars of God;
I will sit enthroned on the mount of assembly,[m]
on the utmost heights[n] of the sacred mountain.[c]
14I will ascend above the tops of the clouds;[o]
I will make myself like the Most High."[p]
15But you are brought down[q] to the grave,[r]
to the depths[s] of the pit.[t]

16Those who see you stare at you,
they ponder your fate:[u]
"Is this the man who shook[v] the earth
and made kingdoms tremble,
17the man who made the world a desert,[w]
who overthrew[x] its cities
and would not let his captives go home?"[y]

18All the kings of the nations lie in state,
each in his own tomb.[z]
19But you are cast out[a] of your tomb
like a rejected branch;
you are covered with the slain,[b]
with those pierced by the sword,[c]

11 [d]**Nu 16:30; Pr 30:16;** [e]Isa 5:12; Eze 26:13; Am 6:5; [f]**Job 7:5;** 24:20; Isa 51:8; 66:24; [g]**Job 21:26**
12 [h]Lk 10:18; [i]2Pe 1:19; Rev 2:28; 8:10; 9:1; [j]Eze 26:17
13 [k]Da 5:23; 8:10; Ob 4; Mt 11:23; [l]Eze 28:2; 2Th 2:4; [m]Ps 82:1; [n]Isa 37:24
14 [o]**Job 20:6;** [p]**Ge 3:5; Nu 24:16;** Isa 10:13; 47:8; Jer 50:29; 51:53; Da 11:36; 2Th 2:4
15 [q]Isa 13:6; 45:7; 47:11; Jer 51:8,43; [r]**Job 21:13;** [s]Mt 11:23; Lk 10:15; [t]**Ps 55:23;** Eze 31:16; 32:23
16 [u]Jer 50:23; Rev 18:9; [v]**Isa 2:19;** 13:13; Joel 3:16; Hag 2:6,21
17 [w]Isa 15:6; Joel 2:3; [x]Ps 52:7; [y]Ex 7:14; **2Ki 15:29;** Jer 50:33; Rev 18:18 *18* [z]Job 21:32
19 [a]Isa 22:16–18; Jer 8:1; 36:30; [b]Isa 34:3; [c]**Isa 13:15**

[a]4 Dead Sea Scrolls, Septuagint and Syriac; the meaning of the word in the Masoretic Text is uncertain. [b]9 Hebrew *Sheol*; also in verses 11 and 15
[c]13 Or *the north*; Hebrew *Zaphon*

those who descend to the stones of
the pit.[d]
Like a corpse trampled underfoot,
20 you will not join them in burial,[e]
for you have destroyed your land
and killed your people.

The offspring[f] of the wicked[g]
will never be mentioned[h] again.
21Prepare a place to slaughter his sons[i]
for the sins of their forefathers;[j]
they are not to rise to inherit the land
and cover the earth with their cities.
22"I will rise up[k] against them,"
declares the LORD Almighty.
"I will cut off from Babylon her name[l]
and survivors,
her offspring and descendants,[m]"
declares the LORD.
23"I will turn her into a place for owls[n]
and into swampland;
I will sweep her with the broom of
destruction,[o]"
declares the LORD Almighty.[p]

A Prophecy Against Assyria

24The LORD Almighty has sworn,[q]

"Surely, as I have planned,[r] so it will
be,
and as I have purposed, so it will
stand.[s]
25I will crush the Assyrian[t] in my land;
on my mountains I will trample him
down.
His yoke[u] will be taken from my
people,
and his burden removed from their
shoulders.[v]"

26This is the plan[w] determined for the
whole world;
this is the hand[x] stretched out over
all nations.
27For the LORD Almighty has purposed,[y]
and who can thwart him?
His hand[z] is stretched out, and who
can turn it back?[a]

A Prophecy Against the Philistines

28This oracle[b] came in the year[c] King
Ahaz[d] died:

29Do not rejoice, all you Philistines,[e]
that the rod that struck you is
broken;
from the root of that snake will spring
up a viper,[f]
its fruit will be a darting, venomous
serpent.[g]

30The poorest of the poor will find
pasture,
and the needy[h] will lie down in
safety.[i]
But your root I will destroy by famine;[j]
it will slay[k] your survivors.[l]

31Wail,[m] O gate![n] Howl, O city!
Melt away, all you Philistines![o]
A cloud of smoke comes from the
north,[p]
and there is not a straggler in its
ranks.[q]
32What answer shall be given
to the envoys[r] of that nation?
"The LORD has established Zion,[s]
and in her his afflicted people will
find refuge.[t]"

A Prophecy Against Moab

16:6–12pp—Jer 48:29–36

15

An oracle[a] concerning Moab:[b]

Ar[c] in Moab is ruined,[d]
destroyed in a night!
Kir[e] in Moab is ruined,
destroyed in a night!
2Dibon[f] goes up to its temple,
to its high places[g] to weep;
Moab wails[h] over Nebo[i] and
Medeba.
Every head is shaved[j]
and every beard cut off.[k]
3In the streets they wear sackcloth;[l]
on the roofs[m] and in the public
squares[n]
they all wail,[o]
prostrate with weeping.[p]
4Heshbon[q] and Elealeh[r] cry out,
their voices are heard all the way to
Jahaz.[s]
Therefore the armed men of Moab cry
out,
and their hearts are faint.

5My heart cries out[t] over Moab;[u]
her fugitives[v] flee as far as Zoar,[w]
as far as Eglath Shelishiyah.
They go up the way to Luhith,
weeping as they go;
on the road to Horonaim[x]
they lament their destruction.[y]

19 [d]Jer 41:7–9
20 [e]**1Ki 21:19;** [f]**Job 18:19;** [g]**Isa 1:4;** [h]**Dt 32:26**
21 [i]**Nu 16:27;** [j]**Ge 9:25; Lev 26:39**
22 [k]**Ps 94:16;** [l]**Job 18:17;** Ps 109:13; Na 1:14; [m]2Sa 18:18; 1Ki 14:10; Job 18:19; **Ps 9:6; Isa 13:18**
23 [n]**Lev 11:16–18;** Isa 34:11–15; Zep 2:14; [o]**Isa 10:3;** Jer 25:12; [p]Jer 50:3; 51:62
24 [q]Isa 45:23; 49:18; 54:9; 62:8; [r]Isa 19:12,17; 23:8–9; 25:1; Da 4:35; [s]**Job 9:3; Isa 7:7;** 46:10–11; Eze 12:25; Ac 4:28
25 [t]**Isa 10:5,**12; 37:36–38; [u]**Isa 9:4;** [v]**Isa 10:27**
26 [w]Isa 23:9; [x]Ex 15:12; **Job 30:21**
27 [y]Jer 49:20; [z]**Ex 14:21;** [a]**2Ch 20:6;** Isa 43:13; Da 4:35
28 [b]**Isa 13:1;** [c]**2Ki 15:7;** [d]**2Ki 16:1**
29 [e]**Jos 13:3; 2Ki 1:2; 2Ch 26:6;** [f]**Isa 11:8;** [g]**Dt 8:15**
30 [h]Isa 3:15; 25:4; [i]**Isa 7:21–22;** [j]Isa 8:21; 9:20; 51:19; [k]Jer 25:16; Zec 9:5–6; [l]Eze 25:15–17; Zep 2:5
31 [m]**Isa 13:6;** [n]**Isa 3:26;** [o]**Ge 10:14;** [p]Isa 41:25; Jer 1:14; 4:6; 6:1,22; 10:22; 13:20; 25:9; 46:20,24; 47:2; 50:41; Eze 32:30; [q]**Isa 5:27**
32 [r]Isa 37:9; [s]**Ps 51:18;** 87:2,5; Isa 2:2; 26:1; 28:16; 31:5; 33:5,20; 44:28; 51:21; 54:11; [t]**Isa 4:6;** Jas 2:5

Ch. 15

1 [a]**Isa 13:1;** [b]Nu 22:3–6; **Dt 23:6; Isa 11:14;** [c]**Nu 21:15;** [d]**Nu 17:12;** Isa 25:12; 26:5; Jer 48:24,41; 51:58; [e]**2Ki 3:25**
2 [f]**Nu 21:30;** [g]1Ki 11:7; Isa 16:12; Jer 48:35; [h]**Isa 13:6;** 65:14; [i]**Nu 32:38;** [j]**Lev 13:40; Job 1:20;** [k]**2Sa 10:4**
3 [l]**Isa 3:24;** [m]**Jos 2:8;** [n]Jer 48:38; [o]Isa 14:31; Jer 47:2; [p]ver 5; Isa 16:9; 22:4; La 2:11; Eze 7:18; Mic 1:8
4 [q]**Nu 21:25; Jos 13:26;** [r]**Nu 32:3;** [s]**Nu 21:23**
5 [t]**ver 3;** [u]Isa 16:11; Jer 48:31; [v]**Nu 21:29;** [w]**Ge 13:10;** [x]Jer 48:3,34; [y]Jer 4:20; 48:5

6The waters of Nimrim are dried up[z]
and the grass is withered;[a]
the vegetation is gone[b]
and nothing green is left.[c]
7So the wealth they have acquired[d] and stored up
they carry away over the Ravine of the Poplars.
8Their outcry echoes along the border of Moab;
their wailing reaches as far as Eglaim,
their lamentation as far as Beer[e] Elim.
9Dimon's[a] waters are full of blood,
but I will bring still more upon Dimon[a]—
a lion[f] upon the fugitives of Moab[g]
and upon those who remain in the land.

16 Send lambs[a] as tribute[b] to the ruler of the land,
from Sela,[c] across the desert,
to the mount of the Daughter of Zion.[d]
2Like fluttering birds
pushed from the nest,[e]
so are the women of Moab[f]
at the fords[g] of the Arnon.[h]

3"Give us counsel,
render a decision.
Make your shadow like night—
at high noon.
Hide the fugitives,[i]
do not betray the refugees.
4Let the Moabite fugitives stay with you;
be their shelter[j] from the destroyer."

The oppressor[k] will come to an end,
and destruction will cease;[l]
the aggressor will vanish from the land.
5In love a throne[m] will be established;[n]
in faithfulness a man will sit on it—
one from the house[a] of David[o]—
one who in judging seeks justice[p]
and speeds the cause of righteousness.

6We have heard of Moab's[q] pride[r]—
her overweening pride and conceit,
her pride and her insolence—
but her boasts are empty.
7Therefore the Moabites wail,[s]
they wail together for Moab.
Lament and grieve
for the men[b t] of Kir Hareseth.[u]
8The fields of Heshbon[v] wither,[w]
the vines of Sibmah[x] also.
The rulers of the nations
have trampled down the choicest vines,[y]
which once reached Jazer[z]
and spread towards the desert.
Their shoots spread out[a]
and went as far as the sea.[b]
9So I weep,[c] as Jazer weeps,
for the vines of Sibmah.
O Heshbon, O Elealeh,[d]
I drench you with tears![e]
The shouts of joy[f] over your ripened fruit
and over your harvests[g] have been stilled.
10Joy and gladness are taken away from the orchards;[h]
no-one sings or shouts[i] in the vineyards;
no-one treads[j] out wine at the presses,[k]
for I have put an end to the shouting.
11My heart laments for Moab[l] like a harp,[m]
my inmost being[n] for Kir Hareseth.
12When Moab appears at her high place,[o]
she only wears herself out;
when she goes to her shrine[p] to pray,
it is to no avail.[q]

13This is the word the LORD has
already spoken concerning Moab. 14But
now the LORD says: "Within three
years,[r] as a servant bound by contract[s]
would count them,[t] Moab's splendour
and all her many people will be despised,[u] and her survivors will be very
few and feeble."[v]

An Oracle Against Damascus

17 An oracle[a] concerning Damascus:[b]

"See, Damascus will no longer be a city
but will become a heap of ruins.[c]
2The cities of Aroer[d] will be deserted
and left to flocks,[e] which will lie down,[f]
with no-one to make them afraid.[g]
3The fortified[h] city will disappear from Ephraim,
and royal power from Damascus;

6 [z]Isa 19:5–7; Jer 48:34; [a]Ps 37:2; Isa 16:8; 24:4,7,11; 33:9; 34:4; 37:27; 40:7; 51:6,12; Hos 4:3; Joel 1:12; [b]**Isa 14:17;** [c]Jer 14:5
7 [d]Isa 30:6; Jer 48:36
8 [e]**Nu 21:16**
9 [f]**2Ki 17:25;** [g]Eze 25:8–11

Ch. 16

1 [a]**2Ki 3:4;** [b]**2Ch 32:23;** [c]**Jdg 1:36;** Ob 3 *fn;* [d]**Isa 10:32**
2 [e]Pr 27:8; [f]Nu 21:29; [g]Jdg 12:5; [h]Nu 21:13–14; Jer 48:20
3 [i]**1Ki 18:4**
4 [j]Isa 58:7; [k]**Isa 9:4;** [l]Isa 2:2–4
5 [m]**1Sa 13:14;** Da 7:14; Mic 4:7; [n]**Pr 20:28;** [o]**Isa 7:2;** Lk 1:32; [p]**Isa 9:7**
6 [q]Jer 25:21; Eze 25:8; Am 2:1; Zep 2:8; [r]**Lev 26:19; Job 20:6;** Jer 49:16; Ob 3; Zep 2:10
7 [s]**Isa 13:6;** Jer 48:20; 49:3; [t]**1Ch 16:3;** [u]**2Ki 3:25**
8 [v]**Nu 21:25;** [w]**Isa 15:6;** [x]**Nu 32:3;** [y]**Isa 5:2;** [z]**Nu 21:32;** [a]**Job 8:16;** [b]Ps 80:11
9 [c]**Isa 15:3;** Eze 27:31; [d]**Nu 32:3;** [e]**Job 7:3;** [f]**Ezr 3:13;** [g]Jer 40:12
10 [h]Isa 24:7–8; [i]Jer 25:30; [j]**Jdg 9:27;** [k]**Job 24:11; Isa 5:2**
11 [l]**Isa 15:5;** [m]**Job 30:31;** [n]Isa 63:15; Hos 11:8; Php 2:1
12 [o]1Ki 11:7; [p]**Isa 15:2;** [q]**1Ki 18:29;** Ps 115:4–7; Isa 44:17–18; 1Co 8:4
14 [r]Isa 20:3; 37:30; [s]**Lev 25:50;** [t]**Lev 19:13;** [u]Isa 25:10; Jer 48:42; [v]Isa 21:17

Ch. 17

1 [a]Isa 13:1; [b]**Ge 14:15;** Ac 9:2; [c]**Dt 13:16; Isa 25:2**
2 [d]**2Ki 10:33;** [e]**Isa 5:17;** 7:21; Eze 25:5; [f]Isa 27:10; [g]**Lev 26:6;** Jer 7:33; Mic 4:4
3 [h]Isa 25:2,12; Hos 10:14

a9 Masoretic Text; Dead Sea Scrolls, some Septuagint manuscripts and Vulgate *Dibon*
a5 Hebrew *tent*
b7 Or *"raisin cakes,"* a wordplay

the remnant of Aram will be
like the glory[i] of the Israelites,"[j]
declares the LORD Almighty.

4 "In that day[k] the glory[l] of Jacob will fade;
the fat of his body will waste[m] away.
5 It will be as when a reaper gathers the standing corn
and harvests[n] the corn with his arm—
as when a man gleans ears of corn[o]
in the Valley of Rephaim.[p]
6 Yet some gleanings will remain,[q]
as when an olive tree is beaten,[r]
leaving two or three olives on the topmost branches,
four or five on the fruitful boughs,"
declares the LORD,
the God of Israel.

7 In that day[s] men will look[t] to their Maker[u]
and turn their eyes to the Holy One[v] of Israel.
8 They will not look to the altars,[w]
the work of their hands,[x]
and they will have no regard for the Asherah poles[a][y]
and the incense altars their fingers[z] have made.

9 In that day their strong cities, which
they left because of the Israelites, will be
like places abandoned to thickets and
undergrowth.[a] And all will be deso-
lation.

10 You have forgotten[b] God your Saviour;[c]
you have not remembered the Rock,[d] your fortress.[e]
Therefore, though you set out the finest plants
and plant imported vines,[f]
11 though on the day you set them out,
you make them grow,
and on the morning[g] when you plant them, you bring them to bud,
yet the harvest[h] will be as nothing[i]
in the day of disease and incurable[j] pain.[k]

12 Oh, the raging[l] of many nations—
they rage like the raging sea![m]
Oh, the uproar[n] of the peoples—
they roar like the roaring of great waters![o]
13 Although the peoples roar[p] like the roar of surging waters,
when he rebukes[q] them they flee[r] far away,
driven before the wind like chaff[s] on the hills,
like tumble-weed before a gale.[t]
14 In the evening, sudden[u] terror![v]
Before the morning, they are gone![w]
This is the portion of those who loot us,
the lot of those who plunder us.

A Prophecy Against Cush

18 Woe[a] to the land of whirring wings[a]
along the rivers of Cush,[b][b]
2 which sends envoys[c] by sea
in papyrus[d] boats over the water.

Go, swift messengers,
to a people tall and smooth-skinned,[e]
to a people feared far and wide,
an aggressive[f] nation of strange speech,
whose land is divided by rivers.[g]
3 All you people of the world,[h]
you who live on the earth,
when a banner[i] is raised on the mountains,
you will see it,
and when a trumpet[j] sounds,
you will hear it.
4 This is what the LORD says to me:
"I will remain quiet[k] and will look on from my dwelling-place,[l]
like shimmering heat in the sunshine,[m]
like a cloud of dew[n] in the heat of harvest."
5 For, before the harvest, when the blossom is gone
and the flower becomes a ripening grape,
he will cut off[o] the shoots with pruning knives,
and cut down and take away the spreading branches.[p]
6 They will all be left to the mountain birds of prey[q]
and to the wild animals;[r]
the birds will feed on them all summer,
the wild animals all winter.

3 [i]ver 4; Isa 21:16; Hos 9:11; [j]Isa 7:8, 16; 8:4
4 [k]**Isa 2:11;** [l]ver 3; [m]**Isa 10:16**
5 [n]ver 11; Isa 33:4; Jer 51:33; Joel 3:13; Mt 13:30; [o]Job 24:24; [p]**Jos 17:15; 1Ch 11:15**
6 [q]**Dt 4:27; Isa 10:19; 24:13;** [r]ver 11; Isa 27:12
7 [s]**Isa 2:11;** [t]**Isa 9:13; 10:20;** [u]**Ps 95:6;** [v]**Isa 12:6**
8 [w]**Lev 26:30;** [x]**2Ch 32:19;** Isa 2:18,20; 30:22; 46:6; Rev 9:20; [y]**Jdg 3:7; 2Ki 17:10;** [z]Isa 2:8
9 [a]**Isa 7:19**
10 [b]**Dt 6:12;** 8:11; Ps 50:22; 106:21; Isa 51:13; 57:11; Jer 2:32; 3:21; 13:25; 18:15; Eze 22:12; 23:35; Hos 8:14; 13:6; [c]**Isa 12:2; Lk 1:47;** [d]**Ge 49:24;** [e]**Ps 18:2;** [f]**Isa 5:7**
11 [g]Ps 90:6; [h]**ver 5;** [i]**Lev 26:20;** Hos 8:7; Joel 1:11; Hag 1:6; [j]Jer 10:19; 30:12; [k]**Dt 28:39; Job 4:8**
12 [l]ver 13; Isa 41:11; [m]**Ps 18:4;** Lk 21:25; [n]**Ps 46:6;** Isa 8:9; [o]Isa 8:7
13 [p]**Ps 46:3;** [q]**Dt 28:20; Ps 9:5;** [r]**Ps 68:1; Isa 13:14;** [s]**Job 13:25; Isa 2:22;** 41:2, 15–16; Da 2:35; [t]Job 21:18; **Ps 65:7**
14 [u]Isa 29:5; 30:13; 47:11; 48:3; [v]Isa 33:18; 54:14; [w]**2Ki 19:35**

Ch. 18

1 [a]Isa 5:8; [b]**Ge 10:6; Ps 68:31; Eze 29:10**
2 [c]Ob 1; [d]Ex 2:3; Job 9:26; [e]**Ge 41:14;** [f]**Ge 10:8–9; 2Ch 12:3;** [g]ver 7
3 [h]**Ps 33:8;** [i]**Ps 60:4;** Isa 5:26; 11:10; 13:2; 31:9; Jer 4:21; [j]**Jos 6:20; Jdg 3:27**
4 [k]Isa 62:1; 64:12; [l]Isa 26:21; Hos 5:15; Mic 1:3; [m]**Jdg 5:31; Ps 18:12;** Hab 3:4; [n]**2Sa 1:21; Ps 133:3;** Isa 26:19; Hos 14:5 *5* [o]**Isa 10:33;** [p]Isa 17:10–11; Eze 17:6
6 [q]**Isa 8:8;** [r]Isa 37:36; 56:9; Jer 7:33; Eze 32:4; 39:17

[a]*8* That is, symbols of the goddess Asherah
[a]*1* Or *of locusts*
[b]*1* That is, the upper Nile region

[7]At that time gifts[s] will be brought to the LORD Almighty

from a people tall and smooth-
skinned,[t]
from a people feared[u] far and wide,
an aggressive nation of strange
speech,
whose land is divided by rivers[v]—

the gifts will be brought to Mount Zion, the place of the Name of the LORD Almighty.[w]

A Prophecy About Egypt

19

An oracle[a] concerning Egypt:[b c]

See, the LORD rides on a swift cloud[d]
and is coming to Egypt.
The idols of Egypt tremble before him,
and the hearts of the Egyptians
melt[e] within them.

2"I will stir up Egyptian against
Egyptian—
brother will fight against brother,[f]
neighbour against neighbour,
city against city,
kingdom against kingdom.[g]
3The Egyptians will lose heart,[h]
and I will bring their plans[i] to
nothing;[j]
they will consult the idols and the
spirits of the dead,
the mediums and the spiritists.[k]
4I will hand the Egyptians over
to the power of a cruel master,
and a fierce king[l] will rule over them,"
declares the Lord, the LORD
Almighty.

5The waters of the river will dry up,[m]
and the river bed will be parched
and dry.[n]
6The canals will stink;[o]
the streams of Egypt will dwindle
and dry up.[p]
The reeds[q] and rushes will wither,[r]
7 also the plants[s] along the Nile,
at the mouth of the river.
Every sown field[t] along the Nile
will become parched, will blow
away and be no more.[u]
8The fishermen[v] will groan and lament,
all who cast hooks[w] into the Nile;
those who throw nets on the water
will pine away.
9Those who work with combed flax[x]
will despair,
the weavers of fine linen[y] will lose
hope.
10The workers in cloth will be dejected,
and all the wage earners will be sick
at heart.
11The officials of Zoan[z] are nothing but
fools;
the wise counsellors[a] of Pharaoh
give senseless advice.[b]
How can you say to Pharaoh,
"I am one of the wise men,[c]
a disciple of the ancient kings"?
12Where are your wise men[d] now?
Let them show you and make
known
what the LORD Almighty
has planned[e] against Egypt.
13The officials of Zoan[f] have become
fools,
the leaders of Memphis[a][g] are
deceived;
the cornerstones[h] of her peoples
have led Egypt astray.
14The LORD has poured into them
a spirit of dizziness;[i]
they make Egypt stagger in all that she
does,
as a drunkard staggers[j] around in
his vomit.
15There is nothing Egypt can do—
head or tail, palm branch or reed.[k]

16In that day[l] the Egyptians will be
like women.[m] They will shudder with
fear[n] at the uplifted hand[o] that the LORD
Almighty raises against them. 17And the
land of Judah will bring terror to the
Egyptians; everyone to whom Judah is
mentioned will be terrified,[p] because of
what the LORD Almighty is planning[q]
against them.
18In that day[r] five cities[s] in Egypt will
speak the language of Canaan and
swear allegiance[t] to the LORD Almighty.
One of them will be called the City of
Destruction.[b][u]
19In that day[v] there will be an altar[w] to
the LORD in the heart of Egypt,[x] and a
monument[y] to the LORD at its border. 20It
will be a sign and witness[z] to the LORD
Almighty in the land of Egypt. When
they cry out to the LORD because of their
oppressors, he will send them a saviour[a]
and defender, and he will rescue[b] them.
21So the LORD will make himself known

7 [s]**2Ch 9:24; Isa 60:7**; [t]**Ge 41:14**; [u]Hab 1:7; [v]ver 2; [w]Ps 68:31
Ch. 19
1 [a]Isa 13:1; [b]Isa 20:3; Joel 3:19; [c]**Ex 12:12**; **Jer 44:3**; [d]**Dt 10:14**; **2Sa 22:10**; **Rev 1:7**; [e]**Jos 2:11**
2 [f]**Jdg 7:22**; **12:4**; Mt 10:21, 36; [g]**2Ch 15:6**; 20:23; Mt 24:7; Mk 13:8; Lk 21:10
3 [h]Ps 18:45; [i]ver 11; **Job 5:12**; [j]2Ch 10:13; [k]**Lev 19:31**; Isa 47:13; Da 2:2,10; 3:8; 5:7
4 [l]Isa 20:4; Jer 46:26; Eze 29:19; 32:11
5 [m]Isa 44:27; 50:2; Jer 50:38; 51:36; [n]**2Sa 14:14**
6 [o]Ex 7:18; [p]Isa 37:25; Eze 30:12; [q]**Ge 41:2**; **Job 8:11**; [r]Isa 15:6
7 [s]Nu 11:5; [t]Dt 29:23; Isa 23:3; [u]Zec 10:11
8 [v]Nu 11:5; Eze 47:10; [w]Am 4:2; Hab 1:15
9 [x]**Jos 2:6**; [y]Pr 7:16; Eze 16:10; 27:7
11 [z]**Nu 13:22**; [a]**Ge 41:37**; [b]**ver 3**; [c]**1Ki 4:30**; Ac 7:22
12 [d]1Co 1:20; [e]**Isa 14:24**; Ro 9:17
13 [f]**Nu 13:22**; [g]Jer 2:16; 44:1; 46:14,19; Eze 30:13,16; Hos 9:6; [h]**Ps 118:22**
14 [i]**Pr 12:8**; Mt 17:17; [j]**Ps 107:27**
15 [k]**Isa 9:14**
16 [l]Isa 2:17; 11:10; [m]Jer 50:37; 51:30; Na 3:13; [n]**Dt 2:25**; Heb 10:31; [o]**Isa 11:15**
17 [p]**Ge 35:5**; [q]**Isa 14:24**
18 [r]**Isa 10:20**; [s]Jer 44:1; [t]Ps 22:27; **63:11**; Isa 48:1; Jer 4:2; Zep 3:9; [u]Isa 17:1; 24:12; 32:19; *fn* Jer 43:13
19 [v]**Isa 10:20**; [w]**Jos 22:10**; [x]**Ps 68:31**; [y]**Ge 28:18**
20 [z]**Ge 21:30**; [a]**Dt 28:29**; **Jdg 2:18**; **Isa 25:9**; [b]Isa 49:24–26

[a]*13* Hebrew *Noph*
[b]*18* Most manuscripts of the Masoretic Text; some manuscripts of the Masoretic Text, Dead Sea Scrolls and Vulgate *City of the Sun* (that is, Heliopolis)

to the Egyptians, and in that day they
will acknowledge[c] the LORD. They will
worship[d] with sacrifices and grain offer-
ings; they will make vows to the LORD
and keep them.[e] 22The LORD will strike[f]
Egypt with a plague;[g] he will strike them
and heal them. They will turn[h] to the
LORD, and he will respond to their pleas
and heal[i] them.

23In that day[j] there will be a highway[k]
from Egypt to Assyria.[l] The Assyrians
will go to Egypt and the Egyptians to
Assyria. The Egyptians and Assyrians
will worship[m] together. 24In that day[n]
Israel will be the third, along with Egypt
and Assyria,[o] a blessing[p] on the earth.
25The LORD Almighty will bless[q] them,
saying, "Blessed be Egypt my people,[r]
Assyria my handiwork,[s] and Israel my
inheritance.[t]"

A Prophecy Against Egypt and Cush

20 In the year that the supreme
commander,[a] sent by Sargon
king of Assyria, came to Ashdod[b] and
attacked and captured it— 2at that time
the LORD spoke through Isaiah son of
Amoz.[c] He said to him, "Take off the
sackcloth[d] from your body and the san-
dals[e] from your feet." And he did so,
going around stripped[f] and barefoot.[g]

3Then the LORD said, "Just as my
servant[h] Isaiah has gone stripped and
barefoot for three years,[i] as a sign[j] and
portent[k] against Egypt[l] and Cush,[a][m]
4so the king[n] of Assyria will lead away
stripped[o] and barefoot the Egyptian
captives[p] and Cushite[q] exiles, young
and old, with buttocks bared[r]—to
Egypt's shame.[s] 5Those who trusted[t]
in Cush[u] and boasted in Egypt[v] will be
afraid and put to shame.[w] 6In that day[x]
the people who live on this coast will
say, 'See what has happened[y] to those
we relied on,[z] those we fled to for
help[a] and deliverance from the king of
Assyria! How then can we escape?[b]' "

A Prophecy Against Babylon

21 An oracle[a] concerning the
Desert[b] by the Sea:

Like whirlwinds[c] sweeping through
the southland,[d]
an invader comes from the desert,
from a land of terror.

2A dire[e] vision has been shown to me:
The traitor betrays,[f] the looter takes
loot.
Elam,[g] attack! Media,[h] lay siege!
I will bring to an end all the
groaning she caused.

3At this my body is racked with pain,[i]
pangs seize me, like those of a
woman in labour;[j]
I am staggered by what I hear,
I am bewildered[k] by what I see.
4My heart[l] falters,
fear makes me tremble;[m]
the twilight I longed for
has become a horror[n] to me.

5They set the tables,
they spread the rugs,
they eat, they drink![o]
Get up, you officers,
oil the shields![p]

6This is what the LORD says to me:

"Go, post a lookout[q]
and have him report what he sees.
7When he sees chariots[r]
with teams of horses,
riders on donkeys
or riders on camels,[s]
let him be alert,
fully alert."

8And the lookout[a][t] shouted,

"Day after day, my lord, I stand on the
watchtower;
every night I stay at my post.
9Look, here comes a man in a chariot[u]
with a team of horses.
And he gives back the answer:
'Babylon[v] has fallen,[w] has fallen!
All the images of its gods[x]
lie shattered[y] on the ground!' "

10O my people, crushed on the
threshing-floor,[z]
I tell you what I have heard
from the LORD Almighty,
from the God of Israel.

21 [c]**Isa 11:9; 43:10;** [d]ver 19; **Ge 27:29; Ps 86:9;** Isa 56:7; 60:7; Mal 1:11; [e]**Nu 30:2; Dt 23:21**
22 [f]Ex 12:23; Heb 12:11; [g]Ex 11:10; [h]Isa 45:14; Eze 33:11; Hos 6:1; 10:12; 12:6; 14:1; Joel 2:13; [i]**Dt 32:39**
23 [j]**ver 16**,24; Isa 20:6; [k]**Isa 11:16;** [l]Mic 7:12; [m]**Ge 27:29;** Isa 2:3; 27:13; 66:23
24 [n]**ver 23;** [o]**Isa 11:11;** [p]**Ge 12:2**
25 [q]**Ge 12:3;** Eph 2:11–14; [r]Ps 87:4; **100:3;** [s]Isa 29:23; 43:7; 45:11; 60:21; 64:8; Eph 2:10; [t]**Ex 34:9;** Jer 30:22; Hos 2:23

Ch. 20

1 [a]2Ki 18:17; [b]**Jos 11:22; 13:3**
2 [c]**Isa 13:1;** [d]2Ki 1:8; **Isa 3:24;** Zec 13:4; Mt 3:4; [e]Eze 24:17,23; [f]**1Sa 19:24;** [g]Eze 4:1–12; Mic 1:8
3 [h]Isa 22:20; 41:8–9; 42:1; 43:10; 49:3, 5–7; 50:10; 52:13; 53:11; Jer 7:25; Hag 2:23; Zec 4:14; [i]**Isa 16:14;** [j]**Ex 3:12; Isa 8:18;** 37:30; 38:7; Ac 21:11; [k]**Dt 28:46;** [l]**Isa 19:1;** [m]ver 5; **Ge 10:6;** Isa 37:9; 43:3
4 [n]**Isa 19:4;** [o]**Job 12:17;** [p]Jer 46:19; Na 3:10; [q]Isa 18:1; Zep 2:12; [r]**Isa 3:24;** [s]Isa 47:3; Jer 13:22,26; Na 3:5
5 [t]**Isa 8:12;** [u]**ver 3;** [v]**2Ki 18:21; Isa 30:5;** [w]Eze 29:16
6 [x]Isa 2:11; **19:23;** [y]**2Ki 18:21;** [z]Jer 46:25; [a]**Isa 10:3;** [b]Jer 30:15–17; 31:2; Mt 23:33; 1Th 5:3; Heb 2:3

Ch. 21

1 [a]**Isa 13:1;** [b]Isa 13:21; Jer 50:12; 51:43; [c]**Job 1:19;** [d]Da 11:40; Zec 9:14
2 [e]Ps 60:3; [f]Isa 24:16; 33:1; [g]**Ge 10:22;** Isa 22:6; [h]**Isa 13:3;** Jer 25:25; 51:28
3 [i]**Job 14:22;** [j]**Ge 3:16;** Ps 48:6; Isa 26:17; 37:3; Jer 30:6; 48:41; 49:22; Jn 16:21; [k]Da 7:28; 8:27; 10:16
4 [l]Isa 7:4; 35:4; [m]**Isa 13:8;** Da 5:9; [n]**Ps 55:5**
5 [o]Isa 5:12; 22:2,13; 23:7; 24:8; 32:13; Jer 25:16,27; 51:39,57; Da 5:2; [p]2Sa 1:21; 1Ki 10:16–17; Jer 46:3; 51:11
6 [q]**2Ki 9:17** 7 [r]ver 9; [s]**Jdg 6:5**
8 [t]Mic 7:7; Hab 2:1
9 [u]ver 7; [v]**Isa 13:1;** 47:1,5; **Rev 14:8;** [w]**Isa 47:11;** Jer 51:8; Da 5:30; [x]**Lev 26:30;** Isa 46:1; Jer 50:2; 51:44; [y]**Isa 2:18**
10 [z]Isa 27:12; 28:27–28; 41:15; Jer 51:33; Mic 4:13; Hab 3:12; Mt 3:12

[a]3 That is, the upper Nile region; also in verse 5
[a]8 Dead Sea Scrolls and Syriac; Masoretic Text *A lion*

A Prophecy Against Edom

11An oracle concerning Dumah:[b] [a]

Someone calls to me from Seir,[b]
"Watchman, what is left of the night?
Watchman, what is left of the night?"
12The watchman replies,
"Morning is coming, but also the night.
If you would ask, then ask;
and come back yet again."

A Prophecy Against Arabia

13An oracle[c] concerning Arabia:[d]

You caravans of Dedanites,[e]
who camp in the thickets of Arabia,
14 bring water for the thirsty;
you who live in Tema,[f]
bring food for the fugitives.
15They flee[g] from the sword,[h]
from the drawn sword,
from the bent bow
and from the heat of battle.

16This is what the LORD says to me:
"Within one year, as a servant bound by
contract[i] would count it, all the pomp[j] of
Kedar[k] will come to an end. 17The sur-
vivors of the bowmen, the warriors of
Kedar, will be few.[l]" The LORD, the God
of Israel, has spoken.[m]

A Prophecy About Jerusalem

22 An oracle[a] concerning the Valley[b] of Vision:[c]

What troubles you now,
that you have all gone up on the roofs,[d]
2O town full of commotion,
O city of tumult[e] and revelry?[f]
Your slain[g] were not killed by the sword,[h]
nor did they die in battle.
3All your leaders have fled[i] together;
they have been captured[j] without using the bow.
All you who were caught were taken prisoner together,
having fled while the enemy was still far away.
4Therefore I said, "Turn away from me;
let me weep[k] bitterly.
Do not try to console me
over the destruction of my people."[l]
5The Lord, the LORD Almighty, has a day[m]
of tumult and trampling[n] and terror[o]
in the Valley of Vision,[p]
a day of battering down walls[q]
and of crying out to the mountains.
6Elam[r] takes up the quiver,[s]
with her charioteers and horses;
Kir[t] uncovers the shield.
7Your choicest valleys[u] are full of chariots,
and horsemen are posted at the city gates;[v]
8 the defences of Judah are stripped away.

And you looked in that day[w]
to the weapons[x] in the Palace of the Forest;[y]
9you saw that the City of David
had many breaches[z] in its defences;
you stored up water
in the Lower Pool.[a]
10You counted the buildings in Jerusalem
and tore down houses[b] to strengthen the wall.[c]
11You built a reservoir between the two walls[d]
for the water of the Old Pool,[e]
but you did not look to the One who made it,
or have regard[f] for the One who planned[g] it long ago.
12The Lord, the LORD Almighty,
called you on that day[h]
to weep[i] and to wail,
to tear out your hair[j] and put on sackcloth.[k]
13But see, there is joy and revelry,[l]
slaughtering of cattle and killing of sheep,
eating of meat and drinking of wine![m]
"Let us eat and drink," you say,
"for tomorrow we die!"[n]

14The LORD Almighty has revealed this in my hearing:[o] "Till your dying day this sin will not be atoned[p] for," says the Lord, the LORD Almighty.

15This is what the Lord, the LORD Almighty, says:

"Go, say to this steward,
to Shebna,[q] who is in charge[r] of the palace:[s]

11 [a]Ge 25:14; Isa 34:11; [b]Ge 32:3
13 [c]Isa 13:1; [d]2Ch 9:14; [e]Ge 10:7; 25:3
14 [f]Ge 25:15
15 [g]Isa 13:14; [h]Isa 31:8
16 [i]Lev 25:50; [j]Isa 17:3; [k]Ge 25:13
17 [l]Dt 4:27; Isa 10:19; [m]Isa 1:20; 16:14

Ch. 22

1 [a]Isa 13:1; [b]Ps 125:2; Jer 21:13; Joel 3:2,12,14; [c]Isa 1:1; [d]Jos 2:8; Jer 48:38
2 [e]Eze 22:5; [f]Isa 5:14; 21:5; [g]Isa 10:4; [h]2Ki 25:3
3 [i]Isa 13:14; [j]2Ki 25:6
4 [k]Isa 15:3; La 1:16; Eze 21:6; Lk 19:41; [l]Jer 9:1
5 [m]Isa 2:12; [n]Job 40:12; Ps 108:13; [o]2Sa 22:43; Isa 13:3; Jer 30:7; La 1:5; Eze 8:17–18; 9:9–10; Joel 2:31; Am 5:18–20; Zep 1:15; [p]Isa 1:1; [q]Ne 6:15; Ps 89:40; Isa 5:5; Jer 39:8; Eze 13:14
6 [r]Isa 21:2; [s]Ps 46:9; Jer 49:35; 51:56; [t]2Ki 16:9
7 [u]Jos 15:8; [v]2Ch 32:1–2
8 [w]Isa 2:12; [x]2Ch 32:5; [y]1Ki 7:2
9 [z]Ne 1:3; [a]2Ki 18:17; 2Ch 32:4
10 [b]Jer 33:4; [c]2Ch 32:5
11 [d]2Ki 25:4; 2Ch 32:5; Jer 39:4; [e]2Ch 32:4; [f]1Sa 12:24; [g]2Ki 19:25
12 [h]Isa 2:12; [i]Joel 1:9; 2:17; [j]Lev 13:40; Mic 1:16; [k]Isa 3:24
13 [l]Isa 21:5; [m]1Sa 25:36; Ecc 8:15; Isa 5:22; 28:7–8; 56:12; Lk 17:26–29; [n]1Co 15:32*
14 [o]Isa 5:9; [p]1Sa 2:25; Isa 13:11; 26:21; 30:13–14; Eze 24:13
15 [q]2Ki 6:30; 18:18; [r]ver 21; [s]Ge 41:40

b11 *Dumah* means *silence* or *stillness*, a wordplay on *Edom*.

16What are you doing here and who
gave you permission
to cut out a grave[t] for yourself[u] here,
hewing your grave on the height
and chiselling your resting place in
the rock?

17"Beware, the LORD is about to take
firm hold of you
and hurl[v] you away, O you mighty
man.
18He will roll you up tightly like a ball
and throw[w] you into a large country.
There you will die
and there your splendid chariots[x]
will remain—
you disgrace to your master's
house!
19I will depose you from your office,
and you will be ousted[y] from your
position.[z]

20"In that day[a] I will summon my
servant,[b] Eliakim[c] son of Hilkiah. 21I will
clothe him with your robe and fasten
your sash[d] around him and hand your
authority[e] over to him. He will be a
father to those who live in Jerusalem
and to the house of Judah. 22I will place
on his shoulder[f] the key[g] to the house of
David;[h] what he opens no-one can shut,
and what he shuts no-one can open.[i] 23I
will drive him like a peg[j] into a firm
place;[k] he will be a seat[a] of honour[l] for
the house of his father. 24All the glory of
his family will hang on him: its offspring
and offshoots—all its lesser vessels,
from the bowls to all the jars.

25"In that day," [m] declares the LORD
Almighty, "the peg[n] driven into the
firm place will give way; it will be
sheared off and will fall, and the load
hanging on it will be cut down." The
LORD has spoken.[o]

A Prophecy About Tyre

23 An oracle concerning Tyre:[a]

Wail,[b] O ships[c] of Tarshish![d]
For Tyre is destroyed[e]
and left without house or harbour.
From the land of Cyprus[a]
word has come to them.

2Be silent,[f] you people of the island
and you merchants[g] of Sidon,[h]
whom the seafarers have enriched.
3On the great waters
came the grain of the Shihor;[i]
the harvest of the Nile[b] [j] was the
revenue of Tyre,[k]
and she became the market-place of
the nations.

4Be ashamed, O Sidon,[l] and you, O
fortress of the sea,
for the sea has spoken:
"I have neither been in labour nor
given birth;[m]
I have neither reared sons nor
brought up daughters."
5When word comes to Egypt,
they will be in anguish[n] at the report
from Tyre.[o]

6Cross over to Tarshish;[p]
wail, you people of the island.
7Is this your city of revelry,[q]
the old, old city,
whose feet have taken her
to settle in far-off lands?
8Who planned this against Tyre,
the bestower of crowns,
whose merchants[r] are princes,
whose traders[s] are renowned in the
earth?
9The LORD Almighty planned[t] it,
to bring low[u] the pride of all glory
and to humble[v] all who are
renowned[w] on the earth.

10Till[c] your land as along the Nile,
O Daughter of Tarshish,
for you no longer have a harbour.
11The LORD has stretched out his hand[x]
over the sea
and made its kingdoms tremble.[y]
He has given an order concerning
Phoenicia[d]
that her fortresses be destroyed.[z]
12He said, "No more of your revelling,[a]
O Virgin Daughter[b] of Sidon, now
crushed!

"Up, cross over to Cyprus;[e] [c]
even there you will find no rest."
13Look at the land of the Babylonians,[f] [d]
this people that is now of no
account!
The Assyrians[e] have made it
a place for desert creatures;[f]
they raised up their siege towers,[g]
they stripped its fortresses bare
and turned it into a ruin.[h]

14Wail, you ships[i] of Tarshish;[j]
your fortress is destroyed![k]

16 [t]Mt 27:60; [u]**Ge 50:5; Nu 32:42**
17 [v]Jer 10:18; 13:18; 22:26
18 [w]**Job 18:11;** Isa 14:19; 17:13; [x]**Ge 41:43**
19 [y]**1Sa 2:7; Ps 52:5;** [z]Lk 16:3
20 [a]ver 25; [b]**Isa 20:3;** [c]**2Ki 18:18; Isa 36:3**
21 [d]**Isa 5:27;** [e]ver 15
22 [f]Isa 9:6; [g]1Ch 9:27; Mt 16:19; Rev 3:7; [h]**Isa 7:2;** [i]**Job 12:14**
23 [j]ver 25; Eze 15:3; Zec 10:4; [k]**Ezr 9:8; Job 6:25;** [l]**1Sa 2:7–8; Job 36:7**
25 [m]ver 20; [n]**ver 23;** [o]Isa 46:11; Mic 4:4

Ch. 23

1 [a]Jos 19:29; 1Ki 5:1; Jer 47:4; Joel 3:4–8; Am 1:9–10; Zec 9:2–4; [b]**Isa 13:6;** [c]**1Ki 10:22;** [d]**Ge 10:4;** Isa 2:16 *fn*; [e]**Ge 1:2;** Eze 26:4
2 [f]**Job 2:13;** [g]Eze 27:5–24; [h]Jdg 1:31
3 [i]**Ge 41:5;** [j]**Isa 19:7;** [k]**Ps 83:7**
4 [l]**Ge 10:15**,19; [m]Isa 54:1
5 [n]Eze 30:9; [o]Eze 26:17–18
6 [p]**Ge 10:4**
7 [q]ver 12; **Isa 5:14; 21:5;** 32:13; Eze 26:13
8 [r]Na 3:16; [s]Eze 28:5; Rev 18:23
9 [t]**Isa 14:24;** [u]**Job 40:11;** [v]**Isa 13:11;** [w]Isa 5:13; 9:15; Eze 27:3
11 [x]**Ex 14:21;** [y]**Ps 46:6;** [z]ver 14; Isa 25:2; Eze 26:4; Zec 9:3–4
12 [a]**ver 7;** Rev 18:22; [b]Isa 37:22; 47:1; Jer 14:17; 46:11; La 2:13; Zep 3:14; Zec 2:10; [c]**Ge 10:4**
13 [d]Isa 43:14; Jer 51:12; [e]Isa 10:5; [f]**Ps 74:14;** Isa 18:6; [g]**2Ki 25:1;** [h]Isa 10:7
14 [i]**1Ki 10:22;** [j]**Ge 10:4;** Isa 2:16 *fn*; [k]**ver 11**

[a]23 Or *throne* [a]1 Hebrew *Kittim*
[b]2,3 Masoretic Text; one Dead Sea Scroll *Sidon, / who cross over the sea; / your envoys* [3]*are on the great waters. / The grain of the Shihor, / the harvest of the Nile,*
[c]10 Dead Sea Scrolls and some Septuagint manuscripts; Masoretic Text *Go through*
[d]11 Hebrew *Canaan* [e]12 Hebrew *Kittim*
[f]13 Or *Chaldeans*

15At that time Tyre[l] will be forgotten
for seventy years,[m] the span of a king's
life. But at the end of these seventy
years, it will happen to Tyre as in the
song of the prostitute:

16"Take up a harp, walk through the
 city,
 O prostitute[n] forgotten;
play the harp well, sing many a song,
 so that you will be remembered."

17At the end of seventy years,[o] the
LORD will deal with Tyre. She will return
to her hire as a prostitute[p] and will ply
her trade with all the kingdoms on the
face of the earth.[q] 18Yet her profit and
her earnings will be set apart for the
LORD;[r] they will not be stored up or
hoarded. Her profits will go to those
who live before the LORD,[s] for abundant
food and fine clothes.[t]

The LORD's Devastation of the Earth

24 See, the LORD is going to lay
 waste the earth[a]
 and devastate[b] it;
he will ruin its face
 and scatter[c] its inhabitants—
2it will be the same
 for priest as for people,[d]
 for master as for servant,
 for mistress as for maid,
 for seller as for buyer,[e]
 for borrower as for lender,
 for debtor as for creditor.[f]
3The earth will be completely laid
 waste[g]
 and totally plundered.[h]
 The LORD has spoken[i]
 this word.

4The earth dries up[j] and withers,[k]
 the world languishes and withers,
 the exalted[l] of the earth languish.[m]
5The earth is defiled[n] by its people;
 they have disobeyed[o] the laws,
violated the statutes
 and broken the everlasting
 covenant.[p]
6Therefore a curse[q] consumes the
 earth;
 its people must bear their guilt.
Therefore earth's inhabitants are
 burned up,[r]
 and very few are left.
7The new wine dries up[s] and the vine
 withers;[t]
 all the merrymakers groan.[u]
8The gaiety of the tambourines[v] is
 stilled,
 the noise[w] of the revellers[x] has
 stopped,
 the joyful harp[y] is silent.[z]
9No longer do they drink wine[a] with a
 song;
 the beer is bitter[b] to its drinkers.
10The ruined city[c] lies desolate;[d]
 the entrance to every house is
 barred.
11In the streets they cry out[e] for wine;[f]
 all joy turns to gloom,[g]
 all gaiety is banished from the earth.
12The city is left in ruins,[h]
 its gate[i] is battered to pieces.
13So will it be on the earth
 and among the nations,
as when an olive tree is beaten,[j]
 or as when gleanings are left after
 the grape harvest.[k]

14They raise their voices, they shout for
 joy;[l]
 from the west[m] they acclaim the
 LORD's majesty.
15Therefore in the east[n] give glory[o] to the
 LORD;
 exalt[p] the name[q] of the LORD, the
 God of Israel,
 in the islands[r] of the sea.
16From the ends of the earth[s] we hear
 singing:[t]
 "Glory[u] to the Righteous One."[v]

But I said, "I waste away, I waste
 away![w]
 Woe[x] to me!
The treacherous[y] betray!
 With treachery the treacherous
 betray![z]"
17Terror[a] and pit and snare[b] await you,
 O people of the earth.[c]
18Whoever flees[d] at the sound of terror
 will fall into a pit;[e]
whoever climbs out of the pit
 will be caught in a snare.[f]

The floodgates of the heavens[g] are
 opened,
 the foundations of the earth shake.[h]
19The earth is broken up,[i]
 the earth is split asunder,[j]
 the earth is thoroughly shaken.
20The earth reels like a drunkard,[k]
 it sways like a hut[l] in the wind;

23:15 [l]Jer 25:22; [m]**Ps 90:10**
16 [n]Pr 7:10
17 [o]**Ps 90:10**; [p]Dt 23:17–18; Eze 16:26; Na 3:4; Rev 17:1; 18:3,9; [q]Jer 25:26
18 [r]Ex 28:36; **39:30**; Jos 6:17–19; Ps 72:10; [s]Isa 18:7; 60:5–9; 61:6; Mic 4:13; [t]Am 1:9–10; Zec 14:1,14

Ch. 24
1 [a]ver 20; Isa 2:19–21; 33:9; Jer 25:29; [b]**Jos 6:17; Isa 13:5**; [c]**Ge 11:9**
2 [d]Hos 4:9; [e]Eze 7:12; 1Co 7:29–31; [f]**Lev 25:35–37**; Dt 23:19–20; Isa 3:1–7
3 [g]**Ge 6:13**; [h]Isa 6:11–12; 10:6; [i]**Isa 7:7**
4 [j]Jer 12:11; 14:4; Joel 1:10; [k]**Isa 15:6**; [l]**Isa 2:12**; [m]**Isa 3:26**
5 [n]**Ge 3:17**; [o]**Isa 1:2**; 9:17; 10:6; 59:12; Jer 7:28; [p]**Ge 9:11; Jer 11:10**
6 [q]**Jos 23:15**; [r]**Isa 1:31**
7 [s]Jer 48:33; Joel 1:5; [t]Isa 7:23; **15:6**; 32:10; [u]**Isa 3:26**; 16:8–10
8 [v]**Ge 31:27; Isa 5:12**; [w]Jer 7:34; 16:9; 25:10; 33:11; Hos 2:11; [x]**Isa 5:14; 21:5**; [y]**Ps 137:2**; Rev 18:22; [z]La 5:14; Eze 26:13
9 [a]Isa 5:11,22; [b]Isa 5:20
10 [c]Isa 25:2; 26:5; [d]**Ge 1:2; Isa 6:11**
11 [e]**Ps 144:14**; [f]La 2:12; [g]**Isa 15:6**; 16:10; 32:13; Jer 14:3
12 [h]**Isa 19:18**; [i]**Isa 3:26; 13:2**
13 [j]**Dt 30:4; Isa 17:6**; [k]Ob 5; Mic 7:1
14 [l]**Isa 12:6**; [m]Isa 43:5; 49:12
15 [n]**Ps 113:3**; [o]Isa 42:12; 66:19; 2Th 1:12; [p]**Ex 15:2**; Isa 25:3; 59:19; Mal 1:11; [q]**Isa 12:4**; [r]**Isa 11:11**
16 [s]**Ps 48:10**; [t]**Ps 65:8**; [u]Isa 28:5; 60:1,19; [v]**Ezr 9:15**; [w]**Lev 26:39**; [x]1Sa 4:8; **Isa 5:8**; Jer 10:19; 45:3; [y]**Ps 25:3**; [z]Isa 21:2; 33:1; Jer 3:6,20; 5:11; 9:2; Hos 5:7; 9:1
17 [a]Dt 32:23–25; [b]Isa 8:14; Jer 48:43; [c]Lk 21:35
18 [d]**Job 20:24**; [e]Isa 42:22; [f]**Job 18:9; Isa 8:14**; La 3:47; Eze 12:13; [g]**Ge 7:11**; [h]**Jdg 5:4; Job 9:6; Ps 11:3; Eze 38:19**
19 [i]**Ps 46:2**; [j]**Dt 11:6**
20 [k]**Job 12:25**; [l]**Job 27:18**

so heavy upon it is the guilt of its
rebellion[m]
that it falls[n]—never to rise again.[o]
21In that day[p] the LORD will punish[q]
the powers[r] in the heavens above
and the kings[s] on the earth below.
22They will be herded together
like prisoners[t] bound in a dungeon;[u]
they will be shut up in prison
and be punished[a] after many days.[v]
23The moon will be abashed, the sun[w]
ashamed;
for the LORD Almighty will reign[x]
on Mount Zion[y] and in Jerusalem,
and before its elders, gloriously.[z]

Praise to the LORD

25 O LORD, you are my God;[a]
I will exalt you and praise your
name,[b]
for in perfect faithfulness[c]
you have done marvellous things,[d]
things planned[e] long ago.
2You have made the city a heap of
rubble,[f]
the fortified[g] town a ruin,[h]
the foreigners' stronghold[i] a city no
more;
it will never be rebuilt.[j]
3Therefore strong peoples will honour
you;[k]
cities of ruthless[l] nations will revere
you.
4You have been a refuge[m] for the poor,[n]
a refuge for the needy[o] in his
distress,
a shelter from the storm[p]
and a shade from the heat.
For the breath of the ruthless[q]
is like a storm driving against a wall
5 and like the heat of the desert.
You silence[r] the uproar of foreigners;[s]
as heat is reduced by the shadow of
a cloud,
so the song of the ruthless[t] is stilled.

6On this mountain[u] the LORD Almighty
will prepare
a feast[v] of rich food for all peoples,
a banquet of aged wine—
the best of meats and the finest of
wines.[w]
7On this mountain he will destroy
the shroud[x] that enfolds all
peoples,[y]
the sheet that covers all nations;
8 he will swallow up death[z] for ever.
The Sovereign LORD will wipe away
the tears[a]
from all faces;
he will remove the disgrace[b] of his
people
from all the earth.
The LORD has spoken.[c]

9In that day[d] they will say,

"Surely this is our God;[e]
we trusted[f] in him, and he saved[g]
us.
This is the LORD, we trusted in him;
let us rejoice[h] and be glad in his
salvation."[i]
10The hand of the LORD will rest on this
mountain;[j]
but Moab[k] will be trampled under
him
as straw is trampled down in the
manure.
11They will spread out their hands in it,
as a swimmer spreads out his hands
to swim.
God will bring down[l] their pride[m]
despite the cleverness[a] of their
hands.
12He will bring down your high fortified
walls[n]
and lay them low;[o]
he will bring them down to the
ground,
to the very dust.

A Song of Praise

26 In that day[a] this song will be
sung[b] in the land of Judah:

We have a strong city;[c]
God makes salvation
its walls[d] and ramparts.[e]
2Open the gates[f]
that the righteous[g] nation may
enter,
the nation that keeps faith.

20 [m]**Isa 1:2**,28; 43:27; 58:1; [n]**Ps 46:2**; [o]**Job 12:14**
21 [p]**Isa 2:11**; **10:20**; Rev 16:14; [q]Isa 10:12; 13:11; Jer 25:29; [r]1Co 6:3; Eph 6:11–12; [s]**Isa 2:12**
22 [t]**Isa 10:4**; [u]Isa 42:7,22; Lk 8:31; Rev 20:7–10; [v]Eze 38:8
23 [w]**Isa 13:10**; [x]**Ps 97:1**; Rev 22:5; [y]**Isa 2:2**; Heb 12:22; [z]Isa 28:5; 41:16; 45:25; 60:19; Eze 48:35; Zec 2:5; Rev 21:23

Ch. 25

1 [a]**Isa 7:13**; [b]**Ps 145:2**; **Isa 12:1**,**4**; [c]Isa 11:5; [d]Ps 40:5; 98:1; Joel 2:21,26; [e]Nu 23:19; **Isa 14:24**; 37:26; 46:11; Eph 1:11
2 [f]Isa 17:1; 26:5; 37:26; [g]**Isa 17:3**; [h]**Dt 13:16**; [i]**Isa 13:22**; [j]**Job 12:14**
3 [k]**Ex 6:2**; **Ps 22:23**; **Isa 11:14**; [l]**Isa 13:11**
4 [m]**2Sa 22:3**; **Ps 118:8**; **Isa 4:6**; 17:10; 27:5; 33:16; Joel 3:16; [n]**Isa 3:14**; [o]**Isa 14:30**; 29:19; [p]**Ps 55:8**; [q]Isa 29:5; 49:25
5 [r]Jer 51:55; [s]**Ps 18:44**; [t]**Isa 13:11**
6 [u]**Isa 2:2**; [v]**Ge 29:22**; 1Ki 1:25; Isa 1:19; 55:1–2; 66:11; Joel 3:18; Mt 8:11; 22:4; Rev 19:9; [w]**Ps 36:8**; **Pr 9:2**
7 [x]2Co 3:15–16; Eph 4:18; [y]**Job 4:9**
8 [z]Isa 26:19; Hos 13:14; 1Co 15:54–55*; [a]Isa 15:3; 30:19; 35:10; 51:11; 65:19; Jer 31:16; Rev 7:17; 21:4; [b]**Ge 30:23**; **Ps 119:39**; Mt 5:11; 1Pe 4:14; Rev 7:14; [c]**Isa 7:7**
9 [d]**Isa 2:11**; **10:20**; [e]Isa 40:9; [f]**Ps 22:5**; **Isa 12:2**; [g]Ps 145:19; Isa 19:20; 33:22; 35:4; 43:3,11; 45:15,21; 49:25–26; 60:16; 63:8; Jer 14:8; [h]**Dt 32:43**; **Ps 9:2**; Isa 9:3; 35:2,10; 41:16; 51:3; 61:7,10; 66:14; [i]**Ps 13:5**; **Isa 12:2**
10 [j]**Isa 2:2**; [k]**Ge 19:37**; **Nu 21:29**; **Dt 23:6**; **Isa 11:14**; Am 2:1–3
11 [l]Isa 5:25; 14:26; 16:14; [m]**Lev 26:19**; **Job 40:12**
12 [n]**Isa 2:15**; [o]**Job 40:11**; **Isa 15:1**; **Jer 51:44**

Ch. 26

1 [a]**Isa 10:20**; [b]Isa 30:29; [c]**Isa 14:32**; [d]Isa 32:18; 60:18; Zec 2:5; 9:8; [e]**Ps 48:13**
2 [f]**Ps 24:7**; [g]Ps 24:3–4; 85:13; **Isa 1:26**; **4:3**; 9:7; 50:8; 53:11; 54:14; 58:8; 62:2

[a]*22* Or *released*
[a]*11* The meaning of the Hebrew for this word is uncertain.

[3]You will keep in perfect peace[h]
him whose mind is steadfast,
because he trusts[i] in you.
[4]Trust[j] in the LORD for ever,[k]
for the LORD, the LORD, is the Rock[l]
eternal.
[5]He humbles those who dwell on high,
he lays the lofty city low;
he levels it to the ground[m]
and casts it down to the dust.[n]
[6]Feet trample[o] it down—
the feet of the oppressed,[p]
the footsteps of the poor.[q]

[7]The path of the righteous is level;[r]
O upright One,[s] you make the way
of the righteous smooth.[t]
[8]Yes, LORD, walking in the way of your
laws,[a] [u]
we wait[v] for you;
your name[w] and renown
are the desire of our hearts.
[9]My soul yearns for you in the night;[x]
in the morning my spirit longs[y] for
you.
When your judgments[z] come upon
the earth,
the people of the world learn
righteousness.[a]
[10]Though grace is shown to the wicked,[b]
they do not learn righteousness;
even in a land of uprightness they go
on doing evil[c]
and regard[d] not the majesty of the
LORD.
[11]O LORD, your hand is lifted high,[e]
but they do not see[f] it.
Let them see your zeal[g] for your
people and be put to shame;[h]
let the fire[i] reserved for your
enemies consume them.

[12]LORD, you establish peace[j] for us;
all that we have accomplished you
have done[k] for us.
[13]O LORD, our God, other lords[l] besides
you have ruled over us,
but your name[m] alone do we
honour.[n]
[14]They are now dead,[o] they live no
more;
those departed spirits[p] do not rise.
You punished them and brought them
to ruin;[q]
you wiped out all memory of them.[r]
[15]You have enlarged the nation, O LORD;
you have enlarged the nation.[s]
You have gained glory for yourself;
you have extended all the borders[t]
of the land.

[16]LORD, they came to you in their
distress;[u]
when you disciplined[v] them,
they could barely whisper[w] a
prayer.[b]
[17]As a woman with child and about to
give birth[x]
writhes and cries out in her pain,
so were we in your presence, O
LORD.
[18]We were with child, we writhed in
pain,
but we gave birth[y] to wind.
We have not brought salvation[z] to the
earth;
we have not given birth to people of
the world.[a]

[19]But your dead[b] will live;
their bodies will rise.
You who dwell in the dust,[c]
wake up and shout for joy.
Your dew[d] is like the dew of the
morning;
the earth will give birth to her dead.[e]

[20]Go, my people, enter your rooms
and shut the doors[f] behind you;
hide[g] yourselves for a little while
until his wrath[h] has passed by.[i]
[21]See, the LORD is coming[j] out of his
dwelling[k]
to punish[l] the people of the earth for
their sins.
The earth will disclose the blood[m] shed
upon her;
she will conceal her slain no longer.

Deliverance of Israel

27

In that day,[a]
the LORD will punish with his
sword,[b]
his fierce, great and powerful
sword,
Leviathan[c] the gliding serpent,[d]
Leviathan the coiling serpent;
he will slay the monster[e] of the sea.

[2]In that day[f]—

"Sing[g] about a fruitful vineyard:[h]

3 [h]**Job 22:21; Isa 9:6–7;** Php 4:7; [i]**1Ch 5:20; Ps 22:5; 28:7; Isa 12:2**
4 [j]**Isa 12:2;** 50:10; [k]**Ps 62:8;** [l]**Ge 49:24**
5 [m]**Isa 25:12;** Eze 26:11; [n]**Isa 25:2**
6 [o]**Isa 5:5;** [p]Isa 49:26; [q]**Isa 3:15; 14:30**
7 [r]**Ps 26:12;** [s]**Ps 25:8;** [t]**Ex 14:19;** Isa 40:4; 42:16
8 [u]**Dt 18:18;** Ps 1:2; Isa 56:1; 64:5; [v]**Ps 37:9; 130:5;** [w]**Ps 145:2; Isa 12:4**
9 [x]**Ps 119:55;** [y]Ps 42:1–3; 63:1; 78:34; Isa 55:6; [z]**1Ch 16:14;** [a]Mt 6:33
10 [b]Mt 5:45; [c]Isa 32:6; 59:7,13; [d]**1Sa 12:24;** Isa 22:12–13; Jer 2:19; Hos 11:7; Jn 5:37–38; Ro 2:4
11 [e]**Ps 10:12;** [f]Isa 18:3; 44:9,18; [g]**Isa 9:7;** Joel 2:18; Zec 1:14; [h]Mic 7:16; [i]**Isa 1:31;** Heb 10:27
12 [j]**Ps 119:165; Isa 9:6;** [k]**Ps 68:28**
13 [l]Isa 2:8; 10:5, 11; [m]**Isa 12:4;** [n]Isa 42:8; 63:7
14 [o]**Dt 4:28;** [p]**Job 26:5;** [q]**Ps 9:5; Isa 10:3;** [r]**Ps 9:6**
15 [s]**Job 12:23; Isa 14:2;** [t]Isa 33:17
16 [u]**Jdg 6:2; Isa 5:30;** [v]**Ps 39:11;** [w]Isa 29:4
17 [x]**Isa 21:3; Jn 16:21;** Rev 12:2
18 [y]Isa 33:11; 59:4; [z]**Ge 49:10;** Ps 17:14; [a]Isa 42:6; 49:6; 51:4; Jer 12:16
19 [b]**Isa 25:8;** Eph 5:14; [c]Ps 22:29; [d]**Ge 27:28; Isa 18:4;** [e]Isa 66:24; Eze 37:1–14; Da 12:2
20 [f]Ex 12:23; [g]Ps 91:1,4; [h]**Isa 10:25; 30:27;** [i]**Job 14:13**
21 [j]Isa 29:6; Jude 14; [k]**Isa 18:4;** [l]**Isa 13:9**,11; 30:12–14; [m]**Job 16:18;** Lk 11:50–51

Ch. 27
1 [a]ver 13; **Isa 2:11;** 28:5; [b]**Ge 3:24; Dt 32:41;** Isa 31:8; 34:6; 65:12; 66:16; Eze 21:3; Na 3:15; [c]**Job 3:8;** [d]Job 26:13; [e]**Ps 68:30; 74:13;** Rev 12:9
2 [f]Isa 24:21; [g]**Isa 5:1;** [h]Jer 2:21

[a]8 Or *judgments*
[b]16 The meaning of the Hebrew for this clause is uncertain.

3 I, the LORD, watch over it;
I water[i] it continually.
I guard[j] it day and night
so that no-one may harm[k] it.
4 I am not angry.
If only there were briers and thorns
confronting me!
I would march against them in
battle;
I would set them all on fire.[l]
5 Or else let them come to me for
refuge;[m]
let them make peace[n] with me,
yes, let them make peace with me."

6 In days to come Jacob will take root,[o]
Israel will bud and blossom[p]
and fill all the world with fruit.[q]

7 Has ⌊the LORD⌋ struck her
as he struck[r] down those who struck
her?
Has she been killed
as those were killed who killed her?
8 By warfare[a] and exile[s] you contend
with her—
with his fierce blast he drives her
out,
as on a day the east wind[t] blows.
9 By this, then, will Jacob's guilt be
atoned[u] for,
and this will be the full fruitage of
the removal of his sin:[v]
When he makes all the altar stones[w]
to be like chalk stones crushed to
pieces,
no Asherah poles[b] [x] or incense altars[y]
will be left standing.
10 The fortified city stands desolate,[z]
an abandoned settlement, forsaken[a]
like the desert;
there the calves graze,[b]
there they lie down;[c]
they strip its branches bare.
11 When its twigs are dry, they are
broken off[d]
and women come and make fires[e]
with them.
For this is a people without
understanding;[f]
so their Maker has no compassion
on them,
and their Creator[g] shows them no
favour.[h]

12 In that day the LORD will thresh[i]
from the flowing Euphrates[c] to the Wadi
of Egypt,[j] and you, O Israelites, will be
gathered[k] up one by one.
13 And in that
day[l] a great trumpet[m] will sound. Those
who were perishing in Assyria and
those who were exiled[n] in Egypt[o] will
come and worship[p] the LORD on the holy
mountain[q] in Jerusalem.

3 [i]Isa 58:11; [j]Ps 91:4; Isa 5:2; [k]Jn 6:39
4 [l]ver 11; Isa 10:17; Mt 3:12; Heb 6:8
5 [m]Isa 25:4; [n]Job 22:21; Ps 119:165; Ro 5:1; 2Co 5:20
6 [o]2Ki 19:30; Isa 11:10; [p]Ge 40:10; [q]Ps 72:16; Isa 11:1; 37:31; Eze 17:23; 36:8; Hos 14:8
7 [r]Isa 10:26; 11:4; 37:36–38
8 [s]Isa 49:14; 50:1; 54:7; [t]Ge 41:6
9 [u]Ps 78:38; [v]Ro 11:27*; [w]Ex 23:24; [x]Ex 34:13; [y]Lev 26:30; 2Ch 14:5
10 [z]Ge 1:2; Dt 13:16; Isa 5:6; 32:14; Jer 10:22; 26:6; La 1:4; 5:18; [a]Isa 5:5; [b]Isa 5:17; [c]Isa 17:2
11 [d]Isa 10:33; [e]ver 4; Isa 33:12; [f]Dt 32:28; Isa 1:3; [g]Dt 32:18; Isa 41:8; 43:1,7, 15; 44:1–2,21, 24; [h]Isa 9:17; Jer 11:16
12 [i]Isa 21:10; Mt 3:12; [j]Ge 15:18; [k]Dt 30:4; Isa 1:9; 11:12; 17:6
13 [l]ver 1; [m]Lev 25:9; Jdg 3:27; Mt 24:31; [n]Ps 106:47; [o]Isa 10:19; 19:21, 25; [p]Ge 27:29; Ps 22:29; 86:9; [q]Isa 2:2

Ch. 28

1 [a]Isa 10:5; 29:1; 30:1; 31:1; 33:1; [b]ver 3; Isa 7:2; 9:9; [c]ver 4; [d]Lev 10:9; Isa 5:11; Hos 7:5; Am 6:6
2 [e]Isa 40:10; [f]Jos 10:11; [g]Isa 29:6; [h]Isa 8:7; Da 9:26
3 [i]ver 1; [j]Job 40:12; Isa 5:5
4 [k]ver 1; [l]SS 2:13; Hos 9:10; Na 3:12
5 [m]Isa 10:20; 27:1; 29:18; 30:23; [n]Isa 24:16,23; [o]Isa 62:3; Jer 13:18; Eze 16:12; 21:26; Zec 9:16; [p]Isa 1:9

Woe to Ephraim

28

Woe[a] to that wreath, the pride
of Ephraim's[b] drunkards,
to the fading flower, his glorious
beauty,
set on the head of a fertile valley[c]—
to that city, the pride of those laid
low by wine![d]
2 See, the Lord has one who is
powerful[e] and strong.
Like a hailstorm[f] and a destructive
wind,[g]
like a driving rain and a flooding[h]
downpour,
he will throw it forcefully to the
ground.
3 That wreath, the pride of Ephraim's[i]
drunkards,
will be trampled[j] underfoot.
4 That fading flower, his glorious
beauty,
set on the head of a fertile valley,[k]
will be like a fig[l] ripe before harvest—
as soon as someone sees it and takes
it in his hand,
he swallows it.

5 In that day[m] the LORD Almighty
will be a glorious[n] crown,[o]
a beautiful wreath
for the remnant[p] of his people.
6 He will be a spirit of justice[q]
to him who sits in judgment,[r]
a source of strength
to those who turn back the battle[s] at
the gate.

7 And these also stagger[t] from wine[u]
and reel[v] from beer:
Priests[w] and prophets[x] stagger from
beer
and are befuddled with wine;
they reel from beer,
they stagger when seeing visions,[y]
they stumble when rendering
decisions.
8 All the tables are covered with vomit[z]
and there is not a spot without filth.

9 "Who is it he is trying to teach?[a]
To whom is he explaining his
message?[b]

6 [q]2Sa 14:20; Isa 11:2–4; 32:1,16; 33:5; [r]Isa 4:4; Jn 5:30; [s]Jdg 9:44–45; 2Ch 32:8
7 [t]Isa 3:12; [u]Lev 10:9; Isa 22:13; Eph 5:18; [v]Ps 107:27; [w]Isa 24:2; [x]Isa 9:15; [y]Isa 1:1; 29:11 *8* [z]Jer 48:26
9 [a]ver 26; Ps 32:8; Isa 2:3; 30:20; 48:17; 50:4; 54:13; Jer 31:34; 32:33; [b]Isa 52:7; 53:1

[a]8 See Septuagint; the meaning of the Hebrew for this word is uncertain.
[b]9 That is, symbols of the goddess Asherah
[c]12 Hebrew *River*

To children weaned[c] from their milk,[d]
to those just taken from the breast?
10For it is:
Do and do, do and do,
rule on rule, rule on rule;[a]
a little here, a little there.[e]"

11Very well then, with foreign lips and
strange tongues[f]
God will speak to this people,[g]
12to whom he said,
"This is the resting-place, let the
weary rest";[h]
and, "This is the place of repose"—
but they would not listen.
13So then, the word of the LORD to them
will become:
Do and do, do and do,
rule on rule, rule on rule;
a little here, a little there[i]—
so that they will go and fall backwards,
be injured[j] and snared and
captured.[k]

14Therefore hear the word of the LORD,[l]
you scoffers[m]
who rule this people in Jerusalem.
15You boast, "We have entered into a
covenant with death,[n]
with the grave[b] we have made an
agreement.
When an overwhelming scourge
sweeps by,[o]
it cannot touch us,
for we have made a lie[p] our refuge
and falsehood[c] our hiding-place.[q]"

16So this is what the Sovereign LORD
says:

"See, I lay a stone in Zion,[r]
a tested stone,[s]
a precious cornerstone for a sure
foundation;[t]
the one who trusts will never be
dismayed.[u]
17I will make justice[v] the measuring line
and righteousness the plumb-line;[w]
hail[x] will sweep away your refuge, the
lie,
and water will overflow[y] your
hiding-place.
18Your covenant with death will be
annulled;
your agreement with the grave will
not stand.[z]
When the overwhelming scourge
sweeps by,[a]
you will be beaten down[b] by it.
19As often as it comes it will carry you
away;[c]
morning after morning,[d] by day and
by night,
it will sweep through."

9 [c]Ps 131:2; [d]Heb 5:12–13; 1Pe 2:2
10 [e]ver 13
11 [f]**Ge 11:7**; Isa 33:19; Jer 5:15; [g]Eze 3:5; 1Co 14:21*
12 [h]**Ex 14:14; Jos 1:13; Job 11:18; Isa 11:10**; Mt 11:28–29
13 [i]ver 10; [j]Mt 21:44; [k]**Isa 8:15**
14 [l]Isa 1:10; [m]2Ch 36:16
15 [n]**Job 5:23**; Isa 8:19; [o]ver 2, 18; Isa 8:7–8; 10:26; 29:6; 30:28; Da 11:22; [p]**Isa 9:15**; [q]**Jdg 9:35**; Isa 29:15; Jer 23:24
16 [r]**Isa 14:32**; [s]Ps 118:22; Isa 8:14–15; Da 2:34–35,45; Zec 12:3; **Ac 4:11**; [t]Jer 51:26; 1Co 3:11; 2Ti 2:19; [u]Isa 29:22; 45:17; 50:7; 54:4; Ro 9:33*; 10:11*; 1Pe 2:6*
17 [v]**Ps 11:7; Isa 5:16**; [w]**2Ki 21:13**; [x]**Jos 10:11**; [y]**Isa 8:7**
18 [z]**Isa 7:7**; [a]**ver 15**; [b]**Isa 5:5**; 63:18; Da 8:13
19 [c]2Ki 24:2; [d]**Ps 5:3**; [e]**Job 18:11**
20 [f]Isa 59:6
21 [g]**Ge 38:29; 1Ch 14:11**; [h]**Jos 9:3**; [i]Isa 10:12; 65:7; Lk 19:41–44
22 [j]**2Ch 36:16**; Jer 29:18; La 2:15; Zep 2:15; [k]**Isa 10:22**; [l]**Isa 10:23**
23 [m]Isa 32:9
24 [n]Ecc 3:2
25 [o]Mt 23:23; [p]**Ex 9:31**; [q]Ex 9:32; Eze 4:9
26 [r]**Ps 94:10**
27 [s]**Isa 21:10**; [t]**Job 41:30**; [u]Isa 10:5
28 [v]**Isa 21:10**
29 [w]**Isa 9:6**; [x]**Ps 92:5**; Ro 11:33

Ch. 29

1 [a]Isa 22:12–13; **28:1**; [b]ver 2, 7; [c]**2Sa 5:7**; [d]**Isa 1:14**

The understanding of this message
will bring sheer terror.[e]
20The bed is too short to stretch out on,
the blanket too narrow to wrap
around you.[f]
21The LORD will rise up as he did at
Mount Perazim,[g]
he will rouse himself as in the Valley
of Gibeon[h]—
to do his work,[i] his strange work,
and perform his task, his alien task.
22Now stop your mocking,[j]
or your chains will become heavier;
the Lord, the LORD Almighty, has told
me
of the destruction decreed[k] against
the whole land.[l]

23Listen[m] and hear my voice;
pay attention and hear what I say.
24When a farmer ploughs for planting,[n]
does he plough continually?
Does he keep on breaking up and
harrowing the soil?
25When he has levelled the surface,
does he not sow caraway and scatter
cummin?[o]
Does he not plant wheat in its place,[d]
barley[p] in its plot,[d]
and spelt[q] in its field?
26His God instructs him
and teaches[r] him the right way.

27Caraway is not threshed[s] with a
sledge,[t]
nor is a cartwheel rolled over
cummin;
caraway is beaten out with a rod,[u]
and cummin with a stick.
28Grain must be ground to make bread;
so one does not go on threshing it
for ever.
Though he drives the wheels of his
threshing-cart[v] over it,
his horses do not grind it.
29All this also comes from the LORD
Almighty,
wonderful in counsel[w] and
magnificent in wisdom.[x]

Woe to David's City

29 Woe[a] to you, Ariel, Ariel,[b]
the city[c] where David settled!
Add year to year
and let your cycle of festivals[d] go on.

[a]*10* Hebrew / *sav lasav sav lasav / kav lakav kav lakav* (possibly meaningless sounds; perhaps a mimicking of the prophet's words); also in verse 13
[b]*15* Hebrew *Sheol*; also in verse 18
[c]*15* Or *false gods*
[d]*25* The meaning of the Hebrew for this word is uncertain.

2Yet I will besiege Ariel;[e]
she will mourn and lament,[f]
she will be to me like an altar
hearth.[a][g]
3I will encamp against you all around;
I will encircle[h] you with towers
and set up my siege works[i] against
you.
4Brought low, you will speak from the
ground;
your speech will mumble[j] out of the
dust.[k]
Your voice will come ghostlike[l] from
the earth;
out of the dust your speech will
whisper.[m]

5But your many enemies will become
like fine dust,[n]
the ruthless[o] hordes like blown
chaff.[p]
Suddenly,[q] in an instant,
6 the LORD Almighty will come[r]
with thunder[s] and earthquake[t] and
great noise,
with windstorm and tempest[u] and
flames of a devouring fire.[v]
7Then the hordes of all the nations[w]
that fight against Ariel,[x]
that attack her and her fortress and
besiege her,
will be as it is with a dream,[y]
with a vision in the night—
8as when a hungry man dreams that he
is eating,
but he awakens,[z] and his hunger
remains;
as when a thirsty man dreams that he
is drinking,
but he awakens faint, with his thirst
unquenched.[a]
So will it be with the hordes of all the
nations
that fight against Mount Zion.[b]

9Be stunned and amazed,[c]
blind yourselves and be sightless;[d]
be drunk,[e] but not from wine,[f]
stagger,[g] but not from beer.
10The LORD has brought over you a deep
sleep:[h]
He has sealed your eyes[i] (the
prophets);[j]
he has covered your heads (the
seers).[k]

11For you this whole vision[l] is nothing
but words sealed[m] in a scroll. And if
you give the scroll to someone who
can read, and say to him, "Read this,
please," he will answer, "I can't; it is
sealed." 12Or if you give the scroll to
someone who cannot read, and say,
"Read this, please," he will answer, "I
don't know how to read."

13The Lord says:

"These people[n] come near to me with
their mouth
and honour me with their lips,[o]
but their hearts are far from me.[p]
Their worship of me
is made up only of rules taught by
men.[b][q]
14Therefore once more I will astound
these people
with wonder upon wonder;[r]
the wisdom of the wise[s] will perish,
the intelligence of the intelligent will
vanish."[t]
15Woe to those who go to great depths
to hide[u] their plans from the LORD,
who do their work in darkness and
think,
"Who sees us?[v] Who will know?"[w]
16You turn things upside down,
as if the potter were thought to be
like the clay![x]
Shall what is formed[y] say to him who
formed it,
"He did not make me"?
Can the pot say of the potter,[z]
"He knows nothing"?[a]

17In a very short time,[b] will not Lebanon[c]
be turned into a fertile field[d]
and the fertile field seem like a
forest?[e]
18In that day[f] the deaf[g] will hear the
words of the scroll,
and out of gloom and darkness[h]
the eyes of the blind will see.[i]
19Once more the humble[j] will rejoice in
the LORD;
the needy[k] will rejoice in the Holy
One[l] of Israel.
20The ruthless[m] will vanish,[n]
the mockers[o] will disappear,
and all who have an eye for evil[p] will
be cut down—

2 [e]ver 1; [f]Isa 3:26; La 2:5; [g]Eze 43:15
3 [h]Lk 19:43–44; [i]2Ki 25:1
4 [j]Isa 8:19; [k]Isa 47:1; 52:2; [l]Lev 19:31; [m]Isa 26:16
5 [n]Dt 9:21; Ps 78:39; 103:15; Isa 2:22; 37:27; 40:6; 51:12; [o]Isa 13:11; [p]Isa 17:13; [q]Ps 55:15; Isa 17:14; 1Th 5:3
6 [r]Isa 26:21; Zec 14:1–5; [s]Ex 19:16; [t]Mt 24:7; Mk 13:8; Lk 21:11; Rev 6:12; 11:19; [u]Ps 50:3; 55:8; Isa 28:15; [v]Lev 10:2; Ps 83:13–15
7 [w]Mic 4:11–12; Zec 12:9; [x]ver 1; [y]Job 20:8
8 [z]Ps 73:20; [a]ver 5,7; Isa 41:11,15; Jer 30:16; Zec 12:3; [b]Isa 17:12–14; 54:17
9 [c]ver 14; Jer 4:9; Hab 1:5; [d]Isa 6:10; [e]Isa 51:17; 63:6; Jer 13:13; 25:27; [f]Lev 10:9; Isa 28:1; 51:21–22; [g]Ps 60:3; Isa 3:12
10 [h]Jdg 4:21; Jnh 1:5; [i]Ps 69:23; Isa 6:9–10; 44:18; Ro 11:8*; 2Th 2:9–11; [j]Mic 3:6; [k]1Sa 9:9
11 [l]Isa 28:7; [m]Isa 8:16; Da 8:26; 12:9; Mt 13:11; Rev 5:1–2
13 [n]Jer 14:11; Hag 1:2; 2:14; [o]Ps 50:16; [p]Ps 119:70; Isa 58:2; Jer 12:2; Eze 33:31; [q]Mt 15:8–9*; Mk 7:6–7*; Col 2:22
14 [r]Job 10:16; [s]Job 5:13; Jer 8:9; 49:7; [t]Isa 6:9–10; 1Co 1:19*
15 [u]Ge 3:8; Isa 28:15; [v]Job 8:3; Ps 10:11–13; 94:7; Isa 47:10; 57:12; Eze 8:12; 9:9; [w]2Ki 21:16; Job 22:13
16 [x]Job 10:9; Isa 10:15; [y]Ge 2:7; [z]Isa 45:9; 64:8; Jer 18:6; Ro 9:20–21*; [a]Job 9:12
17 [b]Isa 10:25; [c]Isa 2:13; [d]Ps 84:6; 107:33; [e]Isa 32:15
18 [f]Isa 28:5; [g]Mk 7:37; [h]Ps 107:14; [i]Ps 146:8; Isa 32:3; Mt 11:5; Lk 7:22
19 [j]Ps 25:9; 37:11; Isa 61:1; Mt 5:5; 11:29; [k]Ps 72:4; Isa 3:15; 14:30; Mt 11:5; Lk 7:22; Jas 1:9; 2:5; [l]ver 23; Isa 1:4; 5:19; 12:6; 30:11
20 [m]Isa 9:4; 13:11; [n]Isa 34:12; [o]2Ch 36:16; Isa 28:22; [p]Job 15:35; Ps 7:14; Isa 32:7; 33:11; 59:4; Eze 11:2; Mic 2:1; Na 1:11

[a]2 The Hebrew for *altar hearth* sounds like the Hebrew for *Ariel*.
[b]13 Hebrew; Septuagint *They worship me in vain; / their teachings are but rules taught by men.*

21those who with a word make a man
out to be guilty,
who ensnare the defender in court[q]
and with false testimony[r] deprive
the innocent of justice.[s]

22Therefore this is what the LORD,
who redeemed[t] Abraham,[u] says to the
house of Jacob:

"No longer will Jacob be ashamed;[v]
no longer will their faces grow
pale.[w]
23When they see among them their
children,[x]
the work of my hands,[y]
they will keep my name holy;[z]
they will acknowledge the holiness
of the Holy One[a] of Jacob,
and will stand in awe of the God of
Israel.
24Those who are wayward[b] in spirit will
gain understanding;[c]
those who complain will accept
instruction."[d]

Woe to the Obstinate Nation

30 "Woe[a] to the obstinate
children,"[b]
declares the LORD,
"to those who carry out plans that are
not mine,
forming an alliance,[c] but not by my
Spirit,
heaping sin upon sin;
2who go down to Egypt[d]
without consulting[e] me;
who look for help to Pharaoh's
protection,[f]
to Egypt's shade for refuge.[g]
3But Pharaoh's protection will be to
your shame,
Egypt's shade[h] will bring you
disgrace.[i]
4Though they have officials in Zoan[j]
and their envoys have arrived in
Hanes,
5everyone will be put to shame
because of a people[k] useless[l] to
them,
who bring neither help[m] nor
advantage,
but only shame and disgrace."[n]

6An oracle[o] concerning the animals of
the Negev:[p]

Through a land of hardship and
distress,[q]
of lions[r] and lionesses,
of adders and darting snakes,[s]
the envoys carry their riches on
donkeys'[t] backs,
their treasures[u] on the humps of
camels,
to that unprofitable nation,
7 to Egypt, whose help is utterly
useless.[v]
Therefore I call her
Rahab[w] the Do-Nothing.

8Go now, write it on a tablet[x] for them,
inscribe it on a scroll,[y]
that for the days to come
it may be an everlasting witness.[z]
9These are rebellious[a] people,
deceitful[b] children,
children unwilling to listen to the
LORD's instruction.[c]
10They say to the seers,[d]
"See no more visions[e]!"
and to the prophets,
"Give us no more visions of what is
right!
Tell us pleasant things,[f]
prophesy illusions.[g]
11Leave this way,[h]
get off this path,
and stop confronting[i] us
with the Holy One[j] of Israel!"

12Therefore, this is what the Holy
One[k] of Israel says:

"Because you have rejected this
message,[l]
relied on oppression[m]
and depended on deceit,
13this sin will become for you
like a high wall,[n] cracked and
bulging,
that collapses[o] suddenly,[p] in an
instant.
14It will break in pieces like pottery,[q]
shattered so mercilessly
that among its pieces not a fragment
will be found
for taking coals from a hearth
or scooping water out of a cistern."

15This is what the Sovereign[r] LORD,
the Holy One[s] of Israel, says:

"In repentance and rest[t] is your
salvation,

21 [q]Am 5:10,15; [r]Pr 21:28; [s]Isa 5:23; 32:7; Hab 1:4
22 [t]Ex 6:6; [u]Ge 17:16; Isa 41:8; 51:2; 63:16; [v]Ps 22:5; 25:3; Isa 28:16; 49:23; 61:7; Joel 2:26; Zep 3:11; [w]Jer 30:6,10; Joel 2:6,21; Na 2:10
23 [x]Isa 49:20–26; 53:10; 54:1–3; [y]Ps 8:6; Isa 19:25; [z]Mt 6:9; [a]ver 19; Isa 5:19
24 [b]Ps 95:10; Pr 12:8; Isa 28:7; Heb 5:2; [c]Isa 1:3; 32:4; 41:20; 60:16; [d]Isa 30:21; 42:16

Ch. 30

1 [a]Isa 28:1; [b]Dt 21:18; Isa 1:2; [c]2Ki 17:4; Isa 8:12
2 [d]2Ki 25:26; Isa 31:1; 36:6; Jer 2:18,36; 42:14; Eze 17:15; 29:16; [e]Ge 25:22; Nu 27:21; [f]Isa 36:9; [g]Isa 4:6
3 [h]Jdg 9:8–15; [i]ver 5; Ps 44:13; Isa 20:4–5; 36:6
4 [j]Nu 13:22
5 [k]ver 7; Isa 20:5; 31:1; 36:6; [l]2Ki 18:21; [m]Ps 108:12; Jer 37:3–5; [n]ver 3; 2Ki 18:21; Eze 17:15
6 [o]Isa 13:1; [p]Jdg 1:9; [q]Ex 1:13; 5:10,21; Isa 5:30; 8:22; Jer 11:4; [r]Isa 5:29; 35:9; [s]Dt 8:15; [t]Ge 42:26; 1Sa 25:18; [u]Isa 15:7
7 [v]2Ki 18:21; Jer 2:36; [w]Job 9:13
8 [x]Dt 27:8; [y]Ex 17:14; Isa 8:1; Jer 25:13; 30:2; 36:28; Hab 2:2; [z]Jos 24:26–27
9 [a]Ps 78:8; Isa 1:2; Eze 2:6; [b]Isa 28:15; 59:3–4; [c]Isa 1:10
10 [d]1Sa 9:9; [e]Jer 11:21; 32:3; Am 7:13; [f]1Ki 22:8; Jer 4:10; [g]Jer 23:26; 25:9; 26:9; 36:29; Eze 13:7; Ro 16:18; 2Ti 4:3–4
11 [h]ver 21; Pr 3:6; Isa 35:8–9; 48:17; [i]Job 21:14; [j]Isa 29:19
12 [k]ver 15; Isa 5:19; 31:1; [l]Isa 5:24; [m]Ps 10:7; 12:5; Isa 5:7
13 [n]Ne 2:17; Ps 62:3; 80:12; [o]1Ki 20:30; [p]Isa 17:14
14 [q]Ps 2:9
15 [r]Jer 7:20; Eze 3:11; [s]ver 12; [t]Ex 14:14; Jos 1:13

in quietness and trust[u] is your
strength,
but you would have none of it.[v]
16You said, 'No, we will flee[w] on
horses.'[x]
Therefore you will flee!
You said, 'We will ride off on swift
horses.'
Therefore your pursuers will be
swift!
17A thousand will flee
at the threat of one;
at the threat of five[y]
you will all flee[z] away,
till you are left[a]
like a flagstaff on a mountaintop,
like a banner[b] on a hill."

18Yet the LORD longs[c] to be gracious to
you;
he rises to show you compassion.[d]
For the LORD is a God of justice.[e]
Blessed are all who wait for him![f]

19O people of Zion, who live in Jeru-
salem, you will weep no more.[g] How
gracious he will be when you cry for
help![h] As soon as he hears, he will
answer[i] you. 20Although the LORD gives
you the bread[j] of adversity and the
water of affliction, your teachers[k] will be
hidden[l] no more; with your own eyes
you will see them. 21Whether you turn
to the right or to the left, your ears will
hear a voice[m] behind you, saying, "This
is the way;[n] walk in it." 22Then you will
defile your idols[o] overlaid with silver
and your images covered with gold;[p]
you will throw them away like a men-
strual[q] cloth and say to them, "Away
with you!"[r]

23He will also send you rain[s] for the
seed you sow in the ground, and the
food that comes from the land will be
rich[t] and plentiful.[u] In that day[v] your
cattle will graze in broad meadows.[w]
24The oxen[x] and donkeys that work the
soil will eat fodder[y] and mash, spread
out with fork[z] and shovel. 25In the day
of great slaughter,[a] when the towers[b]
fall, streams of water will flow[c] on
every high mountain and every lofty
hill. 26The moon will shine like the
sun,[d] and the sunlight will be seven
times brighter, like the light of seven
full days, when the LORD binds up the
bruises of his people and heals[e] the
wounds he inflicted.

27See, the Name[f] of the LORD comes
from afar,
with burning anger[g] and dense
clouds of smoke;

15 [u]2Ch 20:12; Isa 32:17; [v]Isa 8:6; 42:24; 57:17
16 [w]Jer 46:6; [x]Dt 17:16; 1Ki 10:28–29; Ps 20:7; Isa 31:1,3; 36:8
17 [y]Lev 26:8; [z]Lev 26:36; Dt 28:25; 2Ki 7:7; [a]Isa 1:8; [b]Ps 20:5
18 [c]Ge 43:31; Isa 42:14; 2Pe 3:9, 15; [d]Ps 78:38; Isa 48:9; Jnh 3:10; [e]Ps 11:7; Isa 5:16; [f]Ps 27:14; Isa 25:9; 33:2; 40:31; 64:4; La 3:25; Da 12:12
19 [g]Isa 25:8; 60:20; 61:3; [h]Job 24:12; [i]Job 22:27; Ps 50:15; 86:7; Isa 41:17; 58:9; 65:24; Zec 13:9; Mt 7:7–11
20 [j]1Ki 22:27; [k]Isa 28:9; [l]Ps 74:9; Am 8:11
21 [m]Isa 29:24; [n]ver 11; Job 33:11
22 [o]Ex 32:4; Isa 17:8; [p]Job 22:24; Isa 31:7; [q]Lev 15:19–23; [r]Eze 7:19–20
23 [s]Dt 28:12; Isa 65:21–22; [t]Isa 25:6; 55:2; Jer 31:14; [u]Job 36:31; Isa 62:8; [v]Isa 28:5; [w]Ps 65:13
24 [x]Isa 32:14,20; [y]Job 6:5; [z]Mt 3:12; Lk 3:17
25 [a]Isa 13:5; 34:6; 65:12; Jer 25:32; 50:27; [b]Isa 2:15; [c]Ex 17:6; Isa 32:2; 41:18; Joel 3:18; Zec 14:8
26 [d]Isa 24:23; 60:19–20; Zec 14:7; Rev 21:23; 22:5; [e]Dt 32:39; 2Ch 7:14; Ps 107:20; Isa 1:5; Jer 3:22; 17:14; Hos 14:4
27 [f]1Ki 18:24; Ps 20:1; Isa 59:19; 64:2; [g]Isa 26:20; 66:14; Eze 22:31; [h]Isa 10:5; 13:5; [i]ver 30; Job 41:21

his lips are full of wrath,[h]
and his tongue is a consuming fire.[i]
28His breath[j] is like a rushing torrent,[k]
rising up to the neck.[l]
He shakes the nations in the sieve[m] of
destruction;
he places in the jaws of the peoples
a bit[n] that leads them astray.
29And you will sing
as on the night you celebrate a holy
festival;[o]
your hearts will rejoice[p]
as when people go up with flutes[q]
to the mountain[r] of the LORD,
to the Rock[s] of Israel.
30The LORD will cause men to hear his
majestic voice[t]
and will make them see his arm[u]
coming down
with raging anger[v] and consuming
fire,[w]
with cloudburst, thunderstorm[x]
and hail.[y]
31The voice of the LORD will shatter
Assyria;[z]
with his sceptre he will strike[a] them
down.
32Every stroke the LORD lays on them
with his punishing rod[b]
will be to the music of tambourines[c]
and harps,
as he fights them in battle with the
blows of his arm.[d]
33Topheth[e] has long been prepared;
it has been made ready for the king.
Its fire pit has been made deep and
wide,
with an abundance of fire and
wood;
the breath[f] of the LORD,
like a stream of burning sulphur,[g]
sets it ablaze.[h]

Woe to Those Who Rely on Egypt

31 Woe[a] to those who go down to
Egypt[b] for help,
who rely on horses,[c]
who trust in the multitude of their
chariots[d]
and in the great strength of their
horsemen,

28 [j]Isa 11:4; [k]Ps 50:3; Isa 28:15; [l]Isa 8:8; [m]Am 9:9; [n]2Ki 19:28
29 [o]Isa 25:6; [p]Isa 12:1; [q]1Sa 10:5; [r]Ps 42:4; Mt 26:30; [s]Ge 49:24
30 [t]Ps 68:33; [u]Isa 9:12; 40:10; 51:9; 52:10; 53:1; 59:16; 62:8; 63:12; [v]ver 27; [w]Isa 10:25; [x]Isa 4:4; 47:14; [y]Ex 20:18; Ps 29:3; Ex 9:18
31 [z]Isa 10:5,12; [a]Isa 11:4
32 [b]Isa 10:26; [c]Ex 15:20; [d]Isa 11:15; Eze 32:10
33 [e]2Ki 23:10; [f]Ex 15:10; 2Sa 22:16; [g]Ge 19:24; Rev 9:17; [h]Isa 1:31

Ch. 31
1 [a]Isa 28:1; [b]Dt 17:16; Isa 30:2,5; Jer 37:5; [c]Isa 30:16; [d]Isa 2:7

but do not look to the Holy One[e] of Israel,
or seek help from the LORD.[f]
2Yet he too is wise[g] and can bring disaster;[h]
he does not take back his words.[i]
He will rise up against the house of the wicked,[j]
against those who help evildoers.
3But the Egyptians[k] are men and not God;[l]
their horses[m] are flesh and not spirit.
When the LORD stretches out his hand,[n]
he who helps will stumble,
he who is helped[o] will fall;
both will perish together.[p]

4This is what the LORD says to me:

"As a lion[q] growls,
a great lion over his prey—
and though a whole band of shepherds[r]
is called together against him,
he is not frightened by their shouts
or disturbed by their clamour[s]—
so the LORD Almighty will come down[t]
to do battle on Mount Zion and on its heights.
5Like birds hovering[u] overhead,
the LORD Almighty will shield[v] Jerusalem;
he will shield it and deliver[w] it,
he will 'pass over'[x] it and will rescue it."

6Return[y] to him you have so greatly
revolted[z] against, O Israelites. 7For in
that day[a] every one of you will reject the
idols of silver and gold[b] your sinful
hands have made.[c]

8"Assyria[d] will fall by a sword that is not of man;
a sword, not of mortals, will devour[e] them.
They will flee before the sword
and their young men will be put to forced labour.[f]
9Their stronghold[g] will fall because of terror;
at sight of the battle standard[h] their commanders will panic,[i]"
declares the LORD,
whose fire[j] is in Zion,
whose furnace[k] is in Jerusalem.

The Kingdom of Righteousness

32 See, a king[a] will reign in righteousness
and rulers will rule with justice.[b]

1 [e]Job 6:10; **Isa 1:4; 30:12;** [f]**Dt 20:1; Pr 21:31; Isa 9:13;** Jer 46:9; Eze 29:16
2 [g]**Ps 92:5;** Ro 16:27; [h]Isa 45:7; 47:11; Am 3:6; [i]Nu 23:19; **Pr 19:21;** [j]**Isa 1:4;** 29:15; 32:6
3 [k]Isa 20:5; 36:9; [l]**Ps 9:20;** Eze 28:9; 2Th 2:4; [m]**Isa 30:16;** [n]Ne 1:10; **Job 30:21;** Isa 9:17, 21; Jer 51:25; Eze 20:34; [o]Isa 10:3; 30:5–7; [p]**Isa 20:6;** Jer 17:5
4 [q]Nu 24:9; **1Sa 17:34;** Hos 11:10; Am 3:8; [r]Jer 3:15; 23:4; Eze 34:23; Na 3:18; [s]Ps 74:23; [t]Isa 42:13
5 [u]**Ge 1:2; Mt 23:37;** [v]**Ps 91:4; Isa 5:2; Zec 9:15;** [w]**Ps 34:7;** Isa 37:35; 38:6; [x]**Ex 12:23**
6 [y]**Job 22:23; Isa 1:27;** [z]**Isa 1:5**
7 [a]Isa 29:18; [b]**Isa 30:22;** [c]**Ps 135:15**
8 [d]**Isa 10:12;** [e]**Ex 12:12;** Isa 10:12; 14:25; **27:1;** 33:1; 37:7; Jer 25:12; Hab 2:8; [f]**Ge 49:15; Dt 20:11**
9 [g]Dt 32:31,37; [h]**Isa 18:3; Jer 4:6;** [i]Jer 51:9; Na 3:7; [j]**Isa 10:17;** [k]Ps 21:9; Mal 4:1

Ch. 32

1 [a]**Ps 149:2; Isa 6:5;** 55:4; Eze 37:24; [b]Ps 72:1–4; **Isa 9:7; 28:6**
2 [c]**1Ki 18:4;** [d]**Ps 55:8;** [e]**Ps 23:2; Isa 30:25;** 49:10; Jer 31:9; [f]**Ps 107:35;** Isa 44:3
3 [g]**Isa 29:18;** 35:5; 42:7,16; [h]**Dt 29:4**
4 [i]Isa 6:10; **29:24;** [j]Isa 35:6
5 [k]**1Sa 25:25**
6 [l]**Pr 19:3;** [m]**Pr 24:2; Isa 26:10;** [n]**Isa 9:17;** [o]Isa 3:12; 9:16; [p]**Isa 3:15**

2Each man will be like a shelter[c] from the wind
and a refuge from the storm,[d]
like streams of water[e] in the desert[f]
and the shadow of a great rock in a thirsty land.

3Then the eyes of those who see will no longer be closed,[g]
and the ears[h] of those who hear will listen.
4The mind of the rash will know and understand,[i]
and the stammering tongue[j] will be fluent and clear.
5No longer will the fool[k] be called noble
nor the scoundrel be highly respected.
6For the fool speaks folly,[l]
his mind is busy with evil:[m]
He practises ungodliness[n]
and spreads error[o] concerning the LORD;
the hungry he leaves empty[p]
and from the thirsty he withholds water.
7The scoundrel's methods are wicked,[q]
he makes up evil schemes[r]
to destroy the poor with lies,
even when the plea of the needy[s] is just.[t]
8But the noble man makes noble plans,
and by noble deeds[u] he stands.[v]

The Women of Jerusalem

9You women[w] who are so complacent,
rise up and listen[x] to me;
you daughters who feel secure,[y]
hear what I have to say!
10In little more than a year[z]
you who feel secure will tremble;
the grape harvest will fail,[a]
and the harvest of fruit will not come.
11Tremble,[b] you complacent women;
shudder, you daughters who feel secure![c]
Strip off your clothes,[d]
put sackcloth[e] round your waists.
12Beat your breasts[f] for the pleasant fields,
for the fruitful vines[g]
13and for the land of my people,
a land overgrown with thorns and briers[h]—

7 [q]Jer 5:26–28; Da 12:10; [r]**Isa 29:20;** Mic 7:3; [s]**Ps 72:4;** Isa 29:19; 61:1; [t]**Isa 29:21**
8 [u]1Ch 29:9; **Pr 11:25;** [v]Isa 14:24
9 [w]**Isa 4:1;** [x]Isa 28:23; [y]ver 11; Isa 47:8; Da 4:4; Am 6:1; Zep 2:15
10 [z]Isa 37:30; [a]Isa 5:5–6; **24:7**
11 [b]Isa 33:14; [c]**ver 9;** [d]Isa 47:2; Mic 1:8; Na 3:5; [e]**Isa 3:24**
12 [f]Na 2:7; [g]Isa 16:9 **13** [h]**Isa 5:6;** Hos 10:8

yes, mourn[i] for all houses of
merriment
and for this city of revelry.[j]
14The fortress[k] will be abandoned,
the noisy city deserted;[l]
citadel and watchtower[m] will become a
wasteland for ever,
the delight of donkeys,[n] a pasture
for flocks,[o]
15till the Spirit[p] is poured upon us from
on high,
and the desert becomes a fertile
field,[q]
and the fertile field seems like a
forest.[r]
16Justice[s] will dwell in the desert[t]
and righteousness[u] live in the fertile
field.
17The fruit of righteousness[v] will be
peace;[w]
the effect of righteousness will be
quietness and confidence[x] for
ever.
18My people will live in peaceful[y]
dwelling-places,
in secure homes,[z]
in undisturbed places of rest.[a]
19Though hail[b] flattens the forest[c]
and the city is levelled[d] completely,
20how blessed you will be,
sowing[e] your seed by every stream,[f]
and letting your cattle and donkeys
range free.[g]

Distress and Help

33 Woe[a] to you, O destroyer,
you who have not been
destroyed!
Woe to you, O traitor,
you who have not been betrayed!
When you stop destroying,
you will be destroyed;[b]
when you stop betraying,
you will be betrayed.[c]

2O LORD, be gracious[d] to us;
we long for you.
Be our strength[e] every morning,
our salvation[f] in time of distress.[g]
3At the thunder of your voice,[h] the
peoples flee;[i]
when you rise up,[j] the nations
scatter.
4Your plunder,[k] O nations, is
harvested[l] as by young locusts;[m]
like a swarm of locusts men pounce
on it.

5The LORD is exalted,[n] for he dwells on
high;[o]
he will fill Zion with justice[p] and
righteousness.[q]
6He will be the sure foundation for
your times,
a rich store of salvation[r] and
wisdom and knowledge;
the fear[s] of the LORD is the key to this
treasure.[a t]

7Look, their brave men[u] cry aloud in
the streets;
the envoys[v] of peace weep bitterly.
8The highways are deserted,
no travellers[w] are on the roads.[x]
The treaty is broken,[y]
its witnesses[b] are despised,
no-one is respected.
9The land mourns[c z] and wastes away,
Lebanon[a] is ashamed and withers;[b]
Sharon[c] is like the Arabah,
and Bashan[d] and Carmel[e] drop their
leaves.

10"Now will I arise,[f]" says the LORD.
"Now will I be exalted;[g]
now will I be lifted up.
11You conceive[h] chaff,
you give birth[i] to straw;
your breath is a fire[j] that consumes
you.
12The peoples will be burned as if to
lime;[k]
like cut thornbushes[l] they will be set
ablaze.[m]"

13You who are far away,[n] hear[o] what I
have done;
you who are near, acknowledge my
power!
14The sinners[p] in Zion are terrified;
trembling[q] grips the godless:
"Who of us can dwell with the
consuming fire?[r]
Who of us can dwell with
everlasting burning?"
15He who walks righteously[s]
and speaks what is right,[t]
who rejects gain from extortion[u]
and keeps his hand from accepting
bribes,[v]
who stops his ears against plots of
murder
and shuts his eyes[w] against
contemplating evil—

13 [i]Isa 24:11; [j]Isa 23:7 **14** [k]Isa 13:22; [l]Isa 6:11; 27:10; [m]Isa 2:15; 34:13; [n]Ps 104:11; [o]Isa 5:17 **15** [p]Isa 11:2; Eze 37:9; [q]Ps 107:35; Isa 35:1–2; [r]Isa 29:17 **16** [s]Isa 9:7; 28:6; [t]Isa 35:1,6; 42:11; [u]Ps 48:1; Isa 1:26 **17** [v]Ps 85:10; [w]Ps 119:165; Isa 9:7; Ro 14:17; Heb 12:11; Jas 3:18; [x]Isa 30:15 **18** [y]Isa 2:4; [z]Isa 26:1; 33:20; 37:33; 65:21; 66:14; Am 9:14; [a]Jos 1:13; Job 11:18; Hos 2:18–23 **19** [b]Isa 28:17; [c]Isa 10:19; Zec 11:2; [d]Job 40:11; Isa 19:18; 24:10; 27:10 **20** [e]Ecc 11:1; [f]Dt 28:12; [g]Job 39:8; Isa 30:24

Ch. 33

1 [a]2Ki 19:21; Isa 28:1; [b]Isa 31:8; Mt 7:2; [c]Isa 21:2; Jer 30:16; Eze 39:10 **2** [d]Ge 43:29; Ezr 9:8; [e]Isa 40:10; 51:9; 59:16; 63:5; [f]Ps 13:5; Isa 12:2; [g]Isa 5:30 **3** [h]Ps 46:6; 68:33; [i]Ps 68:1; Isa 13:14; [j]ver 10; Nu 10:35; Ps 12:5; Isa 59:16–18 **4** [k]Nu 14:3; 2Ki 7:16; [l]Isa 17:5; Joel 3:13; [m]Joel 1:4 **5** [n]Isa 5:16; [o]Job 16:19; [p]Isa 9:7; 28:6; [q]Isa 1:26 **6** [r]Isa 12:2; 26:1; 51:6; 60:18; [s]Pr 1:7; Isa 11:2–3; Mt 6:33; [t]Ge 39:3; Job 22:25 **7** [u]Isa 10:34; [v]2Ki 18:37 **8** [w]Isa 60:15; Zec 7:14; [x]Jdg 5:6; Isa 30:21; 35:8; [y]2Ki 18:14

9 [z]Isa 3:26; [a]2Ki 19:23; Isa 2:13; 35:2; 37:24; Jer 22:6; [b]Isa 15:6; [c]1Ch 27:29; [d]Mic 7:14; [e]1Ki 18:19; Isa 35:2; Na 1:4 **10** [f]ver 3; Isa 2:21; [g]Isa 5:16
11 [h]Ps 7:14; Isa 59:4; Jas 1:15; [i]Isa 26:18; [j]Isa 1:31
12 [k]Am 2:1; [l]Isa 5:6; [m]Isa 10:17; 27:11
13 [n]Ps 48:10; 49:1; [o]Isa 34:1; 48:16; 49:1
14 [p]Isa 1:28; [q]Isa 32:11; [r]Isa 1:31; 30:30; Zec 13:9; Heb 12:29
15 [s]Isa 58:8; [t]Ps 15:2; 24:4; [u]Eze 22:13; 33:31; [v]Pr 15:27; [w]Ps 119:37

[a]6 Or *is a treasure from him*
[b]8 Dead Sea Scrolls; Masoretic Text / *the cities*
[c]9 Or *dries up*

16this is the man who will dwell on the
heights,[x]
whose refuge[y] will be the mountain
fortress.[z]
His bread will be supplied,
and water will not fail[a] him.

17Your eyes will see the king[b] in his
beauty[c]
and view a land that stretches afar.[d]
18In your thoughts you will ponder the
former terror:[e]
"Where is that chief officer?
Where is the one who took the
revenue?
Where is the officer in charge of the
towers?[f]"
19You will see those arrogant people[g] no
more,
those people of an obscure speech,
with their strange,
incomprehensible tongue.[h]

20Look upon Zion,[i] the city of our
festivals;
your eyes will see Jerusalem,
a peaceful abode,[j] a tent[k] that will
not be moved;[l]
its stakes will never be pulled up,
nor any of its ropes broken.
21There the LORD will be our Mighty[m]
One.
It will be like a place of broad rivers
and streams.[n]
No galley with oars will ride them,
no mighty ship[o] will sail them.
22For the LORD is our judge,[p]
the LORD is our lawgiver,[q]
the LORD is our king;[r]
it is he who will save[s] us.

23Your rigging hangs loose:
The mast is not held secure,
the sail is not spread.
Then an abundance of spoils will be
divided
and even the lame[t] will carry off
plunder.[u]
24No-one living in Zion will say, "I am
ill";[v]
and the sins of those who dwell
there will be forgiven.[w]

Judgment Against the Nations

34 Come near, you nations, and
listen;[a]
pay attention, you peoples![b]
Let the earth[c] hear, and all that is in it,
the world, and all that comes out of
it![d]
2The LORD is angry with all nations;
his wrath[e] is upon all their armies.
He will totally destroy[a][f] them,

16 [x]Dt 32:13; [y]Ps 46:1; Isa 25:4; [z]Ps 18:1–2; Isa 26:1; [a]Isa 48:21; 49:10; 65:13
17 [b]Isa 6:5; [c]Isa 4:2; [d]Isa 26:15
18 [e]Isa 17:14; [f]Isa 2:15
19 [g]Ps 5:5; [h]Ge 11:7; Isa 28:11
20 [i]Ps 125:1; [j]Isa 32:18; [k]Ge 26:22; [l]ver 6; Ps 46:5
21 [m]Isa 10:34; [n]Ex 17:6; Ps 1:3; Isa 32:2; 41:18; 48:18; 49:10; 66:12; Na 3:8; [o]Isa 23:1
22 [p]Isa 11:4; [q]Isa 2:3; Jas 4:12; [r]Ps 89:18; [s]Isa 25:9
23 [t]2Ki 7:8; [u]2Ki 7:16
24 [v]Isa 30:26; [w]Nu 23:21; 2Ch 6:21; Isa 43:1; 48:20; Jer 31:34; 33:8; 1Jn 1:7–9

Ch. 34

1 [a]Isa 33:13; [b]Isa 41:1; 43:9; [c]Dt 4:26; Ps 49:1; [d]Ps 24:1
2 [e]Isa 10:25; [f]Isa 13:5; Zec 5:3; [g]Isa 30:25
3 [h]Isa 5:25; 10:4; [i]Ps 110:6; Eze 39:11; [j]Joel 2:20; Am 4:10; [k]ver 7; 2Sa 1:22; Isa 63:6; Eze 5:17; 14:19; 32:6; 35:6; 38:22
4 [l]Job 9:7; Isa 13:13; 2Pe 3:10; [m]Isa 38:12; Heb 1:12; [n]Mt 24:29*; Mk 13:24–25*; [o]Job 8:12; Isa 15:6; Mt 21:19
5 [p]Dt 32:41–42; Jer 47:6; Eze 21:5; Zec 13:7; [q]2Sa 8:13–14; 2Ch 28:17; Am 1:11–12; [r]Dt 13:15; Jos 6:17; Isa 24:6; Am 3:14–15; 6:11; Mal 1:4
6 [s]Dt 32:41; Isa 27:1; [t]Lev 3:9; [u]Ge 36:33; [v]Isa 30:25; Jer 25:34; Rev 19:17
7 [w]Nu 23:22; [x]Ps 68:30; [y]2Sa 1:22

he will give them over to slaughter.[g]
3Their slain[h] will be thrown out,
their dead bodies[i] will send up a
stench;[j]
the mountains will be soaked with
their blood.[k]
4All the stars of the heavens will be
dissolved[l]
and the sky rolled up[m] like a scroll;
all the starry host will fall[n]
like withered[o] leaves from the vine,
like shrivelled figs from the fig-tree.
5My sword[p] has drunk its fill in the
heavens;
see, it descends in judgment on
Edom,[q]
the people I have totally destroyed.[r]
6The sword[s] of the LORD is bathed in
blood,
it is covered with fat—
the blood of lambs and goats,
fat from the kidneys of rams.
For the LORD has a sacrifice[t] in Bozrah[u]
and a great slaughter[v] in Edom.
7And the wild oxen[w] will fall with
them,
the bull calves and the great bulls.[x]
Their land will be drenched with
blood,[y]
and the dust will be soaked with fat.

8For the LORD has a day[z] of vengeance,[a]
a year of retribution,[b] to uphold
Zion's cause.
9Edom's streams will be turned into
pitch,
her dust into burning sulphur;[c]
her land will become blazing pitch!
10It will not be quenched[d] night and day;
its smoke will rise for ever.[e]
From generation to generation[f] it will
lie desolate;[g]
no-one will ever pass through it
again.
11The desert owl[b][h] and screech owl[b] will
possess it;
the great owl[b] and the raven[i] will
nest there.
God will stretch out over Edom[j]
the measuring line of chaos[k]
and the plumb-line[l] of desolation.

8 [z]Isa 2:12; [a]Isa 1:24; 35:4; 47:3; 63:4; [b]Isa 59:18; Eze 25:12–17; Joel 3:4; Am 1:6–8,9–10
9 [c]Ge 19:24
10 [d]Isa 1:31; [e]Rev 14:10–11; 19:3; [f]ver 17; [g]Isa 13:20; 24:1; Jer 49:18; Eze 29:12; 35:3; Mal 1:3
11 [h]Lev 11:16–18; Dt 14:15–17; Rev 18:2; [i]Ge 8:7; [j]Isa 21:11; Eze 35:15; Joel 3:19; Ob 1; Mal 1:4; [k]Ge 1:2; [l]2Ki 21:13; Am 7:8

[a]2 The Hebrew term refers to the irrevocable giving over of things or persons to the LORD, often by totally destroying them; also in verse 5.
[b]11 The precise identification of these birds is uncertain.

12Her nobles will have nothing there to
be called a kingdom,
all her princes[m] will vanish[n] away.
13Thorns[o] will overrun her citadels,
nettles and brambles her
strongholds.[p]
She will become a haunt for jackals,[q]
a home for owls.[r]
14Desert creatures[s] will meet with
hyenas,[t]
and wild goats will bleat to each
other;
there the night creatures[u] will also
repose
and find for themselves places of
rest.
15The owl will nest there and lay eggs,
she will hatch them, and care for her
young under the shadow of her
wings;[v]
there also the falcons[w] will gather,
each with its mate.

16Look in the scroll[x] of the LORD and
read:

None of these will be missing,[y]
not one will lack her mate.
For it is his mouth[z] that has given the
order,[a]
and his Spirit will gather them
together.
17He allots their portions;[b]
his hand distributes them by
measure.
They will possess it for ever
and dwell there from generation to
generation.[c]

Joy of the Redeemed

35 The desert[a] and the parched
land will be glad;
the wilderness will rejoice and
blossom.[b]
Like the crocus,[c] 2it will burst into
bloom;
it will rejoice greatly and shout for
joy.[d]
The glory of Lebanon[e] will be given to
it,
the splendour of Carmel[f] and
Sharon;[g]
they will see the glory[h] of the LORD,
the splendour of our God.[i]

3Strengthen the feeble hands,
steady the knees[j] that give way;
4say[k] to those with fearful hearts,[l]
"Be strong, do not fear;[m]
your God will come,[n]
he will come with vengeance;[o]
with divine retribution
he will come to save[p] you."

12 [m]Job 12:21; Ps 107:40; Isa 40:23; Jer 21:7; 27:20; 39:6; Eze 24:5; [n]Isa 29:20; 41:11–12
13 [o]Isa 5:6; 7:19; [p]Isa 13:22; [q]Ps 44:19; Isa 13:22; Jer 9:11; 10:22; [r]Lev 11:16–18
14 [s]Ps 74:14; [t]Isa 13:22; [u]Rev 18:2
15 [v]Ps 17:8; [w]Dt 14:13
16 [x]Isa 30:8; [y]Isa 40:26; 48:13; [z]Isa 1:20; 58:14; [a]Isa 1:20
17 [b]Isa 17:14; Jer 13:25; [c]ver 10

Ch. 35
1 [a]Isa 27:10; 32:15–16; 41:18–19; [b]Isa 27:6; 51:3; [c]SS 2:1
2 [d]Ge 21:6; Ps 105:43; Isa 12:6; 25:9; 44:23; 51:11; 52:9; 55:12; [e]Ezr 3:7; Isa 33:9; [f]SS 7:5; [g]1Ch 27:29; Isa 65:10; [h]Ex 16:7; Isa 4:5; 59:19; [i]Isa 25:9
3 [j]Job 4:4; Heb 12:12
4 [k]2Ch 32:6; Isa 40:2; Zec 1:13; [l]Dt 20:3; Isa 21:4; [m]Jos 1:9; Isa 7:4; Da 10:19; [n]Isa 40:9–11; 51:5; 62:11; Rev 22:12; [o]Isa 1:24; 34:8; [p]Isa 25:9
5 [q]Ps 146:8; Jn 9:6–7; Ac 26:18; [r]Isa 29:18; 42:18; 50:4
6 [s]Mt 15:30; Lk 7:22; Jn 5:8–9; Ac 3:8; [t]2Sa 22:34; [u]Isa 32:4; Mt 9:32–33; 12:22; Mk 7:35; Lk 11:14; [v]Ps 20:5; [w]Ex 17:6; Jn 7:38
7 [x]Ps 68:6; Isa 41:17; 44:3; 55:1; [y]Ps 107:35; Isa 49:10; 58:11; [z]Isa 13:22; [a]Job 8:11; 40:21

5Then will the eyes of the blind be
opened[q]
and the ears of the deaf[r] unstopped.
6Then will the lame[s] leap like a deer,[t]
and the mute tongue[u] shout for joy.[v]
Water will gush forth in the
wilderness
and streams[w] in the desert.
7The burning sand will become a pool,
the thirsty ground[x] bubbling
springs.[y]
In the haunts where jackals[z] once lay,
grass and reeds[a] and papyrus will
grow.

8And a highway[b] will be there;
it will be called the Way of
Holiness.[c]
The unclean[d] will not journey on it;
it will be for those who walk in that
Way;
wicked fools will not go about on it.[a]
9No lion[e] will be there,
nor will any ferocious beast[f] get up
on it;
they will not be found there.
But only the redeemed[g] will walk
there,
10 and the ransomed[h] of the LORD will
return.
They will enter Zion with singing;[i]
everlasting joy[j] will crown their
heads.
Gladness[k] and joy will overtake them,
and sorrow and sighing will flee
away.[l]

Sennacherib Threatens Jerusalem

36:1–22pp—2Ki 18:13, 17–37; 2Ch 32:9–19

36 In the fourteenth year of King
Hezekiah's[a] reign, Senna-
cherib[b] king of Assyria attacked all the
fortified cities of Judah and captured
them.[c] 2Then the king of Assyria sent
his field commander with a large army
from Lachish[d] to King Hezekiah at Jeru-
salem. When the commander stopped
at the aqueduct of the Upper Pool, on
the road to the Washerman's Field,[e]
3Eliakim[f] son of Hilkiah the palace ad-
ministrator,[g] Shebna[h] the secretary,[i] and

8 [b]Isa 11:16; 33:8; Jer 31:21; Mt 7:13–14; [c]Isa 4:3; 1Pe 1:15; [d]Isa 52:1
9 [e]Isa 30:6; [f]Isa 11:6; 13:22; 34:14; [g]Ex 6:6; Lev 25:47–55; Isa 51:11; 62:12; 63:4
10 [h]Job 19:25; Isa 1:27; [i]Isa 30:29; [j]Ps 4:7; 126:5; Isa 25:9; Ps 51:8; [k]Isa 51:3; [l]Isa 30:19; Rev 7:17; 21:4

Ch. 36
1 [a]2Ki 18:9; [b]2Ch 32:1; [c]Ps 109:11
2 [d]Jos 10:3; [e]Isa 7:3
3 [f]Isa 22:20–21; 37:2; [g]Ge 41:40; [h]2Ki 18:18; [i]2Sa 8:17

[a]8 Or / *the simple will not stray from it*

Joah[j] son of Asaph the recorder[k] went
out to him.
4The field commander said to them,
"Tell Hezekiah,

" 'This is what the great king, the
king of Assyria, says: On what are
you basing this confidence of
yours? 5You say you have strategy
and military strength—but you
speak only empty words. On
whom are you depending, that you
rebel[l] against me? 6Look now, you
are depending[m] on Egypt,[n o] that
splintered reed[p] of a staff, which
pierces a man's hand and wounds
him if he leans on it! Such is Phar-
aoh king of Egypt to all who de-
pend on him. 7And if you say to
me, "We are depending[q] on the
LORD our God"—isn't he the one
whose high places and altars Heze-
kiah removed,[r] saying to Judah and
Jerusalem, "You must worship
before this altar"?[s]
8" 'Come now, make a bargain
with my master, the king of Assy-
ria: I will give you two thousand
horses[t]—if you can put riders
on them! 9How then can you re-
pulse one officer of the least of
my master's officials, even though
you are depending on Egypt[u]
for chariots[v] and horsemen?[w]
10Furthermore, have I come to
attack and destroy this land with-
out the LORD? The LORD himself
told[x] me to march against this coun-
try and destroy it.' "

11Then Eliakim, Shebna and Joah[y]
said to the field commander, "Please
speak to your servants in Aramaic,[z]
since we understand it. Don't speak to
us in Hebrew in the hearing of the
people on the wall."
12But the commander replied, "Was it
only to your master and you that my
master sent me to say these things, and
not to the men sitting on the wall—
who, like you, will have to eat their own
filth and drink their own urine?[a]"
13Then the commander stood and
called out in Hebrew,[b] "Hear the
words of the great king, the king of
Assyria![c] 14This is what the king says:
Do not let Hezekiah deceive[d] you. He
cannot deliver you! 15Do not let
Hezekiah persuade you to trust in
the LORD when he says, 'The LORD will
surely deliver[e] us; this city will not
be given into the hand of the king of
Assyria.'[f]

16"Do not listen to Hezekiah. This is
what the king of Assyria says: Make
peace with me and come out to me.
Then every one of you will eat from his
own vine and fig-tree[g] and drink water
from his own cistern,[h] 17until I come and
take you to a land like your own[i]—a
land of corn and new wine,[j] a land of
bread and vineyards.
18"Do not let Hezekiah mislead you
when he says, 'The LORD will deliver
us.' Has the god of any nation ever
delivered his land from the hand of the
king of Assyria? 19Where are the gods of
Hamath and Arpad?[k] Where are the
gods of Sepharvaim?[l] Have they res-
cued Samaria[m] from my hand? 20Who of
all the gods[n] of these countries has been
able to save his land from me? How then
can the LORD deliver Jerusalem from my
hand?"[o]
21But the people remained silent and
said nothing in reply, because the king
had commanded, "Do not answer
him."[p]
22Then Eliakim[q] son of Hilkiah the
palace administrator, Shebna the sec-
retary, and Joah son of Asaph the
recorder[r] went to Hezekiah, with their
clothes torn,[s] and told him what the
field commander had said.

Jerusalem's Deliverance Foretold

37:1–13pp—2Ki 19:1–13

37 When King Hezekiah heard
this, he tore his clothes[a] and put
on sackcloth[b] and went into the temple[c]
of the LORD. 2He sent Eliakim[d] the palace
administrator, Shebna[e] the secretary,
and the leading priests, all wearing
sackcloth, to the prophet Isaiah son of
Amoz.[f] 3They told him, "This is what
Hezekiah says: This day is a day of
distress[g] and rebuke and disgrace, as
when children come to the point of
birth[h] and there is no strength to deliver
them. 4It may be that the LORD your God
will hear the words of the field comman-
der, whom his master, the king of
Assyria, has sent to ridicule[i] the living
God,[j] and that he will rebuke him for the
words the LORD your God has heard.[k]
Therefore pray[l] for the remnant[m] that
still survives."
5When King Hezekiah's officials came
to Isaiah, 6Isaiah said to them, "Tell
your master, 'This is what the LORD
says: Do not be afraid[n] of what you have
heard—those words with which the
underlings of the king of Assyria have
blasphemed[o] me. 7Listen! I am going to
put a spirit[p] in him so that when he

3 [j]ver 11; [k]2Sa 8:16
5 [l]2Ki 18:7
6 [m]2Ki 17:4; Isa 8:12; [n]Eze 17:17; [o]Isa 30:2,5; [p]Isa 42:3; 58:5; Eze 29:6–7
7 [q]Ps 22:8; Mt 27:43; [r]2Ki 18:4; [s]Dt 12:2–5; 2Ch 31:1
8 [t]Ps 20:7; Isa 30:16
9 [u]Isa 31:3; [v]Isa 37:24; [w]Ps 20:7; Isa 30:2–5
10 [x]1Ki 13:18; Isa 10:5–7
11 [y]ver 3; [z]Ezr 4:7
12 [a]2Ki 6:25; Eze 4:12
13 [b]2Ch 32:18; [c]Isa 37:4
14 [d]2Ch 32:15
15 [e]Ps 3:2,7; [f]Isa 37:10
16 [g]1Ki 4:25; [h]Pr 5:15
17 [i]2Ki 15:29; [j]Ge 27:28; Dt 28:51
19 [k]2Ki 18:34; [l]2Ki 17:24; [m]2Ki 15:29
20 [n]1Ki 20:23; [o]Ex 5:2; 2Ch 25:15; Isa 10:8–11; 37:10–13, 18–20; 40:18; Da 3:15
21 [p]Pr 9:7–8; 26:4
22 [q]2Ki 18:18; [r]2Sa 8:16; [s]Ge 37:29; 2Ch 34:19

Ch. 37

1 [a]Ge 37:29; 2Ch 34:19; [b]Ge 37:34; [c]ver 14; 1Ki 8:33; Mt 21:13
2 [d]2Ki 18:18; Isa 36:3; [e]2Ki 18:18; [f]ver 21; Isa 1:1; 13:1; 38:1
3 [g]Jdg 6:2; Isa 5:30; [h]Isa 26:18; 66:9; Hos 13:13
4 [i]ver 23–24; 2Ch 32:17; [j]Jos 3:10; [k]Isa 36:13, 18–20; [l]1Sa 7:8; [m]Isa 1:9; Am 7:2
6 [n]Jos 1:9; Isa 7:4; [o]Nu 15:30
7 [p]1Ch 5:26

hears a certain report,[q] he will return to
his own country, and there I will have
him cut down[r] with the sword.' "
8When the field commander heard
that the king of Assyria had left Lach-
ish,[s] he withdrew and found the king
fighting against Libnah.[t]
9Now Sennacherib[u] received a report[v]
that Tirhakah, the Cushite[a][w] king ⌞of
Egypt⌟, was marching out to fight
against him. When he heard it, he sent
messengers to Hezekiah with this word:
10"Say to Hezekiah king of Judah: Do
not let the god you depend on deceive[x]
you when he says, 'Jerusalem will not
be handed over to the king of Assyria.'[y]
11Surely you have heard what the kings
of Assyria have done to all the coun-
tries, destroying them completely. And
will you be delivered?[z] 12Did the gods of
the nations that were destroyed by my
forefathers[a] deliver them—the gods of
Gozan, Haran,[b] Rezeph and the people
of Eden[c] who were in Tel Assar?
13Where is the king of Hamath, the king
of Arpad,[d] the king of the city of Sephar-
vaim,[e] or of Hena or Ivvah?"[f]

Hezekiah's Prayer

37:14–20pp—2Ki 19:14–19

14Hezekiah received the letter[g] from
the messengers and read it. Then he
went up to the temple[h] of the LORD and
spread it out before the LORD. 15And
Hezekiah prayed[i] to the LORD: 16"O
LORD Almighty, God of Israel, en-
throned[j] between the cherubim,[k] you
alone are God[l] over all the kingdoms[m] of
the earth. You have made heaven and
earth.[n] 17Give ear, O LORD, and hear;[o]
open your eyes, O LORD, and see;[p] listen
to all the words Sennacherib[q] has sent to
insult[r] the living God.[s]
18"It is true, O LORD, that the Assyrian
kings have laid waste all these peoples
and their lands.[t] 19They have thrown
their gods into the fire[u] and destroyed
them,[v] for they were not gods[w] but only
wood and stone, fashioned by human
hands.[x] 20Now, O LORD our God,
deliver[y] us from his hand, so that all
kingdoms on earth[z] may know that you
alone, O LORD, are God."[b][a]

Sennacherib's Fall

37:21–38pp—2Ki 19:20–37; 2Ch 32:20–21

21Then Isaiah son of Amoz[b] sent a
message to Hezekiah: "This is what the
LORD, the God of Israel, says: Because
you have prayed to me concerning
Sennacherib king of Assyria, 22this is
the word the LORD has spoken against
him:

"The Virgin Daughter[c] of Zion[d]
despises and mocks you.
The Daughter of Jerusalem
tosses her head[e] as you flee.
23Who is it you have insulted and
blasphemed?[f]
Against whom have you raised your
voice[g]
and lifted your eyes in pride?[h]
Against the Holy One[i] of Israel!
24By your messengers
you have heaped insults on the
Lord.
And you have said,
'With my many chariots[j]
I have ascended the heights of the
mountains,
the utmost heights[k] of Lebanon.[l]
I have cut down its tallest cedars,
the choicest of its pines.[m]
I have reached its remotest heights,
the finest of its forests.
25I have dug wells in foreign lands[c]
and drunk the water there.
With the soles of my feet
I have dried up[n] all the streams of
Egypt.[o]'

26"Have you not heard?
Long ago I ordained[p] it.
In days of old I planned[q] it;
now I have brought it to pass,
that you have turned fortified cities
into piles of stone.[r]
27Their people, drained of power,
are dismayed and put to shame.
They are like plants in the field,
like tender green shoots,
like grass[s] sprouting on the roof,[t]
scorched[d] before it grows up.

28"But I know where you stay
and when you come and go[u]
and how you rage[v] against me.
29Because you rage against me
and because your insolence[w] has
reached my ears,

7 [q]ver 9; [r]Isa 31:8
8 [s]**Jos 10:3;** [t]**Nu 33:20**
9 [u]**2Ch 32:1;** [v]ver 7; [w]**Isa 20:3**
10 [x]2Ch 32:11, 15; [y]Isa 36:15
11 [z]Isa 36:18–20
12 [a]2Ki 18:11; [b]Ge 11:31; 12:1–4; Ac 7:2; [c]Eze 27:23; Am 1:5
13 [d]Isa 10:9; [e]**2Ki 17:24;** [f]**Isa 36:20**
14 [g]2Ch 32:17; [h]ver 1,38; **1Ki 8:33**
15 [i]**2Ch 32:20**
16 [j]**Ps 2:4;** [k]**Ge 3:24;** [l]Dt 10:17; **Ps 46:10;** 86:10; 136:2–3; [m]Da 4:34; [n]**Ge 1:1; Isa 11:12;** 41:9; 43:6; Ac 4:24
17 [o]**1Ki 8:29; 2Ch 6:40;** [p]Jer 25:29; Da 9:18; [q]**2Ch 32:1;** [r]**2Ch 32:17;** [s]**Jos 3:10**
18 [t]**2Ki 15:29;** Na 2:11–12
19 [u]**Jos 7:15;** [v]Isa 26:14; 36:20; [w]2Ch 13:9; [x]Isa 40:17; 41:24,29; Jer 2:11; 5:7; 16:20; Gal 4:8; [x]**2Ch 32:19; Ps 135:15;** Isa 40:18–20; 44:9–11
20 [y]**Ps 3:2,**7; **Pr 20:22;** [z]**Jos 4:24;** [a]**1Sa 17:46; Ps 46:10**
21 [b]**ver 2**
22 [c]**Isa 23:12;** [d]**Isa 10:32;** [e]**Job 16:4**
23 [f]ver 4; **Nu 15:30;** Isa 52:5; Eze 36:20,23; Da 7:25; [g]**Job 15:25;** [h]**Isa 2:11;** [i]**Isa 1:4; 12:6**
24 [j]Isa 36:9; [k]Isa 14:13; [l]**1Ki 7:2; Isa 14:8; 33:9;** [m]1Ki 5:8–10; Isa 41:19; 55:13; 60:13; Hos 14:8
25 [n]**Isa 19:6;** 44:27; [o]**Dt 11:10; Isa 10:14;** Da 4:30

26 [p]Ac 2:23; 4:27–28; 1Pe 2:8; [q]Isa 10:6; **25:1;** [r]**Dt 13:16; Isa 25:2** *27* [s]**Isa 15:6;** [t]Ps 129:6
28 [u]Ps 139:1–3; [v]Ps 2:1 *29* [w]Isa 10:12

[a]9 That is, from the upper Nile region
[b]20 Dead Sea Scrolls (see also 2 Kings 19:19); Masoretic Text *alone are the LORD*
[c]25 Dead Sea Scrolls (see also 2 Kings 19:24); Masoretic Text does not have *in foreign lands.*
[d]27 Some manuscripts of the Masoretic Text, Dead Sea Scrolls and some Septuagint manuscripts (see also 2 Kings 19:26); most manuscripts of the Masoretic Text *housetops / and terraced fields*

I will put my hook[x] in your nose[y]
and my bit in your mouth,
and I will make you return
by the way you came.[z]

30"This will be the sign[a] for you, O
Hezekiah:

"This year[b] you will eat what grows by
itself,
and the second year what springs
from that.
But in the third year[c] sow and reap,
plant vineyards[d] and eat their fruit.[e]
31Once more a remnant of the house of
Judah
will take root[f] below and bear fruit[g]
above.
32For out of Jerusalem will come a
remnant,[h]
and out of Mount Zion a band of
survivors.[i]
The zeal[j] of the LORD Almighty
will accomplish this.

33"Therefore this is what the LORD
says concerning the king of Assyria:

"He will not enter this city[k]
or shoot an arrow here.
He will not come before it with shield
or build a siege ramp[l] against it.
34By the way that he came he will
return;[m]
he will not enter this city,"
declares the LORD.
35"I will defend[n] this city and save it,
for my sake[o] and for the sake of
David[p] my servant!"

36Then the angel[q] of the LORD went
out and put to death[r] a hundred and
eighty-five thousand men in the As-
syrian[s] camp. When the people got up
the next morning—there were all the
dead bodies! 37So Sennacherib[t] king of
Assyria broke camp and withdrew. He
returned to Nineveh[u] and stayed
there.
38One day, while he was worshipping
in the temple[v] of his god Nisroch, his
sons Adrammelech and Sharezer cut
him down with the sword, and they
escaped to the land of Ararat.[w] And
Esarhaddon[x] his son succeeded him as
king.[y]

Hezekiah's Illness

38:1–8pp—2Ki 20:1–11; 2Ch 32:24–26

38 In those days Hezekiah became
ill and was at the point of death.
The prophet Isaiah son of Amoz[a] went
to him and said, "This is what the LORD
says: Put your house in order,[b] because
you are going to die; you will not
recover."[c]
2Hezekiah turned his face to the wall
and prayed to the LORD, 3"Remember,
O LORD, how I have walked[d] before you
faithfully and with wholehearted de-
votion[e] and have done what is good in
your eyes.[f]" And Hezekiah wept[g]
bitterly.
4Then the word[h] of the LORD came to
Isaiah: 5"Go and tell Hezekiah, 'This is
what the LORD, the God of your father
David,[i] says: I have heard your prayer
and seen your tears;[j] I will add fifteen
years[k] to your life. 6And I will deliver
you and this city from the hand of the
king of Assyria. I will defend[l] this city.
7" 'This is the LORD's sign[m] to you that
the LORD will do what he has promised:
8I will make the shadow cast by the sun
go back the ten steps it has gone down
on the stairway of Ahaz.' " So the sun-
light went back the ten steps it had gone
down.[n]

9A writing of Hezekiah king of Judah
after his illness and recovery:

10I said, "In the prime of my life[o]
must I go through the gates of
death[a][p]
and be robbed of the rest of my
years?[q]"
11I said, "I will not again see the LORD,
the LORD,[r] in the land of the living;[s]
no longer will I look on mankind,
or be with those who now dwell in
this world.[b]
12Like a shepherd's tent[t] my house
has been pulled down[u] and taken
from me.
Like a weaver I have rolled[v] up my life,
and he has cut me off from the
loom;[w]
day and night[x] you made an end of
me.
13I waited patiently[y] till dawn,
but like a lion he broke[z] all my
bones;[a]
day and night[b] you made an end of
me.
14I cried like a swift or thrush,
I moaned like a mourning dove.[c]
My eyes grew weak[d] as I looked to the
heavens.
I am troubled; O Lord, come to my
aid!"[e]

29 [x]2Ch 33:11; [y]Job 40:24; [z]ver 34
30 [a]Isa 20:3; [b]Isa 32:10; [c]Isa 16:14; [d]Lev 25:4; [e]Ps 107:37; Isa 30:23; 65:21; Jer 31:5
31 [f]Isa 11:10; [g]Isa 27:6
32 [h]Isa 11:11; [i]Isa 1:9; [j]Isa 9:7
33 [k]Isa 32:18; [l]2Sa 20:15
34 [m]ver 29
35 [n]Isa 31:5; [o]Isa 43:25; 48:9,11; Eze 36:21–22; [p]1Ch 17:19
36 [q]Ex 12:23; [r]Ex 12:12; [s]Isa 10:12
37 [t]2Ch 32:1; [u]Ge 10:11; Na 1:1
38 [v]ver 14; [w]Ge 8:4; Jer 51:27; [x]2Ki 17:24; [y]Isa 9:4; 10:26; 14:25

Ch. 38

1 [a]Isa 37:2; [b]2Sa 17:23; [c]2Ki 8:10
3 [d]Ps 26:3; [e]1Ki 8:61; 1Ch 29:19; [f]Dt 6:18; 10:20; [g]Ps 6:8
4 [h]1Sa 13:13; Isa 39:5
5 [i]2Ki 18:3; [j]Ps 6:6; [k]2Ki 18:2
6 [l]Isa 31:5
7 [m]Ge 24:14; 2Ch 32:31; Isa 7:11,14; 20:3
8 [n]Jos 10:13
10 [o]Ps 102:24; [p]Job 17:16; Ps 107:18; 2Co 1:9; [q]Job 17:11
11 [r]Isa 12:2; [s]Job 28:13; Ps 116:9
12 [t]Isa 33:20; 2Co 5:1,4; 2Pe 1:13–14; [u]Job 4:21; [v]Isa 34:4; Heb 1:12; [w]Nu 11:15; Job 7:6; Ps 31:22; [x]ver 13; Ps 32:4; 73:14
13 [y]Ps 37:7; [z]Job 9:17; Ps 51:8; [a]Job 10:16; Jer 34:17; La 3:4; Da 6:24; [b]ver 12
14 [c]Ge 8:8; Isa 59:11; [d]Ps 6:7; [e]Ge 50:24; Job 17:3

[a]*10* Hebrew *Sheol*
[b]*11* A few Hebrew manuscripts; most Hebrew manuscripts *in the place of cessation*

15 But what can I say?[f]
He has spoken to me, and he
himself has done this.[g]
I will walk humbly[h] all my years
because of this anguish of my soul.[i]
16 Lord, by such things men live;
and my spirit finds life in them too.
You restored me to health
and let me live.[j]
17 Surely it was for my benefit[k]
that I suffered such anguish.[l]
In your love you kept me
from the pit[m] of destruction;
you have put all my sins[n]
behind your back.[o]
18 For the grave[c][p] cannot praise you,
death cannot sing your praise;[q]
those who go down to the pit[r]
cannot hope for your faithfulness.
19 The living, the living—they praise[s]
you,
as I am doing today;
fathers tell their children[t]
about your faithfulness.

20 The LORD will save me,
and we will sing[u] with stringed
instruments[v]
all the days of our lives[w]
in the temple[x] of the LORD.

21 Isaiah had said, "Prepare a poultice
of figs and apply it to the boil, and he
will recover."
22 Hezekiah had asked, "What will be
the sign[y] that I will go up to the temple
of the LORD?"

Envoys From Babylon

39:1–8pp—2Ki 20:12–19

39 At that time Merodach-Baladan
son of Baladan king of Babylon[a]
sent Hezekiah letters and a gift, because
he had heard of his illness and recovery.
2 Hezekiah received the envoys[b] gladly
and showed them what was in his store-
houses—the silver, the gold,[c] the
spices, the fine oil, his entire armoury
and everything found among his
treasures.[d] There was nothing in his
palace or in all his kingdom that Heze-
kiah did not show them.
3 Then Isaiah the prophet went to
King Hezekiah and asked, "What did
those men say, and where did they
come from?"
"From a distant land,[e]" Hezekiah
replied. "They came to me from Bab-
ylon."
4 The prophet asked, "What did they
see in your palace?"
"They saw everything in my palace,"
Hezekiah said. "There is nothing
among my treasures that I did not show
them."
5 Then Isaiah said to Hezekiah, "Hear
the word[f] of the LORD Almighty: 6 The
time will surely come when everything
in your palace, and all that your fathers
have stored up until this day, will be
carried off to Babylon.[g] Nothing will be
left, says the LORD. 7 And some of your
descendants, your own flesh and blood
who will be born to you, will be taken
away, and they will become eunuchs in
the palace of the king of Babylon.[h]"
8 "The word of the LORD you have
spoken is good,[i]" Hezekiah replied. For
he thought, "There will be peace and
security in my lifetime.[j]"

Comfort for God's People

40 Comfort, comfort[a] my people,
says your God.
2 Speak tenderly[b] to Jerusalem,
and proclaim to her
that her hard service[c] has been
completed,[d]
that her sin has been paid for,[e]
that she has received from the LORD's
hand
double[f] for all her sins.

3 A voice of one calling:
"In the desert prepare
the way[g] for the LORD;[a]
make straight[h] in the wilderness
a highway for our God.[b][i]
4 Every valley shall be raised up,[j]
every mountain and hill[k] made low;
the rough ground shall become level,[l]
the rugged places a plain.
5 And the glory[m] of the LORD will be
revealed,
and all mankind together will see
it.[n]
For the mouth of the LORD
has spoken."[o]

6 A voice says, "Cry out."
And I said, "What shall I cry?"

"All men are like grass,[p]
and all their glory is like the flowers
of the field.

15 [f]2Sa 7:20; [g]**Ps 39:9**; [h]1Ki 21:27; [i]**Job 7:11**
16 [j]Ps 119:25; Heb 12:9
17 [k]Ro 8:28; Heb 12:11; [l]**Job 7:11**; Ps 119:71,75; [m]**Job 17:16**; **Ps 30:3**; [n]Ps 103:3; Jer 31:34; [o]**Ps 103:12**; Isa 43:25; Mic 7:19
18 [p]**Nu 16:30**; **Ecc 9:10**; [q]Ps 6:5; 88:10–11; 115:17; [r]**Ps 30:9**
19 [s]Ps 118:17; 119:175; [t]**Dt 11:19**
20 [u]Ps 68:25; [v]**Ps 33:2; 45:8**; [w]Ps 23:6; **63:4**; 116:2; [x]Ps 116:17–19
22 [y]2Ch 32:31

Ch. 39

1 [a]**2Ch 32:31**
2 [b]2Ch 32:31; [c]**2Ki 18:15**; [d]2Ch 32:27–29
3 [e]**Dt 28:49**
5 [f]**Isa 38:4**
6 [g]**Jdg 6:4; 2Ki 24:13**
7 [h]**2Ki 24:15**; Da 1:1–7
8 [i]**Jdg 10:15**; Job 1:21; Ps 39:9; [j]**2Ch 32:26**

Ch. 40

1 [a]Isa 12:1; 49:13; 51:3,12; 52:9; 57:18; 61:2; 66:13; Jer 31:13; Zep 3:14–17; Zec 1:17; 2Co 1:3
2 [b]**Ge 34:3; Isa 35:4**; [c]**Job 7:1**; [d]Isa 41:11–13; 49:25; [e]**Lev 26:41**; [f]Isa 51:19; 61:7; Jer 16:18; 17:18; Zec 9:12; Rev 18:6
3 [g]**Isa 11:16**; 43:19; Mal 3:1; [h]**Pr 3:5–6**; Mt 3:3*; [i]Mk 1:3*; Jn 1:23*
4 [j]Isa 49:11; [k]**Isa 2:14**; [l]**Ps 26:12; Isa 26:7**; 45:2,13; Jer 31:9
5 [m]**Ex 16:7; Nu 14:21; Isa 59:19**; [n]Isa 52:10; 62:2; Lk 2:30; 3:4–6*; [o]**Isa 1:20**; 58:14
6 [p]**Ge 6:3; Isa 29:5**

[c]18 Hebrew *Sheol*
[a]3 Or *A voice of one calling in the desert: / "Prepare the way for the LORD*
[b]3 Hebrew; Septuagint *make straight the paths of our God*

[7]The grass withers[q] and the flowers fall,
because the breath[r] of the LORD blows[s] on them.
Surely the people are grass.
[8]The grass withers and the flowers[t] fall,
but the word[u] of our God stands[v] for ever.[w]"

[9]You who bring good tidings[x] to Zion,
go up on a high mountain.
You who bring good tidings to Jerusalem,[c y]
lift up your voice with a shout,
lift it up, do not be afraid;
say to the towns of Judah,
"Here is your God!"[z]
[10]See, the Sovereign LORD comes[a] with power,[b]
and his arm[c] rules[d] for him.
See, his reward[e] is with him,
and his recompense accompanies him.
[11]He tends his flock like a shepherd:[f]
He gathers the lambs in his arms[g]
and carries them close to his heart;[h]
he gently leads[i] those that have young.[j]

[12]Who has measured the waters[k] in the hollow of his hand,[l]
or with the breadth of his hand marked off the heavens?[m]
Who has held the dust of the earth in a basket,
or weighed the mountains on the scales
and the hills in a balance?[n]
[13]Who has understood the mind[d o] of the LORD,
or instructed him as his counsellor?[p]
[14]Whom did the LORD consult to enlighten him,
and who taught him the right way?
Who was it that taught him knowledge[q]
or showed him the path of understanding?[r]
[15]Surely the nations are like a drop in a bucket;
they are regarded as dust on the scales;[s]
he weighs the islands as though they were fine dust.[t]
[16]Lebanon[u] is not sufficient for altar fires,
nor its animals[v] enough for burnt offerings.
[17]Before him all the nations[w] are as nothing;[x]
they are regarded by him as worthless
and less than nothing.[y]

[18]To whom, then, will you compare God?[z]
What image[a] will you compare him to?
[19]As for an idol,[b] a craftsman casts it,
and a goldsmith[c] overlays it with gold[d]
and fashions silver chains for it.
[20]A man too poor to present such an offering
selects wood[e] that will not rot.
He looks for a skilled craftsman
to set up an idol[f] that will not topple.[g]

[21]Do you not know?
Have you not heard?[h]
Has it not been told[i] you from the beginning?[j]
Have you not understood[k] since the earth was founded?[l]
[22]He sits enthroned[m] above the circle of the earth,
and its people are like grasshoppers.[n]
He stretches out the heavens[o] like a canopy,[p]
and spreads them out like a tent[q] to live in.[r]
[23]He brings princes[s] to naught
and reduces the rulers of this world to nothing.[t]
[24]No sooner are they planted,
no sooner are they sown,
no sooner do they take root[u] in the ground,
than he blows[v] on them and they wither,[w]
and a whirlwind sweeps them away like chaff.[x]

[25]"To whom will you compare me?[y]
Or who is my equal?" says the Holy One.[z]
[26]Lift your eyes and look to the heavens:[a]
Who created[b] all these?
He who brings out the starry host[c] one by one,
and calls them each by name.

7 [q]Job 8:12; Isa 15:6; [r]Ex 15:10; Job 41:21; [s]Ps 103:16; Eze 22:21
8 [t]Isa 5:24; Jas 1:10; [u]Isa 55:11; 59:21; [v]Pr 19:21; Isa 7:7,9; Jer 39:16; [w]Ps 119:89; Mt 5:18; 1Pe 1:24–25*
9 [x]Isa 41:27; 44:28; 52:7–10; 61:1; Na 1:15; Ac 13:32; Ro 10:15; 1Co 15:1–4; [y]Isa 1:1; [z]Isa 25:9
10 [a]Isa 35:4; 59:20; Mt 21:5; Rev 22:7; [b]Isa 28:2; [c]Ps 44:3; Isa 30:30; 33:2; [d]Isa 9:6–7; [e]Isa 35:4; Rev 22:12
11 [f]Ge 48:15; Ps 28:9; Mic 5:4; Jn 10:11; [g]Nu 11:12; [h]Dt 26:19; [i]Isa 49:10; [j]Ge 33:13; Dt 30:4
12 [k]Job 12:15; 38:10; [l]Pr 30:4; [m]Job 38:5; Heb 1:10–12; [n]Job 38:18; Pr 16:11
13 [o]Isa 11:2; 42:1; [p]Job 15:8; Ro 11:34*; 1Co 2:16*
14 [q]Job 21:22; Col 2:3; [r]Job 12:13; 34:13; Isa 55:9
15 [s]Ps 62:9; [t]Dt 9:21; Isa 2:22
16 [u]Isa 33:9; 37:24; [v]Ps 50:9–11; Mic 6:7; Heb 10:5–9
17 [w]Isa 30:28; [x]Job 12:19; Isa 29:7; [y]Isa 37:19; Da 4:35
18 [z]Ex 8:10; 1Sa 2:2; [a]Dt 4:15; Ac 17:29
19 [b]Ex 20:4; Ps 115:4; Isa 37:19; 42:17; Jer 2:8,28; 10:8; 16:19; Hab 2:18; Zec 10:2; [c]Isa 41:7; 46:6; Jer 10:3; [d]Isa 2:20; 31:7
20 [e]Isa 44:19; [f]1Sa 12:21; [g]1Sa 5:3
21 [h]ver 28; 2Ki 19:25; Isa 41:22; 42:9; 44:8; 48:3,5; [i]Ps 19:1; 50:6; Ac 14:17; [j]Ge 1:1; [k]Ro 1:19; [l]Isa 48:13; 51:13
22 [m]2Ch 6:18; Ps 2:4; [n]Nu 13:33; [o]Ge 1:1; Isa 48:13; [p]Ge 1:8; Job 22:14; [q]Job 36:29; [r]Job 26:7
23 [s]Job 12:18; Isa 34:12; [t]Job 12:19; Am 2:3
24 [u]Job 5:3; [v]2Sa 22:16; Isa 11:4; 41:16; [w]Job 8:12; 18:16; [x]Job 24:24; Isa 41:2
25 [y]1Sa 2:2; 1Ch 16:25; [z]Isa 1:4; 37:23
26 [a]Isa 51:6; [b]ver 28; Ps 89:11–13; Isa 42:5; 66:2; [c]2Ki 17:16; Ne 9:6; Job 38:32

[c]9 Or *O Zion, bringer of good tidings, / go up on a high mountain. / O Jerusalem, bringer of good tidings*
[d]13 Or *Spirit*; or *spirit*

Because of his great power and mighty
strength,[d]
not one of them is missing.[e]

27Why do you say, O Jacob,
and complain, O Israel,
"My way is hidden from the LORD;
my cause is disregarded by my
God"?[f]
28Do you not know?
Have you not heard?[g]
The LORD is the everlasting[h] God,
the Creator[i] of the ends of the earth.[j]
He will not grow tired or weary,[k]
and his understanding no-one can
fathom.[l]
29He gives strength[m] to the weary[n]
and increases the power of the
weak.
30Even youths grow tired and weary,
and young men[o] stumble and fall;[p]
31but those who hope[q] in the LORD
will renew their strength.[r]
They will soar on wings like eagles;[s]
they will run and not grow weary,
they will walk and not be faint.[t]

The Helper of Israel

41 "Be silent[a] before me, you
islands![b]
Let the nations renew their
strength![c]
Let them come forward[d] and speak;
let us meet together[e] at the place of
judgment.

2"Who has stirred[f] up one from the
east,[g]
calling him in righteousness[h] to his
service?[a][i]
He hands nations over to him
and subdues kings before him.
He turns them to dust[j] with his sword,
to wind-blown chaff[k] with his bow.[l]
3He pursues them and moves on
unscathed,[m]
by a path his feet have not travelled
before.
4Who has done this and carried it
through,
calling[n] forth the generations from
the beginning?[o]
I, the LORD—with the first of them
and with the last[p]—I am he.[q]"

5The islands[r] have seen it and fear;
the ends of the earth[s] tremble.
They approach and come forward;
6 each helps the other
and says to his brother, "Be
strong![t]"

7The craftsman[u] encourages the
goldsmith,[v]
and he who smooths with the
hammer
spurs on him who strikes the anvil.
He says of the welding, "It is good."
He nails down the idol so that it will
not topple.[w]

8"But you, O Israel, my servant,[x]
Jacob, whom I have chosen,[y]
you descendants of Abraham[z] my
friend,[a]
9I took you from the ends of the earth,[b]
from its farthest corners I called[c]
you.
I said, 'You are my servant';[d]
I have chosen[e] you and have not
rejected you.
10So do not fear,[f] for I am with you;[g]
do not be dismayed, for I am your
God.
I will strengthen[h] you and help[i] you;
I will uphold you[j] with my righteous
right hand.[k]

11"All who rage[l] against you
will surely be ashamed and
disgraced;[m]
those who oppose[n] you
will be as nothing and perish.[o]
12Though you search for your enemies,
you will not find them.[p]
Those who wage war against you
will be as nothing[q] at all.
13For I am the LORD, your God,
who takes hold of your right hand[r]
and says to you, Do not fear;
I will help[s] you.
14Do not be afraid,[t] O worm[u] Jacob,
O little Israel,
for I myself will help[v] you," declares
the LORD,
your Redeemer,[w] the Holy One[x] of
Israel.
15"See, I will make you into a
threshing-sledge,[y]
new and sharp, with many teeth.
You will thresh the mountains[z] and
crush them,
and reduce the hills to chaff.[a]

26 [d]**Job 9:4; Isa 45:24;** Eph 1:19; [e]**Isa 34:16**
27 [f]**Job 6:29; 27:2;** Lk 18:7–8
28 [g]**ver 21;** [h]**Dt 33:27; Ps 90:2;** [i]**ver 26;** [j]**Isa 37:16;** [k]Isa 44:12; [l]**Ps 147:5;** Ro 11:33
29 [m]**Ge 18:14; Ps 68:35; 119:28;** [n]Isa 50:4; 57:19; Jer 31:25
30 [o]Isa 9:17; Jer 6:11; 9:21; [p]**Ps 20:8;** Isa 5:27
31 [q]**Ps 37:9;** 40:1; **Isa 30:18;** Lk 18:1; [r]**1Sa 2:4; 2Ki 6:33; 2Co 4:16;** [s]**Ex 19:4;** [t]2Co 4:1; Heb 12:1–3

Ch. 41

1 [a]Ps 37:7; Hab 2:20; Zep 1:7; Zec 2:13; [b]**Isa 11:11;** [c]**1Sa 2:4;** [d]Isa 48:16; 57:3; [e]**Isa 1:18;** 34:1; 50:8
2 [f]**Ezr 1:2;** [g]ver 25; Isa 13:4, 17; 44:28; 45:1,13; 48:14; Jer 50:3; 51:11; [h]Isa 45:8,13; [i]Isa 44:28; Jer 25:9; [j]**2Sa 22:43;** [k]Ps 1:4; Isa 40:24; [l]**Isa 13:18**
3 [m]Da 8:4
4 [n]ver 9; Isa 43:7; [o]ver 26; **Ge 1:1;** Isa 46:10; [p]Isa 44:6; 48:12; Rev 1:8,17; [q]**Dt 32:39**
5 [r]**Isa 11:11;** Eze 26:17–18; [s]**Dt 30:4; Isa 11:12**
6 [t]**Jos 1:6**
7 [u]Isa 44:13; Jer 10:3–5; [v]**Isa 40:19;** [w]**1Sa 5:3;** Isa 46:7
8 [x]**Ps 136:22; Isa 27:11;** [y]**Isa 14:1;** [z]**Isa 29:22;** 51:2; 63:16; [a]2Ch 20:7; Jas 2:23
9 [b]Isa 11:12; **37:16;** [c]**ver 4;** [d]**Isa 20:3;** [e]**Dt 7:6**
10 [f]**Ge 15:1;** [g]**Dt 3:22;** Jos 1:9; Isa 43:2,5; Jer 30:10; 46:27–28; Ro 8:31; [h]**Ps 68:35; 119:28;** [i]ver 13–14; Isa 44:2; 49:8; 50:7,9; [j]**Ps 18:35; 119:117;** [k]**Ex 3:20; Job 40:14**
11 [l]**Isa 17:12;** [m]Isa 29:22; 45:24; 54:17; [n]**Ex 23:22;** [o]**Isa 29:8; Jer 2:3**
12 [p]Ps 37:35–36; **Isa 34:12;** [q]**Job 7:8;** Isa 17:14; 29:20
13 [r]Ps 73:23; Isa 42:6; 45:1; 51:18; [s]ver 10
14 [t]**Ge 15:1;** [u]**Job 4:19; Ps 22:6;** [v]**ver 10;** [w]**Ex 15:13; Job 19:25; Isa 1:27;** [x]ver 16,20; **Isa 1:4**
15 [y]**Job 41:30; Isa 10:5; 21:10;** [z]Ex 19:18; **Ps 107:33;** Jer 9:10; Eze 33:28; [a]**ver 2**

[a]2 Or / *whom victory meets at every step*

16 You will winnow[b] them, the wind will
pick them up,
and a gale[c] will blow them away.[d]
But you will rejoice[e] in the LORD
and glory[f] in the Holy One[g] of Israel.

17 "The poor and needy search for
water,[h]
but there is none;
their tongues are parched with
thirst.[i]
But I the LORD will answer[j] them;
I, the God of Israel, will not forsake[k]
them.
18 I will make rivers flow[l] on barren
heights,
and springs within the valleys.
I will turn the desert[m] into pools of
water,[n]
and the parched ground into
springs.[o]
19 I will put in the desert[p]
the cedar and the acacia,[q] the myrtle
and the olive.
I will set pines[r] in the wasteland,
the fir and the cypress[s] together,[t]
20 so that people may see and know,[u]
may consider and understand,[v]
that the hand[w] of the LORD has done
this,
that the Holy One[x] of Israel has
created[y] it.

21 "Present your case,[z]" says the LORD.
"Set forth your arguments," says
Jacob's King.[a]
22 "Bring in ⌞your idols⌟ to tell us
what is going to happen.[b]
Tell us what the former things[c] were,
so that we may consider them
and know their final outcome.
Or declare to us the things to come,[d]
23 tell us what the future holds,
so that we may know[e] you are gods.
Do something, whether good or bad,[f]
so that we will be dismayed[g] and
filled with fear.
24 But you are less than nothing[h]
and your works are utterly
worthless;[i]
he who chooses you is detestable.[j]

25 "I have stirred[k] up one from the north,[l]
and he comes—
one from the rising sun who calls on
my name.
He treads[m] on rulers as if they were
mortar,
as if he were a potter treading the
clay.
26 Who told of this from the beginning,[n]
so that we could know,
or beforehand, so that we could say,
'He was right'?
No-one told of this,
no-one foretold[o] it,
no-one heard any words[p] from you.
27 I was the first to tell[q] Zion, 'Look, here
they are!'
I gave to Jerusalem a messenger of
good tidings.[r]
28 I look but there is no-one[s]—
no-one among them to give
counsel,[t]
no-one to give answer[u] when I ask
them.
29 See, they are all false!
Their deeds amount to nothing;[v]
their images[w] are but wind[x] and
confusion.

The Servant of the LORD

42 "Here is my servant,[a] whom I
uphold,
my chosen one[b] in whom I delight;[c]
I will put my Spirit[d] on him
and he will bring justice[e] to the
nations.[f]
2 He will not shout or cry out,[g]
or raise his voice in the streets.
3 A bruised reed[h] he will not break,[i]
and a smouldering wick he will not
snuff out.[j]
In faithfulness he will bring forth
justice;[k]
4 he will not falter or be discouraged
till he establishes justice[l] on earth.
In his law[m] the islands[n] will put their
hope."[o]

5 This is what God the LORD says—
he who created the heavens[p] and
stretched them out,
who spread out the earth[q] and all
that comes out of it,[r]
who gives breath[s] to its people,
and life to those who walk on it:
6 "I, the LORD, have called[t] you in
righteousness;[u]
I will take hold of your hand.[v]
I will keep[w] you and will make you
to be a covenant[x] for the people
and a light[y] for the Gentiles,[z]

16 [b]Jer 15:7; 51:2; [c]Isa 40:24; [d]Da 2:35; [e]**Isa 25:9**; [f]Isa 45:25; 60:19; [g]**ver 14**; **Mk 1:24**
17 [h]Isa 43:20; [i]**Isa 35:7**; [j]**Isa 30:19**; [k]**Dt 31:6**; **Ps 27:9**
18 [l]**Isa 30:25**; [m]Isa 43:19; [n]**2Ki 3:17**; [o]**Job 38:26**; **Isa 35:7**
19 [p]**Isa 35:1**; 51:3; [q]Ex 25:5, 10,13; [r]**Isa 37:24**; [s]Isa 44:14; [t]Isa 60:13
20 [u]**Ex 6:7**; [v]**Isa 29:24**; [w]Ezr 7:6; 8:31; Isa 50:2; 51:9; 59:1; 66:14; Jer 32:17; [x]**ver 14**; Isa 43:3,14; [y]**Isa 4:5**
21 [z]**ver 1**; [a]Isa 43:15; 44:6
22 [b]ver 26; Isa 43:9; 44:7; 45:21; 48:14; [c]Isa 43:18,26; 46:9; 48:3; [d]Isa 42:9; 43:19; 46:10; 48:6; 65:17; Jn 13:19
23 [e]Isa 45:3; [f]Jer 10:5; [g]**2Ki 19:26**
24 [h]**Isa 37:19**; 1Co 8:4; [i]**1Sa 12:21**; Jer 8:19; 10:5,8,15; [j]**Ps 109:7**; **Isa 1:13**; **48:8**
25 [k]**Ezr 1:2**; [l]**ver 2**; Jer 50:9,41; 51:48; [m]**2Sa 22:43**; **Isa 5:5**; Na 3:14
26 [n]**ver 4**; [o]**ver 22**; Isa 52:6; [p]**1Ki 18:26**; Hab 2:18–19
27 [q]Isa 48:3,16; [r]**Isa 40:9**
28 [s]Ps 22:11; Isa 50:2; 59:16; 63:5; 64:7; Eze 22:30; [t]Isa 40:13–14; **1Ki 18:26**; [u]Isa 65:12; 66:4; Jer 25:4
29 [v]**1Sa 12:21**; [w]**Isa 37:19**; [x]Jer 5:13

Ch. 42

1 [a]**Isa 20:3**; **Mt 20:28**; [b]**Isa 14:1**; Lk 9:35; 23:35; 1Pe 2:4,6; [c]Mt 3:17; [d]**Isa 11:2**; **44:3**; Mt 3:16–17; **Jn 3:34**; [e]**Isa 9:7**; [f]**Ge 49:10**
2 [g]Pr 8:1–4
3 [h]**Isa 36:6**; [i]**Job 30:24**; [j]**Job 13:25**; [k]Ps 72:2; 96:13
4 [l]**Isa 2:4**; [m]ver 21; Ex 34:29; Isa 51:4; [n]**Isa 11:11**; [o]**Ge 49:10**; Mt 12:18–21*
5 [p]**Ge 1:6**; Ps 102:25; Isa 48:13; [q]**Ge 1:1**; [r]Ps 24:2; Ac 17:24; [s]**Ge 2:7**; Ac 17:25
6 [t]Ex 31:2; **Jdg 4:10**; Isa 41:9–10; 43:1; [u]Isa 45:24; Jer 23:6; Da 9:7; [v]Isa 41:13; 45:1; [w]Isa 26:3; 27:3; [x]Isa 49:8; 54:10; 59:21; 61:8; Jer 31:31; 32:40; Mal 3:1; **Lk 22:20**; [y]**Isa 9:2**; [z]**Isa 26:18**; **Lk 2:32**

7to open eyes that are blind,[a]
to free[b] captives from prison[c]
and to release from the dungeon
those who sit in darkness.[d]

8"I am the LORD;[e] that is my name![f]
I will not give my glory to another[g]
or my praise to idols.[h]
9See, the former things[i] have taken
place,
and new things I declare;
before they spring into being
I announce[j] them to you."

Song of Praise to the LORD

10Sing[k] to the LORD a new song,[l]
his praise[m] from the ends of the
earth,[n]
you who go down to the sea, and all
that is in it,[o]
you islands,[p] and all who live in
them.
11Let the desert[q] and its towns raise their
voices;
let the settlements where Kedar[r]
lives rejoice.
Let the people of Sela[s] sing for joy;
let them shout from the
mountaintops.[t]
12Let them give glory[u] to the LORD
and proclaim his praise[v] in the
islands.[w]
13The LORD will march out like a mighty[x]
man,
like a warrior[y] he will stir up his
zeal;[z]
with a shout[a] he will raise the battle cry
and will triumph over his enemies.[b]

14"For a long time I have kept silent,[c]
I have been quiet and held myself
back.[d]
But now, like a woman in childbirth,
I cry out, I gasp and pant.[e]
15I will lay waste[f] the mountains[g] and
hills
and dry up all their vegetation;
I will turn rivers into islands
and dry up[h] the pools.
16I will lead[i] the blind[j] by ways they have
not known,
along unfamiliar paths I will guide
them;
I will turn the darkness into light[k]
before them
and make the rough places smooth.[l]
These are the things I will do;
I will not forsake[m] them.
17But those who trust in idols,
who say to images, 'You are our
gods,'[n]
will be turned back in utter shame.[o]

7 [a]Ps 146:8; Isa 32:3; Mt 11:5; [b]Isa 49:9; 51:14; 52:2; Zec 2:7; [c]Ps 66:11; Isa 24:22; 48:20; Zec 9:11; Lk 4:19; 2Ti 2:26; Heb 2:14–15; [d]Ps 107:10,14; Ac 26:18
8 [e]Ps 81:10; Isa 43:3,11,15; 46:9; 49:23; [f]Ex 3:15; 6:3; [g]Isa 48:11; [h]Ex 8:10; 20:4
9 [i]Isa 41:22; [j]Isa 40:21; Eze 2:4
10 [k]Ex 15:1; [l]Ps 96:1; [m]1Ki 10:9; Isa 60:6; [n]Dt 30:4; Ps 48:10; 65:5; Isa 49:6; [o]1Ch 16:32; Ps 96:11; [p]Isa 11:11
11 [q]Isa 32:16; [r]Ge 25:13; Isa 60:7; [s]Jdg 1:36; [t]Isa 52:7; Na 1:15
12 [u]1Ch 16:24; Isa 24:15; [v]Ps 26:7; 66:2; 1Pe 2:9; [w]Isa 11:11
13 [x]Isa 9:6; [y]Ex 14:14; [z]Isa 26:11; [a]Jos 6:5; Jer 25:30; Hos 11:10; Joel 3:16; Am 1:2; 3:4,8; [b]Isa 66:14
14 [c]Est 4:14; Ps 50:21; [d]Ge 43:31; Lk 18:7; 2Pe 3:9; [e]Jer 4:31
15 [f]Eze 38:20; [g]Ps 107:33; [h]Isa 11:15; 50:2; Na 1:4–6
16 [i]Isa 29:24; 40:11; 57:18; 58:11; Jer 31:8–9; Lk 1:78–79; [j]Isa 32:3; [k]Ps 18:28; Isa 58:8,10; Ac 26:18; [l]Isa 26:7; Lk 3:5; [m]Dt 4:31; Heb 13:5
17 [n]Ex 32:4; [o]Ps 97:7; Isa 1:29
18 [p]Isa 35:5
19 [q]Isa 43:8; Eze 12:2; [r]Isa 41:8–9; [s]Isa 44:26; Hag 1:13; [t]Isa 26:3
20 [u]Isa 6:9–10; 43:8; Jer 5:21; 6:10
21 [v]Isa 43:25; [w]ver 4; 2Co 3:7

Israel Blind and Deaf

18"Hear, you deaf;[p]
look, you blind, and see!
19Who is blind[q] but my servant,[r]
and deaf like the messenger[s] I send?
Who is blind like the one committed[t]
to me,
blind like the servant of the LORD?
20You have seen many things, but have
paid no attention;
your ears are open, but you hear
nothing."[u]
21It pleased the LORD
for the sake[v] of his righteousness
to make his law[w] great and glorious.
22But this is a people plundered[x] and
looted,
all of them trapped in pits[y]
or hidden away in prisons.[z]
They have become plunder,
with no-one to rescue them;[a]
they have been made loot,
with no-one to say, "Send them
back."

23Which of you will listen to this
or pay close attention[b] in time to
come?
24Who handed Jacob over to become
loot,
and Israel to the plunderers?[c]
Was it not the LORD,[d]
against whom we have sinned?
For they would not follow[e] his ways;
they did not obey his law.[f]
25So he poured out on them his burning
anger,[g]
the violence of war.
It enveloped them in flames,[h] yet they
did not understand;[i]
it consumed them, but they did not
take it to heart.[j]

Israel's Only Saviour

43 But now, this is what the LORD
says—
he who created[a] you, O Jacob,
he who formed[b] you, O Israel:[c]
"Fear not, for I have redeemed[d] you;
I have summoned you by name;[e]
you are mine.[f]

22 [x]Jdg 6:4; 2Ki 24:13; [y]Isa 24:18; [z]Ps 66:11; Isa 24:22; [a]Isa 5:29
23 [b]Dt 32:29; Ps 81:13; Isa 47:7; 48:18; 57:11
24 [c]2Ki 17:6; Isa 43:28; 47:6; [d]Isa 10:5–6; [e]Isa 30:15; [f]Jos 1:7; Ps 119:136; Isa 5:24; Jer 44:10
25 [g]2Ki 22:13; Job 40:11; Isa 51:17; Eze 7:19; [h]2Ki 25:9; Isa 66:15; Jer 4:4; 21:12; La 2:3; Na 1:6; [i]Isa 1:3; [j]Isa 29:13; 47:7; 57:1,11; Hos 7:9

Ch. 43

1 [a]Isa 27:11; [b]ver 7; Ge 2:7; [c]Ge 32:28; Isa 44:21; [d]Ex 6:6; Job 19:25; [e]Isa 42:6; 45:3–4; 49:1; [f]Dt 7:6; Mal 3:17

[2]When you pass through the waters,[g]
I will be with you;[h]
and when you pass through the rivers,
they will not sweep over you.
When you walk through the fire,[i]
you will not be burned;
the flames will not set you ablaze.[j]
[3]For I am the LORD, your God,[k]
the Holy One[l] of Israel, your Saviour;[m]
I give Egypt[n] for your ransom,
Cush[a][o] and Seba[p] in your stead.[q]
[4]Since you are precious and honoured[r]
in my sight,
and because I love[s] you,
I will give men in exchange for you,
and people in exchange for your life.
[5]Do not be afraid,[t] for I am with you;[u]
I will bring your children[v] from the east
and gather[w] you from the west.[x]
[6]I will say to the north, 'Give them up!'
and to the south,[y] 'Do not hold them back.'
Bring my sons from afar
and my daughters[z] from the ends of the earth[a]—
[7]everyone who is called by my name,[b]
whom I created[c] for my glory,[d]
whom I formed and made.[e]"
[8]Lead out those who have eyes but are blind,[f]
who have ears but are deaf.[g]
[9]All the nations gather together[h]
and the peoples assemble.
Which of them foretold[i] this
and proclaimed to us the former things?
Let them bring in their witnesses to prove they were right,
so that others may hear and say, "It is true."
[10]"You are my witnesses,[j]" declares the LORD,
"and my servant[k] whom I have chosen,
so that you may know[l] and believe me
and understand that I am he.
Before me no god[m] was formed,
nor will there be one after me.[n]
[11]I, even I, am the LORD,[o]
and apart from me there is no saviour.[p]
[12]I have revealed and saved and proclaimed—
I, and not some foreign god[q] among you.
You are my witnesses,[r]" declares the LORD, "that I am God.
13 Yes, and from ancient days[s] I am he.[t]
No-one can deliver out of my hand.
When I act, who can reverse it?"[u]

God's Mercy and Israel's Unfaithfulness

[14]This is what the LORD says—
your Redeemer,[v] the Holy One[w] of Israel:
"For your sake I will send to Babylon
and bring down as fugitives[x] all the Babylonians,[b][y]
in the ships in which they took pride.
[15]I am the LORD,[z] your Holy One,
Israel's Creator,[a] your King.[b]"

[16]This is what the LORD says—
he who made a way through the sea,
a path through the mighty waters,[c]
[17]who drew out[d] the chariots and horses,[e]
the army and reinforcements together,[f]
and they lay[g] there, never to rise again,
extinguished, snuffed out like a wick:[h]
[18]"Forget the former things;[i]
do not dwell on the past.
[19]See, I am doing a new thing![j]
Now it springs up; do you not perceive it?
I am making a way in the desert[k]
and streams in the wasteland.[l]
[20]The wild animals[m] honour me,
the jackals[n] and the owls,
because I provide water[o] in the desert
and streams in the wasteland,
to give drink to my people, my chosen,
21 the people I formed[p] for myself[q]
that they may proclaim my praise.[r]

[22]"Yet you have not called upon me, O Jacob,
you have not wearied[s] yourselves for me, O Israel.[t]
[23]You have not brought me sheep for burnt offerings,[u]
nor honoured[v] me with your sacrifices.[w]

2 [g]Isa 8:7; [h]Ge 26:3; Ex 14:22; [i]Isa 29:6; 30:27; [j]Ps 66:12; Da 3:25–27
3 [k]Ex 20:2; [l]Isa 41:20; [m]Ex 14:30; Jdg 2:18; Ps 3:8; Isa 25:9; [n]Ps 68:31; Isa 19:1; Eze 29:20; [o]Isa 20:3; [p]Ge 10:7; [q]Pr 21:18
4 [r]Ex 19:5; Isa 49:5; [s]Isa 63:9; Rev 3:9
5 [t]Ge 15:1; Isa 44:2; [u]Ge 21:22; Ex 14:22; Jer 30:10–11; [v]Isa 41:8; 54:3; 61:9; 66:22; [w]Isa 11:12; 49:18; [x]Isa 24:14; Zec 8:7; Mt 8:11
6 [y]Ps 107:3; [z]Isa 60:4; Eze 16:61; 2Co 6:18; [a]Dt 30:4; Isa 11:12; Jer 23:8; Eze 36:24
7 [b]Isa 48:1; 56:5; 62:2; 63:19; 65:1; Jer 15:16; Jas 2:7; [c]Isa 27:11; [d]Ps 86:9; [e]ver 1, 21; Ps 100:3; Isa 19:25
8 [f]Isa 6:9–10; [g]Isa 42:20; Eze 12:2
9 [h]Isa 41:1; 45:20; 48:14; [i]Isa 41:26
10 [j]ver 12; Jos 24:22; [k]Isa 20:3; 41:8–9; [l]Ex 6:7; [m]ver 11; Ps 86:10; Isa 19:21; 44:6,8; 45:5–6,14; [n]Dt 4:35; 32:39; Jer 14:22
11 [o]Ex 6:2; Isa 42:8; [p]ver 10; Ps 3:8; 18:31; Isa 25:9; 64:4
12 [q]Dt 32:12; [r]ver 10
13 [s]Ps 90:2; [t]Dt 32:39; Isa 46:4; 48:12; [u]Nu 23:8; Job 9:12
14 [v]Ex 15:13; Job 19:25; [w]Isa 1:4; 41:20; [x]Isa 13:14–15; [y]Isa 23:13
15 [z]Isa 42:8; [a]Isa 27:11; 45:11; [b]Isa 41:21
16 [c]Ex 14:29; 15:8; Isa 11:15
17 [d]Ps 118:12; Isa 1:31; [e]Ex 14:22; [f]Ex 14:9; [g]Ps 76:5–6; [h]Job 13:25; Jer 51:21; Eze 38:4
18 [i]Isa 41:22
19 [j]Isa 41:22; Jer 16:14–15; 23:7–8; 2Co 5:17; Rev 21:5; [k]Isa 40:3; [l]Ps 126:4; Isa 33:21; 35:7
20 [m]Ps 148:10; [n]Isa 13:22; [o]Nu 20:8
21 [p]ver 7; Ge 2:7; [q]Mal 3:17; [r]Ps 66:2; 102:18; 1Pe 2:9
22 [s]Jos 22:5; Isa 1:14; [t]Isa 30:11
23 [u]Ex 29:41; [v]Zec 7:5–6; Mal 1:6–8; [w]Am 5:25

[a]3 That is, the upper Nile region
[b]14 Or *Chaldeans*

I have not burdened[x] you with grain
offerings
nor wearied you with demands[y] for
incense.[z]
24You have not bought any fragrant
calamus[a] for me,
or lavished on me the fat[b] of your
sacrifices.
But you have burdened me with your
sins
and wearied[c] me with your
offences.[d]

25"I, even I, am he who blots out
your transgressions,[e] for my own
sake,[f]
and remembers your sins[g] no
more.[h]
26Review the past for me,
let us argue the matter together;[i]
state the case[j] for your innocence.
27Your first father[k] sinned;
your spokesmen[l] rebelled[m] against
me.
28So I will disgrace the dignitaries of
your temple,
and I will consign Jacob to
destruction[c] [n]
and Israel to scorn.[o]

Israel the Chosen

44 "But now listen, O Jacob, my
servant,[a]
Israel, whom I have chosen.[b]
2This is what the LORD says—
he who made[c] you, who formed you
in the womb,[d]
and who will help[e] you:
Do not be afraid,[f] O Jacob, my
servant,[g]
Jeshurun,[h] whom I have chosen.
3For I will pour water[i] on the thirsty
land,
and streams on the dry ground;[j]
I will pour out my Spirit[k] on your
offspring,
and my blessing[l] on your
descendants.[m]
4They will spring up like grass[n] in a
meadow,
like poplar trees[o] by flowing
streams.[p]
5One will say, 'I belong[q] to the LORD';
another will call himself by the
name of Jacob;
still another will write on his hand,[r]
'The LORD's',[s]
and will take the name Israel.

The LORD, Not Idols

6"This is what the LORD says—
Israel's King[t] and Redeemer,[u] the
LORD Almighty:
I am the first and I am the last;[v]
apart from me there is no God.[w]
7Who then is like me?[x] Let him
proclaim it.
Let him declare and lay out before
me
what has happened since I established
my ancient people,
and what is yet to come—
yes, let him foretell[y] what will come.
8Do not tremble, do not be afraid.
Did I not proclaim[z] this and foretell
it long ago?
You are my witnesses. Is there any
God[a] besides me?
No, there is no other Rock;[b] I know
not one."
9All who make idols[c] are nothing,
and the things they treasure are
worthless.[d]
Those who would speak up for them
are blind;[e]
they are ignorant, to their own
shame.[f]
10Who shapes a god and casts an idol,[g]
which can profit him nothing?[h]
11He and his kind will be put to shame;[i]
craftsmen are nothing but men.
Let them all come together and take
their stand;
they will be brought down to terror
and infamy.[j]
12The blacksmith[k] takes a tool
and works with it in the coals;
he shapes an idol with hammers,
he forges it with the might of his arm.[l]
He gets hungry and loses his strength;
he drinks no water and grows faint.[m]
13The carpenter[n] measures with a line
and makes an outline with a marker;
he roughs it out with chisels
and marks it with compasses.
He shapes it in the form of man,[o]
of man in all his glory,
that it may dwell in a shrine.[p]
14He cut down cedars,
or perhaps took a cypress or oak.
He let it grow among the trees of the
forest,
or planted a pine,[q] and the rain
made it grow.
15It is man's fuel[r] for burning;
some of it he takes and warms
himself,

23 [x]Mic 6:3; Mal 1:12–13; [y]Jer 7:22; [z]Ex 30:35; **Lev 2:1**
24 [a]**Ex 30:23;** [b]Lev 3:9; [c]**Isa 1:14; 7:13; Jer 8:21;** [d]Jer 44:22; Mal 2:17
25 [e]**2Sa 12:13; 2Ch 6:21;** Mk 2:7; Lk 5:21; Ac 3:19; [f]**Isa 37:35; Eze 20:44;** [g]Isa 64:9; Mic 7:18; [h]**Job 7:21; Isa 38:17**
26 [i]**Isa 1:18;** [j]**Isa 41:1;** 49:25; 50:8
27 [k]**Ge 12:18;** [l]Isa 9:15; 28:7; Jer 5:31; [m]**Isa 24:20; 48:8**
28 [n]**Nu 5:27; Dt 13:15; Isa 42:24; Zec 5:3;** [o]**Ps 39:8;** Jer 24:9; Eze 5:15

Ch. 44

1 [a]ver 21; [b]**Ge 16:11; Isa 14:1**
2 [c]ver 21; **Ps 149:2;** [d]**Ge 2:7; Ps 139:13; Isa 27:11;** [e]**Isa 41:10;** [f]**Isa 43:5;** [g]Jer 30:10; 46:27; [h]**Nu 23:21; Dt 32:15**
3 [i]**Joel 3:18;** Jn 4:10; [j]**Pr 9:5; Isa 32:2; 35:7;** [k]**Isa 11:2;** Eze 36:27; **Mk 1:8; Ac 2:17;** [l]Mal 3:10; [m]Isa 61:9; 65:23
4 [n]**Job 5:25; Ps 72:16;** [o]**Lev 23:40;** [p]**Job 40:22**
5 [q]Ps 116:16; Isa 19:21; Jer 50:5; [r]Ex 13:9; [s]Isa 60:3; 66:23; Zec 8:20–22; 13:9; 14:16
6 [t]**Isa 41:21;** [u]**Job 19:25;** Isa 43:1; [v]**Isa 41:4;** Rev 1:8, 17; [w]**Dt 6:4; 1Ch 17:20; Ps 18:31; Isa 43:10**
7 [x]**Dt 32:39;** [y]**Isa 41:22,**26
8 [z]**Isa 40:21; 42:9;** [a]**Isa 43:10;** [b]**Ge 49:24**
9 [c]**Ex 20:4; Lev 19:4;** Isa 40:19; [d]**Isa 41:24;** [e]**Isa 26:11;** [f]**Isa 1:29;** 65:13; 66:5; Jer 22:22
10 [g]**Isa 40:19;** [h]Isa 41:29; Jer 10:5; Ac 19:26
11 [i]**ver 9; Isa 1:29;** [j]**2Ki 19:18; Isa 37:19**
12 [k]**Isa 40:19;** 41:6–7; 54:16; [l]Ac 17:29; [m]Isa 40:28
13 [n]**Isa 41:7;** [o]Ps 115:4–7; [p]**Jdg 17:4–5**
14 [q]**Isa 41:19** 15 [r]ver 19

[c]28 The Hebrew term refers to the irrevocable giving over of things or persons to the LORD, often by totally destroying them.

he kindles a fire and bakes bread.
But he also fashions a god and
worships[s] it;
he makes an idol and bows[t] down to
it.
16Half of the wood he burns in the fire;
over it he prepares his meal,
he roasts his meat and eats his fill.
He also warms himself and says,
"Ah! I am warm; I see the fire.[u]"
17From the rest he makes a god, his idol;
he bows down to it and worships.[v]
He prays[w] to it and says,
"Save[x] me; you are my god."
18They know nothing, they understand[y]
nothing;
their eyes[z] are plastered over so that
they cannot see,
and their minds closed so that they
cannot understand.
19No-one stops to think,
no-one has the knowledge or
understanding[a] to say,
"Half of it I used for fuel;[b]
I even baked bread over its coals,
I roasted meat and I ate.
Shall I make a detestable[c] thing from
what is left?
Shall I bow down to a block of
wood?"[d]
20He feeds on ashes,[e] a deluded[f] heart
misleads him;
he cannot save himself, or say,
"Is not this thing in my right hand a
lie?[g h]"

21"Remember[i] these things, O Jacob,
for you are my servant, O Israel.[j]
I have made you, you are my servant;[k]
O Israel, I will not forget you.[l]
22I have swept away[m] your offences like
a cloud,
your sins like the morning mist.
Return[n] to me,
for I have redeemed[o] you."

23Sing for joy,[p] O heavens, for the LORD
has done this;
shout aloud, O earth[q] beneath.
Burst into song, you mountains,[r]
you forests and all your trees,[s]
for the LORD has redeemed[t] Jacob,
he displays his glory[u] in Israel.

Jerusalem to Be Inhabited

24"This is what the LORD says—
your Redeemer,[v] who formed[w] you
in the womb:[x]

I am the LORD,
who has made all things,
who alone stretched out the heavens,[y]
who spread out the earth[z] by myself,
25who foils[a] the signs of false prophets
and makes fools of diviners,[b]
who overthrows the learning of the
wise[c]
and turns it into nonsense,[d]
26who carries out the words[e] of his
servants
and fulfils[f] the predictions of his
messengers,

who says of Jerusalem,[g] 'It shall be
inhabited,'
of the towns of Judah, 'They shall be
built,'
and of their ruins,[h] 'I will restore
them,'[i]
27who says to the watery deep, 'Be dry,
and I will dry up[j] your streams,'
28who says of Cyrus,[k] 'He is my
shepherd
and will accomplish all that I please;
he will say of Jerusalem,[l] "Let it be
rebuilt,"
and of the temple,[m] "Let its
foundations[n] be laid."'

45

"This is what the LORD says to
his anointed,[a]
to Cyrus,[b] whose right hand I take
hold[c] of
to subdue nations[d] before him
and to strip kings of their armour,
to open doors before him
so that gates will not be shut:
2I will go before you[e]
and will level[f] the mountains;[a]
I will break down gates[g] of bronze
and cut through bars of iron.[h]
3I will give you the treasures[i] of
darkness,
riches stored in secret places,[j]
so that you may know[k] that I am the
LORD,
the God of Israel, who summons
you by name.[l]
4For the sake of Jacob my servant,[m]
of Israel my chosen,

15 [s]**Ex 20:5**; Rev 9:20; [t]**2Ch 25:14**
16 [u]Isa 47:14
17 [v]**Ex 20:5**; Isa 2:8; Jer 1:16; [w]**1Ki 18:26**; [x]**Jdg 10:14**; Isa 45:20; 46:7; 47:15
18 [y]Isa 1:3; **16:12**; Jer 4:22; 10:8,14–15; [z]**Isa 6:9–10**; **29:10**
19 [a]ver 18–19; Isa 5:13; 27:11; 45:20; [b]ver 15; [c]**Dt 27:15**; [d]Isa 40:20
20 [e]Ps 102:9; [f]**Job 15:31**; Ro 1:21–23, 28; 2Th 2:11; 2Ti 3:13; [g]**Dt 4:28**; Hos 10:5; 13:2; [h]Isa 59:3–4,13; Jer 9:3; 10:14; 51:17; Ro 1:25
21 [i]Isa 46:8; Zec 10:9; [j]**Isa 43:1**; [k]**Ps 136:22**; **Isa 27:11**; [l]Ps 27:10; Isa 49:15; Jer 31:20
22 [m]**2Sa 12:13**; **2Ch 6:21**; Ac 3:19; [n]**Job 22:23**; Isa 45:22; 55:7; Jer 36:3; Mal 3:7; [o]**Isa 33:24**; **Mt 20:28**; 1Co 6:20
23 [p]**Ps 98:4**; **Isa 12:6**; [q]**1Ch 16:31**; Ps 148:7; [r]**Ps 98:8**; [s]**Ps 65:13**; [t]**Ex 6:6**; Isa 51:11; 62:12; [u]**Ex 16:7**; **Lev 10:3**; **Isa 4:2**; 43:7; 46:13; 49:3; 52:1; 55:5; 60:9,21; 61:3; Jer 30:19
24 [v]**Job 19:25**; Isa 43:14; [w]**Isa 27:11**; [x]**Ps 139:13**; [y]**Ge 2:1**; **Isa 42:5**; [z]**Ge 1:1**
25 [a]Ps 33:10; [b]Lev 19:26; 1Sa 6:2; Isa 2:6; 8:19; 47:13; Jer 27:9; Da 2:2,10; 4:7; Mic 3:7; Zec 10:2; [c]**Job 5:13**; 1Co 1:27; [d]2Sa 15:31; 1Co 1:19–20
26 [e]Isa 59:21; Zec 1:6; [f]Isa 46:10; 55:11; Jer 23:20; 39:16; La 2:17; Da 9:12; **Mt 5:18**; [g]**Isa 1:1**; [h]**Ps 74:3**; **Isa 51:3**; [i]**Ezr 9:9**; **Ps 51:18**; Isa 49:8–21; **61:4**
27 [j]**Isa 11:15**; **19:5**; Rev 16:12
28 [k]**2Ch 36:22**; **Isa 41:2**; [l]**Isa 14:32**; [m]Ezr 1:2–4; [n]**Isa 28:16**; 58:12

Ch. 45

1 [a]**Ps 45:7**; [b]**2Ch 36:22**; **Isa 41:2**; [c]Ps 73:23; Isa 41:13; 42:6; [d]Isa 48:14; Jer 50:35; 51:20,24; Mic 4:13
2 [e]Ex 23:20; [f]**Isa 40:4**; [g]**Isa 13:2**; [h]Ps 107:16; 147:13; Jer 51:30; La 2:9; Na 3:13
3 [i]**2Ki 24:13**; Jer 50:37; 51:13; [j]Jer 41:8; [k]Isa 41:23; [l]**Ex 33:12**; **Isa 43:1** *4* [m]**Isa 14:1**; 41:8–9

[a]2 Dead Sea Scrolls and Septuagint; the meaning of the word in the Masoretic Text is uncertain.

I summon you by name
and bestow on you a title of honour,
though you do not acknowledge[n]
me.
5I am the LORD, and there is no other;[o]
apart from me there is no God.[p]
I will strengthen you,[q]
though you have not acknowledged
me,
6so that from the rising of the sun
to the place of its setting[r]
men may know[s] there is none besides
me.[t]
I am the LORD, and there is no other.
7I form the light and create darkness,[u]
I bring prosperity and create
disaster;[v]
I, the LORD, do all these things.

8"You heavens above, rain[w] down
righteousness;[x]
let the clouds shower it down.
Let the earth open wide,
let salvation[y] spring up,
let righteousness grow with it;
I, the LORD, have created it.

9"Woe to him who quarrels[z] with his
Maker,[a]
to him who is but a potsherd[b]
among the potsherds on the
ground.
Does the clay say to the potter,[c]
'What are you making?'[d]
Does your work say,
'He has no hands'?[e]
10Woe to him who says to his father,
'What have you begotten?'
or to his mother,
'What have you brought to birth?'

11"This is what the LORD says—
the Holy One[f] of Israel, and its
Maker:[g]
Concerning things to come,
do you question me about my
children,
or give me orders about the work of
my hands?[h]
12It is I who made the earth[i]
and created mankind upon it.
My own hands stretched out the
heavens;[j]
I marshalled their starry hosts.[k]
13I will raise up Cyrus[b][l] in my
righteousness:
I will make all his ways straight.[m]
He will rebuild my city[n]
and set my exiles free,
but not for a price or reward,[o]
says the LORD Almighty."

14This is what the LORD says:

"The products[p] of Egypt and the
merchandise of Cush,[c]
and those tall Sabeans[q]—
they will come over to you[r]
and will be yours;
they will trudge behind you,[s]
coming over to you in chains.[t]
They will bow down before you
and plead[u] with you, saying,
'Surely God is with you,[v] and there is
no other;
there is no other god.[w]' "

15Truly you are a God who hides[x]
himself,
O God and Saviour[y] of Israel.
16All the makers of idols will be put to
shame and disgraced;[z]
they will go off into disgrace
together.
17But Israel will be saved[a] by the LORD
with an everlasting salvation;[b]
you will never be put to shame or
disgraced,[c]
to ages everlasting.

18For this is what the LORD says—
he who created the heavens,
he is God;
he who fashioned and made the
earth,[d]
he founded it;
he did not create it to be empty,[e]
but formed it to be inhabited[f]—
he says:
"I am the LORD,
and there is no other.[g]
19I have not spoken in secret,[h]
from somewhere in a land of
darkness;[i]
I have not said to Jacob's descendants,[j]
'Seek[k] me in vain.'
I, the LORD, speak the truth;
I declare what is right.[l]

20"Gather together[m] and come;
assemble, you fugitives from the
nations.
Ignorant[n] are those who carry[o] about
idols of wood,
who pray to gods that cannot save.[p]
21Declare what is to be, present it—
let them take counsel together.
Who foretold[q] this long ago,
who declared it from the distant
past?[r]

4 [n]Ac 17:23
5 [o]Isa 44:8; [p]Dt 32:12; Ps 18:31; Isa 43:10; [q]Ps 18:39; Eze 30:24–25
6 [r]Ps 113:3; Isa 43:5; [s]Isa 11:9; [t]ver 5,18; Isa 14:13–14; 47:8,10; Zep 2:15
7 [u]Ge 1:4; Ex 10:22; [v]Isa 14:15; 31:2; La 3:38
8 [w]Ps 72:6; 133:3; Joel 3:18; [x]ver 24; Ps 85:11; Isa 41:2; 46:13; 48:18; 60:21; 61:10–11; 62:1; Hos 10:12; Joel 2:23; Am 5:24; Mal 4:2; [y]Ps 85:9; Isa 12:3
9 [z]Job 12:13; 15:25; 27:2; 1Co 10:22; [a]Job 33:13; [b]Ps 22:15; [c]Isa 29:16; Ro 9:20–21*; [d]Job 9:12; Da 4:35; [e]Isa 10:15
11 [f]Isa 1:4; [g]Ps 149:2; Isa 51:13; [h]Ps 8:6; Isa 19:25
12 [i]Ge 1:1; [j]Ge 2:1; Isa 48:13; [k]Ne 9:6; Job 38:32
13 [l]2Ch 36:22; Isa 41:2; [m]1Ki 8:36; Ps 26:12; Isa 40:4; [n]Ezr 1:2; [o]Isa 52:3
14 [p]2Sa 8:2; Isa 18:7; 60:5; [q]Isa 2:3; 60:11; 62:2; Zec 8:20–22; [r]Isa 2:3; [s]Ge 27:29; [t]2Sa 3:34; Isa 14:1–2; [u]Jer 16:19; Zec 8:20–23; [v]1Co 14:25; [w]Ps 18:31; Isa 11:9; 43:10
15 [x]Dt 31:17; Ps 44:24; Isa 1:15; [y]Isa 25:9
16 [z]Ps 35:4; Isa 1:29
17 [a]Jer 23:6; 33:16; Ro 11:26; [b]Isa 12:2; [c]Ge 30:23; Isa 29:22; 41:11
18 [d]Ge 1:1; [e]Ge 1:2; [f]Ge 1:26; [g]ver 5; Dt 4:35
19 [h]Isa 48:16; 65:4; [i]Jer 2:31; [j]ver 25; Isa 41:8; 65:9; Jer 31:36; [k]Dt 4:29; 2Ch 15:2; [l]Dt 30:11
20 [m]Isa 43:9; [n]Isa 44:19; [o]Ps 115:7; Isa 46:1; Jer 10:5; [p]Dt 32:37; Isa 44:17; Jer 1:16; 2:28
21 [q]Isa 41:22; [r]Isa 46:10

b13 Hebrew *him*
c14 That is, the upper Nile region

Was it not I, the LORD?
And there is no God apart from me,[s]
a righteous God[t] and a Saviour;[u]
there is none but me.

22"Turn[v] to me and be saved,[w]
all you ends of the earth;[x]
for I am God, and there is no other.[y]
23By myself I have sworn,[z]
my mouth has uttered in all integrity[a]
a word that will not be revoked:[b]
Before me every knee will bow;[c]
by me every tongue will swear.[d]
24They will say of me, 'In the LORD alone
are righteousness[e] and strength.[f]'"
All who have raged against him
will come to him and be put to shame.[g]
25But in the LORD all the descendants[h] of Israel
will be found righteous[i] and will exult.[j]

Gods of Babylon

46 Bel[a] bows down, Nebo stoops low;
their idols[b] are borne by beasts of burden.[a]
The images that are carried[c] about are burdensome,
a burden for the weary.
2They stoop and bow down together;
unable to rescue the burden,
they themselves go off into captivity.[d]

3"Listen[e] to me, O house of Jacob,
all you who remain[f] of the house of Israel,
you whom I have upheld since you were conceived,[g]
and have carried[h] since your birth.[i]
4Even to your old age and grey hairs[j]
I am he,[k] I am he who will sustain you.
I have made you and I will carry you;
I will sustain[l] you and I will rescue you.

5"To whom will you compare me or count me equal?
To whom will you liken me that we may be compared?[m]
6Some pour out gold from their bags
and weigh out silver on the scales;
they hire a goldsmith[n] to make it into a god,
and they bow down and worship it.[o]
7They lift it to their shoulders and carry[p] it;
they set it up in its place, and there it stands.
From that spot it cannot move.[q]
Though one cries out to it, it does not answer;[r]
it cannot save[s] him from his troubles.

8"Remember[t] this, fix it in mind,
take it to heart, you rebels.[u]
9Remember the former things,[v] those of long ago;[w]
I am God, and there is no other;
I am God, and there is none like me.[x]
10I make known the end from the beginning,[y]
from ancient times,[z] what is still to come.[a]
I say: My purpose will stand,[b]
and I will do all that I please.
11From the east I summon[c] a bird of prey;[d]
from a far-off land, a man to fulfil my purpose.
What I have said, that will I bring about;
what I have planned,[e] that will I do.[f]
12Listen[g] to me, you stubborn-hearted,[h]
you who are far from righteousness.[i]
13I am bringing my righteousness[j] near,
it is not far away;
and my salvation[k] will not be delayed.
I will grant salvation to Zion,[l]
my splendour[m] to Israel.

The Fall of Babylon

47 "Go down, sit in the dust,[a]
Virgin Daughter[b] of Babylon;
sit on the ground without a throne,
Daughter of the Babylonians.[a][c]
No more will you be called
tender or delicate.[d]
2Take millstones[e] and grind[f] flour;
take off your veil.[g]
Lift up your skirts,[h] bare your legs,
and wade through the streams.

21 [s]ver 5; Ps 46:10; Isa 46:9; Mk 12:32; [t]Ps 11:7; [u]Ps 3:8; Isa 25:9
22 [v]Isa 44:22; Zec 12:10; [w]Nu 21:8–9; 2Ch 20:12; [x]Ge 49:10; Isa 11:9,12; 49:6, 12; [y]Hos 13:4
23 [z]Ge 22:16; Isa 14:24; [a]Dt 30:11; Heb 6:13; [b]Isa 55:11; [c]ver 14; [d]Ps 63:11; Isa 19:18; Ro 14:11*; Php 2:10–11
24 [e]ver 8; Jer 33:16; [f]Dt 33:29; Ps 18:39; Isa 40:26; 63:1; [g]Isa 41:11
25 [h]ver 19; [i]Isa 4:3; 49:4; [j]Isa 24:23; 41:16

Ch. 46
1 [a]Isa 21:9; Jer 50:2; 51:44; [b]1Sa 5:2; [c]ver 7; Isa 45:20
2 [d]Jdg 18:17–18; 2Sa 5:21; Jer 51:47
3 [e]ver 12; Isa 48:12; 51:1; [f]Isa 1:9; [g]Ps 139:13; Isa 44:2; [h]Dt 1:31; Ps 28:9; [i]Ps 22:10
4 [j]Ps 71:18; [k]Dt 32:39; Isa 43:13; [l]Ps 18:35; 119:117
5 [m]Ex 15:11; Job 41:10; Isa 40:18,25; Jer 49:19
6 [n]Isa 40:19; [o]Ex 20:5; Isa 44:17; Hos 13:2
7 [p]ver 1; [q]1Sa 5:3; Isa 41:7; [r]1Ki 18:26; [s]Isa 44:17; 47:13
8 [t]Isa 44:21; [u]Isa 1:2
9 [v]Isa 41:22; [w]Dt 32:7; [x]Ex 8:10; Isa 45:21; Mk 12:32
10 [y]Isa 41:4; [z]Isa 45:21; [a]Isa 41:22; [b]Pr 19:21; Isa 7:7,9; 44:26; Ac 5:39; Eph 1:11
11 [c]Jdg 4:10; Ezr 1:2; [d]Isa 8:8; [e]Isa 25:1; [f]Ge 41:25; Jer 44:28
12 [g]ver 3; [h]Ex 32:9; Isa 9:9; [i]Ps 119:150; Isa 48:1; Jer 2:5
13 [j]Isa 1:26; 45:8; Ro 3:21; [k]Ps 85:9; [l]Ps 74:2; Joel 2:32; [m]Isa 44:23

Ch. 47
1 [a]Job 2:13; Isa 29:4; [b]Isa 21:9; 23:12; [c]Ps 137:8; Jer 50:42; 51:33; Zec 2:7; [d]Dt 28:56
2 [e]Ex 11:5; Mt 24:41; [f]Jdg 16:21; [g]Ge 24:65; [h]Isa 32:11

a1 Or *are but beasts and cattle*
a1 Or *Chaldeans;* also in verse 5

3Your nakedness[i] will be exposed
and your shame[j] uncovered.
I will take vengeance;[k]
I will spare no-one."[l]

4Our Redeemer[m]—the LORD Almighty[n]
is his name[o]—
is the Holy One[p] of Israel.

5"Sit in silence,[q] go into darkness,[r]
Daughter of the Babylonians;[s]
no more will you be called
queen[t] of kingdoms.[u]
6I was angry[v] with my people
and desecrated my inheritance;[w]
I gave them into your hand,[x]
and you showed them no mercy.[y]
Even on the aged
you laid a very heavy yoke.
7You said, 'I will continue for ever[z]—
the eternal queen!'[a]
But you did not consider these things
or reflect[b] on what might happen.[c]

8"Now then, listen, you wanton
creature,
lounging in your security[d]
and saying to yourself,
'I am, and there is none besides me.[e]
I will never be a widow[f]
or suffer the loss of children.'
9Both of these will overtake you
in a moment,[g] on a single day:
loss of children[h] and widowhood.[i]
They will come upon you in full
measure,
in spite of your many sorceries[j]
and all your potent spells.[k]
10You have trusted[l] in your wickedness
and have said, 'No-one sees me.'[m]
Your wisdom[n] and knowledge
mislead[o] you
when you say to yourself,
'I am, and there is none besides me.'
11Disaster[p] will come upon you,
and you will not know how to
conjure it away.
A calamity will fall upon you
that you cannot ward off with a
ransom;
a catastrophe you cannot foresee
will suddenly[q] come upon you.

12"Keep on, then, with your magic
spells
and with your many sorceries,[r]
which you have laboured at since
childhood.
Perhaps you will succeed,
perhaps you will cause terror.
13All the counsel you have received has
only worn you out![s]
Let your astrologers[t] come forward,
those stargazers who make
predictions month by month,
let them save[u] you from what is
coming upon you.
14Surely they are like stubble;[v]
the fire[w] will burn them up.
They cannot even save themselves
from the power of the flame.[x]
Here are no coals to warm anyone;
here is no fire to sit by.
15That is all they can do for you—
these you have laboured with
and trafficked[y] with since
childhood.
Each of them goes on in his error;
there is not one that can save[z] you.

Stubborn Israel

48 "Listen to this, O house of
Jacob,
you who are called by the name of
Israel[a]
and come from the line of Judah,[b]
you who take oaths[c] in the name of the
LORD[d]
and invoke[e] the God of Israel—
but not in truth[f] or righteousness—
2you who call yourselves citizens of the
holy city[g]
and rely[h] on the God of Israel—
the LORD Almighty is his name:[i]
3I foretold the former things[j] long ago,
my mouth announced[k] them and I
made them known;
then suddenly[l] I acted, and they
came to pass.
4For I knew how stubborn[m] you were;
the sinews of your neck[n] were iron,
your forehead[o] was bronze.
5Therefore I told you these things long
ago;
before they happened I announced[p]
them to you
so that you could not say,
'My idols did them;[q]
my wooden image and metal god
ordained them.'
6You have heard these things; look at
them all.
Will you not admit them?

"From now on I will tell you of new
things,[r]
of hidden things unknown to you.

3 [i]Ge 2:25; Eze 16:37; Na 3:5; [j]Isa 20:4; [k]Isa 1:24; 34:8; [l]Isa 13:18–19
4 [m]Job 19:25; [n]Isa 13:4; [o]Isa 48:2; Jer 50:34; Am 4:13; [p]Isa 1:4; 48:17
5 [q]Job 2:13; [r]Isa 9:2; 13:10; [s]Isa 21:9; [t]ver 7; La 1:1; Rev 18:7; [u]Isa 13:19; Rev 17:18
6 [v]2Ch 28:9; [w]Dt 13:15; Isa 42:24; Jer 2:7; 50:11; [x]Isa 10:13; [y]Isa 14:6
7 [z]Isa 10:13; Da 4:30; [a]ver 5; Rev 18:7; [b]Isa 42:23,25; [c]Dt 32:29
8 [d]Isa 32:9; [e]Isa 45:6; [f]Isa 49:21; 54:4; La 1:1; Rev 18:7
9 [g]Ps 55:15; 73:19; 1Th 5:3; Rev 18:8–10; [h]Isa 13:18; [i]Isa 4:1; Jer 15:8; 18:21; [j]ver 12; Na 3:4; Mal 3:5; [k]Dt 18:10–11; Rev 9:21; 18:23
10 [l]Job 15:31; Ps 52:7; 62:10; [m]2Ki 21:16; Isa 29:15; [n]Isa 5:21; [o]Isa 44:20
11 [p]Isa 10:3; 14:15; 21:9; 31:2; Lk 17:27; [q]Ps 55:15; Isa 17:14; 1Th 5:3
12 [r]ver 9; Ex 7:11
13 [s]Isa 57:10; Jer 51:58; Hab 2:13; [t]Isa 19:3; 44:25; [u]ver 15; Isa 5:29; 43:13; 46:7
14 [v]Isa 5:24; [w]Isa 30:30; [x]Isa 10:17; Jer 51:30,32,58
15 [y]Rev 18:11; [z]ver 13; Isa 44:17

Ch. 48

1 [a]Ge 17:5; [b]Ge 29:35; [c]Isa 19:18; [d]1Sa 20:42; Isa 43:7; [e]Ex 23:13; 2Sa 14:11; Ps 50:16; Isa 58:2; Jer 7:9–10; 44:26; [f]Isa 59:14; Jer 4:2; 5:2; Da 8:12; Zec 8:3

2 [g]Ne 11:1; Isa 1:26; Mt 4:5; [h]Isa 10:20; Ro 2:17; [i]Isa 47:4
3 [j]Isa 41:22; [k]Isa 40:21; 45:21; [l]Isa 17:14; 30:13
4 [m]Isa 9:9; [n]Ex 32:9; Dt 9:27; Ac 7:51; [o]Eze 3:9
5 [p]Isa 40:21; 42:9; [q]Jer 44:15–18
6 [r]Isa 41:22; Ro 16:25

7They are created[s] now, and not long
ago;[t]
you have not heard of them before
today.
So you cannot say,
'Yes, I knew[u] of them.'
8You have neither heard nor
understood;[v]
from of old your ear[w] has not been
open.
Well do I know how treacherous[x] you
are;
you were called a rebel[y] from birth.
9For my own name's sake[z] I delay my
wrath;[a]
for the sake of my praise I hold it
back from you,
so as not to cut you off.[b]
10See, I have refined[c] you, though not as
silver;
I have tested[d] you in the furnace[e] of
affliction.
11For my own sake,[f] for my own sake, I
do this.
How can I let myself be defamed?[g]
I will not yield my glory to another.[h]

Israel Freed

12"Listen[i] to me, O Jacob,
Israel, whom I have called:[j]
I am he;[k]
I am the first and I am the last.[l]
13My own hand laid the foundations of
the earth,[m]
and my right hand spread out the
heavens;[n]
when I summon them,
they all stand up together.[o]

14"Come together,[p] all of you, and
listen:
Which of ⌊the idols⌋ has foretold[q]
these things?
The LORD's chosen ally[r]
will carry out his purpose[s] against
Babylon;[t]
his arm will be against the
Babylonians.[a]
15I, even I, have spoken;
yes, I have called[u] him.
I will bring him,
and he will succeed[v] in his mission.

16"Come near[w] me and listen[x] to this:

"From the first announcement I have
not spoken in secret;[y]
at the time it happens, I am there."

And now the Sovereign LORD[z] has
sent[a] me,
with his Spirit.[b]

7 [s]Isa 65:18; [t]Isa 45:21; [u]Ex 6:7
8 [v]Isa 1:3; [w]Dt 29:4; [x]Isa 41:24; Mal 2:11,14; [y]Dt 9:7,24; Ps 58:3; Isa 1:2; 43:27; 58:1
9 [z]1Sa 12:22; Isa 37:35; [a]Job 9:13; Isa 30:18; [b]Ne 9:31
10 [c]Isa 1:25; Zec 13:9; Mal 3:3; 1Pe 1:7; [d]Ex 15:25; [e]Ex 1:13; 1Ki 8:51
11 [f]1Sa 12:22; Isa 37:35; [g]Lev 18:21; Dt 32:27; Jer 14:7, 21; Eze 20:9, 14,22,44; [h]Isa 42:8
12 [i]Isa 46:3; [j]Isa 41:8; 42:6; 43:1; [k]Isa 43:13; [l]Isa 41:4; Rev 1:17
13 [m]Heb 1:10–12; [n]Ge 2:1; Ex 20:11; Job 9:8; Isa 40:22; 42:5; 45:18; 51:16; 65:17; [o]Isa 34:16
14 [p]Isa 43:9; [q]Isa 41:22; [r]Isa 41:2; [s]Isa 46:10–11; [t]Isa 21:9; 45:1; Jer 50:45
15 [u]Jdg 4:10; Isa 45:1; [v]Isa 44:28–45:4
16 [w]Isa 41:1; [x]Isa 33:13; [y]Isa 45:19; [z]Isa 50:5,7,9; [a]Zec 2:9,11; [b]Isa 11:2
17 [c]Job 19:25; Isa 49:7; 54:8; [d]Isa 47:4; [e]Isa 28:9; Jer 7:13; [f]Isa 49:10; 57:18; 58:11; [g]Isa 30:11
18 [h]Isa 42:23; [i]Ps 147:14; Isa 9:7; 54:13; 66:12; [j]Isa 33:21; [k]Isa 1:26; 45:8
19 [l]Isa 43:5; 44:3; 61:9; [m]Ge 12:2; [n]Job 5:25; [o]Isa 56:5; 65:23; 66:22; Jer 35:19

17This is what the LORD says—
your Redeemer,[c] the Holy One[d] of
Israel:
"I am the LORD your God,
who teaches[e] you what is best for
you,
who directs[f] you in the way[g] you
should go.
18If only you had paid attention[h] to my
commands,
your peace[i] would have been like a
river,[j]
your righteousness[k] like the waves
of the sea.
19Your descendants[l] would have been
like the sand,[m]
your children like its numberless
grains;[n]
their name would never be cut off[o]
nor destroyed from before me."

20Leave Babylon,
flee[p] from the Babylonians!
Announce this with shouts of joy[q]
and proclaim it.
Send it out to the ends of the earth;[r]
say, "The LORD has redeemed[s] his
servant Jacob."
21They did not thirst[t] when he led them
through the deserts;
he made water flow[u] for them from
the rock;
he split the rock
and water gushed out.[v]

22"There is no peace,"[w] says the LORD,
"for the wicked."[x]

The Servant of the LORD

49 Listen[a] to me, you islands;[b]
hear this, you distant nations:
Before I was born[c] the LORD called[d] me;
from my birth he has made mention
of my name.[e]
2He made my mouth[f] like a sharpened
sword,[g]
in the shadow of his hand[h] he hid
me;
he made me into a polished arrow[i]
and concealed me in his quiver.

20 [p]Isa 52:11; Jer 48:6; 50:8; 51:6,45; Zec 2:6–7; Rev 18:4; [q]Isa 12:6; 49:13; 51:11; [r]Ge 49:10; Dt 30:4; Jer 25:22; [s]Ex 6:6; Isa 33:24; 52:9; 63:9; Mic 4:10
21 [t]Isa 33:16; [u]Isa 30:25; [v]Nu 20:11; Isa 35:6
22 [w]Job 3:26; [x]Isa 3:11; 57:21

Ch. 49

1 [a]Isa 33:13; [b]Isa 11:11; [c]Isa 44:24; 46:3; Mt 1:20; [d]Isa 7:14; 9:6; 44:2; Jer 1:5; Gal 1:15; [e]Ex 33:12; Isa 43:1
2 [f]Job 40:18; [g]Ps 64:3; Eph 6:17; Rev 1:16; [h]Ex 33:22; Ps 91:1; [i]Dt 32:23; Zec 9:13

---

[a]14 Or *Chaldeans*; also in verse 20

3He said to me, "You are my servant,[j]
Israel, in whom I will display my
splendour.[k]"
4But I said, "I have laboured to no
purpose;
I have spent my strength in vain[l]
and for nothing.
Yet what is due to me is in the LORD's
hand,[m]
and my reward[n] is with my God."[o]

5And now the LORD says—
he who formed me in the womb[p] to
be his servant
to bring Jacob back to him
and gather Israel[q] to himself,
for I am honoured[r] in the eyes of the
LORD
and my God has been my
strength[s]—
6he says:
"It is too small a thing for you to be my
servant[t]
to restore the tribes of Jacob
and bring back those of Israel I have
kept.[u]
I will also make you a light[v] for the
Gentiles,[w]
that you may bring my salvation to
the ends of the earth."[x]

7This is what the LORD says—
the Redeemer and Holy One of
Israel[y]—
to him who was despised[z] and
abhorred by the nation,
to the servant of rulers:
"Kings[a] will see you and rise up,
princes will see and bow down,[b]
because of the LORD, who is faithful,[c]
the Holy One of Israel, who has
chosen[d] you."

Restoration of Israel

8This is what the LORD says:

"In the time of my favour[e] I will
answer you,
and in the day of salvation I will
help you;[f]
I will keep[g] you and will make you
to be a covenant for the people,[h]
to restore the land[i]
and to reassign its desolate
inheritances,[j]
9to say to the captives,[k] 'Come out,'
and to those in darkness,[l] 'Be free!'

"They will feed beside the roads
and find pasture on every barren
hill.[m]
10They will neither hunger nor thirst,[n]
nor will the desert heat or the sun
beat upon them.[o]
He who has compassion[p] on them will
guide[q] them
and lead them beside springs[r] of
water.
11I will turn all my mountains into
roads,
and my highways[s] will be raised
up.[t]
12See, they will come from afar[u]—
some from the north, some from the
west,[v]
some from the region of Aswan."[a]

13Shout for joy,[w] O heavens;
rejoice, O earth;[x]
burst into song, O mountains![y]
For the LORD comforts[z] his people
and will have compassion[a] on his
afflicted ones.[b]

14But Zion[c] said, "The LORD has
forsaken[d] me,
the Lord has forgotten me."
15"Can a mother forget the baby at her
breast
and have no compassion on the
child[e] she has borne?
Though she may forget,
I will not forget you![f]
16See, I have engraved[g] you on the
palms of my hands;
your walls[h] are ever before me.
17Your sons hasten back,
and those who laid you waste[i]
depart from you.
18Lift up your eyes and look around;
all your sons gather[j] and come to
you.
As surely as I live,[k]" declares the LORD,
"you will wear[l] them all as
ornaments;
you will put them on, like a bride.
19"Though you were ruined and made
desolate[m]
and your land laid waste,[n]
now you will be too small for your
people,[o]
and those who devoured[p] you will
be far away.
20The children born during your
bereavement
will yet say in your hearing,

3 [j]Isa 20:3; Zec 3:8; [k]Lev 10:3; Isa 44:23
4 [l]Lev 26:20; Isa 55:2; 65:23; [m]Isa 45:25; 50:8; 53:10; 54:17; [n]Isa 35:4; [o]Job 27:2
5 [p]Ps 139:13; Gal 1:15; [q]Dt 30:4; Isa 11:12; [r]Isa 43:4; [s]Ps 18:1
6 [t]ver 3; [u]Isa 1:9; [v]Isa 9:2; Jn 1:9; [w]Isa 26:18; 55:5; Zec 8:22; Lk 2:32; [x]Dt 30:4; Ps 48:10; Mt 28:19; Jn 11:52; Ac 13:47*
7 [y]Isa 48:17; [z]Ps 22:6; 69:7–9; [a]Ezr 1:2; Isa 52:15; [b]Ge 27:29; Ps 22:29; 86:9; [c]Dt 7:9; 1Co 1:9; [d]Isa 14:1
8 [e]Ps 69:13; Isa 60:10; 61:2; [f]Isa 41:10; 2Co 6:2*; [g]Isa 5:2; 26:3; [h]Isa 42:6; [i]Lev 25:10; Ps 37:9; Isa 44:26; 58:12; 61:4; Eze 36:10,33; Am 9:11,14; [j]Nu 34:13; Isa 60:21
9 [k]Isa 42:7; 61:1; Lk 4:19; [l]Ps 107:10; [m]Isa 41:18
10 [n]Isa 33:16; [o]Ps 121:6; Rev 7:16; [p]Isa 14:1; [q]Ps 48:14; Isa 42:16; 48:17; [r]Isa 33:21; 35:7
11 [s]Isa 11:16; [t]Isa 40:4; Jer 31:9
12 [u]Isa 2:3; 11:11; 43:5–6; [v]Isa 59:19; Mt 8:11
13 [w]Isa 48:20; [x]Ps 96:11; [y]Ps 65:12–13; 98:4; Isa 44:23; [z]Ps 71:21; Isa 40:1; 2Co 1:4; [a]Isa 14:1; [b]Ps 9:12
14 [c]Isa 40:9; [d]Ps 9:10; 71:11; Isa 27:8
15 [e]1Ki 3:26; Isa 66:13; [f]Isa 44:21
16 [g]Ge 38:18; Ex 28:9; [h]Ps 48:12–13; Isa 62:6
17 [i]Isa 5:6; 10:6; 37:18
18 [j]Isa 11:12; 14:1; 43:5; 51:3; 54:7; [k]Nu 14:21; Isa 45:23; 54:9; 62:8; Ro 14:11*; [l]Isa 52:1; 61:10; Jer 2:32
19 [m]Lev 26:33; Isa 54:1,3; 60:18; 62:4; [n]Isa 5:6; [o]Eze 36:10–11; Zec 10:10; [p]Isa 1:20

[a]12 Dead Sea Scrolls; Masoretic Text *Sinim*

'This place is too small for us;
give us more space to live in.'[q]
21Then you will say in your heart,
'Who bore me these?[r]
I was bereaved[s] and barren;
I was exiled and rejected.[t]
Who brought these[u] up?
I was left[v] all alone,[w]
but these—where have they come
from?' "

22This is what the Sovereign LORD[x]
says:

"See, I will beckon to the Gentiles,
I will lift up my banner[y] to the
peoples;
they will bring[z] your sons in their arms
and carry your daughters on their
shoulders.[a]
23Kings[b] will be your foster fathers,
and their queens your nursing
mothers.[c]
They will bow down[d] before you with
their faces to the ground;
they will lick the dust[e] at your feet.
Then you will know that I am the
LORD;[f]
those who hope[g] in me will not be
disappointed.[h]"

24Can plunder be taken from warriors,[i]
or captives rescued from the fierce?[b]

25But this is what the LORD says:

"Yes, captives[j] will be taken from
warriors,[k]
and plunder retrieved from the
fierce;[l]
I will contend with those who contend
with you,[m n]
and your children I will save.[o]
26I will make your oppressors[p] eat[q] their
own flesh;
they will be drunk on their own
blood,[r] as with wine.
Then all mankind will know[s]
that I, the LORD, am your Saviour,[t]
your Redeemer,[u] the Mighty One of
Jacob.[v]"

Israel's Sin and the Servant's Obedience

50 This is what the LORD says:

"Where is your mother's certificate of
divorce[a]
with which I sent her away?
Or to which of my creditors
did I sell[b] you?
Because of your sins[c] you were sold;[d]
because of your transgressions your
mother was sent away.
2When I came, why was there no-one?
When I called, why was there
no-one to answer?[e]
Was my arm too short[f] to ransom you?
Do I lack the strength[g] to rescue
you?
By a mere rebuke[h] I dry up the sea,[i]
I turn rivers into a desert;[j]
their fish rot for lack of water
and die of thirst.
3I clothe the sky with darkness[k]
and make sackcloth[l] its covering."

4The Sovereign LORD[m] has given me an
instructed tongue,[n]
to know the word that sustains the
weary.[o]
He wakens me morning by morning,[p]
wakens my ear to listen like one
being taught.[q]
5The Sovereign LORD[r] has opened my
ears,[s]
and I have not been rebellious;[t]
I have not drawn back.
6I offered my back to those who beat[u]
me,
my cheeks to those who pulled out
my beard;[v]
I did not hide my face
from mocking and spitting.[w]
7Because the Sovereign LORD[x] helps[y]
me,
I will not be disgraced.
Therefore have I set my face like flint,[z]
and I know I will not be put to
shame.[a]
8He who vindicates[b] me is near.[c]
Who then will bring charges against
me?[d]
Let us face each other![e]
Who is my accuser?
Let him confront me!
9It is the Sovereign LORD[f] who helps[g]
me.
Who is he who will condemn[h] me?
They will all wear out like a garment;
the moths[i] will eat them up.

10Who among you fears[j] the LORD
and obeys[k] the word of his servant?[l]

20 [q]Isa 54:1–3; Zec 2:4; 10:10
21 [r]Isa 29:23; 66:7–8; [s]**Isa 47:8**; 54:1; [t]Isa 5:13; 54:6; [u]Isa 60:8; [v]**Isa 1:8**; [w]**Ps 142:4**; Isa 51:18; Jer 10:20
22 [x]**Ge 15:2**; [y]**Isa 11:10**; [z]**Isa 11:12; 14:2**; [a]Lk 15:5
23 [b]Isa 60:3, 10–11; [c]**Nu 11:12; Isa 60:16**; [d]**Ge 27:29**; Rev 3:9; [e]**Ge 3:14**; Ps 72:9; [f]**Ex 6:2; Ps 22:23; Isa 42:8**; [g]**Ps 37:9; 130:5**; [h]**Ps 22:5; Isa 29:22; 41:11**
24 [i]Mt 12:29; Mk 3:27; Lk 11:21
25 [j]**Isa 14:2**; [k]Jer 50:33–34; Mk 3:27; [l]**Isa 13:11; 25:4**; [m]Isa 25:5; **43:26**; 51:22; Jer 50:34; [n]**1Sa 24:15**; [o]Isa 25:9; 33:32; 35:4
26 [p]**Isa 9:4; 13:11**; [q]**Isa 9:20**; [r]Nu 23:24; Jer 25:27; Na 1:10; 3:11; Rev 16:6; [s]Ex 6:7; **Isa 11:9**; Eze 39:7; [t]**Isa 25:9**; [u]**Job 19:25; Isa 48:17**; [v]**Ge 49:24; Ps 132:2**

Ch. 50

1 [a]**Dt 24:1**; Hos 2:2; Mt 19:7; Mk 10:4; [b]**Ne 5:5; Mt 18:25**; [c]**Isa 1:28**; [d]**Dt 32:30; Jdg 3:8**
2 [e]**1Sa 8:19; Isa 41:28**; [f]Nu 11:23; Isa 59:1; [g]**Ge 18:14; Ps 68:35**; Jer 14:9; [h]**Ps 18:15**; [i]Ex **14:22**; [j]**Ps 107:33**
3 [k]**Ex 10:22; Isa 5:30**; [l]Rev 6:12
4 [m]ver 5; Isa 61:1; [n]**Ex 4:12**; [o]**Isa 40:29**; Mt 11:28; [p]Ps 5:3; 88:13; 119:147; 143:8; [q]**Isa 28:9**
5 [r]**Isa 48:16**; [s]Isa 35:5; [t]Eze 2:8; 24:3; **Mt 26:39**; Jn 8:29; 14:31; 15:10; Ac 26:19; Heb 5:8
6 [u]Isa 53:5; Mt 27:30; Mk 14:65; 15:19; Lk 22:63; Jn 19:1; [v]**2Sa 10:4**; [w]**Nu 12:14**; La 3:30; Mt 26:67; Mk 10:34
7 [x]**Isa 48:16**; [y]**Isa 41:10**; 42:1; [z]Jer 1:18; 15:20; Eze 3:8–9; [a]**Isa 28:16; 29:22**
8 [b]**Isa 26:2; 49:4**; [c]**Ps 34:18**; [d]**Job 13:19**; [e]**Isa 43:26**; Ro 8:32–34; **Isa 41:1**
9 [f]**Isa 48:16**; [g]**Isa 41:10**; [h]Ro 8:1,34; [i]**Job 13:28; Isa 51:8**
10 [j]**Pr 1:7**; [k]Isa 1:19; Hag 1:12; [l]**Isa 49:3**

b24 Dead Sea Scrolls, Vulgate and Syriac (see also Septuagint and verse 25); Masoretic Text *righteous*

Let him who walks in the dark,
who has no light,[m]
trust[n] in the name of the LORD
and rely on his God.
11But now, all you who light fires
and provide yourselves with
flaming torches,[o]
go, walk in the light of your fires[p]
and of the torches you have set
ablaze.
This is what you shall receive from my
hand:[q]
You will lie down in torment.[r]

Everlasting Salvation for Zion

51 "Listen[a] to me, you who
pursue righteousness[b]
and who seek[c] the LORD:
Look to the rock[d] from which you were
cut
and to the quarry from which you
were hewn;
2look to Abraham,[e] your father,
and to Sarah, who gave you birth.
When I called him he was but one,
and I blessed him and made him
many.[f]
3The LORD will surely comfort[g] Zion[h]
and will look with compassion on all
her ruins;[i]
he will make her deserts like Eden,[j]
her wastelands[k] like the garden of
the LORD.
Joy and gladness[l] will be found in her,
thanksgiving[m] and the sound of
singing.

4"Listen to me, my people;[n]
hear me,[o] my nation:
The law[p] will go out from me;
my justice[q] will become a light to the
nations.[r]
5My righteousness draws near
speedily,
my salvation[s] is on the way,[t]
and my arm[u] will bring justice to the
nations.
The islands[v] will look to me
and wait in hope[w] for my arm.
6Lift up your eyes to the heavens,
look at the earth beneath;
the heavens will vanish like smoke,[x]
the earth will wear out like a
garment[y]
and its inhabitants die like flies.
But my salvation[z] will last for ever,[a]
my righteousness will never fail.[b]

7"Hear me, you who know what is
right,[c]
you people who have my law in
your hearts:[d]
Do not fear the reproach of men
or be terrified by their insults.[e]
8For the moth will eat them up like a
garment;[f]
the worm[g] will devour them like
wool.
But my righteousness will last for
ever,[h]
my salvation through all
generations."

9Awake, awake![i] Clothe yourself with
strength,[j]
O arm[k] of the LORD;
awake, as in days gone by,
as in generations of old.[l]
Was it not you who cut Rahab[m] to
pieces,
who pierced that monster[n]
through?
10Was it not you who dried up the sea,[o]
the waters of the great deep,[p]
who made a road in the depths of the
sea[q]
so that the redeemed[r] might cross
over?
11The ransomed[s] of the LORD will return.
They will enter Zion with singing;[t]
everlasting joy will crown their
heads.
Gladness and joy[u] will overtake them,
and sorrow and sighing will flee
away.[v]

12"I, even I, am he who comforts[w] you.
Who are you that you fear[x] mortal
men,[y]
the sons of men, who are but grass,[z]
13that you forget[a] the LORD your Maker,[b]
who stretched out the heavens[c]
and laid the foundations of the
earth,
that you live in constant terror[d] every
day
because of the wrath of the
oppressor,
who is bent on destruction?
For where is the wrath of the
oppressor?[e]
14 The cowering prisoners will soon be
set free;[f]
they will not die in their dungeon,
nor will they lack bread.[g]

10 [m]Ps 107:14; Ac 26:18; [n]Isa 10:20; 26:4
11 [o]Pr 26:18; [p]Isa 1:31; Jas 3:6; [q]Dt 21:22–23; Pr 26:27; [r]Job 15:20; Isa 65:13–15

Ch. 51

1 [a]Isa 46:3; [b]ver 7; Dt 7:13; 16:20; Ps 94:15; Isa 63:8; Ro 9:30–31; [c]Isa 55:6; 65:10; [d]Isa 17:10
2 [e]Ge 17:6; Isa 29:22; Ro 4:16; Heb 11:11; [f]Ge 12:2
3 [g]Isa 40:1; [h]Ps 51:18; Isa 61:4; [i]Isa 44:26; 52:9; 61:4; [j]Ge 2:8; [k]Isa 5:6; 41:19; [l]Isa 25:9; 35:10; 65:18; 66:10; Jer 16:9; [m]Jer 17:26; 30:19; 33:11
4 [n]Ex 6:7; Ps 50:7; Isa 3:15; 63:8; 64:9; [o]Ps 78:1; [p]Dt 18:18; [q]Isa 2:4; [r]Isa 26:18; 49:6
5 [s]Ps 85:9; Isa 12:2; [t]Isa 35:4; [u]Ps 98:1; Isa 40:10; 50:2; 52:10; 59:16; 63:1,5; [v]Isa 11:11; [w]Ge 49:10; Ps 37:9
6 [x]Ps 37:20; 102:26; Mt 24:35; Lk 21:33; 2Pe 3:10; [y]Ps 102:25–26; Heb 1:10–12; [z]Isa 12:2; [a]ver 8; Ps 119:89; [b]Ps 89:33; Isa 54:10
7 [c]ver 1; [d]Dt 6:6; Ps 119:11; [e]Ps 119:39; Isa 50:7; 54:4; Mt 5:11; Lk 6:22; Ac 5:41
8 [f]Job 13:28; Jas 5:2; [g]Isa 14:11; [h]ver 6
9 [i]Jdg 5:12; [j]Ge 18:14; Ps 65:6; Isa 40:31; 52:1; [k]Ps 98:1; Isa 30:30; 33:2; [l]Ex 6:6; Dt 4:34; 32:7; [m]Job 9:13; [n]Ps 68:30; 74:13

10 [o]Ex 14:22; Zec 10:11; Rev 16:12; [p]Ex 15:5,8; [q]Job 36:30; [r]Ex 15:13
11 [s]Isa 35:9; 44:23; [t]Ps 109:28; Isa 65:14; Jer 30:19; Zep 3:14; [u]Isa 48:20; Jer 33:11; [v]Isa 30:19; Jer 31:13; Rev 7:17
12 [w]Isa 40:1; 2Co 1:4; [x]2Ki 1:15; [y]Isa 2:22; [z]Isa 15:6; 40:6–7; 1Pe 1:24
13 [a]Job 8:13; Isa 17:10; [b]Job 4:17; Isa 17:7; 45:11; 54:5; [c]Ge 1:1; Isa 48:13; [d]Isa 7:4; [e]Isa 9:4
14 [f]Isa 42:7; [g]Isa 49:10

15For I am the LORD your God,
who churns up the sea[h] so that its waves roar[i]—
the LORD Almighty[j] is his name.
16I have put my words in your mouth[k]
and covered you with the shadow of my hand[l]—
I who set the heavens in place,
who laid the foundations of the earth,[m]
and who say to Zion, 'You are my people.[n]' "

The Cup of the LORD's Wrath

17Awake, awake![o]
Rise up, O Jerusalem,
you who have drunk from the hand of the LORD
the cup[p] of his wrath,[q]
you who have drained to its dregs[r]
the goblet that makes men stagger.[s]
18Of all the sons[t] she bore
there was none to guide her;[u]
of all the sons she brought up
there was none to take her by the hand.[v]
19These double calamities[w] have come upon you—
who can comfort you?[x]—
ruin and destruction,[y] famine[z] and sword[a]—
who can[a] console you?
20Your sons have fainted;
they lie at the head of every street,[b]
like antelope caught in a net.[c]
They are filled with the wrath[d] of the LORD
and the rebuke[e] of your God.

21Therefore hear this, you afflicted[f] one,
made drunk,[g] but not with wine.
22This is what your Sovereign LORD says,
your God, who defends[h] his people:
"See, I have taken out of your hand
the cup[i] that made you stagger;
from that cup, the goblet of my wrath,
you will never drink again.
23I will put it into the hands of your tormentors,[j]
who said to you,
'Fall prostrate[k] that we may walk[l] over you.'
And you made your back like the ground,
like a street to be walked over."[m]

52 Awake, awake,[a] O Zion,
clothe yourself with strength.[b]
Put on your garments of splendour,[c]
O Jerusalem, the holy city.[d]
The uncircumcised[e] and defiled[f]
will not enter you again.[g]
2Shake off your dust;[h]
rise up,[i] sit enthroned, O Jerusalem.
Free yourself from the chains on your neck,[j]
O captive Daughter of Zion.[k]
3For this is what the LORD says:

"You were sold for nothing,[l]
and without money[m] you will be redeemed.[n]"

4For this is what the Sovereign LORD says:

"At first my people went down to Egypt[o] to live;
lately, Assyria[p] has oppressed them.

5"And now what do I have here?"
declares the LORD.

"For my people have been taken away for nothing,
and those who rule them mock,"[a]
declares the LORD.
"And all day long
my name is constantly blasphemed.[q]
6Therefore my people will know[r] my name;[s]
therefore in that day[t] they will know
that it is I who foretold[u] it.
Yes, it is I."

7How beautiful on the mountains[v]
are the feet of those who bring good news,[w]
who proclaim peace,[x]
who bring good tidings,
who proclaim salvation,
who say to Zion,
"Your God reigns!"[y]
8Listen! Your watchmen[z] lift up their voices;[a]
together they shout for joy.[b]
When the LORD returns[c] to Zion,[d]
they will see it with their own eyes.
9Burst into songs of joy[e] together,
you ruins[f] of Jerusalem,
for the LORD has comforted[g] his people,
he has redeemed Jerusalem.[h]

15 [h]Ex 14:21; [i]Ps 93:3; [j]Isa 13:4
16 [k]Ex 4:12,15; [l]Ex 33:22; [m]Isa 48:13; [n]Jer 7:23; 11:4; 24:7; Eze 14:11; Zec 8:8
17 [o]Jdg 5:12; Isa 52:1; [p]ver 22; Ps 16:5; Mt 20:22; [q]ver 20; Job 21:20; Isa 42:25; 66:15; Rev 14:10; 16:19; [r]Ps 75:8; [s]ver 23; Ps 60:3
18 [t]Ps 88:18; [u]Job 31:18; Isa 49:21; [v]Isa 41:13
19 [w]Isa 40:2; 47:9; [x]Isa 49:13; 54:11; Jer 15:5; Na 3:7; [y]Isa 60:18; 62:4; Jer 48:3; La 3:47; [z]Isa 14:30; [a]Jer 14:12; 24:10
20 [b]Isa 5:25; Jer 14:16; La 2:19; [c]Job 18:10; [d]ver 17; Job 40:11; Jer 44:6; [e]Dt 28:20
21 [f]Isa 14:32; [g]ver 17; Isa 29:9
22 [h]Isa 49:25; [i]ver 17; Jer 25:15; 51:7; Hab 2:16; Mt 20:22
23 [j]Isa 14:4; 49:26; Jer 25:15–17,26, 28; 49:12; [k]ver 17; Zec 12:2; [l]Jos 10:24; [m]Ps 66:12; Mic 7:10

Ch. 52

1 [a]Isa 51:17; [b]1Sa 2:4; Isa 51:9; [c]Ex 28:2, 40; Est 6:8; Ps 110:3; Isa 49:18; 61:10; Zec 3:4; [d]Ne 11:1; Isa 1:26; Mt 4:5; Rev 21:2; [e]Ge 34:14; [f]Isa 35:8; [g]Joel 3:17; Na 1:15; Zec 9:8; Rev 21:27
2 [h]Isa 29:4; [i]Isa 60:1; [j]Ps 81:6; Isa 10:27; [k]Ps 9:14
3 [l]Ps 44:12; [m]Isa 45:13; [n]Isa 1:27; 1Pe 1:18
4 [o]Ge 46:6; [p]Isa 10:24
5 [q]Isa 37:23; Ro 2:24*
6 [r]Isa 49:23; [s]Ex 6:3; [t]Isa 10:20; [u]Isa 41:26
7 [v]Isa 42:11; [w]2Sa 18:26; Isa 40:9; Ro 10:15*; [x]Na 1:15; Lk 2:14; Eph 6:15; [y]1Ch 16:31; Ps 97:1; 1Co 15:24–25
8 [z]1Sa 14:16; Isa 56:10; 62:6; Jer 6:17; 31:6; Eze 3:17; 33:7; [a]Isa 40:9; [b]Isa 12:6; [c]Nu 10:36; [d]Isa 59:20; Zec 8:3
9 [e]Ps 98:4; Isa 35:2; [f]Ps 74:3; Isa 51:3; [g]Isa 40:1; Lk 2:25; [h]Ezr 9:9; Isa 48:20

[a]*19* Dead Sea Scrolls, Septuagint, Vulgate and Syriac; Masoretic Text / *how can I*
[a]*5* Dead Sea Scrolls and Vulgate; Masoretic Text *wail*

10The LORD will lay bare his holy arm[i]
in the sight of all the nations,[j]
and all the ends of the earth[k] will see
the salvation[l] of our God.

11Depart,[m] depart, go out from there!
Touch no unclean thing![n]
Come out from it and be pure,[o]
you who carry the vessels[p] of the
LORD.
12But you will not leave in haste[q]
or go in flight;
for the LORD will go before you,[r]
the God of Israel will be your rear
guard.[s]

The Suffering and Glory of the Servant

13See, my servant[t] will act wisely;[b]
he will be raised and lifted up and
highly exalted.[u]
14Just as there were many who were
appalled[v] at him[c]—
his appearance was so disfigured[w]
beyond that of any man
and his form marred beyond human
likeness[x]—
15so will he sprinkle[y] many nations,[d]
and kings[z] will shut their mouths[a]
because of him.
For what they were not told, they will
see,
and what they have not heard, they
will understand.[b]

53

Who has believed our message[a]
and to whom has the arm[b] of the
LORD been revealed?[c]
2He grew up before him like a tender
shoot,[d]
and like a root[e] out of dry ground.
He had no beauty or majesty to attract
us to him,
nothing in his appearance[f] that we
should desire him.
3He was despised and rejected by men,
a man of sorrows,[g] and familiar with
suffering.[h]
Like one from whom men hide[i] their
faces
he was despised,[j] and we esteemed
him not.

4Surely he took up our infirmities
and carried our sorrows,[k]
yet we considered him stricken by
God,[l]
smitten by him, and afflicted.[m]
5But he was pierced[n] for our
transgressions,[o]
he was crushed[p] for our iniquities;
the punishment[q] that brought us
peace[r] was upon him,

10 [i]2Ch 32:8; Ps 44:3; Isa 30:30; [j]Isa 66:18; [k]Jos 4:24; Isa 11:9; [l]Ps 67:2; Lk 2:30; 3:6
11 [m]Isa 48:20; [n]Isa 1:16; 2Co 6:17*; [o]Nu 8:6; 2Ti 2:19; [p]2Ch 36:10
12 [q]Ex 12:11; [r]Mic 2:13; Jn 10:4; [s]Ex 14:19
13 [t]Jos 1:8; Isa 4:2; 20:3; [u]Isa 6:1; 57:15; Ac 3:13; Php 2:9
14 [v]Lev 26:32; Job 18:20; [w]2Sa 10:4; [x]Job 2:12; 16:16
15 [y]Lev 14:7; 16:14–15; [z]Isa 49:7; [a]Jdg 18:19; Ps 107:42; [b]Ro 15:21*; Eph 3:4–5

Ch. 53

1 [a]Isa 28:9; Ro 10:16*; [b]Ps 98:1; Isa 30:30; [c]Jn 12:38*
2 [d]2Ki 19:26; Job 14:7; Isa 4:2; [e]Isa 11:10; [f]Isa 52:14
3 [g]Ps 69:29; [h]ver 4,10; Ex 1:10; Mt 16:21; Lk 18:31–33; Heb 5:8; [i]Dt 31:17; Isa 1:15; [j]1Sa 2:30; Ps 22:6; Mt 27:29; Jn 1:10–11
4 [k]Mt 8:17*; [l]Dt 5:24; Job 4:5; Jer 23:5–6; 25:34; Eze 34:23–24; Mic 5:2–4; Zec 13:7; Jn 19:7; [m]ver 3; Ge 12:17; Ru 1:21
5 [n]Ps 22:16; [o]Ex 28:38; Ps 39:8; Jn 3:17; Ro 4:25; 1Co 15:3; Heb 9:28; [p]Ps 34:18; [q]Isa 50:6; [r]Isa 9:6; Ro 5:1; [s]Isa 1:6; Mt 27:26; Jn 19:1; [t]Dt 32:39; 2Ch 7:14; 1Pe 2:24–25
6 [u]Ps 95:10; 1Pe 2:24–25; [v]1Sa 8:3; Isa 56:11; 57:17; Mic 3:5; [w]ver 12; Ex 28:38; Ro 4:25

and by his wounds[s] we are healed.[t]
6We all, like sheep, have gone astray,[u]
each of us has turned to his own
way;[v]
and the LORD has laid on him
the iniquity[w] of us all.

7He was oppressed[x] and afflicted,
yet he did not open his mouth;[y]
he was led like a lamb[z] to the
slaughter,[a]
and as a sheep before her shearers is
silent,
so he did not open his mouth.
8By oppression[a] and judgment[b] he was
taken away.
And who can speak of his
descendants?
For he was cut off from the land of the
living;[c]
for the transgression[d] of my people
he was stricken.[b]
9He was assigned a grave with the
wicked,[e]
and with the rich[f] in his death,
though he had done no violence,[g]
nor was any deceit in his mouth.[h]

10Yet it was the LORD's will[i] to crush[j] him
and cause him to suffer,[k]
and though the LORD makes[c] his life
a guilt offering,[l]
he will see his offspring[m] and prolong
his days,
and the will of the LORD will
prosper[n] in his hand.
11After the suffering[o] of his soul,
he will see the light[p] ⌊of life⌋[d] and be
satisfied;[e]
by his knowledge[f] my righteous
servant[q] will justify[r] many,
and he will bear their iniquities.[s]

7 [x]Isa 49:26; [y]Mk 14:61; 1Pe 2:23; [z]Mt 27:31; Jn 1:29; [a]Ps 44:22
8 [b]Mk 14:49; [c]Ps 88:5; Da 9:26; Ac 8:32–33*; [d]ver 12; Ps 39:8
9 [e]Mt 27:38; Mk 15:27; Lk 23:32; Jn 19:18; [f]Mt 27:57–60; Mk 15:43–46; Lk 23:50–53; Jn 19:38–41; [g]Isa 42:1–3; [h]Job 16:17; 1Pe 2:22*; 1Jn 3:5; Rev 14:5
10 [i]Isa 46:10; 55:11; Ac 2:23; [j]ver 5; [k]ver 3; Ge 12:17; [l]Lev 5:15; Jn 3:17; [m]Ps 22:30; [n]Jos 1:8; Isa 49:4
11 [o]Jn 10:14–18; [p]Job 33:30; [q]Isa 20:3; Ac 7:52; [r]Isa 6:7; Jn 1:29; Ac 10:43; Ro 4:25; [s]Ex 28:38

b13 Or *will prosper* c14 Hebrew *you*
d15 Hebrew; Septuagint *so will many nations marvel at him* a8 Or *From arrest*
b8 Or *away. / Yet who of his generation considered / that he was cut off from the land of the living / for the transgression of my people, / to whom the blow was due?*
c10 Hebrew *though you make*
d11 Dead Sea Scrolls (see also Septuagint); Masoretic Text does not have *the light ⌊of life⌋*.
e11 Or (with Masoretic Text) [11]*He will see the result of the suffering of his soul / and be satisfied*
f11 Or *by knowledge of him*

[12]Therefore I will give him a portion
among the great,[g t]
and he will divide the spoils[u] with
the strong,[h]
because he poured out his life unto
death,[v]
and was numbered with the
transgressors.[w]
For he bore[x] the sin of many,[y]
and made intercession[z] for the
transgressors.

The Future Glory of Zion

54 "Sing, O barren woman,[a]
you who never bore a child;
burst into song, shout for joy,[b]
you who were never in labour;[c]
because more are the children[d] of the
desolate[e] woman
than of her who has a husband,[f]"
says the LORD.
[2]"Enlarge the place of your tent,[g]
stretch your tent curtains wide,
do not hold back;
lengthen your cords,
strengthen your stakes.[h]
[3]For you will spread out to the right
and to the left;
your descendants[i] will dispossess
nations[j]
and settle in their desolate[k] cities.

[4]"Do not be afraid;[l] you will not suffer
shame.[m]
Do not fear disgrace;[n] you will not
be humiliated.
You will forget the shame of your
youth[o]
and remember no more the
reproach[p] of your widowhood.[q]
[5]For your Maker[r] is your husband[s]—
the LORD Almighty is his name—
the Holy One[t] of Israel is your
Redeemer;[u]
he is called the God of all the earth.[v]
[6]The LORD will call you back[w]
as if you were a wife deserted[x] and
distressed in spirit—
a wife who married young,[y]
only to be rejected," says your God.
[7]"For a brief moment[z] I abandoned[a]
you,
but with deep compassion[b] I will
bring you back.[c]
[8]In a surge of anger[d]
I hid[e] my face from you for a
moment,
but with everlasting kindness[f]
I will have compassion[g] on you,"
says the LORD your Redeemer.[h]
[9]"To me this is like the days of Noah,
when I swore that the waters of
Noah would never again cover
the earth.[i]
So now I have sworn[j] not to be angry[k]
with you,
never to rebuke[l] you again.
[10]Though the mountains be shaken[m n]
and the hills be removed,
yet my unfailing love[o] for you will not
be shaken[p]
nor my covenant[q] of peace[r] be
removed,"
says the LORD, who has compassion[s]
on you.

[11]"O afflicted[t] city, lashed by storms[u]
and not comforted,[v]
I will build you with stones of
turquoise,[a w]
your foundations[x] with
sapphires.[b y]
[12]I will make your battlements of rubies,
your gates[z] of sparkling jewels,
and all your walls of precious
stones.
[13]All your sons will be taught by the
LORD,[a]
and great will be your children's
peace.[b]
[14]In righteousness[c] you will be
established:[d]
Tyranny[e] will be far from you;
you will have nothing to fear.[f]
Terror[g] will be far removed;
it will not come near you.
[15]If anyone does attack you, it will not be
my doing;
whoever attacks you will surrender[h]
to you.

[16]"See, it is I who created the
blacksmith[i]
who fans the coals into flame
and forges a weapon[j] fit for its work.
And it is I who have created the
destroyer[k] to work havoc;
[17] no weapon forged against you will
prevail,[l]

12 [t]**Isa 6:1; Php 2:9;** [u]**Ex 15:9; Ps 119:162;** Lk 11:22; [v]Mt 26:28,38–39, 42; [w]Mt 27:38; Mk 15:27*; Lk 22:37*; 23:32; [x]**ver 6;** 1Pe 2:24; [y]Heb 9:28; [z]Isa 59:16; **Ro 8:34**

Ch. 54

1 [a]**Ge 30:1;** [b]**Ge 21:6; Ps 98:4;** [c]Isa 66:7; [d]**Isa 49:20;** [e]**Isa 49:19;** [f]**1Sa 2:5;** Gal 4:27*
2 [g]**Ge 26:22;** Isa 26:15; 49:19–20; [h]Ex 35:18; 39:40
3 [i]**Ge 13:14; Isa 48:19;** [j]**Job 12:23; Isa 14:2;** 60:4–11; [k]**Isa 49:19**
4 [l]Jer 30:10; Joel 2:21; [m]**Isa 28:16; 29:22;** [n]**Ge 30:23; Ps 119:39; Isa 41:11;** [o]**Ps 25:7; Jer 2:2; 22:21;** [p]**Isa 51:7;** [q]**Isa 47:8**
5 [r]**Ps 95:6; 149:2; Isa 51:13;** [s]**SS 3:11;** Jer 3:14; 31:32; Hos 2:7,16; [t]**Isa 1:4;** 49:7; 55:5; 60:9; [u]**Isa 48:17;** [v]**Isa 6:3; 12:4**
6 [w]Isa 49:14–21; [x]ver 6–7; Isa 1:4; 50:1–2; 60:15; 62:4,12; Jer 44:2; Hos 1:10; [y]**Ex 20:14;** Mal 2:15
7 [z]**Job 14:13;** Isa 26:20; [a]**Ps 71:11; Isa 27:8;** [b]**Ps 51:1;** [c]**Isa 49:18**
8 [d]Isa 9:12; 26:20; 60:10; [e]**Isa 1:15;** [f]ver 10; **Ps 25:6;** 92:2; Isa 55:3; 63:7; [g]**Ps 102:13; Isa 14:1;** Hos 2:19; [h]**Isa 48:17**
9 [i]**Ge 8:21;** [j]**Isa 14:24; 49:18;** [k]Ps 13:1; 103:9; Isa 12:1; 57:16; Jer 3:5,12; Eze 39:29; Mic 7:18; [l]**Dt 28:20**
10 [m]Rev 6:14; [n]**Ps 46:2;** [o]**Ps 6:4;** [p]**Isa 51:6;** Heb 12:27; [q]**Ge 9:16;** Ex 34:10; Ps 89:34; **Isa 42:6;** [r]**Nu 25:12;** [s]ver 8; **Isa 14:1;** 55:7
11 [t]**Isa 14:32;** [u]Isa 28:2; 29:6; [v]**Isa 51:19;** [w]1Ch 29:2; Rev 21:18; [x]**Isa 28:16;** Rev 21:19–20; [y]**Ex 24:10; Job 28:6**
12 [z]Rev 21:21
13 [a]**Isa 28:9;** Mic 4:2; Jn 6:45*; Heb 8:11; [b]**Lev 26:6; Isa 48:18**
14 [c]**Isa 26:2;** [d]Jer 30:20; [e]**2Sa 7:10; Isa 9:4;** [f]Zep 3:15; Zec 9:8; [g]**Isa 17:14** **15** [h]Isa 41:11–16
16 [i]**Isa 44:12;** [j]**Isa 10:5;** [k]**Isa 13:5** **17** [l]**Isa 29:8**

[g]*12* Or *many* [h]*12* Or *numerous*
[a]*11* The meaning of the Hebrew for this word is uncertain. [b]*11* Or *lapis lazuli*

and you will refute[m] every tongue
that accuses you.
This is the heritage of the servants[n] of
the LORD,
and this is their vindication[o] from
me,"
declares the LORD.

Invitation to the Thirsty

55 "Come, all you who are
thirsty,[a]
come to the waters;[b]
and you who have no money,
come, buy[c] and eat!
Come, buy wine and milk[d]
without money and without cost.[e]
2Why spend money on what is not
bread,
and your labour on what does not
satisfy?[f]
Listen, listen to me, and eat what is
good,[g]
and your soul will delight in the
richest[h] of fare.
3Give ear and come to me;
hear[i] me, that your soul may live.[j]
I will make an everlasting covenant[k]
with you,
my faithful love[l] promised to
David.[m]
4See, I have made him a witness[n] to the
peoples,
a leader and commander[o] of the
peoples.
5Surely you will summon nations[p] you
know not,
and nations that do not know you
will hasten to you,[q]
because of the LORD your God,
the Holy One[r] of Israel,
for he has endowed you with
splendour."[s]

6Seek[t] the LORD while he may be
found;[u]
call[v] on him while he is near.
7Let the wicked forsake[w] his way
and the evil man his thoughts.[x]
Let him turn[y] to the LORD, and he will
have mercy[z] on him,
and to our God, for he will freely
pardon.[a]
8"For my thoughts[b] are not your
thoughts,
neither are your ways my ways,"[c]
declares the LORD.
9"As the heavens are higher than the
earth,[d]
so are my ways higher than your
ways
and my thoughts than your
thoughts.[e]
10As the rain[f] and the snow
come down from heaven,
and do not return to it
without watering the earth
and making it bud and flourish,[g]
so that it yields seed[h] for the sower
and bread for the eater,[i]
11so is my word[j] that goes out from my
mouth:
It will not return to me empty,[k]
but will accomplish what I desire
and achieve the purpose[l] for which I
sent it.
12You will go out in joy[m]
and be led forth in peace;[n]
the mountains and hills
will burst into song[o] before you,
and all the trees[p] of the field
will clap their hands.[q]
13Instead of the thornbush will grow the
pine tree,
and instead of briers[r] the myrtle[s]
will grow.
This will be for the LORD's renown,[t]
for an everlasting sign,
which will not be destroyed."

Salvation for Others

56 This is what the LORD says:

"Maintain justice[a]
and do what is right,[b]
for my salvation[c] is close at hand
and my righteousness[d] will soon be
revealed.
2Blessed[e] is the man who does this,
the man who holds it fast,
who keeps the Sabbath[f] without
desecrating it,
and keeps his hand from doing any
evil."

3Let no foreigner[g] who has bound
himself to the LORD say,
"The LORD will surely exclude me
from his people."[h]
And let not any eunuch[i] complain,
"I am only a dry tree."

4For this is what the LORD says:

"To the eunuchs[j] who keep my
Sabbaths,

17 [m]Isa 41:11; [n]Isa 56:6–8; 63:17; 65:8–9, 13–15; 66:14; [o]Ps 17:2; Zec 1:20–21

Ch. 55

1 [a]Pr 9:5; Isa 35:7; Mt 5:6; Lk 6:21; Jn 4:14; 7:37; [b]Jer 2:13; Eze 47:1, 12; Zec 14:8; [c]La 5:4; Mt 13:44; Rev 3:18; [d]SS 5:1; 1Pe 2:2; [e]Hos 14:4; Mt 10:8; Rev 21:6; 22:17
2 [f]Ps 22:26; Ecc 6:2; Isa 49:4; Jer 12:13; Hos 4:10; 8:7; Mic 6:14; Hag 1:6; [g]Isa 1:19; [h]Isa 30:23
3 [i]Ps 78:1; [j]Lev 18:5; Jn 6:27; Ro 10:5; [k]Ge 9:16; [l]Isa 54:10; Heb 13:20; Isa 54:8; [m]Ac 13:34*
4 [n]Rev 1:5; [o]1Sa 13:14; 2Ch 7:18; Isa 32:1
5 [p]Isa 49:6; [q]Isa 2:3; [r]Isa 12:6; 54:5; [s]Isa 44:23
6 [t]Dt 4:29; 2Ch 15:2; Isa 9:13; [u]Ps 32:6; Isa 49:8; Ac 17:27; 2Co 6:1–2; [v]Ps 50:15; Isa 65:24; Jer 29:12; 33:3
7 [w]2Ch 7:14; 30:9; Eze 18:27–28; [x]Isa 32:7; 59:7; [y]Isa 44:22; Jer 26:3; Eze 18:32; [z]Isa 54:10; [a]2Ch 6:21; Isa 1:18; 40:2
8 [b]Php 2:5; 4:8; [c]Isa 53:6; Mic 4:12
9 [d]Job 11:8; Ps 103:11; [e]Nu 23:19; Isa 40:13–14
10 [f]Isa 30:23; [g]Lev 25:19; Job 14:9; Ps 67:6; [h]Ge 47:23; [i]2Co 9:10
11 [j]Dt 32:2; Jn 1:1; [k]Isa 40:8; 45:23; Mt 5:18; Heb 4:12; [l]Pr 19:21; Isa 44:26; Eze 12:25
12 [m]Ps 98:4; Isa 35:2; [n]Isa 54:10,13; [o]Ps 65:12–13; 96:12–13; [p]1Ch 16:33; [q]Ps 98:8
13 [r]Nu 33:55; Isa 5:6; [s]Isa 41:19; [t]Ps 102:12; Isa 63:12; Jer 32:20; 33:9

Ch. 56

1 [a]Ps 11:7; Isa 1:17; Jer 22:3; [b]Isa 26:8; [c]Ps 85:9; [d]Jer 23:6; Da 9:24 **2** [e]Ps 119:2; [f]Ex 20:8,10
3 [g]Ex 12:43; 1Ki 8:41; Isa 11:10; Zec 8:20–23; [h]Dt 23:3; [i]Lev 21:20; Jer 38:7 *fn*; Ac 8:27 **4** [j]Jer 38:7 *fn*

who choose what pleases me
and hold fast to my covenant[k]—
5 to them I will give within my temple
and its walls[l]
a memorial[m] and a name
better than sons and daughters;
I will give them an everlasting name[n]
that will not be cut off.[o]
6 And foreigners[p] who bind themselves
to the LORD
to serve[q] him,
to love the name[r] of the LORD,
and to worship him,
all who keep the Sabbath[s] without
desecrating it
and who hold fast to my covenant—
7 these I will bring to my holy mountain[t]
and give them joy in my house of
prayer.
Their burnt offerings and sacrifices[u]
will be accepted on my altar;
for my house will be called
a house of prayer for all nations."[v][w]
8 The Sovereign LORD declares—
he who gathers the exiles of Israel:
"I will gather[x] still others to them
besides those already gathered."

God's Accusation Against the Wicked

9 Come, all you beasts of the field,[y]
come and devour, all you beasts of
the forest!
10 Israel's watchmen[z] are blind,
they all lack knowledge;[a]
they are all mute dogs,
they cannot bark;
they lie around and dream,
they love to sleep.[b]
11 They are dogs with mighty appetites;
they never have enough.
They are shepherds[c] who lack
understanding;[d]
they all turn to their own way,[e]
each seeks his own gain.[f]
12 "Come," each one cries, "let me get
wine![g]
Let us drink our fill of beer!
And tomorrow will be like today,
or even far better."[h]

57 The righteous perish,[a]
and no-one ponders it in his
heart;[b]
devout men are taken away,
and no-one understands
that the righteous are taken away
to be spared from evil.[c]
2 Those who walk uprightly[d]
enter into peace;
they find rest[e] as they lie in death.

3 "But you—come here, you sons of a
sorceress,[f]
you offspring of adulterers[g] and
prostitutes![h]
4 Whom are you mocking?
At whom do you sneer
and stick out your tongue?
Are you not a brood of rebels,[i]
the offspring of liars?
5 You burn with lust among the oaks[j]
and under every spreading tree;[k]
you sacrifice your children[l] in the
ravines
and under the overhanging crags.

6 ⌊The idols⌋[m] among the smooth stones
of the ravines are your portion;
they, they are your lot.
Yes, to them you have poured out
drink offerings[n]
and offered grain offerings.
In the light of these things, should I
relent?[o]
7 You have made your bed on a high
and lofty hill;[p]
there you went up to offer your
sacrifices.[q]
8 Behind your doors and your
doorposts
you have put your pagan symbols.
Forsaking me, you uncovered your
bed,
you climbed into it and opened it
wide;
you made a pact with those whose
beds you love,[r]
and you looked on their
nakedness.[s]
9 You went to Molech[a][t] with olive oil
and increased your perfumes.[u]
You sent your ambassadors[b][v] far
away;
you descended to the grave[c][w] itself!
10 You were wearied[x] by all your ways,
but you would not say, 'It is
hopeless.'[y]
You found renewal of your strength,[z]
and so you did not faint.

11 "Whom have you so dreaded and
feared[a]
that you have been false to me,
and have neither remembered[b] me
nor pondered[c] this in your hearts?
Is it not because I have long been
silent[d]
that you do not fear me?

4 [k]Ex 31:13
5 [l]Isa 26:1; 60:18; [m]Nu 32:42; 1Sa 15:12; [n]Isa 43:7; [o]Isa 48:19; 55:13
6 [p]Ex 12:43; 1Ki 8:41; [q]1Ch 22:2; Isa 60:7, 10; 61:5; [r]Mal 1:11; [s]ver 2,4
7 [t]Isa 2:2; Eze 20:40; [u]Isa 19:21; Ro 12:1; Php 4:18; Heb 13:15; [v]Mt 21:13*; Lk 19:46*; [w]Mk 11:17*
8 [x]Dt 30:4; Isa 1:9; 11:12; 60:3–11; Eze 34:12; Jn 10:16
9 [y]Isa 18:6; Jer 12:9; Eze 34:5,8; 39:17–20
10 [z]Isa 52:8; 62:6; Jer 6:17; 31:6; Eze 3:17; 33:7; [a]Jer 2:8; 10:21; 14:13–14; [b]Na 3:18
11 [c]Jer 23:1; Eze 34:2; [d]Isa 1:3; [e]Isa 53:6; Hos 4:7–8; [f]Isa 57:17; Jer 6:13; 8:10; 22:17; Eze 13:19; Mic 3:11
12 [g]Lev 10:9; Pr 23:20; Isa 22:13; [h]Ps 10:6; Lk 12:18–19

Ch. 57

1 [a]Ps 12:1; Eze 21:3; [b]Isa 42:25; [c]2Ki 22:20
2 [d]Isa 26:7; [e]Da 12:13
3 [f]Ex 22:18; Mal 3:5; [g]ver 7–8; Mt 16:4; Jas 4:4; [h]Isa 1:21; Jer 2:20
4 [i]Isa 1:2
5 [j]Isa 1:29; [k]Dt 12:2; 2Ki 16:4; [l]Lev 18:21; Dt 18:10; Ps 106:37–38; Eze 16:20
6 [m]2Ki 17:10; Jer 3:9; Hab 2:19; [n]Jer 7:18; 19:13; 44:18; [o]Jer 5:9,29; 9:9
7 [p]Jer 3:6; Eze 6:3; 16:16; 20:29; [q]Isa 65:7; Jer 13:27; Eze 6:13; 20:27–28
8 [r]Eze 16:26; 23:7; [s]Eze 16:15,36; 23:18
9 [t]Lev 18:21; 1Ki 11:5; [u]SS 4:10; [v]Eze 23:16,40; [w]Isa 8:19
10 [x]Isa 47:13; [y]Jer 2:25; 18:12; Mal 3:14; [z]Isa 2:4
11 [a]2Ki 1:15; Pr 29:25; Isa 7:2; [b]Isa 17:10; Jer 2:32; 3:21; 13:25; 18:15; Eze 22:12; [c]Isa 42:23; [d]Est 4:14; Ps 50:21; 83:1

[a]9 Or *to the king* [b]9 Or *idols* [c]9 Hebrew *Sheol*

12I will expose your righteousness and
your works,[e]
and they will not benefit you.
13When you cry out[f] for help,
let your collection ⌞of idols⌟ save[g]
you!
The wind will carry all of them off,
a mere breath will blow[h] them away.
But the man who makes me his refuge[i]
will inherit the land[j]
and possess my holy mountain."[k]

Comfort for the Contrite

14And it will be said:

"Build up, build up, prepare the road![l]
Remove the obstacles out of the way
of my people."[m]
15For this is what the high and lofty[n]
One says—
he who lives for ever,[o] whose name
is holy:
"I live in a high[p] and holy place,
but also with him who is contrite[q]
and lowly in spirit,[r]
to revive the spirit of the lowly
and to revive the heart of the
contrite.[s]
16I will not accuse[t] for ever,
nor will I always be angry,[u]
for then the spirit of man would grow
faint before me—
the breath[v] of man that I have
created.
17I was enraged by his sinful greed;[w]
I punished him, and hid[x] my face in
anger,
yet he kept on in his wilful ways.[y]
18I have seen his ways, but I will heal[z]
him;
I will guide[a] him and restore
comfort[b] to him,
19 creating praise on the lips[c] of the
mourners in Israel.
Peace, peace,[d] to those far and near,"[e]
says the LORD. "And I will heal
them."
20But the wicked[f] are like the tossing
sea,[g]
which cannot rest,
whose waves cast up mire[h] and
mud.
21"There is no peace,"[i] says my God,
"for the wicked."[j]

True Fasting

58 "Shout it aloud,[a] do not hold
back.
Raise your voice like a trumpet.[b]
Declare to my people their rebellion[c]
and to the house of Jacob their sins.[d]

12 [e]Isa 29:15; 58:1; 59:6,12; 65:7; 66:18; Eze 16:2; Mic 3:2–4,8
13 [f]Jer 22:20; 30:15; [g]**Jdg 10:14;** [h]Isa 40:7,24; [i]**Ps 118:8;** [j]**Ps 37:9;** [k]Isa 2:2–3; 56:7; 65:9–11
14 [l]**Isa 11:16;** [m]Isa 62:10; Jer 18:15
15 [n]**Isa 52:13;** [o]**Dt 33:27; Ps 90:2;** [p]**Job 16:19;** [q]Ps 147:3; [r]Ps 34:18; 51:17; Isa 66:2; Mic 6:8; Mt 5:3; [s]**2Ki 22:19; Job 5:18; Mt 23:12**
16 [t]**Ps 50:21;** Isa 3:13–14; [u]**Ps 103:9; Isa 54:9;** [v]**Ge 2:7;** Zec 12:1
17 [w]**Isa 56:11;** Jer 8:10; [x]**Isa 1:15;** [y]Isa 1:4; **30:15; 53:6;** 66:3
18 [z]**Dt 32:39; 2Ch 7:14; Isa 30:26;** [a]**Ps 48:14; Isa 42:16; 48:17;** [b]Isa 49:13; 61:1–3
19 [c]Isa 6:7; 51:16; 59:21; Heb 13:15; [d]**Isa 2:4;** 26:3,12; 32:17; **Lk 2:14;** [e]Ac 2:39
20 [f]Job 18:5–21; [g]**Ge 49:4;** Eph 4:14; Jude 13; [h]Ps 69:14
21 [i]**Isa 26:3;** 59:8; Eze 13:16; [j]**Isa 48:22**

Ch. 58

1 [a]Isa 40:6; [b]**Ex 20:18;** [c]**Isa 24:20; 48:8;** [d]**Isa 57:12;** Eze 3:17
2 [e]**Isa 48:1;** Tit 1:16; Jas 4:8; [f]**Dt 32:15; Ps 119:87;** [g]Isa 29:13
3 [h]**Lev 16:29;** [i]**Ex 10:3; 2Ch 6:37;** Jer 44:10; [j]Mal 3:14; [k]Isa 22:13; Zec 7:5–6
4 [l]1Ki 21:9–13; Isa 59:6; Jer 6:7; Eze 7:11; Mal 2:16; [m]**1Sa 8:18;** Isa 59:2; La 3:44; Eze 8:18; Mic 3:4

2For day after day they seek[e] me out;
they seem eager to know my ways,
as if they were a nation that does what
is right
and has not forsaken[f] the
commands of its God.
They ask me for just decisions
and seem eager for God to come
near[g] them.
3'Why have we fasted,'[h] they say,
'and you have not seen it?
Why have we humbled[i] ourselves,
and you have not noticed?'[j]

"Yet on the day of your fasting, you do
as you please[k]
and exploit all your workers.
4Your fasting ends in quarrelling and
strife,[l]
and in striking each other with
wicked fists.
You cannot fast as you do today
and expect your voice to be heard[m]
on high.
5Is this the kind of fast[n] I have chosen,
only a day for a man to humble[o]
himself?
Is it only for bowing one's head like a
reed[p]
and for lying on sackcloth and
ashes?[q]
Is that what you call a fast,
a day acceptable to the LORD?

6"Is not this the kind of fasting[r] I have
chosen:
to loose the chains of injustice[s]
and untie the cords of the yoke,
to set the oppressed[t] free
and break every yoke?[u]
7Is it not to share your food with the
hungry[v]
and to provide the poor wanderer
with shelter[w]—
when you see the naked, to clothe[x]
him,
and not to turn away from your own
flesh and blood?[y]
8Then your light will break forth like
the dawn,[z]
and your healing[a] will quickly
appear;
then your righteousness[a][b] will go
before you,

5 [n]Zec 7:5; [o]1Ki 21:27; Mt 6:16; [p]**Isa 36:6;** [q]**Job 2:8**
6 [r]Joel 2:12–14; [s]Ne 5:10–11; [t]**Dt 14:29;** Isa 61:1; Jer 34:9; Am 4:1; **Lk 4:19;** [u]**Isa 9:4**
7 [v]**Job 22:7;** Eze 18:16; Lk 3:11; [w]Isa 16:4; Heb 13:2; [x]Job 31:19–20; **Mt 25:36;** [y]**Ge 29:14;** Lk 10:31–32
8 [z]**Job 11:17; Isa 9:2;** [a]**Isa 1:5; 30:26;** [b]**Isa 26:2**

[a]8 Or *your righteous One*

and the glory of the LORD will be
your rear guard.[c]
9Then you will call,[d] and the LORD will
answer;[e]
you will cry for help, and he will
say: Here am I.

"If you do away with the yoke of
oppression,
with the pointing finger[f] and
malicious talk,[g]
10and if you spend yourselves on behalf
of the hungry
and satisfy the needs of the
oppressed,[h]
then your light[i] will rise in the
darkness,
and your night will become like the
noonday.[j]
11The LORD will guide[k] you always;
he will satisfy your needs[l] in a
sun-scorched land[m]
and will strengthen[n] your frame.
You will be like a well-watered
garden,[o]
like a spring[p] whose waters never
fail.
12Your people will rebuild the ancient
ruins[q]
and will raise up the age-old
foundations;[r]
you will be called Repairer of Broken
Walls,[s]
Restorer of Streets with Dwellings.

13"If you keep your feet from breaking
the Sabbath[t]
and from doing as you please on my
holy day,
if you call the Sabbath a delight[u]
and the LORD's holy day
honourable,
and if you honour it by not going your
own way
and not doing as you please or
speaking idle words,[v]
14then you will find your joy[w] in the
LORD,
and I will cause you to ride on the
heights[x] of the land
and to feast on the inheritance[y] of
your father Jacob."
The mouth of the LORD
has spoken.[z]

Sin, Confession and Redemption

59 Surely the arm[a] of the LORD is
not too short[b] to save,
nor his ear too dull to hear.[c]
2But your iniquities have separated[d]
you from your God;
your sins have hidden his face from
you,
so that he will not hear.[e]
3For your hands are stained with
blood,[f]
your fingers with guilt.[g]
Your lips have spoken lies,[h]
and your tongue mutters wicked
things.
4No-one calls for justice;[i]
no-one pleads his case with
integrity.
They rely[j] on empty arguments and
speak lies;[k]
they conceive trouble and give birth
to evil.[l]
5They hatch the eggs of vipers[m]
and spin a spider's web.[n]
Whoever eats their eggs will die,
and when one is broken, an adder is
hatched.
6Their cobwebs are useless for clothing;
they cannot cover themselves with
what they make.[o]
Their deeds are evil deeds,
and acts of violence[p] are in their
hands.
7Their feet rush into sin;
they are swift to shed innocent
blood.[q]
Their thoughts are evil thoughts;[r]
ruin and destruction mark their
ways.[s]
8The way of peace they do not know;[t]
there is no justice in their paths.
They have turned them into crooked
roads;[u]
no-one who walks in them will
know peace.[v]

9So justice is far from us,
and righteousness does not reach
us.
We look for light, but all is darkness;[w]
for brightness, but we walk in deep
shadows.
10Like the blind[x] we grope along the
wall,
feeling our way like men without
eyes.
At midday we stumble[y] as if it were
twilight;
among the strong, we are like the
dead.[z]
11We all growl like bears;
we moan mournfully like doves.[a]
We look for justice, but find none;
for deliverance, but it is far away.

12For our offences[b] are many in your
sight,
and our sins testify[c] against us.
Our offences are ever with us,

8 [c]Ex 14:19
9 [d]Ps 50:15; [e]Job 8:6; Isa 30:19; Da 9:20; Zec 10:6; [f]Pr 6:13; [g]Ps 12:2; Isa 59:13
10 [h]Dt 15:7–8; [i]Isa 42:16; [j]Job 11:17
11 [k]Ps 48:14; Isa 42:16; 48:17; [l]Ps 104:28; 107:9; [m]Ps 68:6; [n]Ps 72:16; [o]SS 4:15; [p]Isa 35:7; Jn 4:14
12 [q]Isa 49:8; [r]Isa 44:28; [s]Ne 2:17
13 [t]Ex 20:8; [u]Ps 37:4; 42:4; 84:2,10; [v]Isa 59:3
14 [w]Job 22:26; [x]Dt 32:13; [y]Ps 105:10–11; [z]Isa 1:20

Ch. 59

1 [a]Isa 41:20; [b]Isa 50:2; [c]Isa 30:19; 58:9; 65:24
2 [d]Jer 5:25; Eze 39:23; [e]Ps 18:41; Isa 58:4; Jer 11:11; Jn 9:31
3 [f]2Ki 21:16; Isa 1:15; Eze 22:9; [g]Ps 7:3; [h]Isa 3:8
4 [i]Isa 5:23; [j]Job 15:31; [k]Isa 44:20; [l]Job 4:8; Isa 29:20; Jas 1:15
5 [m]Isa 11:8; Mt 3:7; [n]Job 8:14
6 [o]Isa 28:20; [p]Ps 55:9; Pr 4:17; Isa 58:4
7 [q]2Ki 21:16; Pr 6:17; Mic 3:10; [r]Pr 24:2; Isa 26:10; Mk 7:21–22; [s]Ro 3:15–17*
8 [t]Ro 3:15–17*; [u]Jdg 5:6; [v]Isa 57:21; Lk 1:79
9 [w]Job 19:8; Ps 107:14; Isa 5:30; 8:20; Lk 1:79
10 [x]Dt 28:29; Isa 6:9–10; 56:10; La 4:14; Zep 1:17; [y]Job 3:23; Isa 8:15; Jn 11:9–10; [z]La 3:6
11 [a]Ge 8:8; Ps 74:19; Isa 38:14; Jer 48:28; Eze 7:16; Na 2:7
12 [b]Ezr 9:6; Isa 57:12; [c]Ge 4:7; Isa 3:9; Jer 2:19

and we acknowledge our iniquities:[d]
13rebellion[e] and treachery against the
LORD,
turning our backs[f] on our God,
fomenting oppression[g] and revolt,
uttering lies[h] our hearts have
conceived.
14So justice[i] is driven back,
and righteousness[j] stands at a
distance;
truth[k] has stumbled in the streets,
honesty cannot enter.
15Truth[l] is nowhere to be found,
and whoever shuns evil becomes a
prey.

The LORD looked and was displeased
that there was no justice.[m]
16He saw that there was no-one,[n]
he was appalled that there was
no-one to intervene;[o]
so his own arm worked salvation[p] for
him,
and his own righteousness[q]
sustained him.
17He put on righteousness as his
breastplate,[r]
and the helmet[s] of salvation on his
head;
he put on the garments[t] of vengeance[u]
and wrapped himself in zeal[v] as in a
cloak.
18According to what they have done,
so will he repay[w]
wrath to his enemies
and retribution to his foes;
he will repay the islands[x] their due.
19From the west,[y] men will fear the
name of the LORD,
and from the rising of the sun,[z] they
will revere his glory.[a]
For he will come like a pent-up flood
that the breath[b] of the LORD drives
along.[a]
20"The Redeemer[c] will come to Zion,[d]
to those in Jacob who repent of their
sins,"[e]
declares the LORD.

21"As for me, this is my covenant[f]
with them," says the LORD. "My Spirit,[g]
who is on you, and my words that I
have put in your mouth[h] will not depart
from your mouth,[i] or from the mouths
of your children, or from the mouths of
their descendants from this time on and
for ever," says the LORD.

The Glory of Zion

60 "Arise,[a] shine, for your light[b]
has come,
and the glory[c] of the LORD rises
upon you.
2See, darkness[d] covers the earth
and thick darkness[e] is over the
peoples,
but the LORD rises upon you
and his glory appears over you.
3Nations[f] will come to your light,[g]
and kings[h] to the brightness of your
dawn.

4"Lift up your eyes and look about you:
All assemble[i] and come to you;
your sons come from afar,[j]
and your daughters[k] are carried on
the arm.[l]
5Then you will look and be radiant,[m]
your heart will throb and swell with
joy;[n]
the wealth[o] on the seas will be brought
to you,
to you the riches of the nations will
come.
6Herds of camels[p] will cover your land,
young camels of Midian[q] and
Ephah.[r]
And all from Sheba[s] will come,
bearing gold and inc[illegible]
[illegible] of the
LORD.
7All Kedar's[v] flocks will be gathered to
you,
the rams of Nebaioth will serve you;
they will be accepted as offerings[w] on
my altar,[x]
and I will adorn my glorious
temple.[y]

8"Who are these[z] that fly along like
clouds,[a]
like doves to their nests?
9Surely the islands[b] look to me;
in the lead are the ships of
Tarshish,[a c]
bringing[d] your sons from afar,
with their silver and gold,[e]
to the honour[f] of the LORD your God,
the Holy One[g] of Israel,
for he has endowed you with
splendour.[h]

10"Foreigners[i] will rebuild your walls,
and their kings[j] will serve you.

12 [d]Ps 51:3
13 [e]Isa 46:8; 48:8; [f]**Nu 11:20; Pr 30:9**; Mt 10:33; Tit 1:16; [g]**Ps 12:5; Isa 5:7**; [h]**Isa 3:8; 44:20**; Mk 7:21–22
14 [i]**Isa 29:21**; [j]**Isa 1:21**; [k]**Isa 48:1; Jer 33:16**
15 [l]Jer 7:28; 9:5; Da 8:12; [m]**Isa 5:7**
16 [n]**Isa 41:28**; [o]**Isa 53:12**; [p]**Isa 51:5**; [q]Isa 45:8,13; 46:13
17 [r]Eph 6:14; 1Th 5:8; [s]Eph 6:17; 1Th 5:8; [t]**Job 27:6**; Isa 63:3; [u]**Isa 1:24**; [v]**Isa 9:7**; Eze 5:13
18 [w]**Lev 26:28; Nu 10:35; Isa 34:8; Mt 16:27**; [x]Isa 11:11; 41:5
19 [y]**Isa 49:12; Mt 8:11**; [z]**Ps 113:3**; [a]Ps 97:6; **Isa 24:15**; [illegible]; 40:5; 52:10; 66:18; [b]**Isa 11:4**
20 [c]**Job 19:25**; Isa 60:16; 63:16; [d]**Isa 52:8; Joel 3:21**; [e]**Job 22:23; Isa 1:27; Jer 35:15**; Ac 2:38–39; Ro 11:26–27*
21 [f]**Ge 9:16; Dt 29:14; Isa 42:6**; [g]**Isa 11:2; 44:3**; [h]**Ex 4:15**; [i]**Jos 1:8**

Ch. 60

1 [a]Isa 52:2; [b]**Ps 36:9; 118:27; Isa 9:2**; Jn 8:12; Eph 5:14; [c]**Ex 16:7; Isa 4:5**; Rev 21:11
2 [d]**1Sa 2:9; Ps 82:5; 107:14; Isa 8:20**; [e]Jer 13:16; Col 1:13
3 [f]**Isa 44:5; 45:14**; Mt 2:1–11; Rev 21:24; [g]**Isa 9:2**; 42:6; [h]**Isa 49:23**
4 [i]**Isa 11:12**; [j]**Isa 2:3**; Jer 30:10; [k]**Isa 43:6**; [l]49:20–22
5 [m]**Ex 34:29**; [n]Isa 35:2; 65:13; 66:14; Zec 10:7; [o]**Dt 33:19; Jdg 3:15**; Rev 21:26
6 [p]**Jdg 6:5**; [q]**Ge 25:2**; [r]Ge 25:4; [s]**Ge 10:7**,28; [t]Isa 43:23; Jer 6:20; Mt 2:11; [u]**1Ki 5:7; Isa 42:10**
7 [v]**Ge 25:13**; [w]Isa 18:7; Eze 20:40; 43:27; Zep 3:10; [x]**Isa 19:21**; [y]ver 13; Hag 2:3,7,9
8 [z]Isa 49:21; [a]Isa 19:1
9 [b]**Isa 11:11**; [c]**Ge 10:4**; Isa 2:16 *fn*; [d]**Isa 14:2; 43:6**; [e]**1Ki 10:22**; [f]**Ps 22:23**; [g]ver 14; Isa 1:4; **54:5**; [h]**Isa 44:23**; 55:5; Jer 30:19
10 [i]**Ex 1:11; Isa 14:1–2; 56:6**; [j]**Ezr 1:2**; Rev 21:24

[a]19 Or *When the enemy comes in like a flood, / the Spirit of the LORD will put him to flight*
[a]9 Or *the trading ships*

Though in anger I struck you,
in favour[k] I will show you
compassion.[l]
11Your gates[m] will always stand open,
they will never be shut, day or
night,
so that men may bring you the wealth
of the nations[n]—
their kings[o] led in triumphal
procession.
12For the nation or kingdom that will not
serve[p] you will perish;
it will be utterly ruined.[q]

13"The glory of Lebanon[r] will come to
you,
the pine, the fir and the cypress
together,[s]
to adorn the place of my sanctuary;[t]
and I will glorify the place of my
feet.[u]
14The sons of your oppressors[v] will
come bowing before you;
all who despise you will bow down[w]
at your feet
and will call you the City[x] of the LORD,
Zion[y] of the Holy One[z] of Israel.

15"Although you have been forsaken[a]
and hated,
with no-one travelling[b] through,
I will make you the everlasting pride[c]
and the joy[d] of all generations.
16You will drink the milk of nations
and be nursed[e] at royal breasts.
Then you will know[f] that I, the LORD,
am your Saviour,[g]
your Redeemer,[h] the Mighty One of
Jacob.[i]
17Instead of bronze I will bring you
gold,[j]
and silver in place of iron.
Instead of wood I will bring you
bronze,
and iron in place of stones.
I will make peace[k] your governor
and righteousness your ruler.[l]
18No longer will violence[m] be heard in
your land,
nor ruin or destruction[n] within your
borders,
but you will call your walls Salvation[o]
and your gates Praise.[p]
19The sun will no more be your light by
day,
nor will the brightness of the moon
shine on you,
for the LORD will be your everlasting
light,[q]
and your God will be your glory.[r]
20Your sun[s] will never set again,
and your moon will wane no more;

10 [k]Isa 49:8; [l]Ps 102:13
11 [m]ver 18; Ps 24:7; Isa 62:10; Mic 2:13; Rev 21:25; [n]ver 5; Isa 61:6; Rev 21:26; [o]Ps 149:8; Isa 2:12
12 [p]Isa 11:14; 14:2; [q]Ge 27:29; Ps 110:5; Da 2:34
13 [r]Ezr 3:7; [s]Isa 41:19; [t]ver 7; [u]1Ch 28:2
14 [v]Isa 14:2; [w]Ge 27:29; Isa 2:3; Rev 3:9; [x]Ge 32:28; Isa 1:26; [y]Heb 12:22; [z]ver 9
15 [a]Isa 1:7–9; 6:12; 54:6; [b]Isa 33:8; [c]Isa 4:2; [d]Ps 126:5; Isa 65:18
16 [e]Ex 6:2; Isa 49:23; 66:11–12; [f]Ex 6:7; [g]Ex 14:30; Isa 25:9; [h]Job 19:25; Isa 59:20; [i]Ge 49:24; Ps 132:2
17 [j]1Ki 10:21; [k]Ps 85:8; Isa 66:12; Hag 2:9; [l]Isa 9:7
18 [m]Lev 26:6; 2Sa 7:10; Isa 9:4; [n]Isa 49:19; 51:19; [o]Isa 33:6; [p]Isa 61:11; 62:7; Jer 33:9; Zep 3:20
19 [q]Ps 36:9; 118:27; Rev 22:5; [r]Ps 85:9; Isa 24:16,23; Rev 21:23
20 [s]Isa 30:26; [t]Isa 30:19; 35:10; Rev 7:17
21 [u]Isa 4:3; 26:2; Rev 21:27; [v]Ps 37:11,22; Isa 49:8; 57:13; 61:7; 65:9; Zec 8:12; [w]Ex 15:17; Ps 44:2; 80:8–11; Jer 32:41; Am 9:15; Mt 15:13; [x]Job 10:3; Ps 8:6; Isa 19:25; Eph 2:10; [y]Lev 10:3; Isa 44:23
22 [z]Ge 12:2; Dt 1:10; [a]Isa 5:19

the LORD will be your everlasting light,
and your days of sorrow[t] will end.
21Then will all your people be righteous[u]
and they will possess[v] the land for
ever.
They are the shoot I have planted,[w]
the work of my hands,[x]
for the display of my splendour.[y]
22The least of you will become a
thousand,
the smallest a mighty nation.[z]
I am the LORD;
in its time I will do this swiftly."[a]

The Year of the LORD's Favour

61 The Spirit[a] of the Sovereign
LORD[b] is on me,
because the LORD has anointed[c] me
to preach good news[d] to the poor.[e]
He has sent me to bind up[f] the
broken-hearted,
to proclaim freedom[g] for the
captives[h]
and release from darkness for the
prisoners,[a]
2to proclaim the year of the LORD's
favour[i]
and the day of vengeance[j] of our
God,
to comfort[k] all who mourn,[l]
3 and provide for those who grieve in
Zion—
to bestow on them a crown[m] of beauty
instead of ashes,[n]
the oil[o] of gladness
instead of mourning,[p]
and a garment of praise
instead of a spirit of despair.
They will be called oaks of
righteousness,
a planting[q] of the LORD
for the display of his splendour.[r]
4They will rebuild the ancient ruins[s]
and restore the places long
devastated;
they will renew the ruined cities
that have been devastated for
generations.

Ch. 61
1 [a]Isa 11:2; 2Co 3:17; [b]Isa 50:4; [c]Ps 45:7; Da 9:24–26; Ac 4:26; [d]2Sa 18:26; Isa 40:9; [e]Job 5:16; Mt 11:5; Lk 7:22; [f]2Ki 22:19; Job 5:18; [g]Lev 25:10; [h]Ps 68:6; Isa 49:9
2 [i]Isa 49:8; Lk 4:18–19*; [j]Isa 1:24; [k]Isa 40:1; Mt 5:4; [l]Job 5:11; Lk 6:21
3 [m]Isa 3:23; [n]Job 2:8; [o]Ru 3:3; Isa 1:6; Heb 1:9; [p]Jer 31:13; Mt 5:4; [q]Ps 1:3; 92:12–13; Mt 15:13; 1Co 3:9; [r]Isa 44:23
4 [s]Isa 44:26; 51:3; 65:21; Eze 36:33; Am 9:14; Zec 1:16–17

[a]1 Hebrew; Septuagint *the blind*

5Aliens[t] will shepherd your flocks;
foreigners will work your fields and vineyards.
6And you will be called priests[u] of the LORD,
you will be named ministers of our God.
You will feed on the wealth[v] of nations,
and in their riches you will boast.

7Instead of their shame[w]
my people will receive a double[x] portion,
and instead of disgrace
they will rejoice in their inheritance;
and so they will inherit[y] a double portion in their land,
and everlasting joy[z] will be theirs.

8For I, the LORD, love justice;[a]
I hate robbery and iniquity.
In my faithfulness I will reward them
and make an everlasting covenant[b] with them.
9Their descendants[c] will be known among the nations
and their offspring among the peoples.
All who see them will acknowledge
that they are a people the LORD has blessed."[d]

10I delight greatly in the LORD;
my soul rejoices[e] in my God.
For he has clothed me with garments of salvation
and arrayed me in a robe of righteousness,[f]
as a bridegroom adorns his head[g] like a priest,
and as a bride[h] adorns herself with her jewels.
11For as the soil makes the young plant come up
and a garden[i] causes seeds to grow,
so the Sovereign LORD will make righteousness[j] and praise
spring up before all nations.

Zion's New Name

62 For Zion's sake I will not keep silent,[a]
for Jerusalem's sake I will not remain quiet,
till her righteousness[b] shines out like the dawn,[c]
her salvation[d] like a blazing torch.
2The nations[e] will see your righteousness,
and all kings your glory;
you will be called by a new name[f]
that the mouth of the LORD will bestow.
3You will be a crown[g] of splendour in the LORD's hand,
a royal diadem in the hand of your God.
4No longer will they call you Deserted,[h]
or name your land Desolate.[i]
But you will be called Hephzibah,[a] [j]
and your land Beulah;[b]
for the LORD will take delight[k] in you,
and your land will be married.[l]
5As a young man marries a maiden,
so will your sons[c] marry you;
as a bridegroom[m] rejoices over his bride,
so will your God rejoice[n] over you.

6I have posted watchmen[o] on your walls, O Jerusalem;
they will never be silent day or night.
You who call on the LORD,
give yourselves no rest,[p]
7and give him no rest[q] till he establishes Jerusalem
and makes her the praise[r] of the earth.

8The LORD has sworn[s] by his right hand
and by his mighty arm:
"Never again will I give your grain[t]
as food for your enemies,
and never again will foreigners drink
the new wine
for which you have toiled;
9but those who harvest it will eat[u] it
and praise the LORD,[v]
and those who gather the grapes will drink it
in the courts of my sanctuary."[w]

10Pass through, pass through the gates![x]
Prepare the way for the people.
Build up, build up the highway![y] [z]
Remove the stones.
Raise a banner[a] for the nations.

11The LORD has made proclamation
to the ends of the earth:[b]
"Say to the Daughter of Zion,[c]
'See, your Saviour comes![d]
See, his reward is with him,
and his recompense accompanies him.'"[e]

5 [t]Isa 14:1–2; 56:6
6 [u]Ex 19:6; 1Pe 2:5; [v]Dt 33:19; Isa 60:11
7 [w]Isa 29:22; 41:11; [x]Dt 21:17; Isa 40:2; [y]Isa 60:21; [z]Ps 126:5; Isa 25:9
8 [a]Ps 11:7; Isa 1:17; 5:16; [b]Ge 9:16; Isa 42:6; Heb 13:20
9 [c]Isa 43:5; 48:19; [d]Ge 12:2; Dt 28:3–12
10 [e]Ps 2:11; Isa 7:13; 25:9; Hab 3:18; Lk 1:47; [f]Job 27:6; Ps 132:9; Isa 52:1; Rev 19:8; [g]Ex 39:28; [h]Isa 49:18; Rev 21:2
11 [i]Ge 47:23; Isa 58:11; [j]Isa 45:8

Ch. 62

1 [a]Est 4:14; Ps 50:21; 83:1; [b]Isa 1:26; 45:8; [c]Job 11:17; [d]Ps 67:2
2 [e]Ps 67:2; Isa 40:5; 45:14; 52:10; [f]Ge 32:28; Isa 1:26; Rev 2:17; 3:12
3 [g]Isa 28:5; 1Th 2:19
4 [h]Lev 26:43; Isa 6:12; 54:6; [i]Isa 49:19; 51:19; [j]2Ki 21:1; [k]Isa 65:19; Jer 32:41; Zep 3:17; Mal 3:12; [l]Isa 54:5; Jer 3:14; Hos 2:19
5 [m]SS 3:11; [n]Dt 28:63; Isa 65:19; Jer 31:12; Zep 3:17
6 [o]Isa 52:8; Heb 13:17; [p]Ps 132:4
7 [q]Mt 15:21–28; Lk 18:1–8; [r]Dt 26:19; Isa 60:18
8 [s]Ge 22:16; Isa 14:24; 49:18; [t]Dt 28:30–33; Isa 1:7
9 [u]Isa 1:19; Am 9:14; [v]Dt 12:7; Joel 2:26; [w]Lev 23:39
10 [x]Ps 24:7; Isa 60:11; [y]Isa 57:14; [z]Isa 11:16; [a]Isa 11:10
11 [b]Dt 30:4; [c]Ps 9:14; Zec 9:9; Mt 21:5; [d]Isa 35:4; Rev 22:12; [e]Isa 40:10

a4 *Hephzibah* means *my delight is in her.*
b4 *Beulah* means *married.*
c5 Or *Builder*

[12]They will be called[f] the Holy People,[g]
the Redeemed[h] of the LORD;
and you will be called Sought After,
the City No Longer Deserted.[i]

God's Day of Vengeance and Redemption

63 Who is this coming from Edom,[a]
from Bozrah,[b] with his garments
stained crimson?[c]
Who is this, robed in splendour,
striding forward in the greatness of
his strength?[d]

"It is I, speaking in righteousness,
mighty to save."[e]

[2]Why are your garments red,
like those of one treading the
winepress?[f]

[3]"I have trodden the winepress[g] alone;
from the nations no-one was with
me.
I trampled[h] them in my anger
and trod them down in my wrath;[i]
their blood spattered my garments,[j]
and I stained all my clothing.
[4]For the day of vengeance[k] was in my
heart,
and the year of my redemption has
come.
[5]I looked, but there was no-one[l] to
help,
I was appalled that no-one gave
support;
so my own arm[m] worked salvation for
me,
and my own wrath sustained me.[n]
[6]I trampled[o] the nations in my anger;
in my wrath I made them drunk[p]
and poured their blood[q] on the
ground."

Praise and Prayer

[7]I will tell of the kindnesses[r] of the
LORD,
the deeds for which he is to be
praised,
according to all the LORD has done
for us—
yes, the many good things[s] he has
done
for the house of Israel,
according to his compassion[t] and
many kindnesses.
[8]He said, "Surely they are my people,[u]
sons who will not be false to me";
and so he became their Saviour.[v]
[9]In all their distress he too was
distressed,
and the angel[w] of his presence[x]
saved them.
In his love and mercy he redeemed[y]
them;
he lifted them up and carried[z] them
all the days of old.[a]
[10]Yet they rebelled[b]
and grieved his Holy Spirit.[c]
So he turned and became their enemy[d]
and he himself fought[e] against
them.

[11]Then his people recalled[a] the days of
old,
the days of Moses and his people—
where is he who brought them
through the sea,[f]
with the shepherd of his flock?[g]
Where is he who set
his Holy Spirit[h] among them,
[12]who sent his glorious arm[i] of power
to be at Moses' right hand,
who divided the waters[j] before them,
to gain for himself everlasting
renown,[k]
[13]who led[l] them through the depths?[m]
Like a horse in open country,
they did not stumble;[n]
[14]like cattle that go down to the plain,
they were given rest[o] by the Spirit of
the LORD.
This is how you guided your people
to make for yourself a glorious
name.

[15]Look down from heaven[p] and see
from your lofty throne,[q] holy and
glorious.
Where are your zeal[r] and your might?
Your tenderness and compassion[s]
are withheld[t] from us.
[16]But you are our Father,[u]
though Abraham does not know us
or Israel acknowledge[v] us;
you, O LORD, are our Father,
our Redeemer[w] from of old is your
name.
[17]Why, O LORD, do you make us
wander[x] from your ways
and harden our hearts[y] so that we
do not revere[z] you?
Return[a] for the sake of your servants,
the tribes that are your inheritance.[b]
[18]For a little while[c] your people
possessed your holy place,

12 [f]Ge 32:28; [g]Ex 19:6; 1Pe 2:9; [h]Ps 106:10; Isa 35:9; 44:23; [i]Ps 27:9; Isa 42:16; 54:6
Ch. 63
1 [a]2Ch 28:17; Isa 11:14; [b]Ge 36:33; Am 1:12; [c]Rev 19:13; [d]Job 9:4; Isa 45:24; [e]ver 5; Isa 46:13; 51:5; Jer 42:11; Zep 3:17
2 [f]Ge 49:11
3 [g]Jdg 6:11; Rev 14:20; [h]Job 40:12; Ps 108:13; Isa 5:5; [i]Isa 22:5; [j]Rev 19:13
4 [k]Isa 1:24; Jer 50:15
5 [l]2Ki 14:26; Isa 41:28; [m]Ps 44:3; 98:1; Isa 33:2; [n]Isa 59:16
6 [o]Job 40:12; Ps 108:13; [p]Isa 29:9; La 4:21; [q]Isa 34:3
7 [r]Isa 54:8; [s]Ex 18:9; [t]Ps 51:1; Eph 2:4
8 [u]Ps 100:3; Isa 51:4; [v]Ex 14:30; Isa 25:9
9 [w]Ex 14:19; [x]Ex 33:14; [y]Dt 7:7–8; Ezr 9:9; Isa 48:20; [z]Dt 1:31; Ps 28:9; [a]Dt 32:7; Job 37:23
10 [b]Ps 78:17; Eze 20:8; Ac 7:39–42; [c]Ps 51:11; Ac 7:51; Eph 4:30; [d]Ps 106:40; Isa 10:4; [e]Jos 10:14
11 [f]Ex 14:22,30; [g]Ps 77:20; [h]Nu 11:17
12 [i]Ge 49:24; Ex 3:20; [j]Ex 14:21–22; Isa 11:15; [k]Ps 102:12; Isa 55:13; Jer 13:11
13 [l]Dt 32:12; [m]Ex 14:22; [n]Ps 119:11; Jer 31:9
14 [o]Ex 33:14; Dt 12:9
15 [p]Dt 26:15; La 3:50; [q]1Ki 22:19; Ps 123:1; [r]Isa 9:7; 26:11; [s]1Ki 3:26; Ps 25:6; [t]Ge 43:31; Isa 64:12
16 [u]Ex 4:22; Jer 3:4; Jn 8:41; [v]Job 14:21; [w]Isa 41:14; 44:6; 59:20
17 [x]Ge 20:13; La 3:9; [y]Ex 4:21; [z]Isa 29:13; [a]Nu 10:36; [b]Ex 34:9 *18* [c]Dt 4:26; 11:17

[a]*11* Or *But may he recall*

but now our enemies have
trampled[d] down your
sanctuary.[e]
19We are yours from of old;
but you have not ruled over them,
they have not been called by your
name.[b][f]

64 Oh, that you would rend the
heavens[a] and come down,[b]
that the mountains[c] would tremble
before you!
2As when fire sets twigs ablaze
and causes water to boil,
come down to make your name[d]
known to your enemies
and cause the nations to quake[e]
before you!
3For when you did awesome[f] things
that we did not expect,
you came down, and the mountains
trembled[g] before you.
4Since ancient times no-one has heard,
no ear has perceived,
no eye has seen any God besides you,[h]
who acts on behalf of those who
wait for him.[i]
5You come to the help of those who
gladly do right,[j]
who remember your ways.
But when we continued to sin against
them,
you were angry.[k]
How then can we be saved?
6All of us have become like one who is
unclean,[l]
and all our righteous[m] acts are like
filthy rags;
we all shrivel up like a leaf,[n]
and like the wind our sins sweep us
away.[o]
7No-one[p] calls on your name[q]
or strives to lay hold of you;
for you have hidden[r] your face from us
and made us waste away[s] because
of our sins.

8Yet, O LORD, you are our Father.[t]
We are the clay, you are the potter;[u]
we are all the work of your hand.[v]
9Do not be angry[w] beyond measure, O
LORD;
do not remember our sins[x] for ever.
Oh, look upon us we pray,
for we are all your people.[y]
10Your sacred cities[z] have become a
desert;
even Zion is a desert, Jerusalem a
desolation.[a]
11Our holy and glorious temple,[b] where
our fathers praised you,
has been burned with fire,

18 [d]**Isa 28:18;** Da 8:13; **Lk 21:24;** [e]**Lev 26:31; 2Ki 25:9**
19 [f]**Isa 43:7; Jer 14:9**

Ch. 64

1 [a]Ps 18:9; 144:5; [b]ver 3; Mic 1:3; [c]Ex **19:18**
2 [d]**Isa 30:27;** [e]Ps 99:1; 119:120; Jer 5:22; 33:9
3 [f]**Ps 65:5;** [g]**Ps 18:7**
4 [h]**Isa 43:10–11;** [i]**Isa 30:18;** 1Co 2:9*
5 [j]**Isa 26:8;** [k]**Isa 10:4**
6 [l]**Lev 5:2; 12:2;** [m]Isa 46:12; 48:1; [n]**Ps 1:3;** 90:5–6; [o]Ps 1:4; Jer 4:12
7 [p]**Isa 41:28;** 59:4; 63:5; Jer 8:6; Eze 22:30; [q]**Ps 14:4;** [r]Dt 31:18; Isa 1:15; 54:8; [s]**Isa 9:18;** Eze 22:18–22
8 [t]**Ex 4:22; Jer 3:4;** [u]**Isa 29:16;** Ro 9:20–21; [v]**Job 10:3; Isa 19:25**
9 [w]Isa 54:8; 57:17; 60:10; La 5:22; [x]**Isa 43:25;** [y]**Ps 100:3; Isa 51:4**
10 [z]Ps 78:54; **Isa 1:26;** [a]**Dt 29:23**
11 [b]**Lev 26:31; 2Ki 25:9;** Ps 74:3–7; La 2:7; [c]ver 10–11; La 1:7,10
12 [d]**Ge 43:31;** Ps 74:10–11; [e]**Est 4:14; Ps 50:21; 83:1**

Ch. 65

1 [a]Hos 1:10; Ro 9:24–26; 10:20*; [b]Ro 9:30; Eph 2:12; [c]**Ps 14:4; Isa 43:7**
2 [d]**Ps 78:8; Isa 1:2,**23; Ro 10:21*; [e]Ps 81:11–12; **Pr 24:2;** Isa 66:18
3 [f]**Job 1:11;** [g]**Isa 1:29;** [h]**Lev 2:2;** Jer 41:5; 44:17; Eze 23:41
4 [i]**Lev 19:31; Isa 8:19;** [j]**Lev 11:7**
5 [k]**Ps 40:4;** Mt 9:11; Lk 7:39; 18:9–12; [l]Pr 10:26

and all that we treasured[c] lies in
ruins.
12After all this, O LORD, will you hold
yourself back?[d]
Will you keep silent[e] and punish us
beyond measure?

Judgment and Salvation

65 "I revealed myself to those who
did not ask for me;
I was found by those who did not
seek me.[a]
To a nation[b] that did not call on my
name,[c]
I said, 'Here am I, here am I.'
2All day long I have held out my hands
to an obstinate people,[d]
who walk in ways not good,
pursuing their own imaginations[e]—
3a people who continually provoke me
to my very face,[f]
offering sacrifices in gardens[g]
and burning incense[h] on altars of
brick;
4who sit among the graves[i]
and spend their nights keeping
secret vigil;
who eat the flesh of pigs,[j]
and whose pots hold broth of
unclean meat;
5who say, 'Keep away; don't come near
me,
for I am too sacred[k] for you!'
Such people are smoke[l] in my nostrils,
a fire that keeps burning all day.

6"See, it stands written before me;
I will not keep silent[m] but will pay
back[n] in full;
I will pay it back into their laps[o]—
7both your sins[p] and the sins of your
fathers,"[q]
says the LORD.
"Because they burned sacrifices on the
mountains
and defied me on the hills,[r]
I will measure into their laps
the full payment[s] for their former
deeds."

8This is what the LORD says:

"As when juice is still found in a
cluster of grapes[t]

6 [m]**Ps 50:3;** [n]**2Ch 6:23;** Isa 59:18; Jer 16:18; [o]**Ps 79:12;** Eze 9:10; Lk 6:38
7 [p]**Isa 22:14;** [q]Ex 20:5; Jer 32:18; [r]**Isa 57:7;** [s]**Pr 10:24; Isa 10:12** *8* [t]Isa 5:2

b19 Or *We are like those you have never ruled, / like those never called by your name*

and men say, 'Don't destroy it,
there is yet some good in it,'
so will I do on behalf of my servants;[u]
I will not destroy them all.
9I will bring forth descendants[v] from Jacob,
and from Judah those who will possess[w] my mountains;
my chosen[x] people will inherit them,
and there will my servants live.[y]
10Sharon[z] will become a pasture for flocks,[a]
and the Valley of Achor[b] a resting place for herds,
for my people who seek[c] me.

11"But as for you who forsake[d] the LORD
and forget my holy mountain,[e]
who spread a table for Fortune
and fill bowls of mixed wine[f] for Destiny,
12I will destine you for the sword,[g]
and you will all bend down for the slaughter;[h]
for I called but you did not answer,[i]
I spoke but you did not listen.[j]
You did evil in my sight
and chose what displeases me."[k]

13Therefore this is what the Sovereign LORD says:

"My servants will eat,[l]
but you will go hungry;[m]
my servants will drink,[n]
but you will go thirsty;[o]
my servants will rejoice,[p]
but you will be put to shame.[q]
14My servants will sing[r]
out of the joy of their hearts,
but you will cry out[s]
from anguish of heart
and wail in brokenness of spirit.
15You will leave your name
to my chosen ones as a curse;[t]
the Sovereign LORD will put you to death,
but to his servants he will give another name.[u]
16Whoever invokes a blessing[v] in the land
will do so by the God of truth;[w]
he who takes an oath in the land
will swear[x] by the God of truth.
For the past troubles[y] will be forgotten
and hidden from my eyes.

New Heavens and a New Earth

17"Behold, I will create
new heavens and a new earth.[z]
The former things will not be remembered,[a]
nor will they come to mind.
18But be glad and rejoice[b] for ever
in what I will create,
for I will create Jerusalem[c] to be a delight
and its people a joy.
19I will rejoice[d] over Jerusalem
and take delight[e] in my people;
the sound of weeping and of crying[f]
will be heard in it no more.

20"Never again will there be in it
an infant[g] who lives but a few days,
or an old man who does not live out his years;[h]
he who dies at a hundred
will be thought a mere youth;
he who fails to reach[a] a hundred
will be considered accursed.
21They will build houses[i] and dwell in them;
they will plant vineyards and eat their fruit.[j]
22No longer will they build houses and others live in them,[k]
or plant and others eat.
For as the days of a tree,[l]
so will be the days[m] of my people;
my chosen[n] ones will long enjoy
the works of their hands.
23They will not toil in vain[o]
or bear children doomed to misfortune;[p]
for they will be a people blessed[q] by the LORD,
they and their descendants[r] with them.
24Before they call[s] I will answer;[t]
while they are still speaking[u] I will hear.
25The wolf and the lamb[v] will feed together,
and the lion will eat straw like the ox,[w]
but dust will be the serpent's[x] food.
They will neither harm nor destroy
on all my holy mountain,"[y]
says the LORD.

8 [u]Isa 54:17
9 [v]Isa 45:19; [w]Nu 34:13; Isa 60:21; Jer 50:19; Am 9:11–15; [x]Isa 14:1; [y]Isa 32:18
10 [z]1Ch 27:29; Isa 35:2; Ac 9:35; [a]Jer 31:12; 33:12; Eze 34:13–14; [b]Jos 7:26; [c]Isa 51:1
11 [d]Dt 28:20; 29:24–25; 32:15; Isa 1:28; Jer 2:13; 19:4; [e]Dt 33:19; Ps 137:5; [f]Isa 5:22
12 [g]Isa 1:20; 27:1; [h]Isa 30:25; [i]Pr 1:24–25; Isa 41:28; 66:4; Jer 7:27; [j]2Ch 36:15–16; Jer 7:13; 13:11; 25:3; 26:5; [k]Ps 149:7; Isa 1:24; 66:4; Mic 5:15
13 [l]Isa 1:19; [m]Job 18:12; Lk 6:25; [n]Isa 33:16; [o]Isa 3:1; 41:17; [p]Isa 60:5; [q]Isa 61:7; Isa 44:9
14 [r]Ps 109:28; Zep 3:14–20; Jas 5:13; [s]Isa 15:2; Mt 8:12; Lk 13:28
15 [t]Nu 5:27; Ps 102:8; [u]Ge 32:28; Rev 2:17
16 [v]Dt 29:19; [w]Ps 31:5; Rev 3:14; [x]Ps 63:11; Isa 19:18; [y]Job 11:16
17 [z]Isa 41:22; 66:22; 2Co 5:17; 2Pe 3:13; [a]Isa 43:18; Jer 3:16; Rev 7:17
18 [b]Dt 32:43; Ps 98:1–9; Isa 25:9; [c]Rev 21:2
19 [d]Isa 35:10; 62:5; [e]Dt 30:9; [f]Isa 25:8; Rev 7:17
20 [g]Isa 11:8; [h]Ge 5:1–32; 15:15; Ecc 8:13; Zec 8:4
21 [i]Isa 32:18; 61:4; [j]2Ki 19:29; Isa 37:30; Eze 28:26; Am 9:14
22 [k]Dt 28:30; [l]Ps 1:3; 92:12–14; [m]Ps 21:4; 91:16; [n]Isa 14:1
23 [o]Isa 49:4; 1Co 15:58; [p]Dt 28:32,41; Jer 16:3–4; [q]Ge 12:2; Dt 28:3–12; [r]Isa 44:3; Ac 2:39
24 [s]Isa 55:6; Mt 6:8; [t]Job 8:6; Isa 30:19; Zec 10:6; [u]Da 9:20–23; 10:12
25 [v]Isa 11:6; [w]Job 40:15; [x]Ge 3:14; Mic 7:17; [y]Job 5:23; Isa 2:4

[a]20 Or / *the sinner who reaches*

Judgment and Hope

66 This is what the LORD says:
"Heaven is my throne,[a]
and the earth is my footstool.[b]
Where is the house[c] you will build for me?
Where will my resting place be?
2Has not my hand made all these things,[d]
and so they came into being?"
declares the LORD.

"This is the one I esteem:
he who is humble and contrite in spirit,[e]
and trembles at my word.[f]
3But whoever sacrifices a bull[g]
is like one who kills a man,
and whoever offers a lamb,
like one who breaks a dog's neck;
whoever makes a grain offering
is like one who presents pig's[h] blood,
and whoever burns memorial incense,[i]
like one who worships an idol.
They have chosen their own ways,[j]
and their souls delight in their abominations;[k]
4so I also will choose harsh treatment for them
and will bring upon them what they dread.[l]
For when I called, no-one answered,[m]
when I spoke, no-one listened.
They did evil[n] in my sight
and chose what displeases me."[o]

5Hear the word of the LORD,
you who tremble at his word;[p]
"Your brothers who hate[q] you,
and exclude you because of my name, have said,
'Let the LORD be glorified,
that we may see your joy!'
Yet they will be put to shame.[r]
6Hear that uproar from the city,
hear that noise from the temple!
It is the sound[s] of the LORD
repaying[t] his enemies all they deserve.

7"Before she goes into labour,[u]
she gives birth;
before the pains come upon her,
she delivers a son.[v]
8Who has ever heard of such a thing?
Who has ever seen[w] such things?
Can a country be born in a day[x]
or a nation be brought forth in a moment?

Ch. 66
1 [a]2Ch 6:18; Ps 2:4; 9:7; Mt 23:22; [b]1Ki 8:27; Mt 5:34–35; [c]2Sa 7:7; Jn 4:20–21; Ac 7:48; 17:24
2 [d]Isa 40:26; Ac 7:50*; 17:24; [e]Isa 57:15; Mt 5:3–4; Lk 18:13–14; [f]Ezr 9:4
3 [g]Isa 1:11; [h]Lev 11:7; [i]Lev 2:2; [j]Isa 57:17; [k]ver 17; Dt 27:15; Eze 8:9–13
4 [l]Pr 10:24; Isa 10:12; [m]1Sa 8:19; Isa 41:28; [n]2Ki 21:2,4,6; Isa 59:12; [o]Isa 65:12
5 [p]Ezr 9:4; [q]Ps 38:20; Isa 60:15; Jn 15:21; [r]Isa 44:9; Lk 13:17
6 [s]1Sa 2:10; Ps 68:33; [t]Lev 26:28; Isa 65:6; Joel 3:7
7 [u]Isa 54:1; [v]Rev 12:5
8 [w]Isa 64:4; Jer 18:13; [x]Isa 49:20; [y]Isa 49:21
9 [z]Isa 37:3
10 [a]Dt 32:43; Isa 25:9; Ro 15:10; [b]Ps 26:8; [c]Isa 57:19; 61:2
11 [d]Nu 11:12; Isa 60:16; [e]Ge 49:25; [f]Nu 25:1; Isa 25:6
12 [g]Ps 119:165; Isa 9:6; [h]Isa 33:21; [i]Ps 72:3; Isa 60:5; 61:6; [j]Nu 11:12; Isa 60:4
13 [k]Isa 49:15; 1Th 2:7; [l]Isa 40:1; 2Co 1:4
14 [m]Isa 25:9; 60:5; Joel 2:23; [n]Ps 72:16; [o]Ezr 5:5; Isa 41:20; [p]Isa 54:17; [q]Isa 10:5; 30:27
15 [r]Isa 1:31; 42:25; [s]2Ki 2:11; Ps 68:17; [t]2Ki 2:1; [u]Dt 28:20; Ps 9:5; 39:11
16 [v]Isa 30:30; Am 7:4; Mal 4:1; [w]Isa 1:20; 27:1; Eze 14:21; [x]Isa 13:9,11; Jer 2:35; Eze 36:5; [y]Isa 10:4

Yet no sooner is Zion in labour
than she gives birth to her children.[y]
9Do I bring to the moment of birth[z]
and not give delivery?" says the LORD.
"Do I close up the womb
when I bring to delivery?" says your God.
10"Rejoice[a] with Jerusalem and be glad for her,
all you who love[b] her;
rejoice greatly with her,
all you who mourn[c] over her.
11For you will nurse[d] and be satisfied
at her comforting breasts;[e]
you will drink deeply
and delight in her overflowing abundance."[f]

12For this is what the LORD says:

"I will extend peace[g] to her like a river,[h]
and the wealth[i] of nations like a flooding stream;
you will nurse and be carried[j] on her arm
and dandled on her knees.
13As a mother comforts her child,[k]
so will I comfort[l] you;
and you will be comforted over Jerusalem."

14When you see this, your heart will rejoice[m]
and you will flourish[n] like grass;
the hand[o] of the LORD will be made known to his servants,[p]
but his fury[q] will be shown to his foes.
15See, the LORD is coming with fire,[r]
and his chariots[s] are like a whirlwind;[t]
he will bring down his anger with fury,
and his rebuke[u] with flames of fire.
16For with fire[v] and with his sword[w]
the LORD will execute judgment[x]
upon all men,
and many will be those slain[y] by the LORD.

17"Those who consecrate and purify
themselves to go into the gardens,[z] fol-
lowing the one in the midst of[a] those
who eat the flesh of pigs[a] and rats[b] and
other abominable things—they will
meet their end[c] together," declares the
LORD.

17 [z]Isa 1:29; [a]Lev 11:7; [b]Lev 11:29; [c]Ps 37:20; Isa 1:28

[a]17 Or *gardens behind one of your temples, and*

18"And I, because of their actions and
their imaginations,[d] am about to come[b]
and gather all nations[e] and tongues, and
they will come and see my glory.[f]
19"I will set a sign[g] among them, and
I will send some of those who survive[h]
to the nations—to Tarshish,[i] to the
Libyans[c] and Lydians[j] (famous as
archers), to Tubal[k] and Greece,[l] and to
the distant islands[m] that have not heard
of my fame or seen my glory.[n] They will
proclaim my glory among the nations.
20And they will bring[o] all your brothers,
from all the nations, to my holy moun-
tain[p] in Jerusalem as an offering to the
LORD—on horses, in chariots and
wagons, and on mules and camels,"[q]
says the LORD. "They will bring them, as
the Israelites bring their grain offerings,
to the temple of the LORD in ceremonial-
ly clean vessels.[r] 21And I will select some
of them also to be priests[s] and Levites,"
says the LORD.

18 [d]**Pr 24:2; Isa 65:2;** [e]**Isa 2:3; Zec 12:3;** [f]**Ex 16:7; Isa 59:19**
19 [g]Isa 11:10; 49:22; Mt 24:30; [h]**2Ki 19:31;** [i]**Isa 2:16;** [j]Jer 46:9; Eze 27:10; [k]**Ge 10:2;** [l]Jer 31:10; Da 11:18; [m]Isa 11:11; [n]**1Ch 16:24; Isa 24:15**
20 [o]**Isa 11:12; Jer 25:22;** Eze 34:13; [p]**Dt 33:19; Isa 2:2;** Jer 31:23; [q]**Ezr 2:66;** [r]Isa 52:11
21 [s]**Ex 19:6;** 1Pe 2:5,9

22"As the new heavens and the new
earth[t] that I make will endure before
me," declares the LORD, "so will your
name and descendants endure.[u] 23From
one New Moon to another and from one
Sabbath[v] to another, all mankind will
come and bow down[w] before me," says
the LORD. 24"And they will go out and
look upon the dead bodies[x] of those
who rebelled[y] against me; their worm[z]
will not die, nor will their fire be
quenched,[a] and they will be loathsome
to all mankind."

22 [t]**Isa 65:17;** Heb 12:26-27; **2Pe 3:13;** [u]**Isa 48:19;** Jn 10:27-29; 1Pe 1:4-5
23 [v]Eze 46:1-3; [w]**Ps 22:29; Isa 19:21; 44:5;** Rev 15:4
24 [x]**Ps 110:6;** [y]**Isa 1:2;** [z]**Isa 14:11;** [a]**Isa 1:31; Mt 25:41;** Mk 9:48*

[b]*18* The meaning of the Hebrew for this clause is uncertain.
[c]*19* Some Septuagint manuscripts *Put* (Libyans); Hebrew *Pul*

Jeremiah

1 The words of Jeremiah son of
Hilkiah, one of the priests at
Anathoth[a] in the territory of Benjamin.
2The word of the LORD came[b] to him in
the thirteenth year of the reign of Josiah[c]
son of Amon king of Judah, 3and
through the reign of Jehoiakim[d] son of
Josiah king of Judah, down to the fifth
month of the eleventh year of Zedekiah[e]
son of Josiah king of Judah, when the
people of Jerusalem went into exile.[f]

The Call of Jeremiah

4The word of the LORD came to me,
saying,

5"Before I formed you in the womb[g] I
knew[a][h] you,
before you were born[i] I set you
apart;[j]
I appointed you as a prophet to the
nations.[k]"

6"Ah, Sovereign LORD," I said, "I do
not know how to speak;[l] I am only a
child."[m]
7But the LORD said to me, "Do not say,
'I am only a child.' You must go to
everyone I send you to and say what-
ever I command you. 8Do not be afraid[n]
of them, for I am with you[o] and will
rescue[p] you," declares the LORD.[q]
9Then the LORD reached out his hand
and touched[r] my mouth and said to me,
"Now, I have put my words in your
mouth.[s] 10See, today I appoint you over
nations[t] and kingdoms to uproot[u] and
tear down, to destroy and overthrow, to
build and to plant."[v]
11The word of the LORD came to me:
"What do you see, Jeremiah?"[w]
"I see the branch of an almond tree," I
replied.
12The LORD said to me, "You have
seen correctly, for I am watching[b][x] to
see that my word is fulfilled."
13The word of the LORD came to me
again: "What do you see?"[y]
"I see a boiling pot, tilting away from
the north," I answered.
14The LORD said to me, "From the
north[z] disaster will be poured out on all
who live in the land. 15I am about to
summon all the peoples of the northern
kingdoms," declares the LORD.

"Their kings will come and set up their
thrones
in the entrance of the gates of
Jerusalem;
they will come against all her
surrounding walls
and against all the towns of Judah.[a]
16I will pronounce my judgments[b] on
my people
because of their wickedness[c] in
forsaking me,[d]
in burning incense to other gods[e]
and in worshipping[f] what their
hands have made.[g]

17"Get yourself ready! Stand up and
say[h] to them whatever I command you.
Do not be terrified[i] by them, or I will
terrify you before them. 18Today I have
made you[j] a fortified city, an iron pillar
and a bronze wall to stand against the
whole land—against the kings of
Judah, its officials, its priests and the
people of the land. 19They will fight
against you but will not overcome[k] you,
for I am with you[l] and will rescue[m]
you," declares the LORD.

Israel Forsakes God

2 The word[a] of the LORD came to me:
2"Go and proclaim in the hearing
of Jerusalem:

"'I remember the devotion of your
youth,[b]
how as a bride you loved me
and followed me through the desert,[c]
through a land not sown.

Ch. 1

1 [a]**Jos 21:18**
2 [b]Eze 1:3; Hos 1:1; Joel 1:1; [c]**2Ki 22:1**
3 [d]**2Ki 23:34;** [e]**2Ki 24:17;** [f]Ezr 5:12; Jer 52:15
5 [g]**Ps 139:13;** [h]Ps 139:16; [i]**Isa 49:1;** [j]Jn 10:36; [k]ver 10; Jer 25:15–26
6 [l]**Ex 3:11; 6:12;** [m]1Ki 3:7
8 [n]**Ge 15:1; Jos 8:1;** [o]**Ge 26:3; Jos 1:5;** Jer 15:20; [p]ver 19; Jer 15:21; 26:24; 36:26; 42:11; [q]Jer 20:11
9 [r]**Isa 6:7;** [s]**Ex 4:12**
10 [t]Jer 25:17; 46:1; [u]Jer 12:17; [v]Jer 18:7–10; 24:6; 31:4,28
11 [w]Jer 24:3; Am 7:8
12 [x]**Job 29:2;** Jer 44:27
13 [y]Jer 24:3; Zec 4:2; 5:2
14 [z]**Isa 14:31**
15 [a]Jer 4:16; 9:11; 10:22
16 [b]Jer 4:12; [c]**Ge 6:5;** Jer 44:5; [d]Jer 2:13; 17:13; [e]**Ex 20:3;** Jer 7:9; 19:4; 44:3; [f]**Nu 25:3;** [g]Ps 115:4–8; **135:15**
17 [h]ver 7; Jer 7:27; 26:2,15; 42:4; [i]**Dt 31:6; 2Ki 1:15**
18 [j]**Isa 50:7**
19 [k]**Ps 129:2;** [l]**Ge 26:3;** Isa 43:2; Jer 20:11; [m]**ver 8; Pr 20:22;** Ac 26:17

Ch. 2

1 [a]Isa 38:4; Eze 1:3; Mic 1:1
2 [b]Ps 71:17; Isa 54:4; Jer 3:4; Eze 16:8–14,60; Hos 2:15; 11:1; Rev 2:4; [c]**Ex 13:21; Dt 1:19**

[a]5 Or *chose*
[b]12 The Hebrew for *watching* sounds like the Hebrew for *almond tree*.

3Israel was holy[d] to the LORD,[e]
the firstfruits[f] of his harvest;
all who devoured[g] her were held guilty,[h]
and disaster overtook them,' "
declares the LORD.

4Hear the word of the LORD, O house of Jacob,
all you clans of the house of Israel.

5This is what the LORD says:

"What fault did your fathers find in me,
that they strayed so far from me?
They followed worthless idols[i]
and became worthless[j] themselves.
6They did not ask, 'Where is the LORD,
who brought us up out of Egypt[k]
and led us through the barren wilderness,
through a land of deserts[l] and rifts,[m]
a land of drought and darkness,[a]
a land where no-one travels[n] and no-one lives?'
7I brought you into a fertile land
to eat its fruit and rich produce.[o]
But you came and defiled my land
and made my inheritance detestable.[p]
8The priests did not ask,
'Where is the LORD?'
Those who deal with the law did not know me;[q]
the leaders[r] rebelled against me.
The prophets prophesied by Baal,[s]
following worthless idols.[t]

9"Therefore I bring charges[u] against you again,"
declares the LORD.
"And I will bring charges against your children's children.
10Cross over to the coasts of Kittim[b][v]
and look,
send to Kedar[c][w] and observe closely;
see if there has ever been anything like this:
11Has a nation ever changed its gods?
(Yet they are not gods[x] at all.)
But my people have exchanged their[d] Glory[y]
for worthless idols.
12Be appalled at this, O heavens,
and shudder with great horror,"
declares the LORD.
13"My people have committed two sins:
They have forsaken[z] me,
the spring of living water,[a]
and have dug their own cisterns,
broken cisterns that cannot hold water.
14Is Israel a servant, a slave[b] by birth?
Why then has he become plunder?
15Lions[c] have roared;
they have growled at him.
They have laid waste[d] his land;
his towns are burned[e] and deserted.[f]
16Also, the men of Memphis[e][g] and Tahpanhes[h]
have shaved the crown of your head.[f]
17Have you not brought this on yourselves[i]
by forsaking[j] the LORD your God
when he led you in the way?
18Now why go to Egypt[k]
to drink water from the Shihor[g]?[l]
And why go to Assyria[m]
to drink water from the River[h]?[n]
19Your wickedness will punish you;
your backsliding[o] will rebuke[p] you.
Consider then and realise
how evil and bitter[q] it is for you
when you forsake[r] the LORD your God
and have no awe[s] of me,"
declares the Lord,
the LORD Almighty.

20"Long ago you broke off your yoke[t]
and tore off your bonds;[u]
you said, 'I will not serve you!'[v]
Indeed, on every high hill[w]
and under every spreading tree[x]
you lay down as a prostitute.[y]
21I had planted[z] you like a choice vine[a]
of sound and reliable stock.
How then did you turn against me
into a corrupt,[b] wild vine?
22Although you wash[c] yourself with soda[d]
and use an abundance of soap,
the stain of your guilt is still before me,"
declares the Sovereign LORD.[e]
23"How can you say, 'I am not defiled;[f]
I have not run after the Baals'?[g]
See how you behaved in the valley;[h]
consider what you have done.
You are a swift she-camel
running[i] here and there,
24a wild donkey[j] accustomed to the desert,[k]

3 [d]**Dt 7:6;** [e]**Ex 19:6; Dt 7:6;** [f]Lev 23:9–14; Jas 1:18; Rev 14:4; [g]Isa 41:11; Jer 10:25; 30:16; [h]Jer 50:7
5 [i]**Dt 32:21; 1Sa 12:21;** Ps 31:6; [j]2Ki 17:15
6 [k]**Ex 6:6;** Hos 13:4; [l]**Dt 1:19;** [m]**Dt 32:10;** [n]Jer 51:43
7 [o]**Nu 13:27;** Dt 8:7–9; 11:10–12; [p]Ps 106:34–39; Jer 3:9; 7:30; 16:18; Eze 11:21; 36:17
8 [q]**1Sa 2:12;** Jer 4:22; [r]Jer 3:15; 23:1; 25:34; 50:6; [s]**1Ki 18:22;** [t]ver 25; **Isa 40:19; 56:10;** Jer 5:19; 9:14; 16:19; 22:9
9 [u]Jer 25:31; Hos 4:1; Mic 6:2
10 [v]**Ge 10:4;** [w]**Ge 25:13**
11 [x]**Isa 37:19;** Jer 16:20; Gal 4:8; [y]**1Sa 4:21;** Ro 1:23
13 [z]**Dt 31:16; Isa 65:11;** [a]**Isa 12:3;** Jn 4:14
14 [b]Ex 4:22; Jer 31:9
15 [c]Jer 4:7; 50:17; [d]**Isa 1:7;** [e]**2Ki 25:9;** [f]**Lev 26:43**
16 [g]**Isa 19:13;** [h]Jer 43:7–9
17 [i]Jer 4:18; [j]**Isa 1:28;** Jer 17:13; 19:4
18 [k]**Isa 30:2;** [l]**Jos 13:3;** [m]**2Ki 16:7;** Hos 5:13; 7:11; 8:9; [n]**Isa 7:20**
19 [o]Jer 3:11,22; 7:24; 11:10; 14:7; Hos 14:4; [p]Isa 3:9; 59:12; Hos 5:5; [q]**Job 20:14;** Am 8:10; [r]Jer 19:4; [s]**Ps 36:1**
20 [t]**Lev 26:13;** [u]Ps 2:3; Jer 5:5; [v]**Job 21:14;** [w]Isa 57:7; Jer 3:23; 17:2; [x]**Dt 12:2;** [y]**Isa 1:21;** Eze 16:15
21 [z]**Ex 15:17;** [a]**Ps 80:8;** [b]**Isa 5:4**
22 [c]**Ps 51:2;** La 1:8,17; [d]**Job 9:30;** [e]Jer 17:1
23 [f]**Pr 30:12;** [g]ver 25; Jer 9:14; 23:27; [h]**2Ki 23:10;** Jer 7:31; 19:2; 31:40; [i]ver 33; Jer 31:22
24 [j]**Ge 16:12;** Jer 14:6; [k]**Job 39:6**

[a]6 Or *and the shadow of death*
[b]10 That is, Cyprus and western coastlands
[c]10 The home of Bedouin tribes in the Syro-Arabian desert
[d]11 Masoretic Text; an ancient Hebrew scribal tradition *my*
[e]16 Hebrew *Noph*
[f]16 Or *have cracked your skull*
[g]18 That is, a branch of the Nile
[h]18 That is, the Euphrates

sniffing the wind in her craving—
in her heat who can restrain her?
Any males that pursue her need not
tire themselves;
at mating time they will find her.
25Do not run until your feet are bare
and your throat is dry.
But you said, 'It's no use![l]
I love foreign gods,[m]
and I must go after them.'[n]

26"As a thief is disgraced[o] when he is
caught,
so the house of Israel is disgraced—
they, their kings and their officials,
their priests[p] and their prophets.[q]
27They say to wood,[r] 'You are my
father,'
and to stone,[s] 'You gave me birth.'
They have turned their backs[t] to me
and not their faces;[u]
yet when they are in trouble,[v] they
say,
'Come and save[w] us!'
28Where then are the gods[x] you made
for yourselves?
Let them come if they can save you
when you are in trouble![y]
For you have as many gods
as you have towns,[z] O Judah.

29"Why do you bring charges against
me?
You have all[a] rebelled against me,"
declares the LORD.
30"In vain I punished your people;
they did not respond to correction.[b]
Your sword has devoured your
prophets[c]
like a ravening lion.

31"You of this generation, consider
the word of the LORD:

"Have I been a desert to Israel
or a land of great darkness?[d]
Why do my people say, 'We are free to
roam;
we will come to you no more'?[e]
32Does a maiden forget her jewellery,
a bride her wedding ornaments?
Yet my people have forgotten[f] me,
days without number.
33How skilled you are at pursuing[g] love!
Even the worst of women can learn
from your ways.
34On your clothes men find
the lifeblood[h] of the innocent poor,
though you did not catch them
breaking in.[i]
Yet in spite of all this
35 you say, 'I am innocent;[j]
he is not angry with me.'
But I will pass judgment[k] on you
because you say, 'I have not
sinned.'[l]
36Why do you go about so much,
changing[m] your ways?
You will be disappointed by Egypt[n]
as you were by Assyria.
37You will also leave that place
with your hands on your head,[o]
for the LORD has rejected those you
trust;
you will not be helped[p] by them.

3 "If a man divorces[a] his wife
and she leaves him and marries
another man,
should he return to her again?
Would not the land be completely
defiled?[b]
But you have lived as a prostitute with
many lovers[c]—
would you now return to me?"[d]
declares the LORD.
2"Look up to the barren heights[e] and
see.
Is there any place where you have
not been ravished?
By the roadside[f] you sat waiting for
lovers,
sat like a nomad[a] in the desert.
You have defiled the land[g]
with your prostitution[h] and
wickedness.
3Therefore the showers have been
withheld,[i]
and no spring rains[j] have fallen.
Yet you have the brazen[k] look of a
prostitute;
you refuse to blush with shame.[l]
4Have you not just called to me:
'My Father,[m] my friend from my
youth,[n]
5will you always be angry?[o]
Will your wrath continue for ever?'
This is how you talk,
but you do all the evil you can."

Unfaithful Israel

6During the reign of King Josiah,[p] the
LORD said to me, "Have you seen what
faithless[q] Israel has done? She has gone
up on every high hill and under every
spreading tree[r] and has committed
adultery[s] there. 7I thought that after she
had done all this she would return to me
but she did not, and her unfaithful sis-
ter[t] Judah saw it.[u] 8I gave faithless Israel[v]

25 [l]**Isa 57:10;** [m]Dt 32:16; Jer 3:13; 14:10; [n]**ver 8,23**
26 [o]Jer 48:27; La 1:7; Eze 16:54; 36:4; [p]Eze 22:26; [q]Jer 32:32; 44:17,21
27 [r]Jer 10:8; [s]Jer 3:9; [t]**1Ki 14:9; 2Ch 29:6;** Ps 14:3; Eze 8:16; [u]Jer 18:17; 32:33; Eze 7:22; [v]Jdg 10:10; Isa 26:16; [w]Isa 37:20; Hos 5:15
28 [x]**Isa 45:20;** [y]**Dt 32:37; Isa 40:19;** [z]**2Ki 17:29**
29 [a]Jer 5:1; 6:13; Da 9:11; Mic 3:11; 7:2
30 [b]**Lev 26:23;** [c]**Ne 9:26; Jer 11:21;** Ac 7:52; 1Th 2:15
31 [d]Isa 45:19; [e]**Job 21:14**
32 [f]**Dt 32:18; Isa 57:11**
33 [g]**ver 23**
34 [h]**2Ki 21:16; Pr 6:17;** [i]**Ex 22:2**
35 [j]**Pr 30:12;** [k]Isa 66:16; Jer 25:31; 39:7; 45:5; Eze 17:20; 20:35; Joel 3:2; [l]**2Sa 12:13;** 1Jn 1:8,10
36 [m]Jer 31:22; [n]**Ps 108:12; Isa 30:2–3,7;** Jer 37:7
37 [o]2Sa 13:19; [p]Jer 37:7

Ch. 3

1 [a]Dt 24:1–4; [b]**Ge 3:17;** [c]**2Ki 16:7; Isa 1:21;** Jer 2:25; 4:30; La 1:2; Eze 16:26,29; Hos 2:5,12; 3:1; [d]Hos 2:7
2 [e]ver 21; [f]Ge 38:14; Eze 16:25; [g]ver 9; [h]**Nu 15:39; Isa 1:21**
3 [i]Lev 26:19; Jer 5:25; Am 4:7; [j]**Dt 11:14;** Jer 14:4; Joel 1:10; [k]Eze 3:7; 16:30; [l]Jer 6:15; 8:12; Zep 2:1; 3:5
4 [m]ver 19; **Dt 32:6; Ps 89:26;** Isa 63:16; 64:8; Jer 31:9; [n]**Jer 2:2**
5 [o]**Ps 103:9; Isa 54:9**

6 [p]**1Ch 3:14;** [q]ver 12,22; **Isa 24:16;** Jer 31:22; 49:4; [r]**Dt 12:2;** Jer 17:2; Eze 20:28; Hos 4:13; [s]**Lev 17:7;** Jer 2:20 *7* [t]Eze 16:46; 23:2,11; [u]Am 4:8
8 [v]Jer 11:10

[a]2 Or *an Arab*

her certificate of divorce[w] and sent her
away because of all her adulteries. Yet I
saw that her unfaithful sister Judah had
no fear;[x] she also went out and commit-
ted adultery. 9Because Israel's immoral-
ity mattered so little to her, she defiled
the land[y] and committed adultery[z] with
stone[a] and wood.[b] 10In spite of all this,
her unfaithful sister Judah did not re-
turn[c] to me with all her heart, but only in
pretence,[d]" declares the LORD.[e]
11The LORD said to me, "Faithless
Israel is more righteous[f] than unfaith-
ful[g] Judah.[h] 12Go, proclaim this message
towards the north:[i]

" 'Return,[j] faithless[k] Israel,' declares
the LORD,
'I will frown on you no longer,
for I am merciful,'[l] declares the LORD,
'I will not be angry[m] for ever.
13Only acknowledge[n] your guilt—
you have rebelled against the LORD
your God,
you have scattered your favours to
foreign gods[o]
under every spreading tree,[p]
and have not obeyed[q] me,' "
declares the LORD.

14"Return,[r] faithless people," de-
clares the LORD, "for I am your hus-
band.[s] I will choose you—one from a
town and two from a clan—and bring
you to Zion. 15Then I will give you
shepherds[t] after my own heart,[u] who
will lead you with knowledge and
understanding. 16In those days, when
your numbers have increased greatly in
the land," declares the LORD, "men will
no longer say, 'The ark[v] of the covenant
of the LORD.' It will never enter their
minds or be remembered;[w] it will not
be missed, nor will another one be
made. 17At that time they will call
Jerusalem The Throne[x] of the LORD, and
all nations[y] will gather in Jerusalem to
honour[z] the name of the LORD. No
longer will they follow the stubborn-
ness of their evil hearts.[a] 18In those days
the house of Judah will join the house
of Israel,[b] and together[c] they will come
from a northern[d] land to the land[e] I gave
your forefathers as an inheritance.
19"I myself said,

" 'How gladly would I treat you like
sons
and give you a desirable land,[f]
the most beautiful inheritance[g] of
any nation.'
I thought you would call me 'Father'[h]
and not turn away from following
me.

8 [w]**Dt 4:27; 24:1;** [x]Eze 16:47; 23:11
9 [y]ver 2; [z]**Lev 17:7; Isa 1:21;** [a]**Isa 57:6;** [b]Jer 2:27
10 [c]Isa 31:6; Am 4:9; Hag 2:17; [d]Jer 12:2; Eze 33:31; [e]**2Ki 17:19**
11 [f]Eze 16:52; 23:11; [g]ver 7; [h]**Jer 2:19**
12 [i]2Ki 17:3–6; [j]ver 14; **Dt 4:30;** Jer 31:21–22; Eze 14:6; 33:11; Hos 14:1; [k]**ver 6;** [l]**1Ki 3:26; Ps 6:2;** [m]**Ps 103:9; Isa 54:9**
13 [n]Dt 30:1–3; Jer 14:20; 1Jn 1:9; [o]**Jer 2:25;** [p]**Dt 12:2;** [q]ver 25; Jer 22:21
14 [r]**ver 12; Job 22:23;** Jer 4:1; [s]**Isa 54:5**
15 [t]**Isa 31:4;** [u]Ac 13:22
16 [v]**Nu 3:31; 1Ch 15:25;** [w]**Isa 65:17**
17 [x]**Ps 47:8;** Jer 17:12; 33:16; Eze 1:26; 43:7; 48:35; [y]**Isa 2:3;** Mic 4:1; [z]**Ps 22:23;** Jer 13:11; 33:9; [a]Ps 81:12; Jer 7:24; 9:14; 11:8; 13:10; 16:12; 18:12
18 [b]Jer 30:3; Eze 37:19; [c]**Isa 11:13;** Jer 50:4; [d]Jer 16:15; 31:8; [e]Dt 31:7; **Isa 14:1;** Eze 11:17; 37:22; Am 9:15
19 [f]**Dt 8:7;** [g]Ps 106:24; Eze 20:6; [h]**ver 4; Ex 4:22; 2Sa 7:14**
20 [i]**Isa 24:16**
21 [j]ver 2; [k]Jer 31:18; [l]**Isa 57:11**
22 [m]**ver 12; Job 22:23;** [n]**Isa 30:26;** 57:18; Jer 33:6; Hos 6:1; [o]**Jer 2:19**
23 [p]**Jer 2:20;** [q]Ps 3:8; Jer 17:14
24 [r]Jer 11:13; Hos 9:10

20But like a woman unfaithful to her
husband,
so you have been unfaithful[i] to me,
O house of Israel,"
declares the LORD.

21A cry is heard on the barren heights,[j]
the weeping[k] and pleading of the
people of Israel,
because they have perverted their
ways
and have forgotten[l] the LORD their
God.

22"Return,[m] faithless people;
I will cure[n] you of backsliding."[o]

"Yes, we will come to you,
for you are the LORD our God.
23Surely the ⌊idolatrous⌋ commotion on
the hills[p]
and mountains is a deception;
surely in the LORD our God
is the salvation[q] of Israel.
24From our youth shameful[r] gods have
consumed
the fruits of our fathers' labour—
their flocks and herds,
their sons and daughters.
25Let us lie down in our shame,[s]
and let our disgrace cover us.
We have sinned[t] against the LORD our
God,
both we and our fathers;[u]
from our youth[v] till this day
we have not obeyed[w] the LORD our
God."

4

"If you will return,[a] O Israel,
return to me,"
declares the LORD.
"If you put your detestable idols[b] out
of my sight
and no longer go astray,
2and if in a truthful, just and righteous
way
you swear,[c] 'As surely as the LORD
lives,'[d]
then the nations will be blessed[e] by
him
and in him they will glory.[f]"

3This is what the LORD says to the men
of Judah and to Jerusalem:

"Break up your unploughed ground[g]
and do not sow among thorns.[h]

25 [s]**Ezr 9:6;** Jer 31:19; Da 9:7; [t]**Jdg 10:10; 1Ki 8:47;** [u]Jer 14:20; [v]**Ps 25:7; Jer 22:21;** [w]**ver 13;** Eze 2:3

Ch. 4

1 [a]**Dt 4:30; 2Ki 17:13; Hos 12:6;** [b]**2Ki 21:4;** Jer 16:18; 35:15; Eze 8:5
2 [c]Dt 10:20; **Isa 19:18;** 65:16; [d]**Nu 14:21;** Jer 5:2; 12:16; 44:26; Hos 4:15; [e]**Ge 12:2;** Gal 3:8; [f]Jer 9:24
3 [g]Hos 10:12; [h]Mk 4:18

4Circumcise yourselves to the LORD,
circumcise your hearts,[i]
you men of Judah and people of Jerusalem,
or my wrath[j] will break out and burn like fire[k]
because of the evil[l] you have done—
burn with no-one to quench[m] it.

Disaster From the North

5"Announce in Judah and proclaim[n] in Jerusalem and say:
'Sound the trumpet[o] throughout the land!'
Cry aloud and say:
'Gather together!
Let us flee to the fortified cities!'[p]
6Raise the signal[q] to go to Zion!
Flee for safety without delay!
For I am bringing disaster[r] from the north,[s]
even terrible destruction."

7A lion[t] has come out of his lair;[u]
a destroyer[v] of nations has set out.
He has left his place
to lay waste[w] your land.
Your towns will lie in ruins[x]
without inhabitant.
8So put on sackcloth,[y]
lament[z] and wail,
for the fierce anger[a] of the LORD
has not turned away from us.

9"In that day," declares the LORD,
"the king and the officials will lose heart,[b]
the priests will be horrified,
and the prophets will be appalled."[c]

10Then I said, "Ah, Sovereign LORD,
how completely you have deceived[d] this
people and Jerusalem by saying, 'You
will have peace,'[e] when the sword is at
our throats."
11At that time this people and Jeru-
salem will be told, "A scorching wind[f]
from the barren heights in the desert
blows towards my people, but not to
winnow or cleanse; 12a wind[g] too strong
for that comes from me.[a] Now I pro-
nounce my judgments[h] against them."

13Look! He advances like the clouds,[i]
his chariots[j] come like a whirlwind,[k]
his horses[l] are swifter than eagles.[m]
Woe to us! We are ruined![n]
14O Jerusalem, wash[o] the evil from your heart and be saved.[p]
How long[q] will you harbour wicked thoughts?

15A voice is announcing from Dan,[r]
proclaiming disaster from the hills of Ephraim.[s]
16"Tell this to the nations,
proclaim it to Jerusalem:
'A besieging army is coming from a distant land,[t]
raising a war cry[u] against the cities of Judah.[v]
17They surround[w] her like men guarding a field,
because she has rebelled[x] against me,'"
declares the LORD.
18"Your own conduct and actions[y]
have brought this upon you.[z]
This is your punishment.
How bitter[a] it is!
How it pierces to the heart!"

19Oh, my anguish, my anguish![b]
I writhe in pain.[c]
Oh, the agony of my heart!
My heart pounds[d] within me,
I cannot keep silent.[e]
For I have heard the sound of the trumpet;[f]
I have heard the battle cry.[g]
20Disaster follows disaster;[h]
the whole land lies in ruins.[i]
In an instant my tents[j] are destroyed,
my shelter in a moment.
21How long must I see the battle standard[k]
and hear the sound of the trumpet?[l]

22"My people are fools;[m]
they do not know me.[n]
They are senseless children;
they have no understanding.[o]
They are skilled in doing evil;[p]
they know not how to do good."[q]

23I looked at the earth,
and it was formless and empty;[r]
and at the heavens,
and their light[s] was gone.
24I looked at the mountains,
and they were quaking;[t]
all the hills were swaying.
25I looked, and there were no people;

4 [i]**Lev 26:41;** [j]Zep 1:18; 2:2; [k]**Job 41:21;** [l]**Ex 32:22;** [m]Isa 1:31; Am 5:6
5 [n]Jer 5:20; 11:2,6; [o]**ver 21; Nu 10:2**,7; **Job 39:24;** [p]**Jos 10:20**
6 [q]ver 21; Ps 74:4; **Isa 11:10**; 31:9; Jer 50:2; [r]Jer 11:11; 18:11; [s]**Isa 14:31**; Jer 50:3
7 [t]**2Ki 24:1; Jer 2:15;** [u]Jer 25:38; Hos 5:14; 13:7; Na 2:12; [v]Jer 6:26; 15:8; 22:7; 48:8; 51:1,53; Eze 21:31; 25:7; [w]**Isa 1:7**; Eze 12:20; [x]ver 29; **Lev 26:31; Isa 6:11**
8 [y]1Ki 21:27; **Isa 3:24**; Jer 6:26; Eze 7:18; Joel 1:8; [z]Jer 7:29; 9:20; Am 5:1; [a]**Isa 10:4; Jer 30:24**
9 [b]**1Sa 17:32;** [c]**Isa 29:9**
10 [d]**Ex 5:23;** 2Th 2:11; [e]Isa 30:10; Jer 6:14; 8:11; 14:13; 23:17; Eze 13:10; Mic 3:5; 1Th 5:3
11 [f]**Ge 41:6; Lev 26:33; Job 1:19**
12 [g]**Isa 64:6;** [h]Jer 1:16
13 [i]2Sa 22:10; Isa 19:1; [j]Isa 66:15; Eze 26:10; Na 2:4; [k]**2Ki 2:1;** [l]Hab 3:8; [m]**Dt 28:49;** Hab 1:8; [n]ver 20, 27; Isa 6:11; 24:3; Jer 7:34; 9:11,19; 12:11; 25:11; 44:6; Mic 2:4
14 [o]**Ru 3:3; Ps 51:2;** Jas 4:8; [p]Isa 45:22; [q]**Ps 6:3**
15 [r]**Ge 30:6;** [s]Jer 31:6
16 [t]**Dt 28:49;** [u]ver 19; Eze 21:22; [v]**Jer 1:15**
17 [w]**2Ki 25:1**,4; [x]**1Sa 12:15;** Jer 5:23
18 [y]Ps 107:17; **Isa 1:28;** Jer 5:25; [z]Jer 2:17; [a]Jer 2:19
19 [b]Isa 22:4; Jer 6:24; 9:10; La 1:20; [c]**Job 6:10; 14:22;** Jer 10:19; [d]**Job 37:1;** Jer 23:9; [e]**Job 4:2;** Jer 20:9; [f]**ver 21; Nu 10:2; Job 39:24;** [g]**ver 16;** Nu 10:9; Jer 49:2; Zep 1:16
20 [h]**Dt 31:17;** [i]**ver 13;** [j]**Nu 24:5;** Jer 10:20; La 2:4
21 [k]**ver 6; Nu 2:2; Isa 18:3;** [l]ver 5,19; **Jos 6:20;** Jer 6:1; Hos 5:8; Am 3:6; Zep 1:16
22 [m]Jer 5:21; 10:8; [n]**Isa 1:3**; 27:11; Jer 2:8; 8:7; Hos 5:4; 6:6; [o]**Ps 14:4; 53:2;** [p]Jer 13:23; **1Co 14:20;** [q]**Ps 36:3**
23 [r]**Ge 1:2;** [s]ver 28; **Job 9:7;** 30:26; **Isa 5:30;** 59:9; La 3:2
24 [t]**Ex 19:18; Job 9:6**

[a]12 Or *comes at my command*

every bird in the sky had flown
away.[u]
26I looked, and the fruitful land was a
desert;[v]
all its towns lay in ruins[w]
before the LORD, before his fierce
anger.[x]

27This is what the LORD says:

"The whole land will be ruined,[y]
though I will not destroy[z] it
completely.
28Therefore the earth will mourn[a]
and the heavens above grow dark,[b]
because I have spoken and will not
relent,[c]
I have decided and will not turn
back.[d]"

29At the sound of horsemen and
archers[e]
every town takes to flight.[f]
Some go into the thickets;
some climb up among the rocks.[g]
All the towns are deserted;[h]
no-one lives in them.

30What are you doing,[i] O devastated
one?
Why dress yourself in scarlet
and put on jewels[j] of gold?
Why shade your eyes with paint?[k]
You adorn yourself in vain.
Your lovers[l] despise you;
they seek your life.[m]

31I hear a cry as of a woman in labour,[n]
a groan as of one bearing her first
child—
the cry of the Daughter of Zion[o]
gasping for breath,[p]
stretching out her hands[q] and
saying,
"Alas! I am fainting;
my life is given over to murderers."[r]

Not One Is Upright

5 "Go up and down[a] the streets of
Jerusalem,
look around and consider,[b]
search through her squares.
If you can find but one person[c]
who deals honestly[d] and seeks the
truth,
I will forgive[e] this city.
2Although they say, 'As surely as the
LORD lives,'[f]
still they are swearing falsely.[g]"

3O LORD, do not your eyes[h] look for
truth?
You struck[i] them, but they felt no
pain;
you crushed them but they refused
correction.[j]
They made their faces harder than
stone[k]
and refused to repent.[l]
4I thought, "These are only the poor;
they are foolish,[m]
for they do not know[n] the way of the
LORD,
the requirements of their God.
5So I will go to the leaders[o]
and speak to them;
surely they know the way of the LORD,
the requirements of their God."
But with one accord they too had
broken off the yoke
and torn off the bonds.[p]
6Therefore a lion from the forest[q] will
attack them,
a wolf from the desert will ravage[r]
them,
a leopard[s] will lie in wait near their
towns
to tear to pieces any who venture
out,
for their rebellion is great
and their backslidings many.[t]

7"Why should I forgive you?
Your children have forsaken me
and sworn[u] by gods that are not
gods.[v]
I supplied all their needs,
yet they committed adultery[w]
and thronged to the houses of
prostitutes.[x]
8They are well-fed, lusty stallions,
each neighing for another man's
wife.[y]
9Should I not punish them for this?"[z]
declares the LORD.
"Should I not avenge[a] myself
on such a nation as this?

10"Go through her vineyards and
ravage them,
but do not destroy them
completely.[b]
Strip off her branches,
for these people do not belong to the
LORD.
11The house of Israel and the house of
Judah
have been utterly unfaithful[c] to
me,"
declares the LORD.

25 [u]Jer 7:20; 9:10; 12:4; Hos 4:3; Zep 1:3
26 [v]**Ge 13:10**; Jer 12:4; 23:10; [w]**Isa 6:11**; [x]Jer 12:13; 25:38
27 [y]**ver 13**; [z]**Lev 26:44**; Jer 5:10,18; 12:12; 30:11; 46:28; Eze 20:17; Am 9:8
28 [a]Jer 12:4,11; 14:2; Hos 4:3; [b]**ver 23**; [c]**Nu 23:19**; [d]ver 8; Jer 23:20; 30:24
29 [e]**ver 13**; Jer 6:23; 8:16; [f]2Ki 25:4; [g]**Ex 33:22; 1Sa 26:20**; [h]**ver 7; Isa 6:12**
30 [i]Isa 10:3–4; [j]Eze 16:11; 23:40; [k]**2Ki 9:30**; [l]Job 19:14; La 1:2; Eze 23:9,22; [m]**Ps 35:4**
31 [n]**Ge 3:16**; Jer 6:24; 13:21; 22:23; 30:6; Mic 4:10; [o]**Ps 9:14**; [p]Isa 42:14; [q]Isa 1:15; La 1:17; [r]**Dt 32:25**; La 2:21

Ch. 5

1 [a]2Ch 16:9; Eze 22:30; [b]Ps 45:10; [c]Ge 18:32; **Jer 2:29**; [d]ver 31; Jer 14:14; Eze 13:6; [e]**Ge 18:24**
2 [f]**Jer 4:2**; [g]**Lev 19:12**
3 [h]2Ch 16:9; [i]**Isa 9:13**; [j]**Lev 26:23**; [k]Jer 7:26; 19:15; Eze 3:8–9; 36:26; Zec 7:12; [l]**2Ch 28:22; Isa 1:5**; Eze 2:4–5; Am 4:6; Zec 7:11
4 [m]**ver 21; Jer 4:22**; [n]**Pr 10:21; Isa 1:3**
5 [o]Mic 3:1,9; [p]**Jer 2:20**
6 [q]**Ps 17:12**; [r]**Lev 26:22**; [s]Hos 13:7; [t]Jer 14:7; 30:14
7 [u]**Jos 23:7**; [v]Dt 32:21; Jer 2:11; 16:20; Gal 4:8; [w]**Nu 25:1**; [x]Jer 13:27
8 [y]Jer 29:23; Eze 22:11; 33:26
9 [z]ver 29; Jer 9:9; [a]**Isa 57:6**
10 [b]**Jer 4:27**; Am 9:8
11 [c]**1Ki 19:10; Ps 73:27; Isa 24:16**

12They have lied[d] about the LORD;
they said, "He will do nothing!
No harm will come to us;[e]
we will never see sword or famine.[f]
13The prophets[g] are but wind[h]
and the word is not in them;
so let what they say be done to
them."

14Therefore this is what the LORD God
Almighty says:

"Because the people have spoken
these words,
I will make my words in your
mouth[i] a fire[j]
and these people the wood it
consumes.[k]
15O house of Israel," declares the LORD,
"I am bringing a distant nation[l]
against you—
an ancient and enduring nation,
a people whose language[m] you do
not know,
whose speech you do not
understand.
16Their quivers[n] are like an open grave;
all of them are mighty warriors.
17They will devour[o p] your harvests and
food,
devour[q r] your sons and daughters;
they will devour[s] your flocks and
herds,
devour your vines and fig-trees.[t]
With the sword[u] they will destroy
the fortified cities[v] in which you
trust.[w]

18"Yet even in those days," declares
the LORD, "I will not destroy[x] you com-
pletely. 19And when the people ask,[y]
'Why has the LORD our God done all this
to us?' you will tell them, 'As you have
forsaken me and served foreign gods[z] in
your own land, so now you will serve
foreigners[a] in a land not your own.'

20"Announce this to the house of Jacob
and proclaim[b] it in Judah:
21Hear this, you foolish and senseless
people,[c]
who have eyes[d] but do not see,
who have ears but do not hear:[e]
22Should you not fear[f] me?" declares the
LORD.
"Should you not tremble[g] in my
presence?
I made the sand a boundary for the
sea,[h]
an everlasting barrier it cannot
cross.
The waves may roll, but they cannot
prevail;
they may roar,[i] but they cannot
cross it.
23But these people have stubborn and
rebellious[j] hearts;
they have turned aside[k] and gone
away.
24They do not say to themselves,
'Let us fear[l] the LORD our God,
who gives autumn and spring rains[m]
in season,
who assures us of the regular weeks
of harvest.'[n]
25Your wrongdoings have kept these
away;
your sins have deprived you of
good.[o]

26"Among my people are wicked[p] men
who lie in wait[q] like men who snare
birds
and like those who set traps[r] to catch
men.
27Like cages full of birds,
their houses are full of deceit;[s]
they have become rich[t] and powerful
28 and have grown fat[u] and sleek.
Their evil deeds have no limit;
they do not plead the case of the
fatherless[v] to win it,
they do not defend the rights of the
poor.[w]
29Should I not punish them for this?"
declares the LORD.
"Should I not avenge[x] myself
on such a nation as this?

30"A horrible[y] and shocking thing
has happened in the land:
31The prophets prophesy lies,[z]
the priests[a] rule by their own
authority,
and my people love it this way.
But what will you do in the end?[b]

Jerusalem Under Siege

6 "Flee for safety, people of
Benjamin!
Flee from Jerusalem!
Sound the trumpet[a] in Tekoa![b]
Raise the signal over Beth
Hakkerem![c]
For disaster looms out of the north,[d]
even terrible destruction.
2I will destroy the Daughter of Zion,[e]
so beautiful and delicate.[f]
3Shepherds[g] with their flocks will come
against her;
they will pitch their tents round[h]
her,
each tending his own portion."

12 [d]Isa 28:15; [e]Jer 23:17; [f]Jer 14:13; 27:8
13 [g]Jer 14:15; [h]2Ch 36:16; Job 6:26
14 [i]Hos 6:5; [j]Ps 39:3; Jer 23:29; [k]Isa 1:31
15 [l]Dt 28:49; 2Ki 24:2; [m]Ge 11:7; Isa 28:11
16 [n]Job 39:23
17 [o]Isa 1:7; Jer 8:16; 30:16; [p]Lev 26:16; [q]Jer 50:7,17; [r]Dt 28:32; [s]Dt 28:31; [t]Nu 16:14; Jer 8:13; Hos 2:12; [u]Lev 26:25; [v]Jos 10:20; [w]Dt 28:33
18 [x]Jer 4:27
19 [y]Dt 4:28; 1Ki 9:9; [z]Jer 2:8; 15:14; 16:13; 17:4; [a]Dt 28:48
20 [b]Jer 4:5
21 [c]ver 4; Dt 32:6; Jer 4:22; Hab 2:18; [d]Isa 6:10; Eze 12:2; [e]Dt 29:4; Isa 42:20; Mt 13:15; Mk 8:18
22 [f]Dt 28:58; [g]Job 4:14; Isa 64:2; [h]Ge 1:9; [i]Ps 46:3
23 [j]Dt 21:18; [k]Ps 14:3
24 [l]Dt 6:24; [m]Lev 26:4; 2Sa 1:21; Jas 5:7; [n]Ge 8:22; Ac 14:17
25 [o]Ps 84:11
26 [p]Mt 7:15; [q]Ps 10:8; [r]Ecc 9:12; Jer 9:8; Hos 5:1; Mic 7:2
27 [s]Jer 5:8; 9:6; [t]Jer 12:1
28 [u]Dt 32:15; [v]Zec 7:10; [w]Ex 22:21–24; Ps 82:3; Isa 1:23; Jer 7:6; Eze 16:49; Am 5:12
29 [x]Isa 57:6
30 [y]ver 30–31; Jer 18:13; 23:14; Hos 6:10
31 [z]ver 1; Mic 2:11; [a]La 4:13; [b]Hos 9:5

Ch. 6

1 [a]Nu 10:7; Jer 4:21; [b]2Ch 11:6; Am 1:1; [c]Ne 3:14; [d]Jer 4:6
2 [e]Ps 9:14; [f]La 4:5
3 [g]Jer 12:10; [h]2Ki 25:4; Lk 19:43

4"Prepare for battle against her!
Arise, let us attack at noon![i]
But, alas, the daylight is fading,
and the shadows of evening grow
long.
5So arise, let us attack at night
and destroy her fortresses!"

6This is what the LORD Almighty says:

"Cut down the trees[j]
and build siege ramps[k] against
Jerusalem.
This city must be punished;
it is filled with oppression.[l]
7As a well pours out its water,
so she pours out her wickedness.
Violence[m] and destruction[n] resound in
her;
her sickness and wounds are ever
before me.
8Take warning, O Jerusalem,
or I will turn away[o] from you
and make your land desolate
so that no-one can live in it."

9This is what the LORD Almighty says:

"Let them glean the remnant[p] of Israel
as thoroughly as a vine;
pass your hand over the branches
again,
like one gathering grapes."

10To whom can I speak and give
warning?
Who will listen[q] to me?
Their ears are closed[a r]
so that they cannot hear.[s]
The word[t] of the LORD is offensive to
them;
they find no pleasure in it.
11But I am full of the wrath[u] of the LORD,
and I cannot hold it in.[v]

"Pour it out on the children in the
street
and on the young men[w] gathered
together;
both husband and wife will be caught
in it,
and the old, those weighed down
with years.[x]
12Their houses will be turned over to
others,[y]
together with their fields and their
wives,[z]
when I stretch out my hand[a]
against those who live in the land,"
declares the LORD.
13"From the least to the greatest,
all[b] are greedy for gain;[c]
prophets and priests alike,
all practise deceit.[d]
14They dress the wound of my people
as though it were not serious.
'Peace, peace,' they say,
when there is no peace.[e]
15Are they ashamed of their loathsome
conduct?
No, they have no shame at all;
they do not even know how to
blush.[f]
So they will fall among the fallen;
they will be brought down when I
punish[g] them,"
says the LORD.

16This is what the LORD says:

"Stand at the crossroads and look;
ask for the ancient paths,[h]
ask where the good way[i] is, and walk
in it,
and you will find rest[j] for your
souls.
But you said, 'We will not walk
in it.'
17I appointed watchmen[k] over you and
said,
'Listen to the sound of the trumpet!'[l]
But you said, 'We will not listen.'[m]
18Therefore hear, O nations;
observe, O witnesses,
what will happen to them.
19Hear, O earth:[n]
I am bringing disaster[o] on this people,
the fruit of their schemes,[p]
because they have not listened to my
words[q]
and have rejected my law.[r]
20What do I care about incense from
Sheba[s]
or sweet calamus[t] from a distant
land?
Your burnt offerings are not
acceptable;[u]
your sacrifices[v] do not please me."[w]

21Therefore this is what the LORD says:

"I will put obstacles before this
people.
Fathers and sons alike will stumble[x]
over them;
neighbours and friends will
perish."

22This is what the LORD says:

"Look, an army is coming
from the land of the north;[y]
a great nation is being stirred up
from the ends of the earth.[z]

4 [i]Jer 15:8; 22:7
6 [j]Dt 20:19–20; [k]**2Sa 20:15**; Jer 32:24; 52:4; Eze 26:8; [l]**Dt 28:33**; Jer 25:38; Zep 3:1
7 [m]**Ps 55:9; Isa 58:4**; [n]Jer 20:8
8 [o]Eze 23:18
9 [p]**Ge 45:7**
10 [q]Jer 7:13,24; 35:15; [r]Jer 4:4; Ac 7:51; [s]**Isa 42:20**; [t]Jer 15:10,15; 20:8
11 [u]Jer 7:20; 15:17; [v]Job 32:20; Jer 20:9; [w]**2Ch 36:17; Isa 40:30**; [x]La 2:21
12 [y]**Dt 28:30**; Mic 2:4; [z]1Ki 11:4; Jer 8:10; 29:23; 38:22; 43:6; 44:9,15; [a]Isa 5:25; Jer 21:5; 32:21; Eze 6:14; 35:3; Zep 1:4
13 [b]**Jer 2:29**; [c]**Isa 56:11**; [d]La 4:13
14 [e]**Isa 30:10; Jer 4:10**
15 [f]Jer 3:3; 8:10–12; Mic 3:7; Zec 13:4; [g]2Ch 25:16; Jer 27:15
16 [h]Jer 18:15; [i]**1Ki 8:36; Ps 119:3**; [j]**Jos 1:13; Isa 11:10**; Mt 11:29
17 [k]**Isa 52:8**; [l]**Ex 20:18**; [m]Jer 11:7–8; Eze 33:4; Zec 1:4
19 [n]**Dt 4:26**; Jer 22:29; Mic 1:2; [o]**Jos 23:15**; Jer 11:11; 19:3; [p]Pr 1:31; [q]Jer 29:19; [r]Jer 8:9; Eze 20:13; Am 2:4
20 [s]**Ge 10:7**; [t]**Ex 30:23**; [u]Am 5:22; Mal 1:9; [v]Ps 50:8–10; Jer 7:21; Mic 6:7–8; [w]**Isa 1:11**; Jer 14:12; Hos 8:13; 9:4
21 [x]**Lev 26:37; Isa 8:14**
22 [y]**Jer 4:6**; [z]**Dt 28:49**

[a]*10* Hebrew *uncircumcised*

23They are armed with bow and spear;
they are cruel and show no mercy.[a]
They sound like the roaring sea[b]
as they ride on their horses;[c]
they come like men in battle formation
to attack you, O Daughter of Zion.[d]"

24We have heard reports about them,
and our hands hang limp.[e]
Anguish[f] has gripped us,
pain like that of a woman in labour.[g]
25Do not go out to the fields
or walk on the roads,
for the enemy has a sword,
and there is terror on every side.[h]
26O my people, put on sackcloth[i]
and roll in ashes;[j]
mourn with bitter wailing[k]
as for an only son,[l]
for suddenly the destroyer[m]
will come upon us.

27"I have made you a tester[n] of metals
and my people the ore,
that you may observe
and test their ways.
28They are all hardened rebels,[o]
going about to slander.[p]
They are bronze and iron;[q]
they all act corruptly.
29The bellows blow fiercely
to burn away the lead with fire,
but the refining[r] goes on in vain;
the wicked are not purged out.
30They are called rejected silver,[s]
because the LORD has rejected
them."[t]

False Religion Worthless

7 This is the word that came to Jere-
miah from the LORD: 2"Stand[a] at
the gate of the LORD's house and there
proclaim this message:
" 'Hear the word of the LORD, all you
people of Judah who come through
these gates to worship the LORD. 3This is
what the LORD Almighty, the God of
Israel, says: Reform your ways[b] and
your actions, and I will let you live[c] in
this place. 4Do not trust[d] in deceptive[e]
words and say, "This is the temple of
the LORD, the temple of the LORD, the
temple of the LORD!" 5If you really
change[f] your ways and your actions and
deal with each other justly,[g] 6if you do
not oppress[h] the alien, the fatherless or
the widow and do not shed innocent
blood[i] in this place, and if you do not
follow other gods[j] to your own harm,
7then I will let you live in this place, in
the land[k] I gave to your forefathers[l]
for ever and ever. 8But look, you are
trusting[m] in deceptive[n] words that are
worthless.
9" 'Will you steal[o] and murder,[p] com-
mit adultery[q] and perjury,[a] [r] burn in-
cense to Baal[s] [t] and follow other gods[u]
you have not known, 10and then come
and stand[v] before me in this house,[w]
which bears my Name, and say, "We
are safe"—safe to do all these detestable
things?[x] 11Has this house,[y] which bears
my Name, become a den of robbers[z]
to you? But I have been watching![a]
declares the LORD.
12" 'Go now to the place in Shiloh[b]
where I first made a dwelling[c] for my
Name,[d] and see what I did[e] to it because
of the wickedness of my people Israel.
13While you were doing all these things,
declares the LORD, I spoke[f] to you again
and again,[g] but you did not listen;[h] I
called[i] you, but you did not answer.[j]
14Therefore, what I did to Shiloh[k] I will
now do to the house that bears my
Name,[l] the temple[m] you trust in, the
place I gave to you and your fathers. 15I
will thrust you from my presence,[n] just
as I did all your brothers, the people of
Ephraim.'[o]
16"So do not pray for this people nor
offer any plea[p] or petition for them; do
not plead with me, for I will not listen[q] to
you. 17Do you not see what they are
doing in the towns of Judah and in the
streets of Jerusalem? 18The children
gather wood, the fathers light the fire,
and the women knead the dough and
make cakes of bread for the Queen of
Heaven.[r] They pour out drink offerings[s]
to other gods to provoke[t] me to anger.
19But am I the one they are provoking?[u]
declares the LORD. Are they not rather
harming themselves, to their own
shame?[v]
20" 'Therefore this is what the
Sovereign[w] LORD says: My anger[x] and
my wrath will be poured[y] out on this
place, on man and beast, on the trees of
the field and on the fruit of the ground,
and it will burn and not be quenched.[z]
21" 'This is what the LORD Almighty,
the God of Israel, says: Go ahead, add

23 [a]Isa 13:18; [b]Ps 18:4; 93:3; [c]Jer 4:29; [d]Isa 10:32
24 [e]Isa 13:7; [f]Jer 4:19; [g]Jer 4:31; 50:41–43
25 [h]Job 15:21; Ps 31:13; Jer 49:29
26 [i]Jer 4:8; [j]Job 2:8; Jer 25:34; Eze 27:30; Jnh 3:6; [k]Jer 9:1; 18:22; 20:16; 25:36; [l]Ge 21:16; [m]Ex 12:23; Jer 4:7
27 [n]Jer 9:7; Zec 13:9
28 [o]Jer 5:23; [p]Lev 19:16; [q]Eze 22:18
29 [r]Mal 3:3
30 [s]Pr 17:3; Eze 22:18; [t]Ps 53:5; 119:119; Jer 7:29; La 5:22; Hos 9:17

Ch. 7

2 [a]Jer 17:19
3 [b]Jer 18:11; 26:13; 35:15; [c]ver 7
4 [d]Job 15:31; [e]ver 8; Jer 28:15; Mic 3:11
5 [f]ver 3; Jer 18:11; 26:13; 35:15; [g]Ex 22:22; Lev 25:17; Isa 1:17
6 [h]Jer 5:28; Eze 22:7; [i]2Ki 21:16; Jer 2:34; 19:4; 22:3; [j]Ex 20:3; Dt 8:19
7 [k]Dt 4:40; [l]Jos 1:6
8 [m]Job 15:31; [n]ver 4
9 [o]Ex 20:15; [p]Ex 20:13; [q]Ex 20:14; Nu 25:1; [r]Ex 20:16; Lev 19:12; Zec 8:17; Mal 3:5; [s]Isa 1:13; [t]Jer 11:13,17; 32:29; [u]Ex 20:3; Hos 2:13
10 [v]Isa 48:1; [w]ver 30; 2Ki 21:4–5; Jer 23:11; 32:34; Eze 23:38–39; [x]Eze 33:25
11 [y]Isa 56:7; [z]Mt 21:13*; Mk 11:17*; Lk 19:46; [a]Ge 31:50; Jdg 11:10; Jer 29:23; 42:5
12 [b]Jos 18:1; 1Sa 2:32; [c]Ex 40:2; Jos 18:10; [d]Da 9:18; [e]1Sa 4:10–11,22; Ps 78:60–64
13 [f]Ps 71:17; Isa 48:17; Jer 32:33; [g]2Ch 36:15; [h]ver 26; Isa 65:12; [i]Pr 1:24; [j]Jer 35:17
14 [k]Jdg 18:31; 1Sa 2:32; [l]1Ki 9:7; [m]ver 4; Eze 24:21
15 [n]Ge 4:14; Ex 33:15; 2Ki 17:20; Jer 23:39; [o]Ps 78:67
16 [p]Ex 32:10; Dt 9:14; Jer 15:1; [q]Nu 23:19
18 [r]Jer 44:17–19; [s]Isa 57:6; [t]Dt 31:17; 1Ki 14:9
19 [u]Dt 32:21; Jer 44:3; [v]Job 7:20; Jer 9:19; 20:11; 22:22
20 [w]Isa 30:15; [x]Job 40:11; Jer 42:18; La 2:3–5; [y]Jer 6:11–12; La 4:11; [z]Isa 1:31; Jer 11:16; 13:14; 15:6,14; 17:4,27; Eze 20:47–48

[a]9 Or *and swear by false gods*

your burnt offerings to your other sacri-
fices[a] and eat[b] the meat yourselves! 22For
when I brought your forefathers out of
Egypt and spoke to them, I did not just
give them commands[c] about burnt
offerings and sacrifices,[d] 23but I gave
them this command:[e] Obey[f] me, and I
will be your God and you will be my
people.[g] Walk in all the ways[h] I com-
mand you, that it may go well[i] with you.
24But they did not listen[j] or pay atten-
tion;[k] instead, they followed the stub-
born inclinations of their evil hearts.[l]
They went backward[m] and not forward.
25From the time your forefathers left
Egypt until now, day after day, again
and again[n] I sent you my servants[o] the
prophets.[p] 26But they did not listen to
me or pay attention.[q] They were stiff-
necked[r] and did more evil than their
forefathers.'[s]

27"When you tell[t] them all this, they
will not listen[u] to you; when you
call to them, they will not answer.[v]
28Therefore say to them, 'This is the
nation that has not obeyed the LORD its
God or responded to correction.[w] Truth[x]
has perished; it has vanished from their
lips. 29Cut off[y] your hair and throw it
away; take up a lament[z] on the barren
heights, for the LORD has rejected and
abandoned[a] this generation that is
under his wrath.

The Valley of Slaughter

30"'The people of Judah have done
evil[b] in my eyes, declares the LORD.
They have set up their detestable idols[c]
in the house that bears my Name and
have defiled[d] it. 31They have built the
high places of Topheth[e] in the Valley of
Ben Hinnom[f] to burn their sons and
daughters[g] in the fire—something I did
not command, nor did it enter my
mind.[h] 32So beware, the days are com-
ing, declares the LORD, when people
will no longer call it Topheth or the
Valley of Ben Hinnom, but the Valley of
Slaughter,[i] for they will bury[j] the dead
in Topheth until there is no more room.
33Then the carcasses[k] of this people will
become food[l] for the birds of the air and
the beasts of the earth, and there will be
no-one to frighten them away.[m] 34I will
bring an end to the sounds[n] of joy and
gladness and to the voices of bride and
bridegroom[o] in the towns of Judah
and the streets of Jerusalem,[p] for the
land will become desolate.[q]

8 "'At that time, declares the LORD,
the bones of the kings and officials
of Judah, the bones of the priests and
prophets, and the bones[a] of the people
of Jerusalem will be removed[b] from their
graves. 2They will be exposed to the sun
and the moon and all the stars of the
heavens, which they have loved and
served[c] and which they have followed
and consulted and worshipped.[d] They
will not be gathered up or buried,[e] but
will be like refuse lying on the ground.[f]
3Wherever I banish them,[g] all the survi-
vors of this evil nation will prefer death
to life,[h] declares the LORD Almighty.'

Sin and Punishment

4"Say to them, 'This is what the LORD
says:

"'When men fall down, do they not
get up?[i]
When a man turns away,[j] does he
not return?
5Why then have these people turned
away?
Why does Jerusalem always turn
away?
They cling to deceit;[k]
they refuse to return.[l]
6I have listened[m] attentively,
but they do not say what is right.
No-one repents[n] of his wickedness,
saying, "What have I done?"
Each pursues his own course[o]
like a horse charging into battle.
7Even the stork in the sky
knows her appointed seasons,
and the dove, the swift and the thrush
observe the time of their migration.
But my people do not know[p]
the requirements of the LORD.

8"'How can you say, "We are wise,
for we have the law[q] of the LORD,"
when actually the lying pen of the
scribes
has handled it falsely?
9The wise[r] will be put to shame;
they will be dismayed[s] and
trapped.[t]
Since they have rejected the word[u] of
the LORD,
what kind of wisdom[v] do they have?
10Therefore I will give their wives to
other men
and their fields to new owners.[w]
From the least to the greatest,
all are greedy for gain;[x]

21 [a]**Jer 6:20;** Am 5:21–22; [b]**1Sa 2:12–17;** Hos 8:13
22 [c]Isa 43:23; [d]**1Sa 15:22**
23 [e]1Jn 3:23; [f]**Ex 19:5;** [g]**Lev 26:12; Isa 51:16;** [h]**1Ki 8:36; Ps 119:3;** [i]**Dt 5:33**
24 [j]**Jer 6:10;** [k]Jer 11:8; 17:23; 34:14; [l]**Jer 3:17;** [m]**Jer 2:19;** Eze 37:23
25 [n]**2Ch 36:15;** [o]**Isa 20:3;** [p]**Nu 11:29;** Jer 25:4; 35:15
26 [q]ver 13,24; **2Ch 36:16;** Ps 81:11; Jer 13:11; 22:21; 25:3; 35:15; Eze 20:8,21; [r]**Ex 32:9;** Ac 7:51; [s]Jer 16:12; Mal 3:7; Lk 11:47
27 [t]Eze 2:7; [u]ver 13; Eze 3:7; Zec 7:13; [v]**Isa 65:12**
28 [w]**Lev 26:23;** Zep 3:7; [x]**Ps 15:2; Isa 59:15**
29 [y]**Lev 21:5; Job 1:20;** [z]**Jer 4:8; Eze 19:1;** [a]**Jer 6:30;** 12:7; Hos 11:8; Mic 5:3
30 [b]**ver 10; Lev 18:21;** [c]**Jer 2:7; 4:1;** Eze 7:20–22; [d]**Lev 20:3;** Jer 32:34
31 [e]**2Ki 23:10;** [f]**Jos 15:8;** 2Ch 33:6; [g]**Lev 18:21;** Eze 16:20; [h]Jer 19:5; 32:35; Eze 20:31; Mic 6:7
32 [i]Jer 19:6; [j]Jer 19:11
33 [k]**Ge 15:11;** [l]**Dt 28:26;** Eze 29:5; [m]Jer 6:11; 14:16
34 [n]**Isa 24:8;** [o]Rev 18:23; [p]Isa 24:7–12; Jer 33:10; [q]**Lev 26:34;** Zec 7:14; Mt 23:38

Ch. 8

1 [a]**Ps 53:5;** [b]**Isa 14:19**
2 [c]**2Ki 23:5;** Jer 19:13; Zep 1:5; Ac 7:42; [d]**Job 31:27;** [e]Jer 14:16; Eze 29:5; 37:1; [f]**2Ki 9:37;** Jer 31:40; 36:30

3 [g]Dt 29:28; [h]**Job 3:22;** Rev 9:6
4 [i]Pr 24:16; Mic 7:8; [j]Ps 119:67; Jer 31:19
5 [k]**Jer 5:27;** [l]Zec 7:11
6 [m]Mal 3:16; [n]Rev 9:20; [o]Ps 14:1–3
7 [p]**Dt 32:28; Jer 4:22** *8* [q]Ro 2:17
9 [r]**Isa 29:14;** [s]**2Ki 19:26;** [t]**Job 5:13;** [u]**Jer 6:19;** [v]Pr 1:7; 1Co 1:20 *10* [w]**Jer 6:12;** [x]**Isa 56:11**

prophets[y] and priests alike,
all practise deceit.[z]
11They dress the wound of my people
as though it were not serious.
"Peace, peace," they say,
when there is no peace.[a]
12Are they ashamed of their loathsome
conduct?
No, they have no shame[b] at all;
they do not even know how to
blush.
So they will fall among the fallen;
they will be brought down when
they are punished,[c]
says the LORD.[d]

13" 'I will take away their harvest,
declares the LORD.
There will be no grapes on the vine.[e]
There will be no figs[f] on the tree,
and their leaves will wither.[g]
What I have given them
will be taken[h] from them.' "[a]

14"Why are we sitting here?
Gather together!
Let us flee to the fortified cities[i]
and perish there!
For the LORD our God has doomed us
to perish
and given us poisoned water[j] to
drink,
because we have sinned[k] against
him.
15We hoped for peace[l]
but no good has come,
for a time of healing
but there was only terror.[m]
16The snorting of the enemy's horses[n]
is heard from Dan;[o]
at the neighing of their stallions
the whole land trembles.[p]
They have come to devour[q]
the land and everything in it,
the city and all who live there."

17"See, I will send venomous snakes[r]
among you,
vipers that cannot be charmed,[s]
and they will bite you,"
declares the LORD.

18O my Comforter[b] in sorrow,
my heart is faint[t] within me.
19Listen to the cry of my people
from a land far away:[u]
"Is the LORD not in Zion?
Is her King[v] no longer there?"

"Why have they provoked[w] me to
anger with their images,
with their worthless[x] foreign
idols?"[y]

20"The harvest is past,
the summer has ended,
and we are not saved."

21Since my people are crushed,[z] I am
crushed;
I mourn,[a] and horror grips me.
22Is there no balm in Gilead?[b]
Is there no physician[c] there?
Why then is there no healing[d]
for the wound of my people?

9 1Oh, that my head were a spring of
water
and my eyes a fountain of tears![a]
I would weep[b] day and night
for the slain of my people.[c]
2Oh, that I had in the desert[d]
a lodging place for travellers,
so that I might leave my people
and go away from them;
for they are all adulterers,[e]
a crowd of unfaithful[f] people.

3"They make ready their tongue
like a bow, to shoot lies;[g]
it is not by truth
that they triumph[a] in the land.
They go from one sin to another;
they do not acknowledge[h] me,"
declares the LORD.
4"Beware of your friends;[i]
do not trust your brothers.[j]
For every brother is a deceiver,[b k]
and every friend a slanderer.[l]
5Friend deceives friend,[m]
and no-one speaks the truth.[n]
They have taught their tongues to lie;[o]
they weary themselves with
sinning.
6You[c] live in the midst of deception;[p]
in their deceit they refuse to
acknowledge me,"
declares the LORD.

7Therefore this is what the LORD Almighty says:

"See, I will refine[q] and test[r] them,
for what else can I do
because of the sin of my people?
8Their tongue[s] is a deadly arrow;
it speaks with deceit.
With his mouth each speaks cordially
to his neighbour,[t]
but in his heart he sets a trap[u] for
him.[v]

10 [y]Jer 14:14; La 2:14; [z]Jer 23:11,15
11 [a]ver 15; **Jer 4:10**; Eze 7:25
12 [b]**Jer 3:3**; [c]Ps 52:5–7; Isa 3:9; [d]**Jer 6:15**
13 [e]Hos 2:12; Joel 1:7; [f]Lk 13:6; [g]Mt 21:19; [h]**Jer 5:17**
14 [i]**Jos 10:20**; Jer 35:11; [j]**Dt 29:18**; Jer 9:15; 23:15; [k]Jer 14:7,20; Da 9:5
15 [l]**ver 11**; [m]**Job 19:8**; Jer 14:19
16 [n]**Jer 4:29**; [o]**Ge 30:6**; [p]Jer 51:29; [q]**Jer 5:17**
17 [r]Nu 21:6; **Dt 32:24**; [s]**Ps 58:5; Isa 3:3**
18 [t]La 5:17
19 [u]Dt 28:64; Jer 9:16; [v]Mic 4:9; [w]Jer 44:3; [x]**Isa 41:24**; [y]**Dt 32:21**
21 [z]**Ps 94:5**; [a]Ps 78:40; Isa 43:24; Jer 4:19; 10:19; 14:17; 30:14; La 2:13; Eze 6:9
22 [b]**Ge 37:25**; [c]Job 13:4; [d]**Isa 1:6**; Jer 30:12

Ch. 9

1 [a]**Ps 119:136**; [b]Jer 13:17; 14:17; La 2:11, 18; 3:48; [c]Isa 22:4
2 [d]Ps 55:7; [e]**Nu 25:1**; Jer 23:10; Hos 4:2; 7:4; [f]**1Ki 19:10**; **Isa 24:16**
3 [g]ver 8; **Ex 20:16**; Ps 64:3; **Isa 44:20**; Jer 18:18; Mic 6:12; [h]**Isa 1:3**
4 [i]**2Sa 15:12**; [j]Mic 7:5–6; [k]**Ge 27:35**; [l]**Ex 20:16**; **Lev 19:16**
5 [m]**Lev 6:2**; [n]**Ps 15:2; Isa 59:15**; [o]**Ps 52:3**
6 [p]**Jer 5:27**
7 [q]**Job 28:1; Isa 1:25**; [r]**Jer 6:27**
8 [s]**ver 3**; **Ps 35:20**; [t]**Isa 3:5**; [u]**Jer 5:26**; [v]ver 4

[a]*13* The meaning of the Hebrew for this sentence is uncertain.
[b]*18* The meaning of the Hebrew for this word is uncertain.
[a]3 Or *lies; / they are not valiant for truth*
[b]4 Or *a deceiving Jacob*
[c]6 That is, Jeremiah (the Hebrew is singular)

9"Should I not punish them for this?"
declares the LORD.
"Should I not avenge[w] myself
on such a nation as this?"

10I will weep and wail for the mountains
and take up a lament concerning the
desert pastures.[x]
They are desolate and untravelled,
and the lowing of cattle is not heard.
The birds of the air[y] have fled
and the animals are gone.

11"I will make Jerusalem a heap[z] of
ruins,
a haunt of jackals;[a]
and I will lay waste the towns of
Judah[b]
so that no-one can live there."[c]

12What man is wise[d] enough to under-
stand this? Who has been instructed by
the LORD and can explain it? Why has
the land been ruined and laid waste like
a desert that no-one can cross?
13The LORD said, "It is because they
have forsaken my law, which I set be-
fore them; they have not obeyed me or
followed my law.[e] 14Instead, they have
followed[f] the stubbornness of their
hearts;[g] they have followed the Baals, as
their fathers taught them." 15Therefore,
this is what the LORD Almighty, the God
of Israel, says: "See, I will make this
people eat bitter food[h] and drink
poisoned water.[i] 16I will scatter them
among nations[j] that neither they nor
their fathers have known,[k] and I will
pursue them with the sword[l] until I
have destroyed them."[m]

17This is what the LORD Almighty
says:

"Consider now! Call for the wailing
women[n] to come;
send for the most skilful of them.
18Let them come quickly
and wail over us
till our eyes overflow with tears
and water streams from our
eyelids.[o]
19The sound of wailing is heard from
Zion:
'How ruined[p] we are!
How great is our shame!
We must leave our land
because our houses are in ruins.'"

20Now, O women, hear the word of the
LORD;
open your ears to the words of his
mouth.[q]
Teach your daughters how to wail;
teach one another a lament.[r]
21Death has climbed in through our
windows[s]
and has entered our fortresses;
it has cut off the children from the
streets
and the young men[t] from the public
squares.

22Say, "This is what the LORD de-
clares:

" 'The dead bodies of men will lie
like refuse[u] on the open field,
like cut corn behind the reaper,
with no-one to gather them.' "

23This is what the LORD says:

"Let not the wise man boast of his
wisdom[v]
or the strong man boast of his
strength[w]
or the rich man boast of his riches,[x]
24but let him who boasts boast[y] about
this:
that he understands and knows[z]
me,
that I am the LORD,[a] who exercises
kindness,[b]
justice and righteousness[c] on earth,
for in these I delight,"
declares the LORD.

25"The days are coming," declares
the LORD, "when I will punish all who
are circumcised only in the flesh[d]—
26Egypt, Judah, Edom, Ammon, Moab
and all who live in the desert in distant
places.[d][e] For all these nations are really
uncircumcised,[f] and even the whole
house of Israel is uncircumcised in
heart.[g]"

God and Idols

10:12–16pp—Jer 51:15–19

10

Hear what the LORD says to you,
O house of Israel. 2This is what
the LORD says:

"Do not learn the ways of the nations[a]
or be terrified by signs[b] in the sky,
though the nations are terrified by
them.
3For the customs of the peoples are
worthless;
they cut a tree out of the forest,
and a craftsman[c] shapes it with his
chisel.[d]

9 [w]**Dt 32:43; Isa 10:3**
10 [x]Jer 23:10; Joel 1:19; [y]**Jer 4:25**; 12:4; Hos 4:3; Joel 1:18
11 [z]Jer 26:18; [a]**Job 30:29; Isa 34:13**; [b]**Jer 1:15**; [c]**Lev 26:31**; Isa 25:2; **Jer 4:13**; 26:9; 33:10; 50:3,13; 51:62; La 1:4
12 [d]**Ps 107:43**
13 [e]**2Ch 7:19; Ps 89:30–32**
14 [f]**Jer 2:8**,23; Am 2:4; [g]**Jer 3:17; 7:24**
15 [h]La 3:15; [i]**Jer 8:14**
16 [j]**Lev 26:33**; [k]**Dt 4:32; Jer 8:19**; [l]Jer 14:12; 24:10; Eze 5:2; [m]Jer 44:27; Eze 5:12
17 [n]**Ecc 12:5**
18 [o]**Ps 119:136**; La 3:48
19 [p]**Jer 4:13**
20 [q]Jer 23:16; [r]Isa 32:9–13
21 [s]Joel 2:9; [t]**2Ch 36:17; Isa 40:30; Jer 16:6**
22 [u]**2Ki 9:37**
23 [v]**Job 4:12; Ecc 9:11**; [w]**1Ki 20:11**; [x]Ps 62:10; **Pr 11:28**; Jer 48:7; 49:4; Eze 28:4–5
24 [y]**Ps 34:2**; 1Co 1:31*; Gal 6:14; [z]**Ps 36:10**; [a]2Co 10:17*; [b]Ps 51:1; [c]Ps 36:6
25 [d]**Lev 26:41**; Ro 2:25
26 [e]Jer 25:23; 49:32; [f]**1Sa 14:6**; Eze 31:18; [g]Ac 7:51

Ch. 10

2 [a]**Ex 23:24; Lev 20:23**; [b]**Ge 1:14**
3 [c]**Isa 40:19**; [d]Dt 9:21; **1Ki 8:36**; Jer 44:8; Eze 7:20

d26 Or *desert and who clip the hair by their foreheads*

4They adorn it with silver[e] and gold;
they fasten it with hammer and nails
so that it will not totter.[f]
5Like a scarecrow in a melon patch,
their idols cannot speak;[g]
they must be carried
because they cannot walk.[h]
Do not fear them;
they can do no harm[i]
nor can they do any good."[j]

6No-one is like you,[k] O LORD;
you are great,[l]
and your name is mighty in power.
7Who should not revere[m] you,
O King of the nations?[n]
This is your due.
Among all the wise men of the nations
and in all their kingdoms,
there is no-one like you.
8They are all senseless[o] and foolish;[p]
they are taught by worthless wooden idols.[q]
9Hammered silver is brought from Tarshish[r]
and gold from Uphaz.
What the craftsman and goldsmith have made[s]
is then dressed in blue and purple—
all made by skilled workers.
10But the LORD is the true God;
he is the living God,[t] the eternal King.[u]
When he is angry,[v] the earth trembles;[w]
the nations cannot endure his wrath.[x]

11"Tell them this: 'These gods, who
did not make the heavens and the earth,
will perish[y] from the earth and from
under the heavens.'"[a]

12But God made[z] the earth[a] by his power;
he founded the world by his wisdom[b]
and stretched out the heavens[c] by his understanding.
13When he thunders,[d] the waters in the heavens roar;
he makes clouds rise from the ends of the earth.
He sends lightning[e] with the rain[f]
and brings out the wind from his storehouses.[g]

14Everyone is senseless and without knowledge;
every goldsmith is shamed[h] by his idols.
His images are a fraud;[i]
they have no breath in them.
15They are worthless,[j] the objects of mockery;
when their judgment comes, they will perish.
16He who is the Portion[k] of Jacob is not like these,
for he is the Maker of all things,[l]
including Israel, the tribe of his inheritance[m]—
the LORD Almighty is his name.[n]

Coming Destruction

17Gather up your belongings[o] to leave the land,
you who live under siege.
18For this is what the LORD says:
"At this time I will hurl[p] out
those who live in this land;
I will bring distress[q] on them
so that they may be captured."
19Woe to me because of my injury!
My wound[r] is incurable!
Yet I said to myself,
"This is my sickness, and I must endure[s] it."
20My tent[t] is destroyed;
all its ropes are snapped.
My sons are gone from me and are no more;[u]
no-one is left now to pitch my tent
or to set up my shelter.
21The shepherds[v] are senseless[w]
and do not enquire of the LORD;[x]
so they do not prosper[y]
and all their flock is scattered.[z]
22Listen! The report is coming—
a great commotion from the land of the north![a]
It will make the towns of Judah desolate,[b]
a haunt of jackals.[c]

Jeremiah's Prayer

23I know, O LORD, that a man's life is not his own;
it is not for man to direct his steps.[d]
24Correct me, LORD, but only with justice—
not in your anger,[e]
lest you reduce me to nothing.[f][g]
25Pour out your wrath on the nations[h]
that do not acknowledge you,
on the peoples who do not call on your name.[i]

4 [e]Ps 135:15; Hos 13:2; Hab 2:19; [f]**1Sa 5:3**; Isa 41:7
5 [g]**1Ki 18:26**; 1Co 12:2; [h]**Isa 45:20**; [i]Isa 41:23; [j]**Isa 41:24**; 44:9–20; 46:7; Ac 19:26
6 [k]**Ex 8:10**; [l]**2Sa 7:22; Ps 48:1**
7 [m]Jer 5:22; [n]Ps 22:28; **Isa 12:4**; Rev 15:4
8 [o]**Isa 44:18**; [p]**Isa 40:19; Jer 4:22**; [q]**Dt 32:21**
9 [r]**Ge 10:4**; [s]Ps 115:4; **Isa 40:19**
10 [t]**Jos 3:10; Mt 16:16**; [u]**Ge 21:33**; Da 6:26; [v]**Ps 18:7**; [w]**Jdg 5:4; Job 9:6**; Ps 29:8; [x]Ps 76:7; Jer 21:12; Na 1:6
11 [y]**Isa 2:18**
12 [z]**1Sa 2:8**; [a]**ver 16**; [b]**Ge 1:31**; [c]**Ge 1:1,8**
13 [d]**Job 36:29**; [e]**Job 36:30**; [f]**Ps 104:13; 135:7**; [g]**Dt 28:12**
14 [h]**Ps 97:7; Isa 1:29**; [i]**Isa 44:20**
15 [j]**Isa 41:24; Jer 14:22**
16 [k]**Dt 32:9; Ps 119:57**; [l]ver 12; Jer 32:17; 33:2; [m]**Ex 34:9**; Ps 74:2; [n]Jer 31:35; 32:18
17 [o]Eze 12:3–12
18 [p]**1Sa 25:29; Isa 22:17**; [q]**Dt 28:52**
19 [r]Job 34:6; Jer 14:17; 15:18; 30:12,15; La 2:13; Mic 1:9; Na 3:19; [s]Mic 7:9
20 [t]**Jer 4:20**; [u]Jer 31:15; La 1:5
21 [v]Jer 22:22; 23:1; 25:34; 50:6; [w]ver 8; [x]**Isa 56:10**; [y]Jer 22:30; [z]Jer 23:2; Eze 34:6
22 [a]Jer 6:22; 27:6; 49:28,30; [b]Eze 12:19; [c]**Isa 34:13**
23 [d]**Job 33:29; Pr 3:5–6**; 20:24
24 [e]Ps 6:1; 38:1; **Jer 7:20**; 18:23; [f]Jer 46:28; [g]Jer 30:11
25 [h]**Ps 69:24**; Zep 2:2; 3:8; [i]**Ps 14:4**

[a]*11* The text of this verse is in Aramaic.

For they have devoured[j] Jacob;
they have devoured him completely
and destroyed his homeland.[k]

The Covenant Is Broken

11 This is the word that came
to Jeremiah from the LORD:
2"Listen to the terms of this covenant[a]
and tell them to the people of Judah and
to those who live in Jerusalem. 3Tell
them that this is what the LORD, the God
of Israel, says: 'Cursed[b] is the man who
does not obey the terms of this covenant
—4the terms I commanded your fore-
fathers when I brought them out of
Egypt,[c] out of the iron-smelting fur-
nace.[d]' I said, 'Obey[e] me and do every-
thing I command you, and you will be
my people,[f] and I will be your God.
5Then I will fulfil the oath I swore[g] to
your forefathers, to give them a land
flowing with milk and honey'[h]—the
land you possess today."

I answered, "Amen,[i] LORD."

6The LORD said to me, "Proclaim[j] all
these words in the towns of Judah and
in the streets of Jerusalem: 'Listen to the
terms of this covenant and follow[k]
them. 7From the time I brought your
forefathers up from Egypt until today, I
warned them again and again,[l] saying,
"Obey me." 8But they did not listen or
pay attention;[m] instead, they followed
the stubbornness of their evil hearts.[n]
So I brought on them all the curses[o] of
the covenant I had commanded them to
follow but that they did not keep.[p]'"

9Then the LORD said to me, "There is a
conspiracy[q] among the people of Judah
and those who live in Jerusalem. 10They
have returned to the sins of their fore-
fathers,[r] who refused to listen to my
words.[s] They have followed other gods[t]
to serve them.[u] Both the house of Israel
and the house of Judah have broken the
covenant[v] I made with their forefathers.
11Therefore this is what the LORD says: 'I
will bring on them a disaster[w] they can-
not escape.[x] Although they cry[y] out to
me, I will not listen[z] to them. 12The
towns of Judah and the people of Jeru-
salem will go and cry out to the gods to
whom they burn incense,[a] but they will
not help them at all when disaster[b]
strikes. 13You have as many gods[c] as
you have towns,[d] O Judah; and the
altars you have set up to burn incense[e]
to that shameful[f] god Baal are as many
as the streets of Jerusalem.'

14"Do not pray[g] for this people nor
offer any plea or petition for them, be-
cause I will not listen[h] when they call to
me in the time of their distress.

15"What is my beloved doing in my
temple
as she works out her evil schemes
with many?
Can consecrated meat[i] avert ⌊your
punishment⌋?[j]
When you engage in your
wickedness,
then you rejoice."[a]

16The LORD called you a thriving olive
tree[k]
with fruit beautiful in form.
But with the roar of a mighty storm
he will set it on fire,[l]
and its branches will be broken.[m]

17The LORD Almighty, who planted[n]
you, has decreed disaster[o] for you, be-
cause the house of Israel and the house
of Judah have done evil and provoked[p]
me to anger by burning incense to Baal.[q]

Plot Against Jeremiah

18Because the LORD revealed their plot
to me, I knew it, for at that time he
showed me what they were doing. 19I
had been like a gentle lamb led to the
slaughter;[r] I did not realise that they had
plotted[s] against me, saying,

"Let us destroy the tree and its fruit;
let us cut him off from the land of
the living,[t]
that his name be remembered[u] no
more."
20But, O LORD Almighty, you who judge
righteously[v]
and test the heart[w] and mind,[x]
let me see your vengeance[y] upon
them,
for to you I have committed my
cause.

21"Therefore this is what the LORD
says about the men of Anathoth[z] who
are seeking your life[a] and saying, 'Do
not prophesy[b] in the name of the LORD
or you will die[c] by our hands'—
22therefore this is what the LORD
Almighty says: 'I will punish them.
Their young men[d] will die by the sword,
their sons and daughters by famine.

25 [j]Ps 79:7; Jer 2:3; [k]Ps 79:6–7
Ch. 11
2 [a]Dt 5:2
3 [b]Dt 11:26–28; 27:26; 28:15–68; Gal 3:10
4 [c]ver 7; [d]1Ki 8:51; [e]Ex 24:8; Jer 7:23; [f]Jer 7:23; 31:33; Eze 11:20
5 [g]Ex 6:8; 13:5; Dt 7:12; Ps 105:8–11; [h]Ex 3:8; [i]Dt 27:26
6 [j]Jer 4:5; [k]Ex 15:26; Dt 15:5; Jas 1:22
7 [l]2Ch 36:15
8 [m]Jer 7:26; [n]Ecc 9:3; Jer 3:17; [o]Lev 26:14–43; Dt 28:15–68; Jos 23:15; [p]2Ch 7:19; Ps 78:10; Jer 26:4; 32:23; 44:10
9 [q]Eze 22:25
10 [r]Dt 9:7; 2Ch 30:7; [s]Zec 7:11; [t]Jdg 2:12–13; 10:13; [u]Jer 16:11; Eze 20:8; [v]Isa 24:5; Jer 34:18; Hos 6:7; 8:1
11 [w]2Ki 22:16; Jer 4:6; [x]Job 11:20; La 2:22; [y]Job 27:9; Jer 14:12; Eze 8:18; Mal 2:13; [z]ver 14; Ps 66:18; Pr 1:28; Isa 1:15; 59:2; Eze 8:8; Zec 7:13
12 [a]Dt 32:38; Jer 44:17; [b]Dt 32:37; Jdg 10:14
13 [c]Ex 20:3; Jer 19:4; [d]2Ki 17:29; [e]Jer 7:9; 44:21; [f]Jer 3:24
14 [g]Ex 32:10; [h]ver 11
15 [i]Hag 2:12; [j]Jer 7:9–10
16 [k]Ps 1:3; Hos 14:6; [l]Jer 7:20; 21:14; [m]Isa 27:11; Ro 11:17–24
17 [n]Ex 15:17; Isa 5:2; Jer 12:2; 45:4; [o]ver 11; [p]Jer 7:18; [q]Jer 7:9
19 [r]Ps 44:22; [s]ver 21; Ps 44:16; 54:3; 71:10; Jer 18:18; 20:10; [t]Job 28:13; Ps 116:9; Isa 53:8; [u]Ps 83:4
20 [v]Ps 7:11; [w]1Sa 2:3; 1Ch 29:17; [x]Ps 26:2; [y]Ps 58:10; La 3:60
21 [z]Jos 21:18; [a]ver 19; Jer 12:6; 21:7; 34:20; [b]Isa 30:10; [c]Jer 2:30; 18:23; 26:8,11; 38:4
22 [d]Isa 9:17; Jer 18:21

[a]15 Or *Could consecrated meat avert your punishment? / Then you would rejoice*

23Not even a remnant[e] will be left to them, because I will bring disaster on the men of Anathoth in the year of their punishment.[f]"

Jeremiah's Complaint

12 You are always righteous,[a] O LORD,
when I bring a case[b] before you.
Yet I would speak with you about your justice:[c]
Why does the way of the wicked prosper?[d]
Why do all the faithless live at ease?
2You have planted[e] them, and they have taken root;
they grow and bear fruit.[f]
You are always on their lips
but far from their hearts.[g]
3Yet you know me, O LORD;
you see me and test[h] my thoughts about you.
Drag them off like sheep[i] to be butchered!
Set them apart for the day of slaughter![j]
4How long will the land lie parched[a] [k]
and the grass in every field be withered?[l]
Because those who live in it are wicked,
the animals and birds have perished.[m]
Moreover, the people are saying,
"He will not see what happens to us."

God's Answer

5"If you have raced with men on foot
and they have worn you out,
how can you compete with horses?
If you stumble in safe country,[b]
how will you manage in the thickets[n] by[c] the Jordan?
6Your brothers, your own family—
even they have betrayed you;
they have raised a loud cry against you.[o]
Do not trust them,
though they speak well of you.[p]

7"I will forsake[q] my house,
abandon[r] my inheritance;
I will give the one I love[s]
into the hands of her enemies.[t]
8My inheritance has become to me
like a lion[u] in the forest.
She roars at me;
therefore I hate her.[v]
9Has not my inheritance become to me
like a speckled bird of prey
that other birds of prey surround and attack?
Go and gather all the wild beasts;
bring them to devour.[w]
10Many shepherds[x] will ruin my vineyard
and trample down my field;
they will turn my pleasant field
into a desolate wasteland.[y]
11It will be made a wasteland,[z]
parched and desolate before me;[a]
the whole land will be laid waste
because there is no-one who cares.
12Over all the barren heights in the desert
destroyers will swarm,
for the sword[b] of the LORD[c] will devour[d]
from one end of the land to the other;[e]
no-one will be safe.[f]
13They will sow wheat but reap thorns;
they will wear themselves out but gain nothing.[g]
So bear the shame of your harvest
because of the LORD's fierce anger."[h]

14This is what the LORD says: "As for
all my wicked neighbours who seize the
inheritance[i] I gave to my people Israel, I
will uproot[j] them from their lands and I
will uproot[k] the house of Judah from
among them. 15But after I uproot them, I
will again have compassion[l] and will
bring[m] each of them back to his own
inheritance and his own country. 16And
if they learn[n] well the ways of my people
and swear by my name, saying, 'As
surely as the LORD lives'[o]—even as they
once taught my people to swear by Baal[p]
—then they will be established among
my people.[q] 17But if any nation does not
listen, I will completely uproot and
destroy[r] it," declares the LORD.

A Linen Belt

13 This is what the LORD said to
me: "Go and buy a linen belt
and put it round your waist, but do not
let it touch water." 2So I bought a belt, as
the LORD directed, and put it round my
waist.
3Then the word of the LORD came to
me a second time:[a] 4"Take the belt you
bought and are wearing round your
waist, and go now to Perath[a] [b] and hide

11:23 [e] Jer 6:9; [f] Jer 23:12

Ch. 12

1 [a] **Ezr 9:15**; Job 8:3; Da 9:14; [b] **Job 5:8**; [c] Eze 18:25; [d] **Job 21:7**,13; Ps 37:7; Jer 5:27–28
2 [e] **Jer 11:17**; [f] **Job 5:3**; [g] **Isa 29:13**; **Jer 3:10**; **Eze 22:27**; Mt 15:8; Mk 7:6; Tit 1:16
3 [h] Ps 7:9; 11:5; 139:1–4; [i] **Ps 44:11**; [j] Jer 16:18; 17:18; 20:11
4 [k] **Jer 4:28**; [l] **ver 11**; **Jer 4:26**; Joel 1:10–12; Am 1:2; [m] Dt 28:15–18; **Jer 4:25**; **9:10**
5 [n] Jer 49:19; 50:44
6 [o] **Pr 26:24–25**; Jer 9:4; [p] Ps 12:2
7 [q] **2Ki 21:14**; [r] **Jer 7:29**; [s] Isa 5:1; [t] Jer 17:4
8 [u] **Ps 17:12**; [v] Ps 5:5; Hos 9:15; Am 6:8
9 [w] **Dt 28:26**; Isa 56:9; Jer 15:3; Eze 23:25; 39:17–20
10 [x] Jer 23:1; 25:34; Eze 34:2–10; [y] Isa 5:1–7; Jer 9:10; 25:11
11 [z] **Isa 5:6**; **24:4**; [a] ver 4; Jer 9:12; 14:4; 23:10
12 [b] Eze 21:3–4; [c] **Dt 32:41**; Isa 31:8; Jer 46:10; 47:6; Eze 14:17; 21:28; 33:2; [d] **Dt 32:42**; [e] Jer 3:2; [f] Jer 7:10
13 [g] **Lev 26:20**; **Dt 28:38**; [h] **Ex 15:7**; **Jer 4:26**
14 [i] **Dt 29:28**; **2Ch 7:20**; [j] **Ps 9:6**; Zec 2:7–9; [k] **Dt 28:63**
15 [l] **Ps 6:2**; [m] **Dt 30:3**; Am 9:14–15
16 [n] Jer 18:8; [o] **Jer 4:2**; [p] **Jos 23:7**; [q] **Isa 26:18**; 49:6; Jer 3:17
17 [r] **Ge 27:29**

Ch. 13

3 [a] Jer 33:1
4 [b] **Ge 2:14**

---

[a]4 Or *land mourn*
[b]5 Or *If you put your trust in a land of safety*
[c]5 Or *the flooding of*
[a]4 Or possibly *the Euphrates;* also in verses 5–7

it there in a crevice in the rocks." 5So I
went and hid it at Perath, as the LORD
told me.[c]
6Many days later the LORD said to me,
"Go now to Perath and get the belt I told
you to hide there." 7So I went to Perath
and dug up the belt and took it from the
place where I had hidden it, but now it
was ruined and completely useless.
8Then the word of the LORD came to
me: 9"This is what the LORD says: 'In the
same way I will ruin the pride of Judah
and the great pride[d] of Jerusalem.
10These wicked people, who refuse to
listen[e] to my words, who follow the
stubbornness of their hearts[f] and go
after other gods[g] to serve and worship
them,[h] will be like this belt—completely
useless![i] 11For as a belt is bound round a
man's waist, so I bound the whole
house of Israel and the whole house of
Judah to me,' declares the LORD, 'to be
my people for my renown[j] and praise
and honour.[k] But they have not
listened.'[l]

Wineskins

12"Say to them: 'This is what the
LORD, the God of Israel, says: Every
wineskin should be filled with wine.'
And if they say to you, 'Don't we know
that every wineskin should be filled
with wine?' 13then tell them, 'This is
what the LORD says: I am going to fill
with drunkenness[m] all who live in this
land, including the kings who sit on
David's throne, the priests, the
prophets and all those living in Jeru-
salem. 14I will smash them one against
the other, fathers and sons alike, de-
clares the LORD. I will allow no pity[n] or
mercy or compassion[o] to keep me from
destroying[p] them.'"

Threat of Captivity

15Hear and pay attention,
do not be arrogant,
for the LORD has spoken.[q]
16Give glory[r] to the LORD your God
before he brings the darkness,
before your feet stumble[s]
on the darkening hills.
You hope for light,
but he will turn it to thick darkness
and change it to deep gloom.[t]
17But if you do not listen,[u]
I will weep in secret
because of your pride;
my eyes will weep bitterly,
overflowing with tears,[v]
because the LORD's flock[w] will be
taken captive.[x]
18Say to the king[y] and to the queen
mother,[z]
"Come down from your thrones,
for your glorious crowns[a]
will fall from your heads."
19The cities in the Negev will be shut up,
and there will be no-one to open
them.
All Judah[b] will be carried into exile,
carried completely away.
20Lift up your eyes and see
those who are coming from the
north.[c]
Where is the flock[d] that was entrusted
to you,
the sheep of which you boasted?
21What will you say when ⌊the LORD⌋
sets over you
those you cultivated as your special
allies?[e]
Will not pain grip you
like that of a woman in labour?[f]
22And if you ask yourself,
"Why has this happened to
me?"[g]—
it is because of your many sins[h]
that your skirts have been torn off[i]
and your body ill-treated.[j]
23Can the Ethiopian[b] change his skin
or the leopard its spots?
Neither can you do good
who are accustomed to doing evil.[k]
24"I will scatter you like chaff[l]
driven by the desert wind.[m]
25This is your lot,
the portion[n] I have decreed for
you,"
declares the LORD,
"because you have forgotten[o] me
and trusted in false gods.[p]
26I will pull up your skirts over your face
that your shame may be seen[q]—
27your adulteries and lustful neighings,
your shameless prostitution![r]
I have seen your detestable acts
on the hills and in the fields.[s]
Woe to you, O Jerusalem!
How long will you be unclean?"[t]

Drought, Famine, Sword

14 This is the word of the LORD
to Jeremiah concerning the
drought:[a]

5 [c]Ex 40:16
9 [d]**Lev 26:19; Mt 23:12; Lk 1:51**
10 [e]Jer 22:21; [f]**Ecc 9:3; Jer 3:17;** [g]**Dt 8:19;** Jer 9:14; [h]**Jdg 10:13;** [i]Eze 15:3
11 [j]Isa 63:12; Jer 32:20; [k]Ex 19:5–6; Isa 43:21; **Jer 3:17;** [l]**Isa 65:12; Jer 7:26**
13 [m]Ps 60:3; 75:8; **Isa 29:9;** Jer 25:18; 51:57
14 [n]Eze 7:4; 8:18; 9:5,10; 24:14; Zec 11:6; [o]**Isa 9:17;** Jer 16:5; [p]Dt 29:20; Isa 9:19–21; **Jer 7:20;** 49:32,36; La 2:21; Eze 5:10
15 [q]**Ex 23:21;** Ps 95:7–8
16 [r]**Jos 7:19;** [s]**Lev 26:37; Job 3:23;** Isa 51:17; Jer 23:12; [t]**1Sa 2:9; Job 3:5; Ps 82:5**
17 [u]Mal 2:2; [v]**Jer 9:1;** [w]Ps 80:1; Jer 23:1; [x]Jer 14:18; 29:1
18 [y]Jer 21:11; 22:1; [z]**1Ki 2:19; 2Ki 24:8; Isa 22:17;** [a]**2Sa 12:30;** La 5:16; Eze 16:12; 21:26
19 [b]Jer 20:4; 52:30; La 1:3
20 [c]Jer 6:22; Hab 1:6; [d]Jer 23:2
21 [e]**Ps 41:9;** Jer 4:30; 20:10; 38:22; Ob 7; [f]**Jer 4:31**
22 [g]**1Ki 9:9;** [h]Jer 9:2–6; 16:10–12; [i]**Isa 20:4;** [j]La 1:8; Eze 16:37; 23:26; Na 3:5–6
23 [k]**2Ch 6:36**
24 [l]**Ps 1:4;** [m]**Lev 26:33; Job 1:19; 27:21**
25 [n]**Job 20:29;** Mt 24:51; [o]**Isa 17:10;** [p]**Dt 31:20; Ps 4:2;** 106:19–21
26 [q]La 1:8; Eze 16:37; Na 3:5
27 [r]Eze 23:29; [s]**Isa 57:7;** Eze 6:13; [t]Hos 8:5

Ch. 14

1 [a]**Dt 28:22; Isa 5:6**

b23 Hebrew *Cushite* (probably a person from the upper Nile region)

2"Judah mourns,[b]
her cities languish;
they wail for the land,
and a cry goes up from Jerusalem.
3The nobles send their servants for
water;
they go to the cisterns
but find no water.[c]
They return with their jars unfilled;
dismayed and despairing,
they cover their heads.[d]
4The ground is cracked
because there is no rain in the land;[e]
the farmers are dismayed
and cover their heads.
5Even the doe in the field
deserts her newborn fawn
because there is no grass.[f]
6Wild donkeys stand on the barren
heights[g]
and pant like jackals;
their eyesight fails
for lack of pasture."[h]

7Although our sins testify[i] against us,
O LORD, do something for the sake
of your name.[j]
For our backsliding[k] is great;
we have sinned[l] against you.
8O Hope[m] of Israel,
its Saviour[n] in times of distress,[o]
why are you like a stranger in the land,
like a traveller who stays only a
night?
9Why are you like a man taken by
surprise,
like a warrior powerless to save?[p]
You are among[q] us, O LORD,
and we bear your name;[r]
do not forsake[s] us!

10This is what the LORD says about this
people:

"They greatly love to wander;
they do not restrain their feet.[t]
So the LORD does not accept[u] them;
he will now remember[v] their
wickedness
and punish them for their sins."[w]

11Then the LORD said to me, "Do not
pray[x] for the well-being of this people.
12Although they fast, I will not listen to
their cry;[y] though they offer burnt offer-
ings[z] and grain offerings,[a] I will not
accept[b] them. Instead, I will destroy
them with the sword,[c] famine[d] and
plague."[e]
13But I said, "Ah, Sovereign LORD, the
prophets[f] keep telling them, 'You will
not see the sword or suffer famine.[g]
Indeed, I will give you lasting peace[h] in
this place.'"

14Then the LORD said to me, "The
prophets are prophesying lies[i] in my
name. I have not sent[j] them or
appointed them or spoken to them.
They are prophesying to you false
visions,[k] divinations,[l] idolatries[a] and
the delusions of their own minds.
15Therefore, this is what the LORD says
about the prophets who are prophesy-
ing in my name: I did not send them, yet
they are saying, 'No sword or famine
will touch this land.' Those same
prophets will perish[m] by sword and
famine.[n]
16And the people they are
prophesying to will be thrown out into
the streets of Jerusalem because of the
famine and sword. There will be no-one
to bury[o] them or their wives, their sons
or their daughters.[p] I will pour out on
them the calamity they deserve.[q]
17"Speak this word to them:

"'Let my eyes overflow with tears[r]
night and day without ceasing;
for my virgin[s] daughter—my
people—
has suffered a grievous wound,
a crushing blow.[t]
18If I go into the country,
I see those slain by the sword;
if I go into the city,
I see the ravages of famine.[u]
Both prophet and priest
have gone to a land they know
not.[v]'"

19Have you rejected Judah completely?[w]
Do you despise Zion?
Why have you afflicted us
so that we cannot be healed?[x]
We hoped for peace
but no good has come,
for a time of healing
but there is only terror.[y]
20O LORD, we acknowledge[z] our
wickedness
and the guilt of our fathers;[a]
we have indeed sinned[b] against
you.
21For the sake of your name[c] do not
despise us;
do not dishonour your glorious
throne.[d]
Remember your covenant[e] with us
and do not break it.
22Do any of the worthless idols[f] of the
nations bring rain?[g]

2 [b]**Isa 3:26**
3 [c]**Dt 28:48; 2Ki 18:31;** Job 6:19–20; [d]**Est 6:12**
4 [e]**Jer 3:3; 12:11;** Am 4:8; Zec 14:17
5 [f]Isa 15:6
6 [g]**Job 39:5–6; Ps 104:11; Jer 2:24;** [h]**Ge 47:4**
7 [i]**Isa 3:9;** Hos 5:5; [j]**1Sa 12:22; Ps 79:9;** [k]**Jer 2:19;** 5:6; [l]**Jer 8:14**
8 [m]**Ps 9:18;** Jer 17:13; 50:7; [n]Ps 18:46; **Isa 25:9;** [o]Ps 46:1
9 [p]**Isa 50:2;** [q]**Ge 17:7;** Jer 8:19; [r]Isa 63:19; Jer 15:16; [s]**Ps 27:9**
10 [t]Ps 119:101; Jer 2:25; [u]Jer 6:20; Am 5:22; [v]Hos 7:2; 9:9; Am 8:7; [w]Jer 44:21–23; Hos 8:13; Am 3:2
11 [x]**Ex 32:10; 1Sa 2:25**
12 [y]**Dt 1:45; 1Sa 8:18; Jer 11:11;** [z]Lev 1:1–17; Jer 7:21; [a]**Lev 2:1–16;** [b]Am 5:22; [c]**Isa 51:19; Jer 9:16;** [d]Jer 15:2; 16:4; [e]Jer 21:6; 27:8,13; 32:24; 34:17; Eze 14:21
13 [f]Dt 18:22; Jer 27:14; 37:19; [g]**Jer 5:12;** [h]**Isa 30:10; Jer 4:10**
14 [i]**Jer 5:1;** 23:25; 27:14; Eze 13:2; [j]Jer 23:21,32; 29:31; Eze 13:6; [k]Jer 23:16; La 2:9; [l]Eze 12:24
15 [m]Jer 20:6; Eze 14:9; [n]Jer 5:12–13; 16:4; La 1:19
16 [o]Ps 79:3; [p]Jer 7:33; [q]Pr 1:31; **Jer 17:10**
17 [r]Ps 119:136; [s]**2Ki 19:21; Isa 23:12;** [t]**Jer 8:21**
18 [u]Eze 7:15; [v]**2Ch 36:10; Jer 13:17**
19 [w]Jer 7:29; [x]**Isa 1:6;** Jer 30:12–13; [y]**Job 19:8; Jer 8:15**
20 [z]**Jer 3:13;** [a]**Lev 26:40; 1Ki 8:47; Ezr 9:6;** [b]**Jdg 10:10;** Da 9:7–8
21 [c]ver 7; **Jos 7:9;** [d]Isa 62:7; Jer 3:17; [e]**Ex 2:24**
22 [f]**Isa 41:24; 44:10;** Jer 10:15; 16:19; Hab 2:18; [g]**1Ki 8:36; Ps 135:7**

[a]14 Or *visions, worthless divinations*

Do the skies themselves send down
showers?
No, it is you, O LORD our God.
Therefore our hope is in you,
for you are the one who does all
this.[h]

15 Then the LORD said to me:
"Even if Moses[a] and Samuel[b]
were to stand before me, my heart
would not go out to this people.[c] Send
them away from my presence![d] Let
them go! 2And if they ask you, 'Where
shall we go?' tell them, 'This is what the
LORD says:

"'Those destined for death, to death;
those for the sword, to the sword;[e]
those for starvation, to starvation;[f]
those for captivity, to captivity.'[g]

3"I will send four kinds of destroyers[h]
against them," declares the LORD, "the
sword[i] to kill and the dogs[j] to drag away
and the birds[k] of the air and the beasts of
the earth to devour and destroy.[l] 4I will
make them abhorrent[m] to all the king-
doms of the earth[n] because of what
Manasseh[o] son of Hezekiah king of
Judah did in Jerusalem.

5"Who will have pity[p] on you, O
Jerusalem?
Who will mourn for you?
Who will stop to ask how you are?
6You have rejected[q] me," declares the
LORD.
"You keep on backsliding.
So I will lay hands[r] on you and destroy
you;
I can no longer show compassion.[s]
7I will winnow[t] them with a
winnowing fork
at the city gates of the land.
I will bring bereavement[u] and
destruction on my people,[v]
for they have not changed their
ways.[w]
8I will make their widows[x] more
numerous
than the sand of the sea.
At midday I will bring a destroyer[y]
against the mothers of their young
men;
suddenly I will bring down on them
anguish and terror.[z]
9The mother of seven will grow faint[a]
and breathe her last.[b]
Her sun will set while it is still day;
she will be disgraced[c] and
humiliated.
I will put the survivors to the sword[d]
before their enemies,"[e]
declares the LORD.

10Alas, my mother, that you gave me
birth,[f]
a man with whom the whole land
strives and contends![g]
I have neither lent[h] nor borrowed,
yet everyone curses[i] me.

11The LORD said,

"Surely I will deliver you[j] for a good
purpose;
surely I will make your enemies
plead[k] with you
in times of disaster and times of
distress.

12"Can a man break iron—
iron from the north[l]—or bronze?
13Your wealth[m] and your treasures
I will give as plunder,[n] without
charge,[o]
because of all your sins
throughout your country.[p]
14I will enslave you to your enemies
in[a] a land you do not know,[q]
for my anger will kindle a fire[r]
that will burn against you."

15You understand, O LORD;
remember me and care for me.
Avenge me on my persecutors.[s]
You are long-suffering[t]—do not take
me away;
think of how I suffer reproach for
your sake.[u]
16When your words came, I ate[v] them;
they were my joy and my heart's
delight,[w]
for I bear your name,[x]
O LORD God Almighty.
17I never sat[y] in the company of
revellers,
never made merry with them;
I sat alone because your hand[z] was on
me
and you had filled me with
indignation.
18Why is my pain unending
and my wound grievous and
incurable?[a]
Will you be to me like a deceptive
brook,
like a spring that fails?[b]

19Therefore this is what the LORD
says:

22 [h]Isa 43:10
Ch. 15
1 [a]Ex 32:11; Nu 14:13–20; [b]1Sa 1:20; 7:8; [c]1Sa 2:25; Jer 7:16; [d]2Ki 17:20; Jer 16:13
2 [e]Jer 42:22; 43:11; 44:13; [f]Dt 28:26; Jer 14:12; La 4:9; [g]Eze 12:11; Rev 13:10
3 [h]Nu 33:4; [i]Lev 26:25; [j]1Ki 21:19; 2Ki 9:36; [k]Dt 28:26; [l]Lev 26:22; Eze 14:21; 33:27
4 [m]Jer 24:9; 29:18; 34:17; [n]Dt 28:25; Job 17:6; [o]2Ki 21:2; 23:26–27
5 [p]Isa 27:11; 51:19; Jer 13:14; 16:13; 21:7; Na 3:7
6 [q]Dt 32:15; Jer 6:19; [r]Isa 31:3; Zep 1:4; [s]Jer 7:20; Am 7:8
7 [t]Isa 41:16; [u]Isa 3:26; [v]Jer 18:21; [w]2Ch 28:22
8 [x]Isa 47:9; [y]Jer 4:7; 6:4; [z]Job 18:11
9 [a]1Sa 2:5; [b]Job 8:13; [c]Jer 7:19; [d]Jer 21:7; 25:31; [e]2Ki 25:7; Jer 19:7
10 [f]Job 3:1; 10:18–19; [g]Jer 1:19; [h]Lev 25:36; Ne 5:1–12; [i]Jer 6:10
11 [j]ver 21; Jer 40:4; [k]Jer 21:1–2; 37:3; 42:1–3
12 [l]Dt 28:48; Jer 28:14; La 1:14; Hos 10:11
13 [m]2Ki 25:15; [n]2Ki 24:13; Eze 38:12–13; [o]Ps 44:12; [p]Jer 17:3
14 [q]Dt 28:36; Jer 5:19; [r]Ps 21:9
15 [s]Jdg 16:28; Ps 119:84; [t]Ex 34:6; [u]Ps 44:22; 69:7–9; Jer 6:10
16 [v]Eze 2:8; 3:3; Rev 10:10; [w]Job 15:11; Ps 119:72,103; [x]Isa 43:7; Jer 14:9
17 [y]Ru 3:3; Ps 1:1; 26:4–5; Jer 16:8; [z]2Ki 3:15
18 [a]Job 6:4; Jer 10:19; 30:12; Mic 1:9; [b]Job 6:15; Ps 9:10

[a]14 Some Hebrew manuscripts, Septuagint and Syriac (see also Jer. 17:4); most Hebrew manuscripts *I will cause your enemies to bring you / into*

"If you repent, I will restore you
that you may serve[c] me;
if you utter worthy, not worthless,
words,
you will be my spokesman.[d]
Let this people turn to you,
but you must not turn to them.
20I will make you a wall[e] to this people,
a fortified wall of bronze;
they will fight against you
but will not overcome[f] you,
for I am with you
to rescue and save you,"[g]
declares the LORD.
21"I will save[h] you from the hands of the
wicked[i]
and redeem[j] you from the grasp of
the cruel."[k]

Day of Disaster

16 Then the word of the LORD came
to me: 2"You must not marry[a]
and have sons or daughters in this
place." 3For this is what the LORD says
about the sons and daughters born in
this land and about the women who are
their mothers and the men who are their
fathers:[b] 4"They will die of deadly dis-
eases. They will not be mourned or
buried[c] but will be like refuse lying on
the ground.[d] They will perish by sword
and famine,[e] and their dead bodies will
become food for the birds of the air and
the beasts of the earth."[f]
5For this is what the LORD says: "Do
not enter a house where there is a fu-
neral meal; do not go to mourn or show
sympathy, because I have withdrawn
my blessing, my love and my pity[g] from
this people," declares the LORD. 6"Both
high and low will die in this land.[h] They
will not be buried or mourned,[i] and
no-one will cut[j] himself or shave[k] his
head for them. 7No-one will offer food[l]
to comfort those who mourn[m] for the
dead—not even for a father or a mother
—nor will anyone give them a drink to
console[n] them.
8"And do not enter a house where
there is feasting and sit down to eat and
drink.[o] 9For this is what the LORD
Almighty, the God of Israel, says: Be-
fore your eyes and in your days I will
bring an end to the sounds[p] of joy and
gladness and to the voices of bride[q] and
bridegroom in this place.[r]
10"When you tell these people all this
and they ask you, 'Why has the LORD
decreed such a great disaster against us?
What wrong have we done? What sin
have we committed against the LORD
our God?'[s] 11then say to them, 'It is
because your fathers forsook me,' de-
clares the LORD, 'and followed other
gods and served and worshipped[t]
them. They forsook me and did not
keep my law.[u] 12But you have behaved
more wickedly than your fathers.[v] See
how each of you is following the stub-
bornness of his evil heart[w] instead of
obeying me. 13So I will throw you out of
this land[x] into a land neither you nor
your fathers have known,[y] and there
you will serve other gods[z] day and
night, for I will show you no favour.'[a]
14"However, the days are coming,"[b]
declares the LORD, "when men will no
longer say, 'As surely as the LORD lives,
who brought the Israelites up out of
Egypt,'[c] 15but they will say, 'As surely as
the LORD lives, who brought the
Israelites up out of the land of the north[d]
and out of all the countries where he
had banished them.'[e] For I will restore[f]
them to the land I gave to their fore-
fathers.[g]
16"But now I will send for many
fishermen," declares the LORD, "and
they will catch them.[h] After that I will
send for many hunters, and they will
hunt[i] them down on every mountain
and hill and from the crevices of the
rocks.[j] 17My eyes are on all their ways;
they are not hidden[k] from me, nor is
their sin concealed from my eyes.[l] 18I
will repay[m] them double[n] for their wick-
edness and their sin, because they have
defiled my land[o] with the lifeless forms
of their vile images[p] and have filled
my inheritance with their detestable
idols.[q]"[r]

19O LORD, my strength and my fortress,
my refuge[s] in time of distress,
to you the nations will come[t]
from the ends of the earth and say,
"Our fathers possessed nothing but
false gods,[u]
worthless idols[v] that did them no
good.[w]
20Do men make their own gods?
Yes, but they are not gods!"[x]

21"Therefore I will teach them—
this time I will teach them
my power and might.
Then they will know
that my name[y] is the LORD.

19 [c]Zec 3:7; [d]**Ex 4:16**
20 [e]**Isa 50:7**; [f]**Ps 129:2**; [g]**Jer 1:8**; 20:11; 42:11; Eze 3:8
21 [h]**Jer 1:8**; [i]**Ps 97:10**; [j]Jer 50:34; [k]**Ge 48:16**

Ch. 16

2 [a]Mt 19:12; 1Co 7:26–27
3 [b]Jer 6:21
4 [c]ver 6; Jer 25:33; [d]**Jer 9:22**; [e]**Jer 14:15**; [f]**Dt 28:26**; Ps 79:1–3; **Jer 14:12**; 19:7
5 [g]**Jer 15:5**
6 [h]Jer 9:21; Eze 9:5–6; [i]**ver 4**; [j]**Lev 19:28**; [k]**Lev 21:5**; **Job 1:20**
7 [l]**2Sa 3:35**; [m]Jer 22:10; Eze 24:17; Hos 9:4; [n]La 1:9,16
8 [o]**Ex 32:6**; **Ecc 7:2–4**; **Jer 15:17**
9 [p]**Isa 24:8**; **51:3**; Eze 26:13; Am 6:4–7; [q]**Ps 78:63**; [r]Isa 22:12–14; Rev 18:23
10 [s]**Dt 29:24**; Jer 5:19
11 [t]**Job 31:27**; [u]Dt 29:25–26; **1Ki 9:9**; Ps 106:35–43
12 [v]**Ex 32:8**; **Jer 7:26**; Eze 20:30; Am 2:4; [w]**Ecc 9:3**; **Jer 3:17**
13 [x]**2Ch 7:20**; [y]**Dt 28:36**; **Jer 5:19**; [z]**Dt 4:28**; **1Ki 9:9**; [a]**Jer 15:5**
14 [b]Jer 29:10; 30:3; 31:27,38; [c]**Dt 15:15**
15 [d]**Jer 3:18**; [e]**Isa 11:11**; Jer 23:8; [f]Ps 53:6; **Isa 11:12**; Jer 30:3; 32:44; Eze 38:14; Joel 3:1; [g]**Dt 30:3**; **Isa 14:1**
16 [h]Am 4:2; Hab 1:14–15; [i]Am 9:3; Mic 7:2; [j]**1Sa 26:20**
17 [k]**Ge 3:8**; **Ecc 12:14**; **Mk 4:22**; 1Co 4:5; **Heb 4:13**; [l]**Ps 51:9**; Pr 15:3; Zep 1:12
18 [m]**Isa 65:6**; [n]**Isa 40:2**; **Jer 12:3**; Rev 18:6; [o]Nu 35:34; Jer 2:7; [p]**Ps 101:3**; [q]**1Ki 14:24**; [r]**Jer 2:7**; **4:1**; Eze 5:11; 8:10
19 [s]**2Sa 22:3**; **Ps 46:1**; [t]**Isa 2:2**; Jer 3:17; [u]**Ps 4:2**; [v]**Dt 32:21**; **1Sa 12:21**; [w]**Isa 40:19**; **Jer 14:22**
20 [x]Ps 115:4–7; **Jer 2:11**; Ro 1:23
21 [y]**Ex 3:15**

17 "Judah's sin is engraved with an iron tool,[a]
inscribed with a flint point,
on the tablets of their hearts[b]
and on the horns[c] of their altars.
2Even their children remember
their altars and Asherah poles[a] [d]
beside the spreading trees
and on the high hills.[e]
3My mountain in the land
and your[b] wealth and all your treasures
I will give away as plunder,[f]
together with your high places,[g]
because of sin throughout your country.[h]
4Through your own fault you will lose
the inheritance[i] I gave you.
I will enslave you to your enemies[j]
in a land[k] you do not know,
for you have kindled my anger,
and it will burn[l] for ever."

5This is what the LORD says:

"Cursed is the one who trusts in man,[m]
who depends on flesh for his strength
and whose heart turns away from the LORD.[n]
6He will be like a bush in the wastelands;
he will not see prosperity when it comes.
He will dwell in the parched places[o] of the desert,
in a salt[p] land where no-one lives.

7"But blessed[q] is the man who trusts[r] in the LORD,
whose confidence is in him.
8He will be like a tree planted by the water
that sends out its roots by the stream.[s]
It does not fear when heat comes;
its leaves are always green.
It has no worries in a year of drought[t]
and never fails to bear fruit."[u]

9The heart[v] is deceitful above all things
and beyond cure.
Who can understand it?

10"I the LORD search the heart[w]
and examine the mind,[x]
to reward[y] a man according to his conduct,
according to what his deeds deserve."[z]

11Like a partridge that hatches eggs it did not lay
is the man who gains riches by unjust means.
When his life is half gone, they will desert him,
and in the end he will prove to be a fool.[a]

12A glorious throne,[b] exalted from the beginning,
is the place of our sanctuary.
13O LORD, the hope[c] of Israel,
all who forsake[d] you will be put to shame.
Those who turn away from you will be written in the dust[e]
because they have forsaken the LORD,
the spring of living water.[f]

14Heal me, O LORD, and I shall be healed;[g]
save[h] me and I shall be saved,
for you are the one I praise.[i]
15They keep saying to me,
"Where is the word of the LORD?
Let it now be fulfilled!"[j]
16I have not run away from being your shepherd;
you know I have not desired the day of despair.
What passes my lips[k] is open before you.
17Do not be a terror[l] to me;
you are my refuge[m] in the day of disaster.[n]
18Let my persecutors be put to shame,
but keep me from shame;
let them be terrified,
but keep me from terror.
Bring on them the day of disaster;
destroy them with double destruction.[o]

Keeping the Sabbath Holy

19This is what the LORD said to me:
"Go and stand at the gate of the people,
through which the kings of Judah go in
and out; stand also at all the other gates
of Jerusalem.[p] 20Say to them, 'Hear the
word of the LORD, O kings of Judah and
all people of Judah and everyone living
in Jerusalem[q] who come through these
gates.[r] 21This is what the LORD says: Be
careful not to carry a load on the Sab-
bath[s] day or bring it through the gates of
Jerusalem. 22Do not bring a load out of
your houses or do any work on the
Sabbath, but keep the Sabbath day holy,
as I commanded your forefathers.[t] 23Yet

Ch. 17
1 [a]Job 19:24; [b]**Dt 6:6; 2Co 3:3**; [c]**Ex 27:2**
2 [d]**2Ch 24:18**; [e]**Jer 2:20**
3 [f]**2Ki 24:13**; [g]Jer 26:18; Mic 3:12; [h]Jer 15:13
4 [i]La 5:2; [j]Dt 28:48; **Jer 12:7**; [k]Jer 16:13; 22:28; [l]**Jer 7:20**
5 [m]**Ps 108:12**; **Isa 2:22**; [n]2Co 1:9
6 [o]Job 30:3; [p]Dt 29:23; **Job 39:6**; Ps 107:34; Jer 48:9
7 [q]**Ps 146:5**; [r]**Ps 26:1**; 34:8; 40:4; Pr 16:20; Jer 39:18
8 [s]**Job 14:9**; [t]Jer 14:1–6; [u]Ps 1:3; 92:12–14; Eze 19:10; 47:12
9 [v]**Ecc 9:3**; Mt 13:15; Mk 7:21–22
10 [w]**Jos 22:22**; **2Ch 6:30**; **Rev 2:23**; [x]Ps 17:3; 139:23; Jer 11:20; 20:12; Eze 11:5; 38:10; [y]**Lev 26:28**; Ps 62:12; Jer 32:19; **Mt 16:27**; [z]Jer 12:13; 14:16; 21:14; 32:19
11 [a]Lk 12:20
12 [b]**Jer 3:17**
13 [c]Ps 71:5; Jer 14:8; [d]**Jer 2:17**; [e]**Ps 69:28**; 87:6; Eze 13:9; Da 12:1; [f]**Isa 12:3**; Jn 4:10
14 [g]**Isa 30:26**; Jer 15:18; [h]**Ps 119:94**; [i]**Ex 15:2; Ps 109:1**
15 [j]**Isa 5:19**; 2Pe 3:4
16 [k]Ps 139:4
17 [l]Ps 88:15–16; [m]**Ps 46:1**; Jer 16:19; Na 1:7; [n]**Ps 18:18**
18 [o]Ps 35:1–8; **Isa 40:2**; **Jer 12:3**
19 [p]Jer 7:2; 26:2
20 [q]Jer 19:3; [r]Jer 22:2
21 [s]Nu 15:32–36; **Dt 5:14**; Ne 13:15–21; Jn 5:10
22 [t]**Ge 2:3**; **Ex 20:8**; Isa 56:2–6

[a]2 That is, symbols of the goddess Asherah
[b]2, 3 Or *hills* / [3]*and the mountains of the land. / Your*

they did not listen or pay attention;[u]
they were stiff-necked[v] and would not
listen or respond to discipline.[w] 24But if
you are careful to obey me, declares the
LORD, and bring no load through the
gates of this city on the Sabbath, but
keep the Sabbath day holy[x] by not doing
any work on it, 25then kings who sit on
David's throne[y] will come through the
gates of this city with their officials.
They and their officials will come riding
in chariots and on horses, accompanied
by the men of Judah and those living in
Jerusalem, and this city will be in-
habited for ever.[z] 26People will come
from the towns of Judah and the villages
around Jerusalem, from the territory of
Benjamin and the western foothills,
from the hill country and the Negev,[a]
bringing burnt offerings and sacrifices,
grain offerings, incense and thank-
offerings to the house of the LORD. 27But
if you do not obey[b] me to keep the
Sabbath[c] day holy by not carrying any
load as you come through the gates of
Jerusalem on the Sabbath day, then I
will kindle an unquenchable fire[d] in the
gates of Jerusalem that will consume her
fortresses.'"[e]

At the Potter's House

18 This is the word that came to
Jeremiah from the LORD: 2"Go
down to the potter's house, and there I
will give you my message." 3So I went
down to the potter's house, and I saw
him working at the wheel. 4But the pot
he was shaping from the clay was mar-
red in his hands; so the potter formed it
into another pot, shaping it as seemed
best to him.

5Then the word of the LORD came to
me: 6"O house of Israel, can I not do
with you as this potter does?" declares
the LORD. "Like clay[a] in the hand of the
potter, so are you in my hand,[b] O house
of Israel. 7If at any time I announce that
a nation or kingdom is to be uprooted,[c]
torn down and destroyed, 8and if that
nation I warned repents of its evil, then I
will relent[d] and not inflict on it the dis-
aster[e] I had planned. 9And if at another
time I announce that a nation or king-
dom is to be built[f] up and planted, 10and
if it does evil[g] in my sight and does not
obey me, then I will reconsider[h] the
good I had intended to do for it.[i]

11"Now therefore say to the people of
Judah and those living in Jerusalem,
'This is what the LORD says: Look! I
am preparing a disaster[j] for you and
devising a plan[k] against you. So turn[l]
from your evil ways,[m] each one of you,
and reform your ways and your
actions.'[n] 12But they will reply, 'It's no
use.[o] We will continue with our own
plans; each of us will follow the stub-
bornness of his evil heart.[p]'"

13Therefore this is what the LORD says:

"Enquire among the nations:
Who has ever heard anything like
this?[q]
A most horrible[r] thing has been done
by Virgin[s] Israel.
14Does the snow of Lebanon
ever vanish from its rocky slopes?
Do its cool waters from distant sources
ever cease to flow?[a]
15Yet my people have forgotten[t] me;
they burn incense[u] to worthless
idols,[v]
which made them stumble[w] in their
ways
and in the ancient paths.[x]
They made them walk in bypaths
and on roads not built up.[y]
16Their land will be laid waste,[z]
an object of lasting scorn;[a]
all who pass by will be appalled[b]
and will shake their heads.[c]
17Like a wind[d] from the east,
I will scatter them before their
enemies;
I will show them my back and not my
face[e]
in the day of their disaster."

18They said, "Come, let's make plans[f]
against Jeremiah; for the teaching of the
law by the priest[g] will not be lost, nor
will counsel from the wise,[h] nor the
word from the prophets.[i] So come, let's
attack him with our tongues[j] and pay no
attention to anything he says."

19Listen to me, O LORD;
hear what my accusers[k] are saying!
20Should good be repaid with evil?[l]
Yet they have dug a pit[m] for me.
Remember that I stood[n] before you
and spoke on their behalf[o]
to turn your wrath away from them.
21So give their children over to famine;[p]
hand them over to the power of the
sword.[q]

17:23 [u]Jer 7:26; [v]Jer 19:15; [w]**2Ch 28:22; Jer 7:28**; Zec 7:11
24 [x]ver 22
25 [y]**2Sa 7:13**; Isa 9:7; Jer 22:2,4; Lk 1:32; [z]Jer 30:10; 33:16; Eze 28:26
26 [a]Jer 32:44; 33:13; Zec 7:7
27 [b]**1Ki 9:6**; Jer 22:5; [c]**Ne 10:31**; [d]**Jer 7:20**; [e]**2Ki 25:9**; Hos 8:14; Am 2:5

Ch. 18

6 [a]**Isa 29:16**; 45:9; Ro 9:20–21; [b]**Ge 2:7**
7 [c]Jer 1:10
8 [d]**Ex 32:14**; Ps 25:11; Jer 26:13; 36:3; Jnh 3:8–10; [e]Jer 31:28; 42:10; Da 9:14; Hos 11:8–9; Joel 2:13; Jnh 4:2
9 [f]Jer 1:10; 31:28
10 [g]Eze 33:18; [h]1Sa 2:29–30; 13:13; [i]**Jer 1:10**
11 [j]**2Ki 22:16; Jer 4:6**; [k]ver 18; [l]**Dt 4:30; 2Ki 17:13**; Isa 1:16–19; [m]**Jer 7:3**; [n]**Job 16:17**
12 [o]**Isa 57:10**; [p]**Jer 3:17**
13 [q]**Isa 66:8**; [r]**Jer 5:30**; [s]**2Ki 19:21**
15 [t]**Isa 17:10**; [u]**Isa 1:13**; Jer 44:15,19; [v]Jer 10:15; 51:18; Hos 11:2; [w]Eze 44:12; Mal 2:8; [x]Jer 6:16; [y]**Isa 57:14**; 62:10
16 [z]**Dt 28:37**; Jer 25:9; Eze 33:28–29; [a]Jer 19:8; 42:18; [b]**Lev 26:32**; [c]**2Ki 19:21; Job 16:4**; Ps 22:7; La 1:12
17 [d]**Job 7:10**; Jer 13:24; [e]**2Ch 29:6; Jer 2:27**
18 [f]ver 11; Jer 11:19; [g]Jer 2:8; Hag 2:11; Mal 2:7; [h]**Job 5:13**; Eze 7:26; [i]Jer 5:13; [j]Ps 52:2; 64:2–8; **Jer 9:3**
19 [k]Ps 71:13
20 [l]**Ge 44:4**; [m]Ps 35:7; 57:6; **119:85**; [n]Jer 15:1; [o]**Ge 20:7; Dt 9:19**; Ps 106:23; Jer 14:7–9
21 [p]Jer 11:22; 14:16; [q]**Ps 63:10**

[a]*14* The meaning of the Hebrew for this sentence is uncertain.

Let their wives be made childless and
widows;[r]
let their men be put to death,
their young men[s] slain by the sword
in battle.
22Let a cry[t] be heard from their houses
when you suddenly bring invaders
against them,
for they have dug a pit[u] to capture me
and have hidden snares[v] for my
feet.
23But you know, O LORD,
all their plots to kill[w] me.
Do not forgive[x] their crimes
or blot out their sins from your
sight.
Let them be overthrown before you;
deal with them in the time of your
anger.[y]

19

This is what the LORD says: "Go
and buy a clay jar from a potter.[a]
Take along some of the elders[b] of the
people and of the priests 2and go out to
the Valley of Ben Hinnom,[c] near the
entrance of the Potsherd Gate. There
proclaim the words I tell you, 3and say,
'Hear the word of the LORD, O kings[d] of
Judah and people of Jerusalem. This is
what the LORD Almighty, the God of
Israel, says: Listen! I am going to bring
a disaster[e] on this place that will make
the ears of everyone who hears of it
tingle.[f] 4For they have forsaken[g] me and
made this a place of foreign gods[h]; they
have burned sacrifices[i] in it to gods that
neither they nor their fathers nor the
kings of Judah ever knew, and they
have filled this place with the blood of
the innocent.[j] 5They have built the high
places of Baal to burn their sons[k] in the
fire as offerings to Baal—something I
did not command or mention, nor did it
enter my mind.[l] 6So beware, the days
are coming, declares the LORD, when
people will no longer call this place
Topheth[m] or the Valley of Ben Hinnom,[n]
but the Valley of Slaughter.[o]
7" 'In this place I will ruin[a] the plans[p]
of Judah and Jerusalem. I will make
them fall by the sword before their ene-
mies,[q] at the hands of those who seek
their lives, and I will give their car-
casses[r] as food[s] to the birds of the air and
the beasts of the earth. 8I will devastate
this city and make it an object of scorn;[t]
all who pass by will be appalled[u] and
will scoff because of all its wounds.[v] 9I
will make them eat[w] the flesh of their
sons and daughters, and they will eat
one another's flesh during the stress
of the siege imposed on them by the
enemies[x] who seek their lives.'
10"Then break the jar[y] while those
who go with you are watching, 11and
say to them, 'This is what the LORD
Almighty says: I will smash[z] this nation
and this city just as this potter's jar is
smashed and cannot be repaired. They
will bury[a] the dead in Topheth until
there is no more room. 12This is what I
will do to this place and to those who
live here, declares the LORD. I will make
this city like Topheth. 13The houses[b] in
Jerusalem and those of the kings of
Judah will be defiled[c] like this place,
Topheth—all the houses where they
burned incense on the roofs[d] to all
the starry hosts[e] and poured out drink
offerings[f] to other gods.' "
14Jeremiah then returned from
Topheth, where the LORD had sent him
to prophesy, and stood in the court[g]
of the LORD's temple and said to all
the people, 15"This is what the LORD
Almighty, the God of Israel, says:
'Listen! I am going to bring on this
city and the villages around it every
disaster[h] I pronounced against them,
because they were stiff-necked[i] and
would not listen[j] to my words.' "

Jeremiah and Pashhur

20

When the priest Pashhur son of
Immer,[a] the chief officer[b] in the
temple of the LORD, heard Jeremiah
prophesying these things, 2he had Jere-
miah the prophet beaten[c] and put in the
stocks[d] at the Upper Gate of Benjamin[e]
at the LORD's temple. 3The next day,
when Pashhur released him from the
stocks, Jeremiah said to him, "The
LORD's name[f] for you is not Pashhur, but
Magor-Missabib.[a][g] 4For this is what the
LORD says: 'I will make you a terror to
yourself and to all your friends; with
your own eyes[h] you will see them fall by
the sword of their enemies. I will hand[i]
all Judah over to the king of Babylon,
who will carry[j] them away to Babylon or
put them to the sword. 5I will hand over
to their enemies all the wealth[k] of this
city—all its products, all its valuables
and all the treasures of the kings of
Judah. They will take it away[l] as plun-
der and carry it off to Babylon. 6And

21 [r]1Sa 15:33; Ps 109:9; **Isa 47:9**; La 5:3; [s]**Isa 9:17**
22 [t]**Jer 6:26**; [u]**Ps 119:85**; [v]Ps 35:15; 140:5; Jer 5:26; 20:10
23 [w]**Jer 11:21**; 37:15; [x]**Ne 4:5**; [y]Ps 59:5; **Jer 10:24**

Ch. 19

1 [a]Jer 18:2; [b]**Nu 11:17**; 1Ki 8:1
2 [c]**Jos 15:8**
3 [d]Jer 17:20; [e]**Jer 6:19**; [f]**1Sa 3:11**
4 [g]**Dt 31:16**; **Isa 65:11**; [h]**Ex 20:3**; **Jer 1:16**; [i]**Lev 18:21**; [j]**2Ki 21:16**
5 [k]**Lev 18:21**; **2Ki 3:27**; Ps 106:37–38; [l]**Jer 7:31**; Eze 16:36
6 [m]**2Ki 23:10**; [n]**Jos 15:8**; [o]Jer 7:32
7 [p]Ps 33:10–11; [q]**ver 9**; **Lev 26:17**; **Dt 28:25**; [r]**Jer 16:4**; 34:20; [s]**Dt 28:26**
8 [t]**Dt 28:37**; **Jer 18:16**; 25:9; [u]**Lev 26:32**; La 2:15–16; [v]**Dt 29:22**
9 [w]**Lev 26:29**; Dt 28:49–57; La 4:10; [x]**ver 7**; Jer 21:7; 34:20
10 [y]ver 1; **Ps 2:9**; Jer 13:14
11 [z]Ps 2:9; Isa 30:14; [a]Jer 7:32
13 [b]Jer 32:29; 52:13; Eze 16:41; [c]Ps 74:7; [d]**2Ki 23:12**; [e]Dt 4:19; **2Ki 17:16**; **Job 38:32**; Jer 8:2; Ac 7:42; [f]**Isa 57:6**; Eze 20:28
14 [g]2Ch 20:5; **Jer 7:2**; 26:2
15 [h]ver 3; Jer 11:11; [i]**Ne 9:16**; Ac 7:51; [j]Jer 22:21

Ch. 20

1 [a]**1Ch 24:14**; [b]2Ki 25:18; Lk 22:52
2 [c]Dt 25:2–3; **Jer 1:19**; 15:15; 37:15; 2Co 11:24; [d]**Job 13:27**; Jer 29:26; Ac 16:24; Heb 11:36; [e]**Job 29:7**; Jer 37:13; 38:7; Zec 14:10
3 [f]Hos 1:4; [g]**ver 10**; **Ps 31:13**
4 [h]Jer 29:21; [i]Jer 21:10; 25:9; [j]Jer 13:19; 39:9; 52:27
5 [k]**2Ki 25:15**; Jer 17:3; [l]**2Ki 20:17**

[a]7 The Hebrew for *ruin* sounds like the Hebrew for *jar* (see verses 1 and 10).
[a]3 *Magor-Missabib* means *terror on every side*.

you, Pashhur, and all who live in your house will go into exile to Babylon. There you will die and be buried, you and all your friends to whom you have prophesied[m] lies.' "

Jeremiah's Complaint

7O LORD, you deceived[b] [n] me, and I was
deceived;[b]
you overpowered[o] me and
prevailed.
I am ridiculed[p] all day long;
everyone mocks[q] me.
8Whenever I speak, I cry out
proclaiming violence and
destruction.[r]
So the word of the LORD has brought
me
insult and reproach[s] all day long.
9But if I say, "I will not mention him
or speak any more in his name,"[t]
his word is in my heart like a fire,[u]
a fire shut up in my bones.
I am weary of holding it in;[v]
indeed, I cannot.
10I hear many whispering,
"Terror[w] on every side!
Report[x] him! Let's report him!"
All my friends[y]
are waiting for me to slip,[z] saying,
"Perhaps he will be deceived;
then we will prevail[a] over him
and take our revenge[b] on him."

11But the LORD[c] is with me like a mighty
warrior;
so my persecutors[d] will stumble and
not prevail.[e]
They will fail and be thoroughly
disgraced;[f]
their dishonour will never be
forgotten.
12O LORD Almighty, you who examine
the righteous
and probe the heart and mind,[g]
let me see your vengeance[h] upon
them,
for to you I have committed[i] my
cause.

13Sing[j] to the LORD!
Give praise to the LORD!
He rescues[k] the life of the needy
from the hands of the wicked.[l]

14Cursed be the day I was born![m]
May the day my mother bore me not
be blessed!
15Cursed be the man who brought my
father the news,
who made him very glad, saying,
"A child is born to you—a son!"
16May that man be like the towns[n]
the LORD overthrew without pity.
May he hear wailing[o] in the morning,
a battle cry at noon.
17For he did not kill me in the womb,[p]
with my mother as my grave,
her womb enlarged for ever.
18Why did I ever come out of the womb[q]
to see trouble[r] and sorrow
and to end my days in shame?[s]

God Rejects Zedekiah's Request

21 The word came to Jeremiah
from the LORD when King Zede-
kiah[a] sent to him Pashhur[b] son of Malki-
jah and the priest Zephaniah[c] son of
Maaseiah. They said: 2"Enquire[d] now of
the LORD for us because Nebuchadnez-
zar[a] [e] king of Babylon[f] is attacking us.
Perhaps the LORD will perform won-
ders[g] for us as in times past so that he
will withdraw from us."
3But Jeremiah answered them, "Tell
Zedekiah, 4'This is what the LORD, the
God of Israel, says: I am about to turn[h]
against you the weapons of war that are
in your hands, which you are using to
fight the king of Babylon and the
Babylonians[b] who are outside the wall
besieging[i] you. And I will gather them
inside this city. 5I myself will fight[j]
against you with an outstretched hand[k]
and a mighty arm[l] in anger and fury and
great wrath. 6I will strike[m] down those
who live in this city—both men and
animals—and they will die of a terrible
plague.[n] 7After that, declares the LORD, I
will hand over Zedekiah[o] king of Judah,
his officials and the people in this city
who survive the plague,[p] sword and
famine, to Nebuchadnezzar king of
Babylon[q] and to their enemies[r] who seek
their lives.[s] He will put them to the
sword;[t] he will show them no mercy or
pity or compassion.'[u]
8"Furthermore, tell the people, 'This
is what the LORD says: See, I am setting
before you the way of life[v] and the way
of death. 9Whoever stays in this city will
die by the sword, famine or plague.[w]
But whoever goes out and surrenders[x]

6 [m]Jer 14:15; La 2:14
7 [n]Ex 5:23; 22:16; [o]Isa 8:11; Am 3:8; 1Co 9:16; [p]Job 12:4; [q]Job 17:2; Ps 119:21
8 [r]Jer 6:7; 28:8; [s]2Ch 36:16; Jer 6:10
9 [t]Jer 44:16; [u]Ps 39:3; Jer 4:19; [v]Job 4:2; Jer 6:11; Am 3:8; Ac 4:20
10 [w]Jer 6:25; [x]Ne 6:6–13; Isa 29:21; [y]Job 19:14; Jer 13:21; [z]Ps 57:4; Jer 18:22; Lk 11:53–54; [a]1Ki 19:2; [b]1Sa 18:25; Jer 11:19
11 [c]Jer 1:8; Ro 8:31; [d]Jer 15:15; 17:18; [e]Ps 129:2; [f]Jer 7:19; 23:40
12 [g]Ps 7:9; Jer 17:10; [h]Dt 32:35; Ro 12:19; [i]Ps 62:8; Jer 11:20
13 [j]Isa 12:6; [k]Ps 34:6; 35:10; [l]Ps 97:10
14 [m]Job 3:8,16; Jer 15:10
16 [n]Ge 19:25; [o]Jer 6:26
17 [p]Job 3:16; 10:18–19
18 [q]Job 3:10–11; Ecc 4:2; [r]Ge 3:17; Job 5:7; [s]1Ki 19:4; Ps 90:9; 102:3

Ch. 21

1 [a]2Ki 24:18; Jer 52:1; [b]1Ch 9:12; [c]2Ki 25:18
2 [d]Ge 25:22; 2Ki 22:18; [e]2Ki 25:1; [f]Ge 10:10; [g]Ps 44:1–4; Jer 32:17
4 [h]Jer 32:5; [i]Jer 37:8–10
5 [j]Jos 10:14; Eze 5:8; [k]2Ki 22:13; Jer 6:12; [l]Ex 3:20
6 [m]Jer 7:20; [n]Jer 14:12
7 [o]2Ki 25:7; Jer 52:9; Eze 12:14; [p]Jer 14:12; 27:8; [q]2Ch 36:10; Jer 27:6; 32:4; 34:3; 37:17; 38:18; 39:5; Eze 29:19; [r]Lev 26:17; Jer 19:9; [s]Jer 11:21; [t]Jer 15:9; [u]2Ch 36:17; Jer 15:5; Eze 7:9; Hab 1:6
8 [v]Dt 30:15
9 [w]Jer 14:12; Eze 5:12; [x]Jer 27:11; 40:9

[b]7 Or *persuaded*
[a]2 Hebrew *Nebuchadrezzar,* of which *Nebuchadnezzar* is a variant; here and often in Jeremiah and Ezekiel
[b]4 Or *Chaldeans;* also in verse 9

to the Babylonians who are besieging you will live; he will escape with his life.[y] 10I have determined to do this city harm[z] and not good, declares the LORD. It will be given into the hands[a] of the king of Babylon, and he will destroy it with fire.'[b]

11"Moreover, say to the royal house[c] of Judah, 'Hear the word of the LORD; 12O house of David, this is what the LORD says:

"'Administer justice[d] every morning;
rescue from the hand of his oppressor[e]
the one who has been robbed,
or my wrath will break out and burn like fire[f]
because of the evil[g] you have done—
burn with no-one to quench[h] it.
13I am against[i] you, ⌞Jerusalem,⌟
you who live above this valley[j]
on the rocky plateau,
declares the LORD—
you who say, "Who can come against us?
Who can enter our refuge?"[k]
14I will punish you as your deeds[l] deserve,
declares the LORD.
I will kindle a fire[m] in your forests[n]
that will consume everything around you.'"

Judgment Against Evil Kings

22 This is what the LORD says: "Go down to the palace of the king[a] of Judah and proclaim this message there: 2'Hear[b] the word of the LORD, O king of Judah, you who sit on David's throne[c]—you, your officials and your people who come through these gates.[d] 3This is what the LORD says: Do what is just[e] and right. Rescue from the hand of his oppressor[f] the one who has been robbed. Do no wrong or violence to the alien, the fatherless or the widow,[g] and do not shed innocent blood[h] in this place. 4For if you are careful to carry out these commands, then kings[i] who sit on David's throne will come through the gates of this palace, riding in chariots and on horses, accompanied by their officials and their people. 5But if you do not obey[j] these commands, declares the LORD, I swear[k] by myself that this palace will become a ruin.'"

6For this is what the LORD says about the palace of the king of Judah:

"Though you are like Gilead[l] to me,
like the summit of Lebanon,[m]
I will surely make you like a desert,[n]
like towns not inhabited.
7I will send destroyers[o] against you,
each man with his weapons,
and they will cut[p] up your fine cedar beams
and throw them into the fire.[q]

8"People from many nations will pass by this city and will ask one another, 'Why has the LORD done such a thing to this great city?'[r] 9And the answer will be: 'Because they have forsaken the covenant of the LORD their God and have worshipped and served other gods.'[s]"

10Do not weep for the dead[t] ⌞king⌟ or mourn[u] his loss;
rather, weep bitterly for him who is exiled,
because he will never return[v]
nor see his native land again.

11For this is what the LORD says about Shallum[a][w] son of Josiah, who succeeded his father as king of Judah but has gone from this place: "He will never return. 12He will die[x] in the place where they have led him captive; he will not see this land again."

13"Woe[y] to him who builds[z] his palace by unrighteousness,
his upper rooms by injustice,
making his countrymen work for nothing,
not paying[a] them for their labour.
14He says, 'I will build myself a great palace[b]
with spacious upper rooms.'
So he makes large windows in it,
panels it with cedar[c]
and decorates it in red.[d]

15Does it make you a king
to have more and more cedar?
Did not your father have food and drink?
He did what was right and just,[e]
so all went well[f] with him.
16He defended the cause of the poor and needy,[g]
and so all went well.
Is that not what it means to know[h] me?"
declares the LORD.

9 [y]Jer 27:12; 38:2,17; 39:18; 45:5
10 [z]Jer 44:27; Am 9:4; [a]**Jer 20:4**; 32:28; 38:2–3; [b]**2Ki 25:9; 2Ch 36:19**
11 [c]**Jer 13:18**
12 [d]**Ex 22:22; Lev 25:17**; [e]**Ps 27:11**; [f]**Isa 42:25; Jer 10:10**; [g]Jer 23:2; [h]**Isa 1:31**
13 [i]Jer 23:30; 50:31; 51:25; Eze 5:8; 13:8; 21:3; 29:10; 34:10; Na 2:13; 3:5; [j]Ps 125:2; [k]2Sa 5:6–7; Jer 49:4; La 4:12; Ob 3–4
14 [l]**Pr 1:31; Isa 3:10–11; Jer 17:10**; [m]**2Ch 36:19**; La 2:3; [n]**2Ki 19:23**; Eze 20:47

Ch. 22

1 [a]**Jer 13:18**; 34:2
2 [b]Am 7:16; [c]**Jer 17:25**; Lk 1:32; [d]Jer 17:20
3 [e]**Lev 25:17**; Isa 56:1; Jer 5:1; Eze 33:14; 45:9; Hos 12:6; Am 5:24; Mic 6:8; Zec 7:9; [f]Ps 72:4; Jer 21:12; [g]**Ex 22:22; Isa 1:17**; Jer 5:28; [h]**Jer 7:6**
4 [i]**Jer 17:25**
5 [j]**Jer 17:27**; [k]**Ge 22:16**; Heb 6:13
6 [l]**Ge 31:21; SS 4:1**; [m]**1Ki 7:2; Isa 33:9**; [n]Mic 3:12
7 [o]**Jer 4:7; 6:4**; [p]Ps 74:5; Isa 10:34; [q]**2Ch 36:19**; Zec 11:1
8 [r]Dt 29:25–26; 1Ki 9:8–9; Jer 16:10–11
9 [s]**1Ki 9:9**; Jer 16:11; Eze 39:23
10 [t]**Ecc 4:2**; [u]ver 18; Eze 24:16; [v]ver 27; Jer 24:9; 29:18; 42:18
11 [w]**2Ki 23:31**
12 [x]2Ki 23:34
13 [y]**Isa 5:8**; [z]Mic 3:10; Hab 2:9; [a]**Lev 19:13**; Jas 5:4
14 [b]Isa 5:8–9; [c]**2Sa 7:2**; [d]Eze 23:14
15 [e]2Ki 23:25; [f]Ps 128:2; **Isa 3:10**
16 [g]Ps 72:1–4, 12–13; **82:3; Pr 24:23**; [h]**Ps 36:10**

[a]*11* Also called *Jehoahaz*

17"But your eyes and your heart
are set only on dishonest gain,[i]
on shedding innocent blood[j]
and on oppression and extortion."[k]

18Therefore this is what the LORD says
about Jehoiakim son of Josiah king of
Judah:

"They will not mourn[l] for him:
'Alas, my brother! Alas, my sister!'
They will not mourn for him:
'Alas, my master! Alas, his
splendour!'
19He will have the burial[m] of a donkey—
dragged away and thrown[n]
outside the gates of Jerusalem."

20"Go up to Lebanon and cry out,[o]
let your voice be heard in Bashan,[p]
cry out from Abarim,[q]
for all your allies[r] are crushed.
21I warned you when you felt secure,[s]
but you said, 'I will not listen!'
This has been your way from your
youth;[t]
you have not obeyed[u] me.
22The wind[v] will drive all your
shepherds[w] away,
and your allies[x] will go into exile.
Then you will be ashamed and
disgraced[y]
because of all your wickedness.
23You who live in 'Lebanon,[b][z]'
who are nestled in cedar buildings,
how you will groan when pangs come
upon you,
pain[a] like that of a woman in labour!

24"As surely as I live," declares the
LORD, "even if you, Jehoiachin[c][b] son of
Jehoiakim king of Judah, were a signet
ring[c] on my right hand, I would still pull
you off. 25I will hand you over[d] to those
who seek your life, those you fear—to
Nebuchadnezzar king of Babylon and to
the Babylonians.[d] 26I will hurl[e] you and
the mother[f] who gave you birth into
another country, where neither of you
was born, and there you both will die.
27You will never come back to the land
you long to return[g] to."

28Is this man Jehoiachin[h] a despised,
broken pot,[i]
an object no-one wants?
Why will he and his children be
hurled[j] out,
cast into a land[k] they do not know?
29O land,[l] land, land,
hear the word of the LORD!
30This is what the LORD says:
"Record this man as if childless,[m]
a man who will not prosper[n] in his
lifetime,
for none of his offspring[o] will prosper,
none will sit on the throne[p] of David
or rule any more in Judah."

The Righteous Branch

23 "Woe to the shepherds[a] who
are destroying and scattering[b]
the sheep of my pasture!"[c] declares the
LORD. 2Therefore this is what the LORD,
the God of Israel, says to the shepherds[d]
who tend my people: "Because you
have scattered my flock[e] and driven
them away and have not bestowed care
on them, I will bestow punishment on
you for the evil[f] you have done," de-
clares the LORD. 3"I myself will gather
the remnant[g] of my flock out of all the
countries where I have driven them and
will bring them back to their pasture,[h]
where they will be fruitful and increase
in number. 4I will place shepherds[i] over
them who will tend them, and they will
no longer be afraid[j] or terrified, nor will
any be missing,[k]" declares the LORD.

5"The days are coming," declares the
LORD,
"when I will raise up to David[a] a
righteous Branch,[l]
a King[m] who will reign[n] wisely
and do what is just and right[o] in the
land.
6In his days Judah will be saved
and Israel will live in safety.[p]
This is the name[q] by which he will be
called:
The LORD Our Righteousness.[r]

7"So then, the days are coming,"[s] de-
clares the LORD, "when people will no
longer say, 'As surely as the LORD lives,
who brought the Israelites up out of
Egypt,'[t] 8but they will say, 'As surely as
the LORD lives, who brought the descen-
dants of Israel up out of the land of the
north and out of all the countries where
he had banished them.' Then they will
live in their own land."[u]

17 [i]**Isa 56:11;** [j]2Ki 24:4; [k]**Dt 28:33;** Eze 18:12; Mic 2:2
18 [l]**2Sa 1:26**
19 [m]2Ki 24:6; [n]Jer 8:2; 36:30
20 [o]**Isa 57:13;** [p]**Ps 68:15;** [q]**Nu 27:12;** [r]ver 22; Jer 30:14; La 1:19; Eze 16:33–34; Hos 8:9
21 [s]Zec 7:7; [t]Dt 9:7; Ps 25:7; Isa 54:4; Jer 3:25; 31:19; 32:30; [u]**Jer 3:13;** 7:23–28; Zep 3:2
22 [v]**Dt 28:64; Job 27:21;** [w]**Jer 10:21;** [x]**ver 20;** [y]**Jer 7:19**
23 [z]**1Ki 7:2;** Eze 17:3; [a]**Jer 4:31**
24 [b]**2Ki 24:6,**8; [c]**Ge 38:18**
25 [d]**2Ki 24:16; 2Ch 36:10**
26 [e]**1Sa 25:29; 2Ki 24:8;** 2Ch 36:10; **Isa 22:17;** Eze 19:9–14; [f]**1Ki 2:19**
27 [g]**ver 10**
28 [h]**2Ki 24:6;** [i]Ps 31:12; **Jer 19:10;** 25:34; 48:38; [j]Jer 15:1; [k]**Jer 17:4**
29 [l]**Jer 6:19**
30 [m]1Ch 3:18; Jer 38:23; 52:10; Mt 1:12; [n]Jer 10:21; [o]**Job 18:19;** [p]**Ps 94:20**

Ch. 23

1 [a]Jer 10:21; 12:10; 25:36; Eze 34:1–10; Zec 10:2; 11:15–17; [b]**Isa 56:11;** [c]Ps 100:3; **Jer 13:17;** Eze 34:31
2 [d]Jn 10:8; [e]**Jer 10:21;** 13:20; [f]Jer 21:12; Eze 34:8–10
3 [g]Isa 11:10–12; Jer 32:37; Eze 34:11–16; [h]**1Ki 8:48**
4 [i]**Ge 48:15; Isa 31:4;** Jer 31:10; [j]Jer 30:10; 46:27–28; [k]**Jn 6:39**
5 [l]**2Ki 19:26; Isa 4:2;** Eze 17:22; [m]**Mt 2:2;** [n]Isa 9:7; **Mt 1:1;** [o]**Ge 18:19**
6 [p]**Lev 25:18; Dt 32:8;** Hos 2:18; [q]Ex 23:21; Jer 33:16; Mt 1:21–23; [r]**Ezr 9:15; Isa 42:6;** Ro 3:21–22; **1Co 1:30**
7 [s]Jer 30:3; [t]**Dt 15:15**
8 [u]**Isa 14:1; 43:5–6;** Jer 30:10; Eze 20:42; 34:13; Am 9:14–15

b23 That is, the palace in Jerusalem (see 1 Kings 7:2)
c24 Hebrew *Coniah,* a variant of *Jehoiachin;* also in verse 28
d25 Or *Chaldeans*
a5 Or *up from David's line*

Lying Prophets

9Concerning the prophets:

My heart[v] is broken within me;
all my bones tremble.[w]
I am like a drunken man,
like a man overcome by wine,
because of the LORD
and his holy words.[x]
10The land is full of adulterers;[y]
because of the curse[b] [z] the land lies
parched[c]
and the pastures[a] in the desert are
withered.[b]
The ⌞prophets⌟ follow an evil course
and use their power unjustly.

11"Both prophet and priest are godless;[c]
even in my temple[d] I find their
wickedness,"
declares the LORD.
12"Therefore their path will become
slippery;[e]
they will be banished to darkness
and there they will fall.
I will bring disaster on them
in the year they are punished,[f]"
declares the LORD.

13"Among the prophets of Samaria
I saw this repulsive thing:
They prophesied by Baal[g]
and led my people Israel astray.[h]
14And among the prophets of Jerusalem
I have seen something horrible:[i]
They commit adultery and live a lie.[j]
They strengthen the hands of
evildoers,[k]
so that no-one turns from his
wickedness.[l]
They are all like Sodom[m] to me;
the people of Jerusalem are like
Gomorrah."[n]

15Therefore, this is what the LORD Almighty says concerning the prophets:

"I will make them eat bitter food
and drink poisoned water,[o]
because from the prophets of
Jerusalem
ungodliness[p] has spread
throughout the land."

16This is what the LORD Almighty says:

"Do not listen[q] to what the prophets
are prophesying to you;
they fill you with false hopes.
They speak visions[r] from their own
minds,
not from the mouth[s] of the LORD.
17They keep saying[t] to those who
despise me,
'The LORD says: You will have
peace.'[u]
And to all who follow the
stubbornness[v] of their hearts
they say, 'No harm[w] will come to
you.'
18But which of them has stood in the
council[x] of the LORD
to see or to hear his word?
Who has listened and heard his
word?
19See, the storm[y] of the LORD
will burst out in wrath,
a whirlwind[z] swirling down
on the heads of the wicked.
20The anger[a] of the LORD will not turn
back[b]
until he fully accomplishes
the purposes of his heart.
In days to come
you will understand it clearly.
21I did not send[c] these prophets,
yet they have run with their
message;
I did not speak to them,
yet they have prophesied.
22But if they had stood in my council,[d]
they would have proclaimed[e] my
words to my people
and would have turned[f] them from
their evil ways
and from their evil deeds.[g]

23"Am I only a God nearby,[h]"
declares the LORD,
"and not a God far away?
24Can anyone hide[i] in secret places
so that I cannot see him?"
declares the LORD.
"Do not I fill heaven and earth?"[j]
declares the LORD.

25"I have heard what the prophets say
who prophesy lies[k] in my name. They
say, 'I had a dream![l] I had a dream!'
26How long will this continue in the
hearts of these lying prophets, who
prophesy the delusions[m] of their own
minds?[n] 27They think the dreams they
tell one another will make my people
forget[o] my name, just as their fathers
forgot[p] my name through Baal wor-
ship.[q] 28Let the prophet who has a
dream[r] tell his dream, but let the one
who has my word[s] speak it faithfully.
For what has straw to do with grain?"

9 [v]Jer 4:19; [w]Job 4:14; [x]Jer 20:8–9
10 [y]Jer 9:2; [z]Dt 28:23–24; [a]Ps 107:34; Jer 9:10; [b]Jer 4:26; 12:11
11 [c]Jer 6:13; 8:10; Zep 3:4; [d]2Ki 21:4; Jer 7:10
12 [e]Dt 32:35; Job 3:23; Jer 13:16; [f]Jer 11:23
13 [g]1Ki 18:22; [h]ver 32; Isa 3:12; Eze 13:10
14 [i]Jer 5:30; Hos 6:10; [j]Jer 29:23; [k]ver 22; [l]Isa 5:18; [m]Ge 18:20; Mt 11:24; [n]Jer 20:16; Am 4:11
15 [o]Jer 8:14; 9:15; [p]Jer 8:10
16 [q]Jer 27:9–10, 14; Mt 7:15; [r]Jer 14:14; Eze 13:3; [s]Jer 9:20
17 [t]ver 31; [u]1Ki 22:8; Jer 4:10; [v]Jer 13:10; [w]Jer 5:12; Am 9:10; Mic 3:11
18 [x]1Ki 22:19; Ro 11:34
19 [y]Isa 30:30; Jer 25:32; 30:23; [z]Zec 7:14
20 [a]2Ki 23:26; [b]Jer 4:28
21 [c]Jer 14:14; 27:15
22 [d]1Ki 22:19; [e]Dt 33:10; [f]2Ki 17:13; Jer 25:5; Zec 1:4; [g]ver 14; Am 3:7
23 [h]Ps 139:1–10
24 [i]Ge 3:8; Job 11:20; 22:12–14; Ecc 12:14; Isa 28:15; 1Co 4:5; [j]1Ki 8:27
25 [k]ver 16; Jer 14:14; 27:10; [l]ver 28,32; Dt 13:1; Jer 27:9; 29:8
26 [m]Isa 30:10; 1Ti 4:1–2; [n]Jer 14:14; Eze 13:2
27 [o]Dt 13:1–3; Jer 29:8; [p]Jdg 3:7; 8:33–34; [q]Jer 2:23
28 [r]ver 25; [s]1Sa 3:17

b*10* Or *because of these things*
c*10* Or *land mourns*

declares the LORD. 29 "Is not my word like fire,"[t] declares the LORD, "and like a hammer[u] that breaks a rock in pieces?

30 "Therefore," declares the LORD, "I am against[v] the prophets[w] who steal from one another words supposedly from me. 31 Yes," declares the LORD, "I am against the prophets who wag their own tongues and yet declare, 'The LORD declares.'[x] 32 Indeed, I am against those who prophesy false dreams,[y]" declares the LORD. "They tell them and lead my people astray[z] with their reckless lies,[a] yet I did not send[b] or appoint them. They do not benefit[c] these people in the least," declares the LORD.

False Oracles and False Prophets

33 "When these people, or a prophet or a priest, ask you, 'What is the oracle[d][d] of the LORD?' say to them, 'What oracle?[e] I will forsake[e] you, declares the LORD.' 34 If a prophet or a priest or anyone else claims, 'This is the oracle[f] of the LORD,' I will punish[g] that man and his household. 35 This is what each of you keeps on saying to his friend or relative: 'What is the LORD's answer?'[h] or 'What has the LORD spoken?' 36 But you must not mention 'the oracle of the LORD' again, because every man's own word becomes his oracle and so you distort[i] the words of the living God,[j] the LORD Almighty, our God. 37 This is what you keep saying to a prophet: 'What is the LORD's answer to you?' or 'What has the LORD spoken?' 38 Although you claim, 'This is the oracle of the LORD,' this is what the LORD says: You used the words, 'This is the oracle of the LORD,' even though I told you that you must not claim, 'This is the oracle of the LORD.' 39 Therefore, I will surely forget you and cast[k] you out of my presence along with the city I gave to you and your fathers. 40 I will bring upon you everlasting disgrace[l]—everlasting shame that will not be forgotten."

Two Baskets of Figs

24 After Jehoiachin[a][a] son of Jehoiakim king of Judah and the officials, the craftsmen and the artisans of Judah were carried into exile from Jerusalem to Babylon by Nebuchadnezzar king of Babylon, the LORD showed me two baskets of figs[b] placed in front of the temple of the LORD. 2 One basket had very good figs, like those that ripen early;[c] the other basket had very poor[d] figs, so bad that they could not be eaten.

3 Then the LORD asked me, "What do you see,[e] Jeremiah?"

"Figs," I answered. "The good ones are very good, but the poor ones are so bad that they cannot be eaten."

4 Then the word of the LORD came to me: 5 "This is what the LORD, the God of Israel, says: 'Like these good figs, I regard as good the exiles from Judah, whom I sent[f] away from this place to the land of the Babylonians.[b] 6 My eyes will watch over them for their good, and I will bring them back[g] to this land. I will build[h] them up and not tear them down; I will plant[i] them and not uproot them. 7 I will give them a heart to know[j] me, that I am the LORD. They will be my people,[k] and I will be their God, for they will return[l] to me with all their heart.[m]

8 " 'But like the poor[n] figs, which are so bad that they cannot be eaten,' says the LORD, 'so will I deal with Zedekiah[o] king of Judah, his officials[p] and the survivors[q] from Jerusalem, whether they remain in this land or live in Egypt.[r] 9 I will make them abhorrent[s] and an offence to all the kingdoms of the earth, a reproach and a byword,[t] an object of ridicule and cursing,[u] wherever I banish[v] them. 10 I will send the sword,[w] famine[x] and plague[y] against them until they are destroyed from the land I gave to them and their fathers.[z]' "

Seventy Years of Captivity

25 The word came to Jeremiah concerning all the people of Judah in the fourth year of Jehoiakim[a] son of Josiah king of Judah, which was the first year of Nebuchadnezzar[b] king of Babylon. 2 So Jeremiah the prophet said to all the people of Judah[c] and to all those living in Jerusalem: 3 For twenty-three years—from the thirteenth year of Josiah[d] son of Amon king of Judah until this very day—the word of the LORD has come to me and I have spoken to you again and again,[e] but you have not listened.[f]

4 And though the LORD has sent all his servants the prophets[g] to you again and again, you have not listened or paid any attention.[h] 5 They said, "Turn[i] now, each of you, from your evil ways and

29 [t]**Ps 39:3**; Jer 5:14; **1Co 3:13**; [u]Heb 4:12
30 [v]**Ps 34:16**; [w]ver 2; Dt 18:20; Jer 14:15; **21:13**
31 [x]ver 17
32 [y]**ver 25**; [z]**ver 13; Jer 50:6**; [a]**Job 13:4**; Eze 13:3; 22:28; [b]**Jer 14:14**; [c]Jer 7:8; La 2:14
33 [d]Mal 1:1; [e]**2Ki 21:14**
34 [f]La 2:14; [g]Zec 13:3
35 [h]Jer 33:3; 42:4
36 [i]Gal 1:7–8; 2Pe 3:16; [j]**Jos 3:10**
39 [k]**Jer 7:15**
40 [l]**Jer 20:11**; Eze 5:14–15

Ch. 24

1 [a]**2Ki 24:16; 2Ch 36:9**; [b]Ex 23:19; Dt 26:2; Am 8:1–2
2 [c]**SS 2:13**; [d]**Isa 5:4**
3 [e]Jer 1:11; Am 8:2
5 [f]Jer 29:4,20
6 [g]**Dt 30:3**; Jer 27:22; 29:10; 30:3; Eze 11:17; [h]Jer 33:7; 42:10; [i]**Dt 30:9; Jer 1:10**; Am 9:14–15
7 [j]**Isa 11:9**; [k]**Lev 26:12; Isa 51:16; Zec 2:11**; Heb 8:10; [l]Jer 32:40; [m]**2Ch 6:37**; Eze 11:19
8 [n]Jer 29:17; [o]Jer 32:4–5; 38:18,23; 39:5; 44:30; [p]Jer 39:6; [q]Jer 39:9; [r]Jer 44:1,26; 46:14
9 [s]**Jer 15:4**; 25:18; [t]**Dt 28:25; 1Ki 9:7**; [u]**2Ki 22:19; Jer 29:18**; [v]**Dt 28:37**; Da 9:7
10 [w]**Isa 51:19; Jer 9:16**; Rev 6:8; [x]Jer 15:2; [y]Jer 27:8; [z]**Dt 28:21**

Ch. 25

1 [a]2Ki 24:2; [b]2Ki 24:1
2 [c]Jer 18:11
3 [d]1Ch 3:14; [e]Jer 11:7; 26:5; [f]**Isa 65:12; Jer 7:26**
4 [g]Jer 6:17; **7:25**; 29:19; [h]**Jer 7:26**; 34:14; 44:5
5 [i]**Jdg 6:8; 2Ch 7:14; 30:9; Jer 23:22**

d33 Or *burden* (see Septuagint and Vulgate)
e33 Hebrew; Septuagint and Vulgate *'You are the burden*; the Hebrew for *oracle* and *burden* is the same.
a1 Hebrew *Jeconiah*, a variant of *Jehoiachin*
b5 Or *Chaldeans*

your evil practices, and you can stay in the land[j] the LORD gave to you and your fathers for ever and ever. 6 Do not follow other gods[k] to serve and worship them; do not provoke me to anger with what your hands have made. Then I will not harm you."

7 "But you did not listen to me," declares the LORD, "and you have provoked[l] me with what your hands have made,[m] and you have brought harm[n] to yourselves."

8 Therefore the LORD Almighty says this: "Because you have not listened to my words, 9 I will summon[o] all the peoples of the north[p] and my servant[q] Nebuchadnezzar[r] king of Babylon," declares the LORD, "and I will bring them against this land and its inhabitants and against all the surrounding nations. I will completely destroy[a] [s] them and make them an object of horror and scorn,[t] and an everlasting ruin.[u] 10 I will banish from them the sounds[v] of joy and gladness, the voices of bride and bridegroom,[w] the sound of millstones[x] and the light of the lamp.[y] 11 This whole country will become a desolate wasteland,[z] and these nations will serve[a] the king of Babylon for seventy years.[b]

12 "But when the seventy years[c] are fulfilled, I will punish the king of Babylon[d] and his nation, the land of the Babylonians,[b] for their guilt," declares the LORD, "and will make it desolate[e] for ever. 13 I will bring upon that land all the things I have spoken against it, all that are written[f] in this book and prophesied by Jeremiah against all the nations. 14 They themselves will be enslaved[g] by many nations[h] and great kings; I will repay[i] them according to their deeds and the work of their hands."

The Cup of God's Wrath

15 This is what the LORD, the God of Israel, said to me: "Take from my hand this cup[j] filled with the wine of my wrath and make all the nations to whom I send[k] you drink it. 16 When they drink[l] it, they will stagger[m] and go mad[n] because of the sword[o] I will send among them."

17 So I took the cup from the LORD's hand and made all the nations to whom he sent[p] me drink it: 18 Jerusalem[q] and the towns of Judah, its kings and officials, to make them a ruin[r] and an object of horror and scorn[s] and cursing,[t] as they are today;[u] 19 Pharaoh king[v] of Egypt,[w] his attendants, his officials and all his people, 20 and all the foreign people there; all the kings of Uz;[x] all the kings of the Philistines[y] (those of Ashkelon,[z] Gaza,[a] Ekron, and the people left at Ashdod); 21 Edom,[b] Moab[c] and Ammon;[d] 22 all the kings of Tyre[e] and Sidon;[f] the kings of the coastlands[g] across the sea; 23 Dedan,[h] Tema,[i] Buz[j] and all who are in distant places[c];[k] 24 all the kings of Arabia[l] and all the kings of the foreign people[m] who live in the desert; 25 all the kings of Zimri,[n] Elam[o] and Media;[p] 26 and all the kings of the north,[q] near and far, one after the other—all the kingdoms[r] on the face of the earth. And after all of them, the king of Sheshach[d] [s] will drink it too.

27 "Then tell them, 'This is what the LORD Almighty, the God of Israel, says: Drink, get drunk[t] and vomit, and fall to rise no more because of the sword[u] I will send among you.' 28 But if they refuse to take the cup from your hand and drink[v], tell them, 'This is what the LORD Almighty says: You must drink it! 29 See, I am beginning to bring disaster[w] on the city that bears my Name,[x] and will you indeed go unpunished?[y] You will not go unpunished, for I am calling down a sword[z] upon all[a] who live on the earth,[b] declares the LORD Almighty.'

30 "Now prophesy all these words against them and say to them:

"'The LORD will roar[c] from on high;
he will thunder[d] from his holy
dwelling[e]
and roar mightily against his land.
He will shout like those who tread[f] the
grapes,
shout against all who live on the
earth.
31 The tumult[g] will resound to the ends
of the earth,
for the LORD will bring charges[h]
against the nations;

5 [j]**Ge 12:7; Dt 4:40**
6 [k]**Ex 20:3; Dt 8:19**
7 [l]Jer 30:14; 32:35; 44:5; [m]Dt 32:21; [n]2Ki 17:20; 21:15
9 [o]Isa 13:3–5; [p]**Isa 14:31;** [q]**Isa 41:2;** Jer 27:6; [r]**2Ch 36:6;** [s]**Nu 21:2;** [t]**2Ch 29:8;** [u]**Jer 19:8; 20:4;** Eze 12:20
10 [v]**Isa 24:8;** Eze 26:13; [w]Jer 7:34; 33:11; [x]Ecc 12:3–4; [y]**Job 18:5;** La 5:15; Rev 18:22–23
11 [z]**Lev 26:31–32;** Jer 4:26–27; 12:11–12; [a]Jer 28:14; [b]**2Ch 36:21**
12 [c]Jer 27:7; 29:10; [d]**Ge 10:10; Ps 137:8;** [e]**Isa 13:19–22;** 14:22–23
13 [f]**Isa 30:8**
14 [g]Isa 14:6; Jer 27:7; [h]Jer 50:9; 51:27–28; [i]**Dt 32:41; Job 21:19; Jer 51:6**
15 [j]**Isa 51:17;** Jer 49:12; La 4:21; Eze 23:31; Rev 14:10; [k]Jer 1:5
16 [l]ver 26; [m]**Ps 60:3;** [n]Jer 51:7; [o]ver 27–29
17 [p]Jer 1:10; 27:3
18 [q]**Jer 13:13;** [r]**Job 12:19;** [s]**2Ch 29:8;** [t]**Jer 24:9;** [u]**Ge 19:13;** Jer 44:22
19 [v]**2Ki 18:21;** [w]Isa 19:1; 20:3; Jer 44:30; Eze 29:2
20 [x]**Ge 10:23;** [y]**Jos 13:3; 2Ch 26:6; 28:18;** Zep 2:4–7; [z]Jer 47:5; Am 1:7–8; [a]**Ge 10:19**
21 [b]**Ge 25:30;** [c]**Ge 19:37; Dt 23:6;** [d]**Ge 19:38;** Jer 27:3; 49:1
22 [e]**Jos 19:29;** [f]**Ge 10:15;** [g]Isa 11:11; 48:20; 66:20; Jer 31:10; Eze 27:15; 39:6; Da 11:18
23 [h]**Ge 25:3;** [i]**Ge 25:15;** [j]**Ge 22:21;** [k]Jer 9:26; 49:32
24 [l]**2Ch 9:14;** [m]ver 20
25 [n]Ge 25:2; [o]**Ge 10:22;** [p]**Isa 21:2**
26 [q]ver 9; Jer 50:3,9; 51:11,48; [r]Isa 23:17; [s]Jer 51:41
27 [t]ver 16,28; **Isa 29:9; 49:26;** Jer 51:57; Eze 23:32–34; Na 3:18; Hab 2:16; [u]**Jer 12:12;** Eze 14:17; 21:4
28 [v]**Isa 51:23**
29 [w]**2Sa 5:7;** Isa 10:12; Jer 13:12–14; 39:1; [x]**Dt 28:10; Isa 37:17;** [y]**Pr 11:31;** [z]ver 27; [a]ver 30–31; Isa 34:2; [b]**Isa 24:1**
30 [c]Isa 16:10; **42:13;** [d]**Ps 46:6;** [e]**Ps 68:5;** [f]Isa 63:3; Joel 3:13; Rev 14:19–20
31 [g]Jer 23:19; [h]**Jer 2:9**

[a]9 The Hebrew term refers to the irrevocable giving over of things or persons to the LORD, often by totally destroying them.
[b]12 Or *Chaldeans*
[c]23 Or *who clip the hair by their foreheads*
[d]26 *Sheshach* is a cryptogram for Babylon.

he will bring judgment[i] on all[j]
  mankind
and put the wicked to the sword,[k]'"
  declares the LORD.

32 This is what the LORD Almighty says:

"Look! Disaster[l] is spreading
  from nation to nation;[m]
a mighty storm[n] is rising
  from the ends of the earth."[o]

33 At that time those slain[p] by the LORD will be everywhere—from one end of the earth to the other. They will not be mourned or gathered[q] up or buried,[r] but will be like refuse lying on the ground.

34 Weep and wail, you shepherds;[s]
  roll[t] in the dust, you leaders of the
    flock.
For your time to be slaughtered[u] has
    come;
  you will fall and be shattered like
    fine pottery.[v]
35 The shepherds will have nowhere to
    flee,
  the leaders of the flock no place to
    escape.[w]
36 Hear the cry[x] of the shepherds,[y]
  the wailing of the leaders of the
    flock,
  for the LORD is destroying their
    pasture.
37 The peaceful meadows will be laid
    waste
  because of the fierce anger of the
    LORD.
38 Like a lion[z] he will leave his lair,
  and their land will become desolate[a]
because of the sword[e] of the
    oppressor[b]
  and because of the LORD's fierce
    anger.[c]

Jeremiah Threatened With Death

26 Early in the reign of Jehoiakim[a] son of Josiah king of Judah, this word came from the LORD: 2 "This is what the LORD says: Stand in the courtyard[b] of the LORD's house and speak to all the people of the towns of Judah who come to worship in the house of the LORD.[c] Tell[d] them everything I command you; do not omit[e] a word. 3 Perhaps they will listen and each will turn[f] from his evil way. Then I will relent[g] and not bring on them the disaster I was planning because of the evil they have done. 4 Say to them, 'This is what the LORD says: If you do not listen[h] to me and follow my law,[i] which I have set before you, 5 and if you do not listen to the words of my servants the prophets, whom I have sent to you again and again (though you have not listened[j]), 6 then I will make this house like Shiloh[k] and this city an object of cursing[l] among all the nations of the earth.'"

7 The priests, the prophets and all the people heard Jeremiah speak these words in the house of the LORD. 8 But as soon as Jeremiah finished telling all the people everything the LORD had commanded[m] him to say, the priests, the prophets and all the people seized[n] him and said, "You must die![o] 9 Why do you prophesy in the LORD's name that this house will be like Shiloh and this city will be desolate and deserted?"[p] And all the people crowded[q] around Jeremiah in the house of the LORD.

10 When the officials[r] of Judah heard about these things, they went up from the royal palace to the house of the LORD and took their places at the entrance of the New Gate[s] of the LORD's house. 11 Then the priests and the prophets said to the officials and all the people, "This man should be sentenced to death[t] because he has prophesied against this city. You have heard it with your own ears!"[u]

12 Then Jeremiah said to all the officials[v] and all the people: "The LORD sent me to prophesy[w] against this house and this city all the things you have heard.[x] 13 Now reform[y] your ways and your actions and obey[z] the LORD your God. Then the LORD will relent[a] and not bring the disaster he has pronounced against you. 14 As for me, I am in your hands;[b] do with me whatever you think is good and right. 15 Be assured, however, that if you put me to death, you will bring the guilt of innocent blood[c] on yourselves and on this city and on those who live in it, for in truth the LORD has sent me to you to speak all these words[d] in your hearing."

16 Then the officials[e] and all the people said to the priests and the prophets, "This man should not be sentenced to death![f] He has spoken to us in the name of the LORD our God."

17 Some of the elders of the land stepped forward and said to the entire assembly of people, 18 "Micah[g] of Moresheth prophesied in the days of

31 [i]**1Sa 12:7; Jer 2:35;** Eze 36:5; [j]ver 29; [k]**Jer 15:9**
32 [l]**Isa 30:25;** [m]Isa 34:2; [n]**Jer 23:19;** [o]**Dt 28:49**
33 [p]Isa 66:16; Eze 39:17–20; [q]**Jer 8:2;** [r]**Ps 79:3**
34 [s]**Jer 2:8;** Zec 10:3; [t]**Jer 6:26;** [u]**Ps 44:22; Isa 34:6;** Jer 50:27; 51:40; Zec 11:4,7; [v]**Jer 22:28**
35 [w]**Job 11:20**
36 [x]**Jer 6:26;** [y]**Jer 23:1;** Zec 11:3
38 [z]**Job 10:16; Jer 4:7;** [a]**Jer 44:22;** [b]Jer 46:16; 50:16; [c]**Ex 15:7; Jer 4:26**

Ch. 26

1 [a]2Ki 23:36
2 [b]Jer 19:14; [c]**Jer 17:19;** [d]**ver 12; Jer 1:17;** Mt 28:20; Ac 20:27; [e]Dt 4:2
3 [f]Dt 30:2; 2Ch 33:12–13; Isa 55:7; Jer 35:15; 36:7; [g]**Jer 18:8**
4 [h]Lev 26:14; Jer 25:3; [i]Ex 20:1–23:33; **1Ki 9:6; Jer 11:8**
5 [j]**Pr 1:24; Isa 65:12;** Jer 25:4; 44:5
6 [k]**Jos 18:1; Jdg 18:31;** [l]**Dt 28:25; 2Ki 22:19**
8 [m]Jer 43:1; [n]Ac 6:12; 21:27; [o]Lev 24:15–16; **Ne 9:26; Jer 11:21**
9 [p]**Lev 26:32; Jer 9:11;** [q]Ac 21:32
10 [r]ver 16; Jer 34:19; Eze 22:27; [s]**Ge 23:10**
11 [t]Dt 18:20; **Jer 11:21;** 18:23; Mt 26:66; Ac 6:11; [u]**Ps 44:1**
12 [v]Jer 1:18; [w]**Isa 6:8;** Am 7:15; Ac 4:18–20; 5:29; [x]**ver 2,**15
13 [y]**Jer 7:5;** Joel 2:12–14; [z]Jer 11:4; [a]**Jer 18:8**
14 [b]Jos 9:25; Jer 38:5
15 [c]**Dt 19:10;** [d]**ver 12; Jer 1:17**
16 [e]**ver 10; Ac 23:9;** [f]Ac 23:29
18 [g]Mic 1:1

[e]38 Some Hebrew manuscripts and Septuagint (see also Jer. 46:16 and 50:16); most Hebrew manuscripts *anger*

Hezekiah king of Judah. He told all the
people of Judah, 'This is what the LORD
Almighty says:

"'Zion[h] will be ploughed like a field,
Jerusalem will become a heap of
rubble,[i]
the temple hill[j] a mound overgrown
with thickets.'[a][k]

19"Did Hezekiah king of Judah or any-
one else in Judah put him to death? Did
not Hezekiah[l] fear the LORD and seek[m]
his favour? And did not the LORD
relent,[n] so that he did not bring the
disaster[o] he pronounced against them?
We are about to bring a terrible disaster[p]
on ourselves!"
20(Now Uriah son of Shemaiah from
Kiriath Jearim[q] was another man who
prophesied in the name of the LORD; he
prophesied the same things against this
city and this land as Jeremiah did.
21When King Jehoiakim[r] and all his
officers and officials[s] heard his words,
the king sought to put him to death.[t] But
Uriah heard of it and fled[u] in fear to
Egypt. 22King Jehoiakim, however, sent
Elnathan[v] son of Acbor to Egypt, along
with some other men. 23They brought
Uriah out of Egypt and took him to King
Jehoiakim, who had him struck down
with a sword[w] and his body thrown
into the burial place of the common
people.)[x]
24Furthermore, Ahikam[y] son of
Shaphan supported Jeremiah, and so he
was not handed over to the people to be
put to death.

Judah to Serve Nebuchadnezzar

27 Early in the reign of Zedekiah[a][a]
son of Josiah king of Judah, this
word came to Jeremiah from the LORD:
2This is what the LORD said to me:
"Make a yoke[b] out of straps and cross-
bars and put it on your neck. 3Then
send[c] word to the kings of Edom, Moab,
Ammon,[d] Tyre and Sidon[e] through the
envoys who have come to Jerusalem to
Zedekiah king of Judah. 4Give them a
message for their masters and say, 'This
is what the LORD Almighty, the God of
Israel, says: "Tell this to your masters:
5With my great power and outstretched
arm[f] I made[g] the earth and its people
and the animals[h] that are on it, and I
give[i] it to anyone I please. 6Now I will
hand all your countries over to my ser-
vant[j] Nebuchadnezzar[k] king of Babylon;
I will make even the wild animals sub-
ject to him.[l] 7All nations will serve[m] him
and his son and his grandson until the
time[n] for his land comes; then many
nations and great kings will subjugate[o]
him.
8"'"If, however, any nation or king-
dom will not serve Nebuchadnezzar
king of Babylon or bow its neck under
his yoke, I will punish[p] that nation with
the sword,[q] famine[r] and plague,[s]
declares the LORD, until I destroy it by
his hand. 9So do not listen to your
prophets,[t] your diviners,[u] your inter-
preters of dreams,[v] your mediums[w] or
your sorcerers[x] who tell you, 'You will
not serve[y] the king of Babylon.' 10They
prophesy lies[z] to you that will only serve
to remove[a] you far from your lands; I
will banish you and you will perish.
11But if any nation will bow its neck
under the yoke[b] of the king of Babylon
and serve him, I will let that nation
remain in its own land to till it and to
live[c] there, declares the LORD."'"
12I gave the same message to Zede-
kiah king of Judah. I said, "Bow your
neck under the yoke[d] of the king of
Babylon; serve him and his people, and
you will live.[e] 13Why will you and your
people die[f] by the sword, famine and
plague[g] with which the LORD has
threatened any nation that will not
serve the king of Babylon? 14Do not lis-
ten[h] to the words of the prophets[i] who
say to you, 'You will not serve the king
of Babylon,' for they are prophesying
lies[j] to you. 15'I have not sent[k] them,'
declares the LORD. 'They are prophesy-
ing lies in my name.[l] Therefore, I will
banish you and you will perish,[m] both
you and the prophets who prophesy to
you.'"
16Then I said to the priests and all
these people, "This is what the LORD
says: Do not listen to the prophets who
say, 'Very soon now the articles[n] from
the LORD's house will be brought back
from Babylon.' They are prophesying
lies to you. 17Do not listen[o] to them.
Serve the king of Babylon, and you will
live.[p] Why should this city become a
ruin? 18If they are prophets and have the
word of the LORD, let them plead[q] with
the LORD Almighty that the furnishings
remaining in the house of the LORD and
in the palace of the king of Judah and in
Jerusalem not be taken to Babylon. 19For
this is what the LORD Almighty says

18 [h]Isa 2:3; [i]2Ki 25:9; Ne 4:2; Jer 9:11; [j]Mic 4:1; Zec 8:3; [k]Jer 17:3
19 [l]1Ch 3:13; 2Ch 32:24–26; Isa 37:14–20; [m]1Sa 13:12; [n]Ex 32:14; Jer 18:8; [o]Jer 44:7; [p]Hab 2:10
20 [q]Jos 9:17
21 [r]1Ki 19:2; [s]ver 10; [t]Jer 2:30; Mt 23:37; [u]Ge 31:21; Mt 10:23
22 [v]Jer 36:12,25
23 [w]Heb 11:37; [x]2Ki 23:6
24 [y]2Ki 22:12

Ch. 27

1 [a]2Ch 36:11
2 [b]Lev 26:13; 1Ki 22:11
3 [c]Jer 25:17; [d]Jer 25:21; [e]Ge 10:15; Jer 25:22
5 [f]Dt 9:29; [g]Ge 1:1; [h]Ge 1:25; [i]Ps 115:16; Da 4:17
6 [j]Jer 25:9; [k]Jer 21:7; [l]Jer 28:14; Da 2:37–38
7 [m]2Ch 36:20; Da 5:18; [n]Jer 25:12; [o]Jer 25:14; 51:47; Da 5:28
8 [p]Jer 9:16; [q]Jer 21:9; [r]Jer 5:12; [s]Jer 14:12
9 [t]Eze 13:1–23; [u]Ge 30:27; Isa 44:25; [v]Dt 13:1; Jer 23:25; [w]Dt 18:11; [x]Ex 7:11; [y]Jer 6:14
10 [z]Jer 23:25; Mk 13:5; [a]2Ki 23:27
11 [b]Jer 21:9; [c]Dt 6:2
12 [d]Jer 17:4; [e]Jer 21:9
13 [f]Eze 18:31; [g]Jer 14:12
14 [h]Jer 23:16; [i]Jer 14:13; [j]Jer 14:14; Mt 7:15
15 [k]Jer 23:21; [l]Jer 29:9; 44:16; [m]Jer 6:15; Mt 15:12–14
16 [n]1Ki 7:48–50; 2Ki 24:13
17 [o]Jer 23:16; [p]Jer 42:11
18 [q]Nu 21:7; 1Sa 7:8

[a]*18* Micah 3:12
[a]*1* A few Hebrew manuscripts and Syriac (see also Jer. 27:3,12 and 28:1); most Hebrew manuscripts *Jehoiakim* (most Septuagint manuscripts do not have this verse.)

about the pillars, the Sea,[r] the movable stands and the other furnishings[s] that are left in this city, 20which Nebuchadnezzar king of Babylon did not take away when he carried[t] Jehoiachin[b] [u] son of Jehoiakim king of Judah into exile from Jerusalem to Babylon, along with all the nobles of Judah and Jerusalem —21yes, this is what the LORD Almighty, the God of Israel, says about the things that are left in the house of the LORD and in the palace of the king of Judah and in Jerusalem: 22'They will be taken[v] to Babylon and there they will remain until the day[w] I come for them,' declares the LORD. 'Then I will bring[x] them back and restore them to this place.'"

The False Prophet Hananiah

28 In the fifth month of that same year, the fourth year, early in the reign of Zedekiah[a] king of Judah, the prophet Hananiah son of Azzur, who was from Gibeon,[b] said to me in the house of the LORD in the presence of the priests and all the people: 2"This is what the LORD Almighty, the God of Israel, says: 'I will break the yoke[c] of the king of Babylon. 3Within two years I will bring back to this place all the articles[d] of the LORD's house that Nebuchadnezzar king of Babylon removed from here and took to Babylon. 4I will also bring back to this place Jehoiachin[e] son of Jehoiakim king of Judah and all the other exiles from Judah who went to Babylon,' declares the LORD, 'for I will break the yoke of the king of Babylon.'"[f]

5Then the prophet Jeremiah replied to the prophet Hananiah before the priests and all the people who were standing in the house of the LORD. 6He said, "Amen! May the LORD do so! May the LORD fulfil the words you have prophesied by bringing the articles of the LORD's house and all the exiles back to this place from Babylon.[g] 7Nevertheless, listen to what I have to say in your hearing and in the hearing of all the people: 8From early times the prophets who preceded you and me have prophesied war, disaster and plague[h] against many countries and great kingdoms. 9But the prophet who prophesies peace will be recognised as one truly sent by the LORD only if his prediction comes true.[i]"

10Then the prophet Hananiah took the yoke[j] off the neck of the prophet Jeremiah and broke it, 11and he said[k] before all the people, "This is what the LORD says: 'In the same way will I break the yoke of Nebuchadnezzar king of Babylon off the neck of all the nations within two years.'" At this, the prophet Jeremiah went on his way.

12Shortly after the prophet Hananiah had broken the yoke off the neck of the prophet Jeremiah, the word of the LORD came to Jeremiah: 13"Go and tell Hananiah, 'This is what the LORD says: You have broken a wooden yoke, but in its place you will get a yoke of iron. 14This is what the LORD Almighty, the God of Israel, says: I will put an iron yoke[l] on the necks of all these nations to make them serve[m] Nebuchadnezzar[n] king of Babylon, and they will serve him. I will even give him control over the wild animals.[o]'"

15Then the prophet Jeremiah said to Hananiah the prophet, "Listen, Hananiah! The LORD has not sent[p] you, yet you have persuaded this nation to trust in lies.[q] 16Therefore, this is what the LORD says: 'I am about to remove you from the face of the earth.[r] This very year you are going to die,[s] because you have preached rebellion[t] against the LORD.'"

17In the seventh month of that same year, Hananiah the prophet died.[u]

A Letter to the Exiles

29 This is the text of the letter[a] that the prophet Jeremiah sent from Jerusalem to the surviving elders among the exiles and to the priests, the prophets and all the other people Nebuchadnezzar had carried into exile from Jerusalem to Babylon.[b] 2(This was after King Jehoiachin[c] and the queen mother,[d] the court officials and the leaders of Judah and Jerusalem, the craftsmen and the artisans had gone into exile from Jerusalem.) 3He entrusted the letter to Elasah son of Shaphan and to Gemariah son of Hilkiah, whom Zedekiah king of Judah sent to King Nebuchadnezzar in Babylon. It said:

> 4This is what the LORD Almighty, the God of Israel, says to all those I carried[e] into exile from Jerusalem to Babylon: 5"Build[f] houses and settle down; plant gardens and eat what they produce. 6Marry and have sons and daughters; find wives for your sons and give your daughters in marriage, so that they too may have sons and daughters. Increase

19 [r]1Ki 7:23–26; [s]**1Ki 7:51**; Jer 52:17–23
20 [t]**Dt 28:36**; **2Ch 36:10**; [u]**Jer 22:24**; Mt 1:11
22 [v]**2Ki 20:17**; 25:13; [w]**2Ch 36:21**; **Jer 24:6**; [x]**Ezr 7:19**

Ch. 28

1 [a]**2Ch 36:11**; [b]**Jos 9:3**
2 [c]Jer 27:12
3 [d]**2Ki 24:13**
4 [e]**2Ki 25:30**; Jer 22:24–27; [f]Hos 7:3
6 [g]Zec 6:10
8 [h]Lev 26:14–17; Isa 5:5–7; Na 1:14
9 [i]**Dt 18:22**; Eze 33:33
10 [j]**Lev 26:13**; **1Ki 22:11**
11 [k]Jer 14:14; 27:10
14 [l]**Dt 28:48**; **Jer 15:12**; [m]Jer 25:11; [n]Jer 39:1; Da 1:1; 5:18; [o]**Jer 27:6**
15 [p]Jer 29:31; [q]**Jer 7:4**; 20:6; 29:21; La 2:14; Eze 13:6
16 [r]**Ge 7:4**; [s]Dt 18:20; Zec 13:3; [t]Dt 13:5; Jer 29:32
17 [u]**2Ki 1:17**

Ch. 29

1 [a]ver 28; [b]**2Ch 36:10**; **Jer 13:17**
2 [c]**2Ki 24:12**; [d]**2Ki 24:8**
4 [e]**Jer 24:5**
5 [f]ver 28

[b]20 Hebrew *Jeconiah*, a variant of *Jehoiachin*; also in 28:4 and 29:2

in number there; do not decrease.[g]
7Also, seek[h] the peace and pros-
perity of the city to which I have
carried you into exile. Pray[i] to the
LORD for it, because if it prospers,
you too will prosper." 8Yes, this is
what the LORD Almighty, the God
of Israel, says: "Do not let the
prophets[j] and diviners among you
deceive[k] you. Do not listen to the
dreams[l] you encourage them to
have.[m] 9They are prophesying lies[n]
to you in my name. I have not
sent[o] them," declares the LORD.
10This is what the LORD says:
"When seventy years[p] are com-
pleted for Babylon, I will come
to you[q] and fulfil my gracious
promise[r] to bring you back[s] to this
place. 11For I know the plans[t] I have
for you," declares the LORD, "plans
to prosper[u] you and not to harm
you, plans to give you hope and a
future.[v] 12Then you will call[w] upon
me and come and pray[x] to me, and I
will listen[y] to you. 13You will seek[z]
me and find me when you seek me
with all your heart.[a] 14I will be
found by you," declares the LORD,
"and will bring you back[b] from cap-
tivity.[a] I will gather you from all the
nations and places where I have
banished you," declares the LORD,
"and will bring you back to the
place from which I carried you into
exile."[c]
15You may say, "The LORD has
raised up prophets for us in Bab-
ylon," 16but this is what the LORD
says about the king who sits on
David's throne and all the people
who remain in this city, your coun-
trymen who did not go with you
into exile—17yes, this is what the
LORD Almighty says: "I will send
the sword, famine and plague[d]
against them and I will make them
like poor figs[e] that are so bad they
cannot be eaten. 18I will pursue
them with the sword, famine and
plague and will make them abhor-
rent[f] to all the kingdoms of the
earth and an object of cursing[g] and
horror,[h] of scorn[i] and reproach,
among all the nations where I drive
them. 19For they have not listened
to my words,"[j] declares the LORD,
"words that I sent to them again
and again[k] by my servants the
prophets.[l] And you exiles have not
listened either," declares the LORD.
20Therefore, hear the word of the
LORD, all you exiles whom I have
sent[m] away from Jerusalem to Bab-
ylon. 21This is what the LORD
Almighty, the God of Israel, says
about Ahab son of Kolaiah and
Zedekiah son of Maaseiah, who are
prophesying lies[n] to you in my
name: "I will hand them over to
Nebuchadnezzar king of Babylon,
and he will put them to death be-
fore your very eyes. 22Because of
them, all the exiles from Judah who
are in Babylon will use this curse:
'The LORD treat you like Zedekiah
and Ahab, whom the king of Bab-
ylon burned[o] in the fire.' 23For they
have done outrageous things in
Israel; they have committed adul-
tery[p] with their neighbours' wives
and in my name have spoken lies,
which I did not tell them to do. I
know[q] it and am a witness[r] to it,"
declares the LORD.

Message to Shemaiah

24Tell Shemaiah the Nehelamite,
25"This is what the LORD Almighty, the
God of Israel, says: You sent letters in
your own name to all the people in
Jerusalem, to Zephaniah[s] son of
Maaseiah the priest, and to all the other
priests. You said to Zephaniah, 26'The
LORD has appointed you priest in place
of Jehoiada to be in charge of the house
of the LORD; you should put any mad-
man[t] who acts like a prophet into the
stocks[u] and neck-irons. 27So why have
you not reprimanded Jeremiah from
Anathoth, who poses as a prophet
among you? 28He has sent this message[v]
to us in Babylon: It will be a long time.[w]
Therefore build[x] houses and settle
down; plant gardens and eat what they
produce.' "
29Zephaniah[y] the priest, however,
read the letter to Jeremiah the prophet.
30Then the word of the LORD came to
Jeremiah: 31"Send this message to all the
exiles: 'This is what the LORD says about
Shemaiah[z] the Nehelamite: Because
Shemaiah has prophesied to you, even
though I did not send[a] him, and has led
you to believe a lie, 32this is what the
LORD says: I will surely punish She-
maiah the Nehelamite and his descen-
dants.[b] He will have no-one left among
this people, nor will he see the good[c]
things I will do for my people, declares
the LORD, because he has preached
rebellion[d] against me.' "

6 [g]Jer 30:19
7 [h]**Est 3:8;** [i]1Ti 2:1–2
8 [j]1Jn 4:1; [k]Jer 37:9; [l]**Dt 13:1; Jer 23:25;** [m]**Jer 23:27**
9 [n]**Jer 27:15;** La 2:14; Eze 13:6; [o]Jer 23:21
10 [p]**2Ch 36:21; Da 9:2;** [q]**Ru 1:6;** [r]1Ki 8:56; Jer 32:42; 33:14; [s]**Jer 16:14; 24:6**
11 [t]Ps 40:5; [u]Isa 55:12; [v]**Job 8:7;** Zec 8:15
12 [w]Hos 2:23; Zep 3:12; Zec 13:9; [x]**1Ki 8:30;** [y]Ps 145:19; **Isa 55:6**
13 [z]Mt 7:7; [a]**Dt 4:29; 2Ch 6:37**
14 [b]**Dt 30:3;** Jer 30:3; Eze 39:25; Am 9:14; Zep 3:20; [c]Jer 23:3–4; 30:10; 46:27; Eze 37:21
17 [d]Jer 27:8; [e]**Isa 5:4**
18 [f]Jer 15:4; [g]**Nu 5:27; Jer 18:16; 22:10;** 44:12 [h]**Dt 28:25;** [i]**Dt 28:37; Isa 28:22; Mic 2:6**
19 [j]Jer 6:19; [k]Jer 7:25; [l]**Jer 25:4**
20 [m]**Jer 24:5**
21 [n]ver 9; Jer 14:14
22 [o]Da 3:6
23 [p]**Jer 23:14;** [q]**Heb 4:13;** [r]**Ge 31:48; Jer 7:11**
25 [s]**2Ki 25:18**
26 [t]**1Sa 10:11;** Hos 9:7; **Jn 10:20;** [u]Jer 20:2
28 [v]ver 1; [w]ver 10; [x]ver 5
29 [y]Jer 21:1
31 [z]ver 24; [a]**Jer 14:14**
32 [b]**1Sa 2:30–33;** [c]ver 10; [d]**Jer 28:16**

[a]14 Or *will restore your fortunes*

Restoration of Israel

30 This is the word that came to
Jeremiah from the LORD: 2"This
is what the LORD, the God of Israel, says:
'Write[a] in a book all the words I have
spoken to you. 3The days[b] are coming,'
declares the LORD, 'when I will bring[c]
my people Israel and Judah back from
captivity[a] and restore[d] them to the land I
gave to their forefathers to possess,'
says the LORD."
4These are the words the LORD spoke
concerning Israel and Judah: 5"This is
what the LORD says:

"'Cries of fear[e] are heard—
terror, not peace.
6Ask and see:
Can a man bear children?
Then why do I see every strong man
with his hands on his stomach like a
woman in labour,[f]
every face turned deathly pale?[g]
7How awful that day[h] will be!
None will be like it.
It will be a time of trouble[i] for Jacob,
but he will be saved[j] out of it.

8"'In that day,' declares the LORD
Almighty,
'I will break the yoke[k] off their necks
and will tear off their bonds;[l]
no longer will foreigners enslave
them.[m]
9Instead, they will serve the LORD their
God
and David[n] their king,[o]
whom I will raise up for them.

10"'So do not fear,[p] O Jacob my servant;[q]
do not be dismayed, O Israel,'
declares the LORD.
'I will surely save[r] you out of a distant
place,
your descendants from the land of
their exile.
Jacob will again have peace and
security,[s]
and no-one will make him afraid.[t]
11I am with you[u] and will save you,'
declares the LORD.
'Though I completely destroy all the
nations
among which I scatter you,
I will not completely destroy[v] you.
I will discipline[w] you but only with
justice;
I will not let you go entirely
unpunished.'[x]

12"This is what the LORD says:

"'Your wound[y] is incurable,
your injury beyond healing.[z]
13There is no-one to plead your cause,[a]
no remedy for your sore,
no healing[b] for you.
14All your allies[c] have forgotten you;
they care nothing for you.
I have struck you as an enemy[d] would
and punished you as would the
cruel,[e]
because your guilt is so great
and your sins[f] so many.
15Why do you cry out over your wound,
your pain that has no cure?[g]
Because of your great guilt and many
sins
I have done these things to you.[h]

16"'But all who devour[i] you will be
devoured;
all your enemies will go into exile.[j]
Those who plunder[k] you will be
plundered;
all who make spoil of you I will
despoil.
17But I will restore you to health
and heal[l] your wounds,'
declares the LORD,
'because you are called an outcast,[m]
Zion for whom no-one cares.'[n]

18"This is what the LORD says:

"'I will restore the fortunes[o] of Jacob's
tents[p]
and have compassion[q] on his
dwellings;
the city will be rebuilt[r] on her ruins,
and the palace will stand in its
proper place.
19From them will come songs[s] of
thanksgiving[t]
and the sound of rejoicing.[u]
I will add to their numbers,[v]
and they will not be decreased;
I will bring them honour,[w]
and they will not be disdained.
20Their children[x] will be as in days of
old,
and their community will be
established[y] before me;
I will punish[z] all who oppress them.
21Their leader[a] will be one of their own;
their ruler will arise from among
them.[b]
I will bring him near[c] and he will come
close to me,

Ch. 30

2 [a]Isa 30:8; Jer 36:2
3 [b]Jer 16:14; 24:6; [c]Jer 29:14; [d]Jer 16:15
5 [e]Jer 6:25
6 [f]Jer 4:31; [g]Isa 29:22
7 [h]Isa 2:12; [i]Isa 22:5; Zep 1:15; [j]ver 10; Jer 23:3
8 [k]Isa 9:4; [l]Ps 107:14; [m]Jer 25:14; 27:7; Eze 34:27
9 [n]Mt 1:1; [o]ver 21; 1Sa 13:14; Jer 33:15; Eze 34:23–24; 37:24; Hos 1:11; 3:5
10 [p]Isa 41:10; [q]Isa 44:2; [r]ver 7; Jer 29:14; [s]Isa 35:9; Jer 17:25; [t]Isa 29:22; 54:4; Jer 23:4; Eze 34:25–28
11 [u]Jos 1:5; [v]Lev 26:44; Jer 5:18; 46:28; [w]Jer 10:24; [x]Hos 11:9; Am 9:8
12 [y]Job 6:4; Jer 10:19; [z]Jer 8:22
13 [a]Jdg 6:31; [b]Jer 8:22; 14:19; 46:11; Na 3:19
14 [c]Jer 22:20; La 1:2; [d]Job 13:24; [e]Job 30:21; [f]Jer 25:7
15 [g]Jer 10:19; [h]Pr 1:31; La 1:5
16 [i]Isa 29:8; 33:1; Jer 2:3; [j]Isa 14:2; Joel 3:4–8; [k]Jer 49:2; 50:10
17 [l]Isa 1:5; Hos 6:1; [m]Isa 6:12; Jer 33:24; [n]Ps 142:4
18 [o]ver 3; Dt 30:3; Jer 31:23; 32:44; [p]Nu 24:5; [q]Ps 102:13; Jer 33:26; Eze 39:25; [r]Jer 31:4,24,38; 33:7; Eze 36:10,33; Am 9:14
19 [s]Ps 9:2; Isa 35:10; 51:11; [t]Isa 51:3; [u]Ps 126:1–2; Jer 31:4; [v]Ge 15:5; 22:17; Jer 33:22; Eze 37:26; Zec 2:4; [w]Isa 44:23; 60:9
20 [x]Isa 54:13; Jer 31:17; Zec 8:5; [y]Isa 54:14; [z]Ex 23:22
21 [a]ver 9; Jer 23:5–6; [b]Dt 17:15; [c]Nu 16:5

[a]3 Or *will restore the fortunes of my people Israel and Judah*

for who is he who will devote
himself
to be close to me?'
declares the LORD.
22"'So you will be my people,[d]
and I will be your God.[e]'"
23See, the storm[f] of the LORD
will burst out in wrath,
a driving wind swirling down
on the heads of the wicked.
24The fierce anger[g] of the LORD will not
turn back[h]
until he fully accomplishes
the purposes of his heart.
In days to come
you will understand[i] this.

31 "At that time," declares the
LORD, "I will be the God[a] of all
the clans of Israel, and they will be my
people."
2This is what the LORD says:

"The people who survive the sword
will find favour[b] in the desert;
I will come to give rest[c] to Israel."

3The LORD appeared to us in the past,[a]
saying:

"I have loved[d] you with an everlasting
love;
I have drawn[e] you with
loving-kindness.
4I will build you up again
and you will be rebuilt,[f] O Virgin[g]
Israel.
Again you will take up your
tambourines[h]
and go out to dance[i] with the joyful.[j]
5Again you will plant[k] vineyards
on the hills of Samaria;[l]
the farmers will plant them
and enjoy their fruit.[m]
6There will be a day when watchmen[n]
cry out
on the hills of Ephraim,
'Come, let us go up to Zion,
to the LORD our God.'"[o]

7This is what the LORD says:

"Sing[p] with joy for Jacob;
shout for the foremost[q] of the
nations.
Make your praises heard, and say,
'O LORD, save[r] your people,
the remnant[s] of Israel.'
8See, I will bring them from the land of
the north[t]
and gather[u] them from the ends of
the earth.
Among them will be the blind[v] and the
lame,[w]
expectant mothers and women in
labour;
a great throng will return.
9They will come with weeping;[x]
they will pray as I bring them back.
I will lead[y] them beside streams of
water[z]
on a level[a] path where they will not
stumble,
because I am Israel's father,[b]
and Ephraim is my firstborn son.

10"Hear the word of the LORD, O
nations;
proclaim it in distant coastlands:[c]
'He who scattered[d] Israel will gather[e]
them
and will watch over his flock like a
shepherd.'[f]
11For the LORD will ransom Jacob
and redeem[g] them from the hand of
those stronger[h] than they.
12They will come and shout for joy[i] on
the heights[j] of Zion;
they will rejoice in the bounty[k] of the
LORD—
the grain, the new wine and the oil,[l]
the young of the flocks[m] and herds.
They will be like a well-watered
garden,[n]
and they will sorrow[o] no more.
13Then maidens will dance and be glad,
young men and old as well.
I will turn their mourning[p] into
gladness;
I will give them comfort[q] and joy[r]
instead of sorrow.
14I will satisfy[s] the priests[t] with
abundance,
and my people will be filled with my
bounty,[u]"
declares the LORD.

15This is what the LORD says:

"A voice is heard in Ramah,[v]
mourning and great weeping,
Rachel weeping for her children
and refusing to be comforted,[w]
because her children are no more."[x]

16This is what the LORD says:

"Restrain your voice from weeping
and your eyes from tears,[y]
for your work will be rewarded,[z]"
declares the LORD.
"They will return[a] from the land of
the enemy.

22 [d]Isa 19:25; Hos 2:23; [e]Lev 26:12
23 [f]Jer 23:19
24 [g]Jer 4:8; La 1:12; [h]Jer 4:28; [i]Jer 23:19–20
Ch. 31
1 [a]Lev 26:12
2 [b]Nu 14:20; [c]Ex 33:14; Dt 12:9
3 [d]Dt 4:37; [e]Hos 11:4; Jn 6:44
4 [f]Jer 1:10; 30:18; [g]2Ki 19:21; [h]Ge 31:27; [i]Ex 15:20; [j]Jer 30:19
5 [k]Dt 20:6; [l]Jer 33:13; 50:19; Ob 19; [m]Isa 37:30; Am 9:14
6 [n]Isa 52:8; 56:10; [o]ver 12; Dt 33:19; Jer 50:4–5; Mic 4:2
7 [p]Isa 12:6; [q]Dt 28:13; Isa 61:9; [r]Ps 14:7; 28:9; [s]Isa 37:31
8 [t]Jer 3:18; [u]Ge 33:13; Dt 30:4; Ps 106:47; Eze 34:12–14; [v]Isa 42:16; [w]Eze 34:16; Mic 4:6
9 [x]Ezr 3:12; Ps 126:5; [y]Isa 63:13; [z]Nu 20:8; Ps 1:3; Isa 32:2; [a]Isa 40:4; 49:11; [b]Ex 4:22; Jer 3:4
10 [c]Isa 49:1; 66:19; Jer 25:22; [d]Lev 26:33; [e]Dt 30:4; Isa 11:12; Jer 50:19; [f]Isa 40:11; Eze 34:12
11 [g]Ex 6:6; Zec 9:16; [h]Ps 142:6
12 [i]Ps 126:5; [j]Eze 17:23; 20:40; 40:2; Mic 4:1; [k]Ps 36:8; Joel 3:18; [l]Nu 18:12; Hos 2:21–22; Joel 2:19; [m]ver 24; Isa 65:10; [n]SS 4:15; [o]Isa 30:19; 62:5; Jn 16:22; Rev 7:17
13 [p]Isa 61:3; [q]Isa 40:1; [r]Ps 30:11; Isa 51:11
14 [s]ver 25; [t]Lev 7:35–36; [u]Ps 36:8; Isa 30:23
15 [v]Jos 18:25; [w]Ge 37:35; [x]Jer 10:20; Mt 2:17–18*
16 [y]Ps 30:5; Isa 25:8; 30:19; [z]Ru 2:12; 2Ch 15:7; [a]Jer 30:3; Eze 11:17

[a]3 Or *LORD has appeared to us from afar*

17So there is hope[b] for your future,"
declares the LORD.
"Your children[c] will return to their
own land.

18"I have surely heard Ephraim's
moaning:
'You disciplined[d] me like an unruly
calf,[e]
and I have been disciplined.
Restore[f] me, and I will return,
because you are the LORD my God.
19After I strayed,[g]
I repented;
after I came to understand,
I beat[h] my breast.
I was ashamed[i] and humiliated
because I bore the disgrace of my
youth.'[j]
20Is not Ephraim my dear son,
the child[k] in whom I delight?
Though I often speak against him,
I still remember[l] him.
Therefore my heart yearns for him;
I have great compassion[m] for him,"
declares the LORD.

21"Set up road signs;
put up guideposts.[n]
Take note of the highway,[o]
the road that you take.
Return,[p] O Virgin[q] Israel,
return to your towns.
22How long will you wander,[r]
O unfaithful[s] daughter?
The LORD will create a new thing[t] on
earth—
a woman will surround[b] [u] a man."

23This is what the LORD Almighty, the
God of Israel, says: "When I bring them
back from captivity,[c] [v] the people in the
land of Judah and in its towns will once
again use these words: 'The LORD bless[w]
you, O righteous dwelling,[x] O sacred
mountain.'[y] 24People will live[z] together
in Judah and all its towns—farmers
and those who move about with their
flocks.[a] 25I will refresh the weary[b] and
satisfy the faint."[c]
26At this I awoke[d] and looked around.
My sleep had been pleasant to me.
27"The days are coming,"[e] declares
the LORD, "when I will plant[f] the house
of Israel and the house of Judah with the
offspring of men and of animals. 28Just
as I watched[g] over them to uproot[h] and
tear down, and to overthrow, destroy
and bring disaster,[i] so I will watch over
them to build and to plant,"[j] declares
the LORD. 29"In those days people will
no longer say,

'The fathers[k] have eaten sour grapes,
and the children's teeth are set on
edge.'[l]

30Instead, everyone will die for his own
sin;[m] whoever eats sour grapes—his
own teeth will be set on edge.

31"The time is coming," declares the
LORD,
"when I will make a new covenant[n]
with the house of Israel
and with the house of Judah.
32It will not be like the covenant[o]
I made with their forefathers[p]
when I took them by the hand
to lead them out of Egypt,[q]
because they broke my covenant,
though I was a husband[r] to[d] them,"[e]
declares the LORD.
33"This is the covenant that I will make
with the house of Israel
after that time," declares the LORD.
"I will put my law in their minds[s]
and write it on their hearts.[t]
I will be their God,
and they will be my people.[u]
34No longer will a man teach[v] his
neighbour,
or a man his brother, saying, 'Know
the LORD,'
because they will all know[w] me,
from the least of them to the
greatest,"
declares the LORD.
"For I will forgive[x] their wickedness
and will remember their sins[y] no
more."

35This is what the LORD says,

he who appoints[z] the sun
to shine by day,
who decrees the moon and stars
to shine by night,[a]
who stirs up the sea[b]
so that its waves roar[c]—
the LORD Almighty is his name:[d]
36"Only if these decrees[e] vanish from
my sight,"
declares the LORD,
"will the descendants[f] of Israel ever
cease
to be a nation before me."

37This is what the LORD says:

17 [b]**Job 8:7**; La 3:29; [c]**Jer 30:20**
18 [d]**Job 5:17**; [e]Jer 50:11; Hos 4:16; 10:11; [f]**Ps 80:3**
19 [g]**Ps 95:10; Jer 8:4**; Eze 36:31; [h]Eze 21:12; Lk 18:13; [i]Ezr 9:6; [j]**Ps 25:7; Jer 22:21**
20 [k]La 3:33; [l]**Isa 44:21**; [m]**1Ki 3:26; Ps 6:2**; Isa 55:7; Mic 7:18
21 [n]Eze 21:19; [o]Isa 35:8; Jer 50:5; [p]Isa 52:11; **Jer 3:12**; [q]ver 4
22 [r]**Jer 2:23**; [s]**Jer 3:6**; [t]Isa 43:19; [u]**Dt 32:10**
23 [v]**Jer 30:18**; [w]**Ge 28:3; Nu 6:24**; [x]**Isa 1:26**; [y]**Ps 48:1; Isa 2:2**
24 [z]**Jer 30:18**; Zec 8:4–8; [a]**ver 12**
25 [b]**Isa 40:29**; [c]Jn 4:14
26 [d]Zec 4:1
27 [e]**Jer 16:14**; [f]Hos 2:23
28 [g]**Job 29:2**; [h]**Dt 29:28**; [i]**Jer 18:8**; [j]**Dt 28:63; 30:9; Jer 1:10**; Eze 36:10–11; Am 9:14
29 [k]**Ge 9:25**; Dt 24:16; La 5:7; [l]Eze 18:2
30 [m]**2Ki 14:6; Isa 3:11**; Gal 6:7
31 [n]**Dt 29:14; Isa 42:6; 54:10; Lk 22:20**; Heb 8:8–12*; 10:16–17
32 [o]**Ex 24:8**; [p]Dt 5:3; [q]Jer 11:4; [r]**Isa 54:5**
33 [s]**Ex 4:15**; [t]**Dt 6:6; 2Co 3:3**; [u]**Jer 11:4**; Heb 10:16
34 [v]1Jn 2:27; [w]**Isa 11:9; Jn 6:45**; [x]Ps 85:2; 130:4; Jer 33:8; 50:20; [y]**Job 7:21; Isa 38:17**; Mic 7:19; Heb 10:17*
35 [z]Ps 136:7–9; [a]**Ge 1:16**; [b]**Ex 14:21**; [c]**Ps 93:3**; [d]**Jer 10:16**
36 [e]**Job 38:33**; Jer 33:20–26; [f]Ps 89:36–37

b22 Or *will go about* ⌞*seeking*⌟; or *will protect*
c23 Or *I restore their fortunes*
d32 Hebrew; Septuagint and Syriac *covenant, / and I turned away from*
e32 Or *was their master*

"Only if the heavens above can be
measured[g]
and the foundations of the earth
below be searched out
will I reject[h] all the descendants of
Israel
because of all they have done,"
declares the LORD.

38"The days are coming," declares the
LORD, "when this city will be rebuilt[i] for
me from the Tower of Hananel[j] to the
Corner Gate.[k] 39The measuring line[l] will
stretch from there straight to the hill of
Gareb and then turn to Goah. 40The
whole valley[m] where dead bodies[n] and
ashes are thrown, and all the terraces
out to the Kidron Valley[o] on the east as
far as the corner of the Horse Gate,[p] will
be holy[q] to the LORD. The city will never
again be uprooted or demolished."

Jeremiah Buys a Field

32 This is the word that came to
Jeremiah from the LORD in the
tenth[a] year of Zedekiah king of Judah,
which was the eighteenth[b] year of
Nebuchadnezzar. 2The army of the king
of Babylon was then besieging[c] Jeru-
salem, and Jeremiah the prophet was
confined[d] in the courtyard of the guard[e]
in the royal palace of Judah.
3Now Zedekiah king of Judah had
imprisoned him there, saying, "Why do
you prophesy[f] as you do? You say, 'This
is what the LORD says: I am about to
hand this city over to the king of Bab-
ylon, and he will capture[g] it. 4Zedekiah[h]
king of Judah will not escape[i] out of the
hands of the Babylonians[a][j] but will
certainly be handed over to the king of
Babylon, and will speak with him face to
face and see him with his own eyes.
5He will take[k] Zedekiah to Babylon,
where he will remain until I deal with
him,[l] declares the LORD. If you fight
against the Babylonians, you will not
succeed.'"[m]
6Jeremiah said, "The word of the
LORD came to me: 7Hanamel son of Shal-
lum your uncle is going to come to you
and say, 'Buy my field at Anathoth,[n]
because as nearest relative it is your
right and duty[o] to buy it.'
8"Then, just as the LORD had said, my
cousin Hanamel came to me in the
courtyard of the guard and said, 'Buy
my field[p] at Anathoth in the territory
of Benjamin. Since it is your right to
redeem it and possess it, buy it for
yourself.'
"I knew that this was the word of the
LORD; 9so I bought the field[q] at Anathoth
from my cousin Hanamel and weighed
out for him seventeen shekels[b] of
silver.[r] 10I signed and sealed the deed,[s]
had it witnessed,[t] and weighed out the
silver on the scales. 11I took the deed of
purchase—the sealed copy containing
the terms and conditions, as well as the
unsealed copy—12and I gave this deed
to Baruch[u] son of Neriah,[v] the son of
Mahseiah, in the presence of my cousin
Hanamel and of the witnesses who had
signed the deed and of all the Jews
sitting in the courtyard of the guard.
13"In their presence I gave Baruch
these instructions: 14'This is what the
LORD Almighty, the God of Israel, says:
Take these documents, both the sealed[w]
and unsealed copies of the deed of
purchase, and put them in a clay jar so
that they will last a long time. 15For this
is what the LORD Almighty, the God
of Israel, says: Houses, fields and
vineyards will again be bought in this
land.'[x]
16"After I had given the deed of pur-
chase to Baruch[y] son of Neriah, I prayed
to the LORD:

17"Ah, Sovereign LORD,[z] you have
made the heavens and the earth[a] by
your great power and outstretched
arm.[b] Nothing is too hard[c] for you.
18You show love[d] to thousands but
bring the punishment for the
fathers' sins into the laps[e] of their
children[f] after them. O great and
powerful God,[g] whose name is the
LORD Almighty,[h] 19great are your
purposes and mighty are your
deeds.[i] Your eyes are open to all the
ways of men;[j] you reward everyone
according to his conduct and as his
deeds deserve.[k] 20You performed
miraculous signs and wonders[l] in
Egypt[m] and have continued them to
this day, both in Israel and among
all mankind, and have gained the
renown[n] that is still yours. 21You
brought your people Israel out of
Egypt with signs and wonders, by a
mighty hand[o] and an outstretched
arm[p] and with great terror.[q] 22You
gave them this land you had sworn
to give to their forefathers, a land
flowing with milk and honey.[r]

37 [g]**Job 38:5**; Jer 33:22; [h]Jer 33:24–26; Ro 11:1–5
38 [i]**Jer 30:18**; [j]**Ne 3:1**; [k]**2Ki 14:13; 2Ch 25:23**
39 [l]**1Ki 7:23**
40 [m]**Jer 2:23**; 7:31–32; [n]**Jer 8:2**; [o]**2Sa 15:23**; Jn 18:1; [p]**2Ki 11:16**; [q]**Isa 4:3**; Joel 3:17; Zec 14:21

Ch. 32

1 [a]2Ki 25:1; [b]Jer 25:1
2 [c]**2Ki 25:1**; [d]**Ps 88:8**; [e]**Ne 3:25**
3 [f]Jer 26:8–9; [g]ver 28; Jer 21:4; 34:2–3
4 [h]Jer 34:21; 44:30; [i]**Jer 21:7**; 38:18,23; 39:5–7; 52:9; [j]ver 24
5 [k]Jer 39:7; Eze 12:13; [l]**2Ki 25:7**; [m]Jer 21:4; La 1:14
7 [n]**Jos 21:18**; [o]Lev 25:24–25; **Ru 4:3–4**; Mt 27:10*
8 [p]ver 25
9 [q]Jer 37:12; [r]**Ge 23:16**
10 [s]Ge 23:20; [t]**Ru 4:9; Isa 8:2**
12 [u]ver 16; Jer 36:4; 43:3,6; 45:1; [v]Jer 51:59
14 [w]**Isa 8:16**
15 [x]ver 43–44; Isa 44:26; Jer 30:18; Eze 28:26; Am 9:14–15
16 [y]**ver 12**
17 [z]Jer 1:6; [a]**Ge 1:1; Jer 10:16**; [b]**Dt 9:29**; 2Ki 19:15; Ps 102:25; [c]**2Ki 3:18**; Jer 51:15; **Mt 19:26**
18 [d]**Dt 5:10**; [e]**Ps 79:12**; [f]**Ex 20:5; Ps 109:14**; [g]Jer 10:6; [h]**Jer 10:16**
19 [i]**Job 12:13**; Da 2:20; [j]**Job 14:16; Pr 5:21**; Jer 16:17; [k]**Job 34:11; Mt 16:27**
20 [l]**Ex 3:20; Job 9:10**; [m]Ex 9:16; [n]**Isa 55:13; Jer 13:11**
21 [o]**Ex 6:6**; Da 9:15; [p]**Dt 5:15; Jer 6:12**; [q]**Dt 26:8**
22 [r]**Ex 3:8**; Eze 20:6

a4 Or *Chaldeans;* also in verses 5, 24, 25, 28, 29 and 43
b9 That is, about 7 ounces (about 200 grams)

23They came in and took possession[s] of it, but they did not obey you or follow your law;[t] they did not do what you commanded them to do. So you brought all this disaster[u] upon them.

24"See how the siege ramps[v] are built up to take the city. Because of the sword, famine and plague,[w] the city will be handed over to the Babylonians who are attacking it. What you said[x] has happened,[y] as you now see. 25And though the city will be handed over to the Babylonians, you, O Sovereign LORD, say to me, 'Buy the field[z] with silver and have the transaction witnessed.[a]' "

26Then the word of the LORD came to Jeremiah: 27"I am the LORD, the God of all mankind.[b] Is anything too hard for me?[c] 28Therefore, this is what the LORD says: I am about to hand this city over to the Babylonians and to Nebuchadnezzar[d] king of Babylon, who will capture it.[e] 29The Babylonians who are attacking this city will come in and set it on fire; they will burn it down,[f] along with the houses[g] where the people provoked me to anger by burning incense on the roofs to Baal and by pouring out drink offerings[h] to other gods.[i]

30"The people of Israel and Judah have done nothing but evil in my sight from their youth;[j] indeed, the people of Israel have done nothing but provoke[k] me with what their hands have made,[l] declares the LORD. 31From the day it was built until now, this city[m] has so aroused my anger and wrath that I must remove[n] it from my sight. 32The people of Israel and Judah have provoked[o] me by all the evil[p] they have done—they, their kings and officials,[q] their priests and prophets, the men of Judah and the people of Jerusalem. 33They turned their backs[r] to me and not their faces; though I taught[s] them again and again, they would not listen or respond to discipline.[t] 34They set up their abominable idols[u] in the house that bears my Name[v] and defiled[w] it. 35They built high places for Baal in the Valley of Ben Hinnom[x] to sacrifice their sons and daughters[c] to Molech,[y] though I never commanded, nor did it enter my mind,[z] that they should do such a detestable[a] thing and so make Judah sin.[b]

36"You are saying about this city, 'By the sword, famine and plague[c] it will be handed over to the king of Babylon'; but this is what the LORD, the God of Israel, says: 37I will surely gather[d] them from all the lands where I banish them in my furious anger[e] and great wrath; I will bring them back to this place and let them live in safety.[f] 38They will be my people,[g] and I will be their God. 39I will give them singleness[h] of heart and action, so that they will always fear[i] me for their own good and the good of their children after them. 40I will make an everlasting covenant[j] with them: I will never stop doing good to them, and I will inspire[k] them to fear me, so that they will never turn away from me.[l] 41I will rejoice[m] in doing them good[n] and will assuredly plant[o] them in this land with all my heart and soul.[p]

42"This is what the LORD says: As I have brought all this great calamity[q] on this people, so I will give them all the prosperity I have promised[r] them. 43Once more fields will be bought[s] in this land of which you say, 'It is a desolate[t] waste, without men or animals, for it has been handed over to the Babylonians.' 44Fields will be bought for silver, and deeds[u] will be signed, sealed and witnessed[v] in the territory of Benjamin, in the villages around Jerusalem, in the towns of Judah and in the towns of the hill country, of the western foothills and of the Negev,[w] because I will restore[x] their fortunes,[d] declares the LORD."

Promise of Restoration

33 While Jeremiah was still confined[a] in the courtyard[b] of the guard, the word of the LORD came to him a second time:[c] 2"This is what the LORD says, he who made the earth,[d] the LORD who formed it and established it—the LORD is his name:[e] 3'Call[f] to me and I will answer you and tell you great and unsearchable[g] things you do not know.' 4For this is what the LORD, the God of Israel, says about the houses in this city and the royal palaces of Judah that have been torn down to be used against the siege[h] ramps[i] and the sword 5in the fight with the Babylonians:[a] 'They will be filled with the dead bodies

23 [s]**Ps 44:2;** 78:54–55; [t]**Ex 16:28; Jos 1:7; 1Ki 9:6; Jer 11:8;** [u]**Dt 28:64;** 31:29; Da 9:14
24 [v]**2Sa 20:15; Jer 6:6;** [w]**Jer 14:12;** [x]Dt 4:25–26; Jos 23:15–16; [y]**Dt 28:2**
25 [z]**ver 8;** [a]**Isa 8:2**
27 [b]**Nu 16:22;** [c]**Ge 18:14; 2Ki 3:18**
28 [d]**2Ch 36:17;** [e]**ver 3; Jer 21:10**
29 [f]**2Ch 36:19;** [g]**Jer 19:13;** [h]**Jer 44:18;** [i]**Jer 7:9**
30 [j]**Ps 25:7; Jer 22:21;** [k]Jer 8:19; [l]Jer 25:7
31 [m]1Ki 11:7–8; 2Ki 21:4–5; Mt 23:37; [n]**2Ki 23:27**
32 [o]**1Ki 14:9;** [p]Da 9:8; [q]**Jer 2:26; 44:9**
33 [r]**1Ki 14:9; Ps 14:3;** Jer 2:27; Eze 8:16; Zec 7:11; [s]**Dt 4:5; Isa 28:9; Jer 7:13;** [t]**Jer 7:28**
34 [u]**2Ki 21:4;** Eze 8:3–16; [v]Jer 7:10; 34:15; [w]**Jer 7:30**
35 [x]Jer 19:2; [y]**Lev 18:21;** [z]**Jer 19:5;** [a]**1Ki 14:24;** [b]**Jer 25:7**
36 [c]ver 24
37 [d]**Isa 11:12;** [e]Jer 21:5; [f]**Lev 25:18;** Eze 34:28; 39:26
38 [g]Jer 24:7; 2Co 6:16*
39 [h]**2Ch 30:12; Ps 86:11;** Jn 17:21; Ac 4:32; [i]**Dt 6:24; 10:16**
40 [j]**Ge 9:16; Isa 42:6;** [k]**Dt 4:10;** [l]**Jer 24:7**
41 [m]**Dt 28:63; Isa 62:4;** [n]**Dt 28:3–12;** [o]Jer 24:6; 31:28; [p]Mic 7:18
42 [q]La 3:38; [r]**Jer 29:10**
43 [s]ver 15; [t]Jer 33:12
44 [u]ver 10; [v]**Ru 4:9; Isa 8:2;** [w]**Jer 17:26;** [x]**Ezr 9:9;** Ps 14:7

Ch. 33
1 [a]**Ps 88:8;** [b]Jer 37:21; 38:28; [c]Jer 13:3
2 [d]**Ps 136:6; Jer 10:16;** [e]**Ex 3:15**
3 [f]**Isa 55:6;** [g]**Job 28:11**
4 [h]**2Ki 25:1;** Eze 4:2; [i]Jer 32:24; Eze 26:8; Hab 1:10

[c]35 Or *to make their sons and daughters pass through ⌊the fire⌋*
[d]44 Or *will bring them back from captivity*
[a]5 Or *Chaldeans*

of the men I will slay in my anger and wrath.[j] I will hide my face[k] from this city because of all its wickedness.

[6]'"Nevertheless, I will bring health and healing to it; I will heal[l] my people and will let them enjoy abundant peace[m] and security. [7]I will bring Judah[n] and Israel back from captivity[b][o] and will rebuild[p] them as they were before.[q] [8]I will cleanse[r] them from all the sin they have committed against me and will forgive[s] all their sins of rebellion against me. [9]Then this city will bring me renown,[t] joy, praise[u] and honour[v] before all nations on earth that hear of all the good things I do for it; and they will be in awe and will tremble[w] at the abundant prosperity and peace I provide for it.'

[10]"This is what the LORD says: 'You say about this place, "It is a desolate waste, without men or animals."[x] Yet in the towns of Judah and the streets of Jerusalem that are deserted,[y] inhabited by neither men nor animals, there will be heard once more [11]the sounds of joy and gladness,[z] the voices of bride and bridegroom, and the voices of those who bring thank-offerings[a] to the house of the LORD, saying,

"Give thanks to the LORD Almighty,
for the LORD is good;[b]
his love endures for ever."[c]

For I will restore the fortunes[d] of the land as they were before,[e]' says the LORD.

[12]"This is what the LORD Almighty says: 'In this place, desolate[f] and without men or animals[g]—in all its towns there will again be pastures for shepherds to rest their flocks.[h] [13]In the towns of the hill[i] country, of the western foothills and of the Negev,[j] in the territory of Benjamin, in the villages around Jerusalem and in the towns of Judah, flocks will again pass under the hand[k] of the one who counts them,' says the LORD.

[14]'"The days are coming,' declares the LORD, 'when I will fulfil the gracious promise[l] I made to the house of Israel and to the house of Judah.

[15]'"In those days and at that time
I will make a righteous[m] Branch[n]
sprout from David's line;[o]
he will do what is just and right in
the land.
[16]In those days Judah will be saved[p]
and Jerusalem will live in safety.[q]
This is the name by which it[c] will be
called:[r]
The LORD Our Righteousness.'[s]

[17]For this is what the LORD says: 'David will never fail[t] to have a man to sit on the throne of the house of Israel, [18]nor will the priests,[u] who are Levites,[v] ever fail to have a man to stand before me continually to offer burnt offerings, to burn grain offerings and to present sacrifices.[w]'"

[19]The word of the LORD came to Jeremiah: [20]"This is what the LORD says: 'If you can break my covenant with the day[x] and my covenant with the night, so that day and night no longer come at their appointed time,[y] [21]then my covenant[z] with David my servant—and my covenant with the Levites[a] who are priests ministering before me—can be broken and David will no longer have a descendant to reign on his throne.[b] [22]I will make the descendants of David my servant and the Levites who minister before me as countless[c] as the stars of the sky and as measureless as the sand on the seashore.'"

[23]The word of the LORD came to Jeremiah: [24]"Have you not noticed that these people are saying, 'The LORD has rejected the two kingdoms[d][d] he chose'? So they despise[e] my people and no longer regard them as a nation.[f] [25]This is what the LORD says: 'If I have not established my covenant with day and night[g] and the fixed laws[h] of heaven and earth,[i] [26]then I will reject[j] the descendants of Jacob[k] and David my servant and will not choose one of his sons to rule over the descendants of Abraham, Isaac and Jacob. For I will restore their fortunes[e][l] and have compassion[m] on them.'"

Warning to Zedekiah

34 While Nebuchadnezzar king of Babylon and all his army and all the kingdoms and peoples[a] in the empire he ruled were fighting against Jerusalem[b] and all its surrounding towns, this word came to Jeremiah from the LORD: [2]"This is what the LORD, the God of Israel, says: Go to Zedekiah[c] king of Judah and tell him, 'This is what the LORD says: I am about to hand this

5 [j]Jer 21:4–7; [k]Dt 31:17; Isa 8:17
6 [l]Dt 32:39; Isa 30:26; [m]Isa 9:6
7 [n]Jer 32:44; [o]Jer 30:3; Eze 39:25; Am 9:14; [p]Jer 24:6; [q]Isa 1:26
8 [r]Lev 16:30; Heb 9:13–14; [s]2Sa 24:14; Jer 31:34
9 [t]Isa 55:13; [u]Isa 60:18; [v]Jer 3:17; [w]Isa 64:2
10 [x]Jer 32:43; [y]Lev 26:32; Jer 9:11
11 [z]Ps 51:8; Isa 24:8; 51:3; [a]Lev 7:12; [b]2Ch 7:3; Ps 25:8; 136:1; Na 1:7; [c]1Ch 16:34; 2Ch 5:13; Ps 100:4–5; [d]Ps 14:7; [e]Isa 1:26
12 [f]Jer 32:43; [g]ver 10; [h]Isa 65:10; Eze 34:11–15
13 [i]Jer 31:5; [j]Jer 17:26; Ob 20; [k]Lev 27:32
14 [l]Dt 28:1–14; Jos 23:15; Jer 29:10
15 [m]Ps 72:2; [n]Isa 4:2; [o]2Sa 7:12
16 [p]Isa 45:17; [q]Jer 17:25; 32:37; [r]Isa 59:14; Jer 3:17; Eze 48:35; Zep 3:13; Zec 8:3,16; [s]1Co 1:30
17 [t]2Sa 7:13; 2Ch 7:18; Ps 89:29–37; Lk 1:33
18 [u]Nu 25:11–13; Heb 7:17–22; [v]Dt 18:1; [w]Heb 13:15
20 [x]Ps 89:36; [y]Ge 1:14
21 [z]Ps 89:34; [a]Dt 18:1; [b]2Sa 7:13; 2Ch 7:18
22 [c]Ge 12:2; Jer 30:19; Hos 1:10
24 [d]Eze 37:22; [e]Ne 4:4; [f]Jer 30:17; Eze 36:20
25 [g]Ge 1:18; [h]Ps 148:6; [i]Ps 74:16–17
26 [j]Lev 26:44; [k]Isa 14:1; [l]ver 7; Ps 14:7; [m]Jer 30:18

Ch. 34
1 [a]Jer 27:7; [b]2Ki 25:1; Jer 39:1
2 [c]2Ch 36:11

[b]7 Or *will restore the fortunes of Judah and Israel*
[c]16 Or *he* [d]24 Or *families*
[e]26 Or *will bring them back from captivity*

city over to the king of Babylon, and he will burn it down.[d] 3You will not escape from his grasp but will surely be captured and handed over[e] to him. You will see the king of Babylon with your own eyes, and he will speak with you face to face. And you will go to Babylon.

4" 'Yet hear the promise of the LORD, O Zedekiah king of Judah. This is what the LORD says concerning you: You will not die by the sword;[f] 5you will die peacefully. As people made a funeral fire[g] in honour of your fathers, the former kings who preceded you, so they will make a fire in your honour and lament, "Alas,[h] O master!" I myself make this promise, declares the LORD.' "

6Then Jeremiah the prophet told all this to Zedekiah king of Judah, in Jerusalem, 7while the army of the king of Babylon was fighting against Jerusalem and the other cities of Judah that were still holding out—Lachish[i] and Azekah.[j] These were the only fortified cities left in Judah.

Freedom for Slaves

8The word came to Jeremiah from the LORD after King Zedekiah had made a covenant with all the people[k] in Jerusalem to proclaim freedom[l] for the slaves. 9Everyone was to free his Hebrew slaves, both male and female; no-one was to hold a fellow Jew in bondage.[m] 10So all the officials and people who entered into this covenant agreed that they would free their male and female slaves and no longer hold them in bondage. They agreed, and set them free. 11But afterwards they changed their minds[n] and took back the slaves they had freed and enslaved them again.

12Then the word of the LORD came to Jeremiah: 13"This is what the LORD, the God of Israel, says: I made a covenant with your forefathers[o] when I brought them out of Egypt, out of the land of slavery.[p] I said, 14'Every seventh year each of you must free any fellow Hebrew who has sold himself to you. After he has served you for six years, you must let him go free.'[a][q] Your fathers, however, did not listen to me or pay attention[r] to me. 15Recently you repented and did what is right in my sight: Each of you proclaimed freedom to his countrymen.[s] You even made a covenant before me in the house that bears my Name.[t] 16But now you have turned round[u] and profaned[v] my name; each of you has taken back the male and female slaves you had set free to go where they wished. You have forced them to become your slaves again.

17"Therefore, this is what the LORD says: You have not obeyed me; you have not proclaimed freedom for your fellow countrymen. So I now proclaim 'freedom' for you,[w] declares the LORD —'freedom' to fall by the sword, plague[x] and famine.[y] I will make you abhorrent to all the kingdoms of the earth.[z] 18The men who have violated my covenant[a] and have not fulfilled the terms of the covenant they made before me, I will treat like the calf they cut in two and then walked between its pieces.[b] 19The leaders of Judah and Jerusalem, the court officials,[c] the priests and all the people of the land who walked between the pieces of the calf, 20I will hand over[d] to their enemies who seek their lives.[e] Their dead bodies will become food for the birds of the air and the beasts of the earth.[f]

21"I will hand Zedekiah[g] king of Judah and his officials[h] over to their enemies[i] who seek their lives, to the army of the king of Babylon,[j] which has withdrawn[k] from you. 22I am going to give the order, declares the LORD, and I will bring them back to this city. They will fight against it, take[l] it and burn[m] it down. And I will lay waste[n] the towns of Judah so that no-one can live there."

The Recabites

35 This is the word that came to Jeremiah from the LORD during the reign of Jehoiakim[a] son of Josiah king of Judah: 2"Go to the Recabite[b] family and invite them to come to one of the side rooms[c] of the house of the LORD and give them wine to drink."

3So I went to get Jaazaniah son of Jeremiah, the son of Habazziniah, and his brothers and all his sons—the whole family of the Recabites. 4I brought them into the house of the LORD, into the room of the sons of Hanan son of Igdaliah the man of God.[d] It was next to the room of the officials, which was over that of Maaseiah son of Shallum[e] the door-keeper.[f] 5Then I set bowls full of wine and some cups before the men of the Recabite family and said to them, "Drink some wine."

6But they replied, "We do not drink wine, because our forefather Jonadab[g] son of Recab gave us this command: 'Neither you nor your descendants

2 [d]ver 22; Jer 32:29; 37:8
3 [e]**2Ki 25:7; Jer 21:7**
4 [f]Jer 52:11
5 [g]**2Ch 16:14;** [h]Jer 22:18
7 [i]**Jos 10:3;** [j]Jos 10:10; 2Ch 11:9
8 [k]**2Ki 11:17;** [l]**Ex 21:2;** Lev 25:39–41; Ne 5:5–8
9 [m]Dt 15:12–18
11 [n]Ps 78:37
13 [o]**Ex 24:8;** [p]**Dt 15:15**
14 [q]**Ex 21:2;** [r]2Ki 17:14; **Jer 7:26**
15 [s]ver 8; [t]**Jer 32:34**
16 [u]Eze 3:20; 18:24; [v]**Lev 19:12**
17 [w]**Mt 7:2;** Gal 6:7; [x]Jer 21:7; [y]**Jer 14:12;** [z]Jer 15:4; **24:9; 29:18**
18 [a]**Jer 11:10;** [b]**Ge 15:10**
19 [c]**Jer 26:10;** Zep 3:3–4
20 [d]Jer 21:7; Eze 16:27; 23:28; [e]**Jer 11:21;** [f]**Dt 28:26**
21 [g]**Jer 32:4;** [h]2Ki 25:21; Jer 39:6; 52:24–27; [i]**Jer 21:7;** [j]**2Ch 36:10;** [k]Jer 37:5
22 [l]Jer 39:1–2; [m]**Ne 2:17;** Jer 38:18; 39:8; Eze 23:47; [n]**Lev 26:32; Isa 1:7**

Ch. 35

1 [a]**2Ch 36:5**
2 [b]**2Ki 10:15;** [c]**1Ki 6:5**
4 [d]**Dt 33:1;** [e]1Ch 9:19; [f]**2Ki 12:9; 23:4**
6 [g]**2Ki 10:15**

[a]14 Deut. 15:12

must ever drink wine.[h] 7Also you must
never build houses, sow seed or plant
vineyards; you must never have any of
these things, but must always live in
tents.[i] Then you will live a long time in
the land[j] where you are nomads.' 8We
have obeyed everything our forefather[k]
Jonadab son of Recab commanded us.
Neither we nor our wives nor our sons
and daughters have ever drunk wine 9or
built houses to live in or had vineyards,
fields or crops.[l] 10We have lived in tents
and have fully obeyed everything our
forefather Jonadab commanded us.
11But when Nebuchadnezzar king of
Babylon invaded[m] this land, we said,
'Come, we must go to Jerusalem[n] to
escape the Babylonian[a] and Aramean
armies.' So we have remained in
Jerusalem."
12Then the word of the LORD came to
Jeremiah, saying: 13"This is what the
LORD Almighty, the God of Israel, says:
Go and tell[o] the men of Judah and the
people of Jerusalem, 'Will you not learn
a lesson[p] and obey my words?' declares
the LORD. 14'Jonadab son of Recab
ordered his sons not to drink wine and
this command has been kept. To this
day they do not drink wine, because
they obey their forefather's command.[q]
But I have spoken to you again and
again,[r] yet you have not obeyed[s] me.
15Again and again I sent all my servants
the prophets[t] to you. They said, "Each
of you must turn[u] from your wicked
ways and reform[v] your actions; do not
follow other gods[w] to serve them. Then
you shall live in the land[x] I have given to
you and your fathers." But you have not
paid attention or listened[y] to me. 16The
descendants of Jonadab son of Recab
have carried out the command their
forefather[z] gave them, but these people
have not obeyed me.'
17"Therefore, this is what the LORD
God Almighty, the God of Israel, says:
'Listen! I am going to bring on Judah
and on everyone living in Jerusalem
every disaster[a] I pronounced against
them. I spoke to them, but they did not
listen;[b] I called to them, but they did not
answer.'"[c]
18Then Jeremiah said to the family of
the Recabites, "This is what the LORD
Almighty, the God of Israel, says: 'You
have obeyed the command of your fore-
father[d] Jonadab and have followed all
his instructions and have done every-
thing he ordered.' 19Therefore, this is
what the LORD Almighty, the God of
Israel, says: 'Jonadab son of Recab shall
never fail[e] to have a man to serve[f] me.'"

6 [h]**Lev 10:9**; Nu 6:2–4; **Lk 1:15**
7 [i]Heb 11:9; [j]**Ex 20:12**; Eph 6:2–3
8 [k]Pr 1:8; Col 3:20
9 [l]1Ti 6:6
11 [m]2Ki 24:1; [n]**Jos 10:20**; Jer 8:14
13 [o]Jer 11:6; [p]Jer 6:10; 32:33
14 [q]ver 6–10,16; [r]**Jer 7:13**; [s]Isa 30:9
15 [t]**Jer 7:25**; [u]**2Ki 17:13**; **Jer 26:3**; [v]**Isa 1:16–17**; **59:20**; Jer 4:1; 18:11; Eze 14:6; 18:30; [w]**Ex 20:3**; [x]**Dt 4:40**; Jer 25:5; [y]**Jer 6:10**; **7:26**; 44:4–5
16 [z]**Lev 20:9**; Mal 1:6
17 [a]**Jos 23:15**; **1Ki 13:34**; Jer 21:4–7; [b]**Pr 1:24**; Ro 10:21; [c]Jer 7:13
18 [d]**Ge 31:35**
19 [e]**Isa 48:19**; Jer 33:17; [f]Jer 15:19

Ch. 36

1 [a]**2Ch 36:5**
2 [b]**ver 4**; **Ex 17:14**; **Ps 40:7**; Jer 30:2; Hab 2:2; [c]Eze 2:7; [d]Jer 1:2; 25:3
3 [e]ver 7; Eze 12:3; Am 5:15; [f]Isa 6:9; Mk 4:12; [g]**2Ki 17:13**; **Isa 44:22**; **Jer 26:3**; Ac 3:19; [h]**Jer 18:8**
4 [i]**Jer 32:12**; [j]Jer 51:59; [k]ver 18; [l]ver 2; Eze 2:9; Da 7:1; Zec 5:1
6 [m]ver 9; [n]**Ex 4:16**; [o]2Ch 20:4
7 [p]Jer 37:20; 42:2; [q]**Jer 26:3**; [r]**Dt 31:17**
9 [s]ver 22; [t]**2Ch 20:3**
10 [u]ver 12,25; Jer 29:3; [v]Jer 26:24; [w]Jer 52:25; [x]**Ge 23:10**
12 [y]**2Sa 8:17**; [z]**Jer 26:22**; [a]Jer 38:4
14 [b]ver 21

Jehoiakim Burns Jeremiah's Scroll

36 In the fourth year of Jehoiakim[a]
son of Josiah king of Judah, this
word came to Jeremiah from the LORD:
2"Take a scroll[b] and write on it all the
words[c] I have spoken to you concerning
Israel, Judah and all the other nations
from the time I began speaking to you in
the reign of Josiah[d] till now. 3Perhaps[e]
when the people of Judah hear[f] about
every disaster I plan to inflict on them,
each of them will turn[g] from his wicked
way; then I will forgive[h] their wicked-
ness and their sin."
4So Jeremiah called Baruch[i] son of
Neriah,[j] and while Jeremiah dictated[k] all
the words the LORD had spoken to him,
Baruch wrote them on the scroll.[l] 5Then
Jeremiah told Baruch, "I am restricted; I
cannot go to the LORD's temple. 6So you
go to the house of the LORD on a day of
fasting[m] and read to the people from the
scroll the words of the LORD that you
wrote as I dictated.[n] Read them to all the
people of Judah[o] who come in from their
towns. 7Perhaps they will bring their
petition[p] before the LORD, and each will
turn[q] from his wicked ways, for the
anger[r] and wrath pronounced against
this people by the LORD are great."
8Baruch son of Neriah did everything
Jeremiah the prophet told him to do; at
the LORD's temple he read the words of
the LORD from the scroll. 9In the ninth
month[s] of the fifth year of Jehoiakim son
of Josiah king of Judah, a time of fasting[t]
before the LORD was proclaimed for all
the people in Jerusalem and those who
had come from the towns of Judah.
10From the room of Gemariah[u] son of
Shaphan[v] the secretary,[w] which was in
the upper courtyard at the entrance of
the New Gate[x] of the temple, Baruch
read to all the people at the LORD's
temple the words of Jeremiah from
the scroll.
11When Micaiah son of Gemariah, the
son of Shaphan, heard all the words of
the LORD from the scroll, 12he went
down to the secretary's[y] room in the
royal palace, where all the officials were
sitting: Elishama the secretary, Delaiah
son of Shemaiah, Elnathan[z] son of
Acbor, Gemariah son of Shaphan,
Zedekiah son of Hananiah, and all the
other officials.[a] 13After Micaiah told
them everything he had heard Baruch
read to the people from the scroll, 14all
the officials sent Jehudi[b] son of Nethan-
iah, the son of Shelemiah, the son of

[a]11 Or *Chaldean*

Cushi, to say to Baruch, "Bring the scroll[c] from which you have read to the people and come." So Baruch son of Neriah went to them with the scroll in his hand. 15They said to him, "Sit down, please, and read it to us."

So Baruch read it to them. 16When they heard all these words, they looked at each other in fear[d] and said to Baruch, "We must report all these words to the king." 17Then they asked Baruch, "Tell us, how did you come to write[e] all this? Did Jeremiah dictate it?"

18"Yes," Baruch replied, "he dictated[f] all these words to me, and I wrote them in ink on the scroll."

19Then the officials[g] said to Baruch, "You and Jeremiah, go and hide.[h] Don't let anyone know where you are."

20After they put the scroll in the room of Elishama the secretary, they went to the king in the courtyard and reported everything to him. 21The king sent Jehudi[i] to get the scroll, and Jehudi brought it from the room of Elishama the secretary and read it to the king[j] and all the officials standing beside him. 22It was the ninth month and the king was sitting in the winter apartment,[k] with a fire burning in the brazier in front of him. 23Whenever Jehudi had read three or four columns of the scroll,[l] the king cut them off with a scribe's knife and threw them into the brazier, until the entire scroll was burned in the fire.[m] 24The king and all his attendants who heard all these words showed no fear,[n] nor did they tear their clothes.[o] 25Even though Elnathan, Delaiah[p] and Gemariah[q] urged the king not to burn the scroll, he would not listen to them. 26Instead, the king commanded Jerahmeel, a son of the king, Seraiah son of Azriel and Shelemiah son of Abdeel to arrest[r] Baruch the scribe and Jeremiah the prophet. But the LORD had hidden[s] them.

27After the king burned the scroll containing the words that Baruch had written at Jeremiah's dictation,[t] the word of the LORD came to Jeremiah: 28"Take another scroll[u] and write on it all the words that were on the first scroll, which Jehoiakim king of Judah burned up. 29Also tell Jehoiakim king of Judah, 'This is what the LORD says: You burned that scroll and said, "Why did you write on it that the king of Babylon would certainly come and destroy this land and cut off both men and animals[v] from it?"[w] 30Therefore, this is what the LORD says about Jehoiakim[x] king of Judah: He will have no-one to sit on the throne of David; his body will be thrown out[y] and exposed[z] to the heat by day and the frost by night.[a] 31I will punish him and his children[b] and his attendants for their wickedness; I will bring on them and those living in Jerusalem and the people of Judah every disaster[c] I pronounced against them, because they have not listened.[d]' "

32So Jeremiah took another scroll and gave it to the scribe Baruch son of Neriah, and as Jeremiah dictated,[e] Baruch wrote[f] on it all the words of the scroll that Jehoiakim king of Judah had burned[g] in the fire. And many similar words were added to them.

14 [c]ver 4
16 [d]**Ps 36:1**
17 [e]Jer 30:2
18 [f]ver 4
19 [g]Jer 26:16; [h]**1Ki 17:3**
21 [i]ver 14; [j]2Ki 22:10
22 [k]Am 3:15
23 [l]ver 2; [m]1Ki 22:8
24 [n]**Ps 36:1**; [o]**Ge 37:29; Nu 14:6**
25 [p]ver 12; [q]**ver 10**
26 [r]Mt 23:34; [s]**1Ki 17:3**; Ps 11:1; **Jer 1:8**; 15:21
27 [t]ver 4
28 [u]ver 2
29 [v]Jer 33:12; [w]**Isa 30:10**
30 [x]Jer 52:2; [y]**Isa 14:19**; [z]**2Ki 24:6**; [a]**Jer 8:2**
31 [b]Ex 20:5; [c]**Pr 29:1**; [d]**Pr 1:24**
32 [e]ver 4; [f]Ex 34:1; Jer 30:2; [g]ver 23

Ch. 37

1 [a]**2Ki 24:17**; [b]1Sa 11:1; Eze 17:13; [c]**2Ki 24:8**,12; Jer 22:24
2 [d]**2Ki 24:19**
3 [e]ver 17; Jer 38:14; [f]Jer 38:1; [g]**2Ki 25:18**; Jer 29:25; 52:24; [h]**Ex 8:28; Nu 21:7**; 1Sa 12:19; 1Ki 13:6; 2Ki 19:4; Jer 42:2
4 [i]ver 15; Jer 32:2
5 [j]**Ge 15:18**; Isa 31:1; Eze 17:15; [k]Jer 34:21; [l]**Isa 30:5**; Jer 34:11
7 [m]**Ge 25:22; 2Ki 22:18**; [n]ver 5; [o]**2Ki 18:21; Jer 2:36**; La 1:7; 4:17
8 [p]Jer 38:3; [q]Jer 21:10; 38:18; 39:8
9 [r]Jer 29:8; **Mk 13:5**
10 [s]Jer 21:10

Jeremiah in Prison

37 Zedekiah[a] son of Josiah was made king[b] of Judah by Nebuchadnezzar king of Babylon; he reigned in place of Jehoiachin[a][c] son of Jehoiakim. 2Neither he nor his attendants nor the people of the land paid any attention[d] to the words the LORD had spoken through Jeremiah the prophet.

3King Zedekiah, however, sent[e] Jehucal[f] son of Shelemiah with the priest Zephaniah[g] son of Maaseiah to Jeremiah the prophet with this message: "Please pray[h] to the LORD our God for us."

4Now Jeremiah was free to come and go among the people, for he had not yet been put in prison.[i] 5Pharaoh's army had marched out of Egypt,[j] and when the Babylonians[b] who were besieging Jerusalem heard the report about them, they withdrew[k] from Jerusalem.[l]

6Then the word of the LORD came to Jeremiah the prophet: 7"This is what the LORD, the God of Israel, says: Tell the king of Judah, who sent you to enquire[m] of me, 'Pharaoh's army, which has marched[n] out to support you, will go back to its own land, to Egypt.[o] 8Then the Babylonians will return and attack this city; they will capture[p] it and burn[q] it down.'

9"This is what the LORD says: Do not deceive[r] yourselves, thinking, 'The Babylonians will surely leave us.' They will not! 10Even if you were to defeat the entire Babylonian[c] army that is attacking you and only wounded men were left in their tents, they would come out and burn[s] this city down."

---

[a]*1* Hebrew *Coniah*, a variant of *Jehoiachin*
[b]*5* Or *Chaldeans*; also in verses 8, 9, 13 and 14
[c]*10* Or *Chaldean*; also in verse 11

11After the Babylonian army had
withdrawn[t] from Jerusalem because of
Pharaoh's army, 12Jeremiah started to
leave the city to go to the territory of
Benjamin to get his share of the prop-
erty[u] among the people there. 13But
when he reached the Benjamin Gate,[v]
the captain of the guard, whose name
was Irijah son of Shelemiah, the son of
Hananiah, arrested him and said, "You
are deserting to the Babylonians!"[w]
14"That's not true!" Jeremiah said. "I
am not deserting to the Babylonians."
But Irijah would not listen to him;
instead, he arrested[x] Jeremiah and
brought him to the officials. 15They were
angry with Jeremiah and had him
beaten[y] and imprisoned[z] in the house[a]
of Jonathan the secretary, which they
had made into a prison.
16Jeremiah was put into a vaulted cell
in a dungeon, where he remained a long
time. 17Then King Zedekiah sent[b] for
him and had him brought to the palace,
where he asked[c] him privately,[d] "Is
there any word from the LORD?"
"Yes," Jeremiah replied, "you will be
handed over[e] to the king of Babylon."
18Then Jeremiah said to King Zede-
kiah, "What crime[f] have I committed
against you or your officials or this
people, that you have put me in prison?
19Where are your prophets[g] who
prophesied to you, 'The king of Babylon
will not attack you or this land'? 20But
now, my lord the king, please listen. Let
me bring my petition before you: Do not
send me back to the house of Jonathan
the secretary, or I shall die there."[h]
21King Zedekiah then gave orders for
Jeremiah to be placed in the courtyard of
the guard and given bread from the
street of the bakers each day until all the
bread[i] in the city was gone.[j] So Jeremiah
remained in the courtyard of the guard.[k]

Jeremiah Thrown Into a Cistern

38 Shephatiah son of Mattan,
Gedaliah son of Pashhur[a], Jehu-
cal[a][b] son of Shelemiah, and Pashhur son
of Malkijah heard what Jeremiah was
telling all the people when he said,
2"This is what the LORD says: 'Whoever
stays in this city will die by the sword,
famine or plague,[c] but whoever goes
over to the Babylonians[b] will live. He
will escape with his life; he will live.'[d]
3And this is what the LORD says: 'This
city will certainly be handed over to the
army of the king of Babylon, who will
capture it.'"[e]
4Then the officials[f] said to the king,
"This man should be put to death.[g] He
is discouraging[h] the soldiers who are left
in this city, as well as all the people, by
the things he is saying to them. This
man is not seeking the good of these
people but their ruin."
5"He is in your hands,"[i] King Zede-
kiah answered. "The king can do
nothing[j] to oppose you."
6So they took Jeremiah and put him
into the cistern of Malkijah, the king's
son, which was in the courtyard of the
guard.[k] They lowered Jeremiah by
ropes[l] into the cistern; it had no water in
it,[m] only mud, and Jeremiah sank down
into the mud.[n]
7But Ebed-Melech,[o] a Cushite,[c] an
official[d][p] in the royal palace, heard that
they had put Jeremiah into the cistern.
While the king was sitting in the Ben-
jamin Gate,[q] 8Ebed-Melech went out of
the palace and said to him, 9"My lord
the king, these men have acted wicked-
ly in all they have done to Jeremiah the
prophet. They have thrown him into a
cistern,[r] where he will starve to death
when there is no longer any bread[s] in
the city."
10Then the king commanded Ebed-
Melech the Cushite, "Take thirty men
from here with you and lift Jeremiah the
prophet out of the cistern before he
dies."
11So Ebed-Melech took the men with
him and went to a room under the treas-
ury in the palace. He took some old rags
and worn-out clothes from there and let
them down with ropes[t] to Jeremiah in
the cistern. 12Ebed-Melech the Cushite
said to Jeremiah, "Put these old rags
and worn-out clothes under your arms
to pad the ropes." Jeremiah did so,
13and they pulled him up with the ropes
and lifted him out of the cistern. And
Jeremiah remained in the courtyard of
the guard.[u]

Zedekiah Questions Jeremiah Again

14Then King Zedekiah sent[v] for Jere-
miah the prophet and had him brought
to the third entrance to the temple of the
LORD. "I am going to ask you some-
thing," the king said to Jeremiah. "Do
not hide[w] anything from me."
15Jeremiah said to Zedekiah, "If I give
you an answer, will you not kill me?

11 [t]ver 5
12 [u]**Jer 32:9**
13 [v]**Jer 20:2;** [w]Jer 21:9
14 [x]Isa 58:6; Jer 40:4
15 [y]**Jer 20:2;** Heb 11:36; [z]**1Ki 22:27;** [a]ver 20; Jer 38:26
17 [b]**ver 3;** [c]**Ge 25:22;** Jer 15:11; [d]Jer 38:16; [e]**Jer 21:7**
18 [f]**1Sa 26:18;** Jn 10:32; Ac 25:8
19 [g]**Jer 14:13;** Eze 13:2
20 [h]**ver 15**
21 [i]**Lev 26:26;** Isa 33:16; Jer 38:9; La 1:11; [j]**2Ki 25:3;** [k]Jer 32:2; 38:6,13,28; 39:13–14
Ch. 38
1 [a]**1Ch 9:12;** [b]Jer 37:3
2 [c]Jer 34:17; [d]ver 17; **Jer 21:9;** 39:18; 45:5
3 [e]**Jer 21:4**,10
4 [f]**Jer 36:12;** [g]**Jer 11:21;** [h]**1Sa 17:32**
5 [i]**Jer 26:14;** [j]1Sa 15:24
6 [k]**Jer 37:21;** [l]**Jos 2:15;** [m]**Ge 37:24;** [n]**Job 30:19;** La 3:53
7 [o]Jer 39:16; [p]*fn* Isa 56:3–5; Ac 8:27; [q]**Job 29:7**
9 [r]**Ge 37:20;** [s]**Jer 37:21**
11 [t]**Jos 2:15**
13 [u]**Jer 37:21**
14 [v]**Jer 37:3;** [w]**1Sa 3:17**

[a]1 Hebrew *Jucal*, a variant of *Jehucal*
[b]2 Or *Chaldeans*; also in verses 18, 19 and 23
[c]7 Probably from the upper Nile region
[d]7 Or *a eunuch*

Even if I did give you counsel, you would not listen to me."

16But King Zedekiah swore this oath secretly[x] to Jeremiah: "As surely as the LORD lives, who has given us breath,[y] I will neither kill you nor hand you over to those who are seeking your life."[z]

17Then Jeremiah said to Zedekiah, "This is what the LORD God Almighty, the God of Israel, says: 'If you surrender[a] to the officers of the king of Babylon, your life will be spared and this city will not be burned down; you and your family will live.[b] 18But if you will not surrender to the officers of the king of Babylon, this city will be handed over[c] to the Babylonians and they will burn[d] it down; you yourself will not escape[e] from their hands.'"

19King Zedekiah said to Jeremiah, "I am afraid[f] of the Jews who have gone over[g] to the Babylonians, for the Babylonians may hand me over to them and they will ill-treat me."

20"They will not hand you over," Jeremiah replied. "Obey[h] the LORD by doing what I tell you. Then it will go well[i] with you, and your life[j] will be spared. 21But if you refuse to surrender, this is what the LORD has revealed to me: 22All the women[k] left in the palace of the king of Judah will be brought out to the officials of the king of Babylon. Those women will say to you:

"'They misled you and overcame
you—
those trusted friends[l] of yours.
Your feet are sunk in the mud;[m]
your friends have deserted you.'

23"All your wives and children[n] will be brought out to the Babylonians. You yourself will not escape[o] from their hands but will be captured[p] by the king of Babylon; and this city will[e] be burned down."[q]

24Then Zedekiah said to Jeremiah, "Do not let anyone know[r] about this conversation, or you may die. 25If the officials hear that I talked with you, and they come to you and say, 'Tell us what you said to the king and what the king said to you; do not hide it from us or we will kill you,' 26then tell[s] them, 'I was pleading with the king not to send me back to Jonathan's house[t] to die there.'"

27All the officials did come to Jeremiah and question him, and he told them everything the king had ordered him to say. So they said no more to him, for no-one had heard his conversation with the king.

28And Jeremiah remained in the courtyard of the guard[u] until the day Jerusalem was captured.

The Fall of Jerusalem

39:1–10pp—2Ki 25:1–12; Jer 52:4–16

This is how Jerusalem[a] was taken:

39 1In the ninth year of Zedekiah[b] king of Judah, in the tenth month, Nebuchadnezzar[c] king of Babylon marched against Jerusalem with his whole army and laid siege[d] to it. 2And on the ninth day of the fourth[e] month of Zedekiah's eleventh year, the city wall[f] was broken through.[g] 3Then all the officials[h] of the king of Babylon came and took seats in the Middle Gate: Nergal-Sharezer of Samgar, Nebo-Sarsekim[a] a chief officer, Nergal-Sharezer a high official and all the other officials of the king of Babylon. 4When Zedekiah king of Judah and all the soldiers saw them, they fled; they left the city at night by way of the king's garden, through the gate between the two walls,[i] and headed towards the Arabah.[b][j]

5But the Babylonian[c] army pursued them and overtook Zedekiah[k] in the plains of Jericho. They captured[l] him and took him to Nebuchadnezzar king of Babylon at Riblah[m] in the land of Hamath, where he pronounced sentence on him. 6There at Riblah the king of Babylon slaughtered the sons of Zedekiah before his eyes and also killed all the nobles[n] of Judah. 7Then he put out Zedekiah's eyes[o] and bound him with bronze shackles to take him to Babylon.[p]

8The Babylonians[d] set fire[q] to the royal palace and the houses of the people and broke down the walls[r] of Jerusalem. 9Nebuzaradan commander of the imperial guard carried into exile to Babylon the people who remained in the city, along with those who had gone over to him,[s] and the rest of the people.[t] 10But Nebuzaradan the commander of the guard left behind in the land of Judah some of the poor people, who owned nothing; and at that time he gave them vineyards and fields.

11Now Nebuchadnezzar king of Babylon had given these orders about Jeremiah through Nebuzaradan commander of the imperial guard: 12"Take

16 [x]Jer 37:17; [y]Isa 42:5; 57:16; [z]ver 4
17 [a]Jer 27:8; [b]**Jer 21:9**
18 [c]ver 3; [d]**Jer 37:8**; [e]**Jer 24:8; 32:4**
19 [f]Isa 51:12; Jn 12:42; [g]Jer 39:9; 52:15
20 [h]Jer 11:4; [i]**Dt 5:33**; Jer 40:9; [j]Isa 55:3
22 [k]**Jer 6:12**; [l]**Job 19:14; Jer 13:21**; [m]**Job 30:19**; Ps 69:14
23 [n]**2Ki 25:6**; [o]**Jer 32:4**; Eze 17:15; [p]**Jer 24:8**; [q]Jer 21:10; 37:8
24 [r]Jer 37:17
26 [s]1Sa 16:2; [t]**Jer 37:15**
28 [u]**Jer 37:21**

Ch. 39

1 [a]**Jer 25:29**; [b]**2Ch 36:11**; [c]**2Ki 24:1; Jer 28:14**; [d]**2Ki 25:1**; Jer 52:4; Eze 4:3; 24:2
2 [e]Zec 8:19; [f]**2Ki 14:13**; [g]Eze 33:21
3 [h]ver 13; Jer 21:4
4 [i]**Isa 22:11**; [j]Eze 12:12
5 [k]**Jer 24:8; 32:4**; [l]**Jer 21:7**; [m]**Nu 34:11**
6 [n]**Isa 34:12**
7 [o]**Nu 16:14**; Eze 12:13; [p]**Jer 2:35**
8 [q]**Jer 34:22**; [r]**Ne 1:3; Ps 80:12; Isa 22:5**; La 2:8
9 [s]Jer 21:9; [t]Jer 40:1; La 1:5

[e]23 Or *and you will cause this city to*
[a]3 Or *Nergal-Sharezer, Samgar-Nebo, Sarsekim*
[b]4 Or *the Jordan Valley*
[c]5 Or *Chaldean*
[d]8 Or *Chaldeans*

him and look after him; don't harm[u] him but do for him whatever he asks." 13So Nebuzaradan the commander of the guard, Nebushazban a chief officer, Nergal-Sharezer a high official and all the other officers[v] of the king of Babylon 14sent and had Jeremiah taken out of the courtyard of the guard.[w] They handed him over to Gedaliah[x] son of Ahikam,[y] the son of Shaphan,[z] to take him back to his home. So he remained among his own people.[a]

15While Jeremiah had been confined in the courtyard of the guard, the word of the LORD came to him: 16"Go and tell Ebed-Melech[b] the Cushite, 'This is what the LORD Almighty, the God of Israel, says: I am about to fulfil my words[c] against this city through disaster,[d] not prosperity. At that time they will be fulfilled before your eyes. 17But I will rescue[e] you on that day, declares the LORD; you will not be handed over to those you fear. 18I will save[f] you; you will not fall by the sword[g] but will escape with your life,[h] because you trust[i] in me, declares the LORD.'"

Jeremiah Freed

40 The word came to Jeremiah from the LORD after Nebuzaradan commander of the imperial guard had released him at Ramah.[a] He had found Jeremiah bound in chains among all the captives[b] from Jerusalem and Judah who were being carried into exile to Babylon. 2When the commander[c] of the guard found Jeremiah, he said to him, "The LORD your God decreed[d] this disaster[e] for this place.[f] 3And now the LORD has brought it about; he has done just as he said he would. All this happened because you people sinned[g] against the LORD and did not obey[h] him. 4But today I am freeing[i] you from the chains[j] on your wrists. Come with me to Babylon, if you like, and I will look after you; but if you do not want to, then don't come. Look, the whole country lies before you; go wherever you please."[k] 5However, before Jeremiah turned to go,[a] Nebuzaradan added, "Go back to Gedaliah[l] son of Ahikam,[m] the son of Shaphan, whom the king of Babylon has appointed[n] over the towns[o] of Judah, and live with him among the people, or go anywhere else you please."[p]

Then the commander gave him provisions and a present[q] and let him go. 6So Jeremiah went to Gedaliah son of Ahikam at Mizpah[r] and stayed with him among the people who were left behind in the land.

Gedaliah Assassinated

40:7–9; 41:1–3pp—2Ki 25:22–26

7When all the army officers and their men who were still in the open country heard that the king of Babylon had appointed Gedaliah son of Ahikam as governor[s] over the land and had put him in charge of the men, women and children who were the poorest[t] in the land and who had not been carried into exile to Babylon, 8they came to Gedaliah at Mizpah[u]—Ishmael[v] son of Nethaniah, Johanan[w] and Jonathan the sons of Kareah, Seraiah son of Tanhumeth, the sons of Ephai the Netophathite,[x] and Jaazaniah[b] the son of the Maacathite,[y] and their men. 9Gedaliah son of Ahikam, the son of Shaphan, took an oath to reassure them and their men. "Do not be afraid to serve[z] the Babylonians,[c]"[a] he said. "Settle down in the land and serve the king of Babylon, and it will go well with you.[b] 10I myself will stay in Mizpah[c] to represent you before the Babylonians who come to us, but you are to harvest the wine,[d] summer fruit and oil, and put them in your storage jars,[e] and live in the towns you have taken over."[f]

11When all the Jews in Moab,[g] Ammon, Edom[h] and all the other countries[i] heard that the king of Babylon had left a remnant in Judah and had appointed Gedaliah son of Ahikam, the son of Shaphan, as governor over them, 12they all came back to the land of Judah, to Gedaliah at Mizpah, from all the countries where they had been scattered.[j] And they harvested an abundance of wine and summer fruit.

13Johanan[k] son of Kareah and all the army officers still in the open country came to Gedaliah at Mizpah[l] 14and said to him, "Don't you know that Baalis king of the Ammonites[m] has sent Ishmael[n] son of Nethaniah to take your life?" But Gedaliah son of Ahikam did not believe them.

15Then Johanan[o] son of Kareah said privately to Gedaliah in Mizpah, "Let me go and kill[p] Ishmael son of Nethaniah, and no-one will know it. Why

12 [u]Pr 16:7; Jer 15:20–21; 1Pe 3:13
13 [v]ver 3
14 [w]Ne 3:25; Jer 37:21; [x]2Ki 25:22; [y]2Ki 22:12; [z]2Ki 22:3; [a]Jer 40:5
16 [b]Jer 38:7; [c]Ps 33:11; Isa 14:27; 40:8; Jer 44:28; La 2:17; Mt 1:22; [d]Jos 23:15; Jer 21:10
17 [e]Ps 34:22; 41:1–2
18 [f]1Sa 17:47; Ac 16:31; [g]Job 5:20; [h]Jer 21:9; 38:2; [i]Jer 17:7; Ro 10:11

Ch. 40

1 [a]Jos 18:25; 1Sa 8:4; Mt 2:18; [b]Dt 21:10; 2Ki 24:1; 2Ch 36:10; Na 3:10
2 [c]Ro 13:4; [d]Isa 10:22; [e]2Ch 34:24; Ps 18:18; Pr 8:36; Gal 6:7–8; [f]Jos 23:15
3 [g]Pr 13:21; Ro 6:23; Jas 1:15; [h]Lev 26:33; Dt 28:45–52; 29:24–28; 31:17–18; 1Ki 9:9; Jer 22:8–9; Da 9:14; Ac 7:39; Ro 2:5–9
4 [i]Ps 105:18–20; Jer 37:14; [j]La 3:7; [k]Ge 13:9
5 [l]2Ki 25:22; [m]2Ki 22:12–14; [n]Ne 5:14; Jer 41:2; [o]Jer 44:22; Zec 1:12; [p]Jer 39:14; [q]Ge 32:20; 1Sa 9:7
6 [r]ver 10; Jdg 20:1; 1Sa 7:5–17
7 [s]Ge 41:41; Ne 5:14; [t]2Ki 24:14; Ac 24:17; Jas 2:5
8 [u]ver 13; [v]ver 14; Jer 41:1–2; [w]ver 15; Jer 41:11; [x]2Sa 23:28; [y]Dt 3:14
9 [z]Jer 5:19; 27:11; Ro 13:1–2; Eph 6:5–8; [a]Eze 23:23; [b]Jer 38:20; La 1:1

10 [c]ver 6; [d]Ge 27:28; Ex 23:16; [e]Ex 7:19; 2Co 4:7; [f]Dt 1:39 11 [g]Nu 21:11; 25:1; [h]Ge 25:30; [i]Jer 12:14
12 [j]Jer 43:5 13 [k]Jer 42:1; [l]ver 8
14 [m]Ge 19:38; 2Sa 10:1–19; Jer 25:21; 41:10; 49:1; [n]ver 8
15 [o]ver 8; [p]Dt 5:17; Mt 5:21–22

[a]5 Or *Jeremiah answered*
[b]8 Hebrew *Jezaniah,* a variant of *Jaazaniah*
[c]9 Or *Chaldeans;* also in verse 10

should he take your life and cause all the
Jews who are gathered around you to be
scattered[q] and the remnant[r] of Judah to
perish?"
16But Gedaliah son of Ahikam said to
Johanan[s] son of Kareah, "Don't do such
a thing! What you are saying about
Ishmael is not true."

41 In the seventh month Ishmael[a]
son of Nethaniah, the son of
Elishama, who was of royal blood and
had been one of the king's officers,
came with ten men to Gedaliah son of
Ahikam at Mizpah. While they were
eating together there, 2Ishmael[b] son of
Nethaniah and the ten men who were
with him got up and struck down Geda-
liah son of Ahikam, the son of Shaphan,
with the sword,[c] killing the one whom
the king of Babylon had appointed[d]
as governor over the land.[e] 3Ishmael
also killed all the Jews who were with
Gedaliah at Mizpah, as well as the
Babylonian[a] soldiers who were there.
4The day after Gedaliah's assassin-
ation, before anyone knew about it,
5eighty men who had shaved off their
beards,[f] torn their clothes[g] and cut[h]
themselves came from Shechem,[i] Shi-
loh[j] and Samaria,[k] bringing grain offer-
ings and incense[l] with them to the
house of the LORD.[m] 6Ishmael son of
Nethaniah went out from Mizpah to
meet them, weeping[n] as he went. When
he met them, he said, "Come to Geda-
liah son of Ahikam."[o] 7When they went
into the city, Ishmael son of Nethaniah
and the men who were with him
slaughtered them and threw them into a
cistern.[p] 8But ten of them said to
Ishmael, "Don't kill us! We have wheat
and barley, oil and honey, hidden in a
field."[q] So he let them alone and did not
kill them with the others. 9Now the
cistern where he threw all the bodies of
the men he had killed along with Geda-
liah was the one King Asa[r] had made as
part of his defence[s] against Baasha[t] king
of Israel. Ishmael son of Nethaniah
filled it with the dead.
10Ishmael made captives of all the rest
of the people[u] who were in Mizpah
—the king's daughters[v] along with all
the others who were left there, over
whom Nebuzaradan commander of the
imperial guard had appointed Gedaliah
son of Ahikam. Ishmael son of Nethan-
iah took them captive and set out to
cross over to the Ammonites.[w]
11When Johanan[x] son of Kareah and
all the army officers who were with him
heard about all the crimes Ishmael son
of Nethaniah had committed, 12they
took all their men and went to fight[y]
Ishmael son of Nethaniah. They caught
up with him near the great pool[z] in
Gibeon. 13When all the people[a] Ishmael
had with him saw Johanan son of
Kareah and the army officers who were
with him, they were glad. 14All the
people Ishmael had taken captive at
Mizpah[b] turned and went over to
Johanan son of Kareah. 15But Ishmael
son of Nethaniah and eight of his men
escaped[c] from Johanan and fled to the
Ammonites.

Flight to Egypt

16Then Johanan son of Kareah and all
the army officers[d] who were with him
led away all the survivors[e] from Mizpah
whom he had recovered from Ishmael
son of Nethaniah after he had assassin-
ated Gedaliah son of Ahikam: the
soldiers, women, children and court
officials he had brought from Gibeon.
17And they went on, stopping at Geruth
Kimham[f] near Bethlehem[g] on their way
to Egypt[h] 18to escape the Babylonians.[b]
They were afraid[i] of them because
Ishmael son of Nethaniah had killed
Gedaliah[j] son of Ahikam, whom the
king of Babylon had appointed as
governor over the land.

42 Then all the army officers, in-
cluding Johanan[a] son of Kareah
and Jezaniah[a] son of Hoshaiah,[b] and all
the people from the least to the greatest[c]
approached 2Jeremiah the prophet and
said to him, "Please hear our petition
and pray[d] to the LORD your God for this
entire remnant.[e] For as you now see,
though we were once many, now only a
few[f] are left. 3Pray that the LORD your
God will tell us where we should go and
what we should do."[g]
4"I have heard you," replied Jeremiah
the prophet. "I will certainly pray[h] to
the LORD your God as you have re-
quested; I will tell[i] you everything the
LORD says and will keep nothing back
from you."[j]
5Then they said to Jeremiah, "May
the LORD be a true[k] and faithful[l] wit-
ness[m] against us if we do not act in
accordance with everything the LORD
your God sends you to tell us. 6Whether
it is favourable or unfavourable, we will

15 [q]Ge 11:4; Lev 26:33; Mt 26:31; Jn 11:52; Jas 1:1; [r]2Ki 21:14; Isa 1:9; Ro 11:5
16 [s]Jer 43:2

Ch. 41

1 [a]Jer 40:8
2 [b]Ps 41:9; 109:5; [c]Jos 11:10; Jer 40:15; Heb 11:37; [d]Jer 40:5; [e]2Sa 3:27; 20:9–10; Jer 40:8
5 [f]Lev 19:27; Jer 47:5; 48:37; [g]Ge 37:29; Lev 10:6; Mk 14:63; [h]Lev 19:28; [i]Ge 12:6; 33:18; Jdg 9:1–57; 1Ki 12:1; [j]Jos 18:1; [k]1Ki 16:24; [l]Nu 16:40; Lk 1:9; [m]1Ki 3:2; 6:38; 2Ki 25:9
6 [n]2Sa 3:16; [o]Ps 5:9; Hos 7:11; Rev 20:10
7 [p]Ge 37:24; 2Ki 10:14
8 [q]Isa 45:3
9 [r]1Ki 15:22; 2Ch 16:6; [s]Jdg 6:2; [t]2Ch 16:1
10 [u]Jer 40:7,12; [v]Jer 38:23; [w]Jer 40:14
11 [x]Jer 40:8
12 [y]Ex 14:14; Jn 18:36; [z]Jos 9:3; Jn 9:7
13 [a]ver 10
14 [b]Jer 40:6
15 [c]Job 21:30; Pr 28:17
16 [d]Jer 42:1; 43:2; [e]Isa 1:9; Jer 43:4; Eze 7:16; 14:22; Zep 2:9
17 [f]2Sa 19:37; [g]Ge 35:19; Mic 5:2; [h]Jer 42:14
18 [i]Nu 14:9; Isa 51:12; Jer 42:16; Lk 12:4–5; [j]2Ki 25:22

Ch. 42

1 [a]Jer 40:13; [b]Jer 41:16; [c]Jer 6:13; 44:12
2 [d]Ge 20:7; Jer 36:7; Ac 8:24; Jas 5:16; [e]Isa 1:9; [f]Lev 26:22; La 1:1
3 [g]ver 20; Ps 86:11; Pr 3:6; Jer 15:11
4 [h]Ex 8:29; 1Sa 12:23; [i]Jer 1:17; [j]Nu 22:18; 1Sa 3:17
5 [k]1Ki 22:16; Ps 119:160; Ro 3:4; [l]Dt 7:9; Jn 8:26; 1Co 1:9; [m]Ge 31:48; Dt 4:26; Isa 1:2; Ro 1:9; Rev 1:5

[a]3 Or *Chaldean* [b]18 Or *Chaldeans*
[a]1 Hebrew; Septuagint (see also 43:2) *Azariah*

obey the LORD our God, to whom we are
sending you, so that it will go well[n] with
us, for we will obey[o] the LORD our God."
7Ten days later the word of the LORD
came to Jeremiah. 8So he called together
Johanan son of Kareah and all the army
officers[p] who were with him and all the
people from the least to the greatest.[q]
9He said to them, "This is what the
LORD, the God of Israel, to whom you
sent me to present your petition,[r] says:[s]
10'If you stay in this land,[t] I will build[u]
you up and not tear you down; I will
plant[v] you and not uproot you,[w] for I am
grieved over the disaster I have inflicted
on you.[x] 11Do not be afraid of the king of
Babylon,[y] whom you now fear.[z] Do not
be afraid of him, declares the LORD, for I
am with you and will save[a] you and
deliver you from his hands.[b] 12I will
show you compassion[c] so that he will
have compassion on you and restore
you to your land.'[d]
13"However, if you say, 'We will not
stay in this land,' and so disobey[e] the
LORD your God, 14and if you say, 'No,
we will go and live in Egypt,[f] where we
will not see war or hear the trumpet[g] or
be hungry for bread,'[h] 15then hear the
word of the LORD,[i] O remnant of Judah.
This is what the LORD Almighty, the
God of Israel, says: 'If you are deter-
mined to go to Egypt and you do go to
settle there, 16then the sword[j] you fear[k]
will overtake you there, and the famine[l]
you dread will follow you into Egypt,
and there you will die.[m] 17Indeed, all
who are determined to go to Egypt to
settle there will die by the sword,
famine and plague;[n] not one of them
will survive or escape the disaster I will
bring on them.' 18This is what the LORD
Almighty, the God of Israel, says: 'As
my anger and wrath[o] have been poured
out on those who lived in Jerusalem,[p] so
will my wrath be poured out on you
when you go to Egypt. You will be an
object of cursing[q] and horror,[r] of con-
demnation and reproach;[s] you will
never see this place again.'[t]
19"O remnant[u] of Judah, the LORD has
told you, 'Do not go to Egypt.'[v] Be sure
of this: I warn you today 20that you
made a fatal mistake[b] when you sent me
to the LORD your God and said, 'Pray to
the LORD our God for us; tell us every-
thing he says and we will do it.'[w] 21I
have told you today, but you still have
not obeyed the LORD your God in all he
sent me to tell you.[x] 22So now, be sure of
this: You will die by the sword, famine[y]
and plague[z] in the place where you
want to go to settle."[a]

6 [n]Dt 5:29; 6:3; Jer 7:23; 22:15; [o]ver 19; **Ex 24:7; Jos 24:24**
8 [p]ver 1; [q]Jer 41:16; **Mk 9:35**; Lk 7:28; Heb 8:11
9 [r]ver 2; [s]2Ki 22:15
10 [t]Jer 43:4; [u]**Jer 24:6**; [v]**Dt 30:9**; [w]**Dt 29:28**; Ecc 3:2; Jer 45:4; Eze 36:36; Da 11:4; [x]**2Ch 34:24**; Isa 30:26; **Jer 18:8**
11 [y]Jer 27:11; [z]**Nu 14:9; 1Sa 15:24**; Ps 23:4; Mt 10:28; 2Ti 1:7; [a]Ps 18:27; 69:35; **119:94; Isa 63:1**; Heb 7:25; [b]**Ps 3:7; Pr 20:22; Jer 1:8**; Ro 8:31
12 [c]**Ex 3:21; 2Sa 24:14**; 2Co 1:3; [d]**Ge 31:3; Ne 1:9**; Ps 106:44–46
13 [e]**Dt 11:28**
14 [f]Nu 11:4–5; **Dt 17:16; Isa 30:2**; [g]**Jos 6:20; Mt 24:31**; [h]**Dt 8:3**; 1Sa 2:5; Pr 10:3; Isa 65:13; Mt 4:2–4
15 [i]Jer 44:24
16 [j]**Lev 26:33**; Eze 11:8; 14:17; [k]**Jer 41:18**; [l]**Ge 41:55**; [m]**Ge 2:17**; 2Ch 25:4; **Job 21:20**; Eze 3:19; 18:4
17 [n]ver 22; **Jer 21:7**; 44:13
18 [o]Dt 29:18–20; **2Ch 12:7**; [p]**2Ch 36:19**; Jer 39:1–9; [q]**Nu 5:27; Jer 25:18**; [r]**Dt 28:25**,37; [s]**Ps 44:13**; [t]**Jer 22:10**
19 [u]Jer 40:15; [v]**ver 6**; Dt 17:16; Isa 30:7; Jer 43:2; 44:16
20 [w]ver 2; Eze 14:7–8
21 [x]**Ex 24:7**; Jer 40:3; Eze 2:7; 12:2; Zec 7:11–12
22 [y]**Isa 1:28**; [z]**ver 17**; Jer 24:10; Eze 6:11; [a]**Jer 15:2**; Hos 9:6

43 When Jeremiah finished telling
the people all the words of the
LORD their God—everything the LORD
had sent him to tell them[a]—2Azariah
son of Hoshaiah[b] and Johanan[c] son of
Kareah and all the arrogant[d] men said to
Jeremiah, "You are lying![e] The LORD our
God has not sent you to say, 'You must
not go to Egypt to settle there.'[f] 3But
Baruch[g] son of Neriah is inciting you
against us to hand us over to the Babylo-
nians,[a] so that they may kill us or carry
us into exile to Babylon."[h]
4So Johanan son of Kareah and all the
army officers and all the people[i] dis-
obeyed the LORD's command[j] to stay in
the land of Judah.[k] 5Instead, Johanan
son of Kareah and all the army officers
led away all the remnant of Judah who
had come back to live in the land of
Judah from all the nations where they
had been scattered.[l] 6They also led away
all the men, women[m] and children and
the king's daughters whom Nebuzara-
dan commander of the imperial guard
had left with Gedaliah son of Ahikam,
the son of Shaphan, and Jeremiah the
prophet and Baruch[n] son of Neriah. 7So
they entered Egypt[o] in disobedience to
the LORD and went as far as Tahpanhes.[p]
8In Tahpanhes[q] the word of the LORD
came to Jeremiah: 9"While the Jews are
watching, take some large stones[r] with
you and bury them in clay in the brick[s]
pavement at the entrance to Pharaoh's
palace[t] in Tahpanhes. 10Then say to
them, 'This is what the LORD Almighty,
the God of Israel, says: I will send for
my servant[u] Nebuchadnezzar[v] king of
Babylon, and I will set his throne[w] over
these stones I have buried here; he will
spread his royal canopy[x] above them.
11He will come and attack Egypt,[y] bring-
ing death[z] to those destined[a] for death,
captivity to those destined for capti-
vity,[b] and the sword to those destined

Ch. 43
1 [a]Jer 26:8; 42:9–22
2 [b]**Jer 41:16**; [c]Jer 40:16; [d]**Ne 9:29**; 1Co 4:18–21; [e]**Ge 19:14; Dt 13:3**; Ro 9:1; 2Co 11:31; 1Ti 2:7; [f]**Ex 24:7**; 2Ki 25:24; Jer 18:19; **42:19**; Eze 37:14
3 [g]**Jer 32:12**; [h]Jer 38:4; 41:18; 52:30
4 [i]**Jer 41:16**; [j]2Ch 25:16; Jer 42:5–6; [k]Jer 42:10
5 [l]Jer 40:12
6 [m]**Jer 6:12**; [n]**Jer 32:12**
7 [o]**2Ki 25:26**; [p]Jer 2:16; 44:1; 46:14; Eze 30:18
8 [q]Ps 139:7; Jer 2:16
9 [r]Ge 31:45–53; Jos 4:1–7; 1Ki 18:31–32; [s]**Ge 11:3**; [t]**Ge 47:14**
10 [u]Isa 44:28; 45:1; Jer 25:9; 27:6; [v]Jer 46:13; [w]Jer 49:38; [x]**Ps 18:11**
11 [y]Jer 46:13–26; Eze 29:19–20; [z]**Pr 11:19**; Ro 6:23; [a]**Ps 49:14**; Heb 9:27; [b]**Dt 28:64**; Rev 13:10

b20 Or *you erred in your hearts*
a3 Or *Chaldeans*

for the sword.[c] 12He[b] will set fire[d] to the temples[e] of the gods[f] of Egypt; he will burn their temples and take their gods captive.[g] As a shepherd wraps[h] his garment round him, so will he wrap Egypt round himself and depart from there unscathed. 13There in the temple of the sun[c][i] in Egypt he will demolish the sacred pillars[j] and will burn down the temples of the gods of Egypt.'"

Disaster Because of Idolatry

44 This word came to Jeremiah concerning all the Jews living in Lower Egypt[a]—in Migdol,[b] Tahpanhes[c] and Memphis[a][d]—and in Upper Egypt[b]:[e] 2"This is what the LORD Almighty, the God of Israel, says: You saw the great disaster[f] I brought on Jerusalem and on all the towns of Judah.[g] Today they lie deserted and in ruins[h] 3because of the evil[i] they have done. They provoked me to anger[j] by burning incense[k] and by worshipping other gods[l] that neither they nor you nor your fathers[m] ever knew. 4Again and again[n] I sent my servants the prophets,[o] who said, 'Do not do this detestable[p] thing that I hate!' 5But they did not listen or pay attention;[q][r] they did not turn from their wickedness[s] or stop burning incense[t] to other gods.[u] 6Therefore, my fierce anger was poured out;[v] it raged against the towns of Judah and the streets of Jerusalem and made them the desolate ruins[w] they are today.

7"Now this is what the LORD God Almighty, the God of Israel, says: Why bring such great disaster[x] on yourselves by cutting off from Judah the men and women,[y] the children and infants, and so leave yourselves without a remnant?[z] 8Why provoke me to anger with what your hands have made,[a] burning incense[b] to other gods in Egypt,[c] where you have come to live?[d] You will destroy yourselves and make yourselves an object of cursing and reproach[e] among all the nations on earth. 9Have you forgotten the wickedness committed by your fathers[f] and by the kings[g] and queens[h] of Judah and the wickedness committed by you and your wives[i] in the land of Judah and the streets of Jerusalem?[j] 10To this day they have not humbled[k] themselves or shown reverence,[l] nor have they followed my law[m] and the decrees[n] I set before you and your fathers.[o]

11"Therefore, this is what the LORD Almighty,[p] the God of Israel, says: I am determined to bring disaster[q] on you and to destroy all Judah. 12I will take away the remnant[r] of Judah who were determined to go to Egypt to settle there. They will all perish in Egypt; they will fall by the sword or die from famine. From the least to the greatest,[s] they will die by sword or famine.[t] They will become an object of cursing and horror, of condemnation and reproach.[u] 13I will punish[v] those who live in Egypt with the sword,[w] famine and plague,[x] as I punished Jerusalem. 14None of the remnant of Judah who have gone to live in Egypt will escape or survive to return to the land of Judah, to which they long to return and live; none will return except a few fugitives."[y]

15Then all the men who knew that their wives[z] were burning incense[a] to other gods, along with all the women[b] who were present—a large assembly—and all the people living in Lower and Upper Egypt,[c][c] said to Jeremiah, 16"We will not listen[d] to the message you have spoken to us in the name of the LORD![e] 17We will certainly do everything we said we would:[f] We will burn incense[g] to the Queen of Heaven[h] and will pour out drink offerings to her just as we and our fathers, our kings and our officials[i] did in the towns of Judah and in the streets of Jerusalem.[j] At that time we had plenty of food[k] and were well off and suffered no harm.[l] 18But ever since we stopped burning incense to the Queen of Heaven and pouring out drink offerings[m] to her, we have had nothing and have been perishing by sword and famine."[n][o]

19The women added, "When we burned incense[p] to the Queen of Heaven[q] and poured out drink offerings to her, did not our husbands[r] know that we were making cakes[s] like her image[t] and pouring out drink offerings to her?"

20Then Jeremiah said to all the people, both men and women, who were

11 [c]**Jer 15:2;** Eze 32:11; Zec 11:9
12 [d]**Jos 7:15;** [e]**1Ki 16:32;** [f]ver 13; **Ex 12:12; Isa 2:18;** Jer 46:25; Eze 30:13; Zec 13:2; [g]Da 11:8; [h]**Ps 104:2;** 109:18–19
13 [i]**Ge 1:16;** Isa 19:18 *fn;* **Dt 4:19;** [j]Jer 52:17; Eze 26:11

Ch. 44

1 [a]**Dt 32:42; Jer 24:8;** [b]**Ex 14:2;** [c]**Jer 43:7–8;** [d]**Isa 19:13;** [e]**Isa 11:11**
2 [f]**2Ch 34:24;** [g]**Jer 40:5;** [h]**Lev 26:31; Dt 29:23; Isa 6:11**
3 [i]**Ex 32:22;** [j]**Nu 11:33;** [k]**Nu 16:40;** [l]ver 8; **Nu 25:3;** Dt 13:6–11; 29:26; Isa 19:1; [m]**Jdg 2:19**
4 [n]**Jer 7:13;** [o]**Nu 11:29;** [p]**Dt 18:9; 1Ki 14:24;** 1Pe 4:3
5 [q]Da 9:6; [r]**Jer 25:4;** [s]**Ge 6:5;** Ro 1:18; 2Ti 2:19; [t]ver 21; Jer 1:16; Eze 8:11; 16:18; 23:41; [u]Jer 11:8–10; **25:7**
6 [v]Eze 8:18; 20:34; [w]**Lev 26:31,34; Dt 29:23;** La 1:13; Zec 7:14
7 [x]Jer 26:19; [y]Jer 51:22; [z]**2Ki 21:14**
8 [a]**Isa 40:18–20; Jer 10:3;** Ro 1:23; [b]ver 17–25; Jer 41:5; [c]**ver 3; Ex 12:12;** [d]**1Co 10:22;** [e]**Ps 44:13**
9 [f]**Jdg 2:19;** [g]**2Ki 23:11;** [h]1Ki 21:25; [i]**Pr 31:10; Jer 6:12;** [j]ver 17, 21; Jer 11:12; 32:32
10 [k]**Dt 8:3; Mt 23:12;** Php 2:8; [l]**Dt 6:13; Ps 5:7;** [m]**Jos 1:7; Jer 11:8;** Mt 5:17–20; Gal 3:19; 1Jn 3:4; [n]**Lev 18:4;** [o]1Ki 9:6–9; 2Ki 17:17
11 [p]Rev 4:8; [q]**2Ch 34:24;** Am 9:4
12 [r]ver 7; Jer 40:15; [s]**Jer 42:1;** [t]**Isa 1:28;** [u]**Dt 28:25; Jer 29:18**
13 [v]**Ex 32:34;** Lev 26:14–17; [w]**Jer 15:2;** [x]**Jer 42:17**
14 [y]Jer 22:24–27; 49:5; La 4:15; Eze 6:8; **Ro 9:27**
15 [z]**Pr 31:10; Jer 6:12;** [a]**Jer 18:15;** [b]**Ge 3:6;** 1Ti 2:14; [c]**Isa 11:11**
16 [d]**1Sa 8:19;** Job 15:25–26; Jer 11:8–10; [e]**Jer 42:19**
17 [f]ver 28; Dt 23:23; Zec 1:6; [g]**Isa 65:3;** [h]ver 25; Jer 11:12; [i]Ne 9:34; [j]**ver 9; Jer 2:26;** [k]**Ex 16:3;** Nu 11:4–6; [l]**Job 21:15;** Isa 3:9; Hos 2:5–13; 9:1
18 [m]Lev 23:18; [n]Mal 3:13–15; [o]Jer 42:16
19 [p]**Jer 18:15;** [q]Jer 7:18; [r]**Ge 3:6;** Eph 5:22; [s]Lev 7:12; [t]**Lev 26:1;** Ac 17:29

[b]*12* Or *I* [c]*13* Or *in Heliopolis*
[a]*1* Hebrew *Noph* [b]*1* Hebrew *in Pathros*
[c]*15* Hebrew *in Egypt and Pathros*

answering him, 21 "Did not the LORD
remember[u] and think about the incense[v]
burned in the towns of Judah and the
streets of Jerusalem[w] by you and your
fathers,[x] your kings and your officials
and the people of the land?[y] 22 When the
LORD could no longer endure[z] your
wicked actions and the detestable
things you did, your land became an
object of cursing[a] and a desolate waste[b]
without inhabitants, as it is today.[c]
23 Because you have burned incense and
have sinned against the LORD and have
not obeyed him or followed[d] his law or
his decrees[e] or his stipulations, this dis-
aster[f] has come upon you, as you now
see."[g]

24 Then Jeremiah said to all the people,
including the women,[h] "Hear the word
of the LORD, all you people of Judah
in Egypt.[i] 25 This is what the LORD
Almighty, the God of Israel, says: You
and your wives[j] have shown by your
actions what you promised when you
said, 'We will certainly carry out the
vows we made to burn incense and
pour out drink offerings to the Queen of
Heaven.'[k]

"Go ahead then, do what you prom-
ised! Keep your vows![l] 26 But hear the
word of the LORD, all Jews living in
Egypt:[m] 'I swear[n] by my great name,'
says the LORD, 'that no-one from Judah
living anywhere in Egypt shall ever
again invoke my name or swear, "As
surely as the Sovereign[o] LORD lives."[p]
27 For I am watching[q] over them for
harm,[r] not for good; the Jews in Egypt
will perish[s] by sword and famine[t] until
they are all destroyed.[u] 28 Those who
escape the sword[v] and return to the land
of Judah from Egypt will be very few.[w]
Then the whole remnant[x] of Judah who
came to live in Egypt will know whose
word will stand[y]—mine or theirs.[z]

29 " 'This will be the sign[a] to you that I
will punish[b] you in this place,' declares
the LORD, 'so that you will know that my
threats of harm against you will surely
stand.'[c] 30 This is what the LORD says: 'I
am going to hand Pharaoh[d] Hophra
king of Egypt over to his enemies who
seek his life, just as I handed Zedekiah[e]
king of Judah over to Nebuchadnezzar
king of Babylon, the enemy who was
seeking his life.' "[f]

A Message to Baruch

45 This is what Jeremiah the
prophet told Baruch[a] son of
Neriah[b] in the fourth year of Jehoiakim[c]
son of Josiah king of Judah, after Baruch
had written on a scroll[d] the words Jere-
miah was then dictating: 2 "This is what
the LORD, the God of Israel, says to you,
Baruch: 3 You said, 'Woe[e] to me! The
LORD has added sorrow[f] to my pain;[g] I
am worn out with groaning[h] and find no
rest.' "[i]

4 ⌊The LORD said,⌋ "Say this to him:
'This is what the LORD says: I will over-
throw what I have built and uproot[j]
what I have planted,[k] throughout the
land.[l] 5 Should you then seek great[m]
things for yourself? Seek them not.[n] For
I will bring disaster[o] on all people,[p] de-
clares the LORD, but wherever you go I
will let you escape[q] with your life.' "[r]

A Message About Egypt

46 This is the word of the LORD that
came to Jeremiah the prophet
concerning the nations:[a]

2 Concerning Egypt:[b]

This is the message against the army
of Pharaoh Neco[c] king of Egypt, which
was defeated at Carchemish[d] on the
Euphrates[e] River by Nebuchadnezzar
king of Babylon in the fourth year of
Jehoiakim[f] son of Josiah king of Judah:

3 "Prepare your shields,[g] both large and
 small,
 and march out for battle!
4 Harness the horses,
 mount the steeds!
Take your positions
 with helmets on!
Polish[h] your spears,
 put on your armour![i]
5 What do I see?
 They are terrified,
they are retreating,
 their warriors are defeated.
They flee[j] in haste
 without looking back,
 and there is terror[k] on every side,"
 declares the LORD.
6 "The swift cannot flee[l]
 nor the strong escape.
In the north by the River Euphrates[m]
 they stumble and fall.[n]

21 [u]Isa 64:9; Jer 14:10; Hos 8:13; [v]Jer 11:13; [w]ver 9; [x]Ps 79:8; [y]Jer 2:26
22 [z]Isa 1:14; [a]Jer 25:18; [b]Lev 26:31–32; [c]Ge 19:13; Ps 107:33–34; Eze 33:28–29
23 [d]1Ki 9:6; [e]Lev 18:4; [f]Jer 40:2; [g]Lev 26:33; 1Ki 9:9; Jer 7:13–15; Eze 39:23; Da 9:11–12
24 [h]Ge 3:6; [i]Jer 43:7
25 [j]Pr 31:10; [k]ver 17; Dt 32:38; [l]Pr 20:25; Eze 20:39; Jas 1:13–15
26 [m]Jer 24:8; [n]Ge 22:16; Isa 48:1; Ac 19:13; Heb 6:13–17; [o]Ge 15:2; [p]Dt 32:40; Ps 50:16; Jer 4:2
27 [q]Jer 1:12; [r]Jer 21:10; [s]Lev 26:38; Job 15:22; 2Pe 3:9; [t]Ge 41:55; [u]Jer 9:16; Da 9:14; Am 9:8
28 [v]Jer 45:5; Eze 6:8; [w]ver 13–14; Isa 10:19; [x]2Ki 21:14; [y]Isa 7:9; Jer 39:16; 42:15–18; [z]ver 17,25–26
29 [a]Ge 24:14; Ex 3:12; Nu 16:38; Mt 12:38; 24:3; [b]Ex 32:34; [c]Pr 19:21
30 [d]Jer 25:19; 46:26; Eze 30:21; 32:32; [e]2Ki 25:1–7; Jer 24:8; [f]Jer 43:9–13

Ch. 45
1 [a]Jer 32:12; [b]Jer 51:59; [c]2Ch 36:5; [d]Ex 17:14; Ps 40:7
3 [e]Isa 24:16; 1Co 9:16; [f]Ps 119:28; Mk 14:34; Ro 9:2; [g]Job 6:10; [h]Job 23:2; Ps 69:3; [i]Jos 1:13; Mt 11:28; Heb 4:3
4 [j]Jer 42:10; [k]Jer 11:17; [l]Dt 28:63; 30:9; Isa 5:5–7; Jer 18:7–10
5 [m]Ps 131:1; [n]Mt 6:25–27,33; [o]Jer 11:11; 40:2; [p]Jer 2:35; [q]Ps 68:20; Jer 44:28; [r]Jer 21:9

Ch. 46
1 [a]Jer 1:10
2 [b]Ex 1:8; [c]2Ki 23:29; [d]2Ch 35:20; [e]Ge 2:14; [f]Jer 1:3; 25:1; 35:1; 36:1; 45:1; Da 1:1 3 [g]Isa 21:5
4 [h]Eze 21:9–11; [i]1Sa 17:5,38; 2Ch 26:14; Ne 4:16
5 [j]ver 21; Jer 48:44; [k]Ps 31:13; 48:5
6 [l]Isa 30:16; [m]Ge 2:14; 15:18; [n]ver 12,16; Ps 20:8

7"Who is this that rises like the Nile,
like rivers of surging waters?[o]
8Egypt rises like the Nile,[p]
like rivers of surging waters.
She says, 'I will rise and cover the
earth;
I will destroy cities and their
people.'[q]
9Charge, O horses!
Drive furiously, O charioteers![r]
March on, O warriors—
men of Cush[a][s] and Put who carry
shields,
men of Lydia[t] who draw the bow.
10But that day[u] belongs to the Lord, the
LORD Almighty—
a day of vengeance[v], for vengeance
on his foes.
The sword will devour[w] till it is
satisfied,
till it has quenched its thirst with
blood.[x]
For the Lord, the LORD Almighty, will
offer sacrifice[y]
in the land of the north by the River
Euphrates.[z]

11"Go up to Gilead and get balm,[a]
O Virgin[b] Daughter of Egypt.
But you multiply remedies in vain;
there is no healing[c] for you.
12The nations will hear of your shame;
your cries will fill the earth.
One warrior will stumble over
another;
both will fall[d] down together."

13This is the message the LORD spoke
to Jeremiah the prophet about the com-
ing of Nebuchadnezzar king of Babylon[e]
to attack Egypt:[f]

14"Announce this in Egypt, and
proclaim it in Migdol;
proclaim it also in Memphis[b][g] and
Tahpanhes:[h]
'Take your positions and get ready,
for the sword devours[i] those around
you.'
15Why will your warriors be laid low?
They cannot stand, for the LORD will
push them down.[j]
16They will stumble[k] repeatedly;
they will fall[l] over each other.
They will say, 'Get up, let us go back
to our own people[m] and our native
lands,
away from the sword of the
oppressor.'[n]
17There they will exclaim,
'Pharaoh king of Egypt is only a
loud noise;[o]
he has missed his opportunity.[p]'

18"As surely as I live," declares the
King,[q]
whose name is the LORD Almighty,
"one will come who is like Tabor[r]
among the mountains,
like Carmel[s] by the sea.
19Pack your belongings for exile,[t]
you who live in Egypt,
for Memphis[u] will be laid waste[v]
and lie in ruins without inhabitant.

20"Egypt is a beautiful heifer,
but a gadfly is coming
against her from the north.[w]
21The mercenaries[x] in her ranks
are like fattened calves.[y]
They too will turn and flee[z] together,
they will not stand their ground,
for the day[a] of disaster is coming upon
them,
the time[b] for them to be punished.
22Egypt will hiss like a fleeing serpent
as the enemy advances in force;
they will come against her with axes,
like men who cut down trees.[c]
23They will chop down her forest,"
declares the LORD,
"dense though it be.
They are more numerous than
locusts,[d]
they cannot be counted.
24The Daughter of Egypt will be put to
shame,
handed over to the people of the
north.[e]"

25The LORD Almighty, the God of
Israel, says: "I am about to bring
punishment on Amon god of Thebes,[c][f]
on Pharaoh,[g] on Egypt and her gods[h]
and her kings, and on those who rely[i]
on Pharaoh. 26I will hand them over[j]
to those who seek their lives, to
Nebuchadnezzar king[k] of Babylon and
his officers. Later, however, Egypt will
be inhabited[l] as in times past," declares
the LORD.

27"Do not fear,[m] O Jacob[n] my servant;[o]
do not be dismayed, O Israel.
I will surely save you out of a distant
place,
and your descendants from the land
of their exile.[p]
Jacob will again have peace and
security,
and no-one will make him afraid.
28Do not fear, O Jacob my servant,
for I am with you,"[q] declares the
LORD.

7 [o]Jer 47:2
8 [p]Eze 29:3,9; 30:12; Am 8:8; [q]Da 11:10
9 [r]Jer 47:3; Eze 26:10; Na 3:2; [s]**Ge 10:6;** [t]**Isa 66:19**
10 [u]Eze 32:10; Joel 1:15; Ob 15; [v]**Nu 31:3; Dt 32:41;** 2Ki 23:29–30; [w]**Dt 32:42; 2Sa 2:26;** Zep 2:12; [x]**Dt 32:42;** [y]**Lev 3:9;** Zep 1:7; [z]Ge 2:14; 15:18
11 [a]**Ge 37:25;** [b]**2Ki 19:21;** [c]**Jer 30:13; Mic 1:9**
12 [d]**ver 6;** Isa 19:4; Na 3:8–10
13 [e]ver 26; Eze 32:11; [f]Isa 19:1; Jer 27:7
14 [g]**Isa 19:13;** [h]**Jer 43:8;** [i]**Dt 32:42; 2Sa 2:26; Jer 24:8**
15 [j]**Jos 23:5;** Isa 66:15–16
16 [k]**Lev 26:37;** [l]**ver 6;** [m]**Isa 13:14;** [n]**Jer 25:38**
17 [o]1Ki 20:10–11; [p]Isa 19:11–16
18 [q]Jer 48:15; [r]**Jos 19:22;** [s]1Ki 18:42
19 [t]**Isa 20:4;** [u]**Isa 19:13;** [v]Eze 29:10,12; 35:7
20 [w]ver 24; **Isa 14:31;** Jer 47:2
21 [x]**2Ki 7:6;** [y]Lk 15:27; [z]**ver 5; Job 20:24;** [a]Ps 18:18; 37:13; Jer 18:17; [b]**Job 18:20**
22 [c]Ps 74:5
23 [d]**Dt 28:42; Jdg 7:12**
24 [e]**2Ki 24:7**
25 [f]Eze 30:14; Na 3:8; [g]2Ki 24:7; Eze 30:22; [h]**Jer 43:12;** [i]Isa 20:6
26 [j]**Jer 44:30;** [k]**ver 13; Isa 19:4;** [l]Eze 29:11–16
27 [m]Isa 43:5; Jer 51:46; [n]Isa 41:8; 44:1; Mal 1:2; [o]**Isa 44:2;** [p]**Isa 11:11; Jer 29:14;** 50:19
28 [q]**Ex 14:22; Nu 14:9;** Isa 8:9–10

[a]9 That is, the upper Nile region
[b]14 Hebrew *Noph*; also in verse 19
[c]25 Hebrew *No*

"Though I completely destroy[r] all the
nations
among which I scatter you,
I will not completely destroy you.
I will discipline you but only with
justice;
I will not let you go entirely
unpunished."

A Message About the Philistines

47 This is the word of the LORD that came to Jeremiah the prophet concerning the Philistines[a] before Pharaoh attacked Gaza:[b]

2 This is what the LORD says:

"See how the waters are rising in the
north;[c]
they will become an overflowing
torrent.
They will overflow the land and
everything in it,
the towns and those who live in
them.
The people will cry out;
all who dwell in the land will wail[d]
3 at the sound of the hoofs of galloping
steeds,
at the noise of enemy chariots[e]
and the rumble of their wheels.
Fathers will not turn to help their
children;
their hands will hang limp.[f]
4 For the day has come
to destroy all the Philistines
and to cut off all survivors
who could help Tyre[g] and Sidon.[h]
The LORD is about to destroy the
Philistines,[i]
the remnant from the coasts of
Caphtor.[a][j]
5 Gaza will shave[k] her head in
mourning;
Ashkelon[l] will be silenced.
O remnant on the plain,
how long will you cut[m] yourselves?

6 " 'Ah, sword[n] of the LORD,' ⌞you cry,⌟
'how long till you rest?
Return to your scabbard;
cease and be still.'[o]
7 But how can it rest
when the LORD has commanded it,
when he has ordered it
to attack Ashkelon and the coast?"[p]

A Message About Moab

48:29–36pp—Isa 16:6–12

48 Concerning Moab:[a]

This is what the LORD Almighty, the God of Israel, says:

"Woe to Nebo,[b] for it will be ruined.
Kiriathaim[c] will be disgraced and
captured;
the stronghold[a] will be disgraced
and shattered.
2 Moab will be praised[d] no more;
in Heshbon[b][e] men will plot her
downfall:
'Come, let us put an end to that
nation.'[f]
You too, O Madmen,[c] will be silenced;
the sword will pursue you.
3 Listen to the cries from Horonaim,[g]
cries of great havoc and destruction.
4 Moab will be broken;
her little ones will cry out.[d]
5 They go up the way to Luhith,[h]
weeping bitterly as they go;
on the road down to Horonaim[i]
anguished cries over the
destruction are heard.
6 Flee![j] Run for your lives;
become like a bush[e] in the desert.[k]
7 Since you trust in your deeds and
riches,[l]
you too will be taken captive,
and Chemosh[m] will go into exile,[n]
together with his priests and
officials.[o]
8 The destroyer[p] will come against every
town,
and not a town will escape.
The valley will be ruined
and the plateau[q] destroyed,
because the LORD has spoken.
9 Put salt[r] on Moab,
for she will be laid waste[f];[s]
her towns will become desolate,
with no-one to live in them.

10 "A curse on him who is lax in doing
the LORD's work!
A curse on him who keeps his
sword[t] from bloodshed![u]

11 "Moab has been at rest[v] from youth,
like wine left on its dregs,[w]
not poured from one jar to another—
she has not gone into exile.
So she tastes as she did,
and her aroma is unchanged.
12 But days are coming,"
declares the LORD,
"when I will send men who pour from
jars,

28 [r]Jer 4:27

Ch. 47

1 [a]Ge 10:14; Jdg 3:31; [b]Ge 10:19; Zec 9:5–7
2 [c]Isa 14:31; [d]Isa 15:3
3 [e]Jer 46:9; Eze 23:24; [f]Isa 13:7; Jer 50:43; Eze 7:17; 21:7
4 [g]Isa 23:1; Am 1:9–10; Zec 9:2–4; [h]Ge 10:15; Jer 25:22; [i]Ge 10:14; Joel 3:4; [j]Dt 2:23
5 [k]Jer 41:5; [l]Jer 25:20; [m]Lev 19:28
6 [n]Isa 34:5; Jer 12:12; 48:10; 50:35; [o]Eze 21:30
7 [p]Eze 25:15–17

Ch. 48

1 [a]Ge 19:37; Dt 23:6; [b]Nu 32:38; [c]Nu 32:37; Jos 13:19
2 [d]Isa 16:14; [e]Nu 21:25; Jos 13:26; [f]ver 42
3 [g]Isa 15:5
5 [h]Isa 15:5; [i]ver 3
6 [j]Ge 19:17; [k]Jer 17:6
7 [l]Ps 49:6; Pr 11:28; [m]Nu 21:29; [n]Isa 46:1–2; Jer 49:3; [o]Am 2:3
8 [p]Ex 12:23; Jer 4:7; [q]Jos 13:9
9 [r]Jdg 9:45; [s]Jer 51:29
10 [t]Jer 47:6; [u]1Sa 15:11; 1Ki 20:42; 2Ki 13:15–19
11 [v]Zec 1:15; [w]Zep 1:12

a4 That is, Crete   a1 Or / *Misgab*

b2 The Hebrew for *Heshbon* sounds like the Hebrew for *plot*.

c2 The name of the Moabite town Madmen sounds like the Hebrew for *be silenced*.

d4 Hebrew; Septuagint / *proclaim it to Zoar*

e6 Or *like Aroer*

f9 Or *Give wings to Moab, / for she will fly away*

and they will pour her out;
they will empty her jars
and smash her jugs.
13Then Moab will be ashamed[x] of
Chemosh,[y]
as the house of Israel was ashamed
when they trusted in Bethel.[z]

14"How can you say, 'We are warriors,[a]
men valiant in battle'?
15Moab will be destroyed and her towns
invaded;
her finest young men[b] will go down
in the slaughter,[c]"
declares the King,[d] whose name is
the LORD Almighty.[e]
16"The fall of Moab is at hand;[f]
her calamity will come quickly.
17Mourn for her, all who live around
her,
all who know her fame;[g]
say, 'How broken is the mighty
sceptre,[h]
how broken the glorious staff!'

18"Come down from your glory
and sit on the parched ground,[i]
O inhabitants of the Daughter of
Dibon,[j]
for he who destroys Moab
will come up against you
and ruin your fortified cities.[k]
19Stand by the road and watch,
you who live in Aroer.[l]
Ask the man fleeing and the woman
escaping,
ask them, 'What has happened?'
20Moab is disgraced, for she is
shattered.
Wail[m] and cry out!
Announce by the Arnon[n]
that Moab is destroyed.
21Judgment has come to the plateau[o]—
to Holon,[p] Jahzah[q] and Mephaath,[r]
22 to Dibon,[s] Nebo[t] and Beth
Diblathaim,
23 to Kiriathaim,[u] Beth Gamul and
Beth Meon,[v]
24 to Kerioth[w] and Bozrah[x]—
to all the towns[y] of Moab, far and
near.
25Moab's horn[g][z] is cut off;
her arm[a] is broken,"
declares the LORD.

26"Make her drunk,[b]
for she has defied[c] the LORD.
Let Moab wallow in her vomit;[d]
let her be an object of ridicule.[e]
27Was not Israel the object of your
ridicule?[f]
Was she caught among thieves,[g]
that you shake your head[h] in scorn[i]
whenever you speak of her?
28Abandon your towns and dwell
among the rocks,
you who live in Moab.
Be like a dove[j] that makes its nest
at the mouth of a cave.[k]

29"We have heard of Moab's pride[l]—
her overweening pride and conceit,
her pride and arrogance
and the haughtiness[m] of her heart.
30I know her insolence but it is futile,"
declares the LORD,
"and her boasts[n] accomplish
nothing.
31Therefore I wail[o] over Moab,
for all Moab I cry out,
I moan for the men of Kir Hareseth.[p]
32I weep for you, as Jazer[q] weeps,
O vines of Sibmah.[r]
Your branches spread as far as the sea;
they reached as far as the sea of
Jazer.
The destroyer has fallen
on your ripened fruit and grapes.
33Joy and gladness are gone
from the orchards and fields of
Moab.
I have stopped the flow of wine[s] from
the presses;
no-one treads them with shouts of
joy.[t]
Although there are shouts,
they are not shouts of joy.

34"The sound of their cry rises
from Heshbon[u] to Elealeh[v] and
Jahaz,[w]
from Zoar[x] as far as Horonaim[y] and
Eglath Shelishiyah,
for even the waters of Nimrim are
dried up.[z]
35In Moab I will put an end
to those who make offerings on the
high places[a]
and burn incense[b] to their gods,"
declares the LORD.
36"So my heart laments[c] for Moab like a
flute;
it laments like a flute for the men of
Kir Hareseth.[d]
The wealth they acquired[e] is gone.
37Every head is shaved[f]
and every beard[g] cut off;
every hand is slashed
and every waist is covered with
sackcloth.[h]
38On all the roofs in Moab
and in the public squares[i]
there is nothing but mourning,

13 [x]Hos 10:6; [y]ver 7; [z]**Jos 7:2**
14 [a]Ps 33:16
15 [b]**Isa 9:17;** [c]Jer 51:40; [d]**Jer 46:18;** [e]Jer 51:57
16 [f]Isa 13:22
17 [g]2Ki 3:4–5; [h]**Ps 110:2**
18 [i]Isa 47:1; [j]**Nu 21:30; Jos 13:9;** [k]ver 8
19 [l]**Nu 32:34**
20 [m]**Isa 16:7;** [n]**Nu 21:13**
21 [o]**Jos 13:9,**21; [p]**Jos 15:51;** [q]**Nu 21:23; Isa 15:4;** [r]**Jos 13:18**
22 [s]**Nu 21:30;** Jos 13:9,17; [t]**Nu 32:38**
23 [u]**Nu 32:37; Jos 13:19;** [v]**Jos 13:17**
24 [w]Am 2:2; [x]Jer 49:13; [y]**Isa 15:1**
25 [z]Ps 75:10; [a]Ps 10:15; 37:17; Eze 30:21
26 [b]Jer 25:16,27; 51:39; [c]ver 42; 1Sa 17:26; [d]Isa 28:8; [e]ver 39
27 [f]**Jer 2:26;** [g]2Ki 17:3–6; [h]**Job 16:4;** Ps 44:14; Jer 18:16; [i]**Dt 28:37;** Mic 7:8–10; Zep 2:8,10
28 [j]**Ge 8:8; SS 1:15;** [k]**Jdg 6:2**
29 [l]**Lev 26:19; Job 40:12;** [m]**Ps 10:5; Pr 16:18**
30 [n]**Ps 10:3**
31 [o]ver 36; Isa 15:5–8; [p]**2Ki 3:25**
32 [q]**Jos 13:25;** [r]**Nu 32:3**
33 [s]**Isa 24:7;** [t]Joel 1:12; Am 5:17
34 [u]**Nu 21:25; Jos 13:26;** [v]**Nu 32:3;** [w]**Nu 21:23; Isa 15:4;** [x]**Ge 13:10;** [y]**Isa 15:5;** [z]**Isa 15:6**
35 [a]**Isa 15:2;** [b]Jer 11:13
36 [c]**ver 31;** [d]**2Ki 3:25;** [e]**Isa 15:7**
37 [f]Isa 15:2; **Jer 41:5;** Eze 27:31; 29:18; [g]**Lev 19:27; 2Sa 10:4;** [h]**Ge 37:34; Isa 3:24;** Jer 16:6; Am 8:10
38 [i]**Isa 15:3**

[g]25 *Horn* here symbolises strength.

for I have broken Moab
like a jar[j] that no-one wants,"
declares the LORD.
39"How shattered[k] she is! How they wail!
How Moab turns her back in shame!
Moab has become an object of ridicule,[l]
an object of horror to all those around her."

40This is what the LORD says:

"Look! An eagle is swooping[m] down,
spreading its wings[n] over Moab.
41Kerioth[h][o] will be captured
and the strongholds taken.
In that day the hearts of Moab's warriors[p]
will be like the heart of a woman in labour.[q]
42Moab will be destroyed[r] as a nation[s]
because she defied[t] the LORD.
43Terror[u] and pit and snare[v] await you,
O people of Moab,"
declares the LORD.
44"Whoever flees[w] from the terror
will fall into a pit,
whoever climbs out of the pit
will be caught in a snare;
for I will bring upon Moab
the year[x] of her punishment,"
declares the LORD.

45"In the shadow of Heshbon
the fugitives stand helpless,
for a fire has gone out from Heshbon,
a blaze from the midst of Sihon;[y]
it burns the foreheads of Moab,
the skulls[z] of the noisy boasters.
46Woe to you, O Moab![a]
The people of Chemosh are destroyed;
your sons are taken into exile
and your daughters into captivity.

47"Yet I will restore[b] the fortunes of Moab
in days to come,"
declares the LORD.

Here ends the judgment on Moab.

A Message About Ammon

49 Concerning the Ammonites:[a]
This is what the LORD says:

"Has Israel no sons?
Has she no heirs?
Why then has Molech[a][b] taken possession of Gad?[c]

38 [j]Jer 22:28
39 [k]Jer 50:23; [l]ver 26
40 [m]Dt 28:49; Hab 1:8; [n]Isa 8:8
41 [o]Isa 15:1; [p]Am 2:16; [q]Isa 21:3
42 [r]Isa 16:14; [s]ver 2; [t]ver 26
43 [u]Jer 49:5; [v]Isa 24:17
44 [w]1Ki 19:17; Job 20:24; Isa 24:18; Jer 46:5; [x]Jer 11:23; 23:12
45 [y]Nu 21:21, 26–28; Jos 12:2; [z]Nu 24:17
46 [a]Nu 21:29
47 [b]Ps 14:7; Isa 11:11; Jer 12:15; 49:6,39; Eze 16:53; Da 11:41

Ch. 49

1 [a]Ge 19:38; 1Sa 11:1–11; 2Sa 10:1–19; [b]Lev 18:21; [c]Ge 30:11
2 [d]Jer 4:19; [e]Dt 3:11; [f]Dt 13:16; [g]Isa 14:2; Jer 30:16; Eze 21:28–32; 25:2–11
3 [h]Jos 13:26; [i]Ge 12:8; Jos 8:28; [j]Ge 37:34; [k]Zep 1:5; [l]Jer 48:7
4 [m]Jer 3:6; [n]Jer 9:23; 1Ti 6:17; [o]Jer 21:13
5 [p]Jer 44:14
6 [q]Jer 12:14–17; 48:47
7 [r]Ge 25:30; Ps 83:6; [s]Ge 36:11,15,34
8 [t]Jdg 6:2; [u]Ge 10:7; 25:3

Why do his people live in its towns?
2But the days are coming,"
declares the LORD,
"when I will sound the battle cry[d]
against Rabbah[e] of the Ammonites;
it will become a mound of ruins,[f]
and its surrounding villages will be set on fire.
Then Israel will drive out
those who drove her out,[g]"
says the LORD.
3"Wail, O Heshbon,[h] for Ai[i] is destroyed!
Cry out, O inhabitants of Rabbah!
Put on sackcloth[j] and mourn;
rush here and there inside the walls,
for Molech[k] will go into exile,[l]
together with his priests and officials.
4Why do you boast of your valleys,
boast of your valleys so fruitful?
O unfaithful daughter,[m]
you trust in your riches[n] and say,
'Who will attack me?'[o]
5I will bring terror on you
from all those around you,"
declares the Lord,
the LORD Almighty.
"Every one of you will be driven away,
and no-one will gather the fugitives.[p]

6"Yet afterwards, I will restore[q] the fortunes of the Ammonites,"
declares the LORD.

A Message About Edom

49:9–10pp—Ob 5–6
49:14–16pp—Ob 1–4

7Concerning Edom:[r]

This is what the LORD Almighty says:

"Is there no longer wisdom in Teman?[s]
Has counsel perished from the prudent?
Has their wisdom decayed?
8Turn and flee, hide in deep caves,[t]
you who live in Dedan,[u]
for I will bring disaster on Esau
at the time I punish him.
9If grape-pickers came to you,
would they not leave a few grapes?
If thieves came during the night,
would they not steal only as much as they wanted?

---

[h]41 Or *The cities*
[a]1 Or *their king;* Hebrew *malcam;* also in verse 3

10But I will strip Esau bare;
I will uncover his hiding-places,[v]
so that he cannot conceal himself.
His children, relatives and neighbours
will perish,
and he will be no more.[w]
11Leave your orphans;[x] I will protect
their lives.
Your widows[y] too can trust in me."

12This is what the LORD says: "If those
who do not deserve to drink the cup[z]
must drink it, why should you go
unpunished?[a] You will not go un-
punished, but must drink it. 13I swear[b]
by myself," declares the LORD, "that
Bozrah[c] will become a ruin and an object
of horror,[d] of reproach[e] and of cursing;
and all its towns will be in ruins for
ever."[f]

14I have heard a message from the LORD:
An envoy was sent to the nations to
say,
"Assemble yourselves to attack it!
Rise up for battle!"

15"Now I will make you small among
the nations,
despised among men.
16The terror you inspire
and the pride[g] of your heart have
deceived you,
you who live in the clefts of the rocks,[h]
who occupy the heights of the hill.
Though you build your nest[i] as high as
the eagle's,
from there I will bring you down,"
declares the LORD.
17"Edom will become an object of
horror;[j]
all who pass by will be appalled and
will scoff
because of all its wounds.[k]
18As Sodom[l] and Gomorrah[m] were
overthrown,
along with their neighbouring
towns,"
says the LORD,
"so no-one will live there;
no man will dwell[n] in it.

19"Like a lion[o] coming up from Jordan's
thickets[p]
to a rich pasture-land,
I will chase Edom from its land in an
instant.
Who is the chosen one I will appoint
for this?
Who is like[q] me and who can challenge
me?[r]
And what shepherd[s] can stand
against me?"

20Therefore, hear what the LORD has
planned against Edom,[t]
what he has purposed[u] against
those who live in Teman:[v]
The young of the flock[w] will be
dragged away;
he will completely destroy[x] their
pasture because of them.[y]
21At the sound of their fall the earth will
tremble;[z]
their cry[a] will resound to the Red
Sea.[b]
22Look! An eagle will soar and swoop[b]
down,
spreading its wings over Bozrah.[c]
In that day the hearts of Edom's
warriors[d]
will be like the heart of a woman in
labour.[e]

A Message About Damascus

23Concerning Damascus:[f]

"Hamath[g] and Arpad[h] are dismayed,
for they have heard bad news.
They are disheartened,
troubled like[c] the restless sea.[i]
24Damascus has become feeble,
she has turned to flee
and panic has gripped her;
anguish and pain have seized her,
pain like that of a woman in labour.[j]
25Why has the city of renown not been
abandoned,
the town in which I delight?
26Surely, her young men will fall[k] in the
streets;
all her soldiers will be silenced[l] in
that day,"
declares the LORD Almighty.
27"I will set fire[m] to the walls of
Damascus;[n]
it will consume[o] the fortresses of
Ben-Hadad."[p]

A Message About Kedar and Hazor

28Concerning Kedar[q] and the king-
doms of Hazor,[r] which Nebuchadnez-
zar[s] king of Babylon attacked:

This is what the LORD says:

"Arise, and attack Kedar
and destroy the people of the East.[t]
29Their tents and their flocks[u] will be
taken;

10 [v]**Ge 3:8;** [w]Isa 34:10–12; **Jer 11:23;** Eze 35:4; Ob 18; Mal 1:2–5
11 [x]Hos 14:3; [y]**Dt 10:18;** Jas 1:27
12 [z]**Isa 51:23; Jer 25:15;** Mt 20:22; [a]**Pr 11:31**
13 [b]**Ge 22:16;** [c]**Ge 36:33;** [d]ver 17; [e]Jer 42:18; [f]**Jer 19:8;** Eze 35:9
16 [g]Eze 35:13; Ob 12; [h]**Job 39:28;** [i]**Job 39:27**
17 [j]ver 13; [k]**Dt 29:22;** Eze 35:7
18 [l]Jer 23:14; [m]**Ge 19:24;** [n]ver 33; **Isa 34:10**
19 [o]**1Sa 17:34;** [p]**Jer 12:5;** [q]**Ex 8:10; 2Ch 20:6; Isa 46:5;** [r]**Job 9:19;** Jer 50:44; [s]1Sa 17:35
20 [t]Isa 34:5; [u]Isa 14:27; [v]ver 7; **Ge 36:11;** [w]Jer 50:45; [x]ver 10; Ob 10; Mal 1:3–4; [y]Jer 50:45
21 [z]Ps 114:7; Eze 26:15; 27:28; 31:16; [a]Jer 50:46; 51:29; Eze 26:18
22 [b]**Dt 28:49;** Hos 8:1; Hab 1:8; [c]**Ge 36:33;** [d]Jer 50:36; Na 3:13; [e]Isa 13:8
23 [f]**Ge 14:15;** 2Ki 14:28; 2Ch 16:2; Ac 9:2; [g]1Ki 8:65; Isa 10:9; Eze 47:16; Am 6:2; Zec 9:2; [h]**2Ki 18:34; 19:13;** [i]**Ge 49:4**
24 [j]Jer 13:21
26 [k]**Isa 9:17; 13:18;** [l]Isa 17:12–14
27 [m]Jer 21:14; 43:12; 50:32; Eze 30:8; 39:6; Am 1:4; [n]**Ge 14:15;** [o]Isa 17:1; [p]**1Ki 15:18**
28 [q]**Ge 25:13;** [r]**Jos 11:1;** [s]**Jer 10:22;** [t]**Jdg 6:3**
29 [u]ver 32

b21 Hebrew *Yam Suph;* that is, Sea of Reeds
c23 Hebrew *on* or *by*

their shelters will be carried off
with all their goods and camels.
Men will shout to them,
'Terror[v] on every side!'

30"Flee quickly away!
Stay in deep caves,[w] you who live in
Hazor,[x]"
declares the LORD.
"Nebuchadnezzar[y] king of Babylon
has plotted against you;
he has devised a plan against you.

31"Arise and attack a nation at ease,
which lives in confidence,"
declares the LORD,
"a nation that has neither gates nor
bars;[z]
its people live alone.
32Their camels[a] will become plunder,
and their large herds[b] will be booty.
I will scatter to the winds[c] those who
are in distant places[d] [d]
and will bring disaster on them from
every side,"
declares the LORD.
33"Hazor[e] will become a haunt of
jackals,[f]
a desolate[g] place for ever.
No-one will live there;
no man will dwell[h] in it."

A Message About Elam

34This is the word of the LORD that
came to Jeremiah the prophet concern-
ing Elam,[i] early in the reign of Zedekiah[j]
king of Judah:

35This is what the LORD Almighty
says:

"See, I will break the bow[k] of Elam,
the mainstay of their might.
36I will bring against Elam the four
winds[l]
from the four quarters of the
heavens;[m]
I will scatter them to the four winds,
and there will not be a nation
where Elam's exiles do not go.
37I will shatter Elam before their foes,
before those who seek their lives;
I will bring disaster upon them,
even my fierce anger,"[n]
declares the LORD.
"I will pursue them with the sword[o]
until I have made an end of them.
38I will set my throne in Elam
and destroy her king and officials,"
declares the LORD.

39"Yet I will restore[p] the fortunes of
Elam
in days to come,"
declares the LORD.

A Message About Babylon

51:15–19pp—Jer 10:12–16

50 This is the word the LORD spoke
through Jeremiah the prophet
concerning Babylon[a] and the land of the
Babylonians:[a]

2"Announce and proclaim[b] among the
nations,
lift up a banner[c] and proclaim it;
keep nothing back, but say,
'Babylon will be captured;[d]
Bel[e] will be put to shame,[f]
Marduk[g] filled with terror.
Her images will be put to shame
and her idols[h] filled with terror.'
3A nation from the north[i] will attack
her
and lay waste her land.
No-one will live[j] in it;
both men and animals[k] will flee
away.

4"In those days, at that time,"
declares the LORD,
"the people of Israel and the people of
Judah together[l]
will go in tears[m] to seek[n] the LORD
their God.
5They will ask the way[o] to Zion
and turn their faces towards it.
They will come[p] and bind themselves
to the LORD
in an everlasting covenant[q]
that will not be forgotten.

6"My people have been lost sheep;[r]
their shepherds[s] have led them
astray[t]
and caused them to roam on the
mountains.
They wandered over mountain and
hill[u]
and forgot their own resting place.[v]
7Whoever found them devoured[w]
them;
their enemies said, 'We are not
guilty,[x]
for they sinned against the LORD, their
true pasture,
the LORD, the hope[y] of their fathers.'

8"Flee[z] out of Babylon;[a]
leave the land of the Babylonians,

d32 Or *who clip the hair by their foreheads*
a1 Or *Chaldeans*; also in verses 8, 25, 35 and 45

29 [v]**Jer 6:25**
30 [w]**Jdg 6:2;** [x]Jos 11:1; [y]**Jer 10:22**
31 [z]Eze 38:11
32 [a]**Jdg 6:5;** [b]ver 29; [c]ver 36; Jer 13:24; [d]**Jer 9:26**
33 [e]**Jos 11:1;** [f]**Isa 13:22;** [g]Jer 48:9; [h]**ver 18;** Jer 51:37
34 [i]**Ge 10:22;** [j]2Ki 24:18
35 [k]**Ps 37:15;** **Isa 22:6**
36 [l]**ver 32;** [m]Da 11:4
37 [n]Jer 30:24; [o]Jer 9:16; Eze 32:24
39 [p]**Jer 48:47**

Ch. 50

1 [a]**Ge 10:10; Ps 137:8**
2 [b]**Dt 30:4;** Jer 4:16; [c]**Ps 20:5; Isa 13:2;** [d]ver 9; Jer 51:31; [e]**Isa 21:9; 46:1;** [f]Ps 97:7; Jer 51:52; [g]ver 38; Isa 46:6; Jer 51:47; [h]**Lev 26:30**
3 [i]**ver 26; Isa 41:25; Jer 25:26;** [j]**ver 13; Isa 14:22–23; Jer 9:11;** [k]Zep 1:3
4 [l]**Jer 3:18;** Eze 37:22; [m]**Ezr 3:12;** [n]**Isa 9:13;** Eze 37:17; Hos 3:5
5 [o]**Isa 11:16; Jer 31:21;** [p]**1Sa 29:1;** Jer 33:7; [q]**Dt 29:14;** Isa 55:3; Jer 32:40; Heb 8:6–10
6 [r]**Ps 119:176;** Mt 9:36; 10:6; [s]**Jer 2:8; 10:21;** [t]**Ps 95:10;** Jer 23:32; Eze 13:10; [u]Jer 3:6; Eze 34:6; [v]ver 19
7 [w]**Jer 5:17;** 10:25; Eze 35:12; [x]Jer 2:3; [y]**Jer 14:8**
8 [z]**Isa 48:20;** [a]ver 28

and be like the goats that lead the
flock.
9 For I will stir[b] up and bring against
Babylon
an alliance of great nations[c] from the
land of the north.[d]
They will take up their positions
against her,
and from the north she will be
captured.[e]
Their arrows[f] will be like skilled
warriors
who do not return empty-handed.
10 So Babylonia[b] will be plundered;[g]
all who plunder her will have their
fill,"
declares the LORD.

11 "Because you rejoice and are glad,
you who pillage my inheritance,[h]
because you frolic like a heifer[i]
threshing corn
and neigh like stallions,
12 your mother will be greatly ashamed;
she who gave you birth will be
disgraced.[j]
She will be the least of the nations—
a wilderness, a dry land, a desert.[k]
13 Because of the LORD's anger she will
not be inhabited
but will be completely desolate.[l]
All who pass Babylon will be
horrified[m] and scoff[n]
because of all her wounds.[o]

14 "Take up your positions round
Babylon,
all you who draw the bow.[p]
Shoot at her! Spare no arrows,[q]
for she has sinned against the LORD.
15 Shout[r] against her on every side!
She surrenders, her towers fall,
her walls[s] are torn down.
Since this is the vengeance[t] of the
LORD,
take vengeance on her;
do to her[u] as she has done to others.[v]
16 Cut off from Babylon the sower,
and the reaper with his sickle at
harvest.
Because of the sword[w] of the
oppressor
let everyone return to his own
people,[x]
let everyone flee to his own land.[y]

17 "Israel is a scattered flock[z]
that lions[a] have chased away.
The first to devour[b] him
was the king[c] of Assyria;
the last to crush his bones[d]
was Nebuchadnezzar[e] king[f] of
Babylon."

18 Therefore this is what the LORD
Almighty, the God of Israel, says:

"I will punish the king of Babylon and
his land
as I punished the king[g] of
Assyria.[h]
19 But I will bring[i] Israel back to his own
pasture
and he will graze on Carmel and
Bashan;
his appetite will be satisfied[j]
on the hills[k] of Ephraim and
Gilead.[l]
20 In those days, at that time,"
declares the LORD,
"search will be made for Israel's guilt,
but there will be none,[m]
and for the sins[n] of Judah,
but none will be found,
for I will forgive[o] the remnant[p] I
spare.

21 "Attack the land of Merathaim
and those who live in Pekod.[q]
Pursue, kill and completely destroy[c]
them,"
declares the LORD.
"Do everything I have commanded
you.
22 The noise[r] of battle is in the land,
the noise of great destruction!
23 How broken and shattered
is the hammer[s] of the whole earth![t]
How desolate[u] is Babylon
among the nations!
24 I set a trap[v] for you, O Babylon,
and you were caught before you
knew it;
you were found and captured[w]
because you opposed[x] the LORD.
25 The LORD has opened his arsenal
and brought out the weapons[y] of his
wrath,
for the Sovereign LORD Almighty has
work to do
in the land of the Babylonians.[z]
26 Come against her from afar.[a]
Break open her granaries;
pile her up like heaps of grain.[b]
Completely destroy[c] her
and leave her no remnant.
27 Kill all her young bulls;[d]
let them go down to the slaughter![e]
Woe to them! For their day[f] has come,
the time[g] for them to be punished.
28 Listen to the fugitives[h] and refugees
from Babylon

9 [b]**Isa 13:17;** [c]**Jer 25:14;** [d]**Isa 41:25; Jer 25:26;** [e]**ver 2;** [f]**Isa 13:18**
10 [g]Isa 47:11; **Jer 30:16**
11 [h]**Isa 47:6;** [i]**Jer 31:18**
12 [j]Jer 51:47; [k]ver 13; **Isa 21:1;** Jer 25:12; 51:26
13 [l]ver 3,12; **Jer 9:11;** 48:9; 51:62; [m]Jer 51:41; [n]**Jer 18:16;** 51:37; Eze 27:36; Hab 2:6; [o]**Dt 29:22**
14 [p]ver 29,42; [q]**Isa 13:18**
15 [r]Jer 51:14; [s]**2Ki 25:4; Jer 51:44;** [t]ver 28; **Isa 10:3;** 63:4; Jer 51:6; [u]ver 29; Ps 137:8; Rev 18:6; [v]Jer 51:24; Hab 2:7-8
16 [w]**Jer 25:38;** [x]**Isa 13:14;** [y]Jer 51:9
17 [z]**Lev 26:33; Ps 119:176;** [a]**2Ki 24:1; Jer 2:15;** [b]**Jer 5:17;** [c]**Dt 4:27; 2Ki 15:29;** [d]**Nu 24:8;** La 3:4; [e]Jer 51:34; [f]**2Ki 24:17; 25:7**
18 [g]**Isa 10:12;** [h]Eze 31:3; Zep 2:13
19 [i]**Jer 31:10;** Eze 34:13; [j]Jer 31:14; [k]**Jer 31:5;** [l]Mic 7:14; Zec 10:10
20 [m]**Ps 17:3;** [n]Ps 103:12; **Isa 38:17;** Eze 33:16; Mic 7:18-19; Zec 3:4,9; [o]**Isa 33:24;** [p]**Ge 45:7;** Isa 1:9; 10:20-22; **Ro 9:27**
21 [q]Eze 23:23
22 [r]Jer 4:19-21; 51:54
23 [s]**Isa 10:5;** [t]Jer 51:25; [u]**Isa 14:16**
24 [v]Jer 51:12; [w]Jer 51:31; [x]Job 9:4
25 [y]**Isa 13:5;** [z]Jer 51:25,55
26 [a]ver 3,41; Jer 51:11; [b]**Ru 3:7;** [c]**Isa 14:22-23**
27 [d]**Ps 68:30;** Jer 48:15; [e]**Isa 30:25; Jer 25:34;** [f]**Job 18:20;** [g]Jer 51:6
28 [h]ver 8

[b]*10* Or *Chaldea*
[c]*21* The Hebrew term refers to the irrevocable giving over of things or persons to the LORD, often by totally destroying them; also in verse 26.

declaring in Zion[i]
how the LORD our God has taken
vengeance,[j]
vengeance for his temple.[k]

29"Summon archers against Babylon,
all those who draw the bow.[l]
Encamp all round her;
let no-one escape.[m]
Repay[n] her for her deeds;[o]
do to her as she has done.
For she defied[p] the LORD,
the Holy One[q] of Israel.
30Therefore, her young men[r] will fall in
the streets;
all her soldiers will be silenced in
that day,"
declares the LORD.
31"See, I am against[s] you, O arrogant
one,"
declares the Lord, the LORD
Almighty,
"for your day[t] has come,
the time for you to be punished.
32The arrogant[u] one will stumble and
fall[v]
and no-one will help her up;[w]
I will kindle a fire[x] in her towns
that will consume all who are
around her."

33This is what the LORD Almighty
says:

"The people of Israel are oppressed,[y]
and the people of Judah as well.
All their captors hold them fast,
refusing to let them go.[z]
34Yet their Redeemer[a] is strong;
the LORD Almighty[b] is his name.
He will vigorously defend their cause[c]
so that he may bring rest[d] to their
land,
but unrest to those who live in
Babylon.

35"A sword[e] against the Babylonians!"[f]
declares the LORD—
"against those who live in Babylon
and against her officials and wise[g]
men!
36A sword against her false prophets!
They will become fools.
A sword against her warriors![h]
They will be filled with terror.[i]
37A sword against her horses and
chariots[j]
and all the foreigners in her ranks!
They will become women.[k]
A sword against her treasures![l]
They will be plundered.
38A drought on[d] her waters![m]
They will dry[n] up.

28 [i]Isa 48:20; Jer 51:10; [j]**ver 15**; [k]2Ki 24:13; Jer 51:11; 52:13
29 [l]**ver 14**; [m]**Isa 13:18**; Jer 51:3; [n]**Dt 32:41**; **Job 21:19**; **Jer 51:6**; Rev 18:6; [o]Eze 35:11; Ob 15; [p]**Isa 14:13–14**; 47:10; Da 5:23; [q]Ps 78:41; Isa 41:20; Jer 51:5
30 [r]**Isa 13:18**
31 [s]**Jer 21:13**; [t]**Job 18:20**; Rev 18:7–8
32 [u]**Ps 119:21**; [v]**Ps 20:8**; [w]Am 5:2; [x]**Jer 49:27**
33 [y]Isa 58:6; [z]**Isa 14:17**
34 [a]**Ex 6:6; Job 19:25**; [b]Jer 31:35; 51:19; [c]**Ps 119:154**; **Isa 49:25**; Jer 15:21; 51:36; La 3:58; [d]Isa 14:7
35 [e]**Jer 47:6**; [f]**Isa 45:1**; [g]Da 5:7
36 [h]**Jer 49:22**; [i]Jer 51:30,32
37 [j]**2Ki 19:23**; Jer 51:21; [k]**Isa 19:16**; [l]**Isa 45:3**
38 [m]Ps 137:1; Jer 51:13; [n]**Isa 11:15**; Jer 51:36; [o]**ver 2**
39 [p]**Ps 74:14**; [q]Isa 13:19–22; 34:13–15; Jer 51:37; Rev 18:2
40 [r]**Ge 19:24**; **Mt 10:15**; [s]Jer 51:62
41 [t]**ver 26**; **Isa 41:25**; [u]**Isa 13:17**; [v]**Isa 13:4**; Jer 51:22–28
42 [w]**ver 14**; [x]**Job 30:21**; [y]**Isa 13:18**; [z]**Isa 5:30**; [a]**Isa 47:1**
43 [b]**Jer 47:3**; [c]Jer 6:22–24
44 [d]**Jer 12:5**; [e]**Nu 16:5**; [f]**Job 41:10**; Isa 46:9; **Jer 49:19**
45 [g]Ps 33:11; Jer 51:11; [h]**Isa 48:14**
46 [i]**Jdg 5:4**; **Jer 49:21**; [j]**Job 24:12**; Rev 18:9–10

For it is a land of idols,[o]
idols that will go mad with terror.

39"So desert creatures[p] and hyenas will
live there,
and there the owl will dwell.
It will never again be inhabited
or lived in from generation to
generation.[q]
40As God overthrew Sodom and
Gomorrah[r]
along with their neighbouring
towns,"
declares the LORD,
"so no-one will live there;
no man will dwell in it.[s]

41"Look! An army is coming from the
north;[t]
a great nation and many kings
are being stirred[u] up from the ends
of the earth.[v]
42They are armed with bows[w] and
spears;
they are cruel[x] and without mercy.[y]
They sound like the roaring sea[z]
as they ride on their horses;
they come like men in battle formation
to attack you, O Daughter of
Babylon.[a]
43The king of Babylon has heard reports
about them,
and his hands hang limp.[b]
Anguish has gripped him,
pain like that of a woman in labour.[c]
44Like a lion coming up from Jordan's
thickets[d]
to a rich pasture-land,
I will chase Babylon from its land in an
instant.
Who is the chosen[e] one I will
appoint for this?
Who is like me and who can challenge
me?[f]
And what shepherd can stand
against me?"
45Therefore, hear what the LORD has
planned against Babylon,
what he has purposed[g] against the
land of the Babylonians:[h]
The young of the flock will be dragged
away;
he will completely destroy their
pasture because of them.
46At the sound of Babylon's capture the
earth will tremble;[i]
its cry[j] will resound among the
nations.

d38 Or *A sword against*

51

This is what the LORD says:

"See, I will stir[a] up the spirit of a destroyer
against Babylon[b] and the people of Leb Kamai.[a]
2 I will send foreigners[c] to Babylon
to winnow[d] her and to devastate her land;
they will oppose her on every side
in the day[e] of her disaster.
3 Let not the archer string his bow,[f]
nor let him put on his armour.[g]
Do not spare her young men;
completely destroy[b] her army.
4 They will fall[h] down slain in Babylon,[c]
fatally wounded in her streets.[i]
5 For Israel and Judah have not been forsaken[j]
by their God, the LORD Almighty,
though their land[d] is full of guilt[k]
before the Holy One of Israel.

6 "Flee[l] from Babylon!
Run for your lives!
Do not be destroyed because of her sins.[m]
It is time[n] for the LORD's vengeance;[o]
he will pay[p] her what she deserves.
7 Babylon was a gold cup[q] in the LORD's hand;
she made the whole earth drunk.
The nations drank her wine;
therefore they have now gone mad.
8 Babylon will suddenly fall[r] and be broken.
Wail over her!
Get balm[s] for her pain;
perhaps she can be healed.

9 " 'We would have healed Babylon,
but she cannot be healed;
let us leave[t] her and each go to his own land,
for her judgment[u] reaches to the skies,
it rises as high as the clouds.'

10 " 'The LORD has vindicated[v] us;
come, let us tell in Zion
what the LORD our God has done.'[w]

11 "Sharpen the arrows,[x]
take up the shields![y]
The LORD has stirred up the kings[z] of the Medes,[a]
because his purpose[b] is to destroy Babylon.
The LORD will take vengeance,[c]
vengeance for his temple.[d]
12 Lift up a banner[e] against the walls of Babylon!
Reinforce the guard,
station the watchmen,[f]
prepare an ambush![g]
The LORD will carry out his purpose,[h]
his decree against the people of Babylon.
13 You who live by many waters[i]
and are rich in treasures,[j]
your end has come,
the time for you to be cut off.[k]
14 The LORD Almighty has sworn by himself:[l]
I will surely fill you with men, as with a swarm of locusts,[m]
and they will shout[n] in triumph over you.

15 "He made the earth by his power;
he founded the world by his wisdom[o]
and stretched[p] out the heavens by his understanding.[q]
16 When he thunders,[r] the waters in the heavens roar;
he makes clouds rise from the ends of the earth.
He sends lightning with the rain[s]
and brings out the wind from his storehouses.[t]

17 "Every man is senseless and without knowledge;
every goldsmith is shamed by his idols.
His images are a fraud;[u]
they have no breath in them.
18 They are worthless,[v] the objects of mockery;
when their judgment comes, they will perish.
19 He who is the Portion[w] of Jacob is not like these,
for he is the Maker of all things,
including the tribe of his inheritance[x]—
the LORD Almighty is his name.

20 "You are my war club,[y]
my weapon for battle—
with you I shatter[z] nations,[a]
with you I destroy kingdoms,
21 with you I shatter horse and rider,[b]
with you I shatter chariot[c] and driver,

Ch. 51

1 [a]**Isa 13:17**; [b]Jer 25:12
2 [c]Isa 13:5; [d]**Isa 41:16**; Mt 3:12; [e]**Isa 13:9**
3 [f]**Jer 50:29**; [g]Jer 46:4
4 [h]Isa 13:15; [i]**Isa 13:18**
5 [j]**Lev 26:44**; Isa 54:6–8; [k]Hos 4:1
6 [l]**Isa 48:20**; [m]Nu 16:26; Rev 18:4; [n]Jer 50:27; [o]**Isa 1:24; Jer 50:15**; [p]ver 24,56; Dt 32:35; **Job 21:19**; Jer 25:14; 50:29; La 3:64
7 [q]**Isa 51:22**; Jer 25:15–16; 49:12; Rev 14:8–10
8 [r]**Isa 14:15; 21:9; Rev 14:8**; [s]Jer 8:22; 46:11
9 [t]**Isa 13:14; 31:9**; Jer 50:16; [u]Rev 18:4–5
10 [v]Mic 7:9; [w]Ps 64:9; **Jer 50:28**
11 [x]Jer 50:9; [y]**Isa 21:5**; [z]**Isa 41:2**; [a]ver 28; **Isa 13:3; 41:25**; [b]**Jer 50:45**; [c]**Lev 26:25**; [d]**Jer 50:28**
12 [e]ver 27; **Ps 20:5**; [f]2Sa 18:24; Eze 33:2; [g]Jer 50:24; [h]**Ps 33:11**
13 [i]**Jer 50:38**; [j]**Isa 45:3**; Eze 22:27; Hab 2:9; [k]Jer 50:3
14 [l]**Ge 22:16**; Am 6:8; [m]ver 27; Am 7:1; Na 3:15; [n]Jer 50:15
15 [o]Ps 104:24; [p]**Ge 1:1; Ps 104:2**; [q]**Ps 136:5**
16 [r]Ps 18:11–13; [s]**Job 28:26**; [t]**Dt 28:12; Ps 135:7**; Jnh 1:4
17 [u]**Isa 44:20**; Hab 2:18–19
18 [v]**Jer 18:15**
19 [w]**Ps 119:57**; [x]**Ex 34:9**
20 [y]**Isa 10:5**; Zec 9:13; [z]**Job 34:24**; Mic 4:13; [a]**Isa 45:1**
21 [b]**Ex 15:1**; [c]**Isa 43:17; Jer 50:37**

---

a1 *Leb Kamai* is a cryptogram for Chaldea, that is, Babylonia.
b3 The Hebrew term refers to the irrevocable giving over of things or persons to the LORD, often by totally destroying them.
c4 Or *Chaldea*
d5 Or / *and the land* ⌞*of the Babylonians*⌟

[22]with you I shatter man and woman,
with you I shatter old man and youth,
with you I shatter young man and maiden,[d]
[23]with you I shatter shepherd and flock,
with you I shatter farmer and oxen,
with you I shatter governors and officials.[e]

[24]"Before your eyes I will repay[f]
Babylon[g] and all who live in Babylonia[e]
for all the wrong they have done in
Zion," declares the LORD.

[25]"I am against[h] you, O destroying mountain,
you who destroy the whole earth,"[i]
declares the LORD.
"I will stretch out my hand[j] against you,
roll you off the cliffs,
and make you a burnt-out mountain.[k]
[26]No rock will be taken from you for a cornerstone,
nor any stone for a foundation,
for you will be desolate[l] for ever,"
declares the LORD.

[27]"Lift up a banner[m] in the land!
Blow the trumpet among the nations!
Prepare the nations for battle against her;
summon against her these kingdoms:[n]
Ararat,[o] Minni and Ashkenaz.[p]
Appoint a commander against her;
send up horses like a swarm of locusts.[q]
[28]Prepare the nations for battle against her—
the kings of the Medes,[r]
their governors and all their officials,
and all the countries they rule.[s]
[29]The land trembles[t] and writhes,
for the LORD's purposes[u] against Babylon stand—
to lay waste[v] the land of Babylon
so that no-one will live there.[w]
[30]Babylon's warriors[x] have stopped fighting;
they remain in their strongholds.
Their strength is exhausted;
they have become like women.[y]
Her dwellings are set on fire;[z]
the bars[a] of her gates are broken.
[31]One courier[b] follows another
and messenger follows messenger
to announce to the king of Babylon
that his entire city is captured,[c]
[32]the river crossings seized,
the marshes set on fire,[d]
and the soldiers terrified."[e]

[33]This is what the LORD Almighty, the
God of Israel, says:

"The Daughter of Babylon[f] is like a threshing-floor[g]
at the time it is trampled;
the time to harvest[h] her will soon come."[i]

[34]"Nebuchadnezzar[j] king of Babylon
has devoured[k] us,[l]
he has thrown us into confusion,
he has made us an empty jar.
Like a serpent he has swallowed us
and filled his stomach with our delicacies,
and then has spewed[m] us out.
[35]May the violence[n] done to our flesh[f] be upon Babylon,"
say the inhabitants of Zion.
"May our blood be on those who live in Babylonia,"
says Jerusalem.[o]

[36]Therefore, this is what the LORD
says:

"See, I will defend your cause[p]
and avenge[q] you;
I will dry up[r] her sea
and make her springs dry.
[37]Babylon will be a heap of ruins,
a haunt[s] of jackals,
an object of horror and scorn,[t]
a place where no-one lives.[u]
[38]Her people all roar like young lions,[v]
they growl like lion cubs.
[39]But while they are aroused,
I will set out a feast for them
and make them drunk,[w]
so that they shout with laughter—
then sleep for ever[x] and not awake,"
declares the LORD.[y]
[40]"I will bring them down
like lambs to the slaughter,
like rams and goats.[z]

[41]"How Sheshach[g][a] will be captured,[b]
the boast of the whole earth seized!
What a horror[c] Babylon will be
among the nations!
[42]The sea will rise over Babylon;
its roaring waves[d] will cover her.
[43]Her towns will be desolate,

22 [d]**2Ch 36:17**; Isa 13:17–18
23 [e]ver 57
24 [f]**ver 6**,35; **Dt 32:41**; **Jer 50:15**; La 3:64; [g]**Isa 45:1**
25 [h]**Jer 21:13**; [i]Jer 50:23; [j]**Ex 3:20**; [k]Zec 4:7
26 [l]ver 29; **Isa 13:19–22**; **Jer 50:12**
27 [m]**Ps 20:5**; **Isa 13:2**; [n]**Jer 25:14**; [o]**Ge 8:4**; [p]Ge 10:3; [q]**ver 14**
28 [r]**ver 11**; [s]ver 48
29 [t]**Jdg 5:4**; **Jer 49:21**; [u]**Ps 33:11**; [v]Jer 48:9; [w]ver 43; **Isa 13:20**
30 [x]**Jer 50:36**; [y]**Isa 19:16**; [z]**Isa 47:14**; [a]**Isa 45:2**
31 [b]2Sa 18:19–31; [c]**Jer 50:2**; Da 5:30
32 [d]**Isa 47:14**; [e]**Jer 50:36**
33 [f]**Isa 47:1**; [g]**Isa 21:10**; [h]**Isa 17:5**; [i]**Isa 13:22**
34 [j]**Jer 50:17**; [k]Na 2:12; [l]Hos 8:8; [m]ver 44; **Lev 18:25**
35 [n]Joel 3:19; Hab 2:17; [o]**ver 24**; Ps 137:8
36 [p]Ps 140:12; Jer 50:34; La 3:58; [q]ver 6; Jer 20:12; **Ro 12:19**; [r]**Isa 11:15**; **19:5**; Hos 13:15
37 [s]**Isa 13:22**; Rev 18:2; [t]Na 3:6; Mal 2:9; [u]**Jer 50:13**,**39**
38 [v]**Isa 5:29**
39 [w]**Isa 21:5**; [x]**Ps 13:3**; [y]ver 57; **Jer 50:24**
40 [z]Eze 39:18
41 [a]**Jer 25:26**; [b]Isa 13:19; [c]Jer 50:13
42 [d]**Ps 18:4**; Isa 8:7

[e]24 Or *Chaldea;* also in verse 35
[f]35 Or *done to us and to our children*
[g]41 *Sheshach* is a cryptogram for Babylon.

a dry and desert[e] land,
a land where no-one lives,
through which no man travels.[f]
44I will punish Bel[g] in Babylon
and make him spew out[h] what he
has swallowed.
The nations will no longer stream to
him.
And the wall[i] of Babylon will fall.

45"Come out[j] of her, my people!
Run[k] for your lives!
Run from the fierce anger[l] of the
LORD.
46Do not lose heart[m] or be afraid[n]
when rumours[o] are heard in the
land;
one rumour comes this year, another
the next,
rumours of violence in the land
and of ruler against ruler.
47For the time will surely come
when I will punish the idols[p] of
Babylon;
her whole land will be disgraced[q]
and her slain will all lie fallen within
her.[r]
48Then heaven and earth and all that is
in them
will shout[s] for joy over Babylon,
for out of the north[t]
destroyers[u] will attack her,"
declares the LORD.

49"Babylon must fall because of Israel's
slain,
just as the slain in all the earth
have fallen because of Babylon.[v]
50You who have escaped the sword,
leave[w] and do not linger!
Remember[x] the LORD in a distant
land,[y]
and think on Jerusalem."

51"We are disgraced,[z]
for we have been insulted
and shame covers our faces,
because foreigners have entered
the holy places of the LORD's
house."[a]

52"But days are coming," declares the
LORD,
"when I will punish her idols,[b]
and throughout her land
the wounded will groan.[c]
53Even if Babylon reaches the sky[d]
and fortifies her lofty stronghold,
I will send destroyers[e] against her,"
declares the LORD.

54"The sound of a cry[f] comes from
Babylon,
the sound of great destruction[g]
from the land of the Babylonians.[h]
55The LORD will destroy Babylon;
he will silence[h] her noisy din.
Waves[i] ⌊of enemies⌋ will rage like
great waters;
the roar of their voices will resound.
56A destroyer[j] will come against
Babylon;
her warriors will be captured,
and their bows will be broken.[k]
For the LORD is a God of retribution;
he will repay[l] in full.
57I will make her officials[m] and wise[n]
men drunk,[o]
her governors, officers and warriors
as well;
they will sleep[p] for ever and not
awake,"
declares the King,[q] whose name is
the LORD Almighty.

58This is what the LORD Almighty
says:

"Babylon's thick wall[r] will be levelled
and her high gates[s] set on fire;
the peoples[t] exhaust[u] themselves for
nothing,
the nations' labour is only fuel for
the flames."[v]

59This is the message Jeremiah gave to
the staff officer Seraiah son of Neriah,[w]
the son of Mahseiah, when he went to
Babylon with Zedekiah[x] king of Judah
in the fourth[y] year of his reign.
60Jeremiah had written on a scroll[z] about
all the disasters that would come upon
Babylon—all that had been recorded
concerning Babylon. 61He said to
Seraiah, "When you get to Babylon, see
that you read all these words aloud.
62Then say, 'O LORD, you have said you
will destroy this place, so that neither
man nor animal will live in it; it will be
desolate[a] for ever.' 63When you finish
reading this scroll, tie a stone to it and
throw it into the Euphrates.[b] 64Then say,
'So will Babylon sink to rise no more[c]
because of the disaster I will bring upon
her. And her people[d] will fall.'"[e]

The words of Jeremiah end[f] here.

43 [e]Isa 21:1; [f]ver 29,62; Isa 13:20; Jer 2:6
44 [g]Isa 21:9; 46:1; [h]ver 34; [i]ver 58; 2Ki 25:4; Isa 25:12; Jer 50:15
45 [j]ver 50; [k]Isa 48:20; [l]Ps 76:10; 79:6
46 [m]Ps 18:45; [n]Jer 46:27; [o]2Ki 19:7
47 [p]Isa 46:1–2; Jer 50:2; [q]Jer 50:12; [r]Jer 27:7
48 [s]Job 3:7; Ps 149:2; Rev 18:20; [t]ver 11; Isa 41:25; Jer 25:26; [u]ver 53,56
49 [v]Ps 137:8; Jer 50:29
50 [w]ver 45; [x]Ps 137:6; [y]Jer 23:23
51 [z]Ps 44:13–16; 79:4; [a]La 1:10
52 [b]ver 47; [c]Job 24:12
53 [d]Ge 11:4; Isa 14:13–14; [e]ver 48; Job 15:21
54 [f]Job 24:12; [g]Jer 50:22
55 [h]Isa 25:5; [i]Ps 18:4
56 [j]ver 48; Job 15:21; [k]Ps 46:9; [l]ver 6; Ge 4:24; Dt 32:41; Ps 94:1–2; Hab 2:8
57 [m]ver 23; [n]Job 5:13; [o]Isa 21:5; [p]ver 39; Ps 76:5; Jer 25:27; [q]Isa 6:5
58 [r]ver 44; 2Ki 25:4; Isa 15:1; [s]Isa 13:2; [t]ver 64; [u]Isa 47:13; [v]Isa 47:14
59 [w]Jer 36:4; [x]Jer 52:1; [y]Jer 28:1
60 [z]Ex 17:14; Jer 30:2; 36:2
62 [a]Isa 13:20; Jer 9:11; 50:13
63 [b]Ge 2:14
64 [c]Eze 26:21; 28:19; [d]ver 58; [e]Rev 18:21; [f]Job 31:40

h54 Or *Chaldeans*

The Fall of Jerusalem

52:1–3pp—2Ki 24:18–20; 2Ch 36:11–16
52:4–16pp—Jer 39:1–10
52:4–21pp—2Ki 25:1–21; 2Ch 36:17–20

52 Zedekiah[a] was twenty-one years old when he became king, and he reigned in Jerusalem for eleven years. His mother's name was Hamutal daughter of Jeremiah; she was from Libnah.[b] 2He did evil in the eyes of the LORD, just as Jehoiakim[c] had done. 3It was because of the LORD's anger that all this happened to Jerusalem and Judah,[d] and in the end he thrust them from his presence.[e]

Now Zedekiah rebelled[f] against the king of Babylon.

4So in the ninth year of Zedekiah's reign, on the tenth[g] day of the tenth month, Nebuchadnezzar king of Babylon marched against Jerusalem[h] with his whole army. They camped outside the city and built siege works[i] all around it.[j] 5The city was kept under siege until the eleventh year of King Zedekiah.

6By the ninth day of the fourth month the famine in the city had become so severe that there was no food for the people to eat.[k] 7Then the city wall was broken through, and the whole army fled.[l] They left the city at night through the gate between the two walls near the king's garden, though the Babylonians[a] were surrounding the city. They fled towards the Arabah,[b] 8but the Babylonian[c] army pursued King Zedekiah and overtook him in the plains of Jericho. All his soldiers were separated from him and scattered, 9and he was captured.[m]

He was taken to the king of Babylon at Riblah[n] in the land of Hamath,[o] where he pronounced sentence on him. 10There at Riblah the king of Babylon slaughtered the sons[p] of Zedekiah before his eyes; he also killed all the officials of Judah. 11Then he put out Zedekiah's eyes, bound him with bronze shackles and took him to Babylon, where he put him in prison till the day of his death.[q]

12On the tenth day of the fifth[r] month, in the nineteenth year of Nebuchadnezzar king of Babylon, Nebuzaradan[s] commander of the imperial guard, who served the king of Babylon, came to Jerusalem. 13He set fire[t] to the temple[u] of the LORD, the royal palace and all the houses[v] of Jerusalem. Every important building he burned down. 14The whole Babylonian army under the commander of the imperial guard broke down all the walls[w] around Jerusalem. 15Nebuzaradan the commander of the guard carried into exile[x] some of the poorest people and those who remained in the city, along with the rest of the craftsmen[d] and those who had gone over[y] to the king of Babylon. 16But Nebuzaradan left behind[z] the rest of the poorest people of the land to work the vineyards and fields.

17The Babylonians broke up the bronze pillars,[a] the movable stands[b] and the bronze Sea[c] that were at the temple of the LORD and they carried all the bronze to Babylon.[d] 18They also took away the pots, shovels, wick trimmers, sprinkling bowls,[e] dishes and all the bronze articles used in the temple service.[f] 19The commander of the imperial guard took away the basins, censers,[g] sprinkling bowls, pots, lampstands,[h] dishes[i] and bowls used for drink offerings[j]—all that were made of pure gold or silver.[k]

20The bronze from the two pillars, the Sea and the twelve bronze bulls[l] under it, and the movable stands, which King Solomon had made for the temple of the LORD, was more than could be weighed.[m] 21Each of the pillars was eighteen cubits high and twelve cubits in circumference;[e] each was four fingers thick, and hollow.[n] 22The bronze capital[o] on the top of the one pillar was five cubits[f] high and was decorated with a network and pomegranates[p] of bronze all around. The other pillar, with its pomegranates, was similar. 23There were ninety-six pomegranates on the sides; the total number of pomegranates[q] above the surrounding network was a hundred.[r]

24The commander of the guard took as prisoners Seraiah[s] the chief priest, Zephaniah[t] the priest next in rank and the three doorkeepers.[u] 25Of those still in the city, he took the officer in charge of the fighting men, and seven royal advisers. He also took the secretary[v] who was chief officer in charge of conscripting the people of the land and sixty of his men who were found in the city. 26Nebuzaradan[w] the commander took them all and brought them to the king of Babylon at Riblah. 27There at Riblah,[x] in the land of Hamath, the king had them executed.

So Judah went into captivity, away[y]

Ch. 52

1 [a]**2Ki 24:17;** [b]**Nu 33:20;** Jos 10:29; 2Ki 8:22
2 [c]**Jer 36:30**
3 [d]Isa 3:1; [e]**Ge 4:14; Ex 33:15;** [f]Eze 17:12–16
4 [g]Zec 8:19; [h]Jer 34:1; [i]**Jer 6:6;** [j]Eze 24:1–2
6 [k]**Lev 26:26; Isa 3:1;** La 1:11
7 [l]La 4:19
9 [m]**Jer 21:7; 32:4;** [n]**Nu 34:11;** [o]**Nu 13:21**
10 [p]**Jer 22:30**
11 [q]Jer 34:4; Eze 12:13; 17:16
12 [r]Zec 7:5; 8:19; [s]ver 26
13 [t]**2Ch 36:19; Ps 74:8;** La 2:6; [u]**Dt 29:24;** Ps 79:1; Mic 3:12; [v]**Dt 13:16; Jer 19:13**
14 [w]**Ne 1:3;** La 2:8
15 [x]**2Ki 24:1; Jer 1:3;** [y]**Jer 38:19**
16 [z]Jer 40:6
17 [a]**1Ki 7:15;** [b]1Ki 7:27–37; [c]**1Ki 7:23;** [d]Jer 27:19–22
18 [e]**Nu 4:14;** [f]**Ex 27:3;** 1Ki 7:45
19 [g]**Lev 10:1; 1Ki 7:50;** [h]**Nu 3:31;** [i]Ex 25:29; [j]**Nu 4:7;** [k]Ezr 1:7; Da 5:2
20 [l]1Ki 7:25; [m]**1Ki 7:47**
21 [n]**1Ki 7:15**
22 [o]**1Ki 7:16;** [p]**Ex 28:33**
23 [q]1Ki 7:20; [r]**ver 17; Jer 27:19**
24 [s]**2Ki 25:18;** [t]**2Ki 25:18; Jer 37:3;** [u]**2Ki 12:9**
25 [v]Jer 36:10
26 [w]**ver 12**
27 [x]**Nu 34:11;** [y]**Jer 20:4**

[a]7 Or *Chaldeans;* also in verse 17
[b]7 Or *the Jordan Valley*
[c]8 Or *Chaldean;* also in verse 14
[d]15 Or *populace*
[e]21 That is, about 27 feet (about 8.1 metres) high and 18 feet (about 5.5 metres) in circumference
[f]22 That is, about 7½ feet (about 2.3 metres)

from her land. 28This is the number of
the people Nebuchadnezzar carried
into exile:[z]

in the seventh year, 3,023 Jews;
29in Nebuchadnezzar's eighteenth year,
832 people from Jerusalem;
30in his twenty-third year,
745 Jews taken into exile[a] by
Nebuzaradan the commander
of the imperial guard.
There were 4,600 people in all.[b]

Jehoiachin Released
52:31–34pp—2Ki 25:27–30.

31In the thirty-seventh year of the
exile of Jehoiachin[c] king of Judah, in the
year Evil-Merodach[g] became king of
Babylon, he released Jehoiachin king of
Judah and freed him from prison on the
twenty-fifth day of the twelfth month.
32He spoke kindly to him and gave him
a seat of honour higher than those of
the other kings who were with him in
Babylon. 33So Jehoiachin put aside his
prison clothes and for the rest of his
life ate regularly at the king's table.[d]
34Day by day the king of Babylon gave
Jehoiachin a regular allowance[e] as long
as he lived, till the day of his death.

28 [z]Dt 28:36; 2Ch 36:20; Ne 1:2
30 [a]Jer 43:3; [b]Jer 13:19
31 [c]2Ch 36:9
33 [d]2Sa 9:7
34 [e]2Sa 9:10

g31 Also called *Amel-Marduk*

Lamentations

1 [a] How deserted[a] lies the city,
once so full of people![b]
How like a widow[c] is she,
who once was great[d] among the
nations!
She who was queen among the
provinces
has now become a slave.[e]

2 Bitterly she weeps[f] at night,
tears are upon her cheeks.
Among all her lovers[g]
there is none to comfort her.
All her friends have betrayed[h] her;
they have become her enemies.[i]

3 After affliction and harsh labour,
Judah has gone into exile.[j]
She dwells among the nations;
she finds no resting place.[k]
All who pursue her have overtaken
her[l]
in the midst of her distress.

4 The roads to Zion mourn,[m]
for no-one comes to her appointed
feasts.
All her gateways are desolate,[n]
her priests groan,
her maidens grieve,
and she is in bitter anguish.[o]

5 Her foes have become her masters;
her enemies are at ease.
The LORD has brought her grief[p]
because of her many sins.[q]
Her children have gone into exile,[r]
captive before the foe.[s]

6 All the splendour has departed
from the Daughter of Zion.[t]
Her princes are like deer
that find no pasture;
in weakness they have fled[u]
before the pursuer.

7 In the days of her affliction and
wandering
Jerusalem remembers all the
treasures
that were hers in days of old.

Ch. 1

1 [a]**Lev 26:43;** [b]**Jer 42:2;** [c]Isa **47:8;** [d]**1Ki 4:21;** [e]Isa 3:26; **Jer 40:9;** Eze 5:5
2 [f]Ps 6:6; [g]**Jer 3:1;** [h]**Jer 4:30;** Mic 7:5; [i]ver 16; **Jer 30:14**
3 [j]**Jer 13:19;** [k]Dt 28:65; [l]**Ex 15:9**
4 [m]**Ps 137:1;** [n]**Isa 27:10; Jer 9:11;** [o]ver 21; Joel 1:8–13
5 [p]**Isa 22:5; Jer 30:15;** [q]**Ps 5:10;** [r]**Jer 10:20; 39:9;** 52:28–30; [s]**Ps 137:3;** La 2:17
6 [t]**Ps 9:14;** Jer 13:18; [u]**Lev 26:36**
7 [v]**2Ki 14:26; Jer 37:7;** La 4:17; [w]**Jer 2:26**
8 [x]ver 20; Isa 59:2–13; [y]**Jer 2:22;** [z]**Jer 13:22,**26; [a]ver 21–22; **Ps 6:6; 38:8**
9 [b]Dt 32:28–29; Eze 24:13; [c]Jer 13:18; [d]**Ecc 4:1; Jer 16:7;** [e]Ps 25:18
10 [f]Isa 64:11; [g]Ps 74:7–8; 79:1; Jer 51:51; [h]Dt 23:3
11 [i]Ps 6:6; 38:8; [j]**Jer 37:21; 52:6**
12 [k]**Jer 18:16;** [l]ver 18; [m]**Isa 10:4;** 13:13; **Jer 30:24**
13 [n]**Job 30:30;** Ps 102:3; [o]**Job 18:8;** [p]**Jer 44:6;** [q]Hab 3:16

When her people fell into enemy
hands,
there was no-one to help her.[v]
Her enemies looked at her
and laughed[w] at her destruction.

8 Jerusalem has sinned[x] greatly
and so has become unclean.[y]
All who honoured her despise her,
for they have seen her nakedness;[z]
she herself groans[a]
and turns away.

9 Her filthiness clung to her skirts;
she did not consider her future.[b]
Her fall[c] was astounding;
there was none to comfort[d] her.
"Look, O LORD, on my affliction,[e]
for the enemy has triumphed."

10 The enemy laid hands
on all her treasures;[f]
she saw pagan nations
enter her sanctuary[g]—
those you had forbidden[h]
to enter your assembly.

11 All her people groan[i]
as they search for bread;[j]
they barter their treasures for food
to keep themselves alive.
"Look, O LORD, and consider,
for I am despised."

12 "Is it nothing to you, all you who pass
by?[k]
Look around and see.
Is any suffering like my suffering[l]
that was inflicted on me,
that the LORD brought on me
in the day of his fierce anger?[m]

13 "From on high he sent fire,
sent it down into my bones.[n]
He spread a net[o] for my feet
and turned me back.
He made me desolate,[p]
faint[q] all the day long.

[a]This chapter is an acrostic poem, the verses of which begin with the successive letters of the Hebrew alphabet.

14"My sins have been bound into a
yoke[b];[r]
by his hands they were woven
together.
They have come upon my neck
and the Lord has sapped my
strength.
He has handed me over[s]
to those I cannot withstand.

15"The Lord has rejected
all the warriors in my midst;[t]
he has summoned an army[u] against
me
to[c] crush my young men.[v]
In his winepress[w] the Lord has
trampled[x]
the Virgin Daughter[y] of Judah.

16"This is why I weep
and my eyes overflow with tears.[z]
No-one is near to comfort[a] me,
no-one to restore my spirit.
My children are destitute
because the enemy has prevailed."[b]

17Zion stretches out her hands,[c]
but there is no-one to comfort her.
The LORD has decreed for Jacob
that his neighbours become his
foes;[d]
Jerusalem has become
an unclean[e] thing[f] among them.

18"The LORD is righteous,[g]
yet I rebelled[h] against his command.
Listen, all you peoples;
look upon my suffering.[i]
My young men and maidens
have gone into exile.[j]

19"I called to my allies[k]
but they betrayed me.
My priests and my elders
perished[l] in the city
while they searched for food
to keep themselves alive.

20"See, O LORD, how distressed[m] I am!
I am in torment[n] within,
and in my heart I am disturbed,[o]
for I have been most rebellious.[p]
Outside, the sword bereaves;
inside, there is only death.[q]

21"People have heard my groaning,[r]
but there is no-one to comfort me.[s]
All my enemies have heard of my
distress;
they rejoice[t] at what you have done.
May you bring the day[u] you have
announced
so that they may become like me.

14 [r]**Dt 28:48; Isa 47:6; Jer 15:12;** [s]**Jer 32:5**
15 [t]Jer 37:10; [u]Isa 41:2; [v]Isa 28:18; **Jer 18:21;** [w]**Jdg 6:11;** [x]**Isa 5:5;** [y]Jer 14:17
16 [z]**Job 7:3; Ps 119:136; Isa 22:4;** La 2:11, 18; 3:48–49; [a]**Ps 69:20;** Ecc 4:1; **Jer 16:7;** [b]**ver 2;** Jer 13:17; 14:17
17 [c]**Jer 4:31;** [d]**Ex 23:21;** [e]Jer 2:22; [f]**Lev 18:25–28**
18 [g]**Ex 9:27; Ezr 9:15;** [h]**1Sa 12:14;** [i]ver 12; [j]Dt 28:32, 41
19 [k]**Jer 22:20;** [l]**Jer 14:15;** La 2:20
20 [m]**Jer 4:19;** [n]La 2:11; [o]**Job 20:2;** [p]**ver 8;** [q]**Dt 32:25;** Eze 7:15
21 [r]**ver 8; Ps 6:6; 38:8;** [s]ver 4; [t]La 2:15; [u]Isa 47:11; Jer 30:16
22 [v]Ne 4:5; [w]**ver 8; Ps 6:6**

Ch. 2

1 [a]La 3:44; [b]Ps 99:5; 132:7; [c]**Jer 12:7**
2 [d]ver 17; La 3:43; [e]Ps 21:9; [f]Ps 89:39–40; Mic 5:11; [g]**Isa 25:12**
3 [h]Ps 75:5, 10; [i]Ps 74:11; [j]**Isa 42:25;** Jer 21:4–5, 14
4 [k]**Job 3:23;** 16:13; La 3:12–13; [l]**Ps 48:2;** Eze 24:16, 25; [m]**2Ch 34:21;** Eze 20:34; [n]Isa 42:25; **Jer 7:20;** [o]**Jer 4:20**
5 [p]**Job 13:24;** [q]ver 2; [r]Isa 29:2; [s]**Jer 7:20;** 9:17–20

22"Let all their wickedness come before
you;
deal with them
as you have dealt with me
because of all my sins.[v]
My groans[w] are many
and my heart is faint."

2 [a] How the Lord has covered the
Daughter of Zion
with the cloud of his anger[b]![a]
He has hurled down the splendour of
Israel
from heaven to earth;
he has not remembered his footstool[b]
in the day of his anger.[c]

2Without pity[d] the Lord has swallowed[e]
up
all the dwellings of Jacob;
in his wrath he has torn down
the strongholds[f] of the Daughter of
Judah.
He has brought her kingdom and its
princes
down to the ground[g] in dishonour.

3In fierce anger he has cut off
every horn[c][h] of Israel.
He has withdrawn his right hand[i]
at the approach of the enemy.
He has burned in Jacob like a flaming
fire
that consumes everything around
it.[j]

4Like an enemy he has strung his bow;[k]
his right hand is ready.
Like a foe he has slain
all who were pleasing to the eye;[l]
he has poured out his wrath[m] like fire[n]
on the tent[o] of the Daughter of Zion.

5The Lord is like an enemy;[p]
he has swallowed up Israel.
He has swallowed up all her palaces
and destroyed her strongholds.[q]
He has multiplied mourning and
lamentation[r]
for the Daughter of Judah.[s]

6He has laid waste his dwelling like a
garden;

b14 Most Hebrew manuscripts; Septuagint *He kept watch over my sins*
c15 Or *has set a time for me / when he will*
aThis chapter is an acrostic poem, the verses of which begin with the successive letters of the Hebrew alphabet.
b1 Or *How the* LORD *in his anger / has treated the Daughter of Zion with contempt!*
c3 Or / *all the strength*; or *every king; horn* here symbolises strength.

he has destroyed[t] his place of
meeting.[u]
The LORD has made Zion forget
her appointed feasts and her
Sabbaths;[v]
in his fierce anger he has spurned
both king and priest.[w]

7The Lord has rejected his altar
and abandoned his sanctuary.[x]
He has handed over to the enemy
the walls of her palaces;[y]
they have raised a shout in the house
of the LORD
as on the day of an appointed feast.[z]

8The LORD determined to tear down
the wall around the Daughter of
Zion.[a]
He stretched out a measuring line[b]
and did not withhold his hand from
destroying.
He made ramparts[c] and walls lament;
together they wasted away.[d]

9Her gates[e] have sunk into the ground;
their bars[f] he has broken and
destroyed.
Her king and her princes are exiled[g]
among the nations,
the law[h] is no more,
and her prophets[i] no longer find
visions[j] from the LORD.

10The elders of the Daughter of Zion
sit on the ground in silence;[k]
they have sprinkled dust[l] on their
heads[m]
and put on sackcloth.[n]
The young women of Jerusalem
have bowed their heads to the
ground.[o]

11My eyes fail from weeping,[p]
I am in torment within,[q]
my heart[r] is poured out[s] on the ground
because my people are destroyed,[t]
because children and infants faint[u]
in the streets of the city.

12They say to their mothers,
"Where is bread and wine?"[v]
as they faint like wounded men
in the streets of the city,
as their lives ebb away[w]
in their mothers' arms.[x]

13What can I say for you?[y]
With what can I compare you,
O Daughter[z] of Jerusalem?
To what can I liken you,
that I may comfort you,
O Virgin Daughter of Zion?[a]
Your wound is as deep as the sea.[b]
Who can heal you?

14The visions of your prophets
were false[c] and worthless;
they did not expose your sin
to ward off your captivity.[d]
The oracles they gave you
were false and misleading.[e]

15All who pass your way
clap their hands at you;[f]
they scoff[g] and shake their heads[h]
at the Daughter of Jerusalem:[i]
"Is this the city that was called
the perfection of beauty,[j]
the joy of the whole earth?"[k]

16All your enemies open their mouths
wide against you;[l]
they scoff and gnash their teeth[m]
and say, "We have swallowed her
up.[n]
This is the day we have waited for;
we have lived to see it."[o]

17The LORD has done what he planned;
he has fulfilled[p] his word,
which he decreed long ago.[q]
He has overthrown you without pity,[r]
he has let the enemy gloat over you,[s]
he has exalted the horn[d] of your
foes.[t]

18The hearts of the people
cry out to the Lord.[u]
O wall of the Daughter of Zion,[v]
let your tears[w] flow like a river
day and night;[x]
give yourself no relief,
your eyes no rest.[y]

19Arise, cry out in the night,
as the watches of the night begin;
pour out your heart[z] like water
in the presence of the Lord.[a]
Lift up your hands[b] to him
for the lives of your children,
who faint[c] from hunger
at the head of every street.

20"Look, O LORD, and consider:
Whom have you ever treated like
this?
Should women eat their offspring,[d]
the children they have cared for?[e]
Should priest and prophet be killed[f]
in the sanctuary of the Lord?[g]

6 [t]2Ch 36:19; [u]**Jer 52:13;** [v]Zep 3:18; [w]Isa 43:28; **Jer 7:14;** La 4:16; 5:12
7 [x]**Lev 26:31; Eze 7:24;** [y]Ps 74:7–8; **Isa 64:11;** Jer 33:4–5; Eze 7:21–22; [z]Jer 21:4; 52:13
8 [a]ver 18; [b]**2Ki 21:13;** [c]**Ps 48:13;** [d]Isa 3:26; **Jer 39:8; 52:14**
9 [e]**Ne 1:3;** [f]**Isa 45:2;** Hos 11:6; [g]Dt 28:36; **2Ki 24:15;** Jer 16:13; Hos 3:4; [h]**2Ch 15:3;** [i]**1Sa 3:1;** [j]**Jer 14:14**
10 [k]La 3:28; [l]**Jos 7:6;** [m]Job 2:12; [n]**Isa 3:24;** [o]**Job 2:13; Isa 3:26;** Eze 27:30–31
11 [p]**Ps 119:82; Isa 15:3; La 1:16;** 3:48–51; [q]**Job 30:27;** La 1:20; [r]**Isa 1:5;** [s]ver 19; Ps 22:14; [t]**Jer 9:1;** [u]La 4:4
12 [v]Isa 24:11; [w]**Job 3:24;** [x]La 4:4
13 [y]**Isa 1:6;** [z]**2Ki 19:21;** [a]Isa 37:22; [b]Jer 14:17; 30:12–15; La 1:12
14 [c]**Jer 28:15;** [d]Jer 8:11; [e]Jer 2:8; **20:6;** 23:25–40; **29:9;** Eze 13:3; 22:28
15 [f]**Nu 24:10;** Eze 25:6; [g]**Dt 28:37; Isa 28:22;** Jer 19:8; **Na 3:19;** [h]**Job 16:4;** [i]**La 1:21;** [j]Ps 45:11; **48:2;** 50:2; Eze 16:14; [k]Ps 48:2
16 [l]Ps 22:13; La 3:46; [m]**Job 16:9;** [n]**Ps 35:25;** [o]Eze 36:3; Mic 4:11
17 [p]**Jer 39:16;** [q]Dt 28:15–45; [r]**ver 2;** Eze 5:11; 7:9; 8:18; [s]**Ps 22:17;** [t]Ps 89:42; **Isa 44:26; La 1:5;** Zec 1:6
18 [u]**Ps 119:145;** [v]ver 8; [w]**La 1:16;** [x]**Jer 9:1;** [y]La 3:49
19 [z]1Sa 1:15; [a]**ver 11;** Isa 26:9; [b]**Ps 28:2;** [c]**Isa 51:20**
20 [d]**Dt 28:53;** Jer 19:9; Eze 5:10; [e]La 4:10; [f]Ps 78:64; **Jer 14:15;** 23:11–12; [g]**La 1:19**

d17 *Horn* here symbolises strength.

21"Young and old lie together
in the dust of the streets;
my young men and maidens
have fallen by the sword.[h]
You have slain them in the day of your
anger;
you have slaughtered them without
pity.[i]

22"As you summon to a feast day,
so you summoned against me
terrors[j] on every side.
In the day of the LORD's anger
no-one escaped[k] or survived;
those I cared for and reared,[l]
my enemy has destroyed."

3 [a] I am the man who has seen
affliction[a]
by the rod of his wrath.[b]
2He has driven me away and made me
walk
in darkness[c] rather than light;
3indeed, he has turned his hand
against me[d]
again and again, all day long.

4He has made my skin and my flesh
grow old[e]
and has broken my bones.[f]
5He has besieged me and surrounded
me
with bitterness[g] and hardship.[h]
6He has made me dwell in darkness
like those long dead.[i]

7He has walled me in so that I cannot
escape;[j]
he has weighed me down with
chains.[k]
8Even when I call out or cry for help,[l]
he shuts out my prayer.[m]
9He has barred[n] my way with blocks of
stone;
he has made my paths crooked.[o]

10Like a bear lying in wait,
like a lion[p] in hiding,[q]
11he dragged me from the path and
mangled[r] me
and left me without help.
12He drew his bow[s]
and made me the target[t] for his
arrows.[u]

13He pierced[v] my heart
with arrows from his quiver.[w]
14I became the laughing-stock[x] of all my
people;[y]
they mock me in song[z] all day long.
15He has filled me with bitter herbs
and sated me with gall.[a]

16He has broken my teeth with gravel;[b]
he has trampled me in the dust.[c]
17I have been deprived of peace;
I have forgotten what prosperity is.
18So I say, "My splendour is gone
and all that I had hoped from the
LORD."[d]

19I remember my affliction and my
wandering,
the bitterness[e] and the gall.[f]
20I well remember them,
and my soul is downcast[g] within
me.[h]
21Yet this I call to mind
and therefore I have hope:

22Because of the LORD's great love[i] we
are not consumed,[j]
for his compassions never fail.[k]
23They are new every morning;
great is your faithfulness.[l]
24I say to myself, "The LORD is my
portion;[m]
therefore I will wait for him."

25The LORD is good to those whose hope
is in him,
to the one who seeks him;[n]
26it is good to wait quietly[o]
for the salvation of the LORD.[p]
27It is good for a man to bear the yoke
while he is young.

28Let him sit alone in silence,[q]
for the LORD has laid it on him.
29Let him bury his face in the dust[r]—
there may yet be hope.[s]
30Let him offer his cheek to one who
would strike him,[t]
and let him be filled with disgrace.[u]

31For men are not cast off
by the Lord for ever.[v]
32Though he brings grief, he will show
compassion,
so great is his unfailing love.[w]
33For he does not willingly bring
affliction
or grief to the children of men.[x]

34To crush underfoot
all prisoners in the land,
35to deny a man his rights
before the Most High,[y]

21 [h]**Dt 32:25; 2Ch 36:17**; Ps 78:62–63; Jer 6:11; [i]**Jer 13:14**; La 3:43; Zec 11:6
22 [j]**Ps 31:13; Jer 20:10**; [k]**Jer 11:11**; [l]Job 27:14; Hos 9:13

Ch. 3

1 [a]Jer 15:17–18; [b]**Job 19:21**; Ps 88:7
2 [c]**Job 19:8; Ps 82:5; Jer 4:23**
3 [d]Ps 38:2; Isa 5:25
4 [e]**Job 30:30**; La 4:8; [f]**Ps 51:8; Isa 38:13; Jer 50:17**
5 [g]ver 19; [h]Jer 23:15
6 [i]Ps 88:5–6; 143:3; Isa 59:10
7 [j]**Job 3:23**; [k]Jer 40:4
8 [l]Ps 5:2; [m]ver 44; **Dt 1:45; Job 30:20**; Ps 22:2
9 [n]**Job 19:8**; [o]**Job 9:24; Isa 63:17**; Hos 2:6
10 [p]**Job 10:16**; [q]Hos 13:8; Am 5:18–19
11 [r]Hos 6:1
12 [s]**La 2:4**; [t]Job 7:20; [u]**Job 16:12**; Ps 7:12–13; 38:2
13 [v]**Job 16:13**; [w]Job 6:4
14 [x]**Ge 38:23**; Ps 22:6–7; Jer 20:7; [y]**Job 17:2**; [z]**Job 30:9**
15 [a]ver 19; Jer 9:15
16 [b]**Pr 20:17**; [c]**Ps 7:5**
18 [d]**ver 54; Job 17:15**
19 [e]ver 5; [f]**ver 15**
20 [g]**Ps 42:5**; [h]Ps 42:11; 43:5
22 [i]**Ps 103:11**; [j]**Job 34:15; Hos 11:9**; [k]Ps 78:38; 130:7
23 [l]**Ex 34:6**; Zep 3:5
24 [m]**Ps 119:57**
25 [n]**Ps 33:18**; Isa 25:9; **30:18**
26 [o]**Isa 7:4**; [p]Ps 37:7; 40:1
28 [q]Jer 15:17; La 2:10
29 [r]**Job 2:8**; [s]**Jer 31:17**
30 [t]**Job 16:10; Isa 50:6**; [u]Mic 5:1
31 [v]Ps 94:14; Isa 54:7
32 [w]Ps 78:38; 106:43–45; Hos 11:8; Na 1:12
33 [x]**Job 37:23; Jer 31:20**; Eze 18:23; 33:11
35 [y]Ge 14:18–20,22

[a]This chapter is an acrostic poem; the verses of each stanza begin with the successive letters of the Hebrew alphabet, and the verses within each stanza begin with the same letter.

36to deprive a man of justice—
would not the Lord see such
things?[z]

37Who can speak and have it happen
if the Lord has not decreed it?[a]
38Is it not from the mouth of the Most
High
that both calamities and good things
come?[b]
39Why should any living man complain
when punished for his sins?[c]

40Let us examine our ways and test
them,[d]
and let us return to the LORD.[e]
41Let us lift up our hearts and our hands
to God in heaven,[f] and say:
42"We have sinned and rebelled[g]
and you have not forgiven.[h]

43"You have covered yourself with
anger and pursued[i] us;
you have slain without pity.[j]
44You have covered yourself with a
cloud[k]
so that no prayer[l] can get through.[m]
45You have made us scum[n] and refuse
among the nations.

46"All our enemies have opened their
mouths
wide[o] against us.[p]
47We have suffered terror and pitfalls,[q]
ruin and destruction."[r]
48Streams of tears[s] flow from my eyes[t]
because my people are destroyed.[u]

49My eyes will flow unceasingly,
without relief,[v]
50until the LORD looks down
from heaven and sees.[w]
51What I see brings grief to my soul
because of all the women of my city.

52Those who were my enemies without
cause
hunted me like a bird.[x]
53They tried to end my life in a pit[y]
and threw stones at me;
54the waters closed over my head,[z]
and I thought I was about to be cut
off.[a]

55I called on your name, O LORD,
from the depths[b] of the pit.[c]
56You heard my plea:[d] "Do not close
your ears
to my cry for relief."
57You came near[e] when I called you,
and you said, "Do not fear."[f]

58O Lord, you took up my case;[g]
you redeemed my life.[h]

36 [z]Ps 140:12; **Pr 17:15; Jer 22:3;** Hab 1:13
37 [a]Ps 33:9–11; **Pr 19:21; 21:30**
38 [b]**Job 2:10; Isa 45:7;** Jer 32:42
39 [c]**Jer 30:15;** Mic 7:9
40 [d]2Co 13:5; [e]Ps 119:59; 139:23–24
41 [f]**Ps 25:1; 28:2**
42 [g]Jer 14:20; Da 9:5; [h]**2Ki 24:4;** Jer 5:7–9
43 [i]ver 66; Ps 35:6; [j]**La 2:2,** 17, 21
44 [k]Ps 97:2; La 2:1; [l]**ver 8;** Zec 7:13; [m]**Isa 58:4**
45 [n]1Co 4:13
46 [o]Ps 22:13; [p]La 2:16
47 [q]Jer 48:43; [r]**Isa 24:17–18; 51:19**
48 [s]**Ps 119:136;** [t]**Jer 9:1,** 18; La 1:16; [u]La 2:11
49 [v]Jer 14:17; **La 2:18**
50 [w]**Ps 14:2;** 80:14; **Isa 63:15**
52 [x]Ps 35:7
53 [y]Jer 37:16; **38:6**
54 [z]Ps 69:2; Jnh 2:3–5; [a]ver 18; Ps 88:5; Eze 37:11
55 [b]**Ps 88:6;** [c]Ps 130:1; Jnh 2:2
56 [d]**Ps 55:1;** 116:1–2
57 [e]**Ps 46:1;** [f]Isa 41:10
58 [g]**Jer 51:36;** [h]Ps 34:22; **Jer 50:34**
59 [i]Jer 18:19–20; [j]Ps 35:23; 43:1
60 [k]**Jer 11:20;** 18:18
61 [l]Ps 89:50; Zep 2:8
62 [m]Eze 36:3
63 [n]**Job 30:9**
64 [o]**Ps 28:4; Jer 51:6**
65 [p]Ex 14:8; Dt 2:30; Isa 6:10
66 [q]**ver 43**

Ch. 4

1 [a]Eze 7:19
2 [b]Isa 51:18
3 [c]**Job 39:16**
4 [d]**Dt 28:48; 2Ki 18:31;** [e]**Ps 22:15;** [f]La 2:11–12
5 [g]Jer 6:2; [h]**Isa 3:26;** Am 6:3–7
6 [i]**Ge 19:25**

59You have seen, O LORD, the wrong
done to me.[i]
Uphold my cause![j]
60You have seen the depth of their
vengeance,
all their plots against me.[k]

61O LORD, you have heard their insults,[l]
all their plots against me—
62what my enemies whisper and mutter
against me all day long.[m]
63Look at them! Sitting or standing,
they mock me in their songs.[n]

64Pay them back what they deserve, O
LORD,
for what their hands have done.[o]
65Put a veil over their hearts,[p]
and may your curse be on them!
66Pursue[q] them in anger and destroy
them
from under the heavens of the LORD.

4 [a] How the gold has lost its lustre,
the fine gold become dull!
The sacred gems are scattered
at the head of every street.[a]

2How the precious sons of Zion,[b]
once worth their weight in gold,
are now considered as pots of clay,
the work of a potter's hands!

3Even jackals offer their breasts
to nurse their young,
but my people have become heartless
like ostriches in the desert.[c]

4Because of thirst[d] the infant's tongue
sticks to the roof of its mouth;[e]
the children beg for bread,
but no-one gives it to them.[f]

5Those who once ate delicacies
are destitute in the streets.
Those nurtured in purple[g]
now lie on ash heaps.[h]

6The punishment of my people
is greater than that of Sodom,[i]
which was overthrown in a moment
without a hand turned to help her.

7Their princes were brighter than snow
and whiter than milk,
their bodies more ruddy than rubies,
their appearance like sapphires.[b]

[a]This chapter is an acrostic poem, the verses of which begin with the successive letters of the Hebrew alphabet. [b]7 Or *lapis lazuli*

[8]But now they are blacker[j] than soot;
they are not recognised in the streets.
Their skin has shrivelled on their bones;[k]
it has become as dry as a stick.

[9]Those killed by the sword are better off
than those who die of famine;[l]
racked with hunger, they waste away
for lack of food from the field.[m]

[10]With their own hands compassionate women
have cooked their own children,[n]
who became their food
when my people were destroyed.

[11]The LORD has given full vent to his wrath;[o]
he has poured out[p] his fierce anger.[q]
He kindled a fire[r] in Zion
that consumed her foundations.[s]

[12]The kings of the earth did not believe,
nor did any of the world's people,
that enemies and foes could enter
the gates of Jerusalem.[t]

[13]But it happened because of the sins of her prophets
and the iniquities of her priests,[u]
who shed within her
the blood[v] of the righteous.

[14]Now they grope through the streets
like men who are blind.[w]
They are so defiled with blood[x]
that no-one dares to touch their garments.

[15]"Go away! You are unclean!" men cry to them.
"Away! Away! Don't touch us!"
When they flee and wander[y] about,
people among the nations say,
"They can stay here no longer."[z]

[16]The LORD himself has scattered them;
he no longer watches over them.[a]
The priests are shown no honour,
the elders[b] no favour.[c]

[17]Moreover, our eyes failed,
looking in vain[d] for help;[e]
from our towers we watched
for a nation[f] that could not save us.

[18]Men stalked us at every step,
so we could not walk in our streets.
Our end was near, our days were numbered,
for our end had come.[g]

8 [j]**Job 30:28**; [k]Ps 102:3–5; **La 3:4**
9 [l]**2Ki 25:3**; [m]**Jer 15:2; 16:4**; La 5:10
10 [n]**Lev 26:29**; Dt 28:53–57; Jer 19:9; La 2:20; Eze 5:10
11 [o]**Job 20:23**; [p]**2Ch 34:21**; [q]Na 1:6; Zep 2:2; 3:8; [r]Jer 17:27; [s]**Dt 32:22; Jer 7:20**; Eze 22:31
12 [t]**1Ki 9:9; Jer 21:13**
13 [u]Jer 5:31; 6:13; Eze 22:28; Mic 3:11; [v]**2Ki 21:16**
14 [w]**Isa 59:10**; [x]Jer 19:4
15 [y]**Jer 44:14**; [z]Lev 13:46; Mic 2:10
16 [a]Isa 9:14–16; [b]La 5:12; [c]**La 2:6**
17 [d]**Ge 15:18; Isa 20:5**; Eze 29:16; [e]**La 1:7**; [f]Jer 37:7
18 [g]Eze 7:2–12; Am 8:2
19 [h]**Dt 28:49**; [i]**Lev 26:36**; Isa 5:26–28; [j]Jer 52:7
20 [k]**1Sa 26:9**; 2Sa 19:21; [l]Jer 39:5; Eze 12:12–13; 19:4,8; [m]**Ps 91:1**
21 [n]**Ge 10:23**; [o]**Ps 16:5; Jer 25:15**; [p]Isa 34:6–10; **63:6**; Eze 35:15; Am 1:11–12; Ob 16; Hab 2:16
22 [q]Isa 40:2; Jer 33:8; [r]**Ps 137:7**; Eze 25:12–14; Mal 1:4

Ch. 5

1 [a]Ps 44:13–16; 89:50
2 [b]Ps 79:1; [c]**Ps 109:11**; [d]Zep 1:13; [e]Jer 17:4
3 [f]**Ex 22:24**; Jer 15:8; **18:21**
4 [g]**Isa 55:1**; Eze 4:16–17; [h]Isa 3:1
5 [i]**Ne 9:37**; Isa 47:6; [j]**Jos 1:13**
6 [k]Jer 2:36; Hos 5:13; 7:11; 9:3
7 [l]**Jer 31:29**; [m]Jer 14:20; 16:12
8 [n]Ne 5:15; [o]Zec 11:6

[19]Our pursuers were swifter
than eagles[h] in the sky;
they chased us[i] over the mountains
and lay in wait for us in the desert.[j]

[20]The LORD's anointed,[k] our very life breath,
was caught in their traps.[l]
We thought that under his shadow[m]
we would live among the nations.

[21]Rejoice and be glad, O Daughter of Edom,
you who live in the land of Uz.[n]
But to you also the cup[o] will be passed;
you will be drunk and stripped naked.[p]

[22]O Daughter of Zion, your punishment will end;[q]
he will not prolong your exile.
But, O Daughter of Edom, he will punish your sin
and expose your wickedness.[r]

5

Remember, O LORD, what has happened to us;
look, and see our disgrace.[a]
[2]Our inheritance[b] has been turned over to aliens,[c]
our homes[d] to foreigners.[e]
[3]We have become orphans and fatherless,
our mothers like widows.[f]
[4]We must buy the water we drink;[g]
our wood can be had only at a price.[h]
[5]Those who pursue us are at our heels;
we are weary[i] and find no rest.[j]
[6]We submitted to Egypt and Assyria[k]
to get enough bread.
[7]Our fathers[l] sinned and are no more,
and we bear their punishment.[m]
[8]Slaves[n] rule over us,
and there is none to free us from their hands.[o]
[9]We get our bread at the risk of our lives
because of the sword in the desert.
[10]Our skin is hot as an oven,
feverish from hunger.[p]
[11]Women have been ravished[q] in Zion,
and virgins in the towns of Judah.
[12]Princes have been hung up by their hands;
elders[r] are shown no respect.[s]
[13]Young men toil at the millstones;
boys stagger under loads of wood.
[14]The elders are gone from the city gate;
the young men have stopped their music.[t]

10 [p]**Job 30:30**; La 4:8–9 *11* [q]**Ge 34:29**; Zec 14:2
12 [r]**Lev 19:32**; [s]**La 2:6**; 4:16 *14* [t]**Isa 24:8**; Jer 7:34

15Joy is gone from our hearts;
our dancing has turned to mourning.[u]
16The crown[v] has fallen from our head.[w]
Woe to us, for we have sinned![x]
17Because of this our hearts[y] are faint;[z]
because of these things our eyes[a] grow dim[b]
18for Mount Zion,[c] which lies desolate,[d]
with jackals prowling over it.

19You, O LORD, reign for ever;[e]
your throne endures[f] from generation to generation.
20Why do you always forget us?[g]
Why do you forsake[h] us so long?
21Restore[i] us to yourself, O LORD, that we may return;
renew our days as of old
22unless you have utterly rejected us[j]
and are angry with us beyond measure.[k]

15 [u]**Jer 25:10**; Am 8:10
16 [v]Ps 89:39; **Jer 13:18**; [w]**Job 19:9**; [x]**Isa 3:11**; Jer 14:20
17 [y]**Isa 1:5**; [z]**Jer 8:18**; [a]Ps 6:7; [b]**Job 16:8**
18 [c]Ps 74:2–3; [d]**Isa 27:10**; Mic 3:12
19 [e]**1Ch 16:31**; [f]**Ps 45:6**; 102:12,24–27
20 [g]**Ps 13:1**; 44:24; [h]**Ps 71:11**
21 [i]**Ps 80:3**; Isa 60:20–22
22 [j]**Ps 53:5**; 60:1–2; **Jer 6:30**; [k]**Isa 64:9**

Ezekiel

The Living Creatures and the Glory of the LORD

1 In the[a] thirtieth year, in the fourth
month on the fifth day, while I was
among the exiles[a] by the Kebar River,[b]
the heavens were opened[c] and I saw
visions[d] of God.
2On the fifth of the month—it was the
fifth year of the exile of King Jehoiachin[e]
—3the word of the LORD came to Ezekiel[f]
the priest, the son of Buzi,[b] by the Kebar
River in the land of the Babylonians.[c]
There the hand of the LORD was upon
him.[g]
4I looked, and I saw a windstorm[h]
coming out of the north[i]—an immense
cloud with flashing lightning and sur-
rounded by brilliant light. The centre of
the fire looked like glowing metal,[j] 5and
in the fire was what looked like four
living creatures.[k] In appearance their
form was that of a man,[l] 6but each of
them had four faces[m] and four wings.
7Their legs were straight; their feet were
like those of a calf and gleamed like
burnished bronze.[n] 8Under their wings
on their four sides they had the hands of
a man.[o] All four of them had faces and
wings, 9and their wings touched one
another. Each one went straight ahead;
they did not turn as they moved.[p]
10Their faces looked like this: Each of
the four had the face of a man, and on
the right side each had the face of a lion,
and on the left the face of an ox; each
also had the face of an eagle.[q] 11Such
were their faces. Their wings[r] were
spread out upwards; each had two
wings, one touching the wing of
another creature on either side, and two
wings covering its body. 12Each one
went straight ahead. Wherever the
spirit would go, they would go, without
turning as they went.[s] 13The appearance
of the living creatures was like burning
coals[t] of fire or like torches. Fire moved
back and forth among the creatures; it
was bright, and lightning[u] flashed out
of it. 14The creatures sped back and forth
like flashes of lightning.[v]
15As I looked at the living creatures,[w] I
saw a wheel[x] on the ground beside each
creature with its four faces. 16This was
the appearance and structure of the
wheels: They sparkled like chrysolite,[y]
and all four looked alike. Each appeared
to be made like a wheel intersecting a
wheel. 17As they moved, they would go
in any one of the four directions the
creatures faced; the wheels did not turn[z]
about[d] as the creatures went. 18Their
rims were high and awesome, and all
four rims were full of eyes[a] all around.
19When the living creatures moved,
the wheels beside them moved; and
when the living creatures rose from
the ground, the wheels also rose.
20Wherever the spirit would go, they
would go,[b] and the wheels would rise
along with them, because the spirit of
the living creatures was in the wheels.
21When the creatures moved, they also
moved; when the creatures stood still,
they also stood still; and when the crea-
tures rose from the ground, the wheels
rose along with them, because the spirit
of the living creatures was in the
wheels.[c]
22Spread out above the heads of the
living creatures was what looked like an
expanse,[d] sparkling like ice, and awe-
some. 23Under the expanse their wings
were stretched out one towards the
other, and each had two wings covering
its body. 24When the creatures moved, I
heard the sound of their wings, like the
roar of rushing[e] waters, like the voice[f]
of the Almighty,[e] like the tumult of
an army.[g] When they stood still, they
lowered their wings.
25Then there came a voice from above
the expanse over their heads as they
stood with lowered wings. 26Above the
expanse over their heads was what
looked like a throne[h] of sapphire,[f] [i] and
high above on the throne was a figure
like that of a man.[j] 27I saw that from
what appeared to be his waist up he
looked like glowing metal, as if full of

Ch. 1
1 [a]**Dt 21:10;** Eze 11:24–25; [b]**Ps 137:1;** [c]**Mt 3:16;** [d]**Ex 24:10**
2 [e]**2Ki 24:15**
3 [f]Eze 24:24; [g]**2Ki 3:15;** Isa 8:11; Eze 3:14, 22; 8:1; 33:22; 37:1; 40:1
4 [h]**Job 38:1;** [i]Jer 1:14; [j]Eze 8:2
5 [k]**Isa 6:2;** Rev 4:6; [l]ver 26; Da 7:13
6 [m]Eze 10:14
7 [n]Eze 40:3; Da 10:6; **Rev 1:15**
8 [o]Eze 10:8
9 [p]Eze 10:22
10 [q]Eze 10:14; Rev 4:7
11 [r]Isa 6:2
12 [s]Eze 10:16–19
13 [t]**2Sa 22:9;** [u]Rev 4:5
14 [v]**Ps 29:7**
15 [w]Eze 3:13; [x]Eze 10:2; Da 7:9
16 [y]**Ex 28:20**
17 [z]ver 9
18 [a]Rev 4:6
20 [b]ver 12
21 [c]Eze 10:9–12
22 [d]Eze 10:1
24 [e]**Ps 46:3;** Eze 3:13; [f]Eze 10:5; 43:2; Da 10:6; Rev 1:15; 14:2; 19:6; [g]**2Ki 7:6**
26 [h]**1Ki 22:19;** Isa 6:1; **Jer 3:17;** [i]**Ex 24:10;** [j]**ver 5; Eze 2:1; Rev 1:13**

[a]*1* Or ⌞*my*⌟ [b]3 Or *Ezekiel son of Buzi the priest*
[c]3 Or *Chaldeans* [d]17 Or *aside*
[e]24 Hebrew *Shaddai* [f]26 Or *lapis lazuli*

fire, and that from there down he looked like fire; and brilliant light surrounded him.[k] 28Like the appearance of a rainbow[l] in the clouds on a rainy day, so was the radiance around him.[m]

This was the appearance of the likeness of the glory[n] of the LORD. When I saw it, I fell face down,[o] and I heard the voice of one speaking.

Ezekiel's Call

2 He said to me, "Son of man,[a] stand[b] up on your feet and I will speak to you.[c]" 2As he spoke, the Spirit came into me and raised me[d] to my feet, and I heard him speaking to me.

3He said: "Son of man, I am sending you to the Israelites, to a rebellious nation that has rebelled against me; they and their fathers have been in revolt against me to this very day.[e] 4The people to whom I am sending you are obstinate and stubborn.[f] Say to them, 'This is what the Sovereign LORD says.'[g] 5And whether they listen or fail to listen[h]—for they are a rebellious house[i]—they will know that a prophet has been among them.[j] 6And you, son of man, do not be afraid[k] of them or their words. Do not be afraid, though briers and thorns[l] are all around you and you live among scorpions. Do not be afraid of what they say or terrified by them, though they are a rebellious house.[m] 7You must speak[n] my words to them, whether they listen or fail to listen, for they are rebellious.[o] 8But you, son of man, listen to what I say to you. Do not rebel[p q] like that rebellious house;[r] open your mouth and eat[s] what I give you."

9Then I looked, and I saw a hand[t] stretched out to me. In it was a scroll,[u] 10which he unrolled before me. On both sides of it were written words of lament and mourning and woe.[v]

3 And he said to me, "Son of man, eat what is before you, eat this scroll; then go and speak to the house of Israel." 2So I opened my mouth, and he gave me the scroll to eat.

3Then he said to me, "Son of man, eat this scroll I am giving you and fill your stomach with it." So I ate[a] it, and it tasted as sweet as honey[b] in my mouth.

4He then said to me: "Son of man, go now to the house of Israel and speak my words to them.[c] 5You are not being sent to a people of obscure speech and difficult language,[d] but to the house of Israel—6not to many peoples of obscure speech and difficult language, whose words you cannot understand. Surely if I had sent you to them, they would have listened to you.[e] 7But the house of Israel is not willing to listen[f] to you because they are not willing to listen to me, for the whole house of Israel is hardened and obstinate.[g] 8But I will make you as unyielding and hardened as they are.[h] 9I will make your forehead[i] like the hardest stone, harder than flint.[j] Do not be afraid of them or terrified by them, though they are a rebellious house.[k]"

10And he said to me, "Son of man, listen carefully[l] and take to heart[l] all the words I speak to you. 11Go[m] now to your countrymen in exile and speak to them. Say to them, 'This is what the Sovereign LORD says,'[n] whether they listen or fail to listen.[o]"

12Then the Spirit lifted me up,[p] and I heard behind me a loud rumbling sound—May the glory of the LORD be praised in his dwelling-place!—13the sound of the wings of the living creatures[q] brushing against each other and the sound of the wheels beside them, a loud rumbling sound.[r] 14The Spirit[s] then lifted me up[t] and took me away, and I went in bitterness and in the anger of my spirit, with the strong hand of the LORD[u] upon me. 15I came to the exiles who lived at Tel Abib near the Kebar River.[v] And there, where they were living, I sat among them for seven days[w]—overwhelmed.

Warning to Israel

16At the end of seven days the word of the LORD came to me:[x] 17"Son of man, I have made you a watchman[y] for the house of Israel; so hear the word I speak and give them warning from me.[z] 18When I say to a wicked man, 'You will surely die,'[a'] and you do not warn him or speak out to dissuade him from his evil ways in order to save his life, that wicked man will die for[a] his sin, and I will hold you accountable for his blood.[b] 19But if you do warn the wicked man and he does not turn[c] from his wickedness[d] or from his evil ways, he will die[e] for his sin; but you will have saved yourself.[f]

20"Again, when a righteous man turns[g] from his righteousness and does evil, and I put a stumbling-block[h] before

27 [k]Eze 8:2
28 [l]Ge 9:13; Rev 10:1; [m]Rev 4:2; [n]Ex 16:7; 24:16; Lk 2:9; [o]Ge 17:3; Nu 14:5

Ch. 2

1 [a]Job 25:6; Ps 8:4; Eze 1:26; Da 7:13; 8:15; [b]Da 10:11; Ac 14:10; 26:16; [c]Ac 9:6
2 [d]Eze 3:24; Da 8:18
3 [e]Jer 3:25; Eze 5:6; 20:8–24; 24:3
4 [f]Ex 32:9; Isa 9:9; Eze 3:7; [g]Am 7:15
5 [h]Eze 3:11; [i]Eze 3:27; [j]Jer 5:3; Eze 33:33; Jn 15:22
6 [k]Dt 31:6; 2Ki 1:15; [l]Nu 33:55; Isa 9:18; Mic 7:4; [m]Isa 1:2; 30:9; Eze 24:3; 44:6
7 [n]Jer 7:27; [o]Jer 1:7; 42:21; Eze 3:10–11
8 [p]Nu 20:10–13; [q]Isa 8:11; [r]Isa 50:5; [s]Ps 81:10; Jer 15:16; Rev 10:9
9 [t]Eze 8:3; [u]Ps 40:7; Jer 36:4; Rev 5:1–5; 10:8–10
10 [v]Isa 3:11; Rev 8:13

Ch. 3

3 [a]Jer 15:16; [b]Ps 19:10; Rev 10:9–10
4 [c]Eze 11:4,25
5 [d]Isa 28:11; Jnh 1:2
6 [e]Jnh 3:5–10; Mt 11:21–23; Ac 13:46–48
7 [f]Jer 7:27; [g]Isa 48:4; Jer 3:3; Eze 2:4; Jn 15:20–23
8 [h]Jer 1:18; 15:20
9 [i]Isa 48:4; [j]Jer 5:3; [k]Isa 50:7; Eze 2:6; 44:6; Mic 3:8
10 [l]Job 22:22
11 [m]Isa 6:9; [n]ver 27; [o]Eze 2:4–5,7; 11:24–25
12 [p]ver 14; Eze 8:3; 43:5
13 [q]Eze 1:15; [r]Eze 1:24; 10:5,16–17
14 [s]1Ki 18:12; [t]ver 12; [u]ver 22; Isa 8:11; Eze 37:1
15 [v]Ps 137:1; [w]Ge 50:10 16 [x]Jer 42:7
17 [y]Isa 52:8; [z]Isa 58:1; Jer 1:17; Eze 11:4; Hab 2:1
18 [a]Ge 2:17; Jn 8:21,24; [b]ver 20
19 [c]Ps 7:12; [d]Ge 6:5; [e]Jer 42:16; [f]2Ki 17:13; Eze 14:14, 20; Ac 18:6; 20:26; 1Ti 4:14–16
20 [g]Jer 34:16; [h]Lev 26:37; Isa 8:14; Eze 7:19

[a]18 Or *in;* also in verses 19 and 20

him, he will die. Since you did not warn
him, he will die for his sin. The right-
eous things he did will not be remem-
bered, and I will hold you accountable
for his blood.[i] 21But if you do warn the
righteous man not to sin and he does
not sin, he will surely live because he
took warning, and you will have saved
yourself.[j]"

22The hand of the LORD[k] was upon me
there, and he said to me, "Get up and
go[l] out to the plain,[m] and there I will
speak to you." 23So I got up and went
out to the plain. And the glory of the
LORD was standing there, like the glory I
had seen by the Kebar River,[n] and I fell
face down.[o]

24Then the Spirit came into me and
raised me[p] to my feet. He spoke to me
and said: "Go, shut yourself inside your
house.[q] 25And you, son of man, they
will tie with ropes; you will be bound
so that you cannot go out among the
people.[r] 26I will make your tongue stick
to the roof[s] of your mouth so that you
will be silent and unable to rebuke
them, though they are a rebellious
house.[t] 27But when I speak to you, I will
open your mouth and you shall say to
them, 'This is what the Sovereign LORD
says.'[u] Whoever will listen let him
listen, and whoever will refuse let him
refuse; for they are a rebellious house.[v]

Siege of Jerusalem Symbolised

4 "Now, son of man, take a clay tab-
let, put it in front of you and draw
the city of Jerusalem on it. 2Then lay
siege to it: Erect siege works against it,
build a ramp[a] up to it, set up camps
against it and put battering-rams
around it.[b] 3Then take an iron pan,[c]
place it as an iron wall between you and
the city and turn your face towards[d] it. It
will be under siege, and you shall be-
siege it. This will be a sign[e] to the house
of Israel.[f]

4"Then lie on your left side and put
the sin of the house of Israel upon
yourself.[a] You are to bear their sin for
the number of days you lie on your side.
5I have assigned you the same number
of days as the years of their sin. So for
390 days you will bear the sin of the
house of Israel.

6"After you have finished this, lie
down again, this time on your right
side, and bear the sin[g] of the house of
Judah. I have assigned you 40 days, a
day for each year.[h] 7Turn your face[i] to-
wards the siege of Jerusalem and with
bared arm prophesy against her. 8I will
tie you up with ropes so that you cannot
turn from one side to the other until you
have finished the days of your siege.[j]

9"Take wheat and barley, beans and
lentils, millet and spelt;[k] put them in a
storage jar and use them to make bread
for yourself. You are to eat it during the
390 days you lie on your side. 10Weigh
out twenty shekels[b] [l] of food to eat each
day and eat it at set times. 11Also
measure out a sixth of a hin[c] of water
and drink it at set times.[m] 12Eat the food
as you would a barley cake; bake it in the
sight of the people, using human ex-
crement[n] for fuel." 13The LORD said, "In
this way the people of Israel will eat
defiled food among the nations where I
will drive them."[o]

14Then I said, "Not so, Sovereign
LORD![p] I have never defiled myself.
From my youth until now I have never
eaten anything found dead[q] or torn by
wild animals. No unclean meat has ever
entered my mouth."[r]

15"Very well," he said, "I will let you
bake your bread over cow manure in-
stead of human excrement."

16He then said to me: "Son of man, I
will cut off[s] the supply of food in Jeru-
salem. The people will eat rationed food
in anxiety and drink rationed water in
despair,[t] 17for food and water will be
scarce.[u] They will be appalled at the
sight of each other and will waste away
because of[d] their sin.[v]

5 "Now, son of man, take a sharp
sword and use it as a barber's
razor[a] to shave[b] your head and your
beard.[c] Then take a set of scales and
divide up the hair. 2When the days of
your siege come to an end, burn a third[d]
of the hair with fire[e] inside the city. Take
a third and strike it with the sword all
around the city. And scatter a third to
the wind.[f] For I will pursue them with
drawn sword.[g] 3But take a few strands
of hair and tuck them away in the folds
of your garment.[h] 4Again, take a few of
these and throw them into the fire[i] and
burn them up. A fire will spread from
there to the whole house of Israel.

5"This is what the Sovereign LORD
says: This is Jerusalem, which I have set
in the centre of the nations, with coun-
tries all around her.[j] 6Yet in her wicked-
ness she has rebelled against my laws
and decrees more than the nations and
countries around her. She has rejected

20 [i]ver 18; Ps 125:5; Eze 18:24; 33:12, 18
21 [j]Ac 20:31
22 [k]**ver 14; Eze 1:3;** [l]Ac 9:6; [m]Eze 8:4
23 [n]Eze 1:1; [o]**Ge 17:3**
24 [p]**Eze 2:2;** [q]Jer 15:17
25 [r]Eze 4:8
26 [s]**Ps 22:15;** [t]Eze 2:5; 24:27; 33:22; Hos 4:4
27 [u]ver 11; [v]Eze 2:5; 12:3; 24:27; 29:21; 33:22; Rev 22:11

Ch. 4

2 [a]**Jer 6:6;** Eze 17:17; Da 11:15; [b]**Jer 33:4;** Eze 21:22
3 [c]**Lev 2:5;** [d]ver 7; Eze 20:46; 21:2; [e]**Isa 8:18; 20:3;** Jer 13:1–7; 18:1–4; 19:1–2; Eze 5:1–4; 12:3–6; [f]**Jer 39:1**
6 [g]**Ex 28:38;** [h]Nu 14:34; Da 9:24–26; 12:11–12
7 [i]ver 3; Eze 6:2; **13:17**
8 [j]Eze 3:25
9 [k]**Isa 28:25**
10 [l]**Ex 30:13**
11 [m]ver 16
12 [n]**Isa 36:12**
13 [o]Hos 9:3; Am 7:17
14 [p]Jer 1:6; Eze 9:8; 20:49; [q]**Lev 11:39;** [r]**Ex 22:31;** Dt 14:3; 32:37–38; Da 1:8; Hos 9:3–4
16 [s]**Ps 105:16;** [t]ver 10–11; **Lev 26:26;** Isa 3:1; Eze 12:19
17 [u]La 5:4; Eze 5:16; 12:18–19; Am 4:8; [v]**Lev 26:39;** Eze 24:23; 33:10

Ch. 5

1 [a]**Nu 6:5;** [b]Eze 44:20; [c]**Lev 21:5; 2Sa 10:4**
2 [d]Zec 13:8; [e]Jer 21:10; Eze 15:7; [f]ver 10; Jer 13:24; [g]ver 12; **Lev 26:33; Jer 9:16; 39:1–2**
3 [h]2Ki 25:12; **Ps 74:11;** Jer 39:10
4 [i]Eze 10:7; 15:7
5 [j]**Dt 4:6; La 1:1;** Eze 16:14

[a]4 Or *your side*
[b]10 That is, about 8 ounces (about 0.2 kilogram)
[c]11 That is, about 1 pint (about 0.6 litre)
[d]17 Or *away in*

my laws and has not followed my
decrees.[k]
7"Therefore this is what the
Sovereign LORD says: You have been
more unruly than the nations around
you and have not followed my decrees
or kept my laws. You have not even[a]
conformed to the standards of the
nations around you.[l]
8"Therefore this is what the
Sovereign LORD says: I myself am
against you, Jerusalem, and I will inflict
punishment on you in the sight of the
nations.[m] 9Because of all your detestable
idols, I will do to you what I have never
done before and will never do again.[n]
10Therefore in your midst fathers will
eat their children, and children will eat
their fathers.[o] I will inflict punishment
on you and will scatter all your survi-
vors to the winds.[p] 11Therefore as surely
as I live,[q] declares the Sovereign[r] LORD,
because you have defiled my sanctuary[s]
with all your vile images[t] and detestable
practices,[u] I myself will withdraw my
favour; I will not look on you with pity
or spare you.[v] 12A third of your people
will die of the plague or perish by
famine inside you; a third will fall by the
sword outside your walls; and a third I
will scatter to the winds[w] and pursue
with drawn sword.[x]
13"Then my anger will cease and my
wrath[y] against them will subside, and I
will be avenged.[z] And when I have
spent my wrath upon them, they will
know that I the LORD have spoken in my
zeal.[a]
14"I will make you a ruin and a re-
proach among the nations around you,
in the sight of all who pass by.[b] 15You
will be a reproach[c] and a taunt, a warn-
ing[d] and an object of horror to the na-
tions around you when I inflict punish-
ment on you in anger and in wrath and
with stinging rebuke.[e] I the LORD have
spoken.[f] 16When I shoot at you with
my deadly and destructive arrows of
famine, I will shoot to destroy you. I will
bring more and more famine upon you
and cut off your supply of food.[g] 17I will
send famine and wild beasts[h] against
you, and they will leave you childless.
Plague and bloodshed[i] will sweep
through you, and I will bring the sword
against you. I the LORD have spoken.[j]"

A Prophecy Against the Mountains of Israel

6 The word of the LORD came to me:
2"Son of man, set your face[a]
against the mountains[b] of Israel;
prophesy against them[c] 3and say: 'O
mountains of Israel, hear the word of
the Sovereign LORD. This is what the
Sovereign LORD says to the mountains
and hills, to the ravines and valleys:[d] I
am about to bring a sword against you,
and I will destroy your high places.[e]
4Your altars will be demolished and
your incense altars[f] will be smashed;
and I will slay your people in front of
your idols.[g] 5I will lay the dead bodies of
the Israelites in front of their idols, and I
will scatter your bones[h] around your
altars.[i] 6Wherever you live,[j] the towns
will be laid waste and the high places[k]
demolished, so that your altars will be
laid waste and devastated, your idols[l]
smashed and ruined, your incense
altars[m] broken down, and what you
have made wiped out.[n] 7Your people
will fall slain[o] among you, and you will
know that I am the LORD.[p]
8" 'But I will spare some, for some of
you will escape[q] the sword when you
are scattered among the lands and
nations.[r] 9Then in the nations where
they have been carried captive, those
who escape will remember[s] me—how I
have been grieved[t] by their adulterous
hearts, which have turned away from
me, and by their eyes, which have
lusted after their idols.[u] They will loathe
themselves for the evil[v] they have done
and for all their detestable practices.[w]
10And they will know that I am the
LORD;[x] I did not threaten in vain to bring
this calamity on them.[y]
11" 'This is what the Sovereign LORD
says: Strike your hands together and
stamp your feet and cry out "Alas!"
because of all the wicked and detestable
practices of the house of Israel, for they
will fall by the sword, famine and
plague.[z] 12He that is far away will die of
the plague, and he that is near will fall
by the sword, and he that survives and
is spared will die of famine. So will I
spend my wrath[a] upon them.[b] 13And
they will know that I am the LORD, when
their people lie slain among their idols[c]
around their altars, on every high hill

6 [k]**2Ki 17:15;** Ne 9:17; Jer 11:10; **Eze 2:3;** 16:47–51; Zec 7:11
7 [l]**2Ki 21:9; 2Ch 33:9;** Jer 2:10–11; Eze 16:47
8 [m]**Jer 21:5,**13; 24:9; Eze 11:9; 15:7; Zec 14:2
9 [n]Da 9:12; **Mt 24:21**
10 [o]**Lev 26:29; La 2:20;** [p]**Lev 26:33; Ps 44:11; Jer 13:14;** Eze 12:14
11 [q]**Nu 14:21;** [r]**Ge 15:2;** [s]**Lev 15:31;** [t]Eze 7:20; 11:18; [u]2Ch 36:14; Eze 8:6; [v]**Job 27:22; Jer 16:18; La 2:17;** Eze 7:4,9; 8:18; 9:5
12 [w]ver 10; Jer 13:24; [x]**ver 2,** 17; **Ps 107:39; Jer 15:2; 21:9;** Eze 6:11–12; 7:15; 12:14; Am 9:4; Zec 13:8; Rev 6:8
13 [y]**2Ch 12:7; Job 20:23;** Eze 21:17; 24:13; [z]**Isa 1:24;** [a]**Isa 59:17;** Eze 16:42; 38:19; Hos 10:10; Zec 6:8
14 [b]**Lev 26:32;** Ne 2:17; Ps 74:3–10; 79:1–4; Isa 64:11; Eze 6:6; 22:4; Da 9:16; Mic 3:12
15 [c]**Isa 43:28;** [d]**Dt 28:46;** [e]**Dt 28:20; 1Ki 9:7; Jer 22:8–9;** 24:9; Eze 14:8; [f]**Jer 23:40**
16 [g]**Lev 26:26; Dt 32:24**
17 [h]Eze 14:15; [i]Eze 38:22; [j]ver 12; **Lev 26:25;** Eze 14:21; 28:23

Ch. 6

2 [a]**Eze 4:7;** [b]Eze 18:6; Mic 6:1; [c]ver 13
3 [d]Eze 36:4; [e]**Lev 26:30**
4 [f]**2Ch 14:5;** [g]Eze 9:6; 14:3; 20:16
5 [h]**Nu 19:16; Ps 53:5;** Jer 8:1–2; [i]ver 13; **Lev 26:30**
6 [j]**Ex 12:20;** [k]Hos 10:8; [l]Eze 30:13; Mic 1:7; Zec 13:2; [m]**Lev 26:30;** [n]**1Sa 5:4;** Isa 6:11; **Eze 5:14**
7 [o]Eze 9:7; [p]ver 10,13–14; Eze 11:10–12
8 [q]**Ps 68:20; Jer 44:28;** [r]**Ge 11:4; Ps 44:11;** Isa 6:13; **Jer 44:14;** Eze 7:16; 12:16; 14:22
9 [s]**Ps 137:6;** Zec 10:9; [t]**Isa 7:13; Jer 8:21;** [u]**Ex 22:20;** Eze 20:7,24; Mic 5:13; [v]**Ex 32:22;** [w]**Job 42:6;** Eze 20:43; 23:14–16; 36:31
10 [x]ver 7; [y]**Dt 28:52;** Jer 40:2
11 [z]**Jer 42:22;** Eze 21:14,17; 22:13; 25:6
12 [a]**Job 20:23;** [b]**Eze 5:12;** 7:15 13 [c]**Lev 26:30**

[a]7 Most Hebrew manuscripts; some Hebrew manuscripts and Syriac *You have*

and on all the mountaintops, under
every spreading tree and every leafy
oak[d]—places where they offered fra-
grant incense to all their idols.[e] 14And I
will stretch out my hand[f] against them
and make the land a desolate waste
from the desert to Diblah[a]—wherever
they live. Then they will know that I am
the LORD.[g]'"

The End Has Come

7 The word of the LORD came to me:
2"Son of man, this is what the
Sovereign LORD says to the land of
Israel: The end![a] The end has come upon
the four corners[b] of the land. 3The end is
now upon you and I will unleash my
anger against you. I will judge you
according to your conduct[c] and repay
you for all your detestable practices.[d] 4I
will not look on you with pity[e] or spare
you; I will surely repay you for your
conduct and the detestable practices
among you. Then you will know that I
am the LORD.[f]

5"This is what the Sovereign LORD
says: Disaster![g] An unheard-of[a] disaster
is coming. 6The end[h] has come! The end
has come! It has roused itself against
you. It has come! 7Doom has come upon
you—you who dwell in the land. The
time has come, the day[i] is near;[j] there is
panic, not joy, upon the mountains. 8I
am about to pour out my wrath[k] on you
and spend my anger against you; I will
judge you according to your conduct
and repay you for all your detestable
practices.[l] 9I will not look on you with
pity or spare you;[m] I will repay you in
accordance with your conduct and the
detestable practices among you.[n] Then
you will know that it is I the LORD who
strikes the blow.[o]

10"The day is here! It has come! Doom
has burst forth, the rod[p] has budded,
arrogance has blossomed! 11Violence[q]
has grown into[b] a rod to punish wicked-
ness; none of the people will be left,
none of that crowd—no wealth,
nothing of value.[r] 12The time has come,
the day has arrived. Let not the buyer[s]
rejoice nor the seller grieve, for wrath is
upon the whole crowd.[t] 13The seller will
not recover the land he has sold as long
as both of them live, for the vision con-
cerning the whole crowd will not be
reversed. Because of their sins, not one
of them will preserve his life.[u] 14Though
they blow the trumpet[v] and get every-
thing ready, no-one will go into battle,
for my wrath[w] is upon the whole crowd.

15"Outside is the sword, inside are
plague and famine; those in the country
will die by the sword, and those in the
city will be devoured by famine and
plague.[x] 16All who survive[y] and escape
will be in the mountains, moaning like
doves[z] of the valleys, each because of
his sins.[a] 17Every hand will go limp,[b]
and every knee will become as weak as
water.[c] 18They will put on sackcloth[d]
and be clothed with terror.[e] Their faces
will be covered with shame and their
heads will be shaved.[f] 19They will throw
their silver into the streets,[g] and their
gold will be an unclean thing. Their
silver and gold will not be able to save
them in the day of the LORD's wrath.[h]
They will not satisfy[i] their hunger or fill
their stomachs with it, for it has made
them stumble[j] into sin.[k] 20They were
proud of their beautiful jewellery and
used it to make[l] their detestable idols
and vile images.[m] Therefore I will turn
these into an unclean thing for them.[n]
21I will hand it all over as plunder[o] to
foreigners and as loot to the wicked of
the earth, and they will defile it.[p] 22I will
turn my face[q] away from them, and they
will desecrate my treasured place;
robbers will enter it and desecrate it.[r]

23"Prepare chains, because the land is
full of bloodshed[s] and the city is full of
violence.[t] 24I will bring the most wicked
of the nations to take possession of their
houses; I will put an end to the pride of
the mighty, and their sanctuaries[u] will
be desecrated.[v] 25When terror comes,
they will seek peace, but there will be
none.[w] 26Calamity upon calamity[x] will
come, and rumour upon rumour. They
will try to get a vision from the prophet;[y]
the teaching of the law by the priest will
be lost, as will the counsel of the elders.[z]
27The king will mourn, the prince will be
clothed with despair,[a] and the hands of
the people of the land will tremble. I will
deal with them according to their con-
duct,[b] and by their own standards I will
judge them. Then they will know that I
am the LORD.[c]"

13 [d]**Isa 1:29;** [e]**1Ki 14:23; Jer 2:20;** Eze 18:6; 20:28; Hos 4:13
14 [f]**Ex 7:5; Job 30:21; Jer 6:12;** 51:25; Eze 20:34; [g]Eze 12:19; 14:13

Ch. 7

2 [a]Am 8:2,10; [b]Rev 7:1; 20:8
3 [c]Eze 18:30; [d]**Ge 6:13**
4 [e]**Jer 13:14; Eze 5:11;** [f]**Eze 5:11;** 23:49
5 [g]**2Ki 21:12**
6 [h]Eze 39:8
7 [i]**Job 18:20; Isa 2:12;** Am 5:18–20; [j]Eze 12:23; 30:3; Zep 1:14; Mal 3:2
8 [k]Isa 42:25; Eze 9:8; 14:19; 22:22; Hos 5:10; Na 1:6; [l]Eze 20:8,21; 36:19
9 [m]**Jer 21:7; Eze 5:11;** [n]Eze 22:31; [o]Dt 32:35; **Ps 39:10; Isa 9:13**
10 [p]Ps 89:32; Isa 10:5
11 [q]**Ps 55:9; Isa 58:4;** [r]Jer 16:6; Zep 1:18
12 [s]**Isa 24:2;** [t]ver 7; Isa 5:13–14; Eze 30:3
13 [u]Lev 25:24–28
14 [v]**Job 39:24;** [w]Jer 25:38
15 [x]**Dt 32:25;** Jer 14:18; **La 1:20; Eze 5:12;** 33:27
16 [y]**Isa 10:20; Jer 41:16;** 42:17; [z]**Ge 8:8; Isa 59:11;** [a]**Ezr 9:15;** Jer 9:19; **Eze 6:8**
17 [b]**2Ki 19:26; Jer 47:3;** Eze 21:7; 22:14; [c]Da 5:6
18 [d]**Jer 4:8;** 48:37; 49:3; [e]**Ps 55:5;** [f]**Isa 15:2–3;** Eze 27:31; Am 8:10
19 [g]**La 4:1;** [h]Isa 42:25; Eze 13:5; 30:3; Joel 1:15; 2:1; Zep 1:7,18; 2:2; [i]Isa 55:2; [j]Eze 3:20; 14:3; Hos 4:5; [k]**Pr 11:4**
20 [l]**Jer 10:3;** [m]**Eze 5:11;** [n]**Isa 2:20;** 30:22; Eze 16:17
21 [o]**Nu 14:3;** [p]**2Ki 24:13**
22 [q]**Jer 2:27;** Eze 39:23–24; [r]Ps 74:7–8; Jer 19:13; **La 2:7**
23 [s]**2Ki 21:16; Isa 1:15; Eze 22:9;** [t]**Ge 6:11;** Eze 11:6
24 [u]La 2:7; Eze 24:21; [v]2Ch 7:20; Eze 28:7
25 [w]Jer 6:14; **8:11;** Eze 13:10,16
26 [x]**Dt 29:21; 31:17;** [y]**1Sa 3:1;** [z]Isa 47:11; **Jer 18:18;** Eze 20:1–3; Am 8:11; Mic 3:6
27 [a]**Ps 109:19;** Eze 26:16; [b]**Isa 3:11;** Eze 18:20; [c]**ver 4**

[a]14 Most Hebrew manuscripts; a few Hebrew manuscripts *Riblah*
[a]5 Most Hebrew manuscripts; some Hebrew manuscripts and Syriac *Disaster after*
[b]11 Or *The violent one has become*

Idolatry in the Temple

8 In the sixth year, in the sixth
month on the fifth day, while I was
sitting in my house and the elders[a] of
Judah were sitting before[b] me, the hand
of the Sovereign LORD came upon me
there.[c] 2I looked, and I saw a figure like
that of a man.[a] From what appeared to
be his waist down he was like fire, and
from there up his appearance was as
bright as glowing metal.[d] 3He stretched
out what looked like a hand[e] and took
me by the hair of my head. The Spirit
lifted me up[f] between earth and heaven
and in visions[g] of God he took me to
Jerusalem, to the entrance to the north
gate of the inner court,[h] where the idol
that provokes to jealousy[i] stood. 4And
there before me was the glory[j] of the
God of Israel, as in the vision I had seen
in the plain.[k]
5Then he said to me, "Son of man,
look towards the north." So I looked,
and in the entrance north of the gate of
the altar I saw this idol[l] of jealousy.
6And he said to me, "Son of man,
do you see what they are doing—the
utterly detestable[m] things the house of
Israel is doing here, things that will
drive me far from my sanctuary?[n] But
you will see things that are even more
detestable."
7Then he brought me to the entrance
to the court. I looked, and I saw a hole in
the wall. 8He said to me, "Son of man,
now dig into the wall." So I dug into the
wall and saw a doorway there.
9And he said to me, "Go in and see
the wicked and detestable things they
are doing here." 10So I went in and
looked, and I saw portrayed all over the
walls[o] all kinds of crawling things and
detestable[p] animals and all the idols of
the house of Israel.[q] 11In front of them
stood seventy elders[r] of the house of
Israel, and Jaazaniah son of Shaphan
was standing among them. Each had a
censer[s] in his hand, and a fragrant cloud
of incense[t] was rising.[u]
12He said to me, "Son of man, have
you seen what the elders of the house of
Israel are doing in the darkness,[v] each at
the shrine of his own idol? They say,
'The LORD does not see[w] us; the LORD
has forsaken the land.'" 13Again, he
said, "You will see them doing things
that are even more detestable."
14Then he brought me to the entrance
to the north gate of the house of the
LORD, and I saw women sitting there,
mourning for Tammuz.[x] 15He said to
me, "Do you see this, son of man? You
will see things that are even more de-
testable than this."
16He then brought me into the inner
court[y] of the house of the LORD, and
there at the entrance to the temple, be-
tween the portico and the altar,[z] were
about twenty-five men. With their
backs towards the temple of the LORD
and their faces towards the east, they
were bowing down to the sun[a] in the
east.[b]
17He said to me, "Have you seen this,
son of man? Is it a trivial matter for the
house of Judah to do the detestable
things[c] they are doing here? Must they
also fill the land with violence[d] and con-
tinually provoke me to anger?[e] Look at
them putting the branch to their nose!
18Therefore I will deal with them in
anger;[f] I will not look on them with pity[g]
or spare them. Although they shout in
my ears, I will not listen[h] to them."

Idolaters Killed

9 Then I heard him call out in a loud
voice, "Bring the guards of the city
here, each with a weapon in his hand."
2And I saw six men coming from the
direction of the upper gate, which faces
north, each with a deadly weapon in his
hand. With them was a man clothed in
linen[a] who had a writing kit at his side.
They came in and stood beside the
bronze altar.
3Now the glory[b] of the God of Israel
went up from above the cherubim,[c]
where it had been, and moved to the
threshold of the temple. Then the LORD
called to the man clothed in linen who
had the writing kit at his side 4and said
to him, "Go throughout the city of Jeru-
salem[d] and put a mark[e] on the foreheads
of those who grieve and lament[f] over all
the detestable things that are done in
it.[g]"
5As I listened, he said to the others,
"Follow him through the city and kill,
without showing pity[h] or compassion.[i]
6Slaughter[j] old men, young men and
maidens, women and children,[k] but do
not touch anyone who has the mark.[l]
Begin at my sanctuary." So they began
with the elders[m] who were in front of
the temple.[n]
7Then he said to them, "Defile the
temple and fill the courts with the slain.[o]

Ch. 8

1 [a]**2Ki 6:32**; Eze 14:1; [b]Eze 33:31; [c]Eze 1:1–3; 24:1; 40:1
2 [d]Eze 1:4, 26–27
3 [e]**Eze 2:9**; [f]**Eze 3:12**; 11:1; [g]**Ex 24:10**; [h]ver 16; [i]ver 5; Ex 20:5; Dt 32:16
4 [j]**Ex 24:16**; [k]Eze 3:22
5 [l]Ps 78:58; **Jer 4:1**; 32:34
6 [m]Ps 78:60; **Eze 5:11**; [n]Hos 5:6
10 [o]**Jdg 17:4–5**; Eze 23:14; [p]Jer 44:4; [q]Ex 20:4; Dt 4:15–18; **Jer 16:18**; Eze 11:12
11 [r]**Ex 3:16**; [s]**Lev 10:1**; Nu 16:17; [t]Nu 16:35; **Jer 44:5**; [u]Eze 11:1–2
12 [v]**Job 22:13**; [w]**2Ki 21:16**; Ps 10:11; **Isa 29:15**; Eze 9:9; Zep 1:12
14 [x]Eze 11:12
16 [y]ver 3; [z]Joel 2:17; [a]**Ge 1:16**; [b]Dt 4:19; **17:3**; **Job 31:28**; **Jer 2:27**; Eze 9:6; 11:1,12; 40:6; 43:1
17 [c]Eze 16:2; [d]**Ge 6:11**; [e]**Nu 11:33**; **1Ki 14:9**; Eze 16:26
18 [f]**Jer 44:6**; [g]**Jer 13:14**; **Eze 5:11**; 9:10; 24:14; [h]**1Sa 8:18**; **Isa 58:4**; **Jer 11:11**

Ch. 9

2 [a]**Lev 16:4**; Eze 10:2; Da 10:5; 12:6; Rev 15:6
3 [b]**1Sa 4:21**; Eze 10:4; [c]Eze 11:22
4 [d]Jer 25:29; [e]**Ge 4:15**; Ex 12:7; 2Co 1:22; **Rev 7:3**; [f]Ps 119:136; Jer 7:29; 13:17; Eze 21:6; Am 6:6; [g]Ps 119:53
5 [h]**Jer 13:14**; **Eze 5:11**; [i]**Ex 32:27**; Isa 13:18
6 [j]Jer 7:32; [k]**Jer 16:6**; [l]**Ge 4:15**; **Ex 12:7**; [m]Eze 8:11–13, 16; [n]**2Ch 36:17**; Jer 25:29; **Eze 6:4**; 1Pe 4:17
7 [o]Eze 6:7

[a]2 Or *saw a fiery figure*

"Go!" So they went out and began killing throughout the city. 8While they were killing and I was left alone, I fell face down,[p] crying out, "Ah, Sovereign LORD![q] Are you going to destroy the entire remnant of Israel in this outpouring of your wrath[r] on Jerusalem?[s]"

9He answered me, "The sin of the house of Israel and Judah is exceedingly great; the land is full of bloodshed and the city is full of injustice.[t] They say, 'The LORD has forsaken the land; the LORD does not see.'[u] 10So I will not look on them with pity[v] or spare them, but I will bring down on their own heads what they have done.[w]"

11Then the man in linen with the writing kit at his side brought back word, saying, "I have done as you commanded."

The Glory Departs From the Temple

10 I looked, and I saw the likeness of a throne[a] of sapphire[a][b] above the expanse[c] that was over the heads of the cherubim.[d] 2The LORD said to the man clothed in linen,[e] "Go in among the wheels[f] beneath the cherubim. Fill[g] your hands with burning coals[h] from among the cherubim and scatter them over the city." And as I watched, he went in.

3Now the cherubim were standing on the south side of the temple when the man went in, and a cloud filled the inner court. 4Then the glory of the LORD[i] rose from above the cherubim and moved to the threshold of the temple. The cloud filled the temple, and the court was full of the radiance of the glory of the LORD. 5The sound of the wings of the cherubim could be heard as far away as the outer court, like the voice[j] of God Almighty[b] when he speaks.[k]

6When the LORD commanded the man in linen, "Take fire from among the wheels,[l] from among the cherubim," the man went in and stood beside a wheel. 7Then one of the cherubim reached out his hand to the fire[m] that was among them. He took up some of it and put it into the hands of the man in linen, who took it and went out. 8(Under the wings of the cherubim could be seen what looked like the hands of a man.)[n]

9I looked, and I saw beside the cherubim four wheels, one beside each of the cherubim; the wheels sparkled like chrysolite.[o] 10As for their appearance, the four of them looked alike; each was like a wheel intersecting a wheel. 11As they moved, they would go in any one of the four directions the cherubim faced; the wheels did not turn about[c] as the cherubim went. The cherubim went in whatever direction the head faced, without turning as they went. 12Their entire bodies, including their backs, their hands and their wings, were completely full of eyes,[p] as were their four wheels.[q] 13I heard the wheels being called "the whirling wheels". 14Each of the cherubim[r] had four faces:[s] One face was that of a cherub, the second the face of a man, the third the face of a lion,[t] and the fourth the face of an eagle.[u]

15Then the cherubim rose upwards. These were the living creatures[v] I had seen by the Kebar River.[w] 16When the cherubim moved, the wheels beside them moved; and when the cherubim spread their wings to rise from the ground, the wheels did not leave their side. 17When the cherubim stood still, they also stood still; and when the cherubim rose, they rose with them, because the spirit of the living creatures was in them.[x]

18Then the glory[y] of the LORD departed from over the threshold of the temple and stopped above the cherubim.[z] 19While I watched, the cherubim spread their wings and rose from the ground, and as they went, the wheels went with them.[a] They stopped at the entrance to the east gate of the LORD's house, and the glory[b] of the God of Israel was above them.

20These were the living creatures I had seen beneath the God of Israel by the Kebar River,[c] and I realised that they were cherubim. 21Each had four faces[d] and four wings,[e] and under their wings were what looked like the hands of a man. 22Their faces had the same appearance as those I had seen by the Kebar River.[f] Each one went straight ahead.

Judgment on Israel's Leaders

11 Then the Spirit lifted me up and brought me to the gate of the house of the LORD that faces east. There at the entrance to the gate were twenty-five men, and I saw among them Jaazaniah son of Azzur and Pelatiah[a] son of Benaiah, leaders[b] of the people.[c] 2The LORD said to me, "Son of man, these are the men who are plotting evil[d] and giving wicked advice in this city.[e] 3They say, 'Will it not soon be time to build

8 [p]**Jos 7:6;** [q]**Eze 4:14;** [r]**Eze 7:8;** [s]Eze 11:13; Am 7:1–6
9 [t]**Ps 58:2;** Jer 12:1; Eze 22:29; Hab 1:4; [u]**Job 22:13; Eze 8:12;** 14:23
10 [v]**Jer 13:14; Eze 8:18;** [w]**Isa 22:5;** 65:6; Eze 11:21; 23:49

Ch. 10

1 [a]**Rev 4:2;** [b]**Ex 24:10;** [c]Eze 1:22; [d]**Ge 3:24**
2 [e]**Eze 9:2;** [f]**Eze 1:15;** [g]Rev 8:5; [h]**2Sa 22:9**
4 [i]**Ex 24:16;** Eze 9:3; 44:4
5 [j]**Job 40:9;** [k]**Eze 3:13**
6 [l]Da 7:9
7 [m]**Eze 5:4**
8 [n]Eze 1:8
9 [o]**Ex 28:20;** Rev 21:20
12 [p]Rev 4:6–8; [q]Eze 1:15–21
14 [r]1Ki 7:36; [s]Eze 1:6; [t]1Ki 7:29; [u]Eze 1:10; 41:19; Rev 4:7
15 [v]**Isa 6:2;** [w]**Ps 137:1**
17 [x]**Eze 3:13**
18 [y]**1Sa 4:21;** [z]**Ps 18:10**
19 [a]Eze 11:1,22; [b]Eze 43:4
20 [c]Eze 1:1
21 [d]Eze 41:18; [e]Eze 1:6
22 [f]Eze 1:1

Ch. 11

1 [a]ver 13; [b]Jer 5:5; [c]**Eze 8:16; 10:19;** 43:4–5
2 [d]**Isa 29:20;** Na 1:11; [e]Eze 8:11

[a]1 Or *lapis lazuli* [b]5 Hebrew *El-Shaddai*
[c]11 Or *aside*

houses?[a] This city is a cooking pot,[f] and we are the meat.'[g] 4Therefore prophesy[h] against them; prophesy, son of man."

5Then the Spirit of the LORD came upon me, and he told me to say: "This is what the LORD says: That is what you are saying, O house of Israel, but I know what is going through your mind.[i] 6You have killed many people in this city and filled its streets with the dead.[j]

7"Therefore this is what the Sovereign LORD says: The bodies you have thrown there are the meat and this city is the pot,[k] but I will drive you out of it.[l] 8You fear the sword,[m] and the sword is what I will bring against you, declares the Sovereign LORD.[n] 9I will drive you out of the city and hand you over[o] to foreigners and inflict punishment on you.[p] 10You will fall by the sword, and I will execute judgment on you at the borders of Israel.[q] Then you will know that I am the LORD. 11This city will not be a pot[r] for you, nor will you be the meat in it; I will execute judgment on you at the borders of Israel. 12And you will know that I am the LORD,[s] for you have not followed my decrees[t] or kept my laws but have conformed to the standards of the nations around you.[u]"

13Now as I was prophesying, Pelatiah[v] son of Benaiah died. Then I fell face down and cried out in a loud voice, "Ah, Sovereign LORD! Will you completely destroy the remnant of Israel?[w]"

14The word of the LORD came to me: 15"Son of man, your brothers—your brothers who are your blood-relatives[b] and the whole house of Israel—are those of whom the people of Jerusalem have said, 'They are[c] far away from the LORD; this land was given to us as our possession.'[x]

Promised Return of Israel

16"Therefore say: 'This is what the Sovereign LORD says: Although I sent them far away among the nations and scattered them among the countries, yet for a little while I have been a sanctuary[y] for them in the countries where they have gone.'

17"Therefore say: 'This is what the Sovereign LORD says: I will gather you from the nations and bring you back from the countries where you have been scattered, and I will give you back the land of Israel again.'[z]

18"They will return to it and remove all its vile images[a] and detestable idols.[b] 19I will give them an undivided heart[c] and put a new spirit in them; I will remove from them their heart of stone[d] and give them a heart of flesh.[e] 20Then they will follow my decrees and be careful to keep my laws.[f] They will be my people,[g] and I will be their God.[h] 21But as for those whose hearts are devoted to their vile images and detestable idols,[i] I will bring down on their own heads what they have done, declares the Sovereign LORD.[j]"

22Then the cherubim, with the wheels beside them, spread their wings, and the glory[k] of the God of Israel was above them.[l] 23The glory[m] of the LORD went up from within the city and stopped above the mountain[n] east of it. 24The Spirit[o] lifted me up and brought me to the exiles in Babylonia[d] in the vision[p] given by the Spirit of God.

Then the vision I had seen went up from me, 25and I told the exiles everything the LORD had shown me.[q]

The Exile Symbolised

12 The word of the LORD came to me: 2"Son of man, you are living among a rebellious people.[a] They have eyes to see but do not see and ears to hear but do not hear, for they are a rebellious people.[b]

3"Therefore, son of man, pack your belongings for exile and in the daytime, as they watch, set out and go from where you are to another place. Perhaps[c] they will understand,[d] though they are a rebellious house.[e] 4During the daytime, while they watch, bring out your belongings packed for exile. Then in the evening, while they are watching, go out like those who go into exile.[f] 5While they watch, dig through the wall[g] and take your belongings out through it. 6Put them on your shoulder as they are watching and carry them out at dusk. Cover your face so that you cannot see the land, for I have made you a sign[h] to the house of Israel."

7So I did as I was commanded.[i] During the day I brought out my things packed for exile. Then in the evening I dug through the wall with my hands. I took my belongings out at dusk, carrying them on my shoulders while they watched.

8In the morning the word of the LORD came to me: 9"Son of man, did not that

---

3 [f]Jer 1:13; Eze 24:3; [g]ver 7, 11; Eze 12:22, 27; Mic 3:3
4 [h]**Eze 3:4**,17
5 [i]**Ps 26:2; Jer 17:10**
6 [j]**Eze 7:23**; 22:6
7 [k]Jer 1:13; [l]ver 3; Eze 24:3–13; Mic 3:2–3
8 [m]**Lev 26:25; Jer 42:16**; [n]**Pr 10:24**; Isa 66:4
9 [o]Ps 106:41; [p]Dt 28:36; **Eze 5:8**
10 [q]2Ki 14:25
11 [r]ver 3; Eze 24:6
12 [s]**Eze 6:7**; [t]**Lev 18:4**; Eze 18:9; [u]Eze 8:10
13 [v]ver 1; [w]**Eze 9:8**; Am 7:2
15 [x]Eze 33:24
16 [y]Ps 31:20; 90:1; 91:9; **Isa 4:6**
17 [z]**Ne 1:9; Jer 3:18**; 24:5–6; **31:16**; Eze 20:41; 28:25; 34:13; 36:28
18 [a]**Eze 5:11**; [b]Eze 37:23
19 [c]**2Ch 30:12; Ps 86:11**; [d]Zec 7:12; Ro 2:5; [e]Eze 18:31; **2Co 3:3**
20 [f]**Ps 1:2**; [g]**Jer 11:4**; 32:38; [h]**Ex 6:7**; Eze 14:11; 34:30; 36:26–28; Hos 1:9; Zec 8:8; Heb 8:10
21 [i]Jer 16:18; [j]Jer 16:11; **Eze 9:10**; 16:43
22 [k]**Ex 24:16**; [l]Eze 9:3; **10:19**
23 [m]Eze 1:28; **10:4**; [n]Zec 14:4
24 [o]Eze 37:1; 43:5; [p]2Co 12:2–4
25 [q]**Eze 3:4**,11

Ch. 12

2 [a]Ps 78:40; **Jer 42:21**; [b]**Isa 6:10; Mt 13:15**; Mk 4:12; 8:18
3 [c]**Jer 36:3**; [d]Jer 26:3; [e]ver 11; **Eze 3:27**; 2Ti 2:25–26
4 [f]ver 12; 2Ki 25:4; **Jer 39:4**
5 [g]Jer 52:7; Am 4:3
6 [h]ver 12; **Isa 8:18; 20:3**
7 [i]Eze 24:18; 37:10

---

[a]3 Or *This is not the time to build houses.*
[b]15 Or *are in exile with you* (see Septuagint and Syriac)
[c]15 Or *those to whom the people of Jerusalem have said, 'Stay*
[d]24 Or *Chaldea*

rebellious house of Israel ask you,
'What are you doing?'[j]
10"Say to them, 'This is what the
Sovereign LORD says: This oracle con-
cerns the prince in Jerusalem and the
whole house of Israel who are there.'
11Say to them, 'I am a sign[k] to you.'
"As I have done, so it will be done
to them. They will go into exile as
captives.[l]
12"The prince among them will put
his things on his shoulder at dusk[m] and
leave, and a hole will be dug in the wall
for him to go through. He will cover his
face so that he cannot see the land.[n] 13I
will spread my net[o] for him, and he will
be caught in my snare;[p] I will bring him
to Babylonia, the land of the Chal-
deans,[q] but he will not see[r] it, and there
he will die.[s] 14I will scatter to the winds
all those around him—his staff and all
his troops—and I will pursue them with
drawn sword.[t]
15"They will know that I am the LORD,
when I disperse them among the
nations[u] and scatter them through the
countries. 16But I will spare a few of
them from the sword, famine and
plague, so that in the nations where
they go they may acknowledge all their
detestable practices. Then they will
know that I am the LORD.[v]"
17The word of the LORD came to me:
18"Son of man, tremble as you eat your
food,[w] and shudder in fear as you drink
your water. 19Say to the people of the
land: 'This is what the Sovereign LORD
says about those living in Jerusalem and
in the land of Israel: They will eat their
food in anxiety and drink their water in
despair, for their land will be stripped of
everything[x] in it because of the violence
of all who live there.[y] 20The inhabited
towns will be laid waste and the land
will be desolate. Then you will know
that I am the LORD.[z]' "
21The word of the LORD came to me:
22"Son of man, what is this proverb[a] you
have in the land of Israel: 'The days go
by and every vision comes to nothing'?[b]
23Say to them, 'This is what the
Sovereign LORD says: I am going to put
an end to this proverb, and they will no
longer quote it in Israel.' Say to them,
'The days are near[c] when every vision
will be fulfilled.[d] 24For there will be no
more false visions or flattering divina-
tions[e] among the people of Israel. 25But I
the LORD will speak what I will, and it
shall be fulfilled without delay.[f] For in
your days, you rebellious house, I will
fulfil[g] whatever I say, declares the
Sovereign LORD.[h]' "
26The word of the LORD came to me:
27"Son of man, the house of Israel is
saying, 'The vision he sees is for many
years from now, and he prophesies
about the distant future.'[i]
28"Therefore say to them, 'This is
what the Sovereign LORD says: None of
my words will be delayed any longer;
whatever I say will be fulfilled, declares
the Sovereign LORD.' "

False Prophets Condemned

13 The word of the LORD came to
me: 2"Son of man, prophesy
against the prophets[a] of Israel who are
now prophesying. Say to those who
prophesy out of their own imagination:[b]
'Hear the word of the LORD![c] 3This is
what the Sovereign LORD says: Woe to
the foolish[a] prophets[d] who follow their
own spirit and have seen nothing![e]
4Your prophets, O Israel, are like jackals
among ruins. 5You have not gone up to
the breaks in the wall to repair[f] it for the
house of Israel so that it will stand firm
in the battle on the day of the LORD.[g]
6Their visions are false[h] and their divi-
nations a lie. They say, "The LORD
declares", when the LORD has not sent[i]
them; yet they expect their words to be
fulfilled.[j] 7Have you not seen false
visions[k] and uttered lying divinations
when you say, "The LORD declares",
though I have not spoken?
8" 'Therefore this is what the
Sovereign LORD says: Because of your
false words and lying visions, I am
against you,[l] declares the Sovereign
LORD. 9My hand will be against the
prophets who see false visions and utter
lying[m] divinations. They will not belong
to the council of my people or be listed
in the records[n] of the house of Israel, nor
will they enter the land of Israel. Then
you will know that I am the Sovereign
LORD.[o]
10" 'Because they lead my people
astray,[p] saying, "Peace",[q] when there is
no peace, and because, when a flimsy
wall is built, they cover it with
whitewash,[r] 11therefore tell those who
cover it with whitewash that it is going
to fall. Rain will come in torrents, and I
will send hailstones[s] hurtling down,[t]
and violent winds will burst forth.[u]
12When the wall collapses, will people
not ask you, "Where is the whitewash
you covered it with?"

9 [j]Eze 17:12; 20:49; 24:19
11 [k]Isa 8:18; Zec 3:8; [l]**2Ki 25:7; Jer 15:2**; 52:15
12 [m]**Jer 39:4**; [n]Jer 52:7
13 [o]Eze 17:20; 19:8; 32:3; Hos 7:12; [p]**Isa 24:17–18**; [q]Eze 1:3; [r]**Jer 39:7**; [s]**Jer 24:8; 52:11; La 4:20**; Eze 17:16
14 [t]**2Ki 25:5; Jer 21:7; Eze 5:10**,12; 17:21
15 [u]**Lev 26:33**
16 [v]**Jer 22:8–9**; Eze 6:8–10; 14:22; 36:20
18 [w]La 5:9
19 [x]Jer 10:22; **Eze 6:6–14**; Mic 7:13; Zec 7:14; [y]**Eze 4:16**; 23:33
20 [z]Isa 7:23–24; **Jer 4:7; 25:9**
22 [a]**Ps 49:4**; [b]**Isa 5:19**; Eze 11:3; Am 6:3; 2Pe 3:4
23 [c]**Eze 7:7**; [d]**Ps 37:13**; Eze 18:3; Joel 2:1; Zep 1:14
24 [e]Jer 14:14; Eze 13:23; Mic 3:6; Zec 13:2–4
25 [f]Hab 2:3; [g]**Nu 11:23**; Eze 13:6; [h]Nu 14:28–34; **Isa 14:24; 55:11**; Jer 16:9; Hab 1:5
27 [i]**Eze 11:3**; Da 10:14; Mt 24:48–50; 2Pe 3:4

Ch. 13

2 [a]**Isa 9:15**; [b]Jer 28:15; [c]ver 17; **Jer 23:16; 37:19**; Eze 22:28
3 [d]**La 2:14**; Hos 9:7; [e]**Jer 23:25–32**
5 [f]Isa 58:12; Eze 22:30; [g]**Eze 7:19**; 30:3
6 [h]**Jer 5:1**; 23:16; [i]**Jer 14:14**; [j]**Jer 28:15; 29:9**; Eze 12:24–25; 22:28
7 [k]**Isa 30:10**
8 [l]**Jer 21:13**
9 [m]**Dt 13:3**; [n]**Ex 32:32; Jer 17:13**; [o]**Ex 6:2**; Jer 20:3–6; Eze 20:38
10 [p]**Jer 23:13; 50:6**; [q]**Jer 4:10**; [r]**Eze 7:25**; 22:28
11 [s]**Jos 10:11**; [t]**Job 38:23**; [u]Ps 11:6; Eze 38:22

[a]3 Or *wicked*

13"'Therefore this is what the Sovereign LORD says: In my wrath I will unleash a violent wind, and in my anger hailstones[v] and torrents of rain[w] will fall with destructive fury.[x] 14I will tear down the wall[y] you have covered with whitewash and will level it to the ground so that its foundation[z] will be laid bare. When it[b] falls,[a] you will be destroyed in it; and you will know that I am the LORD. 15So I will spend my wrath against the wall and against those who covered it with whitewash. I will say to you, "The wall is gone and so are those who whitewashed it, 16those prophets of Israel who prophesied to Jerusalem and saw visions of peace for her when there was no peace, declares the Sovereign LORD.[b]"'

17"Now, son of man, set your face[c] against the daughters[d] of your people who prophesy out of their own imagination. Prophesy against them[e] 18and say, 'This is what the Sovereign LORD says: Woe to the women who sew magic charms on all their wrists and make veils of various lengths for their heads in order to ensnare people. Will you ensnare the lives of my people but preserve your own? 19You have profaned[f] me among my people for a few handfuls of barley and scraps of bread.[g] By lying to my people, who listen to lies, you have killed those who should not have died and have spared those who should not live.[h]

20"'Therefore this is what the Sovereign LORD says: I am against your magic charms with which you ensnare people like birds and I will tear them from your arms; I will set free the people that you ensnare like birds.[i] 21I will tear off your veils and save my people from your hands, and they will no longer fall prey to your power. Then you will know that I am the LORD.[j] 22Because you disheartened the righteous with your lies,[k] when I had brought them no grief, and because you encouraged the wicked not to turn from their evil ways and so save their lives,[l] 23therefore you will no longer see false visions[m] or practise divination.[n] I will save[o] my people from your hands. And then you will know that I am the LORD.[p]'"

Idolaters Condemned

14 Some of the elders of Israel came to me and sat down in front of me.[a] 2Then the word of the LORD came to me: 3"Son of man, these men have set up idols in their hearts[b] and put wicked stumbling-blocks[c] before their faces. Should I let them enquire of me at all?[d] 4Therefore speak to them and tell them, 'This is what the Sovereign LORD says: When any Israelite sets up idols in his heart and puts a wicked stumbling-block before his face and then goes to a prophet, I the LORD will answer him myself in keeping with his great idolatry. 5I will do this to recapture the hearts of the people of Israel, who have all deserted[e] me for their idols.'[f]

6"Therefore say to the house of Israel, 'This is what the Sovereign LORD says: Repent![g] Turn from your idols and renounce all your detestable practices![h]

7"'When any Israelite or any alien[i] living in Israel separates himself from me and sets up idols in his heart and puts a wicked stumbling-block[j] before his face and then goes to a prophet to enquire[k] of me, I the LORD will answer him myself. 8I will set my face against[l] that man and make him an example[m] and a byword.[n] I will cut him off from my people. Then you will know that I am the LORD.[o]

9"'And if the prophet[p] is enticed[q] to utter a prophecy, I the LORD have enticed that prophet, and I will stretch out my hand against him and destroy him from among my people Israel.[r] 10They will bear their guilt—the prophet will be as guilty as the one who consults him. 11Then the people of Israel will no longer stray[s] from me, nor will they defile themselves any more with all their sins. They will be my people,[t] and I will be their God, declares the Sovereign LORD.[u]'"

Judgment Inescapable

12The word of the LORD came to me: 13"Son of man, if a country sins[v] against me by being unfaithful and I stretch out my hand against it to cut off its food supply[w] and send famine upon it and kill its men and their animals,[x] 14even if these three men—Noah,[y] Daniel[a][z] and Job[a]—were in it, they could save only themselves by their righteousness,[b] declares the Sovereign LORD.

15"Or if I send wild beasts[c] through that country and they leave it childless and it becomes desolate so that no-one can pass through it because of the beasts,[d] 16as surely as I live, declares the

13 [v]**Jos 10:11**; Rev 11:19; 16:21; [w]Job 14:19; [x]**Ex 9:25; Job 38:23**; Isa 30:30
14 [y]**Isa 22:5**; [z]Mic 1:6; [a]Jer 6:15
16 [b]**Isa 57:21**; Jer 6:14; **Eze 7:25**
17 [c]**Eze 4:7**; 25:2; 28:21; [d]**Ex 15:20**; Rev 2:20; [e]**ver 2**
19 [f]Jer 44:26; Eze 20:39; 22:26; 36:20; 39:7; [g]**Isa 56:11**; [h]Pr 28:21; Mic 3:11
20 [i]Ps 124:7
21 [j]Ps 91:3
22 [k]**Isa 9:15**; [l]Jer 23:14; Eze 18:21; 33:14-16
23 [m]Ne 6:12; [n]**Eze 12:24**; [o]**Ps 72:14**; [p]Mic 3:6

Ch. 14

1 [a]**Eze 8:1**; 20:1
3 [b]**Eze 6:4**; [c]**ver 7; Eze 7:19**; [d]Isa 1:15; Eze 20:31
5 [e]**Dt 32:15**; Eze 16:45; Hos 5:7; Zec 11:8; [f]Jer 2:11
6 [g]Ne 1:9; **Jer 3:12; 35:15**; [h]**Isa 2:20; 30:22**
7 [i]Ex 12:48; 20:10; [j]ver 3; **Isa 8:14**; Hos 4:5; 5:5; [k]**Ge 25:22**
8 [l]Eze 15:7; [m]**Nu 16:38**; [n]**Ps 102:8; Eze 5:15**; [o]**Jer 42:20**
9 [p]**Jer 14:15**; [q]Isa 63:17; Jer 4:10; [r]1Ki 22:23; **2Ch 18:22**; Zec 13:3
11 [s]Eze 48:11; [t]**Isa 51:16**; [u]**Eze 11:19-20**; 37:23
13 [v]**Pr 13:21**; [w]**Lev 26:26**; [x]**Eze 5:16**; 6:14; 15:8
14 [y]Ge 6:8; [z]ver 20; Eze 28:3; Da 1:6; 6:13; [a]**Job 1:1**; [b]**Ge 6:9; Job 42:9**; Jer 15:1; **Eze 3:19**; 18:20
15 [c]Eze 5:17; [d]**Lev 26:22**

[b]14 Or *the city*

[a]14 Or *Danel*; the Hebrew spelling may suggest a person other than the prophet Daniel; also in verse 20.

Sovereign LORD, even if these three men were in it, they could not save their own sons or daughters. They alone would be saved, but the land would be desolate.[e]

17"Or if I bring a sword[f] against that country and say, 'Let the sword pass throughout the land,' and I kill its men and their animals,[g] 18as surely as I live, declares the Sovereign LORD, even if these three men were in it, they could not save their own sons or daughters. They alone would be saved.

19"Or if I send a plague into that land and pour out my wrath[h] upon it through bloodshed,[i] killing its men and their animals,[j] 20as surely as I live, declares the Sovereign LORD, even if Noah, Daniel and Job were in it, they could save neither son nor daughter. They would save only themselves by their righteousness.[k]

21"For this is what the Sovereign LORD says: How much worse will it be when I send against Jerusalem my four dreadful judgments[l]—sword[m] and famine[n] and wild beasts and plague[o]—to kill its men and their animals![p] 22Yet there will be some survivors[q]—sons and daughters who will be brought out of it.[r] They will come to you, and when you see their conduct[s] and their actions, you will be consoled[t] regarding the disaster I have brought upon Jerusalem—every disaster I have brought upon it. 23You will be consoled when you see their conduct and their actions, for you will know that I have done nothing in it without cause, declares the Sovereign LORD.[u]"

Jerusalem, a Useless Vine

15 The word of the LORD came to me: 2"Son of man, how is the wood of a vine[a] better than that of a branch on any of the trees in the forest? 3Is wood ever taken from it to make anything useful?[b] Do they make pegs[c] from it to hang things on? 4And after it is thrown on the fire as fuel and the fire burns both ends and chars the middle, is it then useful for anything?[d] 5If it was not useful for anything when it was whole, how much less can it be made into something useful when the fire has burned it and it is charred?

6"Therefore this is what the Sovereign LORD says: As I have given the wood of the vine among the trees of the forest as fuel for the fire, so will I treat the people living in Jerusalem. 7I will set my face against[e] them. Although they have come out of the fire[f][g], the fire will yet consume them. And when I set my face against them, you will know that I am the LORD.[h] 8I will make the land desolate[i] because they have been unfaithful,[j] declares the Sovereign LORD."

An Allegory of Unfaithful Jerusalem

16 The word of the LORD came to me: 2"Son of man, confront[a] Jerusalem with her detestable practices[b] 3and say, 'This is what the Sovereign LORD says to Jerusalem: Your ancestry[c] and birth were in the land of the Canaanites; your father[d] was an Amorite[e] and your mother a Hittite.[f] 4On the day you were born[g] your cord was not cut, nor were you washed with water to make you clean, nor were you rubbed with salt or wrapped in cloths. 5No-one looked on you with pity or had compassion enough to do any of these things for you. Rather, you were thrown out into the open field, for on the day you were born you were despised.

6" 'Then I passed by and saw you kicking about in your blood, and as you lay there in your blood I said to you, "Live!"[a][h] 7I made you grow[i] like a plant of the field. You grew up and developed and became the most beautiful of jewels.[b] Your breasts were formed and your hair grew, you who were naked and bare.[j]

8" 'Later I passed by, and when I looked at you and saw that you were old enough for love, I spread the corner of my garment[k] over you and covered your nakedness. I gave you my solemn oath and entered into a covenant[l] with you, declares the Sovereign LORD, and you became mine.[m]

9" 'I bathed[c] you with water and washed[n] the blood from you and put ointments on you. 10I clothed you with an embroidered[o] dress and put leather sandals on you. I dressed you in fine linen[p] and covered you with costly garments.[q] 11I adorned you with jewellery:[r] I put bracelets[s] on your arms and a necklace[t] around your neck, 12and I put a ring on your nose,[u] ear-rings[v] on your ears and a beautiful crown[w] on your head.[x] 13So you were adorned with gold and silver; your clothes[y] were of fine linen and costly fabric and embroidered cloth. Your food was fine flour, honey

16 [e]Ge 19:29; Eze 18:20
17 [f]Lev 26:25; Jer 25:27; 42:16; [g]Eze 25:13; Zep 1:3
19 [h]Eze 7:8; [i]Isa 34:3; [j]Jer 14:12; Eze 38:22
20 [k]ver 14
21 [l]Nu 33:4; [m]Isa 31:8; 34:6; 66:16; Eze 21:3,19; [n]2Sa 24:13; [o]Jer 14:12; 27:8; [p]Jer 15:3; Eze 5:17; 33:27; Am 4:6–10; Rev 6:8
22 [q]Jer 41:16; [r]Eze 12:16; [s]Eze 20:43; [t]Eze 31:16; 32:31
23 [u]Jer 22:8–9; Eze 8:6–18; 9:9

Ch. 15

2 [a]Ps 80:8–16; Isa 5:1–7; 27:2–6; Jer 2:21; Hos 10:1; Jn 15:2
3 [b]Jer 13:10; [c]Isa 22:23
4 [d]Eze 17:3–10; 19:14; Jn 15:6
7 [e]Lev 26:17; Ps 34:16; Eze 14:8; [f]Eze 5:2; [g]Eze 5:4; [h]Isa 24:18; Am 9:1–4
8 [i]Eze 14:13; [j]Eze 17:20; 18:24

Ch. 16

2 [a]Isa 57:12; Eze 23:36; [b]Eze 8:17; 20:4; 22:2
3 [c]Ge 11:25–29; Eze 21:30; [d]Ge 12:18; [e]Ge 15:16; [f]ver 45; Ge 10:15; Dt 7:1; Jos 24:14–15
4 [g]Hos 2:3
6 [h]ver 22; Ex 19:4; Eze 18:23,32
7 [i]Dt 1:10; [j]Ex 1:7
8 [k]Ru 3:9; [l]ver 59; Jer 11:10; Mal 2:14; [m]Jer 2:2; Hos 2:7, 19–20
9 [n]Ru 3:3
10 [o]Ex 26:36; Isa 19:9; [p]Eze 27:16; [q]ver 18; Isa 3:23
11 [r]Jer 4:30; Eze 23:40; [s]Isa 3:19; Eze 23:42; [t]Ge 41:42; Ps 73:6
12 [u]Isa 3:21; [v]Ge 35:4; [w]Isa 28:5; Jer 13:18; [x]Pr 1:9; Isa 3:19 13 [y]Est 5:1

[a]6 A few Hebrew manuscripts, Septuagint and Syriac; most Hebrew manuscripts *"Live!" And as you lay there in your blood I said to you, "Live!"*
[b]7 Or *became mature* [c]9 Or *I had bathed*

and olive oil.[z] You became very beautiful and rose to be a queen.[a] 14And your fame[b] spread among the nations on account of your beauty,[c] because the splendour I had given you made your beauty perfect, declares the Sovereign LORD.[d]

15" 'But you trusted in your beauty and used your fame to become a prostitute. You lavished your favours on anyone who passed by[e] and your beauty became his.[d][f] 16You took some of your garments to make gaudy high places,[g] where you carried on your prostitution.[h] Such things should not happen, nor should they ever occur. 17You also took the fine jewellery I gave you, the jewellery made of my gold and silver, and you made for yourself male idols and engaged in prostitution with them.[i] 18And you took your embroidered clothes to put on them, and you offered my oil and incense[j] before them. 19Also the food I provided for you—the fine flour, olive oil and honey I gave you to eat—you offered as fragrant incense before them. That is what happened, declares the Sovereign LORD.[k]

20" 'And you took your sons and daughters[l] whom you bore to me[m] and sacrificed them as food to the idols. Was your prostitution not enough?[n] 21You slaughtered my children and sacrificed them[e] to the idols.[o] 22In all your detestable practices and your prostitution you did not remember the days of your youth,[p] when you were naked and bare,[q] kicking about in your blood.[r]

23" 'Woe![s] Woe to you, declares the Sovereign LORD. In addition to all your other wickedness, 24you built a mound for yourself and made a lofty shrine[t] in every public square.[u] 25At the head of every street[v] you built your lofty shrines and degraded your beauty, offering your body with increasing promiscuity to anyone who passed by.[w] 26You engaged in prostitution[x] with the Egyptians,[y] your lustful neighbours, and provoked[z] me to anger with your increasing promiscuity.[a] 27So I stretched out my hand[b] against you and reduced your territory; I gave you over[c] to the greed of your enemies, the daughters of the Philistines,[d] who were shocked by your lewd conduct. 28You engaged in prostitution with the Assyrians[e] too, because you were insatiable; and even after that, you still were not satisfied.[f] 29Then you increased your promiscuity to include Babylonia,[f][g] a land of merchants, but even with this you were not satisfied.[h]

30" 'How weak-willed you are, declares the Sovereign LORD, when you do all these things, acting like a brazen prostitute![i] 31When you built your mounds at the head of every street and made your lofty shrines[j] in every public square, you were unlike a prostitute, because you scorned payment.

32" 'You adulterous wife! You prefer strangers to your own husband! 33Every prostitute receives a fee,[k] but you give gifts[l] to all your lovers, bribing them to come to you from everywhere for your illicit favours.[m] 34So in your prostitution you are the opposite of others; no-one runs after you for your favours. You are the very opposite, for you give payment and none is given to you.

35" 'Therefore, you prostitute, hear the word of the LORD! 36This is what the Sovereign LORD says: Because you poured out your wealth[g] and exposed your nakedness in your promiscuity with your lovers, and because of all your detestable idols, and because you gave them your children's blood,[n] 37therefore I am going to gather all your lovers, with whom you found pleasure, those you loved as well as those you hated. I will gather them against you from all around and will strip[o] you in front of them, and they will see all your nakedness.[p] 38I will sentence you to the punishment of women who commit adultery and who shed blood;[q] I will bring upon you the blood vengeance of my wrath and jealous anger.[r] 39Then I will hand you over[s] to your lovers, and they will tear down your mounds and destroy your lofty shrines. They will strip you of your clothes and take your fine jewellery and leave you naked and bare.[t] 40They will bring a mob against you, who will stone[u] you and hack you to pieces with their swords. 41They will burn down[v] your houses and inflict punishment on you in the sight of many women.[w] I will put a stop[x] to your prostitution, and you will no longer pay your lovers. 42Then my wrath against you will subside and my jealous anger will turn away from you; I will be calm and no longer angry.[y]

43" 'Because you did not remember[z] the days of your youth but enraged me

13 [z]1Sa 10:1; [a]Dt 32:13–14; **1Ki 4:21;** Est 2:9,17
14 [b]1Ki 10:24; [c]**Est 1:11; Ps 48:2; La 2:15;** [d]**Eze 5:5**
15 [e]ver 25; [f]**Isa 57:8; Jer 2:20;** Eze 23:3; 27:3
16 [g]**Isa 57:7;** [h]**2Ki 23:7**
17 [i]**Eze 7:20;** Hos 2:13
18 [j]**Jer 44:5**
19 [k]Hos 2:8
20 [l]**Jer 7:31;** [m]Ex 13:2; [n]Ps 106:37–38; **Isa 57:5;** Eze 23:37
21 [o]**2Ki 17:17; Jer 19:5**
22 [p]**Ps 25:7; 88:15;** Jer 2:2; Hos 2:15; 11:1; [q]Hos 2:3; [r]ver 6
23 [s]Eze 24:6
24 [t]ver 31; Isa 57:7; [u]Ps 78:58; **Jer 2:20;** 3:2; **44:21;** Eze 20:28
25 [v]**Jer 3:2;** [w]ver 15; **Pr 9:14**
26 [x]**Isa 23:17;** [y]**Jer 3:1;** [z]**1Ki 14:9; Eze 8:17;** [a]**Isa 57:8;** Jer 11:15; Eze 20:8; 23:19–21
27 [b]Eze 20:33; 25:13; [c]**Jer 34:20;** [d]**2Ch 28:18**
28 [e]**2Ki 16:7;** [f]Isa 57:8
29 [g]**Jer 3:1;** Eze 23:14–17; [h]Na 3:4
30 [i]**Jer 3:3**
31 [j]**ver 24**
33 [k]**Ge 30:15;** [l]Isa 30:6; 57:9; [m]Hos 8:9–10
36 [n]**Jer 19:5;** Eze 23:10
37 [o]Hos 2:3; [p]**Isa 47:3; Jer 13:22;** Eze 23:22; Hos 2:10; 8:10; Rev 17:16
38 [q]**Ge 38:24;** [r]**Lev 20:10;** Ps 79:3,5; Eze 23:25; Zep 1:17
39 [s]**2Ki 18:11;** [t]Eze 21:31; Hos 2:3
40 [u]Jn 8:5,7
41 [v]**Dt 13:16; Jer 19:13;** [w]Eze 23:10; [x]Eze 22:15; 23:27,48
42 [y]2Sa 24:25; Isa 40:1–2; 54:9; **Eze 5:13;** 39:29
43 [z]**Ex 15:24;** Ps 78:42

[d]*15* Most Hebrew manuscripts; one Hebrew manuscript (see some Septuagint manuscripts) *by. Such a thing should not happen*
[e]*21* Or *and made them pass through* ⌞*the fire*⌟
[f]*29* Or *Chaldea* [g]*36* Or *lust*

with all these things, I will surely bring down[a] on your head what you have done, declares the Sovereign LORD. Did you not add lewdness to all your other detestable practices?[b]

44"'Everyone who quotes proverbs[c] will quote this proverb about you: "Like mother, like daughter." 45You are a true daughter of your mother, who despised[d] her husband[e] and her children; and you are a true sister of your sisters, who despised their husbands and their children. Your mother was a Hittite and your father an Amorite.[f] 46Your older sister[g] was Samaria, who lived to the north of you with her daughters; and your younger sister, who lived to the south of you with her daughters, was Sodom.[h] 47You not only walked in their ways and copied their detestable practices, but in all your ways you soon became more depraved than they.[i] 48As surely as I live, declares the Sovereign[j] LORD, your sister Sodom[k] and her daughters never did what you and your daughters have done.[l]

49"'Now this was the sin of your sister Sodom:[m] She and her daughters were arrogant,[n] overfed and unconcerned;[o] they did not help the poor and needy.[p] 50They were haughty[q] and did detestable things before me. Therefore I did away with them as you have seen.[r] 51Samaria did not commit half the sins you did. You have done more detestable things than they, and have made your sisters seem righteous by all these things you have done.[s] 52Bear your disgrace, for you have furnished some justification for your sisters. Because your sins were more vile than theirs, they appear more righteous[t] than you. So then, be ashamed and bear[u] your disgrace, for you have made your sisters appear righteous.

53"'However, I will restore[v] the fortunes of Sodom and her daughters and of Samaria and her daughters, and your fortunes along with them,[w] 54so that you may bear your disgrace[x] and be ashamed of all you have done in giving them comfort. 55And your sisters, Sodom with her daughters and Samaria with her daughters, will return to what they were before; and you and your daughters will return to what you were before.[y] 56You would not even mention your sister Sodom in the day of your pride, 57before your wickedness was uncovered. Even so, you are now scorned[z] by the daughters of Edom[h][a] and all her neighbours and the daughters of the Philistines—all those around you who despise you. 58You will bear the consequences of your lewdness and your detestable practices, declares the LORD.[b]

59"'This is what the Sovereign LORD says: I will deal with you as you deserve, because you have despised my oath by breaking the covenant.[c] 60Yet I will remember the covenant[d] I made with you in the days of your youth,[e] and I will establish an everlasting covenant[f] with you. 61Then you will remember your ways and be ashamed[g] when you receive your sisters, both those who are older than you and those who are younger. I will give them to you as daughters,[h] but not on the basis of my covenant with you. 62So I will establish my covenant[i] with you, and you will know that I am the LORD.[j] 63Then, when I make atonement[k] for you for all you have done, you will remember and be ashamed[l] and never again open your mouth[m] because of your humiliation, declares the Sovereign LORD.[n]'"

Two Eagles and a Vine

17 The word of the LORD came to me: 2"Son of man, set forth an allegory and tell the house of Israel a parable.[a] 3Say to them, 'This is what the Sovereign LORD says: A great eagle[b] with powerful wings, long feathers and full plumage of varied colours came to Lebanon.[c] Taking hold of the top of a cedar, 4he broke off[d] its topmost shoot and carried it away to a land of merchants, where he planted it in a city of traders.

5"'He took some of the seed of your land and put it in fertile soil. He planted it like a willow by abundant water,[e] 6and it sprouted and became a low, spreading vine. Its branches[f] turned towards him, but its roots remained under it. So it became a vine and produced branches and put out leafy boughs.[g]

7"'But there was another great eagle with powerful wings and full plumage. The vine now sent out its roots towards him from the plot where it was planted and stretched out its branches to him for water.[h] 8It had been planted in good soil by abundant water so that it would produce branches,[i] bear fruit and become a splendid vine.'

9"Say to them, 'This is what the Sovereign LORD says: Will it thrive? Will it not be uprooted and stripped of its

43 [a]Eze 22:31; [b]Eze 11:21
44 [c]**Ps 49:4**
45 [d]**Eze 14:5**; [e]Jer 44:19; [f]ver 3; Eze 23:2
46 [g]**Jer 3:7**; [h]Ge 13:10–13; **18:20**; Jer 3:8–11; Eze 23:4; Rev 11:8
47 [i]**Eze 5:7**
48 [j]**Ge 15:2**; [k]**Ge 19:25**; [l]Mt 10:15; 11:23–24
49 [m]**Isa 1:10**; [n]Ps 138:6; Eze 28:2; [o]Isa 22:13; [p]**Ge 13:13**; 19:9; **Jer 5:28**; Eze 18:7,12,16; Am 6:4–6; Lk 12:16–20; 16:19; Jas 5:5
50 [q]Ps 18:27; [r]Ge 18:20–21; **19:5**
51 [s]Jer 3:8–11; Eze 5:6–7; 23:11
52 [t]**Jer 3:11**; [u]Eze 23:35
53 [v]**Dt 30:3**; Isa 19:24–25; **Jer 48:47**; [w]Eze 39:25
54 [x]**Jer 2:26**
55 [y]Eze 36:11; Mal 3:4
57 [z]**Ps 137:3**; [a]2Ki 16:6
58 [b]Eze 23:49
59 [c]**ver 8**; Eze 17:19
60 [d]**Ge 6:18**; **9:15**; [e]**Ps 25:7**; **Jer 2:2**; [f]**Ge 9:16**; Eze 37:26
61 [g]ver 63; Eze 20:43; 43:10; 44:13; [h]**Isa 43:6**
62 [i]**Dt 29:14**; [j]**Jer 24:7**; Eze 20:37,43–44; 34:25; 37:26; Hos 2:19–20
63 [k]Ps 65:3; 78:38; 79:9; [l]Eze 36:31–32; [m]Ro 3:19; [n]Ps 39:9; Da 9:7–8

Ch. 17

2 [a]**Jdg 14:12**; **Eze 20:49**
3 [b]**Dt 28:49**; Jer 49:22; Da 7:4; Hos 8:1; [c]**Jer 22:23**
4 [d]**Isa 10:33**
5 [e]Dt 8:7–9; Ps 1:3; Isa 44:4; Eze 31:5
6 [f]**Isa 18:5**; [g]**Job 5:3**
7 [h]Eze 31:4
8 [i]Job 18:19; Mal 4:1

[h]57 Many Hebrew manuscripts and Syriac; most Hebrew manuscripts, Septuagint and Vulgate *Aram*

fruit so that it withers? All its new growth will wither. It will not take a strong arm or many people to pull it up by the roots.[j] 10 Even if it[k] is transplanted, will it thrive? Will it not wither completely when the east wind strikes it—wither away in the plot where it grew?[l]' "

11 Then the word of the LORD came to me: 12 "Say to this rebellious house, 'Do you not know what these things mean?[m]' Say to them: 'The king of Babylon went to Jerusalem and carried off her king and her nobles,[n] bringing them back with him to Babylon.[o] 13 Then he took a member of the royal family and made a treaty[p] with him, putting him under oath.[q] He also carried away the leading men[r] of the land, 14 so that the kingdom would be brought low,[s] unable to rise again, surviving only by keeping his treaty. 15 But the king rebelled[t] against him by sending his envoys to Egypt[u] to get horses and a large army.[v] Will he succeed? Will he who does such things escape? Will he break the treaty and yet escape?[w]

16 " 'As surely as I live, declares the Sovereign LORD, he shall die[x] in Babylon, in the land of the king who put him on the throne, whose oath he despised and whose treaty he broke.[y] 17 Pharaoh[z] with his mighty army and great horde will be of no help to him in war, when ramps[a] are built and siege works erected to destroy many lives.[b] 18 He despised the oath by breaking the covenant. Because he had given his hand in pledge[c] and yet did all these things, he shall not escape.

19 " 'Therefore this is what the Sovereign LORD says: As surely as I live, I will bring down on his head my oath that he despised and my covenant that he broke.[d] 20 I will spread my net[e] for him, and he will be caught in my snare. I will bring him to Babylon and execute judgment[f] upon him there because he was unfaithful[g] to me. 21 All his fleeing troops will fall by the sword,[h] and the survivors[i] will be scattered to the winds.[j] Then you will know that I the LORD have spoken.[k]

22 " 'This is what the Sovereign LORD says: I myself will take a shoot[l] from the very top of a cedar and plant it; I will break off a tender sprig from its topmost shoots and plant it on a high and lofty mountain.[m] 23 On the mountain heights[n] of Israel I will plant it; it will produce branches and bear fruit[o] and become a splendid cedar. Birds of every kind will nest in it; they will find shelter in the shade of its branches.[p] 24 All the trees of the field[q] will know that I the LORD bring down[r] the tall tree and make the low tree grow tall. I dry up the green tree and make the dry tree flourish.[s]

" 'I the LORD have spoken, and I will do it.[t]' "

The Soul Who Sins Will Die

18 The word of the LORD came to me: 2 "What do you people mean by quoting this proverb about the land of Israel:

" 'The fathers eat sour grapes,
and the children's teeth are set on edge'?[a]

3 "As surely as I live, declares the Sovereign LORD, you will no longer quote this proverb[b] in Israel. 4 For every living soul belongs to me, the father as well as the son—both alike belong to me. The soul who sins[c] is the one who will die.[d]

5 "Suppose there is a righteous man
who does what is just and right.
6 He does not eat at the mountain[e] shrines
or look to the idols[f] of the house of Israel.
He does not defile his neighbour's wife
or lie with a woman during her period.[g]
7 He does not oppress[h] anyone,
but returns what he took in pledge[i] for a loan.
He does not commit robbery,[j]
but gives his food to the hungry[k]
and provides clothing for the naked.[l]
8 He does not lend at usury
or take excessive interest.[a][m]
He withholds his hand from doing wrong
and judges fairly[n] between man and man.
9 He follows my decrees[o]
and faithfully keeps my laws.
That man is righteous;[p]
he will surely live,[q]
declares the Sovereign LORD.

9 [j]Jer 42:10; Am 2:9
10 [k]**Job 1:19;** Hos 12:1; 13:15; [l]**Eze 15:4**
12 [m]**Eze 12:9;** [n]**2Ki 24:15;** [o]**Dt 21:10; 2Ch 36:10;** Eze 24:19
13 [p]**Ex 23:32; Jer 37:1;** [q]2Ch 36:13; [r]Isa 3:2
14 [s]Eze 29:14
15 [t]Jer 52:3; [u]**Isa 30:2; Jer 37:5;** [v]**Dt 17:16;** [w]**Ps 56:7; Isa 30:5;** Jer 34:3; 38:18; Eze 29:16
16 [x]**Jer 52:11;** Eze 12:13; [y]**2Ki 24:17**
17 [z]Jer 37:7; [a]**Eze 4:2;** [b]**Isa 36:6;** Jer 37:5; Eze 29:6–7
18 [c]**2Ki 10:15;** 1Ch 29:24
19 [d]Jer 7:9; **Eze 16:59;** 21:23; Hos 10:4
20 [e]**Eze 12:13;** 32:3; [f]**Jer 2:35;** [g]**Eze 15:8**
21 [h]**Eze 12:14;** [i]2Ki 25:11; [j]**Lev 26:33; 2Ki 25:5;** Zec 2:6; [k]**Jer 27:8**
22 [l]**2Ki 19:30; Isa 4:2;** [m]ver 23; Isa 2:2; **Jer 23:5;** Eze 20:40; 36:1,36; 37:22; 40:2; 43:12
23 [n]**ver 22; Jer 31:12;** [o]**Isa 27:6;** [p]Ps 92:12; **Isa 2:2;** Eze 31:6; Da 4:12; Hos 14:5–7; **Mt 13:32**
24 [q]**Ps 96:12;** Isa 2:13; [r]**Ps 52:5;** [s]**Nu 17:8;** Da 5:21; [t]**1Sa 2:7–8;** Eze 19:12; 21:26; 22:14; 37:13; Am 9:11

Ch. 18

2 [a]**Job 21:19;** Isa 3:15; Jer 31:29
3 [b]**Ps 49:4**
4 [c]**2Ki 14:6; Pr 13:21;** [d]ver 20; **Ge 18:23; Ex 17:14; Job 21:20;** Isa 42:5; Eze 33:8; **Ro 6:23**
6 [e]**Eze 6:2;** [f]Dt 4:19; **Eze 6:13;** 20:24; Am 5:26; [g]**Lev 12:2; 15:24**
7 [h]Ex 22:21; Mal 3:5; Jas 5:4; [i]**Ex 22:26;** [j]**Ex 20:15;** [k]**Job 22:7;** [l]Dt 15:11; **Eze 16:49; Mt 25:36;** Lk 3:11
8 [m]**Ex 18:21;** 22:25; **Lev 25:35–37;** Dt 23:19–20; [n]**Jer 22:3;** Zec 8:16
9 [o]**Lev 19:37;** [p]Hab 2:4; [q]**Lev 18:5; Eze 11:12;** 20:11; Am 5:4

[a]8 Or *take interest;* similarly in verses 13 and 17

10"Suppose he has a violent son, who
sheds blood[r] or does any of these other
things[b] 11(though the father has done
none of them):

"He eats at the mountain shrines.[s]
He defiles his neighbour's wife.
12He oppresses the poor[t] and needy.
He commits robbery.
He does not return what he took in
pledge.[u]
He looks to the idols.
He does detestable things.[v]
13He lends at usury and takes excessive
interest.[w]

Will such a man live? He will not! Be-
cause he has done all these detestable
things, he will surely be put to death
and his blood will be on his own head.[x]
14"But suppose this son has a son who
sees all the sins his father commits, and
though he sees them, he does not do
such things:[y]

15"He does not eat at the mountain
shrines[z]
or look to the idols[a] of the house of
Israel.
He does not defile his neighbour's
wife.
16He does not oppress anyone
or require a pledge for a loan.
He does not commit robbery,
but gives his food to the hungry[b]
and provides clothing for the
naked.[c]
17He withholds his hand from sin[c]
and takes no usury or excessive
interest.
He keeps my laws[d] and follows my
decrees.

He will not die for his father's sin; he
will surely live. 18But his father will die
for his own sin, because he practised
extortion, robbed his brother and did
what was wrong among his people.
19"Yet you ask, 'Why does the son not
share the guilt of his father?' Since the
son has done what is just and right and
has been careful to keep all my decrees,
he will surely live.[e] 20The soul who sins
is the one who will die.[f] The son will not
share the guilt of the father, nor will the
father share the guilt of the son. The
righteousness of the righteous man will
be credited to him, and the wickedness
of the wicked will be charged against
him.[g]
21"But if[h] a wicked man turns away
from all the sins he has committed and
keeps all my decrees[i] and does what is
just and right, he will surely live; he will
not die.[j] 22None of the offences he has
committed will be remembered against
him. Because of the righteous things he
has done, he will live.[k] 23Do I take any
pleasure in the death of the wicked?
declares the Sovereign LORD. Rather,
am I not pleased[l] when they turn from
their ways and live?[m]
24"But if a righteous man turns[n] from
his righteousness and commits sin and
does the same detestable things the
wicked man does, will he live? None of
the righteous things he has done will be
remembered. Because of the unfaithful-
ness[o] he is guilty of and because of the
sins he has committed, he will die.[p]
25"Yet you say, 'The way of the LORD
is not just.'[q] Hear, O house of Israel: Is
my way unjust?[r] Is it not your ways that
are unjust? 26If a righteous man turns
from his righteousness and commits
sin, he will die for it; because of the sin
he has committed he will die. 27But if a
wicked man turns away from the wick-
edness he has committed and does
what is just and right, he will save his
life.[s] 28Because he considers all the
offences he has committed and turns
away from them, he will surely live; he
will not die.[t] 29Yet the house of Israel
says, 'The way of the LORD is not just.'
Are my ways unjust, O house of Israel?
Is it not your ways that are unjust?
30"Therefore, O house of Israel, I will
judge you, each one according to his
ways, declares the Sovereign LORD. Re-
pent![u] Turn away from all your offences;
then sin will not be your downfall.[v]
31Rid[w] yourselves of all the offences you
have committed, and get a new heart[x]
and a new spirit. Why[y] will you die, O
house of Israel?[z] 32For I take no pleasure
in the death of anyone, declares the
Sovereign LORD. Repent[a] and live![b]

A Lament for Israel's Princes

19 "Take up a lament[a] concerning
the princes[b] of Israel 2and say:

" 'What a lioness[c] was your mother
among the lions!
She lay down among the young lions
and reared her cubs.[d]
3She brought up one of her cubs,
and he became a strong lion.

10 [r]Ex 21:12; Eze 22:6
11 [s]Eze 22:9
12 [t]Ex 22:22; Job 24:9; Am 4:1; [u]Ex 22:27; [v]2Ki 21:11; Isa 59:6–7; Jer 22:17; Eze 16:49; Hab 2:6
13 [w]Ex 22:25; [x]Lev 20:9; Eze 33:4–5; Hos 12:14
14 [y]2Ch 34:21; Pr 23:24
15 [z]Eze 22:9; [a]Ps 24:4
16 [b]Isa 58:7; [c]Ex 22:27; Ps 41:1; Isa 58:10; Eze 16:49
17 [d]Ps 1:2
19 [e]Ex 20:5; Dt 5:9; Jer 15:4; Zec 1:3–6
20 [f]Nu 15:31; [g]Dt 24:16; 1Ki 8:32; 2Ki 14:6; Isa 3:11; Eze 7:27; 14:14; Mt 16:27; Jn 9:2
21 [h]Jer 18:8; [i]Ge 26:5; [j]Eze 13:22; 36:27
22 [k]Ps 18:20–24; Isa 43:25; Da 4:27; Mic 7:19
23 [l]Ps 147:11; [m]Job 37:23; La 3:33; Eze 16:6; Mic 7:18; 1Ti 2:4
24 [n]Jer 34:16; [o]Eze 15:8; [p]1Sa 15:11; 2Ch 24:17–20; Job 35:8; Pr 21:16; Eze 3:20; 20:27; 2Pe 2:20–22
25 [q]Jer 2:29; [r]Ge 18:25; Jer 12:1; Eze 33:17; Zep 3:5; Mal 2:17; 3:13–15
27 [s]Isa 1:18; Eze 13:22
28 [t]Isa 55:7
30 [u]Isa 1:27; Jer 35:15; Mt 3:2; [v]Eze 7:3; 24:14; 33:20; Hos 12:6; 1Pe 1:17
31 [w]Jdg 6:8; [x]Ps 51:10; [y]Jer 27:13; [z]Isa 1:16–17; Eze 11:19; 36:26
32 [a]Job 22:23; Isa 55:7; Mal 3:7; [b]2Ch 7:14; Job 37:23; Eze 16:6; 33:11

Ch. 19

1 [a]ver 14; Jer 7:29; 9:10,20; Eze 26:17; 27:2,32; 28:12; 32:2,16; Am 5:1; [b]2Ki 24:6
2 [c]Nu 23:24; [d]Ge 49:9

b10 Or *things to a brother*
c17 Septuagint (see also verse 8); Hebrew *from the poor*

He learned to tear the prey
and he devoured men.
4The nations heard about him,
and he was trapped in their pit.
They led him with hooks[e]
to the land of Egypt.[f]

5" 'When she saw her hope unfulfilled,
her expectation gone,
she took another of her cubs[g]
and made him a strong lion.[h]
6He prowled among the lions,
for he was now a strong lion.
He learned to tear the prey
and he devoured men.[i]
7He broke down[a] their strongholds
and devastated[j] their towns.
The land and all who were in it
were terrified by his roaring.
8Then the nations[k] came against him,
those from regions round about.
They spread their net[l] for him,
and he was trapped in their pit.[m]
9With hooks[n] they pulled him into a cage
and brought him to the king of Babylon.[o]
They put him in prison,
so his roar[p] was heard no longer
on the mountains of Israel.[q]

10" 'Your mother was like a vine in your vineyard[b] [r]
planted by the water;[s]
it was fruitful and full of branches
because of abundant water.[t]
11Its branches were strong,
fit for a ruler's sceptre.
It towered high
above the thick foliage,
conspicuous for its height
and for its many branches.[u]
12But it was uprooted[v] in fury
and thrown to the ground.
The east wind[w] made it shrivel,
it was stripped of its fruit;
its strong branches withered
and fire consumed them.[x]
13Now it is planted in the desert,[y]
in a dry and thirsty land.[z]
14Fire spread from one of its main[c] branches
and consumed[a] its fruit.
No strong branch is left on it
fit for a ruler's sceptre.'[b]

This is a lament[c] and is to be used as a lament."

Rebellious Israel

20 In the seventh year, in the fifth month on the tenth day, some of the elders of Israel came to enquire[a] of
the LORD, and they sat down in front of
me.[b]
2Then the word of the LORD came to
me: 3"Son of man, speak to the elders[c] of
Israel and say to them, 'This is what the
Sovereign LORD says: Have you come to
enquire[d] of me? As surely as I live, I will
not let you enquire of me, declares the
Sovereign LORD.[e]'
4"Will you judge them? Will you
judge them, son of man? Then confront
them with the detestable practices of
their fathers[f] 5and say to them: 'This is
what the Sovereign LORD says: On the
day I chose[g] Israel, I swore with uplifted
hand[h] to the descendants of the house
of Jacob and revealed myself to them in
Egypt. With uplifted hand I said to
them, "I am the LORD your God.[i]" 6On
that day I swore[j] to them that I would
bring them out of Egypt into a land I had
searched out for them, a land flowing
with milk and honey,[k] the most beauti-
ful of all lands.[l] 7And I said to them,
"Each of you, get rid of the vile images[m]
you have set your eyes on, and do not
defile yourselves with the idols[n] of
Egypt. I am the LORD your God.[o]"
8" 'But they rebelled against me and
would not listen to me;[p] they did not get
rid of the vile images they had set their
eyes on, nor did they forsake the idols of
Egypt.[q] So I said I would pour out my
wrath on them and spend my anger
against them in Egypt.[r] 9But for the sake
of my name I did what would keep it
from being profaned[s] in the eyes of the
nations they lived among and in whose
sight I had revealed myself to the
Israelites by bringing them out of
Egypt.[t] 10Therefore I led them out of
Egypt and brought them into the des-
ert.[u] 11I gave them my decrees and made
known to them my laws, for the man
who obeys them will live by them.[v]
12Also I gave them my Sabbaths[w] as a
sign[x] between us,[y] so they would know
that I the LORD made them holy.[z]
13" 'Yet the people of Israel rebelled[a]
against me in the desert. They did not
follow my decrees but rejected my
laws[b]—although the man who obeys
them will live by them—and they utterly
desecrated my Sabbaths.[c] So I said I
would pour out my wrath[d] on them and
destroy[e] them in the desert.[f] 14But for

4 [e]**Job 41:2**; [f]2Ki 23:33–34; 2Ch 36:4; **La 4:20**
5 [g]**Ge 49:9**; [h]2Ki 23:34
6 [i]2Ki 24:9; 2Ch 36:9
7 [j]Eze 29:10; 30:12
8 [k]2Ki 24:2; [l]**Eze 12:13**; [m]2Ki 24:11; **La 4:20**
9 [n]**2Ki 19:28**; [o]**2Ki 25:7**; **2Ch 36:6**; [p]Zec 11:3; [q]**2Ki 24:15**
10 [r]**Ge 49:22**; [s]**Jer 17:8**; [t]Ps 80:8–11
11 [u]Eze 31:3; Da 4:11
12 [v]**Dt 29:28**; [w]**Ge 41:6**; [x]**Isa 27:11**; **Eze 17:24**; 28:17; Hos 13:15
13 [y]Eze 20:35; Hos 2:14; [z]Hos 2:3
14 [a]Eze 20:47; [b]**Eze 15:4**; [c]**ver 1**

Ch. 20
1 [a]**Ge 25:22**; [b]Eze 1:1–2; **8:1**; 21:1
3 [c]**Eze 7:26**; [d]**Ge 25:22**; Eze 14:3; [e]**1Sa 28:6**; Isa 1:15; Am 8:12; Mic 3:7
4 [f]**Eze 16:2**; 22:2; Mt 23:32
5 [g]**Dt 7:6**; [h]**Ge 14:22**; **Nu 14:30**; [i]**Lev 11:44**
6 [j]**Ex 6:8**; [k]**Ex 3:8**; [l]**Dt 8:7**; Da 8:9; 11:41; Mal 3:12
7 [m]Ex 20:4; [n]**Eze 6:9**; [o]**Ex 20:2**; Lev 18:3; Dt 29:18
8 [p]**Jer 7:26**; [q]**Jer 11:10**; **Eze 7:8**; **16:26**; [r]**Ex 32:7**; Dt 9:7; **Isa 63:10**
9 [s]**Isa 48:11**; [t]Eze 36:22; 39:7
10 [u]**Ex 13:18**; 19:1
11 [v]Ex 20:1–23; Lev 18:5; Dt 4:7–8; **Eze 18:9**; **Ro 10:5**
12 [w]**Ex 20:10**; [x]**Ex 31:13**; [y]Jer 17:22; [z]**Lev 20:8**
13 [a]Ps 78:40; [b]**Jer 6:19**; 11:8; [c]ver 24; [d]**Dt 9:8**; [e]**Ex 32:10**; [f]Lev 26:15,43; **Nu 14:29**; Ps 95:8–10; Isa 56:6

[a]7 Targum (see Septuagint); Hebrew *He knew*
[b]10 Two Hebrew manuscripts; most Hebrew manuscripts *your blood*
[c]14 Or *from under its*

the sake of my name I did what would keep it from being profaned[g] in the eyes of the nations in whose sight I had brought them out.[h] 15Also with uplifted hand I swore[i] to them in the desert that I would not bring them into the land I had given them—a land flowing with milk and honey, most beautiful of all lands[j]— 16because they rejected my laws[k] and did not follow my decrees and desecrated my Sabbaths. For their hearts[l] were devoted to their idols.[m] 17Yet I looked on them with pity and did not destroy[n] them or put an end to them in the desert. 18I said to their children in the desert, "Do not follow the statutes of your fathers[o] or keep their laws or defile yourselves[p] with their idols. 19I am the LORD your God;[q] follow my decrees and be careful to keep my laws.[r] 20Keep my Sabbaths[s] holy, that they may be a sign[t] between us. Then you will know that I am the LORD your God.[u]"

21" 'But the children rebelled against me: They did not follow my decrees, they were not careful to keep my laws[v]—although the man who obeys them will live by them—and they desecrated my Sabbaths. So I said I would pour out my wrath on them and spend my anger[w] against them in the desert.[x] 22But I withheld[y] my hand, and for the sake of my name[z] I did what would keep it from being profaned in the eyes of the nations in whose sight I had brought them out. 23Also with uplifted hand I swore to them in the desert that I would disperse them among the nations and scatter[a] them through the countries, 24because they had not obeyed my laws but had rejected my decrees[b] and desecrated my Sabbaths,[c] and their eyes ⌊lusted⌋ after[d] their fathers' idols.[e] 25I also gave them over[f] to statutes that were not good and laws they could not live by;[g] 26I let them become defiled through their gifts—the sacrifice[h] of every firstborn[a]—that I might fill them with horror so that they would know that I am the LORD.'[i]

27"Therefore, son of man, speak to the people of Israel and say to them, 'This is what the Sovereign LORD says: In this also your fathers[j] blasphemed[k] me by forsaking me:[l] 28When I brought them into the land[m] I had sworn to give them and they saw any high hill or any leafy tree, there they offered their sacrifices, made offerings that provoked me to anger, presented their fragrant incense and poured out their drink offerings.[n] 29Then I said to them: What is this high place[o] you go to?' " (It is called Bamah[b] to this day.)

Judgment and Restoration

30"Therefore say to the house of Israel: 'This is what the Sovereign LORD says: Will you defile yourselves[p] the way your fathers did and lust after their vile images?[q] 31When you offer your gifts—the sacrifice of your sons[r] in[c] the fire—you continue to defile yourselves with all your idols to this day. Am I to let you enquire of me, O house of Israel? As surely as I live, declares the Sovereign LORD, I will not let you enquire of me.[s]

32" 'You say, "We want to be like the nations, like the peoples of the world, who serve wood and stone." But what you have in mind will never happen. 33As surely as I live, declares the Sovereign LORD, I will rule over you with a mighty hand and an outstretched arm[t] and with outpoured wrath.[u] 34I will bring you from the nations[v] and gather[w] you from the countries where you have been scattered—with a mighty hand[x] and an outstretched arm and with outpoured wrath.[y] 35I will bring you into the desert[z] of the nations and there, face to face, I will execute judgment[a] upon you. 36As I judged your fathers in the desert of the land of Egypt, so I will judge you, declares the Sovereign LORD.[b] 37I will take note of you as you pass under my rod,[c] and I will bring you into the bond of the covenant.[d] 38I will purge[e] you of those who revolt and rebel against me. Although I will bring them out of the land where they are living, yet they will not enter the land of Israel. Then you will know that I am the LORD.[f]

39" 'As for you, O house of Israel, this is what the Sovereign LORD says: Go and serve your idols,[g] every one of you! But afterwards you will surely listen to me and no longer profane my holy name[h] with your gifts and idols.[i] 40For on my holy mountain, the high mountain of Israel,[j] declares the Sovereign LORD, there in the land the entire house of Israel will serve me, and there I will accept them. There I will require your offerings[k] and your choice gifts,[d] along with all your holy sacrifices.[l] 41I will

14 [g]Isa 48:11; [h]Eze 36:23
15 [i]Dt 1:34; [j]Nu 14:22–23; Ps 95:11; 106:26; Heb 3:11
16 [k]Jer 11:8; Am 2:4; [l]Nu 15:39; [m]ver 24; Eze 6:4; Am 5:26
17 [n]Jer 4:27
18 [o]2Ch 30:7; Zec 1:4; [p]Ps 106:39
19 [q]Ex 20:2; [r]Dt 5:32–33; 6:1–2; 8:1; 11:1; 12:1
20 [s]Ex 20:10; [t]Ex 31:13; [u]Jer 17:22
21 [v]Jer 7:26; [w]Nu 25:3; [x]Eze 7:8
22 [y]Ps 78:38; [z]Isa 48:11
23 [a]Lev 26:33; Ps 9:11
24 [b]Am 2:4; [c]ver 13; [d]Eze 6:9; [e]ver 16; Eze 2:3; 18:6
25 [f]Ps 81:12; Ro 1:28; [g]Isa 66:4; 2Th 2:11
26 [h]Lev 18:21; [i]Lev 20:2–5; 2Ki 17:17
27 [j]Ps 78:57; [k]Nu 15:30; Ro 2:24; [l]Eze 18:24
28 [m]Ne 9:23; Ps 78:55,58; [n]Jer 2:7; 3:6; 19:13; Eze 6:13
29 [o]Eze 16:16; 43:7
30 [p]ver 43; [q]Jdg 2:16–19; Jer 16:12
31 [r]Eze 16:20; [s]Ps 106:37–39; Jer 7:31; Eze 14:3; Am 8:12; Zec 7:13
33 [t]Eze 16:27; [u]Jer 21:5; Eze 25:16
34 [v]2Co 6:17*; [w]Dt 30:4; Ps 106:47; [x]Isa 31:3; [y]Isa 27:12–13; Jer 44:6; La 2:4; Eze 6:14
35 [z]Eze 19:13; [a]1Sa 12:7; Job 22:4; Jer 2:35
36 [b]Nu 11:1–35; 14:28–30; 1Co 10:5–10
37 [c]Lev 27:32; [d]Eze 16:62
38 [e]Eze 34:17–22; Am 9:9–10; [f]Ps 95:11; Jer 44:14; Eze 13:9; 23:49; Hos 2:14; Zec 13:8–9; Mal 3:3; 4:1–3; Heb 4:3
39 [g]Jer 44:25; [h]Ex 20:7; Eze 13:19; [i]Eze 43:7; Am 4:4
40 [j]Eze 17:22; 34:14; [k]Isa 60:7; [l]Isa 56:7; Mal 3:4

[a]26 Or—*making every firstborn pass through ⌊the fire⌋*
[b]29 *Bamah* means *high place.*
[c]31 Or—*making your sons pass through*
[d]40 Or *and the gifts of your firstfruits*

accept you as fragrant incense[m] when I
bring you out from the nations and
gather[n] you from the countries where
you have been scattered, and I will
show myself holy[o] among you in the
sight of the nations.[p] 42Then you will
know that I am the LORD,[q] when I bring
you into the land of Israel,[r] the land I
had sworn with uplifted hand to give to
your fathers.[s] 43There you will remem-
ber your conduct[t] and all the actions by
which you have defiled yourselves, and
you will loathe yourselves[u] for all the
evil you have done.[v] 44You will know
that I am the LORD, when I deal with you
for my name's sake[w] and not according
to your evil ways and your corrupt prac-
tices, O house of Israel, declares the
Sovereign LORD.[x]''

Prophecy Against the South

45The word of the LORD came to me:
46"Son of man, set your face towards[y]
the south; preach against the south and
prophesy against[z] the forest of the
southland.[a] 47Say to the southern
forest:[b] 'Hear the word of the LORD. This
is what the Sovereign LORD says: I am
about to set fire to you, and it will con-
sume[c] all your trees, both green and
dry. The blazing flame will not be
quenched, and every face from south to
north[d] will be scorched by it.[e]
48Everyone will see that I the LORD have
kindled it; it will not be quenched.[f]' "
49Then I said, "Ah, Sovereign LORD![g]
They are saying of me, 'Isn't he just
telling parables?[h]' "

Babylon, God's Sword of Judgment

21 The word of the LORD came to
me:[a] 2"Son of man, set your face
against[b] Jerusalem and preach against
the sanctuary.[c] Prophesy against[d] the
land of Israel 3and say to her: 'This is
what the LORD says: I am against you.[e] I
will draw my sword[f] from its scabbard
and cut off from you both the righteous
and the wicked.[g] 4Because I am going to
cut off the righteous and the wicked,
my sword[h] will be unsheathed against
everyone from south to north.[i] 5Then all
people will know that I the LORD have
drawn my sword[j] from its scabbard; it
will not return[k] again.'[l]
6"Therefore groan, son of man! Groan
before them with broken heart and bit-
ter grief.[m] 7And when they ask you,
'Why are you groaning?[n]' you shall say,
'Because of the news that is coming.
Every heart will melt[o] and every hand
go limp;[p] every spirit will become faint[q]
and every knee become as weak as
water.'[r] It is coming! It will surely take
place, declares the Sovereign LORD."
8The word of the LORD came to me:
9"Son of man, prophesy and say, 'This
is what the Lord says:

" 'A sword, a sword,
sharpened and polished—
10sharpened for the slaughter,[s]
polished to flash like lightning!

" 'Shall we rejoice in the sceptre of my
son ⌞Judah⌟? The sword despises every
such stick.[t]

11" 'The sword is appointed to be
polished,[u]
to be grasped with the hand;
it is sharpened and polished,
made ready for the hand of the
slayer.
12Cry out and wail, son of man,
for it is against my people;
it is against all the princes of Israel.
They are thrown to the sword
along with my people.
Therefore beat your breast.[v]

13" 'Testing will surely come. And
what if the sceptre ⌞of Judah⌟, which the
sword despises, does not continue?
declares the Sovereign LORD.'

14"So then, son of man, prophesy
and strike your hands[w] together.
Let the sword strike twice,
even three times.
It is a sword for slaughter—
a sword for great slaughter,
closing in on them from every side.[x]
15So that hearts may melt[y]
and the fallen be many,
I have stationed the sword for
slaughter[a]
at all their gates.
Oh! It is made to flash like lightning,
it is grasped for slaughter.[z]
16O sword, slash to the right,
then to the left,
wherever your blade is turned.
17I too will strike my hands[a] together,
and my wrath[b] will subside.
I the LORD have spoken."

18The word of the LORD came to me:
19"Son of man, mark out two roads for
the sword[d] of the king of Babylon to
take, both starting from the same coun-
try. Make a signpost[e] where the road

41 [m]2Co 2:14; [n]Dt 30:4; [o]Eze 28:25; 36:23; [p]Isa 5:16; Eze 11:17; 2Co 6:17
42 [q]Eze 38:23; [r]Jer 23:8; Eze 34:13; 36:24; [s]Jer 30:3; Eze 34:27; 37:21
43 [t]Eze 14:22; [u]Lev 26:41; [v]Eze 6:9; 16:61; Hos 5:15
44 [w]Ps 109:21; Isa 43:25; Eze 36:22; [x]Eze 16:62; 36:32
46 [y]Eze 4:3; 13:17; [z]Eze 21:2; Am 7:16; [a]Isa 30:6; Jer 13:19
47 [b]2Ki 19:23; [c]Eze 19:14; [d]Eze 21:4; [e]Isa 9:18–19; 13:8
48 [f]Jer 7:20; Eze 21:5,32; 23:25
49 [g]Eze 4:14; [h]Jdg 14:12; Ps 78:2; Eze 12:9; Mt 13:13; Jn 16:25

Ch. 21

1 [a]Eze 20:1
2 [b]Eze 13:17; [c]Eze 9:6; [d]Jer 26:11–12; Eze 20:46
3 [e]Jer 21:13; [f]Isa 27:1; Eze 14:21; [g]ver 9–11; Job 9:22; Isa 57:1; Jer 47:6–7
4 [h]Lev 26:25; Jer 25:27; [i]Eze 20:47
5 [j]Isa 34:5; [k]ver 30; [l]Eze 20:47–48; Na 1:9
6 [m]ver 12; Isa 22:4; Jer 30:6; Eze 9:4
7 [n]Job 23:2; [o]Jos 7:5; [p]Jer 47:3; Eze 22:14; [q]Ps 6:2; [r]Lev 26:36; Job 11:16
10 [s]Ps 110:5–6; Isa 34:5–6; [t]Dt 32:41
11 [u]Jer 46:4
12 [v]Jer 31:19
14 [w]ver 17; Nu 24:10; [x]Eze 6:11; 30:24
15 [y]2Sa 17:10; [z]Ps 22:14
17 [a]ver 14; Eze 22:13; [b]Eze 5:13; [c]Eze 6:11; 16:42
19 [d]Eze 14:21; 32:11; [e]Jer 31:21

[a]15 Septuagint; the meaning of the Hebrew for this word is uncertain.

branches off to the city. 20 Mark out one
road for the sword to come against Rab-
bah of the Ammonites[f] and another
against Judah and fortified Jerusalem.
21 For the king of Babylon will stop at the
fork in the road, at the junction of the
two roads, to seek an omen: He will cast
lots[g] with arrows, he will consult his
idols,[h] he will examine the liver.[i] 22 Into
his right hand will come the lot for
Jerusalem, where he is to set up
battering-rams, to give the command to
slaughter, to sound the battle cry,[j] to set
battering-rams against the gates, to
build a ramp[k] and to erect siege works.[l]
23 It will seem like a false omen to those
who have sworn allegiance to him, but
he will remind[m] them of their guilt[n] and
take them captive.

24 "Therefore this is what the
Sovereign LORD says: 'Because you
people have brought to mind your guilt
by your open rebellion, revealing your
sins in all that you do—because you
have done this, you will be taken
captive.

25 " 'O profane and wicked prince of
Israel, whose day has come,[o] whose
time of punishment has reached its
climax,[p] 26 this is what the Sovereign
LORD says: Take off the turban, remove
the crown.[q] It will not be as it was: The
lowly will be exalted and the exalted will
be brought low.[r] 27 A ruin! A ruin! I will
make it a ruin! It will not be restored
until he comes to whom it rightfully
belongs;[s] to him I will give it.'[t]

28 "And you, son of man, prophesy
and say, 'This is what the Sovereign
LORD says about the Ammonites[u] and
their insults:

" 'A sword,[v] a sword,
drawn for the slaughter,
polished to consume
and to flash like lightning!
29 Despite false visions concerning you
and lying divinations[w] about you,
it will be laid on the necks
of the wicked who are to be slain,
whose day has come,
whose time of punishment has
reached its climax.[x]
30 Return the sword to its scabbard.[y]
In the place where you were
created,
in the land of your ancestry,[z]
I will judge you.
31 I will pour out my wrath upon you
and breathe[a] out my fiery anger[b]
against you;
I will hand you over to brutal men,
men skilled in destruction.[c]

20 [f]Dt 3:11
21 [g]Pr 16:33; [h]Zec 10:2; [i]Nu 22:7; 23:23
22 [j]Jer 4:16; [k]Jer 32:24; [l]2Ki 25:1; Eze 4:2; 26:9
23 [m]Nu 5:15; [n]Eze 17:19
25 [o]Eze 22:4; [p]Eze 35:5
26 [q]Isa 28:5; Jer 13:18; [r]Ps 75:7; Isa 40:4; Eze 17:24; Mt 23:12
27 [s]Ge 49:10; [t]Ps 2:6; Jer 23:5–6; Eze 37:24; Hag 2:21–22
28 [u]Ge 19:38; Zep 2:8; [v]Jer 12:12
29 [w]Jer 27:9; [x]ver 25; Eze 22:28; 35:5
30 [y]ver 5; Jer 47:6; [z]Eze 16:3
31 [a]Ps 18:15; Isa 11:4; [b]Ps 79:6; Eze 22:20–21; [c]Jer 4:7; 51:20–23; Eze 16:39
32 [d]Eze 20:47–48; Mal 4:1; [e]Eze 25:10

Ch. 22

2 [a]Eze 24:6,9; Hos 4:2; Na 3:1; Hab 2:12; [b]Eze 16:2; 23:36
3 [c]ver 6,13,27; Eze 23:37,45; 24:6
4 [d]2Ki 21:16; [e]Eze 21:25; [f]Ps 137:3; [g]Ps 44:13–14; Eze 5:14
5 [h]Isa 22:2
6 [i]Eze 11:6; 18:10; 33:25
7 [j]Dt 5:16; Mic 7:6; [k]Ex 23:9; [l]Ex 22:21–22
8 [m]Ex 20:8; Eze 23:38–39
9 [n]Lev 19:16; [o]Isa 59:3; Eze 11:6; Hos 4:2; 6:9; [p]Eze 18:11; [q]Eze 23:29; Hos 4:10,14
10 [r]Lev 18:7; [s]Lev 12:2; [t]Lev 18:8,19
11 [u]Jer 5:8; [v]Ge 11:31; Lev 18:15; [w]Lev 18:9; 2Sa 13:14; [x]Eze 18:6

32 You will be fuel for the fire,[d]
your blood will be shed in your
land,
you will be remembered[e] no more;
for I the LORD have spoken.' "

Jerusalem's Sins

22 The word of the LORD came to
me: 2 "Son of man, will you
judge her? Will you judge this city of
bloodshed?[a] Then confront her with all
her detestable practices[b] 3 and say: 'This
is what the Sovereign LORD says: O city
that brings on herself doom by shed-
ding blood[c] in her midst and defiles
herself by making idols, 4 you have be-
come guilty because of the blood you
have shed[d] and have become defiled by
the idols you have made. You have
brought your days to a close, and the
end of your years has come.[e] Therefore I
will make you an object of scorn[f] to the
nations and a laughing-stock to all the
countries.[g] 5 Those who are near and
those who are far away will mock you,
O infamous city, full of turmoil.[h]

6 " 'See how each of the princes of
Israel who are in you uses his power to
shed blood.[i] 7 In you they have treated
father and mother with contempt;[j] in
you they have oppressed the alien[k]
and ill-treated the fatherless and the
widow.[l] 8 You have despised my holy
things and desecrated my Sabbaths.[m]
9 In you are slanderous men[n] bent on
shedding blood;[o] in you are those who
eat at the mountain shrines[p] and com-
mit lewd acts.[q] 10 In you are those who
dishonour their fathers' bed;[r] in you are
those who violate women during their
period,[s] when they are ceremonially un-
clean.[t] 11 In you one man commits a de-
testable offence with his neighbour's
wife,[u] another shamefully defiles his
daughter-in-law,[v] and another violates
his sister,[w] his own father's daughter.[x]
12 In you men accept bribes[y] to shed
blood; you take usury[z] and excessive
interest[a] and make unjust gain from
your neighbours[a] by extortion. And
you have forgotten[b] me, declares the
Sovereign LORD.[c]

13 " 'I will surely strike my hands[d]
together at the unjust gain[e] you have
made and at the blood[f] you have shed in

12 [y]Ex 18:21; Dt 27:25; Ps 26:10; Isa 5:23; Am 5:12; Mic 7:3; [z]Eze 18:8; [a]Lev 19:13; [b]Ps 106:21; Isa 17:10; 57:11; [c]Eze 11:6
13 [d]Nu 24:10; Eze 21:17; [e]ver 27; Isa 33:15; [f]ver 3

[a]12 Or *usury and interest*

your midst.[g] 14Will your courage en-
dure[h] or your hands[i] be strong in the
day I deal with you? I the LORD have
spoken,[j] and I will do it.[k] 15I will dis-
perse you among the nations and scat-
ter[l] you through the countries; and I will
put an end to[m] your uncleanness.[n]
16When you have been defiled[b] in the
eyes of the nations, you will know that I
am the LORD.'"

17Then the word of the LORD came to
me: 18"Son of man, the house of Israel
has become dross[o] to me; all of them are
the copper, tin, iron and lead left inside
a furnace.[p] They are but the dross of
silver.[q] 19Therefore this is what the
Sovereign LORD says: 'Because you have
all become dross,[r] I will gather you into
Jerusalem. 20As men gather silver, cop-
per, iron, lead and tin into a furnace to
melt it with a fiery blast, so will I gather
you in my anger and my wrath and put
you inside the city and melt you.[s] 21I will
gather you and I will blow[t] on you with
my fiery wrath, and you will be melted
inside her.[u] 22As silver is melted[v] in a
furnace, so you will be melted inside
her, and you will know that I the LORD
have poured out my wrath[w] upon
you.'"[x]

23Again the word of the LORD came to
me: 24"Son of man, say to the land, 'You
are a land that has had no rain or
showers[c] in the day of wrath.'[y] 25There
is a conspiracy[z] of her princes[d] within
her like a roaring lion[a] tearing its prey;
they devour people,[b] take treasures and
precious things and make many
widows[c] within her. 26Her priests do
violence to my law[d] and profane my
holy things; they do not distinguish be-
tween the holy and the common;[e] they
teach that there is no difference be-
tween the unclean and the clean;[f] and
they shut their eyes to the keeping of
my Sabbaths, so that I am profaned[g]
among them.[h] 27Her officials[i] within
her are like wolves[j] tearing their prey;
they shed blood and kill people[k] to
make unjust gain.[l] 28Her prophets
whitewash[m] these deeds for them by
false visions and lying divinations.[n]
They say, 'This is what the Sovereign
LORD says'—when the LORD has not
spoken.[o] 29The people of the land prac-
tise extortion and commit robbery;[p] they
oppress the poor and needy and ill-treat
the alien,[q] denying them justice.[r]

30"I looked for a man among them
who would build up the wall[s] and stand
before me in the gap on behalf of the
land so that I would not have to destroy
it, but I found none.[t] 31So I will pour out
my wrath on them and consume them
with my fiery anger,[u] bringing down[v]
on their own heads all they have done,
declares the Sovereign LORD."[w]

Two Adulterous Sisters

23 The word of the LORD came to
me: 2"Son of man, there were
two women, daughters of the same
mother.[a] 3They became prostitutes in
Egypt,[b] engaging in prostitution[c] from
their youth.[d] In that land their breasts
were fondled and their virgin bosoms
caressed.[e] 4The older was named Oho-
lah, and her sister was Oholibah. They
were mine and gave birth to sons and
daughters. Oholah is Samaria, and
Oholibah is Jerusalem.[f]

5"Oholah engaged in prostitution
while she was still mine; and she lusted
after her lovers, the Assyrians[g]—
warriors[h] 6clothed in blue, governors
and commanders, all of them hand-
some young men, and mounted horse-
men. 7She gave herself as a prostitute to
all the elite of the Assyrians and defiled
herself with all the idols of everyone she
lusted after.[i] 8She did not give up the
prostitution she began in Egypt,[j] when
during her youth men slept with her,
caressed her virgin bosom and poured
out their lust upon her.[k]

9"Therefore I handed her over[l] to her
lovers,[m] the Assyrians, for whom she
lusted.[n] 10They stripped[o] her naked,
took away her sons and daughters and
killed her with the sword. She became a
byword among women,[p] and punish-
ment was inflicted[q] on her.[r]

11"Her sister Oholibah saw this,[s] yet
in her lust and prostitution she was
more depraved than her sister.[t] 12She
too lusted after the Assyrians—
governors and commanders, warriors
in full dress, mounted horsemen, all
handsome young men.[u] 13I saw that she
too defiled herself; both of them went
the same way.[v]

14"But she carried her prostitution
still further. She saw men portrayed on
a wall,[w] figures of Chaldeans[a] portrayed
in red,[x] 15with belts[y] round their waists

13 [g]**Eze 6:11**
14 [h]Ps 76:7; Joel 2:11; Na 1:6; Mal 3:2; [i]**Eze 7:17**; [j]Eze 24:14; [k]**Eze 17:24**
15 [l]**Lev 26:33**; Dt 4:27; Zec 7:14; [m]**Eze 16:41**; [n]Eze 24:11
18 [o]**Ps 119:119**; [p]Isa 48:10; [q]Jer 6:28–30
19 [r]**Ps 119:119**
20 [s]Hos 8:10; Mal 3:2
21 [t]Isa 40:7; Hag 1:9; [u]Ps 68:2; Eze 21:31
22 [v]**Isa 1:25**; [w]**Eze 7:8**; [x]**Isa 64:7**
24 [y]Eze 24:13
25 [z]Jer 11:9; [a]**Ps 22:13**; [b]Hos 6:9; [c]Jer 15:8; 18:21
26 [d]Hos 9:7–8; Zep 3:4; Mal 2:7–8; [e]Eze 42:20; 44:23; [f]**Lev 20:25**; [g]**Lev 18:21**; **Eze 13:19**; [h]ver 8; **1Sa 2:12–17**; Jer 2:8,26; Hag 2:11–14
27 [i]Jer 26:10; Zep 3:3; [j]Mt 7:15; [k]**ver 3**; **Eze 11:6**; 33:25; 34:2–3; Mic 3:2,10; [l]ver 13; **Ge 37:24**; **Isa 1:23**; **Jer 12:2**; **51:13**; Eze 33:31
28 [m]**Eze 13:10**; [n]**La 2:14**; **4:13**; **Eze 21:29**; [o]**Eze 13:2,6–7**
29 [p]**Ps 62:10**; [q]**Ex 22:21**; [r]**Isa 5:7**
30 [s]**Eze 13:5**; [t]Ps 106:23; **Isa 64:7**; Jer 5:1
31 [u]**Isa 30:27**; **La 4:11**; [v]Eze 16:43; [w]Eze 7:8–9; Ro 2:8

Ch. 23

2 [a]**Jer 3:7**; **Eze 16:45**
3 [b]Jos 24:14; [c]**Lev 17:7**; **Isa 1:21**; [d]**Ps 25:7**; [e]**Eze 16:15**
4 [f]**Eze 16:46**
5 [g]**2Ki 16:7**; Hos 5:13; [h]Hos 8:9
7 [i]Isa 57:8; Hos 5:3; 6:10
8 [j]Ex 32:4; [k]**Eze 16:15**
9 [l]**2Ki 18:11**; [m]**Jer 4:30**; [n]Hos 11:5
10 [o]Hos 2:10; [p]Eze 16:41; [q]Jer 42:10; [r]Eze 16:36
11 [s]**Jer 3:7**; [t]Jer 3:8–11; **Eze 16:51**
12 [u]2Ki 16:7–15; **2Ch 28:16**; **Eze 16:15**,28
13 [v]**2Ki 17:19**; Hos 12:2
14 [w]**Eze 8:10**; [x]Jer 22:14; Na 2:3
15 [y]**Isa 5:27**

[b]16 Or *When I have allotted you your inheritance*
[c]24 Septuagint; Hebrew *has not been cleansed or rained on*
[d]25 Septuagint; Hebrew *prophets*
[a]14 Or *Babylonians*

and flowing turbans on their heads; all
of them looked like Babylonian chariot
officers, natives of Chaldea.[b] 16As soon
as she saw them, she lusted after them
and sent messengers[z] to them in Chal-
dea.[a] 17Then the Babylonians[b] came to
her, to the bed of love, and in their lust
they defiled her. After she had been
defiled by them, she turned away from
them in disgust.[c] 18When she carried on
her prostitution openly and exposed
her nakedness,[d] I turned away[e] from her
in disgust, just as I had turned away
from her sister.[f] 19Yet she became more
and more promiscuous as she recalled
the days of her youth, when she was a
prostitute in Egypt. 20There she lusted
after her lovers, whose genitals were
like those of donkeys and whose
emission was like that of horses. 21So
you longed for the lewdness of your
youth, when in Egypt your bosom was
caressed and your young breasts
fondled.[c][g]

22"Therefore, Oholibah, this is what
the Sovereign LORD says: I will stir up
your lovers[h] against you, those you
turned away from in disgust, and I will
bring them against you from every side[i]
—23the Babylonians[j] and all the Chal-
deans,[k] the men of Pekod[l] and Shoa and
Koa, and all the Assyrians with them,
handsome young men, all of them
governors and commanders, chariot
officers and men of high rank, all
mounted on horses.[m] 24They will come
against you with weapons,[d] chariots
and wagons[n] and with a throng of
people; they will take up positions
against you on every side with large and
small shields and with helmets. I will
turn you over to them for punishment,[o]
and they will punish you according to
their standards. 25I will direct my
jealous anger[p] against you, and they
will deal with you in fury. They will cut
off your noses and your ears, and those
of you who are left will fall by the
sword. They will take away your sons
and daughters,[q] and those of you who
are left will be consumed by fire.[r] 26They
will also strip[s] you of your clothes and
take your fine jewellery.[t] 27So I will put a
stop[u] to the lewdness and prostitution
you began in Egypt. You will not look
on these things with longing or remem-
ber Egypt any more.

28"For this is what the Sovereign LORD
says: I am about to hand you over[v] to
those you hate, to those you turned
away from in disgust. 29They will deal
with you in hatred and take away every-
thing you have worked for. They will
leave you naked[w] and bare, and the
shame of your prostitution will be
exposed.[x] Your lewdness[y] and prom-
iscuity[z] 30have brought this upon you,
because you lusted after the nations and
defiled yourself with their idols.[a] 31You
have gone the way of your sister; so I
will put her cup[b] into your hand.[c]

32"This is what the Sovereign LORD
says:

"You will drink your sister's cup,
a cup large and deep;
it will bring scorn and derision,[d]
for it holds so much.[e]
33You will be filled with drunkenness
and sorrow,
the cup of ruin and desolation,
the cup of your sister Samaria.[f]
34You will drink it[g] and drain it dry;
you will dash it to pieces
and tear your breasts.

I have spoken, declares the Sovereign
LORD.[h]

35"Therefore this is what the
Sovereign LORD says: Since you have
forgotten[i] me and thrust me behind
your back,[j] you must bear[k] the con-
sequences of your lewdness and
prostitution."

36The LORD said to me: "Son of man,
will you judge Oholah and Oholibah?
Then confront[l] them with their detest-
able practices,[m] 37for they have commit-
ted adultery and blood is on their
hands. They committed adultery with
their idols; they even sacrificed their
children, whom they bore to me,[e] as
food for them.[n] 38They have also done
this to me: At that same time they de-
filed my sanctuary[o] and desecrated my
Sabbaths.[p] 39On the very day they sac-
rificed their children to their idols, they
entered my sanctuary and desecrated[q]
it. That is what they did in my house.[r]

40"They even sent messengers for
men who came from far away,[s] and
when they arrived you bathed yourself
for them, painted your eyes[t] and put on
your jewellery.[u] 41You sat on an elegant
couch,[v] with a table[w] spread before it on
which you had placed the incense[x] and
oil that belonged to me.[y]

16 [z]**Isa 57:9**; [a]**Eze 6:9**
17 [b]Jer 40:9; [c]**Eze 16:29**
18 [d]**Isa 57:8**; [e]Ps 78:59; 106:40; Jer 6:8; [f]Jer 12:8; Am 5:21
21 [g]**Eze 16:26**
22 [h]**Jer 4:30**; [i]**Eze 16:37**
23 [j]2Ki 20:14–18; **Jer 40:9**; [k]**Ge 11:28**; [l]Jer 50:21; [m]**2Ki 24:2**
24 [n]Jer 47:3; Eze 26:7,10; Na 2:4; [o]Jer 39:5–6
25 [p]**Dt 29:20**; [q]ver 47; Eze 24:21; [r]**Jer 12:9**; **Eze 16:38**; **20:47–48**
26 [s]**Jer 13:22**; [t]**Isa 3:18–23**; **Eze 16:39**
27 [u]**Eze 16:41**
28 [v]**Jer 34:20**
29 [w]Mic 1:11; [x]**Jer 13:27**; [y]**Eze 22:9**; [z]Dt 28:48; **Eze 16:36**
30 [a]Ps 106:37–38; Zep 3:1
31 [b]**Jer 25:15**; [c]2Ki 21:13
32 [d]Ps 44:13; Hos 7:16; [e]Ps 60:3; Isa 51:17; Jer 25:15
33 [f]Jer 25:15–16; **Eze 12:19**
34 [g]**Ps 16:5**; [h]**Jer 25:27**
35 [i]**Dt 32:18**; **Isa 17:10**; [j]**1Ki 14:9**; **2Ch 29:6**; [k]Eze 16:52
36 [l]**Eze 16:2**; [m]Isa 58:1; Eze 22:2; Mic 3:8
37 [n]**Eze 16:36**
38 [o]**Lev 15:31**; [p]**Ne 10:31**
39 [q]**2Ki 21:4**; [r]Jer 7:10; Eze 22:8
40 [s]**Isa 57:9**; [t]2Ki 9:30; [u]**Jer 4:30**; Eze 16:13–19; Hos 2:13
41 [v]**Est 1:6**; **Pr 7:17**; [w]Isa 65:11; Eze 41:22; 44:16; Mal 1:7,12; [x]Isa 57:9; **65:3**; **Jer 44:5**; [y]**Nu 18:12**

---

b15 Or *Babylonia;* also in verse 16
c21 Syriac (see also verse 3); Hebrew *caressed because of your young breasts*
d24 The meaning of the Hebrew for this word is uncertain.
e37 Or *even made the children they bore to me pass through* ⌞*the fire*⌟

42"The noise of a carefree[z] crowd was
around her; Sabeans[f][a] were brought
from the desert along with men from
the rabble, and they put bracelets[b] on
the arms of the woman and her sister
and beautiful crowns on their heads.[c]
43Then I said about the one worn out by
adultery, 'Now let them use her as a
prostitute,[d] for that is all she is.' 44And
they slept with her. As men sleep with a
prostitute, so they slept with those lewd
women, Oholah and Oholibah. 45But
righteous men will sentence them to the
punishment of women who commit
adultery and shed blood,[e] because they
are adulterous and blood is on their
hands.[f]

46"This is what the Sovereign LORD
says: Bring a mob[g] against them and
give them over to terror and plunder.[h]
47The mob will stone them and cut them
down with their swords; they will kill
their sons and daughters[i] and burn[j]
down their houses.[k]

48"So I will put an end[l] to lewdness in
the land, that all women may take warn-
ing and not imitate you.[m] 49You will
suffer the penalty for your lewdness
and bear the consequences of your sins
of idolatry.[n] Then you will know that I
am the Sovereign LORD.[o]"

The Cooking Pot

24 In the ninth year, in the tenth
month on the tenth day, the
word of the LORD came to me:[a] 2"Son of
man, record[b] this date, this very date,
because the king of Babylon has laid
siege to Jerusalem this very day.[c] 3Tell
this rebellious house[d] a parable[e] and say
to them: 'This is what the Sovereign
LORD says:

"'Put on the cooking pot;[f] put it on
and pour water into it.
4Put into it the pieces of meat,
all the choice pieces—the leg and
the shoulder.
Fill it with the best of these bones;[g]
5 take the pick of the flock.[h]
Pile wood beneath it for the bones;
bring it to the boil
and cook the bones in it.[i]

6"'For this is what the Sovereign LORD
says:

"'Woe[j] to the city of bloodshed,[k]
to the pot now encrusted,
whose deposit will not go away!
Empty it piece by piece
without casting lots[l] for them.[m]

42 [z]**Ps 73:5;** [a]**2Ch 9:1;** [b]**Ge 24:30;** [c]**Eze 16:11–12**
43 [d]ver 3
45 [e]**Eze 22:3;** [f]**Lev 20:10; Eze 16:38;** Hos 2:2; 6:5
46 [g]Eze 16:40; [h]**Dt 28:25; Jer 25:9**
47 [i]ver 25; [j]2Ch 36:19; **Jer 34:22;** [k]**2Ch 36:17**
48 [l]Eze 16:41; [m]2Pe 2:6
49 [n]Eze 24:13; [o]**Eze 7:4; 9:10;** 16:58; **20:38**

Ch. 24

1 [a]**Eze 8:1;** 26:1; 29:17
2 [b]Isa 30:8; Hab 2:2; [c]2Ki 25:1; **Jer 39:1**
3 [d]**Isa 1:2;** Eze 2:3,6; [e]**Eze 20:49;** [f]**Eze 11:3**
4 [g]**Eze 11:7**
5 [h]**Isa 34:12;** Jer 52:10; [i]Jer 52:24–27; Mic 3:2–3
6 [j]**Eze 16:23;** [k]**Eze 22:2;** [l]Job 6:27; Joel 3:3; Ob 11; Na 3:10; [m]**Eze 11:11**
7 [n]**Lev 17:13**
11 [o]Jer 21:10
13 [p]**Isa 22:14;** [q]Jer 6:28–30; La 1:9; **Eze 16:42;** 22:24; 23:36–49; Hos 7:1; Zec 6:8
14 [r]Eze 22:14; [s]**Nu 11:23;** [t]**Eze 8:18;** [u]**Job 27:22;** [v]Eze 36:19; Zec 8:14; [w]**Isa 3:11; Eze 18:30**
16 [x]**Ps 39:10;** [y]ver 21; Ps 84:1; **La 2:4;** [z]Jer 13:17; 16:5; **22:10**
17 [a]Ps 39:9; [b]**Ex 28:39; Isa 3:20;** [c]**Isa 20:2;** [d]**Lev 13:45;** [e]ver 22; **Jer 16:7**
18 [f]**Eze 12:7**

7"'For the blood she shed is in her
midst:
She poured it on the bare rock;
she did not pour it on the ground,
where the dust would cover it.[n]
8To stir up wrath and take revenge
I put her blood on the bare rock,
so that it would not be covered.

9"'Therefore this is what the Sov-
ereign LORD says:

"'Woe to the city of bloodshed!
I, too, will pile the wood high.
10So heap on the wood
and kindle the fire.
Cook the meat well,
mixing in the spices;
and let the bones be charred.
11Then set the empty pot on the coals
till it becomes hot and its copper
glows
so its impurities may be melted
and its deposit burned away.[o]
12It has frustrated all efforts;
its heavy deposit has not been
removed,
not even by fire.

13"'Now your impurity is lewdness.
Because I tried to cleanse you but you
would not be cleansed[p] from your im-
purity, you will not be clean again until
my wrath against you has subsided.[q]

14"'I the LORD have spoken.[r] The time
has come for me to act.[s] I will not hold
back; I will not have pity,[t] nor will I
relent.[u] You will be judged according
to your conduct and your actions,[v]
declares the Sovereign LORD.[w]'"

Ezekiel's Wife Dies

15The word of the LORD came to me:
16"Son of man, with one blow[x] I am
about to take away from you the delight
of your eyes.[y] Yet do not lament or weep
or shed any tears.[z] 17Groan quietly;[a] do
not mourn for the dead. Keep your tur-
ban[b] fastened and your sandals[c] on your
feet; do not cover the lower part of your
face[d] or eat the customary food ⌞of
mourners⌟.[e]"

18So I spoke to the people in the morn-
ing, and in the evening my wife died.
The next morning I did as I had been
commanded.[f]

19Then the people asked me, "Won't

---

f42 Or *drunkards*

you tell us what these things have to do with us?[g]"

20 So I said to them, "The word of the LORD came to me: 21 Say to the house of Israel, 'This is what the Sovereign LORD says: I am about to desecrate my sanctuary[h]—the stronghold in which you take pride,[i] the delight of your eyes,[j] the object of your affection. The sons and daughters[k] you left behind will fall by the sword.[l] 22 And you will do as I have done. You will not cover the lower part of your face[m] or eat the customary food ⌞of mourners⌟.[n] 23 You will keep your turbans[o] on your heads and your sandals[p] on your feet. You will not mourn[q] or weep but will waste away[r] because of[a] your sins and groan among yourselves.[s] 24 Ezekiel[t] will be a sign[u] to you; you will do just as he has done. When this happens, you will know that I am the Sovereign LORD.'

25 "And you, son of man, on the day I take away their stronghold, their joy and glory, the delight of their eyes,[v] their heart's desire,[w] and their sons and daughters[x] as well— 26 on that day a fugitive will come to tell you[y] the news. 27 At that time your mouth will be opened; you will speak with him and will no longer be silent.[z] So you will be a sign to them, and they will know that I am the LORD.[a]"

A Prophecy Against Ammon

25 The word of the LORD came to me: 2 "Son of man, set your face against[a] the Ammonites[b] and prophesy against them.[c] 3 Say to them, 'Hear the word of the Sovereign LORD. This is what the Sovereign LORD says: Because you said "Aha![d]" over my sanctuary when it was desecrated[e] and over the land of Israel when it was laid waste and over the people of Judah when they went into exile,[f] 4 therefore I am going to give you to the people of the East[g] as a possession. They will set up their camps[h] and pitch their tents among you; they will eat your fruit and drink your milk.[i] 5 I will turn Rabbah[j] into a pasture for camels and Ammon into a resting place for sheep.[k] Then you will know that I am the LORD. 6 For this is what the Sovereign LORD says: Because you have clapped your hands[l] and stamped your feet, rejoicing with all the malice of your heart against the land of Israel,[m] 7 therefore I will stretch out my hand[n] against you and give you as plunder[o] to the nations. I will cut you off from the nations and exterminate you from the countries. I will destroy[p] you, and you will know that I am the LORD.[q]'"

A Prophecy Against Moab

8 "This is what the Sovereign LORD says: 'Because Moab[r] and Seir[s] said, "Look, the house of Judah has become like all the other nations," 9 therefore I will expose the flank of Moab, beginning at its frontier towns—Beth Jeshimoth[t], Baal Meon[u] and Kiriathaim[v]—the glory of that land. 10 I will give Moab along with the Ammonites to the people of the East as a possession, so that the Ammonites will not be remembered[w] among the nations; 11 and I will inflict punishment on Moab. Then they will know that I am the LORD.'"[x]

A Prophecy Against Edom

12 "This is what the Sovereign LORD says: 'Because Edom[y] took revenge on the house of Judah and became very guilty by doing so, 13 therefore this is what the Sovereign LORD says: I will stretch out my hand[z] against Edom and kill its men and their animals.[a] I will lay it waste, and from Teman[b] to Dedan[c] they will fall by the sword.[d] 14 I will take vengeance on Edom by the hand of my people Israel, and they will deal with Edom in accordance with my anger[e] and my wrath; they will know my vengeance, declares the Sovereign LORD.'"[f]

A Prophecy Against Philistia

15 "This is what the Sovereign LORD says: 'Because the Philistines[g] acted in vengeance and took revenge with malice[h] in their hearts, and with ancient hostility sought to destroy Judah, 16 therefore this is what the Sovereign LORD says: I am about to stretch out my hand against the Philistines,[i] and I will cut off the Kerethites[j] and destroy those remaining along the coast.[k] 17 I will carry out great vengeance[l] on them and punish[m] them in my wrath. Then they will know that I am the LORD,[n] when I take vengeance on them.[o][p]'"

19 [g]Eze 12:9; 37:18
21 [h]**Lev 26:31; Eze 7:24;** [i]**Lev 26:19;** [j]**ver 16;** Ps 27:4; [k]**Eze 23:25;** [l]Jer 7:14–15; Hos 9:12,16; Mal 2:12
22 [m]**Lev 13:45;** [n]Jer 16:7
23 [o]**Ex 28:39; Isa 3:20;** [p]**Isa 20:2;** [q]Ex 33:4; [r]**Lev 26:16;** [s]Ps 78:64
24 [t]Eze 1:3; [u]**Isa 20:3;** Eze 12:11
25 [v]**La 2:4;** [w]**Ps 20:4;** [x]Dt 28:32; Jer 11:22
26 [y]**1Sa 4:12;** Job 1:15–19
27 [z]Da 10:15; [a]**Eze 3:26;** 33:22

Ch. 25

2 [a]**Eze 13:17;** 29:2; [b]**Eze 21:28;** [c]Jer 49:1–6
3 [d]**Ps 35:21;** Eze 26:2; 36:2; [e]Zep 2:8; [f]**Pr 17:5**
4 [g]**Ge 25:6; Jdg 6:3;** [h]**Nu 31:10;** [i]Dt 28:33,51; **Jdg 6:33**
5 [j]**Dt 3:11;** [k]**Isa 17:2**
6 [l]**Nu 24:10;** [m]**Eze 6:11;** Ob 12; Zep 2:8
7 [n]Zep 1:4; [o]**Nu 14:3;** [p]Eze 21:31; [q]ver 13–14,17; Am 1:14–15
8 [r]**Ge 19:37; Dt 23:6; Isa 16:6;** [s]**Ge 14:6**
9 [t]**Nu 33:49;** [u]**Nu 32:3; Jos 13:17;** [v]**Nu 32:37; Jos 13:19**
10 [w]Eze 21:32
11 [x]Isa 15:9; 16:1–14; Jer 48:1; Am 2:1–3
12 [y]**2Sa 8:13–14; 2Ch 28:17; Isa 11:14**
13 [z]**Ex 7:5; Eze 16:27;** [a]Eze 29:8; [b]**Ge 36:11,**15,34; [c]Jer 25:23; [d]**Jer 49:10; Eze 14:17**
14 [e]Eze 35:11; [f]**Ps 137:7;** Eze 32:29; 35:2–3; 36:5; Am 1:11; Ob 1,10–16; Mal 1:4
15 [g]**Jos 13:3; 2Ch 28:18;** [h]**Ps 73:8**
16 [i]**2Ch 26:6;** Am 1:8; [j]**1Sa 30:14;** [k]**Eze 20:33**
17 [l]**Nu 31:3;** [m]**Jer 44:13;** [n]**Ex 6:2; 8:22;** [o]**Isa 11:14;** [p]**Isa 14:30;** Jer 47:7; Joel 3:4

[a]23 Or *away in*

A Prophecy Against Tyre

26 In the eleventh year, on the first day of the month, the word of the LORD came to me:[a] 2"Son of man, because Tyre[b] has said of Jerusalem, 'Aha![c] The gate to the nations is broken, and its doors have swung open to me; now that she lies in ruins I will prosper,' 3therefore this is what the Sovereign LORD says: I am against you, O Tyre, and I will bring many nations against you, like the sea[d] casting up its waves. 4They will destroy[e] the walls of Tyre[f] and pull down her towers; I will scrape away her rubble and make her a bare rock. 5Out in the sea[g] she will become a place to spread fishing nets,[h] for I have spoken, declares the Sovereign LORD. She will become plunder[i] for the nations,[j] 6and her settlements on the mainland will be ravaged by the sword. Then they will know that I am the LORD.

7"For this is what the Sovereign LORD says: From the north I am going to bring against Tyre Nebuchadnezzar[a][k] king of Babylon, king of kings,[l] with horses and chariots,[m] with horsemen and a great army. 8He will ravage your settlements on the mainland with the sword; he will set up siege works[n] against you, build a ramp[o] up to your walls and raise his shields against you. 9He will direct the blows of his battering-rams against your walls and demolish your towers with his weapons.[p] 10His horses will be so many that they will cover you with dust. Your walls will tremble at the noise of the war horses, wagons and chariots[q] when he enters your gates as men enter a city whose walls have been broken through. 11The hoofs[r] of his horses will trample all your streets; he will kill your people with the sword, and your strong pillars[s] will fall to the ground.[t] 12They will plunder your wealth and loot your merchandise; they will break down your walls and demolish your fine houses and throw your stones, timber and rubble into the sea.[u] 13I will put an end[v] to your noisy songs,[w] and the music of your harps[x] will be heard no more.[y] 14I will make you a bare rock, and you will become a place to spread fishing nets. You will never be rebuilt,[z] for I the LORD have spoken, declares the Sovereign LORD.

15"This is what the Sovereign LORD says to Tyre: Will not the coastlands[a] tremble[b] at the sound of your fall, when the wounded groan[c] and the slaughter takes place in you? 16Then all the princes of the coast will step down from their thrones and lay aside their robes and take off their embroidered[d] garments. Clothed[e] with terror, they will sit on the ground,[f] trembling[g] every moment, appalled[h] at you. 17Then they will take up a lament[i] concerning you and say to you:

"'How you are destroyed, O city of
  renown,
 peopled by men of the sea!
You were a power on the seas,
 you and your citizens;
you put your terror
 on all who lived there.[j]
18Now the coastlands tremble[k]
 on the day of your fall;
the islands in the sea
 are terrified at your collapse.'[l]

19"This is what the Sovereign LORD says: When I make you a desolate city, like cities no longer inhabited, and when I bring the ocean depths[m] over you and its vast waters cover you,[n] 20then I will bring you down with those who go down to the pit,[o] to the people of long ago. I will make you dwell in the earth below, as in ancient ruins, with those who go down to the pit, and you will not return or take your place[b] in the land of the living.[p] 21I will bring you to a horrible end and you will be no more.[q] You will be sought, but you will never again be found, declares the Sovereign LORD."[r]

A Lament for Tyre

27 The word of the LORD came to me: 2"Son of man, take up a lament[a] concerning Tyre. 3Say to Tyre,[b] situated at the gateway to the sea,[c] merchant of peoples on many coasts, 'This is what the Sovereign LORD says:

"'You say, O Tyre,
 "I am perfect in beauty."[d]
4Your domain was on the high seas;
 your builders brought your beauty
  to perfection.[e]
5They made all your timbers
 of pine trees from Senir;[a][f]
they took a cedar from Lebanon[g]
 to make a mast for you.
6Of oaks[h] from Bashan
 they made your oars;

Ch. 26

1 [a]**Eze 24:1**; 29:1; 30:20
2 [b]**Jos 19:29**; 2Sa 5:11; [c]**Eze 25:3**
3 [d]ver 19; Isa 5:30; Jer 50:42; 51:42
4 [e]**Isa 23:1**,11; [f]Am 1:10
5 [g]Eze 27:32; [h]Eze 47:10; [i]**Nu 14:3**; Eze 29:19; [j]Zec 9:2–4
7 [k]Jer 27:6; 39:1; [l]**Ezr 7:12**; [m]**Eze 23:24**; Na 2:3–4
8 [n]**Jer 6:6**; [o]**Jer 33:4**
9 [p]**Eze 21:22**
10 [q]**Jer 4:13**; **46:9**; **Eze 23:24**
11 [r]Isa 5:28; [s]**Jer 43:13**; [t]**Isa 26:5**
12 [u]Isa 23:8; **Jer 4:7**; Eze 27:3–27; 28:8; Hab 1:8
13 [v]**Jer 7:34**; [w]**Isa 23:7**; [x]**Ps 137:2**; **Isa 14:11**; [y]**Job 30:31**; **Jer 16:9**; **25:10**; Rev 18:22
14 [z]**Job 12:14**; Mal 1:4
15 [a]Isa 41:5; Eze 27:35; [b]**Jer 49:21**; [c]**Job 24:12**
16 [d]**Ex 26:36**; [e]**Job 8:22**; [f]**Job 2:8**,13; [g]Hos 11:10; [h]**Lev 26:32**; Eze 32:10
17 [i]**Eze 19:1**; [j]Isa 14:12
18 [k]**Ps 46:6**; **Jer 49:21**; [l]Isa 23:5; **41:5**; Eze 27:35
19 [m]**Ge 7:11**; [n]**ver 3**; Isa 8:7–8
20 [o]Nu 16:30; Ps 28:1; 88:6; Eze 31:14; 32:18; Am 9:2; Jnh 2:2,6; [p]**Job 28:13**; **Isa 14:9–10**; Eze 32:24,30
21 [q]**Jer 51:64**; Da 11:19; [r]Jer 20:4; Eze 27:36; 28:19; Rev 18:21

Ch. 27

2 [a]**Eze 19:1**
3 [b]**Ps 83:7**; [c]ver 33; Hos 9:13; [d]**Isa 23:9**; **Eze 16:15**
4 [e]Eze 28:12
5 [f]**Dt 3:9**; [g]**Isa 2:13**
6 [h]Nu 21:33; **Ps 29:9**; Jer 22:20; Zec 11:2

[a]7 Hebrew *Nebuchadrezzar*, of which *Nebuchadnezzar* is a variant; here and often in Ezekiel and Jeremiah
[b]20 Septuagint; Hebrew *return, and I will give glory*
[a]5 That is, Hermon

of cypress wood[b] from the coasts of
Cyprus[c][i]
they made your deck, inlaid with
ivory.
7Fine embroidered linen[j] from Egypt
was your sail
and served as your banner;
your awnings were of blue and
purple[k]
from the coasts of Elishah.[l]
8Men of Sidon and Arvad[m] were your
oarsmen;
your skilled men, O Tyre, were
aboard as your seamen.[n]
9Veteran craftsmen of Gebal[d][o] were on
board
as shipwrights to caulk your seams.
All the ships of the sea[p] and their
sailors
came alongside to trade for your
wares.

10" 'Men of Persia,[q] Lydia[r] and Put[s]
served as soldiers in your army.
They hung their shields[t] and helmets
on your walls,
bringing you splendour.
11Men of Arvad and Helech
manned your walls on every side;
men of Gammad
were in your towers.
They hung their shields around your
walls;
they brought your beauty to
perfection.[u]

12" 'Tarshish[v] did business with you
because of your great wealth of goods;[w]
they exchanged silver, iron, tin and lead
for your merchandise.
13" 'Greece,[x] Tubal and Meshech[y]
traded with you; they exchanged slaves[z]
and articles of bronze for your wares.
14" 'Men of Beth Togarmah[a] ex-
changed work horses, war horses and
mules for your merchandise.
15" 'The men of Rhodes[e][b] traded with
you, and many coastlands[c] were your
customers; they paid you with ivory[d]
tusks and ebony.
16" 'Aram[f][e] did business with you
because of your many products; they
exchanged turquoise,[f] purple fabric,
embroidered work, fine linen,[g] coral[h]
and rubies for your merchandise.
17" 'Judah and Israel traded with you;
they exchanged wheat[i] from Minnith[j]
and confections,[g] honey, oil and balm[k]
for your wares.[l]
18" 'Damascus,[m] because of your
many products and great wealth of
goods,[n] did business with you in wine
from Helbon and wool from Zahar.
19" 'Danites and Greeks[o] from Uzal[p]
bought your merchandise; they
exchanged wrought iron, cassia[q] and
calamus for your wares.
20" 'Dedan[r] traded in saddle blankets
with you.
21" 'Arabia[s] and all the princes of
Kedar[t] were your customers; they did
business with you in lambs, rams and
goats.
22" 'The merchants of Sheba[u] and
Raamah traded with you; for your mer-
chandise they exchanged the finest of
all kinds of spices[v] and precious stones,
and gold.[w]
23" 'Haran,[x] Canneh and Eden[y] and
merchants of Sheba, Asshur[z] and Kil-
mad traded with you. 24In your market-
place they traded with you beautiful
garments, blue fabric, embroidered
work and multicoloured rugs with
cords twisted and tightly knotted.

25" 'The ships of Tarshish[a] serve
as carriers for your wares.
You are filled with heavy cargo
in the heart of the sea.[b]
26Your oarsmen take you
out to the high seas.
But the east wind[c] will break you to
pieces
in the heart of the sea.
27Your wealth,[d] merchandise and
wares,
your mariners, seamen and
shipwrights,
your merchants and all your soldiers,
and everyone else on board
will sink into the heart of the sea[e]
on the day of your shipwreck.
28The shorelands will quake[f]
when your seamen cry out.
29All who handle the oars
will abandon their ships;
the mariners and all the seamen
will stand on the shore.
30They will raise their voice
and cry bitterly over you;
they will sprinkle dust[g] on their heads
and roll[h] in ashes.[i]
31They will shave their heads[j] because of
you
and will put on sackcloth.

6 [i]Ge 10:4; Isa 23:12
7 [j]Ex 26:36; Isa 19:9; [k]Ex 25:4; Jer 10:9; [l]Ge 10:4
8 [m]Ge 10:18; [n]1Ki 9:27
9 [o]Jos 13:5; [p]Ps 104:26
10 [q]2Ch 36:20; Ezr 1:1; Eze 38:5; Da 8:20; [r]Isa 66:19; [s]Ge 10:6; Eze 30:5; Na 3:9; [t]SS 4:4
11 [u]ver 27
12 [v]Ge 10:4; [w]ver 18,33
13 [x]Joel 3:6; [y]Ge 10:2; Isa 66:19; Eze 32:26; 38:2; 39:1; [z]Rev 18:13
14 [a]Ge 10:3
15 [b]Ge 10:7; [c]Jer 25:22; [d]1Ki 10:22; Rev 18:12
16 [e]Jdg 10:6; Isa 7:1–8; [f]Ex 28:18; 39:11; Eze 28:13; [g]Eze 16:10; [h]Job 28:18
17 [i]1Ki 5:9; [j]Jdg 11:33; [k]Ge 43:11; [l]Ac 12:20
18 [m]Ge 14:15; Eze 47:16–18; [n]ver 12
19 [o]Ge 10:2; [p]Ge 10:27; [q]Ex 30:24
20 [r]Ge 10:7
21 [s]2Ch 9:14; [t]Ge 25:13; Isa 21:17
22 [u]Ge 10:7,28; [v]Ge 43:11; [w]Rev 18:12
23 [x]Ge 11:26; [y]Isa 37:12; [z]Ge 10:22; Nu 24:24
25 [a]Ge 10:4; Isa 2:16 *fn*; [b]Rev 18:3
26 [c]Ge 41:6; Jer 18:17
27 [d]Pr 11:4; [e]Eze 28:8
28 [f]Jer 49:21
30 [g]Jos 7:6; 2Sa 1:2; [h]Jer 6:26; [i]Rev 18:18–19
31 [j]Lev 13:40; Job 1:20; Isa 3:17; Jer 48:37

---

b6 Targum; the Masoretic Text has a different division of the consonants.
c6 Hebrew *Kittim* d9 That is, Byblos
e15 Septuagint; Hebrew *Dedan*
f16 Most Hebrew manuscripts; some Hebrew manuscripts and Syriac *Edom*
g17 The meaning of the Hebrew for this word is uncertain.

They will weep[k] over you with
anguish of soul
and with bitter mourning.[l]
32As they wail and mourn over you,
they will take up a lament[m]
concerning you:
"Who was ever silenced like Tyre,
surrounded by the sea?[n]"
33When your merchandise went out on
the seas,[o]
you satisfied many nations;
with your great wealth[p] and your
wares
you enriched the kings of the earth.
34Now you are shattered by the sea
in the depths of the waters;
your wares and all your company
have gone down with you.[q]
35All who live in the coastlands[r]
are appalled[s] at you;
their kings shudder with horror
and their faces are distorted with
fear.[t]
36The merchants among the nations hiss
at you;[u]
you have come to a horrible end
and will be no more.[v]' "

A Prophecy Against the King of Tyre

28 The word of the LORD came to
me: 2"Son of man[a], say to the
ruler of Tyre, 'This is what the
Sovereign LORD says:

" 'In the pride of your heart
you say, "I am a god;
I sit on the throne[b] of a god
in the heart of the seas."[c]
But you are a man and not a god,
though you think you are as wise as
a god.[d]
3Are you wiser than Daniel?[a][e]
Is no secret hidden from you?
4By your wisdom and understanding
you have gained wealth for yourself
and amassed gold and silver
in your treasuries.[f]
5By your great skill in trading[g]
you have increased your wealth,[h]
and because of your wealth
your heart has grown proud.[i]

6" 'Therefore this is what the
Sovereign LORD says:

" 'Because you think you are wise,
as wise as a god,
7I am going to bring foreigners against
you,
the most ruthless of nations;[j]
they will draw their swords against
your beauty and wisdom[k]
and pierce your shining splendour.[l]
8They will bring you down to the pit,[m]
and you will die a violent death[n]
in the heart of the seas.[o]
9Will you then say, "I am a god,"
in the presence of those who kill
you?
You will be but a man, not a god,[p]
in the hands of those who slay you.[q]
10You will die the death of the
uncircumcised[r]
at the hands of foreigners.

I have spoken, declares the Sovereign
LORD.' "

11The word of the LORD came to me:
12"Son of man, take up a lament[s] con-
cerning the king of Tyre and say to him:
'This is what the Sovereign LORD says:

" 'You were the model of perfection,
full of wisdom and perfect in
beauty.[t]
13You were in Eden,[u]
the garden of God;[v]
every precious stone[w] adorned you:
ruby, topaz and emerald,
chrysolite, onyx and jasper,
sapphire,[b] turquoise[x] and beryl.[c]
Your settings and mountings[d] were
made of gold;
on the day you were created they
were prepared.[y]
14You were anointed[z] as a guardian
cherub,[a]
for so I ordained you.
You were on the holy mount of God;
you walked among the fiery stones.
15You were blameless in your ways
from the day you were created
till wickedness was found in you.
16Through your widespread trade
you were filled with violence,[b]
and you sinned.
So I drove you in disgrace from the
mount of God,
and I expelled you, O guardian
cherub,[c]
from among the fiery stones.
17Your heart became proud[d]
on account of your beauty,
and you corrupted your wisdom
because of your splendour.
So I threw you to the earth;

31 [k]**Isa 16:9**; Rev 18:15; [l]**Est 4:1**; Job 3:20; Isa 22:12; Jer 6:26; **La 2:10**; **Eze 7:18**
32 [m]**Eze 19:1**; [n]Isa 23:1–6; Eze 26:5
33 [o]**ver 3**; [p]**ver 12**; Eze 28:4–5
34 [q]Zec 9:4
35 [r]**Eze 26:15**; [s]**Lev 26:32**; **Job 18:20**; [t]**Eze 26:17–18**; 32:10
36 [u]Jer 19:8; **49:17**; **50:13**; Zep 2:15; [v]**Ps 37:10,36**; **Eze 26:21**
Ch. 28
2 [a]**Isa 13:11**; [b]**Isa 14:13**; [c]Zep 2:15; [d]**Ge 3:5**; **Ps 9:20**; 82:6–7; **Eze 16:49**; 2Th 2:4
3 [e]**Eze 14:14**; Da 1:20; 2:20–23, 28; 5:11–12
4 [f]Isa 10:13; Zec 9:3
5 [g]**Isa 23:8**; [h]**Jer 9:23**; **Eze 27:33**; [i]**Job 31:25**; Ps 52:7; 62:10; Hos 12:8; 13:6
7 [j]Eze 30:11; 31:12; 32:12; Hab 1:6; [k]Jer 9:23; [l]**Eze 7:24**
8 [m]**Ps 55:23**; Eze 32:30; [n]Rev 18:7; [o]**Eze 26:12**; 27:27
9 [p]Isa 31:3; [q]**Eze 16:49**
10 [r]**1Sa 14:6**; **Jer 9:26**; Eze 32:19,24
12 [s]**Eze 19:1**; [t]Eze 27:2–4
13 [u]**Ge 2:8**; [v]Eze 31:8–9; [w]Rev 17:4; [x]**Eze 27:16**; [y]Isa 14:11; Rev 21:20
14 [z]Ex 30:26; 40:9; [a]Ex 25:17–20
16 [b]**Ge 6:11**; Hab 2:17; [c]**Ge 3:24**
17 [d]Isa 10:12; Eze 16:49; 31:10

[a]3 Or *Danel;* the Hebrew spelling may suggest a person other than the prophet Daniel.
[b]13 Or *lapis lazuli*
[c]13 The precise identification of some of these precious stones is uncertain.
[d]13 The meaning of the Hebrew for this phrase is uncertain.

I made a spectacle of you before
kings.[e]
18By your many sins and dishonest
trade
you have desecrated your
sanctuaries.
So I made a fire[f] come out from you,
and it consumed you,
and I reduced you to ashes[g] on the
ground
in the sight of all who were
watching.[h]
19All the nations who knew you
are appalled[i] at you;
you have come to a horrible end
and will be no more.[j]' "

A Prophecy Against Sidon

20The word of the LORD came to me:
21"Son of man, set your face against[k]
Sidon;[l] prophesy against her 22and say:
'This is what the Sovereign LORD says:

" 'I am against you, O Sidon,
and I will gain glory[m] within you.
They will know that I am the LORD,
when I inflict punishment[n] on her
and show myself holy[o] within her.
23I will send a plague upon her
and make blood flow in her streets.
The slain will fall within her,
with the sword against her on every
side.
Then they will know that I am the
LORD.[p]

24" 'No longer will the people of Israel
have malicious neighbours who are
painful briers and sharp thorns.[q] Then
they will know that I am the Sovereign
LORD.
25" 'This is what the Sovereign LORD
says: When I gather[r] the people of Israel
from the nations where they have been
scattered,[s] I will show myself holy[t]
among them in the sight of the nations.
Then they will live in their own land,
which I gave to my servant Jacob.[u]
26They will live there in safety[v] and will
build houses and plant[w] vineyards; they
will live in safety when I inflict punish-
ment[x] on all their neighbours who
maligned them. Then they will know
that I am the LORD their God.[y]' "

A Prophecy Against Egypt

29 In the tenth year, in the tenth
month on the twelfth day, the
word of the LORD came to me:[a] 2"Son of
man, set your face against[b] Pharaoh
king of Egypt[c] and prophesy against

17 [e]Eze 19:12
18 [f]Ob 18; [g]Mal 4:3; [h]Zec 9:2–4
19 [i]Lev 26:32; [j]Jer 51:64; Eze 26:21
21 [k]Eze 13:17; [l]Ge 10:15; Jer 25:22
22 [m]Eze 39:13; [n]Eze 30:19; [o]Lev 10:3
23 [p]Eze 5:17; 38:22
24 [q]Isa 5:6; Eze 2:6
25 [r]Ps 106:47; Jer 32:37; [s]Isa 11:12; [t]Eze 20:41; [u]Jer 12:15; 23:8; Eze 11:17; 34:27; 37:25
26 [v]Lev 25:18; 1Ki 4:25; Jer 17:25; [w]Dt 20:6; [x]Ps 149:9; [y]Isa 65:21; Jer 32:15; Eze 38:8; 39:26–27; Hos 2:15; 11:11; Am 9:14–15

Ch. 29

1 [a]ver 17; Eze 26:1
2 [b]Eze 25:2; [c]Jer 25:19; [d]Isa 19:1–17; Jer 46:2; Eze 30:1–26; 31:1–18; 32:1–32
3 [e]Jer 44:30; [f]Ps 68:30; 74:13; Eze 32:2; [g]Jer 46:8
4 [h]2Ki 19:28; Job 41:2; [i]Eze 38:4
5 [j]Jer 8:2; [k]Jer 7:33; 34:20; Eze 31:13; 32:4–6; 39:4
6 [l]2Ki 18:21
7 [m]2Ki 18:21; Isa 36:6; [n]Jer 17:5; Eze 17:15–17
8 [o]Eze 25:13; 32:11–13
9 [p]Jer 46:8; [q]Eze 30:7–8, 13–19
10 [r]Jer 21:13; [s]Ex 3:22; [t]Jer 46:19; [u]Ex 14:2; [v]Eze 30:6; [w]Isa 18:1; Eze 30:4
11 [x]Eze 32:13
12 [y]Isa 34:10; [z]Jer 46:19; Eze 30:7,23, 26

him and against all Egypt.[d] 3Speak to
him and say: 'This is what the Sovereign
LORD says:

" 'I am against you, Pharaoh[e] king of
Egypt,
you great monster[f] lying among
your streams.
You say, "The Nile[g] is mine;
I made it for myself."
4But I will put hooks[h] in your jaws
and make the fish of your streams
stick to your scales.
I will pull you out from among your
streams,
with all the fish sticking to your
scales.[i]
5I will leave you in the desert,
you and all the fish of your streams.
You will fall on the open field
and not be gathered[j] or picked up.
I will give you as food
to the beasts of the earth and the
birds of the air.[k]

6Then all who live in Egypt will know
that I am the LORD.

" 'You have been a staff of reed[l] for the
house of Israel. 7When they grasped
you with their hands, you splintered[m]
and you tore open their shoulders;
when they leaned on you, you broke
and their backs were wrenched.[a] [n]
8" 'Therefore this is what the
Sovereign LORD says: I will bring a
sword against you and kill your men
and their animals.[o] 9Egypt will become a
desolate wasteland. Then they will
know that I am the LORD.
" 'Because you said, "The Nile[p] is
mine; I made it,[q]" 10therefore I am
against you[r] and against your streams,
and I will make the land of Egypt[s] a ruin
and a desolate waste[t] from Migdol[u] to
Aswan,[v] as far as the border of Cush.[b] [w]
11No foot of man or animal will pass
through it; no-one will live there for
forty years.[x] 12I will make the land of
Egypt desolate[y] among devastated
lands, and her cities will lie desolate for
forty years among ruined cities. And I
will disperse the Egyptians among the
nations and scatter them through the
countries.[z]
13" 'Yet this is what the Sovereign
LORD says: At the end of forty years I
will gather the Egyptians from the
nations where they were scattered. 14I

[a]7 Syriac (see also Septuagint and Vulgate); Hebrew *and you caused their backs to stand*
[b]10 That is, the upper Nile region

will bring them back from captivity and
return them to Upper Egypt,[c][a] the land
of their ancestry. There they will be a
lowly[b] kingdom.[c] 15It will be the lowliest
of kingdoms and will never again exalt
itself above the other nations.[d] I will
make it so weak that it will never again
rule over the nations. 16Egypt will no
longer be a source of confidence[e] for the
people of Israel but will be a reminder[f] of
their sin in turning to her for help.[g]
Then they will know that I am the
Sovereign LORD.[h]'"

17In the twenty-seventh year, in the
first month on the first day, the word of
the LORD came to me:[i] 18"Son of man,
Nebuchadnezzar[j] king of Babylon drove
his army in a hard campaign against
Tyre; every head was rubbed bare[k] and
every shoulder made raw.[l] Yet he and
his army got no reward from the cam-
paign he led against Tyre. 19Therefore
this is what the Sovereign LORD says: I
am going to give Egypt to Nebuchad-
nezzar king[m] of Babylon, and he will
carry off its wealth. He will loot and
plunder[n] the land as pay for his army.[o]
20I have given him Egypt[p] as a reward
for his efforts because he and his army
did it for me, declares the Sovereign
LORD.[q]

21"On that day I will make a horn[d][r]
grow for the house of Israel, and I will
open your mouth[s] among them. Then
they will know that I am the LORD.[t]"

A Lament for Egypt

30 The word of the LORD came to
me: 2"Son of man, prophesy
and say: 'This is what the Sovereign
LORD says:

"'Wail[a] and say,
"Alas for that day!"
3For the day is near,[b]
the day of the LORD[c] is near—
a day of clouds,
a time of doom for the nations.
4A sword will come against Egypt,[d]
and anguish will come upon
Cush.[a][e]
When the slain fall in Egypt,
her wealth will be carried away
and her foundations torn down.[f]

5Cush and Put,[g] Lydia and all Arabia,[h]
Libya[b] and the people[i] of the covenant
land will fall by the sword along with
Egypt.[j]
6"'This is what the LORD says:

"'The allies of Egypt will fall
and her proud strength will fail.
From Migdol to Aswan[k]
they will fall by the sword within
her,
declares the Sovereign LORD.
7"'They will be desolate
among desolate lands,
and their cities will lie
among ruined cities.[l]
8Then they will know that I am the
LORD,
when I set fire[m] to Egypt
and all her helpers are crushed.[n]

9"'On that day messengers will go
out from me in ships to frighten Cush[o]
out of her complacency. Anguish[p] will
take hold of them on the day of Egypt's
doom, for it is sure to come.[q]

10"'This is what the Sovereign LORD
says:

"'I will put an end to the hordes of
Egypt
by the hand of Nebuchadnezzar[r]
king of Babylon.[s]
11He and his army—the most ruthless
of nations[t]—
will be brought in to destroy the
land.
They will draw their swords against
Egypt
and fill the land with the slain.[u]
12I will dry up[v] the streams of the Nile[w]
and sell the land to evil men;
by the hand of foreigners
I will lay waste[x] the land and
everything in it.

I the LORD have spoken.

13"'This is what the Sovereign LORD
says:

"'I will destroy the idols[y]
and put an end to the images in
Memphis.[c][z]
No longer will there be a prince in
Egypt,[a]
and I will spread fear throughout
the land.
14I will lay[b] waste Upper Egypt,[d]
set fire to Zoan[c]
and inflict punishment on Thebes.[e][d]

14 [a]**Isa 11:11**; Eze 30:14; [b]Eze 17:14; [c]**Isa 19:22**; Jer 46:26
15 [d]Zec 10:11
16 [e]2Ch 32:10; [f]**Nu 5:15**; [g]**La 4:17**; [h]Isa 20:5; **30:2**; Hos 8:13
17 [i]**ver 1; Eze 24:1**; 30:20; 40:1
18 [j]Jer 27:6; 39:1; [k]**Lev 13:40**; **Job 1:20**; **Jer 48:37**; [l]Ge 49:15
19 [m]**Isa 19:4**; [n]**Eze 26:5**; [o]Jer 43:10–13; Eze 30:4,10, 24–25; 32:11
20 [p]**Isa 43:3**; [q]Isa 10:6–7; 45:1; **Jer 25:9**
21 [r]**Ps 132:17**; **Lk 1:69**; [s]Eze 33:22; [t]**Eze 3:27**

Ch. 30

2 [a]**Isa 13:6**; Jas 5:1
3 [b]**Eze 7:7**; Joel 1:15; 2:1,11; Ob 15; [c]ver 18; **Eze 7:12**, 19; 32:7; 34:12
4 [d]Jer 25:19; Da 11:43; [e]**Ge 10:6**; **Eze 29:10**; [f]**Eze 29:19**
5 [g]**Eze 27:10**; [h]**2Ch 9:14**; [i]Jer 25:20; [j]Na 3:9
6 [k]Eze 29:10
7 [l]**Eze 29:12**
8 [m]**Jer 49:27**; Eze 39:6; Am 1:4,7,10; Na 1:6; [n]**Eze 29:9**
9 [o]**Ge 10:6**; [p]Isa 23:5; [q]Eze 32:9–10; Zep 2:12
10 [r]Jer 39:1; [s]**Eze 29:19**
11 [t]**Eze 28:7**; [u]ver 24–25
12 [v]**Isa 19:6**; [w]**Jer 46:8**; Eze 29:9; [x]**Eze 19:7**
13 [y]**Jer 43:12**; **Eze 6:6**; [z]**Isa 19:13**; [a]Zec 10:11
14 [b]**Eze 29:14**; [c]**Nu 13:22**; [d]**Jer 46:25**

[c]14 Hebrew *to Pathros*
[d]21 *Horn* here symbolises strength.
[a]4 That is, the upper Nile region; also in verses 5 and 9 [b]5 Hebrew *Cub*
[c]13 Hebrew *Noph*; also in verse 16
[d]14 Hebrew *waste Pathros*
[e]14 Hebrew *No*; also in verses 15 and 16

15I will pour out my wrath on Pelusium,[f]
the stronghold of Egypt,
and cut off the hordes of Thebes.
16I will set fire[e] to Egypt;
Pelusium will writhe in agony.
Thebes will be taken by storm;
Memphis[f] will be in constant
distress.
17The young men of Heliopolis[g] [g] and
Bubastis[h]
will fall by the sword,
and the cities themselves will go
into captivity.
18Dark will be the day at Tahpanhes[h]
when I break the yoke of Egypt;[i]
there her proud strength will come
to an end.
She will be covered with clouds,
and her villages will go into
captivity.[j]
19So I will inflict punishment[k] on Egypt,
and they will know that I am the
LORD.' "

20In the eleventh year, in the first
month on the seventh day, the word of
the LORD came to me:[l] 21"Son of man, I
have broken the arm[m] of Pharaoh[n] king
of Egypt. It has not been bound up for
healing[o] or put in a splint so as to be-
come strong enough to hold a sword.
22Therefore this is what the Sovereign
LORD says: I am against Pharaoh king of
Egypt.[p] I will break both his arms, the
good arm as well as the broken one, and
make the sword fall from his hand.[q] 23I
will disperse the Egyptians among the
nations and scatter them through the
countries.[r] 24I will strengthen[s] the arms
of the king of Babylon and put my
sword[t] in his hand, but I will break the
arms of Pharaoh, and he will groan[u]
before him like a mortally wounded
man. 25I will strengthen the arms of the
king of Babylon, but the arms of Phar-
aoh will fall limp. Then they will know
that I am the LORD, when I put my
sword[v] into the hand of the king of
Babylon and he brandishes it against
Egypt.[w] 26I will disperse the Egyptians
among the nations and scatter them
through the countries. Then they will
know that I am the LORD.[x]"

A Cedar in Lebanon

31 In the eleventh year,[a] in the
third month on the first day, the
word of the LORD came to me:[b] 2"Son of
man, say to Pharaoh king of Egypt and
to his hordes:

" 'Who can be compared with you in
majesty?
3Consider Assyria,[c] once a cedar in
Lebanon,[d]
with beautiful branches
overshadowing the forest;
it towered on high,
its top above the thick foliage.[e]
4The waters[f] nourished it,
deep springs made it grow tall;
their streams flowed
all around its base
and sent their channels
to all the trees of the field.[g]
5So it towered higher[h]
than all the trees of the field;
its boughs increased
and its branches grew long,
spreading because of abundant
waters.[i]
6All the birds of the air
nested in its boughs,
all the beasts of the field
gave birth[j] under its branches;
all the great nations
lived in its shade.[k]
7It was majestic in beauty,
with its spreading boughs,
for its roots went down
to abundant waters.[l]
8The cedars[m] in the garden of God
could not rival it,
nor could the pine trees
equal its boughs,
nor could the plane trees[n]
compare with its branches—
no tree in the garden of God
could match its beauty.[o]
9I made it beautiful
with abundant branches,
the envy of all the trees of Eden[p]
in the garden of God.[q]

10" 'Therefore this is what the
Sovereign LORD says: Because it
towered on high, lifting its top above
the thick foliage, and because it was
proud[r] of its height, 11I handed it over to
the ruler of the nations, for him to deal
with according to its wickedness. I cast
it aside,[s] 12and the most ruthless of
foreign nations[t] cut it down and left it.
Its boughs fell on the mountains and in
all the valleys;[u] its branches lay broken
in all the ravines of the land. All the
nations of the earth came out from
under its shade and left it.[v] 13All the
birds of the air settled on the fallen tree,
and all the beasts of the field were
among its branches.[w] 14Therefore no
other trees by the waters are ever to

16 [e]**Jos 7:15;** [f]**Isa 19:13**
17 [g]Ge 41:45
18 [h]**Jer 43:7;** [i]**Lev 26:13; Isa 9:4;** [j]**ver 3**
19 [k]Eze 28:22
20 [l]Eze 26:1; 29:17; 31:1; 32:1
21 [m]**Jer 48:25;** [n]**Jer 44:30;** [o]Jer 30:13; 46:11
22 [p]**Ge 15:18; Jer 46:25;** [q]Ps 37:17; Zec 11:17
23 [r]**Eze 29:12**
24 [s]Zec 10:6,12; 12:5; [t]**Eze 21:14;** Zep 2:12; [u]Jer 51:52
25 [v]1Ch 21:12; [w]**Isa 10:5;** 45:1,5; **Eze 29:19**
26 [x]**Eze 29:12**

Ch. 31

1 [a]Jer 52:5; [b]**Eze 30:20;** 32:17
3 [c]**Jer 50:18;** [d]**2Ki 19:23;** Hab 2:17; Zec 11:1; [e]Isa 10:34; **Eze 19:11**
4 [f]Eze 17:7; [g]Da 4:10
5 [h]ver 10; [i]**Nu 24:6; Eze 17:5**
6 [j]**Ge 31:7–9;** [k]**Eze 17:23; Mt 13:32**
7 [l]**Job 14:9**
8 [m]Ps 80:10; [n]**Ge 30:37;** [o]Ge 2:8–9
9 [p]**Ge 2:8;** [q]**Ge 13:10;** Eze 28:13
10 [r]**Isa 2:11; 14:13–14; Eze 28:17**
11 [s]Da 5:20
12 [t]**Eze 28:7;** [u]Eze 32:5; 35:8; [v]Eze 32:11–12; Da 4:14
13 [w]**Isa 18:6; Eze 29:5;** 32:4

[f]*15* Hebrew *Sin*; also in verse 16
[g]*17* Hebrew *Awen* (or *On*)
[h]*17* Hebrew *Pi Beseth*

tower proudly on high, lifting their tops
above the thick foliage. No other trees
so well-watered are ever to reach such a
height; they are all destined[x] for death,[y]
for the earth below, among mortal men,
with those who go down to the pit.[z]
15" 'This is what the Sovereign LORD
says: On the day it was brought down to
the grave[a] I covered the deep springs
with mourning for it; I held back its
streams, and its abundant waters were
restrained. Because of it I clothed Leba-
non with gloom, and all the trees of the
field withered away.[a] 16I made the
nations tremble[b] at the sound of its fall
when I brought it down to the grave
with those who go down to the pit.
Then all the trees[c] of Eden,[d] the choicest
and best of Lebanon, all the trees that
were well-watered, were consoled[e] in
the earth below.[f] 17Those who lived in
its shade, its allies among the nations,
had also gone down to the grave with it,
joining those killed by the sword.[g]
18" 'Which of the trees of Eden can be
compared with you in splendour and
majesty? Yet you, too, will be brought
down with the trees of Eden to the earth
below; you will lie among the uncircum-
cised,[h] with those killed by the sword.

" 'This is Pharaoh and all his hordes,
declares the Sovereign LORD.' "

A Lament for Pharaoh

32

In the twelfth year, in the
twelfth month on the first day,
the word of the LORD came to me:[a] 2"Son
of man, take up a lament[b] concerning
Pharaoh king of Egypt and say to him:

" 'You are like a lion[c] among the nations;
you are like a monster[d] in the seas[e]
thrashing about in your streams,
churning the water with your feet
and muddying the streams.[f]

3" 'This is what the Sovereign LORD says:

" 'With a great throng of people
I will cast my net over you,
and they will haul you up in my net.[g]
4I will throw you on the land
and hurl you on the open field.
I will let all the birds of the air settle on you
and all the beasts of the earth gorge themselves on you.[h]
5I will spread your flesh on the mountains
and fill the valleys[i] with your remains.
6I will drench the land with your flowing blood[j]
all the way to the mountains,
and the ravines will be filled with your flesh.[k]
7When I snuff you out, I will cover the heavens
and darken their stars;
I will cover the sun with a cloud,
and the moon will not give its light.[l]
8All the shining lights in the heavens
I will darken[m] over you;
I will bring darkness over your land,[n]
declares the Sovereign LORD.
9I will trouble the hearts of many peoples
when I bring about your destruction among the nations,
among[a] lands you have not known.
10I will cause many peoples to be appalled at you,
and their kings will shudder with horror because of you
when I brandish my sword[o] before them.
On the day[p] of your downfall
each of them will tremble
every moment for his life.[q]

11" 'For this is what the Sovereign LORD says:

" 'The sword[r] of the king of Babylon[s]
will come against you.[t]
12I will cause your hordes to fall
by the swords of mighty men—
the most ruthless of all nations.[u]
They will shatter the pride of Egypt,
and all her hordes will be overthrown.[v]
13I will destroy all her cattle
from beside abundant waters
no longer to be stirred by the foot of man
or muddied by the hoofs of cattle.[w]
14Then I will let her waters settle
and make her streams flow like oil,
declares the Sovereign LORD.
15When I make Egypt desolate
and strip the land of everything in it,
when I strike down all who live there,
then they will know that I am the LORD.[x]'

16"This is the lament[y] they will chant
for her. The daughters of the nations

14 [x]**Ps 49:14**; [y]**Ps 82:7**; [z]**Nu 14:11**; Ps 63:9; **Eze 26:20**; 32:24
15 [a]**2Sa 1:21**
16 [b]**Jer 49:21**; [c]**Isa 14:8**; [d]**Ge 2:8**; [e]**Eze 14:22**; [f]**Isa 14:15**; Eze 32:18
17 [g]Ps 9:17
18 [h]**Jer 9:26**

Ch. 32

1 [a]**Eze 31:1**; 33:21
2 [b]2Sa 1:17; 3:33; 2Ch 35:25; **Eze 19:1**; [c]**2Ki 24:1**; Na 2:11–13; [d]**Job 3:8; Ps 74:13**; [e]**Ge 1:21**; [f]ver 13; Job 41:31; **Eze 29:3**; 34:18
3 [g]**Eze 12:13**; Hab 1:15
4 [h]**Isa 18:6**; Eze 31:12–13; 39:4–5,17
5 [i]**Eze 31:12**
6 [j]**Isa 34:3**; [k]**Eze 29:5**
7 [l]**Isa 13:10**; 34:4; **Eze 30:3**; Joel 2:2, 31; 3:15; **Mt 24:29**; Rev 8:12
8 [m]**Ps 102:26**; [n]**Job 9:7; Jer 4:23**; Joel 2:10
10 [o]**Isa 30:32**; [p]**Jer 46:10**; [q]**Eze 26:16**; **27:35**; 30:9; Rev 18:9–10
11 [r]**Eze 21:19**; [s]**Isa 19:4**; **Jer 46:13**; [t]**Eze 29:19**
12 [u]**Eze 28:7**; [v]Eze 31:11–12
13 [w]**ver 2**; **Eze 29:8**,11
15 [x]Ex 7:5; **14:4**,18; Ps 107:33–34
16 [y]**Ge 50:10**; **Eze 19:1**

[a]*15* Hebrew *Sheol;* also in verses 16 and 17
[a]*9* Hebrew; Septuagint *bring you into captivity among the nations, / to*

will chant it; for Egypt and all her
hordes they will chant it, declares the
Sovereign LORD."

17 In the twelfth year, on the fifteenth
day of the month, the word of the LORD
came to me:[z] 18 "Son of man, wail for the
hordes of Egypt and consign[a] to the
earth below both her and the daughters
of mighty nations, with those who go
down to the pit.[b] 19 Say to them, 'Are you
more favoured than others? Go down
and be laid among the uncircumcised.'[c]
20 They will fall among those killed by
the sword. The sword is drawn; let her
be dragged[d] off with all her hordes.[e]
21 From within the grave[b][f] the mighty
leaders will say of Egypt and her allies,
'They have come down and they lie
with the uncircumcised,[g] with those
killed by the sword.'
22 "Assyria is there with her whole
army; she is surrounded by the graves
of all her slain, all who have fallen by the
sword. 23 Their graves are in the depths
of the pit[h] and her army lies around her
grave.[i] All who had spread terror in the
land of the living are slain, fallen by the
sword.
24 "Elam[j] is there, with all her hordes
around her grave. All of them are slain,
fallen by the sword.[k] All who had
spread terror in the land of the living[l]
went down uncircumcised to the earth
below. They bear their shame with
those who go down to the pit.[m] 25 A bed
is made for her among the slain, with all
her hordes around her grave. All of
them are uncircumcised,[n] killed by the
sword. Because their terror had spread
in the land of the living, they bear their
shame with those who go down to the
pit; they are laid among the slain.
26 "Meshech and Tubal[o] are there,
with all their hordes around their
graves. All of them are uncircumcised,
killed by the sword because they spread
their terror in the land of the living. 27 Do
they not lie with the other uncircum-
cised[p] warriors who have fallen, who
went down to the grave with their
weapons of war, whose swords were
placed under their heads? The punish-
ment for their sins rested on their
bones, though the terror of these
warriors had stalked through the land
of the living.
28 "You too, O Pharaoh, will be broken
and will lie among the uncircumcised,
with those killed by the sword.
29 "Edom[q] is there, her kings and all
her princes; despite their power, they
are laid with those killed by the sword.
They lie with the uncircumcised, with
those who go down to the pit.[r]
30 "All the princes of the north[s] and all
the Sidonians[t] are there; they went
down with the slain in disgrace despite
the terror caused by their power. They
lie uncircumcised[u] with those killed by
the sword and bear their shame with
those who go down to the pit.[v]
31 "Pharaoh—he and all his army—
will see them and he will be consoled[w]
for all his hordes that were killed by the
sword, declares the Sovereign LORD.
32 Although I had him spread terror in
the land of the living, Pharaoh[x] and all
his hordes will be laid among the uncir-
cumcised, with those killed by the
sword, declares the Sovereign LORD."[y]

Ezekiel a Watchman

33 The word of the LORD came to
me: 2 "Son of man, speak to
your countrymen and say to them:
'When I bring the sword[a] against a land,
and the people of the land choose one of
their men and make him their watch-
man,[b] 3 and he sees the sword coming
against the land and blows the trumpet[c]
to warn the people, 4 then if anyone
hears the trumpet but does not take
warning[d] and the sword comes and
takes his life, his blood will be on his
own head.[e] 5 Since he heard the sound of
the trumpet but did not take warning,
his blood will be on his own head.[f] If he
had taken warning, he would have
saved himself.[g] 6 But if the watchman
sees the sword coming and does not
blow the trumpet to warn the people
and the sword comes and takes the life
of one of them, that man will be taken
away because of his sin, but I will hold
the watchman accountable for his
blood.'[h]
7 "Son of man, I have made you a
watchman[i] for the house of Israel; so
hear the word I speak and give them
warning from me.[j] 8 When I say to the
wicked, 'O wicked man, you will surely
die,[k]' and you do not speak out to dis-
suade him from his ways, that wicked
man will die for[a] his sin, and I will hold
you accountable for his blood.[l] 9 But if
you do warn the wicked man to turn
from his ways and he does not do so,[m]
he will die for his sin, but you will be
saved yourself.[n]
10 "Son of man, say to the house of
Israel, 'This is what you are saying:

17 [z]**ver 1**
18 [a]Jer 1:10; [b]Eze 26:20; **31:14**, 16; Mic 1:8
19 [c]ver 29-30; **Eze 28:10**
20 [d]Ps 28:3; [e]Eze 31:17–18
21 [f]**Isa 14:9**; [g]Eze 28:10
23 [h]**Isa 14:15**; [i]Na 1:14
24 [j]**Ge 10:22**; [k]**Jer 49:37**; [l]**Job 28:13**; [m]**Eze 26:20**
25 [n]Eze 28:10
26 [o]**Eze 27:13**
27 [p]Eze 28:10
29 [q]**Ps 137:7**; Isa 34:5–15; Jer 49:7; Eze 35:15; Ob 1; [r]Eze 25:12–14
30 [s]**Isa 14:31**; Jer 25:26; Eze 38:6; 39:2; [t]**Ge 10:15**; **Jer 25:22**; [u]Eze 28:10; [v]**Eze 26:20**; **28:8**
31 [w]**Eze 14:22**
32 [x]**Jer 44:30**; [y]**Job 3:14**

Ch. 33

2 [a]**Lev 26:25**; **Jer 12:12**; [b]**1Sa 14:16**; Isa 21:6–9; **Jer 51:12**
3 [c]**Ex 20:18**; **Nu 10:7**; Hos 5:8; 8:1
4 [d]2Ch 25:16; [e]**Lev 20:9**; **Jer 6:17**; Zec 1:4; Ac 18:6
5 [f]**Lev 20:9**; [g]**Ex 9:21**
6 [h]Isa 56:10–11; **Eze 3:18**
7 [i]**Isa 52:8**; [j]Jer 1:17; 26:2
8 [k]ver 14; [l]**Isa 3:11**; **Eze 18:4**
9 [m]**Ps 7:12**; [n]Eze 3:17–19

[b]*21* Hebrew *Sheol*; also in verse 27
[a]*8* Or *in*; also in verse 9

"Our offences and sins weigh us down, and we are wasting away[o] because of[b] them. How then can we live?[p]"' 11Say to them, 'As surely as I live, declares the Sovereign LORD, I take no pleasure in the death of the wicked, but rather that they turn from their ways and live.[q] Turn![r] Turn from your evil ways! Why will you die, O house of Israel?'[s]

12"Therefore, son of man, say to your countrymen,[t] 'The righteousness of the righteous man will not save him when he disobeys, and the wickedness of the wicked man will not cause him to fall when he turns from it. The righteous man, if he sins, will not be allowed to live because of his former righteousness.'[u] 13If I tell the righteous man that he will surely live, but then he trusts in his righteousness and does evil, none of the righteous things he has done will be remembered; he will die for the evil he has done.[v] 14And if I say to the wicked man, 'You will surely die,' but he then turns away from his sin and does what is just[w] and right—15if he gives back what he took in pledge[x] for a loan, returns what he has stolen,[y] follows the decrees that give life, and does no evil, he will surely live; he will not die.[z] 16None of the sins[a] he has committed will be remembered against him. He has done what is just and right; he will surely live.[b]

17"Yet your countrymen say, 'The way of the LORD is not just.' But it is their way that is not just. 18If a righteous man turns from his righteousness and does evil,[c] he will die for it.[d] 19And if a wicked man turns away from his wickedness and does what is just and right, he will live by doing so.[e] 20Yet, O house of Israel, you say, 'The way of the LORD is not just.' But I will judge each of you according to his own ways."[f]

Jerusalem's Fall Explained

21In the twelfth year of our exile, in the tenth month on the fifth day, a man who had escaped[g] from Jerusalem came to me and said, "The city has fallen![h]" 22Now the evening before the man arrived, the hand of the LORD was upon me,[i] and he opened my mouth[j] before the man came to me in the morning. So my mouth was opened and I was no longer silent.[k]

23Then the word of the LORD came to me: 24"Son of man, the people living in those ruins[l] in the land of Israel are saying, 'Abraham was only one man, yet he possessed the land. But we are many;[m] surely the land has been given to us as our possession.'[n] 25Therefore say to them, 'This is what the Sovereign LORD says: Since you eat[o] meat with the blood[p] still in it and look to your idols and shed blood, should you then possess the land?[q] 26You rely on your sword, you do detestable things,[r] and each of you defiles his neighbour's wife.[s] Should you then possess the land?'

27"Say this to them: 'This is what the Sovereign LORD says: As surely as I live, those who are left in the ruins will fall by the sword, those out in the country I will give to the wild animals to be devoured, and those in strongholds and caves will die of a plague.[t] 28I will make the land a desolate waste, and her proud strength will come to an end, and the mountains[u] of Israel will become desolate so that no-one will cross them.[v] 29Then they will know that I am the LORD, when I have made the land a desolate[w] waste because of all the detestable things they have done.'[x]

30"As for you, son of man, your countrymen are talking together about you by the walls and at the doors of the houses, saying to each other, 'Come and hear the message that has come from the LORD.' 31My people come to you, as they usually do, and sit before[y] you to listen to your words, but they do not put them into practice. With their mouths they express devotion, but their hearts are greedy[z] for unjust gain.[a] 32Indeed, to them you are nothing more than one who sings love songs[b] with a beautiful voice and plays an instrument well, for they hear your words but do not put them into practice.[c]

33"When all this comes true—and it surely will—then they will know that a prophet has been among them.[d]"

Shepherds and Sheep

34 The word of the LORD came to me: 2"Son of man, prophesy against the shepherds of Israel; prophesy and say to them: 'This is what the Sovereign LORD says: Woe to the shepherds of Israel who only take care of themselves! Should not shepherds take care of the flock?[a] 3You eat the curds, clothe yourselves with the wool and slaughter the choice animals, but you do not take care of the flock.[b] 4You

10 [o]Lev 26:16; [p]Lev 26:39; Eze 4:17
11 [q]La 3:33; [r]2Ch 30:9; Isa 19:22; Jer 3:12; [s]Jer 44:7–8; Eze 18:23; Hos 11:8; Joel 2:12; 1Ti 2:4
12 [t]ver 2; [u]2Ch 7:14; Eze 3:20; 18:21
13 [v]Heb 10:38; 2Pe 2:20–21
14 [w]Jer 22:3
15 [x]Ex 22:26; [y]Ex 22:1–4; Lev 6:2–5; [z]Isa 55:7; Jer 18:7–8; Lk 19:8
16 [a]Jer 50:20; [b]Isa 43:25
18 [c]Jer 18:10; [d]Eze 3:20
19 [e]ver 14-15
20 [f]Job 34:11
21 [g]Eze 24:26; [h]2Ki 25:4,10; Jer 39:1–2; 52:4–7; Eze 32:1
22 [i]Eze 1:3; [j]Eze 29:21; Lk 1:64; [k]Eze 3:26–27; 24:27
24 [l]Eze 36:4; [m]Dt 1:10; [n]Isa 51:2; Jer 40:7; Eze 11:15; Lk 3:8; Ac 7:5
25 [o]Jer 7:21; [p]Ge 9:4; [q]Jer 7:9–10; Eze 22:6,27
26 [r]Jer 41:7; [s]Eze 22:11
27 [t]1Sa 13:6; Isa 2:19; Jer 42:22; Eze 7:15; 14:21; 39:4
28 [u]Isa 41:15; [v]Ge 6:7; Jer 9:10
29 [w]Lev 26:34; [x]Jer 18:16; 44:22; Eze 36:4; Mic 7:13
31 [y]Eze 8:1; [z]Ps 119:36; [a]Ps 78:36–37; Isa 29:13; 33:15; Jer 3:10; 6:17; Eze 22:27; Mt 13:22; 1Jn 3:18
32 [b]1Ki 4:32; [c]Mk 6:20
33 [d]1Sa 3:20; Jer 28:9; Eze 2:5

Ch. 34

2 [a]Ps 78:70–72; Isa 40:11; Jer 3:15; 23:1; Mic 3:11; Jn 10:11; 21:15–17; Jude 12
3 [b]Isa 56:11; Eze 22:27; Am 6:4; Zec 11:5

[b]10 Or *away in*

have not strengthened the weak or healed[c] the sick or bound up[d] the injured. You have not brought back the strays or searched for the lost. You have ruled them harshly and brutally.[e] 5So they were scattered because there was no shepherd,[f] and when they were scattered they became food for all the wild animals.[g] 6My sheep wandered over all the mountains and on every high hill.[h] They were scattered[i] over the whole earth, and no-one searched or looked for them.[j]

7"'Therefore, you shepherds, hear the word of the LORD: 8As surely as I live, declares the Sovereign LORD, because my flock lacks a shepherd and so has been plundered[k] and has become food for all the wild animals,[l] and because my shepherds did not search for my flock but cared for themselves rather than for my flock,[m] 9therefore, O shepherds, hear the word of the LORD: 10This is what the Sovereign LORD says: I am against[n] the shepherds and will hold them accountable for my flock. I will remove them from tending the flock so that the shepherds can no longer feed themselves. I will rescue[o] my flock from their mouths, and it will no longer be food for them.[p]

11"'For this is what the Sovereign LORD says: I myself will search for my sheep[q] and look after them. 12As a shepherd[r] looks after his scattered flock when he is with them, so will I look after my sheep. I will rescue them from all the places where they were scattered on a day of clouds and darkness.[s] 13I will bring them out from the nations and gather[t] them from the countries, and I will bring them into their own land.[u v w x] I will pasture them on the mountains of Israel, in the ravines and in all the settlements in the land.[y z a] 14I will tend them in a good pasture, and the mountain heights of Israel[b] will be their grazing land. There they will lie down in good grazing land, and there they will feed in a rich pasture[c] on the mountains of Israel.[d] 15I myself will tend my sheep and make them lie down,[e] declares the Sovereign LORD.[f] 16I will search for the lost and bring back the strays. I will bind up[g] the injured and strengthen the weak,[h] but the sleek and the strong I will destroy.[i] I will shepherd the flock with justice.[j]

17"'As for you, my flock, this is what the Sovereign LORD says: I will judge between one sheep and another, and between rams and goats.[k] 18Is it not enough[l] for you to feed on the good pasture? Must you also trample the rest of your pasture with your feet?[m] Is it not enough for you to drink clear water? Must you also muddy the rest with your feet? 19Must my flock feed on what you have trampled and drink what you have muddied with your feet?

20"'Therefore this is what the Sovereign LORD says to them: See, I myself will judge between the fat sheep and the lean sheep.[n] 21Because you shove with flank and shoulder, butting all the weak sheep with your horns[o] until you have driven them away, 22I will save my flock, and they will no longer be plundered. I will judge between one sheep and another.[p] 23I will place over them one shepherd, my servant David, and he will tend[q] them; he will tend them and be their shepherd.[r] 24I the LORD will be their God,[s] and my servant David[t] will be prince among them.[u] I the LORD have spoken.[v]

25"'I will make a covenant[w] of peace[x] with them and rid the land of wild beasts[y] so that they may live in the desert and sleep in the forests in safety.[z] 26I will bless[a] them and the places surrounding my hill.[a] I will send down showers in season;[b] there will be showers of blessing.[c] 27The trees of the field will yield their fruit[d] and the ground will yield its crops;[e] the people will be secure[f] in their land. They will know that I am the LORD, when I break the bars of their yoke[g] and rescue them from the hands of those who enslaved them.[h] 28They will no longer be plundered by the nations, nor will wild animals devour them. They will live in safety,[i] and no-one will make them afraid.[j] 29I will provide for them a land renowned[k] for its crops, and they will no longer be victims of famine[l] in the land or bear the scorn[m] of the nations.[n] 30Then they will know that I, the LORD their God, am with them and that they, the house of Israel, are my people, declares the Sovereign LORD.[o] 31You my sheep,[p] the sheep of my pasture,[q] are people, and I am your God, declares the Sovereign LORD.'"

4 [c]**Isa 3:7**; [d]**Isa 1:6**; [e]ver 16; **Lev 25:43**; Mic 3:3; Zec 11:15–17
5 [f]**Nu 27:17**; [g]ver 28; **Isa 56:9**; Ac 20:29
6 [h]**Jer 50:6**; [i]**Lev 26:33**; **Ps 95:10**; **Jer 10:21**; [j]2Ch 18:16; Ps 142:4; Hos 7:13; **Mt 9:36**; 18:12–13; Lk 15:5; 1Pe 2:25
8 [k]**Jdg 2:14**; [l]**Isa 56:9**; [m]Jude 12
10 [n]**Jer 21:13**; [o]**Ps 72:14**; [p]1Sa 2:29–30; **Jer 23:2**; Zec 10:3
11 [q]**Ps 119:176**
12 [r]Isa 40:11; **Jer 31:10**; Zec 10:3; Lk 19:10; [s]**Eze 32:7**
13 [t]**Ge 48:21**; **Dt 30:4**; [u]Mic 4:6; [v]**Eze 11:17**; [w]**Jer 23:8**; [x]**Isa 66:20**; [y]**Eze 28:25**; 36:24; [z]**Jer 50:19**; [a]Jer 23:3
14 [b]**Eze 20:40**; [c]Ps 23:2; **37:3**; [d]**Isa 65:10**; Eze 36:29–30; 37:22; Am 9:14; Mic 7:14
15 [e]Zep 3:13; [f]Ps 23:1–2; **Jer 33:12**; Mic 5:4
16 [g]**Ps 147:3**; [h]Mic 4:6; Zep 3:19; [i]Lk 19:10; [j]Isa 10:16; **Jer 31:8**; Lk 5:32
17 [k]Mt 25:32–33
18 [l]**Ge 30:15**; [m]**Eze 32:2**
20 [n]Mt 25:32
21 [o]**Dt 33:17**
22 [p]Ps 72:12–14; Jer 23:2–3; Eze 20:37–38
23 [q]Isa 40:11; [r]**Isa 31:4**; Mic 5:4
24 [s]Eze 36:28; [t]Ps 89:49; [u]**Isa 53:4**; Zec 13:7; [v]Jer 23:4–5; **30:9**; **33:14**; Jn 10:16; Rev 7:17
25 [w]**Eze 16:62**; [x]**Nu 25:12**; [y]Lev 26:6; [z]**Lev 25:18**; Isa 11:6–9; Hos 2:18
26 [a]**Ge 12:2**; [b]Ps 68:9; Joel 2:23; [c]Dt 11:13–15; **28:12**; Isa 44:3
27 [d]**Ps 72:16**; [e]**Job 14:9**; **Ps 67:6**; [f]**Nu 24:21**; [g]**Lev 26:13**; [h]**Jer 30:8**; **Eze 20:42**; **28:25**
28 [i]**Jer 32:37**; [j]**Jer 30:10**; **Eze 28:26**; 39:26; Hos 11:11; Am 9:15; Zep 3:13; Zec 14:11
29 [k]**Isa 4:2**; [l]Eze 36:29; [m]**Ps 137:3**; Eze 36:6; Joel 2:19; [n]Eze 36:15
30 [o]**Eze 14:11**; 37:27
31 [p]**Ps 28:9**; [q]**Jer 23:1**

[a]26 Or *I will make them and the places surrounding my hill a blessing*

A Prophecy Against Edom

35 The word of the LORD came to me: 2"Son of man, set your face against Mount Seir;[a] prophesy against it 3and say: 'This is what the Sovereign LORD says: I am against you, Mount Seir, and I will stretch out my hand[b] against you and make you a desolate waste.[c] 4I will turn your towns into ruins[d] and you will be desolate. Then you will know that I am the LORD.[e]

5" 'Because you harboured an ancient hostility and delivered the Israelites over to the sword[f] at the time of their calamity,[g] the time their punishment reached its climax,[h] 6therefore as surely as I live, declares the Sovereign LORD, I will give you over to bloodshed[i] and it will pursue you.[j] Since you did not hate bloodshed, bloodshed will pursue you. 7I will make Mount Seir a desolate waste[k] and cut off from it all who come and go.[l] 8I will fill your mountains with the slain; those killed by the sword will fall on your hills and in your valleys and in all your ravines.[m] 9I will make you desolate for ever;[n] your towns will not be inhabited. Then you will know that I am the LORD.[o]

10" 'Because you have said, "These two nations and countries will be ours and we will take possession[p] of them," even though I the LORD was there, 11therefore as surely as I live, declares the Sovereign LORD, I will treat you in accordance with the anger[q] and jealousy you showed in your hatred of them and I will make myself known among them when I judge you.[r] 12Then you will know that I the LORD have heard all the contemptible things you have said against the mountains of Israel. You said, "They have been laid waste and have been given over to us to devour.[s]" 13You boasted[t] against me and spoke against me without restraint, and I heard it.[u] 14This is what the Sovereign LORD says: While the whole earth rejoices, I will make you desolate.[v] 15Because you rejoiced[w] when the inheritance of the house of Israel became desolate, that is how I will treat you. You will be desolate, O Mount Seir,[x] you and all of Edom.[y] Then they will know that I am the LORD.' "

A Prophecy to the Mountains of Israel

36 "Son of man, prophesy to the mountains of Israel[a] and say, 'O mountains of Israel, hear the word of the LORD. 2This is what the Sovereign LORD says:[b] The enemy said of you, "Aha![c] The ancient heights[d] have become our possession.[e]" ' 3Therefore prophesy and say, 'This is what the Sovereign LORD says: Because they ravaged[f] and hounded you from every side so that you became the possession of the rest of the nations and the object of people's malicious talk and slander,[g] 4therefore, O mountains of Israel, hear the word of the Sovereign LORD: This is what the Sovereign LORD says to the mountains and hills, to the ravines and valleys,[h] to the desolate ruins[i] and the deserted[j] towns that have been plundered and ridiculed[k] by the rest of the nations around you[l]—5this is what the Sovereign LORD says: In my burning[m] zeal I have spoken against the rest of the nations, and against Edom, for with glee and with malice in their hearts they made my land their own possession so that they might plunder its pastureland.'[n] 6Therefore prophesy concerning the land of Israel and say to the mountains and hills, to the ravines and valleys: 'This is what the Sovereign LORD says: I speak in my jealous wrath because you have suffered the scorn of the nations.[o] 7Therefore this is what the Sovereign LORD says: I swear with uplifted hand[p] that the nations around you will also suffer scorn.[q]

8" 'But you, O mountains of Israel, will produce branches and fruit[r] for my people Israel, for they will soon come home. 9I am concerned for you and will look on you with favour; you will be ploughed and sown,[s] 10and I will multiply the number of people upon you, even the whole house of Israel. The towns will be inhabited and the ruins[t] rebuilt.[u] 11I will increase the number of men and animals upon you, and they will be fruitful[v] and become numerous. I will settle people[w] on you as in the past[x] and will make you prosper more than before.[y] Then you will know that I am the LORD. 12I will cause people, my people Israel, to walk upon you. They will possess you, and you will be their inheritance;[z] you will never again deprive them of their children.

13" 'This is what the Sovereign LORD says: Because people say to you, "You devour men[a] and deprive your nation of its children," 14therefore you will no longer devour men or make your nation childless, declares the Sovereign LORD. 15No longer will I make you hear the taunts of the nations, and no longer will you suffer the scorn of the peoples or

Ch. 35

2 [a]Ge 14:6
3 [b]Jer 6:12; [c]Isa 34:10; Eze 25:12–14
4 [d]Jer 44:2; [e]ver 9; Jer 49:10
5 [f]Ps 63:10; [g]Ob 13; [h]Ps 137:7; Eze 21:29
6 [i]Isa 34:3; [j]Isa 63:2–6
7 [k]Jer 46:19; [l]Jer 49:17
8 [m]Eze 31:12
9 [n]Ob 10; [o]Isa 34:5–6; Jer 49:13
10 [p]Ps 83:12; Eze 36:2,5
11 [q]Eze 25:14; [r]Ps 9:16; Ob 15; Mt 7:2
12 [s]Jer 50:7
13 [t]Jer 49:16; [u]Da 11:36
14 [v]Jer 51:48
15 [w]Eze 36:5; Ob 12; [x]ver 3; [y]Isa 34:5–6,11; Jer 50:11–13; La 4:21; Eze 32:29

Ch. 36

1 [a]Eze 17:22
2 [b]Eze 6:2–3; [c]Eze 25:3; [d]Dt 32:13; [e]Eze 35:10
3 [f]Ob 13; [g]Ps 44:13–14; La 2:16; 3:62
4 [h]Eze 6:3; [i]Eze 33:24; [j]Lev 26:43; [k]Jer 2:26; [l]Dt 11:11; Ps 79:4; Eze 33:28–29
5 [m]Dt 29:20; [n]Isa 66:16; Jer 25:31; 50:11; Eze 25:12–14; 35:10,15; 38:22; Joel 3:2,14
6 [o]Ps 123:3–4; Eze 34:29
7 [p]Nu 14:30; [q]Jer 25:9
8 [r]Isa 4:2; 27:6; Eze 47:12
9 [s]ver 34–36; Jer 31:27
10 [t]Isa 49:8; [u]Isa 49:17–23; Jer 30:18
11 [v]Ge 1:22; [w]Isa 49:19; [x]Mic 7:14; [y]Lev 26:9; Job 42:13; Jer 31:28; Eze 16:55; Zec 10:8
12 [z]Eze 47:14,22
13 [a]Nu 13:32

cause your nation to fall, declares the
Sovereign LORD.[b]' "
16Again the word of the LORD came to
me: 17"Son of man, when the people of
Israel were living in their own land,
they defiled it by their conduct and their
actions. Their conduct was like a
woman's monthly uncleanness[c] in my
sight.[d] 18So I poured out[e] my wrath on
them because they had shed blood in
the land and because they had defiled it
with their idols. 19I dispersed them
among the nations, and they were scat-
tered[f] through the countries; I judged
them according to their conduct and
their actions.[g] 20And wherever they
went among the nations they profaned[h]
my holy name, for it was said of them,
'These are the LORD's people, and yet
they had to leave his land.'[i] 21I had
concern for my holy name, which the
house of Israel profaned among the
nations where they had gone.[j]
22"Therefore say to the house of
Israel, 'This is what the Sovereign LORD
says: It is not for your sake, O house of
Israel, that I am going to do these
things, but for the sake of my holy
name,[k] which you have profaned[l]
among the nations where you have
gone.[m] 23I will show the holiness of my
great name,[n] which has been profaned[o]
among the nations, the name you have
profaned among them. Then the
nations will know that I am the LORD,[p]
declares the Sovereign LORD, when I
show myself holy[q] through you before
their eyes.[r]
24" 'For I will take you out of the
nations; I will gather you from all the
countries and bring you back into your
own land.[s] 25I will sprinkle[t] clean water
on you, and you will be clean; I will
cleanse[u] you from all your impurities[v]
and from all your idols.[w] 26I will give you
a new heart[x] and put a new spirit in you;
I will remove from you your heart of
stone[y] and give you a heart of flesh.[z]
27And I will put my Spirit[a] in you and
move you to follow my decrees[b] and be
careful to keep my laws.[c] 28You will live
in the land I gave your forefathers; you
will be my people,[d] and I will be your
God.[e] 29I will save you from all your
uncleanness. I will call for the corn and
make it plentiful and will not bring
famine[f] upon you. 30I will increase the
fruit of the trees and the crops of the
field, so that you will no longer suffer
disgrace among the nations because of
famine.[g] 31Then you will remember
your evil ways and wicked deeds, and
you will loathe yourselves for your sins
and detestable practices.[h] 32I want you
to know that I am not doing this for your
sake, declares the Sovereign LORD. Be
ashamed[i] and disgraced for your con-
duct, O house of Israel![j]
33" 'This is what the Sovereign LORD
says: On the day I cleanse[k] you from all
your sins, I will resettle your towns, and
the ruins[l] will be rebuilt.[m] 34The desolate
land will be cultivated instead of lying
desolate in the sight of all who pass
through it. 35They will say, "This land
that was laid waste has become like the
garden of Eden;[n] the cities that were
lying in ruins, desolate and destroyed,
are now fortified and inhabited.[o]"
36Then the nations around you that re-
main will know that I the LORD have
rebuilt what was destroyed and have
replanted what was desolate. I the LORD
have spoken, and I will do it.'[p]
37"This is what the Sovereign LORD
says: Once again I will yield to the plea[q]
of the house of Israel and do this for
them: I will make their people as numer-
ous as sheep,[r] 38as numerous as the
flocks for offerings[s] at Jerusalem during
her appointed feasts. So will the ruined
cities be filled with flocks of people.
Then they will know that I am the
LORD.[t]"

The Valley of Dry Bones

37 The hand of the LORD was upon
me,[a] and he brought me out by
the Spirit[b] of the LORD and set me in the
middle of a valley;[c] it was full of bones.[d]
2He led me to and fro among them, and I
saw a great many bones on the floor of
the valley, bones that were very dry.
3He asked me, "Son of man, can these
bones live?"
I said, "O Sovereign LORD, you alone
know.[e]"
4Then he said to me, "Prophesy to
these bones and say to them, 'Dry
bones, hear the word of the LORD![f] 5This
is what the Sovereign LORD says to these
bones: I will make breath[a] enter you,
and you will come to life.[g] 6I will attach
tendons to you and make flesh come
upon you and cover you with skin; I will
put breath in you, and you will come to
life. Then you will know that I am the
LORD.[h]' "

15 [b]Ps 89:50–51; Isa 54:4; **Eze 34:29**
17 [c]**Lev 5:2; 12:2;** [d]Ps 106:37–38; **Jer 2:7**
18 [e]**2Ch 34:21**
19 [f]Dt 28:64; [g]Lev 18:24–28; **Eze 7:8; 24:14;** 39:24
20 [h]**Lev 18:21; Eze 13:19;** Ro 2:24; [i]Isa 52:5; **Jer 33:24; Eze 12:16**
21 [j]Ps 74:18; Isa 48:9
22 [k]**Isa 37:35; Eze 20:44;** [l]Ro 2:24*; [m]Dt 9:5–6; Ps 106:8; **Eze 20:9**
23 [n]**Nu 6:27;** [o]**Isa 37:23;** [p]**Ps 46:10;** [q]**Eze 20:41;** [r]Ps 126:2; **Isa 5:16;** Eze 20:14; 38:23; 39:7,27–28
24 [s]**Isa 43:5–6; Eze 34:13;** 37:21
25 [t]**Lev 14:7; 16:14–15;** Heb 9:13; [u]**Ps 51:2,** 7; [v]**Ezr 6:21;** [w]Isa 2:18; Joel 3:21; Zec 3:4; 13:2; **Ac 22:16**
26 [x]Jer 24:7; [y]**Jer 5:3;** [z]**Ps 51:10; Eze 18:31; 2Co 3:3**
27 [a]**Isa 44:3;** Joel 2:29; Jn 3:5; [b]**Eze 18:21;** [c]Jer 50:20; 1Th 4:8
28 [d]Jer 30:22; 31:33; [e]**Eze 11:17; 14:11;** 34:24; 37:14, 27; Zec 8:8
29 [f]Eze 34:29
30 [g]Lev 26:4–5; **Eze 34:13–14;** Hos 2:21–22
31 [h]Isa 6:5; **Jer 31:19; Eze 6:9**
32 [i]Eze 16:63; [j]Dt 9:5
33 [k]**Lev 16:30;** [l]**Lev 26:31;** [m]**Isa 49:8**
35 [n]**Ge 2:8;** [o]Am 9:14
36 [p]**Jer 42:10; Eze 17:22;** 37:14; 39:27–28
37 [q]Zec 10:6; 13:9; [r]Ps 102:17; Jer 29:12–14
38 [s]1Ki 8:63; 2Ch 35:7–9; [t]**Ex 6:2**

Ch. 37

1 [a]**Eze 1:3;** [b]**Eze 11:24;** Lk 4:1; Ac 8:39; [c]Jer 7:32; [d]**Jer 8:2;** Eze 40:1
3 [e]Dt 32:39; **1Sa 2:6;** Isa 26:19; 1Co 15:35
4 [f]Jer 22:29 **5** [g]**Ge 2:7;** Ps 104:29–30; Rev 11:11
6 [h]**Ex 6:2;** Eze 38:23

[a]5 The Hebrew for this word can also mean *wind* or *spirit* (see verses 6–14).

7So I prophesied as I was comman-
ded. And as I was prophesying, there
was a noise, a rattling sound, and the
bones came together, bone to bone.
8I looked, and tendons and flesh
appeared on them and skin covered
them, but there was no breath in them.
9Then he said to me, "Prophesy to the
breath;[i] prophesy, son of man, and say
to it, 'This is what the Sovereign LORD
says: Come from the four winds,[j] O
breath, and breathe into these slain,
that they may live.'" 10So I prophesied
as he commanded[k] me, and breath
entered them; they came to life and
stood up on their feet—a vast army.[l]
11Then he said to me: "Son of man,
these bones are the whole house of
Israel. They say, 'Our bones are dried
up and our hope is gone; we are cut
off.'[m] 12Therefore prophesy and say to
them: 'This is what the Sovereign LORD
says: O my people, I am going to open
your graves and bring you up from
them; I will bring you back to the land of
Israel.[n] 13Then you, my people, will
know that I am the LORD,[o] when I open
your graves and bring you up from
them.[p] 14I will put my Spirit[q] in you and
you will live, and I will settle[r] you in
your own land. Then you will know that
I the LORD have spoken, and I have done
it, declares the LORD.[s]'"

One Nation Under One King

15The word of the LORD came to me:
16"Son of man, take a stick of wood and
write on it, 'Belonging to Judah and the
Israelites[t] associated with him.[u]' Then
take another stick of wood, and write on
it, 'Ephraim's stick, belonging to Joseph
and all the house of Israel associated
with him.' 17Join them together into one
stick so that they will become one in
your hand.[v]
18"When your countrymen ask you,
'Won't you tell us what you mean by
this?'[w] 19say to them, 'This is what the
Sovereign LORD says: I am going to take
the stick of Joseph—which is in
Ephraim's hand—and of the Israelite
tribes associated with him, and join it to
Judah's stick, making them a single
stick of wood, and they will become one
in my hand.'[x] 20Hold before their eyes
the sticks you have written on 21and say
to them, 'This is what the Sovereign
LORD says: I will take the Israelites out of
the nations where they have gone. I will
gather them from all around and bring
them back into their own land.[y] 22I will
make them one nation in the land, on
the mountains of Israel.[z] There will be
one king over all of them and they will
never again be two nations or be
divided into two kingdoms.[a] 23They will
no longer defile[b] themselves with their
idols and vile images or with any of their
offences, for I will save them from all
their sinful backsliding,[b][c] and I will
cleanse them. They will be my people,
and I will be their God.[d]
24"'My servant David[e] will be king[f]
over them, and they will all have one
shepherd.[g] They will follow my laws
and be careful to keep my decrees.[h]
25They will live in the land I gave to my
servant Jacob, the land where your
fathers lived.[i] They and their children
and their children's children will live
there for ever,[j] and David my servant
will be their prince for ever.[k] 26I will
make a covenant of peace[l] with them; it
will be an everlasting covenant.[m] I will
establish them and increase their num-
bers,[n] and I will put my sanctuary
among them[o] for ever.[p] 27My dwelling-
place[q] will be with them; I will be their
God, and they will be my people.[r]
28Then the nations will know that I the
LORD make Israel holy,[s] when my sanc-
tuary is among them for ever.[t][u]'"

A Prophecy Against Gog

38 The word of the LORD came to
me: 2"Son of man, set your face
against Gog,[a] of the land of Magog,[b] the
chief prince of[a] Meshech and Tubal;[c]
prophesy against him 3and say: 'This is
what the Sovereign LORD says: I am
against you, O Gog, chief prince of[b]
Meshech and Tubal.[d] 4I will turn you
around, put hooks[e] in your jaws and
bring you out with your whole army
—your horses, your horsemen fully
armed, and a great horde with large and
small shields, all of them brandishing
their swords.[f] 5Persia, Cush[c][g] and Put[h]
will be with them, all with shields and
helmets, 6also Gomer[i] with all its troops,
and Beth Togarmah[j] from the far north[k]
with all its troops—the many nations
with you.

9 [i]ver 14; Ps 104:30; Isa 32:15; Eze 39:29; Zec 12:10; [j]Jer 49:36; Da 7:2; 8:8; 11:4; Zec 2:6; 6:5; Rev 7:1
10 [k]**Eze 12:7;** [l]Rev 11:11
11 [m]**Job 17:15; La 3:54**
12 [n]ver 21; Dt 32:39; 1Sa 2:6; Isa 26:19; Jer 29:14; Hos 13:14; Am 9:14–15; Zep 3:20; Zec 8:8
13 [o]**Ex 6:2;** [p]**Eze 17:24;** Hos 13:14
14 [q]**ver 9; Isa 11:2;** Joel 2:28–29; [r]**Jer 43:2;** [s]Eze 36:27–28,36; Rev 11:11
16 [t]**1Ki 12:20;** 2Ch 10:17–19; [u]Nu 17:2–3; 2Ch 15:9
17 [v]ver 24; Isa 11:13; **Jer 50:4;** Hos 1:11
18 [w]**Eze 24:19**
19 [x]Zec 10:6
21 [y]**ver 12; Isa 43:5–6; Eze 20:42;** 39:27; Mic 4:6
22 [z]**Eze 17:22; 34:13–14;** [a]Isa 11:13; Jer 33:24; **50:4;** Hos 1:11
23 [b]Eze 43:7; [c]**Jer 7:24;** [d]Eze 11:18; **36:28;** Na 2:2
24 [e]Isa 55:4; Hos 3:5; [f]**1Sa 13:14; Isa 32:1;** [g]Zec 13:7; [h]Ps 78:70–71; **Jer 30:21; Eze 21:27**
25 [i]**Eze 28:25;** [j]**Ezr 9:12;** Am 9:15; [k]**Ps 89:3–4;** Isa 11:1; **Eze 34:23–24**
26 [l]**Nu 25:12;** [m]**Ge 9:16; Dt 29:14; Heb 13:20;** [n]**Jer 30:19;** [o]Lev 26:11; [p]**Eze 16:62**
27 [q]**Lev 26:11;** [r]**Eze 34:30; 36:28; 2Co 6:16***
28 [s]**Ex 31:13;** [t]Hos 1:10–11; [u]Eze 43:9; Zep 3:15

Ch. 38
2 [a]ver 14; Eze 39:11; [b]**Ge 10:2;** [c]**Eze 27:13**
3 [d]Eze 39:1
4 [e]**2Ki 19:28;** [f]**Isa 43:17;** Eze 29:4; 39:2; Da 11:40
5 [g]**Ge 10:6;** [h]**Ge 10:6; Eze 27:10**
6 [i]**Ge 10:2;** [j]**Ge 10:3;** [k]**Eze 32:30**

[b]23 Many Hebrew manuscripts (see also Septuagint); most Hebrew manuscripts *all their dwelling-places where they sinned* [a]2 Or *the prince of Rosh,* [b]3 Or *Gog, prince of Rosh,* [c]5 That is, the upper Nile region

7"'Get ready; be prepared,[l] you and
all the hordes gathered about you, and
take command of them. 8After many
days[m] you will be called to arms. In
future years you will invade a land that
has recovered from war, whose people
were gathered from many nations[n] to
the mountains of Israel, which had long
been desolate. They had been brought
out from the nations, and now all of
them live in safety.[o] 9You and all your
troops and the many nations with you
will go up, advancing like a storm;[p] you
will be like a cloud[q] covering the land.[r]

10"'This is what the Sovereign LORD
says: On that day thoughts will come
into your mind[s] and you will devise an
evil scheme.[t] 11You will say, "I will in-
vade a land of unwalled villages; I will
attack a peaceful and unsuspecting
people[u]—all of them living without
walls and without gates and bars.[v] 12I
will plunder and loot and turn my hand
against the resettled ruins and the
people gathered from the nations, rich
in livestock and goods, living at the
centre of the land." 13Sheba[w] and
Dedan[x] and the merchants of Tarshish[y]
and all her villages[d] will say to you,
"Have you come to plunder? Have you
gathered your hordes to loot, to carry
off silver and gold, to take away live-
stock and goods and to seize much
plunder?[z]"'

14"Therefore, son of man, prophesy
and say to Gog: 'This is what the
Sovereign LORD says: In that day, when
my people Israel are living in safety,[a]
will you not take notice of it? 15You will
come from your place in the far north,[b]
you and many nations with you, all of
them riding on horses, a great horde, a
mighty army.[c] 16You will advance
against my people Israel like a cloud[d]
that covers the land.[e] In days to come, O
Gog, I will bring you against my land, so
that the nations may know me when I
show myself holy[f] through you before
their eyes.[g]

17"'This is what the Sovereign LORD
says: Are you not the one I spoke of in
former days by my servants the
prophets of Israel? At that time they
prophesied for years that I would bring
you against them. 18This is what will
happen in that day: When Gog attacks
the land of Israel, my hot anger will be
aroused, declares the Sovereign LORD.
19In my zeal and fiery wrath I declare
that at that time there shall be a great
earthquake[h] in the land of Israel.[i] 20The
fish of the sea, the birds of the air, the
beasts of the field, every creature that
moves along the ground, and all the
people on the face of the earth will
tremble[j] at my presence. The mountains
will be overturned,[k] the cliffs will
crumble[l] and every wall will fall to the
ground.[m] 21I will summon a sword[n]
against Gog on all my mountains, de-
clares the Sovereign LORD. Every man's
sword will be against his brother.[o] 22I
will execute judgment[p] upon him with
plague and bloodshed;[q] I will pour
down torrents of rain, hailstones[r] and
burning sulphur[s] on him and on his
troops and on the many nations with
him.[t] 23And so I will show my greatness
and my holiness, and I will make myself
known in the sight of many nations.
Then they will know that I am the
LORD.[u]

39 "Son of man, prophesy against
Gog[a] and say: 'This is what the
Sovereign LORD says: I am against you,
O Gog, chief prince of[a] Meshech[b] and
Tubal.[c] 2I will turn you around and drag
you along. I will bring you from the far
north[d] and send you against the moun-
tains of Israel.[e] 3Then I will strike your
bow[f] from your left hand and make your
arrows[g] drop from your right hand. 4On
the mountains of Israel you will fall, you
and all your troops and the nations with
you. I will give you as food to all kinds of
carrion birds[h] and to the wild animals.[i]
5You will fall in the open field, for I have
spoken, declares the Sovereign LORD.[j] 6I
will send fire[k] on Magog[l] and on those
who live in safety in the coastlands,[m]
and they will know[n] that I am the LORD.

7"'I will make known my holy name
among my people Israel. I will no longer
let my holy name be profaned,[o] and the
nations will know[p] that I the LORD am
the Holy One in Israel.[q] 8It is coming! It
will surely take place, declares the
Sovereign LORD. This is the day[r] I have
spoken of.

9"'Then those who live in the towns
of Israel will go out and use the
weapons for fuel and burn them up
—the small and large shields, the bows
and arrows,[s] the war clubs and spears.
For seven years they will use them for
fuel.[t] 10They will not need to gather
wood from the fields or cut it from the
forests, because they will use the
weapons for fuel. And they will plun-
der[u] those who plundered them and
loot those who looted them, declares
the Sovereign LORD.[v]

7 [l]**Isa 8:9**
8 [m]Isa 24:22; [n]**Isa 11:11;** [o]ver 14; Jer 23:6; **Eze 28:26;** Joel 3:1
9 [p]Isa 25:4; 28:2; [q]ver 16; Jer 4:13; Joel 2:2; [r]Rev 20:8
10 [s]**Jer 17:10;** [t]Ps 36:4; Mic 2:1
11 [u]**Ge 34:25;** [v]Jer 49:31; Zec 2:4
13 [w]**Ge 10:7;** [x]**Ge 25:3;** [y]**Ge 10:4;** [z]Isa 10:6; 33:23; **Jer 15:13**
14 [a]**ver 8; Lev 25:18; Jer 16:15;** Zec 2:5
15 [b]**Eze 32:30;** [c]Eze 39:2; Rev 20:8
16 [d]**ver 9;** [e]Joel 3:11; [f]**Lev 10:3;** [g]Isa 29:23; Eze 39:21
19 [h]Isa 24:18; Joel 2:10; 3:16; **Rev 6:12;** [i]Ps 18:7; **Eze 5:13;** Hag 2:6,21
20 [j]**Ex 15:14;** [k]Isa 42:15; [l]Job 14:18; [m]**Ps 76:8;** Hos 4:3; Na 1:5
21 [n]Isa 66:16; Jer 25:29; [o]**1Sa 14:20; 2Ch 20:23;** Hag 2:22
22 [p]Isa 66:16; Jer 25:31; **Eze 36:5;** [q]**Eze 14:19; 28:23;** [r]**Ex 9:18;** Ps 18:12; Rev 16:21; [s]**Ge 19:24; Rev 9:17;** [t]**Eze 13:11**
23 [u]Eze 20:42; **36:23; 37:6**

Ch. 39

1 [a]Rev 20:8; [b]**Ge 10:2;** [c]**Eze 27:13; 38:2–3**
2 [d]**Eze 32:30;** [e]**Eze 38:4**,15
3 [f]Hos 1:5; Am 2:15; [g]Ps 76:3
4 [h]**Ge 40:19;** [i]ver 17–20; **Jer 25:33; Eze 29:5; 33:27**
5 [j]**Eze 32:4**
6 [k]**Eze 30:8;** Rev 20:9; [l]**Ge 10:2;** [m]**Jer 25:22;** [n]**Ex 6:7**
7 [o]**Ex 20:7; Eze 13:19;** [p]**Isa 49:26;** [q]**Isa 12:6; 54:5; Eze 20:9; 36:23**
8 [r]Eze 7:6
9 [s]Ps 76:3; [t]**Ps 46:9**
10 [u]**Ex 3:22;** [v]**Isa 14:2;** 33:1; Hab 2:8

d13 Or *her strong lions*

a1 Or *Gog, prince of Rosh,*

11"'On that day I will give Gog a
burial place in Israel, in the valley of
those who travel east towards[b] the Sea.[c]
It will block the way of travellers, be-
cause Gog and all his hordes will be
buried[w] there. So it will be called the
Valley of Hamon Gog.[d x]

12"'For seven months the house of
Israel will be burying them in order to
cleanse the land.[y] 13All the people of the
land will bury them, and the day I am
glorified[z] will be a memorable day for
them, declares the Sovereign LORD.

14"'Men will be regularly employed to
cleanse the land. Some will go through-
out the land and, in addition to them,
others will bury those that remain on
the ground. At the end of the seven
months they will begin their search.
15As they go through the land and one
of them sees a human bone, he will set
up a marker beside it until the grave-
diggers have buried it in the Valley of
Hamon Gog. 16(Also a town called
Hamonah[e] will be there.) And so they
will cleanse the land.'

17"Son of man, this is what the
Sovereign LORD says: Call out to every
kind of bird[a] and all the wild animals:
'Assemble and come together from all
around to the sacrifice I am preparing
for you, the great sacrifice on the moun-
tains of Israel. There you will eat flesh
and drink blood.[b] 18You will eat the flesh
of mighty men and drink the blood of
the princes of the earth as if they were
rams and lambs, goats and bulls—all of
them fattened animals from Bashan.[c]
19At the sacrifice[d] I am preparing for
you, you will eat fat till you are glutted
and drink blood till you are drunk. 20At
my table you will eat your fill of horses
and riders, mighty men and soldiers of
every kind,' declares the Sovereign
LORD.[e]

21"I will display my glory among the
nations, and all the nations will see the
punishment I inflict and the hand I lay
upon them.[f] 22From that day forward
the house of Israel will know that I am
the LORD their God. 23And the nations
will know that the people of Israel went
into exile for their sin, because they
were unfaithful to me. So I hid my face
from them and handed them over to
their enemies, and they all fell by the
sword.[g] 24I dealt with them according to
their uncleanness and their offences,
and I hid my face from them.[h]

25"Therefore this is what the
Sovereign LORD says: I will now bring
Jacob back from captivity[f i] and will have
compassion[j] on all the people of Israel,
and I will be zealous for my holy name.[k]
26They will forget their shame and all
the unfaithfulness they showed to-
wards me when they lived in safety[l] in
their land with no-one to make them
afraid.[m] 27When I have brought them
back from the nations and have
gathered them from the countries of
their enemies, I will show myself holy
through them in the sight of many
nations.[n] 28Then they will know that I
am the LORD their God, for though I sent
them into exile among the nations, I will
gather them[o] to their own land, not leav-
ing any behind.[p] 29I will no longer hide
my face[q] from them, for I will pour out
my Spirit[r] on the house of Israel,
declares the Sovereign LORD.[s]"

The New Temple Area

40 In the twenty-fifth year of our
exile, at the beginning of the
year, on the tenth of the month, in the
fourteenth year after the fall of the city[a]
—on that very day the hand of the LORD
was upon me[b] and he took me there. 2In
visions[c] of God he took me to the land of
Israel and set me on a very high moun-
tain,[d] on whose south side were some
buildings that looked like a city. 3He
took me there, and I saw a man whose
appearance was like bronze;[e] he was
standing in the gateway with a linen
cord and a measuring rod[f] in his hand.
4The man said to me, "Son of man, look
with your eyes and hear with your ears
and pay attention to everything I am
going to show you,[g] for that is why you
have been brought here. Tell[h] the house
of Israel everything you see.[i]"

The East Gate to the Outer Court

5I saw a wall completely surrounding
the temple area. The length of the
measuring rod in the man's hand was
six long cubits, each of which was
a cubit[a] and a handbreadth.[b] He
measured[j] the wall; it was one measur-
ing rod thick and one rod high.

6Then he went to the gate facing east.[k]
He climbed its steps and measured the
threshold of the gate; it was one rod
deep.[c] 7The alcoves[l] for the guards were

11 [w]**Isa 34:3**; [x]**Eze 38:2**
12 [y]Dt 21:23
13 [z]Eze 28:22
17 [a]**Job 15:23**; [b]**Eze 32:4**
18 [c]**Ps 22:12**; Jer 51:40
19 [d]**Lev 3:9**
20 [e]**Isa 56:9**; **Jer 12:9**; Rev 19:17–18
21 [f]Ex 9:16; Isa 37:20; **Eze 38:16**
23 [g]Isa 1:15; 59:2; **Jer 22:8–9**; **44:23**
24 [h]2Ki 17:23; Jer 2:17,19; 4:18; **Eze 7:22**; Da 9:7
25 [i]**Jer 33:7**; [j]**Jer 30:18**; [k]Isa 27:12–13; **Eze 16:53**
26 [l]**1Ki 4:25**; **Jer 32:37**; **Eze 38:8**; [m]Isa 17:2; Eze 34:28; Mic 4:4
27 [n]**Eze 37:21**
28 [o]Ps 147:2; [p]**Eze 36:23**,36
29 [q]**Dt 31:17**; [r]**Isa 11:2**; **Eze 37:9**; **Ac 2:17**; [s]**Eze 16:42**

Ch. 40

1 [a]**2Ki 25:7**; Jer 39:1–10; 52:4–11; [b]**Eze 1:3**; **29:17**
2 [c]**Ex 24:10**; Da 7:1,7; [d]**Jer 31:12**; **Eze 17:22**; Rev 21:10
3 [e]**Eze 1:7**; Rev 1:15; [f]Eze 47:3; Zec 2:1–2; Rev 11:1; 21:15
4 [g]**Dt 6:6**; [h]Jer 26:2; [i]Eze 44:5
5 [j]Eze 42:20
6 [k]**Eze 8:16**
7 [l]ver 36

[b]11 Or *of* [c]11 That is, the Dead Sea
[d]11 *Hamon Gog* means *hordes of Gog*.
[e]16 *Hamonah* means *horde*.
[f]25 Or *now restore the fortunes of Jacob*
[a]5 The common cubit was about 1½ feet (about 0.5 metre).
[b]5 That is, about 3 inches (about 8 centimetres)
[c]6 Septuagint; Hebrew *deep, the first threshold, one rod deep*

one rod long and one rod wide, and the projecting walls between the alcoves were five cubits thick. And the threshold of the gate next to the portico facing the temple was one rod deep.

8Then he measured the portico of the gateway; 9it[d] was eight cubits deep and its jambs were two cubits thick. The portico of the gateway faced the temple.

10Inside the east gate were three alcoves on each side; the three had the same measurements, and the faces of the projecting walls on each side had the same measurements. 11Then he measured the width of the entrance to the gateway; it was ten cubits and its length was thirteen cubits. 12In front of each alcove was a wall one cubit high, and the alcoves were six cubits square. 13Then he measured the gateway from the top of the rear wall of one alcove to the top of the opposite one; the distance was twenty-five cubits from one parapet opening to the opposite one. 14He measured along the faces of the projecting walls all around the inside of the gateway—sixty cubits. The measurement was up to the portico[e] facing the courtyard.[f] [m] 15The distance from the entrance of the gateway to the far end of its portico was fifty cubits. 16The alcoves and the projecting walls inside the gateway were surmounted by narrow parapet openings all round, as was the portico; the openings all round faced inward. The faces of the projecting walls were decorated with palm trees.[n]

The Outer Court

17Then he brought me into the outer court.[o] There I saw some rooms and a pavement that had been constructed all round the court; there were thirty rooms[p] along the pavement.[q] 18It abutted the sides of the gateways and was as wide as they were long; this was the lower pavement. 19Then he measured the distance from the inside of the lower gateway to the outside of the inner court;[r] it was a hundred cubits[s] on the east side as well as on the north.

The North Gate

20Then he measured the length and width of the gate facing north, leading into the outer court. 21Its alcoves[t]—three on each side—its projecting walls and its portico[u] had the same measurements as those of the first gateway. It was fifty cubits long and twenty-five cubits wide. 22Its openings, its portico[v] and its palm tree decorations had the same measurements as those of the gate facing east. Seven steps led up to it, with its portico opposite them.[w] 23There was a gate to the inner court facing the north gate, just as there was on the east. He measured from one gate to the opposite one; it was a hundred cubits.[x]

The South Gate

24Then he led me to the south side and I saw a gate facing south. He measured its jambs and its portico, and they had the same measurements[y] as the others. 25The gateway and its portico had narrow openings all round, like the openings of the others. It was fifty cubits long and twenty-five cubits wide.[z] 26Seven steps led up to it, with its portico opposite them; it had palm tree decorations on the faces of the projecting walls on each side.[a] 27The inner court[b] also had a gate facing south, and he measured from this gate to the outer gate on the south side; it was a hundred cubits.[c]

Gates to the Inner Court

28Then he brought me into the inner court through the south gate, and he measured the south gate; it had the same measurements[d] as the others. 29Its alcoves,[e] its projecting walls and its portico had the same measurements as the others. The gateway and its portico had openings all round. It was fifty cubits long and twenty-five cubits wide.[f] 30(The porticoes[g] of the gateways around the inner court were twenty-five cubits wide and five cubits deep.) 31Its portico[h] faced the outer court; palm trees decorated its jambs, and eight steps led up to it.[i]

32Then he brought me to the inner court on the east side, and he measured the gateway; it had the same measurements[j] as the others. 33Its alcoves,[k] its projecting walls and its portico had the same measurements as the others. The gateway and its portico had openings all round. It was fifty cubits long and twenty-five cubits wide. 34Its portico[l] faced the outer court; palm trees decorated the jambs on either side, and eight steps led up to it.

14 [m]**Ex 27:9**
16 [n]ver 21–22; 2Ch 3:5; Eze 41:26
17 [o]Rev 11:2; [p]Eze 41:6; [q]Eze 42:1
19 [r]Eze 46:1; [s]ver 23,27
21 [t]ver 7; [u]ver 30
22 [v]ver 49; [w]**ver 16,26**
23 [x]**ver 19**
24 [y]ver 32,35
25 [z]ver 33
26 [a]**ver 22**
27 [b]ver 32; [c]**ver 19**
28 [d]ver 35
29 [e]ver 7; [f]ver 25
30 [g]ver 21
31 [h]ver 22; [i]ver 34,37
32 [j]**ver 24**
33 [k]ver 7
34 [l]ver 22

[d]8,9 Many Hebrew manuscripts, Septuagint, Vulgate and Syriac; most Hebrew manuscripts *gateway facing the temple; it was one rod deep. 9Then he measured the portico of the gateway; it*
[e]14 Septuagint; Hebrew *projecting wall*
[f]14 The meaning of the Hebrew for this verse is uncertain.

35Then he brought me to the north
gate[m] and measured it. It had the same
measurements[n] as the others, 36as did
its alcoves,[o] its projecting walls and its
portico, and it had openings all round.
It was fifty cubits long and twenty-five
cubits wide. 37Its portico[g][p] faced the
outer court; palm trees decorated the
jambs on either side, and eight steps led
up to it.[q]

The Rooms for Preparing Sacrifices

38A room with a doorway was by the
portico in each of the inner gateways,
where the burnt offerings[r] were
washed. 39In the portico of the gateway
were two tables on each side, on which
the burnt offerings,[s] sin offerings[t] and
guilt offerings[u] were slaughtered.[v] 40By
the outside wall of the portico of the
gateway, near the steps at the entrance
to the north gateway were two tables,
and on the other side of the steps were
two tables. 41So there were four tables
on one side of the gateway and four on
the other—eight tables in all—on which
the sacrifices were slaughtered. 42There
were also four tables of dressed stone[w]
for the burnt offerings, each a cubit and
a half long, a cubit and a half wide and a
cubit high. On them were placed the
utensils for slaughtering the burnt offer-
ings and the other sacrifices.[x] 43And
double-pronged hooks, each a hand-
breadth long, were attached to the wall
all around. The tables were for the flesh
of the offerings.

Rooms for the Priests

44Outside the inner gate, within the
inner court, were two rooms, one[h] at the
side of the north gate and facing south,
and another at the side of the south[i] gate
and facing north. 45He said to me, "The
room facing south is for the priests who
have charge of the temple,[y] 46and the
room facing north[z] is for the priests who
have charge of the altar.[a] These are the
sons of Zadok,[b] who are the only Levites
who may draw near to the LORD to
minister before him.[c]"
47Then he measured the court: It was
square—a hundred cubits long and a
hundred cubits wide. And the altar was
in front of the temple.[d]

The Temple

48He brought me to the portico of the
temple[e] and measured the jambs of the
portico; they were five cubits wide on
either side. The width of the entrance
was fourteen cubits and its projecting
walls were[j] three cubits wide on either
side. 49The portico[f] was twenty cubits
wide, and twelve[k] cubits from front to
back. It was reached by a flight of stairs,[l]
and there were pillars[g] on each side of
the jambs.

41 Then the man brought me to
the outer sanctuary[a] and
measured the jambs; the width of the
jambs was six cubits[a] on each side.[b]
2The entrance was ten cubits wide, and
the projecting walls on each side of it
were five cubits wide. He also measured
the outer sanctuary; it was forty cubits
long and twenty cubits wide.[b]
3Then he went into the inner sanctu-
ary and measured the jambs of the en-
trance; each was two cubits wide. The
entrance was six cubits wide, and the
projecting walls on each side of it were
seven cubits wide. 4And he measured
the length of the inner sanctuary; it was
twenty cubits, and its width was twenty
cubits across the end of the outer sanc-
tuary.[c] He said to me, "This is the Most
Holy Place.[d]"
5Then he measured the wall of the
temple; it was six cubits thick, and each
side room round the temple was four
cubits wide. 6The side rooms were on
three levels, one above another, thirty[e]
on each level. There were ledges all
round the wall of the temple to serve as
supports for the side rooms, so that the
supports were not inserted into the wall
of the temple.[f] 7The side rooms all round
the temple were wider at each success-
ive level. The structure surrounding
the temple was built in ascending
stages, so that the rooms widened as
one went upward. A stairway[g] went up
from the lowest floor to the top floor
through the middle floor.
8I saw that the temple had a raised
base all round it, forming the founda-
tion of the side rooms. It was the length
of the rod, six long cubits. 9The outer
wall of the side rooms was five cubits
thick. The open area between the side
rooms of the temple 10and the ⌞priests'⌟

35 [m]Eze 44:4; 47:2; [n]**ver 24**
36 [o]ver 7
37 [p]ver 22; [q]ver 34
38 [r]**2Ch 4:6**; Eze 42:13
39 [s]Eze 46:2; [t]Lev 4:3,28; [u]**Lev 7:1**; [v]ver 42
42 [w]Ex 20:25; [x]ver 39
45 [y]1Ch 9:23
46 [z]Eze 42:13; [a]Nu 18:5; [b]**2Sa 8:17; Ezr 7:2**; [c]Nu 16:5; Eze 43:19; 44:15; 45:4; 48:11
47 [d]Eze 41:13–14
48 [e]1Ki 6:2
49 [f]ver 22; 1Ki 6:3; [g]**1Ki 7:15**

Ch. 41

1 [a]ver 23
2 [b]2Ch 3:3
4 [c]1Ki 6:20; [d]**Ex 26:33**; Heb 9:3–8
6 [e]Eze 40:17; [f]**1Ki 6:5**
7 [g]1Ki 6:8

[g]*37* Septuagint (see also verses 31 and 34); Hebrew *jambs*
[h]*44* Septuagint; Hebrew *were rooms for singers, which were* [i]*44* Septuagint; Hebrew *east*
[j]*48* Septuagint; Hebrew *entrance was*
[k]*49* Septuagint; Hebrew *eleven*
[l]*49* Hebrew; Septuagint *Ten steps led up to it*
[a]*1* The common cubit was about 1½ feet (about 0.5 metre)
[b]*1* One Hebrew manuscript and Septuagint; most Hebrew manuscripts *side, the width of the tent*

rooms was twenty cubits wide all round the temple. 11There were entrances to the side rooms from the open area, one on the north and another on the south; and the base adjoining the open area was five cubits wide all round.

12The building facing the temple courtyard on the west side was seventy cubits wide. The wall of the building was five cubits thick all round, and its length was ninety cubits.

13Then he measured the temple; it was a hundred cubits long, and the temple courtyard and the building with its walls were also a hundred cubits long. 14The width of the temple courtyard on the east, including the front of the temple, was a hundred cubits.[h]

15Then he measured the length of the building facing the courtyard at the rear of the temple, including its galleries[i] on each side; it was a hundred cubits.

The outer sanctuary, the inner sanctuary and the portico facing the court, 16as well as the thresholds and the narrow windows[j] and galleries round the three of them—everything beyond and including the threshold was covered with wood. The floor, the wall up to the windows, and the windows were covered.[k] 17In the space above the outside of the entrance to the inner sanctuary and on the walls at regular intervals all round the inner and outer sanctuary 18were carved[l] cherubim[m] and palm trees.[n] Palm trees alternated with cherubim. Each cherub had two faces:[o] 19the face of a man towards the palm tree on one side and the face of a lion towards the palm tree on the other. They were carved all round the whole temple.[p] 20From the floor to the area above the entrance, cherubim and palm trees were carved on the wall of the outer sanctuary.

21The outer sanctuary[q] had a rectangular door-frame, and the one at the front of the Most Holy Place was similar. 22There was a wooden altar[r] three cubits high and two cubits square;[c] its corners, its base[d] and its sides were of wood. The man said to me, "This is the table[s] that is before the LORD." 23Both the outer sanctuary[t] and the Most Holy Place had double doors.[u] 24Each door had two leaves—two hinged leaves[v] for each door. 25And on the doors of the outer sanctuary were carved cherubim and palm trees like those carved on the walls, and there was a wooden overhang on the front of the portico. 26On the side walls of the portico were narrow windows with palm trees carved on each side. The side rooms of the temple also had overhangs.[w]

14 [h]Eze 40:47
15 [i]Eze 42:3
16 [j]1Ki 6:4; [k]ver 25–26; 1Ki 6:15; Eze 42:3
18 [l]**1Ki 6:18;** [m]Ex 37:7; **2Ch 3:7;** [n]**1Ki 6:29;** 7:36; [o]Eze 10:21
19 [p]**Eze 10:14**
21 [q]ver 1
22 [r]**Ex 30:1;** [s]**Ex 25:23; Eze 23:41**
23 [t]ver 1; [u]1Ki 6:32
24 [v]1Ki 6:34
26 [w]ver 15–16; Eze 40:16

Ch. 42

1 [a]ver 13; [b]**Ex 27:9;** Eze 41:12–14; [c]Eze 40:17
3 [d]Eze 41:15; [e]Eze 41:16
4 [f]Eze 46:19
9 [g]Eze 44:5; 46:19
10 [h]Eze 41:12–14; [i]ver 1
13 [j]Eze 40:46; [k]ver 1; [l]Eze 41:12–14

Rooms for the Priests

42 Then the man led me northward into the outer court and brought me to the rooms[a] opposite the temple courtyard[b] and opposite the outer wall on the north side.[c] 2The building whose door faced north was a hundred cubits[a] long and fifty cubits wide. 3Both in the section twenty cubits from the inner court and in the section opposite the pavement of the outer court, gallery[d] faced gallery at the three levels.[e] 4In front of the rooms was an inner passageway ten cubits wide and a hundred cubits[b] long. Their doors were on the north.[f] 5Now the upper rooms were narrower, for the galleries took more space from them than from the rooms on the lower and middle floors of the building. 6The rooms on the third floor had no pillars, as the courts had; so they were smaller in floor space than those on the lower and middle floors. 7There was an outer wall parallel to the rooms and the outer court; it extended in front of the rooms for fifty cubits. 8While the row of rooms on the side next to the outer court was fifty cubits long, the row on the side nearest the sanctuary was a hundred cubits long. 9The lower rooms had an entrance[g] on the east side as one enters them from the outer court.

10On the south side[c] along the length of the wall of the outer court, adjoining the temple courtyard[h] and opposite the outer wall, were rooms[i] 11with a passageway in front of them. These were like the rooms on the north; they had the same length and width, with similar exits and dimensions. Similar to the doorways on the north 12were the doorways of the rooms on the south. There was a doorway at the beginning of the passageway that was parallel to the corresponding wall extending eastward, by which one enters the rooms.

13Then he said to me, "The north[j] and south rooms[k] facing the temple courtyard[l] are the priests' rooms, where the priests who approach the LORD will eat the most holy offerings. There they will

[c]22 Septuagint; Hebrew *long*
[d]22 Septuagint; Hebrew *length*
[a]2 The common cubit was about 1½ feet (about 0.5 metre).
[b]4 Septuagint and Syriac; Hebrew *and one cubit*
[c]10 Septuagint; Hebrew *Eastward*

put the most holy offerings—the grain
offerings,[m] the sin offerings[n] and the
guilt offerings[o]—for the place is holy.[p]
14 Once the priests enter the holy pre-
cincts, they are not to go into the outer
court until they leave behind the gar-
ments[q] in which they minister, for these
are holy. They are to put on other
clothes before they go near the places
that are for the people."[r]
15 When he had finished measuring
what was inside the temple area, he led
me out by the east gate[s] and measured
the area all around: 16 He measured the
east side with the measuring rod; it was
five hundred cubits.[d] 17 He measured
the north side; it was five hundred
cubits[e] by the measuring rod. 18 He
measured the south side; it was five
hundred cubits by the measuring rod.
19 Then he turned to the west side and
measured; it was five hundred cubits by
the measuring rod. 20 So he measured[t]
the area[u] on all four sides. It had a wall
round it,[v] five hundred cubits long and
five hundred cubits wide,[w] to separate
the holy from the common.[x]

The Glory Returns to the Temple

43 Then the man brought me to
the gate facing east,[a] 2 and I saw
the glory of the God of Israel coming
from the east. His voice was like the roar
of rushing waters,[b] and the land was
radiant with his glory.[c] 3 The vision I saw
was like the vision I had seen when he[a]
came to destroy the city and like the
visions I had seen by the Kebar River,
and I fell face down. 4 The glory[d] of the
LORD entered the temple through the
gate facing east.[e] 5 Then the Spirit[f] lifted
me up[g] and brought me into the inner
court, and the glory[h] of the LORD filled
the temple.[i]
6 While the man was standing beside
me, I heard someone speaking to me
from inside the temple. 7 He said: "Son
of man, this is the place of my throne[j]
and the place for the soles of my feet.
This is where I will live among the
Israelites for ever. The house of Israel
will never again defile[k] my holy name
—neither they nor their kings—by their
prostitution[b] and the lifeless idols[c] of
their kings at their high places.[l] 8 When
they placed their threshold next to my
threshold and their doorposts beside
my doorposts, with only a wall between
me and them, they defiled my holy
name by their detestable practices. So I
destroyed them in my anger. 9 Now let
them put away from me their prostitu-
tion and the lifeless idols of their kings,
and I will live among them for ever.[m]
10 "Son of man, describe the temple to
the people of Israel, that they may be
ashamed[n] of their sins. Let them con-
sider the plan, 11 and if they are ashamed
of all they have done, make known to
them the design of the temple—its
arrangement, its exits and entrances—
its whole design and all its regulations[d]
and laws. Write these down before
them so that they may be faithful to its
design and follow all its regulations.[o]
12 "This is the law of the temple: All
the surrounding area[p] on top of the
mountain will be most holy.[q] Such is the
law of the temple.

The Altar

13 "These are the measurements of the
altar[r] in long cubits, that cubit being a
cubit[e] and a handbreadth:[f] Its gutter is a
cubit deep and a cubit wide, with a rim
of one span[g] around the edge. And this
is the height of the altar: 14 From the
gutter on the ground up to the lower
edge it is two cubits high and a cubit
wide, and from the smaller ledge up to
the larger ledge it is four cubits high and
a cubit wide. 15 The altar hearth[s] is four
cubits high, and four horns[t] project up-
ward from the hearth. 16 The altar hearth
is square, twelve cubits long and twelve
cubits wide.[u] 17 The upper ledge[v] also is
square, fourteen cubits long and four-
teen cubits wide, with a rim of half a
cubit and a gutter of a cubit all round.
The steps[w] of the altar face east.[x]"
18 Then he said to me, "Son of man,
this is what the Sovereign LORD says:
These will be the regulations for sacrific-
ing burnt offerings[y] and sprinkling
blood[z] upon the altar when it is built:
19 You are to give a young bull[a] as a sin
offering to the priests, who are Levites,
of the family of Zadok,[b] who come near[c]
to minister before me, declares the
Sovereign LORD. 20 You are to take some
of its blood and put it on the four horns

13 [m]Jer 41:5; [n]**Lev 10:17**; [o]Lev 14:13; [p]**Ex 29:31; Lev 6:29**; 7:6; 10:12–13; Nu 18:9–10
14 [q]Lev 16:23; Eze 44:19; [r]Ex 29:9; **Lev 8:7–9**
15 [s]Eze 43:1
20 [t]Eze 40:5; [u]Eze 43:12; [v]Zec 2:5; [w]Eze 45:2; Rev 21:16; [x]**Eze 22:26**

Ch. 43

1 [a]**1Ch 9:18; Eze 8:16**; 42:15; 44:1
2 [b]**Ps 18:4; Rev 1:15**; [c]Isa 6:3; Rev 18:1; 21:11
4 [d]Eze 1:28; [e]Eze 10:19; 44:2
5 [f]**Eze 11:24**; [g]**Eze 3:12**; [h]Ex 16:7; [i]**Isa 6:4**
7 [j]**Jer 3:17**; [k]**Eze 37:23**; [l]**Lev 26:30; Eze 20:29**,39
9 [m]Eze 37:26–28
10 [n]**Eze 16:61**
11 [o]Eze 44:5
12 [p]Eze 42:20; [q]**Eze 17:22**
13 [r]**Ex 20:24**; 2Ch 4:1
15 [s]Isa 29:2; [t]**Ex 27:2**
16 [u]Rev 21:16
17 [v]ver 20; Eze 45:19; [w]Ex 20:26; [x]**Ex 27:1**
18 [y]Ex 40:29; [z]Lev 1:5,11; Heb 9:21–22
19 [a]**Lev 4:3**; [b]**2Sa 8:17; Ezr 7:2**; [c]Nu 16:40; **Eze 40:46**

[d] *16* See Septuagint of verse 17; Hebrew *rods*; also in verses 18 and 19. [e] *17* Septuagint; Hebrew *rods*
[a] *3* Some Hebrew manuscripts and Vulgate; most Hebrew manuscripts *I*
[b] *7* Or *their spiritual adultery*; also in verse 9
[c] *7* Or *the corpses*; also in verse 9
[d] *11* Some Hebrew manuscripts and Septuagint; most Hebrew manuscripts *regulations and its whole design*
[e] *13* The common cubit was about 1½ feet (about 0.5 metre).
[f] *13* That is, about 3 inches (about 8 centimetres)
[g] *13* That is, about 9 inches (about 23 centimetres)

of the altar[d] and on the four corners of the upper ledge[e] and all round the rim, and so purify the altar[f] and make atonement for it. 21You are to take the bull for the sin offering and burn it in the designated part of the temple area outside the sanctuary.[g]

22"On the second day you are to offer a male goat without defect for a sin offering, and the altar is to be purified as it was purified with the bull. 23When you have finished purifying it, you are to offer a young bull and a ram from the flock, both without defect.[h] 24You are to offer them before the LORD, and the priests are to sprinkle salt[i] on them and sacrifice them as a burnt offering to the LORD.

25"For seven days[j] you are to provide a male goat daily for a sin offering; you are also to provide a young bull and a ram from the flock, both without defect.[k] 26For seven days they are to make atonement for the altar and cleanse it; thus they will dedicate it. 27At the end of these days, from the eighth day[l] on, the priests are to present your burnt offerings[m] and fellowship offerings[h][n] on the altar. Then I will accept you, declares the Sovereign LORD."

The Prince, the Levites, the Priests

44 Then the man brought me back to the outer gate of the sanctuary, the one facing east,[a] and it was shut. 2The LORD said to me, "This gate is to remain shut. It must not be opened; no-one may enter through it.[b] It is to remain shut because the LORD, the God of Israel, has entered through it. 3The prince himself is the only one who may sit inside the gateway to eat in the presence[c] of the LORD. He is to enter by way of the portico of the gateway and go out the same way.[d]"

4Then the man brought me by way of the north gate[e] to the front of the temple. I looked and saw the glory of the LORD filling the temple[f] of the LORD, and I fell face down.[g]

5The LORD said to me, "Son of man, look carefully, listen closely and give attention to everything I tell you concerning all the regulations regarding the temple of the LORD. Give attention to the entrance[h] of the temple and all the exits of the sanctuary.[i] 6Say to the rebellious house[j] of Israel, 'This is what the Sovereign LORD says: Enough of your detestable practices, O house of Israel! 7In addition to all your other detestable practices, you brought foreigners uncircumcised in heart[k] and flesh into my sanctuary, desecrating my temple while you offered me food, fat and blood, and you broke my covenant.[l] 8Instead of carrying out your duty in regard to my holy things, you put others in charge of my sanctuary.[m] 9This is what the Sovereign LORD says: No foreigner uncircumcised in heart and flesh is to enter my sanctuary, not even the foreigners who live among the Israelites.[n]

10" 'The Levites who went far from me when Israel went astray[o] and who wandered from me after their idols must bear the consequences of their sin.[p] 11They may serve in my sanctuary, having charge of the gates of the temple and serving in it; they may slaughter the burnt offerings[q] and sacrifices for the people and stand before the people and serve them.[r] 12But because they served them in the presence of their idols and made the house of Israel fall[s] into sin, therefore I have sworn with uplifted hand[t] that they must bear the consequences of their sin, declares the Sovereign LORD.[u] 13They are not to come near to serve me as priests or come near any of my holy things or my most holy offerings; they must bear the shame[v] of their detestable practices.[w] 14Yet I will put them in charge of the duties of the temple and all the work that is to be done in it.[x]

15" 'But the priests, who are Levites and descendants of Zadok[y] and who faithfully carried out the duties of my sanctuary when the Israelites went astray from me, are to come near to minister before me; they are to stand before me to offer sacrifices of fat[z] and blood, declares the Sovereign LORD.[a] 16They alone are to enter my sanctuary; they alone are to come near my table[b] to minister before me and perform my service.[c]

17" 'When they enter the gates of the inner court, they are to wear linen clothes;[d] they must not wear any woollen garment while ministering at the gates of the inner court or inside the temple. 18They are to wear linen turbans[e] on their heads and linen undergarments[f] round their waists. They must not wear anything that makes them perspire.[g] 19When they go out into the outer court where the people are, they are to take off the clothes they have been ministering in and leave them in

20 [d]**Lev 4:7**; [e]ver **17**; [f]Lev 16:19
21 [g]Ex 29:14; Heb 13:11
23 [h]Ex 29:1; **Lev 22:20**
24 [i]**Lev 2:13**; Mk 9:49–50
25 [j]**Lev 8:33**; [k]**Ex 29:37**
27 [l]Lev 9:1; [m]**Isa 60:7**; [n]**Ex 32:6; Lev 17:5**

Ch. 44

1 [a]**Eze 43:1**
2 [b]Eze 43:4–5
3 [c]**Ex 24:9–11**; [d]Eze 46:2,8
4 [e]**Eze 40:35**; [f]**Isa 6:4; Eze 10:4**; Rev 15:8; [g]Da 8:17
5 [h]**Eze 42:9**; [i]Eze 40:4; 43:10–11
6 [j]**Eze 3:9**
7 [k]**Lev 26:41**; [l]Ge 17:14; Ex 12:48; Lev 22:25
8 [m]Lev 22:2; Nu 18:7
9 [n]Joel 3:17; Zec 14:21
10 [o]Ps 95:10; [p]Nu 18:23
11 [q]2Ch 29:34; [r]Nu 3:5–37; **16:9; 1Ch 26:12–19**
12 [s]**Jer 18:15**; [t]Ps 106:26; [u]2Ki 16:10–16; Jer 14:10
13 [v]**Eze 16:61**; [w]Nu 18:3; Hos 5:1
14 [x]1Sa 2:36; 2Ki 23:9; **1Ch 23:28–32**
15 [y]**2Sa 8:17; Ezr 7:2**; [z]**Ex 29:13**; [a]**Jer 33:18; Eze 40:46**; Zec 3:7
16 [b]**Eze 41:22**; [c]Lev 3:16–17; 17:5–6; Nu 18:5; **1Sa 2:35**; Zec 3:7
17 [d]Rev 19:8
18 [e]**Ex 28:39; Isa 3:20**; [f]**Ex 28:42**; [g]**Lev 16:4**

h27 Traditionally *peace offerings*

the sacred rooms, and put on other
clothes, so that they do not consecrate[h]
the people by means of their garments.[i]
20''They must not shave[j] their heads
or let their hair grow long, but they are
to keep the hair of their heads trimmed.[k]
21No priest is to drink wine when he
enters the inner court.[l] 22They must not
marry widows or divorced women; they
may marry only virgins of Israelite de-
scent or widows of priests.[m] 23They are
to teach my people the difference be-
tween the holy and the common[n] and
show them how to distinguish between
the unclean and the clean.[o]
24''In any dispute, the priests are to
serve as judges[p] and decide it according
to my ordinances. They are to keep my
laws and my decrees for all my
appointed feasts,[q] and they are to keep
my Sabbaths holy.[r]
25''A priest must not defile himself by
going near a dead person; however, if
the dead person was his father or
mother, son or daughter, brother or un-
married sister, then he may defile him-
self.[s] 26After he is cleansed, he must
wait seven days.[t] 27On the day he goes
into the inner court of the sanctuary[u] to
minister in the sanctuary, he is to offer a
sin offering[v] for himself, declares the
Sovereign LORD.
28''I am to be the only inheritance[w]
the priests have. You are to give them
no possession in Israel; I will be their
possession. 29They will eat[x] the grain
offerings, the sin offerings and the guilt
offerings; and everything in Israel de-
voted[a] to the LORD[y] will belong to them.[z]
30The best of all the firstfruits[a] and of all
your special gifts will belong to the
priests. You are to give them the first
portion of your ground meal[b] so that a
blessing[c] may rest on your household.[d]
31The priests must not eat anything,
bird or animal, found dead[e] or torn by
wild animals.[f]

Division of the Land

45 ''When you allot the land as an
inheritance,[a] you are to present
to the LORD a portion of the land as a
sacred district, 25,000 cubits long and
20,000[a] cubits wide; the entire area will
be holy.[b] 2Of this, a section 500 cubits
square[c] is to be for the sanctuary, with
50 cubits around it for open land. 3In the
sacred district, measure off a section
25,000 cubits[b] long and 10,000 cubits[c]
wide. In it will be the sanctuary, the
Most Holy Place. 4It will be the sacred
portion of the land for the priests,[d] who
minister in the sanctuary and who draw
near to minister before the LORD. It will
be a place for their houses as well as a
holy place for the sanctuary.[e] 5An area
25,000 cubits long and 10,000 cubits
wide will belong to the Levites, who
serve in the temple, as their possession
for towns to live in.[d][f]
6''You are to give the city as its prop-
erty an area 5,000 cubits wide and
25,000 cubits long, adjoining the sacred
portion; it will belong to the whole
house of Israel.[g]
7''The prince will have the land
bordering each side of the area formed
by the sacred district and the property
of the city. It will extend westward from
the west side and eastward from the
east side, running lengthwise from the
western to the eastern border parallel to
one of the tribal portions.[h] 8This land
will be his possession in Israel. And my
princes will no longer oppress my
people but will allow the house of Israel
to possess the land according to their
tribes.[i]
9''This is what the Sovereign LORD
says: You have gone far enough, O
princes of Israel! Give up your violence
and oppression[j] and do what is just and
right.[k] Stop dispossessing my people,
declares the Sovereign LORD. 10You are
to use accurate scales,[l] an accurate
ephah[e][m] and an accurate bath.[f] 11The
ephah[n] and the bath are to be the same
size, the bath containing a tenth of a
homer[g] and the ephah a tenth of a
homer; the homer is to be the standard
measure for both. 12The shekel[h] is to
consist of twenty gerahs.[o] Twenty
shekels plus twenty-five shekels plus
fifteen shekels equal one mina.[i]

Offerings and Holy Days

13''This is the special gift you are to
offer: a sixth of an ephah from each
homer of wheat and a sixth of an ephah

19 [h]Lev 6:27; [i]Ex 39:27–29; Lev 6:10–11; Eze 42:14
20 [j]Eze 5:1; [k]Lev 21:5; Nu 6:5
21 [l]Lev 10:9
22 [m]Lev 21:7
23 [n]Eze 22:26; [o]Ge 7:2; Lev 13:50; 15:31; Jer 15:19; Hag 2:11–13
24 [p]Dt 17:8–9; 19:17; 21:5; 1Ch 23:4; [q]Lev 23:2; [r]2Ch 19:8
25 [s]Lev 21:1–4
26 [t]Nu 19:14
27 [u]Nu 3:28; [v]Lev 4:28; Nu 6:11
28 [w]Nu 18:20; Dt 18:1–2; Jos 13:33
29 [x]Lev 6:16; [y]Lev 27:21; [z]Nu 18:9,14; Jos 13:14
30 [a]Nu 18:12–13; 2Ch 31:5; [b]Nu 15:18–21; [c]Lev 25:21; [d]2Ch 31:10; Ne 10:35–37
31 [e]Lev 11:39; [f]Ex 22:31; Lev 11:40

Ch. 45

1 [a]Nu 34:13; [b]Eze 48:8–9, 29
2 [c]Eze 42:20
4 [d]Eze 40:46; [e]Eze 48:10–11
5 [f]Eze 48:13
6 [g]Eze 48:15–18
7 [h]Eze 48:21
8 [i]Nu 26:53; Eze 46:18
9 [j]Ps 12:5; [k]Jer 22:3; Zec 7:9–10; 8:16
10 [l]Dt 25:15; Pr 11:1; Am 8:4–6; Mic 6:10–11; [m]Lev 19:36
11 [n]Isa 5:10
12 [o]Ex 30:13; Lev 27:25; Nu 3:47

[a]29 The Hebrew term refers to the irrevocable giving over of things or persons to the LORD.
[a]1 Septuagint (see also verses 3 and 5 and 48:9); Hebrew *10,000*
[b]3 That is, about 7 miles (about 11 kilometres)
[c]3 That is, about 3 miles (about 5 kilometres)
[d]5 Septuagint; Hebrew *temple; they will have as their possession 20 rooms*
[e]10 An ephah was a dry measure.
[f]10 A bath was a liquid measure.
[g]11 A homer was a dry measure.
[h]12 A shekel weighed about 2/5 ounce (about 11.5 grams).
[i]12 That is, 60 shekels; the common mina was 50 shekels.

from each homer of barley. 14The prescribed portion of oil, measured by the bath, is a tenth of a bath from each cor (which consists of ten baths or one homer, for ten baths are equivalent to a homer). 15Also one sheep is to be taken from every flock of two hundred from the well-watered pastures of Israel. These will be used for the grain offerings, burnt offerings[p] and fellowship offerings[j] to make atonement[q] for the people, declares the Sovereign LORD. 16All the people of the land will participate in this special gift for the use of the prince in Israel. 17It will be the duty of the prince to provide the burnt offerings, grain offerings and drink offerings at the festivals, the New Moons[r] and the Sabbaths[s]—at all the appointed feasts of the house of Israel. He will provide the sin offerings, grain offerings, burnt offerings and fellowship offerings to make atonement for the house of Israel.[t]

18" 'This is what the Sovereign LORD says: In the first month[u] on the first day you are to take a young bull without defect[v] and purify the sanctuary.[w] 19The priest is to take some of the blood of the sin offering and put it on the doorposts of the temple, on the four corners of the upper ledge[x] of the altar[y] and on the gateposts of the inner court. 20You are to do the same on the seventh day of the month for anyone who sins unintentionally[z] or through ignorance; so you are to make atonement for the temple.

21" 'In the first month on the fourteenth day you are to observe the Passover,[a] a feast lasting seven days, during which you shall eat bread made without yeast. 22On that day the prince is to provide a bull as a sin offering for himself and for all the people of the land.[b] 23Every day during the seven days of the Feast he is to provide seven bulls and seven rams[c] without defect as a burnt offering to the LORD, and a male goat for a sin offering.[d] 24He is to provide as a grain offering[e] an ephah for each bull and an ephah for each ram, along with a hin[k] of oil for each ephah.[f]

25" 'During the seven days of the Feast,[g] which begins in the seventh month on the fifteenth day, he is to make the same provision for sin offerings, burnt offerings, grain offerings and oil.[h]

46

" 'This is what the Sovereign LORD says: The gate of the inner court[a] facing east[b] is to be shut on the six working days, but on the Sabbath day and on the day of the New Moon[c] it is to be opened. 2The prince is to enter from the outside through the portico[d] of the gateway and stand by the gatepost. The priests are to sacrifice his burnt offering[e] and his fellowship offerings.[a] He is to worship at the threshold of the gateway and then go out, but the gate will not be shut until evening.[f] 3On the Sabbaths[g] and New Moons the people of the land are to worship in the presence of the LORD at the entrance to that gateway.[h] 4The burnt offering the prince brings to the LORD on the Sabbath day is to be six male lambs and a ram, all without defect. 5The grain offering given with the ram is to be an ephah,[b] and the grain offering with the lambs is to be as much as he pleases, along with a hin[c] of oil for each ephah.[i] 6On the day of the New Moon[j] he is to offer a young bull, six lambs and a ram, all without defect.[k] 7He is to provide as a grain offering one ephah with the bull, one ephah with the ram, and with the lambs as much as he wants to give, along with a hin of oil with each ephah.[l] 8When the prince enters, he is to go in through the portico[m] of the gateway, and he is to come out the same way.[n]

9" 'When the people of the land come before the LORD at the appointed feasts,[o] whoever enters by the north gate to worship is to go out by the south gate; and whoever enters by the south gate is to go out by the north gate. No-one is to return through the gate by which he entered, but each is to go out by the opposite gate. 10The prince is to be among them, going in when they go in and going out when they go out.[p]

11" 'At the festivals and the appointed feasts, the grain offering is to be an ephah with a bull, an ephah with a ram, and with the lambs as much as one pleases, along with a hin of oil for each ephah.[q] 12When the prince provides[r] a freewill offering[s] to the LORD—whether a burnt offering or fellowship offerings—the gate facing east is to be opened for him. He shall offer his burnt offering or his fellowship offerings as he does on the Sabbath day. Then he shall go out, and after he has gone out, the gate will be shut.[t]

13" 'Every day you are to provide a year-old lamb without defect for a burnt offering to the LORD; morning by morning[u] you shall provide it.[v] 14You are also

15 [p]**Lev 1:4;** [q]Lev 6:30
17 [r]**Nu 10:10;** [s]**Lev 23:28;** Isa 66:23; [t]**1Ki 8:62; 2Ch 31:3;** Eze 46:4–12
18 [u]Ex 12:2; [v]**Lev 22:20;** Heb 9:14; [w]**Lev 16:33**
19 [x]**Eze 43:17;** [y]Lev 16:18–19
20 [z]Lev 4:27
21 [a]**Ex 12:11**
22 [b]Lev 4:14
23 [c]**Nu 22:40; Job 42:8;** [d]Nu 28:16–25
24 [e]Nu 28:12–13; [f]Eze 46:5–7
25 [g]Dt 16:13; [h]Lev 23:34–43; Nu 29:12–38

Ch. 46

1 [a]**Eze 40:19;** [b]**1Ch 9:18;** [c]ver 6; Isa 66:23
2 [d]ver 8; [e]Eze 40:39; [f]ver 12; **Eze 44:3**
3 [g]**Isa 66:23;** [h]Lk 1:10
5 [i]ver 11
6 [j]ver 1; **Nu 10:10;** [k]**Lev 22:20**
7 [l]Eze 45:24
8 [m]ver 2; [n]Eze 44:3
9 [o]**Ex 23:14; 34:20**
10 [p]2Sa 6:14–15; Ps 42:4
11 [q]ver 5
12 [r]**Eze 45:17;** [s]**Lev 7:16;** [t]ver 2
13 [u]**Ps 5:3;** [v]Ex 29:38; **Nu 28:3**

[j]15 Traditionally *peace offerings;* also in verse 17
[k]24 That is, probably about 6 pints (about 4 litres)
[a]2 Traditionally *peace offerings;* also in verse 12
[b]5 That is, probably about 3/5 bushel (about 22 litres)
[c]5 That is, probably about 6 pints (about 4 litres)

to provide with it morning by morning a grain offering, consisting of a sixth of an ephah with a third of a hin of oil[w] to moisten the flour. The presenting of this grain offering to the LORD is a lasting ordinance.[x] 15So the lamb and the grain offering and the oil shall be provided morning by morning for a regular[y] burnt offering.[z]

16" 'This is what the Sovereign LORD says: If the prince makes a gift from his inheritance to one of his sons, it will also belong to his descendants; it is to be their property by inheritance.[a] 17If, however, he makes a gift from his inheritance to one of his servants, the servant may keep it until the year of freedom;[b] then it will revert to the prince. His inheritance belongs to his sons only; it is theirs. 18The prince must not take[c] any of the inheritance[d] of the people, driving them off their property. He is to give his sons their inheritance out of his own property, so that none of my people will be separated from his property.' "

19Then the man brought me through the entrance[e] at the side of the gate to the sacred rooms facing north,[f] which belonged to the priests, and showed me a place at the western end. 20He said to me, "This is the place where the priests will cook the guilt offering and the sin offering and bake the grain offering, to avoid bringing them into the outer court and consecrating[g] the people."[h]

21He then brought me to the outer court and led me round to its four corners, and I saw in each corner another court. 22In the four corners of the outer court were enclosed[d] courts, forty cubits long and thirty cubits wide; each of the courts in the four corners was the same size. 23Around the inside of each of the four courts was a ledge of stone, with places for fire built all round under the ledge. 24He said to me, "These are the kitchens where those who minister at the temple will cook the sacrifices of the people."

The River From the Temple

47 The man brought me back to the entrance of the temple, and I saw water[a] coming out from under the threshold of the temple towards the east (for the temple faced east). The water was coming down from under the south side of the temple, south of the altar.[b] 2He then brought me out through the north gate[c] and led me round the outside to the outer gate facing east, and the water was flowing from the south side.

3As the man went eastward with a measuring line[d] in his hand, he measured off a thousand cubits[a] and then led me through water that was ankle-deep. 4He measured off another thousand cubits and led me through water that was knee-deep. He measured off another thousand and led me through water that was up to the waist. 5He measured off another thousand, but now it was a river[e] that I could not cross, because the water had risen and was deep enough to swim in—a river that no-one could cross.[f] 6He asked me, "Son of man, do you see this?"

Then he led me back to the bank of the river. 7When I arrived there, I saw a great number of trees on each side of the river.[g] 8He said to me, "This water flows towards the eastern region and goes down into the Arabah,[b][h] where it enters the Sea.[c] When it empties into the Sea,[c] the water there becomes fresh.[i] 9Swarms of living creatures will live wherever the river flows. There will be large numbers of fish, because this water flows there and makes the salt water fresh; so where the river flows everything will live.[j] 10Fishermen[k] will stand along the shore; from En Gedi[l] to En Eglaim there will be places for spreading nets.[m] The fish will be of many kinds[n]—like the fish of the Great Sea.[d][o] 11But the swamps and marshes will not become fresh; they will be left for salt.[p] 12Fruit trees of all kinds will grow on both banks of the river.[q] Their leaves will not wither, nor will their fruit[r] fail. Every month they will bear, because the water from the sanctuary[s] flows to them. Their fruit will serve for food and their leaves for healing.[t]"

The Boundaries of the Land

13This is what the Sovereign LORD says: "These are the boundaries[u] by which you are to divide the land for an inheritance among the twelve tribes of Israel, with two portions for Joseph.[v] 14You are to divide it equally among them. Because I swore with uplifted

14 [w]Nu 15:6; [x]Da 8:11
15 [y]**Ex 29:42**; [z]**Ex 29:38**; Nu 28:5–6
16 [a]2Ch 21:3
17 [b]**Lev 25:10**
18 [c]1Sa 8:14; [d]**Lev 25:23**; Eze 45:8; Mic 2:1–2
19 [e]**Eze 42:9**; [f]Eze 42:4
20 [g]**Lev 6:27**; [h]ver 24; Zec 14:20

Ch. 47

1 [a]**Isa 55:1**; [b]Ps 46:4; Joel 3:18; Rev 22:1
2 [c]**Eze 40:35**
3 [d]**Eze 40:3**
5 [e]**Ge 2:10**; [f]Isa 11:9; Hab 2:14
7 [g]ver 12; Rev 22:2
8 [h]**Dt 1:1**; **3:17**; [i]Isa 41:18
9 [j]Isa 12:3; 55:1; Jn 4:14; 7:37–38
10 [k]**Isa 19:8**; Mt 4:19; [l]**Jos 15:62**; [m]Eze 26:5; [n]**Ps 104:25**; Mt 13:47; [o]**Nu 34:6**
11 [p]**Dt 29:23**
12 [q]ver 7; Rev 22:2; [r]**Ps 1:3**; [s]**Isa 55:1**; [t]**Ge 2:9**; **Jer 17:8**; Eze 36:8
13 [u]Nu 34:2–12; [v]**Ge 48:16**; **49:26**

---

[d]22 The meaning of the Hebrew for this word is uncertain.
[a]3 That is, about 1,500 feet (about 460 metres)
[b]8 Or *the Jordan Valley*
[c]8 That is, the Dead Sea
[d]10 That is, the Mediterranean; also in verses 15, 19 and 20

hand to give it to your forefathers, this
land will become your inheritance.[w]

15"This is to be the boundary of the
land:[x]

"On the north side it will run from the
Great Sea[y] by the Hethlon road[z]
past Lebo[e] Hamath to Zedad,
16Berothah[f][a] and Sibraim (which
lies on the border between Damas-
cus and Hamath),[b] as far as Hazer
Hatticon, which is on the border of
Hauran. 17The boundary will ex-
tend from the sea to Hazar Enan,[g]
along the northern border of
Damascus, with the border of
Hamath to the north. This will be
the north boundary.[c]
18"On the east side the boundary will
run between Hauran and Damas-
cus, along the Jordan between
Gilead and the land of Israel, to the
eastern sea and as far as Tamar.[h]
This will be the east boundary.[d]
19"On the south side it will run from
Tamar as far as the waters of Meri-
bah Kadesh,[e] then along the Wadi
⌞of Egypt⌟[f] to the Great Sea.[g] This
will be the south boundary.
20"On the west side, the Great Sea will
be the boundary to a point opposite
Lebo[i] Hamath.[h] This will be the
west boundary.[i]

21"You are to distribute this land
among yourselves according to the
tribes of Israel. 22You are to allot it as an
inheritance[j] for yourselves and for the
aliens[k] who have settled among you and
who have children. You are to consider
them as native-born Israelites; along
with you they are to be allotted an in-
heritance among the tribes of Israel.[l]
23In whatever tribe the alien settles,
there you are to give him his inheri-
tance," declares the Sovereign LORD.[m]

The Division of the Land

48 "These are the tribes, listed by
name: At the northern frontier,
Dan[a] will have one portion; it will follow
the Hethlon road[b] to Lebo[a] Hamath;[c]
Hazar Enan and the northern border of
Damascus next to Hamath will be part
of its border from the east side to the
west side.
2"Asher[d] will have one portion; it will
border the territory of Dan from east to
west.
3"Naphtali[e] will have one portion; it
will border the territory of Asher from
east to west.
4"Manasseh[f] will have one portion; it
will border the territory of Naphtali
from east to west.
5"Ephraim[g] will have one portion; it
will border the territory of Manasseh[h]
from east to west.[i]
6"Reuben[j] will have one portion; it
will border the territory of Ephraim
from east to west.
7"Judah[k] will have one portion; it will
border the territory of Reuben from east
to west.
8"Bordering the territory of Judah
from east to west will be the portion you
are to present as a special gift. It will be
25,000 cubits[b] wide, and its length from
east to west will equal one of the tribal
portions; the sanctuary will be in the
centre of it.[l]
9"The special portion you are to offer
to the LORD will be 25,000 cubits long
and 10,000 cubits[c] wide.[m] 10This will be
the sacred portion for the priests. It will
be 25,000 cubits long on the north side,
10,000 cubits wide on the west side,
10,000 cubits wide on the east side and
25,000 cubits long on the south side. In
the centre of it will be the sanctuary of
the LORD.[n] 11This will be for the conse-
crated priests, the Zadokites,[o] who were
faithful in serving me[p] and did not go
astray as the Levites did when the
Israelites went astray.[q] 12It will be a
special gift to them from the sacred
portion of the land, a most holy portion,
bordering the territory of the Levites.
13"Alongside the territory of the
priests, the Levites will have an allot-
ment 25,000 cubits long and 10,000
cubits wide. Its total length will be
25,000 cubits and its width 10,000
cubits.[r] 14They must not sell or exchange
any of it. This is the best of the land, and
must not pass into other hands, because
it is holy to the LORD.[s]
15"The remaining area, 5,000 cubits
wide and 25,000 cubits long, will be for
the common use of the city, for houses
and for pasture-land. The city will be in
the centre of it 16and will have these
measurements: the north side 4,500
cubits, the south side 4,500 cubits, the
east side 4,500 cubits, and the west side

14 [w]**Ge 12:7; Dt 1:8; Eze 36:12**
15 [x]Nu 34:2; [y]ver 19; **Nu 34:6**; [z]Eze 48:1
16 [a]2Sa 8:8; [b]Nu 13:21; **Jer 49:23**; Eze 48:1
17 [c]Eze 48:1
18 [d]**Eze 27:18**
19 [e]Dt 32:51; [f]**Ge 15:18**; Isa 27:12; [g]**ver 15**; Eze 48:28
20 [h]**Nu 13:21**; Eze 48:1; [i]Nu 34:6
22 [j]**Eze 36:12**; [k]**Dt 24:19; Isa 14:1**; Mal 3:5; [l]**Lev 24:22**; Nu 15:29; 26:55–56; Isa 56:6–7; Ro 10:12; Eph 2:12–16; 3:6; Col 3:11
23 [m]**Dt 10:19**

Ch. 48

1 [a]**Ge 30:6**; [b]Eze 47:15–17; [c]**Eze 47:20**
2 [d]Jos 19:24–31
3 [e]Jos 19:32–39
4 [f]Jos 17:1–11
5 [g]Jos 16:5–9; [h]Jos 17:7–10; [i]Jos 17:17
6 [j]Jos 13:15–21
7 [k]Jos 15:1–63
8 [l]ver 21
9 [m]**Eze 45:1**
10 [n]ver 21; **Eze 45:3–4**
11 [o]**2Sa 8:17**; [p]**Lev 8:35**; [q]Eze 14:11; **44:15**
13 [r]Eze 45:5
14 [s]**Lev 25:34**; 27:10,28

[e]15 Or *past the entrance to*
[f]15,16 See Septuagint and Ezekiel 48:1; Hebrew *road to go into Zedad,* [16]*Hamath, Berothah*
[g]17 Hebrew *Enon,* a variant of *Enan*
[h]18 Septuagint and Syriac; Hebrew *Israel. You will measure to the eastern sea*
[i]20 Or *opposite the entrance to*
[a]1 Or *to the entrance to*
[b]8 That is, about 7 miles (about 11 kilometres)
[c]9 That is, about 3 miles (about 5 kilometres)

4,500 cubits.[t] 17The pasture-land for the
city will be 250 cubits on the north, 250
cubits on the south, 250 cubits on the
east, and 250 cubits on the west. 18What
remains of the area, bordering on the
sacred portion and running the length
of it, will be 10,000 cubits on the east
side and 10,000 cubits on the west side.
Its produce will supply food for the
workers of the city.[u] 19The workers from
the city who farm it will come from all
the tribes of Israel. 20The entire portion
will be a square, 25,000 cubits on each
side. As a special gift you will set aside
the sacred portion, along with the
property of the city.

21"What remains on both sides of the
area formed by the sacred portion and
the city property will belong to the
prince. It will extend eastward from the
25,000 cubits of the sacred portion to
the eastern border, and westward from
the 25,000 cubits to the western border.
Both these areas running the length of
the tribal portions will belong to the
prince, and the sacred portion with the
temple sanctuary will be in the centre of
them.[v] 22So the property of the Levites
and the property of the city will lie in the
centre of the area that belongs to the
prince. The area belonging to the prince
will lie between the border of Judah and
the border of Benjamin.

23"As for the rest of the tribes: Benjamin[w] will have one portion; it will
extend from the east side to the west
side.

24"Simeon[x] will have one portion; it
will border the territory of Benjamin
from east to west.

25"Issachar[y] will have one portion; it
will border the territory of Simeon from
east to west.

26"Zebulun[z] will have one portion; it
will border the territory of Issachar from
east to west.

27"Gad[a] will have one portion; it will
border the territory of Zebulun from
east to west.

28"The southern boundary of Gad will
run south from Tamar[b] to the waters of
Meribah Kadesh, then along the Wadi
⌞of Egypt⌟ to the Great Sea.[d][c]

29"This is the land you are to allot as
an inheritance to the tribes of Israel, and
these will be their portions," declares
the Sovereign LORD.[d]

The Gates of the City

30"These will be the exits of the city:
Beginning on the north side, which is
4,500 cubits long, 31the gates of the city
will be named after the tribes of Israel.
The three gates on the north side will be
the gate of Reuben, the gate of Judah
and the gate of Levi.

32"On the east side, which is 4,500
cubits long, will be three gates: the gate
of Joseph, the gate of Benjamin and the
gate of Dan.

33"On the south side, which
measures 4,500 cubits, will be three
gates: the gate of Simeon, the gate of
Issachar and the gate of Zebulun.

34"On the west side, which is 4,500
cubits long, will be three gates: the gate
of Gad, the gate of Asher and the gate of
Naphtali.[e]

35"The distance all around will be
18,000 cubits.

"And the name of the city from that
time on will be:

THE LORD IS THERE.[f]"

[d]28 That is, the Mediterranean

16 [t]Rev 21:16
18 [u]Eze 45:6
21 [v]ver 8,10; Eze 45:7
23 [w]Jos 18:11–28
24 [x]**Ge 29:33**; Jos 19:1–9
25 [y]Jos 19:17–23
26 [z]Jos 19:10–16
27 [a]Jos 13:24–28
28 [b]**Ge 14:7**; [c]**Nu 34:6**; Eze 47:19
29 [d]**Eze 45:1**
34 [e]**2Ch 4:4**; Rev 21:12–13
35 [f]**Isa 12:6; 24:23; Jer 3:17**; 14:9; Joel 3:21; Rev 3:12; **21:3**

Daniel

Daniel's Training in Babylon

1 In the third year of the reign of
Jehoiakim[a] king of Judah,
Nebuchadnezzar[b] king of Babylon[c]
came to Jerusalem and besieged it.[d]
2 And the LORD delivered Jehoiakim king
of Judah into his hand, along with some
of the articles from the temple of God.
These he carried[e] off to the temple of
his god in Babylonia[a] and put in the
treasure-house of his god.[f]
3 Then the king ordered Ashpenaz,
chief of his court officials, to bring in
some of the Israelites from the royal
family and the nobility[g]—4 young men
without any physical defect, hand-
some,[h] showing aptitude for every kind
of learning,[i] well informed, quick to
understand, and qualified to serve in
the king's palace. He was to teach them
the language[j] and literature of the Bab-
ylonians.[b] 5 The king assigned them a
daily amount of food and wine[k] from the
king's table.[l] They were to be trained for
three years,[m] and after that they were to
enter the king's service.[n]
6 Among these were some from Judah:
Daniel,[o] Hananiah, Mishael and Azar-
iah.[p] 7 The chief official gave them new
names: to Daniel, the name Belteshaz-
zar;[q] to Hananiah, Shadrach; to
Mishael, Meshach; and to Azariah,
Abednego.[r]
8 But Daniel resolved not to defile[s]
himself with the royal food and wine,
and he asked the chief official for per-
mission not to defile himself in this way.
9 Now God had caused the official to
show favour[t] and sympathy[u] to Daniel,
10 but the official told Daniel, "I am
afraid of my lord the king, who has
assigned your[c] food and drink.[v] Why
should he see you looking worse than
the other young men of your age? The
king would then have my head because
of you."
11 Daniel then said to the guard whom
the chief official had appointed over
Daniel, Hananiah, Mishael and Azar-
iah, 12 "Please test[w] your servants for ten
days: Give us nothing but vegetables to
eat and water to drink. 13 Then compare
our appearance with that of the young
men who eat the royal food, and treat
your servants in accordance with what
you see."[x] 14 So he agreed to this and
tested[y] them for ten days.
15 At the end of the ten days they
looked healthier and better nourished
than any of the young men who ate the
royal food.[z] 16 So the guard took away
their choice food and the wine they
were to drink and gave them vegetables
instead.[a]
17 To these four young men God gave
knowledge and understanding[b] of all
kinds of literature and learning.[c] And
Daniel could understand visions and
dreams of all kinds.[d]
18 At the end of the time[e] set by the
king to bring them in, the chief official
presented them to Nebuchadnezzar.
19 The king talked with them, and he
found none equal to Daniel, Hananiah,
Mishael and Azariah; so they entered
the king's service.[f] 20 In every matter of
wisdom and understanding about
which the king questioned them, he
found them ten times better than all the
magicians[g] and enchanters in his whole
kingdom.[h]
21 And Daniel remained there until the
first year of King Cyrus.[i]

Nebuchadnezzar's Dream

2 In the second year of his reign,
Nebuchadnezzar had dreams;[a] his
mind was troubled[b] and he could not
sleep.[c] 2 So the king summoned the
magicians,[d] enchanters, sorcerers[e] and
astrologers[a][f] to tell him what he had
dreamed.[g] When they came in and
stood before the king, 3 he said to them,
"I have had a dream that troubles[h] me
and I want to know what it means."[b]
4 Then the astrologers answered the

Ch. 1

1 [a]**Jer 46:2**; [b]**2Ki 24:1**; **Jer 28:14**; [c]Jer 50:1; [d]2Ki 24:1; **2Ch 36:6**; Jer 35:11
2 [e]**2Ki 24:13**; [f]**2Ch 36:7**; Jer 27:19–20; Zec 5:5–11
3 [g]**2Ki 20:18**; **24:15**; Isa 39:7
4 [h]**Ge 39:6**; [i]ver 17; [j]**Ezr 4:7**
5 [k]**ver 8,10**; [l]**Est 2:9**; [m]ver 18; [n]ver 19; **Est 2:5–6**
6 [o]**Eze 14:14**; [p]Da 2:17,25
7 [q]Da 2:26; 4:8; 5:12; 10:1; [r]**Isa 39:7**; Da 2:49; 3:12
8 [s]**Eze 4:13–14**
9 [t]**Ge 39:21**; **Pr 16:7**; [u]**1Ki 8:50**
10 [v]ver 5
12 [w]Rev 2:10
13 [x]ver 16
14 [y]Rev 2:10
15 [z]Ex 23:25
16 [a]ver 12–13
17 [b]**Job 12:13**; [c]Da 2:23; Col 1:9; Jas 1:5; [d]Da 2:19,30; 5:11; 7:1; 8:1
18 [e]ver 5
19 [f]**Ge 41:46**
20 [g]**Ge 41:8**; [h]**1Ki 4:30**; Est 2:15; **Eze 28:3**; Da 2:13,28; 4:18; 6:3
21 [i]**2Ch 36:22**; Da 6:28; 10:1

Ch. 2

1 [a]ver 3; **Ge 20:3**; **Job 33:15**,18; Da 4:5; [b]Ge 41:8; [c]**Est 6:1**
2 [d]**Ge 41:8**; [e]Ex 7:11; Jer 27:9; [f]**ver 10**; **Isa 19:3**; **44:25**; [g]Da 4:6
3 [h]Da 4:5

[a]2 Hebrew *Shinar* [b]4 Or *Chaldeans*
[c]10 The Hebrew for *your* and *you* in this verse is plural.
[a]2 Or *Chaldeans;* also in verses 4, 5 and 10
[b]3 Or *was*

king in Aramaic,[c] [i] "O king, live for ever![j] Tell your servants the dream, and we will interpret it."

5The king replied to the astrologers, "This is what I have firmly decided:[k] If you do not tell me what my dream was and interpret it, I will have you cut into pieces[l] and your houses turned into piles of rubble.[m] 6But if you tell me the dream and explain it, you will receive from me gifts and rewards and great honour.[n] So tell me the dream and interpret it for me."

7Once more they replied, "Let the king tell his servants the dream, and we will interpret it."

8Then the king answered, "I am certain that you are trying to gain time, because you realise that this is what I have firmly decided: 9If you do not tell me the dream, there is just one penalty[o] for you. You have conspired to tell me misleading and wicked things, hoping the situation will change. So then, tell me the dream, and I will know that you can interpret it for me."[p]

10The astrologers[q] answered the king, "There is not a man on earth who can do what the king asks! No king, however great and mighty, has ever asked such a thing of any magician or enchanter or astrologer.[r] 11What the king asks is too difficult. No-one can reveal it to the king except the gods,[s] and they do not live among men."

12This made the king so angry and furious[t] that he ordered the execution[u] of all the wise men of Babylon. 13So the decree was issued to put the wise men to death, and men were sent to look for Daniel and his friends to put them to death.[v]

14When Arioch, the commander of the king's guard, had gone out to put to death the wise men of Babylon, Daniel spoke to him with wisdom and tact. 15He asked the king's officer, "Why did the king issue such a harsh decree?" Arioch then explained the matter to Daniel. 16At this, Daniel went in to the king and asked for time, so that he might interpret the dream for him.

17Then Daniel returned to his house and explained the matter to his friends Hananiah, Mishael and Azariah.[w] 18He urged them to plead for mercy[x] from the God of heaven[y] concerning this mystery,[z] so that he and his friends might not be executed with the rest of the wise men of Babylon. 19During the night the mystery[a] was revealed to Daniel in a vision.[b] Then Daniel praised the God of heaven[c] 20and said:

"Praise be to the name of God for ever
 and ever;[d]
 wisdom and power[e] are his.
21He changes times and seasons;[f]
 he sets up kings[g] and deposes[h]
 them.
He gives wisdom[i] to the wise
 and knowledge to the discerning.[j]
22He reveals deep and hidden things;[k]
 he knows what lies in darkness,[l]
 and light[m] dwells with him.
23I thank and praise you, O God of my
 fathers:[n]
 You have given me wisdom[o] and
 power,
you have made known to me what we
 asked of you,
 you have made known to us the
 dream of the king."[p]

Daniel Interprets the Dream

24Then Daniel went to Arioch,[q] whom the king had appointed to execute the wise men of Babylon, and said to him, "Do not execute the wise men of Babylon. Take me to the king, and I will interpret his dream for him."

25Arioch took Daniel to the king at once and said, "I have found a man among the exiles[r] from Judah[s] who can tell the king what his dream means."

26The king asked Daniel (also called Belteshazzar),[t] "Are you able to tell me what I saw in my dream and interpret it?"

27Daniel replied, "No wise man, enchanter, magician or diviner can explain to the king the mystery he has asked about,[u] 28but there is a God in heaven who reveals mysteries.[v] He has shown King Nebuchadnezzar what will happen in days to come.[w] Your dream and the visions that passed through your mind[x] as you lay on your bed[y] are these:[z]

29"As you were lying there, O king, your mind turned to things to come, and the revealer of mysteries showed you what is going to happen.[a] 30As for me, this mystery has been revealed[b] to me, not because I have greater wisdom than other living men, but so that you, O king, may know the interpretation and that you may understand what went through your mind.

31"You looked, O king, and there before you stood a large statue—an enormous, dazzling statue,[c] awesome[d] in appearance. 32The head of the statue

4 [i]Ezr 4:7; [j]Ne 2:3
5 [k]Ge 41:32; [l]ver 12; [m]Ezr 6:11; Da 3:29
6 [n]ver 48; Da 5:7,16
9 [o]Est 4:11; [p]Isa 41:22–24
10 [q]ver 2; Da 3:8; 4:7; [r]ver 27; Da 5:8
11 [s]Ge 41:38
12 [t]Da 3:13,19; [u]ver 5
13 [v]Da 1:20; 5:19
17 [w]Da 1:6
18 [x]Isa 37:4; [y]Ezr 1:2; Ne 1:4; Jnh 1:9; Rev 11:13; [z]ver 23; Jer 33:3
19 [a]ver 28; [b]Job 33:15; Da 1:17; [c]Jos 22:33
20 [d]Ps 113:2; 145:1–2; [e]Job 9:4; Jer 32:19
21 [f]Da 7:25; [g]Da 4:17; [h]Job 12:19; Ps 75:6–7; Ro 13:1; [i]Ps 119:34; Jas 1:5; [j]2Sa 14:17
22 [k]Ge 40:8; Job 12:22; Da 5:11; 1Co 2:10; [l]Job 12:22; Ps 139:11–12; Jer 23:24; Heb 4:13; [m]Isa 45:7; Jas 1:17
23 [n]Ge 31:5; Ex 3:15; [o]Da 1:17; [p]Eze 28:3
24 [q]ver 14
25 [r]Dt 21:10; [s]Da 1:6; 5:13; 6:13
26 [t]Da 1:7
27 [u]ver 10; Ge 41:8
28 [v]Ge 40:8; Jer 10:7; Am 4:13; [w]Ge 49:1; Da 10:14; Mt 24:6; Rev 1:1; 22:6; [x]Da 4:5; [y]Ps 4:4; [z]Eze 28:3; Da 1:20
29 [a]Ge 41:25
30 [b]Isa 45:3; Da 1:17; Am 4:13
31 [c]Hab 1:7; [d]Isa 25:3–5

[c]4 The text from here through chapter 7 is in Aramaic.

was made of pure gold, its chest and
arms of silver, its belly and thighs of
bronze, 33its legs of iron, its feet partly of
iron and partly of baked clay. 34While
you were watching, a rock was cut out,
but not by human hands.[e] It struck the
statue on its feet of iron and clay and
smashed[f] them.[g] 35Then the iron, the
clay, the bronze, the silver and the gold
were broken to pieces at the same time
and became like chaff on a threshing-
floor in the summer. The wind swept
them away[h] without leaving a trace. But
the rock that struck the statue became a
huge mountain[i] and filled the whole
earth.[j]

36"This was the dream, and now we
will interpret it to the king.[k] 37You, O
king, are the king of kings.[l] The God of
heaven has given you dominion[m] and
power and might and glory; 38in your
hands he has placed mankind and the
beasts of the field and the birds of the
air. Wherever they live, he has made
you ruler over them all.[n] You are that
head of gold.

39"After you, another kingdom will
rise, inferior to yours. Next, a third
kingdom, one of bronze, will rule over
the whole earth.[o] 40Finally, there will be
a fourth kingdom, strong as iron—for
iron breaks and smashes everything—
and as iron breaks things to pieces, so it
will crush and break all the others.[p]
41Just as you saw that the feet and toes
were partly of baked clay and partly of
iron, so this will be a divided kingdom;
yet it will have some of the strength of
iron in it, even as you saw iron mixed
with clay. 42As the toes were partly iron
and partly clay, so this kingdom will be
partly strong and partly brittle. 43And
just as you saw the iron mixed with
baked clay, so the people will be a mix-
ture and will not remain united, any
more than iron mixes with clay.

44"In the time of those kings, the God
of heaven will set up a kingdom that will
never be destroyed, nor will it be left to
another people. It will crush[q] all those
kingdoms[r] and bring them to an end,
but it will itself endure for ever.[s] 45This is
the meaning of the vision of the rock[t] cut
out of a mountain, but not by human
hands[u]—a rock that broke the iron, the
bronze, the clay, the silver and the gold
to pieces.

"The great God has shown the king
what will take place in the future.[v] The
dream is true[w] and the interpretation is
trustworthy."

46Then King Nebuchadnezzar fell
prostrate[x] before Daniel and paid him
honour and ordered that an offering[y]
and incense be presented to him. 47The
king said to Daniel, "Surely your God is
the God of gods[z] and the Lord of kings[a]
and a revealer of mysteries,[b] for you
were able to reveal this mystery.[c]"

48Then the king placed Daniel in a
high[d] position and lavished many gifts
on him. He made him ruler over the
entire province of Babylon and placed
him in charge of all its wise men.[e]
49Moreover, at Daniel's request the king
appointed Shadrach, Meshach and
Abednego administrators over the prov-
ince of Babylon,[f] while Daniel himself
remained at the royal court.[g]

The Image of Gold and the Fiery Furnace

3 King Nebuchadnezzar made an
image[a] of gold, ninety feet high
and nine feet[a] wide, and set it up on the
plain of Dura in the province of Bab-
ylon. 2He then summoned the satraps,[b]
prefects, governors, advisers, treasur-
ers, judges, magistrates and all the
other provincial officials[c] to come to the
dedication of the image he had set up.
3So the satraps, prefects, governors,
advisers, treasurers, judges, magis-
trates and all the other provincial of-
ficials assembled for the dedication of
the image that King Nebuchadnezzar
had set up, and they stood before it.

4Then the herald loudly proclaimed,
"This is what you are commanded to
do, O peoples, nations and men of
every language:[d] 5As soon as you hear
the sound of the horn, flute, zither, lyre,
harp,[e] pipes and all kinds of music, you
must fall down and worship the image[f]
of gold that King Nebuchadnezzar has
set up.[g] 6Whoever does not fall down
and worship will immediately be
thrown into a blazing furnace."[h]

7Therefore, as soon as they heard the
sound of the horn, flute, zither, lyre,
harp and all kinds of music, all the
peoples, nations and men of every
language fell down and worshipped
the image of gold that King Nebuchad-
nezzar had set up.[i]

8At this time some astrologers[b][j] came
forward and denounced the Jews.
9They said to King Nebuchadnezzar,
"O king, live for ever![k] 10You have
issued a decree,[l] O king, that everyone
who hears the sound of the horn, flute,
zither, lyre, harp, pipes and all kinds of

34 [e]**Job 12:19**; Zec 4:6; [f]**Job 34:24**; [g]ver 44–45; Ps 2:9; **Isa 60:12**; Da 8:25
35 [h]Ps 1:4; 37:10; **Isa 17:13**; 41:15–16; [i]Isa 2:3; Mic 4:1; [j]Zec 12:3
36 [k]**Ge 40:12**
37 [l]**Ezr 7:12**; [m]**Jer 27:7**; Da 4:26
38 [n]**Jer 27:6**; Da 4:21–22; 5:18
39 [o]Da 7:5
40 [p]Da 7:7,23
44 [q]**Ge 27:29**; Ps 2:9; **110:5**; Mt 21:43–44; 1Co 15:24; [r]**1Sa 9:20**; Hag 2:22; [s]Ps 145:13; **Isa 9:7**; Da 4:34; 6:26; 7:14,27; Ob 21; Mic 4:7,13; **Lk 1:33**; Rev 11:15
45 [t]**Isa 28:16**; [u]Da 8:25; [v]**Ge 41:25**; [w]Rev 22:6
46 [x]Da 8:17; Ac 10:25; [y]Ac 14:13
47 [z]**Dt 10:17**; Da 11:36; [a]Da 4:25; 1Ti 6:15; [b]**ver 22**,28; [c]Da 4:9; 1Co 14:25
48 [d]**2Ki 25:28**; [e]**ver 6; Est 8:2; Da 1:20**; 4:9; 5:11; 8:27
49 [f]**Da 1:7**; 3:30; [g]Da 6:2

Ch. 3

1 [a]ver 14; **Isa 46:6**; Jer 16:20; Hab 2:19
2 [b]**Est 1:1**; [c]ver 27; Da 6:7
4 [d]Da 4:1; 6:25; Rev 10:11
5 [e]**Ge 4:21**; [f]Rev 13:12; [g]ver 10,15
6 [h]ver 11,15,21; Jer 29:22; Da 5:19; 6:7; Mt 13:42,50; Rev 13:15
7 [i]ver 5
8 [j]**Isa 19:3; Da 2:10**
9 [k]**Ne 2:3**; Da 5:10; 6:6
10 [l]Da 6:12

[a]*1* Aramaic *sixty cubits high and six cubits wide* (about 27 metres high and 2.7 metres wide)
[b]*8* Or *Chaldeans*

music must fall down and worship the
image of gold,[m] 11and that whoever
does not fall down and worship will be
thrown into a blazing furnace. 12But
there are some Jews whom you have set
over the affairs of the province of Bab-
ylon—Shadrach, Meshach and Abed-
nego[n]—who pay no attention[o] to you,
O king. They neither serve your gods
nor worship the image of gold you have
set up."[p]
13Furious[q] with rage, Nebuchadnez-
zar summoned Shadrach, Meshach and
Abednego. So these men were brought
before the king, 14and Nebuchadnezzar
said to them, "Is it true, Shadrach,
Meshach and Abednego, that you do
not serve my gods[r] or worship the
image[s] of gold I have set up? 15Now
when you hear the sound of the horn,
flute, zither, lyre, harp, pipes and all
kinds of music, if you are ready to fall
down and worship the image I made,
very good. But if you do not worship it,
you will be thrown immediately into a
blazing furnace. Then what god[t] will be
able to rescue[u] you from my hand?"
16Shadrach, Meshach and Abednego[v]
replied to the king, "O Nebuchadnez-
zar, we do not need to defend ourselves
before you in this matter. 17If we are
thrown into the blazing furnace, the
God we serve is able to save[w] us from it,
and he will rescue[x] us from your hand,
O king. 18But even if he does not, we
want you to know, O king, that we will
not serve your gods or worship the
image of gold you have set up.[y]"
19Then Nebuchadnezzar was furious
with Shadrach, Meshach and Abedne-
go, and his attitude towards them
changed. He ordered the furnace to be
heated seven[z] times hotter than usual
20and commanded some of the
strongest soldiers in his army to tie up
Shadrach, Meshach and Abednego[a] and
throw them into the blazing furnace.
21So these men, wearing their robes,
trousers, turbans and other clothes,
were bound and thrown into the blaz-
ing furnace. 22The king's command was
so urgent and the furnace so hot that the
flames of the fire killed the soldiers who
took up Shadrach, Meshach and Abed-
nego,[b] 23and these three men, firmly
tied, fell into the blazing furnace.
24Then King Nebuchadnezzar leaped
to his feet in amazement and asked his
advisers, "Weren't there three men that
we tied up and threw into the fire?"
They replied, "Certainly, O king."
25He said, "Look! I see four men walk-
ing around in the fire, unbound and
unharmed, and the fourth looks like a
son of the gods."
26Nebuchadnezzar then approached
the opening of the blazing furnace and
shouted, "Shadrach, Meshach and
Abednego, servants of the Most High
God,[c] come out! Come here!"
So Shadrach, Meshach and Abed-
nego came out of the fire, 27and the
satraps, prefects, governors and royal
advisers[d] crowded around them.[e] They
saw that the fire[f] had not harmed their
bodies, nor was a hair of their heads
singed; their robes were not scorched,
and there was no smell of fire on them.
28Then Nebuchadnezzar said, "Praise
be to the God of Shadrach, Meshach
and Abednego, who has sent his angel[g]
and rescued[h] his servants! They trusted[i]
in him and defied the king's command
and were willing to give up their lives
rather than serve or worship any god
except their own God.[j] 29Therefore I de-
cree[k] that the people of any nation or
language who say anything against the
God of Shadrach, Meshach and Abed-
nego be cut into pieces and their houses
be turned into piles of rubble,[l] for no
other god can save[m] in this way."
30Then the king promoted Shadrach,
Meshach and Abednego in the province
of Babylon.[n]

Nebuchadnezzar's Dream of a Tree

4 King Nebuchadnezzar,

To the peoples, nations and men
of every language,[a] who live in all
the world:

May you prosper greatly![b]

2It is my pleasure to tell you
about the miraculous signs[c] and
wonders that the Most High God[d]
has performed for me.

3 How great are his signs,
how mighty his wonders![e]
His kingdom is an eternal kingdom;
his dominion endures[f] from
generation to generation.

4I, Nebuchadnezzar, was at
home in my palace, contented[g] and
prosperous. 5I had a dream[h] that
made me afraid. As I was lying in
my bed,[i] the images and visions
that passed through my mind[j] ter-
rified me.[k] 6So I commanded that all
the wise men of Babylon be
brought before me to interpret[l]
the dream for me. 7When the

10 [m]ver 4–6
12 [n]Da 2:49; [o]Da 6:13; [p]Est 3:3
13 [q]Da 2:12
14 [r]Isa 46:1; Jer 50:2; [s]ver 1
15 [t]Isa 36:18–20; [u]2Ch 32:15
16 [v]Da 1:7
17 [w]Ge 48:16; Ps 18:48; 27:1–2; [x]Job 5:19; Jer 1:8; Da 6:20
18 [y]ver 28; Ex 1:17; Jos 24:15
19 [z]Lev 26:18–28
20 [a]Da 1:7
22 [b]Da 1:7
26 [c]Da 4:2,34
27 [d]ver 2; Da 6:7; [e]Ps 91:3–11; Isa 43:2; Heb 11:32–34; [f]Da 6:23
28 [g]Ps 34:7; Da 6:22; Ac 5:19; [h]Ps 97:10; Ac 12:11; [i]Dt 31:20; Job 13:15; Ps 26:1; 84:12; [j]ver 18
29 [k]Da 6:26; [l]Ezr 6:11; [m]Da 6:27
30 [n]Da 2:49

Ch. 4

1 [a]Da 3:4; [b]Da 6:25
2 [c]Ps 74:9; [d]Da 3:26
3 [e]Ps 105:27; Da 6:27; [f]Da 2:44
4 [g]Ps 30:6; Isa 32:9
5 [h]Da 2:1; [i]Ps 4:4; [j]Da 2:28; [k]ver 19; Ge 41:8; Job 3:26; Da 2:3; 5:6
6 [l]Da 2:2

magicians,[m] enchanters, astrolo-
gers[a] and diviners[n] came, I told
them the dream, but they could not
interpret it for me.[o] 8Finally, Daniel
came into my presence and I told
him the dream. (He is called Bel-
teshazzar,[p] after the name of my
god, and the spirit of the holy gods[q]
is in him.)

9I said, "Belteshazzar, chief[r] of
the magicians, I know that the
spirit of the holy gods[s] is in you,
and no mystery is too difficult for
you. Here is my dream; interpret it
for me. 10These are the visions I saw
while lying in my bed:[t] I looked,
and there before me stood a tree in
the middle of the land. Its height
was enormous.[u] 11The tree grew
large and strong and its top
touched the sky; it was visible to
the ends of the earth.[v] 12Its leaves
were beautiful, its fruit abundant,
and on it was food for all. Under it
the beasts of the field found shelter,
and the birds of the air lived in its
branches;[w] from it every creature
was fed.

13"In the visions I saw while lying
in my bed,[x] I looked, and there
before me was a messenger,[b] a holy
one,[y] coming down from heaven.
14He called in a loud voice: 'Cut
down the tree[z] and trim off its bran-
ches; strip off its leaves and scatter
its fruit. Let the animals flee from
under it and the birds from its
branches.[a] 15But let the stump and
its roots, bound with iron and
bronze, remain in the ground, in
the grass of the field.

"'Let him be drenched with the
dew of heaven, and let him live
with the animals among the plants
of the earth. 16Let his mind be
changed from that of a man and let
him be given the mind of an anim-
al, till seven times[c] pass by for him.[b]

17"'The decision is announced by
messengers, the holy ones declare
the verdict, so that the living may
know that the Most High[c] is
sovereign[d] over the kingdoms of
men and gives them to anyone he
wishes and sets over them the
lowliest[e] of men.'

18"This is the dream that I, King
Nebuchadnezzar, had. Now, Belte-
shazzar, tell me what it means, for
none of the wise men in my king-
dom can interpret it for me.[f] But
you can,[g] because the spirit of the
holy gods[h] is in you."[i]

Daniel Interprets the Dream

19Then Daniel (also called Bel-
teshazzar) was greatly perplexed
for a time, and his thoughts
terrified[j] him. So the king said,
"Belteshazzar, do not let the dream
or its meaning alarm you."[k]

Belteshazzar answered, "My
lord, if only the dream applied to
your enemies and its meaning to
your adversaries! 20The tree you
saw, which grew large and strong,
with its top touching the sky,
visible to the whole earth, 21with
beautiful leaves and abundant
fruit, providing food for all, giving
shelter to the beasts of the field,
and having nesting places in its
branches for the birds of the air[l]
—22you, O king, are that tree![m] You
have become great and strong;
your greatness has grown until it
reaches the sky, and your domin-
ion extends to distant parts of the
earth.[n]

23"You, O king, saw a messen-
ger, a holy one,[o] coming down from
heaven and saying, 'Cut down the
tree and destroy it, but leave the
stump, bound with iron and
bronze, in the grass of the field,
while its roots remain in the
ground. Let him be drenched with
the dew of heaven; let him live like
the wild animals, until seven times
pass by for him.'[p q]

24"This is the interpretation, O
king, and this is the decree[r] the
Most High has issued against my
lord the king: 25You will be driven
away from people and will live with
the wild animals; you will eat grass
like cattle and be drenched[s] with
the dew of heaven. Seven times
will pass by for you until you ac-
knowledge that the Most High[t] is
sovereign over the kingdoms of
men and gives them to anyone he
wishes.[u] 26The command to leave
the stump of the tree with its roots[v]
means that your kingdom will
be restored to you when you ac-
knowledge that Heaven rules.[w]
27Therefore, O king, be pleased to
accept my advice: Renounce your
sins by doing what is right, and
your wickedness by being kind to

7 [m]**Ge 41:8;** [n]**Isa 44:25; Da 2:2;** [o]**Da 2:10**
8 [p]**Da 1:7;** [q]**Ge 41:38**
9 [r]Da 2:48; [s]Da 5:11–12
10 [t]**ver 5;** Ps 4:4; [u]Eze 31:3–4
11 [v]**Eze 19:11;** 31:5
12 [w]**Eze 17:23; Mt 13:32**
13 [x]ver 10; Da 7:1; [y]**ver 23; Dt 33:2**
14 [z]**Job 24:20;** [a]**Eze 31:12; Mt 3:10**
16 [b]ver 23,32
17 [c]ver 2,25; Ps 83:18; [d]**Ps 103:19;** Jer 27:5–7; Da 2:21; 5:18–21; Ro 13:1; [e]Da 11:21; Mt 23:12
18 [f]Ge 41:8; Da 5:8,15; [g]**Ge 41:15;** [h]**Ge 41:38;** [i]ver 7–9; **Da 1:20**
19 [j]**ver 5; Ge 41:8;** Da 7:15, 28; 8:27; 10:16–17; [k]**Ge 40:12**
21 [l]**Eze 31:6**
22 [m]**2Sa 12:7;** [n]Jer 27:7; Da 5:18–19
23 [o]ver 13; Da 8:13; [p]Da 5:21; [q]**Eze 31:3–4**
24 [r]Job 40:12; Ps 107:40; Jer 40:2
25 [s]**Job 24:8;** [t]**ver 17;** [u]Jer 27:5; **Da 2:47;** 5:21
26 [v]ver 15; [w]**Da 2:37**

[a]7 Or *Chaldeans*
[b]13 Or *watchman;* also in verses 17 and 23
[c]16 Or *years;* also in verses 23, 25 and 32

the oppressed.[x] It may be that then
your prosperity[y] will continue.[z]"

The Dream Is Fulfilled

28All this happened[a] to King
Nebuchadnezzar. 29Twelve months
later, as the king was walking on
the roof of the royal palace of Bab-
ylon, 30he said, "Is not this the great
Babylon I have built as the royal
residence, by my mighty power
and for the glory[b] of my majesty?"[c]
31The words were still on his lips
when a voice came from heaven,
"This is what is decreed for you,
King Nebuchadnezzar: Your royal
authority has been taken from
you.[d] 32You will be driven away
from people and will live with the
wild animals; you will eat grass like
cattle. Seven times will pass by for
you until you acknowledge that the
Most High is sovereign over the
kingdoms of men and gives them to
anyone he wishes."[e]
33Immediately what had been
said about Nebuchadnezzar was
fulfilled. He was driven away from
people and ate grass like cattle. His
body was drenched[f] with the dew
of heaven until his hair grew like
the feathers of an eagle and his
nails like the claws of a bird.[g]

34At the end of that time, I,
Nebuchadnezzar, raised my eyes
towards heaven, and my sanity[h]
was restored. Then I praised the
Most High; I honoured and
glorified him who lives for ever.[i]

His dominion is an eternal
dominion;
his kingdom[j] endures from
generation to generation.[k]
35 All the peoples of the earth
are regarded as nothing.[l]
He does as he pleases[m]
with the powers of heaven
and the peoples of the earth.
No-one can hold back[n] his hand[o]
or say to him: "What have you
done?"[p]

36At the same time that my sanity
was restored, my honour and
splendour were returned to me for
the glory of my kingdom.[q] My
advisers and nobles sought me out,
and I was restored to my throne
and became even greater than be-
fore. 37Now I, Nebuchadnezzar,

27 [x]Isa 55:6–7; [y]Jer 29:7; [z]**Dt 24:13**; 1Ki 21:29; **Ps 41:3**; **Pr 28:13**; **Eze 18:22**
28 [a]Nu 23:19
30 [b]Isa 13:19; [c]**Isa 10:13**; **37:24–25**; Da 5:20; Hab 1:11; 2:4
31 [d]**2Sa 22:28**; Da 5:20
32 [e]**Job 9:12**
33 [f]**Job 24:8**; [g]Da 5:20–21
34 [h]**Job 12:20**; [i]Da 12:7; [j]Isa 37:16; [k]Ps 145:13; **Da 2:44**; 5:21; 6:26; Lk 1:33
35 [l]**Isa 40:17**; [m]Dt 21:8; Ps 115:3; **135:6**; Jnh 1:14; [n]**Isa 14:27**; [o]**Dt 32:39**; [p]**Job 9:4**; **Isa 14:24**; **45:9**; Da 5:21; Ro 9:20
36 [q]**Pr 22:4**; Da 5:18
37 [r]**Ex 15:2**; [s]**Ps 34:3**; [t]Dt 32:4; Ps 33:4–5; [u]Ps 18:27; **119:21**; [v]**Job 31:4**; 40:11–12; **Isa 13:11**; Da 5:23; Mt 23:12

Ch. 5

1 [a]ver 30; Da 7:1; 8:1; [b]**1Ki 3:15**; [c]Jer 50:35
2 [d]Isa 21:5; [e]**2Ki 24:13**; **2Ch 36:10**; **Jer 52:19**; [f]**Est 2:14**; [g]**Est 1:7**; Da 1:2
4 [h]Jdg 16:24; [i]**Est 1:10**; Ps 135:15–18; Hab 2:19; Rev 9:20
6 [j]**Job 4:15**; [k]**Da 4:5**; [l]**Isa 7:2**; [m]**Ps 22:14**; Eze 7:17
7 [n]**Ge 41:8**; [o]**Isa 19:3**; [p]Isa 44:25; [q]Jer 50:35; Da 4:6–7; [r]**Ge 41:42**; [s]Est 10:3; [t]Da 2:5–6, 48
8 [u]**Ex 8:18**; [v]**Da 2:10**; **4:18**
9 [w]**Ps 48:5**; **Isa 21:4**
10 [x]**Ne 2:3**; **Da 3:9**
11 [y]**Ge 41:38**; [z]ver 14; **Da 1:17**; [a]**Da 2:22**

praise and exalt[r] and glorify[s] the
King of heaven, because every-
thing he does is right and all his
ways are just.[t] And those who walk
in pride[u] he is able to humble.[v]

The Writing on the Wall

5 King Belshazzar[a] gave a great ban-
quet[b] for a thousand of his nobles[c]
and drank wine with them. 2While Bel-
shazzar was drinking[d] his wine, he gave
orders to bring in the gold and silver
goblets[e] that Nebuchadnezzar his
father[a] had taken from the temple in
Jerusalem, so that the king and his
nobles, his wives and his concubines[f]
might drink from them.[g] 3So they
brought in the gold goblets that had
been taken from the temple of God in
Jerusalem, and the king and his nobles,
his wives and his concubines drank
from them. 4As they drank the wine,
they praised the gods[h] of gold and
silver, of bronze, iron, wood and
stone.[i]
5Suddenly the fingers of a human
hand appeared and wrote on the plaster
of the wall, near the lampstand in the
royal palace. The king watched the
hand as it wrote. 6His face turned pale[j]
and he was so frightened[k] that his knees
knocked[l] together and his legs gave
way.[m]
7The king called out for the enchan-
ters,[n] astrologers[b] [o] and diviners[p] to be
brought and said to these wise[q] men of
Babylon, "Whoever reads this writing
and tells me what it means will be
clothed in purple and have a gold chain
placed around his neck,[r] and he will be
made the third[s] highest ruler in the
kingdom."[t]
8Then all the king's wise men[u] came
in, but they could not read the writing
or tell the king what it meant.[v] 9So King
Belshazzar became even more terrified[w]
and his face grew more pale. His nobles
were baffled.
10The queen,[c] hearing the voices of
the king and his nobles, came into the
banquet hall. "O king, live for ever!"[x]
she said. "Don't be alarmed! Don't look
so pale! 11There is a man in your king-
dom who has the spirit of the holy gods[y]
in him. In the time of your father he was
found to have insight and intelligence
and wisdom[z] like that of the gods.[a] King
Nebuchadnezzar your father—your

[a]2 Or *ancestor*; or *predecessor*; also in verses 11, 13 and 18 [b]7 Or *Chaldeans*; also in verse 11
[c]10 Or *queen mother*

father the king, I say—appointed him chief of the magicians, enchanters, astrologers and diviners.[b] 12This man Daniel, whom the king called Belteshazzar,[c] was found to have a keen mind and knowledge and understanding, and also the ability to interpret dreams, explain riddles[d] and solve difficult problems.[e] Call for Daniel, and he will tell you what the writing means.[f]"

13So Daniel was brought before the king, and the king said to him, "Are you Daniel, one of the exiles my father the king brought from Judah?[g] 14I have heard that the spirit of the gods[h] is in you and that you have insight, intelligence and outstanding wisdom.[i] 15The wise men and enchanters were brought before me to read this writing and tell me what it means, but they could not explain it.[j] 16Now I have heard that you are able to give interpretations and to solve difficult problems.[k] If you can read this writing and tell me what it means, you will be clothed in purple and have a gold chain placed around your neck,[l] and you will be made the third highest ruler in the kingdom."[m]

17Then Daniel answered the king, "You may keep your gifts for yourself and give your rewards to someone else.[n] Nevertheless, I will read the writing for the king and tell him what it means.

18"O king, the Most High God gave your father Nebuchadnezzar[o] sovereignty and greatness and glory and splendour.[p] 19Because of the high position he gave him, all the peoples and nations and men of every language dreaded and feared him. Those the king wanted to put to death, he put to death;[q] those he wanted to spare, he spared; those he wanted to promote, he promoted; and those he wanted to humble, he humbled.[r] 20But when his heart became arrogant and hardened with pride,[s] he was deposed from his royal throne[t] and stripped[u] of his glory.[v] 21He was driven away from people and given the mind of an animal; he lived with the wild donkeys and ate grass like cattle; and his body was drenched with the dew of heaven, until he acknowledged that the Most High God is sovereign[w] over the kingdoms of men and sets over them anyone he wishes.[x]

22"But you his son,[d] O Belshazzar, have not humbled[y] yourself, though you knew all this. 23Instead, you have set yourself up against[z] the Lord of heaven. You had the goblets from his temple brought to you, and you and your nobles, your wives[a] and your concubines drank wine from them. You praised the gods of silver and gold, of bronze, iron, wood and stone, which cannot see or hear or understand.[b] But you did not honour the God who holds in his hand your life[c] and all your ways.[d] 24Therefore he sent the hand that wrote the inscription.

25"This is the inscription that was written:

MENE, MENE, TEKEL, PARSIN[e]

26"This is what these words mean:

Mene[f]: God has numbered the days[e] of your reign and brought it to an end.[f]

27*Tekel*[g]: You have been weighed on the scales[g] and found wanting.[h]

28*Peres*[h]: Your kingdom is divided and given to the Medes[i] and Persians."[j]

29Then at Belshazzar's command, Daniel was clothed in purple, a gold chain was placed around his neck,[k] and he was proclaimed the third highest ruler in the kingdom.[l]

30That very night Belshazzar,[m] king[n] of the Babylonians,[i] was slain,[o] 31and Darius[p] the Mede[q] took over the kingdom, at the age of sixty-two.

Daniel in the Den of Lions

6 It pleased Darius[a] to appoint 120 satraps[b] to rule throughout the kingdom, 2with three administrators over them, one of whom was Daniel.[c] The satraps were made accountable[d] to them so that the king might not suffer loss. 3Now Daniel so distinguished himself among the administrators and the satraps by his exceptional qualities that the king planned to set him over the whole kingdom.[e] 4At this, the administrators and the satraps tried to find grounds for charges[f] against Daniel in his conduct of government affairs, but they were unable to do so. They could find no corruption in him, because he was trustworthy and neither corrupt nor negligent. 5Finally these men said,

11 [b]Da 2:47–48
12 [c]Da 1:7; [d]Nu 12:8; [e]ver 14–16; Da 6:3; [f]Eze 28:3
13 [g]Est 2:5–6; Da 6:13
14 [h]Ge 41:38; [i]Da 2:22
15 [j]Da 4:18
16 [k]Ge 41:15, [l]Ge 41:42; [m]Est 5:3; Da 2:6
17 [n]2Ki 5:16
18 [o]Jer 28:14; [p]Jer 27:7; Da 2:37–38; 4:36
19 [q]Da 2:12–13; 3:6; [r]Da 4:22
20 [s]Da 4:30; [t]Jer 43:10; [u]Jer 13:18; Da 4:31; [v]Job 40:12; Isa 14:13–15; Eze 31:10–11; Da 8:8
21 [w]Eze 17:24; [x]Da 4:16–17, 35
22 [y]Ex 10:3
23 [z]Isa 14:13; Jer 50:29; [a]Jer 44:9; [b]Ps 115:4–8; Hab 2:19; Rev 9:20; [c]Job 12:10; Ac 17:28; [d]Job 31:4; Isa 13:11; Jer 10:23; 48:26
26 [e]Jer 27:7; [f]Isa 13:6
27 [g]Job 6:2; [h]Ps 62:9
28 [i]Isa 13:17; [j]Jer 27:7; 50:41–43; Da 6:28
29 [k]Ge 41:42; [l]Da 2:6
30 [m]ver 1; [n]Jer 50:35; [o]Isa 21:9; Jer 51:31
31 [p]Jer 50:41; Da 6:1; 9:1; 11:1; [q]Isa 13:3

Ch. 6

1 [a]Da 5:31; [b]Est 1:1
2 [c]Da 2:48–49; [d]Ezr 4:22
3 [e]Ge 41:41; Est 10:3; Da 1:20; 5:12–14
4 [f]Jer 20:10

[d]22 Or *descendant*; or *successor*
[e]25 Aramaic *UPARSIN* (that is, *AND PARSIN*)
[f]26 *Mene* can mean *numbered* or *mina* (a unit of money). [g]27 *Tekel* can mean *weighed* or *shekel*.
[h]28 *Peres* (the singular of *Parsin*) can mean *divided* or *Persia* or *a half mina* or *a half shekel*.
[i]30 Or *Chaldeans*

"We will never find any basis for
charges against this man Daniel unless
it has something to do with the law of
his God."[g]
6So the administrators and the satraps
went as a group to the king and said: "O
King Darius, live for ever![h] 7The royal
administrators, prefects, satraps, advis-
ers and governors[i] have all agreed that
the king should issue an edict and en-
force the decree that anyone who prays
to any god or man during the next thirty
days, except to you, O king, shall be
thrown into the lions' den.[j] 8Now, O
king, issue the decree and put it in
writing so that it cannot be altered—
in accordance with the laws of the
Medes and Persians, which cannot be
repealed."[k] 9So King Darius put the
decree in writing.
10Now when Daniel learned that the
decree had been published, he went
home to his upstairs room where the
windows opened towards[l] Jerusalem.
Three times a day he got down on his
knees[m] and prayed, giving thanks to his
God, just as he had done before.[n]
11Then these men went as a group and
found Daniel praying and asking God
for help.[o] 12So they went to the king and
spoke to him about his royal decree:
"Did you not publish a decree that dur-
ing the next thirty days anyone who
prays to any god or man except to you,
O king, would be thrown into the lions'
den?"
The king answered, "The decree
stands—in accordance with the laws of
the Medes and Persians, which cannot
be repealed."[p]
13Then they said to the king, "Daniel,
who is one of the exiles from Judah,[q]
pays no attention[r] to you, O king, or to
the decree you put in writing. He still
prays three times a day." 14When the
king heard this, he was greatly dis-
tressed;[s] he was determined to rescue
Daniel and made every effort until sun-
down to save him.
15Then the men went as a group to the
king and said to him, "Remember, O
king, that according to the law of the
Medes and Persians no decree or edict
that the king issues can be changed."[t]
16So the king gave the order, and they
brought Daniel and threw him into the
lions' den.[u] The king said to Daniel,
"May your God, whom you serve
continually, rescue[v] you!"
17A stone was brought and placed
over the mouth of the den, and the king
sealed[w] it with his own signet ring and
with the rings of his nobles, so that
Daniel's situation might not be
changed. 18Then the king returned to
his palace and spent the night without
eating[x] and without any entertainment
being brought to him. And he could not
sleep.[y]
19At the first light of dawn, the king
got up and hurried to the lions' den.
20When he came near the den, he called
to Daniel in an anguished voice,
"Daniel, servant of the living God, has
your God, whom you serve continually,
been able to rescue you from the
lions?"[z]
21Daniel answered, "O king, live for
ever![a] 22My God sent his angel,[b] and he
shut the mouths of the lions.[c] They have
not hurt me, because I was found inno-
cent in his sight.[d] Nor have I ever done
any wrong before you, O king."
23The king was overjoyed and gave
orders to lift Daniel out of the den. And
when Daniel was lifted from the den, no
wound[e] was found on him, because he
had trusted[f] in his God.
24At the king's command, the men
who had falsely accused Daniel were
brought in and thrown into the lions'
den,[g] along with their wives and chil-
dren.[h] And before they reached the
floor of the den, the lions overpowered
them and crushed all their bones.[i]
25Then King Darius wrote to all the
peoples, nations and men of every
language[j] throughout the land:

"May you prosper greatly![k]

26"I issue a decree that in every
part of my kingdom people must
fear and reverence[l] the God of
Daniel.[m]

"For he is the living God[n]
    and he endures for ever;[o]
his kingdom will not be destroyed,
    his dominion will never end.[p]
27 He rescues and he saves;[q]
    he performs signs and wonders[r]
    in the heavens and on the earth.
He has rescued Daniel
    from the power of the lions."[s]

28So Daniel prospered during the
reign of Darius and the reign of Cyrus[a][t]
the Persian.[u]

Daniel's Dream of Four Beasts

7 In the first year of Belshazzar[a] king
of Babylon, Daniel had a dream,
and visions[b] passed through his mind[c]

5 [g]Act 24:13–16
6 [h]**Ne 2:3**
7 [i]**Da 3:2**; [j]Ps 59:3; 64:2–6; **Da 3:6**
8 [k]**Est 1:19**
10 [l]**1Ki 8:29**; [m]Ps 95:6; [n]Mt 6:6; Ac 5:29
11 [o]1Ki 8:48–50; Ps 55:17; 1Th 5:17–18
12 [p]**Est 1:19**; Da 3:8–12
13 [q]**Eze 14:14**; Da 2:25; [r]**Est 3:8**
14 [s]Mk 6:26
15 [t]**Est 8:8**
16 [u]**ver 7**; [v]**Job 5:19**; Ps 37:39–40; **97:10**
17 [w]Mt 27:66
18 [x]**2Sa 12:17**; Da 10:3; [y]**Est 6:1**
20 [z]**Da 3:17**
21 [a]**Ne 2:3**; Da 3:9
22 [b]**Ge 32:1**; **Da 3:28**; [c]ver 27; Ps 91:11–13; Heb 11:33; [d]Ac 12:11; 2Ti 4:17
23 [e]Da 3:27; [f]**1Ch 5:20**; **Isa 12:2**
24 [g]Dt 19:18–19; Est 7:9–10; Ps 54:5; [h]Dt 24:16; 2Ki 14:6; [i]**Isa 38:13**
25 [j]**Da 3:4**; [k]**Da 4:1**
26 [l]**Ps 5:7**; [m]**Est 8:17**; Ps 99:1–3; Da 3:29; [n]**Jos 2:11**; **3:10**; [o]**Jer 10:10**; Da 12:7; Rev 1:18; [p]**Da 2:44**
27 [q]Da 3:29; [r]**Da 4:3**; [s]**ver 22**
28 [t]**2Ch 36:22**; **Da 1:21**; [u]**Da 5:28**

Ch. 7

1 [a]**Da 5:1**; [b]**Eze 40:2**; [c]**Da 1:17**

[a]28 Or *Darius, that is, the reign of Cyrus*

as he was lying on his bed.[d] He wrote[e]
down the substance of his dream.
2Daniel said: "In my vision at night I
looked, and there before me were the
four winds of heaven[f] churning up the
great sea. 3Four great beasts,[g] each dif-
ferent from the others, came up out of
the sea.
4"The first was like a lion,[h] and it had
the wings of an eagle.[i] I watched until its
wings were torn off and it was lifted
from the ground so that it stood on two
feet like a man, and the heart of a man
was given to it.
5"And there before me was a second
beast, which looked like a bear. It was
raised up on one of its sides, and it had
three ribs in its mouth between its teeth.
It was told, 'Get up and eat your fill of
flesh!'[j]
6"After that, I looked, and there be-
fore me was another beast, one that
looked like a leopard.[k] And on its back it
had four wings like those of a bird. This
beast had four heads, and it was given
authority to rule.
7"After that, in my vision[l] at night I
looked, and there before me was a
fourth beast—terrifying and frighten-
ing and very powerful. It had large
iron[m] teeth; it crushed and devoured its
victims and trampled[n] underfoot what-
ever was left.[o] It was different from all
the former beasts, and it had ten horns.[p]
8"While I was thinking about the
horns, there before me was another
horn, a little[q] one, which came up
among them; and three of the first horns
were uprooted before it. This horn had
eyes like the eyes of a man[r] and a mouth
that spoke boastfully.[s]
9"As I looked,

"thrones were set in place,
  and the Ancient of Days[t] took his
    seat.[u]
His clothing was as white as snow;[v]
  the hair of his head was white like
    wool.[w]
His throne was flaming with fire,
  and its wheels[x] were all ablaze.
10A river of fire[y] was flowing,
  coming out from before him.[z]
Thousands upon thousands attended
    him;
  ten thousand times ten thousand
    stood before him.
The court was seated,
  and the books[a] were opened.

11"Then I continued to watch because
of the boastful words the horn was
speaking.[b] I kept looking until the beast
was slain and its body destroyed and
thrown into the blazing fire.[c] 12(The
other beasts had been stripped of their
authority, but were allowed to live for a
period of time.)
13"In my vision at night I looked, and
there before me was one like a son of
man,[d] coming[e] with the clouds of
heaven.[f] He approached the Ancient of
Days and was led into his presence.
14He was given authority,[g] glory and
sovereign power; all peoples, nations
and men of every language worshipped
him.[h] His dominion is an everlasting
dominion that will not pass away, and
his kingdom[i] is one that will never be
destroyed.[j]

The Interpretation of the Dream

15"I, Daniel, was troubled in spirit,
and the visions that passed through my
mind disturbed me.[k] 16I approached one
of those standing there and asked him
the true meaning of all this.
"So he told me and gave me the inter-
pretation[l] of these things: 17'The four
great beasts are four kingdoms that will
rise from the earth. 18But the saints[m] of
the Most High will receive the king-
dom[n] and will possess it for ever—yes,
for ever and ever.'[o]
19"Then I wanted to know the true
meaning of the fourth beast, which was
different from all the others and most
terrifying, with its iron teeth and bronze
claws—the beast that crushed and de-
voured its victims and trampled under-
foot whatever was left. 20I also wanted
to know about the ten horns[p] on its head
and about the other horn that came up,
before which three of them fell—the
horn that looked more imposing than
the others and that had eyes and a
mouth that spoke boastfully.[q] 21As I
watched, this horn was waging war
against the saints and defeating them,[r]
22until the Ancient of Days came and
pronounced judgment in favour of
the saints of the Most High, and the
time came when they possessed the
kingdom.[s]
23"He gave me this explanation: 'The
fourth beast is a fourth kingdom that
will appear on earth. It will be different
from all the other kingdoms and will
devour the whole earth, trampling it
down and crushing it.[t] 24The ten horns[u]
are ten kings who will come from this
kingdom. After them another king will
arise, different from the earlier ones; he
will subdue three kings. 25He will speak
against the Most High[v] and oppress his

1 [d]Ps 4:4; **Da 4:13**; [e]**Jer 36:4**
2 [f]**Eze 37:9**; Da 8:8; 11:4; Rev 7:1
3 [g]Rev 13:1
4 [h]**2Ki 24:1**; Ps 7:2; Jer 4:7; Rev 13:2; [i]**Eze 17:3**
5 [j]Da 2:39
6 [k]Rev 13:2
7 [l]**Eze 40:2**; [m]**Da 2:40**; [n]Da 8:10; [o]Da 8:7; [p]**Rev 12:3**
8 [q]Da 8:9; [r]Rev 9:7; [s]**Ps 12:3**; Rev 13:5–6
9 [t]ver 22; [u]**1Ki 22:19**; 2Ch 18:18; Mt 19:28; Rev 4:2; 20:4; [v]**Mt 28:3**; [w]Rev 1:14; [x]**Eze 1:15**; 10:6
10 [y]Ps 50:3; 97:3; Isa 30:27; [z]**Dt 33:2**; Ps 68:17; Jude 14; Rev 5:11; [a]**Ex 32:32**; **Ps 56:8**; Rev 20:11–15
11 [b]Rev 13:5–6; [c]Rev 19:20
13 [d]**Eze 1:5**; **2:1**; Mt 8:20*; Rev 1:13*; 14:14*; [e]Isa 13:6; Zep 1:14; Mal 3:2; 4:1; [f]**Dt 33:26**; **Rev 1:7**
14 [g]**Mt 28:18**; [h]Ps 72:11; 102:22; [i]**Isa 16:5**; [j]**Da 2:44**; Heb 12:28; Rev 11:15
15 [k]**Job 4:15**; **Da 4:19**
16 [l]Da 8:16; 9:22; Zec 1:9
18 [m]**Ps 16:3**; [n]**Ps 49:14**; [o]Isa 60:12–14; Lk 12:32; Heb 12:28; Rev 2:26; 20:4
20 [p]Rev 17:12; [q]Rev 13:5–6
21 [r]Rev 13:7
22 [s]Mk 8:35
23 [t]**Da 2:40**
24 [u]Rev 17:12
25 [v]**Isa 37:23**; Da 11:36

saints[w] and try to change the set times[x] and the laws. The saints will be handed over to him for a time, times and half a time.[a][y]

26"'But the court will sit, and his power will be taken away and completely destroyed[z] for ever. 27Then the sovereignty, power and greatness of the kingdoms[a] under the whole heaven will be handed over to the saints,[b] the people of the Most High.[c] His kingdom will be an everlasting[d] kingdom, and all rulers will worship[e] and obey him.'

28"This is the end of the matter. I, Daniel, was deeply troubled[f] by my thoughts,[g] and my face turned pale,[h] but I kept the matter to myself."

Daniel's Vision of a Ram and a Goat

8 In the third year of King Belshazzar's[a] reign, I, Daniel, had a vision,[b] after the one that had already appeared to me. 2In my vision I saw myself in the citadel of Susa[c] in the province of Elam;[d] in the vision I was beside the Ulai Canal. 3I looked up,[e] and there before me was a ram[f] with two horns, standing beside the canal, and the horns were long. One of the horns was longer than the other but grew up later. 4I watched the ram as he charged towards the west and the north and the south. No animal could stand against him, and none could rescue from his power.[g] He did as he pleased[h] and became great.

5As I was thinking about this, suddenly a goat with a prominent horn between his eyes came from the west, crossing the whole earth without touching the ground. 6He came towards the two-horned ram I had seen standing beside the canal and charged at him in great rage. 7I saw him attack the ram furiously, striking the ram and shattering his two horns. The ram was powerless to stand against him; the goat knocked him to the ground and trampled on him,[i] and none could rescue the ram from his power.[j] 8The goat became very great, but at the height of his power his large horn was broken off,[k] and in its place four prominent horns grew up towards the four winds of heaven.[l]

9Out of one of them came another horn, which started small[m] but grew in power to the south and to the east and towards the Beautiful Land.[n] 10It grew until it reached[o] the host of the heavens, and it threw some of the starry host down to the earth[p] and trampled[q] on them. 11It set itself up to be as great as the Prince[r] of the host;[s] it took away the daily sacrifice[t] from him, and the place of his sanctuary was brought low.[u] 12Because of rebellion, the host ⌞of the saints⌟[a] and the daily sacrifice were given over to it. It prospered in everything it did, and truth was thrown to the ground.[v]

13Then I heard a holy one[w] speaking, and another holy one said to him, "How long will it take for the vision to be fulfilled[x]—the vision concerning the daily sacrifice, the rebellion that causes desolation, and the surrender of the sanctuary and of the host that will be trampled[y] underfoot?"

14He said to me, "It will take 2,300 evenings and mornings; then the sanctuary will be reconsecrated."[z]

The Interpretation of the Vision

15While I, Daniel, was watching the vision[a] and trying to understand it, there before me stood one who looked like a man.[b] 16And I heard a man's voice from the Ulai[c] calling, "Gabriel,[d] tell this man the meaning of the vision."[e]

17As he came near the place where I was standing, I was terrified and fell prostrate.[f] "Son of man," he said to me, "understand that the vision concerns the time of the end."[g]

18While he was speaking to me, I was in a deep sleep, with my face to the ground.[h] Then he touched me and raised me to my feet.[i]

19He said: "I am going to tell you what will happen later in the time of wrath,[j] because the vision concerns the appointed time[k] of the end.[b][l] 20The two-horned ram that you saw represents the kings of Media and Persia.[m] 21The shaggy goat is the king of Greece,[n] and the large horn between his eyes is the first king.[o] 22The four horns that replaced the one that was broken off represent four kingdoms that will emerge from his nation but will not have the same power.

23"In the latter part of their reign, when rebels have become completely wicked, a stern-faced king, a master of intrigue, will arise. 24He will become very strong, but not by his own power. He will cause astounding devastation and will succeed in whatever he does. He will destroy the mighty men and the

25 [w]Rev 16:6; [x]Da 2:21; Mk 1:15; Lk 21:8; Ac 1:6–7; [y]Da 8:24; 12:7; **Rev 11:2**
26 [z]Rev 19:20
27 [a]**Isa 14:2**; [b]1Co 6:2; [c]Ge 14:18; [d]**2Sa 7:13**; Ps 145:13; **Da 2:44; 4:34; Lk 1:33**; Rev 11:15; 22:5; [e]**Ps 22:27**; 72:11; 86:9
28 [f]**Isa 21:3; Da 4:19**; [g]**Ps 13:2**; [h]**Job 4:15**

Ch. 8

1 [a]**Da 5:1**; [b]**Da 1:17**
2 [c]**Ezr 4:9; Est 2:8**; [d]**Ge 10:22**
3 [e]Da 10:5; [f]Rev 13:11
4 [g]Isa 41:3; [h]Da 11:3,16
7 [i]**Da 7:7**; [j]Da 11:11,16
8 [k]2Ch 26:16–21; **Da 5:20**; [l]**Da 7:2**; Rev 7:1
9 [m]Da 7:8; [n]**Eze 20:6**; Da 11:16
10 [o]**Isa 14:13**; [p]Rev 8:10; 12:4; [q]**Da 7:7**
11 [r]ver 25; [s]Da 11:36–37; [t]Eze 46:13–14; [u]Da 11:31; 12:11
12 [v]**Isa 48:1**
13 [w]**Dt 33:2; Da 4:23**; [x]Da 12:6; [y]**Isa 28:18; Lk 21:24**; Rev 11:2
14 [z]Da 12:11–12
15 [a]ver 1; [b]**Eze 2:1**; Da 10:16–18
16 [c]ver 2; [d]Da 9:21; **Lk 1:19**; [e]**Da 7:16**
17 [f]Eze 1:28; 44:4; **Da 2:46**; Rev 1:17; [g]ver 19; Hab 2:3
18 [h]Da 10:9; [i]**Eze 2:2**; Da 10:16–18; Zec 4:1
19 [j]**Isa 10:25**; [k]**Ps 102:13**; [l]Hab 2:3
20 [m]**Eze 27:10**
21 [n]Da 10:20; [o]Da 11:3

[a]*25* Or *for a year, two years and half a year*
[a]*12* Or *rebellion, the armies*
[b]*19* Or *because the end will be at the appointed time*

holy people.[p] 25He will cause deceit[q] to prosper, and he will consider himself superior. When they feel secure, he will destroy many and take his stand against the Prince of princes.[r] Yet he will be destroyed, but not by human power.[s]

26"The vision of the evenings and mornings that has been given you is true,[t] but seal[u] up the vision, for it concerns the distant future."[v]

27I, Daniel, was exhausted and lay ill[w] for several days. Then I got up and went about the king's business.[x] I was appalled[y] by the vision; it was beyond understanding.

Daniel's Prayer

9 In the first year of Darius[a] son of Xerxes[a][b] (a Mede by descent), who was made ruler over the Babylonian[b] kingdom—2in the first year of his reign, I, Daniel, understood from the Scriptures, according to the word of the LORD given to Jeremiah the prophet, that the desolation of Jerusalem would last seventy[c] years. 3So I turned to the Lord God and pleaded with him in prayer and petition, in fasting,[d] and in sackcloth and ashes.[e]

4I prayed to the LORD my God and confessed:[f]

"O Lord, the great and awesome God,[g] who keeps his covenant of love[h] with all who love him and obey his commands, 5we have sinned[i] and done wrong.[j] We have been wicked and have rebelled; we have turned away[k] from your commands and laws.[l] 6We have not listened[m] to your servants the prophets,[n] who spoke in your name to our kings, our princes and our fathers,[o] and to all the people of the land.

7"Lord, you are righteous,[p] but this day we are covered with shame[q]—the men of Judah and people of Jerusalem and all Israel, both near and far, in all the countries where you have scattered[r] us because of our unfaithfulness[s] to you.[t] 8O LORD, we and our kings, our princes and our fathers are covered with shame because we have sinned against you.[u] 9The Lord our God is merciful and forgiving,[v] even though we have rebelled against him;[w] 10we have not obeyed the LORD our God or kept the laws he gave us through his servants the prophets.[x] 11All Israel has transgressed[y] your law[z] and turned away, refusing to obey you.

"Therefore the curses[a] and sworn judgments[b] written in the Law of Moses, the servant of God, have been poured out on us, because we have sinned[c] against you. 12You have fulfilled[d] the words spoken against us and against our rulers by bringing upon us great disaster.[e] Under the whole heaven nothing has ever been done like[f] what has been done to Jerusalem.[g] 13Just as it is written in the Law of Moses, all this disaster has come upon us, yet we have not sought the favour of the LORD[h] our God by turning from our sins and giving attention to your truth.[i] 14The LORD did not hesitate to bring the disaster[j] upon us, for the LORD our God is righteous in everything he does;[k] yet we have not obeyed him.[l]

15"Now, O Lord our God, who brought your people out of Egypt with a mighty hand[m] and who made for yourself a name[n] that endures to this day, we have sinned, we have done wrong. 16O Lord, in keeping with all your righteous acts,[o] turn away[p] your anger and your wrath[q] from Jerusalem,[r] your city, your holy hill.[s] Our sins and the iniquities of our fathers have made Jerusalem and your people an object of scorn[t] to all those around us.

17"Now, our God, hear the prayers and petitions of your servant. For your sake, O Lord, look with favour[u] on your desolate sanctuary. 18Give ear,[v] O God, and hear;[w] open your eyes and see[x] the desolation of the city that bears your Name.[y] We do not make requests of you because we are righteous, but because of your great mercy.[z] 19O Lord, listen! O Lord, forgive![a] O Lord, hear and act! For your sake,[b] O my God, do not delay, because your city and your people bear your Name."

24 [p]Da 7:25; 11:36
25 [q]Da 11:23; [r]Da 11:36; [s]**Da 2:34**; 11:21
26 [t]Da 10:1; [u]**Isa 8:16; 29:11**; Rev 10:4; 22:10; [v]Da 10:14
27 [w]Da 10:8; [x]**Da 2:48**; [y]**Isa 21:3; Da 4:19**

Ch. 9

1 [a]**Da 5:31**; [b]**Ezr 4:6**
2 [c]**2Ch 36:21**; Jer 29:10; Zec 1:12; 7:5
3 [d]**2Ch 20:3**; [e]**2Sa 13:19; Ne 1:4**; Jer 29:12; Da 10:12; Jnh 3:6
4 [f]**1Ki 8:30**; [g]**Dt 7:21**; [h]Dt 7:9; **1Ki 8:23**
5 [i]**Jer 8:14**; [j]Ps 106:6; [k]Isa 53:6; [l]ver 11; La 1:20; **3:42**
6 [m]**2Ki 18:12**; [n]**2Ch 36:16; Jer 44:5**; Jas 5:10; Rev 10:7; [o]**2Ch 29:6**
7 [p]**Ezr 9:15; Isa 42:6**; [q]Ezr 9:7; Ps 44:15; [r]Dt 4:27; Am 9:9; [s]**Dt 7:3**; [t]**Jer 3:25; 24:9; Eze 39:23–24**
8 [u]**Ne 9:33; Jer 14:20; Eze 16:63**
9 [v]**Ex 34:7; 2Sa 24:14**; Jer 42:12; [w]**Ne 9:17**; Jer 14:7
10 [x]2Ki 17:13–15; **18:12**; Rev 10:7
11 [y]**Jer 2:29**; [z]2Ki 22:16; [a]**Dt 11:26; 13:15; 28:15**; [b]2Ki 17:23; [c]Isa 1:4–6; Jer 8:5–10
12 [d]**Isa 44:26**; Zec 1:6; [e]**Jer 44:23**; [f]Jer 30:7; [g]Jer 44:2–6; Eze 5:9; Da 12:1; Joel 2:2; Zec 7:12
13 [h]**Dt 4:29; Isa 31:1**; [i]**Isa 9:13**; Jer 2:30
14 [j]**Jer 18:8; 44:27**; [k]**Ge 18:25; 2Ch 12:6; Jer 12:1**; [l]**Ne 9:33; Jer 32:23; 40:3**
15 [m]**Ex 3:20; Jer 32:21**; [n]**Ne 9:10**
16 [o]**Jdg 5:11**; Ps 31:1; [p]**Isa 5:25**; [q]**Ps 85:3**; [r]Jer 32:32; [s]**Ex 15:17; Ps 48:1**; [t]**Ps 39:8; Eze 5:14**
17 [u]Nu 6:24–26; Ps 80:19
18 [v]**Ps 5:1**; [w]Ps 116:1; [x]Ps 80:14; [y]**Dt 28:10; Isa 37:17**; Jer 7:10–12; 25:29; [z]Lk 18:13
19 [a]Ps 44:23; [b]**1Sa 12:22**

[a]1 Hebrew *Ahasuerus* [b]1 Or *Chaldean*

The Seventy "Sevens"

20While I was speaking and praying, confessing[c] my sin and the sin of my people Israel and making my request to the LORD my God for his holy hill[d]— 21while I was still in prayer, Gabriel,[e] the man I had seen in the earlier vision, came to me in swift flight about the time of the evening sacrifice.[f] 22He instructed me and said to me, "Daniel, I have now come to give you insight and understanding.[g] 23As soon as you began to pray,[h] an answer was given, which I have come to tell you, for you are highly esteemed.[i] Therefore, consider the message and understand the vision:[j]

24"Seventy 'sevens'[c] are decreed for your people and your holy city[k] to finish[d] transgression, to put an end to sin, to atone[l] for wickedness, to bring in everlasting righteousness,[m] to seal up vision and prophecy and to anoint the most holy.[e]

25"Know and understand this: From the issuing of the decree[f] to restore and rebuild[n] Jerusalem until the Anointed One,[g][o] the ruler,[p] comes, there will be seven 'sevens', and sixty-two 'sevens'. It will be rebuilt with streets and a trench, but in times of trouble.[q] 26After the sixty-two 'sevens', the Anointed One will be cut off[r] and will have nothing.[h] The people of the ruler who will come will destroy the city and the sanctuary. The end will come like a flood:[s] War will continue until the end, and desolations[t] have been decreed.[u] 27He will confirm a covenant with many for one 'seven'.[i] In the middle of the 'seven'[i] he will put an end to sacrifice and offering. And on a wing ⌊of the temple⌋ he will set up an abomination that causes desolation, until the end that is decreed[v] is poured out on him.[j]"[k]

Daniel's Vision of a Man

10 In the third year of Cyrus[a] king of Persia, a revelation was given to Daniel (who was called Belteshazzar).[b] Its message was true[c] and it concerned a great war.[a] The understanding of the message came to him in a vision.

2At that time I, Daniel, mourned[d] for three weeks. 3I ate no choice food; no meat or wine touched my lips;[e] and I used no lotions at all until the three weeks were over.

4On the twenty-fourth day of the first month, as I was standing on the bank[f] of the great river, the Tigris,[g] 5I looked up[h] and there before me was a man dressed in linen,[i] with a belt of the finest gold[j] round his waist. 6His body was like chrysolite,[k] his face like lightning,[l] his eyes like flaming torches,[m] his arms and legs like the gleam of burnished bronze,[n] and his voice[o] like the sound of a multitude.

7I, Daniel, was the only one who saw the vision; the men with me did not see it,[p] but such terror overwhelmed them that they fled and hid themselves. 8So I was left alone,[q] gazing at this great vision; I had no strength left,[r] my face turned deathly pale[s] and I was helpless.[t] 9Then I heard him speaking, and as I listened to him, I fell into a deep sleep, my face to the ground.[u]

10A hand touched me[v] and set me trembling on my hands and knees.[w] 11He said, "Daniel, you who are highly esteemed,[x] consider carefully the words I am about to speak to you, and stand up,[y] for I have now been sent to you." And when he said this to me, I stood up trembling.

12Then he continued, "Do not be afraid,[z] Daniel. Since the first day that you set your mind to gain understanding and to humble[a] yourself before your God, your words[b] were heard, and I have come in response to them.[c] 13But the prince[d] of the Persian kingdom resisted me twenty-one days. Then Michael,[e] one of the chief princes, came to help me, because I was detained there with the king of Persia. 14Now I have come to explain[f] to you what will happen to your people in the future,[g] for the vision concerns a time yet to come.[h]"

15While he was saying this to me, I bowed with my face towards the ground and was speechless.[i] 16Then one who looked like a man[b] touched my lips, and I opened my mouth and began to speak.[j] I said to the one standing before me, "I am overcome with anguish[k] because of the vision, my lord, and I am helpless. 17How can I, your

20 [c]**Ezr 10:1;** [d]ver 3; Ps 145:18; **Isa 58:9**
21 [e]**Da 8:16; Lk 1:19;** [f]**Ex 29:39**
22 [g]**Da 7:16;** 10:14; Am 3:7
23 [h]**Isa 65:24;** [i]Da 10:19; Lk 1:28; [j]Da 10:11–12; Mt 24:15
24 [k]**Isa 1:26;** [l]**Isa 53:10;** [m]**Isa 56:1;** Heb 9:12
25 [n]**Ezr 4:24; 6:15;** [o]Mt 1:17; Jn 4:25; [p]**1Sa 13:14;** [q]**Ezr 3:3**
26 [r]**Isa 53:8;** Mt 16:21; [s]Isa 28:2; Da 11:10; Na 1:8; [t]**Ps 46:8;** [u]Isa 61:1; **Eze 4:5–6;** Hag 2:23; Zec 4:14
27 [v]**Isa 10:22**

Ch. 10

1 [a]**Da 1:21;** [b]**Da 1:7;** [c]Da 8:26
2 [d]**Ezr 9:4**
3 [e]**Da 6:18**
4 [f]Da 12:5; [g]**Ge 2:14**
5 [h]Da 8:3; [i]**Eze 9:2;** Rev 15:6; [j]Jer 10:9
6 [k]**Ex 28:20;** [l]Mt 17:2; **28:3;** [m]Job 41:19; Rev 19:12; [n]**Eze 1:7; Rev 1:15;** [o]**Eze 1:24**
7 [p]2Ki 6:17–20; Ac 9:7
8 [q]Ge 32:24; [r]**Job 4:14;** Da 8:27; [s]**Job 4:15;** [t]Hab 3:16
9 [u]Da 8:18; Mt 17:6
10 [v]Jer 1:9; [w]Rev 1:17
11 [x]**Ge 6:9;** Da 9:23; [y]**Eze 2:1**
12 [z]**Mt 14:27;** [a]**Lev 16:31; Da 9:3;** [b]**Isa 65:24;** [c]Da 9:20
13 [d]Isa 24:21; [e]ver 21; Da 12:1; **Jude 9**
14 [f]**Da 9:22;** [g]**Eze 12:27;** [h]**Da 2:28;** 8:26; Hab 2:3
15 [i]Eze 24:27; Lk 1:20
16 [j]**Isa 6:7;** Jer 1:9; Da 8:15–18; [k]**Isa 21:3**

c24 Or *'weeks'*; also in verses 25 and 26
d24 Or *restrain*
e24 Or *Most Holy Place*; or *most holy One*
f25 Or *word*
g25 Or *an anointed one*; also in verse 26
h26 Or *off and will have no-one*; or *off, but not for himself*
i27 Or *'week'* j27 Or *it*
k27 Or *And one who causes desolation will come upon the pinnacle of the abominable ⌊temple⌋, until the end that is decreed is poured out on the desolated ⌊city⌋*
a1 Or *true and burdensome*
b16 Most manuscripts of the Masoretic Text; one manuscript of the Masoretic Text, Dead Sea Scrolls and Septuagint *Then something that looked like a man's hand*

servant, talk with you, my lord? My
strength is gone and I can hardly
breathe."[l]
18Again the one who looked like a
man touched[m] me and gave me
strength.[n] 19"Do not be afraid, O man
highly esteemed,"[o] he said. "Peace![p] Be
strong now; be strong."[q]
When he spoke to me, I was strength-
ened and said, "Speak, my lord, since
you have given me strength."[r]
20So he said, "Do you know why I
have come to you? Soon I will return to
fight against the prince of Persia, and
when I go, the prince of Greece[s] will
come; 21but first I will tell you what is
written in the Book of Truth.[t] (No-one
supports me against them except
11 Michael,[u] your prince. 1And in
the first year of Darius[a] the
Mede, I took my stand to support and
protect him.)

The Kings of the South and the North

2"Now then, I tell you the truth:[b]
Three more kings will appear in Persia,
and then a fourth, who will be far richer
than all the others. When he has gained
power by his wealth, he will stir up
everyone against the kingdom of
Greece.[c] 3Then a mighty king will
appear, who will rule with great power
and do as he pleases.[d] 4After he has
appeared, his empire will be broken up
and parcelled out towards the four
winds of heaven.[e] It will not go to his
descendants, nor will it have the power
he exercised, because his empire will be
uprooted[f] and given to others.
5"The king of the South will become
strong, but one of his commanders will
become even stronger than he and will
rule his own kingdom with great
power. 6After some years, they will
become allies. The daughter of the king
of the South will go to the king of the
North to make an alliance, but she will
not retain her power, and he and his
power[a] will not last. In those days she
will be handed over, together with her
royal escort and her father[b] and the one
who supported her.
7"One from her family line will arise
to take her place. He will attack the
forces of the king of the North[g] and
enter his fortress; he will fight against
them and be victorious. 8He will also
seize their gods,[h] their metal images and
their valuable articles of silver and gold
and carry them off to Egypt.[i] For some
years he will leave the king of the North
alone. 9Then the king of the North will
invade the realm of the king of the
South but will retreat to his own coun-
try. 10His sons will prepare for war and
assemble a great army, which will
sweep on like an irresistible flood[j] and
carry the battle as far as his fortress.
11"Then the king of the South will
march out in rage and fight against the
king of the North, who will raise a large
army, but it will be defeated.[k] 12When
the army is carried off, the king of the
South will be filled with pride and will
slaughter many thousands, yet he will
not remain triumphant. 13For the king of
the North will muster another army,
larger than the first; and after several
years, he will advance with a huge army
fully equipped.
14"In those times many will rise
against the king of the South. The vio-
lent men among your own people will
rebel in fulfilment of the vision, but
without success. 15Then the king of the
North will come and build up siege
ramps[l] and will capture a fortified city.
The forces of the South will be power-
less to resist; even their best troops will
not have the strength to stand. 16The
invader will do as he pleases;[m] no-one
will be able to stand against him.[n] He
will establish himself in the Beautiful
Land and will have the power to destroy
it.[o] 17He will determine to come with the
might of his entire kingdom and will
make an alliance with the king of the
South. And he will give him a daughter
in marriage in order to overthrow the
kingdom, but his plans[c] will not suc-
ceed[p] or help him. 18Then he will turn
his attention to the coastlands[q] and will
take many of them, but a commander
will put an end to his insolence and will
turn his insolence back upon him.[r]
19After this, he will turn back towards
the fortresses of his own country but
will stumble and fall,[s] to be seen no
more.[t]
20"His successor will send out a tax
collector to maintain the royal splen-
dour.[u] In a few years, however, he will
be destroyed, yet not in anger or in
battle.
21"He will be succeeded by a
contemptible[v] person who has not been
given the honour of royalty.[w] He will
invade the kingdom when its people
feel secure, and he will seize it through
intrigue. 22Then an overwhelming army

17 [l]Da 4:19
18 [m]ver 16; [n]Da 8:18
19 [o]Da 9:23; [p]Jdg 6:23; Isa 35:4; [q]Jos 1:9; [r]Isa 6:1–8
20 [s]Da 8:21; 11:2
21 [t]Da 11:2; [u]ver 13; Jude 9

Ch. 11

1 [a]Da 5:31
2 [b]Da 10:21; [c]Da 10:20
3 [d]Da 8:4,21
4 [e]Da 7:2; 8:22; [f]Jer 42:10
7 [g]ver 6
8 [h]Isa 37:19; 46:1–2; [i]Jer 43:12
10 [j]Isa 8:8; Jer 46:8; Da 9:26
11 [k]Da 8:7–8
15 [l]Eze 4:2
16 [m]Da 8:4; [n]Jos 1:5; Da 8:7; [o]Da 8:9
17 [p]Ps 20:4
18 [q]Isa 66:19; Jer 25:22; [r]Hos 12:14
19 [s]Ps 27:2; 46:2; [t]Ps 37:36; Eze 26:21
20 [u]Isa 60:17
21 [v]Da 4:17; [w]Da 8:25

[a]6 Or *offspring*
[b]6 Or *child* (see Vulgate and Syriac)
[c]17 Or *but she*

will be swept away[x] before him; both it and a prince of the covenant will be destroyed.[y] 23After coming to an agreement with him, he will act deceitfully,[z] and with only a few people he will rise to power. 24When the richest provinces feel secure, he will invade them and will achieve what neither his fathers nor his forefathers did. He will distribute plunder, loot and wealth among his followers.[a] He will plot the overthrow of fortresses—but only for a time.

25"With a large army he will stir up his strength and courage against the king of the South. The king of the South will wage war with a large and very powerful army, but he will not be able to stand because of the plots devised against him. 26Those who eat from the king's provisions will try to destroy him; his army will be swept away, and many will fall in battle. 27The two kings, with their hearts bent on evil,[b] will sit at the same table and lie[c] to each other, but to no avail, because an end will still come at the appointed time.[d] 28The king of the North will return to his own country with great wealth, but his heart will be set against the holy covenant. He will take action against it and then return to his own country.

29"At the appointed time he will invade the South again, but this time the outcome will be different from what it was before. 30Ships of the western coastlands[d][e] will oppose him, and he will lose heart.[f] Then he will turn back and vent his fury[g] against the holy covenant. He will return and show favour to those who forsake the holy covenant.

31"His armed forces will rise up to desecrate the temple fortress and will abolish the daily sacrifice.[h] Then they will set up the abomination that causes desolation.[i] 32With flattery he will corrupt those who have violated the covenant, but the people who know their God will firmly resist[j] him.

33"Those who are wise will instruct[k] many, though for a time they will fall by the sword or be burned or captured or plundered.[l] 34When they fall, they will receive a little help, and many who are not sincere[m] will join them. 35Some of the wise will stumble, so that they may be refined,[n] purified and made spotless until the time of the end, for it will still come at the appointed time.

The King Who Exalts Himself

36"The king will do as he pleases. He will exalt and magnify himself[o] above every god and will say unheard-of things[p] against the God of gods.[q] He will be successful until the time of wrath[r] is completed, for what has been determined must take place.[s] 37He will show no regard for the gods of his fathers or for the one desired by women, nor will he regard any god, but will exalt himself above them all. 38Instead of them, he will honour a god of fortresses; a god unknown to his fathers he will honour with gold and silver, with precious stones and costly gifts. 39He will attack the mightiest fortresses with the help of a foreign god and will greatly honour those who acknowledge him. He will make them rulers over many people and will distribute the land at a price.[e]

40"At the time of the end the king of the South[t] will engage him in battle, and the king of the North will storm[u] out against him with chariots and cavalry and a great fleet of ships. He will invade many countries and sweep through them like a flood.[v] 41He will also invade the Beautiful Land.[w] Many countries will fall, but Edom,[x] Moab[y] and the leaders of Ammon will be delivered from his hand. 42He will extend his power over many countries; Egypt will not escape. 43He will gain control of the treasures of gold and silver and all the riches of Egypt,[z] with the Libyans[a] and Nubians in submission. 44But reports from the east and the north will alarm him, and he will set out in a great rage to destroy and annihilate many. 45He will pitch his royal tents between the seas at[f] the beautiful holy mountain.[b] Yet he will come to his end, and no-one will help him.

The End Times

12 "At that time Michael,[a] the great prince who protects your people, will arise. There will be a time of distress[b] such as has not happened from the beginning of nations until then. But at that time your people—everyone whose name is found written in the book[c]—will be delivered.[d] 2Multitudes who sleep in the dust of the earth will awake:[e] some to everlasting life, others to shame and everlasting contempt.[f] 3Those who are wise[a][g] will shine[h] like the brightness of the heavens, and those who lead many to righteousness,[i] like the stars for ever and ever.[j] 4But you, Daniel, close up and seal[k] the

22 [x]**Isa 28:15**; [y]Da 8:10–11
23 [z]Da 8:25
24 [a]Ne 9:25
27 [b]Ps 64:6; [c]Ps 12:2; Jer 9:5; [d]Hab 2:3
30 [e]**Ge 10:4**; [f]**1Sa 17:32**; [g]**Job 15:13**
31 [h]Hos 3:4; [i]**Jer 19:4**; Da 8:11–13; **9:27**; Mt 24:15*; Mk 13:14*
32 [j]Mic 5:7–9
33 [k]Da 12:3; Mal 2:7; [l]Mt 24:9; Jn 16:2; Heb 11:32–38
34 [m]Mt 7:15; Ro 16:18
35 [n]**Job 28:1**; **Ps 78:38**; **Isa 48:10**; Da 12:10; Zec 13:9; Jn 15:2
36 [o]Jude 16; [p]Rev 13:5–6; [q]**Dt 10:17**; **Isa 14:13–14**; **Da 7:25**; 8:11–12, 25; 2Th 2:4; [r]**Isa 10:25**; 26:20; [s]Eze 35:13; **Da 8:24**
40 [t]**Isa 21:1**; [u]Isa 5:28; [v]**Isa 8:7**; **Eze 38:4**
41 [w]**Eze 20:6**; Mal 3:12; [x]**Isa 11:14**; [y]**Jer 48:47**
43 [z]**Eze 30:4**; [a]2Ch 12:3; Na 3:9
45 [b]**Isa 2:2**,4; Da 8:9

Ch. 12

1 [a]**Da 10:13**; Jude 9; [b]**Da 9:12**; **Mt 24:21**; Mk 13:19; Rev 16:18; [c]**Ex 32:32**; **Ps 56:8**; **Jer 17:13**; **Lk 10:20**; [d]Jer 30:7
2 [e]Jn 11:24; [f]**Isa 26:19**; Mt 25:46
3 [g]**Da 11:33**; [h]Mt 13:43; Jn 5:35; Php 2:15; [i]**Isa 6:7**; [j]**Pr 4:18**; 1Co 15:42
4 [k]**Isa 8:16**

d30 Hebrew *of Kittim*
e39 Or *land for a reward*
f45 Or *the sea and*
a3 Or *who impart wisdom*

words of the scroll until the time of the
end.[l] Many will go here and there[m] to
increase knowledge."

5Then I, Daniel, looked, and there
before me stood two others, one on this
bank of the river and one on the oppo-
site bank.[n] 6One of them said to the man
clothed in linen,[o] who was above the
waters of the river, "How long will it be
before these astonishing things are
fulfilled?"[p]

7The man clothed in linen, who was
above the waters of the river, lifted his
right hand[q] and his left hand towards
heaven, and I heard him swear by him
who lives for ever,[r] saying, "It will be
for a time, times and half a time.[b][s] When
the power of the holy people[t] has been
finally broken, all these things will be
completed."[u]

8I heard, but I did not understand. So
I asked, "My lord, what will the
outcome of all this be?"

9He replied, "Go your way, Daniel,
because the words are closed up and
sealed[v] until the time of the end.[w]
10Many will be purified, made spotless
and refined,[x] but the wicked will con-
tinue to be wicked.[y] None of the wicked
will understand, but those who are wise
will understand.[z]

11"From the time that the daily sac-
rifice[a] is abolished and the abomination
that causes desolation[b] is set up, there
will be 1,290 days.[c] 12Blessed is the one
who waits[d] for and reaches the end of
the 1,335 days.[e]

13"As for you, go your way till the
end.[f] You will rest,[g] and then at the end
of the days you will rise to receive your
allotted inheritance.[h][i]"

4 [l]ver 9,13; Rev 22:10; [m]Jer 5:1
5 [n]Da 10:4
6 [o]**Eze 9:2;** [p]Da 8:13
7 [q]**Ge 14:22;** [r]**Da 6:26;** Rev 10:5–6; [s]**Da 7:25; Rev 11:2;** [t]**Da 8:24;** [u]Lk 21:24; Rev 10:7
9 [v]**Isa 29:11;** [w]**ver 4**
10 [x]**Isa 1:25; Da 11:35;** [y]**Isa 32:7;** Rev 22:11; [z]Hos 14:9
11 [a]**Ex 29:38;** [b]**Da 8:11; 9:27;** Mt 24:15*; Mk 13:14*; [c]Rev 11:2
12 [d]**Isa 30:18;** [e]**Eze 4:5–6;** Da 8:14
13 [f]**ver 4;** [g]Isa 57:2; [h]Ps 16:5; Rev 14:13; [i]Mt 10:22; Jas 1:12

b7 Or *a year, two years and half a year*

Hosea

1 The word of the LORD that came[a] to
Hosea son of Beeri during the
reigns of Uzziah,[b] Jotham,[c] Ahaz[d] and
Hezekiah,[e] kings of Judah,[f] and during
the reign of Jeroboam[g] son of Joash king
of Israel:[h]

Hosea's Wife and Children

2 When the LORD began to speak
through Hosea, the LORD said to him,
"Go, take to yourself an adulterous[i]
wife and children of unfaithfulness,
because the land is guilty of the vilest
adultery[j] in departing from the LORD."
3 So he married Gomer[k] daughter of
Diblaim, and she conceived and bore
him a son.
4 Then the LORD said to Hosea, "Call
him Jezreel,[l] because I will soon punish
the house of Jehu for the massacre at
Jezreel, and I will put an end to the
kingdom of Israel. 5 In that day I will
break Israel's bow in the Valley of
Jezreel.[m]"
6 Gomer[n] conceived again and gave
birth to a daughter. Then the LORD said
to Hosea, "Call her Lo-Ruhamah,[a][o] for I
will no longer show love to the house of
Israel,[p] that I should at all forgive them.
7 Yet I will show love to the house of
Judah; and I will save them—not by
bow,[q] sword or battle, or by horses and
horsemen, but by the LORD their God.[r]"
8 After she had weaned Lo-Ruhamah,[s]
Gomer had another son. 9 Then the LORD
said, "Call him Lo-Ammi,[b] for you are
not my people, and I am not your God.[t]
10 "Yet the Israelites will be like the
sand on the seashore, which cannot be
measured or counted.[u] In the place
where it was said to them, 'You are not
my people', they will be called 'sons of
the living God'.[v][w] 11 The people of Judah
and the people of Israel will be
reunited,[x] and they will appoint one
leader[y] and will come up out of the
land,[z] for great will be the day of
Jezreel.[a]

2 "Say of your brothers, 'My
people', and of your sisters,
'My loved one'.[a]

Israel Punished and Restored

2 "Rebuke your mother,[b] rebuke her,
for she is not my wife,
and I am not her husband.
Let her remove the adulterous[c] look
from her face
and the unfaithfulness from
between her breasts.
3 Otherwise I will strip[d] her naked
and make her as bare as on the day
she was born;[e]
I will make her like a desert,[f]
turn her into a parched land,
and slay her with thirst.
4 I will not show my love to her
children,[g]
because they are the children of
adultery.[h]
5 Their mother has been unfaithful
and has conceived them in disgrace.
She said, 'I will go after my lovers,[i]
who give me my food and my
water,
my wool and my linen, my oil and
my drink.'[j]
6 Therefore I will block her path with
thornbushes;
I will wall her in so that she cannot
find her way.[k]
7 She will chase after her lovers but not
catch them;
she will look for them but not find
them.[l]
Then she will say,
'I will go back to my husband[m] as at
first,[n]
for then I was better off[o] than now.'
8 She has not acknowledged[p] that I was
the one
who gave her the grain, the new
wine and oil,[q]
who lavished on her the silver and
gold[r]—
which they used for Baal.[s]

Ch. 1

1 [a]Jer 1:2; [b]2Ki 14:21; [c]1Ch 3:12; [d]1Ch 3:13; [e]1Ch 3:13; [f]Isa 1:1; Mic 1:1; [g]2Ki 13:13; [h]Am 1:1
2 [i]Jer 3:1; Hos 2:2,5; 3:1; [j]Dt 31:16; Jer 3:14; Eze 23:3–21; Hos 5:3
3 [k]ver 6
4 [l]ver 11; 1Sa 29:1; 1Ki 18:45; 2Ki 10:1–14; Hos 2:22
5 [m]Jos 15:56; 1Sa 29:1; 2Ki 15:29
6 [n]ver 3; [o]ver 8; Hos 2:23; [p]Hos 2:4
7 [q]Ps 44:6; [r]Zec 4:6
8 [s]ver 6
9 [t]ver 10; Eze 11:19–20; 1Pe 2:10
10 [u]Ge 22:17; Jer 33:22; [v]ver 9; Hos 2:23; Ro 9:26*; [w]Jos 3:10
11 [x]Isa 11:12–13; [y]Jer 23:5–8; 30:9; [z]Eze 37:15–28; [a]ver 4

Ch. 2

1 [a]ver 23; 1Pe 2:10
2 [b]ver 5; Isa 50:1; Hos 1:2; 4:5; [c]Isa 1:21; Eze 23:45
3 [d]Eze 16:37; [e]Eze 16:4,22; [f]Isa 32:13–14
4 [g]Eze 8:18; Hos 1:6; [h]Hos 5:7
5 [i]Jer 3:6; Hos 1:2; [j]Jer 44:17–18
6 [k]Job 3:23; 19:8; La 3:9
7 [l]Hos 5:13; [m]Isa 54:5; [n]Jer 2:2; 3:1; [o]Eze 16:8
8 [p]Isa 1:3; [q]Nu 18:12; [r]Dt 8:18; [s]ver 13; Eze 16:15–19; Hos 8:4

[a]6 *Lo-Ruhamah* means *not loved*.
[b]9 *Lo-Ammi* means *not my people*.

9"Therefore I will take away my grain[t]
when it ripens,
and my new wine[u] when it is ready.
I will take back my wool and my linen,
intended to cover her nakedness.
10So now I will expose[v] her lewdness
before the eyes of her lovers;[w]
no-one will take her out of my
hands.[x]
11I will stop[y] all her celebrations:[z]
her yearly festivals, her New
Moons,
her Sabbath days—all her
appointed feasts.[a]
12I will ruin her vines[b] and her fig-trees,[c]
which she said were her pay from
her lovers;[d]
I will make them a thicket,[e]
and wild animals will devour them.[f]
13I will punish her for the days
she burned incense[g] to the Baals;[h]
she decked herself with rings and
jewellery,[i]
and went after her lovers,[j]
but me she forgot,[k]"
declares the LORD.[l]

14"Therefore I am now going to allure
her;
I will lead her into the desert[m]
and speak tenderly to her.
15There I will give her back her
vineyards,
and will make the Valley of Achor[a] [n]
a door of hope.
There she will sing[b] [o] as in the days of
her youth,[p]
as in the day she came up out of
Egypt.[q]

16"In that day," declares the LORD,
"you will call me 'my husband';[r]
you will no longer call me 'my
master'.[c]
17I will remove the names of the Baals
from her lips;[s]
no longer will their names be
invoked.[t]
18In that day I will make a covenant for
them
with the beasts of the field and the
birds of the air
and the creatures that move along
the ground.[u]
Bow and sword and battle
I will abolish[v] from the land,
so that all may lie down in safety.[w]
19I will betroth[x] you to me for ever;
I will betroth you in[d] righteousness
and justice,[y]
in[e] love and compassion.[z]
20I will betroth you in faithfulness,
and you will acknowledge[a] the
LORD.[b]

9 [t]Hos 8:7; [u]Hos 9:2
10 [v]Eze 23:10; [w]Jer 13:26; [x]**Eze 16:37**
11 [y]Jer 7:34; [z]**Isa 24:8**; [a]**Isa 1:14**; Jer 16:9; Hos 3:4; 9:5; Am 5:21; 8:10
12 [b]**Isa 7:23**; **Jer 8:13**; [c]**Jer 5:17**; [d]**Jer 3:1**; [e]**Isa 5:6**; [f]Hos 5:7; 13:8
13 [g]Isa 65:7; [h]ver 8; **Jer 7:9**; Hos 11:2; [i]**Eze 16:17**; **23:40**; [j]Hos 4:13; [k]Hos 4:6; 8:14; 13:6; [l]**Jer 44:17**; Hos 13:1
14 [m]**Eze 19:13**
15 [n]**Jos 7:24**,26; [o]Ex 15:1–18; [p]**Jer 2:2**; **Eze 16:22**; [q]**Eze 28:26**; Hos 12:9
16 [r]**Isa 54:5**
17 [s]Ex 23:13; Ps 16:4; [t]**Jos 23:7**; Zec 13:2
18 [u]**Job 5:22**; [v]**Ps 46:9**; **Isa 2:4**; Zec 9:10; [w]**Job 5:23**; **Jer 23:6**; Eze 34:25
19 [x]**Isa 62:4**; 2Co 11:2; [y]**Isa 1:27**; [z]**Isa 54:8**
20 [a]Jer 31:34; Hos 4:1; 6:6; 13:4; [b]**Eze 16:8**
21 [c]Isa 55:10; Zec 8:12; Mal 3:10–11
22 [d]**Jer 31:12**; Hos 14:7; Joel 2:19; [e]**Eze 36:29–30**; **Hos 1:4**
23 [f]**Jer 31:27**; [g]**Hos 1:6**; [h]**ver 1**; **Isa 19:25**; **Hos 1:10**; [i]**Jer 29:12**; Ro 9:25*; 1Pe 2:10

Ch. 3
1 [a]**Hos 1:2**; [b]**2Sa 6:19**
4 [c]Hos 13:11; [d]Da 11:31; **Hos 2:11**; [e]Hos 10:1; [f]**Ex 25:7**; [g]Jdg 17:5–6; 18:14–17; **La 2:9**; Zec 10:2
5 [h]**Dt 4:29**; **Isa 9:13**; **10:20**; Hos 5:15; Mic 4:1–2; [i]**1Sa 13:14**; [j]**Ps 18:45**; [k]**Dt 4:30**; **Jer 50:4–5**; Hos 11:10

21"In that day I will respond,"
declares the LORD—
"I will respond[c] to the skies,
and they will respond to the earth;
22and the earth will respond to the
grain,
the new wine and oil,[d]
and they will respond to Jezreel.[f] [e]
23I will plant[f] her for myself in the land;
I will show my love to the one I
called 'Not my loved one.[g] [g]'
I will say to those called 'Not my
people',[h] 'You are my people';[h]
and they will say, 'You are my
God.[i]'"

Hosea's Reconciliation With His Wife

3 The LORD said to me, "Go, show
your love to your wife again,
though she is loved by another and is an
adulteress.[a] Love her as the LORD loves
the Israelites, though they turn to other
gods and love the sacred raisin cakes.[b]"
2So I bought her for fifteen shekels[a] of
silver and about a homer and a lethek[b]
of barley. 3Then I told her, "You are to
live with[c] me for many days; you must
not be a prostitute or be intimate with
any man, and I will live with[c] you."
4For the Israelites will live for many
days without king or prince,[c] without
sacrifice[d] or sacred stones,[e] without
ephod[f] or idol.[g] 5Afterwards the Israel-
ites will return and seek[h] the LORD their
God and David their king.[i] They will
come trembling[j] to the LORD and to his
blessings in the last days.[k]

The Charge Against Israel

4 Hear the word of the LORD, you
Israelites,
because the LORD has a charge[a] to
bring
against you who live in the land:[b]
"There is no faithfulness,[c] no love,
no acknowledgment[d] of God in the
land.[e]
2There is only cursing,[a] lying[f] and
murder,[g]

Ch. 4
1 [a]**Job 10:2**; **Jer 2:9**; [b]Joel 1:2,14; [c]**Pr 24:2**; [d]**Pr 10:21**; **Isa 1:3**; Jer 7:28; **Hos 2:20**; [e]**Jer 51:5**
2 [f]Isa 59:3; Hos 7:3; 10:4; 11:12; [g]Hos 5:2; 6:9

[a]15 *Achor* means *trouble.* [b]15 Or *respond*
[c]16 Hebrew *baal* [d]19 Or *with*; also in verse 20
[e]19 Or *with* [f]22 *Jezreel* means *God plants.*
[g]23 Hebrew *Lo-Ruhamah*
[h]23 Hebrew *Lo-Ammi*
[a]2 That is, about 6 ounces (about 170 grams)
[b]2 That is, probably about 9 bushels (about 330 litres) [c]3 Or *wait for*
[a]2 That is, to pronounce a curse upon

stealing[h] and adultery;[i]
they break all bounds,
and bloodshed follows bloodshed.[j]
3Because of this the land mourns,[b][k]
and all who live in it waste away;[l]
the beasts of the field and the birds of the air
and the fish of the sea are dying.[m]

4"But let no man bring a charge,
let no man accuse another,
for your people are like those
who bring charges against a priest.[n]
5You stumble[o] day and night,
and the prophets stumble with you.
So I will destroy your mother[p]—
6 my people are destroyed from lack of knowledge.[q]

"Because you have rejected knowledge,
I also reject you as my priests;
because you have ignored the law[r] of your God,
I also will ignore your children.
7The more the priests increased,
the more they sinned against me;
they exchanged[c] their[d] Glory[s] for
something disgraceful.[t]
8They feed on the sins of my people
and relish their wickedness.[u]
9And it will be: Like people, like priests.[v]
I will punish both of them for their ways
and repay them for their deeds.[w]

10"They will eat but not have enough;[x]
they will engage in prostitution[y] but not increase,
because they have deserted[z] the LORD
to give themselves 11to prostitution,[a]
to old wine[b] and new,
which take away the
understanding[c] 12of my people.
They consult a wooden idol[d]
and are answered by a stick of wood.[e]
A spirit of prostitution[f] leads them astray;[g]
they are unfaithful[h] to their God.
13They sacrifice on the mountaintops
and burn offerings on the hills,
under oak,[i] poplar and terebinth,
where the shade is pleasant.[j]
Therefore your daughters turn to prostitution[k]
and your daughters-in-law to adultery.[l]

14"I will not punish your daughters
when they turn to prostitution,
nor your daughters-in-law
when they commit adultery,
because the men themselves consort with harlots[m]
and sacrifice with
shrine-prostitutes[n]—
a people without understanding[o]
will come to ruin![p]

15"Though you commit adultery,
O Israel,
let not Judah become guilty.

"Do not go to Gilgal;[q]
do not go up to Beth Aven.[e][r]
And do not swear, 'As surely as the LORD lives!'[s]
16The Israelites are stubborn,[t]
like a stubborn heifer.[u]
How then can the LORD pasture them
like lambs[v] in a meadow?
17Ephraim is joined to idols;
leave him alone!
18Even when their drinks are gone,
they continue their prostitution;
their rulers dearly love shameful ways.
19A whirlwind[w] will sweep them away,
and their sacrifices will bring them shame.[x]

Judgment Against Israel

5 "Hear this, you priests!
Pay attention, you Israelites!
Listen, O royal house!
This judgment[a] is against you:
You have been a snare[b] at Mizpah,
a net[c] spread out on Tabor.
2The rebels are deep in slaughter.[d]
I will discipline all of them.[e]
3I know all about Ephraim;
Israel is not hidden[f] from me.
Ephraim, you have now turned to prostitution;
Israel is corrupt.[g]

4"Their deeds do not permit them
to return[h] to their God.
A spirit of prostitution[i] is in their heart;
they do not acknowledge[j] the LORD.
5Israel's arrogance testifies[k] against them;
the Israelites, even Ephraim,
stumble[l] in their sin;

2 [h]Hos 7:1; [i]Jer 9:2; [j]2Ki 21:16; Isa 1:15; Eze 22:2,9; Hos 5:2; 10:13
3 [k]Jer 4:28; [l]Isa 15:6; 33:9; [m]Jer 4:25; 9:10; Eze 38:20; Zep 1:3
4 [n]Dt 17:12; Eze 3:26
5 [o]Eze 7:19; 14:7; [p]Hos 2:2
6 [q]Pr 10:21; Isa 1:3; Hos 2:13; Mal 2:7–8; [r]Hos 8:1,12
7 [s]Hab 2:16; [t]Hos 9:11; 10:1,6; 13:6
8 [u]Isa 56:11; Hos 14:1; Mic 3:11
9 [v]Isa 24:2; [w]Jer 5:31; Hos 8:13; 9:9,15; 10:10; 12:2
10 [x]Lev 26:26; Isa 55:2; Mic 6:14; [y]Eze 22:9; [z]Hos 7:14; 9:17
11 [a]ver 14; Hos 5:4; [b]Lev 10:9; 1Sa 25:36; [c]Pr 20:1
12 [d]Jer 2:27; [e]Hab 2:19; [f]Nu 15:39; [g]Isa 44:20; [h]Ps 73:27
13 [i]Isa 1:29; [j]Jer 3:6; Hos 10:8; 11:2; [k]Jer 2:20; Am 7:17; [l]Hos 2:13
14 [m]ver 11; [n]Ge 38:21; Hos 9:10; [o]Pr 10:21; [p]ver 19
15 [q]Hos 9:15; 12:11; Am 4:4; 5:5; [r]Jos 7:2; Hos 5:8; [s]Jer 4:2
16 [t]Ex 32:9; [u]Jer 31:18; [v]Isa 5:17; 7:25
19 [w]Hos 12:1; 13:15; [x]ver 13–14; Isa 1:29

Ch. 5

1 [a]Job 10:2; [b]Hos 6:9; 9:8; [c]Jer 5:26
2 [d]Hos 4:2; [e]Hos 9:15
3 [f]Am 5:12; [g]Eze 23:7; Hos 1:2; 6:10
4 [h]Hos 7:10; [i]Hos 4:11; [j]Jer 4:22; Hos 4:6
5 [k]Isa 3:9; Jer 2:19; Hos 7:10; [l]Eze 14:7

b3 Or *dries up*
c7 Syriac and an ancient Hebrew scribal tradition; Masoretic Text *I will exchange*
d7 Masoretic Text; an ancient Hebrew scribal tradition *my*
e15 *Beth Aven* means *house of wickedness* (a name for Bethel, which means *house of God*).

Judah also stumbles with them.[m]
6When they go with their flocks and herds
to seek the LORD,[n]
they will not find him;
he has withdrawn[o] himself from them.
7They are unfaithful[p] to the LORD;
they give birth to illegitimate[q] children.
Now their New Moon festivals[r]
will devour[s] them and their fields.

8"Sound the trumpet[t] in Gibeah,[u]
the horn in Ramah.[v]
Raise the battle cry in Beth Aven[a];[w]
lead on, O Benjamin.
9Ephraim will be laid waste[x]
on the day of reckoning.[y]
Among the tribes of Israel
I proclaim what is certain.[z]
10Judah's leaders are like those
who move boundary stones.[a]
I will pour out my wrath[b] on them
like a flood of water.
11Ephraim is oppressed,
trampled in judgment,
intent on pursuing idols.[b][c]
12I am like a moth[d] to Ephraim,
like rot[e] to the people of Judah.

13"When Ephraim[f] saw his sickness,
and Judah his sores,
then Ephraim turned to Assyria,[g]
and sent to the great king for help.[h]
But he is not able to cure[i] you,
not able to heal your sores.[j]
14For I will be like a lion[k] to Ephraim,
like a great lion to Judah.
I will tear them to pieces[l] and go away;
I will carry them off, with no-one to rescue them.[m]
15Then I will go back to my place[n]
until they admit their guilt.[o]
And they will seek my face;[p]
in their misery[q] they will earnestly seek me."[r]

Israel Unrepentant

6 "Come, let us return[a] to the LORD.
He has torn us to pieces[b]
but he will heal us;[c]
he has injured us
but he will bind up our wounds.[d]
2After two days he will revive us;[e]
on the third day[f] he will restore[g] us,
that we may live in his presence.
3Let us acknowledge the LORD;
let us press on to acknowledge him.
As surely as the sun rises,
he will appear;
he will come to us like the winter rains,[h]
like the spring rains that water the earth."[i]

4"What can I do with you, Ephraim?[j]
What can I do with you, Judah?
Your love is like the morning mist,
like the early dew that disappears.[k]
5Therefore I cut you in pieces with my prophets,
I killed you with the words of my mouth;[l]
my judgments flashed like lightning upon you.[m]
6For I desire mercy, not sacrifice,[n]
and acknowledgment[o] of God
rather than burnt offerings.[p]
7Like Adam,[a] they have broken the covenant[q]—
they were unfaithful[r] to me there.
8Gilead is a city of wicked men,[s]
stained with footprints of blood.
9As marauders lie in ambush for a man,[t]
so do bands of priests;
they murder[u] on the road to Shechem,
committing shameful crimes.[v]
10I have seen a horrible[w] thing
in the house of Israel.
There Ephraim is given to prostitution
and Israel is defiled.[x]

11"Also for you, Judah,
a harvest[y] is appointed.

"Whenever I would restore the fortunes[z] of my people,
7 [1]whenever I would heal Israel,
the sins of Ephraim are exposed
and the crimes of Samaria revealed.[a]
They practise deceit,[b]
thieves break into houses,[c]
bandits rob in the streets;[d]
2but they do not realise
that I remember[e] all their evil deeds.[f]
Their sins engulf them;[g]
they are always before me.

3"They delight the king with their wickedness,
the princes with their lies.[h]

5 [m]Hos 14:1
6 [n]Mic 6:6–7; [o]Pr 1:28; Isa 1:15; Eze 8:6; Mal 1:10
7 [p]Isa 24:16; Hos 6:7; [q]Hos 2:4; [r]Isa 1:14; [s]Hos 2:11–12
8 [t]Nu 10:2; Jer 4:21; Eze 33:3; [u]Jdg 19:12; Hos 9:9; 10:9; [v]Isa 10:29; [w]Jos 7:2; Hos 4:15; 10:5
9 [x]Isa 7:16; [y]Isa 37:3; Hos 9:11–17; [z]Isa 46:10; Zec 1:6
10 [a]Dt 19:14; [b]Eze 7:8
11 [c]Hos 9:16; Mic 6:16
12 [d]Job 13:28; Isa 51:8; [e]Job 18:16
13 [f]Isa 7:16; [g]Eze 23:5; Hos 7:11; 8:9; 12:1; [h]La 5:6; Hos 7:8; 10:6; [i]Isa 3:7; Hos 14:3; [j]Hos 2:7
14 [k]Job 10:16; Jer 4:7; Am 3:4; [l]Hos 6:1; [m]Dt 32:39; Mic 5:8
15 [n]Isa 18:4; [o]Lev 26:40; [p]Nu 21:7; Ps 24:6; Hos 3:5; [q]Ps 50:15; Jer 2:27; [r]Isa 64:9; Eze 20:43

Ch. 6

1 [a]Isa 10:20; 19:22; [b]Job 16:9; La 3:11; Hos 5:14; [c]Nu 12:13; Jer 3:22; [d]Dt 32:39; Job 5:18; Jer 30:17; Hos 14:4
2 [e]Ps 30:5; 80:18; [f]Mt 16:21; [g]Ps 71:20
3 [h]Job 4:3; Joel 2:23; [i]Ps 72:6; Hos 11:10; 12:6
4 [j]Hos 11:8; [k]Hos 7:1; 13:3
5 [l]Jer 1:9–10; 5:14; 23:29; [m]Heb 4:12
6 [n]1Sa 15:22; Isa 1:11; Mt 9:13*; 12:7*; Mk 12:33; [o]Jer 4:22; Hos 2:20; [p]Ps 40:6; Mic 6:8
7 [q]Ge 9:11; Jer 11:10; Hos 8:1; [r]Hos 5:7
8 [s]Hos 12:11
9 [t]Ps 10:8; [u]Hos 4:2; [v]Jer 5:30–31; 7:9–10; Eze 22:9; Hos 5:1; 7:1
10 [w]Jer 5:30; [x]Jer 23:14; Eze 23:7; Hos 5:3
11 [y]Jer 51:33; Joel 3:13; [z]Ps 126:1; Zep 2:7

Ch. 7

1 [a]Eze 24:13; Hos 6:4; [b]ver 13; [c]Ex 22:2; Hos 4:2; [d]Hos 6:9; 12:1
2 [e]Jer 14:10; 44:21; Hos 8:13; [f]Job 35:15; Hos 9:15; [g]Jer 2:19; 4:18
3 [h]Jer 28:1–4; Hos 4:2; 10:13; Mic 7:3

[a]8 *Beth Aven* means *house of wickedness* (a name for Bethel, which means *house of God*).
[b]11 The meaning of the Hebrew for this word is uncertain.
[a]7 Or *As at Adam*; or *Like men*

4They are all adulterers,[i]
burning like an oven
whose fire the baker need not stir
from the kneading of the dough till
it rises.
5On the day of the festival of our king
the princes become inflamed with
wine,[j]
and he joins hands with the
mockers.[k]
6Their hearts are like an oven;[l]
they approach him with intrigue.
Their passion smoulders all night;
in the morning it blazes like a
flaming fire.
7All of them are hot as an oven;
they devour their rulers.
All their kings fall,[m]
and none of them calls[n] on me.

8"Ephraim mixes[o] with the nations;
Ephraim is a flat cake not turned
over.
9Foreigners sap his strength,[p]
but he does not realise it.
His hair is sprinkled with grey,
but he does not notice.
10Israel's arrogance testifies against
him,[q]
but despite all this
he does not return[r] to the LORD his
God
or search[s] for him.

11"Ephraim is like a dove,[t]
easily deceived and senseless—
now calling to Egypt,[u]
now turning to Assyria.[v]
12When they go, I will throw my net[w]
over them;
I will pull them down like birds of
the air.
When I hear them flocking together,
I will catch them.
13Woe[x] to them,
because they have strayed[y] from
me!
Destruction to them,
because they have rebelled against
me!
I long to redeem them
but they speak lies[z] against me.[a]
14They do not cry out to me from their
hearts[b]
but wail upon their beds.
They gather together[a] for grain and
new wine[c]
but turn away from me.[d]
15I trained[e] them and strengthened
them,
but they plot evil[f] against me.
16They do not turn to the Most High;[g]
they are like a faulty bow.[h]
Their leaders will fall by the sword
because of their insolent[i] words.
For this they will be ridiculed[j]
in the land of Egypt.[k]

Israel to Reap the Whirlwind

8 "Put the trumpet[a] to your lips!
An eagle[b] is over the house of the
LORD
because the people have broken my
covenant[c]
and rebelled against my law.[d]
2Israel cries out to me,
'O our God, we acknowledge you!'
3But Israel has rejected what is good;
an enemy will pursue him.[e]
4They set up kings without my
consent;
they choose princes without my
approval.[f]
With their silver and gold
they make idols[g] for themselves
to their own destruction.
5Throw out your calf-idol, O Samaria![h]
My anger burns against them.
How long will they be incapable of
purity?[i]
6 They are from Israel!
This calf—a craftsman has made it;
it is not God.[j]
It will be broken in pieces,
that calf[k] of Samaria.[l]

7"They sow the wind
and reap the whirlwind.[m]
The stalk has no head;
it will produce no flour.[n]
Were it to yield grain,
foreigners would swallow it up.[o]
8Israel is swallowed up;[p]
now she is among the nations
like a worthless[q] thing.
9For they have gone up to Assyria[r]
like a wild donkey[s] wandering
alone.
Ephraim has sold herself to lovers.[t]
10Although they have sold themselves
among the nations,
I will now gather them together.[u]
They will begin to waste away[v]
under the oppression of the mighty
king.

11"Though Ephraim built many altars
for sin offerings,
these have become altars for
sinning.[w]
12I wrote for them the many things of
my law,

4 [i]**Jer 9:2**
5 [j]**Isa 28:1**,7; [k]**Ps 1:1**
6 [l]Ps 21:9
7 [m]Hos 13:10; [n]ver 16; **Ps 14:4; Isa 9:13**; Zep 1:6
8 [o]ver 11; Ps 106:35; **Hos 5:13**
9 [p]Isa 1:7; Hos 8:7
10 [q]Hos 5:5; [r]Hos 5:4; [s]ver 14; **Isa 9:13**
11 [t]**Ge 8:8**; [u]ver 16; Hos 9:6; [v]**ver 8; Jer 2:18; La 5:6**; Hos 9:3; 12:1
12 [w]**Eze 12:13; 32:3**
13 [x]Hos 9:12; [y]Jer 14:10; **Eze 34:4–6**; Hos 9:17; [z]**Ps 116:11**; [a]ver 1; Jer 51:9; Mt 23:37
14 [b]Jer 3:10; [c]Am 2:8; [d]**ver 10; Hos 4:10**; 9:1; 13:16
15 [e]Hos 11:3; [f]Ps 2:1; **140:2**; Na 1:9,11
16 [g]**ver 7**; [h]**Ps 78:9**,57; [i]Mal 3:14; [j]**Eze 23:32**; [k]**ver 11**; Hos 9:3; 11:5

Ch. 8

1 [a]**Nu 10:2; Eze 33:3**; [b]**Dt 28:49**; Jer 4:13; [c]**Jer 11:10**; [d]**Hos 4:6; 6:7**
3 [e]**Mt 7:23**; Tit 1:16
4 [f]Hos 13:10; [g]**Hos 2:8**; 13:1–2
5 [h]ver 6; Hos 10:5; [i]Jer 13:27
6 [j]**Jer 16:20**; Hos 14:3; [k]**Ex 32:4**; [l]ver 5
7 [m]**Job 4:8**; Pr 22:8; Isa 66:15; Hos 10:12–13; Na 1:3; Gal 6:8; [n]**Dt 28:38**; **Isa 17:11**; Hos 9:16; [o]Hos 2:9; **7:9**
8 [p]Jer 51:34; [q]Jer 22:28
9 [r]**Jer 2:18**; [s]**Ge 16:12**; [t]**Jer 22:20**; Eze 23:5; **Hos 5:13**
10 [u]**Eze 16:37; 22:20**; [v]Jer 42:2
11 [w]Hos 10:1; 12:11

[a]14 Most Hebrew manuscripts; some Hebrew manuscripts and Septuagint *They slash themselves*

but they regarded them as
something alien.[x]
13They offer sacrifices given to me
and they eat[y] the meat,
but the LORD is not pleased with
them.[z]
Now he will remember[a] their
wickedness
and punish their sins:[b]
They will return to Egypt.[c]
14Israel has forgotten[d] his Maker[e]
and built palaces;
Judah has fortified many towns.
But I will send fire upon their cities
that will consume their fortresses."[f]

Punishment for Israel

9 Do not rejoice, O Israel;
do not be jubilant[a] like the other
nations.
For you have been unfaithful[b] to your
God;
you love the wages of a prostitute[c]
at every threshing-floor.
2Threshing-floors and winepresses will
not feed the people;
the new wine[d] will fail them.
3They will not remain[e] in the LORD's
land;
Ephraim will return to Egypt[f]
and eat unclean[a] food in Assyria.[g]
4They will not pour out wine offerings[h]
to the LORD,
nor will their sacrifices please[i] him.
Such sacrifices will be to them like the
bread of mourners;[j]
all who eat them will be unclean.[k]
This food will be for themselves;
it will not come into the temple of
the LORD.[l]

5What will you do[m] on the day of your
appointed feasts,[n]
on the festival days of the LORD?
6Even if they escape from destruction,
Egypt will gather them,[o]
and Memphis[p] will bury them.[q]
Their treasures of silver[r] will be taken
over by briers,
and thorns[s] will overrun their tents.
7The days of punishment[t] are coming,
the days of reckoning[u] are at hand.
Let Israel know this.
Because your sins[v] are so many
and your hostility so great,
the prophet is considered a fool,[w]
the inspired man a maniac.[x]
8The prophet, along with my God,
is the watchman over Ephraim,[b]
yet snares[y] await him on all his paths,
and hostility in the house of his
God.[z]

12 [x]ver 1
13 [y]Jer 7:21; [z]Jer 6:20; Hos 9:4; [a]Hos 7:2; 9:9; Am 8:7; [b]Hos 4:9; [c]Hos 9:3,6
14 [d]Dt 32:18; Isa 17:10; Hos 2:13; [e]Ps 95:6; [f]Jer 5:17; 17:27; Am 2:5

Ch. 9
1 [a]Isa 22:12–13; [b]Ps 73:27; Isa 24:16; Hos 7:14; 10:5; [c]Ge 30:15
2 [d]Isa 24:7; Hos 2:9; Joel 1:10
3 [e]Lev 25:23; [f]Hos 7:16; 8:13; [g]Eze 4:13; Hos 7:11; 10:5; Am 7:17
4 [h]Joel 1:9,13; 2:14; [i]Hos 8:13; [j]Jer 16:7; [k]Dt 26:14; Hag 2:13–14; [l]Eze 4:13–14
5 [m]Isa 10:3; Jer 5:31; [n]Hos 2:11
6 [o]Hos 7:11; 8:13; [p]Isa 19:13; [q]Jer 42:22; [r]Zep 1:11; [s]Isa 5:6; Hos 10:8
7 [t]Isa 34:8; Jer 10:15; Mic 7:4; Lk 21:22; [u]Job 31:14; [v]Jer 16:18; [w]1Sa 10:11; Isa 44:25; La 2:14; Eze 14:9–10; [x]Jer 29:26; Hos 14:1
8 [y]Hos 5:1; [z]Eze 22:26
9 [a]Zep 3:7; [b]Jdg 19:16–30; Hos 5:8; [c]Hos 8:13; [d]Hos 4:9
10 [e]SS 2:13; [f]Isa 28:4; [g]Nu 25:1–5; Ps 106:28–29; [h]Jer 11:13; Hos 4:14
11 [i]Isa 17:3; [j]Hos 4:7; 10:5; [k]ver 14
12 [l]ver 16; Eze 24:21; [m]Hos 7:13; [n]Dt 31:17
13 [o]Ps 78:67; [p]Eze 27:3; [q]Job 15:22; La 2:22
14 [r]ver 11; Lk 23:29
15 [s]Hos 4:15; [t]Hos 7:2; [u]Jer 12:8; [v]Isa 1:23; Hos 4:9; 5:2

9They have sunk deep into corruption,[a]
as in the days of Gibeah.[b]
God will remember[c] their wickedness
and punish them for their sins.[d]

10"When I found Israel,
it was like finding grapes in the
desert;
when I saw your fathers,
it was like seeing the early fruit[e] on
the fig-tree.[f]
But when they came to Baal Peor,[g]
they consecrated themselves to that
shameful idol[h]
and became as vile as the thing they
loved.
11Ephraim's glory[i] will fly away like a
bird[j]—
no birth, no pregnancy, no
conception.[k]
12Even if they bring up children,
I will bereave[l] them of every one.
Woe[m] to them
when I turn away from them![n]
13I have seen Ephraim,[o] like Tyre,
planted in a pleasant place.[p]
But Ephraim will bring out
their children to the slayer."[q]

14Give them, O LORD—
what will you give them?
Give them wombs that miscarry
and breasts that are dry.[r]

15"Because of all their wickedness in
Gilgal,[s]
I hated them there.
Because of their sinful deeds,[t]
I will drive them out of my house.
I will no longer love them;[u]
all their leaders are rebellious.[v]
16Ephraim[w] is blighted,
their root is withered,
they yield no fruit.[x]
Even if they bear children,
I will slay[y] their cherished
offspring."

17My God will reject[z] them
because they have not obeyed[a] him;
they will be wanderers among the
nations.[b]

10 Israel was a spreading vine;[a]
he brought forth fruit for
himself.

16 [w]Hos 5:11; [x]Job 15:32; Hos 8:7; [y]ver 12
17 [z]Jer 6:30; [a]Hos 4:10; [b]Dt 28:65; Hos 7:13

Ch. 10
1 [a]Eze 15:2

[a]3 That is, ceremonially unclean
[b]8 Or *The prophet is the watchman over Ephraim, / the people of my God*

As his fruit increased,
he built more altars;[b]
as his land prospered,[c]
he adorned his sacred stones.[d]
2Their heart is deceitful,[e]
and now they must bear their guilt.[f]
The LORD will demolish their altars[g]
and destroy their sacred stones.[h]

3Then they will say, "We have no king
because we did not revere the LORD.
But even if we had a king,
what could he do for us?"
4They make many promises,
take false oaths[i]
and make agreements;[j]
therefore lawsuits spring up
like poisonous weeds[k] in a
ploughed field.
5The people who live in Samaria fear
for the calf-idol[l] of Beth Aven.[a] [m]
Its people will mourn over it,
and so will its idolatrous priests,[n]
those who had rejoiced over its
splendour,
because it is taken from them into
exile.[o]
6It will be carried to Assyria[p]
as tribute[q] for the great king.[r]
Ephraim will be disgraced;[s]
Israel will be ashamed[t] of its
wooden idols.[b]
7Samaria and its king will float away[u]
like a twig on the surface of the
waters.
8The high places[v] of wickedness[c] [w] will
be destroyed—
it is the sin of Israel.
Thorns[x] and thistles will grow up
and cover their altars.[y]
Then they will say to the mountains,
"Cover us!"[z]
and to the hills, "Fall on us!"[a]

9"Since the days of Gibeah,[b] you have
sinned,[c] O Israel,
and there you have remained.[d]
Did not war overtake
the evildoers in Gibeah?
10When I please, I will punish[d] them;
nations will be gathered against
them
to put them in bonds for their
double sin.
11Ephraim is a trained heifer
that loves to thresh;
so I will put a yoke[e]
on her fair neck.
I will drive Ephraim,
Judah must plough,
and Jacob must break up the
ground.
12Sow[f] for yourselves righteousness,[g]
reap the fruit of unfailing love,
and break up your unploughed
ground;[h]
for it is time to seek[i] the LORD,
until he comes
and showers righteousness[j] on you.
13But you have planted wickedness,
you have reaped evil,[k]
you have eaten the fruit of
deception.[l]
Because you have depended on your
own strength
and on your many warriors,[m]
14the roar of battle will rise against your
people,
so that all your fortresses will be
devastated[n]—
as Shalman[o] devastated Beth Arbel on
the day of battle,
when mothers were dashed to the
ground with their children.[p]
15Thus will it happen to you, O Bethel,
because your wickedness is great.
When that day dawns,
the king of Israel will be completely
destroyed.[q]

God's Love for Israel

11 "When Israel was a child,[a] I
loved[b] him,
and out of Egypt I called my son.[c]
2But the more I[a] called Israel,
the further they went from me.[b] [d]
They sacrificed to the Baals[e]
and they burned incense to images.[f]
3It was I who taught Ephraim to walk,
taking them by the arms;[g]
but they did not realise
it was I who healed[h] them.
4I led them with cords of human
kindness,
with ties of love;[i]
I lifted the yoke[j] from their neck
and bent down to feed[k] them.[l]

5"Will they not return to Egypt[m]
and will not Assyria[n] rule over them
because they refuse to repent?[o]
6Swords[p] will flash in their cities,
will destroy the bars[q] of their gates
and put an end to their plans.

1 [b]1Ki 14:23; [c]Hos 13:15; [d]Hos 3:4; 4:7; 8:11; 12:11
2 [e]1Ki 18:21; [f]Hos 13:16; [g]ver 8; [h]Mic 5:13
4 [i]Hos 4:2; [j]Eze 17:19; Am 5:7; [k]Am 6:12
5 [l]Ex 32:4; Isa 44:17–20; [m]ver 8; Hos 5:8; [n]2Ki 23:5; Zep 1:4; [o]Jdg 18:17–18; Hos 8:5; 9:1,3,11
6 [p]2Ki 16:7; Hos 11:5; [q]Jdg 3:15; [r]Hos 5:13; [s]Isa 30:3; Hos 4:7; [t]Jer 48:13
7 [u]ver 15; Hos 13:11
8 [v]Eze 6:6; [w]ver 5; 1Ki 12:28–30; Hos 4:13; [x]Hos 9:6; [y]ver 2; Isa 32:13; [z]Job 30:6; Am 3:14–15; [a]Am 7:9; Lk 23:30*; Rev 6:16
9 [b]Hos 5:8; [c]Jos 7:11
10 [d]Eze 5:13; Hos 4:9
11 [e]Jer 15:12; 31:18
12 [f]Ecc 11:1; [g]Pr 11:18; Jas 3:18; [h]Jer 4:3; [i]Isa 19:22; Hos 12:6; [j]Isa 45:8
13 [k]Job 4:8; Hos 7:3; 11:12; Gal 6:7–8; [l]Pr 11:18; Hos 8:7; [m]Ps 33:16
14 [n]Isa 17:3; Mic 5:11; [o]2Ki 17:3; [p]Isa 13:16; Hos 13:16
15 [q]ver 7

Ch. 11

1 [a]Jer 2:2; Eze 16:22; [b]Dt 4:37; [c]Ex 4:22; Hos 12:9,13; 13:4; Mt 2:15*
2 [d]ver 7; [e]Hos 2:13; [f]2Ki 17:15; Isa 65:7; Jer 18:15; Hos 4:13; 13:1
3 [g]Dt 1:31; 32:11; Hos 7:15; [h]Ex 15:26; Jer 30:17
4 [i]Jer 31:2–3; [j]Lev 26:13; [k]Ex 16:32; Ps 78:25; [l]Jer 31:20
5 [m]Hos 7:16; [n]Hos 10:6; [o]Ex 13:17
6 [p]Hos 13:16; [q]La 2:9

[a]5 *Beth Aven* means *house of wickedness* (a name for Bethel, which means *house of God*).
[b]6 Or *its counsel*
[c]8 Hebrew *aven*, a reference to Beth Aven (a derogatory name for Bethel)
[d]9 Or *there a stand was taken*
[a]2 Some Septuagint manuscripts; Hebrew *they*
[b]2 Septuagint; Hebrew *them*

7My people are determined to turn[r]
from me.[s]
Even if they call to the Most High,
he will by no means exalt them.

8"How can I give you up,[t] Ephraim?[u]
How can I hand you over, Israel?
How can I treat you like Admah?
How can I make you like Zeboiim?[v]
My heart is changed within me;
all my compassion[w] is aroused.[x]
9I will not carry out my fierce anger,[y]
nor will I turn and devastate[z]
Ephraim.
For I am God, and not man[a]—
the Holy One[b] among you.
I will not come in wrath.[c]
10They will follow the LORD;
he will roar[c] like a lion.[d]
When he roars,
his children will come trembling[e]
from the west.[f]
11They will come trembling
like birds from Egypt,
like doves[g] from Assyria.[h]
I will settle them in their homes,"[i]
declares the LORD.

Israel's Sin

12Ephraim has surrounded me with
lies,[j]
the house of Israel with deceit.
And Judah is unruly against God,
even against the faithful[k] Holy One.[l]

12

1Ephraim[a] feeds on the wind;[b]
he pursues the east wind all day
and multiplies lies and violence.[c]
He makes a treaty with Assyria[d]
and sends olive oil to Egypt.[e]
2The LORD has a charge[f] to bring
against Judah;[g]
he will punish[h] Jacob[a] according to
his ways
and repay him according to his
deeds.[i]
3In the womb he grasped his brother's
heel;[j]
as a man he struggled[k] with God.
4He struggled with the angel and
overcame him;
he wept and begged for his favour.
He found him at Bethel[l]
and talked with him there—
5the LORD God Almighty,
the LORD is his name[m] of renown!
6But you must return[n] to your God;
maintain love and justice,[o]
and wait for your God always.[p]

7The merchant uses dishonest scales;[q]
he loves to defraud.
8Ephraim boasts,[r]
"I am very rich; I have become
wealthy.[s]
With all my wealth they will not find
in me
any iniquity or sin."

9"I am the LORD your God,
⌞who brought you⌟ out of[b] Egypt;[t]
I will make you live in tents[u] again,
as in the days of your appointed
feasts.
10I spoke to the prophets,
gave them many visions
and told parables[v] through them."[w]

11Is Gilead wicked?[x]
Its people are worthless!
Do they sacrifice bulls in Gilgal?[y]
Their altars will be like piles of
stones
on a ploughed field.[z]
12Jacob fled to the country of Aram[c];[a]
Israel served to get a wife,
and to pay for her he tended sheep.[b]
13The LORD used a prophet to bring
Israel up from Egypt,[c]
by a prophet he cared for him.[d]
14But Ephraim has bitterly provoked
him to anger;
his Lord will leave upon him the
guilt of his bloodshed[e]
and will repay him for his
contempt.[f]

The LORD's Anger Against Israel

13

When Ephraim spoke, men
trembled;[a]
he was exalted[b] in Israel.
But he became guilty of Baal
worship[c] and died.
2Now they sin more and more;
they make[d] idols for themselves
from their silver,[e]
cleverly fashioned images,
all of them the work of craftsmen.[f]
It is said of these people,
"They offer human sacrifice
and kiss[a][g] the calf-idols.[h]"
3Therefore they will be like the
morning mist,
like the early dew that disappears,[i]
like chaff[j] swirling from a
threshing-floor,[k]
like smoke[l] escaping through a
window.

7 [r]**Isa 26:10;** [s]ver 2; Jer 3:6–7; 8:5
8 [t]**Jer 7:29;** [u]Hos 6:4; [v]**Ge 14:8; La 3:32;** [w]**1Ki 3:26; Ps 25:6;** [x]**Eze 33:11;** Am 7:3
9 [y]Dt 13:17; **Jer 18:8; 30:11;** [z]La 3:22; Mal 3:6; [a]**Nu 23:19;** [b]**2Ki 19:22; Isa 31:1**
10 [c]**Isa 42:13;** [d]**Isa 31:4;** [e]**Ps 18:45;** [f]**Hos 3:5; 6:1–3**
11 [g]**Ge 8:8;** [h]**Isa 11:11;** [i]**Eze 28:26; 34:25–28**
12 [j]**Hos 4:2;** [k]**Dt 7:9;** [l]**Hos 10:13**

Ch. 12

1 [a]**Ps 78:67;** [b]**Ge 41:6; Eze 17:10;** [c]**Hos 4:19; 7:1;** [d]Hos 5:13; **7:11;** [e]**2Ki 17:4**
2 [f]**Job 10:2;** Mic 6:2; [g]Am 2:4; [h]**Ex 32:34;** [i]**Hos 4:9; 9:15**
3 [j]Ge 25:26; [k]Ge 32:24–29
4 [l]**Ge 12:8; 35:15**
5 [m]**Ex 3:15**
6 [n]**Isa 19:22;** Jer 4:1; Joel 2:12; [o]**Ps 106:3; Jer 22:3;** [p]**Eze 18:30;** Hos 6:1–3; 10:12; Mic 7:7
7 [q]**Lev 19:36;** Am 8:5
8 [r]**Eze 28:5;** [s]Ps 62:10; Rev 3:17
9 [t]Lev 23:43; **Hos 2:15; 11:1;** [u]**Ne 8:17**
10 [v]**Jdg 14:12; Eze 20:49;** [w]2Ki 17:13; Jer 7:25
11 [x]**Hos 6:8;** [y]**Hos 4:15;** [z]**Hos 8:11**
12 [a]Ge 28:5; [b]**Ge 29:18**
13 [c]**Hos 11:1;** [d]Ex 13:3; 14:19–22; Isa 63:11–14
14 [e]**Eze 18:13;** [f]Da 11:18

Ch. 13

1 [a]Jdg 12:1; [b]**Jdg 8:1;** [c]**Hos 11:2**
2 [d]Jer 44:8; [e]**Isa 46:6; Jer 10:4;** [f]Hos 14:3; [g]1Ki 19:18; [h]**Isa 44:17–20; Hos 8:4**
3 [i]**Hos 6:4;** [j]**Job 13:25;** Ps 1:4; **Isa 17:13;** [k]Da 2:35; [l]Ps 68:2

[c]9 Or *come against any city*
[a]2 *Jacob* means *he grasps the heel* (figuratively, *he deceives*). [b]9 Or *God / ever since you were in*
[c]12 That is, North-west Mesopotamia
[a]2 Or *"Men who sacrifice / kiss*

4"But I am the LORD your God,
⌞who brought you⌟ out of[b] Egypt.[m]
You shall acknowledge[n] no God but me,[o]
no Saviour[p] except me.
5I cared for you in the desert,[q]
in the land of burning heat.
6When I fed them, they were satisfied;
when they were satisfied, they became proud;[r]
then they forgot[s] me.[t]
7So I will come upon them like a lion,[u]
like a leopard I will lurk by the path.
8Like a bear robbed of her cubs,[v]
I will attack them and rip them open.
Like a lion[w] I will devour them;
a wild animal will tear them apart.[x]

9"You are destroyed, O Israel,
because you are against me,[y]
against your helper.[z]
10Where is your king,[a] that he may save you?
Where are your rulers in all your towns,
of whom you said,
'Give me a king and princes'?[b]
11So in my anger I gave you a king,[c]
and in my wrath I took him away.[d]
12The guilt of Ephraim is stored up,
his sins are kept on record.[e]
13Pains as of a woman in childbirth[f]
come to him,
but he is a child without wisdom;
when the time[g] arrives,
he does not come to the opening of the womb.[h]

14"I will ransom them from the power of the grave[c];[i]
I will redeem them from death.[j]
Where, O death, are your plagues?
Where, O grave,[c] is your destruction?[k]

"I will have no compassion,
15 even though he thrives[l] among his brothers.
An east wind[m] from the LORD will come,
blowing in from the desert;
his spring will fail
and his well dry up.[n]
His storehouse will be plundered[o]
of all its treasures.
16The people of Samaria[p] must bear their guilt,[q]
because they have rebelled[r] against their God.
They will fall by the sword;[s]
their little ones will be dashed[t] to the ground,
their pregnant women[u] ripped open."

Repentance to Bring Blessing

14 Return,[a] O Israel, to the LORD your God.
Your sins[b] have been your downfall![c]
2Take words with you
and return to the LORD.
Say to him:
"Forgive[d] all our sins
and receive us graciously,[e]
that we may offer the fruit of our lips.[a][f]
3Assyria cannot save us;[g]
we will not mount war-horses.[h]
We will never again say 'Our gods'[i]
to what our own hands have made,[j]
for in you the fatherless[k] find compassion."

4"I will heal[l] their waywardness[m]
and love them freely,[n]
for my anger has turned away[o] from them.
5I will be like the dew[p] to Israel;
he will blossom like a lily.[q]
Like a cedar of Lebanon[r]
he will send down his roots;[s]
6 his young shoots will grow.
His splendour will be like an olive tree,[t]
his fragrance like a cedar of Lebanon.[u]
7Men will dwell again in his shade.[v]
He will flourish like the corn.
He will blossom[w] like a vine,
and his fame will be like the wine[x]
from Lebanon.[y]
8O Ephraim, what more have I[b] to do with idols?[z]
I will answer him and care for him.
I am like a green pine[a] tree;
your fruitfulness comes from me."
9Who is wise?[b] He will realise these things.
Who is discerning? He will understand them.[c]
The ways of the LORD are right;[d]
the righteous walk[e] in them,
but the rebellious stumble in them.

4 [m]Jer 2:6; Hos 12:9; [n]Hos 2:20; [o]Ex 20:3; [p]Dt 28:29; Ps 18:46; Isa 43:11; 45:21–22
5 [q]Dt 1:19
6 [r]Eze 28:5; [s]Dt 32:18; Isa 17:10; [t]Dt 32:12–15; Pr 30:7–9; Jer 5:7; Hos 2:13; 4:7
7 [u]Job 10:16; Jer 4:7
8 [v]2Sa 17:8; [w]1Sa 17:34; Ps 17:12; [x]Ps 50:22; La 3:10; Hos 2:12
9 [y]Jer 2:17–19; [z]Dt 33:29
10 [a]2Ki 17:4; Hos 7:7; [b]1Sa 8:6; Hos 8:4
11 [c]Nu 11:20; [d]Jos 24:20; 1Sa 13:14; 1Ki 14:10; Hos 3:4; 10:7
12 [e]Dt 32:34
13 [f]Isa 13:8; Mic 4:9–10; [g]2Ki 19:3; [h]Isa 66:9
14 [i]Ps 16:10; 49:15; Eze 37:12–13; [j]Isa 25:8; [k]1Co 15:55*
15 [l]Hos 10:1; [m]Job 1:19; Eze 19:12; Hos 4:19; [n]Jer 51:36; [o]Jer 20:5
16 [p]2Ki 17:5; [q]Hos 10:2; [r]Hos 7:14; [s]Hos 11:6; [t]2Ki 8:12; Hos 10:14; [u]2Ki 15:16; Isa 13:16; Am 1:13

Ch. 14

1 [a]Isa 19:22; Jer 3:12; [b]Hos 4:8; [c]Hos 5:5; 9:7
2 [d]Ex 34:9; [e]Ps 51:16–17; Mic 7:18–19; [f]Heb 13:15
3 [g]Hos 5:13; [h]Ps 33:17; Isa 31:1; Mic 5:10; [i]Hos 8:6; [j]ver 8; Hos 13:2; [k]Ps 10:14; 68:5; Jer 49:11
4 [l]Isa 30:26; Hos 6:1; [m]Jer 2:19; [n]Isa 55:1; Jer 31:20; Zep 3:17; [o]Job 13:16
5 [p]Ge 27:28; Isa 18:4; [q]SS 2:1; [r]Isa 35:2; [s]Job 29:19
6 [t]Ps 52:8; Jer 11:16; [u]Ps 92:12; SS 4:11
7 [v]Ps 91:1–4; [w]Ge 40:10; [x]Hos 2:22; [y]Eze 17:23
8 [z]ver 3; [a]Isa 37:24
9 [b]Ps 107:43; [c]Pr 10:29; Isa 1:28; Da 12:10; [d]Ps 111:7–8; Zep 3:5; Ac 13:10; [e]Isa 26:7

b4 Or *God / ever since you were in*
c14 Hebrew *Sheol*
a2 Or *offer our lips as sacrifices of bulls*
b8 Or *What more has Ephraim*

Joel

1 The word of the LORD that came[a] to
Joel[b] son of Pethuel.

An Invasion of Locusts

[2]Hear this,[c] you elders;[d]
listen, all who live in the land.[e]
Has anything like this ever happened
in your days
or in the days of your forefathers?[f]
[3]Tell it to your children,[g]
and let your children tell it to their
children,
and their children to the next
generation.[h]
[4]What the locust[i] swarm has left
the great locusts have eaten;
what the great locusts have left
the young locusts have eaten;
what the young locusts have left[j]
other locusts[a] have eaten.[k]

[5]Wake up, you drunkards, and weep!
Wail, all you drinkers of wine;[l]
wail because of the new wine,
for it has been snatched[m] from your
lips.
[6]A nation has invaded my land,
powerful and without number;[n]
it has the teeth[o] of a lion,
the fangs of a lioness.
[7]It has laid waste[p] my vines
and ruined my fig-trees.[q]
It has stripped off their bark
and thrown it away,
leaving their branches white.

[8]Mourn like a virgin[b] in sackcloth[r]
grieving for the husband[c] of her
youth.
[9]Grain offerings and drink offerings[s]
are cut off from the house of the
LORD.
The priests are in mourning,[t]
those who minister before the LORD.
[10]The fields are ruined,
the ground is dried up[d];[u]
the grain is destroyed,
the new wine[v] is dried up,
the oil fails.[w]
[11]Despair, you farmers,[x]
wail, you vine growers;
grieve for the wheat and the barley,[y]
because the harvest of the field is
destroyed.[z]
[12]The vine is dried up
and the fig-tree is withered;[a]
the pomegranate,[b] the palm and the
apple tree—
all the trees of the field—are dried
up.[c]
Surely the joy of mankind
is withered away.

A Call to Repentance

[13]Put on sackcloth,[d] O priests, and
mourn;
wail, you who minister[e] before the
altar.
Come, spend the night in sackcloth,
you who minister before my God;
for the grain offerings and drink
offerings[f]
are withheld from the house of your
God.
[14]Declare a holy fast;[g]
call a sacred assembly.
Summon the elders
and all who live in the land[h]
to the house of the LORD your God,
and cry out[i] to the LORD.[j]

[15]Alas for that[k] day!
For the day of the LORD[l] is near;
it will come like destruction from the
Almighty.[e] [m]

[16]Has not the food been cut off[n]
before our very eyes—
joy and gladness[o]
from the house of our God?[p]
[17]The seeds are shrivelled
beneath the clods.[f] [q]
The storehouses are in ruins,
the granaries have been broken
down,
for the grain has dried up.

Ch. 1

1 [a]**Jer 1:2**; [b]Ac 2:16
2 [c]Hos 5:1; [d]Joel 2:16; [e]**Hos 4:1**; [f]Joel 2:2
3 [g]**Ex 10:2**; [h]**Ps 71:18**
4 [i]**Ex 10:14**; [j]**Ex 10:5**; [k]**Ex 10:15**; **Dt 28:39**; Am 7:1; Na 3:15
5 [l]Joel 3:3; [m]**Isa 24:7**
6 [n]Ps 105:34; Joel 2:2,11,25; [o]Rev 9:8
7 [p]Isa 5:6; [q]Am 4:9
8 [r]ver 13; Isa 22:12; Am 8:10
9 [s]**Hos 9:4**; [t]**Isa 22:12**
10 [u]**Isa 5:6; 24:4; Jer 3:3**; [v]**Hos 9:2**; [w]**Nu 18:12**
11 [x]**Job 6:20**; Am 5:16; [y]**Ex 9:31**; [z]**Isa 17:11**
12 [a]**Isa 15:6**; [b]**Ex 28:33**; [c]**Isa 16:8**; Hag 2:19
13 [d]**Ge 37:34**; **Jer 4:8**; [e]Joel 2:17; [f]ver 9; **Hos 9:4**; Joel 2:14
14 [g]**2Ch 20:3**; [h]**Hos 4:1**; [i]Jnh 3:8; [j]2Ch 20:4
15 [k]**Isa 2:12**; Jer 30:7; **46:10**; **Eze 30:3**; Mal 4:5; [l]Joel 2:1, 11,31; 3:14; Am 5:18; Zep 1:14; Zec 14:1; [m]**Ge 17:1**
16 [n]Isa 3:7; [o]Ps 51:8; [p]Dt 12:7
17 [q]**Isa 17:10–11**

[a]4 The precise meaning of the four Hebrew words used here for locusts is uncertain.
[b]8 Or *young woman*
[c]8 Or *betrothed*
[d]10 Or *ground mourns*
[e]15 Hebrew *Shaddai*
[f]17 The meaning of the Hebrew for this word is uncertain.

18 How the cattle moan!
The herds mill about
because they have no pasture;[r]
even the flocks of sheep are
suffering.[s]

19 To you, O LORD, I call,[t]
for fire[u] has devoured the open
pastures[v]
and flames have burned up all the
trees of the field.
20 Even the wild animals pant for you;[w]
the streams of water have dried up[x]
and fire has devoured the open
pastures.[y]

An Army of Locusts

2 Blow the trumpet[a] in Zion;[b]
sound the alarm on my holy hill.[c]
Let all who live in the land tremble,
for the day of the LORD[d] is coming.
It is close at hand[e]—
2 a day of darkness[f] and gloom,[g h]
a day of clouds[i] and blackness.[j]
Like dawn spreading across the
mountains
a large and mighty army[k] comes,
such as never was of old[l]
nor ever will be in ages to come.

3 Before them fire[m] devours,
behind them a flame blazes.
Before them the land is like the garden
of Eden,[n]
behind them, a desert waste[o]—
nothing escapes them.
4 They have the appearance of horses;[p]
they gallop along like cavalry.
5 With a noise like that of chariots[q]
they leap over the mountaintops,
like a crackling fire[r] consuming
stubble,
like a mighty army drawn up for
battle.

6 At the sight of them, nations are in
anguish;[s]
every face turns pale.[t]
7 They charge like warriors;[u]
they scale walls like soldiers.
They all march in line,[v]
not swerving[w] from their course.
8 They do not jostle each other;
each marches straight ahead.
They plunge through defences
without breaking ranks.
9 They rush upon the city;
they run along the wall.
They climb into the houses;[x]
like thieves they enter through the
windows.[y]

18 [r]Ge 47:4; [s]Jer 9:10
19 [t]Ps 50:15; [u]Ps 97:3; Am 7:4; [v]Jer 9:10
20 [w]Ps 42:1; 104:21; [x]1Ki 17:7; [y]Joel 2:22

Ch. 2

1 [a]Nu 10:2,7; [b]ver 15; [c]Ex 15:17; [d]Joel 1:15; Zep 1:14–16; [e]Eze 12:23; 30:3; Ob 15
2 [f]ver 10,31; Job 9:7; Isa 8:22; 13:10; Am 5:18; [g]Da 9:12; Mt 24:21; [h]Eze 34:12; [i]Eze 38:9; [j]Zep 1:15; Rev 9:2; [k]Joel 1:6; [l]Joel 1:2
3 [m]Ps 97:3; Isa 1:31; [n]Ge 2:8; [o]Ex 10:12–15; Ps 105:34–35; Isa 14:17
4 [p]Rev 9:7
5 [q]Rev 9:9; [r]Isa 5:24; 30:30
6 [s]Isa 13:8; [t]Isa 29:22
7 [u]Job 16:14; [v]Pr 30:27; [w]Isa 5:27
9 [x]Ex 10:6; [y]Jer 9:21
10 [z]Ps 18:7; Na 1:5; [a]Eze 38:19; [b]ver 2; Isa 5:30; Mt 24:29; Mk 13:24; Rev 9:2; [c]Job 9:7; Ps 102:26; Isa 13:10; Eze 32:8
11 [d]Isa 2:12; Eze 30:3; Joel 1:15; Ob 15; [e]Ps 29:3; [f]ver 2,25; [g]Zep 1:14; [h]Eze 22:14; Zep 2:11; Rev 6:17
12 [i]Dt 4:30; Eze 33:11; Hos 12:6; [j]1Sa 7:3
13 [k]Ps 51:17; Isa 57:15; [l]Ge 37:29; Nu 14:6; Job 1:20; [m]Isa 19:22; [n]Dt 4:31; [o]Ex 34:6; Ps 86:5, 15; [p]Jer 18:8; Jnh 4:2
14 [q]Jer 26:3; Jnh 3:9; [r]Am 5:15; Jnh 1:6; [s]Jer 31:14; Hag 2:19; Zec 8:13; Mal 3:10; [t]Joel 1:13

10 Before them the earth shakes,[z]
the sky trembles,[a]
the sun and moon are darkened,[b]
and the stars no longer shine.[c]
11 The LORD[d] thunders[e]
at the head of his army;[f]
his forces are beyond number,
and mighty are those who obey his
command.
The day of the LORD is great;[g]
it is dreadful.
Who can endure it?[h]

Rend Your Heart

12 "Even now," declares the LORD,
"return[i] to me with all your heart,[j]
with fasting and weeping and
mourning."

13 Rend your heart[k]
and not your garments.[l]
Return[m] to the LORD your God,
for he is gracious and
compassionate,[n]
slow to anger and abounding in love,[o]
and he relents from sending
calamity.[p]
14 Who knows? He may turn[q] and have
pity[r]
and leave behind a blessing[s]—
grain offerings and drink offerings[t]
for the LORD your God.

15 Blow the trumpet[u] in Zion,[v]
declare a holy fast,[w]
call a sacred assembly.[x]
16 Gather the people,
consecrate[y] the assembly;
bring together the elders,[z]
gather the children,
those nursing at the breast.
Let the bridegroom[a] leave his room
and the bride her chamber.
17 Let the priests, who minister[b] before
the LORD,
weep[c] between the temple porch
and the altar.[d]
Let them say, "Spare your people,
O LORD.
Do not make your inheritance an
object of scorn,[e]
a byword[f] among the nations.
Why should they say among the
peoples,
'Where is their God?[g]' "

15 [u]Nu 10:2; [v]ver 1; [w]2Ch 20:3; Jer 36:9; [x]Ex 32:5; Nu 10:3
16 [y]Ex 19:10,22; [z]Joel 1:2; [a]Ps 19:5
17 [b]Joel 1:13; [c]Isa 22:12; [d]Eze 8:16; Mt 23:35; [e]Dt 9:26–29; Ps 44:13; [f]1Ki 9:7; Job 17:6; [g]Ps 42:3

The LORD'*s Answer*

[18]Then the LORD will be jealous[h] for his
land
and take pity[i] on his people.

[19]The LORD will reply[a] to them:

"I am sending you grain, new wine[j]
and oil,[k]
enough to satisfy you fully;[l]
never again will I make you
an object of scorn[m] to the nations.

[20]"I will drive the northern army[n] far
from you,
pushing it into a parched and barren
land,
with its front columns going into the
eastern[o] sea[b]
and those in the rear into the
western sea.[c]
And its stench[p] will go up;
its smell will rise."

Surely he has done great things.[d]
21 Be not afraid,[q] O land;
be glad and rejoice.[r]
Surely the LORD has done great
things.[s]
22 Be not afraid, O wild animals,
for the open pastures are becoming
green.[t]
The trees are bearing their fruit;
the fig-tree[u] and the vine[v] yield their
riches.[w]
[23]Be glad, O people of Zion,
rejoice[x] in the LORD your God,
for he has given you
the autumn rains in
righteousness.[e y]
He sends you abundant showers,[z]
both autumn[a] and spring rains,[b] as
before.
[24]The threshing-floors will be filled with
grain;
the vats will overflow[c] with new
wine[d] and oil.

[25]"I will repay you for the years the
locusts[e] have eaten[f]—
the great locust and the young
locust,
the other locusts and the locust
swarm[f]—
my great army[g] that I sent among you.
[26]You will have plenty to eat, until you
are full,[h]
and you will praise[i] the name of the
LORD your God,
who has worked wonders[j] for you;
never again will my people be
shamed.[k]
[27]Then you will know[l] that I am in Israel,
that I am the LORD[m] your God,
and that there is no other;
never again will my people be
shamed.[n]

The Day of the LORD

[28]"And afterwards,
I will pour out my Spirit[o] on all
people.[p]
Your sons and daughters will
prophesy,[q]
your old men will dream dreams,[r]
your young men will see visions.
[29]Even on my servants,[s] both men and
women,
I will pour out my Spirit in those
days.[t]
[30]I will show wonders in the heavens[u]
and on the earth,[v]
blood and fire and billows of smoke.
[31]The sun will be turned to darkness[w]
and the moon to blood
before the coming of the great and
dreadful day of the LORD.[x]
[32]And everyone who calls
on the name of the LORD[y] will be
saved;[z]
for on Mount Zion[a] and in Jerusalem
there will be deliverance,[b]
as the LORD has said,
among the survivors[c]
whom the LORD calls.[d]

The Nations Judged

3 "In those days and at that time,
when I restore the fortunes[a] of
Judah[b] and Jerusalem,
[2]I will gather[c] all nations
and bring them down to the Valley
of Jehoshaphat.[a d]
There I will enter into judgment[e]
against them
concerning my inheritance, my
people Israel,
for they scattered[f] my people among
the nations
and divided up my land.

18 [h]**Isa 26:11;** Zec 1:14; 8:2; [i]**Ps 72:13**
19 [j]Ps 4:7; [k]**Jer 31:12;** [l]**Lev 26:5;** [m]**Eze 34:29**
20 [n]Jer 1:14–15; [o]Zec 14:8; [p]**Isa 34:3**
21 [q]**Isa 29:22; 54:4;** Zep 3:16–17; [r]**Ps 9:2;** [s]**Ps 126:3; Isa 25:1**
22 [t]**Ps 65:12;** [u]**1Ki 4:25;** [v]**Nu 16:14;** [w]Joel 1:18–20; Zec 8:12
23 [x]Ps 33:21; 97:12; 149:2; Isa 12:6; 41:16; 66:14; Hab 3:18; Zec 10:7; [y]**Isa 45:8;** [z]**Job 36:28; Eze 34:26;** [a]Ps 84:6; [b]**Lev 26:4; Ps 135:7;** Jas 5:7
24 [c]Lev 26:10; Mal 3:10; [d]**Pr 3:10;** Joel 3:18; Am 9:13
25 [e]**Ex 10:14;** Am 4:9; [f]**Dt 28:39;** [g]**Joel 1:6**
26 [h]**Lev 26:5;** [i]**Lev 23:40; Isa 62:9;** [j]**Ps 126:3; Isa 25:1;** [k]**Isa 29:22**
27 [l]**Ex 6:7;** [m]**Ex 6:2; Isa 44:8;** Joel 3:17; [n]Isa 45:17; 54:4; Zep 3:11
28 [o]**Isa 11:2; 44:3;** [p]**Nu 11:17; Mk 1:8;** Gal 3:14; [q]**1Sa 19:20;** [r]Jer 23:25
29 [s]1Co 12:13; Gal 3:28; [t]**Eze 36:27**
30 [u]Lk 21:11; [v]Mk 13:24–25
31 [w]**ver 2; Isa 22:5; Jer 4:23; Mt 24:29;** [x]**Joel 1:15;** Ob 15; Mal 3:2; 4:1,5
32 [y]**Ge 4:26; Ps 105:1;** [z]**Ps 106:8;** Ac 2:17–21*; Ro 10:13*; [a]**Isa 46:13;** [b]Ob 17; [c]**Isa 1:9;** 11:11; Mic 4:7; 7:18; **Ro 9:27;** [d]Ac 2:39

Ch. 3

1 [a]**Dt 30:3; Jer 16:15; Eze 38:8;** Zep 3:20; [b]Jer 40:5
2 [c]Zep 3:8; [d]ver 12; **Isa 22:1;** [e]**Isa 13:9; Jer 2:35; Eze 36:5;** [f]**Ge 11:4; Lev 26:33**

[a]*18,19* Or LORD *was jealous . . . / and took pity . . . / [19]The* LORD *replied* [b]*20* That is, the Dead Sea
[c]*20* That is, the Mediterranean
[d]*20* Or *rise. / Surely it has done great things."*
[e]*23* Or / *the teacher for righteousness:*
[f]*25* The precise meaning of the four Hebrew words used here for locusts is uncertain.
[a]*2* *Jehoshaphat* means *the* LORD *judges;* also in verse 12.

3They cast lots[g] for my people
and traded boys for prostitutes;
they sold girls for wine[h]
that they might drink.

4"Now what have you against me, O
Tyre and Sidon[i] and all you regions of
Philistia?[j] Are you repaying me for
something I have done? If you are
paying me back, I will swiftly and
speedily return on your own heads
what you have done.[k] 5For you took my
silver and my gold and carried off my
finest treasures to your temples.[l] 6You
sold the people of Judah and Jerusalem
to the Greeks,[m] that you might send
them far from their homeland.
7"See, I am going to rouse them out of
the places to which you sold them,[n] and
I will return[o] on your own heads what
you have done. 8I will sell your sons[p]
and daughters to the people of Judah,[q]
and they will sell them to the Sabeans,[r]
a nation far away." The LORD has
spoken.[s]

9Proclaim this among the nations:
Prepare for war![t]
Rouse the warriors![u]
Let all the fighting men draw near
and attack.
10Beat your ploughshares into swords
and your pruning hooks[v] into
spears.[w]
Let the weakling[x] say,
"I am strong!"[y]
11Come quickly, all you nations from
every side,
and assemble[z] there.

Bring down your warriors,[a] O LORD!

12"Let the nations be roused;
let them advance into the Valley of
Jehoshaphat,[b]
for there I will sit
to judge[c] all the nations on every
side.
13Swing the sickle,[d]
for the harvest[e] is ripe.
Come, trample the grapes,[f]
for the winepress[g] is full
and the vats overflow—
so great is their wickedness!"

3 [g]Job 6:27; Eze 24:6; [h]Joel 1:5; Am 2:6
4 [i]Ge 10:15; Mt 11:21; [j]Ps 87:4; Isa 14:29–31; Jer 47:1–7; [k]Lev 26:28; Isa 34:8; Eze 25:15–17; Zec 9:5–7
5 [l]1Ki 15:18; 2Ch 21:16–17
6 [m]Eze 27:13; Zec 9:13
7 [n]Isa 43:5–6; Jer 23:8; [o]Isa 66:6
8 [p]Isa 60:14; [q]Isa 14:2; [r]Ge 10:7; 2Ch 9:1; [s]Isa 23:1; Jer 30:16
9 [t]Isa 8:9; [u]Jer 46:4
10 [v]Isa 2:4; [w]Nu 25:7; [x]Zec 12:8; [y]Jos 1:6
11 [z]Eze 38:15–16; Zep 3:8; [a]Isa 13:3
12 [b]ver 2; [c]Ps 82:1; Isa 2:4
13 [d]Mk 4:29; [e]Isa 17:5; Hos 6:11; Mt 13:39; Rev 14:15–19; [f]Jer 25:30; [g]Jdg 6:11; Rev 14:20
14 [h]Isa 13:4; [i]Isa 22:1; [j]Isa 34:2–8; Joel 1:15; Zep 1:7; [k]Isa 2:4; Eze 36:5
15 [l]Job 9:7; Eze 32:7
16 [m]Isa 42:13; [n]Am 1:2; [o]Jdg 5:4; Isa 14:16; Eze 38:19; [p]Ps 46:1; Isa 25:4; Zec 12:8; [q]2Sa 22:3; Jer 16:19; Zec 9:12
17 [r]Ex 6:7; [s]Joel 2:27; [t]Ps 74:2; Isa 4:3; [u]Ps 2:6; Isa 2:2; Eze 17:22; [v]Jer 31:40; [w]Isa 52:1; Eze 44:9; Zec 9:8

14Multitudes,[h] multitudes
in the valley[i] of decision!
For the day of the LORD[j] is near
in the valley of decision.[k]
15The sun and moon will be darkened,
and the stars no longer shine.[l]
16The LORD will roar[m] from Zion
and thunder from Jerusalem;[n]
the earth and the sky will tremble.[o]
But the LORD will be a refuge[p] for his
people,
a stronghold[q] for the people of
Israel.

Blessings for God's People

17"Then you will know[r] that I, the LORD
your God,[s]
dwell in Zion,[t] my holy hill.[u]
Jerusalem will be holy;[v]
never again will foreigners invade
her.[w]

18"In that day the mountains will drip
new wine,[x]
and the hills will flow with milk;[y]
all the ravines of Judah will run with
water.[z]
A fountain will flow out of the LORD's
house[a]
and will water the valley of
acacias.[b] [b]
19But Egypt[c] will be desolate,
Edom[d] a desert waste,
because of violence[e] done to the
people of Judah,
in whose land they shed innocent
blood.
20Judah will be inhabited for ever[f]
and Jerusalem through all
generations.
21Their bloodguilt,[g] which I have not
pardoned,
I will pardon.[h]"

The LORD dwells in Zion![i]

18 [x]Joel 2:24; [y]Ex 3:8; SS 5:1; [z]Isa 30:25; 35:6; 44:3; [a]Rev 22:1–2; [b]Nu 25:1; Isa 25:6; Jer 31:12; Eze 47:1; Am 9:13
19 [c]Isa 19:1; [d]Isa 11:14; 34:11; [e]Jer 51:35; Ob 10
20 [f]Ezr 9:12; Am 9:15
21 [g]Isa 1:15; [h]Eze 36:25; [i]Ps 74:2; Isa 59:20; Eze 48:35; Zec 8:3

b18 Or *Valley of Shittim*

Amos

1 The words of Amos, one of the shepherds of Tekoa[a]—what he saw concerning Israel two years before the earthquake,[b] when Uzziah[c] was king of Judah and Jeroboam[d] son of Jehoash**[a]** was king of Israel.[e]

[2]He said:

"The LORD roars[f] from Zion
and thunders[g] from Jerusalem;[h]
the pastures of the shepherds dry up,**[b]**
and the top of Carmel[i] withers."[j]

Judgment on Israel's Neighbours

[3]This is what the LORD says:

"For three sins of Damascus,[k]
even for four, I will not turn back
⌞my wrath⌟.[l]
Because she threshed Gilead
with sledges having iron teeth,
[4]I will send fire[m] upon the house of
Hazael[n]
that will consume the fortresses[o] of
Ben-Hadad.[p]
[5]I will break down the gate[q] of
Damascus;
I will destroy the king who is in**[c]** the
Valley of Aven**[d]**
and the one who holds the sceptre in
Beth Eden.[r]
The people of Aram will go into
exile to Kir,[s]"
says the LORD.[t]

[6]This is what the LORD says:

"For three sins of Gaza,[u]
even for four, I will not turn back
⌞my wrath⌟.[v]
Because she took captive whole
communities
and sold them to Edom,[w]
[7]I will send fire upon the walls of Gaza
that will consume her fortresses.
[8]I will destroy the king**[e]** of Ashdod[x]
and the one who holds the sceptre
in Ashkelon.
I will turn my hand[y] against Ekron,
till the last of the Philistines[z] is
dead,"[a]
says the Sovereign LORD.[b]

[9]This is what the LORD says:

"For three sins of Tyre,[c]
even for four, I will not turn back
⌞my wrath⌟.[d]
Because she sold whole communities
of captives to Edom,
disregarding a treaty of
brotherhood,[e]
[10]I will send fire upon the walls of Tyre
that will consume her fortresses.[f]"

[11]This is what the LORD says:

"For three sins of Edom,[g]
even for four, I will not turn back
⌞my wrath⌟.
Because he pursued his brother with a
sword,[h]
stifling all compassion,**[f]**
because his anger raged continually
and his fury flamed unchecked,[i]
[12]I will send fire upon Teman[j]
that will consume the fortresses of
Bozrah.[k]"

[13]This is what the LORD says:

"For three sins of Ammon,[l]
even for four, I will not turn back
⌞my wrath⌟.
Because he ripped open the pregnant
women[m] of Gilead
in order to extend his borders,
[14]I will set fire to the walls of Rabbah[n]
that will consume[o] her fortresses
amid war cries[p] on the day of battle,
amid violent winds[q] on a stormy
day.
[15]Her king**[g]** will go into exile,
he and his officials together,[r]"
says the LORD.[s]

Ch. 1

1 [a]2Sa 14:2; [b]Zec 14:5; [c]2Ki 14:21; 2Ch 26:23; [d]2Ki 14:23; [e]Hos 1:1
2 [f]Isa 42:13; [g]Ps 29:3; [h]Joel 3:16; [i]Am 9:3; [j]Jer 12:4
3 [k]Isa 7:8; 8:4; 17:1–3; [l]ver 6,9,11,13; Am 2:6
4 [m]Jer 49:27; Eze 30:8; [n]1Ki 19:17; 2Ki 8:7–15; [o]Jer 17:27; [p]1Ki 20:1; 2Ki 6:24; Jer 49:23–27
5 [q]Jer 51:30; [r]Isa 37:12; [s]2Ki 16:9; Isa 22:6; Zec 9:1; [t]Isa 7:16; Jer 49:27
6 [u]Ge 10:19; 1Sa 6:17; Zep 2:4; [v]ver 3; [w]Ge 14:6; Ob 11
8 [x]2Ch 26:6; [y]Ps 81:14; [z]Eze 25:16; [a]Isa 34:8; [b]Isa 14:28–32; Zep 2:4–7
9 [c]1Ki 5:1; 9:11–14; Jer 25:22; Joel 3:4; Mt 11:21; [d]ver 3; [e]1Ki 5:12
10 [f]Isa 23:1–18; 34:8; Jer 47:4; Eze 26:2–4; Zec 9:1–4
11 [g]Nu 20:14–21; 2Ch 28:17; Ps 83:6; [h]Ps 63:10; [i]Eze 25:12–14; Zec 1:15
12 [j]Ge 36:11,15; [k]Isa 34:5; 63:1–6; Jer 25:21; Eze 25:12–14; 35:1–15; Ob 1; Mal 1:2–5
13 [l]Ge 19:38; Eze 21:28; [m]Ge 34:29; 2Ki 8:12; Hos 13:16
14 [n]Dt 3:11; [o]Isa 30:30; [p]Job 39:25; [q]Jer 23:19
15 [r]Jer 25:21; [s]1Ch 20:1; Jer 49:1; Eze 21:28–32; 25:2–7

a1 Hebrew *Joash*, a variant of *Jehoash*
b2 Or *shepherds mourn*
c5 Or *the inhabitants of*
d5 *Aven* means *wickedness.*
e8 Or *inhabitants*
f11 Or *sword / and destroyed his allies*
g15 Or / *Molech;* Hebrew *malcam*

2 This is what the LORD says:

"For three sins of Moab,[a]
even for four, I will not turn back
⌞my wrath⌟.
Because he burned, as if to lime,[b]
the bones of Edom's king,
2 I will send fire upon Moab
that will consume the fortresses of
Kerioth.[a][c]
Moab will go down in great tumult
amid war cries[d] and the blast of the
trumpet.[e]
3 I will destroy her ruler[f]
and kill all her officials with him,"[g]
says the LORD.[h]

4 This is what the LORD says:

"For three sins of Judah,[i]
even for four, I will not turn back
⌞my wrath⌟.
Because they have rejected the law[j] of
the LORD
and have not kept his decrees,[k]
because they have been led astray[l] by
false gods,[b][m]
the gods[c] their ancestors followed,[n]
5 I will send fire[o] upon Judah
that will consume the fortresses[p] of
Jerusalem.[q]"

Judgment on Israel

6 This is what the LORD says:

"For three sins of Israel,
even for four, I will not turn back
⌞my wrath⌟.[r]
They sell the righteous for silver,
and the needy for a pair of sandals.[s]
7 They trample on the heads of the poor
as upon the dust of the ground
and deny justice to the oppressed.
Father and son use the same girl
and so profane my holy name.[t]
8 They lie down beside every altar
on garments taken in pledge.[u]
In the house of their god
they drink wine[v] taken as fines.[w]

9 "I destroyed the Amorite[x] before
them,
though he was tall[y] as the cedars
and strong as the oaks.[z]
I destroyed his fruit above
and his roots[a] below.

10 "I brought you up out of Egypt,[b]
and I led[c] you for forty years in the
desert[d]
to give you the land of the
Amorites.[e]
11 I also raised up prophets[f] from among
your sons
and Nazirites[g] from among your
young men.
Is this not true, people of Israel?"
declares the LORD.
12 "But you made the Nazirites drink
wine
and commanded the prophets not
to prophesy.[h]

13 "Now then, I will crush you
as a cart crushes when loaded with
grain.[i]
14 The swift will not escape,[j]
the strong[k] will not muster their
strength,
and the warrior will not save his
life.[l]
15 The archer[m] will not stand his ground,
the fleet-footed soldier will not get
away,
and the horseman[n] will not save his
life.[o]
16 Even the bravest warriors[p]
will flee naked on that day,"
declares the LORD.

Witnesses Summoned Against Israel

3 Hear this word the LORD has
spoken against you,[a] O people of
Israel—against the whole family I
brought up out of Egypt:[b]

2 "You only have I chosen[c]
of all the families of the earth;
therefore I will punish[d] you
for all your sins.[e]"

3 Do two walk together
unless they have agreed to do so?
4 Does a lion roar[f] in the thicket
when he has no prey?[g]
Does he growl in his den
when he has caught nothing?
5 Does a bird fall into a trap on the
ground
where no snare[h] has been set?
Does a trap spring up from the earth
when there is nothing to catch?
6 When a trumpet[i] sounds in a city,
do not the people tremble?
When disaster[j] comes to a city,
has not the LORD caused it?[k]

7 Surely the Sovereign LORD does
nothing
without revealing his plan[l]
to his servants the prophets.[m]

Ch. 2

1 [a]Isa 16:6; [b]Isa 33:12
2 [c]Jer 48:24; [d]Job 39:25; [e]Jos 6:20
3 [f]Ps 2:10; [g]Isa 40:23; [h]Isa 15:1–9; 16:1–14; 25:10; Jer 48:1; Eze 25:8–11; Zep 2:8–9
4 [i]2Ki 17:19; Hos 12:2; [j]Jer 6:19; [k]Eze 20:24; [l]Isa 9:16; [m]Ex 34:15; Dt 31:20; Ps 4:2; [n]2Ki 22:13; Jer 9:14; 16:12
5 [o]2Ki 25:9; 2Ch 36:19; [p]Am 3:11; [q]Jer 17:27; Hos 8:14
6 [r]Am 1:3; [s]Joel 3:3; Am 8:6
7 [t]Lev 18:21; Am 5:11–12; 8:4
8 [u]Ex 22:26; Dt 24:12–13; [v]Hos 7:14; Am 4:1; 6:6; [w]Hab 2:6
9 [x]Nu 21:23–26; Jos 10:12; [y]Isa 10:33; [z]Ps 29:9; [a]2Ki 19:30; Job 18:16; Eze 17:9
10 [b]Ex 6:6; 20:2; Am 3:1; [c]Dt 8:2; [d]Dt 2:7; [e]Ex 3:8; Nu 21:25; Jos 13:4; Am 9:7
11 [f]Dt 18:18; Jer 7:25; [g]Jdg 13:5
12 [h]Isa 30:10; Jer 11:21; Am 7:12–13; Mic 2:6
13 [i]Am 7:16–17
14 [j]Job 11:20; [k]1Ki 20:11; [l]Ps 33:16; Isa 30:16–17
15 [m]Eze 39:3; [n]Ex 15:21; Zec 10:5; [o]Ecc 9:11
16 [p]Jer 48:41

Ch. 3

1 [a]Zep 2:5; [b]Am 2:10
2 [c]Ex 19:6; Dt 7:6; Lk 12:47; [d]ver 14; [e]Jer 14:10; Mic 2:3; 1Pe 4:17
4 [f]Isa 42:13; [g]Ps 104:21; Hos 5:14
5 [h]Ps 119:110
6 [i]Nu 10:2; Job 39:24; Jer 4:21; [j]Isa 31:2; [k]Isa 14:24–27
7 [l]Ge 18:17; 1Sa 3:7; Da 9:22; Jn 15:15; Rev 10:7; [m]Jer 23:22

[a]2 Or *of her cities* [b]4 Or *by lies* [c]4 Or *lies*

8The lion[n] has roared[o]—
who will not fear?
The Sovereign LORD has spoken—
who can but prophesy?[p]

9Proclaim to the fortresses of Ashdod[q]
and to the fortresses of Egypt:
"Assemble yourselves on the
mountains of Samaria;[r]
see the great unrest within her
and the oppression among her
people."

10"They do not know how to do right,[s]"
declares the LORD,
"who hoard plunder[t] and loot in
their fortresses."[u]

11Therefore this is what the Sovereign
LORD says:

"An enemy will overrun the land;
he will pull down your strongholds
and plunder your fortresses.[v]"

12This is what the LORD says:

"As a shepherd saves from the lion's[w]
mouth
only two leg bones or a piece of an
ear,
so will the Israelites be saved,
those who sit in Samaria
on the edge of their beds
and in Damascus on their
couches.[a][x]"

13"Hear this and testify[y] against the
house of Jacob," declares the Lord, the
LORD God Almighty.

14"On the day I punish[z] Israel for her
sins,
I will destroy the altars of Bethel;[a]
the horns[b] of the altar will be cut off
and fall to the ground.
15I will tear down the winter house[c]
along with the summer house;[d]
the houses adorned with ivory[e] will be
destroyed
and the mansions[f] will be
demolished,[g]"
declares the LORD.[h]

Israel Has Not Returned to God

4 Hear this word, you cows of
Bashan[a] on Mount Samaria,[b]
you women who oppress the poor[c]
and crush the needy[d]
and say to your husbands,[e] "Bring
us some drinks![f]"
2The Sovereign LORD has sworn by his
holiness:

"The time[g] will surely come
when you will be taken away[h] with
hooks,[i]
the last of you with fish-hooks.
3You will each go straight out
through breaks in the wall,[j]
and you will be cast out towards
Harmon,"[a]
declares the LORD.

4"Go to Bethel[k] and sin;
go to Gilgal[l] and sin yet more.
Bring your sacrifices every morning,[m]
your tithes[n] every three years.[b][o]
5Burn leavened bread[p] as a
thank-offering
and brag about your freewill
offerings[q]—
boast about them, you Israelites,
for this is what you love to do,"
declares the Sovereign LORD.

6"I gave you empty stomachs[c] in every
city
and lack of bread in every town,
yet you have not returned to me,"
declares the LORD.[r]

7"I also withheld[s] rain from you
when the harvest was still three
months away.
I sent rain on one town,
but withheld it from another.[t]
One field had rain;
another had none and dried up.
8People staggered from town to town
for water[u]
but did not get enough[v] to drink,
yet you have not returned[w] to me,"
declares the LORD.[x]

9"Many times I struck your gardens
and vineyards,
I struck them with blight and
mildew.[y]
Locusts[z] devoured your fig and olive
trees,[a]
yet you have not returned[b] to me,"
declares the LORD.

10"I sent plagues[c] among you
as I did to Egypt.[d]
I killed your young men[e] with the
sword,
along with your captured horses.
I filled your nostrils with the stench[f] of
your camps,
yet you have not returned to me,"[g]
declares the LORD.[h]

8 [n]Isa 31:4; [o]Isa 42:13; [p]Jer 20:9; Jnh 1:1–3; 3:1–3; Ac 4:20
9 [q]Jos 13:3; 2Ch 26:6; [r]Am 4:1; 6:1
10 [s]Am 5:7; 6:12; [t]Hab 2:8; [u]Ps 36:3; Mic 6:10; Zep 1:9
11 [v]Am 2:5; 6:14
12 [w]1Sa 17:34; [x]Est 1:6; Am 6:4
13 [y]Eze 2:7
14 [z]ver 2; Lev 26:18; [a]Ge 12:8; Am 5:5–6; [b]Ex 27:2
15 [c]Jer 36:22; [d]Jdg 3:20; [e]1Ki 22:39; [f]Am 5:11; 6:11; [g]Isa 34:5; [h]Hos 10:5–8, 14–15

Ch. 4

1 [a]Ps 22:12; [b]Am 3:9; [c]Isa 58:6; Eze 18:12; [d]Dt 24:14; [e]Jer 44:19; [f]Am 2:8; 5:11; 8:6
2 [g]Jer 31:31; [h]Am 6:8; [i]2Ki 19:28; 2Ch 33:11; Isa 19:8
3 [j]Eze 12:5
4 [k]Jos 7:2; [l]Hos 4:15; [m]Nu 28:3; [n]Dt 14:28; [o]Eze 20:39; Am 5:21–22
5 [p]Lev 7:13; [q]Lev 22:18–21
6 [r]Isa 3:1; 9:13; Jer 5:3; Hag 2:17
7 [s]Jer 3:3; Zec 14:17; [t]Ex 9:4,26; Dt 11:17; 2Ch 7:13; Isa 5:6
8 [u]Eze 4:16–17; [v]Hag 1:6; [w]Jer 3:7; [x]Job 36:31; Jer 14:4
9 [y]Dt 28:22; [z]Ex 10:13; Joel 2:25; [a]Joel 1:7; [b]Isa 9:13; Jer 3:10
10 [c]Ex 9:3; [d]Ex 11:5; [e]Isa 9:17; [f]Isa 34:3; [g]Dt 28:21; [h]Isa 9:13

[a]12 The meaning of the Hebrew for this line is uncertain.
[a]3 Masoretic Text; with a different word division of the Hebrew (see Septuagint) *out, O mountain of oppression* [b]4 Or *tithes on the third day*
[c]6 Hebrew *you cleanness of teeth*

11"I overthrew some of you
as I[d] overthrew Sodom and
Gomorrah.[i]
You were like a burning stick[j]
snatched from the fire,
yet you have not returned to me,"
declares the LORD.[k]

12"Therefore this is what I will do to
you, Israel,
and because I will do this to you,
prepare to meet your God, O
Israel."

13He who forms the mountains,[l]
creates the wind,[m]
and reveals his thoughts[n] to man,
he who turns dawn to darkness,
and treads the high places of the
earth[o]—
the LORD God Almighty is his
name.[p]

A Lament and Call to Repentance

5 Hear this word, O house of Israel,
this lament[a] I take up concerning
you:

2"Fallen is Virgin[b] Israel,
never to rise again,
deserted in her own land,
with no-one to lift her up.[c]"

3This is what the Sovereign LORD
says:

"The city that marches out a thousand
strong for Israel
will have only a hundred left;
the town that marches out a hundred
strong
will have only ten left.[d]"

4This is what the LORD says to the
house of Israel:

"Seek[e] me and live;[f]
5 do not seek Bethel,
do not go to Gilgal,[g]
do not journey to Beersheba.[h]
For Gilgal will surely go into exile,
and Bethel will be reduced to
nothing.[a] [i]"
6Seek[j] the LORD and live,[k]
or he will sweep through the house
of Joseph like a fire;[l]
it will devour,
and Bethel[m] will have no-one to
quench it.[n]

7You who turn justice into bitterness[o]
and cast righteousness[p] to the
ground[q]

11 [i]Ge 19:24; Jer 23:14; [j]Isa 7:4; Jude 23; [k]Job 36:13
13 [l]Ps 65:6; [m]Ps 135:7; [n]Da 2:28; [o]Mic 1:3; [p]Isa 47:4; Am 5:8,27; 9:6

Ch. 5

1 [a]Jer 4:8; Eze 19:1
2 [b]2Ki 19:21; Jer 14:17; [c]Jer 50:32; Am 8:14
3 [d]Isa 6:13; Am 6:9
4 [e]Dt 4:29; [f]Dt 32:46–47; Isa 55:3; Jer 29:13; Eze 18:9
5 [g]1Sa 11:14; Hos 4:15; [h]Ge 21:31; Am 8:14; [i]1Sa 7:16; 8:2
6 [j]Ps 22:26; 105:4; Isa 31:1; 55:6; Zep 2:3; [k]ver 14; Lev 18:5; [l]Dt 4:24; [m]Am 3:14; [n]Jer 4:4
7 [o]Isa 5:20; Am 6:12; [p]Am 3:10; [q]Hos 10:4
8 [r]Ge 1:16; Job 38:31; [s]Job 38:12; Isa 42:16; [t]Ps 104:20; Am 8:9; [u]Ps 104:6–9; Jer 16:21; Am 4:13
9 [v]Mic 5:11
10 [w]Isa 29:21; [x]1Ki 22:8; Gal 4:16
11 [y]Am 8:6; [z]Am 3:15; [a]Dt 28:30; Mic 1:6; [b]Jdg 9:27; Am 4:1; 9:14; Mic 6:15; Zep 1:13
12 [c]Hos 5:3; [d]Job 36:18; Isa 1:23; Eze 22:12; [e]Jer 5:28; [f]Job 5:4; Isa 5:23; Am 2:6–7
13 [g]Est 4:14; [h]Mic 2:3
14 [i]ver 6
15 [j]Ps 52:3; 97:10; Ro 12:9; [k]Ge 18:25; [l]Isa 1:17; 29:21; Zec 8:16; [m]Jer 36:3; [n]Joel 2:14; [o]Mic 5:7–8; 7:18
16 [p]Jer 9:17; Am 8:3; Zep 1:10; [q]Jer 7:34; [r]Joel 1:11

8(he who made the Pleiades and
Orion,[r]
who turns blackness into dawn[s]
and darkens day into night,[t]
who calls for the waters of the sea
and pours them out over the face of
the land—
the LORD is his name[u]—
9he flashes destruction on the
stronghold
and brings the fortified city to
ruin),[v]
10you hate the one who reproves in
court[w]
and despise him who tells the
truth.[x]

11You trample on the poor[y]
and force him to give you grain.
Therefore, though you have built
stone mansions,[z]
you will not live in them;[a]
though you have planted lush
vineyards,
you will not drink their wine.[b]
12For I know how many are your
offences
and how great your sins.[c]

You oppress the righteous and take
bribes[d]
and you deprive the poor[e] of justice
in the courts.[f]
13Therefore the prudent man keeps
quiet[g] in such times,
for the times are evil.[h]

14Seek good, not evil,
that you may live.[i]
Then the LORD God Almighty will be
with you,
just as you say he is.
15Hate evil,[j] love good;[k]
maintain justice in the courts.[l]
Perhaps[m] the LORD God Almighty will
have mercy[n]
on the remnant[o] of Joseph.

16Therefore this is what the Lord, the
LORD God Almighty, says:

"There will be wailing[p] in all the
streets[q]
and cries of anguish in every public
square.
The farmers[r] will be summoned to
weep
and the mourners to wail.

[d]11 Hebrew *God*
[a]5 Or *grief*; or *wickedness*; Hebrew *aven*, a reference to Beth Aven (a derogatory name for Bethel)

17There will be wailing[s] in all the
vineyards,
for I will pass through[t] your midst,"
says the LORD.[u]

The Day of the LORD

18Woe to you who long
for the day of the LORD![v]
Why do you long for the day of the
LORD?[w]
That day will be darkness,[x] not
light.[y]
19It will be as though a man fled from a
lion
only to meet a bear,[z]
as though he entered his house
and rested his hand on the wall
only to have a snake bite him.[a]
20Will not the day of the LORD be
darkness,[b] not light—
pitch-dark, without a ray of
brightness?[c]

21"I hate,[d] I despise your religious
feasts;[e]
I cannot stand your assemblies.[f]
22Even though you bring me burnt
offerings[g] and grain offerings,
I will not accept them.[h i]
Though you bring choice fellowship
offerings,[b]
I will have no regard for them.[j k]
23Away with the noise of your songs!
I will not listen to the music of your
harps.[l]
24But let justice[m] roll on like a river,
righteousness[n] like a never-failing
stream![o]

25"Did you bring me sacrifices[p] and
offerings
for forty years[q] in the desert, O
house of Israel?
26You have lifted up the shrine of your
king,
the pedestal of your idols,[r]
the star of your god—[c]
which you made for yourselves.
27Therefore I will send you into exile[s]
beyond Damascus,"
says the LORD, whose name is God
Almighty.[t]

Woe to the Complacent

6 Woe to you[a] who are complacent[b]
in Zion,
and to you who feel secure[c] on
Mount Samaria,[d]
you notable men of the foremost
nation,
to whom the people of Israel come![e]
2Go to Calneh[f] and look at it;
go from there to great Hamath,[g]
and then go down to Gath[h] in
Philistia.
Are they better off than[i] your two
kingdoms?
Is their land larger than yours?
3You put off the evil day
and bring near a reign of terror.[j]
4You lie on beds inlaid with ivory
and lounge on your couches.[k]
You dine on choice lambs
and fattened calves.[l]
5You strum away on your harps[m] like
David
and improvise on musical
instruments.[n]
6You drink wine[o] by the bowlful
and use the finest lotions,
but you do not grieve[p] over the ruin
of Joseph.[q]
7Therefore you will be among the first
to go into exile;[r]
your feasting and lounging will
end.[s]

The LORD Abhors the Pride of Israel

8The Sovereign LORD has sworn by
himself[t]—the LORD God Almighty de-
clares:

"I abhor[u] the pride of Jacob[v]
and detest his fortresses;[w]
I will deliver up[x] the city
and everything in it.[y]"

9If ten[z] men are left in one house, they
too will die. 10And if a relative who is to
burn the bodies[a] comes to carry them
out of the house and asks anyone still
hiding there, "Is anyone with you?"
and he says, "No," then he will say,
"Hush![b] We must not mention the name
of the LORD."

11For the LORD has given the command,
and he will smash[c] the great house[d]
into pieces
and the small house into bits.[e]

12Do horses run on the rocky crags?
Does one plough there with oxen?
But you have turned justice into
poison[f]
and the fruit of righteousness[g] into
bitterness[h]—

17 [s]**Ex 11:6;** [t]Eze 12:12; [u]Isa 16:10; **Jer 48:33**
18 [v]**Isa 2:12; Joel 1:15;** [w]**Jer 30:5;** [x]**1Sa 2:9; Joel 2:2;** [y]**Job 20:28;** Isa 5:19,30; Jer 30:7
19 [z]**La 3:10;** [a]**Dt 32:24;** Job 20:24; **Ecc 10:8;** Isa 24:17–18; Jer 15:2–3; 48:44
20 [b]**1Sa 2:9;** [c]**Isa 13:10; Eze 7:7;** Ob 15; Zep 1:15
21 [d]Jer 44:4; [e]**Lev 26:31; Hos 2:11;** [f]**Eze 23:18**
22 [g]Lev 26:31; [h]**Jer 7:21;** [i]**Ps 40:6;** [j]Jer 14:12; **Am 4:4;** Mic 6:6–7; [k]Isa 1:11–16; **66:3**
23 [l]Am 6:5
24 [m]**Jer 22:3;** [n]Isa 45:8; [o]Mic 6:8
25 [p]**Isa 43:23;** [q]**Ex 16:35**
26 [r]**Eze 18:6; 20:16**
27 [s]Am 6:7; 7:11, 17; Mic 1:16; [t]Dt 32:17–19; Jer 38:17; **Am 4:13;** Ac 7:42–43*

Ch. 6

1 [a]Lk 6:24; [b]Zep 1:12; [c]**Job 24:23;** [d]**Am 3:9;** [e]Isa 32:9–11
2 [f]**Ge 10:10;** [g]**2Ki 17:24; Jer 49:23;** [h]**Jos 11:22;** 2Ch 26:6; [i]Na 3:8
3 [j]**Isa 56:12; Eze 12:22;** Am 9:10
4 [k]**Est 1:6; Pr 7:17;** [l]**Isa 1:11; Eze 34:2–3; Am 3:12**
5 [m]**Ps 137:2; Isa 14:11;** Am 5:23; [n]**1Ch 15:16**
6 [o]**Isa 28:1; Am 2:8;** [p]**Eze 9:4;** [q]**Eze 16:49**
7 [r]**Am 5:27;** [s]**Jer 16:9; La 4:5**
8 [t]**Ge 22:16;** Heb 6:13; [u]**Lev 26:30;** [v]**Ps 47:4;** [w]**Jer 12:8;** [x]Am 4:2; [y]**Lev 26:19;** Dt 32:19
9 [z]**Am 5:3**
10 [a]**1Sa 31:12;** [b]Am 8:3
11 [c]**Isa 34:5;** [d]**Am 3:15;** [e]Isa 55:11
12 [f]Hos 10:4; [g]**Am 3:10;** [h]**Isa 1:21; Am 5:7**

[b]22 Traditionally *peace offerings*
[c]26 Or *lifted up Sakkuth your king / and Kaiwan your idols, / your star-gods;* Septuagint *lifted up the shrine of Molech / and the star of your god Rephan, / their idols*

13you who rejoice in the conquest of Lo
Debar[a]
and say, "Did we not take Karnaim[b]
by our own strength?[i]"

14For the LORD God Almighty declares,
"I will stir up a nation[j] against you,
O house of Israel,
that will oppress you all the way
from Lebo[c] Hamath[k] to the valley of
the Arabah.[l]"

Locusts, Fire and a Plumb-Line

7 This is what the Sovereign LORD
showed me:[a] He was preparing
swarms of locusts[b] after the king's share
had been harvested and just as the
second crop was coming up. 2When
they had stripped the land clean,[c] I cried
out, "Sovereign LORD, forgive! How can
Jacob survive?[d] He is so small![e]"
3So the LORD relented.[f]
"This will not happen," the LORD
said.[g]
4This is what the Sovereign LORD
showed me: The Sovereign LORD was
calling for judgment by fire;[h] it dried up
the great deep and devoured[i] the land.
5Then I cried out, "Sovereign LORD, I
beg you, stop! How can Jacob survive?
He is so small![j]"
6So the LORD relented.[k]
"This will not happen either," the
Sovereign LORD said.[l]

7This is what he showed me: The
LORD was standing by a wall that had
been built true to plumb, with a plumb-
line in his hand. 8And the LORD asked
me, "What do you see,[m] Amos?[n]"
"A plumb-line,[o]" I replied.
Then the LORD said, "Look, I am
setting a plumb-line among my people
Israel; I will spare them no longer.[p]

9"The high places[q] of Isaac will be
destroyed
and the sanctuaries[r] of Israel will be
ruined;
with my sword I will rise against the
house of Jeroboam.[s]"

Amos and Amaziah

10Then Amaziah the priest of Bethel[t]
sent a message to Jeroboam[u] king of
Israel: "Amos is raising a conspiracy[v]
against you in the very heart of Israel.
The land cannot bear all his words.[w]
11For this is what Amos is saying:

" 'Jeroboam will die by the sword,
and Israel will surely go into exile,[x]
away from their native land.' "[y]

12Then Amaziah said to Amos, "Get
out, you seer![z] Go back to the land of
Judah. Earn your bread there and do
your prophesying there.[a] 13Don't
prophesy any more at Bethel,[b] because
this is the king's sanctuary and the
temple[c] of the kingdom.[d]"
14Amos answered Amaziah, "I was
neither a prophet[e] nor a prophet's son,
but I was a shepherd, and I also took
care of sycamore-fig trees.[f] 15But the
LORD took me from tending the flock[g]
and said to me, 'Go,[h] prophesy[i] to my
people Israel.'[j] 16Now then, hear[k] the
word of the LORD. You say,

" 'Do not prophesy against[l] Israel,
and stop preaching against the
house of Isaac.'

17"Therefore this is what the LORD
says:

" 'Your wife will become a prostitute[m]
in the city,
and your sons and daughters will
fall by the sword.
Your land will be measured and
divided up,
and you yourself will die in a pagan[a]
country.
And Israel will certainly go into exile,[n]
away from their native land.[o]' "

A Basket of Ripe Fruit

8 This is what the Sovereign LORD
showed me:[a] a basket of ripe fruit.
2"What do you see,[b] Amos?[c]" he asked.
"A basket[d] of ripe fruit," I answered.
Then the LORD said to me, "The time
is ripe for my people Israel; I will spare
them no longer.[e]
3"In that day," declares the Sovereign
LORD, "the songs in the temple will turn
to wailing.[a][f] Many, many bodies—
flung everywhere! Silence![g]"

4Hear this, you who trample the needy
and do away with the poor[h] of the
land,[i]

5saying,

"When will the New Moon[j] be over
that we may sell grain,

13 [i]Job 8:15; Isa 28:14–15
14 [j]Jer 5:15; [k]Nu 13:21; [l]Am 3:11

Ch. 7

1 [a]ver 7; Am 8:1; [b]Ps 78:46; Jer 51:14; Joel 1:4
2 [c]Ex 10:15; [d]Isa 37:4; [e]Eze 11:13; Am 4:9
3 [f]Ex 32:14; Dt 32:36; Jer 18:8; 26:19; [g]Hos 11:8
4 [h]Isa 66:16; Joel 1:19; [i]Dt 32:22
5 [j]ver 1–2; Joel 2:17
6 [k]Ex 32:14; Jer 18:8; Jnh 3:10; [l]Jer 42:10; Eze 9:8
8 [m]Jer 1:11,13; [n]Am 8:2; [o]2Ki 21:13; [p]Jer 15:6; Eze 7:2–9
9 [q]Lev 26:30; [r]Lev 26:31; [s]1Ki 13:34; 2Ki 15:9; Isa 63:18; Hos 10:8
10 [t]Jos 7:2; [u]2Ki 14:23; [v]Jer 38:4; [w]2Ki 14:24; Jer 26:8–11
11 [x]Am 5:27; [y]Jer 36:16
12 [z]1Sa 9:9; [a]Mt 8:34
13 [b]Jos 7:2; 1Ki 12:29; [c]Jer 36:5; [d]Jer 20:2; Am 2:12; Ac 4:18
14 [e]1Sa 10:5; 2Ki 2:5; 4:38; Zec 13:5; [f]1Ki 10:27; Isa 9:10
15 [g]Ge 37:2; 2Sa 7:8; [h]Isa 6:9; [i]Jer 26:12; [j]Jer 7:1–2; Eze 2:3–4
16 [k]Jer 22:2; [l]Eze 20:46; Mic 2:6
17 [m]Hos 4:13; [n]Am 5:27; [o]2Ki 17:6; Eze 4:13; Hos 9:3; Am 2:12–13

Ch. 8

1 [a]Am 7:1
2 [b]Jer 1:13; 24:3; [c]Am 7:8; [d]Ge 40:16; [e]La 4:18; Eze 7:2–9
3 [f]Am 5:16; [g]Am 6:10
4 [h]Pr 30:14; [i]Job 20:19; Ps 14:4; Am 2:7
5 [j]Nu 10:10

[a]13 *Lo Debar* means *nothing*.
[b]13 *Karnaim* means *horns*; *horn* here symbolises strength.
[c]14 Or *from the entrance to*
[a]17 Hebrew *an unclean*
[a]3 Or *"the temple singers will wail*

and the Sabbath be ended
that we may market[k] wheat?"[l]—
skimping the measure,
boosting the price
and cheating[m] with dishonest
scales,[n]
6buying the poor[o] with silver
and the needy for a pair of sandals,
selling even the sweepings with the
wheat.[p]

7The LORD has sworn by the Pride of
Jacob:[q] "I will never forget[r] anything
they have done.[s]

8"Will not the land tremble[t] for this,
and all who live in it mourn?
The whole land will rise like the Nile;
it will be stirred up and then sink
like the river of Egypt.[u]

9"In that day," declares the Sovereign
LORD,

"I will make the sun go down at noon
and darken the earth in broad
daylight.[v]
10I will turn your religious feasts[w] into
mourning
and all your singing into weeping.[x]
I will make all of you wear sackcloth[y]
and shave[z] your heads.
I will make that time like mourning for
an only son[a]
and the end of it like a bitter day.[b]

11"The days are coming," [c] declares the
Sovereign LORD,
"when I will send a famine through
the land—
not a famine of food or a thirst for
water,
but a famine[d] of hearing the words
of the LORD.[e]
12Men will stagger from sea to sea
and wander from north to east,
searching for the word of the LORD,
but they will not find it.[f]

13"In that day

"the lovely young women and strong
young men[g]
will faint because of thirst.[h]
14They who swear by the shame[b] of
Samaria,[i]
or say, 'As surely as your god lives,
O Dan',[j]
or, 'As surely as the god[c] of
Beersheba[k] lives'—
they will fall,[l]
never to rise again.[m]"

5 [k]Isa 58:13; [l]Ne 10:31; [m]Ge 31:7; [n]Dt 25:15; 2Ki 4:23; Ne 13:15–16; Eze 45:10–12; Hos 12:7; Mic 6:10–11; Zec 5:6
6 [o]Am 5:11; [p]Am 2:6; 4:1
7 [q]Ps 47:4; [r]Hos 8:13; [s]Job 35:15
8 [t]Job 9:6; Jer 51:29; [u]Ps 18:7; Jer 46:8; Am 9:5
9 [v]Job 5:14; Isa 59:9–10; Jer 13:16; 15:9; Eze 32:7; Am 5:8; Mic 3:6; Mt 27:45; Mk 15:33; Lk 23:44–45
10 [w]Lev 26:31; [x]La 5:15; Hos 2:11; [y]Joel 1:8; [z]Lev 13:40; Isa 3:17; [a]Ge 21:16; [b]Jer 2:19; Eze 7:18
11 [c]Jer 30:3; 31:27; [d]Isa 30:20; [e]1Sa 3:1; 28:6; 2Ch 15:3
12 [f]Eze 20:3,31
13 [g]Isa 9:17; [h]Isa 41:17; Hos 2:3
14 [i]Mic 1:5; [j]1Ki 12:29; [k]Am 5:5; [l]Ps 46:2; [m]Am 5:2

Ch. 9

1 [a]Ps 68:21; [b]Jer 11:11
2 [c]Job 7:9; Eze 26:20; [d]Jer 51:53; [e]Ob 4
3 [f]Am 1:2; [g]Ps 139:8–10; [h]Ps 68:22; [i]Isa 27:1; [j]Jer 16:16–17; [k]Ge 49:17; Job 11:20
4 [l]Lev 26:33; Eze 5:12; [m]Jer 21:10; [n]Jer 39:16; Eze 15:7; [o]Jer 44:11
5 [p]Ps 46:2; [q]Am 8:8
6 [r]Jer 43:9; [s]Ps 104:1–3,5–6, 13; Am 5:8
7 [t]2Ch 12:3; Isa 20:4; 43:3; [u]Ge 10:14; [v]Dt 2:23; [w]2Ki 16:9; Isa 22:6; Am 2:10

Israel to Be Destroyed

9 I saw the LORD standing by the
altar, and he said:

"Strike the tops of the pillars
so that the thresholds shake.
Bring them down on the heads[a] of all
the people;
those who are left I will kill with the
sword.
Not one will get away,
none will escape.[b]
2Though they dig down to the depths
of the grave,[a] [c]
from there my hand will take them.
Though they climb up to the heavens,[d]
from there I will bring them down.[e]
3Though they hide themselves on the
top of Carmel,[f]
there I will hunt them down and
seize them.[g]
Though they hide from me at the
bottom of the sea,[h]
there I will command the serpent[i] to
bite them.[j] [k]
4Though they are driven into exile by
their enemies,
there I will command the sword[l] to
slay them.
I will fix my eyes upon them
for evil[m] and not for good.[n]"[o]

5The Lord, the LORD Almighty,
he who touches the earth and it
melts,[p]
and all who live in it mourn—
the whole land rises like the Nile,
then sinks like the river of Egypt[q]—
6he who builds his lofty palace[b] [r] in the
heavens
and sets its foundation[c] on the
earth,
who calls for the waters of the sea
and pours them out over the face of
the land—
the LORD is his name.[s]

7"Are not you Israelites
the same to me as the Cushites[d]?"[t]
declares the LORD.
"Did I not bring Israel up from Egypt,
the Philistines[u] from Caphtor[e] [v]
and the Arameans from Kir?[w]

b14 Or *by Ashima;* or *by the idol* c14 Or *power*
a2 Hebrew *to Sheol*
b6 The meaning of the Hebrew for this phrase is uncertain.
c6 The meaning of the Hebrew for this word is uncertain.
d7 That is, people from the upper Nile region
e7 That is, Crete

8"Surely the eyes of the Sovereign
LORD
are on the sinful kingdom.
I will destroy[x] it
from the face of the earth—
yet I will not totally destroy the house
of Jacob,"
declares the LORD.[y]
9"For I will give the command,
and I will shake the house of Israel
among all the nations
as grain[z] is shaken in a sieve,[a]
and not a pebble will reach the
ground.[b]
10All the sinners among my people
will die by the sword,[c]
all those who say,
'Disaster will not overtake or meet
us.'[d]

Israel's Restoration

11"In that day I will restore
David's[e] fallen tent.[f]
I will repair its broken places,
restore its ruins,[g]
and build it as it used to be,[h]
12so that they may possess the remnant
of Edom[i]
and all the nations that bear my
name,[f][j]"
declares the LORD,
who will do these things.[k]

13"The days are coming,"[l] declares
the LORD,

"when the reaper[m] will be overtaken
by the ploughman[n]
and the planter by the one treading[o]
grapes.
New wine[p] will drip from the
mountains
and flow from all the hills.[q]
14I will bring[r] back my exiled[g][s] people
Israel;
they will rebuild the ruined cities[t]
and live in them.
They will plant vineyards[u] and drink
their wine;
they will make gardens and eat their
fruit.[v]
15I will plant[w] Israel in their own land,[x]
never again to be uprooted[y]
from the land I have given them,"[z]
says the LORD your God.[a]

8 [x]**Jer 4:27**; [y]**Jer 44:27**
9 [z]Lk 22:31; [a]Isa 30:28; [b]**Jer 31:36; Da 9:7**
10 [c]Jer 49:37; [d]Jer 5:12; **23:17; Eze 20:38; Am 6:3**
11 [e]**Isa 7:2**; [f]**Ge 26:22**; [g]Ps 53:6; **Isa 49:8**; [h]Ps 80:12; **Eze 17:24**; Mic 7:8,11; Zec 12:7; 14:10
12 [i]**Nu 24:18**; [j]Isa 43:7; Jer 25:29; [k]Ac 15:16–17*
13 [l]Jer 31:38; 33:14; [m]**Ru 2:3**; [n]Lev 26:5; [o]**Jdg 9:27**; [p]**Joel 2:24**; [q]**Joel 3:18**
14 [r]**Jer 29:14**; [s]**Jer 33:7**; [t]**Isa 32:18; 49:8; 61:4**; [u]**2Ki 19:29**; [v]**Isa 62:9; Jer 30:18; 31:28**; Eze 28:25–26; **34:13–14; Am 5:11**
15 [w]**Ex 15:17; Isa 60:21**; [x]**Jer 23:8**; [y]**Joel 3:20**; [z]**Isa 65:9; Jer 3:18**; Ob 17; [a]**Jer 18:9**; 24:6; **32:15; Eze 28:26; 34:25–28; 37:12**,25

f12 Hebrew; Septuagint *so that the remnant of men / and all the nations that bear my name may seek ⌊the Lord⌋*
g14 Or *will restore the fortunes of my*

Obadiah

[1]The vision[a] of Obadiah.

1–4pp—Jer 49:14–16
5–6pp—Jer 49:9–10

This is what the Sovereign LORD says about Edom[b]—

We have heard a message from the LORD:
An envoy[c] was sent to the nations to say,
"Rise, and let us go against her for battle"[d]—

[2]"See, I will make you small[e] among the nations;
you will be utterly despised.
[3]The pride[f] of your heart has deceived you,
you who live in the clefts of the rocks[a][g]
and make your home on the heights,
you who say to yourself,
'Who can bring me down to the ground?'[h]
[4]Though you soar like the eagle
and make your nest[i] among the stars,
from there I will bring you down,"[j]
declares the LORD.[k]
[5]"If thieves came to you,
if robbers in the night—
Oh, what a disaster awaits you—
would they not steal only as much as they wanted?
If grape pickers came to you,
would they not leave a few grapes?[l]
[6]But how Esau will be ransacked,
his hidden treasures pillaged!
[7]All your allies[m] will force you to the border;
your friends will deceive and overpower you;
those who eat your bread[n] will set a trap for you,[b]
but you will not detect it.

[8]"In that day," declares the LORD,
"will I not destroy[o] the wise men of Edom,
men of understanding in the mountains of Esau?
[9]Your warriors, O Teman,[p] will be terrified,
and everyone in Esau's mountains
will be cut down in the slaughter.
[10]Because of the violence[q] against your brother Jacob,[r]
you will be covered with shame;
you will be destroyed for ever.[s]
[11]On the day you stood aloof
while strangers carried off his wealth
and foreigners entered his gates
and cast lots[t] for Jerusalem,
you were like one of them.[u]
[12]You should not look down[v] on your brother
in the day of his misfortune,[w]
nor rejoice[x] over the people of Judah
in the day of their destruction,[y]
nor boast[z] so much
in the day of their trouble.[a]
[13]You should not march through the gates of my people
in the day of their disaster,
nor look down on them in their calamity[b]
in the day of their disaster,
nor seize their wealth
in the day of their disaster.
[14]You should not wait at the crossroads
to cut down their fugitives,[c]
nor hand over their survivors
in the day of their trouble.

[15]"The day of the LORD is near[d]
for all nations.
As you have done, it will be done to you;
your deeds[e] will return upon your own head.
[16]Just as you drank[f] on my holy hill,[g]
so all the nations will drink[h] continually;
they will drink and drink
and be as if they had never been.[i]

1 [a]**Isa 1:1**; [b]**Ge 25:14; Isa 11:14; 34:11;** 63:1–6; Jer 49:7–22; **Eze 25:12–14; 32:29; Am 1:11–12;** [c]Isa 18:2; [d]Jer 6:4–5
2 [e]Nu 24:18
3 [f]**Isa 16:6;** [g]*fn*Isa 16:1; [h]**2Ch 25:11–12**
4 [i]**Isa 10:14;** [j]**Isa 14:13;** [k]**Job 20:6**
5 [l]**Dt 4:27;** 24:21; **Isa 24:13**
7 [m]Jer 30:14; [n]**Ps 41:9**
8 [o]Job 5:12; Isa 29:14
9 [p]**Ge 36:11,34**
10 [q]**Joel 3:19;** [r]Ps 137:7; Am 1:11–12; [s]**Ps 137:7; Eze 25:12–14;** 35:9
11 [t]**Job 6:27; Eze 24:6;** [u]**Am 1:6**
12 [v]Pr 24:17; [w]**Job 31:29;** [x]**Eze 35:15;** [y]**Pr 17:5;** [z]Ps 137:7; [a]**Eze 25:6;** Mic 4:11; 7:8
13 [b]**Eze 35:5**
14 [c]**1Ki 18:4**
15 [d]**Jer 46:10; Eze 30:3; Joel 2:31; Am 5:18;** [e]Jer 50:29; Hab 2:8
16 [f]Isa 51:17; [g]**Ex 15:17;** [h]Jer 25:15; 49:12; **La 4:21–22;** [i]**La 4:21; Eze 25:12–14**

a3 Or *of Sela*
b7 The meaning of the Hebrew for this clause is uncertain.

[17]But on Mount Zion will be
deliverance;[j]
it will be holy,[k]
and the house of Jacob
will possess its inheritance.[l]
[18]The house of Jacob will be a fire
and the house of Joseph a flame;
the house of Esau will be stubble,
and they will set it on fire[m] and
consume[n] it.
There will be no survivors[o]
from the house of Esau."
The LORD has spoken.

[19]People from the Negev will occupy
the mountains of Esau,
and people from the foothills will
possess
the land of the Philistines.[p]
They will occupy the fields of Ephraim
and Samaria,[q]
and Benjamin[r] will possess Gilead.
[20]This company of Israelite exiles who
are in Canaan
will possess ⌞the land⌟ as far as
Zarephath;[s]
the exiles from Jerusalem who are in
Sepharad
will possess the towns of the
Negev.[t]
[21]Deliverers[u] will go up on[c] Mount Zion
to govern the mountains of Esau.
And the kingdom will be the
LORD'S.[v]

17 [j]**Ps 69:35; Isa 14:1–2;** Joel 2:32; **Am 9:11–15;** [k]**Ps 74:2; Isa 4:3;** [l]Zec 8:12
18 [m]**Isa 1:31;** [n]Zec 12:6; [o]**Jer 49:10**
19 [p]Isa 11:14; [q]**Jer 31:5;** [r]**Nu 1:36**
20 [s]1Ki 17:9–10; Lk 4:26; [t]**Jer 33:13**
21 [u]**Dt 28:29; Jdg 3:9;** [v]**Ps 22:28;** 47:9; 66:4; **Da 2:44;** Zec 14:9,16; Mal 1:14; Rev 11:15

[c]21 Or *from*

Jonah

Jonah Flees From the LORD

1 The word of the LORD came to Jonah[a] son of Amittai:[b] 2"Go to the great city of Nineveh[c] and preach against it, because its wickedness has come up before me."

3But Jonah ran[d] away from the LORD and headed for Tarshish.[e] He went down to Joppa,[f] where he found a ship bound for that port. After paying the fare, he went aboard and sailed for Tarshish to flee from the LORD.[g]

4Then the LORD sent a great wind on the sea, and such a violent storm arose that the ship threatened to break up.[h] 5All the sailors were afraid and each cried out to his own god. And they threw the cargo into the sea to lighten the ship.[i]

But Jonah had gone below deck, where he lay down and fell into a deep sleep. 6The captain went to him and said, "How can you sleep? Get up and call[j] on your god! Maybe he will take notice of us, and we will not perish."[k]

7Then the sailors said to each other, "Come, let us cast lots to find out who is responsible for this calamity."[l] They cast lots and the lot fell on Jonah.[m]

8So they asked him, "Tell us, who is responsible for making all this trouble for us? What do you do? Where do you come from? What is your country? From what people are you?"

9He answered, "I am a Hebrew and I worship the LORD,[n] the God of heaven,[o] who made the sea[p] and the land.[q]"

10This terrified them and they asked, "What have you done?" (They knew he was running away from the LORD, because he had already told them so.)

11The sea was getting rougher and rougher. So they asked him, "What should we do to you to make the sea calm down for us?"

12"Pick me up and throw me into the sea," he replied, "and it will become calm. I know that it is my fault that this great storm has come upon you."[r]

13Instead, the men did their best to row back to land. But they could not, for the sea grew even wilder than before.[s] 14Then they cried to the LORD, "O LORD, please do not let us die for taking this man's life. Do not hold us accountable for killing an innocent man,[t] for you, O LORD, have done as you pleased."[u] 15Then they took Jonah and threw him overboard, and the raging sea grew calm.[v] 16At this the men greatly feared[w] the LORD, and they offered a sacrifice to the LORD and made vows[x] to him.

17But the LORD provided[y] a great fish to swallow Jonah,[z] and Jonah was inside the fish three days and three nights.

Jonah's Prayer

2 From inside the fish Jonah prayed to the LORD his God. 2He said:

"In my distress I called[a] to the LORD,[b]
 and he answered me.
From the depths of the grave[a][c] I called
  for help,
 and you listened to my cry.
3You hurled me into the deep,[d]
 into the very heart of the seas,
 and the currents swirled about me;
all your waves[e] and breakers
 swept over me.[f]
4I said, 'I have been banished
 from your sight;[g]
yet I will look again
 towards your holy temple.'[h]
5The engulfing waters threatened me,[b]
 the deep surrounded me;
 seaweed was wrapped around my
  head.[i]
6To the roots of the mountains[j] I sank
  down;
 the earth beneath barred me in for
  ever.
But you brought my life up from the
  pit,[k]
 O LORD my God.

7"When my life was ebbing away,
 I remembered[l] you, LORD,
and my prayer[m] rose to you,
 to your holy temple.[n]

Ch. 1

1 [a]Mt 12:39–41; 16:4; Lk 11:29–32; [b]2Ki 14:25
2 [c]**Ge 10:11; Na 1:1**
3 [d]Ps 139:7; [e]**Ge 10:4**; [f]**Jos 19:46**; Ac 9:36,43; [g]Ex 4:13; **Jer 20:9; Am 3:8**
4 [h]Ps 107:23–26
5 [i]Ac 27:18–19
6 [j]Jnh 3:8; [k]**Ps 107:28**
7 [l]Nu 32:23; Jos 7:10–18; **1Sa 14:42**; [m]**Pr 16:33**
9 [n]**Ps 96:9**; [o]**Da 2:18**; Ac 17:24; [p]**Ne 9:6**; [q]**Ge 1:9**
12 [r]2Sa 24:17; 1Ch 21:17
13 [s]**Pr 21:30**
14 [t]Dt 21:8; [u]**Da 4:35**
15 [v]**Ps 107:29**; Lk 8:24
16 [w]Mk 4:41; [x]**Nu 30:2**; Ps 66:13–14
17 [y]Jnh 4:6–7; [z]Mt 12:40; 16:4; Lk 11:30

Ch. 2

2 [a]La 3:55; [b]Ps 18:6; 120:1; [c]Ps 86:13
3 [d]**Ps 88:6**; [e]**2Sa 22:5**; [f]**Ps 42:7**
4 [g]Ps 31:22; Jer 7:15; [h]**1Ki 8:48**
5 [i]Ps 69:1–2
6 [j]Job 28:9; [k]**Job 17:16; 33:18; Ps 30:3**
7 [l]Ps 77:11–12; [m]2Ch 30:27; [n]**Ps 11:4**; 18:6

---

a2 Hebrew *Sheol* b5 Or *waters were at my throat*

8"Those who cling to worthless idols[o]
forfeit the grace that could be theirs.
9But I, with a song of thanksgiving,[p]
will sacrifice[q] to you.
What I have vowed[r] I will make good.
Salvation[s] comes from the LORD."

10And the LORD commanded the fish,
and it vomited Jonah onto dry land.

Jonah Goes to Nineveh

3 Then the word of the LORD came to
Jonah[a] a second time: 2"Go to the
great city of Nineveh and proclaim to it
the message I give you."
3Jonah obeyed the word of the LORD
and went to Nineveh. Now Nineveh
was a very important city—a visit
required three days. 4On the first
day, Jonah started into the city. He
proclaimed:[b] "Forty more days and
Nineveh will be overturned." 5The
Ninevites believed God. They declared
a fast, and all of them, from the greatest
to the least, put on sackcloth.[c]
6When the news reached the king of
Nineveh, he rose from his throne, took
off his royal robes, covered himself with
sackcloth and sat down in the dust.[d]
7Then he issued a proclamation in
Nineveh:

"By the decree of the king and his
nobles:

Do not let any man or beast, herd
or flock, taste anything; do not let
them eat or drink.[e] 8But let man and
beast be covered with sackcloth.
Let everyone call[f] urgently on God.
Let them give up[g] their evil ways[h]
and their violence.[i] 9Who knows?[j]
God may yet relent[k] and with compassion turn[l] from his fierce anger[m]
so that we will not perish."

10When God saw what they did and
how they turned from their evil ways,
he had compassion[n] and did not bring
upon them the destruction[o] he had
threatened.[p]

Jonah's Anger at the LORD's Compassion

4 But Jonah was greatly displeased
and became angry.[a] 2He prayed to
the LORD, "O LORD, is this not what I
said when I was still at home? That is
why I was so quick to flee to Tarshish. I
knew[b] that you are a gracious[c] and compassionate God, slow to anger and
abounding in love,[d] a God who relents[e]
from sending calamity.[f] 3Now, O LORD,
take away my life,[g] for it is better for me
to die[h] than to live."[i]
4But the LORD replied, "Have you any
right to be angry?"[j]
5Jonah went out and sat down at a
place east of the city. There he made
himself a shelter, sat in its shade and
waited to see what would happen to the
city. 6Then the LORD God provided[k] a
vine and made it grow up over Jonah to
give shade for his head to ease his discomfort, and Jonah was very happy about the vine. 7But at dawn the next day
God provided a worm, which chewed
the vine so that it withered.[l] 8When the
sun rose, God provided a scorching east
wind, and the sun blazed on Jonah's
head so that he grew faint. He wanted
to die,[m] and said, "It would be better for
me to die than to live."
9But God said to Jonah, "Do you have
a right to be angry about the vine?"[n]
"I do," he said. "I am angry enough
to die."
10But the LORD said, "You have been
concerned about this vine, though you
did not tend it or make it grow. It sprang
up overnight and died overnight. 11But
Nineveh[o] has more than a hundred and
twenty thousand people who cannot
tell their right hand from their left, and
many cattle as well. Should I not be
concerned[p] about that great city?"

8 [o]Dt 32:21; 1Sa 12:21
9 [p]Ps 42:4; [q]Ps 50:14,23; Heb 13:15; [r]Nu 30:2; Ps 116:14; Ecc 5:4–5; [s]Ex 15:2; Ps 3:8

Ch. 3

1 [a]Jnh 1:1
4 [b]Jer 18:7–10
5 [c]Da 9:3; Mt 11:21; 12:41; Lk 11:32
6 [d]Est 4:1–3; Job 2:8,13; Eze 27:30–31
7 [e]2Ch 20:3; Ezr 10:6
8 [f]Ps 130:1; Jnh 1:6; [g]Jer 25:5; [h]Jer 7:3; [i]Job 16:17
9 [j]2Sa 12:22; [k]Jer 18:8; [l]Joel 2:14; [m]Ps 85:3
10 [n]Am 7:6; [o]Jer 18:8; [p]Ex 32:14

Ch. 4

1 [a]ver 4; Mt 20:11; Lk 15:28
2 [b]Jer 20:7–8; [c]Dt 4:31; Ps 103:8; [d]Ex 22:27; Ps 86:5,15; [e]Nu 14:18; [f]Joel 2:13
3 [g]Nu 11:15; [h]Job 7:15; [i]Jer 8:3
4 [j]Ge 4:6; Mt 20:11–15
6 [k]Jnh 1:17
7 [l]Joel 1:12
8 [m]1Ki 19:4
9 [n]ver 4
11 [o]Jnh 1:2; 3:2; [p]Jnh 3:10

Micah

1 The word of the LORD that came to Micah of Moresheth[a] during the reigns of Jotham,[b] Ahaz[c] and Hezekiah,[d] kings of Judah[e]—the vision[f] he saw concerning Samaria and Jerusalem.

2Hear,[g] O peoples, all of you,[h]
listen, O earth[i] and all who are in it,
that the Sovereign LORD may witness[j]
against you,
the Lord from his holy temple.[k]

Judgment Against Samaria and Jerusalem

3Look! The LORD is coming from his
dwelling-place;[l]
he comes down[m] and treads the
high places of the earth.[n]
4The mountains melt[o] beneath him[p]
and the valleys split apart,[q]
like wax before the fire,
like water rushing down a slope.
5All this is because of Jacob's
transgression,
because of the sins of the house of
Israel.
What is Jacob's transgression?
Is it not Samaria?[r]
What is Judah's high place?
Is it not Jerusalem?

6"Therefore I will make Samaria a heap
of rubble,
a place for planting vineyards.[s]
I will pour her stones[t] into the valley
and lay bare her foundations.[u]
7All her idols[v] will be broken to pieces;[w]
all her temple gifts will be burned
with fire;
I will destroy all her images.[x]
Since she gathered her gifts from the
wages of prostitutes,[y]
as the wages of prostitutes they will
again be used."

Weeping and Mourning

8Because of this I will weep[z] and wail;
I will go about barefoot[a] and naked.
I will howl like a jackal
and moan like an owl.
9For her wound[b] is incurable;[c]
it has come to Judah.[d]
It[a] has reached the very gate[e] of my
people,
even to Jerusalem itself.
10Tell it not in Gath;[b]
weep not at all.[c]
In Beth Ophrah[d]
roll in the dust.
11Pass on in nakedness[f] and shame,
you who live in Shaphir.[e]
Those who live in Zaanan[f]
will not come out.
Beth Ezel is in mourning;
its protection is taken from you.
12Those who live in Maroth[g] writhe in
pain,
waiting for relief,[g]
because disaster[h] has come from the
LORD,
even to the gate of Jerusalem.
13You who live in Lachish,[h] [i]
harness the team to the chariot.
You were the beginning of sin
to the Daughter of Zion,[j]
for the transgressions of Israel
were found in you.
14Therefore you will give parting gifts[k]
to Moresheth[l] Gath.
The town of Aczib[i] [m] will prove
deceptive[n]
to the kings of Israel.
15I will bring a conqueror against you
who live in Mareshah.[j] [o]
He who is the glory of Israel
will come to Adullam.[p]
16Shave[q] your heads in mourning
for the children in whom you
delight;
make yourselves as bald as the
vulture,
for they will go from you into exile.[r]

Ch. 1
1 [a]ver 14; Jer 26:18; [b]**1Ch 3:12;** [c]**1Ch 3:13;** [d]**1Ch 3:13;** [e]**Hos** 1:1; [f]Isa 1:1
2 [g]**Dt 32:1;** [h]**Ps** 50:7; [i]**Jer 6:19;** [j]**Ge 31:50; Dt 4:26; Isa 1:2;** [k]**Ps 11:4**
3 [l]**Isa 18:4;** [m]**Isa 64:1;** [n]**Am 4:13**
4 [o]**Ps 46:2,6;** [p]**Job 9:5;** [q]**Nu 16:31;** Na 1:5
5 [r]Am 8:14
6 [s]**Dt 20:6;** [t]**Am 5:11;** [u]Eze 13:14
7 [v]**Eze 6:6;** [w]**Ex 32:20;** [x]**Dt 9:21;** [y]Dt 23:17–18
8 [z]**Isa 15:3;** [a]**Isa** 20:2
9 [b]Jer 46:11; [c]**Jer 10:19;** [d]**2Ki 18:13;** [e]Isa 3:26
11 [f]Eze 23:29
12 [g]Jer 14:19; [h]Jer 40:2
13 [i]**Jos 10:3;** [j]**Ps** 9:14
14 [k]2Ki 16:8; [l]**ver** 1; [m]**Jos 15:44;** [n]Jer 15:18
15 [o]Jos 15:44; [p]**Jos 12:15**
16 [q]**Lev 13:40;** **Job 1:20;** [r]**Dt 4:27; Am 5:27**

[a]9 Or *He*
[b]10 *Gath* sounds like the Hebrew for *tell.*
[c]10 Hebrew; Septuagint may suggest *not in Acco.* The Hebrew for *in Acco* sounds like the Hebrew for *weep.*
[d]10 *Beth Ophrah* means *house of dust.*
[e]11 *Shaphir* means *pleasant.*
[f]11 *Zaanan* sounds like the Hebrew for *come out.*
[g]12 *Maroth* sounds like the Hebrew for *bitter.*
[h]13 *Lachish* sounds like the Hebrew for *team.*
[i]14 *Aczib* means *deception.*
[j]15 *Mareshah* sounds like the Hebrew for *conqueror.*

Man's Plans and God's

2 Woe to those who plan iniquity,
to those who plot evil[a] on their beds![b]
At morning's light they carry it out
because it is in their power to do it.
2They covet fields[c] and seize them,[d]
and houses, and take them.
They defraud[e] a man of his home,
a fellow-man of his inheritance.[f]

3Therefore, the LORD says:

"I am planning disaster[g] against this people,
from which you cannot save yourselves.
You will no longer walk proudly,[h]
for it will be a time of calamity.
4In that day men will ridicule you;
they will taunt you with this mournful song:
'We are utterly ruined;[i]
my people's possession is divided up.[j]
He takes it from me!
He assigns our fields to traitors.'"
5Therefore you will have no-one in the assembly of the LORD
to divide the land[k] by lot.[l]

False Prophets

6"Do not prophesy," their prophets say.
"Do not prophesy about these things;
disgrace[m] will not overtake us.[n]"
7Should it be said, O house of Jacob:
"Is the Spirit of the LORD angry?
Does he do such things?"

"Do not my words do good[o]
to him whose ways are upright?[p]
8Lately my people have risen up
like an enemy.
You strip off the rich robe
from those who pass by without a care,
like men returning from battle.
9You drive the women of my people
from their pleasant homes.[q]
You take away my blessing
from their children for ever.
10Get up, go away!
For this is not your resting place,[r]
because it is defiled,[s]
it is ruined, beyond all remedy.
11If a liar and deceiver[t] comes and says,
'I will prophesy for you plenty of wine and beer,'[u]
he would be just the prophet for this people![v]

Deliverance Promised

12"I will surely gather all of you, O Jacob;
I will surely bring together the remnant[w] of Israel.
I will bring them together like sheep in a pen,
like a flock in its pasture;
the place will throng with people.[x]
13One who breaks open the way will go up before[y] them;
they will break through the gate[z]
and go out.
Their king will pass through before them,
the LORD at their head."

Leaders and Prophets Rebuked

3 Then I said,

"Listen, you leaders[a] of Jacob,
you rulers of the house of Israel.
Should you not know justice,
2 you who hate good and love evil;
who tear the skin from my people
and the flesh from their bones;[b]
3who eat my people's flesh,[c]
strip off their skin
and break their bones in pieces;[d]
who chop[e] them up like meat for the pan,
like flesh for the pot.[f]"

4Then they will cry out to the LORD,
but he will not answer them.[g]
At that time he will hide his face[h] from them
because of the evil they have done.[i]

5This is what the LORD says:

"As for the prophets
who lead my people astray,[j]
if one feeds them,
they proclaim 'peace';[k]
if he does not,
they prepare to wage war against him.
6Therefore night will come over you,
without visions,
and darkness, without divination.[l]
The sun will set for the prophets,[m]
and the day will go dark for them.[n]
7The seers will be ashamed[o]
and the diviners disgraced.[p]
They will all cover[q] their faces[r]
because there is no answer from God.[s]"

Ch. 2

1 [a]Isa 29:20; [b]Ps 36:4
2 [c]Isa 5:8; [d]Pr 30:14; [e]Jer 22:17; [f]1Sa 8:14; Isa 1:23; Eze 46:18
3 [g]Jer 18:11; Am 3:1–2; [h]Isa 2:12
4 [i]Lev 26:31; Jer 4:13; [j]Jer 6:12
5 [k]Dt 32:13; Jos 18:4; [l]Nu 34:13
6 [m]Ps 44:13; Jer 18:16; 19:8; 25:18; 29:18; Mic 6:16; [n]Am 2:12
7 [o]Ps 119:65; [p]Ps 15:2; 84:11
9 [q]Jer 10:20
10 [r]Dt 12:9; [s]Lev 18:25–29; Ps 106:38–39; La 4:15
11 [t]2Ch 36:16; Jer 5:31; [u]Lev 10:9; [v]Isa 30:10
12 [w]Mic 4:7; 5:7; 7:18; [x]Ne 1:9
13 [y]Isa 52:12; [z]Isa 60:11

Ch. 3

1 [a]Jer 5:5
2 [b]Ps 53:4; Eze 22:27
3 [c]Ps 14:4; [d]Eze 34:4; Zep 3:3; [e]Job 24:14; [f]Eze 11:7; 24:4–5
4 [g]Dt 1:45; 1Sa 8:18; Isa 58:4; Jer 11:11; [h]Dt 31:17; [i]Job 15:31; Eze 8:18
5 [j]Isa 3:12; 9:16; 53:6; [k]Jer 4:10
6 [l]Isa 8:19–22; Eze 12:24; [m]Isa 29:10; [n]Eze 7:26; Am 8:11
7 [o]Jer 6:15; Mic 7:16; [p]Isa 44:25; [q]Est 6:12; [r]Lev 13:45; [s]Eze 20:3

8But as for me, I am filled with power,
with the Spirit of the LORD,
and with justice and might,
to declare to Jacob his transgression,
to Israel his sin.[t]
9Hear this, you leaders of the house of Jacob,
you rulers of the house of Israel,
who despise justice
and distort all that is right;[u]
10who build[v] Zion with bloodshed,[w]
and Jerusalem with wickedness.[x]
11Her leaders judge for a bribe,[y]
her priests teach for a price,[z]
and her prophets tell fortunes for money.[a]
Yet they lean[b] upon the LORD and say,
"Is not the LORD among us?
No disaster will come upon us."[c]
12Therefore because of you,
Zion will be ploughed like a field,
Jerusalem will become a heap of rubble,[d]
the temple[e] hill a mound overgrown with thickets.[f]

The Mountain of the LORD

4:1–3pp—Isa 2:1–4

4
In the last days
the mountain[a] of the LORD's temple will be established
as chief among the mountains;
it will be raised above the hills,[b]
and peoples will stream to it.[c]

2Many nations will come and say,

"Come, let us go up to the mountain of the LORD,[d]
to the house of the God of Jacob.[e]
He will teach us[f] his ways,[g]
so that we may walk in his paths."
The law[h] will go out from Zion,
the word of the LORD from Jerusalem.
3He will judge between many peoples
and will settle disputes for strong nations far and wide.[i]
They will beat their swords into ploughshares
and their spears into pruning hooks.[j]
Nation will not take up sword against nation,
nor will they train for war[k] any more.[l]
4Every man will sit under his own vine
and under his own fig-tree,[m]
and no-one will make them afraid,[n]
for the LORD Almighty has spoken.[o]
5All the nations may walk
in the name of their gods;[p]
we will walk in the name of the LORD
our God for ever and ever.[q]

The LORD's Plan

6"In that day," declares the LORD,

"I will gather the lame;[r]
I will assemble the exiles[s]
and those I have brought to grief.[t]
7I will make the lame a remnant,[u]
those driven away a strong nation.[v]
The LORD will rule over them in Mount Zion[w]
from that day and for ever.[x]
8As for you, O watchtower of the flock,
O stronghold[a] of the Daughter of Zion,
the former dominion will be restored[y] to you;
kingship will come to the Daughter of Jerusalem.[z]"

9Why do you now cry aloud—
have you no king?[a]
Has your counsellor perished,
that pain seizes you like that of a woman in labour?[b]
10Writhe in agony, O Daughter of Zion,
like a woman in labour,
for now you must leave the city
to camp in the open field.
You will go to Babylon;[c]
there you will be rescued.
There the LORD will redeem[d] you
out of the hand of your enemies.

11But now many nations
are gathered against you.
They say, "Let her be defiled,
let our eyes gloat[e] over Zion!"
12But they do not know
the thoughts of the LORD;
they do not understand his plan,[f]
he who gathers them like sheaves to the threshing-floor.

13"Rise and thresh,[g] O Daughter of Zion,
for I will give you horns of iron;
I will give you hoofs of bronze
and you will break to pieces many nations."[h]

You will devote their ill-gotten gains to the LORD,[i]
their wealth to the Lord of all the earth.

8 [t]Isa 57:12; 61:2 9 [u]Ps 58:1–2; Isa 1:23 10 [v]Jer 22:13; [w]Isa 59:7; Mic 7:2; Na 3:1; Hab 2:12; [x]Jer 22:17; Eze 22:27 11 [y]Ex 23:8; Lev 19:15; Mal 2:9; [z]Eze 13:19; [a]Isa 1:23; 56:11; Jer 6:13; La 4:13; Hos 4:8,18; [b]Isa 10:20; [c]Jer 7:4; Eze 34:2 12 [d]2Ki 25:9; Isa 6:11; [e]Jer 52:13; [f]Lev 26:31; Jer 17:3; 22:6; La 5:18; Eze 5:14

Ch. 4

1 [a]Ps 48:1; Zec 8:3; [b]Eze 17:22; [c]Ps 22:27; 86:9; Jer 3:17; 31:12; Da 2:35 2 [d]Jer 31:6; Eze 20:40; [e]Zec 2:11; 14:16; [f]Ps 119:171; [g]Ps 25:8–9; Isa 54:13; [h]Dt 18:18 3 [i]Isa 11:4; [j]Joel 3:10; Zec 9:10; [k]Ps 46:9; [l]Zec 8:20–22 4 [m]1Ki 4:25; [n]Lev 26:6; Eze 39:26; [o]Isa 1:20 5 [p]2Ki 17:29; Ac 14:16; [q]Jos 24:14–15; Isa 26:8; Zec 10:12 6 [r]Jer 31:8; [s]Ps 106:47; [t]Eze 34:13,16; 37:21; Zep 3:19 7 [u]Joel 2:32; Mic 2:12; [v]Ge 12:2; [w]Isa 2:2; [x]Da 2:44; 7:14; Lk 1:33; Rev 11:15 8 [y]Isa 1:26; [z]Zec 9:9 9 [a]Jer 8:19; [b]Ge 3:16; Jer 30:6; 48:41 10 [c]Dt 21:10; 2Ki 20:18; Isa 43:14; [d]Isa 48:20 11 [e]La 2:16; Ob 12; Mic 7:8 12 [f]Ge 50:20; Isa 55:8; Ro 11:33–34 13 [g]Isa 21:10; [h]Isa 45:1; Da 2:44; [i]Isa 23:18

[a]8 Or *hill*

A Promised Ruler From Bethlehem

5 Marshal your troops, O city of
troops,[a]
for a siege is laid against us.
They will strike Israel's ruler
on the cheek[a] with a rod.

2 "But you, Bethlehem[b] Ephrathah,[c]
though you are small among the
clans[b] of Judah,
out of you will come for me
one who will be ruler[d] over Israel,
whose origins[c] are from of old,[e]
from ancient times.[d]"[f]

3 Therefore Israel will be abandoned[g]
until the time when she who is in
labour gives birth
and the rest of his brothers return
to join the Israelites.

4 He will stand and shepherd his flock[h]
in the strength of the LORD,
in the majesty of the name of the
LORD his God.
And they will live securely, for then
his greatness[i]
will reach to the ends of the earth.
5 And he will be their peace.[j]

Deliverance and Destruction

When the Assyrian invades[k] our land
and marches through our
fortresses,
we will raise against him seven
shepherds,
even eight leaders of men.[l]
6 They will rule[e] the land of Assyria
with the sword,
the land of Nimrod[m] with drawn
sword.[f][n]
He will deliver us from the Assyrian
when he invades our land
and marches into our borders.[o]

7 The remnant[p] of Jacob will be
in the midst of many peoples
like dew[q] from the LORD,
like showers on the grass,[r]
which do not wait for man
or linger for mankind.
8 The remnant of Jacob will be among
the nations,
in the midst of many peoples,
like a lion among the beasts of the
forest,[s]
like a young lion among flocks of
sheep,
which mauls and mangles[t] as it goes,
and no-one can rescue.[u]

9 Your hand will be lifted up[v] in triumph
over your enemies,
and all your foes will be destroyed.

10 "In that day," declares the LORD,

"I will destroy your horses from
among you
and demolish your chariots.[w]
11 I will destroy the cities[x] of your land
and tear down all your
strongholds.[y]
12 I will destroy your witchcraft
and you will no longer cast spells.[z]
13 I will destroy your carved images[a]
and your sacred stones from among
you;[b]
you will no longer bow down
to the work of your hands.[c]
14 I will uproot from among you your
Asherah poles[g][d]
and demolish your cities.
15 I will take vengeance[e] in anger and
wrath
upon the nations that have not
obeyed me."

The LORD's Case Against Israel

6 Listen to what the LORD says:
"Stand up, plead your case before the
mountains;[a]
let the hills hear what you have to
say.
2 Hear,[b] O mountains, the LORD's
accusation;[c]
listen, you everlasting foundations
of the earth.
For the LORD has a case[d] against his
people;
he is lodging a charge[e] against
Israel.

3 "My people, what have I done to you?
How have I burdened[f] you?[g]
Answer me.
4 I brought you up out of Egypt[h]
and redeemed you from the land of
slavery.[i]
I sent Moses[j] to lead you,
also Aaron[k] and Miriam.[l]
5 My people, remember
what Balak[m] king of Moab
counselled
and what Balaam son of Beor
answered.

Ch. 5
1 [a]La 3:30
2 [b]Jn 7:42; [c]Ge 35:16; 48:7; [d]Nu 24:19; 1Sa 13:14; 2Sa 6:21; 2Ch 7:18; [e]Ps 102:25; [f]Mt 2:6*
3 [g]Jer 7:29
4 [h]Isa 40:11; 49:9; Eze 34:11–15,23; Mic 7:14; [i]Isa 52:13; Lk 1:32
5 [j]Isa 9:6; Lk 2:14; Col 1:19–20; [k]Isa 8:7; [l]Isa 10:24–27
6 [m]Ge 10:8; [n]Zep 2:13; [o]Na 2:11–13
7 [p]Am 5:15; Mic 2:12; [q]Ps 133:3; [r]Isa 44:4
8 [s]Ge 49:9; [t]Mic 4:13; Zec 10:5; [u]Ps 50:22; Isa 5:29; Hos 5:14
9 [v]Ps 10:12
10 [w]Ex 15:4,19; Hos 14:3; Hag 2:22; Zec 9:10
11 [x]Dt 29:23; Isa 6:11; [y]La 2:2; Hos 10:14; Am 5:9
12 [z]Dt 18:10–12; Isa 2:6; 8:19
13 [a]Na 1:14; [b]Hos 10:2; [c]Isa 2:18; Eze 6:9; Zec 13:2
14 [d]Ex 34:13; Jdg 3:7; 2Ki 17:10
15 [e]Isa 65:12

Ch. 6
1 [a]Ps 50:1; Eze 6:2
2 [b]Dt 32:1; [c]Hos 12:2; [d]Isa 3:13; [e]Ps 50:7; Jer 2:9
3 [f]Jer 2:5; [g]Jer 2:5
4 [h]Ex 3:10; 6:6; [i]Dt 7:8; [j]Ex 4:16; [k]Nu 33:1; Ps 77:20; [l]Ex 15:20
5 [m]Nu 22:2

[a]1 Or *Strengthen your walls, O walled city*
[b]2 Or *rulers* [c]2 Hebrew *goings out*
[d]2 Or *from days of eternity* [e]6 Or *crush*
[f]6 Or *Nimrod in its gates*
[g]14 That is, symbols of the goddess Asherah

Remember ⌞your journey⌟ from
Shittim[n] to Gilgal,[o]
that you may know the righteous
acts[p] of the LORD."

6With what shall I come before[q] the
LORD
and bow down before the exalted
God?
Shall I come before him with burnt
offerings,
with calves a year old?[r]
7Will the LORD be pleased with
thousands of rams,[s]
with ten thousand rivers of oil?[t]
Shall I offer my firstborn[u] for my
transgression,
the fruit of my body for the sin of my
soul?[v]
8He has showed you, O man, what is
good.
And what does the LORD require of
you?
To act justly[w] and to love mercy
and to walk humbly[x] with your
God.[y]

Israel's Guilt and Punishment

9Listen! The LORD is calling to the city—
and to fear your name is wisdom—
"Heed the rod[z] and the One who
appointed it.[a]
10Am I still to forget, O wicked house,
your ill-gotten treasures
and the short ephah,[b] which is
accursed?[a]
11Shall I acquit a man with dishonest
scales,[b]
with a bag of false weights?[c]
12Her rich men are violent;[d]
her people are liars[e]
and their tongues speak deceitfully.[f]
13Therefore, I have begun to destroy[g]
you,
to ruin you because of your sins.
14You will eat but not be satisfied;[h]
your stomach will still be empty.[c]
You will store up but save nothing,[i]
because what you save I will give to
the sword.
15You will plant but not harvest;[j]
you will press olives but not use the
oil on yourselves,
you will crush grapes but not drink
the wine.[k]
16You have observed the statutes of
Omri[l]
and all the practices of Ahab's[m]
house,
and you have followed their
traditions.[n]
Therefore I will give you over to ruin[o]
and your people to derision;
you will bear the scorn[p] of the
nations."[d]

Israel's Misery

7 What misery is mine!
I am like one who gathers summer
fruit
at the gleaning of the vineyard;
there is no cluster of grapes to eat,
none of the early figs[a] that I crave.
2The godly have been swept from the
land;[b]
not one[c] upright man remains.
All men lie in wait[d] to shed blood;[e]
each hunts his brother[f] with a net.[g]
3Both hands are skilled in doing evil;[h]
the ruler demands gifts,
the judge accepts bribes,[i]
the powerful dictate what they
desire—
they all conspire together.
4The best of them is like a brier,[j]
the most upright worse than a
thorn[k] hedge.
The day of your watchmen has come,
the day God visits you.
Now is the time of their confusion.[l]
5Do not trust a neighbour;
put no confidence in a friend.[m]
Even with her who lies in your
embrace
be careful of your words.
6For a son dishonours his father,
a daughter rises up against her
mother,[n]
a daughter-in-law against her
mother-in-law—
a man's enemies are the members of
his own household.[o]

7But as for me, I watch[p] in hope[q] for the
LORD,
I wait for God my Saviour;
my God will hear[r] me.

Israel Will Rise

8Do not gloat over me,[s] my enemy!
Though I have fallen, I will rise.[t]
Though I sit in darkness,
the LORD will be my light.[u]
9Because I have sinned against him,
I will bear the LORD's wrath,[v]
until he pleads my case[w]
and establishes my right.

5 [n]Nu 25:1; [o]Dt 11:30; Jos 5:9–10; [p]Jdg 5:11; 1Sa 12:7
6 [q]Ps 95:2; [r]Ps 40:6–8; 51:16–17
7 [s]Isa 1:11; 40:16; [t]Ps 50:8–10; [u]Lev 18:21; 2Ki 3:27; [v]Hos 5:6; Am 5:22
8 [w]Isa 1:17; Jer 22:3; [x]2Ki 22:19; Isa 57:15; [y]Ge 5:22; Dt 10:12–13; 1Sa 15:22; Hos 6:6; Zec 7:9–10; Mt 9:13; 23:23; Mk 12:33; Lk 11:42
9 [z]Ge 17:1; Isa 11:4
10 [a]Eze 45:9–10; Am 3:10; 8:4–6
11 [b]Lev 19:36; [c]Dt 25:13
12 [d]Isa 1:23; [e]Ps 116:11; Isa 3:8; [f]Ps 35:20; Jer 9:3
13 [g]Isa 1:7; 6:11
14 [h]Isa 9:20; Hos 4:10; [i]Isa 30:6
15 [j]Dt 28:38; Jer 12:13; [k]Job 24:11; Am 5:11; Zep 1:13
16 [l]1Ki 16:25; [m]1Ki 16:29–33; [n]Jer 7:24; [o]Jer 25:9; [p]Dt 28:37; Jer 51:51; Mic 2:6

Ch. 7

1 [a]SS 2:13
2 [b]Ps 12:1; [c]Jer 2:29; 8:6; [d]Ps 10:8; [e]Pr 6:17; Mic 3:10; [f]Isa 3:5; [g]Jer 5:26
3 [h]Pr 4:16; [i]Ex 23:8; Eze 22:12
4 [j]Nu 33:55; Eze 2:6; [k]2Sa 23:6; [l]Job 31:14; Isa 22:5; Hos 9:7
5 [m]Jer 9:4
6 [n]Eze 22:7; [o]Mt 10:35–36*; Mk 13:12
7 [p]Isa 21:8; [q]Ps 130:5; Isa 25:9; [r]Ps 4:3
8 [s]Ps 22:17; Pr 24:17; Mic 4:11; [t]Ps 20:8; 37:24; Am 9:11; [u]2Sa 22:29; Isa 9:2
9 [v]La 3:39–40; [w]Ps 119:154

a9 The meaning of the Hebrew for this line is uncertain. b10 An ephah was a dry measure. c14 The meaning of the Hebrew for this word is uncertain.
d16 Septuagint; Hebrew *scorn due to my people*

He will bring me out into the light;[x]
I will see his righteousness.[y]
10Then my enemy will see it
and will be covered with shame,[z]
she who said to me,
"Where is the LORD your God?"[a]
My eyes will see her downfall;[b]
even now she will be trampled[c]
underfoot
like mire in the streets.

11The day for building your walls[d] will
come,
the day for extending your
boundaries.
12In that day people will come to you
from Assyria[e] and the cities of
Egypt,
even from Egypt to the Euphrates
and from sea to sea
and from mountain to mountain.[f]
13The earth will become desolate
because of its inhabitants,
as the result of their deeds.[g]

Prayer and Praise

14Shepherd[h] your people with your
staff,[i]
the flock of your inheritance,
which lives by itself in a forest,
in fertile pasture-lands.[a] [j]
Let them feed in Bashan[k] and Gilead[l]
as in days long ago.[m]

15"As in the days when you came out of
Egypt,
I will show them my wonders.[n]"

16Nations will see and be ashamed,[o]
deprived of all their power.
They will lay their hands on their
mouths[p]
and their ears will become deaf.
17They will lick dust[q] like a snake,
like creatures that crawl on the
ground.
They will come trembling[r] out of their
dens;
they will turn in fear[s] to the LORD
our God
and will be afraid of you.
18Who is a God[t] like you,
who pardons sin[u] and forgives[v] the
transgression
of the remnant[w] of his inheritance?[x]
You do not stay angry[y] for ever
but delight to show mercy.[z]
19You will again have compassion on us;
you will tread our sins underfoot
and hurl all our iniquities[a] into the
depths of the sea.[b]
20You will be true to Jacob,
and show mercy to Abraham,[c]
as you pledged on oath to our fathers[d]
in days long ago.[e]

9 [x]**Ps 107:10;** [y]Isa 46:13
10 [z]**Ps 35:26;** [a]**Ps 42:3;** [b]**Isa 51:23;** [c]**2Sa 22:43; Job 40:12; Isa** 5:5; Zec 10:5
11 [d]Isa 54:11; **Am 9:11**
12 [e]**Isa 11:11;** [f]Isa 19:23–25; 60:4
13 [g]Isa 3:10–11; **Eze 12:19; 33:28–29**
14 [h]**Ps 28:9; Mic 5:4;** [i]Ps 23:4; [j]Ps 95:7; [k]**Isa 33:9;** [l]**SS 4:1; Jer 50:19;** [m]Eze 36:11
15 [n]**Ex 3:20;** Ps 78:12
16 [o]Isa 26:11; [p]**Jdg 18:19**
17 [q]**Ge 3:14;** [r]2Sa 22:46; [s]Isa 25:3; 59:19
18 [t]**Ex 8:10; 1Sa 2:2;** [u]**Isa 43:25; Jer 50:20;** Zec 3:4; [v]**2Ch 6:21;** Ps 103:8–13; [w]**Joel 2:32; Am 5:15; Mic 2:12;** [x]**Ex 34:9;** [y]**Ps 103:9; Isa 54:9;** [z]**2Ch 30:9; Jer 31:20; 32:41; Eze 18:23**
19 [a]**Isa 43:25;** [b]**Jer 31:34**
20 [c]Gal 3:16; [d]Dt 7:8; Lk 1:72; [e]Ps 108:4

[a]14 Or *in the middle of Carmel*

Nahum

1 An oracle[a] concerning Nineveh.[b] The book of the vision[c] of Nahum the Elkoshite.

The LORD's Anger Against Nineveh

2The LORD is a jealous[d] and avenging
God;
the LORD takes vengeance[e] and is
filled with wrath.
The LORD takes vengeance on his foes
and maintains his wrath against his
enemies.[f]
3The LORD is slow to anger[g] and great in
power;
the LORD will not leave the guilty
unpunished.[h]
His way is in the whirlwind[i] and the
storm,[j]
and clouds[k] are the dust of his feet.
4He rebukes[l] the sea and dries it up;[m]
he makes all the rivers run dry.
Bashan and Carmel[n] wither
and the blossoms of Lebanon fade.
5The mountains quake[o] before him
and the hills melt away.[p]
The earth trembles[q] at his presence,
the world and all who live in it.[r]
6Who can withstand[s] his indignation?
Who can endure[t] his fierce anger?[u]
His wrath is poured out like fire;[v]
the rocks are shattered[w] before him.

7The LORD is good,[x]
a refuge in times of trouble.[y]
He cares for[z] those who trust in him,[a]
8 but with an overwhelming flood[b]
he will make an end of ⌞Nineveh⌟;
he will pursue his foes into
darkness.

9Whatever they plot[c] against the LORD
he[a] will bring to an end;
trouble will not come a second time.
10They will be entangled among thorns[d]
and drunk[e] from their wine;
they will be consumed like dry
stubble.[b][f]
11From you, ⌞O Nineveh,⌟ has one come
forth
who plots evil against the LORD
and counsels wickedness.

12This is what the LORD says:

"Although they have allies and are
numerous,
they will be cut off[g] and pass away.
Although I have afflicted you, ⌞O
Judah,⌟
I will afflict you no more.[h]
13Now I will break their yoke[i] from your
neck
and tear your shackles away."[j]

14The LORD has given a command
concerning you, ⌞Nineveh⌟:
"You will have no descendants to
bear your name.[k]
I will destroy the carved images[l] and
cast idols
that are in the temple of your gods.
I will prepare your grave,[m]
for you are vile."

15Look, there on the mountains,
the feet of one who brings good
news,[n]
who proclaims peace![o]
Celebrate your festivals,[p] O Judah,
and fulfil your vows.
No more will the wicked invade you;[q]
they will be completely destroyed.

Nineveh to Fall

2 An attacker[a] advances against
you, ⌞Nineveh⌟.
Guard the fortress,
watch the road,
brace yourselves,
marshal all your strength!

2The LORD will restore[b] the splendour[c]
of Jacob
like the splendour of Israel,
though destroyers have laid them
waste
and have ruined their vines.

[a]9 Or *What do you foes plot against the LORD? / He*
[b]10 The meaning of the Hebrew for this verse is uncertain.

Ch. 1

1 [a]Isa 13:1; 19:1; Jer 23:33–34; [b]Ge 10:11; Jer 50:18; Na 2:8; 3:7; [c]Isa 1:1
2 [d]Ex 20:5; [e]Ge 4:24; Dt 32:41; Ps 94:1; [f]Dt 7:10
3 [g]Ne 9:17; [h]Ex 34:7; [i]Ex 14:21; 2Ki 2:1; [j]Ps 50:3; [k]2Sa 22:10; Ps 104:3
4 [l]2Sa 22:16; [m]Ex 14:22; [n]Isa 33:9
5 [o]Ex 19:18; Job 9:6; [p]Mic 1:4; [q]Joel 2:10; [r]Eze 38:20
6 [s]Ps 130:3; [t]Eze 22:14; [u]Ps 76:7; [v]Isa 5:24–25; 42:25; Jer 10:10; [w]1Ki 19:11
7 [x]Jer 33:11; [y]Jer 17:17; [z]Ps 1:6; [a]Ps 22:9
8 [b]Isa 8:7; Da 9:26
9 [c]Hos 7:15
10 [d]2Sa 23:6; [e]Isa 49:26; [f]Isa 5:24; Mal 4:1
12 [g]Isa 10:34; [h]Isa 54:6–8; La 3:31–32
13 [i]Isa 9:4; [j]Job 12:18; Ps 107:14
14 [k]Isa 14:22; [l]Mic 5:13; [m]Jer 28:8; Eze 32:22–23
15 [n]Isa 40:9; Ro 10:15; [o]Isa 52:7; Ac 10:36; [p]Lev 23:2–4; [q]Isa 52:1

Ch. 2

1 [a]Jer 51:20
2 [b]Eze 37:23; [c]Isa 60·15

[3]The shields of his soldiers are red;
the warriors are clad in scarlet.[d]
The metal on the chariots flashes
on the day they are made ready;
the spears of pine are brandished.[a]
[4]The chariots[e] storm through the
streets,
rushing back and forth through the
squares.
They look like flaming torches;
they dart about like lightning.

[5]He summons his picked troops,
yet they stumble[f] on their way.
They dash to the city wall;
the protective shield is put in place.
[6]The river gates[g] are thrown open
and the palace collapses.
[7]It is decreed[b] that ⌞the city⌟
be exiled and carried away.
Its slave girls moan[h] like doves
and beat upon their breasts.[i]
[8]Nineveh is like a pool,
and its water is draining away.
"Stop! Stop!" they cry,
but no-one turns back.
[9]Plunder the silver!
Plunder the gold!
The supply is endless,
the wealth from all its treasures!
[10]She is pillaged, plundered, stripped!
Hearts melt,[j] knees give way,
bodies tremble, every face grows
pale.[k]

[11]Where now is the lions' den,[l]
the place where they fed their
young,
where the lion and lioness went,
and the cubs, with nothing to fear?
[12]The lion killed[m] enough for his cubs
and strangled the prey for his mate,
filling his lairs[n] with the kill
and his dens with the prey.[o]

[13]"I am against[p] you,"
declares the LORD Almighty.
"I will burn up your chariots in
smoke,[q]
and the sword[r] will devour your
young lions.
I will leave you no prey on the earth.
The voices of your messengers
will no longer be heard."[s]

Woe to Nineveh

3

Woe to the city of blood,[a]
full of lies,[b]
full of plunder,
never without victims!
[2]The crack of whips,
the clatter of wheels,
galloping horses
and jolting chariots!
[3]Charging cavalry,
flashing swords
and glittering spears!
Many casualties,
piles of dead,
bodies without number,
people stumbling over the
corpses[c]—
[4]all because of the wanton lust of a
harlot,
alluring, the mistress of sorceries,[d]
who enslaved nations by her
prostitution[e]
and peoples by her witchcraft.

[5]"I am against[f] you," declares the LORD
Almighty.
"I will lift your skirts[g] over your
face.
I will show the nations your
nakedness[h]
and the kingdoms your shame.
[6]I will pelt you with filth,[i]
I will treat you with contempt[j]
and make you a spectacle.[k]
[7]All who see you will flee[l] from you and
say,
'Nineveh[m] is in ruins[n]—who will
mourn for her?'[o]
Where can I find anyone to comfort[p]
you?"

[8]Are you better than[q] Thebes,[a][r]
situated on the Nile,[s]
with water around her?
The river was her defence,
the waters her wall.
[9]Cush[b][t] and Egypt were her boundless
strength;
Put[u] and Libya[v] were among her
allies.
[10]Yet she was taken captive[w]
and went into exile.
Her infants were dashed[x] to pieces
at the head of every street.
Lots[y] were cast for her nobles,
and all her great men were put in
chains.[z]
[11]You too will become drunk;[a]
you will go into hiding[b]
and seek refuge from the enemy.

[12]All your fortresses are like fig-trees
with their first ripe fruit;[c]
when they are shaken,

3 [d]Eze 23:14–15 **4** [e]Jer 4:13; Eze 23:24 **5** [f]Jer 46:12 **6** [g]Isa 45:1; Na 3:13 **7** [h]Ge 8:8; Isa 59:11; [i]Isa 32:12 **10** [j]Jos 2:11; 7:5; [k]Isa 29:22 **11** [l]Isa 5:29 **12** [m]Jer 51:34; [n]Jer 4:7; [o]Isa 37:18 **13** [p]Isa 10:5–13; Jer 21:13; Na 3:5; [q]Ps 46:9; [r]2Sa 2:26; [s]Mic 5:6

Ch. 3

1 [a]Eze 22:2; Mic 3:10; [b]Ps 12:2 **3** [c]2Ki 19:35; Isa 34:3; Jer 47:3 **4** [d]Isa 47:9; [e]Isa 23:17; Eze 16:25–29 **5** [f]Na 2:13; [g]Isa 20:4; Jer 13:22; [h]Isa 47:3 **6** [i]Ex 29:14; Job 9:31; [j]1Sa 2:30; Jer 51:37; [k]Isa 14:16 **7** [l]Isa 13:14; 31:9; [m]Na 1:1; [n]Job 3:14; [o]Jer 15:5; [p]Isa 51:19 **8** [q]Am 6:2; [r]Jer 46:25; [s]Isa 19:6–9 **9** [t]Ge 10:6; 2Ch 12:3; [u]Eze 27:10; [v]Eze 30:5 **10** [w]Isa 20:4; [x]2Ki 8:12; Isa 13:16; Hos 13:16; [y]Job 6:27; Eze 24:6; [z]Jer 40:1 **11** [a]Isa 49:26; [b]Isa 2:10 **12** [c]SS 2:13

[a]3 Hebrew; Septuagint and Syriac / *the horsemen rush to and fro*
[b]7 The meaning of the Hebrew for this word is uncertain.
[a]8 Hebrew *No Amon*
[b]9 That is, the upper Nile region

the figs[d] fall into the mouth of the
eater.
13Look at your troops—
they are all women![e]
The gates[f] of your land
are wide open to your enemies;
fire has consumed their bars.[g]

14Draw water for the siege,[h]
strengthen your defences![i]
Work the clay,
tread the mortar,
repair the brickwork!
15There the fire[j] will devour you;
the sword[k] will cut you down
and, like grasshoppers, consume
you.
Multiply like grasshoppers,
multiply like locusts![l]
16You have increased the number of
your merchants
till they are more than the stars of
the sky,
but like locusts[m] they strip the land
and then fly away.

12 [d]Isa 28:4
13 [e]Isa 19:16; [f]Na 2:6; [g]Isa 45:2
14 [h]2Ch 32:4; [i]Na 2:1
15 [j]Isa 27:1; [k]2Sa 2:26; [l]Jer 51:14; Joel 1:4
16 [m]Ex 10:13
17 [n]Jer 51:27
18 [o]Ps 76:5–6; Jer 25:27; [p]Isa 56:10; [q]1Ki 22:17
19 [r]Jer 30:13; Mic 1:9; [s]Job 27:23; La 2:15; Zep 2:15; [t]Isa 37:18

17Your guards are like locusts,[n]
your officials like swarms of locusts
that settle in the walls on a cold
day—
but when the sun appears they fly
away,
and no-one knows where.

18O king of Assyria, your shepherds[c]
slumber;[o]
your nobles lie down to rest.[p]
Your people are scattered[q] on the
mountains
with no-one to gather them.
19Nothing can heal your wound;[r]
your injury is fatal.
Everyone who hears the news about
you
claps his hands[s] at your fall,
for who has not felt
your endless cruelty?[t]

[c]18 Or *rulers*

Habakkuk

1 The oracle[a] that Habakkuk the prophet received.

Habakkuk's Complaint

2How long,[b] O LORD, must I call for help,
but you do not listen?[c]
Or cry out to you, "Violence!"
but you do not save?[d]
3Why do you make me look at injustice?
Why do you tolerate[e] wrong?[f]
Destruction and violence[g] are before me;
there is strife,[h] and conflict abounds.
4Therefore the law[i] is paralysed,
and justice never prevails.
The wicked hem in the righteous,
so that justice[j] is perverted.[k]

The LORD's Answer

5"Look at the nations and watch—
and be utterly amazed.[l]
For I am going to do something in your days
that you would not believe,
even if you were told.[m]
6I am raising up the Babylonians,[a][n]
that ruthless and impetuous people,
who sweep across the whole earth[o]
to seize dwelling-places not their own.[p]
7They are a feared and dreaded people;[q]
they are a law to themselves
and promote their own honour.
8Their horses are swifter[r] than leopards,
fiercer than wolves[s] at dusk.
Their cavalry gallops headlong;
their horsemen come from afar.
They fly like a vulture swooping to devour;
9 they all come bent on violence.
Their hordes[b] advance like a desert wind
and gather prisoners[t] like sand.
10They deride kings
and scoff at rulers.[u]
They laugh at all fortified cities;
they build earthen ramps[v] and capture them.
11Then they sweep past like the wind[w]
and go on—
guilty men, whose own strength is their god."[x]

Habakkuk's Second Complaint

12O LORD, are you not from everlasting?[y]
My God, my Holy One,[z] we will not die.[a]
O LORD, you have appointed[b] them to execute judgment;
O Rock,[c] you have ordained them to punish.
13Your eyes are too pure[d] to look on evil;
you cannot tolerate wrong.[e]
Why then do you tolerate[f] the treacherous?[g]
Why are you silent while the wicked
swallow up those more righteous than themselves?[h]
14You have made men like fish in the sea,
like sea creatures that have no ruler.
15The wicked[i] foe pulls all of them up with hooks,[j]
he catches them in his net,[k]
he gathers them up in his drag-net;
and so he rejoices and is glad.
16Therefore he sacrifices to his net
and burns incense[l] to his drag-net,
for by his net he lives in luxury
and enjoys the choicest food.
17Is he to keep on emptying his net,
destroying nations without mercy?[m]

2 I will stand at my watch[a]
and station myself on the ramparts;[b]
I will look to see what he will say[c] to me,
and what answer I am to give to this complaint.[a][d]

Ch. 1

1 [a]Na 1:1
2 [b]Ps 6:3; [c]Ps 13:1–2; 22:1–2; [d]Jer 14:9; Zec 1:12
3 [e]ver 13; [f]Job 9:23; [g]Jer 20:8; [h]Ps 55:9
4 [i]Ps 119:126; [j]Isa 29:21; [k]Job 19:7; Isa 1:23; 5:20; Eze 9:9
5 [l]Isa 29:9; [m]Ac 13:41*
6 [n]Dt 28:49; 2Ki 24:2; [o]Rev 20:9; [p]Jer 13:20; 21:7
7 [q]Isa 18:7; Jer 39:5–9
8 [r]Jer 4:13; [s]Ge 49:27
9 [t]Hab 2:5
10 [u]2Ch 36:6; [v]Jer 33:4
11 [w]Jer 4:11–12; [x]Da 4:30
12 [y]Ge 21:33; [z]Isa 31:1; 37:23; [a]Ps 118:17; [b]Isa 10:6; [c]Ge 49:24; Ex 33:22
13 [d]Ps 18:26; [e]La 3:34–36; [f]ver 3; [g]Ps 25:3; [h]Job 21:7
15 [i]Jer 5:26; [j]Isa 19:8; [k]Job 18:8; Jer 16:16
16 [l]Jer 44:8
17 [m]Isa 14:6; 19:8

Ch. 2

1 [a]Isa 21:8; [b]Ps 48:13; [c]Ps 85:8; [d]Ps 5:3; Eze 3:17

[a]6 Or *Chaldeans*
[b]9 The meaning of the Hebrew for this word is uncertain.
[a]1 Or *and what to answer when I am rebuked*

The LORD's Answer

2Then the LORD replied:

"Write[e] down the revelation
and make it plain on tablets
so that a herald[b] may run with it.
3For the revelation awaits an appointed time;[f]
it speaks of the end[g]
and will not prove false.
Though it linger, wait[h] for it;
it[c] will certainly come and will not delay.[i]

4"See, he is puffed up;
his desires are not upright—
but the righteous[j] will live by his faith[d][k]—
5indeed, wine[l] betrays him;
he is arrogant[m] and never at rest.
Because he is as greedy as the grave[e]
and like death is never satisfied,[n]
he gathers to himself all the nations
and takes captive[o] all the peoples.

6"Will not all of them taunt[p] him with ridicule and scorn, saying,

"'Woe to him who piles up stolen goods
and makes himself wealthy by extortion![q]
How long must this go on?'
7Will not your debtors[f] suddenly arise?
Will they not wake up and make you tremble?
Then you will become their victim.[r]
8Because you have plundered many nations,
the peoples who are left will plunder you.[s]
For you have shed man's blood;[t]
you have destroyed lands and cities
and everyone in them.[u]

9"Woe to him who builds[v] his realm by unjust gain[w]
to set his nest[x] on high,
to escape the clutches of ruin!
10You have plotted the ruin[y] of many peoples,
shaming[z] your own house and forfeiting your life.
11The stones[a] of the wall will cry out,
and the beams of the woodwork will echo it.

12"Woe to him who builds a city with bloodshed[b]
and establishes a town by crime!
13Has not the LORD Almighty determined
that the people's labour is only fuel for the fire,[c]
that nations exhaust themselves for nothing?[d]
14For the earth will be filled with the knowledge of the glory[e] of the LORD,
as the waters cover the sea.[f]

15"Woe to him who gives drink[g] to his neighbours,
pouring it from the wineskin till they are drunk,
so that he can gaze on their naked bodies.
16You will be filled with shame[h] instead of glory.[i]
Now it is your turn! Drink[j] and be exposed![g][k]
The cup[l] from the LORD's right hand is coming round to you,
and disgrace will cover your glory.
17The violence[m] you have done to Lebanon will overwhelm you,
and your destruction of animals will terrify you.[n]
For you have shed man's blood;[o]
you have destroyed lands and cities
and everyone in them.

18"Of what value[p] is an idol,[q] since a man has carved it?
Or an image[r] that teaches lies?
For he who makes it trusts in his own creation;
he makes idols that cannot speak.[s]
19Woe to him who says to wood, 'Come to life!'
Or to lifeless stone, 'Wake up!'[t]
Can it give guidance?
It is covered with gold and silver;[u]
there is no breath in it.[v]
20But the LORD is in his holy temple;[w]
let all the earth be silent[x] before him."

Habakkuk's Prayer

3 A prayer of Habakkuk the prophet. On *shigionoth*.[a][a]

2LORD, I have heard[b] of your fame;
I stand in awe[c] of your deeds, O LORD.[d]

2 [e]Isa 30:8; Jer 36:2; Eze 24:2; Ro 4:24; Rev 1:19
3 [f]Da 11:27; [g]Da 8:17; [h]Ps 27:14; [i]Eze 12:25
4 [j]Eze 18:9; [k]Ro 1:17*; Gal 3:11*; Heb 10:37–38*
5 [l]Pr 20:1; [m]Isa 2:11; [n]Pr 27:20; 30:15–16; [o]Hab 1:9
6 [p]Isa 14:4; [q]Am 2:8
7 [r]Pr 29:1
8 [s]Isa 33:1; Jer 50:17–18; Ob 15; Zec 2:8–9; [t]ver 17; [u]Eze 39:10
9 [v]Jer 22:13; [w]Jer 51:13; [x]Job 39:27; Isa 10:14
10 [y]Jer 26:19; [z]ver 16; Na 3:6
11 [a]Jos 24:27; Zec 5:4; Lk 19:40
12 [b]Eze 22:2; Mic 3:10
13 [c]Isa 50:11; [d]Isa 47:13
14 [e]Ex 16:7; Nu 14:21; [f]Isa 11:9
15 [g]Pr 23:20
16 [h]ver 10; [i]Eze 23:32–34; Hos 4:7; [j]Lev 10:9; [k]La 4:21; [l]Ps 16:5; Isa 51:22
17 [m]Jer 51:35; [n]Jer 50:15; [o]ver 8
18 [p]1Sa 12:21; [q]Jdg 10:14; Isa 40:19; Jer 5:21; 14:22; [r]Lev 26:1; [s]Ps 115:4–5; Jer 10:14; 1Co 12:2
19 [t]1Ki 18:27; [u]Jer 10:4; [v]Da 5:4,23; Hos 4:12
20 [w]Ps 11:4; [x]Isa 41:1

Ch. 3

1 [a]Ps 7 Title
2 [b]Job 26:14; Ps 44:1; [c]Ps 119:120; [d]Ps 90:16

b2 Or *so that whoever reads it*
c3 Or *Though he linger, wait for him; / he*
d4 Or *faithfulness*
e5 Hebrew *Sheol*
f7 Or *creditors*
g16 Masoretic Text; Dead Sea Scrolls, Aquila, Vulgate and Syriac (see also Septuagint) *and stagger*
a1 Probably a literary or musical term

Renew[e] them in our day,
in our time make them known;
in wrath remember mercy.[f]

3God came from Teman,[g]
the Holy One[h] from Mount Paran.[i]
Selah[b]
His glory covered the heavens[j]
and his praise filled the earth.[k]
4His splendour was like the sunrise;[l]
rays flashed from his hand,
where his power[m] was hidden.
5Plague[n] went before him;
pestilence followed his steps.
6He stood, and shook the earth;
he looked, and made the nations
tremble.
The ancient mountains crumbled[o]
and the age-old hills[p] collapsed.[q]
His ways are eternal.[r]
7I saw the tents of Cushan in distress,
the dwellings of Midian[s] in
anguish.[t]

8Were you angry with the rivers,[u] O
LORD?
Was your wrath against the
streams?
Did you rage against the sea[v]
when you rode with your horses
and your victorious chariots?[w]
9You uncovered your bow,
you called for many arrows.[x] *Selah*
You split the earth with rivers;
10 the mountains saw you and
writhed.[y]
Torrents of water swept by;
the deep roared[z]
and lifted its waves[a] on high.

11Sun and moon stood still[b] in the
heavens
at the glint of your flying arrows,[c]
at the lightning[d] of your flashing
spear.
12In wrath you strode through the earth
and in anger you threshed[e] the
nations.
13You came out[f] to deliver[g] your people,
to save your anointed[h] one.
You crushed[i] the leader of the land of
wickedness,
you stripped him from head to foot.
Selah
14With his own spear you pierced his
head
when his warriors stormed out to
scatter us,[j]
gloating as though about to devour
the wretched[k] who were in hiding.
15You trampled the sea[l] with your
horses,
churning the great waters.[m]

16I heard and my heart pounded,
my lips quivered at the sound;
decay crept into my bones,
and my legs trembled.[n]
Yet I will wait patiently[o] for the day of
calamity
to come on the nation invading us.
17Though the fig-tree does not bud
and there are no grapes on the
vines,
though the olive crop fails
and the fields produce no food,[p]
though there are no sheep in the pen
and no cattle in the stalls,[q]
18yet I will rejoice in the LORD,[r]
I will be joyful in God my Saviour.[s]

19The Sovereign LORD is my strength;[t]
he makes my feet like the feet of a
deer,
he enables me to go on the heights.[u]

For the director of music. On my
stringed instruments.

2 [e]Ps 85:6; [f]Isa 54:8
3 [g]**Ge 36:11**, 15; [h]Isa 31:1; [i]**Nu 10:12**; [j]**Ps 8:1**; [k]Ps 48:10
4 [l]**Isa 18:4**; [m]**Job 9:6**
5 [n]**Lev 26:25**
6 [o]**Ps 46:2**; [p]Ge 49:26; [q]**Ex 19:18**; Ps 18:7; 114:1–6; [r]**Ge 21:33**
7 [s]**Ge 25:2**; **Nu 25:15**; Jdg 7:24–25; [t]Ex 15:14
8 [u]**Ex 7:20**; [v]**Ps 77:16**; [w]**2Ki 2:11**; **Ps 68:17**
9 [x]**Dt 32:23**; Ps 7:12–13
10 [y]**Ps 77:16**; [z]Ps 98:7; [a]**Ps 93:3**
11 [b]Jos 10:13; [c]Ps 18:14; [d]**Ps 144:6**; Zec 9:14
12 [e]**Isa 41:15**
13 [f]Ex 13:21; [g]**Ps 20:6**; **28:8**; [h]2Sa 23:1; [i]Ps 68:21; 110:6
14 [j]Jdg 7:22; [k]Ps 64:2–5
15 [l]**Job 9:8**; [m]Ex 15:8
16 [n]**Job 4:14**; [o]**Ps 37:7**
17 [p]Joel 1:10–12, 18; [q]Jer 5:17
18 [r]Ps 97:12; **Isa 61:10**; Php 4:4; [s]**Ex 15:2**; **Lk 1:47**
19 [t]**Dt 33:29**; Ps 46:1–5; [u]**Dt 32:13**; Ps 18:33

b3 A word of uncertain meaning; possibly a musical term; also in verses 9 and 13

Zephaniah

1 The word of the LORD that came to
Zephaniah son of Cushi, the son of
Gedaliah, the son of Amariah, the son
of Hezekiah, during the reign of Josiah[a]
son of Amon[b] king of Judah:

Warning of Coming Destruction

2"I will sweep away everything
from the face of the earth,"[c]
declares the LORD.
3"I will sweep away both men and
animals;[d]
I will sweep away the birds of the
air[e]
and the fish of the sea.
The wicked will have only heaps of
rubble[a]
when I cut off man from the face of
the earth,"[f]
declares the LORD.[g]

Against Judah

4"I will stretch out my hand[h] against
Judah
and against all who live in
Jerusalem.
I will cut off from this place every
remnant of Baal,[i]
the names of the pagan and the
idolatrous priests[j]—
5those who bow down on the roofs
to worship the starry host,[k]
those who bow down and swear by
the LORD
and who also swear by Molech,[b] [l]
6those who turn back from following[m]
the LORD
and neither seek[n] the LORD nor
enquire[o] of him.
7Be silent[p] before the Sovereign LORD,
for the day of the LORD[q] is near.
The LORD has prepared a sacrifice;[r]
he has consecrated those he has
invited.
8On the day of the LORD's sacrifice
I will punish[s] the princes
and the king's sons[t]
and all those clad
in foreign clothes.
9On that day I will punish
all who avoid stepping on the
threshold,[c] [u]
who fill the temple of their gods
with violence and deceit.[v]

10"On that day,[w]" declares the LORD,
"a cry will go up from the Fish
Gate,[x]
wailing[y] from the New Quarter,
and a loud crash from the hills.
11Wail,[z] you who live in the market
district;[d]
all your merchants will be wiped
out,
all who trade with[e] silver will be
ruined.[a]
12At that time I will search Jerusalem
with lamps
and punish those who are
complacent,[b]
who are like wine left on its dregs,[c]
who think, 'The LORD will do
nothing,[d]
either good or bad.'[e]
13Their wealth will be plundered,[f]
their houses demolished.
They will build houses
but not live in them;
they will plant vineyards
but not drink the wine.[g]

The Great Day of the LORD

14"The great day of the LORD[h] is near[i]—
near and coming quickly.
Listen! The cry on the day of the LORD
will be bitter,
the shouting of the warrior there.
15That day will be a day of wrath,
a day of distress and anguish,
a day of trouble and ruin,
a day of darkness[j] and gloom,
a day of clouds and blackness,[k]
16a day of trumpet and battle cry[l]
against the fortified cities
and against the corner towers.[m]

Ch. 1
1 [a]2Ki 22:1; 2Ch 34:1–35:25; [b]**1Ch 3:14**
2 [c]**Ge 6:7**
3 [d]Jer 50:3; [e]**Jer 4:25**; [f]ver 18; **Hos 4:3**; [g]**Eze 14:17**
4 [h]**Jer 6:12**; [i]Mic 5:13; Zep 2:11; [j]**Jer 15:6**; **Hos 10:5**
5 [k]**Jer 8:2**; [l]**Lev 18:21**; Jer 5:7
6 [m]Isa 1:4; Jer 2:13; [n]**Isa 9:13**; [o]**Hos 7:7**
7 [p]**Isa 41:1**; [q]ver 14; Isa 13:6; **Eze 7:19**; **Joel 3:14**; **Am 5:18–20**; [r]**Lev 3:9**; **Jer 46:10**
8 [s]Isa 24:21; [t]Jer 39:6
9 [u]1Sa 5:5; [v]**Am 3:10**
10 [w]Isa 22:5; [x]2Ch 33:14; [y]**Am 5:16**
11 [z]Jas 5:1; [a]Hos 9:6
12 [b]Am 6:1; [c]Jer 48:11; [d]**2Ki 21:16**; **Eze 8:12**; [e]**Job 22:13**
13 [f]2Ki 24:13; Jer 15:13; [g]Dt 28:30,39; La 5:2; **Am 5:11**
14 [h]**ver 7**; **Joel 1:15**; [i]**Eze 7:7**; **Da 7:13**
15 [j]1Sa 2:9; [k]**Isa 22:5**; Joel 2:2; Mk 13:24–25
16 [l]**Jer 4:19**; [m]**Dt 28:52**; **Isa 2:15**; **Joel 2:1**

[a]3 The meaning of the Hebrew for this line is uncertain. [b]5 Hebrew *Malcam*, that is, Milcom [c]9 See 1 Samuel 5:5. [d]11 Or *the Mortar* [e]11 Or *in*

17I will bring distress[n] on the people
and they will walk like blind[o] men,
because they have sinned against
the LORD.
Their blood will be poured out[p] like
dust
and their entrails like filth.[q]
18Neither their silver nor their gold
will be able to save them
on the day of the LORD's wrath.[r]
In the fire of his jealousy[s]
the whole world will be consumed,[t]
for he will make a sudden end
of all who live in the earth.[u]"

2 Gather together,[a] gather
together,
O shameful[b] nation,
2before the appointed time arrives
and that day sweeps on like chaff,[c]
before the fierce anger[d] of the LORD
comes upon you,
before the day of the LORD's wrath[e]
comes upon you.
3Seek[f] the LORD, all you humble of the
land,
you who do what he commands.
Seek righteousness,[g] seek humility;[h]
perhaps you will be sheltered[i]
on the day of the LORD's anger.

Against Philistia

4Gaza[j] will be abandoned
and Ashkelon[k] left in ruins.
At midday Ashdod will be emptied
and Ekron uprooted.
5Woe to you who live by the sea,
O Kerethite[l] people;
the word of the LORD is against you,[m]
O Canaan, land of the Philistines.

"I will destroy you,
and none will be left."[n]

6The land by the sea, where the
Kerethites[a] dwell,
will be a place for shepherds and
sheep pens.[o]
7It will belong to the remnant[p] of the
house of Judah;
there they will find pasture.
In the evening they will lie down
in the houses of Ashkelon.
The LORD their God will care for them;
he will restore their fortunes.[b][q]

Against Moab and Ammon

8"I have heard the insults[r] of Moab[s]
and the taunts of the Ammonites,[t]
who insulted[u] my people
and made threats against their
land.[v]
9Therefore, as surely as I live,"
declares the LORD Almighty, the
God of Israel,
"surely Moab[w] will become like
Sodom,[x]
the Ammonites[y] like Gomorrah—
a place of weeds and salt pits,
a wasteland for ever.
The remnant of my people will
plunder[z] them;
the survivors[a] of my nation will
inherit their land.[b]"

10This is what they will get in return for
their pride,[c]
for insulting[d] and mocking the
people of the LORD Almighty.[e]
11The LORD will be awesome[f] to them
when he destroys all the gods[g] of the
land.[h]
The nations on every shore will
worship him,[i]
every one in its own land.

Against Cush

12"You too, O Cushites,[c][j]
will be slain by my sword.[k]"

Against Assyria

13He will stretch out his hand against
the north
and destroy Assyria,[l]
leaving Nineveh[m] utterly desolate
and dry as the desert.[n]
14Flocks and herds[o] will lie down there,
creatures of every kind.
The desert owl[p] and the screech owl[q][r]
will roost on her columns.
Their calls will echo through the
windows,
rubble will be in the doorways,
the beams of cedar will be exposed.
15This is the carefree[s] city
that lived in safety.[t]
She said to herself,
"I am, and there is none besides
me."[u]
What a ruin she has become,
a lair for wild beasts![v]
All who pass by her scoff[w]
and shake their fists.[x]

17 [n]Dt 28:52; [o]Isa 59:10; [p]Ps 79:3; [q]Ps 83:10
18 [r]Job 20:20; 40:11; Jer 4:4; Eze 7:19; [s]Dt 29:20; [t]ver 2–3; Zep 3:8; [u]Ge 6:7; Eze 7:11

Ch. 2

1 [a]2Ch 20:4; Joel 1:14; [b]Jer 3:3; 6:15
2 [c]Isa 17:13; Hos 13:3; [d]Jer 10:25; La 4:11; [e]Jer 4:4; Eze 7:19
3 [f]Am 5:6; [g]Isa 1:17; [h]Ps 45:4; [i]Ps 57:1
4 [j]Ge 10:19; Am 1:6,7–8; Zec 9:5–7; [k]Jer 47:5
5 [l]1Sa 30:14; [m]Lev 26:31; Am 3:1; [n]Isa 14:30
6 [o]Isa 5:17
7 [p]Ge 45:7; [q]Dt 30:3; Ps 126:4; Jer 32:44; Hos 6:11; Joel 3:1; Am 1:6–8
8 [r]Jer 48:27; [s]Ge 19:37; Isa 16:6; [t]Eze 21:28; [u]Eze 25:3; [v]La 3:61
9 [w]Dt 23:6; Isa 15:1–16:14; Jer 48:1–47; Eze 25:8–11; [x]Dt 29:23; Isa 13:19; Jer 49:18; [y]Jer 49:1–6; Eze 25:1–7; [z]Isa 11:14; [a]2Ki 19:31; [b]Am 2:1–3
10 [c]Job 40:12; Isa 16:6; [d]Jer 48:27; [e]Ps 9:6
11 [f]Joel 2:11; [g]Zep 1:4; [h]1Ch 19:1; Eze 25:6–7; [i]Ps 86:9; Isa 12:4; Zep 3:9
12 [j]Ge 10:6; Isa 20:4; [k]Jer 46:10
13 [l]Isa 10:5; [m]Ge 10:11; Na 1:1; [n]Mic 5:6; Zec 10:11
14 [o]Isa 5:17; [p]Isa 14:23; [q]Rev 18:2; [r]Ps 102:6
15 [s]Isa 32:9; [t]Isa 47:8; [u]Eze 28:2; [v]Jer 49:33; [w]Isa 28:22; Na 3:19; [x]Eze 27:36

[a]6 The meaning of the Hebrew for this word is uncertain. [b]7 Or *will bring back their captives*
[c]12 That is, people from the upper Nile region

The Future of Jerusalem

3 Woe to the city of oppressors,[a]
rebellious[b] and defiled![c]
2She obeys[d] no-one,
she accepts no correction.[e]
She does not trust[f] in the LORD,
she does not draw near[g] to her God.
3Her officials are roaring lions,[h]
her rulers are evening wolves,[i]
who leave nothing for the morning.[j]
4Her prophets are arrogant;
they are treacherous[k] men.
Her priests profane the sanctuary
and do violence to the law.[l]
5The LORD within her is righteous;[m]
he does no wrong.[n]
Morning by morning[o] he dispenses
his justice,
and every new day he does not fail,[p]
yet the unrighteous know no
shame.[q]

6"I have cut off nations;
their strongholds are demolished.
I have left their streets deserted,
with no-one passing through.
Their cities are destroyed;[r]
no-one will be left—no-one at all.
7I said to the city,
'Surely you will fear me
and accept correction!'[s]
Then her dwelling would not be cut
off,
nor all my punishments come upon
her.
But they were still eager
to act corruptly[t] in all they did.
8Therefore wait[u] for me," declares the
LORD,
"for the day I will stand up to
testify.[a]
I have decided to assemble[v] the
nations,[w]
to gather the kingdoms
and to pour out my wrath[x] on them—
all my fierce anger.[y]
The whole world will be consumed[z]
by the fire of my jealous anger.

9"Then will I purify the lips of the
peoples,
that all of them may call[a] on the
name of the LORD[b]
and serve[c] him shoulder to
shoulder.
10From beyond the rivers of Cush[b][d]
my worshippers, my scattered
people,
will bring me offerings.[e]
11On that day you will not be put to
shame[f]
for all the wrongs you have done
to me,[g]
because I will remove from this city
those who rejoice in their pride.[h]
Never again will you be haughty
on my holy hill.[i]
12But I will leave within you
the meek[j] and humble,
who trust[k] in the name of the LORD.
13The remnant[l] of Israel will do no
wrong;[m]
they will speak no lies,[n]
nor will deceit be found in their
mouths.[o]
They will eat and lie down[p]
and no-one will make them afraid.[q]"

14Sing, O Daughter of Zion;[r]
shout aloud,[s] O Israel!
Be glad and rejoice[t] with all your heart,
O Daughter of Jerusalem!
15The LORD has taken away your
punishment,
he has turned back your enemy.
The LORD, the King of Israel, is with
you;[u]
never again will you fear[v] any
harm.[w]
16On that day they will say to Jerusalem,
"Do not fear, O Zion;
do not let your hands hang limp.[x]
17The LORD your God is with you,
he is mighty to save.[y]
He will take great delight[z] in you,
he will quiet you with his love,[a]
he will rejoice over you with
singing."[b]

18"The sorrows for the appointed feasts
I will remove from you;
they are a burden and a reproach to
you.[c]
19At that time I will deal
with all who oppressed[c] you;
I will rescue the lame
and gather those who have been
scattered.[d]
I will give them praise[e] and honour
in every land where they were put
to shame.
20At that time I will gather you;
at that time I will bring[f] you home.
I will give you honour[g] and praise[h]
among all the peoples of the earth
when I restore your fortunes[d][i]
before your very eyes,"
says the LORD.

Ch. 3
1 [a]Jer 6:6; [b]Dt 21:18; [c]Eze 23:30
2 [d]Jer 22:21; [e]Lev 26:23; Jer 7:28; [f]Dt 1:32; [g]Ps 73:28
3 [h]Ps 22:13; [i]Ge 49:27; [j]Mic 3:3
4 [k]Ps 25:3; Isa 48:8; Jer 3:20; 9:4; Mal 2:10; [l]Jer 23:11; Eze 22:26
5 [m]Ezr 9:15; [n]Dt 32:4; [o]Ps 5:3; [p]La 3:23; [q]Jer 3:3; Eze 18:25
6 [r]Lev 26:31
7 [s]Jer 7:28; [t]Hos 9:9
8 [u]Ps 27:14; [v]Joel 3:11; [w]Isa 2:3; [x]Ps 79:6; Rev 16:1; [y]Jer 10:25; La 4:11; [z]Zep 1:18
9 [a]Zep 2:11; [b]Ge 4:26; [c]Isa 19:18
10 [d]Ge 10:6; Ps 68:31; [e]2Ch 32:23; Isa 60:7
11 [f]Isa 29:22; Joel 2:26–27; [g]Ge 50:15; [h]Ps 59:12; [i]Ex 15:17; Lev 26:19
12 [j]Isa 14:32; [k]Jer 29:12; Na 1:7
13 [l]Isa 10:21; [m]Ps 119:3; Isa 4:3; [n]Jer 33:16; Rev 14:5; [o]Job 16:17; [p]Eze 34:15; Zep 2:7; [q]Lev 26:6; Eze 34:25–28
14 [r]Ps 9:14; Zec 2:10; [s]Ps 95:1; Isa 12:6; Zec 2:10; [t]Ps 9:2; Isa 51:11
15 [u]Eze 37:26–28; [v]Isa 54:14; [w]Zec 9:9
16 [x]2Ki 19:26; Job 4:3; Isa 35:3–4; Heb 12:12
17 [y]Isa 63:1; Joel 2:21; [z]Dt 28:63; Isa 62:4; [a]Hos 14:4; [b]Isa 40:1
19 [c]Isa 14:2; [d]Eze 34:16; Mic 4:6; [e]Isa 60:18
20 [f]Jer 29:14; Eze 37:12; [g]Isa 56:5; 66:22; [h]Dt 26:19; Isa 60:18; [i]Joel 3:1

[a]8 Septuagint and Syriac; Hebrew *will rise up to plunder* [b]10 That is, the upper Nile region
[c]18 Or "*I will gather you who mourn for the appointed feasts; / your reproach is a burden to you*
[d]20 Or *I bring back your captives*

Haggai

A Call to Build the House of the LORD

1 In the second year of King Darius,[a]
on the first day of the sixth month,
the word of the LORD came through the
prophet Haggai[b] to Zerubbabel[c] son of
Shealtiel, governor[d] of Judah, and to
Joshua[a][e] son of Jehozadak,[f] the high
priest:[g]
2This is what the LORD Almighty[h]
says: "These people[i] say, 'The time has
not yet come for the LORD's house to be
built.[j]' "
3Then the word of the LORD came
through the prophet Haggai:[k] 4"Is it a
time for you yourselves to be living in
your panelled houses,[l] while this house
remains a ruin?[m]"
5Now this is what the LORD Almighty
says: "Give careful thought[n] to your
ways. 6You have planted much, but
have harvested little.[o] You eat, but nev-
er have enough.[p] You drink, but never
have your fill.[q] You put on clothes, but
are not warm. You earn wages,[r] only to
put them in a purse with holes in it."
7This is what the LORD Almighty says:
"Give careful thought[s] to your ways.
8Go up into the mountains and bring
down timber[t] and build the house, so
that I may take pleasure[u] in it and be
honoured,[v]" says the LORD. 9"You ex-
pected much, but see, it turned out to
be little.[w] What you brought home, I
blew[x] away. Why?" declares the LORD
Almighty. "Because of my house,
which remains a ruin,[y] while each of
you is busy with his own house.
10Therefore, because of you the heavens
have withheld[z] their dew[a] and the earth
its crops.[b] 11I called for a drought[c] on the
fields and the mountains,[d] on the grain,
the new wine,[e] the oil[f] and whatever the
ground produces, on men and cattle,
and on the labour of your hands.[g]"

12Then Zerubbabel[h] son of Shealtiel,
Joshua son of Jehozadak, the high
priest, and the whole remnant[i] of the
people obeyed[j] the voice of the LORD
their God and the message of the
prophet Haggai, because the LORD their
God had sent him. And the people
feared[k] the LORD.
13Then Haggai,[l] the LORD's mess-
enger,[m] gave this message of the LORD to
the people: "I am with[n] you," declares
the LORD. 14So the LORD stirred up[o] the
spirit of Zerubbabel[p] son of Shealtiel,
governor of Judah, and the spirit of
Joshua son of Jehozadak,[q] the high
priest, and the spirit of the whole rem-
nant[r] of the people. They came and
began work on the house of the LORD
Almighty, their God, 15on the twenty-
fourth day of the sixth month[s] in the
second year of King Darius.[t]

The Promised Glory of the New House

2 On the twenty-first day of the
seventh month,[a] the word of the
LORD came through the prophet Hag-
gai:[b] 2"Speak to Zerubbabel[c] son of
Shealtiel, governor of Judah, to Joshua
son of Jehozadak,[d] the high priest, and
to the remnant[e] of the people. Ask
them, 3'Who of you is left who saw this
house[f] in its former glory? How does it
look to you now? Does it not seem to
you like nothing?[g] 4But now be strong,
O Zerubbabel,' declares the LORD. 'Be
strong,[h] O Joshua son of Jehozadak,[i] the
high priest. Be strong, all you people of
the land,' declares the LORD, 'and work.
For I am with[j] you,' declares the LORD
Almighty. 5'This is what I covenanted[k]
with you when you came out of Egypt.[l]
And my Spirit[m] remains among you. Do
not fear.'[n]
6"This is what the LORD Almighty
says: 'In a little while[o] I will once more
shake the heavens and the earth,[p] the
sea and the dry land. 7I will shake all

Ch. 1

1 [a]**Ezr 4:24;** [b]**Ezr 5:1;** [c]**1Ch 3:19;** Mt 1:12–13; [d]Ezr 5:3; **Ne 5:14;** [e]**Ezr 2:2;** [f]**1Ch 6:15; Ezr 3:2;** [g]Zec 3:8
2 [h]Isa 13:4; [i]**Isa 29:13;** [j]Ezr 1:2
3 [k]**Ezr 5:1**
4 [l]**2Sa 7:2;** [m]ver 9; Jer 33:12
5 [n]ver 7; La 3:40; Hag 2:15,18
6 [o]**Lev 26:20; Isa 5:10;** [p]**Isa 9:20; 55:2;** [q]Am 4:8; [r]Hag 2:16; Zec 8:10
7 [s]**ver 5**
8 [t]**1Ch 14:1;** [u]**Job 22:3;** Ps 132:13–14; [v]**Ex 29:43;** Jer 13:11
9 [w]**Dt 28:38; Isa 5:10;** [x]**Ps 103:16; Eze 22:21;** [y]**ver 4; Ne 13:11**
10 [z]**Dt 28:24;** [a]**Ge 27:28;** 1Ki 17:1; [b]Lev 26:19; Dt 28:23
11 [c]**Dt 11:26; 28:22; Ru 1:1; 1Ki 17:1; Isa 5:6;** [d]Isa 7:25; [e]**Dt 28:51;** Ps 4:7; [f]**Nu 18:12;** [g]Hag 2:17
12 [h]ver 1; [i]ver 14; Isa 1:9; Hag 2:2; [j]**Job 36:11; Isa 50:10;** Mt 28:20; [k]**Dt 31:12; Isa 1:2**
13 [l]ver 1; [m]**Nu 27:21; 2Ch 36:15;** [n]**Ge 26:3; Nu 14:9; Mt 28:20;** Ro 8:31
14 [o]**Ezr 1:5;** [p]**Ezr 5:2;** [q]**1Ch 6:15;** [r]**ver 12**
15 [s]ver 1; Hag 2:10,20; [t]**Ezr 4:24**

Ch. 2

1 [a]ver 10,20; **Lev 23:34;** Jn 7:37; [b]**Ezr 5:1**
2 [c]Hag 1:1; [d]**1Ch 6:15;** [e]**Hag 1:12**
3 [f]**Ezr 3:12; Isa 60:7;** [g]Zec 4:10
4 [h]**1Ch 28:20;** Zec 8:9; **Eph 6:10;** [i]**1Ch 6:15;** [j]**Ex 33:14; Nu 14:9; 2Sa 5:10;** Ac 7:9
5 [k]**Ge 6:18;** [l]**Ex 29:46;** [m]**Ne 9:20;** [n]**Ge 15:1;** 1Ch 28:20; **Ezr 5:2;** Zec 8:13
6 [o]**Isa 10:25;** [p]**Ex 19:18; Job 9:6; Isa 14:16; Eze 38:19;** Heb 12:26*

---

a*1* A variant of *Jeshua*; here and elsewhere in Haggai

nations, and the desired[q] of all nations
will come, and I will fill this house[r] with
glory,[s]' says the LORD Almighty. 8'The
silver is mine and the gold[t] is mine,'
declares the LORD Almighty. 9'The
glory[u] of this present house[v] will be
greater than the glory of the former
house,' says the LORD Almighty. 'And
in this place I will grant peace,[w]' de-
clares the LORD Almighty."

Blessings for a Defiled People

10On the twenty-fourth day of the
ninth month,[x] in the second year of
Darius, the word of the LORD came to
the prophet Haggai: 11"This is what the
LORD Almighty says: 'Ask the priests[y]
what the law says: 12If a person carries
consecrated meat[z] in the fold of his gar-
ment, and that fold touches some bread
or stew, some wine, oil or other food,
does it become consecrated?[a]' "
The priests answered, "No."
13Then Haggai said, "If a person
defiled by contact with a dead body
touches one of these things, does it
become defiled?"
"Yes," the priests replied, "it be-
comes defiled.[b]"
14Then Haggai said, " 'So it is with this
people[c] and this nation in my sight,'
declares the LORD. 'Whatever they do
and whatever they offer[d] there is de-
filed.
15" 'Now give careful thought[e] to this
from this day on[a]—consider how things
were before one stone was laid[f] on
another in the LORD's temple.[g] 16When
anyone came to a heap[h] of twenty
measures, there were only ten. When
anyone went to a wine vat[i] to draw fifty
measures, there were only twenty.[j] 17I
struck all the work of your hands[k] with
blight,[l] mildew and hail,[m] yet you did
not turn[n] to me,' declares the LORD.[o]
18'From this day on, from this twenty-
fourth day of the ninth month, give
careful thought[p] to the day when the
foundation[q] of the LORD's temple was
laid. Give careful thought: 19Is there yet
any seed left in the barn? Until now, the
vine and the fig-tree, the pomegranate[r]
and the olive tree have not borne fruit.[s]
" 'From this day on I will bless[t] you.' "

Zerubbabel the LORD's Signet Ring

20The word of the LORD came to Hag-
gai[u] a second time on the twenty-fourth
day of the month:[v] 21"Tell Zerubbabel[w]
governor of Judah that I will shake[x] the
heavens and the earth. 22I will overturn[y]
royal thrones and shatter the power of
the foreign kingdoms.[z] I will overthrow
chariots[a] and their drivers; horses and
their riders[b] will fall, each by the sword
of his brother.[c]
23" 'On that day,[d]' declares the LORD
Almighty, 'I will take you, my servant[e]
Zerubbabel[f] son of Shealtiel,' declares
the LORD, 'and I will make you like my
signet ring,[g] for I have chosen you,'
declares the LORD Almighty."

7 [q]1Sa 9:20; [r]Isa 60:7; [s]Ex 16:7; 29:43; Lk 2:32
8 [t]1Ch 29:2
9 [u]Ps 85:9; Isa 11:10; [v]Ezr 3:12; Isa 60:7; [w]Lev 26:6; Isa 60:17
10 [x]ver 1; Hag 1:15
11 [y]Lev 10:10–11; Dt 17:8–11; 33:8; Jer 18:18
12 [z]Jer 11:15; [a]Ge 7:2; Lev 6:27; Mt 23:19
13 [b]Lev 22:4–6; Nu 19:13
14 [c]Isa 29:13; [d]Ps 51:17; Isa 1:13
15 [e]Hag 1:5; [f]Ezr 3:10; [g]Ezr 4:24
16 [h]Ru 3:7; [i]Job 24:11; Isa 5:2; [j]Dt 28:38; Isa 5:10; Hag 1:6
17 [k]Hag 1:11; [l]Dt 28:22; [m]Ex 9:18; Ps 78:48; [n]Isa 9:13; Jer 3:10; [o]Am 4:6
18 [p]Hag 1:5; [q]Ezr 3:11
19 [r]Ex 28:33; [s]Joel 1:12; [t]Ge 12:2; Lev 25:21; Ps 128:1–6; Joel 2:14
20 [u]Ezr 5:1; [v]ver 1; Hag 1:15
21 [w]Ezr 5:2; [x]Isa 14:16; Eze 38:19–20
22 [y]Ge 19:25; Job 2:13; [z]Da 2:44; [a]Mic 5:10; [b]Ex 15:21; [c]Jdg 7:22; Eze 38:21
23 [d]Isa 2:11; 10:20; Zec 4:10; [e]Isa 20:3; Da 9:24–26; [f]Mt 1:12; [g]Ge 38:18; Ex 28:9; 2Co 1:22

[a]15 Or *to the days past*

Zechariah

A Call to Return to the LORD

1 In the eighth month of the second year of Darius,[a] the word of the LORD came to the prophet Zechariah[b] son of Berekiah,[c] the son of Iddo:[d]

2"The LORD was very angry[e] with your forefathers. 3Therefore tell the people: This is what the LORD Almighty says: 'Return[f] to me,' declares the LORD Almighty, 'and I will return to you,'[g] says the LORD Almighty. 4Do not be like your forefathers,[h] to whom the earlier prophets[i] proclaimed: This is what the LORD Almighty says: 'Turn from your evil ways[j] and your evil practices.' But they would not listen or pay attention to me,[k] declares the LORD.[l] 5Where are your forefathers now? And the prophets, do they live for ever? 6But did not my words[m] and my decrees, which I commanded my servants the prophets, overtake your forefathers?[n]

"Then they repented and said, 'The LORD Almighty has done to us what our ways and practices deserve,[o] just as he determined to do.'"[p]

The Man Among the Myrtle Trees

7On the twenty-fourth day of the eleventh month, the month of Shebat, in the second year of Darius, the word of the LORD came to the prophet Zechariah son of Berekiah, the son of Iddo.[q]

8During the night I had a vision—and there before me was a man riding a red[r] horse! He was standing among the myrtle trees in a ravine. Behind him were red, brown and white horses.[s]

9I asked, "What are these, my lord?"

The angel[t] who was talking with me answered, "I will show you what they are."[u]

10Then the man standing among the myrtle trees explained, "They are the ones the LORD has sent to go throughout the earth."[v]

11And they reported to the angel of the LORD,[w] who was standing among the myrtle trees, "We have gone throughout the earth and found the whole world at rest and in peace."[x]

12Then the angel of the LORD said, "LORD Almighty, how long[y] will you withhold mercy[z] from Jerusalem and from the towns of Judah,[a] which you have been angry with these seventy[b] years?" 13So the LORD spoke[c] kind and comforting words[d] to the angel who talked with me.[e]

14Then the angel who was speaking to me said, "Proclaim this word: This is what the LORD Almighty says: 'I am very jealous[f] for Jerusalem and Zion, 15but I am very angry with the nations that feel secure.[g] I was only a little angry,[h] but they added to the calamity.'[i]

16"Therefore, this is what the LORD says: 'I will return[j] to Jerusalem with mercy, and there my house will be rebuilt. And the measuring line[k] will be stretched out over Jerusalem,' declares the LORD Almighty.[l]

17"Proclaim further: This is what the LORD Almighty says: 'My towns will again overflow with prosperity, and the LORD will again comfort[m] Zion and choose[n] Jerusalem.'"[o]

Four Horns and Four Craftsmen

18Then I looked up—and there before me were four horns! 19I asked the angel who was speaking to me, "What are these?"

He answered me, "These are the horns[p] that scattered Judah, Israel and Jerusalem."

20Then the LORD showed me four craftsmen. 21I asked, "What are these coming to do?"

He answered, "These are the horns that scattered Judah so that no-one could raise his head, but the craftsmen have come to terrify them and throw down these horns of the nations who lifted up their horns[q] against the land of Judah to scatter its people."[r]

A Man With a Measuring Line

2 Then I looked up—and there before me was a man with a measuring line in his hand! 2I asked, "Where are you going?"

Ch. 1

1 [a]**Ezr 4:24; 6:15**; [b]**Ezr 5:1**; [c]Mt 23:35; Lk 11:51; [d]ver 7; **Ne 12:4**
2 [e]**2Ch 36:16**
3 [f]**Job 22:23**; [g]Mal 3:7; Jas 4:8
4 [h]**2Ch 36:15**; [i]Zec 7:7; [j]**2Ki 17:13; 2Ch 7:14**; Ps 106:6; **Jer 23:22**; [k]**2Ch 24:19**; Ps 78:8; **Jer 6:17**; 17:23; [l]**Eze 20:18; 33:4**
6 [m]**Isa 44:26**; [n]**Dt 28:2; Da 9:12; Hos 5:9**; [o]Jer 12:14–17; La 2:17; [p]Jer 23:20; 39:16; **44:17**
7 [q]**ver 1**
8 [r]Rev 6:4; [s]Zec 6:2–7
9 [t]Zec 4:1,4–5; 5:5; [u]**Da 7:16**
10 [v]Zec 6:5–8
11 [w]Ge 16:7; [x]**Isa 14:7**
12 [y]**Ps 6:3**; [z]Ps 40:11; [a]**Jer 40:5**; [b]**2Ch 36:21; Da 9:2**
13 [c]**Isa 35:4**; [d]**Job 15:11**; [e]Zec 4:1
14 [f]**Isa 26:11; Joel 2:18**
15 [g]Jer 48:11; [h]**2Ch 28:9**; [i]Ps 69:26; 123:3–4; **Am 1:11**
16 [j]Zec 8:3; [k]**Job 38:5**; Zec 2:1–2; [l]**Ezr 1:1**
17 [m]**Isa 40:1**; [n]**Isa 14:1**; [o]**Ezr 9:9; Ps 51:18**; Isa 54:8–10; **61:4**
19 [p]Am 6:13
21 [q]**1Ki 22:11**; Ps 75:4; [r]**Ps 75:10; Isa 54:16–17**; Zec 12:9

He answered me, "To measure Jeru-
salem, to find out how wide and how
long it is."[a]
3Then the angel who was speaking to
me left, and another angel came to meet
him 4and said to him: "Run, tell that
young man, 'Jerusalem will be a city
without walls[b] because of the great
number[c] of men and livestock in it.[d]
5And I myself will be a wall[e] of fire[f]
around it,' declares the LORD, 'and I will
be its glory[g] within.'[h][i]
6"Come! Come! Flee from the land of
the north," declares the LORD, "for I
have scattered[j] you to the four winds of
heaven,"[k] declares the LORD.[l]
7"Come, O Zion! Escape,[m] you who
live in the Daughter of Babylon!"[n] 8For
this is what the LORD Almighty says:
"After he has honoured me and has
sent me against the nations that have
plundered you—for whoever touches
you touches the apple of his eye[o]—9I
will surely raise my hand against them
so that their slaves will plunder them.[a][p]
Then you will know that the LORD
Almighty has sent me.[q]
10"Shout[r] and be glad, O Daughter of
Zion.[s] For I am coming,[t] and I will live
among you,"[u] declares the LORD.[v]
11"Many nations will be joined with the
LORD in that day and will become my
people.[w] I will live among you and you
will know that the LORD Almighty has
sent me to you.[x] 12The LORD will inherit[y]
Judah[z] as his portion in the holy land
and will again choose[a] Jerusalem. 13Be
still[b] before the LORD, all mankind, be-
cause he has roused himself from his
holy dwelling."[c]

Clean Garments for the High Priest

3 Then he showed me Joshua[a][a] the
high priest standing before the
angel of the LORD, and Satan[b][b] standing
at his right side to accuse him. 2The
LORD said to Satan, "The LORD rebuke
you,[c] Satan! The LORD, who has chosen[d]
Jerusalem, rebuke you! Is not this man a
burning stick[e] snatched from the fire?"[f]
3Now Joshua was dressed in filthy
clothes as he stood before the angel.
4The angel said to those who were
standing before him, "Take off his filthy
clothes."
Then he said to Joshua, "See, I have
taken away your sin,[g] and I will put rich
garments[h] on you."
5Then I said, "Put a clean turban[i] on
his head." So they put a clean turban on
his head and clothed him, while the
angel of the LORD stood by.
6The angel of the LORD gave this
charge to Joshua: 7"This is what the
LORD Almighty says: 'If you will walk in
my ways and keep my requirements,[j]
then you will govern my house[k] and
have charge[l] of my courts, and I will
give you a place among these standing
here.[m]
8" 'Listen, O high priest[n] Joshua and
your associates seated before you, who
are men symbolic[o] of things to come: I
am going to bring my servant, the
Branch.[p] 9See, the stone I have set in
front of Joshua![q] There are seven eyes[c][r]
on that one stone,[s] and I will engrave
an inscription on it,' says the LORD Al-
mighty, 'and I will remove the sin[t] of
this land in a single day.
10" 'In that day each of you will invite
his neighbour to sit[u] under his vine and
fig-tree,[v]' declares the LORD Almighty."

The Gold Lampstand and the Two Olive Trees

4 Then the angel who talked with me
returned and wakened[a] me, as a
man is wakened from his sleep.[b] 2He
asked me, "What do you see?"[c]
I answered, "I see a solid gold lamp-
stand[d] with a bowl at the top and seven
lights[e] on it, with seven channels to the
lights. 3Also there are two olive trees[f] by
it, one on the right of the bowl and the
other on its left."
4I asked the angel who talked with
me, "What are these, my lord?"
5He answered, "Do you not know
what these are?"
"No, my lord," I replied.[g]
6So he said to me, "This is the word of
the LORD to Zerubbabel:[h] 'Not[i] by might
nor by power,[j] but by my Spirit,'[k] says
the LORD Almighty.
7"What[a] are you, O mighty moun-
tain? Before Zerubbabel you will be-
come level ground.[l] Then he will bring
out the capstone[m] to shouts[n] of 'God
bless it! God bless it!' "
8Then the word of the LORD came to
me: 9"The hands of Zerubbabel have

Ch. 2

2 [a]**Eze 40:3; Zec 1:16**; Rev 21:15
4 [b]**Eze 38:11;** [c]**Isa 49:20; Jer 30:19; 33:22;** [d]Zec 14:11
5 [e]**Isa 26:1;** Eze 42:20; [f]**Isa 10:17;** [g]**Ps 85:9; Isa 11:10; 24:23;** Rev 21:23; [h]**Ps 125:2;** [i]**Ps 46:5; Eze 38:14**
6 [j]**Ps 44:11;** [k]**Eze 17:21; 37:9;** [l]Mt 24:31; Mk 13:27
7 [m]**Isa 42:7;** [n]**Isa 48:20;** Jer 3:18
8 [o]Dt 32:10
9 [p]**Isa 14:2; Jer 12:14; Hab 2:8;** [q]**Isa 48:16;** Zec 4:9; 6:15
10 [r]**Zep 3:14;** [s]**Isa 23:12; Zep 3:14;** [t]Zec 9:9; [u]**Ex 25:8;** Lev 26:12; **Nu 23:21;** Zec 8:3; [v]**Rev 21:3**
11 [w]**Jer 24:7; Mic 4:2;** Zec 8:8, 20–22; [x]Zec 4:9; 6:15
12 [y]Ex 34:9; Ps 33:12; Jer 10:16; [z]Jer 40:5; [a]**Dt 12:5; Isa 14:1**
13 [b]Ex 14:14; **Isa 41:1;** [c]**Dt 26:15**

Ch. 3

1 [a]**Ezr 2:2;** Zec 6:11; [b]**2Sa 24:1; 2Ch 18:21; Ps 109:6; Mt 4:10**
2 [c]Jude 9; [d]**Isa 14:1;** [e]**Isa 7:4;** [f]Jude 23
4 [g]**2Sa 12:13; Eze 36:25; Mic 7:18;** [h]**Ge 41:42; Ps 132:9; Isa 52:1;** Rev 19:8
5 [i]**Ex 29:6**
7 [j]**Lev 8:35;** [k]Dt 17:8–11; **Eze 44:15–16;** [l]2Ch 23:6; [m]Jer 15:19; Zec 6:15
8 [n]Hag 1:1; [o]**Dt 28:46; Eze 12:11;** [p]**Isa 4:2; 49:3; Eze 17:22**
9 [q]**Ezr 2:2;** [r]**2Ch 16:9;** [s]Isa 28:16; [t]**2Sa 12:13; Jer 50:20**
10 [u]**Job 11:18;** [v]**Nu 16:14; 1Ki 4:25;** Mic 4:4

Ch. 4

1 [a]**Da 8:18;** [b]Jer 31:26
2 [c]**Jer 1:13;** [d]**Ex 25:31;** Rev 1:12; [e]**Rev 4:5**
3 [f]ver 11; **Ps 1:3; Rev 11:4**
5 [g]**Zec 1:9**
6 [h]**1Ch 3:19; Ezr 5:2;** [i]**1Sa 13:22; 1Ki 19:12;** [j]**1Sa 2:9;** [k]**Ne 9:20;** Isa 11:2–4; **Da 2:34;** Hos 1:7
7 [l]**Ps 26:12;** Jer 51:25; [m]**Ps 118:22;** [n]**1Ch 15:28**

[a]*8, 9* Or *says after . . . eye: 9"I . . . plunder them."*
[a]*1* A variant of *Jeshua*; here and elsewhere in Zechariah
[b]*1* *Satan* means *accuser*.
[c]*9* Or *facets*
[a]*7* Or *Who*

laid the foundation[o] of this temple; his
hands will also complete it.[p] Then you
will know that the LORD Almighty has
sent me[q] to you.
10"Who despises the day[r] of small
things?[s] Men will rejoice when they see
the plumb-line in the hand of Zerub-
babel.[t]
"(These seven are the eyes[u] of the
LORD, which range throughout the
earth.)"
11Then I asked the angel, "What are
these two olive trees[v] on the right and
the left of the lampstand?"
12Again I asked him, "What are these
two olive branches beside the two gold
pipes that pour out golden oil?"
13He replied, "Do you not know what
these are?"
"No, my lord," I said.
14So he said, "These are the two who
are anointed[w] to[b] serve the Lord of all
the earth."

The Flying Scroll

5 I looked again—and there before
me was a flying scroll![a]
2He asked me, "What do you see?"[b]
I answered, "I see a flying scroll,
thirty feet long and fifteen feet wide."[a]
3And he said to me, "This is the curse[c]
that is going out over the whole land; for
according to what it says on one side,
every thief[d] will be banished, and
according to what it says on the other,
everyone who swears falsely[e] will be
banished. 4The LORD Almighty de-
clares, 'I will send it out, and it will enter
the house of the thief and the house of
him who swears falsely[f] by my name. It
will remain in his house and destroy it,
both its timbers and its stones.[g]'"

The Woman in a Basket

5Then the angel who was speaking
to me came forward and said to me,
"Look up and see what this is that is
appearing."
6I asked, "What is it?"
He replied, "It is a measuring
basket.[b][h]" And he added, "This is the
iniquity[c] of the people throughout
the land."
7Then the cover of lead was raised,
and there in the basket sat a woman!
8He said, "This is wickedness," and he
pushed her back into the basket and
pushed the lead cover down over its
mouth.[i]
9Then I looked up—and there before
me were two women, with the wind in
their wings! They had wings like those
of a stork,[j] and they lifted up the basket
between heaven and earth.
10"Where are they taking the basket?"
I asked the angel who was speaking to
me.
11He replied, "To the country of Bab-
ylonia[d][k] to build a house[l] for it. When it
is ready, the basket will be set there in
its place."[m]

Four Chariots

6 I looked up again—and there be-
fore me were four chariots[a] coming
out from between two mountains—
mountains of bronze! 2The first chariot
had red horses, the second black,[b] 3the
third white,[c] and the fourth dappled
—all of them powerful. 4I asked the
angel who was speaking to me, "What
are these, my lord?"
5The angel answered me, "These are
the four spirits[a][d] of heaven, going out
from standing in the presence of the
Lord of the whole world.[e] 6The one with
the black horses is going towards the
north country, the one with the white
horses towards the west,[b] and the one
with the dappled horses towards the
south."
7When the powerful horses went out,
they were straining to go throughout
the earth.[f] And he said, "Go throughout
the earth!" So they went throughout the
earth.
8Then he called to me, "Look, those
going towards the north country have
given my Spirit[c] rest[g] in the land of the
north."[h]

A Crown for Joshua

9The word of the LORD came to me:
10"Take ⌊silver and gold⌋ from the exiles
Heldai, Tobijah and Jedaiah,' who have
arrived from Babylon.[i] Go the same day
to the house of Josiah son of Zephaniah.
11Take the silver and gold and make a
crown,[j] and set it on the head of the high
priest, Joshua[k] son of Jehozadak.[l] 12Tell
him this is what the LORD Almighty
says: 'Here is the man whose name is
the Branch,[m] and he will branch out
from his place and build the temple of
the LORD.[n] 13It is he who will build the

9 [o]**Ezr 3:11**; [p]Ezr 3:8; **6:15**; Zec 6:12; [q]**Zec 2:9**
10 [r]**Hag 2:23**; [s]Hag 2:3; [t]**Ezr 5:1**; **Ne 12:1**; **Job 38:5**; [u]**2Ch 16:9**; Rev 5:6
11 [v]**ver 3**; **Rev 11:4**
14 [w]Ex 29:7; 40:15; **Ps 45:7**; **Isa 20:3**; **Da 9:24–26**

Ch. 5

1 [a]**Ps 40:7**; **Jer 36:4**; Rev 5:1
2 [b]**Jer 1:13**
3 [c]Isa 24:6; 34:2; 43:28; Mal 3:9; 4:6; [d]Ex 20:15; Mal 3:8; [e]Ex 20:7; Isa 48:1
4 [f]Zec 8:17; [g]Lev 14:34–45; **Pr 3:33**; **Hab 2:9–11**; Mal 3:5
6 [h]Mic 6:10
8 [i]Mic 6:11
9 [j]Lev 11:19
11 [k]**Ge 10:10**; [l]Jer 29:5,28; [m]**Da 1:2**

Ch. 6

1 [a]ver 5; **2Ki 2:11**
2 [b]Rev 6:5
3 [c]Rev 6:2
5 [d]**Eze 37:9**; Mt 24:31; Rev 7:1; [e]**Jos 3:11**
7 [f]Isa 43:6; Zec 1:8
8 [g]**Eze 5:13**; **24:13**; [h]**Zec 1:10**
10 [i]Ezr 7:14–16; Jer 28:6
11 [j]Ps 21:3; [k]**Ezr 2:2**; **Zec 3:1**; [l]**1Ch 6:15**; **Ezr 3:2**
12 [m]**Isa 4:2**; **Eze 17:22**; [n]Ezr 3:8–10; Zec 4:6–9

[b]14 Or *two who bring oil and*
[a]2 Hebrew *twenty cubits long and ten cubits wide* (about 9 metres long and 4.5 metres wide)
[b]6 Hebrew *an ephah*; also in verses 7–11
[c]6 Or *appearance*
[d]11 Hebrew *Shinar*
[a]5 Or *winds*
[b]6 Or *horses after them*
[c]8 Or *spirit*

temple of the LORD, and he will be
clothed with majesty and will sit and
rule on his throne. And he will be a
priest[o] on his throne. And there will be
harmony between the two.' 14The
crown will be given to Heldai,[d] Tobijah,
Jedaiah and Hen[e] son of Zephaniah as a
memorial[p] in the temple of the LORD.
15Those who are far away will come and
help to build the temple of the LORD,[q]
and you will know that the LORD
Almighty has sent me to you.[r] This will
happen if you diligently obey[s] the LORD
your God."

Justice and Mercy, Not Fasting

7 In the fourth year of King Darius,
the word of the LORD came to
Zechariah[a] on the fourth day of the
ninth month, the month of Kislev.[b] 2The
people of Bethel had sent Sharezer and
Regem-Melech, together with their
men, to entreat[c] the LORD[d] 3by asking
the priests of the house of the LORD
Almighty and the prophets, "Should I
mourn[e] and fast in the fifth[f] month, as I
have done for so many years?"
4Then the word of the LORD Almighty
came to me: 5"Ask all the people of the
land and the priests, 'When you fasted[g]
and mourned in the fifth and seventh[h]
months for the past seventy years,[i] was
it really for me that you fasted? 6And
when you were eating and drinking,
were you not just feasting for your-
selves?[j] 7Are these not the words the
LORD proclaimed through the earlier
prophets[k] when Jerusalem and its sur-
rounding towns were at rest[l] and
prosperous, and the Negev and the
western foothills[m] were settled?' "[n]
8And the word of the LORD came
again to Zechariah: 9"This is what the
LORD Almighty says: 'Administer true
justice;[o] show mercy and compassion to
one another.[p] 10Do not oppress the
widow[q] or the fatherless, the alien[r] or
the poor.[s] In your hearts do not think
evil of each other.'[t]
11"But they refused to pay attention;
stubbornly[u] they turned their backs[v]
and stopped up their ears.[w] 12They
made their hearts as hard as flint[x] and
would not listen to the law or to the
words that the LORD Almighty had sent
by his Spirit through the earlier
prophets.[y] So the LORD Almighty was
very angry.[z]
13" 'When I called, they did not listen;[a]
so when they called, I would not lis-
ten,'[b] says the LORD Almighty.[c] 14'I scat-
tered[d] them with a whirlwind[e] among
all the nations, where they were stran-
gers. The land was left so desolate be-
hind them that no-one could come or
go.[f] This is how they made the pleasant
land desolate.[g]' "

The LORD Promises to Bless Jerusalem

8 Again the word of the LORD
Almighty came to me. 2This is
what the LORD Almighty says: "I am
very jealous[a] for Zion; I am burning with
jealousy for her."
3This is what the LORD says: "I will
return[b] to Zion[c] and dwell in Jerusalem.[d]
Then Jerusalem will be called the City of
Truth,[e] and the mountain[f] of the LORD
Almighty will be called the Holy Moun-
tain.[g]"
4This is what the LORD Almighty says:
"Once again men and women of ripe
old age will sit in the streets of Jeru-
salem,[h] each with cane in hand because
of his age. 5The city streets will be filled
with boys and girls playing there.[i]"
6This is what the LORD Almighty says:
"It may seem marvellous to the remnant
of this people at that time,[j] but will it
seem marvellous to me?[k]" declares the
LORD Almighty.
7This is what the LORD Almighty says:
"I will save my people from the coun-
tries of the east and the west.[l] 8I will
bring them back[m] to live[n] in Jerusalem;
they will be my people,[o] and I will be
faithful and righteous to them as their
God.[p]"
9This is what the LORD Almighty says:
"You who now hear these words
spoken by the prophets[q] who were
there when the foundation[r] was laid for
the house of the LORD Almighty, let
your hands be strong[s] so that the temple
may be built. 10Before that time there
were no wages[t] for man or beast. No-
one could go about his business safely[u]
because of his enemy, for I had turned
every man against his neighbour. 11But
now I will not deal with the remnant of
this people as I did in the past,"[v] de-
clares the LORD Almighty.
12"The seed will grow well, the vine
will yield its fruit,[w] the ground will pro-
duce its crops,[x] and the heavens will
drop their dew.[y] I will give all these

13 [o]Ps 110:4
14 [p]Ex 28:12
15 [q]Isa 60:10; [r]Zec 2:9–11; [s]Isa 58:12; Jer 7:23; Zec 3:7

Ch. 7

1 [a]Ezr 5:1; [b]Ne 1:1
2 [c]Jer 26:19; Zec 8:21; [d]Hag 2:10–14
3 [e]Zec 12:12–14; [f]2Ki 25:9; Jer 52:12–14
5 [g]Isa 58:5; [h]2Ki 25:25; [i]Da 9:2
6 [j]Isa 43:23
7 [k]Isa 1:11–20; Zec 1:4; [l]Jer 22:21; [m]Jer 17:26; [n]Jer 44:4–5
9 [o]Jer 22:3; 42:5; Zec 8:16; [p]Dt 22:1
10 [q]Jer 49:11; [r]Ex 22:21; [s]Lev 25:17; Isa 1:23; [t]Ex 22:22; Job 35:8; Isa 1:17; Eze 45:9; Mic 6:8
11 [u]Isa 9:9; [v]Jer 32:33; [w]Jer 5:3; 8:5; 11:10; 17:23; Eze 5:6
12 [x]Jer 5:3; 17:1; Eze 11:19; [y]Ne 9:29; [z]Jer 42:21; Da 9:12
13 [a]Jer 7:27; [b]Isa 1:15; Jer 11:11; 14:12; Mic 3:4; [c]Pr 1:28; La 3:44; Eze 20:31
14 [d]Lev 26:33; Dt 4:27; 28:64–67; Ps 44:11; [e]Jer 23:19; [f]Isa 33:8; [g]Jer 7:34; 44:6; Eze 12:19

Ch. 8

2 [a]Joel 2:18
3 [b]Zec 1:16; [c]Isa 52:8; Joel 3:21; [d]Zec 2:10; [e]Ps 15:2; Isa 1:26; 48:1; Jer 33:16; [f]Jer 26:18; [g]Isa 1:26; Mic 4:1
4 [h]Isa 65:20
5 [i]Jer 30:20; 31:13
6 [j]Ps 118:23; 126:1–3; [k]Jer 32:17,27
7 [l]Ps 107:3; Isa 11:11; 43:5
8 [m]Eze 37:12; Zec 10:10; [n]Jer 31:24; [o]Isa 51:16; Eze 11:19–20; 36:28; Zec 2:11; Heb 8:10; [p]Jer 11:4; Zec 10:6
9 [q]Ezr 5:1; [r]Ezr 3:11; [s]Hag 2:4
10 [t]Isa 5:10; Hag 1:6; [u]2Ch 15:5 11 [v]Isa 12:1
12 [w]Ps 85:12; Joel 2:22; [x]Ps 67:6; [y]Ge 27:28

[d]14 Syriac; Hebrew *Helem*
[e]14 Or *and the gracious one, the*

things as an inheritance[z] to the remnant
of this people.[a] 13As you have been an
object of cursing[b] among the nations, O
Judah and Israel, so will I save[c] you, and
you will be a blessing.[d] Do not be
afraid,[e] but let your hands be strong.[f]"
14This is what the LORD Almighty
says: "Just as I had determined to bring
disaster[g] upon you and showed no pity
when your fathers angered me," says
the LORD Almighty, 15"so now I have
determined to do good[h] again to Jeru-
salem and Judah.[i] Do not be afraid.
16These are the things you are to do:
Speak the truth[j] to each other, and ren-
der true and sound judgment[k] in your
courts;[l] 17do not plot evil[m] against your
neighbour, and do not love to swear
falsely.[n] I hate all this," declares the
LORD.
18Again the word of the LORD Almigh-
ty came to me. 19This is what the LORD
Almighty says: "The fasts of the fourth,[o]
fifth,[p] seventh[q] and tenth[r] months will
become joyful[s] and glad occasions and
happy festivals for Judah. Therefore
love truth[t] and peace."
20This is what the LORD Almighty
says: "Many peoples and the inhabit-
ants of many cities will yet come, 21and
the inhabitants of one city will go to
another and say, 'Let us go at once to
entreat[u] the LORD and seek[v] the LORD
Almighty. I myself am going.' 22And
many peoples and powerful nations
will come to Jerusalem to seek the LORD
Almighty and to entreat him."[w]
23This is what the LORD Almighty
says: "In those days ten men from all
languages and nations will take firm
hold of one Jew by the hem of his robe
and say, 'Let us go with you, because
we have heard that God is with you.'"[x]

Judgment on Israel's Enemies

An Oracle[y]

9 The word of the LORD is against
the land of Hadrach
and will rest upon Damascus[a]—
for the eyes of men and all the tribes of
Israel
are on the LORD—[a]
2and upon Hamath[b] too, which borders
on it,
and upon Tyre[c] and Sidon,[d] though
they are very skilful.
3Tyre has built herself a stronghold;
she has heaped up silver like dust,
and gold like the dirt of the streets.[e]
4But the Lord will take away her
possessions
and destroy[f] her power on the sea,
and she will be consumed by fire.[g]
5Ashkelon[h] will see it and fear;
Gaza will writhe in agony,
and Ekron too, for her hope will
wither.
Gaza will lose her king
and Ashkelon will be deserted.
6Foreigners will occupy Ashdod,
and I will cut off[i] the pride of the
Philistines.
7I will take the blood from their
mouths,
the forbidden food from between
their teeth.
Those who are left will belong to our
God[j]
and become leaders in Judah,
and Ekron will be like the Jebusites.[k]
8But I will defend[l] my house
against marauding forces.[m]
Never again will an oppressor overrun
my people,
for now I am keeping watch.[n]

The Coming of Zion's King

9Rejoice greatly, O Daughter of Zion![o]
Shout,[p] Daughter of Jerusalem!
See, your king[b] comes to you,[q]
righteous and having salvation,[r]
gentle and riding on a donkey,[s]
on a colt, the foal of a donkey.[t]
10I will take away the chariots from
Ephraim
and the war-horses from Jerusalem,
and the battle-bow will be broken.[u]
He will proclaim peace[v] to the nations.
His rule will extend from sea to sea
and from the River[c] to the ends of
the earth.[d] [w]
11As for you, because of the blood of my
covenant[x] with you,
I will free your prisoners[y] from the
waterless pit.[z]
12Return to your fortress,[a] O prisoners
of hope;
even now I announce that I will
restore twice[b] as much to you.

12 [z]**Ps 65:13; Isa 60:21**; Ob 17; [a]**Hos 2:21**
13 [b]**Nu 5:27; Dt 13:15; Ps 102:8;** Jer 42:18; [c]**Ps 48:8;** [d]**Ge 12:2; Joel 2:14;** [e]**Hag 2:5;** [f]ver 9
14 [g]**Eze 24:14**
15 [h]ver 13; **Jer 29:11;** Mic 7:18–20; [i]Jer 31:28; 32:42
16 [j]**Ps 15:2; Jer 33:16; Eph 4:25;** [k]**Eze 18:8;** [l]**Eze 45:9; Am 5:15; Zec 7:9**
17 [m]Pr 3:29; [n]**Pr 6:16–19; Jer 7:9;** Zec 5:4
19 [o]**2Ki 25:7;** Jer 39:2; [p]**Jer 52:12;** [q]2Ki 25:25; [r]Jer 52:4; [s]Ps 30:11; [t]ver 16
21 [u]**Zec 7:2;** [v]Jer 26:19
22 [w]**Ps 86:9;** 117:1; Isa 2:2–3; **44:5; 45:14;** 49:6; **Zec 2:11**
23 [x]**Ps 102:22; Isa 14:1; 45:14; 56:3;** 1Co 14:25; [y]**Isa 13:1;** Jer 23:33

Ch. 9

1 [a]Isa 17:1; **Am 1:5**
2 [b]**Jer 49:23;** [c]Eze 28:1–19; [d]**Ge 10:15**
3 [e]Job 27:16; **Eze 28:4**
4 [f]**Isa 23:11;** [g]**Isa 23:1;** Jer 25:22; Eze 26:3–5; 27:32–36; 28:18
5 [h]Jer 47:5
6 [i]**Isa 14:30**
7 [j]**Job 25:2;** [k]**Jer 47:1; Joel 3:4; Zep 2:4**
8 [l]**Isa 26:1;** [m]Zec 14:21; [n]**Isa 52:1; 54:14; Joel 3:17**
9 [o]**Isa 62:11;** [p]**1Ki 1:39;** [q]**Ps 24:7; 149:2;** Mic 4:8; [r]Isa 9:6–7; 43:3–11; Jer 23:5–6; Zep 3:14–15; Zec 2:10; [s]**Ge 49:11; 1Ki 1:33;** [t]Mt 21:5*; Jn 12:15*
10 [u]Hos 1:7; 2:18; Mic 4:3; 5:10; Zec 10:4; [v]**Isa 2:4;** [w]Ps 72:8
11 [x]**Ex 24:8; Mt 26:28; Lk 22:20;** [y]**Isa 10:4; 42:7;** [z]Jer 38:6
12 [a]**Joel 3:16;** [b]**Dt 21:17; Isa 40:2**

[a]1 Or *Damascus. / For the eye of the LORD is on all mankind, / as well as on the tribes of Israel.*
[b]9 Or *King*
[c]10 That is, the Euphrates
[d]10 Or *the end of the land*

13I will bend Judah as I bend my bow[c]
and fill it with Ephraim.[d]
I will rouse your sons, O Zion,
against your sons, O Greece,[e]
and make you like a warrior's
sword.[f]

The LORD Will Appear

14Then the LORD will appear over them;[g]
his arrow will flash like lightning.[h]
The Sovereign LORD will sound the
trumpet;[i]
he will march in the storms[j] of the
south,
15 and the LORD Almighty will shield[k]
them.
They will destroy
and overcome with slingstones.[l]
They will drink and roar as with
wine;[m]
they will be full like a bowl[n]
used for sprinkling[e] the corners[o] of
the altar.
16The LORD their God will save them on
that day[p]
as the flock of his people.
They will sparkle in his land
like jewels in a crown.[q]
17How attractive and beautiful they will
be!
Grain will make the young men
thrive,
and new wine the young women.

The LORD Will Care for Judah

10 Ask the LORD for rain in the
springtime;
it is the LORD who makes the storm
clouds.
He gives showers of rain[a] to men,
and plants of the field[b] to everyone.
2The idols[c] speak deceit,
diviners[d] see visions that lie;
they tell dreams[e] that are false,
they give comfort in vain.[f]
Therefore the people wander like
sheep
oppressed for lack of a shepherd.[g]

3"My anger burns against the
shepherds,
and I will punish the leaders;[h]
for the LORD Almighty will care
for his flock, the house of Judah,
and make them like a proud horse in
battle.[i]
4From Judah will come the
cornerstone,[j]
from him the tent peg,[k]
from him the battle-bow,[l]
from him every ruler.
5Together they[a] will be like mighty men
trampling the muddy streets in
battle.[m]
Because the LORD is with them,
they will fight and overthrow the
horsemen.[n]

6"I will strengthen[o] the house of Judah
and save the house of Joseph.
I will restore them
because I have compassion[p] on
them.[q]
They will be as though
I had not rejected them,
for I am the LORD their God
and I will answer[r] them.
7The Ephraimites will become like
mighty men,
and their hearts will be glad as with
wine.[s]
Their children will see it and be joyful;
their hearts will rejoice[t] in the LORD.
8I will signal[u] for them
and gather them in.
Surely I will redeem them;
they will be as numerous[v] as before.
9Though I scatter them among the
peoples,
yet in distant lands they will
remember me.[w]
They and their children will survive,
and they will return.
10I will bring them back from Egypt
and gather them from Assyria.[x]
I will bring them to Gilead[y] and
Lebanon,
and there will not be room[z] enough
for them.
11They will pass through the sea of
trouble;
the surging sea will be subdued
and all the depths of the Nile will
dry up.[a]
Assyria's pride[b] will be brought down
and Egypt's sceptre[c] will pass
away.[d]
12I will strengthen[e] them in the LORD
and in his name they will walk,[f]"
declares the LORD.

11 Open your doors, O
Lebanon,[a]
so that fire[b] may devour your
cedars!
2Wail, O pine tree, for the cedar has
fallen;
the stately trees are ruined!
Wail, oaks[c] of Bashan;
the dense forest[d] has been cut
down![e]

13 [c]2Sa 22:35; [d]Isa 49:2; [e]Joel 3:6; [f]Jer 51:20
14 [g]Isa 31:5; [h]Ps 18:14; Hab 3:11; [i]Lev 25:9; Mt 24:31; [j]Isa 21:1; 66:15
15 [k]Isa 31:5; 37:35; Zec 12:8; [l]Zec 14:3; [m]Zec 10:7; [n]Zec 14:20; [o]Ex 27:2
16 [p]Isa 10:20; [q]Jer 31:11

Ch. 10

1 [a]Lev 26:4; 1Ki 8:36; Ps 104:13; 135:7; [b]Job 14:9
2 [c]Eze 21:21; [d]Isa 44:25; [e]Jer 23:16; [f]Isa 40:19; [g]Nu 27:17; Jer 23:1; Hos 3:4; Mt 9:36
3 [h]Isa 14:9; Jer 25:34; [i]Eze 34:8–10
4 [j]Ps 118:22; Ac 4:11; [k]Isa 22:23; [l]Zec 9:10
5 [m]2Sa 22:43; Mic 7:10; [n]Am 2:15; Mic 5:8; Hag 2:22; Zec 12:4
6 [o]Eze 30:24; [p]Ps 102:13; Isa 14:1; [q]Eze 36:37; 37:19; Zec 8:7–8; [r]Ps 34:17; Isa 58:9; 65:24; Zec 13:9
7 [s]Zec 9:15; [t]1Sa 2:1; Isa 60:5; Joel 2:23
8 [u]Isa 5:26; [v]Jer 33:22; Eze 36:11
9 [w]Isa 44:21; Eze 6:9
10 [x]Isa 11:11; Zec 8:8; [y]Jer 50:19; [z]Isa 49:19
11 [a]Isa 19:5–7; 51:10; [b]Zep 2:13; [c]Eze 30:13; [d]Eze 29:15
12 [e]Eze 30:24; [f]Mic 4:5

Ch. 11

1 [a]Eze 31:3; [b]2Ch 36:19; Zec 12:6
2 [c]Isa 2:13; [d]Isa 32:19; [e]Isa 10:34

[e]15 Or *bowl, / like*
[a]4,5 Or *ruler, all of them together. / 5They*

3Listen to the wail of the shepherds:
their rich pastures are destroyed!
Listen to the roar of the lions;[f]
the lush thicket of the Jordan is
ruined![g]

Two Shepherds

4This is what the LORD my God says:
"Pasture the flock marked for slaugh-
ter.[h] 5Their buyers slaughter them and
go unpunished. Those who sell them
say, 'Praise the LORD, I am rich!' Their
own shepherds do not spare them.[i] 6For
I will no longer have pity on the people
of the land," declares the LORD. "I will
hand everyone over to his neighbour[j]
and his king. They will oppress the
land, and I will not rescue them from
their hands."[k]
7So I pastured the flock marked for
slaughter,[l] particularly the oppressed of
the flock. Then I took two staffs and
called one Favour and the other Union,
and I pastured the flock. 8In one month I
got rid of the three shepherds.
The flock detested[m] me, and I grew
weary of them 9and said, "I will not be
your shepherd. Let the dying die, and
the perishing perish.[n] Let those who are
left eat[o] one another's flesh."
10Then I took my staff called Favour[p]
and broke it, revoking[q] the covenant I
had made with all the nations. 11It was
revoked on that day, and so the afflicted
of the flock who were watching me
knew it was the word of the LORD.
12I told them, "If you think it best,
give me my pay; but if not, keep it." So
they paid me thirty pieces of silver.[r]
13And the LORD said to me, "Throw it
to the potter"—the handsome price at
which they priced me! So I took the
thirty pieces of silver[s] and threw them
into the house of the LORD to the potter.[t]
14Then I broke my second staff called
Union, breaking the brotherhood be-
tween Judah and Israel.
15Then the LORD said to me, "Take
again the equipment of a foolish shep-
herd. 16For I am going to raise up a
shepherd over the land who will not
care for the lost, or seek the young, or
heal the injured, or feed the healthy, but
will eat the meat of the choice sheep,
tearing off their hoofs.

17"Woe to the worthless shepherd,[u]
who deserts the flock!
May the sword strike his arm[v] and his
right eye!
May his arm be completely
withered,
his right eye totally blinded!"[w]

3 [f]Isa 5:29; [g]Jer 2:15; 50:44; Eze 19:9
4 [h]Jer 25:34
5 [i]Jer 50:7; Eze 34:2–3
6 [j]Zec 14:13; [k]Isa 9:19–21; Jer 13:14; La 2:21; 5:8; Mic 5:8; 7:2–6
7 [l]Jer 25:34
8 [m]Eze 14:5
9 [n]Jer 43:11; [o]Isa 9:20
10 [p]ver 7; [q]Ps 89:39; Jer 14:21
12 [r]Ge 23:16; Mt 26:15
13 [s]Ex 21:32; [t]Mt 27:9–10*; Ac 1:18–19
17 [u]Jer 23:1; [v]Eze 30:21–22; [w]Jer 23:1; [x]Isa 13:1

Ch. 12

1 [a]Ge 1:8; Ps 104:2; Jer 51:15; [b]Ps 102:25; Heb 1:10; [c]Isa 57:16
2 [d]Ps 75:8; [e]Ps 60:3; Isa 51:23; [f]Zec 14:14
3 [g]Isa 66:18; Zec 14:2; [h]Isa 28:16; Da 2:34–35; [i]Isa 29:8
4 [j]Ps 76:6; Zec 10:5
5 [k]Eze 30:24
6 [l]Isa 10:17–18; Zec 11:1; [m]Ob 18; [n]Zec 14:10
7 [o]Jer 30:18; Am 9:11
8 [p]Ps 91:4; Joel 3:16; Zec 9:15; [q]Joel 3:10; [r]Ps 82:6; [s]Mic 7:8
9 [t]Isa 29:7; [u]Zec 1:21; 14:2–3
10 [v]Eze 37:9; [w]Isa 44:3; Eze 39:29; Joel 2:28–29; [x]Ps 22:16; Jn 19:34,37*; [y]Jdg 11:34; [z]Ge 21:16; Jer 31:19
11 [a]Jer 50:4; [b]2Ki 23:29
12 [c]Mt 24:30; Rev 1:7

Jerusalem's Enemies to Be Destroyed

An Oracle[x]

12 This is the word of the LORD
concerning Israel. The LORD,
who stretches out the heavens,[a] who
lays the foundation of the earth,[b] and
who forms the spirit of man[c] within
him, declares: 2"I am going to make
Jerusalem a cup[d] that sends all the sur-
rounding peoples reeling.[e] Judah[f] will
be besieged as well as Jerusalem. 3On
that day, when all the nations[g] of the
earth are gathered against her, I will
make Jerusalem an immovable rock[h] for
all the nations. All who try to move it
will injure[i] themselves. 4On that day I
will strike every horse with panic and its
rider with madness," declares the LORD.
"I will keep a watchful eye over the
house of Judah, but I will blind all the
horses of the nations.[j] 5Then the leaders
of Judah will say in their hearts, 'The
people of Jerusalem are strong,[k] because
the LORD Almighty is their God.'
6"On that day I will make the leaders
of Judah like a brazier[l] in a woodpile,
like a flaming torch among sheaves.
They will consume[m] right and left all the
surrounding peoples, but Jerusalem
will remain intact[n] in her place.
7"The LORD will save the dwellings of
Judah first, so that the honour of the
house of David and of Jerusalem's in-
habitants may not be greater than that
of Judah.[o] 8On that day the LORD will
shield[p] those who live in Jerusalem, so
that the feeblest[q] among them will be
like David, and the house of David will
be like God,[r] like the Angel of the LORD
going before[s] them. 9On that day I will
set out to destroy all the nations[t] that
attack Jerusalem.[u]

Mourning for the One They Pierced

10"And I will pour out on the house of
David and the inhabitants of Jerusalem
a spirit[a][v] of grace and supplication.[w]
They will look on[b] me, the one they
have pierced,[x] and they will mourn for
him as one mourns for an only child,[y]
and grieve bitterly for him as one
grieves for a firstborn son.[z] 11On that
day the weeping[a] in Jerusalem will be
great, like the weeping of Hadad Rim-
mon in the plain of Megiddo.[b] 12The
land will mourn,[c] each clan by itself,
with their wives by themselves: the clan
of the house of David and their wives,

[a]10 Or *the Spirit* [b]10 Or *to*

the clan of the house of Nathan and their wives, 13the clan of the house of Levi and their wives, the clan of Shimei and their wives, 14and all the rest of the clans and their wives.[d]

Cleansing From Sin

13 "On that day a fountain[a] will be opened to the house of David and the inhabitants of Jerusalem, to cleanse[b] them from sin and impurity.

2"On that day, I will banish the names of the idols[c] from the land, and they will be remembered no more,"[d] declares the LORD Almighty. "I will remove both the prophets[e] and the spirit of impurity from the land. 3And if anyone still prophesies, his father and mother, to whom he was born, will say to him, 'You must die, because you have told lies[f] in the LORD's name.' When he prophesies, his own parents will stab him.[g]

4"On that day every prophet will be ashamed[h] of his prophetic vision. He will not put on a prophet's garment[i] of hair[j] in order to deceive.[k] 5He will say, 'I am not a prophet. I am a farmer; the land has been my livelihood since my youth.[a][l] 6If someone asks him, 'What are these wounds on your body?'[b] he will answer, 'The wounds I was given at the house of my friends.'

The Shepherd Struck, the Sheep Scattered

7"Awake, O sword,[m] against my
shepherd,[n]
against the man who is close to me!"
declares the LORD Almighty.
"Strike the shepherd,
and the sheep will be scattered,[o]
and I will turn my hand against the
little ones.
8In the whole land," declares the LORD,
"two-thirds will be struck down and
perish;
yet one-third will be left in it.[p]
9This third I will bring into the fire;[q]
I will refine them like silver[r]
and test them like gold.[s]
They will call[t] on my name[u]
and I will answer[v] them;
I will say, 'They are my people,'[w]
and they will say, 'The LORD is our
God.'[x]"

The LORD Comes and Reigns

14 A day of the LORD[a] is coming when your plunder[b] will be divided among you.

2I will gather all the nations[c] to Jerusalem to fight against it;[d] the city will be captured, the houses ransacked, and the women raped.[e] Half of the city will go into exile, but the rest of the people will not be taken from the city.[f]

3Then the LORD will go out and fight[g] against those nations, as he fights in the day of battle.[h] 4On that day his feet will stand on the Mount of Olives,[i] east of Jerusalem, and the Mount of Olives will be split[j] in two from east to west, forming a great valley, with half of the mountain moving north and half moving south. 5You will flee by my mountain valley, for it will extend to Azel. You will flee as you fled from the earthquake[a][k] in the days of Uzziah king of Judah. Then the LORD my God will come,[l] and all the holy ones with him.[m]

6On that day there will be no light,[n] no cold or frost. 7It will be a unique[o] day, without daytime or night-time[p]—a day known to the LORD. When evening comes, there will be light.[q]

8On that day living water[r] will flow[s] out from Jerusalem, half to the eastern[t] sea[b] and half to the western sea,[c] in summer and in winter.[u]

9The LORD will be king[v] over the whole earth.[w] On that day there will be one LORD, and his name the only name.[x]

10The whole land, from Geba[y] to Rimmon,[z] south of Jerusalem, will become like the Arabah. But Jerusalem will be raised up[a] and remain in its place,[b] from the Benjamin Gate[c] to the site of the First Gate, to the Corner Gate,[d] and from the Tower of Hananel[e] to the royal winepresses. 11It will be inhabited;[f] never again will it be destroyed. Jerusalem will be secure.[g]

12This is the plague with which the LORD will strike[h] all the nations that fought against Jerusalem: Their flesh will rot while they are still standing on their feet, their eyes will rot in their sockets, and their tongues will rot in their mouths.[i] 13On that day men will be stricken by the LORD with great panic.[j]

12:14 [d]Zec 7:3

Ch. 13

1 [a]Jer 17:13; [b]Lev 16:30; Ps 51:2; Heb 9:14
2 [c]Jer 43:12; Eze 6:6; 36:25; Hos 2:17; [d]Mic 5:13; [e]1Ki 22:22; Jer 23:14–15
3 [f]Jer 28:16; [g]Dt 13:6–11; 18:20; Ne 6:14; Jer 23:34; Eze 14:9
4 [h]Jer 6:15; [i]Mt 3:4; [j]1Ki 18:7; Isa 20:2; [k]Eze 12:24
5 [l]Am 7:14
7 [m]Isa 34:5; Jer 47:6; [n]Isa 40:11; 53:4; Eze 37:24; [o]2Sa 17:2; Mt 26:31*; Mk 14:27*
8 [p]Eze 5:2–4, 12; Zec 14:2
9 [q]Isa 4:4; 33:14; Mal 3:2; [r]Ps 12:6; Da 11:35; 1Pe 1:6–7; [s]Job 6:29; Jer 6:27; [t]Ps 50:15; [u]Ps 105:1; [v]Ps 86:7; Isa 30:19; Zec 10:6; [w]Lev 26:12; Jer 30:22; [x]Isa 44:5; Jer 29:12; Eze 20:38

Ch. 14

1 [a]Isa 13:6; Joel 1:15; Mal 4:1; [b]Isa 23:18
2 [c]Isa 2:3; Zec 12:3; [d]Eze 5:8; [e]Ge 34:29; La 5:11; [f]Isa 13:6; Zec 13:8
3 [g]Zec 9:14–15; [h]Isa 8:9; Zec 12:9
4 [i]Eze 11:23; [j]Nu 16:31
5 [k]Am 1:1; [l]Isa 29:6; 66:15–16; [m]Dt 33:2; Mt 16:27; 25:31; Jude 14
6 [n]Isa 13:10; Jer 4:23
7 [o]Jer 30:7; [p]Rev 21:23–25; 22:5; [q]Isa 13:10; 30:26
8 [r]Eze 47:1–12; Jn 7:38; Rev 22:1–2; [s]Isa 30:25; [t]Joel 2:20; [u]Ge 8:22
9 [v]Ps 22:28; Ob 21; [w]Dt 6:4; Ps 47:7; Isa 45:24; Rev 11:15; [x]Hab 2:14; Eph 4:5–6
10 [y]1Ki 15:22; [z]Jos 15:32; [a]Isa 2:2; Jer 30:18; Am 9:11; [b]Zec 12:6; [c]Jer 20:2; [d]2Ki 14:13; [e]Ne 3:1
11 [f]Zec 2:4; [g]Ps 48:8; Eze 34:25–28
12 [h]Isa 11:4; [i]ver 18; Lev 26:16; Dt 28:22; Job 18:13
13 [j]Ge 35:5

---

[a]5 Or *farmer; a man sold me in my youth*
[b]6 Or *wounds between your hands*
[a]5 Or [5]*My mountain valley will be blocked and will extend to Azel. It will be blocked as it was blocked because of the earthquake*
[b]8 That is, the Dead Sea
[c]8 That is, the Mediterranean

Each man will seize the hand of
another, and they will attack each
other.[k] 14Judah[l] too will fight at Jeru-
salem. The wealth of all the surround-
ing nations will be collected[m]—great
quantities of gold and silver and
clothing. 15A similar plague[n] will strike
the horses and mules, the camels and
donkeys, and all the animals in those
camps.

16Then the survivors[o] from all the na-
tions that have attacked Jerusalem will
go up year after year to worship[p] the
King,[q] the LORD Almighty, and to cele-
brate the Feast of Tabernacles.[r] 17If any
of the peoples of the earth do not go up
to Jerusalem to worship[s] the King, the
LORD Almighty, they will have no rain.[t]
18If the Egyptian people do not go up
and take part, they will have no rain.
The LORD[d] will bring on them the
plague[u] he inflicts on the nations that
do not go up to celebrate the Feast of
Tabernacles.[v] 19This will be the punish-
ment of Egypt and the punishment of
all the nations that do not go up to
celebrate the Feast of Tabernacles.[w]

20On that day HOLY TO THE LORD[x] will
be inscribed on the bells of the horses,
and the cooking pots[y] in the LORD's
house will be like the sacred bowls[z] in
front of the altar. 21Every pot in Jeru-
salem and Judah will be holy[a] to the
LORD Almighty, and all who come to
sacrifice will take some of the pots and
cook in them. And on that day[b] there
will no longer be a Canaanite[e][c] in the
house[d] of the LORD Almighty.[e]

13 [k]Jdg 7:22; Zec 11:6
14 [l]Zec 12:2; [m]Isa 23:18
15 [n]ver 12
16 [o]2Ki 19:31; [p]Ps 22:29; 86:9; Isa 19:21; [q]Ob 21; [r]Ex 23:16; Isa 60:6–9; Mic 4:2
17 [s]2Ch 32:23; [t]Jer 14:4; Am 4:7
18 [u]Ge 27:29; [v]ver 12
19 [w]Ezr 3:4
20 [x]Ex 39:30; [y]Eze 46:20; [z]Zec 9:15
21 [a]Jer 31:40; Ro 14:6–7; 1Co 10:31; [b]Ne 8:10; [c]Zec 9:8; [d]Ne 11:1; [e]Eze 44:9

d18 Or *part, then the LORD* e21 Or *merchant*

Malachi

1 An oracle:[a] The word[b] of the LORD
to Israel through Malachi.[a]

Jacob Loved, Esau Hated

2"I have loved[c] you," says the LORD.
"But you ask,[d] 'How have you loved
us?'
"Was not Esau Jacob's brother?" the
LORD says. "Yet I have loved Jacob,[e] 3but
Esau I have hated,[f] and I have turned his
mountains into a wasteland[g] and left his
inheritance to the desert jackals.[h]"
4Edom[i] may say, "Though we have
been crushed, we will rebuild[j] the
ruins."
But this is what the LORD Almighty
says: "They may build, but I will de-
molish.[k] They will be called the Wicked
Land, a people always under the wrath
of the LORD.[l] 5You will see it with your
own eyes and say, 'Great[m] is the LORD
—even beyond the borders of Israel!'[n]

Blemished Sacrifices

6"A son honours his father,[o] and a
servant his master.[p] If I am a father,
where is the honour due to me? If I am a
master, where is the respect[q] due to
me?" says the LORD Almighty.[r] "It is
you, O priests, who show contempt for
my name.
"But you ask,[s] 'How have we shown
contempt for your name?'
7"You place defiled food[t] on my altar.
"But you ask,[u] 'How have we defiled
you?'
"By saying that the LORD's table[v] is
contemptible. 8When you bring blind
animals for sacrifice, is that not wrong?
When you sacrifice crippled or diseased
animals,[w] is that not wrong? Try offer-
ing them to your governor! Would he be
pleased[x] with you? Would he accept
you?" says the LORD Almighty.[y]
9"Now implore God to be gracious to
us. With such offerings[z] from your
hands, will he accept[a] you?"—says the
LORD Almighty.
10"Oh, that one of you would shut the
temple doors,[b] so that you would not
light useless fires on my altar! I am not
pleased[c] with you," says the LORD
Almighty, "and I will accept[d] no offer-
ing[e] from your hands. 11My name will be
great[f] among the nations,[g] from the
rising to the setting of the sun.[h] In
every place incense[i] and pure offerings[j]
will be brought to my name, because my
name will be great among the nations,"
says the LORD Almighty.
12"But you profane it by saying of the
Lord's table,[k] 'It is defiled', and of its
food,[l] 'It is contemptible.' 13And you
say, 'What a burden!'[m] and you sniff at
it contemptuously,[n]" says the LORD
Almighty.
"When you bring injured, crippled or
diseased animals and offer them as
sacrifices,[o] should I accept them from
your hands?"[p] says the LORD. 14"Cursed
is the cheat who has an acceptable male
in his flock and vows to give it, but then
sacrifices a blemished animal[q] to the
Lord. For I am a great king,[r]" says the
LORD Almighty,[s] "and my name is to be
feared[t] among the nations.[u]

Admonition for the Priests

2 "And now this admonition is for
you, O priests.[a] 2If you do not lis-
ten,[b] and if you do not set your heart to
honour[c] my name," says the LORD
Almighty, "I will send a curse[d] upon
you, and I will curse your blessings.[e]
Yes, I have already cursed them, be-
cause you have not set your heart to
honour me.
3"Because of you I will rebuke[a] your
descendants;[b] I will spread on your
faces the offal[f] from your festival sac-
rifices, and you will be carried off with

Ch. 1

1 [a]**Na 1:1**; [b]Ac 7:38; Ro 3:1–2; 1Pe 4:11
2 [c]**Dt 4:37**; [d]ver 6–7; Mal 2:14,17; 3:7, 13; [e]**Jer 46:27**; Ro 9:13*
3 [f]Lk 14:26; [g]**Isa 34:10**; [h]**Isa 13:22**
4 [i]**Isa 11:14; 34:11**; [j]Isa 9:10; [k]**Isa 34:5**; [l]**La 4:22; Eze 25:12–14; 26:14**
5 [m]Ps 35:27; 48:1; Mic 5:4; [n]Isa 45:22; 52:10; **Am 1:11–12**
6 [o]**Lev 20:9**; Mt 15:4; 23:9; [p]Lk 6:46; [q]**Dt 31:12; Isa 1:2**; [r]Job 5:17; [s]**ver 2**
7 [t]ver 12; Lev 21:6; [u]**ver 2**; [v]**Eze 23:41**
8 [w]**Lev 1:3; Dt 15:21**; [x]**Ge 32:20**; [y]**Isa 43:23**
9 [z]Lev 23:33–44; Ps 51:17; Mic 6:6–8; Ro 12:1; Heb 13:16; [a]**Jer 6:20**
10 [b]2Ch 28:24; [c]**Hos 5:6**; [d]Lev 22:20; [e]ver 13; Isa 1:11–14; Jer 14:12; Mal 2:12
11 [f]**Isa 24:15**; 56:6; [g]**Isa 6:3; 12:4**; [h]**Ps 113:3; Mt 8:11**; [i]Isa 60:6–7; Rev 5:8; 8:3; [j]**Isa 19:21**; Heb 13:15
12 [k]**Eze 41:22**; [l]**ver 7**
13 [m]Isa 43:22–24; [n]**Nu 14:11**; [o]**ver 10**; [p]**Dt 15:21**

14 [q]Ex 12:5; **Lev 22:18–21**; [r]Ps 95:3; **Ob 21**; 1Ti 6:15; [s]Jer 46:18; [t]**Dt 28:58**; [u]Ps 72:8–11

Ch. 2

1 [a]ver 7
2 [b]Jer 13:17; [c]Mt 15:7–9; Jn 5:23; 1Ti 6:16; Rev 5:12–13; [d]**Dt 11:26; 28:20**; [e]Nu 6:23–27
3 [f]**Ex 29:14; Lev 4:11; Job 9:31**

[a]*1* *Malachi* means *my messenger*.
[a]*3* Or *cut off* (see Septuagint)
[b]*3* Or *will blight your corn*

it.[g] 4And you will know that I have sent
you this admonition so that my cov-
enant with Levi[h] may continue," says
the LORD Almighty. 5"My covenant was
with him, a covenant[i] of life and peace,[j]
and I gave them to him; this called for
reverence[k] and he revered me and stood
in awe of my name. 6True instruction[l]
was in his mouth and nothing false was
found on his lips. He walked[m] with me
in peace[n] and uprightness,[o] and turned
many from sin.[p]
7"For the lips of a priest[q] ought to
preserve knowledge, and from his
mouth men should seek instruction[r]—
because he is the messenger[s] of the
LORD Almighty. 8But you have turned
from the way[t] and by your teaching
have caused many to stumble;[u] you
have violated the covenant[v] with
Levi,"[w] says the LORD Almighty. 9"So I
have caused you to be despised[x] and
humiliated[y] before all the people, be-
cause you have not followed my ways
but have shown partiality[z] in matters of
the law."[a]

Judah Unfaithful

10Have we not all one Father[c]?[b] Did
not one God create us?[c] Why do we
profane the covenant[d] of our fathers by
breaking faith[e] with one another?
11Judah has broken faith. A detest-
able[f] thing has been committed in Israel
and in Jerusalem: Judah has desecrated
the sanctuary the LORD loves,[g] by marry-
ing[h] the daughter of a foreign god.[i]
12As for the man who does this, who-
ever he may be, may the LORD cut him
off[j] from the tents of Jacob[d][k]—even
though he brings offerings[l] to the LORD
Almighty.
13Another thing you do: You flood the
LORD's altar with tears.[m] You weep and
wail[n] because he no longer pays atten-
tion[o] to your offerings or accepts them
with pleasure from your hands.[p] 14You
ask,[q] "Why?" It is because the LORD is
acting as the witness[r] between you and
the wife of your youth,[s] because you
have broken faith with her, though she
is your partner, the wife of your mar-
riage covenant.[t]
15Has not ⌞the LORD⌟ made them
one?[u] In flesh and spirit they are his.
And why one? Because he was seeking
godly offspring.[e][v] So guard yourself[w] in
your spirit, and do not break faith[x] with
the wife of your youth.
16"I hate divorce,[y]" says the LORD God
of Israel, "and I hate a man's covering
himself[f] with violence[z] as well as with

3 [g]1Ki 14:10
4 [h]**Nu 3:12**
5 [i]Dt 33:9; Ps 25:10; 103:18; **Mt 26:28; Lk 22:20;** Heb 7:22; [j]**Nu 25:12;** [k]**Dt 14:23; 28:58;** Ps 119:161; Heb 12:28
6 [l]**Dt 33:10;** [m]**Ge 5:22;** [n]Lk 2:14; **Jn 14:27;** Gal 5:22; [o]**Ps 25:21;** [p]**Ro 11:14;** Jas 5:19–20;
7 [q]**Jer 18:18;** [r]**Lev 10:11; 2Ch 17:7;** [s]**Nu 27:21; 2Ch 36:15;** Mt 11:10; Mk 1:2
8 [t]**Ex 32:8;** Jer 2:8; [u]**Jer 18:15;** [v]Jer 33:21; **Eze 22:26;** [w]**Hos 4:6**
9 [x]**1Sa 2:30; Ps 22:6; Jer 51:37;** [y]**Ps 35:4;** Jer 3:25; Ac 8:32–33; [z]**Ex 18:16; Lev 19:15;** Ac 10:34; Ro 2:11; [a]**1Sa 2:17**
10 [b]**Ex 4:22;** Mt 5:16; 6:4,18; Lk 11:2; 1Co 8:6; [c]**Job 4:17;** Isa 43:1; [d]Ex 19:5; **2Ki 17:15;** Jer 31:32; [e]**Zep 3:3–4**
11 [f]**Isa 1:13; 48:8;** [g]**Dt 4:37;** [h]**Ne 13:23;** [i]**Ex 34:16;** Jer 3:7–9
12 [j]**1Sa 2:30–33; Eze 24:21;** [k]**Nu 24:5;** 2Sa 20:1; [l]**Mal 1:10**
13 [m]**Jer 11:11;** [n]Ps 39:12; [o]Ps 66:18; Jer 14:12; [p]Isa 58:2
14 [q]**Mal 1:2;** [r]**Ge 21:30; Jos 24:22;** [s]**Pr 5:18;** [t]**Eze 16:8;** Heb 13:4
15 [u]**Ge 2:24;** Mt 19:4–6; [v]**Dt 14:2;** 1Co 7:14; [w]**Dt 4:15;** [x]**Isa 54:6;** 1Co 7:10; Heb 13:4
16 [y]**Dt 24:1;** Mt 5:31–32; 19:4–9; Mk 10:4–5; [z]**Ge 6:11;** 34:25; **Pr 4:17; Isa 58:4;** [a]Ps 51:10

his garment," says the LORD Almighty.
So guard yourself in your spirit,[a] and
do not break faith.

The Day of Judgment

17You have wearied[b] the LORD with
your words.
"How have we wearied him?" you
ask.[c]
By saying, "All who do evil are good
in the eyes of the LORD, and he is
pleased[d] with them" or "Where is the
God of justice?[e]"

3 "See, I will send my messenger,[a]
who will prepare the way before
me.[b] Then suddenly the Lord[c] you are
seeking will come to his temple; the
messenger of the covenant,[d] whom you
desire,[e] will come," says the Lord
Almighty.
2But who can endure[f] the day of his
coming?[g] Who can stand[h] when he
appears? For he will be like a refiner's
fire[i] or a launderer's soap.[j] 3He will sit as
a refiner and purifier of silver;[k] he will
purify[l] the Levites and refine them like
gold and silver.[m] Then the LORD will
have men who will bring offerings in
righteousness,[n] 4and the offerings[o] of
Judah and Jerusalem will be acceptable
to the LORD, as in days gone by, as in
former years.[p]
5"So I will come near to you for judg-
ment. I will be quick to testify against
sorcerers,[q] adulterers[r] and perjurers,[s]
against those who defraud labourers of
their wages,[t] who oppress the widows[u]
and the fatherless, and deprive aliens[v]
of justice, but do not fear[w] me," says the
LORD Almighty.

17 [b]**Isa 1:14;** [c]**Mal 1:2;** [d]Ps 5:4; [e]**Ge 18:25; Job 8:3; Eze 18:25**

Ch. 3

1 [a]**Nu 27:21; 2Ch 36:15;** [b]**Isa 40:3; Mt 3:3;** 11:10*; Mk 1:2*; Lk 7:27*; [c]Mic 5:2; [d]**Isa 42:6;** [e]**1Sa 9:20**
2 [f]**Eze 22:14;** Rev 6:17; [g]**Eze 7:7; Da 7:13; Joel 2:31; Mt 16:27;** Jas 5:8; 2Pe 3:4; **Rev 1:7;** [h]**1Sa 6:20;** [i]**Isa 1:31; 30:30; Zec 13:9;** Mt 3:10–12; [j]**Job 9:30**
3 [k]**Da 12:10; 1Co 3:13;** [l]**1Ch 23:28; Isa 1:25;** [m]**Job 28:1; Ps 12:6;** 1Pe 1:7; Rev 3:18; [n]**Ps 132:9**
4 [o]2Ch 7:12; Ps 51:19; Mal 1:11; [p]**2Ch 7:3; Eze 20:40**
5 [q]**Ex 7:11; Isa 47:9;** [r]Ex 20:14; Jas 2:11; 2Pe 2:12–14; [s]Lev 19:11–12; **Jer 7:9;** [t]**Lev 19:13;** Jas 5:4; [u]**Ex 22:22;** [v]**Ex 22:21; Dt 24:19; Eze 22:7;** [w]**Dt 31:12; Isa 1:2**

---

c10 Or *father*
d12 Or [12]*May the LORD cut off from the tents of Jacob anyone who gives testimony on behalf of the man who does this*
e15 Or [15]*But the one ⌞who is our father⌟ did not do this, not as long as life remained in him. And what was he seeking? An offspring from God*
f16 Or *his wife*

Robbing God

6"I the LORD do not change.[x] So you,
O descendants of Jacob, are not de-
stroyed.[y] 7Ever since the time of your
forefathers you have turned away[z] from
my decrees and have not kept them.
Return[a] to me, and I will return to
you,"[b] says the LORD Almighty.
"But you ask,[c] 'How are we to re-
turn?'
8"Will a man rob[d] God? Yet you rob
me.
"But you ask, 'How do we rob you?'
"In tithes[e] and offerings. 9You are
under a curse[f]—the whole nation of
you—because you are robbing me.
10Bring the whole tithe[g] into the
storehouse,[h] that there may be food in
my house. Test me in this," says the
LORD Almighty, "and see if I will not
throw open the floodgates[i] of heaven
and pour out[j] so much blessing[k] that
you will not have room enough for it.[l] 11I
will prevent pests from devouring[m]
your crops, and the vines in your fields
will not cast their fruit,[n]" says the LORD
Almighty. 12"Then all the nations will
call you blessed,[o] for yours will be a
delightful land,"[p] says the LORD
Almighty.[q]
13"You have said harsh things[r]
against me," says the LORD.
"Yet you ask,[s] 'What have we said
against you?'
14"You have said, 'It is futile[t] to serve[u]
God. What did we gain by carrying out
his requirements[v] and going about like
mourners[w] before the LORD Almighty?
15But now we call the arrogant[x] blessed.
Certainly the evildoers[y] prosper,[z] and
even those who challenge God
escape.'"
16Then those who feared the LORD
talked with each other, and the LORD
listened and heard.[a] A scroll[b] of re-
membrance was written in his presence
concerning those who feared[c] the LORD
and honoured his name.
17"They will be mine,[d]" says the LORD
Almighty, "in the day when I make up
my treasured possession.[a][e] I will spare[f]
them, just as in compassion a man
spares his son[g] who serves him. 18And
you will again see the distinction be-
tween the righteous[h] and the wicked,
between those who serve God and
those who do not.[i]

The Day of the LORD

4 "Surely the day is coming;[a] it will
burn like a furnace.[b] All the arro-
gant[c] and every evildoer will be stub-
ble,[d] and that day that is coming will set
them on fire,[e]" says the LORD Almighty.
"Not a root or a branch[f] will be left to
them. 2But for you who revere my
name,[g] the sun of righteousness[h] will
rise with healing[i] in its wings. And you
will go out and leap[j] like calves released
from the stall. 3Then you will trample[k]
down the wicked; they will be ashes[l]
under the soles of your feet on the day
when I do these things," says the LORD
Almighty.
4"Remember the law[m] of my servant
Moses, the decrees and laws I gave him
at Horeb[n] for all Israel.[o]
5"See, I will send you the prophet
Elijah[p] before that great and dreadful
day of the LORD comes.[q] 6He will turn
the hearts of the fathers to their chil-
dren,[r] and the hearts of the children to
their fathers; or else I will come and
strike[s] the land with a curse."[t]

6 [x]Nu 23:19; Heb 7:21; Jas 1:17; [y]Job 34:15; Hos 11:9
7 [z]Ex 32:8; Jer 7:26; Ac 7:51; [a]Isa 44:22; Eze 18:32; [b]Zec 1:3; Jas 4:8; [c]Mal 1:2
8 [d]Zec 5:3; [e]Lev 27:30; Nu 18:21; Ne 13:10–12; Lk 18:12
9 [f]Dt 11:26; 28:15–68; Zec 5:3
10 [g]Ex 22:29; [h]Ne 13:12; [i]2Ki 7:2; [j]Isa 44:3; [k]Lev 25:21; Joel 2:14; 2Co 9:8–11; [l]Joel 2:24
11 [m]Ex 10:15; Dt 28:39; [n]Ex 23:26
12 [o]Dt 28:3–12; Isa 61:9; [p]Isa 62:4; Eze 20:6; [q]2Ch 31:10
13 [r]Mal 2:17; [s]Mal 1:2
14 [t]Ps 73:13; Isa 57:10; [u]Ps 100:2; Jn 12:26; Ro 12:11; [v]Jos 22:5; Isa 1:14; [w]Isa 58:3
15 [x]Ps 119:21; [y]Ps 14:1; 36:1–2; Jer 7:10; [z]Job 21:7
16 [a]Ps 34:15; [b]Ex 32:32; Ps 56:8; 87:6; Lk 10:20; [c]Dt 28:58; 31:12; Ps 33:18; Pr 1:7; Rev 11:18
17 [d]Isa 43:21; [e]Ex 8:22; Dt 7:6; Ro 8:14; Tit 2:14; [f]Ne 13:22; Ps 103:13; Isa 26:20; Lk 15:1–32; [g]Ro 8:32
18 [h]Ge 18:25; [i]Dt 32:4; Mt 25:32–33,41

Ch. 4
1 [a]Da 7:13; Joel 2:31; Mt 11:14; Ac 2:20; [b]Isa 31:9; [c]Isa 2:12; [d]Isa 5:24; Na 1:10; [e]Isa 1:31; [f]2Ki 10:11; Eze 17:8; Mt 3:10
2 [g]Dt 28:58; Ps 61:5; 111:9; Rev 14:1; [h]Ps 118:27; Isa 9:2; 45:8; Lk 1:78; Eph 5:14; [i]2Ch 7:14; Isa 30:26; Mt 4:23; Rev 22:2; [j]Isa 35:6
3 [k]Job 40:12; Ps 18:40–42; [l]Eze 28:18
4 [m]Dt 28:61; Ps 147:19; Mt 5:17; 7:12; Ro 2:13; 4:15; Gal 3:24; [n]Ex 3:1; [o]Ex 20:1
5 [p]1Ki 17:1; Mt 11:14; 16:14; [q]Joel 2:31
6 [r]Lk 1:17; [s]Isa 11:4; Rev 19:15; [t]Dt 11:26; 13:15; Jos 6:17; 23:15; Zec 5:3

[a]17 Or *Almighty, "my treasured possession, in the day when I act*

THE NEW TESTAMENT

Matthew

The Genealogy of Jesus

1:1–17pp—Lk 3:23–38
1:3–6pp—Ru 4:18–22
1:7–11pp—1Ch 3:10–17

1 A record of the genealogy of Jesus
Christ the son of David,[a] the son of
Abraham:[b]

2Abraham was the father of Isaac,[c]
Isaac the father of Jacob,[d]
Jacob the father of Judah and his brothers,[e]
3Judah the father of Perez and Zerah, whose mother was Tamar,[f]
Perez the father of Hezron,
Hezron the father of Ram,
4Ram the father of Amminadab,
Amminadab the father of Nahshon,
Nahshon the father of Salmon,
5Salmon the father of Boaz, whose mother was Rahab,[g]
Boaz the father of Obed, whose mother was Ruth,
Obed the father of Jesse,
6and Jesse the father of King David.[h]

David was the father of Solomon, whose mother had been Uriah's wife,[i]
7Solomon the father of Rehoboam,
Rehoboam the father of Abijah,
Abijah the father of Asa,
8Asa the father of Jehoshaphat,
Jehoshaphat the father of Jehoram,
Jehoram the father of Uzziah,
9Uzziah the father of Jotham,
Jotham the father of Ahaz,
Ahaz the father of Hezekiah,
10Hezekiah the father of Manasseh,[j]
Manasseh the father of Amon,
Amon the father of Josiah,
11and Josiah the father of Jeconiah[a] and his brothers at the time of the exile to Babylon.[k]

12After the exile to Babylon:
Jeconiah was the father of Shealtiel,[l]
Shealtiel the father of Zerubbabel,[m]
13Zerubbabel the father of Abiud,
Abiud the father of Eliakim,
Eliakim the father of Azor,
14Azor the father of Zadok,
Zadok the father of Akim,
Akim the father of Eliud,
15Eliud the father of Eleazar,
Eleazar the father of Matthan,
Matthan the father of Jacob,
16and Jacob the father of Joseph, the husband of Mary,[n] of whom was born Jesus, who is called Christ.[o]

17Thus there were fourteen genera-
tions in all from Abraham to David,
fourteen from David to the exile to
Babylon, and fourteen from the exile to
the Christ.[b]

The Birth of Jesus Christ

18This is how the birth of Jesus Christ
came about: His mother Mary was
pledged to be married to Joseph, but
before they came together, she was
found to be with child through the Holy
Spirit.[p]
19Because Joseph her husband
was a righteous man and did not want
to expose her to public disgrace, he had
in mind to divorce[q] her quietly.
20But after he had considered this, an
angel[r] of the Lord appeared to him in a
dream[s] and said, "Joseph son of David,
do not be afraid to take Mary home as
your wife, because what is conceived in
her is from the Holy Spirit.
21She will
give birth to a son, and you are to give
him the name Jesus,[c][t] because he will
save his people from their sins."[u]
22All this took place to fulfil[v] what the
Lord had said through the prophet:
23"The virgin will be with child and will
give birth to a son, and they will call him

Ch. 1

1 [a]2Sa 7:12–16; Isa 9:6–7; 11:1; Jer 23:5–6; **Mt 9:27**; Lk 1:32, 69; Rev 22:16; [b]Ge 22:18; **Gal 3:16**
2 [c]Ge 21:3,12; [d]Ge 25:26; [e]Ge 29:35; 49:10
3 [f]Ge 38:27–30
5 [g]**Heb 11:31**
6 [h]1Sa 16:1; 17:12; [i]2Sa 12:24
10 [j]2Ki 20:21
11 [k]2Ki 24:14–16; Jer 27:20; 40:1; Da 1:1–2
12 [l]1Ch 3:17; [m]1Ch 3:19; Ezr 3:2
16 [n]Lk 1:27; [o]Mt 27:17
18 [p]Lk 1:35
19 [q]Dt 24:1
20 [r]**Ac 5:19**; [s]**Mt 27:19**
21 [t]**Lk 1:31**; [u]Ps 130:8; **Lk 2:11**; **Jn 3:17**; Ac 5:31; **Ro 11:14**; Tit 2:14
22 [v]Mt 2:15,17, 23; 4:14; 8:17; 12:17; 21:4; 26:54,56; 27:9; Lk 4:21; 21:22; 24:44; Jn 13:18; 19:24,28,36

---

[a]*11* That is, Jehoiachin; also in verse 12
[b]*17* Or *Messiah*. "The Christ" (Greek) and "the Messiah" (Hebrew) both mean "the Anointed One".
[c]*21* *Jesus* is the Greek form of *Joshua*, which means *the* LORD *saves*.

Immanuel"[d][w]—which means, "God
with us."
24When Joseph woke up, he did what
the angel[x] of the Lord had commanded
him and took Mary home as his wife.
25But he had no union with her until she
gave birth to a son. And he gave him the
name Jesus.[y]

The Visit of the Magi

2 After Jesus was born in Bethlehem
in Judea,[a] during the time of King
Herod,[b] Magi[a] from the east came to
Jerusalem 2and asked, "Where is the
one who has been born king of the
Jews?[c] We saw his star[d] in the east[b] and
have come to worship him."
3When King Herod heard this he was
disturbed, and all Jerusalem with him.
4When he had called together all the
people's chief priests and teachers of
the law, he asked them where the
Christ[c] was to be born. 5"In Bethlehem[e]
in Judea," they replied, "for this is what
the prophet has written:

6" 'But you, Bethlehem, in the land of
Judah,
are by no means least among the
rulers of Judah;
for out of you will come a ruler
who will be the shepherd of my
people Israel.'[d]"[f]

7Then Herod called the Magi secretly
and found out from them the exact time
the star had appeared. 8He sent them to
Bethlehem and said, "Go and make a
careful search for the child. As soon as
you find him, report to me, so that I too
may go and worship him."
9After they had heard the king, they
went on their way, and the star they had
seen in the east[e] went ahead of them
until it stopped over the place where the
child was. 10When they saw the star,
they were overjoyed. 11On coming to
the house, they saw the child with his
mother Mary, and they bowed down
and worshipped him.[g] Then they
opened their treasures and presented
him with gifts[h] of gold and of incense
and of myrrh. 12And having been
warned[i] in a dream[j] not to go back to
Herod, they returned to their country
by another route.

The Escape to Egypt

13When they had gone, an angel[k] of
the Lord appeared to Joseph in a
dream.[l] "Get up," he said, "take the
child and his mother and escape to
Egypt. Stay there until I tell you, for
Herod is going to search for the child to
kill him."[m]
14So he got up, took the child and his
mother during the night and left for
Egypt, 15where he stayed until the death
of Herod. And so was fulfilled[n] what the
Lord had said through the prophet:
"Out of Egypt I called my son."[f][o]
16When Herod realised that he had
been outwitted by the Magi, he was
furious, and he gave orders to kill all the
boys in Bethlehem and its vicinity who
were two years old and under, in
accordance with the time he had
learned from the Magi. 17Then what was
said through the prophet Jeremiah was
fulfilled:[p]

18"A voice is heard in Ramah,
weeping and great mourning,
Rachel[q] weeping for her children
and refusing to be comforted,
because they are no more."[g][r]

The Return to Nazareth

19After Herod died, an angel[s] of the
Lord appeared in a dream[t] to Joseph in
Egypt 20and said, "Get up, take the child
and his mother and go to the land of
Israel, for those who were trying to take
the child's life are dead."[u]
21So he got up, took the child and his
mother and went to the land of Israel.
22But when he heard that Archelaus was
reigning in Judea in place of his father
Herod, he was afraid to go there.
Having been warned in a dream,[v] he
withdrew to the district of Galilee,[w]
23and he went and lived in a town called
Nazareth.[x] So was fulfilled[y] what was
said through the prophets: "He will be
called a Nazarene."[z]

John the Baptist Prepares the Way

3:1–12pp—Mk 1:3–8; Lk 3:2–17

3 In those days John the Baptist[a]
came, preaching in the Desert of
Judea 2and saying, "Repent, for the
kingdom of heaven[b] is near." 3This is he
who was spoken of through the prophet
Isaiah:

"A voice of one calling in the desert,
'Prepare the way for the Lord,
make straight paths for him.' "[a][c]

23 [w]Isa 7:14; 8:8,10
24 [x]**Ac 5:19**
25 [y]ver 21; **Lk 1:31**

Ch. 2

1 [a]Lk 2:4–7; [b]Lk 1:5
2 [c]Jer 23:5; Mt 27:11; Mk 15:2; Lk 23:38; Jn 1:49; 18:33–37; [d]Nu 24:17
5 [e]Jn 7:42
6 [f]Mic 5:2; 2Sa 5:2
11 [g]Isa 60:3; [h]Ps 72:10
12 [i]Heb 11:7; [j]ver 13,19, 22; **Mt 27:19**
13 [k]**Ac 5:19**; [l]ver 12,19,22; **Mt 27:19**; [m]Rev 12:4
15 [n]ver 17,23; **Mt 1:22**; [o]Hos 11:1; Ex 4:22–23
17 [p]ver 15,23; **Mt 1:22**
18 [q]Ge 35:19; [r]Jer 31:15
19 [s]**Ac 5:19**; [t]ver 12–13,22; **Mt 27:19**
20 [u]Ex 4:19
22 [v]ver 12–13, 19; **Mt 27:19**; [w]Lk 2:39
23 [x]Mk 1:9; 6:1; **1:24**; Lk 1:26; 2:39,51; 4:16, 23; Jn 1:45–46; [y]ver 15,17; **Mt 1:22**; [z]**Mk 1:24**

Ch. 3

1 [a]ver 13–14; Mt 9:14; 11:2–14; 14:1–12; Lk 1:13,57–66; 3:2–19; Ac 19:3–4
2 [b]Da 7:14; Mt 4:17; 6:10; 7:21; **25:34**; Lk 11:20; 17:20–21; 19:11; 21:31; Jn 3:3,5; Ac 1:3,6
3 [c]Isa 40:3; Mal 3:1; Lk 1:76; Jn 1:23

[d]23 Isaiah 7:14 [a]1 Traditionally *Wise Men*
[b]2 Or *star when it rose* [c]4 Or *Messiah*
[d]6 Micah 5:2 [e]9 Or *seen when it rose*
[f]15 Hosea 11:1 [g]18 Jer. 31:15
[a]3 Isaiah 40:3

[4]John's[d] clothes were made of camel's hair, and he had a leather belt round his waist.[e] His food was locusts[f] and wild honey. [5]People went out to him from Jerusalem and all Judea and the whole region of the Jordan. [6]Confessing their sins, they were baptised[g] by him in the Jordan River.

[7]But when he saw many of the Pharisees and Sadducees coming to where he was baptising, he said to them: "You brood of vipers![h] Who warned you to flee from the coming wrath?[i] [8]Produce fruit in keeping with repentance.[j] [9]And do not think you can say to yourselves, 'We have Abraham as our father.'[k] I tell you that out of these stones God can raise up children for Abraham. [10]The axe is already at the root of the trees, and every tree that does not produce good fruit will be cut down and thrown into the fire.[l]

[11]"I baptise you with[b] water for repentance.[m] But after me will come one who is more powerful than I, whose sandals I am not fit to carry. He will baptise you with the Holy Spirit[n] and with fire.[o] [12]His winnowing fork is in his hand, and he will clear his threshing-floor, gathering his wheat into the barn and burning up the chaff with unquenchable fire."[p]

The Baptism of Jesus

3:13–17pp—Mk 1:9–11; Lk 3:21,22; Jn 1:31–34

[13]Then Jesus came from Galilee to the Jordan to be baptised by John.[q] [14]But John tried to deter him, saying, "I need to be baptised by you, and do you come to me?"

[15]Jesus replied, "Let it be so now; it is proper for us to do this to fulfil all righteousness." Then John consented.

[16]As soon as Jesus was baptised, he went up out of the water. At that moment heaven was opened,[r] and he saw the Spirit of God[s] descending like a dove and lighting on him. [17]And a voice from heaven[t] said, "This is my Son,[u] whom I love; with him I am well pleased."[v]

The Temptation of Jesus

4:1–11pp—Mk 1:12,13; Lk 4:1–13

4 Then Jesus was led by the Spirit into the desert to be tempted[a] by the devil.[b] [2]After fasting for forty days and forty nights,[c] he was hungry. [3]The tempter[d] came to him and said, "If you are the Son of God,[e] tell these stones to become bread."

[4]Jesus answered, "It is written: 'Man does not live on bread alone, but on every word that comes from the mouth of God.'[a]"[f]

[5]Then the devil took him to the holy city[g] and had him stand on the highest point of the temple. [6]"If you are the Son of God,"[h] he said, "throw yourself down. For it is written:

"'He will command his angels
concerning you,
and they will lift you up in their
hands,
so that you will not strike your foot
against a stone.'[b]"[i]

[7]Jesus answered him, "It is also written: 'Do not put the Lord your God to the test.'[c]"[j]

[8]Again, the devil took him to a very high mountain and showed him all the kingdoms of the world and their splendour. [9]"All this I will give you," he said, "if you will bow down and worship me."

[10]Jesus said to him, "Away from me, Satan![k] For it is written: 'Worship the Lord your God, and serve him only.'[d]"[l]

[11]Then the devil left him,[m] and angels came and attended him.[n]

Jesus Begins to Preach

[12]When Jesus heard that John had been put in prison,[o] he returned to Galilee.[p] [13]Leaving Nazareth, he went and lived in Capernaum,[q] which was by the lake in the area of Zebulun and Naphtali—[14]to fulfil[r] what was said through the prophet Isaiah:

[15]"Land of Zebulun and land of
Naphtali,
the way to the sea, along the Jordan,
Galilee of the Gentiles—
[16]the people living in darkness
have seen a great light;
on those living in the land of the
shadow of death
a light has dawned."[e][s]

[17]From that time on Jesus began to preach, "Repent, for the kingdom of heaven[t] is near."

4 [d]**Mt 3:1**; [e]2Ki 1:8; [f]Lev 11:22
6 [g]ver 11; **Mk 1:4**
7 [h]Mt 12:34; 23:33; [i]**Ro 1:18**
8 [j]Ac 26:20
9 [k]**Lk 3:8**
10 [l]Mt 7:19; Lk 3:9; 13:6–9; Jn 15:2,6
11 [m]ver 6; **Mk 1:4**; [n]**Mk 1:8**; [o]Isa 4:4; Ac 2:3–4
12 [p]Mt 13:30; **25:41**
13 [q]**Mt 3:1; Mk 1:4**
16 [r]Eze 1:1; Jn 1:51; Ac 7:56; 10:11; Rev 4:1; 19:11; [s]Isa 11:2; 42:1
17 [t]Dt 4:12; Mt 17:5; Jn 12:28; [u]Ps 2:7; Ac 13:33; Heb 1:1–5; 5:5; 2Pe 1:17–18; [v]Isa 42:1; Mt 12:18; 17:5; Mk 1:11; 9:7; Lk 3:22; 9:35; 2Pe 1:17

Ch. 4

1 [a]Heb 4:15; [b]Ge 3:1–7
2 [c]Ex 34:28; 1Ki 19:8
3 [d]1Th 3:5; [e]**Mt 3:17**; 14:33; 16:16; 27:54; Mk 3:11; Lk 1:35; 22:70; Jn 1:34,49; 5:25; 11:27; 20:31; Ac 9:20; Ro 1:4; 1Jn 5:10–13,20; Rev 2:18
4 [f]Dt 8:3; Jn 4:34
5 [g]Ne 11:1; Da 9:24; Mt 27:53
6 [h]**ver 3**; [i]Ps 91:11–12
7 [j]Dt 6:16
10 [k]1Ch 21:1; Job 1:6–9; Mt 16:23; Mk 4:15; Lk 10:18; 13:16; 22:3,31; Ro 16:20; 2Co 2:11; 11:14; 2Th 2:9; Rev 12:9; [l]Dt 6:13
11 [m]Jas 4:7; [n]Mt 26:53; Lk 22:43; Heb 1:14
12 [o]Mt 14:3; [p]Mk 1:14
13 [q]Mk 1:21; 9:33; Lk 4:23, 31; Jn 2:12; 4:46–47
14 [r]**Mt 1:22**
16 [s]Isa 9:1–2; Lk 2:32; Jn 1:4–5,9
17 [t]**Mt 3:2**

[b]*11* Or *in*
[a]*4* Deut. 8:3
[b]*6* Psalm 91:11,12
[c]*7* Deut. 6:16
[d]*10* Deut. 6:13
[e]*16* Isaiah 9:1,2

The Calling of the First Disciples

4:18–22pp—Mk 1:16–20; Lk 5:2–11; Jn 1:35–42

18As Jesus was walking beside the Sea of Galilee,[u] he saw two brothers, Simon called Peter[v] and his brother Andrew. They were casting a net into the lake, for they were fishermen. 19"Come, follow me,"[w] Jesus said, "and I will make you fishers of men." 20At once they left their nets and followed him.[x]

21Going on from there, he saw two other brothers, James son of Zebedee and his brother John.[y] They were in a boat with their father Zebedee, preparing their nets. Jesus called them, 22and immediately they left the boat and their father and followed him.[z]

Jesus Heals the Sick

23Jesus went throughout Galilee,[a] teaching in their synagogues,[b] preaching the good news[c] of the kingdom,[d] and healing every disease and sickness among the people.[e] 24News about him spread all over Syria,[f] and people brought to him all who were ill with various diseases, those suffering severe pain, the demon-possessed,[g] those having seizures,[h] and the paralysed,[i] and he healed them. 25Large crowds from Galilee, the Decapolis,[f] Jerusalem, Judea and the region across the Jordan followed him.[j]

The Beatitudes

5:3–12pp—Lk 6:20–23

5 Now when he saw the crowds, he went up on a mountainside and sat down. His disciples came to him, 2and he began to teach them, saying:

3"Blessed are the poor in spirit,
for theirs is the kingdom of heaven.[a]
4Blessed are those who mourn,
for they will be comforted.[b]
5Blessed are the meek,
for they will inherit the earth.[c]
6Blessed are those who hunger and thirst for righteousness,
for they will be filled.[d]
7Blessed are the merciful,
for they will be shown mercy.[e]
8Blessed are the pure in heart,[f]
for they will see God.[g]
9Blessed are the peacemakers,[h]
for they will be called sons of God.[i]
10Blessed are those who are persecuted because of righteousness,[j]
for theirs is the kingdom of heaven.[k]

11"Blessed are you when people insult you,[l] persecute you and falsely say all kinds of evil against you because of me.[m] 12Rejoice and be glad,[n] because great is your reward in heaven, for in the same way they persecuted the prophets who were before you.[o]

Salt and Light

13"You are the salt of the earth. But if the salt loses its saltiness, how can it be made salty again? It is no longer good for anything, except to be thrown out and trampled by men.[p]

14"You are the light of the world.[q] A city on a hill cannot be hidden. 15Neither do people light a lamp and put it under a bowl. Instead they put it on its stand, and it gives light to everyone in the house.[r] 16In the same way, let your light shine before men,[s] that they may see your good deeds[t] and praise[u] your Father in heaven.

The Fulfilment of the Law

17"Do not think that I have come to abolish the Law or the Prophets; I have not come to abolish them but to fulfil them.[v] 18I tell you the truth, until heaven and earth disappear, not the smallest letter, not the least stroke of a pen, will by any means disappear from the Law until everything is accomplished.[w] 19Anyone who breaks one of the least of these commandments[x] and teaches others to do the same will be called least in the kingdom of heaven, but whoever practises and teaches these commands will be called great in the kingdom of heaven. 20For I tell you that unless your righteousness surpasses that of the Pharisees and the teachers of the law, you will certainly not enter the kingdom of heaven.[y]

Murder

5:25,26pp—Lk 12:58,59

21"You have heard that it was said to the people long ago, 'Do not murder,[a][z] and anyone who murders will be subject to judgment.' 22But I tell you that

18 [u]Mt 15:29; Mk 7:31; Jn 6:1; [v]Mt 16:17–18
19 [w]ver 20,22; Mt 8:22; Mk 10:21,28,52; Lk 5:28; Jn 1:43; 21:19,22
20 [x]**ver 19**
21 [y]Mt 17:1; 20:20; 26:37; Mk 3:17; 13:3; Lk 8:51; Jn 21:2
22 [z]**ver 19**
23 [a]Mk 1:39; Lk 4:15,44; [b]Mt 9:35; 13:54; Mk 1:21; Lk 4:15; Jn 6:59; 18:20; [c]Mk 1:14; [d]**Mt 3:2**; Ac 20:25; 28:23,31; [e]Mt 8:16; 14:14; 15:30; Mk 3:10; Lk 7:22; Ac 10:38
24 [f]**Lk 2:2**; [g]Mt 8:16,28; 9:32; 12:22; 15:22; Mk 1:32; 5:15–16,18; [h]Mt 17:15; [i]Mt 8:6; 9:2; Mk 2:3
25 [j]Mk 3:7–8; Lk 6:17

Ch. 5

3 [a]ver 10,19; **Mt 25:34**
4 [b]Isa 61:2–3; Rev 7:17
5 [c]Ps 37:11; Ro 4:13
6 [d]Isa 55:1–2
7 [e]**Jas 2:13**
8 [f]Ps 24:3–4; 73:1; [g]Ps 17:15; 42:2; Heb 12:14; Rev 22:4
9 [h]Jas 3:18; **Ro 14:19**; [i]ver 44–45; **Ro 8:14**
10 [j]**1Pe 3:14**; [k]ver 3,19; **Mt 25:34**
11 [l]Isa 51:7; [m]**Jn 15:21**
12 [n]Ps 9:2; Ac 5:41; **2Co 6:10**; 12:10; Col 1:24; Jas 1:2; 1Pe 1:6; 4:13, 16; [o]2Ch 36:16; Mt 23:31,37; Ac 7:52; 1Th 2:15; Heb 11:32–38
13 [p]Mk 9:50; Lk 14:34–35
14 [q]Jn 8:12
15 [r]Mk 4:21; Lk 8:16; 11:33
16 [s]1Co 10:31; Php 1:11; [t]**Tit 2:14**; [u]**Mt 9:8**
17 [v]Jn 10:34–35; Ro 3:31
18 [w]Ps 119:89; Isa 40:8; 55:11; Mt 24:35; Mk 13:31; Lk 16:17; 21:33
19 [x]Jas 2:10
20 [y]Isa 26:2; Mt 18:3; Jn 3:5
21 [z]Ex 20:13; 21:12; Dt 5:17

f25 That is, the Ten Cities
a21 Exodus 20:13

anyone who is angry[a] with his brother[b] will be subject to judgment.[b] Again, anyone who says to his brother, 'Raca,'[c] is answerable to the Sanhedrin.[c] But anyone who says, 'You fool!' will be in danger of the fire of hell.[d]

23"Therefore, if you are offering your gift at the altar and there remember that your brother has something against you, 24leave your gift there in front of the altar. First go and be reconciled to your brother; then come and offer your gift.

25"Settle matters quickly with your adversary who is taking you to court. Do it while you are still with him on the way, or he may hand you over to the judge, and the judge may hand you over to the officer, and you may be thrown into prison. 26I tell you the truth, you will not get out until you have paid the last penny.[d]

Adultery

27"You have heard that it was said, 'Do not commit adultery.'[e][e] 28But I tell you that anyone who looks at a woman lustfully has already committed adultery with her in his heart.[f] 29If your right eye causes you to sin,[g] gouge it out and throw it away. It is better for you to lose one part of your body than for your whole body to be thrown into hell. 30And if your right hand causes you to sin,[h] cut it off and throw it away. It is better for you to lose one part of your body than for your whole body to go into hell.

Divorce

31"It has been said, 'Anyone who divorces his wife must give her a certificate of divorce.'[f][i] 32But I tell you that anyone who divorces his wife, except for marital unfaithfulness, causes her to become an adulteress, and anyone who marries the divorced woman commits adultery.[j]

Oaths

33"Again, you have heard that it was said to the people long ago, 'Do not break your oath,[k] but keep the oaths you have made to the Lord.'[l] 34But I tell you, Do not swear at all:[m] either by heaven, for it is God's throne;[n] 35or by the earth, for it is his footstool; or by Jerusalem, for it is the city of the Great King.[o] 36And do not swear by your head, for you cannot make even one hair white or black. 37Simply let your 'Yes' be 'Yes', and your 'No', 'No';[p] anything beyond this comes from the evil one.[q]

An Eye for an Eye

38"You have heard that it was said, 'Eye for eye, and tooth for tooth.'[g][r] 39But I tell you, Do not resist an evil person. If someone strikes you on the right cheek, turn to him the other also.[s] 40And if someone wants to sue you and take your tunic, let him have your cloak as well. 41If someone forces you to go one mile, go with him two miles. 42Give to the one who asks you, and do not turn away from the one who wants to borrow from you.[t]

Love for Enemies

43"You have heard that it was said, 'Love your neighbour[h][u] and hate your enemy.'[v] 44But I tell you: Love your enemies[i] and pray for those who persecute you,[w] 45that you may be sons[x] of your Father in heaven. He causes his sun to rise on the evil and the good, and sends rain on the righteous and the unrighteous.[y] 46If you love those who love you, what reward will you get?[z] Are not even the tax collectors doing that? 47And if you greet only your brothers, what are you doing more than others? Do not even pagans do that? 48Be perfect, therefore, as your heavenly Father is perfect.[a]

Giving to the Needy

6 "Be careful not to do your 'acts of righteousness' before men, to be seen by them.[a] If you do, you will have no reward from your Father in heaven.

2"So when you give to the needy, do not announce it with trumpets, as the hypocrites do in the synagogues and on the streets, to be honoured by men. I tell you the truth, they have received their reward in full. 3But when you give to the needy, do not let your left hand know what your right hand is doing, 4so that your giving may be in secret. Then your Father, who sees what is done in secret, will reward you.[b]

22 [a]Ecc 7:9; 1Co 13:5; Eph 4:26; Jas 1:19–20; [b]1Jn 3:15; [c]Mt 26:59; Jn 11:47; Ac 5:21,27,34,41; 6:12; [d]Mt 18:9; Mk 9:43,48; Lk 16:24; Jas 3:6
27 [e]Ex 20:14; Dt 5:18
28 [f]Pr 6:25; 2Pe 2:14
29 [g]ver 30; Mt 18:6,8–9; Mk 9:42–47; Lk 17:2; Ro 14:21; 1Co 8:13; **2Co 6:3**; 11:29
30 [h]**ver 29**
31 [i]Dt 24:1–4
32 [j]**Lk 16:18**
33 [k]Lev 19:12; [l]Nu 30:2; Dt 23:21; Mt 23:16–22
34 [m]Jas 5:12; [n]Isa 66:1; Mt 23:22
35 [o]Ps 48:2
37 [p]Jas 5:12; [q]Mt 6:13; 13:19,38; Jn 17:15; Eph 6:16; 2Th 3:3; 1Jn 2:13–14; 3:12; 5:18–19
38 [r]Ex 21:24; Lev 24:20; Dt 19:21
39 [s]Lk 6:29; Ro 12:17,19; 1Pe 3:9
42 [t]Dt 15:8; Lk 6:30
43 [u]Lev 19:18; Mt 19:19; 22:39; Mk 12:31; Lk 10:27; Ro 13:9; Gal 5:14; Jas 2:8; [v]Dt 23:6; Ps 139:21–22
44 [w]Lk 6:27–28; 23:34; Jn 15:20; Ac 7:60; Ro 8:35; 12:14; 1Co 4:12; 1Pe 2:23
45 [x]ver 9; Lk 6:35; **Ro 8:14**; [y]Job 25:3
46 [z]Lk 6:32
48 [a]Lev 19:2; 1Pe 1:16

Ch. 6

1 [a]Mt 5:16; 23:5
4 [b]ver 6,18; Col 3:23–24

[b]22 Some manuscripts *brother without cause*
[c]22 An Aramaic term of contempt
[d]26 Greek *kodrantes*
[e]27 Exodus 20:14
[f]31 Deut. 24:1
[g]38 Exodus 21:24; Lev. 24:20 and Deut. 19:21
[h]43 Lev. 19:18
[i]44 Some late manuscripts *enemies, bless those who curse you, do good to those who hate you*

Prayer

6:9–13pp—Lk 11:2–4

5"And when you pray, do not be like the hypocrites, for they love to pray standing[c] in the synagogues and on the street corners to be seen by men. I tell you the truth, they have received their reward in full. 6But when you pray, go into your room, close the door and pray to your Father,[d] who is unseen. Then your Father, who sees what is done in secret, will reward you. 7And when you pray, do not keep on babbling[e] like pagans, for they think they will be heard because of their many words.[f] 8Do not be like them, for your Father knows what you need[g] before you ask him.

9"This, then, is how you should pray:

"'Our Father[h] in heaven,
hallowed be your name,
10your kingdom[i] come,
your will be done[j]
on earth as it is in heaven.
11Give us today our daily bread.[k]
12Forgive us our debts,
as we also have forgiven our
debtors.[l]
13And lead us not into temptation,[m]
but deliver us from the evil one.'[a] [n]

14For if you forgive men when they sin against you, your heavenly Father will also forgive you.[o] 15But if you do not forgive men their sins, your Father will not forgive your sins.[p]

Fasting

16"When you fast,[q] do not look sombre[r] as the hypocrites do, for they disfigure their faces to show men they are fasting. I tell you the truth, they have received their reward in full. 17But when you fast, put oil on your head and wash your face, 18so that it will not be obvious to men that you are fasting, but only to your Father, who is unseen; and your Father, who sees what is done in secret, will reward you.[s]

Treasures in Heaven

6:22,23pp—Lk 11:34–36

19"Do not store up for yourselves treasures on earth,[t] where moth and rust destroy,[u] and where thieves break in and steal. 20But store up for yourselves treasures in heaven,[v] where moth and rust do not destroy, and where thieves do not break in and steal.[w] 21For where your treasure is, there your heart will be also.[x]

22"The eye is the lamp of the body. If your eyes are good, your whole body will be full of light. 23But if your eyes are bad, your whole body will be full of darkness. If then the light within you is darkness, how great is that darkness!

24"No-one can serve two masters. Either he will hate the one and love the other, or he will be devoted to the one and despise the other. You cannot serve both God and Money.[y]

Do Not Worry

6:25–33pp—Lk 12:22–31

25"Therefore I tell you, do not worry[z] about your life, what you will eat or drink; or about your body, what you will wear. Is not life more important than food, and the body more important than clothes? 26Look at the birds of the air; they do not sow or reap or store away in barns, and yet your heavenly Father feeds them.[a] Are you not much more valuable than they?[b] 27Who of you by worrying can add a single hour to his life?[b] [c]

28"And why do you worry about clothes? See how the lilies of the field grow. They do not labour or spin. 29Yet I tell you that not even Solomon in all his splendour[d] was dressed like one of these. 30If that is how God clothes the grass of the field, which is here today and tomorrow is thrown into the fire, will he not much more clothe you, O you of little faith?[e] 31So do not worry, saying, 'What shall we eat?' or 'What shall we drink?' or 'What shall we wear?' 32For the pagans run after all these things, and your heavenly Father knows that you need them.[f] 33But seek first his kingdom[g] and his righteousness, and all these things will be given to you as well.[h] 34Therefore do not worry about tomorrow, for tomorrow will worry about itself. Each day has enough trouble of its own.

Judging Others

7:3–5pp—Lk 6:41,42

7 "Do not judge, or you too will be judged.[a] 2For in the same way as you judge others, you will be judged, and with the measure you use, it will be measured to you.[b]

5 [c]Mk 11:25; Lk 18:10–14
6 [d]2Ki 4:33
7 [e]Ecc 5:2; [f]1Ki 18:26–29
8 [g]ver 32
9 [h]Jer 3:19; Mal 2:10; 1Pe 1:17
10 [i]**Mt 3:2**; [j]**Mt 26:39**
11 [k]Pr 30:8
12 [l]Mt 18:21–35
13 [m]Jas 1:13; [n]**Mt 5:37**
14 [o]Mt 18:21–35; Mk 11:25–26; Eph 4:32; Col 3:13
15 [p]Mt 18:35
16 [q]Lev 16:29, 31; 23:27–32; Nu 29:7; [r]Isa 58:5; Zec 7:5; 8:19
18 [s]ver 4,6
19 [t]Pr 23:4; Lk 12:16–21; Heb 13:5; [u]**Jas 5:2–3**
20 [v]Mt 19:21; Lk 12:33; 16:9; 18:22; 1Ti 6:19; [w]Lk 12:33
21 [x]Lk 12:34
24 [y]Lk 16:13
25 [z]ver 27–28, 31,34; Lk 10:41; 12:11,22
26 [a]Job 38:41; Ps 104:21; 136:25; 145:15; 147:9; [b]Mt 10:29–31
27 [c]Ps 39:5
29 [d]1Ki 10:4–7
30 [e]Mt 8:26; 14:31; 16:8; Lk 12:28
32 [f]ver 8
33 [g]**Mt 3:2**; [h]Ps 37:4; Mt 19:29

Ch. 7

1 [a]Lk 6:37; Ro 14:4,10,13; 1Co 4:5; 5:12; Jas 4:11–12
2 [b]Eze 35:11; Mk 4:24; Lk 6:38; Ro 2:1

[a]13 Or *from evil;* some late manuscripts *one, / for yours is the kingdom and the power and the glory for ever. Amen.* [b]27 Or *single cubit to his height*

3"Why do you look at the speck of
sawdust in your brother's eye and pay
no attention to the plank in your own
eye? 4How can you say to your brother,
'Let me take the speck out of your eye,'
when all the time there is a plank in your
own eye? 5You hypocrite, first take the
plank out of your own eye, and then
you will see clearly to remove the speck
from your brother's eye.
6"Do not give dogs what is sacred; do
not throw your pearls to pigs. If you do,
they may trample them under their feet,
and then turn and tear you to pieces.

Ask, Seek, Knock
7:7–11pp—Lk 11:9–13

7"Ask and it will be given to you;[c]
seek and you will find; knock and the
door will be opened to you. 8For every-
one who asks receives; he who seeks
finds;[d] and to him who knocks, the door
will be opened.
9"Which of you, if his son asks for
bread, will give him a stone? 10Or if he
asks for a fish, will give him a snake? 11If
you, then, though you are evil, know
how to give good gifts to your children,
how much more will your Father in
heaven give good gifts[e] to those who ask
him! 12So in everything, do to others
what you would have them do to you,[f]
for this sums up the Law and the
Prophets.[g]

The Narrow and Wide Gates

13"Enter through the narrow gate.[h]
For wide is the gate and broad is the
road that leads to destruction, and
many enter through it. 14But small is the
gate and narrow the road that leads to
life, and only a few find it.

A Tree and Its Fruit

15"Watch out for false prophets.[i] They
come to you in sheep's clothing, but
inwardly they are ferocious wolves.[j]
16By their fruit you will recognise them.[k]
Do people pick grapes from thorn-
bushes, or figs from thistles?[l] 17Likewise
every good tree bears good fruit, but a
bad tree bears bad fruit. 18A good tree
cannot bear bad fruit, and a bad tree
cannot bear good fruit.[m] 19Every tree
that does not bear good fruit is cut down
and thrown into the fire.[n] 20Thus, by
their fruit you will recognise them.
21"Not everyone who says to me,
'Lord, Lord,'[o] will enter the kingdom of
heaven,[p] but only he who does the will
of my Father who is in heaven.[q] 22Many
will say to me on that day,[r] 'Lord, Lord,
did we not prophesy in your name, and
in your name drive out demons and
perform many miracles?'[s] 23Then I will
tell them plainly, 'I never knew you.
Away from me, you evildoers!'[t]

The Wise and Foolish Builders
7:24–27pp—Lk 6:47–49

24"Therefore everyone who hears
these words of mine and puts them into
practice[u] is like a wise man who built his
house on the rock. 25The rain came
down, the streams rose, and the winds
blew and beat against that house; yet it
did not fall, because it had its founda-
tion on the rock. 26But everyone who
hears these words of mine and does not
put them into practice is like a foolish
man who built his house on sand. 27The
rain came down, the streams rose, and
the winds blew and beat against that
house, and it fell with a great crash."
28When Jesus had finished saying
these things,[v] the crowds were amazed
at his teaching,[w] 29because he taught as
one who had authority, and not as their
teachers of the law.

The Man With Leprosy
8:2–4pp—Mk 1:40–44; Lk 5:12–14

8 When he came down from the
mountainside, large crowds fol-
lowed him. 2A man with leprosy[a][a] came
and knelt before him[b] and said, "Lord, if
you are willing, you can make me
clean."
3Jesus reached out his hand and
touched the man. "I am willing," he
said. "Be clean!" Immediately he was
cured[b] of his leprosy. 4Then Jesus said
to him, "See that you don't tell anyone.[c]
But go, show yourself to the priest[d] and
offer the gift Moses commanded,[e] as a
testimony to them."

The Faith of the Centurion
8:5–13pp—Lk 7:1–10

5When Jesus had entered Caper-
naum, a centurion came to him, asking
for help. 6"Lord," he said, "my servant
lies at home paralysed[f] and in terrible
suffering."

7 [c]1Ki 3:5; Mt 18:19; 21:22; Jn 14:13–14; 15:7,16; 16:23–24; Jas 1:5–8; 4:2–3; 5:16; 1Jn 3:22; 5:14–15
8 [d]Pr 8:17; Jer 29:12–13
11 [e]Jas 1:17
12 [f]Lk 6:31; [g]Ro 13:8–10; Gal 5:14
13 [h]Lk 13:24; Jn 10:7,9
15 [i]Jer 23:16; Mt 24:24; Lk 6:26; 2Pe 2:1; 1Jn 4:1; Rev 16:13; [j]Eze 22:27; Ac 20:29
16 [k]Mt 12:33; Lk 6:44; [l]Jas 3:12
18 [m]Lk 6:43
19 [n]**Mt 3:10**
21 [o]Hos 8:2; Mt 25:11; **Jn 13:13**; 1Co 12:3; [p]**Mt 3:2**; [q]Mt 12:50; Ro 2:13; Jas 1:22; 1Jn 3:18
22 [r]**Mt 10:15**; [s]Lk 10:20; Ac 19:13; 1Co 13:1–3
23 [t]Ps 6:8; Mt 25:12,41; Lk 13:25–27
24 [u]ver 21; Jas 1:22–25
28 [v]Mt 11:1; 13:53; 19:1; 26:1; [w]Mt 13:54; 22:33; Mk 1:22; 6:2; 11:18; Lk 4:32; Jn 7:46

Ch. 8

2 [a]Lev 13:45; Mt 10:8; 11:5; 26:6; Lk 5:12; 17:12; [b]Mt 9:18; 15:25; 18:26; 20:20
4 [c]Mt 9:30; 12:16; Mk 5:43; 7:36; **8:30**; Lk 4:41; [d]Lk 17:14; [e]Lev 14:2–32
6 [f]**Mt 4:24**

[a]2 The Greek word was used for various diseases affecting the skin—not necessarily leprosy.
[b]3 Greek *made clean*

7Jesus said to him, "I will go and heal him."

8The centurion replied, "Lord, I do not deserve to have you come under my roof. But just say the word, and my servant will be healed.[g] 9For I myself am a man under authority, with soldiers under me. I tell this one, 'Go,' and he goes; and that one, 'Come,' and he comes. I say to my servant, 'Do this,' and he does it."

10When Jesus heard this, he was astonished and said to those following him, "I tell you the truth, I have not found anyone in Israel with such great faith.[h] 11I say to you that many will come from the east and the west,[i] and will take their places at the feast with Abraham, Isaac and Jacob in the kingdom of heaven.[j] 12But the subjects of the kingdom[k] will be thrown outside, into the darkness, where there will be weeping and gnashing of teeth."[l]

13Then Jesus said to the centurion, "Go! It will be done just as you believed it would."[m] And his servant was healed at that very hour.

Jesus Heals Many

8:14–16pp—Mk 1:29–34; Lk 4:38–41

14When Jesus came into Peter's house, he saw Peter's mother-in-law lying in bed with a fever. 15He touched her hand and the fever left her, and she got up and began to wait on him.

16When evening came, many who were demon-possessed were brought to him, and he drove out the spirits with a word and healed all the sick.[n] 17This was to fulfil[o] what was spoken through the prophet Isaiah:

"He took up our infirmities
and carried our diseases."[c][p]

The Cost of Following Jesus

8:19–22pp—Lk 9:57–60

18When Jesus saw the crowd around him, he gave orders to cross to the other side of the lake.[q] 19Then a teacher of the law came to him and said, "Teacher, I will follow you wherever you go."

20Jesus replied, "Foxes have holes and birds of the air have nests, but the Son of Man[r] has nowhere to lay his head."

21Another disciple said to him, "Lord, first let me go and bury my father."

22But Jesus told him, "Follow me,[s] and let the dead bury their own dead."

8 [g]Ps 107:20
10 [h]Mt 15:28
11 [i]Ps 107:3; Isa 49:12; 59:19; Mal 1:11; [j]Lk 13:29
12 [k]Mt 13:38; [l]Mt 13:42,50; 22:13; 24:51; 25:30; Lk 13:28
13 [m]**Mt 9:22**
16 [n]**Mt 4:23–24**
17 [o]**Mt 1:22;** [p]Isa 53:4
18 [q]Mk 4:35
20 [r]Da 7:13; Mt 12:8,32,40; 16:13,27–28; 17:9; 19:28; Mk 2:10; 8:31
22 [s]**Mt 4:19**
26 [t]**Mt 6:30;** [u]Ps 65:7; 89:9; 107:29
28 [v]**Mt 4:24**
29 [w]Jdg 11:12; 2Sa 16:10; 1Ki 17:18; Mk 1:24; Lk 4:34; Jn 2:4; [x]2Pe 2:4
34 [y]Lk 5:8; Ac 16:39

Ch. 9

1 [a]Mt 4:13
2 [b]**Mt 4:24;** [c]**ver 22;** [d]Jn 16:33; [e]Lk 7:48
3 [f]Mt 26:65; Jn 10:33
4 [g]Ps 94:11; Mt 12:25; Lk 6:8; 9:47; 11:17; Jn 2:25

Jesus Calms the Storm

8:23–27pp—Mk 4:36–41; Lk 8:22–25
8:23–27Ref—Mt 14:22–33

23Then he got into the boat and his disciples followed him. 24Without warning, a furious storm came up on the lake, so that the waves swept over the boat. But Jesus was sleeping. 25The disciples went and woke him, saying, "Lord, save us! We're going to drown!"

26He replied, "You of little faith,[t] why are you so afraid?" Then he got up and rebuked the winds and the waves, and it was completely calm.[u]

27The men were amazed and asked, "What kind of man is this? Even the winds and the waves obey him!"

The Healing of Two Demon-possessed Men

8:28–34pp—Mk 5:1–17; Lk 8:26–37

28When he arrived at the other side in the region of the Gadarenes,[d] two demon-possessed[v] men coming from the tombs met him. They were so violent that no-one could pass that way. 29"What do you want with us,[w] Son of God?" they shouted. "Have you come here to torture us before the appointed time?"[x]

30Some distance from them a large herd of pigs was feeding. 31The demons begged Jesus, "If you drive us out, send us into the herd of pigs."

32He said to them, "Go!" So they came out and went into the pigs, and the whole herd rushed down the steep bank into the lake and died in the water. 33Those tending the pigs ran off, went into the town and reported all this, including what had happened to the demon-possessed men. 34Then the whole town went out to meet Jesus. And when they saw him, they pleaded with him to leave their region.[y]

Jesus Heals a Paralytic

9:2–8pp—Mk 2:3–12; Lk 5:18–26

9 Jesus stepped into a boat, crossed over and came to his own town.[a] 2Some men brought to him a paralytic,[b] lying on a mat. When Jesus saw their faith,[c] he said to the paralytic, "Take heart,[d] son; your sins are forgiven."[e]

3At this, some of the teachers of the law said to themselves, "This fellow is blaspheming!"[f]

4Knowing their thoughts,[g] Jesus said,

[c]17 Isaiah 53:4
[d]28 Some manuscripts *Gergesenes;* others *Gerasenes*

"Why do you entertain evil thoughts in
your hearts? 5Which is easier: to say,
'Your sins are forgiven,' or to say, 'Get
up and walk'? 6But so that you may
know that the Son of Man[h] has authority
on earth to forgive sins. . . ." Then he
said to the paralytic, "Get up, take your
mat and go home." 7And the man got
up and went home. 8When the crowd
saw this, they were filled with awe; and
they praised God,[i] who had given such
authority to men.

The Calling of Matthew

9:9–13pp—Mk 2:14–17; Lk 5:27–32

9As Jesus went on from there, he saw
a man named Matthew sitting at the tax
collector's booth. "Follow me,"[j] he told
him, and Matthew got up and followed
him.

10While Jesus was having dinner at
Matthew's house, many tax collectors
and "sinners" came and ate with him
and his disciples. 11When the Pharisees
saw this, they asked his disciples, "Why
does your teacher eat with tax collectors
and 'sinners'?"[k]

12On hearing this, Jesus said, "It is not
the healthy who need a doctor, but the
sick. 13But go and learn what this
means: 'I desire mercy, not sacrifice.'[a][l]
For I have not come to call the righteous,
but sinners."[m]

Jesus Questioned About Fasting

9:14–17pp—Mk 2:18–22; Lk 5:33–39

14Then John's[n] disciples came and
asked him, "How is it that we and the
Pharisees fast,[o] but your disciples do not
fast?"

15Jesus answered, "How can the
guests of the bridegroom mourn while
he is with them?[p] The time will come
when the bridegroom will be taken from
them; then they will fast.[q]

16"No-one sews a patch of unshrunk
cloth on an old garment, for the patch
will pull away from the garment, mak-
ing the tear worse. 17Neither do men
pour new wine into old wineskins. If
they do, the skins will burst, the wine
will run out and the wineskins will
be ruined. No, they pour new wine
into new wineskins, and both are
preserved."

A Dead Girl and a Sick Woman

9:18–26pp—Mk 5:22–43; Lk 8:41–56

18While he was saying this, a ruler
came and knelt before him[r] and said,
"My daughter has just died. But come
and put your hand on her,[s] and she will
live." 19Jesus got up and went with him,
and so did his disciples.

20Just then a woman who had been
subject to bleeding for twelve years
came up behind him and touched the
edge of his cloak.[t] 21She said to herself,
"If I only touch his cloak, I will be
healed."

22Jesus turned and saw her. "Take
heart,[u] daughter," he said, "your faith
has healed you."[v] And the woman was
healed from that moment.[w]

23When Jesus entered the ruler's
house and saw the flute players and the
noisy crowd,[x] 24he said, "Go away. The
girl is not dead[y] but asleep."[z] But they
laughed at him. 25After the crowd had
been put outside, he went in and took
the girl by the hand, and she got up.[a]
26News of this spread through all that
region.[b]

Jesus Heals the Blind and Mute

27As Jesus went on from there, two
blind men followed him, calling out,
"Have mercy on us, Son of David!"[c]

28When he had gone indoors, the
blind men came to him, and he asked
them, "Do you believe that I am able to
do this?"

"Yes, Lord," they replied.[d]

29Then he touched their eyes and
said, "According to your faith will it be
done to you";[e] 30and their sight was
restored. Jesus warned them sternly,
"See that no-one knows about this."[f]
31But they went out and spread the
news about him all over that region.[g]

32While they were going out, a man
who was demon-possessed[h] and could
not talk[i] was brought to Jesus. 33And
when the demon was driven out, the
man who had been mute spoke. The
crowd was amazed and said, "Nothing
like this has ever been seen in Israel."[j]

34But the Pharisees said, "It is by the
prince of demons that he drives out
demons."[k]

The Workers Are Few

35Jesus went through all the towns
and villages, teaching in their syna-
gogues, preaching the good news of the
kingdom and healing every disease and
sickness.[l] 36When he saw the crowds,
he had compassion on them,[m] because

6 [h]**Mt 8:20**
8 [i]Mt 5:16; 15:31; Lk 7:16; 13:13; 17:15; 23:47; Jn 15:8; Ac 4:21; 11:18; 21:20
9 [j]**Mt 4:19**
11 [k]Mt 11:19; Lk 5:30; 15:2; 19:7; Gal 2:15
13 [l]Hos 6:6; Mic 6:6–8; Mt 12:7; [m]Lk 19:10; 1Ti 1:15
14 [n]**Mt 3:1**; [o]Mt 11:18–19; Lk 18:12
15 [p]Jn 3:29; [q]Ac 13:2–3; 14:23
18 [r]**Mt 8:2**; [s]**Mk 5:23**
20 [t]Mt 14:36; Mk 3:10; 6:56; Lk 6:19
22 [u]ver 2; Jn 16:33; [v]ver 29; Mt 8:13; Mk 10:52; Lk 7:50; 17:19; 18:42; [w]Mt 15:28
23 [x]2Ch 35:25; Jer 9:17–18
24 [y]Ac 20:10; [z]Da 12:2; Ps 76:5; Jn 11:11–14; Ac 7:60; 13:36; 1Co 11:30; 15:6,18,20; 1Th 4:13–16
25 [a]**Lk 7:14**
26 [b]ver 31; Mt 4:24; 14:1; Mk 1:28,45; Lk 4:14,37; 5:15; 7:17
27 [c]**Mt 1:1**; 12:23; 15:22; 20:30–31; 21:9,15; 22:42; Mk 10:47
28 [d]Ac 14:9
29 [e]**ver 22**
30 [f]**Mt 8:4**
31 [g]**ver 26**; Mk 7:36
32 [h]**Mt 4:24**; [i]Mt 12:22–24
33 [j]Mk 2:12
34 [k]Mt 12:24
35 [l]**Mt 4:23**
36 [m]Mt 14:14; 15:32; Mk 8:2

[a]13 Hosea 6:6

they were harassed and helpless, like
sheep without a shepherd.[n] 37Then he
said to his disciples, "The harvest[o] is
plentiful but the workers are few.[p] 38Ask
the Lord of the harvest, therefore, to
send out workers into his harvest field."

Jesus Sends Out the Twelve

10:2–4pp—Mk 3:16–19; Lk 6:14–16; Ac 1:13
10:9–15pp—Mk 6:8–11; Lk 9:3–5; 10:4–12
10:19–22pp—Mk 13:11–13; Lk 21:12–17
10:26–33pp—Lk 12:2–9
10:34,35pp—Lk 12:51–53

10 He called his twelve disciples to
him and gave them authority to
drive out evil[a] spirits[a] and to heal every
disease and sickness.[b]
2These are the names of the twelve
apostles: first, Simon (who is called
Peter) and his brother Andrew; James
son of Zebedee, and his brother John;
3Philip and Bartholomew; Thomas and
Matthew the tax collector; James son of
Alphaeus, and Thaddaeus; 4Simon the
Zealot and Judas Iscariot, who betrayed
him.[c]
5These twelve Jesus sent out with the
following instructions: "Do not go
among the Gentiles or enter any town of
the Samaritans.[d] 6Go rather to the lost
sheep of Israel.[e] 7As you go, preach this
message: 'The kingdom of heaven[f] is
near.' 8Heal the sick, raise the dead,
cleanse those who have leprosy,[b] drive
out demons. Freely you have received,
freely give. 9Do not take along any gold
or silver or copper in your belts;[g] 10take
no bag for the journey, or extra tunic, or
sandals or a staff; for the worker is
worth his keep.[h]
11"Whatever town or village you
enter, search for some worthy person
there and stay at his house until you
leave. 12As you enter the home, give it
your greeting.[i] 13If the home is deserv-
ing, let your peace rest on it; if it is not,
let your peace return to you. 14If anyone
will not welcome you or listen to your
words, shake the dust off your feet[j]
when you leave that home or town. 15I
tell you the truth, it will be more bear-
able for Sodom and Gomorrah[k] on the
day of judgment[l] than for that town.[m] 16I
am sending you out like sheep among
wolves.[n] Therefore be as shrewd as
snakes and as innocent as doves.[o]
17"Be on your guard against men;
they will hand you over to the local
councils[p] and flog you in their syna-
gogues.[q] 18On my account you will be
brought before governors and kings[r] as
witnesses to them and to the Gentiles.
19But when they arrest you, do not
worry about what to say or how to say
it.[s] At that time you will be given what
to say, 20for it will not be you speaking,
but the Spirit of your Father[t] speaking
through you.
21"Brother will betray brother to
death, and a father his child; children
will rebel against their parents[u] and
have them put to death.[v] 22All men will
hate you because of me,[w] but he who
stands firm to the end will be saved.[x]
23When you are persecuted in one place,
flee to another. I tell you the truth, you
will not finish going through the cities
of Israel before the Son of Man comes.[y]
24"A student is not above his teacher,
nor a servant above his master.[z] 25It is
enough for the student to be like his
teacher, and the servant like his master.
If the head of the house has been called
Beelzebub,[c][a] how much more the mem-
bers of his household!
26"So do not be afraid of them. There
is nothing concealed that will not be
disclosed, or hidden that will not be
made known.[b] 27What I tell you in the
dark, speak in the daylight; what is
whispered in your ear, proclaim from
the roofs. 28Do not be afraid of those
who kill the body but cannot kill the
soul. Rather, be afraid of the One[c] who
can destroy both soul and body in hell.
29Are not two sparrows sold for a
penny?[d] Yet not one of them will fall to
the ground apart from the will of your
Father. 30And even the very hairs of
your head are all numbered.[d] 31So don't
be afraid; you are worth more than
many sparrows.[e]
32"Whoever acknowledges me before
men,[f] I will also acknowledge him
before my Father in heaven. 33But who-
ever disowns me before men, I will dis-
own him before my Father in heaven.[g]
34"Do not suppose that I have come to
bring peace to the earth. I did not come
to bring peace, but a sword. 35For I have
come to turn

"'a man against his father,
a daughter against her mother,
a daughter-in-law against her
mother-in-law[h]—
36 a man's enemies will be the
members of his own
household.'[e][i]

36 [n]Nu 27:17; 1Ki 22:17; Eze 34:5–6; Zec 10:2
37 [o]Jn 4:35; [p]Lk 10:2

Ch. 10

1 [a]Mk 3:13–15; 6:7; Lk 4:36; 9:1; [b]**Mt 4:23**
4 [c]Mt 26:14–16, 25,47; 27:3; Mk 14:10; Jn 6:71; 12:4; 13:2,26–27; Ac 1:16
5 [d]1Ki 16:24; 2Ki 17:24; Lk 9:52; 10:33; 17:16; Jn 4:4–26, 39–40; 8:48; Ac 8:5,25
6 [e]Jer 50:6; Mt 15:24
7 [f]**Mt 3:2**
9 [g]Lk 22:35
10 [h]**1Ti 5:18**
12 [i]1Sa 25:6
14 [j]Ne 5:13; Mk 6:11; Lk 9:5; 10:11; Ac 13:51; 18:6
15 [k]Ge 18:20; 19:24; 2Pe 2:6; Jude 7; [l]Mt 12:36; Ac 17:31; 2Pe 2:9; 3:7; 1Jn 4:17; Jude 6; [m]Mt 11:22,24
16 [n]Lk 10:3; Ac 20:29; [o]**1Co 14:20**
17 [p]**Mt 5:22**; [q]Mt 23:34; Mk 13:9; Ac 5:40; 22:19; 26:11
18 [r]Ac 25:24–26
19 [s]Ex 4:12
20 [t]Lk 12:11–12; Ac 4:8
21 [u]ver 35–36; Mic 7:6; [v]Mk 13:12
22 [w]**Jn 15:21**; [x]Mt 24:13; Mk 13:13; Lk 21:19; Rev 2:10
23 [y]**Lk 17:30**
24 [z]**Jn 13:16**
25 [a]**Mk 3:22**
26 [b]Mk 4:22; Lk 8:17
28 [c]Isa 8:12–13; Heb 10:31
30 [d]1Sa 14:45; 2Sa 14:11; 1Ki 1:52; Lk 21:18; Ac 27:34
31 [e]Mt 6:26; 12:12
32 [f]Ro 10:9
33 [g]Mk 8:38; 2Ti 2:12
35 [h]ver 21
36 [i]Mic 7:6

[a]1 Greek *unclean*
[b]8 The Greek word was used for various diseases affecting the skin—not necessarily leprosy.
[c]25 Greek *Beezeboul* or *Beelzeboul*
[d]29 Greek *an assarion* [e]36 Micah 7:6

37"Anyone who loves his father or mother more than me is not worthy of me; anyone who loves his son or daughter more than me is not worthy of me;[j] 38and anyone who does not take his cross and follow me is not worthy of me.[k] 39Whoever finds his life will lose it, and whoever loses his life for my sake will find it.[l]

40"He who receives you receives me,[m] and he who receives me receives the one who sent me.[n] 41Anyone who receives a prophet because he is a prophet will receive a prophet's reward, and anyone who receives a righteous man because he is a righteous man will receive a righteous man's reward. 42And if anyone gives even a cup of cold water to one of these little ones because he is my disciple, I tell you the truth, he will certainly not lose his reward."[o]

Jesus and John the Baptist

11:2–19pp—Lk 7:18–35

11 After Jesus had finished instructing his twelve disciples,[a] he went on from there to teach and preach in the towns of Galilee.[a]

2When John[b] heard in prison[c] what Christ was doing, he sent his disciples 3to ask him, "Are you the one who was to come,[d] or should we expect someone else?"

4Jesus replied, "Go back and report to John what you hear and see: 5The blind receive sight, the lame walk, those who have leprosy[b] are cured, the deaf hear, the dead are raised, and the good news is preached to the poor.[e] 6Blessed is the man who does not fall away on account of me."[f]

7As John's[g] disciples were leaving, Jesus began to speak to the crowd about John: "What did you go out into the desert[h] to see? A reed swayed by the wind? 8If not, what did you go out to see? A man dressed in fine clothes? No, those who wear fine clothes are in kings' palaces. 9Then what did you go out to see? A prophet?[i] Yes, I tell you, and more than a prophet. 10This is the one about whom it is written:

" 'I will send my messenger ahead of
  you,[j]
 who will prepare your way before
  you.'[c][k]

11I tell you the truth: Among those born of women there has not risen anyone greater than John the Baptist; yet he who is least in the kingdom of heaven is greater than he. 12From the days of John the Baptist until now, the kingdom of heaven has been forcefully advancing, and forceful men lay hold of it. 13For all the Prophets and the Law prophesied until John.[l] 14And if you are willing to accept it, he is the Elijah who was to come.[m] 15He who has ears, let him hear.[n]

16"To what can I compare this generation? They are like children sitting in the market-places and calling out to others:

17" 'We played the flute for you,
  and you did not dance;
 we sang a dirge,
  and you did not mourn.'

18For John came neither eating[o] nor drinking,[p] and they say, 'He has a demon.' 19The Son of Man came eating and drinking, and they say, 'Here is a glutton and a drunkard, a friend of tax collectors and "sinners".'[q] But wisdom is proved right by her actions."

Woe on Unrepentant Cities

11:21–23pp—Lk 10:13–15

20Then Jesus began to denounce the cities in which most of his miracles had been performed, because they did not repent. 21"Woe to you, Korazin! Woe to you, Bethsaida![r] If the miracles that were performed in you had been performed in Tyre and Sidon,[s] they would have repented long ago in sackcloth and ashes.[t] 22But I tell you, it will be more bearable for Tyre and Sidon on the day of judgment than for you.[u] 23And you, Capernaum,[v] will you be lifted up to the skies? No, you will go down to the depths.[d][w] If the miracles that were performed in you had been performed in Sodom, it would have remained to this day. 24But I tell you that it will be more bearable for Sodom on the day of judgment than for you."[x]

Rest for the Weary

11:25–27pp—Lk 10:21,22

25At that time Jesus said, "I praise you, Father,[y] Lord of heaven and earth, because you have hidden these things from the wise and learned, and revealed them to little children.[z] 26Yes, Father, for this was your good pleasure.

37 [j]Lk 14:26
38 [k]Mt 16:24; Lk 14:27
39 [l]**Jn 12:25**
40 [m]Ex 16:8; Mt 18:5; Gal 4:14; [n]Lk 9:48; 10:16; Jn 12:44; 13:20
42 [o]Pr 14:31; 19:17; Mt 25:40; Mk 9:41; Ac 10:4; Heb 6:10

Ch. 11

1 [a]**Mt 7:28**
2 [b]**Mt 3:1**; [c]Mt 14:3
3 [d]Ps 118:26; Jn 11:27; Heb 10:37
5 [e]Isa 35:4–6; 61:1; Mt 15:31; Lk 4:18–19
6 [f]Mt 13:21; 26:31
7 [g]**Mt 3:1**; [h]Mt 3:1
9 [i]Mt 14:5; 21:26; Lk 1:76; 7:26
10 [j]Jn 3:28; [k]Mal 3:1; Mk 1:2; Lk 7:27
13 [l]Lk 16:16
14 [m]Mal 4:5; Mt 17:10–13; Mk 9:11–13; Lk 1:17; Jn 1:21
15 [n]Mt 13:9,43; Mk 4:23; Lk 14:35; **Rev 2:7**
18 [o]Mt 3:4; [p]**Lk 1:15**
19 [q]**Mt 9:11**
21 [r]Mk 6:45; 8:22; Lk 9:10; Jn 1:44; 12:21; [s]Joel 3:4; Am 1:9; Mt 15:21; Mk 3:8; Lk 6:17; Ac 12:20; [t]Jnh 3:5–9
22 [u]ver 24; Mt 10:15
23 [v]**Mt 4:13**; [w]Isa 14:13–15
24 [x]**Mt 10:15**
25 [y]Mt 16:17; Lk 22:42; 23:34; Jn 11:41; 12:27–28; [z]**Mt 13:11**; 1Co 1:26–29

---

[a]*1* Greek *in their towns*
[b]*5* The Greek word was used for various diseases affecting the skin—not necessarily leprosy.
[c]*10* Mal. 3:1 [d]*23* Greek *Hades*

27"All things have been committed to me[a] by my Father.[b] No-one knows the Son except the Father, and no-one knows the Father except the Son and those to whom the Son chooses to reveal him.[c]

28"Come to me,[d] all you who are weary and burdened, and I will give you rest.[e] 29Take my yoke upon you and learn from me,[f] for I am gentle and humble in heart, and you will find rest for your souls.[g] 30For my yoke is easy and my burden is light."[h]

Lord of the Sabbath

12:1–8pp—Mk 2:23–28; Lk 6:1–5
12:9–14pp—Mk 3:1–6; Lk 6:6–11

12 At that time Jesus went through the cornfields on the Sabbath. His disciples were hungry and began to pick some ears of corn[a] and eat them. 2When the Pharisees saw this, they said to him, "Look! Your disciples are doing what is unlawful on the Sabbath."[b]

3He answered, "Haven't you read what David did when he and his companions were hungry?[c] 4He entered the house of God, and he and his companions ate the consecrated bread—which was not lawful for them to do, but only for the priests.[d] 5Or haven't you read in the Law that on the Sabbath the priests in the temple desecrate the day[e] and yet are innocent? 6I tell you that one[a] greater than the temple is here.[f] 7If you had known what these words mean, 'I desire mercy, not sacrifice,'[b][g] you would not have condemned the innocent. 8For the Son of Man[h] is Lord of the Sabbath."

9Going on from that place, he went into their synagogue, 10and a man with a shrivelled hand was there. Looking for a reason to accuse Jesus,[i] they asked him, "Is it lawful to heal on the Sabbath?"[j]

11He said to them, "If any of you has a sheep and it falls into a pit on the Sabbath, will you not take hold of it and lift it out?[k] 12How much more valuable is a man than a sheep![l] Therefore it is lawful to do good on the Sabbath."

13Then he said to the man, "Stretch out your hand." So he stretched it out and it was completely restored, just as sound as the other. 14But the Pharisees went out and plotted how they might kill Jesus.[m]

God's Chosen Servant

15Aware of this, Jesus withdrew from that place. Many followed him, and he healed all their sick,[n] 16warning them not to tell who he was.[o] 17This was to fulfil[p] what was spoken through the prophet Isaiah:

18"Here is my servant whom I have chosen,
the one I love, in whom I delight;[q]
I will put my Spirit on him,[r]
and he will proclaim justice to the nations.
19He will not quarrel or cry out;
no-one will hear his voice in the streets.
20A bruised reed he will not break,
and a smouldering wick he will not snuff out,
till he leads justice to victory.
21 In his name the nations will put their hope."[c][s]

Jesus and Beelzebub

12:25–29pp—Mk 3:23–27; Lk 11:17–22

22Then they brought him a demon-possessed man who was blind and mute, and Jesus healed him, so that he could both talk and see.[t] 23All the people were astonished and said, "Could this be the Son of David?"[u]

24But when the Pharisees heard this, they said, "It is only by Beelzebub,[d][v] the prince of demons, that this fellow drives out demons."[w]

25Jesus knew their thoughts[x] and said to them, "Every kingdom divided against itself will be ruined, and every city or household divided against itself will not stand. 26If Satan[y] drives out Satan, he is divided against himself. How then can his kingdom stand? 27And if I drive out demons by Beelzebub,[z] by whom do your people[a] drive them out? So then, they will be your judges. 28But if I drive out demons by the Spirit of God, then the kingdom of God[b] has come upon you.

29"Or again, how can anyone enter a strong man's house and carry off his possessions unless he first ties up the strong man? Then he can rob his house.

30"He who is not with me is against me, and he who does not gather with me scatters.[c] 31And so I tell you, every sin and blasphemy will be forgiven men, but the blasphemy against the Spirit will not be forgiven.[d] 32Anyone who speaks a word against the Son of Man will be forgiven, but anyone who

27 [a]**Mt 28:18;** [b]**Jn 3:35;** [c]Jn 10:15; 17:25–26
28 [d]Jn 7:37; [e]Ex 33:14
29 [f]Jn 13:15; Php 2:5; 1Pe 2:21; 1Jn 2:6; [g]Ps 116:7; Jer 6:16
30 [h]1Jn 5:3

Ch. 12

1 [a]Dt 23:25
2 [b]ver 10; Ex 20:10; 23:12; Dt 5:14; Lk 13:14; 14:3; Jn 5:10; 7:23; 9:16
3 [c]1Sa 21:6
4 [d]Lev 24:5,9
5 [e]Nu 28:9–10; Jn 7:22–23
6 [f]ver 41–42
7 [g]Hos 6:6; Mic 6:6–8; Mt 9:13
8 [h]**Mt 8:20**
10 [i]Mk 3:2; 12:13; Lk 11:54; 14:1; 20:20; [j]**ver 2**
11 [k]Lk 14:5
12 [l]Mt 6:26; 10:31
14 [m]Ge 37:18; Ps 71:10; Mt 26:4; 27:1; Mk 3:6; Lk 6:11; Jn 5:18; 7:1,19; 11:53
15 [n]**Mt 4:23**
16 [o]**Mt 8:4**
17 [p]**Mt 1:22**
18 [q]**Mt 3:17;** [r]**Jn 3:34**
21 [s]Isa 42:1–4
22 [t]**Mt 4:24**
23 [u]**Mt 9:27**
24 [v]**Mk 3:22;** [w]Mt 9:34
25 [x]**Mt 9:4**
26 [y]**Mt 4:10**
27 [z]ver 24; [a]Ac 19:13
28 [b]**Mt 3:2**
30 [c]Mk 9:40; Lk 11:23
31 [d]Mk 3:28–29; Lk 12:10

[a]6 Or *something;* also in verses 41 and 42
[b]7 Hosea 6:6 [c]21 Isaiah 42:1–4
[d]24 Greek *Beezeboul* or *Beelzeboul;* also in verse 27

speaks against the Holy Spirit will not be forgiven, either in this age[e] or in the age to come.[f]

33 "Make a tree good and its fruit will be good, or make a tree bad and its fruit will be bad, for a tree is recognised by its fruit.[g] 34 You brood of vipers,[h] how can you who are evil say anything good? For out of the overflow of the heart the mouth speaks.[i] 35 The good man brings good things out of the good stored up in him, and the evil man brings evil things out of the evil stored up in him. 36 But I tell you that men will have to give account on the day of judgment for every careless word they have spoken. 37 For by your words you will be acquitted, and by your words you will be condemned."[j]

The Sign of Jonah

12:39–42pp—Lk 11:29–32
12:43–45pp—Lk 11:24–26

38 Then some of the Pharisees and teachers of the law said to him, "Teacher, we want to see a miraculous sign[k] from you."[l]

39 He answered, "A wicked and adulterous generation asks for a miraculous sign! But none will be given it except the sign of the prophet Jonah.[m] 40 For as Jonah was three days and three nights in the belly of a huge fish,[n] so the Son of Man[o] will be three days and three nights in the heart of the earth.[p] 41 The men of Nineveh[q] will stand up at the judgment with this generation and condemn it; for they repented at the preaching of Jonah,[r] and now one[e] greater than Jonah is here. 42 The Queen of the South will rise at the judgment with this generation and condemn it; for she came[s] from the ends of the earth to listen to Solomon's wisdom, and now one greater than Solomon is here.

43 "When an evil[f] spirit comes out of a man, it goes through arid places seeking rest and does not find it. 44 Then it says, 'I will return to the house I left.' When it arrives, it finds the house unoccupied, swept clean and put in order. 45 Then it goes and takes with it seven other spirits more wicked than itself, and they go in and live there. And the final condition of that man is worse than the first.[t] That is how it will be with this wicked generation."

Jesus' Mother and Brothers

12:46–50pp—Mk 3:31–35; Lk 8:19–21

46 While Jesus was still talking to the crowd, his mother[u] and brothers[v] stood outside, wanting to speak to him. 47 Someone told him, "Your mother and brothers are standing outside, wanting to speak to you."[g]

48 He replied to him, "Who is my mother, and who are my brothers?" 49 Pointing to his disciples, he said, "Here are my mother and my brothers. 50 For whoever does the will of my Father in heaven[w] is my brother and sister and mother."

The Parable of the Sower

13:1–15pp—Mk 4:1–12; Lk 8:4–10
13:16,17pp—Lk 10:23,24
13:18–23pp—Mk 4:13–20; Lk 8:11–15

13 That same day Jesus went out of the house[a] and sat by the lake. 2 Such large crowds gathered round him that he got into a boat[b] and sat in it, while all the people stood on the shore. 3 Then he told them many things in parables, saying: "A farmer went out to sow his seed. 4 As he was scattering the seed, some fell along the path, and the birds came and ate it up. 5 Some fell on rocky places, where it did not have much soil. It sprang up quickly, because the soil was shallow. 6 But when the sun came up, the plants were scorched, and they withered because they had no root. 7 Other seed fell among thorns, which grew up and choked the plants. 8 Still other seed fell on good soil, where it produced a crop—a hundred,[c] sixty or thirty times what was sown. 9 He who has ears, let him hear."[d]

10 The disciples came to him and asked, "Why do you speak to the people in parables?"

11 He replied, "The knowledge of the secrets of the kingdom of heaven[e] has been given to you,[f] but not to them. 12 Whoever has will be given more, and he will have an abundance. Whoever does not have, even what he has will be taken from him.[g] 13 This is why I speak to them in parables:

"Though seeing, they do not see;
  though hearing, they do not hear or
    understand.[h]

14 In them is fulfilled[i] the prophecy of Isaiah:

" 'You will be ever hearing but never
    understanding;

32 [e]Tit 2:12; [f]Mk 10:30; Lk 20:34–35; Eph 1:21; Heb 6:5
33 [g]Mt 7:16–17; Lk 6:43–44
34 [h]Mt 3:7; 23:33; [i]Mt 15:18; Lk 6:45
37 [j]Job 15:6; Pr 10:14; 18:21; Jas 3:2
38 [k]**Jn 2:11; 4:48;** [l]Mt 16:1; Mk 8:11–12; Lk 11:16; Jn 2:18; 6:30; 1Co 1:22
39 [m]Mt 16:4; Lk 11:29
40 [n]Jnh 1:17; [o]**Mt 8:20;** [p]**Mt 16:21**
41 [q]Jnh 1:2; [r]Jnh 3:5
42 [s]1Ki 10:1; 2Ch 9:1
45 [t]2Pe 2:20
46 [u]Mt 1:18; 2:11,13–14,20; Lk 1:43; 2:33–34,48, 51; Jn 2:1,5; 19:25–26; [v]Mt 13:55; Jn 2:12; 7:3,5; Ac 1:14; 1Co 9:5; Gal 1:19
50 [w]Mt 6:10; Jn 15:14

Ch. 13

1 [a]ver 36; Mt 9:28
2 [b]Lk 5:3
8 [c]Ge 26:12
9 [d]**Mt 11:15**
11 [e]**Mt 3:2;** [f]Mt 11:25; 16:17; 19:11; Jn 6:65; 1Co 2:10,14; Col 1:27; 1Jn 2:20,27
12 [g]**Mt 25:29**
13 [h]Dt 29:4; Jer 5:21; Eze 12:2
14 [i]ver 35; **Mt 1:22**

[e]*41* Or *something;* also in verse 42
[f]*43* Greek *unclean*
[g]*47* Some manuscripts do not have verse 47.

you will be ever seeing but never
 perceiving.
15For this people's heart has become
 calloused;
they hardly hear with their ears,
and they have closed their eyes.
Otherwise they might see with their
 eyes,
hear with their ears,
understand with their hearts
and turn, and I would heal them.'[a][j]

16"But blessed are your eyes because they see, and your ears because they hear.[k] 17For I tell you the truth, many prophets and righteous men longed to see what you see[l] but did not see it, and to hear what you hear but did not hear it.

18"Listen then to what the parable of the sower means: 19When anyone hears the message about the kingdom[m] and does not understand it, the evil one[n] comes and snatches away what was sown in his heart. This is the seed sown along the path. 20The one who received the seed that fell on rocky places is the man who hears the word and at once receives it with joy. 21But since he has no root, he lasts only a short time. When trouble or persecution comes because of the word, he quickly falls away.[o] 22The one who received the seed that fell among the thorns is the man who hears the word, but the worries of this life and the deceitfulness of wealth[p] choke it, making it unfruitful. 23But the one who received the seed that fell on good soil is the man who hears the word and understands it. He produces a crop, yielding a hundred, sixty or thirty times what was sown."[q]

The Parable of the Weeds

24Jesus told them another parable: "The kingdom of heaven is like[r] a man who sowed good seed in his field. 25But while everyone was sleeping, his enemy came and sowed weeds among the wheat, and went away. 26When the wheat sprouted and formed ears, then the weeds also appeared.

27"The owner's servants came to him and said, 'Sir, didn't you sow good seed in your field? Where then did the weeds come from?'

28" 'An enemy did this,' he replied.

"The servants asked him, 'Do you want us to go and pull them up?'

29" 'No,' he answered, 'because while you are pulling the weeds, you may root up the wheat with them. 30Let both grow together until the harvest. At that time I will tell the harvesters: First collect the weeds and tie them in bundles to be burned; then gather the wheat and bring it into my barn.' "[s]

The Parables of the Mustard Seed and the Yeast

13:31,32pp—Mk 4:30–32
13:31–33pp—Lk 13:18–21

31He told them another parable: "The kingdom of heaven[t] is like a mustard seed,[u] which a man took and planted in his field. 32Though it is the smallest of all your seeds, yet when it grows, it is the largest of garden plants and becomes a tree, so that the birds of the air come and perch in its branches."[v]

33He told them still another parable: "The kingdom of heaven is like[w] yeast that a woman took and mixed into a large amount[b] of flour[x] until it worked all through the dough."[y]

34Jesus spoke all these things to the crowd in parables; he did not say anything to them without using a parable.[z] 35So was fulfilled[a] what was spoken through the prophet:

"I will open my mouth in parables,
 I will utter things hidden since the
 creation of the world."[c][b]

The Parable of the Weeds Explained

36Then he left the crowd and went into the house. His disciples came to him and said, "Explain to us the parable[c] of the weeds in the field."

37He answered, "The one who sowed the good seed is the Son of Man.[d] 38The field is the world, and the good seed stands for the sons of the kingdom. The weeds are the sons of the evil one,[e] 39and the enemy who sows them is the devil. The harvest[f] is the end of the age,[g] and the harvesters are angels.[h]

40"As the weeds are pulled up and burned in the fire, so it will be at the end of the age. 41The Son of Man[i] will send out his angels,[j] and they will weed out of his kingdom everything that causes sin and all who do evil. 42They will throw them into the fiery furnace, where there will be weeping and gnashing of teeth.[k] 43Then the righteous will shine like the sun[l] in the kingdom of

15 [j]Isa 6:9–10; Jn 12:40; Ac 28:26–27; Ro 11:8
16 [k]Mt 16:17
17 [l]Jn 8:56; Heb 11:13; 1Pe 1:10–12
19 [m]Mt 4:23; [n]**Mt 5:37**
21 [o]Mt 11:6; 26:31
22 [p]Mt 19:23; 1Ti 6:9–10,17
23 [q]ver 8
24 [r]ver 31,33,45,47; Mt 18:23; 20:1; 22:2; 25:1; Mk 4:26,30
30 [s]Mt 3:12
31 [t]**ver 24**; [u]Mt 17:20; Lk 17:6
32 [v]Ps 104:12; Eze 17:23; 31:6; Da 4:12
33 [w]**ver 24**; [x]Ge 18:6; [y]Gal 5:9
34 [z]**Jn 16:25**
35 [a]ver 14; **Mt 1:22**; [b]Ps 78:2; Ro 16:25–26; 1Co 2:7; Eph 3:9; Col 1:26
36 [c]Mt 15:15
37 [d]**Mt 8:20**
38 [e]Jn 8:44–45; 1Jn 3:10
39 [f]Joel 3:13; [g]Mt 24:3; 28:20; [h]Rev 14:15
41 [i]**Mt 8:20**; [j]Mt 24:31
42 [k]**Mt 8:12**
43 [l]Da 12:3

[a]*15* Isaiah 6:9,10
[b]*33* Greek *three satas* (probably about 3/5 bushel or 22 litres)
[c]*35* Psalm 78:2

their Father. He who has ears, let him hear.[m]

The Parables of the Hidden Treasure and the Pearl

44"The kingdom of heaven is like[n] treasure hidden in a field. When a man found it, he hid it again, and then in his joy went and sold all he had and bought that field.[o]

45"Again, the kingdom of heaven is like[p] a merchant looking for fine pearls. 46When he found one of great value, he went away and sold everything he had and bought it.

The Parable of the Net

47"Once again, the kingdom of heaven is like[q] a net that was let down into the lake and caught all kinds[r] of fish. 48When it was full, the fishermen pulled it up on the shore. Then they sat down and collected the good fish in baskets, but threw the bad away. 49This is how it will be at the end of the age. The angels will come and separate the wicked from the righteous[s] 50and throw them into the fiery furnace, where there will be weeping and gnashing of teeth.[t]

51"Have you understood all these things?" Jesus asked.

"Yes," they replied.

52He said to them, "Therefore every teacher of the law who has been instructed about the kingdom of heaven is like the owner of a house who brings out of his storeroom new treasures as well as old."

A Prophet Without Honour

13:54–58pp—Mk 6:1–6

53When Jesus had finished these parables,[u] he moved on from there. 54Coming to his home town, he began teaching the people in their synagogue,[v] and they were amazed.[w] "Where did this man get this wisdom and these miraculous powers?" they asked. 55"Isn't this the carpenter's son?[x] Isn't his mother's[y] name Mary, and aren't his brothers[z] James, Joseph, Simon and Judas? 56Aren't all his sisters with us? Where then did this man get all these things?" 57And they took offence[a] at him.

But Jesus said to them, "Only in his home town and in his own house is a prophet without honour."[b]

58And he did not do many miracles there because of their lack of faith.

43 [m]**Mt 11:15**
44 [n]**ver 24;** [o]Isa 55:1; Mt 19:21; Php 3:7–8
45 [p]**ver 24**
47 [q]**ver 24;** [r]Mt 22:10
49 [s]Mt 25:32
50 [t]**Mt 8:12**
53 [u]**Mt 7:28**
54 [v]**Mt 4:23;** [w]**Mt 7:28**
55 [x]Lk 3:23; Jn 6:42; [y]**Mt 12:46;** [z]**Mt 12:46**
57 [a]Jn 6:61; [b]Lk 4:24; Jn 4:44

Ch. 14

1 [a]Mk 8:15; Lk 3:1,19; 13:31; 23:7–8; Ac 4:27; 12:1; [b]Lk 9:7–9
2 [c]**Mt 3:1**
3 [d]Mt 4:12; 11:2; [e]Lk 3:19–20
4 [f]Lev 18:16; 20:21
5 [g]**Mt 11:9**
10 [h]Mt 17:12
12 [i]Ac 8:2
14 [j]**Mt 9:36;** [k]**Mt 4:23**
17 [l]Mt 16:9
19 [m]1Sa 9:13; Mt 26:26; Mk 8:6; Lk 9:16; 24:30; Ac 2:42; 20:7, 11; 27:35; 1Co 10:16; 1Ti 4:4

John the Baptist Beheaded

14:1–12pp—Mk 6:14–29

14 At that time Herod[a] the tetrarch heard the reports about Jesus,[b] 2and he said to his attendants, "This is John the Baptist;[c] he has risen from the dead! That is why miraculous powers are at work in him."

3Now Herod had arrested John and bound him and put him in prison[d] because of Herodias, his brother Philip's wife,[e] 4for John had been saying to him: "It is not lawful for you to have her."[f] 5Herod wanted to kill John, but he was afraid of the people, because they considered him a prophet.[g]

6On Herod's birthday the daughter of Herodias danced for them and pleased Herod so much 7that he promised with an oath to give her whatever she asked. 8Prompted by her mother, she said, "Give me here on a platter the head of John the Baptist." 9The king was distressed, but because of his oaths and his dinner guests, he ordered that her request be granted 10and had John beheaded[h] in the prison. 11His head was brought in on a platter and given to the girl, who carried it to her mother. 12John's disciples came and took his body and buried it.[i] Then they went and told Jesus.

Jesus Feeds the Five Thousand

14:13–21pp—Mk 6:32–44; Lk 9:10–17; Jn 6:1–13
14:13–21Ref—Mt 15:32–38

13When Jesus heard what had happened, he withdrew by boat privately to a solitary place. Hearing of this, the crowds followed him on foot from the towns. 14When Jesus landed and saw a large crowd, he had compassion on them[j] and healed their sick.[k]

15As evening approached, the disciples came to him and said, "This is a remote place, and it's already getting late. Send the crowds away, so that they can go to the villages and buy themselves some food."

16Jesus replied, "They do not need to go away. You give them something to eat."

17"We have here only five loaves[l] of bread and two fish," they answered.

18"Bring them here to me," he said. 19And he directed the people to sit down on the grass. Taking the five loaves and the two fish and looking up to heaven, he gave thanks and broke the loaves.[m] Then he gave them to the disciples, and the disciples gave them to the people.

20They all ate and were satisfied, and the
disciples picked up twelve basketfuls of
broken pieces that were left over. 21The
number of those who ate was about five
thousand men, besides women and
children.

Jesus Walks on the Water

14:22–33pp—Mk 6:45–51; Jn 6:15–21
14:34–36pp—Mk 6:53–56

22Immediately Jesus made the disci-
ples get into the boat and go on ahead of
him to the other side, while he dis-
missed the crowd. 23After he had
dismissed them, he went up on a moun-
tainside by himself to pray.[n] When
evening came, he was there alone, 24but
the boat was already a considerable dis-
tance[a] from land, buffeted by the waves
because the wind was against it.
25During the fourth watch of the night
Jesus went out to them, walking on the
lake. 26When the disciples saw him
walking on the lake, they were terrified.
"It's a ghost,"[o] they said, and cried out
in fear.
27But Jesus immediately said to them:
"Take courage![p] It is I. Don't be afraid."[q]
28"Lord, if it's you," Peter replied,
"tell me to come to you on the water."
29"Come," he said.
Then Peter got down out of the boat,
walked on the water and came towards
Jesus. 30But when he saw the wind, he
was afraid and, beginning to sink, cried
out, "Lord, save me!"
31Immediately Jesus reached out his
hand and caught him. "You of little
faith,"[r] he said, "why did you doubt?"
32And when they climbed into the
boat, the wind died down. 33Then those
who were in the boat worshipped him,
saying, "Truly you are the Son of
God."[s]
34When they had crossed over, they
landed at Gennesaret. 35And when the
men of that place recognised Jesus, they
sent word to all the surrounding coun-
try. People brought all their sick to him
36and begged him to let the sick just
touch the edge of his cloak,[t] and all who
touched him were healed.

Clean and Unclean

15:1–20pp—Mk 7:1–23

15 Then some Pharisees and
teachers of the law came to
Jesus from Jerusalem and asked, 2"Why
do your disciples break the tradition of
the elders? They don't wash their hands
before they eat!"[a]

23 [n]**Lk 3:21**
26 [o]Lk 24:37
27 [p]Mt 9:2; Ac 23:11; [q]Da 10:12; Mt 17:7; 28:10; Lk 1:13,30; 2:10; Ac 18:9; 23:11; Rev 1:17
31 [r]**Mt 6:30**
33 [s]Ps 2:7; **Mt 4:3**
36 [t]**Mt 9:20**

Ch. 15

2 [a]Lk 11:38
4 [b]Ex 20:12; Dt 5:16; Eph 6:2; [c]Ex 21:17; Lev 20:9
9 [d]Col 2:20–22; [e]Isa 29:13; Mal 2:2
11 [f]**Ac 10:14–15;** [g]ver 18
13 [h]Isa 60:21; 61:3
14 [i]Mt 23:16,24; Ro 2:19; [j]Lk 6:39
15 [k]Mt 13:36
16 [l]Mt 16:9
18 [m]Mt 12:34; Lk 6:45; Jas 3:6
19 [n]Gal 5:19–21
20 [o]Ro 14:14
21 [p]**Mt 11:21**

3Jesus replied, "And why do you
break the command of God for the sake
of your tradition? 4For God said, 'Hon-
our your father and mother'[a][b] and 'Any-
one who curses his father or mother
must be put to death.'[b][c] 5But you say
that if a man says to his father or
mother, 'Whatever help you might
otherwise have received from me is a
gift devoted to God,' 6he is not to 'hon-
our his father'[c] with it. Thus you nullify
the word of God for the sake of your
tradition. 7You hypocrites! Isaiah was
right when he prophesied about you:

8" 'These people honour me with their
lips,
but their hearts are far from me.
9They worship me in vain;
their teachings are but rules taught
by men.[d]'[d][e]"

10Jesus called the crowd to him and
said, "Listen and understand. 11What
goes into a man's mouth does not make
him 'unclean',[f] but what comes out of
his mouth, that is what makes him
'unclean'."[g]
12Then the disciples came to him and
asked, "Do you know that the Pharisees
were offended when they heard this?"
13He replied, "Every plant that my
heavenly Father has not planted[h] will be
pulled up by the roots. 14Leave them;
they are blind guides.[e][i] If a blind man
leads a blind man, both will fall into a
pit."[j]
15Peter said, "Explain the parable to
us."[k]
16"Are you still so dull?"[l] Jesus asked
them. 17"Don't you see that whatever
enters the mouth goes into the stomach
and then out of the body? 18But the
things that come out of the mouth come
from the heart,[m] and these make a man
'unclean'. 19For out of the heart come
evil thoughts, murder, adultery, sexual
immorality, theft, false testimony, slan-
der.[n] 20These are what make a man 'un-
clean';[o] but eating with unwashed
hands does not make him 'unclean'."

The Faith of the Canaanite Woman

15:21–28pp—Mk 7:24–30

21Leaving that place, Jesus withdrew
to the region of Tyre and Sidon.[p] 22A

[a]24 Greek *many stadia*
[a]4 Exodus 20:12; Deut. 5:16
[b]4 Exodus 21:17; Lev. 20:9
[c]6 Some manuscripts *father or his mother*
[d]9 Isaiah 29:13
[e]14 Some manuscripts *guides of the blind*

Canaanite woman from that vicinity came to him, crying out, "Lord, Son of David,[q] have mercy on me! My daughter is suffering terribly from demon-possession."[r]

23 Jesus did not answer a word. So his disciples came to him and urged him, "Send her away, for she keeps crying out after us."

24 He answered, "I was sent only to the lost sheep of Israel."[s]

25 The woman came and knelt before him.[t] "Lord, help me!" she said.

26 He replied, "It is not right to take the children's bread and toss it to their dogs."

27 "Yes, Lord," she said, "but even the dogs eat the crumbs that fall from their masters' table."

28 Then Jesus answered, "Woman, you have great faith![u] Your request is granted." And her daughter was healed from that very hour.

Jesus Feeds the Four Thousand

15:29–31pp—Mk 7:31–37
15:32–39pp—Mk 8:1–10
15:32–39Ref—Mt 14:13–21

29 Jesus left there and went along the Sea of Galilee. Then he went up on a mountainside and sat down. 30 Great crowds came to him, bringing the lame, the blind, the crippled, the mute and many others, and laid them at his feet; and he healed them.[v] 31 The people were amazed when they saw the mute speaking, the crippled made well, the lame walking and the blind seeing. And they praised the God of Israel.[w]

32 Jesus called his disciples to him and said, "I have compassion for these people;[x] they have already been with me three days and have nothing to eat. I do not want to send them away hungry, or they may collapse on the way."

33 His disciples answered, "Where could we get enough bread in this remote place to feed such a crowd?"

34 "How many loaves do you have?" Jesus asked.

"Seven," they replied, "and a few small fish."

35 He told the crowd to sit down on the ground. 36 Then he took the seven loaves and the fish, and when he had given thanks, he broke them[y] and gave them to the disciples, and they in turn to the people. 37 They all ate and were satisfied. Afterwards the disciples picked up seven basketfuls of broken pieces that were left over.[z] 38 The number of those who ate was four thousand, besides women and children. 39 After Jesus had sent the crowd away, he got into the boat and went to the vicinity of Magadan.

22 [q]**Mt 9:27**; [r]**Mt 4:24**
24 [s]Mt 10:6,23; Ro 15:8
25 [t]**Mt 8:2**
28 [u]**Mt 9:22**
30 [v]**Mt 4:23**
31 [w]**Mt 9:8**
32 [x]**Mt 9:36**
36 [y]**Mt 14:19**
37 [z]Mt 16:10

Ch. 16

1 [a]**Ac 4:1**; [b]**Mt 12:38**
3 [c]Lk 12:54–56
4 [d]Mt 12:39
6 [e]Lk 12:1
8 [f]**Mt 6:30**
9 [g]Mt 14:17–21
10 [h]Mt 15:34–38
12 [i]**Ac 4:1**
14 [j]**Mt 3:1**

The Demand for a Sign

16:1–12pp—Mk 8:11–21

16 The Pharisees and Sadducees[a] came to Jesus and tested him by asking him to show them a sign from heaven.[b]

2 He replied,[a] "When evening comes, you say, 'It will be fair weather, for the sky is red,' 3 and in the morning, 'Today it will be stormy, for the sky is red and overcast.' You know how to interpret the appearance of the sky, but you cannot interpret the signs of the times.[c] 4 A wicked and adulterous generation looks for a miraculous sign, but none will be given it except the sign of Jonah."[d] Jesus then left them and went away.

The Yeast of the Pharisees and Sadducees

5 When they went across the lake, the disciples forgot to take bread. 6 "Be careful," Jesus said to them. "Be on your guard against the yeast of the Pharisees and Sadducees."[e]

7 They discussed this among themselves and said, "It is because we didn't bring any bread."

8 Aware of their discussion, Jesus asked, "You of little faith,[f] why are you talking among yourselves about having no bread? 9 Do you still not understand? Don't you remember the five loaves for the five thousand, and how many basketfuls you gathered?[g] 10 Or the seven loaves for the four thousand, and how many basketfuls you gathered?[h] 11 How is it you don't understand that I was not talking to you about bread? But be on your guard against the yeast of the Pharisees and Sadducees." 12 Then they understood that he was not telling them to guard against the yeast used in bread, but against the teaching of the Pharisees and Sadducees.[i]

Peter's Confession of Christ

16:13–16pp—Mk 8:27–29; Lk 9:18–20

13 When Jesus came to the region of Caesarea Philippi, he asked his disciples, "Who do people say the Son of Man is?"

14 They replied, "Some say John the Baptist;[j] others say Elijah; and still

a2 Some early manuscripts do not have the rest of verse 2 and all of verse 3.

others, Jeremiah or one of the prophets."[k]

15"But what about you?" he asked. "Who do you say I am?"

16Simon Peter answered, "You are the Christ,[b] the Son of the living God."[l]

17Jesus replied, "Blessed are you, Simon son of Jonah, for this was not revealed to you by man,[m] but by my Father in heaven.[n] 18And I tell you that you are Peter,[c][o] and on this rock I will build my church,[p] and the gates of Hades[d] will not overcome it.[e] 19I will give you the keys[q] of the kingdom of heaven; whatever you bind on earth will be[f] bound in heaven, and whatever you loose on earth will be[f] loosed in heaven."[r] 20Then he warned his disciples not to tell anyone[s] that he was the Christ.

Jesus Predicts His Death

16:21–28pp—Mk 8:31–9:1; Lk 9:22–27

21From that time on Jesus began to explain to his disciples that he must go to Jerusalem[t] and suffer many things[u] at the hands of the elders, chief priests and teachers of the law,[v] and that he must be killed[w] and on the third day[x] be raised to life.[y]

22Peter took him aside and began to rebuke him. "Never, Lord!" he said. "This shall never happen to you!"

23Jesus turned and said to Peter, "Get behind me, Satan![z] You are a stumbling-block to me; you do not have in mind the things of God, but the things of men."

24Then Jesus said to his disciples, "If anyone would come after me, he must deny himself and take up his cross and follow me.[a] 25For whoever wants to save his life[g] will lose it, but whoever loses his life for me will find it.[b] 26What good will it be for a man if he gains the whole world, yet forfeits his soul? Or what can a man give in exchange for his soul? 27For the Son of Man[c] is going to come[d] in his Father's glory with his angels, and then he will reward each person according to what he has done.[e] 28I tell you the truth, some who are standing here will not taste death before they see the Son of Man coming in his kingdom."

The Transfiguration

17:1–8pp—Lk 9:28–36
17:1–13pp—Mk 9:2–13

17 After six days Jesus took with him Peter, James and John[a] the brother of James, and led them up a high mountain by themselves. 2There he was transfigured before them. His face shone like the sun, and his clothes became as white as the light. 3Just then there appeared before them Moses and Elijah, talking with Jesus.

4Peter said to Jesus, "Lord, it is good for us to be here. If you wish, I will put up three shelters—one for you, one for Moses and one for Elijah."

5While he was still speaking, a bright cloud enveloped them, and a voice from the cloud said, "This is my Son, whom I love; with him I am well pleased.[b] Listen to him!"[c]

6When the disciples heard this, they fell face down to the ground, terrified. 7But Jesus came and touched them. "Get up," he said. "Don't be afraid."[d] 8When they looked up, they saw no-one except Jesus.

9As they were coming down the mountain, Jesus instructed them, "Don't tell anyone[e] what you have seen, until the Son of Man[f] has been raised from the dead."[g]

10The disciples asked him, "Why then do the teachers of the law say that Elijah must come first?"

11Jesus replied, "To be sure, Elijah comes and will restore all things.[h] 12But I tell you, Elijah has already come,[i] and they did not recognise him, but have done to him everything they wished.[j] In the same way the Son of Man is going to suffer[k] at their hands." 13Then the disciples understood that he was talking to them about John the Baptist.[l]

The Healing of a Boy With a Demon

17:14–19pp—Mk 9:14–28; Lk 9:37–42

14When they came to the crowd, a man approached Jesus and knelt before him. 15"Lord, have mercy on my son," he said. "He has seizures[m] and is suffering greatly. He often falls into the fire or into the water. 16I brought him to your disciples, but they could not heal him."

17"O unbelieving and perverse generation," Jesus replied, "how long shall I stay with you? How long shall I put up with you? Bring the boy here to me." 18Jesus rebuked the demon, and it came out of the boy, and he was healed from that moment.

19Then the disciples came to Jesus in

14 *k*Mk 6:15; Jn 1:21
16 *l***Mt 4:3**; Ps 42:2; Jer 10:10; Ac 14:15; 2Co 6:16; 1Th 1:9; 1Ti 3:15; Heb 10:31; 12:22
17 *m*1Co 15:50; Eph 6:12; Heb 2:14; *n***Mt 13:11**
18 *o*Jn 1:42; *p***Eph 2:20**
19 *q*Isa 22:22; Rev 3:7; *r*Mt 18:18; Jn 20:23
20 *s***Mk 8:30**
21 *t***Lk 9:51**; *u*Ps 22:6; Isa 53:3; Mt 26:67–68; Mk 10:34; Lk 17:25; Jn 18:22–23; 19:3; *v*Mt 27:1–2; *w*Ac 2:23; 3:13; *x*Hos 6:2; Mt 12:40; Lk 24:21,46; Jn 2:19; 1Co 15:3–4; *y*Mt 17:22–23; Mk 9:31; Lk 9:22; 18:31–33; 24:6–7
23 *z***Mt 4:10**
24 *a*Mt 10:38; Lk 14:27
25 *b***Jn 12:25**
27 *c***Mt 8:20**; *d***Lk 17:30**; Jn 14:3; Ac 1:11; **1Co 1:7; 1Th 2:19**; 4:16; **Rev 1:7**; 22:7,12,20; *e*2Ch 6:23; Job 34:11; Ps 62:12; Jer 17:10; Eze 18:20; 1Co 3:12–15; 2Co 5:10; Rev 22:12

Ch. 17

1 *a***Mt 4:21**
5 *b***Mt 3:17**; *c*Ac 3:22–23
7 *d***Mt 14:27**
9 *e***Mk 8:30**; *f***Mt 8:20**; *g***Mt 16:21**
11 *h*Mal 4:6; Lk 1:16–17
12 *i***Mt 11:14**; *j*Mt 14:3,10; *k***Mt 16:21**
13 *l***Mt 3:1**
15 *m*Mt 4:24

b16 Or *Messiah;* also in verse 20
c18 *Peter* means *rock.* d18 Or *hell*
e18 Or *not prove stronger than it* f19 Or *have been*
g25 The Greek word means either *life* or *soul;* also in verse 26.

private and asked, "Why couldn't we
drive it out?"
20He replied, "Because you have so
little faith. I tell you the truth, if you
have faith[n] as small as a mustard seed,[o]
you can say to this mountain, 'Move
from here to there' and it will move.[p]
Nothing will be impossible for you."[a]
22When they came together in Galilee,
he said to them, "The Son of Man[q] is
going to be betrayed into the hands of
men. 23They will kill him,[r] and on the
third day[s] he will be raised to life."[t] And
the disciples were filled with grief.

The Temple Tax

24After Jesus and his disciples arrived
in Capernaum, the collectors of the two-
drachma tax[u] came to Peter and asked,
"Doesn't your teacher pay the temple
tax?"[b]
25"Yes, he does," he replied.
When Peter came into the house,
Jesus was the first to speak. "What do
you think, Simon?" he asked. "From
whom do the kings of the earth collect
duty and taxes[v]—from their own sons
or from others?"
26"From others," Peter answered.
"Then the sons are exempt," Jesus
said to him. 27"But so that we may not
offend[w] them, go to the lake and throw
out your line. Take the first fish you
catch; open its mouth and you will find
a four-drachma coin. Take it and give it
to them for my tax and yours."

The Greatest in the Kingdom of Heaven

18:1–5pp—Mk 9:33–37; Lk 9:46–48

18 At that time the disciples came
to Jesus and asked, "Who is the
greatest in the kingdom of heaven?"
2He called a little child and had him
stand among them. 3And he said: "I tell
you the truth, unless you change and
become like little children,[a] you will
never enter the kingdom of heaven.[b]
4Therefore, whoever humbles himself
like this child is the greatest in the king-
dom of heaven.[c]
5"And whoever welcomes a little
child like this in my name welcomes
me.[d] 6But if anyone causes one of these
little ones who believe in me to sin,[e] it
would be better for him to have a large
millstone hung around his neck and to
be drowned in the depths of the sea.[f]
7"Woe to the world because of the
things that cause people to sin! Such
things must come, but woe to the man
through whom they come![g] 8If your
hand or your foot causes you to sin,[h] cut
it off and throw it away. It is better for
you to enter life maimed or crippled
than to have two hands or two feet and
be thrown into eternal fire. 9And if your
eye causes you to sin,[i] gouge it out and
throw it away. It is better for you to
enter life with one eye than to have two
eyes and be thrown into the fire of hell.[j]

The Parable of the Lost Sheep

18:12–14pp—Lk 15:4–7

10"See that you do not look down on
one of these little ones. For I tell you that
their angels[k] in heaven always see the
face of my Father in heaven.[a]
12"What do you think? If a man owns
a hundred sheep, and one of them wan-
ders away, will he not leave the ninety-
nine on the hills and go to look for the
one that wandered off? 13And if he finds
it, I tell you the truth, he is happier
about that one sheep than about the
ninety-nine that did not wander off. 14In
the same way your Father in heaven is
not willing that any of these little ones
should be lost.

A Brother Who Sins Against You

15"If your brother sins against you,[b]
go and show him his fault,[l] just between
the two of you. If he listens to you, you
have won your brother over. 16But if he
will not listen, take one or two others
along, so that 'every matter may be
established by the testimony of two or
three witnesses.'[c][m] 17If he refuses to lis-
ten to them, tell it to the church;[n] and if
he refuses to listen even to the church,
treat him as you would a pagan or a tax
collector.[o]
18"I tell you the truth, whatever you
bind on earth will be[d] bound in heaven,
and whatever you loose on earth will
be[d] loosed in heaven.[p]
19"Again, I tell you that if two of you
on earth agree about anything you ask
for, it will be done for you[q] by my Father
in heaven. 20For where two or three
come together in my name, there am I
with them."[r]

20 [n]**Mt 21:21;** [o]Mt 13:31; Lk 17:6; [p]1Co 13:2
22 [q]**Mt 8:20**
23 [r]Ac 2:23; 3:13; [s]**Mt 16:21;** [t]**Mt 16:21**
24 [u]Ex 30:13
25 [v]Mt 22:17–21; Ro 13:7
27 [w]Jn 6:61

Ch. 18

3 [a]Mt 19:14; 1Pe 2:2; [b]**Mt 3:2**
4 [c]**Mk 9:35**
5 [d]Mt 10:40
6 [e]**Mt 5:29;** [f]Mk 9:42; Lk 17:2
7 [g]Lk 17:1
8 [h]**Mt 5:29**
9 [i]**Mt 5:29;** [j]**Mt 5:22**
10 [k]Ge 48:16; Ps 34:7; Ac 12:11, 15; Heb 1:14
15 [l]Lev 19:17; Lk 17:3; Gal 6:1; Jas 5:19–20
16 [m]Nu 35:30; Dt 17:6; 19:15; Jn 8:17; 2Co 13:1; 1Ti 5:19; Heb 10:28
17 [n]1Co 6:1–6; [o]**Ro 16:17**
18 [p]Mt 16:19; Jn 20:23
19 [q]**Mt 7:7**
20 [r]**Mt 28:20**

a20 Some manuscripts *you.* 21*But this kind does not go out except by prayer and fasting.*
b24 Greek *the two drachmas*
a10 Some manuscripts *heaven.* 11*The Son of Man came to save what was lost.*
b15 Some manuscripts do not have *against you.*
c16 Deut. 19:15
d18 Or *have been*

The Parable of the Unmerciful Servant

21Then Peter came to Jesus and asked, "Lord, how many times shall I forgive my brother when he sins against me?[s] Up to seven times?"[t]

22Jesus answered, "I tell you, not seven times, but seventy-seven times.[e][u]

23"Therefore, the kingdom of heaven is like[v] a king who wanted to settle accounts[w] with his servants. 24As he began the settlement, a man who owed him ten thousand talents[f] was brought to him. 25Since he was not able to pay,[x] the master ordered that he and his wife and his children and all that he had be sold[y] to repay the debt.

26"The servant fell on his knees before him.[z] 'Be patient with me,' he begged, 'and I will pay back everything.' 27The servant's master took pity on him, cancelled the debt and let him go.

28"But when that servant went out, he found one of his fellow-servants who owed him a hundred denarii.[g] He grabbed him and began to choke him. 'Pay back what you owe me!' he demanded.

29"His fellow-servant fell to his knees and begged him, 'Be patient with me, and I will pay you back.'

30"But he refused. Instead, he went off and had the man thrown into prison until he could pay the debt. 31When the other servants saw what had happened, they were greatly distressed and went and told their master everything that had happened.

32"Then the master called the servant in. 'You wicked servant,' he said, 'I cancelled all that debt of yours because you begged me to. 33Shouldn't you have had mercy on your fellow-servant just as I had on you?' 34In anger his master turned him over to the jailers to be tortured, until he should pay back all he owed.

35"This is how my heavenly Father will treat each of you unless you forgive your brother from your heart."[a]

Divorce

19:1–9pp—Mk 10:1–12

19 When Jesus had finished saying these things,[a] he left Galilee and went into the region of Judea to the other side of the Jordan. 2Large crowds followed him, and he healed them[b] there.

3Some Pharisees came to him to test him. They asked, "Is it lawful for a man to divorce his wife[c] for any and every reason?"

4"Haven't you read," he replied, "that at the beginning the Creator 'made them male and female',[a][d] 5and said, 'For this reason a man will leave his father and mother and be united to his wife, and the two will become one flesh'[b]?[e] 6So they are no longer two, but one. Therefore what God has joined together, let man not separate."

7"Why then," they asked, "did Moses command that a man give his wife a certificate of divorce and send her away?"[f]

8Jesus replied, "Moses permitted you to divorce your wives because your hearts were hard. But it was not this way from the beginning. 9I tell you that anyone who divorces his wife, except for marital unfaithfulness, and marries another woman commits adultery."[g]

10The disciples said to him, "If this is the situation between a husband and wife, it is better not to marry."

11Jesus replied, "Not everyone can accept this word, but only those to whom it has been given.[h] 12For some are eunuchs because they were born that way; others were made that way by men; and others have renounced marriage[c] because of the kingdom of heaven. The one who can accept this should accept it."

The Little Children and Jesus

19:13–15pp—Mk 10:13–16; Lk 18:15–17

13Then little children were brought to Jesus for him to place his hands on them[i] and pray for them. But the disciples rebuked those who brought them.

14Jesus said, "Let the little children come to me, and do not hinder them, for the kingdom of heaven belongs[j] to such as these."[k] 15When he had placed his hands on them, he went on from there.

The Rich Young Man

19:16–29pp—Mk 10:17–30; Lk 18:18–30

16Now a man came up to Jesus and asked, "Teacher, what good thing must I do to get eternal life[l]?"[m]

17"Why do you ask me about what is good?" Jesus replied. "There is only One who is good. If you want to enter life, obey the commandments."[n]

18"Which ones?" the man enquired.

21 [s]**Mt 6:14;** [t]Lk 17:4
22 [u]Ge 4:24
23 [v]**Mt 13:24;** [w]Mt 25:19
25 [x]Lk 7:42; [y]Lev 25:39; 2Ki 4:1; Ne 5:5,8
26 [z]**Mt 8:2**
35 [a]**Mt 6:14; Jas 2:13**

Ch. 19

1 [a]**Mt 7:28**
2 [b]**Mt 4:23**
3 [c]Mt 5:31
4 [d]Ge 1:27; 5:2
5 [e]Ge 2:24; 1Co 6:16; Eph 5:31
7 [f]Dt 24:1–4; Mt 5:31
9 [g]**Lk 16:18**
11 [h]**Mt 13:11;** 1Co 7:7–9,17
13 [i]**Mk 5:23**
14 [j]**Mt 25:34;** [k]Mt 18:3; 1Pe 2:2
16 [l]**Mt 25:46;** [m]Lk 10:25
17 [n]Lev 18:5

[e]22 Or *seventy times seven*
[f]24 That is, millions of pounds
[g]28 That is, a few pounds
[a]4 Gen. 1:27 [b]5 Gen. 2:24
[c]12 Or *have made themselves eunuchs*

Jesus replied, "'Do not murder, do
not commit adultery,[o] do not steal, do
not give false testimony, 19honour your
father and mother,'[d][p] and 'love your
neighbour as yourself.'[e]"[q]
20"All these I have kept," the young
man said. "What do I still lack?"
21Jesus answered, "If you want to be
perfect,[r] go, sell your possessions and
give to the poor,[s] and you will have
treasure in heaven.[t] Then come, follow
me."
22When the young man heard this, he
went away sad, because he had great
wealth.
23Then Jesus said to his disciples, "I
tell you the truth, it is hard for a rich
man[u] to enter the kingdom of heaven.
24Again I tell you, it is easier for a camel
to go through the eye of a needle than
for a rich man to enter the kingdom of
God."
25When the disciples heard this, they
were greatly astonished and asked,
"Who then can be saved?"
26Jesus looked at them and said,
"With man this is impossible, but with
God all things are possible."[v]
27Peter answered him, "We have left
everything to follow you![w] What then
will there be for us?"
28Jesus said to them, "I tell you the
truth, at the renewal of all things, when
the Son of Man sits on his glorious
throne,[x] you who have followed me will
also sit on twelve thrones, judging the
twelve tribes of Israel.[y] 29And everyone
who has left houses or brothers or sis-
ters or father or mother[f] or children or
fields for my sake will receive a hundred
times as much and will inherit eternal
life.[z] 30But many who are first will be
last, and many who are last will be first.[a]

The Parable of the Workers in the Vineyard

20 "For the kingdom of heaven is
like[a] a landowner who went out
early in the morning to hire men to work
in his vineyard.[b] 2He agreed to pay them
a denarius for the day and sent them
into his vineyard.
3"About the third hour he went out
and saw others standing in the market-
place doing nothing. 4He told them,
'You also go and work in my vineyard,
and I will pay you whatever is right.' 5So
they went.
"He went out again about the sixth
hour and the ninth hour and did the
same thing. 6About the eleventh hour
he went out and found still others
standing around. He asked them, 'Why
have you been standing here all day
long doing nothing?'
7"'Because no-one has hired us,' they
answered.
"He said to them, 'You also go and
work in my vineyard.'
8"When evening came,[c] the owner of
the vineyard said to his foreman, 'Call
the workers and pay them their wages,
beginning with the last ones hired and
going on to the first.'
9"The workers who were hired about
the eleventh hour came and each re-
ceived a denarius. 10So when those
came who were hired first, they ex-
pected to receive more. But each one of
them also received a denarius. 11When
they received it, they began to grumble[d]
against the landowner. 12'These men
who were hired last worked only one
hour,' they said, 'and you have made
them equal to us who have borne the
burden of the work and the heat[e] of the
day.'
13"But he answered one of them,
'Friend,[f] I am not being unfair to you.
Didn't you agree to work for a denarius?
14Take your pay and go. I want to give
the man who was hired last the same as
I gave you. 15Don't I have the right to
do what I want with my own money?
Or are you envious because I am
generous?'[g]
16"So the last will be first, and the first
will be last."[h]

Jesus Again Predicts His Death

20:17–19pp—Mk 10:32–34; Lk 18:31–33

17Now as Jesus was going up to Jeru-
salem, he took the twelve disciples
aside and said to them, 18"We are going
up to Jerusalem,[i] and the Son of Man[j]
will be betrayed to the chief priests and
the teachers of the law.[k] They will con-
demn him to death 19and will turn him
over to the Gentiles to be mocked and
flogged[l] and crucified.[m] On the third
day[n] he will be raised to life!"[o]

A Mother's Request

20:20–28pp—Mk 10:35–45

20Then the mother of Zebedee's sons[p]
came to Jesus with her sons and, kneel-
ing down,[q] asked a favour of him.
21"What is it you want?" he asked.
She said, "Grant that one of these two

18 [o]Jas 2:11
19 [p]Ex 20:12–16; Dt 5:16–20; [q]Lev 19:18; **Mt 5:43**
21 [r]Mt 5:48; [s]**Ac 2:45**; [t]**Mt 6:20**
23 [u]Mt 13:22; 1Ti 6:9–10
26 [v]Ge 18:14; Job 42:2; Jer 32:17; Lk 1:37; 18:27; Ro 4:21
27 [w]**Mt 4:19**
28 [x]Mt 20:21; 25:31; [y]Lk 22:28–30; Rev 3:21; 4:4; 20:4
29 [z]Mt 6:33; **25:46**
30 [a]Mt 20:16; Mk 10:31; Lk 13:30

Ch. 20

1 [a]**Mt 13:24**; [b]Mt 21:28,33
8 [c]Lev 19:13; Dt 24:15
11 [d]Jnh 4:1
12 [e]Jnh 4:8; Lk 12:55; Jas 1:11
13 [f]Mt 22:12; 26:50
15 [g]Dt 15:9; Mk 7:22
16 [h]**Mt 19:30**
18 [i]**Lk 9:51**; [j]**Mt 8:20**; [k]Mt 27:1–2
19 [l]**Mt 16:21**; [m]**Ac 2:23**; [n]**Mt 16:21**; [o]**Mt 16:21**
20 [p]**Mt 4:21**; [q]**Mt 8:2**

[d]19 Exodus 20:12–16; Deut. 5:16–20
[e]19 Lev. 19:18
[f]29 Some manuscripts *mother or wife*

sons of mine may sit at your right and the other at your left in your kingdom."[r]

22"You don't know what you are asking," Jesus said to them. "Can you drink the cup[s] I am going to drink?"

"We can," they answered.

23Jesus said to them, "You will indeed drink from my cup,[t] but to sit at my right or left is not for me to grant. These places belong to those for whom they have been prepared by my Father."

24When the ten heard about this, they were indignant[u] with the two brothers. 25Jesus called them together and said, "You know that the rulers of the Gentiles lord it over them, and their high officials exercise authority over them. 26Not so with you. Instead, whoever wants to become great among you must be your servant,[v] 27and whoever wants to be first must be your slave—28just as the Son of Man[w] did not come to be served, but to serve,[x] and to give his life as a ransom[y] for many."

Two Blind Men Receive Sight

20:29–34pp—Mk 10:46–52; Lk 18:35–43

29As Jesus and his disciples were leaving Jericho, a large crowd followed him. 30Two blind men were sitting by the roadside, and when they heard that Jesus was going by, they shouted, "Lord, Son of David,[z] have mercy on us!"

31The crowd rebuked them and told them to be quiet, but they shouted all the louder, "Lord, Son of David, have mercy on us!"

32Jesus stopped and called them. "What do you want me to do for you?" he asked.

33"Lord," they answered, "we want our sight."

34Jesus had compassion on them and touched their eyes. Immediately they received their sight and followed him.

The Triumphal Entry

21:1–9pp—Mk 11:1–10; Lk 19:29–38
21:4–9pp—Jn 12:12–15

21 As they approached Jerusalem and came to Bethphage on the Mount of Olives,[a] Jesus sent two disciples, 2saying to them, "Go to the village ahead of you, and at once you will find a donkey tied there, with her colt by her. Untie them and bring them to me. 3If anyone says anything to you, tell him that the Lord needs them, and he will send them right away."

4This took place to fulfil[b] what was spoken through the prophet:

5"Say to the Daughter of Zion,
'See, your king comes to you,
gentle and riding on a donkey,
on a colt, the foal of a donkey.' "[a][c]

6The disciples went and did as Jesus had instructed them. 7They brought the donkey and the colt, placed their cloaks on them, and Jesus sat on them. 8A very large crowd spread their cloaks[d] on the road, while others cut branches from the trees and spread them on the road. 9The crowds that went ahead of him and those that followed shouted,

"Hosanna[b] to the Son of David!"[e]

"Blessed is he who comes in the name of the Lord!"[c][f]

"Hosanna[b] in the highest!"[g]

10When Jesus entered Jerusalem, the whole city was stirred and asked, "Who is this?"

11The crowds answered, "This is Jesus, the prophet[h] from Nazareth in Galilee."

Jesus at the Temple

21:12–16pp—Mk 11:15–18; Lk 19:45–47

12Jesus entered the temple area and drove out all who were buying[i] and selling there. He overturned the tables of the money-changers[j] and the benches of those selling doves.[k] 13"It is written," he said to them, " 'My house will be called a house of prayer,'[d][l] but you are making it a 'den of robbers'.[e]"[m]

14The blind and the lame came to him at the temple, and he healed them.[n] 15But when the chief priests and the teachers of the law saw the wonderful things he did and the children shouting in the temple area, "Hosanna to the Son of David,"[o] they were indignant.[p]

16"Do you hear what these children are saying?" they asked him.

"Yes," replied Jesus, "have you never read,

" 'From the lips of children and infants
you have ordained praise'[f]?"[q]

17And he left them and went out of the city to Bethany,[r] where he spent the night.

21 [r]Mt 19:28
22 [s]Isa 51:17,22; Jer 49:12; Mt 26:39,42; Mk 14:36; Lk 22:42; Jn 18:11
23 [t]Ac 12:2; Rev 1:9
24 [u]Lk 22:24–25
26 [v]**Mk 9:35**
28 [w]**Mt 8:20;** [x]Isa 42:1; Lk 12:37; 22:27; Jn 13:13–16; 2Co 8:9; Php 2:7; [y]Ex 30:12; Isa 44:22; 53:10; Mt 26:28; 1Ti 2:6; Tit 2:14; Heb 9:28; 1Pe 1:18–19
30 [z]**Mt 9:27**

Ch. 21

1 [a]Mt 24:3; 26:30; Mk 14:26; Lk 19:37; 21:37; 22:39; Jn 8:1; Ac 1:12
4 [b]**Mt 1:22**
5 [c]Zec 9:9; Isa 62:11
8 [d]2Ki 9:13
9 [e]ver 15; **Mt 9:27;** [f]Ps 118:26; Mt 23:39; [g]Lk 2:14
11 [h]Dt 18:15; Lk 7:16,39; 24:19; Jn 1:21,25; 6:14; 7:40
12 [i]Dt 14:26; [j]Ex 30:13; [k]Lev 1:14
13 [l]Isa 56:7; [m]Jer 7:11
14 [n]**Mt 4:23**
15 [o]ver 9; **Mt 9:27;** [p]Lk 19:39
16 [q]Ps 8:2
17 [r]Mt 26:6; Mk 11:1; Lk 24:50; Jn 11:1, 18; 12:1

a5 Zech. 9:9
b9 A Hebrew expression meaning "Save!" which became an exclamation of praise; also in verse 15
c9 Psalm 118:26 d13 Isaiah 56:7
e13 Jer. 7:11 f16 Psalm 8:2

The Fig-Tree Withers

21:18–22pp—Mk 11:12–14,20–24

18Early in the morning, as he was on his way back to the city, he was hungry. 19Seeing a fig-tree by the road, he went up to it but found nothing on it except leaves. Then he said to it, "May you never bear fruit again!" Immediately the tree withered.[s]

20When the disciples saw this, they were amazed. "How did the fig-tree wither so quickly?" they asked.

21Jesus replied, "I tell you the truth, if you have faith and do not doubt,[t] not only can you do what was done to the fig-tree, but also you can say to this mountain, 'Go, throw yourself into the sea,' and it will be done. 22If you believe, you will receive whatever you ask for[u] in prayer."

The Authority of Jesus Questioned

21:23–27pp—Mk 11:27–33; Lk 20:1–8

23Jesus entered the temple courts, and, while he was teaching, the chief priests and the elders of the people came to him. "By what authority[v] are you doing these things?" they asked. "And who gave you this authority?"

24Jesus replied, "I will also ask you one question. If you answer me, I will tell you by what authority I am doing these things. 25John's baptism—where did it come from? Was it from heaven, or from men?"

They discussed it among themselves and said, "If we say, 'From heaven', he will ask, 'Then why didn't you believe him?' 26But if we say, 'From men'—we are afraid of the people, for they all hold that John was a prophet."[w]

27So they answered Jesus, "We don't know."

Then he said, "Neither will I tell you by what authority I am doing these things.

The Parable of the Two Sons

28"What do you think? There was a man who had two sons. He went to the first and said, 'Son, go and work today in the vineyard.'[x]

29"'I will not,' he answered, but later he changed his mind and went.

30"Then the father went to the other son and said the same thing. He answered, 'I will, sir,' but he did not go.

31"Which of the two did what his father wanted?"

"The first," they answered.

Jesus said to them, "I tell you the truth, the tax collectors[y] and the prostitutes[z] are entering the kingdom of God ahead of you. 32For John came to you to show you the way of righteousness,[a] and you did not believe him, but the tax collectors[b] and the prostitutes[c] did. And even after you saw this, you did not repent[d] and believe him.

The Parable of the Tenants

21:33–46pp—Mk 12:1–12; Lk 20:9–19

33"Listen to another parable: There was a landowner who planted[e] a vineyard. He put a wall around it, dug a winepress in it and built a watchtower.[f] Then he rented the vineyard to some farmers and went away on a journey.[g] 34When the harvest time approached, he sent his servants[h] to the tenants to collect his fruit.

35"The tenants seized his servants; they beat one, killed another, and stoned a third.[i] 36Then he sent other servants[j] to them, more than the first time, and the tenants treated them in the same way. 37Last of all, he sent his son to them. 'They will respect my son,' he said.

38"But when the tenants saw the son, they said to each other, 'This is the heir.[k] Come, let's kill him[l] and take his inheritance.'[m] 39So they took him and threw him out of the vineyard and killed him.

40"Therefore, when the owner of the vineyard comes, what will he do to those tenants?"

41"He will bring those wretches to a wretched end,"[n] they replied, "and he will rent the vineyard to other tenants,[o] who will give him his share of the crop at harvest time."

42Jesus said to them, "Have you never read in the Scriptures:

> "'The stone the builders rejected
>   has become the capstone;[g]
> the Lord has done this,
>   and it is marvellous in our eyes'[h]?[p]

43"Therefore I tell you that the kingdom of God will be taken away from you[q] and given to a people who will produce its fruit. 44He who falls on this stone will be broken to pieces, but he on whom it falls will be crushed."[i][r]

45When the chief priests and the Pharisees heard Jesus' parables, they

19 [s]Isa 34:4; Jer 8:13
21 [t]Mt 17:20; Lk 17:6; 1Co 13:2; Jas 1:6
22 [u]**Mt 7:7**
23 [v]Ac 4:7; 7:27
26 [w]**Mt 11:9**
28 [x]ver 33; Mt 20:1
31 [y]Lk 7:29; [z]Lk 7:50
32 [a]Mt 3:1–12; [b]Lk 3:12–13; 7:29; [c]Lk 7:36–50; [d]Lk 7:30
33 [e]Ps 80:8; [f]Isa 5:1–7; [g]Mt 25:14–15
34 [h]Mt 22:3
35 [i]2Ch 24:21; Mt 23:34,37; Heb 11:36–37
36 [j]Mt 22:4
38 [k]Heb 1:2; [l]**Mt 12:14**; [m]Ps 2:8
41 [n]Mt 8:11–12; [o]**Ac 13:46**
42 [p]Ps 118:22–23; **Ac 4:11**
43 [q]Mt 8:12
44 [r]**Lk 2:34**

g42 Or *cornerstone* h42 Psalm 118:22,23
i44 Some manuscripts do not have verse 44.

knew he was talking about them. 46They looked for a way to arrest him, but they were afraid of the crowd because the people held that he was a prophet.[s]

The Parable of the Wedding Banquet

22:2-14Ref—Lk 14:16-24

22 Jesus spoke to them again in parables, saying: 2"The kingdom of heaven is like[a] a king who prepared a wedding banquet for his son. 3He sent his servants[b] to those who had been invited to the banquet to tell them to come, but they refused to come.

4"Then he sent some more servants[c] and said, 'Tell those who have been invited that I have prepared my dinner: My oxen and fattened cattle have been slaughtered, and everything is ready. Come to the wedding banquet.'

5"But they paid no attention and went off—one to his field, another to his business. 6The rest seized his servants, ill-treated them and killed them. 7The king was enraged. He sent his army and destroyed those murderers[d] and burned their city.

8"Then he said to his servants, 'The wedding banquet is ready, but those I invited did not deserve to come. 9Go to the street corners[e] and invite to the banquet anyone you find.' 10So the servants went out into the streets and gathered all the people they could find, both good and bad,[f] and the wedding hall was filled with guests.

11"But when the king came in to see the guests, he noticed a man there who was not wearing wedding clothes. 12'Friend,'[g] he asked, 'how did you get in here without wedding clothes?' The man was speechless.

13"Then the king told the attendants, 'Tie him hand and foot, and throw him outside, into the darkness, where there will be weeping and gnashing of teeth.'[h]

14"For many are invited, but few are chosen."[i]

Paying Taxes to Caesar

22:15-22pp—Mk 12:13-17; Lk 20:20-26

15Then the Pharisees went out and laid plans to trap him in his words. 16They sent their disciples to him along with the Herodians.[j] "Teacher," they said, "we know you are a man of integrity and that you teach the way of God in accordance with the truth. You aren't swayed by men, because you pay no attention to who they are. 17Tell us

46 [s]**ver 11,26**

Ch. 22

2 [a]**Mt 13:24**
3 [b]Mt 21:34
4 [c]Mt 21:36
7 [d]Lk 19:27
9 [e]Eze 21:21
10 [f]Mt 13:47-48
12 [g]Mt 20:13; 26:50
13 [h]**Mt 8:12**
14 [i]Rev 17:14
16 [j]Mk 3:6
17 [k]Mt 17:25
21 [l]Ro 13:7
22 [m]Mk 12:12
23 [n]**Ac 4:1**; [o]Ac 23:8; 1Co 15:12
24 [p]Dt 25:5-6
29 [q]Jn 20:9
30 [r]Mt 24:38
32 [s]Ex 3:6; Ac 7:32
33 [t]**Mt 7:28**
34 [u]**Ac 4:1**
35 [v]Lk 7:30; 10:25; 11:45; 14:3

then, what is your opinion? Is it right to pay taxes[k] to Caesar or not?"

18But Jesus, knowing their evil intent, said, "You hypocrites, why are you trying to trap me? 19Show me the coin used for paying the tax." They brought him a denarius, 20and he asked them, "Whose portrait is this? And whose inscription?"

21"Caesar's," they replied.

Then he said to them, "Give to Caesar what is Caesar's,[l] and to God what is God's."

22When they heard this, they were amazed. So they left him and went away.[m]

Marriage at the Resurrection

22:23-33pp—Mk 12:18-27; Lk 20:27-40

23That same day the Sadducees,[n] who say there is no resurrection,[o] came to him with a question. 24"Teacher," they said, "Moses told us that if a man dies without having children, his brother must marry the widow and have children for him.[p] 25Now there were seven brothers among us. The first one married and died, and since he had no children, he left his wife to his brother. 26The same thing happened to the second and third brother, right on down to the seventh. 27Finally, the woman died. 28Now then, at the resurrection, whose wife will she be of the seven, since all of them were married to her?"

29Jesus replied, "You are in error because you do not know the Scriptures[q] or the power of God. 30At the resurrection people will neither marry nor be given in marriage;[r] they will be like the angels in heaven. 31But about the resurrection of the dead—have you not read what God said to you, 32'I am the God of Abraham, the God of Isaac, and the God of Jacob'[a]?[s] He is not the God of the dead but of the living."

33When the crowds heard this, they were astonished at his teaching.[t]

The Greatest Commandment

22:34-40pp—Mk 12:28-31

34Hearing that Jesus had silenced the Sadducees,[u] the Pharisees got together. 35One of them, an expert in the law,[v] tested him with this question: 36"Teacher, which is the greatest commandment in the Law?"

[a]32 Exodus 3:6

37Jesus replied: " 'Love the Lord your
God with all your heart and with all
your soul and with all your mind.'[b][w]
38This is the first and greatest command-
ment. 39And the second is like it: 'Love
your neighbour as yourself.'[c][x] 40All the
Law and the Prophets hang on these
two commandments."[y]

Whose Son Is the Christ?

22:41–46pp—Mk 12:35–37; Lk 20:41–44

41While the Pharisees were gathered
together, Jesus asked them, 42"What do
you think about the Christ?[d] Whose son
is he?"
"The son of David,"[z] they replied.
43He said to them, "How is it then that
David, speaking by the Spirit, calls him
'Lord'? For he says,

44" 'The Lord said to my Lord:
"Sit at my right hand
until I put your enemies
under your feet." '[e][a]

45If then David calls him 'Lord', how can
he be his son?" 46No-one could say a
word in reply, and from that day
on no-one dared to ask him any more
questions.[b]

Seven Woes

23:1–7pp—Mk 12:38,39; Lk 20:45,46
23:37–39pp—Lk 13:34,35

23 Then Jesus said to the crowds
and to his disciples: 2"The
teachers of the law[a] and the Pharisees sit
in Moses' seat. 3So you must obey them
and do everything they tell you. But do
not do what they do, for they do not
practise what they preach. 4They tie up
heavy loads and put them on men's
shoulders, but they themselves are not
willing to lift a finger to move them.[b]
5"Everything they do is done for men
to see:[c] They make their phylacteries[a][d]
wide and the tassels on their garments[e]
long; 6they love the place of honour at
banquets and the most important seats
in the synagogues;[f] 7they love to be
greeted in the market-places and to
have men call them 'Rabbi'.[g]
8"But you are not to be called 'Rabbi',
for you have only one Master and you
are all brothers. 9And do not call anyone
on earth 'father', for you have one
Father,[h] and he is in heaven. 10Nor are
you to be called 'teacher', for you have
one Teacher, the Christ.[b] 11The greatest
among you will be your servant.[i] 12For
whoever exalts himself will be hum-
bled, and whoever humbles himself will
be exalted.[j]
13"Woe to you, teachers of the law
and Pharisees, you hypocrites![k] You
shut the kingdom of heaven in men's
faces. You yourselves do not enter, nor
will you let those enter who are trying
to.[c][l]
15"Woe to you, teachers of the law
and Pharisees, you hypocrites! You
travel over land and sea to win a single
convert,[m] and when he becomes one,
you make him twice as much a son of
hell[n] as you are.
16"Woe to you, blind guides![o] You
say, 'If anyone swears by the temple, it
means nothing; but if anyone swears by
the gold of the temple, he is bound by
his oath.'[p] 17You blind fools! Which is
greater: the gold, or the temple that
makes the gold sacred?[q] 18You also say,
'If anyone swears by the altar, it means
nothing; but if anyone swears by the gift
on it, he is bound by his oath.' 19You
blind men! Which is greater: the gift, or
the altar that makes the gift sacred?[r]
20Therefore, he who swears by the altar
swears by it and by everything on it.
21And he who swears by the temple
swears by it and by the one who dwells[s]
in it. 22And he who swears by heaven
swears by God's throne and by the one
who sits on it.[t]
23"Woe to you, teachers of the law
and Pharisees, you hypocrites! You give
a tenth[u] of your spices—mint, dill and
cummin. But you have neglected the
more important matters of the law—
justice, mercy and faithfulness.[v] You
should have practised the latter, with-
out neglecting the former. 24You blind
guides![w] You strain out a gnat but
swallow a camel.
25"Woe to you, teachers of the law
and Pharisees, you hypocrites! You
clean the outside of the cup and dish,[x]
but inside they are full of greed and
self-indulgence.[y] 26Blind Pharisee! First
clean the inside of the cup and dish, and
then the outside also will be clean.
27"Woe to you, teachers of the law
and Pharisees, you hypocrites! You are
like whitewashed tombs,[z] which look

37 [w]Dt 6:5
39 [x]Lev 19:18; **Mt 5:43**
40 [y]Mt 7:12; Lk 10:25–28
42 [z]**Mt 9:27**
44 [a]Ps 110:1; 1Ki 5:3; Ac 2:34–35; 1Co 15:25; Heb 1:13; 10:13
46 [b]Mk 12:34; Lk 20:40

Ch. 23

2 [a]Ezr 7:6,25
4 [b]Lk 11:46; Ac 15:10; Gal 6:13
5 [c]Mt 6:1–2,5, 16; [d]Ex 13:9; Dt 6:8; [e]Nu 15:38; Dt 22:12
6 [f]Lk 11:43; 14:7; 20:46
7 [g]ver 8; Mt 26:25,49; Mk 9:5; 10:51; Jn 1:38,49; 3:2, 26; 20:16
9 [h]Mal 1:6; Mt 6:9; 7:11
11 [i]**Mk 9:35**
12 [j]1Sa 2:8; Ps 18:27; Pr 3:34; Isa 57:15; Eze 21:26; Lk 1:52; 14:11
13 [k]ver 15,23, 25,27,29; [l]Lk 11:52
15 [m]Ac 2:11; 6:5; 13:43; [n]**Mt 5:22**
16 [o]ver 24; Isa 9:16; Mt 15:14; [p]Mt 5:33–35
17 [q]Ex 30:29
19 [r]Ex 29:37
21 [s]1Ki 8:13; Ps 26:8
22 [t]Ps 11:4; Mt 5:34
23 [u]Lev 27:30; [v]Mic 6:8; Lk 11:42
24 [w]ver 16
25 [x]Mk 7:4; [y]Lk 11:39
27 [z]Lk 11:44; Ac 23:3

[b]37 Deut. 6:5 [c]39 Lev. 19:18
[d]42 Or *Messiah* [e]44 Psalm 110:1
[a]5 That is, boxes containing Scripture verses, worn on forehead and arm [b]10 Or *Messiah*
[c]13 Some manuscripts *to.* [14]*Woe to you, teachers of the law and Pharisees, you hypocrites! You devour widows' houses and for a show make lengthy prayers. Therefore you will be punished more severely.*

beautiful on the outside but on the in-
side are full of dead men's bones and
everything unclean. 28In the same way,
on the outside you appear to people as
righteous but on the inside you are full
of hypocrisy and wickedness.
29"Woe to you, teachers of the law
and Pharisees, you hypocrites! You
build tombs for the prophets[a] and deco-
rate the graves of the righteous. 30And
you say, 'If we had lived in the days of
our forefathers, we would not have
taken part with them in shedding the
blood of the prophets.' 31So you testify
against yourselves that you are the de-
scendants of those who murdered the
prophets.[b] 32Fill up, then, the measure[c]
of the sin of your forefathers![d]
33"You snakes! You brood of vipers![e]
How will you escape being condemned
to hell?[f] 34Therefore I am sending you
prophets and wise men and teachers.
Some of them you will kill and crucify;[g]
others you will flog in your synagogues[h]
and pursue from town to town.[i] 35And
so upon you will come all the righteous
blood that has been shed on earth, from
the blood of righteous Abel[j] to the blood
of Zechariah son of Barakiah,[k] whom
you murdered between the temple and
the altar.[l] 36I tell you the truth, all this
will come upon this generation.[m]
37"O Jerusalem, Jerusalem, you who
kill the prophets and stone those sent to
you,[n] how often I have longed to gather
your children together, as a hen gathers
her chicks under her wings,[o] but you
were not willing. 38Look, your house is
left to you desolate.[p] 39For I tell you, you
will not see me again until you say,
'Blessed is he who comes in the name of
the Lord.'[d]"[q]

Signs of the End of the Age

24:1–51pp—Mk 13:1–37; Lk 21:5–36

24 Jesus left the temple and was
walking away when his disci-
ples came up to him to call his attention
to its buildings. 2"Do you see all these
things?" he asked. "I tell you the truth,
not one stone here will be left on
another;[a] every one will be thrown
down."
3As Jesus was sitting on the Mount of
Olives,[b] the disciples came to him pri-
vately. "Tell us," they said, "when will
this happen, and what will be the sign
of your coming[c] and of the end of the
age?"[d]
4Jesus answered: "Watch out that no-
one deceives you.[e] 5For many will come
in my name, claiming, 'I am the Christ,'[a]
and will deceive many.[f] 6You will hear
of wars and rumours of wars, but see to
it that you are not alarmed. Such things
must happen, but the end is still to
come. 7Nation will rise against nation,
and kingdom against kingdom.[g] There
will be famines[h] and earthquakes in
various places. 8All these are the
beginning of birth-pains.
9"Then you will be handed over to be
persecuted[i] and put to death,[j] and you
will be hated by all nations because of
me.[k] 10At that time many will turn away
from the faith and will betray and hate
each other, 11and many false prophets[l]
will appear and deceive many people.[m]
12Because of the increase of wickedness,
the love of most will grow cold, 13but he
who stands firm to the end will be
saved.[n] 14And this gospel of the king-
dom[o] will be preached in the whole
world[p] as a testimony to all nations, and
then the end will come.
15"So when you see standing in the
holy place[q] 'the abomination that causes
desolation',[b][r] spoken of through the
prophet Daniel—let the reader under-
stand—16then let those who are in
Judea flee to the mountains. 17Let no-
one on the roof of his house[s] go down to
take anything out of the house. 18Let
no-one in the field go back to get his
cloak. 19How dreadful it will be in those
days for pregnant women and nursing
mothers![t] 20Pray that your flight will not
take place in winter or on the Sabbath.
21For then there will be great distress,
unequalled from the beginning of the
world until now—and never to be
equalled again.[u] 22If those days had not
been cut short, no-one would survive,
but for the sake of the elect[v] those days
will be shortened. 23At that time if any-
one says to you, 'Look, here is the
Christ!' or, 'There he is!' do not believe
it.[w] 24For false Christs and false
prophets will appear and perform great
signs and miracles[x] to deceive even the
elect—if that were possible. 25See, I
have told you ahead of time.
26"So if anyone tells you, 'There he is,
out in the desert,' do not go out; or,
'Here he is, in the inner rooms,' do not
believe it. 27For as lightning[y] that comes
from the east is visible even in the west,
so will be the coming[z] of the Son of
Man.[a] 28Wherever there is a carcass,
there the vultures will gather.[b]

29 [a]Lk 11:47–48
31 [b]**Mt 5:12**
32 [c]1Th 2:16; [d]Eze 20:4
33 [e]Mt 3:7; 12:34; [f]**Mt 5:22**
34 [g]2Ch 36:15–16; Lk 11:49; [h]**Mt 10:17**; [i]Mt 10:23
35 [j]Ge 4:8; Heb 11:4; [k]Zec 1:1; [l]2Ch 24:21
36 [m]Mt 10:23; 24:34; Lk 11:50–51
37 [n]2Ch 24:21; **Mt 5:12**; [o]Ps 57:1; 61:4; Isa 31:5
38 [p]1Ki 9:7–8; Jer 22:5
39 [q]Ps 118:26; Mt 21:9

Ch. 24

2 [a]Lk 19:44
3 [b]**Mt 21:1**; [c]**Lk 17:30**; [d]Mt 13:39; 28:20
4 [e]**Mk 13:5**
5 [f]ver 11,23–24; 1Jn 2:18
7 [g]Isa 19:2; [h]Ac 11:28
9 [i]Mt 10:17; [j]Jn 16:2; [k]**Jn 15:21**
11 [l]**Mt 7:15**; [m]**Mk 13:5**
13 [n]**Mt 10:22**
14 [o]**Mt 4:23**; [p]**Ro 10:18**; Lk 2:1; 4:5; Ac 11:28; 17:6; Rev 3:10; 16:14
15 [q]**Ac 6:13**; [r]Da 9:27; 11:31; 12:11
17 [s]1Sa 9:25; Mt 10:27; Lk 12:3; Ac 10:9
19 [t]Lk 23:29
21 [u]Eze 5:9; Da 12:1; Joel 2:2
22 [v]ver 24,31
23 [w]Lk 17:23; 21:8
24 [x]Ex 7:11,22; 2Th 2:9–11; Rev 13:13; 16:14; 19:20
27 [y]Lk 17:24; [z]**Lk 17:30**; [a]**Mt 8:20**
28 [b]Lk 17:37

d*39* Psalm 118:26
a*5* Or *Messiah*; also in verse 23
b*15* Daniel 9:27; 11:31; 12:11

29“Immediately after the distress of those days

“ ‘the sun will be darkened,
  and the moon will not give its light;
the stars will fall from the sky,
  and the heavenly bodies will be
    shaken.’[c] [c]

30“At that time the sign of the Son of Man will appear in the sky, and all the nations of the earth will mourn.[d] They will see the Son of Man coming on the clouds of the sky,[e] with power and great glory. 31And he will send his angels[f] with a loud trumpet call,[g] and they will gather his elect from the four winds, from one end of the heavens to the other.

32“Now learn this lesson from the fig-tree: As soon as its twigs get tender and its leaves come out, you know that summer is near. 33Even so, when you see all these things, you know that it[d] is near, right at the door.[h] 34I tell you the truth, this generation[e] will certainly not pass away until all these things have happened.[i] 35Heaven and earth will pass away, but my words will never pass away.[j]

The Day and Hour Unknown

24:37–39pp—Lk 17:26,27
24:45–51pp—Lk 12:42–46

36“No-one knows about that day or hour, not even the angels in heaven, nor the Son,[f] but only the Father.[k] 37As it was in the days of Noah,[l] so it will be at the coming of the Son of Man. 38For in the days before the flood, people were eating and drinking, marrying and giving in marriage,[m] up to the day Noah entered the ark; 39and they knew nothing about what would happen until the flood came and took them all away. That is how it will be at the coming of the Son of Man.[n] 40Two men will be in the field; one will be taken and the other left.[o] 41Two women will be grinding with a hand mill; one will be taken and the other left.[p]

42“Therefore keep watch, because you do not know on what day your Lord will come.[q] 43But understand this: If the owner of the house had known at what time of night the thief was coming,[r] he would have kept watch and would not have let his house be broken into. 44So you also must be ready,[s] because the Son of Man will come at an hour when you do not expect him.

45“Who then is the faithful and wise servant,[t] whom the master has put in charge of the servants in his household to give them their food at the proper time? 46It will be good for that servant whose master finds him doing so when he returns.[u] 47I tell you the truth, he will put him in charge of all his possessions.[v] 48But suppose that servant is wicked and says to himself, ‘My master is staying away a long time,’ 49and he then begins to beat his fellow-servants and to eat and drink with drunkards.[w] 50The master of that servant will come on a day when he does not expect him and at an hour he is not aware of. 51He will cut him to pieces and assign him a place with the hypocrites, where there will be weeping and gnashing of teeth.[x]

29 [c]Isa 13:10; 34:4; Eze 32:7; Joel 2:10,31; Zep 1:15; Rev 6:12–13; 8:12
30 [d]Rev 1:7; [e]**Rev 1:7**
31 [f]Mt 13:41; [g]Isa 27:13; Zec 9:14; 1Co 15:52; 1Th 4:16; Rev 8:2; 10:7; 11:15
33 [h]Jas 5:9
34 [i]Mt 16:28; **23:36**
35 [j]**Mt 5:18**
36 [k]Ac 1:7
37 [l]Ge 6:5; 7:6–23
38 [m]Mt 22:30
39 [n]**Lk 17:30**
40 [o]Lk 17:34
41 [p]Lk 17:35
42 [q]Mt 25:13; Lk 12:40
43 [r]**Lk 12:39**
44 [s]1Th 5:6
45 [t]Mt 25:21,23
46 [u]Rev 16:15
47 [v]Mt 25:21,23
49 [w]Lk 21:34
51 [x]**Mt 8:12**

Ch. 25

1 [a]**Mt 13:24;** [b]Lk 12:35–38; Ac 20:8; Rev 4:5; [c]Rev 19:7; 21:2
2 [d]Mt 24:45
5 [e]1Th 5:6
8 [f]Lk 12:35
10 [g]Rev 19:9
12 [h]ver 41; **Mt 7:23**
13 [i]Mt 24:42,44; Mk 13:35; Lk 12:40
14 [j]Mt 21:33; Lk 19:12

The Parable of the Ten Virgins

25 “At that time the kingdom of heaven will be like[a] ten virgins who took their lamps[b] and went out to meet the bridegroom.[c] 2Five of them were foolish and five were wise.[d] 3The foolish ones took their lamps but did not take any oil with them. 4The wise, however, took oil in jars along with their lamps. 5The bridegroom was a long time in coming, and they all became drowsy and fell asleep.[e]

6“At midnight the cry rang out: ‘Here’s the bridegroom! Come out to meet him!’

7“Then all the virgins woke up and trimmed their lamps. 8The foolish ones said to the wise, ‘Give us some of your oil; our lamps are going out.’[f]

9“ ‘No,’ they replied, ‘there may not be enough for both us and you. Instead, go to those who sell oil and buy some for yourselves.’

10“But while they were on their way to buy the oil, the bridegroom arrived. The virgins who were ready went in with him to the wedding banquet.[g] And the door was shut.

11“Later the others also came. ‘Sir! Sir!’ they said. ‘Open the door for us!’

12“But he replied, ‘I tell you the truth, I don’t know you.’[h]

13“Therefore keep watch, because you do not know the day or the hour.[i]

The Parable of the Talents

25:14–30Ref—Lk 19:12–27

14“Again, it will be like a man going on a journey,[j] who called his servants

[c]29 Isaiah 13:10; 34:4
[d]33 Or *he* [e]34 Or *race*
[f]36 Some manuscripts do not have *nor the Son*.

and entrusted his property to them.
15To one he gave five talents[a] of money,
to another two talents, and to another
one talent, each according to his ability.[k]
Then he went on his journey. 16The man
who had received the five talents went
at once and put his money to work and
gained five more. 17So also, the one with
the two talents gained two more. 18But
the man who had received the one tal-
ent went off, dug a hole in the ground
and hid his master's money.

19"After a long time the master of
those servants returned and settled
accounts with them.[l] 20The man who
had received the five talents brought the
other five. 'Master,' he said, 'you en-
trusted me with five talents. See, I have
gained five more.'

21"His master replied, 'Well done,
good and faithful servant! You have
been faithful with a few things; I will put
you in charge of many things.[m] Come
and share your master's happiness!'

22"The man with the two talents also
came. 'Master,' he said, 'you entrusted
me with two talents; see, I have gained
two more.'

23"His master replied, 'Well done,
good and faithful servant! You have
been faithful with a few things; I will put
you in charge of many things.[n] Come
and share your master's happiness!'

24"Then the man who had received
the one talent came. 'Master,' he said, 'I
knew that you are a hard man, harvest-
ing where you have not sown and
gathering where you have not scattered
seed. 25So I was afraid and went out and
hid your talent in the ground. See, here
is what belongs to you.'

26"His master replied, 'You wicked,
lazy servant! So you knew that I harvest
where I have not sown and gather
where I have not scattered seed? 27Well
then, you should have put my money
on deposit with the bankers, so that
when I returned I would have received
it back with interest.

28" 'Take the talent from him and give
it to the one who has the ten talents.
29For everyone who has will be given
more, and he will have an abundance.
Whoever does not have, even what he
has will be taken from him.[o] 30And
throw that worthless servant outside,
into the darkness, where there will be
weeping and gnashing of teeth.'[p]

The Sheep and the Goats

31"When the Son of Man comes[q] in his
glory, and all the angels with him, he
will sit on his throne[r] in heavenly glory.
32All the nations will be gathered before
him, and he will separate[s] the people
one from another as a shepherd sepa-
rates the sheep from the goats.[t] 33He will
put the sheep on his right and the goats
on his left.

34"Then the King will say to those on
his right, 'Come, you who are blessed
by my Father; take your inheritance, the
kingdom[u] prepared for you since the
creation of the world.[v] 35For I was hun-
gry and you gave me something to eat, I
was thirsty and you gave me something
to drink, I was a stranger and you in-
vited me in,[w] 36I needed clothes and you
clothed me,[x] I was sick and you looked
after me,[y] I was in prison and you came
to visit me.'[z]

37"Then the righteous will answer
him, 'Lord, when did we see you hun-
gry and feed you, or thirsty and give
you something to drink? 38When did we
see you a stranger and invite you in, or
needing clothes and clothe you? 39When
did we see you sick or in prison and go
to visit you?'

40"The King will reply, 'I tell you the
truth, whatever you did for one of the
least of these brothers of mine, you did
for me.'[a]

41"Then he will say to those on his
left, 'Depart from me,[b] you who are
cursed, into the eternal fire[c] prepared
for the devil and his angels.[d] 42For I was
hungry and you gave me nothing to eat,
I was thirsty and you gave me nothing
to drink, 43I was a stranger and you did
not invite me in, I needed clothes and
you did not clothe me, I was sick and in
prison and you did not look after me.'

44"They also will answer, 'Lord,
when did we see you hungry or thirsty
or a stranger or needing clothes or sick
or in prison, and did not help you?'

45"He will reply, 'I tell you the truth,
whatever you did not do for one of the
least of these, you did not do for me.'[e]

46"Then they will go away to eternal
punishment, but the righteous to eter-
nal life."[f][g]

The Plot Against Jesus

26:2–5pp—Mk 14:1,2; Lk 22:1,2

26 When Jesus had finished saying
all these things,[a] he said to his
disciples, 2"As you know, the Passover[b]
is two days away—and the Son of Man
will be handed over to be crucified."

15 [k]Mt 18:24–25
19 [l]Mt 18:23
21 [m]ver 23; Mt 24:45,47; Lk 16:10
23 [n]ver 21
29 [o]Mt 13:12; Mk 4:25; Lk 8:18; 19:26
30 [p]**Mt 8:12**
31 [q]**Lk 17:30;** [r]Mt 19:28
32 [s]Mal 3:18; [t]Eze 34:17,20
34 [u]**Mt 3:2;** 5:3, 10,19; 19:14; **Ac 20:32;** 1Co 15:50; Gal 5:21; Jas 2:5; [v]Heb 4:3; 9:26; Rev 13:8; 17:8
35 [w]Job 31:32; Heb 13:2
36 [x]Isa 58:7; Eze 18:7; Jas 2:15–16; [y]Jas 1:27; [z]2Ti 1:16
40 [a]**Mt 10:40**,42; Heb 13:2
41 [b]**Mt 7:23;** [c]Isa 66:24; Mt 3:12; **5:22;** Mk 9:43,48; Lk 3:17; Jude 7; [d]2Pe 2:4
45 [e]Pr 14:31; 17:5
46 [f]Mt 19:29; Jn 3:15–16,36; 17:2–3; Ro 2:7; Gal 6:8; 1Jn 1:2; 5:11, 13,20; [g]Da 12:2; Jn 5:29; Ac 24:15; Ro 2:7–8; Gal 6:8

Ch. 26

1 [a]**Mt 7:28**
2 [b]**Jn 11:55**

[a]*15* A talent was worth several hundred pounds.

3Then the chief priests and the elders of the people assembled[c] in the palace of the high priest, whose name was Caiaphas,[d] 4and they plotted to arrest Jesus in some sly way and kill him.[e] 5"But not during the Feast," they said, "or there may be a riot[f] among the people."

Jesus Anointed at Bethany

26:6–13pp—Mk 14:3–9
26:6–13Ref—Lk 7:37,38; Jn 12:1–8

6While Jesus was in Bethany[g] in the home of a man known as Simon the Leper, 7a woman came to him with an alabaster jar of very expensive perfume, which she poured on his head as he was reclining at the table.

8When the disciples saw this, they were indignant. "Why this waste?" they asked. 9"This perfume could have been sold at a high price and the money given to the poor."

10Aware of this, Jesus said to them, "Why are you bothering this woman? She has done a beautiful thing to me. 11The poor you will always have with you,[h] but you will not always have me. 12When she poured this perfume on my body, she did it to prepare me for burial.[i] 13I tell you the truth, wherever this gospel is preached throughout the world, what she has done will also be told, in memory of her."

Judas Agrees to Betray Jesus

26:14–16pp—Mk 14:10,11; Lk 22:3–6

14Then one of the Twelve—the one called Judas Iscariot[j]—went to the chief priests 15and asked, "What are you willing to give me if I hand him over to you?" So they counted out for him thirty silver coins.[k] 16From then on Judas watched for an opportunity to hand him over.

The Lord's Supper

26:17–19pp—Mk 14:12–16; Lk 22:7–13
26:20–24pp—Mk 14:17–21
26:26–29pp—Mk 14:22–25; Lk 22:17–20; 1 Co 11:23–25

17On the first day of the Feast of Unleavened Bread,[l] the disciples came to Jesus and asked, "Where do you want us to make preparations for you to eat the Passover?"[m]

18He replied, "Go into the city to a certain man and tell him, 'The Teacher says: My appointed time[n] is near. I am going to celebrate the Passover with my disciples at your house.'" 19So the disciples did as Jesus had directed them and prepared the Passover.

20When evening came, Jesus was reclining at the table with the Twelve. 21And while they were eating, he said, "I tell you the truth, one of you will betray me."[o]

22They were very sad and began to say to him one after the other, "Surely not I, Lord?"

23Jesus replied, "The one who has dipped his hand into the bowl with me will betray me.[p] 24The Son of Man will go just as it is written about him.[q] But woe to that man who betrays the Son of Man! It would be better for him if he had not been born."

25Then Judas, the one who would betray him,[r] said, "Surely not I, Rabbi?"[s]

Jesus answered, "Yes, it is you."[a]

26While they were eating, Jesus took bread, gave thanks and broke it,[t] and gave it to his disciples, saying, "Take and eat; this is my body."

27Then he took the cup,[u] gave thanks and offered it to them, saying, "Drink from it, all of you. 28This is my blood of the[b] covenant,[v] which is poured out for many for the forgiveness of sins.[w] 29I tell you, I will not drink of this fruit of the vine from now on until that day when I drink it anew with you[x] in my Father's kingdom."

30When they had sung a hymn, they went out to the Mount of Olives.[y]

Jesus Predicts Peter's Denial

26:31–35pp—Mk 14:27–31; Lk 22:31–34

31Then Jesus told them, "This very night you will all fall away on account of me,[z] for it is written:

> "'I will strike the shepherd,
> and the sheep of the flock will be
> scattered.'[c][a]

32But after I have risen, I will go ahead of you into Galilee."[b]

33Peter replied, "Even if all fall away on account of you, I never will."

34"I tell you the truth," Jesus answered, "this very night, before the cock crows, you will disown me three times."[c]

35But Peter declared, "Even if I have to die with you,[d] I will never disown

3 [c]Ps 2:2; [d]ver 57; Lk 3:2; Jn 11:47–53; 18:13–14,24, 28; Ac 4:6
4 [e]**Mt 12:14**
5 [f]Mt 27:24
6 [g]**Mt 21:17**
11 [h]Dt 15:11
12 [i]Jn 19:40
14 [j]ver 25,47; **Mt 10:4**
15 [k]Ex 21:32; Zec 11:12
17 [l]Ex 12:18–20; [m]Dt 16:5–8
18 [n]Mk 14:35,41; Jn 7:6,8,30; 8:20; 12:23; 13:1; 17:1
21 [o]Lk 22:21–23; Jn 13:21
23 [p]Ps 41:9; Jn 13:18
24 [q]ver 31,54,56; Isa 53; Da 9:26; Mk 9:12; Lk 24:25–27, 46; Ac 17:2–3; 26:22–23; 1Pe 1:10–11
25 [r]**Mt 10:4**; [s]**Mt 23:7**
26 [t]**Mt 14:19**
27 [u]1Co 10:16
28 [v]Ex 24:6–8; Zec 9:11; Mal 2:5; Heb 9:20; 10:29; **13:20**; [w]**Mt 20:28**; Mk 1:4
29 [x]Ac 10:41
30 [y]**Mt 21:1**
31 [z]Mt 11:6; 13:21; [a]Zec 13:7; Jn 16:32
32 [b]Mt 28:7, 10,16
34 [c]ver 75; Jn 13:38
35 [d]Jn 13:37

[a]25 Or *"You yourself have said it."*
[b]28 Some manuscripts *the new*
[c]31 Zech. 13:7

you." And all the other disciples said the same.

Gethsemane

26:36–46pp—Mk 14:32–42; Lk 22:40–46

36Then Jesus went with his disciples to a place called Gethsemane, and he said to them, "Sit here while I go over there and pray." 37He took Peter and the two sons of Zebedee[e] along with him, and he began to be sorrowful and troubled. 38Then he said to them, "My soul is overwhelmed with sorrow[f] to the point of death. Stay here and keep watch with me."[g]

39Going a little farther, he fell with his face to the ground and prayed, "My Father, if it is possible, may this cup[h] be taken from me. Yet not as I will, but as you will."[i]

40Then he returned to his disciples and found them sleeping. "Could you men not keep watch with me[j] for one hour?" he asked Peter. 41"Watch and pray so that you will not fall into temptation.[k] The spirit is willing, but the body is weak."

42He went away a second time and prayed, "My Father, if it is not possible for this cup to be taken away unless I drink it, may your will be done."[l]

43When he came back, he again found them sleeping, because their eyes were heavy. 44So he left them and went away once more and prayed the third time, saying the same thing.

45Then he returned to the disciples and said to them, "Are you still sleeping and resting? Look, the hour[m] is near, and the Son of Man is betrayed into the hands of sinners. 46Rise, let us go! Here comes my betrayer!"

Jesus Arrested

26:47–56pp—Mk 14:43–50; Lk 22:47–53

47While he was still speaking, Judas,[n] one of the Twelve, arrived. With him was a large crowd armed with swords and clubs, sent from the chief priests and the elders of the people. 48Now the betrayer had arranged a signal with them: "The one I kiss is the man; arrest him." 49Going at once to Jesus, Judas said, "Greetings, Rabbi!"[o] and kissed him.

50Jesus replied, "Friend,[p] do what you came for."[d]

Then the men stepped forward, seized Jesus and arrested him. 51With that, one of Jesus' companions reached for his sword,[q] drew it out and struck the servant of the high priest, cutting off his ear.[r]

52"Put your sword back in its place," Jesus said to him, "for all who draw the sword will die by the sword.[s] 53Do you think I cannot call on my Father, and he will at once put at my disposal more than twelve legions of angels?[t] 54But how then would the Scriptures be fulfilled[u] that say it must happen in this way?"

55At that time Jesus said to the crowd, "Am I leading a rebellion, that you have come out with swords and clubs to capture me? Every day I sat in the temple courts teaching,[v] and you did not arrest me. 56But this has all taken place that the writings of the prophets might be fulfilled."[w] Then all the disciples deserted him and fled.

Before the Sanhedrin

26:57–68pp—Mk 14:53–65; Jn 18:12,13,19–24

57Those who had arrested Jesus took him to Caiaphas,[x] the high priest, where the teachers of the law and the elders had assembled. 58But Peter followed him at a distance, right up to the courtyard of the high priest.[y] He entered and sat down with the guards[z] to see the outcome.

59The chief priests and the whole Sanhedrin[a] were looking for false evidence against Jesus so that they could put him to death. 60But they did not find any, though many false witnesses[b] came forward.

Finally two[c] came forward 61and declared, "This fellow said, 'I am able to destroy the temple of God and rebuild it in three days.'"[d]

62Then the high priest stood up and said to Jesus, "Are you not going to answer? What is this testimony that these men are bringing against you?" 63But Jesus remained silent.[e]

The high priest said to him, "I charge you under oath[f] by the living God:[g] Tell us if you are the Christ,[e][h] the Son of God."[i]

64"Yes, it is as you say,"[j] Jesus replied. "But I say to all of you: In the future you will see the Son of Man sitting at the right hand of the Mighty One[k] and coming on the clouds of heaven."[l]

65Then the high priest tore his clothes[m] and said, "He has spoken blasphemy! Why do we need any more

37 [e]**Mt 4:21**
38 [f]**Jn 12:27;** [g]ver 40–41
39 [h]**Mt 20:22;** [i]ver 42; Ps 40:6–8; Isa 50:5; Mt 6:10; Jn 4:34; 5:30; 6:38
40 [j]ver 38
41 [k]Mt 6:13
42 [l]**ver 39**
45 [m]**ver 18**
47 [n]**Mt 10:4**
49 [o]ver 25; **Mt 23:7**
50 [p]Mt 20:13; 22:12
51 [q]Lk 22:36,38; [r]Jn 18:10
52 [s]Ge 9:6; Ex 21:12; Rev 13:10
53 [t]2Ki 6:17; Da 7:10; Mt 4:11
54 [u]**ver 24; Mt 1:22**
55 [v]Mk 12:35; Lk 21:37; Jn 7:14, 28; 18:20
56 [w]**ver 24; Mt 1:22**
57 [x]**ver 3**
58 [y]ver 69; Mk 14:66; Lk 22:55; Jn 18:15; [z]Mk 15:16; Lk 11:21; Jn 7:32, 45–46
59 [a]**Mt 5:22**
60 [b]Ps 27:12; 35:11; Ac 6:13; [c]Dt 19:15
61 [d]**Jn 2:19**
63 [e]**Mk 14:61;** [f]Lev 5:1; [g]**Mt 16:16;** [h]Lk 22:67; [i]**Mt 4:3**
64 [j]Mt 27:11; Lk 22:70; [k]**Mk 16:19;** [l]**Rev 1:7**
65 [m]**Mk 14:63**

[d]*50* Or *"Friend, why have you come?"*
[e]*63* Or *Messiah;* also in verse 68

witnesses? Look, now you have heard
the blasphemy. 66 What do you think?"
"He is worthy of death,"[n] they
answered.
67Then they spat in his face and struck
him with their fists.[o] Others slapped
him 68and said, "Prophesy to us, Christ.
Who hit you?"[p]

Peter Disowns Jesus

26:69–75pp—Mk 14:66–72; Lk 22:55–62; Jn 18:16–18, 25–27

69Now Peter was sitting out in the
courtyard, and a servant girl came to
him. "You also were with Jesus of
Galilee," she said.
70But he denied it before them all. "I
don't know what you're talking about,"
he said.
71Then he went out to the gateway,
where another girl saw him and said to
the people there, "This fellow was with
Jesus of Nazareth."
72He denied it again, with an oath: "I
don't know the man!"
73After a little while, those standing
there went up to Peter and said, "Surely
you are one of them, for your accent
gives you away."
74Then he began to call down curses
on himself and he swore to them, "I
don't know the man!"
Immediately a cock crowed. 75Then
Peter remembered the word Jesus had
spoken: "Before the cock crows, you
will disown me three times."[q] And he
went outside and wept bitterly.

Judas Hangs Himself

27 Early in the morning, all the
chief priests and the elders of
the people came to the decision to put
Jesus to death.[a] 2They bound him, led
him away and handed him over[b] to
Pilate, the governor.[c]
3When Judas, who had betrayed
him,[d] saw that Jesus was condemned,
he was seized with remorse and re-
turned the thirty silver coins[e] to the
chief priests and the elders. 4"I have
sinned," he said, "for I have betrayed
innocent blood."
"What is that to us?" they replied.
"That's your responsibility."[f]
5So Judas threw the money into the
temple[g] and left. Then he went away
and hanged himself.[h]
6The chief priests picked up the coins
and said, "It is against the law to put
this into the treasury, since it is blood
money." 7So they decided to use the
money to buy the potter's field as a
burial place for foreigners. 8That is why
it has been called the Field of Blood[i] to
this day. 9Then what was spoken by
Jeremiah the prophet was fulfilled:[j]
"They took the thirty silver coins, the
price set on him by the people of Israel,
10and they used them to buy the potter's
field, as the Lord commanded me."[a][k]

Jesus Before Pilate

27:11–26pp—Mk 15:2–15; Lk 23:2,3,18–25; Jn 18:29–19:16

11Meanwhile Jesus stood before the
governor, and the governor asked him,
"Are you the king of the Jews?"[l]
"Yes, it is as you say," Jesus replied.
12When he was accused by the chief
priests and the elders, he gave no
answer.[m] 13Then Pilate asked him,
"Don't you hear the testimony they are
bringing against you?"[n] 14But Jesus
made no reply,[o] not even to a single
charge—to the great amazement of the
governor.
15Now it was the governor's custom at
the Feast to release a prisoner[p] chosen
by the crowd. 16At that time they had a
notorious prisoner, called Barabbas.
17So when the crowd had gathered,
Pilate asked them, "Which one do you
want me to release to you: Barabbas, or
Jesus who is called Christ?"[q] 18For he
knew it was out of envy that they had
handed Jesus over to him.
19While Pilate was sitting on the
judge's seat,[r] his wife sent him this
message: "Don't have anything to do
with that innocent[s] man, for I have suf-
fered a great deal today in a dream[t]
because of him."
20But the chief priests and the elders
persuaded the crowd to ask for Barab-
bas and to have Jesus executed.[u]
21"Which of the two do you want me
to release to you?" asked the governor.
"Barabbas," they answered.
22"What shall I do, then, with Jesus
who is called Christ?"[v] Pilate asked.
They all answered, "Crucify him!"
23"Why? What crime has he commit-
ted?" asked Pilate.
But they shouted all the louder, "Cru-
cify him!"
24When Pilate saw that he was getting
nowhere, but that instead an uproar[w]
was starting, he took water and washed
his hands[x] in front of the crowd. "I am
innocent of this man's blood,"[y] he said.
"It is your responsibility!"[z]

[a]10 See Zech. 11:12,13; Jer. 19:1–13; 32:6–9.

66 [n]Lev 24:16; Jn 19:7
67 [o]**Mt 16:21**
68 [p]Lk 22:63–65
75 [q]ver 34; Jn 13:38

Ch. 27

1 [a]**Mt 12:14**; Mk 15:1; Lk 22:66
2 [b]Mt 20:19; [c]Mk 15:1; Lk 13:1; Ac 3:13; 1Ti 6:13
3 [d]**Mt 10:4**; [e]Mt 26:14–15
4 [f]ver 24
5 [g]Lk 1:9,21; [h]Ac 1:18
8 [i]Ac 1:19
9 [j]**Mt 1:22**
10 [k]Zec 11:12–13; Jer 32:6–9
11 [l]**Mt 2:2**
12 [m]**Mk 14:61**
13 [n]Mt 26:62
14 [o]**Mk 14:61**
15 [p]Jn 18:39
17 [q]ver 22; Mt 1:16
19 [r]Jn 19:13; [s]ver 24; [t]Ge 20:6; Nu 12:6; 1Ki 3:5; Job 33:14–16; Mt 1:20; 2:12–13, 19,22
20 [u]Ac 3:14
22 [v]Mt 1:16
24 [w]Mt 26:5; [x]Ps 26:6; [y]Dt 21:6–8; [z]ver 4

25All the people answered, "Let his
blood be on us and on our children!"[a]
26Then he released Barabbas to them.
But he had Jesus flogged,[b] and handed
him over to be crucified.

The Soldiers Mock Jesus

27:27–31pp—Mk 15:16–20

27Then the governor's soldiers took
Jesus into the Praetorium[c] and gathered
the whole company of soldiers round
him. 28They stripped him and put a
scarlet robe on him,[d] 29and then twisted
together a crown of thorns and set it on
his head. They put a staff in his right
hand and knelt in front of him and
mocked him. "Hail, king of the Jews!"
they said.[e] 30They spat on him, and took
the staff and struck him on the head
again and again.[f] 31After they had
mocked him, they took off the robe and
put his own clothes on him. Then they
led him away to crucify him.[g]

The Crucifixion

27:33–44pp—Mk 15:22–32; Lk 23:33–43; Jn 19:17–24

32As they were going out,[h] they met a
man from Cyrene,[i] named Simon, and
they forced him to carry the cross.[j]
33They came to a place called Golgotha
(which means The Place of the Skull).[k]
34There they offered Jesus wine to
drink, mixed with gall;[l] but after tasting
it, he refused to drink it. 35When they
had crucified him, they divided up his
clothes by casting lots.[b][m] 36And sitting
down, they kept watch[n] over him there.
37Above his head they placed the writ-
ten charge against him: THIS IS JESUS,
THE KING OF THE JEWS. 38Two robbers
were crucified with him,[o] one on his
right and one on his left. 39Those who
passed by hurled insults at him, shak-
ing their heads[p] 40and saying, "You who
are going to destroy the temple and
build it in three days,[q] save yourself![r]
Come down from the cross, if you are
the Son of God!"[s]

41In the same way the chief priests,
the teachers of the law and the elders
mocked him. 42"He saved others," they
said, "but he can't save himself! He's
the King of Israel![t] Let him come down
now from the cross, and we will believe[u]
in him. 43He trusts in God. Let God
rescue him[v] now if he wants him, for he
said, 'I am the Son of God.'" 44In the
same way the robbers who were cru-
cified with him also heaped insults on
him.

The Death of Jesus

27:45–56pp—Mk 15:33–41; Lk 23:44–49

45From the sixth hour until the ninth
hour darkness[w] came over all the land.
46About the ninth hour Jesus cried out in
a loud voice, "*Eloi, Eloi,*[c] *lama sabach-
thani?*"—which means, "My God, my
God, why have you forsaken me?"[d][x]
47When some of those standing there
heard this, they said, "He's calling
Elijah."
48Immediately one of them ran and
got a sponge. He filled it with wine
vinegar,[y] put it on a stick, and offered it
to Jesus to drink. 49The rest said, "Now
leave him alone. Let's see if Elijah comes
to save him."
50And when Jesus had cried out again
in a loud voice, he gave up his spirit.[z]
51At that moment the curtain of the
temple[a] was torn in two from top to
bottom. The earth shook and the rocks
split.[b] 52The tombs broke open and the
bodies of many holy people who had
died were raised to life. 53They came out
of the tombs, and after Jesus' resurrec-
tion they went into the holy city[c] and
appeared to many people.
54When the centurion and those with
him who were guarding[d] Jesus saw the
earthquake and all that had happened,
they were terrified, and exclaimed,
"Surely he was the Son[e] of God!"[e]
55Many women were there, watching
from a distance. They had followed
Jesus from Galilee to care for his needs.[f]
56Among them were Mary Magdalene,
Mary the mother of James and Joses,
and the mother of Zebedee's sons.[g]

The Burial of Jesus

27:57–61pp—Mk 15:42–47; Lk 23:50–56; Jn 19:38–42

57As evening approached, there came
a rich man from Arimathea, named
Joseph, who had himself become a
disciple of Jesus. 58Going to Pilate, he
asked for Jesus' body, and Pilate
ordered that it be given to him. 59Joseph
took the body, wrapped it in a clean
linen cloth, 60and placed it in his own
new tomb[h] that he had cut out of the
rock. He rolled a big stone in front of the
entrance to the tomb and went away.
61Mary Magdalene and the other Mary
were sitting there opposite the tomb.

25 [a]Jos 2:19; **Ac 5:28**
26 [b]Isa 53:5; Jn 19:1
27 [c]Jn 18:28,33; 19:9
28 [d]Jn 19:2
29 [e]Isa 53:3; Jn 19:2–3
30 [f]**Mt 16:21**
31 [g]Isa 53:7
32 [h]Heb 13:12; [i]Ac 2:10; 6:9; 11:20; 13:1; [j]Mk 15:21; Lk 23:26
33 [k]Jn 19:17
34 [l]ver 48; Ps 69:21
35 [m]Ps 22:18
36 [n]ver 54
38 [o]Isa 53:12
39 [p]Ps 22:7; 109:25; La 2:15
40 [q]**Jn 2:19**; [r]ver 42; [s]Mt 4:3,6
42 [t]Jn 1:49; 12:13; [u]**Jn 3:15**
43 [v]Ps 22:8
45 [w]Am 8:9
46 [x]Ps 22:1
48 [y]ver 34; Ps 69:21
50 [z]Jn 19:30
51 [a]Ex 26:31–33; Heb 9:3,8; 10:19–20; [b]ver 54
53 [c]**Mt 4:5**
54 [d]ver 36; [e]**Mt 4:3**; 17:5
55 [f]Lk 8:2–3
56 [g]Mk 15:47; Lk 24:10; Jn 19:25
60 [h]Mt 27:66; 28:2; Mk 16:4; Ac 13:29

---

b35 A few late manuscripts *lots that the word spoken by the prophet might be fulfilled: "They divided my garments among themselves and cast lots for my clothing."* (Psalm 22:18)
c46 Some manuscripts *Eli, Eli*
d46 Psalm 22:1 e54 Or *a son*

The Guard at the Tomb

62The next day, the one after Prepara-
tion Day, the chief priests and the Phari-
sees went to Pilate. 63"Sir," they said,
"we remember that while he was still
alive that deceiver said, 'After three
days I will rise again.'[i] 64So give the
order for the tomb to be made secure
until the third day. Otherwise, his disci-
ples may come and steal the body[j] and
tell the people that he has been raised
from the dead. This last deception will
be worse than the first."
65"Take a guard,"[k] Pilate answered.
"Go, make the tomb as secure as you
know how." 66So they went and made
the tomb secure by putting a seal[l] on the
stone[m] and posting the guard.[n]

The Resurrection

28:1-8pp—Mk 16:1-8; Lk 24:1-10

28 After the Sabbath, at dawn on
the first day of the week, Mary
Magdalene[a] and the other Mary[b] went
to look at the tomb.
2There was a violent earthquake,[c] for
an angel[d] of the Lord came down from
heaven and, going to the tomb, rolled
back the stone[e] and sat on it. 3His
appearance was like lightning, and his
clothes were white as snow.[f] 4The
guards were so afraid of him that they
shook and became like dead men.
5The angel said to the women, "Do
not be afraid,[g] for I know that you are
looking for Jesus, who was crucified.
6He is not here; he has risen, just as he
said.[h] Come and see the place where he
lay. 7Then go quickly and tell his disci-
ples: 'He has risen from the dead and is
going ahead of you into Galilee.[i] There
you will see him.' Now I have told you."
8So the women hurried away from the
tomb, afraid yet filled with joy, and ran
to tell his disciples. 9Suddenly Jesus met
them.[j] "Greetings," he said. They came
to him, clasped his feet and worshipped
him. 10Then Jesus said to them, "Do not
be afraid. Go and tell my brothers[k] to go
to Galilee; there they will see me."

The Guards' Report

11While the women were on their
way, some of the guards[l] went into the
city and reported to the chief priests
everything that had happened. 12When
the chief priests had met with the elders
and devised a plan, they gave the sol-
diers a large sum of money, 13telling
them, "You are to say, 'His disciples
came during the night and stole him
away[m] while we were asleep.' 14If this
report gets to the governor,[n] we will
satisfy him and keep you out of trou-
ble." 15So the soldiers took the money
and did as they were instructed. And
this story has been widely circulated
among the Jews to this very day.

The Great Commission

16Then the eleven disciples went to
Galilee, to the mountain where Jesus
had told them to go.[o] 17When they saw
him, they worshipped him; but some
doubted. 18Then Jesus came to them
and said, "All authority in heaven and
on earth has been given to me.[p]
19Therefore go and make disciples of all
nations,[q] baptising them in[a] the name of
the Father and of the Son and of the
Holy Spirit,[r] 20and teaching[s] them to
obey everything I have commanded
you. And surely I am with you[t] always,
to the very end of the age."[u]

63 [i]Mt 16:21
64 [j]Mt 28:13
65 [k]ver 66; Mt 28:11
66 [l]Da 6:17; [m]ver 60; Mt 28:2 [n]Mt 28:11

Ch. 28

1 [a]Lk 8:2; [b]Mt 27:56
2 [c]Mt 27:51; [d]Jn 20:12; **Ac 5:19;** [e]Mt 27:60
3 [f]Da 7:9; 10:6; Mk 9:3; Jn **20:12**
5 [g]ver 10; **Mt 14:27**
6 [h]**Mt 16:21**
7 [i]ver 10,16; Mt 26:32
9 [j]Jn 20:14–18
10 [k]Mt 12:50; 25:40; Mk 3:34; Jn 20:17; Ro 8:29; Heb 2:11–13,17
11 [l]Mt 27:65–66
13 [m]Mt 27:64
14 [n]**Mt 27:2**
16 [o]ver 7,10; Mt 26:32
18 [p]Da 7:13–14; Lk 10:22; Jn 3:35; **13:13;** 17:2; 1Co 15:27; Eph 1:20–22; Php 2:9–10
19 [q]Isa 49:6; Mk 16:15–16; Lk 24:47; Ac 1:8; 14:21; [r]Ac 1:8, 2:38; 8:16; Ro 6:3–4; Gal 3:27; Col 2:12
20 [s]Jn 14:26; Ac 2:42; [t]Dt 31:6; 1Ki 8:57; Hag 1:13; Mt 18:20; Ac 18:10; [u]Mt 13:39; 24:3

---

[a]*19* Or *into*; see Acts 8:16; 19:5; Rom. 6:3; 1 Cor. 1:13; 10:2 and Gal. 3:27.

Mark

John the Baptist Prepares the Way

1:2–8pp—Mt 3:1–11; Lk 3:2–16

1 The beginning of the gospel about
Jesus Christ, the Son of God.[a][a]

2 It is written in Isaiah the prophet:

"I will send my messenger ahead of
you,
who will prepare your way"[b][b]—
3 "a voice of one calling in the desert,
'Prepare the way for the Lord,
make straight paths for him.' "[c][c]

4 And so John[d] came, baptising in the
desert region and preaching a baptism
of repentance[e] for the forgiveness of
sins.[f] 5 The whole Judean countryside
and all the people of Jerusalem went out
to him. Confessing their sins, they were
baptised by him in the Jordan River.
6 John wore clothing made of camel's
hair, with a leather belt round his
waist,[g] and he ate locusts[h] and wild
honey. 7 And this was his message:
"After me will come one more power-
ful than I, the thongs of whose sandals I
am not worthy to stoop down and un-
tie.[i] 8 I baptise you with[d] water, but he
will baptise you with the Holy Spirit."[j]

The Baptism and Temptation of Jesus

1:9–11pp—Mt 3:13–17; Lk 3:21,22
1:12,13pp—Mt 4:1–11; Lk 4:1–13

9 At that time Jesus came from
Nazareth[k] in Galilee and was baptised
by John[l] in the Jordan. 10 As Jesus was
coming up out of the water, he saw
heaven being torn open and the Spirit
descending on him like a dove.[m] 11 And a
voice came from heaven: "You are my
Son,[n] whom I love; with you I am well
pleased."[o]
12 At once the Spirit sent him out into
the desert, 13 and he was in the desert for
forty days,[p] being tempted by Satan.[q]
He was with the wild animals, and
angels attended him.

The Calling of the First Disciples

1:16–20pp—Mt 4:18–22; Lk 5:2–11; Jn 1:35–42

14 After John[r] was put in prison, Jesus
went into Galilee,[s] proclaiming the
good news of God.[t] 15 "The time has
come,"[u] he said. "The kingdom of God
is near. Repent and believe[v] the good
news!"[w]
16 As Jesus walked beside the Sea of
Galilee, he saw Simon and his brother
Andrew casting a net into the lake, for
they were fishermen. 17 "Come, follow
me," Jesus said, "and I will make you
fishers of men." 18 At once they left their
nets and followed him.[x]
19 When he had gone a little farther, he
saw James son of Zebedee and his
brother John in a boat, preparing their
nets. 20 Without delay he called them,
and they left their father Zebedee in the
boat with the hired men and followed
him.

Jesus Drives Out an Evil Spirit

1:21–28pp—Lk 4:31–37

21 They went to Capernaum, and
when the Sabbath came, Jesus went into
the synagogue and began to teach.[y]
22 The people were amazed at his
teaching, because he taught them as
one who had authority, not as the
teachers of the law.[z] 23 Just then a man in
their synagogue who was possessed by
an evil[e] spirit cried out, 24 "What do you
want with us,[a] Jesus of Nazareth?[b] Have
you come to destroy us? I know who
you are—the Holy One of God!"[c]
25 "Be quiet!" said Jesus sternly.
"Come out of him!"[d] 26 The evil spirit
shook the man violently and came out
of him with a shriek.[e]
27 The people were all so amazed[f] that
they asked each other, "What is this? A
new teaching—and with authority! He
even gives orders to evil spirits and they
obey him." 28 News about him spread

Ch. 1

1 [a]**Mt 4:3**
2 [b]Mal 3:1; Mt 11:10; Lk 7:27
3 [c]Isa 40:3; Jn 1:23
4 [d]**Mt 3:1**; [e]ver 8; Jn 1:26,33; Ac 1:5,22; 13:24; 18:25; 19:3–4; [f]Lk 1:77
6 [g]2Ki 1:8; [h]Lev 11:22
7 [i]Ac 13:25
8 [j]Isa 44:3; Joel 2:28; Jn 1:33; Ac 1:5; 2:4; 11:16; 19:4–6
9 [k]**Mt 2:23**; [l]**Mt 3:1**
10 [m]Jn 1:32
11 [n]**Mt 3:17**; [o]**Mt 3:17**
13 [p]Ex 24:18; 1Ki 19:8; [q]**Mt 4:10**; Heb 4:15
14 [r]**Mt 3:1**; [s]Mt 4:12; [t]Mt 4:23
15 [u]Ro 5:6; Gal 4:4; Eph 1:10; [v]**Jn 3:15**; [w]Ac 20:21
18 [x]**Mt 4:19**
21 [y]ver 39; **Mt 4:23; Mk 10:1**
22 [z]**Mt 7:28–29**
24 [a]**Mt 8:29**; [b]Jdg 13:5; **Mt 2:23**; Lk 24:19; Jn 1:45–46; Ac 4:10; 24:5; [c]Ps 16:10; Isa 41:14,16,20; Lk 1:35; Jn 6:69; Ac 3:14; 1Jn 2:20
25 [d]ver 34
26 [e]Mk 9:20
27 [f]Mk 10:24,32

[a]1 Some manuscripts do not have *the Son of God*.
[b]2 Mal. 3:1 [c]3 Isaiah 40:3 [d]8 Or *in*
[e]23 Greek *unclean*; also in verses 26 and 27

quickly over the whole region[g] of
Galilee.

Jesus Heals Many

1:29–31pp—Mt 8:14,15; Lk 4:38,39
1:32–34pp—Mt 8:16,17; Lk 4:40,41

29As soon as they left the synagogue,[h]
they went with James and John to the
home of Simon and Andrew. 30Simon's
mother-in-law was in bed with a fever,
and they told Jesus about her. 31So he
went to her, took her hand and helped
her up.[i] The fever left her and she began
to wait on them.
32That evening after sunset the people
brought to Jesus all the sick and demon-
possessed.[j] 33The whole town gathered
at the door, 34and Jesus healed many
who had various diseases.[k] He also
drove out many demons, but he would
not let the demons speak because they
knew who he was.[l]

Jesus Prays in a Solitary Place

1:35–38pp—Lk 4:42,43

35Very early in the morning, while it
was still dark, Jesus got up, left the
house and went off to a solitary place,
where he prayed.[m] 36Simon and his
companions went to look for him, 37and
when they found him, they exclaimed:
"Everyone is looking for you!"
38Jesus replied, "Let us go some-
where else—to the nearby villages—so
that I can preach there also. That is why
I have come."[n] 39So he travelled
throughout Galilee, preaching in their
synagogues[o] and driving out demons.[p]

A Man With Leprosy

1:40–44pp—Mt 8:2–4; Lk 5:12–14

40A man with leprosy[f] came to him
and begged him on his knees,[q] "If you
are willing, you can make me clean."
41Filled with compassion, Jesus
reached out his hand and touched the
man. "I am willing," he said. "Be
clean!" 42Immediately the leprosy left
him and he was cured.
43Jesus sent him away at once with a
strong warning: 44"See that you don't
tell this to anyone.[r] But go, show your-
self to the priest[s] and offer the sacrifices
that Moses commanded for your cleans-
ing,[t] as a testimony to them." 45Instead
he went out and began to talk freely,
spreading the news. As a result, Jesus
could no longer enter a town openly but
stayed outside in lonely places.[u] Yet the
people still came to him from every-
where.[v]

28 [g]**Mt 9:26**
29 [h]ver 21,23
31 [i]**Lk 7:14**
32 [j]**Mt 4:24**
34 [k]**Mt 4:23;** [l]Mk 3:12; Ac 16:17–18
35 [m]**Lk 3:21**
38 [n]Isa 61:1
39 [o]**Mt 4:23;** [p]**Mt 4:24**
40 [q]Mk 10:17
44 [r]**Mt 8:4;** [s]Lev 13:49; [t]Lev 14:1–32
45 [u]Lk 5:15–16; [v]Mk 2:13; Lk 5:17; Jn 6:2

Ch. 2

2 [a]ver 13; Mk 1:45
3 [b]**Mt 4:24**
5 [c]Lk 7:48
7 [d]Isa 43:25
10 [e]**Mt 8:20**
12 [f]**Mt 9:8;** [g]Mt 9:33
13 [h]Mk 1:45; Lk 5:15; Jn 6:2
14 [i]**Mt 4:19**
16 [j]Ac 23:9; [k]**Mt 9:11**

Jesus Heals a Paralytic

2:3–12pp—Mt 9:2–8; Lk 5:18–26

2 A few days later, when Jesus again
entered Capernaum, the people
heard that he had come home. 2So
many[a] gathered that there was no room
left, not even outside the door, and he
preached the word to them. 3Some men
came, bringing to him a paralytic,[b] car-
ried by four of them. 4Since they could
not get him to Jesus because of the
crowd, they made an opening in the
roof above Jesus and, after digging
through it, lowered the mat the para-
lysed man was lying on. 5When Jesus
saw their faith, he said to the paralytic,
"Son, your sins are forgiven."[c]
6Now some teachers of the law were
sitting there, thinking to themselves,
7"Why does this fellow talk like that?
He's blaspheming! Who can forgive sins
but God alone?"[d]
8Immediately Jesus knew in his spirit
that this was what they were thinking in
their hearts, and he said to them, "Why
are you thinking these things? 9Which is
easier: to say to the paralytic, 'Your sins
are forgiven,' or to say, 'Get up, take
your mat and walk'? 10But that you may
know that the Son of Man[e] has authority
on earth to forgive sins. . . ." He said to
the paralytic, 11"I tell you, get up, take
your mat and go home." 12He got up,
took his mat and walked out in full view
of them all. This amazed everyone and
they praised God,[f] saying, "We have
never seen anything like this!"[g]

The Calling of Levi

2:14–17pp—Mt 9:9–13; Lk 5:27–32

13Once again Jesus went out beside
the lake. A large crowd came to him,[h]
and he began to teach them. 14As he
walked along, he saw Levi son of
Alphaeus sitting at the tax collector's
booth. "Follow me,"[i] Jesus told him,
and Levi got up and followed him.
15While Jesus was having dinner at
Levi's house, many tax collectors and
"sinners" were eating with him and his
disciples, for there were many who fol-
lowed him. 16When the teachers of the
law who were Pharisees[j] saw him eating
with the "sinners" and tax collectors,
they asked his disciples: "Why does he
eat with tax collectors and 'sinners'?"[k]
17On hearing this, Jesus said to them,
"It is not the healthy who need a doctor,

f*40* The Greek word was used for various diseases affecting the skin—not necessarily leprosy.

but the sick. I have not come to call the
righteous, but sinners."[l]

Jesus Questioned About Fasting

2:18–22pp—Mt 9:14–17; Lk 5:33–38

18Now John's disciples and the Phari-
sees were fasting.[m] Some people came
and asked Jesus, "How is it that John's
disciples and the disciples of the Phari-
sees are fasting, but yours are not?"
19Jesus answered, "How can the
guests of the bridegroom fast while he is
with them? They cannot, so long as they
have him with them. 20But the time will
come when the bridegroom will be
taken from them,[n] and on that day they
will fast.
21"No-one sews a patch of unshrunk
cloth on an old garment. If he does, the
new piece will pull away from the old,
making the tear worse. 22And no-one
pours new wine into old wineskins. If
he does, the wine will burst the skins,
and both the wine and the wineskins
will be ruined. No, he pours new wine
into new wineskins."

Lord of the Sabbath

2:23–28pp—Mt 12:1–8; Lk 6:1–5
3:1–6pp—Mt 12:9–14; Lk 6:6–11

23One Sabbath Jesus was going
through the cornfields, and as his disci-
ples walked along, they began to pick
some ears of corn.[o] 24The Pharisees said
to him, "Look, why are they doing what
is unlawful on the Sabbath?"[p]
25He answered, "Have you never
read what David did when he and his
companions were hungry and in need?
26In the days of Abiathar the high
priest,[q] he entered the house of God and
ate the consecrated bread, which is law-
ful only for priests to eat.[r] And he also
gave some to his companions."[s]
27Then he said to them, "The Sabbath
was made for man,[t] not man for the
Sabbath.[u] 28So the Son of Man[v] is Lord
even of the Sabbath."

3 Another time he went into the
synagogue,[a] and a man with a
shrivelled hand was there. 2Some of
them were looking for a reason to ac-
cuse Jesus, so they watched him closely[b]
to see if he would heal him on the Sab-
bath.[c] 3Jesus said to the man with the
shrivelled hand, "Stand up in front of
everyone."
4Then Jesus asked them, "Which is
lawful on the Sabbath: to do good or to
do evil, to save life or to kill?" But they
remained silent.
5He looked round at them in anger
and, deeply distressed at their stubborn
hearts, said to the man, "Stretch out
your hand." He stretched it out, and his
hand was completely restored. 6Then
the Pharisees went out and began to
plot with the Herodians[d] how they
might kill Jesus.[e]

Crowds Follow Jesus

3:7–12pp—Mt 12:15,16; Lk 6:17–19

7Jesus withdrew with his disciples to
the lake, and a large crowd from Galilee
followed.[f] 8When they heard all he was
doing, many people came to him from
Judea, Jerusalem, Idumea, and the re-
gions across the Jordan and around
Tyre and Sidon.[g] 9Because of the crowd
he told his disciples to have a small boat
ready for him, to keep the people from
crowding him. 10For he had healed
many,[h] so that those with diseases were
pushing forward to touch him.[i]
11Whenever the evil[a] spirits saw him,
they fell down before him and cried out,
"You are the Son of God."[j] 12But he gave
them strict orders not to tell who he
was.[k]

The Appointing of the Twelve Apostles

3:16–19pp—Mt 10:2–4; Lk 6:14–16; Ac 1:13

13Jesus went up on a mountainside
and called to him those he wanted, and
they came to him.[l] 14He appointed
twelve—designating them apostles[b][m]
—that they might be with him and that
he might send them out to preach 15and
to have authority to drive out demons.[n]
16These are the twelve he appointed:
Simon (to whom he gave the name
Peter);[o] 17James son of Zebedee and his
brother John (to them he gave the name
Boanerges, which means Sons of Thun-
der); 18Andrew, Philip, Bartholomew,
Matthew, Thomas, James son of
Alphaeus, Thaddaeus, Simon the
Zealot 19and Judas Iscariot, who be-
trayed him.

Jesus and Beelzebub

3:23–27pp—Mt 12:25–29; Lk 11:17–22

20Then Jesus entered a house, and
again a crowd gathered,[p] so that he and
his disciples were not even able to eat.[q]
21When his family heard about this,

17 [l]Lk 19:10; 1Ti 1:15
18 [m]**Mt 6:16–18;** Ac 13:2
20 [n]Lk 17:22
23 [o]Dt 23:25
24 [p]**Mt 12:2**
26 [q]1Ch 24:6; 2Sa 8:17; [r]Lev 24:5–9; [s]1Sa 21:1–6
27 [t]Ex 23:12; Dt 5:14; [u]Col 2:16
28 [v]**Mt 8:20**

Ch. 3

1 [a]**Mt 4:23;** Mk 1:21
2 [b]**Mt 12:10;** [c]Lk 14:1
6 [d]Mt 22:16; Mk 12:13; [e]**Mt 12:14**
7 [f]Mt 4:25
8 [g]**Mt 11:21**
10 [h]**Mt 4:23;** [i]**Mt 9:20**
11 [j]**Mt 4:3;** Mk 1:23–24
12 [k]**Mt 8:4;** Mk 1:24–25,34; Ac 16:17–18
13 [l]Mt 5:1
14 [m]**Mk 6:30**
15 [n]**Mt 10:1**
16 [o]Jn 1:42
20 [p]ver 7; [q]Mk 6:31

[a]*11* Greek *unclean;* also in verse 30
[b]*14* Some manuscripts do not have *designating them apostles.*

they went to take charge of him, for they said, "He is out of his mind."[r]

22And the teachers of the law who came down from Jerusalem[s] said, "He is possessed by Beelzebub![c][t] By the prince of demons he is driving out demons."[u]

23So Jesus called them and spoke to them in parables:[v] "How can Satan[w] drive out Satan? 24If a kingdom is divided against itself, that kingdom cannot stand. 25If a house is divided against itself, that house cannot stand. 26And if Satan opposes himself and is divided, he cannot stand; his end has come. 27In fact, no-one can enter a strong man's house and carry off his possessions unless he first ties up the strong man. Then he can rob his house.[x] 28I tell you the truth, all the sins and blasphemies of men will be forgiven them. 29But whoever blasphemes against the Holy Spirit will never be forgiven; he is guilty of an eternal sin."[y]

30He said this because they were saying, "He has an evil spirit."

Jesus' Mother and Brothers

3:31–35pp—Mt 12:46–50; Lk 8:19–21

31Then Jesus' mother and brothers arrived.[z] Standing outside, they sent someone in to call him. 32A crowd was sitting around him, and they told him, "Your mother and brothers are outside looking for you."

33"Who are my mother and my brothers?" he asked.

34Then he looked at those seated in a circle around him and said, "Here are my mother and my brothers! 35Whoever does God's will is my brother and sister and mother."

The Parable of the Sower

4:1–12pp—Mt 13:1–15; Lk 8:4–10
4:13–20pp—Mt 13:18–23; Lk 8:11–15

4 Again Jesus began to teach by the lake.[a] The crowd that gathered round him was so large that he got into a boat and sat in it out on the lake, while all the people were along the shore at the water's edge. 2He taught them many things by parables,[b] and in his teaching said: 3"Listen! A farmer went out to sow his seed.[c] 4As he was scattering the seed, some fell along the path, and the birds came and ate it up. 5Some fell on rocky places, where it did not have much soil. It sprang up quickly, because the soil was shallow. 6But when the sun came up, the plants were scorched, and they withered because they had no root. 7Other seed fell among thorns, which grew up and choked the plants, so that they did not bear grain. 8Still other seed fell on good soil. It came up, grew and produced a crop, multiplying thirty, sixty or even a hundred times."[d]

9Then Jesus said, "He who has ears to hear, let him hear."[e]

10When he was alone, the Twelve and the others around him asked him about the parables. 11He told them, "The secret of the kingdom of God[f] has been given to you. But to those on the outside[g] everything is said in parables 12so that,

"'they may be ever seeing but never
perceiving,
and ever hearing but never
understanding;
otherwise they might turn and be
forgiven!'[a]"[h]

13Then Jesus said to them, "Don't you understand this parable? How then will you understand any parable? 14The farmer sows the word.[i] 15Some people are like seed along the path, where the word is sown. As soon as they hear it, Satan[j] comes and takes away the word that was sown in them. 16Others, like seed sown on rocky places, hear the word and at once receive it with joy. 17But since they have no root, they last only a short time. When trouble or persecution comes because of the word, they quickly fall away. 18Still others, like seed sown among thorns, hear the word; 19but the worries of this life, the deceitfulness of wealth[k] and the desires for other things come in and choke the word, making it unfruitful. 20Others, like seed sown on good soil, hear the word, accept it, and produce a crop —thirty, sixty or even a hundred times what was sown."

A Lamp on a Stand

21He said to them, "Do you bring in a lamp to put it under a bowl or a bed? Instead, don't you put it on its stand?[l] 22For whatever is hidden is meant to be disclosed, and whatever is concealed is meant to be brought out into the open.[m] 23If anyone has ears to hear, let him hear."[n]

24"Consider carefully what you hear," he continued. "With the measure you use, it will be measured to you

21 [r]Jn 10:20; Ac 26:24
22 [s]Mt 15:1; [t]Mt 10:25; 11:18; 12:24; Jn 7:20; 8:48,52; 10:20; [u]Mt 9:34
23 [v]Mk 4:2; [w]**Mt 4:10**
27 [x]Isa 49:24–25
29 [y]Mt 12:31–32; Lk 12:10
31 [z]ver 21

Ch. 4

1 [a]Mk 2:13; 3:7
2 [b]ver 11; Mk 3:23
3 [c]ver 26
8 [d]Jn 15:5; Col 1:6
9 [e]ver 23; **Mt 11:15**
11 [f]**Mt 3:2;** [g]1Co 5:12–13; Col 4:5; 1Th 4:12; 1Ti 3:7
12 [h]Isa 6:9–10; **Mt 13:13–15**
14 [i]Mk 16:20; Lk 1:2; Ac 4:31; 8:4; 16:6; 17:11; Php 1:14
15 [j]**Mt 4:10**
19 [k]Mt 19:23; 1Ti 6:9–10,17; 1Jn 2:15–17
21 [l]**Mt 5:15**
22 [m]Jer 16:17; Mt 10:26; Lk 8:17; 12:2
23 [n]ver 9; **Mt 11:15**

[c]*22* Greek *Beezeboul* or *Beelzeboul*
[a]*12* Isaiah 6:9,10

—and even more.[o] 25Whoever has will
be given more; whoever does not have,
even what he has will be taken from
him."[p]

The Parable of the Growing Seed

26He also said, "This is what the king-
dom of God is like.[q] A man scatters seed
on the ground. 27Night and day,
whether he sleeps or gets up, the seed
sprouts and grows, though he does not
know how. 28All by itself the soil pro-
duces corn—first the stalk, then the ear,
then the full grain in the ear. 29As soon
as the grain is ripe, he puts the sickle to
it, because the harvest has come."[r]

The Parable of the Mustard Seed

4:30–32pp—Mt 13:31,32; Lk 13:18,19

30Again he said, "What shall we say
the kingdom of God is like,[s] or what
parable shall we use to describe it? 31It is
like a mustard seed, which is the small-
est seed you plant in the ground. 32Yet
when planted, it grows and becomes
the largest of all garden plants, with
such big branches that the birds of the
air can perch in its shade."
33With many similar parables Jesus
spoke the word to them, as much as
they could understand.[t] 34He did not
say anything to them without using a
parable. But when he was alone with his
own disciples, he explained every-
thing.[u]

Jesus Calms the Storm

4:35–41pp—Mt 8:18,23–27; Lk 8:22–25

35That day when evening came, he
said to his disciples, "Let us go over to
the other side." 36Leaving the crowd
behind, they took him along, just as he
was, in the boat. There were also other
boats with him.[v] 37A furious squall came
up, and the waves broke over the boat,
so that it was nearly swamped. 38Jesus
was in the stern, sleeping on a cushion.
The disciples woke him and said to him,
"Teacher, don't you care if we drown?"
39He got up, rebuked the wind and
said to the waves, "Quiet! Be still!"
Then the wind died down and it was
completely calm.
40He said to his disciples, "Why are
you so afraid? Do you still have no
faith?"[w]
41They were terrified and asked each
other, "Who is this? Even the wind and
the waves obey him!"

24 [o]Mt 7:2
25 [p]**Mt 25:29**
26 [q]**Mt 13:24**
29 [r]Rev 14:15
30 [s]**Mt 13:24**
33 [t]Jn 16:12
34 [u]**Jn 16:25**
36 [v]ver 1; Mk 3:9; 5:2,21; 6:32,45
40 [w]Mt 14:31; Mk 16:14

Ch. 5

2 [a]Mk 4:1; [b]Mk 1:23
7 [c]**Mt 8:29**; [d]**Mt 4:3**; Lk 1:32; 6:35; Ac 16:17; Heb 7:1
9 [e]ver 15
15 [f]ver 9; [g]ver 16,18; **Mt 4:24**
19 [h]**Mt 8:4**

The Healing of a Demon-possessed Man

5:1–17pp—Mt 8:28–34; Lk 8:26–37
5:18–20pp—Lk 8:38,39

5 They went across the lake to the
region of the Gerasenes.[a] 2When
Jesus got out of the boat,[a] a man with an
evil[b] spirit[b] came from the tombs to meet
him. 3This man lived in the tombs, and
no-one could bind him any more, not
even with a chain. 4For he had often
been chained hand and foot, but he tore
the chains apart and broke the irons on
his feet. No-one was strong enough to
subdue him. 5Night and day among the
tombs and in the hills he would cry out
and cut himself with stones.
6When he saw Jesus from a distance,
he ran and fell on his knees in front of
him. 7He shouted at the top of his voice,
"What do you want with me,[c] Jesus,
Son of the Most High God?[d] Swear to
God that you won't torture me!" 8For
Jesus had said to him, "Come out of this
man, you evil spirit!"
9Then Jesus asked him, "What is your
name?"
"My name is Legion,"[e] he replied,
"for we are many." 10And he begged
Jesus again and again not to send them
out of the area.
11A large herd of pigs was feeding on
the nearby hillside. 12The demons
begged Jesus, "Send us among the pigs;
allow us to go into them." 13He gave
them permission, and the evil spirits
came out and went into the pigs. The
herd, about two thousand in number,
rushed down the steep bank into the
lake and were drowned.
14Those tending the pigs ran off and
reported this in the town and country-
side, and the people went out to see
what had happened. 15When they came
to Jesus, they saw the man who had
been possessed by the legion[f] of de-
mons,[g] sitting there, dressed and in his
right mind; and they were afraid.
16Those who had seen it told the people
what had happened to the demon-
possessed man—and told about the
pigs as well. 17Then the people began to
plead with Jesus to leave their region.
18As Jesus was getting into the boat,
the man who had been demon-
possessed begged to go with him.
19Jesus did not let him, but said, "Go
home to your family and tell them[h] how
much the Lord has done for you, and

---

[a]1 Some manuscripts *Gadarenes;* other manuscripts *Gergesenes*
[b]2 Greek *unclean;* also in verses 8 and 13

how he has had mercy on you." 20So the
man went away and began to tell in the
Decapolis[c][i] how much Jesus had done
for him. And all the people were
amazed.

A Dead Girl and a Sick Woman

5:22–43pp—Mt 9:18–26; Lk 8:41–56

21When Jesus had again crossed over
by boat to the other side of the lake,[j] a
large crowd gathered round him while
he was by the lake.[k] 22Then one of the
synagogue rulers,[l] named Jairus, came
there. Seeing Jesus, he fell at his feet
23and pleaded earnestly with him, "My
little daughter is dying. Please come
and put your hands on[m] her so that she
will be healed and live." 24So Jesus went
with him.

A large crowd followed and pressed
around him. 25And a woman was there
who had been subject to bleeding[n] for
twelve years. 26She had suffered a great
deal under the care of many doctors and
had spent all she had, yet instead of
getting better she grew worse. 27When
she heard about Jesus, she came up
behind him in the crowd and touched
his cloak, 28because she thought, "If I
just touch his clothes,[o] I will be healed."
29Immediately her bleeding stopped
and she felt in her body that she was
freed from her suffering.[p]

30At once Jesus realised that power[q]
had gone out from him. He turned
around in the crowd and asked, "Who
touched my clothes?"

31"You see the people crowding
against you," his disciples answered,
"and yet you can ask, 'Who touched
me?'"

32But Jesus kept looking around to see
who had done it. 33Then the woman,
knowing what had happened to her,
came and fell at his feet and, trembling
with fear, told him the whole truth. 34He
said to her, "Daughter, your faith has
healed you.[r] Go in peace[s] and be freed
from your suffering."

35While Jesus was still speaking, some
men came from the house of Jairus, the
synagogue ruler.[t] "Your daughter is
dead," they said. "Why bother the
teacher any more?"

36Ignoring what they said, Jesus told
the synagogue ruler, "Don't be afraid;
just believe."

37He did not let anyone follow him
except Peter, James and John the
brother of James.[u] 38When they came to
the home of the synagogue ruler,[v] Jesus
saw a commotion, with people crying
and wailing loudly. 39He went in and
said to them, "Why all this commotion
and wailing? The child is not dead but
asleep."[w] 40But they laughed at him.

After he put them all out, he took the
child's father and mother and the disci-
ples who were with him, and went in
where the child was. 41He took her by
the hand[x] and said to her, *"Talitha
koum!"* (which means, "Little girl, I say
to you, get up!").[y] 42Immediately the girl
stood up and walked around (she was
twelve years old). At this they were
completely astonished. 43He gave strict
orders not to let anyone know about
this,[z] and told them to give her some-
thing to eat.

A Prophet Without Honour

6:1–6pp—Mt 13:54–58

6 Jesus left there and went to his
home town,[a] accompanied by his
disciples. 2When the Sabbath came,[b] he
began to teach in the synagogue,[c] and
many who heard him were amazed.[d]

"Where did this man get these
things?" they asked. "What's this wis-
dom that has been given him, that he
even does miracles! 3Isn't this the
carpenter? Isn't this Mary's son and the
brother of James, Joseph,[a] Judas and
Simon?[e] Aren't his sisters here with
us?" And they took offence at him.[f]

4Jesus said to them, "Only in his
home town, among his relatives and in
his own house is a prophet without
honour."[g] 5He could not do any mira-
cles there, except lay his hands on[h] a few
sick people and heal them. 6And he was
amazed at their lack of faith.

Jesus Sends Out the Twelve

6:7–11pp—Mt 10:1,9–14; Lk 9:1,3–5

Then Jesus went round teaching from
village to village.[i] 7Calling the Twelve to
him,[j] he sent them out two by two[k] and
gave them authority over evil[b] spirits.[l]

8These were his instructions: "Take
nothing for the journey except a staff
—no bread, no bag, no money in your
belts. 9Wear sandals but not an extra
tunic. 10Whenever you enter a house,
stay there until you leave that town.
11And if any place will not welcome you
or listen to you, shake the dust off your
feet[m] when you leave, as a testimony
against them."

20 [i]Mt 4:25; Mk 7:31
21 [j]Mt 9:1; [k]Mk 4:1
22 [l]ver 35–36,38; Lk 13:14; Ac 13:15; 18:8,17
23 [m]Mt 19:13; Mk 6:5; 7:32; 8:23; 16:18; Lk 4:40; 13:13; **Ac 6:6**
25 [n]Lev 15:25–30
28 [o]**Mt 9:20**
29 [p]ver 34
30 [q]Lk 5:17; 6:19
34 [r]**Mt 9:22**; [s]**Ac 15:33**
35 [t]**ver 22**
37 [u]**Mt 4:21**
38 [v]**ver 22**
39 [w]**Mt 9:24**
41 [x]Mk 1:31; [y]**Lk 7:14**
43 [z]**Mt 8:4**

Ch. 6

1 [a]**Mt 2:23**
2 [b]Mk 1:21; [c]**Mt 4:23**; [d]**Mt 7:28**
3 [e]**Mt 12:46**; [f]Mt 11:6; Jn 6:61
4 [g]Lk 4:24; Jn 4:44
5 [h]**Mk 5:23**
6 [i]Mt 9:35; Mk 1:39; Lk 13:22
7 [j]Mk 3:13; [k]Dt 17:6; Lk 10:1; [l]**Mt 10:1**
11 [m]**Mt 10:14**

[c]20 That is, the Ten Cities
[a]3 Greek *Joses*, a variant of *Joseph*
[b]7 Greek *unclean*

12They went out and preached that
people should repent.[n] 13They drove
out many demons and anointed many
sick people with oil[o] and healed them.

John the Baptist Beheaded

6:14–29pp—Mt 14:1–12
6:14–16pp—Lk 9:7–9

14King Herod heard about this, for
Jesus' name had become well known.
Some were saying,[c] "John the Baptist[p]
has been raised from the dead, and that
is why miraculous powers are at work in
him."
15Others said, "He is Elijah."[q]
And still others claimed, "He is a
prophet,[r] like one of the prophets of
long ago."[s]
16But when Herod heard this, he said,
"John, the man I beheaded, has been
raised from the dead!"
17For Herod himself had given orders
to have John arrested, and he had him
bound and put in prison.[t] He did
this because of Herodias, his brother
Philip's wife, whom he had married.
18For John had been saying to Herod,
"It is not lawful for you to have your
brother's wife."[u] 19So Herodias nursed a
grudge against John and wanted to kill
him. But she was not able to, 20because
Herod feared John and protected him,
knowing him to be a righteous and holy
man.[v] When Herod heard John, he was
greatly puzzled;[d] yet he liked to listen to
him.
21Finally the opportune time came.
On his birthday Herod gave a banquet[w]
for his high officials and military com-
manders and the leading men of
Galilee.[x] 22When the daughter of Hero-
dias came in and danced, she pleased
Herod and his dinner guests.
The king said to the girl, "Ask me for
anything you want, and I'll give it to
you." 23And he promised her with an
oath, "Whatever you ask I will give you,
up to half my kingdom."[y]
24She went out and said to her
mother, "What shall I ask for?"
"The head of John the Baptist," she
answered.
25At once the girl hurried in to the
king with the request: "I want you to
give me right now the head of John the
Baptist on a platter."
26The king was greatly distressed, but
because of his oaths and his dinner
guests, he did not want to refuse her.
27So he immediately sent an executioner
with orders to bring John's head. The
man went, beheaded John in the prison,
28and brought back his head on a plat-
ter. He presented it to the girl, and she
gave it to her mother. 29On hearing of
this, John's disciples came and took his
body and laid it in a tomb.

Jesus Feeds the Five Thousand

6:32–44pp—Mk 14:13–21; Lk 9:10–17; Jn 6:5–13
6:32–44Ref—Mk 8:2–9

30The apostles[z] gathered round Jesus
and reported to him all they had done
and taught.[a] 31Then, because so many
people were coming and going that they
did not even have a chance to eat,[b] he
said to them, "Come with me by
yourselves to a quiet place and get some
rest."
32So they went away by themselves in
a boat[c] to a solitary place. 33But many
who saw them leaving recognised them
and ran on foot from all the towns and
got there ahead of them. 34When Jesus
landed and saw a large crowd, he had
compassion on them, because they
were like sheep without a shepherd.[d] So
he began teaching them many things.
35By this time it was late in the day, so
his disciples came to him. "This is a
remote place," they said, "and it's
already very late. 36Send the people
away so that they can go to the sur-
rounding countryside and villages and
buy themselves something to eat."
37But he answered, "You give them
something to eat."[e]
They said to him, "That would take
eight months of a man's wages![e] Are we
to go and spend that much on bread and
give it to them to eat?"
38"How many loaves do you have?"
he asked. "Go and see."
When they found out, they said,
"Five—and two fish."[f]
39Then Jesus directed them to have all
the people sit down in groups on the
green grass. 40So they sat down in
groups of hundreds and fifties. 41Taking
the five loaves and the two fish and
looking up to heaven, he gave thanks
and broke the loaves.[g] Then he gave
them to his disciples to set before the
people. He also divided the two fish
among them all. 42They all ate and were
satisfied, 43and the disciples picked up
twelve basketfuls of broken pieces of
bread and fish. 44The number of the
men who had eaten was five thousand.

12 [n]Lk 9:6
13 [o]**Jas 5:14**
14 [p]**Mt 3:1**
15 [q]Mal 4:5; [r]**Mt 21:11**; [s]Mt 16:14; Mk 8:28
17 [t]Mt 4:12; 11:2; Lk 3:19–20
18 [u]Lev 18:16; 20:21
20 [v]**Mt 11:9**
21 [w]Est 1:3; 2:18; [x]Lk 3:1
23 [y]Est 5:3,6; 7:2
30 [z]Mt 10:2; Lk 9:10; 17:5; 22:14; 24:10; Ac 1:2,26; [a]Lk 9:10
31 [b]Mk 3:20
32 [c]ver 45; **Mk 4:36**
34 [d]**Mt 9:36**
37 [e]2Ki 4:42–44
38 [f]Mt 15:34; Mk 8:5
41 [g]**Mt 14:19**

[c]14 Some early manuscripts *He was saying*
[d]20 Some early manuscripts *he did many things*
[e]37 Greek *take two hundred denarii*

Jesus Walks on the Water

6:45–51pp—Mt 14:22–32; Jn 6:15–21
6:53–56pp—Mt 14:34–36

45 Immediately Jesus made his disciples get into the boat[h] and go on ahead of him to Bethsaida,[i] while he dismissed the crowd. 46 After leaving them, he went up on a mountainside to pray.[j]

47 When evening came, the boat was in the middle of the lake, and he was alone on land. 48 He saw the disciples straining at the oars, because the wind was against them. About the fourth watch of the night he went out to them, walking on the lake. He was about to pass by them, 49 but when they saw him walking on the lake, they thought he was a ghost.[k] They cried out, 50 because they all saw him and were terrified.

Immediately he spoke to them and said, "Take courage! It is I. Don't be afraid."[l] 51 Then he climbed into the boat[m] with them, and the wind died down.[n] They were completely amazed, 52 for they had not understood about the loaves; their hearts were hardened.[o]

53 When they had crossed over, they landed at Gennesaret and anchored there.[p] 54 As soon as they got out of the boat, people recognised Jesus. 55 They ran throughout that whole region and carried the sick on mats to wherever they heard he was. 56 And wherever he went—into villages, towns or countryside—they placed the sick in the market-places. They begged him to let them touch even the edge of his cloak,[q] and all who touched him were healed.

Clean and Unclean

7:1–23pp—Mt 15:1–20

7 The Pharisees and some of the teachers of the law who had come from Jerusalem gathered round Jesus and 2 saw some of his disciples eating food with hands that were "unclean",[a] that is, unwashed. 3 (The Pharisees and all the Jews do not eat unless they give their hands a ceremonial washing, holding to the tradition of the elders.[b] 4 When they come from the market-place they do not eat unless they wash. And they observe many other traditions, such as the washing of cups, pitchers and kettles.[a])[c]

5 So the Pharisees and teachers of the law asked Jesus, "Why don't your disciples live according to the tradition of the elders[d] instead of eating their food with 'unclean' hands?"

6 He replied, "Isaiah was right when he prophesied about you hypocrites; as it is written:

"'These people honour me with their lips,
but their hearts are far from me.
7 They worship me in vain;
their teachings are but rules taught by men.'[b][e]

8 You have let go of the commands of God and are holding on to the traditions of men."[f]

9 And he said to them: "You have a fine way of setting aside the commands of God in order to observe[c] your own traditions![g] 10 For Moses said, 'Honour your father and your mother,'[d][h] and, 'Anyone who curses his father or mother must be put to death.'[e][i] 11 But you say[j] that if a man says to his father or mother: 'Whatever help you might otherwise have received from me is Corban' (that is, a gift devoted to God), 12 then you no longer let him do anything for his father or mother. 13 Thus you nullify the word of God[k] by your tradition[l] that you have handed down. And you do many things like that."

14 Again Jesus called the crowd to him and said, "Listen to me, everyone, and understand this. 15 Nothing outside a man can make him 'unclean' by going into him. Rather, it is what comes out of a man that makes him 'unclean'."[f]

17 After he had left the crowd and entered the house, his disciples asked him[m] about this parable. 18 "Are you so dull?" he asked. "Don't you see that nothing that enters a man from the outside can make him 'unclean'? 19 For it doesn't go into his heart but into his stomach, and then out of his body." (In saying this, Jesus declared all foods[n] "clean".)[o]

20 He went on: "What comes out of a man is what makes him 'unclean'. 21 For from within, out of men's hearts, come evil thoughts, sexual immorality, theft, murder, adultery, 22 greed,[p] malice, deceit, lewdness, envy, slander, arrogance and folly. 23 All these evils come from inside and make a man 'unclean'."

45 [h]ver 32; [i]**Mt 11:21**
46 [j]**Lk 3:21**
49 [k]Lk 24:37
50 [l]**Mt 14:27**
51 [m]ver 32; [n]Mk 4:39
52 [o]Mk 8:17–21
53 [p]Jn 6:24–25
56 [q]**Mt 9:20**

Ch. 7

2 [a]Ac 10:14,28; 11:8; Ro 14:14
3 [b]ver 5,8–9,13; Lk 11:38
4 [c]Mt 23:25; Lk 11:39
5 [d]**ver 3**; Gal 1:14; Col 2:8
7 [e]Isa 29:13
8 [f]**ver 3**
9 [g]**ver 3**
10 [h]Ex 20:12; Dt 5:16; [i]Ex 21:17; Lev 20:9
11 [j]Mt 23:16,18
13 [k]**Heb 4:12**; [l]**ver 3**
17 [m]Mk 9:28
19 [n]Ro 14:1–12; Col 2:16; 1Ti 4:3–5; [o]**Ac 10:15**
22 [p]Mt 20:15

a4 Some early manuscripts *pitchers, kettles and dining couches*
b6,7 Isaiah 29:13
c9 Some manuscripts *set up*
d10 Exodus 20:12; Deut. 5:16
e10 Exodus 21:17; Lev. 20:9
f15 Some early manuscripts *'unclean'. 16If anyone has ears to hear, let him hear."*

The Faith of a Syro-Phoenician Woman

7:24–30pp—Mt 15:21–28

24 Jesus left that place and went to the
vicinity of Tyre.[g][q] He entered a house
and did not want anyone to know it; yet
he could not keep his presence secret.
25 In fact, as soon as she heard about
him, a woman whose little daughter
was possessed by an evil[h] spirit[r] came
and fell at his feet. 26 The woman was a
Greek, born in Syrian Phoenicia. She
begged Jesus to drive the demon out of
her daughter.
27 "First let the children eat all they
want," he told her, "for it is not right to
take the children's bread and toss it to
their dogs."
28 "Yes, Lord," she replied, "but even
the dogs under the table eat the chil-
dren's crumbs."
29 Then he told her, "For such a reply,
you may go; the demon has left your
daughter."
30 She went home and found her child
lying on the bed, and the demon gone.

The Healing of a Deaf and Mute Man

7:31–37pp—Mt 15:29–31

31 Then Jesus left the vicinity of Tyre[s]
and went through Sidon, down to the
Sea of Galilee[t] and into the region of
the Decapolis.[i][u] 32 There some people
brought to him a man who was deaf and
could hardly talk,[v] and they begged him
to place his hand on[w] the man.
33 After he took him aside, away from
the crowd, Jesus put his fingers into the
man's ears. Then he spat[x] and touched
the man's tongue. 34 He looked up to
heaven[y] and with a deep sigh[z] said to
him, "*Ephphatha!*" (which means, "Be
opened!"). 35 At this, the man's ears
were opened, his tongue was loosened
and he began to speak plainly.[a]
36 Jesus commanded them not to tell
anyone.[b] But the more he did so, the
more they kept talking about it. 37 People
were overwhelmed with amazement.
"He has done everything well," they
said. "He even makes the deaf hear and
the mute speak."

Jesus Feeds the Four Thousand

8:1–9pp—Mt 15:32–39
8:1–9Ref—Mk 6:32–44
8:11–21pp—Mt 16:1–12

8 During those days another large
crowd gathered. Since they had
nothing to eat, Jesus called his disciples
to him and said, 2 "I have compassion
for these people;[a] they have already
been with me three days and have
nothing to eat. 3 If I send them home
hungry, they will collapse on the way,
because some of them have come a long
distance."
4 His disciples answered, "But where
in this remote place can anyone get
enough bread to feed them?"
5 "How many loaves do you have?"
Jesus asked.
"Seven," they replied.
6 He told the crowd to sit down on the
ground. When he had taken the seven
loaves and given thanks, he broke them
and gave them to his disciples to set
before the people, and they did so.
7 They had a few small fish as well; he
gave thanks for them also and told the
disciples to distribute them.[b] 8 The peo-
ple ate and were satisfied. Afterwards
the disciples picked up seven basketfuls
of broken pieces that were left over.[c]
9 About four thousand men were pres-
ent. And having sent them away, 10 he
got into the boat with his disciples and
went to the region of Dalmanutha.
11 The Pharisees came and began to
question Jesus. To test him, they asked
him for a sign from heaven.[d] 12 He
sighed deeply[e] and said, "Why does
this generation ask for a miraculous
sign? I tell you the truth, no sign will be
given to it." 13 Then he left them, got
back into the boat and crossed to the
other side.

The Yeast of the Pharisees and Herod

14 The disciples had forgotten to bring
bread, except for one loaf they had with
them in the boat. 15 "Be careful," Jesus
warned them. "Watch out for the yeast[f]
of the Pharisees[g] and that of Herod."[h]
16 They discussed this with one
another and said, "It is because we have
no bread."
17 Aware of their discussion, Jesus
asked them: "Why are you talking
about having no bread? Do you still not
see or understand? Are your hearts
hardened?[i] 18 Do you have eyes but fail
to see, and ears but fail to hear? And
don't you remember? 19 When I broke
the five loaves for the five thousand,
how many basketfuls of pieces did you
pick up?"
"Twelve,"[j] they replied.
20 "And when I broke the seven loaves

24 [q] **Mt 11:21**
25 [r] **Mt 4:24**
31 [s] ver 24; **Mt 11:21**; [t] **Mt 4:18**; [u] Mt 4:25; Mk 5:20
32 [v] Mt 9:32; Lk 11:14; [w] **Mk 5:23**
33 [x] Mk 8:23
34 [y] Mk 6:41; Jn 11:41; [z] Mk 8:12
35 [a] Isa 35:5–6
36 [b] **Mt 8:4**

Ch. 8

2 [a] **Mt 9:36**
7 [b] Mt 14:19
8 [c] ver 20
11 [d] **Mt 12:38**
12 [e] Mk 7:34
15 [f] 1Co 5:6–8; [g] Lk 12:1; [h] **Mt 14:1**; Mk 12:13
17 [i] Isa 6:9–10; Mk 6:52
19 [j] Mt 14:20; Mk 6:41–44; Lk 9:17; Jn 6:13

[g] 24 Many early manuscripts *Tyre and Sidon*
[h] 25 Greek *unclean*
[i] 31 That is, the Ten Cities

for the four thousand, how many basketfuls of pieces did you pick up?"

They answered, "Seven."[k]

21 He said to them, "Do you still not understand?"[l]

The Healing of a Blind Man at Bethsaida

22 They came to Bethsaida,[m] and some people brought a blind man[n] and begged Jesus to touch him. 23 He took the blind man by the hand and led him outside the village. When he had spat[o] on the man's eyes and put his hands on[p] him, Jesus asked, "Do you see anything?"

24 He looked up and said, "I see people; they look like trees walking around."

25 Once more Jesus put his hands on the man's eyes. Then his eyes were opened, his sight was restored, and he saw everything clearly. 26 Jesus sent him home, saying, "Don't go into the village."[a]

Peter's Confession of Christ

8:27–29pp—Mt 16:13–16; Lk 9:18–20

27 Jesus and his disciples went on to the villages around Caesarea Philippi. On the way he asked them, "Who do people say I am?"

28 They replied, "Some say John the Baptist;[q] others say Elijah;[r] and still others, one of the prophets."

29 "But what about you?" he asked. "Who do you say I am?"

Peter answered, "You are the Christ."[b][s]

30 Jesus warned them not to tell anyone about him.[t]

Jesus Predicts His Death

8:31–9:1pp—Mt 16:21–28; Lk 9:22–27

31 He then began to teach them that the Son of Man[u] must suffer many things[v] and be rejected by the elders, chief priests and teachers of the law,[w] and that he must be killed[x] and after three days[y] rise again.[z] 32 He spoke plainly[a] about this, and Peter took him aside and began to rebuke him.

33 But when Jesus turned and looked at his disciples, he rebuked Peter. "Get behind me, Satan!"[b] he said. "You do not have in mind the things of God, but the things of men."

34 Then he called the crowd to him along with his disciples and said: "If anyone would come after me, he must deny himself and take up his cross and follow me.[c] 35 For whoever wants to save his life[c] will lose it, but whoever loses his life for me and for the gospel will save it.[d] 36 What good is it for a man to gain the whole world, yet forfeit his soul? 37 Or what can a man give in exchange for his soul? 38 If anyone is ashamed of me and my words in this adulterous and sinful generation, the Son of Man[e] will be ashamed of him[f] when he comes[g] in his Father's glory with the holy angels."

9 And he said to them, "I tell you the truth, some who are standing here will not taste death before they see the kingdom of God come[a] with power."[b]

The Transfiguration

9:2–8pp—Lk 9:28–36
9:2–13pp—Mt 17:1–13

2 After six days Jesus took Peter, James and John[c] with him and led them up a high mountain, where they were all alone. There he was transfigured before them. 3 His clothes became dazzling white,[d] whiter than anyone in the world could bleach them. 4 And there appeared before them Elijah and Moses, who were talking with Jesus.

5 Peter said to Jesus, "Rabbi,[e] it is good for us to be here. Let us put up three shelters—one for you, one for Moses and one for Elijah." 6 (He did not know what to say, they were so frightened.)

7 Then a cloud appeared and enveloped them, and a voice came from the cloud:[f] "This is my Son, whom I love. Listen to him!"[g]

8 Suddenly, when they looked round, they no longer saw anyone with them except Jesus.

9 As they were coming down the mountain, Jesus gave them orders not to tell anyone[h] what they had seen until the Son of Man[i] had risen from the dead. 10 They kept the matter to themselves, discussing what "rising from the dead" meant.

11 And they asked him, "Why do the teachers of the law say that Elijah must come first?"

12 Jesus replied, "To be sure, Elijah does come first, and restores all things. Why then is it written that the Son of Man[j] must suffer much[k] and be rejected?[l] 13 But I tell you, Elijah has come,"[m]

20 [k]ver 6–9; Mt 15:37
21 [l]Mk 6:52
22 [m]**Mt 11:21;** [n]Mk 10:46; Jn 9:1
23 [o]Mk 7:33; [p]**Mk 5:23**
28 [q]**Mt 3:1;** [r]Mal 4:5
29 [s]Jn 6:69; 11:27
30 [t]**Mt 8:4;** 16:20; 17:9; Mk 9:9; Lk 9:21
31 [u]**Mt 8:20;** [v]**Mt 16:21;** [w]Mt 27:1–2; [x]Ac 2:23; 3:13; [y]**Mt 16:21;** [z]**Mt 16:21**
32 [a]Jn 18:20
33 [b]**Mt 4:10**
34 [c]Mt 10:38; Lk 14:27
35 [d]**Jn 12:25**
38 [e]**Mt 8:20;** [f]Mt 10:33; Lk 12:9; [g]**1Th 2:19**

Ch. 9

1 [a]Mk 13:30; Lk 22:18; [b]Mt 24:30; 25:31
2 [c]**Mt 4:21**
3 [d]**Mt 28:3**
5 [e]**Mt 23:7**
7 [f]Ex 24:16; [g]**Mt 3:17**
9 [h]**Mk 8:30;** [i]**Mt 8:20**
12 [j]**Mt 8:20;** [k]**Mt 16:21;** [l]Lk 23:11
13 [m]**Mt 11:14**

[a]26 Some manuscripts *Don't go and tell anyone in the village*
[b]29 Or *Messiah*. "The Christ" (Greek) and "the Messiah" (Hebrew) both mean "the Anointed One".
[c]35 The Greek word means either *life* or *soul*; also in verse 36.

and they have done to him everything
they wished, just as it is written about
him."

The Healing of a Boy With an Evil Spirit

9:14–28,30–32pp—Mt 17:14–19,22,23; Lk 9:37–45

14When they came to the other dis-
ciples, they saw a large crowd around
them and the teachers of the law
arguing with them. 15As soon as all the
people saw Jesus, they were over-
whelmed with wonder and ran to greet
him.

16"What are you arguing with them
about?" he asked.

17A man in the crowd answered,
"Teacher, I brought you my son, who is
possessed by a spirit that has robbed
him of speech. 18Whenever it seizes
him, it throws him to the ground. He
foams at the mouth, gnashes his teeth
and becomes rigid. I asked your disci-
ples to drive out the spirit, but they
could not."

19"O unbelieving generation," Jesus
replied, "how long shall I stay with
you? How long shall I put up with you?
Bring the boy to me."

20So they brought him. When the
spirit saw Jesus, it immediately threw
the boy into a convulsion. He fell to the
ground and rolled around, foaming at
the mouth.[n]

21Jesus asked the boy's father, "How
long has he been like this?"

"From childhood," he answered.
22"It has often thrown him into fire or
water to kill him. But if you can do
anything, take pity on us and help us."

23" 'If you can'?" said Jesus. "Every-
thing is possible for him who believes."[o]

24Immediately the boy's father ex-
claimed, "I do believe; help me over-
come my unbelief!"

25When Jesus saw that a crowd was
running to the scene,[p] he rebuked the
evil[a] spirit. "You deaf and mute spirit,"
he said, "I command you, come out of
him and never enter him again."

26The spirit shrieked, convulsed him
violently and came out. The boy looked
so much like a corpse that many said,
"He's dead." 27But Jesus took him by
the hand and lifted him to his feet, and
he stood up.

28After Jesus had gone indoors, his
disciples asked him privately,[q] "Why
couldn't we drive it out?"

29He replied, "This kind can come out
only by prayer."[b]

30They left that place and passed
through Galilee. Jesus did not want
anyone to know where they were,
31because he was teaching his disciples.
He said to them, "The Son of Man[r] is
going to be betrayed into the hands of
men. They will kill him,[s] and after three
days[t] he will rise."[u] 32But they did not
understand what he meant[v] and were
afraid to ask him about it.

Who Is the Greatest?

9:33–37pp—Mt 18:1–5; Lk 9:46–48

33They came to Capernaum.[w] When
he was in the house,[x] he asked them,
"What were you arguing about on the
road?" 34But they kept quiet because on
the way they had argued about who
was the greatest.[y]

35Sitting down, Jesus called the
Twelve and said, "If anyone wants to be
first, he must be the very last, and the
servant of all."[z]

36He took a little child and had him
stand among them. Taking him in his
arms,[a] he said to them, 37"Whoever
welcomes one of these little children in
my name welcomes me; and whoever
welcomes me does not welcome me but
the one who sent me."[b]

Whoever Is Not Against Us Is for Us

9:38–40pp—Lk 9:49,50

38"Teacher," said John, "we saw a
man driving out demons in your name
and we told him to stop, because he was
not one of us."[c]

39"Do not stop him," Jesus said. "No-
one who does a miracle in my name can
in the next moment say anything bad
about me, 40for whoever is not against
us is for us.[d] 41I tell you the truth, any-
one who gives you a cup of water in my
name because you belong to Christ will
certainly not lose his reward.[e]

Causing to Sin

42"And if anyone causes one of these
little ones who believe in me to sin,[f] it
would be better for him to be thrown
into the sea with a large millstone tied
around his neck.[g] 43If your hand causes
you to sin,[h] cut it off. It is better for you
to enter life maimed than with two
hands to go into hell,[i] where the fire
never goes out.[c][j] 45And if your foot
causes you to sin,[k] cut it off. It is better

20 [n]Mk 1:26
23 [o]**Mt 21:21**; Mk 11:23; Jn 11:40
25 [p]ver 15
28 [q]Mk 7:17
31 [r]**Mt 8:20**; [s]ver 12; Ac 2:23; 3:13; [t]**Mt 16:21**; [u]**Mt 16:21**
32 [v]Lk 2:50; 9:45; 18:34; Jn 12:16
33 [w]**Mt 4:13**; [x]Mk 1:29
34 [y]Lk 22:24
35 [z]Mt 18:4; Mk 10:43; Lk 22:26
36 [a]Mk 10:16
37 [b]**Mt 10:40**
38 [c]Nu 11:27–29
40 [d]Mt 12:30; Lk 11:23
41 [e]**Mt 10:42**
42 [f]**Mt 5:29**; [g]Mt 18:6; Lk 17:2
43 [h]**Mt 5:29**; [i]Mt 5:30; 18:8; [j]**Mt 25:41**
45 [k]**Mt 5:29**

[a]25 Greek *unclean*
[b]29 Some manuscripts *prayer and fasting*
[c]43 Some manuscripts *out,* [44]*where / " 'their worm does not die, / and the fire is not quenched.'*

for you to enter life crippled than to
have two feet and be thrown into hell.[d][l]
47And if your eye causes you to sin,[m]
pluck it out. It is better for you to enter
the kingdom of God with one eye than
to have two eyes and be thrown into
hell,[n] 48where

"'their worm does not die,[o]
and the fire is not quenched.'[e]

49Everyone will be salted[p] with fire.
50"Salt is good, but if it loses its salti-
ness, how can you make it salty again?[q]
Have salt in yourselves,[r] and be at peace
with each other."[s]

Divorce

10:1–12pp—Mt 19:1–9

10 Jesus then left that place and
went into the region of Judea
and across the Jordan.[a] Again crowds of
people came to him, and as was his
custom, he taught them.[b]
2Some Pharisees[c] came and tested
him by asking, "Is it lawful for a man to
divorce his wife?"
3"What did Moses command you?"
he replied.
4They said, "Moses permitted a man
to write a certificate of divorce and send
her away."[d]
5"It was because your hearts were
hard[e] that Moses wrote you this law,"
Jesus replied. 6"But at the beginning of
creation God 'made them male and
female'.[a][f] 7'For this reason a man will
leave his father and mother and be
united to his wife,[b] 8and the two will
become one flesh.'[c][g] So they are no
longer two, but one. 9Therefore what
God has joined together, let man not
separate."
10When they were in the house again,
the disciples asked Jesus about this.
11He answered, "Anyone who divorces
his wife and marries another woman
commits adultery against her.[h] 12And if
she divorces her husband and marries
another man, she commits adultery."[i]

The Little Children and Jesus

10:13–16pp—Mt 19:13–15; Lk 18:15–17

13People were bringing little children
to Jesus to have him touch them, but the
disciples rebuked them. 14When Jesus
saw this, he was indignant. He said to
them, "Let the little children come to
me, and do not hinder them, for the
kingdom of God belongs to such as
these.[j] 15I tell you the truth, anyone who
will not receive the kingdom of God like
a little child will never enter it."[k] 16And
he took the children in his arms,[l] put his
hands on them and blessed them.

The Rich Young Man

10:17–31pp—Mt 19:16–30; Lk 18:18–30

17As Jesus started on his way, a man
ran up to him and fell on his knees[m]
before him. "Good teacher," he asked,
"what must I do to inherit eternal life?"[n]
18"Why do you call me good?" Jesus
answered. "No-one is good—except
God alone. 19You know the command-
ments: 'Do not murder, do not commit
adultery, do not steal, do not give false
testimony, do not defraud, honour your
father and mother.'[d]"[o]
20"Teacher," he declared, "all these I
have kept since I was a boy."
21Jesus looked at him and loved him.
"One thing you lack," he said. "Go, sell
everything you have and give to the
poor,[p] and you will have treasure in
heaven.[q] Then come, follow me."[r]
22At this the man's face fell. He went
away sad, because he had great wealth.
23Jesus looked around and said to his
disciples, "How hard it is for the rich[s] to
enter the kingdom of God!"
24The disciples were amazed at his
words. But Jesus said again, "Children,
how hard it is[e] to enter the kingdom of
God![t] 25It is easier for a camel to go
through the eye of a needle than for a
rich man to enter the kingdom of
God."[u]
26The disciples were even more
amazed, and said to each other, "Who
then can be saved?"
27Jesus looked at them and said,
"With man this is impossible, but not
with God; all things are possible with
God."[v]
28Peter said to him, "We have left
everything to follow you!"[w]
29"I tell you the truth," Jesus replied,
"no-one who has left home or brothers
or sisters or mother or father or children
or fields for me and the gospel 30will fail
to receive a hundred times as much[x] in
this present age (homes, brothers, sis-
ters, mothers, children and fields—and
with them, persecutions) and in the age

45 [l]Mt 18:8
47 [m]**Mt 5:29;** [n]Mt 5:29; 18:9
48 [o]Isa 66:24; **Mt 25:41**
49 [p]Lev 2:13
50 [q]Mt 5:13; Lk 14:34–35; [r]Col 4:6; [s]Ro 12:18; 2Co 13:11; 1Th 5:13

Ch. 10

1 [a]Mk 1:5; Jn 10:40; 11:7; [b]**Mt 4:23;** Mk 2:13; 4:2; 6:6,34
2 [c]Mk 2:16
4 [d]Dt 24:1–4; Mt 5:31
5 [e]Ps 95:8; Heb 3:15
6 [f]Ge 1:27; 5:2
8 [g]Ge 2:24; 1Co 6:16
11 [h]**Lk 16:18**
12 [i]Ro 7:3; 1Co 7:10–11
14 [j]**Mt 25:34**
15 [k]Mt 18:3
16 [l]Mk 9:36
17 [m]Mk 1:40; [n]Lk 10:25; **Ac 20:32**
19 [o]Ex 20:12–16; Dt 5:16–20
21 [p]**Ac 2:45;** [q]Mt 6:20; Lk 12:33; [r]**Mt 4:19**
23 [s]Ps 52:7; 62:10; Mk 4:19; 1Ti 6:9–10,17
24 [t]Mt 7:13–14; Jn 3:5
25 [u]Lk 12:16–20; 16:19–31
27 [v]**Mt 19:26**
28 [w]**Mt 4:19**
30 [x]Mt 6:33

[d]45 Some manuscripts *hell,* [46]*where / "'their worm does not die, / and the fire is not quenched.'*
[e]48 Isaiah 66:24 [a]6 Gen. 1:27
[b]7 Some early manuscripts do not have *and be united to his wife.* [c]8 Gen. 2:24
[d]19 Exodus 20:12–16; Deut. 5:16–20
[e]24 Some manuscripts *is for those who trust in riches*

to come,[y] eternal life.[z] 31But many who are first will be last, and the last first."[a]

Jesus Again Predicts His Death

10:32–34pp—Mt 20:17–19; Lk 18:31–33

32They were on their way up to Jerusalem, with Jesus leading the way, and the disciples were astonished, while those who followed were afraid. Again he took the Twelve[b] aside and told them what was going to happen to him. 33"We are going up to Jerusalem,"[c] he said, "and the Son of Man[d] will be betrayed to the chief priests and teachers of the law.[e] They will condemn him to death and will hand him over to the Gentiles, 34who will mock him and spit on him, flog him[f] and kill him.[g] Three days later[h] he will rise."[i]

The Request of James and John

10:35–45pp—Mt 20:20–28

35Then James and John, the sons of Zebedee, came to him. "Teacher," they said, "we want you to do for us whatever we ask."

36"What do you want me to do for you?" he asked.

37They replied, "Let one of us sit at your right and the other at your left in your glory."[j]

38"You don't know what you are asking,"[k] Jesus said. "Can you drink the cup[l] I drink or be baptised with the baptism I am baptised with?"[m]

39"We can," they answered.

Jesus said to them, "You will drink the cup I drink and be baptised with the baptism I am baptised with,[n] 40but to sit at my right or left is not for me to grant. These places belong to those for whom they have been prepared."

41When the ten heard about this, they became indignant with James and John. 42Jesus called them together and said, "You know that those who are regarded as rulers of the Gentiles lord it over them, and their high officials exercise authority over them. 43Not so with you. Instead, whoever wants to become great among you must be your servant,[o] 44and whoever wants to be first must be slave of all. 45For even the Son of Man did not come to be served, but to serve,[p] and to give his life as a ransom for many."[q]

Blind Bartimaeus Receives His Sight

10:46–52pp—Mt 20:29–34; Lk 18:35–43

46Then they came to Jericho. As Jesus and his disciples, together with a large crowd, were leaving the city, a blind man, Bartimaeus (that is, the Son of Timaeus), was sitting by the roadside begging. 47When he heard that it was Jesus of Nazareth,[r] he began to shout, "Jesus, Son of David,[s] have mercy on me!"

48Many rebuked him and told him to be quiet, but he shouted all the more, "Son of David, have mercy on me!"

49Jesus stopped and said, "Call him."

So they called to the blind man, "Cheer up! On your feet! He's calling you." 50Throwing his cloak aside, he jumped to his feet and came to Jesus.

51"What do you want me to do for you?" Jesus asked him.

The blind man said, "Rabbi,[t] I want to see."

52"Go," said Jesus, "your faith has healed you."[u] Immediately he received his sight and followed[v] Jesus along the road.

The Triumphal Entry

11:1–10pp—Mt 21:1–9; Lk 19:29–38
11:7–10pp—Jn 12:12–15

11 As they approached Jerusalem and came to Bethphage and Bethany[a] at the Mount of Olives,[b] Jesus sent two of his disciples, 2saying to them, "Go to the village ahead of you, and just as you enter it, you will find a colt tied there, which no-one has ever ridden.[c] Untie it and bring it here. 3If anyone asks you, 'Why are you doing this?' tell him, 'The Lord needs it and will send it back here shortly.'"

4They went and found a colt outside in the street, tied at a doorway.[d] As they untied it, 5some people standing there asked, "What are you doing, untying that colt?" 6They answered as Jesus had told them to, and the people let them go. 7When they brought the colt to Jesus and threw their cloaks over it, he sat on it. 8Many people spread their cloaks on the road, while others spread branches they had cut in the fields. 9Those who went ahead and those who followed shouted,

"Hosanna!"[a]

"Blessed is he who comes in the name
of the Lord!"[b][e]

30 [y]**Mt 12:32;** [z]**Mt 25:46**
31 [a]**Mt 19:30**
32 [b]Mk 3:16–19
33 [c]**Lk 9:51;** [d]**Mt 8:20;** [e]Mt 27:1–2
34 [f]**Mt 16:21;** [g]Ac 2:23; 3:13; [h]**Mt 16:21;** [i]**Mt 16:21**
37 [j]Mt 19:28
38 [k]Job 38:2; [l]**Mt 20:22;** [m]Lk 12:50
39 [n]Ac 12:2; Rev 1:9
43 [o]**Mk 9:35**
45 [p]**Mt 20:28;** [q]**Mt 20:28**
47 [r]**Mk 1:24;** [s]**Mt 9:27**
51 [t]**Mt 23:7**
52 [u]**Mt 9:22;** [v]**Mt 4:19**

Ch. 11

1 [a]**Mt 21:17;** [b]**Mt 21:1**
2 [c]Nu 19:2; Dt 21:3; 1Sa 6:7
4 [d]Mk 14:16
9 [e]Ps 118:25–26; Mt 23:39

[a]9 A Hebrew expression meaning "Save!" which became an exclamation of praise; also in verse 10.
[b]9 Psalm 118:25,26

10"Blessed is the coming kingdom of our
father David!"
"Hosanna in the highest!"[f]

11Jesus entered Jerusalem and went to
the temple. He looked around at every-
thing, but since it was already late, he
went out to Bethany with the Twelve.[g]

Jesus Clears the Temple
11:12–14pp—Mt 21:18–22
11:15–18pp—Mt 21:12–16; Lk 19:45–47; Jn 2:13–16

12The next day as they were leaving
Bethany, Jesus was hungry. 13Seeing in
the distance a fig-tree in leaf, he went to
find out if it had any fruit. When he
reached it, he found nothing but leaves,
because it was not the season for figs.[h]
14Then he said to the tree, "May no-one
ever eat fruit from you again." And his
disciples heard him say it.
15On reaching Jerusalem, Jesus en-
tered the temple area and began driving
out those who were buying and selling
there. He overturned the tables of the
money-changers and the benches of
those selling doves, 16and would not
allow anyone to carry merchandise
through the temple courts. 17And as he
taught them, he said, "Is it not written:

"'My house will be called
a house of prayer for all nations'[c]?[i]

But you have made it 'a den of
robbers'.[d]"[j]
18The chief priests and the teachers of
the law heard this and began looking for
a way to kill him, for they feared him,[k]
because the whole crowd was amazed
at his teaching.[l]
19When evening came, they[e] went out
of the city.[m]

The Withered Fig-Tree
11:20–24pp—Mt 21:19–22

20In the morning, as they went along,
they saw the fig-tree withered from the
roots. 21Peter remembered and said to
Jesus, "Rabbi,"[n] look! The fig-tree you
cursed has withered!"
22"Have[f] faith in God," Jesus
answered. 23"I tell you the truth, if any-
one says to this mountain, 'Go, throw
yourself into the sea,' and does not
doubt in his heart but believes that what
he says will happen, it will be done for
him.[o] 24Therefore I tell you, whatever
you ask for in prayer, believe that you
have received it, and it will be yours.[p]

10 [f]Lk 2:14
11 [g]Mt 21:12,17
13 [h]Lk 13:6–9
17 [i]Isa 56:7; [j]Jer 7:11
18 [k]Mt 21:46; Mk 12:12; Lk 20:19; [l]Mt 7:28
19 [m]Lk 21:37
21 [n]Mt 23:7
23 [o]Mt 21:21
24 [p]Mt 7:7
25 [q]Mt 6:14
32 [r]Mt 11:9

Ch. 12

1 [a]Isa 5:1–7
6 [b]Heb 1:1–3

25And when you stand praying, if you
hold anything against anyone, forgive
him, so that your Father in heaven may
forgive you your sins."[g][q]

The Authority of Jesus Questioned
11:27–33pp—Mt 21:23–27; Lk 20:1–8

27They arrived again in Jerusalem,
and while Jesus was walking in the tem-
ple courts, the chief priests, the teachers
of the law and the elders came to him.
28"By what authority are you doing
these things?" they asked. "And who
gave you authority to do this?"
29Jesus replied, "I will ask you one
question. Answer me, and I will tell you
by what authority I am doing these
things. 30John's baptism—was it from
heaven, or from men? Tell me!"
31They discussed it among them-
selves and said, "If we say, 'From
heaven', he will ask, 'Then why didn't
you believe him?' 32But if we say, 'From
men'. . . ." (They feared the people, for
everyone held that John really was a
prophet.)[r]
33So they answered Jesus, "We don't
know."
Jesus said, "Neither will I tell you by
what authority I am doing these
things."

The Parable of the Tenants
12:1–12pp—Mt 21:33–46; Lk 20:9–19

12 He then began to speak to them
in parables: "A man planted a
vineyard.[a] He put a wall around it, dug
a pit for the winepress and built a
watchtower. Then he rented the
vineyard to some farmers and went
away on a journey. 2At harvest time he
sent a servant to the tenants to collect
from them some of the fruit of the
vineyard. 3But they seized him, beat
him and sent him away empty-handed.
4Then he sent another servant to them;
they struck this man on the head and
treated him shamefully. 5He sent still
another, and that one they killed. He
sent many others; some of them they
beat, others they killed.
6"He had one left to send, a son,
whom he loved. He sent him last of all,[b]
saying, 'They will respect my son.'

[c]17 Isaiah 56:7 [d]17 Jer. 7:11
[e]19 Some early manuscripts *he*
[f]22 Some early manuscripts *If you have*
[g]25 Some manuscripts *sins.* [26]*But if you do not forgive, neither will your Father who is in heaven forgive your sins.*

7"But the tenants said to one another,
'This is the heir. Come, let's kill him,
and the inheritance will be ours.' 8So
they took him and killed him, and threw
him out of the vineyard.
9"What then will the owner of the
vineyard do? He will come and kill
those tenants and give the vineyard
to others. 10Haven't you read this
scripture:

"'The stone the builders rejected
has become the capstone;[a][c]
11the Lord has done this,
and it is marvellous in our eyes'[b]?"[d]

12Then they looked for a way to arrest
him because they knew he had spoken
the parable against them. But they were
afraid of the crowd;[e] so they left him and
went away.[f]

Paying Taxes to Caesar

12:13–17pp—Mt 22:15–22; Lk 20:20–26

13Later they sent some of the Phari-
sees and Herodians[g] to Jesus to catch
him[h] in his words. 14They came to him
and said, "Teacher, we know you are a
man of integrity. You aren't swayed by
men, because you pay no attention to
who they are; but you teach the way of
God in accordance with the truth. Is it
right to pay taxes to Caesar or not?
15Should we pay or shouldn't we?"
But Jesus knew their hypocrisy.
"Why are you trying to trap me?" he
asked. "Bring me a denarius and let me
look at it." 16They brought the coin, and
he asked them, "Whose portrait is this?
And whose inscription?"
"Caesar's," they replied.
17Then Jesus said to them, "Give to
Caesar what is Caesar's and to God
what is God's."[i]
And they were amazed at him.

Marriage at the Resurrection

12:18–27pp—Mt 22:23–33; Lk 20:27–38

18Then the Sadducees,[j] who say there
is no resurrection,[k] came to him with
a question. 19"Teacher," they said,
"Moses wrote for us that if a man's
brother dies and leaves a wife but no
children, the man must marry the
widow and have children for his
brother.[l] 20Now there were seven
brothers. The first one married and died
without leaving any children. 21The
second one married the widow, but he
also died, leaving no child. It was the
same with the third. 22In fact, none of

10 [c]**Ac 4:11**
11 [d]Ps 118:22–23
12 [e]**Mk 11:18**; [f]Mt 22:22
13 [g]Mt 22:16; Mk 3:6; [h]**Mt 12:10**
17 [i]Ro 13:7
18 [j]**Ac 4:1**; [k]Ac 23:8; 1Co 15:12
19 [l]Dt 25:5
24 [m]2Ti 3:15–17
25 [n]1Co 15:42, 49,52
26 [o]Ex 3:6
28 [p]Lk 10:25–28; 20:39
30 [q]Dt 6:4–5
31 [r]Lev 19:18; **Mt 5:43**
32 [s]Dt 4:35,39; Isa 45:6,14; 46:9
33 [t]1Sa 15:22; Hos 6:6; Mic 6:6–8; Heb 10:8
34 [u]**Mt 3:2**; [v]Mt 22:46; Lk 20:40
35 [w]**Mt 26:55**

the seven left any children. Last of all,
the woman died too. 23At the resurrec-
tion[c] whose wife will she be, since the
seven were married to her?"
24Jesus replied, "Are you not in error
because you do not know the Scrip-
tures[m] or the power of God? 25When the
dead rise, they will neither marry nor
be given in marriage; they will be like
the angels in heaven.[n] 26Now about
the dead rising—have you not read
in the book of Moses, in the account
of the bush, how God said to him, 'I
am the God of Abraham, the God of
Isaac, and the God of Jacob'[d]?[o] 27He is
not the God of the dead, but of the
living. You are badly mistaken!"

The Greatest Commandment

12:28–34pp—Mt 22:34–40

28One of the teachers of the law[p] came
and heard them debating. Noticing that
Jesus had given them a good answer, he
asked him, "Of all the commandments,
which is the most important?"
29"The most important one,"
answered Jesus, "is this: 'Hear, O
Israel, the Lord our God, the Lord is
one.[e] 30Love the Lord your God with all
your heart and with all your soul and
with all your mind and with all your
strength.'[f][q] 31The second is this: 'Love
your neighbour as yourself.'[g][r] There is
no commandment greater than these."
32"Well said, teacher," the man re-
plied. "You are right in saying that God
is one and there is no other but him.[s]
33To love him with all your heart, with
all your understanding and with all
your strength, and to love your neigh-
bour as yourself is more important than
all burnt offerings and sacrifices."[t]
34When Jesus saw that he had
answered wisely, he said to him, "You
are not far from the kingdom of God."[u]
And from then on no-one dared ask him
any more questions.[v]

Whose Son Is the Christ?

12:35–37pp—Mt 22:41–46; Lk 20:41–44
12:38–40pp—Mt 23:1–7; Lk 20:45–47

35While Jesus was teaching in the tem-
ple courts,[w] he asked, "How is it that
the teachers of the law say that the

---

[a]10 Or *cornerstone* [b]11 Psalm 118:22,23
[c]23 Some manuscripts *resurrection, when men rise from the dead,* [d]26 Exodus 3:6
[e]29 Or *the Lord our God is one Lord*
[f]30 Deut. 6:4,5 [g]31 Lev. 19:18

Christ[h] is the son of David?[x] 36David
himself, speaking by the Holy Spirit,[y]
declared:

"'The Lord said to my Lord:
"Sit at my right hand
until I put your enemies
under your feet."'[i][z]

37David himself calls him 'Lord'. How
then can he be his son?"
The large crowd[a] listened to him with
delight.
38As he taught, Jesus said, "Watch
out for the teachers of the law. They like
to walk around in flowing robes and be
greeted in the market-places, 39and
have the most important seats in the
synagogues and the places of honour at
banquets.[b] 40They devour widows'
houses and for a show make lengthy
prayers. Such men will be punished
most severely."

The Widow's Offering

12:41–44pp—Lk 21:1–4

41Jesus sat down opposite the place
where the offerings were put[c] and
watched the crowd putting their money
into the temple treasury. Many rich
people threw in large amounts. 42But a
poor widow came and put in two very
small copper coins,[j] worth only a frac-
tion of a penny.[k]
43Calling his disciples to him, Jesus
said, "I tell you the truth, this poor
widow has put more into the treasury
than all the others. 44They all gave out
of their wealth; but she, out of her
poverty, put in everything—all she
had to live on."[d]

Signs of the End of the Age

13:1–37pp—Mt 24:1–51; Lk 21:5–36

13 As he was leaving the temple,
one of his disciples said to him,
"Look, Teacher! What massive stones!
What magnificent buildings!"
2"Do you see all these great build-
ings?" replied Jesus. "Not one stone
here will be left on another; every one
will be thrown down."[a]
3As Jesus was sitting on the Mount of
Olives[b] opposite the temple, Peter,
James, John[c] and Andrew asked him
privately, 4"Tell us, when will these
things happen? And what will be the
sign that they are all about to be
fulfilled?"
5Jesus said to them: "Watch out that
no-one deceives you.[d] 6Many will come
in my name, claiming, 'I am he,' and
will deceive many. 7When you hear of
wars and rumours of wars, do not be
alarmed. Such things must happen, but
the end is still to come. 8Nation will rise
against nation, and kingdom against
kingdom. There will be earthquakes in
various places, and famines. These are
the beginning of birth-pains.
9"You must be on your guard. You
will be handed over to the local councils
and flogged in the synagogues.[e] On
account of me you will stand before
governors and kings as witnesses to
them. 10And the gospel must first be
preached to all nations. 11Whenever you
are arrested and brought to trial, do not
worry beforehand about what to say.
Just say whatever is given you at the
time, for it is not you speaking, but the
Holy Spirit.[f]
12"Brother will betray brother to
death, and a father his child. Children
will rebel against their parents and have
them put to death.[g] 13All men will hate
you because of me,[h] but he who stands
firm to the end will be saved.[i]
14"When you see 'the abomination
that causes desolation'[a][j] standing
where it[b] does not belong—let the read-
er understand—then let those who are
in Judea flee to the mountains. 15Let
no-one on the roof of his house go down
or enter the house to take anything out.
16Let no-one in the field go back to get
his cloak. 17How dreadful it will be in
those days for pregnant women and
nursing mothers![k] 18Pray that this will
not take place in winter, 19because those
will be days of distress unequalled from
the beginning, when God created the
world,[l] until now—and never to be
equalled again.[m] 20If the Lord had not
cut short those days, no-one would sur-
vive. But for the sake of the elect, whom
he has chosen, he has shortened them.
21At that time if anyone says to you,
'Look, here is the Christ!'[c] or, 'Look,
there he is!' do not believe it.[n] 22For false
Christs and false prophets[o] will appear
and perform signs and miracles[p] to de-
ceive the elect—if that were possible.
23So be on your guard;[q] I have told you
everything ahead of time.
24"But in those days, following that
distress,

"'the sun will be darkened,
and the moon will not give its light;

35 [x]**Mt 9:27**
36 [y]2Sa 23:2; [z]Ps 110:1; **Mt 22:44**
37 [a]Jn 12:9
39 [b]Lk 11:43
41 [c]2Ki 12:9; Jn 8:20
44 [d]2Co 8:12

Ch. 13

2 [a]Lk 19:44
3 [b]**Mt 21:1**; [c]**Mt 4:21**
5 [d]ver 22; Jer 29:8; Eph 5:6; 2Th 2:3, 10–12; 1Ti 4:1; 2Ti 3:13; 1Jn 4:6
9 [e]**Mt 10:17**
11 [f]Mt 10:19–20; Lk 12:11–12
12 [g]Mic 7:6; Mt 10:21; Lk 12:51–53
13 [h]**Jn 15:21**; [i]**Mt 10:22**
14 [j]Da 9:27; 11:31; 12:11
17 [k]Lk 23:29
19 [l]Mk 10:6; [m]Da 9:26; 12:1; Joel 2:2
21 [n]Lk 17:23; 21:8
22 [o]**Mt 7:15**; [p]**Jn 4:48**; 2Th 2:9–10
23 [q]2Pe 3:17

[h]35 Or *Messiah* [i]36 Psalm 110:1
[j]42 Greek *two lepta* [k]42 Greek *kodrantes*
[a]14 Daniel 9:27; 11:31; 12:11
[b]14 Or *he*; also in verse 29 [c]21 Or *Messiah*

25the stars will fall from the sky,
and the heavenly bodies will be
shaken.'[d][r]

26"At that time men will see the Son of
Man coming in clouds[s] with great pow-
er and glory. 27And he will send his
angels and gather his elect from the four
winds, from the ends of the earth to the
ends of the heavens.[t]
28"Now learn this lesson from the fig-
tree: As soon as its twigs get tender and
its leaves come out, you know that sum-
mer is near. 29Even so, when you see
these things happening, you know that
it is near, right at the door. 30I tell you
the truth, this generation[e][u] will certain-
ly not pass away until all these things
have happened.[v] 31Heaven and earth
will pass away, but my words will never
pass away.[w]

The Day and Hour Unknown

32"No-one knows about that day or
hour, not even the angels in heaven,
nor the Son, but only the Father.[x] 33Be
on guard! Be alert[f]![y] You do not know
when that time will come. 34It's like a
man going away: He leaves his house
and puts his servants[z] in charge, each
with his assigned task, and tells the one
at the door to keep watch.
35"Therefore keep watch because you
do not know when the owner of the
house will come back—whether in the
evening, or at midnight, or when the
cock crows, or at dawn. 36If he comes
suddenly, do not let him find you sleep-
ing. 37What I say to you, I say to every-
one: 'Watch!'"[a]

Jesus Anointed at Bethany

14:1–11pp—Mt 26:2–16
14:1,2,10,11pp—Lk 22:1–6
14:3–8Ref—Jn 12:1–8

14 Now the Passover[a] and the
Feast of Unleavened Bread
were only two days away, and the chief
priests and the teachers of the law were
looking for some sly way to arrest Jesus
and kill him.[b] 2"But not during the
Feast," they said, "or the people may
riot."
3While he was in Bethany,[c] reclining
at the table in the home of a man known
as Simon the Leper, a woman came with
an alabaster jar of very expensive per-
fume, made of pure nard. She broke the
jar and poured the perfume on his
head.[d]
4Some of those present were saying
indignantly to one another, "Why this
waste of perfume? 5It could have been
sold for more than a year's wages[a] and
the money given to the poor." And they
rebuked her harshly.
6"Leave her alone," said Jesus. "Why
are you bothering her? She has done a
beautiful thing to me. 7The poor you
will always have with you, and you can
help them any time you want.[e] But you
will not always have me. 8She did what
she could. She poured perfume on my
body beforehand to prepare for my
burial.[f] 9I tell you the truth, wherever
the gospel is preached throughout the
world,[g] what she has done will also be
told, in memory of her."
10Then Judas Iscariot, one of the
Twelve,[h] went to the chief priests to
betray Jesus to them.[i] 11They were de-
lighted to hear this and promised to give
him money. So he watched for an
opportunity to hand him over.

The Lord's Supper

14:12–26pp—Mt 26:17–30; Lk 22:7–23
14:22–25pp—1Co 11:23–25

12On the first day of the Feast of Un-
leavened Bread, when it was customary
to sacrifice the Passover lamb,[j] Jesus'
disciples asked him, "Where do you
want us to go and make preparations for
you to eat the Passover?"
13So he sent two of his disciples, tell-
ing them, "Go into the city, and a man
carrying a jar of water will meet you.
Follow him. 14Say to the owner of the
house he enters, 'The Teacher asks:
Where is my guest room, where I may
eat the Passover with my disciples?'
15He will show you a large upper room,[k]
furnished and ready. Make prepara-
tions for us there."
16The disciples left, went into the city
and found things just as Jesus had told
them. So they prepared the Passover.
17When evening came, Jesus arrived
with the Twelve. 18While they were re-
clining at the table eating, he said, "I tell
you the truth, one of you will betray
me—one who is eating with me."
19They were saddened, and one by
one they said to him, "Surely not I?"
20"It is one of the Twelve," he replied,
"one who dips bread into the bowl with
me.[l] 21The Son of Man[m] will go just as it
is written about him. But woe to that
man who betrays the Son of Man! It

25 [r]Isa 13:10; 34:4; **Mt 24:29**
26 [s]**Rev 1:7**
27 [t]Zec 2:6
30 [u]Mk 9:1; [v]Lk 17:25
31 [w]**Mt 5:18**
32 [x]Ac 1:7; 1Th 5:1–2
33 [y]1Th 5:6
34 [z]Mt 25:14
37 [a]Lk 12:35–40

Ch. 14

1 [a]**Jn 11:55**; [b]**Mt 12:14**
3 [c]**Mt 21:17**; [d]Lk 7:37–39
7 [e]Dt 15:11
8 [f]Jn 19:40
9 [g]**Mt 24:14**; Mk 16:15
10 [h]Mk 3:16–19; [i]**Mt 10:4**
12 [j]Ex 12:1–11; Dt 16:1–4; 1Co 5:7
15 [k]Ac 1:13
20 [l]Jn 13:18–27
21 [m]**Mt 8:20**

[d]25 Isaiah 13:10; 34:4
[e]30 Or *race*
[f]33 Some manuscripts *alert and pray*
[a]5 Greek *than three hundred denarii*

would be better for him if he had not
been born."
22While they were eating, Jesus took
bread, gave thanks and broke it,[n] and
gave it to his disciples, saying, "Take it;
this is my body."
23Then he took the cup, gave thanks
and offered it to them, and they all
drank from it.[o]
24"This is my blood of the[b] covenant,[p]
which is poured out for many," he said
to them. 25"I tell you the truth, I will not
drink again of the fruit of the vine until
that day when I drink it anew in the
kingdom of God."[q]
26When they had sung a hymn, they
went out to the Mount of Olives.[r]

Jesus Predicts Peter's Denial

14:27–31pp—Mt 26:31–35

27"You will all fall away," Jesus told
them, "for it is written:

"'I will strike the shepherd,
and the sheep will be scattered.'[c][s]

28But after I have risen, I will go ahead of
you into Galilee."[t]
29Peter declared, "Even if all fall
away, I will not."
30"I tell you the truth," Jesus an-
swered, "today—yes, tonight—before
the cock crows twice[d] you yourself will
disown me three times."[u]
31But Peter insisted emphatically,
"Even if I have to die with you,[v] I will
never disown you." And all the others
said the same.

Gethsemane

14:32–42pp—Mt 26:36–46; Lk 22:40–46

32They went to a place called Geth-
semane, and Jesus said to his disciples,
"Sit here while I pray." 33He took Peter,
James and John[w] along with him, and he
began to be deeply distressed and trou-
bled. 34"My soul is overwhelmed with
sorrow to the point of death,"[x] he said
to them. "Stay here and keep watch."
35Going a little farther, he fell to the
ground and prayed that if possible the
hour[y] might pass from him. 36"*Abba*,[e]
Father,"[z] he said, "everything is poss-
ible for you. Take this cup[a] from me. Yet
not what I will, but what you will."[b]
37Then he returned to his disciples
and found them sleeping. "Simon," he
said to Peter, "are you asleep? Could
you not keep watch for one hour?
38Watch and pray so that you will not
fall into temptation.[c] The spirit is will-
ing, but the body is weak."[d]
39Once more he went away and
prayed the same thing. 40When he came
back, he again found them sleeping,
because their eyes were heavy. They
did not know what to say to him.
41Returning the third time, he said to
them, "Are you still sleeping and rest-
ing? Enough! The hour[e] has come.
Look, the Son of Man is betrayed into
the hands of sinners. 42Rise! Let us go!
Here comes my betrayer!"

Jesus Arrested

14:43–50pp—Mt 26:47–56; Lk 22:47–50; Jn 18:3–11

43Just as he was speaking, Judas,[f] one
of the Twelve, appeared. With him was
a crowd armed with swords and clubs,
sent from the chief priests, the teachers
of the law, and the elders.
44Now the betrayer had arranged a
signal with them: "The one I kiss is the
man; arrest him and lead him away
under guard." 45Going at once to Jesus,
Judas said, "Rabbi!"[g] and kissed him.
46The men seized Jesus and arrested
him. 47Then one of those standing near
drew his sword and struck the servant
of the high priest, cutting off his ear.
48"Am I leading a rebellion," said
Jesus, "that you have come out with
swords and clubs to capture me?
49Every day I was with you, teaching in
the temple courts,[h] and you did not
arrest me. But the Scriptures must be
fulfilled."[i] 50Then everyone deserted
him and fled.[j]
51A young man, wearing nothing but
a linen garment, was following Jesus.
When they seized him, 52he fled naked,
leaving his garment behind.

Before the Sanhedrin

14:53–65pp—Mt 26:57–68; Jn 18:12,13,19–24
14:61–63pp—Lk 22:67–71

53They took Jesus to the high priest,
and all the chief priests, elders and
teachers of the law came together.
54Peter followed him at a distance, right
into the courtyard of the high priest.[k]
There he sat with the guards and
warmed himself at the fire.[l]
55The chief priests and the whole
Sanhedrin[m] were looking for evidence
against Jesus so that they could put him
to death, but they did not find any.

22 [n]**Mt 14:19**
23 [o]1Co 10:16
24 [p]**Mt 26:28**
25 [q]**Mt 3:2**
26 [r]**Mt 21:1**
27 [s]Zec 13:7
28 [t]Mk 16:7
30 [u]ver 66–72; Lk 22:34; Jn 13:38
31 [v]Lk 22:33; Jn 13:37
33 [w]**Mt 4:21**
34 [x]Jn 12:27
35 [y]ver 41; **Mt 26:18**
36 [z]Ro 8:15; Gal 4:6; [a]**Mt 20:22;** [b]**Mt 26:39**
38 [c]Mt 6:13; [d]Ro 7:22–23
41 [e]ver 35; **Mt 26:18**
43 [f]**Mt 10:4**
45 [g]**Mt 23:7**
49 [h]**Mt 26:55;** [i]Isa 53:7–12; **Mt 1:22**
50 [j]ver 27
54 [k]**Mt 26:3;** [l]Jn 18:18
55 [m]**Mt 5:22**

[b]24 Some manuscripts *the new* [c]27 Zech. 13:7
[d]30 Some early manuscripts do not have *twice*.
[e]36 Aramaic for *Father*

56Many testified falsely against him, but
their statements did not agree.
57Then some stood up and gave this
false testimony against him: 58"We
heard him say, 'I will destroy this man-
made temple and in three days will
build another,[n] not made by man.'"
59Yet even then their testimony did not
agree.
60Then the high priest stood up before
them and asked Jesus, "Are you not
going to answer? What is this testimony
that these men are bringing against
you?" 61But Jesus remained silent and
gave no answer.[o]
Again the high priest asked him,
"Are you the Christ,[f] the Son of the
Blessed One?"[p]
62"I am," said Jesus. "And you will
see the Son of Man sitting at the right
hand of the Mighty One and coming on
the clouds of heaven."[q]
63The high priest tore his clothes.[r]
"Why do we need any more wit-
nesses?" he asked. 64"You have heard
the blasphemy. What do you think?"
They all condemned him as worthy of
death.[s] 65Then some began to spit at
him; they blindfolded him, struck him
with their fists, and said, "Prophesy!"
And the guards took him and beat him.[t]

Peter Disowns Jesus

14:66–72pp—Mt 26:69–75; Lk 22:56–62; Jn 18:16–18, 25–27

66While Peter was below in the court-
yard,[u] one of the servant girls of the
high priest came by. 67When she saw
Peter warming himself,[v] she looked
closely at him.
"You also were with that Nazarene,
Jesus,"[w] she said.
68But he denied it. "I don't know
or understand what you're talking
about,"[x] he said, and went out into the
entrance.[g]
69When the servant girl saw him
there, she said again to those standing
around, "This fellow is one of them."
70Again he denied it.[y]
After a little while, those standing
near said to Peter, "Surely you are one
of them, for you are a Galilean."[z]
71He began to call down curses on
himself, and he swore to them, "I don't
know this man you're talking about."[a]
72Immediately the cock crowed the
second time.[h] Then Peter remembered
the word Jesus had spoken to him:
"Before the cock crows twice[i] you will
disown me three times."[b] And he broke
down and wept.

58 [n]**Jn 2:19**
61 [o]Isa 53:7; Mt 27:12,14; Mk 15:5; Lk 23:9; Jn 19:9; [p]Mt 16:16; Jn 4:25–26
62 [q]**Rev 1:7**
63 [r]Lev 10:6; 21:10; Nu 14:6; Ac 14:14
64 [s]Lev 24:16
65 [t]**Mt 16:21**
66 [u]ver 54
67 [v]ver 54; [w]**Mk 1:24**
68 [x]ver 30,72
70 [y]ver 30,68,72; [z]Ac 2:7
71 [a]ver 30,72
72 [b]ver 30,68

Ch. 15

1 [a]Mt 27:1; Lk 22:66; [b]**Mt 5:22**; [c]**Mt 27:2**
2 [d]ver 9,12,18, 26; **Mt 2:2**
5 [e]**Mk 14:61**
9 [f]**ver 2**
11 [g]Ac 3:14
15 [h]Isa 53:6
16 [i]Jn 18:28,33; 19:9

Jesus Before Pilate

15:2–15pp—Mt 27:11–26; Lk 23:2,3,18–25; Jn 18:29–19:16

15 Very early in the morning, the
chief priests, with the elders,
the teachers of the law[a] and the whole
Sanhedrin,[b] reached a decision. They
bound Jesus, led him away and turned
him over to Pilate.[c]
2"Are you the king of the Jews?"[d]
asked Pilate.
"Yes, it is as you say," Jesus replied.
3The chief priests accused him of
many things. 4So again Pilate asked
him, "Aren't you going to answer? See
how many things they are accusing you
of."
5But Jesus still made no reply,[e] and
Pilate was amazed.
6Now it was the custom at the Feast to
release a prisoner whom the people re-
quested. 7A man called Barabbas was in
prison with the insurrectionists who
had committed murder in the uprising.
8The crowd came up and asked Pilate to
do for them what he usually did.
9"Do you want me to release to you
the king of the Jews?"[f] asked Pilate,
10knowing it was out of envy that the
chief priests had handed Jesus over to
him. 11But the chief priests stirred up
the crowd to have Pilate release Barab-
bas[g] instead.
12"What shall I do, then, with the one
you call the king of the Jews?" Pilate
asked them.
13"Crucify him!" they shouted.
14"Why? What crime has he commit-
ted?" asked Pilate.
But they shouted all the louder, "Cru-
cify him!"
15Wanting to satisfy the crowd, Pilate
released Barabbas to them. He had
Jesus flogged,[h] and handed him over to
be crucified.

The Soldiers Mock Jesus

15:16–20pp—Mt 27:27–31

16The soldiers led Jesus away into the
palace[i] (that is, the Praetorium) and
called together the whole company of
soldiers. 17They put a purple robe on
him, then twisted together a crown of
thorns and set it on him. 18And they
began to call out to him, "Hail, king of

[f]61 Or *Messiah*
[g]68 Some early manuscripts *entrance and the cock crowed*
[h]72 Some early manuscripts do not have *the second time.*
[i]72 Some early manuscripts do not have *twice.*

the Jews!"[j] 19Again and again they struck him on the head with a staff and spat on him. Falling on their knees, they paid homage to him. 20And when they had mocked him, they took off the purple robe and put his own clothes on him. Then they led him out[k] to crucify him.

The Crucifixion

15:22–32pp—Mt 27:33–44; Lk 23:33–43; Jn 19:17–24

21A certain man from Cyrene,[l] Simon, the father of Alexander and Rufus,[m] was passing by on his way in from the country, and they forced him to carry the cross.[n] 22They brought Jesus to the place called Golgotha (which means The Place of the Skull). 23Then they offered him wine mixed with myrrh,[o] but he did not take it. 24And they crucified him. Dividing up his clothes, they cast lots[p] to see what each would get.

25It was the third hour when they crucified him. 26The written notice of the charge against him read: THE KING OF THE JEWS.[q] 27They crucified two robbers with him, one on his right and one on his left.[a] 29Those who passed by hurled insults at him, shaking their heads[r] and saying, "So! You who are going to destroy the temple and build it in three days,[s] 30come down from the cross and save yourself!"

31In the same way the chief priests and the teachers of the law mocked him[t] among themselves. "He saved others," they said, "but he can't save himself! 32Let this Christ,[b][u] this King of Israel,[v] come down now from the cross, that we may see and believe." Those crucified with him also heaped insults on him.

The Death of Jesus

15:33–41pp—Mt 27:45–56; Lk 23:44–49

33At the sixth hour darkness came over the whole land until the ninth hour.[w] 34And at the ninth hour Jesus cried out in a loud voice, *"Eloi, Eloi, lama sabachthani?"*—which means, "My God, my God, why have you forsaken me?"[c][x]

35When some of those standing near heard this, they said, "Listen, he's calling Elijah."

36One man ran, filled a sponge with wine vinegar,[y] put it on a stick, and offered it to Jesus to drink. "Now leave him alone. Let's see if Elijah comes to take him down," he said.

37With a loud cry, Jesus breathed his last.[z]

18 [j]**ver 2**
20 [k]Heb 13:12
21 [l]**Mt 27:32;** [m]Ro 16:13; [n]Mt 27:32; Lk 23:26
23 [o]ver 36; Ps 69:21; Pr 31:6
24 [p]Ps 22:18
26 [q]**ver 2**
29 [r]Ps 22:7; 109:25; [s]**Jn 2:19**
31 [t]Ps 22:7
32 [u]**Mk 14:61;** [v]**ver 2**
33 [w]Am 8:9
34 [x]Ps 22:1
36 [y]ver 23; Ps 69:21
37 [z]Jn 19:30
38 [a]Heb 10:19–20
39 [b]ver 45; [c]Mk 1:1,11; 9:7; **Mt 4:3**
40 [d]Ps 38:11; [e]Mk 16:1; Lk 24:10; Jn 19:25
41 [f]Mt 27:55–56; Lk 8:2–3
42 [g]Mt 27:62; Jn 19:31
43 [h]**Mt 5:22;** [i]**Mt 3:2;** Lk 2:25,38
45 [j]ver 39
46 [k]Mk 16:3
47 [l]ver 40

Ch. 16

1 [a]Lk 23:56; Jn 19:39–40
3 [b]Mk 15:46

38The curtain of the temple was torn in two from top to bottom.[a] 39And when the centurion,[b] who stood there in front of Jesus, heard his cry and[d] saw how he died, he said, "Surely this man was the Son[e] of God!"[c]

40Some women were watching from a distance.[d] Among them were Mary Magdalene, Mary the mother of James the younger and of Joses, and Salome.[e] 41In Galilee these women had followed him and cared for his needs. Many other women who had come up with him to Jerusalem were also there.[f]

The Burial of Jesus

15:42–47pp—Mt 27:57–61; Lk 23:50–56; Jn 19:38–42

42It was Preparation Day (that is, the day before the Sabbath).[g] So as evening approached, 43Joseph of Arimathea, a prominent member of the Council,[h] who was himself waiting for the kingdom of God,[i] went boldly to Pilate and asked for Jesus' body. 44Pilate was surprised to hear that he was already dead. Summoning the centurion, he asked him if Jesus had already died. 45When he learned from the centurion[j] that it was so, he gave the body to Joseph. 46So Joseph bought some linen cloth, took down the body, wrapped it in the linen, and placed it in a tomb cut out of rock. Then he rolled a stone against the entrance of the tomb.[k] 47Mary Magdalene and Mary the mother of Joses[l] saw where he was laid.

The Resurrection

16:1–8pp—Mt 28:1–8; Lk 24:1–10

16 When the Sabbath was over, Mary Magdalene, Mary the mother of James, and Salome bought spices[a] so that they might go to anoint Jesus' body. 2Very early on the first day of the week, just after sunrise, they were on their way to the tomb 3and they asked each other, "Who will roll the stone away from the entrance of the tomb?"[b]

4But when they looked up, they saw that the stone, which was very large, had been rolled away. 5As they entered the tomb, they saw a young man

[a]27 Some manuscripts *left,* [28]*and the scripture was fulfilled which says, "He was counted with the lawless ones"* (Isaiah 53:12) [b]32 Or *Messiah*
[c]34 Psalm 22:1
[d]39 Some manuscripts do not have *heard his cry and.*
[e]39 Or *a son*

dressed in a white robe[c] sitting on the
right side, and they were alarmed.
6"Don't be alarmed," he said. "You
are looking for Jesus the Nazarene,[d]
who was crucified. He has risen! He is
not here. See the place where they laid
him. 7But go, tell his disciples and Peter,
'He is going ahead of you into Galilee.
There you will see him,[e] just as he told
you.' "[f]
8Trembling and bewildered, the
women went out and fled from the
tomb. They said nothing to anyone,
because they were afraid.

[The earliest manuscripts and some other ancient witnesses do not have Mark 16:9–20]

9When Jesus rose early on the first
day of the week, he appeared first to
Mary Magdalene,[g] out of whom he had
driven seven demons. 10She went and
told those who had been with him and
who were mourning and weeping.
11When they heard that Jesus was alive
and that she had seen him, they did not
believe it.[h]
12Afterwards Jesus appeared in a
different form to two of them while they
were walking in the country.[i] 13These
returned and reported it to the rest; but
they did not believe them either.
14Later Jesus appeared to the Eleven
as they were eating; he rebuked them
for their lack of faith and their stubborn
refusal to believe those who had seen
him after he had risen.[j]
15He said to them, "Go into all the
world and preach the good news to all
creation.[k] 16Whoever believes and is
baptised will be saved, but whoever
does not believe will be condemned.[l]
17And these signs[m] will accompany
those who believe: In my name they will
drive out demons;[n] they will speak in
new tongues;[o] 18they will pick up
snakes[p] with their hands; and when
they drink deadly poison, it will not
hurt them at all; they will place their
hands on[q] sick people, and they will get
well."
19After the Lord Jesus had spoken to
them, he was taken up into heaven[r] and
he sat at the right hand of God.[s] 20Then
the disciples went out and preached
everywhere, and the Lord worked with
them and confirmed his word by the
signs[t] that accompanied it.

5 [c]**Jn 20:12**
6 [d]**Mk 1:24**
7 [e]Jn 21:1–23; [f]Mk 14:28
9 [g]Mk 15:47; Jn 20:11–18
11 [h]ver 13–14; Lk 24:11
12 [i]Lk 24:13–32
14 [j]Lk 24:36–43
15 [k]Mt 28:18–20; Lk 24:47–48; Ac 1:8
16 [l]Jn 3:16,18, 36; Ac 16:31
17 [m]**Jn 4:48**; [n]Mk 9:38; Lk 10:17; Ac 5:16; 8:7; 16:18; 19:13–16; [o]Ac 2:4; 10:46; 19:6; 1Co 12:10,28,30; 13:1; 14:2–39
18 [p]Lk 10:19; Ac 28:3–5; [q]**Ac 6:6**
19 [r]Lk 24:50–51; Jn 6:62; Ac 1:9–11; 1Ti 3:16; [s]Ps 110:1; Mt 26:64; Ac 2:33; 5:31; Ro 8:34; Col 3:1; Heb 1:3; 12:2
20 [t]**Jn 4:48**

Luke

Introduction

1:1–4Ref—Ac 1:1

1 Many have undertaken to draw up an account of the things that have been fulfilled[a] among us, 2just as they were handed down to us by those who from the first[a] were eye-witnesses[b] and servants of the word.[c] 3Therefore, since I myself have carefully investigated everything from the beginning, it seemed good also to me to write an orderly account[d] for you, most excellent[e] Theophilus,[f] 4so that you may know the certainty of the things you have been taught.[g]

The Birth of John the Baptist Foretold

5In the time of Herod king of Judea[h] there was a priest named Zechariah, who belonged to the priestly division of Abijah;[i] his wife Elizabeth was also a descendant of Aaron. 6Both of them were upright in the sight of God, observing all the Lord's commandments and regulations blamelessly.[j] 7But they had no children, because Elizabeth was barren; and they were both well on in years.

8Once when Zechariah's division was on duty and he was serving as priest before God,[k] 9he was chosen by lot,[l] according to the custom of the priesthood, to go into the temple of the Lord and burn incense.[m] 10And when the time for the burning of incense came, all the assembled worshippers were praying outside.[n]

11Then an angel[o] of the Lord appeared to him, standing at the right side of the altar of incense.[p] 12When Zechariah saw him, he was startled and was gripped with fear.[q] 13But the angel said to him: "Do not be afraid,[r] Zechariah; your prayer has been heard. Your wife Elizabeth will bear you a son, and you are to give him the name John.[s] 14He will be a joy and delight to you, and many will rejoice because of his birth,[t] 15for he will be great in the sight of the Lord. He is never to take wine or other fermented drink,[u] and he will be filled with the Holy Spirit[v] even from birth.[b][w] 16Many of the people of Israel will he bring back to the Lord their God. 17And he will go on before the Lord,[x] in the spirit and power of Elijah,[y] to turn the hearts of the fathers to their children[z] and the disobedient to the wisdom of the righteous—to make ready a people prepared for the Lord."[a]

18Zechariah asked the angel, "How can I be sure of this?[b] I am an old man and my wife is well on in years."[c]

19The angel answered, "I am Gabriel.[d] I stand in the presence of God, and I have been sent to speak to you and to tell you this good news. 20And now you will be silent and not able to speak[e] until the day this happens, because you did not believe my words, which will come true at their proper time."

21Meanwhile, the people were waiting for Zechariah and wondering why he stayed so long in the temple. 22When he came out, he could not speak to them. They realised he had seen a vision in the temple, for he kept making signs[f] to them but remained unable to speak.

23When his time of service was completed, he returned home. 24After this his wife Elizabeth became pregnant and for five months remained in seclusion. 25"The Lord has done this for me," she said. "In these days he has shown his favour and taken away my disgrace[g] among the people."

The Birth of Jesus Foretold

26In the sixth month, God sent the angel Gabriel[h] to Nazareth,[i] a town in Galilee, 27to a virgin pledged to be married to a man named Joseph,[j] a descendant of David. The virgin's name was Mary. 28The angel went to her and said, "Greetings, you who are highly favoured! The Lord is with you."

Ch. 1

2 [a]Mk 1:1; Jn 15:27; Ac 1:21–22; [b]Heb 2:3; 1Pe 5:1; 2Pe 1:16; 1Jn 1:1; [c]**Mk 4:14**
3 [d]Ac 11:4; [e]Ac 24:3; 26:25; [f]Ac 1:1
4 [g]Jn 20:31; Ac 2:42
5 [h]Mt 2:1; [i]1Ch 24:10
6 [j]Ge 6:9; Dt 5:33; 1Ki 9:4; Lk 2:25
8 [k]1Ch 24:19; 2Ch 8:14
9 [l]Ac 1:26; [m]Ex 30:7–8; 1Ch 23:13; 2Ch 29:11; Ps 141:2
10 [n]Lev 16:17
11 [o]**Ac 5:19**; [p]Ex 30:1–10
12 [q]Jdg 6:22–23; 13:22
13 [r]ver 30; **Mt 14:27**; [s]ver 60, 63; **Mt 3:1**
14 [t]ver 58
15 [u]Nu 6:3; Lev 10:9; Jdg 13:4; Lk 7:33; [v]ver 41,67; Ac 2:4; 4:8,31; 6:3,5; 9:17; 11:24; Eph 5:18; **Ac 10:44**; [w]Jer 1:5; Gal 1:15
17 [x]ver 76; [y]**Mt 11:14**; [z]Mal 4:5–6; [a]**Mt 3:3**
18 [b]Ge 15:8; [c]ver 34; Ge 17:17
19 [d]ver 26; Da 8:16; 9:21
20 [e]Ex 4:11; Eze 3:26
22 [f]ver 62
25 [g]Ge 30:23; Isa 4:1
26 [h]**ver 19**; [i]**Mt 2:23**
27 [j]Mt 1:16,18, 20; Lk 2:4

[a]1 Or *been surely believed*
[b]15 Or *from his mother's womb*

29Mary was greatly troubled at his
words and wondered what kind of
greeting this might be. 30But the angel
said to her, "Do not be afraid, Mary,[k]
you have found favour with God.[l] 31You
will be with child and give birth to a son,
and you are to give him the name
Jesus.[m] 32He will be great and will be
called the Son of the Most High.[n] The
Lord God will give him the throne of his
father David,[o] 33and he will reign over
the house of Jacob for ever; his king-
dom[p] will never end."[q]

34"How will this be," Mary asked the
angel, "since I am a virgin?"

35The angel answered, "The Holy
Spirit will come upon you,[r] and the
power of the Most High[s] will over-
shadow you. So the holy one[t] to be born
will be called[c] the Son of God.[u] 36Even
Elizabeth your relative is going to have a
child[v] in her old age, and she who was
said to be barren is in her sixth month.
37For nothing is impossible with God."[w]

38"I am the Lord's servant," Mary
answered. "May it be to me as you have
said." Then the angel left her.

Mary Visits Elizabeth

39At that time Mary got ready and
hurried to a town in the hill country of
Judea,[x] 40where she entered Zechariah's
home and greeted Elizabeth. 41When
Elizabeth heard Mary's greeting, the
baby leaped in her womb, and Elizabeth
was filled with the Holy Spirit.[y] 42In a
loud voice she exclaimed: "Blessed are
you among women,[z] and blessed is the
child you will bear! 43But why am I so
favoured, that the mother of my Lord[a]
should come to me? 44As soon as the
sound of your greeting reached my
ears, the baby in my womb leaped for
joy. 45Blessed is she who has believed
that what the Lord has said to her will be
accomplished!"

Mary's Song

1:46–53pp—1Sa 2:1–10

46And Mary said:

"My soul glorifies the Lord[b]
47 and my spirit rejoices in God my
Saviour,[c]
48for he has been mindful
of the humble state of his servant.[d]
From now on all generations will call
me blessed,[e]
49 for the Mighty One has done great
things[f] for me—
holy is his name.[g]
50His mercy extends to those who fear
him,
from generation to generation.[h]
51He has performed mighty deeds with
his arm;[i]
he has scattered those who are
proud in their inmost thoughts.[j]
52He has brought down rulers from their
thrones
but has lifted up the humble.[k]
53He has filled the hungry with good
things[l]
but has sent the rich away empty.
54He has helped his servant Israel,
remembering to be merciful[m]
55to Abraham and his descendants[n] for
ever,
even as he said to our fathers."

56Mary stayed with Elizabeth for
about three months and then returned
home.

The Birth of John the Baptist

57When it was time for Elizabeth to
have her baby, she gave birth to a son.
58Her neighbours and relatives heard
that the Lord had shown her great
mercy, and they shared her joy.

59On the eighth day they came to cir-
cumcise[o] the child, and they were going
to name him after his father Zechariah,
60but his mother spoke up and said,
"No! He is to be called John."[p]

61They said to her, "There is no-one
among your relatives who has that
name."

62Then they made signs[q] to his father,
to find out what he would like to name
the child. 63He asked for a writing tablet,
and to everyone's astonishment he
wrote, "His name is John."[r] 64Im-
mediately his mouth was opened and
his tongue was loosed, and he began to
speak,[s] praising God. 65The neighbours
were all filled with awe, and throughout
the hill country of Judea[t] people were
talking about all these things.
66Everyone who heard this wondered
about it, asking, "What then is this child
going to be?" For the Lord's hand was
with him.[u]

Zechariah's Song

67His father Zechariah was filled with
the Holy Spirit[v] and prophesied:[w]

68"Praise be to the Lord, the God of
Israel,[x]

30 [k]ver 13; **Mt 14:27**; [l]Ge 6:8
31 [m]Isa 7:14; Mt 1:21,25; Lk 2:21
32 [n]ver 35,76; **Mk 5:7**; [o]**Mt 1:1**
33 [p]Mt 28:18; [q]2Sa 7:16; Ps 89:3–4; Isa 9:7; Jer 33:17; Da 2:44; 7:14, 27; Mic 4:7; Heb 1:8
35 [r]Mt 1:18; [s]ver 32,76; **Mk 5:7**; [t]**Mk 1:24**; [u]**Mt 4:3**
36 [v]ver 24
37 [w]**Mt 19:26**
39 [x]ver 65
41 [y]**ver 15**
42 [z]Jdg 5:24
43 [a]**Jn 13:13**
46 [b]Ps 34:2–3
47 [c]Ps 18:46; Isa 17:10; 61:10; Hab 3:18; 1Ti 1:1; 2:3; 4:10
48 [d]ver 38; Ps 138:6; [e]Lk 11:27
49 [f]Ps 71:19; [g]Ps 111:9
50 [h]Ex 20:6; Ps 103:17
51 [i]Ps 98:1; Isa 40:10; [j]Ge 11:8; Ex 18:11; 2Sa 22:28; Jer 13:9; 49:16
52 [k]**Mt 23:12**
53 [l]Ps 107:9
54 [m]Ps 98:3
55 [n]**Gal 3:16**
59 [o]Ge 17:12; Lev 12:3; Lk 2:21; Php 3:5
60 [p]ver 13,63; **Mt 3:1**
62 [q]ver 22
63 [r]ver 13,60; **Mt 3:1**
64 [s]ver 20; Eze 24:27
65 [t]ver 39
66 [u]Ge 39:2; Ac 11:21
67 [v]**ver 15**; [w]Joel 2:28
68 [x]Ge 24:27; 1Ki 8:15; Ps 72:18

[c]35 Or *So the child to be born will be called holy,*

because he has come and has
redeemed his people.[y]
69 He has raised up a horn[d][z] of salvation
for us
in the house of his servant David[a]
70 (as he said through his holy prophets
of long ago),[b]
71 salvation from our enemies
and from the hand of all who hate
us—
72 to show mercy to our fathers[c]
and to remember his holy
covenant,[d]
73 the oath he swore to our father
Abraham:[e]
74 to rescue us from the hand of our
enemies,
and to enable us to serve him[f]
without fear[g]
75 in holiness and righteousness[h]
before him all our days.

76 And you, my child, will be called a
prophet[i] of the Most High;[j]
for you will go on before the Lord to
prepare the way for him,[k]
77 to give his people the knowledge of
salvation
through the forgiveness of their
sins,[l]
78 because of the tender mercy of our
God,
by which the rising sun[m] will come
to us from heaven
79 to shine on those living in darkness
and in the shadow of death,[n]
to guide our feet into the path of
peace."[o]

80 And the child grew and became
strong in spirit;[p] and he lived in the
desert until he appeared publicly to
Israel.

The Birth of Jesus

2 In those days Caesar Augustus[a]
issued a decree that a census
should be taken of the entire Roman
world.[b] (2 This was the first census that
took place while Quirinius was gov-
ernor of Syria.)[c] 3 And everyone went to
his own town to register.
4 So Joseph also went up from the
town of Nazareth in Galilee to Judea, to
Bethlehem[d] the town of David, because
he belonged to the house and line of
David. 5 He went there to register with
Mary, who was pledged to be married
to him[e] and was expecting a child.
6 While they were there, the time came
for the baby to be born, 7 and she gave
birth to her firstborn, a son. She
wrapped him in cloths and placed him
in a manger, because there was no room
for them in the inn.

The Shepherds and the Angels

8 And there were shepherds living out
in the fields near by, keeping watch
over their flocks at night. 9 An angel[f] of
the Lord appeared to them, and the
glory of the Lord shone around them,
and they were terrified. 10 But the angel
said to them, "Do not be afraid.[g] I bring
you good news of great joy that will be
for all the people. 11 Today in the town of
David a Saviour[h] has been born to you;
he is Christ[a][i] the Lord.[j] 12 This will be
a sign[k] to you: You will find a baby
wrapped in cloths and lying in a
manger."
13 Suddenly a great company of the
heavenly host appeared with the angel,
praising God and saying,

14 "Glory to God in the highest,
and on earth peace[l] to men on
whom his favour rests."

15 When the angels had left them and
gone into heaven, the shepherds said to
one another, "Let's go to Bethlehem
and see this thing that has happened,
which the Lord has told us about."
16 So they hurried off and found Mary
and Joseph, and the baby, who was
lying in the manger.[m] 17 When they had
seen him, they spread the word con-
cerning what had been told them about
this child, 18 and all who heard it were
amazed at what the shepherds said to
them. 19 But Mary treasured up all these
things and pondered them in her
heart.[n] 20 The shepherds returned, glori-
fying and praising God[o] for all the
things they had heard and seen, which
were just as they had been told.

Jesus Presented in the Temple

21 On the eighth day, when it was time
to circumcise him,[p] he was named
Jesus, the name the angel had given him
before he had been conceived.[q]
22 When the time of their purification
according to the Law of Moses[r] had
been completed, Joseph and Mary took
him to Jerusalem to present him to the
Lord 23 (as it is written in the Law of the

68 [y]Ps 111:9; Lk 7:16
69 [z]1Sa 2:1,10; 2Sa 22:3; Ps 18:2; 89:17; 132:17; Eze 29:21; [a]**Mt 1:1**
70 [b]Jer 23:5; Ac 3:21; Ro 1:2
72 [c]Mic 7:20; [d]Ps 105:8–9; 106:45; Eze 16:60
73 [e]Ge 22:16–18
74 [f]Heb 9:14; [g]1Jn 4:18
75 [h]Eph 4:24
76 [i]**Mt 11:9**; [j]ver 32,35; **Mk 5:7**; [k]ver 17; **Mt 3:3**
77 [l]Jer 31:34; Mt 1:21; Mk 1:4
78 [m]Mal 4:2
79 [n]Ps 107:14; Isa 9:2; 59:9; Mt 4:16; **Ac 26:18**; [o]**Lk 2:14**
80 [p]Lk 2:40,52

Ch. 2

1 [a]Lk 3:1; Mt 22:17; [b]**Mt 24:14**
2 [c]Mt 4:24; Ac 15:23,41; 21:3; Gal 1:21
4 [d]**Jn 7:42**
5 [e]Lk 1:27
9 [f]**Ac 5:19**
10 [g]**Mt 14:27**
11 [h]**Mt 1:21; Jn 3:17**; 4:42; Ac 5:31; 13:23; **Ro 11:14**; 1Ti 4:10; 1Jn 4:14; [i]Mt 1:16; 16:16,20; Jn 11:27; Ac 2:36; 3:20; **9:22**; [j]**Jn 13:13**
12 [k]1Sa 2:34; 10:7; 2Ki 19:29; Ps 86:17; Isa 7:14
14 [l]Isa 9:6; 52:7; 53:5; Mic 5:5; Lk 1:79; **Jn 14:27**; Ro 5:1; Eph 2:14,17
16 [m]ver 7
19 [n]ver 51
20 [o]**Mt 9:8**
21 [p]**Lk 1:59**; [q]**Lk 1:31**
22 [r]Lev 12:2–8

[d]*69* *Horn* here symbolises strength.
[a]*11* Or *Messiah*. "The Christ" (Greek) and "the Messiah" (Hebrew) both mean "the Anointed One"; also in verse 26.

Lord, "Every firstborn male is to be consecrated to the Lord"[b]),[s] 24and to offer a sacrifice in keeping with what is said in the Law of the Lord: "a pair of doves or two young pigeons".[c][t]

25Now there was a man in Jerusalem called Simeon, who was righteous and devout.[u] He was waiting for the consolation of Israel,[v] and the Holy Spirit was upon him. 26It had been revealed to him by the Holy Spirit that he would not die before he had seen the Lord's Christ. 27Moved by the Spirit, he went into the temple courts. When the parents brought in the child Jesus to do for him what the custom of the Law required,[w] 28Simeon took him in his arms and praised God, saying:

29"Sovereign Lord, as you have
promised,[x]
you now dismiss[d] your servant in
peace.[y]
30For my eyes have seen your salvation,[z]
31 which you have prepared in the
sight of all people,
32a light for revelation to the Gentiles
and for glory to your people
Israel."[a]

33The child's father and mother marvelled at what was said about him. 34Then Simeon blessed them and said to Mary, his mother:[b] "This child is destined to cause the falling[c] and rising of many in Israel, and to be a sign that will be spoken against, 35so that the thoughts of many hearts will be revealed. And a sword will pierce your own soul too."

36There was also a prophetess,[d] Anna, the daughter of Phanuel, of the tribe of Asher. She was very old; she had lived with her husband seven years after her marriage, 37and then was a widow until she was eighty-four.[e][e] She never left the temple but worshipped night and day, fasting and praying.[f] 38Coming up to them at that very moment, she gave thanks to God and spoke about the child to all who were looking forward to the redemption of Jerusalem.[g]

39When Joseph and Mary had done everything required by the Law of the Lord, they returned to Galilee to their own town of Nazareth.[h] 40And the child grew and became strong; he was filled with wisdom, and the grace of God was upon him.[i]

The Boy Jesus at the Temple

41Every year his parents went to Jerusalem for the Feast of the Passover.[j] 42When he was twelve years old, they went up to the Feast, according to the custom. 43After the Feast was over, while his parents were returning home, the boy Jesus stayed behind in Jerusalem, but they were unaware of it. 44Thinking he was in their company, they travelled on for a day. Then they began looking for him among their relatives and friends. 45When they did not find him, they went back to Jerusalem to look for him. 46After three days they found him in the temple courts, sitting among the teachers, listening to them and asking them questions. 47Everyone who heard him was amazed[k] at his understanding and his answers. 48When his parents saw him, they were astonished. His mother[l] said to him, "Son, why have you treated us like this? Your father[m] and I have been anxiously searching for you."

49"Why were you searching for me?" he asked. "Didn't you know I had to be in my Father's house?"[n] 50But they did not understand what he was saying to them.[o]

51Then he went down to Nazareth with them[p] and was obedient to them. But his mother treasured all these things in her heart.[q] 52And Jesus grew in wisdom and stature, and in favour with God and men.[r]

John the Baptist Prepares the Way

3:2–10pp—Mt 3:1–10; Mk 1:3–5
3:16,17pp—Mt 3:11,12; Mk 1:7,8

3 In the fifteenth year of the reign of Tiberius Caesar—when Pontius Pilate[a] was governor of Judea, Herod[b] tetrarch of Galilee, his brother Philip tetrarch of Iturea and Traconitis, and Lysanias tetrarch of Abilene—2during the high priesthood of Annas and Caiaphas,[c] the word of God came to John[d] son of Zechariah[e] in the desert. 3He went into all the country around the Jordan, preaching a baptism of repentance for the forgiveness of sins.[f] 4As is written in the book of the words of Isaiah the prophet:

"A voice of one calling in the desert,
'Prepare the way for the Lord,
make straight paths for him.
5Every valley shall be filled in,
every mountain and hill made low.

23 [s]Ex 13:2,12, 15; Nu 3:13
24 [t]Lev 12:8
25 [u]Lk 1:6; [v]ver 38; Isa 52:9; Lk 23:51
27 [w]ver 22
29 [x]ver 26; [y]Ac 2:24
30 [z]Isa 40:5; 52:10; Lk 3:6
32 [a]Isa 42:6; 49:6; Ac 13:47; 26:23
34 [b]**Mt 12:46;** [c]Isa 8:14; Mt 21:44; 1Co 1:23; 2Co 2:16; Gal 5:11; 1Pe 2:7–8
36 [d]**Ac 21:9**
37 [e]1Ti 5:9; [f]Ac 13:3; 14:23; 1Ti 5:5
38 [g]ver 25; Isa 40:2; 52:9; Lk 1:68; 24:21
39 [h]ver 51; **Mt 2:23**
40 [i]ver 52; Lk 1:80
41 [j]Ex 23:15; Dt 16:1–8; Lk 22:8
47 [k]**Mt 7:28**
48 [l]**Mt 12:46;** [m]Lk 3:23; 4:22
49 [n]Jn 2:16
50 [o]**Mk 9:32**
51 [p]ver 39; **Mt 2:23;** [q]ver 19
52 [r]ver 40; 1Sa 2:26; Pr 3:4; Lk 1:80

Ch. 3

1 [a]**Mt 27:2;** [b]**Mt 14:1**
2 [c]**Mt 26:3;** [d]**Mt 3:1;** [e]Lk 1:13
3 [f]ver 16; **Mk 1:4**

[b]23 Exodus 13:2,12 [c]24 Lev. 12:8
[d]29 Or *promised, / now dismiss*
[e]37 Or *widow for eighty-four years*

The crooked roads shall become
straight,
the rough ways smooth.
6And all mankind will see God's
salvation.' "[a][g]

7John said to the crowds coming out to be baptised by him, "You brood of vipers![h] Who warned you to flee from the coming wrath?[i] 8Produce fruit in keeping with repentance. And do not begin to say to yourselves, 'We have Abraham as our father.'[j] For I tell you that out of these stones God can raise up children for Abraham. 9The axe is already at the root of the trees, and every tree that does not produce good fruit will be cut down and thrown into the fire."[k]

10"What should we do then?"[l] the crowd asked.

11John answered, "The man with two tunics should share with him who has none, and the one who has food should do the same."[m]

12Tax collectors also came to be baptised.[n] "Teacher," they asked, "what should we do?"

13"Don't collect any more than you are required to,"[o] he told them.

14Then some soldiers asked him, "And what should we do?"

He replied, "Don't extort money and don't accuse people falsely[p]—be content with your pay."

15The people were waiting expectantly and were all wondering in their hearts if John[q] might possibly be the Christ.[b][r] 16John answered them all, "I baptise you with[c] water.[s] But one more powerful than I will come, the thongs of whose sandals I am not worthy to untie. He will baptise you with the Holy Spirit and with fire.[t] 17His winnowing fork[u] is in his hand to clear his threshing-floor and to gather the wheat into his barn, but he will burn up the chaff with unquenchable fire."[v] 18And with many other words John exhorted the people and preached the good news to them.

19But when John rebuked Herod[w] the tetrarch because of Herodias, his brother's wife, and all the other evil things he had done, 20Herod added this to them all: He locked John up in prison.[x]

The Baptism and Genealogy of Jesus

3:21,22pp—Mt 3:13–17; Mk 1:9–11
3:23–38pp—Mt 1:1–17

21When all the people were being baptised, Jesus was baptised too. And as he was praying,[y] heaven was opened 22and the Holy Spirit descended on him[z] in bodily form like a dove. And a voice came from heaven: "You are my Son,[a] whom I love; with you I am well pleased."[b]

23Now Jesus himself was about thirty years old when he began his ministry.[c] He was the son, so it was thought, of Joseph,[d]

the son of Heli, 24the son of Matthat,
the son of Levi, the son of Melki,
the son of Jannai, the son of Joseph,
25the son of Mattathias, the son of
Amos,
the son of Nahum, the son of Esli,
the son of Naggai, 26the son of Maath,
the son of Mattathias, the son of
Semein,
the son of Josech, the son of Joda,
27the son of Joanan, the son of Rhesa,
the son of Zerubbabel,[e] the son of
Shealtiel,
the son of Neri, 28the son of Melki,
the son of Addi, the son of Cosam,
the son of Elmadam, the son of Er,
29the son of Joshua, the son of Eliezer,
the son of Jorim, the son of Matthat,
the son of Levi, 30the son of Simeon,
the son of Judah, the son of Joseph,
the son of Jonam, the son of Eliakim,
31the son of Melea, the son of Menna,
the son of Mattatha, the son of
Nathan,[f]
the son of David, 32the son of Jesse,
the son of Obed, the son of Boaz,
the son of Salmon,[d] the son of
Nahshon,
33the son of Amminadab, the son of
Ram,[e]
the son of Hezron, the son of Perez,[g]
the son of Judah, 34the son of Jacob,
the son of Isaac, the son of Abraham,
the son of Terah, the son of Nahor,[h]
35the son of Serug, the son of Reu,
the son of Peleg, the son of Eber,
the son of Shelah, 36the son of Cainan,
the son of Arphaxad,[i] the son of
Shem,
the son of Noah, the son of Lamech,[j]
37the son of Methuselah, the son of
Enoch,
the son of Jared, the son of Mahalalel,
the son of Kenan,[k] 38the son of Enosh,
the son of Seth, the son of Adam,
the son of God.[l]

6 [g]Isa 40:3–5; Ps 98:2; Isa 42:16; 52:10; Lk 2:30
7 [h]Mt 12:34; 23:33; [i]**Ro 1:18**
8 [j]Isa 51:2; Lk 19:9; Jn 8:33, 39; Ac 13:26; Ro 4:1,11–12, 16–17; 9:7–8; Gal 3:7
9 [k]**Mt 3:10**
10 [l]ver 12,14; Ac 2:37; 16:30
11 [m]Isa 58:7; Eze 18:7
12 [n]Lk 7:29
13 [o]Lk 19:8
14 [p]Ex 23:1; Lev 19:11
15 [q]**Mt 3:1**; [r]Jn 1:19–20; Ac 13:25
16 [s]ver 3; **Mk 1:4**; [t]Jn 1:26, 33; Ac 1:5; 2:3; 11:16; 19:4
17 [u]Isa 30:24; [v]Mt 13:30; **25:41**
19 [w]ver 1; **Mt 14:1**
20 [x]**Mt 14:3–4**
21 [y]Mt 14:23; Mk 1:35; 6:46; Lk 5:16; 6:12; 9:18,28; 11:1
22 [z]Isa 42:1; Jn 1:32–33; Ac 10:38; [a]**Mt 3:17**; [b]**Mt 3:17**
23 [c]Mt 4:17; Ac 1:1; [d]Lk 1:27
27 [e]Mt 1:12
31 [f]2Sa 5:14; 1Ch 3:5
33 [g]Ru 4:18–22; 1Ch 2:10–12
34 [h]Ge 11:24,26
36 [i]Ge 11:12; [j]Ge 5:28–32
37 [k]Ge 5:12–25
38 [l]Ge 5:1–2,6–9

[a]6 Isaiah 40:3–5 [b]15 Or *Messiah*
[c]16 Or *in* [d]32 Some early manuscripts *Sala*
[e]33 Some manuscripts *Amminadab, the son of Admin, the son of Arni*; other manuscripts vary widely.

The Temptation of Jesus
4:1–13pp—Mt 4:1–11; Mk 1:12,13

4 Jesus, full of the Holy Spirit,[a] re-
turned from the Jordan[b] and was
led by the Spirit[c] in the desert, 2where
for forty days[d] he was tempted by the
devil.[e] He ate nothing during those
days, and at the end of them he was
hungry.
3The devil said to him, "If you are the
Son of God,[f] tell this stone to become
bread."
4Jesus answered, "It is written: 'Man
does not live on bread alone.'[a]"[g]
5The devil led him up to a high place
and showed him in an instant all the
kingdoms of the world.[h] 6And he said to
him, "I will give you all their authority
and splendour, for it has been given to
me,[i] and I can give it to anyone I want
to. 7So if you worship me, it will all be
yours."
8Jesus answered, "It is written:
'Worship the Lord your God and serve
him only.'[b]"[j]
9The devil led him to Jerusalem and
had him stand on the highest point of
the temple. "If you are the Son of God,"
he said, "throw yourself down from
here. 10For it is written:

" 'He will command his angels
concerning you
to guard you carefully;
11they will lift you up in their hands,
so that you will not strike your foot
against a stone.'[c]"[k]

12Jesus answered, "It says: 'Do not
put the Lord your God to the test.'[d]"[l]
13When the devil had finished all this
tempting,[m] he left him[n] until an oppor-
tune time.

Jesus Rejected at Nazareth

14Jesus returned to Galilee[o] in the
power of the Spirit, and news about him
spread through the whole countryside.[p]
15He taught in their synagogues,[q] and
everyone praised him.
16He went to Nazareth,[r] where he had
been brought up, and on the Sabbath
day he went into the synagogue,[s] as was
his custom. And he stood up to read.[t]
17The scroll of the prophet Isaiah was
handed to him. Unrolling it, he found
the place where it is written:

18"The Spirit of the Lord is on me,[u]
because he has anointed me
to preach good news[v] to the poor.
He has sent me to proclaim freedom
for the prisoners
and recovery of sight for the blind,
to release the oppressed,
19 to proclaim the year of the Lord's
favour."[e][w]

20Then he rolled up the scroll, gave it
back to the attendant and sat down.[x]
The eyes of everyone in the synagogue
were fastened on him, 21and he began
by saying to them, "Today this scripture
is fulfilled[y] in your hearing."
22All spoke well of him and were
amazed at the gracious words that came
from his lips. "Isn't this Joseph's son?"
they asked.[z]
23Jesus said to them, "Surely you will
quote this proverb to me: 'Physician,
heal yourself! Do here in your home
town[a] what we have heard that you did
in Capernaum.' "[b]
24"I tell you the truth," he continued,
"no prophet is accepted in his home
town.[c] 25I assure you that there were
many widows in Israel in Elijah's time,
when the sky was shut for three and a
half years and there was a severe famine
throughout the land.[d] 26Yet Elijah was
not sent to any of them, but to a widow
in Zarephath in the region of Sidon.[e]
27And there were many in Israel with
leprosy[f] in the time of Elisha the
prophet, yet not one of them was
cleansed—only Naaman the Syrian."[f]
28All the people in the synagogue
were furious when they heard this.
29They got up, drove him out of the
town,[g] and took him to the brow of the
hill on which the town was built, in
order to throw him down the cliff. 30But
he walked right through the crowd and
went on his way.[h]

Jesus Drives Out an Evil Spirit
4:31–37pp—Mk 1:21–28

31Then he went down to Capernaum,[i]
a town in Galilee, and on the Sabbath
began to teach the people. 32They were
amazed at his teaching,[j] because his
message had authority.[k]
33In the synagogue there was a man
possessed by a demon, an evil[g] spirit.
He cried out at the top of his voice,
34"Ha! What do you want with us,[l] Jesus

Ch. 4

1 [a]ver 14,18; **Lk 1:15**,35; 3:16, 22; 10:21; [b]Lk 3:3,21; [c]Eze 37:1; Lk 2:27
2 [d]Ex 34:28; 1Ki 19:8; [e]Heb 4:15
3 [f]**Mt 4:3**
4 [g]Dt 8:3
5 [h]**Mt 24:14**
6 [i]Jn 12:31; 14:30; 1Jn 5:19
8 [j]Dt 6:13
11 [k]Ps 91:11–12
12 [l]Dt 6:16
13 [m]Heb 4:15; [n]Jn 14:30
14 [o]Mt 4:12; [p]**Mt 9:26**
15 [q]**Mt 4:23**
16 [r]**Mt 2:23**; [s]Mt 13:54; [t]**1Ti 4:13**
18 [u]**Jn 3:34**; [v]Mk 16:15
19 [w]Isa 61:1–2; Lev 25:10; Ps 102:20; 103:6; Isa 42:7; 49:8–9; 58:6
20 [x]ver 17; **Mt 26:55**
21 [y]**Mt 1:22**
22 [z]Mt 13:54–55; Jn 6:42; 7:15
23 [a]ver 16; **Mt 2:23**; [b]Mk 1:21–28; 2:1–12
24 [c]Mt 13:57; Jn 4:44
25 [d]1Ki 17:1; 18:1; Jas 5:17–18; Rev 11:6
26 [e]1Ki 17:8–16; **Mt 11:21**
27 [f]2Ki 5:1–14
29 [g]Nu 15:35; Ac 7:58; Heb 13:12
30 [h]Jn 8:59; 10:39
31 [i]ver 23; **Mt 4:13**
32 [j]**Mt 7:28**; [k]ver 36; Mt 7:29
34 [l]**Mt 8:29**

a4 Deut. 8:3
b8 Deut. 6:13
c11 Psalm 91:11,12
d12 Deut. 6:16
e19 Isaiah 61:1,2
f27 The Greek word was used for various diseases affecting the skin—not necessarily leprosy.
g33 Greek *unclean*; also in verse 36

of Nazareth?[m] Have you come to destroy us? I know who you are[n]—the Holy One of God!"[o]

35"Be quiet!" Jesus said sternly.[p] "Come out of him!" Then the demon threw the man down before them all and came out without injuring him.

36All the people were amazed[q] and said to each other, "What is this teaching? With authority[r] and power he gives orders to evil spirits and they come out!" 37And the news about him spread throughout the surrounding area.[s]

Jesus Heals Many

4:38–41pp—Mt 8:14–17
4:38–43pp—Mk 1:29–38

38Jesus left the synagogue and went to the home of Simon. Now Simon's mother-in-law was suffering from a high fever, and they asked Jesus to help her. 39So he bent over her and rebuked[t] the fever, and it left her. She got up at once and began to wait on them.

40When the sun was setting, the people brought to Jesus all who had various kinds of sickness, and laying his hands on each one,[u] he healed them.[v] 41Moreover, demons came out of many people, shouting, "You are the Son of God!"[w] But he rebuked[x] them and would not allow them to speak,[y] because they knew he was the Christ.[h]

42At daybreak Jesus went out to a solitary place. The people were looking for him and when they came to where he was, they tried to keep him from leaving them. 43But he said, "I must preach the good news of the kingdom of God[z] to the other towns also, because that is why I was sent." 44And he kept on preaching in the synagogues of Judea.[i][a]

The Calling of the First Disciples

5:1–11pp—Mt 4:18–22; Mk 1:16–20; Jn 1:40–42

5 One day as Jesus was standing by the Lake of Gennesaret,[a] with the people crowding round him and listening to the word of God,[a] 2he saw at the water's edge two boats, left there by the fishermen, who were washing their nets. 3He got into one of the boats, the one belonging to Simon, and asked him to put out a little from shore. Then he sat down and taught the people from the boat.[b]

4When he had finished speaking, he said to Simon, "Put out into deep water, and let down[b] the nets for a catch."[c]

5Simon answered, "Master,[d] we've worked hard all night and haven't caught anything.[e] But because you say so, I will let down the nets."

6When they had done so, they caught such a large number of fish that their nets began to break.[f] 7So they signalled to their partners in the other boat to come and help them, and they came and filled both boats so full that they began to sink.

8When Simon Peter saw this, he fell at Jesus' knees and said, "Go away from me, Lord; I am a sinful man!"[g] 9For he and all his companions were astonished at the catch of fish they had taken, 10and so were James and John, the sons of Zebedee, Simon's partners.

Then Jesus said to Simon, "Don't be afraid;[h] from now on you will catch men." 11So they pulled their boats up on shore, left everything and followed him.[i]

The Man With Leprosy

5:12–14pp—Mt 8:2–4; Mk 1:40–44

12While Jesus was in one of the towns, a man came along who was covered with leprosy.[c][j] When he saw Jesus, he fell with his face to the ground and begged him, "Lord, if you are willing, you can make me clean."

13Jesus reached out his hand and touched the man. "I am willing," he said. "Be clean!" And immediately the leprosy left him.

14Then Jesus ordered him, "Don't tell anyone,[k] but go, show yourself to the priest and offer the sacrifices that Moses commanded[l] for your cleansing, as a testimony to them."

15Yet the news about him spread all the more,[m] so that crowds of people came to hear him and to be healed of their sicknesses. 16But Jesus often withdrew to lonely places and prayed.[n]

Jesus Heals a Paralytic

5:18–26pp—Mt 9:2–8; Mk 2:3–12

17One day as he was teaching, Pharisees and teachers of the law,[o] who had come from every village of Galilee and

34 [m]**Mk 1:24**; [n]Jas 2:19; [o]ver 41; **Mk 1:24**
35 [p]ver 39,41; Mt 8:26; Lk 8:24
36 [q]**Mt 7:28**; [r]ver 32; Mt 7:29; **10:1**
37 [s]ver 14; **Mt 9:26**
39 [t]ver 35,41
40 [u]**Mk 5:23**; [v]**Mt 4:23**
41 [w]**Mt 4:3**; [x]**ver 35**; [y]**Mt 8:4**
43 [z]**Mt 3:2**
44 [a]**Mt 4:23**

Ch. 5

1 [a]**Mk 4:14; Heb 4:12**
3 [b]Mt 13:2
4 [c]Jn 21:6
5 [d]Lk 8:24,45; 9:33,49; 17:13; [e]Jn 21:3
6 [f]Jn 21:11
8 [g]Ge 18:27; Job 42:6; Isa 6:5
10 [h]**Mt 14:27**
11 [i]ver 28; **Mt 4:19**
12 [j]**Mt 8:2**
14 [k]**Mt 8:4**; [l]Lev 14:2–32
15 [m]**Mt 9:26**
16 [n]**Lk 3:21**
17 [o]Mt 15:1; Lk 2:46

[h]*41* Or *Messiah*
[i]*44* Or *the land of the Jews*; some manuscripts *Galilee*
[a]*1* That is, Sea of Galilee
[b]*4* The Greek verb is plural.
[c]*12* The Greek word was used for various diseases affecting the skin—not necessarily leprosy.

from Judea and Jerusalem, were sitting
there. And the power of the Lord was
present for him to heal the sick.[p] 18Some
men came carrying a paralytic on a mat
and tried to take him into the house to
lay him before Jesus. 19When they could
not find a way to do this because of the
crowd, they went up on the roof and
lowered him on his mat through the
tiles into the middle of the crowd, right
in front of Jesus.

20When Jesus saw their faith, he said,
"Friend, your sins are forgiven."[q]

21The Pharisees and the teachers of
the law began thinking to themselves,
"Who is this fellow who speaks blas-
phemy? Who can forgive sins but God
alone?"[r]

22Jesus knew what they were thinking
and asked, "Why are you thinking
these things in your hearts? 23Which is
easier: to say, 'Your sins are forgiven,'
or to say, 'Get up and walk'? 24But that
you may know that the Son of Man[s] has
authority on earth to forgive sins. . . ."
He said to the paralysed man, "I tell
you, get up, take your mat and go
home." 25Immediately he stood up in
front of them, took what he had been
lying on and went home praising God.
26Everyone was amazed and gave praise
to God.[t] They were filled with awe and
said, "We have seen remarkable things
today."

The Calling of Levi

5:27–32pp—Mt 9:9–13; Mk 2:14–17

27After this, Jesus went out and saw a
tax collector by the name of Levi sitting
at his tax booth. "Follow me,"[u] Jesus
said to him, 28and Levi got up, left
everything and followed him.[v]

29Then Levi held a great banquet for
Jesus at his house, and a large crowd of
tax collectors[w] and others were eating
with them. 30But the Pharisees and the
teachers of the law who belonged to
their sect[x] complained to his disciples,
"Why do you eat and drink with tax
collectors and 'sinners'?"[y]

31Jesus answered them, "It is not the
healthy who need a doctor, but the sick.
32I have not come to call the righteous,
but sinners to repentance."[z]

Jesus Questioned About Fasting

5:33–39pp—Mt 9:14–17; Mk 2:18–22

33They said to him, "John's disciples[a]
often fast and pray, and so do the
disciples of the Pharisees, but yours
go on eating and drinking."

34Jesus answered, "Can you make the
guests of the bridegroom[b] fast while he
is with them? 35But the time will come
when the bridegroom will be taken from
them;[c] in those days they will fast."

36He told them this parable: "No-one
tears a patch from a new garment and
sews it on an old one. If he does, he will
have torn the new garment, and the
patch from the new will not match the
old. 37And no-one pours new wine into
old wineskins. If he does, the new wine
will burst the skins, the wine will run
out and the wineskins will be ruined.
38No, new wine must be poured into
new wineskins. 39And no-one after
drinking old wine wants the new, for he
says, 'The old is better.'"

Lord of the Sabbath

6:1–11pp—Mt 12:1–14; Mk 2:23–3:6

6 One Sabbath Jesus was going
through the cornfields, and his dis-
ciples began to pick some ears of corn,
rub them in their hands and eat the
grain.[a] 2Some of the Pharisees asked,
"Why are you doing what is unlawful
on the Sabbath?"[b]

3Jesus answered them, "Have you
never read what David did when he and
his companions were hungry?[c] 4He en-
tered the house of God, and taking the
consecrated bread, he ate what is lawful
only for priests to eat.[d] And he also gave
some to his companions." 5Then Jesus
said to them, "The Son of Man[e] is Lord
of the Sabbath."

6On another Sabbath[f] he went into
the synagogue and was teaching, and a
man was there whose right hand was
shrivelled. 7The Pharisees and the
teachers of the law were looking for a
reason to accuse Jesus, so they watched
him closely[g] to see if he would heal on
the Sabbath.[h] 8But Jesus knew what
they were thinking[i] and said to the man
with the shrivelled hand, "Get up and
stand in front of everyone." So he got
up and stood there.

9Then Jesus said to them, "I ask you,
which is lawful on the Sabbath: to do
good or to do evil, to save life or to
destroy it?"

10He looked round at them all, and
then said to the man, "Stretch out your
hand." He did so, and his hand was
completely restored. 11But they were
furious[j] and began to discuss with
one another what they might do to
Jesus.

17 pMk 5:30; Lk 6:19
20 qLk 7:48–49
21 rIsa 43:25
24 sMt 8:20
26 tMt 9:8
27 uMt 4:19
28 vver 11; Mt 4:19
29 wLk 15:1
30 xAc 23:9; yMt 9:11
32 zJn 3:17
33 aLk 7:18; Jn 1:35; 3:25–26
34 bJn 3:29
35 cLk 9:22; 17:22; Jn 16:5–7

Ch. 6

1 aDt 23:25
2 bMt 12:2
3 c1Sa 21:6
4 dLev 24:5,9
5 eMt 8:20
6 fver 1
7 gMt 12:10; hMt 12:2
8 iMt 9:4
11 jJn 5:18

The Twelve Apostles

6:13–16pp—Mt 10:2–4; Mk 3:16–19; Ac 1:13

12One of those days Jesus went out to
a mountainside to pray, and spent the
night praying to God.[k] 13When morning
came, he called his disciples to him and
chose twelve of them, whom he also
designated apostles:[l] 14Simon (whom he
named Peter), his brother Andrew,
James, John, Philip, Bartholomew,
15Matthew,[m] Thomas, James son of
Alphaeus, Simon who was called the
Zealot, 16Judas son of James, and Judas
Iscariot, who became a traitor.

Blessings and Woes

17He went down with them and stood
on a level place. A large crowd of his
disciples was there and a great number
of people from all over Judea, from Jeru-
salem, and from the coast of Tyre and
Sidon,[n] 18who had come to hear him and
to be healed of their diseases. Those
troubled by evil[a] spirits were cured,
19and the people all tried to touch him,[o]
because power was coming from him
and healing them all.[p]
20Looking at his disciples, he said:

"Blessed are you who are poor,
for yours is the kingdom of God.[q]
21Blessed are you who hunger now,
for you will be satisfied.[r]
Blessed are you who weep now,
for you will laugh.[s]
22Blessed are you when men hate you,
when they exclude you[t] and insult
you[u]
and reject your name as evil,
because of the Son of Man.[v]

23"Rejoice in that day and leap for
joy,[w] because great is your reward in
heaven. For that is how their fathers
treated the prophets.[x]

24"But woe to you who are rich,[y]
for you have already received your
comfort.[z]
25Woe to you who are well fed now,
for you will go hungry.[a]
Woe to you who laugh now,
for you will mourn and weep.[b]
26Woe to you when all men speak well of
you,
for that is how their fathers treated
the false prophets.[c]

Love for Enemies

6:29,30pp—Mt 5:39–42

27"But I tell you who hear me: Love
your enemies, do good to those who
hate you,[d] 28bless those who curse you,
pray for those who ill-treat you.[e] 29If
someone strikes you on one cheek, turn
to him the other also. If someone takes
your cloak, do not stop him from taking
your tunic. 30Give to everyone who asks
you, and if anyone takes what belongs
to you, do not demand it back.[f] 31Do to
others as you would have them do to
you.[g]
32"If you love those who love you,
what credit is that to you?[h] Even 'sin-
ners' love those who love them. 33And if
you do good to those who are good to
you, what credit is that to you? Even
'sinners' do that. 34And if you lend to
those from whom you expect repay-
ment, what credit is that to you?[i] Even
'sinners' lend to 'sinners', expecting to
be repaid in full. 35But love your en-
emies, do good to them,[j] and lend to
them without expecting to get anything
back. Then your reward will be great,
and you will be sons[k] of the Most High,[l]
because he is kind to the ungrateful and
wicked. 36Be merciful,[m] just as your
Father[n] is merciful.

Judging Others

6:37–42pp—Mt 7:1–5

37"Do not judge, and you will not be
judged.[o] Do not condemn, and you will
not be condemned. Forgive, and you
will be forgiven.[p] 38Give, and it will be
given to you. A good measure, pressed
down, shaken together and running
over, will be poured into your lap.[q] For
with the measure you use, it will be
measured to you."[r]
39He also told them this parable: "Can
a blind man lead a blind man? Will they
not both fall into a pit?[s] 40A student is
not above his teacher, but everyone
who is fully trained will be like his
teacher.[t]
41"Why do you look at the speck of
sawdust in your brother's eye and pay
no attention to the plank in your own
eye? 42How can you say to your brother,
'Brother, let me take the speck out of
your eye,' when you yourself fail to see
the plank in your own eye? You hypo-
crite, first take the plank out of your eye,
and then you will see clearly to remove
the speck from your brother's eye.

A Tree and Its Fruit

6:43,44pp—Mt 7:16,18,20

43"No good tree bears bad fruit, nor
does a bad tree bear good fruit. 44Each

12 [k]**Lk 3:21**
13 [l]**Mk 6:30**
15 [m]Mt 9:9
17 [n]Mt 4:25; **11:21**; Mk 3:7–8
19 [o]**Mt 9:20**; [p]Mk 5:30; Lk 5:17
20 [q]**Mt 25:34**
21 [r]Isa 55:1–2; Mt 5:6; [s]Isa 61:2–3; Mt 5:4; Rev 7:17
22 [t]Jn 9:22; 16:2; [u]Isa 51:7; [v]**Jn 15:21**
23 [w]**Mt 5:12**; [x]**Mt 5:12**
24 [y]Jas 5:1; [z]Lk 16:25
25 [a]Isa 65:13; [b]Pr 14:13
26 [c]**Mt 7:15**
27 [d]ver 35; Mt 5:44; Ro 12:20
28 [e]**Mt 5:44**
30 [f]Dt 15:7–8,10; Pr 21:26
31 [g]Mt 7:12
32 [h]Mt 5:46
34 [i]Mt 5:42
35 [j]ver 27; [k]**Ro 8:14**; [l]**Mk 5:7**
36 [m]Jas 2:13; [n]Mt 5:48; 6:1; Lk 11:2; 12:32; Ro 8:15; Eph 4:6; 1Pe 1:17; 1Jn 1:3; 3:1
37 [o]**Mt 7:1**; [p]Mt 6:14
38 [q]Ps 79:12; Isa 65:6–7; [r]**Mt 7:2**
39 [s]Mt 15:14
40 [t]**Jn 13:16**

[a]18 Greek *unclean*

tree is recognised by its own fruit.[u] People do not pick figs from thorn-bushes, or grapes from briers. 45The good man brings good things out of the good stored up in his heart, and the evil man brings evil things out of the evil stored up in his heart. For out of the overflow of his heart his mouth speaks.[v]

The Wise and Foolish Builders

6:47–49pp—Mt 7:24–27

46"Why do you call me, 'Lord, Lord,'[w] and do not do what I say?[x] 47I will show you what he is like who comes to me and hears my words and puts them into practice.[y] 48He is like a man building a house, who dug down deep and laid the foundation on rock. When the flood came, the torrent struck that house but could not shake it, because it was well built. 49But the one who hears my words and does not put them into practice is like a man who built a house on the ground without a foundation. The moment the torrent struck that house, it collapsed and its destruction was complete."

The Faith of the Centurion

7:1–10pp—Mt 8:5–13

7 When Jesus had finished saying all this[a] in the hearing of the people, he entered Capernaum. 2There a centurion's servant, whom his master valued highly, was sick and about to die. 3The centurion heard of Jesus and sent some elders of the Jews to him, asking him to come and heal his servant. 4When they came to Jesus, they pleaded earnestly with him, "This man deserves to have you do this, 5because he loves our nation and has built our synagogue." 6So Jesus went with them.

He was not far from the house when the centurion sent friends to say to him: "Lord, don't trouble yourself, for I do not deserve to have you come under my roof. 7That is why I did not even consider myself worthy to come to you. But say the word, and my servant will be healed.[b] 8For I myself am a man under authority, with soldiers under me. I tell this one, 'Go', and he goes; and that one, 'Come', and he comes. I say to my servant, 'Do this', and he does it."

9When Jesus heard this, he was amazed at him, and turning to the crowd following him, he said, "I tell you, I have not found such great faith even in Israel." 10Then the men who had been sent returned to the house and found the servant well.

Jesus Raises a Widow's Son

7:11–16Ref—1Ki 17:17–24; 2Ki 4:32–37; Mk 5:21–24, 35–43; Jn 11:1–44

11Soon afterwards, Jesus went to a town called Nain, and his disciples and a large crowd went along with him. 12As he approached the town gate, a dead person was being carried out—the only son of his mother, and she was a widow. And a large crowd from the town was with her. 13When the Lord[c] saw her, his heart went out to her and he said, "Don't cry."

14Then he went up and touched the coffin, and those carrying it stood still. He said, "Young man, I say to you, get up!"[d] 15The dead man sat up and began to talk, and Jesus gave him back to his mother.

16They were all filled with awe[e] and praised God.[f] "A great prophet[g] has appeared among us," they said. "God has come to help his people."[h] 17This news about Jesus spread throughout Judea[a] and the surrounding country.[i]

Jesus and John the Baptist

7:18–35pp—Mt 11:2–19

18John's[j] disciples[k] told him about all these things. Calling two of them, 19he sent them to the Lord to ask, "Are you the one who was to come, or should we expect someone else?"

20When the men came to Jesus, they said, "John the Baptist sent us to you to ask, 'Are you the one who was to come, or should we expect someone else?' "

21At that very time Jesus cured many who had diseases, sicknesses[l] and evil spirits, and gave sight to many who were blind. 22So he replied to the messengers, "Go back and report to John what you have seen and heard: The blind receive sight, the lame walk, those who have leprosy[b] are cured, the deaf hear, the dead are raised, and the good news is preached to the poor.[m] 23Blessed is the man who does not fall away on account of me."

24After John's messengers left, Jesus began to speak to the crowd about John: "What did you go out into the desert to see? A reed swayed by the wind? 25If not, what did you go out to see? A man dressed in fine clothes? No, those who wear expensive clothes and indulge in luxury are in palaces. 26But what did

44 [u]Mt 12:33
45 [v]Pr 4:23; Mt 12:34–35; Mk 7:20
46 [w]**Jn 13:13;** [x]Mal 1:6; Mt 7:21
47 [y]Lk 8:21; 11:28; Jas 1:22–25

Ch. 7

1 [a]Mt 7:28
7 [b]Ps 107:20
13 [c]ver 19; Lk 10:1; 13:15; 17:5; 22:61; 24:34; Jn 11:2
14 [d]Mt 9:25; Mk 1:31; Lk 8:54; Jn 11:43; Ac 9:40
16 [e]Lk 1:65; [f]**Mt 9:8;** [g]ver 39; **Mt 21:11;** [h]Lk 1:68
17 [i]**Mt 9:26**
18 [j]**Mt 3:1;** [k]**Lk 5:33**
21 [l]**Mt 4:23**
22 [m]Isa 29:18–19; 35:5–6; 61:1–2; Lk 4:18

[a]17 Or *the land of the Jews*
[b]22 The Greek word was used for various diseases affecting the skin—not necessarily leprosy.

you go out to see? A prophet?[n] Yes, I tell
you, and more than a prophet. 27This is
the one about whom it is written:

"'I will send my messenger ahead of
you,
who will prepare your way before
you.'[c][o]

28I tell you, among those born of women
there is no-one greater than John; yet
the one who is least in the kingdom of
God[p] is greater than he."
(29All the people, even the tax collec-
tors, when they heard Jesus' words,
acknowledged that God's way was
right, because they had been baptised
by John.[q] 30But the Pharisees and ex-
perts in the law[r] rejected God's purpose
for themselves, because they had not
been baptised by John.)
31"To what, then, can I compare the
people of this generation? What are
they like? 32They are like children sitting
in the market-place and calling out to
each other:

"'We played the flute for you,
and you did not dance;
we sang a dirge,
and you did not cry.'

33For John the Baptist came neither eat-
ing bread nor drinking wine,[s] and you
say, 'He has a demon.' 34The Son of Man
came eating and drinking, and you say,
'Here is a glutton and a drunkard, a
friend of tax collectors and "sinners".'[t]
35But wisdom is proved right by all her
children."

Jesus Anointed by a Sinful Woman

7:37–39Ref—Mt 26:6–13; Mk 14:3–9; Jn 12:1–8
7:41,42Ref—Mt 18:23–24

36Now one of the Pharisees invited
Jesus to have dinner with him, so he
went to the Pharisee's house and re-
clined at the table. 37When a woman
who had lived a sinful life in that town
learned that Jesus was eating at the
Pharisee's house, she brought an ala-
baster jar of perfume, 38and as she stood
behind him at his feet weeping, she
began to wet his feet with her tears.
Then she wiped them with her hair,
kissed them and poured perfume on
them.
39When the Pharisee who had invited
him saw this, he said to himself, "If this
man were a prophet,[u] he would know
who is touching him and what kind of
woman she is—that she is a sinner."

26 [n]**Mt 11:9**
27 [o]Mal 3:1; Mt 11:10; Mk 1:2
28 [p]**Mt 3:2**
29 [q]Mt 21:32; Mk 1:5; Lk 3:12
30 [r]**Mt 22:35**
33 [s]Lk 1:15
34 [t]Lk 5:29–30; 15:1–2
39 [u]ver 16; **Mt 21:11**
44 [v]Ge 18:4; 19:2; 43:24; Jdg 19:21; Jn 13:4–14; 1Ti 5:10
45 [w]Lk 22:47–48; **Ro 16:16**
46 [x]Ps 23:5; Ecc 9:8
48 [y]Mt 9:2
50 [z]**Mt 9:22;** [a]**Ac 15:33**

Ch. 8

1 [a]**Mt 4:23**
2 [b]Mt 27:55–56
3 [c]**Mt 14:1**

40Jesus answered him, "Simon, I have
something to tell you."
"Tell me, teacher," he said.
41"Two men owed money to a certain
money-lender. One owed him five hun-
dred denarii,[d] and the other fifty.
42Neither of them had the money to pay
him back, so he cancelled the debts of
both. Now which of them will love him
more?"
43Simon replied, "I suppose the one
who had the bigger debt cancelled."
"You have judged correctly," Jesus
said.
44Then he turned towards the woman
and said to Simon, "Do you see this
woman? I came into your house. You
did not give me any water for my feet,[v]
but she wet my feet with her tears and
wiped them with her hair. 45You did not
give me a kiss,[w] but this woman, from
the time I entered, has not stopped kiss-
ing my feet. 46You did not put oil on my
head,[x] but she has poured perfume on
my feet. 47Therefore, I tell you, her
many sins have been forgiven—for she
loved much. But he who has been for-
given little loves little."
48Then Jesus said to her, "Your sins
are forgiven."[y]
49The other guests began to say
among themselves, "Who is this who
even forgives sins?"
50Jesus said to the woman, "Your
faith has saved you;[z] go in peace."[a]

The Parable of the Sower

8:4–15pp—Mt 13:2–23; Mk 4:1–20

8 After this, Jesus travelled about
from one town and village to
another, proclaiming the good news of
the kingdom of God.[a] The Twelve were
with him, 2and also some women who
had been cured of evil spirits and dis-
eases: Mary (called Magdalene)[b] from
whom seven demons had come out;
3Joanna the wife of Chuza, the manager
of Herod's[c] household; Susanna; and
many others. These women were help-
ing to support them out of their own
means.
4While a large crowd was gathering
and people were coming to Jesus from
town after town, he told this parable:
5"A farmer went out to sow his seed. As
he was scattering the seed, some fell
along the path; it was trampled on, and
the birds of the air ate it up. 6Some fell

[c]*27* Mal. 3:1
[d]*41* A denarius was a coin worth about a day's wages.

on rock, and when it came up, the plants withered because they had no moisture. 7Other seed fell among thorns, which grew up with it and choked the plants. 8Still other seed fell on good soil. It came up and yielded a crop, a hundred times more than was sown."

When he said this, he called out, "He who has ears to hear, let him hear."[d]

9His disciples asked him what this parable meant. 10He said, "The knowledge of the secrets of the kingdom of God has been given to you,[e] but to others I speak in parables, so that,

"'though seeing, they may not see;
though hearing, they may not
understand.'[a][f]

11"This is the meaning of the parable: The seed is the word of God.[g] 12Those along the path are the ones who hear, and then the devil comes and takes away the word from their hearts, so that they may not believe and be saved. 13Those on the rock are the ones who receive the word with joy when they hear it, but they have no root. They believe for a while, but in the time of testing they fall away.[h] 14The seed that fell among thorns stands for those who hear, but as they go on their way they are choked by life's worries, riches[i] and pleasures, and they do not mature. 15But the seed on good soil stands for those with a noble and good heart, who hear the word, retain it, and by persevering produce a crop.

A Lamp on a Stand

16"No-one lights a lamp and hides it in a jar or puts it under a bed. Instead, he puts it on a stand, so that those who come in can see the light.[j] 17For there is nothing hidden that will not be disclosed, and nothing concealed that will not be known or brought out into the open.[k] 18Therefore consider carefully how you listen. Whoever has will be given more; whoever does not have, even what he thinks he has will be taken from him."[l]

Jesus' Mother and Brothers

8:19–21pp—Mt 12:46–50; Mk 3:31–35

19Now Jesus' mother and brothers came to see him, but they were not able to get near him because of the crowd. 20Someone told him, "Your mother and brothers[m] are standing outside, wanting to see you."

21He replied, "My mother and brothers are those who hear God's word and put it into practice."[n]

Jesus Calms the Storm

8:22–25pp—Mt 8:23–27; Mk 4:36–41
8:22–25Ref—Mk 6:47–52; Jn 6:16–21

22One day Jesus said to his disciples, "Let's go over to the other side of the lake." So they got into a boat and set out. 23As they sailed, he fell asleep. A squall came down on the lake, so that the boat was being swamped, and they were in great danger.

24The disciples went and woke him, saying, "Master, Master,[o] we're going to drown!"

He got up and rebuked[p] the wind and the raging waters; the storm subsided, and all was calm.[q] 25"Where is your faith?" he asked his disciples.

In fear and amazement they asked one another, "Who is this? He commands even the winds and the water, and they obey him."

The Healing of a Demon-possessed Man

8:26–37pp—Mt 8:28–34
8:26–39pp—Mk 5:1–20

26They sailed to the region of the Gerasenes,[b] which is across the lake from Galilee. 27When Jesus stepped ashore, he was met by a demon-possessed man from the town. For a long time this man had not worn clothes or lived in a house, but had lived in the tombs. 28When he saw Jesus, he cried out and fell at his feet, shouting at the top of his voice, "What do you want with me,[r] Jesus, Son of the Most High God?[s] I beg you, don't torture me!" 29For Jesus had commanded the evil[c] spirit to come out of the man. Many times it had seized him, and though he was chained hand and foot and kept under guard, he had broken his chains and had been driven by the demon into solitary places.

30Jesus asked him, "What is your name?"

"Legion," he replied, because many demons had gone into him. 31And they begged him repeatedly not to order them to go into the Abyss.[t]

32A large herd of pigs was feeding there on the hillside. The demons begged Jesus to let them go into them,

8 [d]**Mt 11:15**
10 [e]**Mt 13:11;** [f]Isa 6:9; **Mt 13:13–14**
11 [g]**Heb 4:12**
13 [h]Mt 11:6
14 [i]Mt 19:23; 1Ti 6:9–10,17
16 [j]**Mt 5:15**
17 [k]Mt 10:26; Mk 4:22; Lk 12:2
18 [l]**Mt 25:29**
20 [m]Jn 7:5
21 [n]Lk 6:47; 11:28; Jn 14:21
24 [o]**Lk 5:5;** [p]Lk 4:35,39,41; [q]Ps 107:29; Jnh 1:15
28 [r]**Mt 8:29;** [s]**Mk 5:7**
31 [t]Rev 9:1–2, 11; 11:7; 17:8; 20:1,3

[a]*10* Isaiah 6:9
[b]*26* Some manuscripts *Gadarenes;* other manuscripts *Gergesenes;* also in verse 37
[c]*29* Greek *unclean*

and he gave them permission. 33When
the demons came out of the man, they
went into the pigs, and the herd rushed
down the steep bank into the lake[u] and
was drowned.
34When those tending the pigs saw
what had happened, they ran off and
reported this in the town and country-
side, 35and the people went out to see
what had happened. When they came
to Jesus, they found the man from
whom the demons had gone out, sitting
at Jesus' feet,[v] dressed and in his right
mind; and they were afraid. 36Those
who had seen it told the people how
the demon-possessed[w] man had been
cured. 37Then all the people of the re-
gion of the Gerasenes asked Jesus to
leave them,[x] because they were over-
come with fear. So he got into the boat
and left.
38The man from whom the demons
had gone out begged to go with him,
but Jesus sent him away, saying,
39"Return home and tell how much God
has done for you." So the man went
away and told all over the town how
much Jesus had done for him.

A Dead Girl and a Sick Woman

8:40–56pp—Mt 9:18–26; Mk 5:22–43

40Now when Jesus returned, a crowd
welcomed him, for they were all expect-
ing him. 41Then a man named Jairus, a
ruler of the synagogue,[y] came and fell at
Jesus' feet, pleading with him to come
to his house 42because his only daugh-
ter, a girl of about twelve, was dying.
As Jesus was on his way, the crowds
almost crushed him. 43And a woman
was there who had been subject to
bleeding[z] for twelve years,[d] but no-one
could heal her. 44She came up behind
him and touched the edge of his cloak,[a]
and immediately her bleeding stopped.
45"Who touched me?" Jesus asked.
When they all denied it, Peter said,
"Master,[b] the people are crowding and
pressing against you."
46But Jesus said, "Someone touched
me;[c] I know that power has gone out
from me."[d]
47Then the woman, seeing that she
could not go unnoticed, came trembling
and fell at his feet. In the presence of all
the people, she told why she had
touched him and how she had been
instantly healed. 48Then he said to her,
"Daughter, your faith has healed you.[e]
Go in peace."[f]
49While Jesus was still speaking,
someone came from the house of Jairus,

33 [u]ver 22–23
35 [v]Lk 10:39
36 [w]**Mt 4:24**
37 [x]Ac 16:39
41 [y]ver 49; **Mk 5:22**
43 [z]Lev 15:25–30
44 [a]**Mt 9:20**
45 [b]**Lk 5:5**
46 [c]Mt 14:36; Mk 3:10; [d]Lk 5:17; 6:19
48 [e]**Mt 9:22;** [f]**Ac 15:33**
49 [g]ver 41
51 [h]**Mt 4:21**
52 [i]Lk 23:27; [j]**Mt 9:24**
54 [k]**Lk 7:14**
56 [l]**Mt 8:4**

Ch. 9

1 [a]**Mt 10:1;** [b]**Mt 4:23**; Lk 5:17
2 [c]**Mt 3:2**
3 [d]Lk 10:4; 22:35
5 [e]**Mt 10:14**
7 [f]**Mt 14:1;** [g]**Mt 3:1;** [h]ver 19
8 [i]**Mt 11:14;** [j]ver 19; Jn 1:21
9 [k]Lk 23:8
10 [l]**Mk 6:30**

the synagogue ruler.[g] "Your daughter is
dead," he said. "Don't bother the
teacher any more."
50Hearing this, Jesus said to Jairus,
"Don't be afraid; just believe, and she
will be healed."
51When he arrived at the house of
Jairus, he did not let anyone go in with
him except Peter, John and James,[h]
and the child's father and mother.
52Meanwhile, all the people were wail-
ing and mourning[i] for her. "Stop wail-
ing," Jesus said. "She is not dead but
asleep."[j]
53They laughed at him, knowing that
she was dead. 54But he took her by the
hand and said, "My child, get up!"[k]
55Her spirit returned, and at once she
stood up. Then Jesus told them to give
her something to eat. 56Her parents
were astonished, but he ordered them
not to tell anyone what had happened.[l]

Jesus Sends Out the Twelve

9:3–5pp—Mt 10:9–15; Mk 6:8–11
9:7–9pp—Mt 14:1,2; Mk 6:14–16

9 When Jesus had called the Twelve
together, he gave them power and
authority to drive out all demons[a] and to
cure diseases,[b] 2and he sent them out to
preach the kingdom of God[c] and to heal
the sick. 3He told them: "Take nothing
for the journey—no staff, no bag, no
bread, no money, no extra tunic.[d]
4Whatever house you enter, stay there
until you leave that town. 5If people do
not welcome you, shake the dust off
your feet when you leave their town, as
a testimony against them."[e] 6So they set
out and went from village to village,
preaching the gospel and healing
people everywhere.
7Now Herod[f] the tetrarch heard about
all that was going on. And he was per-
plexed, because some were saying that
John[g] had been raised from the dead,[h]
8others that Elijah had appeared,[i] and
still others that one of the prophets of
long ago had come back to life.[j] 9But
Herod said, "I beheaded John. Who,
then, is this I hear such things about?"
And he tried to see him.[k]

Jesus Feeds the Five Thousand

9:10–17pp—Mt 14:13–21; Mk 6:32–44; Jn 6:5–13
9:13–17Ref—2Ki 4:42–44

10When the apostles[l] returned, they
reported to Jesus what they had done.

d43 Many manuscripts *years, and she had spent all she had on doctors*

Then he took them with him and they withdrew by themselves to a town called Bethsaida,[m] 11but the crowds learned about it and followed him. He welcomed them and spoke to them about the kingdom of God,[n] and healed those who needed healing.

12Late in the afternoon the Twelve came to him and said, "Send the crowd away so they can go to the surrounding villages and countryside and find food and lodging, because we are in a remote place here."

13He replied, "You give them something to eat."

They answered, "We have only five loaves of bread and two fish—unless we go and buy food for all this crowd." 14(About five thousand men were there.)

But he said to his disciples, "Make them sit down in groups of about fifty each." 15The disciples did so, and everybody sat down. 16Taking the five loaves and the two fish and looking up to heaven, he gave thanks and broke them.[o] Then he gave them to the disciples to set before the people. 17They all ate and were satisfied, and the disciples picked up twelve basketfuls of broken pieces that were left over.

Peter's Confession of Christ

9:18–20pp—Mt 16:13–16; Mk 8:27–29
9:22–27pp—Mt 16:21–28; Mk 8:31–9:1

18Once when Jesus was praying[p] in private and his disciples were with him, he asked them, "Who do the crowds say I am?"

19They replied, "Some say John the Baptist;[q] others say Elijah; and still others, that one of the prophets of long ago has come back to life."[r]

20"But what about you?" he asked. "Who do you say I am?"

Peter answered, "The Christ[a] of God."[s]

21Jesus strictly warned them not to tell this to anyone.[t] 22And he said, "The Son of Man[u] must suffer many things[v] and be rejected by the elders, chief priests and teachers of the law,[w] and he must be killed[x] and on the third day[y] be raised to life."[z]

23Then he said to them all: "If anyone would come after me, he must deny himself and take up his cross daily and follow me.[a] 24For whoever wants to save his life will lose it, but whoever loses his life for me will save it.[b] 25What good is it for a man to gain the whole world, and yet lose or forfeit his very self? 26If anyone is ashamed of me and my words, the Son of Man will be ashamed of him[c] when he comes in his glory and in the glory of the Father and of the holy angels.[d] 27I tell you the truth, some who are standing here will not taste death before they see the kingdom of God."

The Transfiguration

9:28–36pp—Mt 17:1–8; Mk 9:2–8

28About eight days after Jesus said this, he took Peter, John and James[e] with him and went up onto a mountain to pray.[f] 29As he was praying, the appearance of his face changed, and his clothes became as bright as a flash of lightning. 30Two men, Moses and Elijah, 31appeared in glorious splendour, talking with Jesus. They spoke about his departure,[g] which he was about to bring to fulfilment at Jerusalem. 32Peter and his companions were very sleepy,[h] but when they became fully awake, they saw his glory and the two men standing with him. 33As the men were leaving Jesus, Peter said to him, "Master,[i] it is good for us to be here. Let us put up three shelters—one for you, one for Moses and one for Elijah." (He did not know what he was saying.)

34While he was speaking, a cloud appeared and enveloped them, and they were afraid as they entered the cloud. 35A voice came from the cloud, saying, "This is my Son, whom I have chosen;[j] listen to him."[k] 36When the voice had spoken, they found that Jesus was alone. The disciples kept this to themselves, and told no-one at that time what they had seen.[l]

The Healing of a Boy With an Evil Spirit

9:37–42,43–45pp—Mt 17:14–18,22,23; Mk 9:14–27, 30–32

37The next day, when they came down from the mountain, a large crowd met him. 38A man in the crowd called out, "Teacher, I beg you to look at my son, for he is my only child. 39A spirit seizes him and he suddenly screams; it throws him into convulsions so that he foams at the mouth. It scarcely ever leaves him and is destroying him. 40I begged your disciples to drive it out, but they could not."

41"O unbelieving and perverse generation,"[m] Jesus replied, "how long

---

10 [m]**Mt 11:21**
11 [n]ver 2; **Mt 3:2**
16 [o]**Mt 14:19**
18 [p]**Lk 3:21**
19 [q]**Mt 3:1**; [r]ver 7–8
20 [s]Jn 1:49; 6:66–69; 11:27
21 [t]**Mk 8:30**
22 [u]**Mt 8:20**; [v]**Mt 16:21**; [w]Mt 27:1–2; [x]Ac 2:23; 3:13; [y]**Mt 16:21**; [z]**Mt 16:21**
23 [a]Mt 10:38; Lk 14:27
24 [b]**Jn 12:25**
26 [c]Mt 10:33; Lk 12:9; 2Ti 2:12; [d]**Mt 16:27**
28 [e]**Mt 4:21**; [f]**Lk 3:21**
31 [g]2Pe 1:15
32 [h]Mt 26:43
33 [i]**Lk 5:5**
35 [j]Isa 42:1; [k]**Mt 3:17**
36 [l]Mt 17:9
41 [m]Dt 32:5

---

[a]20 Or *Messiah*

shall I stay with you and put up with
you? Bring your son here."
42Even while the boy was coming, the
demon threw him to the ground in a
convulsion. But Jesus rebuked the evil[b]
spirit, healed the boy and gave him back
to his father. 43And they were all
amazed at the greatness of God.
While everyone was marvelling at all
that Jesus did, he said to his disciples,
44"Listen carefully to what I am about to
tell you: The Son of Man is going to be
betrayed into the hands of men."[n] 45But
they did not understand what this
meant. It was hidden from them, so that
they did not grasp it,[o] and they were
afraid to ask him about it.

Who Will Be the Greatest?

9:46–48pp—Mt 18:1–5
9:46–50pp—Mk 9:33–40

46An argument started among the
disciples as to which of them would be
the greatest.[p] 47Jesus, knowing their
thoughts,[q] took a little child and made
him stand beside him. 48Then he said to
them, "Whoever welcomes this little
child in my name welcomes me; and
whoever welcomes me welcomes the
one who sent me.[r] For he who is least
among you all—he is the greatest."[s]
49"Master,"[t] said John, "we saw a
man driving out demons in your name
and we tried to stop him, because he is
not one of us."
50"Do not stop him," Jesus said, "for
whoever is not against you is for you."[u]

Samaritan Opposition

51As the time approached for him to
be taken up to heaven,[v] Jesus resolutely
set out for Jerusalem.[w] 52And he sent
messengers on ahead, who went into a
Samaritan[x] village to get things ready
for him; 53but the people there did not
welcome him, because he was heading
for Jerusalem. 54When the disciples
James and John[y] saw this, they asked,
"Lord, do you want us to call fire down
from heaven to destroy them[c]?"[z] 55But
Jesus turned and rebuked them, 56and[d]
they went to another village.

The Cost of Following Jesus

9:57–60pp—Mt 8:19–22

57As they were walking along the
road,[a] a man said to him, "I will follow
you wherever you go."
58Jesus replied, "Foxes have holes
and birds of the air have nests, but the
Son of Man[b] has nowhere to lay his
head."
59He said to another man, "Follow
me."[c]
But the man replied, "Lord, first let
me go and bury my father."
60Jesus said to him, "Let the dead
bury their own dead, but you go and
proclaim the kingdom of God."[d]
61Still another said, "I will follow you,
Lord; but first let me go back and say
good-bye to my family."[e]
62Jesus replied, "No-one who puts his
hand to the plough and looks back is fit
for service in the kingdom of God."

Jesus Sends Out the Seventy-two

10:4–12pp—Lk 9:3–5
10:13–15,21,22pp—Mt 11:21–23,25–27
10:23,24pp—Mt 13:16,17

10 After this the Lord[a] appointed
seventy-two[a] others[b] and sent
them two by two[c] ahead of him to every
town and place where he was about to
go.[d] 2He told them, "The harvest is
plentiful, but the workers are few. Ask
the Lord of the harvest, therefore, to
send out workers into his harvest field.[e]
3Go! I am sending you out like lambs
among wolves.[f] 4Do not take a purse or
bag or sandals; and do not greet anyone
on the road.
5"When you enter a house, first say,
'Peace to this house.' 6If a man of peace
is there, your peace will rest on him; if
not, it will return to you. 7Stay in that
house, eating and drinking whatever
they give you, for the worker deserves
his wages.[g] Do not move around from
house to house.
8"When you enter a town and are
welcomed, eat what is set before you.[h]
9Heal the sick who are there and tell
them, 'The kingdom of God[i] is near
you.' 10But when you enter a town and
are not welcomed, go into its streets and
say, 11'Even the dust of your town that
sticks to our feet we wipe off against
you.[j] Yet be sure of this: The kingdom of
God is near.'[k] 12I tell you, it will be more
bearable on that day for Sodom[l] than for
that town.[m]
13"Woe to you,[n] Korazin! Woe to you,
Bethsaida! For if the miracles that were
performed in you had been performed

44 [n]ver 22
45 [o]**Mk 9:32**
46 [p]Lk 22:24
47 [q]**Mt 9:4**
48 [r]**Mt 10:40;** [s]**Mk 9:35**
49 [t]**Lk 5:5**
50 [u]Mt 12:30; Lk 11:23
51 [v]**Mk 16:19;** [w]Lk 13:22; 17:11; 18:31; 19:28
52 [x]**Mt 10:5**
54 [y]**Mt 4:21;** [z]2Ki 1:10,12
57 [a]ver 51
58 [b]**Mt 8:20**
59 [c]**Mt 4:19**
60 [d]**Mt 3:2**
61 [e]1Ki 19:20

Ch. 10

1 [a]**Lk 7:13;** [b]Lk 9:1–2,51–52; [c]Mk 6:7; [d]Mt 10:1
2 [e]Mt 9:37–38; Jn 4:35
3 [f]Mt 10:16
7 [g]**1Ti 5:18**
8 [h]1Co 10:27
9 [i]**Mt 3:2**
11 [j]**Mt 10:14;** [k]ver 9
12 [l]**Mt 10:15;** [m]Mt 11:24
13 [n]Lk 6:24–26

[b]42 Greek *unclean*
[c]54 Some manuscripts *them, even as Elijah did*
[d]55,56 Some manuscripts *them. And he said, "You do not know what kind of spirit you are of, for the Son of Man did not come to destroy men's lives, but to save them."* [56]*And*
[a]1 Some manuscripts *seventy;* also in verse 17

in Tyre and Sidon, they would have repented long ago, sitting in sackcloth[o] and ashes. 14But it will be more bearable for Tyre and Sidon at the judgment than for you. 15And you, Capernaum,[p] will you be lifted up to the skies? No, you will go down to the depths.[b]

16"He who listens to you listens to me; he who rejects you rejects me; but he who rejects me rejects him who sent me."[q]

17The seventy-two[r] returned with joy and said, "Lord, even the demons submit to us in your name."[s]

18He replied, "I saw Satan[t] fall like lightning from heaven.[u] 19I have given you authority to trample on snakes[v] and scorpions and to overcome all the power of the enemy; nothing will harm you. 20However, do not rejoice that the spirits submit to you, but rejoice that your names are written in heaven."[w]

21At that time Jesus, full of joy through the Holy Spirit, said, "I praise you, Father, Lord of heaven and earth, because you have hidden these things from the wise and learned, and revealed them to little children.[x] Yes, Father, for this was your good pleasure.

22"All things have been committed to me by my Father.[y] No-one knows who the Son is except the Father, and no-one knows who the Father is except the Son and those to whom the Son chooses to reveal him."[z]

23Then he turned to his disciples and said privately, "Blessed are the eyes that see what you see. 24For I tell you that many prophets and kings wanted to see what you see but did not see it, and to hear what you hear but did not hear it."[a]

The Parable of the Good Samaritan

10:25–28pp—Mt 22:34–40; Mk 12:28–31

25On one occasion an expert in the law stood up to test Jesus. "Teacher," he asked, "what must I do to inherit eternal life?"[b]

26"What is written in the Law?" he replied. "How do you read it?"

27He answered: "'Love the Lord your God with all your heart and with all your soul and with all your strength and with all your mind'[c];[c] and, 'Love your neighbour as yourself.'[d]"[d]

28"You have answered correctly," Jesus replied. "Do this and you will live."[e]

29But he wanted to justify himself,[f] so he asked Jesus, "And who is my neighbour?"

30In reply Jesus said: "A man was going down from Jerusalem to Jericho, when he fell into the hands of robbers. They stripped him of his clothes, beat him and went away, leaving him half-dead. 31A priest happened to be going down the same road, and when he saw the man, he passed by on the other side.[g] 32So too, a Levite, when he came to the place and saw him, passed by on the other side. 33But a Samaritan,[h] as he travelled, came where the man was; and when he saw him, he took pity on him. 34He went to him and bandaged his wounds, pouring on oil and wine. Then he put the man on his own donkey, brought him to an inn and took care of him. 35The next day he took out two silver coins[e] and gave them to the innkeeper. 'Look after him,' he said, 'and when I return, I will reimburse you for any extra expense you may have.'

36"Which of these three do you think was a neighbour to the man who fell into the hands of robbers?"

37The expert in the law replied, "The one who had mercy on him."

Jesus told him, "Go and do likewise."

At the Home of Martha and Mary

38As Jesus and his disciples were on their way, he came to a village where a woman named Martha[i] opened her home to him. 39She had a sister called Mary,[j] who sat at the Lord's feet[k] listening to what he said. 40But Martha was distracted by all the preparations that had to be made. She came to him and asked, "Lord, don't you care[l] that my sister has left me to do the work by myself? Tell her to help me!"

41"Martha, Martha," the Lord answered, "you are worried[m] and upset about many things, 42but only one thing is needed.[f][n] Mary has chosen what is better, and it will not be taken away from her."

Jesus' Teaching on Prayer

11:2–4pp—Mt 6:9–13
11:9–13pp—Mt 7:7–11

11 One day Jesus was praying[a] in a certain place. When he finished, one of his disciples said to him, "Lord,[b] teach us to pray, just as John taught his disciples."

13 [o]**Rev 11:3**
15 [p]**Mt 4:13**
16 [q]**Mt 10:40**
17 [r]ver 1; [s]**Mk 16:17**
18 [t]**Mt 4:10**; [u]Isa 14:12; Rev 9:1; 12:8–9
19 [v]Mk 16:18; Ac 28:3–5
20 [w]**Rev 20:12**
21 [x]1Co 1:26–29
22 [y]**Mt 28:18**; [z]Jn 1:18
24 [a]1Pe 1:10–12
25 [b]Mt 19:16; Lk 18:18
27 [c]Dt 6:5; [d]Lev 19:18; **Mt 5:43**
28 [e]**Ro 7:10**
29 [f]Lk 16:15
31 [g]Lev 21:1–3
33 [h]**Mt 10:5**
38 [i]Jn 11:1; 12:2
39 [j]Jn 11:1; 12:3; [k]Lk 8:35
40 [l]Mk 4:38
41 [m]Mt 6:25–34; Lk 12:11,22
42 [n]Ps 27:4

Ch. 11

1 [a]**Lk 3:21**; [b]**Jn 13:13**

[b]15 Greek *Hades*
[c]27 Deut. 6:5
[d]27 Lev. 19:18
[e]35 Greek *two denarii*
[f]42 Some manuscripts *but few things are needed—or only one*

2He said to them, "When you pray, say:

" 'Father,[a]
hallowed be your name,
your kingdom[c] come.[b]
3Give us each day our daily bread.
4Forgive us our sins,
for we also forgive everyone who sins against us.[c][d]
And lead us not into temptation.' "[d][e]

5Then he said to them, "Suppose one of you has a friend, and he goes to him at midnight and says, 'Friend, lend me three loaves of bread, 6because a friend of mine on a journey has come to me, and I have nothing to set before him.'

7"Then the one inside answers, 'Don't bother me. The door is already locked, and my children are with me in bed. I can't get up and give you anything.' 8I tell you, though he will not get up and give him the bread because he is his friend, yet because of the man's boldness[e] he will get up and give him as much as he needs.[f]

9"So I say to you: Ask and it will be given to you;[g] seek and you will find; knock and the door will be opened to you. 10For everyone who asks receives; he who seeks finds; and to him who knocks, the door will be opened.

11"Which of you fathers, if your son asks for[f] a fish, will give him a snake instead? 12Or if he asks for an egg, will give him a scorpion? 13If you then, though you are evil, know how to give good gifts to your children, how much more will your Father in heaven give the Holy Spirit to those who ask him!"

Jesus and Beelzebub

11:14,15,17–22, 24–26pp—Mt 12:22,24–29, 43–45
11:17–22pp—Mk 3:23–27

14Jesus was driving out a demon that was mute. When the demon left, the man who had been mute spoke, and the crowd was amazed.[h] 15But some of them said, "By Beelzebub,[g][i] the prince of demons, he is driving out demons."[j] 16Others tested him by asking for a sign from heaven.[k]

17Jesus knew their thoughts[l] and said to them: "Any kingdom divided against itself will be ruined, and a house divided against itself will fall. 18If Satan[m] is divided against himself, how can his kingdom stand? I say this because you claim that I drive out demons by Beelzebub. 19Now if I drive out demons by Beelzebub, by whom do your followers drive them out? So then, they will be your judges. 20But if I drive out demons by the finger of God,[n] then the kingdom of God[o] has come to you.

21"When a strong man, fully armed, guards his own house, his possessions are safe. 22But when someone stronger attacks and overpowers him, he takes away the armour in which the man trusted and divides up the spoils.

23"He who is not with me is against me, and he who does not gather with me, scatters.[p]

24"When an evil[h] spirit comes out of a man, it goes through arid places seeking rest and does not find it. Then it says, 'I will return to the house I left.' 25When it arrives, it finds the house swept clean and put in order. 26Then it goes and takes seven other spirits more wicked than itself, and they go in and live there. And the final condition of that man is worse than the first."[q]

27As Jesus was saying these things, a woman in the crowd called out, "Blessed is the mother who gave you birth and nursed you."[r]

28He replied, "Blessed rather are those who hear the word of God[s] and obey it."[t]

The Sign of Jonah

11:29–32pp—Mt 12:39–42

29As the crowds increased, Jesus said, "This is a wicked generation. It asks for a miraculous sign,[u] but none will be given it except the sign of Jonah.[v] 30For as Jonah was a sign to the Ninevites, so also will the Son of Man be to this generation. 31The Queen of the South will rise at the judgment with the men of this generation and condemn them; for she came from the ends of the earth to listen to Solomon's wisdom,[w] and now one[i] greater than Solomon is here. 32The men of Nineveh will stand up at the judgment with this generation and condemn it; for they repented at the preaching of Jonah,[x] and now one greater than Jonah is here.

2 [c]**Mt 3:2**
4 [d]Mt 18:35; Mk 11:25; [e]Mt 26:41; Jas 1:13
8 [f]Lk 18:1–6
9 [g]**Mt 7:7**
14 [h]Mt 9:32–33
15 [i]**Mk 3:22**; [j]Mt 9:34
16 [k]**Mt 12:38**
17 [l]**Mt 9:4**
18 [m]**Mt 4:10**
20 [n]Ex 8:19; [o]**Mt 3:2**
23 [p]Mt 12:30; Mk 9:40; Lk 9:50
26 [q]2Pe 2:20
27 [r]Lk 23:29
28 [s]**Heb 4:12**; [t]Pr 8:32; Lk 6:47; 8:21; Jn 14:21
29 [u]ver 16; **Mt 12:38**; [v]Jnh 1:17; Mt 16:4
31 [w]1Ki 10:1; 2Ch 9:1
32 [x]Jnh 3:5

[a]2 Some manuscripts *Our Father in heaven*
[b]2 Some manuscripts *come. May your will be done on earth as it is in heaven.*
[c]4 Greek *everyone who is indebted to us*
[d]4 Some manuscripts *temptation but deliver us from the evil one*
[e]8 Or *persistence*
[f]11 Some manuscripts *for bread, will give him a stone; or if he asks for*
[g]15 Greek *Beezeboul* or *Beelzeboul*; also in verses 18 and 19
[h]24 Greek *unclean*
[i]31 Or *something*; also in verse 32

The Lamp of the Body

11:34,35pp—Mt 6:22,23

33"No-one lights a lamp and puts it in a place where it will be hidden, or under a bowl. Instead he puts it on its stand, so that those who come in may see the light.[y] 34Your eye is the lamp of your body. When your eyes are good, your whole body also is full of light. But when they are bad, your body also is full of darkness. 35See to it, then, that the light within you is not darkness. 36Therefore, if your whole body is full of light, and no part of it dark, it will be completely lighted, as when the light of a lamp shines on you."

Six Woes

37When Jesus had finished speaking, a Pharisee invited him to eat with him; so he went in and reclined at the table.[z] 38But the Pharisee, noticing that Jesus did not first wash before the meal,[a] was surprised.

39Then the Lord[b] said to him, "Now then, you Pharisees clean the outside of the cup and dish, but inside you are full of greed and wickedness.[c] 40You foolish people![d] Did not the one who made the outside make the inside also? 41But give what is inside ⌞the dish⌟[j] to the poor,[e] and everything will be clean for you.[f]

42"Woe to you Pharisees, because you give God a tenth[g] of your mint, rue and all other kinds of garden herbs, but you neglect justice and the love of God.[h] You should have practised the latter without leaving the former undone.[i]

43"Woe to you Pharisees, because you love the most important seats in the synagogues and greetings in the market-places.[j]

44"Woe to you, because you are like unmarked graves,[k] which men walk over without knowing it."

45One of the experts in the law[l] answered him, "Teacher, when you say these things, you insult us also."

46Jesus replied, "And you experts in the law, woe to you, because you load people down with burdens they can hardly carry, and you yourselves will not lift one finger to help them.[m]

47"Woe to you, because you build tombs for the prophets, and it was your forefathers who killed them. 48So you testify that you approve of what your forefathers did; they killed the prophets, and you build their tombs.[n] 49Because of this, God in his wisdom[o] said, 'I will send them prophets and apostles, some of whom they will kill and others they will persecute.'[p] 50Therefore this generation will be held responsible for the blood of all the prophets that has been shed since the beginning of the world, 51from the blood of Abel[q] to the blood of Zechariah,[r] who was killed between the altar and the sanctuary. Yes, I tell you, this generation will be held responsible for it all.[s]

52"Woe to you experts in the law, because you have taken away the key to knowledge. You yourselves have not entered, and you have hindered those who were entering."[t]

53When Jesus left there, the Pharisees and the teachers of the law began to oppose him fiercely and to besiege him with questions, 54waiting to catch him in something he might say.[u]

33 [y]**Mt 5:15**
37 [z]Lk 7:36; 14:1
38 [a]Mk 7:3–4
39 [b]**Lk 7:13**; [c]Mt 23:25–26; Mk 7:20–23
40 [d]Lk 12:20; 1Co 15:36
41 [e]Lk 12:33; [f]**Ac 10:15**
42 [g]Lk 18:12; [h]Dt 6:5; Mic 6:8; [i]Mt 23:23
43 [j]Mt 23:6–7; Lk 14:7; 20:46
44 [k]Mt 23:27
45 [l]**Mt 22:35**
46 [m]**Mt 23:4**
48 [n]Mt 23:29–32; Ac 7:51–53
49 [o]1Co 1:24,30; Col 2:3; [p]Mt 23:34
51 [q]Ge 4:8; [r]2Ch 24:20–21; [s]Mt 23:35–36
52 [t]Mt 23:13
54 [u]**Mt 12:10**

Ch. 12

1 [a]Mt 16:6, 11–12
2 [b]**Mk 4:22**
4 [c]Jn 15:14–15
5 [d]Heb 10:31
7 [e]**Mt 10:30**; [f]Mt 12:12
8 [g]Lk 15:10
9 [h]Mk 8:38; 2Ti 2:12
10 [i]**Mt 8:20**; [j]Mt 12:31–32; **1Jn 5:16**

Warnings and Encouragements

12:2–9pp—Mt 10:26–33

12 Meanwhile, when a crowd of many thousands had gathered, so that they were trampling on one another, Jesus began to speak first to his disciples, saying: "Be on your guard against the yeast of the Pharisees, which is hypocrisy.[a] 2There is nothing concealed that will not be disclosed, or hidden that will not be made known.[b] 3What you have said in the dark will be heard in the daylight, and what you have whispered in the ear in the inner rooms will be proclaimed from the roofs.

4"I tell you, my friends,[c] do not be afraid of those who kill the body and after that can do no more. 5But I will show you whom you should fear: Fear him who, after the killing of the body, has power to throw you into hell. Yes, I tell you, fear him.[d] 6Are not five sparrows sold for two pennies?[a] Yet not one of them is forgotten by God. 7Indeed, the very hairs of your head are all numbered.[e] Don't be afraid; you are worth more than many sparrows.[f]

8"I tell you, whoever acknowledges me before men, the Son of Man will also acknowledge him before the angels of God.[g] 9But he who disowns me before men will be disowned[h] before the angels of God. 10And everyone who speaks a word against the Son of Man[i] will be forgiven, but anyone who blasphemes against the Holy Spirit will not be forgiven.[j]

---

[j]41 Or *what you have*   [a]6 Greek *two assaria*

11"When you are brought before synagogues, rulers and authorities, do not worry about how you will defend yourselves or what you will say,[k] 12for the Holy Spirit will teach you at that time what you should say."[l]

The Parable of the Rich Fool

13Someone in the crowd said to him, "Teacher, tell my brother to divide the inheritance with me."

14Jesus replied, "Man, who appointed me a judge or an arbiter between you?" 15Then he said to them, "Watch out! Be on your guard against all kinds of greed; a man's life does not consist in the abundance of his possessions."[m]

16And he told them this parable: "The ground of a certain rich man produced a good crop. 17He thought to himself, 'What shall I do? I have no place to store my crops.'

18"Then he said, 'This is what I'll do. I will tear down my barns and build bigger ones, and there I will store all my grain and my goods. 19And I'll say to myself, "You have plenty of good things laid up for many years. Take life easy; eat, drink and be merry." '

20"But God said to him, 'You fool![n] This very night your life will be demanded from you.[o] Then who will get what you have prepared for yourself?'[p]

21"This is how it will be with anyone who stores up things for himself but is not rich towards God."[q]

Do Not Worry

12:22–31pp—Mt 6:25–33

22Then Jesus said to his disciples: "Therefore I tell you, do not worry about your life, what you will eat; or about your body, what you will wear. 23Life is more than food, and the body more than clothes. 24Consider the ravens: They do not sow or reap, they have no storeroom or barn; yet God feeds them.[r] And how much more valuable you are than birds! 25Who of you by worrying can add a single hour to his life?[b] 26Since you cannot do this very little thing, why do you worry about the rest?

27"Consider how the lilies grow. They do not labour or spin. Yet I tell you, not even Solomon in all his splendour[s] was dressed like one of these. 28If that is how God clothes the grass of the field, which is here today, and tomorrow is thrown into the fire, how much more will he clothe you, O you of little faith![t] 29And do not set your heart on what you will eat or drink; do not worry about it. 30For the pagan world runs after all such things, and your Father[u] knows that you need them.[v] 31But seek his kingdom,[w] and these things will be given to you as well.[x]

32"Do not be afraid,[y] little flock, for your Father has been pleased to give you the kingdom.[z] 33Sell your possessions and give to the poor.[a] Provide purses for yourselves that will not wear out, a treasure in heaven[b] that will not be exhausted, where no thief comes near and no moth destroys.[c] 34For where your treasure is, there your heart will be also.[d]

Watchfulness

12:35,36pp—Mt 25:1–13; Mk 13:33–37
12:39,40,42–46pp—Mt 24:43–51

35"Be dressed ready for service and keep your lamps burning, 36like men waiting for their master to return from a wedding banquet, so that when he comes and knocks they can immediately open the door for him. 37It will be good for those servants whose master finds them watching when he comes.[e] I tell you the truth, he will dress himself to serve, will have them recline at the table and will come and wait on them.[f] 38It will be good for those servants whose master finds them ready, even if he comes in the second or third watch of the night. 39But understand this: If the owner of the house had known at what hour the thief[g] was coming, he would not have let his house be broken into. 40You also must be ready,[h] because the Son of Man will come at an hour when you do not expect him."

41Peter asked, "Lord, are you telling this parable to us, or to everyone?"

42The Lord[i] answered, "Who then is the faithful and wise manager, whom the master puts in charge of his servants to give them their food allowance at the proper time? 43It will be good for that servant whom the master finds doing so when he returns. 44I tell you the truth, he will put him in charge of all his possessions. 45But suppose the servant says to himself, 'My master is taking a long time in coming,' and he then begins to beat the menservants and maidservants and to eat and drink and get drunk. 46The master of that servant will come on a day when he does not expect him and at an hour he is not aware of.[j]

11 [k]Mt 10:17,19; Lk 21:12,14
12 [l]Ex 4:12; Mt 10:20; Mk 13:11; Lk 21:15
15 [m]Job 20:20; 31:24; Ps 62:10
20 [n]Jer 17:11; Lk 11:40; [o]Job 27:8; [p]Ps 39:6; 49:10
21 [q]ver 33
24 [r]Job 38:41; Ps 147:9
27 [s]1Ki 10:4–7
28 [t]**Mt 6:30**
30 [u]**Lk 6:36;** [v]Mt 6:8
31 [w]**Mt 3:2;** [x]Mt 19:29
32 [y]**Mt 14:27;** [z]**Mt 25:34**
33 [a]**Ac 2:45;** [b]**Mt 6:20;** [c]**Jas 5:2**
34 [d]Mt 6:21
37 [e]Mt 24:42,46; 25:13; [f]**Mt 20:28**
39 [g]Mt 6:19; 1Th 5:2; 2Pe 3:10; Rev 3:3; 16:15
40 [h]Mk 13:33; Lk 21:36
42 [i]**Lk 7:13**
46 [j]ver 40

b25 Or *single cubit to his height*

He will cut him to pieces and assign him
a place with the unbelievers.
47"That servant who knows his mas-
ter's will and does not get ready or does
not do what his master wants will be
beaten with many blows.[k] 48But the one
who does not know and does things
deserving punishment will be beaten
with few blows.[l] From everyone who
has been given much, much will be
demanded; and from the one who has
been entrusted with much, much more
will be asked.

Not Peace but Division

12:51–53pp—Mt 10:34–36

49"I have come to bring fire on the
earth, and how I wish it were already
kindled! 50But I have a baptism[m] to
undergo, and how distressed I am until
it is completed![n] 51Do you think I came
to bring peace on earth? No, I tell you,
but division. 52From now on there will
be five in one family divided against
each other, three against two and two
against three. 53They will be divided,
father against son and son against
father, mother against daughter and
daughter against mother, mother-in-
law against daughter-in-law and
daughter-in-law against mother-in-
law."[o]

Interpreting the Times

54He said to the crowd: "When you
see a cloud rising in the west, im-
mediately you say, 'It's going to rain,'
and it does.[p] 55And when the south
wind blows, you say, 'It's going to be
hot,' and it is. 56Hypocrites! You know
how to interpret the appearance of the
earth and the sky. How is it that you
don't know how to interpret this pres-
ent time?[q]
57"Why don't you judge for your-
selves what is right? 58As you are going
with your adversary to the magistrate,
try hard to be reconciled to him on the
way, or he may drag you off to the
judge, and the judge turn you over to
the officer, and the officer throw you
into prison.[r] 59I tell you, you will not
get out until you have paid the last
penny.[c]"[s]

Repent or Perish

13 Now there were some present
at that time who told Jesus
about the Galileans whose blood Pilate[a]
had mixed with their sacrifices. 2Jesus
answered, "Do you think that these
Galileans were worse sinners than all
the other Galileans because they suf-
fered this way?[b] 3I tell you, no! But un-
less you repent, you too will all perish.
4Or those eighteen who died when the
tower in Siloam[c] fell on them—do you
think they were more guilty than all the
others living in Jerusalem? 5I tell you,
no! But unless you repent,[d] you too will
all perish."
6Then he told this parable: "A man
had a fig-tree, planted in his vineyard,
and he went to look for fruit on it, but
did not find any.[e] 7So he said to the man
who took care of the vineyard, 'For
three years now I've been coming to
look for fruit on this fig-tree and haven't
found any. Cut it down![f] Why should it
use up the soil?'
8"'Sir,' the man replied, 'leave it
alone for one more year, and I'll dig
round it and fertilise it. 9If it bears fruit
next year, fine! If not, then cut it
down.'"

A Crippled Woman Healed on the Sabbath

10On a Sabbath Jesus was teaching in
one of the synagogues,[g] 11and a woman
was there who had been crippled by a
spirit for eighteen years.[h] She was bent
over and could not straighten up at all.
12When Jesus saw her, he called her
forward and said to her, "Woman, you
are set free from your infirmity." 13Then
he put his hands on her,[i] and im-
mediately she straightened up and
praised God.
14Indignant because Jesus had healed
on the Sabbath,[j] the synagogue ruler[k]
said to the people, "There are six days
for work.[l] So come and be healed on
those days, not on the Sabbath."
15The Lord answered him, "You
hypocrites! Doesn't each of you on the
Sabbath untie his ox or donkey from the
stall and lead it out to give it water?[m]
16Then should not this woman, a
daughter of Abraham,[n] whom Satan[o]
has kept bound for eighteen long years,
be set free on the Sabbath day from
what bound her?"
17When he said this, all his opponents
were humiliated,[p] but the people were
delighted with all the wonderful things
he was doing.

47 [k]Dt 25:2
48 [l]Lev 5:17; Nu 15:27–30
50 [m]Mk 10:38; [n]**Jn 19:30**
53 [o]Mic 7:6; Mt 10:21
54 [p]Mt 16:2
56 [q]Mt 16:3
58 [r]Mt 5:25
59 [s]Mt 5:26; Mk 12:42

Ch. 13

1 [a]**Mt 27:2**
2 [b]Jn 9:2–3
4 [c]Jn 9:7,11
5 [d]Mt 3:2; Ac 2:38
6 [e]Isa 5:2; Jer 8:13; Mt 21:19
7 [f]**Mt 3:10**
10 [g]**Mt 4:23**
11 [h]ver 16
13 [i]**Mk 5:23**
14 [j]Mt 12:2; [k]Mk 5:22; [l]Ex 20:9
15 [m]Lk 14:5
16 [n]**Lk 3:8**; [o]**Mt 4:10**
17 [p]Isa 66:5

[c]59 Greek *lepton*

The Parables of the Mustard Seed and the Yeast

13:18,19pp—Mk 4:30–32
13:18–21pp—Mt 13:31–33

[18]Then Jesus asked, "What is the kingdom of God[q] like?[r] What shall I compare it to? [19]It is like a mustard seed, which a man took and planted in his garden. It grew and became a tree,[s] and the birds of the air perched in its branches."[t]

[20]Again he asked, "What shall I compare the kingdom of God to? [21]It is like yeast that a woman took and mixed into a large amount[a] of flour until it worked all through the dough."[u]

The Narrow Door

[22]Then Jesus went through the towns and villages, teaching as he made his way to Jerusalem.[v] [23]Someone asked him, "Lord, are only a few people going to be saved?"

He said to them, [24]"Make every effort to enter through the narrow door,[w] because many, I tell you, will try to enter and will not be able to. [25]Once the owner of the house gets up and closes the door, you will stand outside knocking and pleading, 'Sir, open the door for us.'

"But he will answer, 'I don't know you or where you come from.'[x]

[26]"Then you will say, 'We ate and drank with you, and you taught in our streets.'

[27]"But he will reply, 'I don't know you or where you come from. Away from me, all you evildoers!'[y]

[28]"There will be weeping there, and gnashing of teeth,[z] when you see Abraham, Isaac and Jacob and all the prophets in the kingdom of God, but you yourselves thrown out. [29]People will come from east and west[a] and north and south, and will take their places at the feast in the kingdom of God. [30]Indeed there are those who are last who will be first, and first who will be last."[b]

Jesus' Sorrow for Jerusalem

13:34,35pp—Mt 23:37–39
13:34,35Ref—Lk 19:41

[31]At that time some Pharisees came to Jesus and said to him, "Leave this place and go somewhere else. Herod[c] wants to kill you."

[32]He replied, "Go tell that fox, 'I will drive out demons and heal people today and tomorrow, and on the third day I will reach my goal.'[d] [33]In any case, I must keep going today and tomorrow and the next day—for surely no prophet[e] can die outside Jerusalem!

[34]"O Jerusalem, Jerusalem, you who kill the prophets and stone those sent to you, how often I have longed to gather your children together, as a hen gathers her chicks under her wings,[f] but you were not willing! [35]Look, your house is left to you desolate.[g] I tell you, you will not see me again until you say, 'Blessed is he who comes in the name of the Lord.'[b]"[h]

Jesus at a Pharisee's House

14:8–10Ref—Pr 25:6,7

14 One Sabbath, when Jesus went to eat in the house of a prominent Pharisee,[a] he was being carefully watched.[b] [2]There in front of him was a man suffering from dropsy. [3]Jesus asked the Pharisees and experts in the law,[c] "Is it lawful to heal on the Sabbath or not?"[d] [4]But they remained silent. So taking hold of the man, he healed him and sent him away.

[5]Then he asked them, "If one of you has a son[a] or an ox that falls into a well on the Sabbath day, will you not immediately pull him out?"[e] [6]And they had nothing to say.

[7]When he noticed how the guests picked the places of honour at the table,[f] he told them this parable: [8]"When someone invites you to a wedding feast, do not take the place of honour, for a person more distinguished than you may have been invited. [9]If so, the host who invited both of you will come and say to you, 'Give this man your seat.' Then, humiliated, you will have to take the least important place. [10]But when you are invited, take the lowest place, so that when your host comes, he will say to you, 'Friend, move up to a better place.' Then you will be honoured in the presence of all your fellow guests. [11]For everyone who exalts himself will be humbled, and he who humbles himself will be exalted."[g]

[12]Then Jesus said to his host, "When you give a luncheon or dinner, do not invite your friends, your brothers or relatives, or your rich neighbours; if you do, they may invite you back and so you will be repaid. [13]But when you give a

18 [q]Mt 3:2; [r]Mt 13:24
19 [s]Lk 17:6; [t]Mt 13:32
21 [u]1Co 5:6
22 [v]Lk 9:51
24 [w]Mt 7:13
25 [x]Mt 7:23; 25:10–12
27 [y]Mt 7:23
28 [z]Mt 8:12
29 [a]Mt 8:11
30 [b]Mt 19:30
31 [c]Mt 14:1
32 [d]Heb 2:10
33 [e]Mt 21:11
34 [f]Mt 23:37
35 [g]Jer 12:17; 22:5; [h]Ps 118:26; Lk 19:38

Ch. 14

1 [a]Lk 7:36; 11:37; [b]Mt 12:10
3 [c]Mt 22:35; [d]Mt 12:2
5 [e]Lk 13:15
7 [f]Lk 11:43
11 [g]Mt 23:12

[a]21 Greek *three satas* (probably about 3/5 bushel or 22 litres) [b]35 Psalm 118:26
[a]5 Some manuscripts *donkey*

banquet, invite the poor, the crippled, the lame, the blind,[h] 14and you will be blessed. Although they cannot repay you, you will be repaid at the resurrection of the righteous."[i]

The Parable of the Great Banquet

14:16–24Ref—Mt 22:2–14

15When one of those at the table with him heard this, he said to Jesus, "Blessed is the man who will eat at the feast[j] in the kingdom of God."[k]

16Jesus replied: "A certain man was preparing a great banquet and invited many guests. 17At the time of the banquet he sent his servant to tell those who had been invited, 'Come, for everything is now ready.'

18"But they all alike began to make excuses. The first said, 'I have just bought a field, and I must go and see it. Please excuse me.'

19"Another said, 'I have just bought five yoke of oxen, and I'm on my way to try them out. Please excuse me.'

20"Still another said, 'I have just got married, so I can't come.'

21"The servant came back and reported this to his master. Then the owner of the house became angry and ordered his servant, 'Go out quickly into the streets and alleys of the town and bring in the poor, the crippled, the blind and the lame.'[l]

22"'Sir,' the servant said, 'what you ordered has been done, but there is still room.'

23"Then the master told his servant, 'Go out to the roads and country lanes and make them come in, so that my house will be full. 24I tell you, not one of those men who were invited will get a taste of my banquet.'"[m]

The Cost of Being a Disciple

25Large crowds were travelling with Jesus, and turning to them he said: 26"If anyone comes to me and does not hate his father and mother, his wife and children, his brothers and sisters—yes, even his own life—he cannot be my disciple.[n] 27And anyone who does not carry his cross and follow me cannot be my disciple.[o]

28"Suppose one of you wants to build a tower. Will he not first sit down and estimate the cost to see if he has enough money to complete it? 29For if he lays the foundation and is not able to finish it, everyone who sees it will ridicule him, 30saying, 'This fellow began to build and was not able to finish.'

31"Or suppose a king is about to go to war against another king. Will he not first sit down and consider whether he is able with ten thousand men to oppose the one coming against him with twenty thousand? 32If he is not able, he will send a delegation while the other is still a long way off and will ask for terms of peace. 33In the same way, any of you who does not give up everything he has cannot be my disciple.[p]

34"Salt is good, but if it loses its saltiness, how can it be made salty again?[q] 35It is fit neither for the soil nor for the manure heap; it is thrown out.[r]

"He who has ears to hear, let him hear."[s]

The Parable of the Lost Sheep

15:4–7pp—Mt 18:12–14

15 Now the tax collectors[a] and "sinners" were all gathering round to hear him. 2But the Pharisees and the teachers of the law muttered, "This man welcomes sinners, and eats with them."[b]

3Then Jesus told them this parable:[c] 4"Suppose one of you has a hundred sheep and loses one of them. Does he not leave the ninety-nine in the open country and go after the lost sheep until he finds it?[d] 5And when he finds it, he joyfully puts it on his shoulders 6and goes home. Then he calls his friends and neighbours together and says, 'Rejoice with me; I have found my lost sheep.'[e] 7I tell you that in the same way there will be more rejoicing in heaven over one sinner who repents than over ninety-nine righteous persons who do not need to repent.[f]

The Parable of the Lost Coin

8"Or suppose a woman has ten silver coins[a] and loses one. Does she not light a lamp, sweep the house and search carefully until she finds it? 9And when she finds it, she calls her friends and neighbours together and says, 'Rejoice with me; I have found my lost coin.'[g] 10In the same way, I tell you, there is rejoicing in the presence of the angels of God over one sinner who repents."[h]

The Parable of the Lost Son

11Jesus continued: "There was a man who had two sons.[i] 12The younger one

13 [h]ver 21
14 [i]Ac 24:15
15 [j]Isa 25:6; Mt 26:29; Lk 13:29; Rev 19:9; [k]**Mt 3:2**
21 [l]ver 13
24 [m]Mt 21:43; Ac 13:46
26 [n]Mt 10:37; **Jn 12:25**
27 [o]Mt 10:38; Lk 9:23
33 [p]Php 3:7–8
34 [q]Mk 9:50
35 [r]Mt 5:13; [s]**Mt 11:15**

Ch. 15

1 [a]Lk 5:29
2 [b]**Mt 9:11**
3 [c]Mt 13:3
4 [d]Ps 23; 119:176; Jer 31:10; Eze 34:11–16; Lk 5:32; 19:10
6 [e]ver 9
7 [f]ver 10
9 [g]ver 6
10 [h]ver 7
11 [i]Mt 21:28

a8 Greek *ten drachmas,* each worth about a day's wages

said to his father, 'Father, give me my share of the estate.'[j] So he divided his property[k] between them.

13"Not long after that, the younger son got together all he had, set off for a distant country and there squandered his wealth[l] in wild living. 14After he had spent everything, there was a severe famine in that whole country, and he began to be in need. 15So he went and hired himself out to a citizen of that country, who sent him to his fields to feed pigs.[m] 16He longed to fill his stomach with the pods that the pigs were eating, but no-one gave him anything.

17"When he came to his senses, he said, 'How many of my father's hired men have food to spare, and here I am starving to death! 18I will set out and go back to my father and say to him: Father, I have sinned[n] against heaven and against you. 19I am no longer worthy to be called your son; make me like one of your hired men.' 20So he got up and went to his father.

"But while he was still a long way off, his father saw him and was filled with compassion for him; he ran to his son, threw his arms around him and kissed him.[o]

21"The son said to him, 'Father, I have sinned against heaven and against you.[p] I am no longer worthy to be called your son.'[b]

22"But the father said to his servants, 'Quick! Bring the best robe[q] and put it on him. Put a ring on his finger[r] and sandals on his feet. 23Bring the fattened calf and kill it. Let's have a feast and celebrate. 24For this son of mine was dead and is alive again;[s] he was lost and is found.' So they began to celebrate.[t]

25"Meanwhile, the older son was in the field. When he came near the house, he heard music and dancing. 26So he called one of the servants and asked him what was going on. 27'Your brother has come,' he replied, 'and your father has killed the fattened calf because he has him back safe and sound.'

28"The older brother became angry[u] and refused to go in. So his father went out and pleaded with him. 29But he answered his father, 'Look! All these years I've been slaving for you and never disobeyed your orders. Yet you never gave me even a young goat so I could celebrate with my friends. 30But when this son of yours who has squandered your property[v] with prostitutes[w] comes home, you kill the fattened calf for him!'

31"'My son,' the father said, 'you are always with me, and everything I have is yours. 32But we had to celebrate and be glad, because this brother of yours was dead and is alive again; he was lost and is found.'"[x]

The Parable of the Shrewd Manager

16 Jesus told his disciples: "There was a rich man whose manager was accused of wasting his possessions.[a] 2So he called him in and asked him, 'What is this I hear about you? Give an account of your management, because you cannot be manager any longer.'

3"The manager said to himself, 'What shall I do now? My master is taking away my job. I'm not strong enough to dig, and I'm ashamed to beg—4I know what I'll do so that, when I lose my job here, people will welcome me into their houses.'

5"So he called in each one of his master's debtors. He asked the first, 'How much do you owe my master?'

6"'Eight hundred gallons[a] of olive oil,' he replied.

"The manager told him, 'Take your bill, sit down quickly, and make it four hundred.'

7"Then he asked the second, 'And how much do you owe?'

"'A thousand bushels[b] of wheat,' he replied.

"He told him, 'Take your bill and make it eight hundred.'

8"The master commended the dishonest manager because he had acted shrewdly. For the people of this world[b] are more shrewd[c] in dealing with their own kind than are the people of the light.[d] 9I tell you, use worldly wealth[e] to gain friends for yourselves, so that when it is gone, you will be welcomed into eternal dwellings.[f]

10"Whoever can be trusted with very little can also be trusted with much,[g] and whoever is dishonest with very little will also be dishonest with much. 11So if you have not been trustworthy in handling worldly wealth,[h] who will trust you with true riches? 12And if you have not been trustworthy with someone else's property, who will give you property of your own?

13"No servant can serve two masters.

12 [j]Dt 21:17; [k]ver 30
13 [l]ver 30; Lk 16:1
15 [m]Lev 11:7
18 [n]Lev 26:40; Mt 3:2
20 [o]Ge 45:14–15; 46:29; Ac 20:37
21 [p]Ps 51:4
22 [q]Zec 3:4; Rev 6:11; [r]Ge 41:42
24 [s]Eph 2:1,5; 5:14; 1Ti 5:6; [t]ver 32
28 [u]Jnh 4:1
30 [v]ver 12–13; [w]Pr 29:3
32 [x]ver 24; Mal 3:17

Ch. 16

1 [a]Lk 15:13,30
8 [b]Ps 17:14; [c]Ps 18:26; [d]Jn 12:36; Eph 5:8; 1Th 5:5
9 [e]ver 11,13; [f]Mt 19:21; Lk 12:33
10 [g]Mt 25:21,23; Lk 19:17
11 [h]ver 9,13

b*21* Some early manuscripts *son. Make me like one of your hired men.*

a*6* Greek *one hundred batous* (probably about 3 kilolitres)

b*7* Greek *one hundred korous* (probably about 35 kilolitres)

Either he will hate the one and love the other, or he will be devoted to the one and despise the other. You cannot serve both God and Money."[i]

14The Pharisees, who loved money,[j] heard all this and were sneering at Jesus.[k] 15He said to them, "You are the ones who justify yourselves[l] in the eyes of men, but God knows your hearts.[m] What is highly valued among men is detestable in God's sight.

Additional Teachings

16"The Law and the Prophets were proclaimed until John.[n] Since that time, the good news of the kingdom of God is being preached,[o] and everyone is forcing his way into it. 17It is easier for heaven and earth to disappear than for the least stroke of a pen to drop out of the Law.[p]

18"Anyone who divorces his wife and marries another woman commits adultery, and the man who marries a divorced woman commits adultery.[q]

The Rich Man and Lazarus

19"There was a rich man who was dressed in purple and fine linen and lived in luxury every day.[r] 20At his gate was laid a beggar[s] named Lazarus, covered with sores 21and longing to eat what fell from the rich man's table.[t] Even the dogs came and licked his sores.

22"The time came when the beggar died and the angels carried him to Abraham's side. The rich man also died and was buried. 23In hell,[c] where he was in torment, he looked up and saw Abraham far away, with Lazarus by his side. 24So he called to him, 'Father Abraham,[u] have pity on me and send Lazarus to dip the tip of his finger in water and cool my tongue, because I am in agony in this fire.'[v]

25"But Abraham replied, 'Son, remember that in your lifetime you received your good things, while Lazarus received bad things,[w] but now he is comforted here and you are in agony.[x] 26And besides all this, between us and you a great chasm has been fixed, so that those who want to go from here to you cannot, nor can anyone cross over from there to us.'

27"He answered, 'Then I beg you, father, send Lazarus to my father's house, 28for I have five brothers. Let him warn them,[y] so that they will not also come to this place of torment.'

29"Abraham replied, 'They have Moses[z] and the Prophets;[a] let them listen to them.'

30"'No, father Abraham,'[b] he said, 'but if someone from the dead goes to them, they will repent.'

31"He said to him, 'If they do not listen to Moses and the Prophets, they will not be convinced even if someone rises from the dead.'"

Sin, Faith, Duty

17 Jesus said to his disciples: "Things that cause people to sin[a] are bound to come, but woe to that person through whom they come.[b] 2It would be better for him to be thrown into the sea with a millstone tied round his neck than for him to cause one of these little ones[c] to sin.[d] 3So watch yourselves.

"If your brother sins, rebuke him,[e] and if he repents, forgive him.[f] 4If he sins against you seven times in a day, and seven times comes back to you and says, 'I repent,' forgive him."[g]

5The apostles[h] said to the Lord,[i] "Increase our faith!"

6He replied, "If you have faith as small as a mustard seed,[j] you can say to this mulberry tree, 'Be uprooted and planted in the sea,' and it will obey you.[k]

7"Suppose one of you had a servant ploughing or looking after the sheep. Would he say to the servant when he comes in from the field, 'Come along now and sit down to eat'? 8Would he not rather say, 'Prepare my supper, get yourself ready and wait on me[l] while I eat and drink; after that you may eat and drink'? 9Would he thank the servant because he did what he was told to do? 10So you also, when you have done everything you were told to do, should say, 'We are unworthy servants; we have only done our duty.'"[m]

Ten Healed of Leprosy

11Now on his way to Jerusalem,[n] Jesus travelled along the border between Samaria and Galilee.[o] 12As he was going into a village, ten men who had leprosy[a][p] met him. They stood at a distance[q] 13and called out in a loud voice, "Jesus, Master,[r] have pity on us!"

14When he saw them, he said, "Go,

13 [i]ver 9,11; Mt 6:24
14 [j]**1Ti 3:3**; [k]Lk 23:35
15 [l]Lk 10:29; [m]**Rev 2:23**
16 [n]Mt 5:17; 11:12–13; [o]**Mt 4:23**
17 [p]**Mt 5:18**
18 [q]Mt 5:31–32; 19:9; Mk 10:11; Ro 7:2–3; 1Co 7:10–11
19 [r]Eze 16:49
20 [s]Ac 3:2
21 [t]Mt 15:27; Lk 15:16
24 [u]ver 30; **Lk 3:8**; [v]**Mt 5:22**
25 [w]Ps 17:14; [x]Lk 6:21, 24–25
28 [y]Ac 2:40; 20:23; 1Th 4:6
29 [z]**Lk 24:27**,44; Jn 1:45; 5:45–47; Ac 15:21; [a]Lk 4:17; 24:27,44; Jn 1:45
30 [b]ver 24; **Lk 3:8**

Ch. 17

1 [a]**Mt 5:29**; [b]Mt 18:7
2 [c]Mk 10:24; Lk 10:21; [d]**Mt 5:29**
3 [e]**Mt 18:15**; [f]Eph 4:32; Col 3:13
4 [g]Mt 18:21–22
5 [h]**Mk 6:30**; [i]**Lk 7:13**
6 [j]Mt 13:31; 17:20; Lk 13:19; [k]**Mt 21:21**; Mk 9:23
8 [l]Lk 12:37
10 [m]1Co 9:16
11 [n]**Lk 9:51**; [o]Lk 9:51–52; Jn 4:3–4
12 [p]**Mt 8:2**; [q]Lev 13:45–46
13 [r]**Lk 5:5**

[c]23 Greek *Hades*
[a]12 The Greek word was used for various diseases affecting the skin—not necessarily leprosy.

show yourselves to the priests."[s] And as they went, they were cleansed.

15One of them, when he saw he was healed, came back, praising God[t] in a loud voice. 16He threw himself at Jesus' feet and thanked him—and he was a Samaritan.[u]

17Jesus asked, "Were not all ten cleansed? Where are the other nine? 18Was no-one found to return and give praise to God except this foreigner?" 19Then he said to him, "Rise and go; your faith has made you well."[v]

The Coming of the Kingdom of God

17:26,27pp—Mt 24:37–39

20Once, having been asked by the Pharisees when the kingdom of God would come,[w] Jesus replied, "The kingdom of God does not come with your careful observation, 21nor will people say, 'Here it is,' or 'There it is,'[x] because the kingdom of God is within[b] you."

22Then he said to his disciples, "The time is coming when you will long to see one of the days of the Son of Man,[y] but you will not see it.[z] 23Men will tell you, 'There he is!' or 'Here he is!' Do not go running off after them.[a] 24For the Son of Man in his day[c] will be like the lightning,[b] which flashes and lights up the sky from one end to the other. 25But first he must suffer many things[c] and be rejected[d] by this generation.[e]

26"Just as it was in the days of Noah,[f] so also will it be in the days of the Son of Man. 27People were eating, drinking, marrying and being given in marriage up to the day Noah entered the ark. Then the flood came and destroyed them all.

28"It was the same in the days of Lot.[g] People were eating and drinking, buying and selling, planting and building. 29But the day Lot left Sodom, fire and sulphur rained down from heaven and destroyed them all.

30"It will be just like this on the day the Son of Man is revealed.[h] 31On that day no-one who is on the roof of his house, with his goods inside, should go down to get them. Likewise, no-one in the field should go back for anything.[i] 32Remember Lot's wife![j] 33Whoever tries to keep his life will lose it, and whoever loses his life will preserve it.[k] 34I tell you, on that night two people will be in one bed; one will be taken and the other left. 35Two women will be grinding grain together; one will be taken and the other left.[d]"[l]

37"Where, Lord?" they asked.

He replied, "Where there is a dead body, there the vultures will gather."[m]

The Parable of the Persistent Widow

18 Then Jesus told his disciples a parable to show them that they should always pray and not give up.[a] 2He said: "In a certain town there was a judge who neither feared God nor cared about men. 3And there was a widow in that town who kept coming to him with the plea, 'Grant me justice[b] against my adversary.'

4"For some time he refused. But finally he said to himself, 'Even though I don't fear God or care about men, 5yet because this widow keeps bothering me, I will see that she gets justice, so that she won't eventually wear me out with her coming!'"[c]

6And the Lord[d] said, "Listen to what the unjust judge says. 7And will not God bring about justice for his chosen ones, who cry out[e] to him day and night? Will he keep putting them off? 8I tell you, he will see that they get justice, and quickly. However, when the Son of Man[f] comes,[g] will he find faith on the earth?"

The Parable of the Pharisee and the Tax Collector

9To some who were confident of their own righteousness[h] and looked down on everybody else,[i] Jesus told this parable: 10"Two men went up to the temple to pray,[j] one a Pharisee and the other a tax collector. 11The Pharisee stood up[k] and prayed about[a] himself: 'God, I thank you that I am not like other men—robbers, evildoers, adulterers—or even like this tax collector. 12I fast[l] twice a week and give a tenth[m] of all I get.'

13"But the tax collector stood at a distance. He would not even look up to heaven, but beat his breast[n] and said, 'God, have mercy on me, a sinner.'[o]

14"I tell you that this man, rather than the other, went home justified before God. For everyone who exalts himself will be humbled, and he who humbles himself will be exalted."[p]

14 [s]Lev 14:2; Mt 8:4
15 [t]**Mt 9:8**
16 [u]**Mt 10:5**
19 [v]**Mt 9:22**
20 [w]**Mt 3:2**
21 [x]ver 23
22 [y]**Mt 8:20;** [z]**Lk 5:35**
23 [a]Mt 24:23; Lk 21:8
24 [b]Mt 24:27
25 [c]**Mt 16:21;** [d]Lk 9:22; 18:32; [e]Mk 13:30; Lk 21:32
26 [f]Ge 6:5–8; 7:6–24
28 [g]Ge 19:1–28
30 [h]Mt 10:23; **16:27;** 24:3, 27,37,39; 25:31; **1Co 1:7; 1Th 2:19;** 2Th 1:7; 2:8; 2Pe 3:4; **Rev 1:7**
31 [i]Mt 24:17–18
32 [j]Ge 19:26
33 [k]**Jn 12:25**
35 [l]Mt 24:41
37 [m]Mt 24:28

Ch. 18

1 [a]Isa 40:31; Lk 11:5–8; **Ac 1:14; Ro 1:10;** 12:12; Eph 6:18; Col 4:2; 1Th 5:17
3 [b]Isa 1:17
5 [c]Lk 11:8
6 [d]**Lk 7:13**
7 [e]Ex 22:23; Ps 88:1; Rev 6:10
8 [f]**Mt 8:20;** [g]**Mt 16:27**
9 [h]Lk 16:15; [i]Isa 65:5
10 [j]Ac 3:1
11 [k]Mt 6:5; Mk 11:25
12 [l]Isa 58:3; Mt 9:14; [m]Mal 3:8; Lk 11:42
13 [n]Isa 66:2; Jer 31:19; Lk 23:48; [o]Lk 5:32; 1Ti 1:15
14 [p]**Mt 23:12**

b21 Or *among*
c24 Some manuscripts do not have *in his day*.
d35 Some manuscripts *left*. 36*Two men will be in the field; one will be taken and the other left.*
a11 Or *to*

The Little Children and Jesus

18:15–17pp—Mt 19:13–15; Mk 10:13–16

15People were also bringing babies to
Jesus to have him touch them. When
the disciples saw this, they rebuked
them. 16But Jesus called the children to
him and said, "Let the little children
come to me, and do not hinder them, for
the kingdom of God belongs to such as
these. 17I tell you the truth, anyone who
will not receive the kingdom of God like
a little child[q] will never enter it."

The Rich Ruler

18:18–30pp—Mt 19:16–29; Mk 10:17–30

18A certain ruler asked him, "Good
teacher, what must I do to inherit eternal life?"[r]

19"Why do you call me good?" Jesus
answered. "No-one is good—except
God alone. 20You know the commandments: 'Do not commit adultery, do not
murder, do not steal, do not give false
testimony, honour your father and
mother.'[b]"[s]

21"All these I have kept since I was a
boy," he said.

22When Jesus heard this, he said to
him, "You still lack one thing. Sell
everything you have and give to the
poor,[t] and you will have treasure in
heaven.[u] Then come, follow me."

23When he heard this, he became very
sad, because he was a man of great
wealth. 24Jesus looked at him and said,
"How hard it is for the rich to enter the
kingdom of God![v] 25Indeed, it is easier
for a camel to go through the eye of a
needle than for a rich man to enter the
kingdom of God."

26Those who heard this asked, "Who
then can be saved?"

27Jesus replied, "What is impossible
with men is possible with God."[w]

28Peter said to him, "We have left all
we had to follow you!"[x]

29"I tell you the truth," Jesus said to
them, "no-one who has left home or
wife or brothers or parents or children
for the sake of the kingdom of God 30will
fail to receive many times as much in
this age and, in the age to come,[y] eternal
life."[z]

Jesus Again Predicts His Death

18:31–33pp—Mt 20:17–19; Mk 10:32–34

31Jesus took the Twelve aside and told
them, "We are going up to Jerusalem,[a]
and everything that is written by the
prophets[b] about the Son of Man[c] will be
fulfilled. 32He will be turned over to the
Gentiles.[d] They will mock him, insult
him, spit on him, flog him[e] and kill him.[f]
33On the third day[g] he will rise again."[h]

34The disciples did not understand
any of this. Its meaning was hidden
from them, and they did not know what
he was talking about.[i]

A Blind Beggar Receives His Sight

18:35–43pp—Mt 20:29–34; Mk 10:46–52

35As Jesus approached Jericho,[j] a
blind man was sitting by the roadside
begging. 36When he heard the crowd
going by, he asked what was happening. 37They told him, "Jesus of Nazareth
is passing by."[k]

38He called out, "Jesus, Son of David,[l]
have mercy[m] on me!"

39Those who led the way rebuked him
and told him to be quiet, but he shouted
all the more, "Son of David, have mercy
on me!"[n]

40Jesus stopped and ordered the man
to be brought to him. When he came
near, Jesus asked him, 41"What do you
want me to do for you?"

"Lord, I want to see," he replied.

42Jesus said to him, "Receive your
sight; your faith has healed you."[o]
43Immediately he received his sight and
followed Jesus, praising God. When all
the people saw it, they also praised
God.[p]

Zacchaeus the Tax Collector

19 Jesus entered Jericho[a] and was
passing through. 2A man was
there by the name of Zacchaeus; he was
a chief tax collector and was wealthy.
3He wanted to see who Jesus was, but
being a short man he could not, because
of the crowd. 4So he ran ahead and
climbed a sycamore-fig[b] tree to see him,
since Jesus was coming that way.[c]

5When Jesus reached the spot, he
looked up and said to him, "Zacchaeus,
come down immediately. I must stay at
your house today." 6So he came down
at once and welcomed him gladly.

7All the people saw this and began to
mutter, "He has gone to be the guest of
a 'sinner'."[d]

8But Zacchaeus stood up and said to
the Lord,[e] "Look, Lord! Here and now I
give half of my possessions to the poor,
and if I have cheated anybody out of
anything,[f] I will pay back four times the
amount."[g]

17 [q]Mt 11:25; 18:3
18 [r]Lk 10:25
20 [s]Ex 20:12–16; Dt 5:16–20; Ro 13:9
22 [t]**Ac 2:45**; [u]**Mt 6:20**
24 [v]Pr 11:28
27 [w]**Mt 19:26**
28 [x]**Mt 4:19**
30 [y]**Mt 12:32**; [z]**Mt 25:46**
31 [a]**Lk 9:51**; [b]Ps 22; Isa 53; [c]**Mt 8:20**
32 [d]Lk 23:1; [e]**Mt 16:21**; [f]**Ac 2:23**
33 [g]**Mt 16:21**; [h]**Mt 16:21**
34 [i]**Mk 9:32**
35 [j]Lk 19:1
37 [k]Lk 19:4
38 [l]ver 39; **Mt 9:27**; [m]Mt 17:15; Lk 18:13
39 [n]ver 38
42 [o]**Mt 9:22**
43 [p]**Mt 9:8**; Lk 13:17

Ch. 19

1 [a]Lk 18:35
4 [b]1Ki 10:27; 1Ch 27:28; Isa 9:10; [c]Lk 18:37
7 [d]**Mt 9:11**
8 [e]**Lk 7:13**; [f]Lk 3:12–13; [g]Ex 22:1; Lev 6:4–5; Nu 5:7; 2Sa 12:6; Eze 33:14–15

b*20* Exodus 20:12–16; Deut. 5:16–20

9Jesus said to him, "Today salvation has come to this house, because this man, too, is a son of Abraham.[h] 10For the Son of Man came to seek and to save what was lost."[i]

The Parable of the Ten Minas

19:12–27Ref—Mt 25:14–30

11While they were listening to this, he went on to tell them a parable, because he was near Jerusalem and the people thought that the kingdom of God[j] was going to appear at once.[k] 12He said: "A man of noble birth went to a distant country to have himself appointed king and then to return. 13So he called ten of his servants[l] and gave them ten minas.[a] 'Put this money to work,' he said, 'until I come back.'

14"But his subjects hated him and sent a delegation after him to say, 'We don't want this man to be our king.'

15"He was made king, however, and returned home. Then he sent for the servants to whom he had given the money, in order to find out what they had gained with it.

16"The first one came and said, 'Sir, your mina has earned ten more.'

17" 'Well done, my good servant!'[m] his master replied. 'Because you have been trustworthy in a very small matter, take charge of ten cities.'[n]

18"The second came and said, 'Sir, your mina has earned five more.'

19"His master answered, 'You take charge of five cities.'

20"Then another servant came and said, 'Sir, here is your mina; I have kept it laid away in a piece of cloth. 21I was afraid of you, because you are a hard man. You take out what you did not put in and reap what you did not sow.'[o]

22"His master replied, 'I will judge you by your own words,[p] you wicked servant! You knew, did you, that I am a hard man, taking out what I did not put in, and reaping what I did not sow?[q] 23Why then didn't you put my money on deposit, so that when I came back, I could have collected it with interest?'

24"Then he said to those standing by, 'Take his mina away from him and give it to the one who has ten minas.'

25" 'Sir,' they said, 'he already has ten!'

26"He replied, 'I tell you that to everyone who has, more will be given, but as for the one who has nothing, even what he has will be taken away.[r] 27But those enemies of mine who did not want me to be a king over them—bring them here and kill them in front of me.' "

The Triumphal Entry

19:29–38pp—Mt 21:1–9; Mk 11:1–10
19:35–38pp—Jn 12:12–15

28After Jesus had said this, he went on ahead, going up to Jerusalem.[s] 29As he approached Bethphage and Bethany[t] at the hill called the Mount of Olives,[u] he sent two of his disciples, saying to them, 30"Go to the village ahead of you, and as you enter it, you will find a colt tied there, which no-one has ever ridden. Untie it and bring it here. 31If anyone asks you, 'Why are you untying it?' tell him, 'The Lord needs it.' "

32Those who were sent ahead went and found it just as he had told them.[v] 33As they were untying the colt, its owners asked them, "Why are you untying the colt?"

34They replied, "The Lord needs it."

35They brought it to Jesus, threw their cloaks on the colt and put Jesus on it. 36As he went along, people spread their cloaks[w] on the road.

37When he came near the place where the road goes down the Mount of Olives,[x] the whole crowd of disciples began joyfully to praise God in loud voices for all the miracles they had seen:

38"Blessed is the king who comes in the
name of the Lord!"[b][y]

"Peace in heaven and glory in the
highest!"[z]

39Some of the Pharisees in the crowd said to Jesus, "Teacher, rebuke your disciples!"[a]

40"I tell you," he replied, "if they keep quiet, the stones will cry out."[b]

41As he approached Jerusalem and saw the city, he wept over it[c] 42and said, "If you, even you, had only known on this day what would bring you peace—but now it is hidden from your eyes. 43The days will come upon you when your enemies will build an embankment against you and encircle you and hem you in on every side.[d] 44They will dash you to the ground, you and the children within your walls.[e] They will not leave one stone on another,[f] because you did not recognise the time of God's coming[g] to you."

9 [h]**Lk 3:8**
10 [i]Eze 34:12,16; **Jn 3:17**
11 [j]**Mt 3:2**; [k]Lk 17:20; Ac 1:6
13 [l]Mk 13:34
17 [m]Pr 27:18; [n]Lk 16:10
21 [o]Mt 25:24
22 [p]2Sa 1:16; Job 15:6; [q]Mt 25:26
26 [r]**Mt 25:29**
28 [s]Mk 10:32; **Lk 9:51**
29 [t]**Mt 21:17**; [u]**Mt 21:1**
32 [v]Lk 22:13
36 [w]2Ki 9:13
37 [x]**Mt 21:1**
38 [y]Ps 118:26; Lk 13:35; [z]**Lk 2:14**
39 [a]Mt 21:15–16
40 [b]Hab 2:11
41 [c]Isa 22:4; Lk 13:34–35
43 [d]Isa 29:3; Jer 6:6; Eze 4:2; 26:8; Lk 21:20
44 [e]Ps 137:9; [f]Lk 21:6; [g]1Pe 2:12

---

[a] *13* A mina was about three months' wages.
[b] *38* Psalm 118:26

Jesus at the Temple

19:45,46pp—Mt 21:12–16; Mk 11:15–18; Jn 2:13–16

45Then he entered the temple area
and began driving out those who were
selling. 46"It is written," he said to
them, "'My house will be a house of
prayer';[c][h] but you have made it 'a den of
robbers'.[d]"[i]

47Every day he was teaching at the
temple.[j] But the chief priests, the
teachers of the law and the leaders
among the people were trying to kill
him.[k] 48Yet they could not find any way
to do it, because all the people hung on
his words.

The Authority of Jesus Questioned

20:1–8pp—Mt 21:23–27; Mk 11:27–33

20 One day as he was teaching the
people in the temple courts[a]
and preaching the gospel,[b] the chief
priests and the teachers of the law,
together with the elders, came up to
him. 2"Tell us by what authority you are
doing these things," they said. "Who
gave you this authority?"[c]

3He replied, "I will also ask you a
question. Tell me, 4John's baptism[d]—
was it from heaven, or from men?"

5They discussed it among themselves
and said, "If we say, 'From heaven', he
will ask, 'Why didn't you believe him?'
6But if we say, 'From men', all the
people[e] will stone us, because they are
persuaded that John was a prophet."[f]

7So they answered, "We don't know
where it was from."

8Jesus said, "Neither will I tell you by
what authority I am doing these
things."

The Parable of the Tenants

20:9–19pp—Mt 21:33–46; Mk 12:1–12

9He went on to tell the people this
parable: "A man planted a vineyard,[g]
rented it to some farmers and went
away for a long time.[h] 10At harvest time
he sent a servant to the tenants so they
would give him some of the fruit of the
vineyard. But the tenants beat him and
sent him away empty-handed. 11He
sent another servant, but that one also
they beat and treated shamefully and
sent away empty-handed. 12He sent still
a third, and they wounded him and
threw him out.

13"Then the owner of the vineyard
said, 'What shall I do? I will send my
son, whom I love;[i] perhaps they will
respect him.'

14"But when the tenants saw him,
they talked the matter over. 'This is the
heir,' they said. 'Let's kill him, and the
inheritance will be ours.' 15So they
threw him out of the vineyard and killed
him.

"What then will the owner of the
vineyard do to them? 16He will come
and kill those tenants[j] and give the
vineyard to others."

When the people heard this, they
said, "May this never be!"

17Jesus looked directly at them and
asked, "Then what is the meaning of
that which is written:

"'The stone the builders rejected
has become the capstone[a]'[b]?[k]

18Everyone who falls on that stone will
be broken to pieces, but he on whom it
falls will be crushed."[l]

19The teachers of the law and the chief
priests looked for a way to arrest him[m]
immediately, because they knew he had
spoken this parable against them. But
they were afraid of the people.[n]

Paying Taxes to Caesar

20:20–26pp—Mt 22:15–22; Mk 12:13–17

20Keeping a close watch on him, they
sent spies, who pretended to be honest.
They hoped to catch Jesus in something
he said[o] so that they might hand him
over to the power and authority of the
governor.[p] 21So the spies questioned
him: "Teacher, we know that you speak
and teach what is right, and that you do
not show partiality but teach the way of
God in accordance with the truth.[q] 22Is it
right for us to pay taxes to Caesar or
not?"

23He saw through their duplicity and
said to them, 24"Show me a denarius.
Whose portrait and inscription are on
it?"

25"Caesar's," they replied.

He said to them, "Then give to Caesar
what is Caesar's,[r] and to God what is
God's."

26They were unable to trap him in
what he had said there in public. And
astonished by his answer, they became
silent.

The Resurrection and Marriage

20:27–40pp—Mt 22:23–33; Mk 12:18–27

27Some of the Sadducees,[s] who say
there is no resurrection,[t] came to Jesus

46 [h]Isa 56:7; [i]Jer 7:11
47 [j]**Mt 26:55;** [k]**Mt 12:14;** Mk 11:18

Ch. 20

1 [a]**Mt 26:55;** [b]Lk 8:1
2 [c]Jn 2:18; Ac 4:7; 7:27
4 [d]**Mk 1:4**
6 [e]Lk 7:29; [f]**Mt 11:9**
9 [g]Isa 5:1–7; [h]Mt 25:14
13 [i]**Mt 3:17**
16 [j]Lk 19:27
17 [k]Ps 118:22; **Ac 4:11**
18 [l]Isa 8:14–15
19 [m]Lk 19:47; [n]**Mk 11:18**
20 [o]**Mt 12:10;** [p]Mt 27:2
21 [q]Jn 3:2
25 [r]Lk 23:2; Ro 13:7
27 [s]**Ac 4:1;** [t]Ac 23:8; 1Co 15:12

[c]46 Isaiah 56:7 [d]46 Jer. 7:11
[a]17 Or *cornerstone* [b]17 Psalm 118:22

with a question. 28"Teacher," they said,
"Moses wrote for us that if a man's
brother dies and leaves a wife but no
children, the man must marry the
widow and have children for his
brother.[u] 29Now there were seven
brothers. The first one married a
woman and died childless. 30The
second 31and then the third married her,
and in the same way the seven died,
leaving no children. 32Finally, the
woman died too. 33Now then, at the
resurrection whose wife will she be,
since the seven were married to her?"
34Jesus replied, "The people of this
age marry and are given in marriage.
35But those who are considered worthy
of taking part in that age[v] and in the
resurrection from the dead will neither
marry nor be given in marriage, 36and
they can no longer die; for they are like
the angels. They are God's children,[w]
since they are children of the resurrec-
tion. 37But in the account of the bush,
even Moses showed that the dead rise,
for he calls the Lord 'the God of Abra-
ham, and the God of Isaac, and the God
of Jacob'.[c][x] 38He is not the God of the
dead, but of the living, for to him all are
alive."
39Some of the teachers of the law re-
sponded, "Well said, teacher!" 40And
no-one dared to ask him any more
questions.[y]

Whose Son Is the Christ?

20:41–47pp—Mt 22:41–23:7; Mk 12:35–40

41Then Jesus said to them, "How is it
that they say the Christ[d] is the Son of
David?[z] 42David himself declares in the
Book of Psalms:

> "'The Lord said to my Lord:
> "Sit at my right hand
> 43until I make your enemies
> a footstool for your feet." '[e][a]

44David calls him 'Lord'. How then can
he be his son?"
45While all the people were listening,
Jesus said to his disciples, 46"Beware of
the teachers of the law. They like to
walk around in flowing robes and love
to be greeted in the market-places and
have the most important seats in the
synagogues and the places of honour at
banquets.[b] 47They devour widows'
houses and for a show make lengthy
prayers. Such men will be punished
most severely."

28 [u]Dt 25:5
35 [v]**Mt 12:32**
36 [w]**Jn 1:12**
37 [x]Ex 3:6
40 [y]Mt 22:46; Mk 12:34
41 [z]**Mt 1:1**
43 [a]Ps 110:1; Mt **22:44**
46 [b]**Lk 11:43**

Ch. 21

1 [a]Mt 27:6; Jn 8:20
4 [b]2Co 8:12
6 [c]Lk 19:44
8 [d]Lk 17:23
10 [e]2Ch 15:6; Isa 19:2
11 [f]Isa 29:6; Joel 2:30
13 [g]Php 1:12
14 [h]Lk 12:11
15 [i]**Lk 12:12**
16 [j]Lk 12:52–53

The Widow's Offering

21:1–4pp—Mk 12:41–44

21 As he looked up, Jesus saw the
rich putting their gifts into the
temple treasury.[a] 2He also saw a poor
widow put in two very small copper
coins.[a] 3"I tell you the truth," he said,
"this poor widow has put in more than
all the others. 4All these people gave
their gifts out of their wealth; but she
out of her poverty put in all she had to
live on."[b]

Signs of the End of the Age

21:5–36pp—Mt 24; Mk 13
21:12–17pp—Mt 10:17–22

5Some of his disciples were remarking
about how the temple was adorned
with beautiful stones and with gifts
dedicated to God. But Jesus said, 6"As
for what you see here, the time will
come when not one stone will be left on
another;[c] every one of them will be
thrown down."
7"Teacher," they asked, "when will
these things happen? And what will be
the sign that they are about to take
place?"
8He replied: "Watch out that you are
not deceived. For many will come in my
name, claiming, 'I am he,' and 'The time
is near.' Do not follow them.[d] 9When
you hear of wars and revolutions, do
not be frightened. These things must
happen first, but the end will not come
right away."
10Then he said to them: "Nation will
rise against nation, and kingdom
against kingdom.[e] 11There will be great
earthquakes, famines and pestilences in
various places, and fearful events and
great signs from heaven.[f]
12"But before all this, they will lay
hands on you and persecute you. They
will deliver you to synagogues and pris-
ons, and you will be brought before
kings and governors, and all on account
of my name. 13This will result in your
being witnesses to them.[g] 14But make up
your mind not to worry beforehand
how you will defend yourselves.[h] 15For I
will give you[i] words and wisdom that
none of your adversaries will be able to
resist or contradict. 16You will be be-
trayed even by parents, brothers, rela-
tives and friends,[j] and they will put

[c]37 Exodus 3:6
[d]41 Or *Messiah*
[e]43 Psalm 110:1
[a]2 Greek *two lepta*

some of you to death. 17All men will hate you because of me.[k] 18But not a hair of your head will perish.[l] 19By standing firm you will gain life.[m]

20"When you see Jerusalem being surrounded by armies,[n] you will know that its desolation is near. 21Then let those who are in Judea flee to the mountains, let those in the city get out, and let those in the country not enter the city.[o] 22For this is the time of punishment[p] in fulfilment[q] of all that has been written. 23How dreadful it will be in those days for pregnant women and nursing mothers! There will be great distress in the land and wrath against this people. 24They will fall by the sword and will be taken as prisoners to all the nations. Jerusalem will be trampled[r] on by the Gentiles until the times of the Gentiles are fulfilled.

25"There will be signs in the sun, moon and stars. On the earth, nations will be in anguish and perplexity at the roaring and tossing of the sea.[s] 26Men will faint from terror, apprehensive of what is coming on the world, for the heavenly bodies will be shaken.[t] 27At that time they will see the Son of Man[u] coming in a cloud[v] with power and great glory. 28When these things begin to take place, stand up and lift up your heads, because your redemption is drawing near."[w]

29He told them this parable: "Look at the fig-tree and all the trees. 30When they sprout leaves, you can see for yourselves and know that summer is near. 31Even so, when you see these things happening, you know that the kingdom of God[x] is near.

32"I tell you the truth, this generation[b][y] will certainly not pass away until all these things have happened. 33Heaven and earth will pass away, but my words will never pass away.[z]

34"Be careful, or your hearts will be weighed down with dissipation, drunkenness and the anxieties of life,[a] and that day will close on you unexpectedly[b] like a trap. 35For it will come upon all those who live on the face of the whole earth. 36Be always on the watch, and pray[c] that you may be able to escape all that is about to happen, and that you may be able to stand before the Son of Man."

37Each day Jesus was teaching at the temple,[d] and each evening he went out[e] to spend the night on the hill called the Mount of Olives,[f] 38and all the people came early in the morning to hear him at the temple.[g]

Judas Agrees to Betray Jesus

22:1,2pp—Mt 26:2–5; Mk 14:1,2,10,11

22 Now the Feast of Unleavened Bread, called the Passover, was approaching,[a] 2and the chief priests and the teachers of the law were looking for some way to get rid of Jesus,[b] for they were afraid of the people. 3Then Satan[c] entered Judas, called Iscariot,[d] one of the Twelve. 4And Judas went to the chief priests and the officers of the temple guard[e] and discussed with them how he might betray Jesus. 5They were delighted and agreed to give him money.[f] 6He consented, and watched for an opportunity to hand Jesus over to them when no crowd was present.

The Last Supper

22:7–13pp—Mt 26:17–19; Mk 14:12–16
22:17–20pp—Mt 26:26–29; Mk 14:22–25; 1Co 11:23–25
22:21–23pp—Mt 26:21–24; Mk 14:18–21; Jn 13:21–30
22:25–27pp—Mt 20:25–28; Mk 10:42–45
22:33,34pp—Mt 26:33–35; Mk 14:29–31; Jn 13:37,38

7Then came the day of Unleavened Bread on which the Passover lamb had to be sacrificed.[g] 8Jesus sent Peter and John,[h] saying, "Go and make preparations for us to eat the Passover."

9"Where do you want us to prepare for it?" they asked.

10He replied, "As you enter the city, a man carrying a jar of water will meet you. Follow him to the house that he enters, 11and say to the owner of the house, 'The Teacher asks: Where is the guest room, where I may eat the Passover with my disciples?' 12He will show you a large upper room, all furnished. Make preparations there."

13They left and found things just as Jesus had told them.[i] So they prepared the Passover.

14When the hour came, Jesus and his apostles[j] reclined at the table.[k] 15And he said to them, "I have eagerly desired to eat this Passover with you before I suffer.[l] 16For I tell you, I will not eat it again until it finds fulfilment in the kingdom of God."[m]

17After taking the cup, he gave thanks and said, "Take this and divide it among you. 18For I tell you I will not drink again of the fruit of the vine until the kingdom of God comes."

19And he took bread, gave thanks and broke it,[n] and gave it to them, saying, "This is my body given for you; do this in remembrance of me."

17 [k]**Jn 15:21**
18 [l]**Mt 10:30**
19 [m]**Mt 10:22**
20 [n]**Lk 19:43**
21 [o]Lk 17:31
22 [p]Isa 63:4; Da 9:24–27; Hos 9:7; [q]**Mt 1:22**
24 [r]Isa 5:5; 63:18; Da 8:13; Rev 11:2
25 [s]2Pe 3:10,12
26 [t]**Mt 24:29**
27 [u]**Mt 8:20;** [v]**Rev 1:7**
28 [w]Lk 18:7
31 [x]**Mt 3:2**
32 [y]Lk 11:50; 17:25
33 [z]**Mt 5:18**
34 [a]Mk 4:19; [b]Lk 12:40,46; 1Th 5:2–7
36 [c]Mt 26:41
37 [d]**Mt 26:55;** [e]Mk 11:19; [f]**Mt 21:1**
38 [g]Jn 8:2

Ch. 22

1 [a]**Jn 11:55**
2 [b]**Mt 12:14**
3 [c]**Mt 4:10;** [d]**Mt 10:4**
4 [e]ver 52; Ac 4:1; 5:24
5 [f]Zec 11:12
7 [g]Ex 12:18–20; Dt 16:5–8; **Mk 14:12**
8 [h]Ac 3:1,11; 4:13,19; 8:14
13 [i]Lk 19:32
14 [j]**Mk 6:30;** [k]Mt 26:20; Mk 14:17–18
15 [l]**Mt 16:21**
16 [m]**Lk 14:15**
19 [n]**Mt 14:19**

b32 Or *race*

20In the same way, after the supper he
took the cup, saying, "This cup is the
new covenant[o] in my blood, which is
poured out for you. 21But the hand of
him who is going to betray me is with
mine on the table.[p] 22The Son of Man[q]
will go as it has been decreed,[r] but woe
to that man who betrays him." 23They
began to question among themselves
which of them it might be who would
do this.

24Also a dispute arose among them as
to which of them was considered to be
greatest.[s] 25Jesus said to them, "The
kings of the Gentiles lord it over them;
and those who exercise authority over
them call themselves Benefactors. 26But
you are not to be like that. Instead, the
greatest among you should be like the
youngest,[t] and the one who rules like
the one who serves.[u] 27For who is great-
er, the one who is at the table or the one
who serves? Is it not the one who is at
the table? But I am among you as one
who serves.[v] 28You are those who have
stood by me in my trials. 29And I confer
on you a kingdom,[w] just as my Father
conferred one on me, 30so that you may
eat and drink at my table in my king-
dom[x] and sit on thrones, judging the
twelve tribes of Israel.[y]

31"Simon, Simon, Satan has asked[z] to
sift you**[a]** as wheat.[a] 32But I have prayed
for you,[b] Simon, that your faith may not
fail. And when you have turned back,
strengthen your brothers."[c]

33But he replied, "Lord, I am ready to
go with you to prison and to death."[d]

34Jesus answered, "I tell you, Peter,
before the cock crows today, you will
deny three times that you know me."

35Then Jesus asked them, "When I
sent you without purse, bag or sandals,[e]
did you lack anything?"

"Nothing," they answered.

36He said to them, "But now if you
have a purse, take it, and also a bag; and
if you don't have a sword, sell your
cloak and buy one. 37It is written: 'And
he was numbered with the transgres-
sors'**[b]**;[f] and I tell you that this must be
fulfilled in me. Yes, what is written
about me is reaching its fulfilment."

38The disciples said, "See, Lord, here
are two swords."

"That is enough," he replied.

Jesus Prays on the Mount of Olives

22:40–46pp—Mt 26:36–46; Mk 14:32–42

39Jesus went out as usual[g] to the
Mount of Olives,[h] and his disciples fol-
lowed him. 40On reaching the place, he
said to them, "Pray that you will not fall
into temptation."[i] 41He withdrew about
a stone's throw beyond them, knelt
down[j] and prayed, 42"Father, if you are
willing, take this cup[k] from me; yet not
my will, but yours be done."[l] 43An angel
from heaven appeared to him and
strengthened him.[m] 44And being in
anguish, he prayed more earnestly, and
his sweat was like drops of blood falling
to the ground.**[c]**

45When he rose from prayer and went
back to the disciples, he found them
asleep, exhausted from sorrow. 46"Why
are you sleeping?" he asked them. "Get
up and pray so that you will not fall into
temptation."[n]

Jesus Arrested

22:47–53pp—Mt 26:47–56; Mk 14:43–50; Jn 18:3–11

47While he was still speaking a crowd
came up, and the man who was called
Judas, one of the Twelve, was leading
them. He approached Jesus to kiss him,
48but Jesus asked him, "Judas, are you
betraying the Son of Man with a kiss?"

49When Jesus' followers saw what
was going to happen, they said, "Lord,
should we strike with our swords?"[o]
50And one of them struck the servant of
the high priest, cutting off his right ear.

51But Jesus answered, "No more of
this!" And he touched the man's ear
and healed him.

52Then Jesus said to the chief priests,
the officers of the temple guard,[p] and
the elders, who had come for him, "Am
I leading a rebellion, that you have come
with swords and clubs? 53Every day I
was with you in the temple courts,[q] and
you did not lay a hand on me. But this is
your hour[r]—when darkness reigns."[s]

Peter Disowns Jesus

22:55–62pp—Mt 26:69–75; Mk 14:66–72; Jn 18:16–18, 25–27

54Then seizing him, they led him
away and took him into the house of the
high priest.[t] Peter followed at a dis-
tance.[u] 55But when they had kindled a
fire in the middle of the courtyard and
had sat down together, Peter sat down
with them. 56A servant girl saw him
seated there in the firelight. She looked
closely at him and said, "This man was
with him."

20 [o]Ex 24:8; Isa 42:6; Jer 31:31–34; Zec 9:11; 2Co 3:6; Heb 8:6; 9:15
21 [p]Ps 41:9
22 [q]**Mt 8:20**; [r]Ac 2:23; 4:28
24 [s]Mk 9:34; Lk 9:46
26 [t]1Pe 5:5; [u]**Mk 9:35**
27 [v]**Mt 20:28**
29 [w]**Mt 25:34**; 2Ti 2:12
30 [x]**Lk 14:15**; [y]**Mt 19:28**
31 [z]Job 1:6–12; [a]Am 9:9
32 [b]Jn 17:9,15; **Ro 8:34**; [c]Jn 21:15–17
33 [d]Jn 11:16
35 [e]Mt 10:9–10; Lk 9:3; 10:4
37 [f]Isa 53:12
39 [g]Lk 21:37; [h]**Mt 21:1**
40 [i]Mt 6:13
41 [j]Lk 18:11
42 [k]**Mt 20:22**; [l]**Mt 26:39**
43 [m]Mt 4:11; Mk 1:13
46 [n]ver 40
49 [o]ver 38
52 [p]ver 4
53 [q]**Mt 26:55**; [r]Jn 12:27; [s]Mt 8:12; Jn 1:5; 3:20
54 [t]Mt 26:57; Mk 14:53; [u]Mt 26:58; Mk 14:54; Jn 18:15

a31 The Greek is plural. **b**37 Isaiah 53:12
c44 Some early manuscripts do not have verses 43 and 44.

57But he denied it. "Woman, I don't
know him," he said.
58A little later someone else saw him
and said, "You also are one of them."
"Man, I am not!" Peter replied.
59About an hour later another
asserted, "Certainly this fellow was
with him, for he is a Galilean."[v]
60Peter replied, "Man, I don't know
what you're talking about!" Just as he
was speaking, the cock crowed. 61The
Lord[w] turned and looked straight at
Peter. Then Peter remembered the
word the Lord had spoken to him: "Be-
fore the cock crows today, you will dis-
own me three times."[x] 62And he went
outside and wept bitterly.

The Soldiers Mock Jesus

22:63–65pp—Mt 26:67,68; Mk 14:65; Jn 18:22,23

63The men who were guarding Jesus
began mocking and beating him. 64They
blindfolded him and demanded,
"Prophesy! Who hit you?" 65And they
said many other insulting things to
him.[y]

Jesus Before Pilate and Herod

22:67–71pp—Mt 26:63–66; Mk 14:61–63; Jn 18:19–21
23:2,3pp—Mt 27:11–14; Mk 15:2–5; Jn 18:29–37
23:18–25pp—Mt 27:15–26; Mk 15:6–15; Jn 18:39–19:16

66At daybreak the council[z] of the
elders of the people, both the chief
priests and teachers of the law, met
together,[a] and Jesus was led before
them. 67"If you are the Christ,"[d] they
said, "tell us."
Jesus answered, "If I tell you, you will
not believe me, 68and if I asked you, you
would not answer.[b] 69But from now on,
the Son of Man will be seated at the right
hand of the mighty God."[c]
70They all asked, "Are you then the
Son of God?"[d]
He replied, "You are right in saying I
am."[e]
71Then they said, "Why do we need
any more testimony? We have heard it
from his own lips."

23 Then the whole assembly rose
and led him off to Pilate.[a] 2And
they began to accuse him, saying, "We
have found this man subverting our
nation.[b] He opposes payment of taxes to
Caesar[c] and claims to be Christ,[a] a
king."[d]
3So Pilate asked Jesus, "Are you the
king of the Jews?"
"Yes, it is as you say," Jesus replied.
4Then Pilate announced to the chief
priests and the crowd, "I find no basis
for a charge against this man."[e]
5But they insisted, "He stirs up the
people all over Judea[b] by his teaching.
He started in Galilee[f] and has come all
the way here."
6On hearing this, Pilate asked if the
man was a Galilean.[g] 7When he learned
that Jesus was under Herod's jurisdic-
tion, he sent him to Herod,[h] who was
also in Jerusalem at that time.
8When Herod saw Jesus, he was
greatly pleased, because for a long time
he had been wanting to see him.[i] From
what he had heard about him, he hoped
to see him perform some miracle. 9He
plied him with many questions, but
Jesus gave him no answer.[j] 10The chief
priests and the teachers of the law were
standing there, vehemently accusing
him. 11Then Herod and his soldiers ridi-
culed and mocked him. Dressing him in
an elegant robe,[k] they sent him back to
Pilate. 12That day Herod and Pilate be-
came friends[l]—before this they had
been enemies.
13Pilate called together the chief
priests, the rulers and the people, 14and
said to them, "You brought me this man
as one who was inciting the people to
rebellion. I have examined him in your
presence and have found no basis for
your charges against him.[m] 15Neither
has Herod, for he sent him back to us; as
you can see, he has done nothing to
deserve death. 16Therefore, I will pun-
ish him[n] and then release him."[c]
18With one voice they cried out,
"Away with this man! Release Barabbas
to us!"[o] (19Barabbas had been thrown
into prison for an insurrection in the
city, and for murder.)
20Wanting to release Jesus, Pilate
appealed to them again. 21But they kept
shouting, "Crucify him! Crucify him!"
22For the third time he spoke to them:
"Why? What crime has this man com-
mitted? I have found in him no grounds
for the death penalty. Therefore I will
have him punished and then release
him."[p]
23But with loud shouts they insistent-
ly demanded that he be crucified, and
their shouts prevailed. 24So Pilate de-
cided to grant their demand. 25He re-
leased the man who had been thrown
into prison for insurrection and murder,

59 [v]Lk 23:6
61 [w]**Lk 7:13;** [x]ver 34
65 [y]**Mt 16:21**
66 [z]**Mt 5:22;** [a]Mt 27:1; Mk 15:1
68 [b]Lk 20:3–8
69 [c]**Mk 16:19**
70 [d]**Mt 4:3;** [e]Mt 27:11; Lk 23:3

Ch. 23

1 [a]**Mt 27:2**
2 [b]ver 14; [c]Lk 20:22; [d]Jn 19:12
4 [e]ver 14,22,41; Mt 27:23; Jn 18:38; 1Ti 6:13; **2Co 5:21**
5 [f]Mk 1:14
6 [g]Lk 22:59
7 [h]**Mt 14:1**
8 [i]Lk 9:9
9 [j]**Mk 14:61**
11 [k]Mk 15:17–19; Jn 19:2–3
12 [l]Ac 4:27
14 [m]**ver 4**
16 [n]ver 22; Mt 27:26; Jn 19:1; Ac 16:37; 2Co 11:23–24
18 [o]Ac 3:13–14
22 [p]ver 16

d67 Or *Messiah*
a2 Or *Messiah;* also in verses 35 and 39
b5 Or *over the land of the Jews*
c16 Some manuscripts *him."* [17]*Now he was obliged to release one man to them at the Feast.*

the one they asked for, and surrendered Jesus to their will.

The Crucifixion

23:33–43pp—Mt 27:33–44; Mk 15:22–32; Jn 19:17–24

26As they led him away, they seized Simon from Cyrene,[q] who was on his way in from the country, and put the cross on him and made him carry it behind Jesus.[r] 27A large number of people followed him, including women who mourned and wailed[s] for him. 28Jesus turned and said to them, "Daughters of Jerusalem, do not weep for me; weep for yourselves and for your children.[t] 29For the time will come when you will say, 'Blessed are the barren women, the wombs that never bore and the breasts that never nursed!'[u] 30Then

> " 'they will say to the mountains, "Fall on us!"
> and to the hills "Cover us!" '[d][v]

31For if men do these things when the tree is green, what will happen when it is dry?"[w]

32Two other men, both criminals, were also led out with him to be executed.[x] 33When they came to the place called the Skull, there they crucified him, along with the criminals—one on his right, the other on his left. 34Jesus said, "Father,[y] forgive them, for they do not know what they are doing."[e][z] And they divided up his clothes by casting lots.[a]

35The people stood watching, and the rulers even sneered at him.[b] They said, "He saved others; let him save himself if he is the Christ of God, the Chosen One."[c]

36The soldiers also came up and mocked him.[d] They offered him wine vinegar[e] 37and said, "If you are the king of the Jews,[f] save yourself."

38There was a written notice above him, which read: THIS IS THE KING OF THE JEWS.[g]

39One of the criminals who hung there hurled insults at him: "Aren't you the Christ? Save yourself and us!"[h]

40But the other criminal rebuked him. "Don't you fear God," he said, "since you are under the same sentence? 41We are punished justly, for we are getting what our deeds deserve. But this man has done nothing wrong."[i]

42Then he said, "Jesus, remember me when you come into your kingdom[f]."[j]

43Jesus answered him, "I tell you the truth, today you will be with me in paradise."[k]

Jesus' Death

23:44–49pp—Mt 27:45–56; Mk 15:33–41

44It was now about the sixth hour, and darkness came over the whole land until the ninth hour,[l] 45for the sun stopped shining. And the curtain of the temple[m] was torn in two.[n] 46Jesus called out with a loud voice,[o] "Father, into your hands I commit my spirit."[p] When he had said this, he breathed his last.[q]

47The centurion, seeing what had happened, praised God[r] and said, "Surely this was a righteous man." 48When all the people who had gathered to witness this sight saw what took place, they beat their breasts[s] and went away. 49But all those who knew him, including the women who had followed him from Galilee,[t] stood at a distance,[u] watching these things.

Jesus' Burial

23:50–56pp—Mt 27:57–61; Mk 15:42–47; Jn 19:38–42

50Now there was a man named Joseph, a member of the Council, a good and upright man, 51who had not consented to their decision and action. He came from the Judean town of Arimathea and he was waiting for the kingdom of God.[v] 52Going to Pilate, he asked for Jesus' body. 53Then he took it down, wrapped it in linen cloth and placed it in a tomb cut in the rock, one in which no-one had yet been laid. 54It was Preparation Day,[w] and the Sabbath was about to begin.

55The women who had come with Jesus from Galilee[x] followed Joseph and saw the tomb and how his body was laid in it. 56Then they went home and prepared spices and perfumes.[y] But they rested on the Sabbath in obedience to the commandment.[z]

The Resurrection

24:1–10pp—Mt 28:1–8; Mk 16:1–8; Jn 20:1–8

24 On the first day of the week, very early in the morning, the women took the spices they had prepared[a] and went to the tomb. 2They found the stone rolled away from the tomb, 3but when they entered, they did

26 [q]**Mt 27:32;** [r]Mk 15:21; Jn 19:17
27 [s]Lk 8:52
28 [t]Lk 19:41–44; 21:23–24
29 [u]Mt 24:19
30 [v]Hos 10:8; Isa 2:19; Rev 6:16
31 [w]Eze 20:47
32 [x]Isa 53:12; Mt 27:38; Mk 15:27; Jn 19:18
34 [y]**Mt 11:25;** [z]**Mt 5:44;** [a]Ps 22:18
35 [b]Ps 22:17; [c]Isa 42:1
36 [d]Ps 22:7; [e]Ps 69:21; Mt 27:48
37 [f]Lk 4:3,9
38 [g]**Mt 2:2**
39 [h]ver 35,37
41 [i]**ver 4**
42 [j]**Mt 16:27**
43 [k]2Co 12:3–4; Rev 2:7
44 [l]Am 8:9
45 [m]Ex 26:31–33; Heb 9:3,8; [n]Heb 10:19–20
46 [o]Mt 27:50; [p]Ps 31:5; 1Pe 2:23; [q]Jn 19:30
47 [r]**Mt 9:8**
48 [s]Lk 18:13
49 [t]Lk 8:2; [u]Ps 38:11
51 [v]Lk 2:25,38
54 [w]Mt 27:62
55 [x]ver 49
56 [y]Mk 16:1; Lk 24:1; [z]Ex 12:16; 20:10

Ch. 24
1 [a]Lk 23:56

d30 Hosea 10:8
e34 Some early manuscripts do not have this sentence.
f42 Some manuscripts *come with your kingly power*

not find the body of the Lord Jesus.[b]
4While they were wondering about this,
suddenly two men in clothes that
gleamed like lightning[c] stood beside
them. 5In their fright the women bowed
down with their faces to the ground, but
the men said to them, "Why do you
look for the living among the dead? 6He
is not here; he has risen! Remember
how he told you, while he was still with
you in Galilee:[d] 7'The Son of Man[e] must
be delivered into the hands of sinful
men, be crucified and on the third day
be raised again.'"[f] 8Then they remem-
bered his words.[g]

9When they came back from the
tomb, they told all these things to the
Eleven and to all the others. 10It was
Mary Magdalene, Joanna, Mary the
mother of James, and the others with
them[h] who told this to the apostles.[i]
11But they did not believe[j] the women,
because their words seemed to them
like nonsense. 12Peter, however, got up
and ran to the tomb. Bending over, he
saw the strips of linen lying by them-
selves,[k] and he went away,[l] wondering
to himself what had happened.

On the Road to Emmaus

13Now that same day two of them
were going to a village called Emmaus,
about seven miles[a] from Jerusalem.[m]
14They were talking with each other
about everything that had happened.
15As they talked and discussed these
things with each other, Jesus himself
came up and walked along with them;[n]
16but they were kept from recognising
him.[o]

17He asked them, "What are you dis-
cussing together as you walk along?"

They stood still, their faces downcast.
18One of them, named Cleopas,[p] asked
him, "Are you only a visitor to Jeru-
salem and do not know the things that
have happened there in these days?"

19"What things?" he asked.

"About Jesus of Nazareth,"[q] they re-
plied. "He was a prophet,[r] powerful in
word and deed before God and all the
people. 20The chief priests and our
rulers[s] handed him over to be sentenced
to death, and they crucified him; 21but
we had hoped that he was the one who
was going to redeem Israel.[t] And what
is more, it is the third day[u] since all this
took place. 22In addition, some of our
women amazed us.[v] They went to the
tomb early this morning 23but didn't
find his body. They came and told us
that they had seen a vision of angels,
who said he was alive. 24Then some of
our companions went to the tomb and
found it just as the women had said, but
him they did not see."[w]

25He said to them, "How foolish you
are, and how slow of heart to believe all
that the prophets have spoken! 26Did
not the Christ[b] have to suffer these
things and then enter his glory?"[x] 27And
beginning with Moses[y] and all the
Prophets,[z] he explained to them what
was said in all the Scriptures concerning
himself.[a]

28As they approached the village to
which they were going, Jesus acted as if
he were going further. 29But they urged
him strongly, "Stay with us, for it is
nearly evening; the day is almost over."
So he went in to stay with them.

30When he was at the table with them,
he took bread, gave thanks, broke it[b]
and began to give it to them. 31Then
their eyes were opened and they recog-
nised him,[c] and he disappeared from
their sight. 32They asked each other,
"Were not our hearts burning within
us[d] while he talked with us on the road
and opened the Scriptures[e] to us?"

33They got up and returned at once to
Jerusalem. There they found the Eleven
and those with them, assembled
together 34and saying, "It is true! The
Lord[f] has risen and has appeared to
Simon."[g] 35Then the two told what had
happened on the way, and how Jesus
was recognised by them when he broke
the bread.[h]

Jesus Appears to the Disciples

36While they were still talking about
this, Jesus himself stood among them
and said to them, "Peace be with you."[i]

37They were startled and frightened,
thinking they saw a ghost.[j] 38He said to
them, "Why are you troubled, and why
do doubts rise in your minds? 39Look at
my hands and my feet. It is I myself!
Touch me and see;[k] a ghost does not
have flesh and bones, as you see I
have."

40When he had said this, he showed
them his hands and feet. 41And while
they still did not believe it because of joy
and amazement, he asked them, "Do
you have anything here to eat?" 42They
gave him a piece of broiled fish, 43and he
took it and ate it in their presence.[l]

44He said to them, "This is what I told

3 [b]ver 23–24
4 [c]**Jn 20:12**
6 [d]Mt 17:22–23; Lk 9:22; 24:44
7 [e]**Mt 8:20;** [f]**Mt 16:21**
8 [g]Jn 2:22
10 [h]Lk 8:1–3; [i]**Mk 6:30**
11 [j]Mk 16:11
12 [k]Jn 20:3–7; [l]Jn 20:10
13 [m]Mk 16:12
15 [n]ver 36
16 [o]Jn 20:14; 21:4
18 [p]Jn 19:25
19 [q]**Mk 1:24;** [r]**Mt 21:11**
20 [s]Lk 23:13
21 [t]Lk 1:68; 2:38; 21:28; [u]**Mt 16:21**
22 [v]ver 1–10
24 [w]ver 12
26 [x]Heb 2:10; 1Pe 1:11
27 [y]Ge 3:15; Nu 21:9; Dt 18:15; [z]Isa 7:14; 9:6; 40:10–11; 53; Eze 34:23; Da 9:24; Mic 7:20; Mal 3:1; [a]Jn 1:45
30 [b]**Mt 14:19**
31 [c]ver 16
32 [d]Ps 39:3; [e]ver 27,45
34 [f]**Lk 7:13;** [g]1Co 15:5
35 [h]ver 30–31
36 [i]Jn 20:19,21, 26; **14:27**
37 [j]Mk 6:49
39 [k]Jn 20:27; 1Jn 1:1
43 [l]Ac 10:41

[a]*13* Greek *sixty stadia* (about 11 kilometres)
[b]*26* Or *Messiah;* also in verse 46

you while I was still with you:[m] Every-
thing must be fulfilled[n] that is written
about me in the Law of Moses,[o] the
Prophets[p] and the Psalms."[q]
45Then he opened their minds so they
could understand the Scriptures. 46He
told them, "This is what is written: The
Christ will suffer[r] and rise from the dead
on the third day,[s] 47and repentance and
forgiveness of sins will be preached in
his name[t] to all nations,[u] beginning at
Jerusalem.[v] 48You are witnesses[w] of
these things. 49I am going to send you
what my Father has promised;[x] but stay
in the city until you have been clothed
with power from on high."

44 [m]Lk 9:45; 18:34; [n]**Mt 1:22**; 16:21; Lk 9:22,44; 18:31–33; 22:37; [o]**ver 27**; [p]**ver 27**; [q]Ps 2; 16; 22; 69; 72; 110; 118
46 [r]**Mt 16:21**; [s]**Mt 16:21**
47 [t]Ac 5:31; 10:43; 13:38; [u]Mt 28:19; Mk 13:10; [v]Isa 2:3

The Ascension

50When he had led them out to the
vicinity of Bethany,[y] he lifted up his
hands and blessed them. 51While he
was blessing them, he left them and was
taken up into heaven.[z] 52Then they wor-
shipped him and returned to Jerusalem
with great joy. 53And they stayed con-
tinually at the temple,[a] praising God.

48 [w]**Jn 15:27**; Ac 1:8; 2:32; 4:20; 5:32; 13:31; 1Pe 5:1
49 [x]**Jn 14:16**; Ac 1:4 *50* [y]**Mt 21:17**
51 [z]2Ki 2:11 *53* [a]**Ac 2:46**

John

The Word Became Flesh

1 In the beginning was the Word,[a]
and the Word was with God,[b] and
the Word was God.[c] 2He was with God
in the beginning.[d]
3Through him all things were made;
without him nothing was made that has
been made.[e] 4In him was life,[f] and that
life was the light[g] of men. 5The light
shines in the darkness,[h] but the dark-
ness has not understood[a] it.[i]
6There came a man who was sent
from God; his name was John.[j] 7He
came as a witness to testify[k] concerning
that light, so that through him all men
might believe.[l] 8He himself was not the
light; he came only as a witness to the
light. 9The true light[m] that gives light to
every man[n] was coming into the world.[b]
10He was in the world, and though
the world was made through him,[o] the
world did not recognise him. 11He came
to that which was his own, but his own
did not receive him.[p] 12Yet to all who
received him, to those who believed[q] in
his name,[r] he gave the right to become
children of God[s]—13children born not of
natural descent,[c] nor of human decision
or a husband's will, but born of God.[t]
14The Word became flesh[u] and made
his dwelling among us. We have seen
his glory,[v] the glory of the One and
Only,[d] who came from the Father, full
of grace[w] and truth.[x]
15John testifies[y] concerning him. He
cries out, saying, "This was he of whom
I said, 'He who comes after me has
surpassed me because he was before
me.' "[z] 16From the fulness[a] of his grace[b]
we have all received one blessing after
another. 17For the law was given
through Moses;[c] grace and truth came
through Jesus Christ.[d] 18No-one has
ever seen God,[e] but God the One and
Only,[e,f][f] who is at the Father's side, has
made him known.

John the Baptist Denies Being the Christ

19Now this was John's[g] testimony
when the Jews[h] of Jerusalem sent priests
and Levites to ask him who he was. 20He
did not fail to confess, but confessed
freely, "I am not the Christ."[g][i]
21They asked him, "Then who are
you? Are you Elijah?"[j]
He said, "I am not."
"Are you the Prophet?"[k]
He answered, "No."
22Finally they said, "Who are you?
Give us an answer to take back to those
who sent us. What do you say about
yourself?"
23John replied in the words of Isaiah
the prophet, "I am the voice of one
calling in the desert,[l] 'Make straight the
way for the Lord.'[h]"[m]
24Now some Pharisees who had been
sent 25questioned him, "Why then do
you baptise if you are not the Christ, nor
Elijah, nor the Prophet?"
26"I baptise with[i] water,"[n] John re-
plied, "but among you stands one you
do not know. 27He is the one who comes
after me,[o] the thongs of whose sandals I
am not worthy to untie."[p]
28This all happened at Bethany on the
other side of the Jordan,[q] where John
was baptising.

Jesus the Lamb of God

29The next day John saw Jesus coming
towards him and said, "Look, the Lamb
of God,[r] who takes away the sin of the
world![s] 30This is the one I meant when I
said, 'A man who comes after me has

Ch. 1

1 [a]Isa 55:11; Rev 19:13; [b]Jn 17:5; 1Jn 1:2; [c]Php 2:6
2 [d]Ge 1:1; Jn 8:58; 17:5,24; 1Jn 1:1; Rev 1:8
3 [e]ver 10; 1Co 8:6; Col 1:16; Heb 1:2
4 [f]**Jn 5:26**; 6:57; 11:25; 14:6; Ac 3:15; Heb 7:16; 1Jn 1:1–2; 5:20; Rev 1:18; [g]Ps 36:9; Jn 3:19; 8:12; 9:5; 12:46
5 [h]Ps 18:28; [i]Jn 3:19
6 [j]**Mt 3:1**
7 [k]ver 15,19,32; Jn 3:26; 5:33; [l]ver 12; **Jn 3:15**
9 [m]1Jn 2:8; [n]Isa 49:6
10 [o]**ver 3**
11 [p]Isa 53:3
12 [q]ver 7; **Jn 3:15**; [r]**1Jn 3:23**; [s]Dt 14:1; **Ro 8:14**,16,21; Eph 5:1; 1Jn 3:1–2
13 [t]Jn 3:6; Tit 3:5; Jas 1:18; 1Pe 1:23; 1Jn 3:9; 4:7; 5:1,4
14 [u]Gal 4:4; Php 2:7–8; 1Ti 3:16; Heb 2:14; 1Jn 1:1–2; 4:2; [v]Ex 33:18; 40:34; [w]**Ro 3:24**; [x]Jn 14:6
15 [y]ver 7; [z]ver 30; Mt 3:11
16 [a]Eph 1:23; Col 1:19; 2:9; [b]**Ro 3:24**
17 [c]Dt 32:46; Jn 7:19; [d]ver 14
18 [e]Ex 33:20; Jn 6:46; Col 1:15; 1Ti 6:16; 1Jn 4:12; [f]Jn 3:16, 18; 1Jn 4:9
19 [g]**Mt 3:1**; [h]Jn 2:18; 5:10,16; 6:41,52; 7:1; 10:24
20 [i]Jn 3:28; Lk 3:15–16

21 [j]**Mt 11:14**; [k]Dt 18:15 23 [l]Mt 3:1; [m]Isa 40:3
26 [n]**Mk 1:4** 27 [o]ver 15,30; [p]Mk 1:7
28 [q]Jn 3:26; 10:40
29 [r]ver 36; Ge 22:8; Isa 53:7; 1Pe 1:19; Rev 5:6; 13:8; [s]**Jn 3:17**

[a]5 Or *darkness, and the darkness has not overcome*
[b]9 Or *This was the true light that gives light to every man who comes into the world* [c]13 Greek *of bloods*
[d]14 Or *the Only Begotten*
[e]18 Or *the Only Begotten*
[f]18 Some manuscripts *but the only* (or *only begotten*) *Son*
[g]20 Or *Messiah.* "The Christ" (Greek) and "the Messiah" (Hebrew) both mean "the Anointed One"; also in verse 25. [h]23 Isaiah 40:3
[i]26 Or *in*; also in verses 31 and 33

surpassed me because he was before
me.'[t] 31I myself did not know him, but
the reason I came baptising with water
was that he might be revealed to Israel."
32Then John gave this testimony: "I
saw the Spirit come down from heaven
as a dove and remain on him.[u] 33I would
not have known him, except that the
one who sent me to baptise with water[v]
told me, 'The man on whom you see the
Spirit come down and remain is he who
will baptise with the Holy Spirit.'[w] 34I
have seen and I testify that this is the
Son of God."[x]

Jesus' First Disciples

1:40–42pp—Mt 4:18–22; Mk 1:16–20; Lk 5:2–11

35The next day John[y] was there again
with two of his disciples. 36When he saw
Jesus passing by, he said, "Look, the
Lamb of God!"[z]
37When the two disciples heard him
say this, they followed Jesus. 38Turning
round, Jesus saw them following and
asked, "What do you want?"
They said, "Rabbi"[a] (which means
Teacher), "where are you staying?"
39"Come," he replied, "and you will
see."
So they went and saw where he was
staying, and spent that day with him. It
was about the tenth hour.
40Andrew, Simon Peter's brother,
was one of the two who heard what
John had said and who had followed
Jesus. 41The first thing Andrew did was
to find his brother Simon and tell him,
"We have found the Messiah" (that is,
the Christ).[b] 42And he brought him to
Jesus.
Jesus looked at him and said, "You
are Simon son of John. You will be
called[c] Cephas" (which, when trans-
lated, is Peter[j]).[d]

Jesus Calls Philip and Nathanael

43The next day Jesus decided to leave
for Galilee. Finding Philip,[e] he said to
him, "Follow me."[f]
44Philip, like Andrew and Peter, was
from the town of Bethsaida.[g] 45Philip
found Nathanael[h] and told him, "We
have found the one Moses wrote about
in the Law,[i] and about whom the
prophets also wrote[j]—Jesus of Naza-
reth,[k] the son of Joseph."[l]
46"Nazareth! Can anything good
come from there?"[m] Nathanael asked.
"Come and see," said Philip.
47When Jesus saw Nathanael
approaching, he said of him, "Here is a
true Israelite,[n] in whom there is nothing
false."[o]
48"How do you know me?" Natha-
nael asked.
Jesus answered, "I saw you while you
were still under the fig-tree before
Philip called you."
49Then Nathanael declared, "Rabbi,[p]
you are the Son of God;[q] you are the
King of Israel."[r]
50Jesus said, "You believe[k] because I
told you I saw you under the fig-tree.
You shall see greater things than that."
51He then added, "I tell you[l] the truth,
you[l] shall see heaven open,[s] and the
angels of God ascending[t] and descend-
ing on the Son of Man."[u]

Jesus Changes Water to Wine

2 On the third day a wedding took
place at Cana in Galilee.[a] Jesus'
mother[b] was there, 2and Jesus and his
disciples had also been invited to the
wedding. 3When the wine was gone,
Jesus' mother said to him, "They have
no more wine."
4"Dear woman,[c] why do you involve
me?"[d] Jesus replied. "My time[e] has not
yet come."
5His mother said to the servants, "Do
whatever he tells you."[f]
6Nearby stood six stone water
jars, the kind used by the Jews for
ceremonial washing,[g] each holding
from twenty to thirty gallons.[a]
7Jesus said to the servants, "Fill the
jars with water"; so they filled them to
the brim.
8Then he told them, "Now draw
some out and take it to the master of the
banquet."
They did so, 9and the master of the
banquet tasted the water that had been
turned into wine.[h] He did not realise
where it had come from, though the
servants who had drawn the water
knew. Then he called the bridegroom
aside 10and said, "Everyone brings out
the choice wine first and then the cheap-
er wine after the guests have had too
much to drink; but you have saved the
best till now."
11This, the first of his miraculous
signs,[i] Jesus performed in Cana of
Galilee. He thus revealed his glory,[j]
and his disciples put their faith in him.[k]

30 [t]ver 15,27
32 [u]Mt 3:16
33 [v]**Mk 1:4;** [w]**Mk 1:8**
34 [x]ver 49; **Mt 4:3**
35 [y]**Mt 3:1**
36 [z]**ver 29**
38 [a]ver 49; **Mt 23:7**
41 [b]Jn 4:25
42 [c]Ge 17:5,15; 32:28; 35:10; [d]Mt 16:18
43 [e]Mt 10:3; Jn 6:5–7; 12:21–22; 14:8–9; [f]**Mt 4:19**
44 [g]**Mt 11:21**
45 [h]Jn 21:2; [i]**Lk 24:27;** [j]**Lk 24:27;** [k]**Mk 1:24;** [l]Lk 3:23
46 [m]Jn 7:41–42, 52
47 [n]Ro 9:4,6; [o]Ps 32:2
49 [p]ver 38; **Mt 23:7;** [q]ver 34; **Mt 4:3;** [r]**Mt 2:2;** 27:42; Jn 12:13
51 [s]**Mt 3:16;** [t]Ge 28:12; [u]**Mt 8:20**

Ch. 2

1 [a]Jn 4:46; 21:2; [b]**Mt 12:46**
4 [c]Jn 19:26; [d]**Mt 8:29;** [e]**Mt 26:18**
5 [f]Ge 41:55
6 [g]Mk 7:3–4; Jn 3:25
9 [h]Jn 4:46
11 [i]ver 23; Mt 12:38; Jn 3:2; **4:48;** 6:2,14, 26,30; 12:37; 20:30; [j]Jn 1:14; [k]Ex 14:31

[j]42 Both *Cephas* (Aramaic) and *Peter* (Greek) mean *rock*. [k]50 Or *Do you believe . . . ?*
[l]51 The Greek is plural.
[a]6 Greek *two to three metretes* (probably about 75 to 115 litres)

Jesus Clears the Temple

2:14–16pp—Mt 21:12,13; Mk 11:15–17; Lk 19:45,46

12After this he went down to Capernaum[l] with his mother[m] and brothers[n] and his disciples. There they stayed for a few days.

13When it was almost time for the Jewish Passover,[o] Jesus went up to Jerusalem.[p] 14In the temple courts he found men selling cattle, sheep and doves,[q] and others sitting at tables exchanging money.[r] 15So he made a whip out of cords, and drove all from the temple area, both sheep and cattle; he scattered the coins of the money-changers and overturned their tables. 16To those who sold doves he said, "Get these out of here! How dare you turn my Father's house[s] into a market!"

17His disciples remembered that it is written, "Zeal for your house will consume me."[b][t]

18Then the Jews[u] demanded of him, "What miraculous sign[v] can you show us to prove your authority to do all this?"[w]

19Jesus answered them, "Destroy this temple, and I will raise it again in three days."[x]

20The Jews replied, "It has taken forty-six years to build this temple, and you are going to raise it in three days?" 21But the temple he had spoken of was his body.[y] 22After he was raised from the dead, his disciples recalled what he had said.[z] Then they believed the Scripture[a] and the words that Jesus had spoken.

23Now while he was in Jerusalem at the Passover Feast,[b] many people saw the miraculous signs[c] he was doing and believed[d] in his name.[c] 24But Jesus would not entrust himself to them, for he knew all men. 25He did not need man's testimony about man,[e] for he knew what was in a man.[f]

Jesus Teaches Nicodemus

3 Now there was a man of the Pharisees named Nicodemus,[a] a member of the Jewish ruling council.[b] 2He came to Jesus at night and said, "Rabbi,[c] we know[d] you are a teacher who has come from God. For no-one could perform the miraculous signs[e] you are doing if God were not with him."[f]

3In reply Jesus declared, "I tell you the truth, no-one can see the kingdom of God unless he is born again."[a][g][h]

4"How can a man be born when he is old?" Nicodemus asked. "Surely he cannot enter a second time into his mother's womb to be born!"

5Jesus answered, "I tell you the truth, no-one can enter the kingdom of God unless he is born of water and the Spirit.[i][j] 6Flesh gives birth to flesh, but the Spirit[b] gives birth to spirit.[k] 7You should not be surprised at my saying, 'You[c] must be born again.' 8The wind blows wherever it pleases. You hear its sound, but you cannot tell where it comes from or where it is going. So it is with everyone born of the Spirit."[l]

9"How can this be?"[m] Nicodemus asked.

10"You are Israel's teacher,"[n] said Jesus, "and do you not understand these things? 11I tell you the truth, we speak of what we know,[o] and we testify to what we have seen, but still you people do not accept our testimony.[p] 12I have spoken to you of earthly things and you do not believe; how then will you believe if I speak of heavenly things? 13No-one has ever gone into heaven[q] except the one who came from heaven[r]—the Son of Man.[d][s] 14Just as Moses lifted up the snake in the desert,[t] so the Son of Man must be lifted up,[u] 15that everyone who believes[v] in him may have eternal life.[e][w]

16"For God so loved[x] the world that he gave[y] his one and only Son,[f][z] that whoever believes[a] in him shall not perish but have eternal life.[b] 17For God did not send his Son into the world[c] to condemn the world, but to save the world through him.[d] 18Whoever believes in him is not condemned,[e] but whoever does not believe stands condemned already because he has not believed in the name of God's one and only Son.[g][f] 19This is the verdict: Light[g] has come into the world, but men loved darkness instead of light because their deeds were evil.[h] 20Everyone who does evil hates the light, and will not come into the light for fear that his deeds will be exposed.[i] 21But whoever lives by the truth comes into the light, so that it may

12 [l]**Mt 4:13;** [m]**Mt 12:46;** [n]**Mt 12:46**
13 [o]**Jn 11:55;** [p]Dt 16:1–6; Lk 2:41
14 [q]Lev 1:14; Dt 14:26; [r]Dt 14:25
16 [s]Lk 2:49
17 [t]Ps 69:9
18 [u]**Jn 1:19;** [v]**ver 11;** [w]**Mt 12:38**
19 [x]**Mt 16:21;** 26:61; 27:40; Mk 14:58; 15:29; Ac 6:14
21 [y]1Co 6:19
22 [z]Lk 24:5–8; Jn 12:16; 14:26; [a]Ps 16:10; **Lk 24:27**
23 [b]ver 13; [c]**ver 11;** [d]**Jn 3:15**
25 [e]Isa 11:3; [f]Dt 31:21; 1Ki 8:39; **Mt 9:4;** Jn 6:61,64; 13:11

Ch. 3

1 [a]Jn 7:50; 19:39; [b]Lk 23:13
2 [c]**Mt 23:7;** [d]ver 11; [e]**Jn 2:11;** [f]Jn 10:38; 14:10–11; Ac 2:22; 10:38
3 [g]**Jn 1:13;** [h]**Mt 3:2**
5 [i]**Ac 22:16;** [j]Tit 3:5
6 [k]**Jn 1:13;** 1Co 15:50
8 [l]1Co 2:14–16
9 [m]Jn 6:52,60
10 [n]Lk 2:46
11 [o]Jn 1:18; 7:16–17; [p]ver 32
13 [q]Pr 30:4; Ac 2:34; Eph 4:8–10; [r]ver 31; Jn 6:38, 42; Heb 4:14; 9:24; [s]**Mt 8:20**
14 [t]Nu 21:8–9; [u]**Jn 12:32**
15 [v]ver 16,36; Ge 15:6; Nu 14:11; Mt 27:42; Mk 1:15; Jn 1:7, 12; 2:23; 5:24; 7:38; 20:29; Ac 13:39; 16:31; Ro 3:22; 10:9–10; 1Jn 5:1,5,10; [w]ver 16,36; **Mt 25:46;** Jn 20:31
16 [x]Ro 5:8; Eph 2:4; 1Jn 4:9–10; [y]Isa 9:6; Ro 8:32; [z]Ge 22:12; Jn 1:18; [a]**ver 15;** [b]ver 36; Jn 6:29,40; 11:25–26
17 [c]Jn 6:29,57; 10:36; 11:42; 17:8,21; 20:21; [d]Isa 53:11; **Mt 1:21; Lk 2:11;** 19:10; Jn 1:29; 12:47; **Ro 11:14;** 1Ti 1:15; 2:5–6; 1Jn 2:2; 3:5
18 [e]Jn 5:24; [f]Jn 1:18; 1Jn 4:9
19 [g]**Jn 1:4;** [h]Ps 52:3; Jn 7:7
20 [i]Eph 5:11,13

[b]17 Psalm 69:9 [c]23 Or *and believed in him*
[a]3 Or *born from above;* also in verse 7
[b]6 Or *but spirit* [c]7 The Greek is plural.
[d]13 Some manuscripts *Man, who is in heaven*
[e]15 Or *believes may have eternal life in him*
[f]16 Or *his only begotten Son*
[g]18 Or *God's only begotten Son*

be seen plainly that what he has done has been done through God."[h]

John the Baptist's Testimony About Jesus

22After this, Jesus and his disciples went out into the Judean countryside, where he spent some time with them, and baptised.[j] 23Now John[k] also was baptising at Aenon near Salim, because there was plenty of water, and people were constantly coming to be baptised. 24(This was before John was put in prison.)[l] 25An argument developed between some of John's disciples and a certain Jew[i] over the matter of ceremonial washing.[m] 26They came to John and said to him, "Rabbi,[n] that man who was with you on the other side of the Jordan—the one you testified[o] about—well, he is baptising, and everyone is going to him."

27To this John replied, "A man can receive only what is given him from heaven. 28You yourselves can testify that I said, 'I am not the Christ[j] but am sent ahead of him.'[p] 29The bride belongs to the bridegroom.[q] The friend who attends the bridegroom waits and listens for him, and is full of joy when he hears the bridegroom's voice. That joy is mine, and it is now complete.[r] 30He must become greater; I must become less.

31"The one who comes from above[s] is above all; the one who is from the earth belongs to the earth, and speaks as one from the earth.[t] The one who comes from heaven is above all. 32He testifies to what he has seen and heard,[u] but no-one accepts his testimony.[v] 33The man who has accepted it has certified that God is truthful. 34For the one whom God has sent[w] speaks the words of God, for God[k] gives the Spirit[x] without limit. 35The Father loves the Son and has placed everything in his hands.[y] 36Whoever believes in the Son has eternal life,[z] but whoever rejects the Son will not see life, for God's wrath remains on him."[l]

Jesus Talks With a Samaritan Woman

4 The Pharisees heard that Jesus was gaining and baptising more disciples than John,[a] 2although in fact it was not Jesus who baptised, but his disciples. 3When the Lord[b] learned of this, he left Judea[c] and went back once more to Galilee.

4Now he had to go through Samaria.[d] 5So he came to a town in Samaria called Sychar, near the plot of ground Jacob had given to his son Joseph.[e] 6Jacob's well was there, and Jesus, tired as he was from the journey, sat down by the well. It was about the sixth hour.

7When a Samaritan woman came to draw water, Jesus said to her, "Will you give me a drink?"[f] 8(His disciples had gone into the town[g] to buy food.)

9The Samaritan woman said to him, "You are a Jew and I am a Samaritan[h] woman. How can you ask me for a drink?" (For Jews do not associate with Samaritans.[a])

10Jesus answered her, "If you knew the gift of God and who it is that asks you for a drink, you would have asked him and he would have given you living water."[i]

11"Sir," the woman said, "you have nothing to draw with and the well is deep. Where can you get this living water? 12Are you greater than our father Jacob, who gave us the well[j] and drank from it himself, as did also his sons and his flocks and herds?"

13Jesus answered, "Everyone who drinks this water will be thirsty again, 14but whoever drinks the water I give him will never thirst.[k] Indeed, the water I give him will become in him a spring of water[l] welling up to eternal life."[m]

15The woman said to him, "Sir, give me this water so that I won't get thirsty[n] and have to keep coming here to draw water."

16He told her, "Go, call your husband and come back."

17"I have no husband," she replied.

Jesus said to her, "You are right when you say you have no husband. 18The fact is, you have had five husbands, and the man you now have is not your husband. What you have just said is quite true."

19"Sir," the woman said, "I can see that you are a prophet.[o] 20Our fathers worshipped on this mountain,[p] but you Jews claim that the place where we must worship is in Jerusalem."[q]

21Jesus declared, "Believe me, woman, a time is coming[r] when you will worship the Father neither on this mountain nor in Jerusalem.[s] 22You Samaritans worship what you do not know;[t] we worship what we do know,

22 [j]Jn 4:2
23 [k]**Mt 3:1**
24 [l]Mt 4:12; 14:3
25 [m]Jn 2:6
26 [n]**Mt 23:7;** [o]Jn 1:7
28 [p]Jn 1:20,23
29 [q]Mt 9:15; [r]Jn 16:24; 17:13; Php 2:2; 1Jn 1:4
31 [s]ver 13; [t]Jn 8:23; 1Jn 4:5
32 [u]Jn 8:26; 15:15; [v]ver 11
34 [w]**ver 17;** [x]Isa 42:1; Mt 12:18; Lk 4:18; Ac 10:38
35 [y]**Mt 28:18**
36 [z]**ver 15;** Jn 5:24; 6:47

Ch. 4

1 [a]Jn 3:22,26
3 [b]**Lk 7:13;** [c]Jn 3:22
4 [d]**Mt 10:5**
5 [e]Ge 33:19; Jos 24:32
7 [f]Ge 24:17; 1Ki 17:10
8 [g]ver 5,39
9 [h]**Mt 10:5**
10 [i]Isa 44:3; 55:1; Jer 2:13; 17:13; Zec 14:8; Jn 7:37–38; Rev 7:17; 21:6; 22:1,17
12 [j]ver 6
14 [k]Jn 6:35; [l]Isa 12:3; 58:11; Jn 7:38; [m]**Mt 25:46**
15 [n]Jn 6:34
19 [o]**Mt 21:11**
20 [p]Dt 11:29; Jos 8:33; [q]Lk 9:53
21 [r]Jn 5:28; 16:2; [s]Mal 1:11; 1Ti 2:8
22 [t]2Ki 17:28–41

[h]*21* Some interpreters end the quotation after verse 15.
[i]*25* Some manuscripts *and certain Jews*
[j]*28* Or *Messiah* [k]*34* Greek *he*
[l]*36* Some interpreters end the quotation after verse 30.
[a]*9* Or *do not use dishes Samaritans have used*

for salvation is from the Jews.[u] 23Yet a time is coming and has now come[v] when the true worshippers will worship the Father in spirit[w] and truth, for they are the kind of worshippers the Father seeks. 24God is spirit,[x] and his worshippers must worship in spirit and in truth."

25The woman said, "I know that Messiah" (called Christ)[y] "is coming. When he comes, he will explain everything to us."

26Then Jesus declared, "I who speak to you am he."[z]

The Disciples Rejoin Jesus

27Just then his disciples returned[a] and were surprised to find him talking with a woman. But no-one asked, "What do you want?" or "Why are you talking with her?"

28Then, leaving her water jar, the woman went back to the town and said to the people, 29"Come, see a man who told me everything I ever did.[b] Could this be the Christ[b]?"[c] 30They came out of the town and made their way towards him.

31Meanwhile his disciples urged him, "Rabbi,[d] eat something."

32But he said to them, "I have food to eat[e] that you know nothing about."

33Then his disciples said to each other, "Could someone have brought him food?"

34"My food," said Jesus, "is to do the will[f] of him who sent me and to finish his work.[g] 35Do you not say, 'Four months more and then the harvest'? I tell you, open your eyes and look at the fields! They are ripe for harvest.[h] 36Even now the reaper draws his wages, even now he harvests[i] the crop for eternal life,[j] so that the sower and the reaper may be glad together. 37Thus the saying 'One sows and another reaps'[k] is true. 38I sent you to reap what you have not worked for. Others have done the hard work, and you have reaped the benefits of their labour."

Many Samaritans Believe

39Many of the Samaritans from that town[l] believed in him because of the woman's testimony, "He told me everything I ever did."[m] 40So when the Samaritans came to him, they urged him to stay with them, and he stayed two days. 41And because of his words many more became believers.

42They said to the woman, "We no longer believe just because of what you said; now we have heard for ourselves, and we know that this man really is the Saviour of the world."[n]

Jesus Heals the Official's Son

43After the two days[o] he left for Galilee. 44(Now Jesus himself had pointed out that a prophet has no honour in his own country.)[p] 45When he arrived in Galilee, the Galileans welcomed him. They had seen all that he had done in Jerusalem at the Passover Feast,[q] for they also had been there.

46Once more he visited Cana in Galilee, where he had turned the water into wine.[r] And there was a certain royal official whose son lay sick at Capernaum. 47When this man heard that Jesus had arrived in Galilee from Judea,[s] he went to him and begged him to come and heal his son, who was close to death.

48"Unless you people see miraculous signs and wonders,"[t] Jesus told him, "you will never believe."

49The royal official said, "Sir, come down before my child dies."

50Jesus replied, "You may go. Your son will live."

The man took Jesus at his word and departed. 51While he was still on the way, his servants met him with the news that his boy was living. 52When he enquired as to the time when his son got better, they said to him, "The fever left him yesterday at the seventh hour."

53Then the father realised that this was the exact time at which Jesus had said to him, "Your son will live." So he and all his household[u] believed.

54This was the second miraculous sign[v] that Jesus performed, having come from Judea to Galilee.

The Healing at the Pool

5 Some time later, Jesus went up to Jerusalem for a feast of the Jews. 2Now there is in Jerusalem near the Sheep Gate[a] a pool, which in Aramaic[b] is called Bethesda[a] and which is surrounded by five covered colonnades. 3Here a great number of disabled people used to lie—the blind, the lame, the paralysed.[b] 5One who was there had

22 [u]Isa 2:3; Ro 3:1–2; 9:4–5; 15:8–9
23 [v]Jn 5:25; 16:32; [w]Php 3:3
24 [x]Php 3:3
25 [y]Mt 1:16; Jn 1:41
26 [z]Jn 8:24; 9:35–37
27 [a]ver 8
29 [b]ver 17–18; [c]Mt 12:23; Jn 7:26,31
31 [d]**Mt 23:7**
32 [e]Job 23:12; Mt 4:4; Jn 6:27
34 [f]**Mt 26:39;** [g]**Jn 19:30**
35 [h]Mt 9:37; Lk 10:2
36 [i]Ro 1:13; [j]**Mt 25:46**
37 [k]Job 31:8; Mic 6:15
39 [l]ver 5; [m]ver 29
42 [n]**Lk 2:11**
43 [o]ver 40
44 [p]Mt 13:57; Lk 4:24
45 [q]Jn 2:23
46 [r]Jn 2:1–11
47 [s]ver 3,54
48 [t]Da 4:2–3; **Jn 2:11;** Ac 2:43; 14:3; Ro 15:19; 2Co 12:12; Heb 2:4
53 [u]**Ac 11:14**
54 [v]**ver 48; Jn 2:11**

Ch. 5

2 [a]Ne 3:1; 12:39; [b]Jn 19:13,17,20; 20:16; Ac 21:40; 22:2; 26:14

b29 Or *Messiah*

a2 Some manuscripts *Bethzatha;* other manuscripts *Bethsaida*

b3 Some less important manuscripts *paralysed—and they waited for the moving of the waters.* [4]*From time to time an angel of the Lord would come down and stir up the waters. The first one into the pool after each such disturbance would be cured of whatever disease he had.*

been an invalid for thirty-eight years.
6When Jesus saw him lying there and
learned that he had been in this condi-
tion for a long time, he asked him, "Do
you want to get well?"
7"Sir," the invalid replied, "I have
no-one to help me into the pool when
the water is stirred. While I am trying to
get in, someone else goes down ahead
of me."
8Then Jesus said to him, "Get up! Pick
up your mat and walk."[c] 9At once the
man was cured; he picked up his mat
and walked.
The day on which this took place was
a Sabbath,[d] 10and so the Jews[e] said to the
man who had been healed, "It is the
Sabbath; the law forbids you to carry
your mat."[f]
11But he replied, "The man who made
me well said to me, 'Pick up your mat
and walk.'"
12So they asked him, "Who is this
fellow who told you to pick it up and
walk?"
13The man who was healed had no
idea who it was, for Jesus had slipped
away into the crowd that was there.
14Later Jesus found him at the temple
and said to him, "See, you are well
again. Stop sinning[g] or something
worse may happen to you." 15The man
went away and told the Jews[h] that it was
Jesus who had made him well.

Life Through the Son

16So, because Jesus was doing these
things on the Sabbath, the Jews perse-
cuted him. 17Jesus said to them, "My
Father[i] is always at his work[j] to this very
day, and I, too, am working." 18For this
reason the Jews tried all the harder to
kill him;[k] not only was he breaking the
Sabbath, but he was even calling God
his own Father, making himself equal
with God.[l]
19Jesus gave them this answer: "I tell
you the truth, the Son can do nothing by
himself;[m] he can do only what he sees
his Father doing, because whatever the
Father does the Son also does. 20For the
Father loves the Son[n] and shows him all
he does. Yes, to your amazement he will
show him even greater things than
these.[o] 21For just as the Father raises the
dead and gives them life,[p] even so the
Son gives life[q] to whom he is pleased to
give it. 22Moreover, the Father judges
no-one, but has entrusted all judgment
to the Son,[r] 23that all may honour the
Son just as they honour the Father. He
who does not honour the Son does not
honour the Father, who sent him.[s]
24"I tell you the truth, whoever hears
my word and believes him who sent me[t]
has eternal life[u] and will not be con-
demned;[v] he has crossed over from
death to life.[w] 25I tell you the truth, a
time is coming and has now come[x]
when the dead will hear[y] the voice of the
Son of God and those who hear will live.
26For as the Father has life in himself, so
he has granted the Son to have life[z] in
himself. 27And he has given him author-
ity to judge[a] because he is the Son of
Man.
28"Do not be amazed at this, for a time
is coming[b] when all who are in their
graves will hear his voice 29and come
out—those who have done good will
rise to live, and those who have done
evil will rise to be condemned.[c] 30By
myself I can do nothing;[d] I judge only as
I hear, and my judgment is just,[e] for I
seek not to please myself but him who
sent me.[f]

Testimonies About Jesus

31"If I testify about myself, my testi-
mony is not valid.[g] 32There is another
who testifies in my favour,[h] and I know
that his testimony about me is valid.
33"You have sent to John and he has
testified[i] to the truth. 34Not that I accept
human testimony;[j] but I mention it that
you may be saved.[k] 35John was a lamp
that burned and gave light,[l] and you
chose for a time to enjoy his light.
36"I have testimony weightier than
that of John.[m] For the very work that the
Father has given me to finish, and
which I am doing,[n] testifies that the
Father has sent me.[o] 37And the Father
who sent me has himself testified con-
cerning me.[p] You have never heard his
voice nor seen his form,[q] 38nor does his
word dwell in you,[r] for you do not be-
lieve[s] the one he sent.[t] 39You diligently
study[c] the Scriptures[u] because you
think that by them you possess eternal
life.[v] These are the Scriptures that testify
about me,[w] 40yet you refuse to come to
me[x] to have life.
41"I do not accept praise from men,[y]
42but I know you. I know that you do not
have the love of God in your hearts. 43I
have come in my Father's name, and
you do not accept me; but if someone
else comes in his own name, you will
accept him. 44How can you believe if
you accept praise from one another, yet
make no effort to obtain the praise that
comes from the only God?[d] [z]

8 [c]Mt 9:5–6
9 [d]Mt 12:1–14; Jn 9:14
10 [e]ver 16; [f]Ne 13:15–22; Jer 17:21; **Mt 12:2**
14 [g]Mk 2:5; Jn 8:11
15 [h]**Jn 1:19**
17 [i]Lk 2:49; [j]Jn 9:4; 14:10
18 [k]**Mt 12:14**; [l]Jn 10:30,33; 19:7
19 [m]ver 30; **Jn 14:24**
20 [n]Jn 3:35; [o]Jn 14:12
21 [p]Ro 4:17; 8:11; 2Co 1:9; Heb 11:19; [q]Jn 11:25
22 [r]ver 27; Ge 18:25; Jdg 11:27; Jn 9:39; **Ac 10:42**
23 [s]Lk 10:16; **1Jn 2:23**
24 [t]**Mt 10:40; Jn 3:15,17;** [u]**Mt 25:46;** [v]Jn 3:18; [w]1Jn 3:14
25 [x]Jn 4:23; 16:32; [y]Jn 8:43,47
26 [z]Dt 30:20; Job 10:12; 33:4; Ps 36:9; **Jn 1:4**
27 [a]**ver 22**
28 [b]Jn 4:21; 16:2
29 [c]**Mt 25:46**
30 [d]ver 19; [e]Isa 28:6; Jn 8:16; [f]**Mt 26:39**
31 [g]Jn 8:14
32 [h]ver 37; Jn 8:18
33 [i]**Jn 1:7**
34 [j]1Jn 5:9; [k]Ac 16:30–31; Eph 2:8; Tit 3:5
35 [l]Da 12:3; 2Pe 1:19
36 [m]1Jn 5:9; [n]Jn 14:11; 15:24; [o]**Jn 3:17**
37 [p]Jn 8:18; [q]Dt 4:12; 1Ti 1:17; **Jn 1:18**
38 [r]1Jn 1:10; 2:14; [s]Isa 26:10; [t]**Jn 3:17**
39 [u]Ro 2:17–18; [v]**Mt 25:46;** [w]**Lk 24:27,44;** Ac 13:27
40 [x]Jn 6:44
41 [y]ver 44
44 [z]**Ro 2:29**

---

c39 Or *Study diligently* (the imperative)
d44 Some early manuscripts *the Only One*

45"But do not think I will accuse you
before the Father. Your accuser is
Moses,[a] on whom your hopes are set.[b]
46If you believed Moses, you would
believe me, for he wrote about me.[c]
47But since you do not believe what he
wrote, how are you going to believe
what I say?"[d]

Jesus Feeds the Five Thousand

6:1–13pp—Mt 14:13–21; Mk 6:32–44; Lk 9:10–17

6 Some time after this, Jesus crossed
to the far shore of the Sea of Galilee
(that is, the Sea of Tiberias), 2and a great
crowd of people followed him because
they saw the miraculous signs[a] he had
performed on the sick. 3Then Jesus
went up on a mountainside[b] and sat
down with his disciples. 4The Jewish
Passover Feast[c] was near.

5When Jesus looked up and saw a
great crowd coming towards him, he
said to Philip,[d] "Where shall we buy
bread for these people to eat?" 6He
asked this only to test him, for he
already had in mind what he was going
to do.

7Philip answered him, "Eight
months' wages[a] would not buy enough
bread for each one to have a bite!"

8Another of his disciples, Andrew,
Simon Peter's brother,[e] spoke up,
9"Here is a boy with five small barley
loaves and two small fish, but how far
will they go among so many?"[f]

10Jesus said, "Make the people sit
down." There was plenty of grass in
that place, and the men sat down, about
five thousand of them. 11Jesus then took
the loaves, gave thanks,[g] and distri-
buted to those who were seated as
much as they wanted. He did the same
with the fish.

12When they had all had enough to
eat, he said to his disciples, "Gather the
pieces that are left over. Let nothing be
wasted." 13So they gathered them and
filled twelve baskets with the pieces of
the five barley loaves left over by those
who had eaten.

14After the people saw the miraculous
sign[h] that Jesus did, they began to say,
"Surely this is the Prophet who is to
come into the world."[i] 15Jesus, knowing
that they intended to come and make
him king[j] by force, withdrew again to a
mountain by himself.[k]

Jesus Walks on the Water

6:16–21pp—Mt 14:22–33; Mk 6:47–51

16When evening came, his disciples
went down to the lake, 17where they got
into a boat and set off across the lake for
Capernaum. By now it was dark, and
Jesus had not yet joined them. 18A
strong wind was blowing and the
waters grew rough. 19When they had
rowed three or three and a half miles,[b]
they saw Jesus approaching the boat,
walking on the water;[l] and they were
terrified. 20But he said to them, "It is I;
don't be afraid."[m] 21Then they were
willing to take him into the boat, and
immediately the boat reached the shore
where they were heading.

22The next day the crowd that had
stayed on the opposite shore of the lake[n]
realised that only one boat had been
there, and that Jesus had not entered it
with his disciples, but that they had
gone away alone.[o] 23Then some boats
from Tiberias[p] landed near the place
where the people had eaten the bread
after the Lord had given thanks.[q] 24Once
the crowd realised that neither Jesus nor
his disciples were there, they got into
the boats and went to Capernaum in
search of Jesus.

Jesus the Bread of Life

25When they found him on the other
side of the lake, they asked him,
"Rabbi,[r] when did you get here?"

26Jesus answered, "I tell you the
truth, you are looking for me,[s] not be-
cause you saw miraculous signs[t] but
because you ate the loaves and had your
fill. 27Do not work for food that spoils,
but for food that endures[u] to eternal
life,[v] which the Son of Man[w] will give
you. On him God the Father has placed
his seal[x] of approval."

28Then they asked him, "What must
we do to do the works God requires?"

29Jesus answered, "The work of God
is this: to believe[y] in the one he has
sent."[z]

30So they asked him, "What miracu-
lous sign[a] then will you give that we
may see it and believe you?[b] What will
you do? 31Our forefathers ate the man-
na[c] in the desert; as it is written: 'He
gave them bread from heaven to eat.'[c]"[d]

32Jesus said to them, "I tell you the
truth, it is not Moses who has given you
the bread from heaven, but it is my
Father who gives you the true bread
from heaven. 33For the bread of God is
he who comes down from heaven[e] and
gives life to the world."

45 [a]Jn 9:28; [b]Ro 2:17
46 [c]Ge 3:15; **Lk 24:27**,44; Ac 26:22
47 [d]Lk 16:29,31

Ch. 6

2 [a]**Jn 2:11**
3 [b]ver 15
4 [c]**Jn 11:55**
5 [d]**Jn 1:43**
8 [e]Jn 1:40
9 [f]2Ki 4:43
11 [g]ver 23; **Mt 14:19**
14 [h]**Jn 2:11**; [i]Dt 18:15,18; Mt 11:3; **21:11**
15 [j]Jn 18:36; [k]Mt 14:23; Mk 6:46
19 [l]Job 9:8
20 [m]**Mt 14:27**
22 [n]ver 2; [o]ver 15–21
23 [p]ver 1; [q]ver 11
25 [r]**Mt 23:7**
26 [s]ver 24; [t]ver 30; **Jn 2:11**
27 [u]Isa 55:2; [v]ver 54; **Mt 25:46**; [w]**Mt 8:20**; [x]Ro 4:11; 1Co 9:2; 2Co 1:22; Eph 1:13; 4:30; 2Ti 2:19; Rev 7:3
29 [y]1Jn 3:23; [z]**Jn 3:17**
30 [a]**Jn 2:11**; [b]**Mt 12:38**
31 [c]Nu 11:7–9; [d]Ex 16:4,15; Ne 9:15; Ps 78:24; 105:40
33 [e]ver 50; Jn 3:13,31

[a]*7* Greek *two hundred denarii*
[b]*19* Greek *rowed twenty-five or thirty stadia* (about 5 or 6 kilometres)
[c]*31* Exodus 16:4; Neh. 9:15; Psalm 78:24,25

34“Sir,” they said, “from now on give us this bread.”[f]

35Then Jesus declared, “I am[g] the bread of life.[h] He who comes to me will never go hungry, and he who believes[i] in me will never be thirsty.[j] 36But as I told you, you have seen me and still you do not believe. 37All that the Father gives me[k] will come to me, and whoever comes to me I will never drive away. 38For I have come down from heaven[l] not to do my will but to do the will[m] of him who sent me.[n] 39And this is the will of him who sent me, that I shall lose none of all that he has given me,[o] but raise them up at the last day.[p] 40For my Father’s will is that everyone who looks to the Son[q] and believes in him shall have eternal life,[r] and I will raise him up at the last day.”

41At this the Jews began to grumble about him because he said, “I am the bread that came down from heaven.” 42They said, “Is this not Jesus, the son of Joseph,[s] whose father and mother we know?[t] How can he now say, ‘I came down from heaven’?”[u]

43“Stop grumbling among yourselves,” Jesus answered. 44“No-one can come to me unless the Father who sent me draws him,[v] and I will raise him up at the last day. 45It is written in the Prophets: ‘They will all be taught by God.’[d][w] Everyone who listens to the Father and learns from him comes to me. 46No-one has seen the Father except the one who is from God;[x] only he has seen the Father. 47I tell you the truth, he who believes has everlasting life.[y] 48I am the bread of life.[z] 49Your forefathers ate the manna in the desert, yet they died.[a] 50But here is the bread that comes down from heaven,[b] which a man may eat and not die. 51I am the living bread[c] that came down from heaven.[d] If anyone eats of this bread, he will live for ever. This bread is my flesh, which I will give for the life of the world.”[e]

52Then the Jews[f] began to argue sharply among themselves,[g] “How can this man give us his flesh to eat?”

53Jesus said to them, “I tell you the truth, unless you can eat the flesh[h] of the Son of Man[i] and drink his blood,[j] you have no life in you. 54Whoever eats my flesh and drinks my blood has eternal life, and I will raise him up at the last day.[k] 55For my flesh is real food and my blood is real drink. 56Whoever eats my flesh and drinks my blood remains in me, and I in him.[l] 57Just as the living Father sent me[m] and I live because of the Father, so the one who feeds on me will live because of me. 58This is the bread that came down from heaven. Your forefathers ate manna and died, but he who feeds on this bread will live for ever.”[n] 59He said this while teaching in the synagogue in Capernaum.

Many Disciples Desert Jesus

60On hearing it, many of his disciples[o] said, “This is a hard teaching. Who can accept it?”[p]

61Aware that his disciples were grumbling about this, Jesus said to them, “Does this offend you?[q] 62What if you see the Son of Man[r] ascend to where he was before![s] 63The Spirit gives life;[t] the flesh counts for nothing. The words I have spoken to you are spirit[e] and they are life. 64Yet there are some of you who do not believe.” For Jesus had known[u] from the beginning which of them did not believe and who would betray him.[v] 65He went on to say, “This is why I told you that no-one can come to me unless the Father has enabled him.”[w]

66From this time many of his disciples[x] turned back and no longer followed him.

67“You do not want to leave too, do you?” Jesus asked the Twelve.[y]

68Simon Peter answered him,[z] “Lord, to whom shall we go? You have the words of eternal life.[a] 69We believe and know that you are the Holy One of God.”[b]

70Then Jesus replied, “Have I not chosen you,[c] the Twelve? Yet one of you is a devil!”[d] 71(He meant Judas, the son of Simon Iscariot,[e] who, though one of the Twelve, was later to betray him.)[f]

Jesus Goes to the Feast of Tabernacles

7 After this, Jesus went around in Galilee, purposely staying away from Judea because the Jews[a] there were waiting to take his life.[b] 2But when the Jewish Feast of Tabernacles[c] was near, 3Jesus’ brothers[d] said to him, “You ought to leave here and go to Judea, so that your disciples may see the miracles you do. 4No-one who wants to become a public figure acts in secret. Since you are doing these things, show yourself to the world.” 5For even his own brothers did not believe in him.[e]

6Therefore Jesus told them, “The

34 [f]Jn 4:15
35 [g]Ex 3:14; Jn 8:12; 10:7,11; 11:25; 14:6; 15:1; [h]ver 48, 51; [i]**Jn 3:15**; [j]Jn 4:14
37 [k]ver 39; Jn 17:2,6,9,24
38 [l]Jn 3:13,31; [m]**Mt 26:39**; [n]**Jn 3:17**
39 [o]Isa 27:3; Jer 23:4; Jn 10:28; 17:12; 18:9; [p]ver 40,44,54
40 [q]Jn 12:45; [r]**Mt 25:46**
42 [s]Lk 4:22; [t]Jn 7:27–28; [u]ver 38,62
44 [v]ver 65; Jer 31:3; Jn 12:32
45 [w]Isa 54:13; Jer 31:33–34; 1Co 2:13; 1Th 4:9; Heb 8:10–11; 10:16; 1Jn 2:27
46 [x]**Jn 1:18**; 5:37; 7:29
47 [y]**Mt 25:46**
48 [z]ver 35,51
49 [a]ver 31,58
50 [b]ver 33
51 [c]ver 35,48; [d]ver 41,58; [e]Heb 10:10
52 [f]**Jn 1:19**; [g]Jn 7:43; 9:16; 10:19
53 [h]Mt 26:26; [i]**Mt 8:20**; [j]Mt 26:28
54 [k]ver 39
56 [l]Jn 15:4–7; 1Jn 2:24; 3:24; 4:15
57 [m]**Jn 3:17**
58 [n]ver 49–51; Jn 3:36; 5:24
60 [o]ver 66; [p]ver 52
61 [q]Mt 13:57
62 [r]**Mt 8:20**; [s]**Mk 16:19; Jn 3:13**; 17:5
63 [t]2Co 3:6
64 [u]**Jn 2:25**; [v]**Mt 10:4**
65 [w]ver 37,44; **Mt 13:11**
66 [x]ver 60
67 [y]Mt 10:2
68 [z]Mt 16:16; [a]ver 63; **Mt 25:46**
69 [b]**Mk 1:24**; 8:29; Lk 9:20
70 [c]Jn 15:16,19; [d]Jn 13:27; 17:12
71 [e]**Mt 26:14**; [f]**Mt 10:4**

Ch. 7

1 [a]**Jn 1:19**; [b]ver 19,25; **Mt 12:14**
2 [c]Lev 23:34; Dt 16:16
3 [d]**Mt 12:46**
5 [e]Ps 69:8; Mk 3:21

d45 Isaiah 54:13 e63 Or *Spirit*

right time[f] for me has not yet come; for you any time is right. 7The world cannot hate you, but it hates me[g] because I testify that what it does is evil.[h] 8You go to the Feast. I am not yet[a] going up to this Feast, because for me the right time[i] has not yet come." 9Having said this, he stayed in Galilee.

10However, after his brothers had left for the Feast, he went also, not publicly, but in secret. 11Now at the Feast the Jews were watching for him[j] and asking, "Where is that man?"

12Among the crowds there was widespread whispering about him. Some said, "He is a good man."

Others replied, "No, he deceives the people."[k] 13But no-one would say anything publicly about him for fear of the Jews.[l]

Jesus Teaches at the Feast

14Not until halfway through the Feast did Jesus go up to the temple courts and begin to teach.[m] 15The Jews[n] were amazed and asked, "How did this man get such learning[o] without having studied?"[p]

16Jesus answered, "My teaching is not my own. It comes from him who sent me.[q] 17If anyone chooses to do God's will, he will find out[r] whether my teaching comes from God or whether I speak on my own. 18He who speaks on his own does so to gain honour for himself,[s] but he who works for the honour of the one who sent him is a man of truth; there is nothing false about him. 19Has not Moses given you the law?[t] Yet not one of you keeps the law. Why are you trying to kill me?"[u]

20"You are demon-possessed,"[v] the crowd answered. "Who is trying to kill you?"

21Jesus said to them, "I did one miracle,[w] and you are all astonished. 22Yet, because Moses gave you circumcision[x] (though actually it did not come from Moses, but from the patriarchs),[y] you circumcise a child on the Sabbath. 23Now if a child can be circumcised on the Sabbath so that the law of Moses may not be broken, why are you angry with me for healing the whole man on the Sabbath? 24Stop judging by mere appearances, and make a right judgment."[z]

Is Jesus the Christ?

25At that point some of the people of Jerusalem began to ask, "Isn't this the man they are trying to kill?[a] 26Here he is, speaking publicly, and they are not saying a word to him. Have the authorities[b] really concluded that he is the Christ?[b][c] 27But we know where this man is from;[d] when the Christ comes, no-one will know where he is from."

28Then Jesus, still teaching in the temple courts,[e] cried out, "Yes, you know me, and you know where I am from.[f] I am not here on my own, but he who sent me is true.[g] You do not know him, 29but I know him[h] because I am from him and he sent me."[i]

30At this they tried to seize him, but no-one laid a hand on him,[j] because his time had not yet come.[k] 31Still, many in the crowd put their faith in him.[l] They said, "When the Christ comes, will he do more miraculous signs[m] than this man?"

32The Pharisees heard the crowd whispering such things about him. Then the chief priests and the Pharisees sent temple guards to arrest him.

33Jesus said, "I am with you for only a short time,[n] and then I go to the one who sent me.[o] 34You will look for me, but you will not find me; and where I am, you cannot come."[p]

35The Jews said to one another, "Where does this man intend to go that we cannot find him? Will he go where our people live scattered[q] among the Greeks,[r] and teach the Greeks? 36What did he mean when he said, 'You will look for me, but you will not find me,' and 'Where I am, you cannot come'?"[s]

37On the last and greatest day of the Feast,[t] Jesus stood and said in a loud voice, "If anyone is thirsty, let him come to me and drink.[u] 38Whoever believes[v] in me, as[c] the Scripture has said,[w] streams of living water[x] will flow from within him."[y] 39By this he meant the Spirit,[z] whom those who believed in him were later to receive.[a] Up to that time the Spirit had not been given, since Jesus had not yet been glorified.[b]

40On hearing his words, some of the people said, "Surely this man is the Prophet."[c]

41Others said, "He is the Christ."

Still others asked, "How can the Christ come from Galilee?[d] 42Does not the Scripture say that the Christ will come from David's family[d][e] and from Bethlehem,[f] the town where David

6 [f]**Mt 26:18**
7 [g]Jn 15:18–19; [h]Jn 3:19–20
8 [i]ver 6; **Mt 26:18**
11 [j]Jn 11:56
12 [k]ver 40,43
13 [l]Jn 9:22; 12:42; 19:38; 20:19
14 [m]ver 28; **Mt 26:55**
15 [n]**Jn 1:19;** [o]Ac 26:24; [p]Mt 13:54
16 [q]**Jn 14:24**
17 [r]Ps 25:14
18 [s]Jn 5:41; 8:50,54
19 [t]Dt 32:46; Jn 1:17; [u]ver 1; **Mt 12:14**
20 [v]**Mk 3:22**
21 [w]ver 23; Jn 5:2–9
22 [x]Lev 12:3; [y]Ge 17:10–14
24 [z]1Sa 16:7; Isa 11:3–4; Jn 8:15; 2Co 10:7
25 [a]ver 1; **Mt 12:14**
26 [b]ver 48; [c]Jn 4:29
27 [d]Mt 13:55; Lk 4:22; Jn 6:42
28 [e]ver 14; [f]Jn 8:14; [g]Jn 8:26,42
29 [h]**Mt 11:27;** [i]**Jn 3:17**
30 [j]ver 32,44; Jn 10:39; [k]**Mt 26:18**
31 [l]Jn 8:30; 10:42; 11:45; 12:11,42; [m]**Jn 2:11**
33 [n]Jn 12:35; 13:33; 16:16; [o]Jn 16:5,10, 17,28
34 [p]ver 36; Jn 8:21; 13:33
35 [q]**Jas 1:1;** [r]Jn 12:20; Ac 17:4; 18:4
36 [s]ver 34
37 [t]Lev 23:36; [u]Isa 55:1; Rev 22:17
38 [v]**Jn 3:15;** [w]Isa 58:11; [x]**Jn 4:10;** [y]**Jn 4:14**
39 [z]Joel 2:28; Jn 1:33; Ac 2:17, 33; [a]**Jn 20:22;** [b]Jn 12:23; 13:31–32
40 [c]**Mt 21:11**
41 [d]ver 52; Jn 1:46
42 [e]**Mt 1:1;** [f]Mic 5:2; Mt 2:5–6; Lk 2:4

a8 Some early manuscripts do not have *yet*.
b26 Or *Messiah;* also in verses 27, 31, 41 and 42
c37,38 Or *If anyone is thirsty, let him come to me. / And let him drink, 38who believes in me. / As*
d42 Greek *seed*

lived?" 43Thus the people were divided[g]
because of Jesus. 44Some wanted to
seize him, but no-one laid a hand on
him.[h]

Unbelief of the Jewish Leaders

45Finally the temple guards went back
to the chief priests and Pharisees, who
asked them, "Why didn't you bring him
in?"
46"No-one ever spoke the way this
man does,"[i] the guards declared.
47"You mean he has deceived you
also?"[j] the Pharisees retorted. 48"Has
any of the rulers or of the Pharisees
believed in him?[k] 49No! But this mob
that knows nothing of the law—there is
a curse on them."
50Nicodemus,[l] who had gone to Jesus
earlier and who was one of their own
number, asked, 51"Does our law con-
demn a man without first hearing him
to find out what he is doing?"
52They replied, "Are you from
Galilee, too? Look into it, and you will
find that a prophet[e] does not come out
of Galilee."[m]

[The earliest manuscripts and other ancient witnesses do not have John 7:53–8:11]

53Then each went to his own home.
8 But Jesus went to the Mount of
Olives.[a] 2At dawn he appeared
again in the temple courts, where all the
people gathered round him, and he sat
down to teach them.[b] 3The teachers of
the law and the Pharisees brought in a
woman caught in adultery. They made
her stand before the group 4and said to
Jesus, "Teacher, this woman was
caught in the act of adultery. 5In the Law
Moses commanded us to stone such
women.[c] Now what do you say?" 6They
were using this question as a trap,[d] in
order to have a basis for accusing him.[e]
But Jesus bent down and started to
write on the ground with his finger.
7When they kept on questioning him,
he straightened up and said to them, "If
any one of you is without sin, let him be
the first to throw a stone[f] at her."[g]
8Again he stooped down and wrote on
the ground.
9At this, those who heard began to go
away one at a time, the older ones first,
until only Jesus was left, with the
woman still standing there. 10Jesus
straightened up and asked her,
"Woman, where are they? Has no-one
condemned you?"

43 [g]Jn 6:52; 9:16; 10:19
44 [h]ver 30
46 [i]**Mt 7:28**
47 [j]ver 12
48 [k]Jn 12:42
50 [l]Jn 3:1; 19:39
52 [m]ver 41

Ch. 8

1 [a]**Mt 21:1**
2 [b]ver 20; **Mt 26:55**
5 [c]Lev 20:10; Dt 22:22; Job 31:11
6 [d]Mt 22:15,18; [e]**Mt 12:10**
7 [f]Dt 17:7; Eze 16:40; [g]Ro 2:1,22
11 [h]Jn 3:17; [i]Jn 5:14
12 [j]**Jn 6:35**; [k]**Jn 1:4**; [l]Pr 4:18; Mt 5:14
13 [m]Jn 5:31
14 [n]Jn 13:3; 16:28; [o]Jn 7:28; 9:29
15 [p]**Jn 7:24**; [q]Jn 3:17
16 [r]Jn 5:30
17 [s]**Mt 18:16**
18 [t]Jn 5:37
19 [u]Jn 16:3; [v]**1Jn 2:23**
20 [w]**Mt 26:55**; [x]Mk 12:41; [y]**Mt 26:18**
21 [z]Eze 3:18; [a]Jn 7:34; 13:33
23 [b]Jn 3:31; 17:14
24 [c]Jn 4:26; 13:19

11"No-one, sir," she said.
"Then neither do I condemn you,"[h]
Jesus declared. "Go now and leave your
life of sin."[i]

The Validity of Jesus' Testimony

12When Jesus spoke again to the
people, he said, "I am[j] the light of the
world.[k] Whoever follows me will never
walk in darkness, but will have the light
of life."[l]
13The Pharisees challenged him,
"Here you are, appearing as your own
witness; your testimony is not valid."[m]
14Jesus answered, "Even if I testify on
my own behalf, my testimony is valid,
for I know where I came from and
where I am going.[n] But you have no idea
where I come from[o] or where I am
going. 15You judge by human stan-
dards;[p] I pass judgment on no-one.[q]
16But if I do judge, my decisions are
right, because I am not alone. I stand
with the Father, who sent me.[r] 17In your
own Law it is written that the testimony
of two men is valid.[s] 18I am one who
testifies for myself; my other witness is
the Father, who sent me."[t]
19Then they asked him, "Where is
your father?"
"You do not know me or my
Father,"[u] Jesus replied. "If you knew
me, you would know my Father also."[v]
20He spoke these words while teaching[w]
in the temple area near the place where
the offerings were put.[x] Yet no-one
seized him, because his time had not yet
come.[y]
21Once more Jesus said to them, "I am
going away, and you will look for me,
and you will die[z] in your sin. Where I
go, you cannot come."[a]
22This made the Jews ask, "Will he kill
himself? Is that why he says, 'Where I
go, you cannot come'?"
23But he continued, "You are from
below; I am from above. You are of this
world; I am not of this world.[b] 24I told
you that you would die in your sins; if
you do not believe that I am ⌞the one I
claim to be⌟,[a][c] you will indeed die in
your sins."
25"Who are you?" they asked.
"Just what I have been claiming all
along," Jesus replied. 26"I have much to
say in judgment of you. But he who sent

[e]52 Two early manuscripts *the Prophet*
[a]24 Or *I am he*; also in verse 28

me is reliable,[d] and what I have heard from him I tell the world."[e]

27They did not understand that he was telling them about his Father. 28So Jesus said, "When you have lifted up the Son of Man,[f] then you will know that I am ⌞the one I claim to be⌟ and that I do nothing on my own but speak just what the Father has taught me.[g] 29The one who sent me is with me; he has not left me alone,[h] for I always do what pleases him."[i] 30Even as he spoke, many put their faith in him.[j]

The Children of Abraham

31To the Jews who had believed him, Jesus said, "If you hold to my teaching,[k] you are really my disciples. 32Then you will know the truth, and the truth will set you free."[l]

33They answered him, "We are Abraham's descendants[b][m] and have never been slaves of anyone. How can you say that we shall be set free?"

34Jesus replied, "I tell you the truth, everyone who sins is a slave to sin.[n] 35Now a slave has no permanent place in the family, but a son belongs to it for ever.[o] 36So if the Son sets you free,[p] you will be free indeed. 37I know you are Abraham's descendants. Yet you are ready to kill me,[q] because you have no room for my word. 38I am telling you what I have seen in the Father's presence,[r] and you do what you have heard from your father."[c][s]

39"Abraham is our father," they answered.

"If you were Abraham's children,"[t] said Jesus, "then you would[d] do the things Abraham did. 40As it is, you are determined to kill me,[u] a man who has told you the truth that I heard from God.[v] Abraham did not do such things. 41You are doing the things your own father does."[w]

"We are not illegitimate children," they protested. "The only Father we have is God himself."[x]

The Children of the Devil

42Jesus said to them, "If God were your Father, you would love me,[y] for I came from God[z] and now am here. I have not come on my own;[a] but he sent me.[b] 43Why is my language not clear to you? Because you are unable to hear what I say. 44You belong to your father, the devil,[c] and you want to carry out your father's desire.[d] He was a murderer from the beginning, not holding to the truth, for there is no truth in him. When he lies, he speaks his native language, for he is a liar and the father of lies.[e] 45Yet because I tell the truth,[f] you do not believe me! 46Can any of you prove me guilty of sin? If I am telling the truth, why don't you believe me? 47He who belongs to God hears what God says.[g] The reason you do not hear is that you do not belong to God."

The Claims of Jesus About Himself

48The Jews answered him, "Aren't we right in saying that you are a Samaritan[h] and demon-possessed?"[i]

49"I am not possessed by a demon," said Jesus, "but I honour my Father and you dishonour me. 50I am not seeking glory for myself;[j] but there is one who seeks it, and he is the judge. 51I tell you the truth, if anyone keeps my word, he will never see death."[k]

52At this the Jews exclaimed, "Now we know that you are demon-possessed![l] Abraham died and so did the prophets, yet you say that if anyone keeps your word, he will never taste death. 53Are you greater than our father Abraham?[m] He died, and so did the prophets. Who do you think you are?"

54Jesus replied, "If I glorify myself,[n] my glory means nothing. My Father, whom you claim as your God, is the one who glorifies me.[o] 55Though you do not know him,[p] I know him.[q] If I said I did not, I would be a liar like you, but I do know him and keep his word.[r] 56Your father Abraham[s] rejoiced at the thought of seeing my day; he saw it[t] and was glad."

57"You are not yet fifty years old," the Jews said to him, "and you have seen Abraham!"

58"I tell you the truth," Jesus answered, "before Abraham was born,[u] I am!"[v] 59At this, they picked up stones to stone him,[w] but Jesus hid himself,[x] slipping away from the temple grounds.

Jesus Heals a Man Born Blind

9 As he went along, he saw a man blind from birth. 2His disciples asked him, "Rabbi,[a] who sinned,[b] this man[c] or his parents,[d] that he was born blind?"

26 [d]Jn 7:28; [e]Jn 3:32; 15:15
28 [f]**Jn 12:32;** [g]**Jn 14:24**
29 [h]ver 16; Jn 16:32; [i]Isa 50:5; Jn 4:34; 5:30; 6:38
30 [j]**Jn 7:31**
31 [k]Jn 15:7; 2Jn 9
32 [l]ver 36; Ro 8:2; 2Co 3:17; Gal 5:1,13
33 [m]ver 37,39; **Lk 3:8**
34 [n]**Ro 6:16**
35 [o]Gal 4:30
36 [p]ver 32
37 [q]ver 39–40
38 [r]Jn 5:19,30; 14:10,24; [s]ver 41,44
39 [t]ver 37; **Lk 3:8**
40 [u]**Mt 12:14;** [v]ver 26
41 [w]ver 38,44; [x]Isa 63:16; 64:8
42 [y]1Jn 5:1; [z]**Jn 13:3;** [a]Jn 7:28; [b]**Jn 3:17**
44 [c]1Jn 3:8; [d]ver 38,41; [e]Ge 3:4; 4:9; 2Ch 18:21; Ps 5:6; 12:2
45 [f]Jn 18:37
47 [g]Jn 18:37; 1Jn 4:6
48 [h]**Mt 10:5;** [i]ver 52; **Mk 3:22**
50 [j]ver 54; Jn 5:41
51 [k]Jn 11:26
52 [l]ver 48; **Mk 3:22**
53 [m]ver 39; Jn 4:12
54 [n]ver 50; [o]Jn 16:14; 17:1,5
55 [p]ver 19; [q]Jn 7:28–29; [r]Jn 15:10
56 [s]ver 37,39; Ge 18:18; [t]**Mt 13:17**
58 [u]**Jn 1:2;** [v]Ex 3:14; 6:3
59 [w]Ex 17:4; Lev 24:16; 1Sa 30:6; Jn 10:31; 11:8; [x]Jn 12:36

Ch. 9

2 [a]**Mt 23:7;** [b]ver 34; Lk 13:2; Ac 28:4; [c]Eze 18:20; [d]Ex 20:5; Job 21:19

[b]33 Greek *seed;* also in verse 37
[c]38 Or *presence. Therefore do what you have heard from the Father.*
[d]39 Some early manuscripts *"If you are Abraham's children," said Jesus, "then*

3"Neither this man nor his parents
sinned," said Jesus, "but this hap-
pened so that the work of God might be
displayed in his life.[e] 4As long as it is
day,[f] we must do the work of him who
sent me. Night is coming, when no-one
can work. 5While I am in the world, I am
the light of the world."[g]
6Having said this, he spat[h] on the
ground, made some mud with the sal-
iva, and put it on the man's eyes. 7"Go,"
he told him, "wash in the Pool of
Siloam"[i] (this word means Sent). So the
man went and washed, and came home
seeing.[j]
8His neighbours and those who had
formerly seen him begging asked, "Isn't
this the same man who used to sit and
beg?"[k] 9Some claimed that he was.
Others said, "No, he only looks like
him."
But he himself insisted, "I am the
man."
10"How then were your eyes
opened?" they demanded.
11He replied, "The man they call Jesus
made some mud and put it on my eyes.
He told me to go to Siloam and wash. So
I went and washed, and then I could
see."[l]
12"Where is this man?" they asked
him.
"I don't know," he said.

The Pharisees Investigate the Healing

13They brought to the Pharisees the
man who had been blind. 14Now the
day on which Jesus had made the mud
and opened the man's eyes was a Sab-
bath.[m] 15Therefore the Pharisees also
asked him how he had received his
sight.[n] "He put mud on my eyes," the
man replied, "and I washed, and now I
see."
16Some of the Pharisees said, "This
man is not from God, for he does not
keep the Sabbath."[o]
But others asked, "How can a sinner
do such miraculous signs?"[p] So they
were divided.[q]
17Finally they turned again to the
blind man, "What have you to say about
him? It was your eyes he opened."
The man replied, "He is a prophet."[r]
18The Jews[s] still did not believe that he
had been blind and had received his
sight until they sent for the man's
parents. 19"Is this your son?" they
asked. "Is this the one you say was born
blind? How is it that now he can see?"
20"We know he is our son," the
parents answered, "and we know he
was born blind. 21But how he can see
now, or who opened his eyes, we don't
know. Ask him. He is of age; he will
speak for himself." 22His parents said
this because they were afraid of the
Jews,[t] for already the Jews had decided
that anyone who acknowledged that
Jesus was the Christ[a] would be put out[u]
of the synagogue.[v] 23That was why his
parents said, "He is of age; ask him."[w]
24A second time they summoned the
man who had been blind. "Give glory
to God,"[b][x] they said. "We know this
man is a sinner."[y]
25He replied, "Whether he is a sinner
or not, I don't know. One thing I do
know. I was blind but now I see!"
26Then they asked him, "What did he
do to you? How did he open your
eyes?"
27He answered, "I have told you
already[z] and you did not listen. Why
do you want to hear it again? Do you
want to become his disciples, too?"
28Then they hurled insults at him and
said, "You are this fellow's disciple! We
are disciples of Moses![a] 29We know that
God spoke to Moses, but as for this
fellow, we don't even know where he
comes from."[b]
30The man answered, "Now that is
remarkable! You don't know where he
comes from, yet he opened my eyes.
31We know that God does not listen to
sinners. He listens to the godly man
who does his will.[c] 32Nobody has ever
heard of opening the eyes of a man
born blind. 33If this man were not from
God,[d] he could do nothing."
34To this they replied, "You were
steeped in sin at birth;[e] how dare you
lecture us!" And they threw him out.[f]

Spiritual Blindness

35Jesus heard that they had thrown
him out, and when he found him, he
said, "Do you believe[g] in the Son of
Man?"[h]
36"Who is he, sir?" the man asked.
"Tell me so that I may believe in him."[i]
37Jesus said, "You have now seen
him; in fact, he is the one speaking with
you."[j]
38Then the man said, "Lord, I be-
lieve," and he worshipped him.[k]
39Jesus said, "For judgment[l] I have
come into this world,[m] so that the blind

3 [e]Jn 11:4
4 [f]Jn 11:9; 12:35
5 [g]**Jn 1:4**
6 [h]Mk 7:33; 8:23
7 [i]ver 11; 2Ki 5:10; Lk 13:4; [j]Isa 35:5; Jn 11:37
8 [k]Ac 3:2,10
11 [l]ver 7
14 [m]Mt 12:1–14; Jn 5:9
15 [n]ver 10
16 [o]**Mt 12:2;** [p]**Jn 2:11;** [q]**Jn 6:52**
17 [r]**Mt 21:11**
18 [s]**Jn 1:19**
22 [t]**Jn 7:13;** [u]ver 34; Lk 6:22; [v]Jn 12:42; 16:2
23 [w]ver 21
24 [x]Jos 7:19; [y]ver 16
27 [z]ver 15
28 [a]Jn 5:45
29 [b]Jn 8:14
31 [c]Ge 18:23–32; Ps 34:15–16; 145:19–20; Pr 15:29; Isa 59:1–2; Jn 15:7; Jas 5:16–18; 1Jn 5:14–15
33 [d]ver 16; Jn 3:2
34 [e]ver 2; [f]ver 22,35; Isa 66:5
35 [g]**Jn 3:15;** [h]**Mt 8:20**
36 [i]Ro 10:14
37 [j]Jn 4:26
38 [k]Mt 28:9
39 [l]**Jn 5:22;** [m]Jn 3:19; 12:47

[a]22 Or *Messiah*
[b]24 A solemn charge to tell the truth (see Joshua 7:19)

will see[n] and those who see will become
blind."[o]
40Some Pharisees who were with him
heard him say this and asked, "What?
Are we blind too?"[p]
41Jesus said, "If you were blind, you
would not be guilty of sin; but now that
you claim you can see, your guilt
remains.[q]

The Shepherd and His Flock

10 "I tell you the truth, the man
who does not enter the sheep
pen by the gate, but climbs in by some
other way, is a thief and a robber.[a] 2The
man who enters by the gate is the
shepherd of his sheep.[b] 3The watchman
opens the gate for him, and the sheep
listen to his voice.[c] He calls his own
sheep by name and leads them out.[d]
4When he has brought out all his own,
he goes on ahead of them, and his sheep
follow him because they know his
voice.[e] 5But they will never follow a
stranger; in fact, they will run away
from him because they do not recognise
a stranger's voice." 6Jesus used this
figure of speech,[f] but they did not
understand what he was telling them.[g]
7Therefore Jesus said again, "I tell you
the truth, I am[h] the gate[i] for the sheep.
8All who ever came before me[j] were
thieves and robbers,[k] but the sheep did
not listen to them. 9I am the gate; who-
ever enters through me will be saved.[a]
He will come in and go out, and find
pasture. 10The thief comes only to steal
and kill and destroy; I have come that
they may have life,[l] and have it to the
full.[m]
11"I am[n] the good shepherd.[o] The
good shepherd lays down his life for the
sheep.[p] 12The hired hand is not the
shepherd who owns the sheep. So
when he sees the wolf coming, he aban-
dons the sheep and runs away.[q] Then
the wolf attacks the flock and scatters it.
13The man runs away because he is a
hired hand and cares nothing for the
sheep.
14"I am the good shepherd;[r] I know
my sheep[s] and my sheep know me—
15just as the Father knows me and I
know the Father[t]—and I lay down my
life for the sheep.[u] 16I have other sheep[v]
that are not of this sheep pen. I must
bring them also. They too will listen to
my voice, and there shall be one flock[w]
and one shepherd.[x] 17The reason my
Father loves me is that I lay down my
life[y]—only to take it up again. 18No-one
takes it from me, but I lay it down of my
own accord.[z] I have authority to lay it
down and authority to take it up again.
This command I received from my
Father."[a]
19At these words the Jews were again
divided.[b] 20Many of them said, "He is
demon-possessed[c] and raving mad.[d]
Why listen to him?"
21But others said, "These are not the
sayings of a man possessed by a de-
mon.[e] Can a demon open the eyes of the
blind?"[f]

The Unbelief of the Jews

22Then came the Feast of Dedication[b]
at Jerusalem. It was winter, 23and Jesus
was in the temple area walking in
Solomon's Colonnade.[g] 24The Jews[h]
gathered round him, saying, "How
long will you keep us in suspense? If
you are the Christ,[c] tell us plainly."[i]
25Jesus answered, "I did tell you,[j] but
you do not believe. The miracles I do in
my Father's name speak for me,[k] 26but
you do not believe because you are not
my sheep.[l] 27My sheep listen to my
voice; I know them,[m] and they follow
me.[n] 28I give them eternal life,[o] and they
shall never perish;[p] no-one can snatch
them out of my hand.[q] 29My Father,
who has given them to me,[r] is greater
than all[d];[s] no-one can snatch them out of
my Father's hand. 30I and the Father are
one."[t]
31Again the Jews picked up stones to
stone him,[u] 32but Jesus said to them, "I
have shown you many great miracles
from the Father. For which of these do
you stone me?"
33"We are not stoning you for any of
these," replied the Jews, "but for blas-
phemy, because you, a mere man, claim
to be God."[v]
34Jesus answered them, "Is it not writ-
ten in your Law,[w] 'I have said you are
gods'[e]?[x] 35If he called them 'gods', to
whom the word of God[y] came—and the
Scripture cannot be broken[z]—36what
about the one whom the Father set
apart[a] as his very own[b] and sent into the
world?[c] Why then do you accuse me of
blasphemy because I said, 'I am God's

39 [n]Lk 4:18; [o]Mt 13:13
40 [p]Ro 2:19
41 [q]Jn 15:22,24

Ch. 10

1 [a]ver 8,10
2 [b]ver 11,14; Mk 6:34
3 [c]ver 4–5,14, 16,27; [d]ver 4, 5,14,16,27
4 [e]**ver 3**
6 [f]**Jn 16:25;** [g]**Mk 9:32**
7 [h]**Jn 6:35;** [i]ver 9
8 [j]Jer 23:1–2; Eze 34:2; [k]ver 1
10 [l]**Jn 1:4;** 3:15–16; 5:40; 20:31; [m]Ps 65:11; Ro 5:17
11 [n]**Jn 6:35;** [o]ver 14; Ps 23:1; Isa 40:11; Eze 34:11–16,23; Mt 2:6; Lk 12:32; Heb 13:20; 1Pe 2:25; 5:4; Rev 7:17; [p]ver 15, 17–18; Jn 15:13; 1Jn 3:16
12 [q]Zec 11:16–17
14 [r]**ver 11;** [s]ver 27; Ex 33:12
15 [t]Mt 11:27; [u]ver 11, 17–18
16 [v]Isa 56:8; Ac 10:34–35; [w]Jn 11:52; 17:20–21; Eph 2:11–19; [x]Eze 34:23; 37:24
17 [y]ver 11,15,18
18 [z]Mt 26:53; [a]Jn 15:10; Php 2:8; Heb 5:8
19 [b]**Jn 6:52**
20 [c]**Mk 3:22;** [d]2Ki 9:11; Jer 29:26; Mk 3:21
21 [e]**Mt 4:24;** [f]Ex 4:11; Jn 9:32–33
23 [g]Ac 3:11; 5:12
24 [h]**Jn 1:19;** [i]Lk 22:67; Jn 16:25,29
25 [j]Jn 4:26; 8:58; [k]Jn 5:36; 14:11
26 [l]Jn 8:47
27 [m]ver 14; [n]ver 4
28 [o]**Mt 25:46;** [p]Isa 66:22; [q]**Jn 6:39**
29 [r]Jn 17:2,6,24; [s]Jn 14:28
30 [t]Dt 6:4; Jn 17:21–23
31 [u]**Jn 8:59**
33 [v]Lev 24:16; Mt 26:63–66; Jn 5:18
34 [w]Jn 8:17; 12:34; 15:25; Ro 3:19; 1Co 14:21; [x]Ps 82:6
35 [y]**Heb 4:12;** [z]**Mt 5:18**
36 [a]Jer 1:5; [b]Jn 6:69; [c]**Jn 3:17**

a9 Or *kept safe*
b22 That is, Hanukkah
c24 Or *Messiah*
d29 Many early manuscripts *What my Father has given me is greater than all*
e34 Psalm 82:6

Son'?[d] 37Do not believe me unless I do
what my Father does.[e] 38But if I do it,
even though you do not believe me,
believe the miracles, that you may know
and understand that the Father is in me,
and I in the Father."[f] 39Again they tried
to seize him,[g] but he escaped their
grasp.[h]

40Then Jesus went back across the Jor-
dan[i] to the place where John had been
baptising in the early days. Here he
stayed 41and many people came to him.
They said, "Though John never per-
formed a miraculous sign,[j] all that John
said about this man was true."[k] 42And in
that place many believed in Jesus.[l]

The Death of Lazarus

11 Now a man named Lazarus was
sick. He was from Bethany,[a] the
village of Mary and her sister Martha.[b]
2This Mary, whose brother Lazarus now
lay sick, was the same one who poured
perfume on the Lord and wiped his feet
with her hair.[c] 3So the sisters sent word
to Jesus, "Lord, the one you love[d] is
sick."

4When he heard this, Jesus said,
"This sickness will not end in death.
No, it is for God's glory[e] so that God's
Son may be glorified through it." 5Jesus
loved Martha and her sister and Lazar-
us. 6Yet when he heard that Lazarus
was sick, he stayed where he was two
more days.

7Then he said to his disciples, "Let us
go back to Judea."[f]

8"But Rabbi,"[g] they said, "a short
while ago the Jews tried to stone you,[h]
and yet you are going back there?"

9Jesus answered, "Are there not
twelve hours of daylight? A man who
walks by day will not stumble, for he
sees by this world's light.[i] 10It is when
he walks by night that he stumbles, for
he has no light."

11After he had said this, he went on to
tell them, "Our friend[j] Lazarus has
fallen asleep;[k] but I am going there to
wake him up."

12His disciples replied, "Lord, if he
sleeps, he will get better." 13Jesus had
been speaking of his death, but his dis-
ciples thought he meant natural sleep.[l]

14So then he told them plainly,
"Lazarus is dead, 15and for your sake I
am glad I was not there, so that you may
believe. But let us go to him."

16Then Thomas[m] (called Didymus)
said to the rest of the disciples, "Let us
also go, that we may die with him."

Jesus Comforts the Sisters

17On his arrival, Jesus found that
Lazarus had already been in the tomb
for four days.[n] 18Bethany[o] was less than
two miles[a] from Jerusalem, 19and many
Jews had come to Martha and Mary to
comfort them in the loss of their
brother.[p] 20When Martha heard that
Jesus was coming, she went out to meet
him, but Mary stayed at home.[q]

21"Lord," Martha said to Jesus, "if
you had been here, my brother would
not have died.[r] 22But I know that even
now God will give you whatever you
ask."[s]

23Jesus said to her, "Your brother will
rise again."

24Martha answered, "I know he will
rise again in the resurrection[t] at the last
day."[u]

25Jesus said to her, "I am[v] the resur-
rection and the life.[w] He who believes[x]
in me will live, even though he dies;
26and whoever lives and believes[y] in me
will never die.[z] Do you believe this?"

27"Yes, Lord," she told him, "I be-
lieve that you are the Christ,[b][a] the Son
of God,[b] who was to come into the
world."[c]

28And after she had said this, she
went back and called her sister Mary
aside. "The Teacher[d] is here," she said,
"and is asking for you." 29When Mary
heard this, she got up quickly and went
to him. 30Now Jesus had not yet entered
the village, but was still at the place
where Martha had met him.[e] 31When
the Jews who had been with Mary in the
house, comforting her,[f] noticed how
quickly she got up and went out, they
followed her, supposing she was going
to the tomb to mourn there.

32When Mary reached the place
where Jesus was and saw him, she fell at
his feet and said, "Lord, if you had been
here, my brother would not have
died."[g]

33When Jesus saw her weeping, and
the Jews who had come along with her
also weeping, he was deeply moved[h] in
spirit and troubled.[i] 34"Where have you
laid him?" he asked.

"Come and see, Lord," they replied.

35Jesus wept.[j]

36Then the Jews said, "See how he
loved him!"[k]

37But some of them said, "Could not
he who opened the eyes of the blind
man[l] have kept this man from dying?"[m]

36 [d]Jn 5:17–18
37 [e]ver 25
38 [f]Jn 14:10–11, 20; 17:21
39 [g]Jn 7:30; [h]Lk 4:30; Jn 8:59
40 [i]Jn 1:28
41 [j]**Jn 2:11**; [k]Jn 1:26–27,30,34
42 [l]**Jn 7:31**

Ch. 11

1 [a]**Mt 21:17**; [b]Lk 10:38
2 [c]Mk 14:3; Lk 7:38; Jn 12:3
3 [d]ver 5,36
4 [e]ver 40
7 [f]Jn 10:40
8 [g]**Mt 23:7**; [h]Jn 8:59; 10:31
9 [i]Jn 9:4; 12:35
11 [j]ver 3; [k]**Mt 9:24**
13 [l]Mt 9:24
16 [m]Mt 10:3; Jn 14:5; 20:24–28; 21:2; Ac 1:13
17 [n]ver 6,39
18 [o]ver 1; **Mt 21:17**
19 [p]ver 31; Job 2:11
20 [q]Lk 10:38–42
21 [r]ver 32,37
22 [s]ver 41–42
24 [t]Da 12:2; Jn 5:28–29; Ac 24:15; [u]Jn 6:39–40
25 [v]**Jn 6:35**; [w]**Jn 1:4**; [x]**Jn 3:15**
26 [y]**Jn 3:15**; [z]**Mt 25:46**
27 [a]**Lk 2:11**; [b]**Mt 4:3**; [c]Jn 6:14
28 [d]Mt 26:18; Jn 13:13
30 [e]ver 20
31 [f]ver 19
32 [g]ver 21
33 [h]ver 38; [i]**Jn 12:27**
35 [j]Lk 19:41
36 [k]ver 3
37 [l]Jn 9:6–7; [m]ver 21,32

[a]*18* Greek *fifteen stadia* (about 3 kilometres)
[b]27 Or *Messiah*

Jesus Raises Lazarus From the Dead

38Jesus, once more deeply moved,[n] came to the tomb. It was a cave with a stone laid across the entrance.[o] 39"Take away the stone," he said.

"But, Lord," said Martha, the sister of the dead man, "by this time there is a bad odour, for he has been there four days."[p]

40Then Jesus said, "Did I not tell you that if you believed,[q] you would see the glory of God?"[r]

41So they took away the stone. Then Jesus looked up[s] and said, "Father,[t] I thank you that you have heard me. 42I knew that you always hear me, but I said this for the benefit of the people standing here,[u] that they may believe that you sent me."[v]

43When he had said this, Jesus called in a loud voice, "Lazarus, come out!"[w] 44The dead man came out, his hands and feet wrapped with strips of linen,[x] and a cloth around his face.[y]

Jesus said to them, "Take off the grave clothes and let him go."

The Plot to Kill Jesus

45Therefore many of the Jews who had come to visit Mary,[z] and had seen what Jesus did,[a] put their faith in him.[b] 46But some of them went to the Pharisees and told them what Jesus had done. 47Then the chief priests and the Pharisees[c] called a meeting[d] of the Sanhedrin.[e]

"What are we accomplishing?" they asked. "Here is this man performing many miraculous signs.[f] 48If we let him go on like this, everyone will believe in him, and then the Romans will come and take away both our place[c] and our nation."

49Then one of them, named Caiaphas,[g] who was high priest that year,[h] spoke up, "You know nothing at all! 50You do not realise that it is better for you that one man die for the people than that the whole nation perish."[i]

51He did not say this on his own, but as high priest that year he prophesied that Jesus would die for the Jewish nation, 52and not only for that nation but also for the scattered children of God, to bring them together and make them one.[j] 53So from that day on they plotted to take his life.[k]

54Therefore Jesus no longer moved about publicly among the Jews.[l] Instead he withdrew to a region near the desert, to a village called Ephraim, where he stayed with his disciples.

55When it was almost time for the Jewish Passover,[m] many went up from the country to Jerusalem for their ceremonial cleansing[n] before the Passover. 56They kept looking for Jesus,[o] and as they stood in the temple area they asked one another, "What do you think? Isn't he coming to the Feast at all?" 57But the chief priests and Pharisees had given orders that if anyone found out where Jesus was, he should report it so that they might arrest him.

Jesus Anointed at Bethany

12:1–8Ref—Mt 26:6–13; Mk 14:3–9; Lk 7:37–39

12 Six days before the Passover,[a] Jesus arrived at Bethany,[b] where Lazarus lived, whom Jesus had raised from the dead. 2Here a dinner was given in Jesus' honour. Martha served,[c] while Lazarus was among those reclining at the table with him. 3Then Mary took about a pint[a] of pure nard, an expensive perfume;[d] she poured it on Jesus' feet and wiped his feet with her hair.[e] And the house was filled with the fragrance of the perfume.

4But one of his disciples, Judas Iscariot, who was later to betray him,[f] objected, 5"Why wasn't this perfume sold and the money given to the poor? It was worth a year's wages."[b] 6He did not say this because he cared about the poor but because he was a thief; as keeper of the money bag,[g] he used to help himself to what was put into it.

7"Leave her alone," Jesus replied. "⌊It was intended⌋ that she should save this perfume for the day of my burial.[h] 8You will always have the poor among you,[i] but you will not always have me."

9Meanwhile a large crowd of Jews found out that Jesus was there and came, not only because of him but also to see Lazarus, whom he had raised from the dead.[j] 10So the chief priests made plans to kill Lazarus as well, 11for on account of him[k] many of the Jews were going over to Jesus and putting their faith in him.[l]

The Triumphal Entry

12:12–15pp—Mt 21:4–9; Mk 11:7–10; Lk 19:35–38

12The next day the great crowd that had come for the Feast heard that Jesus

---

[c]48 Or *temple*

[a]3 Greek *a litra* (probably about 0.5 litre)

[b]5 Greek *three hundred denarii*

---

38 [n]ver 33; [o]Mt 27:60; Lk 24:2; Jn 20:1
39 [p]ver 17
40 [q]ver 23–25; [r]ver 4
41 [s]Jn 17:1; [t]**Mt 11:25**
42 [u]Jn 12:30; [v]**Jn 3:17**
43 [w]**Lk 7:14**
44 [x]Jn 19:40; [y]Jn 20:7
45 [z]ver 19; [a]Jn 2:23; [b]Ex 14:31; **Jn 7:31**
47 [c]ver 57; [d]Mt 26:3; [e]**Mt 5:22;** [f]**Jn 2:11**
49 [g]**Mt 26:3;** [h]ver 51; Jn 18:13–14
50 [i]Jn 18:14
52 [j]Isa 49:6; Jn 10:16
53 [k]**Mt 12:14**
54 [l]Jn 7:1
55 [m]Ex 12:13, 23,27; Mt 26:1–2; Mk 14:1; Jn 13:1; [n]2Ch 30:17–18
56 [o]Jn 7:11

Ch. 12

1 [a]**Jn 11:55;** [b]**Mt 21:17**
2 [c]Lk 10:38–42
3 [d]Mk 14:3; [e]Jn 11:2
4 [f]**Mt 10:4**
6 [g]Jn 13:29
7 [h]Jn 19:40
8 [i]Dt 15:11
9 [j]Jn 11:43–44
11 [k]ver 17–18; Jn 11:45; [l]**Jn 7:31**

was on his way to Jerusalem. 13They took palm branches[m] and went out to meet him, shouting,

"Hosanna!"[c]

"Blessed is he who comes in the name
of the Lord!"[d][n]

"Blessed is the King of Israel!"[o]

14Jesus found a young donkey and sat upon it, as it is written,

15"Do not be afraid, O Daughter of Zion;
see, your king is coming,
seated on a donkey's colt."[e][p]

16At first his disciples did not understand all this.[q] Only after Jesus was glorified[r] did they realise that these things had been written about him and that they had done these things to him.

17Now the crowd that was with him[s] when he called Lazarus from the tomb and raised him from the dead continued to spread the word. 18Many people, because they had heard that he had given this miraculous sign,[t] went out to meet him. 19So the Pharisees said to one another, "See, this is getting us nowhere. Look how the whole world has gone after him!"[u]

Jesus Predicts His Death

20Now there were some Greeks[v] among those who went up to worship at the Feast. 21They came to Philip, who was from Bethsaida[w] in Galilee, with a request. "Sir," they said, "we would like to see Jesus." 22Philip went to tell Andrew; Andrew and Philip in turn told Jesus.

23Jesus replied, "The hour[x] has come for the Son of Man to be glorified.[y] 24I tell you the truth, unless a grain of wheat falls to the ground and dies,[z] it remains only a single seed. But if it dies, it produces many seeds. 25The man who loves his life will lose it, while the man who hates his life in this world will keep it[a] for eternal life.[b] 26Whoever serves me must follow me; and where I am, my servant also will be.[c] My Father will honour the one who serves me.

27"Now my heart is troubled,[d] and what shall I say? 'Father,[e] save me from this hour'?[f] No, it was for this very reason I came to this hour. 28Father, glorify your name!"

Then a voice came from heaven,[g] "I have glorified it, and will glorify it again." 29The crowd that was there and heard it said it had thundered; others said an angel had spoken to him.

30Jesus said, "This voice was for your benefit,[h] not mine. 31Now is the time for judgment on this world;[i] now the prince of this world[j] will be driven out. 32But I, when I am lifted up from the earth,[k] will draw all men to myself."[l] 33He said this to show the kind of death he was going to die.[m]

34The crowd spoke up, "We have heard from the Law[n] that the Christ[f] will remain for ever,[o] so how can you say, 'The Son of Man[p] must be lifted up'?[q] Who is this 'Son of Man'?"

35Then Jesus told them, "You are going to have the light[r] just a little while longer. Walk while you have the light,[s] before darkness overtakes you.[t] The man who walks in the dark does not know where he is going. 36Put your trust in the light while you have it, so that you may become sons of light."[u] When he had finished speaking, Jesus left and hid himself from them.[v]

The Jews Continue in Their Unbelief

37Even after Jesus had done all these miraculous signs[w] in their presence, they still would not believe in him. 38This was to fulfil the word of Isaiah the prophet:

"Lord, who has believed our message
and to whom has the arm of the
Lord been revealed?"[g][x]

39For this reason they could not believe, because, as Isaiah says elsewhere:

40"He has blinded their eyes
and deadened their hearts,
so they can neither see with their eyes,
nor understand with their hearts,
nor turn—and I would heal
them."[h][y]

41Isaiah said this because he saw Jesus' glory[z] and spoke about him.[a]

42Yet at the same time many even among the leaders believed in him.[b] But because of the Pharisees[c] they would not confess their faith for fear they would be put out of the synagogue;[d] 43for they loved praise from men[e] more than praise from God.[f]

13 [m]Lev 23:40; [n]Ps 118:25–26; [o]**Jn 1:49**
15 [p]Zec 9:9
16 [q]**Mk 9:32**; [r]ver 23; Jn 2:22; 7:39
17 [s]Jn 11:42
18 [t]ver 11; Lk 19:37
19 [u]Jn 11:47–48
20 [v]Jn 7:35; Ac 11:20
21 [w]**Mt 11:21**
23 [x]**Mt 26:18**; [y]Jn 13:32; 17:1
24 [z]1Co 15:36
25 [a]Mt 10:39; Mk 8:35; Lk 14:26; 17:33; [b]**Mt 25:46**
26 [c]Jn 14:3; 17:24; 2Co 5:8; Php 1:23; 1Th 4:17
27 [d]Mt 26:38–39; Jn 11:33,38; 13:21; [e]**Mt 11:25**; [f]ver 23
28 [g]**Mt 3:17**
30 [h]Ex 19:9; Jn 11:42
31 [i]Jn 16:11; [j]Jn 14:30; 16:11; 2Co 4:4; Eph 2:2; 1Jn 4:4; 5:19
32 [k]ver 34; Isa 11:10; Jn 3:14; 8:28; [l]Jn 6:44
33 [m]Jn 18:32; 21:19
34 [n]**Jn 10:34**; [o]Ps 110:4; Isa 9:7; Eze 37:25; Da 7:14; [p]**Mt 8:20**; [q]Jn 3:14
35 [r]ver 46; [s]Eph 5:8; [t]1Jn 1:6; 2:11
36 [u]ver 46; **Lk 16:8**; [v]Jn 8:59
37 [w]**Jn 2:11**
38 [x]Isa 53:1; Ro 10:16
40 [y]Isa 6:10; **Mt 13:13**,15
41 [z]Isa 6:1–4; [a]Lk 24:27
42 [b]ver 11; Jn 7:48; [c]**Jn 7:13**; [d]Jn 9:22
43 [e]1Sa 15:30; [f]**Ro 2:29**

c13 A Hebrew expression meaning "Save!" which became an exclamation of praise
d13 Psalm 118:25,26 e15 Zech. 9:9
f34 Or *Messiah* g38 Isaiah 53:1
h40 Isaiah 6:10

44Then Jesus cried out, "When a man believes in me, he does not believe in me only, but in the one who sent me.[g] 45When he looks at me, he sees the one who sent me.[h] 46I have come into the world as a light,[i] so that no-one who believes in me should stay in darkness.

47"As for the person who hears my words but does not keep them, I do not judge him. For I did not come to judge the world, but to save it.[j] 48There is a judge for the one who rejects me and does not accept my words; that very word which I spoke will condemn him[k] at the last day. 49For I did not speak of my own accord, but the Father who sent me commanded me[l] what to say and how to say it. 50I know that his command leads to eternal life.[m] So whatever I say is just what the Father has told me to say."[n]

Jesus Washes His Disciples' Feet

13 It was just before the Passover Feast.[a] Jesus knew that the time had come[b] for him to leave this world and go to the Father.[c] Having loved his own who were in the world, he now showed them the full extent of his love.[a]

2The evening meal was being served, and the devil had already prompted Judas Iscariot, son of Simon, to betray Jesus.[d] 3Jesus knew that the Father had put all things under his power,[e] and that he had come from God[f] and was returning to God; 4so he got up from the meal, took off his outer clothing, and wrapped a towel round his waist.[g] 5After that, he poured water into a basin and began to wash his disciples' feet,[h] drying them with the towel that was wrapped round him.

6He came to Simon Peter, who said to him, "Lord, are you going to wash my feet?"

7Jesus replied, "You do not realise now what I am doing, but later you will understand."[i]

8"No," said Peter, "you shall never wash my feet."

Jesus answered, "Unless I wash you, you have no part with me."

9"Then, Lord," Simon Peter replied, "not just my feet but my hands and my head as well!"

10Jesus answered, "A person who has had a bath needs only to wash his feet; his whole body is clean. And you are clean,[j] though not every one of you."[k] 11For he knew who was going to betray him,[l] and that was why he said not every one was clean.

12When he had finished washing their feet, he put on his clothes and returned to his place. "Do you understand what I have done for you?" he asked them. 13"You call me 'Teacher'[m] and 'Lord',[n] and rightly so, for that is what I am. 14Now that I, your Lord and Teacher, have washed your feet, you also should wash one another's feet.[o] 15I have set you an example that you should do as I have done for you.[p] 16I tell you the truth, no servant is greater than his master,[q] nor is a messenger greater than the one who sent him. 17Now that you know these things, you will be blessed if you do them.[r]

Jesus Predicts His Betrayal

18"I am not referring to all of you;[s] I know those I have chosen.[t] But this is to fulfil the scripture:[u] 'He who shares my bread[v] has lifted up his heel[w] against me.'[b][x]

19"I am telling you now before it happens, so that when it does happen you will believe[y] that I am He.[z] 20I tell you the truth, whoever accepts anyone I send accepts me; and whoever accepts me accepts the one who sent me."[a]

21After he had said this, Jesus was troubled in spirit[b] and testified, "I tell you the truth, one of you is going to betray me."[c]

22His disciples stared at one another, at a loss to know which of them he meant. 23One of them, the disciple whom Jesus loved,[d] was reclining next to him. 24Simon Peter motioned to this disciple and said, "Ask him which one he means."

25Leaning back against Jesus, he asked him, "Lord, who is it?"[e]

26Jesus answered, "It is the one to whom I will give this piece of bread when I have dipped it in the dish." Then, dipping the piece of bread, he gave it to Judas Iscariot,[f] son of Simon. 27As soon as Judas took the bread, Satan entered into him.[g]

"What you are about to do, do quickly," Jesus told him, 28but no-one at the meal understood why Jesus said this to him. 29Since Judas had charge of the money,[h] some thought Jesus was telling him to buy what was needed for the Feast,[i] or to give something to the poor.[j] 30As soon as Judas had taken the bread, he went out. And it was night.[k]

44 [g]**Mt 10:40**; Jn 5:24
45 [h]**Jn 14:9**
46 [i]**Jn 1:4**
47 [j]**Jn 3:17**
48 [k]Jn 5:45
49 [l]Jn 14:31
50 [m]**Mt 25:46**; [n]**Jn 14:24**

Ch. 13

1 [a]**Jn 11:55**; [b]**Mt 26:18**; [c]Jn 16:28
2 [d]**Mt 10:4**
3 [e]**Mt 28:18**; [f]Jn 8:42; 16:27–28,30; 17:8
4 [g]**Mt 20:28**
5 [h]**Lk 7:44**
7 [i]ver 12
10 [j]Jn 15:3; [k]ver 18
11 [l]**Mt 10:4**
13 [m]Mt 26:18; Jn 11:28; [n]**Mt 28:18**; Lk 1:43; 2:11; 6:46; 11:1; Ac 10:36; Ro 10:9,12; 14:9; 1Co 12:3; Php 2:11; Col 2:6
14 [o]1Pe 5:5
15 [p]**Mt 11:29**; **1Ti 4:12**
16 [q]Mt 10:24; Lk 6:40; Jn 15:20
17 [r]Mt 7:24–25; Lk 11:28; Jas 1:25
18 [s]ver 10; [t]Jn 15:16,19; [u]**Mt 1:22**; [v]Mt 26:23; [w]Jn 6:70; [x]Ps 41:9
19 [y]Jn 14:29; 16:4; [z]Jn 4:26; 8:24
20 [a]**Mt 10:40**
21 [b]**Jn 12:27**; [c]Mt 26:21
23 [d]Jn 19:26; 20:2; 21:7,20
25 [e]Mt 26:22; Jn 21:20
26 [f]**Mt 10:4**
27 [g]Lk 22:3
29 [h]Jn 12:6; [i]ver 1; [j]Jn 12:5
30 [k]Lk 22:53

[a]1 *Or he loved them to the last*
[b]18 Psalm 41:9

Jesus Predicts Peter's Denial

13:37,38pp—Mt 26:33–35; Mk 14:29–31; Lk 22:33,34

31 When he was gone, Jesus said, "Now is the Son of Man[l] glorified[m] and God is glorified in him.[n] 32 If God is glorified in him,[c] God will glorify the Son in himself,[o] and will glorify him at once.

33 "My children, I will be with you only a little longer. You will look for me, and just as I told the Jews, so I tell you now: Where I am going, you cannot come.[p]

34 "A new command[q] I give you: Love one another.[r] As I have loved you, so you must love one another.[s] 35 By this all men will know that you are my disciples, if you love one another."[t]

36 Simon Peter asked him, "Lord, where are you going?"[u]

Jesus replied, "Where I am going, you cannot follow now,[v] but you will follow later."[w]

37 Peter asked, "Lord, why can't I follow you now? I will lay down my life for you."

38 Then Jesus answered, "Will you really lay down your life for me? I tell you the truth, before the cock crows, you will disown me three times![x]

Jesus Comforts His Disciples

14 "Do not let your hearts be troubled.[a] Trust[b] in God;[a][c] trust also in me. 2 In my Father's house are many rooms; if it were not so, I would have told you. I am going there[d] to prepare a place for you. 3 And if I go and prepare a place for you, I will come back[e] and take you to be with me that you also may be where I am.[f] 4 You know the way to the place where I am going."

Jesus the Way to the Father

5 Thomas[g] said to him, "Lord, we don't know where you are going, so how can we know the way?"

6 Jesus answered, "I am[h] the way[i] and the truth[j] and the life.[k] No-one comes to the Father except through me.[l] 7 If you really knew me, you would know[b] my Father as well.[m] From now on, you do know him and have seen him."

8 Philip[n] said, "Lord, show us the Father and that will be enough for us."

9 Jesus answered: "Don't you know me, Philip, even after I have been among you such a long time? Anyone who has seen me has seen the Father.[o] How can you say, 'Show us the Father'? 10 Don't you believe that I am in the Father, and that the Father is in me?[p] The words I say to you are not just my own.[q] Rather, it is the Father, living in me, who is doing his work. 11 Believe me when I say that I am in the Father and the Father is in me; or at least believe on the evidence of the miracles themselves.[r] 12 I tell you the truth, anyone who has faith[s] in me will do what I have been doing.[t] He will do even greater things than these, because I am going to the Father. 13 And I will do whatever you ask[u] in my name, so that the Son may bring glory to the Father. 14 You may ask me for anything in my name, and I will do it.

Jesus Promises the Holy Spirit

15 "If you love me, you will obey what I command.[v] 16 And I will ask the Father, and he will give you another Counsellor[w] to be with you for ever—17 the Spirit of truth.[x] The world cannot accept him,[y] because it neither sees him nor knows him. But you know him, for he lives with you and will be[c] in you. 18 I will not leave you as orphans;[z] I will come to you.[a] 19 Before long, the world will not see me any more, but you will see me.[b] Because I live, you also will live.[c] 20 On that day[d] you will realise that I am in my Father,[e] and you are in me, and I am in you.[f] 21 Whoever has my commands and obeys them, he is the one who loves me.[g] He who loves me will be loved by my Father,[h] and I too will love him and show myself to him."

22 Then Judas[i] (not Judas Iscariot) said, "But, Lord, why do you intend to show yourself to us and not to the world?"[j]

23 Jesus replied, "If anyone loves me, he will obey my teaching.[k] My Father will love him, and we will come to him and make our home with him.[l] 24 He who does not love me will not obey my teaching. These words you hear are not my own; they belong to the Father who sent me.[m]

25 "All this I have spoken while still with you. 26 But the Counsellor,[n] the Holy Spirit, whom the Father will send in my name,[o] will teach you all things[p] and will remind you of everything I

31 [l]**Mt 8:20**; [m]Jn 7:39; 12:23; [n]Jn 14:13; 17:4; 1Pe 4:11
32 [o]Jn 17:1
33 [p]**Jn 7:33–34**
34 [q]Jn 15:12; 1Jn 2:7–11; 3:11; [r]Lev 19:18; 1Th 4:9; 1Pe 1:22; [s]Jn 15:12; Eph 5:2; 1Jn 4:10–11
35 [t]1Jn 3:14; 4:20
36 [u]Jn 16:5; [v]ver 33; Jn 14:2; [w]Jn 21:18–19; 2Pe 1:14
38 [x]Jn 18:27

Ch. 14

1 [a]ver 27; [b]**Jn 3:15**; [c]Ps 4:5
2 [d]Jn 13:33,36; 16:5
3 [e]ver 18,28; **Mt 16:27**; [f]**Jn 12:26**
5 [g]**Jn 11:16**
6 [h]**Jn 6:35**; [i]Jn 10:9; Eph 2:18; Heb 10:20; [j]Jn 1:14; [k]**Jn 1:4**; [l]Ac 4:12
7 [m]Jn 1:18; **1Jn 2:23**
8 [n]**Jn 1:43**
9 [o]Isa 9:6; Jn 1:14; 12:45; 2Co 4:4; Php 2:6; Col 1:15; Heb 1:3
10 [p]ver 11,20; Jn 10:38; 17:21; [q]**ver 24**
11 [r]Jn 5:36; 10:38
12 [s]Mt 21:21; [t]Lk 10:17
13 [u]**Mt 7:7**
15 [v]ver 21,23; Ps 103:18; Jn 15:10; 1Jn 2:3–5; 3:22, 24; 5:3; 2Jn 6; Rev 12:17; 14:12
16 [w]ver 26; Jn 15:26; 16:7
17 [x]Jn 15:26; 16:13; 1Jn 4:6; 5:6; [y]1Co 2:14
18 [z]1Ki 6:13; [a]ver 3,28; **Mt 16:27**
19 [b]Jn 7:33–34; 16:16; [c]Jn 6:57
20 [d]Jn 16:23,26; [e]ver 10–11; Jn 10:38; 17:21; [f]**Ro 8:10**
21 [g]**ver 15**; [h]Dt 7:13; Jn 16:27; 1Jn 2:5
22 [i]Lk 6:16; Ac 1:13; [j]Ac 10:41
23 [k]**ver 15**; [l]**Ro 8:10**
24 [m]ver 10; Dt 18:18; Jn 5:19; 7:16; 8:28; 12:49–50
26 [n]ver 16; Jn 15:26; 16:7; [o]Ac 2:33; [p]Jn 16:13; 1Jn 2:20, 27

[c]32 Many early manuscripts do not have *If God is glorified in him.* [a]1 Or *You trust in God*
[b]7 Some early manuscripts *If you really have known me, you will know*
[c]17 Some early manuscripts *and is*

have said to you.[q] 27Peace I leave with you; my peace I give you.[r] I do not give to you as the world gives. Do not let your hearts be troubled[s] and do not be afraid.

28"You heard me say, 'I am going away and I am coming back to you.'[t] If you loved me, you would be glad that I am going to the Father,[u] for the Father is greater than I.[v] 29I have told you now before it happens, so that when it does happen you will believe.[w] 30I will not speak with you much longer, for the prince of this world[x] is coming. He has no hold on me, 31but the world must learn that I love the Father and that I do exactly what my Father has commanded me.[y]

"Come now; let us leave.

The Vine and the Branches

15 "I am[a] the true vine,[b] and my Father is the gardener. 2He cuts off every branch in me that bears no fruit,[c] while every branch that does bear fruit[d] he prunes[a] so that it will be even more fruitful. 3You are already clean because of the word I have spoken to you.[e] 4Remain in me, and I will remain in you.[f] No branch can bear fruit by itself; it must remain in the vine. Neither can you bear fruit unless you remain in me.

5"I am the vine; you are the branches. If a man remains in me and I in him, he will bear much fruit;[g] apart from me you can do nothing. 6If anyone does not remain in me, he is like a branch that is thrown away and withers; such branches are picked up, thrown into the fire and burned.[h] 7If you remain in me[i] and my words remain in you, ask whatever you wish, and it will be given you.[j] 8This is to my Father's glory,[k] that you bear much fruit, showing yourselves to be my disciples.[l]

9"As the Father has loved me,[m] so have I loved you. Now remain in my love. 10If you obey my commands,[n] you will remain in my love, just as I have obeyed my Father's commands and remain in his love. 11I have told you this so that my joy may be in you and that your joy may be complete.[o] 12My command is this: Love each other as I have loved you.[p] 13Greater love has no-one than this, that he lay down his life for his friends.[q] 14You are my friends[r] if you do what I command.[s] 15I no longer call you servants, because a servant does not know his master's business. Instead, I have called you friends, for everything that I learned from my Father I have made known to you.[t] 16You did not choose me, but I chose you and appointed you[u] to go and bear fruit[v]—fruit that will last. Then the Father will give you whatever you ask in my name.[w] 17This is my command: Love each other.[x]

The World Hates the Disciples

18"If the world hates you,[y] keep in mind that it hated me first. 19If you belonged to the world, it would love you as its own. As it is, you do not belong to the world, but I have chosen you[z] out of the world. That is why the world hates you.[a] 20Remember the words I spoke to you: 'No servant is greater than his master.'[b][b] If they persecuted me, they will persecute you also.[c] If they obeyed my teaching, they will obey yours also. 21They will treat you this way because of my name,[d] for they do not know the One who sent me.[e] 22If I had not come and spoken to them,[f] they would not be guilty of sin. Now, however, they have no excuse for their sin.[g] 23He who hates me hates my Father as well. 24If I had not done among them what no-one else did,[h] they would not be guilty of sin.[i] But now they have seen these miracles, and yet they have hated both me and my Father. 25But this is to fulfil what is written in their Law:[j] 'They hated me without reason.'[c][k]

26"When the Counsellor[l] comes, whom I will send to you from the Father,[m] the Spirit of truth[n] who goes out from the Father, he will testify about me.[o] 27And you also must testify,[p] for you have been with me from the beginning.[q]

16 "All this[a] I have told you so that you will not go astray.[b] 2They will put you out of the synagogue;[c] in fact, a time is coming when anyone who kills you will think he is offering a service to God.[d] 3They will do such things because they have not known the Father or me.[e] 4I have told you this, so that when the time comes you will remember[f] that I warned you. I did not tell you this at first because I was with you.[g]

26 [q]Jn 2:22
27 [r]Nu 6:26; Ps 85:8; Mal 2:6; **Lk 2:14**; 24:36; Jn 16:33; Php 4:7; Col 3:15; [s]ver 1
28 [t]ver 2–4,18; **Mt 16:27**; [u]Jn 5:18; [v]Jn 10:29
29 [w]Jn 13:19; 16:4
30 [x]**Jn 12:31**
31 [y]Jn 10:18; 12:49

Ch. 15

1 [a]**Jn 6:35**; [b]Ps 80:8–11; Isa 5:1–7
2 [c]ver 6; **Mt 3:10**; [d]Ps 92:14; Mt 3:8; 7:20; Gal 5:22; Eph 5:9; Php 1:11
3 [e]Jn 13:10; 17:17; Eph 5:26
4 [f]**Jn 6:56**
5 [g]ver 16
6 [h]ver 2; Eze 15:4; **Mt 3:10**
7 [i]ver 4; **Jn 6:56**; [j]**Mt 7:7**
8 [k]**Mt 9:8**; [l]Jn 8:31
9 [m]Jn 17:23–24, 26
10 [n]**Jn 14:15**
11 [o]**Jn 3:29**
12 [p]ver 17; **Jn 13:34**
13 [q]Ge 44:33; Jn 10:11; Ro 5:7–8
14 [r]Job 16:20; Pr 18:24; Lk 12:4; [s]Mt 12:50
15 [t]Jn 8:26
16 [u]ver 19; Jn 13:18; [v]ver 5; [w]**Mt 7:7**
17 [x]ver 12
18 [y]Isa 66:5; Jn 7:7; 1Jn 3:13
19 [z]ver 16; [a]Jn 17:14
20 [b]**Jn 13:16**; [c]2Ti 3:12
21 [d]Isa 66:5; Mt 5:10–11; 10:22; Lk 6:22; Ac 5:41; 1Pe 4:14; Rev 2:3; [e]Jn 16:3
22 [f]Eze 2:5; 3:7; [g]Jn 9:41; Ro 1:20; 2:1
24 [h]Jn 5:36; [i]Jn 9:41
25 [j]**Jn 10:34**; [k]Ps 35:19; 69:4; 109:3
26 [l]Jn 14:16; [m]Jn 14:26; 16:7; [n]**Jn 14:17**; [o]1Jn 5:7
27 [p]**Lk 24:48**; Jn 21:24; 1Jn 1:2; 4:14; [q]**Lk 1:2**

Ch. 16

1 [a]Jn 15:18–27; [b]Mt 11:6
2 [c]Jn 9:22; 12:42; [d]Isa 66:5; Ac 26:9–10; Rev 6:9
3 [e]Jn 15:21; 17:25; 1Jn 3:1
4 [f]Jn 13:19; 14:29; [g]Jn 15:27

[a]2 The Greek for *prunes* also means *cleans*.
[b]20 John 13:16 [c]25 Psalms 35:19; 69:4

The Work of the Holy Spirit

5"Now I am going to him who sent
me,[h] yet none of you asks me, 'Where
are you going?'[i] 6Because I have said
these things, you are filled with grief.[j]
7But I tell you the truth: It is for your
good that I am going away. Unless I go
away, the Counsellor[k] will not come to
you; but if I go, I will send him to you.[l]
8When he comes, he will convict the
world of guilt[a] in regard to sin and right-
eousness and judgment: 9in regard to
sin,[m] because men do not believe in me;
10in regard to righteousness,[n] because I
am going to the Father,[o] where you can
see me no longer; 11and in regard to
judgment, because the prince of this
world[p] now stands condemned.

12"I have much more to say to you,
more than you can now bear.[q] 13But
when he, the Spirit of truth,[r] comes, he
will guide you into all truth.[s] He will not
speak on his own; he will speak only
what he hears, and he will tell you what
is yet to come. 14He will bring glory to
me by taking from what is mine and
making it known to you. 15All that be-
longs to the Father is mine.[t] That is why
I said the Spirit will take from what is
mine and make it known to you.

16"In a little while[u] you will see me no
more, and then after a little while you
will see me."[v]

The Disciples' Grief Will Turn to Joy

17Some of his disciples said to one
another, "What does he mean by
saying, 'In a little while you will see me
no more, and then after a little while
you will see me,'[w] and 'Because I am
going to the Father'?"[x] 18They kept
asking, "What does he mean by 'a little
while'? We don't understand what he is
saying."

19Jesus saw that they wanted to ask
him about this, so he said to them, "Are
you asking one another what I meant
when I said, 'In a little while you will see
me no more, and then after a little while
you will see me'? 20I tell you the truth,
you will weep and mourn[y] while the
world rejoices. You will grieve, but your
grief will turn to joy.[z] 21A woman giving
birth to a child has pain[a] because her
time has come; but when her baby is
born she forgets the anguish because of
her joy that a child is born into the
world. 22So with you: Now is your time
of grief,[b] but I will see you again[c] and
you will rejoice, and no-one will take
away your joy.[d] 23In that day[e] you will
no longer ask me anything. I tell you the
truth, my Father will give you whatever
you ask in my name.[f] 24Until now you
have not asked for anything in my
name. Ask and you will receive,[g] and
your joy will be complete.[h]

25"Though I have been speaking
figuratively,[i] a time is coming[j] when I
will no longer use this kind of language
but will tell you plainly about my
Father. 26In that day you will ask in my
name.[k] I am not saying that I will ask the
Father on your behalf. 27No, the Father
himself loves you because you have
loved me[l] and have believed that I came
from God.[m] 28I came from the Father
and entered the world; now I am leav-
ing the world and going back to the
Father."[n]

29Then Jesus' disciples said, "Now
you are speaking clearly and without
figures of speech.[o] 30Now we can see
that you know all things and that you do
not even need to have anyone ask you
questions. This makes us believe[p] that
you came from God."[q]

31"You believe at last!"[b] Jesus
answered. 32"But a time is coming,[r] and
has come, when you will be scattered,[s]
each to his own home. You will leave
me all alone.[t] Yet I am not alone, for my
Father is with me.[u]

33"I have told you these things, so
that in me you may have peace.[v] In this
world you will have trouble.[w] But take
heart! I have overcome[x] the world."

Jesus Prays for Himself

17 After Jesus said this, he looked
towards heaven[a] and prayed:

"Father, the time has come.[b]
Glorify your Son, that your Son
may glorify you.[c] 2For you granted
him authority over all people[d] that
he might give eternal life[e] to all
those you have given him.[f] 3Now
this is eternal life: that they may
know you,[g] the only true God, and
Jesus Christ, whom you have sent.[h]
4I have brought you glory[i] on earth
by completing the work you gave
me to do.[j] 5And now, Father,
glorify me[k] in your presence with
the glory I had with you[l] before the
world began.[m]

5 [h]ver 10,17,28; Jn 7:33; [i]Jn 13:36; 14:5
6 [j]ver 22
7 [k]Jn 14:16,26; 15:26; [l]Jn 7:39; 14:26
9 [m]Jn 15:22
10 [n]Ac 3:14; 7:52; Ro 1:17; 3:21–22; 1Pe 3:18; [o]**ver 5**
11 [p]**Jn 12:31**
12 [q]Mk 4:33; 1Co 3:2
13 [r]**Jn 14:17;** [s]Ps 25:5; Jn 14:26
15 [t]Jn 17:10
16 [u]**Jn 7:33;** [v]ver 22; Jn 14:18–24
17 [w]ver 16; [x]ver 5
20 [y]Mk 16:10; Lk 23:27; [z]Jn 20:20
21 [a]Isa 13:8; 21:3; 26:17; Mic 4:9; 1Th 5:3
22 [b]ver 6; [c]ver 16; [d]ver 20; Jer 31:12
23 [e]ver 26; Jn 14:20; [f]**Mt 7:7**
24 [g]**Mt 7:7;** [h]**Jn 3:29**
25 [i]ver 29; Ps 78:2; Eze 20:49; Mt 13:34; Mk 4:33–34; Jn 10:6; [j]ver 2
26 [k]ver 23–24
27 [l]Jn 14:21,23; [m]ver 30; **Jn 13:3**
28 [n]ver 5,10,17; Jn 13:3
29 [o]**ver 25**
30 [p]1Ki 17:24; [q]ver 27; **Jn 13:3**
32 [r]ver 2,25; [s]Mt 26:31; [t]Mt 26:56; [u]Jn 8:16, 29
33 [v]**Jn 14:27;** [w]Jn 15:18–21; [x]Ro 8:37; 1Jn 4:4; 5:4; Rev 2:7,11,17,26; 3:5,12,21; 21:7

Ch. 17

1 [a]Jn 11:41; [b]**Mt 26:18;** [c]Jn 12:23; 13:31–32
2 [d]**Mt 28:18;** [e]**Mt 25:46;** [f]ver 6,9,24; Da 7:14; Jn 6:37,39
3 [g]**Php 3:8;** [h]ver 8,18,21,23, 25; **Jn 3:17**
4 [i]Jn 13:31; [j]**Jn 19:30**
5 [k]ver 1; [l]Php 2:6; [m]**Jn 1:2**

[a]8 Or *will expose the guilt of the world*
[b]31 Or *"Do you now believe?"*

Jesus Prays for His Disciples

6"I have revealed you[a][n] to those
whom you gave me[o] out of the
world. They were yours; you gave
them to me and they have obeyed
your word. 7Now they know that
everything you have given me
comes from you. 8For I gave them
the words you gave me[p] and they
accepted them. They knew with
certainty that I came from you,[q] and
they believed that you sent me.[r] 9I
pray for them.[s] I am not praying for
the world, but for those you have
given me,[t] for they are yours. 10All I
have is yours, and all you have is
mine.[u] And glory has come to me
through them. 11I will remain in the
world no longer, but they are still in
the world,[v] and I am coming to
you.[w] Holy Father, protect them by
the power of your name—the
name you gave me—so that they
may be one[x] as we are one.[y] 12While
I was with them, I protected them
and kept them safe by that name
you gave me. None has been
lost[z] except the one doomed to
destruction[a] so that Scripture
would be fulfilled.[b]

13"I am coming to you now,[c] but I
say these things while I am still in
the world, so that they may have
the full measure of my joy[d] within
them. 14I have given them your
word and the world has hated
them,[e] for they are not of the world
any more than I am of the world.[f]
15My prayer is not that you take
them out of the world but that you
protect them from the evil one.[g]
16They are not of the world, even as
I am not of it.[h] 17Sanctify[b] them by
the truth; your word is truth.[i] 18As
you sent me into the world,[j] I have
sent them into the world.[k] 19For
them I sanctify myself, that they
too may be truly sanctified.[l]

Jesus Prays for All Believers

20"My prayer is not for them
alone. I pray also for those who will
believe in me through their mes-
sage, 21that all of them may be
one,[m] Father, just as you are in me
and I am in you.[n] May they also be
in us so that the world may believe
that you have sent me.[o] 22I have
given them the glory that you gave
me,[p] that they may be one as we are
one:[q] 23I in them and you in me.
May they be brought to complete
unity to let the world know that
you sent me[r] and have loved them[s]
even as you have loved me.

24"Father, I want those you have
given me[t] to be with me where I
am,[u] and to see my glory,[v] the glory
you have given me because you
loved me before the creation of the
world.[w]

25"Righteous Father, though the
world does not know you,[x] I know
you, and they know that you have
sent me.[y] 26I have made you known
to them,[z] and will continue to make
you known in order that the love
you have for me may be in them[a]
and that I myself may be in them."

6 [n]ver 26; Jn 1:18; [o]**ver 2**
8 [p]ver 14,26; Jn **14:24**; [q]**Jn 13:3**; [r]ver 3,18,21, 23,25; **Jn 3:17**
9 [s]Lk 22:32; [t]**ver 2**
10 [u]Jn 16:15
11 [v]Jn 13:1; [w]ver 13; Jn 7:33; [x]ver 21–23; Ps 133:1; [y]Jn 10:30
12 [z]**Jn 6:39**; [a]Jn 6:70; [b]**Mt 1:22**
13 [c]ver 11; [d]**Jn 3:29**
14 [e]Jn 15:19; [f]ver 16; Jn 8:23
15 [g]**Mt 5:37**
16 [h]ver 14
17 [i]**Jn 15:3**; 2Sa 7:28; 1Ki 17:24
18 [j]ver 3,8,21, 23,25; **Jn 3:17**; [k]Jn 20:21
19 [l]ver 17
21 [m]Jer 32:39; [n]ver 11; Jn 10:38; [o]ver 3, 8,18,23,25; **Jn 3:17**
22 [p]Jn 1:14; [q]**Jn 14:20**
23 [r]ver 3,8,18, 21,25; **Jn 3:17**; [s]Jn 16:27
24 [t]**ver 2**; [u]**Jn 12:26**; [v]Jn 1:14; [w]ver 5; **Mt 25:34; Jn 1:2**
25 [x]Jn 15:21; 16:3; [y]ver 3, 8,18,21,23; **Jn 3:17**; 16:27
26 [z]ver 6; [a]Jn 15:9

Ch. 18

1 [a]2Sa 15:23; [b]ver 26; **Mt 21:1**; [c]Mt 26:36
2 [d]Lk 21:37; 22:39
3 [e]Ac 1:16; [f]ver 12
4 [g]Jn 6:64; 13:1, 11; [h]ver 7
5 [i]**Mk 1:24**
7 [j]ver 4
9 [k]**Jn 6:39**
11 [l]**Mt 20:22**

Jesus Arrested

18:3–11pp—Mt 26:47–56; Mk 14:43–50; Lk 22:47–53

18 When he had finished praying,
Jesus left with his disciples and
crossed the Kidron Valley.[a] On the
other side there was an olive grove,[b] and
he and his disciples went into it.[c]

2Now Judas, who betrayed him,
knew the place, because Jesus had often
met there with his disciples.[d] 3So Judas
came to the grove, guiding[e] a detach-
ment of soldiers and some officials from
the chief priests and Pharisees.[f] They
were carrying torches, lanterns and
weapons.

4Jesus, knowing all that was going to
happen to him,[g] went out and asked
them, "Who is it you want?"[h]

5"Jesus of Nazareth,"[i] they replied.

"I am he," Jesus said. (And Judas the
traitor was standing there with them.)
6When Jesus said, "I am he," they drew
back and fell to the ground.

7Again he asked them, "Who is it you
want?"[j]

And they said, "Jesus of Nazareth."

8"I told you that I am he," Jesus
answered. "If you are looking for me,
then let these men go." 9This happened
so that the words he had spoken would
be fulfilled: "I have not lost one of those
you gave me."[a][k]

10Then Simon Peter, who had a
sword, drew it and struck the high
priest's servant, cutting off his right ear.
(The servant's name was Malchus.)

11Jesus commanded Peter, "Put your
sword away! Shall I not drink the cup[l]
the Father has given me?"

---

[a]6 Greek *your name*; also in verse 26
[b]17 Greek *hagiazo* (*set apart for sacred use* or *make holy*); also in verse 19 [a]9 John 6:39

Jesus Taken to Annas

18:12,13pp—Mt 26:57

12Then the detachment of soldiers
with its commander and the Jewish
officials[m] arrested Jesus. They bound
him 13and brought him first to Annas,
who was the father-in-law of Caiaphas,[n]
the high priest that year. 14Caiaphas
was the one who had advised the Jews
that it would be good if one man died for
the people.[o]

Peter's First Denial

18:16–18pp—Mt 26:69,70; Mk 14:66–68; Lk 22:55–57

15Simon Peter and another disciple
were following Jesus. Because this disci-
ple was known to the high priest,[p] he
went with Jesus into the high priest's
courtyard,[q] 16but Peter had to wait out-
side at the door. The other disciple, who
was known to the high priest, came
back, spoke to the girl on duty there and
brought Peter in.
17"You are not one of this man's dis-
ciples, are you?" the girl at the door
asked Peter.
He replied, "I am not."[r]
18It was cold, and the servants and
officials stood round a fire[s] they had
made to keep warm. Peter also was
standing with them, warming himself.[t]

The High Priest Questions Jesus

18:19–24pp—Mt 26:59–68; Mk 14:55–65; Lk 22:63–71

19Meanwhile, the high priest ques-
tioned Jesus about his disciples and his
teaching.
20"I have spoken openly to the
world," Jesus replied. "I always taught
in synagogues[u] or at the temple,[v] where
all the Jews come together. I said no-
thing in secret.[w] 21Why question me?
Ask those who heard me. Surely they
know what I said."
22When Jesus said this, one of the
officials[x] near by struck him in the face.[y]
"Is this the way you answer the high
priest?" he demanded.
23"If I said something wrong," Jesus
replied, "testify as to what is wrong. But
if I spoke the truth, why did you strike
me?"[z] 24Then Annas sent him, still
bound, to Caiaphas[a] the high priest.[b]

Peter's Second and Third Denials

18:25–27pp—Mt 26:71–75; Mk 14:69–72; Lk 22:58–62

25As Simon Peter stood warming him-
self,[b] he was asked, "You are not one of
his disciples, are you?"
He denied it, saying, "I am not."[c]
26One of the high priest's servants, a
relative of the man whose ear Peter had
cut off,[d] challenged him, "Didn't I see
you with him in the olive grove?"[e]
27Again Peter denied it, and at that
moment a cock began to crow.[f]

Jesus Before Pilate

18:29–40pp—Mt 27:11–18,20–23; Mk 15:2–15; Lk 23:2, 3,18–25

28Then the Jews led Jesus from
Caiaphas to the palace of the Roman
governor.[g] By now it was early
morning, and to avoid ceremonial
uncleanness the Jews did not enter the
palace;[h] they wanted to be able to eat the
Passover.[i] 29So Pilate came out to them
and asked, "What charges are you
bringing against this man?"
30"If he were not a criminal," they
replied, "we would not have handed
him over to you."
31Pilate said, "Take him yourselves
and judge him by your own law."
"But we have no right to execute any-
one," the Jews objected. 32This hap-
pened so that the words Jesus had
spoken indicating the kind of death he
was going to die[j] would be fulfilled.
33Pilate then went back inside the
palace,[k] summoned Jesus and asked
him, "Are you the king of the Jews?"[l]
34"Is that your own idea," Jesus
asked, "or did others talk to you about
me?"
35"Am I a Jew?" Pilate replied. "It was
your people and your chief priests who
handed you over to me. What is it you
have done?"
36Jesus said, "My kingdom[m] is not of
this world. If it were, my servants
would fight to prevent my arrest by the
Jews.[n] But now my kingdom is from
another place."[o]
37"You are a king, then!" said Pilate.
Jesus answered, "You are right in
saying I am a king. In fact, for this
reason I was born, and for this I came
into the world, to testify to the truth.[p]
Everyone on the side of truth listens to
me."[q]
38"What is truth?" Pilate asked. With
this he went out again to the Jews and
said, "I find no basis for a charge against
him.[r] 39But it is your custom for me to
release to you one prisoner at the time of
the Passover. Do you want me to release
'the king of the Jews'?"

12 [m]ver 3
13 [n]ver 24; **Mt 26:3**
14 [o]Jn 11:49–51
15 [p]**Mt 26:3**; [q]Mt 26:58; Mk 14:54; Lk 22:54
17 [r]ver 25
18 [s]Jn 21:9; [t]Mk 14:54,67
20 [u]**Mt 4:23**; [v]Mt 26:55; [w]Jn 7:26
22 [x]ver 3; [y]Mt 16:21; Jn 19:3
23 [z]Mt 5:39; Ac 23:2–5
24 [a]ver 13; **Mt 26:3**
25 [b]ver 18; [c]ver 17
26 [d]ver 10; [e]ver 1
27 [f]Jn 13:38
28 [g]**Mt 27:2**; [h]ver 33; Jn 19:9; [i]Jn 11:55
32 [j]Mt 20:19; 26:2; Jn 3:14; 8:28; 12:32–33
33 [k]ver 28–29; Jn 19:9; [l]Lk 23:3; **Mt 2:2**
36 [m]**Mt 3:2**; [n]Mt 26:53; [o]Lk 17:21; Jn 6:15
37 [p]Jn 3:32; [q]Jn 8:47; 1Jn 4:6
38 [r]**Lk 23:4**

---

b24 Or (*Now Annas had sent him, still bound, to Caiaphas the high priest.*)

40They shouted back, "No, not him!
Give us Barabbas!" Now Barabbas had
taken part in a rebellion.[s]

Jesus Sentenced to be Crucified

19:1–16pp—Mt 27:27–31; Mk 15:16–20

19 Then Pilate took Jesus and had
him flogged.[a] 2The soldiers
twisted together a crown of thorns and
put it on his head. They clothed him in a
purple robe 3and went up to him again
and again, saying, "Hail, king of the
Jews!"[b] And they struck him in the face.[c]
4Once more Pilate came out and said
to the Jews, "Look, I am bringing him
out[d] to you to let you know that I find no
basis for a charge against him."[e] 5When
Jesus came out wearing the crown of
thorns and the purple robe,[f] Pilate said
to them, "Here is the man!"
6As soon as the chief priests and
their officials saw him, they shouted,
"Crucify! Crucify!"
But Pilate answered, "You take him
and crucify him.[g] As for me, I find no
basis for a charge against him."[h]
7The Jews insisted, "We have a law,
and according to that law he must die,[i]
because he claimed to be the Son of
God."[j]
8When Pilate heard this, he was even
more afraid, 9and he went back inside
the palace.[k] "Where do you come
from?" he asked Jesus, but Jesus gave
him no answer.[l] 10"Do you refuse to
speak to me?" Pilate said. "Don't you
realise I have power either to free you or
to crucify you?"
11Jesus answered, "You would have
no power over me if it were not given to
you from above.[m] Therefore the one
who handed me over to you[n] is guilty of
a greater sin."
12From then on, Pilate tried to set
Jesus free, but the Jews kept shouting,
"If you let this man go, you are no friend
of Caesar. Anyone who claims to be a
king[o] opposes Caesar."
13When Pilate heard this, he brought
Jesus out and sat down on the judge's
seat[p] at a place known as the Stone
Pavement (which in Aramaic[q] is Gab-
batha). 14It was the day of Preparation[r]
of Passover Week, about the sixth
hour.[s]
"Here is your king,"[t] Pilate said to the
Jews.
15But they shouted, "Take him away!
Take him away! Crucify him!"
"Shall I crucify your king?" Pilate
asked.
"We have no king but Caesar," the
chief priests answered.
16Finally Pilate handed him over to
them to be crucified.[u]

The Crucifixion

19:17–24pp—Mt 27:33–44; Mk 15:22–32; Lk 23:33–43

So the soldiers took charge of Jesus.
17Carrying his own cross,[v] he went out
to the place of the Skull[w] (which in Ara-
maic[x] is called Golgotha). 18Here they
crucified him, and with him two others[y]
—one on each side and Jesus in the
middle.
19Pilate had a notice prepared and
fastened to the cross. It read: JESUS OF
NAZARETH,[z] THE KING OF THE JEWS.[a]
20Many of the Jews read this sign, for the
place where Jesus was crucified was
near the city,[b] and the sign was written
in Aramaic, Latin and Greek. 21The chief
priests of the Jews protested to Pilate,
"Do not write 'The King of the Jews',
but that this man claimed to be king of
the Jews."[c]
22Pilate answered, "What I have writ-
ten, I have written."
23When the soldiers crucified Jesus,
they took his clothes, dividing them
into four shares, one for each of them,
with the undergarment remaining. This
garment was seamless, woven in one
piece from top to bottom.
24"Let's not tear it," they said to one
another. "Let's decide by lot who will
get it."
This happened that the scripture
might be fulfilled[d] which said,

"They divided my garments among
them
and cast lots for my clothing."[a][e]

So this is what the soldiers did.
25Near the cross[f] of Jesus stood his
mother,[g] his mother's sister, Mary the
wife of Clopas,[h] and Mary Magdalene.[i]
26When Jesus saw his mother[j] there,
and the disciple whom he loved[k] stand-
ing near by, he said to his mother,
"Dear woman, here is your son," 27and
to the disciple, "Here is your mother."
From that time on, this disciple took her
into his home.

The Death of Jesus

19:29,30pp—Mt 27:48,50; Mk 15:36,37; Lk 23:36

28Later, knowing that all was now
completed,[l] and so that the Scripture

40 [s]Ac 3:14
Ch. 19
1 [a]Dt 25:3; Isa 50:6; 53:5; Mt 27:26
3 [b]Mt 27:29; [c]Jn 18:22
4 [d]Jn 18:38; [e]ver 6; **Lk 23:4**
5 [f]ver 2
6 [g]Ac 3:13; [h]ver 4; **Lk 23:4**
7 [i]Lev 24:16; [j]Mt 26:63–66; Jn 5:18; 10:33
9 [k]Jn 18:33; [l]**Mk 14:61**
11 [m]**Ro 13:1**; [n]Jn 18:28–30; Ac 3:13
12 [o]Lk 23:2
13 [p]Mt 27:19; [q]**Jn 5:2**
14 [r]Mt 27:62; [s]Mk 15:25; [t]ver 19,21
16 [u]Mt 27:26; Mk 15:15; Lk 23:25
17 [v]Ge 22:6; Lk 14:27; 23:26; [w]Lk 23:33; [x]**Jn 5:2**
18 [y]Lk 23:32
19 [z]**Mk 1:24**; [a]ver 14,21
20 [b]Heb 13:12
21 [c]ver 14
24 [d]ver 28, 36–37; **Mt 1:22**; [e]Ps 22:18
25 [f]Mt 27:55–56; [g]**Mt 12:46**; [h]Lk 24:18; [i]Lk 8:2; Jn 20:1,18
26 [j]**Mt 12:46**; [k]**Jn 13:23**
28 [l]**ver 30**; Jn 13:1

[a]24 Psalm 22:18

would be fulfilled,[m] Jesus said, "I am
thirsty." 29A jar of wine vinegar[n] was
there, so they soaked a sponge in it, put
the sponge on a stalk of the hyssop
plant, and lifted it to Jesus' lips. 30When
he had received the drink, Jesus said,
"It is finished."[o] With that, he bowed
his head and gave up his spirit.
31Now it was the day of Preparation,[p]
and the next day was to be a special
Sabbath. Because the Jews did not want
the bodies left on the crosses[q] during the
Sabbath, they asked Pilate to have the
legs broken and the bodies taken down.
32The soldiers therefore came and broke
the legs of the first man who had been
crucified with Jesus, and then those of
the other.[r] 33But when they came to
Jesus and found that he was already
dead, they did not break his legs.
34Instead, one of the soldiers pierced[s]
Jesus' side with a spear, bringing a sud-
den flow of blood and water.[t] 35The man
who saw it[u] has given testimony, and
his testimony is true.[v] He knows that he
tells the truth, and he testifies so that
you also may believe. 36These things
happened so that the scripture would
be fulfilled:[w] "Not one of his bones will
be broken,"[b][x] 37and, as another scrip-
ture says, "They will look on the one
they have pierced."[c][y]

The Burial of Jesus

19:38–42pp—Mt 27:57–61; Mk 15:42–47; Lk 23:50–56

38Later, Joseph of Arimathea asked
Pilate for the body of Jesus. Now Joseph
was a disciple of Jesus, but secretly be-
cause he feared the Jews.[z] With Pilate's
permission, he came and took the body
away. 39He was accompanied by
Nicodemus,[a] the man who earlier had
visited Jesus at night. Nicodemus
brought a mixture of myrrh and aloes,
about seventy-five pounds.[d] 40Taking
Jesus' body, the two of them wrapped
it, with the spices, in strips of linen.[b]
This was in accordance with Jewish
burial customs.[c] 41At the place where
Jesus was crucified, there was a garden,
and in the garden a new tomb, in
which no-one had ever been laid. 42Be-
cause it was the Jewish day of Prep-
aration[d] and since the tomb was near
by,[e] they laid Jesus there.

The Empty Tomb

20:1–8pp—Mt 28:1–8; Mk 16:1–8; Lk 24:1–10

20 Early on the first day of the
week, while it was still dark,
Mary Magdalene[a] went to the tomb and
saw that the stone had been removed
from the entrance.[b] 2So she came run-
ning to Simon Peter and the other disci-
ple, the one Jesus loved,[c] and said,
"They have taken the Lord out of the
tomb, and we don't know where they
have put him!"[d]
3So Peter and the other disciple
started for the tomb.[e] 4Both were run-
ning, but the other disciple outran Peter
and reached the tomb first. 5He bent
over and looked in[f] at the strips of linen[g]
lying there but did not go in. 6Then
Simon Peter, who was behind him, ar-
rived and went into the tomb. He saw
the strips of linen lying there, 7as well as
the burial cloth that had been around
Jesus' head.[h] The cloth was folded up by
itself, separate from the linen. 8Finally
the other disciple, who had reached the
tomb first,[i] also went inside. He saw
and believed. 9(They still did not under-
stand from Scripture[j] that Jesus had to
rise from the dead.)[k]

Jesus Appears to Mary Magdalene

10Then the disciples went back to their
homes, 11but Mary stood outside the
tomb crying. As she wept, she bent over
to look into the tomb[l] 12and saw two
angels in white,[m] seated where Jesus'
body had been, one at the head and the
other at the foot.
13They asked her, "Woman, why are
you crying?"[n]
"They have taken my Lord away,"
she said, "and I don't know where they
have put him."[o] 14At this, she turned
round and saw Jesus standing there,[p]
but she did not realise that it was Jesus.[q]
15"Woman," he said, "why are you
crying?[r] Who is it you are looking for?"
Thinking he was the gardener, she
said, "Sir, if you have carried him away,
tell me where you have put him, and I
will get him."
16Jesus said to her, "Mary."
She turned towards him and cried out
in Aramaic,[s] "Rabboni!"[t] (which means
Teacher).
17Jesus said, "Do not hold on to me,
for I have not yet returned to the Father.
Go instead to my brothers[u] and tell
them, 'I am returning to my Father[v]
and your Father, to my God and your
God.'"
18Mary Magdalene[w] went to the disci-
ples[x] with the news: "I have seen the

28 [m]ver 24, 36–37; **Mt 1:22**
29 [n]Ps 69:21
30 [o]Lk 12:50; Jn 4:34; 17:4
31 [p]ver 14,42; [q]Dt 21:23; Jos 8:29; 10:26–27
32 [r]ver 18
34 [s]Zec 12:10; Rev 1:7; [t]1Jn 5:6,8
35 [u]**Lk 24:48**; [v]Jn 15:27; 21:24
36 [w]ver 24,28, 37; **Mt 1:22**; [x]Ex 12:46; Nu 9:12; Ps 34:20
37 [y]Zec 12:10; Rev 1:7
38 [z]**Jn 7:13**
39 [a]Jn 3:1; 7:50
40 [b]Lk 24:12; Jn 11:44; 20:5,7; [c]Mt 26:12
42 [d]ver 14,31; [e]ver 20,41

Ch. 20

1 [a]ver 18; Lk 8:2; Jn 19:25; [b]Mt 27:60,66
2 [c]**Jn 13:23**; [d]ver 13
3 [e]Lk 24:12
5 [f]ver 11; [g]**Jn 19:40**
7 [h]Jn 11:44
8 [i]ver 4
9 [j]Mt 22:29; Jn 2:22; [k]Lk 24:26,46; Ac 2:24
11 [l]ver 5
12 [m]Mt 28:2–3; Mk 16:5; Lk 24:4; Ac 1:10; **5:9**; 10:30
13 [n]ver 15; [o]ver 2
14 [p]Mk 16:9; [q]Lk 24:16; Jn 21:4
15 [r]ver 13
16 [s]**Jn 5:2**; [t]**Mt 23:7**
17 [u]**Mt 28:10**; [v]Jn 7:33
18 [w]**ver 1**; [x]Lk 24:10,22–23

b36 Exodus 12:46; Num. 9:12; Psalm 34:20
c37 Zech. 12:10
d39 Greek *a hundred litrai* (about 34 kilograms)

Lord!" And she told them that he had
said these things to her.

Jesus Appears to His Disciples

19On the evening of that first day of
the week, when the disciples were
together, with the doors locked for fear
of the Jews,[y] Jesus came and stood
among them and said, "Peace[z] be with
you!"[a] 20After he said this, he showed
them his hands and side.[b] The disciples
were overjoyed[c] when they saw the
Lord.

21Again Jesus said, "Peace be with
you![d] As the Father has sent me,[e] I am
sending you."[f] 22And with that he
breathed on them and said, "Receive
the Holy Spirit.[g] 23If you forgive anyone
his sins, they are forgiven; if you do not
forgive them, they are not forgiven."[h]

Jesus Appears to Thomas

24Now Thomas[i] (called Didymus),
one of the Twelve, was not with the
disciples when Jesus came. 25So the
other disciples told him, "We have seen
the Lord!"

But he said to them, "Unless I see the
nail marks in his hands and put my
finger where the nails were, and put my
hand into his side,[j] I will not believe it."[k]

26A week later his disciples were in
the house again, and Thomas was with
them. Though the doors were locked,
Jesus came and stood among them and
said, "Peace[l] be with you!"[m] 27Then he
said to Thomas, "Put your finger here;
see my hands. Reach out your hand and
put it into my side. Stop doubting and
believe."[n]

28Thomas said to him, "My Lord and
my God!"

29Then Jesus told him, "Because you
have seen me, you have believed;[o]
blessed are those who have not seen
and yet have believed."[p]

30Jesus did many other miraculous
signs[q] in the presence of his disciples,
which are not recorded in this book.[r]
31But these are written that you may[a]
believe[s] that Jesus is the Christ, the Son
of God,[t] and that by believing you may
have life in his name.[u]

Jesus and the Miraculous Catch of Fish

21 Afterwards Jesus appeared
again to his disciples,[a] by the
Sea of Tiberias.[a][b] It happened this way:
2Simon Peter, Thomas[c] (called Didy-
mus), Nathanael[d] from Cana in Galilee,[e]
the sons of Zebedee,[f] and two other
disciples were together. 3"I'm going out
to fish," Simon Peter told them, and
they said, "We'll go with you." So they
went out and got into the boat, but that
night they caught nothing.[g]

4Early in the morning, Jesus stood
on the shore, but the disciples did not
realise that it was Jesus.[h]

5He called out to them, "Friends,
haven't you any fish?"

"No," they answered.

6He said, "Throw your net on the
right side of the boat and you will find
some." When they did, they were un-
able to haul the net in because of the
large number of fish.[i]

7Then the disciple whom Jesus loved[j]
said to Peter, "It is the Lord!" As soon as
Simon Peter heard him say, "It is the
Lord," he wrapped his outer garment
around him (for he had taken it off) and
jumped into the water. 8The other disci-
ples followed in the boat, towing the net
full of fish, for they were not far from
shore, about a hundred yards.[b] 9When
they landed, they saw a fire[k] of burning
coals there with fish on it,[l] and some
bread.

10Jesus said to them, "Bring some of
the fish you have just caught."

11Simon Peter climbed aboard and
dragged the net ashore. It was full of
large fish, 153, but even with so many
the net was not torn. 12Jesus said to
them, "Come and have breakfast."
None of the disciples dared ask him,
"Who are you?" They knew it was the
Lord. 13Jesus came, took the bread and
gave it to them, and did the same with
the fish.[m] 14This was now the third time
Jesus appeared to his disciples[n] after he
was raised from the dead.

Jesus Reinstates Peter

15When they had finished eating,
Jesus said to Simon Peter, "Simon son
of John, do you truly love me more than
these?"

"Yes, Lord," he said, "you know that
I love you."[o]

Jesus said, "Feed my lambs."[p]

16Again Jesus said, "Simon son of
John, do you truly love me?"

He answered, "Yes, Lord, you know
that I love you."

Jesus said, "Take care of my sheep."[q]

17The third time he said to him,

19 [y]**Jn 7:13;** [z]**Jn 14:27;** [a]ver 21,26; Lk 24:36–39
20 [b]Lk 24:39–40; Jn 19:34; [c]Jn 16:20,22
21 [d]ver 19; [e]**Jn 3:17;** [f]Mt 28:19; Jn 17:18
22 [g]Jn 7:39; Ac 2:38; 8:15–17; 19:2; Gal 3:2
23 [h]Mt 16:19; 18:18
24 [i]**Jn 11:16**
25 [j]ver 20; [k]Mk 16:11
26 [l]**Jn 14:27;** [m]ver 21
27 [n]ver 25; Lk 24:40
29 [o]**Jn 3:15;** [p]1Pe 1:8
30 [q]**Jn 2:11;** [r]Jn 21:25
31 [s]**Jn 3:15;** 19:35; [t]**Mt 4:3;** [u]**Mt 25:46**

Ch. 21

1 [a]ver 14; Jn 20:19,26; [b]Jn 6:1
2 [c]**Jn 11:16;** [d]Jn 1:45; [e]Jn 2:1; [f]**Mt 4:21**
3 [g]Lk 5:5
4 [h]Lk 24:16; Jn 20:14
6 [i]Lk 5:4–7
7 [j]**Jn 13:23**
9 [k]Jn 18:18; [l]ver 10,13
13 [m]ver 9
14 [n]Jn 20:19,26
15 [o]Mt 26:33,35; Jn 13:37; [p]Lk 12:32
16 [q]2Sa 5:2; Eze 34:2; Mt 2:6; **Jn 10:11;** Ac 20:28; 1Pe 5:2–3

[a]31 Some manuscripts *may continue to*
[a]1 That is, Sea of Galilee
[b]8 Greek *about two hundred cubits* (about 90 metres)

"Simon son of John, do you love me?"
Peter was hurt because Jesus asked
him the third time, "Do you love me?"[r]
He said, "Lord, you know all things;[s]
you know that I love you."
Jesus said, "Feed my sheep.[t] 18I tell
you the truth, when you were younger
you dressed yourself and went where
you wanted; but when you are old you
will stretch out your hands, and some-
one else will dress you and lead you
where you do not want to go." 19Jesus
said this to indicate the kind of death[u]
by which Peter would glorify God.[v]
Then he said to him, "Follow me!"[w]
20Peter turned and saw that the disci-
ple whom Jesus loved[x] was following
them. (This was the one who had
leaned back against Jesus at the supper
and had said, "Lord, who is going to
betray you?")[y] 21When Peter saw him,
he asked, "Lord, what about him?"
22Jesus answered, "If I want him to
remain alive until I return,[z] what is
that to you? You must follow me."[a]
23Because of this, the rumour spread
among the brothers[b] that this disciple
would not die. But Jesus did not say that
he would not die; he only said, "If I
want him to remain alive until I return,
what is that to you?"
24This is the disciple who testifies to
these things[c] and who wrote them
down. We know that his testimony is
true.[d]
25Jesus did many other things as
well.[e] If every one of them were
written down, I suppose that even the
whole world would not have room for
the books that would be written.

17 [r]Jn 13:38; [s]Jn 16:30; [t]**ver 16**
19 [u]Jn 12:33; 18:32; [v]Jn 13:36; 2Pe 1:14; [w]**Mt 4:19**
20 [x]ver 7; **Jn 13:23;** [y]Jn 13:25
22 [z]**Mt 16:27;** [a]ver 19; **Mt 4:19**
23 [b]**Ac 1:16**
24 [c]**Jn 15:27;** [d]Jn 19:35
25 [e]Jn 20:30

Acts

Jesus Taken Up Into Heaven

1 In my former book,[a] Theophilus, I wrote about all that Jesus began to do and to teach[b] 2until the day he was taken up to heaven,[c] after giving instructions[d] through the Holy Spirit to the apostles[e] he had chosen.[f] 3After his suffering, he showed himself to these men and gave many convincing proofs that he was alive. He appeared to them[g] over a period of forty days and spoke about the kingdom of God.[h] 4On one occasion, while he was eating with them, he gave them this command: "Do not leave Jerusalem, but wait[i] for the gift my Father promised, which you have heard me speak about.[j] 5For John baptised with[a] water,[k] but in a few days you will be baptised with the Holy Spirit."[l]

6So when they met together, they asked him, "Lord, are you at this time going to restore[m] the kingdom to Israel?"

7He said to them: "It is not for you to know the times or dates the Father has set by his own authority.[n] 8But you will receive power when the Holy Spirit comes on you;[o] and you will be my witnesses[p] in Jerusalem, and in all Judea and Samaria,[q] and to the ends of the earth."[r]

9After he said this, he was taken up[s] before their very eyes, and a cloud hid him from their sight.

10They were looking intently up into the sky as he was going, when suddenly two men dressed in white[t] stood beside them. 11"Men of Galilee,"[u] they said, "why do you stand here looking into the sky? This same Jesus, who has been taken from you into heaven, will come back[v] in the same way you have seen him go into heaven."

Matthias Chosen to Replace Judas

12Then they returned to Jerusalem[w] from the hill called the Mount of Olives,[x] a Sabbath day's walk[b] from the city. 13When they arrived, they went upstairs to the room[y] where they were staying. Those present were Peter, John, James and Andrew; Philip and Thomas, Bartholomew and Matthew; James son of Alphaeus and Simon the Zealot, and Judas son of James.[z] 14They all joined together constantly in prayer,[a] along with the women[b] and Mary the mother of Jesus, and with his brothers.[c]

15In those days Peter stood up among the believers[c] (a group numbering about a hundred and twenty) 16and said, "Brothers,[d] the Scripture had to be fulfilled[e] which the Holy Spirit spoke long ago through the mouth of David concerning Judas,[f] who served as guide for those who arrested Jesus—17he was one of our number[g] and shared in this ministry."[h]

18(With the reward[i] he got for his wickedness, Judas bought a field;[j] there he fell headlong, his body burst open and all his intestines spilled out. 19Everyone in Jerusalem heard about this, so they called that field in their language[k] Akeldama, that is, Field of Blood.)

20"For," said Peter, "it is written in the Book of Psalms,

> " 'May his place be deserted;
> let there be no-one to dwell in it,'[d][l]

and,

> " 'May another take his place of
> leadership.'[e][m]

21Therefore it is necessary to choose one of the men who have been with us the whole time the Lord Jesus went in and out among us, 22beginning from John's baptism[n] to the time when Jesus was taken up from us. For one of these must become a witness[o] with us of his resurrection."

23So they proposed two men: Joseph called Barsabbas (also known as Justus)

Ch. 1

1 [a]Lk 1:1–4; [b]Lk 3:23
2 [c]ver 9,11; **Mk 16:19;** [d]Mt 28:19–20; [e]**Mk 6:30;** [f]Jn 13:18; 15:16,19
3 [g]Mt 28:17; Lk 24:34,36; Jn 20:19,26; 21:1,14; 1Co 15:5–7; [h]**Mt 3:2**
4 [i]Ps 27:14; [j]Lk 24:49; Jn 14:16; Ac 2:33
5 [k]**Mk 1:4;** [l]**Mk 1:8**
6 [m]Mt 17:11; Ac 3:21
7 [n]Dt 29:29; Ps 102:13; Mt 24:36
8 [o]Ac 2:1–4; [p]**Lk 24:48;** [q]Ac 8:1–25; [r]**Mt 28:19**
9 [s]ver 2; **Mk 16:19**
10 [t]**Jn 20:12**
11 [u]Ac 2:7; [v]**Mt 16:27**
12 [w]Lk 24:52; [x]**Mt 21:1**
13 [y]Ac 9:37; 20:8; [z]Mt 10:2–4; Mk 3:16–19; Lk 6:14–16
14 [a]Ac 2:42; 4:24; 6:4; **Lk 18:1; Ro 1:10;** [b]Lk 23:49,55; [c]**Mt 12:46**
16 [d]Ac 6:3; 11:1, 12,29; 14:2; 18:18,27; 21:7; **22:5; Ro 7:1;** [e]ver 20; **Mt 1:22;** [f]**Mt 10:4**
17 [g]Jn 6:70–71; [h]ver 25
18 [i]Mt 26:14–15; [j]Mt 27:3–10
19 [k]**Jn 5:2**
20 [l]Ps 69:25; [m]Ps 109:8
22 [n]**Mk 1:4;** [o]ver 8; **Lk 24:48**

---

[a]*5* Or *in*
[b]*12* That is, about ¾ of a mile (about 1,100 metres)
[c]*15* Greek *brothers*
[d]*20* Psalm 69:25
[e]*20* Psalm 109:8

and Matthias. 24Then they prayed,[p]
"Lord, you know everyone's heart.[q]
Show us[r] which of these two you have
chosen 25to take over this apostolic
ministry, which Judas left to go where
he belongs." 26Then they cast lots, and
the lot fell to Matthias; so he was added
to the eleven apostles.[s]

The Holy Spirit Comes at Pentecost

2 When the day of Pentecost[a] came,
they were all together[b] in one
place. 2Suddenly a sound like the blow-
ing of a violent wind came from heaven
and filled the whole house where they
were sitting.[c] 3They saw what seemed to
be tongues of fire that separated and
came to rest on each of them. 4All of
them were filled with the Holy Spirit[d]
and began to speak in other tongues[a][e] as
the Spirit enabled them.

5Now there were staying in Jerusalem
God-fearing[f] Jews from every nation
under heaven. 6When they heard this
sound, a crowd came together in be-
wilderment, because each one heard
them speaking in his own language.
7Utterly amazed,[g] they asked: "Are not
all these men who are speaking
Galileans?[h] 8Then how is it that each of
us hears them in his own native lan-
guage? 9Parthians, Medes and Elamites;
residents of Mesopotamia, Judea and
Cappadocia,[i] Pontus[j] and Asia,[k]
10Phrygia[l] and Pamphylia,[m] Egypt and
the parts of Libya near Cyrene;[n] visitors
from Rome 11(both Jews and converts to
Judaism); Cretans and Arabs—we hear
them declaring the wonders of God in
our own tongues!" 12Amazed and per-
plexed, they asked one another, "What
does this mean?"

13Some, however, made fun of them
and said, "They have had too much
wine.[b]"[o]

Peter Addresses the Crowd

14Then Peter stood up with the
Eleven, raised his voice and addressed
the crowd: "Fellow Jews and all of you
who live in Jerusalem, let me explain
this to you; listen carefully to what I say.
15These men are not drunk, as you sup-
pose. It's only nine in the morning![p]
16No, this is what was spoken by the
prophet Joel:

17" 'In the last days, God says,
I will pour out my Spirit on all
people.[q]
Your sons and daughters will
prophesy,[r]
your young men will see visions,
your old men will dream dreams.
18Even on my servants, both men and
women,
I will pour out my Spirit in those
days,
and they will prophesy.[s]
19I will show wonders in the heaven
above
and signs on the earth below,[t]
blood and fire and billows of smoke.
20The sun will be turned to darkness
and the moon to blood[u]
before the coming of the great and
glorious day of the Lord.
21And everyone who calls
on the name of the Lord[v] will be
saved.'[c][w]

22"Men of Israel, listen to this: Jesus of
Nazareth[x] was a man accredited by God
to you by miracles, wonders and signs,[y]
which God did among you through
him,[z] as you yourselves know. 23This
man was handed over to you by God's
set purpose and foreknowledge;[a] and
you, with the help of wicked men,[d] put
him to death by nailing him to the
cross.[b] 24But God raised him from the
dead,[c] freeing him from the agony of
death, because it was impossible for
death to keep its hold on him.[d] 25David
said about him:

" 'I saw the Lord always before me.
Because he is at my right hand,
I will not be shaken.
26Therefore my heart is glad and my
tongue rejoices;
my body also will live in hope,
27because you will not abandon me to
the grave,
nor will you let your Holy One see
decay.[e]
28You have made known to me the
paths of life;
you will fill me with joy in your
presence.'[e][f]

29"Brothers,[g] I can tell you confidently
that the patriarch[h] David died and was
buried,[i] and his tomb is here[j] to this day.
30But he was a prophet and knew that
God had promised him on oath that he
would place one of his descendants on
his throne.[k] 31Seeing what was ahead,
he spoke of the resurrection of the

24 [p]Ac 6:6; 13:3; 14:23; [q]**Rev 2:23;** [r]1Sa 14:41
26 [s]Ac 2:14

Ch. 2

1 [a]Lev 23:15–16; Ac 20:16; 1Co 16:8; [b]Ac 1:14
2 [c]Ac 4:31
4 [d]**Lk 1:15;** [e]**Mk 16:17**
5 [f]Lk 2:25; Ac 8:2
7 [g]ver 12; [h]Ac 1:11
9 [i]1Pe 1:1; [j]Ac 18:2; 1Pe 1:1; [k]Ac 16:6; 19:10; Ro 16:5; 1Co 16:19; 2Co 1:8; Rev 1:4
10 [l]Ac 16:6; 18:23; [m]Ac 13:13; 14:24; 15:38; [n]**Mt 27:32**
13 [o]1Co 14:23; Eph 5:18
15 [p]1Th 5:7
17 [q]Nu 11:25; Isa 44:3; Eze 39:29; Jn 7:37–39; Ac 10:45; [r]**Ac 21:9**
18 [s]Ac 21:9–12
19 [t]Lk 21:11
20 [u]**Mt 24:29**
21 [v]Ge 4:26; 26:25; Ps 105:1; Ac 9:14; 1Co 1:2; 2Ti 2:22; [w]Joel 2:28–32; Ro 10:13
22 [x]**Mk 1:24;** [y]**Jn 4:48;** [z]**Jn 3:2**
23 [a]Isa 53:10; Ac 3:18; 4:28; [b]Mt 16:21; Lk 24:20; Ac 3:13
24 [c]ver 32; Ac 13:30,33–34, 37; 17:31; Ro 6:4; 8:11; 10:9; 1Co 6:14; 15:15; Eph 1:20; Col 2:12; Heb 13:20; 1Pe 1:21; [d]Jn 20:9
27 [e]ver 31; Ac 13:35
28 [f]Ps 16:8–11
29 [g]**Ac 22:5;** [h]Ac 7:8–9; [i]Ac 13:36; 1Ki 2:10; [j]Ne 3:16
30 [k]**Mt 1:1**

[a]4 Or *languages;* also in verse 11
[b]13 Or *sweet wine*
[c]21 Joel 2:28–32
[d]23 Or *of those not having the law* (that is, Gentiles)
[e]28 Psalm 16:8–11

Christ,[f] that he was not abandoned to
the grave, nor did his body see decay.[l]
32God has raised this Jesus to life,[m] and
we are all witnesses[n] of the fact.
33Exalted[o] to the right hand of God,[p] he
has received from the Father[q] the pro-
mised Holy Spirit[r] and has poured out[s]
what you now see and hear. 34For David
did not ascend to heaven, and yet he
said,

"'The Lord said to my Lord:
"Sit at my right hand
35until I make your enemies
a footstool for your feet."'[g][t]

36"Therefore let all Israel be assured of
this: God has made this Jesus, whom
you crucified, both Lord[u] and Christ."[v]
37When the people heard this, they
were cut to the heart and said to Peter
and the other apostles, "Brothers, what
shall we do?"[w]
38Peter replied, "Repent and be bap-
tised,[x] every one of you, in the name of
Jesus Christ for the forgiveness of your
sins.[y] And you will receive the gift of the
Holy Spirit.[z] 39The promise is for you
and your children[a] and for all who are
far off[b]—for all whom the Lord our God
will call."
40With many other words he warned
them; and he pleaded with them,
"Save yourselves from this corrupt
generation."[c] 41Those who accepted his
message were baptised, and about three
thousand were added to their number[d]
that day.

The Fellowship of the Believers

42They devoted themselves to the
apostles' teaching[e] and to the fellow-
ship, to the breaking of bread[f] and to
prayer.[g] 43Everyone was filled with
awe, and many wonders and miracu-
lous signs were done by the apostles.[h]
44All the believers were together and
had everything in common.[i] 45Selling
their possessions and goods, they gave
to anyone as he had need.[j] 46Every day
they continued to meet together in the
temple courts.[k] They broke bread[l] in
their homes and ate together with glad
and sincere hearts, 47praising God and
enjoying the favour of all the people.[m]
And the Lord added to their number[n]
daily those who were being saved.

Peter Heals the Crippled Beggar

3 One day Peter and John[a] were
going up to the temple[b] at the time
of prayer—at three in the afternoon.[c]
2Now a man crippled from birth[d] was
being carried to the temple gate[e] called
Beautiful, where he was put every day
to beg[f] from those going into the temple
courts. 3When he saw Peter and John
about to enter, he asked them for
money. 4Peter looked straight at him, as
did John. Then Peter said, "Look at us!"
5So the man gave them his attention,
expecting to get something from them.
6Then Peter said, "Silver or gold I do
not have, but what I have I give you. In
the name of Jesus Christ of Nazareth,[g]
walk." 7Taking him by the right hand,
he helped him up, and instantly the
man's feet and ankles became strong.
8He jumped to his feet and began to
walk. Then he went with them into the
temple courts, walking and jumping,[h]
and praising God. 9When all the people[i]
saw him walking and praising God,
10they recognised him as the same man
who used to sit begging at the temple
gate called Beautiful,[j] and they were
filled with wonder and amazement at
what had happened to him.

Peter Speaks to the Onlookers

11While the beggar held on to Peter
and John,[k] all the people were aston-
ished and came running to them in the
place called Solomon's Colonnade.[l]
12When Peter saw this, he said to them:
"Men of Israel, why does this surprise
you? Why do you stare at us as if by our
own power or godliness we had made
this man walk? 13The God of Abraham,
Isaac and Jacob,[m] the God of our
fathers,[n] has glorified his servant Jesus.
You handed him over[o] to be killed, and
you disowned him before Pilate,[p]
though he had decided to let him go.[q]
14You disowned the Holy[r] and Right-
eous One[s] and asked that a murderer be
released to you.[t] 15You killed the author
of life, but God raised him from the
dead.[u] We are witnesses[v] of this. 16By
faith in the name of Jesus,[w] this man
whom you see and know was made
strong. It is Jesus' name and the faith
that comes through him that has given
this complete healing to him, as you can
all see.
17"Now, brothers,[x] I know that you
acted in ignorance,[y] as did your
leaders.[z] 18But this is how God fulfilled[a]
what he had foretold[b] through all the

31 [l]Ps 16:10
32 [m]**ver 24**; [n]**Lk 24:48**
33 [o]**Php 2:9**; [p]**Mk 16:19**; [q]Ac 1:4; [r]Jn 7:39; 14:26; 15:26; [s]Ac 10:45
35 [t]Ps 110:1; **Mt 22:44**
36 [u]**Mt 28:18**; [v]**Lk 2:11**
37 [w]Lk 3:10,12, 14; Ac 16:30
38 [x]ver 41; Ac 8:12,16,36,38; 9:18; 10:48; 16:15,33; 19:5; 22:16; Col 2:12; [y]Jer 36:3; Mk 1:4; **Lk 24:47**; Ac 3:19; [z]**Jn 20:22**
39 [a]Isa 44:3; 65:23; [b]Isa 57:19; Ac 10:45; Eph 2:13
40 [c]Dt 32:5; Php 2:15
41 [d]ver 47; Ac 4:4; 5:14; 6:1,7; 9:31,35,42; 11:21,24; 14:1, 21; 16:5; 17:12
42 [e]Mt 28:20; [f]**Mt 14:19**; [g]**Ac 1:14**
43 [h]Ac 5:12
44 [i]Ac 4:32
45 [j]Mt 19:21; Lk 12:33; 18:22; Ac 4:34–35; 6:1
46 [k]Lk 24:53; Ac 3:1; 5:21,42; [l]ver 42; **Mt 14:19**
47 [m]**Ro 14:18**; [n]**ver 41**

Ch. 3

1 [a]**Lk 22:8**; [b]Ac 2:46; [c]Ps 55:17; Ac 10:30
2 [d]Ac 14:8; [e]Lk 16:20; [f]Jn 9:8
6 [g]ver 16; **Mk 1:24**
8 [h]Isa 35:6; Ac 14:10
9 [i]Ac 4:16,21
10 [j]ver 2
11 [k]**Lk 22:8**; [l]Jn 10:23; Ac 5:12
13 [m]Ex 3:6; [n]Ac 5:30; 7:32; 22:14; [o]Ac 2:23; [p]**Mt 27:2**; [q]**Lk 23:4**
14 [r]**Mk 1:24**; Ac 4:27; [s]Ac 7:52; [t]Mk 15:11; Lk 23:18–25
15 [u]**Ac 2:24**; [v]**Lk 24:48**
16 [w]ver 6
17 [x]**Ac 22:5**; [y]Lk 23:34; [z]Ac 13:27
18 [a]**Mt 1:22**; [b]Ac 2:23

[f]31 Or *Messiah*. "The Christ" (Greek) and "the Messiah" (Hebrew) both mean "the Anointed One"; also in verse 36.
[g]35 Psalm 110:1

prophets,[c] saying that his Christ[a] would
suffer.[d] 19 Repent, then, and turn to
God, so that your sins may be wiped
out,[e] that times of refreshing may come
from the Lord, 20 and that he may send
the Christ,[f] who has been appointed for
you—even Jesus. 21 He must remain in
heaven[g] until the time comes for God to
restore everything,[h] as he promised
long ago through his holy prophets.[i]
22 For Moses said, 'The Lord your God
will raise up for you a prophet like me
from among your own people; you
must listen to everything he tells you.[j]
23 Anyone who does not listen to him
will be completely cut off from among
his people.'[b][k]
24 "Indeed, all the prophets[l] from
Samuel on, as many as have spoken,
have foretold these days. 25 And you are
heirs[m] of the prophets and of the
covenant[n] God made with your fathers.
He said to Abraham, 'Through your
offspring all peoples on earth will be
blessed.'[c][o] 26 When God raised up[p] his
servant, he sent him first[q] to you to bless
you by turning each of you from your
wicked ways."

Peter and John Before the Sanhedrin

4 The priests and the captain of the
temple guard[a] and the Sadducees[b]
came up to Peter and John while they
were speaking to the people. 2 They
were greatly disturbed because the
apostles were teaching the people and
proclaiming in Jesus the resurrection of
the dead.[c] 3 They seized Peter and John,
and because it was evening, they put
them in jail[d] until the next day. 4 But
many who heard the message believed,
and the number of men grew[e] to about
five thousand.
5 The next day the rulers,[f] elders and
teachers of the law met in Jerusalem.
6 Annas the high priest was there, and so
were Caiaphas,[g] John, Alexander and
the other men of the high priest's fam-
ily. 7 They had Peter and John brought
before them and began to question
them: "By what power or what name
did you do this?"
8 Then Peter, filled with the Holy
Spirit,[h] said to them: "Rulers and elders
of the people![i] 9 If we are being called
to account today for an act of kindness
shown to a cripple[j] and are asked how
he was healed, 10 then know this, you
and all the people of Israel: It is by the
name of Jesus Christ of Nazareth,[k]
whom you crucified but whom God
raised from the dead,[l] that this man
stands before you healed. 11 He is

"'the stone you builders rejected,
which has become the
capstone.'[a][b][m]

12 Salvation is found in no-one else, for
there is no other name under heaven
given to men by which we must be
saved."[n]
13 When they saw the courage of Peter
and John[o] and realised that they were
unschooled, ordinary men,[p] they were
astonished and they took note that
these men had been with Jesus.[q] 14 But
since they could see the man who had
been healed standing there with them,
there was nothing they could say. 15 So
they ordered them to withdraw from
the Sanhedrin[r] and then conferred
together. 16 "What are we going to do
with these men?"[s] they asked. "Every-
body living in Jerusalem knows they
have done an outstanding miracle,[t] and
we cannot deny it. 17 But to stop this
thing from spreading any further
among the people, we must warn these
men to speak no longer to anyone in this
name."
18 Then they called them in again and
commanded them not to speak or teach
at all in the name of Jesus.[u] 19 But Peter
and John replied, "Judge for yourselves
whether it is right in God's sight to obey
you rather than God.[v] 20 For we cannot
help speaking[w] about what we have
seen and heard."[x]
21 After further threats they let them
go. They could not decide how to pun-
ish them, because all the people[y] were
praising God[z] for what had happened.
22 For the man who was miraculously
healed was over forty years old.

The Believers' Prayer

23 On their release, Peter and John
went back to their own people and re-
ported all that the chief priests and
elders had said to them. 24 When they
heard this, they raised their voices
together in prayer to God.[a] "Sovereign
Lord," they said, "you made the
heaven and the earth and the sea, and
everything in them.[b] 25 You spoke by the
Holy Spirit through the mouth of your
servant, our father David:[c]

18 [c]**Lk 24:27;** [d]Ac 17:2–3; 26:22–23
19 [e]Ps 51:1; Isa 43:25; 44:22; **Ac 2:38**
20 [f]**Lk 2:11**
21 [g]Ac 1:11; [h]Mt 17:11; Ac 1:6; [i]Lk 1:70
22 [j]Dt 18:15,18; Ac 7:37
23 [k]Dt 18:19
24 [l]**Lk 24:27**
25 [m]Ac 2:39; [n]Ro 9:4–5; [o]Ge 12:3; 22:18; 26:4; 28:14
26 [p]ver 22; **Ac 2:24;** [q]Ac 13:46; Ro 1:16

Ch. 4

1 [a]Lk 22:4; [b]Mt 3:7; 16:1,6; 22:23,34; Ac 5:17; 23:6–8
2 [c]Ac 17:18
3 [d]Ac 5:18
4 [e]**Ac 2:41**
5 [f]Lk 23:13
6 [g]**Mt 26:3**
8 [h]**Lk 1:15;** [i]ver 5; Lk 23:13
9 [j]Ac 3:6
10 [k]**Mk 1:24;** [l]**Ac 2:24**
11 [m]Ps 118:22; Isa 28:16; Zec 10:4; Mt 21:42; Eph 2:20; 1Pe 2:7
12 [n]**Mt 1:21;** Jn 14:6; Ac 10:43; **Ro 11:14;** 1Ti 2:5
13 [o]**Lk 22:8;** [p]Mt 11:25; [q]Mk 3:14
15 [r]**Mt 5:22**
16 [s]Jn 11:47; [t]Ac 3:6–10
18 [u]Am 7:13; Ac 5:40
19 [v]Ac 5:29
20 [w]Job 32:18; Jer 20:9; Am 3:8; [x]**Lk 24:48**
21 [y]Ac 5:26; [z]**Mt 9:8**
24 [a]**Ac 1:14;** [b]Ne 9:6; Job 41:11; Isa 37:16
25 [c]Ac 1:16

[a]*18* Or *Messiah;* also in verse 20
[b]*23* Deut. 18:15,18,19
[c]*25* Gen. 22:18; 26:4
[a]*11* Or *cornerstone*
[b]*11* Psalm 118:22

"'Why do the nations rage
and the peoples plot in vain?
26The kings of the earth take their stand
and the rulers gather together
against the Lord
and against his Anointed One.[c,d]'[d][e]

27Indeed Herod[f] and Pontius Pilate[g] met
together with the Gentiles and the peo-
ple[e] of Israel in this city to conspire
against your holy servant Jesus,[h] whom
you anointed. 28They did what your
power and will had decided beforehand
should happen.[i] 29Now, Lord, consider
their threats and enable your servants to
speak your word with great boldness.[j]
30Stretch out your hand to heal and per-
form miraculous signs and wonders[k]
through the name of your holy servant
Jesus."[l]
31After they prayed, the place where
they were meeting was shaken.[m] And
they were all filled with the Holy Spirit[n]
and spoke the word of God[o] boldly.[p]

The Believers Share Their Possessions

32All the believers were one in heart
and mind. No-one claimed that any of
his possessions was his own, but they
shared everything they had.[q] 33With
great power the apostles continued to
testify[r] to the resurrection[s] of the Lord
Jesus, and much grace[t] was upon them
all. 34There were no needy persons
among them. For from time to time
those who owned lands or houses sold
them,[u] brought the money from the
sales 35and put it at the apostles' feet,[v]
and it was distributed to anyone as he
had need.[w]
36Joseph, a Levite from Cyprus,
whom the apostles called Barnabas[x]
(which means Son of Encouragement),
37sold a field he owned and brought the
money and put it at the apostles' feet.[y]

Ananias and Sapphira

5 Now a man named Ananias,
together with his wife Sapphira,
also sold a piece of property. 2With his
wife's full knowledge he kept back part
of the money for himself,[a] but brought
the rest and put it at the apostles' feet.[b]
3Then Peter said, "Ananias, how is it
that Satan[c] has so filled your heart[d] that
you have lied to the Holy Spirit[e] and
have kept for yourself some of the
money you received for the land?[f]
4Didn't it belong to you before it was
sold? And after it was sold, wasn't the
money at your disposal?[g] What made
you think of doing such a thing? You
have not lied to men but to God."[h]
5When Ananias heard this, he fell
down and died.[i] And great fear[j] seized
all who heard what had happened.
6Then the young men came forward,
wrapped up his body,[k] and carried him
out and buried him.
7About three hours later his wife
came in, not knowing what had hap-
pened. 8Peter asked her, "Tell me, is
this the price you and Ananias got for
the land?"
"Yes," she said, "that is the price."[l]
9Peter said to her, "How could you
agree to test the Spirit of the Lord?[m]
Look! The feet of the men who buried
your husband are at the door, and they
will carry you out also."
10At that moment she fell down at his
feet and died.[n] Then the young men
came in and, finding her dead, carried
her out and buried her beside her hus-
band.[o] 11Great fear[p] seized the whole
church and all who heard about these
events.

The Apostles Heal Many

12The apostles performed many mira-
culous signs and wonders[q] among the
people. And all the believers used
to meet together[r] in Solomon's Col-
onnade.[s] 13No-one else dared join them,
even though they were highly regarded
by the people.[t] 14Nevertheless, more
and more men and women believed in
the Lord and were added to their num-
ber.[u] 15As a result, people brought the
sick into the streets and laid them on
beds and mats so that at least Peter's
shadow might fall on some of them as
he passed by.[v] 16Crowds gathered also
from the towns around Jerusalem,
bringing their sick and those tormented
by evil[a] spirits, and all of them were
healed.[w]

The Apostles Persecuted

17Then the high priest and all his
associates, who were members of the
party[x] of the Sadducees,[y] were filled
with jealousy. 18They arrested the apos-
tles and put them in the public jail.[z]
19But during the night an angel[a] of the
Lord opened the doors of the jail[b] and
brought them out.[c] 20"Go, stand in the
temple courts," he said, "and tell the
people the full message of this new
life."[d]

26 [d]Da 9:25; Lk 4:18; Ac 10:38; [e]Heb 1:9; Ps 2:1–2
27 [f]**Mt 14:1;** [g]**Mt 27:2;** Lk 23:12; [h]ver 30; Ac 3:13–14
28 [i]Ac 2:23
29 [j]ver 13,31; Ps 138:3; Ac 9:27; 13:46; 14:3; 28:31; Eph 6:19; Php 1:14
30 [k]**Jn 4:48;** [l]ver 27
31 [m]Ac 2:2; [n]**Lk 1:15;** [o]**Heb 4:12;** [p]**ver 29**
32 [q]Ac 2:44
33 [r]**Lk 24:48;** [s]Ac 1:22; [t]**Ro 3:24**
34 [u]Mt 19:21; Ac 2:45
35 [v]ver 37; Ac 5:2; [w]Ac 2:45; 6:1
36 [x]Ac 9:27; 11:22,30; 13:2; 1Co 9:6; Gal 2:1,9,13
37 [y]ver 35; Ac 5:2

Ch. 5

2 [a]Jos 7:11; [b]Ac 4:35,37
3 [c]**Mt 4:10;** [d]Jn 13:2,27; [e]ver 9; [f]Dt 23:21
4 [g]Dt 23:22; [h]Lev 6:2
5 [i]ver 10; Ps 5:6; [j]ver 11
6 [k]Jn 19:40
8 [l]ver 2
9 [m]ver 3
10 [n]ver 5; [o]ver 6
11 [p]ver 5; Ac 19:17
12 [q]**Jn 4:48;** Ac 2:43; [r]Ac 4:32; [s]Jn 10:23; Ac 3:11
13 [t]Ac 2:47; 4:21
14 [u]**Ac 2:41**
15 [v]Ac 19:12
16 [w]Mt 8:16; **Mk 16:17**
17 [x]Ac 15:5; [y]**Ac 4:1**
18 [z]Ac 4:3
19 [a]Ge 16:7; Ex 3:2; Mt 1:20; 2:13,19; 28:2; Lk 1:11; 2:9; **Jn 20:12;** Ac 8:26; 10:3; 12:7,23; 27:23; [b]Ac 16:26; [c]Ps 34:7
20 [d]Jn 6:63,68

[c]26 That is, Christ or Messiah [d]26 Psalm 2:1,2
[e]27 The Greek is plural. [a]16 Greek *unclean*

21At daybreak they entered the tem-
ple courts, as they had been told, and
began to teach the people.
When the high priest and his asso-
ciates[e] arrived, they called together the
Sanhedrin[f]—the full assembly of the
elders of Israel—and sent to the jail for
the apostles. 22But on arriving at the jail,
the officers did not find them there.[g] So
they went back and reported, 23"We
found the jail securely locked, with the
guards standing at the doors; but when
we opened them, we found no-one in-
side." 24On hearing this report, the cap-
tain of the temple guard and the chief
priests[h] were puzzled, wondering what
would come of this.
25Then someone came and said,
"Look! The men you put in jail are
standing in the temple courts teaching
the people." 26At that, the captain went
with his officers and brought the apos-
tles. They did not use force, because
they feared that the people[i] would stone
them.
27Having brought the apostles, they
made them appear before the Sanhed-
rin[j] to be questioned by the high priest.
28"We gave you strict orders not to teach
in this name,"[k] he said. "Yet you have
filled Jerusalem with your teaching and
are determined to make us guilty of this
man's blood."[l]
29Peter and the other apostles replied:
"We must obey God rather than men![m]
30The God of our fathers[n] raised Jesus
from the dead[o]—whom you had killed
by hanging him on a tree.[p] 31God exalted
him to his own right hand[q] as Prince and
Saviour[r] that he might give repentance
and forgiveness of sins to Israel.[s] 32We
are witnesses of these things,[t] and so is
the Holy Spirit,[u] whom God has given
to those who obey him."
33When they heard this, they were
furious[v] and wanted to put them to
death. 34But a Pharisee named Gama-
liel,[w] a teacher of the law,[x] who was
honoured by all the people, stood up in
the Sanhedrin and ordered that the men
be put outside for a little while. 35Then
he addressed them: "Men of Israel, con-
sider carefully what you intend to do to
these men. 36Some time ago Theudas
appeared, claiming to be somebody,
and about four hundred men rallied to
him. He was killed, all his followers
were dispersed, and it all came to no-
thing. 37After him, Judas the Galilean
appeared in the days of the census[y] and
led a band of people in revolt. He too
was killed, and all his followers were
scattered. 38Therefore, in the present
case I advise you: Leave these men
alone! Let them go! For if their purpose
or activity is of human origin, it will fail.[z]
39But if it is from God, you will not be
able to stop these men; you will only
find yourselves fighting against God."[a]
40His speech persuaded them. They
called the apostles in and had them
flogged.[b] Then they ordered them not to
speak in the name of Jesus, and let them
go.
41The apostles left the Sanhedrin, re-
joicing[c] because they had been counted
worthy of suffering disgrace for the
Name.[d] 42Day after day, in the temple
courts[e] and from house to house, they
never stopped teaching and proclaim-
ing the good news[f] that Jesus is the
Christ.[b][g]

The Choosing of the Seven

6 In those days when the number of
disciples was increasing,[a] the Gre-
cian Jews[b] among them complained
against the Hebraic Jews because their
widows[c] were being overlooked in the
daily distribution of food.[d] 2So the
Twelve gathered all the disciples[e]
together and said, "It would not be right
for us to neglect the ministry of the
word of God[f] in order to wait on tables.
3Brothers,[g] choose seven men from
among you who are known to be full of
the Spirit[h] and wisdom. We will turn
this responsibility over to them[i] 4and
will give our attention to prayer[j] and the
ministry of the word."
5This proposal pleased the whole
group. They chose Stephen,[k] a man full
of faith and of the Holy Spirit;[l] also
Philip,[m] Procorus, Nicanor, Timon, Par-
menas, and Nicolas from Antioch, a
convert to Judaism. 6They presented
these men to the apostles, who prayed[n]
and laid their hands on them.[o]
7So the word of God spread.[p] The
number of disciples in Jerusalem in-
creased rapidly,[q] and a large number of
priests became obedient to the faith.

Stephen Seized

8Now Stephen, a man full of God's
grace and power, did great wonders
and miraculous signs[r] among the peo-
ple. 9Opposition arose, however, from
members of the Synagogue of the
Freedmen (as it was called)—Jews of
Cyrene[s] and Alexandria as well as the
provinces of Cilicia[t] and Asia.[u] These

21 [e]Ac 4:5–6; [f]ver 27,34,41; **Mt 5:22**
22 [g]Ac 12:18–19
24 [h]Ac 4:1
26 [i]Ac 4:21
27 [j]**Mt 5:22**
28 [k]Ac 4:18; [l]Mt 23:35; 27:25; Ac 2:23,36; 3:14–15; 7:52
29 [m]Ex 1:17; Ac 4:19
30 [n]**Ac 3:13**; [o]**Ac 2:24**; [p]Ac 10:39; 13:29; Gal 3:13
31 [q]**Mk 16:19**; [r]**Lk 2:11**; [s]**Mt 1:21**; Mk 1:4; Lk 24:47; Ac 2:38; 3:19; 10:43
32 [t]**Lk 24:48**; [u]Jn 15:26
33 [v]Ac 2:37; 7:54
34 [w]Ac 22:3; [x]Lk 2:46; 5:17
37 [y]Lk 2:1–2
38 [z]Mt 15:13
39 [a]2Ch 13:12; Pr 21:30; Isa 46:10; Ac 7:51; 11:17
40 [b]**Mt 10:17**
41 [c]**Mt 5:12**; [d]**Jn 15:21**
42 [e]**Ac 2:46**; [f]**Ac 13:32**; [g]**Ac 9:22**

Ch. 6

1 [a]**Ac 2:41**; [b]Ac 9:29; [c]Ac 9:39, 41; 1Ti 5:3; [d]Ac 4:35
2 [e]**Ac 11:26**; [f]**Heb 4:12**
3 [g]**Ac 1:16**; [h]**Lk 1:15**; [i]Ex 18:21; Ne 13:13
4 [j]**Ac 1:14**
5 [k]ver 8; Ac 7:55–60; 11:19; 22:20; [l]**Lk 1:15**; [m]Ac 8:5–40; 21:8
6 [n]**Ac 1:24**; [o]Nu 8:10; 27:18; Ac 9:17; 19:6; 28:8; 1Ti 4:14; **Mk 5:23**
7 [p]Ac 12:24; 19:20; [q]**Ac 2:41**
8 [r]Jn 4:48
9 [s]**Mt 27:32**; [t]Ac 15:23,41; 22:3; 23:34; [u]**Ac 2:9**

[b]42 Or *Messiah*

men began to argue with Stephen, 10but
they could not stand up against his wis-
dom or the Spirit by whom he spoke.[v]
11Then they secretly[w] persuaded
some men to say, "We have heard
Stephen speak words of blasphemy
against Moses and against God."[x]
12So they stirred up the people and
the elders and the teachers of the law.
They seized Stephen and brought him
before the Sanhedrin.[y] 13They produced
false witnesses,[z] who testified, "This
fellow never stops speaking against this
holy place[a] and against the law. 14For we
have heard him say that this Jesus of
Nazareth will destroy this place[b] and
change the customs Moses handed
down to us."[c]
15All who were sitting in the Sanhed-
rin[d] looked intently at Stephen, and
they saw that his face was like the face of
an angel.

Stephen's Speech to the Sanhedrin

7 Then the high priest asked him,
"Are these charges true?"
2To this he replied: "Brothers and
fathers,[a] listen to me! The God of glory[b]
appeared to our father Abraham while
he was still in Mesopotamia, before he
lived in Haran.[c] 3'Leave your country
and your people,' God said, 'and go to
the land I will show you.'[a][d]
4"So he left the land of the Chaldeans
and settled in Haran. After the death of
his father, God sent him to this land
where you are now living.[e] 5He gave
him no inheritance here,[f] not even a foot
of ground. But God promised him that
he and his descendants after him would
possess the land,[g] even though at that
time Abraham had no child. 6God spoke
to him in this way: 'Your descendants
will be strangers in a country not their
own, and they will be enslaved and
ill-treated for four hundred years.[h] 7But
I will punish the nation they serve as
slaves,' God said, 'and afterwards they
will come out of that country and
worship me in this place.'[b][i] 8Then he
gave Abraham the covenant of circum-
cision.[j] And Abraham became the father
of Isaac and circumcised him eight days
after his birth.[k] Later Isaac became the
father of Jacob,[l] and Jacob became the
father of the twelve patriarchs.[m]
9"Because the patriarchs were jealous
of Joseph,[n] they sold him as a slave into
Egypt.[o] But God was with him[p] 10and
rescued him from all his troubles. He
gave Joseph wisdom and enabled him
to gain the goodwill of Pharaoh king of
Egypt; so he made him ruler over Egypt
and all his palace.[q]
11"Then a famine struck all Egypt and
Canaan, bringing great suffering, and
our fathers could not find food.[r] 12When
Jacob heard that there was grain in
Egypt, he sent our fathers on their first
visit.[s] 13On their second visit, Joseph
told his brothers who he was,[t] and Phar-
aoh learned about Joseph's family.[u]
14After this, Joseph sent for his father
Jacob and his whole family,[v] seventy-
five in all.[w] 15Then Jacob went down to
Egypt, where he and our fathers died.[x]
16Their bodies were brought back to
Shechem and placed in the tomb that
Abraham had bought from the sons of
Hamor at Shechem for a certain sum of
money.[y]
17"As the time drew near for God to
fulfil his promise to Abraham, the
number of our people in Egypt greatly
increased.[z] 18Then another king, who
knew nothing about Joseph, became
ruler of Egypt.[a] 19He dealt treacherously
with our people and oppressed our
forefathers by forcing them to throw out
their newborn babies so that they would
die.[b]
20"At that time Moses was born, and
he was no ordinary child.[c] For three
months he was cared for in his father's
house.[c] 21When he was placed outside,
Pharaoh's daughter took him and
brought him up as her own son.[d]
22Moses was educated in all the wisdom
of the Egyptians[e] and was powerful in
speech and action.
23"When Moses was forty years old,
he decided to visit his fellow Israelites.
24He saw one of them being ill-treated
by an Egyptian, so he went to his de-
fence and avenged him by killing the
Egyptian. 25Moses thought that his own
people would realise that God was
using him to rescue them, but they
did not. 26The next day Moses came
upon two Israelites who were fighting.
He tried to reconcile them by saying,
'Men, you are brothers; why do you
want to hurt each other?'
27"But the man who was ill-treating
the other pushed Moses aside and said,
'Who made you ruler and judge over
us?[f] 28Do you want to kill me as you
killed the Egyptian yesterday?'[d] 29When
Moses heard this, he fled to Midian,
where he settled as a foreigner and had
two sons.[g]

10 [v]Lk 21:15
11 [w]1Ki 21:10; [x]Mt 26:59-61
12 [y]**Mt 5:22**
13 [z]Ex 23:1; Ps 27:12; [a]Mt 24:15; Ac 7:48; 21:28
14 [b]**Jn 2:19**; [c]Ac 15:1; 21:21; 26:3; 28:17
15 [d]**Mt 5:22**

Ch. 7

2 [a]Ac 22:1; [b]Ps 29:3; [c]Ge 11:31; 15:7
3 [d]Ge 12:1
4 [e]Ge 12:5
5 [f]Heb 11:13; [g]Ge 12:7; 17:8; 26:3
6 [h]Ex 1:8-11; 12:40
7 [i]Ge 15:13-14; Ex 3:12
8 [j]Ge 17:9-14; [k]Ge 21:2-4; [l]Ge 25:26; [m]Ge 29:31-35; 30:5-13,17-24; 35:16-18, 22-26
9 [n]Ge 37:4,11; [o]Ge 37:28; Ps 105:17; [p]Ge 39:2,21,23; Hag 2:4
10 [q]Ge 41:37-43; Ps 105:20-22
11 [r]Ge 41:54
12 [s]Ge 42:1-2
13 [t]Ge 45:1-4; [u]Ge 45:16
14 [v]Ge 45:9-10; [w]Ge 46:26-27; Ex 1:5; Dt 10:22
15 [x]Ge 46:5-7; 49:33; Ex 1:6
16 [y]Ge 23:16-20; 33:18-19; 50:13; Jos 24:32
17 [z]Ex 1:7; Ps 105:24
18 [a]Ex 1:8
19 [b]Ex 1:10-22
20 [c]Ex 2:2; Heb 11:23
21 [d]Ex 2:3-10
22 [e]1Ki 4:30; Isa 19:11
27 [f]Ge 19:9; Nu 16:13
29 [g]Ex 2:11-15

[a]3 Gen. 12:1 [b]7 Gen. 15:13,14
[c]20 Or *was fair in the sight of God*
[d]28 Exodus 2:14

30"After forty years had passed, an
angel appeared to Moses in the flames
of a burning bush in the desert near
Mount Sinai. 31When he saw this, he
was amazed at the sight. As he went
over to look more closely, he heard the
Lord's voice:[h] 32'I am the God of your
fathers,[i] the God of Abraham, Isaac and
Jacob.'[e] Moses trembled with fear and
did not dare to look.[j]
33"Then the Lord said to him, 'Take
off your sandals; the place where you
are standing is holy ground.[k] 34I have
indeed seen the oppression of my peo-
ple in Egypt. I have heard their groan-
ing and have come down to set them
free. Now come, I will send you back to
Egypt.'[f][l]
35"This is the same Moses whom they
had rejected with the words, 'Who
made you ruler and judge?'[m] He was
sent to be their ruler and deliverer by
God himself, through the angel who
appeared to him in the bush. 36He led
them out of Egypt[n] and did wonders
and miraculous signs[o] in Egypt, at the
Red Sea[g][p] and for forty years in the
desert.[q]
37"This is that Moses who told the
Israelites, 'God will send you a prophet
like me from your own people.'[h][r]
38He was in the assembly in the desert,
with the angel[s] who spoke to him on
Mount Sinai, and with our fathers;[t]
and he received living words[u] to pass
on to us.[v]
39"But our fathers refused to obey
him. Instead, they rejected him and in
their hearts turned back to Egypt.[w]
40They told Aaron, 'Make us gods who
will go before us. As for this fellow
Moses who led us out of Egypt—we
don't know what has happened to
him!'[i][x] 41That was the time they made
an idol in the form of a calf. They
brought sacrifices to it and held a
celebration in honour of what their
hands had made.[y] 42But God turned
away[z] and gave them over to the
worship of the heavenly bodies.[a] This
agrees with what is written in the book
of the prophets:

"'Did you bring me sacrifices and
offerings
for forty years in the desert, O
house of Israel?
43You have lifted up the shrine of
Molech
and the star of your god Rephan,
the idols you made to worship.
Therefore I will send you into exile'[j][b]
beyond Babylon.

44"Our forefathers had the tabernacle
of the Testimony[c] with them in the des-
ert. It had been made as God directed
Moses, according to the pattern he had
seen.[d] 45Having received the tabernacle,
our fathers under Joshua brought it
with them when they took the land
from the nations God drove out before
them.[e] It remained in the land until the
time of David,[f] 46who enjoyed God's
favour and asked that he might provide
a dwelling-place for the God of Jacob.[k][g]
47But it was Solomon who built the
house for him.[h]
48"However, the Most High[i] does not
live in houses made by men.[j] As the
prophet says:

49"'Heaven is my throne,
and the earth is my footstool.[k]
What kind of house will you build for
me?
says the Lord.
Or where will my resting place be?
50Has not my hand made all these
things?'[l]

51"You stiff-necked people,[m] with un-
circumcised hearts[n] and ears! You are
just like your fathers: You always resist
the Holy Spirit! 52Was there ever a
prophet your fathers did not perse-
cute?[o] They even killed those who pre-
dicted the coming of the Righteous
One. And now you have betrayed and
murdered him[p]—53you who have re-
ceived the law that was put into effect
through angels[q] but have not obeyed
it."

The Stoning of Stephen

54When they heard this, they were
furious[r] and gnashed their teeth at him.
55But Stephen, full of the Holy Spirit,[s]
looked up to heaven and saw the glory
of God, and Jesus standing at the right
hand of God.[t] 56"Look," he said, "I see
heaven open[u] and the Son of Man[v]
standing at the right hand of God."
57At this they covered their ears and,
yelling at the top of their voices, they all
rushed at him, 58dragged him out of the
city[w] and began to stone him.[x] Mean-
while, the witnesses[y] laid their clothes[z]
at the feet of a young man named Saul.[a]
59While they were stoning him,

31 h Ex 3:1–4
32 i **Ac 3:13**; j Ex 3:6
33 k Ex 3:5; Jos 5:15
34 l Ex 3:7–10
35 m ver 27
36 n Ex 12:41; 33:1; o Ex 11:10; **Jn 4:48**; p Ex 14:21; q Ex 15:25; 17:5–6
37 r Dt 18:15,18; Ac 3:22
38 s ver 53; t Ex 19:17; Lev 27:34; u Dt 32:45–47; Heb 4:12; v Ro 3:2
39 w Nu 14:3–4
40 x Ex 32:1,23
41 y Ex 32:4–6; Ps 106:19–20; Rev 9:20
42 z Jos 24:20; Isa 63:10; a Jer 19:13
43 b Am 5:25–27
44 c Ex 38:21; Nu 1:50; 17:7; d Ex 25:8–9,40
45 e Jos 3:14–17; 18:1; 23:9; 24:18; Ps 44:2; f 2Sa 7:2,6
46 g 2Sa 7:8–16; 1Ki 8:17; Ps 132:1–5
47 h 1Ki 6:1–38
48 i **Mk 5:7**; j 1Ki 8:27; 2Ch 2:6
49 k Mt 5:34–35
50 l Isa 66:1–2
51 m Ex 32:9; 33:3,5; n Lev 26:41; Dt 10:16; Jer 4:4; 9:26
52 o **Mt 5:12**; p Ac 3:14; 1Th 2:15
53 q ver 38; Gal 3:19; Heb 2:2
54 r Ac 5:33
55 s **Lk 1:15**; t **Mk 16:19**
56 u **Mt 3:16**; v **Mt 8:20**
58 w Lk 4:29; x Lev 24:14,16; y Dt 17:7; z Ac 22:20; a Ac 8:1

e 32 Exodus 3:6
f 34 Exodus 3:5,7,8,10
g 36 That is, Sea of Reeds
h 37 Deut. 18:15
i 40 Exodus 32:1
j 43 Amos 5:25–27
k 46 Some early manuscripts *the house of Jacob*
l 50 Isaiah 66:1,2

Stephen prayed, "Lord Jesus, receive my spirit."[b] 60Then he fell on his knees[c] and cried out, "Lord, do not hold this sin against them."[d] When he had said this, he fell asleep.[e]

8 And Saul[a] was there, giving approval to his death.

The Church Persecuted and Scattered

On that day a great persecution broke out against the church at Jerusalem, and all except the apostles were scattered[b] throughout Judea and Samaria.[c] 2Godly men buried Stephen and mourned deeply for him. 3But Saul[d] began to destroy the church.[e] Going from house to house, he dragged off men and women and put them in prison.

Philip in Samaria

4Those who had been scattered[f] preached the word wherever they went.[g] 5Philip[h] went down to a city in Samaria and proclaimed the Christ[a] there. 6When the crowds heard Philip and saw the miraculous signs he did, they all paid close attention to what he said. 7With shrieks, evil[b] spirits came out of many,[i] and many paralytics and cripples were healed.[j] 8So there was great joy in that city.

Simon the Sorcerer

9Now for some time a man named Simon had practised sorcery[k] in the city and amazed all the people of Samaria. He boasted that he was someone great,[l] 10and all the people, both high and low, gave him their attention and exclaimed, "This man is the divine power known as the Great Power."[m] 11They followed him because he had amazed them for a long time with his magic. 12But when they believed Philip as he preached the good news of the kingdom of God[n] and the name of Jesus Christ, they were baptised,[o] both men and women. 13Simon himself believed and was baptised. And he followed Philip everywhere, astonished by the great signs and miracles[p] he saw.

14When the apostles in Jerusalem heard that Samaria[q] had accepted the word of God,[r] they sent Peter and John[s] to them. 15When they arrived, they prayed for them that they might receive the Holy Spirit,[t] 16because the Holy Spirit had not yet come upon any of them;[u] they had simply been baptised into[c] the name of the Lord Jesus.[v]

17Then Peter and John placed their hands on them,[w] and they received the Holy Spirit.[x]

18When Simon saw that the Spirit was given at the laying on of the apostles' hands, he offered them money 19and said, "Give me also this ability so that everyone on whom I lay my hands may receive the Holy Spirit."

20Peter answered: "May your money perish with you, because you thought you could buy the gift of God with money![y] 21You have no part or share[z] in this ministry, because your heart is not right[a] before God. 22Repent[b] of this wickedness and pray to the Lord. Perhaps he will forgive you for having such a thought in your heart. 23For I see that you are full of bitterness and captive to sin."

24Then Simon answered, "Pray to the Lord for me[c] so that nothing you have said may happen to me."

25When they had testified and proclaimed the word of the Lord,[d] Peter and John returned to Jerusalem, preaching the gospel in many Samaritan villages.[e]

Philip and the Ethiopian

26Now an angel[f] of the Lord said to Philip,[g] "Go south to the road—the desert road—that goes down from Jerusalem to Gaza." 27So he started out, and on his way he met an Ethiopian[d][h] eunuch,[i] an important official in charge of all the treasury of Candace, queen of the Ethiopians. This man had gone to Jerusalem to worship,[j] 28and on his way home was sitting in his chariot reading the book of Isaiah the prophet. 29The Spirit told[k] Philip, "Go to that chariot and stay near it."

30Then Philip ran up to the chariot and heard the man reading Isaiah the prophet. "Do you understand what you are reading?" Philip asked.

31"How can I," he said, "unless someone explains it to me?" So he invited Philip to come up and sit with him.

32The eunuch was reading this passage of Scripture:

"He was led like a sheep to the
 slaughter,
 and as a lamb before the shearer is
 silent,
 so he did not open his mouth.

59 [b]Ps 31:5; Lk 23:46
60 [c]Lk 22:41; Ac 9:40; [d]**Mt 5:44**; [e]**Mt 9:24**

Ch. 8

1 [a]Ac 7:58; [b]ver 4; Ac 11:19; [c]Ac 9:31
3 [d]Ac 7:58; [e]Ac 9:1,13,21; 22:4,19; 26:10–11; 1Co 15:9; Gal 1:13, 23; Php 3:6; 1Ti 1:13
4 [f]ver 1; [g]Ac 15:35
5 [h]Ac 6:5; 21:8
7 [i]**Mk 16:17**; [j]**Mt 4:24**
9 [k]Ac 13:6; [l]Ac 5:36
10 [m]Ac 14:11; 28:6
12 [n]**Mt 3:2**; [o]**Ac 2:38**
13 [p]ver 6; Ac 19:11
14 [q]ver 1; [r]**Heb 4:12**; [s]**Lk 22:8**
15 [t]**Jn 20:22**
16 [u]**Ac 10:44**; 19:2; [v]Mt 28:19; **Ac 2:38**
17 [w]**Ac 6:6**; [x]**Jn 20:22**
20 [y]2Ki 5:16; Da 5:17; Mt 10:8; Ac 2:38
21 [z]Ne 2:20; [a]Ps 78:37
22 [b]Ac 2:38
24 [c]Ex 8:8; Nu 21:7; 1Ki 13:6; Jer 42:2
25 [d]**Ac 13:48**; [e]ver 40
26 [f]**Ac 5:19**; [g]Ac 6:5
27 [h]Ps 68:31; 87:4; Zep 3:10; [i]Isa 56:3–5; [j]1Ki 8:41–43; Jn 12:20
29 [k]Ac 10:19; 11:12; 13:2; 20:23; 21:11

[a]5 Or *Messiah* [b]7 Greek *unclean*
[c]16 Or *in*
[d]27 That is, from the upper Nile region

33In his humiliation he was deprived of
justice.
Who can speak of his descendants?
For his life was taken from the
earth."[e][l]

34The eunuch asked Philip, "Tell me,
please, who is the prophet talking
about, himself or someone else?"
35Then Philip began[m] with that very
passage of Scripture[n] and told him the
good news[o] about Jesus.
36As they travelled along the road,
they came to some water and the
eunuch said, "Look, here is water. Why
shouldn't I be baptised?"[f][p] 38And he
gave orders to stop the chariot. Then
both Philip and the eunuch went down
into the water and Philip baptised him.
39When they came up out of the water,
the Spirit of the Lord suddenly took
Philip away,[q] and the eunuch did not
see him again, but went on his way
rejoicing. 40Philip, however, appeared
at Azotus and travelled about,
preaching the gospel in all the towns[r]
until he reached Caesarea.[s]

Saul's Conversion

9:1–19Ref—Ac 22:4–16; 26:9–18

9 Meanwhile, Saul was still
breathing out murderous threats
against the Lord's disciples.[a] He went to
the high priest 2and asked him for let-
ters to the synagogues in Damascus,[b] so
that if he found any there who belonged
to the Way,[c] whether men or women,
he might take them as prisoners to Jeru-
salem. 3As he neared Damascus on his
journey, suddenly a light from heaven
flashed around him.[d] 4He fell to the
ground and heard a voice[e] say to him,
"Saul, Saul, why do you persecute
me?"
5"Who are you, Lord?" Saul asked.
"I am Jesus, whom you are per-
secuting," he replied. 6"Now get up
and go into the city, and you will be told
what you must do."[f]
7The men travelling with Saul stood
there speechless; they heard the sound[g]
but did not see anyone.[h] 8Saul got up
from the ground, but when he opened
his eyes he could see nothing.[i] So they
led him by the hand into Damascus.
9For three days he was blind, and did
not eat or drink anything.
10In Damascus there was a disciple
named Ananias. The Lord called to him
in a vision,[j] "Ananias!"
"Yes, Lord," he answered.

33 [l]Isa 53:7–8
35 [m]Mt 5:2; [n]Lk 24:27; Ac 17:2; 18:28; 28:23; [o]**Ac 13:32**
36 [p]**Ac 2:38**; 10:47
39 [q]1Ki 18:12; 2Ki 2:16; Eze 3:12,14; 8:3; 11:1,24; 43:5; 2Co 12:2; 1Th 4:17; Rev 12:5
40 [r]ver 25; [s]Ac 10:1,24; 12:19; 21:8,16; 23:23,33; 25:1,4,6,13

Ch. 9

1 [a]**Ac 8:3**
2 [b]Isa 17:1; Jer 49:23; [c]Ac 19:9,23; 22:4; 24:14,22
3 [d]1Co 15:8
4 [e]Isa 6:8
6 [f]ver 16; Eze 3:22
7 [g]Jn 12:29; [h]Da 10:7
8 [i]ver 18
10 [j]Ac 10:3,17,19; 12:9; 16:9–10; 18:9
11 [k]ver 30; Ac 11:25; 21:39; 22:3
12 [l]**Mk 5:23**
13 [m]ver 32; Ac 26:10; Ro 1:7; 15:25–26,31; 16:2,15; Eph 1:1; Php 1:1; [n]**Ac 8:3**
14 [o]ver 2,21; [p]**Ac 2:21**
15 [q]Ac 13:2; Ro 1:1; Gal 1:15; 1Ti 1:12; [r]Ro 11:13; 15:15–16; Gal 1:16; 2:7–8; [s]Ac 25:22–23; 26:1
16 [t]Ac 20:23; 21:11; 2Co 6:4–10; 11:23–27; 2Ti 1:8; 2:3,9
17 [u]**Ac 6:6**; [v]**Lk 1:15**
18 [w]**Ac 2:38**
19 [x]**Ac 11:26**; [y]Ac 26:20
20 [z]Ac 13:5,14; 14:1; 17:2,10,17; 18:4,19; 19:8; [a]**Mt 4:3**
21 [b]**Ac 8:3**; [c]ver 14
22 [d]**Lk 2:11**; Ac 5:42; 17:3; 18:5,28
23 [e]**Ac 20:3**
24 [f]Ac 20:3,19; 23:16,30
25 [g]1Sa 19:12; 2Co 11:32–33
26 [h]Ac 22:17; 26:20; Gal 1:17–18
27 [i]**Ac 4:36**

11The Lord told him, "Go to the house
of Judas on Straight Street and ask for a
man from Tarsus[k] named Saul, for he is
praying. 12In a vision he has seen a man
named Ananias come and place his
hands on[l] him to restore his sight."
13"Lord," Ananias answered, "I have
heard many reports about this man and
all the harm he has done to your saints[m]
in Jerusalem.[n] 14And he has come here
with authority from the chief priests[o] to
arrest all who call on your name."[p]
15But the Lord said to Ananias, "Go!
This man is my chosen instrument[q] to
carry my name before the Gentiles[r] and
their kings[s] and before the people of
Israel. 16I will show him how much he
must suffer for my name."[t]
17Then Ananias went to the house
and entered it. Placing his hands on[u]
Saul, he said, "Brother Saul, the Lord
—Jesus, who appeared to you on the
road as you were coming here—has
sent me so that you may see again and
be filled with the Holy Spirit."[v]
18Immediately, something like scales
fell from Saul's eyes, and he could see
again. He got up and was baptised,[w]
19and after taking some food, he re-
gained his strength.

Saul in Damascus and Jerusalem

Saul spent several days with the dis-
ciples[x] in Damascus.[y] 20At once he began
to preach in the synagogues[z] that Jesus
is the Son of God.[a] 21All those who
heard him were astonished and asked,
"Isn't he the man who caused havoc in
Jerusalem among those who call on this
name?[b] And hasn't he come here to take
them as prisoners to the chief priests?"[c]
22Yet Saul grew more and more power-
ful and baffled the Jews living in Damas-
cus by proving that Jesus is the Christ.[a][d]
23After many days had gone by, the
Jews conspired to kill him,[e] 24but Saul
learned of their plan.[f] Day and night
they kept close watch on the city gates
in order to kill him. 25But his followers
took him by night and lowered him in a
basket through an opening in the wall.[g]
26When he came to Jerusalem,[h] he
tried to join the disciples, but they were
all afraid of him, not believing that he
really was a disciple. 27But Barnabas[i]

[e]33 Isaiah 53:7,8

[f]36 Some late manuscripts *baptised?"* 37*Philip said, "If you believe with all your heart, you may." The eunuch answered, "I believe that Jesus Christ is the Son of God."*

[a]22 Or *Messiah*

took him and brought him to the
apostles. He told them how Saul on his
journey had seen the Lord and that the
Lord had spoken to him,[j] and how in
Damascus he had preached fearlessly in
the name of Jesus.[k] 28So Saul stayed
with them and moved about freely in
Jerusalem, speaking boldly in the name
of the Lord. 29He talked and debated
with the Grecian Jews,[l] but they tried to
kill him.[m] 30When the brothers[n] learned
of this, they took him down to Caesarea[o]
and sent him off to Tarsus.[p]

31Then the church throughout Judea,
Galilee and Samaria[q] enjoyed a time
of peace. It was strengthened; and
encouraged by the Holy Spirit, it grew
in numbers,[r] living in the fear of the
Lord.

Aeneas and Dorcas

32As Peter travelled about the coun-
try, he went to visit the saints[s] in Lydda.
33There he found a man named Aeneas,
a paralytic who had been bedridden for
eight years. 34"Aeneas," Peter said to
him, "Jesus Christ heals you.[t] Get up
and tidy up your mat." Immediately
Aeneas got up. 35All those who lived in
Lydda and Sharon[u] saw him and turned
to the Lord.[v]

36In Joppa[w] there was a disciple
named Tabitha (which, when trans-
lated, is Dorcas[b]), who was always
doing good[x] and helping the poor.
37About that time she became sick and
died, and her body was washed and
placed in an upstairs room.[y] 38Lydda
was near Joppa; so when the disciples[z]
heard that Peter was in Lydda, they sent
two men to him and urged him, "Please
come at once!"

39Peter went with them, and when he
arrived he was taken upstairs to the
room. All the widows[a] stood around
him, crying and showing him the robes
and other clothing that Dorcas had
made while she was still with them.

40Peter sent them all out of the room;[b]
then he got down on his knees[c] and
prayed. Turning towards the dead
woman, he said, "Tabitha, get up."[d]
She opened her eyes, and seeing Peter
she sat up. 41He took her by the hand
and helped her to her feet. Then he
called the believers and the widows and
presented her to them alive. 42This be-
came known all over Joppa, and many
people believed in the Lord.[e] 43Peter
stayed in Joppa for some time with a
tanner named Simon.[f]

Cornelius Calls for Peter

10 At Caesarea[a] there was a man
named Cornelius, a centurion
in what was known as the Italian
Regiment. 2He and all his family were
devout and God-fearing;[b] he gave gen-
erously to those in need and prayed to
God regularly. 3One day at about three
in the afternoon[c] he had a vision.[d] He
distinctly saw an angel[e] of God, who
came to him and said, "Cornelius!"

4Cornelius stared at him in fear.
"What is it, Lord?" he asked.

The angel answered, "Your prayers
and gifts to the poor have come up as a
memorial offering[f] before God.[g] 5Now
send men to Joppa[h] to bring back a man
named Simon who is called Peter. 6He is
staying with Simon the tanner,[i] whose
house is by the sea."

7When the angel who spoke to him
had gone, Cornelius called two of his
servants and a devout soldier who was
one of his attendants. 8He told them
everything that had happened and sent
them to Joppa.[j]

Peter's Vision

10:9–32Ref—Ac 11:5–14

9About noon the following day as
they were on their journey and
approaching the city, Peter went up on
the roof[k] to pray. 10He became hungry
and wanted something to eat, and while
the meal was being prepared, he fell
into a trance.[l] 11He saw heaven opened[m]
and something like a large sheet being
let down to earth by its four corners.
12It contained all kinds of four-footed
animals, as well as reptiles of the earth
and birds of the air. 13Then a voice told
him, "Get up, Peter. Kill and eat."

14"Surely not, Lord!"[n] Peter replied.
"I have never eaten anything impure or
unclean."[o]

15The voice spoke to him a second
time, "Do not call anything impure that
God has made clean."[p]

16This happened three times, and im-
mediately the sheet was taken back to
heaven.

17While Peter was wondering about
the meaning of the vision,[q] the men sent
by Cornelius[r] found out where Simon's
house was and stopped at the gate.
18They called out, asking if Simon who
was known as Peter was staying there.

19While Peter was still thinking about

27 [j]ver 3–6; [k]ver 20,22
29 [l]Ac 6:1; [m]2Co 11:26
30 [n]**Ac 1:16;** [o]**Ac 8:40;** [p]**ver 11**
31 [q]Ac 8:1; [r]**Ac 2:41**
32 [s]**ver 13**
34 [t]Ac 3:6,16; 4:10
35 [u]1Ch 5:16; 27:29; SS 2:1; Isa 33:9; 35:2; 65:10; [v]**Ac 2:41**
36 [w]Jos 19:46; 2Ch 2:16; Ezr 3:7; Jnh 1:3; Ac 10:5; [x]1Ti 2:10; Tit 3:8
37 [y]Ac 1:13; 20:8
38 [z]**Ac 11:26**
39 [a]Ac 6:1; 1Ti 5:3
40 [b]Mt 9:25; [c]Lk 22:41; Ac 7:60; [d]**Lk 7:14**
42 [e]**Ac 2:41**
43 [f]Ac 10:6

Ch. 10

1 [a]**Ac 8:40**
2 [b]ver 22,35; Ac 13:16,26
3 [c]Ps 55:17; Ac 3:1; [d]**Ac 9:10;** [e]**Ac 5:19**
4 [f]Ps 20:3; **Mt 10:42**; 26:13; [g]Rev 8:4
5 [h]**Ac 9:36**
6 [i]Ac 9:43
8 [j]**Ac 9:36**
9 [k]**Mt 24:17**
10 [l]Ac 22:17
11 [m]**Mt 3:16**
14 [n]Ac 9:5; [o]Lev 11:4–8, 13–20; 20:25; Dt 14:3–20; Eze 4:14
15 [p]ver 28; Ge 9:3; Mt 15:11; Lk 11:41; Ac 11:9; Ro 14:14,17,20; 1Co 10:25; 1Ti 4:3–4; Tit 1:15
17 [q]**Ac 9:10;** [r]ver 7–8

b36 Both *Tabitha* (Aramaic) and *Dorcas* (Greek) mean *gazelle*.

the vision,[s] the Spirit said[t] to him,
"Simon, three[a] men are looking for you.
20So get up and go downstairs. Do not
hesitate to go with them, for I have sent
them."[u]
21Peter went down and said to the
men, "I'm the one you're looking for.
Why have you come?"
22The men replied, "We have come
from Cornelius the centurion. He is a
righteous and God-fearing man,[v] who is
respected by all the Jewish people. A
holy angel told him to have you come to
his house so that he could hear what
you have to say."[w] 23Then Peter invited
the men into the house to be his guests.

Peter at Cornelius' House

The next day Peter started out with
them, and some of the brothers[x] from
Joppa went along.[y] 24The following day
he arrived in Caesarea.[z] Cornelius was
expecting them and had called together
his relatives and close friends. 25As
Peter entered the house, Cornelius met
him and fell at his feet in reverence.
26But Peter made him get up. "Stand
up," he said, "I am only a man myself."[a]
27Talking with him, Peter went inside
and found a large gathering of people.[b]
28He said to them: "You are well aware
that it is against our law for a Jew to
associate with a Gentile or visit him.[c]
But God has shown me that I should not
call any man impure or unclean.[d] 29So
when I was sent for, I came without
raising any objection. May I ask why
you sent for me?"
30Cornelius answered: "Four days
ago I was in my house praying at this
hour, at three in the afternoon. Sudden-
ly a man in shining clothes[e] stood before
me 31and said, 'Cornelius, God has
heard your prayer and remembered
your gifts to the poor. 32Send to Joppa
for Simon who is called Peter. He is a
guest in the home of Simon the tanner,
who lives by the sea.' 33So I sent for you
immediately, and it was good of you to
come. Now we are all here in the pres-
ence of God to listen to everything the
Lord has commanded you to tell us."
34Then Peter began to speak: "I now
realise how true it is that God does not
show favouritism[f] 35but accepts men
from every nation who fear him and do
what is right.[g] 36You know the message[h]
God sent to the people of Israel, telling
the good news[i] of peace[j] through Jesus
Christ, who is Lord of all.[k] 37You know
what has happened throughout Judea,
beginning in Galilee after the baptism
that John preached—38how God anoin-
ted[l] Jesus of Nazareth with the Holy
Spirit and power, and how he went
around doing good and healing[m] all
who were under the power of the devil,
because God was with him.[n]
39"We are witnesses[o] of everything he
did in the country of the Jews and in
Jerusalem. They killed him by hanging
him on a tree,[p] 40but God raised him
from the dead[q] on the third day and
caused him to be seen. 41He was not
seen by all the people,[r] but by witnesses
whom God had already chosen—by us
who ate[s] and drank with him after he
rose from the dead. 42He commanded
us to preach to the people[t] and to testify
that he is the one whom God appointed
as judge of the living and the dead.[u]
43All the prophets testify about him[v]
that everyone[w] who believes[x] in him
receives forgiveness of sins through his
name."[y]
44While Peter was still speaking these
words, the Holy Spirit came on[z] all who
heard the message. 45The circumcised
believers who had come with Peter[a]
were astonished that the gift of the Holy
Spirit had been poured out[b] even on the
Gentiles.[c] 46For they heard them speak-
ing in tongues[b][d] and praising God.
Then Peter said, 47"Can anyone keep
these people from being baptised with
water?[e] They have received the Holy
Spirit just as we have."[f] 48So he ordered
that they be baptised in the name of
Jesus Christ.[g] Then they asked Peter to
stay with them for a few days.

Peter Explains His Actions

11 The apostles and the brothers[a]
throughout Judea heard that
the Gentiles also had received the word
of God.[b] 2So when Peter went up to
Jerusalem, the circumcised believers[c]
criticised him 3and said, "You went into
the house of uncircumcised men and ate
with them."[d]
4Peter began and explained every-
thing to them precisely as it had hap-
pened: 5"I was in the city of Joppa
praying, and in a trance I saw a vision.[e] I
saw something like a large sheet being
let down from heaven by its four cor-
ners, and it came down to where I was.
6I looked into it and saw four-footed
animals of the earth, wild beasts, rep-
tiles, and birds of the air. 7Then I heard a

19 [s]**Ac 9:10;** [t]**Ac 8:29**
20 [u]Ac 15:7–9
22 [v]ver 2; [w]Ac 11:14
23 [x]**Ac 1:16;** [y]ver 45; Ac 11:12
24 [z]**Ac 8:40**
26 [a]Ac 14:15; Rev 19:10; 22:8–9
27 [b]ver 24
28 [c]Jn 4:9; 18:28; Ac 11:3; [d]**ver 14–15;** Ac 15:8–9
30 [e]**Jn 20:12**
34 [f]Dt 10:17; 2Ch 19:7; Job 34:19; Mk 12:14; Ro 2:11; Gal 2:6; Eph 6:9; Col 3:25; Jas 2:1; 1Pe 1:17
35 [g]Ac 15:9
36 [h]1Jn 1:5; [i]**Ac 13:32;** [j]**Lk 2:14;** [k]**Mt 28:18**
38 [l]**Ac 4:26;** [m]**Mt 4:23;** [n]**Jn 3:2**
39 [o]ver 41; **Lk 24:48;** [p]**Ac 5:30**
40 [q]**Ac 2:24**
41 [r]Jn 14:17,22; [s]Lk 24:43; Jn 21:13; Ac 1:4
42 [t]Mt 28:19–20; [u]**Jn 5:22;** Ac 17:31; Ro 14:9; 2Co 5:10; 2Ti 4:1; 1Pe 4:5
43 [v]Isa 53:11; Ac 26:22; [w]Ac 15:9; [x]**Jn 3:15;** [y]**Lk 24:27**
44 [z]Ac 8:15–16; 11:15; 15:8; 19:6; **Lk 1:15**
45 [a]ver 23; [b]Ac 2:33,38; [c]Ac 11:18; 15:8
46 [d]**Mk 16:17**
47 [e]Ac 8:36; [f]**Jn 20:22;** Ac 11:17
48 [g]**Ac 2:38**

Ch. 11

1 [a]**Ac 1:16;** [b]**Heb 4:12**
2 [c]Ac 10:45
3 [d]Ac 10:25,28; Gal 2:12
5 [e]Ac 10:9–32; **9:10**

[a]19 One early manuscript *two*; other manuscripts do not have the number.
[b]46 Or *other languages*

voice telling me, 'Get up, Peter. Kill and
eat.'
8"I replied, 'Surely not, Lord!
Nothing impure or unclean has ever
entered my mouth.'
9"The voice spoke from heaven a
second time, 'Do not call anything im-
pure that God has made clean.'[f] 10This
happened three times, and then it was
pulled up to heaven again.
11"Right then three men who had
been sent to me from Caesarea[g] stopped
at the house where I was staying. 12The
Spirit told[h] me to have no hesitation
about going with them.[i] These six
brothers[j] also went with me, and we
entered the man's house. 13He told us
how he had seen an angel[k] appear in his
house and say, 'Send to Joppa for Simon
who is called Peter. 14He will bring you a
message[l] through which you and all
your household[m] will be saved.'
15"As I began to speak, the Holy Spirit
came on[n] them as he had come on us at
the beginning.[o] 16Then I remembered
what the Lord had said: 'John baptised
with[a] water,[p] but you will be baptised
with the Holy Spirit.'[q] 17So if God gave
them the same gift[r] as he gave us,[s] who
believed in the Lord Jesus Christ, who
was I to think that I could oppose God?"
18When they heard this, they had no
further objections and praised God,
saying, "So then, God has granted even
the Gentiles repentance unto life."[t]

The Church in Antioch

19Now those who had been scattered
by the persecution in connection with
Stephen[u] travelled as far as Phoenicia,
Cyprus and Antioch,[v] telling the
message only to Jews. 20Some of
them, however, men from Cyprus[w] and
Cyrene,[x] went to Antioch[y] and began to
speak to Greeks also, telling them the
good news[z] about the Lord Jesus. 21The
Lord's hand was with them,[a] and a great
number of people believed and turned
to the Lord.[b]
22News of this reached the ears of the
church at Jerusalem, and they sent Bar-
nabas[c] to Antioch. 23When he arrived
and saw the evidence of the grace of
God,[d] he was glad and encouraged
them all to remain true to the Lord with
all their hearts.[e] 24He was a good man,
full of the Holy Spirit[f] and faith, and a
great number of people were brought to
the Lord.[g]
25Then Barnabas went to Tarsus[h] to
look for Saul, 26and when he found him,
he brought him to Antioch. So for a
whole year Barnabas and Saul met with
the church and taught great numbers
of people. The disciples[i] were called
Christians first[j] at Antioch.
27During this time some prophets[k]
came down from Jerusalem to Antioch.
28One of them, named Agabus,[l] stood
up and through the Spirit predicted that
a severe famine would spread over the
entire Roman world.[m] (This happened
during the reign of Claudius.)[n] 29The
disciples,[o] each according to his ability,
decided to provide help[p] for the
brothers[q] living in Judea. 30This they
did, sending their gift to the elders[r] by
Barnabas[s] and Saul.[t]

Peter's Miraculous Escape From Prison

12 It was about this time that King
Herod[a] arrested some who be-
longed to the church, intending to
persecute them. 2He had James, the
brother of John,[b] put to death with the
sword.[c] 3When he saw that this pleased
the Jews,[d] he proceeded to seize Peter
also. This happened during the Feast of
Unleavened Bread.[e] 4After arresting
him, he put him in prison, handing him
over to be guarded by four squads of
four soldiers each. Herod intended to
bring him out for public trial after the
Passover.[f]
5So Peter was kept in prison, but the
church was earnestly praying to God for
him.[g]
6The night before Herod was to bring
him to trial, Peter was sleeping between
two soldiers, bound with two chains,[h]
and sentries stood guard at the en-
trance. 7Suddenly an angel[i] of the Lord
appeared and a light shone in the cell.
He struck Peter on the side and woke
him up. "Quick, get up!" he said, and
the chains fell off Peter's wrists.[j]
8Then the angel said to him, "Put on
your clothes and sandals." And Peter
did so. "Wrap your cloak around you
and follow me," the angel told him.
9Peter followed him out of the prison,
but he had no idea that what the angel
was doing was really happening; he
thought he was seeing a vision.[k] 10They
passed the first and second guards and
came to the iron gate leading to the city.
It opened for them by itself,[l] and they
went through it. When they had walked
the length of one street, suddenly the
angel left him.

9 [f]**Ac 10:15**
11 [g]**Ac 8:40**
12 [h]**Ac 8:29;** [i]Ac 15:9; Ro 3:22; [j]ver 1,29; **Ac 1:16**
13 [k]**Ac 5:19**
14 [l]Ac 10:36; [m]Jn 4:53; Ac 16:15, 31–34; 18:8; 1Co 1:11,16
15 [n]**Ac 10:44;** [o]Ac 2:4
16 [p]**Mk 1:4;** [q]**Mk 1:8**
17 [r]Ac 2:38; [s]Ac 10:45,47
18 [t]Ro 10:12–13; 2Co 7:10
19 [u]Ac 8:1,4; [v]ver 26–27; Ac 13:1; 14:26; 18:22; Gal 2:11
20 [w]Ac 4:36; [x]**Mt 27:32;** [y]**ver 19;** [z]**Ac 13:32**
21 [a]Lk 1:66; [b]**Ac 2:41**
22 [c]**Ac 4:36**
23 [d]Ac 13:43; 14:26; 15:40; 20:24; [e]Ac 14:22
24 [f]**Lk 1:15;** [g]**Ac 2:41**
25 [h]**Ac 9:11**
26 [i]ver 29; Ac 6:1–2; 9:19,26, 38; 13:52; [j]Ac 26:28; 1Pe 4:16
27 [k]Ac 13:1; 15:32; 1Co 11:4; 12:28–29; 14:29,32,37; **Eph 4:11**
28 [l]Ac 21:10; [m]**Mt 24:14;** [n]Ac 18:2
29 [o]**ver 26;** [p]Ro 15:26; 2Co 8:1–4; 9:2; [q]ver 1,12; **Ac 1:16**
30 [r]Ac 14:23; 15:2,22; 20:17; 1Ti 5:17; Tit 1:5; Jas 5:14; 1Pe 5:1; 2Jn 1; [s]**Ac 4:36;** [t]Ac 12:25

Ch. 12

1 [a]**Mt 14:1**
2 [b]**Mt 4:21;** [c]Mk 10:39
3 [d]Ac 24:27; 25:9; [e]Ex 12:15; 23:15; Ac 20:6
4 [f]**Jn 11:55**
5 [g]**Ac 1:14;** Ro 15:30–31; Eph 6:18
6 [h]Ac 21:33
7 [i]**Ac 5:19;** [j]Ps 107:14; Ac 16:26
9 [k]**Ac 9:10**
10 [l]Ac 5:19; 16:26

[a]16 Or *in*

11Then Peter came to himself[m] and
said, "Now I know without a doubt
that the Lord sent his angel and rescued
me[n] from Herod's clutches and from
everything the Jewish people were
anticipating."
12When this had dawned on him, he
went to the house of Mary the mother of
John, also called Mark,[o] where many
people had gathered and were
praying.[p] 13Peter knocked at the outer
entrance, and a servant girl named Rho-
da came to answer the door.[q] 14When
she recognised Peter's voice, she was so
overjoyed[r] she ran back without open-
ing it and exclaimed, "Peter is at the
door!"
15"You're out of your mind," they
told her. When she kept insisting that it
was so, they said, "It must be his
angel."[s]
16But Peter kept on knocking, and
when they opened the door and saw
him, they were astonished. 17Peter
motioned with his hand[t] for them to be
quiet and described how the Lord had
brought him out of prison. "Tell James[u]
and the brothers[v] about this," he said,
and then he left for another place.
18In the morning, there was no small
commotion among the soldiers as to
what had become of Peter. 19After
Herod had a thorough search made for
him and did not find him, he cross-
examined the guards and ordered that
they be executed.[w]

Herod's Death

Then Herod went from Judea to
Caesarea[x] and stayed there a while.
20He had been quarrelling with the peo-
ple of Tyre and Sidon;[y] they now joined
together and sought an audience with
him. Having secured the support of
Blastus, a trusted personal servant of
the king, they asked for peace, because
they depended on the king's country for
their food supply.[z]
21On the appointed day Herod, wear-
ing his royal robes, sat on his throne and
delivered a public address to the peo-
ple. 22They shouted, "This is the voice
of a god, not of a man." 23Immediately,
because Herod did not give praise to
God, an angel[a] of the Lord struck him
down,[b] and he was eaten by worms and
died.
24But the word of God[c] continued to
increase and spread.[d]
25When Barnabas[e] and Saul had
finished their mission,[f] they returned
from[a] Jerusalem, taking with them
John, also called Mark.[g]

Barnabas and Saul Sent Off

13 In the church at Antioch[a] there
were prophets[b] and teachers:[c]
Barnabas,[d] Simeon called Niger, Lucius
of Cyrene,[e] Manaen (who had been
brought up with Herod[f] the tetrarch)
and Saul. 2While they were worship-
ping the Lord and fasting, the Holy
Spirit said,[g] "Set apart for me Barnabas
and Saul for the work[h] to which I have
called them."[i] 3So after they had fasted
and prayed, they placed their hands on
them[j] and sent them off.[k]

On Cyprus

4The two of them, sent on their way
by the Holy Spirit,[l] went down to
Seleucia and sailed from there to
Cyprus.[m] 5When they arrived at
Salamis, they proclaimed the word of
God[n] in the Jewish synagogues.[o] John[p]
was with them as their helper.
6They travelled through the whole
island until they came to Paphos. There
they met a Jewish sorcerer[q] and false
prophet[r] named Bar-Jesus, 7who was an
attendant of the proconsul,[s] Sergius
Paulus. The proconsul, an intelligent
man, sent for Barnabas and Saul be-
cause he wanted to hear the word of
God. 8But Elymas the sorcerer[t] (for that
is what his name means) opposed them
and tried to turn the proconsul[u] from
the faith.[v] 9Then Saul, who was also
called Paul, filled with the Holy Spirit,[w]
looked straight at Elymas and said,
10"You are a child of the devil[x] and an
enemy of everything that is right! You
are full of all kinds of deceit and trick-
ery. Will you never stop perverting the
right ways of the Lord?[y] 11Now the hand
of the Lord is against you.[z] You are
going to be blind, and for a time you will
be unable to see the light of the sun."[a]
Immediately mist and darkness came
over him, and he groped about, seeking
someone to lead him by the hand.
12When the proconsul[b] saw what had
happened, he believed, for he was
amazed at the teaching about the Lord.

In Pisidian Antioch

13From Paphos,[c] Paul and his com-
panions sailed to Perga in Pamphylia,[d]

11 [m]Lk 15:17; [n]Ps 34:7; Da 3:28; 6:22; 2Co 1:10; 2Pe 2:9
12 [o]ver 25; Ac 13:5,13; 15:37, 39; Col 4:10; 2Ti 4:11; Phm 24; 1Pe 5:13; [p]ver 5
13 [q]Jn 18:16–17
14 [r]Lk 24:41
15 [s]**Mt 18:10**
17 [t]Ac 13:16; 19:33; 21:40; [u]**Ac 15:13;** [v]**Ac 1:16**
19 [w]Ac 16:27; [x]**Ac 8:40**
20 [y]**Mt 11:21;** [z]1Ki 5:9,11; Eze 27:17
23 [a]**Ac 5:19;** [b]1Sa 25:38; 2Sa 24:16–17; 2Ki 19:35
24 [c]**Heb 4:12;** [d]Ac 6:7; 19:20
25 [e]**Ac 4:36;** [f]Ac 11:30; [g]**ver 12**

Ch. 13

1 [a]**Ac 11:19;** [b]**Ac 11:27;** [c]**Eph 4:11;** [d]**Ac 4:36;** [e]**Mt 27:32;** [f]**Mt 14:1**
2 [g]**Ac 8:29;** [h]Ac 14:26; [i]Ac 9:15; 22:21
3 [j]**Ac 6:6;** [k]Ac 14:26
4 [l]ver 2–3; [m]Ac 4:36
5 [n]**Heb 4:12;** [o]**Ac 9:20;** [p]**Ac 12:12**
6 [q]Ac 8:9; [r]**Mt 7:15**
7 [s]ver 8,12; Ac 18:12; 19:38
8 [t]Ac 8:9; [u]**ver 7;** [v]Isa 30:11; Ac 6:7
9 [w]**Lk 1:15**
10 [x]Mt 13:38; Jn 8:44; [y]Hos 14:9
11 [z]Ex 9:3; 1Sa 5:6–7; Ps 32:4; [a]Ge 19:10–11; 2Ki 6:18
12 [b]**ver 7**
13 [c]ver 6; [d]**Ac 2:10**

[a]25 Some manuscripts *to*

where John[e] left them to return to Jeru-
salem. 14From Perga they went on to
Pisidian Antioch.[f] On the Sabbath[g] they
entered the synagogue[h] and sat down.
15After the reading from the Law[i] and
the Prophets, the synagogue rulers sent
word to them, saying, "Brothers, if you
have a message of encouragement for
the people, please speak."
16Standing up, Paul motioned with
his hand[j] and said: "Men of Israel and
you Gentiles who worship God, listen
to me! 17The God of the people of Israel
chose our fathers; he made the people
prosper during their stay in Egypt, with
mighty power he led them out of that
country,[k] 18he endured their conduct[a][l]
for about forty years in the desert,[m] 19he
overthrew seven nations in Canaan[n]
and gave their land to his people[o] as
their inheritance.[p] 20All this took about
450 years.
"After this, God gave them judges[q]
until the time of Samuel the prophet.[r]
21Then the people asked for a king,[s] and
he gave them Saul[t] son of Kish, of the
tribe of Benjamin,[u] who ruled for forty
years. 22After removing Saul,[v] he made
David their king.[w] He testified concern-
ing him: 'I have found David son of
Jesse a man after my own heart;[x] he will
do everything I want him to do.'[y]
23"From this man's descendants[z] God
has brought to Israel the Saviour[a] Jesus,[b]
as he promised.[c] 24Before the coming of
Jesus, John preached repentance and
baptism to all the people of Israel.[d] 25As
John was completing his work,[e] he said:
'Who do you think I am? I am not that
one.[f] No, but he is coming after me,
whose sandals I am not worthy to
untie.'[g]
26"Brothers,[h] children of Abraham,[i]
and you God-fearing Gentiles, it is to us
that this message of salvation[j] has been
sent. 27The people of Jerusalem and
their rulers did not recognise Jesus,[k] yet
in condemning him they fulfilled the
words of the prophets[l] that are read
every Sabbath. 28Though they found no
proper ground for a death sentence,
they asked Pilate to have him exe-
cuted.[m] 29When they had carried out all
that was written about him,[n] they took
him down from the tree[o] and laid him in
a tomb.[p] 30But God raised him from the
dead,[q] 31and for many days he was seen
by those who had travelled with him
from Galilee to Jerusalem.[r] They are
now his witnesses[s] to our people.
32"We tell you the good news:[t] What
God promised our fathers[u] 33he has ful-
filled for us, their children, by raising up
Jesus.[v] As it is written in the second
Psalm:

"'You are my Son;
today I have become your
Father.'[b][c][w]

34The fact that God raised him from the
dead, never to decay, is stated in these
words:

"'I will give you the holy and sure
blessings promised to David.'[d][x]

35So it is stated elsewhere:

"'You will not let your Holy One see
decay.'[e][y]

36"For when David had served God's
purpose in his own generation, he fell
asleep;[z] he was buried with his fathers[a]
and his body decayed. 37But the one
whom God raised from the dead[b] did
not see decay.
38"Therefore, my brothers, I want you
to know that through Jesus the forgive-
ness of sins is proclaimed to you.[c]
39Through him everyone who believes[d]
is justified from everything you could
not be justified from by the law of
Moses.[e] 40Take care that what the
prophets have said does not happen to
you:

41"'Look, you scoffers,
wonder and perish,
for I am going to do something in your
days
that you would never believe,
even if someone told you.'[f]"[f]

42As Paul and Barnabas were leaving
the synagogue,[g] the people invited
them to speak further about these
things on the next Sabbath. 43When the
congregation was dismissed, many of
the Jews and devout converts to Juda-
ism followed Paul and Barnabas, who
talked with them and urged them to
continue in the grace of God.[h]
44On the next Sabbath almost the
whole city gathered to hear the word of
the Lord. 45When the Jews saw the
crowds, they were filled with jealousy
and talked abusively[i] against what Paul
was saying.[j]
46Then Paul and Barnabas answered

13 [e]**Ac 12:12**
14 [f]Ac 14:19,21; [g]ver 27,42, 44; Ac 16:13; 18:4; [h]**Ac 9:20**
15 [i]Ac 15:21
16 [j]**Ac 12:17**
17 [k]Ex 6:6–7; Dt 7:6–8
18 [l]Dt 1:31; [m]Nu 14:33; Ps 95:10; Ac 7:36
19 [n]Dt 7:1; [o]Jos 19:51; Ac 7:45; [p]Ps 78:55
20 [q]Jdg 2:16; [r]1Sa 3:19–20; Ac 3:24
21 [s]1Sa 8:5,19; [t]1Sa 10:1; [u]1Sa 9:1–2
22 [v]1Sa 15:23,26; [w]1Sa 16:13; Ps 89:20; [x]1Sa 13:14; Jer 3:15; [y]Isa 44:28
23 [z]**Mt 1:1;** [a]**Lk 2:11;** [b]Mt 1:21; [c]ver 32; 2Sa 7:11; 22:51; Jer 30:9
24 [d]**Mk 1:4**
25 [e]Ac 20:24; [f]Jn 1:20; [g]Mt 3:11; Jn 1:27
26 [h]**Ac 22:5;** [i]**Lk 3:8;** [j]Ac 4:12; 28:28
27 [k]Ac 3:17; [l]**Lk 24:27; Mt 1:22**
28 [m]Mt 27:20–25; Ac 3:14
29 [n]**Mt 1:22;** Lk 18:31; [o]**Ac 5:30;** [p]Lk 23:53
30 [q]**Mt 16:21;** 28:6; **Ac 2:24**
31 [r]Mt 28:16; [s]**Lk 24:48**
32 [t]Isa 40:9; 52:7; Ac 5:42; 8:35; 10:36; 14:7, 15,21; 17:18; [u]Ac 26:6; Ro 1:2; 4:13; 9:4
33 [v]**Ac 2:24;** [w]Ps 2:7; **Mt 3:17**
34 [x]Isa 55:3
35 [y]Ps 16:10; Ac 2:27
36 [z]**Mt 9:24;** [a]2Sa 7:12; 1Ki 2:10; 2Ch 29:28; Ac 2:29
37 [b]**Ac 2:24**
38 [c]**Lk 24:47;** Ac 2:38
39 [d]**Jn 3:15;** [e]**Ro 3:28**
41 [f]Hab 1:5
42 [g]ver 14
43 [h]**Ac 11:23;** 14:22; **Ro 3:24**
45 [i]Ac 18:6; 1Pe 4:4; Jude 10; [j]**1Th 2:16**

[a]*18* Some manuscripts *and cared for them*
[b]*33* Or *have begotten you*
[c]*33* Psalm 2:7
[d]*34* Isaiah 55:3
[e]*35* Psalm 16:10
[f]*41* Hab. 1:5

them boldly: "We had to speak the
word of God to you first.[k] Since you
reject it and do not consider yourselves
worthy of eternal life, we now turn to
the Gentiles.[l] 47For this is what the Lord
has commanded us:

"'I have made you[g] a light for the
Gentiles,'[m]
that you[g] may bring salvation to the
ends of the earth.'[h]"[n]

48When the Gentiles heard this, they
were glad and honoured the word of the
Lord;[o] and all who were appointed for
eternal life believed.
49The word of the Lord[p] spread
through the whole region. 50But the
Jews incited the God-fearing women of
high standing and the leading men of
the city. They stirred up persecution
against Paul and Barnabas, and
expelled them from their region.[q]
51So they shook the dust from their feet[r]
in protest against them and went to
Iconium.[s] 52And the disciples[t] were
filled with joy and with the Holy Spirit.[u]

In Iconium

14 At Iconium[a] Paul and Barnabas
went as usual into the Jewish
synagogue.[b] There they spoke so effec-
tively that a great number[c] of Jews and
Gentiles believed. 2But the Jews who
refused to believe stirred up the Gen-
tiles and poisoned their minds against
the brothers.[d] 3So Paul and Barnabas
spent considerable time there, speaking
boldly[e] for the Lord, who confirmed the
message of his grace by enabling them
to do miraculous signs and wonders.[f]
4The people of the city were divided;
some sided with the Jews, others with
the apostles.[g] 5There was a plot afoot
among the Gentiles and Jews,[h] together
with their leaders, to ill-treat them and
stone them.[i] 6But they found out about
it and fled[j] to the Lycaonian cities of
Lystra and Derbe and to the surround-
ing country, 7where they continued to
preach[k] the good news.[l]

In Lystra and Derbe

8In Lystra there sat a man crippled in
his feet, who was lame from birth[m] and
had never walked. 9He listened to Paul
as he was speaking. Paul looked directly
at him, saw that he had faith to be
healed[n] 10and called out, "Stand up on
your feet!"[o] At that, the man jumped up
and began to walk.[p]
11When the crowd saw what Paul had
done, they shouted in the Lycaonian
language, "The gods have come down
to us in human form!"[q] 12Barnabas they
called Zeus, and Paul they called
Hermes because he was the chief
speaker.[r] 13The priest of Zeus, whose
temple was just outside the city,
brought bulls and wreaths to the city
gates because he and the crowd wanted
to offer sacrifices to them.
14But when the apostles Barnabas and
Paul heard of this, they tore their
clothes[s] and rushed out into the crowd,
shouting: 15"Men, why are you doing
this? We too are only men,[t] human like
you. We are bringing you good news,[u]
telling you to turn from these worthless
things[v] to the living God,[w] who made
heaven and earth[x] and sea and every-
thing in them.[y] 16In the past, he let[z] all
nations go their own way.[a] 17Yet he has
not left himself without testimony:[b] He
has shown kindness by giving you rain
from heaven and crops in their seasons;[c]
he provides you with plenty of food and
fills your hearts with joy."[d] 18Even with
these words, they had difficulty keep-
ing the crowd from sacrificing to them.
19Then some Jews[e] came from Anti-
och and Iconium[f] and won the crowd
over. They stoned Paul[g] and dragged
him outside the city, thinking he was
dead. 20But after the disciples[h] had
gathered round him, he got up and
went back into the city. The next day he
and Barnabas left for Derbe.

The Return to Antioch in Syria

21They preached the good news[i] in
that city and won a large number[j] of
disciples. Then they returned to Lystra,
Iconium[k] and Antioch, 22strengthening
the disciples and encouraging them to
remain true to the faith.[l] "We must go
through many hardships[m] to enter the
kingdom of God," they said. 23Paul and
Barnabas appointed elders[a][n] for them in
each church and, with prayer and fast-
ing,[o] committed them to the Lord,[p] in
whom they had put their trust. 24After
going through Pisidia, they came into
Pamphylia,[q] 25and when they had
preached the word in Perga, they went
down to Attalia.
26From Attalia they sailed back to An-
tioch,[r] where they had been committed
to the grace of God[s] for the work they

46 [k]ver 26; Ac 3:26; [l]Mt 21:41; Ac 18:6; 22:21; 26:20; 28:28; Ro 11:11
47 [m]**Lk 2:32**; [n]Isa 49:6
48 [o]ver 49; Ac 8:25; 15:35–36; 19:10,20
49 [p]**ver 48**
50 [q]**1Th 2:16**
51 [r]**Mt 10:14**; [s]Ac 14:1,19, 21; 16:2; 2Ti 3:11
52 [t]**Ac 11:26**; [u]**Lk 1:15**

Ch. 14

1 [a]**Ac 13:51**; [b]**Ac 9:20**; [c]**Ac 2:41**
2 [d]**Ac 1:16**
3 [e]**Ac 4:29**; [f]**Jn 4:48**
4 [g]Ac 17:4–5; 28:24
5 [h]**Ac 20:3**; [i]ver 19
6 [j]Mt 10:23
7 [k]Ac 16:10; [l]ver 15,21; **Ac 13:32**
8 [m]Ac 3:2
9 [n]Mt 9:28–29; 13:58
10 [o]Eze 2:1; [p]Ac 3:8
11 [q]Ac 8:10; 28:6
12 [r]Ex 7:1
14 [s]**Mk 14:63**
15 [t]**Ac 10:26**; [u]ver 7,21; **Ac 13:32**; [v]1Sa 12:21; 1Th 1:9; [w]**Mt 16:16**; [x]Ge 1:1; [y]Ps 146:6; Rev 14:7
16 [z]Ac 17:30; [a]Ps 81:12; Mic 4:5
17 [b]Ro 1:20; [c]Dt 11:14; Job 5:10; Ps 65:10; [d]Ps 4:7
19 [e]Ac 13:45; [f]**Ac 13:51**; [g]2Co 11:25; 2Ti 3:11
20 [h]ver 22,28; **Ac 11:26**
21 [i]**Ac 13:32**; [j]**Ac 2:41**; [k]**Ac 13:51**
22 [l]Ac 11:23; 13:43; [m]Jn 16:33; 1Th 3:3; 2Ti 3:12
23 [n]**Ac 11:30**; [o]Ac 13:3; [p]Ac 20:32
24 [q]**Ac 2:10**
26 [r]**Ac 11:19**; [s]**Ac 11:23**

[g]47 The Greek is singular. [h]47 Isaiah 49:6
[a]23 Or *Barnabas ordained elders*; or *Barnabas had elders elected*

had now completed.[t] 27On arriving
there, they gathered the church
together and reported all that God had
done through them[u] and how he had
opened the door[v] of faith to the Gen-
tiles. 28And they stayed there a long
time with the disciples.[w]

The Council at Jerusalem

15 Some men[a] came down from
Judea to Antioch and were
teaching the brothers:[b] "Unless you are
circumcised,[c] according to the custom
taught by Moses,[d] you cannot be
saved." 2This brought Paul and Barna-
bas into sharp dispute and debate with
them. So Paul and Barnabas were
appointed, along with some other be-
lievers, to go up to Jerusalem[e] to see the
apostles and elders[f] about this question.
3The church sent them on their way,
and as they travelled through Phoeni-
cia[g] and Samaria, they told how the
Gentiles had been converted.[h] This
news made all the brothers very glad.
4When they came to Jerusalem, they
were welcomed by the church and the
apostles and elders, to whom they re-
ported everything God had done
through them.[i]

5Then some of the believers who be-
longed to the party[j] of the Pharisees[k]
stood up and said, "The Gentiles must
be circumcised and required to obey the
law of Moses."[l]

6The apostles and elders met to con-
sider this question. 7After much discus-
sion, Peter got up and addressed them:
"Brothers, you know that some time
ago God made a choice among you that
the Gentiles might hear from my lips the
message of the gospel and believe.[m]
8God, who knows the heart,[n] showed
that he accepted them by giving the
Holy Spirit to them,[o] just as he did to us.
9He made no distinction between us
and them,[p] for he purified their hearts
by faith.[q] 10Now then, why do you try to
test God[r] by putting on the necks of the
disciples a yoke[s] that neither we nor our
fathers have been able to bear? 11No! We
believe it is through the grace[t] of our
Lord Jesus that we are saved, just as
they are."

12The whole assembly became silent
as they listened to Barnabas and Paul
telling about the miraculous signs and
wonders[u] God had done among the
Gentiles through them.[v] 13When they
finished, James[w] spoke up: "Brothers,
listen to me. 14Simon[a] has described to
us how God at first showed his concern
by taking from the Gentiles a people for
himself.[x] 15The words of the prophets
are in agreement with this, as it is
written:

16" 'After this I will return
and rebuild David's fallen tent.
Its ruins I will rebuild,
and I will restore it,
17that the remnant of men may seek the
Lord,
and all the Gentiles who bear my
name,
says the Lord, who does these
things'[b][y]
18 that have been known for ages.[c][z]

19"It is my judgment, therefore, that
we should not make it difficult for the
Gentiles who are turning to God.
20Instead we should write to them, tell-
ing them to abstain from food polluted
by idols,[a] from sexual immorality,[b] from
the meat of strangled animals and from
blood.[c] 21For Moses has been preached
in every city from the earliest times and
is read in the synagogues on every
Sabbath."[d]

The Council's Letter to Gentile Believers

22Then the apostles and elders,[e] with
the whole church, decided to choose
some of their own men and send them
to Antioch[f] with Paul and Barnabas.
They chose Judas (called Barsabbas) and
Silas,[g] two men who were leaders
among the brothers. 23With them they
sent the following letter:

The apostles and elders, your
brothers,

To the Gentile believers in
Antioch,[h] Syria[i] and Cilicia:[j]

Greetings.[k]

24We have heard that some went
out from us without our authorisa-
tion and disturbed you, troubling
your minds by what they said.[l] 25So
we all agreed to choose some men
and send them to you with our dear
friends Barnabas and Paul—26men
who have risked their lives[m] for the
name of our Lord Jesus Christ.
27Therefore we are sending Judas

26 [t]Ac 13:1,3
27 [u]Ac 15:4,12; 21:19; [v]1Co 16:9; 2Co 2:12; Col 4:3; Rev 3:8
28 [w]**Ac 11:26**

Ch. 15

1 [a]ver 24; Gal 2:12; [b]**Ac 1:16**; [c]ver 5; Gal 5:2–3; [d]**Ac 6:14**
2 [e]Gal 2:2; [f]**Ac 11:30**
3 [g]Ac 11:19; [h]Ac 14:27
4 [i]ver 12; Ac 14:27; 21:19
5 [j]Ac 5:17; [k]Mt 3:7; [l]ver 1
7 [m]Ac 10:1–48
8 [n]**Rev 2:23**; [o]**Ac 10:44**,47
9 [p]Ac 10:28,34; 11:12; [q]Ac 10:43
10 [r]Ac 5:9; [s]**Mt 23:4**; Gal 5:1
11 [t]**Ro 3:24**; Gal 2:16; Eph 2:5–8
12 [u]**Jn 4:48**; [v]ver 4; Ac 14:27; 21:19
13 [w]Ac 12:17; 21:18; 1Co 15:7; Gal 1:19; 2:9,12
14 [x]2Pe 1:1
17 [y]Am 9:11–12
18 [z]Isa 45:21
20 [a]1Co 8:7–13; 10:14–28; Rev 2:14,20; [b]1Co 10:7–8; Rev 2:14,20; [c]ver 29; Ge 9:4; Lev 3:17; 7:26; 17:10–13; 19:26; Dt 12:16,23
21 [d]Ac 13:15; 2Co 3:14–15
22 [e]**Ac 11:30**; [f]**Ac 11:19**; [g]ver 27, 32,40; Ac 16:19,25,29; 2Co 1:19; 1Th 1:1; 1Pe 5:12
23 [h]ver 1; **Ac 11:19**; [i]**Lk 2:2**; [j]ver 41; **Ac 6:9**; [k]Ac 23:25–26; Jas 1:1
24 [l]ver 1; Gal 1:7; 5:10
26 [m]Ac 9:23–25; 14:19; 1Co 15:30

[a]*14* Greek *Simeon*, a variant of *Simon*; that is, Peter
[b]*17* Amos 9:11,12
[c]*17,18* Some manuscripts *things'— / [18]known to the Lord for ages is his work*

and Silas[n] to confirm by word of
mouth what we are writing. 28It
seemed good to the Holy Spirit[o]
and to us not to burden you with
anything beyond the following re-
quirements: 29You are to abstain
from food sacrificed to idols, from
blood, from the meat of strangled
animals and from sexual immor-
ality.[p] You will do well to avoid
these things.

Farewell.

30The men were sent off and went
down to Antioch, where they gathered
the church together and delivered the
letter. 31The people read it and were
glad for its encouraging message.
32Judas and Silas,[q] who themselves
were prophets,[r] said much to encourage
and strengthen the brothers. 33After
spending some time there, they were
sent off by the brothers with the bless-
ing of peace[s] to return to those who had
sent them.[d] 35But Paul and Barnabas
remained in Antioch, where they and
many others taught and preached[t] the
word of the Lord.[u]

Disagreement Between Paul and Barnabas

36Some time later Paul said to Barna-
bas, "Let us go back and visit the
brothers in all the towns[v] where we
preached the word of the Lord[w] and see
how they are doing." 37Barnabas
wanted to take John, also called Mark,[x]
with them, 38but Paul did not think it
wise to take him, because he had de-
serted them[y] in Pamphylia and had not
continued with them in the work.
39They had such a sharp disagreement
that they parted company. Barnabas
took Mark and sailed for Cyprus, 40but
Paul chose Silas[z] and left, commended
by the brothers to the grace of the Lord.[a]
41He went through Syria[b] and Cilicia,[c]
strengthening the churches.[d]

Timothy Joins Paul and Silas

16 He came to Derbe and then to
Lystra,[a] where a disciple named
Timothy[b] lived, whose mother was a
Jewess and a believer,[c] but whose father
was a Greek. 2The brothers[d] at Lystra
and Iconium[e] spoke well of him. 3Paul
wanted to take him along on the jour-
ney, so he circumcised him because of
the Jews who lived in that area, for they
all knew that his father was a Greek.[f]
4As they travelled from town to town,
they delivered the decisions reached by
the apostles and elders[g] in Jerusalem[h]
for the people to obey.[i] 5So the churches
were strengthened[j] in the faith and
grew daily in numbers.[k]

Paul's Vision of the Man of Macedonia

6Paul and his companions travelled
throughout the region of Phrygia[l] and
Galatia,[m] having been kept by the Holy
Spirit from preaching the word in the
province of Asia.[n] 7When they came to
the border of Mysia, they tried to enter
Bithynia, but the Spirit of Jesus[o] would
not allow them to. 8So they passed by
Mysia and went down to Troas.[p]
9During the night Paul had a vision[q] of a
man of Macedonia[r] standing and beg-
ging him, "Come over to Macedonia
and help us." 10After Paul had seen the
vision, we[s] got ready at once to leave for
Macedonia, concluding that God had
called us to preach the gospel[t] to them.

Lydia's Conversion in Philippi

11From Troas[u] we put out to sea and
sailed straight for Samothrace, and the
next day on to Neapolis. 12From there
we travelled to Philippi,[v] a Roman col-
ony and the leading city of that district
of Macedonia.[w] And we stayed there
several days.

13On the Sabbath[x] we went outside
the city gate to the river, where we
expected to find a place of prayer. We
sat down and began to speak to the
women who had gathered there. 14One
of those listening was a woman named
Lydia, a dealer in purple cloth from the
city of Thyatira,[y] who was a worshipper
of God. The Lord opened her heart[z] to
respond to Paul's message. 15When she
and the members of her household[a]
were baptised,[b] she invited us to her
home. "If you consider me a believer in
the Lord," she said, "come and stay at
my house." And she persuaded us.

Paul and Silas in Prison

16Once when we were going to the
place of prayer,[c] we were met by a
slave girl who had a spirit[d] by which
she predicted the future. She earned a
great deal of money for her owners by
fortune-telling. 17This girl followed Paul
and the rest of us, shouting, "These
men are servants of the Most High

27 [n]ver 22
28 [o]Ac 5:32
29 [p]ver 20; Ac 21:25
32 [q]ver 22; [r]**Ac 11:27**
33 [s]1Sa 1:17; Mk 5:34; Lk 7:50; Ac 16:36; 1Co 16:11
35 [t]Ac 8:4; [u]**Ac 13:48**
36 [v]Ac 13:4, 13–14,51; 14:1,6,24–25; [w]**Ac 13:48**
37 [x]**Ac 12:12**
38 [y]Ac 13:13
40 [z]**ver 22**; [a]**Ac 11:23**
41 [b]ver 23; **Lk 2:2**; [c]**Ac 6:9**; [d]Ac 16:5

Ch. 16

1 [a]Ac 14:6; [b]1Co 4:17; 16:10; 2Co 1:1,19; Php 1:1; 2:19; 1Th 3:2,6; 1Ti 1:2, 18; 2Ti 1:2, 5–6; [c]2Ti 1:5
2 [d]ver 40; **Ac 1:16**; [e]**Ac 13:51**
3 [f]Gal 2:3
4 [g]**Ac 11:30**; [h]Ac 15:2; [i]Ac 15:28–29
5 [j]Ac 9:31; 15:41; [k]**Ac 2:41**
6 [l]Ac 2:10; 18:23; [m]Ac 18:23; Gal 1:2; 3:1; [n]**Ac 2:9**
7 [o]Ro 8:9; Gal 4:6; Php 1:19; 1Pe 1:11
8 [p]ver 11; Ac 20:5; 2Co 2:12; 2Ti 4:13
9 [q]**Ac 9:10**; [r]Ac 19:21,29; 20:1, 3; Ro 15:26; 1Co 16:5; 1Th 1:7–8
10 [s]ver 10–17; Ac 20:5–15; 21:1–18; 27:1–28:16; [t]Ac 14:7
11 [u]**ver 8**
12 [v]Ac 20:6; Php 1:1; 1Th 2:2; [w]**ver 9**
13 [x]**Ac 13:14**
14 [y]Rev 1:11; 2:18,24; [z]Lk 24:45
15 [a]**Ac 11:14**; [b]**Ac 2:38**
16 [c]ver 13; [d]Dt 18:11; 1Sa 28:3,7

d33 Some manuscripts *them*, 34*but Silas decided to remain there*

God,[e] who are telling you the way to be
saved." 18She kept this up for many
days. Finally Paul became so troubled
that he turned round and said to the
spirit, "In the name of Jesus Christ I
command you to come out of her!" At
that moment the spirit left her.[f]
19When the owners of the slave girl
realised that their hope of making
money[g] was gone, they seized Paul and
Silas[h] and dragged[i] them into the
market-place to face the authorities.
20They brought them before the magis-
trates and said, "These men are Jews,
and are throwing our city into an up-
roar[j] 21by advocating customs unlawful
for us Romans[k] to accept or practise."[l]
22The crowd joined in the attack
against Paul and Silas, and the magis-
trates ordered them to be stripped and
beaten.[m] 23After they had been severely
flogged, they were thrown into prison,
and the jailer[n] was commanded to
guard them carefully. 24Upon receiving
such orders, he put them in the inner
cell and fastened their feet in the
stocks.[o]
25About midnight[p] Paul and Silas[q]
were praying and singing hymns[r] to
God, and the other prisoners were
listening to them. 26Suddenly there was
such a violent earthquake that the
foundations of the prison were shaken.[s]
At once all the prison doors flew open,[t]
and everybody's chains came loose.[u]
27The jailer woke up, and when he saw
the prison doors open, he drew his
sword and was about to kill himself
because he thought the prisoners had
escaped.[v] 28But Paul shouted, "Don't
harm yourself! We are all here!"
29The jailer called for lights, rushed in
and fell trembling before Paul and
Silas.[w] 30He then brought them out and
asked, "Sirs, what must I do to be
saved?"[x]
31They replied, "Believe[y] in the Lord
Jesus, and you will be saved[z]—you and
your household."[a] 32Then they spoke
the word of the Lord to him and to all
the others in his house. 33At that hour of
the night[b] the jailer took them and
washed their wounds; then immediate-
ly he and all his family were baptised.[c]
34The jailer brought them into his house
and set a meal before them; he[d] was
filled with joy because he had come
to believe in God—he and his whole
family.
35When it was daylight, the magis-
trates sent their officers to the jailer with
the order: "Release those men." 36The
jailer[e] told Paul, "The magistrates have
ordered that you and Silas be released.
Now you can leave. Go in peace."[f]
37But Paul said to the officers: "They
beat us publicly without a trial, even
though we are Roman citizens,[g] and
threw us into prison. And now do they
want to get rid of us quietly? No! Let
them come themselves and escort us
out."
38The officers reported this to the
magistrates, and when they heard that
Paul and Silas were Roman citizens,
they were alarmed.[h] 39They came to
appease them and escorted them from
the prison, requesting them to leave the
city.[i] 40After Paul and Silas came out of
the prison, they went to Lydia's house,[j]
where they met with the brothers[k] and
encouraged them. Then they left.

In Thessalonica

17 When they had passed through
Amphipolis and Apollonia,
they came to Thessalonica,[a] where there
was a Jewish synagogue. 2As his custom
was, Paul went into the synagogue,[b]
and on three Sabbath[c] days he reasoned
with them from the Scriptures,[d]
3explaining and proving that the Christ[a]
had to suffer[e] and rise from the dead.[f]
"This Jesus I am proclaiming to you is
the Christ,[a]"[g] he said. 4Some of the Jews
were persuaded and joined Paul and
Silas,[h] as did a large number of God-
fearing Greeks and not a few prominent
women.
5But the Jews were jealous; so they
rounded up some bad characters from
the market-place, formed a mob and
started a riot in the city.[i] They rushed to
Jason's[j] house in search of Paul and Silas
in order to bring them out to the crowd.[b]
6But when they did not find them,
they dragged[k] Jason and some other
brothers[l] before the city officials, shout-
ing: "These men who have caused trou-
ble all over the world[m] have now come
here,[n] 7and Jason has welcomed them
into his house. They are all defying
Caesar's decrees, saying that there is
another king, one called Jesus."[o] 8When
they heard this, the crowd and the city
officials were thrown into turmoil.
9Then they put Jason[p] and the others on
bail and let them go.

In Berea

10As soon as it was night, the brothers
sent Paul and Silas[q] away to Berea.[r] On

17 [e]**Mk 5:7**
18 [f]**Mk 16:17**
19 [g]ver 16; Ac 19:25–26; [h]**Ac 15:22**; [i]Ac 8:3; 17:6; 21:30; Jas 2:6
20 [j]Ac 17:6
21 [k]ver 12; [l]Est 3:8
22 [m]2Co 11:25; 1Th 2:2
23 [n]ver 27,36
24 [o]Job 13:27; 33:11; Jer 20:2–3; 29:26
25 [p]Ps 119:55,62; [q]**Ac 15:22**; [r]**Eph 5:19**
26 [s]Ac 4:31; [t]Ac 5:19; 12:10; [u]Ac 12:7
27 [v]Ac 12:19
29 [w]**Ac 15:22**
30 [x]Ac 2:37
31 [y]**Jn 3:15**; [z]**Ro 11:14**; [a]**Ac 11:14**
33 [b]ver 25; [c]**Ac 2:38**
34 [d]**Ac 11:14**
36 [e]ver 23,27; [f]**Ac 15:33**
37 [g]Ac 22:25–29
38 [h]Ac 22:29
39 [i]Mt 8:34; Lk 8:37
40 [j]ver 14; [k]ver 2; **Ac 1:16**

Ch. 17

1 [a]ver 11,13; Php 4:16; 1Th 1:1; 2Th 1:1; 2Ti 4:10
2 [b]**Ac 9:20**; [c]**Ac 13:14**; [d]Ac 8:35; 18:28
3 [e]Lk 24:26; Ac 3:18; [f]Lk 24:46; **Ac 2:24**; [g]**Ac 9:22**
4 [h]**Ac 15:22**
5 [i]ver 13; **1Th 2:16**; [j]Ro 16:21
6 [k]**Ac 16:19**; [l]**Ac 1:16**; [m]**Mt 24:14**; [n]Ac 16:20
7 [o]Lk 23:2; Jn 19:12
9 [p]ver 5
10 [q]**Ac 15:22**; [r]ver 13; Ac 20:4

[a]3 Or *Messiah* [b]5 Or *the assembly of the people*

arriving there, they went to the Jewish synagogue.[s] 11 Now the Bereans were of more noble character than the Thessalonians,[t] for they received the message with great eagerness and examined the Scriptures[u] every day to see if what Paul said was true.[v] 12 Many of the Jews believed, as did also a number of prominent Greek women and many Greek men.[w]

13 When the Jews in Thessalonica learned that Paul was preaching the word of God at Berea,[x] they went there too, agitating the crowds and stirring them up. 14 The brothers[y] immediately sent Paul to the coast, but Silas[z] and Timothy[a] stayed at Berea. 15 The men who escorted Paul brought him to Athens[b] and then left with instructions for Silas and Timothy to join him as soon as possible.[c]

In Athens

16 While Paul was waiting for them in Athens, he was greatly distressed to see that the city was full of idols. 17 So he reasoned in the synagogue[d] with the Jews and the God-fearing Greeks, as well as in the market-place day by day with those who happened to be there. 18 A group of Epicurean and Stoic philosophers began to dispute with him. Some of them asked, "What is this babbler trying to say?" Others remarked, "He seems to be advocating foreign gods." They said this because Paul was preaching the good news[e] about Jesus and the resurrection.[f] 19 Then they took him and brought him to a meeting of the Areopagus,[g] where they said to him, "May we know what this new teaching[h] is that you are presenting? 20 You are bringing some strange ideas to our ears, and we want to know what they mean." 21 (All the Athenians[i] and the foreigners who lived there spent their time doing nothing but talking about and listening to the latest ideas.)

22 Paul then stood up in the meeting of the Areopagus[j] and said: "Men of Athens! I see that in every way you are very religious.[k] 23 For as I walked around and looked carefully at your objects of worship, I even found an altar with this inscription: TO AN UNKNOWN GOD. Now what you worship as something unknown[l] I am going to proclaim to you.

24 "The God who made the world and everything in it[m] is the Lord of heaven and earth[n] and does not live in temples built by hands.[o] 25 And he is not served by human hands, as if he needed anything, because he himself gives all men life and breath and everything else.[p] 26 From one man he made every nation of men, that they should inhabit the whole earth; and he determined the times set for them and the exact places where they should live.[q] 27 God did this so that men would seek him and perhaps reach out for him and find him, though he is not far from each one of us.[r] 28 'For in him we live and move and have our being.'[s] As some of your own poets have said, 'We are his offspring.'[t]

29 "Therefore since we are God's offspring, we should not think that the divine being is like gold or silver or stone—an image made by man's design and skill.[u] 30 In the past God overlooked[v] such ignorance,[w] but now he commands all people everywhere to repent.[x] 31 For he has set a day when he will judge[y] the world with justice[z] by the man he has appointed.[a] He has given proof of this to all men by raising him from the dead."[b]

32 When they heard about the resurrection of the dead,[c] some of them sneered, but others said, "We want to hear you again on this subject." 33 At that, Paul left the Council. 34 A few men became followers of Paul and believed. Among them was Dionysius, a member of the Areopagus,[d] also a woman named Damaris, and a number of others.

In Corinth

18

After this, Paul left Athens[a] and went to Corinth.[b] 2 There he met a Jew named Aquila, a native of Pontus, who had recently come from Italy with his wife Priscilla,[c] because Claudius[d] had ordered all the Jews to leave Rome. Paul went to see them, 3 and because he was a tentmaker as they were, he stayed and worked with them.[e] 4 Every Sabbath[f] he reasoned in the synagogue,[g] trying to persuade Jews and Greeks.

5 When Silas[h] and Timothy[i] came from Macedonia,[j] Paul devoted himself exclusively to preaching, testifying to the Jews that Jesus was the Christ.[a][k] 6 But when the Jews opposed Paul and became abusive,[l] he shook out his clothes in protest[m] and said to them, "Your blood be on your own heads![n] I am clear of my responsibility.[o] From now on I will go to the Gentiles."[p]

10 [s]**Ac 9:20**
11 [t]**ver 1;** [u]Lk 16:29; Jn 5:39; [v]Dt 29:29
12 [w]**Ac 2:41**
13 [x]**Heb 4:12**
14 [y]**Ac 9:30;** [z]**Ac 15:22;** [a]**Ac 16:1**
15 [b]ver 16, 21–22; Ac 18:1; 1Th 3:1; [c]Ac 18:5
17 [d]**Ac 9:20**
18 [e]**Ac 13:32;** [f]ver 31–32; Ac 4:2
19 [g]ver 22; [h]Mk 1:27
21 [i]**ver 15**
22 [j]ver 19; [k]ver 16
23 [l]Jn 4:22
24 [m]Isa 42:5; Ac 14:15; [n]Dt 10:14; Isa 66:1–2; Mt 11:25; [o]1Ki 8:27; Ac 7:48
25 [p]Ps 50:10–12; Isa 42:5
26 [q]Dt 32:8; Job 12:23
27 [r]Dt 4:7; Isa 55:6; Jer 23:23–24
28 [s]Dt 30:20; Job 12:10; Da 5:23; [t]Epimenides; Aratus, **Phaenomena, 5**
29 [u]Isa 40:18–20; Ro 1:23
30 [v]Ac 14:16; Ro 3:25; [w]ver 23; 1Pe 1:14; [x]Lk 24:47; Tit 2:11–12
31 [y]**Mt 10:15;** [z]Ps 9:8; 96:13; 98:9; [a]**Ac 10:42;** [b]**Ac 2:24**
32 [c]ver 18,31
34 [d]ver 19,22

Ch. 18

1 [a]**Ac 17:15;** [b]Ac 19:1; 1Co 1:2; 2Co 1:1, 23; 2Ti 4:20
2 [c]ver 19,26; Ro 16:3; 1Co 16:19; 2Ti 4:19; [d]Ac 11:28
3 [e]Ac 20:34; 1Co 4:12; 1Th 2:9; 2Th 3:8
4 [f]**Ac 13:14;** [g]**Ac 9:20**
5 [h]**Ac 15:22;** [i]**Ac 16:1;** [j]**Ac 16:9;** 17:14–15; [k]**Ac 9:22**
6 [l]**Ac 13:45;** [m]**Mt 10:14;** [n]2Sa 1:16; Eze 33:4; [o]Eze 3:17–19; Ac 20:26; [p]**Ac 13:46**

[a]5 Or *Messiah;* also in verse 28

7Then Paul left the synagogue and
went next door to the house of Titius
Justus, a worshipper of God.[q] 8Crispus,[r]
the synagogue ruler,[s] and his entire
household[t] believed in the Lord; and
many of the Corinthians who heard him
believed and were baptised.
9One night the Lord spoke to Paul in a
vision:[u] "Do not be afraid;[v] keep on
speaking, do not be silent. 10For I am
with you,[w] and no-one is going to attack
and harm you, because I have many
people in this city." 11So Paul stayed for
a year and a half, teaching them the
word of God.[x]
12While Gallio was proconsul[y] of
Achaia,[z] the Jews made a united attack
on Paul and brought him into court.
13"This man," they charged, "is per-
suading the people to worship God in
ways contrary to the law."
14Just as Paul was about to speak,
Gallio said to the Jews, "If you Jews
were making a complaint about some
misdemeanour or serious crime, it
would be reasonable for me to listen to
you. 15But since it involves questions
about words and names and your own
law[a]—settle the matter yourselves. I
will not be a judge of such things." 16So
he had them ejected from the court.
17Then they all turned on Sosthenes[b] the
synagogue ruler[c] and beat him in front
of the court. But Gallio showed no
concern whatever.

Priscilla, Aquila and Apollos

18Paul stayed on in Corinth for some
time. Then he left the brothers[d] and
sailed for Syria,[e] accompanied by Pris-
cilla and Aquila.[f] Before he sailed, he
had his hair cut off at Cenchrea[g] because
of a vow he had taken.[h] 19They arrived at
Ephesus,[i] where Paul left Priscilla and
Aquila. He himself went into the syna-
gogue and reasoned with the Jews.
20When they asked him to spend more
time with them, he declined. 21But as he
left, he promised, "I will come back if it
is God's will."[j] Then he set sail from
Ephesus. 22When he landed at
Caesarea,[k] he went up and greeted
the church and then went down to
Antioch.[l]
23After spending some time in Anti-
och, Paul set out from there and
travelled from place to place throughout
the region of Galatia[m] and Phrygia,[n]
strengthening all the disciples.[o]
24Meanwhile a Jew named Apollos,[p] a
native of Alexandria, came to Ephesus.[q]
He was a learned man, with a thorough
knowledge of the Scriptures. 25He had
been instructed in the way of the Lord,
and he spoke with great fervour[b][r] and
taught about Jesus accurately, though
he knew only the baptism of John.[s] 26He
began to speak boldly in the synagogue.
When Priscilla and Aquila[t] heard him,
they invited him to their home and ex-
plained to him the way of God more
adequately.
27When Apollos wanted to go to
Achaia,[u] the brothers[v] encouraged him
and wrote to the disciples there to wel-
come him. On arriving, he was a great
help to those who by grace had be-
lieved. 28For he vigorously refuted the
Jews in public debate, proving from the
Scriptures[w] that Jesus was the Christ.[x]

Paul in Ephesus

19 While Apollos[a] was at Corinth,[b]
Paul took the road through the
interior and arrived at Ephesus.[c] There
he found some disciples 2and asked
them, "Did you receive the Holy Spirit[d]
when[a] you believed?"
They answered, "No, we have not
even heard that there is a Holy Spirit."
3So Paul asked, "Then what baptism
did you receive?"
"John's baptism," they replied.
4Paul said, "John's baptism[e] was a
baptism of repentance. He told the peo-
ple to believe in the one coming after
him, that is, in Jesus."[f] 5On hearing this,
they were baptised into[b] the name of the
Lord Jesus.[g] 6When Paul placed his
hands on them,[h] the Holy Spirit came
on them,[i] and they spoke in tongues[c][j]
and prophesied. 7There were about
twelve men in all.
8Paul entered the synagogue[k] and
spoke boldly there for three months,
arguing persuasively about the king-
dom of God.[l] 9But some of them[m] be-
came obstinate; they refused to believe
and publicly maligned the Way.[n] So
Paul left them. He took the disciples[o]
with him and had discussions daily in
the lecture hall of Tyrannus. 10This went
on for two years,[p] so that all the Jews
and Greeks who lived in the province of
Asia[q] heard the word of the Lord.[r]
11God did extraordinary miracles[s]
through Paul, 12so that even hand-
kerchiefs and aprons that had touched
him were taken to the sick, and their
illnesses were cured[t] and the evil spirits
left them.

7 [q]Ac 16:14
8 [r]1Co 1:14; [s]**Mk 5:22**; [t]**Ac 11:14**
9 [u]**Ac 9:10**; [v]**Mt 14:27**
10 [w]**Mt 28:20**
11 [x]**Heb 4:12**
12 [y]Ac 13:7–8, 12; 19:38; [z]ver 27; Ro 15:26; 1Co 16:15; 2Co 9:2; 1Th 1:7–8
15 [a]Ac 23:29; 25:11,19
17 [b]1Co 1:1; [c]ver 8
18 [d]ver 27; **Ac 1:16**; [e]**Lk 2:2**; [f]**ver 2**; [g]Ro 16:1; [h]Nu 6:2, 5,18; Ac 21:24
19 [i]ver 21,24; Ac 19:1,17,26; 1Co 15:32; 16:8; Eph 1:1; 1Ti 1:3; Rev 1:11; 2:1
21 [j]Ro 1:10; 15:32; 1Co 4:19; Jas 4:15
22 [k]**Ac 8:40**; [l]**Ac 11:19**
23 [m]**Ac 16:6**; [n]Ac 2:10; 16:6; [o]Ac 14:22; 15:32,41
24 [p]Ac 19:1; 1Co 1:12; 3:5–6,22; 4:6; 16:12; Tit 3:13; [q]**ver 19**
25 [r]Ro 12:11; [s]**Mk 1:4**
26 [t]**ver 2**
27 [u]**ver 12**; [v]ver 18; **Ac 1:16**
28 [w]Ac 8:35; 17:2; [x]ver 5; **Ac 9:22**

Ch. 19

1 [a]**Ac 18:24**; [b]**Ac 18:1**; [c]**Ac 18:19**
2 [d]**Jn 20:22**
4 [e]**Mk 1:4**; [f]Jn 1:7
5 [g]**Ac 2:38**
6 [h]**Ac 6:6**; [i]**Ac 10:44**; [j]**Mk 16:17**
8 [k]**Ac 9:20**; [l]**Mt 3:2**; Ac 28:23
9 [m]Ac 14:4; [n]ver 23; **Ac 9:2**; [o]ver 30; **Ac 11:26**
10 [p]Ac 20:31; [q]ver 22, 26–27; **Ac 2:9**; [r]**Ac 13:48**
11 [s]Ac 8:13
12 [t]Ac 5:15

b25 Or *with fervour in the Spirit*
a2 Or *after* b5 Or *in*
c6 Or *other languages*

13Some Jews who went around driv-
ing out evil spirits[u] tried to invoke the
name of the Lord Jesus over those who
were demon-possessed. They would
say, "In the name of Jesus,[v] whom Paul
preaches, I command you to come out."
14Seven sons of Sceva, a Jewish chief
priest, were doing this. 15⌞One day⌟ the
evil spirit answered them, "Jesus I
know, and I know about Paul, but who
are you?" 16Then the man who had the
evil spirit jumped on them and over-
powered them all. He gave them such a
beating that they ran out of the house
naked and bleeding.

17When this became known to the
Jews and Greeks living in Ephesus,[w]
they were all seized with fear,[x] and the
name of the Lord Jesus was held in high
honour. 18Many of those who believed
now came and openly confessed their
evil deeds. 19A number who had prac-
tised sorcery brought their scrolls
together and burned them publicly.
When they calculated the value of the
scrolls, the total came to fifty thousand
drachmas.[d] 20In this way the word of
the Lord[y] spread widely and grew
in power.[z]

21After all this had happened, Paul
decided to go to Jerusalem,[a] passing
through Macedonia[b] and Achaia.[c]
"After I have been there," he said, "I
must visit Rome also."[d] 22He sent two
of his helpers,[e] Timothy[f] and Erastus,[g]
to Macedonia, while he stayed in the
province of Asia[h] a little longer.

The Riot in Ephesus

23About that time there arose a great
disturbance about the Way.[i] 24A silver-
smith named Demetrius, who made sil-
ver shrines of Artemis, brought in no
little business for the craftsmen. 25He
called them together, along with the
workmen in related trades, and said:
"Men, you know we receive a good
income from this business.[j] 26And you
see and hear how this fellow Paul has
convinced and led astray large numbers
of people here in Ephesus[k] and in practi-
cally the whole province of Asia.[l] He
says that man-made gods are no gods at
all.[m] 27There is danger not only that our
trade will lose its good name, but also
that the temple of the great goddess
Artemis will be discredited, and the
goddess herself, who is worshipped
throughout the province of Asia and the
world, will be robbed of her divine
majesty."

28When they heard this, they were
furious and began shouting: "Great is
Artemis of the Ephesians!"[n] 29Soon the
whole city was in an uproar. The people
seized Gaius[o] and Aristarchus,[p] Paul's
travelling companions from Macedo-
nia,[q] and rushed as one man into the
theatre. 30Paul wanted to appear before
the crowd, but the disciples[r] would not
let him. 31Even some of the officials of
the province, friends of Paul, sent him a
message begging him not to venture
into the theatre.

32The assembly was in confusion:
Some were shouting one thing, some
another.[s] Most of the people did not
even know why they were there. 33The
Jews pushed Alexander to the front,
and some of the crowd shouted instruc-
tions to him. He motioned[t] for silence in
order to make a defence before the
people. 34But when they realised he
was a Jew, they all shouted in unison
for about two hours: "Great is Artemis
of the Ephesians!"[u]

35The city clerk quietened the crowd
and said: "Men of Ephesus,[v] doesn't all
the world know that the city of Ephesus
is the guardian of the temple of the great
Artemis and of her image, which fell
from heaven? 36Therefore, since these
facts are undeniable, you ought to be
quiet and not do anything rash. 37You
have brought these men here, though
they have neither robbed temples[w] nor
blasphemed our goddess. 38If, then, De-
metrius and his fellow craftsmen[x] have
a grievance against anybody, the courts
are open and there are proconsuls.[y]
They can press charges. 39If there is
anything further you want to bring up,
it must be settled in a legal assembly.
40As it is, we are in danger of being
charged with rioting because of today's
events. In that case we would not be
able to account for this commotion,
since there is no reason for it." 41After
he had said this, he dismissed the
assembly.

Through Macedonia and Greece

20 When the uproar had ended,
Paul sent for the disciples[a] and,
after encouraging them, said good-bye
and set out for Macedonia.[b] 2He
travelled through that area, speaking
many words of encouragement to the
people, and finally arrived in Greece,
3where he stayed three months. Be-
cause the Jews made a plot against him[c]

---

13 [u]Mt 12:27; [v]Mk 9:38
17 [w]**Ac 18:19**; [x]Ac 5:5,11
20 [y]**Ac 13:48**; [z]Ac 6:7; 12:24
21 [a]Ac 20:16,22; 21:4,12,15; Ro 15:25; [b]**Ac 16:9**; [c]**Ac 18:12**; [d]Ro 15:24,28
22 [e]Ac 13:5; [f]**Ac 16:1**; [g]Ro 16:23; 2Ti 4:20; [h]ver 10, 26–27; **Ac 2:9**
23 [i]**Ac 9:2**
25 [j]Ac 16:16, 19–20
26 [k]**Ac 18:19**; [l]**Ac 2:9**; [m]Dt 4:28; Ps 115:4; Isa 44:10–20; Jer 10:3–5; Ac 17:29; 1Co 8:4; Rev 9:20
28 [n]**Ac 18:19**
29 [o]Ac 20:4; Ro 16:23; 1Co 1:14; [p]Ac 20:4; 27:2; Col 4:10; Phm 24; [q]**Ac 16:9**
30 [r]**Ac 11:26**
32 [s]Ac 21:34
33 [t]**Ac 12:17**
34 [u]ver 28
35 [v]**Ac 18:19**
37 [w]Ro 2:22
38 [x]ver 24; [y]Ac 13:7–8,12; 18:12

Ch. 20

1 [a]**Ac 11:26**; [b]**Ac 16:9**
3 [c]ver 19; Ac 9:23–24; 14:5; 23:12,15,30; 25:3; 2Co 11:26; **1Th 2:16**

---

d19 A drachma was a silver coin worth about a day's wages.

just as he was about to sail for Syria,[d] he decided to go back through Macedonia.[e] 4He was accompanied by Sopater son of Pyrrhus from Berea, Aristarchus[f] and Secundus from Thessalonica,[g] Gaius[h] from Derbe, Timothy[i] also, and Tychicus[j] and Trophimus[k] from the province of Asia.[l] 5These men went on ahead and waited for us[m] at Troas.[n] 6But we sailed from Philippi[o] after the Feast of Unleavened Bread, and five days later joined the others at Troas,[p] where we stayed seven days.

Eutychus Raised From the Dead at Troas

7On the first day of the week[q] we came together to break bread.[r] Paul spoke to the people and, because he intended to leave the next day, kept on talking until midnight. 8There were many lamps in the upstairs room[s] where we were meeting. 9Seated in a window was a young man named Eutychus, who was sinking into a deep sleep as Paul talked on and on. When he was sound asleep, he fell to the ground from the third storey and was picked up dead. 10Paul went down, threw himself on the young man[t] and put his arms around him. "Don't be alarmed," he said. "He's alive!"[u] 11Then he went upstairs again and broke bread[v] and ate. After talking until daylight, he left. 12The people took the young man home alive and were greatly comforted.

Paul's Farewell to the Ephesian Elders

13We went on ahead to the ship and sailed for Assos, where we were going to take Paul aboard. He had made this arrangement because he was going there on foot. 14When he met us at Assos, we took him aboard and went on to Mitylene. 15The next day we set sail from there and arrived off Kios. The day after that we crossed over to Samos, and on the following day arrived at Miletus.[w] 16Paul had decided to sail past Ephesus[x] to avoid spending time in the province of Asia,[y] for he was in a hurry to reach Jerusalem,[z] if possible, by the day of Pentecost.[a]

17From Miletus,[b] Paul sent to Ephesus for the elders[c] of the church. 18When they arrived, he said to them: "You know how I lived the whole time I was with you,[d] from the first day I came into the province of Asia.[e] 19I served the Lord with great humility and with tears,[f] although I was severely tested by the plots of the Jews.[g] 20You know that I have not hesitated to preach anything[h] that would be helpful to you but have taught you publicly and from house to house. 21I have declared to both Jews[i] and Greeks that they must turn to God in repentance[j] and have faith in our Lord Jesus.[k]

22"And now, compelled by the Spirit, I am going to Jerusalem,[l] not knowing what will happen to me there. 23I only know that in every city the Holy Spirit warns me[m] that prison and hardships are facing me.[n] 24However, I consider my life worth nothing to me,[o] if only I may finish the race[p] and complete the task[q] the Lord Jesus has given me[r]—the task of testifying to the gospel of God's grace.[s]

25"Now I know that none of you among whom I have gone about preaching the kingdom[t] will ever see me again.[u] 26Therefore, I declare to you today that I am innocent of the blood of all men.[v] 27For I have not hesitated to proclaim to you the whole will of God.[w] 28Keep watch over yourselves and all the flock[x] of which the Holy Spirit has made you overseers.[a][y] Be shepherds of the church of God,[b][z] which he bought[a] with his own blood.[b] 29I know that after I leave, savage wolves[c] will come in among you and will not spare the flock.[d] 30Even from your own number men will arise and distort the truth in order to draw away disciples[e] after them. 31So be on your guard! Remember that for three years[f] I never stopped warning each of you night and day with tears.[g]

32"Now I commit you to God[h] and to the word of his grace, which can build you up and give you an inheritance[i] among all those who are sanctified.[j] 33I have not coveted anyone's silver or gold or clothing.[k] 34You yourselves know that these hands of mine have supplied my own needs and the needs of my companions.[l] 35In everything I did, I showed you that by this kind of hard work we must help the weak, remembering the words the Lord Jesus himself said: 'It is more blessed to give than to receive.'"

36When he had said this, he knelt down with all of them and prayed.[m] 37They all wept as they embraced him and kissed him.[n] 38What grieved them most was his statement that they would never see his face again.[o] Then they accompanied him to the ship.[p]

3 dLk 2:2; eAc 16:9
4 fAc 19:29; gAc 17:1; hAc 19:29; iAc 16:1; jEph 6:21; Col 4:7; Tit 3:12; kAc 21:29; 2Ti 4:20; lAc 2:9
5 mAc 16:10; nAc 16:8
6 oAc 16:12; pAc 16:8
7 q1Co 16:2; Rev 1:10; rMt 14:19
8 sAc 1:13; 9:37
10 t1Ki 17:21; 2Ki 4:34; uMt 9:23–24
11 vver 7; Mt 14:19
15 wver 17; 2Ti 4:20
16 xAc 18:19; yAc 2:9; zAc 19:21; aAc 2:1
17 bver 15; cAc 11:30
18 dAc 18:19–21; 19:1–41; eAc 2:9
19 fPs 6:6; gver 3
20 hver 27; Ps 40:10; Jer 26:2; 42:4
21 iAc 18:5; jAc 2:38; kAc 24:24; 26:18; Eph 1:15; Col 2:5; Phm 5
22 lver 16
23 mAc 8:29; 21:4; nAc 9:16
24 oAc 21:13; p2Ti 4:7; q2Co 4:1; rGal 1:1; Tit 1:3; sAc 11:23
25 tMt 4:23; uver 38
26 vEze 3:17–19; Ac 18:6
27 wver 20
28 xver 29; Jn 21:16; y1Ti 3:1; z1Co 10:32; a1Co 6:20; bRo 3:25
29 cEze 34:5; Mt 7:15; dver 28
30 eAc 11:26
31 fAc 19:10; gver 19
32 hAc 14:23; iEph 1:14; Mt 25:34; Col 1:12; 3:24; Heb 9:15; 1Pe 1:4; jAc 26:18
33 k1Sa 12:3; 1Co 9:12; 2Co 2:17; 7:2; 11:9; 12:14–17; 1Th 2:5
34 lAc 18:3
36 mLk 22:41; Ac 9:40; 21:5
37 nLk 15:20
38 over 25; pAc 21:5

a28 Traditionally *bishops*
b28 Many manuscripts *of the Lord*

On to Jerusalem

21 After we[a] had torn ourselves
away from them, we put out to
sea and sailed straight to Cos. The next
day we went to Rhodes and from there
to Patara. 2We found a ship crossing
over to Phoenicia,[b] went on board and
set sail. 3After sighting Cyprus and pas-
sing to the south of it, we sailed on to
Syria.[c] We landed at Tyre, where our
ship was to unload its cargo. 4Finding
the disciples[d] there, we stayed with
them seven days. Through the Spirit[e]
they urged Paul not to go on to Jeru-
salem. 5But when our time was up, we
left and continued on our way. All the
disciples and their wives and children
accompanied us out of the city, and
there on the beach we knelt to pray.[f]
6After saying good-bye to each other,
we went aboard the ship, and they re-
turned home.

7We continued our voyage from Tyre[g]
and landed at Ptolemais, where we
greeted the brothers[h] and stayed with
them for a day. 8Leaving the next day,
we reached Caesarea[i] and stayed at the
house of Philip[j] the evangelist,[k] one of
the Seven. 9He had four unmarried
daughters who prophesied.[l]

10After we had been there a number of
days, a prophet named Agabus[m] came
down from Judea. 11Coming over to us,
he took Paul's belt, tied his own hands
and feet with it and said, "The Holy
Spirit says,[n] 'In this way the Jews of
Jerusalem will bind[o] the owner of this
belt and will hand him over to the
Gentiles.'"[p]

12When we heard this, we and the
people there pleaded with Paul not to
go up to Jerusalem. 13Then Paul
answered, "Why are you weeping and
breaking my heart? I am ready not only
to be bound, but also to die[q] in Jeru-
salem for the name of the Lord Jesus."[r]
14When he would not be dissuaded, we
gave up[s] and said, "The Lord's will be
done."[t]

15After this, we got ready and went
up to Jerusalem.[u] 16Some of the disciples
from Caesarea[v] accompanied us and
brought us to the home of Mnason,
where we were to stay. He was a man
from Cyprus[w] and one of the early
disciples.

Paul's Arrival at Jerusalem

17When we arrived at Jerusalem, the
brothers[x] received us warmly.[y] 18The
next day Paul and the rest of us went to
see James,[z] and all the elders[a] were pres-
ent. 19Paul greeted them and reported in
detail what God had done among the
Gentiles[b] through his ministry.[c]

20When they heard this, they praised
God. Then they said to Paul: "You see,
brother, how many thousands of Jews
have believed, and all of them are
zealous[d] for the law.[e] 21They have been
informed that you teach all the Jews
who live among the Gentiles to turn
away from Moses,[f] telling them not to
circumcise their children[g] or live accord-
ing to our customs.[h] 22What shall we do?
They will certainly hear that you have
come, 23so do what we tell you. There
are four men with us who have made a
vow.[i] 24Take these men, join in their
purification rites[j] and pay their ex-
penses, so that they can have their
heads shaved.[k] Then everybody will
know there is no truth in these reports
about you, but that you yourself are
living in obedience to the law. 25As for
the Gentile believers, we have written
to them our decision that they should
abstain from food sacrificed to idols,
from blood, from the meat of strangled
animals and from sexual immorality."[l]

26The next day Paul took the men and
purified himself along with them. Then
he went to the temple to give notice of
the date when the days of purification
would end and the offering would be
made for each of them.[m]

Paul Arrested

27When the seven days were nearly
over, some Jews from the province of
Asia saw Paul at the temple. They
stirred up the whole crowd and
seized him,[n] 28shouting, "Men of Israel,
help us! This is the man who teaches all
men everywhere against our people
and our law and this place. And be-
sides, he has brought Greeks into the
temple area and defiled this holy
place."[o] 29(They had previously seen
Trophimus[p] the Ephesian[q] in the city
with Paul and assumed that Paul had
brought him into the temple area.)

30The whole city was aroused, and the
people came running from all direc-
tions. Seizing Paul,[r] they dragged him[s]
from the temple, and immediately the
gates were shut. 31While they were
trying to kill him, news reached the
commander of the Roman troops that
the whole city of Jerusalem was in an
uproar. 32He at once took some officers
and soldiers and ran down to the

Ch. 21

1 [a]**Ac 16:10**
2 [b]Ac 11:19
3 [c]**Lk 2:2**
4 [d]**Ac 11:26;** [e]ver 11; Ac 20:23
5 [f]Lk 22:41; Ac 9:40; 20:36
7 [g]Ac 12:20; [h]**Ac 1:16**
8 [i]**Ac 8:40;** [j]Ac 6:5; 8:5–40; [k]Eph 4:11; 2Ti 4:5
9 [l]Ex 15:20; Jdg 4:4; Ne 6:14; Lk 2:36; Ac 2:17; 1Co 11:5
10 [m]Ac 11:28
11 [n]**Ac 8:29;** [o]ver 33; [p]1Ki 22:11; Isa 20:2–4; Jer 13:1–11; Mt 20:19
13 [q]Ac 20:24; [r]**Jn 15:21; Ac 9:16**
14 [s]Ru 1:18; [t]**Mt 26:39**
15 [u]**Ac 19:21**
16 [v]**Ac 8:40;** [w]ver 3–4
17 [x]**Ac 9:30;** [y]Ac 15:4
18 [z]**Ac 15:13;** [a]**Ac 11:30**
19 [b]Ac 14:27; 15:4,12; [c]Ac 1:17
20 [d]Ac 22:3; Ro 10:2; Gal 1:14; Php 3:6; [e]Ac 15:1,5
21 [f]ver 28; [g]Ac 15:19–21; 1Co 7:18–19; [h]**Ac 6:14**
23 [i]Nu 6:2,5,18; Ac 18:18
24 [j]ver 26; Ac 24:18; [k]Ac 18:18
25 [l]Ac 15:20,29
26 [m]Nu 6:13–20; Ac 24:18
27 [n]Jer 26:8; Ac 24:18; 26:21; **1Th 2:16**
28 [o]Mt 24:15; Ac 6:13; 24:5–6
29 [p]Ac 20:4; 2Ti 4:20; [q]**Ac 18:19**
30 [r]Ac 26:21; [s]**Ac 16:19**

crowd. When the rioters saw the commander and his soldiers, they stopped beating Paul.[t]

33The commander came up and arrested him and ordered him to be bound[u] with two[v] chains.[w] Then he asked who he was and what he had done. 34Some in the crowd shouted one thing and some another,[x] and since the commander could not get at the truth because of the uproar, he ordered that Paul be taken into the barracks.[y] 35When Paul reached the steps,[z] the violence of the mob was so great he had to be carried by the soldiers. 36The crowd that followed kept shouting, "Away with him!"[a]

Paul Speaks to the Crowd

22:3–16pp—Ac 9:1–22; 26:9–18

37As the soldiers were about to take Paul into the barracks,[b] he asked the commander, "May I say something to you?"

"Do you speak Greek?" he replied. 38"Aren't you the Egyptian who started a revolt and led four thousand terrorists out into the desert[c] some time ago?"[d]

39Paul answered, "I am a Jew, from Tarsus[e] in Cilicia,[f] a citizen of no ordinary city. Please let me speak to the people."

40Having received the commander's permission, Paul stood on the steps and motioned[g] to the crowd. When they were all silent, he said to them in Aramaic[a]:[h]

22 1"Brothers and fathers,[a] listen now to my defence."

2When they heard him speak to them in Aramaic,[b] they became very quiet.

Then Paul said: 3"I am a Jew,[c] born in Tarsus[d] of Cilicia,[e] but brought up in this city. Under[f] Gamaliel[g] I was thoroughly trained in the law of our fathers[h] and was just as zealous[i] for God as any of you are today. 4I persecuted[j] the followers of this Way[k] to their death, arresting both men and women and throwing them into prison,[l] 5as also the high priest and all the Council[m] can testify. I even obtained letters from them to their brothers[n] in Damascus,[o] and went there to bring these people as prisoners to Jerusalem to be punished.

6"About noon as I came near Damascus, suddenly a bright light from heaven flashed around me.[p] 7I fell to the ground and heard a voice say to me, 'Saul! Saul! Why do you persecute me?'

8"'Who are you, Lord?' I asked.

"'I am Jesus of Nazareth,[q] whom you are persecuting,' he replied. 9My companions saw the light,[r] but they did not understand the voice[s] of him who was speaking to me.

10"'What shall I do, Lord?' I asked.

"'Get up,' the Lord said, 'and go into Damascus. There you will be told all that you have been assigned to do.'[t] 11My companions led me by the hand into Damascus, because the brilliance of the light had blinded me.[u]

12"A man named Ananias came to see me.[v] He was a devout observer of the law and highly respected by all the Jews living there.[w] 13He stood beside me and said, 'Brother Saul, receive your sight!' And at that very moment I was able to see him.

14"Then he said: 'The God of our fathers[x] has chosen you to know his will and to see[y] the Righteous One[z] and to hear words from his mouth. 15You will be his witness[a] to all men of what you have seen[b] and heard. 16And now what are you waiting for? Get up, be baptised[c] and wash your sins away,[d] calling on his name.'[e]

17"When I returned to Jerusalem[f] and was praying at the temple, I fell into a trance[g] 18and saw the Lord speaking. 'Quick!' he said to me. 'Leave Jerusalem immediately, because they will not accept your testimony about me.'

19"'Lord,' I replied, 'these men know that I went from one synagogue to another to imprison[h] and beat[i] those who believe in you. 20And when the blood of your martyr[a] Stephen was shed, I stood there giving my approval and guarding the clothes of those who were killing him.'[j]

21"Then the Lord said to me, 'Go; I will send you far away to the Gentiles.'"[k]

Paul the Roman Citizen

22The crowd listened to Paul until he said this. Then they raised their voices and shouted, "Rid the earth of him![l] He's not fit to live!"[m]

23As they were shouting and throwing off their cloaks[n] and flinging dust into the air,[o] 24the commander ordered Paul to be taken into the barracks.[p] He directed[q] that he be flogged and questioned in order to find out why the people were shouting at him like this. 25As they stretched him out to flog him, Paul said to the centurion standing

32 [t]Ac 23:27
33 [u]ver 11; [v]Ac 12:6; [w]Ac 20:23; 22:29; Eph 6:20; 2Ti 2:9
34 [x]Ac 19:32; [y]ver 37; Ac 22:24; 23:10, 16,32
35 [z]ver 40
36 [a]Lk 23:18; Jn 19:15; Ac 22:22
37 [b]**ver 34**
38 [c]Mt 24:26; [d]Ac 5:36
39 [e]**Ac 9:11;** [f]**Ac 6:9**
40 [g]**Ac 12:17;** [h]**Jn 5:2**

Ch. 22

1 [a]Ac 7:2
2 [b]Ac 21:40; **Jn 5:2**
3 [c]Ac 21:39; [d]**Ac 9:11;** [e]**Ac 6:9;** [f]Lk 10:39; [g]Ac 5:34; [h]Ac 26:5; [i]1Ki 19:10; **Ac 21:20**
4 [j]**Ac 8:3;** [k]**Ac 9:2;** [l]ver 19–20
5 [m]Lk 22:66; [n]**Ac 1:16;** 2:29; 13:26; 23:1; 28:17, 21; **Ro 7:1;** 9:3; [o]Ac 9:2
6 [p]Ac 9:3
8 [q]**Mk 1:24**
9 [r]Ac 26:13; [s]Ac 9:7
10 [t]Ac 16:30
11 [u]Ac 9:8
12 [v]Ac 9:17; [w]Ac 10:22
14 [x]**Ac 3:13;** [y]**1Co 15:8;** [z]Ac 7:52
15 [a]Ac 23:11; 26:16; [b]ver 14
16 [c]**Ac 2:38;** [d]Lev 8:6; Ps 51:2; Eze 36:25; Jn 3:5; 1Co 6:11; Eph 5:26; Tit 3:5; Heb 10:22; 1Pe 3:21; [e]Ro 10:13
17 [f]Ac 9:26; [g]Ac 10:10
19 [h]ver 4; **Ac 8:3;** [i]**Mt 10:17**
20 [j]Ac 7:57–60; 8:1
21 [k]**Ac 9:15; 13:46**
22 [l]Ac 21:36; [m]Ac 25:24
23 [n]Ac 7:58; [o]2Sa 16:13
24 [p]**Ac 21:34;** [q]ver 29

[a]40 Or possibly *Hebrew;* also in 22:2
[a]20 Or *witness*

there, "Is it legal for you to flog a Roman citizen who hasn't even been found guilty?"[r]

26When the centurion heard this, he went to the commander and reported it. "What are you going to do?" he asked. "This man is a Roman citizen."

27The commander went to Paul and asked, "Tell me, are you a Roman citizen?"

"Yes, I am," he answered.

28Then the commander said, "I had to pay a big price for my citizenship."

"But I was born a citizen," Paul replied.

29Those who were about to question him[s] withdrew immediately. The commander himself was alarmed when he realised that he had put Paul, a Roman citizen,[t] in chains.[u]

Before the Sanhedrin

30The next day, since the commander wanted to find out exactly why Paul was being accused by the Jews,[v] he released him[w] and ordered the chief priests and all the Sanhedrin[x] to assemble. Then he brought Paul and had him stand before them.

23 Paul looked straight at the Sanhedrin[a] and said, "My brothers,[b] I have fulfilled my duty to God in all good conscience[c] to this day." 2At this the high priest Ananias[d] ordered those standing near Paul to strike him on the mouth.[e] 3Then Paul said to him, "God will strike you, you whitewashed wall![f] You sit there to judge me according to the law, yet you yourself violate the law by commanding that I be struck!"[g]

4Those who were standing near Paul said, "You dare to insult God's high priest?"

5Paul replied, "Brothers, I did not realise that he was the high priest; for it is written: 'Do not speak evil about the ruler of your people.'a"[h]

6Then Paul, knowing that some of them were Sadducees[i] and the others Pharisees, called out in the Sanhedrin, "My brothers,[j] I am a Pharisee,[k] the son of a Pharisee. I stand on trial because of my hope in the resurrection of the dead."[l] 7When he said this, a dispute broke out between the Pharisees and the Sadducees, and the assembly was divided. 8(The Sadducees say that there is no resurrection,[m] and that there are neither angels nor spirits, but the Pharisees acknowledge them all.)

9There was a great uproar, and some of the teachers of the law who were Pharisees[n] stood up and argued vigorously. "We find nothing wrong with this man,"[o] they said. "What if a spirit or an angel has spoken to him?"[p] 10The dispute became so violent that the commander was afraid Paul would be torn to pieces by them. He ordered the troops to go down and take him away from them by force and bring him into the barracks.[q]

11The following night the Lord stood near Paul and said, "Take courage![r] As you have testified about me in Jerusalem, so you must also testify in Rome."[s]

The Plot to Kill Paul

12The next morning the Jews formed a conspiracy[t] and bound themselves with an oath not to eat or drink until they had killed Paul.[u] 13More than forty men were involved in this plot. 14They went to the chief priests and elders and said, "We have taken a solemn oath not to eat anything until we have killed Paul.[v] 15Now then, you and the Sanhedrin[w] petition the commander to bring him before you on the pretext of wanting more accurate information about his case. We are ready to kill him before he gets here."

16But when the son of Paul's sister heard of this plot, he went into the barracks[x] and told Paul.

17Then Paul called one of the centurions and said, "Take this young man to the commander; he has something to tell him." 18So he took him to the commander.

The centurion said, "Paul, the prisoner,[y] sent for me and asked me to bring this young man to you because he has something to tell you."

19The commander took the young man by the hand, drew him aside and asked, "What is it you want to tell me?"

20He said: "The Jews have agreed to ask you to bring Paul before the Sanhedrin[z] tomorrow on the pretext of wanting more accurate information about him.[a] 21Don't give in to them, because more than forty[b] of them are waiting in ambush for him. They have taken an oath not to eat or drink until they have killed him.[c] They are ready now, waiting for your consent to their request."

22The commander dismissed the young man and cautioned him, "Don't

a5 Exodus 22:28

25 [r]Ac 16:37
29 [s]ver 24; [t]ver 24–25; Ac 16:38; [u]**Ac 21:33**
30 [v]Ac 23:28; [w]Ac 21:33; [x]**Mt 5:22**

Ch. 23

1 [a]Ac 22:30; [b]**Ac 22:5**; [c]Ac 24:16; 1Co 4:4; 2Co 1:12; 1Ti 1:5,19; 3:9; 2Ti 1:3; Heb 9:14; 10:22; 13:18; 1Pe 3:16,21
2 [d]Ac 24:1; [e]Jn 18:22
3 [f]Mt 23:27; [g]Lev 19:15; Dt 25:1–2; Jn 7:51
5 [h]Ex 22:28
6 [i]ver 7–8; **Ac 4:1**; [j]**Ac 22:5**; [k]Ac 26:5; Php 3:5; [l]Ac 24:15,21; 26:8
8 [m]Mt 22:23; 1Co 15:12
9 [n]Mk 2:16; [o]ver 29; Jer 26:16; **Lk 23:4**; Ac 25:25; 26:31; 28:18; [p]Ac 22:7, 17–18
10 [q]**Ac 21:34**
11 [r]**Mt 14:27**; [s]Ac 19:21; 28:23
12 [t]**Ac 20:3**; [u]ver 14,21,30; Ac 25:3
14 [v]ver 12
15 [w]ver 1; Ac 22:30
16 [x]ver 10; **Ac 21:34**
18 [y]**Eph 3:1**
20 [z]ver 1; [a]ver 14–15
21 [b]ver 13; [c]ver 12,14

tell anyone that you have reported this
to me."

Paul Transferred to Caesarea

23Then he called two of his centurions
and ordered them, "Get ready a detach-
ment of two hundred soldiers, seventy
horsemen and two hundred spearmen[b]
to go to Caesarea[d] at nine tonight.[e]
24Provide mounts for Paul so that he
may be taken safely to Governor Felix."[f]
25He wrote a letter as follows:

26Claudius Lysias,

To His Excellency,[g] Governor Felix:

Greetings.[h]

27This man was seized by the
Jews and they were about to kill
him,[i] but I came with my troops
and rescued him,[j] for I had learned
that he is a Roman citizen.[k] 28I
wanted to know why they were
accusing him, so I brought him to
their Sanhedrin.[l] 29I found that the
accusation had to do with ques-
tions about their law,[m] but there
was no charge against him[n] that
deserved death or imprisonment.
30When I was informed[o] of a plot[p] to
be carried out against the man, I
sent him to you at once. I also
ordered his accusers[q] to present to
you their case against him.

31So the soldiers, carrying out their
orders, took Paul with them during the
night and brought him as far as Antipat-
ris. 32The next day they let the cavalry[r]
go on with him, while they returned
to the barracks.[s] 33When the cavalry[t]
arrived in Caesarea,[u] they delivered the
letter to the governor[v] and handed Paul
over to him. 34The governor read the
letter and asked what province he was
from. Learning that he was from Cili-
cia,[w] 35he said, "I will hear your case
when your accusers[x] get here." Then he
ordered that Paul be kept under guard[y]
in Herod's palace.

The Trial Before Felix

24 Five days later the high priest
Ananias[a] went down to
Caesarea with some of the elders and a
lawyer named Tertullus, and they
brought their charges[b] against Paul
before the governor.[c] 2When Paul was
called in, Tertullus presented his case
before Felix: "We have enjoyed a long
period of peace under you, and your
foresight has brought about reforms in
this nation. 3Everywhere and in every
way, most excellent[d] Felix, we acknowl-
edge this with profound gratitude. 4But
in order not to weary you further, I
would request that you be kind enough
to hear us briefly.

5"We have found this man to be a
troublemaker, stirring up riots[e] among
the Jews[f] all over the world. He is a
ringleader of the Nazarene[g] sect[h] 6and
even tried to desecrate the temple;[i] so
we seized him. 8By[a] examining him
yourself you will be able to learn the
truth about all these charges we are
bringing against him."

9The Jews joined in the accusation,[j]
asserting that these things were true.

10When the governor[k] motioned for
him to speak, Paul replied: "I know that
for a number of years you have been a
judge over this nation; so I gladly make
my defence. 11You can easily verify that
no more than twelve days[l] ago I went up
to Jerusalem to worship. 12My accusers
did not find me arguing with anyone at
the temple,[m] or stirring up a crowd[n] in
the synagogues or anywhere else in the
city. 13And they cannot prove to you the
charges they are now making against
me.[o] 14However, I admit that I worship
the God of our fathers[p] as a follower of
the Way,[q] which they call a sect.[r] I be-
lieve everything that agrees with the
Law and that is written in the Prophets,[s]
15and I have the same hope in God as
these men, that there will be a resurrec-
tion[t] of both the righteous and the wick-
ed.[u] 16So I strive always to keep my
conscience clear[v] before God and man.

17"After an absence of several years, I
came to Jerusalem to bring my people
gifts for the poor[w] and to present offer-
ings. 18I was ceremonially clean[x] when
they found me in the temple courts
doing this. There was no crowd with
me, nor was I involved in any distur-
bance.[y] 19But there are some Jews from
the province of Asia,[z] who ought to be
here before you and bring charges if
they have anything against me.[a] 20Or
these who are here should state what
crime they found in me when I stood
before the Sanhedrin—21unless it was

23 [d]**Ac 8:40;** [e]ver 33
24 [f]ver 26,33; Ac 24:1–3,10; 25:14
26 [g]Lk 1:3; Ac 24:3; 26:25; [h]Ac 15:23
27 [i]Ac 21:32; [j]Ac 21:33; [k]Ac 22:25–29
28 [l]Ac 22:30
29 [m]Ac 18:15; 25:19; [n]**ver 9**
30 [o]ver 20–21; [p]**Ac 20:3;** [q]ver 35; Ac 24:19; 25:16
32 [r]ver 23; [s]**Ac 21:34**
33 [t]ver 23–24; [u]**Ac 8:40;** [v]ver 26
34 [w]**Ac 6:9;** 21:39
35 [x]ver 30; Ac 24:19; 25:16; [y]Ac 24:27

Ch. 24

1 [a]Ac 23:2; [b]Ac 23:30,35; [c]**Ac 23:24**
3 [d]Lk 1:3; Ac 23:26; 26:25
5 [e]Ac 16:20; 17:6; [f]Ac 21:28; [g]**Mk 1:24;** [h]ver 14; Ac 26:5; 28:22
6 [i]Ac 21:28
9 [j]**1Th 2:16**
10 [k]**Ac 23:24**
11 [l]Ac 21:27; ver 1
12 [m]Ac 25:8; 28:17; [n]ver 18
13 [o]Ac 25:7
14 [p]**Ac 3:13;** [q]**Ac 9:2;** [r]**ver 5;** [s]Ac 26:6,22; 28:23
15 [t]Ac 23:6; 28:20; [u]**Mt 25:46**
16 [v]**Ac 23:1**
17 [w]Ac 11:29–30; Ro 15:25–28,31; 1Co 16:1–4,15; 2Co 8:1–4; Gal 2:10
18 [x]Ac 21:26; [y]ver 12
19 [z]**Ac 2:9;** [a]Ac 23:30

b23 The meaning of the Greek for this word is uncertain.
a6–8 Some manuscripts *him and wanted to judge him according to our law. 7But the commander, Lysias, came and with the use of much force snatched him from our hands 8and ordered his accusers to come before you. By*

this one thing I shouted as I stood in
their presence: 'It is concerning the re-
surrection of the dead that I am on trial
before you today.' "[b]
22Then Felix, who was well ac-
quainted with the Way,[c] adjourned the
proceedings. "When Lysias the com-
mander comes," he said, "I will decide
your case." 23He ordered the centurion
to keep Paul under guard[d] but to give
him some freedom[e] and permit his
friends to take care of his needs.[f]
24Several days later Felix came with
his wife Drusilla, who was a Jewess. He
sent for Paul and listened to him as he
spoke about faith in Christ Jesus.[g] 25As
Paul discoursed on righteousness, self-
control[h] and the judgment[i] to come,
Felix was afraid[j] and said, "That's
enough for now! You may leave. When I
find it convenient, I will send for you."
26At the same time he was hoping that
Paul would offer him a bribe, so he sent
for him frequently and talked with him.
27When two years had passed, Felix
was succeeded by Porcius Festus,[k] but
because Felix wanted to grant a favour
to the Jews,[l] he left Paul in prison.[m]

The Trial Before Festus

25 Three days after arriving in the
province, Festus[a] went up from
Caesarea[b] to Jerusalem, 2where the chief
priests and Jewish leaders appeared be-
fore him and presented the charges
against Paul.[c] 3They urgently requested
Festus, as a favour to them, to have Paul
transferred to Jerusalem, for they were
preparing an ambush to kill him along
the way.[d] 4Festus answered, "Paul is
being held[e] at Caesarea,[f] and I myself
am going there soon. 5Let some of your
leaders come with me and press charges
against the man there, if he has done
anything wrong."
6After spending eight or ten days
with them, he went down to Caesarea,
and the next day he convened the court[g]
and ordered that Paul be brought before
him.[h] 7When Paul appeared, the Jews
who had come down from Jerusalem
stood around him, bringing many
serious charges against him,[i] which
they could not prove.[j]
8Then Paul made his defence: "I have
done nothing wrong against the law of
the Jews or against the temple[k] or
against Caesar."
9Festus, wishing to do the Jews a
favour,[l] said to Paul, "Are you willing to
go up to Jerusalem and stand trial before
me there on these charges?"[m]

21 [b]Ac 23:6
22 [c]**Ac 9:2**
23 [d]Ac 23:35; [e]Ac 28:16; [f]Ac 23:16; 27:3
24 [g]**Ac 20:21**
25 [h]Gal 5:23; 1Th 5:6; 1Pe 4:7; 5:8; 2Pe 1:6; [i]Ac 10:42; [j]Jer 36:16
27 [k]Ac 25:1,4,9, 14; [l]Ac 12:3; 25:9; [m]Ac 23:35; 25:14

Ch. 25

1 [a]**Ac 24:27**; [b]**Ac 8:40**
2 [c]ver 15; Ac 24:1
3 [d]**Ac 20:3**
4 [e]Ac 24:23; [f]**Ac 8:40**
6 [g]ver 17; [h]ver 10
7 [i]Mk 15:3; Lk 23:2,10; Ac 24:5–6; [j]Ac 24:13
8 [k]Ac 6:13; 24:12; 28:17
9 [l]Ac 24:27; 12:3; [m]ver 20
10 [n]ver 8
11 [o]ver 21,25; Ac 26:32; 28:19
13 [p]**Ac 8:40**
14 [q]Ac 24:27
15 [r]ver 2; Ac 24:1
16 [s]ver 4–5; Ac 23:30
17 [t]ver 6,10
19 [u]Ac 18:15; 23:29; [v]Ac 17:22
20 [w]ver 9
21 [x]ver 11–12
22 [y]Ac 9:15
23 [z]ver 13; Ac 26:30

10Paul answered: "I am now standing
before Caesar's court, where I ought to
be tried. I have not done any wrong to
the Jews,[n] as you yourself know very
well. 11If, however, I am guilty of doing
anything deserving death, I do not re-
fuse to die. But if the charges brought
against me by these Jews are not true,
no-one has the right to hand me over to
them. I appeal to Caesar!"[o]
12After Festus had conferred with
his council, he declared: "You have
appealed to Caesar. To Caesar you will
go!"

Festus Consults King Agrippa

13A few days later King Agrippa and
Bernice arrived at Caesarea[p] to pay their
respects to Festus. 14Since they were
spending many days there, Festus dis-
cussed Paul's case with the king. He
said: "There is a man here whom Felix
left as a prisoner.[q] 15When I went to
Jerusalem, the chief priests and elders
of the Jews brought charges against
him[r] and asked that he be condemned.
16"I told them that it is not the Roman
custom to hand over any man before he
has faced his accusers and has had an
opportunity to defend himself against
their charges.[s] 17When they came here
with me, I did not delay the case, but
convened the court the next day and
ordered the man to be brought in.[t]
18When his accusers got up to speak,
they did not charge him with any of the
crimes I had expected. 19Instead, they
had some points of dispute[u] with him
about their own religion[v] and about a
dead man named Jesus whom Paul
claimed was alive. 20I was at a loss how
to investigate such matters; so I asked if
he would be willing to go to Jerusalem
and stand trial there on these charges.[w]
21When Paul made his appeal to be held
over for the Emperor's decision, I
ordered him to be held until I could
send him to Caesar."[x]
22Then Agrippa said to Festus, "I
would like to hear this man myself."
He replied, "Tomorrow you will hear
him."[y]

Paul Before Agrippa

26:12–18pp—Ac 9:3–8; 22:6–11

23The next day Agrippa and Bernice[z]
came with great pomp and entered the
audience room with the high ranking
officers and the leading men of the city.
At the command of Festus, Paul was

brought in. 24Festus said: "King Agrip-
pa, and all who are present with us, you
see this man! The whole Jewish com-
munity[a] has petitioned me about him in
Jerusalem and here in Caesarea, shout-
ing that he ought not to live any longer.[b]
25I found he had done nothing deserv-
ing of death,[c] but because he made his
appeal to the Emperor[d] I decided to
send him to Rome. 26But I have nothing
definite to write to His Majesty about
him. Therefore I have brought him be-
fore all of you, and especially before
you, King Agrippa, so that as a result of
this investigation I may have something
to write. 27For I think it is unreasonable
to send on a prisoner without specifying
the charges against him."

26

Then Agrippa said to Paul,
"You have permission to speak
for yourself."[a]

So Paul motioned with his hand[b] and
began his defence: 2"King Agrippa, I
consider myself fortunate to stand be-
fore you[c] today as I make my defence
against all the accusations of the Jews,[d]
3and especially so because you are well
acquainted with all the Jewish customs[e]
and controversies.[f] Therefore, I beg you
to listen to me patiently.

4"The Jews all know the way I have
lived ever since I was a child,[g] from the
beginning of my life in my own country,
and also in Jerusalem. 5They have
known me for a long time[h] and can
testify, if they are willing, that accord-
ing to the strictest sect[i] of our religion, I
lived as a Pharisee.[j] 6And now it is be-
cause of my hope[k] in what God has
promised our fathers[l] that I am on trial
today. 7This is the promise our twelve
tribes[m] are hoping to see fulfilled as they
earnestly serve God day and night.[n] O
King, it is because of this hope that the
Jews are accusing me.[o] 8Why should
any of you consider it incredible that
God raises the dead?[p]

9"I too was convinced[q] that I ought to
do all that was possible to oppose[r] the
name of Jesus of Nazareth.[s] 10And that
is just what I did in Jerusalem. On the
authority of the chief priests I put many
of the saints[t] in prison,[u] and when they
were put to death, I cast my vote against
them.[v] 11Many a time I went from one
synagogue to another to have them
punished,[w] and I tried to force them to
blaspheme. In my obsession against
them, I even went to foreign cities to
persecute them.

12"On one of these journeys I was
going to Damascus with the authority
and commission of the chief priests.
13About noon, O King, as I was on the
road, I saw a light from heaven, brighter
than the sun, blazing around me and
my companions. 14We all fell to the
ground, and I heard a voice[x] saying to
me in Aramaic,[a][y] 'Saul, Saul, why do
you persecute me? It is hard for you to
kick against the goads.'

15"Then I asked, 'Who are you, Lord?'

"'I am Jesus, whom you are persecut-
ing,' the Lord replied. 16'Now get up
and stand on your feet.[z] I have appeared
to you to appoint you as a servant and as
a witness of what you have seen of me
and what I will show you.[a] 17I will res-
cue you[b] from your own people and
from the Gentiles.[c] I am sending you to
them 18to open their eyes[d] and turn
them from darkness to light,[e] and from
the power of Satan to God, so that they
may receive forgiveness of sins[f] and a
place among those who are sanctified
by faith in me.'[g]

19"So then, King Agrippa, I was not
disobedient[h] to the vision from heaven.
20First to those in Damascus,[i] then to
those in Jerusalem[j] and in all Judea, and
to the Gentiles[k] also, I preached that
they should repent[l] and turn to God and
prove their repentance by their deeds.[m]
21That is why the Jews seized me[n] in the
temple courts and tried to kill me.[o] 22But
I have had God's help to this very day,
and so I stand here and testify to small
and great alike. I am saying nothing
beyond what the prophets and Moses
said would happen[p]—23that the Christ[b]
would suffer[q] and, as the first to rise
from the dead,[r] would proclaim light to
his own people and to the Gentiles."[s]

24At this point Festus interrupted
Paul's defence. "You are out of your
mind,[t] Paul!" he shouted. "Your great
learning[u] is driving you insane."

25"I am not insane, most excellent[v]
Festus," Paul replied. "What I am
saying is true and reasonable. 26The
king is familiar with these things,[w] and I
can speak freely to him. I am convinced
that none of this has escaped his notice,
because it was not done in a corner.
27King Agrippa, do you believe the
prophets? I know you do."

28Then Agrippa said to Paul, "Do you
think that in such a short time you can
persuade me to be a Christian?"[x]

29Paul replied, "Short time or long—I
pray God that not only you but all who
are listening to me today may become
what I am, except for these chains."[y]

24 [a]ver 2–3,7; [b]Ac 22:22
25 [c]**Ac 23:9**; [d]**ver 11**

Ch. 26

1 [a]Ac 9:15; 25:22; [b]**Ac 12:17**
2 [c]Ps 119:46; [d]Ac 24:1,5; 25:2,7,11
3 [e]ver 7; **Ac 6:14**; [f]Ac 25:19
4 [g]Gal 1:13–14; Php 3:5
5 [h]Ac 22:3; [i]**Ac 24:5**; [j]Ac 23:6; Php 3:5
6 [k]Ac 23:6; 24:15; 28:20; [l]**Ac 13:32**; Ro 15:8
7 [m]Jas 1:1; [n]1Th 3:10; 1Ti 5:5; [o]ver 2
8 [p]Ac 23:6
9 [q]1Ti 1:13; [r]Jn 16:2; [s]**Jn 15:21**
10 [t]**Ac 9:13**; [u]**Ac 8:3**; 9:2,14, 21; [v]Ac 22:20
11 [w]**Mt 10:17**
14 [x]Ac 9:7; [y]**Jn 5:2**
16 [z]Eze 2:1; Da 10:11; [a]Ac 22:14–15
17 [b]Jer 1:8,19; [c]**Ac 9:15; 13:46**
18 [d]Isa 35:5; [e]Ps 18:28; Isa 42:7, 16; Eph 5:8; Col 1:13; 1Pe 2:9; [f]Lk 24:47; Ac 2:38; [g]**Ac 20:21**
19 [h]Isa 50:5
20 [i]Ac 9:19–25; [j]Ac 9:26–29; 22:17–20; [k]**Ac 9:15; 13:46**; [l]Ac 3:19; [m]Jer 18:11; 35:15; Mt 3:8; Lk 3:8
21 [n]Ac 21:27,30; [o]Ac 21:31
22 [p]**Lk 24:27**,44; Ac 10:43; 24:14
23 [q]**Mt 16:21**; [r]1Co 15:20,23; Col 1:18; Rev 1:5; [s]**Lk 2:32**
24 [t]**Jn 10:20; 1Co 4:10**; [u]Jn 7:15
25 [v]**Ac 23:26**
26 [w]ver 3
28 [x]Ac 11:26
29 [y]**Ac 21:33**

[a]14 Or *Hebrew* [b]23 Or *Messiah*

30The king rose, and with him the
governor and Bernice[z] and those sitting
with them. 31They left the room, and
while talking with one another, they
said, "This man is not doing anything
that deserves death or imprisonment."[a]
32Agrippa said to Festus, "This man
could have been set free[b] if he had not
appealed to Caesar."[c]

Paul Sails for Rome

27 When it was decided that we[a]
would sail for Italy,[b] Paul and
some other prisoners were handed over
to a centurion named Julius, who
belonged to the Imperial Regiment.[c]
2We boarded a ship from Adramyttium
about to sail for ports along the coast of
the province of Asia,[d] and we put out to
sea. Aristarchus,[e] a Macedonian[f] from
Thessalonica,[g] was with us.
3The next day we landed at Sidon;[h]
and Julius, in kindness to Paul,[i] allowed
him to go to his friends so they might
provide for his needs.[j] 4From there we
put out to sea again and passed to the
lee of Cyprus because the winds were
against us.[k] 5When we had sailed across
the open sea off the coast of Cilicia[l] and
Pamphylia,[m] we landed at Myra in
Lycia. 6There the centurion found an
Alexandrian[n] ship sailing for Italy[o] and
put us on board. 7We made slow head-
way for many days and had difficulty
arriving off Cnidus. When the wind did
not allow us to hold our course,[p] we
sailed to the lee of Crete,[q] opposite Sal-
mone. 8We moved along the coast with
difficulty and came to a place called Fair
Havens, near the town of Lasea.
9Much time had been lost, and sailing
had already become dangerous because
by now it was after the Fast.[a][r] So Paul
warned them, 10"Men, I can see that our
voyage is going to be disastrous and
bring great loss to ship and cargo, and to
our own lives also."[s] 11But the centu-
rion, instead of listening to what Paul
said, followed the advice of the pilot
and of the owner of the ship. 12Since the
harbour was unsuitable to winter in, the
majority decided that we should sail on,
hoping to reach Phoenix and winter
there. This was a harbour in Crete,[t]
facing both south-west and north-west.

The Storm

13When a gentle south wind began to
blow, they thought they had obtained
what they wanted; so they weighed
anchor and sailed along the shore of
Crete. 14Before very long, a wind of
hurricane force,[u] called the "north-
easter", swept down from the island.
15The ship was caught by the storm and
could not head into the wind; so we
gave way to it and were driven along.
16As we passed to the lee of a small
island called Cauda, we were hardly
able to make the lifeboat[v] secure.
17When the men had hoisted it aboard,
they passed ropes under the ship itself
to hold it together. Fearing that they
would run aground[w] on the sand-bars
of Syrtis, they lowered the sea anchor
and let the ship be driven along. 18We
took such a violent battering from the
storm that the next day they began to
throw the cargo overboard.[x] 19On the
third day, they threw the ship's tackle
overboard with their own hands.
20When neither sun nor stars appeared
for many days and the storm continued
raging, we finally gave up all hope of
being saved.
21After the men had gone a long time
without food, Paul stood up before
them and said: "Men, you should have
taken my advice[y] not to sail from Crete;[z]
then you would have spared yourselves
this damage and loss. 22But now I urge
you to keep up your courage,[a] because
not one of you will be lost; only the ship
will be destroyed. 23Last night an angel[b]
of the God whose I am and whom I
serve[c] stood beside me[d] 24and said, 'Do
not be afraid, Paul. You must stand trial
before Caesar;[e] and God has graciously
given you the lives of all who sail with
you.'[f] 25So keep up your courage,[g] men,
for I have faith in God that it will happen
just as he told me.[h] 26Nevertheless, we
must run aground[i] on some island."[j]

The Shipwreck

27On the fourteenth night we were
still being driven across the Adriatic[b]
Sea, when about midnight the sailors
sensed they were approaching land.
28They took soundings and found that
the water was one hundred and twenty
feet[c] deep. A short time later they took
soundings again and found it was nine-
ty feet[d] deep. 29Fearing that we would
be dashed against the rocks, they drop-
ped four anchors from the stern and
prayed for daylight. 30In an attempt to

30 [z]Ac 25:23
31 [a]**Ac 23:9**
32 [b]Ac 28:18; [c]**Ac 25:11**

Ch. 27

1 [a]**Ac 16:10**; [b]Ac 18:2; 25:12,25; [c]Ac 10:1
2 [d]**Ac 2:9**; [e]**Ac 19:29**; [f]**Ac 16:9**; [g]**Ac 17:1**
3 [h]Mt 11:21; [i]ver 43; [j]Ac 24:23; 28:16
4 [k]ver 7
5 [l]**Ac 6:9**; [m]**Ac 2:10**
6 [n]Ac 28:11; [o]ver 1; Ac 18:2; 25:12,25
7 [p]ver 4; [q]ver 12–13,21; Tit 1:5
9 [r]Lev 16:29–31; 23:27–29; Nu 29:7
10 [s]ver 21
12 [t]**ver 7**
14 [u]Mk 4:37
16 [v]ver 30
17 [w]ver 26,39
18 [x]ver 19,38; Jnh 1:5
21 [y]ver 10; [z]**ver 7**
22 [a]ver 25,36
23 [b]**Ac 5:19**; [c]Ro 1:9; [d]Ac 18:9; 23:11; 2Ti 4:17
24 [e]Ac 23:11; [f]ver 44
25 [g]ver 22,36; [h]Ro 4:20–21
26 [i]ver 17,39; [j]Ac 28:1

[a]9 That is, the Day of Atonement (Yom Kippur)
[b]27 In ancient times the name referred to an area extending well south of Italy.
[c]28 Greek *twenty orguias* (about 37 metres)
[d]28 Greek *fifteen orguias* (about 27 metres)

escape from the ship, the sailors let the
lifeboat[k] down into the sea, pretending
they were going to lower some anchors
from the bow. 31Then Paul said to the
centurion and the soldiers, "Unless
these men stay with the ship, you can-
not be saved."[l] 32So the soldiers cut the
ropes that held the lifeboat and let it fall
away.

33Just before dawn Paul urged them
all to eat. "For the last fourteen days,"
he said, "you have been in constant
suspense and have gone without food
—you haven't eaten anything. 34Now I
urge you to take some food. You need it
to survive. Not one of you will lose a
single hair from his head."[m] 35After he
said this, he took some bread and gave
thanks to God in front of them all. Then
he broke it[n] and began to eat. 36They
were all encouraged[o] and ate some food
themselves. 37Altogether there were 276
of us on board. 38When they had eaten
as much as they wanted, they lightened
the ship by throwing the grain into the
sea.[p]

39When daylight came, they did not
recognise the land, but they saw a bay
with a sandy beach,[q] where they de-
cided to run the ship aground if they
could. 40Cutting loose the anchors,[r]
they left them in the sea and at the same
time untied the ropes that held the rud-
ders. Then they hoisted the foresail to
the wind and made for the beach. 41But
the ship struck a sand-bar and ran
aground. The bow stuck fast and would
not move, and the stern was broken to
pieces by the pounding of the surf.[s]

42The soldiers planned to kill the pris-
oners to prevent any of them from
swimming away and escaping. 43But the
centurion wanted to spare Paul's life[t]
and kept them from carrying out their
plan. He ordered those who could swim
to jump overboard first and get to land.
44The rest were to get there on planks or
on pieces of the ship. In this way every-
one reached land in safety.[u]

Ashore on Malta

28 Once safely on shore, we[a]
found out that the island[b] was
called Malta. 2The islanders showed us
unusual kindness. They built a fire and
welcomed us all because it was raining
and cold. 3Paul gathered a pile of brush-
wood and, as he put it on the fire, a
viper, driven out by the heat, fastened
itself on his hand. 4When the islanders
saw the snake hanging from his hand,[c]
they said to each other, "This man must
be a murderer; for though he escaped
from the sea, Justice has not allowed
him to live."[d] 5But Paul shook the snake
off into the fire and suffered no ill
effects.[e] 6The people expected him to
swell up or suddenly fall dead, but after
waiting a long time and seeing nothing
unusual happen to him, they changed
their minds and said he was a god.[f]

7There was an estate near by that be-
longed to Publius, the chief official of
the island. He welcomed us to his home
and for three days entertained us hos-
pitably. 8His father was sick in bed,
suffering from fever and dysentery.
Paul went in to see him and, after
prayer,[g] placed his hands on him[h] and
healed him.[i] 9When this had happened,
the rest of the sick on the island came
and were cured. 10They honoured us[j] in
many ways and when we were ready to
sail, they furnished us with the supplies
we needed.

Arrival at Rome

11After three months we put out to sea
in a ship that had wintered in the island.
It was an Alexandrian ship[k] with the
figurehead of the twin gods Castor and
Pollux. 12We put in at Syracuse and
stayed there three days. 13From there
we set sail and arrived at Rhegium. The
next day the south wind came up, and
on the following day we reached
Puteoli. 14There we found some
brothers[l] who invited us to spend a
week with them. And so we came to
Rome. 15The brothers[m] there had heard
that we were coming, and they travelled
as far as the Forum of Appius and the
Three Taverns to meet us. At the sight
of these men Paul thanked God and was
encouraged. 16When we got to Rome,
Paul was allowed to live by himself,
with a soldier to guard him.[n]

Paul Preaches at Rome Under Guard

17Three days later he called together
the leaders of the Jews.[o] When they had
assembled, Paul said to them: "My
brothers,[p] although I have done nothing
against our people[q] or against the cus-
toms of our ancestors,[r] I was arrested in
Jerusalem and handed over to the
Romans. 18They examined me[s] and
wanted to release me,[t] because I was not
guilty of any crime deserving death.[u]
19But when the Jews objected, I was
compelled to appeal to Caesar[v]—not
that I had any charge to bring against
my own people. 20For this reason I have

30 [k]ver 16
31 [l]ver 24
34 [m]**Mt 10:30**
35 [n]**Mt 14:19**
36 [o]ver 22,25
38 [p]ver 18; Jnh 1:5
39 [q]Ac 28:1
40 [r]ver 29
41 [s]2Co 11:25
43 [t]ver 3
44 [u]ver 22,31

Ch. 28

1 [a]**Ac 16:10**; [b]Ac 27:26,39
4 [c]Mk 16:18; [d]Lk 13:2,4
5 [e]Lk 10:19
6 [f]Ac 14:11
8 [g]Jas 5:14–15; [h]**Ac 6:6**; [i]Ac 9:40
10 [j]Ps 15:4
11 [k]Ac 27:6
14 [l]**Ac 1:16**
15 [m]**Ac 1:16**
16 [n]Ac 24:23; 27:3
17 [o]Ac 25:2; [p]**Ac 22:5**; [q]**Ac 25:8**; [r]**Ac 6:14**
18 [s]Ac 22:24; [t]Ac 26:31–32; [u]**Ac 23:9**
19 [v]**Ac 25:11**

asked to see you and talk with you. It is
because of the hope of Israel[w] that I am
bound with this chain."[x]
21They replied, "We have not re-
ceived any letters from Judea concern-
ing you, and none of the brothers[y] who
have come from there has reported or
said anything bad about you. 22But we
want to hear what your views are, for
we know that people everywhere are
talking against this sect."[z]
23They arranged to meet Paul on a
certain day, and came in even larger
numbers to the place where he was
staying. From morning till evening he
explained and declared to them the
kingdom of God[a] and tried to convince
them about Jesus[b] from the Law of
Moses and from the Prophets.[c] 24Some
were convinced by what he said, but
others would not believe.[d] 25They dis-
agreed among themselves and began to
leave after Paul had made this final
statement: "The Holy Spirit spoke the
truth to your forefathers when he said[e]
through Isaiah the prophet:

26" 'Go to this people and say,

"You will be ever hearing but never
understanding;
you will be ever seeing but never
perceiving."
27For this people's heart has become
calloused;[f]
they hardly hear with their ears,
and they have closed their eyes.
Otherwise they might see with their
eyes,
hear with their ears,
understand with their hearts
and turn, and I would heal them.'[a] [g]

28"Therefore I want you to know that
God's salvation[h] has been sent to the
Gentiles,[i] and they will listen!"[b]
30For two whole years Paul stayed
there in his own rented house and
welcomed all who came to see him.
31Boldly[j] and without hindrance he
preached the kingdom of God[k] and
taught about the Lord Jesus Christ.

20 [w]Ac 26:6–7; [x]**Ac 21:33**
21 [y]**Ac 22:5**
22 [z]**Ac 24:5**
23 [a]**Mt 3:2**; Ac 19:8; [b]Ac 17:3; [c]**Ac 8:35**
24 [d]Ac 14:4; 17:4–5
25 [e]**Heb 3:7**
27 [f]Ps 119:70; [g]Isa 6:9–10; **Mt 13:15**
28 [h]Lk 2:30; [i]**Ac 13:46**
31 [j]**Ac 4:29**; [k]ver 23; **Mt 4:23**

---

[a]27 Isaiah 6:9,10
[b]28 Some manuscripts *listen!"* [29]*After he said this, the Jews left, arguing vigorously among themselves.*

Romans

1 Paul, a servant of Christ Jesus,
called to be an apostle[a] and set
apart[b] for the gospel of God[c]—2the gos-
pel he promised beforehand[d] through
his prophets[e] in the Holy Scriptures[f]
3regarding his Son, who as to his human
nature[g] was a descendant of David,[h]
4and who through the Spirit[a] of holiness
was declared with power to be the Son
of God,[b i] by his resurrection from the
dead:[j] Jesus Christ our Lord.[k] 5Through
him and for his name's sake, we re-
ceived grace[l] and apostleship to call
people from among all the Gentiles[m] to
the obedience that comes from faith.[n]
6And you also are among those who are
called to belong to Jesus Christ.[o]

7To all in Rome who are loved by God[p]
and called to be saints:[q]

Grace and peace to you from God our
Father and from the Lord Jesus Christ.[r]

Paul's Longing to Visit Rome

8First, I thank my God through Jesus
Christ for all of you,[s] because your faith
is being reported all over the world.[t]
9God, whom I serve[u] with my whole
heart in preaching the gospel of his Son,
is my witness[v] how constantly I remem-
ber you 10in my prayers at all times;[w]
and I pray that now at last by God's will[x]
the way may be opened for me to come
to you.[y]
11I long to see you[z] so that I may
impart to you some spiritual gift[a] to
make you strong—12that is, that you
and I may be mutually encouraged by
each other's faith. 13I do not want you to
be unaware,[b] brothers,[c] that I planned
many times to come to you (but have
been prevented from doing so until
now)[d] in order that I might have a har-
vest among you, just as I have had
among the other Gentiles.
14I am bound[e] both to Greeks and
non-Greeks, both to the wise and the
foolish. 15That is why I am so eager to
preach the gospel also to you who are at
Rome.[f]

16I am not ashamed of the gospel,[g]
because it is the power of God[h] for the
salvation of everyone who believes:[i]
first for the Jew,[j] then for the Gentile.[k]
17For in the gospel a righteousness from
God is revealed,[l] a righteousness that is
by faith[m] from first to last,[c] just as it is
written: "The righteous will live by
faith."[d n]

God's Wrath Against Mankind

18The wrath of God[o] is being revealed
from heaven against all the godlessness
and wickedness of men who suppress
the truth by their wickedness, 19since
what may be known about God is plain
to them, because God has made it plain
to them.[p] 20For since the creation of the
world God's invisible qualities—his
eternal power and divine nature—have
been clearly seen, being understood
from what has been made,[q] so that men
are without excuse.[r]
21For although they knew God, they
neither glorified him as God nor gave
thanks to him, but their thinking be-
came futile and their foolish hearts were
darkened.[s] 22Although they claimed to
be wise, they became fools[t] 23and ex-
changed the glory of the immortal God
for images[u] made to look like mortal
man and birds and animals and reptiles.
24Therefore God gave them over[v] in
the sinful desires of their hearts to sex-
ual impurity for the degrading of their
bodies with one another.[w] 25They ex-
changed the truth of God for a lie,[x] and
worshipped and served created things[y]
rather than the Creator—who is for ever
praised.[z] Amen.[a]

Ch. 1

1 [a]**1Co 1:1**; [b]**Ac 9:15**; [c]Ro 15:16; **2Co 2:12**; 11:7; 1Th 2:8–9; 1Pe 4:17
2 [d]**Ac 13:32**; Tit 1:2; [e]Lk 1:70; Ro 3:21; [f]Gal 3:8
3 [g]**Jn 1:14**; Ro 9:5; [h]**Mt 1:1**
4 [i]**Mt 4:3**; [j]**Ac 2:24**; [k]1Co 1:2
5 [l]1Ti 1:14; [m]**Ac 9:15**; [n]Ac 6:7; Ro 16:26
6 [o]Jude 1; Rev 17:14
7 [p]Ro 8:39; 1Th 1:4; [q]**Ac 9:13**; [r]1Co 1:3; Eph 1:2; 1Ti 1:2; Tit 1:4; 1Pe 1:2
8 [s]1Co 1:4; Eph 1:16; 1Th 2:13; 2Th 1:3; 2Ti 1:3; [t]**Ro 10:18**; 16:19
9 [u]2Ti 1:3; [v]Job 16:19; Jer 42:5; 2Co 1:23; Gal 1:20; Php 1:8; 1Th 2:5,10
10 [w]1Sa 12:23; **Lk 18:1**; **Ac 1:14**; Eph 1:16; Php 1:4; Col 1:9; 2Th 1:11; 2Ti 1:3; Phm 4; [x]**Ac 18:21**; [y]ver 13; Ro 15:32
11 [z]Ro 15:23; [a]1Co 1:7; 12:1–31
13 [b]**Ro 11:25**; [c]**Ro 7:1**; [d]Ro 15:22–23
14 [e]1Co 9:16
15 [f]Ro 15:20
16 [g]2Ti 1:8; [h]1Co 1:18; [i]**Jn 3:15**; [j]Ac 3:26; 13:46; [k]**Ac 13:46**; Ro 2:9–10
17 [l]Ro 3:21; Php 3:9; [m]**Ro 9:30**; [n]Hab 2:4; Gal 3:11; Heb 10:38

18 [o]Jn 3:36; Ro 5:9; Eph 5:6; Col 3:6; 1Th 1:10; Rev 19:15
19 [p]Ac 14:17 *20* [q]Ps 19:1–6; [r]Ro 2:1
21 [s]Ge 8:21; Jer 2:5; 17:9; Eph 4:17–18
22 [t]1Co 1:20,27; 3:18–19
23 [u]Dt 4:16–17; Ps 106:20; Jer 2:11; Ac 17:29
24 [v]ver 26,28; Ps 81:12; Eph 4:19; [w]1Pe 4:3
25 [x]Isa 44:20; [y]Jer 10:14; 13:25; 16:19–20; [z]Ro 9:5; 2Co 11:31; [a]**Ro 11:36**

a4 Or *who as to his spirit*
b4 Or *was appointed to be the Son of God with power*
c17 Or *is from faith to faith*
d17 Hab. 2:4

26 Because of this, God gave them over[b] to shameful lusts.[c] Even their women exchanged natural relations for unnatural ones.[d] 27 In the same way the men also abandoned natural relations with women and were inflamed with lust for one another. Men committed indecent acts with other men, and received in themselves the due penalty for their perversion.[e]

28 Furthermore, since they did not think it worth while to retain the knowledge of God, he gave them over[f] to a depraved mind, to do what ought not to be done. 29 They have become filled with every kind of wickedness, evil, greed and depravity. They are full of envy, murder, strife, deceit and malice. They are gossips,[g] 30 slanderers, God-haters, insolent, arrogant and boastful; they invent ways of doing evil; they disobey their parents;[h] 31 they are senseless, faithless, heartless,[i] ruthless. 32 Although they know God's righteous decree that those who do such things deserve death,[j] they not only continue to do these very things but also approve[k] of those who practise them.

God's Righteous Judgment

2 You, therefore, have no excuse,[a] you who pass judgment on someone else, for at whatever point you judge[b] the other, you are condemning yourself, because you who pass judgment do the same things.[b] 2 Now we know that God's judgment against those who do such things is based on truth. 3 So when you, a mere man, pass judgment on them and yet do the same things, do you think you will escape God's judgment? 4 Or do you show contempt for the riches[c] of his kindness[d], tolerance[e] and patience,[f] not realising that God's kindness leads you towards repentance?[g]

5 But because of your stubbornness and your unrepentant heart, you are storing up wrath against yourself for the day of God's wrath,[h] when his righteous judgment[i] will be revealed. 6 God "will give to each person according to what he has done".[a][j] 7 To those who by persistence in doing good seek glory, honour[k] and immortality,[l] he will give eternal life.[m] 8 But for those who are self-seeking and who reject the truth and follow evil,[n] there will be wrath and anger.[o] 9 There will be trouble and distress for every human being who does evil:[p] first for the Jew, then for the Gentile;[q] 10 but glory, honour and peace for everyone who does good: first for the Jew, then for the Gentile.[r] 11 For God does not show favouritism.[s]

12 All who sin apart from the law will also perish apart from the law, and all who sin under the law[t] will be judged by the law. 13 For it is not those who hear the law who are righteous in God's sight, but it is those who obey[u] the law who will be declared righteous. 14 (Indeed, when Gentiles, who do not have the law, do by nature things required by the law,[v] they are a law for themselves, even though they do not have the law, 15 since they show that the requirements of the law are written on their hearts, their consciences also bearing witness, and their thoughts now accusing, now even defending them.) 16 This will take place on the day when God will judge men's secrets[w] through Jesus Christ,[x] as my gospel[y] declares.

The Jews and the Law

17 Now you, if you call yourself a Jew; if you rely on the law and brag about your relationship to God;[z] 18 if you know his will and approve of what is superior because you are instructed by the law; 19 if you are convinced that you are a guide for the blind, a light for those who are in the dark, 20 an instructor of the foolish, a teacher of infants, because you have in the law the embodiment of knowledge and truth—21 you, then, who teach others, do you not teach yourself? You who preach against stealing, do you steal?[a] 22 You who say that people should not commit adultery, do you commit adultery? You who abhor idols, do you rob temples?[b] 23 You who brag about the law,[c] do you dishonour God by breaking the law? 24 As it is written: "God's name is blasphemed among the Gentiles because of you."[b][d]

25 Circumcision has value if you observe the law,[e] but if you break the law, you have become as though you had not been circumcised.[f] 26 If those who are not circumcised keep the law's requirements,[g] will they not be regarded as though they were circumcised?[h] 27 The one who is not circumcised physically and yet obeys the law will condemn you[i] who, even though you have the[c] written code and circumcision, are a law-breaker.

26 [b]ver 24,28; [c]Eph 4:19; 1Th 4:5; [d]Lev 18:22–23
27 [e]Lev 18:22; 20:13; 1Co 6:18
28 [f]ver 24,26
29 [g]2Co 12:20; 1Ti 5:13; Jas 3:2; 3Jn 10
30 [h]2Ti 3:2
31 [i]2Ti 3:3
32 [j]**Ro 6:23;** [k]Ps 50:18; Lk 11:48; Ac 8:1; 22:20

Ch. 2

1 [a]Ro 1:20; [b]2Sa 12:5–7; **Mt 7:1–2**
4 [c]Ro 9:23; 11:33; Eph 1:7, 18; 2:7; 3:8,16; Col 2:2; [d]Ro 11:22; [e]Ro 3:25; [f]Ex 34:6; Ro 9:22; 1Ti 1:16; 1Pe 3:20; 2Pe 3:15; [g]2Pe 3:9
5 [h]Ps 110:5; Rev 6:17; [i]Jude 6
6 [j]Ps 62:12; **Mt 16:27**
7 [k]ver 10; [l]1Co 15:53–54; 2Ti 1:10; [m]**Mt 25:46**
8 [n]2Th 2:12; [o]Eze 22:31
9 [p]Ps 32:10; [q]ver 10; Ro 1:16
10 [r]ver 9; Ro 1:16
11 [s]**Ac 10:34**
12 [t]Ro 3:19; 6:14; 1Co 9:20–21; Gal 4:21; 5:18; **Ro 7:4**
13 [u]Jas 1:22–23, 25
14 [v]Ac 10:35
16 [w]Ecc 12:14; 1Co 4:5; [x]Ac 10:42; [y]Ro 16:25; 2Ti 2:8
17 [z]ver 23; Jer 8:8; Mic 3:11; Jn 5:45; Ro 9:4
21 [a]Mt 23:3–4
22 [b]Ac 19:37
23 [c]**ver 17**
24 [d]Isa 52:5; Eze 36:22; 2Pe 2:2
25 [e]ver 13,27; Gal 5:3; [f]Jer 4:4; 9:25–26
26 [g]Ro 8:4; [h]**1Co 7:19**
27 [i]Mt 12:41–42

[a]6 Psalm 62:12; Prov. 24:12
[b]24 Isaiah 52:5; Ezek. 36:22
[c]27 *Or who, by means of a*

28A man is not a Jew if he is only one
outwardly,[j] nor is circumcision merely
outward and physical.[k] 29No, a man is a
Jew if he is one inwardly; and circum-
cision is circumcision of the heart,[l] by
the Spirit,[m] not by the written code.[n]
Such a man's praise is not from men,
but from God.[o]

God's Faithfulness

3 What advantage, then, is there in
being a Jew, or what value is there
in circumcision? 2Much in every way![a]
First of all, they have been entrusted
with the very words of God.[b]
3What if some did not have faith?[c]
Will their lack of faith nullify God's
faithfulness?[d] 4Not at all! Let God be
true,[e] and every man a liar.[f] As it is
written:

"So that you may be proved right
when you speak
and prevail when you judge."[a][g]

5But if our unrighteousness brings
out God's righteousness more clearly,[h]
what shall we say? That God is unjust in
bringing his wrath on us? (I am using a
human argument.)[i] 6Certainly not! If
that were so, how could God judge the
world?[j] 7Someone might argue, "If my
falsehood enhances God's truthfulness
and so increases his glory,[k] why am I
still condemned as a sinner?"[l] 8Why not
say—as we are being slanderously
reported as saying and as some claim
that we say—"Let us do evil that good
may result"?[m] Their condemnation is
deserved.

No-one Is Righteous

9What shall we conclude then? Are
we any better[b]?[n] Not at all! We have
already made the charge that Jews and
Gentiles alike are all under sin.[o] 10As it is
written:

"There is no-one righteous, not even
one;
11 there is no-one who understands,
no-one who seeks God.
12All have turned away,
they have together become
worthless;
there is no-one who does good,
not even one."[c][p]
13"Their throats are open graves;
their tongues practise deceit."[d][q]
"The poison of vipers is on their
lips."[e][r]
14 "Their mouths are full of cursing
and bitterness."[f][s]
15"Their feet are swift to shed blood;
16 ruin and misery mark their ways,
17and the way of peace they do not
know."[g][t]
18 "There is no fear of God before their
eyes."[h][u]

19Now we know that whatever the
law says,[v] it says to those who are under
the law,[w] so that every mouth may be
silenced[x] and the whole world held
accountable to God.[y] 20Therefore no-
one will be declared righteous in his
sight by observing the law;[z] rather,
through the law we become conscious
of sin.[a]

Righteousness Through Faith

21But now a righteousness from God,[b]
apart from law, has been made known,
to which the Law and the Prophets tes-
tify.[c] 22This righteousness from God[d]
comes through faith[e] in Jesus Christ[f] to
all who believe.[g] There is no difference,[h]
23for all have sinned[i] and fall short of the
glory of God, 24and are justified[j] freely
by his grace[k] through the redemption[l]
that came by Christ Jesus. 25God pre-
sented him as a sacrifice of atone-
ment,[i][m] through faith in his blood.[n] He
did this to demonstrate his justice,
because in his forbearance he had
left the sins committed beforehand un-
punished[o] 26—he did it to demonstrate
his justice at the present time, so as
to be just and the one who justifies
those who have faith in Jesus.
27Where, then, is boasting?[p] It is ex-
cluded. On what principle? On that of
observing the law? No, but on that of
faith. 28For we maintain that a man is
justified by faith apart from observing
the law.[q] 29Is God the God of Jews only?
Is he not the God of Gentiles too? Yes, of
Gentiles too,[r] 30since there is only one
God, who will justify the circumcised by
faith and the uncircumcised through

28 [j]Mt 3:9; Jn 8:39; Ro 9:6–7; [k]Gal 6:15
29 [l]Dt 30:6; [m]Php 3:3; Col 2:11; [n]Ro 7:6; 2Co 3:6; [o]Jn 5:44; 12:43; 1Co 4:5; 2Co 10:18; Gal 1:10; 1Th 2:4; 1Pe 3:4

Ch. 3

2 [a]Ro 9:4–5; [b]Dt 4:8; Ps 147:19; Ac 7:38
3 [c]Ro 10:16; Heb 4:2; [d]2Ti 2:13
4 [e]Jn 3:33; [f]Ps 116:11; [g]Ps 51:4
5 [h]Ro 5:8; [i]Ro 6:19; Gal 3:15
6 [j]Ge 18:25; Ro 2:16
7 [k]ver 4; [l]Ro 9:19
8 [m]Ro 6:1
9 [n]ver 1; [o]ver 19,23; 1Ki 8:46; 2Ch 6:36; Ps 106:6; Ro 5:12; 11:32; Gal 3:22
12 [p]Ps 14:1–3; 53:1–3; Ecc 7:20
13 [q]Ps 5:9; [r]Ps 140:3
14 [s]Ps 10:7
17 [t]Isa 59:7–8
18 [u]Ps 36:1
19 [v]**Jn 10:34**; [w]**Ro 2:12**; [x]Ps 63:11; 107:42; Eze 16:63; [y]ver 9
20 [z]Ac 13:39; Gal 2:16; [a]**Ro 4:15**
21 [b]Isa 46:13; Jer 23:6; Ro 1:17; 9:30; [c]Ac 10:43; Ro 1:2
22 [d]Ro 1:17; [e]**Ro 9:30**; [f]Gal 2:16; 3:22; [g]**Jn 3:15**; Ro 4:11; 10:4; [h]Ro 10:12; Gal 3:28; Col 3:11
23 [i]**ver 9**
24 [j]**Ro 4:25**; [k]Jn 1:14,16–17; Ro 4:16; 5:21; 6:14; 11:5; 2Co 12:9; Eph 2:8; 4:7; Tit 2:11; Heb 4:16; [l]Ps 130:7; 1Co 1:30; Gal 4:5; Eph 1:7, 14; Col 1:14; Heb 9:12
25 [m]Ex 25:17; Lev 16:10; Ps 65:3; Heb 2:17; 9:28; 1Jn 4:10; [n]Ac 20:28; Ro 5:9; Eph 1:7; Heb 9:12,14; 13:12; 1Pe 1:19; Rev 1:5; [o]Ac 14:16; 17:30
27 [p]Ro 2:17,23; 4:2; 1Co 1:29–31; Eph 2:9
28 [q]Ac 13:39; Ro 3:20–21; Gal 2:16; 3:11; Eph 2:9; Jas 2:20,24,26
29 [r]Ac 10:34–35; Ro 9:24; 10:12; 15:9; Gal 3:28

[a]4 Psalm 51:4 [b]9 Or *worse*
[c]12 Psalms 14:1–3; 53:1–3; Eccles. 7:20
[d]13 Psalm 5:9 [e]13 Psalm 140:3
[f]14 Psalm 10:7 [g]17 Isaiah 59:7,8
[h]18 Psalm 36:1
[i]25 Or *as the one who would turn aside his wrath, taking away sin*

that same faith.[s] 31Do we, then, nullify
the law by this faith? Not at all! Rather,
we uphold the law.

Abraham Justified by Faith

4 What then shall we say[a] that Abra-
ham, our forefather,[b] discovered in
this matter? 2If, in fact, Abraham was
justified by works, he had something
to boast about—but not before God.[c]
3What does the Scripture say? "Abra-
ham believed God, and it was credited
to him as righteousness."[a][d]
4Now when a man works, his wages
are not credited to him as a gift,[e] but as
an obligation. 5However, to the man
who does not work but trusts God who
justifies the wicked, his faith is credited
as righteousness.[f] 6David says the same
thing when he speaks of the blessed-
ness of the man to whom God credits
righteousness apart from works:

7"Blessed are they
whose transgressions are forgiven,
whose sins are covered.
8Blessed is the man
whose sin the Lord will never count
against him."[b][g]

9Is this blessedness only for the
circumcised, or also for the uncircum-
cised?[h] We have been saying that Abra-
ham's faith was credited to him as right-
eousness.[i] 10Under what circumstances
was it credited? Was it after he was
circumcised, or before? It was not after,
but before! 11And he received the sign of
circumcision, a seal of the righteousness
that he had by faith while he was still
uncircumcised.[j] So then, he is the
father[k] of all who believe[l] but have not
been circumcised, in order that right-
eousness might be credited to them.
12And he is also the father of the circum-
cised who not only are circumcised but
who also walk in the footsteps of the
faith that our father Abraham had
before he was circumcised.
13It was not through law that Abra-
ham and his offspring received the
promise[m] that he would be heir of the
world,[n] but through the righteousness
that comes by faith.[o] 14For if those who
live by law are heirs, faith has no value
and the promise is worthless,[p]
15because law brings wrath.[q] And
where there is no law there is no
transgression.[r]
16Therefore, the promise comes by
faith, so that it may be by grace[s] and
may be guaranteed[t] to all Abraham's

30 [s]Ro 4:11–12; Gal 3:8

Ch. 4

1 [a]Ro 8:31; [b]Lk 3:8
2 [c]1Co 1:31
3 [d]ver 5,9,22; Ge 15:6; Gal 3:6; Jas 2:23
4 [e]Ro 11:6
5 [f]ver 3,9,22; Ro 9:30
8 [g]Ps 32:1–2; 103:12; 2Co 5:19
9 [h]Ro 3:30; [i]ver 3
11 [j]Ge 17:10–11; [k]ver 16–17; Lk 3:8; [l]Ro 3:22
13 [m]Ac 13:32; Gal 3:16,29; [n]Ge 17:4–6; [o]Ro 9:30
14 [p]Gal 3:18
15 [q]Ro 7:7–25; 1Co 15:56; 2Co 3:7; Gal 3:10; Ro 7:12; [r]Ro 3:20; 5:13; 7:7
16 [s]Ro 3:24; [t]Ro 15:8; [u]ver 11; Lk 3:8; Gal 3:16
17 [v]Ge 17:5; [w]Jn 5:21; [x]Isa 48:13; [y]1Co 1:28
18 [z]ver 17; [a]Ge 15:5
19 [b]Heb 11:11–12; [c]Ge 17:17; [d]Ge 18:11
20 [e]1Sa 30:6; [f]Mt 9:8
21 [g]Ge 18:14; Mt 19:26
22 [h]ver 3
24 [i]Ps 102:18; Hab 2:2; Ro 15:4; 1Co 9:10; 10:11; 2Ti 3:16–17; [j]Ro 10:9; 1Pe 1:21; [k]Ac 2:24
25 [l]Isa 53:5–6; Ro 5:6,8; 8:32; 2Co 5:21; [m]Isa 53:11; Ro 3:24; 5:1,9,16, 18; 8:30; 1Co 6:11; 2Co 5:15

Ch. 5

1 [a]Ro 4:25; [b]Ro 3:28; [c]Lk 2:14; [d]ver 10
2 [e]Eph 2:18; 3:12; [f]1Co 15:1; [g]Heb 3:6
3 [h]Mt 5:12; [i]Heb 10:36

offspring—not only to those who are of
the law but also to those who are of the
faith of Abraham. He is the father of us
all.[u] 17As it is written: "I have made you
a father of many nations."[c][v] He is our
father in the sight of God, in whom he
believed—the God who gives life[w] to
the dead and calls[x] things that are not[y]
as though they were.
18Against all hope, Abraham in hope
believed and so became the father of
many nations,[z] just as it had been said to
him, "So shall your offspring be."[d][a]
19Without weakening in his faith, he
faced the fact that his body was as good
as dead[b]—since he was about a hun-
dred years old[c]—and that Sarah's
womb was also dead.[d] 20Yet he did not
waver through unbelief regarding the
promise of God, but was strengthened[e]
in his faith and gave glory to God,[f]
21being fully persuaded that God had
power to do what he had promised.[g]
22This is why "it was credited to him as
righteousness."[h] 23The words "it was
credited to him" were written not for
him alone, 24but also for us,[i] to whom
God will credit righteousness—for us
who believe in him[j] who raised Jesus
our Lord from the dead.[k] 25He was de-
livered over to death for our sins[l] and
was raised to life for our justification.[m]

Peace and Joy

5 Therefore, since we have been jus-
tified[a] through faith,[b] we[a] have
peace[c] with God through our Lord Jesus
Christ,[d] 2through whom we have
gained access[e] by faith into this grace in
which we now stand.[f] And we[a] rejoice
in the hope[g] of the glory of God. 3Not
only so, but we[a] also rejoice in our
sufferings,[h] because we know that
suffering produces perseverance;[i]
4perseverance, character; and character,
hope. 5And hope[j] does not disappoint
us, because God has poured out his
love[k] into our hearts by the Holy Spirit,[l]
whom he has given us.
6You see, at just the right time,[m] when
we were still powerless,[n] Christ died for
the ungodly.[o] 7Very rarely will anyone
die for a righteous man, though for a
good man someone might possibly dare

5 [j]Php 1:20; Heb 3:6; 1Jn 3:2–3; [k]ver 8; Jn 3:16; Ro 8:39; [l]Ac 2:33; 10:45; Tit 3:5–6
6 [m]Mk 1:15; Gal 4:4; Eph 1:10; [n]ver 8,10; [o]Ro 4:25

[a]3 Gen. 15:6; also in verse 22
[b]8 Psalm 32:1,2
[c]17 Gen. 17:5
[d]18 Gen. 15:5
[a]1,2,3 Or *let us*

to die. 8But God demonstrates his own
love for us in this: While we were still
sinners, Christ died for us.[p]
9Since we have now been justified[q] by
his blood,[r] how much more shall we be
saved from God's wrath[s] through him!
10For if, when we were God's enemies,[t]
we were reconciled[u] to him through the
death of his Son, how much more, hav-
ing been reconciled, shall we be saved
through his life![v] 11Not only is this so,
but we also rejoice in God through our
Lord Jesus Christ, through whom we
have now received reconciliation.[w]

Death Through Adam, Life Through Christ

12Therefore, just as sin entered the
world through one man,[x] and death
through sin,[y] and in this way death
came to all men, because all sinned[z]
—13for before the law was given, sin
was in the world. But sin is not taken
into account when there is no law.[a]
14Nevertheless, death reigned from the
time of Adam to the time of Moses, even
over those who did not sin by breaking a
command, as did Adam,[b] who was a
pattern of the one to come.[c]
15But the gift is not like the trespass.
For if the many died by the trespass of
the one man,[d] how much more did
God's grace and the gift that came by
the grace of the one man, Jesus Christ,[e]
overflow to the many! 16Again, the gift
of God is not like the result of the one
man's sin: The judgment followed one
sin and brought condemnation, but the
gift followed many trespasses and
brought justification. 17For if, by the
trespass of the one man, death[f] reigned
through that one man, how much more
will those who receive God's abundant
provision of grace and of the gift of
righteousness reign in life[g] through the
one man, Jesus Christ.
18Consequently, just as the result of
one trespass was condemnation for all
men,[h] so also the result of one act of
righteousness was justification[i] that
brings life[j] for all men. 19For just as
through the disobedience of the one
man[k] the many were made sinners,[l] so
also through the obedience[m] of the one
man the many will be made righteous.
20The law was added so that the tres-
pass might increase.[n] But where sin in-
creased, grace increased all the more,[o]
21so that, just as sin reigned in death,[p] so
also grace[q] might reign through right-
eousness to bring eternal life[r] through
Jesus Christ our Lord.

8 [p]Jn 3:16; 15:13; 1Pe 3:18; 1Jn 3:16; 4:10
9 [q]**Ro 4:25;** [r]**Ro 3:25;** [s]**Ro 1:18**
10 [t]Ro 11:28; Col 1:21; [u]ver 11; Ro 11:15; 2Co 5:18–19; Col 1:20,22; [v]Ro 8:34; Heb 7:25
11 [w]**ver 10**
12 [x]ver 15–17; Ge 3:1–7; 1Co 15:21–22; [y]ver 14,18; Ge 2:17; 3:19; **Ro 6:23;** [z]**Ro 3:9**
13 [a]**Ro 4:15**
14 [b]Ge 3:11–12; [c]1Co 15:22,45
15 [d]ver 12, 18–19; [e]Ac 15:11
17 [f]**ver 12;** [g]Jn 10:10
18 [h]**ver 12;** [i]**Ro 4:25;** [j]Isa 53:11
19 [k]ver 12; [l]**Ro 3:9;** [m]**Php 2:8**
20 [n]Ro 3:20; 7:7–8; Gal 3:19; [o]Ro 6:1; 1Ti 1:13–14
21 [p]ver 12,14; **Ro 6:16;** [q]**Ro 3:24;** [r]**Mt 25:46**

Ch. 6

1 [a]**Ro 8:31;** [b]ver 15; Ro 3:5,8
2 [c]**ver 6,**10–11, **18;** Ro 8:13; Col 3:5; 1Pe 2:24
3 [d]**Mt 28:19**
4 [e]**ver 6;** [f]**Ac 2:24;** [g]Ro 7:6; **2Co 5:17;** Eph 4:22–24; Col 3:10
5 [h]ver 4,8; Ro 8:11; 2Co 4:10; Eph 2:6; Php 3:10–11; Col 2:12; 3:1; 2Ti 2:11
6 [i]**Gal 5:24;** Eph 4:22; Col 3:9; [j]**ver 2,** 3–8; 2Co 4:10; Gal 2:20; 5:24; 6:14; Php 3:10; Col 2:12, 20; 3:3; [k]Ro 7:24; [l]**ver 16**
7 [m]**ver 18**
8 [n]**ver 5**
9 [o]ver 4; **Ac 2:24;** [p]Rev 1:18
10 [q]**ver 2;** [r]**Heb 7:27**
11 [s]**ver 2**
12 [t]ver 16

Dead to Sin, Alive in Christ

6 What shall we say, then?[a] Shall we
go on sinning, so that grace may
increase?[b] 2By no means! We died to
sin;[c] how can we live in it any longer?
3Or don't you know that all of us who
were baptised[d] into Christ Jesus were
baptised into his death? 4We were there-
fore buried with him through baptism
into death[e] in order that, just as Christ
was raised from the dead[f] through the
glory of the Father, we too may live a
new life.[g]
5If we have been united with him like
this in his death, we will certainly also
be united with him in his resurrection.[h]
6For we know that our old self[i] was
crucified with him[j] so that the body of
sin[k] might be done away with,[a] that we
should no longer be slaves to sin[l]—
7because anyone who has died has been
freed from sin.[m]
8Now if we died with Christ, we be-
lieve that we will also live with him.[n]
9For we know that since Christ was
raised from the dead,[o] he cannot die
again; death no longer has mastery over
him.[p] 10The death he died, he died to
sin[q] once for all;[r] but the life he lives, he
lives to God.
11In the same way, count yourselves
dead to sin[s] but alive to God in Christ
Jesus. 12Therefore do not let sin reign[t]
in your mortal body so that you obey
its evil desires. 13Do not offer the parts
of your body to sin, as instruments
of wickedness,[u] but rather offer
yourselves to God, as those who have
been brought from death to life; and
offer the parts of your body to him as
instruments of righteousness.[v] 14For sin
shall not be your master,[w] because you
are not under law,[x] but under grace.[y]

Slaves to Righteousness

15What then? Shall we sin because we
are not under law but under grace?[z] By
no means! 16Don't you know that when
you offer yourselves to someone to obey
him as slaves, you are slaves to the one
whom you obey[a]—whether you are
slaves to sin,[b] which leads to death,[c] or
to obedience, which leads to righteous-
ness? 17But thanks be to God[d] that,

13 [u]ver 16,19; Ro 7:5; [v]Ro 12:1; 2Co 5:14–15; 1Pe 2:24
14 [w]**ver 16;** [x]**Ro 2:12;** [y]**Ro 3:24** *15* [z]ver 1,14
16 [a]2Pe 2:19; [b]ver 6,12,14,17,20; Ge 4:7; Ps 51:5; 119:133; Jn 8:34; Ro 5:21; 7:14,23,25; 8:2; 2Pe 2:19; [c]**ver 23** *17* [d]Ro 1:8; **2Co 2:14**

[a]6 Or *be rendered powerless*

though you used to be slaves to sin,[e]
you wholeheartedly obeyed the form of
teaching[f] to which you were entrusted.
18You have been set free from sin[g] and
have become slaves to righteousness.[h]
19I put this in human terms[i] because
you are weak in your natural selves. Just
as you used to offer the parts of your
body in slavery to impurity and to ever-
increasing wickedness, so now offer
them in slavery to righteousness[j] lead-
ing to holiness. 20When you were slaves
to sin,[k] you were free from the control of
righteousness.[l] 21What benefit did you
reap at that time from the things you are
now ashamed of? Those things result in
death![m] 22But now that you have been
set free from sin[n] and have become
slaves to God,[o] the benefit you reap
leads to holiness, and the result is eter-
nal life.[p] 23For the wages of sin is death,[q]
but the gift of God is eternal life[r] in[b]
Christ Jesus our Lord.

An Illustration From Marriage

7 Do you not know, brothers[a]—for I
am speaking to men who know the
law—that the law has authority over a
man only as long as he lives? 2For exam-
ple, by law a married woman is bound
to her husband as long as he is alive, but
if her husband dies, she is released from
the law of marriage.[b] 3So then, if she
marries another man while her husband
is still alive, she is called an adulteress.[c]
But if her husband dies, she is released
from that law and is not an adulteress,
even though she marries another man.
4So, my brothers, you also died to the
law[d] through the body of Christ,[e] that
you might belong to another,[f] to him
who was raised from the dead, in order
that we might bear fruit to God. 5For
when we were controlled by the sinful
nature,[a][g] the sinful passions aroused by
the law[h] were at work in our bodies,[i] so
that we bore fruit for death.[j] 6But now,
by dying to what once bound us, we
have been released from the law[k] so that
we serve in the new way of the Spirit,
and not in the old way of the written
code.[l]

Struggling With Sin

7What shall we say, then?[m] Is the law
sin? Certainly not![n] Indeed I would not
have known what sin was except
through the law.[o] For I would not have
known what coveting really was if the
law had not said, "Do not covet."[b][p] 8But
sin, seizing the opportunity afforded by
the commandment,[q] produced in me
every kind of covetous desire. For apart
from law, sin is dead.[r] 9Once I was alive
apart from law; but when the com-
mandment came, sin sprang to life and I
died. 10I found that the very command-
ment that was intended to bring life[s]
actually brought death. 11For sin, seiz-
ing the opportunity afforded by the
commandment,[t] deceived me,[u] and
through the commandment put me to
death. 12So then, the law is holy, and the
commandment is holy, righteous and
good.[v]
13Did that which is good, then, be-
come death to me? By no means! But in
order that sin might be recognised as
sin, it produced death in me[w] through
what was good,[x] so that through the
commandment sin might become
utterly sinful.
14We know that the law is spiritual;
but I am unspiritual,[y] sold[z] as a slave to
sin.[a] 15I do not understand what I do.
For what I want to do I do not do, but
what I hate I do.[b] 16And if I do what I do
not want to do, I agree that the law is
good.[c] 17As it is, it is no longer I myself
who do it, but it is sin living in me.[d] 18I
know that nothing good lives in me,
that is, in my sinful nature.[c][e] For I have
the desire to do what is good, but I
cannot carry it out. 19For what I do is not
the good I want to do; no, the evil I do
not want to do—this I keep on doing.[f]
20Now if I do what I do not want to do, it
is no longer I who do it, but it is sin
living in me that does it.[g]
21So I find this law at work:[h] When I
want to do good, evil is right there with
me. 22For in my inner being[i] I delight in
God's law;[j] 23but I see another law at
work in the members of my body,
waging war[k] against the law of my
mind and making me a prisoner of
the law of sin[l] at work within my
members. 24What a wretched man I am!
Who will rescue me from this body of
death?[m] 25Thanks be to God—through
Jesus Christ our Lord![n]
So then, I myself in my mind am a
slave to God's law,[o] but in the sinful
nature a slave to the law of sin.[p]

17 [e]**ver 16**; [f]2Ti 1:13
18 [g]**ver 2**,7,22; Ro 8:2; 1Pe 4:1; **ver 16**; [h]**ver 22**
19 [i]Ro 3:5; Gal 3:15; [j]**ver 13,22**
20 [k]**ver 16**; [l]ver 16
21 [m]**ver 23**
22 [n]**ver 18**; [o]ver 18,19; Ro 7:25; 1Co 7:22; Eph 6:6; 1Pe 2:16; [p]**Mt 25:46**
23 [q]ver 16,21; Ge 2:17; Pr 10:16; Eze 18:4; Ro 1:32; **5:12**; 7:5,13; 8:6,13; Gal 6:7–8; Jas 1:15; [r]**Mt 25:46**

Ch. 7

1 [a]**Ac 1:16; 22:5**; Ro 1:13; 1Co 1:10; 5:11; 6:6; 14:20,26; Gal 3:15; 6:18
2 [b]1Co 7:39
3 [c]**Lk 16:18**
4 [d]ver 6; **Ro 6:6**; 8:2; Gal 2:19; 3:23–25; 4:31; 5:1; [e]Col 1:22; [f]Gal 2:19–20
5 [g]**Gal 5:24**; [h]Ro 7:7–11; [i]Ro 6:13; [j]**Ro 6:23**
6 [k]**ver 4**; [l]Ro 2:29; 2Co 3:6
7 [m]**Ro 8:31**; [n]**ver 12**; [o]**Ro 4:15**; [p]Ex 20:17; Dt 5:21
8 [q]ver 11; [r]**Ro 4:15**
10 [s]Lev 18:5; Lk 10:26–28; **Ro 10:5**; Gal 3:12
11 [t]ver 8; [u]Ge 3:13
12 [v]ver 7,13–14, 16; Ro 8:4; Gal 3:21; 1Ti 1:8; **Ro 4:15**
13 [w]**Ro 6:23**; [x]**ver 12**
14 [y]1Co 3:1; [z]1Ki 21:20,25; 2Ki 17:17; [a]**Ro 6:16**
15 [b]ver 19; Gal 5:17
16 [c]**ver 12**
17 [d]ver 20
18 [e]ver 25; **Gal 5:24**
19 [f]ver 15
20 [g]ver 17
21 [h]ver 23,25
22 [i]Eph 3:16; [j]Ps 1:2; 40:8
23 [k]Gal 5:17; Jas 4:1; 1Pe 2:11; [l]**Ro 6:16**
24 [m]Ro 6:6; 8:2
25 [n]**2Co 2:14**; [o]**Ro 6:22**; [p]**Ro 6:16**

[b]23 Or *through* [a]5 Or *the flesh;* also in verse 25
[b]7 Exodus 20:17; Deut. 5:21 [c]18 Or *my flesh*

Life Through the Spirit

8 Therefore, there is now no con-
demnation[a] for those who are in
Christ Jesus,[a][b] 2because through Christ
Jesus[c] the law of the Spirit of life[d] set me
free[e] from the law of sin[f] and death. 3For
what the law was powerless[g] to do in
that it was weakened by the sinful
nature,[b][h] God did by sending his own
Son in the likeness of sinful man[i] to be a
sin offering.[c][j] And so he condemned sin
in sinful man,[d] 4in order that the right-
eous requirements[k] of the law might be
fully met in us, who do not live accord-
ing to the sinful nature but according to
the Spirit.[l]

5Those who live according to the sin-
ful nature have their minds set on what
that nature desires;[m] but those who live
in accordance with the Spirit have their
minds set on what the Spirit desires.[n]
6The mind of sinful man[e] is death[o], but
the mind controlled by the Spirit is life[p]
and peace; 7the sinful mind[f] is hostile to
God.[q] It does not submit to God's law,
nor can it do so. 8Those controlled by
the sinful nature[r] cannot please God.

9You, however, are controlled not by
the sinful nature[s] but by the Spirit, if the
Spirit of God lives in you.[t] And if any-
one does not have the Spirit of Christ,[u]
he does not belong to Christ. 10But if
Christ is in you,[v] your body is dead
because of sin, yet your spirit is alive
because of righteousness. 11And if the
Spirit of him who raised Jesus from the
dead[w] is living in you, he who raised
Christ from the dead will also give life to
your mortal bodies[x] through his Spirit,
who lives in you.

12Therefore, brothers, we have an
obligation—but it is not to the sinful
nature, to live according to it.[y] 13For if
you live according to the sinful nature,
you will die;[z] but if by the Spirit you put
to death the misdeeds of the body,[a] you
will live,[b] 14because those who are led by
the Spirit of God[c] are sons of God.[d] 15For
you did not receive a spirit[e] that makes
you a slave again to fear,[f] but you re-
ceived the Spirit of sonship.[g] And by
him we cry, "*Abba*,[h] Father."[g] 16The
Spirit himself testifies with our spirit[h]
that we are God's children.[i] 17Now if we
are children, then we are heirs[j]—heirs
of God and co-heirs with Christ, if in-
deed we share in his sufferings[k] in order
that we may also share in his glory.[l]

Future Glory

18I consider that our present suffer-
ings are not worth comparing with the
glory that will be revealed in us.[m] 19The
creation waits in eager expectation for
the sons of God[n] to be revealed. 20For
the creation was subjected to frustra-
tion, not by its own choice, but by the
will of the one who subjected it,[o] in hope
21that[i] the creation itself will be liberated
from its bondage to decay[p] and brought
into the glorious freedom of the chil-
dren of God.[q]

22We know that the whole creation
has been groaning[r] as in the pains of
childbirth right up to the present time.
23Not only so, but we ourselves, who
have the firstfruits of the Spirit,[s] groan[t]
inwardly as we wait eagerly[u] for our
adoption as sons, the redemption of our
bodies.[v] 24For in this hope we were
saved.[w] But hope that is seen is no hope
at all.[x] Who hopes for what he already
has? 25But if we hope for what we do not
yet have, we wait for it patiently.[y]

26In the same way, the Spirit helps us
in our weakness. We do not know what
we ought to pray for, but the Spirit[z]
himself intercedes for us[a] with groans
that words cannot express. 27And he
who searches our hearts[b] knows the
mind of the Spirit, because the Spirit
intercedes[c] for the saints in accordance
with God's will.

More Than Conquerors

28And we know that in all things God
works for the good[d] of those who love
him,[j] who[k] have been called[e] according
to his purpose.[f] 29For those God fore-
knew[g] he also predestined[h] to be con-
formed to the likeness of his Son,[i] that
he might be the firstborn[j] among many
brothers. 30And those he predestined,[k]
he also called;[l] those he called, he also
justified;[m] those he justified, he also
glorified.[n]

31What, then, shall we say in

Ch. 8

1 [a]ver 34; [b]ver 39; **Ro 16:3**
2 [c]Ro 7:25; [d]1Co 15:45; [e]Jn 8:32,36; **Ro 6:18**; [f]**Ro 6:16; 7:4**
3 [g]Heb 7:18; 10:1–4; [h]Ro 7:18–19; **Gal 5:24**; [i]**Php 2:7**; [j]Heb 2:14,17
4 [k]Ro 2:26; [l]**Gal 5:16**
5 [m]Gal 5:19–21; [n]Gal 5:22–25
6 [o]**Ro 6:23**; [p]ver 13; Gal 6:8
7 [q]Jas 4:4
8 [r]**Gal 5:24**
9 [s]**Gal 5:24**; [t]ver 11; 1Co 6:19; 2Ti 1:14; [u]Jn 14:17; **Ac 16:7**; 1Jn 4:13
10 [v]ver 9; Ex 29:45; Jn 14:20,23; 2Co 13:5; Gal 2:20; Eph 3:17; Col 1:27; Rev 3:20
11 [w]**Ac 2:24**; [x]Jn 5:21; **Ro 6:5**
12 [y]ver 4; **Gal 5:24**
13 [z]**Ro 6:23**; [a]**Ro 6:2**; [b]ver 6; Gal 6:8
14 [c]**Gal 5:18**; [d]ver 19; Hos 1:10; Mal 3:17; Mt 5:9; **Jn 1:12** Gal 3:26; 4:5; Eph 1:5; Rev 21:7
15 [e]**Jn 20:22**; [f]**2Ti 1:7**; [g]Mk 14:36; Gal 4:5–6
16 [h]2Co 1:22; Eph 1:13; [i]**ver 14; Jn 1:12**
17 [j]**Ac 20:32**; Gal 3:29; 4:7; Eph 3:6; Tit 3:7; [k]**2Co 1:5**; [l]2Ti 2:12; 1Pe 4:13
18 [m]2Co 4:17; 1Pe 4:13; 5:1
19 [n]**ver 14**
20 [o]Ge 3:17–19; 5:29
21 [p]Ac 3:21; 2Pe 3:13; Rev 21:1; [q]**Jn 1:12**
22 [r]Jer 12:4
23 [s]**2Co 5:5**; [t]2Co 5:2,4; [u]ver 19; Gal 5:5; [v]ver 11; Php 3:21
24 [w]1Th 5:8; Tit 3:7; [x]**2Co 4:18**
25 [y]Ps 37:7
26 [z]ver 15–16; [a]Eph 6:18
27 [b]**Rev 2:23**; [c]**ver 34**

28 [d]Ge 50:20; Isa 38:17; Jer 29:11; [e]ver 30; Ro 11:29; 1Co 1:9; Gal 1:6,15; Eph 4:1,4; 1Th 2:12; 2Ti 1:9; Heb 9:15; 1Pe 2:9; 2Pe 1:10; [f]Eph 1:11; 3:11; Heb 6:17
29 [g]Ro 11:2; 1Pe 1:2; [h]Eph 1:5,11; [i]1Co 15:49; 2Co 3:18; Php 3:21; 1Jn 3:2; [j]**Col 1:18**
30 [k]Eph 1:5,11; [l]**ver 28**; [m]**Ro 4:25**; [n]Ro 9:23

[a]1 Some later manuscripts *Jesus, who do not live according to the sinful nature but according to the Spirit,*
[b]3 Or *the flesh;* also in verses 4, 5, 8, 9, 12 and 13
[c]3 Or *man, for sin*
[d]3 Or *in the flesh*
[e]6 Or *mind set on the flesh*
[f]7 Or *the mind set on the flesh*
[g]15 Or *adoption*
[h]15 Aramaic for *Father*
[i]20,21 Or *subjected it in hope.* 21*For*
[j]28 Some manuscripts *And we know that all things work together for good to those who love God*
[k]28 Or *works together with those who love him to bring about what is good—with those who*

response to this?[o] If God is for us,[p]
who can be against us?[q] 32He who did
not spare his own Son,[r] but gave him up
for us all—how will he not also, along
with him, graciously give us all things?
33Who will bring any charge[s] against
those whom God has chosen? It is God
who justifies. 34Who is he that con-
demns?[t] Christ Jesus, who died[u]—more
than that, who was raised to life[v]—is at
the right hand of God[w] and is also in-
terceding for us.[x] 35Who shall separate
us from the love of Christ?[y] Shall trouble
or hardship or persecution or famine or
nakedness or danger or sword?[z] 36As it
is written:

"For your sake we face death all day
long;
we are considered as sheep to be
slaughtered."[l][a]

37No, in all these things we are more
than conquerors[b] through him who
loved us.[c] 38For I am convinced that
neither death nor life, neither angels
nor demons,[m] neither the present nor
the future,[d] nor any powers,[e] 39neither
height nor depth, nor anything else in
all creation, will be able to separate us
from the love of God[f] that is in Christ
Jesus our Lord.[g]

God's Sovereign Choice

9 I speak the truth in Christ—I am
not lying,[a] my conscience
confirms[b] it in the Holy Spirit—2I have
great sorrow and unceasing anguish in
my heart. 3For I could wish that I myself[c]
were cursed[d] and cut off from Christ for
the sake of my brothers,[e] those of my
own race,[f] 4the people of Israel.[g] Theirs
is the adoption as sons;[h] theirs the
divine glory,[i] the covenants,[j] the
receiving of the law,[k] the temple wor-
ship[l] and the promises.[m] 5Theirs are the
patriarchs,[n] and from them is traced the
human ancestry of Christ,[o] who is God
over all,[p] for ever praised![a][q] Amen.
6It is not as though God's word[r] had
failed. For not all who are descended
from Israel are Israel.[s] 7Nor because
they are his descendants are they all
Abraham's children. On the contrary,
"It is through Isaac that your offspring
will be reckoned."[b][t] 8In other words, it
is not the natural children who are
God's children,[u] but it is the children of
the promise who are regarded as Abra-
ham's offspring.[v] 9For this was how the
promise was stated: "At the appointed
time I will return, and Sarah will have a
son."[c][w]

10Not only that, but Rebekah's chil-
dren had one and the same father, our
father Isaac.[x] 11Yet, before the twins
were born or had done anything good
or bad[y]—in order that God's purpose[z]
in election might stand: 12not by works
but by him who calls—she was told,
"The older will serve the younger."[d][a]
13Just as it is written: "Jacob I loved, but
Esau I hated."[e][b]
14What then shall we say?[c] Is God
unjust? Not at all![d] 15For he says to
Moses,

"I will have mercy on whom I have
mercy,
and I will have compassion on
whom I have compassion."[f][e]

16It does not, therefore, depend on
man's desire or effort, but on God's
mercy.[f] 17For the Scripture says to
Pharaoh: "I raised you up for this very
purpose, that I might display my power
in you and that my name might be pro-
claimed in all the earth."[g][g] 18Therefore
God has mercy on whom he wants to
have mercy, and he hardens whom he
wants to harden.[h]
19One of you will say to me:[i] "Then
why does God still blame us?[j] For who
resists his will?"[k] 20But who are you, O
man, to talk back to God?[l] "Shall what is
formed say to him who formed it,[m]
'Why did you make me like this?'"[h][n]
21Does not the potter have the right to
make out of the same lump of clay some
pottery for noble purposes and some for
common use?[o]
22What if God, choosing to show his
wrath and make his power known, bore
with great patience[p] the objects of his
wrath—prepared for destruction?[q]
23What if he did this to make the riches
of his glory[r] known to the objects of his
mercy, whom he prepared in advance
for glory[s]—24even us, whom he also
called,[t] not only from the Jews but also

31 [o]Ro 4:1; 6:1; 7:7; 9:14,30; [p]Ex 3:12; Isa 41:10; Hag 1:13; [q]Ps 56:9; 118:6; Isa 8:10; Jer 20:11; Heb 13:6
32 [r]Ge 22:13; Mal 3:17; Jn 3:16; Ro 5:8
33 [s]Isa 50:8–9
34 [t]ver 1; [u]Ro 5:6–8; [v]**Ac 2:24**; [w]**Mk 16:19**; [x]ver 27; Job 16:20; Isa 53:12; Heb 7:25; 9:24; 1Jn 2:1
35 [y]ver 37–39; [z]1Co 4:11; 2Co 11:26–27
36 [a]Ps 44:22; 1Co 4:9; 15:30–31; 2Co 4:11; 6:9; 11:23
37 [b]1Co 15:57; [c]Ro 5:8; Gal 2:20; Eph 5:2; Rev 1:5; 3:9
38 [d]1Co 3:22; [e]Eph 1:21; Col 1:16; 1Pe 3:22
39 [f]**Ro 5:8**; [g]ver 1; **Ro 16:3**

Ch. 9

1 [a]Ps 15:2; 2Co 11:10; Gal 1:20; 1Ti 2:7; [b]**Ro 1:9**
3 [c]Ex 32:32; [d]1Co 12:3; 16:22; [e]**Ac 22:5**; [f]Ro 11:14
4 [g]ver 6; [h]Ex 4:22; 6:7; Dt 7:6; [i]Heb 9:5; [j]Ge 17:2; Dt 4:13; Ac 3:25; Eph 2:12; [k]Ps 147:19; [l]Heb 9:1; [m]**Ac 13:32; Gal 3:16**
5 [n]Ro 11:28; [o]Mt 1:1–16; Ro 1:3; [p]Jn 1:1; Col 2:9; [q]Ro 1:25; 2Co 11:31
6 [r]**Heb 4:12**; [s]Ro 2:28–29; Gal 6:16
7 [t]Ge 21:12; Heb 11:18
8 [u]**Ro 8:14**; [v]**Gal 3:16**
9 [w]Ge 18:10,14
10 [x]Ge 25:21
11 [y]ver 16; [z]Ro 8:28
12 [a]Ge 25:23
13 [b]Mal 1:2–3
14 [c]**Ro 8:31**; [d]2Ch 19:7
15 [e]Ex 33:19
16 [f]Eph 2:8; Tit 3:5
17 [g]Ex 9:16; 14:4; Ps 76:10
18 [h]Ex 4:21; 7:3; 14:4,17; Dt 2:30; Jos 11:20; Ro 11:25
19 [i]Ro 11:19; 1Co 15:35; Jas 2:18; [j]Ro 3:7; [k]2Sa 16:10; 2Ch 20:6; Da 4:35
20 [l]Job 1:22; 9:12; 40:2; [m]Isa 64:8; Jer 18:6; [n]Isa 29:16; 45:9; 10:15
21 [o]2Ti 2:20 22 [p]**Ro 2:4**; [q]Pr 16:4
23 [r]**Ro 2:4**; [s]Ro 8:30 24 [t]**Ro 8:28**

[l]36 Psalm 44:22 [m]38 Or *nor heavenly rulers*
[a]5 Or *Christ, who is over all. God be for ever praised!* Or *Christ. God who is over all be for ever praised!*
[b]7 Gen. 21:12 [c]9 Gen. 18:10,14
[d]12 Gen. 25:23 [e]13 Mal. 1:2,3
[f]15 Exodus 33:19 [g]17 Exodus 9:16
[h]20 Isaiah 29:16; 45:9

from the Gentiles?[u] 25As he says in
Hosea:

"I will call them 'my people' who are
not my people;
and I will call her 'my loved one'
who is not my loved one,"[i][v]

26and,

"It will happen that in the very place
where it was said to them,
'You are not my people,'
they will be called 'sons of the living
God'."[j][w]

27Isaiah cries out concerning Israel:

"Though the number of the Israelites
be like the sand by the sea,[x]
only the remnant will be saved.[y]
28For the Lord will carry out
his sentence on earth with speed
and finality."[k][z]

29It is just as Isaiah said previously:

"Unless the Lord Almighty[a]
had left us descendants,
we would have become like Sodom,
we would have been like
Gomorrah."[l][b]

Israel's Unbelief

30What then shall we say?[c] That the
Gentiles, who did not pursue righteous-
ness, have obtained it, a righteousness
that is by faith;[d] 31but Israel, who pur-
sued a law of righteousness,[e] has not
attained it.[f] 32Why not? Because they
pursued it not by faith but as if it were
by works. They stumbled over the
"stumbling-stone".[g] 33As it is written:

"See, I lay in Zion a stone that causes
men to stumble
and a rock that makes them fall,
and the one who trusts in him will
never be put to shame."[m][h]

10 Brothers, my heart's desire[a] and
prayer to God for the Israelites
is that they may be saved. 2For I can
testify about them that they are zealous[b]
for God, but their zeal is not based on
knowledge. 3Since they did not know
the righteousness that comes from God
and sought to establish their own, they
did not submit to God's righteousness.[c]
4Christ is the end of the law[d] so that
there may be righteousness for every-
one who believes.[e]

5Moses describes in this way the
righteousness that is by the law: "The
man who does these things will live by
them."[a][f] 6But the righteousness that is
by faith[g] says: "Do not say in your heart,
'Who will ascend into heaven?'[b]"[h] (that
is, to bring Christ down) 7"or 'Who will
descend into the deep?'[c]"[i] (that is, to
bring Christ up from the dead).[j] 8But
what does it say? "The word is near you;
it is in your mouth and in your heart,"[d][k]
that is, the word of faith we are pro-
claiming: 9That if you confess[l] with your
mouth, "Jesus is Lord,"[m] and believe[n] in
your heart that God raised him from the
dead,[o] you will be saved.[p] 10For it is with
your heart that you believe and are jus-
tified, and it is with your mouth that
you confess and are saved. 11As the
Scripture says, "Anyone who trusts in
him will never be put to shame."[e][q] 12For
there is no difference between Jew and
Gentile[r]—the same Lord is Lord of all[s]
and richly blesses all who call on him,
13for, "Everyone who calls on the name
of the Lord[t] will be saved."[f][u]

14How, then, can they call on the one
they have not believed in? And how can
they believe in the one of whom they
have not heard? And how can they hear
without someone preaching to them?
15And how can they preach unless they
are sent? As it is written, "How beauti-
ful are the feet of those who bring good
news!"[g][v]

16But not all the Israelites accepted the
good news.[w] For Isaiah says, "Lord,
who has believed our message?"[h][x]
17Consequently, faith comes from hear-
ing the message,[y] and the message is
heard through the word of Christ.[z] 18But
I ask: Did they not hear? Of course they
did:

"Their voice has gone out into all the
earth,
their words to the ends of the
world."[i][a]

19Again I ask: Did Israel not under-
stand? First, Moses says,

"I will make you envious[b] by those
who are not a nation;
I will make you angry by a nation
that has no understanding."[j][c]

24 [u]**Ro 3:29**
25 [v]Hos 2:23; 1Pe 2:10
26 [w]Hos 1:10; **Mt 16:16; Ro 8:14**
27 [x]Ge 22:17; Hos 1:10; [y]2Ki 19:4; Jer 44:14; 50:20; Joel 2:32; Ro 11:5
28 [z]Isa 10:22–23
29 [a]Jas 5:4; [b]Isa 1:9; Ge 19:24–29; Dt 29:23; Isa 13:19; Jer 50:40
30 [c]**Ro 8:31**; [d]Ro 1:17; 3:22; 4:5, 13; 10:6; Gal 2:16; Php 3:9; Heb 11:7
31 [e]Dt 6:25; Isa 51:1; Ro 10:2–3; 11:7; [f]Gal 5:4
32 [g]1Pe 2:8
33 [h]Isa 8:14; 28:16; Ro 10:11; 1Pe 2:6,8

Ch. 10

1 [a]Ps 20:4
2 [b]**Ac 21:20**
3 [c]Ro 1:17; **9:31**
4 [d]Gal 3:24; Ro 7:1–4; [e]**Ro 3:22**
5 [f]Lev 18:5; Dt 4:1; 6:24; Ne 9:29; Pr 19:16; Isa 55:3; Eze 20:11,13,21; **Ro 7:10**
6 [g]**Ro 9:30**; [h]Dt 30:12
7 [i]Dt 30:13; [j]**Ac 2:24**
8 [k]Dt 30:14
9 [l]Mt 10:32; [m]**Jn 13:13**; [n]**Jn 3:15**; [o]**Ac 2:24**; [p]**Ro 11:14**
11 [q]Isa 28:16; Ro 9:33
12 [r]**Ro 3:22**,29; [s]**Mt 28:18**
13 [t]**Ac 2:21**; [u]Joel 2:32
15 [v]Isa 52:7; Na 1:15
16 [w]Heb 4:2; [x]Isa 53:1; Jn 12:38
17 [y]Gal 3:2,5; [z]Col 3:16
18 [a]Ps 19:4; **Mt 24:14**; Ro 1:8; Col 1:6,23; 1Th 1:8
19 [b]Ro 11:11,14; [c]Dt 32:21

[i]25 Hosea 2:23 [j]26 Hosea 1:10
[k]28 Isaiah 10:22,23 [l]29 Isaiah 1:9
[m]33 Isaiah 8:14; 28:16 [a]5 Lev. 18:5
[b]6 Deut. 30:12 [c]7 Deut. 30:13
[d]8 Deut. 30:14 [e]11 Isaiah 28:16
[f]13 Joel 2:32 [g]15 Isaiah 52:7
[h]16 Isaiah 53:1 [i]18 Psalm 19:4
[j]19 Deut. 32:21

20And Isaiah boldly says,

"I was found by those who did not
seek me;
I revealed myself to those who did
not ask for me."[k][d]

21But concerning Israel he says,

"All day long I have held out my
hands
to a disobedient and obstinate
people."[l][e]

The Remnant of Israel

11 I ask then: Did God reject his
people? By no means![a] I am an
Israelite myself, a descendant of Abra-
ham,[b] from the tribe of Benjamin.[c] 2God
did not reject his people,[d] whom he
foreknew.[e] Don't you know what the
Scripture says in the passage about Eli-
jah—how he appealed to God against
Israel: 3"Lord, they have killed your
prophets and torn down your altars; I
am the only one left, and they are trying
to kill me"[a]?[f] 4And what was God's
answer to him? "I have reserved for
myself seven thousand who have not
bowed the knee to Baal."[b][g] 5So too, at
the present time there is a remnant[h]
chosen by grace.[i] 6And if by grace, then
it is no longer by works;[j] if it were, grace
would no longer be grace.[c]
7What then? What Israel sought so
earnestly it did not obtain,[k] but the elect
did. The others were hardened,[l] 8as it is
written:

"God gave them a spirit of stupor,
eyes so that they could not see
and ears so that they could not
hear,[m]
to this very day."[d][n]

9And David says:

"May their table become a snare and a
trap,
a stumbling-block and a retribution
for them.
10May their eyes be darkened so they
cannot see,[o]
and their backs be bent for ever."[e][p]

Ingrafted Branches

11Again I ask: Did they stumble so as
to fall beyond recovery? Not at all![q]
Rather, because of their transgression,
salvation has come to the Gentiles[r] to
make Israel envious.[s] 12But if their
transgression means riches for the
world, and their loss means riches for
the Gentiles,[t] how much greater riches
will their fulness bring!
13I am talking to you Gentiles. In-
asmuch as I am the apostle to the Gen-
tiles,[u] I make much of my ministry 14in
the hope that I may somehow arouse
my own people to envy[v] and save[w]
some of them. 15For if their rejection is
the reconciliation[x] of the world, what
will their acceptance be but life from the
dead?[y] 16If the part of the dough offered
as firstfruits[z] is holy, then the whole
batch is holy; if the root is holy, so are
the branches.
17If some of the branches have been
broken off,[a] and you, though a wild
olive shoot, have been grafted in among
the others[b] and now share in the
nourishing sap from the olive root, 18do
not boast over those branches. If you
do, consider this: You do not support
the root, but the root supports you.[c]
19You will say then, "Branches were
broken off so that I could be grafted in."
20Granted. But they were broken off
because of unbelief, and you stand by
faith.[d] Do not be arrogant,[e] but be
afraid.[f] 21For if God did not spare the
natural branches, he will not spare you
either.
22Consider therefore the kindness[g]
and sternness of God: sternness to
those who fell, but kindness to you,
provided that you continue[h] in his kind-
ness. Otherwise, you also will be cut
off.[i] 23And if they do not persist in unbe-
lief, they will be grafted in, for God is
able to graft them in again.[j] 24After all, if
you were cut out of an olive tree that is
wild by nature, and contrary to nature
were grafted into a cultivated olive tree,[k]
how much more readily will these, the
natural branches, be grafted into their
own olive tree!

All Israel Will Be Saved

25I do not want you to be ignorant[l] of
this mystery,[m] brothers, so that you
may not be conceited:[n] Israel has experi-
enced a hardening[o] in part until the full
number of the Gentiles has come in.[p]
26And so all Israel will be saved,[q] as it is
written:

20 [d]Isa 65:1; Ro 9:30
21 [e]Isa 65:2; Jer 35:17

Ch. 11

1 [a]Lev 26:44; 1Sa 12:22; Ps 94:14; Jer 31:37; 33:24–26; [b]2Co 11:22; [c]Php 3:5
2 [d]**ver 1**; [e]**Ro 8:29**
3 [f]1Ki 19:10,14
4 [g]1Ki 19:18
5 [h]**Ro 9:27**; [i]**Ro 3:24**
6 [j]Ro 4:4
7 [k]Ro 9:31; [l]ver 25; **Ro 9:18**
8 [m]**Mt 13:13–15**; [n]Dt 29:4; Isa 29:10
10 [o]ver 8; [p]Ps 69:22–23
11 [q]ver 1; [r]**Ac 13:46**; [s]ver 14; Ro 10:19
12 [t]ver 25
13 [u]**Ac 9:15**
14 [v]ver 11; Ro 10:19; 1Co 10:33; 1Th 2:16; [w]**Mt 1:21**; **Lk 2:11**; **Jn 3:17**; Ac 4:12; 16:31; 1Co 1:21; 1Ti 2:4; Tit 3:5
15 [x]**Ro 5:10**; [y]Lk 15:24,32
16 [z]Lev 23:10, 17; Nu 15:18–21
17 [a]Jer 11:16; Jn 15:2; [b]Ac 2:39; Eph 2:11–13
18 [c]Jn 4:22
20 [d]1Co 10:12; 2Co 1:24; [e]1Ti 6:17; [f]1Pe 1:17
22 [g]Ro 2:4; [h]1Co 15:2; Col 1:23; Heb 3:6; [i]Jn 15:2
23 [j]2Co 3:16
24 [k]Jer 11:16
25 [l]Ro 1:13; 1Co 10:1; 12:1; 2Co 1:8; 1Th 4:13; [m]**Ro 16:25**; [n]Ro 12:16; [o]ver 7; **Ro 9:18**; [p]Lk 21:24
26 [q]Isa 45:17; Jer 31:34

[k]*20* Isaiah 65:1 [l]*21* Isaiah 65:2
[a]*3* 1 Kings 19:10,14 [b]*4* 1 Kings 19:18
[c]*6* Some manuscripts *by grace. But if by works, then it is no longer grace; if it were, work would no longer be work.* [d]*8* Deut. 29:4; Isaiah 29:10
[e]*10* Psalm 69:22,23

"The deliverer will come from Zion;
he will turn godlessness away from
Jacob.
27And this is[f] my covenant with them
when I take away their sins."[g r]

28As far as the gospel is concerned,
they are enemies[s] on your account; but
as far as election is concerned, they are
loved on account of the patriarchs,[t] 29for
God's gifts and his call[u] are irrevocable.[v]
30Just as you who were at one time dis-
obedient[w] to God have now received
mercy as a result of their disobedience,
31so they too have now become disobe-
dient in order that they too may now[h]
receive mercy as a result of God's mercy
to you. 32For God has bound all men
over to disobedience[x] so that he may
have mercy on them all.

Doxology

33Oh, the depth of the riches[y] of the
wisdom and[i] knowledge of
God![z]
How unsearchable his judgments,
and his paths beyond tracing out![a]
34"Who has known the mind of the
Lord?
Or who has been his counsellor?"[j b]
35"Who has ever given to God,
that God should repay him?"[k c]
36For from him and through him and to
him are all things.[d]
To him be the glory for ever! Amen.[e]

Living Sacrifices

12 Therefore, I urge you,[a] bro-
thers, in view of God's mercy,
to offer your bodies as living sacrifices,[b]
holy and pleasing to God—this is your
spiritual[a] act of worship. 2Do not con-
form[c] any longer to the pattern of this
world,[d] but be transformed by the re-
newing of your mind.[e] Then you will be
able to test and approve what God's will
is[f]—his good, pleasing[g] and perfect
will.
3For by the grace given me[h] I say to
every one of you: Do not think of your-
self more highly than you ought, but
rather think of yourself with sober judg-
ment, in accordance with the measure
of faith God has given you. 4Just as each
of us has one body with many mem-
bers, and these members do not all have
the same function,[i] 5so in Christ we who
are many form one body,[j] and each
member belongs to all the others. 6We
have different gifts,[k] according to the
grace given us. If a man's gift is
prophesying,[l] let him use it in propor-
tion to his[b] faith.[m] 7If it is serving, let
him serve; if it is teaching, let him
teach;[n] 8if it is encouraging, let him en-
courage;[o] if it is contributing to the
needs of others, let him give generous-
ly;[p] if it is leadership, let him govern
diligently; if it is showing mercy, let him
do it cheerfully.

Love

9Love must be sincere.[q] Hate what is
evil; cling to what is good.[r] 10Be devoted
to one another in brotherly love.[s] Hon-
our one another above yourselves.[t]
11Never be lacking in zeal, but keep your
spiritual fervour,[u] serving the Lord. 12Be
joyful in hope,[v] patient in affliction,[w]
faithful in prayer.[x] 13Share with God's
people who are in need.[y] Practise
hospitality.[z]
14Bless those who persecute you;[a]
bless and do not curse. 15Rejoice with
those who rejoice; mourn with those
who mourn.[b] 16Live in harmony with
one another.[c] Do not be proud, but be
willing to associate with people of low
position.[c] Do not be conceited.[d]
17Do not repay anyone evil for evil.[e]
Be careful to do what is right in the eyes
of everybody.[f] 18If it is possible, as far as
it depends on you, live at peace with
everyone.[g] 19Do not take revenge,[h] my
friends, but leave room for God's wrath,
for it is written: "It is mine to avenge; I
will repay,"[d i] says the Lord. 20On the
contrary:

"If your enemy is hungry, feed him;
if he is thirsty, give him something
to drink.
In doing this, you will heap burning
coals on his head."[e j]

21Do not be overcome by evil, but over-
come evil with good.

27 [r]Isa 59:20–21; 27:9; Heb 8:10,12
28 [s]Ro 5:10; [t]Dt 7:8; 10:15; Ro 9:5
29 [u]**Ro 8:28**; [v]**Heb 7:21**
30 [w]**Eph 2:2**
32 [x]**Ro 3:9**
33 [y]**Ro 2:4**; [z]Ps 92:5; Eph 3:10; Col 2:3; [a]Job 5:9; 11:7; Ps 139:6; Ecc 8:17; Isa 40:28
34 [b]Isa 40:13–14; Job 15:8; 36:22; Jer 23:18; 1Co 2:16
35 [c]Job 41:11; 35:7
36 [d]1Co 8:6; 11:12; Col 1:16; Heb 2:10; [e]Ro 16:27; Eph 3:21; 1Ti 1:17; 1Pe 5:11; Jude 25; Rev 5:13; 27:12

Ch. 12

1 [a]Eph 4:1; 1Pe 2:11; [b]Ro 6:13, 16,19; 1Co 6:20; 1Pe 2:5
2 [c]1Pe 1:14; [d]1Co 1:20; 2Co 10:2; 1Jn 2:15; [e]Eph 4:23; [f]**Eph 5:17**; [g]**1Ti 5:4**
3 [h]Ro 15:15; 1Co 15:10; Gal 2:9; Eph 3:7; 4:7; 1Pe 4:10–11
4 [i]1Co 12:12–14; Eph 4:16
5 [j]1Co 6:15; 10:17; 12:12, 20,27; Eph 2:16; 4:4,25; 5:30; Col 3:15
6 [k]1Co 7:7; 12:4,8–10; [l]**Eph 4:11**; [m]1Pe 4:10–11
7 [n]**Eph 4:11**
8 [o]Ac 11:23; 13:15; 15:32; [p]2Co 8:2; 9:5–13
9 [q]2Co 6:6; 1Ti 1:5; [r]Ps 97:10; Am 5:15; 1Th 5:21–22
10 [s]Ps 133:1; 1Th 4:9; Heb 13:1; 1Pe 1:22; [t]Php 2:3
11 [u]Ac 18:25
12 [v]Ro 5:2; [w]Heb 10:32, 36; [x]**Lk 18:1**
13 [y]**Ac 24:17**; [z]2Ki 4:10; Job 31:32; 1Ti 3:2; 5:10; Heb 13:2; 1Pe 4:9
14 [a]**Mt 5:44**
15 [b]Job 30:25
16 [c]**Ro 15:5**; [d]ver 3; Ps 131:1; Isa 5:21; Jer 45:5; Ro 11:25
17 [e]ver 19; Pr 20:22; 24:29; [f]2Co 8:21
18 [g]**Mk 9:50; Ro 14:19**
19 [h]ver 17; Lev 19:18; Pr 20:22; 24:29; [i]Dt 32:35; Ge 50:19; 1Sa 26:10; Ps 94:1; Jer 51:36
20 [j]Pr 25:21–22; Ex 23:4; Mt 5:44; Lk 6:27

f27 Or *will be*
g27 Isaiah 59:20,21; 27:9; Jer. 31:33,34
h31 Some manuscripts do not have *now*.
i33 Or *riches and the wisdom and the*
j34 Isaiah 40:13
k35 Job 41:11
a1 Or *reasonable*
b6 Or *in agreement with the*
c16 Or *willing to do menial work*
d19 Deut. 32:35
e20 Prov. 25:21,22

Submission to the Authorities

13 Everyone must submit himself to the governing authorities,[a] for there is no authority except that which God has established.[b] The authorities that exist have been established by God. 2Consequently, he who rebels against the authority is rebelling against what God has instituted,[c] and those who do so will bring judgment on themselves. 3For rulers hold no terror for those who do right, but for those who do wrong. Do you want to be free from fear of the one in authority? Then do what is right and he will commend you.[d] 4For he is God's servant to do you good. But if you do wrong, be afraid, for he does not bear the sword for nothing. He is God's servant, an agent of wrath to bring punishment on the wrongdoer.[e] 5Therefore, it is necessary to submit to the authorities, not only because of possible punishment but also because of conscience.[f]

6This is also why you pay taxes,[g] for the authorities are God's servants, who give their full time to governing. 7Give everyone what you owe him: If you owe taxes, pay taxes;[h] if revenue, then revenue; if respect, then respect; if honour, then honour.

Love, for the Day Is Near

8Let no debt remain outstanding, except the continuing debt to love one another, for he who loves his fellow-man has fulfilled the law.[i] 9The commandments, "Do not commit adultery," "Do not murder," "Do not steal," "Do not covet,"[a][j] and whatever other commandment there may be, are summed up[k] in this one rule: "Love your neighbour as yourself."[b][l] 10Love does no harm to its neighbour. Therefore love is the fulfilment of the law.[m]

11And do this, understanding the present time. The hour has come[n] for you to wake up from your slumber,[o] because our salvation is nearer now than when we first believed. 12The night is nearly over; the day is almost here.[p] So let us put aside the deeds of darkness[q] and put on the armour[r] of light. 13Let us behave decently, as in the daytime, not in orgies and drunkenness,[s] not in sexual immorality and debauchery, not in dissension and jealousy.[t] 14Rather, clothe yourselves with the Lord Jesus Christ,[u] and do not think about how to gratify the desires of the sinful nature.[c][v]

Ch. 13

1 [a]Tit 3:1; 1Pe 2:13–14; [b]Da 2:21; 4:17; Jn 19:11
2 [c]Ex 16:8
3 [d]1Pe 2:14
4 [e]1Th 4:6
5 [f]Pr 24:21–22
6 [g]Mt 22:17
7 [h]Mt 17:25; Mt 22:17,21; Lk 23:2
8 [i]ver 10; **Mt 5:43**; Jn 13:34; Col 3:14
9 [j]Ex 20:13–15, 17; Dt 5:17–19,21; [k]Mt 7:12; [l]Lev 19:18; **Mt 5:43**
10 [m]**ver 8–9**
11 [n]1Co 7:29–31; 10:11; Jas 5:8; 1Pe 4:7; 1Jn 2:18; Rev 22:10; [o]Eph 5:14; 1Th 5:5–6
12 [p]Heb 10:25; 1Jn 2:8; [q]Eph 5:11; [r]Eph 6:11,13; 1Th 5:8
13 [s]**Eph 5:18**; [t]Lk 21:34; Gal 5:20–21; Eph 5:18; 1Pe 4:3
14 [u]Gal 3:27; Eph 4:24; Col 3:10,12; [v]**Gal 5:24**

Ch. 14

1 [a]Ro 15:1; 1Co 8:9–12; 9:22
2 [b]ver 14
3 [c]ver 10; Lk 18:9; [d]ver 10, 13; Col 2:16
4 [e]**Mt 7:1**
5 [f]Gal 4:10; Col 2:16
6 [g]**Mt 14:19**; 1Co 10:30–31; 1Ti 4:3–4
7 [h]2Co 5:15; Gal 2:20
8 [i]Php 1:20
9 [j]Rev 1:18; 2:8; [k]**Ac 10:42**; 2Co 5:15
10 [l]ver 3; **Mt 7:1**; [m]**2Co 5:10**
11 [n]Isa 49:18; [o]Isa 45:23; Php 2:10–11
12 [p]Mt 12:36; 1Pe 4:5
13 [q]ver 1; **Mt 7:1**; [r]**2Co 6:3**
14 [s]ver 20; **Ac 10:15**; [t]1Co 8:7
15 [u]Eph 5:2

The Weak and the Strong

14 Accept him whose faith is weak,[a] without passing judgment on disputable matters. 2One man's faith allows him to eat everything, but another man, whose faith is weak, eats only vegetables.[b] 3The man who eats everything must not look down on[c] him who does not, and the man who does not eat everything must not condemn[d] the man who does, for God has accepted him. 4Who are you to judge someone else's servant?[e] To his own master he stands or falls. And he will stand, for the Lord is able to make him stand.

5One man considers one day more sacred than another;[f] another man considers every day alike. Each one should be fully convinced in his own mind. 6He who regards one day as special, does so to the Lord. He who eats meat, eats to the Lord, for he gives thanks to God;[g] and he who abstains, does so to the Lord and gives thanks to God. 7For none of us lives to himself alone[h] and none of us dies to himself alone. 8If we live, we live to the Lord; and if we die, we die to the Lord. So, whether we live or die, we belong to the Lord.[i]

9For this very reason, Christ died and returned to life[j] so that he might be the Lord of both the dead and the living.[k] 10You, then, why do you judge your brother? Or why do you look down on[l] your brother? For we will all stand before God's judgment seat.[m] 11It is written:

"'As surely as I live,'[n] says the Lord,
'Every knee will bow before me;
every tongue will confess to
God.'"[a][o]

12So then, each of us will give an account of himself to God.[p]

13Therefore let us stop passing judgment[q] on one another. Instead, make up your mind not to put any stumbling-block or obstacle in your brother's way.[r] 14As one who is in the Lord Jesus, I am fully convinced that no food[b] is unclean in itself.[s] But if anyone regards something as unclean, then for him it is unclean.[t] 15If your brother is distressed because of what you eat, you are no longer acting in love.[u] Do not by your eating destroy your brother for whom

---

[a]9 Exodus 20:13–15,17; Deut. 5:17–19,21
[b]9 Lev. 19:18 [c]14 Or *the flesh*
[a]11 Isaiah 45:23 [b]14 Or *that nothing*

Christ died.[v] 16Do not allow what you consider good to be spoken of as evil.[w] 17For the kingdom of God is not a matter of eating and drinking,[x] but of righteousness, peace[y] and joy in the Holy Spirit,[z] 18because anyone who serves Christ in this way is pleasing to God and approved by men.[a]

19Let us therefore make every effort to do what leads to peace[b] and to mutual edification.[c] 20Do not destroy the work of God for the sake of food.[d] All food is clean,[e] but it is wrong for a man to eat anything that causes someone else to stumble.[f] 21It is better not to eat meat or drink wine or to do anything else that will cause your brother to fall.[g]

22So whatever you believe about these things keep between yourself and God. Blessed is the man who does not condemn[h] himself by what he approves. 23But the man who has doubts[i] is condemned if he eats, because his eating is not from faith; and everything that does not come from faith is sin.

15 We who are strong ought to bear with the failings of the weak[a] and not to please ourselves. 2Each of us should please his neighbour for his good,[b] to build him up.[c] 3For even Christ did not please himself[d] but, as it is written: "The insults of those who insult you have fallen on me."[a][e] 4For everything that was written in the past was written to teach us,[f] so that through endurance and the encouragement of the Scriptures we might have hope.

5May the God who gives endurance and encouragement give you a spirit of unity[g] among yourselves as you follow Christ Jesus, 6so that with one heart and mouth you may glorify[h] the God and Father[i] of our Lord Jesus Christ.

7Accept one another,[j] then, just as Christ accepted you, in order to bring praise to God. 8For I tell you that Christ has become a servant of the Jews[b][k] on behalf of God's truth, to confirm the promises[l] made to the patriarchs 9so that the Gentiles[m] may glorify God[n] for his mercy, as it is written:

"Therefore I will praise you among the Gentiles;
I will sing hymns to your name."[c][o]

10Again, it says,

"Rejoice, O Gentiles, with his people."[d][p]

11And again,

"Praise the Lord, all you Gentiles,
and sing praises to him, all you peoples."[e][q]

12And again, Isaiah says,

"The Root of Jesse[r] will spring up,
one who will arise to rule over the nations;
the Gentiles will hope in him."[f][s]

13May the God of hope fill you with all joy and peace[t] as you trust in him, so that you may overflow with hope by the power of the Holy Spirit.[u]

Paul the Minister to the Gentiles

14I myself am convinced, my brothers, that you yourselves are full of goodness,[v] complete in knowledge[w] and competent to instruct one another. 15I have written to you quite boldly on some points, as if to remind you of them again, because of the grace God gave me[x] 16to be a minister of Christ Jesus to the Gentiles[y] with the priestly duty of proclaiming the gospel of God,[z] so that the Gentiles might become an offering[a] acceptable to God, sanctified by the Holy Spirit.

17Therefore I glory in Christ Jesus[b] in my service to God.[c] 18I will not venture to speak of anything except what Christ has accomplished through me in leading the Gentiles[d] to obey God[e] by what I have said and done—19by the power of signs and miracles,[f] through the power of the Spirit.[g] So from Jerusalem[h] all the way round to Illyricum, I have fully proclaimed the gospel of Christ.[i] 20It has always been my ambition to preach the gospel[j] where Christ was not known, so that I would not be building on someone else's foundation.[k] 21Rather, as it is written:

"Those who were not told about him will see,
and those who have not heard will understand."[g][l]

22This is why I have often been hindered from coming to you.[m]

Paul's Plan to Visit Rome

23But now that there is no more place for me to work in these regions, and

15 [v]ver 20; 1Co 8:11
16 [w]1Co 10:30
17 [x]1Co 8:8; [y]Isa 32:17; [z]Ro 15:13; Gal 5:22
18 [a]Lk 2:52; Ac 24:16; 2Co 8:21
19 [b]Ps 34:14; Ro 12:18; 1Co 7:15; 2Ti 2:22; Heb 12:14; [c]Ro 15:2; 1Co 14:3–5,12,17, 26; 2Co 12:19; Eph 4:12,29
20 [d]ver 15; [e]ver 14; **Ac 10:15**; [f]ver 13; 1Co 8:9–12
21 [g]**Mt 5:29**
22 [h]1Jn 3:21
23 [i]ver 5

Ch. 15

1 [a]Ro 14:1; 1Th 5:14
2 [b]**1Co 10:24**; [c]**Ro 14:19**
3 [d]2Co 8:9; [e]Ps 69:9
4 [f]**Ro 4:23–24**
5 [g]Ro 12:16; 1Co 1:10; 2Co 13:11; Eph 4:3; Php 2:2; Col 3:14; 1Pe 3:8
6 [h]Ps 34:3; [i]Rev 1:6
7 [j]Ro 14:1
8 [k]Mt 15:24; Ac 3:25–26; [l]2Co 1:20
9 [m]**Ro 3:29**; [n]**Mt 9:8**; [o]2Sa 22:50; Ps 18:49
10 [p]Dt 32:43; Isa 66:10
11 [q]Ps 117:1
12 [r]**Rev 5:5**; [s]Isa 11:10; Mt 12:21
13 [t]Ro 14:17; [u]ver 19; 1Co 2:4; 4:20; 1Th 1:5
14 [v]Eph 5:9; [w]**2Co 8:7**; 2Pe 1:12
15 [x]**Ro 12:3**
16 [y]**Ac 9:15**; [z]ver 19; **Ro 1:1**; [a]Isa 66:20
17 [b]Php 3:3; [c]Heb 2:17
18 [d]Ac 15:12; 21:19; Ro 1:5; [e]Ro 16:26
19 [f]**Jn 4:48**; Ac 19:11; [g]**ver 13**; [h]Ac 22:17–21; [i]**2Co 2:12**
20 [j]Ro 1:15; [k]2Co 10:15–16
21 [l]Isa 52:15
22 [m]Ro 1:13

[a]3 Psalm 69:9 [b]8 Greek *circumcision*
[c]9 2 Samuel 22:50; Psalm 18:49
[d]10 Deut. 32:43 [e]11 Psalm 117:1
[f]12 Isaiah 11:10 [g]21 Isaiah 52:15

since I have been longing for many
years to see you,[n] 24I plan to do so when
I go to Spain.[o] I hope to visit you while
passing through and to have you assist[p]
me on my journey there, after I have
enjoyed your company for a while.
25Now, however, I am on my way to
Jerusalem[q] in the service[r] of the saints[s]
there. 26For Macedonia[t] and Achaia[u]
were pleased to make a contribution for
the poor among the saints in Jeru-
salem.[v] 27They were pleased to do it,
and indeed they owe it to them. For if
the Gentiles have shared in the Jews'
spiritual blessings, they owe it to the
Jews to share with them their material
blessings.[w] 28So after I have completed
this task and have made sure that they
have received this fruit, I will go to
Spain[x] and visit you on the way. 29I
know that when I come to you,[y] I will
come in the full measure of the blessing
of Christ.

30I urge you, brothers, by our Lord
Jesus Christ and by the love of the Spir-
it,[z] to join me in my struggle by praying
to God for me.[a] 31Pray that I may be
rescued[b] from the unbelievers in Judea
and that my service[c] in Jerusalem may
be acceptable to the saints[d] there, 32so
that by God's will[e] I may come to you[f]
with joy and together with you be re-
freshed.[g] 33The God of peace[h] be with
you all. Amen.

Personal Greetings

16 I commend[a] to you our sister
Phoebe, a servant[a] of the
church in Cenchrea.[b] 2I ask you to re-
ceive her in the Lord[c] in a way worthy of
the saints[d] and to give her any help she
may need from you, for she has been a
great help to many people, including
me.

3Greet Priscilla[b] and Aquila,[e] my
fellow-workers[f] in Christ Jesus.[g]
4They risked their lives for me. Not
only I but all the churches of the
Gentiles are grateful to them.
5Greet also the church that meets at
their house.[h]
Greet my dear friend Epenetus, who
was the first convert[i] to Christ in the
province of Asia.[j]
6Greet Mary, who worked very hard
for you.
7Greet Andronicus and Junias, my
relatives[k] who have been in prison
with me.[l] They are outstanding
among the apostles, and they were
in Christ[m] before I was.
8Greet Ampliatus, whom I love in the
Lord.
9Greet Urbanus, our fellow-worker in
Christ,[n] and my dear friend Stachys.
10Greet Apelles, tested and approved in
Christ.[o]
Greet those who belong to the house-
hold[p] of Aristobulus.
11Greet Herodion, my relative.[q]
Greet those in the household[r] of
Narcissus who are in the Lord.
12Greet Tryphena and Tryphosa, those
women who work hard in the Lord.
Greet my dear friend Persis, another
woman who has worked very hard
in the Lord.
13Greet Rufus,[s] chosen[t] in the Lord, and
his mother, who has been a mother
to me, too.
14Greet Asyncritus, Phlegon, Hermes,
Patrobas, Hermas and the brothers
with them.
15Greet Philologus, Julia, Nereus and
his sister, and Olympas and all the
saints[u] with them.[v]
16Greet one another with a holy kiss.[w]
All the churches of Christ send
greetings.

17I urge you, brothers, to watch out
for those who cause divisions and put
obstacles in your way that are contrary
to the teaching you have learned.[x] Keep
away from them.[y] 18For such people are
not serving our Lord Christ,[z] but their
own appetites.[a] By smooth talk and
flattery they deceive[b] the minds of naïve
people. 19Everyone has heard[c] about
your obedience, so I am full of joy over
you; but I want you to be wise about
what is good, and innocent about what
is evil.[d]
20The God of peace[e] will soon crush[f]
Satan[g] under your feet.
The grace of our Lord Jesus be with
you.[h]
21Timothy,[i] my fellow-worker, sends
his greetings to you, as do Lucius,[j]
Jason[k] and Sosipater, my relatives.[l]
22I, Tertius, who wrote down this let-
ter, greet you in the Lord.
23Gaius,[m] whose hospitality I and the
whole church here enjoy, sends you his
greetings.
Erastus,[n] who is the city's director of

23 [n]Ac 19:21; Ro 1:10–11
24 [o]ver 28; [p]1Co 16:6; Tit 3:13
25 [q]**Ac 19:21**; [r]**Ac 24:17**; [s]**Ac 9:13**
26 [t]**Ac 16:9**; [u]**Ac 18:12**; [v]**Ac 24:17**
27 [w]1Co 9:11
28 [x]ver 24
29 [y]Ro 1:10–11
30 [z]Gal 5:22; Col 1:8; [a]2Co 1:11; Col 4:12
31 [b]2Co 1:10; 2Th 3:2; 2Ti 3:11; 2Pe 2:9; [c]ver 25; **Ac 24:17**; [d]**Ac 9:13**
32 [e]**Ac 18:21**; [f]Ro 1:10,13; [g]1Co 16:18; Phm 7
33 [h]Ro 16:20; 2Co 13:11; Php 4:9; 1Th 5:23; 2Th 3:16; Heb 13:20

Ch. 16

1 [a]**2Co 3:1**; [b]Ac 18:18
2 [c]Php 2:29; [d]**Ac 9:13**
3 [e]**Ac 18:2**; [f]**Php 2:25**; [g]ver 7, 9–10; Ro 8:1, 39; 1Co 1:30; 2Co 5:17; Gal 1:22; 5:6; Eph 1:13
5 [h]1Co 16:19; Col 4:15; Phm 2; [i]1Co 16:15; [j]**Ac 2:9**
7 [k]ver 11,21; [l]Col 4:10; Phm 23; [m]**ver 3**
9 [n]**ver 3**
10 [o]**ver 3**; [p]**Ac 11:14**
11 [q]ver 7,21; [r]**Ac 11:14**
13 [s]Mk 15:21; [t]**2Jn 1**
15 [u]ver 2; **Ac 9:13**; [v]ver 14
16 [w]1Co 16:20; 2Co 13:12; 1Th 5:26; 1Pe 5:14
17 [x]Gal 1:8–9; 1Ti 1:3; 6:3; [y]Mt 18:15–17; 1Co 5:11; 2Th 3:6,14; 2Ti 3:5; Tit 3:10; 2Jn 10
18 [z]Ro 14:18; [a]Php 3:19; [b]2Sa 15:6; Ps 12:2; Isa 30:10; Col 2:4
19 [c]Ro 1:8; [d]**1Co 14:20**

20 [e]**Ro 15:33**; [f]Ge 3:15; [g]**Mt 4:10**; [h]2Co 13:14; **Gal 6:18**; 1Th 5:28; Rev 22:21
21 [i]**Ac 16:1**; [j]Ac 13:1; [k]Ac 17:5; [l]ver 7,11
23 [m]**Ac 19:29**; [n]Ac 19:22; 2Ti 4:20

[a]1 Or *deaconess*
[b]3 Greek *Prisca*, a variant of *Priscilla*

public works, and our brother Quartus
send you their greetings.[c]
25Now to him who is able[o] to establish
you by my gospel[p] and the proclamation
of Jesus Christ, according to the revela-
tion of the mystery[q] hidden for long
ages past, 26but now revealed and made
known through the prophetic writings[r]
by the command of the eternal God, so
that all nations might believe and obey[s]
him—27to the only wise God be glory
for ever through Jesus Christ! Amen.[t]

25 [o]2Co 9:8; Eph 3:20; Jude 24; [p]Ro 2:16; 2Ti 2:8; [q]Isa 48:6; Eph 1:9; 3:3–6,9; Col 1:26–27; 2:2; 1Ti 3:16
26 [r]Ro 1:2; [s]Ro 1:5
27 [t]Ro 11:36

[c]23 Some manuscripts *their greetings.* [24]*May the grace of our Lord Jesus Christ be with all of you. Amen.*

1 Corinthians

1 Paul, called to be an apostle[a] of
Christ Jesus by the will of God,[b]
and our brother Sosthenes,[c]

2To the church of God[d] in Corinth,[e] to
those sanctified in Christ Jesus and
called[f] to be holy, together with all
those everywhere who call on the
name[g] of our Lord Jesus Christ—their
Lord and ours:

3Grace and peace to you from God our
Father and the Lord Jesus Christ.[h]

Thanksgiving

4I always thank God for you[i] because
of his grace given you in Christ Jesus.
5For in him you have been enriched[j] in
every way—in all your speaking and in
all your knowledge[k]—6because our tes-
timony[l] about Christ was confirmed in
you. 7Therefore you do not lack any
spiritual gift[m] as you eagerly wait for our
Lord Jesus Christ to be revealed.[n] 8He
will keep you strong to the end, so that
you will be blameless[o] on the day of our
Lord Jesus Christ.[p] 9God, who has
called you[q] into fellowship with his
Son Jesus Christ our Lord,[r] is faithful.[s]

Divisions in the Church

10I appeal to you, brothers,[t] in the
name of our Lord Jesus Christ, that all of
you agree with one another so that there
may be no divisions among you[u] and
that you may be perfectly united[v] in
mind and thought. 11My brothers, some
from Chloe's household[w] have in-
formed me that there are quarrels
among you. 12What I mean is this: One
of you says, "I follow Paul";[x] another, "I
follow Apollos";[y] another, "I follow
Cephas[a]";[z] still another, "I follow
Christ."
13Is Christ divided? Was Paul cru-
cified for you? Were you baptised into[b]
the name of Paul?[a] 14I am thankful that I
did not baptise any of you except Cris-
pus[b] and Gaius,[c] 15so no-one can say
that you were baptised into my name.
(16Yes, I also baptised the household[d] of
Stephanas;[e] beyond that, I don't re-
member if I baptised anyone else.) 17For
Christ did not send me to baptise,[f] but to
preach the gospel—not with words of
human wisdom,[g] lest the cross of Christ
be emptied of its power.

Christ the Wisdom and Power of God

18For the message of the cross is
foolishness[h] to those who are
perishing,[i] but to us who are being
saved[j] it is the power of God.[k] 19For it is
written:

> "I will destroy the wisdom of the wise;
> the intelligence of the intelligent I
> will frustrate."[c][l]

20Where is the wise man?[m] Where is
the scholar? Where is the philosopher of
this age?[n] Has not God made foolish[o]
the wisdom of the world? 21For since in
the wisdom of God the world[p] through
its wisdom did not know him, God was
pleased through the foolishness of what
was preached to save[q] those who be-
lieve.[r] 22Jews demand miraculous signs[s]
and Greeks look for wisdom, 23but we
preach Christ crucified:[t] a stumbling-
block[u] to Jews and foolishness[v] to Gen-
tiles, 24but to those whom God has
called,[w] both Jews and Greeks, Christ
the power of God[x] and the wisdom of
God.[y] 25For the foolishness[z] of God
is wiser than man's wisdom, and the
weakness[a] of God is stronger than
man's strength.
26Brothers, think of what you were
when you were called.[b] Not many of
you were wise[c] by human standards;
not many were influential; not many
were of noble birth. 27But God chose[d]

Ch. 1

1 [a]Ro 1:1; Eph 1:1; 2Ti 1:1; [b]**2Co 1:1;** [c]Ac 18:17
2 [d]**1Co 10:32;** [e]**Ac 18:1;** [f]Ro 1:7; [g]**Ac 2:21**
3 [h]**Ro 1:7**
4 [i]**Ro 1:8**
5 [j]2Co 9:11; [k]**2Co 8:7**
6 [l]2Th 1:10; 1Ti 2:6; Rev 1:2
7 [m]Ro 1:11; 1Co 12:1–31; [n]**Mt 16:27; Lk 17:30;** 1Th 1:10; **2:19;** Tit 2:13; Jas 5:7–8; 1Pe 1:13; 2Pe 3:12; **Rev 1:7**
8 [o]**1Th 3:13;** [p]Am 5:18; 1Co 5:5; Php 1:6,10; 2:16; 1Th 5:2
9 [q]**Ro 8:28;** [r]1Jn 1:3; [s]Dt 7:9; Isa 49:7; 1Co 10:13; 1Th 5:24; 2Th 3:3; 2Ti 2:13; Heb 10:23; 11:11
10 [t]**Ro 7:1;** [u]1Co 11:18; [v]**Ro 15:5**
11 [w]**Ac 11:14**
12 [x]1Co 3:4,22; [y]**Ac 18:24;** [z]Jn 1:42; 1Co 3:22; 9:5
13 [a]**Mt 28:19**
14 [b]Ac 18:8; [c]**Ac 19:29**
16 [d]**Ac 11:14;** [e]1Co 16:15
17 [f]Jn 4:2; **Ac 2:38;** [g]1Co 2:1,4,13
18 [h]ver 21,23,25; 1Co 2:14; [i]2Co 2:15; 4:3; 2Th 2:10; [j]Ac 2:47; [k]ver 24; Ro 1:16
19 [l]Isa 29:14
20 [m]Isa 19:11–12; [n]1Co 2:6,8; 3:18; 2Co 4:4; Gal 1:4; [o]ver 27; Job 12:17; Isa 44:25; Jer 8:9; Ro 1:22; 1Co 3:18–19
21 [p]ver 27–28; 1Co 6:2; 11:32; [q]**Ro 11:14;** [r]**Ro 3:22**
22 [s]**Mt 12:38; Jn 2:11; 4:48**
23 [t]1Co 2:2; Gal 3:1; [u]**Lk 2:34;** [v]**ver 18**
24 [w]**Ro 8:28;** [x]ver 18; Ro 1:16; [y]ver 30; **Col 2:3**
25 [z]**ver 18;** [a]2Co 13:4
26 [b]**Ro 8:28;** [c]ver 20
27 [d]Jas 2:5

[a]*12* That is, Peter
[b]*13* Or *in;* also in verse 15
[c]*19* Isaiah 29:14

the foolish[e] things of the world to shame
the wise; God chose the weak things of
the world to shame the strong. 28He
chose the lowly things of this world and
the despised things—and the things
that are not[f]—to nullify the things that
are, 29so that no-one may boast before
him.[g] 30It is because of him that you are
in Christ Jesus,[h] who has become for us
wisdom from God—that is, our right-
eousness,[i] holiness[j] and redemption.[k]
31Therefore, as it is written: "Let him
who boasts boast in the Lord."[d] [l]

2 When I came to you, brothers, I did
not come with eloquence or su-
perior wisdom[a] as I proclaimed to you
the testimony about God.[a] 2For I resolved
to know nothing while I was with you
except Jesus Christ and him crucified.[b]
3I came to you[c] in weakness[d] and fear,
and with much trembling.[e] 4My mess-
age and my preaching were not with
wise and persuasive words,[f] but with a
demonstration of the Spirit's power,[g]
5so that your faith might not rest on
men's wisdom, but on God's power.[h]

Wisdom From the Spirit

6We do, however, speak a message of
wisdom among the mature,[i] but not the
wisdom of this age[j] or of the rulers of
this age, who are coming to nothing.[k]
7No, we speak of God's secret wisdom,
a wisdom[l] that has been hidden[m] and
that God destined for our glory before
time began. 8None of the rulers of this
age[n] understood it, for if they had, they
would not have crucified the Lord of
glory.[o] 9However, as it is written:

"No eye has seen,
no ear has heard,
no mind has conceived
what God has prepared for those
who love him"[b] [p]—

10but God has revealed[q] it to us by his
Spirit.[r]
The Spirit searches all things, even
the deep things of God. 11For who
among men knows the thoughts of a
man[s] except the man's spirit[t] within
him? In the same way no-one knows the
thoughts of God except the Spirit of
God. 12We have not received the spirit[u]
of the world[v] but the Spirit who is from
God, that we may understand what
God has freely given us. 13This is what
we speak, not in words taught us by
human wisdom[w] but in words taught by
the Spirit, expressing spiritual truths in
spiritual words.[c] 14The man without the

27 [e]ver 20; Ro 1:22; 1Co 3:18–19
28 [f]Ro 4:17
29 [g]Eph 2:9
30 [h]**Ro 16:3**; [i]Jer 23:5–6; 33:16; 2Co 5:21; Php 3:9; [j]1Co 1:2; [k]**Ro 3:24**
31 [l]Jer 9:23–24; Ps 34:2; 44:8; 2Co 10:17

Ch. 2

1 [a]ver 4,13; 1Co 1:17
2 [b]Gal 6:14; 1Co 1:23
3 [c]Ac 18:1–18; [d]1Co 4:10; 9:22; 2Co 11:29–30; 12:5,9–10; 13:9; [e]**2Co 7:15**
4 [f]ver 1; [g]**Ro 15:13**
5 [h]2Co 4:7; 6:7
6 [i]Eph 4:13; Php 3:15; Col 4:12; Heb 5:14; 6:1; Jas 1:4; [j]ver 8; **1Co 1:20**; [k]Ps 146:4
7 [l]ver 1; [m]Ro 16:25
8 [n]ver 6; **1Co 1:20**; [o]Ps 24:7; Ac 7:2; Jas 2:1
9 [p]Isa 64:4; 65:17
10 [q]**Mt 13:11**; 2Co 12:1,7; Gal 1:12; 2:2; Eph 3:3,5; [r]Jn 14:26
11 [s]Jer 17:9; [t]Pr 20:27
12 [u]Ro 8:15; [v]1Co 1:20,27; Jas 2:5
13 [w]ver 1,4; 1Co 1:17
14 [x]Jn 14:17; [y]**1Co 1:18**
15 [z]1Co 3:1; Gal 6:1
16 [a]Isa 40:13; **Ro 11:34**; [b]Jn 15:15

Ch. 3

1 [a]1Co 2:15; [b]Ro 7:14; 1Co 2:14; [c]1Co 14:20
2 [d]Heb 5:12–14; 1Pe 2:2; [e]Jn 16:12
3 [f]Ro 13:13; 1Co 1:11; Gal 5:20
4 [g]1Co 1:12
5 [h]**Ac 18:24**; [i]1Co 4:1; 2Co 6:4; Eph 3:7; Col 1:23,25
6 [j]Ac 18:4–11; 1Co 4:15; 9:1; 15:1

Spirit does not accept the things that
come from the Spirit of God,[x] for they
are foolishness[y] to him, and he cannot
understand them, because they are
spiritually discerned. 15The spiritual[z]
man makes judgments about all things,
but he himself is not subject to any
man's judgment:

16"For who has known the mind of the
Lord
that he may instruct him?"[d] [a]
But we have the mind of Christ.[b]

On Divisions in the Church

3 Brothers, I could not address you
as spiritual[a] but as worldly[b]—mere
infants[c] in Christ. 2I gave you milk, not
solid food,[d] for you were not yet ready
for it.[e] Indeed, you are still not ready.
3You are still worldly. For since there is
jealousy and quarrelling[f] among you,
are you not worldly? Are you not acting
like mere men? 4For when one says, "I
follow Paul," and another, "I follow
Apollos,"[g] are you not mere men?
5What, after all, is Apollos?[h] And
what is Paul? Only servants,[i] through
whom you came to believe—as the Lord
has assigned to each his task. 6I planted
the seed,[j] Apollos watered it, but God
made it grow. 7So neither he who plants
nor he who waters is anything, but only
God, who makes things grow. 8The man
who plants and the man who waters
have one purpose, and each will be
rewarded according to his own labour.[k]
9For we are God's fellow-workers;[l] you
are God's field,[m] God's building.[n]
10By the grace God has given me,[o] I
laid a foundation[p] as an expert builder,
and someone else is building on it. But
each one should be careful how he
builds. 11For no-one can lay any founda-
tion other than the one already laid,
which is Jesus Christ.[q] 12If any man
builds on this foundation using gold,
silver, costly stones, wood, hay or
straw, 13his work will be shown for what
it is,[r] because the Day[s] will bring it to
light. It will be revealed with fire, and

8 [k]ver 14; Ps 18:20; 62:12; Mt 25:21; 1Co 9:17
9 [l]Mk 16:20; 2Co 6:1; 1Th 3:2; [m]Isa 61:3; [n]Eph 2:20–22; 1Pe 2:5 *10* [o]**Ro 12:3**; [p]Ro 15:20; **Eph 2:20**
11 [q]Isa 28:16; Eph 2:20
13 [r]1Co 4:5; [s]**1Co 1:8**; 2Th 1:7–10; 2Ti 1:12,18; 4:8

d*31* Jer. 9:24
a*1* Some manuscripts *as I proclaimed to you God's mystery* b*9* Isaiah 64:4
c*13* Or *Spirit, interpreting spiritual truths to spiritual men* d*16* Isaiah 40:13

the fire will test the quality of each
man's work.[t] 14If what he has built sur-
vives, he will receive his reward.[u] 15If it
is burned up, he will suffer loss; he
himself will be saved, but only as one
escaping through the flames.[v]
16Don't you know that you yourselves
are God's temple[w] and that God's Spirit
lives in you?[x] 17If anyone destroys God's
temple, God will destroy him; for God's
temple is sacred, and you are that
temple.
18Do not deceive yourselves. If any
one of you thinks he is wise[y] by the
standards of this age,[z] he should be-
come a "fool" so that he may become
wise. 19For the wisdom of this world is
foolishness[a] in God's sight. As it is writ-
ten: "He catches the wise in their craft-
iness";[a][b] 20and again, "The Lord knows
that the thoughts of the wise are
futile."[b][c] 21So then, no more boasting
about men![d] All things are yours,[e]
22whether Paul or Apollos[f] or Cephas[c][g]
or the world or life or death or the
present or the future[h]—all are yours,
23and you are of Christ,[i] and Christ is of
God.

Apostles of Christ

4 So then, men ought to regard us as
servants[a] of Christ and as those
entrusted[b] with the secret things[c] of
God. 2Now it is required that those who
have been given a trust must prove
faithful. 3I care very little if I am judged
by you or by any human court; indeed, I
do not even judge myself. 4My con-
science[d] is clear, but that does not make
me innocent.[e] It is the Lord who judges
me.[f] 5Therefore judge nothing[g] before
the appointed time; wait till the Lord
comes.[h] He will bring to light[i] what is
hidden in darkness and will expose the
motives of men's hearts. At that time
each will receive his praise from God.[j]
6Now, brothers, I have applied these
things to myself and Apollos for your
benefit, so that you may learn from us
the meaning of the saying, "Do not go
beyond what is written."[k] Then you will
not take pride in one man over against
another.[l] 7For who makes you different
from anyone else? What do you have
that you did not receive?[m] And if you
did receive it, why do you boast as
though you did not?
8Already you have all you want!
Already you have become rich![n] You
have become kings—and that without
us! How I wish that you really had be-
come kings so that we might be kings
with you! 9For it seems to me that God
has put us apostles on display at the end
of the procession, like men condemned
to die[o] in the arena. We have been made
a spectacle[p] to the whole universe, to
angels as well as to men. 10We are fools
for Christ,[q] but you are so wise in
Christ![r] We are weak, but you are
strong![s] You are honoured, we are dis-
honoured! 11To this very hour we go
hungry and thirsty, we are in rags, we
are brutally treated, we are homeless.[t]
12We work hard with our own hands.[u]
When we are cursed, we bless;[v] when
we are persecuted,[w] we endure it;
13when we are slandered, we answer
kindly. Up to this moment we have
become the scum of the earth, the
refuse[x] of the world.
14I am not writing this to shame you,[y]
but to warn you, as my dear children.[z]
15Even though you have ten thousand
guardians in Christ, you do not have
many fathers, for in Christ Jesus I be-
came your father[a] through the gospel.[b]
16Therefore I urge you to imitate me.[c]
17For this reason I am sending to you[d]
Timothy,[e] my son[f] whom I love, who is
faithful in the Lord. He will remind you
of my way of life in Christ Jesus, which
agrees with what I teach everywhere in
every church.[g]
18Some of you have become arro-
gant,[h] as if I were not coming to you.[i]
19But I will come to you very soon,[j] if the
Lord is willing,[k] and then I will find out
not only how these arrogant people are
talking, but what power they have.
20For the kingdom of God is not a matter
of[l] talk but of power.[m] 21What do you
prefer? Shall I come to you with a whip,[n]
or in love and with a gentle spirit?

Expel the Immoral Brother!

5 It is actually reported that there is
sexual immorality among you, and
of a kind that does not occur even
among pagans: A man has his father's
wife.[a] 2And you are proud! Shouldn't
you rather have been filled with grief[b]
and have put out of your fellowship[c] the
man who did this? 3Even though I am
not physically present, I am with you in
spirit.[d] And I have already passed judg-
ment on the one who did this, just as if I
were present. 4When you are assembled

13 [t]Nu 31:22–23; Jer 23:28–29; Mal 3:3; 2Th 1:7
14 [u]ver 8
15 [v]Jude 23
16 [w]1Co 6:19; 2Co 6:16; Eph 2:21–22; Heb 3:6; [x]Ro 8:9
18 [y]Isa 5:21; 1Co 8:2; Gal 6:3; [z]1Co 1:20
19 [a]ver 18; Ro 1:22; 1Co 1:20, 27; [b]Job 5:13
20 [c]Ps 94:11
21 [d]1Co 4:6; [e]Ro 8:32
22 [f]ver 5–6; [g]1Co 1:12; [h]Ro 8:38
23 [i]1Co 15:23; 2Co 10:7; Gal 3:29

Ch. 4

1 [a]1Co 3:5; [b]1Co 9:17; Tit 1:7; [c]Ro 16:25
4 [d]Ac 23:1; [e]Ro 2:13; [f]2Co 10:18
5 [g]Mt 7:1–2; [h]1Th 2:19; [i]Job 12:22; Ps 90:8; 1Co 3:13; [j]Ro 2:29
6 [k]1Co 1:19,31; 3:19–20; [l]1Co 1:12; 3:4
7 [m]Jn 3:27; Ro 12:3,6
8 [n]Rev 3:17–18
9 [o]Ro 8:36; [p]Ps 71:7; Heb 10:33
10 [q]1Co 1:18; Ac 17:18; 26:24; [r]1Co 3:18; 2Co 11:19; [s]1Co 2:3
11 [t]Ro 8:35; 2Co 11:23–27
12 [u]Ac 18:3; [v]Ro 12:14; 1Pe 3:9; [w]Mt 5:44
13 [x]Jer 20:18; La 3:45
14 [y]1Co 6:5; 15:34; 2Th 3:14; [z]1Th 2:11
15 [a]ver 14; [b]1Co 9:12,14, 18,23; 15:1
16 [c]1Co 11:1; Php 3:17; 4:9; 1Th 1:6; 2Th 3:7,9
17 [d]1Co 16:10; [e]Ac 16:1; [f]1Ti 1:2; [g]1Co 7:17
18 [h]Jer 43:2; [i]ver 21
19 [j]1Co 16:5–6; 2Co 1:15–16; [k]Ac 18:21
20 [l]Ro 14:17; [m]Ro 15:13
21 [n]2Co 1:23; 2:1; 13:2,10

Ch. 5

1 [a]Lev 18:8; Dt 22:30; 27:20 2 [b]2Co 7:7–11; [c]ver 13
3 [d]Col 2:5; 1Th 2:17

[a]19 Job 5:13 [b]20 Psalm 94:11
[c]22 That is, Peter

in the name of our Lord Jesus[e] and I am with you in spirit, and the power of our Lord Jesus is present, 5hand this man over[f] to Satan,[g] so that the sinful nature[a] may be destroyed and his spirit saved on the day of the Lord.[h]

6Your boasting is not good.[i] Don't you know that a little yeast[j] works through the whole batch of dough?[k] 7Get rid of the old yeast that you may be a new batch without yeast—as you really are. For Christ, our Passover lamb, has been sacrificed.[l] 8Therefore let us keep the Festival, not with the old yeast, the yeast of malice and wickedness, but with bread without yeast,[m] the bread of sincerity and truth.

9I have written to you in my letter not to associate[n] with sexually immoral people—10not at all meaning the people of this world[o] who are immoral, or the greedy and swindlers, or idolaters. In that case you would have to leave this world. 11But now I am writing to you that you must not associate with anyone who calls himself a brother[p] but is sexually immoral or greedy, an idolater[q] or a slanderer, a drunkard or a swindler. With such a man do not even eat.[r]

12What business is it of mine to judge those outside[s] the church? Are you not to judge those inside?[t] 13God will judge those outside. "Expel the wicked man from among you."[b][u]

Lawsuits Among Believers

6 If any of you has a dispute with another, dare he take it before the ungodly for judgment instead of before the saints?[a] 2Do you not know that the saints will judge the world?[b] And if you are to judge the world, are you not competent to judge trivial cases? 3Do you not know that we will judge angels? How much more the things of this life! 4Therefore, if you have disputes about such matters, appoint as judges even men of little account in the church![a] 5I say this to shame you.[c] Is it possible that there is nobody among you wise enough to judge a dispute between believers?[d] 6But instead, one brother[e] goes to law against another—and this in front of unbelievers![f]

7The very fact that you have lawsuits among you means you have been completely defeated already. Why not rather be wronged? Why not rather be cheated?[g] 8Instead, you yourselves cheat and do wrong, and you do this to your brothers.[h]

9Do you not know that the wicked will not inherit the kingdom of God?[i] Do not be deceived:[j] Neither the sexually immoral nor idolaters nor adulterers[k] nor male prostitutes nor homosexual offenders[l] 10nor thieves nor the greedy nor drunkards nor slanderers nor swindlers[m] will inherit the kingdom of God. 11And that is what some of you were.[n] But you were washed,[o] you were sanctified,[p] you were justified[q] in the name of the Lord Jesus Christ and by the Spirit of our God.

Sexual Immorality

12"Everything is permissible for me"—but not everything is beneficial.[r] "Everything is permissible for me"—but I will not be mastered by anything. 13"Food for the stomach and the stomach for food"—but God will destroy them both.[s] The body is not meant for sexual immorality, but for the Lord,[t] and the Lord for the body. 14By his power God raised the Lord from the dead,[u] and he will raise us also.[v] 15Do you not know that your bodies are members of Christ himself?[w] Shall I then take the members of Christ and unite them with a prostitute? Never! 16Do you not know that he who unites himself with a prostitute is one with her in body? For it is said, "The two will become one flesh."[b][x] 17But he who unites himself with the Lord is one with him in spirit.[y]

18Flee from sexual immorality.[z] All other sins a man commits are outside his body, but he who sins sexually sins against his own body.[a] 19Do you not know that your body is a temple[b] of the Holy Spirit, who is in you, whom you have received from God? You are not your own;[c] 20you were bought at a price.[d] Therefore honour God with your body.[e]

Marriage

7 Now for the matters you wrote about: It is good for a man not to marry.[a][a] 2But since there is so much immorality, each man should have his own wife, and each woman her own

4 [e]2Th 3:6
5 [f]1Ti 1:20; [g]**Mt 4:10**; [h]**1Co 1:8**
6 [i]Jas 4:16; [j]Mt 16:6,12; [k]Gal 5:9
7 [l]Ex 12:3–6,21; Mk 14:12; 1Pe 1:19
8 [m]Ex 12:14–15; Dt 16:3
9 [n]Eph 5:11; 2Th 3:6,14
10 [o]1Co 10:27
11 [p]**Ro 7:1**; [q]1Co 10:7,14; [r]**Ro 16:17**
12 [s]**Mk 4:11**; [t]ver 3–5; 1Co 6:1–4
13 [u]Dt 13:5; 17:7; 19:19; 22:21,24; 24:7; Jdg 20:13

Ch. 6

1 [a]Mt 18:17
2 [b]Mt 19:28; Lk 22:30; 1Co 5:12
5 [c]**1Co 4:14**; [d]Ac 1:15
6 [e]**Ro 7:1**; [f]2Co 6:14–15; 1Ti 5:8
7 [g]Mt 5:39–40
8 [h]1Th 4:6
9 [i]**Mt 25:34**; [j]Job 13:9; 1Co 15:33; Gal 6:7; Jas 1:16; [k]Lev 18:20; Dt 22:22; [l]Lev 18:22
10 [m]1Ti 1:10; Rev 21:8; 22:15
11 [n]**Eph 2:2**; [o]**Ac 22:16**; [p]1Co 1:2; [q]**Ro 4:25**
12 [r]1Co 10:23
13 [s]Col 2:22; [t]ver 15,19; Ro 12:1
14 [u]**Ac 2:24**; [v]**Ro 6:5**; Eph 1:19–20; 1Th 4:16
15 [w]**Ro 12:5**
16 [x]Ge 2:24; Mt 19:5; Eph 5:31
17 [y]Jn 17:21–23; Ro 8:9–11; Gal 2:20
18 [z]ver 9; 1Co 5:1; 2Co 12:21; Gal 5:19; Eph 5:3; 1Th 4:3–4; Heb 13:4; [a]Ro 6:12
19 [b]Jn 2:21; [c]Ro 14:7–8
20 [d]Ps 74:2; **Mt 20:28**; Ac 20:28; 1Co 7:23; Rev 5:9; 14:4; [e]Php 1:20

Ch. 7

1 [a]ver 8,26

[a]5 Or *that his body;* or *that the flesh*
[b]13 Deut. 17:7; 19:19; 21:21; 22:21,24; 24:7
[a]4 Or *matters, do you appoint as judges men of little account in the church?* [b]16 Gen. 2:24
[a]1 Or *"It is good for a man not to have sexual relations with a woman."*

husband. 3The husband should fulfil his marital duty to his wife,[b] and likewise the wife to her husband. 4The wife's body does not belong to her alone but also to her husband. In the same way, the husband's body does not belong to him alone but also to his wife. 5Do not deprive each other except by mutual consent and for a time,[c] so that you may devote yourselves to prayer. Then come together again so that Satan[d] will not tempt you[e] because of your lack of self-control. 6I say this as a concession, not as a command.[f] 7I wish that all men were as I am.[g] But each man has his own gift from God; one has this gift, another has that.[h]

8Now to the unmarried and the widows I say: It is good for them to stay unmarried, as I am.[i] 9But if they cannot control themselves, they should marry,[j] for it is better to marry than to burn with passion.

10To the married I give this command (not I, but the Lord): A wife must not separate from her husband.[k] 11But if she does, she must remain unmarried or else be reconciled to her husband.[l] And a husband must not divorce his wife.

12To the rest I say this (I, not the Lord):[m] If any brother has a wife who is not a believer and she is willing to live with him, he must not divorce her. 13And if a woman has a husband who is not a believer and he is willing to live with her, she must not divorce him. 14For the unbelieving husband has been sanctified through his wife, and the unbelieving wife has been sanctified through her believing husband. Otherwise your children would be unclean, but as it is, they are holy.[n]

15But if the unbeliever leaves, let him do so. A believing man or woman is not bound in such circumstances; God has called us to live in peace.[o] 16How do you know, wife, whether you will save[p] your husband?[q] Or, how do you know, husband, whether you will save your wife?

17Nevertheless, each one should retain the place in life that the Lord assigned to him and to which God has called him.[r] This is the rule I lay down in all the churches.[s] 18Was a man already circumcised when he was called? He should not become uncircumcised. Was a man uncircumcised when he was called? He should not be circumcised.[t] 19Circumcision is nothing and uncircumcision is nothing.[u] Keeping God's commands is what counts. 20Each one should remain in the situation which he was in when God called him.[v] 21Were you a slave when you were called? Don't let it trouble you—although if you can gain your freedom, do so. 22For he who was a slave when he was called by the Lord is the Lord's freedman;[w] similarly, he who was a free man when he was called is Christ's slave.[x] 23You were bought at a price;[y] do not become slaves of men. 24Brothers, each man, as responsible to God, should remain in the situation God called him to.[z]

25Now about virgins: I have no command from the Lord,[a] but I give a judgment as one who by the Lord's mercy[b] is trustworthy. 26Because of the present crisis, I think that it is good for you to remain as you are.[c] 27Are you married? Do not seek a divorce. Are you unmarried? Do not look for a wife.[d] 28But if you do marry, you have not sinned;[e] and if a virgin marries, she has not sinned. But those who marry will face many troubles in this life, and I want to spare you this.

29What I mean, brothers, is that the time is short.[f] From now on those who have wives should live as if they had none; 30those who mourn, as if they did not; those who are happy, as if they were not; those who buy something, as if it were not theirs to keep; 31those who use the things of the world, as if not engrossed in them. For this world in its present form is passing away.[g]

32I would like you to be free from concern. An unmarried man is concerned about the Lord's affairs[h]—how he can please the Lord. 33But a married man is concerned about the affairs of this world—how he can please his wife—34and his interests are divided. An unmarried woman or virgin is concerned about the Lord's affairs: Her aim is to be devoted to the Lord in both body and spirit.[i] But a married woman is concerned about the affairs of this world—how she can please her husband. 35I am saying this for your own good, not to restrict you, but that you may live in a right way in undivided[j] devotion to the Lord.

36If anyone thinks he is acting improperly towards the virgin he is engaged to, and if she is getting on in years and he feels he ought to marry, he should do as he wants. He is not sinning.[k] They should get married. 37But the man who has settled the matter in his own mind, who is under no compulsion but has control over his own will, and who has made up his mind not to marry the virgin—this man also does

3 [b]Ex 21:10; 1Pe 3:7
5 [c]Ex 19:15; 1Sa 21:4–5; [d]**Mt 4:10**; [e]1Th 3:5
6 [f]2Co 8:8
7 [g]ver 8; 1Co 9:5; [h]Mt 19:11–12; Ro 12:6; 1Co 12:4,11
8 [i]ver 1,26
9 [j]1Ti 5:14
10 [k]Mal 2:14–16; **Lk 16:18**
11 [l]ver 39; Ro 7:2–3
12 [m]ver 6,10; 2Co 11:17
14 [n]Mal 2:15
15 [o]**Ro 14:19**; 1Co 14:33
16 [p]**Ro 11:14**; [q]1Pe 3:1
17 [r]Ro 12:3; [s]1Co 4:17; 14:33; 2Co 8:18; 11:28
18 [t]Ac 15:1–2
19 [u]Ro 2:25–27; Gal 5:6; 6:15; Col 3:11
20 [v]ver 24
22 [w]Jn 8:32,36; [x]**Ro 6:22**
23 [y]**1Co 6:20**
24 [z]ver 20
25 [a]ver 6; 2Co 8:8; [b]2Co 4:1; 1Ti 1:13,16
26 [c]ver 1,8
27 [d]ver 20–21
28 [e]ver 36
29 [f]ver 31; **Ro 13:11–12**
31 [g]ver 29; **Heb 12:27**
32 [h]1Ti 5:5
34 [i]Lk 2:37
35 [j]Ps 86:11
36 [k]ver 28

the right thing. 38So then, he who marries the virgin does right,[l] but he who does not marry her does even better.[b]

39A woman is bound to her husband as long as he lives.[m] But if her husband dies, she is free to marry anyone she wishes, but he must belong to the Lord.[n] 40In my judgment,[o] she is happier if she stays as she is—and I think that I too have the Spirit of God.

Food Sacrificed to Idols

8 Now about food sacrificed to idols:[a] We know that we all possess knowledge.[a][b] Knowledge puffs up, but love builds up. 2The man who thinks he knows something[c] does not yet know as he ought to know.[d] 3But the man who loves God is known by God.[e]

4So then, about eating food sacrificed to idols:[f] We know that an idol is nothing at all in the world[g] and that there is no God but one.[h] 5For even if there are so-called gods,[i] whether in heaven or on earth (as indeed there are many "gods" and many "lords"), 6yet for us there is but one God,[j] the Father,[k] from whom all things came[l] and for whom we live; and there is but one Lord,[m] Jesus Christ, through whom all things came[n] and through whom we live.

7But not everyone knows this.[o] Some people are still so accustomed to idols that when they eat such food they think of it as having been sacrificed to an idol, and since their conscience is weak,[p] it is defiled. 8But food does not bring us near to God;[q] we are no worse if we do not eat, and no better if we do.

9Be careful, however, that the exercise of your freedom does not become a stumbling-block[r] to the weak.[s] 10For if anyone with a weak conscience sees you who have this knowledge eating in an idol's temple, won't he be emboldened to eat what has been sacrificed to idols?[t] 11So this weak brother, for whom Christ died, is destroyed[u] by your knowledge. 12When you sin against your brothers[v] in this way and wound their weak conscience, you sin against Christ.[w] 13Therefore, if what I eat causes my brother to fall into sin, I will never eat meat again, so that I will not cause him to fall.[x]

The Rights of an Apostle

9 Am I not free?[a] Am I not an apostle?[b] Have I not seen Jesus our Lord?[c] Are you not the result of my work in the Lord?[d] 2Even though I may not be an apostle to others, surely I am to you! For you are the seal[e] of my apostleship in the Lord.

3This is my defence to those who sit in judgment on me. 4Don't we have the right to food and drink?[f] 5Don't we have the right to take a believing wife[g] along with us, as do the other apostles and the Lord's brothers[h] and Cephas?[a][i] 6Or is it only I and Barnabas[j] who must work for a living?

7Who serves as a soldier[k] at his own expense? Who plants a vineyard[l] and does not eat of its grapes? Who tends a flock and does not drink of the milk? 8Do I say this merely from a human point of view? Doesn't the Law say the same thing? 9For it is written in the Law of Moses: "Do not muzzle an ox while it is treading out the grain."[b][m] Is it about oxen that God is concerned?[n] 10Surely he says this for us, doesn't he? Yes, this was written for us,[o] because when the ploughman ploughs and the thresher threshes, they ought to do so in the hope of sharing in the harvest.[p] 11If we have sown spiritual seed among you, is it too much if we reap a material harvest from you?[q] 12If others have this right of support from you, shouldn't we have it all the more?

But we did not use this right.[r] On the contrary, we put up with anything rather than hinder[s] the gospel of Christ. 13Don't you know that those who work in the temple get their food from the temple, and those who serve at the altar share in what is offered on the altar?[t] 14In the same way, the Lord has commanded that those who preach the gospel should receive their living from the gospel.[u]

15But I have not used any of these rights.[v] And I am not writing this in the hope that you will do such things for me. I would rather die than have anyone deprive me of this boast.[w] 16Yet when I preach the gospel, I cannot boast, for I am compelled to preach.[x] Woe to me if I do not preach the gospel! 17If I preach voluntarily, I have a

38 [l]Heb 13:4
39 [m]Ro 7:2–3; [n]2Co 6:14
40 [o]ver 25

Ch. 8

1 [a]ver 4,7,10; Ac 15:20; [b]Ro 15:14
2 [c]1Co 3:18; [d]1Co 13:8–9,12; 1Ti 6:4
3 [e]Jer 1:5; Ro 8:29; Gal 4:9
4 [f]ver 1,7,10; Ex 34:15; [g]Ac 14:15; 1Co 10:19; Gal 4:8; [h]ver 6; Dt 6:4; Ps 86:10; Eph 4:6; 1Ti 2:5
5 [i]2Th 2:4
6 [j]ver 4; [k]Mal 2:10; [l]Ro 11:36; [m]Eph 4:5; [n]Jn 1:3
7 [o]ver 1; [p]Ro 14:14; 1Co 10:28
8 [q]Ro 14:17
9 [r]2Co 6:3; Gal 5:13; [s]Ro 14:1
10 [t]ver 1,4,7
11 [u]Ro 14:15,20
12 [v]Mt 18:6; [w]Mt 25:40,45
13 [x]Mt 5:29

Ch. 9

1 [a]ver 19; [b]1Co 1:1; 2Co 12:12; [c]1Co 15:8; [d]1Co 3:6; 4:15
2 [e]2Co 3:2–3
4 [f]ver 14; Ac 18:3
5 [g]1Co 7:7–8; [h]Mt 12:46; [i]1Co 1:12
6 [j]Ac 4:36
7 [k]2Ti 2:3–4; [l]Dt 20:6; Pr 27:18; 1Co 3:6,8
9 [m]Dt 25:4; 1Ti 5:18; [n]Dt 22:1–4; Pr 12:10
10 [o]Ro 4:23–24; [p]Pr 11:25; 2Ti 2:6
11 [q]ver 14; Ro 15:27; Gal 6:6
12 [r]ver 15,18; Ac 18:3; [s]2Co 6:3; 11:7–12
13 [t]Lev 6:16,26; Dt 18:1
14 [u]1Ti 5:18
15 [v]ver 12,18; Ac 18:3; [w]2Co 11:9–10
16 [x]Ro 1:14; Ac 9:15; 26:16–18

[b]*36–38* Or *36If anyone thinks he is not treating his daughter properly, and if she is getting on in years, and he feels she ought to marry, he should do as he wants. He is not sinning. He should let her get married. 37But the man who has settled the matter in his own mind, who is under no compulsion but has control over his own will, and who has made up his mind to keep the virgin unmarried—this man also does the right thing. 38So then, he who gives his virgin in marriage does right, but he who does not give her in marriage does even better.*

[a]*1* Or *"We all possess knowledge," as you say*

[a]*5* That is, Peter [b]*9* Deut. 25:4

reward;[y] if not voluntarily, I am simply discharging the trust committed to me.[z] 18What then is my reward? Just this: that in preaching the gospel I may offer it free of charge,[a] and so not make use of my rights[b] in preaching it.

19Though I am free[c] and belong to no man, I make myself a slave to everyone,[d] to win as many as possible.[e] 20To the Jews I became like a Jew, to win the Jews.[f] To those under the law I became like one under the law (though I myself am not under the law),[g] so as to win those under the law. 21To those not having the law I became like one not having the law[h] (though I am not free from God's law but am under Christ's law),[i] so as to win those not having the law. 22To the weak I became weak, to win the weak.[j] I have become all things to all men[k] so that by all possible means I might save some.[l] 23I do all this for the sake of the gospel, that I may share in its blessings.

24Do you not know that in a race all the runners run, but only one gets the prize?[m] Run[n] in such a way as to get the prize. 25Everyone who competes in the games goes into strict training. They do it to get a crown[o] that will not last; but we do it to get a crown that will last for ever.[p] 26Therefore I do not run like a man running aimlessly;[q] I do not fight like a man beating the air.[r] 27No, I beat my body[s] and make it my slave so that after I have preached to others, I myself will not be disqualified for the prize.[t]

Warnings From Israel's History

10 For I do not want you to be ignorant[a] of the fact, brothers, that our forefathers were all under the cloud[b] and that they all passed through the sea.[c] 2They were all baptised into[d] Moses in the cloud and in the sea. 3They all ate the same spiritual food[e] 4and drank the same spiritual drink; for they drank from the spiritual rock[f] that accompanied them, and that rock was Christ. 5Nevertheless, God was not pleased with most of them; their bodies were scattered over the desert.[g]

6Now these things occurred as examples[a][h] to keep us from setting our hearts on evil things as they did. 7Do not be idolaters,[i] as some of them were; as it is written: "The people sat down to eat and drink and got up to indulge in pagan revelry."[b][j] 8We should not commit sexual immorality, as some of them did—and in one day twenty-three thousand of them died.[k] 9We should not test the Lord,[l] as some of them did—and were killed by snakes.[m] 10And do not grumble, as some of them did[n]—and were killed[o] by the destroying angel.[p]

11These things happened to them as examples[q] and were written down as warnings for us,[r] on whom the fulfilment of the ages has come.[s] 12So, if you think you are standing firm,[t] be careful that you don't fall! 13No temptation has seized you except what is common to man. And God is faithful;[u] he will not let you be tempted beyond what you can bear.[v] But when you are tempted, he will also provide a way out so that you can stand up under it.

Idol Feasts and the Lord's Supper

14Therefore, my dear friends,[w] flee from idolatry.[x] 15I speak to sensible people; judge for yourselves what I say. 16Is not the cup of thanksgiving for which we give thanks a participation in the blood of Christ? And is not the bread that we break[y] a participation in the body of Christ?[z] 17Because there is one loaf, we, who are many, are one body,[a] for we all partake of the one loaf.

18Consider the people of Israel: Do not those who eat the sacrifices[b] participate in the altar? 19Do I mean then that a sacrifice offered to an idol is anything, or that an idol is anything?[c] 20No, but the sacrifices of pagans are offered to demons,[d] not to God, and I do not want you to be participants with demons. 21You cannot drink the cup of the Lord and the cup of demons too; you cannot have a part in both the Lord's table and the table of demons.[e] 22Are we trying to arouse the Lord's jealousy?[f] Are we stronger than he?[g]

The Believer's Freedom

23"Everything is permissible"—but not everything is beneficial.[h] "Everything is permissible"—but not everything is constructive. 24Nobody should seek his own good, but the good of others.[i]

25Eat anything sold in the meat market without raising questions of

17 [y]1Co 3:8,14; [z]1Co 4:1; Gal 2:7; Col 1:25
18 [a]2Co 11:7; 12:13; [b]ver 12,15
19 [c]ver 1; [d]2Co 4:5; Gal 5:13; [e]Mt 18:15; 1Pe 3:1
20 [f]Ac 16:3; 21:20–26; Ro 11:14; [g]**Ro 2:12**
21 [h]Ro 2:12,14; [i]Gal 6:2
22 [j]**Ro 14:1; 1Co 2:3;** [k]1Co 10:33; [l]**Ro 11:14**
24 [m]Php 3:14; Col 2:18; [n]ver 25–26; Gal 2:2; 5:7; Php 2:16; 2Ti 4:7; Heb 12:1
25 [o]2Ti 2:5; [p]2Ti 4:8; Jas 1:12; 1Pe 5:4; Rev 2:10; 3:11
26 [q]**ver 24;** [r]1Ti 6:12
27 [s]Ro 8:13; [t]ver 24

Ch. 10

1 [a]**Ro 11:25;** [b]Ex 13:21; Ps 105:39; [c]Ex 14:22,29; Ps 66:6
2 [d]Ro 6:3
3 [e]**Jn 6:31**
4 [f]Ex 17:6; Nu 20:11; Ps 78:15; 105:41
5 [g]Nu 14:29; Heb 3:17; Jude 5
6 [h]ver 11
7 [i]ver 14; [j]Ex 32:4,6,19
8 [k]Nu 25:1–9
9 [l]Ex 17:2; Ps 78:18; 95:9; 106:14; [m]Nu 21:5–6
10 [n]Nu 16:41; 17:5,10; [o]Nu 16:49; [p]Ex 12:23; 1Ch 21:15; Heb 11:28
11 [q]ver 6; [r]**Ro 4:24;** [s]**Ro 13:11**
12 [t]Ro 11:20; 2Co 1:24
13 [u]**1Co 1:9;** [v]2Pe 2:9
14 [w]Heb 6:9; 1Pe 2:11; 1Jn 2:7; Jude 3; [x]ver 7; 1Jn 5:21
16 [y]**Mt 14:19;** [z]Mt 26:26–28; 1Co 11:23–25
17 [a]**Ro 12:5**
18 [b]Lev 7:6, 14–15
19 [c]**1Co 8:4**
20 [d]Lev 17:7; Dt 32:17; Ps 106:37; Rev 9:20
21 [e]2Co 6:15–16
22 [f]Dt 32:16,21; 1Ki 14:22; Ps 78:58; Jer 44:8; [g]Ecc 6:10; Isa 45:9
23 [h]1Co 6:12
24 [i]ver 33; **Ro 15:1–2;** 1Co 13:5; Php 2:4,21

[a]6 Or *types;* also in verse 11 [b]7 Exodus 32:6

conscience,[j] 26for, "The earth is the Lord's, and everything in it."[c][k]

27If some unbeliever invites you to a meal and you want to go, eat whatever is put before you[l] without raising questions of conscience. 28But if anyone says to you, "This has been offered in sacrifice," then do not eat it, both for the sake of the man who told you and for conscience' sake[d][m]—29the other man's conscience, I mean, not yours. For why should my freedom[n] be judged by another's conscience? 30If I take part in the meal with thankfulness, why am I denounced because of something I thank God for?[o]

31So whether you eat or drink or whatever you do, do it all for the glory of God.[p] 32Do not cause anyone to stumble,[q] whether Jews, Greeks or the church of God[r]—33even as I try to please everybody in every way.[s] For I am not seeking my own good but the good of many,[t] so that they may be saved.[u]

11 1Follow my example,[a] as I follow the example of Christ.[b]

Propriety in Worship

2I praise you[c] for remembering me in everything[d] and for holding to the teachings,[a] just as I passed them on to you.[e]

3Now I want you to realise that the head of every man is Christ,[f] and the head of the woman is man,[g] and the head of Christ is God.[h] 4Every man who prays or prophesies[i] with his head covered dishonours his head. 5And every woman who prays or prophesies[j] with her head uncovered dishonours her head—it is just as though her head were shaved.[k] 6If a woman does not cover her head, she should have her hair cut off; and if it is a disgrace for a woman to have her hair cut or shaved off, she should cover her head. 7A man ought not to cover his head,[b] since he is the image[l] and glory of God; but the woman is the glory of man. 8For man did not come from woman, but woman from man;[m] 9neither was man created for woman, but woman for man.[n] 10For this reason, and because of the angels, the woman ought to have a sign of authority on her head.

11In the Lord, however, woman is not independent of man, nor is man independent of woman. 12For as woman came from man, so also man is born of woman. But everything comes from God.[o] 13Judge for yourselves: Is it proper for a woman to pray to God with her head uncovered? 14Does not the very nature of things teach you that if a man has long hair, it is a disgrace to him, 15but that if a woman has long hair, it is her glory? For long hair is given to her as a covering. 16If anyone wants to be contentious about this, we have no other practice—nor do the churches of God.[p]

The Lord's Supper

11:23–25pp—Mt 26:26–28; Mk 14:22–24; Lk 22:17–20

17In the following directives I have no praise for you,[q] for your meetings do more harm than good. 18In the first place, I hear that when you come together as a church, there are divisions[r] among you, and to some extent I believe it. 19No doubt there have to be differences among you to show which of you have God's approval.[s] 20When you come together, it is not the Lord's Supper you eat, 21for as you eat, each of you goes ahead without waiting for anybody else.[t] One remains hungry, another gets drunk. 22Don't you have homes to eat and drink in? Or do you despise the church of God[u] and humiliate those who have nothing?[v] What shall I say to you? Shall I praise you[w] for this? Certainly not!

23For I received from the Lord[x] what I also passed on to you:[y] The Lord Jesus, on the night he was betrayed, took bread, 24and when he had given thanks, he broke it and said, "This is my body,[z] which is for you; do this in remembrance of me." 25In the same way, after supper he took the cup, saying, "This cup is the new covenant[a] in my blood;[b] do this, whenever you drink it, in remembrance of me." 26For whenever you eat this bread and drink this cup, you proclaim the Lord's death until he comes.[c]

27Therefore, whoever eats the bread or drinks the cup of the Lord in an unworthy manner will be guilty of sinning against the body and blood of the Lord.[d] 28A man ought to examine himself[e] before he eats of the bread and drinks of the cup. 29For anyone who

25 [j]**Ac 10:15**; 1Co 8:7
26 [k]Ps 24:1; Ex 9:29; 19:5; Job 41:11; Ps 50:12; 1Ti 4:4
27 [l]Lk 10:7
28 [m]1Co 8:7, 10–12
29 [n]1Co 9:1,19
30 [o]**Ro 14:6**
31 [p]Zec 14:21; Col 3:17; 1Pe 4:11
32 [q]**Mt 5:29**; Ac 24:16; **2Co 6:3**; [r]Ac 20:28; 1Co 1:2; 11:16, 22; 15:9; 1Ti 3:5,15
33 [s]Ro 15:2; 1Co 9:22; [t]**ver 24**; [u]**Ro 11:14**

Ch. 11

1 [a]**1Co 4:16**; [b]Ro 15:3; 1Pe 2:21
2 [c]ver 17,22; [d]1Co 4:17; [e]ver 23; 1Co 15:2–3; 2Th 2:15; 3:6
3 [f]**Eph 1:22**; [g]Ge 3:16; Eph 5:23; [h]1Co 3:23
4 [i]**Ac 11:27**
5 [j]**Ac 21:9**; [k]Dt 21:12
7 [l]Ge 1:26; 5:1; 9:6; Jas 3:9
8 [m]Ge 2:21–23; 1Ti 2:13
9 [n]Ge 2:18
12 [o]**Ro 11:36**
16 [p]**1Co 7:17; 10:32**
17 [q]ver 2,22
18 [r]1Co 1:10–12; 3:3
19 [s]1Jn 2:19
21 [t]2Pe 2:13; Jude 12
22 [u]**1Co 10:32**; [v]Jas 2:6; [w]ver 2,17
23 [x]Gal 1:12; [y]**ver 2**
24 [z]1Co 10:16
25 [a]**Lk 22:20**; [b]1Co 10:16
26 [c]**1Co 1:7**
27 [d]Heb 10:29
28 [e]2Co 13:5

c26 Psalm 24:1
d28 Some manuscripts *conscience' sake, for "the earth is the Lord's and everything in it"*
a2 Or *traditions*
b4–7 Or [4]*Every man who prays or prophesies with long hair dishonours his head.* [5]*And every woman who prays or prophesies with no covering ⌊of hair⌋ on her head dishonours her head—she is just like one of the "shorn women".* [6]*If a woman has no covering, let her be for now with short hair, but since it is a disgrace for a woman to have her hair shorn or shaved, she should grow it again.* [7]*A man ought not to have long hair*

eats and drinks without recognising
the body of the Lord eats and drinks
judgment on himself. 30 That is why
many among you are weak and sick,
and a number of you have fallen asleep.[f]
31 But if we judged ourselves, we would
not come under judgment.[g] 32 When we
are judged by the Lord, we are being
disciplined[h] so that we will not be
condemned with the world.[i]
33 So then, my brothers, when you
come together to eat, wait for each
other. 34 If anyone is hungry,[j] he should
eat at home,[k] so that when you meet
together it may not result in judgment.
And when I come[l] I will give further
directions.

Spiritual Gifts

12 Now about spiritual gifts,[a]
brothers, I do not want you to
be ignorant.[b] 2 You know that when you
were pagans,[c] somehow or other you
were influenced and led astray to mute
idols.[d] 3 Therefore I tell you that no-one
who is speaking by the Spirit of God
says, "Jesus be cursed,"[e] and no-one
can say, "Jesus is Lord,"[f] except by the
Holy Spirit.[g]
4 There are different kinds of gifts, but
the same Spirit.[h] 5 There are different
kinds of service, but the same Lord.
6 There are different kinds of working,
but the same God[i] works all of them in
all men.[j]
7 Now to each one the manifestation of
the Spirit is given for the common
good.[k] 8 To one there is given through
the Spirit the message of wisdom,[l] to
another the message of knowledge[m] by
means of the same Spirit, 9 to another
faith[n] by the same Spirit, to another gifts
of healing[o] by that one Spirit, 10 to
another miraculous powers,[p] to another
prophecy,[q] to another distinguishing
between spirits,[r] to another speaking in
different kinds of tongues,[a][s] and to still
another the interpretation of tongues.[a]
11 All these are the work of one and the
same Spirit,[t] and he gives them to each
one, just as he determines.

One Body, Many Parts

12 The body is a unit, though it is made
up of many parts; and though all its
parts are many, they form one body.[u] So
it is with Christ.[v] 13 For we were all
baptised[w] by[b] one Spirit[x] into one body
—whether Jews or Greeks, slave or
free[y]—and we were all given the one
Spirit to drink.[z]
14 Now the body is not made up of one
part but of many.[a] 15 If the foot should
say, "Because I am not a hand, I do not
belong to the body," it would not for
that reason cease to be part of the body.
16 And if the ear should say, "Because I
am not an eye, I do not belong to the
body," it would not for that reason
cease to be part of the body. 17 If the
whole body were an eye, where would
the sense of hearing be? If the whole
body were an ear, where would the
sense of smell be? 18 But in fact God has
arranged[b] the parts in the body, every
one of them, just as he wanted them to
be.[c] 19 If they were all one part, where
would the body be? 20 As it is, there are
many parts, but one body.[d]
21 The eye cannot say to the hand, "I
don't need you!" And the head cannot
say to the feet, "I don't need you!" 22 On
the contrary, those parts of the body
that seem to be weaker are indispens-
able, 23 and the parts that we think are
less honourable we treat with special
honour. And the parts that are unpre-
sentable are treated with special mod-
esty, 24 while our presentable parts need
no special treatment. But God has com-
bined the members of the body and has
given greater honour to the parts that
lacked it, 25 so that there should be no
division in the body, but that its parts
should have equal concern for each
other. 26 If one part suffers, every part
suffers with it; if one part is honoured,
every part rejoices with it.
27 Now you are the body of Christ,[e]
and each one of you is a part of it.[f] 28 And
in the church[g] God has appointed first
of all apostles,[h] second prophets,[i] third
teachers, then workers of miracles, also
those having gifts of healing,[j] those able
to help others, those with gifts of
administration,[k] and those speaking in
different kinds of tongues.[l] 29 Are all
apostles? Are all prophets? Are all
teachers? Do all work miracles? 30 Do all
have gifts of healing? Do all speak in
tongues?[c][m] Do all interpret? 31 But
eagerly desire[d][n] the greater gifts.

Love

And now I will show you the most
excellent way.

13 If I speak in the tongues[a][a] of
men and of angels, but have not
love, I am only a resounding gong or a

30 [f]**Mt 9:24**
31 [g]Ps 32:5; 1Jn 1:9
32 [h]Ps 94:12; 118:18; Pr 3:11–12; Heb 12:7–10; Rev 3:19; [i]Jn 15:18–19
34 [j]ver 21; [k]ver 22; [l]**1Co 4:19**

Ch. 12

1 [a]Ro 1:11; 1Co 1:7; 14:1,37; [b]**Ro 11:25**
2 [c]**Eph 2:2;** [d]Ps 115:5; Jer 10:5; Hab 2:18–19
3 [e]Ro 9:3; 1Co 16:22; [f]**Jn 13:13;** [g]1Jn 4:2–3
4 [h]ver 8–11; Ro 12:4–8; Eph 4:11; Heb 2:4
6 [i]Eph 4:6; [j]**Php 2:13**
7 [k]1Co 14:12; Eph 4:12
8 [l]1Co 2:6; [m]**2Co 8:7**
9 [n]Mt 17:19–20; 1Co 13:2; [o]ver 28,30; Mt 10:1
10 [p]ver 28–30; Gal 3:5; [q]**Eph 4:11;** [r]1Jn 4:1; [s]**Mk 16:17**
11 [t]**ver 4**
12 [u]**Ro 12:5;** [v]ver 27
13 [w]**Mk 1:8;** [x]Eph 2:18; [y]Gal 3:28; Col 3:11; [z]Jn 7:37–39
14 [a]ver 12,20
18 [b]ver 28; [c]ver 11
20 [d]ver 12,14; **Ro 12:5**
27 [e]Eph 1:23; 4:12; Col 1:18,24; [f]**Ro 12:5**
28 [g]**1Co 10:32;** [h]**Eph 4:11;** [i]**Eph 4:11;** [j]ver 9; [k]Ro 12:6–8; [l]ver 10; **Mk 16:17**
30 [m]ver 10
31 [n]1Co 14:1,39

Ch. 13

1 [a]ver 8; **Mk 16:17**

[a]10 Or *languages;* also in verse 28
[b]13 Or *with;* or *in*
[c]30 Or *other languages*
[d]31 Or *But you are eagerly desiring*
[a]1 Or *languages*

clanging cymbal. 2If I have the gift of
prophecy[b] and can fathom all mysteries[c]
and all knowledge,[d] and if I have a faith[e]
that can move mountains,[f] but have not
love, I am nothing. 3If I give all I possess
to the poor[g] and surrender my body to
the flames,[b] [h] but have not love, I gain
nothing.
4Love is patient,[i] love is kind. It does
not envy, it does not boast, it is not
proud.[j] 5It is not rude, it is not self-
seeking,[k] it is not easily angered,[l] it
keeps no record of wrongs.[m] 6Love
does not delight in evil[n] but rejoices
with the truth.[o] 7It always protects,
always trusts, always hopes, always
perseveres.[p]
8Love never fails. But where there are
prophecies,[q] they will cease; where
there are tongues,[r] they will be stilled;
where there is knowledge, it will pass
away. 9For we know in part[s] and we
prophesy in part, 10but when perfection
comes,[t] the imperfect disappears.
11When I was a child, I talked like a
child, I thought like a child, I reasoned
like a child. When I became a man, I put
childish ways[u] behind me. 12Now we
see but a poor reflection as in a mirror;[v]
then we shall see face to face.[w] Now I
know in part; then I shall know fully,
even as I am fully known.[x]
13And now these three remain: faith,
hope and love.[y] But the greatest of these
is love.[z]

Gifts of Prophecy and Tongues

14 Follow the way of love[a] and
eagerly desire[b] spiritual gifts,[c]
especially the gift of prophecy.[d] 2For
anyone who speaks in a tongue[a] [e] does
not speak to men but to God. Indeed,
no-one understands him;[f] he utters
mysteries[g] with his spirit.[b] 3But every-
one who prophesies speaks to men for
their strengthening,[h] encouragement[i]
and comfort. 4He who speaks in a
tongue[j] edifies[k] himself, but he who
prophesies[l] edifies the church. 5I would
like every one of you to speak in
tongues,[c] but I would rather have
you prophesy.[m] He who prophesies is
greater than one who speaks in
tongues,[c] unless he interprets, so that
the church may be edified.[n]
6Now, brothers, if I come to you and
speak in tongues, what good will I be to
you, unless I bring you some revelation[o]
or knowledge[p] or prophecy or word of
instruction?[q] 7Even in the case of lifeless
things that make sounds, such as the
flute or harp, how will anyone know
what tune is being played unless there
is a distinction in the notes? 8Again, if
the trumpet does not sound a clear call,
who will get ready for battle?[r] 9So it is
with you. Unless you speak intelligible
words with your tongue, how will
anyone know what you are saying? You
will just be speaking into the air.
10Undoubtedly there are all sorts of lan-
guages in the world, yet none of them is
without meaning. 11If then I do not
grasp the meaning of what someone is
saying, I am a foreigner to the speaker,
and he is a foreigner to me.[s] 12So it is
with you. Since you are eager to have
spiritual gifts,[t] try to excel in gifts that
build up[u] the church.
13For this reason anyone who speaks
in a tongue should pray that he may
interpret what he says.[v] 14For if I pray in
a tongue, my spirit prays,[w] but my mind
is unfruitful. 15So what shall I do? I will
pray with my spirit,[x] but I will also pray
with my mind; I will sing[y] with my
spirit, but I will also sing with my mind.
16If you are praising God with your
spirit, how can one who finds himself
among those who do not understand[d]
say "Amen"[z] to your thanksgiving,[a]
since he does not know what you are
saying? 17You may be giving thanks well
enough, but the other man is not
edified.[b]
18I thank God that I speak in tongues
more than all of you. 19But in the church
I would rather speak five intelligible
words to instruct others than ten
thousand words in a tongue.[c]
20Brothers, stop thinking like chil-
dren.[d] In regard to evil be infants,[e] but in
your thinking be adults. 21In the Law[f] it
is written:

"Through men of strange tongues
and through the lips of foreigners
I will speak to this people,
but even then they will not listen to
me,"[e] [g]
says the Lord.

22Tongues, then, are a sign, not
for believers but for unbelievers;
prophecy,[h] however, is for believers,
not for unbelievers. 23So if the whole

2 [b]ver 8; **Eph 4:11; Ac 11:27;** [c]1Co 14:2; [d]**2Co 8:7;** [e]1Co 12:9; [f]Mt 17:20; 21:21
3 [g]Lk 19:8; **Ac 2:45;** [h]Da 3:28
4 [i]1Th 5:14; [j]1Co 5:2
5 [k]**1Co 10:24;** [l]**Mt 5:22;** [m]Job 14:16–17; Pr 10:12; 17:9; 1Pe 4:8
6 [n]2Th 2:12; [o]2Jn 4; 3Jn 3–4
7 [p]ver 8,13
8 [q]ver 2; [r]ver 1
9 [s]ver 12; **1Co 8:2**
10 [t]Php 3:12
11 [u]Ps 131:2
12 [v]Job 26:14; 36:26; [w]Ge 32:30; Job 19:26; 1Jn 3:2; [x]1Co 8:3; Gal 4:9
13 [y]Ro 5:2–5; Gal 5:5–6; Eph 4:2–5; Col 1:4–5; 1Th 1:3; 5:8; Heb 6:10–12; [z]Mt 22:37–40; 1Co 16:14; Gal 5:6; 1Jn 4:7–12,16

Ch. 14

1 [a]1Co 16:14; [b]ver 39; 1Co 12:31; [c]**1Co 12:1;** [d]ver 39; **Eph 4:11**
2 [e]**Mk 16:17;** [f]ver 6–11,16; [g]1Co 13:2
3 [h]ver 4–5,12, 17,26; **Ro 14:19;** [i]ver 31
4 [j]**Mk 16:17;** [k]**ver 3;** [l]**1Co 13:2**
5 [m]Nu 11:29; [n]**ver 3**
6 [o]ver 26; Eph 1:17; [p]**2Co 8:7;** [q]Ro 6:17
8 [r]Nu 10:9; Jer 4:19
11 [s]Ge 11:7
12 [t]**1Co 12:1;** [u]**ver 3**
13 [v]ver 5
14 [w]ver 2
15 [x]ver 2,14; [y]**Eph 5:19**
16 [z]Dt 27:15–26; 1Ch 16:36; Ne 8:6; Ps 106:48; Rev 5:14; 7:12; [a]**Mt 14:19;** 1Co 11:24
17 [b]**ver 3**
19 [c]ver 6
20 [d]1Co 3:11; Eph 4:14; Heb 5:12–13; 1Pe 2:2; [e]Jer 4:22; Mt 10:16; Ro 16:19
21 [f]ver 34; **Jn 10:34;** [g]Dt 28:49; Isa 28:11–12
22 [h]ver 1

[b]3 Some early manuscripts *body that I may boast*
[a]2 Or *another language;* also in verses 4, 13, 14, 19, 26 and 27 [b]2 Or *by the Spirit*
[c]5 Or *other languages;* also in verses 6, 18, 22, 23 and 39 [d]16 Or *among the enquirers*
[e]21 Isaiah 28:11,12

church comes together and everyone
speaks in tongues, and some who do
not understand[f] or some unbelievers
come in, will they not say that you are
out of your mind?[i] 24But if an unbeliever
or someone who does not understand[g]
comes in while everybody is prophesy-
ing, he will be convinced by all that he is
a sinner and will be judged by all, 25and
the secrets[j] of his heart will be laid bare.
So he will fall down and worship God,
exclaiming, "God is really among you!"[k]

Orderly Worship

26What then shall we say, brothers?[l]
When you come together, everyone[m]
has a hymn,[n] or a word of instruction,[o] a
revelation, a tongue[p] or an interpreta-
tion.[q] All of these must be done for the
strengthening[r] of the church. 27If any-
one speaks in a tongue, two—or at the
most three—should speak, one at a
time, and someone must interpret. 28If
there is no interpreter, the speaker
should keep quiet in the church and
speak to himself and God.
29Two or three prophets[s] should
speak, and the others should weigh
carefully what is said.[t] 30And if a revela-
tion comes to someone who is sitting
down, the first speaker should stop.
31For you can all prophesy in turn so
that everyone may be instructed and
encouraged. 32The spirits of prophets
are subject to the control of prophets.[u]
33For God is not a God of disorder[v] but of
peace.[w]
As in all the congregations[x] of the
saints,[y] 34women should remain silent
in the churches. They are not allowed to
speak,[z] but must be in submission,[a] as
the Law[b] says. 35If they want to enquire
about something, they should ask their
own husbands at home; for it is dis-
graceful for a woman to speak in the
church.
36Did the word of God[c] originate with
you? Or are you the only people it has
reached? 37If anybody thinks he is a
prophet[d] or spiritually gifted,[e] let him
acknowledge that what I am writing
to you is the Lord's command.[f] 38If
he ignores this, he himself will be
ignored.[h]
39Therefore, my brothers, be eager[g] to
prophesy,[h] and do not forbid speaking
in tongues. 40But everything should be
done in a fitting and orderly[i] way.

The Resurrection of Christ

15 Now, brothers, I want to re-
mind you of the gospel[a] I
preached to you,[b] which you received
and on which you have taken your
stand. 2By this gospel you are saved,[c] if
you hold firmly[d] to the word I preached
to you. Otherwise, you have believed in
vain.
3For what I received[e] I passed on to
you[f] as of first importance:[a] that Christ
died for our sins[g] according to the Scrip-
tures,[h] 4that he was buried,[i] that he was
raised[j] on the third day[k] according to the
Scriptures,[l] 5and that he appeared to
Peter,[b][m] and then to the Twelve.[n] 6After
that, he appeared to more than five
hundred of the brothers at the same
time, most of whom are still living,
though some have fallen asleep.[o] 7Then
he appeared to James,[p] then to all the
apostles,[q] 8and last of all he appeared to
me also,[r] as to one abnormally born.
9For I am the least of the apostles[s] and
do not even deserve to be called an
apostle, because I persecuted[t] the
church of God.[u] 10But by the grace[v] of
God I am what I am, and his grace to
me[w] was not without effect. No, I
worked harder than all of them[x]—yet
not I, but the grace of God that was with
me.[y] 11Whether, then, it was I or they,[z]
this is what we preach, and this is what
you believed.

The Resurrection of the Dead

12But if it is preached that Christ has
been raised from the dead,[a] how can
some of you say that there is no resur-
rection[b] of the dead?[c] 13If there is no
resurrection of the dead, then not even
Christ has been raised. 14And if Christ
has not been raised,[d] our preaching is
useless and so is your faith. 15More than
that, we are then found to be false wit-
nesses about God, for we have testified
about God that he raised Christ from the
dead.[e] But he did not raise him if in fact
the dead are not raised. 16For if the dead
are not raised, then Christ has not been
raised either. 17And if Christ has not
been raised, your faith is futile; you are
still in your sins.[f] 18Then those also who
have fallen asleep[g] in Christ are lost. 19If
only for this life we have hope in Christ,
we are to be pitied more than all men.[h]
20But Christ has indeed been raised

23 [i]Ac 2:13
25 [j]Ro 2:16; [k]Isa 45:14; Zec 8:23
26 [l]**Ro 7:1**; [m]1Co 12:7–10; [n]**Eph 5:19**; [o]ver 6; [p]ver 2; [q]1Co 12:10; [r]**Ro 14:19**
29 [s]ver 32,37; **1Co 13:2**; [t]1Co 12:10
32 [u]1Jn 4:1
33 [v]ver 40; [w]**Ro 15:33**; [x]**1Co 7:17; 10:32**; [y]**Ac 9:13**
34 [z]1Co 11:5,13; [a]**Eph 5:22**; 1Ti 2:11–12; [b]ver 21; Ge 3:16
36 [c]**Heb 4:12**
37 [d]**Ac 11:27**; 1Co 13:2; 2Co 10:7; [e]1Co 2:15; **12:1**; [f]1Jn 4:6
39 [g]ver 1; 1Co 12:31; [h]ver 1; **Eph 4:11**
40 [i]ver 33; Col 2:5

Ch. 15

1 [a]Isa 40:9; Ro 2:16; [b]**1Co 3:6; Gal 1:8**
2 [c]Ro 1:16; [d]**Ro 11:22**
3 [e]Gal 1:12; [f]**1Co 11:2**; [g]Isa 53:5; Jn 1:29; **Gal 1:4**; 1Pe 2:24; [h]**Mt 26:24; Lk 24:27; 24:44**; Ac 17:2; 26:22–23
4 [i]Mt 27:59–60; [j]**Ac 2:24**; [k]**Mt 16:21**; [l]Jn 2:21–22; Ac 2:25,30–31
5 [m]Lk 24:34; [n]Mk 16:14; Lk 24:36–43
6 [o]ver 18,20; **Mt 9:24**
7 [p]**Ac 15:13**; [q]Lk 24:33, 36–37; Ac 1:3–4
8 [r]Ac 9:3–6,17; 1Co 9:1; Gal 1:16
9 [s]2Co 12:11; Eph 3:8; 1Ti 1:15; [t]**Ac 8:3**; [u]**1Co 10:32**
10 [v]**Ro 3:24**; [w]**Ro 12:3**; [x]2Co 11:23; Col 1:29; [y]**Php 2:13**
11 [z]Gal 2:6
12 [a]ver 4; [b]**Jn 11:24**; [c]Ac 17:32; 23:8; 2Ti 2:18
14 [d]1Th 4:14 15 [e]**Ac 2:24** 17 [f]**Ro 4:25**
18 [g]ver 6,20; **Mt 9:24** 19 [h]**1Co 4:9**

[f]23 Or *some enquirers* [g]24 Or *or some enquirer*
[h]38 Some manuscripts *If he is ignorant of this, let him be ignorant*
[a]3 Or *you at the first* [b]5 Greek *Cephas*

from the dead,[i] the firstfruits[j] of those who have fallen asleep.[k] 21 For since death came through a man,[l] the resurrection of the dead[m] comes also through a man. 22 For as in Adam all die, so in Christ all will be made alive.[n] 23 But each in his own turn: Christ, the firstfruits;[o] then, when he comes,[p] those who belong to him.[q] 24 Then the end will come, when he hands over the kingdom[r] to God the Father after he has destroyed all dominion, authority and power.[s] 25 For he must reign[t] until he has put all his enemies under his feet.[u] 26 The last enemy to be destroyed is death.[v] 27 For he "has put everything under his feet".[c][w] Now when it says that "everything" has been put under him, it is clear that this does not include God himself, who put everything under Christ.[x] 28 When he has done this, then the Son himself will be made subject to him who put everything under him,[y] so that God may be all in all.[z]

29 Now if there is no resurrection, what will those do who are baptised for the dead? If the dead are not raised at all, why are people baptised for them? 30 And as for us, why do we endanger ourselves every hour?[a] 31 I die every day[b]—I mean that, brothers—just as surely as I glory over you in Christ Jesus our Lord. 32 If I fought wild beasts[c] in Ephesus[d] for merely human reasons, what have I gained? If the dead are not raised,

"Let us eat and drink,
for tomorrow we die."[d][e]

33 Do not be misled:[f] "Bad company corrupts good character."[g] 34 Come back to your senses as you ought, and stop sinning; for there are some who are ignorant of God[h]—I say this to your shame.[i]

The Resurrection Body

35 But someone may ask,[j] "How are the dead raised? With what kind of body will they come?"[k] 36 How foolish![l] What you sow does not come to life unless it dies.[m] 37 When you sow, you do not plant the body that will be, but just a seed, perhaps of wheat or of something else. 38 But God gives it a body as he has determined, and to each kind of seed he gives its own body.[n] 39 All flesh is not the same: Men have one kind of flesh, animals have another, birds another and fish another. 40 There are also heavenly bodies and there are earthly bodies; but the splendour of the heavenly bodies is one kind, and the splendour of the earthly bodies is another. 41 The sun has one kind of splendour,[o] the moon another and the stars another;[p] and star differs from star in splendour.

42 So will it be[q] with the resurrection of the dead.[r] The body that is sown is perishable, it is raised imperishable;[s] 43 it is sown in dishonour, it is raised in glory;[t] it is sown in weakness, it is raised in power; 44 it is sown a natural body, it is raised a spiritual body.[u]

If there is a natural body, there is also a spiritual body. 45 So it is written: "The first man Adam became a living being";[e][v] the last Adam,[w] a life-giving spirit.[x] 46 The spiritual did not come first, but the natural, and after that the spiritual.[y] 47 The first man was of the dust of the earth,[z] the second man from heaven.[a] 48 As was the earthly man, so are those who are of the earth; and as is the man from heaven, so also are those who are of heaven.[b] 49 And just as we have borne the likeness of the earthly man,[c] so shall we[f] bear the likeness of the man from heaven.[d]

50 I declare to you, brothers, that flesh and blood[e] cannot inherit the kingdom of God,[f] nor does the perishable inherit the imperishable.[g] 51 Listen, I tell you a mystery:[h] We will not all sleep,[i] but we will all be changed[j]—52 in a flash, in the twinkling of an eye, at the last trumpet. For the trumpet will sound,[k] the dead[l] will be raised imperishable, and we will be changed. 53 For the perishable[m] must clothe itself with the imperishable,[n] and the mortal with immortality. 54 When the perishable has been clothed with the imperishable, and the mortal with immortality, then the saying that is written will come true: "Death has been swallowed up in victory."[g][o]

55 "Where, O death, is your victory?
Where, O death, is your sting?"[h][p]

56 The sting of death is sin,[q] and the power of sin is the law.[r] 57 But thanks be to God![s] He gives us the victory through our Lord Jesus Christ.[t]

58 Therefore, my dear brothers, stand firm. Let nothing move you. Always give yourselves fully to the work of the Lord,[u] because you know that your labour in the Lord is not in vain.[v]

20 [i]1Pe 1:3; [j]ver 23; **Ac 26:23;** [k]ver 6,18; **Mt 9:24**
21 [l]**Ro 5:12;** [m]ver 12
22 [n]Ro 5:14–18; **1Co 6:14**
23 [o]ver 20; [p]ver 52; **1Th 2:19;** [q]**1Co 3:23**
24 [r]Da 2:44; 7:14,27; 2Pe 1:11; [s]Ro 8:38
25 [t]Isa 9:7; 52:7; [u]ver 27; **Mt 22:44**
26 [v]2Ti 1:10; Rev 20:14; 21:4
27 [w]ver 25; Ps 8:6; **Mt 22:44;** [x]**Mt 28:18**
28 [y]Php 3:21; [z]1Co 3:23
30 [a]2Co 11:26
31 [b]**Ro 8:36**
32 [c]2Co 1:8; [d]**Ac 18:19;** [e]Isa 22:13; Lk 12:19
33 [f]**1Co 6:9;** [g]Pr 22:24–25
34 [h]**Gal 4:8;** [i]**1Co 4:14**
35 [j]Ro 9:19; [k]Eze 37:3
36 [l]Lk 11:40; 12:20; [m]Jn 12:24
38 [n]Ge 1:11
41 [o]Ps 19:4–6; [p]Ps 8:1,3
42 [q]Da 12:3; Mt 13:43; [r]ver 12; [s]ver 50,53–54
43 [t]Php 3:21; Col 3:4
44 [u]ver 50
45 [v]Ge 2:7; [w]Ro 5:14; [x]Jn 5:21; 6:57–58; Ro 8:2
46 [y]ver 44
47 [z]Ge 2:7; 3:19; Ps 90:3; [a]Jn 3:13,31
48 [b]Php 3:20–21
49 [c]Ge 5:3; [d]**Ro 8:29**
50 [e]Eph 6:12; Heb 2:14; [f]**Mt 25:34;** [g]ver 42,53–54
51 [h]1Co 13:2; 14:2; [i]**Mt 9:24;** [j]2Co 5:4; Php 3:21
52 [k]**Mt 24:31;** [l]Jn 5:25
53 [m]ver 42,50,54; [n]2Co 5:2,4
54 [o]Isa 25:8; Heb 2:14; Rev 20:14
55 [p]Hos 13:14
56 [q]**Ro 5:12;** [r]**Ro 4:15**
57 [s]**2Co 2:14;** [t]Ro 8:37; Heb 2:14–15
58 [u]1Co 16:10; [v]Isa 65:23

[c]27 Psalm 8:6 [d]32 Isaiah 22:13
[e]45 Gen. 2:7
[f]49 Some early manuscripts *so let us*
[g]54 Isaiah 25:8 [h]55 Hosea 13:14

The Collection for God's People

16 Now about the collection[a] for
God's people:[b] Do what I told
the Galatian[c] churches to do. 2On the
first day of every week,[d] each one of you
should set aside a sum of money in
keeping with his income, saving it up,
so that when I come no collections will
have to be made.[e] 3Then, when I arrive,
I will give letters of introduction to the
men you approve[f] and send them with
your gift to Jerusalem. 4If it seems
advisable for me to go also, they will
accompany me.

Personal Requests

5After I go through Macedonia, I will
come to you[g]—for I will be going
through Macedonia.[h] 6Perhaps I will
stay with you awhile, or even spend the
winter, so that you can help me on my
journey,[i] wherever I go. 7I do not want
to see you now and make only a passing
visit; I hope to spend some time with
you, if the Lord permits.[j] 8But I will
stay on at Ephesus[k] until Pentecost,[l]
9because a great door for effective work
has opened to me,[m] and there are many
who oppose me.

10If Timothy[n] comes, see to it that he
has nothing to fear while he is with you,
for he is carrying on the work of the
Lord,[o] just as I am. 11No-one, then,
should refuse to accept him.[p] Send him
on his way[q] in peace[r] so that he may
return to me. I am expecting him along
with the brothers.

12Now about our brother Apollos:[s] I
strongly urged him to go to you with the
brothers. He was quite unwilling to go
now, but he will go when he has the
opportunity.

13Be on your guard; stand firm[t] in the
faith; be men of courage; be strong.[u]
14Do everything in love.[v]

15You know that the household of
Stephanas[w] were the first converts[x] in
Achaia,[y] and they have devoted them-
selves to the service[z] of the saints.[a] I
urge you, brothers, 16to submit[b] to such
as these and to everyone who joins in
the work, and labours at it. 17I was
glad when Stephanas, Fortunatus
and Achaicus arrived, because they
have supplied what was lacking from
you.[c] 18For they refreshed[d] my spirit
and yours also. Such men deserve
recognition.[e]

Final Greetings

19The churches in the province of
Asia[f] send you greetings. Aquila and
Priscilla[a][g] greet you warmly in the Lord,
and so does the church that meets at
their house.[h] 20All the brothers here
send you greetings. Greet one another
with a holy kiss.[i]

21I, Paul, write this greeting in my
own hand.[j]

22If anyone does not love the Lord[k]
—a curse[l] be on him. Come, O Lord![b][m]

23The grace of the Lord Jesus be with
you.[n]

24My love to all of you in Christ Jesus.
Amen.[c]

Ch. 16

1 [a]**Ac 24:17;** [b]**Ac 9:13;** [c]**Ac 16:6**
2 [d]Ac 20:7; [e]2Co 9:4–5
3 [f]2Co 3:1; 8:18–19
5 [g]**1Co 4:19;** [h]**Ac 16:9**
6 [i]Ro 15:24; Tit 3:13
7 [j]**Ac 18:21**
8 [k]**Ac 18:19;** [l]**Ac 2:1**
9 [m]**Ac 14:27**
10 [n]**Ac 16:1;** [o]1Co 15:58
11 [p]1Ti 4:12; [q]2Co 1:16; 3Jn 6; [r]**Ac 15:33**
12 [s]**Ac 18:24**
13 [t]1Co 1:8; 2Co 1:21; Gal 5:1; Php 1:27; 1Th 3:8; **Tit 1:9;** [u]**Eph 6:10**
14 [v]1Co 14:1
15 [w]1Co 1:16; [x]Ro 16:5; [y]**Ac 18:12;** [z]**Ac 24:17;** [a]**Ac 9:13**
16 [b]1Th 5:12; Heb 13:17
17 [c]2Co 11:9; Php 2:30
18 [d]Ro 15:32; Phm 7; [e]Php 2:29
19 [f]**Ac 2:9;** [g]**Ac 18:2;** [h]**Ro 16:5**
20 [i]**Ro 16:16**
21 [j]Gal 6:11; Col 4:18; 2Th 3:17; Phm 19
22 [k]Eph 6:24; [l]Ro 9:3; [m]Rev 22:20
23 [n]**Ro 16:20**

a19 Greek *Prisca,* a variant of *Priscilla*
b22 In Aramaic the expression *Come, O Lord* is *Marana tha.*
c24 Some manuscripts do not have *Amen.*

2 Corinthians

1 Paul, an apostle[a] of Christ Jesus by
the will of God,[b] and Timothy[c] our
brother,

To the church of God[d] in Corinth,[e]
together with all the saints throughout
Achaia:[f]

2Grace and peace to you from God our
Father and the Lord Jesus Christ.[g]

The God of All Comfort

3Praise be to the God and Father of
our Lord Jesus Christ,[h] the Father of
compassion and the God of all comfort,
4who comforts us[i] in all our troubles, so
that we can comfort those in any trouble
with the comfort we ourselves have re-
ceived from God. 5For just as the suffer-
ings of Christ flow over into our lives,[j]
so also through Christ our comfort over-
flows. 6If we are distressed, it is for your
comfort and salvation;[k] if we are com-
forted, it is for your comfort, which
produces in you patient endurance of
the same sufferings we suffer. 7And our
hope for you is firm, because we know
that just as you share in our sufferings,[l]
so also you share in our comfort.

8We do not want you to be unin-
formed,[m] brothers, about the hardships
we suffered[n] in the province of Asia.[o]
We were under great pressure, far
beyond our ability to endure, so that we
despaired even of life. 9Indeed, in our
hearts we felt the sentence of death. But
this happened that we might not rely on
ourselves but on God,[p] who raises the
dead.[q] 10He has delivered us from such a
deadly peril,[r] and he will deliver us. On
him we have set our hope[s] that he will
continue to deliver us, 11as you help us
by your prayers.[t] Then many will give
thanks[u] on our[a] behalf for the gracious
favour granted us in answer to the
prayers of many.

Paul's Change of Plans

12Now this is our boast: Our con-
science[v] testifies that we have con-
ducted ourselves in the world, and
especially in our relations with you, in
the holiness[w] and sincerity[x] that are
from God. We have done so not accord-
ing to worldly wisdom[y] but according to
God's grace. 13For we do not write to
you anything you cannot read or under-
stand. And I hope that, 14as you have
understood us in part, you will come to
understand fully that you can boast of
us just as we will boast of you in the day
of the Lord Jesus.[z]

15Because I was confident of this, I
planned to visit you[a] first so that you
might benefit twice.[b] 16I planned to visit
you on my way[c] to Macedonia[d] and to
come back to you from Macedonia, and
then to have you send me on my way[e] to
Judea.[f] 17When I planned this, did I do it
lightly? Or do I make my plans in a
worldly manner[g] so that in the same
breath I say, "Yes, yes" and "No, no"?

18But as surely as God is faithful,[h] our
message to you is not "Yes" and "No".
19For the Son of God,[i] Jesus Christ, who
was preached among you by me and
Silas[b][j] and Timothy,[k] was not "Yes"
and "No", but in him it has always[l] been
"Yes". 20For no matter how many prom-
ises[m] God has made, they are "Yes" in
Christ. And so through him the
"Amen"[n] is spoken by us to the glory of
God.[o] 21Now it is God who makes both
us and you stand firm[p] in Christ. He
anointed[q] us, 22set his seal[r] of owner-
ship on us, and put his Spirit in our
hearts as a deposit, guaranteeing what
is to come.[s]

23I call God as my witness[t] that it was
in order to spare you[u] that I did not
return to Corinth. 24Not that we lord it
over[v] your faith, but we work with you
for your joy, because it is by faith you

2 stand firm.[w] 1So I made up my
mind that I would not make
another painful visit to you.[a] 2For if I
grieve you,[b] who is left to make me glad

Ch. 1

1 [a]**1Co 1:1;** [b]1Co 1:1; Eph 1:1; Col 1:1; 2Ti 1:1; [c]**Ac 16:1;** [d]**1Co 10:32;** [e]**Ac 18:1;** [f]**Ac 18:12**
2 [g]**Ro 1:7**
3 [h]Eph 1:3; 1Pe 1:3
4 [i]Isa 49:13; 51:12; 66:13; 2Co 7:6–7,13
5 [j]Ro 8:17; 2Co 4:10; Gal 6:17; Php 3:10; Col 1:24; 1Pe 4:13
6 [k]2Co 4:15
7 [l]**ver 5**
8 [m]**Ro 11:25;** [n]1Co 15:32; [o]**Ac 2:9**
9 [p]Jer 17:5,7; [q]**Jn 5:21**
10 [r]**Ro 15:31;** [s]1Ti 4:10
11 [t]Ro 15:30; Php 1:19; [u]2Co 4:15; 9:11
12 [v]**Ac 23:1;** [w]1Th 2:10; [x]2Co 2:17; [y]1Co 1:17; 2:1,4,13
14 [z]**1Co 1:8**
15 [a]**1Co 4:19;** [b]Ro 1:11,13; 15:29
16 [c]1Co 16:5–7; [d]**Ac 16:9;** [e]1Co 16:11; 3Jn 6; [f]Ac 19:21
17 [g]2Co 10:2–3; 11:18
18 [h]**1Co 1:9**
19 [i]**Mt 4:3;** [j]**Ac 15:22;** [k]**Ac 16:1;** [l]Heb 13:8
20 [m]Ro 15:8; [n]**1Co 14:16;** [o]Ro 15:9
21 [p]**1Co 16:13;** [q]1Jn 2:20,27
22 [r]Ge 38:18; Eze 9:4; Hag 2:23; [s]**2Co 5:5**
23 [t]**Ro 1:9;** [u]1Co 4:21; 2Co 2:1,3; 13:2,10
24 [v]1Pe 5:3; [w]Ro 11:20; 1Co 15:1

Ch. 2

1 [a]**2Co 1:23** 2 [b]2Co 7:8

[a]*11* Many manuscripts *your*
[b]*19* Greek *Silvanus*, a variant of *Silas*

but you whom I have grieved? 3I wrote as I did[c] so that when I came I should not be distressed[d] by those who ought to make me rejoice. I had confidence[e] in all of you, that you would all share my joy. 4For I wrote to you[f] out of great distress and anguish of heart and with many tears, not to grieve you but to let you know the depth of my love for you.

Forgiveness for the Sinner

5If anyone has caused grief,[g] he has not so much grieved me as he has grieved all of you, to some extent—not to put it too severely. 6The punishment[h] inflicted on him by the majority is sufficient for him. 7Now instead, you ought to forgive and comfort him,[i] so that he will not be overwhelmed by excessive sorrow. 8I urge you, therefore, to reaffirm your love for him. 9The reason I wrote to you[j] was to see if you would stand the test and be obedient in everything.[k] 10If you forgive anyone, I also forgive him. And what I have forgiven—if there was anything to forgive—I have forgiven in the sight of Christ for your sake, 11in order that Satan[l] might not outwit us. For we are not unaware of his schemes.[m]

Ministers of the New Covenant

12Now when I went to Troas[n] to preach the gospel of Christ[o] and found that the Lord had opened a door[p] for me, 13I still had no peace of mind,[q] because I did not find my brother Titus[r] there. So I said good-bye to them and went on to Macedonia.[s]

14But thanks be to God,[t] who always leads us in triumphal procession in Christ and through us spreads everywhere the fragrance[u] of the knowledge[v] of him. 15For we are to God the aroma[w] of Christ among those who are being saved and those who are perishing.[x] 16To the one we are the smell of death;[y] to the other, the fragrance of life. And who is equal to such a task?[z] 17Unlike so many, we do not peddle the word of God for profit.[a] On the contrary, in Christ we speak before God with sincerity,[b] like men sent from God.[c]

3 Are we beginning to commend ourselves[a] again? Or do we need, like some people, letters of recommendation[b] to you or from you? 2You yourselves are our letter, written on our hearts, known and read by everybody.[c] 3You show that you are a letter from Christ, the result of our ministry, written not with ink but with the Spirit of the living God,[d] not on tablets of stone[e] but on tablets of human hearts.[f]

4Such confidence[g] as this is ours through Christ before God. 5Not that we are competent in ourselves[h] to claim anything for ourselves, but our competence comes from God.[i] 6He has made us competent as ministers of a new covenant[j]—not of the letter[k] but of the Spirit; for the letter kills, but the Spirit gives life.[l]

The Glory of the New Covenant

7Now if the ministry that brought death,[m] which was engraved in letters on stone, came with glory, so that the Israelites could not look steadily at the face of Moses because of its glory,[n] fading though it was, 8will not the ministry of the Spirit be even more glorious? 9If the ministry that condemns men[o] is glorious, how much more glorious is the ministry that brings righteousness![p] 10For what was glorious has no glory now in comparison with the surpassing glory. 11And if what was fading away came with glory, how much greater is the glory of that which lasts!

12Therefore, since we have such a hope,[q] we are very bold.[r] 13We are not like Moses, who would put a veil over his face[s] to keep the Israelites from gazing at it while the radiance was fading away. 14But their minds were made dull,[t] for to this day the same veil remains when the old covenant[u] is read.[v] It has not been removed, because only in Christ is it taken away. 15Even to this day when Moses is read, a veil covers their hearts. 16But whenever anyone turns to the Lord,[w] the veil is taken away.[x] 17Now the Lord is the Spirit,[y] and where the Spirit of the Lord is, there is freedom.[z] 18And we, who with unveiled faces all reflect[a][a] the Lord's glory,[b] are being transformed into his likeness[c] with ever-increasing glory, which comes from the Lord, who is the Spirit.

Treasures in Jars of Clay

4 Therefore, since through God's mercy[a] we have this ministry, we do not lose heart.[b] 2Rather, we have

3 [c]ver 4,9; 2Co 7:8,12; [d]2Co 12:21; [e]2Co 7:16; 8:22; Gal 5:10; 2Th 3:4; Phm 21
4 [f]ver 3,9; 2Co 7:8,12
5 [g]1Co 5:1–2
6 [h]1Co 5:4–5; 2Co 7:11
7 [i]Gal 6:1; Eph 4:32; Col 3:13
9 [j]ver 3–4; 2Co 7:8,12; [k]2Co 7:15; 10:6
11 [l]**Mt 4:10**; [m]Lk 22:31; 2Co 4:4; 1Pe 5:8–9
12 [n]**Ac 16:8**; [o]**Ro 1:1**; 2Co 4:3–4; 8:18; 9:13; 1Th 3:2; [p]**Ac 14:27**
13 [q]2Co 7:5; [r]2Co 7:6,13; 8:6,16,23; 12:18; Gal 2:1,3; Tit 1:4; [s]**Ac 16:9**
14 [t]Ro 6:17; 7:25; 1Co 15:57; 2Co 9:15; [u]Eze 20:41; Eph 5:2; Php 4:18; [v]**2Co 8:7**
15 [w]**ver 14**; Ge 8:21; Ex 29:18; Nu 15:3; [x]**1Co 1:18**
16 [y]**Lk 2:34**; Jn 3:36; [z]2Co 3:5–6
17 [a]**Ac 20:33**; 2Co 4:2; 1Th 2:5; [b]1Co 5:8; [c]2Co 1:12; 12:19

Ch. 3

1 [a]Ro 16:1; 2Co 5:12; 10:12, 18; 12:11; [b]Ac 18:27; Ro 16:1; 1Co 16:3
2 [c]1Co 9:2
3 [d]**Mt 16:16**; [e]ver 7; Ex 24:12; 31:18; 32:15–16; [f]Pr 3:3; 7:3; Jer 31:33; Eze 36:26
4 [g]**Eph 3:12**
5 [h]2Co 2:16; [i]1Co 15:10
6 [j]**Lk 22:20**; [k]Ro 2:29; 7:6; [l]Jn 6:63
7 [m]ver 9; **Ro 4:15**; [n]ver 13; Ex 34:29–35; Isa 42:21
9 [o]ver 7; Dt 27:26; [p]Ro 1:17; 3:21–22
12 [q]Ro 5:4–5; 8:24–25; [r]**Ac 4:29**
13 [s]ver 7; Ex 34:33
14 [t]Ro 11:7–8; 2Co 4:4; [u]Ac 13:15; 15:21; [v]ver 6
16 [w]Ro 11:23; [x]Ex 34:34; Isa 25:7
17 [y]Isa 61:1–2; Gal 4:6–7; [z]**Jn 8:32**
18 [a]1Co 13:12; [b]Jn 17:22,24; 2Co 4:4,6; [c]**Ro 8:29**

Ch. 4

1 [a]1Co 7:25; 1Ti 1:13,16; [b]ver 16; Ps 18:45; Isa 40:31

[a]18 Or *contemplate*

renounced secret and shameful ways;[c]
we do not use deception, nor do we
distort the word of God.[d] On the con-
trary, by setting forth the truth plainly
we commend ourselves to every man's
conscience[e] in the sight of God. 3And
even if our gospel[f] is veiled,[g] it is veiled
to those who are perishing.[h] 4The god[i]
of this age[j] has blinded[k] the minds of
unbelievers, so that they cannot see the
light of the gospel of the glory of Christ,[l]
who is the image of God.[m] 5For we do
not preach ourselves,[n] but Jesus Christ
as Lord,[o] and ourselves as your ser-
vants[p] for Jesus' sake. 6For God, who
said, "Let light shine out of darkness,"[a][q]
made his light shine in our hearts[r] to
give us the light of the knowledge of the
glory of God in the face of Christ.[s]

7But we have this treasure in jars of
clay[t] to show that this all-surpassing
power is from God[u] and not from us.
8We are hard pressed on every side,[v] but
not crushed; perplexed,[w] but not in
despair; 9persecuted,[x] but not aban-
doned;[y] struck down, but not des-
troyed.[z] 10We always carry around in
our body the death of Jesus,[a] so that the
life of Jesus may also be revealed in our
body.[b] 11For we who are alive are always
being given over to death for Jesus'
sake,[c] so that his life may be revealed in
our mortal body. 12So then, death is at
work in us, but life is at work in you.[d]

13It is written: "I believed; therefore I
have spoken."[b][e] With that same spirit
of faith[f] we also believe and therefore
speak, 14because we know that the one
who raised the Lord Jesus from the
dead[g] will also raise us with Jesus[h] and
present us with you in his presence.[i]
15All this is for your benefit, so that the
grace that is reaching more and more
people may cause thanksgiving[j] to over-
flow to the glory of God.

16Therefore we do not lose heart.[k]
Though outwardly we are wasting
away, yet inwardly[l] we are being re-
newed[m] day by day. 17For our light and
momentary troubles are achieving for
us an eternal glory that far outweighs
them all.[n] 18So we fix our eyes not on
what is seen, but on what is unseen.[o]
For what is seen is temporary, but what
is unseen is eternal.

Our Heavenly Dwelling

5 Now we know that if the earthly[a]
tent[b] we live in is destroyed, we
have a building from God, an eternal
house in heaven, not built by human
hands. 2Meanwhile we groan,[c] longing
to be clothed with our heavenly dwell-
ing,[d] 3because when we are clothed, we
will not be found naked. 4For while we
are in this tent, we groan[e] and are bur-
dened, because we do not wish to be
unclothed but to be clothed with our
heavenly dwelling,[f] so that what is mor-
tal may be swallowed up by life. 5Now it
is God who has made us for this very
purpose and has given us the Spirit as a
deposit, guaranteeing what is to come.[g]

6Therefore we are always confident
and know that as long as we are at home
in the body we are away from the Lord.
7We live by faith, not by sight.[h] 8We are
confident, I say, and would prefer to be
away from the body and at home with
the Lord.[i] 9So we make it our goal to
please him,[j] whether we are at home in
the body or away from it. 10For we must
all appear before the judgment seat of
Christ, that each one may receive what
is due to him[k] for the things done while
in the body, whether good or bad.

The Ministry of Reconciliation

11Since, then, we know what it is to
fear the Lord,[l] we try to persuade men.
What we are is plain to God, and I hope
it is also plain to your conscience.[m] 12We
are not trying to commend ourselves to
you again,[n] but are giving you an oppor-
tunity to take pride in us,[o] so that you
can answer those who take pride in
what is seen rather than in what is in the
heart. 13If we are out of our mind,[p] it is
for the sake of God; if we are in our right
mind, it is for you. 14For Christ's love
compels us, because we are convinced
that one died for all, and therefore all
died.[q] 15And he died for all, that those
who live should no longer live for them-
selves[r] but for him who died for them[s]
and was raised again.

16So from now on we regard no-one
from a worldly[t] point of view. Though
we once regarded Christ in this way, we
do so no longer. 17Therefore, if anyone
is in Christ,[u] he is a new creation;[v] the
old has gone, the new has come![w] 18All
this is from God,[x] who reconciled us to
himself through Christ[y] and gave us the
ministry of reconciliation: 19that God
was reconciling the world to himself in
Christ, not counting men's sins against

2 [c]Ro 6:21; **1Co 4:5**; [d]2Co 2:17; **Heb 4:12**; [e]2Co 5:11
3 [f]**2Co 2:12**; [g]2Co 3:14; [h]**1Co 1:18**
4 [i]**Jn 12:31**; [j]**1Co 1:20**; [k]2Co 3:14; [l]ver 6; [m]**Jn 14:9**
5 [n]1Co 1:13; [o]1Co 1:23; [p]1Co 9:19
6 [q]Ge 1:3; Ps 18:28; [r]2Pe 1:19; [s]ver 4
7 [t]Job 4:19; Isa 64:8; 2Ti 2:20; [u]Jdg 7:2; 1Co 2:5; 2Co 6:7
8 [v]2Co 7:5; [w]Gal 4:20
9 [x]Jn 15:20; Ro 8:35; [y]Heb 13:5; [z]Ps 37:24; Pr 24:16
10 [a]**Ro 6:6; 2Co 1:5**; [b]**Ro 6:5**
11 [c]Ro 8:36
12 [d]2Co 13:9
13 [e]Ps 116:10; [f]1Co 12:9
14 [g]**Ac 2:24**; [h]1Th 4:14; [i]Eph 5:27; Col 1:22; Jude 24
15 [j]2Co 1:11; 9:11
16 [k]ver 1; Ps 18:45; [l]Ro 7:22; [m]Ps 103:5; Isa 40:31; Col 3:10
17 [n]Ps 30:5; Ro 8:18; 1Pe 1:6–7
18 [o]2Co 5:7; Ro 8:24; Heb 11:1

Ch. 5

1 [a]1Co 15:47; [b]Isa 38:12; 2Pe 1:13–14
2 [c]ver 4; Ro 8:23; [d]ver 4; 1Co 15:53–54
4 [e]ver 2; Ro 8:23; [f]ver 2; 1Co 15:53–54
5 [g]Ro 8:23; 2Co 1:22; Eph 1:13–14
7 [h]1Co 13:12; **2Co 4:18**
8 [i]**Jn 12:26**
9 [j]Ro 14:18; Eph 5:10; Col 1:10; 1Th 4:1
10 [k]**Mt 16:27**; Ac 10:42; Ro 2:16; 14:10; Eph 6:8
11 [l]Job 23:15; Heb 10:31; 12:29; Jude 23; [m]2Co 4:2
12 [n]**2Co 3:1**; [o]2Co 1:14
13 [p]2Co 11:1,16–17; 12:11
14 [q]Ro 6:6–7; Gal 2:20; Col 3:3
15 [r]Ro 14:7–9; [s]Ro 4:25
16 [t]2Co 10:4; 11:18
17 [u]**Ro 16:3**; [v]**Jn 1:13**; **Ro 6:4**; Gal 6:15; [w]Isa 65:17; Rev 21:4–5
18 [x]**Ro 11:36**; [y]**Ro 5:10**

[a]*6* Gen. 1:3 [b]*13* Psalm 116:10

them.[z] And he has committed to us the message of reconciliation. 20We are therefore Christ's ambassadors,[a] as though God were making his appeal through us.[b] We implore you on Christ's behalf: Be reconciled to God.[c] 21God made him who had no sin[d] to be sin[a] for us, so that in him we might become the righteousness of God.[e]

6 As God's fellow-workers[a] we urge you not to receive God's grace in vain.[b] 2For he says,

"In the time of my favour I heard you,
and in the day of salvation I helped you."[a c]

I tell you, now is the time of God's favour, now is the day of salvation.

Paul's Hardships

3We put no stumbling-block in anyone's path,[d] so that our ministry will not be discredited. 4Rather, as servants of God we commend ourselves in every way: in great endurance; in troubles, hardships and distresses; 5in beatings, imprisonments[e] and riots; in hard work, sleepless nights and hunger;[f] 6in purity, understanding, patience and kindness; in the Holy Spirit[g] and in sincere love;[h] 7in truthful speech[i] and in the power of God;[j] with weapons of righteousness[k] in the right hand and in the left; 8through glory and dishonour,[l] bad report[m] and good report; genuine, yet regarded as impostors;[n] 9known, yet regarded as unknown; dying,[o] and yet we live on;[p] beaten, and yet not killed; 10sorrowful, yet always rejoicing;[q] poor, yet making many rich;[r] having nothing,[s] and yet possessing everything.[t]

11We have spoken freely to you, Corinthians, and opened wide our hearts to you.[u] 12We are not withholding our affection from you, but you are withholding yours from us. 13As a fair exchange—I speak as to my children[v] —open wide your hearts[w] also.

Do Not Be Yoked With Unbelievers

14Do not be yoked together[x] with unbelievers.[y] For what do righteousness and wickedness have in common? Or what fellowship can light have with darkness?[z] 15What harmony is there between Christ and Belial[b]?[a] What does a believer[b] have in common with an unbeliever?[c] 16What agreement is there between the temple of God and idols?[d] For we are the temple[e] of the living God.[f] As God has said: "I will live with them and walk among them, and I will be their God, and they will be my people."[c g]

17"Therefore come out from them[h]
and be separate,
says the Lord.
Touch no unclean thing,
and I will receive you."[d i]
18"I will be a Father to you,
and you will be my sons and daughters,[j]
says the Lord Almighty."[e k]

7 Since we have these promises,[a] dear friends,[b] let us purify ourselves from everything that contaminates body and spirit, perfecting holiness[c] out of reverence for God.

Paul's Joy

2Make room for us in your hearts.[d] We have wronged no-one, we have corrupted no-one, we have exploited no-one. 3I do not say this to condemn you; I have said before that you have such a place in our hearts[e] that we would live or die with you. 4I have great confidence in you; I take great pride in you.[f] I am greatly encouraged;[g] in all our troubles my joy knows no bounds.[h]

5For when we came into Macedonia,[i] this body of ours had no rest, but we were harassed at every turn[j]—conflicts on the outside, fears within.[k] 6But God, who comforts the downcast,[l] comforted us by the coming of Titus,[m] 7and not only by his coming but also by the comfort you had given him. He told us about your longing for me, your deep sorrow, your ardent concern for me, so that my joy was greater than ever.

8Even if I caused you sorrow by my letter,[n] I do not regret it. Though I did regret it—I see that my letter hurt you, but only for a little while—9yet now I am happy, not because you were made sorry, but because your sorrow led you to repentance. For you became sorrowful as God intended and so were not harmed in any way by us. 10Godly sorrow brings repentance that leads to salvation[o] and leaves no regret, but worldly sorrow brings death. 11See what

19 [z]**Ro 4:8**
20 [a]2Co 6:1; Eph 6:20; [b]ver 18; [c]Isa 27:5
21 [d]Heb 4:15; 7:26; 1Pe 2:22,24; 1Jn 3:5; [e]**Ro 1:17; 1Co 1:30**

Ch. 6

1 [a]**1Co 3:9**; 2Co 5:20; [b]1Co 15:2
2 [c]Isa 49:8; Ps 69:13; Isa 55:6
3 [d]**Mt 5:29**; Ro 14:13,20; 1Co 8:9,13; 9:12; 10:32
5 [e]Ac 16:23; 2Co 11:23–25; [f]1Co 4:11
6 [g]1Co 2:4; 1Th 1:5; [h]Ro 12:9; 1Ti 1:5
7 [i]2Co 4:2; [j]2Co 4:7; [k]Ro 13:12; 2Co 10:4; Eph 6:10–18
8 [l]1Co 4:10; [m]1Co 4:13; [n]Mt 27:63
9 [o]**Ro 8:36**; [p]2Co 1:8–10; 4:10–11
10 [q]**Mt 5:12**; 2Co 7:4; Php 2:17; 4:4; Col 1:24; 1Th 1:6; [r]2Co 8:9; [s]Ac 3:6; [t]Ro 8:32; 1Co 3:21
11 [u]2Co 7:3
13 [v]**1Th 2:11**; [w]2Co 7:2
14 [x]Ge 24:3; Dt 22:10; 1Co 5:9–10; [y]1Co 6:6; [z]Eph 5:7,11; 1Jn 1:6
15 [a]1Co 10:21; [b]Ac 5:14; [c]1Co 6:6
16 [d]1Co 10:21; [e]**1Co 3:16**; [f]**Mt 16:16**; [g]Lev 26:12; Jer 32:38; Eze 37:27; Rev 21:3
17 [h]Rev 18:4; [i]Isa 52:11; Eze 20:34,41
18 [j]Ex 4:22; 2Sa 7:14; 1Ch 17:13; Isa 43:6; **Ro 8:14**; [k]2Sa 7:8

Ch. 7

1 [a]2Co 6:17–18; [b]**1Co 10:14**; [c]1Th 4:7; 1Pe 1:15–16
2 [d]2Co 6:12–13
3 [e]2Co 6:11–12; Php 1:7
4 [f]ver 14; 2Co 8:24; [g]ver 13; [h]**2Co 6:10**

5 [i]2Co 2:13; **Ac 16:9**; [j]2Co 4:8; [k]Dt 32:25
6 [l]2Co 1:3–4; [m]ver 13; **2Co 2:13** *8* [n]2Co 2:2,4
10 [o]Ac 11:18

[a]*21* Or *be a sin offering* [a]*2* Isaiah 49:8
[b]*15* Greek *Beliar*, a variant of *Belial*
[c]*16* Lev. 26:12; Jer. 32:38; Ezek. 37:27
[d]*17* Isaiah 52:11; Ezek. 20:34,41
[e]*18* 2 Samuel 7:14; 7:8

this godly sorrow has produced in you: what earnestness, what eagerness to clear yourselves, what indignation, what alarm, what longing, what concern,[p] what readiness to see justice done. At every point you have proved yourselves to be innocent in this matter. 12So even though I wrote to you,[q] it was not on account of the one who did the wrong[r] or of the injured party, but rather that before God you could see for yourselves how devoted to us you are. 13By all this we are encouraged.

In addition to our own encouragement, we were especially delighted to see how happy Titus[s] was, because his spirit has been refreshed by all of you. 14I had boasted to him about you,[t] and you have not embarrassed me. But just as everything we said to you was true, so our boasting about you to Titus[u] has proved to be true as well. 15And his affection for you is all the greater when he remembers that you were all obedient,[v] receiving him with fear and trembling.[w] 16I am glad I can have complete confidence in you.[x]

Generosity Encouraged

8 And now, brothers, we want you to know about the grace that God has given the Macedonian[a] churches. 2Out of the most severe trial, their overflowing joy and their extreme poverty welled up in rich generosity.[b] 3For I testify that they gave as much as they were able,[c] and even beyond their ability. Entirely on their own, 4they urgently pleaded with us for the privilege of sharing[d] in this service[e] to the saints.[f] 5And they did not do as we expected, but they gave themselves first to the Lord and then to us in keeping with God's will. 6So we urged[g] Titus,[h] since he had earlier made a beginning, to bring also to completion[i] this act of grace on your part. 7But just as you excel in everything[j]—in faith, in speech, in knowledge,[k] in complete earnestness and in your love for us[a]—see that you also excel in this grace of giving.

8I am not commanding you,[l] but I want to test the sincerity of your love by comparing it with the earnestness of others. 9For you know the grace[m] of our Lord Jesus Christ,[n] that though he was rich, yet for your sakes he became poor,[o] so that you through his poverty might become rich.[p]

10And here is my advice[q] about what is best for you in this matter: Last year you were the first not only to give but also to have the desire to do so.[r] 11Now finish the work, so that your eager willingness[s] to do it may be matched by your completion of it, according to your means. 12For if the willingness is there, the gift is acceptable according to what one has,[t] not according to what he does not have.

13Our desire is not that others might be relieved while you are hard pressed, but that there might be equality. 14At the present time your plenty will supply what they need,[u] so that in turn their plenty will supply what you need. Then there will be equality, 15as it is written: "He who gathered much did not have too much, and he who gathered little did not have too little."[b][v]

Titus Sent to Corinth

16I thank God,[w] who put into the heart[x] of Titus[y] the same concern I have for you. 17For Titus not only welcomed our appeal, but he is coming to you with much enthusiasm and on his own initiative.[z] 18And we are sending along with him the brother[a] who is praised by all the churches[b] for his service to the gospel.[c] 19What is more, he was chosen by the churches to accompany us[d] as we carry the offering, which we administer in order to honour the Lord himself and to show our eagerness to help.[e] 20We want to avoid any criticism of the way we administer this liberal gift. 21For we are taking pains to do what is right, not only in the eyes of the Lord but also in the eyes of men.[f]

22In addition, we are sending with them our brother who has often proved to us in many ways that he is zealous, and now even more so because of his great confidence in you. 23As for Titus,[g] he is my partner[h] and fellow-worker[i] among you; as for our brothers,[j] they are representatives of the churches and an honour to Christ. 24Therefore show these men the proof of your love and the reason for our pride in you,[k] so that the churches can see it.

9 There is no need[a] for me to write to you about this service[b] to the saints.[c] 2For I know your eagerness to help,[d] and I have been boasting[e] about it to the Macedonians, telling them that since last year[f] you in Achaia[g] were ready to give; and your enthusiasm has stirred most of them to action. 3But I am

---

11 [p]ver 7
12 [q]ver 8; 2Co 2:3,9; [r]1Co 5:1–2
13 [s]ver 6; **2Co 2:13**
14 [t]ver 4; [u]ver 6
15 [v]2Co 2:9; 10:6; [w]Ps 55:5; 1Co 2:3; Php 2:12
16 [x]**2Co 2:3**

Ch. 8

1 [a]**Ac 16:9**
2 [b]Ex 36:5; 2Co 9:11
3 [c]1Co 16:2
4 [d]ver 1; [e]**Ac 24:17;** [f]**Ac 9:13**
6 [g]ver 17; 2Co 12:18; [h]ver 16,23; **2Co 2:13;** [i]ver 10–11
7 [j]2Co 9:8; [k]Ro 15:14; 1Co 1:5; 12:8; 13:1–2; 14:6
8 [l]1Co 7:6
9 [m]**Ro 3:24;** [n]2Co 13:14; [o]Mt 20:28; Php 2:6–8; [p]2Co 6:10
10 [q]1Co 7:25,40; [r]1Co 16:2–3; 2Co 9:2
11 [s]ver 12,19; Ex 25:2; 2Co 9:2
12 [t]Mk 12:43–44; 2Co 9:7
14 [u]Ac 4:34; 2Co 9:12
15 [v]Ex 16:18
16 [w]**2Co 2:14;** [x]Rev 17:17; [y]**2Co 2:13**
17 [z]ver 6
18 [a]2Co 12:18; [b]**1Co 7:17;** [c]**2Co 2:12**
19 [d]Ac 14:23; 1Co 16:3–4; [e]ver 11–12
21 [f]Ro 12:17; **14:18; Tit 2:14**
23 [g]**2Co 2:13;** [h]Phm 17; [i]**Php 2:25;** [j]ver 18,22
24 [k]2Co 7:4,14; 9:2

Ch. 9

1 [a]1Th 4:9; [b]**Ac 24:17;** [c]**Ac 9:13**
2 [d]2Co 8:11–12, 19; [e]2Co 7:4, 14; 8:24; [f]2Co 8:10; [g]**Ac 18:12**

---

a7 Some manuscripts *in our love for you*
b15 Exodus 16:18

sending the brothers[h] in order that our boasting about you in this matter should not prove hollow, but that you may be ready, as I said you would be.[i] 4For if any Macedonians[j] come with me and find you unprepared, we—not to say anything about you—would be ashamed of having been so confident. 5So I thought it necessary to urge the brothers[k] to visit you in advance and finish the arrangements for the generous gift you had promised. Then it will be ready as a generous gift,[l] not as one grudgingly given.[m]

Sowing Generously

6Remember this: Whoever sows sparingly will also reap sparingly, and whoever sows generously will also reap generously.[n] 7Each man should give what he has decided in his heart to give,[o] not reluctantly or under compulsion,[p] for God loves a cheerful giver.[q] 8And God is able[r] to make all grace abound to you, so that in all things at all times, having all that you need,[s] you will abound in every good work. 9As it is written:

"He has scattered abroad his gifts[t] to
  the poor;
his righteousness endures for
  ever."[a][u]

10Now he who supplies seed to the sower and bread for food[v] will also supply and increase your store of seed and will enlarge the harvest of your righteousness.[w] 11You will be made rich[x] in every way so that you can be generous[y] on every occasion, and through us your generosity will result in thanksgiving to God.[z]

12This service that you perform is not only supplying the needs[a] of God's people but is also overflowing in many expressions of thanks to God.[b] 13Because of the service[c] by which you have proved yourselves, men will praise God[d] for the obedience that accompanies your confession[e] of the gospel of Christ,[f] and for your generosity[g] in sharing with them and with everyone else. 14And in their prayers for you their hearts will go out to you, because of the surpassing grace God has given you. 15Thanks be to God[h] for his indescribable gift![i]

Paul's Defence of His Ministry

10 By the meekness and gentleness[a] of Christ, I appeal to you —I, Paul,[b] who am "timid" when face to face with you, but "bold" when away! 2I beg you that when I come I may not have to be as bold[c] as I expect to be towards some people who think that we live by the standards of this world.[d] 3For though we live in the world, we do not wage war as the world does.[e] 4The weapons we fight with[f] are not the weapons of the world. On the contrary, they have divine power[g] to demolish strongholds.[h] 5We demolish arguments and every pretension that sets itself up against the knowledge of God,[i] and we take captive every thought to make it obedient[j] to Christ. 6And we will be ready to punish every act of disobedience, once your obedience is complete.[k]

7You are looking only on the surface of things.[a][l] If anyone is confident that he belongs to Christ,[m] he should consider again that we belong to Christ just as much as he.[n] 8For even if I boast somewhat freely about the authority the Lord gave us[o] for building you up rather than pulling you down,[p] I will not be ashamed of it. 9I do not want to seem to be trying to frighten you with my letters. 10For some say, "His letters are weighty and forceful, but in person he is unimpressive[q] and his speaking amounts to nothing."[r] 11Such people should realise that what we are in our letters when we are absent, we will be in our actions when we are present.

12We do not dare to classify or compare ourselves with some who commend themselves.[s] When they measure themselves by themselves and compare themselves with themselves, they are not wise. 13We, however, will not boast beyond proper limits, but will confine our boasting to the field God has assigned to us,[t] a field that reaches even to you. 14We are not going too far in our boasting, as would be the case if we had not come to you, for we did get as far as you[u] with the gospel of Christ.[v] 15Neither do we go beyond our limits[w] by boasting of work done by others.[b][x] Our hope is that, as your faith continues to grow,[y] our area of activity among you will greatly expand, 16so that we can preach the gospel[z] in the regions beyond you.[a] For we do not want to boast about work already done in

3 [h]2Co 8:23; [i]1Co 16:2
4 [j]Ro 15:26
5 [k]ver 3; [l]Php 4:17; [m]2Co 12:17–18
6 [n]Pr 11:24–25; 22:9; Gal 6:7,9
7 [o]Ex 25:2; 2Co 8:12; [p]Dt 15:10; [q]Ro 12:8
8 [r]Eph 3:20; [s]Php 4:19
9 [t]Mal 3:10; [u]Ps 112:9
10 [v]Isa 55:10; [w]Hos 10:12
11 [x]1Co 1:5; [y]ver 5; [z]2Co 1:11; 4:15
12 [a]2Co 8:14; [b]2Co 1:11
13 [c]2Co 8:4; [d]Mt 9:8; [e]Heb 3:1; [f]2Co 2:12; [g]ver 5
15 [h]2Co 2:14; [i]Ro 5:15–16

Ch. 10

1 [a]Mt 11:29; [b]Gal 5:2; Eph 3:1
2 [c]1Co 4:21; [d]Ro 12:2
3 [e]ver 2
4 [f]2Co 6:7; [g]1Co 2:5; [h]ver 8; Jer 1:10; 23:29; 2Co 13:10
5 [i]Isa 2:11–12; 1Co 1:19; [j]2Co 9:13
6 [k]2Co 2:9; 7:15
7 [l]Jn 7:24; 2Co 5:12; [m]1Co 1:12; 3:23; 14:37; [n]2Co 11:23
8 [o]ver 13,15; [p]ver 4; Jer 1:10; 2Co 13:10
10 [q]ver 1; 1Co 2:3; Gal 4:13–14; [r]1Co 1:17; 2Co 11:6
12 [s]ver 18; 2Co 3:1
13 [t]ver 15–16; Ro 12:3
14 [u]1Co 3:6; [v]2Co 2:12
15 [w]ver 13; [x]Ro 15:20; [y]2Th 1:3
16 [z]Ro 1:1; 2Co 2:12; [a]Ac 19:21

[a]9 Psalm 112:9 [a]7 Or *Look at the obvious facts* [b]13–15 Or [13]*We, however, will not boast about things that cannot be measured, but we will boast according to the standard of measurement that the God of measure has assigned us—a measurement that relates even to you.* [14]. . . [15]*Neither do we boast about things that cannot be measured in regard to the work done by others.*

another man's territory. 17But, "Let him who boasts boast in the Lord."[c][b] 18For it is not the one who commends himself[c] who is approved, but the one whom the Lord commends.[d]

Paul and the False Apostles

11 I hope you will put up with[a] a little of my foolishness;[b] but you are already doing that. 2I am jealous for you with a godly jealousy. I promised you to one husband,[c] to Christ, so that I might present you[d] as a pure virgin to him. 3But I am afraid that just as Eve was deceived by the serpent's cunning,[e] your minds may somehow be led astray from your sincere and pure devotion to Christ. 4For if someone comes to you and preaches a Jesus other than the Jesus we preached,[f] or if you receive a different spirit[g] from the one you received, or a different gospel[h] from the one you accepted, you put up with it[i] easily enough. 5But I do not think I am in the least inferior to those "super-apostles".[j] 6I may not be a trained speaker,[k] but I do have knowledge.[l] We have made this perfectly clear to you in every way.

7Was it a sin[m] for me to lower myself in order to elevate you by preaching the gospel of God[n] to you free of charge?[o] 8I robbed other churches by receiving support from them[p] so as to serve you. 9And when I was with you and needed something, I was not a burden to anyone, for the brothers who came from Macedonia supplied what I needed.[q] I have kept myself from being a burden to you[r] in any way, and will continue to do so. 10As surely as the truth of Christ is in me,[s] nobody in the regions of Achaia[t] will stop this boasting[u] of mine. 11Why? Because I do not love you? God knows[v] I do![w] 12And I will keep on doing what I am doing in order to cut the ground from under those who want an opportunity to be considered equal with us in the things they boast about.

13For such men are false apostles,[x] deceitful[y] workmen, masquerading as apostles of Christ.[z] 14And no wonder, for Satan[a] himself masquerades as an angel of light. 15It is not surprising, then, if his servants masquerade as servants of righteousness. Their end will be what their actions deserve.[b]

Paul Boasts About His Sufferings

16I repeat: Let no-one take me for a fool.[c] But if you do, then receive me just as you would a fool, so that I may do a little boasting. 17In this self-confident boasting I am not talking as the Lord would,[d] but as a fool.[e] 18Since many are boasting in the way the world does,[f] I too will boast.[g] 19You gladly put up with[h] fools since you are so wise![i] 20In fact, you even put up with[j] anyone who enslaves you[k] or exploits you or takes advantage of you or pushes himself forward or slaps you in the face. 21To my shame I admit that we were too weak[l] for that!

What anyone else dares to boast about—I am speaking as a fool—I also dare to boast about.[m] 22Are they Hebrews? So am I.[n] Are they Israelites? So am I.[o] Are they Abraham's descendants? So am I.[p] 23Are they servants of Christ?[q] (I am out of my mind to talk like this.) I am more. I have worked much harder,[r] been in prison more frequently,[s] been flogged more severely,[t] and been exposed to death again and again.[u] 24Five times I received from the Jews the forty lashes[v] minus one. 25Three times I was beaten with rods,[w] once I was stoned,[x] three times I was shipwrecked,[y] I spent a night and a day in the open sea, 26I have been constantly on the move. I have been in danger from rivers, in danger from bandits, in danger from my own countrymen,[z] in danger from Gentiles; in danger in the city,[a] in danger in the country, in danger at sea; and in danger from false brothers.[b] 27I have laboured and toiled[c] and have often gone without sleep; I have known hunger and thirst and have often gone without food;[d] I have been cold and naked. 28Besides everything else, I face daily the pressure of my concern for all the churches.[e] 29Who is weak, and I do not feel weak?[f] Who is led into sin,[g] and I do not inwardly burn?

30If I must boast, I will boast[h] of the things that show my weakness.[i] 31The God and Father of the Lord Jesus, who is to be praised for ever,[j] knows[k] that I am not lying. 32In Damascus the governor under King Aretas had the city of the Damascenes guarded in order to arrest me.[l] 33But I was lowered in a basket from a window in the wall and slipped through his hands.[m]

17 [b]Jer 9:24; Ps 34:2; 44:8; 1Co 1:31
18 [c]ver 12; [d]**Ro 2:29**

Ch. 11

1 [a]ver 4,19–20; Mt 17:17; [b]ver 16–17,21; 2Co 5:13
2 [c]Hos 2:19; Eph 5:26–27; [d]**2Co 4:14**
3 [e]Ge 3:1–6,13; 1Ti 2:14; Rev 12:9
4 [f]1Co 3:11; [g]Ro 8:15; [h]Gal 1:6–9; [i]**ver 1**
5 [j]2Co 12:11; Gal 2:6
6 [k]**1Co 1:17;** [l]**2Co 8:7;** Eph 3:4
7 [m]2Co 12:13; [n]**Ro 1:1;** [o]1Co 9:18
8 [p]Php 4:15,18
9 [q]Php 4:15,18; [r]2Co 12:13–14,16
10 [s]**Ro 9:1;** [t]**Ac 18:12;** [u]1Co 9:15
11 [v]ver 31; **Ro 1:9;** [w]2Co 12:15
13 [x]**Mt 7:15;** [y]Tit 1:10; [z]Rev 2:2
14 [a]**Mt 4:10**
15 [b]**Mt 16:27;** Php 3:19
16 [c]ver 1
17 [d]1Co 7:12,25; [e]ver 21
18 [f]2Co 5:16; 10:4; [g]ver 21; Php 3:3–4
19 [h]**ver 1;** [i]1Co 4:10
20 [j]**ver 1;** [k]Gal 2:4; 4:9; 5:1
21 [l]2Co 10:1,10; [m]ver 17–18; Php 3:4
22 [n]Php 3:5; [o]Ro 9:4; 11:1; [p]**Lk 3:8;** Ro 11:1
23 [q]**1Co 3:5;** [r]**1Co 15:10;** [s]Ac 16:23; 2Co 6:4–5; [t]Ac 16:23; 2Co 6:4–5; [u]**Ro 8:36**
24 [v]Dt 25:3
25 [w]Ac 16:22; [x]Ac 14:19; [y]Ac 27:1–44
26 [z]**Ac 20:3;** [a]Ac 21:31; [b]Gal 2:4
27 [c]**Ac 18:3;** Col 1:29; [d]1Co 4:11–12; 2Co 6:5
28 [e]**1Co 7:17**
29 [f]**Ro 14:1; 1Co 2:3;** [g]**Mt 5:29**
30 [h]ver 16; Gal 6:14; 2Co 12:5,9; [i]**1Co 2:3**
31 [j]Ro 1:25; 9:5; [k]ver 11; **Ro 1:9**
32 [l]Ac 9:24
33 [m]Ac 9:25

[c]17 Jer. 9:24

Paul's Vision and His Thorn

12 I must go on boasting.[a]
Although there is nothing to be
gained, I will go on to visions and
revelations[b] from the Lord. 2I know a
man in Christ[c] who fourteen years ago
was caught up[d] to the third heaven.[e]
Whether it was in the body or out of the
body I do not know—God knows.[f]
3And I know that this man—whether in
the body or apart from the body I do not
know, but God knows—4was caught
up[g] to paradise.[h] He heard inexpressible
things, things that man is not permitted
to tell. 5I will boast about a man like that,
but I will not boast about myself, except
about my weaknesses.[i] 6Even if I should
choose to boast,[j] I would not be a fool,[k]
because I would be speaking the truth.
But I refrain, so no-one will think more
of me than is warranted by what I do or
say.
7To keep me from becoming con-
ceited because of these surpassingly
great revelations,[l] there was given me a
thorn in my flesh,[m] a messenger of
Satan,[n] to torment me. 8Three times I
pleaded with the Lord to take it away
from me.[o] 9But he said to me, "My
grace[p] is sufficient for you, for my
power[q] is made perfect in weakness."[r][s]
Therefore I will boast all the more gladly
about my weaknesses, so that Christ's
power may rest on me. 10That is why,
for Christ's sake, I delight[t] in weak-
nesses, in insults, in hardships,[u] in
persecutions,[v] in difficulties. For
when I am weak, then I am strong.[w]

Paul's Concern for the Corinthians

11I have made a fool of myself,[x] but
you drove me to it. I ought to have been
commended by you, for I am not in the
least inferior to the "super-apostles",[y]
even though I am nothing.[z] 12The things
that mark an apostle—signs, wonders
and miracles[a]—were done among you
with great perseverance. 13How were
you inferior to the other churches,
except that I was never a burden to
you?[b] Forgive me this wrong![c]
14Now I am ready to visit you for the
third time,[d] and I will not be a burden to
you, because what I want is not your
possessions but you. After all, children
should not have to save up for their
parents,[e] but parents for their children.[f]
15So I will very gladly spend for you
everything I have and expend myself as
well.[g] If I love you more,[h] will you love
me less? 16Be that as it may, I have not
been a burden to you.[i] Yet, crafty fellow
that I am, I caught you by trickery! 17Did
I exploit you through any of the men I
sent you? 18I urged[j] Titus[k] to go to you
and I sent our brother[l] with him. Titus
did not exploit you, did he? Did we not
act in the same spirit and follow the
same course?
19Have you been thinking all along
that we have been defending ourselves
to you? We have been speaking in the
sight of God[m] as those in Christ; and
everything we do, dear friends,[n] is for
your strengthening.[o] 20For I am afraid
that when I come[p] I may not find you as I
want you to be, and you may not find
me as you want me to be.[q] I fear that
there may be quarrelling,[r] jealousy, out-
bursts of anger, factions,[s] slander,[t] gos-
sip,[u] arrogance[v] and disorder.[w] 21I am
afraid that when I come again my God
will humble me before you, and I will be
grieved[x] over many who have sinned
earlier[y] and have not repented of the
impurity, sexual sin and debauchery[z] in
which they have indulged.

Final Warnings

13 This will be my third visit to
you.[a] "Every matter must be
established by the testimony of two or
three witnesses."[a][b] 2I already gave you
a warning when I was with you the
second time. I now repeat it while
absent:[c] On my return I will not spare[d]
those who sinned earlier[e] or any of the
others, 3since you are demanding proof
that Christ is speaking through me.[f] He
is not weak in dealing with you, but is
powerful among you. 4For to be sure, he
was crucified in weakness,[g] yet he lives
by God's power.[h] Likewise, we are
weak[i] in him, yet by God's power we
will live with him[j] to serve you.
5Examine yourselves[k] to see whether
you are in the faith; test yourselves.[l] Do
you not realise that Christ Jesus is in
you[m]—unless, of course, you fail the
test? 6And I trust that you will discover
that we have not failed the test. 7Now
we pray to God that you will not do
anything wrong. Not that people will
see that we have stood the test but that
you will do what is right even though
we may seem to have failed. 8For we
cannot do anything against the truth,
but only for the truth. 9We are glad
whenever we are weak[n] but you are

Ch. 12

1 [a]ver 5,9; 2Co 11:16,30; [b]ver 7; **1Co 2:10**
2 [c]**Ro 16:3**; [d]ver 4; **Ac 8:39**; [e]Eph 4:10; [f]2Co 11:11
4 [g]ver 2; [h]Lk 23:43; Rev 2:7
5 [i]ver 9–10; **1Co 2:3**
6 [j]2Co 10:8; [k]ver 11; 2Co 11:16
7 [l]ver 1; **1Co 2:10**; [m]Nu 33:55; [n]**Mt 4:10**
8 [o]Mt 26:39,44
9 [p]**Ro 3:24**; [q]**Php 4:13**; [r]**1Co 2:3**; [s]1Ki 19:12
10 [t]**Mt 5:12**; [u]2Co 6:4; [v]2Th 1:4; [w]2Co 13:4
11 [x]2Co 11:1; [y]2Co 11:5; [z]1Co 15:9–10
12 [a]**Jn 4:48**
13 [b]ver 14; 1Co 9:12,18; [c]2Co 11:7
14 [d]2Co 13:1; [e]1Co 4:14–15; [f]Pr 19:14
15 [g]Php 2:17; 1Th 2:8; [h]2Co 11:11
16 [i]2Co 11:9
18 [j]2Co 8:6,16; [k]**2Co 2:13**; [l]2Co 8:18
19 [m]Ro 9:1; [n]**1Co 10:14**; [o]**Ro 14:19**; 2Co 10:8
20 [p]2Co 2:1–4; [q]1Co 4:21; [r]1Co 1:11; 3:3; [s]Gal 5:20; [t]Ro 1:30; [u]**Ro 1:29**; [v]1Co 4:18; [w]1Co 14:33
21 [x]2Co 2:1,4; [y]2Co 13:2; [z]**1Co 6:18**

Ch. 13

1 [a]2Co 12:14; [b]Dt 19:15; **Mt 18:16**
2 [c]ver 10; [d]2Co 1:23; [e]2Co 12:21
3 [f]Mt 10:20; 1Co 5:4
4 [g]1Co 1:25; Php 2:7–8; 1Pe 3:18; [h]Ro 1:4; 6:4; 1Co 6:14; [i]ver 9; **1Co 2:3**; [j]**Ro 6:5**
5 [k]1Co 11:28; [l]La 3:40; Jn 6:6; [m]**Ro 8:10**
9 [n]**1Co 2:3**

[a]*1* Deut. 19:15

strong;[o] and our prayer is for your per-
fection.[p] 10This is why I write these
things when I am absent, that when I
come I may not have to be harsh[q] in my
use of authority—the authority the
Lord gave me for building you up, not
for tearing you down.[r]

Final Greetings

11Finally, brothers,[s] good-bye. Aim
for perfection, listen to my appeal, be of
one mind, live in peace.[t] And the God of
love[u] and peace[v] will be with you.
12Greet one another with a holy kiss.[w]
13All the saints send their greetings.[x]
14May the grace of the Lord Jesus
Christ,[y] and the love of God,[z] and the
fellowship of the Holy Spirit[a] be with
you all.

9 [o]2Co 4:12; [p]ver 11; Eph 4:13
10 [q]**2Co 1:23**; [r]2Co 10:8
11 [s]1Th 4:1; 2Th 3:1; [t]**Mk 9:50**; [u]1Jn 4:16; [v]**Ro 15:33**; Eph 6:23
12 [w]**Ro 16:16**
13 [x]Php 4:22

14 [y]**Ro 16:20**; 2Co 8:9; [z]Ro 5:5; Jude 21; [a]**Php 2:1**

Galatians

1 Paul, an apostle[a]—sent not from
men nor by man,[b] but by Jesus
Christ[c] and God the Father,[d] who raised
him from the dead[e]—2and all the
brothers with me,[f]

To the churches in Galatia:[g]

3Grace and peace to you from God our
Father and the Lord Jesus Christ,[h] 4who
gave himself for our sins[i] to rescue us
from the present evil age,[j] according to
the will of our God and Father,[k] 5to
whom be glory for ever and ever.
Amen.[l]

No Other Gospel

6I am astonished that you are so
quickly deserting the one who called[m]
you by the grace of Christ and are turn-
ing to a different gospel[n]—7which is
really no gospel at all. Evidently some
people are throwing you into confusion[o]
and are trying to pervert[p] the gospel of
Christ. 8But even if we or an angel from
heaven should preach a gospel other
than the one we preached to you,[q] let
him be eternally condemned![r] 9As we
have already said, so now I say again: If
anybody is preaching to you a gospel
other than what you accepted,[s] let him
be eternally condemned!

10Am I now trying to win the approval
of men, or of God? Or am I trying to
please men?[t] If I were still trying to
please men, I would not be a servant of
Christ.

Paul Called by God

11I want you to know, brothers,[u] that
the gospel I preached[v] is not something
that man made up. 12I did not receive it
from any man,[w] nor was I taught it;
rather, I received it by revelation[x] from
Jesus Christ.[y]

13For you have heard of my previous
way of life in Judaism,[z] how intensely I
persecuted the church of God[a] and tried
to destroy it.[b] 14I was advancing in Juda-
ism beyond many Jews of my own age
and was extremely zealous[c] for the
traditions of my fathers.[d] 15But when
God, who set me apart from birth[a][e] and
called me[f] by his grace, was pleased 16to
reveal his Son in me so that I might
preach him among the Gentiles,[g] I did
not consult any man,[h] 17nor did I go
up to Jerusalem to see those who
were apostles before I was, but I went
immediately into Arabia and later
returned to Damascus.[i]

18Then after three years,[j] I went up to
Jerusalem[k] to get acquainted with Peter[b]
and stayed with him fifteen days. 19I
saw none of the other apostles—only
James,[l] the Lord's brother. 20I assure
you before God[m] that what I am writing
to you is no lie.[n] 21Later I went to Syria[o]
and Cilicia.[p] 22I was personally un-
known to the churches of Judea[q] that are
in Christ.[r] 23They only heard the report:
"The man who formerly persecuted us
is now preaching the faith[s] he once tried
to destroy."[t] 24And they praised God[u]
because of me.

Paul Accepted by the Apostles

2 Fourteen years later I went up
again to Jerusalem,[a] this time with
Barnabas.[b] I took Titus[c] along also. 2I
went in response to a revelation[d] and set
before them the gospel that I preach
among the Gentiles.[e] But I did this
privately to those who seemed to be
leaders, for fear that I was running or
had run my race[f] in vain. 3Yet not
even Titus,[g] who was with me, was
compelled to be circumcised, even
though he was a Greek.[h] 4⌞This matter
arose⌟ because some false brothers[i]
had infiltrated our ranks to spy on[j] the
freedom[k] we have in Christ Jesus and to
make us slaves. 5We did not give in to
them for a moment, so that the truth of
the gospel[l] might remain with you.

Ch. 1

1 [a]**1Co 1:1**; [b]ver 11–12; [c]ver 15–16; **Ac 9:15**; 20:24; [d]ver 15–16; **Ac 9:15**; 20:24; [e]**Ac 2:24**
2 [f]Php 4:21; [g]**Ac 16:6**
3 [h]**Ro 1:7**
4 [i]**Mt 20:28**; **Ro 4:25**; **1Co 15:3**; Gal 2:20; [j]**1Co 1:20**; [k]**Php 4:20**
5 [l]**Ro 11:36**
6 [m]ver 15; **Ro 8:28**; [n]2Co 11:4
7 [o]Ac 15:24; Gal 5:10; [p]Jer 23:16,36
8 [q]ver 11,16; 1Co 15:1; 2Co 11:4; Gal 2:2; [r]Ro 9:3
9 [s]Ro 16:17
10 [t]**Ro 2:29**
11 [u]1Co 15:1; [v]**ver 8**
12 [w]ver 1; [x]ver 16; **1Co 2:10**; [y]1Co 11:23; 15:3
13 [z]Ac 26:4–5; [a]**1Co 10:32**; [b]**Ac 8:3**
14 [c]**Ac 21:20**; [d]Mt 15:2
15 [e]Isa 49:1,5; Jer 1:5; [f]**Ac 9:15**; **Ro 8:28**
16 [g]**Ac 9:15**; Gal 2:9; [h]Mt 16:17
17 [i]Ac 9:2,19–22
18 [j]Ac 9:22–23; [k]Ac 9:26–27
19 [l]Mt 13:55; **Ac 15:13**
20 [m]**Ro 1:9**; [n]**Ro 9:1**
21 [o]**Lk 2:2**; [p]**Ac 6:9**
22 [q]1Th 2:14; [r]**Ro 16:3**
23 [s]Ac 6:7; [t]**Ac 8:3**
24 [u]**Mt 9:8**

Ch. 2

1 [a]Ac 15:2; [b]**Ac 4:36**; [c]**2Co 2:13**
2 [d]**1Co 2:10**; [e]Ac 15:4,12; [f]**1Co 9:24**
3 [g]ver 1; **2Co 2:13**; [h]Ac 16:3; 1Co 9:21
4 [i]**Ac 1:16**; 2Co 11:26; [j]Jude 4; [k]Gal 5:1,13
5 [l]ver 14

[a]15 Or *from my mother's womb*
[b]18 Greek *Cephas*

6 As for those who seemed to be im-
portant[m]—whatever they were makes
no difference to me; God does not judge
by external appearance[n]—those men
added nothing to my message.[o] 7 On the
contrary, they saw that I had been en-
trusted with the task[p] of preaching the
gospel to the Gentiles,[a][q] just as Peter[r]
had been to the Jews.[b] 8 For God, who
was at work in the ministry of Peter as
an apostle[s] to the Jews, was also at work
in my ministry as an apostle[t] to the
Gentiles. 9 James,[u] Peter[c][v] and John,
those reputed to be pillars,[w] gave me
and Barnabas[x] the right hand of
fellowship when they recognised the
grace given to me.[y] They agreed that we
should go to the Gentiles,[z] and they to
the Jews. 10 All they asked was that we
should continue to remember the poor,[a]
the very thing I was eager to do.

Paul Opposes Peter

11 When Peter[b] came to Antioch,[c] I
opposed him to his face, because he was
clearly in the wrong. 12 Before certain
men came from James,[d] he used to eat
with the Gentiles.[e] But when they ar-
rived, he began to draw back and sepa-
rate himself from the Gentiles because
he was afraid of those who belonged to
the circumcision group.[f] 13 The other
Jews joined him in his hypocrisy, so that
by their hypocrisy even Barnabas[g] was
led astray.
14 When I saw that they were not
acting in line with the truth of the
gospel,[h] I said to Peter[i] in front of them
all, "You are a Jew, yet you live like a
Gentile and not like a Jew.[j] How is it,
then, that you force Gentiles to follow
Jewish customs?[k]
15 "We who are Jews by birth[l] and not
'Gentile sinners'[m] 16 know that a man is
not justified by observing the law,[n] but
by faith in Jesus Christ.[o] So we, too,
have put our faith in Christ Jesus that
we may be justified by faith in Christ
and not by observing the law, because
by observing the law no-one will be
justified.[p]
17 "If, while we seek to be justified in
Christ, it becomes evident that we
ourselves are sinners,[q] does that mean
that Christ promotes sin? Absolutely
not![r] 18 If I rebuild what I destroyed, I
prove that I am a law-breaker. 19 For
through the law I died to the law[s] so that
I might live for God.[t] 20 I have been
crucified with Christ[u] and I no longer
live, but Christ lives in me.[v] The life I
live in the body, I live by faith in the
Son of God,[w] who loved me[x] and gave
himself for me.[y] 21 I do not set aside
the grace of God, for if righteousness
could be gained through the law,[z]
Christ died for nothing!"[d]

Faith or Observance of the Law

3 You foolish[a] Galatians![b] Who has
bewitched you?[c] Before your very
eyes Jesus Christ was clearly portrayed
as crucified.[d] 2 I would like to learn just
one thing from you: Did you receive the
Spirit[e] by observing the law,[f] or by be-
lieving what you heard?[g] 3 Are you so
foolish? After beginning with the Spirit,
are you now trying to attain your goal
by human effort? 4 Have you suffered so
much for nothing—if it really was for
nothing? 5 Does God give you his Spirit
and work miracles[h] among you because
you observe the law, or because you
believe what you heard?[i]
6 Consider Abraham: "He believed
God, and it was credited to him as right-
eousness."[a][j] 7 Understand, then, that
those who believe[k] are children of Abra-
ham.[l] 8 The Scripture foresaw that God
would justify the Gentiles by faith, and
announced the gospel in advance to
Abraham: "All nations will be blessed
through you."[b][m] 9 So those who have
faith[n] are blessed along with Abraham,
the man of faith.[o]
10 All who rely on observing the law[p]
are under a curse,[q] for it is written:
"Cursed is everyone who does not con-
tinue to do everything written in the
Book of the Law."[c][r] 11 Clearly no-one
is justified before God by the law,[s]
because, "The righteous will live by
faith."[d][t] 12 The law is not based on faith;
on the contrary, "The man who does
these things will live by them."[e][u]
13 Christ redeemed us from the curse of
the law[v] by becoming a curse for us, for
it is written: "Cursed is everyone who is
hung on a tree."[f][w] 14 He redeemed us
in order that the blessing given to
Abraham might come to the Gentiles
through Christ Jesus,[x] so that by faith
we might receive the promise of the
Spirit.[y]

6 [m]ver 2; [n]**Ac 10:34; Rev 2:23;** [o]1Co 15:11
7 [p]1Th 2:4; 1Ti 1:11; [q]**Ac 9:15;** [r]ver 9,11,14
8 [s]Ac 1:25; [t]**1Co 1:1**
9 [u]**Ac 15:13;** [v]ver 7,11,14; [w]1Ti 3:15; Rev 3:12; [x]ver 1; **Ac 4:36;** [y]**Ro 12:3;** [z]**Ac 9:15**
10 [a]**Ac 24:17**
11 [b]ver 7,9,14; [c]**Ac 11:19**
12 [d]**Ac 15:13;** [e]Ac 11:3; [f]Ac 10:45; 11:2
13 [g]ver 1; **Ac 4:36**
14 [h]ver 5; [i]ver 7, 9,11; [j]Ac 10:28; [k]ver 12
15 [l]Php 3:4–5; [m]1Sa 15:18; Lk 24:7
16 [n]**Ro 3:28;** [o]**Ro 9:30;** [p]**Ro 3:28; 4:25**
17 [q]ver 15; [r]Gal 3:21
19 [s]**Ro 7:4;** [t]Ro 6:10–11,14; 2Co 5:15
20 [u]**Ro 6:6;** [v]**Ro 8:10;** 1Pe 4:2; [w]**Mt 4:3;** [x]**Ro 8:37;** [y]**Gal 1:4**
21 [z]Gal 3:21

Ch. 3

1 [a]Lk 24:25; [b]**Ac 16:6;** [c]Gal 5:7; [d]1Co 1:23
2 [e]**Jn 20:22;** [f]ver 5,10; Gal 2:16; [g]Ro 10:17; Heb 4:2
5 [h]1Co 12:10; [i]ver 2,10; Gal 2:16
6 [j]Ge 15:6; **Ro 4:3**
7 [k]ver 9; [l]**Lk 3:8**
8 [m]Ge 12:3; 18:18; 22:18; 26:4; Ac 3:25
9 [n]ver 7; Ro 4:16; [o]Ro 4:18–22
10 [p]ver 2,5; Gal 2:16; [q]ver 13; **Ro 4:15;** [r]Dt 27:26; Jer 11:3
11 [s]**Ro 3:28;** [t]Hab 2:4; **Ro 9:30;** Heb 10:38
12 [u]Lev 18:5; **Ro 10:5**
13 [v]Gal 4:5; [w]Dt 21:23; **Ac 5:30**
14 [x]Ro 4:9,16; [y]ver 2; Joel 2:28; **Jn 20:22; Ac 2:33**

a7 Greek *uncircumcised*
b7 Greek *circumcised;* also in verses 8 and 9
c9 Greek *Cephas;* also in verses 11 and 14
d21 Some interpreters end the quotation after verse 14.
a6 Gen. 15:6
b8 Gen. 12:3; 18:18; 22:18
c10 Deut. 27:26
d11 Hab. 2:4
e12 Lev. 18:5
f13 Deut. 21:23

The Law and the Promise

15Brothers,[z] let me take an example from everyday life. Just as no-one can set aside or add to a human covenant that has been duly established, so it is in this case. 16The promises were spoken to Abraham and to his seed.[a] The Scripture does not say "and to seeds", meaning many people, but "and to your seed",[g][b] meaning one person, who is Christ. 17What I mean is this: The law, introduced 430 years[c] later, does not set aside the covenant previously established by God and thus do away with the promise. 18For if the inheritance depends on the law, then it no longer depends on a promise;[d] but God in his grace gave it to Abraham through a promise.

19What, then, was the purpose of the law? It was added because of transgressions[e] until the Seed[f] to whom the promise referred had come. The law was put into effect through angels[g] by a mediator.[h] 20A mediator,[i] however, does not represent just one party; but God is one.

21Is the law, therefore, opposed to the promises of God? Absolutely not![j] For if a law had been given that could impart life, then righteousness would certainly have come by the law.[k] 22But the Scripture declares that the whole world is a prisoner of sin,[l] so that what was promised, being given through faith in Jesus Christ, might be given to those who believe.

23Before this faith came, we were held prisoners[m] by the law, locked up until faith should be revealed.[n] 24So the law was put in charge to lead us to Christ[h][o] that we might be justified by faith.[p] 25Now that faith has come, we are no longer under the supervision of the law.[q]

Sons of God

26You are all sons of God[r] through faith in Christ Jesus, 27for all of you who were baptised into Christ[s] have clothed yourselves with Christ.[t] 28There is neither Jew nor Greek, slave nor free,[u] male nor female,[v] for you are all one in Christ Jesus.[w] 29If you belong to Christ,[x] then you are Abraham's seed,[y] and heirs[z] according to the promise.[a]

4 What I am saying is that as long as the heir is a child, he is no different from a slave, although he owns the whole estate. 2He is subject to guardians and trustees until the time set by his father. 3So also, when we were children, we were in slavery[a] under the basic principles of the world.[b] 4But when the time had fully come,[c] God sent his Son,[d] born of a woman,[e] born under law,[f] 5to redeem[g] those under law, that we might receive the full rights[h] of sons.[i] 6Because you are sons, God sent the Spirit of his Son[j] into our hearts,[k] the Spirit who calls out, "*Abba*,[a] Father."[l] 7So you are no longer a slave, but a son; and since you are a son, God has made you also an heir.[m]

Paul's Concern for the Galatians

8Formerly, when you did not know God,[n] you were slaves[o] to those who by nature are not gods.[p] 9But now that you know God—or rather are known by God[q]—how is it that you are turning back to those weak and miserable principles? Do you wish to be enslaved[r] by them all over again?[s] 10You are observing special days and months and seasons and years![t] 11I fear for you, that somehow I have wasted my efforts on you.[u]

12I plead with you, brothers,[v] become like me, for I became like you. You have done me no wrong. 13As you know, it was because of an illness[w] that I first preached the gospel to you. 14Even though my illness was a trial to you, you did not treat me with contempt or scorn. Instead, you welcomed me as if I were an angel of God, as if I were Christ Jesus himself.[x] 15What has happened to all your joy? I can testify that, if you could have done so, you would have torn out your eyes and given them to me. 16Have I now become your enemy by telling you the truth?[y]

17Those people are zealous to win you over, but for no good. What they want is to alienate you ⌞from us⌟, so that you may be zealous for them.[z] 18It is fine to be zealous, provided the purpose is good, and to be so always and not just when I am with you.[a] 19My dear children,[b] for whom I am again in the pains of childbirth until Christ is formed in you,[c] 20how I wish I could be with you now and change my tone, because I am perplexed about you!

15 [z]**Ro 7:1**
16 [a]Ge 17:19; Ps 132:11; Mic 7:20; Lk 1:55; Ro 4:13,16; 9:4,8; Gal 3:29; 4:28; [b]Ge 12:7; 13:15; 17:7–8,10; 24:7
17 [c]Ge 15:13–14; Ex 12:40; Ac 7:6
18 [d]Ro 4:14
19 [e]Ro 5:20; [f]ver 16; [g]Dt 33:2; Ac 7:53; [h]Ex 20:19; Dt 5:5
20 [i]1Ti 2:5; Heb 8:6; 9:15; 12:24
21 [j]Gal 2:17; **Ro 7:12**; [k]Gal 2:21
22 [l]Ro 3:9–19; 11:32
23 [m]Ro 11:32; [n]ver 25
24 [o]ver 19; Ro 10:4; **4:15**; [p]Gal 2:16
25 [q]**Ro 7:4**
26 [r]**Ro 8:14**
27 [s]**Mt 28:19**; [t]**Ro 13:14**
28 [u]1Co 12:13; Col 3:11; [v]Ge 1:27; 5:2; Joel 2:29; [w]Jn 10:16; 17:11; Eph 2:14–15
29 [x]**1Co 3:23**; [y]ver 16; **Lk 3:8**; [z]**Ro 8:17**; [a]**Gal 3:16**

Ch. 4

3 [a]ver 8–9, 24–25; Gal 2:4; [b]Col 2:8,20
4 [c]Mk 1:15; Ro 5:6; Eph 1:10; [d]**Jn 3:17**; [e]**Jn 1:14**; [f]Lk 2:27
5 [g]**Ro 3:24**; [h]Jn 1:12; [i]**Ro 8:14**
6 [j]**Ac 16:7**; [k]Ro 5:5; [l]Ro 8:15–16
7 [m]**Ro 8:17**
8 [n]Ro 1:28; 1Co 1:21; 15:34; 1Th 4:5; 2Th 1:8; [o]**ver 3**; [p]2Ch 13:9; Isa 37:19; Jer 2:11; 5:7; 16:20; 1Co 8:4–5
9 [q]1Co 8:3; [r]**ver 3**; [s]Col 2:20
10 [t]Ro 14:5; Col 2:16
11 [u]1Th 3:5
12 [v]**Ro 7:1**; Gal 6:18
13 [w]1Co 2:3
14 [x]Mt 10:40
16 [y]Am 5:10
17 [z]Gal 2:4,12
18 [a]ver 13–14
19 [b]**1Th 2:11**; [c]Ro 8:29; Eph 4:13

g*16* Gen. 12:7; 13:15; 24:7
h*24* Or *charge until Christ came*
a*6* Aramaic for *Father*

Hagar and Sarah

21Tell me, you who want to be under
the law,[d] are you not aware of what
the law says? 22For it is written that
Abraham had two sons, one by the
slave woman[e] and the other by the
free woman.[f] 23His son by the slave
woman was born in the ordinary way;[g]
but his son by the free woman was
born as the result of a promise.[h]
24These things may be taken
figuratively, for the women represent
two covenants. One covenant is from
Mount Sinai and bears children who are
to be slaves: This is Hagar. 25Now Hagar
stands for Mount Sinai in Arabia and
corresponds to the present city of
Jerusalem, because she is in slavery
with her children. 26But the Jerusalem
that is above[i] is free, and she is our
mother. 27For it is written:

"Be glad, O barren woman,
who bears no children;
break forth and cry aloud,
you who have no labour pains;
because more are the children of the
desolate woman
than of her who has a husband."[b][j]

28Now you, brothers, like Isaac, are
children of promise.[k] 29At that time the
son born in the ordinary way[l] perse-
cuted the son born by the power of the
Spirit.[m] It is the same now. 30But what
does the Scripture say? "Get rid of the
slave woman and her son, for the slave
woman's son will never share in the
inheritance with the free woman's
son."[c][n] 31Therefore, brothers, we are
not children of the slave woman,[o] but of
the free woman.[p]

Freedom in Christ

5 It is for freedom that Christ has set
us free.[a] Stand firm,[b] then, and do
not let yourselves be burdened again by
a yoke of slavery.[c]
2Mark my words! I, Paul, tell you that
if you let yourselves be circumcised,[d]
Christ will be of no value to you at
all. 3Again I declare to every man who
lets himself be circumcised that he is
required to obey the whole law.[e] 4You
who are trying to be justified by law[f]
have been alienated from Christ; you
have fallen away from grace.[g] 5But by
faith we eagerly await through the Spirit
the righteousness for which we hope.[h]
6For in Christ Jesus[i] neither circum-
cision nor uncircumcision has any
value.[j] The only thing that counts is
faith expressing itself through love.[k]
7You were running a good race.[l] Who
cut in on you[m] and kept you from
obeying the truth? 8That kind of per-
suasion does not come from the one
who calls you.[n] 9"A little yeast works
through the whole batch of dough."[o] 10I
am confident[p] in the Lord that you will
take no other view.[q] The one who is
throwing you into confusion[r] will pay
the penalty, whoever he may be.
11Brothers, if I am still preaching cir-
cumcision, why am I still being perse-
cuted?[s] In that case the offence[t] of the
cross has been abolished. 12As for those
agitators,[u] I wish they would go the
whole way and emasculate themselves!
13You, my brothers, were called to be
free.[v] But do not use your freedom to
indulge the sinful nature[a];[w] rather,
serve one another[x] in love. 14The entire
law is summed up in a single command:
"Love your neighbour as yourself."[b][y]
15If you keep on biting and devouring
each other, watch out or you will be
destroyed by each other.

Life by the Spirit

16So I say, live by the Spirit,[z] and you
will not gratify the desires of the sinful
nature.[a] 17For the sinful nature desires
what is contrary to the Spirit, and the
Spirit what is contrary to the sinful
nature.[b] They are in conflict with each
other, so that you do not do what you
want.[c] 18But if you are led by the Spirit,[d]
you are not under law.[e]
19The acts of the sinful nature are
obvious: sexual immorality,[f] impurity
and debauchery; 20idolatry and witch-
craft; hatred, discord, jealousy, fits of
rage, selfish ambition, dissensions,
factions 21and envy; drunkenness,
orgies, and the like.[g] I warn you, as I did
before, that those who live like this will
not inherit the kingdom of God.[h]
22But the fruit[i] of the Spirit is love,[j]
joy, peace,[k] patience, kindness, good-
ness, faithfulness, 23gentleness and self-
control.[l] Against such things there is no
law.[m] 24Those who belong to Christ
Jesus have crucified the sinful nature[n]
with its passions and desires.[o] 25Since
we live by the Spirit,[p] let us keep in step

21 [d]**Ro 2:12**
22 [e]Ge 16:15; [f]Ge 21:2
23 [g]ver 28–29; Ro 9:7–8; [h]Ge 17:16–21; 18:10–14; 21:1; Heb 11:11
26 [i]Heb 12:22; Rev 3:12; 21:2,10
27 [j]Isa 54:1
28 [k]ver 23; **Gal 3:16**
29 [l]ver 23; [m]Ge 21:9
30 [n]Ge 21:10
31 [o]**Ro 7:4**; [p]ver 22

Ch. 5

1 [a]ver 13; Jn 8:32; Gal 2:4; **Ro 7:4**; [b]**1Co 16:13**; [c]**Mt 23:4**; Gal 2:4
2 [d]ver 3,6, 11–12; Ac 15:1
3 [e]Ro 2:25; Gal 3:10; Jas 2:10
4 [f]**Ro 3:28**; [g]Heb 12:15; 2Pe 3:17
5 [h]Ro 8:23–24
6 [i]**Ro 16:3**; [j]**1Co 7:19**; [k]1Th 1:3; Jas 2:22
7 [l]**1Co 9:24**; [m]Gal 3:1
8 [n]**Ro 8:28**
9 [o]1Co 5:6
10 [p]**2Co 2:3**; [q]Php 3:15; [r]ver 12; Gal 1:7
11 [s]Gal 4:29; 6:12; [t]**Lk 2:34**
12 [u]ver 10
13 [v]**ver 1**; [w]**ver 24**; 1Co 8:9; 1Pe 2:16; [x]1Co 9:19; 2Co 4:5; Eph 5:21
14 [y]Lev 19:18; **Mt 5:43**; Gal 6:2
16 [z]ver 18,25; Ro 8:2,4–6,9,14; **2Co 5:17**; [a]**ver 24**
17 [b]Ro 8:5–8; [c]Ro 7:15–23
18 [d]**ver 16**; [e]**Ro 2:12**; 1Ti 1:9
19 [f]**1Co 6:18**
21 [g]Mt 15:19; Ro 13:13; [h]**Mt 25:34**
22 [i]Mt 7:16–20; Eph 5:9; [j]Col 3:12–15; [k]Mal 2:6
23 [l]**Ac 24:25**; [m]ver 18
24 [n]ver 13,16–21; **Ro 6:6**; 7:5,18; 8:3–5,8–9,12–13; 13:14; Gal 6:8; Col 2:11; [o]ver 16–17
25 [p]**ver 16**

[b]27 Isaiah 54:1 [c]30 Gen. 21:10

[a]13 Or *the flesh*; also in verses 16, 17, 19 and 24
[b]14 Lev. 19:18

with the Spirit. 26Let us not become
conceited,[q] provoking and envying each
other.

Doing Good to All

6 Brothers, if someone is caught in a
sin, you who are spiritual[a] should
restore[b] him gently. But watch yourself,
or you also may be tempted. 2Carry each
other's burdens, and in this way you
will fulfil the law of Christ.[c] 3If anyone
thinks he is something[d] when he is no-
thing, he deceives himself.[e] 4Each one
should test his own actions. Then he
can take pride in himself,[f] without com-
paring himself to somebody else,[g] 5for
each one should carry his own load.[h]
6Anyone who receives instruction in
the word must share all good things
with his instructor.[i]
7Do not be deceived:[j] God cannot be
mocked. A man reaps what he sows.[k]
8The one who sows to please his sinful
nature,[l] from that nature[a] will reap de-
struction;[m] the one who sows to please
the Spirit, from the Spirit will reap eter-
nal life.[n] 9Let us not become weary in
doing good,[o] for at the proper time we
will reap a harvest if we do not give up.[p]
10Therefore, as we have opportunity, let
us do good[q] to all people, especially
to those who belong to the family[r] of
believers.

26 [q]Php 2:3

Ch. 6

1 [a]1Co 2:15; 3:1; [b]**Mt 18:15; 2Co 2:7**
2 [c]1Co 9:21; Jas 2:8
3 [d]Ro 12:3; 1Co 8:2; [e]1Co 3:18
4 [f]2Co 13:5; [g]2Co 10:12
5 [h]ver 2; Jer 31:30
6 [i]1Co 9:11,14; 1Ti 5:17–18
7 [j]**1Co 6:9**; [k]Pr 22:8; Jer 34:17; Hos 10:12–13; 2Co 9:6
8 [l]**Gal 5:24**; [m]Job 4:8; Hos 8:7; **Ro 6:23**; [n]Jas 3:18
9 [o]1Co 15:58; 2Co 4:1; [p]Job 42:12; Ps 126:5; Heb 12:3; Rev 2:10
10 [q]Pr 3:27; **Tit 2:14**; [r]Eph 2:19; 1Pe 4:17
11 [s]**1Co 16:21**
12 [t]Mt 23:25–26; [u]Ac 15:1; [v]Gal 5:11
13 [w]Ro 2:25; [x]Php 3:3
14 [y]1Co 2:2; [z]**Ro 6:2,6**
15 [a]**1Co 7:19**; [b]**2Co 5:17**

Not Circumcision but a New Creation

11See what large letters I use as I write
to you with my own hand![s]
12Those who want to make a good
impression outwardly[t] are trying to
compel you to be circumcised.[u] The
only reason they do this is to avoid
being persecuted[v] for the cross of
Christ. 13Not even those who are
circumcised obey the law,[w] yet they
want you to be circumcised that they
may boast about your flesh.[x] 14May I
never boast except in the cross of our
Lord Jesus Christ,[y] through which[b] the
world has been crucified to me, and I
to the world.[z] 15Neither circumcision
nor uncircumcision means anything;[a]
what counts is a new creation.[b] 16Peace
and mercy to all who follow this rule,
even to the Israel of God.
17Finally, let no-one cause me trouble,
for I bear on my body the marks[c] of
Jesus.
18The grace of our Lord Jesus Christ[d]
be with your spirit,[e] brothers. Amen.

17 [c]Isa 44:5; **2Co 1:5**; 11:23
18 [d]**Ro 16:20**; [e]Php 4:23; 2Ti 4:22; Phm 25

[a]8 *Or his flesh, from the flesh* [b]14 *Or whom*

Ephesians

1 Paul, an apostle[a] of Christ Jesus by the will of God,[b]

To the saints[c] in Ephesus,[a][d] the faithful[b][e] in Christ Jesus:

2Grace and peace to you from God our Father and the Lord Jesus Christ.[f]

Spiritual Blessings in Christ

3Praise be to the God and Father of our Lord Jesus Christ,[g] who has blessed us in the heavenly realms[h] with every spiritual blessing in Christ. 4For he chose us[i] in him before the creation of the world[j] to be holy and blameless[k] in his sight. In love[l] 5he[c] predestined[m] us to be adopted as his sons[n] through Jesus Christ, in accordance with his pleasure[o] and will—6to the praise of his glorious grace,[p] which he has freely given us in the One he loves.[q] 7In him we have redemption[r] through his blood,[s] the forgiveness of sins, in accordance with the riches[t] of God's grace 8that he lavished on us with all wisdom and understanding. 9And he[d] made known to us the mystery[u] of his will according to his good pleasure, which he purposed[v] in Christ, 10to be put into effect when the times will have reached their fulfilment[w]—to bring all things in heaven and on earth together under one head, even Christ.[x]

11In him we were also chosen,[e] having been predestined[y] according to the plan of him who works out everything in conformity with the purpose[z] of his will, 12in order that we, who were the first to hope in Christ, might be for the praise of his glory.[a] 13And you also were included in Christ[b] when you heard the word of truth,[c] the gospel of your salvation. Having believed, you were marked in him with a seal,[d] the promised Holy Spirit,[e] 14who is a deposit guaranteeing our inheritance[f] until the redemption[g] of those who are God's possession—to the praise of his glory.[h]

Ch 1

1 [a]**1Co 1:1;** [b]**2Co 1:1;** [c]**Ac 9:13;** [d]**Ac 18:19;** [e]Col 1:2
2 [f]**Ro 1:7**
3 [g]2Co 1:3; 1Pe 1:3; [h]ver 20; Eph 2:6; 3:10; 6:12
4 [i]2Th 2:13; [j]**Mt 25:34;** [k]Lev 11:44; 20:7; 2Sa 22:24; Ps 15:2; Eph 5:27; Col 1:22; [l]Eph 4:2, 15–16
5 [m]ver 11; Ro 8:29–30; [n]**Ro 8:14–15;** [o]Lk 12:32; 1Co 1:21; Col 1:19
6 [p]ver 12,14; [q]Mt 3:17
7 [r]ver 14; **Ro 3:24;** [s]**Ro 3:25;** [t]**Ro 2:4**
9 [u]**Ro 16:25;** [v]**ver 11**
10 [w]Mk 1:15; Ro 5:6; Gal 4:4; [x]Col 1:20
11 [y]ver 5; Ro 8:29–30; [z]ver 9; Ro 8:28; Eph 3:11; Heb 6:17
12 [a]ver 6,14
13 [b]**Ro 16:3;** [c]Eph 4:21; Col 1:5; [d]Eph 4:30; [e]Jn 14:16–17
14 [f]**Ac 20:32; 2Co 5:5;** [g]ver 7; **Ro 3:24;** [h]ver 6,12
15 [i]**Ac 20:21;** [j]**Col 1:4**
16 [k]**Ro 1:8;** [l]**Ro 1:10**
17 [m]Jn 20:17; Ro 15:6; Rev 1:6; [n]Ex 28:3; Isa 11:2; Php 1:9; Col 1:9
18 [o]Job 42:5; 2Co 4:6; Heb 6:4; [p]**Ro 8:28;** [q]ver 7; **Ro 2:4;** [r]ver 11; [s]Col 1:12
19 [t]Eph 3:7; Col 1:29; [u]Isa 40:26; Eph 6:10

Thanksgiving and Prayer

15For this reason, ever since I heard about your faith in the Lord Jesus[i] and your love for all the saints,[j] 16I have not stopped giving thanks for you,[k] remembering you in my prayers.[l] 17I keep asking that the God of our Lord Jesus Christ, the glorious Father,[m] may give you the Spirit[f] of wisdom[n] and revelation, so that you may know him better. 18I pray also that the eyes of your heart may be enlightened[o] in order that you may know the hope to which he has called[p] you, the riches[q] of his glorious inheritance[r] in the saints,[s] 19and his incomparably great power for us who believe. That power[t] is like the working of his mighty strength,[u] 20which he exerted in Christ when he raised him from the dead[v] and seated him at his right hand[w] in the heavenly realms,[x] 21far above all rule and authority, power and dominion,[y] and every title[z] that can be given, not only in the present age but also in the one to come.[a] 22And God placed all things under his feet[b] and appointed him to be head[c] over everything for the church, 23which is his body,[d] the fulness of him[e] who fills everything in every way.[f]

Made Alive in Christ

2 As for you, you were dead in your transgressions and sins,[a] 2in which you used to live[b] when you followed the ways of this world[c] and of the ruler of

20 [v]**Ac 2:24;** [w]**Mk 16:19;** [x]**ver 3**
21 [y]Eph 3:10; Col 1:16; [z]Php 2:9–10; [a]**Mt 12:32**
22 [b]**Mt 22:44; 28:18;** [c]1Co 11:3; Eph 4:15; 5:23; Col 1:18; 2:19
23 [d]**1Co 12:27;** [e]**Jn 1:16;** Eph 3:19; [f]Eph 4:10

Ch. 2

1 [a]ver 5; Col 2:13
2 [b]ver 3,11–13; Ro 11:30; 1Co 6:11; 5:8; Col 3:7; Tit 3:3; 1Pe 4:3; [c]Ro 12:2

a*1* Some early manuscripts do not have *in Ephesus.*
b*1* Or *believers who are*
c*4,5* Or *sight in love.* [5]*He*
d*8,9* Or *us. With all wisdom and understanding,* [9]*he*
e*11* Or *were made heirs*
f*17* Or *a spirit*

the kingdom of the air,[d] the spirit who is now at work in those who are disobedient.[e] 3All of us also lived among them at one time,[f] gratifying the cravings of our sinful nature[a][g] and following its desires and thoughts. Like the rest, we were by nature objects of wrath. 4But because of his great love for us,[h] God, who is rich in mercy, 5made us alive with Christ even when we were dead in transgressions[i]—it is by grace you have been saved.[j] 6And God raised us up with Christ[k] and seated us with him[l] in the heavenly realms[m] in Christ Jesus, 7in order that in the coming ages he might show the incomparable riches of his grace,[n] expressed in his kindness[o] to us in Christ Jesus. 8For it is by grace[p] you have been saved,[q] through faith[r]—and this not from yourselves, it is the gift of God—9not by works,[s] so that no-one can boast.[t] 10For we are God's workmanship,[u] created[v] in Christ Jesus to do good works,[w] which God prepared in advance for us to do.

One in Christ

11Therefore, remember that formerly[x] you who are Gentiles by birth and called "uncircumcised" by those who call themselves "the circumcision" (that done in the body by the hands of men)[y]—12remember that at that time you were separate from Christ, excluded from citizenship in Israel and foreigners[z] to the covenants of the promise,[a] without hope[b] and without God in the world. 13But now in Christ Jesus you who once[c] were far away have been brought near[d] through the blood of Christ.[e]

14For he himself is our peace,[f] who has made the two one[g] and has destroyed the barrier, the dividing wall of hostility, 15by abolishing in his flesh[h] the law with its commandments and regulations.[i] His purpose was to create in himself one[j] new man out of the two, thus making peace, 16and in this one body to reconcile both of them to God through the cross,[k] by which he put to death their hostility. 17He came and preached peace[l] to you who were far away and peace to those who were near.[m] 18For through him we both have access[n] to the Father[o] by one Spirit.[p]

19Consequently, you are no longer foreigners and aliens,[q] but fellow-citizens[r] with God's people and members of God's household,[s] 20built[t] on the foundation[u] of the apostles and prophets,[v] with Christ Jesus himself[w] as the chief cornerstone.[x] 21In him the whole building is joined together and rises to become a holy temple[y] in the Lord. 22And in him you too are being built together to become a dwelling in which God lives by his Spirit.[z]

Paul the Preacher to the Gentiles

3 For this reason I, Paul, the prisoner[a] of Christ Jesus for the sake of you Gentiles—

2Surely you have heard about the administration of God's grace that was given to me[b] for you, 3that is, the mystery[c] made known to me by revelation,[d] as I have already written briefly. 4In reading this, then, you will be able to understand my insight[e] into the mystery of Christ, 5which was not made known to men in other generations as it has now been revealed by the Spirit to God's holy apostles and prophets.[f] 6This mystery is that through the gospel the Gentiles are heirs[g] together with Israel, members together of one body,[h] and sharers together in the promise in Christ Jesus.[i]

7I became a servant of this gospel[j] by the gift of God's grace given me[k] through the working of his power.[l] 8Although I am less than the least of all God's people,[m] this grace was given me: to preach to the Gentiles[n] the unsearchable riches of Christ,[o] 9and to make plain to everyone the administration of this mystery,[p] which for ages past was kept hidden in God, who created all things. 10His intent was that now, through the church, the manifold wisdom of God[q] should be made known[r] to the rulers and authorities[s] in the heavenly realms,[t] 11according to his eternal purpose[u] which he accomplished in Christ Jesus our Lord. 12In him and through faith in him we may approach God[v] with freedom and confidence.[w] 13I ask you, therefore, not to be discouraged because of my sufferings for you, which are your glory.

A Prayer for the Ephesians

14For this reason I kneel[x] before the Father, 15from whom his whole family[a] in heaven and on earth derives its name. 16I pray that out of his glorious riches[y] he may strengthen you with

2 [d]Jn 12:31; [e]Eph 5:6
3 [f]ver 2; [g]Gal 5:24
4 [h]Jn 3:16
5 [i]ver 1; Ps 103:12; [j]ver 8; Jn 5:24; Ac 15:11
6 [k]Ro 6:5; [l]Eph 1:20; [m]Eph 1:3
7 [n]Ro 2:4; [o]Tit 3:4
8 [p]Ro 3:24; [q]ver 5; [r]Ro 9:30
9 [s]Dt 9:5; Ro 4:2; 2Ti 1:9; Tit 3:5; [t]1Co 1:29
10 [u]Isa 29:23; 43:7; 60:21; [v]Eph 4:24; [w]Tit 2:14
11 [x]ver 2; [y]Col 2:11
12 [z]Isa 14:1; 65:1; [a]Gal 3:17; [b]1Th 4:13
13 [c]ver 2; [d]ver 17; [e]Col 1:20
14 [f]ver 15; Jn 14:27; [g]1Co 12:13; Eph 3:6
15 [h]Col 1:21–22; [i]Col 2:14; [j]Gal 3:28
16 [k]2Co 5:18; Col 1:20,22
17 [l]Lk 2:14; [m]ver 13; Ps 148:14; Isa 57:19
18 [n]Eph 3:12; [o]Col 1:12; [p]1Co 12:13; Eph 4:4
19 [q]ver 12; [r]Php 3:20; [s]Gal 6:10
20 [t]1Co 3:9; [u]Mt 16:18; 1Co 3:10; Rev 21:14; [v]Eph 4:11; [w]1Co 3:11; [x]Ac 4:11; 1Pe 2:4–8
21 [y]1Co 3:16–17
22 [z]1Co 3:16

Ch. 3

1 [a]Ac 23:18; Eph 4:1; 2Ti 1:8; Phm 1,9
2 [b]Col 1:25
3 [c]Ro 16:25; [d]1Co 2:10
4 [e]2Co 11:6
5 [f]Ro 16:26; Eph 4:11
6 [g]Ro 8:17; [h]Eph 2:15–16; [i]Eze 47:22
7 [j]1Co 3:5; [k]Ro 12:3; [l]Eph 1:19; Col 1:29
8 [m]1Co 15:9; [n]Ac 9:15; [o]Ro 2:4
9 [p]Ro 16:25

10 [q]Ro 11:33; 1Co 2:7; [r]1Pe 1:12; [s]Eph 1:21; 6:12; Col 2:10,15; [t]Eph 1:3 11 [u]Eph 1:11
12 [v]Eph 2:18; [w]2Co 3:4; Heb 3:14; 4:16; 10:19,35; 1Jn 2:28; 3:21; 4:17 14 [x]Php 2:10
16 [y]ver 8; Ro 2:4

a3 Or *our flesh*
a15 Or *whom all fatherhood*

power[z] through his Spirit in your inner
being,[a] 17so that Christ may dwell in
your hearts[b] through faith. And I pray
that you, being rooted[c] and established
in love, 18may have power, together
with all the saints,[d] to grasp how wide
and long and high and deep[e] is the love
of Christ, 19and to know this love that
surpasses knowledge[f]—that you may
be filled[g] to the measure of all the
fulness of God.[h]
20Now to him who is able[i] to do im-
measurably more than all we ask[j] or
imagine, according to his power[k] that is
at work within us, 21to him be glory in
the church and in Christ Jesus through-
out all generations, for ever and ever!
Amen.[l]

Unity in the Body of Christ

4 As a prisoner[a] for the Lord, then, I
urge you to live a life worthy[b] of the
calling[c] you have received. 2Be com-
pletely humble and gentle; be patient,
bearing with one another[d] in love.[e]
3Make every effort to keep the unity[f] of
the Spirit through the bond of peace.[g]
4There is one body[h] and one Spirit[i]—
just as you were called to one hope
when you were called[j]—5one Lord,[k]
one faith, one baptism; 6one God and
Father of all,[l] who is over all and
through all and in all.[m]
7But to each one of us[n] grace[o] has been
given[p] as Christ apportioned it. 8This is
why it[a] says:

"When he ascended on high,
he led captives[q] in his train
and gave gifts to men."[b][r]

9(What does "he ascended" mean
except that he also descended to the
lower, earthly regions?[c] 10He who de-
scended is the very one who ascended[s]
higher than all the heavens, in order to
fill the whole universe.)[t] 11It was he who
gave[u] some to be apostles,[v] some to be
prophets,[w] some to be evangelists,[x] and
some to be pastors and teachers,[y] 12to
prepare God's people for works of
service, so that the body of Christ[z] may
be built up[a] 13until we all reach unity[b] in
the faith and in the knowledge of the Son
of God[c] and become mature,[d] attaining
to the whole measure of the fulness
of Christ.[e]
14Then we will no longer be infants,[f]
tossed back and forth by the waves,[g]
and blown here and there by every
wind of teaching and by the cunning
and craftiness of men in their deceitful
scheming.[h] 15Instead, speaking the
truth in love,[i] we will in all things grow
up into him who is the Head,[j] that is,
Christ. 16From him the whole body,
joined and held together by every
supporting ligament, grows[k] and builds
itself up[l] in love,[m] as each part does its
work.

Living as Children of Light

17So I tell you this, and insist on it in
the Lord, that you must no longer[n] live
as the Gentiles do, in the futility of their
thinking.[o] 18They are darkened in their
understanding[p] and separated from the
life of God[q] because of the ignorance
that is in them due to the hardening of
their hearts.[r] 19Having lost all sensi-
tivity,[s] they have given themselves
over[t] to sensuality[u] so as to indulge in
every kind of impurity, with a continual
lust for more.
20You, however, did not come to
know Christ that way. 21Surely you
heard of him and were taught in him in
accordance with the truth that is in
Jesus. 22You were taught, with regard to
your former way of life, to put off[v] your
old self,[w] which is being corrupted by its
deceitful desires;[x] 23to be made new in
the attitude of your minds;[y] 24and to put
on[z] the new self,[a] created to be like God
in true righteousness and holiness.[b]
25Therefore each of you must put off
falsehood and speak truthfully[c] to his
neighbour, for we are all members of
one body.[d] 26"In your anger do not
sin"[d]:[e] Do not let the sun go down while
you are still angry, 27and do not give the
devil a foothold.[f] 28He who has been
stealing must steal no longer, but must
work,[g] doing something useful with his
own hands,[h] that he may have some-
thing to share with those in need.[i]
29Do not let any unwholesome talk
come out of your mouths,[j] but only
what is helpful for building others up[k]
according to their needs, that it may
benefit those who listen. 30And do not
grieve the Holy Spirit of God,[l] with

16 [z]**Php 4:13**; [a]Ro 7:22
17 [b]**Ro 8:10**; [c]Col 2:7
18 [d]Eph 1:15; [e]Job 11:8–9; Ps 103:11
19 [f]Php 4:7; [g]Col 2:10; [h]Eph 1:23
20 [i]Ro 16:25; 2Co 9:8; [j]1Ki 3:13; [k]ver 7
21 [l]**Ro 11:36**
Ch. 4
1 [a]**Eph 3:1**; [b]Php 1:27; Col 1:10; 1Th 2:12; [c]**Ro 8:28**
2 [d]Col 3:12–13; [e]ver 15–16; Eph 1:4
3 [f]**Ro 15:5**; [g]Col 3:15
4 [h]**Ro 12:5**; [i]1Co 12:13; Eph 2:18; [j]**Ro 8:28**
5 [k]1Co 8:6
6 [l]Dt 6:4; Zec 14:9; [m]**Ro 11:36**
7 [n]1Co 12:7,11; [o]**Ro 3:24**; [p]**Ro 12:3**
8 [q]Col 2:15; [r]Ps 68:18
10 [s]Pr 30:1–4; [t]Eph 1:23
11 [u]ver 8; [v]1Co 12:28; Eph 2:20; 3:5; 2Pe 3:2; Jude 17; [w]**Ac 11:27**; Ro 12:6; 1Co 12:10,28; 13:2,8; 14:1, 39; Eph 2:20; 3:5; 2Pe 3:2; [x]Ac 21:8; 2Ti 4:5; [y]Ac 13:1; Ro 2:21; 12:7; 1Co 12:28; 14:26; 1Ti 1:7; Jas 3:1
12 [z]**1Co 12:27**; [a]**Ro 14:19**
13 [b]ver 3,5; [c]**Php 3:8**; [d]**1Co 2:6**; Col 1:28; [e]Jn 1:16; Eph 1:23; 3:19
14 [f]**1Co 14:20**; [g]Isa 57:20; Jas 1:6; [h]Eph 6:11
15 [i]ver 2,16; Eph 1:4; [j]**Eph 1:22**
16 [k]Col 2:19; [l]1Co 12:7; [m]ver 2,15; Eph 1:4
17 [n]Eph 2:2; [o]Ro 1:21
18 [p]Dt 29:4; Ro 1:21; [q]Eph 2:12; [r]2Co 3:14
19 [s]1Ti 4:2; [t]Ro 1:24; [u]Col 3:5; 1Pe 4:3
22 [v]ver 25,31; Col 3:5,8–9; Jas 1:21; 1Pe 2:1; [w]**Ro 6:6**; [x]Jer 17:9; Heb 3:13
23 [y]Ro 12:2; Col 3:10
24 [z]**Ro 13:14**; [a]**Ro 6:4**; [b]Eph 2:10
25 [c]Ps 15:2; Lev 19:11; Zec 8:16; Col 3:9; [d]**Ro 12:5**
26 [e]Ps 4:4; **Mt 5:22**
27 [f]2Co 2:10–11
28 [g]Ac 20:35; [h]1Th 4:11; [i]Gal 6:10
29 [j]Mt 12:36; Eph 5:4; Col 3:8; [k]**Ro 14:19**
30 [l]Isa 63:10; 1Th 5:19

a8 Or *God* **b**8 Psalm 68:18
c9 Or *the depths of the earth* **d**26 Psalm 4:4

whom you were sealed[m] for the day of
redemption.[n] 31Get rid of[o] all bitterness,
rage and anger, brawling and slander,
along with every form of malice.[p]
32Be kind and compassionate to one
another,[q] forgiving each other, just as in
Christ God forgave you.[r]

5 Be imitators of God,[a] therefore, as
dearly loved children[b] 2and live a
life of love, just as Christ loved us[c] and
gave himself up for us[d] as a fragrant
offering and sacrifice to God.[e]

3But among you there must not be
even a hint of sexual immorality,[f] or of
any kind of impurity, or of greed,[g] be-
cause these are improper for God's holy
people. 4Nor should there be obscenity,
foolish talk[h] or coarse joking, which are
out of place, but rather thanksgiving.[i]
5For of this you can be sure: No im-
moral, impure or greedy person—such
a man is an idolater[j]—has any inherit-
ance[k] in the kingdom of Christ and of
God.[a][l] 6Let no-one deceive you[m] with
empty words, for because of such
things God's wrath[n] comes on those
who are disobedient.[o] 7Therefore do not
be partners with them.

8For you were once[p] darkness, but
now you are light in the Lord. Live as
children of light[q] 9(for the fruit[r] of the
light consists in all goodness,[s] right-
eousness and truth) 10and find out what
pleases the Lord.[t] 11Have nothing to do
with the fruitless deeds of darkness,[u]
but rather expose them. 12For it is
shameful even to mention what the dis-
obedient do in secret. 13But everything
exposed by the light[v] becomes visible,
14for it is light that makes everything
visible. This is why it is said:

"Wake up, O sleeper,[w]
rise from the dead,[x]
and Christ will shine on you."[y]

15Be very careful, then, how you live[z]
—not as unwise but as wise, 16making
the most of every opportunity,[a] because
the days are evil.[b] 17Therefore do not be
foolish, but understand what the Lord's
will is.[c] 18Do not get drunk on wine,[d]
which leads to debauchery. Instead, be
filled with the Spirit.[e] 19Speak to one
another with psalms, hymns and
spiritual songs.[f] Sing and make music
in your heart to the Lord, 20always
giving thanks[g] to God the Father for
everything, in the name of our Lord
Jesus Christ.

21Submit to one another[h] out of
reverence for Christ.

Wives and Husbands

5:22–6:9pp—Col 3:18–4:1

22Wives, submit to your husbands[i] as
to the Lord.[j] 23For the husband is the
head of the wife as Christ is the head of
the church,[k] his body, of which he is the
Saviour. 24Now as the church submits to
Christ, so also wives should submit to
their husbands[l] in everything.

25Husbands, love your wives,[m] just as
Christ loved the church and gave him-
self up for her[n] 26to make her holy,[o]
cleansing[b] her by the washing[p] with
water through the word, 27and to pre-
sent her to himself[q] as a radiant church,
without stain or wrinkle or any other
blemish, but holy and blameless.[r] 28In
this same way, husbands ought to love
their wives[s] as their own bodies. He
who loves his wife loves himself. 29After
all, no-one ever hated his own body, but
he feeds and cares for it, just as Christ
does the church—30for we are members
of his body.[t] 31"For this reason a man
will leave his father and mother and be
united to his wife, and the two will
become one flesh."[c][u] 32This is a pro-
found mystery—but I am talking about
Christ and the church. 33However, each
one of you also must love his wife[v] as he
loves himself, and the wife must respect
her husband.

Children and Parents

6 Children, obey your parents in the
Lord, for this is right.[a] 2"Honour
your father and mother"—which is the
first commandment with a promise—
3"that it may go well with you and that
you may enjoy long life on the earth."[a][b]

4Fathers, do not exasperate your chil-
dren;[c] instead, bring them up in the
training and instruction of the Lord.[d]

Slaves and Masters

5Slaves, obey your earthly masters
with respect[e] and fear, and with
sincerity of heart,[f] just as you would
obey Christ.[g] 6Obey them not only to
win their favour when their eye is on

30 [m]2Co 1:22; 5:5; Eph 1:13; [n]Ro 8:23
31 [o]**ver 22**; [p]Col 3:8; 1Pe 2:1
32 [q]1Pe 3:8; [r]Mt 6:14–15; Col 3:12–13

Ch. 5

1 [a]Mt 5:48; Lk 6:36; [b]**Jn 1:12**
2 [c]**Jn 13:34**; [d]ver 25; **Gal 1:4**; 2:20; [e]Heb 7:27
3 [f]**1Co 6:18**; [g]Col 3:5
4 [h]Eph 4:29; [i]**ver 20**
5 [j]Col 3:5; [k]**Ac 20:32**; [l]**Mt 25:34**
6 [m]**Mk 13:5**; [n]**Ro 1:18**; [o]Eph 2:2
8 [p]**Eph 2:2**; [q]Jn 8:12; **Lk 16:8**; **Ac 26:18**
9 [r]Mt 7:16–20; Gal 5:22; [s]Ro 15:14
10 [t]**1Ti 5:4**
11 [u]Ro 13:12; 2Co 6:14
13 [v]Jn 3:20–21
14 [w]Ro 13:11; [x]Isa 26:19; Jn 5:25; [y]Isa 60:1; Mal 4:2
15 [z]ver 2
16 [a]Col 4:5; [b]Eph 6:13
17 [c]Ro 12:2; Col 1:9; 1Th 4:3
18 [d]Lev 10:9; Pr 20:1; Isa 28:7; Ro 13:13; [e]**Lk 1:15**
19 [f]Ps 27:6; 95:2; Ac 16:25; 1Co 14:15,26; Col 3:16
20 [g]ver 4; Job 1:21; Ps 34:1; Col 3:17; Heb 13:15
21 [h]Gal 5:13; 1Pe 5:5
22 [i]Ge 3:16; 1Co 14:34; Col 3:18; 1Ti 2:12; Tit 2:5; 1Pe 3:1,5–6; [j]Eph 6:5
23 [k]**Eph 1:22**
24 [l]**ver 22**
25 [m]ver 28,33; Col 3:19; [n]**ver 2**
26 [o]Jn 17:19; Heb 2:11; 10:10, 14; 13:12; [p]**Ac 22:16**
27 [q]**2Co 4:14**; [r]Eph 1:4
28 [s]ver 25
30 [t]**Ro 12:5**; **1Co 12:27**
31 [u]Ge 2:24; Mt 19:5; 1Co 6:16
33 [v]ver 25

Ch. 6

1 [a]Pr 6:20; Col 3:20
3 [b]Ex 20:12; Dt 5:16
4 [c]Col 3:21; [d]Ge 18:19; Dt 6:7; Pr 13:24; 22:6
5 [e]1Ti 6:1; Tit 2:9; 1Pe 2:18; [f]Col 3:22; [g]Eph 5:22

---

[a]5 Or *kingdom of the Christ and God*
[b]26 Or *having cleansed*
[c]*31* Gen. 2:24
[a]3 Deut. 5:16

you, but like slaves of Christ,[h] doing
the will of God from your heart.
7Serve wholeheartedly, as if you were
serving the Lord, not men,[i] 8because
you know that the Lord will reward
everyone for whatever good he does,[j]
whether he is slave or free.
9And masters, treat your slaves in the
same way. Do not threaten them, since
you know that he who is both their
Master and yours[k] is in heaven, and
there is no favouritism[l] with him.

The Armour of God

10Finally, be strong in the Lord[m] and
in his mighty power.[n] 11Put on the full
armour of God[o] so that you can take
your stand against the devil's schemes.
12For our struggle is not against flesh
and blood,[p] but against the rulers,
against the authorities,[q] against the
powers[r] of this dark world and against
the spiritual forces of evil in the heaven-
ly realms.[s] 13Therefore put on the full
armour of God,[t] so that when the day of
evil comes, you may be able to stand
your ground, and after you have done
everything, to stand. 14Stand firm then,
with the belt of truth buckled round
your waist,[u] with the breastplate of
righteousness in place,[v] 15and with your
feet fitted with the readiness that comes
from the gospel of peace.[w] 16In addition
to all this, take up the shield of faith,[x]
with which you can extinguish all the
flaming arrows of the evil one.[y] 17Take
the helmet of salvation[z] and the sword
of the Spirit,[a] which is the word of
God.[b] 18And pray in the Spirit[c] on all
occasions[d] with all kinds of prayers
and requests.[e] With this in mind, be
alert and always keep on praying[f] for
all the saints.
19Pray also for me,[g] that whenever I
open my mouth, words may be given
me so that I will fearlessly[h] make known
the mystery[i] of the gospel, 20for which I
am an ambassador[j] in chains.[k] Pray that
I may declare it fearlessly, as I should.

Final Greetings

21Tychicus,[l] the dear brother and
faithful servant in the Lord, will tell you
everything, so that you also may know
how I am and what I am doing. 22I am
sending him to you for this very
purpose, that you may know how we
are,[m] and that he may encourage you.[n]
23Peace[o] to the brothers, and love with
faith from God the Father and the Lord
Jesus Christ. 24Grace to all who love our
Lord Jesus Christ with an undying love.

6 [h]**Ro 6:22**
7 [i]Col 3:23
8 [j]**Mt 16:27;** Col 3:24
9 [k]Job 31:13–14; [l]**Ac 10:34**
10 [m]2Sa 10:12; Ps 27:14; Hag 2:4; 1Co 16:13; 2Ti 2:1; [n]Eph 1:19
11 [o]ver 13; Ro 13:12; 1Th 5:8
12 [p]1Co 15:50; Heb 2:14; [q]Eph 1:21; 3:10; [r]Ro 8:38; [s]**Eph 1:3**
13 [t]ver 11; **2Co 6:7**
14 [u]Isa 11:5; [v]Ps 132:9; Isa 59:17; 1Th 5:8
15 [w]Isa 52:7; Ro 10:15
16 [x]1Jn 5:4; [y]**Mt 5:37**
17 [z]Isa 59:17; [a]Isa 49:2; [b]**Heb 4:12**
18 [c]Ro 8:26–27; [d]**Lk 18:1;** [e]Mt 26:41; Php 1:4; 4:6; [f]**Ac 1:14;** Col 1:3
19 [g]**1Th 5:25;** [h]**Ac 4:29;** [i]**Ro 16:25**
20 [j]2Co 5:20; [k]**Ac 21:33**
21 [l]**Ac 20:4**
22 [m]Col 4:7–9; [n]Col 2:2; 4:8

23 [o]Gal 6:16; 2Th 3:16; 1Pe 5:14

Philippians

1 Paul and Timothy,[a] servants of
Christ Jesus,

To all the saints[b] in Christ Jesus at
Philippi,[c] together with the overseers[a][d]
and deacons:[e]

2Grace and peace to you from God our
Father and the Lord Jesus Christ.[f]

Thanksgiving and Prayer

3I thank my God every time I remem-
ber you.[g] 4In all my prayers for all of
you, I always pray[h] with joy 5because of
your partnership[i] in the gospel from the
first day[j] until now, 6being confident of
this, that he who began a good work in
you will carry it on to completion[k] until
the day of Christ Jesus.[l]
7It is right[m] for me to feel this way
about all of you, since I have you in my
heart;[n] for whether I am in chains[o] or
defending[p] and confirming the gospel,
all of you share in God's grace with me.
8God can testify[q] how I long for all of you
with the affection of Christ Jesus.
9And this is my prayer: that your love[r]
may abound more and more in knowl-
edge and depth of insight,[s] 10so that you
may be able to discern what is best and
may be pure and blameless until the day
of Christ,[t] 11filled with the fruit of right-
eousness[u] that comes through Jesus
Christ—to the glory and praise of God.

Paul's Chains Advance the Gospel

12Now I want you to know, brothers,
that what has happened to me has really
served to advance the gospel. 13As a
result, it has become clear throughout
the whole palace guard[b] and to every-
one else that I am in chains[v] for Christ.
14Because of my chains,[w] most of the
brothers in the Lord have been
encouraged to speak the word of God
more courageously and fearlessly.[x]
15It is true that some preach Christ out
of envy and rivalry, but others out of
goodwill. 16The latter do so in love,
knowing that I am put here for the
defence of the gospel.[y] 17The former
preach Christ out of selfish ambition,[z]
not sincerely, supposing that they can
stir up trouble for me while I am in
chains.[c][a] 18But what does it matter? The
important thing is that in every way,
whether from false motives or true,
Christ is preached. And because of this I
rejoice.
Yes, and I will continue to rejoice,
19for I know that through your prayers[b]
and the help given by the Spirit of Jesus
Christ,[c] what has happened to me will
turn out for my deliverance.[d][d] 20I eager-
ly expect[e] and hope that I will in no way
be ashamed, but will have sufficient
courage[f] so that now as always Christ
will be exalted in my body,[g] whether by
life or by death.[h] 21For to me, to live is
Christ[i] and to die is gain. 22If I am to go
on living in the body, this will mean
fruitful labour for me. Yet what shall I
choose? I do not know! 23I am torn be-
tween the two: I desire to depart[j] and be
with Christ,[k] which is better by far; 24but
it is more necessary for you that I remain
in the body. 25Convinced of this, I know
that I will remain, and I will continue
with all of you for your progress and joy
in the faith, 26so that through my being
with you again your joy in Christ Jesus
will overflow on account of me.
27Whatever happens, conduct your-
selves in a manner worthy[l] of the gospel
of Christ. Then, whether I come and see
you or only hear about you in my ab-
sence, I will know that you stand firm[m]
in one spirit, contending[n] as one man
for the faith of the gospel 28without
being frightened in any way by those
who oppose you. This is a sign to them
that they will be destroyed, but that you
will be saved—and that by God. 29For it
has been granted to you[o] on behalf of
Christ not only to believe on him, but
also to suffer[p] for him, 30since you are
going through the same struggle[q] you
saw[r] I had, and now hear[s] that I still
have.

Ch. 1
1 [a]**Ac 16:1**; 2Co 1:1; [b]**Ac 9:13**; [c]**Ac 16:12**; [d]**1Ti 3:1**; [e]1Ti 3:8
2 [f]**Ro 1:7**
3 [g]**Ro 1:8**
4 [h]**Ro 1:10**
5 [i]Ac 2:42; Php 4:15; [j]Ac 16:12–40
6 [k]Ps 138:8; [l]ver 10; **1Co 1:8**
7 [m]2Pe 1:13; [n]2Co 7:3; [o]ver 13–14, 17; **Ac 21:33**; [p]ver 16
8 [q]**Ro 1:9**
9 [r]1Th 3:12; [s]**Eph 1:17**
10 [t]ver 6; **1Co 1:8**
11 [u]**Jas 3:18**
13 [v]ver 7, 14, 17; **Ac 21:33**
14 [w]ver 7, 13, 17; **Ac 21:33**; [x]**Ac 4:29**
16 [y]ver 7, 12
17 [z]Php 2:3; [a]ver 7, 13–14; **Ac 21:33**
19 [b]2Co 1:11; [c]**Ac 16:7**; [d]Phm 22
20 [e]Ro 8:19; [f]ver 14; [g]1Co 6:20; [h]Ro 14:8
21 [i]Gal 2:20
23 [j]2Ti 4:6; [k]**Jn 12:26**
27 [l]**Eph 4:1**; [m]**1Co 16:13**; [n]Jude 3
29 [o]Mt 5:11–12; Ac 5:41; [p]**Ac 14:22**
30 [q]1Th 2:2; Heb 10:32; [r]Ac 16:19–40; [s]ver 13

[a]1 Traditionally *bishops*
[b]13 Or *whole palace*
[c]16,17 Some late manuscripts have verses 16 and 17 in reverse order.
[d]19 Or *salvation*

Imitating Christ's Humility

2 If you have any encouragement
from being united with Christ, if
any comfort from his love, if any
fellowship with the Spirit,[a] if any
tenderness and compassion,[b] 2then
make my joy complete[c] by being like-
minded,[d] having the same love, being
one[e] in spirit and purpose. 3Do nothing
out of selfish ambition or vain conceit,[f]
but in humility consider others better
than yourselves.[g] 4Each of you should
look not only to your own interests, but
also to the interests of others.[h]
5Your attitude should be the same as
that of Christ Jesus:[i]

6Who, being in very nature[a] God,[j]
did not consider equality with God[k]
something to be grasped,
7but made himself nothing,[l]
taking the very nature[b] of a
servant,[m]
being made in human likeness.[n]
8And being found in appearance as a
man,
he humbled himself
and became obedient to death[o]—
even death on a cross![p]
9Therefore God exalted him[q] to the
highest place
and gave him the name that is above
every name,[r]
10that at the name of Jesus every knee
should bow,[s]
in heaven and on earth and under
the earth,[t]
11and every tongue confess that Jesus
Christ is Lord,[u]
to the glory of God the Father.

Shining as Stars

12Therefore, my dear friends, as you
have always obeyed—not only in my
presence, but now much more in my
absence—continue to work out your
salvation with fear and trembling,[v] 13for
it is God who works in you[w] to will and
to act according to his good purpose.[x]
14Do everything without com-
plaining[y] or arguing, 15so that you may
become blameless[z] and pure, children
of God[a] without fault in a crooked and
depraved generation,[b] in which you
shine like stars in the universe 16as you
hold out[c] the word of life—in order that
I may boast on the day of Christ[c] that I
did not run[d] or labour for nothing.[e] 17But
even if I am being poured out like a
drink offering[f] on the sacrifice[g] and ser-
vice coming from your faith, I am glad
and rejoice with all of you.[h] 18So you too
should be glad and rejoice with me.

Timothy and Epaphroditus

19I hope in the Lord Jesus to send
Timothy[i] to you soon,[j] that I also may be
cheered when I receive news about you.
20I have no-one else like him,[k] who takes
a genuine interest in your welfare. 21For
everyone looks out for his own in-
terests,[l] not those of Jesus Christ. 22But
you know that Timothy has proved
himself, because as a son with his
father[m] he has served with me in the
work of the gospel. 23I hope, therefore,
to send him as soon as I see how things
go with me.[n] 24And I am confident[o] in
the Lord that I myself will come soon.
25But I think it is necessary to send
back to you Epaphroditus, my brother,
fellow-worker[p] and fellow-soldier,[q]
who is also your messenger, whom you
sent to take care of my needs.[r] 26For he
longs for all of you[s] and is distressed
because you heard he was ill. 27Indeed
he was ill, and almost died. But God had
mercy on him, and not on him only but
also on me, to spare me sorrow upon
sorrow. 28Therefore I am all the more
eager to send him,[t] so that when you see
him again you may be glad and I may
have less anxiety. 29Welcome him in the
Lord with great joy, and honour men
like him,[u] 30because he almost died for
the work of Christ, risking his life to
make up for the help you could not give
me.[v]

No Confidence in the Flesh

3 Finally, my brothers, rejoice in the
Lord! It is no trouble for me to write
the same things to you again,[a] and it is a
safeguard for you.
2Watch out for those dogs,[b] those
men who do evil, those mutilators of the
flesh. 3For it is we who are the circum-
cision,[c] we who worship by the Spirit of
God, who glory in Christ Jesus,[d] and
who put no confidence in the flesh—
4though I myself have reasons for such
confidence.[e]
If anyone else thinks he has reasons
to put confidence in the flesh, I have
more: 5circumcised[f] on the eighth day,
of the people of Israel,[g] of the tribe of
Benjamin,[h] a Hebrew of Hebrews; in
regard to the law, a Pharisee;[i] 6as for

Ch. 2

1 [a]2Co 13:14; [b]Col 3:12
2 [c]**Jn 3:29**; [d]Php 4:2; [e]**Ro 15:5**
3 [f]Gal 5:26; [g]Ro 12:10; 1Pe 5:5
4 [h]**1Co 10:24**
5 [i]**Mt 11:29**
6 [j]Jn 1:1; **14:9**; [k]Jn 5:18
7 [l]2Co 8:9; [m]**Mt 20:28**; [n]**Jn 1:14**; Ro 8:3; Heb 2:17
8 [o]**Mt 26:39**; Jn 10:18; Ro 5:19; Heb 5:8; [p]**1Co 1:23**
9 [q]Isa 52:13; 53:12; Da 7:14; Ac 2:33; Heb 2:9; [r]Eph 1:20–21
10 [s]Ps 95:6; Isa 45:23; Ro 14:11; [t]Mt 28:18; Eph 1:10; Col 1:20
11 [u]**Jn 13:13**
12 [v]**2Co 7:15**
13 [w]Ezr 1:5; 1Co 12:6; 15:10; Gal 2:8; Heb 13:21; [x]Eph 1:5
14 [y]1Co 10:10; 1Pe 4:9
15 [z]**1Th 3:13**; [a]Mt 5:45,48; Eph 5:1; [b]Ac 2:40
16 [c]**1Co 1:8**; [d]**1Co 9:24**; [e]1Th 2:19
17 [f]2Co 12:15; 2Ti 4:6; [g]Ro 15:16; [h]**2Co 6:10**
19 [i]**Ac 16:1**; [j]ver 23
20 [k]1Co 16:10
21 [l]**1Co 10:24**
22 [m]1Co 4:17; 1Ti 1:2
23 [n]ver 19
24 [o]Php 1:25
25 [p]Ro 16:3,9, 21; 2Co 8:23; Php 4:3; Col 4:11; Phm 1; [q]Phm 2; [r]Php 4:18
26 [s]Php 1:8
28 [t]ver 25
29 [u]1Co 16:18; 1Ti 5:17
30 [v]1Co 16:17

Ch. 3

1 [a]Php 2:18
2 [b]Ps 22:16,20; Rev 22:15
3 [c]Ro 2:28–29; Gal 6:15; Col 2:11; [d]Ro 15:17; Gal 6:14
4 [e]2Co 11:21
5 [f]**Lk 1:59**; [g]2Co 11:22; [h]Ro 11:1; [i]Ac 23:6

a6 Or *in the form of* b7 Or *the form*
c16 Or *hold on to*

zeal,[j] persecuting the church;[k] as for legalistic righteousness,[l] faultless.

7But whatever was to my profit I now consider loss[m] for the sake of Christ. 8What is more, I consider everything a loss compared to the surpassing greatness of knowing[n] Christ Jesus my Lord, for whose sake I have lost all things. I consider them rubbish, that I may gain Christ[o] 9and be found in him, not having a righteousness of my own that comes from the law,[p] but that which is through faith in Christ—the righteousness[q] that comes from God and is by faith.[r] 10I want to know[s] Christ and the power of his resurrection and the fellowship of sharing in his sufferings,[t] becoming like him in his death,[u] 11and so, somehow, to attain to the resurrection[v] from the dead.

Pressing on Towards the Goal

12Not that I have already obtained all this, or have already been made perfect,[w] but I press on to take hold[x] of that for which Christ Jesus took hold of me.[y] 13Brothers, I do not consider myself yet to have taken hold of it. But one thing I do: Forgetting what is behind[z] and straining towards what is ahead, 14I press on[a] towards the goal to win the prize[b] for which God has called[c] me heavenwards in Christ Jesus.

15All of us who are mature[d] should take such a view of things.[e] And if on some point you think differently, that too God will make clear to you.[f] 16Only let us live up to what we have already attained.

17Join with others in following my example,[g] brothers, and take note of those who live according to the pattern we gave you.[h] 18For, as I have often told you before and now say again even with tears,[i] many live as enemies of the cross of Christ.[j] 19Their destiny[k] is destruction, their god is their stomach,[l] and their glory is in their shame.[m] Their mind is on earthly things.[n] 20But our citizenship[o] is in heaven.[p] And we eagerly await a Saviour from there, the Lord Jesus Christ,[q] 21who, by the power[r] that enables him to bring everything under his control, will transform our lowly bodies[s] so that they will be like his glorious body.[t]

4 Therefore, my brothers, you whom I love and long for,[a] my joy and crown, that is how you should stand firm[b] in the Lord, dear friends!

Exhortations

2I plead with Euodia and I plead with Syntyche to agree with each other[c] in the Lord. 3Yes, and I ask you, loyal yoke-fellow,[a] help these women who have contended at my side in the cause of the gospel, along with Clement and the rest of my fellow-workers,[d] whose names are in the book of life.[e]

4Rejoice in the Lord always. I will say it again: Rejoice![f] 5Let your gentleness be evident to all. The Lord is near.[g] 6Do not be anxious about anything,[h] but in everything, by prayer and petition, with thanksgiving, present your requests to God.[i] 7And the peace of God,[j] which transcends all understanding,[k] will guard your hearts and your minds in Christ Jesus.

8Finally, brothers, whatever is true, whatever is noble, whatever is right, whatever is pure, whatever is lovely, whatever is admirable—if anything is excellent or praiseworthy—think about such things. 9Whatever you have learned or received or heard from me, or seen in me—put it into practice.[l] And the God of peace[m] will be with you.

Thanks for Their Gifts

10I rejoice greatly in the Lord that at last you have renewed your concern for me.[n] Indeed, you have been concerned, but you had no opportunity to show it. 11I am not saying this because I am in need, for I have learned to be content[o] whatever the circumstances. 12I know what it is to be in need, and I know what it is to have plenty. I have learned the secret of being content in any and every situation, whether well fed or hungry,[p] whether living in plenty or in want.[q] 13I can do everything through him who gives me strength.[r]

14Yet it was good of you to share[s] in my troubles. 15Moreover, as you Philippians know, in the early days[t] of your acquaintance with the gospel, when I set out from Macedonia,[u] not one church shared with me in the matter of giving and receiving, except you only;[v] 16for even when I was in Thessalonica,[w] you sent me aid again and again when I was in need.[x] 17Not that I am looking for a gift, but I am looking for what may be

6 [j]**Ac 21:20;** [k]**Ac 8:3;** [l]ver 9; Ro 10:5
7 [m]Mt 13:44; Lk 14:33
8 [n]ver 10; Jer 9:23–24; Jn 17:3; Eph 4:13; **2Pe 1:2;** [o]Ps 73:25
9 [p]ver 6; Ro 10:5; [q]Jer 33:16; [r]**Ro 9:30**
10 [s]**ver 8;** [t]**2Co 1:5;** [u]**Ro 6:3–5**
11 [v]**Jn 11:24; Ro 6:5;** Rev 20:5–6
12 [w]1Co 13:10; [x]1Ti 6:12; [y]Ac 9:5–6
13 [z]Lk 9:62
14 [a]Heb 6:1; [b]1Co 9:24; [c]**Ro 8:28**
15 [d]**1Co 2:6;** [e]Gal 5:10; [f]Eph 1:17; 1Th 4:9
17 [g]**1Co 4:16;** [h]**1Ti 4:12**
18 [i]Ac 20:31; [j]Gal 6:12
19 [k]Ps 73:17; [l]Ro 16:18; [m]Ro 6:21; Jude 13; [n]Ro 8:5–6; Col 3:2
20 [o]Eph 2:19; [p]Col 3:1; Heb 12:22; [q]**1Co 1:7**
21 [r]Eph 1:19; [s]1Co 15:43–53; [t]Ro 8:29; Col 3:4

Ch. 4

1 [a]Php 1:8; [b]**1Co 16:13**
2 [c]Php 2:2
3 [d]**Php 2:25;** [e]**Lk 10:20**
4 [f]Ps 85:6; 97:12; Hab 3:18; **Mt 5:12;** Ro 12:12; Php 3:1
5 [g]Ps 119:151; 145:18; Heb 10:37; Jas 5:8–9
6 [h]Mt 6:25–34; [i]Eph 6:18; 1Ti 2:1
7 [j]Isa 26:3; **Jn 14:27;** [k]Eph 3:19
9 [l]**1Co 4:16;** [m]**Ro 15:33**
10 [n]2Co 11:9
11 [o]1Ti 6:6,8; Heb 13:5
12 [p]**1Co 4:11;** [q]2Co 11:9
13 [r]2Co 12:9; Eph 3:16; Col 1:11; 1Ti 1:12; 2Ti 4:17
14 [s]Php 1:7
15 [t]Php 1:5; [u]**Ac 16:9;** [v]2Co 11:8–9
16 [w]**Ac 17:1;** [x]1Th 2:9

[a]3 Or *loyal Syzygus*

credited to your account.[y] 18I have
received full payment and even more;
I am amply supplied, now that I have
received from Epaphroditus[z] the gifts
you sent. They are a fragrant[a] offering,
an acceptable sacrifice, pleasing to God.
19And my God will meet all your needs[b]
according to his glorious riches[c] in Christ
Jesus.

20To our God and Father[d] be glory for
ever and ever. Amen.[e]

17 [y]1Co 9:11–12
18 [z]Php 2:25; [a]**2Co 2:14**
19 [b]Ps 23:1; 2Co 9:8; [c]**Ro 2:4**
20 [d]Gal 1:4; 1Th 1:3; 3:11,13; [e]**Ro 11:36**
21 [f]Gal 1:2
22 [g]**Ac 9:13**
23 [h]**Ro 16:20;** [i]**Gal 6:18**

Final Greetings

21Greet all the saints in Christ Jesus.
The brothers who are with me[f] send
greetings. 22All the saints[g] send you
greetings, especially those who belong
to Caesar's household.

23The grace of the Lord Jesus Christ[h]
be with your spirit.[i] Amen.[b]

[b]23 Some manuscripts do not have *Amen.*

Colossians

1 Paul, an apostle[a] of Christ Jesus by the will of God,[b] and Timothy[c] our brother,

2 To the holy and faithful[a] brothers in Christ at Colosse:

Grace[d] and peace to you from God our Father.[b] [e]

Thanksgiving and Prayer

3 We always thank God,[f] the Father of our Lord Jesus Christ, when we pray for you, 4 because we have heard of your faith in Christ Jesus and of the love[g] you have for all the saints[h]— 5 the faith and love that spring from the hope[i] that is stored up for you in heaven[j] and that you have already heard about in the word of truth,[k] the gospel 6 that has come to you. All over the world[l] this gospel is bearing fruit[m] and growing, just as it has been doing among you since the day you heard it and understood God's grace in all its truth. 7 You learned it from Epaphras,[n] our dear fellow-servant, who is a faithful minister[o] of Christ on our[c] behalf, 8 and who also told us of your love in the Spirit.[p]

9 For this reason, since the day we heard about you,[q] we have not stopped praying for you[r] and asking God to fill you with the knowledge of his will[s] through all spiritual wisdom and understanding.[t] 10 And we pray this in order that you may live a life worthy[u] of the Lord and may please him[v] in every way: bearing fruit in every good work, growing in the knowledge of God,[w] 11 being strengthened with all power[x] according to his glorious might so that you may have great endurance and patience,[y] and joyfully 12 giving thanks to the Father,[z] who has qualified you[d] to share in the inheritance[a] of the saints in the kingdom of light.[b] 13 For he has rescued us from the dominion of darkness[c] and brought us into the kingdom[d] of the Son he loves,[e] 14 in whom we have redemption,[e] [f] the forgiveness of sins.[g]

The Supremacy of Christ

15 He is the image[h] of the invisible God,[i] the firstborn[j] over all creation. 16 For by him all things were created:[k] things in heaven and on earth, visible and invisible, whether thrones or powers or rulers or authorities;[l] all things were created by him and for him.[m] 17 He is before all things,[n] and in him all things hold together. 18 And he is the head[o] of the body, the church;[p] he is the beginning and the firstborn[q] from among the dead,[r] so that in everything he might have the supremacy. 19 For God was pleased[s] to have all his fulness[t] dwell in him, 20 and through him to reconcile[u] to himself all things, whether things on earth or things in heaven,[v] by making peace[w] through his blood,[x] shed on the cross.

21 Once you were alienated from God and were enemies[y] in your minds[z] because of[f] your evil behaviour. 22 But now he has reconciled[a] you by Christ's physical body[b] through death to present you[c] holy in his sight, without blemish and free from accusation[d]— 23 if you continue[e] in your faith, established[f] and firm, not moved from the hope[g] held out in the gospel. This is the gospel that you heard and that has been proclaimed to every creature under heaven,[h] and of which I, Paul, have become a servant.[i]

Paul's Labour for the Church

24 Now I rejoice[j] in what was suffered for you, and I fill up in my flesh what is still lacking in regard to Christ's afflictions,[k] for the sake of his body, which is the church.[l] 25 I have become its servant[m] by the commission God gave me[n] to

Ch. 1

1 [a]**1Co 1:1;** [b]**2Co 1:1;** [c]**Ac 16:1**
2 [d]Col 4:18; [e]**Ro 1:7**
3 [f]**Ro 1:8**
4 [g]Gal 5:6; [h]**Ac 9:13;** Eph 1:15; Phm 5
5 [i]ver 23; 1Th 5:8; Tit 1:2; [j]1Pe 1:4; [k]**2Ti 2:15**
6 [l]ver 23; **Ro 10:18;** [m]Jn 15:16
7 [n]Col 4:12; Phm 23; [o]Col 4:7
8 [p]Ro 15:30
9 [q]ver 4; Eph 1:15; [r]**Ro 1:10;** [s]**Eph 5:17;** [t]**Eph 1:17**
10 [u]**Eph 4:1;** [v]**2Co 5:9;** [w]ver 6
11 [x]**Php 4:13;** [y]Eph 4:2
12 [z]Eph 5:20; [a]**Ac 20:32;** [b]**Ac 26:18**
13 [c]**Ac 26:18;** [d]2Pe 1:11; [e]Mt 3:17
14 [f]**Ro 3:24;** [g]Eph 1:7
15 [h]**Jn 14:9;** [i]**Jn 1:18;** 1Ti 1:17; Heb 11:27; [j]**ver 18**
16 [k]**Jn 1:3;** [l]Eph 1:20–21; [m]**Ro 11:36**
17 [n]**Jn 1:2**
18 [o]**Eph 1:22;** [p]ver 24; **1Co 12:27;** [q]ver 15; Ps 89:27; Ro 8:29; Heb 1:6; [r]Ac 26:23; Rev 1:5
19 [s]**Eph 1:5;** [t]**Jn 1:16**
20 [u]**Ro 5:10;** [v]Eph 1:10; [w]**Lk 2:14;** [x]Eph 2:13
21 [y]Ro 5:10; [z]Eph 2:3
22 [a]ver 20; **Ro 5:10;** [b]Ro 7:4; [c]**2Co 4:14;** [d]Eph 1:4; 5:27
23 [e]**Ro 11:22;** [f]Eph 3:17; [g]ver 5; [h]ver 6; **Ro 10:18;** [i]ver 25; **1Co 3:5**
24 [j]**2Co 6:10;** [k]**2Co 1:5;** [l]**1Co 12:27**
25 [m]ver 23; **1Co 3:5;** [n]Eph 3:2

[a]2 Or *believing*
[b]2 Some manuscripts *Father and the Lord Jesus Christ*
[c]7 Some manuscripts *your*
[d]12 Some manuscripts *us*
[e]14 A few late manuscripts *redemption through his blood*
[f]21 Or *minds, as shown by*

present to you the word of God[o] in its
fulness—26the mystery[p] that has been
kept hidden for ages and generations,
but is now disclosed to the saints. 27To
them God has chosen to make known[q]
among the Gentiles the glorious riches[r]
of this mystery, which is Christ in you,[s]
the hope of glory.

28We proclaim him, admonishing[t]
and teaching everyone with all wis-
dom,[u] so that we may present everyone
perfect[v] in Christ. 29To this end I
labour,[w] struggling[x] with all his energy,
which so powerfully works in me.[y]

2 I want you to know how much I am
struggling[a] for you and for those at
Laodicea,[b] and for all who have not met
me personally. 2My purpose is that they
may be encouraged in heart[c] and united
in love, so that they may have the full
riches of complete understanding, in
order that they may know the mystery[d]
of God, namely, Christ, 3in whom are
hidden all the treasures of wisdom and
knowledge.[e] 4I tell you this so that no-
one may deceive you by fine-sounding
arguments.[f] 5For though I am absent
from you in body, I am present with you
in spirit[g] and delight to see how orderly[h]
you are and how firm[i] your faith in
Christ[j] is.

Freedom From Human Regulations Through Life With Christ

6So then, just as you received Christ
Jesus as Lord,[k] continue to live in him,
7rooted[l] and built up in him, strength-
ened in the faith as you were taught,[m]
and overflowing with thankfulness.

8See to it that no-one takes you cap-
tive through hollow and deceptive phil-
osophy,[n] which depends on human
tradition and the basic principles of this
world[o] rather than on Christ.

9For in Christ all the fulness[p] of the
Deity lives in bodily form, 10and you
have been given fulness in Christ, who
is the Head[q] over every power and auth-
ority.[r] 11In him you were also circum-
cised,[s] in the putting off of the sinful
nature,[a][t] not with a circumcision done
by the hands of men but with the
circumcision done by Christ, 12having
been buried with him in baptism[u] and
raised with him[v] through your faith in
the power of God, who raised him from
the dead.[w]

13When you were dead in your sins[x]
and in the uncircumcision of your sinful
nature,[b] God made you[c] alive[y] with
Christ. He forgave us all our sins,[z]
14having cancelled the written code,
with its regulations,[a] that was against us
and that stood opposed to us; he took it
away, nailing it to the cross.[b] 15And
having disarmed the powers and auth-
orities,[c] he made a public spectacle of
them, triumphing over them[d] by the
cross.[d]

16Therefore do not let anyone judge
you[e] by what you eat or drink,[f] or with
regard to a religious festival,[g] a New
Moon celebration[h] or a Sabbath day.[i]
17These are a shadow of the things that
were to come;[j] the reality, however, is
found in Christ. 18Do not let anyone
who delights in false humility[k] and the
worship of angels disqualify you for the
prize.[l] Such a person goes into great
detail about what he has seen, and his
unspiritual mind puffs him up with idle
notions. 19He has lost connection with
the Head,[m] from whom the whole
body,[n] supported and held together by
its ligaments and sinews, grows as God
causes it to grow.[o]

20Since you died with Christ[p] to the
basic principles of this world,[q] why, as
though you still belonged to it, do you
submit to its rules:[r] 21"Do not handle!
Do not taste! Do not touch!"? 22These
are all destined to perish[s] with use, be-
cause they are based on human com-
mands and teachings.[t] 23Such regula-
tions indeed have an appearance of wis-
dom, with their self-imposed worship,
their false humility[u] and their harsh
treatment of the body, but they lack any
value in restraining sensual indulgence.

Rules for Holy Living

3 Since, then, you have been raised
with Christ,[a] set your hearts on
things above, where Christ is seated at
the right hand of God.[b] 2Set your minds
on things above, not on earthly things.[c]
3For you died,[d] and your life is now
hidden with Christ in God. 4When
Christ, who is your[a] life,[e] appears,[f] then
you also will appear with him in glory.[g]

5Put to death,[h] therefore, whatever
belongs to your earthly nature:[i] sexual
immorality,[j] impurity, lust, evil desires
and greed,[k] which is idolatry.[l] 6Because
of these, the wrath of God[m] is coming.[b]
7You used to walk in these ways, in the

25 [o]**Heb 4:12**
26 [p]**Ro 16:25**
27 [q]**Mt 13:11;** [r]**Ro 2:4;** [s]**Ro 8:10**
28 [t]Col 3:16; [u]1Co 2:6–7; [v]Mt 5:48; Eph 5:27
29 [w]1Co 15:10; 2Co 11:23; [x]Col 2:1; [y]Eph 1:19; 3:7

Ch. 2

1 [a]Col 1:29; 4:12; [b]Col 4:13,15–16; Rev 1:11; 3:14
2 [c]Eph 6:22; Col 4:8; [d]**Ro 16:25**
3 [e]Isa 11:2; Jer 23:5; Ro 11:33; 1Co 1:24,30
4 [f]**Ro 16:18**
5 [g]1Co 5:4; 1Th 2:17; [h]1Co 14:40; [i]1Pe 5:9; [j]**Ac 20:21**
6 [k]**Jn 13:13;** Col 1:10
7 [l]Eph 3:17; [m]Eph 4:21
8 [n]1Ti 6:20; [o]ver 20; Gal 4:3
9 [p]**Jn 1:16**
10 [q]**Eph 1:22;** [r]**Mt 28:18**
11 [s]Ro 2:29; Php 3:3; [t]**Gal 5:24**
12 [u]**Mt 28:19;** [v]**Ro 6:5;** [w]**Ac 2:24**
13 [x]Eph 2:1,5; [y]Eph 2:5; [z]Eph 4:32
14 [a]Eph 2:15; [b]1Pe 2:24
15 [c]ver 10; Eph 6:12; [d]Mt 12:29; Lk 10:18; Jn 12:31
16 [e]Ro 14:3–4; [f]Mk 7:19; Ro 14:17; [g]Lev 23:2; Ro 14:5; [h]1Ch 23:31; [i]Mk 2:27–28; Gal 4:10
17 [j]Heb 8:5; 10:1
18 [k]ver 23; [l]1Co 9:24; Php 3:14
19 [m]**Eph 1:22;** [n]**1Co 12:27;** [o]Eph 4:16
20 [p]**Ro 6:6;** [q]ver 8; Gal 4:3,9; [r]ver 14,16
22 [s]1Co 6:13; [t]Isa 29:13; Mt 15:9; Tit 1:14
23 [u]ver 18

Ch. 3

1 [a]**Ro 6:5;** [b]**Mk 16:19**
2 [c]Php 3:19–20
3 [d]**Ro 6:2;** 2Co 5:14
4 [e]Gal 2:20; [f]1Co 1:7; [g]1Pe 1:13; 1Jn 3:2
5 [h]**Ro 6:2; Eph 4:22;** [i]**Gal 5:24;** [j]**1Co 6:18;** [k]Eph 5:3; [l]Gal 5:19–21; Eph 5:5
6 [m]**Ro 1:18**

[a]11 Or *the flesh*
[b]13 Or *your flesh*
[c]13 Some manuscripts *us*
[d]15 Or *them in him*
[a]4 Some manuscripts *our*
[b]6 Some early manuscripts *coming on those who are disobedient*

life you once lived.[n] 8 But now you must rid yourselves[o] of all such things as these: anger, rage, malice, slander[p] and filthy language from your lips.[q] 9 Do not lie to each other,[r] since you have taken off your old self[s] with its practices 10 and have put on the new self,[t] which is being renewed[u] in knowledge in the image of its Creator.[v] 11 Here there is no Greek or Jew,[w] circumcised or uncircumcised,[x] barbarian, Scythian, slave or free,[y] but Christ is all,[z] and is in all.

12 Therefore, as God's chosen people, holy and dearly loved, clothe yourselves[a] with compassion, kindness, humility,[b] gentleness and patience.[c] 13 Bear with each other[d] and forgive whatever grievances you may have against one another. Forgive as the Lord forgave you.[e] 14 And over all these virtues put on love,[f] which binds them all together in perfect unity.[g]

15 Let the peace of Christ[h] rule in your hearts, since as members of one body[i] you were called to peace.[j] And be thankful. 16 Let the word of Christ[k] dwell in you richly as you teach and admonish one another with all wisdom,[l] and as you sing psalms,[m] hymns and spiritual songs with gratitude in your hearts to God.[n] 17 And whatever you do,[o] whether in word or deed, do it all in the name of the Lord Jesus, giving thanks[p] to God the Father through him.

Rules for Christian Households

3:18–4:1pp—Eph 5:22–6:9

18 Wives, submit to your husbands,[q] as is fitting in the Lord.

19 Husbands, love your wives and do not be harsh with them.

20 Children, obey your parents in everything, for this pleases the Lord.

21 Fathers, do not embitter your children, or they will become discouraged.

22 Slaves, obey your earthly masters in everything; and do it, not only when their eye is on you and to win their favour, but with sincerity of heart and reverence for the Lord. 23 Whatever you do, work at it with all your heart, as working for the Lord, not for men, 24 since you know that you will receive an inheritance[r] from the Lord as a reward.[s] It is the Lord Christ you are serving. 25 Anyone who does wrong will be repaid for his wrong, and there is no favouritism.[t]

4 Masters, provide your slaves with what is right and fair,[a] because you know that you also have a Master in heaven.

Further Instructions

2 Devote yourselves to prayer,[b] being watchful and thankful. 3 And pray for us, too, that God may open a door[c] for our message, so that we may proclaim the mystery[d] of Christ, for which I am in chains.[e] 4 Pray that I may proclaim it clearly, as I should. 5 Be wise[f] in the way you act towards outsiders;[g] make the most of every opportunity.[h] 6 Let your conversation be always full of grace,[i] seasoned with salt,[j] so that you may know how to answer everyone.[k]

Final Greetings

7 Tychicus[l] will tell you all the news about me. He is a dear brother, a faithful minister and fellow-servant[m] in the Lord. 8 I am sending him to you for the express purpose that you may know about our[a] circumstances and that he may encourage your hearts.[n] 9 He is coming with Onesimus,[o] our faithful and dear brother, who is one of you.[p] They will tell you everything that is happening here.

10 My fellow-prisoner Aristarchus[q] sends you his greetings, as does Mark,[r] the cousin of Barnabas.[s] (You have received instructions about him; if he comes to you, welcome him.) 11 Jesus, who is called Justus, also sends greetings. These are the only Jews among my fellow-workers[t] for the kingdom of God, and they have proved a comfort to me. 12 Epaphras,[u] who is one of you[v] and a servant of Christ Jesus, sends greetings. He is always wrestling in prayer for you,[w] that you may stand firm in all the will of God, mature[x] and fully assured. 13 I vouch for him that he is working hard for you and for those at Laodicea[y] and Hierapolis. 14 Our dear friend Luke,[z] the doctor, and Demas[a] send greetings. 15 Give my greetings to the brothers at Laodicea,[b] and to Nympha and the church in her house.[c]

16 After this letter has been read to you, see that it is also read[d] in the church of the Laodiceans and that you in turn read the letter from Laodicea.

17 Tell Archippus:[e] "See to it that you complete the work you have received in the Lord."[f]

18 I, Paul, write this greeting in my own hand.[g] Remember[h] my chains.[i] Grace be with you.[j]

7 [n]**Eph 2:2**
8 [o]**Eph 4:22;** [p]Eph 4:31; [q]Eph 4:29
9 [r]**Eph 4:25;** [s]**Ro 6:6**
10 [t]**Ro 6:4; 13:14;** [u]Ro 12:2; **2Co 4:16;** Eph 4:23; [v]Eph 2:10
11 [w]Ro 10:12; 1Co 12:13; [x]**1Co 7:19;** [y]Gal 3:28; [z]Eph 1:23
12 [a]ver 10; [b]Php 2:3; [c]2Co 6:6; Gal 5:22–23; Eph 4:2
13 [d]Eph 4:2; [e]Eph 4:32
14 [f]1Co 13:1–13; [g]**Ro 15:5**
15 [h]**Jn 14:27;** [i]**Ro 12:5;** [j]**Ro 14:19**
16 [k]Ro 10:17; [l]Col 1:28; [m]Ps 47:7; [n]**Eph 5:19**
17 [o]1Co 10:31; [p]**Eph 5:20**
18 [q]**Eph 5:22**
24 [r]**Ac 20:32;** [s]**Mt 16:27**
25 [t]**Ac 10:34**

Ch. 4

1 [a]Lev 25:43,53
2 [b]**Lk 18:1**
3 [c]**Ac 14:27;** [d]**Ro 16:25;** [e]**Ac 21:33**
5 [f]Eph 5:15; [g]**Mk 4:11;** [h]Eph 5:16
6 [i]Eph 4:29; [j]Mk 9:50; [k]1Pe 3:15
7 [l]**Ac 20:4;** [m]Eph 6:21–22; Col 1:7
8 [n]Eph 6:21–22; Col 2:2
9 [o]Phm 10; [p]ver 12
10 [q]**Ac 19:29;** [r]**Ac 12:12;** [s]**Ac 4:36**
11 [t]**Php 2:25**
12 [u]Col 1:7; Phm 23; [v]ver 9; [w]**Ro 15:30;** [x]**1Co 2:6**
13 [y]**Col 2:1**
14 [z]2Ti 4:11; Phm 24; [a]2Ti 4:10; Phm 24
15 [b]**Col 2:1;** [c]**Ro 16:5**
16 [d]2Th 3:14; **1Ti 4:13**
17 [e]Phm 2; [f]2Ti 4:5
18 [g]**1Co 16:21;** [h]Heb 13:3; [i]**Ac 21:33;** [j]1Ti 6:21; 2Ti 4:22; Tit 3:15; Heb 13:25

[a]8 Some manuscripts *that he may know about your*

1 Thessalonians

1 Paul, Silas[a][a] and Timothy,[b]

To the church of the Thessalonians[c] in God the Father and the Lord Jesus Christ:

Grace and peace to you.[b][d]

Thanksgiving for the Thessalonians' Faith

2 We always thank God for all of you,[e] mentioning you in our prayers.[f] 3 We continually remember before our God and Father[g] your work produced by faith,[h] your labour prompted by love,[i] and your endurance inspired by hope[j] in our Lord Jesus Christ.

4 For we know, brothers loved by God,[k] that he has chosen you, 5 because our gospel[l] came to you not simply with words, but also with power,[m] with the Holy Spirit and with deep conviction. You know[n] how we lived among you for your sake. 6 You became imitators of us[o] and of the Lord; in spite of severe suffering,[p] you welcomed the message with the joy[q] given by the Holy Spirit.[r] 7 And so you became a model[s] to all the believers in Macedonia[t] and Achaia.[u] 8 The Lord's message[v] rang out from you not only in Macedonia and Achaia—your faith in God has become known everywhere.[w] Therefore we do not need to say anything about it, 9 for they themselves report what kind of reception you gave us. They tell how you turned[x] to God from idols[y] to serve the living and true God,[z] 10 and to wait for his Son from heaven,[a] whom he raised from the dead[b]—Jesus, who rescues us from the coming wrath.[c]

Paul's Ministry in Thessalonica

2 You know, brothers, that our visit to you[a] was not a failure.[b] 2 We had previously suffered[c] and been insulted in Philippi,[d] as you know, but with the help of our God we dared to tell you his gospel in spite of strong opposition.[e] 3 For the appeal we make does not spring from error or impure motives,[f] nor are we trying to trick you.[g] 4 On the contrary, we speak as men approved by God to be entrusted with the gospel.[h] We are not trying to please men[i] but God, who tests our hearts.[j] 5 You know we never used flattery, nor did we put on a mask to cover up greed[k]—God is our witness.[l] 6 We were not looking for praise from men,[m] not from you or anyone else.

As apostles[n] of Christ we could have been a burden to you,[o] 7 but we were gentle among you, like a mother caring for her little children.[p] 8 We loved you so much that we were delighted to share with you not only the gospel of God[q] but our lives as well,[r] because you had become so dear to us. 9 Surely you remember, brothers, our toil and hardship; we worked[s] night and day in order not to be a burden to anyone[t] while we preached the gospel of God to you.

10 You are witnesses,[u] and so is God,[v] of how holy,[w] righteous and blameless we were among you who believed. 11 For you know that we dealt with each of you as a father deals with his own children,[x] 12 encouraging, comforting and urging you to live lives worthy[y] of God, who calls[z] you into his kingdom and glory.

13 And we also thank God continually[a] because, when you received the word of God,[b] which you heard from us, you accepted it not as the word of men, but as it actually is, the word of God, which is at work in you who believe. 14 For you, brothers, became imitators[c] of God's churches in Judea,[d] which are in Christ Jesus: You suffered from your own countrymen[e] the same things those churches suffered from the Jews, 15 who killed the Lord Jesus[f] and the prophets[g] and also drove us out. They displease God and are hostile to all men 16 in their

Ch. 1

1 [a]**Ac 15:22;** [b]**Ac 16:1**; 2Th 1:1; [c]**Ac 17:1;** [d]**Ro 1:7**
2 [e]**Ro 1:8**; Eph 5:20; [f]**Ro 1:10**
3 [g]**Php 4:20;** [h]Gal 5:6; 2Th 1:11; Jas 2:14–26; [i]1Th 3:6; 2Th 1:3; **1Co 13:13;** [j]Ro 8:25
4 [k]Col 3:12; 2Th 2:13
5 [l]**2Co 2:12;** 2Th 2:14; [m]Ro 1:16; **15:13;** [n]1Th 2:10
6 [o]**1Co 4:16;** [p]Ac 17:5–10; [q]**2Co 6:10;** [r]Ac 13:52
7 [s]**1Ti 4:12;** [t]**Ac 16:9;** [u]**Ac 18:12**
8 [v]2Th 3:1; [w]Ro 1:8
9 [x]Ac 14:15; [y]1Co 12:2; Gal 4:8; [z]**Mt 16:16**
10 [a]**1Co 1:7;** [b]**Ac 2:24;** [c]**Ro 1:18**

Ch. 2

1 [a]1Th 1:5,9; [b]2Th 1:10
2 [c]Ac 14:19; 16:22; Php 1:30; [d]**Ac 16:12;** [e]Ac 17:1–9
3 [f]2Co 2:17; [g]2Co 4:2
4 [h]Gal 2:7; 1Ti 1:11; [i]**Ro 2:29;** [j]**Rev 2:23**
5 [k]**Ac 20:33;** [l]ver 10; **Ro 1:9**
6 [m]Jn 5:41,44; [n]1Co 9:1–2; [o]2Co 11:7–11
7 [p]**ver 11**
8 [q]**Ro 1:1;** [r]2Co 12:15; 1Jn 3:16
9 [s]**Ac 18:3;** [t]**2Co 11:9;** 2Th 3:8
10 [u]1Th 1:5; [v]ver 5; **Ro 1:9;** [w]2Co 1:12
11 [x]ver 7; 1Co 4:14; Gal 4:19; **1Ti 1:2;** Phm 10; **1Jn 2:1**
12 [y]**Eph 4:1;** [z]**Ro 8:28**
13 [a]1Th 1:2; **Ro 1:8;** [b]**Heb 4:12**
14 [c]1Th 1:6; [d]Gal 1:22; [e]Ac 17:5; 2Th 1:4
15 [f]Lk 24:20; Ac 2:23; [g]**Mt 5:12**

[a]*1* Greek *Silvanus*, a variant of *Silas*
[b]*1* Some early manuscripts *you from God our Father and the Lord Jesus Christ*

effort to keep us from speaking to the
Gentiles[h] so that they may be saved. In
this way they always heap up their sins
to the limit.[i] The wrath of God has come
upon them at last.[a]

Paul's Longing to See the Thessalonians

17But, brothers, when we were torn
away from you for a short time (in
person, not in thought),[j] out of our
intense longing we made every effort
to see you.[k] 18For we wanted to come to
you—certainly I, Paul, did, again and
again—but Satan[l] stopped us.[m] 19For
what is our hope, our joy, or the
crown[n] in which we will glory[o] in the
presence of our Lord Jesus Christ when
he comes?[p] Is it not you? 20Indeed,
you are our glory[q] and joy.

3 So when we could stand it no
longer,[a] we thought it best to be left
by ourselves in Athens.[b] 2We sent
Timothy,[c] who is our brother and God's
fellow-worker[a] [d] in spreading the gospel
of Christ,[e] to strengthen and encourage
you in your faith, 3so that no-one would
be unsettled by these trials.[f] You know
quite well that we were destined for
them.[g] 4In fact, when we were with you,
we kept telling you that we would be
persecuted. And it turned out that way,
as you well know.[h] 5For this reason,
when I could stand it no longer,[i] I sent to
find out about your faith.[j] I was afraid
that in some way the tempter[k] might
have tempted you and our efforts might
have been useless.[l]

Timothy's Encouraging Report

6But Timothy[m] has just now come to
us from you[n] and has brought good
news about your faith and love.[o] He has
told us that you always have pleasant
memories of us and that you long to see
us, just as we also long to see you.[p]
7Therefore, brothers, in all our distress
and persecution we were encouraged
about you because of your faith. 8For
now we really live, since you are
standing firm[q] in the Lord. 9How can
we thank God enough for you[r] in return
for all the joy we have in the presence of
our God because of you?[s] 10Night and
day we pray[t] most earnestly that we may
see you again[u] and supply what is
lacking in your faith.

11Now may our God and Father[v] him-
self and our Lord Jesus clear the way for
us to come to you. 12May the Lord make
your love increase and overflow for
each other[w] and for everyone else, just
as ours does for you. 13May he streng-
then your hearts so that you will be
blameless[x] and holy in the presence of
our God and Father[y] when our Lord
Jesus comes[z] with all his holy ones.[a]

Living to Please God

4 Finally, brothers,[a] we instructed
you how to live[b] in order to please
God,[c] as in fact you are living. Now we
ask you and urge you in the Lord Jesus
to do this more and more. 2For you
know what instructions we gave you by
the authority of the Lord Jesus.

3It is God's will[d] that you should be
sanctified: that you should avoid sexual
immorality;[e] 4that each of you should
learn to control his own body[a] [f] in a way
that is holy and honourable, 5not in
passionate lust[g] like the heathen,[h] who
do not know God;[i] 6and that in this
matter no-one should wrong his brother
or take advantage of him.[j] The Lord will
punish men[k] for all such sins,[l] as we
have already told you and warned you.
7For God did not call us to be impure,
but to live a holy life.[m] 8Therefore, he
who rejects this instruction does not
reject man but God, who gives you his
Holy Spirit.[n]

9Now about brotherly love[o] we do
not need to write to you,[p] for you
yourselves have been taught by God[q]
to love each other.[r] 10And in fact, you
do love all the brothers throughout
Macedonia.[s] Yet we urge you, brothers,
to do so more and more.[t]

11Make it your ambition to lead a quiet
life, to mind your own business and to
work with your hands,[u] just as we told
you, 12so that your daily life may win the
respect of outsiders[v] and so that you will
not be dependent on anybody.

The Coming of the Lord

13Brothers, we do not want you to be
ignorant[w] about those who fall asleep,[x]
or to grieve like the rest of men, who
have no hope.[y] 14We believe that Jesus
died and rose again[z] and so we believe
that God will bring with Jesus those
who have fallen asleep in him.[a]

16 [h]Ac 13:45,50; 17:5; **20:3**; 21:27; 24:9; [i]Mt 23:32
17 [j]1Co 5:3; Col 2:5; [k]1Th 3:10
18 [l]**Mt 4:10**; [m]Ro 1:13; 15:22
19 [n]Isa 62:3; Php 4:1; [o]2Co 1:14; [p]**Mt 16:27; Lk 17:30; 1Co 1:7**; 4:5; 1Th 3:13; 2Th 1:8–10; 1Pe 1:7; 1Jn 2:28; **Rev 1:7**
20 [q]2Co 1:14

Ch. 3

1 [a]ver 5; [b]**Ac 17:15**
2 [c]**Ac 16:1**; [d]**1Co 3:9**; [e]**2Co 2:12**
3 [f]Mk 4:17; Jn 16:33; Ro 5:3; 2Co 1:4; 4:17; 2Ti 3:12; [g]**Ac 9:16**; 14:22
4 [h]1Th 2:14
5 [i]ver 1; [j]ver 2; [k]Mt 4:3; [l]Gal 2:2; Php 2:16
6 [m]**Ac 16:1**; [n]Ac 18:5; [o]1Th 1:3; [p]1Th 2:17–18
8 [q]**1Co 16:13**
9 [r]1Th 1:2; [s]1Th 2:19–20
10 [t]2Ti 1:3; [u]1Th 2:17
11 [v]ver 13; **Php 4:20**
12 [w]Php 1:9; 1Th 4:9–10; 2Th 1:3
13 [x]Ps 15:2; 1Co 1:8; Php 2:15; 1Th 5:23; 1Ti 6:14; 2Pe 3:14; [y]ver 11; **Php 4:20**; [z]**1Th 2:19**; [a]Mt 25:31; 2Th 1:7

Ch. 4

1 [a]2Co 13:11; 2Th 3:1; [b]**Eph 4:1**; [c]**2Co 5:9**
3 [d]**Eph 5:17**; [e]**1Co 6:18**
4 [f]1Co 7:2,9
5 [g]Ro 1:26; [h]Eph 4:17; [i]**Gal 4:8**
6 [j]Lev 25:17; 1Co 6:8; [k]Dt 32:35; Ps 94:1; Ro 2:5–11; 12:19; Heb 10:30–31; [l]Heb 13:4
7 [m]Lev 11:44; 1Pe 1:15
8 [n]Eze 36:27; Ro 5:5; 2Co 1:22; Gal 4:6; 1Jn 3:24
9 [o]**Ro 12:10**; [p]1Th 5:1; [q]**Jn 6:45**; [r]**Jn 13:34**
10 [s]**Ac 16:9**; [t]**1Th 3:12** *11* [u]Eph 4:28; 2Th 3:10–12
12 [v]**Mk 4:11** *13* [w]**Ro 11:25**; [x]**Mt 9:24**; [y]Eph 2:12
14 [z]Ro 14:9; 1Co 15:3–4; 2Co 5:15; [a]1Co 15:18

[a]16 Or *them fully*
[a]2 Some manuscripts *brother and fellow-worker;* other manuscripts *brother and God's servant*
[a]4 Or *learn to live with his own wife;* or *learn to acquire a wife*

15According to the Lord's own word, we
tell you that we who are still alive, who
are left till the coming of the Lord,[b] will
certainly not precede those who have
fallen asleep.[c] 16For the Lord himself
will come down from heaven,[d] with a
loud command, with the voice of the
archangel[e] and with the trumpet call of
God,[f] and the dead in Christ will rise
first.[g] 17After that, we who are still alive
and are left[h] will be caught up together
with them in the clouds[i] to meet the
Lord in the air. And so we will be with
the Lord[j] for ever. 18Therefore encour-
age each other[k] with these words.

5 Now, brothers, about times and
dates[a] we do not need to write to
you,[b] 2for you know very well that the
day of the Lord[c] will come like a thief in
the night.[d] 3While people are saying,
"Peace and safety",[e] destruction will
come on them suddenly,[f] as labour
pains on a pregnant woman, and they
will not escape.[g]

4But you, brothers, are not in dark-
ness[h] so that this day should surprise
you like a thief.[i] 5You are all sons of the
light[j] and sons of the day. We do not
belong to the night or to the darkness.
6So then, let us not be like others, who
are asleep,[k] but let us be alert[l] and self-
controlled.[m] 7For those who sleep, sleep
at night, and those who get drunk, get
drunk at night.[n] 8But since we belong to
the day,[o] let us be self-controlled, put-
ting on faith and love as a breastplate,[p]
and the hope of salvation[q] as a helmet.[r]
9For God did not appoint us to suffer
wrath[s] but to receive salvation through
our Lord Jesus Christ.[t] 10He died for us
so that, whether we are awake or
asleep, we may live together with him.[u]
11Therefore encourage one another[v] and
build each other up,[w] just as in fact you
are doing.

15 [b]**1Co 1:7;** [c]1Co 15:52
16 [d]**Mt 16:27;** [e]Jude 9; [f]**Mt 24:31;** [g]1Co 15:23; 2Th 2:1; Rev 14:13
17 [h]1Co 15:52; [i]Ac 1:9; **8:39; Rev 1:7;** 11:12; [j]**Jn 12:26**
18 [k]1Th 5:11

Ch. 5

1 [a]Ac 1:7; [b]1Th 4:9
2 [c]**1Co 1:8;** [d]**Lk 12:39**
3 [e]Jer 4:10; 6:14; Eze 13:10; [f]Job 15:21; Ps 35:8; 55:15; Isa 29:5; 47:9,11; [g]2Th 1:9
4 [h]**Ac 26:18;** 1Jn 2:8; [i]ver 2
5 [j]**Lk 16:8**
6 [k]Ro 13:11; [l]**Mt 25:13;** [m]**Ac 24:25**
7 [n]Ac 2:15; Ro 13:13; 2Pe 2:13
8 [o]ver 5; [p]**Eph 6:14;** [q]Ro 8:24; [r]Isa 59:17; Eph 6:17
9 [s]1Th 1:10; [t]2Th 2:13–14
10 [u]Ro 14:9; 2Co 5:15
11 [v]1Th 4:18; [w]Eph 4:29
12 [x]Ro 16:6,12; 1Co 15:10; [y]1Ti 5:17; Heb 13:17
13 [z]**Mk 9:50**
14 [a]2Th 3:6–7, 11; [b]Ro 14:1; 1Co 8:7–12
15 [c]Ro 12:17; 1Pe 3:9; [d]Eph 4:32
16 [e]Php 4:4

Final Instructions

12Now we ask you, brothers, to
respect those who work hard[x] among
you, who are over you in the Lord[y] and
who admonish you. 13Hold them in the
highest regard in love because of their
work. Live in peace with each other.[z]
14And we urge you, brothers, warn
those who are idle,[a] encourage the
timid, help the weak,[b] be patient with
everyone. 15Make sure that nobody
pays back wrong for wrong,[c] but always
try to be kind to each other[d] and to
everyone else.

16Be joyful always;[e] 17pray continu-
ally;[f] 18give thanks in all circumstances,[g]
for this is God's will for you in Christ
Jesus.

19Do not put out the Spirit's fire;[h] 20do
not treat prophecies[i] with contempt.
21Test everything.[j] Hold on to the good.[k]
22Avoid every kind of evil.

23May God himself, the God of peace,[l]
sanctify you through and through. May
your whole spirit, soul[m] and body be
kept blameless[n] at the coming of our
Lord Jesus Christ.[o] 24The one who calls[p]
you is faithful[q] and he will do it.[r]

25Brothers, pray for us.[s] 26Greet all the
brothers with a holy kiss.[t] 27I charge you
before the Lord to have this letter read
to all the brothers.[u]

28The grace of our Lord Jesus Christ
be with you.[v]

17 [f]**Lk 18:1** *18* [g]**Eph 5:20** *19* [h]Eph 4:30
20 [i]1Co 14:1–40 *21* [j]1Co 14:29; 1Jn 4:1; [k]Ro 12:9
23 [l]**Ro 15:33;** [m]Heb 4:12; [n]**1Th 3:13;** [o]**1Th 2:19**
24 [p]**Ro 8:28;** [q]**1Co 1:9;** [r]Nu 23:19; Php 1:6
25 [s]Eph 6:19; Col 4:3; 2Th 3:1; Heb 13:18
26 [t]**Ro 16:16** *27* [u]2Th 3:14; **1Ti 4:13**
28 [v]**Ro 16:20**

2 Thessalonians

1 Paul, Silas[a][a] and Timothy,[b]

To the church of the Thessalonians[c] in God our Father and the Lord Jesus Christ:

2Grace and peace to you from God the Father and the Lord Jesus Christ.[d]

Thanksgiving and Prayer

3We ought always to thank God for you,[e] brothers, and rightly so, because your faith is growing more and more, and the love every one of you has for each other is increasing.[f] 4Therefore, among God's churches we boast[g] about your perseverance and faith[h] in all the persecutions and trials you are enduring.[i]

5All this is evidence[j] that God's judgment is right, and as a result you will be counted worthy[k] of the kingdom of God, for which you are suffering. 6God is just:[l] He will pay back trouble to those who trouble you[m] 7and give relief to you who are troubled, and to us as well. This will happen when the Lord Jesus is revealed from heaven[n] in blazing fire[o] with his powerful angels.[p] 8He will punish[q] those who do not know God[r] and do not obey the gospel of our Lord Jesus.[s] 9They will be punished with everlasting destruction[t] and shut out from the presence of the Lord[u] and from the majesty of his power[v] 10on the day[w] he comes to be glorified[x] in his holy people and to be marvelled at among all those who have believed. This includes you, because you believed our testimony to you.[y]

11With this in mind, we constantly pray for you,[z] that our God may count you worthy[a] of his calling,[b] and that by his power he may fulfil every good purpose[c] of yours and every act prompted by your faith.[d] 12We pray this so that the name of our Lord Jesus may be glorified in you,[e] and you in him, according to the grace of our God and the Lord Jesus Christ.[b]

Ch. 1

1 [a]**Ac 15:22**; [b]**Ac 16:1**; 1Th 1:1; [c]**Ac 17:1**
2 [d]**Ro 1:7**
3 [e]**Ro 1:8**; Eph 5:20; [f]**1Th 3:12**
4 [g]2Co 7:14; [h]1Th 1:3; [i]1Th 1:6; 2:14; **3:3**
5 [j]Php 1:28; [k]Lk 20:35
6 [l]Lk 18:7–8; [m]Ro 12:19; Col 3:25; **Rev 6:10**
7 [n]**Lk 17:30**; [o]Heb 10:27; **12:29**; 2Pe 3:7; **Rev 1:14**; [p]Jude 14
8 [q]Ps 79:6; Isa 66:15; Jer 10:25; [r]**Gal 4:8**; [s]Ro 2:8; **2Co 2:12**
9 [t]Php 3:19; 1Th 5:3; 2Pe 3:7; [u]2Ki 17:18; [v]Isa 2:10,19; 2Th 2:8
10 [w]1Co 3:13; [x]Jn 17:10; [y]1Co 1:6
11 [z]**Ro 1:10**; [a]ver 5; [b]**Ro 8:28**; [c]Ro 15:14; [d]1Th 1:3
12 [e]Isa 24:15; Php 2:9–11

Ch. 2

1 [a]**1Th 2:19**; [b]Mk 13:27; 1Th 4:15–17
2 [c]ver 15; 2Th 3:17; [d]**1Co 1:8**; [e]2Ti 2:18
3 [f]**Mk 13:5**; [g]Mt 24:10–12; [h]ver 8; Da 7:25; 8:25; 11:36; Rev 13:5–6
4 [i]1Co 8:5; [j]Isa 14:13–14; Eze 28:2
5 [k]1Th 3:4
6 [l]ver 7
7 [m]ver 6
8 [n]**ver 3**; [o]Isa 11:4; Rev 2:16; 19:15; [p]**Lk 17:30**

The Man of Lawlessness

2 Concerning the coming of our Lord Jesus Christ[a] and our being gathered to him,[b] we ask you, brothers, 2not to become easily unsettled or alarmed by some prophecy, report or letter[c] supposed to have come from us, saying that the day of the Lord[d] has already come.[e] 3Don't let anyone deceive you[f] in any way, for ⌞that day will not come⌟ until the rebellion[g] occurs and the man of lawlessness[a] is revealed,[h] the man doomed to destruction. 4He will oppose and will exalt himself over everything that is called God[i] or is worshipped, so that he sets himself up in God's temple, proclaiming himself to be God.[j]

5Don't you remember that when I was with you I used to tell you these things?[k] 6And now you know what is holding him back,[l] so that he may be revealed at the proper time. 7For the secret power of lawlessness is already at work; but the one who now holds it back[m] will continue to do so till he is taken out of the way. 8And then the lawless one will be revealed,[n] whom the Lord Jesus will overthrow with the breath of his mouth[o] and destroy by the splendour of his coming.[p] 9The coming of the lawless one will be in accordance with the work of Satan[q] displayed in all kinds of counterfeit miracles, signs and wonders,[r] 10and in every sort of evil that deceives those who are perishing.[s] They perish because they refused to love the truth and so be saved.[t] 11For this reason God sends them[u] a powerful delusion[v] so that they will believe the lie[w] 12and so that all will be condemned who have not believed the truth but have delighted in wickedness.[x]

9 [q]**Mt 4:10**; [r]Mt 24:24; Rev 13:13; **Jn 4:48**
10 [s]**1Co 1:18**; [t]Pr 4:6; Jn 3:17–19
11 [u]Ro 1:28; [v]Mt 24:5; **Mk 13:5**; [w]Ro 1:25
12 [x]Ro 1:32; 2:8

---

[a]*1* Greek *Silvanus*, a variant of *Silas*
[b]*12* Or *God and Lord, Jesus Christ*
[a]*3* Some manuscripts *sin*

Stand Firm

13But we ought always to thank God
for you,[y] brothers loved by the Lord,
because from the beginning God chose
you[b][z] to be saved[a] through the
sanctifying work of the Spirit[b] and
through belief in the truth. 14He called
you[c] to this through our gospel,[d] that
you might share in the glory of our
Lord Jesus Christ. 15So then, brothers,
stand firm[e] and hold to the teachings[c]
we passed on to you,[f] whether by word
of mouth or by letter.

16May our Lord Jesus Christ himself
and God our Father,[g] who loved us[h] and
by his grace gave us eternal encourage-
ment and good hope, 17encourage[i] your
hearts and strengthen[j] you in every
good deed and word.

Request for Prayer

3 Finally, brothers,[a] pray for us[b] that
the message of the Lord[c] may
spread rapidly and be honoured, just as
it was with you.[d] 2And pray that we may
be delivered from wicked and evil men,[e]
for not everyone has faith. 3But the Lord
is faithful,[f] and he will strengthen and
protect you from the evil one.[g] 4We have
confidence[h] in the Lord that you are
doing and will continue to do the things
we command. 5May the Lord direct
your hearts[i] into God's love and Christ's
perseverance.

Warning Against Idleness

6In the name of the Lord Jesus Christ,[j]
we command you, brothers, to keep
away from[k] every brother who is idle[l]
and does not live according to the
teaching[a] you received from us.[m] 7For
you yourselves know how you ought to
follow our example.[n] We were not idle
when we were with you, 8nor did we eat
anyone's food without paying for it. On
the contrary, we worked[o] night and
day, labouring and toiling so that we
would not be a burden to any of you.
9We did this, not because we do not
have the right to such help,[p] but in order
to make ourselves a model for you to
follow.[q] 10For even when we were with
you,[r] we gave you this rule: "If a man
will not work,[s] he shall not eat."

11We hear that some among you are
idle. They are not busy; they are busy-
bodies.[t] 12Such people we command
and urge in the Lord Jesus Christ[u] to
settle down and earn the bread they
eat.[v] 13And as for you, brothers, never
tire of doing what is right.[w]

14If anyone does not obey our instruc-
tion in this letter, take special note of
him. Do not associate with him,[x] in
order that he may feel ashamed.[y] 15Yet
do not regard him as an enemy, but
warn him as a brother.[z]

Final Greetings

16Now may the Lord of peace[a] himself
give you peace at all times and in every
way. The Lord be with all of you.[b]

17I, Paul, write this greeting in my
own hand,[c] which is the distinguishing
mark in all my letters. This is how I
write.

18The grace of our Lord Jesus Christ
be with you all.[d]

13 [y]**Ro 1:8**; [z]Eph 1:4; [a]1Th 5:9; [b]1Pe 1:2
14 [c]**Ro 8:28; 11:29**; [d]1Th 1:5
15 [e]**1Co 16:13**; [f]**1Co 11:2**
16 [g]**Php 4:20**; [h]**Jn 3:16**
17 [i]1Th 3:2; [j]2Th 3:3

Ch. 3

1 [a]1Th 4:1; [b]**1Th 5:25**; [c]1Th 1:8; [d]1Th 2:13
2 [e]**Ro 15:31**
3 [f]**1Co 1:9**; [g]**Mt 5:37**
4 [h]**2Co 2:3**
5 [i]1Ch 29:18
6 [j]1Co 5:4; [k]ver 14; **Ro 16:17**; [l]ver 7,11; [m]**1Co 11:2**
7 [n]ver 9; **1Co 4:16**
8 [o]**Ac 18:3**; Eph 4:28
9 [p]1Co 9:4–14; [q]ver 7; **1Co 4:16**
10 [r]1Th 3:4; [s]1Th 4:11
11 [t]ver 6–7; 1Ti 5:13
12 [u]1Th 4:1; [v]1Th 4:11; Eph 4:28
13 [w]Gal 6:9
14 [x]ver 6; **Ro 16:17**; [y]**1Co 4:14**
15 [z]Gal 6:1; 1Th 5:14; Phm 16
16 [a]**Ro 15:33**; [b]Ru 2:4
17 [c]**1Co 16:21**
18 [d]**Ro 16:20**

[b]13 Some manuscripts *because God chose you as his firstfruits* [c]15 Or *traditions* [a]6 Or *tradition*

1 Timothy

1 Paul, an apostle of Christ Jesus by the command of God[a] our Saviour[b] and of Christ Jesus our hope,[c]

2To Timothy[d] my true son[e] in the faith:

Grace, mercy and peace from God the Father and Christ Jesus our Lord.[f]

Warning Against False Teachers of the Law

3As I urged you when I went into Macedonia,[g] stay there in Ephesus[h] so that you may command certain men not to teach false doctrines[i] any longer 4nor to devote themselves to myths[j] and endless genealogies.[k] These promote controversies[l] rather than God's work —which is by faith. 5The goal of this command is love, which comes from a pure heart[m] and a good conscience[n] and a sincere faith.[o] 6Some have wandered away from these and turned to meaningless talk. 7They want to be teachers[p] of the law, but they do not know what they are talking about or what they so confidently affirm.[q]

8We know that the law is good[r] if one uses it properly. 9We also know that law**[a]** is made not for the righteous[s] but for lawbreakers and rebels,[t] the ungodly and sinful, the unholy and irreligious; for those who kill their fathers or mothers, for murderers, 10for adulterers and perverts, for slave traders and liars and perjurers—and for whatever else is contrary to the sound doctrine[u] 11that conforms to the glorious gospel of the blessed God, which he entrusted to me.[v]

The Lord's Grace to Paul

12I thank Christ Jesus our Lord, who has given me strength,[w] that he considered me faithful, appointing me to his service.[x] 13Even though I was once a blasphemer and a persecutor[y] and a violent man, I was shown mercy[z] because I acted in ignorance and unbelief.[a] 14The grace of our Lord was poured out on me abundantly,[b] along with the faith and love that are in Christ Jesus.[c]

15Here is a trustworthy saying[d] that deserves full acceptance: Christ Jesus came into the world to save sinners[e]—of whom I am the worst. 16But for that very reason I was shown mercy[f] so that in me, the worst of sinners, Christ Jesus might display his unlimited patience[g] as an example for those who would believe[h] on him and receive eternal life.[i] 17Now to the King[j] eternal, immortal,[k] invisible,[l] the only God,[m] be honour and glory for ever and ever. Amen.[n]

18Timothy, my son,[o] I give you this instruction in keeping with the prophecies once made about you,[p] so that by following them you may fight the good fight,[q] 19holding on to faith and a good conscience.[r] Some have rejected these and so have shipwrecked their faith.[s] 20Among them are Hymenaeus[t] and Alexander,[u] whom I have handed over to Satan[v] to be taught not to blaspheme.

Instructions on Worship

2 I urge, then, first of all, that requests, prayers,[a] intercession and thanksgiving be made for everyone— 2for kings and all those in authority,[b] that we may live peaceful and quiet lives in all godliness[c] and holiness. 3This is good, and pleases[d] God our Saviour,[e] 4who wants[f] all men[g] to be saved[h] and to come to a knowledge of the truth.[i] 5For there is one God[j] and one mediator[k] between God and men, the man Christ Jesus,[l] 6who gave himself as a ransom[m] for all men—the testimony[n] given in its proper time.[o] 7And for this purpose I was appointed a herald and an apostle —I am telling the truth, I am not lying[p] —and a teacher[q] of the true faith to the Gentiles.[r]

8I want men everywhere to lift up

Ch. 1

1 [a]**2Co 1:1**; Tit 1:3; [b]**Lk 1:47**; [c]Col 1:27
2 [d]**Ac 16:1**; [e]ver 18; 1Co 4:17; **1Th 2:11**; 2Ti 1:2; Tit 1:4; [f]**Ro 1:7**
3 [g]**Ac 16:9**; [h]**Ac 18:19**; [i]Gal 1:6–7; 1Ti 6:3
4 [j]1Ti 4:7; 2Ti 4:4; Tit 1:14; [k]Tit 3:9; [l]**2Ti 2:14**
5 [m]2Ti 2:22; [n]**Ac 23:1**; 1Ti 4:2; [o]Gal 5:6; 2Ti 1:5
7 [p]**Eph 4:11**; [q]Job 38:2
8 [r]Ro 7:12
9 [s]Gal 5:23; [t]Gal 3:19
10 [u]1Ti 6:3; 2Ti 1:13; 4:3; Tit 1:9; 2:1
11 [v]Gal 2:7; 1Th 2:4; Tit 1:3
12 [w]**Php 4:13**; [x]**Ac 9:15**
13 [y]**Ac 8:3**; [z]ver 16; [a]Ac 26:9
14 [b]2Co 4:15; [c]2Ti 1:13; **1Th 1:3**
15 [d]1Ti 3:1; 4:9; 2Ti 2:11; Tit 3:8; [e]Mk 2:17; **Jn 3:17**
16 [f]ver 13; [g]**Ro 2:4**; [h]**Jn 3:15**; [i]**Mt 25:46**
17 [j]Rev 15:3; [k]1Ti 6:16; [l]**Col 1:15**; [m]Jude 25; [n]**Ro 11:36**
18 [o]**ver 2**; [p]1Ti 4:14; [q]1Ti 6:12; 2Ti 2:3; 4:7
19 [r]ver 5; **Ac 23:1**; [s]1Ti 6:21; 2Ti 2:18
20 [t]2Ti 2:17; [u]2Ti 4:14; [v]1Co 5:5

Ch. 2

1 [a]Eph 6:18
2 [b]Ezr 6:10; Ro 13:1; [c]1Ti 3:16; 4:7–8; 6:3, 5–6,11; 2Ti 3:5; Tit 1:1
3 [d]**1Ti 5:4**; [e]**Lk 1:47**
4 [f]Eze 18:23,32; 33:11; [g]1Ti 4:10; Tit 2:11; 2Pe 3:9; [h]**Jn 3:17**; **Ro 11:14**; [i]2Ti 2:25; Tit 1:1; Heb 10:26
5 [j]Dt 6:4; Ro 3:29–30; 10:12; [k]**Gal 3:20**; [l]Ro 1:3
6 [m]**Mt 20:28**; [n]**1Co 1:6**; [o]1Ti 6:15; Tit 1:3
7 [p]**Ro 9:1**; [q]2Ti 1:11; [r]**Ac 9:15**

[a]9 Or *that the law*

holy hands[s] in prayer, without anger or
disputing.
9I also want women to dress mod-
estly, with decency and propriety,
not with braided hair or gold or pearls
or expensive clothes,[t] 10but with good
deeds,[u] appropriate for women who
profess to worship God.
11A woman should learn in quietness
and full submission.[v] 12I do not permit a
woman to teach or to have authority
over a man; she must be silent.[w] 13For
Adam was formed first, then Eve.[x]
14And Adam was not the one deceived;
it was the woman who was deceived
and became a sinner.[y] 15But women[a]
will be saved[b] through childbearing—
if they continue in faith, love[z] and
holiness with propriety.

Overseers and Deacons

3 Here is a trustworthy saying:[a] If
anyone sets his heart on being an
overseer,[a][b] he desires a noble task.
2Now the overseer must be above re-
proach,[c] the husband of but one wife,[d]
temperate,[e] self-controlled, respectable,
hospitable,[f] able to teach,[g] 3not given to
drunkenness,[h] not violent but gentle,
not quarrelsome,[i] not a lover of money.[j]
4He must manage his own family well
and see that his children obey him with
proper respect.[k] 5(If anyone does not
know how to manage his own family,
how can he take care of God's church?)[l]
6He must not be a recent convert, or he
may become conceited[m] and fall under
the same judgment[n] as the devil. 7He
must also have a good reputation with
outsiders,[o] so that he will not fall into
disgrace and into the devil's trap.[p]
8Deacons,[q] likewise, are to be men
worthy of respect, sincere, not indulg-
ing in much wine,[r] and not pursuing
dishonest gain. 9They must keep hold of
the deep truths of the faith with a clear
conscience.[s] 10They must first be tested;[t]
and then if there is nothing against
them, let them serve as deacons.
11In the same way, their wives[b] are
to be women worthy of respect, not
malicious talkers[u] but temperate[v] and
trustworthy in everything.
12A deacon must be the husband of
but one wife[w] and must manage his
children and his household well.[x]
13Those who have served well gain an
excellent standing and great assurance
in their faith in Christ Jesus.
14Although I hope to come to you
soon, I am writing you these instruc-
tions so that, 15if I am delayed, you will
know how people ought to conduct
themselves in God's household, which
is the church[y] of the living God,[z] the
pillar and foundation of the truth.
16Beyond all question, the mystery[a] of
godliness[b] is great:

He[c] appeared in a body,[d][c]
was vindicated by the Spirit,
was seen by angels,
was preached among the nations,[d]
was believed on in the world,
was taken up in glory.[e]

Instructions to Timothy

4 The Spirit[a] clearly says that in later
times[b] some will abandon the faith
and follow deceiving spirits[c] and things
taught by demons. 2Such teachings
come through hypocritical liars, whose
consciences have been seared as with a
hot iron.[d] 3They forbid people to marry[e]
and order them to abstain from certain
foods,[f] which God created[g] to be re-
ceived with thanksgiving[h] by those who
believe and who know the truth. 4For
everything God created is good,[i] and
nothing is to be rejected[j] if it is received
with thanksgiving, 5because it is conse-
crated by the word of God[k] and prayer.
6If you point these things out to the
brothers, you will be a good minister of
Christ Jesus, brought up in the truths of
the faith[l] and of the good teaching that
you have followed.[m] 7Have nothing to
do with godless myths and old wives'
tales;[n] rather, train yourself to be godly.[o]
8For physical training is of some value,
but godliness has value for all things,[p]
holding promise for both the present
life[q] and the life to come.[r]
9This is a trustworthy saying[s] that
deserves full acceptance 10(and for this
we labour and strive), that we have put
our hope in the living God,[t] who is
the Saviour of all men,[u] and especially
of those who believe.
11Command and teach these things.[v]
12Don't let anyone look down on you[w]
because you are young, but set an exam-
ple[x] for the believers in speech, in life, in
love, in faith[y] and in purity. 13Until I
come,[z] devote yourself to the public
reading of Scripture,[a] to preaching and

8 [s]Ps 24:4; 63:4; 134:2; 141:2; Lk 24:50
9 [t]1Pe 3:3
10 [u]Pr 31:13
11 [v]1Pe 3:3–4
12 [w]**Eph 5:22**
13 [x]Ge 2:7,22; 1Co 11:8
14 [y]Ge 3:1–6,13; 2Co 11:3
15 [z]1Ti 1:14

Ch. 3

1 [a]**1Ti 1:15**; [b]Ac 20:28; Php 1:1; Tit 1:7
2 [c]Tit 1:6–8; [d]ver 12; [e]ver 11; Tit 2:2; [f]**Ro 12:13**; [g]2Ti 2:24
3 [h]Tit 1:7; [i]2Ti 2:24; [j]Lk 16:14; 1Ti 6:10; 2Ti 3:2; Heb 13:5; 1Pe 5:2
4 [k]ver 12; Tit 1:6
5 [l]**1Co 10:32**
6 [m]1Ti 6:4; 2Ti 3:4; [n]**2Pe 2:4**
7 [o]**Mk 4:11**; [p]2Ti 2:26
8 [q]Php 1:1; [r]1Ti 5:23; Tit 1:7; 2:3
9 [s]**Ac 23:1**
10 [t]1Ti 5:22
11 [u]2Ti 3:3; Tit 2:3; [v]ver 2
12 [w]ver 2; [x]ver 4
15 [y]ver 5; **1Co 10:32**; [z]**Mt 16:16**
16 [a]**Ro 16:25**; [b]**1Ti 2:2**; [c]**Jn 1:14**; [d]Ps 9:11; Col 1:23; [e]**Mk 16:19**

Ch. 4

1 [a]Jn 16:13; **Ac 8:29**; 1Co 2:10; [b]2Ti 3:1; 2Pe 3:3; [c]**Mk 13:5**
2 [d]Eph 4:19
3 [e]Heb 13:4; [f]Col 2:16; [g]Ge 1:29; 9:3; [h]ver 4; Ro 14:6; 1Co 10:30
4 [i]Ge 1:10,12, 18,21,25,31; Mk 7:18–19; Ro 14:14–18; [j]**Ac 10:15**
5 [k]**Heb 4:12**
6 [l]1Ti 1:10; [m]2Ti 3:15
7 [n]1Ti 1:4; 2Ti 2:16; [o]**1Ti 2:2**
8 [p]1Ti 6:6; [q]Ps 37:9,11; Pr 22:4; Mt 6:33; Mk 10:29–30; [r]Mk 10:29–30
9 [s]**1Ti 1:15**
10 [t]**Mt 16:16**; [u]**Lk 1:47; 2:11**
11 [v]1Ti 5:7; 6:2
12 [w]**2Ti 1:7**; Tit 2:15; [x]Php 3:17; 1Th 1:7; 2Th 3:9; Tit 2:7; 1Pe 5:3; [y]1Ti 1:14
13 [z]1Ti 3:14; [a]Lk 4:16; Ac 13:14–16; Col 4:16; 1Th 5:27

a15 Greek *she* **b**15 Or *restored*
a1 Traditionally *bishop;* also in verse 2
b11 Or *way, deaconesses*
c16 Some manuscripts *God* **d**16 Or *in the flesh*

to teaching. 14Do not neglect your
gift, which was given you through a
prophetic message[b] when the body
of elders[c] laid their hands on you.[d]
15Be diligent in these matters; give
yourself wholly to them, so that every-
one may see your progress. 16Watch
your life and doctrine closely. Persevere
in them, because if you do, you will
save[e] both yourself and your hearers.

Advice About Widows, Elders and Slaves

5 Do not rebuke an older man[a]
harshly,[b] but exhort him as if he
were your father. Treat younger men[c]
as brothers, 2older women as mothers,
and younger women as sisters, with
absolute purity.
3Give proper recognition to those
widows who are really in need.[d] 4But if a
widow has children or grandchildren,
these should learn first of all to put their
religion into practice by caring for their
own family and so repaying their par-
ents and grandparents,[e] for this is pleas-
ing to God.[f] 5The widow who is really in
need[g] and left all alone puts her hope in
God[h] and continues night and day to
pray[i] and to ask God for help. 6But the
widow who lives for pleasure is dead
even while she lives.[j] 7Give the people
these instructions,[k] too, so that no-one
may be open to blame. 8If anyone does
not provide for his relatives, and
especially for his immediate family,
he has denied[l] the faith and is worse
than an unbeliever.
9No widow may be put on the list of
widows unless she is over sixty, has
been faithful to her husband,[a] 10and is
well known for her good deeds,[m] such
as bringing up children, showing hospi-
tality,[n] washing the feet[o] of the saints,
helping those in trouble[p] and devoting
herself to all kinds of good deeds.
11As for younger widows, do not put
them on such a list. For when their
sensual desires overcome their
dedication to Christ, they want to
marry. 12Thus they bring judgment on
themselves, because they have broken
their first pledge. 13Besides, they get
into the habit of being idle and going
about from house to house. And not
only do they become idlers, but also
gossips[q] and busybodies,[r] saying
things they ought not to. 14So I counsel
younger widows to marry,[s] to have
children, to manage their homes and
to give the enemy no opportunity for
slander.[t] 15Some have in fact already
turned away to follow Satan.[u]
16If any woman who is a believer has
widows in her family, she should help
them and not let the church be
burdened with them, so that the church
can help those widows who are really
in need.[v]
17The elders[w] who direct the affairs of
the church well are worthy of double
honour,[x] especially those whose work is
preaching and teaching. 18For the Scrip-
ture says, "Do not muzzle the ox while
it is treading out the grain,"[b y] and "The
worker deserves his wages."[c z] 19Do not
entertain an accusation against an elder[a]
unless it is brought by two or three
witnesses.[b] 20Those who sin are to be
rebuked[c] publicly, so that the others
may take warning.[d]
21I charge you, in the sight of God and
Christ Jesus[e] and the elect angels, to
keep these instructions without par-
tiality, and to do nothing out of
favouritism.
22Do not be hasty in the laying on of
hands,[f] and do not share in the sins of
others.[g] Keep yourself pure.[h]
23Stop drinking only water, and use a
little wine[i] because of your stomach and
your frequent illnesses.
24The sins of some men are obvious,
reaching the place of judgment ahead of
them; the sins of others trail behind
them. 25In the same way, good deeds
are obvious, and even those that are not
cannot be hidden.

6 All who are under the yoke of
slavery should consider their
masters worthy of full respect,[a] so that
God's name and our teaching may not
be slandered.[b] 2Those who have
believing masters are not to show less
respect for them because they are
brothers.[c] Instead, they are to serve
them even better, because those who
benefit from their service are believers,
and dear to them. These are the things
you are to teach and urge on them.[d]

Love of Money

3If anyone teaches false doctrines[e]
and does not agree to the sound instruc-
tion[f] of our Lord Jesus Christ and to
godly teaching, 4he is conceited[g] and
understands nothing. He has an un-
healthy interest in controversies and
quarrels about words[h] that result in
envy, strife, malicious talk, evil sus-
picions 5and constant friction between

14 [b]1Ti 1:18; [c]**Ac 11:30;** [d]**Ac 6:6;** 2Ti 1:6
16 [e]**Ro 11:14**

Ch. 5

1 [a]Tit 2:2; [b]Lev 19:32; [c]Tit 2:6
3 [d]ver 5,16
4 [e]ver 8; Eph 6:1–2; [f]Ro 12:2; Eph 5:10; 1Ti 2:3
5 [g]ver 3,16; [h]1Co 7:34; 1Pe 3:5; [i]Lk 2:37; **Ro 1:10**
6 [j]**Lk 15:24**
7 [k]1Ti 4:11; 6:2
8 [l]2Pe 2:1; Jude 4
10 [m]Ac 9:36; 1Ti 6:18; 1Pe 2:12; [n]**Ro 12:13;** [o]**Lk 7:44;** [p]ver 16
13 [q]**Ro 1:29;** [r]2Th 3:11
14 [s]1Co 7:9; [t]1Ti 6:1
15 [u]**Mt 4:10**
16 [v]ver 3–5
17 [w]**Ac 11:30;** [x]Php 2:29; 1Th 5:12
18 [y]Dt 25:4; 1Co 9:7–9; [z]Lk 10:7; Lev 19:13; Dt 24:14–15; Mt 10:10; 1Co 9:14
19 [a]**Ac 11:30;** [b]**Mt 18:16**
20 [c]2Ti 4:2; Tit 1:13; 2:15; [d]Dt 13:11
21 [e]1Ti 6:13; 2Ti 4:1
22 [f]**Ac 6:6;** [g]Eph 5:11; [h]Ps 18:26
23 [i]1Ti 3:8

Ch. 6

1 [a]**Eph 6:5;** [b]1Ti 5:14; Tit 2:5,8
2 [c]Phm 16; [d]1Ti 4:11
3 [e]1Ti 1:3; [f]**1Ti 1:10**
4 [g]1Ti 3:6; 2Ti 3:4; [h]**2Ti 2:14**

[a]*9* Or *has had but one husband* [b]*18* Deut. 25:4
[c]*18* Luke 10:7

men of corrupt mind, who have been robbed of the truth[i] and who think that godliness is a means to financial gain.
6But godliness with contentment[j] is great gain.[k] 7For we brought nothing into the world, and we can take nothing out of it.[l] 8But if we have food and clothing, we will be content with that.[m] 9People who want to get rich[n] fall into temptation and a trap[o] and into many foolish and harmful desires that plunge men into ruin and destruction. 10For the love of money[p] is a root of all kinds of evil. Some people, eager for money, have wandered from the faith[q] and pierced themselves with many griefs.[r]

Paul's Charge to Timothy

11But you, man of God,[s] flee from all this, and pursue righteousness, godliness,[t] faith, love,[u] endurance and gentleness. 12Fight the good fight[v] of the faith. Take hold of[w] the eternal life[x] to which you were called when you made your good confession[y] in the presence of many witnesses. 13In the sight of God, who gives life to everything, and of Christ Jesus, who while testifying before Pontius Pilate[z] made the good confession,[a] I charge you[b] 14to keep this command without spot or blame[c] until the appearing of our Lord Jesus Christ,[d] 15which God will bring about in his own time[e]—God, the blessed[f] and only Ruler,[g] the King of kings and Lord of lords,[h] 16who alone is immortal[i] and who lives in unapproachable light,[j] whom no-one has seen or can see.[k] To him be honour and might for ever. Amen.[l]

17Command those who are rich[m] in this present world not to be arrogant nor to put their hope in wealth,[n] which is so uncertain, but to put their hope in God,[o] who richly provides us with everything for our enjoyment.[p] 18Command them to do good, to be rich in good deeds,[q] and to be generous and willing to share.[r] 19In this way they will lay up treasure for themselves[s] as a firm foundation for the coming age, so that they may take hold of[t] the life that is truly life.

20Timothy, guard what has been entrusted[u] to your care. Turn away from godless chatter[v] and the opposing ideas of what is falsely called knowledge, 21which some have professed and in so doing have wandered from the faith.[w]

Grace be with you.[x]

5 [i]2Ti 3:8; Tit 1:15
6 [j]Php 4:11; Heb 13:5; [k]1Ti 4:8
7 [l]Job 1:21; Ps 49:17; Ecc 5:15
8 [m]Pr 30:8; Heb 13:5
9 [n]Pr 15:27; 28:20; [o]1Ti 3:7
10 [p]**1Ti 3:3**; [q]ver 21; Jas 5:19; [r]Jos 7:21
11 [s]2Ti 3:17; [t]ver 3,5–6; **1Ti 2:2**; [u]1Ti 1:14; 2Ti 2:22; 3:10
12 [v]1Co 9:25–26; **1Ti 1:18**; [w]ver 19; Php 3:12; [x]**Mt 25:46**; [y]**Heb 3:1**
13 [z]Jn 18:33–37; [a]ver 12; [b]1Ti 5:21; 2Ti 4:1
14 [c]**1Th 3:13**; [d]**1Co 1:7**; 2Ti 1:10; 4:1,8
15 [e]1Ti 2:6; Tit 1:3; [f]1Ti 1:11; [g]1Ti 1:17; [h]Dt 10:17; Ps 136:3; Da 2:47; Rev 1:5; 17:14; 19:16
16 [i]1Ti 1:17; [j]Ps 104:2; 1Jn 1:7; [k]**Jn 1:18**; [l]**Ro 11:36**

17 [m]ver 9; [n]Ps 62:10; Jer 49:4; Lk 12:20–21; [o]1Ti 4:10; [p]Ac 14:17 *18* [q]1Ti 5:10; [r]Ro 12:8,13; Eph 4:28
19 [s]**Mt 6:20**; [t]ver 12; Php 3:12
20 [u]2Ti 1:12,14; [v]2Ti 2:16
21 [w]ver 10; 2Ti 2:18; [x]**Col 4:18**

2 Timothy

1 Paul, an apostle[a] of Christ Jesus by the will of God,[b] according to the promise of life that is in Christ Jesus,[c]

2To Timothy,[d] my dear son:[e]

Grace, mercy and peace from God the Father and Christ Jesus our Lord.[f]

Encouragement to Be Faithful

3I thank God,[g] whom I serve, as my forefathers did, with a clear conscience,[h] as night and day I constantly remember you in my prayers.[i] 4Recalling your tears,[j] I long to see you,[k] so that I may be filled with joy. 5I have been reminded of your sincere faith,[l] which first lived in your grandmother Lois and in your mother Eunice[m] and, I am persuaded, now lives in you also. 6For this reason I remind you to fan into flame the gift of God, which is in you through the laying on of my hands.[n] 7For God did not give us a spirit of timidity,[o] but a spirit of power,[p] of love and of self-discipline.

8So do not be ashamed[q] to testify about our Lord, or ashamed of me his prisoner.[r] But join with me in suffering for the gospel,[s] by the power of God, 9who has saved[t] us and called[u] us to a holy life—not because of anything we have done[v] but because of his own purpose and grace. This grace was given us in Christ Jesus before the beginning of time, 10but it has now been revealed[w] through the appearing of our Saviour, Christ Jesus,[x] who has destroyed death[y] and has brought life and immortality to light through the gospel. 11And of this gospel[z] I was appointed[a] a herald and an apostle and a teacher.[b] 12That is why I am suffering as I am. Yet I am not ashamed,[c] because I know whom I have believed, and am convinced that he is able to guard[d] what I have entrusted to him for that day.[e]

13What you heard from me,[f] keep[g] as the pattern[h] of sound teaching,[i] with faith and love in Christ Jesus.[j] 14Guard[k] the good deposit that was entrusted to you—guard it with the help of the Holy Spirit who lives in us.[l]

15You know that everyone in the province of Asia[m] has deserted me,[n] including Phygelus and Hermogenes.

16May the Lord show mercy to the household of Onesiphorus,[o] because he often refreshed me and was not ashamed[p] of my chains.[q] 17On the contrary, when he was in Rome, he searched hard for me until he found me. 18May the Lord grant that he will find mercy from the Lord on that day![r] You know very well in how many ways he helped me[s] in Ephesus.[t]

2 You then, my son,[a] be strong[b] in the grace that is in Christ Jesus. 2And the things you have heard me say[c] in the presence of many witnesses[d] entrust to reliable men who will also be qualified to teach others. 3Endure hardship with us[e] like a good soldier[f] of Christ Jesus. 4No-one serving as a soldier gets involved in civilian affairs—he wants to please his commanding officer. 5Similarly, if anyone competes as an athlete, he does not receive the victor's crown[g] unless he competes according to the rules. 6The hardworking farmer should be the first to receive a share of the crops.[h] 7Reflect on what I am saying, for the Lord will give you insight into all this.

8Remember Jesus Christ, raised from the dead,[i] descended from David.[j] This is my gospel,[k] 9for which I am suffering[l] even to the point of being chained[m] like a criminal. But God's word[n] is not chained. 10Therefore I endure everything[o] for the sake of the elect,[p] that they too may obtain the salvation[q] that is in Christ Jesus, with eternal glory.[r]

11Here is a trustworthy saying:[s]

If we died with him,
    we will also live with him;[t]
12if we endure,
    we will also reign with him.[u]

Ch. 1

1 [a]**1Co 1:1;** [b]**2Co 1:1;** [c]Eph 3:6; Tit 1:2; 1Ti 6:19
2 [d]**Ac 16:1;** [e]**1Ti 1:2;** [f]**Ro 1:7**
3 [g]**Ro 1:8;** [h]**Ac 23:1;** [i]**Ro 1:10**
4 [j]Ac 20:37; [k]2Ti 4:9
5 [l]1Ti 1:5; [m]Ac 16:1; 2Ti 3:15
6 [n]**Ac 6:6;** 1Ti 4:14
7 [o]Jer 42:11; Ro 8:15; 1Co 16:10–11; 1Ti 4:12; Heb 2:15; [p]Isa 11:2
8 [q]ver 12,16; Mk 8:38; [r]**Eph 3:1;** [s]2Ti 2:3,9; 4:5
9 [t]**Ro 11:14;** [u]**Ro 8:28;** [v]**Eph 2:9**
10 [w]Eph 1:9; [x]**1Ti 6:14;** [y]1Co 15:26,54
11 [z]ver 8; [a]**Ac 9:15;** [b]1Ti 2:7
12 [c]ver 8,16; Mk 8:38; [d]ver 14; 1Ti 6:20; [e]ver 18; **1Co 1:8;** 2Ti 4:8
13 [f]2Ti 2:2; [g]**Tit 1:9;** [h]Ro 6:17; [i]**1Ti 1:10;** [j]**1Th 1:3;** 1Ti 1:14
14 [k]ver 12; [l]**Ro 8:9**
15 [m]**Ac 2:9;** [n]2Ti 4:10–11,16
16 [o]2Ti 4:19; [p]ver 8,12; Mk 8:38; [q]**Ac 21:33**
18 [r]**ver 12;** [s]Heb 6:10; [t]**Ac 18:19**

Ch. 2

1 [a]**1Ti 1:2;** [b]**Eph 6:10**
2 [c]2Ti 1:13; [d]1Ti 6:12
3 [e]ver 9; 2Ti 1:8; 4:5; [f]**1Ti 1:18**
5 [g]**1Co 9:25**
6 [h]1Co 9:10
8 [i]**Ac 2:24;** [j]**Mt 1:1;** [k]Ro 2:16; 16:25

9 [l]**Ac 9:16;** [m]**Ac 21:33;** [n]**Heb 4:12**
10 [o]Col 1:24; [p]Tit 1:1; [q]2Co 1:6; [r]2Co 4:17; 1Pe 5:10
11 [s]**1Ti 1:15;** [t]Ro 6:2–11 12 [u]Ro 8:17; 1Pe 4:13

If we disown him,
he will also disown us;[v]
13if we are faithless,
he will remain faithful,[w]
for he cannot disown himself.

A Workman Approved by God

14Keep reminding them of these
things. Warn them before God against
quarrelling about words;[x] it is of no
value, and only ruins those who listen.
15Do your best to present yourself to
God as one approved, a workman who
does not need to be ashamed and who
correctly handles the word of truth.[y]
16Avoid godless chatter,[z] because those
who indulge in it will become more and
more ungodly. 17Their teaching will
spread like gangrene. Among them are
Hymenaeus[a] and Philetus, 18who have
wandered away from the truth. They
say that the resurrection has already
taken place,[b] and they destroy the faith
of some.[c] 19Nevertheless, God's solid
foundation stands firm,[d] sealed with
this inscription: "The Lord knows those
who are his,"[a][e] and, "Everyone who
confesses the name of the Lord[f] must
turn away from wickedness."
20In a large house there are articles not
only of gold and silver, but also of wood
and clay; some are for noble purposes
and some for ignoble.[g] 21If a man
cleanses himself from the latter, he will
be an instrument for noble purposes,
made holy, useful to the Master and
prepared to do any good work.[h]
22Flee the evil desires of youth, and
pursue righteousness, faith, love[i] and
peace, along with those who call on the
Lord[j] out of a pure heart.[k] 23Don't have
anything to do with foolish and stupid
arguments, because you know they
produce quarrels.[l] 24And the Lord's ser-
vant must not quarrel; instead, he must
be kind to everyone, able to teach, not
resentful.[m] 25Those who oppose him he
must gently instruct, in the hope that
God will grant them repentance leading
them to a knowledge of the truth,[n] 26and
that they will come to their senses and
escape from the trap of the devil,[o] who
has taken them captive to do his will.

Godlessness in the Last Days

3 But mark this: There will be terrible
times in the last days.[a] 2People will
be lovers of themselves, lovers of
money,[b] boastful, proud,[c] abusive,[d] dis-
obedient to their parents,[e] ungrateful,
unholy, 3without love, unforgiving,
slanderous, without self-control,
brutal, not lovers of the good, 4treacher-
ous,[f] rash, conceited,[g] lovers of pleasure
rather than lovers of God—5having a
form of godliness[h] but denying its
power. Have nothing to do with them.[i]
6They are the kind who worm their
way[j] into homes and gain control over
weak-willed women, who are loaded
down with sins and are swayed by all
kinds of evil desires, 7always learning
but never able to acknowledge the
truth.[k] 8Just as Jannes and Jambres
opposed Moses,[l] so also these men
oppose[m] the truth—men of depraved
minds,[n] who, as far as the faith is
concerned, are rejected. 9But they will
not get very far because, as in the case
of those men,[o] their folly will be clear
to everyone.

Paul's Charge to Timothy

10You, however, know all about my
teaching,[p] my way of life, my purpose,
faith, patience, love, endurance,
11persecutions, sufferings—what kinds
of things happened to me in Antioch,[q]
Iconium[r] and Lystra,[s] the persecutions
I endured.[t] Yet the Lord rescued[u] me
from all of them.[v] 12In fact, everyone
who wants to live a godly life in Christ
Jesus will be persecuted,[w] 13while evil
men and impostors will go from bad to
worse,[x] deceiving and being deceived.[y]
14But as for you, continue in what
you have learned and have become
convinced of, because you know those
from whom you learned it,[z] 15and how
from infancy[a] you have known the
holy Scriptures,[b] which are able to make
you wise[c] for salvation through faith
in Christ Jesus. 16All Scripture is
God-breathed[d] and is useful for
teaching,[e] rebuking, correcting and
training in righteousness,[f] 17so that
the man of God[g] may be thoroughly
equipped for every good work.[h]

4 In the presence of God and of
Christ Jesus, who will judge the
living and the dead,[a] and in view of his
appearing[b] and his kingdom, I give you
this charge:[c] 2Preach[d] the Word;[e] be
prepared in season and out of season;
correct, rebuke[f] and encourage[g]—with
great patience and careful instruction.
3For the time will come when men will
not put up with sound doctrine.[h]
Instead, to suit their own desires, they
will gather around them a great number

12 [v]Mt 10:33
13 [w]Ro 3:3; **1Co 1:9**
14 [x]ver 23; 1Ti 1:4; 6:4; Tit 3:9
15 [y]Eph 1:13; Col 1:5; Jas 1:18
16 [z]Tit 3:9; 1Ti 6:20
17 [a]1Ti 1:20
18 [b]2Th 2:2; [c]1Ti 1:19; 6:21
19 [d]Isa 28:16; [e]Ex 33:12; Nu 16:5; Jn 10:14; 1Co 8:3; Gal 4:9; [f]1Co 1:2
20 [g]Ro 9:21
21 [h]2Co 9:8; Eph 2:10; 2Ti 3:17
22 [i]1Ti 1:14; 6:11; [j]**Ac 2:21**; [k]1Ti 1:5
23 [l]**ver 14**
24 [m]1Ti 3:2–3
25 [n]**1Ti 2:4**
26 [o]1Ti 3:7

Ch. 3

1 [a]1Ti 4:1; 2Pe 3:3
2 [b]**1Ti 3:3**; [c]Ro 1:30; [d]2Pe 2:10–12; [e]Ro 1:30
4 [f]Ps 25:3; [g]1Ti 3:6; 6:4
5 [h]**1Ti 2:2**; [i]**Ro 16:17**
6 [j]Jude 4
7 [k]**1Ti 2:4**
8 [l]Ex 7:11; [m]Ac 13:8; [n]1Ti 6:5
9 [o]Ex 7:12; 8:18; 9:11
10 [p]1Ti 4:6
11 [q]Ac 13:14,50; [r]**Ac 13:51**; [s]Ac 14:6; [t]2Co 11:23–27; [u]**Ro 15:31**; [v]Ps 34:19
12 [w]Jn 15:20; **Ac 14:22**
13 [x]2Ti 2:16; [y]**Mk 13:5**
14 [z]2Ti 1:13
15 [a]2Ti 1:5; [b]Jn 5:39; [c]Dt 4:6; Ps 119:98–99
16 [d]2Pe 1:20–21; [e]**Ro 4:23–24**; [f]Dt 29:29
17 [g]1Ti 6:11; [h]2Ti 2:21

Ch. 4

1 [a]**Ac 10:42**; [b]ver 8; **1Ti 6:14**; [c]1Ti 5:21; 6:13
2 [d]1Ti 4:13; [e]Gal 6:6; [f]1Ti 5:20; Tit 1:13; 2:15; [g]Tit 2:15
3 [h]1Ti 1:10

[a]*19* Num. 16:5 (see Septuagint)

of teachers to say what their itching ears
want to hear.[i] 4They will turn their ears
away from the truth and turn aside to
myths.[j] 5But you, keep your head in all
situations, endure hardship,[k] do the
work of an evangelist,[l] discharge all the
duties of your ministry.
6For I am already being poured out
like a drink offering,[m] and the time has
come for my departure.[n] 7I have fought
the good fight,[o] I have finished the
race,[p] I have kept the faith. 8Now there
is in store for me[q] the crown of right-
eousness,[r] which the Lord, the right-
eous Judge, will award to me on that
day[s]—and not only to me, but also to all
who have longed for his appearing.[t]

Personal Remarks

9Do your best to come to me quickly,[u]
10for Demas,[v] because he loved this
world,[w] has deserted me and has gone
to Thessalonica.[x] Crescens has gone to
Galatia,[y] and Titus[z] to Dalmatia. 11Only
Luke[a] is with me.[b] Get Mark[c] and bring
him with you, because he is helpful
to me in my ministry. 12I sent Tychicus[d]
to Ephesus.[e] 13When you come, bring
the cloak that I left with Carpus at
Troas,[f] and my scrolls, especially the
parchments.
14Alexander[g] the metalworker did me
a great deal of harm. The Lord will
repay him for what he has done.[h] 15You
too should be on your guard against
him, because he strongly opposed our
message.
16At my first defence, no-one came to
my support, but everyone deserted me.
May it not be held against them.[i] 17But
the Lord stood at my side[j] and gave me
strength,[k] so that through me the mess-
age might be fully proclaimed and all
the Gentiles might hear it.[l] And I was
delivered from the lion's mouth.[m] 18The
Lord will rescue me from every evil
attack[n] and will bring me safely to his
heavenly kingdom.[o] To him be glory for
ever and ever. Amen.[p]

Final Greetings

19Greet Priscilla[a] and Aquila[q] and the
household of Onesiphorus.[r] 20Erastus[s]
stayed in Corinth, and I left Trophimus[t]
sick in Miletus.[u] 21Do your best to get
here before winter.[v] Eubulus greets
you, and so do Pudens, Linus, Claudia
and all the brothers.
22The Lord be with your spirit.[w] Grace
be with you.[x]

3 [i]Isa 30:10
4 [j]**1Ti 1:4**
5 [k]2Ti 1:8; 2:3,9; [l]Ac 21:8; Eph 4:11
6 [m]Nu 15:1–12; 28:7,24; Php 2:17; [n]Php 1:23
7 [o]**1Ti 1:18;** [p]**1Co 9:24;** Ac 20:24
8 [q]Col 1:5; 1Pe 1:4; [r]**1Co 9:25;** [s]**2Ti 1:12;** [t]**1Ti 6:14**
9 [u]ver 21; Tit 3:12
10 [v]Col 4:14; Phm 24; [w]1Jn 2:15; [x]**Ac 17:1;** [y]**Ac 16:6;** [z]**2Co 2:13**
11 [a]Col 4:14; Phm 24; [b]2Ti 1:15; [c]**Ac 12:12**
12 [d]**Ac 20:4;** [e]**Ac 18:19**
13 [f]**Ac 16:8**
14 [g]Ac 19:33; 1Ti 1:20; [h]Ps 28:4; 109:20; Ro 2:6; 12:19
16 [i]Ac 7:60
17 [j]Ac 23:11; [k]**Php 4:13;** [l]**Ac 9:15;** [m]1Sa 17:37; Ps 22:21; Da 6:22; 1Co 15:32
18 [n]Ps 121:7; 2Pe 2:9; [o]ver 1; [p]**Ro 11:36**

19 [q]**Ac 18:2;** [r]2Ti 1:16
20 [s]Ac 19:22; [t]Ac 20:4; 21:29; [u]Ac 20:15,17
21 [v]ver 9; Tit 3:12 *22* [w]**Gal 6:18;** [x]**Col 4:18**

[a]*19* Greek *Prisca,* a variant of *Priscilla*

Titus

1 Paul, a servant of God[a] and an
apostle[b] of Jesus Christ for the faith
of God's elect and the knowledge of the
truth[c] that leads to godliness[d]—2a faith
and knowledge resting on the hope of
eternal life,[e] which God, who does not
lie,[f] promised before the beginning of
time,[g] 3and at his appointed season[h] he
brought his word to light[i] through the
preaching entrusted to me[j] by the
command of God[k] our Saviour,[l]

4To Titus,[m] my true son[n] in our
common faith:

Grace and peace from God the Father
and Christ Jesus our Saviour.[o]

Titus' Task on Crete

1:6–8Ref—1Ti 3:2–4

5The reason I left you in Crete[p] was
that you might straighten out what was
left unfinished and appoint**a** elders[q] in
every town, as I directed you. 6An elder
must be blameless,[r] the husband of but
one wife, a man whose children believe
and are not open to the charge of being
wild and disobedient. 7Since an over-
seer**b**[s] is entrusted with God's work,[t] he
must be blameless—not overbearing,
not quick-tempered, not given to
drunkenness, not violent, not pursuing
dishonest gain.[u] 8Rather he must be
hospitable,[v] one who loves what is
good,[w] who is self-controlled,[x] upright,
holy and disciplined. 9He must hold
firmly[y] to the trustworthy message as
it has been taught, so that he can
encourage others by sound doctrine[z]
and refute those who oppose it.

10For there are many rebellious peo-
ple, mere talkers[a] and deceivers, espe-
cially those of the circumcision group.[b]
11They must be silenced, because they
are ruining whole households[c] by
teaching things they ought not to teach
—and that for the sake of dishonest
gain. 12Even one of their own prophets[d]
has said, "Cretans[e] are always liars, evil
brutes, lazy gluttons." 13This testimony
is true. Therefore, rebuke[f] them
sharply, so that they will be sound
in the faith[g] 14and will pay no attention
to Jewish myths[h] or to the commands[i]
of those who reject the truth.[j] 15To the
pure, all things are pure,[k] but to those
who are corrupted and do not believe,
nothing is pure.[l] In fact, both their
minds and consciences are corrupted.[m]
16They claim to know God, but by
their actions they deny him.[n] They are
detestable, disobedient and unfit for
doing anything good.[o]

What Must Be Taught to Various Groups

2 You must teach what is in accord
with sound doctrine.[a] 2Teach the
older men[b] to be temperate,[c] worthy of
respect, self-controlled,[d] and sound in
faith,[e] in love and in endurance.

3Likewise, teach the older women to
be reverent in the way they live, not to
be slanderers[f] or addicted to much
wine,[g] but to teach what is good. 4Then
they can train the younger women[h] to
love their husbands and children, 5to be
self-controlled[i] and pure, to be busy at
home,[j] to be kind, and to be subject to
their husbands,[k] so that no-one will
malign the word of God.[l]

6Similarly, encourage the young
men[m] to be self-controlled.[n] 7In every-
thing set them an example[o] by doing
what is good.[p] In your teaching show
integrity, seriousness 8and soundness
of speech that cannot be condemned, so
that those who oppose you may be
ashamed because they have nothing
bad to say about us.[q]

9Teach slaves to be subject to their
masters in everything,[r] to try to please
them, not to talk back to them, 10and not
to steal from them, but to show that
they can be fully trusted, so that in
every way they will make the teaching
about God our Saviour[s] attractive.[t]

Ch. 1

1 [a]Ro 1:1; Jas 1:1; [b]**1Co 1:1**; [c]**1Ti 2:4**; [d]**1Ti 2:2**
2 [e]Tit 3:7; 2Ti 1:1; [f]Nu 23:19; Heb 6:18; [g]2Ti 1:9
3 [h]1Ti 2:6; 6:15; [i]2Ti 1:10; [j]**1Ti 1:11**; [k]**2Co 1:1**; 1Ti 1:1; [l]**Lk 1:47**
4 [m]**2Co 2:13**; [n]**1Ti 1:2**; [o]**Ro 1:7**
5 [p]Ac 27:7; [q]**Ac 11:30**
6 [r]**1Th 3:13**; 1Ti 3:2
7 [s]**1Ti 3:1**; [t]1Co 4:1; [u]**1Ti 3:3**,8
8 [v]**Ro 12:13**; [w]2Ti 3:3; [x]Tit 2:2,5–6,12
9 [y]**1Co 16:13**; 1Ti 1:19; 2Ti 1:13; 3:14; [z]**1Ti 1:10**
10 [a]1Ti 1:6; [b]Ac 10:45; 11:2
11 [c]1Ti 5:13
12 [d]Ac 17:28; [e]Ac 2:11
13 [f]**1Ti 5:20**; [g]Tit 2:2
14 [h]**1Ti 1:4**; [i]**Col 2:22**; [j]2Ti 4:4
15 [k]Ps 18:26; Mt 15:10–11; Mk 7:14–19; Ac 10:9–16,28; Col 2:20–22; [l]Ro 14:14,23; [m]1Ti 6:5
16 [n]Jer 5:2; 12:2; 1Jn 2:4; [o]Hos 8:2–3

Ch. 2

1 [a]**1Ti 1:10**
2 [b]1Ti 5:1; [c]1Ti 3:2; [d]ver 5–6, 12; Tit 1:8; [e]Tit 1:13
3 [f]1Ti 3:11; [g]1Ti 3:8
4 [h]1Ti 5:2
5 [i]ver 2,6,12; Tit 1:8; [j]1Ti 5:14; [k]**Eph 5:22**; [l]1Ti 6:1; **Heb 4:12**
6 [m]1Ti 5:1; [n]ver 2,5,12; Tit 1:8
7 [o]**1Ti 4:12**; [p]**ver 14**
8 [q]**1Pe 2:12**
9 [r]**Eph 6:5**
10 [s]**Lk 1:47**; [t]Mt 5:16

a5 Or *ordain* **b**7 Traditionally *bishop*

11For the grace[u] of God that brings
salvation has appeared[v] to all men.[w] 12It
teaches us to say "No" to ungodliness
and worldly passions,[x] and to live self-
controlled,[y] upright and godly lives[z] in
this present age, 13while we wait for the
blessed hope—the glorious appearing[a]
of our great God and Saviour, Jesus
Christ,[b] 14who gave himself for us[c] to
redeem us from all wickedness[d] and to
purify[e] for himself a people that are his
very own,[f] eager to do what is good.[g]
15These, then, are the things you
should teach. Encourage and rebuke
with all authority. Do not let anyone
despise you.

Doing What is Good

3 Remind the people to be subject to
rulers and authorities,[a] to be obedi-
ent, to be ready to do whatever is good,[b]
2to slander no-one,[c] to be peaceable and
considerate, and to show true humility
towards all men.
3At one time[d] we too were foolish,
disobedient, deceived and enslaved by
all kinds of passions and pleasures. We
lived in malice and envy, being hated
and hating one another. 4But when the
kindness[e] and love of God our Saviour[f]
appeared,[g] 5he saved us,[h] not because
of righteous things we had done,[i] but
because of his mercy.[j] He saved us
through the washing[k] of rebirth and
renewal[l] by the Holy Spirit, 6whom he
poured out on us[m] generously through
Jesus Christ our Saviour, 7so that,
having been justified by his grace,[n] we
might become heirs[o] having the hope[p]
of eternal life.[q] 8This is a trustworthy
saying.[r] And I want you to stress these
things, so that those who have trusted
in God may be careful to devote them-
selves to doing what is good.[s] These
things are excellent and profitable for
everyone.
9But avoid[t] foolish controversies and
genealogies and arguments and quar-
rels[u] about the law,[v] because these are
unprofitable and useless.[w] 10Warn a
divisive person once, and then warn
him a second time. After that, have
nothing to do with him.[x] 11You may
be sure that such a man is warped and
sinful; he is self-condemned.

Final Remarks

12As soon as I send Artemas or Tychi-
cus[y] to you, do your best to come to me
at Nicopolis, because I have decided to
winter there.[z] 13Do everything you can
to help Zenas the lawyer and Apollos[a]
on their way and see that they have
everything they need. 14Our people
must learn to devote themselves to
doing what is good,[b] in order that they
may provide for daily necessities and
not live unproductive lives.
15Everyone with me sends you
greetings. Greet those who love us
in the faith.[c]
Grace be with you all.[d]

11 [u]**Ro 3:24**; [v]2Ti 1:10; [w]**1Ti 2:4**
12 [x]Tit 3:3; [y]ver 2,5–6; Tit 1:8; [z]2Ti 3:12
13 [a]**1Co 1:7; 1Ti 6:14**; [b]2Pe 1:1
14 [c]**Mt 20:28**; [d]**Mt 1:21**; [e]Heb 1:3; 1Jn 1:7; [f]Ex 19:5; Dt 4:20; 14:2; Ps 135:4; Mal 3:17; 1Pe 2:9; [g]ver 7; Pr 16:7; Mt 5:16; 2Co 8:21; Eph 2:10; Tit 3:1,8,14; 1Pe 2:12,15; 3:13

Ch. 3

1 [a]Ro 13:1; 1Pe 2:13–14; [b]**2Ti 2:21; Tit 2:14**
2 [c]Eph 4:31
3 [d]**Eph 2:2**
4 [e]Eph 2:7; [f]**Lk 1:47**; [g]Tit 2:11
5 [h]**Ro 11:14**; [i]**Eph 2:9**; [j]1Pe 1:3; [k]**Ac 22:16**; [l]Ro 12:2
6 [m]**Ro 5:5**
7 [n]**Ro 3:24**; [o]**Ro 8:17**; [p]Ro 8:24; [q]**Mt 25:46**; Tit 1:2
8 [r]**1Ti 1:15**; [s]**Tit 2:14**
9 [t]2Ti 2:16; [u]**2Ti 2:14**; [v]Tit 1:10–16; [w]2Ti 2:14
10 [x]**Ro 16:17**
12 [y]**Ac 20:4**; [z]2Ti 4:9,21
13 [a]**Ac 18:24**
14 [b]**Tit 2:14**
15 [c]1Ti 1:2; [d]**Col 4:18**

Philemon

1Paul, a prisoner[a] of Christ Jesus, and
Timothy[b] our brother,[c]

To Philemon our dear friend and
fellow-worker,[d] 2to Apphia our sister,
to Archippus[e] our fellow-soldier[f] and to
the church that meets in your home:[g]

3Grace to you and peace from God our
Father and the Lord Jesus Christ.[h]

Thanksgiving and Prayer

4I always thank my God[i] as I
remember you in my prayers,[j] 5because
I hear about your faith in the Lord
Jesus[k] and your love for all the saints.[l]
6I pray that you may be active in sharing
your faith, so that you will have a full
understanding of every good thing we
have in Christ. 7Your love has given
me great joy and encouragement,[m]
because you, brother, have refreshed[n]
the hearts of the saints.

Paul's Plea for Onesimus

8Therefore, although in Christ I could
be bold and order you to do what you
ought to do, 9yet I appeal to you[o] on the
basis of love. I then, as Paul—an old
man and now also a prisoner[p] of Christ
Jesus—10I appeal to you for my son[q]
Onesimus,[a] [r] who became my son while
I was in chains.[s] 11Formerly he was
useless to you, but now he has
become useful both to you and to me.

12I am sending him—who is my very
heart—back to you. 13I would have
liked to keep him with me so that he
could take your place in helping me
while I am in chains[t] for the gospel.
14But I did not want to do anything
without your consent, so that any
favour you do will be spontaneous and
not forced.[u] 15Perhaps the reason he
was separated from you for a little while
was that you might have him back for
good—16no longer as a slave,[v] but better
than a slave, as a dear brother.[w] He is
very dear to me but even dearer to you,
both as a man and as a brother in the
Lord.

17So if you consider me a partner,[x]
welcome him as you would welcome
me. 18If he has done you any wrong or
owes you anything, charge it to me.[y] 19I,
Paul, am writing this with my own
hand.[z] I will pay it back—not to men-
tion that you owe me your very self. 20I
do wish, brother, that I may have some
benefit from you in the Lord; refresh[a]
my heart in Christ. 21Confident[b] of your
obedience, I write to you, knowing that
you will do even more than I ask.

22And one thing more: Prepare a
guest room for me, because I hope to be[c]
restored to you in answer to your
prayers.[d]

23Epaphras,[e] my fellow-prisoner[f] in
Christ Jesus, sends you greetings.
24And so do Mark,[g] Aristarchus,[h]
Demas[i] and Luke, my fellow-workers.[j]

25The grace of the Lord Jesus Christ be
with your spirit.[k]

1 [a]ver 9,23; **Eph 3:1**; [b]**Ac 16:1**; [c]2Co 1:1; [d]**Php 2:25**
2 [e]Col 4:17; [f]Php 2:25; [g]**Ro 16:5**
3 [h]**Ro 1:7**
4 [i]**Ro 1:8**; [j]**Ro 1:10**
5 [k]**Ac 20:21**; [l]**Col 1:4**; 1Th 3:6
7 [m]2Co 7:4,13; [n]ver 20; Ro 15:32; 1Co 16:18
9 [o]1Co 1:10; [p]ver 1,23; **Eph 3:1**
10 [q]**1Th 2:11**; [r]Col 4:9; [s]**Ac 21:33**
13 [t]ver 10; **Ac 21:33**
14 [u]2Co 9:7; 1Pe 5:2
16 [v]1Co 7:22; [w]Mt 23:8; **Ac 1:16**; 1Ti 6:2
17 [x]2Co 8:23
18 [y]Ge 43:9
19 [z]**1Co 16:21**
20 [a]ver 7; 1Co 16:18
21 [b]**2Co 2:3**
22 [c]Php 1:25; 2:24; Heb 13:19; [d]2Co 1:11; Php 1:19
23 [e]Col 1:7; [f]ver 1; Ro 16:7; Col 4:10
24 [g]**Ac 12:12**; [h]**Ac 19:29**; [i]Col 4:14; 2Ti 4:10; [j]ver 1
25 [k]**Gal 6:18**

---

[a]*10 Onesimus* means *useful.*

Hebrews

The Son Superior to Angels

1 In the past God spoke[a] to our forefathers through the prophets[b] at many times and in various ways,[c] 2but in these last days[d] he has spoken to us by his Son,[e] whom he appointed heir[f] of all things, and through whom[g] he made the universe.[h] 3The Son is the radiance of God's glory[i] and the exact representation of his being,[j] sustaining all things[k] by his powerful word. After he had provided purification for sins,[l] he sat down at the right hand of the Majesty in heaven.[m] 4So he became as much superior to the angels as the name he has inherited is superior to theirs.[n]

5For to which of the angels did God ever say,

"You are my Son;
 today I have become your
  Father[a]"[b]?[o]

Or again,

"I will be his Father,
 and he will be my Son"[c]?[p]

6And again, when God brings his firstborn[q] into the world,[r] he says,

"Let all God's angels worship him."[d][s]

7In speaking of the angels he says,

"He makes his angels winds,
 his servants flames of fire."[e][t]

8But about the Son he says,

"Your throne, O God, will last for ever
  and ever,[u]
 and righteousness will be the
  sceptre of your kingdom.
9You have loved righteousness and
  hated wickedness;
 therefore God, your God, has set
  you above your companions[v]
 by anointing you with the oil[w] of
  joy."[f][x]

10He also says,

"In the beginning, O Lord, you laid
  the foundations of the earth,
 and the heavens are the work of
  your hands.[y]
11They will perish, but you remain;
 they will all wear out like a
  garment.[z]
12You will roll them up like a robe;
 like a garment they will be changed.
 But you remain the same,[a]
 and your years will never end."[g][b]

13To which of the angels did God ever say,

"Sit at my right hand[c]
 until I make your enemies
  a footstool[d] for your feet"[h]?[e]

14Are not all angels ministering spirits[f] sent to serve those who will inherit[g] salvation?[h]

Warning to Pay Attention

2 We must pay more careful attention, therefore, to what we have heard, so that we do not drift away.[a] 2For if the message spoken[b] by angels[c] was binding, and every violation and disobedience received its just punishment,[d] 3how shall we escape if we ignore such a great salvation?[e] This salvation, which was first announced by the Lord,[f] was confirmed to us by those who heard him.[g] 4God also testified to it by signs, wonders and various miracles,[h] and gifts of the Holy Spirit[i] distributed according to his will.[j]

Jesus Made Like His Brothers

5It is not to angels that he has subjected the world to come, about which

Ch. 1

1 [a]Jn 9:29; Heb 2:2–3; 4:8; 12:25; [b]Lk 1:70; Ac 2:30; [c]Nu 12:6,8
2 [d]Dt 4:30; Heb 9:26; 1Pe 1:20; [e]ver 5; **Mt 3:17**; Heb 3:6; 5:8; 7:28; [f]Ps 2:8; Mt 11:27; **28:18**; [g]**Jn 1:3**; [h]Heb 11:3
3 [i]Jn 1:14; [j]**Jn 14:9**; [k]Col 1:17; [l]Tit 2:14; Heb 7:27; 9:11–14; [m]**Mk 16:19**
4 [n]Eph 1:21; Php 2:9–10; Heb 8:6
5 [o]Ps 2:7; **Mt 3:17**; [p]2Sa 7:14
6 [q]Jn 3:16; **Col 1:18**; [r]Heb 10:5; [s]Dt 32:43 *fn*; Ps 97:7
7 [t]Ps 104:4
8 [u]**Lk 1:33**
9 [v]Php 2:9; [w]Isa 61:1,3; [x]Ps 45:6–7
10 [y]Ps 8:6; Zec 12:1
11 [z]Isa 34:4; 51:6; **Heb 12:27**
12 [a]Heb 13:8; [b]Ps 102:25–27
13 [c]ver 3; **Mk 16:19**; [d]Jos 10:24; Heb 10:13; [e]Ps 110:1; **Mt 22:44**
14 [f]Ps 91:11; 103:20; Da 7:10; [g]Mt 25:34; Mk 10:17; **Ac 20:32**; [h]**Ro 11:14**; Heb 2:3; 5:9; 9:28

Ch. 2

1 [a]**Ro 11:22**
2 [b]**Heb 1:1**; [c]Dt 33:2; Ac 7:53; Gal 3:19; [d]Heb 10:28
3 [e]Heb 10:29; 12:25; [f]Heb 1:2; [g]**Lk 1:2**
4 [h]Mk 16:20; **Jn 4:48**; [i]1Co 12:4; [j]**Eph 1:5**

---

a5 Or *have begotten you* b5 Psalm 2:7
c5 2 Samuel 7:14; 1 Chron. 17:13
d6 Deut. 32:43 (see Dead Sea Scrolls and Septuagint) e7 Psalm 104:4
f9 Psalm 45:6,7 g12 Psalm 102:25–27
h13 Psalm 110:1

we are speaking. 6But there is a place
where someone[k] has testified:

"What is man that you are mindful of
him,
the son of man that you care for
him?[l]
7You made him a little[a] lower than the
angels;
you crowned him with glory and
honour
8 and put everything under his
feet."[b][m]

In putting everything under him, God
left nothing that is not subject to him.
Yet at present we do not see everything
subject to him. 9But we see Jesus, who
was made a little lower than the angels,
now crowned with glory and honour[n]
because he suffered death,[o] so that by
the grace of God he might taste death
for everyone.[p]
10In bringing many sons to glory, it
was fitting that God, for whom and
through whom everything exists,[q]
should make the author of their salva-
tion perfect through suffering.[r] 11Both
the one who makes men holy[s] and those
who are made holy[t] are of the same
family. So Jesus is not ashamed to call
them brothers.[u] 12He says,

"I will declare your name to my
brothers;
in the presence of the congregation
I will sing your praises."[c][v]

13And again,

"I will put my trust in him."[d][w]

And again he says,

"Here am I, and the children God has
given me."[e][x]

14Since the children have flesh and
blood,[y] he too shared in their humanity[z]
so that by his death he might destroy[a]
him who holds the power of death—
that is, the devil[b]—15and free those who
all their lives were held in slavery by
their fear[c] of death. 16For surely it is not
angels he helps, but Abraham's
descendants.[d] 17For this reason he had
to be made like his brothers[e] in every
way, in order that he might become a
merciful[f] and faithful high priest[g] in ser-
vice to God,[h] and that he might make
atonement for[f] the sins of the people.[i]
18Because he himself suffered when he
was tempted, he is able to help those
who are being tempted.[j]

6 [k]Heb 4:4; [l]Job 7:17; Ps 144:3
8 [m]Ps 8:4–6; **Mt 22:44**
9 [n]ver 7; Ac 3:13; **Php 2:9**; [o]Php 2:7–9; [p]2Co 5:15
10 [q]**Ro 11:36**; [r]Lk 24:26; Heb 5:8–9; 7:28
11 [s]Heb 13:12; [t]**Eph 5:26**; [u]**Mt 28:10**
12 [v]Ps 22:22; 68:26
13 [w]Isa 8:17; [x]Isa 8:18; Jn 10:29
14 [y]1Co 15:50; Eph 6:12; [z]**Jn 1:14**; [a]Ge 3:15; 1Co 15:54–57; 2Ti 1:10; [b]1Jn 3:8
15 [c]**2Ti 1:7**
16 [d]**Lk 3:8**
17 [e]ver 14; **Php 2:7**; [f]Heb 5:2; [g]Heb 3:1; 4:14–15; 5:5, 10; 7:26,28; 8:1,3; 9:11; [h]Heb 5:1; [i]**Ro 3:25**
18 [j]Heb 4:15

Ch. 3

1 [a]Heb 2:11; [b]**Ro 8:28**; [c]**Heb 2:17**; [d]1Ti 6:12; Heb 4:14; 10:23; 2Co 9:13
2 [e]ver 5; Nu 12:7
3 [f]Dt 34:12
4 [g]Ge 1:1
5 [h]Ex 14:31; [i]ver 2; Nu 12:7
6 [j]**Heb 1:2**; [k]**1Co 3:16**; 1Ti 3:15; [l]ver 14; **Ro 11:22**; Heb 4:14; [m]Ro 5:2; Heb 6:11,18–19; 7:19; 11:1
7 [n]Ac 28:25; Heb 9:8; 10:15
8 [o]ver 15; Heb 4:7
9 [p]Nu 14:33; Dt 1:3; Ac 7:36
11 [q]Dt 1:34–35; [r]Heb 4:3,5; [s]Ps 95:7–11
12 [t]**Mt 16:16**
13 [u]Heb 10:24–25; [v]Jer 17:9; Eph 4:22
14 [w]ver 6; [x]**Eph 3:12**
15 [y]Ps 95:7–8; ver 7–8; Heb 4:7

Jesus Greater Than Moses

3 Therefore, holy brothers,[a] who
share in the heavenly calling,[b] fix
your thoughts on Jesus, the apostle and
high priest[c] whom we confess.[d] 2He was
faithful to the one who appointed him,
just as Moses was faithful in all God's
house.[e] 3Jesus has been found worthy of
greater honour than Moses,[f] just as the
builder of a house has greater honour
than the house itself. 4For every house is
built by someone, but God is the builder
of everything.[g] 5Moses was faithful as a
servant[h] in all God's house,[i] testifying to
what would be said in the future. 6But
Christ is faithful as a son[j] over God's
house. And we are his house,[k] if we
hold on[l] to our courage and the hope[m] of
which we boast.

Warning Against Unbelief

7So, as the Holy Spirit says:[n]

"Today, if you hear his voice,
8 do not harden your hearts[o]
as you did in the rebellion,
during the time of testing in the
desert,
9where your fathers tested and tried
me
and for forty years saw what I did.[p]
10That is why I was angry with that
generation,
and I said, 'Their hearts are always
going astray,
and they have not known my ways.'
11So I declared on oath in my anger,[q]
'They shall never enter my rest.'"[r][a][s]

12See to it, brothers, that none of you
has a sinful, unbelieving heart that
turns away from the living God.[t] 13But
encourage one another daily,[u] as long as
it is called Today, so that none of you
may be hardened by sin's deceitful-
ness.[v] 14We have come to share in Christ
if we hold firmly[w] till the end the con-
fidence[x] we had at first. 15As has just
been said:

"Today, if you hear his voice,
do not harden your hearts
as you did in the rebellion."[b][y]

16Who were they who heard and re-
belled? Were they not all those Moses

---

[a]*7* Or *him for a little while;* also in verse 9
[b]*8* Psalm 8:4–6 [c]*12* Psalm 22:22
[d]*13* Isaiah 8:17 [e]*13* Isaiah 8:18
[f]*17* Or *and that he might turn aside God's wrath, taking away*
[a]*11* Psalm 95:7–11
[b]*15* Psalm 95:7,8

led out of Egypt?[z] 17And with whom was he angry for forty years? Was it not with those who sinned, whose bodies fell in the desert?[a] 18And to whom did God swear that they would never enter his rest[b] if not to those who disobeyed[c]?[c] 19So we see that they were not able to enter, because of their unbelief.[d]

A Sabbath-rest for the People of God

4 Therefore, since the promise of entering his rest still stands, let us be careful that none of you be found to have fallen short of it.[a] 2For we also have had the gospel preached to us, just as they did; but the message they heard was of no value to them, because those who heard did not combine it with faith.[a][b] 3Now we who have believed enter that rest, just as God has said,

"So I declared on oath in my anger,
'They shall never enter my rest.'"[b][c]

And yet his work has been finished since the creation of the world. 4For somewhere he has spoken about the seventh day in these words: "And on the seventh day God rested from all his work."[c][d] 5And again in the passage above he says, "They shall never enter my rest."[e]

6It still remains that some will enter that rest, and those who formerly had the gospel preached to them did not go in, because of their disobedience.[f] 7Therefore God again set a certain day, calling it Today, when a long time later he spoke through David, as was said before:

"Today, if you hear his voice,
do not harden your hearts."[d][g]

8For if Joshua had given them rest,[h] God would not have spoken[i] later about another day. 9There remains, then, a Sabbath-rest for the people of God; 10for anyone who enters God's rest also rests from his own work,[j] just as God did from his.[k] 11Let us, therefore, make every effort to enter that rest, so that no-one will fall by following their example of disobedience.[l]

12For the word of God[m] is living[n] and active.[o] Sharper than any double-edged sword,[p] it penetrates even to dividing soul and spirit, joints and marrow; it judges the thoughts and attitudes of the heart.[q] 13Nothing in all creation is hidden from God's sight.[r] Everything is uncovered and laid bare before the eyes of him to whom we must give account.

16 [z]Nu 14:2
17 [a]Nu 14:29; Ps 106:26; 1Co 10:5
18 [b]Nu 14:20–23; Dt 1:34–35; [c]Heb 4:6
19 [d]Ps 78:22; 106:24; Jn 3:36

Ch. 4

1 [a]Heb 12:15
2 [b]1Th 2:13
3 [c]Ps 95:11; Dt 1:34–35; Heb 3:11
4 [d]Ge 2:2–3; Ex 20:11
5 [e]Ps 95:11; **ver 3**
6 [f]ver 11; Heb 3:18
7 [g]Ps 95:7–8; Heb 3:7–8,15
8 [h]Jos 22:4; [i]**Heb 1:1**
10 [j]Lev 23:3; Rev 14:13; [k]ver 4
11 [l]ver 6; Heb 3:18
12 [m]**Mk 4:14**; Lk 5:1; 11:28; Jn 10:35; Ac 12:24; 1Th 2:13; 2Ti 2:9; 1Pe 1:23; 1Jn 2:14; Rev 1:2, 9; [n]Ac 7:38; 1Pe 1:23; [o]Isa 55:11; Jer 23:29; 1Th 2:13; [p]Eph 6:17; **Rev 1:16**; [q]1Co 14:24–25
13 [r]Ps 33:13–15; Pr 5:21; Jer 16:17; 23:24; Da 2:22
14 [s]**Heb 2:17**; [t]Heb 6:20; 8:1; 9:24; [u]**Mt 4:3**; [v]**Heb 3:1**
15 [w]**Heb 2:17**; [x]Heb 2:18; [y]**2Co 5:21**
16 [z]**Heb 7:19**; [a]**Eph 3:12**

Ch. 5

1 [a]Heb 2:17; [b]Heb 8:3; 9:9; [c]Heb 7:27
2 [d]Isa 29:24; Heb 2:18; 4:15; [e]Heb 7:28
3 [f]Lev 9:7; 16:6; Heb 7:27; 9:7
4 [g]Ex 28:1; Nu 14:40; 18:7
5 [h]Jn 8:54; [i]**Heb 2:17**; [j]**Heb 1:1**; [k]Ps 2:7; **Mt 3:17**
6 [l]ver 10; Ge 14:18; Heb 6:20; 7:1–22; [m]Ps 110:4; Heb 7:17,21

Jesus the Great High Priest

14Therefore, since we have a great high priest[s] who has gone through the heavens,[e][t] Jesus the Son of God,[u] let us hold firmly to the faith we profess.[v] 15For we do not have a high priest[w] who is unable to sympathise with our weaknesses, but we have one who has been tempted in every way, just as we are[x]—yet was without sin.[y] 16Let us then approach[z] the throne of grace with confidence,[a] so that we may receive mercy and find grace to help us in our time of need.

5 Every high priest is selected from among men and is appointed to represent them in matters related to God,[a] to offer gifts and sacrifices[b] for sins.[c] 2He is able to deal gently with those who are ignorant and are going astray,[d] since he himself is subject to weakness.[e] 3This is why he has to offer sacrifices for his own sins, as well as for the sins of the people.[f]

4No-one takes this honour upon himself; he must be called by God, just as Aaron was.[g] 5So Christ also did not take upon himself the glory[h] of becoming a high priest.[i] But God said[j] to him,

"You are my Son;
today I have become your
Father.[a]"[b][k]

6And he says in another place,

"You are a priest for ever,
in the order of Melchizedek."[l][c][m]

7During the days of Jesus' life on earth, he offered up prayers and petitions[n] with loud cries and tears[o] to the one who could save him from death, and he was heard[p] because of his reverent submission.[q] 8Although he was a son,[r] he learned obedience from what he suffered[s] 9and, once made perfect,[t] he became the source of eternal salvation for all who obey him 10and was designated by God to be high priest[u] in the order of Melchizedek.[v]

7 [n]Lk 22:41–44; [o]Mt 27:46,50; Lk 23:46; [p]Ps 22:24; [q]Mk 14:36 *8* [r]**Heb 1:2**; [s]**Php 2:8**
9 [t]**Heb 2:10** *10* [u]ver 5; **Heb 2:17**; [v]**ver 6**

---

c18 Or *disbelieved*
a2 Many manuscripts *because they did not share in the faith of those who obeyed*
b3 Psalm 95:11; also in verse 5
c4 Gen. 2:2
d7 Psalm 95:7,8
e14 Or *gone into heaven*
a5 Or *have begotten you*
b5 Psalm 2:7
c6 Psalm 110:4

Warning Against Falling Away

6:4–6Ref—Heb 10:26–31

11We have much to say about this, but
it is hard to explain because you are
slow to learn. 12In fact, though by this
time you ought to be teachers, you need
someone to teach you the elementary
truths[w] of God's word all over again.
You need milk, not solid food![x]
13Anyone who lives on milk, being still
an infant,[y] is not acquainted with the
teaching about righteousness. 14But
solid food is for the mature,[z] who by
constant use have trained themselves to
distinguish good from evil.[a]

6 Therefore let us leave[a] the
elementary teachings[b] about Christ
and go on to maturity, not laying again
the foundation of repentance from acts
that lead to death,[a][c] and of faith in God,
2instruction about baptisms,[d] the laying
on of hands,[e] the resurrection of the
dead,[f] and eternal judgment. 3And God
permitting,[g] we will do so.

4It is impossible for those who
have once been enlightened,[h] who have
tasted the heavenly gift,[i] who have
shared in the Holy Spirit,[j] 5who
have tasted the goodness[k] of the word of
God[l] and the powers of the coming age,
6if they fall away, to be brought back
to repentance,[m] because[b] to their loss
they are crucifying the Son of God[n] all
over again and subjecting him to public
disgrace.

7Land that drinks in the rain often
falling on it and that produces a crop
useful to those for whom it is farmed
receives the blessing of God. 8But land
that produces thorns and thistles is
worthless and is in danger of being
cursed.[o] In the end it will be burned.

9Even though we speak like this, dear
friends,[p] we are confident of better
things in your case—things that accom-
pany salvation. 10God is not unjust; he
will not forget your work and the love
you have shown him as you have
helped his people and continue to help
them.[q] 11We want each of you to show
this same diligence to the very end, in
order to make your hope[r] sure. 12We
do not want you to become lazy, but
to imitate[s] those who through faith
and patience[t] inherit what has been
promised.[u]

The Certainty of God's Promise

13When God made his promise to
Abraham, since there was no-one
greater for him to swear by, he swore
by himself,[v] 14saying, "I will surely bless
you and give you many descendants."[c][w]
15And so after waiting patiently, Abra-
ham received what was promised.[x]

16Men swear by someone greater than
themselves, and the oath confirms what
is said and puts an end to all argument.[y]
17Because God wanted to make the un-
changing[z] nature of his purpose very
clear to the heirs of what was promised,[a]
he confirmed it with an oath. 18God
did this so that, by two unchangeable
things in which it is impossible for God
to lie,[b] we who have fled to take hold of
the hope[c] offered to us may be greatly
encouraged. 19We have this hope as an
anchor for the soul, firm and secure. It
enters the inner sanctuary behind the
curtain,[d] 20where Jesus, who went be-
fore us, has entered on our behalf.[e] He
has become a high priest[f] for ever, in the
order of Melchizedek.[g]

Melchizedek the Priest

7 This Melchizedek was king of
Salem[a] and priest of God Most
High.[b] He met Abraham returning
from the defeat of the kings and
blessed him,[c] 2and Abraham gave him
a tenth of everything. First, his name
means "king of righteousness"; then
also, "king of Salem" means "king of
peace". 3Without father or mother,
without genealogy,[d] without beginning
of days or end of life, like the Son of
God[e] he remains a priest for ever.

4Just think how great he was: Even
the patriarch[f] Abraham gave him a
tenth of the plunder![g] 5Now the law
requires the descendants of Levi who
become priests to collect a tenth from the
people[h]—that is, their brothers—even
though their brothers are descended
from Abraham. 6This man, however,
did not trace his descent from Levi, yet
he collected a tenth from Abraham and
blessed[i] him who had the promises.[j]
7And without doubt the lesser person is
blessed by the greater. 8In the one case,
the tenth is collected by men who die;
but in the other case, by him who is
declared to be living.[k] 9One might even
say that Levi, who collects the tenth,
paid the tenth through Abraham,
10because when Melchizedek met Abra-
ham, Levi was still in the body of his
ancestor.

12 [w]Heb 6:1; [x]1Co 3:2; 1Pe 2:2
13 [y]**1Co 14:20**
14 [z]**1Co 2:6**; [a]Isa 7:15

Ch. 6

1 [a]Php 3:12–14; [b]Heb 5:12; [c]Heb 9:14
2 [d]Jn 3:25; [e]**Ac 6:6**; [f]**Ac 2:24**; 17:18,32
3 [g]Ac 18:21
4 [h]Heb 10:32; [i]Eph 2:8; [j]Gal 3:2
5 [k]Ps 34:8; [l]**Heb 4:12**
6 [m]2Pe 2:21; 1Jn 5:16; [n]**Mt 4:3**
8 [o]Ge 3:17–18; Isa 5:6; 27:4
9 [p]**1Co 10:14**
10 [q]**Mt 10:40**,42; 1Th 1:3
11 [r]**Heb 3:6**
12 [s]Heb 13:7; [t]2Th 1:4; Jas 1:3; Rev 13:10; 14:12; [u]Heb 10:36
13 [v]Ge 22:16; Lk 1:73
14 [w]Ge 22:17
15 [x]Ge 21:5
16 [y]Ex 22:11
17 [z]ver 18; Ps 110:4; [a]Ro 4:16; Heb 11:9
18 [b]Nu 23:19; Tit 1:2; [c]**Heb 3:6**
19 [d]Lev 16:2; Heb 9:2–3,7
20 [e]**Heb 4:14**; [f]**Heb 2:17**; [g]**Heb 5:6**

Ch. 7

1 [a]Ps 76:2; [b]**Mk 5:7**; [c]ver 6; Ge 14:18–20
3 [d]ver 6; [e]**Mt 4:3**
4 [f]Ac 2:29; [g]Ge 14:20
5 [h]Nu 18:21,26
6 [i]Ge 14:19–20; [j]Ro 4:13
8 [k]Heb 5:6; 6:20

[a]*1* Or *from useless rituals* [b]*6* Or *repentance while* [c]*14* Gen. 22:17

Jesus Like Melchizedek

[11]If perfection could have been
attained through the Levitical priest-
hood (for on the basis of it the law was
given to the people),[l] why was there still
need for another priest to come[m]—one
in the order of Melchizedek,[n] not in the
order of Aaron? [12]For when there is a
change of the priesthood, there must
also be a change of the law. [13]He of
whom these things are said belonged to
a different tribe,[o] and no-one from that
tribe has ever served at the altar.[p] [14]For
it is clear that our Lord descended
from Judah,[q] and in regard to that tribe
Moses said nothing about priests. [15]And
what we have said is even more clear
if another priest like Melchizedek
appears, [16]one who has become a priest
not on the basis of a regulation as to his
ancestry but on the basis of the power of
an indestructible life. [17]For it is declared:

"You are a priest for ever,
in the order of Melchizedek."[a][r]

[18]The former regulation is set aside
because it was weak and useless[s] [19](for
the law made nothing perfect),[t] and a
better hope[u] is introduced, by which we
draw near to God.[v]
[20]And it was not without an oath!
Others became priests without any
oath, [21]but he became a priest with an
oath when God said to him:

"The Lord has sworn
and will not change his mind:[w]
'You are a priest for ever.'"[b][x]

[22]Because of this oath, Jesus has become
the guarantee of a better covenant.[y]
[23]Now there have been many of those
priests, since death prevented them
from continuing in office; [24]but because
Jesus lives for ever, he has a permanent
priesthood.[z] [25]Therefore he is able to
save[a] completely[c] those who come to
God[b] through him, because he always
lives to intercede for them.[c]
[26]Such a high priest[d] meets our need
—one who is holy, blameless, pure, set
apart from sinners,[e] exalted above the
heavens.[f] [27]Unlike the other high
priests, he does not need to offer sacri-
fices[g] day after day, first for his own
sins,[h] and then for the sins of the peo-
ple. He sacrificed for their sins once for
all[i] when he offered himself.[j] [28]For the
law appoints as high priests men who
are weak;[k] but the oath, which came
after the law, appointed the Son,[l] who
has been made perfect[m] for ever.

The High Priest of a New Covenant

8 The point of what we are saying
is this: We do have such a high
priest,[a] who sat down at the right hand
of the throne of the Majesty in heaven,[b]
[2]and who serves in the sanctuary, the
true tabernacle[c] set up by the Lord, not
by man.
[3]Every high priest[d] is appointed to
offer both gifts and sacrifices,[e] and so it
was necessary for this one also to have
something to offer.[f] [4]If he were on earth,
he would not be a priest, for there are
already men who offer the gifts pre-
scribed by the law.[g] [5]They serve at a
sanctuary that is a copy[h] and shadow[i] of
what is in heaven. This is why Moses
was warned[j] when he was about to
build the tabernacle: "See to it that you
make everything according to the pat-
tern shown you on the mountain."[a][k]
[6]But the ministry Jesus has received is as
superior to theirs as the covenant[l] of
which he is mediator[m] is superior to the
old one, and it is founded on better
promises.
[7]For if there had been nothing wrong
with that first covenant, no place would
have been sought for another.[n] [8]But
God found fault with the people and
said:[b]

"The time is coming, declares the
Lord,
when I will make a new covenant[o]
with the house of Israel
and with the house of Judah.
[9]It will not be like the covenant
I made with their forefathers[p]
when I took them by the hand
to lead them out of Egypt,
because they did not remain faithful to
my covenant,
and I turned away from them,
declares the Lord.
[10]This is the covenant[q] I will make with
the house of Israel
after that time, declares the Lord.
I will put my laws in their minds
and write them on their hearts.[r]
I will be their God,
and they will be my people.[s]
[11]No longer will a man teach his
neighbour,
or a man his brother, saying, 'Know
the Lord,'

11 [l]ver 18–19; Heb 8:7; [m]Heb 10:1; [n]ver 17; **Heb 5:6**
13 [o]ver 11; [p]ver 14
14 [q]Isa 11:1; Mt 1:3; 2:6; Lk 3:33; Rev 5:5
17 [r]Ps 110:4; ver 21; **Heb 5:6**
18 [s]Ro 8:3
19 [t]ver 11; Ro 3:20; 7:7–8; Gal 3:21; Heb 9:9; 10:1; [u]**Heb 3:6;** [v]ver 25; Heb 4:16; 10:1,22; Jas 4:8
21 [w]Nu 23:19; 1Sa 15:29; Mal 3:6; Ro 11:29; [x]Ps 110:4; **Heb 5:6**
22 [y]**Lk 22:20**
24 [z]ver 28
25 [a]**Ro 11:14;** [b]**ver 19;** [c]**Ro 8:34**
26 [d]**Heb 2:17;** [e]**2Co 5:21;** [f]**Heb 4:14**
27 [g]Heb 5:1; [h]**Heb 5:3;** [i]Ro 6:10; Heb 9:12, 26,28; 10:10; 1Pe 3:18; [j]Eph 5:2; Heb 9:14,28
28 [k]Heb 5:2; [l]**Heb 1:2;** [m]**Heb 2:10**

Ch. 8

1 [a]**Heb 2:17;** [b]**Mk 16:19; Heb 4:14**
2 [c]Heb 9:11,24
3 [d]**Heb 2:17;** [e]Heb 5:1; 9:9; [f]Heb 9:14
4 [g]Heb 5:1; 9:9
5 [h]Heb 9:23; [i]Col 2:17; Heb 10:1; [j]Heb 11:7; 12:25; [k]Ex 25:40
6 [l]ver 8,13; **Lk 22:20;** [m]**Gal 3:20**
7 [n]Heb 7:11,18; 10:1
8 [o]ver 6,13; **Lk 22:20**
9 [p]Ex 19:5–6; 20:1–17
10 [q]Ro 11:27; [r]2Co 3:3; Heb 10:16; [s]Eze 11:20; Zec 8:8

[a]*17* Psalm 110:4 [b]*21* Psalm 110:4
[c]*25* Or *for ever* [a]*5* Exodus 25:40
[b]*8* Some manuscripts may be translated *fault and said to the people.*

because they will all know me,[t]
from the least of them to the greatest.
12For I will forgive their wickedness
and will remember their sins no more."[u][c][v]

13By calling this covenant "new",[w] he has made the first one obsolete;[x] and what is obsolete and ageing will soon disappear.

Worship in the Earthly Tabernacle

9 Now the first covenant had regulations for worship and also an earthly sanctuary.[a] 2A tabernacle[b] was set up. In its first room were the lampstand,[c] the table[d] and the consecrated bread;[e] this was called the Holy Place.[f] 3Behind the second curtain was a room called the Most Holy Place,[g] 4which had the golden altar of incense[h] and the gold-covered ark of the covenant.[i] This ark contained the gold jar of manna,[j] Aaron's staff that had budded,[k] and the stone tablets of the covenant.[l] 5Above the ark were the cherubim of the Glory,[m] overshadowing the atonement cover.[a][n] But we cannot discuss these things in detail now.

6When everything had been arranged like this, the priests entered regularly[o] into the outer room to carry on their ministry. 7But only the high priest entered[p] the inner room,[q] and that only once a year,[r] and never without blood,[s] which he offered for himself[t] and for the sins the people had committed in ignorance.[u] 8The Holy Spirit was showing[v] by this that the way[w] into the Most Holy Place had not yet been disclosed as long as the first tabernacle was still standing. 9This is an illustration[x] for the present time, indicating that the gifts and sacrifices being offered[y] were not able to clear the conscience[z] of the worshipper. 10They are only a matter of food[a] and drink[b] and various ceremonial washings[c]—external regulations[d] applying until the time of the new order.

The Blood of Christ

11When Christ came as high priest[e] of the good things that are already here,[b][f] he went through the greater and more perfect tabernacle[g] that is not man-made,[h] that is to say, not a part of this creation. 12He did not enter by means of the blood of goats and calves;[i] but he entered the Most Holy Place[j] once for all[k] by his own blood,[l] having obtained eternal redemption. 13The blood of goats and bulls[m] and the ashes of a heifer[n] sprinkled on those who are ceremonially unclean sanctify them so that they are outwardly clean. 14How much more, then, will the blood of Christ, who through the eternal Spirit[o] offered himself[p] unblemished to God, cleanse our consciences[q] from acts that lead to death,[c][r] so that we may serve the living God![s]

15For this reason Christ is the mediator[t] of a new covenant,[u] that those who are called[v] may receive the promised[w] eternal inheritance[x]—now that he has died as a ransom to set them free from the sins committed under the first covenant.[y]

16In the case of a will,[d] it is necessary to prove the death of the one who made it, 17because a will is in force only when somebody has died; it never takes effect while the one who made it is living. 18This is why even the first covenant was not put into effect without blood.[z] 19When Moses had proclaimed[a] every commandment of the law to all the people, he took the blood of calves,[b] together with water, scarlet wool and branches of hyssop, and sprinkled the scroll and all the people.[c] 20He said, "This is the blood of the covenant, which God has commanded you to keep."[e][d] 21In the same way, he sprinkled with the blood both the tabernacle and everything used in its ceremonies. 22In fact, the law requires that nearly everything be cleansed with blood,[e] and without the shedding of blood there is no forgiveness.[f]

23It was necessary, then, for the copies[g] of the heavenly things to be purified with these sacrifices, but the heavenly things themselves with better sacrifices than these. 24For Christ did not enter a man-made sanctuary that was only a copy of the true one;[h] he entered heaven itself,[i] now to appear for us in God's presence.[j] 25Nor did he enter heaven to offer himself again and again, the way the high priest enters the Most Holy Place[k] every year with blood that is not his own.[l] 26Then Christ would have had to suffer many times

11 [t]Isa 54:13; Jn **6:45**
12 [u]Heb 10:17; [v]Jer 31:31–34
13 [w]ver 6,8; **Lk 22:20**; [x]2Co 5:17

Ch. 9

1 [a]Ex 25:8
2 [b]Ex 25:8–9; [c]Ex 25:31–39; [d]Ex 25:23–29; [e]Ex 25:30; Lev 24:5–8; [f]Ex 26:33–34
3 [g]Ex 26:31–33
4 [h]Ex 30:1–5; [i]Ex 25:10–22; [j]Ex 16:32–33; [k]Nu 17:10; [l]Ex 31:18; 32:15
5 [m]Ex 25:17–19; [n]Ex 25:20–22; 26:34
6 [o]Nu 28:3
7 [p]Lev 16:11–19; [q]ver 2–3; [r]Lev 16:34; [s]Lev 16:11,14; [t]Lev 16:11; Heb 5:2–3; [u]Heb 5:2–3
8 [v]**Heb 3:7**; [w]Jn 14:6; Heb 10:19–20
9 [x]Heb 10:1; [y]Heb 5:1; 8:3; [z]**Heb 7:19**
10 [a]Lev 11:2–23; [b]Nu 6:3; Col 2:16; [c]Lev 11:25,28,40; [d]Heb 7:16
11 [e]**Heb 2:17**; [f]Heb 10:1; [g]ver 24; Heb 8:2; [h]**Jn 2:19**
12 [i]ver 19; Lev 16:6,15; Heb 10:4; [j]ver 24; [k]ver 26,28; **Heb 7:27**; [l]ver 14; **Ro 3:25**
13 [m]Heb 10:4; [n]Nu 19:9, 17–18
14 [o]1Pe 3:18; [p]**Eph 5:2**; [q]Ps 51:2; 65:3; Jer 33:8; Zec 13:1; **Tit 2:14**; Heb 10:2,22; [r]Heb 6:1; [s]**Mt 16:16**
15 [t]**Gal 3:20**; [u]**Lk 22:20**; [v]**Ro 8:28**; **11:29**; [w]Heb 6:15; 10:36; [x]**Ac 20:32**; [y]Heb 7:22
18 [z]Ex 24:6–8
19 [a]Heb 1:1; [b]ver 12; [c]Ex 24:6–8
20 [d]Ex 24:8; **Mt 26:28**
22 [e]Ex 29:21; Lev 8:15; [f]Lev 17:11
23 [g]Heb 8:5
24 [h]Heb 8:2; [i]ver 12; **Heb 4:14**; [j]**Ro 8:34**
25 [k]Heb 10:19; [l]ver 7–8

c*12* Jer. 31:31–34
a*5* Traditionally *the mercy seat*
b*11* Some early manuscripts *are to come*
c*14* Or *from useless rituals*
d*16* Same Greek word as *covenant*; also in verse 17
e*20* Exodus 24:8

since the creation of the world.[m] But
now he has appeared[n] once for all[o] at the
end of the ages to do away with sin by
the sacrifice of himself.[p] 27Just as man is
destined to die once,[q] and after that to
face judgment,[r] 28so Christ was sac-
rificed once[s] to take away the sins of
many people; and he will appear a
second time,[t] not to bear sin,[u] but to
bring salvation[v] to those who are wait-
ing for him.[w]

Christ's Sacrifice Once for All

10 The law is only a shadow[a] of the
good things[b] that are coming
—not the realities themselves.[c] For this
reason it can never, by the same sac-
rifices repeated endlessly year after
year, make perfect[d] those who draw
near to worship.[e] 2If it could, would
they not have stopped being offered?
For the worshippers would have been
cleansed once for all, and would no
longer have felt guilty for their sins.[f]
3But those sacrifices are an annual re-
minder of sins,[g] 4because it is impossible
for the blood of bulls and goats[h] to take
away sins.[i]
5Therefore, when Christ came into
the world,[j] he said:

"Sacrifice and offering you did not
desire,
but a body you prepared for me;[k]
6with burnt offerings and sin offerings
you were not pleased.
7Then I said, 'Here I am—it is written
about me in the scroll[l]—
I have come to do your will, O
God.' "[a][m]

8First he said, "Sacrifices and offerings,
burnt offerings and sin offerings you
did not desire, nor were you pleased
with them" [n] (although the law required
them to be made). 9Then he said, "Here
I am, I have come to do your will."[o] He
sets aside the first to establish the
second. 10And by that will, we have
been made holy[p] through the sacrifice of
the body[q] of Jesus Christ once for all.[r]
11Day after day every priest stands
and performs his religious duties; again
and again he offers the same sacrifices,[s]
which can never take away sins.[t] 12But
when this priest had offered for all time
one sacrifice for sins,[u] he sat down at the
right hand of God.[v] 13Since that time he
waits for his enemies to be made his
footstool,[w] 14because by one sacrifice he
has made perfect[x] for ever those who
are being made holy.[y]
15The Holy Spirit also testifies[z] to us
about this. First he says:

16"This is the covenant I will make with
them
after that time, says the Lord.
I will put my laws in their hearts,
and I will write them on their
minds."[b][a]

17Then he adds:

"Their sins and lawless acts
I will remember no more."[c][b]

18And where these have been forgiven,
there is no longer any sacrifice for sin.

A Call to Persevere

19Therefore, brothers, since we have
confidence[c] to enter the Most Holy
Place[d] by the blood of Jesus, 20by a new
and living way[e] opened for us through
the curtain,[f] that is, his body, 21and
since we have a great priest[g] over the
house of God,[h] 22let us draw near
to God[i] with a sincere heart in full
assurance of faith,[j] having our hearts
sprinkled to cleanse us from a guilty
conscience[k] and having our bodies
washed with pure water.[l] 23Let us hold
unswervingly to the hope[m] we pro-
fess,[n] for he who promised is faithful.[o]
24And let us consider how we may spur
one another on towards love and good
deeds.[p] 25Let us not give up meeting
together,[q] as some are in the habit of
doing, but let us encourage one
another[r]—and all the more as you see
the Day approaching.[s]
26If we deliberately keep on sinning[t]
after we have received the knowledge of
the truth,[u] no sacrifice for sins is left,
27but only a fearful expectation of judg-
ment and of raging fire[v] that will con-
sume the enemies of God. 28Anyone
who rejected the law of Moses died
without mercy on the testimony of two
or three witnesses.[w] 29How much more
severely do you think a man deserves to
be punished who has trampled the Son
of God[x] under foot,[y] who has treated as
an unholy thing the blood of the cov-
enant[z] that sanctified him,[a] and who
has insulted the Spirit[b] of grace?[c] 30For
we know him who said, "It is mine to

26 [m]Heb 4:3; [n]1Jn 3:5; [o]ver 12,28; **Heb 7:27**; [p]ver 12
27 [q]Ge 3:19; [r]2Co 5:10
28 [s]ver 12,26; **Heb 7:27**; [t]**Mt 16:27**; [u]1Pe 2:24; [v]Heb 5:9; [w]**1Co 1:7**

Ch. 10

1 [a]Col 2:17; Heb 8:5; [b]Heb 9:11; [c]Heb 9:23; [d]ver 4, 11; **Heb 7:19**; [e]**Heb 7:19**
2 [f]Heb 9:9
3 [g]Lev 16:34; Heb 9:7
4 [h]Heb 9:12–13; [i]ver 1,11
5 [j]Heb 1:6; [k]Heb 2:14; 1Pe 2:24
7 [l]Ezr 6:2; Jer 36:2; [m]Ps 40:6–8; **Mt 26:39**
8 [n]ver 5–6; **Mk 12:33**
9 [o]ver 7
10 [p]ver 14; **Eph 5:26**; [q]Heb 2:14; 1Pe 2:24; [r]**Heb 7:27**
11 [s]Heb 5:1; [t]ver 1,4
12 [u]Heb 5:1; [v]**Mk 16:19**
13 [w]Jos 10:24; Heb 1:13
14 [x]ver 1; [y]ver 10; **Eph 5:26**
15 [z]**Heb 3:7**
16 [a]Jer 31:33; Heb 8:10
17 [b]Jer 31:34; Heb 8:12
19 [c]**Eph 3:12**; [d]Lev 16:2; Eph 2:18; Heb 9:8, 12,25
20 [e]Heb 9:8; [f]Heb 6:19; 9:3
21 [g]**Heb 2:17**; [h]**Heb 3:6**
22 [i]ver 1; **Heb 7:19**; [j]Eph 3:12; [k]Eze 36:25; Heb 9:14; 12:24; 1Pe 1:2; [l]**Ac 22:16**
23 [m]**Heb 3:6**; [n]**Heb 3:1**; [o]**1Co 1:9**
24 [p]**Tit 2:14**
25 [q]Ac 2:42; [r]Heb 3:13; [s]**1Co 3:13**
26 [t]Ex 21:14; Nu 15:30; Heb 5:2; 6:4–8; 2Pe 2:20; [u]**1Ti 2:4**
27 [v]Isa 26:11; 2Th 1:7; Heb 9:27; 12:29
28 [w]Dt 17:6–7; **Mt 18:16**; Heb 2:2
29 [x]**Mt 4:3**; [y]Heb 6:6; [z]**Mt 26:28**; [a]1Co 6:11; Rev 1:5; [b]Eph 4:30; Heb 6:4; [c]Heb 2:3; 12:25

[a]7 Psalm 40:6–8 (see Septuagint)
[b]16 Jer. 31:33 [c]17 Jer. 31:34

avenge; I will repay,"[d][d] and again, "The
Lord will judge his people."[e][e] 31 It is a
dreadful thing[f] to fall into the hands[g] of
the living God.[h]
32 Remember those earlier days after
you had received the light,[i] when you
stood your ground in a great contest in
the face of suffering.[j] 33 Sometimes you
were publicly exposed to insult and
persecution;[k] at other times you stood
side by side with those who were so
treated.[l] 34 You sympathised with those
in prison[m] and joyfully accepted the
confiscation of your property, because
you knew that you yourselves had
better and lasting possessions.[n]
35 So do not throw away your confi-
dence;[o] it will be richly rewarded. 36 You
need to persevere[p] so that when you
have done the will of God, you will
receive what he has promised.[q] 37 For in
just a very little while,

"He who is coming[r] will come and will
not delay.[s]
38 But my righteous one[f] will live by
faith.[t]
And if he shrinks back,
I will not be pleased with him."[g][u]

39 But we are not of those who shrink
back and are destroyed, but of those
who believe and are saved.

By Faith

11 Now faith is being sure of what
we hope for[a] and certain of
what we do not see.[b] 2 This is what the
ancients were commended for.[c]
3 By faith we understand that the uni-
verse was formed at God's command,[d]
so that what is seen was not made out of
what was visible.
4 By faith Abel offered God a better
sacrifice than Cain did. By faith he was
commended[e] as a righteous man, when
God spoke well of his offerings.[f] And by
faith he still speaks, even though he is
dead.[g]
5 By faith Enoch was taken from this
life, so that he did not experience death;
he could not be found, because God had
taken him away.[h] For before he was
taken, he was commended as one who
pleased God. 6 And without faith it is
impossible to please God, because any-
one who comes to him[i] must believe
that he exists and that he rewards those
who earnestly seek him.
7 By faith Noah, when warned about
things not yet seen,[j] in holy fear built an
ark[k] to save his family.[l] By his faith he
condemned the world and became heir
of the righteousness that comes by
faith.[m]
8 By faith Abraham, when called to go
to a place he would later receive as his
inheritance,[n] obeyed and went,[o] even
though he did not know where he was
going. 9 By faith he made his home in the
promised land[p] like a stranger in a
foreign country; he lived in tents,[q] as
did Isaac and Jacob, who were heirs
with him of the same promise.[r] 10 For he
was looking forward to the city[s] with
foundations,[t] whose architect and
builder is God.[u]
11 By faith Abraham, even though he
was past age—and Sarah herself was
barren[v]—was enabled to become a
father[w] because he[a] considered him
faithful[x] who had made the promise.
12 And so from this one man, and he as
good as dead,[y] came descendants as
numerous as the stars in the sky and as
countless as the sand on the seashore.[z]
13 All these people were still living by
faith when they died. They did not re-
ceive the things promised;[a] they only
saw them and welcomed them from a
distance.[b] And they admitted that they
were aliens and strangers on earth.[c]
14 People who say such things show that
they are looking for a country of their
own. 15 If they had been thinking of the
country they had left, they would have
had opportunity to return.[d] 16 Instead,
they were longing for a better country
—a heavenly one.[e] Therefore God is not
ashamed[f] to be called their God,[g] for he
has prepared a city[h] for them.
17 By faith Abraham, when God tested
him, offered Isaac as a sacrifice.[i] He who
had received the promises was about to
sacrifice his one and only son, 18 even
though God had said to him, "It is
through Isaac that your offspring[b] will
be reckoned."[c][j] 19 Abraham reasoned
that God could raise the dead,[k] and
figuratively speaking, he did receive
Isaac back from death.
20 By faith Isaac blessed Jacob and
Esau in regard to their future.[l]
21 By faith Jacob, when he was dying,
blessed each of Joseph's sons,[m] and
worshipped as he leaned on the top of
his staff.
22 By faith Joseph, when his end was

30 [d]Dt 32:35; Ro 12:19; [e]Dt 32:36; Ps 135:14
31 [f]**2Co 5:11**; [g]Isa 19:16; [h]**Mt 16:16**
32 [i]Heb 6:4; [j]Php 1:29–30
33 [k]1Co 4:9; [l]Php 4:14; 1Th 2:14
34 [m]Heb 13:3; [n]Heb 11:16; 1Pe 1:4–5
35 [o]**Eph 3:12**
36 [p]Ro 5:3; Heb 12:1; Jas 1:3–4,12; 5:11; 2Pe 1:6; [q]Heb 6:15; 9:15
37 [r]Mt 11:3; [s]Rev 22:20
38 [t]Ro 1:17; Gal 3:11; [u]Hab 2:3–4

Ch. 11

1 [a]**Heb 3:6**; [b]**2Co 4:18**
2 [c]ver 4,39
3 [d]Ge 1; Jn 1:3; Heb 1:2; 2Pe 3:5
4 [e]ver 2,39; [f]Ge 4:4; 1Jn 3:12; [g]Heb 12:24
5 [h]Ge 5:21–24
6 [i]Heb 7:19
7 [j]**ver 1**; [k]Ge 6:13–22; [l]1Pe 3:20; [m]Ge 6:9; Eze 14:14,20; **Ro 9:30**
8 [n]Ge 12:7; [o]Ge 12:1–4; Ac 7:2–4
9 [p]Ac 7:5; [q]Ge 12:8; 18:1,9; [r]Heb 6:17
10 [s]Heb 12:22; 13:14; [t]Rev 21:2,14; [u]ver 16
11 [v]Ge 17:17–19; 18:11–14; [w]Ge 21:2; [x]**1Co 1:9**
12 [y]Ro 4:19; [z]Ge 22:17
13 [a]ver 39; [b]**Mt 13:17**; [c]Ge 23:4; Lev 25:23; Php 3:20; 1Pe 1:17; 2:11
15 [d]Ge 24:6–8
16 [e]2Ti 4:18; [f]Mk 8:38; [g]Ge 26:24; 28:13; Ex 3:6,15; [h]ver 10; Heb 13:14
17 [i]Ge 22:1–10; Jas 2:21
18 [j]Ge 21:12; Ro 9:7
19 [k]Ro 4:21; **Jn 5:21**
20 [l]Ge 27:27–29, 39–40
21 [m]Ge 48:1, 8–22

[d]30 Deut. 32:35 [e]30 Deut. 32:36; Psalm 135:14
[f]38 One early manuscript *But the righteous*
[g]38 Hab. 2:3,4
[a]11 Or *By faith even Sarah, who was past age, was enabled to bear children because she*
[b]18 Greek *seed* [c]18 Gen. 21:12

near, spoke about the exodus of the
Israelites from Egypt and gave instruc-
tions about his bones.[n]
23By faith Moses' parents hid him for
three months after he was born,[o] be-
cause they saw he was no ordinary
child, and they were not afraid of the
king's edict.[p]
24By faith Moses, when he had grown
up, refused to be known as the son of
Pharaoh's daughter.[q] 25He chose to be
ill-treated[r] along with the people of God
rather than to enjoy the pleasures of sin
for a short time. 26He regarded disgrace[s]
for the sake of Christ[t] as of greater value
than the treasures of Egypt, because he
was looking ahead to his reward.[u] 27By
faith he left Egypt,[v] not fearing the
king's anger; he persevered because he
saw him who is invisible. 28By faith he
kept the Passover and the sprinkling of
blood, so that the destroyer[w] of the
firstborn would not touch the firstborn
of Israel.[x]
29By faith the people passed through
the Red Sea[d] as on dry land; but when
the Egyptians tried to do so, they were
drowned.[y]
30By faith the walls of Jericho fell, after
the people had marched around them
for seven days.[z]
31By faith the prostitute Rahab, be-
cause she welcomed the spies, was
not killed with those who were
disobedient.[e][a]
32And what more shall I say? I do not
have time to tell about Gideon,[b] Barak,[c]
Samson,[d] Jephthah,[e] David,[f] Samuel[g]
and the prophets, 33who through faith
conquered kingdoms,[h] administered
justice, and gained what was promised;
who shut the mouths of lions,[i]
34quenched the fury of the flames,[j] and
escaped the edge of the sword;[k] whose
weakness was turned to strength;[l] and
who became powerful in battle and
routed foreign armies.[m] 35Women re-
ceived back their dead, raised to life
again.[n] Others were tortured and re-
fused to be released, so that they might
gain a better resurrection. 36Some faced
jeers and flogging,[o] while still others
were chained and put in prison.[p] 37They
were stoned;[f][q] they were sawn in two;
they were put to death by the sword.[r]
They went about in sheepskins and
goatskins,[s] destitute, persecuted and ill-
treated—38the world was not worthy of
them. They wandered in deserts and
mountains, and in caves[t] and holes in
the ground.
39These were all commended[u] for
their faith, yet none of them received
what had been promised.[v] 40God had
planned something better for us so that
only together with us[w] would they be
made perfect.[x]

God Disciplines His Sons

12 Therefore, since we are sur-
rounded by such a great cloud
of witnesses, let us throw off everything
that hinders and the sin that so easily
entangles, and let us run[a] with
perseverance[b] the race marked out for
us. 2Let us fix our eyes on Jesus,[c] the
author[d] and perfecter of our faith, who
for the joy set before him endured the
cross,[e] scorning its shame,[f] and sat
down at the right hand of the throne of
God.[g] 3Consider him who endured such
opposition from sinful men, so that you
will not grow weary[h] and lose heart.
4In your struggle against sin, you
have not yet resisted to the point of
shedding your blood.[i] 5And you have
forgotten that word of encouragement
that addresses you as sons:

"My son, do not make light of the
Lord's discipline,
and do not lose heart[j] when he
rebukes you,
6because the Lord disciplines those he
loves,[k]
and he punishes everyone he
accepts as a son."[a][l]

7Endure hardship as discipline; God
is treating you as sons.[m] For what son is
not disciplined by his father? 8If you are
not disciplined (and everyone under-
goes discipline),[n] then you are illegiti-
mate children and not true sons.
9Moreover, we have all had human
fathers who disciplined us and we re-
spected them for it. How much more
should we submit to the Father of our
spirits[o] and live![p] 10Our fathers disci-
plined us for a little while as they
thought best; but God disciplines us for
our good, that we may share in his
holiness.[q] 11No discipline seems
pleasant at the time, but painful. Later
on, however, it produces a harvest of
righteousness and peace[r] for those who
have been trained by it.
12Therefore, strengthen your feeble
arms and weak knees![s] 13"Make level
paths for your feet,"[b][t] so that the lame
may not be disabled, but rather healed.[u]

22 [n]Ge 50:24–25; Ex 13:19; Jos 24:32
23 [o]Ex 2:2; [p]Ex 1:16,22
24 [q]Ex 2:10–11
25 [r]ver 37
26 [s]Heb 13:13; [t]Lk 14:33; [u]Heb 10:35
27 [v]Ex 12:50–51
28 [w]1Co 10:10; [x]Ex 12:21–23
29 [y]Ex 14:21–31
30 [z]Jos 6:12–20
31 [a]Jos 2:1,9–14; 6:22–25; Jas 2:25
32 [b]Jdg 6–8; [c]Jdg 4–5; [d]Jdg 13–16; [e]Jdg 11–12; [f]1Sa 16:1,13; [g]1Sa 1:20
33 [h]2Sa 8:1–3; [i]Da 6:22
34 [j]Da 3:19–27; [k]Ex 18:4; [l]2Ki 20:7; [m]Jdg 15:8
35 [n]1Ki 17:22–23; 2Ki 4:36–37
36 [o]Jer 20:2; 37:15; [p]Ge 39:20
37 [q]2Ch 24:21; [r]1Ki 19:10; Jer 26:23; [s]2Ki 1:8
38 [t]1Ki 18:4; 19:9
39 [u]ver 2,4; [v]ver 13; Heb 10:36
40 [w]Rev 6:11; [x]**Heb 2:10**

Ch. 12

1 [a]**1Co 9:24**; [b]**Heb 10:36**
2 [c]Ps 25:15; [d]Heb 2:10; [e]Php 2:8–9; Heb 2:9; [f]Heb 13:13; [g]**Mk 16:19**
3 [h]Gal 6:9; Rev 2:3
4 [i]Heb 10:32–34; 13:13
5 [j]ver 3
6 [k]Ps 94:12; 119:75; Rev 3:19; [l]Pr 3:11–12
7 [m]Dt 8:5; 2Sa 7:14; Pr 13:24
8 [n]1Pe 5:9
9 [o]Nu 16:22; 27:16; Rev 22:6; [p]Isa 38:16
10 [q]**2Pe 1:4**
11 [r]Isa 32:17; Jas 3:17–18
12 [s]Isa 35:3
13 [t]Pr 4:26; [u]Gal 6:1

[d]29 That is, Sea of Reeds [e]31 Or *unbelieving* [f]37 Some early manuscripts *stoned; they were put to the test;* [a]6 Prov. 3:11,12 [b]13 Prov. 4:26

Warning Against Refusing God

14Make every effort to live in peace with all men[v] and to be holy;[w] without holiness no-one will see the Lord.[x] 15See to it that no-one misses the grace of God[y] and that no bitter root[z] grows up to cause trouble and defile many. 16See that no-one is sexually immoral,[a] or is godless like Esau, who for a single meal sold his inheritance rights as the oldest son.[b] 17Afterwards, as you know, when he wanted to inherit this blessing, he was rejected. He could bring about no change of mind, though he sought the blessing with tears.[c]

18You have not come to a mountain that can be touched and that is burning with fire; to darkness, gloom and storm;[d] 19to a trumpet blast[e] or to such a voice speaking words[f] that those who heard it begged that no further word be spoken to them,[g] 20because they could not bear what was commanded: "If even an animal touches the mountain, it must be stoned."[c][h] 21The sight was so terrifying that Moses said, "I am trembling with fear."[d][i]

22But you have come to Mount Zion,[j] to the heavenly Jerusalem,[k] the city[l] of the living God.[m] You have come to thousands upon thousands of angels in joyful assembly, 23to the church of the firstborn,[n] whose names are written in heaven.[o] You have come to God, the judge of all men,[p] to the spirits of righteous men made perfect,[q] 24to Jesus the mediator[r] of a new covenant, and to the sprinkled blood[s] that speaks a better word than the blood of Abel.[t]

25See to it that you do not refuse[u] him who speaks.[v] If they did not escape when they refused him who warned[w] them on earth, how much less will we, if we turn away from him who warns us from heaven?[x] 26At that time his voice shook the earth,[y] but now he has promised, "Once more I will shake not only the earth but also the heavens."[e][z] 27The words "once more" indicate the removing of what can be shaken[a]—that is, created things—so that what cannot be shaken may remain.

28Therefore, since we are receiving a kingdom that cannot be shaken,[b] let us be thankful, and so worship God acceptably with reverence and awe,[c] 29for our "God is a consuming fire."[f][d]

Concluding Exhortations

13 Keep on loving each other as brothers.[a] 2Do not forget to entertain strangers,[b] for by so doing some people have entertained angels without knowing it.[c] 3Remember those in prison[d] as if you were their fellow-prisoners, and those who are ill-treated as if you yourselves were suffering.

4Marriage should be honoured by all,[e] and the marriage bed kept pure, for God will judge the adulterer and all the sexually immoral.[f] 5Keep your lives free from the love of money[g] and be content with what you have,[h] because God has said,

"Never will I leave you;
never will I forsake you."[a][i]

6So we say with confidence,

"The Lord is my helper; I will not be afraid.
What can man do to me?"[b][j]

7Remember your leaders,[k] who spoke the word of God[l] to you. Consider the outcome of their way of life and imitate[m] their faith. 8Jesus Christ is the same yesterday and today and for ever.[n]

9Do not be carried away by all kinds of strange teachings.[o] It is good for our hearts to be strengthened[p] by grace, not by ceremonial foods,[q] which are of no value to those who eat them.[r] 10We have an altar from which those who minister at the tabernacle[s] have no right to eat.[t]

11The high priest carries the blood of animals into the Most Holy Place as a sin offering,[u] but the bodies are burned outside the camp.[v] 12And so Jesus also suffered outside the city gate[w] to make the people holy[x] through his own blood.[y] 13Let us, then, go to him[z] outside the camp, bearing the disgrace he bore.[a] 14For here we do not have an enduring city,[b] but we are looking for the city that is to come.[c]

15Through Jesus, therefore, let us continually offer to God a sacrifice[d] of praise—the fruit of lips[e] that confess his name. 16And do not forget to do good and to share with others,[f] for with such sacrifices[g] God is pleased.

17Obey your leaders[h] and submit to

14 [v]**Ro 14:19;** [w]Ro 6:22; [x]**Mt 5:8**
15 [y]Gal 5:4; Heb 3:12; 4:1; [z]Dt 29:18
16 [a]**1Co 6:18;** [b]Ge 25:29–34
17 [c]Ge 27:30–40
18 [d]Ex 19:12–22; 20:18; Dt 4:11
19 [e]Ex 20:18; [f]Dt 4:12; [g]Ex 20:19; Dt 5:5, 25; 18:16
20 [h]Ex 19:12–13
21 [i]Dt 9:19
22 [j]Isa 24:23; 60:14; Rev 14:1; [k]**Gal 4:26;** [l]Heb 11:10; 13:14; [m]**Mt 16:16**
23 [n]Ex 4:22; [o]**Lk 10:20;** [p]Ge 18:25; Ps 94:2; [q]Php 3:12
24 [r]**Gal 3:20;** [s]Heb 9:19; 10:22; 1Pe 1:2; [t]Ge 4:10; Heb 11:4
25 [u]Heb 3:12; [v]**Heb 1:1;** [w]Heb 8:5; 11:7; [x]Dt 18:19; Heb 2:2–3; 10:29
26 [y]Ex 19:18; [z]Hag 2:6
27 [a]Isa 34:4; 54:10; 1Co 7:31; Heb 1:11–12; 2Pe 3:10; 1Jn 2:17
28 [b]Ps 15:5; Da 2:44; [c]Mal 2:5; 4:2; Heb 13:15
29 [d]Ex 24:17; Dt 4:24; 9:3; Ps 97:3; Isa 33:14; **2Th 1:7**

Ch. 13

1 [a]**Ro 12:10**
2 [b]Job 31:32; Mt 25:35; **Ro 12:13;** [c]Ge 18:1–33; 19:1–3
3 [d]Mt 25:36; Col 4:18; Heb 10:34
4 [e]Mal 2:15; 1Co 7:38; 1Ti 4:3; [f]Dt 22:22; 1Co 6:9; Rev 22:15
5 [g]**1Ti 3:3;** [h]Php 4:11; 1Ti 6:6,8; [i]Dt 31:6,8; Jos 1:5
6 [j]Ps 118:6–7
7 [k]ver 17,24; 1Co 16:16; [l]**Heb 4:12;** [m]Heb 6:12
8 [n]Ps 102:27; Heb 1:12
9 [o]Eph 4:14; [p]Col 2:7; [q]Col 2:16; [r]Heb 9:10
10 [s]Heb 8:5; [t]1Co 9:13; 10:18
11 [u]Lev 16:15; [v]Ex 29:14; Lev 4:12,21; 9:11; 16:27
12 [w]Jn 19:17; [x]**Eph 5:26;** [y]**Ro 3:25**
13 [z]Lk 9:23; [a]Heb 11:26
14 [b]Heb 12:27; [c]Php 3:20; Heb 11:10,27; 12:22
15 [d]1Pe 2:5; [e]Isa 57:19; Hos 14:2
16 [f]Ro 12:13; [g]Php 4:18 *17* [h]ver 7,24

[c]*20* Exodus 19:12,13 [d]*21* Deut. 9:19
[e]*26* Haggai 2:6 [f]*29* Deut. 4:24
[a]*5* Deut. 31:6 [b]*6* Psalm 118:6,7

their authority. They keep watch over
you[i] as men who must give an account.
Obey them so that their work will be a
joy, not a burden, for that would be of
no advantage to you.

18Pray for us.[j] We are sure that we
have a clear conscience[k] and desire to
live honourably in every way. 19I parti-
cularly urge you to pray so that I may be
restored to you soon.[l]

20May the God of peace,[m] who
through the blood of the eternal cov-
enant[n] brought back from the dead[o] our
Lord Jesus, that great Shepherd of the
sheep,[p] 21equip you with everything
good for doing his will,[q] and may he
work in us[r] what is pleasing to him,[s]
through Jesus Christ, to whom be glory
for ever and ever. Amen.[t]

22Brothers, I urge you to bear with my
word of exhortation, for I have written
you only a short letter.[u]

23I want you to know that our brother
Timothy[v] has been released. If he
arrives soon, I will come with him to
see you.

24Greet all your leaders[w] and all God's
people. Those from Italy[x] send you their
greetings.

25Grace be with you all.[y]

17 [i]Isa 62:6; Ac 20:28
18 [j]1Th 5:25; [k]**Ac 23:1**
19 [l]Phm 22
20 [m]**Ro 15:33;** [n]Ge 9:16; 17:7, 13,19; Isa 55:3; 61:8; Eze 37:26; **Mt 26:28;** [o]**Ac 2:24;** [p]**Jn 10:11**
21 [q]2Co 9:8; [r]**Php 2:13;** [s]1Jn 3:22; [t]**Ro 11:36**
22 [u]1Pe 5:12
23 [v]**Ac 16:1**
24 [w]ver 7,17; [x]Ac 18:2
25 [y]**Col 4:18**

James

1 James,[a] a servant of God[b] and of
the Lord Jesus Christ,

To the twelve tribes[c] scattered[d]
among the nations:

Greetings.[e]

Trials and Temptations

2Consider it pure joy, my brothers,
whenever you face trials of many kinds,[f]
3because you know that the testing of
your faith[g] develops perseverance.[h]
4Perseverance must finish its work so
that you may be mature[i] and complete,
not lacking anything. 5If any of you
lacks wisdom, he should ask God,[j] who
gives generously to all without finding
fault, and it will be given to him.[k] 6But
when he asks, he must believe and not
doubt,[l] because he who doubts is like a
wave of the sea, blown and tossed by
the wind. 7That man should not think
he will receive anything from the Lord;
8he is a double-minded man,[m] unstable[n]
in all he does.

9The brother in humble circum-
stances ought to take pride in his high
position.[o] 10But the one who is rich
should take pride in his low position,
because he will pass away like a wild
flower.[p] 11For the sun rises with
scorching heat[q] and withers[r] the plant;
its blossom falls and its beauty is de-
stroyed.[s] In the same way, the rich man
will fade away even while he goes about
his business.

12Blessed is the man who perseveres
under trial,[t] because when he has stood
the test, he will receive the crown of life[u]
that God has promised to those who
love him.[v]

13When tempted, no-one should say,
"God is tempting me." For God cannot
be tempted by evil, nor does he tempt
anyone; 14but each one is tempted
when, by his own[w] evil desire, he is
dragged away and enticed. 15Then, after
desire has conceived, it gives birth to
sin;[x] and sin, when it is full-grown,
gives birth to death.[y]

16Don't be deceived,[z] my dear
brothers.[a] 17Every good and perfect gift
is from above,[b] coming down from the
Father of the heavenly lights,[c] who does
not change[d] like shifting shadows. 18He
chose to give us birth[e] through the word
of truth,[f] that we might be a kind of
firstfruits[g] of all he created.

Listening and Doing

19My dear brothers,[h] take note of this:
Everyone should be quick to listen, slow
to speak[i] and slow to become angry,
20for man's anger[j] does not bring about
the righteous life that God desires.
21Therefore, get rid of[k] all moral filth and
the evil that is so prevalent, and humbly
accept the word planted in you,[l] which
can save you.

22Do not merely listen to the word,
and so deceive yourselves. Do what it
says.[m] 23Anyone who listens to the
word but does not do what it says is like
a man who looks at his face in a mirror
24and, after looking at himself, goes
away and immediately forgets what he
looks like. 25But the man who looks
intently into the perfect law that gives
freedom,[n] and continues to do this, not
forgetting what he has heard, but doing
it—he will be blessed in what he does.[o]

26If anyone considers himself reli-
gious and yet does not keep a tight rein
on his tongue,[p] he deceives himself and
his religion is worthless. 27Religion that
God our Father accepts as pure and
faultless is this: to look after[q] orphans
and widows[r] in their distress and to
keep oneself from being polluted by the
world.[s]

Favouritism Forbidden

2 My brothers, as believers in our
glorious[a] Lord Jesus Christ, don't
show favouritism.[b] 2Suppose a man

Ch. 1

1 [a]**Ac 15:13**; [b]Ro 1:1; Tit 1:1; [c]Ac 26:7; [d]Dt 32:26; Jn 7:35; 1Pe 1:1 [e]Ac 15:23
2 [f]ver 12; **Mt 5:12**; Heb 10:34; 12:11
3 [g]1Pe 1:7; [h]**Heb 10:36**
4 [i]**1Co 2:6**
5 [j]1Ki 3:9–10; Pr 2:3–6; [k]Ps 51:6; Da 1:17; 2:21; **Mt 7:7**
6 [l]**Mt 21:21**; Mk 11:24
8 [m]Ps 119:113; Jas 4:8; [n]2Pe 2:14; 3:16
9 [o]**Mt 23:12**
10 [p]Job 14:2; Ps 103:15–16; Isa 40:6–7; 1Co 7:31; 1Pe 1:24
11 [q]Mt 20:12; [r]Ps 102:4,11; [s]Isa 40:6–8
12 [t]ver 2; Ge 22:1; Jas 5:11; 1Pe 3:14; [u]**1Co 9:25**; [v]Ex 20:6; 1Co 2:9; 8:3; Jas 2:5
14 [w]Pr 19:3
15 [x]Ge 3:6; Job 15:35; Ps 7:14; Isa 59:4; [y]**Ro 6:23**
16 [z]**1Co 6:9**; [a]ver 19; Jas 2:5
17 [b]Ps 85:12; Jn 3:27; Jas 3:15, 17; [c]Ge 1:16; Ps 136:7; Da 2:22; 1Jn 1:5; [d]Nu 23:19; Ps 102:27; Mal 3:6
18 [e]**Jn 1:13**; [f]**2Ti 2:15**; [g]Jer 2:3; Rev 14:4
19 [h]ver 16; Jas 2:5; [i]Pr 10:19; Jas 3:3–12
20 [j]**Mt 5:22**
21 [k]**Eph 4:22**; [l]Eph 1:13
22 [m]**Mt 7:21**; Jas 2:14–20
25 [n]Ps 19:7; Jn 8:32; Gal 2:4; Jas 2:12; [o]**Jn 13:17**

26 [p]Ps 34:13; 39:1; 141:3; Jas 3:2–12; 1Pe 3:10
27 [q]Mt 25:36; [r]Dt 14:29; Job 31:16–17,21; Ps 146:9; Isa 1:17,23; [s]Ro 12:2; Jas 4:4; 2Pe 1:4; 2:20

Ch. 2

1 [a]Ac 7:2; 1Co 2:8; [b]ver 9; Dt 1:17; Lev 19:15; Pr 24:23; **Ac 10:34**

comes into your meeting wearing a gold
ring and fine clothes, and a poor man in
shabby clothes also comes in. 3If you
show special attention to the man wear-
ing fine clothes and say, "Here's a good
seat for you," but say to the poor man,
"You stand there" or "Sit on the floor by
my feet," 4have you not discriminated
among yourselves and become judges[c]
with evil thoughts?

5Listen, my dear brothers:[d] Has not
God chosen those who are poor in the
eyes of the world[e] to be rich in faith[f] and
to inherit the kingdom[g] he promised
those who love him?[h] 6But you have
insulted the poor.[i] Is it not the rich who
are exploiting you? Are they not the
ones who are dragging you into court?[j]
7Are they not the ones who are slander-
ing the noble name of him to whom you
belong?

8If you really keep the royal law found
in Scripture, "Love your neighbour as
yourself,"[a][k] you are doing right. 9But if
you show favouritism,[l] you sin and are
convicted by the law as law-breakers.[m]
10For whoever keeps the whole law and
yet stumbles[n] at just one point is guilty
of breaking all of it.[o] 11For he who said,
"Do not commit adultery,"[b][p] also said,
"Do not murder."[c][q] If you do not com-
mit adultery but do commit murder,
you have become a law-breaker.

12Speak and act as those who are
going to be judged[r] by the law that gives
freedom,[s] 13because judgment without
mercy will be shown to anyone who has
not been merciful.[t] Mercy triumphs
over judgment!

Faith and Deeds

14What good is it, my brothers, if a
man claims to have faith but has no
deeds?[u] Can such faith save him?
15Suppose a brother or sister is without
clothes and daily food.[v] 16If one of you
says to him, "Go, I wish you well; keep
warm and well fed," but does nothing
about his physical needs, what good is
it?[w] 17In the same way, faith by itself, if it
is not accompanied by action, is dead.[x]

18But someone will say, "You have
faith; I have deeds."

Show me your faith without deeds,[y]
and I will show you my faith[z] by what I
do.[a] 19You believe that there is one
God.[b] Good! Even the demons believe
that[c]—and shudder.

20You foolish man, do you want
evidence that faith without deeds is
useless[d]?[d] 21Was not our ancestor Abra-
ham considered righteous for what he
did when he offered his son Isaac on the
altar?[e] 22You see that his faith and his
actions were working together,[f] and his
faith was made complete by what he
did.[g] 23And the scripture was fulfilled
that says, "Abraham believed God, and
it was credited to him as righteous-
ness,"[e][h] and he was called God's friend.[i]
24You see that a person is justified by
what he does and not by faith alone.

25In the same way, was not even
Rahab the prostitute considered right-
eous for what she did when she gave
lodging to the spies and sent them off in
a different direction?[j] 26As the body
without the spirit is dead, so faith with-
out deeds is dead.[k]

Taming the Tongue

3 Not many of you should presume
to be teachers,[a] my brothers, be-
cause you know that we who teach will
be judged[b] more strictly.[c] 2We all stum-
ble[d] in many ways. If anyone is never at
fault in what he says,[e] he is a perfect
man,[f] able to keep his whole body in
check.[g]

3When we put bits into the mouths of
horses to make them obey us, we can
turn the whole animal.[h] 4Or take ships
as an example. Although they are so
large and are driven by strong winds,
they are steered by a very small rudder
wherever the pilot wants to go.
5Likewise the tongue is a small part of
the body, but it makes great boasts.[i]
Consider what a great forest is set on
fire by a small spark. 6The tongue also is
a fire,[j] a world of evil among the parts of
the body. It corrupts the whole person,[k]
sets the whole course of his life on fire,
and is itself set on fire by hell.[l]

7All kinds of animals, birds, reptiles
and creatures of the sea are being tamed
and have been tamed by man, 8but no
man can tame the tongue. It is a restless
evil, full of deadly poison.[m]

9With the tongue we praise our Lord
and Father, and with it we curse
men, who have been made in God's
likeness.[n] 10Out of the same mouth
come praise and cursing. My brothers,
this should not be. 11Can both fresh
water and salt[a] water flow from the
same spring? 12My brothers, can a fig-
tree bear olives, or a grapevine bear

4 [c]Jn 7:24
5 [d]Jas 1:16,19; [e]Job 34:19; 1Co 1:26–28; [f]Lk 12:21; Rev 2:9; [g]**Mt 25:34**; [h]**Jas 1:12**
6 [i]1Co 11:22; [j]Ac 8:3; 16:19
8 [k]Lev 19:18; **Mt 5:43**
9 [l]ver 1; [m]Dt 1:17
10 [n]Jas 3:2; [o]Mt 5:19; Gal 3:10; 5:3
11 [p]Ex 20:14; Dt 5:18; [q]Ex 20:13; Dt 5:17
12 [r]**Mt 16:27**; [s]**Jas 1:25**
13 [t]Mt 5:7; 9:13; 12:7; 18:32–35; Lk 6:37
14 [u]Mt 7:26; Jas 1:22–25
15 [v]Mt 25:35–36
16 [w]Lk 3:11; 1Jn 3:17–18
17 [x]ver 20,26; Gal 5:6
18 [y]Ro 3:28; [z]Heb 11; [a]Mt 7:16–17; Jas 3:13
19 [b]Dt 6:4; Mk 12:29; 1Co 8:4–6; [c]Mt 8:29; Lk 4:34
20 [d]ver 17,26
21 [e]Ge 22:9,12
22 [f]Heb 11:17; [g]1Th 1:3
23 [h]Ge 15:6; **Ro 4:3**; [i]2Ch 20:7; Isa 41:8
25 [j]**Heb 11:31**
26 [k]ver 17,20

Ch. 3

1 [a]**Eph 4:11**; [b]**Mt 7:1**; [c]Ro 2:21
2 [d]1Ki 8:46; Ro 3:9–20; Jas 2:10; 1Jn 1:8; [e]Ps 39:1; Pr 10:19; 1Pe 3:10; [f]**Mt 12:37**; [g]Jas 1:26
3 [h]Ps 32:9
5 [i]Ps 12:3–4; 73:8–9
6 [j]Pr 16:27; [k]Mt 15:11,18–19; [l]**Mt 5:22**
8 [m]Ps 140:3; Ro 3:13
9 [n]Ge 1:26–27; 1Co 11:7

[a]*8* Lev. 19:18 [b]*11* Exodus 20:14; Deut. 5:18
[c]*11* Exodus 20:13; Deut. 5:17
[d]*20* Some early manuscripts *dead*
[e]*23* Gen. 15:6
[a]*11* Greek *bitter* (see also verse 14)

figs?[o] Neither can a salt spring produce fresh water.

Two Kinds of Wisdom

13Who is wise and understanding among you? Let him show it[p] by his good life, by deeds[q] done in the humility that comes from wisdom. 14But if you harbour bitter envy and selfish ambition[r] in your hearts, do not boast about it or deny the truth.[s] 15Such "wisdom" does not come down from heaven[t] but is earthly, unspiritual, of the devil.[u] 16For where you have envy and selfish ambition,[v] there you find disorder and every evil practice.

17But the wisdom that comes from heaven[w] is first of all pure; then peace-loving,[x] considerate, submissive, full of mercy[y] and good fruit, impartial and sincere.[z] 18Peacemakers[a] who sow in peace raise a harvest of righteousness.[b]

Submit Yourselves to God

4 What causes fights and quarrels[a] among you? Don't they come from your desires that battle[b] within you? 2You want something but don't get it. You kill[c] and covet, but you cannot have what you want. You quarrel and fight. You do not have, because you do not ask God. 3When you ask, you do not receive,[d] because you ask with wrong motives,[e] that you may spend what you get on your pleasures.

4You adulterous[f] people, don't you know that friendship with the world[g] is hatred towards God?[h] Anyone who chooses to be a friend of the world becomes an enemy of God.[i] 5Or do you think Scripture says without reason that the spirit he caused to live in us[j] envies intensely?[a] 6But he gives us more grace. That is why Scripture says:

"God opposes the proud
but gives grace to the humble."[b][k]

7Submit yourselves, then, to God. Resist the devil,[l] and he will flee from you. 8Come near to God and he will come near to you.[m] Wash your hands,[n] you sinners, and purify your hearts,[o] you double-minded.[p] 9Grieve, mourn and wail. Change your laughter to mourning and your joy to gloom.[q] 10Humble yourselves before the Lord, and he will lift you up.[r]

11Brothers, do not slander one another.[s] Anyone who speaks against his brother or judges him[t] speaks against the law[u] and judges it. When you judge the law, you are not keeping it,[v] but sitting in judgment on it. 12There is only one Lawgiver and Judge,[w] the one who is able to save and destroy.[x] But you—who are you to judge your neighbour?[y]

Boasting About Tomorrow

13Now listen,[z] you who say, "Today or tomorrow we will go to this or that city, spend a year there, carry on business and make money."[a] 14Why, you do not even know what will happen tomorrow. What is your life? You are a mist that appears for a little while and then vanishes.[b] 15Instead, you ought to say, "If it is the Lord's will,[c] we will live and do this or that." 16As it is, you boast and brag. All such boasting is evil.[d] 17Anyone, then, who knows the good he ought to do and doesn't do it, sins.[e]

Warning to Rich Oppressors

5 Now listen,[a] you rich people,[b] weep and wail[c] because of the misery that is coming upon you. 2Your wealth has rotted, and moths have eaten your clothes.[d] 3Your gold and silver are corroded. Their corrosion will testify against you and eat your flesh like fire. You have hoarded wealth in the last days.[e] 4Look! The wages you failed to pay the workmen[f] who mowed your fields are crying out against you. The cries[g] of the harvesters have reached the ears of the Lord Almighty.[h] 5You have lived on earth in luxury and self-indulgence. You have fattened yourselves[i] in the day of slaughter.[a][j] 6You have condemned and murdered[k] innocent men,[l] who were not opposing you.

Patience in Suffering

7Be patient, then, brothers, until the Lord's coming.[m] See how the farmer waits for the land to yield its valuable crop and how patient he is[n] for the autumn and spring rains.[o] 8You too, be patient and stand firm, because the Lord's coming[p] is near.[q] 9Don't grumble

12 [o]Mt 7:16
13 [p]Jas 2:18; [q]**1Pe 2:12**
14 [r]ver 16; 2Co 12:20; [s]Jas 5:19
15 [t]ver 17; Jas 1:17; [u]1Ti 4:1
16 [v]ver 14; Gal 5:20–21
17 [w]1Co 2:6; Jas 1:17; [x]Heb 12:11; [y]Lk 6:36; [z]Ro 12:9
18 [a]Mt 5:9; **Ro 14:19**; [b]Pr 11:18; Isa 32:17; Hos 10:12; Php 1:11

Ch. 4

1 [a]Tit 3:9; [b]**Ro 7:23**
2 [c]Mt 5:21–22; Jas 5:6; 1Jn 3:15
3 [d]Ps 18:41; **Mt 7:7**; [e]Ps 66:18; 1Jn 3:22; 5:14
4 [f]Isa 54:5; Jer 3:20; Hos 2:2–5; 3:1; 9:1; [g]**Jas 1:27**; [h]Ro 8:7; 1Jn 2:15; [i]Jn 15:19
5 [j]1Co 6:19
6 [k]Pr 3:34; **Mt 23:12**
7 [l]Eph 4:27; 6:11; 1Pe 5:6–9
8 [m]Ps 73:28; Zec 1:3; Mal 3:7; Heb 7:19; [n]Isa 1:16; [o]Ps 24:4; Jer 4:14; [p]Ps 119:113; Jas 1:8
9 [q]Lk 6:25
10 [r]ver 6; Job 5:11; 1Pe 5:6
11 [s]Ro 1:30; 2Co 12:20; 1Pe 2:1; [t]**Mt 7:1**; [u]Jas 2:8; [v]Jas 1:22
12 [w]Isa 33:22; **Jas 5:9**; [x]Mt 10:28; [y]**Mt 7:1**
13 [z]Jas 5:1; [a]Pr 27:1; Lk 12:18–20
14 [b]Job 7:7; Ps 39:5; 102:3; 144:4; Isa 2:22
15 [c]**Ac 18:21**
16 [d]1Co 5:6
17 [e]Lk 12:47; Jn 9:41

Ch. 5

1 [a]Jas 4:13; [b]Lk 6:24; 1Ti 6:9; Jas 2:2–6; [c]Isa 13:6; Eze 30:2
2 [d]Job 13:28; Ps 39:11; Isa 50:9; Mt 6:19–20
3 [e]ver 7–8
4 [f]Lev 19:13; Jer 22:13; Mal 3:5; [g]Dt 24:15; [h]Ro 9:29
5 [i]Eze 16:49; Am 6:1; Lk 16:19; [j]Jer 12:3; 25:34
6 [k]Jas 4:2; [l]Heb 10:38
7 [m]**1Co 1:7**; [n]Gal 6:9; [o]Dt 11:14; Jer 5:24; Joel 2:23
8 [p]**1Co 1:7**; [q]**Ro 13:11**

[a]5 Or *that God jealously longs for the spirit that he made to live in us; or that the Spirit he caused to live in us longs jealously* [b]6 Prov. 3:34
[a]5 Or *yourselves as in a day of feasting*

against each other, brothers,[r] or you
will be judged. The Judge[s] is standing at
the door![t]
10Brothers, as an example of patience
in the face of suffering, take the
prophets[u] who spoke in the name of the
Lord. 11As you know, we consider bles-
sed[v] those who have persevered. You
have heard of Job's perseverance[w] and
have seen what the Lord finally brought
about.[x] The Lord is full of compassion
and mercy.[y]
12Above all, my brothers, do not
swear—not by heaven or by earth or
by anything else. Let your "Yes" be
yes, and your "No", no, or you will be
condemned.[z]

The Prayer of Faith

13Is any one of you in trouble? He
should pray.[a] Is anyone happy? Let him
sing songs of praise.[b] 14Is any one of you
sick? He should call the elders[c] of the
church to pray over him and anoint him
with oil[d] in the name of the Lord. 15And
the prayer offered in faith[e] will make the
sick person well; the Lord will raise him
up. If he has sinned, he will be for-
given. 16Therefore confess your sins[f]
to each other and pray for each other
so that you may be healed.[g] The
prayer of a righteous man is powerful
and effective.[h]
17Elijah was a man just like us.[i] He
prayed earnestly that it would not rain,
and it did not rain on the land for three
and a half years.[j] 18Again he prayed,
and the heavens gave rain, and the
earth produced its crops.[k]
19My brothers, if one of you should
wander from the truth[l] and someone
should bring him back,[m] 20remember
this: Whoever turns a sinner from the
error of his way will save[n] him from
death and cover over a multitude of
sins.[o]

9 [r]Jas 4:11; [s]Ps 94:2; 1Co 4:5; Jas 4:12; 1Pe 4:5; [t]Mt 24:33
10 [u]**Mt 5:12**
11 [v]Mt 5:10; [w]Job 1:21–22; 2:10; **Heb 10:36;** [x]Job 42:10,12–17; [y]Ex 34:6; Nu 14:18; Ps 103:8
12 [z]Mt 5:34–37
13 [a]Ps 50:15; [b]Col 3:16
14 [c]**Ac 11:30;** [d]Ps 23:5; Isa 1:6; Mk 6:13; 16:18; Lk 10:34
15 [e]Jas 1:6

16 [f]Mt 3:6; Ac 19:18; [g]Heb 12:13; 1Pe 2:24; [h]**Mt 7:7; Jn 9:31** *17* [i]Ac 14:15; [j]1Ki 17:1; Lk 4:25
18 [k]1Ki 18:41–45 *19* [l]Jas 3:14; [m]**Mt 18:15**
20 [n]**Ro 11:14;** [o]1Pe 4:8

1 Peter

1 Peter, an apostle of Jesus Christ,[a]

To God's elect,[b] strangers in the world,[c] scattered[d] throughout Pontus,[e] Galatia,[f] Cappadocia, Asia and Bithynia,[g] 2who have been chosen according to the foreknowledge[h] of God the Father, through the sanctifying work of the Spirit,[i] for obedience[j] to Jesus Christ and sprinkling by his blood:[k]

Grace and peace be yours in abundance.[l]

Praise to God for a Living Hope

3Praise be to the God and Father of our Lord Jesus Christ![m] In his great mercy[n] he has given us new birth[o] into a living hope[p] through the resurrection of Jesus Christ from the dead,[q] 4and into an inheritance[r] that can never perish, spoil or fade[s]—kept in heaven for you,[t] 5who through faith are shielded by God's power[u] until the coming of the salvation[v] that is ready to be revealed[w] in the last time. 6In this you greatly rejoice,[x] though now for a little while[y] you may have had to suffer grief in all kinds of trials.[z] 7These have come so that your faith—of greater worth than gold, which perishes even though refined by fire[a]—may be proved genuine[b] and may result in praise, glory and honour[c] when Jesus Christ is revealed.[d] 8Though you have not seen him, you love him; and even though you do not see him now, you believe in him[e] and are filled with an inexpressible and glorious joy, 9for you are receiving the goal of your faith, the salvation of your souls.[f]

10Concerning this salvation, the prophets, who spoke[g] of the grace that was to come to you,[h] searched intently and with the greatest care,[i] 11trying to find out the time and circumstances to which the Spirit of Christ[j] in them was pointing when he predicted[k] the sufferings of Christ and the glories that would follow. 12It was revealed to them that they were not serving themselves but you,[l] when they spoke of the things that have now been told you by those who have preached the gospel to you[m] by the Holy Spirit sent from heaven.[n] Even angels long to look into these things.

Be Holy

13Therefore, prepare your minds for action; be self-controlled;[o] set your hope[p] fully on the grace to be given you[q] when Jesus Christ is revealed.[r] 14As obedient[s] children, do not conform[t] to the evil desires you had when you lived in ignorance.[u] 15But just as he who called you is holy, so be holy in all you do;[v] 16for it is written: "Be holy, because I am holy."[a][w]

17Since you call on a Father[x] who judges each man's work[y] impartially,[z] live your lives as strangers[a] here in reverent fear.[b] 18For you know that it was not with perishable things such as silver or gold that you were redeemed[c] from the empty way of life[d] handed down to you from your forefathers, 19but with the precious blood[e] of Christ, a lamb[f] without blemish or defect.[g] 20He was chosen before the creation of the world,[h] but was revealed in these last times[i] for your sake. 21Through him you believe in God,[j] who raised him from the dead[k] and glorified him,[l] and so your faith and hope[m] are in God.

22Now that you have purified[n] yourselves by obeying[o] the truth so that you have sincere love for your brothers, love one another deeply,[p] from the heart.[b] 23For you have been born again,[q] not of perishable seed, but of imperishable,[r] through the living and enduring word of God.[s] 24For,

Ch. 1

1 [a]2Pe 1:1; [b]Mt 24:22; [c]**Heb 11:13**; [d]**Jas 1:1**; [e]Ac 2:9; 18:2; [f]**Ac 16:6**; [g]Ac 16:7
2 [h]Ro 8:29; [i]2Th 2:13; [j]ver 14, 22; [k]Heb 10:22; 12:24; [l]**Ro 1:7**
3 [m]2Co 1:3; Eph 1:3; [n]Tit 3:5; [o]ver 23; **Jn 1:13**; [p]ver 13,21; **Heb 3:6**; [q]1Co 15:20; 1Pe 3:21
4 [r]**Ac 20:32; Ro 8:17**; [s]1Pe 5:4; [t]Col 1:5; 2Ti 4:8
5 [u]1Sa 2:9; Jn 10:28; [v]**Ro 11:14**; [w]**Ro 8:18**
6 [x]Ro 5:2; [y]1Pe 5:10; [z]Jas 1:2; 1Pe 4:12
7 [a]Job 23:10; Ps 66:10; Pr 17:3; Isa 48:10; [b]Jas 1:3; [c]2Co 4:17; [d]ver 13; **1Th 2:19**; 1Pe 4:13
8 [e]Jn 20:29
9 [f]Ro 6:22
10 [g]**Mt 26:24**; [h]ver 13; [i]**Mt 13:17**
11 [j]**Ac 16:7**; 2Pe 1:21; [k]**Mt 26:24**
12 [l]**Ro 4:24**; [m]ver 25; [n]**Lk 24:49**
13 [o]**Ac 24:25**; [p]ver 3,21; **Heb 3:6**; [q]ver 10; [r]ver 7; **1Co 1:7**
14 [s]ver 2,22; [t]Ro 12:2; [u]Eph 4:18
15 [v]Isa 35:8; 1Th 4:7; 1Jn 3:3
16 [w]Lev 11:44-45; 19:2; 20:7
17 [x]**Mt 6:9**; [y]**Mt 16:27**; [z]**Ac 10:34**; [a]**Heb 11:13**; [b]Heb 12:28
18 [c]**Mt 20:28**; **1Co 6:20**; [d]Gal 4:3
19 [e]**Ro 3:25**; [f]**Jn 1:29**; [g]Ex 12:5
20 [h]Eph 1:4; **Mt 25:34**; [i]Heb 9:26
21 [j]Ro 4:24; 10:9; [k]**Ac 2:24**; [l]Php 2:7-9; Heb 2:9; [m]ver 3,13; **Heb 3:6**
22 [n]Jas 4:8; [o]ver,2,14; [p]**Jn 13:34**; **Ro 12:10**
23 [q]ver 3; **Jn 1:13**; [r]Jn 1:13; [s]**Heb 4:12**

[a]*16* Lev. 11:44,45; 19:2; 20:7
[b]22 Some early manuscripts *from a pure heart*

"All men are like grass,
and all their glory is like the flowers
of the field;
the grass withers and the flowers fall,
25 but the word of the Lord stands for
ever."[c][t]

And this is the word that was preached
to you.

2 Therefore, rid yourselves[a] of all
malice and all deceit, hypocrisy,
envy, and slander[b] of every kind. 2Like
newborn babies, crave pure spiritual
milk,[c] so that by it you may grow up[d] in
your salvation, 3now that you have
tasted that the Lord is good.[e]

The Living Stone and a Chosen People

4As you come to him, the living
Stone[f]—rejected by men but chosen by
God[g] and precious to him—5you also,
like living stones, are being built[h] into
a spiritual house[i] to be a holy priest-
hood,[j] offering spiritual sacrifices accept-
able to God through Jesus Christ.[k] 6For
in Scripture it says:

"See, I lay a stone in Zion,
a chosen and precious cornerstone,[l]
and the one who trusts in him
will never be put to shame."[a][m]

7Now to you who believe, this stone
is precious. But to those who do not
believe,[n]

"The stone the builders rejected[o]
has become the capstone,[b]"[c][p]

8and,

"A stone that causes men to stumble
and a rock that makes them fall."[d][q]

They stumble because they disobey the
message—which is also what they were
destined for.[r]

9But you are a chosen people,[s] a royal
priesthood,[t] a holy nation,[u] a people
belonging to God,[v] that you may declare
the praises of him who called you out of
darkness into his wonderful light.[w]
10Once you were not a people, but now
you are the people of God;[x] once you
had not received mercy, but now you
have received mercy.

11Dear friends,[y] I urge you, as aliens
and strangers in the world,[z] to abstain
from sinful desires,[a] which war against
your soul.[b] 12Live such good lives
among the pagans that, though they
accuse you of doing wrong, they may
see your good deeds[c] and glorify God[d]
on the day he visits us.

Submission to Rulers and Masters

13Submit yourselves for the Lord's
sake to every authority[e] instituted
among men: whether to the king, as the
supreme authority, 14or to governors,
who are sent by him to punish those
who do wrong[f] and to commend those
who do right.[g] 15For it is God's will[h] that
by doing good you should silence the
ignorant talk of foolish men.[i] 16Live as
free men,[j] but do not use your freedom
as a cover-up for evil;[k] live as servants of
God.[l] 17Show proper respect to every-
one: Love the brotherhood of be-
lievers,[m] fear God, honour the king.[n]

18Slaves, submit yourselves to your
masters with all respect,[o] not only to
those who are good and considerate,[p]
but also to those who are harsh. 19For it
is commendable if a man bears up under
the pain of unjust suffering because he
is conscious of God.[q] 20But how is it to
your credit if you receive a beating for
doing wrong and endure it? But if you
suffer for doing good and you endure it,
this is commendable before God.[r] 21To
this[s] you were called,[t] because Christ
suffered for you,[u] leaving you an exam-
ple,[v] that you should follow in his steps.

22"He committed no sin,[w]
and no deceit was found in his
mouth."[e][x]

23When they hurled their insults at
him,[y] he did not retaliate; when he suf-
fered, he made no threats.[z] Instead, he
entrusted himself[a] to him who judges
justly.[b] 24He himself bore our sins[c] in his
body on the tree,[d] so that we might die
to sins[e] and live for righteousness; by
his wounds you have been healed.[f]
25For you were like sheep going astray,[g]
but now you have returned to the
Shepherd[h] and Overseer of your souls.[i]

Wives and Husbands

3 Wives, in the same way be submis-
sive[a] to your husbands[b] so that, if
any of them do not believe the word,

25 [t]Isa 40:6–8; **Jas 1:10–11**

Ch. 2

1 [a]**Eph 4:22;** [b]**Jas 4:11**
2 [c]1Co 3:2; Heb 5:12–13; [d]Eph 4:15–16
3 [e]Ps 34:8; Heb 6:5
4 [f]ver 7; [g]Isa 42:1
5 [h]Pr 9:1; 1Co 3:9; Eph 2:20–22; [i]1Ti 3:15; [j]ver 9; Ex 19:6; Isa 61:6; Rev 1:6; 5:10; 20:6; [k]Php 4:18; Heb 13:15
6 [l]Eph 2:20; [m]Isa 28:16; Ro 9:32–33; 10:11
7 [n]2Co 2:16; [o]ver 4; [p]Ps 118:22; **Ac 4:11**
8 [q]Isa 8:14; **Lk 2:34;** [r]Ro 9:22
9 [s]Dt 10:15; 1Sa 12:22; [t]ver 5; [u]Ex 19:6; Dt 7:6; Isa 62:12; [v]**Tit 2:14;** [w]**Ac 26:18**
10 [x]Hos 1:9–10; 2:23; Ro 9:25–26
11 [y]**1Co 10:14;** [z]**Heb 11:13;** [a]Ro 13:14; Gal 5:16; [b]Jas 4:1
12 [c]Php 2:15; Tit 2:8; **Tit 2:14;** 1Pe 3:16; [d]**Mt 9:8**
13 [e]Ro 13:1; Tit 3:1
14 [f]Ro 13:4; [g]Ro 13:3
15 [h]1Pe 3:17; 4:19; [i]**ver 12**
16 [j]**Jn 8:32;** [k]Gal 5:13; [l]**Ro 6:22**
17 [m]**Ro 12:10;** [n]Pr 24:21; Ro 13:7
18 [o]**Eph 6:5;** [p]Jas 3:17
19 [q]1Pe 3:14,17
20 [r]1Pe 3:17
21 [s]**Ac 14:22;** Php 1:29; 1Pe 3:9; [t]**Ro 8:28;** [u]1Pe 3:18; 4:1,13; [v]**Mt 11:29;** 16:24
22 [w]**2Co 5:21;** [x]Isa 53:9
23 [y]Heb 12:3; 1Pe 3:9; [z]Isa 53:7; [a]Lk 23:46; [b]Ps 9:4
24 [c]Isa 53:4,11; Heb 9:28; [d]**Ac 5:30;** [e]**Ro 6:2;** [f]Dt 32:39; Ps 103:3; Isa 53:5; Heb 12:13; Jas 5:16
25 [g]Isa 53:6; [h]**Jn 10:11;** [i]Job 10:12

Ch. 3

1 [a]1Pe 2:18; [b]**Eph 5:22**

[c]25 Isaiah 40:6–8
[a]6 Isaiah 28:16
[b]7 Or *cornerstone*
[c]7 Psalm 118:22
[d]8 Isaiah 8:14
[e]22 Isaiah 53:9

they may be won over[c] without words
by the behaviour of their wives, 2when
they see the purity and reverence of
your lives. 3Your beauty should not
come from outward adornment, such as
braided hair and the wearing of gold
jewellery and fine clothes.[d] 4Instead, it
should be that of your inner self,[e] the
unfading beauty of a gentle and quiet
spirit, which is of great worth in God's
sight.[f] 5For this is the way the holy
women of the past who put their hope
in God[g] used to make themselves
beautiful.[h] They were submissive to
their own husbands, 6like Sarah, who
obeyed Abraham and called him her
master.[i] You are her daughters if you do
what is right and do not give way to
fear.

7Husbands,[j] in the same way be con-
siderate as you live with your wives,
and treat them with respect as the
weaker partner and as heirs with you
of the gracious gift of life, so that
nothing will hinder your prayers.

Suffering for Doing Good

8Finally, all of you, live in harmony
with one another;[k] be sympathetic, love
as brothers,[l] be compassionate and
humble.[m] 9Do not repay evil with evil[n]
or insult with insult,[o] but with blessing,[p]
because to this[q] you were called[r] so that
you may inherit a blessing.[s] 10For,

"Whoever would love life
  and see good days
must keep his tongue from evil
  and his lips from deceitful speech.
11He must turn from evil and do good;
  he must seek peace and pursue it.
12For the eyes of the Lord are on the
    righteous
  and his ears are attentive to their
    prayer,
but the face of the Lord is against those
    who do evil."[a][t]

13Who is going to harm you if you are
eager to do good?[u] 14But even if you
should suffer for what is right, you are
blessed.[v] "Do not fear what they fear[b];
do not be frightened."[c][w] 15But in your
hearts set apart Christ as Lord. Always
be prepared to give an answer[x] to every-
one who asks you to give the reason for
the hope[y] that you have. But do this
with gentleness and respect, 16keeping
a clear conscience,[z] so that those who
speak maliciously against your good be-
haviour in Christ may be ashamed of
their slander.[a] 17It is better, if it is God's

1 [c]1Co 7:16; 9:19
3 [d]Isa 3:18–23; 1Ti 2:9
4 [e]Ro 7:22; Eph 3:16; [f]**Ro 2:29**
5 [g]1Ti 5:5; [h]Est 2:15
6 [i]Ge 18:12
7 [j]Eph 5:25–33; Col 3:19
8 [k]**Ro 15:5**; [l]**Ro 12:10**; [m]Eph 4:2; 1Pe 5:5
9 [n]Ro 12:17; 1Th 5:15; [o]1Pe 2:23; [p]**Mt 5:44**; [q]**1Pe 2:21**; [r]**Ro 8:28**; [s]Heb 6:14
12 [t]Ps 34:12–16
13 [u]**Tit 2:14**
14 [v]ver 17; 1Pe 2:19–20; 4:15–16; [w]Isa 8:12–13
15 [x]Col 4:6; [y]**Heb 3:6**
16 [z]ver 21; **Ac 23:1**; [a]1Pe 2:12,15
17 [b]1Pe 2:15; 4:19; [c]1Pe 2:20; 4:15–16
18 [d]1Pe 2:21; 4:1, 13; [e]**Heb 7:27**; [f]**Ro 5:2**; [g]Col 1:22; 1Pe 4:1; [h]1Pe 4:6
19 [i]1Pe 4:6
20 [j]**Ro 2:4**; [k]Ge 6:3,5,13–14; [l]Ge 8:18; [m]Heb 11:7
21 [n]**Ac 22:16**; [o]ver 16; **Ac 23:1**; [p]1Pe 1:3
22 [q]**Heb 4:14**; [r]**Mk 16:19**; [s]**Mt 28:18**; **Ro 8:38**

Ch. 4

1 [a]**1Pe 2:21**; [b]**Ro 6:18**
2 [c]Ro 6:2; 1Pe 1:14
3 [d]**Eph 2:2**; [e]**Ro 13:13**
4 [f]1Pe 3:16
5 [g]**Ac 10:42**
6 [h]1Pe 3:19
7 [i]**Ro 13:11**; [j]**Ac 24:25**
8 [k]**1Pe 1:22**; [l]Pr 10:12; Jas 5:20
9 [m]**Ro 12:13**; [n]Php 2:14
10 [o]Ro 12:6–7; [p]1Co 4:2
11 [q]1Th 2:4

will,[b] to suffer for doing good[c] than for
doing evil. 18For Christ died for sins[d]
once for all,[e] the righteous for the un-
righteous, to bring you to God.[f] He was
put to death in the body[g] but made alive
by the Spirit,[h] 19through whom[d] also he
went and preached to the spirits in
prison[i] 20who disobeyed long ago when
God waited patiently[j] in the days of
Noah while the ark was being built.[k] In
it only a few people, eight in all,[l] were
saved[m] through water, 21and this water
symbolises baptism that now saves
you[n] also—not the removal of dirt from
the body but the pledge[e] of a good con-
science[o] towards God. It saves you by
the resurrection of Jesus Christ,[p] 22who
has gone into heaven[q] and is at God's
right hand[r]—with angels, authorities
and powers in submission to him.[s]

Living for God

4 Therefore, since Christ suffered in
his body,[a] arm yourselves also
with the same attitude, because he who
has suffered in his body is done with
sin.[b] 2As a result, he does not live the
rest of his earthly life for evil human
desires,[c] but rather for the will of God.
3For you have spent enough time in the
past[d] doing what pagans choose to do
—living in debauchery, lust, drunken-
ness, orgies, carousing and detestable
idolatry.[e] 4They think it strange that you
do not plunge with them into the same
flood of dissipation, and they heap
abuse on you.[f] 5But they will have to
give account to him who is ready to
judge the living and the dead.[g] 6For this
is the reason the gospel was preached
even to those who are now dead,[h] so
that they might be judged according to
men in regard to the body, but live
according to God in regard to the spirit.

7The end of all things is near.[i] There-
fore be clear minded and self-controlled[j]
so that you can pray. 8Above all, love
each other deeply,[k] because love covers
over a multitude of sins.[l] 9Offer hospi-
tality[m] to one another without grum-
bling.[n] 10Each one should use whatever
gift he has received to serve others,[o]
faithfully[p] administering God's grace in
its various forms. 11If anyone speaks, he
should do it as one speaking the very
words of God.[q] If anyone serves, he

[a]12 Psalm 34:12–16
[b]14 Or *not fear their threats* [c]14 Isaiah 8:12
[d]18,19 Or *alive in the spirit,* [19]*through which*
[e]21 Or *response*

should do it with the strength God provides,[r] so that in all things God may be praised[s] through Jesus Christ. To him be the glory and the power for ever and ever. Amen.[t]

Suffering for Being a Christian

12Dear friends, do not be surprised at the painful trial you are suffering,[u] as though something strange were happening to you. 13But rejoice[v] that you participate in the sufferings of Christ,[w] so that you may be overjoyed when his glory is revealed.[x] 14If you are insulted because of the name of Christ,[y] you are blessed,[z] for the Spirit of glory and of God rests on you. 15If you suffer, it should not be as a murderer or thief or any other kind of criminal, or even as a meddler. 16However, if you suffer as a Christian, do not be ashamed, but praise God that you bear that name.[a] 17For it is time for judgment to begin with the family of God;[b] and if it begins with us, what will the outcome be for those who do not obey the gospel of God?[c] 18And,

"If it is hard for the righteous to be
  saved,
 what will become of the ungodly
  and the sinner?"[a][d]

19So then, those who suffer according to God's will[e] should commit themselves to their faithful Creator and continue to do good.

To Elders and Young Men

5 To the elders among you, I appeal as a fellow-elder,[a] a witness[b] of Christ's sufferings and one who also will share in the glory to be revealed:[c] 2Be shepherds of God's flock[d] that is under your care, serving as overseers —not because you must, but because you are willing, as God wants you to be;[e] not greedy for money,[f] but eager to serve; 3not lording it over[g] those entrusted to you, but being examples[h] to the flock. 4And when the Chief Shepherd[i] appears, you will receive the crown of glory[j] that will never fade away.[k]

5Young men, in the same way be submissive[l] to those who are older. All of you, clothe yourselves with humility[m] towards one another, because,

"God opposes the proud
 but gives grace to the humble."[a][n]

6Humble yourselves, therefore, under God's mighty hand, that he may lift you up in due time.[o] 7Cast all your anxiety on him[p] because he cares for you.[q]

8Be self-controlled[r] and alert. Your enemy the devil prowls around[s] like a roaring lion[t] looking for someone to devour. 9Resist him,[u] standing firm in the faith,[v] because you know that your brothers throughout the world are undergoing the same kind of sufferings.[w]

10And the God of all grace, who called you[x] to his eternal glory[y] in Christ, after you have suffered a little while,[z] will himself restore you and make you strong,[a] firm and steadfast. 11To him be the power for ever and ever. Amen.[b]

Final Greetings

12With the help of Silas,[b][c] whom I regard as a faithful brother, I have written to you briefly,[d] encouraging you and testifying that this is the true grace of God. Stand fast in it.[e]

13She who is in Babylon, chosen together with you, sends you her greetings, and so does my son Mark.[f] 14Greet one another with a kiss of love.[g]

Peace[h] to all of you who are in Christ.

11 [r]Eph 6:10; [s]1Co 10:31; [t]**Ro 11:36**
12 [u]1Pe 1:6–7
13 [v]**Mt 5:12**; [w]**2Co 1:5**; [x]Ro 8:17; 1Pe 1:7; 5:1
14 [y]**Jn 15:21**; [z]Mt 5:11
16 [a]Ac 5:41
17 [b]Jer 25:29; Eze 9:6; Am 3:2; 1Ti 3:15; [c]2Th 1:8
18 [d]Pr 11:31; Lk 23:31
19 [e]1Pe 2:15; 3:17

Ch. 5

1 [a]**Ac 11:30**; [b]**Lk 24:48**; [c]1Pe 1:5,7; 4:13; Rev 1:9
2 [d]**Jn 21:16**; [e]2Co 9:7; Phm 14; [f]**1Ti 3:3**
3 [g]Eze 34:4; Mt 20:25–28; [h]**1Ti 4:12**
4 [i]**Jn 10:11**; [j]**1Co 9:25**; [k]1Pe 1:4
5 [l]Eph 5:21; [m]1Pe 3:8; [n]Pr 3:34; **Mt 23:12**
6 [o]Job 5:11; Jas 4:10
7 [p]Ps 37:5; Mt 6:25; [q]Ps 55:22; Heb 13:5
8 [r]**Ac 24:25**; [s]Job 1:7; [t]2Ti 4:17
9 [u]**Jas 4:7**; [v]Col 2:5; [w]**Ac 14:22**
10 [x]**Ro 8:28**; [y]2Co 4:17; 2Ti 2:10; [z]1Pe 1:6; [a]Ps 18:32; 2Th 2:17
11 [b]**Ro 11:36**
12 [c]**Ac 15:22**; [d]Heb 13:22; [e]**1Co 16:13**
13 [f]**Ac 12:12**
14 [g]**Ro 16:16**; [h]**Eph 6:23**

[a]*18* Prov. 11:31 [a]*5* Prov. 3:34
[b]*12* Greek *Silvanus*, a variant of *Silas*

2 Peter

1 Simon Peter, a servant[a] and apostle
of Jesus Christ,[b]

To those who through the righteous-
ness[c] of our God and Saviour Jesus
Christ[d] have received a faith as precious
as ours:

2Grace and peace be yours in abun-
dance[e] through the knowledge of God
and of Jesus our Lord.[f]

Making One's Calling and Election Sure

3His divine power[g] has given us
everything we need for life and godli-
ness through our knowledge of him[h]
who called us[i] by his own glory and
goodness. 4Through these he has given
us his very great and precious prom-
ises,[j] so that through them you may
participate in the divine nature[k] and
escape the corruption in the world
caused by evil desires.[l]
5For this very reason, make every
effort to add to your faith goodness; and
to goodness, knowledge;[m] 6and to
knowledge, self-control;[n] and to self-
control, perseverance;[o] and to persever-
ance, godliness;[p] 7and to godliness,
brotherly kindness; and to brotherly
kindness, love.[q] 8For if you possess
these qualities in increasing measure,
they will keep you from being ineffec-
tive and unproductive[r] in your know-
ledge of our Lord Jesus Christ.[s] 9But if
anyone does not have them, he is short-
sighted and blind,[t] and has forgotten
that he has been cleansed from his past
sins.[u]
10Therefore, my brothers, be all the
more eager to make your calling[v] and
election sure. For if you do these things,
you will never fall,[w] 11and you will re-
ceive a rich welcome into the eternal
kingdom[x] of our Lord and Saviour Jesus
Christ.[y]

Prophecy of Scripture

12So I will always remind you of these
things,[z] even though you know them
and are firmly established in the truth[a]
you now have. 13I think it is right to
refresh your memory[b] as long as I live in
the tent of this body,[c] 14because I know
that I will soon put it aside,[d] as our Lord
Jesus Christ has made clear to me.[e]
15And I will make every effort to see that
after my departure[f] you will always be
able to remember these things.
16We did not follow cleverly invented
stories when we told you about the
power and coming of our Lord Jesus
Christ,[g] but we were eye-witnesses of
his majesty.[h] 17For he received honour
and glory from God the Father when the
voice came to him from the Majestic
Glory, saying, "This is my Son, whom I
love; with him I am well pleased."[a][i]
18We ourselves heard this voice that
came from heaven when we were with
him on the sacred mountain.[j]
19And we have the word of the
prophets made more certain,[k] and you
will do well to pay attention to it, as to a
light[l] shining in a dark place, until the
day dawns[m] and the morning star[n] rises
in your hearts.[o] 20Above all, you must
understand[p] that no prophecy of Scrip-
ture came about by the prophet's own
interpretation. 21For prophecy never
had its origin in the will of man, but men
spoke from God[q] as they were carried
along by the Holy Spirit.[r]

False Teachers and Their Destruction

2 But there were also false prophets[a]
among the people, just as there
will be false teachers among you.[b] They
will secretly introduce destructive
heresies, even denying the sovereign
Lord[c] who bought them[d]—bringing
swift destruction on themselves. 2Many
will follow their shameful ways[e] and
will bring the way of truth into disre-
pute. 3In their greed[f] these teachers will
exploit you[g] with stories they have
made up. Their condemnation has long

Ch. 1

1 [a]Ro 1:1; [b]1Pe 1:1; [c]Ro 3:21–26; [d]Tit 2:13
2 [e]**Ro 1:7**; [f]ver 3,8; 2Pe 2:20; 3:18; **Php 3:8**
3 [g]1Pe 1:5; [h]**ver 2**; [i]**Ro 8:28**
4 [j]2Co 7:1; [k]Eph 4:24; Heb 12:10; 1Jn 3:2; [l]Jas 1:27; 2Pe 2:18–20
5 [m]**ver 2**; Col 2:3
6 [n]**Ac 24:25**; [o]**Heb 10:36**; [p]ver 3
7 [q]**Ro 12:10**; 1Th 3:12
8 [r]Jn 15:2; Col 1:10; Tit 3:14; [s]**ver 2**
9 [t]1Jn 2:11; [u]Eph 5:26; **Mt 1:21**
10 [v]**Ro 8:28**; [w]Ps 15:5; 2Pe 3:17; Jude 24
11 [x]Ps 145:13; 2Ti 4:18; [y]2Pe 2:20; 3:18
12 [z]Php 3:1; 1Jn 2:21; Jude 5; [a]2Jn 2
13 [b]2Pe 3:1; [c]Isa 38:12; 2Co 5:1,4
14 [d]2Ti 4:6; [e]Jn 13:36; 21:18–19
15 [f]Lk 9:31
16 [g]Mk 13:26; 14:62; [h]Mt 17:1–8
17 [i]**Mt 3:17**
18 [j]Mt 17:6
19 [k]1Pe 1:10–11; [l]Ps 119:105; [m]Lk 1:78; [n]Rev 22:16; [o]2Co 4:6
20 [p]2Pe 3:3
21 [q]2Ti 3:16; [r]2Sa 23:2; Ac 1:16; 3:18; 1Pe 1:11

Ch. 2

1 [a]Dt 13:1–3; Jer 6:13; **Mt 7:15**; [b]1Ti 4:1; [c]Jude 4; [d]**1Co 6:20**
2 [e]Jude 4
3 [f]ver 14; [g]2Co 2:17; 1Th 2:5

[a]17 Matt. 17:5; Mark 9:7; Luke 9:35

been hanging over them, and their des-
truction has not been sleeping.
4For if God did not spare angels when
they sinned,[h] but sent them to hell,[a]
putting them into gloomy dungeons[b] to
be held for judgment;[i] 5if he did not
spare the ancient world[j] when he
brought the flood on its ungodly peo-
ple,[k] but protected Noah, a preacher of
righteousness, and seven others;[l] 6if he
condemned the cities of Sodom and
Gomorrah by burning them to ashes,[m]
and made them an example[n] of what is
going to happen to the ungodly;[o] 7and if
he rescued Lot,[p] a righteous man, who
was distressed by the filthy lives of
lawless men[q] 8(for that righteous man,[r]
living among them day after day, was
tormented in his righteous soul by the
lawless deeds he saw and heard)—9if
this is so, then the Lord knows how to
rescue godly men from trials[s] and to
hold the unrighteous for the day of
judgment,[t] while continuing their
punishment.[c] 10This is especially true
of those who follow the corrupt desire[u]
of the sinful nature[d] and despise
authority.

Bold and arrogant, these men are not
afraid to slander celestial beings;[v] 11yet
even angels, although they are stronger
and more powerful, do not bring
slanderous accusations against such
beings in the presence of the Lord.[w]
12But these men blaspheme in matters
they do not understand. They are like
brute beasts, creatures of instinct, born
only to be caught and destroyed, and
like beasts they too will perish.[x]
13They will be paid back with harm for
the harm they have done. Their idea of
pleasure is to carouse in broad day-
light.[y] They are blots and blemishes,
revelling in their pleasures while they
feast with you.[e z] 14With eyes full of
adultery, they never stop sinning; they
seduce[a] the unstable;[b] they are experts
in greed[c]—an accursed brood![d] 15They
have left the straight way and wandered
off to follow the way of Balaam[e] son of
Beor, who loved the wages of wicked-
ness. 16But he was rebuked for his
wrongdoing by a donkey—a beast
without speech—who spoke with a
man's voice and restrained the
prophet's madness.[f]
17These men are springs without
water[g] and mists driven by a storm.
Blackest darkness is reserved for them.[h]
18For they mouth empty, boastful
words[i] and, by appealing to the lustful
desires of sinful human nature, they
entice people who are just escaping[j]
from those who live in error. 19They
promise them freedom, while they
themselves are slaves of depravity—for
a man is a slave to whatever has
mastered him.[k] 20If they have escaped the
corruption of the world by knowing[l] our
Lord and Saviour Jesus Christ[m] and are
again entangled in it and overcome,
they are worse off at the end than they
were at the beginning.[n] 21It would have
been better for them not to have known
the way of righteousness, than to have
known it and then to turn their backs on
the sacred command that was passed on
to them.[o] 22Of them the proverbs are
true: "A dog returns to its vomit,"[f p]
and, "A sow that is washed goes back to
her wallowing in the mud."

The Day of the Lord

3 Dear friends,[a] this is now my
second letter to you. I have written
both of them as reminders[b] to stimulate
you to wholesome thinking. 2I want you
to recall the words spoken in the past by
the holy prophets[c] and the command
given by our Lord and Saviour through
your apostles.[d]
3First of all, you must understand that
in the last days[e] scoffers will come,
scoffing and following their own evil
desires.[f] 4They will say, "Where is this
'coming' he promised?[g] Ever since our
fathers died, everything goes on as it
has since the beginning of creation."[h]
5But they deliberately forget that long
ago by God's word[i] the heavens existed
and the earth was formed out of water
and by water.[j] 6By these waters also the
world of that time[k] was deluged and
destroyed.[l] 7By the same word the pres-
ent heavens and earth are reserved for
fire,[m] being kept for the day of judg-
ment[n] and destruction of ungodly men.
8But do not forget this one thing, dear
friends: With the Lord a day is like a
thousand years, and a thousand years
are like a day.[o] 9The Lord is not slow in
keeping his promise,[p] as some under-
stand slowness. He is patient[q] with you,
not wanting anyone to perish, but
everyone to come to repentance.[r]
10But the day of the Lord will come
like a thief.[s] The heavens will disappear
with a roar;[t] the elements will be

4 [h]Ge 6:1–4; [i]1Ti 3:6; Jude 6; Rev 20:1–2
5 [j]2Pe 3:6; [k]Ge 6:5–8:19; [l]Heb 11:7; 1Pe 3:20
6 [m]Ge 19:24–25; [n]Nu 26:10; Jude 7; [o]Mt 10:15; 11:23–24; Ro 9:29
7 [p]Ge 19:16; [q]2Pe 3:17
8 [r]Heb 11:4
9 [s]Ps 37:33; **Ro 15:31**; Rev 3:10; [t]**Mt 10:15**
10 [u]2Pe 3:3; Jude 16,18; [v]Jude 8
11 [w]Jude 9
12 [x]Ps 49:12; Jude 10
13 [y]**Ro 13:13**; 1Th 5:7; [z]1Co 11:20–21; Jude 12
14 [a]ver 18; [b]Jas 1:8; 2Pe 3:16; [c]ver 3; [d]Eph 2:3
15 [e]Nu 22:4–20; 31:16; Dt 23:4; Jude 11; Rev 2:14
16 [f]Nu 22:21–30
17 [g]Jude 12; [h]Jude 13
18 [i]Jude 16; [j]ver 20; 2Pe 1:4
19 [k]**Ro 6:16**
20 [l]**2Pe 1:2**; [m]2Pe 1:11; 3:18; [n]Mt 12:45
21 [o]Eze 18:24; Heb 6:4–6; 10:26–27
22 [p]Pr 26:11

Ch. 3

1 [a]**1Co 10:14**; [b]2Pe 1:13
2 [c]Lk 1:70; Ac 3:21; [d]**Eph 4:11**
3 [e]1Ti 4:1; 2Ti 3:1; [f]2Pe 2:10; Jude 18
4 [g]Isa 5:19; Eze 12:22; Mt 24:48; **Lk 17:30**; [h]Mk 10:6
5 [i]Ge 1:6,9; Heb 11:3; [j]Ps 24:2
6 [k]2Pe 2:5; [l]Ge 7:21–22
7 [m]ver 10,12; **2Th 1:7**; [n]**Mt 10:15**
8 [o]Ps 90:4
9 [p]Hab 2:3; Heb 10:37; [q]**Ro 2:4**; [r]**1Ti 2:4**; Rev 2:21
10 [s]**Lk 12:39**; [t]Isa 34:4

a4 Greek *Tartarus*
b4 Some manuscripts *into chains of darkness*
c9 Or *unrighteous for punishment until the day of judgment*
d10 Or *the flesh*
e13 Some manuscripts *in their love feasts*
f22 Prov. 26:11

destroyed by fire,[u] and the earth and
everything in it will be laid bare.[a v]
11Since everything will be destroyed
in this way, what kind of people ought
you to be? You ought to live holy and
godly lives 12as you look forward[w] to the
day of God and speed its coming.[b x]
That day will bring about the destruction
of the heavens by fire, and the
elements will melt in the heat.[y] 13But in
keeping with his promise we are looking
forward to a new heaven and a new
earth,[z] the home of righteousness.
14So then, dear friends, since you are
looking forward to this, make every
effort to be found spotless, blameless[a]
and at peace with him. 15Bear in mind
that our Lord's patience[b] means salvation,[c]
just as our dear brother Paul also
wrote to you with the wisdom that God
gave him.[d] 16He writes the same way in
all his letters, speaking in them of these
matters. His letters contain some things
that are hard to understand, which
ignorant and unstable[e] people distort,[f]
as they do the other Scriptures,[g] to their
own destruction.
17Therefore, dear friends, since you
already know this, be on your guard[h] so
that you may not be carried away by the
error[i] of lawless men[j] and fall from your
secure position.[k] 18But grow in the grace[l]
and knowledge[m] of our Lord and
Saviour Jesus Christ.[n] To him be glory
both now and for ever! Amen.[o]

10 [u]ver 7,12; **2Th 1:7**; [v]Mt 24:35; **Heb 12:27**; Rev 21:1
12 [w]**1Co 1:7**; [x]Ps 50:3; [y]ver 10
13 [z]Isa 65:17; 66:22; Rev 21:1
14 [a]**1Th 3:13**
15 [b]**Ro 2:4**; [c]ver 9; [d]Eph 3:3
16 [e]Jas 1:8; [f]2Pe 2:14; Ps 56:5; Jer 23:36; [g]ver 2
17 [h]1Co 10:12; [i]2Pe 2:18; [j]2Pe 2:7; [k]Rev 2:5
18 [l]**Ro 3:24**; [m]**2Pe 1:2**; [n]2Pe 1:11; 2:20; [o]**Ro 11:36**

---

[a]*10* Some manuscripts *be burned up*
[b]*12* Or *as you wait eagerly for the day of God to come*

1 John

The Word of Life

1 That which was from the begin-
ning,[a] which we have heard,
which we have seen with our eyes,[b]
which we have looked at and our hands
have touched[c]—this we proclaim con-
cerning the Word of life. 2The life
appeared;[d] we have seen it and testify to
it,[e] and we proclaim to you the eternal
life,[f] which was with the Father and has
appeared to us. 3We proclaim to you
what we have seen and heard,[g] so that
you also may have fellowship with us.
And our fellowship is with the Father
and with his Son, Jesus Christ.[h] 4We
write this[i] to make our[a] joy complete.[j]

Walking in the Light

5This is the message we have heard[k]
from him and declare to you: God is
light;[l] in him there is no darkness at all.
6If we claim to have fellowship with him
yet walk in the darkness,[m] we lie and do
not live by the truth.[n] 7But if we walk in
the light,[o] as he is in the light, we have
fellowship with one another, and the
blood of Jesus, his Son, purifies us from
all[b] sin.[p]

8If we claim to be without sin,[q] we
deceive ourselves and the truth is not in
us.[r] 9If we confess our sins, he is faithful
and just and will forgive us our sins[s] and
purify us from all unrighteousness.[t] 10If
we claim we have not sinned,[u] we make
him out to be a liar[v] and his word has no
place in our lives.[w]

2 My dear children,[a] I write this to
you so that you will not sin. But if
anybody does sin, we have one who
speaks to the Father in our defence[b]
—Jesus Christ, the Righteous One. 2He
is the atoning sacrifice for our sins,[c] and
not only for ours but also for[a] the sins of
the whole world.[d]

3We know[e] that we have come to
know him[f] if we obey his commands.[g]
4The man who says, "I know him,"[h] but
does not do what he commands is a liar,
and the truth is not in him.[i] 5But if
anyone obeys his word,[j] God's love[b] is
truly made complete in him.[k] This is
how we know[l] we are in him: 6Whoever
claims to live in him must walk as Jesus
did.[m]

7Dear friends,[n] I am not writing you a
new command but an old one, which
you have had since the beginning.[o] This
old command is the message you have
heard. 8Yet I am writing you a new
command;[p] its truth is seen in him and
you, because the darkness is passing[q]
and the true light[r] is already shining.[s]

9Anyone who claims to be in the light
but hates his brother[t] is still in the dark-
ness.[u] 10Whoever loves his brother lives
in the light,[v] and there is nothing in
him[c] to make him stumble.[w] 11But who-
ever hates his brother[x] is in the darkness
and walks around in the darkness;[y] he
does not know where he is going, be-
cause the darkness has blinded him.[z]

12I write to you, dear children,[a]
because your sins have been
forgiven on account of his
name.[b]
13I write to you, fathers,
because you have known him who
is from the beginning.[c]
I write to you, young men,
because you have overcome[d] the
evil one.[e]
I write to you, dear children,[f]
because you have known the
Father.
14I write to you, fathers,
because you have known him who
is from the beginning.[g]
I write to you, young men,
because you are strong,[h]

Ch. 1

1 [a]**Jn 1:2**; [b]**Lk 24:48**; Jn 1:14; 19:35; Ac 4:20; 2Pe 1:16; 1Jn 4:14; [c]Jn 20:27
2 [d]Jn 1:1–4; 11:25; 14:6; 1Ti 3:16; 1Pe 1:20; 1Jn 3:5,8; [e]**Jn 15:27**; [f]**Mt 25:46**
3 [g]**ver 1**; [h]1Co 1:9
4 [i]1Jn 2:1; [j]**Jn 3:29**
5 [k]1Jn 3:11; [l]1Ti 6:16
6 [m]Jn 3:19–21; 8:12; 2Co 6:14; Eph 5:8; 1Jn 2:11; [n]Jn 3:19–21; 1Jn 2:4; 4:20
7 [o]Isa 2:5; [p]Heb 9:14; Rev 1:5; 7:14
8 [q]Pr 20:9; Jer 2:35; Ro 3:9–19; Jas 3:2; [r]Jn 8:44; 1Jn 2:4
9 [s]Ps 32:5; 51:2; Pr 28:13; [t]ver 7; Mic 7:18–20; Heb 10:22
10 [u]ver 8; [v]1Jn 5:10; [w]Jn 5:38; 1Jn 2:14

Ch. 2

1 [a]ver 12–13, 28; 1Jn 3:7, 18; 4:4; 5:21; **1Th 2:11**; [b]**Ro 8:34**; 1Ti 2:5
2 [c]Ro 3:25; 1Jn 4:10; [d]**Mt 1:21**; **Jn 3:17**
3 [e]ver 5; 1Jn 3:24; 4:13; 5:2; [f]**ver 4**; [g]**Jn 14:15**
4 [h]ver 3; Tit 1:16; 1Jn 3:6; 4:7–8; [i]1Jn 1:6,8
5 [j]**Jn 14:15**; [k]1Jn 4:12; [l]**ver 3**
6 [m]**Mt 11:29**
7 [n]**1Co 10:14**; [o]ver 24; 1Jn 3:11,23; 4:21; 2Jn 5–6
8 [p]**Jn 13:34**; [q]Ro 13:12; Heb 10:25; [r]Jn 1:9; [s]**Eph 5:8**; 1Th 5:5
9 [t]ver 11; Lev 19:17; 1Jn 3:10,15–16; 4:20–21; [u]1Jn 1:5
10 [v]1Jn 3:14; [w]ver 11; Ps 119:165
11 [x]**ver 9**; [y]**1Jn 1:6**; [z]Jn 11:9; 12:35
12 [a]**ver 1**; [b]**1Jn 3:23**
13 [c]**Jn 1:1**; [d]**Jn 16:33**; [e]ver 14; **Mt 5:37**; [f]**ver 1**
14 [g]**Jn 1:1**; [h]Eph 6:10

[a]4 Some manuscripts *your* [b]7 Or *every*
[a]2 Or *He is the one who turns aside God's wrath, taking away our sins, and not only ours but also*
[b]5 Or *word, love for God* [c]10 Or *it*

and the word of God[i] lives in you,[j]
and you have overcome the evil
one.[k]

Do Not Love the World

15Do not love the world or anything in
the world.[l] If anyone loves the world,
the love of the Father is not in him.[m]
16For everything in the world—the
cravings of sinful man,[n] the lust of his
eyes[o] and the boasting of what he has
and does—comes not from the Father
but from the world. 17The world and its
desires pass away,[p] but the man who
does the will of God[q] lives for ever.

Warning Against Antichrists

18Dear children, this is the last hour;[r]
and as you have heard that the anti-
christ is coming,[s] even now many anti-
christs have come.[t] This is how we
know it is the last hour. 19They went out
from us,[u] but they did not really belong
to us. For if they had belonged to us,
they would have remained with us; but
their going showed that none of them
belonged to us.[v]
20But you have an anointing[w] from the
Holy One,[x] and all of you know the
truth.[d][y] 21I do not write to you because
you do not know the truth, but because
you do know it[z] and because no lie
comes from the truth. 22Who is the liar?
It is the man who denies that Jesus is the
Christ. Such a man is the antichrist—he
denies the Father and the Son.[a] 23No-
one who denies the Son has the Father;
whoever acknowledges the Son has the
Father also.[b]
24See that what you have heard from
the beginning[c] remains in you. If it
does, you also will remain in the Son
and in the Father.[d] 25And this is what he
promised us—even eternal life.[e]
26I am writing these things to you
about those who are trying to lead you
astray.[f] 27As for you, the anointing[g] you
received from him remains in you, and
you do not need anyone to teach you.
But as his anointing teaches you about
all things[h] and as that anointing is real,
not counterfeit—just as it has taught
you, remain in him.[i]

Children of God

28And now, dear children,[j] continue
in him, so that when he appears[k] we
may be confident[l] and unashamed be-
fore him at his coming.[m]
29If you know that he is righteous,[n]
you know that everyone who does what
is right has been born of him.[o]

3 How great is the love[a] the Father
has lavished on us, that we should
be called children of God![b] And that is
what we are! The reason the world does
not know us is that it did not know him.[c]
2Dear friends,[d] now we are children of
God,[e] and what we will be has not yet
been made known. But we know that
when he appears,[a][f] we shall be like
him,[g] for we shall see him as he is.[h]
3Everyone who has this hope in him
purifies himself,[i] just as he is pure.[j]
4Everyone who sins breaks the law; in
fact, sin is lawlessness.[k] 5But you know
that he appeared so that he might take
away our sins.[l] And in him is no sin.[m]
6No-one who lives in him keeps on sin-
ning.[n] No-one who continues to sin has
either seen him[o] or known him.[p]
7Dear children,[q] do not let anyone
lead you astray.[r] He who does what is
right is righteous, just as he is right-
eous.[s] 8He who does what is sinful is of
the devil,[t] because the devil has been
sinning from the beginning. The reason
the Son of God[u] appeared was to de-
stroy the devil's work.[v] 9No-one who is
born of God[w] will continue to sin,[x] be-
cause God's seed[y] remains in him; he
cannot go on sinning, because he has
been born of God. 10This is how we
know who the children of God[z] are and
who the children of the devil[a] are: Any-
one who does not do what is right is not
a child of God; nor is anyone who does
not love[b] his brother.[c]

Love One Another

11This is the message you heard[d] from
the beginning:[e] We should love one
another.[f] 12Do not be like Cain, who
belonged to the evil one[g] and murdered
his brother.[h] And why did he murder
him? Because his own actions were evil
and his brother's were righteous.[i] 13Do
not be surprised, my brothers, if the
world hates you.[j] 14We know that we
have passed from death to life,[k] because
we love our brothers. Anyone who does
not love remains in death.[l] 15Anyone
who hates his brother[m] is a murderer,[n]
and you know that no murderer has
eternal life in him.[o]

14 [i]**Heb 4:12**; Jn 5:38; [j]1Jn 1:10; [k]**ver 13**
15 [l]Ro 12:2; [m]Jas 4:4
16 [n]Ge 3:6; Ro 13:14; Eph 2:3; [o]Pr 27:20
17 [p]**Heb 12:27**; [q]Mt 12:50
18 [r]**Ro 13:11**; [s]ver 22; 1Jn 4:3; 2Jn 7; [t]1Jn 4:1
19 [u]Ac 20:30; [v]1Co 11:19
20 [w]ver 27; 2Co 1:21; [x]**Mk 1:24**; [y]Jer 31:34; Mt 13:11; Jn 14:26
21 [z]2Pe 1:12; Jude 5
22 [a]1Jn 4:3; 2Jn 7
23 [b]Jn 8:19; 14:7; 1Jn 4:15; 5:1; 2Jn 9
24 [c]**ver 7**; [d]Jn 14:23; 15:4; 1Jn 1:3; 2Jn 9
25 [e]**Mt 25:46**
26 [f]1Jn 3:7
27 [g]ver 20; [h]1Co 2:12; [i]Jn 15:4
28 [j]**ver 1**; [k]1Jn 3:2; Col 3:4; [l]**Eph 3:12**; [m]**1Th 2:19**
29 [n]1Jn 3:7; [o]**Jn 1:13**

Ch. 3

1 [a]**Jn 3:16**; [b]ver 2,10; **Jn 1:12**; [c]Jn 15:21; 16:3
2 [d]**1Co 10:14**; [e]ver 1,10; **Jn 1:12**; [f]Col 3:4; 1Jn 2:28; [g]Ro 8:29; 2Pe 1:4; [h]Ps 17:15; Jn 17:24; 2Co 3:18
3 [i]2Co 7:1; 2Pe 3:13–14; [j]Ps 18:26
4 [k]1Jn 5:17
5 [l]ver 8; **Jn 3:17**; [m]**2Co 5:21**
6 [n]ver 9; 1Jn 5:18; [o]3Jn 11; [p]**1Jn 2:4**
7 [q]**1Jn 2:1**; [r]1Jn 2:26; [s]1Jn 2:29
8 [t]ver 10; Jn 8:44; [u]**Mt 4:3**; [v]Heb 2:14
9 [w]**Jn 1:13**; [x]ver 6; Ps 119:3; 1Jn 5:18; [y]1Pe 1:23
10 [z]ver 1–2; **Jn 1:12**; [a]ver 8; [b]1Jn 4:8; [c]**1Jn 2:9**
11 [d]1Jn 1:5; [e]**1Jn 2:7**; [f]Jn 13:34–35; 15:12; 1Jn 4:7,11,21; 2Jn 5
12 [g]**Mt 5:37**; [h]Ge 4:8; [i]Ps 38:20; Pr 29:10
13 [j]Jn 15:18–19; 17:14
14 [k]Jn 5:24; [l]**1Jn 2:9**
15 [m]**1Jn 2:9**; [n]Mt 5:21–22; Jn 8:44; [o]Gal 5:20–21; Rev 21:8

d20 Some manuscripts *and you know all things*
a2 Or *when it is made known*

16This is how we know what love is:
Jesus Christ laid down his life for us.[p]
And we ought to lay down our lives for
our brothers.[q] 17If anyone has material
possessions and sees his brother in
need but has no pity on him,[r] how can
the love of God be in him?[s] 18Dear chil-
dren,[t] let us not love with words or
tongue but with actions and in truth.[u]
19This then is how we know that we
belong to the truth, and how we set our
hearts at rest in his presence 20whenever
our hearts condemn us. For God is
greater than our hearts, and he knows
everything.
21Dear friends,[v] if our hearts do not
condemn us, we have confidence before
God[w] 22and receive from him anything
we ask,[x] because we obey his com-
mands[y] and do what pleases him.[z]
23And this is his command: to believe[a] in
the name of his Son, Jesus Christ,[b] and
to love one another as he commanded
us.[c] 24Those who obey his commands[d]
live in him,[e] and he in them. And this is
how we know that he lives in us: We
know it by the Spirit he gave us.[f]

Test the Spirits

4 Dear friends,[a] do not believe every
spirit,[b] but test the spirits to see
whether they are from God, because
many false prophets have gone out into
the world.[c] 2This is how you can recog-
nise the Spirit of God: Every spirit that
acknowledges that Jesus Christ has
come in the flesh[d] is from God,[e] 3but
every spirit that does not acknowledge
Jesus is not from God. This is the spirit
of the antichrist,[f] which you have heard
is coming and even now is already in the
world.[g]
4You, dear children,[h] are from God
and have overcome them,[i] because the
one who is in you[j] is greater than the
one who is in the world.[k] 5They are from
the world[l] and therefore speak from the
viewpoint of the world, and the world
listens to them. 6We are from God, and
whoever knows God listens to us; but
whoever is not from God does not listen
to us.[m] This is how we recognise
the Spirit[a] of truth[n] and the spirit of
falsehood.[o]

God's Love and Ours

7Dear friends, let us love one
another,[p] for love comes from God.
Everyone who loves has been born of
God[q] and knows God.[r] 8Whoever does
not love does not know God, because

16 [p]Jn 10:11; [q]Jn 15:13; Php 2:17; 1Th 2:8
17 [r]Dt 15:7–8; Jas 2:15–16; [s]1Jn 4:20
18 [t]**1Jn 2:1**; [u]Eze 33:31; Ro 12:9
21 [v]**1Co 10:14**; [w]**Eph 3:12**; 1Jn 5:14
22 [x]**Mt 7:7**; [y]**Jn 14:15**; [z]Jn 8:29; Heb 13:21
23 [a]Jn 6:29; [b]**Lk 24:47**; Jn 1:12; 3:18; 20:31; 1Co 6:11; 1Jn 5:13; [c]**Jn 13:34**
24 [d]1Jn 2:3; [e]1Jn 2:6; 4:15; [f]1Th 4:8; 1Jn 4:13

Ch. 4

1 [a]**1Co 10:14**; [b]Jer 29:8; 1Co 12:10; 2Th 2:2; [c]**Mt 7:15**; 1Jn 2:18
2 [d]**Jn 1:14**; 1Jn 2:23; [e]1Co 12:3
3 [f]1Jn 2:22; 2Jn 7; [g]1Jn 2:18
4 [h]**1Jn 2:1**; [i]**Jn 16:33**; [j]Ro 8:31; [k]2Ki 6:16; **Jn 12:31**
5 [l]Jn 15:19; 17:14,16
6 [m]Jn 8:47; [n]**Jn 14:17**; [o]**Mk 13:5**
7 [p]**1Jn 3:11**; [q]**Jn 1:13**; [r]**1Jn 2:4**
8 [s]ver 7,16
9 [t]Jn 1:18; [u]Jn 3:16–17; 1Jn 5:11
10 [v]Ro 5:8,10; [w]**Ro 3:25**
11 [x]**1Co 10:14**; [y]**Jn 3:16**; [z]Jn 15:12; **1Jn 3:11**
12 [a]**Jn 1:18**; [b]ver 17; 1Jn 2:5
13 [c]**1Jn 2:3**; [d]1Jn 3:24
14 [e]**Jn 15:27**; [f]**Lk 2:11**; **Jn 3:17**
15 [g]**1Jn 2:23**; 5:5; [h]1Jn 3:24
16 [i]ver 8; [j]ver 12–13; 1Jn 3:24
17 [k]ver 12; 1Jn 2:5; [l]**Eph 3:12**; [m]**Mt 10:15**
18 [n]Ro 8:15
19 [o]ver 10
20 [p]**1Jn 2:9**; [q]**1Jn 1:6**; 2:4; [r]1Jn 3:17; [s]ver 12; **Jn 1:18**
21 [t]1Jn 2:7; [u]**Mt 5:43**; **1Jn 2:9**

Ch. 5

1 [a]**Jn 3:15**; [b]1Jn 2:22; 4:2,15; [c]**Jn 1:13**; **1Jn 2:23**; [d]Jn 8:42

God is love.[s] 9This is how God showed
his love among us: He sent his one and
only Son[b][t] into the world that we might
live through him.[u] 10This is love: not
that we loved God, but that he loved us[v]
and sent his Son as an atoning sacrifice
for[c] our sins.[w] 11Dear friends,[x] since God
so loved us,[y] we also ought to love one
another.[z] 12No-one has ever seen God;[a]
but if we love one another, God lives in
us and his love is made complete in us.[b]
13We know[c] that we live in him and he
in us, because he has given us of his
Spirit.[d] 14And we have seen and testify[e]
that the Father has sent his Son to be
the Saviour of the world.[f] 15If anyone
acknowledges that Jesus is the Son of
God,[g] God lives in him and he in God.[h]
16And so we know and rely on the love
God has for us.
God is love.[i] Whoever lives in love
lives in God, and God in him.[j] 17In this
way, love is made complete[k] among us
so that we will have confidence[l] on the
day of judgment,[m] because in this world
we are like him. 18There is no fear in
love. But perfect love drives out fear,[n]
because fear has to do with punish-
ment. The one who fears is not made
perfect in love.
19We love because he first loved us.[o]
20If anyone says, "I love God," yet hates
his brother,[p] he is a liar.[q] For anyone
who does not love his brother, whom he
has seen,[r] cannot love God, whom he
has not seen.[s] 21And he has given us this
command:[t] Whoever loves God must
also love his brother.[u]

Faith in the Son of God

5 Everyone who believes[a] that Jesus
is the Christ[b] is born of God,[c] and
everyone who loves the father loves his
child as well.[d] 2This is how we know[e]
that we love the children of God:[f] by
loving God and carrying out his com-
mands. 3This is love for God: to obey his
commands.[g] And his commands are not
burdensome,[h] 4for everyone born of
God[i] overcomes[j] the world. This is the
victory that has overcome the world,
even our faith. 5Who is it that over-
comes the world? Only he who believes
that Jesus is the Son of God.[k]
6This is the one who came by water

2 [e]**1Jn 2:3**; [f]1Jn 3:14 *3* [g]**Jn 14:15**; [h]Mt 11:30; 23:4
4 [i]**Jn 1:13**; [j]**Jn 16:33** *5* [k]ver 1; **1Jn 2:23**

a6 Or *spirit* b9 Or *his only begotten Son*
c10 Or *as the one who would turn aside his wrath, taking away*

and blood[l]—Jesus Christ. He did not
come by water only, but by water and
blood. And it is the Spirit who testifies,
because the Spirit is the truth.[m] 7For
there are three[n] that testify: 8the[a] Spirit,
the water and the blood; and the three
are in agreement. 9We accept man's tes-
timony,[o] but God's testimony is greater
because it is the testimony of God,[p]
which he has given about his Son.
10Anyone who believes in the Son of
God has this testimony in his heart.[q]
Anyone who does not believe God has
made him out to be a liar,[r] because he
has not believed the testimony God has
given about his Son. 11And this is the
testimony: God has given us eternal
life,[s] and this life is in his Son.[t] 12He who
has the Son has life; he who does not
have the Son of God does not have life.[u]

Concluding Remarks

13I write these things to you who be-
lieve in the name of the Son of God[v] so
that you may know that you have eter-
nal life.[w] 14This is the confidence[x] we
have in approaching God: that if we ask
anything according to his will, he hears
us.[y] 15And if we know that he hears
us—whatever we ask—we know[z] that
we have what we asked of him.[a]

16If anyone sees his brother commit a
sin that does not lead to death, he
should pray and God will give him life.[b]
I refer to those whose sin does not lead
to death. There is a sin that leads to
death.[c] I am not saying that he should
pray about that.[d] 17All wrongdoing is
sin,[e] and there is sin that does not lead
to death.[f]

18We know that anyone born of God[g]
does not continue to sin; the one who
was born of God keeps him safe, and
the evil one[h] cannot harm him.[i] 19We
know that we are children of God,[j] and
that the whole world is under the con-
trol of the evil one.[k] 20We know also that
the Son of God has come[l] and has given
us understanding,[m] so that we may
know him who is true.[n] And we are in
him who is true—even in his Son Jesus
Christ. He is the true God and eternal
life.[o]

21Dear children,[p] keep yourselves
from idols.[q]

6 [l]Jn 19:34; [m]**Jn 14:17**
7 [n]**Mt 18:16**
9 [o]Jn 5:34; [p]Mt 3:16–17; Jn 5:32,37; 8:17–18
10 [q]Ro 8:16; Gal 4:6; [r]Jn 3:33; 1Jn 1:10
11 [s]**Mt 25:46**; [t]**Jn 1:4**
12 [u]Jn 3:15–16, 36
13 [v]**1Jn 3:23**; [w]ver 11; **Mt 25:46**
14 [x]**Eph 3:12**; 1Jn 3:21; [y]**Mt 7:7**
15 [z]ver 18–20; [a]1Ki 3:12
16 [b]Jas 5:15; [c]Ex 23:21; Heb 6:4–6; 10:26; [d]Jer 7:16; 14:11
17 [e]1Jn 3:4; [f]ver 16; 1Jn 2:1
18 [g]**Jn 1:13**; [h]**Mt 5:37**; [i]Jn 14:30
19 [j]1Jn 4:6; [k]Jn 12:31; 14:30; 17:15
20 [l]ver 5; [m]Lk 24:45; [n]Jn 17:3; [o]ver 11; **Mt 25:46**
21 [p]**1Jn 2:1**; [q]1Co 10:14; 1Th 1:9

[a]7,8 Late manuscripts of the Vulgate *testify in heaven: the Father, the Word and the Holy Spirit, and these three are one.* 8*And there are three that testify on earth: the* (not found in any Greek manuscript before the sixteenth century)

2 John

1 The elder,[a]

To the chosen[b] lady and her children,
whom I love in the truth[c]—and not I
only, but also all who know the truth[d]
—2 because of the truth,[e] which lives in
us[f] and will be with us for ever:

3 Grace, mercy and peace from God
the Father and from Jesus Christ,[g] the
Father's Son, will be with us in truth
and love.

4 It has given me great joy to find some
of your children walking in the truth,[h]
just as the Father commanded us. 5 And
now, dear lady, I am not writing you a
new command but one we have had
from the beginning.[i] I ask that we love
one another. 6 And this is love:[j] that we
walk in obedience to his commands.[k] As
you have heard from the beginning,[l] his
command is that you walk in love.

7 Many deceivers, who do not
acknowledge Jesus Christ[m] as coming in
the flesh,[n] have gone out into the
world.[o] Any such person is the deceiver
and the antichrist.[p] 8 Watch out that you
do not lose what you have worked for,
but that you may be rewarded fully.[q]
9 Anyone who runs ahead and does not
continue in the teaching of Christ[r] does
not have God; whoever continues in the
teaching has both the Father and the
Son.[s] 10 If anyone comes to you and does
not bring this teaching, do not take him
into your house or welcome[t] him.
11 Anyone who welcomes him shares[u] in
his wicked work.

12 I have much to write to you, but I do
not want to use paper and ink. Instead,
I hope to visit you and talk with you
face to face,[v] so that our joy may be
complete.[w]

13 The children of your chosen[x] sister
send their greetings.

1 [a]**Ac 11:30**; 3Jn 1; [b]ver 13; Ro 16:13; 1Pe 5:13; [c]ver 3; [d]Jn 8:32; 1Ti 2:4
2 [e]2Pe 1:12; [f]Jn 14:17; 1Jn 1:8
3 [g]**Ro 1:7**
4 [h]3Jn 3:4
5 [i]**1Jn 2:7**
6 [j]1Jn 2:5; [k]**Jn 14:15**; [l]**1Jn 2:7**
7 [m]1Jn 2:22; 4:2–3; [n]**Jn 1:14**; [o]1Jn 4:1; [p]**1Jn 2:18**
8 [q]**Mt 10:42**; Mk 10:29–30; 1Co 3:8; Heb 10:35–36; 11:26
9 [r]Jn 8:31; [s]**1Jn 2:23**
10 [t]**Ro 16:17**
11 [u]1Ti 5:22
12 [v]3Jn 13–14; [w]**Jn 3:29**
13 [x]ver 1

3 John

1 The elder,[a]

To my dear friend Gaius, whom I love
in the truth.

2 Dear friend, I pray that you may
enjoy good health and that all may go
well with you, even as your soul is
getting along well. 3 It gave me great joy
to have some brothers[b] come and tell
about your faithfulness to the truth and
how you continue to walk in the truth.[c]
4 I have no greater joy than to hear that
my children[d] are walking in the truth.[e]
5 Dear friend, you are faithful in what
you are doing for the brothers,[f] even
though they are strangers to you.[g]
6 They have told the church about your
love. You will do well to send them on
their way[h] in a manner worthy[i] of God.
7 It was for the sake of the Name[j] that
they went out, receiving no help from
the pagans.[k] 8 We ought therefore to
show hospitality to such men so that we
may work together for the truth.

9 I wrote to the church, but Diotre-
phes, who loves to be first, will have
nothing to do with us. 10 So if I come,[l] I
will call attention to what he is doing,
gossiping maliciously about us. Not sat-
isfied with that, he refuses to welcome
the brothers.[m] He also stops those who
want to do so and puts them out of the
church.[n]
11 Dear friend, do not imitate what is
evil but what is good.[o] Anyone who
does what is good is from God.[p] Anyone
who does what is evil has not seen
God.[q] 12 Demetrius is well spoken of by
everyone[r]—and even by the truth itself.
We also speak well of him, and you
know that our testimony is true.[s]
13 I have much to write to you, but I do
not want to do so with pen and ink. 14 I
hope to see you soon, and we will talk
face to face.[t]

Peace to you.[u] The friends here send
their greetings. Greet the friends there
by name.[v]

1 [a]**Ac 11:30**; 2Jn 1
3 [b]ver 5,10; **Ac 1:16**; [c]2Jn 4
4 [d]**1Jn 2:1**; [e]ver 3
5 [f]**ver 3**; [g]Ro 12:13; Heb 13:2
6 [h]1Co 16:11; 2Co 1:16; [i]**Eph 4:1**
7 [j]**Jn 15:21**; [k]Ac 20:33,35
10 [l]ver 14; 2Jn 12; [m]ver 5; [n]Jn 9:22,34
11 [o]Ps 34:14; 37:27; [p]1Jn 2:29; [q]1Jn 3:6, 9–10
12 [r]1Ti 3:7; [s]Jn 19:35; 21:24
14 [t]2Jn 12; [u]**Ro 1:7; Eph 6:23**; [v]Jn 10:3

Jude

1Jude,[a] a servant of Jesus Christ[b] and a brother of James,

To those who have been called,[c] who are loved by God the Father and kept by[a] Jesus Christ:[d]

2Mercy, peace[e] and love be yours in abundance.[f]

The Sin and Doom of Godless Men

3Dear friends,[g] although I was very eager to write to you about the salvation we share,[h] I felt I had to write and urge you to contend[i] for the faith[j] that was once for all entrusted to the saints.[k] 4For certain men whose condemnation was written about[b] long ago have secretly slipped in among you.[l] They are godless men, who change the grace of our God into a licence for immorality and deny Jesus Christ our only Sovereign and Lord.[m]

5Though you already know all this,[n] I want to remind you[o] that the Lord[c] delivered his people out of Egypt, but later destroyed those who did not believe.[p] 6And the angels who did not keep their positions of authority but abandoned their own home—these he has kept in darkness, bound with everlasting chains for judgment on the great Day.[q] 7In a similar way, Sodom and Gomorrah[r] and the surrounding towns[s] gave themselves up to sexual immorality and perversion. They serve as an example of those who suffer the punishment of eternal fire.[t]

8In the very same way, these dreamers pollute their own bodies, reject authority and slander celestial beings.[u] 9But even the archangel[v] Michael,[w] when he was disputing with the devil about the body of Moses,[x] did not dare to bring a slanderous accusation against him, but said, "The Lord rebuke you!"[y] 10Yet these men speak abusively against whatever they do not understand; and what things they do understand by instinct, like unreasoning animals—these are the very things that destroy them.[z]

11Woe to them! They have taken the way of Cain;[a] they have rushed for profit into Balaam's error;[b] they have been destroyed in Korah's rebellion.[c]

12These men are blemishes at your love feasts,[d] eating with you without the slightest qualm—shepherds who feed only themselves.[e] They are clouds without rain,[f] blown along by the wind;[g] autumn trees, without fruit and uprooted[h]—twice dead. 13They are wild waves of the sea,[i] foaming up their shame;[j] wandering stars, for whom blackest darkness has been reserved for ever.[k]

14Enoch,[l] the seventh from Adam, prophesied about these men: "See, the Lord is coming[m] with thousands upon thousands of his holy ones[n] 15to judge[o] everyone, and to convict all the ungodly of all the ungodly acts they have done in the ungodly way, and of all the harsh words ungodly sinners have spoken against him."[p] 16These men are grumblers[q] and fault-finders; they follow their own evil desires;[r] they boast[s] about themselves and flatter others for their own advantage.

A Call to Persevere

17But, dear friends, remember what the apostles[t] of our Lord Jesus Christ foretold.[u] 18They said to you, "In the last times[v] there will be scoffers who will follow their own ungodly desires."[w] 19These are the men who divide you, who follow mere natural instincts and do not have the Spirit.[x]

20But you, dear friends, build yourselves up[y] in your most holy faith[z]

1 [a]Mt 13:55; Jn 14:22; Ac 1:13; [b]Ro 1:1; [c]Ro 1:6–7; [d]Jn 17:12
2 [e]Gal 6:16; 1Ti 1:2; [f]**Ro 1:7**
3 [g]**1Co 10:14**; [h]Tit 1:4; [i]1Ti 6:12; [j]ver 20; Ac 6:7; [k]**Ac 9:13**
4 [l]Gal 2:4; [m]Tit 1:16; 2Pe 2:1; 1Jn 2:22
5 [n]**1Jn 2:20**; [o]2Pe 1:12–13; 3:1–2; [p]Nu 14:29; Dt 1:32; 2:15; Ps 106:26; 1Co 10:1–5; Heb 3:16–17
6 [q]**2Pe 2:4**,9
7 [r]**Mt 10:15**; [s]Dt 29:23; [t]**Mt 25:41**; 2Pe 3:7
8 [u]2Pe 2:10
9 [v]1Th 4:16; [w]Da 10:13, 21; 12:1; Rev 12:7; [x]Dt 34:6; [y]Zec 3:2
10 [z]2Pe 2:12
11 [a]Ge 4:3–8; Heb 11:4; 1Jn 3:12; [b]**2Pe 2:15**; [c]Nu 16:1–3,31–35
12 [d]2Pe 2:13; 1Co 11:20–22; [e]Eze 34:2,8, 10; [f]Pr 25:14; 2Pe 2:17; [g]Eph 4:14; [h]Mt 15:13
13 [i]Isa 57:20; [j]Php 3:19; [k]2Pe 2:17
14 [l]Ge 5:18, 21–24; [m]**Mt 16:27**; [n]Dt 33:2; Da 7:10; Zec 14:5; Heb 12:22
15 [o]2Pe 2:6–9; [p]1Ti 1:9
16 [q]1Co 10:10; [r]ver 18; 2Pe 2:10; [s]2Pe 2:18
17 [t]**Eph 4:11**; [u]Heb 2:3; 2Pe 3:2
18 [v]1Ti 4:1; 2Ti 3:1; 2Pe 3:3; [w]ver 16; 2Pe 2:1; 3:3
19 [x]1Co 2:14–15
20 [y]Col 2:7; 1Th 5:11; [z]ver 3

---

[a]*1* Or *for*; or *in*
[b]4 Or *men who were marked out for condemnation*
[c]5 Some early manuscripts *Jesus*

and pray in the Holy Spirit.[a] 21Keep
yourselves in God's love as you wait[b] for
the mercy of our Lord Jesus Christ to
bring you to eternal life.[c]
22Be merciful to those who doubt;
23snatch others from the fire and save
them;[d] to others show mercy, mixed
with fear—hating even the clothing
stained by corrupted flesh.[e]

Doxology

24To him who is able[f] to keep you
from falling and to present you before
his glorious presence[g] without fault[h]
and with great joy—25to the only God[i]
our Saviour be glory, majesty, power
and authority, through Jesus Christ our
Lord, before all ages, now and for ever-
more![j] Amen.[k]

20 [a]Eph 6:18
21 [b]Tit 2:13; Heb 9:28; 2Pe 3:12; [c]**Mt 25:46**
23 [d]Am 4:11; Zec 3:2–5; 1Co 3:15; [e]Rev 3:4
24 [f]**Ro 16:25;** [g]**2Co 4:14;** [h]Col 1:22
25 [i]Jn 5:44; 1Ti 1:17; [j]Heb 13:8; [k]**Ro 11:36**

Revelation

Prologue

1 The revelation of Jesus Christ,
which God gave[a] him to show his
servants what must soon take place.[b] He
made it known by sending his angel[c] to
his servant John,[d] 2who testifies to
everything he saw—that is, the word of
God[e] and the testimony of Jesus Christ.[f]
3Blessed is the one who reads the words
of this prophecy, and blessed are those
who hear it and take to heart what is
written in it,[g] because the time is near.[h]

Greetings and Doxology

4John,

To the seven churches[i] in the province of Asia:

Grace and peace to you[j] from him
who is, and who was, and who is to
come,[k] and from the seven spirits[a][l]
before his throne, 5and from Jesus
Christ, who is the faithful witness,[m] the
firstborn from the dead,[n] and the ruler
of the kings of the earth.[o]

To him who loves us[p] and has freed us
from our sins by his blood,[q] 6and has
made us to be a kingdom and priests[r] to
serve his God and Father[s]—to him be
glory and power for ever and ever!
Amen.[t]

7Look, he is coming with the clouds,[u]
and every eye will see him,
even those who pierced him;[v]
and all the peoples of the earth will
mourn[w] because of him.
So shall it be! Amen.

8"I am the Alpha and the Omega,"[x]
says the Lord God, "who is, and
who was, and who is to come,[y] the
Almighty."[z]

One Like a Son of Man

9I, John,[a] your brother and companion in the suffering[b] and kingdom[c] and
patient endurance[d] that are ours in
Jesus, was on the island of Patmos because of the word of God[e] and the testimony of Jesus.[f] 10On the Lord's Day[g] I
was in the Spirit,[h] and I heard behind
me a loud voice like a trumpet,[i] 11which
said: "Write on a scroll what you see[j]
and send it to the seven churches:[k]
to Ephesus,[l] Smyrna,[m] Pergamum,[n]
Thyatira,[o] Sardis,[p] Philadelphia[q] and
Laodicea."[r]

12I turned round to see the voice that
was speaking to me. And when I turned
I saw seven golden lampstands,[s] 13and
among the lampstands[t] was someone
"like a son of man",[b][u] dressed in a robe
reaching down to his feet[v] and with a
golden sash round his chest.[w] 14His
head and hair were white like wool, as
white as snow, and his eyes were like
blazing fire.[x] 15His feet were like bronze
glowing in a furnace,[y] and his voice was
like the sound of rushing waters.[z] 16In
his right hand he held seven stars,[a] and
out of his mouth came a sharp double-edged sword.[b] His face was like the sun[c]
shining in all its brilliance.

17When I saw him, I fell at his feet[d] as
though dead. Then he placed his right
hand on me[e] and said: "Do not be
afraid.[f] I am the First and the Last.[g] 18I
am the Living One; I was dead,[h] and
behold I am alive for ever and ever![i] And
I hold the keys of death and Hades.[j]

19"Write, therefore, what you have
seen,[k] what is now and what will take
place later. 20The mystery of the seven
stars that you saw in my right hand[l] and
of the seven golden lampstands[m] is this:
The seven stars are the angels[c] of the

Ch. 1

1 [a]Jn 12:49; 17:8; [b]ver 19; Da 2:28–29; Rev 22:6; [c]Rev 22:16; [d]ver 4,9; Rev 22:8
2 [e]ver 9; **Heb 4:12**; [f]ver 9; 1Co 1:6; Rev 6:9; 12:17; 19:10
3 [g]Lk 11:28; Rev 22:7; [h]**Ro 13:11**
4 [i]ver 11,20; [j]**Ro 1:7**; [k]ver 8; Rev 4:8; 11:17; 16:5; [l]Isa 11:2; Rev 3:1; 4:5; 5:6
5 [m]Isa 55:4; Jn 18:37; Rev 3:14; [n]Ps 89:27; Col 1:18; [o]**1Ti 6:15**; [p]**Ro 8:37**; [q]**Ro 3:25**
6 [r]**1Pe 2:5**; Rev 5:10; 20:6; [s]Ro 15:6; [t]**Ro 11:36**
7 [u]Da 7:13; **Mt 16:27**; 24:30; 26:64; **Lk 17:30; 1Co 1:7; 1Th 2:19**; 4:16–17; [v]Jn 19:34,37; [w]Zec 12:10; Mt 24:30
8 [x]**ver 17**; Rev 21:6; 22:13; [y]**ver 4**; [z]Rev 4:8; 15:3; 19:6
9 [a]ver 1; [b]**Ac 14:22**; 2Co 1:7; Php 4:14; [c]ver 6; [d]2Ti 2:12; [e]ver 2; **Heb 4:12**; [f]**ver 2**
10 [g]Ac 20:7; [h]Rev 4:2; 17:3; 21:10; [i]Ex 20:18; Rev 4:1
11 [j]ver 19; [k]ver 4,20; [l]**Ac 18:19**; [m]Rev 2:8; [n]Rev 2:12; [o]Ac 16:14; Rev 2:18,24; [p]Rev 3:1; [q]Rev 3:7; [r]**Col 2:1**; Rev 3:14
12 [s]ver 20; Ex 25:31–40; Zec 4:2; Rev 2:1
13 [t]Rev 2:1; [u]Eze 1:26; Da 7:13; 10:16; Rev 14:14; [v]Isa 6:1; [w]Da 10:5; Rev 15:6
14 [x]Da 7:9; 10:6; Rev 2:18; 19:12
15 [y]Eze 1:7; Da 10:6; Rev 2:18; [z]Eze 43:2; Rev 14:2; 19:6
16 [a]ver 20; Rev 2:1; 3:1; [b]Isa 1:20; 49:2; Heb 4:12; Rev 2:12,16; 19:15,21; [c]Jdg 5:31; Mt 17:2
17 [d]Eze 1:28; Da 8:17–18; [e]Da 8:18; [f]**Mt 14:27**; [g]Isa 41:4; 44:6; 48:12; Rev 2:8; 22:13
18 [h]Ro 6:9; Rev 2:8; [i]Dt 32:40; Da 4:34; 12:7; Rev 4:9–10; 10:6; 15:7; [j]Rev 9:1; 20:1
19 [k]ver 11; Hab 2:2
20 [l]**ver 16**; [m]**ver 12**

[a]*4* Or *the sevenfold Spirit*
[b]*13* Daniel 7:13
[c]*20* Or *messengers*

seven churches,[n] and the seven lamp-
stands are the seven churches.[o]

To the Church in Ephesus

2 "To the angel[a] of the church in
Ephesus[a] write:

These are the words of him who
holds the seven stars in his right
hand[b] and walks among the seven
golden lampstands:[c] 2I know your
deeds,[d] your hard work and your
perseverance. I know that you can-
not tolerate wicked men, that you
have tested[e] those who claim to be
apostles but are not, and have
found them false.[f] 3You have perse-
vered and have endured hardships
for my name,[g] and have not grown
weary.
4Yet I hold this against you: You
have forsaken your first love.[h]
5Remember the height from which
you have fallen! Repent[i] and do the
things you did at first. If you do not
repent, I will come to you and
remove your lampstand[j] from its
place. 6But you have this in your
favour: You hate the practices of
Nicolaitans,[k] which I also hate.
7He who has an ear, let him hear[l]
what the Spirit says to the chur-
ches. To him who overcomes,[m] I
will give the right to eat from the
tree of life,[n] which is in the para-
dise[o] of God.

To the Church in Smyrna

8"To the angel of the church in Smyrna[p]
write:

These are the words of him who
is the First and the Last,[q] who died
and came to life again.[r] 9I know
your afflictions and your poverty
—yet you are rich![s] I know the slan-
der of those who say they are Jews
and are not,[t] but are a synagogue of
Satan.[u] 10Do not be afraid of what
you are about to suffer. I tell you,
the devil will put some of you in
prison to test you,[v] and you will
suffer persecution for ten days.[w] Be
faithful,[x] even to the point of death,
and I will give you the crown of
life.[y]
11He who has an ear, let him
hear[z] what the Spirit says to the
churches. He who overcomes will
not be hurt at all by the second
death.[a]

To the Church in Pergamum

12"To the angel of the church in Perga-
mum[b] write:

These are the words of him who
has the sharp, double-edged
sword.[c] 13I know where you live
—where Satan has his throne. Yet
you remain true to my name. You
did not renounce your faith in me,[d]
even in the days of Antipas, my
faithful witness,[e] who was put to
death in your city—where Satan
lives.[f]
14Nevertheless, I have a few
things against you:[g] You have peo-
ple there who hold to the teaching
of Balaam,[h] who taught Balak to
entice the Israelites to sin by eating
food sacrificed to idols[i] and by
committing sexual immorality.[j]
15Likewise you also have those who
hold to the teaching of the Nico-
laitans.[k] 16Repent[l] therefore! Other-
wise, I will soon come to you and
will fight against them with the
sword of my mouth.[m]
17He who has an ear, let him
hear[n] what the Spirit says to the
churches. To him who overcomes,[o]
I will give some of the hidden
manna.[p] I will also give him a
white stone with a new name[q] writ-
ten on it, known only to him who
receives it.[r]

To the Church in Thyatira

18"To the angel of the church in Thya-
tira[s] write:

These are the words of the Son of
God,[t] whose eyes are like blazing
fire and whose feet are like bur-
nished bronze.[u] 19I know your
deeds,[v] your love and faith, your
service and perseverance, and that
you are now doing more than you
did at first.
20Nevertheless, I have this
against you: You tolerate that
woman Jezebel,[w] who calls herself
a prophetess. By her teaching she
misleads my servants into sexual
immorality and the eating of food
sacrificed to idols.[x] 21I have given
her time[y] to repent of her immoral-
ity, but she is unwilling.[z] 22So I will
cast her on a bed of suffering, and I

20 [n]ver 4,11; [o]Mt 5:14–15

Ch. 2

1 [a]**Ac 18:19;** [b]Rev 1:16; [c]Rev 1:12–13
2 [d]ver 19; Rev 3:1,8,15; [e]1Jn 4:1; [f]2Co 11:13
3 [g]**Jn 15:21**
4 [h]Jer 2:2; Mt 24:12
5 [i]ver 16,22; Rev 3:3,19; [j]Rev 1:20
6 [k]ver 15
7 [l]**Mt 11:15;** ver 11,17,29; Rev 3:6,13, 22; 13:9; [m]**Jn 16:33;** [n]Ge 2:9; 3:22–24; Rev 22:2,14, 19; [o]Lk 23:43
8 [p]Rev 1:11; [q]**Rev 1:17;** [r]Rev 1:18
9 [s]2Co 6:10; Jas 2:5; [t]Rev 3:9; [u]ver 13,24; **Mt 4:10**
10 [v]Rev 3:10; [w]Da 1:12,14; [x]ver 13; Rev 17:14; [y]**Mt 10:22; 1Co 9:25**
11 [z]**ver 7;** [a]Rev 20:6,14; 21:8
12 [b]Rev 1:11; [c]ver 16; **Rev 1:16**
13 [d]Rev 14:12; [e]Rev 1:5; 11:3; [f]ver 9,24; **Mt 4:10**
14 [g]ver 20; [h]**2Pe 2:15;** [i]**Ac 15:20;** [j]1Co 6:13
15 [k]ver 6
16 [l]ver 5; [m]2Th 2:8; **Rev 1:16**
17 [n]**ver 7;** [o]**Jn 16:33;** [p]Jn 6:49–50; [q]Isa 56:5; 62:2; 65:15; [r]Rev 19:12
18 [s]ver 24; Ac 16:14; Rev 1:11; [t]**Mt 4:3;** [u]**Rev 1:14–15**
19 [v]**ver 2**
20 [w]1Ki 16:31; 21:25; 2Ki 9:7; [x]ver 14; **Ac 15:20**
21 [y]Ro 2:4; 2Pe 3:9; [z]Ro 2:5; Rev 9:20; 16:9,11

a1 Or *messenger;* also in verses 8, 12 and 18

will make those who commit adul-
tery[a] with her suffer intensely, un-
less they repent of her ways. 23I will
strike her children dead. Then all
the churches will know that I am he
who searches hearts and minds,[b]
and I will repay each of you accord-
ing to your deeds.[c] 24Now I say to
the rest of you in Thyatira, to you
who do not hold to her teaching
and have not learned Satan's so-
called deep secrets (I will not im-
pose any other burden on you):[d]
25Only hold on to what you have[e]
until I come.[f]
26To him who overcomes[g] and
does my will to the end,[h] I will give
authority over the nations[i]—

27'He will rule them with an iron
sceptre;[j]
he will dash them to pieces like
pottery'[b][k]—

just as I have received authority
from my Father. 28I will also give
him the morning star.[l] 29He who
has an ear, let him hear[m] what the
Spirit says to the churches.

To the Church in Sardis

3 "To the angel[a] of the church in
Sardis[a] write:

These are the words of him who
holds the seven spirits[b][b] of God
and the seven stars.[c] I know your
deeds;[d] you have a reputation of
being alive, but you are dead.[e]
2Wake up! Strengthen what re-
mains and is about to die, for I have
not found your deeds complete in
the sight of my God. 3Remember,
therefore, what you have received
and heard; obey it, and repent.[f] But
if you do not wake up, I will come
like a thief,[g] and you will not know
at what time[h] I will come to you.
4Yet you have a few people in
Sardis who have not soiled their
clothes.[i] They will walk with me,
dressed in white,[j] for they are
worthy. 5He who overcomes[k] will,
like them, be dressed in white.[l] I
will never blot out his name from
the book of life,[m] but will acknowl-
edge his name before my Father[n]
and his angels. 6He who has an ear,
let him hear[o] what the Spirit says to
the churches.

To the Church in Philadelphia

7"To the angel of the church in Phil-
adelphia[p] write:

These are the words of him who
is holy[q] and true,[r] who holds the
key of David.[s] What he opens no-
one can shut, and what he shuts
no-one can open. 8I know your
deeds.[t] See, I have placed before
you an open door[u] that no-one can
shut. I know that you have little
strength, yet you have kept my
word and have not denied my
name.[v] 9I will make those who are
of the synagogue of Satan,[w] who
claim to be Jews though they are
not,[x] but are liars—I will make
them come and fall down at your
feet[y] and acknowledge that I have
loved you.[z] 10Since you have kept
my command to endure patiently, I
will also keep you[a] from the hour of
trial that is going to come upon the
whole world[b] to test[c] those who live
on the earth.[d]
11I am coming soon.[e] Hold on to
what you have,[f] so that no-one will
take your crown.[g] 12Him who over-
comes[h] I will make a pillar[i] in the
temple of my God. Never again will
he leave it. I will write on him the
name of my God[j] and the name of
the city of my God,[k] the new Jeru-
salem,[l] which is coming down out
of heaven from my God; and I will
also write on him my new name.
13He who has an ear, let him
hear[m] what the Spirit says to the
churches.

To the Church in Laodicea

14"To the angel of the church in Laodi-
cea[n] write:

These are the words of the
Amen, the faithful and true wit-
ness,[o] the ruler of God's creation.[p]
15I know your deeds,[q] that you are
neither cold nor hot.[r] I wish you
were either one or the other! 16So,
because you are lukewarm—
neither hot nor cold—I am about to
spit you out of my mouth. 17You
say, 'I am rich; I have acquired
wealth and do not need a thing.'[s]
But you do not realise that you are

22 [a]Rev 17:2; 18:9
23 [b]1Sa 16:7; 1Ki 8:39; Ps 139:1–2,23; Pr 21:2; Jer 17:10; Lk 16:15; Ro 8:27; 1Th 2:4; [c]**Mt 16:27**
24 [d]Ac 15:28
25 [e]Rev 3:11; [f]**Mt 16:27**
26 [g]**Jn 16:33**; [h]Mt 10:22; [i]Ps 2:8; Rev 3:21
27 [j]Rev 12:5; 19:15; [k]Ps 2:9; Isa 30:14; Jer 19:11
28 [l]Rev 22:16
29 [m]**ver 7**

Ch. 3

1 [a]Rev 1:11; [b]**Rev 1:4**; [c]**Rev 1:16**; [d]**Rev 2:2**; [e]1Ti 5:6
3 [f]**Rev 2:5**; [g]**Lk 12:39**; [h]Lk 12:39
4 [i]Jude 23; [j]ver 5,18; Rev 4:4; 6:11; 7:9, 13–14; 19:14
5 [k]**Jn 16:33**; [l]**ver 4**; [m]**Rev 20:12**; [n]Mt 10:32
6 [o]**Rev 2:7**
7 [p]Rev 1:11; [q]**Mk 1:24**; [r]1Jn 5:20; Rev 6:10; 19:11; [s]Isa 22:22; Mt 16:19
8 [t]**Rev 2:2**; [u]**Ac 14:27**; [v]Rev 2:13
9 [w]Rev 2:9; [x]Rev 2:9; [y]Isa 49:23; [z]Isa 43:4; **Ro 8:37**
10 [a]2Pe 2:9; [b]**Mt 24:14**; [c]Rev 2:10; [d]Rev 6:10; 8:13; 11:10; 13:8,14; 17:8
11 [e]**Mt 16:27**; [f]Rev 2:25; [g]**1Co 9:25**
12 [h]**Jn 16:33**; [i]Gal 2:9; [j]Rev 14:1; 22:4; [k]Eze 48:35; [l]Gal 4:26; Rev 21:2,10
13 [m]**Rev 2:7**
14 [n]**Col 2:1**; Rev 1:11; [o]Jn 18:37; Rev 1:5; [p]Pr 8:22; Jn 1:3; Col 1:16,18
15 [q]**Rev 2:2**; [r]Ro 12:11
17 [s]Hos 12:8; 1Co 4:8

b27 Psalm 2:9
a1 Or *messenger;* also in verses 7 and 14
b1 Or *the sevenfold Spirit*

wretched, pitiful, poor, blind and
naked.[t] 18 I counsel you to buy from
me gold refined in the fire,[u] so that
you can become rich; and white
clothes[v] to wear, so that you can
cover your shameful nakedness;[w]
and salve to put on your eyes, so
that you can see.
19 Those whom I love I rebuke and
discipline.[x] So be earnest, and re-
pent.[y] 20 Here I am! I stand at the
door[z] and knock. If anyone hears
my voice and opens the door,[a] I will
come in[b] and eat with him, and he
with me.
21 To him who overcomes,[c] I will
give the right to sit with me on my
throne,[d] just as I overcame[e] and sat
down with my Father on his
throne. 22 He who has an ear, let
him hear[f] what the Spirit says to the
churches."

The Throne in Heaven

4 After this I looked, and there be-
fore me was a door standing open[a]
in heaven. And the voice I had first
heard speaking to me like a trumpet[b]
said, "Come up here,[c] and I will show
you what must take place after this."[d]
2 At once I was in the Spirit,[e] and there
before me was a throne in heaven[f] with
someone sitting on it. 3 And the one who
sat there had the appearance of jasper[g]
and carnelian.[h] A rainbow,[i] resembling
an emerald,[j] encircled the throne.
4 Surrounding the throne were twenty-
four other thrones, and seated on them
were twenty-four elders.[k] They were
dressed in white[l] and had crowns of
gold on their heads. 5 From the throne
came flashes of lightning, rumblings
and peals of thunder.[m] Before the
throne, seven lamps[n] were blazing.
These are the seven spirits[a][o] of God.
6 Also before the throne there was what
looked like a sea of glass,[p] clear as
crystal.
In the centre, around the throne,
were four living creatures,[q] and they
were covered with eyes, in front and
behind.[r] 7 The first living creature was
like a lion, the second was like an ox, the
third had a face like a man, the fourth
was like a flying eagle.[s] 8 Each of the four
living creatures[t] had six wings[u] and was
covered with eyes all around,[v] even
under his wings. Day and night[w] they
never stop saying:

"Holy, holy, holy
is the Lord God Almighty,[x]
who was, and is, and is to come."[y]

17 [t]Pr 13:7
18 [u]**1Pe 1:7**; [v]**ver 4**; [w]Rev 16:15
19 [x]Dt 8:5; Pr 3:12; 1Co 11:32; Heb 12:5–6; [y]**Rev 2:5**
20 [z]Mt 24:33; Jas 5:9; [a]Lk 12:36; [b]**Ro 8:10**
21 [c]**Jn 16:33**; [d]**Mt 19:28**; [e]Rev 5:5
22 [f]**Rev 2:7**

Ch. 4

1 [a]**Mt 3:16**; [b]Rev 1:10; [c]Rev 11:12; [d]Rev 1:19; 22:6
2 [e]**Rev 1:10**; [f]ver 9–10; 1Ki 22:19; Isa 6:1; Eze 1:26–28; Da 7:9; Rev 20:11
3 [g]Rev 21:11; [h]Rev 21:20; [i]Eze 1:28; Rev 10:1; [j]Rev 21:19
4 [k]ver 10; Rev 5:6,8,14; 11:16; 19:4; [l]**Rev 3:4–5**
5 [m]Ex 19:16; Rev 8:5; 11:19; 16:18; [n]Zec 4:2; [o]**Rev 1:4**
6 [p]Rev 15:2; [q]ver 8–9; Eze 1:5; Rev 5:6; 6:1; 7:11; 14:3; 15:7; 19:4; [r]Eze 1:18; 10:12
7 [s]Eze 1:10; 10:14
8 [t]**ver 6**; [u]Isa 6:2; [v]Eze 1:18; [w]Rev 14:11; [x]Isa 6:3; **Rev 1:8**; [y]**Rev 1:4**
9 [z]ver 2; Ps 47:8; **Rev 5:1**; [a]**Rev 1:18**
10 [b]**ver 4**; [c]Dt 33:3; Rev 5:8, 14; 7:11; 11:16; [d]**ver 2**
11 [e]Rev 1:6; 5:12; [f]Ac 14:15; Rev 10:6

Ch. 5

1 [a]ver 7,13; Rev 4:2,9; 6:16; [b]Eze 2:9–10; [c]Isa 29:11; Da 12:4
2 [d]Rev 10:1
5 [e]Ge 49:9; [f]**Heb 7:14**; [g]Isa 11:1,10; Ro 15:12; Rev 22:16

9 Whenever the living creatures give
glory, honour and thanks to him who
sits on the throne[z] and who lives for
ever and ever,[a] 10 the twenty-four elders[b]
fall down before him[c] who sits on the
throne,[d] and worship him who lives for
ever and ever. They lay their crowns
before the throne and say:

11 "You are worthy, our Lord and God,
to receive glory and honour and
power,[e]
for you created all things,
and by your will they were created
and have their being."[f]

The Scroll and the Lamb

5 Then I saw in the right hand of him
who sat on the throne[a] a scroll with
writing on both sides[b] and sealed[c] with
seven seals. 2 And I saw a mighty angel[d]
proclaiming in a loud voice, "Who is
worthy to break the seals and open the
scroll?" 3 But no-one in heaven or on
earth or under the earth could open the
scroll or even look inside it. 4 I wept and
wept because no-one was found who
was worthy to open the scroll or look
inside. 5 Then one of the elders said to
me, "Do not weep! See, the Lion[e] of the
tribe of Judah,[f] the Root of David,[g] has
triumphed. He is able to open the scroll
and its seven seals."
6 Then I saw a Lamb,[h] looking as if it
had been slain, standing in the centre of
the throne, encircled by the four living
creatures[i] and the elders.[j] He had seven
horns and seven eyes,[k] which are the
seven spirits[a][l] of God sent out into all
the earth. 7 He came and took the scroll
from the right hand of him who sat on
the throne.[m] 8 And when he had taken it,
the four living creatures[n] and the
twenty-four elders[o] fell down before the
Lamb. Each one had a harp[p] and they
were holding golden bowls full of in-
cense, which are the prayers[q] of the
saints. 9 And they sang a new song:[r]

"You are worthy[s] to take the scroll
and to open its seals,
because you were slain,
and with your blood[t] you
purchased[u] men for God

6 [h]ver 8–9,12–13; **Jn 1:29**; [i]**Rev 4:6**; [j]**Rev 4:4**; [k]Zec 4:10; [l]**Rev 1:4** *7* [m]**ver 1**
8 [n]**Rev 4:6**; [o]**Rev 4:4**; [p]Rev 14:2; 15:2; [q]Ps 141:2; Rev 8:3–4
9 [r]Ps 40:3; 98:1; 149:1; Isa 42:10; Rev 14:3–4; [s]Rev 4:11; [t]Heb 9:12; [u]**1Co 6:20**

[a]5 Or *the sevenfold Spirit*
[a]6 Or *the sevenfold Spirit*

from every tribe and language and
people and nation.[v]
10You have made them to be a kingdom
and priests[w] to serve our God,
and they will reign on the earth."[x]

11Then I looked and heard the voice of
many angels, numbering thousands
upon thousands, and ten thousand
times ten thousand.[y] They encircled the
throne and the living creatures[z] and the
elders.[a] 12In a loud voice they sang:

"Worthy is the Lamb,[b] who was slain,[c]
to receive power and wealth and
wisdom and strength
and honour and glory and praise!"[d]

13Then I heard every creature in
heaven and on earth and under the
earth[e] and on the sea, and all that is in
them, singing:

"To him who sits on the throne[f] and to
the Lamb[g]
be praise and honour and glory and
power,
for ever and ever!"[h]

14The four living creatures[i] said,
"Amen",[j] and the elders[k] fell down and
worshipped.[l]

The Seals

6 I watched as the Lamb[a] opened the
first of the seven seals.[b] Then I
heard one of the four living creatures[c]
say in a voice like thunder,[d] "Come!" 2I
looked, and there before me was a white
horse![e] Its rider held a bow, and he was
given a crown,[f] and he rode out as a
conqueror bent on conquest.[g]
3When the Lamb opened the second
seal, I heard the second living creature[h]
say, "Come!" 4Then another horse
came out, a fiery red one.[i] Its rider was
given power to take peace from the
earth[j] and to make men slay each other.
To him was given a large sword.
5When the Lamb opened the third
seal, I heard the third living creature[k]
say, "Come!" I looked, and there before
me was a black horse![l] Its rider was
holding a pair of scales in his hand.
6Then I heard what sounded like a voice
among the four living creatures,[m]
saying, "A quart[a] of wheat for a day's
wages,[b] and three quarts of barley for a
day's wages,[b][n] and do not damage[o] the
oil and the wine!"
7When the Lamb opened the fourth
seal, I heard the voice of the fourth liv-
ing creature[p] say, "Come!" 8I looked, and
there before me was a pale horse![q] Its
rider was named Death, and Hades[r] was
following close behind him. They were
given power over a fourth of the earth
to kill by sword, famine and plague,
and by the wild beasts of the earth.[s]
9When he opened the fifth seal, I saw
under[t] the altar[u] the souls of those who
had been slain[v] because of the word of
God[w] and the testimony they had main-
tained. 10They called out in a loud voice,
"How long,[x] Sovereign Lord,[y] holy and
true,[z] until you judge the inhabitants of
the earth[a] and avenge our blood?"[b]
11Then each of them was given a white
robe,[c] and they were told to wait a little
longer, until the number of their fellow-
servants and brothers who were to be
killed as they had been was completed.[d]
12I watched as he opened the sixth
seal. There was a great earthquake.[e] The
sun turned black[f] like sackcloth[g] made
of goat hair, the whole moon turned
blood red, 13and the stars in the sky fell
to earth,[h] as late figs drop from a fig-tree[i]
when shaken by a strong wind. 14The
sky receded like a scroll, rolling up,[j]
and every mountain and island was
removed from its place.[k]
15Then the kings of the earth, the
princes, the generals, the rich, the
mighty, and every slave and every free
man[l] hid in caves and among the rocks
of the mountains.[m] 16They called to the
mountains and the rocks, "Fall on us"[n]
and hide us from the face of him who
sits on the throne[o] and from the wrath of
the Lamb! 17For the great day[p] of their
wrath has come, and who can stand?"[q]

144,000 Sealed

7 After this I saw four angels stand-
ing at the four corners[a] of the earth,
holding back the four winds[b] of the
earth to prevent[c] any wind from blow-
ing on the land or on the sea or on any
tree. 2Then I saw another angel coming
up from the east, having the seal[d] of the
living God.[e] He called out in a loud voice
to the four angels who had been given
power to harm the land and the sea:[f]

9 [v]**Rev 13:7**
10 [w]**1Pe 2:5;** [x]Rev 3:21; 20:4
11 [y]Da 7:10; Heb 12:22; Jude 14; [z]**Rev 4:6;** [a]**Rev 4:4**
12 [b]ver 13; [c]ver 9; [d]Rev 1:6; 4:11
13 [e]ver 3; Php 2:10; [f]**ver 1**,7; [g]ver 6; Rev 6:16; 7:10; [h]1Ch 29:11; Mal 1:6; 2:2; **Ro 11:36**
14 [i]**Rev 4:6;** [j]Rev 4:9; [k]**Rev 4:4;** [l]Rev 4:10

Ch. 6

1 [a]**Rev 5:6;** [b]Rev 5:1; [c]**Rev 4:6–7;** [d]Rev 14:2; 19:6
2 [e]Zec 1:8; 6:3; Rev 19:11; [f]Zec 6:11; Rev 14:14; 19:12; [g]Ps 45:4
3 [h]Rev 4:7
4 [i]Zec 1:8; 6:2; [j]Mt 10:34
5 [k]Rev 4:7; [l]Zec 6:2
6 [m]**Rev 4:6–7;** [n]Eze 4:16; [o]Rev 7:1,3; 9:4
7 [p]Rev 4:7
8 [q]Zec 6:3; [r]Hos 13:14; Rev 1:18; 20:13–14; [s]Jer 15:2–3; 24:10; Eze 5:12,17
9 [t]Ex 29:12; Lev 4:7; [u]Rev 14:18; 16:7; [v]Rev 20:4; [w]Ro 1:2; **Heb 4:12**
10 [x]Ps 119:84; Zec 1:12; [y]Lk 2:29; 2Pe 2:1; [z]**Rev 3:7;** [a]**Rev 3:10;** [b]Dt 32:43; 2Ki 9:7; Ps 79:10; Rev 16:6; 18:20; 19:2
11 [c]**Rev 3:4;** [d]Heb 11:40
12 [e]Ps 97:4; Isa 29:6; Eze 38:19; Rev 8:5; 11:13; 16:18; [f]**Mt 24:29;** [g]Isa 50:3
13 [h]**Mt 24:29;** Rev 8:10; 9:1; [i]Isa 34:4
14 [j]**2Pe 3:10;** Rev 20:11; 21:1; [k]Ps 46:2; Isa 54:10; Jer 4:24; Eze 38:20; Na 1:5; Rev 16:20; 21:1
15 [l]Rev 19:18; [m]Isa 2:10,19,21
16 [n]Hos 10:8; Lk 23:30; [o]**Rev 5:1**
17 [p]Joel 1:15; 2:1–2,11,31; Zep 1:14–15; Rev 16:14; [q]Ps 76:7; Na 1:6; Mal 3:2

Ch. 7

1 [a]Isa 11:12; [b]Jer 49:36; Eze 37:9; Da 7:2; Zec 6:5; Mt 24:31; [c]**Rev 6:6** **2** [d]Rev 9:4; [e]**Mt 16:16;** [f]ver 1

[a]6 Greek *a choinix* (probably about a litre)
[b]6 Greek *a denarius*

3"Do not harm[g] the land or the sea or the trees until we put a seal on the foreheads[h] of the servants of our God." 4Then I heard the number[i] of those who were sealed: 144,000[j] from all the tribes of Israel.

5From the tribe of Judah 12,000 were sealed,
from the tribe of Reuben 12,000,
from the tribe of Gad 12,000,
6from the tribe of Asher 12,000,
from the tribe of Naphtali 12,000,
from the tribe of Manasseh 12,000,
7from the tribe of Simeon 12,000,
from the tribe of Levi 12,000,
from the tribe of Issachar 12,000,
8from the tribe of Zebulun 12,000,
from the tribe of Joseph 12,000,
from the tribe of Benjamin 12,000.

The Great Multitude in White Robes

9After this I looked and there before me was a great multitude that no-one could count, from every nation, tribe, people and language,[k] standing before the throne[l] and in front of the Lamb. They were wearing white robes[m] and were holding palm branches in their hands. 10And they cried out in a loud voice:

"Salvation belongs to our God,[n]
who sits on the throne,[o]
and to the Lamb."

11All the angels were standing round the throne and around the elders[p] and the four living creatures.[q] They fell down on their faces[r] before the throne and worshipped God, 12saying:

"Amen!
Praise and glory
and wisdom and thanks and honour
and power and strength
be to our God for ever and ever.
Amen!"[s]

13Then one of the elders asked me, "These in white robes[t]—who are they, and where did they come from?"

14I answered, "Sir, you know."

And he said, "These are they who have come out of the great tribulation; they have washed their robes[u] and made them white in the blood of the Lamb.[v] 15Therefore,

"they are before the throne of God[w]
and serve him[x] day and night in his temple;[y]
and he who sits on the throne[z] will spread his tent over them.[a]
16Never again will they hunger;
never again will they thirst.[b]
The sun will not beat upon them,
nor any scorching heat.[c]
17For the Lamb at the centre of the throne will be their shepherd;[d]
he will lead them to springs of living water.[e]
And God will wipe away every tear from their eyes."[f]

The Seventh Seal and the Golden Censer

8 When he opened the seventh seal,[a] there was silence in heaven for about half an hour.

2And I saw the seven angels[b] who stand before God, and to them were given seven trumpets.[c]

3Another angel,[d] who had a golden censer, came and stood at the altar. He was given much incense to offer, with the prayers of all the saints,[e] on the golden altar[f] before the throne. 4The smoke of the incense, together with the prayers of the saints, went up before God[g] from the angel's hand. 5Then the angel took the censer, filled it with fire from the altar,[h] and hurled it on the earth; and there came peals of thunder,[i] rumblings, flashes of lightning and an earthquake.[j]

The Trumpets

6Then the seven angels who had the seven trumpets[k] prepared to sound them.

7The first angel[l] sounded his trumpet, and there came hail and fire[m] mixed with blood, and it was hurled down upon the earth. A third[n] of the earth was burned up, a third of the trees were burned up, and all the green grass was burned up.[o]

8The second angel sounded his trumpet, and something like a huge mountain,[p] all ablaze, was thrown into the sea. A third[q] of the sea turned into blood,[r] 9a third[s] of the living creatures in the sea died, and a third of the ships were destroyed.

10The third angel sounded his trumpet, and a great star, blazing like a torch, fell from the sky[t] on a third of the rivers and on the springs of water[u]—11the name of the star is Wormwood.[a] A

3 [g]**Rev 6:6**; [h]Eze 9:4; Rev 9:4; 14:1; 22:4
4 [i]Rev 9:16; [j]Rev 14:1,3
9 [k]**Rev 13:7**; [l]ver 15; [m]**Rev 3:4**
10 [n]Ps 3:8; Rev 12:10; 19:1; [o]**Rev 5:1**
11 [p]**Rev 4:4**; [q]**Rev 4:6**; [r]**Rev 4:10**
12 [s]**Ro 11:36**; Rev 5:12–14
13 [t]**Rev 3:4**
14 [u]Rev 22:14; [v]Heb 9:14; 1Jn 1:7; Rev 12:11
15 [w]ver 9; [x]Rev 22:3; [y]Rev 11:19; [z]**Rev 5:1**; [a]Isa 4:5–6; Rev 21:3
16 [b]Jn 6:35; [c]Isa 49:10
17 [d]**Jn 10:11**; [e]**Jn 4:10**; [f]Isa 25:8; 35:10; 51:11; 65:19; Rev 21:4

Ch. 8

1 [a]Rev 6:1
2 [b]ver 6–13; Rev 9:1,13; 11:15; [c]**Mt 24:31**
3 [d]Rev 7:2; [e]Rev 5:8; [f]ver 5; Ex 30:1–6; Heb 9:4; Rev 9:13
4 [g]Ps 141:2
5 [h]Lev 16:12–13; [i]**Rev 4:5**; [j]**Rev 6:12**
6 [k]**ver 2**
7 [l]**ver 2**; [m]Eze 38:22; [n]ver 7–12; Rev 9:15,18; 12:4; [o]Rev 9:4
8 [p]Jer 51:25; [q]ver 7; [r]Rev 16:3
9 [s]**ver 7**
10 [t]Isa 14:12; Rev 6:13; 9:1; [u]Rev 14:7; 16:4

[a]*11* That is, Bitterness

third[v] of the waters turned bitter, and many people died from the waters that had become bitter.[w]

12The fourth angel sounded his trumpet, and a third of the sun was struck, a third of the moon, and a third of the stars, so that a third[x] of them turned dark.[y] A third of the day was without light, and also a third of the night.[z]

13As I watched, I heard an eagle that was flying in mid-air[a] call out in a loud voice: "Woe! Woe! Woe[b] to the inhabitants of the earth,[c] because of the trumpet blasts about to be sounded by the other three angels!"

9 The fifth angel sounded his trumpet, and I saw a star that had fallen from the sky to the earth.[a] The star was given the key[b] to the shaft of the Abyss.[c] 2When he opened the Abyss, smoke rose from it like the smoke from a gigantic furnace.[d] The sun and sky were darkened[e] by the smoke from the Abyss.[f] 3And out of the smoke locusts[g] came down upon the earth and were given power like that of scorpions[h] of the earth. 4They were told not to harm[i] the grass of the earth or any plant or tree,[j] but only those people who did not have the seal of God on their foreheads.[k] 5They were not given power to kill them, but only to torture them for five months.[l] And the agony they suffered was like that of the sting of a scorpion[m] when it strikes a man. 6During those days men will seek death, but will not find it; they will long to die, but death will elude them.[n]

7The locusts looked like horses prepared for battle.[o] On their heads they wore something like crowns of gold, and their faces resembled human faces.[p] 8Their hair was like women's hair, and their teeth were like lions' teeth.[q] 9They had breastplates like breastplates of iron, and the sound of their wings was like the thundering of many horses and chariots rushing into battle.[r] 10They had tails and stings like scorpions, and in their tails they had power to torment people for five months.[s] 11They had as king over them the angel of the Abyss,[t] whose name in Hebrew[u] is Abaddon,[v] and in Greek, Apollyon.[a]

12The first woe is past; two other woes are yet to come.[w]

13The sixth angel sounded his trumpet, and I heard a voice coming from the horns[b] [x] of the golden altar that is before God.[y] 14It said to the sixth angel who had the trumpet, "Release the four angels[z] who are bound at the great river Euphrates."[a] 15And the four angels who had been kept ready for this very hour and day and month and year were released[b] to kill a third[c] of mankind.[d] 16The number of the mounted troops was two hundred million. I heard their number.[e]

17The horses and riders I saw in my vision looked like this: Their breastplates were fiery red, dark blue, and yellow as sulphur. The heads of the horses resembled the heads of lions, and out of their mouths[f] came fire, smoke and sulphur.[g] 18A third[h] of mankind was killed[i] by the three plagues of fire, smoke and sulphur[j] that came out of their mouths. 19The power of the horses was in their mouths and in their tails; for their tails were like snakes, having heads with which they inflict injury.

20The rest of mankind that were not killed by these plagues still did not repent[k] of the work of their hands;[l] they did not stop worshipping demons,[m] and idols of gold, silver, bronze, stone and wood—idols that cannot see or hear or walk.[n] 21Nor did they repent[o] of their murders, their magic arts,[p] their sexual immorality[q] or their thefts.

The Angel and the Little Scroll

10 Then I saw another mighty angel[a] coming down from heaven.[b] He was robed in a cloud, with a rainbow[c] above his head; his face was like the sun,[d] and his legs were like fiery pillars.[e] 2He was holding a little scroll,[f] which lay open in his hand. He planted his right foot on the sea and his left foot on the land,[g] 3and he gave a loud shout like the roar of a lion.[h] When he shouted, the voices of the seven thunders[i] spoke. 4And when the seven thunders spoke, I was about to write;[j] but I heard a voice from heaven[k] say, "Seal up what the seven thunders have said and do not write it down."[l]

5Then the angel I had seen standing on the sea and on the land[m] raised his right hand to heaven.[n] 6And he swore[o] by him who lives for ever and ever,[p] who created the heavens and all that is

11 [v]ver 7; [w]Jer 9:15; 23:15
12 [x]ver 7; [y]Ex 10:21–23; Rev 6:12–13; [z]Eze 32:7
13 [a]Rev 14:6; 19:17; [b]Rev 9:12; 11:14; 12:12; [c]**Rev 3:10**

Ch. 9
1 [a]Rev 8:10; [b]Rev 1:18; [c]ver 2,11; **Lk 8:31**
2 [d]Ge 19:28; Ex 19:18; [e]Joel 2:2,10; [f]ver 1, 11; **Lk 8:31**
3 [g]Ex 10:12–15; [h]ver 5,10
4 [i]**Rev 6:6**; [j]Rev 8:7; [k]**Rev 7:2–3**
5 [l]ver 10; [m]ver 3
6 [n]Job 3:21; 7:15; Jer 8:3; Rev 6:16
7 [o]Joel 2:4; [p]Da 7:8
8 [q]Joel 1:6
9 [r]Joel 2:5
10 [s]ver 3,5,19
11 [t]ver 1–2; **Lk 8:31**; [u]Rev 16:16; [v]Job 26:6; 28:22; 31:12; Ps 88:11
12 [w]**Rev 8:13**
13 [x]Ex 30:1–3; [y]Rev 8:3
14 [z]Rev 7:1; [a]Ge 15:18; Dt 1:7; Jos 1:4; Isa 11:15; Rev 16:12
15 [b]Rev 20:7; [c]**Rev 8:7**; [d]ver 18
16 [e]Rev 5:11; 7:4
17 [f]Rev 11:5; [g]ver 18; Ps 11:6; Isa 30:33; Eze 38:22; Rev 14:10; 19:20; 20:10; 21:8
18 [h]**Rev 8:7**; [i]ver 15; [j]**ver 17**
20 [k]**Rev 2:21**; [l]Dt 4:28; 31:29; Jer 1:16; Mic 5:13; Ac 7:41; [m]**1Co 10:20**; [n]Ps 115:4–7; 135:15–17; Da 5:23
21 [o]**Rev 2:21**; [p]Isa 47:9,12; Rev 18:23; [q]Rev 17:2,5

Ch. 10
1 [a]Rev 5:2; [b]Rev 18:1; 20:1; [c]Eze 1:28; Rev 4:3; [d]Mt 17:2; Rev 1:16; [e]Rev 1:15
2 [f]ver 8–10; Rev 5:1; [g]ver 5,8
3 [h]Hos 11:10; [i]Rev 4:5
4 [j]Rev 1:11,19; [k]ver 8; [l]Da 8:26; 12:4,9; Rev 22:10
5 [m]ver 1–2; [n]Dt 32:40; Da 12:7
6 [o]Ge 14:22; Ex 6:8; Nu 14:30; [p]**Rev 1:18**

[a]*11* *Abaddon* and *Apollyon* mean *Destroyer*.
[b]*13* That is, projections

in them, the earth and all that is in it,
and the sea and all that is in it,[q] and said,
"There will be no more delay![r] 7But in
the days when the seventh angel is
about to sound his trumpet,[s] the mys-
tery[t] of God will be accomplished, just
as he announced to his servants the
prophets."[u]
8Then the voice that I had heard from
heaven[v] spoke to me once more: "Go,
take the scroll[w] that lies open in the
hand of the angel who is standing on
the sea and on the land."
9So I went to the angel and asked him
to give me the little scroll. He said to me,
"Take it and eat it. It will turn your
stomach sour, but in your mouth it will
be as sweet as honey."[x] 10I took the little
scroll from the angel's hand and ate it. It
tasted as sweet as honey in my mouth,[y]
but when I had eaten it, my stomach
turned sour. 11Then I was told, "You
must prophesy[z] again about many peo-
ples, nations, languages and kings."[a]

The Two Witnesses

11 I was given a reed like a measur-
ing rod[a] and was told, "Go and
measure the temple of God and the
altar, and count the worshippers there.
2But exclude the outer court;[b] do not
measure it, because it has been given to
the Gentiles.[c] They will trample on the
holy city[d] for 42 months.[e] 3And I will
give power to my two witnesses,[f] and
they will prophesy for 1,260 days,[g]
clothed in sackcloth."[h] 4These are the
two olive trees[i] and the two lampstands
that stand before the Lord of the earth.[j]
5If anyone tries to harm them, fire
comes from their mouths and devours
their enemies.[k] This is how anyone
who wants to harm them must die.[l]
6These men have power to shut up the
sky[m] so that it will not rain during the
time they are prophesying;[n] and they
have power to turn the waters into
blood[o] and to strike the earth with every
kind of plague as often as they want.
7Now when they have finished their
testimony, the beast[p] that comes up
from the Abyss[q] will attack them,[r] and
overpower and kill them. 8Their bodies
will lie in the street of the great city,[s]
which is figuratively called Sodom[t] and
Egypt, where also their Lord was cru-
cified.[u] 9For three and a half days men
from every people, tribe, language and
nation[v] will gaze on their bodies and
refuse them burial.[w] 10The inhabitants
of the earth[x] will gloat over them and
will celebrate by sending each other
gifts,[y] because these two prophets had
tormented those who live on earth.
11But after the three and a half days[z] a
breath of life from God entered them,[a]
and they stood on their feet, and terror
struck those who saw them. 12Then they
heard a loud voice from heaven saying
to them, "Come up here."[b] And they
went up to heaven in a cloud,[c] while
their enemies looked on.
13At that very hour there was a severe
earthquake[d] and a tenth of the city col-
lapsed. Seven thousand people were
killed in the earthquake, and the sur-
vivors were terrified and gave glory[e]
to the God of heaven.[f]
14The second woe has passed; the
third woe is coming soon.[g]

The Seventh Trumpet

15The seventh angel sounded his
trumpet,[h] and there were loud voices[i] in
heaven, which said:

"The kingdom of the world has
become the kingdom of our Lord
and of his Christ,[j]
and he will reign for ever and
ever."[k]

16And the twenty-four elders,[l] who
were seated on their thrones before
God, fell on their faces[m] and worship-
ped God, 17saying:

"We give thanks[n] to you, Lord God
Almighty,[o]
the One who is and who was,[p]
because you have taken your great
power
and have begun to reign.[q]
18The nations were angry;[r]
and your wrath has come.
The time has come for judging the
dead,[s]
and for rewarding your servants the
prophets[t]
and your saints and those who
reverence your name,
both small and great[u]—
and for destroying those who destroy
the earth."

19Then God's temple[v] in heaven was
opened, and within his temple was seen
the ark of his covenant.[w] And there
came flashes of lightning, rumblings,
peals of thunder,[x] an earthquake and a
great hailstorm.[y]

6 [q]Ps 115:15; 146:6; Rev 4:11; 14:7; [r]Rev 16:17
7 [s]**Mt 24:31;** [t]**Ro 16:25;** [u]Am 3:7
8 [v]ver 4; [w]ver 2
9 [x]Jer 15:16; Eze 2:8–3:3
10 [y]**ver 9**
11 [z]Eze 37:4,9; [a]Da 3:4; **Rev 13:7**

Ch. 11

1 [a]Eze 40:3; Rev 21:15
2 [b]Eze 40:17,20; [c]Lk 21:24; [d]**Rev 21:2;** [e]ver 3; Da 7:25; 12:7; Rev 12:6,14; 13:5
3 [f]Rev 1:5; 2:13; [g]**ver 2;** [h]Ge 37:34; 2Sa 3:31; Ne 9:1; Jnh 3:5
4 [i]Ps 52:8; Jer 11:16; Zec 4:3, 11; [j]Zec 4:14
5 [k]2Sa 22:9; 2Ki 1:10; Jer 5:14; Rev 9:17–18; [l]Nu 16:29,35
6 [m]**Lk 4:25;** [n]ver 3; [o]Ex 7:17,19; Rev 8:8
7 [p]Rev 13:1–4; [q]**Lk 8:31;** [r]Da 7:21; Rev 13:7
8 [s]Rev 16:19; [t]Isa 1:9; Jer 23:14; Eze 16:46; [u]Heb 13:12
9 [v]**Rev 13:7;** [w]Ps 79:2–3
10 [x]**Rev 3:10;** [y]Ne 8:10,12; Est 9:19,22
11 [z]ver 9; [a]Eze 37:5,9–10,14
12 [b]Rev 4:1; [c]2Ki 2:11; Ac 1:9
13 [d]**Rev 6:12;** [e]Rev 14:7; 16:9; 19:7; [f]Rev 16:11
14 [g]**Rev 8:13**
15 [h]**Mt 24:31;** [i]Rev 16:17; 19:1; [j]Rev 12:10; [k]Ps 145:13; Da 2:44; 7:14,27; Mic 4:7; Zec 14:9; Lk 1:33
16 [l]**Rev 4:4;** [m]**Rev 4:10**
17 [n]Ps 30:12; [o]**Rev 1:8;** [p]**Rev 1:4;** [q]Rev 19:6
18 [r]Ps 2:1; [s]Rev 20:12; [t]Rev 10:7; [u]**Rev 19:5**
19 [v]Rev 15:5,8; [w]Ex 25:10–22; 2Ch 5:7; Heb 9:4; [x]**Rev 4:5;** [y]Rev 16:21

The Woman and the Dragon

12 A great and wondrous sign[a]
appeared in heaven:[b] a woman
clothed with the sun, with the moon
under her feet and a crown of twelve
stars[c] on her head. 2She was pregnant
and cried out in pain[d] as she was about
to give birth. 3Then another sign
appeared in heaven:[e] an enormous red
dragon[f] with seven heads[g] and ten
horns[h] and seven crowns[i] on his heads.
4His tail swept a third[j] of the stars out of
the sky and flung them to the earth.[k]
The dragon stood in front of the woman
who was about to give birth, so that he
might devour her child[l] the moment it
was born. 5She gave birth to a son, a
male child, who will rule all the nations
with an iron sceptre.[m] And her child
was snatched up[n] to God and to his
throne. 6The woman fled into the desert
to a place prepared for her by God,
where she might be taken care of for
1,260 days.[o]
7And there was war in heaven.
Michael[p] and his angels fought against
the dragon,[q] and the dragon and his
angels[r] fought back. 8But he was not
strong enough, and they lost their place
in heaven. 9The great dragon was
hurled down—that ancient serpent[s]
called the devil[t], or Satan,[u] who leads
the whole world astray.[v] He was hurled
to the earth,[w] and his angels with him.
10Then I heard a loud voice in heaven[x]
say:

"Now have come the salvation[y] and
the power and the kingdom of
our God,
and the authority of his Christ.
For the accuser of our brothers,[z]
who accuses them before our God
day and night,
has been hurled down.
11They overcame[a] him
by the blood of the Lamb[b]
and by the word of their testimony;[c]
they did not love their lives so much
as to shrink from death.[d]
12Therefore rejoice, you heavens[e]
and you who dwell in them!
But woe[f] to the earth and the sea,[g]
because the devil has gone down to
you!
He is filled with fury,
because he knows that his time is
short."

13When the dragon[h] saw that he had
been hurled to the earth, he pursued the
woman who had given birth to the male
child.[i] 14The woman was given the two
wings of a great eagle,[j] so that she might
fly to the place prepared for her in the
desert, where she would be taken care
of for a time, times and half a time,[k] out
of the serpent's reach. 15Then from his
mouth the serpent[l] spewed water like a
river, to overtake the woman and sweep
her away with the torrent. 16But the
earth helped the woman by opening its
mouth and swallowing the river that the
dragon had spewed out of his mouth.
17Then the dragon was enraged at the
woman and went off to make war[m]
against the rest of her offspring[n]—those
who obey God's commandments[o] and
hold to the testimony of Jesus.[p]

13 1And the dragon[a] stood on the
shore of the sea.

The Beast out of the Sea

And I saw a beast coming out of the
sea.[a] He had ten horns and seven
heads,[b] with ten crowns on his horns,
and on each head a blasphemous
name.[c] 2The beast I saw resembled a
leopard,[d] but had feet like those of a
bear[e] and a mouth like that of a lion.[f] The
dragon gave the beast his power and his
throne and great authority.[g] 3One of the
heads of the beast seemed to have had a
fatal wound, but the fatal wound had
been healed.[h] The whole world was
astonished[i] and followed the beast.
4Men worshipped the dragon because
he had given authority to the beast, and
they also worshipped the beast and
asked, "Who is like[j] the beast? Who
can make war against him?"
5The beast was given a mouth to utter
proud words and blasphemies[k] and to
exercise his authority for forty-two
months.[l] 6He opened his mouth to blas-
pheme God, and to slander his name
and his dwelling-place and those who
live in heaven.[m] 7He was given power to
make war[n] against the saints and to
conquer them. And he was given auth-
ority over every tribe, people, language
and nation.[o] 8All inhabitants of the
earth[p] will worship the beast—all
whose names have not been written in
the book of life[q] belonging to the Lamb[r]
that was slain from the creation of the
world.[b] [s]
9He who has an ear, let him hear.[t]

Ch. 12

1 [a]ver 3; [b]Rev 11:19; [c]Ge 37:9
2 [d]Isa 26:17; Gal 4:19
3 [e]ver 1; Rev 15:1; [f]ver 9,13, 16–17; Rev 13:1; [g]Rev 13:1; 17:3,7,9; [h]Da 7:7,20; Rev 13:1; 17:3,7,12,16; [i]Rev 19:12
4 [j]**Rev 8:7**; [k]Da 8:10; [l]Mt 2:16
5 [m]Ps 2:9; Rev 2:27; 19:15; [n]**Ac 8:39**
6 [o]**Rev 11:2**
7 [p]**Jude 9**; [q]ver 3; [r]Mt 25:41
9 [s]ver 15; Ge 3:1–7; [t]Mt 25:41; Rev 20:2; [u]**Mt 4:10**; [v]Rev 20:3,8, 10; [w]Lk 10:18; Jn 12:31
10 [x]Rev 11:15; [y]Rev 7:10; [z]Job 1:9–11; Zec 3:1; 1Pe 5:8
11 [a]**Jn 16:33**; Rev 15:2; [b]**Rev 7:14**; [c]Rev 6:9; [d]Lk 14:26; Rev 2:10
12 [e]Ps 96:11; Isa 44:23; 49:13; Rev 18:20; [f]**Rev 8:13**; [g]Rev 10:6
13 [h]ver 3; [i]ver 5
14 [j]Ex 19:4; [k]**Rev 11:2**
15 [l]ver 9
17 [m]Rev 11:7; 13:7; [n]Ge 3:15; [o]**Jn 14:15**; [p]**Rev 1:2**

Ch. 13

1 [a]Da 7:1–6; Rev 15:2; 16:13; [b]**Rev 12:3**; [c]Da 11:36; Rev 17:3
2 [d]Da 7:6; [e]Da 7:5; [f]Da 7:4; [g]Rev 2:13; 16:10
3 [h]ver 12,14; [i]Rev 17:8
4 [j]Ex 15:11
5 [k]Da 7:8,11, 20,25; 11:36; 2Th 2:4; [l]**Rev 11:2**
6 [m]Rev 12:12
7 [n]Da 7:21; Rev 11:7; [o]Rev 5:9; 7:9; 10:11; 17:15
8 [p]**ver 12,14; Rev 3:10**; [q]**Rev 20:12**; [r]**Jn 1:29**; [s]**Mt 25:34**
9 [t]**Rev 2:7**

[a]1 Some late manuscripts *And I*
[b]8 Or *written from the creation of the world in the book of life belonging to the Lamb that was slain*

10If anyone is to go into captivity,
into captivity he will go.
If anyone is to be killed[c] with the
sword,
with the sword he will be killed.[u]

This calls for patient endurance and
faithfulness[v] on the part of the saints.[w]

The Beast out of the Earth

11Then I saw another beast, coming
out of the earth.[x] He had two horns like
a lamb, but he spoke like a dragon.[y] 12He
exercised all the authority[z] of the first
beast on his behalf,[a] and made the earth
and its inhabitants worship the first
beast,[b] whose fatal wound had been
healed.[c] 13And he performed great and
miraculous signs,[d] even causing fire to
come down from heaven[e] to earth in full
view of men. 14Because of the signs[f] he
was given power to do on behalf of the
first beast, he deceived[g] the inhabitants
of the earth.[h] He ordered them to set up
an image in honour of the beast who
was wounded by the sword and yet
lived.[i] 15He was given power to give
breath to the image of the first beast, so
that it could speak and cause all who
refused to worship[j] the image to be
killed.[k] 16He also forced everyone,
small and great,[l] rich and poor, free and
slave, to receive a mark on his right
hand or on his forehead,[m] 17so that no-
one could buy or sell unless he had the
mark,[n] which is the name of the beast or
the number of his name.[o]
18This calls for wisdom.[p] If anyone has
insight, let him calculate the number of
the beast, for it is man's number.[q] His
number is 666.

The Lamb and the 144,000

14 Then I looked, and there before
me was the Lamb,[a] standing on
Mount Zion,[b] and with him 144,000[c]
who had his name and his Father's
name[d] written on their foreheads.[e] 2And
I heard a sound from heaven like the
roar of rushing waters[f] and like a loud
peal of thunder.[g] The sound I heard was
like that of harpists playing their harps.[h]
3And they sang a new song[i] before the
throne and before the four living crea-
tures[j] and the elders.[k] No-one could
learn the song except the 144,000[l] who
had been redeemed from the earth.
4These are those who did not defile
themselves with women, for they kept
themselves pure.[m] They follow the
Lamb wherever he goes.[n] They were
purchased from among men[o] and
offered as firstfruits[p] to God and the
Lamb. 5No lie was found in their
mouths;[q] they are blameless.[r]

The Three Angels

6Then I saw another angel flying in
mid-air,[s] and he had the eternal gospel
to proclaim to those who live on the
earth[t]—to every nation, tribe, language
and people.[u] 7He said in a loud voice,
"Fear God[v] and give him glory,[w] be-
cause the hour of his judgment has
come. Worship him who made[x] the
heavens, the earth, the sea and the
springs of water."[y]
8A second angel followed and said,
"Fallen! Fallen is Babylon the Great,[z]
which made all the nations drink the
maddening wine of her adulteries."[a]
9A third angel followed them and said
in a loud voice: "If anyone worships the
beast[b] and his image[c] and receives his
mark on the forehead[d] or on the hand,
10he, too, will drink of the wine of God's
fury,[e] which has been poured full
strength into the cup of his wrath.[f] He
will be tormented with burning sul-
phur[g] in the presence of the holy angels
and of the Lamb. 11And the smoke of
their torment rises for ever and ever.[h]
There is no rest day or night[i] for those
who worship the beast and his image,[j]
or for anyone who receives the mark
of his name."[k] 12This calls for patient
endurance[l] on the part of the saints[m]
who obey God's commandments[n] and
remain faithful to Jesus.
13Then I heard a voice from heaven
say, "Write: Blessed are the dead who
die in the Lord[o] from now on."
"Yes," says the Spirit,[p] "they will rest
from their labour, for their deeds will
follow them."

The Harvest of the Earth

14I looked, and there before me was a
white cloud,[q] and seated on the cloud
was one "like a son of man"[a][r] with a
crown[s] of gold on his head and a sharp
sickle in his hand. 15Then another angel
came out of the temple[t] and called in a
loud voice to him who was sitting on the

10 [u]Jer 15:2; 43:11; [v]**Heb 6:12**; [w]Rev 14:12
11 [x]ver 1–2; [y]Rev 16:13
12 [z]ver 4; [a]ver 14; Rev 19–20; [b]ver 15; Rev 14:9,11; 16:2; 19:20; 20:4; [c]ver 3
13 [d]**Mt 24:24**; [e]1Ki 18:38; 2Ki 1:10; Lk 9:54; Rev 20:9
14 [f]2Th 2:9–10; [g]Rev 12:9; [h]**Rev 3:10**; [i]ver 3,12
15 [j]**ver 12**; [k]Da 3:3–6
16 [l]**Rev 19:5**; [m]Rev 7:3; 14:9; 20:4
17 [n]Rev 14:9; [o]ver 18; Rev 14:11; 15:2
18 [p]Rev 17:9; [q]Rev 15:2; 21:17

Ch. 14

1 [a]**Rev 5:6**; [b]Ps 2:6; Heb 12:22; [c]ver 3; Rev 7:4; [d]Rev 3:12; 22:4; [e]**Rev 7:3**
2 [f]**Rev 1:15**; [g]Rev 6:1; [h]Rev 5:8; 15:2
3 [i]**Rev 5:9**; [j]**Rev 4:6**; [k]**Rev 4:4**; [l]ver 1
4 [m]2Co 11:2; Rev 3:4; [n]Rev 7:17; [o]Rev 5:9; [p]Jer 2:3; Jas 1:18
5 [q]Ps 32:2; Zep 3:13; Jn 1:47; 1Pe 2:22; [r]Eph 5:27
6 [s]Rev 8:13; 19:17; [t]**Rev 3:10**; [u]**Rev 13:7**
7 [v]Ps 34:9; Rev 15:4; [w]**Rev 11:13**; [x]**Rev 10:6**; [y]Rev 8:10; 16:4
8 [z]Isa 21:9; Jer 51:8; Rev 16:19; 17:5; 18:2,10; [a]Rev 17:2,4; 18:3,9
9 [b]**Rev 13:12**; [c]Rev 13:14; [d]**Rev 13:16**
10 [e]Isa 51:17; [f]Jer 25:15; [f]Jer 51:7; Rev 18:6; [g]**Rev 9:17**
11 [h]Isa 34:10; Rev 19:3; [i]Rev 4:8; [j]ver 9; **Rev 13:12**; [k]Rev 13:17

12 [l]**Heb 6:12**; [m]Rev 13:10; [n]**Jn 14:15**
13 [o]1Co 15:18; 1Th 4:16; [p]Rev 2:7; 22:17
14 [q]Mt 17:5; [r]Da 7:13; **Rev 1:13**; [s]**Rev 6:2**
15 [t]ver 17; Rev 11:19

[c]10 Some manuscripts *anyone kills*
[a]14 Daniel 7:13

cloud, "Take your sickle[u] and reap, be-
cause the time to reap has come, for the
harvest[v] of the earth is ripe." 16So he
who was seated on the cloud swung his
sickle over the earth, and the earth was
harvested.
17Another angel came out of the tem-
ple in heaven, and he too had a sharp
sickle.[w] 18Still another angel, who had
charge of the fire, came from the altar[x]
and called in a loud voice to him who
had the sharp sickle, "Take your sharp
sickle[y] and gather the clusters of grapes
from the earth's vine, because its grapes
are ripe." 19The angel swung his sickle
on the earth, gathered its grapes and
threw them into the great winepress of
God's wrath.[z] 20They were trampled in
the winepress[a] outside the city,[b] and
blood[c] flowed out of the press, rising as
high as the horses' bridles for a distance
of 1,600 stadia.[b]

Seven Angels With Seven Plagues

15 I saw in heaven another great
and marvellous sign:[a] seven
angels[b] with the seven last plagues[c]—
last, because with them God's wrath is
completed. 2And I saw what looked like
a sea of glass[d] mixed with fire and,
standing beside the sea, those who had
been victorious[e] over the beast[f] and his
image[g] and over the number of his
name.[h] They held harps[i] given them by
God 3and sang the song of Moses[j] the
servant of God[k] and the song of the
Lamb:[l]

"Great and marvellous are your
deeds,[m]
Lord God Almighty.[n]
Just and true are your ways,[o]
King of the ages.
4Who will not fear you, O Lord,[p]
and bring glory to your name?[q]
For you alone are holy.
All nations will come
and worship before you,[r]
for your righteous acts[s] have been
revealed."

5After this I looked and in heaven the
temple,[t] that is, the tabernacle of the
Testimony,[u] was opened.[v] 6Out of the
temple[w] came the seven angels with the
seven plagues.[x] They were dressed in
clean, shining linen[y] and wore golden
sashes round their chests.[z] 7Then one of
the four living creatures[a] gave to the
seven angels[b] seven golden bowls filled
with the wrath of God, who lives for
ever and ever.[c] 8And the temple was
filled with smoke[d] from the glory of
God and from his power, and no-one
could enter the temple[e] until the seven
plagues of the seven angels were
completed.

The Seven Bowls of God's Wrath

16 Then I heard a loud voice from
the temple[a] saying to the seven
angels,[b] "Go, pour out the seven bowls
of God's wrath on the earth."[c]
2The first angel went and poured out
his bowl on the land,[d] and ugly and
painful sores[e] broke out on the people
who had the mark of the beast and
worshipped his image.[f]
3The second angel poured out his
bowl on the sea, and it turned into blood
like that of a dead man, and every living
thing in the sea died.[g]
4The third angel poured out his bowl
on the rivers and springs of water,[h] and
they became blood.[i] 5Then I heard the
angel in charge of the waters say:

"You are just in these judgments,[j]
you who are and who were,[k] the
Holy One,[l]
because you have so judged;[m]
6for they have shed the blood of your
saints and prophets,[n]
and you have given them blood to
drink[o] as they deserve."

7And I heard the altar[p] respond:

"Yes, Lord God Almighty,[q]
true and just are your judgments."[r]

8The fourth angel[s] poured out his
bowl on the sun,[t] and the sun was given
power to scorch people with fire.[u] 9They
were seared by the intense heat and
they cursed the name of God,[v] who had
control over these plagues, but they
refused to repent[w] and glorify him.[x]
10The fifth angel poured out his bowl
on the throne of the beast,[y] and his
kingdom was plunged into darkness.[z]
Men gnawed their tongues in agony
11and cursed[a] the God of heaven[b] be-
cause of their pains and their sores,[c] but
they refused to repent of what they had
done.[d]
12The sixth angel poured out his bowl
on the great river Euphrates,[e] and its

15 [u]ver 18; Joel 3:13; Mk 4:29; [v]Jer 51:33
17 [w]**ver 15**
18 [x]Rev 6:9; 8:5; 16:7; [y]**ver 15**
19 [z]Rev 19:15
20 [a]ver 19; Isa 63:3; Joel 3:13; Rev 19:15; [b]Heb 13:12; Rev 11:8; [c]Ge 49:11; Dt 32:14

Ch. 15

1 [a]Rev 12:1,3; [b]ver 6–8; Rev 16:1; 17:1; 21:9; [c]Lev 26:21; Rev 9:20
2 [d]Rev 4:6; [e]Rev 12:11; [f]Rev 13:1; [g]Rev 13:14; [h]Rev 13:17; [i]Rev 5:8; 14:2
3 [j]Ex 15:1; [k]Jos 1:1; [l]**Rev 5:9;** [m]Ps 111:2; [n]**Rev 1:8;** [o]Ps 145:17
4 [p]Jer 10:7; [q]Ps 86:9; [r]Isa 66:23; [s]Rev 19:8
5 [t]Rev 11:19; [u]Ex 38:21; Nu 1:50; [v]**Mt 3:16**
6 [w]Rev 14:15; [x]**ver 1**; [y]Eze 9:2; Da 10:5; [z]Rev 1:13
7 [a]**Rev 4:6**; [b]**ver 1**; [c]**Rev 1:18**
8 [d]Isa 6:4; [e]Ex 40:34–35; 1Ki 8:10–11; 2Ch 5:13–14

Ch. 16

1 [a]Rev 11:19; [b]**Rev 15:1;** [c]ver 2–21; Ps 79:6; Zep 3:8
2 [d]Rev 8:7; [e]ver 11; Ex 9:9–11; Dt 28:35; [f]Rev 13:15–17; 14:9
3 [g]Ex 7:17–21; Rev 8:8–9; 11:6
4 [h]Rev 8:10; [i]Ex 7:17–21
5 [j]Rev 15:3; [k]**Rev 1:4**; [l]Rev 15:4; [m]Rev 6:10
6 [n]Lk 11:49–51; [o]Isa 49:26; Rev 17:6; 18:24
7 [p]Rev 6:9; 14:18; [q]**Rev 1:8**; [r]Rev 15:3; 19:2
8 [s]Rev 8:12; [t]Rev 6:12; [u]Rev 14:18
9 [v]ver 11,21; [w]**Rev 2:21**; [x]**Rev 11:13**
10 [y]Rev 13:2; [z]Ex 10:21–23; Isa 8:22; Rev 8:12; 9:2
11 [a]ver 9,21; [b]Rev 11:13; [c]ver 2; [d]**Rev 2:21**
12 [e]**Rev 9:14**

b20 That is, about 180 miles (about 300 kilometres)

water was dried up to prepare the way[f]
for the kings from the East.[g] 13Then I
saw three evil[a] spirits[h] that looked like
frogs;[i] they came out of the mouth of the
dragon,[j] out of the mouth of the beast[k]
and out of the mouth of the false
prophet.[l] 14They are spirits of demons[m]
performing miraculous signs,[n] and they
go out to the kings of the whole world,[o]
to gather them for the battle[p] on the
great day[q] of God Almighty.

15"Behold, I come like a thief![r] Blessed
is he who stays awake[s] and keeps his
clothes with him, so that he may not go
naked and be shamefully exposed."[t]

16Then they gathered the kings
together[u] to the place that in Hebrew[v] is
called Armageddon.[w]

17The seventh angel poured out his
bowl into the air,[x] and out of the temple[y]
came a loud voice[z] from the throne,
saying, "It is done!"[a] 18Then there came
flashes of lightning, rumblings, peals of
thunder[b] and a severe earthquake.[c] No
earthquake like it has ever occurred
since man has been on earth,[d] so
tremendous was the quake. 19The great
city[e] split into three parts, and the cities
of the nations collapsed. God remem-
bered[f] Babylon the Great[g] and gave her
the cup filled with the wine of the fury
of his wrath.[h] 20Every island fled away
and the mountains could not be found.[i]
21From the sky huge hailstones[j] of about
a hundred pounds each fell upon men.
And they cursed God[k] on account of the
plague of hail,[l] because the plague was
so terrible.

The Woman on the Beast

17 One of the seven angels[a] who
had the seven bowls[b] came and
said to me, "Come, I will show you the
punishment[c] of the great prostitute,[d]
who sits on many waters.[e] 2With her the
kings of the earth committed adultery
and the inhabitants of the earth were
intoxicated with the wine of her
adulteries."[f]

3Then the angel carried me away in
the Spirit[g] into a desert.[h] There I saw a
woman sitting on a scarlet[i] beast that
was covered with blasphemous names[j]
and had seven heads and ten horns.[k]
4The woman was dressed in purple and
scarlet, and was glittering with gold,
precious stones and pearls.[l] She held a
golden cup[m] in her hand, filled with
abominable things and the filth of her
adulteries.[n] 5This title was written on
her forehead:

MYSTERY[o]
BABYLON THE GREAT[p]
THE MOTHER OF PROSTITUTES[q]
AND OF THE ABOMINATIONS
OF THE EARTH.

6I saw that the woman was drunk with
the blood of the saints,[r] the blood of
those who bore testimony to Jesus.

When I saw her, I was greatly aston-
ished. 7Then the angel said to me: "Why
are you astonished? I will explain to you
the mystery[s] of the woman and of the
beast she rides, which has the seven
heads and ten horns.[t] 8The beast, which
you saw, once was, now is not, and will
come up out of the Abyss[u] and go to his
destruction.[v] The inhabitants of the
earth[w] whose names have not been
written in the book of life[x] from the
creation of the world will be astonished[y]
when they see the beast, because he
once was, now is not, and yet will come.

9"This calls for a mind with wisdom.[z]
The seven heads[a] are seven hills on
which the woman sits. 10They are also
seven kings. Five have fallen, one is, the
other has not yet come; but when he
does come, he must remain for a little
while. 11The beast who once was, and
now is not,[b] is an eighth king. He be-
longs to the seven and is going to his
destruction.

12"The ten horns[c] you saw are ten
kings who have not yet received a king-
dom, but who for one hour[d] will receive
authority as kings along with the beast.
13They have one purpose and will give
their power and authority to the beast.[e]
14They will make war[f] against the Lamb,
but the Lamb will overcome[g] them be-
cause he is Lord of lords and King of
kings[h]—and with him will be his called,
chosen[i] and faithful followers."

15Then the angel said to me, "The
waters[j] you saw, where the prostitute
sits, are peoples, multitudes, nations
and languages.[k] 16The beast and the ten
horns[l] you saw will hate the prostitute.[m]
They will bring her to ruin[n] and leave
her naked;[o] they will eat her flesh[p] and
burn her with fire.[q] 17For God has put it
into their hearts[r] to accomplish his pur-
pose by agreeing to give the beast their
power to rule,[s] until God's words are
fulfilled.[t] 18The woman you saw is the

12 [f]Isa 11:15-16; [g]Isa 41:2; 46:11
13 [h]Rev 18:2; [i]Ex 8:6; [j]**Rev 12:3;** [k]**Rev 13:1;** [l]Rev 19:20; 20:10
14 [m]1Ti 4:1; [n]**Mt 24:24;** [o]**Mt 24:14;** [p]Rev 17:14; 19:19; 20:8; [q]**Rev 6:17**
15 [r]**Lk 12:39;** [s]Lk 12:37; [t]Rev 3:18
16 [u]ver 14; [v]Rev 9:11; [w]Jdg 5:19; 2Ki 23:29-30; Zec 12:11
17 [x]Eph 2:2; [y]Rev 14:15; [z]Rev 11:15; [a]Rev 21:6
18 [b]**Rev 4:5;** [c]**Rev 6:12;** [d]Da 12:1; Mt 24:21
19 [e]**Rev 17:18;** [f]Rev 18:5; [g]**Rev 14:8;** [h]Rev 14:10
20 [i]**Rev 6:14**
21 [j]Eze 13:13; 38:22; Rev 8:7; 11:19; [k]ver 9, 11; [l]Ex 9:23-25

Ch. 17

1 [a]**Rev 15:1;** [b]Rev 15:7; [c]Rev 16:19; [d]ver 5,15-16; Isa 23:17; Rev 19:2; [e]Jer 51:13
2 [f]**Rev 14:8**
3 [g]**Rev 1:10;** [h]Rev 12:6,14; [i]Rev 18:12,16; [j]Rev 13:1; [k]**Rev 12:3**
4 [l]Eze 28:13; Rev 18:16; [m]Jer 51:7; Rev 18:6; [n]ver 2; **Rev 14:8**
5 [o]ver 7; [p]**Rev 14:8;** [q]ver 1-2
6 [r]Rev 16:6; 18:24
7 [s]ver 5; [t]ver 3; **Rev 12:3**
8 [u]**Lk 8:31;** [v]Rev 13:10; [w]**Rev 3:10;** [x]**Rev 20:12;** [y]Rev 13:3
9 [z]Rev 13:18; [a]ver 3
11 [b]ver 8
12 [c]**Rev 12:3;** [d]Rev 18:10, 17,19
13 [e]ver 17
14 [f]**Rev 16:14;** [g]**Jn 16:33;** [h]**1Ti 6:15;** [i]Mt 22:14
15 [j]ver 1; Isa 8:7; Jer 47:2; [k]**Rev 13:7**
16 [l]**Rev 12:3;** [m]ver 1; [n]Rev 18:17,19; [o]Eze 16:37,39; [p]Rev 19:18; [q]Rev 18:8
17 [r]2Co 8:16; [s]ver 13; [t]Jer 39:16; Rev 10:7

[a]13 Greek *unclean*

great city[u] that rules over the kings of
the earth."

The Fall of Babylon

18 After this I saw another angel[a]
coming down from heaven.[b] He
had great authority, and the earth was
illuminated by his splendour.[c] 2With a
mighty voice he shouted:

"Fallen! Fallen is Babylon the Great![d]
She has become a home for demons
and a haunt for every evil[a] spirit,[e]
a haunt for every unclean and
detestable bird.[f]
3For all the nations have drunk
the maddening wine of her
adulteries.[g]
The kings of the earth committed
adultery with her,[h]
and the merchants of the earth grew
rich[i] from her excessive
luxuries."[j]

4Then I heard another voice from
heaven say:

"Come out of her, my people,[k]
so that you will not share in her sins,
so that you will not receive any of
her plagues;[l]
5for her sins are piled up to heaven,[m]
and God has remembered[n] her
crimes.
6Give back to her as she has given;
pay her back[o] double[p] for what she
has done.
Mix her a double portion from her
own cup.[q]
7Give her as much torture and grief
as the glory and luxury she gave
herself.[r]
In her heart she boasts,
'I sit as queen; I am not a widow,
and I will never mourn.'[s]
8Therefore in one day[t] her plagues will
overtake her:
death, mourning and famine.
She will be consumed by fire,[u]
for mighty is the Lord God who
judges her.

9"When the kings of the earth who
committed adultery with her[v] and
shared her luxury[w] see the smoke of her
burning,[x] they will weep and mourn
over her.[y] 10Terrified at her torment,
they will stand far off[z] and cry:

"'Woe! Woe, O great city,[a]
O Babylon, city of power!
In one hour[b] your doom has come!'

11"The merchants[c] of the earth will
weep and mourn[d] over her because no-
one buys their cargoes any more[e]—
12cargoes of gold, silver, precious stones
and pearls; fine linen, purple, silk and
scarlet cloth; every sort of citron wood,
and articles of every kind made of ivory,
costly wood, bronze, iron and marble;[f]
13cargoes of cinnamon and spice, of in-
cense, myrrh and frankincense, of wine
and olive oil, of fine flour and wheat;
cattle and sheep; horses and carriages;
and bodies and souls of men.[g]

14"They will say, 'The fruit you
longed for is gone from you. All your
riches and splendour have vanished,
never to be recovered.' 15The merchants
who sold these things and gained their
wealth from her[h] will stand far off,[i] ter-
rified at her torment. They will weep
and mourn[j] 16and cry out:

"'Woe! Woe, O great city,[k]
dressed in fine linen, purple and
scarlet,
and glittering with gold, precious
stones and pearls![l]
17In one hour[m] such great wealth has
been brought to ruin!'[n]

"Every sea captain, and all who travel
by ship, the sailors, and all who earn
their living from the sea,[o] will stand far
off.[p] 18When they see the smoke of her
burning,[q] they will exclaim, 'Was there
ever a city like this great city[r]?'[s] 19They
will throw dust on their heads,[t] and
with weeping and mourning[u] cry out:

"'Woe! Woe, O great city,[v]
where all who had ships on the sea
became rich through her wealth!
In one hour she has been brought to
ruin![w]
20Rejoice over her, O heaven![x]
Rejoice, saints and apostles and
prophets!
God has judged her for the way she
treated you.'"[y]

21Then a mighty angel[z] picked up a
boulder the size of a large millstone and
threw it into the sea,[a] and said:

"With such violence
the great city[b] of Babylon will be
thrown down,
never to be found again.

18 [u]Rev 16:19; 18:10,18–19, 21

Ch. 18

1 [a]Rev 17:1; [b]Rev 10:1; 20:1; [c]Eze 43:2
2 [d]**Rev 14:8;** [e]Rev 16:13; [f]Isa 13:21–22; 34:11,13–15; Jer 50:39; 51:37; Zep 2:14–15
3 [g]**Rev 14:8;** [h]Rev 17:2; [i]ver 11,15,23; Eze 27:9–25; [j]ver 7,9
4 [k]Isa 48:20; Jer 50:8; 51:6,9, 45; 2Co 6:17; [l]Ge 19:15
5 [m]2Ch 28:9; Ezr 9:6; [n]Jer 51:9; Rev 16:19
6 [o]Ps 137:8; Jer 50:15,29; [p]Isa 40:2; [q]Rev 14:10; 16:19; 17:4
7 [r]Eze 28:2–8; [s]Ps 10:6; Isa 47:7–8; Zep 2:15
8 [t]ver 10; Isa 9:14; 47:9; Jer 50:31–32; [u]Rev 17:16
9 [v]ver 3; Rev 14:8; 17:2,4; [w]ver 3,7; [x]ver 18; Rev 14:11; 19:3; [y]Jer 51:8; Eze 26:17–18
10 [z]ver 15,17; [a]ver 16,19; [b]ver 17; Rev 17:12
11 [c]Eze 27:27; [d]ver 15,19; Eze 27:31; [e]**ver 3**
12 [f]Eze 27:12–22; Rev 17:4
13 [g]Eze 27:13; 1Ti 1:10
15 [h]**ver 3;** [i]ver 10,17; [j]ver 11,19; Eze 27:31
16 [k]ver 10,19; [l]Rev 17:4
17 [m]ver 10; Rev 17:12; [n]Rev 17:16; [o]Eze 27:28–30; [p]ver 10,15
18 [q]ver 9; Rev 19:3; [r]**Rev 17:18;** [s]Eze 27:32; Rev 13:4
19 [t]Jos 7:6; La 2:10; Eze 27:30; [u]ver 11,15; Eze 27:31; [v]ver 10,16; Rev 17:18; [w]Rev 17:16
20 [x]Jer 51:48; **Rev 12:12;** [y]Rev 19:2
21 [z]Rev 5:2; 10:1; [a]Jer 51:63; [b]**Rev 17:18**

a2 Greek *unclean*

22The music of harpists and musicians,
flute players and trumpeters,
will never be heard in you again.[c]
No workman of any trade
will ever be found in you again.
The sound of a millstone
will never be heard in you again.[d]
23The light of a lamp
will never shine in you again.
The voice of bridegroom and bride
will never be heard in you again.[e]
Your merchants were the world's
great men.[f]
By your magic spell[g] all the nations
were led astray.
24In her was found the blood of
prophets and of the saints,[h]
and of all who have been killed on
the earth."[i]

Hallelujah!

19 After this I heard what sounded
like the roar of a great multi-
tude[a] in heaven shouting:

"Hallelujah![b]
Salvation[c] and glory and power[d]
belong to our God,
2 for true and just are his judgments.[e]
He has condemned the great
prostitute[f]
who corrupted the earth by her
adulteries.
He has avenged on her the blood of his
servants."[g]

3And again they shouted:

"Hallelujah![h]
The smoke from her goes up for ever
and ever."[i]

4The twenty-four elders[j] and the four
living creatures[k] fell down[l] and wor-
shipped God, who was seated on the
throne. And they cried:

"Amen, Hallelujah!"[m]

5Then a voice came from the throne,
saying:

"Praise our God,
all you his servants,[n]
you who fear him,
both small and great!"[o]

6Then I heard what sounded like a
great multitude,[p] like the roar of rushing
waters[q] and like loud peals of thunder,
shouting:

"Hallelujah![r]
For our Lord God Almighty[s] reigns.[t]
7Let us rejoice and be glad
and give him glory![u]
For the wedding of the Lamb[v] has
come,
and his bride[w] has made herself
ready.
8Fine linen,[x] bright and clean,
was given her to wear."
(Fine linen stands for the righteous acts[y]
of the saints.)

9Then the angel said to me,[z] "Write:[a]
'Blessed are those who are invited to the
wedding supper of the Lamb!'"[b] And
he added, "These are the true words of
God."[c]

10At this I fell at his feet to worship
him.[d] But he said to me, "Do not do it! I
am a fellow-servant with you and with
your brothers who hold to the testi-
mony of Jesus. Worship God![e] For the
testimony of Jesus[f] is the spirit of
prophecy."

The Rider on the White Horse

11I saw heaven standing open[g] and
there before me was a white horse,
whose rider[h] is called Faithful and True.[i]
With justice he judges and makes war.[j]
12His eyes are like blazing fire,[k] and on
his head are many crowns.[l] He has a
name written on him[m] that no-one
knows but he himself.[n] 13He is dressed
in a robe dipped in blood,[o] and his name
is the Word of God.[p] 14The armies of
heaven were following him, riding on
white horses and dressed in fine linen,[q]
white[r] and clean. 15Out of his mouth
comes a sharp sword[s] with which to
strike down[t] the nations. "He will rule
them with an iron sceptre."[a][u] He treads
the winepress[v] of the fury of the wrath
of God Almighty. 16On his robe and on
his thigh he has this name written:[w]

KING OF KINGS AND LORD OF LORDS.[x]

17And I saw an angel standing in the
sun, who cried in a loud voice to all the
birds[y] flying in mid-air,[z] "Come,[a] gather
together for the great supper of God,[b]
18so that you may eat the flesh of kings,
generals, and mighty men, of horses
and their riders, and the flesh of all

22 [c]Isa 24:8; Eze 26:13; [d]Jer 25:10
23 [e]Jer 7:34; 16:9; 25:10; [f]ver 3; Isa 23:8; [g]Na 3:4
24 [h]Rev 16:6; 17:6; [i]Jer 51:49; Mt 23:35

Ch. 19

1 [a]ver 6; Rev 11:15; [b]ver 3–4,6; [c]Rev 7:10; 12:10; [d]Rev 4:11; 7:12
2 [e]Rev 16:7; [f]**Rev 17:1**; [g]**Rev 6:10**
3 [h]ver 1,4,6; [i]Isa 34:10; Rev 14:11
4 [j]**Rev 4:4**; [k]**Rev 4:6**; [l]**Rev 4:10**; [m]ver 1,3,6
5 [n]Ps 134:1; [o]ver 18; Ps 115:13; Rev 11:18; 13:16; 20:12
6 [p]ver 1; Rev 11:15; [q]**Rev 1:15**; [r]ver 1, 3–4; [s]**Rev 1:8**; [t]Rev 11:15
7 [u]**Rev 11:13**; [v]ver 9; Mt 22:2; 25:10; Eph 5:32; [w]Rev 21:2,9; 22:17
8 [x]ver 14; Rev 15:6; [y]Isa 61:10; Eze 44:17; Zec 3:4; Rev 15:4
9 [z]ver 10; [a]Rev 1:19; [b]Lk 14:15; [c]Rev 21:5; 22:6
10 [d]Rev 22:8; [e]Ac 10:25–26; Rev 22:9; [f]**Rev 1:2**
11 [g]**Mt 3:16**; [h]ver 19,21; Rev 6:2; [i]Rev 3:14; [j]Ex 15:3; Ps 96:13; Isa 11:4
12 [k]**Rev 1:14**; [l]Rev 6:2; 12:3; [m]ver 16; [n]**Rev 2:17**
13 [o]Isa 63:2–3; [p]Jn 1:1
14 [q]ver 8; [r]**Rev 3:4**
15 [s]ver 21; **Rev 1:16**; [t]Isa 11:4; 2Th 2:8; [u]Ps 2:9; Rev 2:27; 12:5; [v]**Rev 14:20**
16 [w]ver 12; [x]**1Ti 6:15**
17 [y]ver 21; [z]Rev 8:13; 14:6; [a]Jer 12:9; Eze 39:17; [b]Isa 34:6; Jer 46:10

[a]15 Psalm 2:9

people,[c] free and slave,[d] small and
great."[e]
19Then I saw the beast[f] and the kings
of the earth[g] and their armies gathered
together to make war against the rider
on the horse[h] and his army. 20But the
beast was captured, and with him the
false prophet[i] who had performed the
miraculous signs[j] on his behalf.[k] With
these signs he had deluded[l] those who
had received the mark of the beast[m] and
worshipped his image.[n] The two of
them were thrown alive into the fiery
lake[o] of burning sulphur.[p] 21The rest of
them were killed with the sword[q] that
came out of the mouth of the rider on
the horse,[r] and all the birds[s] gorged
themselves on their flesh.

The Thousand Years

20 And I saw an angel coming
down out of heaven,[a] having
the key[b] to the Abyss[c] and holding in his
hand a great chain. 2He seized the dra-
gon, that ancient serpent, who is the
devil, or Satan,[d] and bound him for a
thousand years.[e] 3He threw him into the
Abyss,[f] and locked and sealed[g] it over
him, to keep him from deceiving the
nations[h] any more until the thousand
years were ended. After that, he must
be set free for a short time.
4I saw thrones[i] on which were seated
those who had been given authority to
judge.[j] And I saw the souls of those who
had been beheaded[k] because of their
testimony for Jesus[l] and because of the
word of God.[m] They had not worship-
ped the beast[n] or his image and had not
received his mark on their foreheads
or their hands.[o] They came to life and
reigned[p] with Christ for a thousand
years. 5(The rest of the dead did not
come to life until the thousand years
were ended.) This is the first resur-
rection.[q] 6Blessed[r] and holy are those
who have part in the first resurrection.
The second death[s] has no power over
them, but they will be priests[t] of God
and of Christ and will reign with him[u]
for a thousand years.

Satan's Doom

7When the thousand years are over,[v]
Satan will be released from his prison
8and will go out to deceive the nations[w]
in the four corners of the earth[x]—Gog
and Magog[y]—to gather them for battle.[z]
In number they are like the sand on the
seashore.[a] 9They marched across the
breadth of the earth and surrounded[b]

18 [c]Eze 39:18–20; [d]Rev 6:15; [e]**ver 5**
19 [f]**Rev 13:1;** [g]Rev 16:14,16; [h]ver 11,21
20 [i]Rev 16:13; [j]**Mt 24:24;** [k]Rev 13:12; [l]Rev 13:14; [m]Rev 13:16; [n]Rev 13:15; [o]Da 7:11; Rev 20:10,14–15; 21:8; [p]**Rev 9:17**
21 [q]ver 15; **Rev 1:16;** [r]ver 11, 19; [s]ver 17

Ch. 20

1 [a]Rev 10:1; 18:1; [b]Rev 1:18; [c]**Lk 8:31**
2 [d]**Mt 4:10;** [e]Isa 24:22; **2Pe 2:4**
3 [f]ver 1; [g]Da 6:17; Mt 27:66; [h]ver 8, 10; Rev 12:9
4 [i]Da 7:9; [j]Mt 19:28; Rev 3:21; [k]Rev 6:9; [l]**Rev 1:2;** [m]**Heb 4:12;** [n]**Rev 13:12;** [o]**Rev 13:16;** [p]ver 6; Rev 22:5
5 [q]ver 6; Lk 14:14; Php 3:11; 1Th 4:16
6 [r]Rev 14:13; [s]**Rev 2:11;** [t]**1Pe 2:5;** [u]ver 4; Rev 22:5
7 [v]ver 2
8 [w]ver 3,10; Rev 12:9; [x]Isa 11:12; Eze 7:2; Rev 7:1; [y]Eze 38:2; 39:1; [z]**Rev 16:14;** [a]Eze 38:9,15; Heb 11:12
9 [b]Eze 38:9,16; [c]Ps 87:2; [d]Eze 38:22; 39:6; **Rev 13:13**
10 [e]ver 3,8; Rev 12:9; 19:20; [f]**Rev 9:17;** [g]Rev 16:13; [h]Rev 16:13; [i]Rev 14:10–11
11 [j]**Rev 4:2;** [k]**Rev 6:14**
12 [l]**Rev 19:5;** [m]Da 7:10; [n]ver 15; Ex 32:32; Dt 29:20; Da 12:1; Mal 3:16; Lk 10:20; Rev 3:5; 21:27; [o]Rev 11:18; [p]Jer 17:10; **Mt 16:27**
13 [q]Rev 1:18; 6:8; [r]Isa 26:19; [s]**Mt 16:27**

the camp of God's people, the city he
loves.[c] But fire came down from
heaven[d] and devoured them. 10And the
devil, who deceived them,[e] was thrown
into the lake of burning sulphur,[f] where
the beast[g] and the false prophet[h] had
been thrown. They will be tormented
day and night for ever and ever.[i]

The Dead Are Judged

11Then I saw a great white throne[j] and
him who was seated on it. Earth and sky
fled from his presence,[k] and there was
no place for them. 12And I saw the dead,
great and small,[l] standing before the
throne, and books were opened.[m]
Another book was opened, which is the
book of life.[n] The dead were judged[o]
according to what they had done[p] as
recorded in the books. 13The sea gave up
the dead that were in it, and death and
Hades[q] gave up the dead[r] that were in
them, and each person was judged
according to what he had done.[s] 14Then
death[t] and Hades[u] were thrown into the
lake of fire.[v] The lake of fire is the second
death.[w] 15If anyone's name was not
found written in the book of life,[x] he
was thrown into the lake of fire.

The New Jerusalem

21 Then I saw a new heaven and a
new earth,[a] for the first heaven
and the first earth had passed away,[b]
and there was no longer any sea. 2I saw
the Holy City,[c] the new Jerusalem, com-
ing down out of heaven from God,[d]
prepared as a bride[e] beautifully dressed
for her husband. 3And I heard a loud
voice from the throne saying, "Now the
dwelling of God is with men, and he
will live with them.[f] They will be his
people, and God himself will be with
them and be their God.[g] 4He will wipe
every tear from their eyes.[h] There will be
no more death[i] or mourning or crying or
pain,[j] for the old order of things has
passed away."[k]
5He who was seated on the throne[l]
said, "I am making everything new!"[m]
Then he said, "Write this down, for
these words are trustworthy and true."[n]

14 [t]1Co 15:26; [u]ver 13; [v]**Rev 19:20;** [w]**Rev 2:11**
15 [x]**ver 12**

Ch. 21

1 [a]**2Pe 3:13;** [b]**Rev 6:14**
2 [c]ver 10; Ne 11:18; Isa 52:1; Rev 11:2; 22:19; [d]ver 10; Heb 11:10; 12:22; Rev 3:12; [e]**Rev 19:7**
3 [f]Ex 25:8; 2Ch 6:18; Eze 48:35; Zec 2:10; [g]**2Co 6:16**
4 [h]**Rev 7:17;** [i]Isa 25:8; 1Co 15:26; Rev 20:14; [j]Isa 35:10; 65:19; [k]**2Co 5:17**
5 [l]Rev 4:9; 20:11; [m]ver 4; [n]Rev 19:9; 22:6

6He said to me: "It is done.[o] I am the
Alpha and the Omega,[p] the Beginning
and the End. To him who is thirsty I will
give to drink without cost[q] from the
spring of the water of life.[r] 7He who
overcomes[s] will inherit all this, and I
will be his God and he will be my son.[t]
8But the cowardly, the unbelieving, the
vile, the murderers, the sexually im-
moral, those who practise magic arts,
the idolaters and all liars[u]—their place
will be in the fiery lake of burning sul-
phur.[v] This is the second death."[w]

9One of the seven angels who had the
seven bowls full of the seven last
plagues[x] came and said to me, "Come, I
will show you the bride,[y] the wife of the
Lamb." 10And he carried me away[z] in
the Spirit[a] to a mountain great and high,
and showed me the Holy City, Jeru-
salem, coming down out of heaven
from God.[b] 11It shone with the glory of
God,[c] and its brilliance was like that of a
very precious jewel, like a jasper,[d] clear
as crystal.[e] 12It had a great, high wall
with twelve gates,[f] and with twelve
angels at the gates. On the gates were
written the names of the twelve tribes of
Israel.[g] 13There were three gates on the
east, three on the north, three on the
south and three on the west. 14The wall
of the city had twelve foundations,[h] and
on them were the names of the twelve
apostles[i] of the Lamb.

15The angel who talked with me had a
measuring rod[j] of gold to measure the
city, its gates[k] and its walls. 16The city
was laid out like a square, as long as it
was wide. He measured the city with
the rod and found it to be 12,000 stadia[a]
in length, and as wide and high as it is
long. 17He measured its wall and it was
144 cubits[b] thick,[c] by man's[l] measure-
ment, which the angel was using. 18The
wall was made of jasper,[m] and the city of
pure gold, as pure as glass.[n] 19The
foundations of the city walls were dec-
orated with every kind of precious
stone.[o] The first foundation was jasper,[p]
the second sapphire, the third chalce-
dony, the fourth emerald, 20the fifth
sardonyx, the sixth carnelian,[q] the
seventh chrysolite, the eighth beryl, the
ninth topaz, the tenth chrysoprase,
the eleventh jacinth, and the twelfth
amethyst.[d] 21The twelve gates[r] were
twelve pearls,[s] each gate made of a
single pearl. The great street of the city
was of pure gold, like transparent
glass.[t]

22I did not see a temple[u] in the city,
because the Lord God Almighty[v] and
the Lamb[w] are its temple. 23The city does
not need the sun or the moon to shine
on it, for the glory of God[x] gives it light,[y]
and the Lamb[z] is its lamp. 24The nations
will walk by its light, and the kings of
the earth will bring their splendour into
it.[a] 25On no day will its gates[b] ever be
shut,[c] for there will be no night there.[d]
26The glory and honour of the nations
will be brought into it.[e] 27Nothing im-
pure will ever enter it, nor will anyone
who does what is shameful or deceitful,[f]
but only those whose names are written
in the Lamb's book of life.[g]

The River of Life

22 Then the angel showed me the
river[a] of the water of life,[b] as
clear as crystal,[c] flowing[d] from the
throne of God and of the Lamb 2down
the middle of the great street of the city.
On each side of the river stood the tree
of life,[e] bearing twelve crops of fruit,
yielding its fruit every month. And the
leaves of the tree are for the healing of
the nations.[f] 3No longer will there be
any curse.[g] The throne of God and of the
Lamb will be in the city, and his ser-
vants will serve him.[h] 4They will see his
face,[i] and his name will be on their
foreheads.[j] 5There will be no more
night.[k] They will not need the light of a
lamp or the light of the sun, for the Lord
God will give them light.[l] And they will
reign for ever and ever.[m]

6The angel said to me,[n] "These words
are trustworthy and true.[o] The Lord, the
God of the spirits of the prophets,[p] sent
his angel[q] to show his servants the
things that must soon take place."

Jesus Is Coming

7"Behold, I am coming soon![r] Blessed[s]
is he who keeps the words of the
prophecy in this book."[t]

8I, John, am the one who heard and
saw these things.[u] And when I had
heard and seen them, I fell down to
worship at the feet[v] of the angel who
had been showing them to me. 9But he

6 [o]Rev 16:17; [p]Rev 1:8; 22:13; [q]Isa 55:1; [r]**Jn 4:10**
7 [s]**Jn 16:33**; [t]ver 3; 2Sa 7:14; 2Co 6:16; **Ro 8:14**
8 [u]ver 27; Ps 5:6; 1Co 6:9; Heb 12:14; Rev 22:15; [v]**Rev 9:17**; [w]**Rev 2:11**
9 [x]**Rev 15:1**, 6–7; [y]**Rev 19:7**
10 [z]Eze 40:2; Rev 17:3; [a]**Rev 1:10**; [b]**ver 2**
11 [c]ver 23; Isa 60:1–2; Eze 43:2; Rev 15:8; 22:5; [d]ver 18–19; Rev 4:3; [e]Rev 4:6
12 [f]ver 15,21,25; Rev 22:14; [g]Eze 48:30–34
14 [h]**Eph 2:20**; Heb 11:10; [i]Ac 1:26; Eph 2:20
15 [j]Eze 40:3; Rev 11:1; [k]**ver 12**
17 [l]Rev 13:18
18 [m]**ver 11**; [n]ver 21
19 [o]Ex 28:17–20; Isa 54:11–12; Eze 28:13; [p]**ver 11**
20 [q]Rev 4:3
21 [r]**ver 12**; [s]Isa 54:12; [t]ver 18
22 [u]Jn 4:21,23; [v]**Rev 1:8**; [w]**Rev 5:6**
23 [x]**ver 11**; [y]Isa 24:23; 60:19–20; Rev 22:5; [z]**Rev 5:6**
24 [a]ver 26; Isa 60:3,5
25 [b]**ver 12**; [c]Isa 60:11; [d]Zec 14:7; Rev 22:5
26 [e]ver 24
27 [f]Isa 52:1; Joel 3:17; Rev 22:14–15; [g]**Rev 20:12**

Ch. 22

1 [a]Ps 36:8; 46:4 [b]ver 17; **Jn 4:10**; [c]Rev 4:6; [d]Eze 47:1; Zec 14:8
2 [e]**Rev 2:7**; [f]Eze 47:12
3 [g]Zec 14:11; [h]Rev 7:15
4 [i]**Mt 5:8**; [j]**Rev 7:3**
5 [k]Rev 21:25; Zec 14:7; [l]Isa 60:19–20; Rev 21:23; [m]Da 7:27; Rev 20:4
6 [n]Rev 1:1; [o]Rev 21:5; [p]1Co 14:32; Heb 12:9; [q]ver 16; Rev 1:1
7 [r]ver 12,20; **Mt 16:27**; [s]Rev 1:3; 16:15; [t]ver 10,18–19
8 [u]**Rev 1:1**; [v]Rev 19:10

[a]*16* That is, about 1,400 miles (about 2,200 kilometres)
[b]*17* That is, about 200 feet (about 65 metres)
[c]*17* Or *high*
[d]*20* The precise identification of some of these precious stones is uncertain.

said to me, "Do not do it! I am a fellow-
servant with you and with your
brothers the prophets and of all who
keep the words of this book.[w] Worship
God!"[x]
10 Then he told me, "Do not seal up[y]
the words of the prophecy of this book,[z]
because the time is near.[a] 11 Let him who
does wrong continue to do wrong; let
him who is vile continue to be vile; let
him who does right continue to do right;
and let him who is holy continue to be
holy."[b]

12 "Behold, I am coming soon![c] My
reward is with me,[d] and I will give to
everyone according to what he has
done.[e] 13 I am the Alpha and the Omega,[f]
the First and the Last,[g] the Beginning
and the End.[h]
14 "Blessed are those who wash their
robes,[i] that they may have the right to
the tree of life[j] and may go through the
gates[k] into the city.[l] 15 Outside[m] are the
dogs,[n] those who practise magic arts,
the sexually immoral, the murderers,
the idolaters and everyone who loves
and practises falsehood.
16 "I, Jesus,[o] have sent my angel[p]
to give you[a] this testimony for the
churches.[q] I am the Root[r] and the
Offspring of David,[s] and the bright
Morning Star."[t]

17 The Spirit[u] and the bride[v] say,
"Come!" And let him who hears say,
"Come!" Whoever is thirsty, let him
come; and whoever wishes, let him take
the free gift of the water of life.[w]

18 I warn everyone who hears the
words of the prophecy of this book:[x] If
anyone adds anything to them,[y] God
will add to him the plagues described in
this book.[z] 19 And if anyone takes words
away[a] from this book of prophecy,[b] God
will take away from him his share in the
tree of life[c] and in the holy city, which
are described in this book.
20 He who testifies to these things[d]
says, "Yes, I am coming soon."[e]
Amen. Come, Lord Jesus.[f]
21 The grace of the Lord Jesus be with
God's people.[g] Amen.

9 [w]ver 10, 18–19; [x]Rev 19:10
10 [y]Da 8:26; Rev 10:4; [z]ver 7, 18–19; [a]**Ro 13:11**
11 [b]Eze 3:27; Da 12:10
12 [c]ver 7,20; **Mt 16:27**; [d]Isa 40:10; 62:11; [e]**Mt 16:27**
13 [f]Rev 1:8; [g]**Rev 1:17**; [h]Rev 21:6
14 [i]Rev 7:14 [j]**Rev 2:7**; [k]**Rev 21:12**; [l]**Rev 21:27**
15 [m]Dt 23:18; 1Co 6:9–10; Gal 5:19–21; Col 3:5–6; Rev 21:8; [n]Php 3:2
16 [o]Rev 1:1; [p]ver 6; [q]Rev 1:4; [r]**Rev 5:5**; [s]**Mt 1:1**; [t]2Pe 1:19; Rev 2:28
17 [u]Rev 2:7; 14:13; [v]**Rev 19:7**; [w]**Jn 4:10**
18 [x]ver 7,10,19; [y]Dt 4:2; 12:32; Pr 30:6; [z]Rev 15:6–16:21
19 [a]Dt 4:2; 12:32; Pr 30:6; [b]ver 7, 10,18; [c]**Rev 2:7**
20 [d]Rev 1:2; [e]ver 7,12; **Mt 16:27**; [f]1Co 16:22
21 [g]**Ro 16:20**

[a]*16* The Greek is plural.

Table of Weights and Measures

BIBLICAL UNIT		APPROXIMATE IMPERIAL EQUIVALENT	APPROXIMATE METRIC EQUIVALENT
		WEIGHTS	
talent	*(60 minas)*	75 pounds	34 kilograms
mina	*(50 shekels)*	1¼ pounds	0.6 kilogram
shekel	*(2 bekas)*	⅖ ounce	11.5 grams
pim	*(⅔ shekel)*	¼ ounce	7.7 grams
beka	*(10 gerahs)*	⅕ ounce	5.8 grams
gerah		1/50 ounce	0.6 gram
		LENGTH	
cubit		18 inches	0.5 metre
span		9 inches	23 centimetres
handbreadth		3 inches	8 centimetres
		CAPACITY	
		Dry Measure	
cor [homer]	*(10 ephahs)*	6 bushels	220 litres
lethek	*(5 ephahs)*	3 bushels	110 litres
ephah	*(10 omers)*	⅗ bushel	22 litres
seah	*(⅓ ephah)*	13 pints	7.3 litres
omer	*(1/10 ephah)*	4 pints	2 litres
cab	*(1/18 ephah)*	2 pints	1 litre
		Liquid Measure	
bath	*(1 ephah)*	5 gallons	22 litres
hin	*(⅙ bath)*	7 pints	4 litres
log	*(1/72 bath)*	½ pint	0.3 litre

The figures of the table are calculated on the basis of a shekel equalling 11.5 grams, a cubit equalling 18 inches and an ephah equalling 22 litres. It is based upon the best available information, but it is not intended to be mathematically precise; like the measurement equivalents in the footnotes, it merely gives approximate amounts and distances. Weights and measures differed somewhat at various times and places in the ancient world. There is uncertainty particularly about the ephah and the bath; further discoveries may give more light on these units of capacity.

A Concordance

to the

NEW INTERNATIONAL VERSION

INTRODUCTION

This NIV Concordance is an abridgement of *The NIV Complete Concordance*, taking over 35,000 references from the latter's 250,000. These 35,000 references have been selected as the most helpful for the average Bible reader.

When determining whether or not to include a verse reference, we gave careful consideration to the passage in which the verse is located. We also encourage you to always consider the larger context of the passage, giving special attention to the flow of the thought from beginning to end. Whenever you look up a verse, your goal should be to discover the intended meaning of the verse in context. Do not use this concordance, or any concordance, merely as a *verse-finder*; it should also be used as a *passage-finder*. The contexts surrounding each entry are helpful; but even so, the context excerpts are too brief for study purposes. They serve only to help you locate familiar verses.

In some cases the usual short contextual phrases are ineffective in helping you locate a passage. This is especially true in studying key events in a Bible character's life. Therefore, we have incorporated 260 "block entries" in which we use descriptive phrases that mark the breadth of a passage containing episodes of that person's life. The descriptive phrases replace the brief context surrounding each occurrence of the name.

Often more than one Bible character has the same name. For example, there are more than thirty Zechariahs in the Bible. In these cases we have given the name a block entry, assigning each person a number (1), (2), etc., and have included a descriptive phrase to distinguish each. Less significant names are not included.

In a few instances, where two words with the same spelling have widely-divergent meanings, two entries are made in the concordance, and the words are distinguished by a number in square brackets. For example, BEAR [1] indexes all occurrences of BEAR where it means "carry". The creature, BEAR, is indexed under BEAR [2].

In this concordance there are 1,239 key word entries that have an exhaustive list of every appearance of that word. When this occurs, the word or block entry is marked with an asterisk (*). Note that the asterisk for the entry *LORD has a different significance, explained in a footnote.

Since this concordance can only serve one translation—the New International Version—it is difficult for readers familiar with the Authorised Version to make the transition from its older, more archaic language to that of the NIV. We have tried, therefore, to make this transition a bit easier by including some forty-four prominent Authorised Version words and linking them to NIV words that have taken their place. We wish to thank Dr. Daniel E. Sauerwein of Multnomah School of the Bible for supplying the data for these additional words.

We pray that this concordance will be used by NIV readers to introduce them to the full scope of God's truth in every book of the Bible.

John R. Kohlenberger III
Edward W. Goodrick

AARON

Genealogy of (Ex 6:16-20; Jos 21:4, 10; 1Ch 6:3-15).

Priesthood of (Ex 28:1; Nu 17; Heb 5:1-4; 7), garments (Ex 28; 39), consecration (Ex 29), ordination (Lev 8).

Spokesman for Moses (Ex 4:14-16, 27-31; 7:1-2). Supported Moses' hands in battle (Ex 17:8-13). Built golden calf (Ex 32; Dt 9:20). Talked against Moses (Nu 12). Priesthood opposed (Nu 16); staff budded (Nu 17). Forbidden to enter land (Nu 20:1-12). Death (Nu 20:22-29; 33:38-39).

ABADDON*

Rev 9: 11 whose name in Hebrew is *A*,

ABANDON (ABANDONED)

Dt 4: 31 he will not *a* or destroy you
1Ki 6: 13 and will not *a* my people Israel."
Ne 9: 19 compassion you did not *a* them
9: 31 an end to them or *a* them,
Ps 16: 10 you will not *a* me to the grave,
Ac 2: 27 you will not *a* me to the grave,
1Ti 4: 1 in later times some will *a* the faith

ABANDONED (ABANDON)

Ge 24: 27 who has not *a* his kindness
2Co 4: 9 persecuted, but not *a*; struck down,

ABBA*

Mk 14: 36 "*A*, Father," he said, "everything is
Ro 8: 15 And by him we cry, "*A*, Father."
Gal 4: 6 the Spirit who calls out, "*A*, Father

ABEDNEGO

Deported to Babylon with Daniel (Da 1:1-6). Name changed from Azariah (Da 1:7). Refused defilement by food (Da 1:8-20). Refused idol worship (Da 3:1-12); saved from furnace (Da 3:13-30).

ABEL

Second son of Adam (Ge 4:2). Offered proper sacrifice (Ge 4:4; Heb 11:4). Murdered by Cain (Ge 4:8; Mt 23:35; Lk 11:51; 1Jn 3:12).

ABHOR (ABHORS)

Lev 26: 30 of your idols, and I will *a* you.
Dt 7: 26 Utterly *a* and detest it,
Ps 26: 5 I *a* the assembly of evildoers
119: 163 I hate and *a* falsehood
139: 21 and *a* those who rise up against you
Am 6: 8 "I *a* the pride of Jacob
Ro 2: 22 You who *a* idols, do you rob

ABHORS (ABHOR)

Pr 11: 1 The LORD *a* dishonest scales,

ABIATHAR

High priest in days of Saul and David (1Sa 22; 2Sa 15; 1Ki 1-2; Mk 2:26). Escaped Saul's slaughter of priests (1Sa 22:18-23). Supported David in Absalom's revolt (2Sa 15:24-29). Supported Adonijah (1Ki 1:7-32); deposed by Solomon (1Ki 2:22-35; cf. 1Sa 2:31-35).

ABIDE see REMAIN

ABIGAIL

1. Sister of David (1Ch 2:16-17).
2. Wife of Nabal (1Sa 25:30); pleaded for his life with David (1Sa 25:14-35). Became David's wife after Nabal's death (1Sa 25:36-42); bore him Kileab (2Sa 3:3) also known as Daniel (1Ch 3:1).

ABIHU

Son of Aaron (Ex 6:23; 24:1, 9); killed for offering unauthorised fire (Lev 10; Nu 3:2-4; 1Ch 24:1-2).

ABIJAH

1. Second son of Samuel (1Ch 6:28); a corrupt judge (1Sa 8:1-5).
2. An Aaronic priest (1Ch 24:10; Lk 1:5).
3. Son of Jeroboam I of Israel; died as prophesied by Ahijah (1Ki 14:1-18).
4. Son of Rehoboam; king of Judah who fought Jeroboam I attempting to reunite the kingdom (1Ki 14:31-15:8; 2Ch 12:16-14:1; Mt 1:7).

ABILITY (ABLE)

Ex 35: 34 tribe of Dan, the *a* to teach others.
Dt 8: 18 for it is he who gives you the *a*
Ezr 2: 69 According to their *a* they gave
Mt 25: 15 one talent, each according to his *a*.
Ac 11: 29 disciples, each according to his *a*,
2Co 1: 8 far beyond our *a* to endure,
8: 3 were able, and even beyond their *a*.

ABIMELECH

1. King of Gerar who took Abraham's wife Sarah, believing her to be his sister (Ge 20). Later made a covenant with Abraham (Ge 21:22-33).
2. King of Gerar who took Isaac's wife Rebekah, believing her to be his sister (Ge 26:1-11). Later made a covenant with Isaac (Ge 26:12-31).
3. Son of Gideon (Jdg 8:31). Attempted to make himself king (Jdg 9).

ABISHAG*

Shunammite virgin; attendant of David in his old age (1Ki 1:1-15; 2:17-22).

ABISHAI

Son of Zeruiah, David's sister (1Sa 26:6; 1Ch 2:16). One of David's chief warriors (1Ch 11:15-21): against Edom (1Ch 18:12-13), Ammon (2Sa 10), Absalom (2Sa 18), Sheba (2Sa 20). Wanted to kill Saul (1Sa 26), killed Abner (2Sa 2:18-27; 3:22-39), wanted to kill Shimei (2Sa 16:5-13; 19:16-23).

ABLE (ABILITY ENABLE ENABLED ENABLES ENABLING)

Nu 14: 16 'The LORD was not *a*
1Ch 29: 14 that we should be *a* to give
2Ch 2: 6 who is *a* to build a temple for him,
Eze 7: 19 and gold will not be *a* to save them
Da 3: 17 the God we serve is *a* to save us
4: 37 walk in pride he is *a* to humble.
Mt 9: 28 "Do you believe that I am *a*
Lk 13: 24 will try to enter and will not be *a* to
14: 30 to build and was not *a* to finish.'
21: 15 none of your adversaries will be *a*
21: 36 and that you may be *a* to stand
Ac 5: 39 you will not be *a* to stop these men;
Ro 8: 39 will be *a* to separate us
14: 4 for the Lord is *a* to make him stand
16: 25 to him who is *a* to establish you
2Co 9: 8 God is *a* to make all grace abound
Eph 3: 20 him who is *a* to do immeasurably
6: 13 you may be *a* to stand your ground,
1Ti 3: 2 respectable, hospitable, *a* to teach,
2Ti 1: 12 and am convinced that he is *a*
2: 24 kind to everyone, *a* to teach,
3: 15 which are *a* to make you wise
Heb 2: 18 he is *a* to help those who are being
7: 25 he is *a* to save completely
Jas 3: 2 *a* to keep his whole body in check.
Jude : 24 To him who is *a* to keep you
Rev 5: 5 He is *a* to open the scroll

ABNER

Cousin of Saul and commander of his army (1Sa 14:50; 17:55-57; 26). Made Ish-Bosheth king after Saul (2Sa 2:8-10), but later defected to David (2Sa 3:6-21). Killed Asahel (2Sa 2:18-32), for which he was killed by Joab and Abishai (2Sa 3:22-39).

ABOLISH (ABOLISHED ABOLISHING)

Hos 2: 18 I will *a* from the land,
Mt 5: 17 that I have come to *a* the Law

ABOLISHED (ABOLISH)

Gal 5: 11 the offence of the cross has been *a*.

ABOLISHING* (ABOLISH)

Eph 2: 15 by *a* in his flesh the law

ABOMINATION* (ABOMINATIONS)

Da 11: 31 set up the *a* that causes desolation.
12: 11 *a* that causes desolation is set up,
Mt 24: 15 the holy place 'the *a* that causes
Mk 13: 14 you see 'the *a* that causes

ABOMINATIONS (ABOMINATION)

Da 9: 27 who causes desolation will place *a*

ABOUND (ABOUNDING)

2Co 9: 8 able to make all grace *a* to you,
9: 8 you will *a* in every good work.
Php 1: 9 that your love may *a* more

ABOUNDING (ABOUND)

Ex 34: 6 slow to anger, *a* in love
Nu 14: 18 *a* in love and forgiving sin
Ne 9: 17 slow to anger and *a* in love.
Ps 86: 5 *a* in love to all who call to you.
86: 15 slow to anger, *a* in love
103: 8 slow to anger, *a* in love.
Joel 2: 13 slow to anger and *a* in love,
Jnh 4: 2 slow to anger and *a* in love,

ABRAHAM

Abram, son of Terah (Ge 11:26-27), husband of Sarah (Ge 11:29).

Covenant relation with the LORD (Ge 12:1-3; 13:14-17; 15; 17; 22:15-18; Ex 2:24; Ne 9:8; Ps 105; Mic 7:20; Lk 1:68-75; Ro 4; Heb 6:13-15).

Called from Ur, via Haran, to Canaan (Ge 12:1; Ac 7:2-4; Heb 11:8-10). Moved to Egypt, nearly lost Sarah to Pharaoh (Ge 12:10-20). Divided the land with Lot; settled in Hebron (Ge 13). Saved Lot from four kings (Ge 14:1-16); blessed by Melchizedek (Ge 14:17-20; Heb 7:1-20). Declared righteous by faith (Ge 15:6; Ro 4:3; Gal 3:6-9). Fathered Ishmael by Hagar (Ge 16).

Name changed from Abram (Ge 17:5; Ne 9:7). Circumcised (Ge 17; Ro 4:9-12). Entertained three visitors (Ge 18); promised a son by Sarah (Ge 18:9-15; 17:16). Questioned destruction of Sodom and Gomorrah (Ge 18:16-33). Moved to Gerar; nearly lost Sarah to Abimelech (Ge 20). Fathered Isaac by Sarah (Ge 21:1-7; Ac 7:8; Heb 11:11-12); sent away Hagar and Ishmael (Ge 21:8-21; Gal 4:22-30). Covenant with Abimelech (Ge 21:22-32). Tested by offering Isaac (Ge 22; Heb 11:17-19; Jas 2:21-24). Sarah died; bought field of Ephron for burial (Ge 23). Secured wife for Isaac (Ge 24). Fathered children by Keturah (Ge 25:1-6; 1Ch 1:32-33). Death (Ge 25:7-11).

Called servant of God (Ge 26:24), friend of God (2Ch 20:7; Isa 41:8; Jas 2:23), prophet (Ge 20:7), father of Israel (Ex 3:15; Isa 51:2; Mt 3:9; Jn 8:39-58).

ABRAM see ABRAHAM

ABSALOM

Son of David by Maacah (2Sa 3:3; 1Ch 3:2). Killed Amnon for rape of his sister Tamar; banished by David (2Sa 13). Returned to Jerusalem; received by David (2Sa 14). Rebelled against David; seized kingdom (2Sa 15-17). Killed (2Sa 18).

ABSENT

Col 2: 5 though I am *a* from you in body,

ABSOLUTE*

1Ti 5: 2 women as sisters, with *a* purity.

ABSTAIN (ABSTAINS)

Ex 19: 15 *A* from sexual relations."
Nu 6: 3 he must *a* from wine and other
Ac 15: 20 them to *a* from food polluted
1Pe 2: 11 to *a* from sinful desires,

ABSTAINS* (ABSTAIN)

Ro 14: 6 thanks to God; and he who *a*,

ABUNDANCE (ABUNDANT)
Ge 41: 29 Seven years of great *a* are coming
Job 36: 31 and provides food in *a*.
Ps 66: 12 but you brought us to a place of *a*.
Ecc 5: 12 but the *a* of a rich man
Isa 66: 11 and delight in her overflowing *a*."
Jer 2: 22 and use an *a* of soap,
Mt 13: 12 given more, and he will have an *a*.
25: 29 given more, and he will have an *a*.
Lk 12: 15 consist in the *a* of his possessions."
1Pe 1: 2 Grace and peace be yours in *a*.
2Pe 1: 2 yours in *a* through the knowledge
Jude : 2 peace and love be yours in *a*.

ABUNDANT (ABUNDANCE)
Dt 28: 11 will grant you *a* prosperity—
32: 2 like *a* rain on tender plants.
Job 36: 28 and *a* showers fall on mankind.
Ps 68: 9 You gave *a* showers, O God;
78: 15 gave them water as *a* as the seas;
132: 15 I will bless her with *a* provisions;
145: 7 will celebrate your *a* goodness
Pr 12: 11 works his land will have *a* food,
28: 19 works his land will have *a* food,
Jer 33: 9 and will tremble at the *a* prosperity
Ro 5: 17 who receive God's *a* provision

ABUSIVE
2Ti 3: 2 *a*, disobedient to their parents,

ABYSS*
Lk 8: 31 not to order them to go into the *A*.
Rev 9: 1 the key to the shaft of the *A*.
9: 2 When he opened the *A*, smoke rose
9: 2 darkened by the smoke from the *A*.
9: 11 king over them the angel of the *A*,
11: 7 up from the *A* will attack them,
17: 8 and will come up out of the *A*
20: 1 having the key to the *A*
20: 3 He threw him into the *A*,

ACCEPT (ACCEPTABLE ACCEPTANCE ACCEPTED ACCEPTS)
Ex 23: 8 "Do not *a* a bribe,
Dt 16: 19 Do not *a* a bribe, for a bribe blinds
Job 42: 8 and I will *a* his prayer and not deal
Pr 10: 8 The wise in heart *a* commands,
19: 20 Listen to advice and *a* instruction,
Ro 15: 7 *A* one another, then, just
Jas 1: 21 humbly *a* the word planted in you,

ACCEPTABLE (ACCEPT)
Pr 21: 3 is more *a* to the LORD

ACCEPTANCE* (ACCEPT)
Ro 11: 15 what will their *a* be but life
1Ti 1: 15 saying that deserves full *a*:
4: 9 saying that deserves full *a*

ACCEPTED (ACCEPT)
Ge 4: 7 will you not be *a*? But if you do not
Job 42: 9 and the LORD *a* Job's prayer.
Lk 4: 24 "no prophet is *a* in his home town.
Gal 1: 9 you a gospel other than what you *a*,

ACCEPTS (ACCEPT)
Ps 6: 9 the LORD *a* my prayer.
Jn 13: 20 whoever *a* anyone I send *a* me;
13: 20 whoever *a* me *a* the one who sent

ACCESS
Ro 5: 2 through whom we have gained *a*
Eph 2: 18 For through him we both have *a*

ACCOMPANIED (ACCOMPANY)
1Co 10: 4 from the spiritual rock that *a* them,
Jas 2: 17 if it is not *a* by action, is dead.

ACCOMPANIES (ACCOMPANY)
2Co 9: 13 obedience that *a* your confession

ACCOMPANY (ACCOMPANIED ACCOMPANIES)
Dt 28: 2 *a* you if you obey the LORD your
Mk 16: 17 these signs will *a* those who believe
Heb 6: 9 your case—things that *a* salvation.

ACCOMPLISH
Ecc 2: 2 And what does pleasure *a*?"
Isa 44: 28 and will *a* all that I please;
55: 11 but will *a* what I desire

ACCORD
Nu 24: 13 not do anything of my own *a*,
Jn 10: 18 but I lay it down of my own *a*.
12: 49 For I did not speak of my own *a*,

ACCOUNT (ACCOUNTABLE)
Ge 2: 4 This is the *a* of the heavens
5: 1 This is the written *a* of Adam's line
6: 9 This is the *a* of Noah.
10: 1 This is the *a* of Shem, Ham
11: 10 This is the *a* of Shem.
11: 27 This is the *a* of Terah.
25: 12 This is the *a* of Abraham's son
25: 19 This is the *a* of Abraham's son
36: 1 This is the *a* of Esau (that is, Edom
36: 9 This is the *a* of Esau the father
37: 2 This is the *a* of Jacob.
Mt 12: 36 to give *a* on the day of judgment
Lk 16: 2 Give an *a* of your management,
Ro 14: 12 each of us will give an *a* of himself
Heb 4: 13 of him to whom we must give *a*.

ACCOUNTABLE* (ACCOUNT)
Eze 3: 18 and I will hold you *a* for his blood.
3: 20 and I will hold you *a* for his blood.
33: 6 but I will hold the watchman *a*
33: 8 and I will hold you *a* for his blood.
34: 10 and will hold them *a* for my flock.
Da 6: 2 The satraps were made *a* to them
Jnh 1: 14 Do not hold us *a* for killing
Ro 3: 19 and the whole world held *a* to God.

ACCURATE
Dt 25: 15 You must have *a* and honest
Pr 11: 1 but *a* weights are his delight.

ACCURSED (CURSE)
2Pe 2: 14 experts in greed—an *a* brood!

ACCUSATION (ACCUSE)
1Ti 5: 19 Do not entertain an *a*

ACCUSATIONS (ACCUSE)
2Pe 2: 11 do not bring slanderous *a*

ACCUSE (ACCUSATION ACCUSATIONS ACCUSER ACCUSES ACCUSING)
Pr 3: 30 Do not *a* a man for no reason—
Lk 3: 14 and don't *a* people falsely—

ACCUSER (ACCUSE)
Jn 5: 45 Your *a* is Moses, on whom your
Rev 12: 10 For the *a* of our brothers,

ACCUSES (ACCUSE)
Job 40: 2 Let him who *a* God answer him!"
Rev 12: 10 who *a* them before our God day

ACCUSING (ACCUSE)
Ro 2: 15 and their thoughts now *a*,

ACHAN*
Sin at Jericho caused defeat at Ai; stoned (Jos 7; 22:20; 1Ch 2:7).

ACHE*
Pr 14: 13 Even in laughter the heart may *a*,

ACHIEVE
Isa 55: 11 *a* the purpose for which I sent it.

ACHISH
King of Gath before whom David feigned insanity (1Sa 21:10-15). Later "ally" of David (2Sa 27-29).

ACKNOWLEDGE (ACKNOWLEDGED ACKNOWLEDGES)
Pr 3: 6 in all your ways *a* him,
Jer 3: 13 Only *a* your guilt—
Hos 6: 3 let us press on to *a* him.
Mt 10: 32 *a* him before my Father in heaven.
Lk 12: 8 *a* him before the angels of God.
1Jn 4: 3 spirit that does not *a* Jesus is not

ACKNOWLEDGED (ACKNOWLEDGE)
Lk 7: 29 *a* that God's way was right,

ACKNOWLEDGES* (ACKNOWLEDGE)
Ps 91: 14 for he *a* my name.
Mt 10: 32 "Whoever *a* me before men,
Lk 12: 8 whoever *a* me before men,
1Jn 2: 23 whoever *a* the Son has the Father
4: 2 Every spirit that *a* that Jesus Christ
4: 15 If anyone *a* that Jesus is the Son

ACQUIRES (ACQUIRING)
Pr 18: 15 of the discerning *a* knowledge;

ACQUIRING* (ACQUIRES)
Pr 1: 3 for *a* a disciplined and prudent life,

ACQUIT (ACQUITTING)
Ex 23: 7 to death, for I will not *a* the guilty.

ACQUITTING* (ACQUIT)
Dt 25: 1 *a* the innocent and condemning
Pr 17: 15 *A* the guilty and condemning

ACT (ACTION ACTIONS ACTIVE ACTIVITY ACTS)
Ps 119: 126 It is time for you to *a*, O LORD;

ACTION (ACT)
2Co 9: 2 has stirred most of them to *a*.
Jas 2: 17 if it is not accompanied by *a*,
1Pe 1: 13 minds for *a*; be self-controlled;

ACTIONS (ACT)
Mt 11: 19 wisdom is proved right by her *a*."
Gal 6: 4 Each one should test his own *a*.
Tit 1: 16 but by their *a* they deny him.

ACTIVE* (ACT)
Phm : 6 I pray that you may be *a*
Heb 4: 12 For the word of God is living and *a*

ACTIVITY (ACT)
Ecc 3: 1 a season for every *a* under heaven:
3: 17 for there will be a time for every *a*,

ACTS (ACT)
1Ch 16: 9 tell of all his wonderful *a*.
Ps 71: 16 proclaim your mighty *a*,
71: 24 tell of your righteous *a*
105: 2 tell of all his wonderful *a*.
106: 2 Who can proclaim the mighty *a*
145: 4 they will tell of your mighty *a*.
145: 12 all men may know of your mighty *a*
150: 2 Praise him for his *a* of power;
Isa 64: 6 all our righteous *a* are like filthy
Mt 6: 1 not to do your '*a* of righteousness'

ADAM
1. First man (Ge 1:26-2:25; Ro 5:14; 1Ti 2:13). Sin of (Ge 3; Hos 6:7; Ro 5:12-21). Children of (Ge 4:1-5:5). Death of (Ge 5:5; Ro 5:12-21; 1Co 15:22).
2. City (Jos 3:16).

ADD (ADDED)
Dt 4: 2 Do not *a* to what I command you
12: 32 do not *a* to it or take away from it.
Pr 1: 5 let the wise listen and *a*
9: 9 he will *a* to his learning.
30: 6 Do not *a* to his words,
Mt 6: 27 by worrying can *a* a single hour
Lk 12: 25 by worrying can *a* a single hour
Rev 22: 18 God will *a* to him the plagues

ADDED (ADD)
Ecc 3: 14 nothing can be *a* to it and nothing
Ac 2: 47 Lord *a* to their number daily those
Ro 5: 20 The law was *a* so that the trespass
Gal 3: 19 It was *a* because of transgressions

ADDICTED*
Tit 2: 3 to be slanderers or *a* to much wine,

ADMINISTRATION*
1Co 12: 28 with gifts of *a*, and those speaking
Eph 3: 2 Surely you have heard about the *a*
3: 9 to everyone the *a* of this mystery,

ADMIRABLE*
Php 4: 8 whatever is lovely, whatever is *a*—

ADMIT
Hos 5: 15 until they *a* their guilt.

ADMONISH* (ADMONISHING)
Col 3: 16 and *a* one another with all wisdom,
1Th 5: 12 you in the Lord and who *a* you.

ADMONISHING* (ADMONISH)
Col 1: 28 *a* and teaching everyone

ADONIJAH
1. Son of David by Haggith (2Sa 3:4; 1Ch 3:2). Attempted to be king after David; killed by Solomon's order (1Ki 1-2).
2. Levite; teacher of the Law (2Ch 17:8).

ADOPTED (ADOPTION)
Eph 1: 5 In love he predestined us to be *a*

ADOPTION* (ADOPTED)
Ro 8: 23 as we wait eagerly for our *a* as sons,
9: 4 Theirs is the *a* as sons; theirs

ADORE*
SS 1: 4 How right they are to *a* you!

ADORNMENT* (ADORNS)
1Pe 3: 3 should not come from outward *a*,

ADORNS* (ADORNMENT)
Ps 93: 5 holiness *a* your house
Isa 61: 10 as a bride *a* herself with her jewels.
61: 10 bridegroom *a* his head like a priest,

ADULTERER (ADULTERY)
Lev 20: 10 both the *a* and the adulteress must
Heb 13: 4 for God will judge the *a*

ADULTERERS (ADULTERY)
1Co 6: 9 idolaters nor *a* nor male prostitutes
1Ti 1: 10 for murderers, for *a* and perverts,

ADULTERESS (ADULTERY)
Hos 3: 1 she is loved by another and is an *a*.
Mt 5: 32 causes her to become an *a*.

ADULTERIES (ADULTERY)
Jer 3: 8 sent her away because of all her *a*.

ADULTEROUS (ADULTERY)
Mk 8: 38 in this *a* and sinful generation,
Jas 4: 4 You *a* people, don't you know that

ADULTERY (ADULTERER ADULTERERS ADULTERESS ADULTERIES ADULTEROUS)
Ex 20: 14 "You shall not commit *a*.
Dt 5: 18 "You shall not commit *a*.
Mt 5: 27 that it was said, 'Do not commit *a*.'
5: 28 lustfully has already committed *a*
5: 32 a woman so divorced commits *a*.
15: 19 murder, *a*, sexual immorality, theft
19: 9 marries another woman commits *a*
19: 18 do not commit *a*, do not steal,
Mk 7: 21 theft, murder, *a*, greed, malice,
10: 11 marries another woman commits *a*
10: 12 another man, she commits *a*."
10: 19 do not commit *a*, do not steal,
Lk 16: 18 a divorced woman commits *a*.
16: 18 marries another woman commits *a*
18: 20 'Do not commit *a*, do not murder,
Jn 8: 4 woman was caught in the act of *a*.
Rev 18: 3 of the earth committed *a* with her,

ADULTS*
1Co 14: 20 but in your thinking be *a*.

ADVANCE (ADVANCED)
Ps 18: 29 With your help I can *a*
Php 1: 12 has really served to *a* the gospel.

ADVANCED (ADVANCE)
Job 32: 7 *a* years should teach wisdom.

ADVANTAGE
Ex 22: 22 "Do not take *a* of a widow
Dt 24: 14 Do not take *a* of a hired man who is
Ro 3: 1 What *a*, then, is there
2Co 11: 20 or exploits you or takes *a* of you
1Th 4: 6 should wrong his brother or take *a*

ADVERSITY*
Pr 17: 17 and a brother is born for *a*.
Isa 30: 20 the Lord gives you the bread of *a*

ADVICE (ADVISERS)
1Ki 12: 8 rejected the *a* the elders
12: 14 he followed the *a* of the young men
2Ch 10: 8 rejected the *a* the elders
Pr 12: 5 but the *a* of the wicked is deceitful.
12: 15 but a wise man listens to *a*.
19: 20 Listen to *a* and accept instruction,
20: 18 Make plans by seeking *a*;

ADVISERS (ADVICE)
Pr 11: 14 but many *a* make victory sure.

ADVOCATE*
Job 16: 19 my *a* is on high.

AFFLICTED (AFFLICTION)
Job 2: 7 and *a* Job with painful sores
36: 6 but gives the *a* their rights.
Ps 9: 12 he does not ignore the cry of the *a*.
9: 18 nor the hope of the *a* ever perish.
119: 67 Before I was *a* I went astray,
119: 71 It was good for me to be *a*
119: 75 and in faithfulness you have *a* me.
Isa 49: 13 will have compassion on his *a* ones.
53: 4 smitten by him, and *a*.
53: 7 He was oppressed and *a*,
Na 1: 12 Although I have *a* you, ₍O Judah,₎

AFFLICTION (AFFLICTED AFFLICTIONS)
Dt 16: 3 bread of *a*, because you left Egypt
Ps 107: 41 he lifted the needy out of their *a*
Isa 30: 20 of adversity and the water of *a*,
48: 10 in the furnace of *a*.
La 3: 33 For he does not willingly bring *a*
Ro 12: 12 patient in *a*, faithful in prayer.

AFFLICTIONS (AFFLICTION)
Col 1: 24 lacking in regard to Christ's *a*,

AFRAID (FEAR)
Ge 3: 10 and I was *a* because I was naked;
26: 24 Do not be *a*, for I am with you;
Ex 2: 14 Then Moses was *a* and thought,
3: 6 because he was *a* to look at God.
Dt 1: 21 Do not be *a*; do not be discouraged
1: 29 "Do not be terrified; do not be *a*
20: 1 do not be *a* of them,
20: 3 Do not be faint-hearted or *a*;
2Ki 25: 24 "Do not be *a* of the Babylonian
1Ch 13: 12 David was *a* of God that day
Ps 27: 1 of whom shall I be *a*?
56: 3 When I am *a*, / I will trust in you.
56: 4 in God I trust; I will not be *a*.
Pr 3: 24 lie down, you will not be *a*;
Isa 10: 24 do not be *a* of the Assyrians,
12: 2 I will trust and not be *a*.
44: 8 Do not tremble, do not be *a*.
Jer 1: 8 Do not be *a* of them, for I am
Mt 8: 26 You of little faith, why are you so *a*
10: 28 be *a* of the one who can destroy
10: 31 So don't be *a*; you are worth more
Mk 5: 36 "Don't be *a*; just believe."
Lk 9: 34 and they were *a* as they entered
Jn 14: 27 hearts be troubled and do not be *a*.
Ac 27: 24 beside me and said, 'Do not be *a*,
Ro 11: 20 Do not be arrogant, but be *a*.
Heb 13: 6 Lord is my helper; I will not be *a*.

AGAG (AGAGITE)
King of Amalekites not killed by Saul (1Sa 15).

AGAGITE (AGAG)
Est 8: 3 to the evil plan of Haman the *A*,

AGED (AGES)
Job 12: 12 Is not wisdom found among the *a*?
Pr 17: 6 children are a crown to the *a*,

AGES (AGED)
Ro 16: 25 the mystery hidden for long *a* past,
Eph 2: 7 that in the coming *a* he might show
3: 9 which for *a* past was kept hidden
Col 1: 26 that has been kept hidden for *a*
Rev 15: 3 King of the *a*.

AGONY
Lk 16: 24 because I am in *a* in this fire.'
Rev 16: 10 Men gnawed their tongues in *a*

AGREE (AGREEMENT AGREES)
Mt 18: 19 on earth *a* about anything you ask
Ro 7: 16 want to do, I *a* that the law is good.
Php 4: 2 with Syntyche to *a* with each other

AGREEMENT (AGREE)
2Co 6: 16 What *a* is there between the temple

AGREES* (AGREE)
Ac 7: 42 This *a* with what is written
24: 14 I believe anything that *a*
1Co 4: 17 which *a* with what I teach

AGRIPPA*
Descendant of Herod; king before whom Paul pleaded his case in Caesarea (Ac 25:13-26:32).

AHAB
1. Son of Omri; king of Israel (1Ki 16:28-22:40), husband of Jezebel (1Ki 16:31). Promoted Baal worship (1Ki 16:31-33); opposed by Elijah (1Ki 17:1; 18; 21), a prophet (1Ki 20:35-43), Micaiah (1Ki 22:1-28). Defeated Ben-Hadad (1Ki 20). Killed for failing to kill Ben-Hadad and for murder of Naboth (1Ki 20:35-21:40).
2. A false prophet (Jer 29:21-22).

AHAZ
1. Son of Jotham; king of Judah, (2Ki 16; 2Ch 28). Idolatry of (2Ki 16:3-4, 10-18; 2Ch 28:1-4, 22-25). Defeated by Aram and Israel (2Ki 16:5-6; 2Ch 28:5-15). Sought help from Assyria rather than the LORD (2Ki 16:7-9; 2Ch 28:16-21; Isa 7).
2. Benjamite, descendant of Saul (1Ch 8:35-36).

AHAZIAH
1. Son of Ahab; king of Israel (1Ki 22:51-2Ki 1:18; 2Ch 20:35-37). Made an unsuccessful alliance with Jehoshaphat of Judah (2Ch 20:35-37). Died for seeking Baal rather than the LORD (1Ki 1).
2. Son of Jehoram; king of Judah (2Ki 8:25-29; 9:14-29), also called Jehoahaz (2Ch 21:17-22:9; 25:23). Killed by Jehu while visiting Joram (2Ki 9:14-29; 2Ch 22:1-9).

AHIJAH
1Sa 14: 18 Saul said to *A*, "Bring the ark

1Ki 14: 2 *A* the prophet is there—the one

AHIMELECH

1. Priest who helped David in his flight from Saul (1Sa 21-22).
2. One of David's warriors (1Sa 26:6).

AHITHOPHEL

One of David's counsellors who sided with Absalom (2Sa 15:12, 31-37; 1Ch 27:33-34); committed suicide when his advice was ignored (2Sa 16:15-17:23).

AI

Jos 7: 4 they were routed by the men of *A*,
8: 28 So Joshua burned *A* and made it

AID

Isa 38: 14 troubled; O Lord, come to my *a*!"
Php 4: 16 you sent me *a* again and again

AIM

1Co 7: 34 Her *a* is to be devoted to the Lord
2Co 13: 11 *A* for perfection, listen

AIR

Mt 8: 20 and birds of the *a* have nests,
Lk 9: 58 and birds of the *a* have nests,
1Co 9: 26 not fight like a man beating the *a*.
14: 9 You will just be speaking into the *a*
Eph 2: 2 of the ruler of the kingdom of the *a*,
1Th 4: 17 clouds to meet the Lord in the *a*.

ALABASTER*

Mt 26: 7 came to him with an *a* jar
Mk 14: 3 a woman came with an *a* jar
Lk 7: 37 she brought an *a* jar of perfume,

ALARM (ALARMED)

2Co 7: 11 indignation, what *a*, what longing,

ALARMED (ALARM)

Mk 13: 7 and rumours of wars, do not be *a*.
2Th 2: 2 not to become easily unsettled or *a*

ALERT*

Jos 8: 4 All of you be on the *a*.
Ps 17: 11 with eyes *a*, to throw me
Isa 21: 7 let him be *a*, / fully *a*."
Mk 13: 33 Be *a*! You do not know
Eph 6: 18 be *a* and always keep on praying
1Th 5: 6 but let us be *a* and self-controlled.
1Pe 5: 8 Be self-controlled and *a*.

ALIEN (ALIENATED ALIENS)

Ex 22: 21 "Do not ill-treat an *a*
Lev 24: 22 are to have the same law for the *a*
Ps 146: 9 The LORD watches over the *a*

ALIENATED (ALIEN)

Gal 5: 4 by law have been *a* from Christ;
Col 1: 21 Once you were *a* from God

ALIENS (ALIEN)

Ex 23: 9 know how it feels to be *a*,
1Pe 2: 11 as *a* and strangers in the world,

ALIVE (LIVE)

1Sa 2: 6 LORD brings death and makes *a*;
Lk 24: 23 vision of angels, who said he was *a*.
Ac 1: 3 convincing proofs that he was *a*.
Ro 6: 11 but *a* to God in Christ Jesus.
1Co 15: 22 so in Christ all will be made *a*.
Eph 2: 5 made us *a* with Christ

ALMIGHTY (MIGHT)

Ge 17: 1 "I am God *A*; walk before me
Ex 6: 3 to Isaac and to Jacob as God *A*,
Ru 1: 20 the *A* has made my life very bitter.
Job 11: 7 Can you probe the limits of the *A*?
33: 4 the breath of the *A* gives me life.
Ps 89: 8 O LORD God *A*, who is like you?
91: 1 will rest in the shadow of the *A*.
Isa 6: 3 "Holy, holy, holy is the LORD *A*;
45: 13 says the LORD *A*."
47: 4 the LORD *A* is his name—
48: 2 the LORD *A* is his name:
51: 15 the LORD *A* is his name.
54: 5 the LORD *A* is his name—
Am 5: 14 the LORD God *A* will be with you,
5: 15 the LORD God *A* will have mercy
Rev 4: 8 holy is the Lord God *A*, who was,
19: 6 For our Lord God *A* reigns.

ALMS see GIVING, (acts of) RIGHTEOUSNESS

ALPHA*

Rev 1: 8 "I am the *A* and the Omega,"
21: 6 I am the *A* and the Omega,
22: 13 I am the *A* and the Omega,

ALTAR

Ge 8: 20 Then Noah built an *a* to the LORD
12: 7 So he built an *a* there to the LORD
13: 18 where he built an *a* to the LORD.
22: 9 Abraham built an *a* there
22: 9 his son Isaac and laid him on the *a*;
26: 25 Isaac built an *a* there and called
35: 1 and build an *a* there to God,
Ex 17: 15 Moses built an *a* and called it
27: 1 "Build an *a* of acacia wood,
30: 1 "Make an *a* of acacia wood
37: 25 They made the *a* of incense out
Dt 27: 5 an *a* to the LORD your God, an *a*
Jos 8: 30 on Mount Ebal an *a* to the LORD,
22: 10 built an imposing *a* there
Jdg 6: 24 So Gideon built an *a* to the LORD
21: 4 the next day the people built an *a*
1Sa 7: 17 he built an *a* there to the LORD.
14: 35 Then Saul built an *a* to the LORD;
2Sa 24: 25 David built an *a* to the LORD
1Ki 12: 33 sacrifices on the *a* he had built
13: 2 "O *a*, *a*! This is what the LORD
16: 32 He set up an *a* for Baal
18: 30 and he repaired the *a* of the LORD
2Ki 16: 11 So Uriah the priest built an *a*
1Ch 21: 26 David built an *a* to the LORD
2Ch 4: 1 made a bronze *a* twenty cubits
4: 19 the golden *a*; the tables
15: 8 He repaired the *a* of the LORD
32: 12 'You must worship before one *a*
33: 16 he restored the *a* of the LORD
Ezr 3: 2 to build the *a* of the God of Israel
Isa 6: 6 taken with tongs from the *a*.
Eze 40: 47 the *a* was in front of the temple.
Mt 5: 23 if you are offering your gift at the *a*
Ac 17: 23 found an *a* with this inscription:
Heb 13: 10 We have an *a* from which those
Rev 6: 9 I saw under the *a* the souls

ALTER*

Ps 89: 34 or *a* what my lips have uttered.

ALWAYS

Dt 15: 11 There will *a* be poor people
Ps 16: 8 I have set the LORD *a* before me.
51: 3 and my sin is *a* before me.
Pr 23: 7 who is *a* thinking about the cost.
Mt 26: 11 The poor you will *a* have with you,
28: 20 And surely I will be with you *a*,
Mk 14: 7 The poor you will *a* have with you,
Jn 12: 8 You will *a* have the poor
1Co 13: 7 *a* protects, *a* trusts, *a* hopes, *a*
Php 4: 4 Rejoice in the Lord *a*.
1Pe 3: 15 *A* be prepared to give an answer

AMALEKITES

Ex 17: 8 *A* came and attacked the Israelites
1Sa 15: 2 'I will punish the *A*

AMASA

Nephew of David (1Ch 2:17). Commander of Absalom's forces (2Sa 17:24-27). Returned to David (2Sa 19:13). Killed by Joab (2Sa 20:4-13).

AMASSES*

Pr 28: 8 *a* it for another, who will be kind

AMAZED

Mt 7: 28 the crowds were *a* at his teaching,
Mk 6: 6 And he was *a* at their lack of faith.
10: 24 The disciples were *a* at his words.
Ac 2: 7 Utterly *a*, they asked: "Are not all
13: 12 for he was *a* at the teaching about

AMAZIAH

1. Son of Joash; king of Judah (2Ki 14; 2Ch 25). Defeated Edom (2Ki 14:7; 2Ch 25:5-13); defeated by Israel for worshipping Edom's gods (2Ki 14:8-14; 2Ch 25:14-24).
2. Idolatrous priest who opposed Amos (Am 7:10-17).

AMBASSADOR* (AMBASSADORS)

Eph 6: 20 for which I am an *a* in chains.

AMBASSADORS (AMBASSADOR)

2Co 5: 20 We are therefore Christ's *a*,

AMBITION*

Ro 15: 20 It has always been my *a*
Gal 5: 20 fits of rage, selfish *a*, dissensions,
Php 1: 17 preach Christ out of selfish *a*,
2: 3 Do nothing out of selfish *a*
1Th 4: 11 Make it your *a* to lead a quiet life,
Jas 3: 14 and selfish *a* in your hearts,
3: 16 where you have envy and selfish *a*,

AMENDS

Pr 14: 9 Fools mock at making *a* for sin,

AMNON

Firstborn of David (2Sa 3:2; 1Ch 3:1). Killed by Absalom for raping his sister Tamar (2Sa 13).

AMON

1. Son of Manasseh; king of Judah (2Ki 21:18-26; 1Ch 3:14; 2Ch 33:21-25).
2. Ruler of Samaria under Ahab (1Ki 22:26; 2Ch 18:25).

AMOS

1. Prophet from Tekoa (Am 1:1; 7:10-17).
2. Ancestor of Jesus (Lk 3:25).

ANAK (ANAKITES)

Nu 13: 28 even saw descendants of *A* there.

ANAKITES (ANAK)

Dt 1: 28 We even saw the *A* there.'"
2: 10 and numerous, and as tall as the *A*.
9: 2 "Who can stand up against the *A*?"

ANANIAS

1. Husband of Sapphira; died for lying to God (Ac 5:1-11).
2. Disciple who baptised Saul (Ac 9:10-19).
3. High priest at Paul's arrest (Ac 22:30-24:1).

ANCESTORS (ANCESTRY)

1Ki 19: 4 I am no better than my *a*."

ANCESTRY (ANCESTORS)

Ro 9: 5 from them is traced the human *a*

ANCHOR

Heb 6: 19 We have this hope as an *a*

ANCIENT

Da 7: 9 and the *A* of Days took his seat.
7: 13 He approached the *A* of Days
7: 22 until the *A* of Days came

ANDREW*

Apostle; brother of Simon Peter (Mt 4:18; 10:2; Mk 1:16-18, 29; 3:18; 13:3; Lk 6:14; Jn 1:35-44; 6:8-9; 12:22; Ac 1:13).

ANGEL (ANGELS ARCHANGEL)

Ge 16: 7 The *a* of the LORD found Hagar
22: 11 But the *a* of the LORD called out

- Ex 23: 20 I am sending an *a* ahead of you
- Nu 22: 23 When the donkey saw the *a*
- Jdg 2: 1 The *a* of the LORD went up
- 6: 22 Gideon realised that it was the *a*
- 13: 15 Manoah said to the *a* of the LORD
- 2Sa 24: 16 The *a* of the LORD was then
- 1Ki 19: 7 The *a* of the LORD came back
- 2Ki 19: 35 That night the *a* of the LORD went
- Ps 34: 7 The *a* of the LORD encamps
- Hos 12: 4 He struggled with the *a*
- Mt 2: 13 an *a* of the Lord appeared
- 28: 2 for an *a* of the Lord came
- Lk 1: 26 God sent the *a* Gabriel
- 2: 9 An *a* of the Lord appeared to them,
- 22: 43 An *a* from heaven appeared to him
- Ac 6: 15 his face was like the face of an *a*.
- 12: 7 Suddenly an *a* of the Lord
- 2Co 11: 14 Satan himself masquerades as an *a*
- Gal 1: 8 or an *a* from heaven should preach

ANGELS (ANGEL)

- Ps 91: 11 command his *a* concerning you
- Mt 4: 6 command his *a* concerning you,
- 13: 39 of the age, and the harvesters are *a*.
- 13: 49 The *a* will come and separate
- 18: 10 For I tell you that their *a*
- 25: 41 prepared for the devil and his *a*.
- Lk 4: 10 command his *a* concerning you
- 20: 36 for they are like the *a*.
- 1Co 6: 3 you not know that we will judge *a*?
- 13: 1 in the tongues of men and of *a*,
- Col 2: 18 and the worship of *a* disqualify you
- Heb 1: 4 as much superior to the *a*
- 1: 6 "Let all God's *a* worship him."
- 1: 7 "He makes his *a* winds,
- 1: 14 Are not all *a* ministering spirits
- 2: 7 made him a little lower than the *a*;
- 2: 9 was made a little lower than the *a*,
- 13: 2 some people have entertained *a*
- 1Pe 1: 12 Even *a* long to look
- 2Pe 2: 4 For if God did not spare *a*
- Jude : 6 *a* who did not keep their positions

ANGER (ANGERED ANGRY)

- Ex 15: 7 You unleashed your burning *a*;
- 22: 24 My *a* will be aroused, and I will kill
- 32: 10 alone so that my *a* may burn
- 32: 11 "why should your *a* burn
- 32: 12 Turn from your fierce *a*; relent
- 32: 19 his *a* burned and he threw
- 34: 6 slow to *a*, abounding in love
- Lev 26: 28 then in my *a* I will be hostile
- Nu 14: 18 slow to *a*, abounding in love
- 25: 11 has turned my *a* away
- 32: 10 LORD's *a* was aroused that day
- 32: 13 The LORD's *a* burned
- Dt 9: 19 I feared the *a* and wrath
- 29: 28 In furious *a* and in great wrath
- Jdg 14: 19 Burning with *a*, he went up
- 2Sa 12: 5 David burned with *a*
- 2Ki 22: 13 Great is the LORD's *a* that burns
- Ne 9: 17 slow to *a* and abounding in love.
- Ps 30: 5 For his *a* lasts only a moment,
- 78: 38 Time after time he restrained his *a*
- 86: 15 slow to *a*, abounding in love
- 90: 7 We are consumed by your *a*
- 103: 8 slow to *a*, abounding in love.
- Pr 15: 1 but a harsh word stirs up *a*.
- 29: 11 A fool gives full vent to his *a*,
- 30: 33 so stirring up *a* produces strife."
- Jnh 4: 2 slow to *a* and abounding in love,
- Eph 4: 26 "In your *a* do not sin": Do not let
- Jas 1: 20 for man's *a* does not bring about

ANGERED (ANGER)

- Pr 22: 24 do not associate with one easily *a*,
- 1Co 13: 5 it is not easily *a*, it keeps no record

ANGRY (ANGER)

- Ps 2: 12 Kiss the Son, lest he be *a*
- 95: 10 For forty years I was *a*
- Pr 29: 22 An *a* man stirs up dissension,
- Mt 5: 22 But I tell you that anyone who is *a*
- Jas 1: 19 slow to speak and slow to become *a*

ANGUISH

- Ps 118: 5 In my *a* I cried to the LORD,
- Jer 4: 19 Oh, my *a*, my *a*!
- Zep 1: 15 a day of distress and *a*,
- Lk 21: 25 nations will be in *a* and perplexity
- 22: 24 in *a*, he prayed more earnestly,
- Ro 9: 2 and unceasing *a* in my heart.

ANIMALS

- Ge 1: 24 wild *a*, each according to its kind."
- 7: 16 The *a* going in were male
- Dt 14: 4 These are the *a* you may eat: the ox
- Job 12: 7 ask the *a*, and they will teach you,
- Isa 43: 20 The wild *a* honour me,

ANNOUNCE (ANNOUNCED)

- Mt 6: 2 give to the needy, do not *a* it

ANNOUNCED (ANNOUNCE)

- Isa 48: 5 before they happened I *a* them
- Gal 3: 8 and *a* the gospel in advance

ANNOYANCE*

- Pr 12: 16 A fool shows his *a* at once,

ANNUAL*

- Ex 30: 10 This *a* atonement must be made
- Jdg 21: 19 there is the *a* festival of the LORD
- 1Sa 1: 21 family to offer the *a* sacrifice
- 2: 19 husband to offer the *a* sacrifice.
- 20: 6 an *a* sacrifice is being made there
- 2Ch 8: 13 New Moons and the three *a* feasts
- Heb 10: 3 those sacrifices are an *a* reminder

ANOINT (ANOINTED ANOINTING)

- Ex 30: 26 use it to *a* the Tent of Meeting,
- 30: 30 "*A* Aaron and his sons
- 1Sa 9: 16 *A* him leader over my people Israel
- 15: 1 to *a* you king over his people Israel;
- 2Ki 9: 3 what the LORD says: I *a* you king
- Ps 23: 5 You *a* my head with oil;
- Da 9: 24 prophecy and to *a* the most holy.
- Jas 5: 14 and *a* him with oil in the name

ANOINTED (ANOINT)

- 1Ch 16: 22 "Do not touch my *a* ones;
- Ps 105: 15 "Do not touch my *a* ones;
- Isa 61: 1 because the LORD has *a* me
- Da 9: 26 the *A* One will be cut off
- Lk 4: 18 because he has *a* me
- Ac 10: 38 how God *a* Jesus of Nazareth

ANOINTING (ANOINT)

- Lev 8: 12 some of the *a* oil on Aaron's head
- 1Ch 29: 22 *a* him before the LORD to be ruler
- Ps 45: 7 by *a* you with the oil of joy.
- Heb 1: 9 by *a* you with the oil of joy."
- 1Jn 2: 20 you have an *a* from the Holy One,
- 2: 27 about all things and as that *a* is real,

ANT* (ANTS)

- Pr 6: 6 Go to the *a*, you sluggard;

ANTICHRIST* (ANTICHRISTS)

- 1Jn 2: 18 have heard that the *a* is coming,
- 2: 22 a man is the *a*—he denies
- 4: 3 of the *a*, which you have heard is
- 2Jn : 7 person is the deceiver and the *a*.

ANTICHRISTS* (ANTICHRIST)

- 1Jn 2: 18 even now many *a* have come.

ANTIOCH

- Ac 11: 26 were first called Christians at *A*.

ANTS* (ANT)

- Pr 30: 25 *A* are creatures of little strength,

ANXIETIES* (ANXIOUS)

- Lk 21: 34 drunkenness and the *a* of life,

ANXIETY (ANXIOUS)

- 1Pe 5: 7 Cast all your *a* on him

ANXIOUS (ANXIETIES ANXIETY)

- Pr 12: 25 An *a* heart weighs a man down,
- Php 4: 6 Do not be *a* about anything,

APOLLOS*

Christian from Alexandria, learned in the Scriptures; instructed by Aquila and Priscilla (Ac 18:24-28). Ministered with Paul at Corinth (Ac 19:1; 1Co 1:12; 3; Tit 3:13).

APOLLYON*

- Rev 9: 11 is Abaddon, and in Greek, *A*.

APOSTLE (APOSTLES APOSTLES')

- Ro 11: 13 as I am the *a* to the Gentiles,
- 1Co 9: 1 Am I not an *a*? Have I not seen
- 2Co 12: 12 The things that mark an *a*—signs,
- Gal 2: 8 of Peter as an *a* to the Jews,
- 1Ti 2: 7 was appointed a herald and an *a*—
- 2Ti 1: 11 I was appointed a herald and an *a*
- Heb 3: 1 *a* and high priest whom we confess.

APOSTLES (APOSTLE)

See also Andrew, Bartholomew, James, John, Judas, Matthew, Matthias, Nathanael, Paul, Peter, Philip, Simon, Thaddaeus, Thomas.

- Mk 3: 14 twelve—designating them *a*—
- Lk 11: 49 'I will send them prophets and *a*,
- Ac 1: 26 so he was added to the eleven *a*.
- 2: 43 signs were done by the *a*.
- 1Co 12: 28 God has appointed first of all *a*,
- 15: 9 For I am the least of the *a*
- 2Co 11: 13 masquerading as *a* of Christ.
- Eph 2: 20 built on the foundation of the *a*
- 4: 11 It was he who gave some to be *a*,
- Rev 21: 14 names of the twelve *a* of the Lamb.

APOSTLES' (APOSTLE)

- Ac 5: 2 the rest and put it at the *a* feet.
- 8: 18 at the laying on of the *a* hands,

APPEAL

- Ac 25: 11 I *a* to Caesar!" After Festus had
- Phm : 9 yet I *a* to you on the basis of love.

APPEAR (APPEARANCE APPEARANCES APPEARED APPEARING APPEARS)

- Ge 1: 9 to one place, and let dry ground *a*."
- Lev 16: 2 I *a* in the cloud over the atonement
- Mt 24: 30 of the Son of Man will *a* in the sky,
- Mk 13: 22 false prophets will *a* and perform
- Lk 19: 11 of God was going to *a* at once.
- 2Co 5: 10 we must all *a* before the judgment
- Col 3: 4 also will *a* with him in glory.
- Heb 9: 24 now to *a* for us in God's presence.
- 9: 28 and he will *a* a second time,

APPEARANCE (APPEAR)

- 1Sa 16: 7 Man looks at the outward *a*,
- Isa 52: 14 his *a* was so disfigured beyond that
- 53: 2 in his *a* that we should desire him.
- Gal 2: 6 God does not judge by external *a*—

APPEARANCES* (APPEAR)

- Jn 7: 24 Stop judging by mere *a*,

APPEARED (APPEAR)

- Nu 14: 10 glory of the LORD *a* at the Tent
- Mt 1: 20 an angel of the Lord *a* to him
- Lk 2: 9 An angel of the Lord *a* to them,
- 1Co 15: 5 and that he *a* to Peter,
- Heb 9: 26 now he has *a* once for all at the end

APPEARING (APPEAR)

- 1Ti 6: 14 until the *a* of our Lord Jesus Christ,
- 2Ti 1: 10 through the *a* of our Saviour,
- 4: 8 to all who have longed for his *a*.
- Tit 2: 13 the glorious *a* of our great God

APPEARS (APPEAR)
Mal 3: 2 Who can stand when he *a*?
Col 3: 4 When Christ, who is your life, *a*,
1Pe 5: 4 And when the Chief Shepherd *a*,
1Jn 3: 2 But we know that when he *a*,

APPETITE
Pr 16: 26 The labourer's *a* works for him;
Ecc 6: 7 yet his *a* is never satisfied.
Jer 50: 19 his *a* will be satisfied

APPLES
Pr 25: 11 is like *a* of gold in settings of silver.

APPLY (APPLYING)
Pr 22: 17 *a* your heart to what I teach,
23: 12 *A* your heart to instruction

APPLYING (APPLY)
Pr 2: 2 and *a* your heart to understanding,

APPOINT (APPOINTED)
Ps 61: 7 *a* your love and faithfulness
1Th 5: 9 For God did not *a* us
Tit 1: 5 and *a* elders in every town,

APPOINTED (APPOINT)
Dt 1: 15 *a* them to have authority over you
Pr 8: 23 I was *a* from eternity,
Da 11: 27 an end will still come at the *a* time.
Hab 2: 3 For the revelation awaits an *a* time;
Ro 9: 9 "At the *a* time I will return,

APPROACH (APPROACHING)
Ex 24: 2 but Moses alone is to *a* the LORD;
Eph 3: 12 in him we may *a* God with freedom
Heb 4: 16 Let us then *a* the throne of grace

APPROACHING (APPROACH)
Heb 10: 25 all the more as you see the Day *a*.
1Jn 5: 14 is the confidence we have in *a* God:

APPROPRIATE
1Ti 2: 10 *a* for women who profess

APPROVAL (APPROVE)
Jdg 18: 6 Your journey has the LORD's *a*."
Jn 6: 27 the Father has placed his seal of *a*."
1Co 11: 19 to show which of you have God's *a*
Gal 1: 10 trying to win the *a* of men,

APPROVE (APPROVAL APPROVED APPROVES)
Ro 2: 18 if you know his will and *a*
12: 2 and *a* what God's will is—

APPROVED* (APPROVE)
Ro 14: 18 pleasing to God and *a* by men.
16: 10 Greet Apelles, tested and *a*
2Co 10: 18 who commends himself who is *a*,
1Th 2: 4 as men *a* by God to be entrusted
2Ti 2: 15 to present yourself to God as one *a*,

APPROVES* (APPROVE)
Ro 14: 22 not condemn himself by what he *a*.

APT*
Pr 15: 23 A man finds joy in giving an *a* reply

AQUILA*
Husband of Priscilla; co-worker with Paul, instructor of Apollos (Ac 18; Ro 16:3; 1Co 16:19; 2Ti 4:19).

ARABIA
Gal 1: 17 but I went immediately into *A*
4: 25 Hagar stands for Mount Sinai in *A*

ARARAT
Ge 8: 4 came to rest on the mountains of *A*.

ARAUNAH
2Sa 24: 16 threshing-floor of *A* the Jebusite.

ARBITER* (ARBITRATE)
Lk 12: 14 who appointed me a judge or an *a*

ARBITRATE* (ARBITER)
Job 9: 33 If only there were someone to *a*

ARCHANGEL* (ANGEL)
1Th 4: 16 with the voice of the *a*
Jude : 9 *a* Michael, when he was disputing

ARCHER
Pr 26: 10 Like an *a* who wounds at random

ARCHIPPUS*
Col 4: 17 Tell *A*: "See to it that you complete
Phm : 2 to *A* our fellow soldier

ARCHITECT*
Heb 11: 10 whose *a* and builder is God.

AREOPAGUS*
Ac 17: 19 brought him to a meeting of the *A*,
17: 22 up in the meeting of the *A*
17: 34 of the *A*, also a woman named

ARGUE (ARGUMENT ARGUMENTS)
Job 13: 3 and to *a* my case with God.
13: 8 Will you *a* the case for God?
Pr 25: 9 If you *a* your case with a neighbour,

ARGUMENT (ARGUE)
Heb 6: 16 is said and puts an end to all *a*.

ARGUMENTS (ARGUE)
Isa 41: 21 "Set forth your *a*," says Jacob's
Col 2: 4 you by fine-sounding *a*.
2Ti 2: 23 to do with foolish and stupid *a*,
Tit 3: 9 and *a* and quarrels about the law,

ARK [1]
Ge 6: 14 So make yourself an *a*

ARK [2]
Ex 25: 21 and put in the *a* the Testimony,
Dt 10: 5 put the tablets in the *a* I had made,
1Sa 4: 11 The *a* of God was captured,
7: 2 that the *a* remained at Kiriath
2Sa 6: 17 They brought the *a* of the LORD
1Ki 8: 9 There was nothing in the *a*
1Ch 13: 9 out his hand to steady the *a*,
2Ch 35: 3 "Put the sacred *a* in the temple that
Heb 9: 4 This *a* contained the gold jar
11: 7 in holy fear built an *a*
Rev 11: 19 within his temple was seen the *a*

ARM [1] (ARMS)
Nu 11: 23 "Is the LORD's *a* too short?
Dt 4: 34 hand and an outstretched *a*,
7: 19 mighty hand and outstretched *a*,
Ps 44: 3 it was your right hand, your *a*,
98: 1 his right hand and his holy *a*
Jer 27: 5 outstretched *a* I made the earth

ARM [2] (ARMY)
1Pe 4: 1 *a* yourselves also with the same

ARMAGEDDON*
Rev 16: 16 that in Hebrew is called *A*.

ARMIES (ARMY)
1Sa 17: 26 Philistine that he should defy the *a*
Rev 19: 14 *a* of heaven were following him,

ARMOUR (ARMY)
1Ki 20: 11 on his *a* should not boast like one
Jer 46: 4 put on your *a*!
Ro 13: 12 deeds of darkness and put on the *a*
Eph 6: 11 Put on the full *a* of God
6: 13 Therefore put on the full *a* of God,

ARMS [1] (ARM)
Dt 33: 27 underneath are the everlasting *a*.
Pr 31: 17 her *a* are strong for her tasks.
Pr 31: 20 She opens her *a* to the poor
Isa 40: 11 He gathers the lambs in his *a*
Mk 10: 16 And he took the children in his *a*,
Heb 12: 12 strengthen your feeble *a*

ARMS [2] (ARMY)
Ps 18: 32 It is God who *a* me with strength

ARMY (ARM ARMIES ARMOUR ARMS)
Ps 33: 16 No king is saved by the size of his *a*
Joel 2: 2 a large and mighty *a* comes,
2: 5 like a mighty *a* drawn up for battle.
2: 11 thunders at the head of his *a*;
Rev 19: 19 the rider on the horse and his *a*.

AROMA
Ge 8: 21 The LORD smelled the pleasing *a*
Ex 29: 18 a pleasing *a*, an offering made
Lev 3: 16 made by fire, a pleasing *a*.
2Co 2: 15 For we are to God the *a* of Christ

AROUSE (AROUSED)
Ro 11: 14 I may somehow *a* my own people

AROUSED (AROUSE)
Ps 78: 58 they *a* his jealousy with their idols.

ARRANGED
1Co 12: 18 But in fact God has *a* the parts

ARRAYED*
Ps 110: 3 *A* in holy majesty,
Isa 61: 10 and *a* me in a robe of righteousness

ARREST
Mt 10: 19 But when they *a* you, do not worry

ARROGANCE (ARROGANT)
1Sa 2: 3 or let your mouth speak such *a*,
Pr 8: 13 I hate pride and *a*,
Mk 7: 22 lewdness, envy, slander, *a* and folly
2Co 12: 20 slander, gossip, *a* and disorder.

ARROGANT (ARROGANCE)
Ps 5: 5 The *a* cannot stand
119: 78 May the *a* be put to shame
Pr 17: 7 *A* lips are unsuited to a fool—
21: 24 a man—"Mocker" is his name;
Ro 1: 30 God-haters, insolent, *a*
11: 20 Do not be *a*, but be afraid.
1Ti 6: 17 in this present world not to be *a*

ARROW (ARROWS)
Ps 91: 5 nor the *a* that flies by day,
Pr 25: 18 Like a club or a sword or a sharp *a*

ARROWS (ARROW)
Ps 64: 3 and aim their words like deadly *a*.
64: 7 But God will shoot them with *a*;
127: 4 Like *a* in the hands of a warrior
Pr 26: 18 firebrands or deadly *a*
Eph 6: 16 you can extinguish all the flaming *a*

ARTAXERXES
King of Persia; allowed rebuilding of temple under Ezra (Ezr 4; 7), and of walls of Jerusalem under his cupbearer Nehemiah (Ne 2; 5:14; 13:6).

ARTEMIS
Ac 19: 28 "Great is *A* of the Ephesians!"

ASA
King of Judah (1Ki 15:8-24; 1Ch 3:10; 2Ch 14-16). Godly reformer (2Ch 15); in later years defeated Israel with help of Aram, not the LORD (1Ki 15:16-22; 2Ch 16).

ASAHEL
1. Nephew of David, one of his warriors (2Sa 23:24; 1Ch 2:16; 11:26; 27:7). Killed by Abner (2Sa 2); avenged by Joab (2Sa 3:22-39).
2. Levite; teacher (2Ch 17:8).

ASAPH

1. Recorder to Hezekiah (2Ki 18:18, 37; Isa 36:3, 22).
2. Levitical musician (1Ch 6:39; 15:17-19; 16:4-7, 37). Sons of (1Ch 25; 2Ch 5:12; 20:14; 29:13; 35:15; Ezr 2:41; 3:10; Ne 7:44; 11:17; 12:27-47). Psalms of (2Ch 29:30; Ps 50; 73-83).

ASCEND* (ASCENDED ASCENDING)

Dt 30: 12 "Who will *a* into heaven to get it
Ps 24: 3 Who may *a* the hill of the LORD?
Isa 14: 13 "I will *a* to heaven;
14: 14 I will *a* above the tops of the clouds
Jn 6: 62 of Man *a* to where he was before!
Ac 2: 34 For David did not *a* to heaven,
Ro 10: 6 'Who will *a* into heaven?'" (that is,

ASCENDED (ASCEND)

Ps 68: 18 When you *a* on high,
Eph 4: 8 "When he *a* on high,

ASCENDING (ASCEND)

Ge 28: 12 and the angels of God were *a*
Jn 1: 51 and the angels of God *a*

ASCRIBE*

1Ch 16: 28 *A* to the LORD, O families
16: 28 *a* to the LORD glory and strength,
16: 29 *a* to the LORD the glory due his
Job 36: 3 I will *a* justice to my Maker.
Ps 29: 1 *A* to the LORD, O mighty ones,
29: 1 *a* to the LORD glory and strength.
29: 2 *A* to the LORD the glory due his
96: 7 *A* to the LORD, O families
96: 7 *a* to the LORD glory and strength.
96: 8 *A* to the LORD the glory due his

ASHAMED (SHAME)

Mk 8: 38 If anyone is *a* of me and my words
Lk 9: 26 If anyone is *a* of me and my words,
Ro 1: 16 I am not *a* of the gospel,
2Ti 1: 8 So do not be *a* to testify about our
2: 15 who does not need to be *a*

ASHER

Son of Jacob by Zilpah (Ge 30:13; 35:26; 46:17; Ex 1:4; 1Ch 2:2). Tribe of blessed (Ge 49:20; Dt 33:24-25), numbered (Nu 1:40-41; 26:44-47), allotted land (Jos 10:24-31; Eze 48:2), failed to fully possess (Jdg 1:31-32), failed to support Deborah (Jdg 5:17), supported Gideon (Jdg 6:35; 7:23) and David (1Ch 12:36), 12,000 from (Rev 7:6).

ASHERAH (ASHERAHS)

Ex 34: 13 and cut down their *A* poles.
1Ki 18: 19 the four hundred prophets of *A*,

ASHERAHS* (ASHERAH)

Jdg 3: 7 and served the Baals and the *A*.

ASHES

Job 42: 6 and repent in dust and *a*."
Mt 11: 21 ago in sackcloth and *a*.

ASHTORETHS

Jdg 2: 13 and served Baal and the *A*.
1Sa 7: 4 put away their Baals and *A*,

ASLEEP (SLEEP)

1Co 15: 18 who have fallen *a* in Christ are lost.
1Th 4: 13 be ignorant about those who fall *a*,

ASSEMBLY

Ps 1: 5 nor sinners in the *a* of the righteous
35: 18 I will give you thanks in the great *a*
82: 1 God presides in the great *a*;
149: 1 his praise in the *a* of the saints.

ASSIGNED

1Ki 7: 14 and did all the work *a* to him.
Mk 13: 34 with his *a* task, and tells the one
1Co 3: 5 as the Lord has *a* to each his task.
7: 17 place in life that the Lord *a* to him
2Co 10: 13 to the field God has *a* to us,

ASSOCIATE

Pr 22: 24 do not *a* with one easily angered,
Jn 4: 9 (For Jews do not *a* with Samaritans
Ac 10: 28 law for a Jew to *a* with a Gentile
Ro 12: 16 but be willing to *a* with people
1Co 5: 9 to *a* with sexually immoral people
5: 11 am writing to you that you must not *a*
2Th 3: 14 Do not *a* with him,

ASSURANCE (ASSURED)

Heb 10: 22 with a sincere heart in full *a* of faith

ASSURED (ASSURANCE)

Col 4: 12 the will of God, mature and fully *a*.

ASTRAY

Ps 119: 67 Before I was afflicted I went *a*,
Pr 10: 17 ignores correction leads others *a*.
20: 1 whoever is led *a* by them is not
Isa 53: 6 We all, like sheep, have gone *a*,
Jer 50: 6 their shepherds have led them *a*
Jn 16: 1 you so that you will not go *a*.
1Pe 2: 25 For you were like sheep going *a*,
1Jn 3: 7 do not let anyone lead you *a*.

ASTROLOGERS

Isa 47: 13 Let your *a* come forward,
Da 2: 2 *a* to tell him what he had dreamed.

ATE (EAT)

Ge 3: 6 wisdom, she took some and *a* it.
27: 25 Jacob brought it to him and he *a*;
2Sa 9: 11 Mephibosheth *a* at David's table
Ps 78: 25 Men *a* the bread of angels;
Jer 15: 16 When your words came, I *a* them;
Eze 3: 3 So I *a* it, and it tasted as sweet
Mt 14: 20 They all *a* and were satisfied,
15: 37 They all *a* and were satisfied.
Mk 6: 42 They all *a* and were satisfied,
Lk 9: 17 They all *a* and were satisfied,

ATHALIAH

Granddaughter of Omri; wife of Jehoram and mother of Ahaziah; encouraged their evil ways (2Ki 8:18, 27; 2Ch 22:2). At death of Ahaziah she made herself queen, killing all his sons but Joash (2Ki 11:1-3; 2Ch 22:10-12); killed six years later when Joash was revealed (2Ki 11:4-16; 2Ch 23:1-15).

ATHLETE*

2Ti 2: 5 if anyone competes as an *a*,

ATONE* (ATONEMENT)

Ex 30: 15 to the LORD to *a* for your lives.
2Ch 29: 24 for a sin offering to *a* for all Israel,
Da 9: 24 an end to sin, to *a* for wickedness,

ATONED* (ATONEMENT)

Dt 21: 8 And the bloodshed will be *a* for.
1Sa 3: 14 guilt of Eli's house will never be *a*
Pr 16: 6 faithfulness sin is *a* for;
Isa 6: 7 guilt is taken away and your sin *a*
22: 14 your dying day this sin will not be *a*
27: 9 then, will Jacob's guilt be *a* for,

ATONEMENT (ATONE ATONED)

Ex 25: 17 "Make an *a* cover of pure gold—
30: 10 Once a year Aaron shall make *a*
Lev 17: 11 it is the blood that makes *a*
23: 27 this seventh month is the Day of *A*.
Nu 25: 13 and made *a* for the Israelites."
Ro 3: 25 presented him as a sacrifice of *a*,
Heb 2: 17 that he might make *a* for the sins

ATTACK

Ps 109: 3 they *a* me without cause.

ATTAINED

Php 3: 16 up to what we have already *a*.
Heb 7: 11 If perfection could have been *a*

ATTENTION (ATTENTIVE)

Pr 4: 1 pay *a* and gain understanding.
4: 20 My son, pay *a* to what I say;
5: 1 My son, pay *a* to my wisdom,
7: 24 pay *a* to what I say.
22: 17 Pay *a* and listen to the sayings
Ecc 7: 21 Do not pay *a* to every word people
Isa 42: 20 many things, but have paid no *a*;
Tit 1: 14 and will pay no *a* to Jewish myths
Heb 2: 1 We must pay more careful *a*,

ATTENTIVE (ATTENTION)

Ne 1: 11 let your ear be *a* to the prayer
1Pe 3: 12 and his ears are *a* to their prayer,

ATTITUDE (ATTITUDES)

Eph 4: 23 new in the *a* of your minds;
Php 2: 5 Your *a* should be the same
1Pe 4: 1 yourselves also with the same *a*,

ATTITUDES (ATTITUDE)

Heb 4: 12 it judges the thoughts and *a*

ATTRACTIVE

Tit 2: 10 teaching about God our Saviour *a*.

AUDIENCE

Pr 29: 26 Many seek an *a* with a ruler,

AUTHORITIES (AUTHORITY)

Ro 13: 1 *a* that exist have been established
13: 5 it is necessary to submit to the *a*,
13: 6 for the *a* are God's servants,
Eph 3: 10 and *a* in the heavenly realms,
6: 12 but against the rulers, against the *a*,
Col 1: 16 thrones or powers or rulers or *a*;
2: 15 having disarmed the powers and *a*,
Tit 3: 1 people to be subject to rulers and *a*,
1Pe 3: 22 *a* and powers in submission to him.

AUTHORITY (AUTHORITIES)

Mt 7: 29 because he taught as one who had *a*
9: 6 the Son of Man has *a* on earth
28: 18 "All *a* in heaven and on earth has
Mk 1: 22 he taught them as one who had *a*,
2: 10 the Son of Man has *a* on earth
Lk 4: 32 because his message had *a*.
5: 24 the Son of Man has *a* on earth
Jn 10: 18 *a* to lay it down and *a*
Ac 1: 7 the Father has set by his own *a*.
Ro 7: 1 that the law has *a* over a man only
13: 1 for there is no *a* except that which
13: 2 rebels against the *a* is rebelling
1Co 11: 10 to have a sign of *a* on her head.
15: 24 he has destroyed all dominion, *a*
1Ti 2: 2 for kings and all those in *a*,
2: 12 to teach or to have *a* over a man;
Tit 2: 15 Encourage and rebuke with all *a*.
Heb 13: 17 your leaders and submit to their *a*.

AUTUMN*

Dt 11: 14 both *a* and spring rains,
Ps 84: 6 the *a* rains also cover it with pools.
Jer 5: 24 who gives *a* and spring rains
Joel 2: 23 both *a* and spring rains, as before.
Jas 5: 7 and how patient he is for the *a*
Jude : 12 blown along by the wind; *a* trees,

AVENGE (VENGEANCE)

Lev 26: 25 sword upon you to *a* the breaking
Dt 32: 35 It is mine to *a*; I will repay.
32: 43 for he will *a* the blood
Ro 12: 19 "It is mine to *a*; I will repay,"
Heb 10: 30 "It is mine to *a*; I will repay,"
Rev 6: 10 of the earth and *a* our blood?"

AVENGER (VENGEANCE)

Nu 35: 27 the *a* of blood may kill the accused
Jos 20: 3 find protection from the *a* of blood.
Ps 8: 2 to silence the foe and the *a*.

AVENGES (VENGEANCE)
Ps 94: 1 O LORD, the God who *a*,

AVENGING (VENGEANCE)
1Sa 25: 26 and from *a* yourself with your own
Na 1: 2 The LORD is a jealous and *a* God;

AVOID (AVOIDS)
Pr 4: 15 *A* it, do not travel on it;
20: 3 It is to a man's honour to *a* strife,
20: 19 so *a* a man who talks too much.
Ecc 7: 18 who fears God will *a* all ⌊extremes⌋.
1Th 4: 3 you should *a* sexual immorality;
5: 22 *A* every kind of evil.
2Ti 2: 16 *A* godless chatter, because those
Tit 3: 9 But *a* foolish controversies

AVOIDS* (AVOID)
Pr 16: 6 of the LORD a man *a* evil.
16: 17 The highway of the upright *a* evil;

AWAITS (WAIT)
Pr 15: 10 Stern discipline *a* him who leaves
28: 22 and is unaware that poverty *a* him.

AWAKE (WAKE)
Ps 17: 15 when I *a*, I will be satisfied
Pr 6: 22 when you *a*, they will speak to you.

AWARD*
2Ti 4: 8 will *a* to me on that day—

AWARE
Ex 34: 29 he was not *a* that his face was
Mt 24: 50 and at an hour he is not *a* of.
Lk 12: 46 and at an hour he is not *a* of.

AWE* (AWESOME OVERAWED)
1Sa 12: 18 So all the people stood in *a*
1Ki 3: 28 they held the king in *a*,
Job 25: 2 "Dominion and *a* belong to God;
Ps 119: 120 I stand in *a* of your laws.
Ecc 5: 7 Therefore stand in *a* of God.
Isa 29: 23 will stand in *a* of the God of Israel.
Jer 2: 19 and have no *a* of me,"
33: 9 they will be in *a* and will tremble
Hab 3: 2 I stand in *a* of your deeds,
Mal 2: 5 and stood in *a* of my name.
Mt 9: 8 they were filled with *a*;
Lk 1: 65 The neighbours were all filled with *a*
5: 26 They were filled with *a* and said,
7: 16 They were all filled with *a*
Ac 2: 43 Everyone was filled with *a*,
Heb 12: 28 acceptably with reverence and *a*,

AWESOME* (AWE)
Ge 28: 17 and said, "How *a* is this place!
Ex 15: 11 *a* in glory,
34: 10 among will see how *a* is the work
Dt 4: 34 or by great and *a* deeds,
7: 21 is among you, is a great and *a* God.
10: 17 the great God, mighty and *a*,
10: 21 and *a* wonders you saw
28: 58 revere this glorious and *a* name—
34: 12 performed the *a* deeds that Moses
Jdg 13: 6 like an angel of God, very *a*.
2Sa 7: 23 *a* wonders by driving out nations
1Ch 17: 21 *a* wonders by driving out nations
Ne 1: 5 of heaven, the great and *a* God,
4: 14 and *a*, and fight for your brothers,
9: 32 the great, mighty and *a* God,
Job 10: 16 again display your *a* power
37: 22 God comes in *a* majesty.
Ps 45: 4 let your right hand display *a* deeds.
47: 2 How *a* is the LORD Most High,
65: 5 us with *a* deeds of righteousness,
66: 3 to God, "How *a* are your deeds!
66: 5 how *a* his works on man's behalf!
68: 35 You are *a*, O God,
89: 7 he is more *a* than all who surround
99: 3 praise your great and *a* name—
106: 22 and *a* deeds by the Red Sea.
111: 9 holy and *a* is his name.
145: 6 of the power of your *a* works,
Isa 64: 3 when you did *a* things that we did
Eze 1: 18 Their rims were high and *a*,
1: 22 expanse, sparkling like ice and *a*.
Da 2: 31 dazzling statue, *a* in appearance.
9: 4 "O Lord, the great and *a* God,
Zep 2: 11 The LORD will be *a* to them

AXE
Mt 3: 10 The *a* is already at the root
Lk 3: 9 The *a* is already at the root

BAAL
Jdg 6: 25 Tear down your father's altar to *B*
1Ki 16: 32 *B* in the temple of *B* that he built
18: 25 Elijah said to the prophets of *B*,
19: 18 knees have not bowed down to *B*
2Ki 10: 28 Jehu destroyed *B* worship in Israel.
Jer 19: 5 places of *B* to burn their sons
Ro 11: 4 have not bowed the knee to *B*."

BAASHA
King of Israel (1Ki 15:16-16:7; 2Ch 16:1-6).

BABBLER* (BABBLING)
Ac 17: 18 "What is this *b* trying to say?"

BABBLING* (BABBLER)
Mt 6: 7 do not keep on *b* like pagans,

BABIES* (BABY)
Ge 25: 22 The *b* jostled each other within her
Ex 2: 6 "This is one of the Hebrew *b*,"
Lk 18: 15 also bringing *b* to Jesus
Ac 7: 19 them to throw out their newborn *b*
1Pe 2: 2 Like newborn *b*, crave pure

BABY* (BABIES BABY'S)
Ex 2: 6 She opened it and saw the *b*.
2: 7 women to nurse the *b* for you?"
2: 9 So the woman took the *b*
2: 9 "Take this *b* and nurse him for me,
1Ki 3: 17 I had a *b* while she was there
3: 18 was born, this woman also had a *b*.
3: 26 give her the living *b*! Don't kill him
3: 27 Give the living *b* to the first woman
Isa 49: 15 "Can a mother forget the *b*
Lk 1: 41 the *b* leaped in her womb,
1: 44 the *b* in my womb leaped for joy.
1: 57 time for Elizabeth to have her *b*,
2: 6 the time came for the *b* to be born,
2: 12 You will find a *b* wrapped in cloths
2: 16 the *b*, who was lying in the manger.
Jn 16: 21 but when her *b* is born she forgets

BABY'S* (BABY)
Ex 2: 8 the girl went and got the *b* mother.

BABYLON
Ps 137: 1 By the rivers of *B* we sat and wept
Jer 29: 10 seventy years are completed for *B*,
51: 37 *B* will be a heap of ruins,
Rev 14: 8 "Fallen! Fallen is *B* the Great,
17: 5 MYSTERY *B* THE GREAT

BACKS
2Pe 2: 21 and then to turn their *b*

BACKSLIDING* (BACKSLIDINGS)
Jer 2: 19 your *b* will rebuke you.
3: 22 I will cure you of *b*."
14: 7 For our *b* is great;
15: 6 "You keep on *b*.
Eze 37: 23 them from all their sinful *b*,

BACKSLIDINGS* (BACKSLIDING)
Jer 5: 6 and their *b* many.

BALAAM
Prophet who attempted to curse Israel (Nu 22-24; Dt 23:4-5; 2Pe 2:15; Jude 11). Killed in Israel's vengeance on Midianites (Nu 31:8; Jos 13:22).

BALAK
Moabite king who hired Balaam to curse Israel (Nu 22-24; Jos 24:9).

BALDHEAD
2Ki 2: 23 "Go on up, you *b*!" they said.

BALM
Jer 8: 22 Is there no *b* in Gilead?

BANISH (BANISHED)
Jer 25: 10 I will *b* from them the sounds of joy

BANISHED (BANISH)
Dt 30: 4 Even if you have been *b*

BANNER
Ex 17: 15 and called it The LORD is my *B*.
SS 2: 4 and his *b* over me is love.
Isa 11: 10 the Root of Jesse will stand as a *b*

BANQUET
SS 2: 4 He has taken me to the *b* hall,
Lk 14: 13 when you give a *b*, invite the poor,

BAPTISE* (BAPTISED BAPTISING BAPTISM BAPTISMS)
Mt 3: 11 He will *b* you with the Holy Spirit
3: 11 "I *b* you with water for repentance.
Mk 1: 8 I *b* you with water, but he will
1: 8 he will *b* you with the Holy Spirit."
Lk 3: 16 He will *b* you with the Holy Spirit
3: 16 John answered them all, "I *b* you
Jn 1: 25 "Why then do you *b*
1: 26 nor the Prophet?" "I *b* with water,"
1: 33 and remain is he who will *b*
1: 33 me to *b* with water told me,
1Co 1: 14 I am thankful that I did not *b* any
1: 17 For Christ did not send me to *b*,

BAPTISED* (BAPTISE)
Mt 3: 6 they were *b* by him in the Jordan
3: 13 to the Jordan to be *b* by John.
3: 14 saying, "I need to be *b* by you,
3: 16 as Jesus was *b*, he went up out
Mk 1: 5 they were *b* by him in the Jordan
1: 9 and was *b* by John in the Jordan.
10: 38 or be *b* with the baptism I am
10: 38 with the baptism I am *b* with?"
10: 39 and be *b* with the baptism I am
10: 39 with the baptism I am *b* with,
16: 16 believes and is *b* will be saved,
Lk 3: 7 to the crowds coming out to be *b*
3: 12 Tax collectors also came to be *b*.
3: 21 were being *b*, Jesus was *b* too.
7: 29 because they had been *b* by John.
7: 30 they had not been *b* by John.)
Jn 3: 22 spent some time with them, and *b*.
3: 23 were constantly coming to be *b*.
4: 2 in fact it was not Jesus who *b*,
Ac 1: 5 For John *b* with water,
1: 5 but in a few days you will be *b*
2: 38 Repent and be *b*, every one of you,
2: 41 who accepted his message were *b*,
8: 12 they were *b*, both men and women.
8: 13 Simon himself believed and was *b*.
8: 16 they had simply been *b*
8: 36 Why shouldn't I be *b*?"
8: 38 into the water and Philip *b* him.
9: 18 was *b*, and after taking some food,
10: 47 people from being *b* with water?
10: 48 So he ordered that they be *b*
11: 16 what the Lord had said, 'John *b*
11: 16 you will be *b* with the Holy Spirit.'
16: 15 members of her household were *b*,
16: 33 he and all his family were *b*.
18: 8 heard him believed and were *b*.
19: 5 they were *b* into the name
22: 16 be *b* and wash your sins away,
Ro 6: 3 *b* into Christ Jesus were *b*
1Co 1: 13 Were you *b* into the name of Paul?
1: 15 so no-one can say that you were *b*
1: 16 I also *b* the household of Stephanas

1Co 1:16 I don't remember if I *b* anyone else
10:2 They were all *b* into Moses
12:13 For we were all *b* by one Spirit
15:29 what will those do who are *b*
15:29 why are people *b* for them?
Gal 3:27 all of you who were *b*

BAPTISING* (BAPTISE)
Mt 3:7 coming to where he was *b*,
28:19 *b* them in the name of the Father
Mk 1:4 *b* in the desert region
Jn 1:28 of the Jordan, where John was *b*.
1:31 but the reason I came *b*
3:23 also was *b* at Aenon near Salim,
3:26 he is *b*, and everyone is going
4:1 and *b* more disciples than John,
10:40 to the place where John had been *b*

BAPTISM* (BAPTISE)
Mt 21:25 John's *b*—where did it come from?
Mk 1:4 and preaching a *b* of repentance
10:38 baptised with the *b* I am baptised
10:39 baptised with the *b* I am baptised
11:30 John's *b*—was it from heaven,
Lk 3:3 preaching a *b* of repentance
12:50 But I have a *b* to undergo,
20:4 John's *b*—was it from heaven,
Ac 1:22 beginning from John's *b*
10:37 after the *b* that John preached—
13:24 and *b* to all the people of Israel.
18:25 though he knew only the *b* of John.
19:3 did you receive?" "John's *b*,"
19:3 "Then what *b* did you receive?"
19:4 "John's *b* was a *b* of repentance.
Ro 6:4 with him through *b* into death
Eph 4:5 one Lord, one faith, one *b*;
Col 2:12 having been buried with him in *b*
1Pe 3:21 this water symbolises *b* that now

BAPTISMS* (BAPTISE)
Heb 6:2 instruction about *b*, the laying

BAR-JESUS*
Ac 13:6 and false prophet named *B*,

BARABBAS
Mt 27:26 Then he released *B* to them.

BARAK*
Judge who fought with Deborah against Canaanites (Jdg 4-5; 1Sa 12:11; Heb 11:32).

BARBARIAN*
Col 3:11 circumcised or uncircumcised, *b*,

BARBS*
Nu 33:55 allow to remain will become *b*

BARE
Hos 2:3 as *b* as on the day she was born;
Heb 4:13 and laid *b* before the eyes of him

BARNABAS*
Disciple, originally Joseph (Ac 4:36), prophet (Ac 13:1), apostle (Ac 14:14). Brought Paul to apostles (Ac 9:27), Antioch (Ac 11:22-29; Gal 2:1-13), on the first missionary journey (Ac 13-14). Together at Jerusalem Council, they separated over John Mark (Ac 15). Later co-workers (1Co 9:6; Col 4:10).

BARREN
Ge 11:30 Sarai was *b*; she had no children.
29:31 her womb, but Rachel was *b*.
Ps 113:9 He settles the *b* woman
Isa 54:1 "Sing, O *b* woman,
Lk 1:7 children, because Elizabeth was *b*;
Gal 4:27 "Be glad, O *b* woman,
Heb 11:11 and Sarah herself was *b*—

BARTHOLOMEW*
Apostle (Mt 10:3; Mk 3:18; Lk 6:14; Ac 1:13). Possibly also known as Nathanael (Jn 1:45-49; 21:2).

BARUCH
Jeremiah's secretary (Jer 32:12-16; 36; 43:1-6; 45:1-2).

BARZILLAI
1. Gileadite who aided David during Absalom's revolt (2Sa 17:27; 19:31-39).
2. Son-in-law of 1. (Ezr 2:61; Ne 7:63).

BASHAN
Jos 22:7 Moses had given land in *B*,
Ps 22:12 strong bulls of *B* encircle me.

BASIN
Ex 30:18 "Make a bronze *b*,

BASKET
Ex 2:3 she got a papyrus *b* for him
Ac 9:25 him in a *b* through an opening
2Co 11:33 I was lowered in a *b* from a window

BATCH*
Ro 11:16 then the whole *b* is holy;
1Co 5:6 through the whole *b* of dough?
5:7 old yeast that you may be a new *b*
Gal 5:9 through the whole *b* of dough."

BATH (BATHING)
Jn 13:10 person who has had a *b* needs only

BATHING (BATH)
2Sa 11:2 From the roof he saw a woman *b*.

BATHSHEBA*
Wife of Uriah who committed adultery with and became wife of David (2Sa 11), mother of Solomon (2Sa 12:24; 1Ki 1-2; 1Ch 3:5).

BATTLE (BATTLES)
1Sa 17:47 for the *b* is the LORD's,
2Ch 20:15 For the *b* is not yours, but God's.
Ps 24:8 the LORD mighty in *b*.
Ecc 9:11 or the *b* to the strong,
Isa 31:4 down to do *b* on Mount Zion
Eze 13:5 in the *b* on the day of the LORD.
Rev 16:14 them for the *b* on the great day
20:8 and Magog—to gather them for *b*.

BATTLES* (BATTLE)
1Sa 8:20 to go out before us and fight our *b*."
18:17 and fight the *b* of the LORD."
25:28 because he fights the LORD's *b*.
2Ch 32:8 God to help us and to fight our *b*."

BEAR [1] (BEARING BEARS BIRTH BIRTHRIGHT BORE BORN CHILDBEARING CHILDBIRTH FIRSTBORN NEWBORN REBIRTH)
Ge 4:13 punishment is more than I can *b*.
Ps 38:4 like a burden too heavy to *b*.
Isa 53:11 and he will *b* their iniquities.
Mt 7:18 A good tree cannot *b* bad fruit,
Jn 15:2 branch that does *b* fruit he trims
15:8 glory, that you *b* much fruit,
15:16 but I chose you to go and *b* fruit—
Ro 7:4 in order that we might *b* fruit
15:1 ought to *b* with the failings
1Co 10:13 tempted beyond what you can *b*.
Col 3:13 *B* with each other and forgive

BEAR [2]
Isa 11:7 The cow will feed with the *b*,
Da 7:5 beast, which looked like a *b*.

BEARD
Lev 19:27 or clip off the edges of your *b*.
Isa 50:6 to those who pulled out my *b*;

BEARING (BEAR [1])
Eph 4:2 *b* with one another in love.
Col 1:6 *b* fruit and growing,
1:10 *b* fruit in every good work,
Heb 13:13 outside the camp, *b* the disgrace he

BEARS (BEAR [1])
1Ki 8:43 house I have built *b* your Name.
Ps 68:19 who daily *b* our burdens.

BEAST (BEASTS)
Rev 13:18 him calculate the number of the *b*,
16:2 people who had the mark of the *b*
19:20 who had received the mark of the *b*

BEASTS (BEAST)
Da 7:3 Four great *b*, each different
1Co 15:32 If I fought wild *b* in Ephesus

BEAT (BEATEN BEATING BEATINGS)
Isa 2:4 They will *b* their swords
Joel 3:10 *B* your ploughshares into swords
Mic 4:3 They will *b* their swords
1Co 9:27 I *b* my body and make it my slave

BEATEN (BEAT)
Lk 12:47 do what his master wants will be *b*
12:48 deserving punishment will be *b*
2Co 11:25 Three times I was *b* with rods,

BEATING (BEAT)
1Co 9:26 I do not fight like a man *b* the air.
1Pe 2:20 if you receive a *b* for doing wrong

BEATINGS (BEAT)
Pr 19:29 and *b* for the backs of fools.

BEAUTIFUL* (BEAUTY)
Ge 6:2 that the daughters of men were *b*,
12:11 "I know what a *b* woman you are.
12:14 saw that she was a very *b* woman.
24:16 The girl was very *b*, a virgin;
26:7 of Rebekah, because she is *b*."
29:17 Rachel was lovely in form, and *b*.
49:21 that bears *b* fawns.
Nu 24:5 "How *b* are your tents, O Jacob,
Dt 21:11 among the captives a *b* woman
Jos 7:21 saw in the plunder a *b* robe
1Sa 25:3 was an intelligent and *b* woman,
2Sa 11:2 The woman was very *b*,
13:1 the *b* sister of Absalom son
14:27 and she became a *b* woman.
1Ki 1:3 throughout Israel for a *b* girl
1:4 The girl was very *b*; she took care
Est 2:2 for *b* young virgins for the king.
2:3 realm to bring all these *b* girls
Job 38:31 "Can you bind the *b* Pleiades?
42:15 land were there found women as *b*
Ps 48:2 It is *b* in its loftiness,
Pr 11:22 is a *b* woman who shows no
24:4 filled with rare and *b* treasures.
Ecc 3:11 He has made everything *b*
SS 1:8 If you do not know, most *b*
1:10 Your cheeks are *b* with ear-rings,
1:15 Oh, how *b*!
1:15 How *b* you are, my darling!
2:10 my *b* one, and come with me.
2:13 my *b* one, come with me."
4:1 How *b* you are, my darling!
4:1 Oh, how *b*!
4:7 All *b* you are, my darling;
5:9 most *b* of women?
6:1 most *b* of women?
6:4 You are *b*, my darling,
7:1 How *b* your sandalled feet,
7:6 How *b* you are and how pleasing,
Isa 4:2 of the LORD will be *b*
28:5 a *b* wreath
52:7 How *b* on the mountains
Jer 3:19 the most *b* inheritance
6:2 so *b* and delicate.
11:16 with fruit *b* in form.
46:20 "Egypt is a *b* heifer,

Eze 7: 20 They were proud of their *b* jewellery
16: 7 and became the most *b* of jewels.
16: 12 and a *b* crown on your head.
16: 13 You became very *b* and rose
20: 6 and honey, the most *b* of all lands.
20: 15 and honey, most *b* of all lands—
23: 42 and *b* crowns on their heads
27: 24 traded with you *b* garments,
31: 3 with *b* branches overshadowing
31: 9 I made it *b*
33: 32 who sings love songs with a *b* voice
Da 4: 12 Its leaves were *b*, its fruit abundant
4: 21 with *b* leaves and abundant fruit,
8: 9 to the east and towards the *B* Land.
11: 16 will establish himself in the *B* Land
11: 41 He will also invade the *B* Land.
11: 45 the seas at the *b* holy mountain.
Zec 9: 17 How attractive and *b* they will be!
Mt 23: 27 which look *b* on the outside
26: 10 She has done a *b* thing to me.
Mk 14: 6 She has done a *b* thing to me.
Lk 21: 5 temple was adorned with *b* stones
Ac 3: 2 carried to the temple gate called *B*,
3: 10 at the temple gate called *B*,
Ro 10: 15 "How *b* are the feet
1Pe 3: 5 in God used to make themselves *b*.

BEAUTY* (BEAUTIFUL)

Est 1: 11 order to display her *b* to the people
2: 3 let *b* treatments be given to them.
2: 9 her with her *b* treatments
2: 12 months of *b* treatments prescribed
Ps 27: 4 to gaze upon the *b* of the LORD
37: 20 LORD's enemies will be like the *b*
45: 11 The king is enthralled by your *b*;
50: 2 From Zion, perfect in *b*,
Pr 6: 25 lust in your heart after her *b*
31: 30 is deceptive, and *b* is fleeting;
Isa 3: 24 instead of *b*, branding.
28: 1 to the fading flower, his glorious *b*,
28: 4 That fading flower, his glorious *b*,
33: 17 Your eyes will see the king in his *b*
53: 2 He had no *b* or majesty
61: 3 to bestow on them a crown of *b*
La 2: 15 the perfection of *b*,
Eze 16: 14 had given you made your *b* perfect,
16: 14 the nations on account of your *b*,
16: 15 passed by and your *b* became his.
16: 15 "'But you trusted in your *b*
16: 25 lofty shrines and degraded your *b*,
27: 3 "I am perfect in *b*."
27: 4 your builders brought your *b*
27: 11 they brought your *b* to perfection.
28: 7 draw their swords against your *b*
28: 12 full of wisdom and perfect in *b*.
28: 17 proud on account of your *b*,
31: 7 It was majestic in *b*,
31: 8 could match its *b*.
Jas 1: 11 blossom falls and its *b* is destroyed.
1Pe 3: 3 Your *b* should not come
3: 4 the unfading *b* of a gentle

BED (SICKBED)

Isa 28: 20 The *b* is too short to stretch out on,
Lk 11: 7 and my children are with me in *b*.
17: 34 night two people will be in one *b*;
Heb 13: 4 and the marriage *b* kept pure,

BEELZEBUB*

Mt 10: 25 of the house has been called *B*,
12: 24 "It is only by *B*, the prince
12: 27 And if I drive out demons by *B*,
Mk 3: 22 possessed by *B*! By the prince
Lk 11: 15 "By *B*, the prince of demons,
11: 18 claim that I drive out demons by *B*.
11: 19 Now if I drive out demons by *B*,

BEER

Pr 20: 1 Wine is a mocker and *b* a brawler;

BEERSHEBA

Ge 21: 14 and wandered in the desert of *B*.
Jdg 20: 1 all the Israelites from Dan to *B*
1Sa 3: 20 to *B* recognised that Samuel was
2Sa 3: 10 and Judah from Dan to *B*"
17: 11 Let all Israel, from Dan to *B*—
24: 2 the tribes of Israel from Dan to *B*
24: 15 of the people from Dan to *B* died.
1Ki 4: 25 from Dan to *B*, lived in safety,
1Ch 21: 2 count the Israelites from *B* to Dan.
2Ch 30: 5 throughout Israel, from *B* to Dan,

BEFALLS*

Pr 12: 21 No harm *b* the righteous,

BEGGING

Ps 37: 25 or their children *b* bread.
Ac 16: 9 of Macedonia standing and *b* him,

BEGINNING

Ge 1: 1 In the *b* God created the heavens
Ps 102: 25 In the *b* you laid the foundations
111: 10 of the LORD is the *b* of wisdom;
Pr 1: 7 of the LORD is the *b* of knowledge
9: 10 of the LORD is the *b* of wisdom,
Ecc 3: 11 fathom what God has done from *b*
Isa 40: 21 Has it not been told you from the *b*
46: 10 I make known the end from the *b*,
Mt 24: 8 All these are the *b* of birth-pains.
Lk 1: 3 investigated everything from the *b*,
Jn 1: 1 In the *b* was the Word,
1Jn 1: 1 That which was from the *b*,
Rev 21: 6 and the Omega, the *B* and the End.
22: 13 and the Last, the *B* and the End.

BEHAVE (BEHAVIOUR)

Ro 13: 13 Let us *b* decently, as in the daytime

BEHAVIOUR (BEHAVE)

1Pe 3: 1 without talk by the *b* of their wives,
3: 16 maliciously against your good *b*

BEHEMOTH*

Job 40: 15 "Look at the *b*,

BELIEVE (BELIEVED BELIEVER BELIEVERS BELIEVES BELIEVING)

Ex 4: 1 "What if they do not *b* me
1Ki 10: 7 I did not *b* these things until I came
2Ch 9: 6 But I did not *b* what they said
Ps 78: 32 of his wonders, they did not *b*.
Hab 1: 5 that you would not *b*,
Mt 18: 6 one of these little ones who *b* in me
21: 22 If you *b*, you will receive whatever
27: 42 from the cross, and we will *b* in him
Mk 1: 15 Repent and *b* the good news!"
5: 36 ruler, "Don't be afraid; just *b*."
9: 24 "I do *b*; help me overcome my
9: 42 one of these little ones who *b* in me
11: 24 *b* that you have received it,
15: 32 the cross, that we may see and *b*."
16: 16 but whoever does not *b* will be
16: 17 signs will accompany those who *b*:
Lk 8: 12 so that they may not *b* and be saved.
8: 13 They *b* for a while, but in the time
8: 50 just *b*, and she will be healed."
22: 67 you will not *b* me,
24: 25 to *b* all that the prophets have
Jn 1: 7 that through him all men might *b*.
3: 18 does not *b* stands condemned
4: 42 "We no longer *b* just
5: 38 for you do not *b* the one he sent.
5: 46 believed Moses, you would *b* me,
6: 29 to *b* in the one he has sent."
6: 69 We *b* and know that you are
7: 5 his own brothers did not *b* in him.
8: 24 if you do not *b* that I am ⌊the one I
9: 35 "Do you *b* in the Son of Man?"
9: 36 "Tell me so that I may *b* in him."
9: 38 "Lord, I *b*," and he worshipped him.
10: 26 you do not *b* because you are not
10: 37 Do not *b* me unless I do what my
10: 38 you do not *b* me, *b* the miracles,
11: 27 "I *b* that you are the Christ,
12: 37 they still would not *b* in him.
12: 39 For this reason they could not *b*,
Jn 12: 44 in me, he does not *b* in me only,
13: 19 does happen you will *b* that I am
14: 10 Don't you *b* that I am in the Father
14: 11 *B* me when I say that I am
14: 11 or at least *b* on the evidence
16: 30 This makes us *b* that you came
16: 31 "You *b* at last!" Jesus answered.
17: 21 that the world may *b* that you have
19: 35 he testifies so that you also may *b*.
20: 27 Stop doubting and *b*."
20: 31 written that you may *b* that Jesus is
Ac 16: 31 They replied, "*B* in the Lord Jesus,
19: 4 the people to *b* in the one coming
24: 14 I *b* everything that agrees
26: 27 Agrippa, do you *b* the prophets?
Ro 3: 22 faith in Jesus Christ to all who *b*.
4: 11 he is the father of all who *b*
10: 9 *b* in your heart that God raised him
10: 10 For it is with your heart that you *b*
10: 14 And how can they *b* in the one
16: 26 so that all nations might *b*
1Co 1: 21 preached to save those who *b*.
Gal 3: 22 might be given to those who *b*.
Php 1: 29 of Christ not only to *b* on him,
1Th 4: 14 We *b* that Jesus died and rose again
2Th 2: 11 delusion so that they will *b* the lie
1Ti 4: 10 and especially of those who *b*.
Tit 1: 6 a man whose children *b*
Heb 11: 6 comes to him must *b* that he exists
Jas 1: 6 But when he asks, he must *b*
2: 19 Even the demons *b* that—
2: 19 You *b* that there is one God.
1Pe 2: 7 to you who *b*, this stone is precious
1Jn 3: 23 to *b* in the name of his Son,
4: 1 Dear friends, do not *b* every spirit,
5: 13 things to you who *b* in the name

BELIEVED (BELIEVE)

Ge 15: 6 Abram *b* the LORD, and he
Ex 4: 31 signs before the people, and they *b*.
Isa 53: 1 Who has *b* our message
Jnh 3: 5 The Ninevites *b* God.
Lk 1: 45 is she who has *b* that what the Lord
Jn 1: 12 to those who *b* in his name,
2: 22 Then they *b* the Scripture
3: 18 because he has not *b* in the name
5: 46 If you *b* Moses, you would believe
7: 39 whom those who *b*
11: 40 "Did I not tell you that if you *b*,
12: 38 "Lord, who has *b* our message
20: 8 He saw and *b*.
20: 29 who have not seen and yet have *b*."
Ac 13: 48 were appointed for eternal life *b*.
19: 2 the Holy Spirit when you *b*?"
Ro 4: 3 Scripture say? "Abraham *b* God,
10: 14 call on the one they have not *b* in?
10: 16 "Lord, who has *b* our message?"
1Co 15: 2 Otherwise, you have *b* in vain.
Gal 3: 6 Consider Abraham: "He *b* God,
2Th 2: 12 who have not *b* the truth
1Ti 3: 16 was *b* on in the world,
2Ti 1: 12 because I know whom I have *b*,
Jas 2: 23 that says, "Abraham *b* God,

BELIEVER* (BELIEVE)

1Ki 18: 3 (Obadiah was a devout *b*
Ac 16: 1 whose mother was a Jewess and a *b*
16: 15 "If you consider me a *b* in the Lord
1Co 7: 12 brother has a wife who is not a *b*
7: 13 has a husband who is not a *b*
2Co 6: 15 What does a *b* have in common
1Ti 5: 16 any woman who is a *b* has widows

BELIEVERS* (BELIEVE)

Jn 4: 41 of his words many more became *b*.
Ac 1: 15 among the *b* (a group numbering
2: 44 All the *b* were together
4: 32 All the *b* were one in heart
5: 12 And all the *b* used to meet together
9: 41 he called the *b* and the widows
10: 45 The circumcised *b* who had come
11: 2 the circumcised *b* criticised him

Ac 15: 2 along with some other *b*,
15: 5 Then some of the *b* who belonged
15: 23 To the Gentile *b* in Antioch,
21: 25 for the Gentile *b*, we have written
1Co 6: 5 to judge a dispute between *b*?
14: 22 is for *b*, not for unbelievers.
14: 22 not for *b* but for unbelievers;
Gal 6: 10 who belong to the family of *b*.
1Th 1: 7 a model to all the *b* in Macedonia
1Ti 4: 12 set an example for the *b* in speech,
6: 2 benefit from their service are *b*,
Jas 2: 1 *b* in our glorious Lord Jesus Christ,
1Pe 2: 17 Love the brotherhood of *b*,

BELIEVES* (BELIEVE)
Pr 14: 15 A simple man *b* anything,
Mk 9: 23 is possible for him who *b*."
11: 23 *b* that what he says will happen,
16: 16 Whoever *b* and is baptised will be
Jn 3: 15 that everyone who *b*
3: 16 that whoever *b* in him shall not
3: 18 Whoever *b* in him is not
3: 36 Whoever *b* in the Son has eternal
5: 24 *b* him who sent me has eternal life
6: 35 and he who *b* in me will never be
6: 40 and *b* in him shall have eternal life,
6: 47 he who *b* has everlasting life.
7: 38 Whoever *b* in me, as the Scripture
11: 25 He who *b* in me will live, even
11: 26 and *b* in me will never die.
12: 44 Jesus cried out, "When a man *b*
12: 46 so that no-one who *b*
Ac 10: 43 about him that everyone who *b*
13: 39 him everyone who *b* is justified
Ro 1: 16 for the salvation of everyone who *b*
10: 4 righteousness for everyone who *b*.
1Jn 5: 1 Everyone who *b* that Jesus is
5: 5 Only he who *b* that Jesus is the Son
5: 10 Anyone who *b* in the Son

BELIEVING* (BELIEVE)
Jn 20: 31 and that by *b* you may have life
Ac 9: 26 not *b* that he really was a disciple.
1Co 7: 14 sanctified through her *b* husband.
7: 15 A *b* man or woman is not bound
9: 5 right to take a *b* wife along with us,
Gal 3: 2 or by *b* what you heard? Are you
1Ti 6: 2 Those who have *b* masters are not

BELLY
Ge 3: 14 You will crawl on your *b*
Da 2: 32 its *b* and thighs of bronze,
Mt 12: 40 three nights in the *b* of a huge fish,

BELONG (BELONGING BELONGS)
Ge 40: 8 "Do not interpretations *b* to God?
Lev 25: 55 for the Israelites *b* to me
Dt 10: 14 LORD your God *b* the heavens,
29: 29 The secret things *b*
Job 12: 13 "To God *b* wisdom and power;
12: 16 to him *b* strength and victory;
25: 2 "Dominion and awe *b* to God;
Ps 47: 9 for the kings of the earth *b* to God;
95: 4 and the mountain peaks *b* to him.
115: 16 The highest heavens *b*
Jer 5: 10 for these people do not *b*
Jn 8: 44 You *b* to your father, the devil,
15: 19 As it is, you do not *b* to the world,
Ro 1: 6 called to *b* to Jesus Christ.
7: 4 that you might *b* to another,
8: 9 of Christ, he does not *b* to Christ.
14: 8 we live or die, we *b* to the Lord.
1Co 7: 39 but he must *b* to the Lord.
15: 23 when he comes, those who *b*
Gal 3: 29 If you *b* to Christ, then you are
5: 24 Those who *b* to Christ Jesus have
1Th 5: 5 We do not *b* to the night
5: 8 But since we *b* to the day, let us be
1Jn 3: 19 then is how we know that we *b*

BELONGING (BELONG)
1Pe 2: 9 a holy nation, a people *b* to God,

BELONGS (BELONG)
Lev 27: 30 *b* to the LORD; it is holy
Dt 1: 17 of any man, for judgment *b* to God.
Job 41: 11 Everything under heaven *b* to me.
Ps 22: 28 for dominion *b* to the LORD
89: 18 Indeed, our shield *b* to the LORD,
111: 10 To him *b* eternal praise.
Eze 18: 4 For every living soul *b* to me,
Jn 8: 47 He who *b* to God hears what God
Ro 12: 5 each member *b* to all the others.
Rev 7: 10 "Salvation *b* to our God,

BELOVED* (LOVE)
Dt 33: 12 "Let the *b* of the LORD rest secure
SS 5: 9 How is your *b* better than others,
5: 9 How is your *b* better
Jer 11: 15 "What is my *b* doing in my temple

BELSHAZZAR
King of Babylon in days of Daniel (Da 5).

BELT
Ex 12: 11 with your cloak tucked into your *b*,
1Ki 18: 46 and, tucking his cloak into his *b*,
2Ki 4: 29 "Tuck your cloak into your *b*,
9: 1 "Tuck your cloak into your *b*,
Isa 11: 5 Righteousness will be his *b*
Eph 6: 14 with the *b* of truth buckled

BENEFICIAL* (BENEFIT)
1Co 6: 12 for me"—but not everything is *b*.
10: 23 but not everything is *b*.

BENEFIT (BENEFICIAL BENEFITS)
Job 22: 2 "Can a man be of *b* to God?
Isa 38: 17 Surely it was for my *b*
Ro 6: 22 the *b* you reap leads to holiness,
2Co 4: 15 All this is for your *b*,

BENEFITS (BENEFIT)
Ps 103: 2 and forget not all his *b*.
Jn 4: 38 you have reaped the *b* of their labour

BENJAMIN
Twelfth son of Jacob by Rachel (Ge 35:16-24; 46:19-21; 1Ch 2:2). Jacob refused to send him to Egypt, but relented (Ge 42-45). Tribe of blessed (Ge 49:27; Dt 33:12), numbered (Nu 1:37; 26:41), allotted land (Jos 18:11-28; Eze 48:23), failed to fully possess (Jdg 1:21), nearly obliterated (Jdg 20-21), sided with Ish-Bosheth (2Sa 2), but turned to David (1Ch 12:2, 29). 12,000 from (Rev 7:8).

BEREANS*
Ac 17: 11 the *B* were of more noble character

BESTOWING* (BESTOWS)
Pr 8: 21 *b* wealth on those who love me

BESTOWS (BESTOWING)
Ps 84: 11 the LORD *b* favour and honour;

BETHANY
Mk 11: 1 and *B* at the Mount of Olives,

BETHEL
Ge 28:19 He called that place *B*,

BETHLEHEM
Ru 1:19 went on until they came to *B*.
1Sa 16: 1 I am sending you to Jesse of *B*.
2Sa 23: 15 from the well near the gate of *B*!"
Mic 5: 2 "But you, *B* Ephrathah,
Mt 2: 1 After Jesus was born in *B* in Judea,
2: 6 "'But you, *B*, in the land of Judah,

BETHPHAGE
Mt 21: 1 came to *B* on the Mount of Olives,

BETHSAIDA
Jn 12: 21 who was from *B* in Galilee,

BETRAY (BETRAYED BETRAYS)
Ps 89: 33 nor will I ever *b* my faithfulness.
Pr 25: 9 do not *b* another man's confidence,
Mt 10: 21 "Brother will *b* brother to death,
26: 21 the truth, one of you will *b* me."

BETRAYED (BETRAY)
Mt 27: 4 "for I have *b* innocent blood."

BETRAYS (BETRAY)
Pr 11: 13 A gossip *b* a confidence,
20: 19 A gossip *b* a confidence;

BEULAH*
Isa 62: 4 and your land *B*;

BEWITCHED*
Gal 3: 1 foolish Galatians! Who has *b* you?

BEZALEL
Judahite craftsman in charge of building the tabernacle (Ex 31:1-11; 35:30-39:31).

BIDDING*
Ps 103: 20 you mighty ones who do his *b*,
148: 8 stormy winds that do his *b*,

BILDAD
One of Job's friends (Job 8; 18; 25).

BILHAH
Servant of Rachel, mother of Jacob's sons Dan and Naphtali (Ge 30:1-7; 35:25; 46:23-25).

BIND (BINDS BOUND)
Dt 6: 8 and *b* them on your foreheads.
Pr 3: 3 *b* them around your neck,
6: 21 *B* them upon your heart for ever;
7: 3 *B* them on your fingers;
Isa 61: 1 me to *b* up the broken-hearted,
Mt 16: 19 whatever you *b* on earth will be

BINDS (BIND)
Ps 147: 3 and *b* up their wounds.
Isa 30: 26 when the LORD *b* up the bruises

BIRD (BIRDS)
Pr 27: 8 Like a *b* that strays from its nest
Ecc 10: 20 a *b* of the air may carry your words,

BIRDS (BIRD)
Mt 8: 20 and *b* of the air have nests,
Lk 9: 58 and *b* of the air have nests,

BIRTH (BEAR [1])
Ps 51: 5 Surely I have been a sinner from *b*,
58: 3 Even from *b* the wicked go astray;
Isa 26: 18 but we gave *b* to wind.
Mt 1: 18 This is how the *b* of Jesus Christ
24: 8 these are the beginning of *b*-pains.
Jn 3: 6 Flesh gives *b* to flesh, but the Spirit
1Pe 1: 3 great mercy he has given us new *b*

BIRTHRIGHT (BEAR [1])
Ge 25: 34 So Esau despised his *b*.

BISHOP see OVERSEER

BITTEN
Nu 21: 8 anyone who is *b* can look at it

BITTER (BITTERNESS EMBITTER)
Ex 12: 8 along with *b* herbs, and bread made
Pr 27: 7 what is *b* tastes sweet.

BITTERNESS (BITTER)
Pr 14: 10 Each heart knows its own *b*,
17: 25 and *b* to the one who bore him.
Ro 3: 14 full of cursing and *b*."
Eph 4: 31 Get rid of all *b*, rage and anger,

BLACK
Zec 6: 6 The one with the *b* horses is going

Rev 6: 5 and there before me was a *b* horse!

BLAMELESS* (BLAMELESSLY)

Ge 6: 9 *b* among the people of his time,
17: 1 walk before me and be *b*.
Dt 18: 13 You must be *b* before the LORD
2Sa 22: 24 I have been *b* before him
22: 26 to the *b* you show yourself *b*,
Job 1: 1 This man was *b* and upright;
1: 8 one on earth like him; he is *b*
2: 3 one on earth like him; he is *b*
4: 6 and your *b* ways your hope?
8: 20 God does not reject a *b* man
9: 20 if I were *b*, it would pronounce me
9: 21 "Although I am *b*,
9: 22 'He destroys both the *b*
12: 4 though righteous and *b*!
22: 3 gain if your ways were *b*?
31: 6 and he will know that I am *b*—
Ps 15: 2 He whose walk is *b*
18: 23 I have been *b* before him
18: 25 to the *b* you show yourself *b*,
19: 13 Then will I be *b*,
26: 1 for I have led a *b* life;
26: 11 But I lead a *b* life;
37: 18 The days of the *b* are known
37: 37 Consider the *b*, observe the upright
84: 11 from those whose walk is *b*.
101: 2 I will be careful to lead a *b* life—
101: 2 house with *b* heart.
101: 6 he whose walk is *b*
119: 1 Blessed are they whose ways are *b*,
119: 80 May my heart be *b*
Pr 2: 7 a shield to those whose walk is *b*,
2: 21 and the *b* will remain in it;
11: 5 of the *b* makes a straight way
11: 20 in those whose ways are *b*.
19: 1 Better a poor man whose walk is *b*
20: 7 The righteous man leads a *b* life;
28: 6 Better a poor man whose walk is *b*
28: 10 *b* will receive a good inheritance.
28: 18 He whose walk is *b* is kept safe,
Eze 28: 15 You were *b* in your ways
1Co 1: 8 so that you will be *b* on the day
Eph 1: 4 world to be holy and *b* in his sight.
5: 27 any other blemish, but holy and *b*.
Php 1: 10 and *b* until the day of Christ,
2: 15 so that you may become *b* and pure
1Th 2: 10 and *b* we were among you who
3: 13 hearts so that you will be *b*
5: 23 and body be kept *b* at the coming
Tit 1: 6 An elder must be *b*, the husband of
1: 7 he must be *b*—not overbearing,
Heb 7: 26 *b*, pure, set apart from sinners,
2Pe 3: 14 effort to be found spotless, *b*
Rev 14: 5 found in their mouths; they are *b*.

BLAMELESSLY* (BLAMELESS)

Lk 1: 6 commandments and regulations *b*.

BLASPHEME* (BLASPHEMED BLASPHEMER BLASPHEMES BLASPHEMIES BLASPHEMING BLASPHEMOUS BLASPHEMY)

Ex 22: 28 "Do not *b* God or curse the ruler
Ac 26: 11 and I tried to force them to *b*.
1Ti 1: 20 over to Satan to be taught not to *b*.
2Pe 2: 12 these men *b* in matters they do not
Rev 13: 6 He opened his mouth to *b* God,

BLASPHEMED* (BLASPHEME)

Lev 24: 11 of the Israelite woman *b* the name
2Ki 19: 6 of the king of Assyria have *b* me.
19: 22 Who is it you have insulted and *b*?
Isa 37: 6 of the king of Assyria have *b* me.
37: 23 Who is it you have insulted and *b*?
52: 5 my name is constantly *b*.
Eze 20: 27 your fathers *b* me by forsaking me:
Ac 19: 37 robbed temples nor *b* our goddess.
Ro 2: 24 name is *b* among the Gentiles

BLASPHEMER* (BLASPHEME)

Lev 24: 14 "Take the *b* outside the camp.
24: 23 they took the *b* outside the camp
1Ti 1: 31 I was once a *b* and a persecutor

BLASPHEMES* (BLASPHEME)

Lev 24: 16 anyone who *b* the name
24: 16 native-born, when he *b* the Name,
Nu 15: 30 native-born or alien, *b* the LORD,
Mk 3: 29 whoever *b* against the Holy Spirit
Lk 12: 10 but anyone who *b* against the Holy

BLASPHEMIES* (BLASPHEME)

Ne 9: 18 or when they committed awful *b*.
9: 26 to you; they committed awful *b*.
Mk 3: 28 and *b* of men will be forgiven them.
Rev 13: 5 and *b* and to exercise his authority

BLASPHEMING* (BLASPHEME)

Mt 9: 3 "This fellow is *b*!" Knowing their
Mk 2: 7 He's *b*! Who can forgive sins

BLASPHEMOUS* (BLASPHEME)

Rev 13: 1 and on each head a *b* name.
17: 3 that was covered with *b* names

BLASPHEMY* (BLASPHEME)

Mt 12: 31 and *b* will be forgiven men,
12: 31 the *b* against the Spirit will not be
26: 65 Look, now you have heard the *b*.
26: 65 "He has spoken *b*! Why do we,
Mk 14: 64 "You have heard the *b*.
Lk 5: 21 "Who is this fellow who speaks *b*?
Jn 10: 33 replied the Jews, "but for *b*,
10: 36 Why then do you accuse me of *b*
Ac 6: 11 words of *b* against Moses

BLAST*

Ex 15: 8 By the *b* of your nostrils
19: 13 horn sounds a long *b* may they go
19: 16 and a very loud trumpet *b*.
Nu 10: 5 When a trumpet *b* is sounded,
10: 6 At the sounding of a second *b*,
10: 6 The *b* will be the signal
10: 9 sound a *b* on the trumpets.
Jos 6: 5 you hear them sound a long *b*
6: 16 the priests sounded the trumpet *b*,
2Sa 22: 16 at the *b* of breath from his nostrils.
Job 4: 9 at the *b* of his anger they perish.
39: 25 At the *b* of the trumpet he snorts,
Ps 18: 15 the *b* of breath from your nostrils.
98: 6 and the *b* of the ram's horn—
147: 17 Who can withstand his icy *b*?
Isa 27: 8 with his fierce *b* he drives her out,
Eze 22: 20 a furnace to melt it with a fiery *b*,
Am 2: 2 tumult amid war cries and the *b*
Heb 12: 19 to a trumpet *b* or to such a voice

BLEATING*

1Sa 15: 14 "What then is this *b* of sheep

BLEMISH (BLEMISHES)

Lev 22: 21 be without defect or *b*
Eph 5: 27 or wrinkle or any other *b*,
Col 1: 22 without *b* and free from accusation
1Pe 1: 19 a lamb without *b* or defect.

BLEMISHES* (BLEMISH)

2Pe 2: 13 and *b*, revelling in their pleasures
Jude : 12 These men are *b* at your love feasts

BLESS (BLESSED BLESSES BLESSING BLESSINGS)

Ge 12: 3 I will *b* those who *b* you,
32: 26 not let you go unless you *b* me."
Dt 7: 13 He will love you and *b* you
33: 11 *B* all his skills, O LORD,
Ps 72: 15 and *b* him all day long.
Ro 12: 14 *B* those who persecute you; *b*

BLESSED (BLESS)

Ge 1: 22 God *b* them and said, "Be fruitful
2: 3 And God *b* the seventh day
22: 18 nations on earth will be *b*,
Nu 24: 9 "May those who bless you be *b*
1Ch 17: 27 have *b* it, and it will be *b* for ever."
Ps 1: 1 *B* is the man
2: 12 *B* are all who take refuge in him.
32: 2 *B* is the man
33: 12 *B* is the nation whose God is
40: 4 *B* is the man
41: 1 *B* is he who has regard for the weak
84: 5 *B* are those whose strength is
89: 15 *B* are those who have learned
94: 12 *B* is the man you discipline,
106: 3 *B* are they who maintain justice,
112: 1 *B* is the man who fears the LORD,
118: 26 *B* is he who comes in the name
119: 1 *B* are they whose ways are
119: 2 *B* are they who keep his statutes
127: 5 *B* is the man
Pr 3: 13 *B* is the man who finds wisdom,
8: 34 *B* is the man who listens to me,
28: 20 A faithful man will be richly *b*,
29: 18 but *b* is he who keeps the law.
31: 28 Her children arise and call her *b*;
Isa 30: 18 *B* are all who wait for him!
Mal 3: 12 Then all the nations will call you *b*,
3: 15 But now we call the arrogant *b*.
Mt 5: 3 saying: "*B* are the poor in spirit,
5: 4 *B* are those who mourn,
5: 5 *B* are the meek,
5: 6 *B* are those who hunger
5: 7 *B* are the merciful,
5: 8 *B* are the pure in heart,
5: 9 *B* are the peacemakers,
5: 10 *B* are those who are persecuted
5: 11 "*B* are you when people insult you,
Lk 1: 48 on all generations will call me *b*,
Jn 12: 13 "*B* is he who comes in the name
Ac 20: 35 'It is more *b* to give than to receive
Tit 2: 13 while we wait for the *b* hope—
Jas 1: 12 *B* is the man who perseveres
Rev 1: 3 *B* is the one who reads the words
22: 7 *B* is he who keeps the words
22: 14 "*B* are those who wash their robes,

BLESSES (BLESS)

Ps 29: 11 the LORD *b* his people with peace.
Ro 10: 12 and richly *b* all who call on him,

BLESSING (BLESS)

Ge 27: 4 so that I may give you my *b*
Dt 23: 5 turned the curse into a *b* for you,
33: 1 This is the *b* that Moses the man
Pr 10: 22 The *b* of the LORD brings wealth,
Eze 34: 26 there will be showers of *b*.

BLESSINGS (BLESS)

Dt 11: 29 proclaim on Mount Gerizim the *b*,
Jos 8: 34 all the words of the law—the *b*
Pr 10: 6 *B* crown the head of the righteous,
Ro 15: 27 shared in the Jews' spiritual *b*,

BLIND (BLINDED)

Mt 15: 14 a *b* man leads a *b* man, both will fall
23: 16 "Woe to you, *b* guides! You say,
Mk 10: 46 a *b* man, Bartimaeus (that is,
Lk 6: 39 "Can a *b* man lead a *b* man?
Jn 9: 25 I was *b* but now I see!"

BLINDED (BLIND)

Jn 12: 40 elsewhere: "He has *b* their eyes
2Co 4: 4 The god of this age has *b* the minds

BLOOD (BLOODSHED BLOODTHIRSTY)

Ge 4: 10 Your brother's *b* cries out to me
9: 6 "Whoever sheds the *b* of man,
Ex 12: 13 and when I see the *b*, I will pass
24: 8 "This is the *b* of the covenant that
Lev 16: 15 and take its *b* behind the curtain
17: 11 For the life of a creature is in the *b*,
Dt 12: 23 eat the *b*, because the *b* is the life,
Ps 72: 14 for precious is their *b* in his sight.
Pr 6: 17 hands that shed innocent *b*,
Isa 1: 11 pleasure in the *b* of bulls and lambs

Mt 26: 28 This is my *b* of the covenant,
27: 24 "I am innocent of this man's *b*,"
Mk 14: 24 "This is my *b* of the covenant,
Lk 22: 44 drops of *b* falling to the ground.
Jn 6: 53 of the Son of Man and drink his *b*,
Ac 15: 20 of strangled animals and from *b*.
20: 26 innocent of the *b* of all men.
Ro 3: 25 of atonement, through faith in his *b*
5: 9 have now been justified by his *b*,
1Co 11: 25 cup is the new covenant in my *b*;
Eph 1: 7 we have redemption through his *b*,
2: 13 near through the *b* of Christ.
Col 1: 20 by making peace through his *b*,
Heb 9: 7 once a year, and never without *b*,
9: 12 once for all by his own *b*,
9: 20 "This is the *b* of the covenant,
9: 22 of *b* there is no forgiveness.
12: 24 word than the *b* of Abel.
1Pe 1: 19 but with the precious *b* of Christ,
1Jn 1: 7 and the *b* of Jesus, his Son,
Rev 1: 5 has freed us from our sins by his *b*,
5: 9 with your *b* you purchased men
7: 14 white in the *b* of the Lamb.
12: 11 him by the *b* of the Lamb
19: 13 He is dressed in a robe dipped in *b*,

BLOODSHED (BLOOD)
Jer 48: 10 on him who keeps his sword from *b*
Eze 35: 6 did not hate *b*, *b* will pursue you.
Hab 2: 12 to him who builds a city with *b*

BLOODTHIRSTY* (BLOOD)
Ps 5: 6 *b* and deceitful men
26: 9 or my life with *b* men,
55: 23 *b* and deceitful men
59: 2 and save me from *b* men.
139: 19 Away from me, you *b* men!
Pr 29: 10 *B* men hate a man of integrity

BLOSSOM
Isa 35: 1 the wilderness will rejoice and *b*.

BLOT (BLOTS)
Ex 32: 32 then *b* me out of the book you have
Ps 51: 1 *b* out my transgressions.
Rev 3: 5 I will never *b* out his name

BLOTS (BLOT)
Isa 43: 25 "I, even I, am he who *b* out

BLOWN
Eph 4: 14 and *b* here and there by every wind
Jas 1: 6 doubts is like a wave of the sea, *b*
Jude : 12 without rain, *b* along by the wind;

BLUSH
Jer 6: 15 they do not even know how to *b*.

BOAST (BOASTS)
1Ki 20: 11 armour should not *b* like one who
Ps 34: 2 My soul will *b* in the LORD;
44: 8 In God we make our *b* all day long,
Pr 27: 1 Do not *b* about tomorrow,
Jer 9: 23 or the rich man *b* of his riches,
1Co 1: 31 Let him who boasts *b* in the Lord."
2Co 10: 17 Let him who boasts *b* in the Lord."
11: 30 I do not inwardly burn? If I must *b*,
Gal 6: 14 May I never *b* except in the cross
Eph 2: 9 not by works, so that no-one can *b*.

BOASTS (BOAST)
Jer 9: 24 but let him who *b* boast about this:

BOAZ
Wealthy Bethlehemite who showed favour to Ruth (Ru 2), married her (Ru 4). Ancestor of David (Ru 4:18-22; 1Ch 2:12-15), Jesus (Mt 1:5-16; Lk 3:23-32).

BODIES (BODY)
Isa 26: 19 their *b* will rise.
Ro 12: 1 to offer your *b* as living sacrifices,
1Co 6: 15 not know that your *b* are members
Eph 5: 28 to love their wives as their own *b*.

BODILY (BODY)
Col 2: 9 of the Deity lives in *b* form

BODY (BODIES BODILY EMBODIMENT)
Zec 13: 6 What are these wounds on your *b*?'
Mt 10: 28 afraid of those who kill the *b*
26: 26 saying, "Take and eat; this is my *b*
26: 41 spirit is willing, but the *b* is weak."
Mk 14: 22 saying, "Take it; this is my *b*."
Lk 22: 19 saying, "This is my *b* given for you;
Jn 13: 10 wash his feet; his whole *b* is clean.
Ro 6: 13 Do not offer the parts of your *b*
12: 4 us has one *b* with many members,
1Co 6: 19 not know that your *b* is a temple
6: 20 Therefore honour God with your *b*.
11: 24 "This is my *b*, which is for you;
12: 12 The *b* is a unit, though it is made up
12: 13 baptised by one Spirit into one *b*—
15: 44 a natural *b*, it is raised a spiritual *b*.
Eph 1: 23 which is his *b*, the fulness
4: 25 for we are all members of one *b*.
5: 30 for we are members of his *b*.
Php 1: 20 Christ will be exalted in my *b*,
Col 1: 24 sake of his *b*, which is the church.

BOLD (BOLDNESS)
Ps 138: 3 you made me *b* and stout-hearted.
Pr 21: 29 A wicked man puts up a *b* front,
28: 1 but the righteous are as *b* as a lion.

BOLDNESS* (BOLD)
Lk 11: 8 because of the man's *b*
Ac 4: 29 to speak your word with great *b*.

BONDAGE
Ezr 9: 9 God has not deserted us in our *b*.

BONES
Ge 2: 23 "This is now bone of my *b*
Ps 22: 14 and all my *b* are out of joint.
22: 17 I can count all my *b*;
Eze 37: 1 middle of a valley; it was full of *b*.
Jn 19: 36 "Not one of his *b* will be broken,"

BOOK (BOOKS)
Ex 32: 33 against me I will blot out of my *b*.
Jos 1: 8 Do not let this *B* of the Law depart
2Ki 22: 8 "I have found the *B* of the Law
2Ch 34: 15 "I have found the *B* of the Law
Ne 8: 8 They read from the *B* of the Law
Ps 69: 28 May they be blotted out of the *b*
Da 12: 1 name is found written in the *b*—
Jn 20: 30 which are not recorded in this *b*.
Php 4: 3 whose names are in the *b* of life.
Rev 3: 5 never erase his name from the *b*
20: 12 *b* was opened, which is the *b*
20: 15 was not found written in the *b*
21: 27 written in the Lamb's *b* of life.
22: 18 him the plagues described in this *b*.

BOOKS* (BOOK)
Ecc 12: 12 Of making many *b* there is no end,
Da 7: 10 and the *b* were opened.
Jn 21: 25 for the *b* that would be written.
Rev 20: 12 the throne, and *b* were opened.
20: 12 they had done as recorded in the *b*.

BORE (BEAR [1])
Isa 53: 12 For he *b* the sin of many,
1Pe 2: 24 He himself *b* our sins in his body

BORN (BEAR [1])
Ecc 3: 2 a time to be *b* and a time to die,
Isa 9: 6 For to us a child is *b*,
66: 8 Can a country be *b* in a day
Lk 2: 11 of David a Saviour has been *b* to you
Jn 3: 3 a man is *b* again, he cannot see
3: 4 How can a man be *b* when he is old
3: 5 unless a man is *b* of water
3: 7 at my saying, 'You must be *b* again
3: 8 it is with everyone *b* of the Spirit."
1Pe 1: 23 For you have been *b* again,
1Jn 3: 9 because he has been *b* of God.
4: 7 Everyone who loves has been *b*
5: 1 believes that Jesus is the Christ is *b*
5: 4 for everyone *b* of God overcomes
5: 18 We know that anyone *b*

BORROWER
Pr 22: 7 and the *b* is servant to the lender.

BOTHER (BOTHERING)
Lk 11: 7 one inside answers, 'Don't *b* me.

BOTHERING (BOTHER)
Lk 18: 5 yet because this widow keeps *b* me,

BOUGHT (BUY)
Ac 20: 28 which he *b* with his own blood.
1Co 6: 20 You are not your own; you were *b*
7: 23 You were *b* at a price; do not
2Pe 2: 1 the sovereign Lord who *b* them—

BOUND (BIND)
Isa 56: 3 Let no foreigner who has *b* himself
Mt 16: 19 bind on earth will be *b* in heaven,
18: 18 bind on earth will be *b* in heaven,
Ro 7: 2 by law a married woman is *b*
1Co 7: 39 A woman is *b* to her husband
Jude : 6 *b* with everlasting chains
Rev 20: 2 and *b* him for a thousand years.

BOUNDARY (BOUNDS)
Nu 34: 3 your southern *b* will start
Pr 23: 10 Do not move an ancient *b* stone
Hos 5: 10 who move *b* stones.

BOUNDS (BOUNDARY)
2Co 7: 4 all our troubles my joy knows no *b*.

BOUNTY*
Ge 49: 26 than the *b* of the age-old hills.
Dt 28: 12 heavens, the storehouse of his *b*,
1Ki 10: 13 he had given her out of his royal *b*.
Ps 65: 11 You crown the year with your *b*,
68: 10 from your *b*, O God, you provided
Jer 31: 12 rejoice in the *b* of the LORD—
31: 14 my people will be filled with my *b*

BOW [1]
1Ki 22: 34 But someone drew his *b* at random
Ps 44: 6 I do not trust in my *b*,

BOW [2] (BOWED BOWS)
Dt 5: 9 You shall not *b* down to them
Ps 5: 7 in reverence will I *b* down
95: 6 Come, let us *b* down in worship,
138: 2 I will *b* down towards your holy
Isa 44: 19 Shall I *b* down to a block of wood?"
45: 23 Before me every knee will *b*;
Ro 14: 11 'Every knee will *b* before me;
Php 2: 10 name of Jesus every knee should *b*,

BOWED (BOW [2])
Ps 145: 14 and lifts up all who are *b* down.
146: 8 the LORD lifts up those who are *b*

BOWS (BOW [2])
Isa 44: 15 he makes an idol and *b* down to it.
44: 17 he *b* down to it and worships.

BOY (BOY'S BOYS)
Ge 21: 17 God heard the *b* crying,
22: 12 not lay a hand on the *b*
Jdg 13: 5 *b* is to be a Nazirite,
1Sa 2: 11 *b* ministered before the LORD.
3: 8 the LORD was calling the *b*.
Isa 7: 16 before the *b* knows enough
Mt 17: 18 demon, and it came out of the *b*
Lk 2: 43 the *b* Jesus stayed behind

BOY'S (BOY)
1Ki 17: 22 the *b* life returned to him

2Ki 4:34 the *b* body grew warm

BOYS (BOY)

Ge 25:24 twin *b* in her womb
Ex 1:18 they let the *b* live.

BRACE*

Job 38:3 *B* yourself like a man;
40:7 out of the storm: "*B* yourself like
Na 2:1 *b* yourselves,

BRAG*

Am 4:5 and *b* about your freewill offerings
Ro 2:17 *b* about your relationship to God;
2:23 temples? You who *b* about the law,
Jas 4:16 As it is, you boast and *b*.

BRAIDED

1Ti 2:9 not with *b* hair or gold or pearls
1Pe 3:3 as *b* hair and the wearing

BRANCH (BRANCHES)

Isa 4:2 In that day the *B* of the LORD will
Jer 23:5 up to David a righteous *B*,
33:15 I will make a righteous *B* sprout
Zec 3:8 going to bring my servant, the *B*.
6:12 is the man whose name is the *B*,
Jn 15:2 while every *b* that does bear fruit
15:4 No *b* can bear fruit by itself;

BRANCHES (BRANCH)

Jn 15:5 "I am the vine; you are the *b*.
Ro 11:21 if God did not spare the natural *b*,

BRAVE

2Sa 2:7 Now then, be strong and *b*,
13:28 you this order? Be strong and *b*."

BREACH (BREAK)

Ps 106:23 stood in the *b* before him

BREACHING (BREAK)

Pr 17:14 Starting a quarrel is like *b* a dam;

BREAD

Ex 12:8 and *b* made without yeast.
23:15 the Feast of Unleavened *B*;
25:30 Put the *b* of the Presence
Dt 8:3 that man does not live on *b* alone
Ps 78:25 Men ate the *b* of angels;
Pr 30:8 but give me only my daily *b*.
Ecc 11:1 Cast your *b* upon the waters,
Isa 55:2 Why spend money on what is not *b*
Mt 4:3 tell these stones to become *b*."
4:4 'Man does not live on *b* alone,
6:11 Give us today our daily *b*.
26:26 Jesus took *b*, gave thanks
Mk 14:22 Jesus took *b*, gave thanks
Lk 4:3 tell this stone to become *b*."
4:4 'Man does not live on *b* alone.'"
9:13 "We have only five loaves of *b*
11:3 Give us each day our daily *b*.
22:19 And he took *b*, gave thanks
Jn 6:33 For the *b* of God is he who comes
6:35 Jesus declared, "I am the *b* of life.
6:41 "I am the *b* that came
6:48 I am the *b* of life.
6:51 I am the living *b* that came
6:51 This *b* is my flesh, which I will give
21:13 took the *b* and gave it to them,
1Co 10:16 And is not the *b* that we break
11:23 took *b*, and when he had given
11:26 For whenever you eat this *b*

BREAK (BREACH BREACHING BREAKERS BREAKING BREAKS BROKE BROKEN BROKENNESS)

Nu 30:2 he must not *b* his word
Jdg 2:1 'I will never *b* my covenant
Pr 25:15 and a gentle tongue can *b* a bone.
Isa 42:3 A bruised reed he will not *b*,
Mal 2:15 and do not *b* faith with the wife
Mt 12:20 A bruised reed he will not *b*,
Ac 20:7 week we came together to *b* bread.
1Co 10:16 the bread that we *b* a participation
Rev 5:2 "Who is worthy to *b* the seals

BREAKERS* (BREAK)

Ps 42:7 all your waves and *b*
93:4 mightier than the *b* of the sea—
Jnh 2:3 all your waves and *b*

BREAKING (BREAK)

Jos 9:20 fall on us for *b* the oath we swore
Eze 16:59 oath by *b* the covenant.
17:18 the oath by *b* the covenant.
Ac 2:42 to the *b* of bread and to prayer.
Jas 2:10 at just one point is guilty of *b* all

BREAKS (BREAK)

Jer 23:29 "and like a hammer that *b* a rock
1Jn 3:4 Everyone who sins *b* the law;

BREASTPIECE (BREASTPLATE)

Ex 28:15 Fashion a *b* for making decisions—

BREASTPLATE* (BREASTPIECE)

Isa 59:17 He put on righteousness as his *b*,
Eph 6:14 with the *b* of righteousness in place
1Th 5:8 putting on faith and love as a *b*,

BREASTS

La 4:3 Even jackals offer their *b*

BREATH (BREATHED GOD-BREATHED)

Ge 2:7 into his nostrils the *b* of life,

BREATHED (BREATH)

Ge 2:7 *b* into his nostrils the breath of life,
Mk 15:37 With a loud cry, Jesus *b* his last.
Jn 20:22 And with that he *b* on them

BREEDS*

Pr 13:10 Pride only *b* quarrels,

BRIBE

Ex 23:8 "Do not accept a *b*,
Dt 16:19 for a *b* blinds the eyes of the wise
27:25 "Cursed is the man who accepts a *b*
Pr 6:35 will refuse the *b*, however great it

BRIDE

Isa 62:5 as a bridegroom rejoices over his *b*,
Rev 19:7 and his *b* has made herself ready.
21:2 as a *b* beautifully dressed
21:9 I will show you the *b*, the wife
22:17 The Spirit and the *b* say, "Come!"

BRIDEGROOM

Ps 19:5 which is like a *b* coming forth
Mt 25:1 and went out to meet the *b*.
25:5 The *b* was a long time in coming,

BRIGHTENS* (BRIGHTNESS)

Pr 16:15 When a king's face *b*, it means life;
Ecc 8:1 Wisdom *b* a man's face

BRIGHTER (BRIGHTNESS)

Pr 4:18 shining ever *b* till the full light

BRIGHTNESS* (BRIGHTENS BRIGHTER)

2Sa 22:13 Out of the *b* of his presence
23:4 like the *b* after rain
Ps 18:12 of the *b* of his presence clouds
Isa 59:9 for *b*, but we walk in deep shadows.
60:3 and kings to the *b* of your dawn.
60:19 will the *b* of the moon shine on you
Da 12:3 who are wise will shine like the *b*
Am 5:20 pitch-dark, without a ray of *b*?

BRILLIANCE* (BRILLIANT)

Ac 22:11 the *b* of the light had blinded me.
Rev 1:16 was like the sun shining in all its *b*.
21:11 its *b* was like that of a very precious

BRILLIANT* (BRILLIANCE)

Ecc 9:11 or wealth to the *b*
Eze 1:4 and surrounded by *b* light.
1:27 and *b* light surrounded him.

BRINK*

Pr 5:14 I have come to the *b* of utter ruin

BRITTLE

Da 2:42 will be partly strong and partly *b*.

BROAD

Mt 7:13 and *b* is the road that leads

BROKE (BREAK)

Mt 26:26 took bread, gave thanks and *b* it,
Mk 14:22 took bread, gave thanks and *b* it,
Ac 2:46 They *b* bread in their homes
20:11 he went upstairs again and *b* bread
1Co 11:24 when he had given thanks, he *b* it

BROKEN (BREAK)

Ps 34:20 not one of them will be *b*.
51:17 The sacrifices of God are a *b* spirit;
Ecc 4:12 of three strands is not quickly *b*.
Lk 20:18 on that stone will be *b* to pieces,
Jn 7:23 the law of Moses may not be *b*,
10:35 and the Scripture cannot be *b*—
19:36 "Not one of his bones will be *b*,"
Ro 11:20 they were *b* off because of unbelief,

BROKEN-HEARTED* (HEART)

Ps 34:18 The LORD is close to the *b*
109:16 and the needy and the *b*.
147:3 He heals the *b*
Isa 61:1 He has sent me to bind up the *b*,

BROKENNESS* (BREAK)

Isa 65:14 and wail in *b* of spirit.

BRONZE

Ex 27:2 and overlay the altar with *b*.
30:18 "Make a *b* basin, with its *b* stand,
Nu 21:9 So Moses made a *b* snake
Da 2:32 and thighs of *b*, its legs of iron,
10:6 legs like the gleam of burnished *b*,
Rev 1:15 His feet were like *b* glowing
2:18 whose feet are like burnished *b*.

BROTHER (BROTHER'S BROTHERHOOD BROTHERLY BROTHERS)

Pr 17:17 and a *b* is born for adversity.
18:24 a friend who sticks closer than a *b*.
27:10 neighbour nearby than a *b* far away.
Mt 5:24 and be reconciled to your *b*;
18:15 "If your *b* sins against you,
Mk 3:35 Whoever does God's will is my *b*
Lk 17:3 "If your *b* sins, rebuke him,
Ro 14:15 not by your eating destroy your *b*
14:21 anything else that will cause your *b*
1Co 8:13 if what I eat causes my *b* to fall
2Th 3:6 away from every *b* who is idle
3:15 as an enemy, but warn him as a *b*.
Phm :16 but better than a slave, as a dear *b*.
Jas 2:15 Suppose a *b* or sister is
4:11 Anyone who speaks against his *b*
1Jn 2:9 hates his *b* is still in the darkness.
2:10 Whoever loves his *b* lives
2:11 But whoever hates his *b* is
3:10 is anyone who does not love his *b*.
3:15 who hates his *b* is a murderer,
3:17 material possessions and sees his *b*
4:20 For anyone who does not love his *b*
4:20 yet hates his *b*, he is a liar.
4:21 loves God must also love his *b*.
5:16 If anyone sees his *b* commit a sin

BROTHER'S (BROTHER)

Ge 4:9 "Am I my *b* keeper?" The LORD
Mt 7:5 remove the speck from your *b* eye.
Ro 14:13 or obstacle in your *b* way.

BROTHERHOOD (BROTHER)

1Pe 2:17 Love the *b* of believers, fear God,

BROTHERLY* (BROTHER)
Ro 12: 10 devoted to one another in *b* love.
1Th 4: 9 Now about *b* love we do not need
2Pe 1: 7 and to godliness, *b* kindness;
1: 7 kindness; and to *b* kindness,

BROTHERS (BROTHER)
Jos 1: 14 You are to help your *b*
Ps 133: 1 is when *b* live together in unity!
Pr 6: 19 who stirs up dissension among *b*.
Mt 12: 49 "Here are my mother and my *b*.
19: 29 everyone who has left houses or *b*
25: 40 one of the least of these *b* of mine,
Mk 3: 33 "Who are my mother and my *b*?"
10: 29 or *b* or sisters or mother or father
Lk 21: 16 You will be betrayed by parents, *b*,
22: 32 turned back, strengthen your *b*."
Jn 7: 5 his own *b* did not believe in him.
Ac 15: 32 to encourage and strengthen the *b*.
Ro 9: 3 off from Christ for the sake of my *b*
1Co 8: 12 sin against your *b* in this way
2Co 11: 26 and in danger from false *b*.
Gal 2: 4 some false *b* had infiltrated our
1Th 4: 10 you do love all the *b*
5: 26 Greet all the *b* with a holy kiss.
1Ti 6: 2 for them because they are *b*.
Heb 2: 11 Jesus is not ashamed to call them *b*.
2: 17 to be made like his *b* in every way,
13: 1 Keep on loving each other as *b*.
1Pe 1: 22 you have sincere love for your *b*,
3: 8 be sympathetic, love as *b*,
1Jn 3: 14 death to life, because we love our *b*.
3: 16 to lay down our lives for our *b*.
3Jn : 10 he refuses to welcome the *b*.
Rev 12: 10 For the accuser of our *b*,

BROW
Ge 3: 19 By the sweat of your *b*

BRUISED (BRUISES)
Isa 42: 3 A *b* reed he will not break,
Mt 12: 20 A *b* reed he will not break,

BRUISES (BRUISED)
Isa 30: 26 when the LORD binds up the *b*

BRUTAL (BRUTE)
2Ti 3: 3 slanderous, without self-control, *b*,

BRUTE* (BRUTAL)
Ps 73: 22 I was a *b* beast before you.
2Pe 2: 12 They are like *b* beasts, creatures

BUBBLING*
Pr 18: 4 the fountain of wisdom is a *b* brook
Isa 35: 7 the thirsty ground *b* springs.

BUCKET*
Isa 40: 15 the nations are like a drop in a *b*;

BUCKLED* (BUCKLER)
Eph 6: 14 belt of truth *b* around your waist,

BUCKLER* (BUCKLED)
Ps 35: 2 Take up shield and *b*;

BUD (BUDDED)
Isa 27: 6 Israel will *b* and blossom

BUDDED (BUD)
Heb 9: 4 Aaron's staff that had *b*,

BUILD (BUILDER BUILDERS BUILDING BUILDS BUILT REBUILD REBUILT)
2Sa 7: 5 Are you the one to *b* me a house
1Ki 6: 1 he began to *b* the temple
Ecc 3: 3 a time to tear down and a time to *b*,
Mt 16: 18 and on this rock I will *b* my church,
Ac 20: 32 which can *b* you up and give you
Ro 15: 2 neighbour for his good, to *b* him up.
1Co 14: 12 excel in gifts that *b* up the church.
1Th 5: 11 one another and *b* each other up,
Jude : 20 *b* yourselves up in your most holy

BUILDER* (BUILD)
1Co 3: 10 I laid a foundation as an expert *b*,
Heb 3: 3 the *b* of a house has greater honour
3: 4 but God is the *b* of everything.
11: 10 whose architect and *b* is God.

BUILDERS (BUILD)
Ps 118: 22 The stone the *b* rejected
Mt 21: 42 "'The stone the *b* rejected
Mk 12: 10 "'The stone the *b* rejected
Lk 20: 17 "'The stone the *b* rejected
Ac 4: 11 "'the stone you *b* rejected,
1Pe 2: 7 "The stone the *b* rejected

BUILDING (BUILD)
Ezr 3: 8 to supervise the *b* of the house
Ne 4: 17 of Judah who were *b* the wall.
Ro 15: 20 so that I would not be *b*
1Co 3: 9 you are God's field, God's *b*.
2Co 5: 1 we have a *b* from God, an eternal
10: 8 us for *b* you up rather
13: 10 the Lord gave me for *b* you up,
Eph 2: 21 him the whole *b* is joined together
4: 29 helpful for *b* others up according

BUILDS (BUILD)
Ps 127: 1 Unless the LORD *b* the house,
Pr 14: 1 The wise woman *b* her house,
1Co 3: 10 one should be careful how he *b*.
3: 12 If any man *b* on this foundation
8: 1 Knowledge puffs up, but love *b* up.
Eph 4: 16 grows and *b* itself up in love,

BUILT (BUILD)
1Ki 6: 14 So Solomon *b* the temple
Mt 7: 24 is like a wise man who *b* his house
Lk 6: 49 is like a man who *b* a house
Ac 17: 24 does not live in temples *b* by hands.
1Co 3: 14 If what he has *b* survives, he will.
2Co 5: 1 in heaven, not *b* by human hands.
Eph 2: 20 *b* on the foundation of the apostles
4: 12 the body of Christ may be *b* up
Col 2: 7 live in him, rooted and *b* up in him,
1Pe 2: 5 are being *b* into a spiritual house

BULL (BULLS)
Lev 4: 3 bring to the LORD a young *b*

BULLS (BULL)
1Ki 7: 25 The Sea stood on twelve *b*,
Heb 10: 4 it is impossible for the blood of *b*

BURDEN (BURDENED BURDENS BURDENSOME)
Ps 38: 4 like a *b* too heavy to bear.
Ecc 1: 13 What a heavy *b* God has laid
Mt 11: 30 my yoke is easy and my *b* is light."
Ac 15: 28 to us not to *b* you with anything
2Co 11: 9 from being a *b* to you in any way,
12: 14 and I will not be a *b* to you,
1Th 2: 9 day in order not to be a *b* to anyone
2Th 3: 8 so that we would not be a *b* to any
Heb 13: 17 not a *b*, for that would be

BURDENED* (BURDEN)
Isa 43: 23 have not *b* you with grain offerings
43: 24 But you have *b* me with your sins
Mic 6: 3 How have I *b* you? Answer me.
Mt 11: 28 all you who are weary and *b*,
2Co 5: 4 are in this tent, we groan and are *b*,
Gal 5: 1 do not let yourselves be *b* again
1Ti 5: 16 not let the church be *b* with them,

BURDENS (BURDEN)
Ps 68: 19 who daily bears our *b*.
Lk 11: 46 down with *b* they can hardly carry,
Gal 6: 2 Carry each other's *b*,

BURDENSOME (BURDEN)
1Jn 5: 3 And his commands are not *b*,

BURIED (BURY)
Ru 1: 17 die I will die, and there I will be *b*.
Ro 6: 4 *b* with him through baptism
1Co 15: 4 that he was *b*, that he was raised
Col 2: 12 having been *b* with him in baptism

BURN (BURNING BURNT)
Dt 7: 5 and *b* their idols in the fire.
Ps 79: 5 long will your jealousy *b* like fire?
1Co 7: 9 to marry than to *b* with passion.

BURNING (BURN)
Ex 27: 20 so that the lamps may be kept *b*.
Lev 6: 9 the fire must be kept *b* on the altar.
Ps 18: 28 You, O LORD, keep my lamp *b*;
Pr 25: 22 you will heap *b* coals on his head,
Ro 12: 20 you will heap *b* coals on his head."
Rev 19: 20 alive into the fiery lake of *b* sulphur.

BURNISHED*
1Ki 7: 45 of the LORD were of *b* bronze.
Eze 1: 7 and gleamed like *b* bronze.
Da 10: 6 and legs like the gleam of *b* bronze,
Rev 2: 18 and whose feet are like *b* bronze.

BURNT (BURN)
Ge 8: 20 he sacrificed *b* offerings on it.
22: 2 as a *b* offering on one
Ex 10: 25 and *b* offerings to present
18: 12 brought a *b* offering and other
40: 6 Place the altar of *b* offering in front
Lev 1: 3 "'If the offering is a *b* offering
Jos 8: 31 offered to the LORD *b* offerings
Jdg 6: 26 offer the second bull as a *b* offering
13: 16 But if you prepare a *b* offering,
1Ki 3: 4 offered a thousand *b* offerings
9: 25 year Solomon sacrificed *b* offerings
10: 5 and the *b* offerings he made
Ezr 3: 2 Israel to sacrifice *b* offerings on it,
Eze 43: 18 for sacrificing *b* offerings

BURST
Ps 98: 4 *b* into jubilant song with music;
Isa 44: 23 *B* into song, you mountains,
49: 13 *b* into song, O mountains!
52: 9 *B* into songs of joy together,
54: 1 *b* into song, shout for joy,
55: 12 will *b* into song before you,

BURY (BURIED)
Mt 8: 22 and let the dead *b* their own dead."
Lk 9: 60 "Let the dead *b* their own dead,

BUSH
Ex 3: 2 the *b* was on fire it did not burn up.
Mk 12: 26 the account of the *b*, how God said
Lk 20: 37 But in the account of the *b*,
Ac 7: 35 who appeared to him in the *b*.

BUSINESS
Ecc 4: 8 a miserable *b*!
Da 8: 27 and went about the king's *b*.
1Co 5: 12 What *b* is it of mine to judge those
1Th 4: 11 to mind your own *b* and to work
Jas 1: 11 even while he goes about his *b*.

BUSY*
1Ki 18: 27 Perhaps he is deep in thought, or *b*,
20: 40 While your servant was *b* here
Isa 32: 6 his mind is *b* with evil:
Hag 1: 9 of you is *b* with his own house.
2Th 3: 11 They are not *b*; they are
Tit 2: 5 to be *b* at home, to be kind,

BUSYBODIES*
2Th 3: 11 They are not busy; they are *b*.
1Ti 5: 13 *b*, saying things they ought not to.

BUY (BOUGHT BUYS)
Pr 23: 23 *B* the truth and do not sell it;
Isa 55: 1 Come, *b* wine and milk
Rev 13: 17 so that no-one could *b* or sell

BUYS (BUY)
Pr 31: 16 She considers a field and *b* it;

BYWORD (WORD)
1Ki 9: 7 Israel will then become a *b*
Ps 44: 14 You have made us a *b*
Joel 2: 17 a *b* among the nations.

CAESAR
Mt 22: 21 "Give to *C* what is Caesar's,

CAIN
Firstborn of Adam (Ge 4:1), murdered brother Abel (Ge 4:1-16; 1Jn 3:12).

CAKE
Hos 7: 8 Ephraim is a flat *c* not turned over.

CALEB
Judahite who spied out Canaan (Nu 13:6); allowed to enter land because of faith (Nu 13:30-14:38; Dt 1:36). Possessed Hebron (Jdg 14:6-15:19).

CALF
Ex 32: 4 into an idol cast in the shape of a *c*,
Pr 15: 17 than a fattened *c* with hatred.
Lk 15: 23 Bring the fattened *c* and kill it.
Ac 7: 41 made an idol in the form of a *c*.

CALL (CALLED CALLING CALLS)
1Ki 18: 24 I will *c* on the name of the LORD.
2Ki 5: 11 *c* on the name of the LORD his
1Ch 16: 8 to the LORD, *c* on his name;
Ps 105: 1 to the LORD, *c* on his name;
116: 13 and *c* on the name of the LORD.
116: 17 and *c* on the name of the LORD.
145: 18 near to all who *c* on him,
Pr 31: 28 children arise and *c* her blessed;
Isa 5: 20 Woe to those who *c* evil good
12: 4 to the LORD, *c* on his name;
55: 6 *c* on him while he is near.
65: 24 Before they *c* I will answer;
Jer 33: 3 '*C* to me and I will answer you
Zep 3: 9 that all of them may *c* on the name
Zec 13: 9 They will *c* on my name
Mt 9: 13 come to *c* the righteous,
Mk 2: 17 I have not come to *c* the righteous,
Lk 5: 32 I have not come to *c* the righteous,
Ac 2: 39 all whom the Lord our God will *c*."
9: 14 to arrest all who *c* on your name."
9: 21 among those who *c* on this name?
Ro 10: 12 and richly blesses all who *c* on him,
11: 29 gifts and his *c* are irrevocable.
1Co 1: 2 with all those everywhere who *c*
1Th 4: 7 For God did not *c* us to be impure,
2Ti 2: 22 along with those who *c*

CALLED (CALL)
Ge 2: 23 she shall be *c* 'woman',
5: 2 he blessed them and *c* them "man
12: 8 and *c* on the name of the LORD.
21: 33 and there he *c* upon the name
26: 25 and *c* on the name of the LORD.
1Sa 3: 5 and said, "Here I am; you *c* me."
2Ch 7: 14 if my people, who are *c*
Ps 34: 6 This poor man *c*, and the LORD
116: 4 Then I *c* on the name of the LORD
Isa 56: 7 for my house will be *c*
La 3: 55 I *c* on your name, O LORD,
Hos 11: 1 and out of Egypt I *c* my son.
Mt 1: 16 was born Jesus, who is *c* Christ.
2: 15 "Out of Egypt I *c* my son."
21: 13 " 'My house will be *c* a house
Mk 11: 17 " 'My house will be *c*
Lk 1: 32 will be *c* the Son of the Most High.
1: 35 to be born will be *c* the Son of God.
Ro 1: 1 *c* to be an apostle and set apart
1: 6 among those who are *c* to belong
1: 7 loved by God and *c* to be saints:
8: 28 who have been *c* according
8: 30 And those he predestined, he also *c*
1Co 1: 1 *c* to be an apostle of Christ Jesus
1: 2 in Christ Jesus and *c* to be holy,
1: 24 but to those whom God has *c*,
1Co 1: 26 of what you were when you were *c*.
7: 15 God has *c* us to live in peace.
7: 17 and to which God has *c* him.
Gal 1: 6 deserting the one who *c* you
1: 15 from birth and *c* me by his grace,
5: 13 You, my brothers, were *c* to be free
Eph 1: 18 the hope to which he has *c* you,
4: 4 as you were *c* to one hope
Col 3: 15 of one body you were *c* to peace.
2Th 2: 14 He *c* you to this through our gospel
1Ti 6: 12 life to which you were *c*
2Ti 1: 9 who has saved us and *c* us
Heb 9: 15 that those who are *c* may receive
1Pe 1: 15 But just as he who *c* you is holy,
2: 9 of him who *c* you out of darkness
3: 9 to this you were *c* so that you may
5: 10 who *c* you to his eternal glory
2Pe 1: 3 of him who *c* us by his own glory
Jude : 1 To those who have been *c*,

CALLING (CALL)
Isa 40: 3 A voice of one *c*:
Mt 3: 3 "A voice of one *c* in the desert,
Mk 1: 3 "a voice of one *c* in the desert,
10: 49 Cheer up! On your feet! He's *c* you
Lk 3: 4 "A voice of one *c* in the desert,
Jn 1: 23 I am the voice of one *c* in the desert
Ac 22: 16 wash your sins away, *c* on his name
Eph 4: 1 worthy of the *c* you have received.
2Th 1: 11 may count you worthy of his *c*,
2Pe 1: 10 all the more eager to make your *c*

CALLOUS* (CALLOUSED)
Ps 17: 10 They close up their *c* hearts,
73: 7 From their *c* hearts comes iniquity;
119: 70 Their hearts are *c* and unfeeling,

CALLOUSED* (CALLOUS)
Isa 6: 10 Make the heart of this people *c*;
Mt 13: 15 this people's heart has become *c*;
Ac 28: 27 this people's heart has become *c*;

CALLS (CALL)
Ps 147: 4 and *c* them each by name.
Isa 40: 26 and *c* them each by name.
Joel 2: 32 And everyone who *c*
Mt 22: 43 speaking by the Spirit, *c* him 'Lord
Jn 10: 3 He *c* his own sheep by name
Ac 2: 21 And everyone who *c*
Ro 10: 13 "Everyone who *c* on the name
1Th 2: 12 who *c* you into his kingdom
5: 24 The one who *c* you is faithful

CALM (CALMS)
Ps 107: 30 They were glad when it grew *c*,
Isa 7: 4 keep *c* and don't be afraid.
Eze 16: 42 I will be *c* and no longer angry.

CALMS* (CALM)
Pr 15: 18 but a patient man *c* a quarrel.

CAMEL
Mt 19: 24 it is easier for a *c* to go
23: 24 strain out a gnat but swallow a *c*.
Mk 10: 25 It is easier for a *c* to go
Lk 18: 25 it is easier for a *c* to go

CAMP (ENCAMPS)
Heb 13: 13 outside the *c*, bearing the disgrace

CANAAN (CANAANITE CANAANITES)
Ge 10: 15 *C* was the father of Sidon his
Lev 14: 34 "When you enter the land of *C*,
25: 38 of Egypt to give you the land of *C*
Nu 13: 2 men to explore the land of *C*,
33: 51 'When you cross the Jordan into *C*,
Jdg 4: 2 a king of *C*, who reigned in Hazor.
1Ch 16: 18 "To you I will give the land of *C*
Ps 105: 11 "To you I will give the land of *C*
Ac 13: 19 He overthrew seven nations in *C*

CANAANITE (CANAAN)
Ge 10: 18 Later the *C* clans scattered
Ge 28: 1 "Do not marry a *C* woman.
Jos 5: 1 all the *C* kings along the coast
Jdg 1: 32 lived among the *C* inhabitants

CANAANITES (CANAAN)
Ex 33: 2 before you and drive out the *C*,

CANCEL (CANCELLED)
Dt 15: 1 seven years you must *c* debts.

CANCELLED (CANCEL)
Mt 18: 27 pity on him, *c* the debt
Lk 7: 42 so he *c* the debts of both.
Col 2: 14 having *c* the written code,

CANDLESTICKS see LAMPSTANDS

CANOPY*
2Sa 22: 12 He made darkness his *c*
2Ki 16: 18 away the Sabbath *c* that had been
Ps 18: 11 made darkness his covering, his *c*
Isa 4: 5 over all the glory will be a *c*.
40: 22 stretches out the heavens like a *c*,
Jer 43: 10 he will spread his royal *c*

CAPERNAUM
Mt 4: 13 Nazareth, he went and lived in *C*,
Jn 6: 59 teaching in the synagogue in *C*.

CAPITAL
Dt 21: 22 guilty of a *c* offence is put to death

CAPSTONE* (STONE)
Ps 118: 22 has become the *c*;
Zec 4: 7 he will bring out the *c* to shouts
Mt 21: 42 has become the *c*;
Mk 12: 10 has become the *c*;
Lk 20: 17 has become the *c*'?
Ac 4: 11 which has become the *c*.'
1Pe 2: 7 has become the *c*,"

CAPTIVATE* (CAPTIVE)
Pr 6: 25 or let her *c* you with her eyes,

CAPTIVATED* (CAPTIVE)
Pr 5: 19 may you ever be *c* by her love.
5: 20 Why be *c*, my son, by an adulteress

CAPTIVE (CAPTIVATE CAPTIVATED CAPTIVES CAPTIVITY CAPTURED)
Ac 8: 23 full of bitterness and *c* to sin."
2Co 10: 5 and we take *c* every thought
Col 2: 8 See to it that no-one takes you *c*
2Ti 2: 26 who has taken them *c* to do his will.

CAPTIVES (CAPTIVE)
Ps 68: 18 you led *c* in your train;
Isa 61: 1 to proclaim freedom for the *c*
Eph 4: 8 he led *c* in his train

CAPTIVITY (CAPTIVE)
Dt 28: 41 because they will go into *c*.
2Ki 25: 21 So Judah went into *c*, away
Jer 30: 3 Israel and Judah back from *c*
52: 27 So Judah went into *c*, away
Eze 29: 14 I will bring them back from *c*

CAPTURED (CAPTIVE)
1Sa 4: 11 The ark of God was *c*,
2Sa 5: 7 David *c* the fortress of Zion,
2Ki 17: 6 the king of Assyria *c* Samaria

CARCASS
Jdg 14: 9 taken the honey from the lion's *c*.
Mt 24: 28 there is a *c*, there the vultures

CARE (CAREFUL CARES CARING)
Ps 8: 4 the son of man that you *c* for him?
65: 9 You *c* for the land and water it;
144: 3 what is man that you *c* for him,
Pr 29: 7 The righteous *c* about justice
Mk 5: 26 deal under the *c* of many doctors
Lk 10: 34 him to an inn and took *c* of him.

Lk 18: 4 I don't fear God or *c* about men,
Jn 21: 16 Jesus said, "Take *c* of my sheep."
1Ti 3: 5 how can he take *c* of God's church
6: 20 what has been entrusted to your *c*.
Heb 2: 6 the son of man that you *c* for him?
1Pe 5: 2 of God's flock that is under your *c*,

CAREFUL* (CARE)

Ge 31: 24 "Be *c* not to say anything to Jacob,
31: 29 'Be *c* not to say anything to Jacob,
Ex 19: 12 'Be *c* that you do not go up
23: 13 "Be *c* to do everything I have said
34: 12 Be *c* not to make a treaty
34: 15 "Be *c* not to make a treaty
Lev 18: 4 and be *c* to follow my decrees.
25: 18 " 'Follow my decrees and be *c*
26: 3 and are *c* to obey my commands,
Dt 2: 4 afraid of you, but be very *c*.
4: 9 before you today? Only be *c*,
4: 23 Be *c* not to forget the covenant
5: 32 So be *c* to do what the LORD your
6: 3 be *c* to obey so that it may go well
6: 12 be *c* that you do not forget
6: 25 And if we are *c* to obey all this law
7: 12 attention to these laws and are *c*
8: 1 Be *c* to follow every command I am
8: 11 Be *c* that you do not forget
11: 16 Be *c*, or you will be enticed
12: 1 and laws you must be *c* to follow
12: 13 Be *c* not to sacrifice your burnt
12: 19 Be *c* not to neglect the Levites
12: 28 Be *c* to obey all these regulations I
12: 30 be *c* not to be ensnared
15: 5 are *c* to follow all these commands
15: 9 Be *c* not to harbour this wicked
17: 10 Be *c* to do everything they direct
24: 8 cases of leprous diseases be very *c*
Jos 1: 7 Be *c* to obey all the law my servant
1: 8 so that you may be *c*
22: 5 But be very *c* to keep
23: 6 be *c* to obey all that is written
23: 11 be very *c* to love the LORD your
1Ki 8: 25 if only your sons are *c* in all they do
2Ki 10: 31 Yet Jehu was not *c* to keep the law
17: 37 You must always be *c*
21: 8 if only they will be *c*
1Ch 22: 13 if you are *c* to observe the decrees
28: 8 Be *c* to follow all the commands
2Ch 6: 16 if only your sons are *c* in all they do
33: 8 if only they will be *c*
Ezr 4: 22 Be *c* not to neglect this matter.
Job 36: 18 Be *c* that no-one entices you
Ps 101: 2 I will be *c* to lead a blameless life—
Pr 13: 24 he who loves him is *c*
27: 23 give *c* attention to your herds;
Isa 7: 4 Be *c*, keep calm and don't be afraid.
Jer 17: 21 Be *c* not to carry a load
17: 24 But if you are *c* to obey me,
22: 4 For if you are *c* to carry out these
Eze 11: 20 will follow my decrees and be *c*
18: 19 has been *c* to keep all my decrees,
20: 19 follow my decrees and be *c*
20: 21 they were not *c* to keep my laws—
36: 27 you to follow my decrees and be *c*
37: 24 and be *c* to keep my decrees.
Mic 7: 5 be *c* of your words.
Hag 1: 5 "Give *c* thought to your ways.
1: 7 "Give *c* thought to your ways.
2: 15 give *c* thought to this from this day
2: 18 Give *c* thought: Is there yet any
2: 18 give *c* thought to the day
Mt 2: 8 and make a *c* search for the child.
6: 1 "Be *c* not to do your 'acts
16: 6 "Be *c*," Jesus said to them.
Mk 8: 15 "Be *c*," Jesus warned them.
Lk 21: 34 Be *c*, or your hearts will be weighed
Ro 12: 17 Be *c* to do what is right in the eyes
1Co 3: 10 each one should be *c* how he builds
8: 9 Be *c*, however, that the exercise
10: 12 standing firm, be *c* that you don't
Eph 5: 15 Be very *c*, then, how you live—
2Ti 4: 2 great patience and *c* instruction.
Tit 3: 8 may be *c* to devote themselves

Heb 2: 1 We must pay more *c* attention,
4: 1 let us be *c* that none

CARELESS*

Mt 12: 36 for every *c* word they have spoken.

CARES* (CARE)

Dt 11: 12 It is a land the LORD your God *c*
Job 39: 16 she *c* not that her labour was in vain,
Ps 55: 22 Cast your *c* on the LORD
142: 4 no-one *c* for my life.
Pr 12: 10 A righteous man *c* for the needs
Ecc 5: 3 when there are many *c*,
Jer 12: 11 because there is no-one who *c*.
30: 17 Zion for whom no-one *c*.'
Na 1: 7 He *c* for those who trust in him,
Jn 10: 13 and *c* nothing for the sheep.
Eph 5: 29 but he feeds and *c* for it, just
1Pe 5: 7 on him because he *c* for you.

CARING* (CARE)

1Th 2: 7 like a mother *c* for her little
1Ti 5: 4 practice by *c* for their own family

CARNAL see SINFUL, UNSPIRITUAL, WORLDLY

CARPENTER (CARPENTER'S)

Mk 6: 3 does miracles! Isn't this the *c*?

CARPENTER'S* (CARPENTER)

Mt 13: 55 "Isn't this the *c* son? Isn't his

CARRIED (CARRY)

Ex 19: 4 and how I *c* you on eagles' wings
Dt 1: 31 How the LORD your God *c* you,
Isa 53: 4 and *c* our sorrows,
63: 9 he lifted them up and *c* them
Mt 8: 17 and *c* our diseases."
Heb 13: 9 Do not be *c* away by all kinds
2Pe 1: 21 as they were *c* along by the Holy
3: 17 so that you may not be *c* away

CARRIES (CARRY)

Dt 32: 11 and *c* them on its pinions.
Isa 40: 11 and *c* them close to his heart;

CARRY (CARRIED CARRIES CARRYING)

Lev 16: 22 goat will *c* on itself all their sins
26: 15 and fail to *c* out all my commands
Isa 46: 4 I have made you and I will *c* you;
Lk 14: 27 anyone who does not *c* his cross
Gal 6: 2 *C* each other's burdens,
6: 5 for each one should *c* his own load.

CARRYING (CARRY)

Jn 19: 17 *C* his own cross, he went out
1Jn 5: 2 loving God and *c* out his

CARVED (CARVES)

Ne 33: 52 Destroy all their *c* images
Mic 5: 13 I will destroy your *c* images

CARVES* (CARVED)

Dt 27: 15 "Cursed is the man who *c* an image

CASE

Pr 18: 17 to present his *c* seems right,
22: 23 for the LORD will take up their *c*
23: 11 he will take up their *c* against you.

CAST (CASTING)

Ex 34: 17 "Do not make *c* idols.
Lev 16: 8 He is to *c* lots for the two goats—
Ps 22: 18 and *c* lots for my clothing.
55: 22 *C* your cares on the LORD
Pr 16: 33 The lot is *c* into the lap,
Ecc 11: 1 *C* your bread upon the waters,
Jn 19: 24 and *c* lots for my clothing."
1Pe 5: 7 *C* all your anxiety on him

CASTING (CAST)

Pr 18: 18 *C* the lot settles disputes
Mt 27: 35 divided up his clothes by *c* lots.

CATCH (CATCHES CAUGHT)

Lk 5: 4 and let down the nets for a *c*."
5: 10 from now on you will *c* men."

CATCHES (CATCH)

Job 5: 13 He *c* the wise in their craftiness,
1Co 3: 19 "He *c* the wise in their craftiness";

CATTLE

Ps 50: 10 and the *c* on a thousand hills.

CAUGHT (CATCH)

Ge 22: 13 there in a thicket he saw a ram *c*
2Co 12: 2 who fourteen years ago was *c* up
1Th 4: 17 and are left will be *c* up with them

CAUSE (CAUSES)

Pr 24: 28 against your neighbour without *c*,
Ecc 8: 3 Do not stand up for a bad *c*,
Mt 18: 7 of the things that *c* people to sin!
Ro 14: 21 else that will *c* your brother
1Co 10: 32 Do not *c* anyone to stumble,

CAUSES (CAUSE)

Ps 7: 16 The trouble he *c* recoils on himself;
Isa 8: 14 a stone that *c* men to stumble
Mt 5: 29 If your right eye *c* you to sin,
5: 30 And if your right hand *c* you to sin,
18: 6 if anyone *c* one of these little ones
18: 8 or your foot *c* you to sin,
Ro 14: 20 to eat anything that *c* someone else
1Co 8: 13 if what I eat *c* my brother to fall
1Pe 2: 8 "A stone that *c* men to stumble

CAUTIOUS*

Pr 12: 26 A righteous man is *c* in friendship,

CEASE

Ps 46: 9 He makes wars *c* to the ends

CELEBRATE*

Ex 10: 9 we are to *c* a festival to the LORD
12: 14 generations to come you shall *c* it
12: 17 *C* this day as a lasting ordinance
12: 17 "*C* the Feast of Unleavened Bread,
12: 47 community of Israel must *c* it.
12: 48 to *c* the LORD's Passover must
23: 14 are to *c* a festival to me.
23: 15 "*C* the Feast of Unleavened Bread;
23: 16 "*C* the Feast of Harvest
23: 16 "*C* the Feast of Ingathering
34: 18 "*C* the Feast of Unleavened Bread.
34: 22 "*C* the Feast of Weeks
Lev 23: 39 *c* the festival to the LORD
23: 41 *C* this as a festival to the LORD
23: 41 for the generations to come; *c* it
Nu 9: 2 "Have the Israelites *c* the Passover
9: 3 *C* it at the appointed time,
9: 4 told the Israelites to *c* the Passover,
9: 6 of them could not *c* the Passover
9: 10 they may still *c* the LORD's
9: 11 are to *c* it on the fourteenth day
9: 12 When they *c* the Passover,
9: 13 on a journey fails to *c* the Passover,
9: 14 to *c* the LORD's Passover must do
29: 12 *C* a festival to the LORD
Dt 16: 1 *c* the Passover of the LORD your
16: 10 Then *c* the Feast of Weeks
16: 13 *C* the Feast of Tabernacles
16: 15 For seven days *c* the Feast
Jdg 16: 23 to Dagon their god and to *c*,
2Sa 6: 21 the LORD's people Israel—I will *c*
2Ki 23: 21 "*C* the Passover to the LORD your
2Ch 30: 1 and *c* the Passover to the LORD,
30: 2 decided to *c* the Passover
30: 3 able to *c* it at the regular time
30: 5 and *c* the Passover to the LORD,
30: 13 in Jerusalem to *c* the Feast
30: 23 to *c* the festival seven more days;
Ne 8: 12 of food and to *c* with great joy,
12: 27 to *c* joyfully the dedication
Est 9: 21 to have them *c* annually
Ps 145: 7 They will *c* your abundant

Isa 30: 29 as on the night you *c* a holy festival
Na 1: 15 *C* your festivals, O Judah,
Zec 14: 16 and to *c* the Feast of Tabernacles.
14: 18 up to *c* the Feast of Tabernacles.
14: 19 up to *c* the Feast of Tabernacles.
Mt 26: 18 I am going to *c* the Passover
Lk 15: 23 Let's have a feast and *c*.
15: 24 So they began to *c*.
15: 29 goat so I could *c* with my friends.
15: 32 But we had to *c* and be glad,
Rev 11: 10 will *c* by sending each other gifts,

CELESTIAL*
2Pe 2: 10 afraid to slander *c* beings;
Jude : 8 authority and slander *c* beings.

CENSER (CENSERS)
Lev 16: 12 is to take a *c* full of burning coals
Rev 8: 3 Another angel, who had a golden *c*,

CENSERS (CENSER)
Nu 16: 6 Take *c* and tomorrow put fire

CENTURION
Mt 8: 5 had entered Capernaum, a *c* came
27: 54 When the *c* and those
Mk 15: 39 And when the *c*, who stood there
Lk 7: 3 The *c* heard of Jesus and sent some
23: 47 The *c*, seeing what had happened,
Ac 10: 1 a *c* in what was known
27: 1 handed over to a *c* named Julius,

CEPHAS* (PETER)
Jn 1: 42 You will be called *C*" (which,
1Co 1: 12 another, "I follow *C*"; still another,
3: 22 Paul or Apollos or *C* or the world
9: 5 and the Lord's brothers and *C*?

CEREMONIAL* (CEREMONY)
Lev 14: 2 at the time of his *c* cleansing,
15: 13 off seven days for his *c* cleansing;
Mk 7: 3 they give their hands a *c* washing,
Jn 2: 6 used by the Jews for *c* washing,
3: 25 Jew over the matter of *c* washing.
11: 55 to Jerusalem for their *c* cleansing
18: 28 to avoid *c* uncleanness the Jews did
Heb 9: 10 drink and various *c* washings—
13: 9 not by *c* foods, which are

CEREMONIALLY* (CEREMONY)
Lev 4: 12 outside the camp to a place *c* clean,
5: 2 touches anything *c* unclean—
6: 11 the camp to a place that is *c* clean.
7: 19 anyone *c* clean may eat it.
7: 19 touches anything *c* unclean must
10: 14 Eat them in a *c* clean place;
11: 4 not have a split hoof; it is *c* unclean
12: 2 birth to a son will be *c* unclean
12: 7 and then she will be *c* clean
13: 3 he shall pronounce him *c* unclean.
14: 8 with water; then he will be *c* clean.
15: 28 and after that she will be *c* clean.
15: 33 lies with a woman who is *c* unclean.
21: 1 must not make himself *c* unclean
22: 3 of your descendants is *c* unclean
27: 11 he vowed is a *c* unclean animal—
Nu 5: 2 who is *c* unclean because of a dead
6: 7 must not make himself *c* unclean
8: 6 Israelites and make them *c* clean.
9: 6 they were *c* unclean on account
9: 13 But if a man who is *c* clean
18: 11 household who is *c* clean may eat
18: 13 household who is *c* clean may eat
19: 7 but he will be *c* unclean till evening
19: 9 and put them in a *c* clean place
19: 18 Then a man who is *c* clean is
Dt 12: 15 Both the *c* unclean and the clean
12: 22 Both the *c* unclean and the clean
14: 7 they are *c* unclean for you.
15: 22 Both the *c* unclean and the clean
1Sa 20: 26 to David to make him *c* unclean—
2Ch 13: 11 the bread on the *c* clean table
30: 17 for all those who were not *c* clean
Ezr 6: 20 themselves and were all *c* clean.
Ne 12: 30 Levites had purified themselves *c*,
Isa 66: 20 of the LORD in *c* clean vessels.
Eze 22: 10 period when they are *c* unclean.
Mk 7: 2 that is, *c* unwashed—hands.
Ac 24: 18 I was *c* clean when they found me
Heb 9: 13 those who are *c* unclean sanctify

CEREMONY* (CEREMONIAL CEREMONIALLY)
Ge 50: 11 Egyptians are holding a solemn *c*
Ex 12: 25 as he promised, observe this *c*.
12: 26 'What does this *c* mean to you?'
13: 5 are to observe this *c* in this month:

CERTAIN (CERTAINTY)
2Pe 1: 19 word of the prophets made more *c*,

CERTAINTY* (CERTAIN)
Lk 1: 4 so that you may know the *c*
Jn 17: 8 They knew with *c* that I came

CERTIFICATE* (CERTIFIED)
Dt 24: 1 and he writes her a *c* of divorce,
24: 3 and writes her a *c* of divorce,
Isa 50: 1 "Where is your mother's *c*
Jer 3: 8 I gave faithless Israel her *c*
Mt 5: 31 divorces his wife must give her a *c*
19: 7 that a man give his wife a *c*
Mk 10: 4 a man to write a *c* of divorce

CERTIFIED* (CERTIFICATE)
Jn 3: 33 has accepted it has *c* that God is

CHAFF
Ps 1: 4 They are like *c*
35: 5 May they be like *c* before the wind,
Da 2: 35 became like *c* on a threshing floor
Mt 3: 12 up the *c* with unquenchable fire."

CHAINED (CHAINS)
2Ti 2: 9 But God's word is not *c*.

CHAINS (CHAINED)
Eph 6: 20 for which I am an ambassador in *c*.
Col 4: 18 Remember my *c*.
2Ti 1: 16 and was not ashamed of my *c*.
Jude : 6 with everlasting *c* for judgment

CHAMPION
Ps 19: 5 like a *c* rejoicing to run his course.

CHANCE
Ecc 9: 11 but time and *c* happen to them all.

CHANGE (CHANGED)
1Sa 15: 29 of Israel does not lie or *c* his mind;
Ps 110: 4 and will not *c* his mind:
Jer 7: 5 If you really *c* your ways
Mal 3: 6 "I the LORD do not *c*.
Mt 18: 3 unless you *c* and become like little
Heb 7: 21 and will not *c* his mind:
Jas 1: 17 who does not *c* like shifting

CHANGED (CHANGE)
1Sa 10: 6 you will be *c* into a different person
Hos 11: 8 My heart is *c* within me;
1Co 15: 51 but we will all be *c*—in a flash,

CHARACTER*
Ru 3: 11 that you are a woman of noble *c*.
Pr 12: 4 of noble *c* is her husband's crown,
31: 10 A wife of noble *c* who can find?
Ac 17: 11 noble *c* than the Thessalonians,
Ro 5: 4 perseverance, *c*; and *c*, hope.
1Co 15: 33 "Bad company corrupts good *c*."

CHARGE (CHARGES)
Job 34: 13 him in *c* of the whole world?
Ro 8: 33 Who will bring any *c*
1Co 9: 18 the gospel I may offer it free of *c*,
2Co 11: 7 the gospel of God to you free of *c*?
2Ti 4: 1 I give you this *c*: Preach the Word;
Phm : 18 or owes you anything, *c* it to me.

CHARGES (CHARGE)
Isa 50: 8 Who then will bring *c* against me?

CHARIOT (CHARIOTS)
2Ki 2: 11 suddenly a *c* of fire and horses
Ps 104: 3 He makes the clouds his *c*
Ac 8: 28 sitting in his *c* reading the book

CHARIOTS (CHARIOT)
2Ki 6: 17 and *c* of fire all around Elisha.
Ps 20: 7 Some trust in *c* and some in horses,
68: 17 The *c* of God are tens of thousands

CHARITY see LOVE

CHARM* (CHARMING)
Pr 17: 8 bribe is a *c* to the one who gives it;
31: 30 *C* is deceptive, and beauty is

CHARMING* (CHARM)
Pr 26: 25 his speech is *c*, do not believe
SS 1: 16 Oh, how *c*!

CHASE (CHASES)
Lev 26: 8 Five of you will *c* a hundred,

CHASES* (CHASE)
Pr 12: 11 he who *c* fantasies lacks judgment.
28: 19 one who *c* fantasies will have his

CHASM*
Lk 16: 26 and you a great *c* has been fixed,

CHATTER* (CHATTERING)
1Ti 6: 20 Turn away from godless *c*
2Ti 2: 16 Avoid godless *c*, because those

CHATTERING* (CHATTER)
Pr 10: 8 but a *c* fool comes to ruin.
10: 10 and a *c* fool comes to ruin.

CHEAT* (CHEATED CHEATING CHEATS)
Mal 1: 14 "Cursed is the *c* who has
1Co 6: 8 you yourselves *c* and do wrong,

CHEATED* (CHEAT)
Ge 31: 7 yet your father has *c* me
1Sa 12: 3 Whom have I *c*? Whom have I
12: 4 "You have not *c* or oppressed us,"
Lk 19: 8 if I have *c* anybody out of anything,
1Co 6: 7 Why not rather be *c*? Instead,

CHEATING* (CHEAT)
Am 8: 5 and *c* with dishonest scales,

CHEATS* (CHEAT)
Lev 6: 2 or if he *c* him, or if he finds lost

CHEEK (CHEEKS)
Mt 5: 39 someone strikes you on the right *c*,
Lk 6: 29 If someone strikes you on one *c*,

CHEEKS (CHEEK)
Isa 50: 6 my *c* to those who pulled out my

CHEERFUL* (CHEERS)
Pr 15: 13 A happy heart makes the face *c*,
15: 15 but the *c* heart has a continual feast
15: 30 A *c* look brings joy to the heart,
17: 22 A *c* heart is good medicine,
2Co 9: 7 for God loves a *c* giver.

CHEERS (CHEERFUL)
Pr 12: 25 but a kind word *c* him up.

CHEMOSH
2Ki 23: 13 for *C* the vile god of Moab,

CHERISH (CHERISHED CHERISHES)
Ps 17: 14 You still the hunger of those you *c*;

CHERISHED (CHERISH)
Ps 66: 18 If I had *c* sin in my heart,

CHERISHES* (CHERISH)
Pr 19: 8 he who *c* understanding prospers.

CHERUB (CHERUBIM)
Ex 25: 19 Make one *c* on one end
Eze 28: 14 You were anointed as a guardian *c*,

CHERUBIM (CHERUB)
Ge 3: 24 side of the Garden of Eden *c*
1Sa 4: 4 who is enthroned between the *c*.
2Sa 6: 2 enthroned between the *c* that are
22: 11 He mounted the *c* and flew;
1Ki 6: 23 a pair of *c* of olive wood,
2Ki 19: 15 of Israel, enthroned between the *c*,
1Ch 13: 6 who is enthroned between the *c*—
Ps 18: 10 He mounted the *c* and flew;
80: 1 who sit enthroned between the *c*,
99: 1 he sits enthroned between the *c*,
Isa 37: 16 of Israel, enthroned between the *c*,
Eze 10: 1 was over the heads of the *c*.

CHEST
Ex 25: 10 "Have them make a *c*
2Ki 12: 9 Jehoiada the priest took a *c*
Da 2: 32 its *c* and arms of silver, its belly
Rev 1: 13 with a golden sash around his *c*.

CHEWS
Lev 11: 3 divided and that *c* the cud.

CHIEF
1Pe 5: 4 And when the *C* Shepherd appears,

CHILD (CHILDISH CHILDREN CHILDREN'S GRANDCHILDREN)
Pr 20: 11 Even a *c* is known by his actions,
22: 6 Train a *c* in the way he should go,
22: 15 Folly is bound up in the heart of a *c*
23: 13 not withhold discipline from a *c*;
29: 15 *c* left to itself disgraces his mother.
Isa 7: 14 The virgin will be with *c*
9: 6 For to us a *c* is born,
11: 6 and a little *c* will lead them.
66: 13 As a mother comforts her *c*,
Mt 1: 23 "The virgin will be with *c*
18: 2 He called a little *c* and had him
Lk 1: 42 and blessed is the *c* you will bear!
1: 80 And the *c* grew and became strong
1Co 13: 11 When I was a *c*, I talked like a *c*,
1Jn 5: 1 who loves the father loves his *c*

CHILDBEARING (BEAR [1])
Ge 3: 16 greatly increase your pains in *c*;

CHILDBIRTH (BEAR [1])
Gal 4: 19 the pains of *c* until Christ is formed

CHILDISH* (CHILD)
1Co 13: 11 When I became a man, I put *c* ways

CHILDREN (CHILD)
Ex 20: 5 punishing the *c* for the sin
Dt 4: 9 Teach them to your *c*
6: 7 Impress them on your *c*.
11: 19 them to your *c*, talking about them
14: 1 You are the *c* of the LORD your
24: 16 nor *c* put to death for their fathers;
30: 19 so that you and your *c* may live
32: 46 so that you may command your *c*
Job 1: 5 "Perhaps my *c* have sinned
Ps 8: 2 From the lips of *c* and infants
78: 5 forefathers to teach their *c*,
Pr 17: 6 Children's *c* are a crown
20: 7 blessed are his *c* after him.
31: 28 Her *c* arise and call her blessed;
Joel 1: 3 Tell it to your *c*,
Mal 4: 6 the hearts of the fathers to their *c*,
Mt 7: 11 how to give good gifts to your *c*,
11: 25 and revealed them to little *c*.
18: 3 you change and become like little *c*
19: 14 "Let the little *c* come to me,
Mt 21: 16 " 'From the lips of *c* and infants
Mk 9: 37 one of these little *c* in my name
10: 14 "Let the little *c* come to me,
10: 16 And he took the *c* in his arms,
13: 12 *C* will rebel against their parents
Lk 10: 21 and revealed them to little *c*.
18: 16 "Let the little *c* come to me,
Jn 1: 12 the right to become *c* of God—
Ac 2: 39 The promise is for you and your *c*
Ro 8: 16 with our spirit that we are God's *c*.
1Co 14: 20 Brothers, stop thinking like *c*.
2Co 12: 14 parents, but parents for their *c*.
Eph 6: 1 *C*, obey your parents in the Lord,
6: 4 do not exasperate your *c*; instead,
Col 3: 20 *C*, obey your parents in everything,
3: 21 Fathers, do not embitter your *c*,
1Ti 3: 4 and see that his *c* obey him
3: 12 and must manage his *c* and his
5: 10 bringing up *c*, showing hospitality,
Heb 2: 13 and the *c* God has given me."
1Jn 3: 1 that we should be called *c* of God!

CHILDREN'S (CHILD)
Isa 54: 13 and great will be your *c* peace.

CHOKE
Mk 4: 19 come in and *c* the word,

CHOOSE (CHOOSES CHOSE CHOSEN)
Dt 30: 19 Now *c* life, so that you
Jos 24: 15 then *c* for yourselves this day
Pr 8: 10 *C* my instruction instead of silver,
16: 16 to *c* understanding rather
Jn 15: 16 You did not *c* me, but I chose you

CHOOSES (CHOOSE)
Mt 11: 27 to whom the Son *c* to reveal him.
Lk 10: 22 to whom the Son *c* to reveal him."
Jn 7: 17 If anyone *c* to do God's Will,

CHOSE (CHOOSE)
Ge 13: 11 So Lot *c* for himself the whole plain
Ps 33: 12 the people he *c* for his inheritance.
Jn 15: 16 but I *c* you and appointed you to go
1Co 1: 27 But God *c* the foolish things
Eph 1: 4 he *c* us in him before the creation
2Th 2: 13 from the beginning God *c* you

CHOSEN (CHOOSE)
Isa 41: 8 Jacob, whom I have *c*,
Mt 22: 14 For many are invited, but few are *c*
Lk 10: 42 Mary has *c* what is better,
23: 35 the Christ of God, the *C* One."
Jn 15: 19 but I have *c* you out of the world.
1Pe 1: 20 He was *c* before the creation
2: 9 But you are a *c* people, a royal

CHRIST (CHRIST'S CHRISTIAN CHRISTIANS CHRISTS)
Mt 1: 16 was born Jesus, who is called *C*.
16: 16 Peter answered, "You are the *C*,
22: 42 "What do you think about the *C*?
Mk 1: 1 of the gospel about Jesus *C*,
8: 29 Peter answered, "You are the *C*."
14: 61 "Are you the *C*, the Son
Lk 9: 20 Peter answered, "The *C* of God."
Jn 1: 41 found the Messiah" (that is, the *C*).
20: 31 you may believe that Jesus is the *C*,
Ac 2: 36 you crucified, both Lord and *C*."
5: 42 the good news that Jesus is the *C*.
9: 22 by proving that Jesus is the *C*.
9: 34 said to him, "Jesus *C* heals you.
17: 3 proving that the *C* had to suffer
18: 28 the Scriptures that Jesus was the *C*.
26: 23 that the *C* would suffer and,
Ro 1: 4 from the dead: Jesus *C* our Lord.
3: 22 comes through faith in Jesus *C*
5: 1 God through our Lord Jesus *C*,
5: 6 we were still powerless, *C* died
5: 8 While we were still sinners, *C* died
Ro 5: 11 in God through our Lord Jesus *C*,
5: 17 life through the one man, Jesus *C*.
6: 4 as *C* was raised from the dead
6: 9 that since *C* was raised
6: 23 life in *C* Jesus our Lord.
7: 4 to the law through the body of *C*,
8: 1 for those who are in *C* Jesus,
8: 9 Spirit of *C*, he does not belong to *C*.
8: 17 heirs of God and co-heirs with *C*,
8: 34 Who is he that condemns? *C* Jesus,
8: 35 us from the love of *C*?
9: 5 is traced the human ancestry of *C*,
10: 4 *C* is the end of the law
12: 5 so in *C* we who are many form one
13: 14 yourselves with the Lord Jesus *C*,
14: 9 *C* died and returned to life
15: 3 For even *C* did not please himself
15: 5 yourselves as you follow *C* Jesus,
15: 7 then, just as *C* accepted you,
16: 18 people are not serving our Lord *C*,
1Co 1: 2 to those sanctified in *C* Jesus
1: 7 for our Lord Jesus *C* to be revealed.
1: 13 Is *C* divided? Was Paul crucified
1: 17 For *C* did not send me to baptise,
1: 23 but we preach *C* crucified:
1: 30 of him that you are in *C* Jesus,
2: 2 except Jesus *C* and him crucified.
3: 11 one already laid, which is Jesus *C*.
5: 7 For *C*, our Passover lamb,
6: 15 bodies are members of *C* himself?
8: 6 and there is but one Lord, Jesus *C*,
8: 12 conscience, you sin against *C*.
10: 4 them, and that rock was *C*.
11: 1 as I follow the example of *C*.
11: 3 the head of every man is *C*,
12: 27 Now you are the body of *C*,
15: 3 that *C* died for our sins according
15: 14 And if *C* has not been raised,
15: 22 so in *C* all will be made alive.
15: 57 victory through our Lord Jesus *C*.
2Co 1: 5 as the sufferings of *C* flow
2: 14 us in triumphal procession in *C*
3: 3 show that you are a letter from *C*,
3: 14 because only in *C* is it taken away.
4: 4 light of the gospel of the glory of *C*,
4: 5 not preach ourselves, but Jesus *C*
4: 6 of the glory of God in the face of *C*.
5: 10 before the judgment seat of *C*,
5: 17 Therefore, if anyone is in *C*,
6: 15 What harmony is there between *C*
10: 1 the meekness and gentleness of *C*,
11: 2 you to one husband, to *C*,
Gal 1: 7 are trying to pervert the gospel of *C*
2: 4 on the freedom we have in *C* Jesus
2: 16 but by faith in Jesus *C*.
2: 17 does that mean that *C* promotes sin
2: 20 I have been crucified with *C*
2: 21 *C* died for nothing!" You foolish
3: 13 *C* redeemed us from the curse
3: 16 meaning one person, who is *C*.
3: 26 of God through faith in *C* Jesus,
4: 19 of childbirth until *C* is formed
5: 1 for freedom that *C* has set us free.
5: 4 by law have been alienated from *C*;
5: 24 to *C* Jesus have crucified the sinful
6: 14 in the cross of our Lord Jesus *C*,
Eph 1: 3 with every spiritual blessing in *C*.
1: 10 together under one head, even *C*.
1: 20 which he exerted in *C*
2: 5 made us alive with *C*
2: 10 created in *C* Jesus
2: 12 time you were separate from *C*,
2: 20 with *C* Jesus himself as the chief
3: 8 the unsearchable riches of *C*,
3: 17 so that *C* may dwell in your hearts
4: 7 has been given as *C* apportioned it.
4: 13 measure of the fulness of *C*.
4: 15 into him who is the Head, that is, *C*
4: 32 just as in *C* God forgave you.
5: 2 as *C* loved us and gave himself up
5: 21 out of reverence for *C*.
5: 23 as *C* is the head of the church,
5: 25 just as *C* loved the church

Php 1: 18 motives or true, C is preached.
1: 21 to live is C and to die is gain.
1: 23 I desire to depart and be with C,
1: 27 worthy of the gospel of C.
1: 29 on behalf of C not only to believe
2: 5 be the same as that of C Jesus:
3: 7 now consider loss for the sake of C.
3: 10 I want to know C and the power
3: 18 as enemies of the cross of C.
4: 19 to his glorious riches in C Jesus.
Col 1: 4 heard of your faith in C Jesus
1: 27 which is C in you, the hope of glory
1: 28 may present everyone perfect in C.
2: 2 the mystery of God, namely, C,
2: 6 as you received C Jesus as Lord,
2: 9 For in C all the fulness
2: 13 God made you alive with C.
2: 17 the reality, however, is found in C.
3: 1 then, you have been raised with C,
3: 3 and your life is now hidden with C
3: 15 Let the peace of C rule
1Th 5: 9 through our Lord Jesus C.
2Th 2: 1 the coming of our Lord Jesus C
2: 14 in the glory of our Lord Jesus C.
1Ti 1: 12 I thank C Jesus our Lord, who has
1: 15 C Jesus came into the world
1: 16 C Jesus might display his unlimited
2: 5 the man C Jesus, who gave himself
2Ti 1: 9 us in C Jesus before the beginning
1: 10 appearing of our Saviour, C Jesus,
2: 1 in the grace that is in C Jesus.
2: 3 us like a good soldier of C Jesus.
2: 8 Remember Jesus C, raised
2: 10 the salvation that is in C Jesus,
3: 12 life in C Jesus will be persecuted,
3: 15 salvation through faith in C Jesus.
4: 1 presence of God and of C Jesus,
Tit 2: 13 our great God and Saviour, Jesus C,
Heb 3: 6 But C is faithful as a son
3: 14 to share in C if we hold firmly
5: 5 So C also did not take
6: 1 the elementary teachings about C
9: 11 When C came as high priest
9: 14 more, then, will the blood of C,
9: 15 For this reason C is the mediator
9: 24 For C did not enter a man-made
9: 26 Then C would have had
9: 28 so C was sacrificed once
10: 10 of the body of Jesus C once for all.
13: 8 Jesus C is the same yesterday
1Pe 1: 2 for obedience to Jesus C
1: 3 of Jesus C from the dead,
1: 11 he predicted the sufferings of C
1: 19 but with the precious blood of C,
2: 21 because C suffered for you,
3: 15 in your hearts set apart C as Lord.
3: 18 For C died for sins once for all,
3: 21 you by the resurrection of Jesus C,
4: 13 participate in the sufferings of C,
4: 14 insulted because of the name of C,
2Pe 1: 1 and Saviour Jesus C have received
1: 16 and coming of our Lord Jesus C,
1Jn 2: 1 Jesus C, the Righteous One.
2: 22 man who denies that Jesus is the C.
3: 16 Jesus C laid down his life for us.
3: 23 in the name of his Son, Jesus C,
4: 2 that Jesus C has come
5: 1 believes that Jesus is the C is born
5: 20 even in his Son Jesus C.
2Jn : 9 teaching of C does not have God;
Jude : 4 deny Jesus C our only Sovereign
Rev 1: 1 The revelation of Jesus C,
1: 5 from Jesus C, who is the faithful
11: 15 kingdom of our Lord and of his C,
20: 4 reigned with C a thousand years.
20: 6 they will be priests of God and of C

CHRIST'S (CHRIST)
1Co 9: 21 from God's law but am under C law
2Co 5: 14 For C love compels us,
5: 20 We are therefore C ambassadors,
12: 9 so that C power may rest on me.
Col 1: 22 by C physical body through death

CHRISTIAN* (CHRIST)
Ac 26: 28 you can persuade me to be a C?"
1Pe 4: 16 as a C, do not be ashamed,

CHRISTIANS* (CHRIST)
Ac 11: 26 The disciples were first called C

CHRISTS* (CHRIST)
Mt 24: 24 For false C and false prophets will
Mk 13: 22 For false C and false prophets will

CHURCH
Mt 16: 18 and on this rock I will build my c,
18: 17 if he refuses to listen even to the c,
Ac 20: 28 Be shepherds of the c of God,
1Co 5: 12 of mine to judge those outside the c
14: 4 but he who prophesies edifies the c.
14: 12 to excel in gifts that build up the c.
14: 26 done for the strengthening of the c.
15: 9 because I persecuted the c of God.
Gal 1: 13 how intensely I persecuted the c
Eph 5: 23 as Christ is the head of the c,
Col 1: 18 he is the head of the body, the c;
1: 24 the sake of his body, which is the c.

CHURNING
Pr 30: 33 For as c the milk produces butter,

CIRCLE
Isa 40: 22 enthroned above the c of the earth,

CIRCUMCISE (CIRCUMCISED CIRCUMCISION)
Dt 10: 16 C your hearts, therefore,

CIRCUMCISED (CIRCUMCISE)
Ge 17: 10 Every male among you shall be c.
17: 12 who is eight days old must be c,
Jos 5: 3 and c the Israelites at Gibeath
Gal 5: 2 that if you let yourselves be c,

CIRCUMCISION (CIRCUMCISE)
Ro 2: 25 C has value if you observe the law,
2: 29 and c is c of the heart, by the Spirit,
1Co 7: 19 C is nothing and uncircumcision is

CIRCUMSTANCES
Php 4: 11 to be content whatever the c.
1Th 5: 18 continually; give thanks in all c,

CITIES (CITY)
Lk 19: 17 small matter, take charge of ten c.'
19: 19 'You take charge of five c.'

CITIZENSHIP* (FELLOW-CITIZENS)
Ac 22: 28 "I had to pay a big price for my c."
Eph 2: 12 excluded from c in Israel
Php 3: 20 But our c is in heaven.

CITY (CITIES)
Mt 5: 14 A c on a hill cannot be hidden.
Ac 18: 10 I have many people in this c."
Heb 13: 14 here we do not have an enduring c,
Rev 21: 2 saw the Holy C, the new

CIVILIAN*
2Ti 2: 4 a soldier gets involved in c affairs—

CLAIM (CLAIMS RECLAIM)
Pr 25: 6 do not c a place among great men;
1Jn 1: 6 If we c to have fellowship
1: 8 If we c to be without sin, we
1: 10 If we c we have not sinned,

CLAIMS (CLAIM)
Jas 2: 14 if a man c to have faith
1Jn 2: 6 Whoever c to live in him must walk
2: 9 Anyone who c to be in the light

CLANGING*
1Co 13: 1 a resounding gong or a c cymbal.

CLAP* (CLAPPED CLAPS)
Job 21: 5 c your hand over your mouth.
Ps 47: 1 C your hands, all you nations;
98: 8 Let the rivers c their hands,
Pr 30: 32 c your hand over your mouth!
Isa 55: 12 will c their hands.
La 2: 15 c their hands at you;

CLAPPED* (CLAP)
2Ki 11: 12 and the people c their hands
Eze 25: 6 Because you have c your hands

CLAPS* (CLAP)
Job 27: 23 It c its hands in derision
34: 37 scornfully he c his hands among us
Na 3: 19 c his hands at your fall,

CLASSIFY*
2Co 10: 12 dare to c or compare ourselves

CLAUDIUS
Ac 11: 28 happened during the reign of C.)
18: 2 because C had ordered all the Jews

CLAY
Isa 45: 9 Does the c say to the potter,
64: 8 We are the c, you are the potter;
Jer 18: 6 "Like c in the hand of the potter,
La 4: 2 are now considered as pots of c,
Da 2: 33 partly of iron and partly of baked c.
Ro 9: 21 of the same lump of c some pottery
2Co 4: 7 we have this treasure in jars of c
2Ti 2: 20 and c; some are for noble purposes

CLEAN (CLEANNESS CLEANSE CLEANSED CLEANSES CLEANSING)
Ge 7: 2 seven of every kind of c animal,
Lev 4: 12 the camp to a place ceremonially c,
16: 30 you will be c from all your sins.
Ps 24: 4 He who has c hands and a pure
51: 7 with hyssop, and I will be c;
Pr 20: 9 I am c and without sin"?
Eze 36: 25 I will sprinkle c water on you,
Mt 8: 2 are willing, you can make me c."
12: 44 the house unoccupied, swept c
23: 25 You c the outside of the cup
Mk 7: 19 Jesus declared all foods "c.")
Jn 13: 10 to wash his feet; his whole body is c
15: 3 are already c because of the word
Ac 10: 15 impure that God has made c."
Ro 14: 20 All food is c, but it is wrong

CLEANNESS (CLEAN)
2Sa 22: 25 according to my c in his sight.

CLEANSE (CLEAN)
Ps 51: 2 and c me from my sin.
51: 7 C me with hyssop, and I will be
Pr 20: 30 Blows and wounds c away evil,
Heb 9: 14 c our consciences from acts that
10: 22 having our hearts sprinkled to c us

CLEANSED (CLEAN)
Heb 9: 22 requires that nearly everything be c
2Pe 1: 9 has forgotten that he has been c

CLEANSES* (CLEAN)
2Ti 2: 21 If a man c himself from the latter,

CLEANSING (CLEAN)
Eph 5: 26 c her by the washing with water

CLEFT*
Ex 33: 22 I will put you in a c in the rock

CLEVER
Isa 5: 21 and c in their own sight.

CLING
Ro 12: 9 Hate what is evil; c to what is good.

CLOAK
Ex 12: 11 with your c tucked into your belt,

2Ki 4: 29 "Tuck your *c* into your belt,
9: 1 "Tuck your *c* into your belt,
Mt 5: 40 let him have your *c* as well.

CLOSE (CLOSER)
2Ki 11: 8 Stay *c* to the king wherever he goes
2Ch 23: 7 Stay *c* to the king wherever he goes
Ps 34: 18 LORD is *c* to the broken-hearted
148: 14 of Israel, the people *c* to his heart.
Isa 40: 11 and carries them *c* to his heart;
Jer 30: 21 himself to be *c* to me?'

CLOSER (CLOSE)
Ex 3: 5 "Do not come any *c*," God said.
Pr 18: 24 there is a friend who sticks *c*

CLOSES
Pr 28: 27 he who *c* his eyes to them receives

CLOTHE (CLOTHED CLOTHES CLOTHING CLOTHS)
Ps 45: 3 *c* yourself with splendour
Isa 52: 1 *c* yourself with strength.
Ro 13: 14 *c* yourselves with the Lord Jesus
Col 3: 12 *c* yourselves with compassion,
1Pe 5: 5 *C* yourselves with humility

CLOTHED (CLOTHE)
Ps 30: 11 removed my sackcloth and *c* me
104: 1 you are *c* with splendour
Pr 31: 22 she is *c* in fine linen and purple.
31: 25 She is *c* with strength and dignity;
Isa 61: 10 For he has *c* me with garments
Lk 24: 49 until you have been *c* with power
Gal 3: 27 into Christ have *c* yourselves

CLOTHES (CLOTHE)
Dt 8: 4 Your *c* did not wear out
Mt 6: 25 the body more important than *c*?
6: 28 "And why do you worry about *c*?
27: 35 they divided up his *c* by casting lots
Jn 11: 44 Take off the grave *c* and let him go

CLOTHING (CLOTHE)
Dt 22: 5 A woman must not wear men's *c*,
Job 29: 14 I put on righteousness as my *c*;
Ps 22: 18 and cast lots for my *c*.
Mt 7: 15 They come to you in sheep's *c*,
1Ti 6: 8 But if we have food and *c*,

CLOTHS (CLOTHE)
Lk 2: 12 You will find a baby wrapped in *c*

CLOUD (CLOUDS)
Ex 13: 21 them in a pillar of *c* to guide them
1Ki 18: 44 *c* as small as a man's hand is rising
Pr 16: 15 his favour is like a rain *c* in spring.
Isa 19: 1 See, the LORD rides on a swift *c*
Lk 21: 27 of Man coming in a *c* with power
Heb 12: 1 by such a great *c* of witnesses,
Rev 14: 14 seated on the *c* was one "like a son

CLOUDS (CLOUD)
Dt 33: 26 and on the *c* in his majesty.
Ps 68: 4 extol him who rides on the *c*—
104: 3 He makes the *c* his chariot
Pr 25: 14 Like *c* and wind without rain
Da 7: 13 coming with the *c* of heaven.
Mt 24: 30 of Man coming on the *c* of the sky,
26: 64 and coming on the *c* of heaven."
Mk 13: 26 coming in *c* with great power
1Th 4: 17 with them in the *c* to meet the Lord
Rev 1: 7 Look, he is coming with the *c*,

CLUB
Pr 25: 18 Like a *c* or a sword or a sharp arrow

CO-HEIRS* (INHERIT)
Ro 8: 17 heirs of God and *c* with Christ,

COALS
Pr 25: 22 you will heap burning *c* on his head
Ro 12: 20 you will heap burning *c* on his head

COARSE*
Eph 5: 4 or *c* joking, which are out of place,

COCK
Mt 26: 34 this very night, before the *c* crows,

CODE*
Ro 2: 27 even though you have the written *c*
2: 29 by the Spirit, not by the written *c*.
7: 6 not in the old way of the written *c*.
Col 2: 14 having cancelled the written *c*,

COINS
Mt 26: 15 out for him thirty silver *c*.
Lk 15: 8 suppose a woman has ten silver *c*

COLD
Pr 25: 25 Like *c* water to a weary soul
Mt 10: 42 if anyone gives a cup of *c* water
24: 12 the love of most will grow *c*,

COLLECTION
1Co 16: 1 Now about the *c* for God's people:

COLT
Zec 9: 9 on a *c*, the foal of a donkey.
Mt 21: 5 on a *c*, the foal of a donkey.'"

COMB
Ps 19: 10 than honey from the *c*.

COMFORT* (COMFORTED COMFORTER COMFORTERS COMFORTING COMFORTS)
Ge 5: 29 "He will *c* us in the labour
37: 35 and daughters came to *c* him,
Ru 2: 13 "You have given me *c*
1Ch 7: 22 and his relatives came to *c* him.
Job 2: 11 sympathise with him and *c* him.
7: 13 When I think my bed will *c* me
16: 5 *c* from my lips would bring you
36: 16 to the *c* of your table laden
Ps 23: 4 rod and your staff, they *c* me.
71: 21 and *c* me once again.
119: 50 My *c* in my suffering is this:
119: 52 and I find *c* in them.
119: 76 May your unfailing love be my *c*,
119: 82 I say, "When will you *c* me?"
Isa 40: 1 *C*, *c* my people,
51: 3 The LORD will surely *c* Zion
51: 19 who can *c* you?—
57: 18 I will guide him and restore *c*
61: 2 to *c* all who mourn,
66: 13 so will I *c* you;
Jer 16: 7 food to *c* those who mourn
31: 13 I will give them *c* and joy instead
La 1: 2 there is none to *c* her.
1: 9 there was none to *c* her.
1: 16 No-one is near to *c* me,
1: 17 but there is no-one to *c* her.
1: 21 but there is no-one to *c* me.
2: 13 that I may *c* you,
Eze 16: 54 all you have done in giving them *c*.
Na 3: 7 Where can I find anyone to *c* you?"
Zec 1: 17 and the LORD will again *c* Zion
10: 2 they give *c* in vain.
Lk 6: 24 you have already received your *c*.
Jn 11: 19 and Mary to *c* them in the loss
1Co 14: 3 encouragement and *c*.
2Co 1: 3 of compassion and the God of all *c*,
1: 4 so that we can *c* those
1: 4 with the *c* we ourselves have
1: 5 through Christ our *c* overflows.
1: 6 if we are comforted, it is for your *c*,
1: 6 it is for your *c* and salvation;
1: 7 so also you share in our *c*.
2: 7 you ought to forgive and *c* him,
7: 7 also by the *c* you had given him.
Php 2: 1 if any *c* from his love,
Col 4: 11 and they have proved a *c* to me.

COMFORTED* (COMFORT)
Ge 24: 67 Isaac was *c* after his mother's death
37: 35 comfort him, but he refused to be *c*.
2Sa 12: 24 Then David *c* his wife Bathsheba,
Job 42: 11 They *c* and consoled him
Ps 77: 2 and my soul refused to be *c*.
86: 17 have helped me and *c* me.
Isa 12: 1 and you have *c* me.
52: 9 for the LORD has *c* his people,
54: 11 lashed by storms and not *c*,
66: 13 and you will be *c* over Jerusalem."
Jer 31: 15 and refusing to be *c*,
Mt 2: 18 and refusing to be *c*,
5: 4 for they will be *c*.
Lk 16: 25 but now he is *c* here and you are
Ac 20: 12 man home alive and were greatly *c*.
2Co 1: 6 if we are *c*, it is for your comfort,
7: 6 *c* us by the coming of Titus,

COMFORTER* (COMFORT)
Ecc 4: 1 and they have no *c*;
Jer 8: 18 O my *C* in sorrow,

COMFORTERS* (COMFORT)
Job 16: 2 miserable *c* are you all!
Ps 69: 20 for *c*, but I found none.

COMFORTING* (COMFORT)
Isa 66: 11 satisfied at her *c* breasts;
Zec 1: 13 *c* words to the angel who talked
Jn 11: 31 *c* her, noticed how quickly she got
1Th 2: 12 *c* and urging you to live lives

COMFORTS* (COMFORT)
Job 29: 25 I was like one who *c* mourners.
Isa 49: 13 For the LORD *c* his people
51: 12 "I, even I, am he who *c* you.
66: 13 As a mother *c* her child,
2Co 1: 4 who *c* us in all our troubles,
7: 6 But God, who *c* the downcast,

COMMAND (COMMANDED COMMANDING COMMANDMENT COMMANDMENTS COMMANDS)
Ex 7: 2 You are to say everything I *c* you,
Nu 14: 41 are you disobeying the LORD's *c*?
24: 13 to go beyond the *c* of the LORD—
Dt 4: 2 Do not add to what I *c* you
8: 1 To follow every *c* I am giving you
12: 32 See that you do all I *c* you;
15: 11 I *c* you to be open-handed
30: 16 For I *c* you today to love
32: 46 so that you may *c* your children
Ps 91: 11 For he will *c* his angels concerning
Pr 13: 13 but he who respects a *c* is rewarded
Ecc 8: 2 Obey the king's *c*, I say,
Jer 1: 7 you to and say whatever I *c* you.
1: 17 and say to them whatever I *c* you.
7: 23 Walk in all the ways I *c* you,
11: 4 Obey me and do everything I *c* you
26: 2 Tell them everything I *c* you;
Joel 2: 11 mighty are those who obey his *c*.
Mt 4: 6 He will *c* his angels concerning you
15: 3 why do you break the *c* of God
Lk 4: 10 "'He will *c* his angels concerning
Jn 13: 34 "A new *c* I give you: Love one
14: 15 love me, you will obey what I *c*.
15: 12 My *c* is this: Love each other
15: 14 friends if you do what I *c*.
15: 17 This is my *c*: Love each other.
1Co 14: 37 writing to you is the Lord's *c*.
Gal 5: 14 law is summed up in a single *c*:
1Ti 1: 5 goal of this *c* is love, which comes
6: 14 you to keep this *c* without spot
6: 17 *C* those who are rich
Heb 11: 3 universe was formed at God's *c*,
2Pe 2: 21 on the sacred *c* that was passed
3: 2 and the *c* given by our Lord
1Jn 2: 7 I am not writing you a new *c*
3: 23 this is his *c*: to believe in the name
4: 21 And he has given us this *c*:
2Jn : 6 his *c* is that you walk in love.

COMMANDED (COMMAND)
Ge 2: 16 And the LORD God *c* the man,

Ge 7: 5 Noah did all that the LORD *c* him.
50: 12 Jacob's sons did as he had *c* them:
Ex 7: 6 did just as the LORD *c* them.
19: 7 all the words the LORD had *c* him
Dt 4: 5 laws as the LORD my God *c* me,
6: 24 The LORD *c* us to obey all these
Jos 1: 9 Have I not *c* you? Be strong
1: 16 Whatever you have *c* us we will do,
2Sa 5: 25 So David did as the LORD *c* him,
2Ki 17: 13 the entire Law that I *c* your fathers
21: 8 careful to do everything I *c* them
2Ch 33: 8 do everything I *c* them concerning
Ps 33: 9 he *c*, and it stood firm.
78: 5 which he *c* our forefathers
148: 5 for he *c* and they were created.
Mt 28: 20 to obey everything I have *c* you.
1Co 9: 14 Lord has *c* that those who preach
1Jn 3: 23 and to love one another as he *c* us.
2Jn : 4 in the truth, just as the Father *c* us.

COMMANDING (COMMAND)

2Ti 2: 4 he wants to please his *c* officer.

COMMANDMENT* (COMMAND)

Jos 22: 5 But be very careful to keep the *c*
Mt 22: 36 which is the greatest *c* in the Law?"
22: 38 This is the first and greatest *c*.
Mk 12: 31 There is no *c* greater than these."
Lk 23: 56 the Sabbath in obedience to the *c*.
Ro 7: 8 the opportunity afforded by the *c*,
7: 9 when the *c* came, sin sprang to life
7: 10 that the very *c* that was intended
7: 11 and through the *c* put me to death.
7: 11 the opportunity afforded by the *c*,
7: 12 and the *c* is holy, righteous
7: 13 through the *c* sin might become
13: 9 and whatever other *c* there may be,
Eph 6: 2 which is the first *c* with a promise
Heb 9: 19 Moses had proclaimed every *c*

COMMANDMENTS* (COMMAND)

Ex 20: 6 who love me and keep my *c*.
34: 28 of the covenant—the Ten *C*.
Dt 4: 13 to you his covenant, the Ten *C*,
5: 10 who love me and keep my *c*.
5: 22 These are the *c* the LORD
6: 6 These *c* that I give you today are
9: 10 were all the *c* the LORD
10: 4 The Ten *C* he had proclaimed
Ecc 12: 13 Fear God and keep his *c*,
Mt 5: 19 one of the least of these *c*
19: 17 If you want to enter life, obey the *c*
22: 40 the Prophets hang on these two *c*."
Mk 10: 19 You know the *c*: 'Do not murder,
12: 28 "Of all the *c*, which is the most
Lk 1: 6 observing all the Lord's *c*
18: 20 You know the *c*: 'Do not commit
Ro 13: 9 The *c*, "Do not commit adultery,"
Eph 2: 15 in his flesh the law with its *c*
Rev 12: 17 those who obey God's *c*
14: 12 part of the saints who obey God's *c*

COMMANDS (COMMAND)

Ex 24: 12 and *c* I have written for their
25: 22 give you all my *c* for the Israelites.
34: 32 gave them all the *c* the LORD had
Lev 22: 31 "Keep my *c* and follow them.
Nu 15: 39 and so you will remember all the *c*
Dt 7: 9 those who love him and keep his *c*.
7: 11 Therefore, take care to follow the *c*
11: 1 decrees, his laws and his *c* always.
11: 27 the blessing if you obey the *c*
28: 1 carefully follow all his *c* I give you
30: 10 LORD your God and keep his *c*
Jos 22: 5 to walk in all his ways, to obey his *c*
1Ki 2: 3 and keep his decrees and *c*,
8: 58 in all his ways and to keep the *c*,
8: 61 to live by his decrees and obey his *c*
1Ch 28: 7 unswerving in carrying out my *c*
29: 19 devotion to keep your *c*,
2Ch 31: 21 in obedience to the law and the *c*,
Ne 1: 5 those who love him and obey his *c*,
Ps 78: 7 but would keep his *c*.
Ps 112: 1 who finds great delight in his *c*.
119: 10 do not let me stray from your *c*.
119: 32 I run in the path of your *c*,
119: 35 Direct me in the path of your *c*,
119: 47 for I delight in your *c*
119: 48 lift up my hands to your *c*,
119: 73 me understanding to learn your *c*.
119: 86 All your *c* are trustworthy;
119: 96 but your *c* are boundless.
119: 98 Your *c* make me wiser
119: 115 that I may keep the *c* of my God!
119: 127 Because I love your *c*
119: 131 longing for your *c*.
119: 143 but your *c* are my delight.
119: 151 and all your *c* are true.
119: 172 for all your *c* are righteous.
119: 176 for I have not forgotten your *c*.
Pr 2: 1 and store up my *c* within you,
3: 1 but keep my *c* in your heart,
6: 23 For these *c* are a lamp,
10: 8 The wise in heart accept *c*,
Isa 48: 18 you had paid attention to my *c*,
Da 9: 4 all who love him and obey his *c*,
Mt 5: 19 teaches these *c* will be called great
Mk 7: 8 You have let go of the *c* of God
7: 9 way of setting aside the *c* of God
Jn 14: 21 Whoever has my *c* and obeys them,
15: 10 If you obey my *c*, you will remain
Ac 17: 30 but now he *c* all people everywhere
1Co 7: 19 Keeping God's *c* is what counts.
1Jn 2: 3 come to know him if we obey his *c*.
2: 4 but does not do what he *c* is a liar,
3: 22 we obey his *c* and do what pleases
3: 24 Those who obey his *c* live in him,
5: 2 loving God and carrying out his *c*.
5: 3 And his *c* are not burdensome,
5: 3 This is love for God: to obey his *c*.
2Jn : 6 that we walk in obedience to his *c*.

COMMEMORATE

Ex 12: 14 "This is a day you are to *c*;

COMMEND* (COMMENDABLE COMMENDED COMMENDS)

Ps 145: 4 One generation will *c* your works
Ecc 8: 15 So I *c* the enjoyment of life,
Ro 13: 3 do what is right and he will *c* you.
16: 1 I *c* to you our sister Phoebe,
2Co 3: 1 beginning to *c* ourselves again?
4: 2 the truth plainly we *c* ourselves
5: 12 trying to *c* ourselves to you again,
6: 4 as servants of God we *c* ourselves
10: 12 with some who *c* themselves.
1Pe 2: 14 and to *c* those who do right.

COMMENDABLE* (COMMEND)

1Pe 2: 19 For it is *c* if a man bears up
2: 20 you endure it, this is *c* before God.

COMMENDED* (COMMEND)

Ne 11: 2 The people *c* all the men who
Job 29: 11 and those who saw me *c* me,
Lk 16: 8 master *c* the dishonest manager
Ac 15: 40 *c* by the brothers to the grace
2Co 12: 11 I ought to have been *c* by you,
Heb 11: 2 This is what the ancients were *c* for
11: 4 By faith he was *c* as a righteous
11: 5 he was *c* as one who pleased God.
11: 39 These were all *c* for their faith,

COMMENDS* (COMMEND)

Pr 15: 2 of the wise *c* knowledge,
2Co 10: 18 but the one whom the Lord *c*.
10: 18 not the one who *c* himself who is

COMMIT (COMMITS COMMITTED)

Ex 20: 14 "You shall not *c* adultery.
Dt 5: 18 "You shall not *c* adultery.
1Sa 7: 3 and *c* yourselves to the LORD
Ps 31: 5 Into your hands I *c* my spirit;
37: 5 *C* your way to the LORD;
Pr 16: 3 *C* to the LORD whatever you do,
Mt 5: 27 that it was said, 'Do not *c* adultery.'
Mt 5: 32 causes her to *c* adultery,
19: 18 do not *c* adultery, do not steal,
Mk 10: 19 do not *c* adultery, do not steal,
Lk 18: 20 'Do not *c* adultery, do not murder,
23: 46 into your hands I *c* my spirit."
Ac 20: 32 I *c* you to God and to the word
Ro 2: 22 do you *c* adultery? You who abhor
2: 22 that people should not *c* adultery,
13: 9 "Do not *c* adultery,"
1Co 10: 8 We should not *c* sexual immorality,
Jas 2: 11 do not *c* adultery but do *c* murder,
1Pe 4: 19 to God's will should *c* themselves
Rev 2: 22 I will make those who *c* adultery

COMMITS (COMMIT)

Pr 6: 32 man who *c* adultery lacks
29: 22 a hot-tempered one *c* many sins.
Ecc 8: 12 a wicked man *c* a hundred crimes
Eze 18: 12 He *c* robbery.
18: 14 who sees all the sins his father *c*,
18: 24 from his righteousness and *c* sin
18: 26 from his righteousness and *c* sin,
22: 11 you one man *c* a detestable offence
Mt 5: 32 a woman so divorced *c* adultery.
19: 9 marries another woman *c* adultery
Mk 10: 11 marries another woman *c* adultery
10: 12 another man, she *c* adultery."
Lk 16: 18 a divorced woman *c* adultery.
16: 18 marries another woman *c* adultery,

COMMITTED (COMMIT)

Nu 5: 7 and must confess the sin he has *c*.
1Ki 8: 61 But your hearts must be fully *c*
15: 14 Asa's heart was fully *c*
2Ch 16: 9 those whose hearts are fully *c*
Mt 5: 28 lustfully has already *c* adultery
11: 27 "All things have been *c* to me
Lk 10: 22 "All things have been *c* to me
Ac 14: 23 *c* them to the Lord
14: 26 where they had been *c* to the grace
1Co 9: 17 I am simply discharging the trust *c*
2Co 5: 19 And he has *c* to us the message
1Pe 2: 22 "He *c* no sin,
Rev 17: 2 the kings of the earth *c* adultery
18: 3 of the earth *c* adultery with her,
18: 9 kings of the earth who *c* adultery

COMMON

Ge 11: 1 had one language and a *c* speech.
Lev 10: 10 distinguish between the holy and the *c*,
Pr 22: 2 Rich and poor have this in *c*:
29: 13 the oppressor have this in *c*:
Ac 2: 44 together and had everything in *c*,
1Co 10: 13 has seized you except what is *c*
2Co 6: 14 and wickedness have in *c*?

COMPANION (COMPANIONS)

Ps 55: 13 my *c*, my close friend,
55: 20 My *c* attacks his friends;
Pr 13: 20 but a *c* of fools suffers harm.
28: 7 a *c* of gluttons disgraces his father.
29: 3 *c* of prostitutes squanders his
Rev 1: 9 your brother and *c* in the suffering

COMPANIONS (COMPANION)

Ps 45: 7 your God, has set you above your *c*
Pr 18: 24 A man of many *c* may come to ruin
Heb 1: 9 your God, has set you above your *c*

COMPANY

Ps 14: 5 present in the *c* of the righteous.
Pr 21: 16 comes to rest in the *c* of the dead.
24: 1 do not desire their *c*;
Jer 15: 17 I never sat in the *c* of revellers,
1Co 15: 33 "Bad *c* corrupts good character."

COMPARE* (COMPARED COMPARING COMPARISON)

Job 28: 17 Neither gold nor crystal can *c*
28: 19 The topaz of Cush cannot *c* with it;
39: 13 but they cannot *c* with the pinions
Ps 86: 8 no deeds can *c* with yours.
89: 6 skies above can *c* with the LORD?

Pr 3: 15 nothing you desire can *c* with her.
8: 11 nothing you desire can *c* with her.
Isa 40: 18 To whom, then, will you *c* God?
40: 18 What image will you *c* him to?
40: 25 "To whom will you *c* me?
46: 5 "To whom will you *c* me
La 2: 13 With what can I *c* you,
Eze 31: 8 *c* with its branches—
Da 1: 13 Then *c* our appearance with that
Mt 11: 16 "To what can I *c* this generation?
Lk 7: 31 I *c* the people of this generation?
13: 18 What shall I *c* it to? It is like
13: 20 What shall I *c* the kingdom of God
2Co 10: 12 and *c* themselves with themselves,
10: 12 or *c* ourselves with some who

COMPARED* (COMPARE)

Jdg 8: 2 What have I accomplished *c* to you
8: 3 What was I able to do *c* to you?"
Isa 46: 5 you liken me that we may be *c*?
Eze 31: 2 Who can be *c* with you in majesty?
31: 18 the trees of Eden can be *c* with you
Php 3: 8 I consider everything a loss *c*

COMPARING* (COMPARE)

Ro 8: 18 present sufferings are not worth *c*
2Co 8: 8 the sincerity of your love by *c* it
Gal 6: 4 without *c* himself to somebody else

COMPARISON* (COMPARE)

2Co 3: 10 now in *c* with the surpassing glory.

COMPASSION* (COMPASSIONATE COMPASSIONS)

Ex 33: 19 I will have *c* on whom I will have *c*.
Dt 13: 17 he will show you mercy, have *c*
28: 54 man among you will have no *c*
30: 3 restore your fortunes and have *c*
32: 36 and have *c* on his servants
Jdg 2: 18 for the LORD had *c* on them
1Ki 3: 26 son was alive was filled with *c*
2Ki 13: 23 and had *c* and showed concern
2Ch 30: 9 and your children will be shown *c*
Ne 9: 19 of your great *c* you did not
9: 27 and in your great *c* you gave them
9: 28 in your *c* you delivered them time
Ps 51: 1 according to your great *c*
77: 9 Has he in anger withheld his *c*?"
90: 13 Have *c* on your servants.
102: 13 You will arise and have *c* on Zion,
103: 4 and crowns me with love and *c*.
103: 13 As a father has *c* on his children,
103: 13 so the LORD has *c*
116: 5 our God is full of *c*.
119: 77 Let your *c* come to me that I may
119: 156 Your *c* is great, O LORD;
135: 14 and have *c* on his servants.
145: 9 he has *c* on all he has made.
Isa 13: 18 will they look with *c* on children.
14: 1 The LORD will have *c* on Jacob;
27: 11 so their Maker has no *c* on them,
30: 18 he rises to show you *c*.
49: 10 He who has *c* on them will guide
49: 13 and will have *c* on his afflicted ones
49: 15 and have no *c* on the child she has
51: 3 and will look with *c* on all her ruins
54: 7 with deep *c* I will bring you back.
54: 8 I will have *c* on you,"
54: 10 says the LORD, who has *c* on you.
60: 10 in favour I will show you *c*.
63: 7 to his *c* and many kindnesses.
63: 15 and *c* are withheld from us.
Jer 12: 15 I will again have *c* and will bring
13: 14 *c* to keep me from destroying them
15: 6 I can no longer show *c*.
21: 7 show them no mercy or pity or *c*.'
30: 18 and have *c* on his dwellings;
31: 20 I have great *c* for him,"
33: 26 restore their fortunes and have *c*
42: 12 I will show you *c* so that he will
42: 12 so that he will have *c* on you
La 3: 32 he brings grief, he will show *c*,
Eze 9: 5 without showing pity or *c*.
16: 5 or had *c* enough to do any
39: 25 and will have *c* on all the people
Hos 2: 19 in love and *c*.
11: 8 all my *c* is aroused.
13: 14 "I will have no *c*,
14: 3 for in you the fatherless find *c*."
Am 1: 11 stifling all *c*,
Jnh 3: 9 with *c* turn from his fierce anger
3: 10 he had *c* and did not bring
Mic 7: 19 You will again have *c* on us;
Zec 7: 9 show mercy and *c* to one another.
10: 6 because I have *c* on them.
Mal 3: 17 as in *c* a man spares his son who
Mt 9: 36 When he saw the crowds, he had *c*
14: 14 he had *c* on them and healed their
15: 32 "I have *c* for these people;
20: 34 Jesus had *c* on them and touched
Mk 1: 41 with *c*, Jesus reached out his hand
6: 34 and saw a large crowd, he had *c*
8: 2 "I have *c* for these people;
Lk 15: 20 and was filled with *c* for him;
Ro 9: 15 and I will have *c* on whom I have *c*
2Co 1: 3 the Father of *c* and the God
Php 2: 1 and *c*, then make my joy complete
Col 3: 12 clothe yourselves with *c*, kindness,
Jas 5: 11 The Lord is full of *c* and mercy.

COMPASSIONATE* (COMPASSION)

Ex 22: 27 out to me, I will hear, for I am *c*.
34: 6 the LORD, the *c* and gracious God
2Ch 30: 9 LORD your God is gracious and *c*.
Ne 9: 17 gracious and *c*, slow to anger
Ps 86: 15 O Lord, are a *c* and gracious God,
103: 8 The LORD is *c* and gracious,
111: 4 the LORD is gracious and *c*.
112: 4 the gracious and *c* and righteous
145: 8 The LORD is gracious and *c*,
La 4: 10 With their own hands *c* women
Joel 2: 13 for he is gracious and *c*,
Jnh 4: 2 that you are a gracious and *c* God,
Eph 4: 32 Be kind and *c* to one another,
1Pe 3: 8 love as brothers, be *c* and humble.

COMPASSIONS* (COMPASSION)

La 3: 22 for his *c* never fail.

COMPELLED (COMPULSION)

Ac 20: 22 "And now, *c* by the Spirit,
1Co 9: 16 I cannot boast, for I am *c* to preach.

COMPELS (COMPULSION)

Job 32: 18 and the spirit within me *c* me;
2Co 5: 14 For Christ's love *c* us, because we

COMPETENCE* (COMPETENT)

2Co 3: 5 but our *c* comes from God.

COMPETENT* (COMPETENCE)

Ro 15: 14 and *c* to instruct one another.
1Co 6: 2 are you not *c* to judge trivial cases?
2Co 3: 5 Not that we are *c* to claim anything
3: 6 He has made us *c* as ministers

COMPETES*

1Co 9: 25 Everyone who *c* in the games goes
2Ti 2: 5 Similarly, if anyone *c* as an athlete,
2: 5 unless he *c* according to the rules.

COMPLACENCY* (COMPLACENT)

Pr 1: 32 and the *c* of fools will destroy them
Eze 30: 9 ships to frighten Cush out of her *c*.

COMPLACENT* (COMPLACENCY)

Isa 32: 9 You women who are so *c*,
32: 11 Tremble, you *c* women;
Am 6: 1 Woe to you who are *c* in Zion,
Zep 1: 12 and punish those who are *c*,

COMPLAINING*

Php 2: 14 Do everything without *c* or arguing

COMPLETE

Dt 16: 15 your hands, and your joy will be *c*.
Jn 3: 29 That joy is mine, and it is now *c*.
15: 11 and that your joy may be *c*.
16: 24 will receive, and your joy will be *c*.
17: 23 May they be brought to *c* unity
Ac 20: 24 *c* the task the Lord Jesus has given
Php 2: 2 then make my joy *c*
Col 4: 17 to it that you *c* the work you have
Jas 1: 4 so that you may be mature and *c*,
2: 22 his faith was made *c* by what he did
1Jn 1: 4 We write this to make our joy *c*.
2: 5 God's love is truly made *c* in him.
4: 12 and his love is made *c* in us.
4: 17 Love is made *c* among us
2Jn : 12 to face, so that our joy may be *c*.

COMPLIMENTS*

Pr 23: 8 and will have wasted your *c*.

COMPREHEND* (COMPREHENDED)

Job 28: 13 Man does not *c* its worth;
Ecc 8: 17 No-one can *c* what goes
8: 17 he knows, he cannot really *c* it.

COMPREHENDED* (COMPREHEND)

Job 38: 18 Have you *c* the vast expanses

COMPULSION (COMPELLED COMPELS)

2Co 9: 7 not reluctantly or under *c*,

CONCEAL (CONCEALED CONCEALS)

Ps 40: 10 I do not *c* your love and your truth
Pr 25: 2 It is the glory of God to *c* a matter;

CONCEALED (CONCEAL)

Jer 16: 17 nor is their sin *c* from my eyes.
Mt 10: 26 There is nothing *c* that will not be
Mk 4: 22 and whatever is *c* is meant
Lk 8: 17 nothing *c* that will not be known
12: 2 There is nothing *c* that will not be

CONCEALS* (CONCEAL)

Pr 10: 18 He who *c* his hatred has lying lips,
28: 13 He who *c* his sins does not prosper,

CONCEIT* (CONCEITED CONCEITS)

Isa 16: 6 her overweening pride and *c*,
Jer 48: 29 her overweening pride and *c*,
Php 2: 3 out of selfish ambition or vain *c*,

CONCEITED* (CONCEIT)

1Sa 17: 28 I know how *c* you are and how
Ro 11: 25 brothers, so that you may not be *c*:
12: 16 Do not be *c*.
2Co 12: 7 To keep me from becoming *c*
Gal 5: 26 Let us not become *c*, provoking
1Ti 3: 6 or he may become *c* and fall
6: 4 he is *c* and understands nothing.
2Ti 3: 4 of the good, treacherous, rash, *c*,

CONCEITS* (CONCEIT)

Ps 73: 7 evil *c* of their minds know no

CONCEIVED (CONCEIVES)

Ps 51: 5 from the time my mother *c* me.
Mt 1: 20 what is *c* in her is from the Holy
1Co 2: 9 no mind has *c*
Jas 1: 15 after desire has *c*, it gives birth

CONCEIVES* (CONCEIVED)

Ps 7: 14 *c* trouble gives birth

CONCERN* (CONCERNED)

Ge 39: 6 he did not *c* himself with anything
39: 8 "my master does not *c* himself
1Sa 23: 21 "The LORD bless you for your *c*
2Ki 13: 23 and had compassion and showed *c*
Job 9: 21 have no *c* for myself;
19: 4 my error remains my *c* alone.
Ps 131: 1 I do not *c* myself with great matters
Pr 29: 7 but the wicked have no such *c*.
Eze 36: 21 I had *c* for my holy name, which
Ac 15: 14 God at first showed his *c* by taking
18: 17 But Gallio showed no *c* whatever.

1Co 7: 32 I would like you to be free from *c*.
12: 25 that its parts should have equal *c*
2Co 7: 7 your deep sorrow, your ardent *c*
7: 11 what alarm, what longing, what *c*,
8: 16 of Titus the same *c* I have for you.
11: 28 of my *c* for all the churches.
Php 4: 10 at last you have renewed your *c*

CONCERNED (CONCERN)

Ex 2: 25 Israelites and was *c* about them.
Ps 142: 4 no-one is *c* for me.
Jnh 4: 10 "You have been *c* about this vine,
4: 11 Should I not be *c* about that great
1Co 7: 32 An unmarried man is *c* about
9: 9 Is it about oxen that God is *c*?
Php 4: 10 you have been *c*, but you had no

CONCESSION*

1Co 7: 6 I say this as a *c*, not as a command.

CONDEMN* (CONDEMNATION CONDEMNED CONDEMNING CONDEMNS)

Job 9: 20 innocent, my mouth would *c* me;
10: 2 I will say to God: Do not *c* me,
34: 17 Will you *c* the just and mighty One
34: 29 if he remains silent, who can *c* him?
40: 8 Would you *c* me to justify yourself?
Ps 94: 21 and *c* the innocent to death.
109: 7 and may his prayers *c* him.
109: 31 from those who *c* him.
Isa 50: 9 Who is he that will *c* me?
Mt 12: 41 with this generation and *c* it;
12: 42 with this generation and *c* it;
20: 18 They will *c* him to death
Mk 10: 33 They will *c* him to death
Lk 6: 37 Do not *c*, and you will not be
11: 31 men of this generation and *c* them,
11: 32 with this generation and *c* it,
Jn 3: 17 Son into the world to *c* the world,
7: 51 "Does our law *c* a man
8: 11 "Then neither do I *c* you,"
12: 48 very word which I spoke will *c* him
Ro 2: 27 yet obeys the law will *c* you who,
14: 3 everything must not *c* the man who
14: 22 is the man who does not *c* himself
2Co 7: 3 this to *c* you; I have said
1Jn 3: 20 presence whenever our hearts *c* us.
3: 21 if our hearts do not *c* us,

CONDEMNATION* (CONDEMN)

Jer 42: 18 of *c* and reproach; you will never
44: 12 and horror, of *c* and reproach.
Ro 3: 8 may result"? Their *c* is deserved.
5: 16 followed one sin and brought *c*,
5: 18 of one trespass was *c* for all men,
8: 1 there is now no *c* for those who are
2Pe 2: 3 Their *c* has long been hanging
Jude : 4 certain men whose *c* was written

CONDEMNED* (CONDEMN)

Dt 13: 17 of those *c* things shall be found
Job 32: 3 to refute Job, and yet had *c* him.
Ps 34: 21 the foes of the righteous will be *c*.
34: 22 who takes refuge in him will be *c*.
37: 33 let them be *c* when brought to trial.
79: 11 preserve those *c* to die.
102: 20 and release those *c* to death."
Mt 12: 7 you would not have *c* the innocent.
12: 37 and by your words you will be *c*."
23: 33 How will you escape being *c* to hell
27: 3 betrayed him, saw that Jesus was *c*,
Mk 14: 64 They all *c* him as worthy of death.
16: 16 whoever does not believe will be *c*.
Lk 6: 37 condemn, and you will not be *c*.
Jn 3: 18 Whoever believes in him is not *c*,
3: 18 does not believe stands *c* already
5: 24 has eternal life and will not be *c*;
5: 29 who have done evil will rise to be *c*.
8: 10 Has no-one *c* you?" "No-one, sir,"
16: 11 prince of this world now stands *c*.
Ac 25: 15 against him and asked that he be *c*.
Ro 3: 7 why am I still *c* as a sinner?"
8: 3 And so he *c* sin in sinful man,

Ro 14: 23 But the man who has doubts is *c*
1Co 4: 9 like men *c* to die in the arena.
11: 32 disciplined so that we will not be *c*
Gal 1: 8 let him be eternally *c*! As we have
1: 9 let him be eternally *c*! Am I now
2Th 2: 12 that all will be *c* who have not
Tit 2: 8 of speech that cannot be *c*,
Heb 11: 7 By his faith he *c* the world
Jas 5: 6 You have *c* and murdered innocent
5: 12 and your "No," no, or you will be *c*
2Pe 2: 6 if he *c* the cities of Sodom
Rev 19: 2 He has *c* the great prostitute

CONDEMNING* (CONDEMN)

Dt 25: 1 the innocent and *c* the guilty.
1Ki 8: 32 *c* the guilty and bringing
Pr 17: 15 the guilty and *c* the innocent—
Ac 13: 27 yet in *c* him they fulfilled the words
Ro 2: 1 judge the other, you are *c* yourself,

CONDEMNS* (CONDEMN)

Job 15: 6 Your own mouth *c* you, not mine;
Pr 12: 2 but the LORD *c* a crafty man.
Ro 8: 34 Who is he that *c*? Christ Jesus,
2Co 3: 9 the ministry that *c* men is glorious,

CONDITION

Pr 27: 23 Be sure you know the *c*

CONDUCT (CONDUCTED CONDUCTS)

Pr 10: 23 A fool finds pleasure in evil *c*,
20: 11 by whether his *c* is pure and right.
21: 8 but the *c* of the innocent is upright.
Ecc 6: 8 how to *c* himself before others?
Jer 4: 18 "Your own *c* and actions
17: 10 to reward a man according to his *c*,
Eze 7: 3 I will judge you according to your *c*
Php 1: 27 *c* yourselves in a manner worthy
1Ti 3: 15 to *c* themselves in God's household

CONDUCTED* (CONDUCT)

2Co 1: 12 testifies that we have *c* ourselves

CONDUCTS* (CONDUCT)

Ps 112: 5 who *c* his affairs with justice.

CONFESS* (CONFESSED CONFESSES CONFESSING CONFESSION)

Lev 5: 5 he must *c* in what way he has
16: 21 and *c* over it all the wickedness
26: 40 "'But if they will *c* their sins
Nu 5: 7 must *c* the sin he has committed.
1Ki 8: 33 back to you and *c* your name,
8: 35 towards this place and *c* your name
2Ch 6: 24 they turn back and *c* your name,
6: 26 towards this place and *c* your name
Ne 1: 6 I *c* the sins we Israelites, including
Ps 32: 5 I said, "I will *c*
38: 18 I *c* my iniquity;
Jn 1: 20 fail to *c*, but confessed freely,
12: 42 they would not *c* their faith
Ro 10: 9 That if you *c* with your mouth,
10: 10 it is with your mouth that you *c*
14: 11 every tongue will *c* to God.'"
Php 2: 11 every tongue *c* that Jesus Christ is
Heb 3: 1 and high priest whom we *c*.
13: 15 the fruit of lips that *c* his name.
Jas 5: 16 Therefore *c* your sins to each other
1Jn 1: 9 if we *c* our sins, he is faithful

CONFESSED* (CONFESS)

1Sa 7: 6 day they fasted and there they *c*,
Ne 9: 2 in their places and *c* their sins
Da 9: 4 to the LORD my God and *c*:
Jn 1: 20 but *c* freely, "I am not the Christ."
Ac 19: 18 and openly *c* their evil deeds.

CONFESSES* (CONFESS)

Pr 28: 13 whoever *c* and renounces them
2Ti 2: 19 and, "Everyone who *c* the name

CONFESSING* (CONFESS)

Ezr 10: 1 While Ezra was praying and *c*,

Da 9: 20 *c* my sin and the sin
Mt 3: 6 *C* their sins, they were baptised
Mk 1: 5 *C* their sins, they were baptised

CONFESSION* (CONFESS)

Ezr 10: 11 Now make *c* to the LORD,
Ne 9: 3 and spent another fourth in *c*
2Co 9: 13 obedience that accompanies your *c*
1Ti 6: 12 called when you made your good *c*
6: 13 Pontius Pilate made the good *c*,

CONFIDENCE* (CONFIDENT)

Jdg 9: 26 and its citizens put their *c* in him.
2Ki 18: 19 On what are you basing this *c*
2Ch 32: 8 And the people gained *c*
32: 10 On what are you basing your *c*,
Job 4: 6 Should not your piety be your *c*
Ps 71: 5 my *c* since my youth.
Pr 3: 26 for the LORD will be your *c*
3: 32 but takes the upright into his *c*.
11: 13 A gossip betrays a *c*,
20: 19 A gossip betrays a *c*;
25: 9 do not betray another man's *c*,
31: 11 Her husband has full *c* in her
Isa 32: 17 will be quietness and *c* for ever.
36: 4 On what are you basing this *c*
Jer 17: 7 whose *c* is in him.
49: 31 which lives in *c*,"
Eze 29: 16 a source of *c* for the people of Israel
Mic 7: 5 put no *c* in a friend.
2Co 2: 3 I had *c* in all of you, that you would
3: 4 Such *c* as this is ours
7: 4 I have great *c* in you; I take great
7: 16 I am glad I can have complete *c*
8: 22 so because of his great *c* in you.
Eph 3: 12 God with freedom and *c*.
Php 3: 3 and who put no *c* in the flesh—
3: 4 I myself have reasons for such *c*.
3: 4 reasons to put *c* in the flesh,
2Th 3: 4 We have *c* in the Lord that you are
Heb 3: 14 till the end the *c* we had at first.
4: 16 the throne of grace with *c*,
10: 19 since we have *c* to enter the Most
10: 35 So do not throw away your *c*;
13: 6 So we say with *c*,
1Jn 3: 21 we have *c* before God and receive
4: 17 us so that we will have *c* on the day
5: 14 the *c* we have in approaching God:

CONFIDENT* (CONFIDENCE)

Job 6: 20 because they had been *c*;
Ps 27: 3 even then will I be *c*.
27: 13 I am still *c* of this:
Lk 18: 9 To some who were *c*
2Co 1: 15 Because I was *c* of this, I planned
5: 6 Therefore we are always *c*
5: 8 We are *c*, I say, and would prefer
9: 4 ashamed of having been so *c*.
10: 7 If anyone is *c* that he belongs
Gal 5: 10 I am *c* in the Lord that you will
Php 1: 6 day until now, being *c* of this,
2: 24 I am *c* in the Lord that I myself will
Phm : 21 *C* of your obedience, I write to you,
Heb 6: 9 we are *c* of better things
1Jn 2: 28 that when he appears we may be *c*

CONFIDES*

Ps 25: 14 The LORD *c* in those who fear him

CONFORM* (CONFORMED CONFORMITY CONFORMS)

Ro 12: 2 Do not *c* any longer to the pattern
1Pe 1: 14 do not *c* to the evil desires you had

CONFORMED* (CONFORM)

Eze 5: 7 *c* to the standards of the nations
11: 12 but have *c* to the standards
Ro 8: 29 predestined to be *c* to the likeness

CONFORMITY* (CONFORM)

Eph 1: 11 in *c* with the purpose of his will,

CONFORMS* (CONFORM)

1Ti 1: 11 to the sound doctrine that *c*

CONQUEROR* (CONQUERORS)

Mic 1: 15 I will bring a *c* against you
Rev 6: 2 he rode out as a *c* bent on conquest.

CONQUERORS (CONQUEROR)

Ro 8: 37 than *c* through him who loved us.

CONSCIENCE* (CONSCIENCE-STRICKEN CONSCIENCES CONSCIENTIOUS)

Ge 20: 5 I have done this with a clear *c*
20: 6 I know you did this with a clear *c*,
1Sa 25: 31 have on his *c* the staggering burden
Job 27: 6 my *c* will not reproach me as long
Ac 23: 1 to God in all good *c* to this day."
24: 16 to keep my *c* clear before God
Ro 9: 1 my *c* confirms it in the Holy Spirit
13: 5 punishment but also because of *c*.
1Co 4: 4 My *c* is clear, but that does not
8: 7 since their *c* is weak, it is defiled.
8: 10 with a weak *c* sees you who have
8: 12 in this way and wound their weak *c*
10: 25 without raising questions of *c*,
10: 27 you without raising questions of *c*.
10: 28 man who told you and for *c*' sake—
10: 29 freedom be judged by another's *c*?
10: 29 the other man's *c*, I mean,
2Co 1: 12 Our *c* testifies that we have
4: 2 to every man's *c* in the sight of God
5: 11 and I hope it is also plain to your *c*.
1Ti 1: 5 and a good *c* and a sincere faith.
1: 19 holding on to faith and a good *c*.
3: 9 truths of the faith with a clear *c*.
2Ti 1: 3 as my forefathers did, with a clear *c*
Heb 9: 9 able to clear the *c* of the worshipper.
10: 22 to cleanse us from a guilty *c*
13: 18 We are sure that we have a clear *c*
1Pe 3: 16 and respect, keeping a clear *c*,
3: 21 the pledge of a good *c* towards God.

CONSCIENCE-STRICKEN* (CONSCIENCE)

1Sa 24: 5 David was *c* for having cut
2Sa 24: 10 David was *c* after he had counted

CONSCIENCES* (CONSCIENCE)

Ro 2: 15 their *c* also bearing witness,
1Ti 4: 2 whose *c* have been seared
Tit 1: 15 their minds and *c* are corrupted.
Heb 9: 14 cleanse our *c* from acts that lead

CONSCIENTIOUS* (CONSCIENCE)

2Ch 29: 34 for the Levites had been more *c*

CONSCIOUS*

Ro 3: 20 through the law we become *c* of sin
1Pe 2: 19 of unjust suffering because he is *c*

CONSECRATE (CONSECRATED)

Ex 13: 2 "*C* to me every firstborn male.
40: 9 *c* it and all its furnishings,
Lev 20: 7 "'*C* yourselves and be holy,
25: 10 *C* the fiftieth year and proclaim
1Ch 15: 12 fellow Levites are to *c* yourselves

CONSECRATED (CONSECRATE)

Ex 29: 43 and the place will be *c* by my glory.
Lev 8: 30 So he *c* Aaron and his garments
2Ch 7: 16 *c* this temple so that my Name may
Lk 2: 23 is to be *c* to the Lord"),
1Ti 4: 5 because it is *c* by the word of God

CONSENT

1Co 7: 5 except by mutual *c* and for a time,

CONSIDER (CONSIDERATE CONSIDERED CONSIDERS)

1Sa 12: 24 *c* what great things he has done
16: 7 "Do not *c* his appearance
2Ch 19: 6 "*C* carefully what you do,
Job 37: 14 stop and *c* God's wonders.
Ps 8: 3 When I *c* your heavens,
77: 12 and *c* all your mighty deeds.
107: 43 and *c* the great love of the LORD.
143: 5 and *c* what your hands have done.
Pr 6: 6 *c* its ways and be wise!
20: 25 and only later to *c* his vows.
Ecc 7: 13 *C* what God has done:
Lk 12: 24 *C* the ravens: They do not sow
12: 27 about the rest? "*C* how the lilies
Php 2: 3 but in humility *c* others better
3: 8 I *c* everything a loss compared
Heb 10: 24 And let us *c* how we may spur one
Jas 1: 2 *C* it pure joy, my brothers,

CONSIDERATE* (CONSIDER)

Tit 3: 2 to be peaceable and *c*,
Jas 3: 17 then peace loving, *c*, submissive,
1Pe 2: 18 only to those who are good and *c*,
3: 7 in the same way be *c* as you live

CONSIDERED (CONSIDER)

Job 1: 8 "Have you *c* my servant Job?
2: 3 "Have you *c* my servant Job?
Ps 44: 22 we are *c* as sheep to be slaughtered.
Isa 53: 4 yet we *c* him stricken by God,
Ro 8: 36 we are *c* as sheep to be slaughtered

CONSIDERS (CONSIDER)

Pr 31: 16 She *c* a field and buys it;
Ro 14: 5 One man *c* one day more sacred
Jas 1: 26 If anyone *c* himself religious

CONSIST (CONSISTS)

Lk 12: 15 a man's life does not *c*

CONSISTS (CONSIST)

Eph 5: 9 fruit of the light *c* in all goodness,

CONSOLATION

Ps 94: 19 your *c* brought joy to my soul.

CONSPIRE

Ps 2: 1 Why do the nations *c*

CONSTANT

Dt 28: 66 You will live in *c* suspense,
Pr 19: 13 wife is like a *c* dripping.
27: 15 a *c* dripping on a rainy day;
Ac 27: 33 "you have been in *c* suspense
Heb 5: 14 by *c* use have trained themselves

CONSTRUCTIVE*

1Co 10: 23 but not everything is *c*.

CONSULT

Pr 15: 12 he will not *c* the wise.
Gal 1: 16 I did not *c* any man, nor did I go up

CONSUME (CONSUMES CONSUMING)

Jn 2: 17 "Zeal for your house will *c* me."

CONSUMES (CONSUME)

Ps 69: 9 for zeal for your house *c* me,

CONSUMING (CONSUME)

Dt 4: 24 For the LORD your God is a *c* fire,
Heb 12: 29 and awe, for our God is a *c* fire.

CONTAIN* (CONTAINED CONTAINS)

1Ki 8: 27 the highest heaven, cannot *c* you.
2Ch 2: 6 the highest heavens, cannot *c* him?
6: 18 the highest heavens, cannot *c* you.
Ecc 8: 8 power over the wind to *c* it;
2Pe 3: 16 His letters *c* some things that are

CONTAINED (CONTAIN)

Heb 9: 4 This ark *c* the gold jar of manna,

CONTAINS (CONTAIN)

Pr 15: 6 of the righteous *c* great treasure,

CONTAMINATES*

2Co 7: 1 from everything that *c* body

CONTEMPT

Pr 14: 31 He who oppresses the poor shows *c*
17: 5 He who mocks the poor shows *c*
18: 3 When wickedness comes, so does *c*
Da 12: 2 others to shame and everlasting *c*.
Mal 1: 6 O priests, who show *c* for my name.
Ro 2: 4 Or do you show *c* for the riches
Gal 4: 14 you did not treat me with *c*
1Th 5: 20 do not treat prophecies with *c*.

CONTEND (CONTENDED CONTENDING CONTENTIOUS)

Ge 6: 3 "My Spirit will not *c*
Ps 35: 1 *C*, O LORD, with those who
Isa 49: 25 I will *c* with those who *c* with you,
Jude : 3 you to *c* for the faith that was once

CONTENDED (CONTEND)

Php 4: 3 help these women who have *c*

CONTENDING* (CONTEND)

Php 1: 27 *c* as one man for the faith

CONTENT* (CONTENTMENT)

Jos 7: 7 If only we had been *c* to stay
Pr 13: 25 The righteous eat to their hearts' *c*,
19: 23 one rests *c*, untouched by trouble.
Ecc 4: 8 yet his eyes were not *c*
Lk 3: 14 don't accuse people falsely—be *c*
Php 4: 11 to be *c* whatever the circumstances
4: 12 I have learned the secret of being *c*
1Ti 6: 8 and clothing, we will be *c* with that.
Heb 13: 5 and be *c* with what you have,

CONTENTIOUS* (CONTEND)

1Co 11: 16 If anyone wants to be *c* about this,

CONTENTMENT* (CONTENT)

Job 36: 11 and their years in *c*.
SS 8: 10 like one bringing *c*.
1Ti 6: 6 But godliness with *c* is great gain.

CONTEST*

Heb 10: 32 in a great *c* in the face of suffering.

CONTINUAL (CONTINUE)

Pr 15: 15 but the cheerful heart has a *c* feast.
Eph 4: 19 of impurity, with a *c* lust for more.

CONTINUE (CONTINUAL CONTINUES CONTINUING)

1Ki 8: 23 servants who *c* wholeheartedly
2Ch 6: 14 servants who *c* wholeheartedly
Ps 36: 10 *C* your love to those who know you
Ac 13: 43 urged them to *c* in the grace of God
Ro 11: 22 provided that you *c* in his kindness.
Gal 3: 10 Cursed is everyone who does not *c*
Php 2: 12 *c* to work out your salvation
Col 1: 23 if you *c* in your faith, established
2: 6 received Christ Jesus as Lord, *c*
1Ti 2: 15 if they *c* in faith, love and holiness
2Ti 3: 14 *c* in what you have learned
1Jn 2: 28 And now, dear children, *c* in him,
3: 9 born of God will *c* to sin,
5: 18 born of God does not *c* to sin;
2Jn : 9 and does not *c* in the teaching
Rev 22: 11 and let him who is holy *c* to be holy
22: 11 let him who does right *c* to do right;

CONTINUES (CONTINUE)

Ps 100: 5 *c* through all generations.
119: 90 Your faithfulness *c*
2Co 10: 15 Our hope is that, as your faith *c*
1Jn 3: 6 No-one who *c* to sin has

CONTINUING (CONTINUE)

Ro 13: 8 the *c* debt to love one another,

CONTRIBUTION (CONTRIBUTIONS)

Ro 15: 26 pleased to make a *c* for the poor

CONTRIBUTIONS (CONTRIBUTION)

2Ch 24: 10 all the people brought their *c* gladly

2Ch 31: 12 they faithfully brought in the *c*,

CONTRITE*

Ps 51: 17 a broken and *c* heart,
Isa 57: 15 also with him who is *c* and lowly
57: 15 and to revive the heart of the *c*.
66: 2 he who is humble and *c* in spirit,

CONTROL (CONTROLLED CONTROLS SELF-CONTROL SELF-CONTROLLED)

Pr 29: 11 a wise man keeps himself under *c*.
1Co 7: 9 But if they cannot *c* themselves,
7: 37 but has *c* over his own will,
1Th 4: 4 you should learn to *c* his own body

CONTROLLED (CONTROL)

Ps 32: 9 but must be *c* by bit and bridle
Ro 8: 6 but the mind *c* by the Spirit is life
8: 8 Those *c* by the sinful nature cannot

CONTROLS* (CONTROL)

Job 37: 15 you know how God *c* the clouds
Pr 16: 32 a man who *c* his temper

CONTROVERSIES*

Ac 26: 3 with all the Jewish customs and *c*.
1Ti 1: 4 These promote *c* rather
6: 4 He has an unhealthy interest in *c*
Tit 3: 9 But avoid foolish *c* and genealogies

CONVERSATION

Col 4: 6 Let your *c* be always full of grace,

CONVERT

1Ti 3: 6 He must not be a recent *c*,

CONVICT (CONVICTION)

Pr 24: 25 with those who *c* the guilty,
Jn 16: 8 he will *c* the world of guilt in regard
Jude : 15 and to *c* all the ungodly

CONVICTION* (CONVICT)

1Th 1: 5 the Holy Spirit and with deep *c*.

CONVINCE* (CONVINCED CONVINCING)

Ac 28: 23 and tried to *c* them about Jesus

CONVINCED* (CONVINCE)

Ge 45: 28 "I'm *c*! My son Joseph is still alive.
Lk 16: 31 will not be *c* even if someone rises
Ac 19: 26 and hear how this fellow Paul has *c*
26: 9 "I too was *c* that I ought
26: 26 I am *c* that none of this has escaped
28: 24 Some were *c* by what he said,
Ro 2: 19 if you are *c* that you are a guide
8: 38 For I am *c* that neither death
14: 5 Each one should be fully *c*
14: 14 I am fully *c* that no food is unclean
15: 14 I myself am *c*, my brothers,
1Co 14: 24 he will be *c* by all that he is a sinner
2Co 5: 14 we are *c* that one died for all,
Php 1: 25 *C* of this, I know that I will remain,
2Ti 1: 12 and am *c* that he is able
3: 14 have learned and have become *c*

CONVINCING* (CONVINCE)

Ac 1: 3 and gave many *c* proofs that he was

COOLNESS*

Pr 25: 13 Like the *c* of snow at harvest time

COPIES (COPY)

Heb 9: 23 for the *c* of the heavenly things

COPY (COPIES)

Dt 17: 18 for himself on a scroll a *c* of this law
Heb 8: 5 They serve at a sanctuary that is a *c*
9: 24 sanctuary that was only a *c*

CORBAN*

Mk 7: 11 received from me is *C*' (that is,

CORD (CORDS)

Jos 2: 18 you have tied this scarlet *c*
Ecc 4: 12 *c* of three strands is not quickly

CORDS (CORD)

Pr 5: 22 the *c* of his sin hold him fast.
Isa 54: 2 lengthen your *c*,
Hos 11: 4 them with *c* of human kindness,

CORINTH

Ac 18: 1 Paul left Athens and went to *C*.
1Co 1: 2 To the church of God in *C*,
2Co 1: 1 To the church of God in *C*,

CORNELIUS*

Roman to whom Peter preached; first Gentile Christian (Ac 10).

CORNER (CORNERS)

Ru 3: 9 "Spread the *c* of your garment
Pr 21: 9 Better to live on a *c* of the roof
25: 24 Better to live on a *c* of the roof
Ac 26: 26 because it was not done in a *c*.

CORNERS (CORNER)

Mt 6: 5 on the street *c* to be seen by men.
22: 9 Go to the street *c* and invite

CORNERSTONE* (STONE)

Job 38: 6 or who laid its *c*—
Isa 28: 16 a precious *c* for a sure foundation;
Jer 51: 26 rock will be taken from you for a *c*,
Zec 10: 4 From Judah will come the *c*,
Eph 2: 20 Christ Jesus himself as the chief *c*.
1Pe 2: 6 a chosen and precious *c*,

CORRECT* (CORRECTED CORRECTING CORRECTION CORRECTIONS CORRECTS)

Job 6: 26 Do you mean to *c* what I say,
40: 2 contends with the Almighty *c* him?
Jer 10: 24 *C* me, LORD, but only with justice
2Ti 4: 2 *c*, rebuke and encourage—

CORRECTED* (CORRECT)

Pr 29: 19 A servant cannot be *c*

CORRECTING* (CORRECT)

2Ti 3: 16 *c* and training in righteousness,

CORRECTION* (CORRECT)

Lev 26: 23 things you do not accept my *c*
Job 36: 10 He makes them listen to *c*
Pr 5: 12 How my heart spurned *c*!
10: 17 whoever ignores *c* leads others
12: 1 but he who hates *c* is stupid.
13: 18 but whoever heeds *c* is honoured.
15: 5 whoever heeds *c* shows prudence.
15: 10 he who hates *c* will die.
15: 12 A mocker resents *c*;
15: 32 whoever heeds *c* gains
29: 15 The rod of *c* imparts wisdom,
Jer 2: 30 they did not respond to *c*.
5: 3 crushed them, but they refused *c*.
7: 28 LORD its God or responded to *c*.
Zep 3: 2 she accepts no *c*.
3: 7 you will fear me / and accept *c*!'

CORRECTIONS* (CORRECT)

Pr 6: 23 and the *c* of discipline

CORRECTS* (CORRECT)

Job 5: 17 "Blessed is the man whom God *c*;
Pr 9: 7 Whoever *c* a mocker invites insult;

CORRUPT (CORRUPTED CORRUPTION CORRUPTS)

Ge 6: 11 Now the earth was *c* in God's sight
Ps 14: 1 They are *c*, their deeds are vile;
14: 3 they have together become *c*;
Pr 4: 24 keep *c* talk far from your lips.
6: 12 who goes about with a *c* mouth,
19: 28 A *c* witness mocks at justice,

CORRUPTED (CORRUPT)

2Co 7: 2 wronged no-one, we have *c* no-one,
Tit 1: 15 but to those who are *c* and do not

CORRUPTION (CORRUPT)

2Pe 1: 4 escape the *c* in the world caused
2: 20 If they have escaped the *c*

CORRUPTS* (CORRUPT)

Ecc 7: 7 and a bribe *c* the heart.
1Co 15: 33 "Bad company *c* good character."
Jas 3: 6 It *c* the whole person, sets

COST (COSTS)

Nu 16: 38 sinned at the *c* of their lives.
Pr 4: 7 Though it *c* all you have, get
7: 23 little knowing it will *c* him his life.
Isa 55: 1 milk without money and without *c*.
Lk 14: 28 and estimate the *c* to see
Rev 21: 6 to drink without *c* from the spring

COSTS (COST)

Pr 6: 31 it *c* him all the wealth of his house.

COUNCIL

Ps 89: 7 In the *c* of the holy ones God is
107: 32 and praise him in the *c* of the elders

COUNSEL (COUNSELLOR COUNSELS)

1Ki 22: 5 "First seek the *c* of the LORD."
2Ch 18: 4 "First seek the *c* of the LORD."
Job 38: 2 "Who is this that darkens my *c*
42: 3 'Who is this that obscures my *c*
Ps 1: 1 walk in the *c* of the wicked
73: 24 You guide me with your *c*,
107: 11 despised the *c* of the Most High.
Pr 8: 14 *C* and sound judgment are mine;
15: 22 Plans fail for lack of *c*,
27: 9 from his earnest *c*.
Isa 28: 29 wonderful in *c* and magnificent
1Ti 5: 14 So I *c* younger widows to marry,
Rev 3: 18 I *c* you to buy from me gold refined

COUNSELLOR (COUNSEL)

Isa 9: 6 Wonderful *C*, Mighty God,
Jn 14: 16 he will give you another *C* to be
14: 26 But the *C*, the Holy Spirit,
15: 26 "When the *C* comes, whom I will
16: 7 the *C* will not come to you;
Ro 11: 34 Or who has been his *c*?"

COUNSELS (COUNSEL)

Ps 16: 7 I will praise the LORD, who *c* me;

COUNT (COUNTED COUNTING COUNTS)

Ps 22: 17 I can *c* all my bones;
Ro 4: 8 whose sin the Lord will never *c*
6: 11 *c* yourselves dead to sin
2Th 1: 11 that our God may *c* you worthy

COUNTED (COUNT)

Ac 5: 41 because they had been *c* worthy
2Th 1: 5 and as a result you will be *c* worthy

COUNTERFEIT*

2Th 2: 9 displayed in all kinds of *c* miracles,
1Jn 2: 27 not *c*—just as it has taught you,

COUNTING (COUNT)

2Co 5: 19 not *c* men's sins against them.

COUNTRY

Pr 28: 2 When a *c* is rebellious, it has many
29: 4 By justice a king gives a *c* stability,
Isa 66: 8 Can a *c* be born in a day
Lk 15: 13 off for a distant *c* and there
Jn 4: 44 prophet has no honour in his own *c*.)
2Co 11: 26 in danger in the *c*, in danger at sea;
Heb 11: 14 looking for a *c* of their own.

COUNTRYMEN

2Co 11: 26 danger from my own *c*, in danger

COUNTS (COUNT)
Jn 6: 63 The Spirit gives life; the flesh *c*
1Co 7: 19 God's commands is what *c*.
Gal 5: 6 only thing that *c* is faith expressing

COURAGE* (COURAGEOUS)
Jos 2: 11 everyone's *c* failed because of you,
5: 1 and they no longer had the *c*
2Sa 4: 1 he lost *c*, and all Israel became
7: 27 So your servant has found *c*
1Ch 17: 25 So your servant has found *c* to pray
2Ch 15: 8 son of Oded the prophet, he took *c*.
19: 11 Act with *c*, and may the LORD be
Ezr 7: 28 I took *c* and gathered leading men
10: 4 We will support you, so take *c*
Ps 107: 26 in their peril their *c* melted away.
Eze 22: 14 Will your *c* endure or your hands
Da 11: 25 and *c* against the king of the South.
Mt 14: 27 said to them: "Take *c*!
Mk 6: 50 spoke to them and said, "Take *c*!
Ac 4: 13 When they saw the *c* of Peter
23: 11 "Take *c*! As you have testified
27: 22 now I urge you to keep up your *c*,
27: 25 So keep up your *c*, men,
1Co 16: 13 stand firm in the faith; be men of *c*;
Php 1: 20 will have sufficient *c* so that now
Heb 3: 6 if we hold on to our *c* and the hope

COURAGEOUS* (COURAGE)
Dt 31: 6 Be strong and *c*.
31: 7 of all Israel, "Be strong and *c*,
31: 23 son of Nun: "Be strong and *c*,
Jos 1: 6 and *c*, because you will lead these
1: 7 Be strong and very *c*.
1: 9 commanded you? Be strong and *c*.
1: 18 Only be strong and *c*!"
10: 25 Be strong and *c*.
1Ch 22: 13 Be strong and *c*.
28: 20 "Be strong and *c*, and do the work.
2Ch 26: 17 priest with eighty other *c* priests
32: 7 with these words: "Be strong and *c*.

COURSE
Ps 19: 5 a champion rejoicing to run his *c*.
Pr 2: 8 for he guards the *c* of the just
15: 21 of understanding keeps a straight *c*.
16: 9 In his heart a man plans his *c*,
17: 23 to pervert the *c* of justice.
Jas 3: 6 sets the whole *c* of his life on fire,

COURT (COURTS)
Pr 22: 22 and do not crush the needy in *c*,
25: 8 do not bring hastily to *c*,
Mt 5: 25 adversary who is taking you to *c*.
1Co 4: 3 judged by you or by any human *c*;

COURTS (COURT)
Ps 84: 10 Better is one day in your *c*
100: 4 and his *c* with praise;
Am 5: 15 maintain justice in the *c*.
Zec 8: 16 and sound judgment in your *c*;

COURTYARD
Ex 27: 9 "Make a *c* for the tabernacle.

COUSIN
Col 4: 10 as does Mark, the *c* of Barnabas.

COVENANT (COVENANTS)
Ge 9: 9 "I now establish my *c* with you
17: 2 I will confirm my *c* between me
Ex 19: 5 if you obey me fully and keep my *c*,
24: 7 Then he took the Book of the *C*
Dt 4: 13 declared to you his *c*, the Ten
29: 1 in addition to the *c* he had made
Jdg 2: 1 'I will never break my *c* with you,
1Sa 23: 18 of them made a *c* before the LORD
1Ki 8: 21 in which is the *c* of the LORD that
8: 23 you who keep your *c* of love
2Ki 23: 2 the words of the Book of the *C*,
1Ch 16: 15 He remembers his *c* for ever,
2Ch 6: 14 you who keep your *c* of love
34: 30 the words of the Book of the *C*,
Ne 1: 5 who keeps his *c* of love
Job 31: 1 "I made a *c* with my eyes
Ps 105: 8 He remembers his *c* for ever,
Pr 2: 17 ignored the *c* she made before God
Isa 42: 6 you to be a *c* for the people
61: 8 make an everlasting *c* with them.
Jer 11: 2 "Listen to the terms of this *c*
31: 31 "when I will make a new *c*
31: 32 It will not be like the *c*
31: 33 "This is the *c* I will make
Eze 37: 26 I will make a *c* of peace with them;
Da 9: 27 He will confirm a *c* with many
Hos 6: 7 Like Adam, they have broken the *c*
Mal 2: 14 the wife of your marriage *c*.
3: 1 of the *c*, whom you desire,
Mt 26: 28 blood of the *c*, which is poured out
Mk 14: 24 "This is my blood of the *c*,
Lk 22: 20 "This cup is the new *c* in my blood,
1Co 11: 25 "This cup is the new *c* in my blood;
2Co 3: 6 as ministers of a new *c*—
Gal 4: 24 One *c* is from Mount Sinai
Heb 8: 6 as the *c* of which he is mediator is
8: 8 when I will make a new *c*
9: 15 Christ is the mediator of a new *c*,
12: 24 to Jesus the mediator of a new *c*,

COVENANTS (COVENANT)
Ro 9: 4 theirs the divine glory, the *c*,
Gal 4: 24 for the women represent two *c*.

COVER (COVER-UP COVERED COVERING COVERINGS COVERS)
Ex 25: 17 "Make an atonement *c* of pure gold
25: 21 Place the *c* on top of the ark
33: 22 and *c* you with my hand
Lev 16: 2 in the cloud over the atonement *c*.
Ps 32: 5 and did not *c* up my iniquity.
91: 4 He will *c* you with his feathers,
Hos 10: 8 say to the mountains, "*C* us!"
Lk 23: 30 and to the hills, "*C* us!"'
1Co 11: 6 If a woman does not *c* her head,
11: 6 shaved off, she should *c* her head.
11: 7 A man ought not to *c* his head,
Jas 5: 20 and *c* over a multitude of sins.

COVER-UP* (COVER)
1Pe 2: 16 but do not use your freedom as a *c*

COVERED (COVER)
Ps 32: 1 whose sins are *c*.
85: 2 and *c* all their sins.
Isa 6: 2 With two wings they *c* their faces,
51: 16 *c* you with the shadow of my hand
Ro 4: 7 whose sins are *c*.
1Co 11: 4 with his head *c* dishonours his head.

COVERING (COVER)
1Co 11: 15 For long hair is given to her as a *c*.

COVERINGS (COVER)
Ge 3: 7 and made *c* for themselves.
Pr 31: 22 She makes *c* for her bed;

COVERS (COVER)
Pr 10: 12 but love *c* over all wrongs.
17: 9 He who *c* over an offence promotes
2Co 3: 15 Moses is read, a veil *c* their hearts.
1Pe 4: 8 love *c* over a multitude of sins.

COVET* (COVETED COVETOUS)
Ex 20: 17 You shall not *c* your neighbour's
20: 17 "You shall not *c* your neighbour's
34: 24 and no-one will *c* your land
Dt 5: 21 "You shall not *c* your neighbour's
7: 25 Do not *c* the silver and gold
Mic 2: 2 They *c* fields and seize them,
Ro 7: 7 if the law had not said, "Do not *c*."
7: 7 was to *c* if the law had not said,
13: 9 "Do not steal," "Do not *c*,"
Jas 4: 2 *c*, but you cannot have what you

COVETED* (COVET)
Jos 7: 21 weighing fifty shekels, I *c* them
Ac 20: 33 I have not *c* anyone's silver or gold

COVETOUS* (COVET)
Ro 7: 8 in me every kind of *c* desire.

COWARDLY*
Rev 21: 8 But the *c*, the unbelieving, the vile,

COWS
Ge 41: 2 of the river there came up seven *c*,
Ex 25: 5 skins dyed red and hides of sea *c*;
Nu 4: 6 are to cover this with hides of sea *c*,
1Sa 6: 7 Hitch the *c* to the cart,

CRAFTINESS* (CRAFTY)
Job 5: 13 He catches the wise in their *c*,
1Co 3: 19 "He catches the wise in their *c*";
Eph 4: 14 and *c* of men in their deceitful

CRAFTSMAN
Pr 8: 30 Then I was the *c* at his side.

CRAFTY* (CRAFTINESS)
Ge 3: 1 the serpent was more *c* than any
1Sa 23: 22 They tell me he is very *c*.
Job 5: 12 He thwarts the plans of the *c*,
15: 5 you adopt the tongue of the *c*.
Pr 7: 10 like a prostitute and with *c* intent.
12: 2 but the LORD condemns a *c* man.
14: 17 and a *c* man is hated.
2Co 12: 16 *c* fellow that I am, I caught you

CRAVE* (CRAVED CRAVES CRAVING CRAVINGS)
Nu 11: 4 with them began to *c* other food,
Dt 12: 20 you *c* meat and say, "I would like
Pr 23: 3 Do not *c* his delicacies,
23: 6 do not *c* his delicacies;
31: 4 not for rulers to *c* beer;
Mic 7: 1 none of the early figs that I *c*.
1Pe 2: 2 newborn babies, *c* pure spiritual

CRAVED* (CRAVE)
Nu 11: 34 the people who had *c* other food.
Ps 78: 18 by demanding the food they *c*.
78: 29 for he had given them what they *c*.
78: 30 turned from the food they *c*,

CRAVES* (CRAVE)
Pr 13: 4 The sluggard *c* and gets nothing,
21: 10 The wicked man *c* evil;
21: 26 All day long he *c* for more,

CRAVING* (CRAVE)
Job 20: 20 he will have no respite from his *c*;
Ps 106: 14 In the desert they gave in to their *c*;
Pr 10: 3 but he thwarts the *c* of the wicked.
13: 2 the unfaithful have a *c* for violence.
21: 25 The sluggard's *c* will be the death
Jer 2: 24 sniffing the wind in her *c*—

CRAVINGS* (CRAVE)
Ps 10: 3 He boasts of the *c* of his heart;
Eph 2: 3 gratifying the *c* of our sinful nature
1Jn 2: 16 in the world—the *c* of sinful man,

CRAWL
Ge 3: 14 You will *c* on your belly

CREATE* (CREATED CREATES CREATING CREATION CREATOR)
Ps 51: 10 *C* in me a pure heart, O God,
Isa 4: 5 Then the LORD will *c* over all
45: 7 I bring prosperity and *c* disaster;
45: 7 I form the light and *c* darkness,
45: 18 he did not *c* it to be empty,
65: 17 "Behold, I will *c* / new heavens
65: 18 for I will *c* Jerusalem to be a delight
65: 18 for ever in what I will *c*,
Jer 31: 22 The LORD will *c* a new thing
Mal 2: 10 one Father? Did not one God *c* us?
Eph 2: 15 His purpose was to *c*

CREATED* (CREATE)
Ge 1: 1 In the beginning God *c* the heavens
1: 21 God *c* the great creatures of the sea
1: 27 So God *c* man in his own image,
1: 27 in the image of God he *c* him;
1: 27 male and female he *c* them.
2: 4 and the earth when they were *c*.
5: 1 When God *c* man, he made him
5: 2 He *c* them male and female;
5: 2 when they were *c*, he called them
6: 7 whom I have *c*, from the face
Dt 4: 32 from the day God *c* man
Ps 89: 12 You *c* the north and the south;
89: 47 what futility you have *c* all men!
102: 18 a people not yet *c* may praise
104: 30 you send your Spirit, / they are *c*,
139: 13 For you *c* my inmost being;
148: 5 for he commanded and they were *c*
Isa 40: 26 Who *c* all these?
41: 20 that the Holy One of Israel has *c* it.
42: 5 he who *c* the heavens and stretched
43: 1 he who *c* you, O Jacob,
43: 7 whom I *c* for my glory,
45: 8 I, the LORD, have *c* it.
45: 12 and *c* mankind upon it.
45: 18 he who *c* the heavens,
48: 7 They are *c* now, and not long ago;
54: 16 And it is I who have *c* the destroyer
54: 16 "See, it is I who *c* the blacksmith
57: 16 the breath of man that I have *c*.
Eze 21: 30 In the place where you were *c*,
28: 13 the day you were *c* they were
28: 15 ways from the day you were *c*
Mk 13: 19 when God *c* the world, until now—
Ro 1: 25 and served *c* things rather
1Co 11: 9 neither was man *c* for woman,
Eph 2: 10 *c* in Christ Jesus to do good works,
3: 9 hidden in God, who *c* all things.
4: 24 *c* to be like God in true
Col 1: 16 For by him all things were *c*:
1: 16 all things were *c* by him
1Ti 4: 3 which God *c* to be received
4: 4 For everything God *c* is good,
Heb 12: 27 *c* things—so that what cannot be
Jas 1: 18 a kind of firstfruits of all he *c*.
Rev 4: 11 and by your will they were *c*
4: 11 for you *c* all things,
10: 6 who *c* the heavens and all that is

CREATES* (CREATE)
Am 4: 13 *c* the wind,

CREATING* (CREATE)
Ge 2: 3 the work of *c* that he had done.
Isa 57: 19 *c* praise on the lips of the mourners

CREATION* (CREATE)
Hab 2: 18 he who makes it trusts in his own *c*;
Mt 13: 35 hidden since the *c* of the world."
25: 34 for you since the *c* of the world.
Mk 10: 6 of *c* God 'made them male
16: 15 and preach the good news to all *c*.
Jn 17: 24 me before the *c* of the world.
Ro 1: 20 For since the *c* of the world God's
8: 19 The *c* waits in eager expectation
8: 20 For the *c* was subjected
8: 21 in hope that the *c* itself will be
8: 22 that the whole *c* has been groaning
8: 39 depth, nor anything else in all *c*,
2Co 5: 17 he is a new *c*; the old has gone,
Gal 6: 15 anything; what counts is a new *c*.
Eph 1: 4 us in him before the *c* of the world
Col 1: 15 God, the firstborn over all *c*.
Heb 4: 3 finished since the *c* of the world.
4: 13 Nothing in all *c* is hidden
9: 11 that is to say, not a part of this *c*.
9: 26 times since the *c* of the world.
1Pe 1: 20 chosen before the *c* of the world,
2Pe 3: 4 as it has since the beginning of *c*."
Rev 3: 14 true witness, the ruler of God's *c*.
13: 8 slain from the *c* of the world.
17: 8 life from the *c* of the world will be

CREATOR* (CREATE)
Ge 14: 19 *C* of heaven and earth.
14: 22 God Most High, *C* of heaven
Dt 32: 6 Is he not your Father, your *C*,
Ecc 12: 1 Remember your *C*
Isa 27: 11 and their *C* shows them no favour.
40: 28 the *C* of the ends of the earth.
43: 15 Israel's *C*, your King."
Mt 19: 4 the beginning the *C* 'made them
Ro 1: 25 created things rather than the *C*—
Col 3: 10 in knowledge in the image of its *C*.
1Pe 4: 19 themselves to their faithful *C*

CREATURE (CREATURES)
Lev 17: 11 For the life of a *c* is in the blood,
17: 14 the life of every *c* is its blood.
Ps 136: 25 and who gives food to every *c*.
Eze 1: 15 beside each *c* with its four faces.
Rev 4: 7 The first living *c* was like a lion,

CREATURES (CREATURE)
Ge 6: 19 bring into the ark two of all living *c*,
8: 21 again will I destroy all living *c*,
Ps 104: 24 the earth is full of your *c*.
Eze 1: 5 was what looked like four living *c*.

CREDIT (CREDITED CREDITOR CREDITS)
Lk 6: 33 what *c* is that to you? Even
Ro 4: 24 to whom God will *c* righteousness
1Pe 2: 20 it to your *c* if you receive a beating

CREDITED (CREDIT)
Ge 15: 6 and he *c* it to him as righteousness.
Ps 106: 31 This was *c* to him as righteousness
Eze 18: 20 of the righteous man will be *c*
Ro 4: 3 and it was *c* to him as righteousness
4: 4 his wages are not *c* to him as a gift,
4: 5 his faith is *c* as righteousness.
4: 9 saying that Abraham's faith was *c*
4: 23 The words "it was *c*
Gal 3: 6 and it was *c* to him as righteousness
Php 4: 17 for what may be *c* to your account.
Jas 2: 23 and it was *c* to him as righteousness

CREDITOR (CREDIT)
Dt 15: 2 Every *c* shall cancel the loan he has

CREDITS (CREDIT)
Ro 4: 6 whom God *c* righteousness apart

CRETANS (CRETE)
Tit 1: 12 "*C* are always liars, evil brutes,

CRETE (CRETANS)
Ac 27: 12 harbour in *C*, facing both south-west

CRIED (CRY)
Ex 2: 23 groaned in their slavery and *c* out,
14: 10 They were terrified and *c* out
Nu 20: 16 but when we *c* out to the LORD,
Jos 24: 7 But they *c* to the LORD for help,
Jdg 3: 9 But when they *c* out to the LORD,
3: 15 Again the Israelites *c* out
4: 3 they *c* to the LORD for help.
6: 6 the Israelites that they *c* out
10: 12 Maonites oppressed you and you *c*
1Sa 7: 9 He *c* out to the LORD
12: 8 they *c* to the LORD for help,
12: 10 they *c* out to the LORD and said,
Ps 18: 6 I *c* to my God for help.

CRIMINALS
Lk 23: 32 both *c*, were also led out with him

CRIMSON
Isa 1: 18 though they are red as *c*,
63: 1 with his garments stained *c*?

CRIPPLED
2Sa 9: 3 of Jonathan; he is *c* in both feet."
Mk 9: 45 better for you to enter life *c*

CRISIS*
1Co 7: 26 of the present *c*, I think that it is

CRITICISM*
2Co 8: 20 We want to avoid any *c*

CROOKED*
Dt 32: 5 but a warped and *c* generation.
2Sa 22: 27 to the *c* you show yourself shrewd.
Ps 18: 26 to the *c* you show yourself shrewd.
125: 5 But those who turn to *c* ways
Pr 2: 15 whose paths are *c*
5: 6 her paths are *c*, but she knows it
8: 8 none of them is *c* or perverse.
10: 9 he who takes *c* paths will be found
Ecc 7: 13 what he has made *c*?
Isa 59: 8 have turned them into *c* roads;
La 3: 9 he has made my paths *c*.
Lk 3: 5 The *c* roads shall become straight,
Php 2: 15 children of God without fault in a *c*

CROP (CROPS)
Mt 13: 8 where it produced a *c*—a hundred,
21: 41 share of the *c* at harvest time."

CROPS (CROP)
Pr 3: 9 with the firstfruits of all your *c*;
10: 5 He who gathers *c* in summer is
28: 3 like a driving rain that leaves no *c*.
2Ti 2: 6 the first to receive a share of the *c*.

CROSS [1] (CROSSED CROSSING)
Dt 4: 21 Swore that I would not *c* the Jordan
12: 10 But you will *c* the Jordan

CROSS [2]
Mt 10: 38 and anyone who does not take his *c*
16: 24 and take up his *c* and follow me.
Mk 8: 34 and take up his *c* and follow me.
Lk 9: 23 take up his *c* daily and follow me.
14: 27 anyone who does not carry his *c*
Jn 19: 17 Carrying his own *c*, he went out
Ac 2: 23 to death by nailing him to the *c*.
1Co 1: 17 lest the *c* of Christ be emptied
1: 18 the message of the *c* is foolishness
Gal 5: 11 offence of the *c* has been abolished.
6: 12 persecuted for the *c* of Christ.
6: 14 in the *c* of our Lord Jesus Christ,
Eph 2: 16 both of them to God through the *c*,
Php 2: 8 even death on a *c*!
3: 18 as enemies of the *c* of Christ.
Col 1: 20 through his blood, shed on the *c*.
2: 14 he took it away, nailing it to the *c*.
2: 15 triumphing over them by the *c*.
Heb 12: 2 set before him endured the *c*,

CROSSED (CROSS [1])
Jos 4: 7 When it *c* the Jordan, the waters
Jn 5: 24 he has *c* over from death to life.

CROSSING (CROSS [1])
Ge 48: 14 he was the younger, and *c* his arms,

CROSSROADS (ROAD)
Jer 6: 16 "Stand at the *c* and look;

CROUCHING
Ge 4: 7 sin is *c* at your door; it desires

CROWD (CROWDS)
Ex 23: 2 Do not follow the *c* in doing wrong.

CROWDS (CROWD)
Mt 9: 36 he saw the *c*, he had compassion

CROWED (CROWS)
Mt 26: 74 the man!" Immediately a cock *c*.

CROWN (CROWNED CROWNS)
Pr 4: 9 present you with a *c* of splendour."
10: 6 Blessings *c* the head
12: 4 noble character is her husband's *c*,
16: 31 Grey hair is a *c* of splendour;

Pr 17: 6 Children's children are a *c*
Isa 35: 10 everlasting joy will *c* their heads.
51: 11 everlasting joy will *c* their heads.
61: 3 to bestow on them a *c* of beauty
62: 3 You will be a *c* of splendour
Eze 16: 12 and a beautiful *c* on your head.
Zec 9: 16 like jewels in a *c*.
Mt 27: 29 and then twisted together a *c* of thorns
Mk 15: 17 then twisted together a *c* of thorns
Jn 19: 2 The soldiers twisted together a *c*
19: 5 When Jesus came out wearing the *c*
1Co 9: 25 it to get a *c* that will last for ever.
9: 25 it to get a *c* that will not last;
Php 4: 1 and long for, my joy and *c*,
1Th 2: 19 or the *c* in which we will glory
2Ti 2: 5 he does not receive the victor's *c*
4: 8 store for me the *c* of righteousness,
Jas 1: 12 he will receive the *c*
1Pe 5: 4 you will receive the *c*
Rev 2: 10 and I will give you the *c* of life.
3: 11 so that no-one will take your *c*.
14: 14 a son of man" with a *c* of gold

CROWNED* (CROWN)

Ps 8: 5 and *c* him with glory and honour.
Pr 14: 18 the prudent are *c* with knowledge.
SS 3: 11 crown with which his mother *c* him
Heb 2: 7 you *c* him with glory and honour
2: 9 now *c* with glory and honour

CROWNS (CROWN)

Ps 103: 4 and *c* me with love and compassion
149: 4 he *c* the humble with salvation.
Pr 11: 26 blessing *c* him who is willing to sell.
Rev 4: 4 and had *c* of gold on their heads.
4: 10 They lay their *c* before the throne
12: 3 ten horns and seven *c* on his heads.
19: 12 and on his head are many *c*.

CROWS (CROWED)

Mt 26: 34 this very night, before the cock *c*

CRUCIFIED* (CRUCIFY)

Mt 20: 19 to be mocked and flogged and *c*.
26: 2 of Man will be handed over to be *c*
27: 26 and handed him over to be *c*.
27: 35 When they had *c* him, they divided
27: 38 Two robbers were *c* with him,
27: 44 same way the robbers who were *c*
28: 5 looking for Jesus, who was *c*.
Mk 15: 15 and handed him over to be *c*.
15: 24 And they *c* him.
15: 25 the third hour when they *c* him.
15: 27 They *c* two robbers with him,
15: 32 Those *c* with him also heaped
16: 6 for Jesus the Nazarene, who was *c*.
Lk 23: 23 insistently demanded that he be *c*,
23: 33 *c* him, along with the criminals—
24: 7 be *c* and on the third day be raised
24: 20 sentenced to death, and they *c* him;
Jn 19: 16 him over to them to be *c*.
19: 18 Here they *c* him, and with him two
19: 20 for the place where Jesus was *c* was
19: 23 When the soldiers *c* Jesus,
19: 32 of the first man who had been *c*
19: 41 At the place where Jesus was *c*,
Ac 2: 36 whom you *c*, both Lord and Christ
4: 10 whom you *c* but whom God raised
Ro 6: 6 For we know that our old self was *c*
1Co 1: 13 Is Christ divided? Was Paul *c*
1: 23 but we preach Christ *c*: a stumbling
2: 2 except Jesus Christ and him *c*.
2: 8 they would not have *c* the Lord
2Co 13: 4 to be sure, he was *c* in weakness,
Gal 2: 20 I have been *c* with Christ
3: 1 Christ was clearly portrayed as *c*.
5: 24 Christ Jesus have *c* the sinful
6: 14 which the world has been *c*
Rev 11: 8 where also their Lord was *c*.

CRUCIFY* (CRUCIFIED CRUCIFYING)

Mt 23: 34 Some of them you will kill and *c*;
27: 22 They all answered, "*C* him!" "Why
27: 23 they shouted all the louder, "*C* him
27: 31 Then they led him away to *c* him.
Mk 15: 13 "*C* him!" they shouted.
15: 14 they shouted all the louder, "*C* him
15: 20 Then they led him out to *c* him.
Lk 23: 21 they kept shouting, "*C* him! *C* him
Jn 19: 6 they shouted, "*C*! *C*!"
19: 6 "You take him and *c* him.
19: 10 either to free you or to *c* you?"
19: 15 *C* him!" "Shall I *c* your king
19: 15 away! Take him away! *C* him!"

CRUCIFYING* (CRUCIFY)

Heb 6: 6 to their loss they are *c* the Son

CRUSH (CRUSHED)

Ge 3: 15 he will *c* your head,
Isa 53: 10 it was the LORD's will to *c* him
Ro 16: 20 The God of peace will soon *c* Satan

CRUSHED (CRUSH)

Ps 34: 18 and saves those who are *c* in spirit.
Pr 17: 22 but a *c* spirit dries up the bones.
18: 14 but a *c* spirit who can bear?
Isa 53: 5 he was *c* for our iniquities;
2Co 4: 8 not *c*; perplexed, but not in despair;

CRY (CRIED)

Ex 2: 23 *c* for help because of their slavery
Ps 5: 2 Listen to my *c* for help,
34: 15 and his ears are attentive to their *c*;
40: 1 he turned to me and heard my *c*.
130: 1 Out of the depths I *c* to you,
Pr 21: 13 to the *c* of the poor,
La 2: 18 *c* out to the Lord.
Hab 2: 11 The stones of the wall will *c* out,
Lk 19: 40 keep quiet, the stones will *c* out."

CUNNING

2Co 11: 3 deceived by the serpent's *c*,
Eph 4: 14 and by the *c* and craftiness of men

CUP

Ps 23: 5 my *c* overflows.
Isa 51: 22 from that *c*, the goblet of my wrath,
51: 22 the *c* that made you stagger;
Mt 10: 42 if anyone gives a *c* of cold water
20: 22 "Can you drink the *c* I am going
23: 25 You clean the outside of the *c*
23: 26 First clean the inside of the *c*
26: 27 Then he took the *c*, gave thanks
26: 39 may this *c* be taken from me.
26: 42 possible for this *c* to be taken away
Mk 9: 41 anyone who gives you a *c* of water
10: 38 "Can you drink the *c* I drink
10: 39 "You will drink the *c* I drink
14: 23 Then he took the *c*, gave thanks
14: 36 Take this *c* from me.
Lk 11: 39 Pharisees clean the outside of the *c*
22: 17 After taking the *c*, he gave thanks
22: 20 after the supper he took the *c*,
22: 20 "This *c* is the new covenant
22: 42 if you are willing, take this *c*
Jn 18: 11 I not drink the *c* the Father has
1Co 10: 16 Is not the *c* of thanksgiving
10: 21 the *c* of the Lord and the *c*
11: 25 after supper he took the *c*, saying,
11: 25 "This *c* is the new covenant

CUPBEARER

Ge 40: 1 the *c* and the baker of the king
Ne 1: 11 I was *c* to the king.

CURE (CURED)

Jer 17: 9 and beyond *c*.
30: 15 your pain that has no *c*?
Hos 5: 13 But he is not able to *c* you,
Lk 9: 1 out all demons and to *c* diseases,

CURED (CURE)

Mt 11: 5 those who have leprosy are *c*,
Lk 6: 18 troubled by evil spirits were *c*,

CURSE (ACCURSED CURSED CURSES CURSING)

Ge 4: 11 Now you are under a *c*
8: 21 "Never again will I *c* the ground
12: 3 and whoever curses you I will *c*;
Dt 11: 26 before you today a blessing and a *c*
11: 28 the *c* if you disobey the commands
21: 23 hung on a tree is under God's *c*.
23: 5 turned the *c* into a blessing for you,
Job 1: 11 he will surely *c* you to your face."
2: 5 he will surely *c* you to your face."
2: 9 *C* God and die!" He replied,
Ps 109: 28 They may *c*, but you will bless;
Pr 3: 33 The LORD's *c* is on the house
24: 24 peoples will *c* him and nations
Mal 2: 2 and I will *c* your blessings.
Lk 6: 28 bless those who *c* you, pray
Ro 12: 14 persecute you; bless and do not *c*.
Gal 3: 10 on observing the law are under a *c*,
3: 13 of the law by becoming a *c* for us,
Jas 3: 9 with it we *c* men, who have been
Rev 22: 3 No longer will there be any *c*.

CURSED (CURSE)

Ge 3: 17 "*C* is the ground because of you;
Dt 27: 15 "*C* is the man who carves an image
27: 16 "*C* is the man who dishonours his
27: 17 "*C* is the man who moves his
27: 18 "*C* is the man who leads the blind
27: 19 *C* is the man who withholds justice
27: 20 "*C* is the man who sleeps
27: 21 "*C* is the man who has sexual
27: 22 "*C* is the man who sleeps
27: 23 "*C* is the man who sleeps
27: 24 "*C* is the man who kills his
27: 25 "*C* is the man who accepts a bribe
27: 26 "*C* is the man who does not uphold
Jer 17: 5 "*C* is the one who trusts in man,
Mal 1: 14 "*C* is the cheat who has
Ro 9: 3 I could wish that I myself were *c*
1Co 4: 12 When we are *c*, we bless;
12: 3 "Jesus be *c*," and no-one can say,
Gal 3: 10 "*C* is everyone who does not
3: 13 *C* is everyone who is hung on a tree

CURSES (CURSE)

Ex 21: 17 "Anyone who *c* his father
Lev 20: 9 "'If anyone *c* his father or mother,
Nu 5: 23 is to write these *c* on a scroll
Jos 8: 34 the blessings and the *c*—just
Pr 20: 20 If a man *c* his father or mother,
28: 27 to them receives many *c*.
Mt 15: 4 and 'Anyone who *c* his father
Mk 7: 10 and, 'Anyone who *c* his father

CURSING (CURSE)

Ps 109: 18 He wore *c* as his garment;
Ro 3: 14 "Their mouths are full of *c*
Jas 3: 10 the same mouth come praise and *c*.

CURTAIN

Ex 26: 31 "Make a *c* of blue, purple
26: 33 The *c* will separate the Holy Place
Mt 27: 51 At that moment the *c*
Mk 15: 38 The *c* of the temple was torn in two
Lk 23: 45 the *c* of the temple was torn in two.
Heb 6: 19 the inner sanctuary behind the *c*,
9: 3 Behind the second *c* was a room
10: 20 opened for us through the *c*,

CUSTOM

Job 1: 5 This was Job's regular *c*.
Mk 10: 1 and as was his *c*, he taught them.
Lk 4: 16 into the synagogue, as was his *c*.
Ac 17: 2 As his *c* was, Paul went

CUT

Lev 19: 27 "'Do not *c* the hair at the sides
21: 5 of their beards or *c* their bodies.
1Ki 3: 25 "*C* the living child in two
Isa 51: 1 to the rock from which you were *c*
53: 8 For he was *c* off from the land

Da 2: 45 of the rock *c* out of a mountain,
9: 26 the Anointed One will be *c* off
Mt 3: 10 not produce good fruit will be *c*
24: 22 If those days had not been *c* short,
1Co 11: 6 for a woman to have her hair *c*

CYMBAL* (CYMBALS)

1Co 13: 1 a resounding gong or a clanging *c*.

CYMBALS (CYMBAL)

1Ch 15: 16 instruments: lyres, harps and *c*.
2Ch 5: 12 dressed in fine linen and playing *c*,
Ps 150: 5 praise him with resounding *c*.

CYRUS

Persian king who allowed exiles to return (2Ch 36:22-Ezr 1:8), to rebuild temple (Ezr 5:13-6:14), as appointed by the LORD (Isa 44:28-45:13).

DAGON

Jdg 16: 23 offer a great sacrifice to *D* their god
1Sa 5: 2 *D*'s temple and set it beside *D*.

DAMASCUS

Ac 9: 3 As he neared *D* on his journey,

DAN

1. Son of Jacob by Bilhah (Ge 30:4-6; 35:25; 46:23). Tribe of blessed (Ge 49:16-17; Dt 33:22), numbered (Nu 1:39; 26:43), allotted land (Jos 19:40-48; Eze 48:1), failed to fully possess (Jdg 1:34-35), failed to support Deborah (Jdg 5:17), possessed Laish/Dan (Jdg 18).

2. Northernmost city in Israel (Ge 14:14; Jdg 18; 20:1).

DANCE (DANCED DANCING)

Ecc 3: 4 a time to mourn and a time to *d*,
Mt 11: 17 and you did not *d*;

DANCED (DANCE)

2Sa 6: 14 *d* before the LORD
Mk 6: 22 of Herodias came in and *d*,

DANCING (DANCE)

Ps 30: 11 You turned my wailing into *d*;
149: 3 Let them praise his name with *d*

DANGER

Pr 22: 3 A prudent man sees *d*
27: 12 The prudent see *d* and take refuge,
Mt 5: 22 will be in *d* of the fire of hell.
Ro 8: 35 famine or nakedness or *d* or sword?
2Co 11: 26 I have been in *d* from rivers,

DANIEL

1. Hebrew exile to Babylon, name changed to Belteshazzar (Da 1:6-7). Refused to eat unclean food (Da 1:8-21). Interpreted Nebuchadnezzar's dreams (Da 2; 4), writing on the wall (Da 5). Thrown into lions' den (Da 6). Visions of (Da 7-12).

2. Son of David (1Ch 3:1).

DARIUS

1. King of Persia (Ezr 4:5), allowed rebuilding of temple (Ezr 5-6).

2. Mede who conquered Babylon (Da 5:31).

DARK (DARKENED DARKENS DARKNESS)

Job 34: 22 There is no *d* place, no deep
Ps 18: 9 *d* clouds were under his feet.
Pr 31: 15 She gets up while it is still *d*;
SS 1: 6 Do not stare at me because I am *d*,
Jn 12: 35 in the *d* does not know where he is
Ro 2: 19 a light for those who are in the *d*,
2Pe 1: 19 as to a light shining in a *d* place,

DARKENED (DARK)

Joel 2: 10 the sun and moon are *d*,
Mt 24: 29 " 'the sun will be *d*,
Ro 1: 21 and their foolish hearts were *d*.
Eph 4: 18 They are *d* in their understanding

DARKENS (DARK)

Job 38: 2 "Who is this that *d* my counsel

DARKNESS (DARK)

Ge 1: 2 *d* was over the surface of the deep,
1: 4 he separated the light from the *d*.
Ex 10: 22 and total *d* covered all Egypt
20: 21 approached the thick *d* where God
2Sa 22: 29 the LORD turns my *d* into light.
Ps 18: 28 my God turns my *d* into light.
91: 6 the pestilence that stalks in the *d*,
112: 4 Even in *d* light dawns
139: 12 even the *d* will not be dark to you;
Pr 4: 19 the way of the wicked is like deep *d*
Isa 5: 20 and light for *d*,
42: 16 I will turn the *d* into light
45: 7 I form the light and create *d*,
58: 10 then your light will rise in the *d*,
61: 1 release from *d* for the prisoners,
Joel 2: 31 The sun will be turned to *d*
Mt 4: 16 the people living in *d*
6: 23 how great is that *d*! "No-one can
Lk 11: 34 are bad, your body also is full of *d*.
23: 44 and *d* came over the whole land
Jn 1: 5 The light shines in the *d*,
3: 19 but men loved *d* instead of light
Ac 2: 20 The sun will be turned to *d*
2Co 4: 6 who said, "Let light shine out of *d*
6: 14 fellowship can light have with *d*?
Eph 5: 8 For you were once *d*, but now you
5: 11 to do with the fruitless deeds of *d*,
1Pe 2: 9 out of *d* into his wonderful light.
2Pe 2: 17 Blackest *d* is reserved for them.
1Jn 1: 5 in him there is no *d* at all.
2: 9 but hates his brother is still in the *d*.
Jude : 6 in *d*, bound with everlasting chains
: 13 for whom blackest *d* has been

DASH

Ps 2: 9 you will *d* them to pieces like

DAUGHTER (DAUGHTERS)

Ex 1: 10 she took him to Pharaoh's *d*
Jdg 11: 48 to commemorate the *d* of Jephthah
Est 2: 7 Mordecai had taken her as his own *d*
Ps 9: 14 praises in the gates of the *D* of Zion
137: 8 O *D* of Babylon, doomed
Isa 62: 11 "Say to the *D* of Zion
Zec 9: 9 Shout, *D* of Jerusalem!
Mk 5: 34 "*D*, your faith has healed you.
7: 29 the demon has left your *d*.

DAUGHTERS (DAUGHTER)

Ge 6: 2 the *d* of men were beautiful,
19: 36 Lot's *d* became pregnant
Nu 36: 10 Zelophehad's *d* did as the LORD
Joel 2: 28 sons and *d* will prophesy,

DAVID

Son of Jesse (Ru 4:17-22; 1Ch 2:13-15), ancestor of Jesus (Mt 1:1-17; Lk 3:31). Wives and children (1Sa 18; 25:39-44; 2Sa 3:2-5; 5:13-16; 11:27; 1Ch 3:1-9).

Anointed king by Samuel (1Sa 16:1-13). Musician to Saul (1Sa 16:14-23; 18:10). Killed Goliath (1Sa 17). Relation with Jonathan (1Sa 18:1-4; 19-20; 23:16-18; 2Sa 1). Disfavour of Saul (1Sa 18:6-23:29). Spared Saul's life (1Sa 24; 26). Among Philistines (1Sa 21:10-14; 27-30). Lament for Saul and Jonathan (2Sa 1).

Anointed king of Judah (2Sa 2:1-11). Conflict with house of Saul (2Sa 2-4). Anointed king of Israel (2Sa 5:1-4; 1Ch 11:1-3). Conquered Jerusalem (2Sa 6; 1Ch 13; 15-16). The LORD promised eternal dynasty (2Sa 7; 1Ch 17; Ps 132). Showed kindness to Mephibosheth (2Sa 9). Adultery with Bathsheba, murder of Uriah (2Sa 11-12). Son Amnon raped daughter Tamar; killed by Absalom (2Sa 13). Absalom's revolt (2Sa 14-17); death (2Sa 18). Sheba's revolt (2Sa 20). Victories: Philistines (2Sa 5:17-25; 1Ch 14:8-17; 2Sa 21:15-22; 1Ch 20:4-8), Ammonites (2Sa 10; 1Ch 19), various (2Sa 8; 1Ch 18). Mighty men (2Sa 23:8-39; 1Ch 11-12). Punished for numbering army (2Sa 24; 1Ch 21). Appointed Solomon king (1Ki 1:28-2:9). Prepared for building of temple (1Ch 22-29). Last words (2Sa 23:1-7). Death (1Ki 2:10-12; 1Ch 29:28).

Psalmist (Mt 22:43-45), musician (Am 6:5), prophet (2Sa 23:2-7; Ac 1:16; 2:30).

Psalms of: 2 (Ac 4:25), 3-32, 34-41, 51-65, 68-70, 86, 95 (Heb 4:7), 101, 103, 108-110, 122, 124, 131, 133, 138-145.

DAWN (DAWNED DAWNS)

Ps 37: 6 your righteousness shine like the *d*,
Pr 4: 18 is like the first gleam of *d*,
Isa 14: 12 O morning star, son of the *d*!
Am 4: 13 he who turns *d* to darkness,
5: 8 who turns blackness into *d*

DAWNED (DAWN)

Isa 9: 2 a light has *d*.
Mt 4: 16 a light has *d*."

DAWNS* (DAWN)

Ps 65: 8 where morning *d* and evening
112: 4 in darkness light *d* for the upright,
Hos 10: 15 When that day *d*,
2Pe 1: 19 until the day *d* and the morning

DAY (DAYS)

Ge 1: 5 God called the light "*d*"
1: 5 and there was morning—the first *d*
1: 8 there was morning—the second *d*.
1: 13 there was morning—the third *d*.
1: 19 there was morning—the fourth *d*.
1: 23 there was morning—the fifth *d*.
1: 31 there was morning—the sixth *d*.
2: 2 so on the seventh *d* he rested
8: 22 *d* and night
Ex 16: 30 the people rested on the seventh *d*.
20: 8 "Remember the Sabbath *d*
Lev 16: 30 on this *d* atonement will be made
23: 28 because it is the *D* of Atonement,
Nu 14: 14 before them in a pillar of cloud by *d*
Jos 1: 8 meditate on it *d* and night,
2Ki 7: 9 This is a *d* of good news
25: 30 *D* by *d* the king gave Jehoiachin
1Ch 16: 23 proclaim his salvation *d* after *d*.
Ne 8: 18 *D* after *d*, from the first *d*
Ps 84: 10 Better is one *d* in your courts
96: 2 proclaim his salvation *d* after *d*.
118: 24 This is the *d* the LORD has made;
Pr 27: 1 not know what a *d* may bring forth.
Isa 13: 9 a cruel *d*, with wrath and fierce
Jer 46: 10 But that *d* belongs to the LORD,
50: 31 "for your *d* has come,
Eze 30: 2 "Alas for that *d*!"
Joel 2: 31 and dreadful *d* of the LORD.
Am 3: 14 On the *d* I punish Israel for her sins
5: 20 Will not the *d* of the LORD be
Ob : 15 "The *d* of the LORD is near
Zep 1: 14 The great *d* of the LORD is near—
Zec 2: 11 joined with the LORD in that *d*
14: 1 A *d* of the LORD is coming
14: 7 It will be a unique *d*,
Mal 4: 5 dreadful *d* of the LORD comes.
Mt 24: 38 up to the *d* Noah entered the ark;
Lk 11: 3 Give us each *d* our daily bread.
17: 24 in his *d* will be like the lightning,
Ac 5: 42 *D* after *d*, in the temple courts
17: 11 examined the Scriptures every *d*
17: 17 as in the market-place *d* by *d*
Ro 14: 5 man considers every *d* alike.
1Co 5: 5 his spirit saved on the *d* of the Lord
2Co 4: 16 we are being renewed *d* by *d*.
11: 25 I spent a night and a *d*
1Th 5: 2 for you know very well that the *d*
5: 4 so that this *d* should surprise you
2Th 2: 2 saying that the *d* of the Lord has
Heb 7: 27 need to offer sacrifices *d* after *d*,
2Pe 3: 8 With the Lord a *d* is like
3: 10 *d* of the Lord will come like a thief.

Rev 6: 17 For the great *d* of their wrath has
16: 14 on the great *d* of God Almighty.

DAYS (DAY)

Dt 17: 19 he is to read it all the *d* of his life
32: 7 Remember the *d* of old;
Ps 23: 6 all the *d* of my life,
34: 12 and desires to see many good *d*,
39: 5 have made my *d* a mere
90: 10 The length of our *d* is seventy years
90: 12 Teach us to number our *d* aright,
103: 15 As for man, his *d* are like grass,
128: 5 all the *d* of your life;
Pr 31: 12 all the *d* of her life.
Ecc 9: 9 all the *d* of this meaningless life
12: 1 Creator in the *d* of your youth,
Isa 38: 20 all the *d* of our lives
Da 7: 9 and the Ancient of *D* took his seat.
7: 13 He approached the Ancient of *D*
7: 22 until the Ancient of *D* came
Hos 3: 5 and to his blessings in the last *d*.
Joel 2: 29 I will pour out my Spirit in those *d*.
Mic 4: 1 In the last *d*
Lk 19: 43 The *d* will come upon you
Ac 2: 17 by the prophet Joel: "'In the last *d*,
2Ti 3: 1 will be terrible times in the last *d*.
Heb 1: 2 in these last *d* he has spoken to us
2Pe 3: 3 that in the last *d* scoffers will come,

DAZZLING*

Da 2: 31 *d* statue, awesome in appearance.
Mk 9: 3 His clothes became *d* white,

DEACON* (DEACONS)

1Ti 3: 12 A *d* must be the husband of

DEACONS* (DEACON)

Php 1: 1 together with the overseers and *d*:
1Ti 3: 8 *D*, likewise, are to be men worthy
3: 10 against them, let them serve as *d*.

DEAD (DIE)

Lev 17: 15 who eats anything found *d*
Dt 18: 11 or spiritist or who consults the *d*.
Isa 8: 19 Why consult the *d* on behalf
Mt 8: 22 and let the *d* bury their own *d*."
28: 7 'He has risen from the *d*
Lk 15: 24 For this son of mine was *d*
24: 46 rise from the *d* on the third day,
Ro 6: 11 count yourselves *d* to sin
1Co 15: 29 do who are baptised for the *d*?
Eph 2: 1 you were *d* in your transgressions
1Th 4: 16 and the *d* in Christ will rise first.
Jas 2: 17 is not accompanied by action, is *d*.
2: 26 so faith without deeds is *d*.
Rev 14: 13 Blessed are the *d* who die
20: 12 And I saw the *d*, great and small,

DEADENED* (DIE)

Jn 12: 40 and *d* their hearts,

DEAR* (DEARER)

2Sa 1: 26 you were very *d* to me.
Ps 102: 14 For her stones are *d*
Jer 31: 20 Is not Ephraim my *d* son,
Jn 2: 4 "*D* woman, why do you involve me
19: 26 he said to his mother, "*D* woman,
Ac 15: 25 to you with our *d* friends Barnabas
Ro 16: 5 Greet my *d* friend Epenetus,
16: 9 in Christ, and my *d* friend Stachys.
16: 12 Greet my *d* friend Persis, another
1Co 4: 14 but to warn you, as my *d* children.
10: 14 my *d* friends, flee from idolatry.
15: 58 Therefore, my *d* brothers,
2Co 7: 1 we have these promises, *d* friends,
12: 19 and everything we do, *d* friends,
Gal 4: 19 My *d* children, for whom I am
Eph 6: 21 the *d* brother and faithful servant
Php 2: 12 my *d* friends, as you have always
4: 1 firm in the Lord, *d* friends!
Col 1: 7 Epaphras, our *d* fellow-servant,
Col 4: 7 He is a *d* brother, a faithful
4: 9 our faithful and *d* brother,
4: 14 Our *d* friend Luke, the doctor,
1Th 2: 8 because you had become so *d* to us.
1Ti 6: 2 their service are believers, and *d*
2Ti 1: 2 To Timothy, my *d* son: Grace,
Phm : 1 To Philemon our *d* friend
: 16 He is very *d* to me but
: 16 better than a slave, as a *d* brother.
Heb 6: 9 we speak like this, *d* friends,
Jas 1: 16 Don't be deceived, my *d* brothers.
1: 19 My *d* brothers, take note of this:
2: 5 thoughts? Listen, my *d* brothers:
1Pe 2: 11 *D* friends, I urge you, as aliens
4: 12 *D* friends, do not be surprised
2Pe 3: 1 *D* friends, this is now my second
3: 8 not forget this one thing, *d* friends:
3: 14 *d* friends, since you are looking
3: 15 just as our *d* brother Paul
3: 17 *d* friends, since you already know
1Jn 2: 1 My *d* children, I write this to you
2: 7 *D* friends, I am not writing you
2: 12 I write to you, *d* children,
2: 13 I write to you, *d* children,
2: 18 *D* children, this is the last hour;
2: 28 *d* children, continue in him,
3: 2 *D* friends, now we are children
3: 7 *D* children, do not let anyone lead
3: 18 love of God be in him? *D* children,
3: 21 *D* friends, if our hearts do not
4: 1 *D* friends, do not believe every
4: 4 *d* children, are from God
4: 7 *D* friends, let us love one another,
4: 11 *D* friends, since God so loved us,
5: 21 *D* children, keep yourselves
2Jn : 5 *d* lady, I am not writing you a new
3Jn : 1 The elder, To my *d* friend Gaius,
: 2 *D* friend, I pray that you may enjoy
: 5 *D* friend, you are faithful
: 11 *D* friend, do not imitate what is evil
Jude : 3 *D* friends, although I was very
: 17 But, *d* friends, remember what
: 20 *d* friends, build yourselves up

DEARER* (DEAR)

Phm : 16 dear to me but even *d* to you,

DEATH (DIE)

Ex 21: 12 kills him shall surely be put to *d*.
Nu 35: 16 the murderer shall be put to *d*.
Dt 30: 19 set before you life and *d*,
Ru 1: 17 if anything but *d* separates you
2Ki 4: 40 O man of God, there is *d* in the pot
Job 26: 6 *D* is naked before God;
Ps 23: 4 the valley of the shadow of *d*,
44: 22 for your sake we face *d* all day long
89: 48 What man can live and not see *d*,
116: 15 is the *d* of his saints.
Pr 8: 36 all who hate me love *d*."
11: 19 he who pursues evil goes to his *d*.
14: 12 but in the end it leads to *d*.
15: 11 *D* and Destruction lie open
16: 25 but in the end it leads to *d*.
18: 21 tongue has the power of life and *d*,
19: 18 do not be a willing party to his *d*.
23: 14 and save his soul from *d*.
Ecc 7: 2 for *d* is the destiny of every man;
Isa 25: 8 he will swallow up *d* for ever.
53: 12 he poured out his life unto *d*,
Eze 18: 23 pleasure in the *d* of the wicked?
18: 32 pleasure in the *d* of anyone,
33: 11 pleasure in the *d* of the wicked,
Hos 13: 14 Where, O *d*, are your plagues?
Jn 5: 24 he has crossed over from *d* to life.
Ro 4: 25 delivered over to *d* for our sins
5: 12 and in this way *d* came to all men,
5: 14 *d* reigned from the time of Adam
6: 3 Jesus were baptised into his *d*?
6: 23 For the wages of sin is *d*,
7: 24 me from this body of *d*?
8: 13 put to *d* the misdeeds of the body,
8: 36 your sake we face *d* all day long;
15: 21 For since *d* came through a man,
1Co 15: 26 The last enemy to be destroyed is *d*
15: 55 Where, O *d*, is your sting?"
2Ti 1: 10 who has destroyed *d* and has
Heb 2: 14 him who holds the power of *d*—
1Jn 5: 16 There is a sin that leads to *d*.
Rev 1: 18 And I hold the keys of *d* and Hades
2: 11 hurt at all by the second *d*.
20: 6 The second *d* has no power
20: 14 The lake of fire is the second *d*.
20: 14 Then *d* and Hades were thrown
21: 4 There will be no more *d*
21: 8 This is the second *d*."

DEBAUCHERY*

Ro 13: 13 not in sexual immorality and *d*,
2Co 12: 21 and *d* in which they have indulged.
Gal 5: 19 impurity and *d*; idolatry
Eph 5: 18 drunk on wine, which leads to *d*.
1Pe 4: 3 living in *d*, lust, drunkenness,

DEBORAH*

1. Prophetess who led Israel to victory over Canaanites (Jdg 4-5).
2. Rebekah's nurse (Ge 35:8).

DEBT* (DEBTOR DEBTORS DEBTS)

Dt 15: 3 must cancel any *d* your brother
24: 6 the upper one—as security for a *d*,
1Sa 22: 2 or in *d* or discontented gathered
Job 24: 9 of the poor is seized for a *d*.
Mt 18: 25 that he had be sold to repay the *d*.
18: 27 cancelled the *d* and let him go.
18: 30 into prison until he could pay the *d*.
18: 32 'I cancelled all that *d* of yours
Lk 7: 43 who had the bigger *d* cancelled."
Ro 13: 8 Let no *d* remain outstanding,
13: 8 continuing *d* to love one another,

DEBTOR* (DEBT)

Isa 24: 2 for *d* as for creditor.

DEBTORS* (DEBT)

Hab 2: 7 Will not your *d* suddenly rise?
Mt 6: 12 as we also have forgiven our *d*.
Lk 16: 5 called in each one of his master's *d*.

DEBTS* (DEBT)

Dt 15: 1 seven years you must cancel *d*.
15: 2 time for cancelling *d* has been
15: 9 the year for cancelling *d*, is near,"
31: 10 in the year for cancelling *d*,
2Ki 4: 7 "Go, sell the oil and pay your *d*.
Ne 10: 31 the land and will cancel all *d*.
Pr 22: 26 or puts up security for *d*;
Mt 6: 12 Forgive us our *d*,
Lk 7: 42 so he cancelled the *d* of both.

DECAY*

Ps 16: 10 will you let your Holy One see *d*.
49: 9 and not see *d*.
49: 14 their forms will *d* in the grave,
Pr 12: 4 a disgraceful wife is like *d*
Isa 5: 24 so their roots will *d*
Hab 3: 16 *d* crept into my bones,
Ac 2: 27 will you let your Holy One see *d*,
2: 31 to the grave, nor did his body see *d*.
13: 34 never to *d*, is stated in these words:
13: 35 will not let your Holy One see *d*.'
13: 37 raised from the dead did not see *d*.
Ro 8: 21 liberated from its bondage to *d*

DECEIT (DECEIVE)

Ps 5: 9 with their tongue they speak *d*.
Isa 53: 9 nor was any *d* in his mouth.
Da 8: 25 He will cause *d* to prosper,
Zep 3: 13 nor will *d* be found in their mouths.
Mk 7: 22 greed, malice, *d*, lewdness, envy,
Ac 13: 10 You are full of all kinds of *d*
Ro 1: 29 murder, strife, *d* and malice.
3: 13 their tongues practise *d*."
1Pe 2: 1 yourselves of all malice and all *d*,
2: 22 and no *d* was found in his mouth."

DECEITFUL (DECEIVE)
Jer 17: 9 The heart is *d* above all things
Hos 10: 2 Their heart is *d*,
2Co 11: 13 men are false apostles, *d* workmen,
Eph 4: 14 of men in their *d* scheming.
4: 22 is being corrupted by its *d* desires;
1Pe 3: 10 and his lips from *d* speech.
Rev 21: 27 who does what is shameful or *d*,

DECEITFULNESS* (DECEIVE)
Ps 119: 118 for their *d* is in vain.
Mt 13: 22 and the *d* of wealth choke it,
Mk 4: 19 the *d* of wealth and the desires
Heb 3: 13 of you may be hardened by sin's *d*.

DECEIVE (DECEIT DECEITFUL DECEITFULNESS DECEIVED DECEIVER DECEIVERS DECEIVES DECEIVING DECEPTION DECEPTIVE)
Lev 19: 11 "'Do not *d* one another.
Pr 14: 5 A truthful witness does not *d*,
24: 28 or use your lips to *d*.
Jer 37: 9 Do not *d* yourselves, thinking,
Zec 13: 4 garment of hair in order to *d*.
Mt 24: 5 'I am the Christ,' and will *d* many.
24: 11 will appear and *d* many people.
24: 24 and miracles to *d* even the elect—
Mk 13: 6 'I am he,' and will *d* many.
13: 22 and miracles to *d* the elect—
Ro 16: 18 and flattery they *d* the minds
1Co 3: 18 Do not *d* yourselves.
Eph 5: 6 Let no-one *d* you with empty words
Col 2: 4 this so that no-one may *d* you
2Th 2: 3 Don't let anyone *d* you in any way,
Jas 1: 22 to the word, and so *d* yourselves.
1Jn 1: 8 we *d* ourselves and the truth is not
Rev 20: 8 and will go out to *d* the nations

DECEIVED (DECEIVE)
Ge 3: 13 "The serpent *d* me, and I ate."
Lk 21: 8 "Watch out that you are not *d*.
1Co 6: 9 the kingdom of God? Do not be *d*:
2Co 11: 3 Eve was *d* by the serpent's cunning
Gal 6: 7 Do not be *d*: God cannot be
1Ti 2: 14 And Adam was not the one *d*;
2Ti 3: 13 to worse, deceiving and being *d*.
Tit 3: 3 *d* and enslaved by all kinds
Jas 1: 16 Don't be *d*, my dear brothers.
Rev 13: 14 he *d* the inhabitants of the earth.
20: 10 And the devil, who *d* them,

DECEIVER (DECEIVE)
Mt 27: 63 while he was still alive that *d* said,
2Jn : 7 Any such person is the *d*

DECEIVERS* (DECEIVE)
Ps 49: 5 when wicked *d* surround me—
Tit 1: 10 and *d*, especially those
2Jn : 7 Many *d*, who do not acknowledge

DECEIVES (DECEIVE)
Pr 26: 19 is a man who *d* his neighbour
Mt 24: 4 "Watch out that no-one *d* you.
Mk 13: 5 "Watch out that no-one *d* you.
Gal 6: 3 when he is nothing, he *d* himself.
2Th 2: 10 sort of evil that *d* those who are
Jas 1: 26 he *d* himself and his religion is

DECEIVING* (DECEIVE)
Lev 6: 2 by *d* his neighbour about something
1Ti 4: 1 follow *d* spirits and things taught
2Ti 3: 13 go from bad to worse, *d*
Rev 20: 3 him from *d* the nations any more

DECENCY* (DECENTLY)
1Ti 2: 9 women to dress modestly, with *d*

DECENTLY* (DECENCY)
Ro 13: 13 Let us behave *d*, as in the daytime,

DECEPTION (DECEIVE)
Pr 14: 8 but the folly of fools is *d*.
26: 26 His malice may be concealed by *d*,
Mt 27: 64 This last *d* will be worse
2Co 4: 2 we do not use *d*, nor do we distort

DECEPTIVE (DECEIVE)
Pr 11: 18 The wicked man earns *d* wages,
31: 30 Charm is *d*, and beauty is fleeting;
Jer 7: 4 Do not trust in *d* words and say,
Col 2: 8 through hollow and *d* philosophy,

DECIDED (DECISION)
2Co 9: 7 man should give what he has *d*

DECISION (DECIDED)
Ex 28: 29 heart on the breastpiece of *d*
Joel 3: 14 multitudes in the valley of *d*!

DECLARE (DECLARED DECLARING)
1Ch 16: 24 *D* his glory among the nations,
Ps 19: 1 The heavens *d* the glory of God;
96: 3 *D* his glory among the nations,
Isa 42: 9 and new things I *d*;

DECLARED (DECLARE)
Mk 7: 19 Jesus *d* all foods "clean".)
Ro 2: 13 the law who will be *d* righteous.
3: 20 no-one will be *d* righteous

DECLARING (DECLARE)
Ps 71: 8 *d* your splendour all day long.
Ac 2: 11 we hear them *d* the wonders

DECREE (DECREED DECREES)
Ex 15: 25 There the LORD made a *d*
1Ch 16: 17 He confirmed it to Jacob as a *d*,
Ps 2: 7 I will proclaim the *d* of the LORD:
7: 6 Awake, my God; *d* justice.
81: 4 this is a *d* for Israel,
148: 6 he gave a *d* that will never pass
Da 4: 24 and this is the *d* the Most High has
Lk 2: 1 Augustus issued a *d* that a census
Ro 1: 32 know God's righteous *d* that those

DECREED (DECREE)
Ps 78: 5 He *d* statutes for Jacob
Jer 40: 2 LORD your God *d* this disaster
La 3: 37 happen if the Lord has not *d* it?
Da 9: 24 "Seventy 'sevens' are *d*
9: 26 and desolations have been *d*.
Lk 22: 22 Son of Man will go as it has been *d*,

DECREES (DECREE)
Ge 26: 5 my commands, my *d* and my laws
Ex 15: 26 to his commands and keep all his *d*,
18: 16 inform them of God's *d* and laws."
18: 20 Teach them the *d* and laws,
Lev 10: 11 Israelites all the *d* the LORD has
18: 4 and be careful to follow my *d*.
18: 5 Keep my *d* and laws,
18: 26 you must keep my *d* and my laws.
Ps 119: 12 teach me your *d*.
119: 16 I delight in your *d*;
119: 48 and I meditate on your *d*.
119: 112 My heart is set on keeping your *d*

DEDICATE (DEDICATED DEDICATION)
Nu 6: 12 He must *d* himself to the LORD
Pr 20: 25 for a man to *d* something rashly

DEDICATED (DEDICATE)
Lev 21: 12 he has been *d* by the anointing oil
Nu 6: 9 thus defiling the hair he has *d*,
6: 18 shave off the hair that he *d*.
18: 6 *d* to the LORD to do the work
1Ki 8: 63 and all the Israelites *d* the temple
2Ch 29: 31 "You have now *d* yourselves
Ne 3: 1 They *d* it and set its doors in place,

DEDICATION (DEDICATE)
Nu 6: 19 shaved off the hair of his *d*,
Jn 10: 22 came the Feast of *D* at Jerusalem.
1Ti 5: 11 sensual desires overcome their *d*

DEED [1]
Jer 32: 10 and sealed the *d*, had it witnessed,
32: 16 After I had given the *d* of purchase

DEED [2] (DEEDS)
Col 3: 17 you do, whether in word or *d*,
2Th 2: 17 and strengthen you in every good *d*

DEEDS (DEED [2])
Dt 3: 24 or on earth who can do the *d*
4: 34 or by great and awesome *d*,
34: 12 the awesome *d* that Moses
1Sa 2: 3 and by him *d* are weighed.
1Ch 16: 24 his marvellous *d* among all peoples.
Job 34: 25 Because he takes note of their *d*,
Ps 26: 7 and telling of all your wonderful *d*.
45: 4 right hand display awesome *d*.
65: 5 with awesome *d* of righteousness,
66: 3 "How awesome are your *d*!
71: 17 day I declare your marvellous *d*.
72: 18 who alone does marvellous *d*.
73: 28 I will tell of all your *d*.
75: 1 men tell of your wonderful *d*.
77: 11 I will remember the *d* of the LORD
77: 12 and consider all your mighty *d*.
78: 4 the praiseworthy *d* of the LORD,
78: 7 and would not forget his *d*
86: 8 no *d* can compare with yours.
86: 10 you are great and do marvellous *d*;
88: 12 or your righteous *d* in the land
90: 16 May your *d* be shown
92: 4 For you make me glad by your *d*,
96: 3 his marvellous *d* among all peoples.
107: 8 and his wonderful *d* for men,
107: 15 and his wonderful *d* for men,
107: 21 and his wonderful *d* for men.
107: 24 his wonderful *d* in the deep.
107: 31 and his wonderful *d* for men.
111: 3 Glorious and majestic are his *d*,
145: 6 and I will proclaim your great *d*.
Jer 32: 19 purposes and mighty are your *d*.
Hab 3: 2 I stand in awe of your *d*, O LORD.
Mt 5: 16 that they may see your good *d*
Lk 1: 51 He has performed mighty *d*
23: 41 we are getting what our *d* deserve.
Ac 26: 20 prove their repentance by their *d*.
1Ti 6: 18 rich in good *d*, and to be generous
Heb 10: 24 on towards love and good *d*.
Jas 2: 14 claims to have faith but has no *d*?
2: 18 Show me your faith without *d*,
2: 20 faith without *d* is useless?
2: 26 so faith without *d* is dead.
1Pe 2: 12 they may see your good *d*
Rev 2: 19 I know your *d*, your love and faith,
2: 23 each of you according to your *d*.
3: 1 I know your *d*; you have
3: 2 I have not found your *d* complete
3: 8 I know your *d*.
3: 15 I know your *d*, that you are neither
14: 13 for their *d* will follow them."
15: 3 "Great and marvellous are your *d*,

DEEP (DEPTH DEPTHS)
Ge 1: 2 was over the surface of the *d*,
8: 2 Now the springs of the *d*
Ps 42: 7 *D* calls to *d*
Lk 5: 4 to Simon, "Put out into *d* water,
1Co 2: 10 all things, even the *d* things
1Ti 3: 9 hold of the *d* truths of the faith

DEER
Ps 42: 1 As the *d* pants for streams of water,

DEFAMED*
Isa 48: 11 How can I let myself be *d*?

DEFEATED
1Co 6: 7 have been completely *d* already.

DEFENCE (DEFEND)
Ps 35: 23 Awake, and rise to my *d*!
Php 1: 16 here for the *d* of the gospel.
1Jn 2: 1 speaks to the Father in our *d*—

DEFEND (DEFENCE DEFENDED DEFENDER DEFENDING DEFENDS)

Ps 72: 4 He will *d* the afflicted
74: 22 Rise up, O God, and *d* your cause;
82: 2 "How long will you *d* the unjust
82: 3 *D* the cause of the weak
119: 154 *D* my cause and redeem me;
Pr 31: 9 *d* the rights of the poor and needy
Isa 1: 17 *D* the cause of the fatherless,
1: 23 They do not *d* the cause
Jer 5: 28 they do not *d* the rights of the poor.
50: 34 He will vigorously *d* their cause

DEFENDED (DEFEND)

Jer 22: 16 He *d* the cause of the poor

DEFENDER (DEFEND)

Ex 22: 2 the *d* is not guilty of bloodshed,
Ps 68: 5 to the fatherless, a *d* of widows,
Pr 23: 11 for their *D* is strong;

DEFENDING (DEFEND)

Ps 10: 18 *d* the fatherless and the oppressed,
Ro 2: 15 now accusing, now even *d* them.)
Php 1: 7 or *d* and confirming the gospel,

DEFENDS* (DEFEND)

Dt 10: 18 He *d* the cause of the fatherless
33: 7 With his own hands he *d* his cause.
Isa 51: 22 your God, who *d* his people:

DEFERRED*

Pr 13: 12 Hope *d* makes the heart sick,

DEFIED

1Sa 17: 45 armies of Israel, whom you have *d*.
1Ki 13: 26 the man of God who *d* the word

DEFILE (DEFILED)

Da 1: 8 Daniel resolved not to *d* himself
Rev 14: 4 are those who did not *d* themselves

DEFILED (DEFILE)

Isa 24: 5 The earth is *d* by its people;

DEFRAUD

Lev 19: 13 Do not *d* your neighbour or rob him.
Mk 10: 19 do not *d*, honour your father

DEITY*

Col 2: 9 of the *D* lives in bodily form,

DELAY

Ecc 5: 4 vow to God, do not *d* in fulfilling it.
Isa 48: 9 my own name's sake I *d* my wrath;
Heb 10: 37 is coming will come and will not *d*.
Rev 10: 6 and said, "There will be no more *d*!

DELICACIES

Ps 141: 4 let me not eat of their *d*.
Pr 23: 3 Do not crave his *d*,
23: 6 do not crave his *d*;

DELICIOUS*

Pr 9: 17 food eaten in secret is *d*!"

DELIGHT* (DELIGHTED DELIGHTFUL DELIGHTING DELIGHTS)

Lev 26: 31 and I will take no *d* in the pleasing
Dt 30: 9 The LORD will again *d* in you
1Sa 2: 1 for I *d* in your deliverance.
15: 22 "Does the LORD *d*
Ne 1: 11 the prayer of your servants who *d*
Job 22: 26 Surely then you will find *d*
27: 10 Will he find *d* in the Almighty?
Ps 1: 2 But his *d* is in the law of the LORD
16: 3 in whom is all my *d*.
35: 9 and *d* in his salvation.
35: 27 those who *d* in my vindication
37: 4 *D* yourself in the LORD
43: 4 to God, my joy and my *d*.
51: 16 You do not *d* in sacrifice,
51: 19 whole burnt offerings to *d* you;
Ps 62: 4 they take *d* in lies.
68: 30 Scatter the nations who *d* in war.
111: 2 by all who *d* in them.
112: 1 who finds great *d* in his commands.
119: 16 I *d* in your decrees;
119: 24 Your statutes are my *d*;
119: 35 for there I find *d*.
119: 47 for I *d* in your commands
119: 70 but I *d* in your law.
119: 77 for your law is my *d*.
119: 92 If your law had not been my *d*,
119: 143 but your commands are my *d*.
119: 174 and your law is my *d*.
147: 10 nor his *d* in the legs of a man;
149: 4 For the LORD takes *d*
Pr 1: 22 How long will mockers *d*
2: 14 who *d* in doing wrong
8: 30 I was filled with *d* day after day,
11: 1 but accurate weights are his *d*.
29: 17 he will bring *d* to your soul.
Ecc 2: 10 My heart took *d* in all my work,
SS 1: 4 We rejoice and *d* in you;
2: 3 I *d* to sit in his shade,
Isa 5: 7 are the garden of his *d*.
11: 3 he will *d* in the fear of the LORD.
13: 17 and have no *d* in gold.
32: 14 the *d* of donkeys, a pasture
42: 1 my chosen one in whom I *d*;
55: 2 and your soul will *d* in the richest
58: 13 if you call the Sabbath a *d*
61: 10 I *d* greatly in the LORD;
62: 4 for the LORD will take *d* in you,
65: 18 for I will create Jerusalem to be a *d*
65: 19 and take *d* in my people;
66: 3 their souls *d* in their abominations;
66: 11 *d* in her overflowing abundance."
Jer 9: 24 for in these I *d*,"
15: 16 they were my joy and my heart's *d*,
31: 20 the child in whom I *d*?
49: 25 the town in which I *d*?
Eze 24: 16 away from you the *d* of your eyes.
24: 21 in which you take pride, the *d*
24: 25 and glory, the *d* of their eyes,
Hos 7: 3 *d* the king with their wickedness,
Mic 1: 16 for the children in whom you *d*;
7: 18 but *d* to show mercy.
Zep 3: 17 He will take great *d* in you,
Mt 12: 18 the one I love, in whom I *d*;
Mk 12: 37 large crowd listened to him with *d*.
Lk 1: 14 He will be a joy and *d* to you,
Ro 7: 22 in my inner being I *d* in God's law;
1Co 13: 6 Love does not *d* in evil
2Co 12: 10 for Christ's sake, I *d* in weaknesses,
Col 2: 5 and *d* to see how orderly you are

DELIGHTED (DELIGHT)

2Sa 22: 20 he rescued me because he *d* in me.
1Ki 10: 9 who has *d* in you and placed you
2Ch 9: 8 who has *d* in you and placed you
Ps 18: 19 he rescued me because he *d* in me.
Lk 13: 17 but the people were *d* with all

DELIGHTFUL* (DELIGHT)

Ps 16: 6 surely I have a *d* inheritance.
SS 1: 2 for your love is more *d* than wine.
4: 10 How *d* is your love, my sister,
Mal 3: 12 for yours will be a *d* land,"

DELIGHTING* (DELIGHT)

Pr 8: 31 and *d* in mankind.

DELIGHTS (DELIGHT)

Est 6: 6 for the man the king *d* to honour?"
Ps 22: 8 since he *d* in him."
35: 27 who *d* in the well-being
36: 8 from your river of *d*.
37: 23 The LORD *d* in the way of the man
147: 11 the LORD *d* in those who fear him,
Pr 3: 12 as a father the son he *d* in.
10: 23 of understanding *d* in wisdom.
11: 20 he *d* in those whose ways are
12: 22 but he *d* in men who are truthful.
14: 35 A king *d* in a wise servant,
Pr 18: 2 but *d* in airing his own opinions.
23: 24 he who has a wise son *d* in him.
Col 2: 18 Do not let anyone who *d*

DELILAH*

Woman who betrayed Samson (Jdg 16:4-22).

DELIVER (DELIVERANCE DELIVERED DELIVERER DELIVERS)

Dt 32: 39 and no-one can *d* out of my hand.
Ps 22: 8 Let him *d* him,
72: 12 For he will *d* the needy who cry out
79: 9 *d* us and atone for our sins
109: 21 of the goodness of your love, *d* me.
119: 170 *d* me according to your promise.
Mt 6: 13 but *d* us from the evil one.'
2Co 1: 10 hope that he will continue to *d* us,

DELIVERANCE (DELIVER)

1Sa 2: 1 for I delight in your *d*.
Ps 3: 8 From the LORD comes *d*.
32: 7 and surround me with songs of *d*.
33: 17 A horse is a vain hope for *d*;
Ob : 17 But on Mount Zion will be *d*;

DELIVERED (DELIVER)

Ps 34: 4 he *d* me from all my fears.
107: 6 and he *d* them from their distress.
116: 8 have *d* my soul from death,
Da 12: 1 written in the book—will be *d*.
Ro 4: 25 He was *d* over to death for our sins

DELIVERER* (DELIVER)

Jdg 3: 9 for them a *d*, Othniel son of Kenaz,
3: 15 and he gave them a *d*—Ehud,
2Sa 22: 2 is my rock, my fortress and my *d*;
2Ki 13: 5 The LORD provided a *d* for Israel,
Ps 18: 2 is my rock, my fortress and my *d*;
40: 17 You are my help and my *d*;
70: 5 You are my help and my *d*;
140: 7 O Sovereign LORD, my strong *d*,
144: 2 my stronghold and my *d*,
Ac 7: 35 sent to be their ruler and *d*
Ro 11: 26 "The *d* will come from Zion;

DELIVERS (DELIVER)

Ps 34: 17 he *d* them from all their troubles.
34: 19 but the LORD *d* him from them all
37: 40 The LORD helps them and *d* them
37: 40 he *d* them from the wicked

DELUSION*

2Th 2: 11 God sends them a powerful *d*

DEMAND (DEMANDED)

Lk 6: 30 belongs to you, do not *d* it back.

DEMANDED (DEMAND)

Lk 12: 20 This very night your life will be *d*
12: 48 been given much, much will be *d*;

DEMETRIUS

Ac 19: 24 A silversmith named *D*, who made

DEMON* (DEMONS)

Mt 9: 33 And when the *d* was driven out,
11: 18 and they say, 'He has a *d*.'
17: 18 Jesus rebuked the *d*, and it came
Mk 7: 26 to drive the *d* out of her daughter.
7: 29 the *d* has left your daughter."
7: 30 lying on the bed, and the *d* gone.
Lk 4: 33 there was a man possessed by a *d*,
4: 35 Then the *d* threw the man
7: 33 wine, and you say, 'He has a *d*.'
8: 29 driven by the *d* into solitary places.
9: 42 the *d* threw him to the ground
11: 14 When the *d* left, the man who had
11: 14 was driving out a *d* that was mute.
Jn 8: 49 "I am not possessed by a *d*,"
10: 21 Can a *d* open the eyes of the blind
10: 21 sayings of a man possessed by a *d*.

DEMON-POSSESSED* (DEMON-POSSESSION)

Mt 4:24 those suffering severe pain, the *d*,
8:16 many who were *d* were brought
8:28 two *d* men coming
8:33 what had happened to the *d* men.
9:32 man who was *d* and could not talk
12:22 they brought him a *d* man who was
Mk 1:32 brought to Jesus all the sick and *d*.
5:16 what had happened to the *d* man—
5:18 the man who had been *d* begged
Lk 8:27 met by a *d* man from the town.
8:36 the people how the *d* man had been
Jn 7:20 "You are *d*," the crowd answered.
8:48 that you are a Samaritan and *d*?"
8:52 "Now we know that you are *d*!
10:20 Many of them said, "He is *d*
Ac 19:13 Jesus over those who were *d*.

DEMON-POSSESSION* (DEMON-POSSESSED)

Mt 15:22 is suffering terribly from *d*."

DEMONS* (DEMON)

Dt 32:17 to *d*, which are not God—
Ps 106:37 and their daughters to *d*.
Mt 7:22 and in your name drive out *d*
8:31 *d* begged Jesus, "If you drive us
9:34 prince of *d* that he drives out *d*."
10:8 who have leprosy, drive out *d*.
12:24 of *d*, that this fellow drives out
12:24 that this fellow drives out *d*."
12:27 And if I drive out *d* by Beelzebub,
12:28 if I drive out *d* by the Spirit of God,
Mk 1:34 He also drove out many *d*,
1:34 but he would not let the *d* speak
1:39 their synagogues and driving out *d*.
3:15 to have authority to drive out *d*.
3:22 the prince of *d* he is driving out *d*."
5:12 The *d* begged Jesus, "Send us
5:15 possessed by the legion of *d*,
6:13 They drove out many *d*
9:38 "we saw a man driving out *d*
16:9 out of whom he had driven seven *d*
16:17 In my name they will drive out *d*;
Lk 4:41 *d* came out of many people,
8:2 from whom seven *d* had come out;
8:30 because many *d* had gone into him.
8:32 The *d* begged Jesus to let them go
8:33 When the *d* came out of the man,
8:35 from whom the *d* had gone out,
8:38 from whom the *d* had gone out
9:1 and authority to drive out all *d*
9:49 "we saw a man driving out *d*
10:17 the *d* submit to us in your name."
11:15 the prince of *d*, he is driving out *d*."
11:18 you claim that I drive out *d*
11:19 Now if I drive out *d* by Beelzebub,
11:20 if I drive out *d* by the finger of God,
13:32 'I will drive out *d* and heal people
Ro 8:38 neither angels nor *d*, neither
1Co 10:20 of pagans are offered to *d*,
10:20 you to be participants with *d*.
10:21 of the Lord and the cup of *d* too;
10:21 the Lord's table and the table of *d*.
1Ti 4:1 spirits and things taught by *d*.
Jas 2:19 Good! Even the *d* believe that—
Rev 9:20 they did not stop worshipping *d*,
16:14 of *d* performing miraculous signs,
18:2 She has become a home for *d*

DEMONSTRATE* (DEMONSTRATES DEMONSTRATION)

Ro 3:25 He did this to *d* his justice,
3:26 he did it to *d* his justice

DEMONSTRATES* (DEMONSTRATE)

Ro 5:8 God *d* his own love for us in this:

DEMONSTRATION* (DEMONSTRATE)

1Co 2:4 but with a *d* of the Spirit's power,

DEN

Da 6:16 and threw him into the lions' *d*.
Mt 21:13 you are making it a '*d* of robbers.'"
Mk 11:17 you have made it 'a *d* of robbers.'"
Lk 19:46 but you have made it 'a *d* of robbers

DENARII* (DENARIUS)

Mt 18:28 who owed him a hundred *d*.
Lk 7:41 One owed him five hundred *d*,

DENARIUS (DENARII)

Mt 20:2 agreed to pay them a *d* for the day
Mk 12:15 Bring me a *d* and let me look at it."

DENIED (DENY)

Mt 26:70 But he *d* it before them all.
Mk 14:68 But he *d* it.
Lk 22:57 But he *d* it.
Jn 18:25 He *d* it, saying, "I am not."
1Ti 5:8 he has *d* the faith and is worse
Rev 3:8 my word and have not *d* my name.

DENIES (DENY)

1Jn 2:22 It is the man who *d* that Jesus is
2:23 No-one who *d* the Son has

DENY (DENIED DENIES DENYING)

Ex 23:6 "Do not *d* justice to your poor
Job 27:5 till I die, I will not *d* my integrity.
Isa 5:23 but *d* justice to the innocent.
La 3:35 to *d* a man his rights
Am 2:7 and *d* justice to the oppressed.
Mt 16:24 he must *d* himself and take up his
Mk 8:34 he must *d* himself and take up his
Lk 9:23 he must *d* himself and take up his
22:34 you will *d* three times that you
Ac 4:16 miracle, and we cannot *d* it.
Tit 1:16 but by their actions they *d* him.
Jas 3:14 do not boast about it or *d* the truth.
Jude :4 *d* Jesus Christ our only Sovereign

DENYING* (DENY)

Eze 22:29 mistreat the alien, *d* them justice.
2Ti 3:5 a form of godliness but *d* its power.
2Pe 2:1 *d* the sovereign Lord who bought

DEPART (DEPARTED DEPARTS DEPARTURE)

Ge 49:10 The sceptre will not *d* from Judah,
Job 1:21 and naked I will *d*.
Mt 25:41 '*D* from me, you who are cursed,
Php 1:23 I desire to *d* and be with Christ,

DEPARTED (DEPART)

1Sa 4:21 "The glory has *d* from Israel"—
Ps 119:102 I have not *d* from your laws,

DEPARTS (DEPART)

Ecc 5:15 and as he comes, so he *d*.

DEPARTURE (DEPART)

Lk 9:31 spoke about his *d*, which he was
2Ti 4:6 and the time has come for my *d*.
2Pe 1:15 after my *d* you will always be able

DEPEND

Ps 62:7 My salvation and my honour *d*

DEPOSES*

Da 2:21 he sets up kings and *d* them.

DEPOSIT

Mt 25:27 money on *d* with the bankers,
Lk 19:23 didn't you put my money on *d*,
2Co 1:22 put his Spirit in our hearts as a *d*,
5:5 and has given us the Spirit as a *d*,
Eph 1:14 who is a *d* guaranteeing our
2Ti 1:14 Guard the good *d* that was

DEPRAVED* (DEPRAVITY)

Eze 16:47 ways you soon became more *d*
23:11 and prostitution she was more *d*
Ro 1:28 he gave them over to a *d* mind,
Php 2:15 fault in a crooked and *d* generation,
2Ti 3:8 oppose the truth—men of *d* minds,

DEPRAVITY* (DEPRAVED)

Ro 1:29 of wickedness, evil, greed and *d*.
2Pe 2:19 they themselves are slaves of *d*—

DEPRIVE

Dt 24:17 Do not *d* the alien or the fatherless
Pr 18:5 or to *d* the innocent of justice.
31:5 *d* all the oppressed of their rights.
Isa 10:2 to *d* the poor of their rights
29:21 with false testimony *d* the innocent
La 3:36 to *d* a man of justice—
1Co 7:5 Do not *d* each other
9:15 die than have anyone *d* me

DEPTH (DEEP)

Ro 8:39 any powers, neither height nor *d*,
11:33 the *d* of the riches of the wisdom

DEPTHS (DEEP)

Ps 130:1 Out of the *d* I cry to you, O LORD;

DERIDES*

Pr 11:12 who lacks judgment *d* his neighbour,

DERIVES*

Eph 3:15 in heaven and on earth *d* its name.

DESCEND (DESCENDED DESCENDING)

Ro 10:7 "or 'Who will *d* into the deep?'"

DESCENDED (DESCEND)

Eph 4:9 except that he also *d* to the lower,
Heb 7:14 For it is clear that our Lord *d*

DESCENDING (DESCEND)

Ge 28:12 of God were ascending and *d* on it.
Mt 3:16 the Spirit of God *d* like a dove
Mk 1:10 and the Spirit *d* on him like a dove.
Jn 1:51 and *d* on the Son of Man."

DESECRATING*

Ne 13:17 you are doing—*d* the Sabbath day?
13:18 against Israel by *d* the Sabbath."
Isa 56:2 who keeps the Sabbath without *d* it
56:6 who keep the Sabbath without *d* it
Eze 44:7 *d* my temple while you offered me

DESERT

Nu 32:13 wander in the *d* forty years,
Dt 8:16 He gave you manna to eat in the *d*,
29:5 years that I led you through the *d*,
Ne 9:19 you did not abandon them in the *d*.
Ps 78:19 "Can God spread a table in the *d*?
78:52 led them like sheep through the *d*.
Pr 21:19 Better to live in a *d*
Isa 32:2 like streams of water in the *d*
32:15 and the *d* becomes a fertile field,
35:6 and streams in the *d*.
43:20 because I provide water in the *d*
Mk 1:3 "a voice of one calling in the *d*,
1:13 and he was in the *d* forty days,
Rev 12:6 fled into the *d* to a place prepared

DESERTED (DESERTS)

Ezr 9:9 our God has not *d* us
Mt 26:56 all the disciples *d* him and fled.
2Ti 1:15 in the province of Asia has *d* me,

DESERTING (DESERTS)

Gal 1:6 are so quickly *d* the one who called

DESERTS (DESERTED DESERTING)

Zec 11:17 who *d* the flock!

DESERVE* (DESERVED DESERVES)

Ge 40:15 to *d* being put in a dungeon."
Lev 26:21 times over, as your sins *d*.
Jdg 20:10 it can give them what they *d*
1Sa 26:16 you and your men *d* to die,
1Ki 2:26 You *d* to die, but I will not put you
Ps 28:4 bring back upon them what they *d*.
94:2 pay back to the proud what they *d*.
103:10 he does not treat us as our sins *d*

Pr 3: 27 from those who *d* it,
Ecc 8: 14 men who get what the righteous *d*.
8: 14 men who get what the wicked *d*,
Isa 66: 6 repaying his enemies all they *d*.
Jer 14: 16 out on them the calamity they *d*.
17: 10 according to what his deeds *d*."
21: 14 I will punish you as your deeds *d*,
32: 19 to his conduct and as his deeds *d*.
49: 12 "If those who do not *d*
La 3: 64 Pay them back what they *d*,
Eze 16: 59 I will deal with you as you *d*,
Zec 1: 6 to us what our ways and practices *d*
Mt 8: 8 I do not *d* to have you come
22: 8 those I invited did not *d* to come.
Lk 7: 6 for I do not *d* to have you come
23: 15 he has done nothing to *d* death.
23: 41 for we are getting what our deeds *d*
Ro 1: 32 those who do such things *d* death,
1Co 15: 9 even *d* to be called an apostle,
16: 18 Such men *d* recognition.
2Co 11: 15 end will be what their actions *d*.
Rev 16: 6 blood to drink as they *d*."

DESERVED* (DESERVE)
2Sa 19: 28 descendants *d* nothing
Ezr 9: 13 less than our sins have *d*
Job 33: 27 but I did not get what I *d*.
Ac 23: 29 charge against him that *d* death
Ro 3: 8 Their condemnation is *d*.

DESERVES* (DESERVE)
Nu 35: 31 the life of a murderer, who *d* to die.
Dt 25: 2 If the guilty man *d* to be beaten,
25: 2 the number of lashes his crime *d*,
Jdg 9: 16 and if you have treated him as he *d*
2Sa 12: 5 the man who did this *d* to die!
Job 34: 11 upon him what his conduct *d*.
Jer 51: 6 he will pay her what she *d*.
Lk 7: 4 "This man *d* to have you do this,
10: 7 for the worker *d* his wages.
Ac 26: 31 is not doing anything that *d* death
1Ti 1: 15 saying that *d* full acceptance:
4: 9 saying that *d* full acceptance
5: 18 and "The worker *d* his wages."
Heb 10: 29 severely do you think a man *d*

DESIGNATED
Lk 6: 13 also *d* apostles: Simon (whom he
Heb 5: 10 and was *d* by God to be high priest

DESIRABLE* (DESIRE)
Ge 3: 6 and also *d* for gaining wisdom,
Pr 22: 1 A good name is more *d*
Jer 3: 19 and give you a *d* land,

DESIRE* (DESIRABLE DESIRED DESIRES)
Ge 3: 16 Your *d* will be for your husband,
Dt 5: 21 You shall not set your *d*
1Sa 9: 20 to whom is all the *d* of Israel turned
2Sa 19: 38 anything you *d* from me I will do
23: 5 and grant me my every *d*?
1Ch 29: 18 keep this *d* in their hearts
2Ch 1: 11 "Since this is your heart's *d*
9: 8 and his *d* to uphold them for ever,
Job 13: 3 But I *d* to speak to the Almighty
21: 14 We have no *d* to know your ways.
Ps 10: 17 O LORD, the *d* of the afflicted;
20: 4 May he give you the *d*
21: 2 You have granted him the *d*
27: 12 me over to the *d* of my foes,
40: 6 Sacrifice and offering you did not *d*
40: 8 I *d* to do your will, O my God;
40: 14 may all who *d* my ruin
41: 2 him to the *d* of his foes.
51: 6 Surely you *d* truth
70: 2 may all who *d* my ruin
73: 25 being with you, I *d* nothing
Pr 3: 15 nothing you *d* can compare
8: 11 and nothing you *d* can compare
10: 24 what the righteous *d* will be
11: 23 The *d* of the righteous ends only
12: 12 The wicked *d* the plunder
17: 16 since he has no *d* to get wisdom?
Pr 24: 1 do not *d* their company;
Ecc 12: 5 and *d* no longer is stirred.
SS 6: 12 my *d* set me among the royal
7: 10 and his *d* is for me.
Isa 26: 8 are the *d* of our hearts.
53: 2 appearance that we should *d* him.
55: 11 but will accomplish what I *d*
Eze 24: 25 delight of their eyes, their heart's *d*,
Hos 6: 6 For I *d* mercy, not sacrifice,
Mic 7: 3 the powerful dictate what they *d*—
Mal 3: 1 whom you *d*, will come," says
Mt 9: 13 learn what this means: 'I *d* mercy,
12: 7 what these words mean, 'I *d* mercy,
Jn 8: 44 want to carry out your father's *d*.
Ro 7: 8 in me every kind of covetous *d*.
7: 18 For I have the *d* to do what is good,
9: 16 depend on man's *d* or effort,
10: 1 my heart's *d* and prayer to God
1Co 12: 31 But eagerly *d* the greater gifts.
14: 1 and eagerly *d* spiritual gifts,
2Co 8: 10 but also to have the *d* to do so.
8: 13 Our *d* is not that others might be
Php 1: 23 I *d* to depart and be with Christ,
Heb 10: 5 Sacrifice and offering you did not *d*
10: 8 and sin offerings you did not *d*,
13: 18 *d* to live honourably in every way.
Jas 1: 14 by his own evil *d*, he is dragged
1: 15 Then, after *d* has conceived,
2Pe 2: 10 of those who follow the corrupt *d*

DESIRED (DESIRE)
Hag 2: 7 and the *d* of all nations will come,
Lk 22: 15 "I have eagerly *d* to eat this

DESIRES* (DESIRE)
Ge 4: 7 at your door; it *d* to have you,
41: 16 will give Pharaoh the answer he *d*."
2Sa 3: 21 rule over all that your heart *d*."
1Ki 11: 37 rule over all that your heart *d*;
Job 17: 11 and so are the *d* of my heart.
31: 16 "If I have denied the *d* of the poor
Ps 34: 12 and *d* to see many good days,
37: 4 he will give you the *d* of your heart.
103: 5 He satisfies my *d* with good things,
140: 8 do not grant the wicked their *d*,
145: 16 satisfy the *d* of every living thing.
145: 19 He fulfils the *d* of those who fear
Pr 11: 6 the unfaithful are trapped by evil *d*.
13: 4 *d* of the diligent are fully satisfied.
19: 22 What a man *d* is unfailing love;
Ecc 6: 2 so that he lacks nothing his heart *d*,
SS 2: 7 or awaken love/until it so *d*.
3: 5 or awaken love/until it so *d*.
8: 4 or awaken love/until it so *d*.
Hab 2: 4 his *d* are not upright—
Mk 4: 19 and the *d* for other things come in
Ro 1: 24 over in the sinful *d* of their hearts
6: 12 body so that you obey its evil *d*.
8: 5 set on what that nature *d*;
8: 5 set on what the Spirit *d*.
13: 14 to gratify the *d* of the sinful nature.
Gal 5: 16 and you will not gratify the *d*
5: 17 the sinful nature *d* what is contrary
5: 24 nature with its passions and *d*.
Eph 2: 3 and following its *d* and thoughts.
4: 22 being corrupted by its deceitful *d*;
Col 3: 5 impurity, lust, evil *d* and greed,
1Ti 3: 1 an overseer, he *d* a noble task.
5: 11 their sensual *d* overcome their
6: 9 and harmful *d* that plunge men
2Ti 2: 22 Flee the evil *d* of youth,
3: 6 are swayed by all kinds of evil *d*,
4: 3 Instead, to suit their own *d*,
Jas 1: 20 about the righteous life that God *d*.
4: 1 from your *d* that battle within you?
1Pe 1: 14 conform to the evil *d* you had
2: 11 to abstain from sinful *d*, which war
4: 2 of his earthly life for evil human *d*,
2Pe 1: 4 in the world caused by evil *d*.
2: 18 to the lustful *d* of sinful human
3: 3 and following their own evil *d*.
1Jn 2: 17 The world and its *d* pass away,
Jude : 16 they follow their own evil *d*;
Jude : 18 will follow their own ungodly *d*."

DESOLATE (DESOLATION)
Isa 54: 1 are the children of the *d* woman
Gal 4: 27 are the children of the *d* woman

DESOLATION (DESOLATE)
Da 11: 31 up the abomination that causes *d*.
12: 11 abomination that causes *d* is set up,
Mt 24: 15 'the abomination that causes *d*,'

DESPAIR (DESPAIRED)
Isa 61: 3 instead of a spirit of *d*.
2Co 4: 8 perplexed, but not in *d*; persecuted,

DESPAIRED* (DESPAIR)
2Co 1: 8 ability to endure, so that we *d*

DESPERATE*
2Sa 12: 18 He may do something *d*."
Ps 60: 3 have shown your people *d* times;
79: 8 for we are in *d* need.
142: 6 for I am in *d* need;

DESPISE (DESPISED DESPISES)
2Sa 12: 9 Why did you *d* the word
Job 5: 17 so do not *d* the discipline
36: 5 God is mighty, but does not *d* men;
42: 6 Therefore I *d* myself
Ps 51: 17 O God, you will not *d*.
102: 17 he will not *d* their plea.
Pr 1: 7 but fools *d* wisdom and discipline.
3: 11 do not *d* the LORD's discipline
6: 30 Men do not *d* a thief if he steals
23: 22 do not *d* your mother
Jer 14: 21 of your name do not *d* us;
Am 5: 10 and *d* him who tells the truth.
5: 21 "I hate, I *d* your religious feasts;
Mt 6: 24 devoted to the one and *d* the other.
Lk 16: 13 devoted to the one and *d* the other.
1Co 11: 22 Or do you *d* the church of God
Tit 2: 15 Do not let anyone *d* you.
2Pe 2: 10 of the sinful nature and *d* authority.

DESPISED (DESPISE)
Ge 25: 34 So Esau *d* his birthright.
Ps 22: 6 by men and *d* by the people.
Pr 12: 8 but men with warped minds are *d*.
Isa 53: 3 He was *d* and rejected by men,
53: 3 he was *d*, and we esteemed him not
1Co 1: 28 of this world and the *d* things—

DESPISES (DESPISE)
Pr 14: 21 He who *d* his neighbour sins,
15: 20 but a foolish man *d* his mother.
15: 32 who ignores discipline *d* himself,
Zec 4: 10 "Who *d* the day of small things?

DESTINED (DESTINY)
Lk 2: 34 "This child is *d* to cause the falling
1Co 2: 7 and that God *d* for our glory
Col 2: 22 These are all *d* to perish with use,
1Th 3: 3 know quite well that we were *d*
Heb 9: 27 Just as man is *d* to die once,
1Pe 2: 8 which is also what they were *d* for.

DESTINY* (DESTINED PREDESTINED)
Job 8: 13 Such is the *d* of all who forget God;
Ps 73: 17 then I understood their final *d*.
Ecc 7: 2 for death is the *d* of every man;
9: 2 share a common *d*—the righteous
9: 3 the sun: The same *d* overtakes all.
Isa 65: 11 and fill bowls of mixed wine for *D*,
Php 3: 19 Their *d* is destruction, their god is

DESTITUTE
Ps 102: 17 to the prayer of the *d*;
Pr 31: 8 for the rights of all who are *d*.
Heb 11: 37 *d*, persecuted and ill-treated—

DESTROY (DESTROYED DESTROYING DESTROYS DESTRUCTION DESTRUCTIVE)
Ge 6: 17 floodwaters on the earth to *d* all life

Ge 9:11 will there be a flood to *d* the earth."
Pr 1:32 complacency of fools will *d* them;
Mt 10:28 of the one who can *d* both soul
Mk 14:58 'I will *d* this man-made temple
Lk 4:34 to *d* us? I know who you are—
Jn 10:10 only to steal and kill and *d*;
Ac 8:3 But Saul began to *d* the church.
Rev 11:18 destroying those who *d* the earth."

DESTROYED (DESTROY)

Dt 8:19 you today that you will surely be *d*.
Job 19:26 And after my skin has been *d*,
Pr 6:15 he will suddenly be *d*—
11:3 the unfaithful are *d*
21:28 listens to him will be *d* for ever.
29:1 will suddenly be *d*—
Isa 55:13 which will not be *d*."
Da 2:44 up a kingdom that will never be *d*,
6:26 his kingdom will not be *d*,
1Co 5:5 so that the sinful nature may be *d*
8:11 for whom Christ died, is *d*
15:24 Father after he has *d* all dominion,
15:26 The last enemy to be *d* is death.
2Co 4:9 abandoned; struck down, but not *d*.
5:1 if the earthly tent we live in is *d*,
Gal 5:15 or you will be *d* by each other.
Eph 2:14 the two one and has *d* the barrier,
2Ti 1:10 who has *d* death and has brought
Heb 10:39 of those who shrink back and are *d*,
2Pe 2:12 born only to be caught and *d*,
3:10 the elements will be *d* by fire,
3:11 Since everything will be *d*
Jude :5 later *d* those who did not believe.
:11 have been *d* in Korah's rebellion.

DESTROYING (DESTROY)

Jer 23:1 "Woe to the shepherds who are *d*

DESTROYS (DESTROY)

Pr 6:32 whoever does so *d* himself.
11:9 mouth the godless *d* his neighbour,
18:9 is brother to one who *d*.
28:24 he is partner to him who *d*.
Ecc 9:18 but one sinner *d* much good.
1Co 3:17 If anyone *d* God's temple,

DESTRUCTION (DESTROY)

Nu 32:15 and you will be the cause of their *d*
Pr 16:18 Pride goes before *d*,
17:19 he who builds a high gate invites *d*.
24:22 for those two will send sudden *d*
Hos 13:14 Where, O grave, is your *d*?
Mt 7:13 broad is the road that leads to *d*,
Lk 6:49 it collapsed and its *d* was complete
Jn 17:12 except the one doomed to *d*
Ro 9:22 of his wrath—prepared for *d*?
Gal 6:8 from that nature will reap *d*;
Php 3:19 Their destiny is *d*, their god is their
1Th 5:3 *d* will come on them suddenly,
2Th 1:9 punished with everlasting *d*
2:3 is revealed, the man doomed to *d*.
1Ti 6:9 that plunge men into ruin and *d*.
2Pe 2:1 bringing swift *d* on themselves.
2:3 and their *d* has not been sleeping.
3:7 of judgment and *d* of ungodly men.
3:12 That day will bring about the *d*
3:16 other Scriptures, to their own *d*.
Rev 17:8 out of the Abyss and go to his *d*.
17:11 to the seven and is going to his *d*.

DESTRUCTIVE (DESTROY)

2Pe 2:1 will secretly introduce *d* heresies,

DETERMINED (DETERMINES)

Job 14:5 Man's days are *d*;
Isa 14:26 This is the plan *d* for the whole
Da 11:36 for what has been *d* must take place
Ac 17:26 and he *d* the times set for them

DETERMINES* (DETERMINED)

Ps 147:4 He *d* the number of the stars
Pr 16:9 but the LORD *d* his steps.

1Co 12:11 them to each one, just as he *d*.

DETEST (DETESTABLE DETESTED DETESTS)

Lev 11:10 in the water—you are to *d*.
Pr 8:7 for my lips *d* wickedness.
13:19 but fools *d* turning from evil.
16:12 Kings *d* wrongdoing,
24:9 and men *d* a mocker.
29:27 The righteous *d* the dishonest;
29:27 the wicked *d* the upright.

DETESTABLE (DETEST)

Pr 6:16 seven that are *d* to him:
21:27 The sacrifice of the wicked is *d*—
28:9 even his prayers are *d*.
Isa 1:13 Your incense is *d* to me.
41:24 he who chooses you is *d*.
44:19 Shall I make a *d* thing
Jer 44:4 'Do not do this *d* thing that I hate!'
Eze 8:13 doing things that are even more *d*."
Lk 16:15 among men is *d* in God's sight.
Tit 1:16 They are *d*, disobedient
1Pe 4:3 orgies, carousing and *d* idolatry.

DETESTED* (DETEST)

Zec 11:8 The flock *d* me, and I grew weary

DETESTS* (DETEST)

Dt 22:5 LORD your God *d* anyone who
23:18 the LORD your God *d* them both.
25:16 LORD your God *d* anyone who
Pr 3:32 for the LORD *d* a perverse man
11:20 The LORD *d* men
12:22 The LORD *d* lying lips,
15:8 The LORD *d* the sacrifice
15:9 The LORD *d* the way
15:26 The LORD *d* the thoughts
16:5 The LORD *d* all the proud of heart
17:15 the LORD *d* them both.
20:10 the LORD *d* them both.
20:23 The LORD *d* differing weights,

DEVIATE*

2Ch 8:15 They did not *d* from the king's

DEVICES*

Ps 81:12 to follow their own *d*.

DEVIL* (DEVIL'S)

Mt 4:1 the desert to be tempted by the *d*.
4:5 the *d* took him to the holy city
4:8 *d* took him to a very high mountain
4:11 the *d* left him, and angels came
13:39 the enemy who sows them is the *d*.
25:41 the eternal fire prepared for the *d*
Lk 4:2 forty days he was tempted by the *d*.
4:3 *d* said to him, "If you are the Son
4:5 The *d* led him up to a high place
4:9 The *d* led him to Jerusalem
4:13 When the *d* had finished all this
8:12 then the *d* comes and takes away
Jn 6:70 of you is a *d*!" (He meant Judas,
8:44 You belong to your father, the *d*,
13:2 the *d* had already prompted Judas
Ac 10:38 were under the power of the *d*,
13:10 "You are a child of the *d*
Eph 4:27 and do not give the *d* a foothold.
1Ti 3:6 under the same judgment as the *d*.
2Ti 2:26 and escape from the trap of the *d*,
Heb 2:14 the *d*—and free those who all their
Jas 3:15 but is earthly, unspiritual, of the *d*.
4:7 Resist the *d*, and he will flee
1Pe 5:8 Your enemy the *d* prowls
1Jn 3:8 because the *d* has been sinning
3:8 who does what is sinful is of the *d*,
3:10 and who the children of the *d* are:
Jude :9 with the *d* about the body of Moses
Rev 2:10 the *d* will put some of you in prison
12:9 that ancient serpent called the *d*
12:12 the *d* has gone down to you!
20:2 that ancient serpent, who is the *d*,
20:10 And the *d*, who deceived them,

DEVIL'S* (DEVIL)

Eph 6:11 stand against the *d* schemes.
1Ti 3:7 into disgrace and into the *d* trap.
1Jn 3:8 was to destroy the *d* work.

DEVILS see DEMONS

DEVIOUS*

Pr 2:15 and who are *d* in their ways.
14:2 he whose ways are *d* despises him.
21:8 The way of the guilty is *d*,

DEVOTE* (DEVOTED DEVOTING DEVOTION DEVOUT)

1Ch 22:19 Now *d* your heart and soul
2Ch 31:4 Levites so they could *d* themselves
Job 11:13 "Yet if you *d* your heart to him
Jer 30:21 for who is he who will *d* himself
Mic 4:13 You will *d* their ill-gotten gains
1Co 7:5 so that you may *d* yourselves
Col 4:2 *D* yourselves to prayer, being
1Ti 1:4 nor to *d* themselves to myths
4:13 *d* yourself to the public reading
Tit 3:8 may be careful to *d* themselves
3:14 people must learn to *d* themselves

DEVOTED (DEVOTE)

1Ki 11:4 and his heart was not fully *d*
Ezr 7:10 For Ezra had *d* himself to the study
Ps 86:2 Guard my life, for I am *d* to you.
Mt 6:24 or he will be *d* to the one
Mk 7:11 from me is Corban' (that is, a gift *d*
Ac 2:42 They *d* themselves
18:5 Paul *d* himself exclusively
Ro 12:10 Be *d* to one another
1Co 7:34 Her aim is to be *d* to the Lord
16:15 and they have *d* themselves
2Co 7:12 for yourselves how *d* to us you are.

DEVOTING* (DEVOTE)

1Ti 5:10 *d* herself to all kinds of good deeds.

DEVOTION* (DEVOTE)

2Ki 20:3 and with wholehearted *d* and have
1Ch 28:9 and serve him with wholehearted *d*
29:3 in my *d* to the temple
29:19 son Solomon the wholehearted *d*
2Ch 32:32 and his acts of *d* are written
35:26 of Josiah's reign and his acts of *d*,
Job 6:14 despairing man should have the *d*
15:4 and hinder *d* to God.
Isa 38:3 and with wholehearted *d* and have
Jer 2:2 " 'I remember the *d* of your youth,
Eze 33:31 With their mouths they express *d*,
1Co 7:35 way in undivided *d* to the Lord.
2Co 11:3 from your sincere and pure *d*

DEVOUR (DEVOURED DEVOURING DEVOURS)

2Sa 2:26 "Must the sword *d* for ever?
Mk 12:40 They *d* widows' houses
1Pe 5:8 lion looking for someone to *d*.

DEVOURED (DEVOUR)

Jer 30:16 But all who devour you will be *d*;

DEVOURING (DEVOUR)

Gal 5:15 keep on biting and *d* each other,

DEVOURS (DEVOUR)

2Sa 11:25 the sword *d* one as well as another.
Pr 21:20 but a foolish man *d* all he has.

DEVOUT* (DEVOTE)

1Ki 18:3 (Obadiah was a *d* believer
Isa 57:1 *d* men are taken away,
Lk 2:25 Simeon, who was righteous and *d*.
Ac 10:2 his family were *d* and God-fearing;
10:7 a *d* soldier who was one
13:43 and *d* converts to Judaism followed
22:12 He was a *d* observer of the law

DEW

Jdg 6:37 If there is *d* only on the fleece

DICTATED
Jer 36: 4 and while Jeremiah *d* all the words

DIE (DEAD DEADENED DEATH DIED DIES DYING)
Ge 2: 17 when you eat of it you will surely *d*
3: 3 you must not touch it, or you will *d*
3: 4 will not surely *d*," the serpent said
Ex 11: 5 Every firstborn son in Egypt will *d*,
Ru 1: 17 Where you *d* I will *d*, and there I
2Ki 14: 6 each is to *d* for his own sins."
Job 2: 9 Curse God and *d*!" He replied,
Pr 5: 23 He will *d* for lack of discipline,
10: 21 but fools *d* for lack of judgment.
15: 10 he who hates correction will *d*.
23: 13 with the rod, he will not *d*.
Ecc 3: 2 a time to be born and a time to *d*,
Isa 22: 13 "for tomorrow we *d*!"
66: 24 their worm will not *d*, nor will their
Jer 31: 30 everyone will *d* for his own sin;
Eze 3: 18 that wicked man will *d* for his sin,
3: 19 he will *d* for his sin; but you will
3: 20 block before him, he will *d*.
18: 4 soul who sins is the one who will *d*.
18: 20 soul who sins is the one who will *d*.
18: 31 Why will you *d*, O house of Israel?
33: 8 'O wicked man, you will surely *d*,'
Mt 26: 52 "for all who draw the sword will *d*
Mk 9: 48 " 'their worm does not *d*,
Jn 8: 21 and you will *d* in your sin.
11: 26 and believes in me will never *d*.
Ro 5: 7 Very rarely will anyone *d*
14: 8 and if we *d*, we *d* to the Lord.
1Co 15: 22 in Adam all *d*, so in Christ all will
15: 31 I *d* every day—I mean that,
15: 32 for tomorrow we *d*."
Php 1: 21 to live is Christ and to *d* is gain.
Heb 9: 27 Just as man is destined to *d* once,
1Pe 2: 24 so that we might *d* to sins
Rev 14: 13 Blessed are the dead who *d*

DIED (DIE)
1Ki 16: 18 So he *d*, because of the sins he had
1Ch 1: 51 Hadad also *d*.
10: 13 Saul *d* because he was unfaithful
Lk 16: 22 "The time came when the beggar *d*
Ro 5: 6 we were still powerless, Christ *d*
5: 8 we were still sinners, Christ *d*
6: 2 By no means! We *d* to sin;
6: 7 anyone who has *d* has been freed
6: 8 if we *d* with Christ, we believe that
6: 10 The death he *d*, he *d* to sin once
14: 9 Christ *d* and returned to life
14: 15 brother for whom Christ *d*.
1Co 8: 11 for whom Christ *d*, is destroyed
15: 3 that Christ *d* for our sins according
2Co 5: 14 *d* for all, and therefore all *d*.
5: 15 he *d* for all, that those who live
Col 2: 20 Since you *d* with Christ
3: 3 For you *d*, and your life is now
1Th 4: 14 We believe that Jesus *d*
5: 10 He *d* for us so that, whether we are
2Ti 2: 11 If we *d* with him,
Heb 9: 15 now that he has *d* as a ransom
9: 17 in force only when somebody has *d*
1Pe 3: 18 For Christ *d* for sins once for all,
Rev 2: 8 who *d* and came to life again.

DIES (DIE)
Job 14: 14 If a man *d*, will he live again?
Pr 11: 7 a wicked man *d*, his hope perishes;
26: 20 without gossip a quarrel *d* down.
Jn 11: 25 in me will live, even though he *d*;
12: 24 But if it *d*, it produces many seeds.
Ro 7: 2 but if her husband *d*, she is released
14: 7 and none of us *d* to himself alone.
1Co 7: 39 But if her husband *d*, she is free
15: 36 does not come to life unless it *d*.

DIFFERENCE* (DIFFERENT)
2Sa 19: 35 Can I tell the *d* between what is
2Ch 12: 8 so that they may learn the *d*
Eze 22: 26 they teach that there is no *d*
44: 23 are to teach my people the *d*
Ro 3: 22 There is no *d*, for all have sinned
10: 12 For there is no *d* between Jew
Gal 2: 6 whatever they were makes no *d*

DIFFERENCES* (DIFFERENT)
1Co 11: 19 to be *d* among you to show which

DIFFERENT* (DIFFERENCE DIFFERENCES DIFFERING DIFFERS)
Lev 19: 19 " 'Do not mate *d* kinds of animals.
Nu 14: 24 my servant Caleb has a *d* spirit
1Sa 10: 6 you will be changed into a *d* person
Est 1: 7 each one *d* from the other,
3: 8 Their customs are *d* from those
Da 7: 3 Four great beasts, each *d*
7: 7 It was *d* from all the former beasts,
7: 19 which was *d* from all the others
7: 23 It will be *d* from all the other
7: 24 them another king will arise, *d*
11: 29 but this time the outcome will be *d*
Mk 16: 12 Jesus appeared in a *d* form
Ro 12: 6 We have *d* gifts, according
1Co 4: 7 For who makes you *d*
12: 4 There are *d* kinds of gifts,
12: 5 There are *d* kinds of service,
12: 6 There are *d* kinds of working.
12: 10 to speak in *d* kinds of tongues,
12: 28 and those speaking in *d* kinds
2Co 11: 4 or a *d* gospel from the one you
11: 4 or if you receive a *d* spirit
Gal 1: 6 and are turning to a *d* gospel—
4: 1 he is no *d* from a slave,
Heb 7: 13 are said belonged to a *d* tribe,
Jas 2: 25 and sent them off in a *d* direction?

DIFFERING* (DIFFERENT)
Dt 25: 13 Do not have two *d* weights
25: 14 Do not have two *d* measures
Pr 20: 10 *D* weights and *d* measures
20: 23 The LORD detests *d* weights,

DIFFERS* (DIFFERENT)
1Co 15: 41 and star *d* from star in splendour.

DIFFICULT (DIFFICULTIES)
Ex 18: 22 but have them bring every *d* case
Dt 30: 11 commanding you today is not too *d*
2Ki 2: 10 "You have asked a *d* thing,"
Eze 3: 5 of obscure speech and *d* language,
Ac 15: 19 that we should not make it *d*

DIFFICULTIES* (DIFFICULT)
Dt 31: 17 and *d* will come upon them,
31: 21 when many disasters and *d* come
2Co 12: 10 in hardships, in persecutions, in *d*.

DIGNITY
Pr 31: 25 She is clothed with strength and *d*;

DIGS
Pr 26: 27 If a man *d* a pit, he will fall into it;

DILIGENCE (DILIGENT)
Ezr 5: 8 The work is being carried on with *d*
Heb 6: 11 to show this same *d* to the very end

DILIGENT (DILIGENCE)
Pr 10: 4 but *d* hands bring wealth.
12: 24 *D* hands will rule,
12: 27 the *d* man prizes his possessions.
13: 4 of the *d* are fully satisfied.
21: 5 The plans of the *d* lead to profit
1Ti 4: 15 Be *d* in these matters; give yourself

DINAH*
Only daughter of Jacob, by Leah (Ge 30:21; 46:15). Raped by Shechem; avenged by Simeon and Levi (Ge 34).

DINE
Pr 23: 1 When you sit to *d* with a ruler,

DIOTREPHES*
3Jn : 9 but *D*, who loves to be first,

DIRECT (DIRECTED DIRECTIVES DIRECTS)
Ge 18: 19 so that he will *d* his children
Dt 17: 10 to do everything they *d* you to do.
Ps 119: 35 *D* me in the path of your
119: 133 *D* my footsteps according
Jer 10: 23 it is not for man to *d* his steps.
2Th 3: 5 May the Lord *d* your hearts
1Ti 5: 17 The elders who *d* the affairs

DIRECTED (DIRECT)
Ge 24: 51 master's son, as the LORD has *d*."
Nu 16: 40 as the LORD *d* him through Moses
Dt 2: 1 Sea, as the LORD had *d* me.
6: 1 laws the LORD your God *d* me
Jos 11: 9 did to them as the LORD had *d*:
11: 23 just as the LORD had *d* Moses,
Pr 20: 24 A man's steps are *d* by the LORD.
Jer 13: 2 as the LORD *d*, and put it
Ac 7: 44 It had been made as God *d* Moses,
Tit 1: 5 elders in every town, as I *d* you.

DIRECTIVES* (DIRECT)
1Co 11: 17 In the following *d* I have no praise

DIRECTS (DIRECT)
Ps 42: 8 By day the LORD *d* his love,
Isa 48: 17 who *d* you in the way you should

DIRGE*
Mt 11: 17 we sang a *d*,
Lk 7: 32 we sang a *d*,

DISABLED*
Jn 5: 3 number of *d* people used to lie—
Heb 12: 13 so that the lame may not be *d*,

DISAGREEMENT*
Ac 15: 39 had such a sharp *d* that they parted

DISAPPEAR (DISAPPEARED DISAPPEARS)
Mt 5: 18 will by any means *d* from the Law
Lk 16: 17 earth to *d* than for the least stroke
Heb 8: 13 is obsolete and aging will soon *d*.
2Pe 3: 10 The heavens will *d* with a roar;

DISAPPEARED (DISAPPEAR)
1Ki 20: 40 busy here and there, the man *d*."

DISAPPEARS (DISAPPEAR)
1Co 13: 10 perfection comes, the imperfect *d*.

DISAPPOINT* (DISAPPOINTED)
Ro 5: 5 And hope does not *d* us,

DISAPPOINTED (DISAPPOINT)
Ps 22: 5 in you they trusted and were not *d*.

DISAPPROVE*
Pr 24: 18 or the LORD will see and *d*

DISARMED*
Col 2: 15 And having *d* the powers

DISASTER
Ex 32: 12 and do not bring *d* on your people.
Ps 57: 1 wings until the *d* has passed.
Pr 1: 26 I in turn will laugh at your *d*;
3: 25 Have no fear of sudden *d*
6: 15 Therefore *d* will overtake him
16: 4 even the wicked for a day of *d*.
17: 5 over *d* will not go unpunished.
27: 10 house when *d* strikes you—
Isa 45: 7 I bring prosperity and create *d*;
Jer 17: 17 you are my refuge in the day of *d*.
Eze 7: 5 An unheard-of *d* is coming.

DISCERN (DISCERNED DISCERNING DISCERNMENT)
Ps 19: 12 Who can *d* his errors?
139: 3 You *d* my going out and my lying

Php 1: 10 you may be able to *d* what is best

DISCERNED (DISCERN)

1Co 2: 14 because they are spiritually *d*.

DISCERNING (DISCERN)

1Ki 3: 9 So give your servant a *d* heart
3: 12 I will give you a wise and *d* heart,
Pr 1: 5 and let the *d* get guidance—
8: 9 To the *d* all of them are right;
10: 13 on the lips of the *d*,
14: 6 knowledge comes easily to the *d*.
14: 33 in the heart of the *d*
15: 14 The *d* heart seeks knowledge,
16: 21 The wise in heart are called *d*,
17: 24 A *d* man keeps wisdom in view.
17: 28 and *d* if he holds his tongue.
18: 15 heart of the *d* acquires knowledge;
19: 25 rebuke a *d* man, and he will gain
28: 7 He who keeps the law is a *d* son,

DISCERNMENT (DISCERN)

Ps 119: 125 I am your servant; give me *d*
Pr 3: 21 preserve sound judgment and *d*,
17: 10 A rebuke impresses a man of *d*
28: 11 a poor man who has *d* sees

DISCHARGED* (DISCHARGING)

Ecc 8: 8 As no-one is *d* in time of war,

DISCHARGING* (DISCHARGED)

1Co 9: 17 I am simply *d* the trust committed

DISCIPLE (DISCIPLES DISCIPLES')

Mt 10: 42 these little ones because he is my *d*,
Lk 14: 26 his own life—he cannot be my *d*.
14: 27 and follow me cannot be my *d*.
14: 33 everything he has cannot be my *d*.
Jn 13: 23 of them, the *d* whom Jesus loved,
19: 26 and the *d* whom he loved standing
21: 7 Then the *d* whom Jesus loved said
21: 20 saw that the *d* whom Jesus loved

DISCIPLES (DISCIPLE)

Mt 10: 1 He called his twelve *d* to him
26: 56 Then all the *d* deserted him
28: 19 Therefore go and make *d*
Mk 3: 7 withdrew with his *d* to the lake,
16: 20 Then the *d* went out and preached
Lk 6: 13 he called his *d* to him and chose
Jn 2: 11 and his *d* put their faith in him.
6: 66 many of his *d* turned back
8: 31 to my teaching, you are really my *d*
12: 16 At first his *d* did not understand all
13: 35 men will know that you are my *d*
15: 8 showing yourselves to be my *d*.
20: 20 The *d* were overjoyed
Ac 6: 1 the number of *d* was increasing,
11: 26 The *d* were first called Christians
14: 22 strengthening the *d*
18: 23 Phrygia, strengthening all the *d*.

DISCIPLES' (DISCIPLE)

Jn 13: 5 and began to wash his *d* feet,

DISCIPLINE* (DISCIPLINED DISCIPLINES SELF-DISCIPLINE)

Dt 4: 36 made you hear his voice to *d* you.
11: 2 and experienced the *d*
21: 18 listen to them when they *d* him,
Job 5: 17 so do not despise the *d*
Ps 6: 1 or *d* me in your wrath.
38: 1 or *d* me in your wrath.
39: 11 You rebuke and *d* men for their sin;
94: 12 Blessed is the man you *d*, O LORD
Pr 1: 2 for attaining wisdom and *d*;
1: 7 but fools despise wisdom and *d*.
3: 11 do not despise the LORD's *d*
5: 12 You will say, "How I hated *d*!
5: 23 He will die for lack of *d*,
6: 23 and the corrections of *d*
10: 17 He who heeds *d* shows the way
12: 1 Whoever loves *d* loves knowledge,
13: 18 He who ignores *d* comes to poverty
13: 24 who loves him is careful to *d* him.
15: 5 A fool spurns his father's *d*,
15: 10 Stern *d* awaits him who leaves
15: 32 He who ignores *d* despises himself,
19: 18 *D* your son, for in that there is hope
22: 15 the rod of *d* will drive it far
23: 13 Do not withhold *d* from a child;
23: 23 get wisdom, *d* and understanding.
29: 17 *D* your son, and he will give you
Jer 17: 23 would not listen or respond to *d*.
30: 11 I will *d* you but only with justice;
32: 33 would not listen or respond to *d*.
46: 28 I will *d* you but only with justice;
Hos 5: 2 I will *d* all of them.
Heb 12: 5 do not make light of the Lord's *d*.
12: 7 as *d*; God is treating you
12: 8 (and everyone undergoes *d*),
12: 11 No *d* seems pleasant at the time,
Rev 3: 19 Those whom I love I rebuke and *d*.

DISCIPLINED* (DISCIPLINE)

Pr 1: 3 for acquiring a *d* and prudent life,
Isa 26: 16 when you *d* them,
Jer 31: 18 and I have been *d*.
31: 18 'You *d* me like an unruly calf,
1Co 11: 32 we are being *d* so that we will not
Tit 1: 8 upright, holy and *d*.
Heb 12: 7 For what son is not *d* by his father?
12: 8 you are not *d* (and everyone
12: 9 all had human fathers who *d* us
12: 10 Our fathers *d* us for a little while

DISCIPLINES* (DISCIPLINE)

Dt 8: 5 so the LORD your God *d* you.
8: 5 your heart that as a man *d* his son,
Ps 94: 10 Does he who *d* nations not punish?
Pr 3: 12 the LORD *d* those he loves,
Heb 12: 6 because the Lord *d* those he loves,
12: 10 but God *d* us for our good,

DISCLOSED

Lk 8: 17 is nothing hidden that will not be *d*,
Col 1: 26 and generations, but is now *d*
Heb 9: 8 Holy Place had not yet been *d*

DISCORD

Gal 5: 20 idolatry and witchcraft; hatred, *d*,

DISCOURAGED* (DISCOURAGEMENT)

Nu 32: 9 they *d* the Israelites
Dt 1: 21 Do not be afraid; do not be *d*."
31: 8 Do not be afraid; do not be *d*."
Jos 1: 9 Do not be terrified; do not be *d*,
8: 1 "Do not be afraid; do not be *d*.
10: 25 "Do not be afraid; do not be *d*.
1Ch 22: 13 Do not be afraid or *d*.
28: 20 or *d*, for the LORD God,
2Ch 20: 15 or *d* because of this vast army.
20: 17 Do not be afraid; do not be *d*.
32: 7 or *d* because of the king of Assyria
Job 4: 5 to you, and you are *d*;
Isa 42: 4 he will not falter or be *d*
Eph 3: 13 to be *d* because of my sufferings
Col 3: 21 children, or they will become *d*.

DISCOURAGEMENT* (DISCOURAGED)

Ex 6: 9 of their *d* and cruel bondage.

DISCOVERED

2Ki 23: 24 book that Hilkiah the priest had *d*

DISCREDIT* (DISCREDITED)

Ne 6: 13 would give me a bad name to *d* me.
Job 40: 8 "Would you *d* my justice?

DISCREDITED (DISCREDIT)

2Co 6: 3 so that our ministry will not be *d*.

DISCRETION*

1Ch 22: 12 May the LORD give you *d*
Pr 1: 4 knowledge and *d* to the young—
2: 11 *D* will protect you,
5: 2 that you may maintain *d*
8: 12 I possess knowledge and *d*.
11: 22 a beautiful woman who shows no *d*.

DISCRIMINATED*

Jas 2: 4 have you not *d* among yourselves

DISEASE (DISEASES)

Mt 4: 23 and healing every *d* and sickness
9: 35 and healing every *d* and sickness.
10: 1 and to heal every *d* and sickness.

DISEASES (DISEASE)

Ps 103: 3 and heals all my *d*;
Mt 8: 17 and carried our *d*."
Mk 3: 10 those with *d* were pushing forward
Lk 9: 1 drive out all demons and to cure *d*,

DISFIGURE* (DISFIGURED)

Mt 6: 16 for they *d* their faces

DISFIGURED (DISFIGURE)

Isa 52: 14 his appearance was so *d*

DISGRACE (DISGRACEFUL DISGRACES)

Ps 44: 15 My *d* is before me all day long,
52: 1 you who are a *d* in the eyes of God?
74: 21 not let the oppressed retreat in *d*;
Pr 6: 33 Blows and *d* are his lot,
11: 2 When pride comes, then comes *d*,
14: 34 but sin is a *d* to any people.
19: 26 is a son who brings shame and *d*.
Mt 1: 19 want to expose her to public *d*,
Ac 5: 41 of suffering *d* for the Name.
1Co 11: 6 and if it is a *d* for a woman
11: 14 it is a *d* to him, but that
1Ti 3: 7 so that he will not fall into *d*
Heb 6: 6 and subjecting him to public *d*.
11: 26 He regarded *d* for the sake
13: 13 the camp, bearing the *d* he bore.

DISGRACEFUL (DISGRACE)

Pr 10: 5 during harvest is a *d* son.
12: 4 a *d* wife is like decay in his bones.
17: 2 wise servant will rule over a *d* son,
1Co 14: 35 for it is *d* for a woman to speak

DISGRACES (DISGRACE)

Pr 28: 7 of gluttons *d* his father.
29: 15 but a child left to itself *d* his mother

DISGUISES*

Pr 26: 24 A malicious man *d* himself

DISH

Pr 19: 24 sluggard buries his hand in the *d*;
Mt 23: 25 the outside of the cup and *d*,

DISHONEST*

Ex 18: 21 trustworthy men who hate *d* gain
Lev 19: 35 " 'Do not use *d* standards
1Sa 8: 3 They turned aside after *d* gain
Pr 11: 1 The LORD abhors *d* scales,
13: 11 *D* money dwindles away,
20: 23 and *d* scales do not please him.
29: 27 The righteous detest the *d*;
Jer 22: 17 are set only on *d* gain,
Eze 28: 18 By your many sins and *d* trade
Hos 12: 7 The merchant uses *d* scales;
Am 8: 5 and cheating with *d* scales,
Mic 6: 11 Shall I acquit a man with *d* scales,
Lk 16: 8 master commended the *d* manager
16: 10 whoever is *d* with very little will
16: 10 with very little will also be *d*
1Ti 3: 8 wine, and not pursuing *d* gain.
Tit 1: 7 not violent, not pursuing *d* gain.
1: 11 and that for the sake of *d* gain.

DISHONOUR* (DISHONOURED DISHONOURS)

Lev 18: 7 " 'Do not *d* your father
18: 8 wife; that would *d* your father.
18: 10 daughter; that would *d* you.

Lev 18: 14 "'Do not *d* your father's brother
18: 16 that would *d* your brother.
20: 19 for that would *d* a close relative;
Dt 22: 30 he must not *d* his father's bed.
Pr 30: 9 and so *d* the name of my God.
Jer 14: 21 do not *d* your glorious throne.
20: 11 their *d* will never be forgotten.
La 2: 2 princes down to the ground in *d*.
Eze 22: 10 are those who *d* their fathers' bed;
Jn 8: 49 I honour my Father and you *d* me.
Ro 2: 23 do you *d* God by breaking the law?
1Co 15: 43 it is sown in *d*, it is raised in glory;
2Co 6: 8 through glory and *d*, bad report

DISHONOURED* (DISHONOUR)
Lev 20: 11 father's wife, he has *d* his father.
20: 17 He has *d* his sister and will be held
20: 20 with his aunt, he has *d* his uncle.
20: 21 of impurity; he has *d* his brother.
Dt 21: 14 as a slave, since you have *d* her.
Ezr 4: 14 proper for us to see the king *d*,
1Co 4: 10 You are honoured, we are *d*!

DISHONOURS* (DISHONOUR)
Dt 27: 16 Cursed is the man who *d* his father
27: 20 for he *d* his father's bed."
Job 20: 3 I hear a rebuke that *d* me,
Mic 7: 6 For a son *d* his father,
1Co 11: 4 with his head covered *d* his head.
11: 5 her head uncovered *d* her head—

DISILLUSIONMENT*
Ps 7: 14 conceives trouble gives birth to *d*.

DISMAYED
Isa 28: 16 the one who trusts will never be *d*.
41: 10 do not be *d*, for I am your God.

DISOBEDIENCE* (DISOBEY)
Jos 22: 22 in rebellion or *d* to the LORD,
Jer 43: 7 So they entered Egypt in *d*
Ro 5: 19 as through the *d* of the one man
11: 30 mercy as a result of their *d*,
11: 32 to *d* so that he may have mercy
2Co 10: 6 ready to punish every act of *d*,
Heb 2: 2 and *d* received its just punishment,
4: 6 go in, because of their *d*.
4: 11 fall by following their example of *d*.

DISOBEDIENT* (DISOBEY)
Ne 9: 26 "But they were *d* and rebelled
Lk 1: 17 and the *d* to the wisdom
Ac 26: 19 I was not *d* to the vision
Ro 10: 21 hands to a *d* and obstinate people."
11: 30 as you who were at one time *d*
11: 31 so they too have now become *d*
Eph 2: 2 now at work in those who are *d*.
5: 6 comes on those who are *d*.
5: 12 to mention what the *d* do in secret.
2Ti 3: 2 proud, abusive, *d* to their parents,
Tit 1: 6 to the charge of being wild and *d*.
1: 16 *d* and unfit for doing anything
3: 3 At one time we too were foolish, *d*,
Heb 11: 31 killed with those who were *d*.

DISOBEY* (DISOBEDIENCE DISOBEDIENT DISOBEYED DISOBEYING DISOBEYS)
Dt 11: 28 the curse if you *d* the commands
2Ch 24: 20 'Why do you *d* the LORD's
Est 3: 3 Why do you *d* the king's command
Jer 42: 13 and so *d* the LORD your God,
Ro 1: 30 they *d* their parents; they are
1Pe 2: 8 because they *d* the message—

DISOBEYED* (DISOBEY)
Nu 14: 22 and in the desert but who *d* me
27: 14 both of you *d* my command
Jdg 2: 2 Yet you have *d* me.
Ne 9: 29 arrogant and *d* your commands.
Isa 24: 5 they have *d* the laws,
Jer 43: 4 and all the people *d* the LORD's
Lk 15: 29 for you and never *d* your orders.
Heb 3: 18 rest if not to those who *d*?

1Pe 3: 20 the spirits in prison who *d* long ago

DISOBEYING* (DISOBEY)
Nu 14: 41 "Why are you *d* the LORD's

DISOBEYS* (DISOBEY)
Eze 33: 12 man will not save him when he *d*,

DISORDER
1Co 14: 33 For God is not a God of *d*
2Co 12: 20 slander, gossip, arrogance and *d*.
Jas 3: 16 there you find *d* and every evil

DISOWN (DISOWNS)
Pr 30: 9 I may have too much and *d* you
Mt 10: 33 I will *d* him before my Father
26: 35 to die with you, I will never *d* you."
2Ti 2: 12 If we *d* him,

DISOWNS (DISOWN)
Lk 12: 9 he who *d* me before men will be

DISPENSATION see ADMINISTRATION, TRUST

DISPLACES
Pr 30: 23 a maidservant who *d* her mistress.

DISPLAY (DISPLAYED DISPLAYS)
Ps 45: 4 your right hand *d* awesome deeds.
Eze 39: 21 I will *d* my glory among the nations
Ro 9: 17 that I might *d* my power in you
1Co 4: 9 on *d* at the end of the procession,
1Ti 1: 16 Christ Jesus might *d* his unlimited

DISPLAYED (DISPLAY)
Jn 9: 3 work of God might be *d* in his life.
2Th 2: 9 the work of Satan *d* in all kinds

DISPLAYS (DISPLAY)
Isa 44: 23 he *d* his glory in Israel.

DISPLEASE (DISPLEASED)
1Th 2: 15 They *d* God and are hostile

DISPLEASED (DISPLEASE)
2Sa 11: 27 David had done *d* the LORD.

DISPUTABLE* (DISPUTE)
Ro 14: 1 passing judgment on *d* matters.

DISPUTE (DISPUTABLE DISPUTES DISPUTING)
Pr 17: 14 before a *d* breaks out.
1Co 6: 1 If any of you has a *d* with another,

DISPUTES (DISPUTE)
Pr 18: 18 Casting the lot settles *d*

DISPUTING (DISPUTE)
1Ti 2: 8 in prayer, without anger or *d*.

DISQUALIFIED*
1Co 9: 27 I myself will not be *d* for the prize.

DISREPUTE*
2Pe 2: 2 will bring the way of truth into *d*.

DISSENSION* (DISSENSIONS)
Pr 6: 14 he always stirs up *d*.
6: 19 and a man who stirs up *d*
10: 12 Hatred stirs up *d*,
15: 18 A hot-tempered man stirs up *d*,
16: 28 A perverse man stirs up *d*,
28: 25 A greedy man stirs up *d*,
29: 22 An angry man stirs up *d*,
Ro 13: 13 debauchery, not in *d* and jealousy.

DISSENSIONS* (DISSENSION)
Gal 5: 20 selfish ambition, *d*, factions

DISSIPATION*
Lk 21: 34 will be weighed down with *d*,

1Pe 4: 4 with them into the same flood of *d*,

DISTINCTION
Ac 15: 9 He made no *d* between us

DISTINGUISH
1Ki 3: 9 and to *d* between right and wrong.
1Co 12: 10 the ability to *d* between spirits,
Heb 5: 14 themselves to *d* good from evil.

DISTORT
Ac 20: 30 and *d* the truth in order
2Co 4: 2 nor do we *d* the word of God.
2Pe 3: 16 ignorant and unstable people *d*,

DISTRACTED*
Lk 10: 40 But Martha was *d* by all

DISTRESS (DISTRESSED)
2Ch 15: 4 in their *d* they turned to the LORD
Ps 18: 6 In my *d* I called to the LORD;
81: 7 In your *d* you called and I rescued
120: 1 I call on the LORD in my *d*,
Jnh 2: 2 "In my *d* I called to the LORD,
Mt 24: 21 For then there will be great *d*,
Jas 1: 27 after orphans and widows in their *d*

DISTRESSED (DISTRESS)
Lk 12: 50 how *d* I am until it is completed!
Ro 14: 15 If your brother is *d*

DIVIDE (DIVIDED DIVIDING DIVISION DIVISIONS DIVISIVE)
Ps 22: 18 They *d* my garments among them

DIVIDED (DIVIDE)
Mt 12: 25 household *d* against itself will not
Lk 23: 34 they *d* up his clothes by casting lots
1Co 1: 13 Is Christ *d*? Was Paul crucified

DIVIDING (DIVIDE)
Eph 2: 14 destroyed the barrier, the *d* wall
Heb 4: 12 it penetrates even to *d* soul

DIVINATION
Lev 19: 26 "'Do not practise *d* or sorcery.

DIVINE
Ro 1: 20 his eternal power and *d* nature—
2Co 10: 4 they have *d* power
2Pe 1: 4 you may participate in the *d* nature

DIVISION (DIVIDE)
Lk 12: 51 on earth? No, I tell you, but *d*.
1Co 12: 25 so that there should be no *d*

DIVISIONS (DIVIDE)
Ro 16: 17 to watch out for those who cause *d*
1Co 1: 10 another so that there may be no *d*
11: 18 there are *d* among you,

DIVISIVE* (DIVIDE)
Tit 3: 10 Warn a *d* person once,

DIVORCE* (DIVORCED DIVORCES)
Dt 22: 19 he must not *d* her as long as he lives
22: 29 He can never *d* her as long
24: 1 and he writes her a certificate of *d*,
24: 3 and writes her a certificate of *d*,
Isa 50: 1 is your mother's certificate of *d*
Jer 3: 8 faithless Israel her certificate of *d*
Mal 2: 16 "I hate *d*," says the LORD God
Mt 1: 19 he had in mind to *d* her quietly.
5: 31 must give her a certificate of *d*.'
19: 3 for a man to *d* his wife for any
19: 7 man give his wife a certificate of *d*
19: 8 permitted you to *d* your wives
Mk 10: 2 Is it lawful for a man to *d* his wife?"
10: 4 a man to write a certificate of *d*
1Co 7: 11 And a husband must not *d* his wife.
7: 12 to live with him, he must not *d* her.
7: 13 to live with her, she must not *d* him
7: 27 Are you married? Do not seek a *d*.

DIVORCED* (DIVORCE)
Lev 21: 7 or *d* from their husbands,
21: 14 not marry a widow, a *d* woman,
22: 13 daughter becomes a widow or is *d*,
Nu 30: 9 or *d* woman will be binding on her.
Dt 24: 4 then her first husband, who *d* her,
1Ch 8: 8 after he had *d* his wives Hushim
Eze 44: 22 not marry widows or *d* women;
Mt 5: 32 a woman so *d* commits adultery.
Lk 16: 18 who marries a *d* woman commits

DIVORCES* (DIVORCE)
Jer 3: 1 "If a man *d* his wife
Mt 5: 31 'Anyone who *d* his wife must give
5: 32 tell you that anyone who *d* his wife,
19: 9 tell you that anyone who *d* his wife,
Mk 10: 11 "Anyone who *d* his wife
10: 12 And if she *d* her husband
Lk 16: 18 "Anyone who *d* his wife

DOCTOR
Mt 9: 12 "It is not the healthy who need a *d*,

DOCTRINE* (DOCTRINES)
1Ti 1: 10 to the sound *d* that conforms
4: 16 Watch your life and *d* closely.
2Ti 4: 3 men will not put up with sound *d*.
Tit 1: 9 can encourage others by sound *d*
2: 1 is in accord with sound *d*.

DOCTRINES* (DOCTRINE)
1Ti 1: 3 not to teach false *d* any longer
6: 3 If anyone teaches false *d*

DOEG*
Edomite; Saul's head shepherd; responsible for murder of priests at Nob (1Sa 21:7; 22:6-23; Ps 52).

DOG (DOGS)
Pr 26: 11 As a *d* returns to its vomit,
Ecc 9: 4 a live *d* is better off than a dead lion
2Pe 2: 22 "A *d* returns to its vomit," and,

DOGS (DOG)
Mt 7: 6 "Do not give *d* what is sacred;
15: 26 bread and toss it to their *d*."

DOMINION
Job 25: 2 "*D* and awe belong to God;
Ps 22: 28 for *d* belongs to the LORD

DONKEY
Nu 22: 30 *d* said to Balaam, "Am I not your
Zec 9: 9 gentle and riding on a *d*,
Mt 21: 5 gentle and riding on a *d*,
2Pe 2: 16 for his wrongdoing by a *d*—

DOOR (DOORS)
Job 31: 32 for my *d* was always open
Ps 141: 3 keep watch over the *d* of my lips.
Mt 6: 6 close the *d* and pray to your Father
7: 7 and the *d* will be opened to you.
Ac 14: 27 how he had opened the *d* of faith
1Co 16: 9 a great *d* for effective work has
2Co 2: 12 found that the LORD had opened a *d*
Rev 3: 20 I stand at the *d* and knock.

DOOR-FRAMES
Dt 6: 9 Write them on the *d* of your houses

DOORKEEPER
Ps 84: 10 I would rather be a *d* in the house

DOORS (DOOR)
Ps 24: 7 be lifted up, you ancient *d*,

DORCAS
Ac 9: 36 is *D*), who was always doing good

DOUBLE
2Ki 2: 9 "Let me inherit a *d* portion
1Ti 5: 17 church well are worthy of *d* honour,

DOUBLE-EDGED (EDGE)
Heb 4: 12 Sharper than any *d* sword,
Rev 1: 16 of his mouth came a sharp *d* sword.
2: 12 of him who has the sharp, *d* sword.

DOUBLE-MINDED* (MIND)
Ps 119: 113 I hate *d* men,
Jas 1: 8 he is a *d* man, unstable
4: 8 and purify your hearts, you *d*.

DOUBT (DOUBTING DOUBTS)
Mt 14: 31 he said, "why did you *d*?"
21: 21 if you have faith and do not *d*,
Mk 11: 23 and does not *d* in his heart
Jas 1: 6 he must believe and not *d*,
Jude : 22 Be merciful to those who *d*;

DOUBTING* (DOUBT)
Jn 20: 27 Stop *d* and believe."

DOUBTS* (DOUBT)
Lk 24: 38 and why do *d* rise in your minds?
Ro 14: 23 the man who has *d* is condemned
Jas 1: 6 he who *d* is like a wave of the sea,

DOVE (DOVES)
Ge 8: 8 Then he sent out a *d* to see
Mt 3: 16 Spirit of God descending like a *d*

DOVES (DOVE)
Lev 12: 8 is to bring two *d* or two young
Mt 10: 16 as snakes and as innocent as *d*.
Lk 2: 24 "a pair of *d* or two young pigeons."

DOWNCAST
Ps 42: 5 Why are you *d*, O my soul?
2Co 7: 6 But God, who comforts the *d*,

DOWNFALL
Hos 14: 1 Your sins have been your *d*!

DRAGON
Rev 12: 7 and his angels fought against the *d*,
13: 2 The *d* gave the beast his power
20: 2 He seized the *d*, that ancient

DRAW (DRAWING DRAWS)
Mt 26: 52 "for all who *d* the sword will die
Jn 12: 32 up from the earth, will *d* all men
Heb 10: 22 let us *d* near to God

DRAWING (DRAW)
Lk 21: 28 because your redemption is *d* near

DRAWS (DRAW)
Jn 6: 44 the Father who sent me *d* him,

DREAD (DREADFUL)
Ps 53: 5 they were, overwhelmed with *d*,

DREADFUL (DREAD)
Mt 24: 19 How *d* it will be in those days
Heb 10: 31 It is a *d* thing to fall into the hands

DREAM
Joel 2: 28 your old men will *d* dreams,
Ac 2: 17 your old men will *d* dreams.

DRESS
1Ti 2: 9 I also want women to *d* modestly,

DRIFT*
Heb 2: 1 so that we do not *d* away.

DRINK (DRINKING DRINKS DRUNK DRUNKARD DRUNKARD'S DRUNKARDS DRUNKENNESS)
Ex 29: 40 of a hin of wine as a *d* offering.
Nu 6: 3 He must not *d* grape juice
Jdg 7: 5 from those who kneel down to *d*."
2Sa 23: 15 that someone would get me a *d*
Pr 5: 15 *D* water from your own cistern,
Mt 20: 22 "Can you *d* the cup I am going to *d*
26: 27 saying, "*D* from it, all of you.
Mk 16: 18 and when they *d* deadly poison,
Lk 12: 19 Take life easy; eat, *d* and be merry
Jn 7: 37 let him come to me and *d*.
18: 11 Shall I not *d* the cup the Father has
1Co 10: 4 and drank the same spiritual *d*;
12: 13 were all given the one Spirit to *d*.
Php 2: 17 being poured out like a *d* offering
2Ti 4: 6 being poured out like a *d* offering,
Rev 14: 10 too, will *d* of the wine of God's fury
21: 6 to *d* without cost from the spring

DRINKING (DRINK)
Ro 14: 17 God is not a matter of eating and *d*,

DRINKS (DRINK)
Isa 5: 22 and champions at mixing *d*,
Jn 4: 13 "Everyone who *d* this water will be
6: 54 and *d* my blood has eternal life,
1Co 11: 27 or *d* the cup of the Lord

DRIPPING
Pr 19: 13 wife is like a constant *d*.
27: 15 a constant *d* on a rainy day;

DRIVE (DRIVES)
Ex 23: 30 Little by little I will *d* them out
Nu 33: 52 *d* out all the inhabitants of the land
Jos 13: 13 Israelites did not *d* out the people
23: 13 will no longer *d* out these nations
Pr 22: 10 *D* out the mocker, and out goes
Mt 10: 1 authority to *d* out evil spirits
Jn 6: 37 comes to me I will never *d* away.

DRIVES (DRIVE)
Mt 12: 26 If Satan *d* out Satan, he is divided
1Jn 4: 18 But perfect love *d* out fear,

DROP (DROPS)
Pr 17: 14 so *d* the matter before a dispute
Isa 40: 15 Surely the nations are like a *d*

DROPS (DROP)
Lk 22: 44 his sweat was like *d* of blood falling

DROSS
Ps 119: 119 of the earth you discard like *d*;
Pr 25: 4 Remove the *d* from the silver,

DROUGHT
Jer 17: 8 It has no worries in a year of *d*

DROWNED
Ex 15: 4 are *d* in the Red Sea.
Mt 18: 6 and to be *d* in the depths of the sea.
Heb 11: 29 tried to do so, they were *d*.

DROWSINESS*
Pr 23: 21 and *d* clothes them in rags.

DRUNK (DRINK)
1Sa 1: 13 Eli thought she was *d* and said
Ac 2: 15 men are not *d*, as you suppose.
Eph 5; 18 Do not get *d* on wine, which leads

DRUNKARD (DRINK)
Mt 11: 19 and a *d*, a friend of tax collectors
1Co 5: 11 or a slanderer, a *d* or a swindler.

DRUNKARD'S* (DRINK)
Pr 26: 9 Like a thornbush in a *d* hand

DRUNKARDS (DRINK)
Pr 23: 21 for *d* and gluttons become poor,
1Co 6: 10 nor the greedy nor *d* nor slanderers

DRUNKENNESS (DRINK)
Lk 21: 34 weighed down with dissipation, *d*
Ro 13: 13 and *d*, not in sexual immorality
Gal 5: 21 factions and envy; *d*, orgies,
1Ti 3: 3 not given to *d*,
Tit 1: 7 not given to *d*,
1Pe 4: 3 living in debauchery, lust, *d*, orgies,

DRY
Ge 1: 9 place, and let *d* ground appear."
Ex 14: 16 go through the sea on *d* ground.
Jos 3: 17 the crossing on *d* ground.
Isa 53: 2 and like a root out of *d* ground.
Eze 37: 4 '*D* bones, hear the word

DULL
Isa 6: 10 make their ears *d*
2Co 3: 14 But their minds were made *d*,

DUST
Ge 2: 7 man from the *d* of the ground
3: 19 for *d* you are
Job 42: 6 and repent in *d* and ashes."
Ps 22: 15 you lay me in the *d* of death.
103: 14 he remembers that we are *d*.
Ecc 3: 20 all come from *d*, and to *d* all return.
Mt 10: 14 shake the *d* off your feet
1Co 15: 47 was of the *d* of the earth,

DUTIES (DUTY)
2Ti 4: 5 discharge all the *d* of your ministry

DUTY (DUTIES)
Ecc 12: 13 for this is the whole *d* of man.
Ac 23: 1 I have fulfilled my *d* to God
1Co 7: 3 husband should fulfil his marital *d*

DWELL (DWELLING DWELLINGS DWELLS DWELT)
Ex 25: 8 for me, and I will *d* among them.
2Sa 7: 5 the one to build me a house to *d* in?
1Ki 8: 27 "But will God really *d* on earth?
Ps 23: 6 I will *d* in the house of the LORD
37: 3 *d* in the land and enjoy safe pasture
61: 4 I long to *d* in your tent for ever
Pr 8: 12 wisdom, *d* together with prudence;
Isa 33: 14 of us can *d* with the consuming fire
43: 18 do not *d* on the past.
Jn 5: 38 nor does his word *d* in you,
Eph 3: 17 so that Christ may *d* in your hearts
Col 1: 19 to have all his fulness *d* in him,
3: 16 the word of Christ *d* in you richly

DWELLING (DWELL)
2Co 5: 2 to be clothed with our heavenly *d*,
Eph 2: 22 to become a *d* in which God lives

DWELLING-PLACE
Lev 26: 11 I will put my *d* among you
Dt 26: 15 from heaven, your holy *d*,
Ps 90: 1 Lord, you have been our *d*

DWELLINGS (DWELL)
Lk 16: 9 will be welcomed into eternal *d*.

DWELLS (DWELL)
Ps 46: 4 holy place where the Most High *d*.
91: 1 He who *d* in the shelter

DWELT (DWELL)
Dt 33: 16 of him who *d* in the burning bush.

DYING (DIE)
Ro 7: 6 by *d* to what once bound us,
2Co 6: 9 yet regarded as unknown; *d*,

EAGER
Pr 31: 13 and works with *e* hands
Ro 8: 19 The creation waits in *e* expectation
1Co 14: 12 Since you are *e* to have spiritual
14: 39 my brothers, be *e* to prophesy,
Tit 2: 14 a people that are his very own, *e*
1Pe 5: 2 greedy for money, but *e* to serve;

EAGLE (EAGLE'S EAGLES)
Dt 32: 11 like an *e* that stirs up its nest
Eze 1: 10 each also had the face of an *e*.
Rev 4: 7 the fourth was like a flying *e*.
12: 14 given the two wings of a great *e*,

EAGLE'S (EAGLE)
Ps 103: 5 my youth is renewed like the *e*.

EAGLES (EAGLE)
Isa 40: 31 They will soar on wings like *e*;

EAR (EARS)
Ex 21: 6 and pierce his *e* with an awl.
Ps 5: 1 Give *e* to my words, O LORD,
Pr 2: 2 turning your *e* to wisdom
1Co 2: 9 no *e* has heard,
12: 16 if the *e* should say, "Because I am
Rev 2: 7 He who has an *e*, let him hear what

EAR-RING (EAR-RINGS)
Pr 25: 12 Like an *e* of gold or an ornament

EAR-RINGS (EAR-RING)
Ex 32: 2 Take off the gold *e* that your wives,

EARN (EARNED EARNINGS)
2Th 3: 12 down and *e* the bread they eat.

EARNED (EARN)
Pr 31: 31 Give her the reward she has *e*,

EARNEST see DEPOSIT

EARNESTNESS
2Co 7: 11 what *e*, what eagerness
8: 7 in complete *e* and in your love

EARNINGS (EARN)
Pr 31: 16 out of her *e* she plants a vineyard.

EARS (EAR)
Job 42: 5 My *e* had heard of you
Ps 34: 15 and his *e* are attentive to their cry;
Pr 21: 13 If a man shuts his *e* to the cry
26: 17 Like one who seizes a dog by the *e*
Isa 6: 10 hear with their *e*,
Mt 11: 15 He who has *e*, let him hear.
2Ti 4: 3 to say what their itching *e* want
1Pe 3: 12 his *e* are attentive to their prayer,

EARTH (EARTH'S EARTHLY)
Ge 1: 1 God created the heavens and the *e*.
1: 2 Now the *e* was formless and empty,
7: 24 The waters flooded the *e*
14: 19 Creator of heaven and *e*.
1Ki 8: 27 "But will God really dwell on *e*?
Job 26: 7 he suspends the *e* over nothing.
Ps 24: 1 *e* is the LORD's, and everything
46: 6 he lifts his voice, the *e* melts.
90: 2 or you brought forth the *e*
97: 5 before the Lord of all the *e*.
102: 25 you laid the foundations of the *e*,
108: 5 and let your glory be over all the *e*.
Pr 8: 26 before he made the *e* or its fields
Isa 6: 3 the whole *e* is full of his glory."
24: 20 The *e* reels like a drunkard,
37: 16 You have made heaven and *e*.
40: 22 enthroned above the circle of the *e*,
51: 6 the *e* will wear out like a garment
54: 5 he is called the God of all the *e*.
55: 9 the heavens are higher than the *e*,
65: 17 new heavens and a new *e*.
66: 1 and the *e* is my footstool.
Jer 10: 10 When he is angry, the *e* trembles;
23: 24 "Do not I fill heaven and *e*?"
33: 25 and the fixed laws of heaven and *e*,
Hab 2: 20 let all the *e* be silent before him."
Mt 5: 5 for they will inherit the *e*.
5: 35 or by the *e*, for it is his footstool;
6: 10 done on *e* as it is in heaven.
16: 19 bind on *e* will be bound
24: 35 Heaven and *e* will pass away,
28: 18 and on *e* has been given to me.
Lk 2: 14 on *e* peace to men
Jn 12: 32 when I am lifted up from the *e*,
Ac 4: 24 "you made the heaven and the *e*
7: 49 and the *e* is my footstool.
1Co 10: 26 The *e* is the Lord's, and everything
Eph 3: 15 in heaven and on *e* derives its name
Php 2: 10 in heaven and on *e* and under the *e*,
Heb 1: 10 you laid the foundations of the *e*,
2Pe 3: 13 to a new heaven and a new *e*,
Rev 8: 7 A third of the *e* was burned up,
12: 12 But woe to the *e* and the sea,
20: 11 *E* and sky fled from his presence,
21: 1 I saw a new heaven and a new *e*,
21: 1 and the first *e* had passed away,

EARTH'S (EARTH)
Job 38: 4 when I laid the *e* foundation?

EARTHENWARE
Pr 26: 23 Like a coating of glaze over *e*

EARTHLY (EARTH)
Eph 4: 9 descended to the lower, *e* regions?
Php 3: 19 Their mind is on *e* things.
Col 3: 2 on things above, not on *e* things.
3: 5 whatever belongs to your *e* nature:

EARTHQUAKE (EARTHQUAKES)
Eze 38: 19 at that time there shall be a great *e*
Mt 28: 2 There was a violent *e*, for an angel
Rev 6: 12 There was a great *e*.

EARTHQUAKES (EARTHQUAKE)
Mt 24: 7 There will be famines and *e*

EASE
Pr 1: 33 and be at *e*, without fear of harm."

EASIER (EASY)
Lk 16: 17 It is *e* for heaven and earth
18: 25 it is *e* for a camel to go

EAST
Ge 2: 8 God had planted a garden in the *e*,
Ps 103: 12 as far as the *e* is from the west,
Eze 43: 2 God of Israel coming from the *e*.
Mt 2: 1 Magi from the *e* came to Jerusalem
2: 2 We saw his star in the *e*

EASY (EASIER)
Mt 11: 30 For my yoke is *e* and my burden is

EAT (ATE EATEN EATER EATING EATS)
Ge 2: 16 "You are free to *e* from any tree
2: 17 but you must not *e* from the tree
3: 19 you will *e* your food
Ex 12: 11 *E* it in haste; it is the LORD's
Lev 11: 2 these are the ones you may *e*:
17: 12 "None of you may *e* blood,
Dt 8: 16 He gave you manna to *e*
14: 4 These are the animals you may *e*:
Jdg 14: 14 "Out of the eater, something to *e*;
2Sa 9: 7 and you will always *e* at my table."
Pr 31: 27 and does not *e* the bread of idleness
Isa 55: 1 come, buy and *e*!
65: 25 and the lion will *e* straw like the ox,
Eze 3: 1 *e* what is before you, *e* this scroll;
Mt 14: 16 You give them something to *e*."
15: 2 wash their hands before they *e*!"
26: 26 "Take and *e*; this is my body."
Mk 14: 14 where I may *e* the Passover
Lk 10: 8 and are welcomed, *e* what is set
12: 19 Take life easy; *e*, drink
12: 22 what you will *e*; or about your body
Jn 4: 32 to *e* that you know nothing about."
6: 31 bread from heaven to *e*.' "
6: 52 can this man give us his flesh to *e*?"
Ac 10: 13 Kill and *e*."
Ro 14: 2 faith allows him to *e* everything,
14: 15 is distressed because of what you *e*,
14: 20 to *e* anything that causes someone
14: 21 It is better not to *e* meat
1Co 5: 11 With such a man do not even *e*.
8: 13 if what I *e* causes my brother to fall
10: 25 *E* anything sold in the meat market
10: 27 *e* whatever is put before you
10: 31 So whether you *e* or drink
11: 26 For whenever you *e* this bread

2Th 3: 10 man will not work, he shall not *e*."
Rev 2: 7 the right to *e* from the tree of life,
3: 20 I will come in and *e* with him,

EATEN (EAT)

Ge 3: 11 Have you *e* from the tree that I
Ac 10: 14 "I have never *e* anything impure
Rev 10: 10 when I had *e* it, my stomach turned

EATER (EAT)

Isa 55: 10 for the sower and bread for the *e*,

EATING (EAT)

Ex 34: 28 and forty nights without *e* bread
Ro 14: 15 not by your *e* destroy your brother
14: 17 kingdom of God is not a matter of *e*
14: 23 because his *e* is not from faith;
1Co 8: 4 about *e* food sacrificed to idols:
8: 10 you who have this knowledge *e*
Jude : 12 *e* with you without the slightest

EATS (EAT)

1Sa 14: 24 "Cursed be any man who *e* food
Lk 15: 2 "This man welcomes sinners and *e*
Jn 6: 51 If a man *e* of this bread, he will live
6: 54 Whoever *e* my flesh and drinks my
Ro 14: 2 faith is weak, *e* only vegetables.
14: 3 man who *e* everything must not
14: 6 He who *e* meat, *e* to the Lord,
14: 23 has doubts is condemned if he *e*,
1Co 11: 27 whoever *e* the bread or drinks

EBAL

Dt 11: 29 and on Mount *E* the curses.
Jos 8: 30 Joshua built on Mount *E* an altar

EBENEZER

1Sa 7: 12 He named it *E*, saying, "Thus far

EDEN

Ge 2: 8 in *E*; and there he put the man
Eze 28: 13 You were in *E*,

EDGE (DOUBLE-EDGED)

Mt 9: 20 and touched the *e* of his cloak.

EDICT

Heb 11: 23 they were not afraid of the king's *e*.

EDIFICATION (EDIFIED EDIFIES)

Ro 14: 19 leads to peace and to mutual *e*.

EDIFIED* (EDIFICATION)

1Co 14: 5 so that the church may be *e*.
14: 17 but the other man is not *e*.

EDIFIES* (EDIFICATION)

1Co 14: 4 but he who prophesies *e* the church
14: 4 speaks in a tongue *e* himself,

EDOM

Ge 36: 1 the account of Esau (that is, *E*).
36: 8 *E*) settled in the hill country of Seir
Isa 63: 1 Who is this coming from *E*,
Ob : 1 Sovereign LORD says about *E*—

EDUCATED*

Ac 7: 22 Moses was *e* in all the wisdom

EFFECT* (EFFECTIVE)

Job 41: 26 sword that reaches him has no *e*,
Isa 32: 17 *e* of righteousness will be quietness
Ac 7: 53 put into *e* through angels
1Co 15: 10 his grace to me was not without *e*.
Gal 3: 19 put into *e* through angels
Eph 1: 10 put into *e* when the times will have
Heb 9: 17 it never takes *e* while the one who
9: 18 put into *e* without blood.

EFFECTIVE* (EFFECT)

1Co 16: 9 a great door for *e* work has opened
Jas 5: 16 a righteous man is powerful and *e*.

EFFORT*

Ecc 2: 19 into which I have poured my *e*
Da 6: 14 and made every *e* until sundown
Lk 13: 24 "Make every *e* to enter
Jn 5: 44 yet make no *e* to obtain the praise
Ro 9: 16 depend on man's desire or *e*,
14: 19 make every *e* to do what leads
Gal 3: 3 to attain your goal by human *e*?
Eph 4: 3 Make every *e* to keep the unity
1Th 2: 16 to all men in their *e* to keep us
2: 17 intense longing we made every *e*
Heb 4: 11 make every *e* to enter that rest,
12: 14 Make every *e* to live in peace
2Pe 1: 5 make every *e* to add
1: 15 And I will make every *e* to see that
3: 14 make every *e* to be found spotless,

EGG

Lk 11: 12 for an *e*, will give him a scorpion?

EGLON

1. Fat king of Moab killed by Ehud (Jdg 3:12-30).
2. City in Canaan (Jos 10).

EGYPT (EGYPTIANS)

Ge 12: 10 went down to *E* to live there
37: 28 Ishmaelites, who took him to *E*.
42: 3 went down to buy grain from *E*.
45: 20 the best of all *E* will be yours.'"
46: 6 and all his offspring went to *E*.
47: 27 Now the Israelites settled in *E*
Ex 3: 11 and bring the Israelites out of *E*?"
12: 40 lived in *E* was 430 years.
12: 41 all the LORD's divisions left *E*.
32: 1 Moses who brought us up out of *E*,
Nu 11: 18 We were better off in *E*!"
14: 4 choose a leader and go back to *E*."
24: 8 "God brought them out of *E*;
Dt 6: 21 "We were slaves of Pharaoh in *E*,
1Ki 4: 30 greater than all the wisdom of *E*.
10: 28 horses were imported from *E*
11: 40 but Jeroboam fled to *E*,
14: 25 king of *E* attacked Jerusalem.
2Ch 35: 20 Neco king of *E* went up to fight
36: 3 The king of *E* dethroned him
Isa 19: 23 a highway from *E* to Assyria.
Hos 11: 1 and out of *E* I called my son.
Mt 2: 15 "Out of *E* I called my son."
Heb 11: 27 By faith he left *E*, not fearing
Rev 11: 8 is figuratively called Sodom and *E*,

EGYPTIANS (EGYPT)

Nu 14: 13 "Then the *E* will hear about it!

EHUD

Left-handed judge who delivered Israel from Moabite king, Eglon (Jdg 3:12-30).

EKRON

1Sa 5: 10 So they sent the ark of God to *E*.

ELAH

Son of Baasha; king of Israel (1Ki 16:6-14).

ELATION

Pr 28: 12 righteous triumph, there is great *e*;

ELDER* (ELDERLY ELDERS FELLOW-ELDER)

Isa 3: 2 the soothsayer and *e*,
1Ti 5: 19 an accusation against an *e*
Tit 1: 6 *e* must be blameless, the husband
2Jn : 1 The *e*, To the chosen lady
3Jn : 1 The *e*, To my dear friend Gaius,

ELDERLY* (ELDER)

Lev 19: 32 show respect for the *e*

ELDERS (ELDER)

1Ki 12: 8 rejected the advice the *e* gave him
Mt 15: 2 break the tradition of the *e*?
Mk 7: 3 holding to the tradition of the *e*.
7: 5 to the tradition of the *e* instead
Ac 11: 30 gift to the *e* by Barnabas
14: 23 and Barnabas appointed *e* for them
15: 2 the apostles and *e* about this
15: 4 the church and the apostles and *e*,
15: 6 and *e* met to consider this question.
15: 22 and *e*, with the whole church,
15: 23 The apostles and *e*, your brothers,
16: 4 and *e* in Jerusalem for the people
20: 17 to Ephesus for the *e* of the church.
21: 18 and all the *e* were present.
23: 14 They went to the chief priests and *e*
24: 1 to Caesarea with some of the *e*
1Ti 4: 14 when the body of *e* laid their hands
5: 17 The *e* who direct the affairs
Tit 1: 5 and appoint *e* in every town,
Jas 5: 14 He should call the *e* of the church
1Pe 5: 1 To the *e* among you, I appeal
Rev 4: 4 seated on them were twenty-four *e*.
4: 10 the twenty-four *e* fall

ELEAZAR

Third son of Aaron (Ex 6:23-25). Succeeded Aaron as high priest (Nu 20:26; Dt 10:6). Allotted land to tribes (Jos 14:1). Death (Jos 24:33).

ELECT* (ELECTION)

Mt 24: 22 the sake of the *e* those days will be
24: 24 miracles to deceive even the *e*—
24: 31 and they will gather his *e*
Mk 13: 20 sake of the *e*, whom he has chosen,
13: 22 and miracles to deceive the *e*—
13: 27 gather his *e* from the four winds,
Ro 11: 7 it did not obtain, but the *e* did.
1Ti 5: 21 and Christ Jesus and the *e* angels,
2Ti 2: 10 everything for the sake of the *e*,
Tit 1: 1 Christ for the faith of God's *e*
1Pe 1: 1 To God's *e*, strangers in the world,

ELECTION* (ELECT)

Ro 9: 11 God's purpose in *e* might stand:
11: 28 but as far as *e* is concerned,
2Pe 1: 10 to make your calling and *e* sure.

ELEMENTARY* (ELEMENTS)

Heb 5: 12 someone to teach you the *e* truths
6: 1 us leave the *e* teachings about

ELEMENTS* (ELEMENTARY)

2Pe 3: 10 the *e* will be destroyed by fire,
3: 12 and the *e* will melt in the heat.

ELEVATE*

2Co 11: 7 to *e* you by preaching the gospel

ELI

High priest in youth of Samuel (1Sa 1-4). Blessed Hannah (1Sa 1:12-18); raised Samuel (1Sa 2:11-26). Prophesied against because of wicked sons (1Sa 2:27-36). Death of Eli and sons (1Sa 4:11-22).

ELIHU

One of Job's friends (Job 32-37).

ELIJAH

Prophet; predicted famine in Israel (1Ki 17:1; Jas 5:17). Fed by ravens (1Ki 17:2-6). Raised Sidonian widow's son (1Ki 17:7-24). Defeated prophets of Baal at Carmel (1Ki 18:16-46). Ran from Jezebel (1Ki 19:1-9). Prophesied death of Azariah (2Ki 1). Succeeded by Elisha (1Ki 19:19-21; 2Ki 2:1-18). Taken to heaven in whirlwind (2Ki 2:11-12).

Return prophesied (Mal 4:5-6); equated with John the Baptist (Mt 17:9-13; Mk 9:9-13; Lk 1:17) Appeared with Moses in transfiguration of Jesus (Mt 17:1-8; Mk 9:1-8).

ELIMELECH

Ru 1: 3 Now *E*, Naomi's husband, died,

ELIPHAZ

1. Firstborn of Esau (Ge 36).
2. One of Job's friends (Job 4-5; 15; 22).

ELISHA

Prophet; successor of Elijah (1Ki 19:16-21); inherited his cloak (2Ki 2:1-18). Purified bad water (2Ki 2:19-22). Cursed young men (2Ki 2:23-25). Aided Israel's defeat of Moab (2Ki 3). Provided widow with oil (2Ki 4:1-7). Raised Shunammite woman's son (2Ki 4:8-37). Purified food (2Ki 4:38-41). Fed 100 men (2Ki 4:42-44). Healed Naaman's leprosy (2Ki 5). Made axe-head float (2Ki 6:1-7). Captured Arameans (2Ki 6:8-23). Political adviser to Israel (2Ki 6:24-8:6; 9:1-3; 13:14-19), Damascus (2Ki 8:7-15). Death (2Ki 13:20).

ELIZABETH*

Mother of John the Baptist, relative of Mary (Lk 1:5-58).

ELKANAH

Husband of Hannah, father of Samuel (1Sa 1-2).

ELOI*

Mt 27: 46 "E, E, *lama sabachthani*?"—
Mk 15: 34 "E, E, *lama sabachthani*?"—

ELOQUENCE* (ELOQUENT)

1Co 2: 1 come with *e* or superior wisdom

ELOQUENT* (ELOQUENCE)

Ex 4: 10 "O Lord, I have never been *e*,

ELYMAS

Ac 13: 8 *E* the sorcerer (for that is what his

EMBEDDED*

Ecc 12: 11 sayings like firmly *e* nails—

EMBERS

Pr 26: 21 As charcoal to *e* and as wood to fire

EMBITTER* (BITTER)

Col 3: 21 Fathers, do not *e* your children,

EMBODIMENT* (BODY)

Ro 2: 20 have in the law the *e* of knowledge

EMPTIED (EMPTY)

1Co 1: 17 the cross of Christ be *e* of its power.

EMPTY (EMPTIED)

Ge 1: 2 Now the earth was formless and *e*,
Job 26: 7 the northern ⌞skies⌟ over *e* space;
Isa 45: 18 he did not create it to be *e*,
55: 11 It will not return to me *e*,
Jer 4: 23 and it was formless and *e*;
Lk 1: 53 but has sent the rich away *e*.
Eph 5: 6 no-one deceive you with *e* words,
1Pe 1: 18 from the *e* way of life handed
2Pe 2: 18 For they mouth *e*, boastful words

ENABLE (ABLE)

Lk 1: 74 to *e* us to serve him without fear
Ac 4: 29 *e* your servants to speak your word

ENABLED* (ABLE)

Lev 26: 13 *e* you to walk with heads held high.
Ru 4: 13 And the LORD *e* her to conceive,
Jn 6: 65 unless the Father has *e* him."
Ac 2: 4 other tongues as the Spirit *e* them.
7: 10 and *e* him to gain the goodwill
Heb 11: 11 was *e* to become a father

ENABLES (ABLE)

Php 3: 21 by the power that *e* him

ENABLING* (ABLE)

Ac 14: 3 the message of his grace by *e* them

ENCAMPS* (CAMP)

Ps 34: 7 The angel of the LORD *e*

ENCOURAGE* (ENCOURAGED ENCOURAGEMENT ENCOURAGES ENCOURAGING)

Dt 1: 38 *E* him, because he will lead Israel
3: 28 and *e* and strengthen him,
2Sa 11: 25 Say this to *e* Joab."
19: 7 Now go out and *e* your men.
Job 16: 5 But my mouth would *e* you;
Ps 10: 17 you *e* them, and you listen
64: 5 They *e* each other in evil plans,
Isa 1: 17 *e* the oppressed.
Jer 29: 8 to the dreams you *e* them to have.
Ac 15: 32 to *e* and strengthen the brothers.
Ro 12: 8 if it is encouraging, let him *e*;
Eph 6: 22 how we are, and that he may *e* you.
Col 4: 8 and that he may *e* your hearts.
1Th 3: 2 to strengthen and *e* you
4: 18 Therefore *e* each other
5: 11 Therefore *e* one another
5: 14 those who are idle, *e* the timid,
2Th 2: 17 *e* your hearts and strengthen you
2Ti 4: 2 rebuke and *e*—with great patience
Tit 1: 9 so that he can *e* others
2: 6 *e* the young men to be
2: 15 *E* and rebuke with all authority.
Heb 3: 13 But *e* one another daily, as long
10: 25 but let us *e* one another—

ENCOURAGED* (ENCOURAGE)

Jdg 7: 11 you will be *e* to attack the camp."
20: 22 But the men of Israel *e* one another
2Ch 22: 3 for his mother *e* him
32: 6 and *e* them with these words:
35: 2 and *e* them in the service
Eze 13: 22 you *e* the wicked not to turn
Ac 9: 31 It was strengthened; and *e*
11: 23 and *e* them all to remain true
16: 40 met with the brothers and *e* them.
18: 27 the brothers *e* him and wrote
27: 36 They were all *e* and ate some food
28: 15 men Paul thanked God and was *e*.
Ro 1: 12 and I may be mutually *e*
1Co 14: 31 everyone may be instructed and *e*.
2Co 7: 4 I am greatly *e*; in all our troubles
7: 13 By all this we are *e*.
Php 1: 14 brothers in the Lord have been *e*
Col 2: 2 My purpose is that they may be *e*
1Th 3: 7 persecution we were *e* about you
Heb 6: 18 offered to us may be greatly *e*.

ENCOURAGEMENT* (ENCOURAGE)

Ac 4: 36 Barnabas (which means Son of *E*),
13: 15 a message of *e* for the people,
20: 2 speaking many words of *e*
Ro 15: 4 *e* of the Scriptures we might have
15: 5 and *e* give you a spirit of unity
1Co 14: 3 to men for their strengthening, *e*
2Co 7: 13 to our own *e*, we were especially
Php 2: 1 If you have any *e* from being united
2Th 2: 16 and by his grace gave us eternal *e*
Phm : 7 love has given me great joy and *e*,
Heb 12: 5 word of *e* that addresses you

ENCOURAGES* (ENCOURAGE)

Isa 41: 7 The craftsman *e* the goldsmith,

ENCOURAGING* (ENCOURAGE)

Ac 14: 22 *e* them to remain true to the faith.
15: 31 and were glad for its *e* message.
20: 1 for the disciples and, after *e* them,
Ro 12: 8 if it is *e*, let him encourage;
1Th 2: 12 *e*, comforting and urging you
1Pe 5: 12 *e* you and testifying that this is

ENCROACH

Pr 23: 10 or *e* on the fields of the fatherless,

END (ENDS)

Ps 119: 33 then I will keep them to the *e*.
119: 112 to the very *e*.
Pr 1: 19 Such is the *e* of all who go
5: 4 but in the *e* she is bitter as gall,
5: 11 At the *e* of your life you will groan,
14: 12 but in the *e* it leads to death.
14: 13 and joy may *e* in grief.
16: 25 but in the *e* it leads to death.
19: 20 and in the *e* you will be wise.
20: 21 will not be blessed at the *e*.
23: 32 In the *e* it bites like a snake
25: 8 for what will you do in the *e*
28: 23 in the *e* gain more favour
29: 21 he will bring grief in the *e*.
Ecc 3: 11 done from beginning to *e*.
7: 8 The *e* of a matter is better
12: 12 making many books there is no *e*,
Eze 7: 2 The *e*! The *e* has come
Mt 10: 22 firm to the *e* will be saved.
24: 13 firm to the *e* will be saved.
24: 14 nations, and then the *e* will come.
Lk 21: 9 but the *e* will not come right away
Ro 10: 4 Christ is the *e* of the law
1Co 15: 24 the *e* will come, when he hands
Rev 21: 6 Omega, the Beginning and the *E*.
22: 13 the Last, the Beginning and the *E*.

ENDS (END)

Ps 19: 4 their words to the *e* of the world.
Pr 20: 17 he *e* up with a mouth full of gravel.
Isa 49: 6 salvation to the *e* of the earth."
62: 11 proclamation to the *e* of the earth:
Ac 13: 47 salvation to the *e* of the earth.'"
Ro 10: 18 their words to the *e* of the world."

ENDURANCE* (ENDURE)

Ro 15: 4 through *e* and the encouragement
15: 5 May the God who gives *e*
2Co 1: 6 which produces in you patient *e*
6: 4 in great *e*; in troubles, hardships
Col 1: 11 might so that you may have great *e*
1Th 1: 3 and your *e* inspired by hope
1Ti 6: 11 faith, love, *e* and gentleness.
2Ti 3: 10 patience, love, *e*, persecutions,
Tit 2: 2 and sound in faith, in love and in *e*.
Rev 1: 9 and patient *e* that are ours in Jesus,
13: 10 This calls for patient *e*
14: 12 This calls for patient *e* on the part

ENDURE (ENDURANCE ENDURED ENDURES ENDURING)

Ps 72: 17 May his name *e* for ever;
Pr 12: 19 Truthful lips *e* for ever,
27: 24 for riches do not *e* for ever,
Ecc 3: 14 everything God does will *e* for ever;
Da 2: 44 to an end, but it will itself *e* for ever.
Mal 3: 2 who can *e* the day of his coming?
1Co 4: 12 when we are persecuted, we *e* it;
2Co 1: 8 far beyond our ability to *e*,
2Ti 2: 3 *E* hardship with us like a good
2: 10 Therefore I *e* everything
2: 12 if we *e*, / we will also reign
4: 5 head in all situations, *e* hardship,
Heb 12: 7 *E* hardship as discipline; God is
1Pe 2: 20 a beating for doing wrong and *e* it?
2: 20 suffer for doing good and you *e* it,
Rev 3: 10 kept my command to *e* patiently,

ENDURED* (ENDURE)

Ps 123: 3 for we have *e* much contempt.
123: 4 We have *e* much ridicule
132: 1 and all the hardships he *e*.
Ac 13: 18 and *e* their conduct forty years
2Ti 3: 11 and Lystra, the persecutions I *e*.
Heb 12: 2 set before him *e* the cross,
12: 3 him who *e* such opposition
Rev 2: 3 and have *e* hardships for my name,

ENDURES (ENDURE)

Ps 102: 12 renown *e* through all generations.
112: 9 his righteousness *e* for ever;
136: 1 *His love e for ever.*
Da 9: 15 made for yourself a name that *e*
2Co 9: 9 his righteousness *e* for ever."

ENDURING (ENDURE)
2Th 1: 4 persecutions and trials you are *e*.
1Pe 1: 23 through the living and *e* word

ENEMIES (ENEMY)
Ps 23: 5 in the presence of my *e*.
110: 1 hand until I make your *e*
Pr 16: 7 his *e* live at peace with him.
Isa 59: 18 wrath to his *e*
Mic 7: 6 a man's *e* are the members
Mt 5: 44 Love your *e* and pray
10: 36 a man's *e* will be the members
Lk 6: 27 Love your *e*, do good
6: 35 But love your *e*, do good to them,
20: 43 hand until I make your *e*
Ro 5: 10 For if, when we were God's *e*,
1Co 15: 25 reign until he has put all his *e*
Php 3: 18 many live as *e* of the cross of Christ
Heb 1: 13 hand until I make your *e*
10: 13 for his *e* to be made his footstool,

ENEMY (ENEMIES ENMITY)
Pr 24: 17 Do not gloat when your *e* falls;
25: 21 If your *e* is hungry, give him food
27: 6 but an *e* multiplies kisses.
29: 24 of a thief is his own *e*;
Lk 10: 19 to overcome all the power of the *e*;
Ro 12: 20 "If your *e* is hungry, feed him;
1Co 15: 26 The last *e* to be destroyed is death.
1Ti 5: 14 and to give the *e* no opportunity
1Pe 5: 8 Your *e* the devil prowls

ENERGY*
Col 1: 29 struggling with all his *e*, which

ENGRAVED
Isa 49: 16 I have *e* you on the palms
2Co 3: 7 which was *e* in letters on stone,

ENHANCES*
Ro 3: 7 my falsehood *e* God's truthfulness

ENJOY (JOY)
Dt 6: 2 and so that you may *e* long life.
Ps 37: 3 dwell in the land and *e* safe pasture.
Pr 28: 16 ill-gotten gain will *e* a long life.
Ecc 3: 22 better for a man than to *e* his work,
Eph 6: 3 and that you may *e* long life
Heb 11: 25 rather than to *e* the pleasures of sin
3Jn : 2 I pray that you may *e* good health

ENJOYMENT (JOY)
Ecc 5: 8 and why am I depriving myself of *e*
1Ti 6: 17 us with everything for our *e*.

ENLARGE (ENLARGES)
2Co 9: 10 *e* the harvest of your righteousness.

ENLARGES (ENLARGE)
Dt 33: 20 Blessed is he who *e* Gad's domain!

ENLIGHTENED* (LIGHT [2])
Eph 1: 18 that the eyes of your heart may be *e*
Heb 6: 4 for those who have once been *e*,

ENMITY* (ENEMY)
Ge 3: 15 And I will put *e*

ENOCH
1. Son of Cain (Ge 4:17-18).
2. Descendant of Seth; walked with God and taken by him (Ge 5:18-24; Heb 11:5). Prophet (Jude 14).

ENQUIRE
Isa 8: 19 should not a people *e* of their God?

ENSLAVED (SLAVE)
Gal 4: 9 Do you wish to be *e* by them all
Tit 3: 3 and *e* by all kinds of passions

ENSNARE (SNARE)
Pr 5: 22 of a wicked man *e* him;
Ecc 7: 26 but the sinner she will *e*.

ENSNARED* (SNARE)
Dt 7: 25 for yourselves, or you will be *e* by it
12: 30 be careful not to be *e*
Ps 9: 16 the wicked are *e* by the work
Pr 6: 2 *e* by the words of your mouth,
22: 25 and get yourself *e*.

ENTANGLED (ENTANGLES)
2Pe 2: 20 and are again *e* in it and overcome,

ENTANGLES* (ENTANGLED)
Heb 12: 1 and the sin that so easily *e*,

ENTER (ENTERED ENTERING ENTERS ENTRANCE)
Ps 95: 11 "They shall never *e* my rest."
100: 4 *E* his gates with thanksgiving
Pr 2: 10 For wisdom will *e* your heart,
Mt 5: 20 will certainly not *e* the kingdom
7: 13 "*E* through the narrow gate.
7: 21 Lord,' will *e* the kingdom of heaven
18: 3 you will never *e* the kingdom
18: 8 It is better for you to *e* life maimed
19: 17 to *e* life, obey the commandments
19: 23 men to *e* the kingdom of heaven.
Mk 9: 43 It is better for you to *e* life maimed
9: 45 It is better for you to *e* life crippled
9: 47 for you to *e* the kingdom of God
10: 15 like a little child will never *e* it."
10: 23 is for the rich to *e* the kingdom
Lk 13: 24 will try to *e* and will not be able to.
13: 24 "Make every effort to *e*
18: 17 like a little child will never *e* it."
18: 24 is for the rich to *e* the kingdom
Jn 3: 5 he cannot *e* the kingdom of God.
Heb 3: 11 'They shall never *e* my rest.'"
4: 11 make every effort to *e* that rest,

ENTERED (ENTER)
Ps 73: 17 me till I *e* the sanctuary of God;
Eze 4: 14 meat has ever *e* my mouth."
Ac 11: 8 or unclean has ever *e* my mouth.'
Ro 5: 12 as sin *e* the world through one man,
Heb 9: 12 but he *e* the Most Holy Place once

ENTERING (ENTER)
Mt 21: 31 the prostitutes are *e* the kingdom
Lk 11: 52 have hindered those who were *e*."
Heb 4: 1 the promise of *e* his rest still stands,

ENTERS (ENTER)
Mk 7: 18 you see that nothing that *e* a man
Jn 10: 2 The man who *e* by the gate is

ENTERTAIN* (ENTERTAINED ENTERTAINMENT)
Jdg 16: 25 "Bring out Samson to *e* us."
Mt 9: 4 "Why do you *e* evil thoughts
1Ti 5: 19 Do not *e* an accusation
Heb 13: 2 Do not forget to *e* strangers,

ENTERTAINED* (ENTERTAIN)
Ac 28: 7 and for three days *e* us hospitably.
Heb 13: 2 so doing some people have *e* angels

ENTERTAINMENT* (ENTERTAIN)
Da 6: 18 without any *e* being brought to him

ENTHRALLED*
Ps 45: 11 The king is *e* by your beauty;

ENTHRONED* (THRONE)
1Sa 4: 4 who is *e* between the cherubim.
2Sa 6: 2 who is *e* between the cherubim that
2Ki 19: 15 of Israel, *e* between the cherubim,
1Ch 13: 6 who is *e* between the cherubim—
Ps 2: 4 The One *e* in heaven laughs;
9: 11 to the LORD; *e* in Zion;
22: 3 Yet you are *e* as the Holy One;
29: 10 The LORD sits *e* over the flood;
29: 10 the LORD is *e* as King for ever.
55: 19 God, who is *e* for ever,
61: 7 May he be *e* in God's presence
80: 1 who sit *e* between the cherubim,
99: 1 he sits *e* between the cherubim,
102: 12 But you, O LORD, sit *e* for ever;
113: 5 the One who sits *e* on high,
132: 14 here I will sit *e*, for I have desired it
Isa 14: 13 I will sit *e* on the mount
37: 16 of Israel, *e* between the cherubim,
40: 22 He sits *e* above the circle
52: 2 rise up, sit *e*, O Jerusalem.

ENTHRONES* (THRONE)
Job 36: 7 he *e* them with kings

ENTHUSIASM*
2Co 8: 17 he is coming to you with much *e*
9: 2 and your *e* has stirred most of them

ENTICE* (ENTICED ENTICES)
Pr 1: 10 My son, if sinners *e* you,
2Pe 2: 18 they *e* people who are just escaping
Rev 2: 14 who taught Balak to *e* the Israelites

ENTICED* (ENTICE)
Dt 4: 19 do not be *e* into bowing
11: 16 or you will be *e* to turn away
2Ki 17: 21 Jeroboam *e* Israel away
Job 31: 9 If my heart has been *e* by a woman,
31: 27 so that my heart was secretly *e*
Jas 1: 14 desire, he is dragged away and *e*.

ENTICES* (ENTICE)
Dt 13: 6 your closest friend secretly *e* you,
Job 36: 18 Be careful that no-one *e* you
Pr 16: 29 A violent man *e* his neighbour

ENTIRE
Gal 5: 14 The *e* law is summed up

ENTRANCE (ENTER)
Mt 27: 60 stone in front of the *e* to the tomb
Mk 15: 46 a stone against the *e* of the tomb.
16: 3 away from the *e* of the tomb?"
Jn 11: 38 cave with a stone laid across the *e*.
20: 1 had been removed from the *e*.

ENTRUST (TRUST)
Jn 2: 24 Jesus would not *e* himself to them,
2Ti 2: 2 the presence of many witnesses *e*

ENTRUSTED (TRUST)
Jer 13: 20 Where is the flock that was *e* to you
Jn 5: 22 but has *e* all judgment to the Son,
Ro 3: 2 they have been *e* with the very
6: 17 of teaching to which you were *e*.
1Co 4: 1 as those *e* with the secret things
Gal 2: 7 I had been *e* with the task
1Th 2: 4 by God to be *e* with the gospel.
1Ti 1: 11 of the blessed God, which he *e*
6: 20 guard what has been *e* to your care.
2Ti 1: 12 able to guard what I have *e* to him
1: 14 Guard the good deposit that was *e*
Tit 1: 3 light through the preaching *e* to me
1: 7 Since an overseer is *e*
1Pe 2: 23 he *e* himself to him who judges
5: 3 not lording it over those *e* to you,
Jude : 3 once for all *e* to the saints.

ENVIES (ENVY)
Jas 4: 5 he caused to live in us *e* intensely?

ENVIOUS (ENVY)
Dt 32: 21 I will make them *e*
Pr 24: 19 or be *e* of the wicked,
Ro 10: 19 "I will make you *e*

ENVOY
Pr 13: 17 but a trustworthy *e* brings healing.

ENVY (ENVIES ENVIOUS ENVYING)
Pr 3: 31 Do not *e* a violent man
14: 30 but *e* rots the bones.

Pr 23: 17 Do not let your heart *e* sinners,
24: 1 Do not *e* wicked men,
Mk 7: 22 malice, deceit, lewdness, *e*, slander
Ro 1: 29 They are full of *e*, murder, strife,
11: 14 arouse my own people to *e*
1Co 13: 4 It does not *e*, it does not boast,
Gal 5: 21 factions and *e*; drunkenness, orgies
Php 1: 15 that some preach Christ out of *e*
1Ti 6: 4 quarrels about words that result in *e*,
Tit 3: 3 lived in malice and *e*, being hated
Jas 3: 14 But if you harbour bitter *e*
3: 16 where you have *e* and selfish
1Pe 2: 1 *e*, and slander of every kind.

ENVYING* (ENVY)

Gal 5: 26 provoking and *e* each other.

EPHAH

Eze 45: 11 The *e* and the bath are

EPHESUS

Ac 18: 19 at *E*, where Paul left Priscilla
19: 1 the interior and arrived at *E*.
Eph 1: 1 To the saints in *E*, the faithful
Rev 2: 1 the angel of the church in *E* write:

EPHRAIM

1. Second son of Joseph (Ge 41:52; 46:20). Blessed as firstborn by Jacob (Ge 48). Tribe of numbered (Nu 1:33; 26:37), blessed (Dt 33:17), allotted land (Jos 16:4-9; Eze 48:5), failed to fully possess (Jos 16:10; Jdg 1:29).

2. Synonymous with Northern Kingdom (Isa 7:17; Hos 5).

EQUAL (EQUALITY EQUITY)

Dt 33: 25 and your strength will *e* your days.
1Sa 9: 2 without *e* among the Israelites—
Isa 40: 25 who is my *e*?" says the Holy One.
46: 5 you compare me or count me *e*?
Da 1: 19 and he found none *e* to Daniel,
Jn 5: 18 making himself *e* with God.
1Co 12: 25 that its parts should have *e* concern
2Co 2: 16 And who is *e* to such a task?

EQUALITY* (EQUAL)

2Co 8: 13 pressed, but that there might be *e*.
8: 14 Then there will be *e*, as it is written:
Php 2: 6 did not consider *e*

EQUIP* (EQUIPPED)

Heb 13: 21 *e* you with everything good

EQUIPPED (EQUIP)

2Ti 3: 17 man of God may be thoroughly *e*

EQUITY* (EQUAL)

Ps 96: 10 he will judge the peoples with *e*.
98: 9 and the peoples with *e*.
99: 4 you have established *e*;

ERODES*

Job 14: 18 "But as a mountain *e* and crumbles

ERROR (ERRORS)

Jas 5: 20 Whoever turns a sinner from the *e*
2Pe 2: 18 escaping from those who live in *e*.

ERRORS* (ERROR)

Ps 19: 12 Who can discern his *e*?
Ecc 10: 4 calmness can lay great *e* to rest.

ESAU

Firstborn of Isaac, twin of Jacob (Ge 25:21-26). Also called Edom (Ge 25:30). Sold Jacob his birthright (Ge 25:29-34); lost blessing (Ge 27). Married Hittites (Ge 26:34), Ishmaelites (Ge 28:6-9). Reconciled to Jacob (Ge 22). Genealogy (Ge 36). The LORD chose Jacob over Esau (Mal 1:2-3), but gave Esau land (Dt 2:2-12). Descendants eventually obliterated (Ob 1-21; Jer 49:7-22).

ESCAPE (ESCAPED ESCAPES ESCAPING)

Ps 68: 20 from the Sovereign LORD comes *e*
Pr 11: 9 through knowledge the righteous *e*.
Ro 2: 3 think you will *e* God's judgment?
1Th 5: 3 woman, and they will not *e*.
2Ti 2: 26 and *e* from the trap of the devil,
Heb 2: 3 how shall we *e* if we ignore such
12: 25 If they did not *e* when they refused
2Pe 1: 4 and *e* the corruption in the world

ESCAPED (ESCAPE)

2Pe 2: 20 If they have *e* the corruption

ESCAPES (ESCAPE)

Pr 12: 13 but a righteous man *e* trouble.

ESCAPING (ESCAPE)

1Co 3: 15 only as one *e* through the flames.
2Pe 2: 18 they entice people who are just *e*

ESTABLISH (ESTABLISHED ESTABLISHES)

Ge 6: 18 But I will *e* my covenant with you,
17: 21 But my covenant I will *e* with Isaac
2Sa 7: 11 the LORD himself will *e* a house
1Ki 9: 5 I will *e* your royal throne
1Ch 28: 7 I will *e* his kingdom for ever
Ps 90: 17 *e* the work of our hands for us—
Isa 26: 12 LORD, you *e* peace for us;
Ro 10: 3 God and sought to *e* their own,
16: 25 able to *e* you by my gospel
Heb 10: 9 sets aside the first to *e* the second.

ESTABLISHED (ESTABLISH)

Ge 9: 17 the sign of the covenant I have *e*
Ex 6: 4 also *e* my covenant with them
Pr 16: 12 a throne is *e* through righteousness.

ESTABLISHES (ESTABLISH)

Job 25: 2 he *e* order in the heights of heaven.
Isa 42: 4 till he *e* justice on earth.

ESTATE

Ps 136: 23 who remembered us in our low *e*

ESTEEMED

Pr 22: 1 to be *e* is better than silver or gold.
Isa 53: 3 he was despised, and we *e* him not.

ESTHER

Jewess, originally named Hadassah, who lived in Persia; cousin of Mordecai (Est 2:7). Chosen queen of Xerxes (Est 2:8-18). Persuaded by Mordecai to foil Haman's plan to exterminate the Jews (Est 3-4). Revealed Haman's plans to Xerxes, resulting in Haman's death (Est 7), the Jews' preservation (Est 8-9), Mordecai's exaltation (Est 8:15; 9:4; 10). Decreed celebration of Purim (Est 9:18-32).

ETERNAL* (ETERNALLY ETERNITY)

Ge 21: 33 the name of the LORD, the *E* God.
Dt 33: 27 The *e* God is your refuge,
1Ki 10: 9 of the LORD's *e* love for Israel,
Ps 16: 11 with *e* pleasures at your right hand.
21: 6 you have granted him *e* blessings
111: 10 To him belongs *e* praise.
119: 89 Your word, O LORD, is *e*;
119: 160 all your righteous laws are *e*.
Ecc 12: 5 Then man goes to his *e* home
Isa 26: 4 LORD, the LORD, is the Rock *e*.
47: 7 the *e* queen!'
Jer 10: 10 he is the living God, the *e* King.
Da 4: 3 His kingdom is an *e* kingdom;
4: 34 His dominion is an *e* dominion;
Hab 3: 6 His ways are *e*.
Mt 18: 8 two feet and be thrown into *e* fire.
19: 16 good thing must I do to get *e* life?"
19: 29 as much and will inherit *e* life.
25: 41 into the *e* fire prepared for the devil
25: 46 but the righteous to *e* life."
25: 46 they will go away to *e* punishment,
Mk 3: 29 be forgiven; he is guilty of an *e* sin."
10: 17 "what must I do to inherit *e* life?"
10: 30 and in the age to come, *e* life.
Lk 10: 25 "what must I do to inherit *e* life?"
16: 9 will be welcomed into *e* dwellings.
18: 18 what must I do to inherit *e* life?"
18: 30 and, in the age to come, *e* life."
Jn 3: 15 believes in him may have *e* life.
3: 16 him shall not perish but have *e* life.
3: 36 believes in the Son has *e* life,
4: 14 spring of water welling up to *e* life."
4: 36 now he harvests the crop for *e* life,
5: 24 believes him who sent me has *e* life
5: 39 that by them you possess *e* life.
6: 27 but for food that endures to *e* life,
6: 40 believes in him shall have *e* life,
6: 54 and drinks my blood has *e* life,
6: 68 You have the words of *e* life.
10: 28 I give them *e* life, and they shall
12: 25 in this world will keep it for *e* life.
12: 50 that his command leads to *e* life.
17: 2 all people that he might give *e* life
17: 3 this is *e* life: that they may know
Ac 13: 46 yourselves worthy of *e* life,
13: 48 were appointed for *e* life believed.
Ro 1: 20 his *e* power and divine nature—
2: 7 and immortality, he will give *e* life.
5: 21 righteousness to bring *e* life
6: 22 to holiness, and the result is *e* life.
6: 23 but the gift of God is *e* life
16: 26 by the command of the *e* God,
2Co 4: 17 for us an *e* glory that far outweighs
4: 18 temporary, but what is unseen is *e*.
5: 1 from God, an *e* house in heaven,
Gal 6: 8 from the Spirit will reap *e* life.
Eph 3: 11 to his *e* purpose which he
2Th 2: 16 his grace gave us *e* encouragement
1Ti 1: 16 believe on him and receive *e* life.
1: 17 Now to the King *e*, immortal,
6: 12 Take hold of the *e* life
2Ti 2: 10 is in Christ Jesus, with *e* glory.
Tit 1: 2 resting on the hope of *e* life,
3: 7 heirs having the hope of *e* life.
Heb 5: 9 he became the source of *e* salvation
6: 2 of the dead, and *e* judgment.
9: 12 having obtained *e* redemption.
9: 14 through the *e* Spirit offered himself
9: 15 the promised *e* inheritance—
13: 20 of the *e* covenant brought back
1Pe 5: 10 you to his *e* glory in Christ,
2Pe 1: 11 into the *e* kingdom of our Lord
1Jn 1: 2 and we proclaim to you the *e* life,
2: 25 what he promised us—even *e* life.
3: 15 know that no murderer has *e* life
5: 11 God has given us *e* life,
5: 13 you may know that you have *e* life.
5: 20 He is the true God and *e* life.
Jude : 7 who suffer the punishment of *e* fire.
: 21 Christ to bring you to *e* life.
Rev 14: 6 and he had the *e* gospel to proclaim

ETERNALLY* (ETERNAL)

Gal 1: 8 let him be *e* condemned! As we
1: 9 let him be *e* condemned! Am I now

ETERNITY* (ETERNAL)

Ps 93: 2 you are from all *e*.
Pr 8: 23 I was appointed from *e*,
Ecc 3: 11 also set *e* in the hearts of men;

ETHIOPIAN*

Jer 13: 23 Can the *E* change his skin
Ac 8: 27 and on his way he met an *E* eunuch

EUNUCH (EUNUCHS)

Ac 8: 27 on his way he met an Ethiopian *e*,

EUNUCHS (EUNUCH)

Isa 56: 4 "To the *e* who keep my Sabbaths,
Mt 19: 12 For some are *e* because they were

EUTYCHUS*

Ac 20: 9 was a young man named *E*,

EVANGELIST* (EVANGELISTS)

Ac 21: 8 stayed at the house of Philip the *e*,

2Ti 4: 5 hardship, do the work of an e,

EVANGELISTS* (EVANGELIST)
Eph 4: 11 some to be prophets, some to be e,

EVE*
Ge 3: 20 Adam named his wife E,
4: 1 Adam lay with his wife E,
2Co 11: 3 as E was deceived by the serpent's
1Ti 2: 13 For Adam was formed first, then E

EVEN-TEMPERED* (TEMPER)
Pr 17: 27 and a man of understanding is e.

EVENING
Ge 1: 5 there was e, and there was morning

EVER (EVERLASTING EVERMORE)
Ge 3: 22 the tree of life and eat, and live for e.
6: 3 Spirit will not contend with man for e,
Ex 3: 15 This is my name for e, the name
15: 18 Lord will reign for e and e.
Dt 8: 19 If you e forget the Lord your
2Sa 7: 26 so that your name will be great for e.
1Ki 2: 33 may there be the LORD's peace for e.
3: 12 anyone like you, nor will there e be.
9: 3 by putting my Name there for e.
1Ch 16: 15 He remembers his covenant for e,
16: 34 his love endures for e.
16: 41 "for his love endures for e."
17: 24 and that your name will be great for e.
2Ch 5: 13 his love endures for e.
20: 21 for his love endures for e.
Job 4: 7 were the upright e destroyed?
Ps 5: 11 let them e sing for joy.
9: 7 The LORD reigns for e
10: 16 The LORD is King for e and e
21: 4 length of days, for e and e
23: 6 dwell in the house of the LORD for e
25: 3 will e be put to shame
25: 15 My eyes are e on the LORD,
26: 3 for your Love is e before me,
28: 9 be their shepherd and carry them for e
29: 10 The Lord is enthroned as King for e.
33: 11 the plans of the LORD stand firm for e
37: 28 They will be protected for e
44: 8 and we will praise your name for e
45: 6 O God, will last for e and e
45: 17 nations will praise you for e and e.
46: 1 an e present help in trouble
48: 14 For this God is our God for e and e.
52: 8 God's unfailing love for e and e
61: 4 I long to dwell in your tent for e
61: 8 will I e sing praise to your name
71: 6 I will e praise your
72: 19 Praise be to his glorious name for e
73: 26 and my portion for e
77: 8 Has his unfailing love vanished for e?
79: 13 will praise you for e;
81: 15 and their punishment would last for e.
84: 4 they are e praising you
86: 12 I will glorify your name for e
89: 1 of the LORD's great love for e
89: 33 nor will I e betray my faithfulness.
92: 8 But you, O LORD, are exalted for e.
100: 5 is good and his love endures for e.
102: 12 But you, O LORD, sit enthroned for e
104: 31 of the LORD endure for e
107: 1 his love endures for e
110: 4 "You are a priest for e
111: 3 and his righteousness endures for e.
111: 8 They are steadfast for e and e
112: 6 man will be remembered for e.
117: 2 of the LORD endures for e
118: 1 his love endures for e
119: 44 your law, for e and e
119: 98 for they are e with me
119: 111 Your statutes are my heritage for e
119: 152 that you established them to last for e
132: 12 sit on your throne for e and e
136: 1 *His love endures for* e.
145: 1 I will praise your name for e and e
145: 2 and extol your name for e and e
Ps 145: 21 his holy name for e and e
146: 6 the LORD, who remains faithful for e
Pr 4: 18 shining e brighter till the full light
5: 19 may you e be captivated
10: 25 but the righteous stand firm for e.
27: 24 for riches do not endure for e
Isa 25: 8 he will swallow up death for e
26: 4 Trust in the LORD for e,
32: 17 will be quietness and confidence for e
40: 8 but the word of our God stands for e
51: 6 But my salvation will last for e
51: 8 But my righteousness will last for e
57: 15 he who lives for e, whose name is holy:
59: 21 from this time on and for e
66: 8 Who has e heard of such a thing?
66: 8 Who has e seen such things?
Jer 7: 7 I gave your forefathers for e and e.
25: 5 and your fathers for e and e
31: 36 the descendants of Israel e cease
33: 11 his love endures for e
Eze 37: 26 put my sanctuary among them for e
Da 2: 20 be to the name of God for e and e
2: 44 to an end, but it will itself endure for e
3: 9 live for e! You have issued a decree,
7: 18 for e—yes, for e and e
12: 3 like the stars for e and e
Mic 4: 5 our God for e and e
Mt 13: 14 you will be e seeing but never
13: 14 you will be e hearing
Mk 4: 12 e hearing but never understanding
Jn 1: 18 No-one has e seen God
6: 51 eats of this bread, he will live for e
14: 16 Counsellor to be with you for e—
Ro 9: 5 who is God over all, for e praised!
16: 27 to the only wise God be glory for e
1Co 9: 25 to get a crown that will last for e
Gal 1: 5 to whom be glory for e and e
Eph 3: 21 all generations, for e and e!
Php 4: 20 and Father be glory for e and e
1Th 4: 17 And so we will be with the Lord for e
1Ti 1: 17 be honour and glory for e and e
2Ti 4: 18 To him be glory for e and e
Heb 1: 8 O God, will last for e and e
5: 6 You are a priest for e
7: 17 You are a priest for e
7: 24 Jesus lives for e, he has a permanent
13: 8 same yesterday and today and for e
13: 21 to whom be glory for e and e
1Pe 1: 25 but the word of the Lord stands for e
4: 11 the glory and the power for e and e
5: 11 To him be the power for e and e
Jn 2: 17 who does the will of God lives for e
4: 12 No-one has e seen God;
2Jn : 2 lives in us and will be with us for e
Rev 1: 6 him be glory and power for e and e!
1: 18 and behold I am alive for e and e!
21: 27 Nothing impure will e enter it
22: 5 And they will reign for e and e

EVER-INCREASING* (INCREASE)
Ro 6: 19 to impurity and to e wickedness,
2Co 3: 18 into his likeness with e glory,

EVERLASTING* (EVER)
Ge 9: 16 and remember the e covenant
17: 7 an e covenant between me and you
17: 8 I will give as an e possession to you
17: 13 in your flesh is to be an e covenant.
17: 19 an e covenant for his descendants
48: 4 e possession to your descendants
Nu 18: 19 It is an e covenant of salt
Dt 33: 15 and the fruitfulness of the e hills;
33: 27 and underneath are the e arms.
2Sa 23: 5 made with me an e covenant,
1Ch 16: 17 to Israel as an e covenant:
16: 36 from e to e.
29: 10 from e to e.
Ezr 9: 12 to your children as an e inheritance
Ne 9: 5 your God, who is from e to e."
Ps 41: 13 from e to e.
52: 5 God will bring you down to e ruin:
74: 3 through these e ruins,
78: 66 he put them to e shame.
Ps 90: 2 from e to e you are God.
103: 17 But from e to e
105: 10 to Israel as an e covenant:
106: 48 from e to e.
119: 142 Your righteousness is e
139: 24 and lead me in the way e.
145: 13 Your kingdom is an e kingdom,
Isa 9: 6 E Father, Prince of Peace.
24: 5 and broken the e covenant.
30: 8 it may be an e witness.
33: 14 Who of us can dwell with e burning
35: 10 e joy will crown their heads.
40: 28 The LORD is the e God,
45: 17 the LORD with an e salvation;
45: 17 to ages e.
51: 11 e joy will crown their heads.
54: 8 but with e kindness
55: 3 I will make an e covenant with you,
55: 13 for an e sign,
56: 5 I will give them an e name
60: 15 I will make you the e pride
60: 19 for the LORD will be your e light,
60: 20 the LORD will be your e light,
61: 7 and e joy will be theirs.
61: 8 and make an e covenant with them.
63: 12 to gain for himself e renown,
Jer 5: 22 an e barrier it cannot cross.
23: 40 I will bring upon you e disgrace—
23: 40 e shame that will not be forgotten."
25: 9 of horror and scorn, and an e ruin.
31: 3 "I have loved you with an e love;
32: 40 I will make an e covenant
50: 5 the LORD in an e covenant
Eze 16: 60 and I will establish an e covenant
37: 26 with them; it will be an e covenant.
Da 7: 14 dominion is an e dominion that will
7: 27 His kingdom will be an e kingdom,
9: 24 to bring in e righteousness,
12: 2 others to shame and e contempt.
12: 2 some to e life, others to shame
Mic 6: 2 you e foundations of the earth.
Hab 1: 12 O LORD, are you not from e?
Jn 6: 47 the truth, he who believes has e life.
2Th 1: 9 punished with e destruction
Jude : 6 bound with e chains for judgment

EVERMORE
Ps 113: 2 both now and for e.

EVIDENCE (EVIDENT)
Jn 14: 11 on the e of the miracles themselves.
Ac 11: 23 and saw the e of the grace of God,
2Th 1: 5 All this is e that God's judgment is
Jas 2: 20 do you want e that faith

EVIDENT (EVIDENCE)
Php 4: 5 Let your gentleness be e to all.

EVIL (EVILDOER EVILDOERS EVILS)
Ge 2: 9 of the knowledge of good and e.
3: 5 be like God, knowing good and e."
6: 5 of his heart was only e all the time.
Ex 32: 22 how prone these people are to e.
Jdg 2: 11 Then the Israelites did e in the eyes
3: 7 The Israelites did e in the eyes
3: 12 Once again the Israelites did e
4: 1 the Israelites once again did e
6: 1 Again the Israelites did e
10: 6 Again the Israelites did e
13: 1 Again the Israelites did e
1Ki 11: 6 So Solomon did e in the eyes
16: 25 But Omri did e in the eyes
2Ki 15: 24 Pekahiah did e in the eyes
Job 1: 1 he feared God and shunned e.
1: 8 a man who fears God and shuns e."
34: 10 Far be it from God to do e,
36: 21 Beware of turning to e,
Ps 5: 4 not a God who takes pleasure in e;
23: 4 I will fear no e,
34: 13 keep your tongue from e
34: 14 Turn from e and do good;
34: 16 is against those who do e,
37: 1 Do not fret because of e men

Ps 37: 8 do not fret—it leads only to *e*.
37: 27 Turn from *e* and do good;
49: 5 fear when *e* days come,
51: 4 and done what is *e* in your sight,
97: 10 those who love the LORD hate *e*,
101: 4 I will have nothing to do with *e*.
141: 4 not my heart be drawn to what is *e*,
Pr 4: 27 keep your foot from *e*.
8: 13 To fear the LORD is to hate *e*;
10: 23 A fool finds pleasure in *e* conduct,
11: 19 he who pursues *e* goes to his death.
11: 27 *e* comes to him who searches for it.
14: 16 man fears the LORD and shuns *e*,
17: 13 If a man pays back *e* for good,
20: 30 Blows and wounds cleanse away *e*,
24: 19 Do not fret because of *e* men
24: 20 for the *e* man has no future hope,
26: 23 are fervent lips with an *e* heart.
28: 5 *E* men do not understand justice,
29: 6 An *e* man is snared by his own sin,
Ecc 12: 14 whether it is good or *e*.
Isa 5: 20 Woe to those who call *e* good
13: 11 I will punish the world for its *e*,
55: 7 and the *e* man his thoughts.
Jer 4: 14 wash the *e* from your heart
18: 8 nation I warned repents of its *e*,
18: 11 So turn from your *e* ways,
Eze 33: 11 Turn! Turn from your *e* ways!
33: 13 he will die for the *e* he has done.
33: 15 and does no *e*, he will surely live;
Am 5: 13 for the times are *e*.
Hab 1: 13 Your eyes are too pure to look on *e*;
Zec 8: 17 do not plot *e* against your neighbour,
Mt 5: 45 He causes his sun to rise on the *e*
6: 13 but deliver us from the *e* one.'
7: 11 If you, then, though you are *e*,
12: 34 you who are *e* say anything good?
12: 35 and the *e* man brings *e* things out
12: 35 out of the *e* stored up in him.
12: 43 "When an *e* spirit comes out
15: 19 out of the heart come *e* thoughts,
Mk 7: 21 come *e* thoughts, sexual
Lk 6: 45 and the *e* man brings *e* things out
11: 13 If you then, though you are *e*,
Jn 3: 19 of light because their deeds were *e*.
3: 20 Everyone who does *e* hates
17: 15 you protect them from the *e* one.
Ro 1: 30 they invent ways of doing *e*;
2: 8 who reject the truth and follow *e*,
2: 9 for every human being who does *e*:
3: 8 "Let us do *e* that good may result"?
6: 12 body so that you obey its *e* desires.
7: 19 no, the *e* I do not want to do—
7: 21 to do good, *e* is right there with me.
12: 9 Hate what is *e*; cling
12: 17 Do not repay anyone *e* for *e*.
12: 21 Do not be overcome by *e*,
14: 16 good to be spoken of as *e*.
16: 19 and innocent about what is *e*.
1Co 13: 6 Love does not delight in *e*
14: 20 In regard to *e* be infants,
Eph 5: 16 because the days are *e*.
6: 12 forces of *e* in the heavenly realms.
6: 16 all the flaming arrows of the *e* one.
Col 3: 5 impurity, lust, *e* desires and greed,
1Th 5: 22 Avoid every kind of *e*.
2Th 3: 3 and protect you from the *e* one.
1Ti 6: 10 of money is a root of all kinds of *e*.
2Ti 2: 22 Flee the *e* desires of youth,
3: 6 are swayed by all kinds of *e* desires,
3: 13 while *e* men and impostors will go
Heb 5: 14 to distinguish good from *e*.
Jas 1: 13 For God cannot be tempted by *e*,
1: 21 and the *e* that is so prevalent,
3: 6 a world of *e* among the parts
3: 8 It is a restless *e*, full
1Pe 2: 16 your freedom as a cover-up for *e*;
3: 9 Do not repay *e* with *e* or insult
3: 10 must keep his tongue from *e*
3: 17 for doing good than for doing *e*.
1Jn 2: 13 you have overcome the *e* one.
2: 14 and you have overcome the *e* one.
3: 12 who belonged to the *e* one
5: 18 and the *e* one cannot harm him.
5: 19 is under the control of the *e* one.
3Jn : 11 do not imitate what is *e*

EVILDOER* (EVIL)

2Sa 3: 39 the LORD repay the *e* according
Ps 101: 8 I will cut off every *e*
Mal 4: 1 and every *e* will be stubble,

EVILDOERS* (EVIL)

1Sa 24: 13 saying goes, 'From *e* come evil
Job 8: 20 or strengthen the hands of *e*.
34: 8 He keeps company with *e*;
34: 22 where *e* can hide.
Ps 14: 4 Will *e* never learn—
14: 6 You *e* frustrate the plans
26: 5 I abhor the assembly of *e*
36: 12 See how the *e* lie fallen—
53: 4 Will the *e* never learn—
59: 2 Deliver me from *e*
64: 2 from that noisy crowd of *e*,
92: 7 and all *e* flourish,
92: 9 all *e* will be scattered.
94: 4 all the *e* are full of boasting.
94: 16 will take a stand for me against *e*?
119: 115 Away from me, you *e*,
125: 5 the LORD will banish with the *e*.
141: 4 deeds with men who are *e*;
141: 5 ever against the deeds of *e*;
141: 9 from the traps set by *e*.
Pr 21: 15 but terror to *e*.
Isa 1: 4 a brood of *e*,
31: 2 against those who help *e*.
Jer 23: 14 They strengthen the hands of *e*,
Hos 10: 9 the *e* in Gibeah?
Mal 3: 15 Certainly the *e* prosper, and
Mt 7: 23 you *e*!' "Therefore everyone who
Lk 13: 27 Away from me, all you *e*!'
18: 11 *e*, adulterers—or even like this tax

EVILS* (EVIL)

Mk 7: 23 All these *e* come from inside

EWE

2Sa 12: 3 one little *e* lamb he had bought.

EXACT*

Ge 43: 21 the *e* weight—in the mouth
Est 4: 7 including the *e* amount
Mt 2: 7 from them the *e* time the star had
Jn 4: 53 realised that this was the *e* time
Ac 17: 26 the *e* places where they should live.
Heb 1: 3 the *e* representation of his being,

EXALT* (EXALTED EXALTS)

Ex 15: 2 my father's God, and I will *e* him.
Jos 3: 7 begin to *e* you in the eyes
1Sa 2: 10 and *e* the horn of his anointed."
1Ch 25: 5 the promises of God to *e* him.
29: 12 power to *e* and give strength to all.
Job 19: 5 If indeed you would *e* yourselves
Ps 30: 1 I will *e* you, O LORD,
34: 3 let us *e* his name together.
35: 26 may all who *e* themselves over me
37: 34 He will *e* you to inherit the land;
38: 16 *e* themselves over me
75: 6 or from the desert can *e* a man.
89: 17 and by your favour you *e* our horn.
99: 5 *E* the LORD our God
99: 9 *E* the LORD our God
107: 32 Let them *e* him in the assembly
118: 28 you are my God, and I will *e* you.
145: 1 I will *e* you, my God the King;
Pr 4: 8 Esteem her, and she will *e* you;
25: 6 Do not *e* yourself in the king's
Isa 24: 15 *e* the name of the LORD, the God
25: 1 I will *e* you and praise your name,
Eze 29: 15 and will never again *e* itself
Da 4: 37 *e* and glorify the King of heaven,
11: 36 He will *e* and magnify himself
11: 37 but will *e* himself above them all.
Hos 11: 7 he will by no means *e* them.

EXALTED* (EXALT)

Ex 15: 1 for he is highly *e*.
15: 21 for he is highly *e*.
Nu 24: 7 their kingdom will be *e*.
Jos 4: 14 That day the LORD *e* Joshua
2Sa 5: 12 and had *e* his kingdom for the sake
22: 47 *E* be God, the Rock, my Saviour!
22: 49 You *e* me above my foes;
23: 1 of the man *e* by the Most High,
1Ch 14: 2 that his kingdom had been highly *e*
17: 17 as though I were the most *e* of men,
29: 11 you are *e* as head over all.
29: 25 The LORD highly *e* Solomon
Ne 9: 5 and may it be *e* above all blessing
Job 24: 24 For a little while they are *e*,
36: 22 "God is *e* in his power.
37: 23 beyond our reach and *e* in power;
Ps 18: 46 *E* be God my Saviour!
18: 48 You *e* me above my foes;
21: 13 Be *e*, O LORD, in your strength;
27: 6 Then my head will be *e*
35: 27 they always say, "The LORD be *e*,
40: 16 "The LORD be *e*!"
46: 10 I will be *e* among the nations,
46: 10 I will be *e* in the earth."
47: 9 he is greatly *e*.
57: 5 Be *e*, O God, above the heavens;
57: 11 Be *e*, O God, above the heavens;
70: 4 "Let God be *e*!"
89: 13 hand is strong, your right hand *e*.
89: 19 I have *e* a young man
89: 24 through my name his horn will be *e*
89: 27 the most *e* of the kings of the earth.
89: 42 You have *e* the right hand
92: 8 But you, O LORD, are *e* for ever.
92: 10 You have *e* my horn like that
97: 9 you are *e* far above all gods.
99: 2 he is *e* over all the nations.
108: 5 Be *e*, O God, above the heavens,
113: 4 The LORD is *e* over all the nations
138: 2 for you have *e* above all things
148: 13 for his name alone is *e*;
Pr 11: 11 of the upright a city is *e*,
30: 32 have played the fool and *e* yourself,
Isa 2: 11 the LORD alone will be *e*
2: 12 for all that is *e*
2: 17 the LORD alone will be *e*
5: 16 the LORD Almighty will be *e*
6: 1 *e*, and the train of his robe filled
12: 4 and proclaim that his name is *e*.
24: 4 the *e* of the earth languish.
33: 5 The LORD is *e*, for he dwells
33: 10 "Now will I be *e*;
52: 13 be raised and lifted up and highly *e*.
Jer 17: 12 A glorious throne, *e*
La 2: 17 he has *e* the horn of your foes.
Eze 21: 26 The lowly will be *e* and the *e* will be
Hos 13: 1 he was *e* in Israel.
Mic 6: 6 and bow down before the *e* God?
Mt 23: 12 whoever humbles himself will be *e*.
Lk 14: 11 he who humbles himself will be *e*."
18: 14 he who humbles himself will be *e*."
Ac 2: 33 *E* to the right hand of God,
5: 31 God *e* him to his own right hand
Php 1: 20 always Christ will be *e* in my body,
2: 9 Therefore God *e* him
Heb 7: 26 from sinners, *e* above the heavens.

EXALTS* (EXALT)

1Sa 2: 7 he humbles and he *e*.
Job 36: 7 and *e* them for ever.
Ps 75: 7 He brings one down, he *e* another.
Pr 14: 34 Righteousness *e* a nation,
Mt 23: 12 For whoever *e* himself will be
Lk 14: 11 For everyone who *e* himself will be
18: 14 For everyone who *e* himself will be
2Th 2: 4 *e* himself over everything that is

EXAMINE (EXAMINED EXAMINES)

Ps 11: 4 his eyes *e* them.
17: 3 you probe my heart and *e* me
26: 2 *e* my heart and my mind;
Jer 17: 10 and *e* the mind,

Jer 20:12 Almighty, you who *e* the righteous
La 3:40 Let us *e* our ways and test them,
1Co 11:28 A man ought to *e* himself
2Co 13:5 *E* yourselves to see whether you

EXAMINED (EXAMINE)
Job 13:9 Would it turn out well if he *e* you?
Ac 17:11 *e* the Scriptures every day to see

EXAMINES (EXAMINE)
Ps 11:5 The LORD *e* the righteous,
Pr 5:21 and he *e* all his paths.

EXAMPLE* (EXAMPLES)
2Ki 14:3 In everything he followed the *e*
Ecc 9:13 also saw under the sun this *e*
Eze 14:8 and make him an *e* and a byword.
Jn 13:15 have set you an *e* that you should
Ro 7:2 as long as he lives? For *e*,
1Co 11:1 Follow my *e*, as I follow
11:1 as I follow the *e* of Christ.
Gal 3:15 let me take an *e* from everyday life.
Php 3:17 Join with others in following my *e*,
2Th 3:7 how you ought to follow our *e*.
1Ti 1:16 as an *e* for those who would believe
4:12 set an *e* for the believers in speech,
Tit 2:7 In everything set them an *e*
Heb 4:11 fall by following their *e*
Jas 3:4 Or take ships as an *e*.
5:10 as an *e* of patience in the face
1Pe 2:21 leaving you an *e*, that you should
2Pe 2:6 made them an *e* of what is going
Jude :7 as an *e* of those who suffer

EXAMPLES* (EXAMPLE)
1Co 10:6 Now these things occurred as *e*,
10:11 as *e* and were written down
1Pe 5:3 to you, but being *e* to the flock.

EXASPERATE*
Eph 6:4 Fathers, do not *e* your children;

EXCEL* (EXCELLENT)
Ge 49:4 as the waters, you will no longer *e*,
1Co 14:12 to *e* in gifts that build up the church
2Co 8:7 But just as you *e* in everything—
8:7 also *e* in this grace of giving.

EXCELLENT (EXCEL)
1Co 12:31 now I will show you the most *e* way
Php 4:8 if anything is *e* or praiseworthy—
1Ti 3:13 have served well gain an *e* standing
Tit 3:8 These things are *e* and profitable

EXCESSIVE
Eze 18:8 or take *e* interest.
2Co 2:7 not be overwhelmed by *e* sorrow.

EXCHANGE (EXCHANGED)
Mt 16:26 Or what can a man give in *e*
Mk 8:37 Or what can a man give in *e*
2Co 6:13 As a fair *e*—I speak

EXCHANGED (EXCHANGE)
Ps 106:20 They *e* their Glory
Jer 2:11 But my people have *e* their Glory
Hos 4:7 they *e* their Glory
Ro 1:23 *e* the glory of the immortal God
1:25 They *e* the truth of God for a lie,
1:26 their women *e* natural relations

EXCLAIM
Ps 35:10 My whole being will *e*,

EXCUSE* (EXCUSES)
Ps 25:3 who are treacherous without *e*.
Lk 14:18 Please *e* me.'
14:19 Please *e* me.'
Jn 15:22 they have no *e* for their sin.
Ro 1:20 so that men are without *e*.
2:1 You, therefore, have no *e*,

EXCUSES* (EXCUSE)
Lk 14:18 "But they all alike began to make *e*.

EXERTED*
Eph 1:20 which he *e* in Christ

EXHORT*
1Ti 5:1 but *e* him as if he were your father.

EXILE
2Ki 17:23 taken from their homeland into *e*
25:11 into *e* the people who remained

EXISTED* (EXISTS)
2Pe 3:5 ago by God's word the heavens *e*

EXISTS (EXISTED)
Heb 2:10 and through whom everything *e*,
11:6 to him must believe that he *e*

EXPANSE
Ge 1:7 So God made the *e* and separated
1:8 God called the *e* "sky".

EXPECT (EXPECTATION EXPECTED EXPECTING)
Mt 24:44 at an hour when you do not *e* him.
Lk 12:40 at an hour when you do not *e* him."
Php 1:20 I eagerly *e* and hope that I will

EXPECTATION (EXPECT)
Ro 8:19 waits in eager *e* for the sons
Heb 10:27 but only a fearful *e* of judgment

EXPECTED (EXPECT)
Pr 11:7 all he *e* from his power comes
Hag 1:9 "You *e* much, but see, it turned out

EXPECTING (EXPECT)
Lk 6:35 and lend to them without *e*

EXPEL* (EXPELLED)
1Co 5:13 *E* the wicked man from among you

EXPELLED (EXPEL)
Eze 28:16 and I *e* you, O guardian cherub,

EXPENSE (EXPENSIVE)
1Co 9:7 Who serves as a soldier at his own *e*

EXPENSIVE* (EXPENSE)
Mt 26:7 jar of very *e* perfume,
Mk 14:3 jar of very *e* perfume,
Lk 7:25 those who wear *e* clothes
Jn 12:3 a pint of pure nard, an *e* perfume;
1Ti 2:9 or gold or pearls or *e* clothes,

EXPERT
1Co 3:10 I laid a foundation as an *e* builder,

EXPLAINING (EXPLAINS)
Ac 17:3 *e* and proving that the Christ had

EXPLAINS* (EXPLAINING)
Ac 8:31 he said, "unless someone *e* it to me

EXPLOIT* (EXPLOITED EXPLOITING EXPLOITS)
Pr 22:22 Do not *e* the poor because they are
Isa 58:3 and *e* all your workers.
2Co 12:17 Did I *e* you through any
12:18 Titus did not *e* you, did he?
2Pe 2:3 greed these teachers will *e* you

EXPLOITED* (EXPLOIT)
2Co 7:2 no-one, we have *e* no-one.

EXPLOITING* (EXPLOIT)
Jas 2:6 Is it not the rich who are *e* you?

EXPLOITS (EXPLOIT)
2Co 11:20 or *e* you or takes advantage of you

EXPLORE
Nu 13:2 "Send some men to *e* the land

EXPOSE (EXPOSED)
1Co 4:5 will *e* the motives of men's hearts.
Eph 5:11 of darkness, but rather *e* them.

EXPOSED (EXPOSE)
Jn 3:20 for fear that his deeds will be *e*.
Eph 5:13 everything *e* by the light becomes

EXPRESS (EXPRESSING)
Ro 8:26 us with groans that words cannot *e*.

EXPRESSING* (EXPRESS)
1Co 2:13 *e* spiritual truths in spiritual words.
Gal 5:6 thing that counts is faith *e* itself

EXTENDS (EXTENT)
Pr 31:20 and *e* her hands to the needy.
Lk 1:50 His mercy *e* to those who fear him,

EXTENT (EXTENDS)
Jn 13:1 he now showed them the full *e*

EXTERNAL
Gal 2:6 judge by *e* appearance—

EXTINGUISH (EXTINGUISHED)
Eph 6:16 which you can *e* all the flaming

EXTINGUISHED (EXTINGUISH)
2Sa 21:17 the lamp of Israel will not be *e*."

EXTOL*
Job 36:24 Remember to *e* his work,
Ps 34:1 I will *e* the LORD at all times;
68:4 *e* him who rides on the clouds—
95:2 and *e* him with music and song.
109:30 mouth I will greatly *e* the LORD;
111:1 I will *e* the LORD with all my heart
115:18 it is we who *e* the LORD,
117:1 *e* him, all you peoples.
145:2 and *e* your name for ever and ever.
145:10 your saints will *e* you.
147:12 *E* the LORD, O Jerusalem;

EXTORT*
Lk 3:14 "Don't *e* money and don't accuse

EXTRAORDINARY*
Ac 19:11 God did *e* miracles through Paul.

EXTREME (EXTREMES)
2Co 8:2 and their *e* poverty welled up

EXTREMES* (EXTREME)
Ecc 7:18 who fears God will avoid ⌞*e*⌟.

EXULT
Ps 89:16 they *e* in your righteousness.
Isa 45:25 will be found righteous and will *e*.

EYE (EYES)
Ge 3:6 good for food and pleasing to the *e*,
Ex 21:24 you are to take life for life, *e* for *e*,
Dt 19:21 life for life, *e* for *e*, tooth for tooth,
Ps 94:9 Does he who formed the *e* not see?
Mt 5:29 If your right *e* causes you to sin,
5:38 '*E* for *e*, and tooth for tooth.'
6:22 "The *e* is the lamp of the body.
7:3 of sawdust in your brother's *e*
1Co 2:9 "No *e* has seen,
12:16 I am not an *e*, I do not belong
15:52 of an *e*, at the last trumpet.
Eph 6:6 favour when their *e* is on you,
Col 3:22 not only when their *e* is on you
Rev 1:7 and every *e* will see him,

EYE-WITNESSES* (WITNESS)
Lk 1:2 by those who from the first were *e*
2Pe 1:16 but we were *e* of his majesty.

EYES (EYE)
Nu 15:39 the lusts of your own hearts and *e*.
33:55 remain will become barbs in your *e*

Dt 11: 12 the *e* of the LORD your God are
12: 25 right in the *e* of the LORD.
16: 19 of a bribe blinds the *e* of the wise
Jos 23: 13 on your backs and thorns in your *e*,
1Sa 15: 17 you were once small in your own *e*,
1Ki 10: 7 I came and saw with my own *e*.
2Ki 9: 30 heard about it, she painted her *e*,
2Ch 16: 9 For the *e* of the LORD range
Job 31: 1 "I made a covenant with my *e*
36: 7 He does not take his *e*
Ps 25: 15 My *e* are ever on the LORD,
36: 1 God before his *e*.
101: 6 My *e* will be on the faithful
118: 23 and it is marvellous in our *e*.
119: 18 Open my *e* that I may see
119: 37 my *e* away from worthless things;
121: 1 I lift up my *e* to the hills—
123: 1 I lift up my *e* to you,
139: 16 your *e* saw my unformed body.
141: 8 But my *e* are fixed on you,
Pr 3: 7 Do not be wise in your own *e*;
4: 25 Let your *e* look straight ahead,
15: 3 The *e* of the LORD are everywhere
17: 24 a fool's *e* wander to the ends
Isa 6: 5 and my *e* have seen the King,
33: 17 Your *e* will see the king
42: 7 to open *e* that are blind,
Jer 24: 6 My *e* will watch over them
Hab 1: 13 Your *e* are too pure to look on evil;
Mt 6: 22 If your *e* are good, your whole
21: 42 and it is marvellous in our *e*'?
Lk 16: 15 ones who justify yourselves in the *e*
24: 31 Then their *e* were opened
Jn 4: 35 open your *e* and look at the fields!
Ac 1: 9 he was taken up before their very *e*,
2Co 4: 18 So we fix our *e* not on what is seen,
8: 21 not only in the *e* of the Lord but
Eph 1: 18 also that the *e* of your heart may be
Heb 12: 2 Let us fix our *e* on Jesus, the author
Jas 2: 5 poor in the *e* of the world to be rich
1Pe 3: 12 For the *e* of the Lord are
Rev 7: 17 wipe away every tear from their *e*."
21: 4 He will wipe every tear from their *e*

EZEKIEL*

Priest called to be prophet to the exiles (Eze 1-3). Symbolically acted out destruction of Jerusalem (Eze 4-5; 12; 24).

EZRA*

Priest and teacher of the Law who led a return of exiles to Israel to re-establish temple and worship (Ezr 7-8). Corrected intermarriage of priests (Ezr 9-10). Read Law at celebration of Feast of Tabernacles (Ne 8). Participated in dedication of Jerusalem's walls (Ne 12).

FACE (FACES)

Ge 32: 30 "It is because I saw God *f* to *f*,
Ex 3: 6 Moses hid his *f*, because he was
33: 11 would speak to Moses *f* to *f*,
33: 20 But," he said, "you cannot see my *f*
34: 29 was not aware that his *f* was radiant
Nu 6: 25 the LORD make his *f* shine
12: 8 With him I speak *f* to *f*,
14: 14 O LORD, have been seen *f* to *f*,
Dt 5: 4 The LORD spoke to you *f* to *f* out
31: 17 I will hide my *f* from them,
34: 10 whom the LORD knew *f* to *f*,
Jdg 6: 22 the angel of the LORD *f* to *f*!"
2Ki 14: 8 challenge: "Come, meet me *f* to *f*."
1Ch 16: 11 seek his *f* always.
2Ch 7: 14 and seek my *f* and turn
25: 17 of Israel: "Come, meet me *f* to *f*."
Ezr 9: 6 and disgraced to lift up my *f* to you,
Ps 4: 6 Let the light of your *f* shine upon us
27: 8 Your *f*, LORD, I will seek.
31: 16 Let your *f* shine on your servant;
44: 3 and the light of your *f*,
44: 22 Yet for your sake we *f* death all day
51: 9 Hide your *f* from my sins
67: 1 and make his *f* shine upon us; *Selah*
80: 3 make your *f* shine upon us,
Ps 105: 4 seek his *f* always.
119: 135 Make your *f* shine
SS 2: 14 and your *f* is lovely.
Isa 50: 7 Therefore have I set my *f* like flint,
50: 8 Let us *f* each other!
54: 8 I hid my *f* from you for a moment,
Jer 32: 4 and will speak with him *f* to *f*
34: 3 and he will speak with you *f* to *f*.
Eze 1: 10 Each of the four had the *f* of a man,
20: 35 *f* to *f*, I will execute judgment
Mt 17: 2 His *f* shone like the sun,
18: 10 angels in heaven always see the *f*
Lk 9: 29 the appearance of his *f* changed,
Ro 8: 36 "For your sake we *f* death all day
1Co 13: 12 reflection; then we shall see *f* to *f*.
2Co 3: 7 could not look steadily at the *f*
4: 6 the glory of God in the *f* of Christ.
10: 1 who am "timid" when *f* to *f*
1Pe 3: 12 but the *f* of the Lord is
2Jn : 12 to visit you and talk with you *f* to *f*,
3Jn : 14 see you soon, and we will talk *f* to *f*.
Rev 1: 16 His *f* was like the sun shining
22: 4 They will see his *f*, and his name

FACES (FACE)

2Co 3: 18 who with unveiled *f* all reflect

FACTIONS

2Co 12: 20 outbursts of anger, *f*, slander,
Gal 5: 20 selfish ambition, dissensions, *f*

FADE (FADING)

Jas 1: 11 the rich man will *f* away
1Pe 5: 4 of glory that will never *f* away.

FADING (FADE)

2Co 3: 7 *f* though it was, will not
3: 11 if what was *f* away came with glory,
3: 13 at it while the radiance was *f* away.

FAIL (FAILED FAILING FAILINGS FAILS FAILURE)

Lev 26: 15 and *f* to carry out all my commands
1Ki 2: 4 you will never *f* to have a man
1Ch 28: 20 He will not *f* you or forsake you
2Ch 34: 33 they did not *f* to follow the LORD,
Ps 89: 28 my covenant with him will never *f*.
Pr 15: 22 Plans *f* for lack of counsel,
Isa 51: 6 my righteousness will never *f*.
La 3: 22 for his compassions never *f*.
Lk 22: 32 Simon, that your faith may not *f*.
2Co 13: 5 unless, of course, you *f* the test?

FAILED (FAIL)

Jos 23: 14 has been fulfilled; not one has *f*.
1Ki 8: 56 Not one word has *f*
Ps 77: 8 Has his promise *f* for all time?
Ro 9: 6 as though God's word had *f*.
2Co 13: 6 discover that we have not *f* the test.

FAILING (FAIL)

1Sa 12: 23 sin against the LORD by *f* to pray

FAILINGS (FAIL)

Ro 15: 1 ought to bear with the *f* of the weak

FAILS (FAIL)

Jer 14: 6 their eyesight *f*
Joel 1: 10 the oil *f*.
1Co 13: 8 Love never *f*.

FAILURE* (FAIL)

1Th 2: 1 that our visit to you was not a *f*.

FAINT

Isa 40: 31 they will walk and not be *f*.

FAINT-HEARTED* (HEART)

Dt 20: 3 Do not be *f* or afraid; do not be
20: 8 shall add, "Is any man afraid or *f*?

FAIR (FAIRNESS)

Pr 1: 3 doing what is right and just and *f*;
Col 4: 1 slaves with what is right and *f*,

FAIRNESS* (FAIR)

Pr 29: 14 If a king judges the poor with *f*,

FAITH* (FAITHFUL FAITHFULLY FAITHFULNESS FAITHLESS)

Ex 21: 8 because he has broken *f* with her.
Dt 32: 51 both of you broke *f* with me
Jos 22: 16 'How could you break *f*
Jdg 9: 16 and in good *f* when you made
9: 19 and in good *f* towards Jerub-Baal
1Sa 14: 33 "You have broken *f*," he said.
2Ch 20: 20 Have *f* in the LORD your God
20: 20 have *f* in his prophets and you will
Isa 7: 9 If you do not stand firm in your *f*,
26: 2 the nation that keeps *f*.
Hab 2: 4 but the righteous will live by his *f*—
Mal 2: 10 by breaking *f* with one another?
2: 11 one another? Judah has broken *f*.
2: 14 because you have broken *f* with her
2: 15 and do not break *f* with the wife
2: 16 in your spirit, and do not break *f*.
Mt 6: 30 O you of little *f*? So do not worry,
8: 10 anyone in Israel with such great *f*.
8: 26 He replied, "You of little *f*,
9: 2 When Jesus saw their *f*, he said
9: 22 he said, "your *f* has healed you."
9: 29 According to your *f* will it be done
13: 58 there because of their lack of *f*.
14: 31 of little *f*," he said, "why did you
15: 28 "Woman, you have great *f*!
16: 8 Jesus asked, "You of little *f*,
17: 20 if you have *f* as small as a mustard
17: 20 "Because you have so little *f*.
21: 21 if you have *f* and do not doubt,
24: 10 many will turn away from the *f*
Mk 2: 5 When Jesus saw their *f*, he said
4: 40 still have no *f*?" They were
5: 34 "Daughter, your *f* has healed you.
6: 6 he was amazed at their lack of *f*.
10: 52 said Jesus, "your *f* has healed you."
11: 22 "Have *f* in God," Jesus answered.
16: 14 he rebuked them for their lack of *f*
Lk 5: 20 When Jesus saw their *f*, he said,
7: 9 I have not found such great *f*
7: 50 the woman, "Your *f* has saved you;
8: 25 "Where is your *f*?" he asked his
8: 48 "Daughter, your *f* has healed you.
12: 28 will he clothe you, O you of little *f*!
17: 5 "Increase our *f*!" He replied,
17: 6 "If you have *f* as small
17: 19 your *f* has made you well."
18: 8 will he find *f* on the earth?"
18: 42 your sight; your *f* has healed you."
22: 32 Simon, that your *f* may not fail.
Jn 2: 11 and his disciples put their *f* in him.
7: 31 in the crowd put their *f* in him.
8: 30 he spoke, many put their *f* in him.
11: 45 had seen what Jesus did, put their *f*
12: 11 to Jesus and putting their *f* in him.
12: 42 they would not confess their *f*
14: 12 anyone who has *f* in me will do
Ac 3: 16 By *f* in the name of Jesus, this man
3: 16 *f* that comes through him that has
6: 5 full of *f* and of the Holy Spirit;
6: 7 of priests became obedient to the *f*.
11: 24 full of the Holy Spirit and *f*,
13: 8 to turn the proconsul from the *f*.
14: 9 saw that he had *f* to be healed
14: 22 them to remain true to the *f*.
14: 27 the door of *f* to the Gentiles.
15: 9 for he purified their hearts by *f*.
16: 5 were strengthened in the *f*
20: 21 and have *f* in our Lord Jesus.
24: 24 as he spoke about *f* in Christ Jesus.
26: 18 those who are sanctified by *f*
27: 25 for I have *f* in God that it will
Ro 1: 5 to the obedience that comes from *f*.
1: 8 because your *f* is being reported all
1: 12 encouraged by each other's *f*.

Ro 1: 17 is by *f* from first to last,
1: 17 "The righteous will live by *f*."
3: 3 What if some did not have *f*?
3: 3 lack of *f* nullify God's faithfulness?
3: 22 comes through *f* in Jesus Christ
3: 25 a sacrifice of atonement, through *f*
3: 26 one who justifies those who have *f*
3: 27 the law? No, but on that of *f*.
3: 28 by *f* apart from observing the law.
3: 30 through that same *f*.
3: 30 will justify the circumcised by *f*
3: 31 nullify the law by this *f*? Not at all!
4: 5 his *f* is credited as righteousness.
4: 9 that Abraham's *f* was credited
4: 11 had by *f* while he was still
4: 12 of the *f* that our father Abraham
4: 13 the righteousness that comes by *f*.
4: 14 *f* has no value and the promise is
4: 16 Therefore, the promise comes by *f*,
4: 16 are of the *f* of Abraham.
4: 19 Without weakening in his *f*,
4: 20 but was strengthened in his *f*
5: 1 we have been justified through *f*,
5: 2 access by *f* into this grace
9: 30 a righteousness that is by *f*;
9: 32 Because they pursued it not by *f*
10: 6 the righteousness that is by *f* says:
10: 8 the word of *f* we are proclaiming:
10: 17 *f* comes from hearing the message,
11: 20 of unbelief, and you stand by *f*.
12: 3 measure of *f* God has given you.
12: 6 let him use it in proportion to his *f*.
14: 1 Accept him whose *f* is weak,
14: 2 One man's *f* allows him
14: 2 but another man, whose *f* is weak,
14: 23 because his eating is not from *f*;
14: 23 that does not come from *f* is sin.
1Co 2: 5 so that your *f* might not rest
12: 9 to another *f* by the same Spirit,
13: 2 and if I have a *f* that can move
13: 13 And now these three remain: *f*,
15: 14 is useless and so is your *f*.
15: 17 has not been raised, your *f* is futile;
16: 13 stand firm in the *f*; be men
2Co 1: 24 Not that we lord it over your *f*,
1: 24 because it is by *f* you stand firm.
4: 13 With that same spirit of *f* we
5: 7 We live by *f*, not by sight.
8: 7 in *f*, in speech, in knowledge,
10: 15 as your *f* continues to grow,
13: 5 to see whether you are in the *f*;
Gal 1: 23 now preaching the *f* he once tried
2: 16 Jesus that we may be justified by *f*
2: 16 but by *f* in Jesus Christ.
2: 16 have put our *f* in Christ Jesus that
2: 20 I live by *f* in the Son of God,
3: 8 would justify the Gentiles by *f*,
3: 9 So those who have *f* are blessed
3: 9 along with Abraham, the man of *f*.
3: 11 "The righteous will live by *f*."
3: 12 based on *f*; on the contrary,
3: 14 by *f* we might receive the promise.
3: 22 being given through *f*
3: 23 Before this *f* came, we were held
3: 23 up until *f* should be revealed.
3: 24 that we might be justified by *f*.
3: 25 that *f* has come, we are no longer
3: 26 of God through *f* in Christ Jesus,
5: 5 But by *f* we eagerly await
5: 6 that counts is *f* expressing itself
Eph 1: 15 ever since I heard about your *f*
2: 8 through *f*—and this not
3: 12 through *f* in him we may approach
3: 17 dwell in your hearts through *f*.
4: 5 one Lord, one *f*, one baptism;
4: 13 up until we all reach unity in the *f*
6: 16 to all this, take up the shield of *f*,
6: 23 love with *f* from God the Father
Php 1: 25 for your progress and joy in the *f*,
1: 27 as one man for the *f* of the gospel
2: 17 and service coming from your *f*,
3: 9 comes from God and is by *f*.
3: 9 that which is through *f* in Christ—

Col 1: 4 heard of your *f* in Christ Jesus
1: 5 the *f* and love that spring
1: 23 continue in your *f*, established
2: 5 and how firm your *f* in Christ is.
2: 7 in the *f* as you were taught,
2: 12 him through your *f* in the power
1Th 1: 3 Father your work produced by *f*,
1: 8 your *f* in God has become known
3: 2 and encourage you in your *f*,
3: 5 I sent to find out about your *f*.
3: 6 brought good news about your *f*
3: 7 about you because of your *f*.
3: 10 supply what is lacking in your *f*.
5: 8 on *f* and love as a breastplate,
2Th 1: 3 because your *f* is growing more
1: 4 and *f* in all the persecutions
1: 11 and every act prompted by your *f*.
3: 2 evil men, for not everyone has *f*.
1Ti 1: 2 To Timothy my true son in the *f*:
1: 4 than God's work—which is by *f*.
1: 5 a good conscience and a sincere *f*.
1: 14 along with the *f* and love that are
1: 19 and so have shipwrecked their *f*.
1: 19 on to *f* and a good conscience.
2: 7 of the true *f* to the Gentiles.
2: 15 if they continue in *f*, love
3: 9 of the *f* with a clear conscience.
3: 13 assurance in their *f* in Christ Jesus.
4: 1 later times some will abandon the *f*
4: 6 brought up in the truths of the *f*
4: 12 in life, in love, in *f* and in purity.
5: 8 he has denied the *f* and is worse
6: 10 have wandered from the *f*
6: 11 pursue righteousness, godliness, *f*,
6: 12 Fight the good fight of the *f*.
6: 21 so doing have wandered from the *f*.
2Ti 1: 5 been reminded of your sincere *f*,
1: 13 with *f* and love in Christ Jesus.
2: 18 and they destroy the *f* of some.
2: 22 and pursue righteousness, *f*,
3: 8 as far as the *f* is concerned,
3: 10 my purpose, *f*, patience, love,
3: 15 wise for salvation through *f*
4: 7 finished the race, I have kept the *f*.
Tit 1: 1 Christ for the *f* of God's elect
1: 2 a *f* and knowledge resting
1: 4 my true son in our common *f*:
1: 13 so that they will be sound in the *f*
2: 2 self-controlled, and sound in *f*,
3: 15 Greet those who love us in the *f*.
Phm : 5 because I hear about your *f*
: 6 may be active in sharing your *f*,
Heb 4: 2 heard did not combine it with *f*.
4: 14 firmly to the *f* we profess.
6: 1 and of *f* in God, instruction about
6: 12 but to imitate those who through *f*
10: 22 heart in full assurance of *f*,
10: 38 But my righteous one will live by *f*.
11: 1 *f* is being sure of what we hope for
11: 3 By *f* we understand that
11: 4 And by *f* he still speaks, even
11: 4 By *f* Abel offered God a better
11: 4 By *f* he was commended
11: 5 By *f* Enoch was taken from this life
11: 6 And without *f* it is impossible
11: 7 By his *f* he condemned the world
11: 7 By *f* Noah, when warned about
11: 7 the righteousness that comes by *f*.
11: 8 By *f* Abraham, when called to go
11: 9 By *f* he made his home
11: 11 By *f* Abraham, even though he was
11: 13 living by *f* when they died.
11: 17 By *f* Abraham, when God tested
11: 20 By *f* Isaac blessed Jacob
11: 21 By *f* Jacob, when he was dying,
11: 22 By *f* Joseph, when his end was near
11: 23 By *f* Moses' parents hid him
11: 24 By *f* Moses, when he had grown up
11: 27 By *f* he left Egypt, not fearing
11: 28 By *f* he kept the Passover
11: 29 By *f* the people passed
11: 30 By *f* the walls of Jericho fell,
11: 31 By *f* the prostitute Rahab,

Heb 11: 33 through *f* conquered kingdoms,
11: 39 were all commended for their *f*,
12: 2 the author and perfecter of our *f*,
13: 7 way of life and imitate their *f*.
Jas 1: 3 of your *f* develops perseverance.
2: 5 the eyes of the world to be rich in *f*
2: 14 has no deeds? Can such *f* save him?
2: 14 if a man claims to have *f*
2: 17 In the same way, *f* by itself,
2: 18 I will show you my *f* by what I do.
2: 18 Show me your *f* without deeds,
2: 18 "You have *f*; I have deeds."
2: 20 do you want evidence that *f*
2: 22 You see that his *f* and his actions
2: 22 and his *f* was made complete
2: 24 by what he does and not by *f* alone.
2: 26 so *f* without deeds is dead.
5: 15 in *f* will make the sick person well;
1Pe 1: 5 who through *f* are shielded
1: 7 These have come so that your *f*—
1: 9 you are receiving the goal of your *f*,
1: 21 and so your *f* and hope are in God.
5: 9 Resist him, standing firm in the *f*,
2Pe 1: 1 Jesus Christ have received a *f*
1: 5 effort to add to your *f* goodness;
1Jn 5: 4 overcome the world, even our *f*.
Jude : 3 to contend for the *f* that was once
: 20 up in your most holy *f*
Rev 2: 13 You did not renounce your *f* in me,
2: 19 your love and *f*, your service

FAITHFUL* (FAITH)

Nu 12: 7 he is *f* in all my house.
Dt 7: 9 your God is God; he is the *f* God,
32: 4 A *f* God who does no wrong,
1Sa 2: 35 I will raise up for myself a *f* priest,
2Sa 20: 19 We are the peaceful and *f* in Israel.
22: 26 "To the *f* you show yourself *f*,
1Ki 3: 6 because he was *f* to you
2Ch 31: 18 were *f* in consecrating themselves.
31: 20 and *f* before the LORD his God.
Ne 9: 8 You found his heart *f* to you,
Ps 12: 1 the *f* have vanished
18: 25 To the *f* you show yourself *f*,
25: 10 of the LORD are loving and *f*
31: 23 The LORD preserves the *f*,
33: 4 he is *f* in all he does.
37: 28 and will not forsake his *f* ones.
78: 8 whose spirits were not *f* to him.
78: 37 they were not *f* to his covenant.
89: 19 to your *f* people you said:
89: 24 My *f* love will be with him,
89: 37 the *f* witness in the sky."
97: 10 for he guards the lives of his *f* ones
101: 6 My eyes will be on the *f* in the land,
111: 7 The works of his hands are *f*
145: 13 The LORD is *f* to all his promises
146: 6 the LORD, who remains *f* for ever.
Pr 2: 8 and protects the way of his *f* ones.
20: 6 but a *f* man who can find?
27: 6 but *f* are the wounds of a friend.
28: 20 A *f* man will be richly blessed,
31: 26 and *f* instruction is on her tongue.
Isa 1: 21 See how the *f* city has become
1: 26 The *F* City."
49: 7 because of the LORD, who is *f*,
55: 3 my *f* love promised to David.
Jer 42: 5 *f* witness against us if we do not act
Eze 43: 11 so that they may be *f* to its design
48: 11 who were *f* in serving me
Hos 11: 12 even against the *f* Holy One.
Zec 8: 8 I will be *f* and righteous to them
Mt 24: 45 Who then is the *f* and wise servant,
25: 21 'Well done, good and *f* servant!
25: 21 You have been *f* with a few things;
25: 23 You have been *f* with a few things;
25: 23 'Well done, good and *f* servant!
Lk 12: 42 then is the *f* and wise manager,
Ro 12: 12 patient in affliction, *f* in prayer.
1Co 1: 9 his Son Jesus Christ our Lord, is *f*.
4: 2 been given a trust must prove *f*.
4: 17 my son whom I love, who is *f*
10: 13 And God is *f*; he will not let you be

2Co 1: 18 no"? But as surely as God is *f*,
Eph 1: 1 in Ephesus, the *f* in Christ Jesus:
6: 21 the dear brother and *f* servant
Col 1: 2 and *f* brothers in Christ at Colosse:
1: 7 who is a *f* minister of Christ
4: 7 a *f* minister and fellow-servant
4: 9 He is coming with Onesimus, our *f*
1Th 5: 24 The one who calls you is *f*
2Th 3: 3 the Lord is *f*, and he will strengthen
1Ti 1: 12 he considered me *f*, appointing me
5: 9 has been *f* to her husband,
2Ti 2: 13 he will remain *f*,
Heb 2: 17 and *f* high priest in service to God,
3: 2 He was *f* to the one who appointed
3: 2 as Moses was *f* in all God's house.
3: 5 Moses was *f* as a servant
3: 6 But Christ is *f* as a son
8: 9 because they did not remain *f*
10: 23 for he who promised is *f*.
11: 11 he considered him *f* who had made
1Pe 4: 19 themselves to their *f* Creator
5: 12 whom I regard as a *f* brother,
1Jn 1: 9 he is *f* and just and will forgive us
3Jn : 5 you are *f* in what you are doing
Rev 1: 5 who is the *f* witness, the firstborn
2: 10 Be *f*, even to the point of death,
2: 13 the days of Antipas, my *f* witness,
3: 14 the words of the Amen, the *f*
14: 12 commandments and remain *f*
17: 14 his called, chosen and *f* followers."
19: 11 whose rider is called *F* and True.

FAITHFULLY* (FAITH)

Dt 11: 13 if you *f* obey the commands I am
Jos 2: 14 *f* when the LORD gives us the land
1Sa 12: 24 and serve him *f* with all your heart;
1Ki 2: 4 and if they walk *f* before me
2Ki 20: 3 how I have walked before you *f*
22: 7 because they are acting *f*."
2Ch 19: 9 must serve *f* and wholeheartedly
31: 12 they *f* brought in the contributions,
31: 15 and Shecaniah assisted him *f*
32: 1 all that Hezekiah had so *f* done,
34: 12 The men did the work *f*.
Ne 9: 33 you have acted *f*, while we did
13: 14 so *f* done for the house of my God
Isa 38: 3 how I have walked before you *f*
Jer 23: 28 one who has my word speak it *f*.
Eze 18: 9 and *f* keeps my laws.
44: 15 and who *f* carried out the duties
1Pe 4: 10 *f* administering God's grace

FAITHFULNESS* (FAITH)

Ge 24: 27 not abandoned his kindness and *f*
24: 49 if you will show kindness and *f*
32: 10 and *f* you have shown your servant.
47: 29 you will show me kindness and *f*.
Ex 34: 6 *f*, maintaining love to thousands,
Jos 24: 14 the LORD and serve him with all *f*.
1Sa 26: 23 man for his righteousness and *f*.
2Sa 2: 6 now show you kindness and *f*,
15: 20 May kindness and *f* be with you."
Ps 30: 9 Will it proclaim your *f*?
36: 5 your *f* to the skies.
40: 10 I speak of your *f* and salvation.
54: 5 in your *f* destroy them.
57: 3 God sends his love and his *f*.
57: 10 your *f* reaches to the skies.
61: 7 appoint your love and *f*
71: 22 the harp for your *f*, O my God;
85: 10 Love and *f* meet together;
85: 11 *F* springs forth from the earth,
86: 15 to anger, abounding in love and *f*.
88: 11 your *f* in Destruction?
89: 1 mouth I will make your *f* known
89: 2 that you established your *f*
89: 5 your *f* too, in the assembly
89: 8 and your *f* surrounds you.
89: 14 love and *f* go before you.
89: 33 nor will I ever betray my *f*.
89: 49 which in your *f* you swore to David
91: 4 his *f* will be your shield
92: 2 and your *f* at night,
Ps 98: 3 and his *f* to the house of Israel;
100: 5 *f* continues through all
108: 4 your *f* reaches to the skies.
111: 8 done in *f* and uprightness.
115: 1 because of your love and *f*.
117: 2 the *f* of the LORD endures for ever.
119: 75 and in *f* you have afflicted me.
119: 90 *f* continues through all
138: 2 name for your love and your *f*,
143: 1 in your *f* and righteousness
Pr 3: 3 Let love and *f* never leave you;
14: 22 plan what is good find love and *f*.
16: 6 Through love and *f* sin is atoned for
20: 28 Love and *f* keep a king safe;
Isa 11: 5 and *f* the sash around his waist.
16: 5 in *f* a man will sit on it—
25: 1 for in perfect *f*
38: 18 cannot hope for your *f*.
38: 19 about your *f*.
42: 3 In *f* he will bring forth justice;
61: 8 In my *f* I will reward them
La 3: 23 great is your *f*.
Hos 2: 20 I will betroth you in *f*,
4: 1 "There is no *f*, no love,
Mt 23: 23 of the law—justice, mercy and *f*.
Ro 3: 3 lack of faith nullify God's *f*?
Gal 5: 22 patience, kindness, goodness, *f*,
3Jn : 3 and tell about your *f* to the truth
Rev 13: 10 and *f* on the part of the saints.

FAITHLESS* (FAITH)

Ps 78: 57 fathers they were disloyal and *f*,
101: 3 The deeds of *f* men I hate;
119: 158 I look on the *f* with loathing,
Pr 14: 14 The *f* will be fully repaid
Jer 3: 6 you seen what *f* Israel has done?
3: 8 I gave *f* Israel her certificate
3: 11 "*F* Israel is more righteous
3: 12 *f* Israel,' declares the LORD,
3: 14 *f* people," declares the LORD,
3: 22 "Return, *f* people;
12: 1 Why do all the *f* live at ease?
Ro 1: 31 they are senseless, *f*, heartless,
2Ti 2: 13 if we are *f*,

FALL (FALLEN FALLING FALLS)

Ps 37: 24 though he stumble, he will not *f*,
55: 22 he will never let the righteous *f*.
69: 9 of those who insult you *f* on me.
145: 14 The LORD upholds all those who *f*
Pr 11: 28 Whoever trusts in his riches will *f*,
Isa 40: 7 The grass withers and the flowers *f*,
Mt 7: 25 yet it did not *f*, because it had its
Lk 10: 18 "I saw Satan *f* like lightning
11: 17 a house divided against itself will *f*.
23: 30 say to the mountains, "*F* on us!"
Ro 3: 23 and *f* short of the glory of God,
Heb 6: 6 if they *f* away, to be brought back

FALLEN (FALL)

2Sa 1: 19 How the mighty have *f*!
Isa 14: 12 How you have *f* from heaven,
1Co 11: 30 and a number of you have *f* asleep.
15: 6 though some have *f* asleep.
15: 18 who have *f* asleep in Christ are lost.
15: 20 of those who have *f* asleep.
Gal 5: 4 you have *f* away from grace.
1Th 4: 15 precede those who have *f* asleep.

FALLING (FALL)

Jude : 24 able to keep you from *f*

FALLS (FALL)

Pr 11: 14 For lack of guidance a nation *f*,
24: 17 Do not gloat when your enemy *f*;
28: 14 he who hardens his heart *f*
Mt 13: 21 of the word, he quickly *f* away.
21: 44 He who *f* on this stone will be
Jn 12: 24 a grain of wheat *f* to the ground
Ro 14: 4 To his own master he stands or *f*.

FALSE (FALSEHOOD FALSELY)

Ex 20: 16 "You shall not give *f* testimony
Ex 23: 1 "Do not spread *f* reports.
23: 7 Have nothing to do with a *f* charge
Dt 5: 20 "You shall not give *f* testimony
Pr 12: 17 but a *f* witness tells lies.
13: 5 The righteous hate what is *f*,
14: 5 but a *f* witness pours out lies.
14: 25 but a *f* witness is deceitful.
19: 5 A *f* witness will not go unpunished,
19: 9 A *f* witness will not go unpunished,
21: 28 A *f* witness will perish,
25: 18 is the man who gives *f* testimony
Isa 44: 25 who foils the signs of *f* prophets
Jer 23: 16 they fill you with *f* hopes.
Mt 7: 15 "Watch out for *f* prophets.
15: 19 theft, *f* testimony, slander.
19: 18 not steal, do not give *f* testimony,
24: 11 and many *f* prophets will appear
24: 24 For *f* Christs and *f* prophets will
Mk 10: 19 do not give *f* testimony, do not
13: 22 For *f* Christs and *f* prophets will
Lk 6: 26 their fathers treated the *f* prophets.
18: 20 not steal, do not give *f* testimony,
Jn 1: 47 in whom there is nothing *f*."
1Co 15: 15 found to be *f* witnesses about God,
2Co 11: 13 For such men are *f* apostles,
11: 26 and in danger from *f* brothers.
Gal 2: 4 some *f* brothers had infiltrated our
Php 1: 18 whether from *f* motives or true,
Col 2: 18 anyone who delights in *f* humility
2: 23 their *f* humility and their harsh
1Ti 1: 3 not to teach *f* doctrines any longer
6: 3 If anyone teaches *f* doctrines
2Pe 2: 1 also *f* prophets among the people,
2: 1 there will be *f* teachers among you.
1Jn 4: 1 many *f* prophets have gone out
Rev 16: 13 out of the mouth of the *f* prophet.
19: 20 with him the *f* prophet who had
20: 10 and the *f* prophet had been thrown.

FALSEHOOD* (FALSE)

Job 21: 34 left of your answers but *f*!"
31: 5 "If I have walked in *f*
Ps 52: 3 *f* rather than speaking the truth.
119: 163 I hate and abhor *f*
Pr 30: 8 Keep *f* and lies far from me;
Isa 28: 15 and *f* our hiding place."
Ro 3: 7 "If my *f* enhances God's
Eph 4: 25 each of you must put off *f*
1Jn 4: 6 Spirit of truth and the spirit of *f*.
Rev 22: 15 everyone who loves and practises *f*

FALSELY (FALSE)

Lev 19: 12 "'Do not swear *f* by my name
Mt 5: 11 *f* say all kinds of evil against you
Lk 3: 14 and don't accuse people *f*—
1Ti 6: 20 ideas of what is *f* called knowledge,

FALTER*

Pr 24: 10 If you *f* in times of trouble,
Isa 42: 4 he will not *f* or be discouraged

FAME

Jos 9: 9 of the *f* of the LORD your God.
Isa 66: 19 islands that have not heard of my *f*
Hab 3: 2 LORD, I have heard of your *f*;

FAMILIES (FAMILY)

Ps 68: 6 God sets the lonely in *f*,

FAMILY (FAMILIES)

Pr 15: 27 greedy man brings trouble to his *f*,
31: 15 she provides food for her *f*
Mk 5: 19 to your *f* and tell them how much
Lk 9: 61 go back and say good-bye to my *f*."
12: 52 in one *f* divided against each other,
Ac 10: 2 He and all his *f* were devout
16: 33 and all his *f* were baptised.
16: 34 and the whole *f* was filled with joy,
1Ti 3: 4 He must manage his own *f* well
3: 5 how to manage his own *f*,
5: 4 practice by caring for their own *f*
5: 8 and especially for his immediate *f*,

FAMINE
Ge 12: 10 Now there was a *f* in the land,
26: 1 Now there was a *f* in the land—
41: 30 seven years of *f* will follow them.
Ru 1: 1 the judges ruled, there was a *f*
1Ki 18: 2 Now the *f* was severe in Samaria,
Am 8: 11 but a *f* of hearing the words
Ro 8: 35 or persecution or *f* or nakedness

FAN*
2Ti 1: 6 you to *f* into flame the gift of God,

FANTASIES*
Ps 73: 20 you will despise them as *f*.
Pr 12: 11 but he who chases *f* lacks judgment
28: 19 one who chases *f* will have his fill

FAST [1]
Dt 10: 20 Hold *f* to him and take your oaths
11: 22 in all his ways and to hold *f* to him
13: 4 serve him and hold *f* to him.
30: 20 to his voice, and hold *f* to him.
Jos 22: 5 to hold *f* to him and to serve him
23: 8 to hold *f* to the LORD your God,
2Ki 18: 6 He held *f* to the LORD
Ps 119: 31 I hold *f* to your statutes, O LORD;
139: 10 your right hand will hold me *f*.
1Pe 5: 12 Stand *f* in it.

FAST [2] (FASTING)
Mt 6: 16 "When you *f*, do not look sombre

FASTING (FAST [2])
Ps 35: 13 and humbled myself with *f*.
Ac 13: 2 were worshipping the Lord and *f*,
14: 23 and *f*, committed them to the Lord

FATHER (FATHER'S FATHERED FATHERLESS FATHERS FOREFATHERS)
Ge 2: 24 this reason a man will leave his *f*
17: 4 You will be the *f* of many nations.
Ex 20: 12 "Honour your *f* and your mother,
21: 15 "Anyone who attacks his *f*
21: 17 "Anyone who curses his *f*
Lev 18: 7 "'Do not dishonour your *f*
19: 3 you must respect his mother and *f*,
20: 9 "'If anyone curses his *f* or mother,
Dt 1: 31 carried you, as a *f* carries his son,
5: 16 "Honour your *f* and your mother,
21: 18 son who does not obey his *f*
32: 6 Is he not your *F*, your Creator,
2Sa 7: 14 I will be his *f*, and he will be my son
1Ch 17: 13 I will be his *f*, and he will be my son
22: 10 will be my son, and I will be his *f*.
28: 6 to be my son, and I will be his *f*.
Job 38: 28 Does the rain have a *f*?
Ps 2: 7 today I have become your *F*.
27: 10 Though my *f* and mother forsake
68: 5 A *f* to the fatherless, a defender
89: 26 to me, 'You are my *F*,
103: 13 As a *f* has compassion
Pr 3: 12 as a *f* the son he delights in.
10: 1 A wise son brings joy to his *f*,
17: 21 there is no joy for the *f* of a fool.
17: 25 A foolish son brings grief to his *f*
23: 22 Listen to your *f*, who gave you life,
23: 24 *f* of a righteous man has great joy;
28: 7 of gluttons disgraces his *f*.
28: 24 He who robs his *f* or mother
29: 3 loves wisdom brings joy to his *f*,
Isa 9: 6 Everlasting *F*, Prince of Peace.
45: 10 Woe to him who says to his *f*,
63: 16 But you are our *F*,
Jer 2: 27 They say to wood, 'You are my *f*,'
3: 19 I thought you would call me '*F*'
31: 9 because I am Israel's *f*,
Eze 18: 19 the son not share the guilt of his *f*?'
Mic 7: 6 For a son dishonours his *f*,
Mal 1: 6 If I am a *f*, where is the honour due
2: 10 we not all one *F*? Did not one God
Mt 3: 9 'We have Abraham as our *f*.'
5: 16 and praise your *F* in heaven.
Mt 6: 9 "'Our *F* in heaven,
6: 26 yet your heavenly *F* feeds them.
10: 37 "Anyone who loves his *f*
11: 27 no-one knows the *F* except the Son
15: 4 'Honour your *f* and mother'
18: 10 the face of my *F* in heaven.
19: 5 this reason a man will leave his *f*
19: 19 honour your *f* and mother,'
19: 29 or brothers or sisters or *f* or mother
23: 9 And do not call anyone on earth '*f*,'
Mk 7: 10 'Honour your *f* and mother,' and,
Lk 9: 59 "Lord, first let me go and bury my *f*
12: 53 *f* against son and son against *f*,
14: 26 and does not hate his *f* and mother,
18: 20 honour your *f* and mother.'"
23: 34 Jesus said, "*F*, forgive them,
Jn 3: 35 The *F* loves the Son and has placed
4: 21 you will worship the *F* neither
5: 17 "My *F* is always at his work
5: 18 he was even calling God his own *F*,
5: 20 For the *F* loves the Son
6: 44 the *F* who sent me draws him,
6: 46 No-one has seen the *F*
8: 19 "You do not know me or my *F*,"
8: 28 speak just what the *F* has taught me
8: 41 The only *F* we have is God himself
8: 42 God were your *F*, you would love
8: 44 You belong to your *f*, the devil,
10: 17 reason my *F* loves me is that I lay
10: 30 I and the *F* are one."
10: 38 and understand that the *F* is in me,
14: 6 No-one comes to the *F*
14: 9 who has seen me has seen the *F*.
14: 28 for the *F* is greater than I.
15: 9 "As the *F* has loved me,
15: 23 He who hates me hates my *F*
20: 17 'I am returning to my *F* and your *F*,
Ac 13: 33 today I have become your *F*.'
Ro 4: 11 he is the *f* of all who believe
4: 16 He is the *f* of us all.
8: 15 And by him we cry, "*Abba*, *F*."
1Co 4: 15 for in Christ Jesus I became your *f*
2Co 6: 18 "I will be a *F* to you,
Eph 5: 31 this reason a man will leave his *f*
6: 2 "Honour your *f* and mother"—
Php 2: 11 to the glory of God the *F*.
Heb 1: 5 today I have become your *F*"?
12: 7 what son is not disciplined by his *f*?
1Jn 1: 3 And our fellowship is with the *F*
2: 15 the love of the *F* is not in him.
2: 22 he denies the *F* and the Son.

FATHER'S (FATHER)
Pr 13: 1 A wise son heeds his *f* instruction,
15: 5 A fool spurns his *f* discipline,
19: 13 A foolish son is his *f* ruin,
Mt 16: 27 going to come in his *F* glory
Lk 2: 49 had to be in my *F* house?"
Jn 2: 16 How dare you turn my *F* house
10: 29 can snatch them out of my *F* hand.
14: 2 In my *F* house are many rooms;
15: 8 to my *F* glory, that you bear much

FATHERED (FATHER)
Dt 32: 18 You deserted the Rock, who *f* you;

FATHERLESS (FATHER)
Dt 10: 18 He defends the cause of the *f*
14: 29 the *f* and the widows who live
24: 17 Do not deprive the alien or the *f*
24: 19 Leave it for the alien, the *f*
26: 12 the alien, the *f* and the widow,
Ps 68: 5 A father to the *f*, a defender
82: 3 Defend the cause of the weak and *f*
Pr 23: 10 or encroach on the fields of the *f*,

FATHERS (FATHER)
Ex 20: 5 for the sin of the *f* to the third
Jer 31: 29 'The *f* have eaten sour grapes,
Mal 4: 6 the hearts of the children to their *f*;
Lk 1: 17 the hearts of the *f* to their children
11: 11 "Which of you *f*, if your son asks
Jn 4: 20 Our *f* worshipped on this mountain,
1Co 4: 15 you do not have many *f*,
Eph 6: 4 *F*, do not exasperate your children;
Col 3: 21 *F*, do not embitter your children,
Heb 12: 9 all had human *f* who disciplined us

FATHOM* (FATHOMED)
Job 11: 7 "Can you *f* the mysteries of God?
Ps 145: 3 his greatness no-one can *f*.
Ecc 3: 11 yet they cannot *f* what God has
Isa 40: 28 and his understanding no-one can *f*
1Co 13: 2 and can *f* all mysteries and all

FATHOMED* (FATHOM)
Job 5: 9 performs wonders that cannot be *f*,
9: 10 performs wonders that cannot be *f*,

FATTENED
Pr 15: 17 than a *f* calf with hatred.
Lk 15: 23 Bring the *f* calf and kill it.

FAULT (FAULTS)
1Sa 29: 3 I have found no *f* in him."
Mt 18: 15 and show him his *f*, just
Php 2: 15 of God without *f* in a crooked
Jas 1: 5 generously to all without finding *f*,
Jude : 24 his glorious presence without *f*

FAULT-FINDERS*
Jude : 16 These men are grumblers and *f*;

FAULTLESS*
Pr 8: 9 they are *f* to those who have
Php 3: 6 as for legalistic righteousness, *f*.
Jas 1: 27 Father accepts as pure and *f* is this:

FAULTS* (FAULT)
Job 10: 6 that you must search out my *f*
Ps 19: 12 Forgive my hidden *f*.

FAVOUR (FAVOURITISM)
Ge 4: 4 The LORD looked with *f* on Abel
6: 8 But Noah found *f* in the eyes
Ex 33: 12 and you have found *f* with me.'
34: 9 if I have found *f* in your eyes,"
Lev 26: 9 "'I will look on you with *f*
Nu 11: 15 if I have found *f* in your eyes—
Jdg 6: 17 "If now I have found *f* in your eyes,
1Sa 2: 26 in *f* with the LORD and with men.
2Sa 2: 6 and I too will show you the same *f*
2Ki 13: 4 Jehoahaz sought the LORD's *f*,
2Ch 33: 12 In his distress he sought the *f*
Est 7: 3 "If I have found *f* with you, O king,
Ps 90: 17 May the *f* of the Lord our God rest
Pr 8: 35 and receives *f* from the LORD.
18: 22 and receives *f* from the LORD.
19: 6 Many curry *f* with a ruler,
Isa 61: 2 proclaim the year of the LORD's *f*
Zec 11: 7 called one *F* and the other Union,
Lk 1: 30 Mary, you have found *f* with God.
2: 14 to men on whom his *f* rests."
2: 52 and in *f* with God and men.
4: 19 to proclaim the year of the Lord's *f*
2Co 6: 2 now is the time of God's *f*,

FAVOURITISM* (FAVOUR)
Ex 23: 3 and do not show *f* to a poor man
Lev 19: 15 to the poor or *f* to the great,
Ac 10: 34 true it is that God does not show *f*
Ro 2: 11 For God does not show *f*.
Eph 6: 9 and there is no *f* with him.
Col 3: 25 for his wrong, and there is no *f*.
1Ti 5: 21 and to do nothing out of *f*.
Jas 2: 1 Lord Jesus Christ, don't show *f*.
2: 9 But if you show *f*, you sin

FEAR (AFRAID FEARED FEARS FRIGHTENED GOD-FEARING)
Dt 6: 13 *F* the LORD your God, serve him
10: 12 but to *f* the LORD your God,
31: 12 and learn to *f* the LORD your God
31: 13 and learn to *f* the LORD your God
Jos 4: 24 you might always *f* the LORD

Jos 24: 14 "Now f the LORD and serve him
1Sa 12: 14 If you f the LORD and serve
12: 24 But be sure to f the LORD
2Sa 23: 3 when he rules in the f of God,
2Ch 19: 7 let the f of the LORD be upon you.
26: 5 who instructed him in the f of God.
Job 1: 9 "Does Job f God for nothing?"
Ps 2: 11 Serve the LORD with f
19: 9 The f of the LORD is pure,
23: 4 I will f no evil,
27: 1 whom shall I f?
33: 8 Let all the earth f the LORD;
34: 7 around those who f him,
34: 9 F the LORD, you his saints,
46: 2 Therefore we will not f,
86: 11 that I may f your name.
90: 11 great as the f that is due you.
91: 5 You will not f the terror of night,
111: 10 f of the LORD is the beginning
118: 4 Let those who f the LORD say:
128: 1 Blessed are all who f the LORD,
145: 19 of those who f him;
147: 11 delights in those who f him,
Pr 1: 7 f of the LORD is the beginning
1: 33 and be at ease, without f of harm."
8: 13 To f the LORD is to hate evil;
9: 10 f of the LORD is the beginning
10: 27 The f of the LORD adds length
14: 27 The f of the LORD is a fountain
15: 33 f of the LORD teaches a man
16: 6 through the f of the LORD a man
19: 23 The f of the LORD leads to life:
22: 4 Humility and the f of the LORD
29: 25 F of man will prove to be a snare,
31: 21 she has no f for her household;
Ecc 12: 13 F God and keep his
Isa 11: 3 delight in the f of the LORD.
33: 6 the f of the LORD is the key
35: 4 "Be strong, do not f;
41: 10 So do not f, for I am with you;
41: 13 and says to you, Do not f;
43: 1 "F not, for I have redeemed you;
51: 7 Do not f the reproach of men
54: 14 you will have nothing to f.
Jer 17: 8 It does not f when heat comes;
Lk 12: 5 I will show you whom you should f:
2Co 5: 11 we know what it is to f the Lord,
Php 2: 12 to work out your salvation with f
1Jn 4: 18 But perfect love drives out f,
Jude :23 to others show mercy, mixed with f
Rev 14: 7 "F God and give him glory,

FEARED (FEAR)
Job 1: 1 he f God and shunned evil.
Ps 76: 7 You alone are to be f.
Mal 3: 16 those who f the LORD talked

FEARS (FEAR)
Job 1: 8 a man who f God and shuns evil."
2: 3 a man who f God and shuns evil.
Ps 34: 4 he delivered me from all my f.
112: 1 is the man who f the LORD,
Pr 14: 16 A wise man f the LORD
14: 26 He who f the LORD has a secure
31: 30 a woman who f the LORD is
2Co 7: 5 conflicts on the outside, f within.
1Jn 4: 18 The one who f is not made perfect

FEAST (FEASTING FEASTS)
Pr 15: 15 the cheerful heart has a continual f.
2Pe 2: 13 pleasures while they f with you.

FEASTING (FEAST)
Pr 17: 1 than a house full of f, with strife.

FEASTS (FEAST)
Am 5: 21 "I hate, I despise your religious f;
Jude :12 men are blemishes at your love f,

FEATHERS
Ps 91: 4 He will cover you with his f,

FEEBLE
Job 4: 3 you have strengthened f hands.
Isa 35: 3 Strengthen the f hands,
Heb 12: 12 strengthen your f arms

FEED (FEEDS)
Jn 21: 15 Jesus said, "F my lambs."
21: 17 Jesus said, "F my sheep.
Ro 12: 20 "If your enemy is hungry, f him;
Jude :12 shepherds who f only themselves.

FEEDS (FEED)
Pr 15: 14 but the mouth of a fool f on folly.
Mt 6: 26 yet your heavenly Father f them.
Jn 6: 57 so the one who f on me will live

FEEL
Jdg 16: 26 me where I can f the pillars that
Ps 115: 7 they have hands, but cannot f;

FEET (FOOT)
Ru 3: 8 discovered a woman lying at his f.
Ps 8: 6 you put everything under his f:
22: 16 have pierced my hands and my f.
40: 2 he set my f on a rock
56: 13 and my f from stumbling,
66: 9 and kept our f from slipping.
73: 2 as for me, my f had almost slipped;
110: 1 a footstool for your f."
119: 105 Your word is a lamp to my f
Pr 4: 26 Make level paths for your f
Isa 52: 7 are the f of those who bring good
Da 2: 33 its f partly of iron and partly
Na 1: 15 the f of one who brings good news,
Mt 10: 14 shake the dust off your f
22: 44 enemies under your f."'
Lk 1: 79 to guide our f into the path of peace
20: 43 a footstool for your f."'
24: 39 Look at my hands and my f.
Jn 13: 5 and began to wash his disciples' f,
13: 14 also should wash one another's f.
Ro 3: 15 "Their f are swift to shed blood;
10: 15 "How beautiful are the f
16: 20 will soon crush Satan under your f.
1Co 12: 21 And the head cannot say to the f,
15: 25 has put all his enemies under his f.
Eph 1: 22 God placed all things under his f
1Ti 5: 10 washing the f of the saints,
Heb 1: 13 a footstool for your f"?
2: 8 and put everything under his f."
12: 13 "Make level paths for your f,"
Rev 1: 15 His f were like bronze glowing

FELIX
Governor before whom Paul was tried (Ac 23:23-24:27).

FELLOW-CITIZENS (CITIZENSHIP)
Eph 2: 19 but F with God's people

FELLOW-ELDER (ELDER)
1Pe 5: 1 among you, I appeal as a f

FELLOW-WORKERS (WORK)
1Co 3: 9 For we are God's f

FELLOWSHIP
Ex 20: 24 burnt offerings and f offerings,
Lev 3: 1 If someone's offering is a f offering,
1Co 1: 9 who has called you into f
5: 2 out of your f the man who did this?
2Co 6: 14 what f can light have with darkness
13: 14 and the f of the Holy Spirit be
Gal 2: 9 and Barnabas the right hand of f
Php 2: 1 if any f with the Spirit,
3: 10 the f of sharing in his sufferings,
1Jn 1: 3 And our f is with the Father
1: 3 so that you also may have f with us.
1: 6 claim to have f with him yet walk
1: 7 we have f with one another,

FEMALE
Ge 1: 27 male and f he created them.
5: 2 He created them male and f;
Mt 19: 4 Creator 'made them male and f,'
Mk 10: 6 God 'made them male and f.'
Gal 3: 28 f, for you are all one in Christ Jesus

FEROCIOUS
Mt 7: 15 but inwardly they are f wolves.

FERTILE (FERTILISE)
Isa 32: 15 and the desert becomes a f field,
Jer 2: 7 I brought you into a f land

FERTILISE* (FERTILE)
Lk 13: 8 and I'll dig around it and f it.

FERVOUR*
Ac 18: 25 and he spoke with great f
Ro 12: 11 but keep your spiritual f, serving

FESTIVAL
1Co 5: 8 Therefore let us keep the F,
Col 2: 16 or with regard to a religious f.

FESTUS
Successor of Felix; sent Paul to Caesar (Ac 25-26).

FEVER
Job 30: 30 my body burns with f.
Mt 8: 14 mother-in-law lying in bed with a f.
Lk 4: 38 was suffering from a high f,
Jn 4: 52 "The f left him yesterday
Ac 28: 8 suffering from f and dysentery.

FIELD (FIELDS)
Ge 4: 8 Abel, "Let's go out to the f."
Lev 19: 9 reap to the very edges of your f
19: 19 Do not plant your f with two kinds
Pr 31: 16 She considers a f and buys it;
Isa 40: 6 glory is like the flowers of the f.
Mt 6: 28 See how the lilies of the f grow.
6: 30 how God clothes the grass of the f,
13: 38 f is the world, and the good seed
13: 44 is like treasure hidden in a f.
Lk 14: 18 I have just bought a f, and I must go
1Co 3: 9 you are God's f, God's building.
1Pe 1: 24 glory is like the flowers of the f;

FIELDS (FIELD)
Ru 2: 2 go to the f and pick up the leftover
Lk 2: 8 were shepherds living out in the f
Jn 4: 35 open your eyes and look at the f!

FIG (FIG-TREE FIGS SYCAMORE-FIG)
Ge 3: 7 so they sewed f leaves together

FIG-TREE (FIG)
Jdg 9: 10 "Next, the trees said to the f,
1Ki 4: 25 man under his own vine and f.
Pr 27: 18 He who tends a f will eat its
Mic 4: 4 and under his own f,
Zec 3: 10 to sit under his vine and f,'
Mt 21: 19 Seeing a f by the road,
Lk 13: 6 "A man had a f, planted
Jas 3: 12 brothers, can a f bear olives,
Rev 6: 13 drop from a f when shaken

FIGHT (FIGHTING FIGHTS FOUGHT)
Ex 14: 14 The LORD will f for you; you need
Dt 1: 30 going before you, will f for you,
3: 22 the LORD your God himself will f
Ne 4: 20 Our God will f for us!"
Ps 35: 1 f against those who f against me.
Jn 18: 36 my servants would f
1Co 9: 26 I do not f like a man beating the air.
2Co 10: 4 The weapons we f
1Ti 1: 18 them you may f the good f,
6: 12 F the good f of the faith.
2Ti 4: 7 fought the good f, I have finished

FIGHTING (FIGHT)
Jos 10: 14 Surely the LORD was *f* for Israel!

FIGHTS (FIGHT)
Jos 23: 10 the LORD your God *f* for you,
1Sa 25: 28 because he *f* the LORD's battles.
Jas 4: 1 What causes *f* and quarrels

FIGS (FIG)
Lk 6: 44 People do not pick *f*
Jas 3: 12 grapevine bear *f*? Neither can a salt

FILL (FILLED FILLING FILLS FULL FULLY FULNESS)
Ge 1: 28 and increase in number; *f* the earth
Ps 16: 11 you will *f* me with joy
81: 10 wide your mouth and I will *f* it.
Pr 28: 19 who chases fantasies will have his *f*
Hag 2: 7 and I will *f* this house with glory,'
Jn 6: 26 you ate the loaves and had your *f*.
Ac 2: 28 you will *f* me with joy
Ro 15: 13 the God of hope *f* you with all joy

FILLED (FILL)
Ex 31: 3 I have *f* him with the Spirit of God,
35: 31 he has *f* him with the Spirit of God,
Dt 34: 9 son of Nun was *f* with the spirit
1Ki 8: 10 the cloud *f* the temple
8: 11 glory of the LORD *f* his temple.
2Ch 5: 14 of the LORD *f* the temple of God.
7: 1 the glory of the LORD *f* the temple
Ps 72: 19 may the whole earth be *f*
119: 64 The earth is *f* with your love,
Isa 6: 4 and the temple was *f* with smoke.
Eze 10: 3 and a cloud *f* the inner court.
10: 4 The cloud *f* the temple,
43: 5 the glory of the LORD *f* the temple
Hab 2: 14 For the earth will be *f*
3: 3 and his praise *f* the earth.
Mt 5: 6 for they will be *f*.
Lk 1: 15 and he will be *f* with the Holy Spirit
1: 41 and Elizabeth was *f* with the Holy
1: 67 His father Zechariah was *f*
2: 40 and became strong; he was *f*
Jn 12: 3 the house was *f* with the fragrance
Ac 2: 2 *f* the whole house where they were
2: 4 All of them were *f*
4: 8 Then Peter, *f* with the Holy Spirit,
4: 31 they were all *f* with the Holy Spirit
9: 17 and be *f* with the Holy Spirit."
13: 9 called Paul, *f* with the Holy Spirit,
Eph 5: 18 Instead, be *f* with the Spirit.
Php 1: 11 *f* with the fruit of righteousness
Rev 15: 8 And the temple was *f* with smoke

FILLING (FILL)
Eze 44: 4 the glory of the LORD *f* the temple

FILLS (FILL)
Nu 14: 21 of the LORD *f* the whole earth,
Ps 107: 9 and *f* the hungry with good things.
Eph 1: 23 fulness of him who *f* everything

FILTH (FILTHY)
Isa 4: 4 The LORD will wash away the *f*
Jas 1: 21 rid of all moral *f* and the evil that is

FILTHY (FILTH)
Isa 64: 6 all our righteous acts are like *f* rags;
Col 3: 8 and *f* language from your lips.
2Pe 2: 7 by the *f* lives of lawless men

FINAL (FINALITY)
Ps 73: 17 then I understood their *f* destiny.

FINALITY* (FINAL)
Ro 9: 28 on earth with speed and *f*."

FINANCIAL*
1Ti 6: 5 that godliness is a means to *f* gain.

FIND (FINDS FOUND)
Nu 32: 23 be sure that your sin will *f* you out.
Dt 4: 29 you will *f* him if you look for him
1Sa 23: 16 and helped him *f* strength in God.
Job 23: 3 If only I knew where to *f* him;
Ps 36: 7 *f* refuge in the shadow
62: 5 *F* rest, O my soul, in God alone;
91: 4 under his wings you will *f* refuge;
Pr 8: 17 and those who seek me *f* me.
14: 22 those who plan what is good *f* love
20: 6 but a faithful man who can *f*?
24: 14 if you *f* it, there is a future hope
31: 10 A wife of noble character who can *f*
Jer 6: 16 and you will *f* rest for your souls.
29: 13 and *f* me when you seek me
Mt 7: 7 seek and you will *f*; knock
11: 29 and you will *f* rest for your souls.
16: 25 loses his life for me will *f* it.
22: 9 invite to the banquet anyone you *f*.'
Lk 11: 9 seek and you will *f*; knock
18: 8 will he *f* faith on the earth?"
Jn 10: 9 come in and go out, and *f* pasture.

FINDS (FIND)
Ps 62: 1 My soul *f* rest in God alone;
112: 1 who *f* great delight
119: 162 like one who *f* great spoil.
Pr 3: 13 Blessed is the man who *f* wisdom.
8: 35 For whoever *f* me *f* life
11: 27 He who seeks good *f* good will,
18: 22 He who *f* a wife *f* what is good
Mt 7: 8 he who seeks *f*; and to him who
10: 39 Whoever *f* his life will lose it,
Lk 11: 10 he who seeks *f*, and to him who
12: 37 whose master *f* them watching
12: 43 servant whom the master *f* doing
15: 4 go after the lost sheep until he *f* it?
15: 8 and search carefully until she *f* it?

FINE-SOUNDING* (SOUND)
Col 2: 4 may deceive you by *f* arguments.

FINGER
Ex 8: 19 to Pharaoh, "This is the *f* of God,"
31: 18 of stone inscribed by the *f* of God.
Dt 9: 10 two stone tablets inscribed by the *f*
Lk 11: 20 But if I drive out demons by the *f*
16: 24 to dip the tip of his *f* in water
Jn 8: 6 to write on the ground with his *f*.
20: 25 and put my *f* where the nails were,

FINISH (FINISHED)
Jn 4: 34 him who sent me and to *f* his work.
5: 36 that the Father has given me to *f*,
Ac 20: 24 if only I may *f* the race
2Co 8: 11 Now *f* the work, so that your eager
Jas 1: 4 Perseverance must *f* its work

FINISHED (FINISH)
Ge 2: 2 seventh day God had *f* the work he
Jn 19: 30 the drink, Jesus said, "It is *f*."
2Ti 4: 7 I have *f* the race, I have kept

FIRE
Ex 3: 2 in flames of *f* from within a bush.
13: 21 in a pillar of *f* to give them light,
Lev 6: 12 *f* on the altar must be kept burning;
9: 24 *F* came out from the presence
1Ki 18: 38 Then the *f* of the LORD fell
2Ki 2: 11 suddenly a chariot of *f*
Isa 5: 24 as tongues of *f* lick up straw
30: 27 and his tongue is a consuming *f*.
Jer 23: 29 my word like *f*," declares
Da 3: 25 four men walking around in the *f*,
Zec 3: 2 stick snatched from the *f*?"
Mal 3: 2 For he will be like a refiner's *f*
Mt 3: 11 you with the Holy Spirit and with *f*.
3: 12 the chaff with unquenchable *f*."
5: 22 will be in danger of the *f* of hell.
18: 8 and be thrown into eternal *f*.
25: 41 into the eternal *f* prepared
Mk 9: 43 where the *f* never goes out.
9: 48 and the *f* is not quenched.'
9: 49 Everyone will be salted with *f*.
Lk 3: 16 you with the Holy Spirit and with *f*.
12: 49 I have come to bring *f* on the earth,
Ac 2: 3 to be tongues of *f* that separated
1Co 3: 13 It will be revealed with *f*,
1Th 5: 19 Do not put out the Spirit's *f*;
Heb 12: 29 for our God is a consuming *f*.
Jas 3: 5 set on *f* by a small spark.
3: 6 also is a *f*, a world of evil
2Pe 3: 10 the elements will be destroyed by *f*,
Jude : 7 suffer the punishment of eternal *f*.
: 23 snatch others from the *f*
Rev 1: 14 and his eyes were like blazing *f*.
20: 14 The lake of *f* is the second death.

FIRM*
Ex 14: 13 Stand *f* and you will see
15: 8 surging waters stood *f* like a wall;
Jos 3: 17 the covenant of the LORD stood *f*
2Ch 20: 17 stand *f* and see the deliverance
Ezr 9: 8 giving us a *f* place in his sanctuary,
Job 11: 15 you will stand *f* and without fear.
36: 5 he is mighty, and *f* in his purpose.
41: 23 they are *f* and immovable.
Ps 20: 8 but we rise up and stand *f*.
30: 7 you made my mountain stand *f*;
33: 9 he commanded, and it stood *f*.
33: 11 of the LORD stand *f* for ever,
37: 23 whose steps he has made *f*;
40: 2 and gave me a *f* place to stand.
75: 3 it is I who hold its pillars *f*.
78: 13 made the water stand *f* like a wall.
89: 2 that your love stands *f* for ever,
89: 4 and make your throne *f*
93: 5 Your statutes stand *f*;
119: 89 it stands *f* in the heavens.
Pr 4: 26 and take only ways that are *f*.
10: 25 but the righteous stand *f* for ever.
12: 7 the house of the righteous stands *f*.
Isa 7: 9 If you do not stand *f* in your faith,
22: 17 about to take *f* hold of you
22: 23 drive him like a peg into a *f* place;
22: 25 into the *f* place will give way;
Eze 13: 5 so that it will stand *f* in the battle
Zec 8: 23 nations will take *f* hold of one Jew
Mt 10: 22 he who stands *f* to the end will be
24: 13 he who stands *f* to the end will be
Mk 13: 13 he who stands *f* to the end will be
Lk 21: 19 By standing *f* you will gain life.
1Co 10: 12 So, if you think you are standing *f*,
15: 58 my dear brothers, stand *f*.
16: 13 on your guard; stand *f* in the faith;
2Co 1: 7 for you is *f*, because we know that
1: 21 who makes both us and you stand *f*
1: 24 because it is by faith you stand *f*.
Gal 5: 1 Stand *f*, then, and do not let
Eph 6: 14 Stand *f* then, with the belt
Php 1: 27 I will know that you stand *f*
4: 1 that is how you should stand *f*
Col 1: 23 in your faith, established and *f*,
2: 5 and how *f* your faith in Christ is.
4: 12 that you may stand *f* in all the will
1Th 3: 8 since you are standing *f* in the Lord
2Th 2: 15 stand *f* and hold to the teachings
1Ti 6: 19 a *f* foundation for the coming age,
2Ti 2: 19 God's solid foundation stands *f*,
Heb 6: 19 an anchor for the soul, *f* and secure
Jas 5: 8 You too, be patient and stand *f*,
1Pe 5: 9 Resist him, standing *f* in the faith,
5: 10 make you strong, *f* and steadfast.

FIRMAMENT see EXPANSE, HEAVENS, SKIES

FIRST
Ge 1: 5 and there was morning—the *f* day.
13: 4 and where he had *f* built an altar.
Ex 34: 19 *f* offspring of every womb belongs
1Ki 22: 5 "*F* seek the counsel of the LORD."
Pr 18: 17 *f* to present his case seems right,
Isa 44: 6 I am the *f* and I am the last;
48: 12 I am the *f* and I am the last.
Mt 5: 24 *F* go and be reconciled
6: 33 But seek *f* his kingdom
7: 5 *f* take the plank out

Mt 19: 30 But many who are *f* will be last,
20: 16 last will be *f*, and the *f* will be last."
20: 27 wants to be *f* must be your slave—
22: 38 This is the *f* and greatest
23: 26 *F* clean the inside of the cup
Mk 9: 35 to be *f*, he must be the very last,
10: 31 are *f* will be last, and the last *f*."
10: 44 wants to be *f* must be slave
13: 10 And the gospel must *f* be preached
Lk 13: 30 will be *f*, and *f* who will be last."
Jn 8: 7 let him be the *f* to throw a stone
Ac 11: 26 disciples were *f* called Christians
Ro 1: 16 *f* for the Jew, then for the Gentile.
1: 17 is by faith from *f* to last,
2: 9 *f* for the Jew, then for the Gentile;
2: 10 *f* for the Jew, then for the Gentile.
1Co 12: 28 in the church God has appointed *f*
15: 45 "The *f* man Adam became a living
2Co 8: 5 they gave themselves *f* to the Lord
Eph 6: 2 which is the *f* commandment
1Th 4: 16 and the dead in Christ will rise *f*.
1Ti 2: 13 For Adam was formed *f*, then Eve.
Heb 10: 9 He sets aside the *f*
Jas 3: 17 comes from heaven is *f* of all pure;
1Jn 4: 19 We love because he *f* loved us.
3Jn : 9 but Diotrephes, who loves to be *f*,
Rev 1: 17 I am the *F* and the Last.
2: 4 You have forsaken your *f* love.
22: 13 and the Omega, the *F* and the Last,

FIRSTBORN (BEAR [1])
Ex 11: 5 Every *f* son in Egypt will die,
34: 20 Redeem all your *f* sons.
Ps 89: 27 I will also appoint him my *f*,
Lk 2: 7 and she gave birth to her *f*, a son.
Ro 8: 29 that he might be the *f*
Col 1: 15 image of the invisible God, the *f*
1: 18 and the *f* from among the dead,
Heb 1: 6 when God brings his *f*
12: 23 of the *f*, whose names are written
Rev 1: 5 who is the faithful witness, the *f*

FIRSTFRUITS
Ex 23: 16 the Feast of Harvest with the *f*
23: 19 "Bring the best of the *f* of your soil
Ro 8: 23 who have the *f* of the Spirit,
1Co 15: 23 Christ, the *f*; then, when he comes,
Rev 14: 4 offered as *f* to God and the Lamb.

FISH (FISHERS)
Ge 1: 26 let them rule over the *f* of the sea
Jnh 1: 17 But the LORD provided a great *f*
Mt 7: 10 asks for a *f*, will give him a snake?
12: 40 three nights in the belly of a huge *f*,
14: 17 loaves of bread and two *f*."
Mk 6: 38 they said, "Five—and two *f*."
Lk 5: 6 of *f* that their nets began to break.
9: 13 loaves of bread and two *f*—
Jn 6: 9 small barley loaves and two small *f*,
21: 5 haven't you any *f*?" "No,"
21: 11 It was full of large *f*, 153, but

FISH-HOOK*
Job 41: 1 pull in the leviathan with a *f*

FISHERMEN
Mk 1: 16 a net into the lake, for they were *f*.

FISHERS (FISH)
Mt 4: 19 "and I will make you *f* of men."
Mk 1: 17 "and I will make you *f* of men."

FISTS
Mt 26: 67 and struck him with their *f*.

FIT (FITTING)
Jdg 17: 6 no king; everyone did as he saw *f*.
21: 25 no king; everyone did as he saw *f*.

FITTING* (FIT)
Ps 33: 1 it is *f* for the upright to praise him.
147: 1 how pleasant and *f* to praise him!
Pr 10: 32 of the righteous know what is *f*,
19: 10 It is not *f* for a fool to live in luxury
26: 1 honour is not *f* for a fool.
1Co 14: 40 everything should be done in a *f*
Col 3: 18 to your husbands, as is *f* in the Lord
Heb 2: 10 sons to glory, it was *f* that God,

FIX* (FIXED)
Dt 11: 18 *F* these words of mine
Job 14: 3 Do you *f* your eye on such a one?
Pr 4: 25 *f* your gaze directly before you.
Isa 46: 8 "Remember this, *f* it in mind,
Am 9: 4 I will *f* my eyes upon them
2Co 4: 18 we *f* our eyes not on what is seen,
Heb 3: 1 heavenly calling, *f* your thoughts
12: 2 Let us *f* our eyes on Jesus,

FIXED* (FIX)
2Ki 8: 11 stared at him with a *f* gaze
Job 38: 10 when I *f* limits for it
Ps 141: 8 my eyes are *f* on you, O Sovereign
Pr 8: 28 *f* securely the fountains of the deep
Jer 33: 25 and night and the *f* laws of heaven
Lk 16: 26 and you a great chasm has been *f*,

FLAME (FLAMES FLAMING)
2Ti 1: 6 you to fan into *f* the gift of God,

FLAMES (FLAME)
1Co 3: 15 only as one escaping through the *f*.
13: 3 and surrender my body to the *f*,

FLAMING (FLAME)
Eph 6: 16 you can extinguish all the *f* arrows

FLANK
Eze 34: 21 Because you shove with *f*

FLASH
1Co 15: 52 in a *f*, in the twinkling of an eye,

FLATTER* (FLATTERING FLATTERS FLATTERY)
Job 32: 21 nor will I *f* any man;
Ps 78: 36 But then they would *f* him
Jude : 16 *f* others for their own advantage.

FLATTERING* (FLATTER)
Ps 12: 2 their *f* lips speak with deception.
12: 3 May the LORD cut off all *f* lips
Pr 26: 28 and a *f* mouth works ruin.
28: 23 than he who has a *f* tongue.
Eze 12: 24 or *f* divinations among the people

FLATTERS* (FLATTER)
Ps 36: 2 For in his own eyes he *f* himself
Pr 29: 5 Whoever *f* his neighbour

FLATTERY* (FLATTER)
Job 32: 22 for if I were skilled in *f*,
Da 11: 32 With *f* he will corrupt those who
Ro 16: 18 and *f* they deceive the minds
1Th 2: 5 You know we never used *f*,

FLAWLESS*
2Sa 22: 31 the word of the LORD is *f*.
Job 11: 4 You say to God, 'My beliefs are *f*
Ps 12: 6 And the words of the LORD are *f*,
18: 30 the word of the LORD is *f*.
Pr 30: 5 "Every word of God is *f*;
SS 5: 2 my dove, my *f* one.

FLEE (FLEES)
Ps 139: 7 Where can I *f* from your presence?
1Co 6: 18 *F* from sexual immorality.
10: 14 my dear friends, *f* from idolatry.
1Ti 6: 11 But you, man of God, *f* from all this
2Ti 2: 22 *F* the evil desires of youth,
Jas 4: 7 Resist the devil, and he will *f*

FLEECE
Jdg 6: 37 I will place a wool *f*

FLEES (FLEE)
Pr 28: 1 The wicked man *f* though no-one

FLEETING*
Job 14: 2 like a *f* shadow, he does not endure
Ps 39: 4 let me know how *f* is my life.
89: 47 Remember how *f* is my life.
144: 4 his days are like a *f* shadow.
Pr 21: 6 is a *f* vapour and a deadly snare.
31: 30 Charm is deceptive, and beauty is *f*

FLESH see also BODY, MANKIND, PEOPLE, SINFUL (nature)
Ge 2: 23 and *f* of my *f*;
2: 24 and they will become one *f*.
2Ch 32: 8 With him is only the arm of *f*,
Job 19: 26 yet in my *f* I will see God;
Eze 11: 19 of stone and give them a heart of *f*.
36: 26 of stone and give you a heart of *f*.
Mt 19: 5 and the two will become one *f*'?
Mk 10: 8 and the two will become one *f*.'
Jn 1: 14 The Word became *f* and made his
6: 51 This bread is my *f*, which I will give
1Co 6: 16 "The two will become one *f*."
15: 39 All *f* is not the same: Men have one
Eph 5: 31 and the two will become one *f*."
6: 12 For our struggle is not against *f*
Php 3: 2 do evil, those mutilators of the *f*.
1Jn 4: 2 come in the *f* is from God,
Jude : 23 the clothing stained by corrupted *f*.

FLIGHT
Dt 32: 30 or two put ten thousand to *f*,

FLINT
Isa 50: 7 Therefore have I set my face like *f*,
Zec 7: 12 They made their hearts as hard as *f*

FLIRTING*
Isa 3: 16 *f* with their eyes,

FLOCK (FLOCKS)
Ps 77: 20 You led your people like a *f*
78: 52 he brought his people out like a *f*;
95: 7 the *f* under his care.
Isa 40: 11 He tends his *f* like a shepherd:
Jer 10: 21 and all their *f* is scattered.
23: 2 "Because you have scattered my *f*
31: 10 watch over his *f* like a shepherd.'
Eze 34: 2 not shepherds take care of the *f*?
Zec 11: 17 who deserts the *f*!
Mt 26: 31 the sheep of the *f* will be scattered.'
Lk 12: 32 little *f*, for your Father has been
Jn 10: 16 shall be one *f* and one shepherd.
Ac 20: 28 all the *f* of which the Holy Spirit
1Co 9: 7 Who tends a *f* and does not drink
1Pe 5: 2 Be shepherds of God's *f* that is
5: 3 but being examples to the *f*.

FLOCKS (FLOCK)
Lk 2: 8 keeping watch over their *f* at night.

FLOG (FLOGGED FLOGGING)
Pr 19: 25 *F* a mocker, and the simple will
Ac 22: 25 to *f* a Roman citizen who hasn't

FLOGGED (FLOG)
Jn 19: 1 Pilate took Jesus and had him *f*.
Ac 5: 40 the apostles in and had them *f*.
16: 23 After they had been severely *f*,
2Co 11: 23 frequently, been *f* more severely,

FLOGGING (FLOG)
Heb 11: 36 *f*, while still others were chained

FLOOD (FLOODGATES)
Ge 7: 7 ark to escape the waters of the *f*.
Mal 2: 13 You *f* the LORD's altar with tears.
Mt 24: 38 For in the days before the *f*,
2Pe 2: 5 world when he brought the *f*

FLOODGATES (FLOOD)
Ge 7: 11 the *f* of the heavens were opened.

Mal 3: 10 see if I will not throw open the *f*

FLOOR

Jas 2: 3 or "Sit on the *f* by my feet,"

FLOUR

Lev 2: 1 his offering is to be of fine *f*.
Nu 7: 13 filled with fine *f* mixed with oil
28: 9 of an ephah of fine *f* mixed with oil.

FLOURISH (FLOURISHES FLOURISHING)

Ps 72: 7 In his days the righteous will *f*;
92: 7 and all evildoers *f*,
92: 12 The righteous will *f* like a palm tree
Pr 14: 11 but the tent of the upright will *f*.

FLOURISHES (FLOURISH)

Pr 12: 12 but the root of the righteous *f*.

FLOURISHING (FLOURISH)

Ps 52: 8 *f* in the house of God;

FLOW (FLOWING)

Nu 13: 27 and it does *f* with milk and honey!
Jn 7: 38 streams of living water will *f*

FLOWER (FLOWERS)

Job 14: 2 up like a *f* and withers away;
Ps 103: 15 he flourishes like a *f* of the field;
Jas 1: 10 he will pass away like a wild *f*.

FLOWERS (FLOWER)

Isa 40: 6 and all their glory is like the *f*
40: 7 The grass withers and the *f* fall,
1Pe 1: 24 and all their glory is like the *f*

FLOWING (FLOW)

Ex 3: 8 a land *f* with milk and honey—
33: 3 Go up to the land *f* with milk
Nu 16: 14 us into a land *f* with milk
Jos 5: 6 a land *f* with milk and honey.
Ps 107: 33 *f* springs into thirsty ground,
107: 35 the parched ground into *f* springs;
Jer 32: 22 a land *f* with milk and honey.
Eze 20: 6 a land *f* with milk and honey,
Rev 22: 1 *f* from the throne of God

FLUTE

Ps 150: 4 praise him with the strings and *f*,
Mt 11: 17 "'We played the *f* for you,
1Co 14: 7 that make sounds, such as the *f*

FOAL*

Zec 9: 9 on a colt, the *f* of a donkey.
Mt 21: 5 on a colt, the *f* of a donkey.'"

FOILS*

Ps 33: 10 The LORD *f* the plans
Isa 44: 25 who *f* the signs of false prophets

FOLDING* (FOLDS)

Pr 6: 10 a little *f* of the hands to rest—
24: 33 a little *f* of the hands to rest—

FOLDS (FOLDING)

Ecc 4: 5 The fool *f* his hands

FOLLOW (FOLLOWED FOLLOWING FOLLOWS)

Ex 23: 2 Do not *f* the crowd in doing wrong.
Lev 18: 4 and be careful to *f* my decrees.
Dt 5: 1 Learn them and be sure to *f* them.
17: 19 *f* carefully all the words of this law
1Ki 11: 6 he did not *f* the LORD completely,
2Ch 34: 33 they did not fail to *f* the LORD,
Ps 23: 6 Surely goodness and love will *f* me
119: 166 and I *f* your commands.
Mt 4: 19 *f* me," Jesus said, "and I will make
8: 19 I will *f* you wherever you go."
8: 22 But Jesus told him, "*F* me,
16: 24 and take up his cross and *f* me.
19: 27 "We have left everything to *f* you!
Lk 9: 23 take up his cross daily and *f* me.
9: 61 Still another said, "I will *f* you,
Jn 10: 4 his sheep *f* him because they know
10: 5 But they will never *f* a stranger;
10: 27 I know them, and they *f* me.
12: 26 Whoever serves me must *f* me;
21: 19 Then he said to him, "*F* me!"
1Co 1: 12 One of you says, "I *f* Paul";
11: 1 *F* my example, as I *f*
14: 1 *F* the way of love and eagerly
2Th 3: 9 ourselves a model for you to *f*.
1Pe 2: 21 that you should *f* in his steps.
Rev 14: 4 They *f* the Lamb wherever he goes.

FOLLOWED (FOLLOW)

Nu 32: 11 they have not *f* me wholeheartedly,
Dt 1: 36 he *f* the LORD wholeheartedly."
Jos 14: 14 he *f* the LORD, the God of Israel,
2Ch 10: 14 he *f* the advice of the young men
Mt 4: 20 once they left their nets and *f* him.
9: 9 and Matthew got up and *f* him.
26: 58 But Peter *f* him at a distance,
Lk 18: 43 he received his sight and *f* Jesus,

FOLLOWING (FOLLOW)

Ps 119: 14 I rejoice in *f* your statutes
Php 3: 17 Join with others in *f* my example,
1Ti 1: 18 by *f* them you may fight the good

FOLLOWS (FOLLOW)

Jn 8: 12 Whoever *f* me will never walk

FOLLY (FOOL)

Pr 14: 29 a quick-tempered man displays *f*.
19: 3 A man's own *f* ruins his life,
Ecc 10: 1 so a little *f* outweighs wisdom
Mk 7: 22 envy, slander, arrogance and *f*.
2Ti 3: 9 their *f* will be clear to everyone.

FOOD (FOODS)

Ge 1: 30 I give every green plant for *f*."
Pr 12: 9 to be somebody and have no *f*.
12: 11 his land will have abundant *f*,
20: 13 you will have *f* to spare.
20: 17 *F* gained by fraud tastes sweet
21: 20 of the wise are stores of choice *f*
22: 9 for he shares his *f* with the poor.
23: 3 for that *f* is deceptive.
23: 6 Do not eat the *f* of a stingy man,
25: 21 If your enemy is hungry, give him *f*
31: 14 bringing her *f* from afar.
31: 15 she provides *f* for her family
Isa 58: 7 not to share your *f* with the hungry
Eze 18: 7 but gives his *f* to the hungry
Da 1: 8 to defile himself with the royal *f*
Mt 3: 4 His *f* was locusts and wild honey.
6: 25 Is not life more important than *f*,
Jn 4: 32 "I have *f* to eat that you know
4: 34 have brought him *f*?" "My *f*,"
6: 27 Do not work for *f* that spoils,
6: 55 my flesh is real *f* and my blood is
Ac 15: 20 to abstain from *f* polluted by idols,
Ro 14: 14 fully convinced that no *f* is unclean
1Co 8: 1 Now about *f* sacrificed to idols:
8: 8 But *f* does not bring us near to God
2Co 11: 27 and have often gone without *f*;
1Ti 6: 8 But if we have *f* and clothing,
Heb 5: 14 But solid *f* is for the mature,
Jas 2: 15 sister is without clothes and daily *f*.

FOODS (FOOD)

Mk 7: 19 Jesus declared all *f* "clean".)

FOOL (FOLLY FOOL'S FOOLISH FOOLISHNESS FOOLS)

1Sa 25: 25 his name is *F*, and folly goes
Ps 14: 1 The *f* says in his heart,
Pr 10: 10 and a chattering *f* comes to ruin.
10: 18 and whoever spreads slander is a *f*.
12: 15 The way of a *f* seems right to him,
12: 16 A *f* shows his annoyance at once,
14: 16 but a *f* is hotheaded and reckless.
15: 5 A *f* spurns his father's discipline,
17: 12 than a *f* in his folly.
17: 16 use is money in the hand of a *f*,
17: 21 To have a *f* for a son brings grief;
17: 28 Even a *f* is thought wise
18: 2 A *f* finds no pleasure
20: 3 but every *f* is quick to quarrel.
23: 9 Do not speak to a *f*,
24: 7 Wisdom is too high for a *f*;
26: 4 Do not answer a *f* according
26: 5 Answer a *f* according to his folly,
26: 7 is a proverb in the mouth of a *f*.
26: 11 so a *f* repeats his folly.
26: 12 for a *f* than for him.
27: 22 Though you grind a *f* in a mortar,
28: 26 He who trusts in himself is a *f*,
29: 11 A *f* gives full vent to his anger,
29: 20 for a *f* than for him.
Mt 5: 22 But anyone who says, 'You *f*!'
Lk 12: 20 "But God said to him, 'You *f*!
1Co 3: 18 he should become a "*f*"
2Co 11: 21 I am speaking as a *f*—I

FOOL'S (FOOL)

Pr 14: 3 A *f* talk brings a rod to his back,
18: 7 A *f* mouth is his undoing,

FOOLISH (FOOL)

Pr 10: 1 but a *f* son grief to his mother.
14: 1 her own hands the *f* one tears hers
15: 20 but a *f* man despises his mother.
17: 25 A *f* son brings grief to his father
19: 13 A *f* son is his father's ruin,
Mt 7: 26 practice is like a *f* man who built
25: 2 of them were *f* and five were wise.
Lk 11: 40 You *f* people! Did not the one who
24: 25 He said to them, "How *f* you are,
1Co 1: 20 Has not God made *f* the wisdom
1: 27 God chose the *f* things of the world
Gal 3: 1 died for nothing!" You *f* Galatians!
Eph 5: 4 should there be obscenity, *f* talk
5: 17 Therefore do not be *f*,
Tit 3: 9 But avoid *f* controversies

FOOLISHNESS (FOOL)

1Co 1: 18 of the cross is *f* to those who are
1: 21 through the *f* of what was preached
1: 23 block to Jews and *f* to Gentiles,
1: 25 For the *f* of God is wiser
2: 14 for they are *f* to him, and he cannot
3: 19 of this world is *f* in God's sight.

FOOLS (FOOL)

Pr 1: 7 but *f* despise wisdom and discipline
3: 35 but *f* he holds up to shame.
12: 23 but the heart of *f* blurts out folly.
13: 19 but *f* detest turning from evil.
13: 20 but a companion of *f* suffers harm.
14: 9 *F* mock at making amends for sin,
14: 24 but the folly of *f* yields folly.
Ecc 7: 5 than to listen to the song of *f*.
7: 6 so is the laughter of *f*.
10: 6 *F* are put in many high positions,
Mt 23: 17 You blind *f*! Which is greater:
Ro 1: 22 they became *f* and exchanged
1Co 4: 10 We are *f* for Christ, but you are

FOOT (FEET FOOTHOLD)

Jos 1: 3 every place where you set your *f*,
Ps 121: 3 He will not let your *f* slip—
Pr 3: 23 and your *f* will not stumble;
4: 27 keep your *f* from evil.
25: 17 Seldom set *f* in your neighbour's
Isa 1: 6 From the sole of your *f* to the top
Mt 18: 8 or your *f* causes you to sin,
Lk 4: 11 so that you will not strike your *f*
1Co 12: 15 If the *f* should say, "Because I am
Rev 10: 2 He planted his right *f* on the sea

FOOTHOLD* (FOOT)

Ps 69: 2 where there is no *f*.
73: 2 I had nearly lost my *f*.
Eph 4: 27 and do not give the devil a *f*.

FOOTSTEPS (STEP)
Ps 119: 133 Direct my *f* according

FOOTSTOOL
Ps 99: 5 and worship at his *f*;
110: 1 a *f* for your feet."
Isa 66: 1 and the earth is my *f*.
Mt 5: 35 for it is his *f*; or by Jerusalem,
Ac 7: 49 and the earth is my *f*.
Heb 1: 13 a *f* for your feet"?
10: 13 for his enemies to be made his *f*,

FORBEARANCE*
Ro 3: 25 because in his *f* he had left the sins

FORBID
1Co 14: 39 and do not *f* speaking in tongues.
1Ti 4: 3 They *f* people to marry

FORCE (FORCED FORCEFUL FORCES FORCING)
Jn 6: 15 to come and make him king by *f*,
Ac 26: 11 and I tried to *f* them to blaspheme.
Gal 2: 14 that you *f* Gentiles

FORCED (FORCE)
Mt 27: 32 and they *f* him to carry the cross.
Phm : 14 do will be spontaneous and not *f*.

FORCEFUL* (FORCE)
Mt 11: 12 forcefully advancing, and *f* men lay
2Co 10: 10 "His letters are weighty and *f*,

FORCES [1] (FORCE)
Mt 5: 41 If someone *f* you to go one mile,

FORCES [2] (FORCE)
Eph 6: 12 and against the spiritual *f* of evil

FORCING (FORCE)
Lk 16: 16 and everyone is *f* his way into it.

FOREFATHERS (FATHER)
Heb 1: 1 spoke to our *f* through the prophets
1Pe 1: 18 handed down to you from your *f*,

FOREHEAD (FOREHEADS)
Ex 13: 9 a reminder on your *f* that the law
13: 16 on your *f* that the LORD brought
1Sa 17: 49 and struck the Philistine on the *f*.
Rev 13: 16 a mark on his right hand or on his *f*,

FOREHEADS (FOREHEAD)
Dt 6: 8 hands and bind them on your *f*.
Rev 9: 4 not have the seal of God on their *f*.
14: 1 his Father's name written on their *f*

FOREIGN (FOREIGNER FOREIGNERS)
Ge 35: 2 "Get rid of the *f* gods you have
2Ch 14: 3 He removed the *f* altars
33: 15 He got rid of the *f* gods
Isa 28: 11 with *f* lips and strange tongues

FOREIGNER (FOREIGN)
Lk 17: 18 give praise to God except this *f*?"
1Co 14: 11 I am a *f* to the speaker,

FOREIGNERS (FOREIGN)
Eph 2: 12 *f* to the covenants of the promise,
2: 19 you are no longer *f* and aliens,

FOREKNEW* (KNOWN)
Ro 8: 29 For those God *f* he
11: 2 not reject his people, whom he *f*.

FOREKNOWLEDGE* (KNOW)
Ac 2: 23 to you by God's set purpose and *f*;
1Pe 1: 2 to the *f* of God the Father,

FORESAW*
Gal 3: 8 Scripture *f* that God would justify

FOREST
Jas 3: 5 Consider what a great *f* is set

FORFEIT
Mk 8: 36 the whole world, yet *f* his soul?
Lk 9: 25 and yet lose or *f* his very self?

FORGAVE (FORGIVE)
Ps 32: 5 and you *f*,
65: 3 you *f* our transgressions
78: 3 he *f* their iniquities
Eph 4: 32 just as in Christ God *f* you.
Col 2: 13 He *f* us all our sins, having
3: 13 Forgive as the Lord *f* you.

FORGET (FORGETS FORGETTING FORGOT FORGOTTEN)
Dt 4: 23 Be careful not to *f* the covenant
6: 12 that you do not *f* the LORD,
2Ki 17: 38 Do not *f* the covenant I have made
Ps 9: 17 all the nations that *f* God.
10: 12 Do not *f* the helpless.
50: 22 "Consider this, you who *f* God,
78: 7 and would not *f* his deeds
103: 2 and *f* not all his benefits.
119: 93 I will never *f* your precepts,
137: 5 may my right hand *f* ₁its skill₁.
Pr 3: 1 My son, do not *f* my teaching,
4: 5 do not *f* my words or swerve
Isa 49: 15 "Can a mother *f* the baby
51: 13 that you *f* the LORD your Maker,
Jer 2: 32 Does a maiden *f* her jewellery,
23: 39 I will surely *f* you and cast you out
Heb 6: 10 he will not *f* your work
13: 2 Do not *f* to entertain strangers,
13: 16 And do not *f* to do good
2Pe 3: 8 But do not *f* this one thing,

FORGETS (FORGET)
Jn 16: 21 her baby is born she *f* the anguish
Jas 1: 24 immediately *f* what he looks like.

FORGETTING* (FORGET)
Php 3: 13 *F* what is behind and straining
Jas 1: 25 to do this, not *f* what he has heard,

FORGIVE* (FORGAVE FORGIVENESS FORGIVES FORGIVING)
Ge 50: 17 I ask you to *f* your brothers the sins
50: 17 please *f* the sins of the servants
Ex 10: 17 Now *f* my sin once more
23: 21 he will not *f* your rebellion,
32: 32 But now, please *f* their sin—
34: 9 *f* our wickedness and our sin,
Nu 14: 19 with your great love, *f* the sin
Dt 29: 20 will never be willing to *f* him;
Jos 24: 19 He will not *f* your rebellion
1Sa 15: 25 *f* my sin and come back with me,
25: 28 Please *f* your servant's offence,
1Ki 8: 30 place, and when you hear, *f*.
8: 34 and *f* the sin of your people Israel
8: 36 and *f* the sin of your servants,
8: 39 *F* and act; deal with each man
8: 50 *f* all the offences they have
8: 50 *f* your people, who have sinned
2Ki 5: 18 But may the LORD *f* your servant
5: 18 may the LORD *f* your servant
24: 4 and the LORD was not willing to *f*.
2Ch 6: 21 place; and when you hear, *f*.
6: 25 and *f* the sin of your people Israel
6: 27 and *f* the sin of your servants,
6: 30 *F*, and deal with each man
6: 39 *f* your people, who have sinned
7: 14 will *f* their sin and will heal their
Job 7: 21 and *f* my sins?
Ps 19: 12 *F* my hidden faults.
25: 11 *f* my iniquity, though it is great.
79: 9 deliver us and *f* our sins
Isa 2: 9 do not *f* them.
Jer 5: 1 I will *f* this city.
5: 7 "Why should I *f* you?
18: 23 Do not *f* their crimes
31: 34 "For I will *f* their wickedness
Jer 33: 8 and will *f* all their sins of rebellion
36: 3 then I will *f* their wickedness
50: 20 for I will *f* the remnant I spare.
Da 9: 19 O Lord, listen! O Lord, *f*! O Lord,
Hos 1: 6 that I should at all *f* them.
14: 2 "*F* all our sins
Am 7: 2 *f*! How can Jacob survive?
Mt 6: 12 *F* us our debts,
6: 14 For if you *f* men when they sin
6: 14 heavenly Father will also *f* you.
6: 15 But if you do not *f* men their sins,
6: 15 your Father will not *f* your sins.
9: 6 authority on earth to *f* sins . . .
18: 21 many times shall I *f* my brother
18: 35 you *f* your brother from your heart
Mk 2: 7 Who can *f* sins but God alone?"
2: 10 authority on earth to *f* sins
11: 25 anything against anyone, *f* him,
11: 25 in heaven may *f* you your sins."
Lk 5: 21 Who can *f* sins but God alone?"
5: 24 authority on earth to *f* sins . . .
6: 37 *F*, and you will be forgiven.
11: 4 *F* us our sins,
11: 4 *f* everyone who sins against us.
17: 3 rebuke him, and if he repents, *f* him
17: 4 and says, 'I repent,' *f* him."
23: 34 Jesus said, "Father, *f* them,
Jn 20: 23 If you *f* anyone his sins, they are
20: 23 if you do not *f* them, they are not
Ac 8: 22 Perhaps he will *f* you
2Co 2: 7 you ought to *f* and comfort him,
2: 10 If you *f* anyone, I also *f* him.
2: 10 if there was anything to *f*—
12: 13 a burden to you? *F* me this wrong!
Col 3: 13 and *f* whatever grievances you may
3: 13 *F* as the Lord forgave you.
Heb 8: 12 For I will *f* their wickedness
1Jn 1: 9 and just and will *f* us our sins

FORGIVENESS* (FORGIVE)
Ps 130: 4 But with you there is *f*;
Mt 26: 28 out for many for the *f* of sins.
Mk 1: 4 of repentance for the *f* of sins.
Lk 1: 77 salvation through the *f* of their sins,
3: 3 of repentance for the *f* of sins.
24: 47 and *f* of sins will be preached
Ac 5: 31 that he might give repentance and *f*
10: 43 believes in him receives *f* of sins
13: 38 that through Jesus the *f*
26: 18 so that they may receive *f* of sins
Eph 1: 7 through his blood, the *f* of sins,
Col 1: 14 in whom we have redemption, the *f*
Heb 9: 22 the shedding of blood there is no *f*.

FORGIVES* (FORGIVE)
Ps 103: 3 He *f* all my sins
Mic 7: 18 pardons sin and *f* the transgression
Lk 7: 49 "Who is this who even *f* sins?"

FORGIVING* (FORGIVE)
Ex 34: 7 and *f* wickedness, rebellion and sin.
Nu 14: 18 abounding in love and *f* sin
Ne 9: 17 But you are a *f* God, gracious
Ps 86: 5 You are *f* and good, O Lord,
99: 8 you were to Israel a *f* God,
Da 9: 9 The Lord our God is merciful and *f*
Eph 4: 32 to one another, *f* each other,

FORGOT (FORGET)
Dt 32: 18 you *f* the God who gave you birth.
Ps 78: 11 They *f* what he had done,
106: 13 But they soon *f* what he had done

FORGOTTEN (FORGET)
Job 11: 6 God has even *f* some of your sin.
Ps 44: 20 If we had *f* the name of our God
Isa 17: 10 You have *f* God your Saviour;
Hos 8: 14 Israel has *f* his Maker
Lk 12: 6 Yet not one of them is *f* by God.
2Pe 1: 9 and has *f* that he has been cleansed

FORM (FORMED)
Isa 52: 14 *f* marred beyond human likeness—

2Ti 3: 5 having a *f* of godliness

FORMED (FORM)

Ge 2: 7 And the LORD God *f* man
2: 19 Now the LORD God had *f* out
Ps 103: 14 for he knows how we are *f*,
Ecc 11: 5 or how the body is *f* in a mother's
Isa 29: 16 Shall what is *f* say to him who *f* it,
45: 18 but *f* it to be inhabited—
49: 5 he who *f* me in the womb
Jer 1: 5 "Before I *f* you in the womb I knew
Ro 9: 20 "Shall what is *f* say to him who *f* it,
Gal 4: 19 of childbirth until Christ is *f* in you,
1Ti 2: 13 For Adam was *f* first, then Eve.
Heb 11: 3 understand that the universe was *f*
2Pe 3: 5 and the earth was *f* out of water

FORMLESS*

Ge 1: 2 Now the earth was *f* and empty,
Jer 4: 23 and it was *f* and empty;

FORNICATION see IMMORALITY, UNFAITHFULNESS

FORSAKE (FORSAKEN)

Dt 31: 6 he will never leave you nor *f* you."
Jos 1: 5 I will never leave you or *f* you.
24: 16 "Far be it from us to *f* the LORD
2Ch 15: 2 but if you *f* him, he will *f* you.
Ps 27: 10 Though my father and mother *f* me
94: 14 he will never *f* his inheritance.
Isa 55: 7 Let the wicked *f* his way
Heb 13: 5 never will I *f* you."

FORSAKEN (FORSAKE)

Ps 22: 1 my God, why have you *f* me?
37: 25 I have never seen the righteous *f*
Mt 27: 46 my God, why have you *f* me?"
Rev 2: 4 You have *f* your first love.

FORTRESS

2Sa 22: 2 "The LORD is my rock, my *f*
Ps 18: 2 The LORD is my rock, my *f*
31: 2 a strong *f* to save me.
59: 16 for you are my *f*,
71: 3 for you are my rock and my *f*.
Pr 14: 26 who fears the LORD has a secure *f*,

FORTUNE-TELLING*

Ac 16: 16 deal of money for her owners by *f*.

FORTY

Ge 7: 4 on the earth for *f* days and *f* nights,
18: 29 "What if only *f* are found there?"
Ex 16: 35 The Israelites ate manna *f* years,
24: 18 on the mountain *f* days and *f* nights
Nu 14: 34 For *f* years—one year for each
Jos 14: 7 I was *f* years old when Moses
1Sa 4: 18 He had led Israel *f* years.
2Sa 5: 4 king, and he reigned *f* years.
1Ki 19: 8 he travelled *f* days and *f* nights
2Ki 12: 1 and he reigned in Jerusalem *f* years
2Ch 9: 30 in Jerusalem over all Israel *f* years.
Eze 29: 12 her cities will lie desolate *f* years
Jnh 3: 4 "*F* more days and Nineveh will be
Mt 4: 2 After fasting *f* days and *f* nights,

FOUGHT (FIGHT)

1Co 15: 32 If I *f* wild beasts in Ephesus
2Ti 4: 7 I have *f* the good fight, I have

FOUND (FIND)

2Ki 22: 8 "I have *f* the Book of the Law
1Ch 28: 9 If you seek him, he will be *f* by you;
2Ch 15: 15 sought God eagerly, and he was *f*
Isa 55: 6 Seek the LORD while he may be *f*;
65: 1 I was *f* by those who did not seek
Da 5: 27 on the scales and *f* wanting.
Mt 1: 18 she was *f* to be with child
Lk 15: 6 with me; I have *f* my lost sheep.'
15: 9 with me; I have *f* my lost coin.'
15: 24 is alive again; he was lost and is *f*.'
Ac 4: 12 Salvation is *f* in no-one else,
Ro 10: 20 "I was *f* by those who did not seek
Jas 2: 8 If you really keep the royal law *f*
Rev 5: 4 no-one was *f* who was worthy

FOUNDATION (FOUNDATIONS FOUNDED)

Isa 28: 16 a precious cornerstone for a sure *f*;
Mt 7: 25 because it had its *f* on the rock.
Lk 14: 29 For if he lays the *f* and is not able
Ro 15: 20 building on someone else's *f*.
1Co 3: 10 I laid a *f* as an expert builder,
3: 11 For no-one can lay any *f* other
Eph 2: 20 built on the *f* of the apostles
1Ti 3: 15 the pillar and *f* of the truth.
2Ti 2: 19 God's solid *f* stands firm,
Heb 6: 1 not laying again the *f* of repentance

FOUNDATIONS (FOUNDATION)

Ps 102: 25 In the beginning you laid the *f*
Heb 1: 10 O Lord, you laid the *f* of the earth,

FOUNDED (FOUNDATION)

Jer 10: 12 he *f* the world by his wisdom
Heb 8: 6 and it is *f* on better promises.

FOUNTAIN

Ps 36: 9 For with you is the *f* of life;
Pr 14: 27 The fear of the LORD is a *f* of life,
18: 4 the *f* of wisdom is a bubbling brook.
Zec 13: 1 "On that day a *f* will be opened

FOX (FOXES)

Lk 13: 32 He replied, "Go tell that *f*,

FOXES (FOX)

SS 2: 15 the little *f*
Mt 8: 20 "*F* have holes and birds

FRAGRANCE (FRAGRANT)

Ex 30: 38 it to enjoy its *f* must be cut
Jn 12: 3 filled with the *f* of the perfume.
2Co 2: 14 us spreads everywhere the *f*
2: 16 of death; to the other, the *f* of life.

FRAGRANT (FRAGRANCE)

Eph 5: 2 as a *f* offering and sacrifice to God.
Php 4: 18 They are a *f* offering, an acceptable

FREE (FREED FREEDOM FREELY)

Ge 2: 16 "You are *f* to eat from any tree
Ps 118: 5 and he answered by setting me *f*.
119: 32 for you have set my heart *f*.
146: 7 The LORD sets prisoners *f*,
Pr 6: 3 then do this, my son, to *f* yourself,
Jn 8: 32 and the truth will set you *f*."
8: 36 if the Son sets you *f*, you will be *f*
Ro 6: 18 You have been set *f* from sin
8: 2 of life set me *f* from the law of sin
1Co 12: 13 whether Jews or Greeks, slave or *f*
Gal 3: 28 slave nor *f*, male nor female,
5: 1 for freedom that Christ has set us *f*.
1Pe 2: 16 *f* men, but do not use your freedom

FREED (FREE)

Ps 116: 16 you have *f* me from my chains.
Ro 6: 7 anyone who has died has been *f*
Rev 1: 5 has *f* us from our sins by his blood,

FREEDOM (FREE)

Ps 119: 45 I will walk about in *f*,
Isa 61: 1 to proclaim *f* for the captives
Lk 4: 18 me to proclaim *f* for the prisoners
Ro 8: 21 into the glorious *f* of the children
1Co 7: 21 although if you can gain your *f*,
2Co 3: 17 the Spirit of the Lord is, there is *f*.
Gal 2: 4 ranks to spy on the *f* we have
5: 13 But do not use your *f* to indulge
Jas 1: 25 into the perfect law that gives *f*,
1Pe 2: 16 but do not use your *f* as a cover-up

FREELY (FREE)

Isa 55: 7 and to our God, for he will *f* pardon
Mt 10: 8 *F* you have received, *f* give.
Ro 3: 24 and are justified *f* by his grace
Eph 1: 6 which he has *f* given us

FRESH

Jas 3: 11 Can both *f* water and salt water

FRET*

Ps 37: 1 Do not *f* because of evil men
37: 7 do not *f* when men succeed
37: 8 do not *f*—it leads only to evil.
Pr 24: 19 Do not *f* because of evil men

FRICTION

1Ti 6: 5 and constant *f* between men

FRIEND (FRIENDS FRIENDSHIP)

Ex 33: 11 as a man speaks with his *f*.
2Ch 20: 7 descendants of Abraham your *f*?
Pr 17: 17 A *f* loves at all times,
18: 24 there is a *f* who sticks closer
27: 6 wounds from a *f* can be trusted,
27: 10 Do not forsake your *f* and the *f*
Isa 41: 8 you descendants of Abraham my *f*,
Mt 11: 19 a *f* of tax collectors and "sinners".'
Lk 11: 8 him the bread because he is his *f*,
Jn 19: 12 "If you let this man go, you are no *f*
Jas 2: 23 and he was called God's *f*.
4: 4 Anyone who chooses to be a *f*

FRIENDS (FRIEND)

Pr 16: 28 and a gossip separates close *f*.
17: 9 the matter separates close *f*.
Zec 13: 6 given at the house of my *f*.'
Jn 15: 13 that one lay down his life for his *f*.
15: 14 You are my *f* if you do what I

FRIENDSHIP (FRIEND)

Jas 4: 4 don't you know that *f*

FRIGHTENED (FEAR)

Php 1: 28 gospel without being *f* in any way
1Pe 3: 14 fear what they fear; do not be *f*."

FROGS

Ex 8: 2 plague your whole country with *f*.
Rev 16: 13 three evil spirits that looked like *f*;

FRUIT (FRUITFUL)

Jdg 9: 11 'Should I give up my *f*, so good
Ps 1: 3 which yields its *f* in season
Pr 11: 30 The *f* of the righteous is a tree
12: 14 From the *f* of his lips a man is filled
27: 18 He who tends a fig-tree will eat its *f*
Isa 11: 1 from his roots a Branch will bear *f*.
27: 6 and fill all the world with *f*.
32: 17 The *f* of righteousness will be peace
Jer 17: 8 and never fails to bear *f*."
Hos 10: 12 reap the *f* of unfailing love,
14: 2 that we may offer the *f* of our lips.
Am 8: 1 showed me: a basket of ripe *f*.
Mt 3: 8 Produce *f* in keeping
3: 10 does not produce good *f* will be cut
7: 16 By their *f* you will recognise them.
7: 17 good *f*, but a bad tree bears bad *f*.
7: 20 by their *f* you will recognise them.
12: 33 a tree good and its *f* will be good,
Lk 3: 9 does not produce good *f* will be cut
6: 43 nor does a bad tree bear good *f*.
13: 6 and he went to look for *f* on it,
Jn 15: 2 branch in me that bears no *f*,
15: 16 and bear *f*—*f* that will last.
Ro 7: 4 in order that we might bear *f*
Gal 5: 22 But the *f* of the Spirit is love, joy,
Php 1: 11 with the *f* of righteousness that
Col 1: 10 bearing *f* in every good work,
Heb 13: 15 the *f* of lips that confess his name.
Jas 3: 17 and good *f*, impartial and sincere.
Jude : 12 autumn trees, without *f*
Rev 22: 2 of *f*, yielding its *f* every month.

FRUITFUL (FRUIT)

Ge 1: 22 "Be *f* and increase in number

Ge 9: 1 "Be *f* and increase in number
35: 11 be *f* and increase in number.
Ex 1: 7 the Israelites were *f* and multiplied
Ps 128: 3 Your wife will be like a *f* vine
Jn 15: 2 clean so that it will be even more *f*.
Php 1: 22 this will mean *f* labour for me.

FRUITLESS*
Eph 5: 11 to do with the *f* deeds of darkness,

FRUSTRATION
Ro 8: 20 For the creation was subjected to *f*,

FUEL
Isa 44: 19 "Half of it I used for *f*;

FULFIL (FULFILLED FULFILMENT FULFILS)
Nu 23: 19 Does he promise and not *f*?
Ps 61: 8 and *f* my vows day after day.
116: 14 I will *f* my vows to the LORD
138: 8 The LORD will *f* ₍his purpose₎
Ecc 5: 5 than to make a vow and not *f* it.
Isa 46: 11 far-off land, a man to *f* my purpose.
Jer 33: 14 'when I will *f* the gracious promise
Mt 1: 22 place to *f* what the Lord had said
3: 15 us to do this to *f* all righteousness."
4: 14 *f* what was said
5: 17 come to abolish them but to *f* them.
8: 17 This was to *f* what was spoken
12: 17 This was to *f* what was spoken
21: 4 place to *f* what was spoken
Jn 12: 38 This was to *f* the word
13: 18 But this is to *f* the scripture:
15: 25 But this is to *f* what is written
1Co 7: 3 husband should *f* his marital duty

FULFILLED (FULFIL)
Jos 21: 45 of Israel failed; every one was *f*.
23: 14 Every promise has been *f*;
Pr 13: 12 but a longing *f* is a tree of life.
13: 19 A longing *f* is sweet to the soul,
Mt 2: 15 so was *f* what the Lord had said
2: 17 the prophet Jeremiah was *f*:
2: 23 So was *f* what was said
13: 14 In them is *f* the prophecy of Isaiah:
13: 35 So was *f* what was spoken
26: 54 would the Scriptures be *f* that say it
26: 56 of the prophets might be *f*."
27: 9 by Jeremiah the prophet was *f*:
Mk 13: 4 that they are all about to be *f*?"
14: 49 But the Scriptures must be *f*."
Lk 4: 21 "Today this scripture is *f*
18: 31 about the Son of Man will be *f*.
24: 44 Everything must be *f* that is
Jn 18: 9 words he had spoken would be *f*:
19: 24 the Scripture might be *f* which said,
19: 28 and so that the Scripture would be *f*
19: 36 so that the Scripture would be *f*:
Ac 1: 16 to be *f* which the Holy Spirit spoke
Ro 13: 8 loves his fellow-man has *f* the law
Jas 2: 23 And the scripture was *f* that says,

FULFILMENT (FULFIL)
Ro 13: 10 Therefore love is the *f* of the law.

FULFILS (FULFIL)
Ps 57: 2 to God, who *f* ₍his purpose₎ for me.
145: 19 He *f* the desires of those who fear

FULL (FILL)
2Ch 24: 10 them into the chest until it was *f*.
Ps 127: 5 whose quiver is *f* of them.
Pr 27: 7 He who is *f* loathes honey,
31: 11 Her husband has *f* confidence
Isa 6: 3 the whole earth is *f* of his glory."
11: 9 for the earth will be *f*
Lk 4: 1 Jesus, *f* of the Holy Spirit,
Jn 10: 10 may have life, and have it to the *f*.
Ac 6: 3 known to be *f* of the Spirit
6: 5 a man *f* of faith and of the Holy
7: 55 But Stephen, *f* of the Holy Spirit,
11: 24 *f* of the Holy Spirit and faith,

FULL-GROWN* (GROW)
Jas 1: 15 when it is *f*, gives birth to death.

FULLY (FILL)
1Ki 8: 61 your hearts must be *f* committed
2Ch 16: 9 whose hearts are *f* committed
Ps 119: 4 that are to be *f* obeyed.
119: 138 they are *f* trustworthy.
Pr 13: 4 of the diligent are *f* satisfied.
Lk 6: 40 everyone who is *f* trained will be
Ro 4: 21 being *f* persuaded that God had
14: 5 Each one should be *f* convinced
1Co 13: 12 shall know *f*, even as I am *f* known.
15: 58 Always give yourselves *f*
2Ti 4: 17 the message might be *f* proclaimed

FULNESS* (FILL)
Dt 33: 16 gifts of the earth and its *f*
Jn 1: 16 From the *f* of his grace we have all
Ro 11: 12 greater riches will their *f* bring!
Eph 1: 23 the *f* of him who fills everything
3: 19 to the measure of all the *f* of God.
4: 13 to the whole measure of the *f*
Col 1: 19 to have all his *f* dwell in him,
1: 25 to you the word of God in its *f*—
2: 9 in Christ all the *f* of the Deity lives
2: 10 and you have been given *f* in Christ

FURIOUS (FURY)
Dt 29: 28 In *f* anger and in great wrath
Jer 32: 37 where I banish them in my *f* anger

FURNACE
Isa 48: 10 in the *f* of affliction.
Da 3: 6 be thrown into a blazing *f*."
Mt 13: 42 will throw them into the fiery *f*,

FURY (FURIOUS)
Isa 14: 6 and in *f* subdued nations
Jer 21: 5 and a mighty arm in anger and *f*
Rev 14: 10 will drink of the wine of God's *f*,
16: 19 with the wine of the *f* of his wrath.
19: 15 the winepress of the *f* of the wrath

FUTILE (FUTILITY)
Mal 3: 14 You have said, 'It is *f* to serve God.
1Co 3: 20 that the thoughts of the wise are *f*."

FUTILITY (FUTILE)
Eph 4: 17 in the *f* of their thinking.

FUTURE
Ps 37: 37 there is a *f* for the man of peace.
Pr 23: 18 There is surely a *f* hope for you,
Ecc 7: 14 anything about his *f*.
8: 7 Since no man knows the *f*,
Jer 29: 11 plans to give you hope and a *f*.
31: 17 So there is hope for your *f*,"
Ro 8: 38 neither the present nor the *f*,
1Co 3: 22 life or death or the present or the *f*

GABRIEL*

Angel who interpreted Daniel's visions (Da 8:16-26; 9:20-27); announced births of John (Lk 1:11-20), Jesus (Lk 1:26-38).

GAD

1. Son of Jacob by Zilpah (Ge 30:9-11; 35:26; 1Ch 2:2). Tribe of blessed (Ge 49:19; Dt 33:20-21), numbered (Nu 1:25; 26:18), allotted land east of the Jordan (Nu 32; 34:14; Jos 18:7; 22), west (Eze 48:27-28), 12,000 from (Rev 7:5).

2. Prophet; seer of David (1Sa 22:5; 2Sa 24:11-19; 1Ch 29:29).

GAIN (GAINED GAINS)
Ex 14: 17 And I will *g* glory through Pharaoh
Ps 60: 12 With God we will *g* the victory,
Pr 4: 1 pay attention and *g* understanding.
8: 5 You who are simple, *g* prudence;
28: 16 he who hates ill-gotten *g* will enjoy
28: 23 in the end *g* more favour
Isa 63: 12 to *g* for himself everlasting renown
Da 2: 8 that you are trying to *g* time,
Mk 8: 36 it for a man to *g* the whole world,
Lk 9: 25 it for a man to *g* the whole world,
1Co 13: 3 but have not love, I *g* nothing.
Php 1: 21 to live is Christ and to die is *g*.
3: 8 that I may *g* Christ and be found
1Ti 3: 13 have served well *g* an excellent
6: 5 godliness is a means to financial *g*.
6: 6 with contentment is great *g*.

GAINED (GAIN)
Jer 32: 20 have *g* the renown that is still yours
Ro 5: 2 through whom we have *g* access

GAINS (GAIN)
Pr 3: 13 the man who *g* understanding,
11: 16 A kindhearted woman *g* respect,
15: 32 heeds correction *g* understanding.
29: 23 but a man of lowly spirit *g* honour.
Mt 16: 26 for a man if he *g* the whole world,

GALILEE
Isa 9: 1 but in the future he will honour *G*
Mt 4: 15 *G* of the Gentiles—
26: 32 I will go ahead of you into *G*."
28: 10 Go and tell my brothers to go to *G*;

GALL
Mt 27: 34 mixed with *g*; but after tasting it,

GALLIO
Ac 18: 12 While *G* was proconsul of Achaia,

GALLOWS
Est 7: 10 Haman on the *g* he had prepared

GAMALIEL
Ac 5: 34 But a Pharisee named *G*, a teacher

GAMES
1Co 9: 25 in the *g* goes into strict training.

GAP
Eze 22: 30 stand before me in the *g* on behalf

GAPE*
Ps 35: 21 They *g* at me and say, "Aha! Aha!

GARDEN (GARDENER)
Ge 2: 8 the LORD God had planted a *g*
2: 15 put him in the *G* of Eden to work it
SS 4: 12 You are a *g* locked up, my sister,
Isa 58: 11 You will be like a well-watered *g*,
Jer 31: 12 They will be like a well-watered *g*,
Eze 28: 13 the *g* of God;
31: 9 Eden in the *g* of God.

GARDENER (GARDEN)
Jn 15: 1 true vine and my Father is the *g*.

GARLAND*
Pr 1: 9 They will be a *g* to grace your head
4: 9 She will set a *g* of grace

GARMENT (GARMENTS)
Ps 102: 26 they will all wear out like a *g*.
Isa 50: 9 They will all wear out like a *g*;
51: 6 the earth will wear out like a *g*
61: 3 and a *g* of praise
Mt 9: 16 of unshrunk cloth on an old *g*,
Jn 19: 23 This *g* was seamless, woven
Heb 1: 11 they will all wear out like a *g*.

GARMENTS (GARMENT)
Ge 3: 21 The LORD God made *g* of skin
Ex 28: 2 Make sacred *g* for your brother
Lev 16: 23 and take off the linen *g* he put
16: 24 holy place and put on his regular *g*.
Isa 61: 10 me with *g* of salvation
63: 1 with his *g* stained crimson?
Joel 2: 13 and not your *g*.
Zec 3: 4 and I will put rich *g* on you."
Jn 19: 24 "They divided my *g* among them

GATE (GATES)

Ps 118: 20 This is the g of the LORD
Pr 31: 23 husband is respected at the city g,
31: 31 works bring her praise at the city g.
Mt 7: 13 For wide is the g and broad is
7: 13 "Enter through the narrow g.
Jn 10: 1 not enter the sheep pen by the g,
10: 2 enters by the g is the shepherd
10: 7 "I tell you the truth, I am the g
10: 9 I am the g; whoever enters
Heb 13: 12 also suffered outside the city g
Rev 21: 21 each g made of a single pearl.

GATES (GATE)

Ps 24: 7 Lift up your heads, O you g;
24: 9 Lift up your heads, O you g;
100: 4 Enter his g with thanksgiving
118: 19 Open for me the g of righteousness
Isa 60: 11 Your g will always stand open,
60: 18 and your g Praise.
62: 10 Pass through, pass through the g!
Mt 16: 18 the g of Hades will not overcome it
Rev 21: 12 On the g were written the names
21: 21 The twelve g were twelve pearls,
21: 25 On no day will its g ever be shut,
22: 14 may go through the g into the city.

GATH

1Sa 17: 23 the Philistine champion from G,
2Sa 1: 20 "Tell it not in G,
Mic 1: 10 Tell it not in G;

GATHER (GATHERED GATHERS)

Ps 106: 47 and g us from the nations,
Isa 11: 12 and g the exiles of Israel;
Jer 3: 17 and all nations will g in Jerusalem
23: 3 "I myself will g the remnant
31: 10 who scattered Israel will g them
Zep 2: 1 G together, g together,
3: 20 At that time I will g you;
Zec 14: 2 I will g all the nations to Jerusalem
Mt 12: 30 he who does not g with me scatters
13: 30 then g the wheat and bring it
23: 37 longed to g your children together,
24: 31 and they will g his elect
25: 26 g where I have not scattered seed?
Mk 13: 27 and g his elect from the four winds,
Lk 3: 17 and to g the wheat into his barn,
11: 23 and he who does not g with me,
13: 34 longed to g your children together,

GATHERED (GATHER)

Ex 16: 18 and he who g little did not have too
Pr 30: 4 Who has g up the wind
Mt 25: 32 All the nations will be g before him
2Co 8: 15 and he that g little did not have too
2Th 2: 1 Lord Jesus Christ and our being g
Rev 16: 16 Then they g the kings together

GATHERS (GATHER)

Ps 147: 2 he g the exiles of Israel.
Pr 10: 5 He who g crops in summer is a wise
Isa 40: 11 He g the lambs in his arms
Mt 23: 37 a hen g her chicks under her wings,

GAVE (GIVE)

Ge 2: 20 man g names to all the livestock,
3: 6 She also g some to her husband,
14: 20 Abram g him a tenth of everything.
28: 4 the land God g to Abraham."
35: 12 The land I g to Abraham
39: 23 g him success in whatever he did.
47: 11 g them property in the best part
Ex 4: 11 to him, "Who g man his mouth?
31: 18 he g him the two tablets
Dt 2: 12 did in the land the LORD g them
2: 36 The LORD our God g us all
3: 12 I g the Reubenites and the Gadites
3: 13 I g to the half tribe of Manasseh.
3: 15 And I g Gilead to Makir.
3: 16 Gadites I g the territory extending
8: 16 He g you manna to eat in the desert
26: 9 us to this place and g us this land,
Dt 32: 8 the Most High g the nations their
Jos 11: 23 and he g it as an inheritance
13: 14 tribe of Levi he g no inheritance,
14: 13 g him Hebron as his inheritance.
21: 44 The LORD g them rest
24: 13 I g you a land on which you did not
1Sa 27: 6 So on that day Achish g him Ziklag
2Sa 12: 8 I g you the house of Israel
1Ki 4: 29 God g Solomon wisdom
5: 12 The LORD g Solomon wisdom,
Ezr 2: 69 According to their ability they g
Ne 9: 15 In their hunger you g them bread
9: 20 You g your good Spirit
9: 22 You g them kingdoms and nations,
9: 27 compassion you g them deliverers,
Job 1: 21 LORD g and the LORD has taken
42: 10 prosperous again and g him twice
Ps 69: 21 and g me vinegar for my thirst.
135: 12 he g their land as an inheritance,
Ecc 12: 7 the spirit returns to God who g it.
Eze 3: 2 and he g me the scroll to eat.
Mt 1: 25 And he g him the name Jesus.
25: 35 and you g me something to drink,
25: 42 and you g me nothing to drink,
26: 26 Jesus took bread, g thanks
27: 50 in a loud voice, he g up his spirit.
Mk 6: 7 g them authority over evil spirits.
Jn 1: 12 he g the right to become children
3: 16 so loved the world that he g his one
17: 4 by completing the work you g me
17: 6 you g them to me and they have
19: 30 bowed his head and g up his spirit.
Ac 1: 3 g many convincing proofs that he
2: 45 they g to anyone as he had need.
11: 17 g them the same gift as he g us,
Ro 1: 24 Therefore God g them
1: 26 God g them over to shameful lusts.
1: 28 he g them over to a depraved mind,
8: 32 not spare his own Son, but g him up
2Co 5: 18 g us the ministry of reconciliation:
8: 3 For I testify that they g as much
8: 5 they g themselves first to the Lord
Gal 1: 4 who g himself for our sins
2: 20 who loved me and g himself for me
Eph 4: 8 and g gifts to men."
5: 2 as Christ loved us and g himself up
5: 25 and g himself up for her
2Th 2: 16 and by his grace g us eternal
1Ti 2: 6 who g himself as a ransom
Tit 2: 14 who g himself for us to redeem us
1Jn 3: 24 We know it by the Spirit he g us.

GAZE

Ps 27: 4 to g upon the beauty of the LORD
Pr 4: 25 fix your g directly before you.

GEDALIAH

Governor of Judah appointed by Nebuchadnezzar (2Ki 25:22-26; Jer 39-41).

GEHAZI*

Servant of Elisha (2Ki 4:12-5:27; 8:4-5).

GENEALOGIES

1Ti 1: 4 themselves to myths and endless g.
Tit 3: 9 avoid foolish controversies and g

GENERATION (GENERATIONS)

Ex 3: 15 am to be remembered from g to g.
Nu 32: 13 until the whole g of those who had
Dt 1: 35 of this evil g shall see the good land
Jdg 2: 10 After that whole g had been
Ps 24: 6 Such is the g of those who seek him
48: 13 tell of them to the next g.
71: 18 I declare your power to the next g,
78: 4 we will tell the next g
102: 18 Let this be written for a future g,
112: 2 each g of the upright will be blessed
145: 4 One g will commend your works
La 5: 19 your throne endures from g to g.
Da 4: 3 his dominion endures from g to g.
4: 34 his kingdom endures from g to g.
Joel 1: 3 and their children to the next g.
Mt 12: 39 adulterous g asks for a miraculous
17: 17 "O unbelieving and perverse g,"
23: 36 all this will come upon this g.
24: 34 this g will certainly not pass away
Mk 9: 19 "O unbelieving g," Jesus replied,
13: 30 this g will certainly not pass away
Lk 1: 50 who fear him, from g to g.
11: 29 Jesus said, "This is a wicked g.
11: 30 will the Son of Man be to this g.
11: 50 Therefore this g will be held
21: 32 this g will certainly not pass away
Ac 2: 40 Save yourselves from this corrupt g
Php 2: 15 fault in a crooked and depraved g,

GENERATIONS (GENERATION)

Ge 9: 12 a covenant for all g to come:
17: 7 after you for the g to come,
17: 9 after you for the g to come.
Ex 31: 13 and you for the g to come,
Dt 7: 9 covenant of love to a thousand g
32: 7 consider the g long past.
1Ch 16: 15 he commanded, for a thousand g,
Job 8: 8 "Ask the former g
Ps 22: 30 future g will be told about the Lord
33: 11 of his heart through all g.
45: 17 your memory through all g;
89: 1 faithfulness known through all g.
90: 1 throughout all g.
100: 5 continues through all g.
102: 12 your renown endures through all g.
105: 8 he commanded, for a thousand g,
119: 90 continues through all g;
135: 13 renown, O LORD, through all g.
145: 13 dominion endures through all g.
146: 10 your God, O Zion, for all g.
Pr 27: 24 and a crown is not secure for all g.
Isa 41: 4 forth the g from the beginning?
51: 8 my salvation through all g."
Lk 1: 48 now on all g will call me blessed,
Eph 3: 5 not made known to men in other g
3: 21 in Christ Jesus throughout all g,
Col 1: 26 been kept hidden for ages and g,

GENEROSITY* (GENEROUS)

2Co 8: 2 poverty welled up in rich g.
9: 11 and through us your g will result
9: 13 and for your g in sharing with them

GENEROUS* (GENEROSITY)

Ps 37: 26 They are always g and lend freely;
112: 5 Good will come to him who is g
Pr 11: 25 A g man will prosper;
22: 9 A g man will himself be blessed,
Mt 20: 15 Or are you envious because I am g
2Co 9: 5 Then it will be ready as a g gift,
9: 5 for the g gift you had promised.
9: 11 way so that you can be g
1Ti 6: 18 and to be g and willing to share.

GENTILE (GENTILES)

Ac 21: 25 As for the G believers, we have
Ro 1: 16 first for the Jew, then for the G.
2: 9 first for the Jew, then for the G;
2: 10 first for the Jew, then for the G.
10: 12 difference between Jew and G—

GENTILES (GENTILE)

Isa 42: 6 and a light for the G,
49: 6 also make you a light for the G,
49: 22 "See, I will beckon to the G,
Lk 2: 32 a light for revelation to the G
21: 24 on by the G until the times
Ac 9: 15 to carry my name before the G
10: 45 been poured out even on the G.
11: 18 granted the G repentance unto life
13: 16 and you G who worship God,
13: 46 of eternal life, we now turn to the G
13: 47 I have made you a light for the G,
14: 27 opened the door of faith to the G.
15: 14 by taking from the G a people
18: 6 From now on I will go to the G."
22: 21 I will send you far away to the G.'"
26: 20 and in all Judea, and to the G also,

Ac 28: 28 salvation has been sent to the *G*,
Ro 2: 14 when *G*, who do not have the law,
3: 9 and *G* alike are all under sin.
3: 29 Is he not the God of *G* too? Yes,
9: 24 from the Jews but also from the *G*?
11: 11 to the *G* to make Israel envious.
11: 12 their loss means riches for the *G*,
11: 13 as I am the apostle to the *G*,
15: 9 I will praise you among the *G*;
15: 9 so that the *G* may glorify God
1Co 1: 23 block to Jews and foolishness to *G*,
Gal 1: 16 I might preach him among the *G*,
2: 2 gospel that I preach among the *G*.
2: 8 my ministry as an apostle to the *G*.
2: 9 agreed that we should go to the *G*,
3: 8 that God would justify the *G*
3: 14 to the *G* through Christ Jesus,
Eph 3: 6 the gospel the *G* are heirs together
3: 8 to the *G* the unsearchable riches
Col 1: 27 among the *G* the glorious riches
1Ti 2: 7 a teacher of the true faith to the *G*.
2Ti 4: 17 and all the *G* might hear it.

GENTLE* (GENTLENESS)

Dt 28: 54 Even the most *g* and sensitive man
28: 56 The most *g* and sensitive woman
28: 56 and *g* that she would not venture
2Sa 18: 5 Be *g* with the young man Absalom
1Ki 19: 12 And after the fire came a *g* whisper
Job 41: 3 Will he speak to you with *g* words?
Pr 15: 1 A *g* answer turns away wrath,
25: 15 and a *g* tongue can break a bone.
Jer 11: 19 I had been like a *g* lamb led
Zec 9: 9 *g* and riding on a donkey,
Mt 11: 29 for I am *g* and humble in heart,
21: 5 *g* and riding on a donkey,
Ac 27: 13 When a *g* south wind began
1Co 4: 21 or in love and with a *g* spirit?
Eph 4: 2 Be completely humble and *g*;
1Th 2: 7 but we were *g* among you,
1Ti 3: 3 not violent but *g*, not quarrelsome,
1Pe 3: 4 the unfading beauty of a *g*

GENTLENESS* (GENTLE)

2Co 10: 1 By the meekness and *g* of Christ,
Gal 5: 23 faithfulness, *g* and self-control.
Php 4: 5 Let your *g* be evident to all.
Col 3: 12 kindness, humility, *g* and patience.
1Ti 6: 11 faith, love, endurance and *g*.
1Pe 3: 15 But do this with *g* and respect,

GENUINE*

2Co 6: 8 *g*, yet regarded as impostors;
Php 2: 20 who takes a *g* interest
1Pe 1: 7 may be proved *g* and may result

GERIZIM

Dt 27: 12 on Mount *G* to bless the people:

GERSHOM

Ex 2: 22 and Moses named him *G*, saying,

GETHSEMANE*

Mt 26: 36 disciples to a place called *G*,
Mk 14: 32 They went to a place called *G*,

GHOST see also SPIRIT

Lk 24: 39 a *g* does not have flesh and bones,

GIBEON

Jos 10: 12 "O sun, stand still over *G*,

GIDEON*

Judge, also called Jerub-Baal; freed Israel from Midianites (Jdg 6-8; Heb 11:32). Given sign of fleece (Jdg 8:36-40).

GIFT (GIFTED GIFTS)

Pr 18: 16 A *g* opens the way for the giver
21: 14 A *g* given in secret soothes anger,
Ecc 3: 13 in all his toil—this is the *g* of God.
Mt 5: 23 if you are offering your *g*
Jn 4: 10 "If you knew the *g* of God
Ac 1: 4 wait for the *g* my Father promised,
2: 38 And you will receive the *g*
11: 17 So if God gave them the same *g*
Ro 6: 23 but the *g* of God is eternal life
12: 6 If a man's *g* is prophesying,
1Co 7: 7 each man has his own *g* from God;
2Co 8: 12 the *g* is acceptable according
9: 15 be to God for his indescribable *g*!
Eph 2: 8 it is the *g* of God—not by works,
1Ti 4: 14 not neglect your *g*, which was
2Ti 1: 6 you to fan into flame the *g* of God,
Heb 6: 4 who have tasted the heavenly *g*,
Jas 1: 17 and perfect *g* is from above,
1Pe 3: 7 with you of the gracious *g* of life,
4: 10 should use whatever *g* he has
Rev 22: 17 let him take the free *g* of the water

GIFTED* (GIFT)

1Co 14: 37 he is a prophet or spiritually *g*,

GIFTS (GIFT)

Ps 76: 11 bring *g* to the One to be feared.
112: 9 He has scattered abroad his *g*
Pr 25: 14 of *g* he does not give.
Mt 2: 11 and presented him with *g* of gold
7: 11 Father in heaven give good *g*
7: 11 to give good *g* to your children,
Lk 11: 13 to give good *g* to your children,
Ac 10: 4 and *g* to the poor have come up
Ro 11: 29 for God's *g* and his call are
12: 6 We have different *g*, according
1Co 12: 1 Now about spiritual *g*, brothers,
12: 4 There are different kinds of *g*,
12: 28 those with *g* of administration,
12: 30 all work miracles? Do all have *g*
12: 31 But eagerly desire the greater *g*.
14: 1 and eagerly desire spiritual *g*,
14: 12 eager to have spiritual *g*,
14: 12 excel in *g* that build up the church.
2Co 9: 9 "He has scattered abroad his *g*
Eph 4: 8 and gave *g* to men."
Heb 2: 4 and *g* of the Holy Spirit distributed
9: 9 indicating that the *g* and sacrifices

GILEAD

1Ch 27: 21 the half-tribe of Manasseh in *G*:
Jer 8: 22 Is there no balm in *G*?
46: 11 "Go up to *G* and get balm,

GILGAL

Jos 5: 9 So the place has been called *G*

GIRD*

Ps 45: 3 *G* your sword upon your side,

GIRL

Ge 24: 16 *g* was very beautiful, a virgin;
2Ki 5: 2 a young *g* from Israel.
Mk 5: 41 Little *g*, I say to you, get up!

GIVE (GAVE GIVEN GIVER GIVES GIVING LIFE-GIVING)

Ge 28: 22 that you *g* me I will *g* you a tenth."
Ex 20: 16 "You shall not *g* false testimony
30: 15 The rich are not to *g* more
Nu 6: 26 and *g* you peace."'
Dt 5: 20 "You shall not *g* false testimony
15: 10 *G* generously to him and do
15: 14 *G* to him as the LORD your God
1Sa 1: 11 then I will *g* him to the LORD
1: 28 So now I *g* him to the LORD.
2Ch 15: 7 be strong and do not *g* up,
Pr 21: 26 but the righteous *g* without sparing
23: 26 My son, *g* me your heart
25: 21 if he is thirsty, *g* him water to drink
30: 8 but *g* me only my daily bread.
31: 31 *G* her the reward she has earned,
Ecc 3: 6 a time to search and a time to *g* up,
Isa 42: 8 I will not *g* my glory to another
Eze 36: 26 I will *g* you a new heart
Mt 6: 11 *G* us today our daily bread.
7: 11 know how to *g* good gifts
Mt 10: 8 Freely you have received, freely *g*.
16: 19 I will *g* you the keys
22: 21 "*G* to Caesar what is Caesar's,
Mk 8: 37 Or what can a man *g* in exchange
10: 19 not steal, do not *g* false testimony,
Lk 6: 38 *G*, and it will be given to you.
11: 3 *G* us each day our daily bread.
11: 13 Father in heaven *g* the Holy Spirit
14: 33 who does not *g* up everything he
Jn 10: 28 I *g* them eternal life, and they shall
13: 34 "A new commandment I *g* you:
14: 16 he will *g* you another Counsellor
14: 27 I do not *g* to you as the world gives.
14: 27 leave with you; my peace I *g* you.
17: 2 people that he might *g* eternal life
Ac 20: 35 blessed to *g* than to receive.'"
Ro 2: 7 immortality, he will *g* eternal life.
8: 32 with him, graciously *g* us all things
12: 8 let him *g* generously;
13: 7 *G* everyone what you owe him:
14: 12 each of us will *g* an account
2Co 9: 7 Each man should *g* what he has
Gal 2: 5 We did not *g* in to them
6: 9 reap a harvest if we do not *g* up.
Heb 10: 25 Let us not *g* up meeting together,
Rev 14: 7 "Fear God and *g* him glory,

GIVEN (GIVE)

Nu 8: 16 are to be *g* wholly to me.
Dt 26: 11 things the LORD your God has *g*
Job 3: 23 Why is life *g* to a man
Ps 115: 16 but the earth he has *g* to man.
Isa 9: 6 to us a son is *g*,
Mt 6: 33 and all these things will be *g* to you
7: 7 "Ask and it will be *g* to you;
13: 12 Whoever has will be *g* more,
22: 30 people will neither marry nor be *g*
25: 29 everyone who has will be *g* more,
Lk 6: 38 Give, and it will be *g* to you.
8: 10 kingdom of God has been *g* to you,
11: 9 Ask and it will be *g* to you;
22: 19 saying, "This is my body *g* for you;
Jn 3: 27 man can receive only what is *g* him
15: 7 you wish, and it will be *g* you.
17: 24 I want those you have *g* me to be
17: 24 the glory you have *g* me
18: 11 the cup the Father has *g* me?"
Ac 5: 32 whom God has *g* to those who
20: 24 the task the Lord Jesus has *g* me—
Ro 5: 5 the Holy Spirit, whom he has *g* us.
1Co 4: 2 those who have been *g* a trust must
11: 24 and when he had *g* thanks,
12: 13 we were all *g* the one Spirit to drink
2Co 5: 5 and has *g* us the Spirit as a deposit,
Eph 1: 6 which he has freely *g* us
4: 7 to each one of us grace has been *g*
1Ti 4: 14 was *g* you through a prophetic
1Jn 4: 13 because he has *g* us of his Spirit.

GIVER* (GIVE)

Pr 18: 16 A gift opens the way for the *g*
2Co 9: 7 for God loves a cheerful *g*.

GIVES (GIVE)

Job 35: 10 who *g* songs in the night,
Ps 119: 130 The entrance of your words *g* light;
Pr 3: 34 but *g* grace to the humble.
11: 24 One man *g* freely, yet gains
14: 30 A heart at peace *g* life to the body,
15: 30 good news *g* health to the bones.
19: 6 of a man who *g* gifts.
25: 26 is a righteous man who *g* way
28: 27 He who *g* to the poor will lack
29: 4 justice a king *g* a country stability,
Isa 40: 29 He *g* strength to the weary
Hab 2: 15 "Woe to him who *g* drink
Mt 10: 42 And if anyone *g* a cup of cold water
Jn 5: 21 even so the Son *g* life to whom he is
6: 63 The Spirit *g* life; the flesh counts
1Co 15: 57 He *g* us the victory
2Co 3: 6 the letter kills, but the Spirit *g* life.
1Th 4: 8 who *g* you his Holy Spirit.
Jas 1: 25 into the perfect law that *g* freedom,

Jas 4: 6 but *g* grace to the humble."
1Pe 5: 5 but *g* grace to the humble."

GIVING (GIVE)

Ne 8: 8 *g* the meaning so that the people
Est 9: 19 a day for *g* presents to each other.
Ps 19: 8 *g* joy to the heart.
Pr 15: 23 A man finds joy in *g* an apt reply—
Mt 6: 4 so that your *g* may be in secret.
24: 38 marrying and *g* in marriage,
Ac 15: 8 them by *g* the Holy Spirit to them,
2Co 8: 7 also excel in this grace of *g*.
Php 4: 15 shared with me in the matter of *g*

GLAD* (GLADDENS GLADNESS)

Ex 4: 14 his heart will be *g* when he sees you
Jos 22: 33 They were *g* to hear the report
Jdg 8: 25 "We'll be *g* to give them."
18: 20 household?" Then the priest was *g*.
1Sa 19: 5 and you saw it and were *g*.
2Sa 1: 20 daughters of the Philistines be *g*,
1Ki 8: 66 and *g* in heart for all the good
1Ch 16: 31 heavens rejoice, let the earth be *g*;
2Ch 7: 10 and *g* in heart for the good things
Ps 5: 11 let all who take refuge in you be *g*;
9: 2 I will be *g* and rejoice in you;
14: 7 let Jacob rejoice and Israel be *g*!
16: 9 Therefore my heart is *g*
21: 6 made him *g* with the joy
31: 7 I will be *g* and rejoice in your love,
32: 11 Rejoice in the LORD and be *g*,
40: 16 rejoice and be *g* in you;
45: 8 music of the strings makes you *g*.
46: 4 whose streams make *g* the city
48: 11 the villages of Judah are *g*
53: 6 let Jacob rejoice and Israel be *g*!
58: 10 The righteous will be *g*
67: 4 May the nations be *g* and sing
68: 3 But may the righteous be *g*
69: 32 The poor will see and be *g*—
70: 4 rejoice and be *g* in you;
90: 14 for joy and be *g* all our days.
90: 15 Make us *g* for as many days
92: 4 For you make me *g* by your deeds,
96: 11 heavens rejoice, let the earth be *g*;
97: 1 LORD reigns, let the earth be *g*;
97: 8 and the villages of Judah are *g*
105: 38 Egypt was *g* when they left,
107: 30 They were *g* when it grew calm,
118: 24 let us rejoice and be *g* in it.
149: 2 of Zion be *g* in their King.
Pr 23: 15 then my heart will be *g*;
23: 25 May your father and mother be *g*;
29: 6 a righteous one can sing and be *g*.
Ecc 8: 15 sun than to eat and drink and be *g*.
Isa 25: 9 let us rejoice and be *g*
35: 1 and the parched land will be *g*;
65: 18 But be *g* and rejoice for ever
66: 10 with Jerusalem and be *g* for her,
Jer 20: 15 who made him very *g*, saying,
31: 13 Then maidens will dance and be *g*,
41: 13 were with him, they were *g*.
50: 11 "Because you rejoice and are *g*,
La 4: 21 be *g*, O Daughter of Edom,
Joel 2: 21 be *g* and rejoice.
2: 23 Be *g*, O people of Zion,
Hab 1: 15 and so he rejoices and is *g*.
Zep 3: 14 Be *g* and rejoice with all your heart
Zec 2: 10 and be *g*, O Daughter of Zion.
8: 19 will become joyful and *g* occasions
10: 7 their hearts will be *g* as with wine.
Mt 5: 12 be *g*, because great is your reward
Lk 15: 32 But we had to celebrate and be *g*,
Jn 4: 36 and the reaper may be *g* together.
8: 56 my day; he saw it and was *g*."
11: 15 for your sake I am *g* I was not there
14: 28 you would be *g* that I am going
Ac 2: 26 Therefore my heart is *g*
2: 46 together with *g* and sincere hearts,
11: 23 he was *g* and encouraged them all
13: 48 they were *g* and honoured the word
15: 3 news made all the brothers very *g*.
15: 31 were *g* for its encouraging message.
1Co 16: 17 was *g* when Stephanas, Fortunatus
2Co 2: 2 who is left to make me *g*
7: 16 I am *g* I can have complete
13: 9 We are *g* whenever we are weak
Gal 4: 27 "Be *g*, O barren woman,
Php 2: 17 I am *g* and rejoice with all of you.
2: 18 So you too should be *g* and rejoice
2: 28 you see him again you may be *g*
Rev 19: 7 Let us rejoice and be *g*

GLADDENS* (GLAD)

Ps 104: 15 wine that *g* the heart of man,

GLADNESS* (GLAD)

2Ch 29: 30 So they sang praises with *g*
Est 8: 16 a time of happiness and joy, *g*
8: 17 there was joy and *g*
Job 3: 22 who are filled with *g*
Ps 35: 27 shout for joy and *g*;
45: 15 They are led in with joy and *g*;
51: 8 Let me hear joy and *g*;
65: 12 the hills are clothed with *g*.
100: 2 Worship the LORD with *g*;
Ecc 5: 20 God keeps him occupied with *g*
9: 7 Go, eat your food with *g*,
Isa 16: 10 *g* are taken away from the orchards
35: 10 *G* and joy will overtake them,
51: 3 Joy and *g* will be found in her,
51: 11 *G* and joy will overtake them,
61: 3 the oil of *g* / instead of mourning,
Jer 7: 34 and *g* and to the voices of bride
16: 9 and *g* and to the voices of bride
25: 10 from them the sounds of joy and *g*,
31: 13 I will turn their mourning into *g*;
33: 11 once more the sounds of joy and *g*,
48: 33 Joy and *g* are gone
Joel 1: 16 joy and *g*

GLAZE*

Pr 26: 23 of *g* over earthenware

GLEAM*

Pr 4: 18 of the righteous is like the first *g*
Da 10: 6 legs like the *g* of burnished bronze,

GLOAT (GLOATS)

Pr 24: 17 Do not *g* when your enemy falls;

GLOATS* (GLOAT)

Pr 17: 5 whoever *g* over disaster will not go

GLORIES* (GLORY)

1Pe 1: 11 and the *g* that would follow.

GLORIFIED* (GLORY)

Isa 66: 5 'Let the LORD be *g*,
Eze 39: 13 day I am *g* will be a memorable day
Da 4: 34 and *g* him who lives for ever.
Jn 7: 39 since Jesus had not yet been *g*.
11: 4 glory so that God's Son may be *g*
12: 16 after Jesus was *g* did they realise
12: 23 come for the Son of Man to be *g*.
12: 28 "I have *g* it, and will glorify it again
13: 31 Son of Man *g* and God is *g* in him.
13: 32 If God is *g* in him, God will glorify
Ac 3: 13 our fathers, has *g* his servant Jesus.
Ro 1: 21 they neither *g* him as God
8: 30 those he justified, he also *g*.
2Th 1: 10 comes to be *g* in his holy people
1: 12 of our Lord Jesus may be *g* in you,
1Pe 1: 21 him from the dead and *g* him,

GLORIFIES* (GLORY)

Lk 1: 46 My soul *g* the Lord
Jn 8: 54 as your God, is the one who *g* me.

GLORIFY* (GLORY)

Ps 34: 3 *G* the LORD with me;
63: 3 my lips will *g* you.
69: 30 and *g* him with thanksgiving.
86: 12 I will *g* your name for ever.
Isa 60: 13 and I will *g* the place of my feet.
Da 4: 37 and exalt and *g* the King of heaven,
Jn 8: 54 Jesus replied, "If I *g* myself,
12: 28 glorified it, and will *g* it again."
12: 28 *g* your name!" Then a voice came
13: 32 God will *g* the Son in himself,
13: 32 in himself, and will *g* him at once.
17: 1 *G* your Son, that your Son may
17: 1 your Son, that your Son may *g* you.
17: 5 *g* me in your presence
21: 19 death by which Peter would *g* God.
Ro 15: 6 and mouth you may *g* the God
15: 9 so that the Gentiles may *g* God
1Pe 2: 12 and *g* God on the day he visits us.
Rev 16: 9 they refused to repent and *g* him.

GLORIFYING* (GLORY)

Lk 2: 20 *g* and praising God

GLORIOUS* (GLORY)

Dt 28: 58 not revere this *g* and awesome
33: 29 and your *g* sword.
1Ch 29: 13 and praise your *g* name.
Ne 9: 5 "Blessed be your *g* name,
Ps 3: 3 my *G* One, who lifts up my head.
16: 3 they are the *g* ones
45: 13 All *g* is the princess
72: 19 Praise be to his *g* name for ever;
87: 3 *G* things are said of you,
111: 3 *G* and majestic are his deeds,
145: 5 of the *g* splendour of your majesty,
145: 12 the *g* splendour of your kingdom.
Isa 3: 8 defying his *g* presence.
4: 2 the LORD will be beautiful and *g*,
11: 10 and his place of rest will be *g*.
12: 5 for he has done *g* things;
28: 1 to the fading flower, his *g* beauty,
28: 4 That fading flower, his *g* beauty,
28: 5 will be a *g* crown,
42: 21 to make his law great and *g*.
60: 7 and I will adorn my *g* temple.
63: 12 who sent his *g* arm of power
63: 14 to make for yourself a *g* name.
63: 15 from your lofty throne, holy and *g*.
64: 11 *g* temple, where our fathers praised
Jer 13: 18 for your *g* crowns
14: 21 do not dishonour your *g* throne.
17: 12 A *g* throne, exalted
48: 17 how broken the *g* staff!'
Mt 19: 28 the Son of Man sits on his *g* throne,
Lk 9: 31 appeared in *g* splendour, talking
Ac 2: 20 of the great and *g* day of the Lord.
Ro 8: 21 and brought into the *g* freedom
2Co 3: 8 of the Spirit be even more *g*?
3: 9 how much more *g* is the ministry
3: 9 ministry that condemns men is *g*,
3: 10 For what was *g* has no glory now
Eph 1: 6 to the praise of his *g* grace,
1: 17 *g* Father, may give you the Spirit
1: 18 the riches of his *g* inheritance
3: 16 of his *g* riches he may strengthen
Php 3: 21 so that they will be like his *g* body.
4: 19 to his *g* riches in Christ Jesus.
Col 1: 11 all power according to his *g* might
1: 27 among the Gentiles the *g* riches
1Ti 1: 11 to the *g* gospel of the blessed God,
Tit 2: 13 the *g* appearing of our great God
Jas 2: 1 believers in our *g* Lord Jesus Christ
1Pe 1: 8 with an inexpressible and *g* joy,
Jude : 24 before his *g* presence without fault

GLORIOUSLY* (GLORY)

Isa 24: 23 and before its elders, *g*.

GLORY (GLORIES GLORIFIED GLORIFIES GLORIFY GLORIFYING GLORIOUS GLORIOUSLY)

Ex 14: 4 But I will gain *g* for myself
14: 17 And I will gain *g* through Pharaoh
15: 11 awesome in *g*,
16: 10 and there was the *g* of the LORD
24: 16 and the *g* of the LORD settled
33: 18 Moses said, "Now show me your *g*
40: 34 and the *g* of the LORD filled

Nu 14:21 the g of the LORD fills the whole
Dt 5:24 LORD our God has shown us his g
Jos 7:19 "My son, give g to the LORD.
1Sa 4:21 "The g has departed from Israel"—
1Ch 16:10 G in his holy name;
16:24 Declare his g among the nations,
16:28 ascribe to the LORD g
29:11 and the g and the majesty
Ps 8:1 You have set your g
8:5 and crowned him with g and honour
19:1 The heavens declare the g of God;
24:7 that the King of g may come in.
26:8 the place where your g dwells.
29:1 ascribe to the LORD g
29:9 And in his temple all cry, "G!"
57:5 let your g be over all the earth.
66:2 Sing the g of his name;
72:19 the whole earth be filled with his g.
96:3 Declare his g among the nations,
102:15 of the earth will revere your g.
108:5 and let your g be over all the earth.
149:9 This is the g of all his saints.
Pr 19:11 it is to his g to overlook an offence.
25:2 It is the g of God to conceal
Isa 4:5 over all the g will be a canopy.
6:3 the whole earth is full of his g."
24:16 "G to the Righteous One."
26:15 You have gained g for yourself;
35:2 they will see the g of the LORD,
40:5 the g of the LORD will be revealed
42:8 I will not give my g to another
42:12 Let them give g to the LORD
43:7 whom I created for my g,
44:23 he displays his g in Israel.
48:11 I will not yield my g to another.
66:18 and they will come and see my g.
66:19 They will proclaim my g
Eze 1:28 the likeness of the g of the LORD.
10:4 the radiance of the g of the LORD.
43:2 and the land was radiant with his g.
44:4 and saw the g of the LORD filling
Hab 2:14 knowledge of the g of the LORD,
3:3 His g covered the heavens
Zec 2:5 'and I will be its g within.'
Mt 16:27 in his Father's g with his angels,
24:30 of the sky, with power and great g.
25:31 sit on his throne in heavenly g.
25:31 the Son of Man comes in his g,
Mk 8:38 in his Father's g with the holy
13:26 in clouds with great power and g.
Lk 2:9 and the g of the Lord shone
2:14 saying, "G to God in the highest,
9:26 and in the g of the Father
9:26 of him when he comes in his g
9:32 they saw his g and the two men
19:38 in heaven and g in the highest!"
21:27 in a cloud with power and great g.
24:26 these things and then enter his g?"
Jn 1:14 We have seen his g, the g of the one
2:11 He thus revealed his g,
8:50 I am not seeking g for myself;
8:54 myself, my g means nothing.
11:4 for God's g so that God's Son may
11:40 you would see the g of God?"
12:41 he saw Jesus' g and spoke about
14:13 so that the Son may bring g
15:8 is to my Father's g, that you bear
16:14 He will bring g to me by taking
17:4 I have brought you g on earth
17:5 presence with the g I had with you
17:10 g has come to me through them.
17:22 given them the g that you gave
17:24 to see my g, the g you have given
Ac 7:2 The God of g appeared
7:55 up to heaven and saw the g of God,
Ro 1:23 exchanged the g of the immortal
2:7 by persistence in doing good seek g
2:10 then for the Gentile; but g,
3:7 truthfulness and so increases his g,
3:23 and fall short of the g of God,
4:20 in his faith and gave g to God,
8:17 that we may also share in his g.
8:18 with the g that will be revealed
Ro 9:4 theirs the divine g, the covenants,
9:23 riches of his g known to the objects
9:23 whom he prepared in advance for g
11:36 To him be the g for ever! Amen.
15:17 Therefore I g in Christ Jesus
16:27 to the only wise God be g for ever
1Co 2:7 for our g before time began
10:31 whatever you do, do it all for the g
11:7 but the woman is the g of man.
11:7 since he is the image and g of God;
11:15 it is her g? For long hair is given
15:43 it is raised in g; it is sown
2Co 1:20 spoken by us to the g of God.
3:7 in letters on stone, came with g,
3:7 the face of Moses because of its g,
3:10 comparison with the surpassing g.
3:10 what was glorious has no g now
3:11 how much greater is the g
3:11 what was fading away came with g,
3:18 faces all reflect the Lord's g,
3:18 likeness with ever-increasing g,
4:4 of the gospel of the g of Christ,
4:6 of the knowledge of the g of God
4:15 to overflow to the g of God.
4:17 us an eternal g that far outweighs
Gal 1:5 to whom be g for ever and ever.
Eph 1:12 might be for the praise of his g.
1:14 to the praise of his g.
3:13 for you, which are your g.
3:21 to him be g in the church
Php 1:11 to the g and praise of God.
2:11 to the g of God the Father.
3:3 of God, who g in Christ Jesus,
4:20 and Father be g for ever and ever.
Col 1:27 Christ in you, the hope of g.
3:4 also will appear with him in g.
1Th 2:12 you into his kingdom and g.
2:19 in which we will g in the presence
2:20 Indeed, you are our g and joy.
2Th 2:14 in the g of our Lord Jesus Christ.
1Ti 1:17 be honour and g for ever and ever.
3:16 was taken up in g.
2Ti 2:10 is in Christ Jesus, with eternal g.
4:18 To him be g for ever and ever.
Heb 1:3 The Son is the radiance of God's g
2:7 you crowned him with g and honour
2:9 now crowned with g and honour
2:10 In bringing many sons to g,
5:5 take upon himself the g
9:5 the ark were the cherubim of the G,
13:21 to whom be g for ever and ever.
1Pe 1:7 g and honour when Jesus Christ is
1:24 and all their g is like the flowers
4:11 To him be the g and the power
4:13 overjoyed when his g is revealed.
4:14 for the Spirit of g and of God rests
5:1 will share in the g to be revealed:
5:4 of g that will never fade away.
5:10 you to his eternal g in Christ,
2Pe 1:3 of him who called us by his own g
1:17 and g from God the Father
1:17 came to him from the Majestic G,
3:18 To him be g both now and for ever!
Jude :25 to the only God our Saviour be g,
Rev 1:6 to him be g and power for ever
4:9 the living creatures give g,
4:11 to receive g and honour and power,
5:12 and honour and g and praise!"
5:13 and honour and g and power,
7:12 Praise and g
11:13 and gave g to the God of heaven.
14:7 "Fear God and give him g,
15:4 and bring g to your name?
15:8 with smoke from the g of God
19:1 g and power belong to our God,
19:7 and give him g!
21:11 It shone with the g of God,
21:23 for the g of God gives it light,
21:26 g and honour of the nations will be

GLOWING
Eze 8:2 was as bright as g metal.
Rev 1:15 His feet were like bronze g

GLUTTONS* (GLUTTONY)
Pr 23:21 for drunkards and g become poor,
28:7 of g disgraces his father.
Tit 1:12 always liars, evil brutes, lazy g."

GLUTTONY* (GLUTTONS)
Pr 23:2 throat if you are given to g.

GNASHING
Mt 8:12 where there will be weeping and g

GNAT* (GNATS)
Mt 23:24 You strain out a g but swallow

GNATS (GNAT)
Ex 8:16 of Egypt the dust will become g."

GOADS
Ecc 12:11 The words of the wise are like g,
Ac 26:14 hard for you to kick against the g.'

GOAL*
Lk 13:32 on the third day I will reach my g.'
2Co 5:9 So we make it our g to please him,
Gal 3:3 to attain your g by human effort?
Php 3:14 on towards the g to win the prize
1Ti 1:5 The g of this command is love,
1Pe 1:9 for you are receiving the g

GOAT (GOATS SCAPEGOAT)
Ge 15:9 "Bring me a heifer, a g and a ram,
30:32 and every spotted or speckled g,
37:31 slaughtered a g and dipped
Ex 26:7 Make curtains of g hair for the tent
Lev 16:9 shall bring the g whose lot falls
Nu 7:16 one male g for a sin offering;
Isa 11:6 the leopard will lie down with the g
Da 8:5 suddenly a g with a prominent

GOATS (GOAT)
Nu 7:17 five male g and five male lambs
Mt 25:32 separates the sheep from the g.
Heb 10:4 of bulls and g to take away sins.

GOD (GOD'S GODLINESS GODLY GODS)
Ge 1:1 In the beginning G created
1:2 and the Spirit of G was hovering
1:3 And G said, "Let there be light,"
1:7 So G made the expanse
1:9 And G said, "Let the water
1:11 Then G said, "Let the land produce
1:20 And G said, "Let the water teem
1:21 So G created the great creatures
1:25 G made the wild animals according
1:26 Then G said, "Let us make man
1:27 So G created man in his own image
1:31 G saw all that he had made,
2:3 And G blessed the seventh day
2:7 And the LORD G formed man
2:8 the LORD G had planted a garden
2:18 The LORD G said, "It is not good
2:22 Then the LORD G made a woman
3:1 to the woman, "Did G really say,
3:5 you will be like G, knowing good
3:8 from the LORD G among the trees
3:9 But the LORD G called to the man
3:21 The LORD G made garments
3:22 LORD G said, "The man has now
3:23 So the LORD G banished him
5:1 When G created man, he made him
5:22 Enoch walked with G 300 years
5:24 because G took him away.
6:2 sons of G saw that the daughters
6:9 of his time, and he walked with G.
6:12 G saw how corrupt the earth had
8:1 But G remembered Noah
9:1 Then G blessed Noah and his sons,
9:6 for in the image of G
9:16 everlasting covenant between G
14:18 He was priest of G Most High,
14:19 Blessed be Abram by G Most High,
16:13 "You are the G who sees me,"

Ge 17: 1 "I am *G* Almighty; walk before me
17: 7 to be your *G* and the *G*
21: 4 him, as *G* commanded him.
21: 6 "*G* has brought me laughter,
21: 20 *G* was with the boy as he grew up.
21: 22 *G* is with you in everything you do.
21: 33 name of the LORD, the Eternal *G*.
22: 1 Some time later *G* tested Abraham.
22: 8 "*G* himself will provide the lamb
22: 12 Now I know that you fear *G*,
25: 11 Abraham's death, *G* blessed his
28: 12 and the angels of *G* were ascending
28: 17 other than the house of *G*;
31: 42 But *G* has seen my hardship
31: 50 remember that *G* is a witness
32: 1 and the angels of *G* met him.
32: 28 because you have struggled with *G*
32: 30 "It is because I saw *G* face to face,
33: 11 for *G* has been gracious to me
35: 1 and build an altar there to *G*,
35: 5 and the terror of *G* fell
35: 10 *G* said to him, "Your name is Jacob
35: 11 *G* said to him, "I am *G* Almighty;
41: 51 *G* has made me forget all my
41: 52 *G* has made me fruitful in the land
50: 20 but *G* intended it for good
50: 24 But *G* will surely come to your aid
Ex 2: 24 *G* heard their groaning
3: 5 "Do not come any closer," *G* said.
3: 6 because he was afraid to look at *G*.
3: 12 And *G* said, "I will be with you.
3: 14 what shall I tell them?" *G* said
4: 27 he met Moses at the mountain of *G*
6: 7 own people, and I will be your *G*.
8: 10 is no-one like the LORD our *G*.
10: 16 sinned against the LORD your *G*
13: 18 So *G* led the people
15: 2 He is my *G*, and I will praise him,
16: 12 that I am the LORD your *G*.'"
17: 9 with the staff of *G* in my hands."
18: 5 camped near the mountain of *G*.
19: 3 Then Moses went up to *G*,
20: 1 And *G* spoke all these words:
20: 2 the LORD your *G*, who brought
20: 5 the LORD your *G*, am a jealous *G*,
20: 7 the name of the LORD your *G*,
20: 10 a Sabbath to the LORD your *G*.
20: 12 the LORD your *G* is giving you.
20: 19 But do not have *G* speak to us
20: 20 the fear of *G* will be with you
22: 20 "Whoever sacrifices to any *g* other
22: 28 "Do not blaspheme *G*
23: 19 to the house of the LORD your *G*.
31: 18 inscribed by the finger of *G*.
34: 6 the compassionate and gracious *G*,
34: 14 name is Jealous, is a jealous *G*.
Lev 2: 13 salt of the covenant of your *G* out
11: 44 the LORD your *G*; consecrate
18: 21 not profane the name of your *G*.
19: 2 the LORD your *G*, am holy.
20: 7 because I am the LORD your *G*.
21: 6 They must be holy to their *G*
22: 33 out of Egypt to be your *G*.
26: 12 walk among you and be your *G*,
Nu 15: 40 and will be consecrated to your *G*.
22: 18 the command of the LORD my *G*.
22: 38 I must speak only what *G* puts
23: 19 *G* is not a man, that he should lie,
25: 13 zealous for the honour of his *G*
Dt 1: 17 for judgment belongs to *G*.
1: 21 the LORD your *G* has given you
1: 30 The LORD your *G*, who is going
3: 22 LORD your *G* himself will fight
3: 24 For what *g* is there in heaven
4: 24 is a consuming fire, a jealous *G*.
4: 29 there you seek the LORD your *G*,
4: 31 the LORD your *G* is a merciful *G*;
4: 39 heart this day that the LORD is *G*
5: 9 the LORD your *G*, am a jealous *G*,
5: 11 the name of the LORD your *G*,
5: 12 the LORD your *G* has commanded
5: 14 a Sabbath to the LORD your *G*.
5: 15 the LORD your *G* brought you out

Dt 5: 16 the LORD your *G* has commanded
5: 16 the LORD your *G* is giving you.
5: 24 LORD our *G* has shown us his
5: 26 of the living *G* speaking out of fire,
6: 2 them may fear the LORD your *G*
6: 4 LORD our *G*, the LORD is one.
6: 5 Love the LORD your *G*
6: 13 the LORD your *G*, serve him only
6: 16 Do not test the LORD your *G*
7: 6 holy to the LORD your *G*.
7: 9 your *G* is *G*; he is the faithful *G*,
7: 12 the LORD your *G* will keep his
7: 19 LORD your *G* will do the same
7: 21 is a great and awesome *G*.
8: 5 the LORD your *G* disciplines you.
8: 11 do not forget the LORD your *G*,
8: 18 But remember the LORD your *G*,
9: 10 inscribed by the finger of *G*.
10: 12 but to fear the LORD your *G*,
10: 14 the LORD your *G* belong
10: 17 For the LORD your *G* is *G* of gods
10: 21 He is your praise; he is your *G*,
11: 1 Love the LORD your *G*
11: 13 to love the LORD your *G*
12: 12 rejoice before the LORD your *G*,
12: 28 in the eyes of the LORD your *G*.
13: 3 The LORD your *G* is testing you
13: 4 the LORD your *G* you must
15: 6 the LORD your *G* will bless you
15: 19 the LORD your *G* every firstborn
16: 11 rejoice before the LORD your *G*
16: 17 the LORD your *G* has blessed you.
18: 13 before the LORD your *G*.
18: 15 The LORD your *G* will raise up
19: 9 to love the LORD your *G*
22: 5 the LORD your *G* detests anyone
23: 5 the LORD your *G* loves you.
23: 14 the LORD your *G* moves about
23: 21 a vow to the LORD your *G*,
25: 16 the LORD your *G* detests anyone
26: 5 declare before the LORD your *G*:
29: 13 that he may be your *G*
29: 29 belong to the LORD our *G*,
30: 2 return to the LORD your *G*
30: 4 the LORD your *G* will gather you
30: 6 The LORD your *G* will circumcise
30: 16 today to love the LORD your *G*,
30: 20 you may love the LORD your *G*,
31: 6 for the LORD your *G* goes
32: 3 Oh, praise the greatness of our *G*!
32: 4 A faithful *G* who does no wrong,
33: 27 The eternal *G* is your refuge,
Jos 1: 9 for the LORD your *G* will be
14: 8 the LORD my *G* wholeheartedly.
14: 9 the LORD my *G* wholeheartedly.'
14: 14 the *G* of Israel, wholeheartedly.
22: 5 to love the LORD your *G*,
22: 22 The Mighty One, *G*, the LORD!
22: 34 BETWEEN US THAT THE LORD IS *G*.
23: 8 to hold fast to the LORD your *G*,
23: 11 careful to love the LORD your *G*.
23: 14 the LORD your *G* gave you has
23: 15 of the LORD your *G* has come true
24: 19 He is a holy *G*; he is a jealous *G*.
24: 23 to the LORD, the *G* of Israel."
Jdg 5: 3 to the LORD, the *G* of Israel.
16: 28 O *G*, please strengthen me just
Ru 1: 16 be my people and your *G* my *G*.
2: 12 by the LORD, the *G* of Israel,
1Sa 2: 2 there is no Rock like our *G*.
2: 3 for the LORD is a *G* who knows,
2: 25 another man, *G* may mediate
10: 26 men whose hearts *G* had touched.
12: 12 the LORD your *G* was your king.
16: 15 spirit from *G* is tormenting you.
17: 26 defy the armies of the living *G*?"
17: 36 defied the armies of the living *G*.
17: 45 the *G* of the armies of Israel,
17: 46 world will know that there is a *G*
23: 16 and helped him find strength in *G*.
28: 15 and *G* has turned away from me.
30: 6 strength in the LORD his *G*.
2Sa 7: 22 and there is no *G* but you,

2Sa 7: 23 on earth that *G* went out to redeem
14: 14 But *G* does not take away life;
21: 14 *G* answered prayer on behalf
22: 3 my *G* is my rock, in whom I take
22: 31 "As for *G*, his way is perfect;
22: 32 And who is the Rock except our *G*
22: 33 It is *G* who arms me with strength
22: 47 Exalted be *G*, the Rock, my Saviour!
1Ki 2: 3 what the LORD your *G* requires:
4: 29 *G* gave Solomon wisdom
5: 5 for the Name of the LORD my *G*,
8: 23 there is no *G* like you in heaven
8: 27 "But will *G* really dwell on earth?
8: 60 may know that the LORD is *G*
8: 61 committed to the LORD our *G*,
10: 24 to hear the wisdom *G* had put
15: 30 he provoked the LORD, the *G*
18: 21 If the LORD is *G*, follow him;
18: 36 it be known today that you are *G*
18: 37 are *G*, and that you are turning
20: 28 a *g* of the hills and not a *g*
2Ki 5: 15 "Now I know that there is no *G*
18: 5 in the LORD, the *G* of Israel.
19: 15 *G* of Israel, enthroned
19: 19 Now, O LORD our *G*, deliver us
1Ch 12: 18 for your *G* will help you."
13: 2 if it is the will of the LORD our *G*,
16: 35 Cry out, "Save us, O *G* our Saviour;
17: 20 and there is no *G* but you,
17: 24 the *G* over Israel, is Israel's *G*!'
21: 8 said to *G*, "I have sinned greatly
22: 1 house of the LORD *G* is to be here,
22: 19 soul to seeking the LORD your *G*.
28: 2 for the footstool of our *G*,
28: 9 acknowledge the *G* of your father,
28: 20 for the LORD *G*, my *G*, is with you
29: 1 not for man but for the LORD *G*.
29: 2 provided for the temple of my *G*—
29: 3 of my *G* I now give my personal
29: 10 *G* of our father Israel,
29: 13 Now, our *G*, we give you thanks,
29: 16 O LORD our *G*, as for all this
29: 17 my *G*, that you test the heart
29: 18 *G* of our fathers Abraham,
2Ch 2: 4 for the Name of the LORD my *G*
5: 14 of the LORD filled the temple of *G*
6: 4 be to the LORD, the *G* of Israel,
6: 14 there is no *G* like you in heaven
6: 18 "But will *G* really dwell on earth
10: 15 for this turn of events was from *G*,
13: 12 *G* is with us; he is our leader.
15: 3 was without the true *G*,
15: 12 the *G* of their fathers,
15: 15 They sought *G* eagerly,
18: 13 I can tell him only what my *G* says
19: 3 have set your heart on seeking *G*."
19: 7 with the LORD our *G* there is no
20: 6 are you not the *G* who is in heaven?
20: 20 Have faith in the LORD your *G*
25: 8 for *G* has the power to help
26: 5 sought the LORD, *G* gave him
30: 9 for the LORD your *G* is gracious
30: 19 who sets his heart on seeking *G*—
31: 21 he sought his *G* and worked
32: 31 *G* left him to test him
33: 12 the favour of the LORD his *G*
34: 33 fail to follow the LORD, the *G*
Ezr 6: 21 to seek the LORD, the *G* of Israel.
7: 18 accordance with the will of your *G*.
7: 23 Whatever the *G* of heaven has
8: 22 "The gracious hand of our *G* is
8: 31 The hand of our *G* was on us,
9: 6 "O my *G*, I am too ashamed
9: 9 our *G* has not deserted us
9: 13 our *G*, you have punished us less
9: 15 *G* of Israel, you are righteous!
Ne 1: 5 the great and awesome *G*,
5: 9 fear of our *G* to avoid the reproach
5: 15 for *G* I did not act like that.
7: 2 feared *G* more than most men do.
8: 8 from the Book of the Law of *G*,
8: 18 from the Book of the Law of *G*.
9: 5 and praise the LORD your *G*,

Ne 9:17 But you are a forgiving *G*,
9:31 you are a gracious and merciful *G*.
9:32 the great, mighty and awesome *G*,
10:29 oath to follow the Law of *G* given
10:39 not neglect the house of our *G*."
12:43 *G* had given them great joy.
13:11 Why is the house of *G* neglected?"
13:26 He was loved by his *G*,
13:31 Remember me with favour, O my *G*
Job 1:1 he feared *G* and shunned evil.
1:22 by charging *G* with wrongdoing.
2:10 Shall we accept good from *G*,
4:17 a mortal be more righteous than *G*?
5:17 is the man whom *G* corrects;
8:3 Does *G* pervert justice?
8:20 "Surely *G* does not reject
9:2 a mortal be righteous before *G*?
11:7 Can you fathom the mysteries of *G*
12:13 "To *G* belong wisdom and power;
16:7 Surely, O *G*, you have worn me out
19:26 yet in my flesh I will see *G*;
21:19 '*G* stores up a man's punishment
21:22 Can anyone teach knowledge to *G*,
22:12 "Is not *G* in the heights of heaven?
22:13 Yet you say, 'What does *G* know?
22:21 "Submit to *G* and be at peace
25:2 "Dominion and awe belong to *G*;
25:4 can a man be righteous before *G*?
26:6 Death is naked before *G*;
30:20 O *G*, but you do not answer;
31:6 let *G* weigh me in honest scales
31:14 do when *G* confronts me?
32:13 let *G* refute him, not man.'
33:6 I am just like you before *G*;
33:14 For *G* does speak—now one way,
33:26 He prays to *G* and finds favour
34:10 Far be it from *G* to do evil,
34:12 is unthinkable that *G* would do
34:23 *G* has no need to examine men
34:33 Should *G* then reward you
36:5 "*G* is mighty, but does not despise
36:26 is *G*—beyond our understanding!
37:22 *G* comes in awesome majesty.
Ps 5:4 You are not a *G* who takes pleasure
7:11 *G* is a righteous judge,
10:14 O *G*, do see trouble and grief;
14:5 for *G* is present in the company
18:2 my *G* is my rock, in whom I take
18:28 my *G* turns my darkness into light.
18:30 As for *G*, his way is perfect;
18:31 And who is the Rock except our *G*
18:32 It is *G* who arms me with strength
18:46 Exalted be *G* my Saviour!
19:1 The heavens declare the glory of *G*;
22:1 *G*, my *G*, why have you forsaken
22:10 womb you have been my *G*.
27:9 O *G* my Saviour.
29:3 The *G* of glory thunders,
31:5 redeem me, O LORD, the *G*
31:14 I say, "You are my *G*."
33:12 the nation whose *G* is the LORD,
35:24 righteousness, O LORD my *G*;
37:31 The law of his *G* is in his heart;
40:3 a hymn of praise to our *G*.
40:8 I desire to do your will, O my *G*;
42:1 so my soul pants for you, O *G*.
42:2 thirsts for *G*, for the living *G*.
42:5 Put your hope in *G*,
42:8 a prayer to the *G* of my life.
42:11 Put your hope in *G*,
43:4 to *G*, my joy and my delight.
44:8 In *G* we make our boast all day
45:6 O *G*, will last for ever and ever;
45:7 therefore *G*, your *G*, has set you
46:1 *G* is our refuge and strength,
46:5 *G* will help her at break of day.
46:10 "Be still, and know that I am *G*;
47:1 shout to *G* with cries of joy.
47:6 Sing praises to *G*, sing praises;
47:7 For *G* is the King of all the earth;
48:9 Within your temple, O *G*,
49:7 or give to *G* a ransom for him—
50:2 *G* shines forth.
Ps 50:3 Our *G* comes and will not be silent;
51:1 Have mercy on me, O *G*,
51:10 Create in me a pure heart, O *G*,
51:17 O *G*, you will not despise.
53:2 any who seek *G*.
54:4 Surely *G* is my help;
55:19 *G*, who is enthroned for ever,
56:4 In *G*, whose word I praise,
56:10 In *G*, whose word I praise,
56:13 that I may walk before *G*
57:3 *G* sends his love and his
57:7 My heart is steadfast, O *G*,
59:17 are my fortress, my loving *G*.
62:1 My soul finds rest in *G* alone;
62:7 my honour depend on *G*;
62:8 for *G* is our refuge.
62:11 One thing *G* has spoken,
63:1 O *G*, you are my *G*,
65:5 O *G* our Saviour,
66:1 Shout with joy to *G*, all the earth!
66:3 Say to *G*, "How awesome are your
66:5 Come and see what *G* has done,
66:16 listen, all you who fear *G*;
66:20 Praise be to *G*,
68:4 Sing to *G*, sing praise to his name,
68:6 *G* sets the lonely in families,
68:20 Our *G* is a *G* who saves;
68:24 has come into view, O *G*,
68:35 You are awesome, O *G*,
69:5 You know my folly, O *G*;
70:1 Hasten, O *G*, to save me;
70:4 "Let *G* be exalted!"
70:5 come quickly to me, O *G*.
71:17 my youth, O *G*, you have taught
71:18 do not forsake me, O *G*,
71:19 reaches to the skies, O *G*,
71:22 harp for your faithfulness, O my *G*;
73:17 me till I entered the sanctuary of *G*;
73:26 but *G* is the strength of my heart
76:11 Make vows to the LORD your *G*
77:13 What *g* is so great as our *G*?
77:14 You are the *G* who performs
78:19 Can *G* spread a table in the desert?
79:9 Help us, O *G* our Saviour,
81:1 Sing for joy to *G* our strength;
82:1 *G* presides in the great assembly;
84:2 out for the living *G*.
84:10 a doorkeeper in the house of my *G*
84:11 For the LORD *G* is a sun
86:12 O Lord my *G*, with all my heart;
86:15 a compassionate and gracious *G*,
87:3 O city of *G*: *Selah*
89:7 of the holy ones *G* is greatly feared;
90:2 to everlasting you are *G*.
91:2 my *G*, in whom I trust."
94:22 my *G* the rock in whom I take
95:7 for he is our *G*
99:8 you were to Israel a forgiving *G*,
99:9 Exalt the LORD our *G*
100:3 Know that the LORD is *G*.
108:1 My heart is steadfast, O *G*;
113:5 Who is like the LORD our *G*,
115:3 Our *G* is in heaven;
116:5 our *G* is full of compassion.
123:2 look to the LORD our *G*,
136:2 Give thanks to the *G* of gods.
136:26 Give thanks to the *G* of heaven.
139:17 to me are your thoughts, O *G*!
139:23 Search me, O *G*, and know my
143:10 for you are my *G*;
144:2 He is my loving *G* and my fortress,
147:1 is to sing praises to our *G*,
Pr 3:4 in the sight of *G* and man.
14:31 to the needy honours *G*.
25:2 of *G* to conceal a matter;
30:5 "Every word of *G* is flawless;
Ecc 2:26 *G* gives wisdom, knowledge
3:11 cannot fathom what *G* has done
3:13 in all his toil—this is the gift of *G*.
3:14 *G* does it, so men will revere him.
5:4 When you make a vow to *G*,
5:19 in his work—this is a gift of *G*.
8:12 who are reverent before *G*.
Ecc 11:5 cannot understand the work of *G*,
12:7 the spirit returns to *G* who gave it.
12:13 Fear *G* and keep his
Isa 5:16 the holy *G* will show himself holy
9:6 Wonderful Counsellor, Mighty *G*,
12:2 Surely *G* is my salvation;
25:9 "Surely this is our *G*;
28:11 *G* will speak to this people,
29:23 will stand in awe of the *G* of Israel.
30:18 For the LORD is a *G* of justice.
35:4 your *G* will come,
37:16 you alone are *G* over all
40:1 says your *G*.
40:3 a highway for our *G*.
40:8 the word of our *G* stands for ever."
40:18 then, will you compare *G*?
40:28 The LORD is the everlasting *G*,
41:10 not be dismayed, for I am your *G*.
41:13 For I am the LORD, your *G*,
43:10 Before me no *g* was formed,
44:6 apart from me there is no *G*.
44:15 he also fashions a *g* and worships it;
45:18 he is *G*;
48:17 "I am the LORD your *G*,
52:7 "Your *G* reigns!"
52:12 *G* of Israel will be your rear guard.
55:7 to our *G*, for he will freely pardon.
57:21 says my *G*, "for the wicked."
59:2 you from your *G*;
60:19 and your *G* will be your glory.
61:2 and the day of vengeance of our *G*,
61:10 my soul rejoices in my *G*.
62:5 so will your *G* rejoice over you.
Jer 7:23 I will be your *G* and you will be my
10:10 But the LORD is the true *G*;
10:12 But *G* made the earth by his power;
23:23 "Am I only a *G* near by,"
23:36 distort the words of the living *G*,
31:33 I will be their *G*,
32:27 "I am the LORD, the *G*
42:6 for we will obey the LORD our *G*."
51:10 what the LORD our *G* has done.'
51:56 For the LORD is a *G* of retribution
Eze 28:13 the garden of *G*;
34:31 and I am your *G*, declares
Da 2:28 there is a *G* in heaven who reveals
3:17 the *G* we serve is able to save us
3:29 for no other *g* can save in this way
6:16 "May your *G*, whom you serve
9:4 O Lord, the great and awesome *G*,
10:12 to humble yourself before your *G*,
11:36 things against the *G* of gods.
Hos 1:9 my people, and I am not your *G*.
1:10 will be called 'sons of the living *G*'.
4:6 you have ignored the law of your *G*
6:6 acknowledgment of *G* rather
9:8 The prophet, along with my *G*,
12:6 and wait for your *G* always.
Joel 2:13 Return to the LORD your *G*,
2:23 rejoice in the LORD your *G*,
Am 4:12 prepare to meet your *G*, O Israel."
4:13 the LORD *G* Almighty is his name
Jnh 1:6 Get up and call on your *g*!
4:2 a gracious and compassionate *G*,
Mic 6:8 and to walk humbly with your *G*.
7:7 I wait for *G* my Saviour;
7:18 Who is a *G* like you,
Na 1:2 LORD is a jealous and avenging *G*;
Hab 3:18 I will be joyful in *G* my Saviour.
Zep 3:17 The LORD your *G* is with you,
Zec 14:5 Then the LORD my *G* will come,
Mal 2:10 Father? Did not one *G* create us?
2:16 says the LORD *G* of Israel,
3:8 Will a man rob *G*? Yet you rob me.
Mt 1:23 which means, "*G* with us."
4:4 comes from the mouth of *G*.'"
4:7 'Do not put the Lord your *G*
4:10 'Worship the Lord your *G*,
5:8 for they will see *G*.
6:24 You cannot serve both *G*
19:6 Therefore what *G* has joined
19:26 but with *G* all things are possible."
22:21 and to *G* what is God's."

Mt 22: 32 He is not the *G* of the dead
22: 37 "'Love the Lord your *G*
27: 46 which means, "My *G*, my *G*,
Mk 2: 7 Who can forgive sins but *G* alone?"
7: 13 Thus you nullify the word of *G*
10: 6 of creation *G* 'made them male
10: 9 Therefore what *G* has joined
10: 18 "No-one is good—except *G* alone.
10: 27 all things are possible with *G*."
11: 22 "Have faith in *G*," Jesus answered.
12: 17 and to *G* what is God's."
12: 29 the Lord our *G*, the Lord is one.
12: 30 Love the Lord your *G*
15: 34 which means, "My *G*, my *G*,
16: 19 and he sat at the right hand of *G*.
Lk 1: 30 Mary, you have found favour with *G*
1: 37 For nothing is impossible with *G*."
1: 47 my spirit rejoices in *G* my Saviour,
2: 14 "Glory to *G* in the highest,
2: 52 and in favour with *G* and men.
4: 8 'Worship the Lord your *G*
5: 21 Who can forgive sins but *G* alone?"
8: 39 tell how much *G* has done for you."
10: 9 'The kingdom of *G* is near you.'
10: 27 "'Love the Lord your *G*
13: 18 "What is the kingdom of *G* like?
18: 19 "No-one is good—except *G* alone.
18: 27 with men is possible with *G*."
20: 25 and to *G* what is God's."
20: 38 He is not the *G* of the dead,
22: 69 at the right hand of the mighty *G*."
Jn 1: 1 was with *G*, and the Word was *G*.
1: 18 ever seen *G*, but *G* the only ⌊Son⌋,
1: 29 Lamb of *G*, who takes away the sin
3: 16 "For *G* so loved the world that he
3: 34 the one whom *G* has sent speaks
4: 24 *G* is spirit, and his worshippers must
5: 44 praise that comes from the only *G*?
6: 29 answered, "The work of *G* is this:
7: 17 my teaching comes from *G* or
8: 42 to them, "If *G* were your Father,
8: 47 belongs to *G* hears what *G* says.
11: 40 you would see the glory of *G*?"
13: 3 from *G* and was returning to *G*;
13: 31 of Man glorified and *G* is glorified
14: 1 Trust in *G*; trust also in me.
17: 3 the only true *G*, and Jesus Christ,
20: 17 your Father, to my *G* and your *G*
20: 28 "My Lord and my *G*!"
20: 31 the Son of *G*, and that
Ac 2: 11 wonders of *G* in our own tongues!"
2: 24 But *G* raised him from the dead,
2: 33 Exalted to the right hand of *G*,
2: 36 *G* has made this Jesus, whom you
3: 15 but *G* raised him from the dead.
3: 19 Repent, then, and turn to *G*,
4: 31 and spoke the word of *G* boldly.
5: 4 You have not lied to men but to *G*
5: 29 "We must obey *G* rather than men!
5: 31 *G* exalted him to his own right
5: 32 whom *G* has given
7: 55 to heaven and saw the glory of *G*,
8: 21 your heart is not right before *G*.
11: 9 anything impure that *G* has made
12: 24 But the word of *G* continued
13: 32 What *G* promised our fathers he
15: 10 to test *G* by putting on the necks
17: 23 TO AN UNKNOWN *G*.
17: 30 In the past *G* overlooked such
20: 27 to you the whole will of *G*.
20: 32 "Now I commit you to *G*
24: 16 keep my conscience clear before *G*
Ro 1: 16 the power of *G* for the salvation
1: 17 a righteousness from *G* is revealed,
1: 18 The wrath of *G* is being revealed
1: 24 Therefore *G* gave them
1: 26 *G* gave them over to shameful lusts
2: 11 For *G* does not show favouritism.
2: 16 when *G* will judge men's secrets
3: 4 Let *G* be true, and every man a liar.
3: 19 world held accountable to *G*.
3: 23 and fall short of the glory of *G*,
3: 29 Is *G* the *G* of Jews only? Is he not
Ro 4: 3 say? "Abraham believed *G*,
4: 6 to whom *G* credits righteousness
4: 17 the *G* who gives life to the dead
4: 24 to whom *G* will credit
5: 1 we have peace with *G*
5: 5 because *G* has poured out his love
5: 8 *G* demonstrates his own love for us
6: 22 and have become slaves to *G*,
6: 23 but the gift of *G* is eternal life
8: 7 the sinful mind is hostile to *G*.
8: 17 heirs of *G* and co-heirs with Christ,
8: 28 in all things *G* works for the good
9: 14 What then shall we say? Is *G* unjust
9: 18 Therefore *G* has mercy
10: 9 in your heart that *G* raised him
11: 2 *G* did not reject his people,
11: 22 the kindness and sternness of *G*:
11: 32 For *G* has bound all men
13: 1 exist have been established by *G*.
14: 12 give an account of himself to *G*.
16: 20 *G* of peace will soon crush Satan
1Co 1: 18 are being saved it is the power of *G*.
1: 20 Has not *G* made foolish
1: 25 For the foolishness of *G* is wiser
1: 27 But *G* chose the foolish things
2: 9 what *G* has prepared
2: 11 of *G* except the Spirit of *G*.
3: 6 watered it, but *G* made it grow.
3: 17 God's temple, *G* will destroy
6: 20 Therefore honour *G* with your body.
7: 7 each man has his own gift from *G*;
7: 15 *G* has called us to live in peace.
7: 20 was in when *G* called him.
7: 24 each man, as responsible to *G*,
8: 3 man who loves *G* is known by *G*.
8: 8 food does not bring us near to *G*;
10: 13 *G* is faithful; he will not let you be
10: 31 do it all for the glory of *G*.
12: 24 But *G* has combined the members
14: 33 For *G* is not a *G* of disorder
15: 24 over the kingdom to *G* the Father
15: 28 so that *G* may be all in all.
15: 34 are some who are ignorant of *G*—
15: 57 be to *G*! He gives us the victory
2Co 1: 9 rely on ourselves but on *G*,
2: 14 be to *G*, who always leads us
2: 15 For we are to *G* the aroma of Christ
2: 17 we do not peddle the word of *G*
3: 5 but our competence comes from *G*.
4: 2 nor do we distort the word of *G*.
4: 7 this all-surpassing power is from *G*
5: 5 Now it is *G* who has made us
5: 19 that *G* was reconciling the world
5: 20 though *G* were making his appeal
5: 21 *G* made him who had no sin
6: 16 we are the temple of the living *G*.
9: 7 for *G* loves a cheerful giver.
9: 8 *G* is able to make all grace abound
10: 13 to the field *G* has assigned to us,
Gal 2: 6 *G* does not judge by external
3: 5 Does *G* give you his Spirit
3: 6 Abraham: "He believed *G*,
3: 11 justified before *G* by the law,
3: 26 You are all sons of *G* through faith
6: 7 not be deceived: *G* cannot be
Eph 1: 22 *G* placed all things under his feet
2: 8 it is the gift of *G*—not by works,
2: 10 which *G* prepared in advance for us
2: 22 in which *G* lives by his Spirit.
4: 6 one baptism; one *G* and Father
4: 24 to be like *G* in true righteousness
5: 1 Be imitators of *G*, therefore,
6: 6 doing the will of *G* from your heart.
Php 2: 6 Who, being in very nature *G*,
2: 9 Therefore *G* exalted him
2: 13 for it is *G* who works in you to will
4: 7 peace of *G*, which transcends all
4: 19 And my *G* will meet all your needs
Col 1: 19 For *G* was pleased
2: 13 *G* made you alive with Christ.
1Th 2: 4 trying to please men but *G*.
2: 13 but as it actually is, the word of *G*,
3: 9 How can we thank *G* enough
1Th 4: 7 For *G* did not call us to be impure,
4: 9 taught by *G* to love each other.
5: 9 For *G* did not appoint us
1Ti 2: 5 one mediator between *G* and men,
4: 4 For everything *G* created is good,
5: 4 for this is pleasing to *G*.
2Ti 1: 6 you to fan into flame the gift of *G*,
Tit 1: 2 which *G*, who does not lie,
2: 13 glorious appearing of our great *G*
Heb 1: 1 In the past *G* spoke
3: 4 but *G* is the builder of everything.
4: 4 "And on the seventh day *G* rested
4: 12 For the word of *G* is living
6: 10 *G* is not unjust; he will not forget
6: 18 in which it is impossible for *G* to lie
7: 19 by which we draw near to *G*.
7: 25 come to *G* through him,
10: 22 draw near to *G* with a sincere heart
10: 31 to fall into the hands of the living *G*
11: 5 commended as one who pleased *G*.
11: 6 faith it is impossible to please *G*,
12: 7 as discipline; *G* is treating you
12: 10 but *G* disciplines us for our good,
12: 29 for our *G* is a consuming fire.
13: 15 offer to *G* a sacrifice of praise—
Jas 1: 12 crown of life that *G* has promised
1: 13 For *G* cannot be tempted by evil,
1: 27 religion that *G* our Father accepts
2: 19 You believe that there is one *G*.
2: 23 "Abraham believed *G*,
4: 4 the world becomes an enemy of *G*.
4: 6 "*G* opposes the proud
4: 8 Come near to *G* and he will come
1Pe 1: 23 the living and enduring word of *G*.
2: 20 this is commendable before *G*.
3: 18 the unrighteous, to bring you to *G*.
4: 11 it with the strength *G* provides,
5: 5 because, "*G* opposes the proud
2Pe 1: 21 but men spoke from *G*
2: 4 For if *G* did not spare angels
1Jn 1: 5 *G* is light; in him there is no
2: 17 the will of *G* lives for ever.
3: 1 we should be called children of *G*!
3: 9 born of *G* will continue to sin,
3: 10 we know who the children of *G* are
3: 20 For *G* is greater than our hearts,
4: 7 for love comes from *G*.
4: 8 not know *G*, because *G* is love.
4: 9 This is how *G* showed his love
4: 11 Dear friends, since *G* so loved us,
4: 12 No-one has ever seen *G*;
4: 15 *G* lives in him and he in *G*.
4: 16 *G* is love.
4: 20 "I love *G*," yet hates his brother,
4: 21 Whoever loves *G* must
5: 2 that we love the children of *G*:
5: 3 love for *G*: to obey his commands.
5: 4 born of *G* overcomes the world.
5: 10 does not believe *G* has made him
5: 14 have in approaching *G*:
5: 18 born of *G* does not continue to sin;
Rev 4: 8 holy is the Lord *G* Almighty,
7: 12 be to our *G* for ever and ever.
7: 17 *G* will wipe away every tear
11: 16 fell on their faces and worshipped *G*,
15: 3 Lord *G* Almighty.
17: 17 For *G* has put it into their hearts
19: 6 For our Lord *G* Almighty reigns.
21: 3 Now the dwelling of *G* is with men,
21: 23 for the glory of *G* gives it light,

GOD-BREATHED* (BREATH)

2Ti 3: 16 All Scripture is *G* and is useful

GOD-FEARING* (FEAR)

Ecc 8: 12 that it will go better with *G* men,
Ac 2: 5 staying in Jerusalem *G* Jews
10: 2 all his family were devout and *G*;
10: 22 He is a righteous and *G* man,
13: 26 of Abraham, and you *G* Gentiles,
13: 50 But the Jews incited the *G* women
17: 4 as did a large number of *G* Greeks
17: 17 with the Jews and the *G* Greeks,

GOD-HATERS* (HATE)
Ro 1:30 They are gossips, slanderers, *G*,

GOD'S (GOD)
2Ch 20:15 For the battle is not yours, but *G*.
Job 37:14 stop and consider *G* wonders.
Ps 52:8 I trust in *G* unfailing love
69:30 I will praise *G* name in song
Mk 3:35 Whoever does *G* will is my brother
Jn 7:17 If anyone chooses to do *G* will,
10:36 'I am *G* Son'? Do not believe me
Ro 2:3 think you will escape *G* judgment?
2:4 not realising that *G* kindness leads
3:3 lack of faith nullify *G* faithfulness?
7:22 in my inner being I delight in *G* law
9:16 or effort, but on *G* mercy.
11:29 for *G* gifts and his call are
12:2 and approve what *G* will is—
12:13 Share with *G* people who are
13:6 for the authorities are *G* servants,
1Co 7:19 Keeping *G* commands is what
2Co 6:2 now is the time of *G* favour,
Eph 1:7 riches of *G* grace that he lavished
1Th 4:3 It is *G* will that you should be sanctified:
5:18 for this is *G* will for you
1Ti 6:1 so that *G* name and our teaching
2Ti 2:19 *G* solid foundation stands firm,
Tit 1:7 overseer is entrusted with *G* work,
Heb 1:3 The Son is the radiance of *G* glory
9:24 now to appear for us in *G* presence.
11:3 was formed at *G* command,
1Pe 2:15 For it is *G* will that
3:4 which is of great worth in *G* sight.
1Jn 2:5 *G* love is truly made complete

GODLESS
Job 20:5 the joy of the *g* lasts but a moment.
1Ti 6:20 Turn away from *g* chatter

GODLINESS (GOD)
1Ti 2:2 and quiet lives in all *g* and holiness.
4:8 but *g* has value for all things,
6:5 and who think that *g* is a means
6:6 *g* with contentment is great gain.
6:11 and pursue righteousness, *g*, faith,
2Pe 1:6 and to perseverance, *g*;

GODLY (GOD)
Ps 4:3 that the LORD has set apart the *g*
2Co 7:10 *G* sorrow brings repentance that
11:2 jealous for you with a *g* jealousy.
2Ti 3:12 everyone who wants to live a *g* life
2Pe 3:11 You ought to live holy and *g* lives

GODS (GOD)
Ex 20:3 "You shall have no other *g*
Dt 5:7 "You shall have no other *g*
1Ch 16:26 For all the *g* of the nations are idols
Ps 82:6 "I said, 'You are "*g*";
Jn 10:34 have said you are *g*'? If he called
Ac 19:26 He says that man-made *g* are no *g*

GOG
Eze 38:18 When *G* attacks the land of Israel,
Rev 20:8 *G* and Magog—to gather them

GOLD
1Ki 20:3 'Your silver and *g* are mine,
Job 22:25 then the Almighty will be your *g*,
23:10 tested me, I will come forth as *g*.
28:15 cannot be bought with the finest *g*,
31:24 "If I have put my trust in *g*
Ps 19:10 They are more precious than *g*,
119:127 more than *g*, more than pure *g*,
Pr 3:14 and yields better returns than *g*.
22:1 esteemed is better than silver or *g*.
Hag 2:8 The silver is mine and the *g* is mine
Mt 2:11 and presented him with gifts of *g*
Rev 3:18 to buy from me *g* refined in the fire,

GOLGOTHA*
Mt 27:33 to a place called *G* (which means
Mk 15:22 to the place called *G* (which means
Jn 19:17 (which in Aramaic is called *G*).

GOLIATH
Philistine giant killed by David (1Sa 17; 21:9).

GOMORRAH
Ge 19:24 sulphur on Sodom and *G*—
Mt 10:15 and *G* on the day of judgment
2Pe 2:6 and *G* by burning them to ashes,
Jude :7 *G* and the surrounding towns gave

GOOD
Ge 1:4 God saw that the light was *g*,
1:10 And God saw that it was *g*.
1:12 And God saw that it was *g*.
1:18 And God saw that it was *g*.
1:21 And God saw that it was *g*.
1:25 And God saw that it was *g*.
1:31 he had made, and it was very *g*.
2:9 and the tree of the knowledge of *g*
2:9 pleasing to the eye and *g* for food.
2:18 "It is not *g* for the man to be alone.
3:22 become like one of us, knowing *g*
50:20 but God intended it for *g*
2Ch 7:3 "He is *g*; / his love endures
31:20 doing what was *g* and right
Job 2:10 Shall we accept *g* from God,
Ps 14:1 there is no-one who does *g*.
34:8 Taste and see that the LORD is *g*;
34:14 Turn from evil and do *g*;
37:3 Trust in the LORD and do *g*;
37:27 Turn from evil and do *g*;
52:9 for your name is *g*.
53:3 there is no-one who does *g*,
84:11 no *g* thing does he withhold
100:5 For the LORD is *g* and his love
103:5 satisfies my desires with *g* things,
112:5 *G* will come to him who is
119:68 You are *g*, and what you do is *g*;
133:1 How *g* and pleasant it is
145:9 The LORD is *g* to all;
147:1 How *g* it is to sing praises
Pr 3:4 you will win favour and a *g* name
3:27 Do not withhold *g*
11:27 He who seeks *g* finds goodwill,
13:22 A *g* man leaves an inheritance
14:22 those who plan what is *g* find love
15:3 on the wicked and the *g*.
15:23 and how *g* is a timely word!
15:30 *g* news gives health to the bones.
17:22 A cheerful heart is *g* medicine,
18:22 He who finds a wife finds what is *g*
19:2 It is not *g* to have zeal
22:1 A *g* name is more desirable
31:12 She brings him *g*, not harm,
Ecc 12:14 whether it is *g* or evil.
Isa 5:20 Woe to those who call evil *g*
40:9 You who bring *g* tidings
52:7 the feet of those who bring *g* news,
61:1 me to preach *g* news to the poor.
Jer 6:16 ask where the *g* way is,
13:23 Neither can you do *g*
32:39 the *g* of their children after them.
Eze 34:14 I will tend them in a *g* pasture,
Mic 6:8 has showed you, O man, what is *g*.
Na 1:15 the feet of one who brings *g* news,
Mt 5:45 sun to rise on the evil and the *g*,
7:11 Father in heaven give *g* gifts
7:17 Likewise every *g* tree bears *g* fruit,
7:18 A *g* tree cannot bear bad fruit,
12:35 The *g* man brings *g* things out
13:8 Still other seed fell on *g* soil,
13:24 is like a man who sowed *g* seed
13:48 and collected the *g* fish in baskets,
19:17 "There is only One who is *g*.
22:10 both *g* and bad, and the wedding
25:21 'Well done, *g* and faithful servant!
Mk 1:15 Repent and believe the *g* news!'
3:4 lawful on the Sabbath: to do *g*
4:8 Still other seed fell on *g* soil.
8:36 What *g* is it for a man
10:18 "No-one is *g*—except God alone.
16:15 preach the *g* news to all creation.
Lk 2:10 I bring you *g* news
3:9 does not produce *g* fruit will be
6:27 do *g* to those who hate you,
6:43 nor does a bad tree bear *g* fruit.
6:45 The *g* man brings *g* things out
8:8 Still other seed fell on *g* soil.
9:25 What *g* is it for a man
14:34 "Salt is *g* but if it loses its saltiness,
18:19 "No-one is *g*—except God alone.
19:17 "'Well done, my *g* servant!'
Jn 10:11 "I am the *g* shepherd.
Ro 3:12 there is no-one who does *g*,
7:12 is holy, righteous and *g*.
7:16 want to do, I agree that the law is *g*.
7:18 I have the desire to do what is *g*,
8:28 for the *g* of those who love him,
10:15 feet of those who bring *g* news!"
12:2 his *g*, pleasing and perfect will.
12:9 Hate what is evil; cling to what is *g*.
13:4 For he is God's servant to do you *g*
16:19 you to be wise about what is *g*,
1Co 7:1 It is *g* for a man not to marry.
10:24 should seek his own *g*, but the *g*
15:33 Bad company corrupts *g* character
2Co 9:8 you will abound in every *g* work.
Gal 4:18 provided the purpose is *g*,
6:9 us not become weary in doing *g*,
6:10 as we have opportunity, let us do *g*
Eph 2:10 in Christ Jesus to do *g* works,
6:8 everyone for whatever *g* he does,
Php 1:6 that he who began a *g* work
Col 1:10 bearing fruit in every *g* work,
1Th 5:21 Hold on to the *g*.
1Ti 3:7 have a *g* reputation with outsiders,
4:4 For everything God created is *g*,
6:12 Fight the *g* fight of the faith.
6:18 them to do *g*, to be rich in *g* deeds,
2Ti 3:17 equipped for every *g* work.
4:7 I have fought the *g* fight, I have
Tit 1:8 loves what is *g*, who is
2:7 an example by doing what is *g*.
2:14 his very own, eager to do what is *g*.
Heb 5:14 to distinguish *g* from evil.
10:24 on towards love and *g* deeds.
12:10 but God disciplines us for our *g*,
13:16 do not forget to do *g* and to share
Jas 4:17 who knows the *g* he ought to do
1Pe 2:3 you have tasted that the Lord is *g*.
2:12 Live such *g* lives among the pagans
2:18 not only to those who are *g*
3:17 to suffer for doing *g*

GOODS
Ecc 5:11 As *g* increase,

GORGE
Pr 23:20 or *g* themselves on meat,

GOSHEN
Ge 45:10 You shall live in the region of *G*
Ex 8:22 differently with the land of *G*,

GOSPEL
Ro 1:16 I am not ashamed of the *g*,
15:16 duty of proclaiming the *g* of God,
15:20 to preach the *g* where Christ was
1Co 1:17 to preach the *g*—not with words
9:12 rather than hinder the *g* of Christ.
9:14 who preach the *g* should receive
9:16 Woe to me if I do not preach the *g*!
15:1 you of the *g* I preached to you,
15:2 By this *g* you are saved,
2Co 4:4 light of the *g* of the glory of Christ,
9:13 your confession of the *g*
Gal 1:7 a different *g*—which is really no *g*
Eph 6:15 comes from the *g* of peace.
Php 1:27 in a manner worthy of the *g*
Col 1:23 This is the *g* that you heard
1Th 2:4 by God to be entrusted with the *g*.
2Th 1:8 do not obey the *g* of our Lord Jesus
2Ti 1:10 immortality to light through the *g*.
Rev 14:6 he had the eternal *g* to proclaim

GOSSIP*
Pr 11:13 A *g* betrays a confidence,

Pr 16: 28 and a *g* separates close friends.
18: 8 of a *g* are like choice morsels;
20: 19 A *g* betrays a confidence;
26: 20 without *g* a quarrel dies down.
26: 22 of a *g* are like choice morsels;
2Co 12: 20 slander, *g*, arrogance and disorder.

GOVERN (GOVERNMENT)

Ge 1: 16 the greater light to *g* the day
Job 34: 17 Can he who hates justice *g*?
Ro 12: 8 it is leadership, let him *g* diligently;

GOVERNMENT (GOVERN)

Isa 9: 6 and the *g* will be on his shoulders.

GRACE* (GRACIOUS)

Ps 45: 2 lips have been anointed with *g*,
Pr 1: 9 will be a garland to *g* your head
3: 22 an ornament to *g* your neck.
3: 34 but gives *g* to the humble.
4: 9 She will set a garland of *g*
Isa 26: 10 Though *g* is shown to the wicked,
Jnh 2: 8 forfeit the *g* that could be theirs.
Zec 12: 10 of Jerusalem a spirit of *g*
Lk 2: 40 and the *g* of God was upon him.
Jn 1: 14 who came from the Father, full of *g*
1: 16 of his *g* we have all received one
1: 17 *g* and truth came through Jesus
Ac 4: 33 and much *g* was upon them all.
6: 8 a man full of God's *g* and power,
11: 23 saw the evidence of the *g* of God,
13: 43 them to continue in the *g* of God.
14: 3 message of his *g* by enabling them
14: 26 they had been committed to the *g*
15: 11 We believe it is through the *g*
15: 40 by the brothers to the *g* of the Lord
18: 27 to those who by *g* had believed.
20: 24 testifying to the gospel of God's *g*.
20: 32 to God and to the word of his *g*,
Ro 1: 5 we received *g* and apostleship
1: 7 *G* and peace to you
3: 24 and are justified freely by his *g*
4: 16 be by *g* and may be guaranteed
5: 2 access by faith into this *g*
5: 15 came by the *g* of the one man,
5: 15 how much more did God's *g*
5: 17 God's abundant provision of *g*
5: 20 where sin increased, *g* increased all
5: 21 also *g* might reign
6: 1 on sinning so that *g* may increase?
6: 14 you are not under law, but under *g*.
6: 15 we are not under law but under *g*?
11: 5 there is a remnant chosen by *g*.
11: 6 if by *g*, then it is no longer by works
11: 6 if it were, *g* would no longer be *g*.
12: 3 For by the *g* given me I say
12: 6 according to the *g* given us.
15: 15 because of the *g* God gave me
16: 20 The *g* of our Lord Jesus be
1Co 1: 3 *G* and peace to you
1: 4 of his *g* given you in Christ Jesus.
3: 10 By the *g* God has given me,
15: 10 But by the *g* of God I am what I am
15: 10 but the *g* of God that was with me.
15: 10 his *g* to me was not without effect.
16: 23 The *g* of the Lord Jesus be with you
2Co 1: 2 *G* and peace to you
1: 12 wisdom but according to God's *g*.
4: 15 so that the *g* that is reaching more
6: 1 not to receive God's *g* in vain.
8: 1 to know about the *g* that God has
8: 6 also to completion this act of *g*
8: 7 also excel in this *g* of giving.
8: 9 For you know the *g*
9: 8 able to make all *g* abound to you,
9: 14 of the surpassing *g* God has given
12: 9 "My *g* is sufficient for you,
13: 14 May the *g* of the Lord Jesus Christ,
Gal 1: 3 *G* and peace to you
1: 6 the one who called you by the *g*
1: 15 from birth and called me by his *g*,
2: 9 when they recognised the *g* given
Gal 2: 21 I do not set aside the *g* of God,
3: 18 God in his *g* gave it to Abraham
5: 4 you have fallen away from *g*.
6: 18 The *g* of our Lord Jesus Christ be
Eph 1: 2 *G* and peace to you
1: 6 to the praise of his glorious *g*,
1: 7 riches of God's *g* that he lavished
2: 5 it is by *g* you have been saved.
2: 7 the incomparable riches of his *g*,
2: 8 For it is by *g* you have been saved,
3: 2 of God's *g* that was given to me
3: 7 by the gift of God's *g* given me
3: 8 God's people, this *g* was given me:
4: 7 to each one of us *g* has been given
6: 24 *G* to all who love our Lord Jesus
Php 1: 2 *G* and peace to you
1: 7 all of you share in God's *g* with me.
4: 23 The *g* of the Lord Jesus Christ be
Col 1: 2 *G* and peace to you
1: 6 understood God's *g* in all its truth.
4: 6 conversation be always full of *g*,
4: 18 *G* be with you.
1Th 1: 1 and the Lord Jesus Christ: *G*
5: 28 The *g* of our Lord Jesus Christ be
2Th 1: 2 *G* and peace to you
1: 12 according to the *g* of our God
2: 16 and by his *g* gave us eternal
3: 18 The *g* of our Lord Jesus Christ be
1Ti 1: 2 my true son in the faith: *G*,
1: 14 The *g* of our Lord was poured out
6: 21 *G* be with you.
2Ti 1: 2 To Timothy, my dear son: *G*,
1: 9 This *g* was given us in Christ Jesus
1: 9 because of his own purpose and *g*.
2: 1 be strong in the *g* that is
4: 22 *G* be with you.
Tit 1: 4 *G* and peace from God the Father
2: 11 For the *g* of God that brings
3: 7 having been justified by his *g*,
3: 15 *G* be with you all.
Phm : 3 *G* to you and peace
: 25 The *g* of the Lord Jesus Christ be
Heb 2: 9 that by the *g* of God he might taste
4: 16 find *g* to help us in our time of need
4: 16 the throne of *g* with confidence,
10: 29 and who has insulted the Spirit of *g*
12: 15 See to it that no-one misses the *g*
13: 9 hearts to be strengthened by *g*,
13: 25 *G* be with you all.
Jas 4: 6 but gives *g* to the humble."
4: 6 But he gives us more *g*. That is why
1Pe 1: 2 *G* and peace be yours in abundance
1: 10 who spoke of the *g* that was
1: 13 fully on the *g* to be given you
4: 10 faithfully administering God's *g*
5: 5 but gives *g* to the humble."
5: 10 the God of all *g*, who called you
5: 12 and testifying that this is the true *g*
2Pe 1: 2 *G* and peace be yours in abundance
3: 18 But grow in the *g* and knowledge
2Jn : 3 and will be with us for ever: *G*,
Jude : 4 who change the *g* of our God
Rev 1: 4 *G* and peace to you
22: 21 The *g* of the Lord Jesus be

GRACIOUS (GRACE)

Ex 34: 6 the compassionate and *g* God,
Nu 6: 25 and be *g* to you;
Ne 9: 17 But you are a forgiving God, *g*
Ps 67: 1 May God be *g* to us and bless us
Pr 22: 11 a pure heart and whose speech is *g*
Isa 30: 18 Yet the LORD longs to be *g* to you

GRAIN

Lev 2: 1 When someone brings a *g* offering
Mk 4: 28 then the full *g* in the ear.
Lk 17: 35 women will be grinding *g* together;
Jn 12: 24 a *g* of wheat falls to the ground
1Co 9: 9 ox while it is treading out the *g*."

GRANDCHILDREN (CHILD)

1Ti 5: 4 But if a widow has children or *g*,

GRANDMOTHER (MOTHER)

2Ti 1: 5 which first lived in your *g* Lois

GRANT (GRANTED)

Ps 20: 5 May the LORD *g* all your requests
51: 12 *g* me a willing spirit, to sustain me.

GRANTED (GRANT)

Pr 10: 24 what the righteous desire will be *g*.
Mt 15: 28 great faith! Your request is *g*."
Php 1: 29 For it has been *g* to you on behalf

GRAPES

Nu 13: 23 branch bearing a single cluster of *g*
Jer 31: 29 'The fathers have eaten sour *g*,
Eze 18: 2 "'The fathers eat sour *g*,
Mt 7: 16 Do people pick *g* from thornbushes
Rev 14: 18 and gather the clusters of *g*

GRASPED

Php 2: 6 with God something to be *g*,

GRASS

Ps 103: 15 As for man, his days are like *g*,
Isa 40: 6 "All men are like *g*,
Mt 6: 30 If that is how God clothes the *g*
1Pe 1: 24 "All men are like *g*,

GRASSHOPPERS

Nu 13: 33 We seemed like *g* in our own eyes,

GRATIFY* (GRATITUDE)

Ro 13: 14 think about how to *g* the desires
Gal 5: 16 and you will not *g* the desires

GRATITUDE (GRATIFY)

Col 3: 16 and spiritual songs with *g*

GRAVE (GRAVES)

Nu 19: 16 who touches a human bone or a *g*,
Dt 34: 6 day no-one knows where his *g* is.
Ps 5: 9 Their throat is an open *g*;
49: 15 will redeem my soul from the *g*;
Pr 7: 27 Her house is a highway to the *g*,
Hos 13: 14 Where, O *g*, is your destruction?
Jn 11: 44 "Take off the *g* clothes
Ac 2: 27 you will not abandon me to the *g*,

GRAVES (GRAVE)

Eze 37: 12 I am going to open your *g*
Jn 5: 28 are in their *g* will hear his voice
Ro 3: 13 "Their throats are open *g*;

GREAT (GREATER GREATEST GREATNESS)

Ge 12: 2 I will make your name *g*,
12: 2 "I will make you into a *g* nation
Ex 32: 11 out of Egypt with *g* power
Nu 14: 19 In accordance with your *g* love,
Dt 4: 32 so *g* as this ever happened,
10: 17 the *g* God, mighty and awesome,
29: 28 in *g* wrath the LORD uprooted
Jos 7: 9 do for your own *g* name?'
Jdg 16: 5 you the secret of his *g* strength
2Sa 7: 22 "How *g* you are, O Sovereign
22: 36 you stoop down to make me *g*.
24: 14 for his mercy is *g*; but do not let me
1Ch 17: 19 made known all these *g* promises.
Ps 18: 35 you stoop down to make me *g*.
19: 11 in keeping them there is *g* reward.
47: 2 the *g* King over all the earth!
57: 10 For *g* is your love, reaching
68: 11 and *g* was the company
89: 1 of the LORD's *g* love for ever;
103: 11 so *g* is his love for those who fear
107: 43 consider the *g* love of the LORD.
108: 4 For *g* is your love, higher
117: 2 For *g* is his love towards us.
119: 165 *G* peace have they who love your
145: 3 *G* is the LORD and most worthy
Pr 22: 1 is more desirable than *g* riches;
23: 24 of a righteous man has *g* joy;
Isa 42: 21 to make his law *g* and glorious.
Jer 27: 5 With my *g* power and outstretched

Jer 32: 19 *g* are your purposes and mighty are
La 3: 23 *g* is your faithfulness.
Da 9: 4 "O Lord, the *g* and awesome God,
Joel 2: 11 The day of the LORD is *g*;
2: 20 Surely he has done *g* things.
Zep 1: 14 "The *g* day of the LORD is near—
Mal 1: 11 My name will be *g*
4: 5 the prophet Elijah before that *g*
Mt 20: 26 Whoever wants to become *g*
Mk 10: 43 whoever wants to become *g*
Lk 6: 23 because *g* is your reward in heaven.
6: 35 Then your reward will be *g*,
21: 27 in a cloud with power and *g* glory.
Eph 1: 19 and his incomparably *g* power
2: 4 But because of his *g* love for us,
1Ti 6: 6 with contentment is *g* gain.
Tit 2: 13 glorious appearing of our *g* God
Heb 2: 3 if we ignore such a *g* salvation?
1Jn 3: 1 How *g* is the love the Father has
Rev 6: 17 For the *g* day of their wrath has
20: 11 Then I saw a *g* white throne

GREATER (GREAT)
Mt 11: 11 there has not risen anyone *g*
12: 6 I tell you that one *g*
12: 41 and now one *g* than Jonah is here.
12: 42 now one *g* than Solomon is here.
Mk 12: 31 There is no commandment *g*
Jn 1: 50 You shall see *g* things than that."
3: 30 He must become *g*; I must become
14: 12 He will do even *g* things than these
15: 13 *G* love has no-one than this,
1Co 12: 31 But eagerly desire the *g* gifts.
2Co 3: 11 how much *g* is the glory
Heb 3: 3 the builder of a house has *g* honour
3: 3 worthy of *g* honour than Moses,
7: 7 lesser person is blessed by the *g*.
11: 26 as of *g* value than the treasures
1Jn 3: 20 For God is *g* than our hearts,
4: 4 is in you is *g* than the one who is

GREATEST (GREAT)
Mt 22: 38 is the first and *g* commandment.
23: 11 *g* among you will be your servant.
Lk 9: 48 least among you all—he is the *g*."
1Co 13: 13 But the *g* of these is love.

GREATNESS* (GREAT)
Ex 15: 7 In the *g* of your majesty
Dt 3: 24 to show to your servant your *g*
32: 3 Oh, praise the *g* of our God!
1Ch 29: 11 O LORD, is the *g* and the power
2Ch 9: 6 half the *g* of your wisdom was told
Est 10: 2 account of the *g* of Mordecai
Ps 145: 3 his *g* no-one can fathom.
150: 2 praise him for his surpassing *g*.
Isa 63: 1 forward in the *g* of his strength?
Eze 38: 23 I will show my *g* and my holiness,
Da 4: 22 your *g* has grown until it reaches
5: 18 and *g* and glory and splendour.
7: 27 and *g* of the kingdoms
Mic 5: 4 will live securely, for then his *g*
Lk 9: 43 And they were all amazed at the *g*
Php 3: 8 compared to the surpassing *g*

GREED (GREEDY)
Lk 12: 15 on your guard against all kinds of *g*
Ro 1: 29 kind of wickedness, evil, *g*
Eph 5: 3 or of any kind of impurity, or of *g*,
Col 3: 5 evil desires and *g*, which is idolatry
2Pe 2: 14 experts in *g*—an accursed brood!

GREEDY (GREED)
Pr 15: 27 A *g* man brings trouble
1Co 6: 10 nor thieves nor the *g* nor drunkards
Eph 5: 5 No immoral, impure or *g* person—
1Pe 5: 2 not *g* for money, but eager to serve;

GREEK (GREEKS)
Gal 3: 28 There is neither Jew nor *G*,
Col 3: 11 Here there is no *G* or Jew,

GREEKS (GREEK)
1Co 1: 22 miraculous signs and *G* look

GREEN
Ps 23: 2 makes me lie down in *g* pastures,

GREW (GROW)
Lk 1: 80 And the child *g* and became strong
2: 52 And Jesus *g* in wisdom and stature,
Ac 9: 31 by the Holy Spirit, it *g* in numbers,
16: 5 in the faith and *g* daily in numbers.

GREY
Pr 16: 31 *G* hair is a crown of splendour;
20: 29 *g* hair the splendour of the old.

GRIEF (GRIEFS GRIEVANCES GRIEVE GRIEVED)
Ps 10: 14 O God, do see trouble and *g*;
Pr 10: 1 but a foolish son *g* to his mother.
14: 13 and joy may end in *g*.
17: 21 To have a fool for a son brings *g*;
Ecc 1: 18 the more knowledge, the more *g*.
La 3: 32 Though he brings *g*, he will show
Jn 16: 20 but your *g* will turn to joy.
1Pe 1: 6 had to suffer *g* in all kinds of trials.

GRIEFS* (GRIEF)
1Ti 6: 10 pierced themselves with many *g*.

GRIEVANCES* (GRIEF)
Col 3: 13 forgive whatever *g* you may have

GRIEVE (GRIEF)
Eph 4: 30 do not *g* the Holy Spirit of God,
1Th 4: 13 or to *g* like the rest of men,

GRIEVED (GRIEF)
Isa 63: 10 and *g* his Holy Spirit.

GRINDING
Lk 17: 35 women will be *g* grain together;

GROAN (GROANING GROANS)
Ro 8: 23 *g* inwardly as we wait eagerly
2Co 5: 4 For while we are in this tent, we *g*

GROANING (GROAN)
Ex 2: 24 God heard their *g* and he
Eze 21: 7 'Why are you *g*?' you shall say,
Ro 8: 22 that the whole creation has been *g*

GROANS (GROAN)
Ro 8: 26 with *g* that words cannot express.

GROUND
Ge 1: 10 God called the dry *g* "land",
3: 17 "Cursed is the *g* because of you;
4: 10 blood cries out to me from the *g*.
Ex 3: 5 where you are standing is holy *g*."
15: 19 walked through the sea on dry *g*.
Isa 53: 2 and like a root out of dry *g*.
Mt 10: 29 fall to the *g* apart from the will
25: 25 and hid your talent in the *g*.
Jn 8: 6 to write on the *g* with his finger.
Eph 6: 13 you may be able to stand your *g*,

GROW (FULL-GROWN GREW GROWING GROWS)
Pr 13: 11 by little makes it *g*.
20: 13 not love sleep or you will *g* poor;
Isa 40: 31 they will run and not *g* weary,
Mt 6: 28 See how the lilies of the field *g*.
1Co 3: 6 watered it, but God made it *g*.
2Pe 3: 18 But *g* in the grace and knowledge

GROWING (GROW)
Col 1: 6 this gospel is bearing fruit and *g*,
1: 10 *g* in the knowledge of God,
2Th 1: 3 your faith is *g* more and more,

GROWS (GROW)
Eph 4: 16 *g* and builds itself up in love,
Col 2: 19 *g* as God causes it to grow.

GRUMBLE (GRUMBLED GRUMBLERS GRUMBLING)
1Co 10: 10 And do not *g*, as some of them did
Jas 5: 9 Don't *g* against each other,

GRUMBLED (GRUMBLE)
Ex 15: 24 So the people *g* against Moses,
Nu 14: 29 and who has *g* against me.

GRUMBLERS* (GRUMBLE)
Jude : 16 These men are *g* and fault-finders;

GRUMBLING (GRUMBLE)
Jn 6: 43 "Stop *g* among yourselves,"
1Pe 4: 9 to one another without *g*.

GUARANTEE (GUARANTEEING)
Heb 7: 22 Jesus has become the *g*

GUARANTEEING* (GUARANTEE)
2Co 1: 22 as a deposit, *g* what is to come.
5: 5 as a deposit, *g* what is to come.
Eph 1: 14 who is a deposit *g* our inheritance

GUARD (GUARDS)
1Sa 2: 9 He will *g* the feet of his saints,
Ps 141: 3 Set a *g* over my mouth, O LORD;
Pr 2: 11 and understanding will *g* you.
4: 13 *g* it well, for it is your life.
4: 23 Above all else, *g* your heart,
7: 2 *g* my teachings as the apple
Isa 52: 12 the God of Israel will be your rear *g*
Mk 13: 33 Be on *g*! Be alert! You do not know
Lk 12: 1 "Be on your *g* against the yeast
12: 15 Be on your *g* against all kinds
Ac 20: 31 So be on your *g*! Remember that
1Co 16: 13 Be on your *g*; stand firm in the faith
Php 4: 7 will *g* your hearts and your minds
1Ti 6: 20 *g* what has been entrusted
2Ti 1: 14 *G* the good deposit that was

GUARDS (GUARD)
Pr 13: 3 He who *g* his lips *g* his life,
19: 16 who obeys instructions *g* his life,
21: 23 He who *g* his mouth and his tongue
22: 5 he who *g* his soul stays far

GUIDANCE (GUIDE)
Pr 1: 5 and let the discerning get *g*—
11: 14 For lack of *g* a nation falls,
24: 6 for waging war you need *g*,

GUIDE (GUIDANCE GUIDED GUIDES)
Ex 13: 21 of cloud to *g* them on their way
15: 13 In your strength you will *g* them
Ne 9: 19 cease to *g* them on their path,
Ps 25: 5 *g* me in your truth and teach me,
43: 3 let them *g* me;
48: 14 he will be our *g* even to the end.
67: 4 and *g* the nations of the earth.
73: 24 You *g* me with your counsel,
139: 10 even there your hand will *g* me,
Pr 4: 11 I *g* you in the way of wisdom
6: 22 When you walk, they will *g* you;
Isa 58: 11 The LORD will *g* you always;
Jn 16: 13 comes, he will *g* you into all truth.

GUIDED (GUIDE)
Ps 107: 30 he *g* them to their desired haven.

GUIDES (GUIDE)
Ps 23: 3 He *g* me in paths of righteousness
25: 9 He *g* the humble in what is right
Pr 11: 3 The integrity of the upright *g* them,
16: 23 A wise man's heart *g* his mouth,
Mt 23: 16 "Woe to you, blind *g*! You say,
23: 24 You blind *g*! You strain out a gnat

GUILT (GUILTY)
Lev 5: 15 It is a *g* offering.
Ps 32: 5 the *g* of my sin.
38: 4 My *g* has overwhelmed me
Isa 6: 7 your *g* is taken away and your sin

Jer 2: 22 the stain of your *g* is still before me
Eze 18: 19 'Why does the son not share the *g*

GUILTY (GUILT)

Ex 34: 7 does not leave the *g* unpunished;
Mk 3: 29 Spirit will never be forgiven; he is *g*
Jn 8: 46 Can any of you prove me *g* of sin?
1Co 11: 27 in an unworthy manner will be *g*
Heb 10: 2 and would no longer have felt *g*
10: 22 to cleanse us from a *g* conscience
Jas 2: 10 at just one point is *g* of breaking all

HABAKKUK*

Prophet to Judah (Hab 1:1; 3:1).

HABIT

1Ti 5: 13 they get into the *h* of being idle
Heb 10: 25 as some are in the *h* of doing,

HADAD

Edomite adversary of Solomon (1Ki 11:14-25).

HADES*

Mt 16: 18 the gates of *H* will not overcome it.
Rev 1: 18 And I hold the keys of death and *H*
6: 8 *H* was following close behind him.
20: 13 and *H* gave up the dead that were
20: 14 *H* were thrown into the lake of fire.

HAGAR

Servant of Sarah, wife of Abraham, mother of Ishmael (Ge 16:1-6; 25:12). Driven away by Sarah while pregnant (Ge 16:5-16); after birth of Isaac (Ge 21:9-21; Gal 4:21-31).

HAGGAI*

Post-exilic prophet who encouraged rebuilding of the temple (Ezr 5:1; 6:14; Hag 1-2).

HAIL

Ex 9: 19 the *h* will fall on every man
Rev 8: 7 and there came *h* and fire mixed

HAIR (HAIRS HAIRY)

Lev 19: 27 "'Do not cut the *h* at the sides
Nu 6: 5 he must let the *h* of his head grow
Pr 16: 31 Grey *h* is a crown of splendour;
20: 29 grey *h* the splendour of the old.
Lk 7: 44 and wiped them with her *h*.
21: 18 But not a *h* of your head will perish
Jn 11: 2 and wiped his feet with her *h*.
12: 3 and wiped his feet with her *h*.
1Co 11: 6 for a woman to have her *h* cut
11: 6 she should have her *h* cut off;
11: 14 that if a man has long *h*,
11: 15 For long *h* is given to her
11: 15 but that if a woman has long *h*,
1Ti 2: 9 not with braided *h* or gold or pearls
1Pe 3: 3 as braided *h* and the wearing
Rev 1: 14 and *h* were white like wool,

HAIRS (HAIR)

Mt 10: 30 even the very *h* of your head are all
Lk 12: 7 the very *h* of your head are all

HAIRY (HAIR)

Ge 27: 11 "But my brother Esau is a *h* man,

HALF

Ex 30: 13 This *h* shekel is an offering
Jos 8: 33 *H* of the people stood in front
1Ki 3: 25 give *h* to one and *h* to the other."
10: 7 Indeed, not even *h* was told me;
Est 5: 3 Even up to *h* the kingdom,
Da 7: 25 him for a time, times and *h* a time.
Mk 6: 23 up to *h* my kingdom."

HALF-TRIBE (TRIBE)

Nu 32: 33 and the *h* of Manasseh son

HALLELUJAH*

Rev 19: 1, 3, 4, 6.

HALLOWED* (HOLY)

Mt 6: 9 *h* be your name,
Lk 11: 2 *h* be your name,

HALT

Job 38: 11 here is where your proud waves *h*'?

HALTER*

Pr 26: 3 for the horse, a *h* for the donkey,

HAM

Son of Noah (Ge 5:32; 1Ch 1:4), father of Canaan (Ge 9:18; 10:6-20; 1Ch 1:8-16). Saw Noah's nakedness (Ge 9:20-27).

HAMAN

Agagite nobleman honoured by Xerxes (Est 3:1-2). Plotted to exterminate the Jews because of Mordecai (Est 3:3-15). Forced to honour Mordecai (Est 5-6). Plot exposed by Esther (Est 5:1-8; 7:1-8). Hanged (Est 7:9-10).

HAMPERED*

Pr 4: 12 you walk, your steps will not be *h*;

HAND (HANDED HANDFUL HANDS OPEN-HANDED)

Ge 24: 2 "Put your *h* under my thigh.
47: 29 put your *h* under my thigh
Ex 13: 3 out of it with a mighty *h*.
15: 6 Your right *h*, O LORD,
33: 22 and cover you with my *h*
Dt 12: 7 in everything you have put your *h*
1Ki 8: 42 and your mighty *h* and your
13: 4 But the *h* he stretched out
1Ch 29: 14 you only what comes from your *h*.
29: 16 it comes from your *h*, and all
2Ch 6: 15 with your *h* you have fulfilled it—
Ne 4: 17 materials did their work with one *h*
Job 40: 4 I put my *h* over my mouth.
Ps 16: 8 Because he is at my right *h*,
32: 4 your *h* was heavy upon me;
37: 24 the LORD upholds him with his *h*.
44: 3 it was your right *h*, your arm,
45: 9 at your right *h* is the royal bride
63: 8 your right *h* upholds me.
75: 8 In the *h* of the LORD is a cup
91: 7 ten thousand at your right *h*,
98: 1 his right *h* and his holy arm
109: 31 at the right *h* of the needy one,
110: 1 "Sit at my right *h*
137: 5 may my right *h* forget ⌊its skill⌋.
139: 10 even there your *h* will guide me,
145: 16 You open your *h*
Pr 27: 16 or grasping oil with the *h*.
Ecc 5: 15 that he can carry in his *h*.
9: 10 Whatever your *h* finds to do,
Isa 11: 8 the young child put his *h*
40: 12 the waters in the hollow of his *h*,
41: 13 who takes hold of your right *h*
44: 5 still another will write on his *h*,
48: 13 My own *h* laid the foundations
64: 8 we are all the work of your *h*.
La 3: 3 he has turned his *h* against me
Da 10: 10 *h* touched me and set me trembling
Jnh 4: 11 people who cannot tell their right *h*
Hab 3: 4 rays flashed from his *h*,
Mt 5: 30 if your right *h* causes you to sin,
6: 3 know what your right *h* is doing,
12: 10 a man with a shrivelled *h* was there.
18: 8 If your *h* or your foot causes you
22: 44 "Sit at my right *h*
26: 64 at the right *h* of the Mighty One
Mk 3: 1 a man with a shrivelled *h* was there.
9: 43 If your *h* causes you to sin, cut it off
12: 36 "Sit at my right *h*
16: 19 and he sat at the right *h* of God.
Lk 6: 6 there whose right *h* was shrivelled.
20: 42 "Sit at my right *h*
22: 69 at the right *h* of the mighty God."
Jn 10: 28 one can snatch them out of my *h*.
20: 27 Reach out your *h* and put it
Ac 7: 55 Jesus standing at the right *h* of God
1Co 12: 15 I am not a *h*, I do not belong
Heb 1: 13 "Sit at my right *h*
Rev 13: 16 to receive a mark on his right *h*

HANDED (HAND)

Da 7: 25 The saints will be *h* over to him
1Ti 1: 20 whom I have *h* over to Satan

HANDFUL (HAND)

Ecc 4: 6 Better one *h* with tranquillity

HANDLE (HANDLES)

Col 2: 21 "Do not *h*! Do not taste! Do not

HANDLES (HANDLE)

2Ti 2: 15 who correctly *h* the word of truth.

HANDS (HAND)

Ge 27: 22 but the *h* are the *h* of Esau."
Ex 17: 11 As long as Moses held up his *h*,
29: 10 his sons shall lay their *h* on its head
Dt 6: 8 Tie them as symbols on your *h*
Jdg 7: 6 lapped with their *h* to their mouths.
2Ki 11: 12 and the people clapped their *h*
2Ch 6: 4 who with his *h* has fulfilled what he
Ps 22: 16 they have pierced my *h*
24: 4 He who has clean *h* and a pure
31: 5 Into your *h* I commit my spirit;
31: 15 My times are in your *h*;
47: 1 Clap your *h*, all you nations;
63: 4 and in your name I will lift up my *h*
Pr 10: 4 Lazy *h* make a man poor,
21: 25 because his *h* refuse to work.
31: 13 and works with eager *h*.
31: 20 and extends her *h* to the needy.
Ecc 10: 18 if his *h* are idle, the house leaks.
Isa 35: 3 Strengthen the feeble *h*,
49: 16 you on the palms of my *h*;
55: 12 will clap their *h*.
65: 2 All day long I have held out my *h*
La 3: 41 Let us lift up our hearts and our *h*
Lk 23: 46 into your *h* I commit my spirit."
Ac 6: 6 who prayed and laid their *h*
8: 18 at the laying on of the apostles' *h*,
13: 3 they placed their *h* on them
19: 6 When Paul placed his *h* on them,
28: 8 placed his *h* on him and healed him
1Th 4: 11 and to work with your *h*,
1Ti 2: 8 to lift up holy *h* in prayer,
4: 14 body of elders laid their *h* on you.
5: 22 hasty in the laying on of *h*,
2Ti 1: 6 you through the laying on of my *h*.
Heb 6: 2 the laying on of *h*, the resurrection

HANDSOME*

Ge 39: 6 Now Joseph was well-built and *h*,
1Sa 16: 12 a fine appearance and *h* features.
17: 42 ruddy and *h*, and he despised him.
2Sa 14: 25 praised for his *h* appearance
1Ki 1: 6 also very *h* and was born next
SS 1: 16 How *h* you are, my lover!
Eze 23: 6 all of them *h* young men,
23: 12 horsemen, all *h* young men.
23: 23 with them, *h* young men,
Da 1: 4 without any physical defect, *h*,
Zec 11: 13 the *h* price at which they priced me

HANG (HANGED HANGING HUNG)

Mt 22: 40 and the Prophets *h* on these two

HANGED (HANG)

Mt 27: 5 Then he went away and *h* himself.

HANGING (HANG)

Ac 10: 39 They killed him by *h* him on a tree,

HANNAH*

Wife of Elkanah, mother of Samuel (1Sa 1). Prayer at dedication of Samuel (1Sa 2:1-10). Blessed (1Sa 2:18-21).

HAPPIER (HAPPY)

Mt 18: 13 he is *h* about that one sheep

1Co 7: 40 she is *h* if she stays as she is—

HAPPINESS* (HAPPY)

Dt 24: 5 bring *h* to the wife he has married.
Est 8: 16 For the Jews it was a time of *h*
Job 7: 7 my eyes will never see *h* again.
Ecc 2: 26 gives wisdom, knowledge and *h*,
Mt 25: 21 Come and share your master's *h*!'
25: 23 Come and share your master's *h*!'

HAPPY* (HAPPIER HAPPINESS)

Ge 30: 13 The women will call me *h*."
30: 13 Then Leah said, "How *h* I am!
1Ki 4: 20 they drank and they were *h*.
10: 8 How *h* your men must be!
10: 8 men must be! How *h* your officials,
2Ch 9: 7 How *h* your men must be!
9: 7 men must be! How *h* your officials,
Est 5: 9 Haman went out that day *h*
5: 14 the king to the dinner and be *h*."
Ps 10: 6 I'll always be *h* and never have
68: 3 may they be *h* and joyful.
113: 9 as a *h* mother of children.
137: 8 *h* is he who repays you
Pr 15: 13 A *h* heart makes the face cheerful,
Ecc 3: 12 better for men than to be *h*
5: 19 to accept his lot and be *h*
7: 14 When times are good, be *h*;
11: 9 Be *h*, young man, while you are
Jnh 4: 6 Jonah was very *h* about the vine.
Zec 8: 19 and glad occasions and *h* festivals
1Co 7: 30 those who are *h*, as if they were not
2Co 7: 9 yet now I am *h*, not because you
7: 13 delighted to see how *h* Titus was,
Jas 5: 13 Is anyone *h*? Let him sing songs

HARD (HARDEN HARDENED HARDENING HARDENS HARDER HARDSHIP HARDSHIPS)

Ge 18: 14 Is anything too *h* for the LORD?
1Ki 10: 1 came to test him with *h* questions.
Pr 14: 23 All *h* work brings a profit,
Jer 32: 17 Nothing is too *h* for you.
Zec 7: 12 They made their hearts as *h* as flint
Mt 19: 23 it is *h* for a rich man
Mk 10: 5 your hearts were *h* that Moses
Jn 6: 60 disciples said, "This is a *h* teaching.
Ac 20: 35 of *h* work we must help the weak,
26: 14 It is *h* for you to kick
Ro 16: 12 woman who has worked very *h*
1Co 4: 12 We work *h* with our own hands.
2Co 6: 5 imprisonments and riots; in *h* work
1Th 5: 12 to respect those who work *h*
Rev 2: 2 your *h* work and your

HARD-HEARTED* (HEART)

Dt 15: 7 do not be *h* or tight-fisted

HARDEN (HARD)

Ex 4: 21 I will *h* his heart so that he will not
Ps 95: 8 do not *h* your hearts as you did
Ro 9: 18 he hardens whom he wants to *h*.
Heb 3: 8 do not *h* your hearts

HARDENED (HARD)

Ex 10: 20 But the LORD *h* Pharaoh's heart,

HARDENING* (HARD)

Ro 11: 25 Israel has experienced a *h* in part
Eph 4: 18 in them due to the *h* of their hearts.

HARDENS* (HARD)

Pr 28: 14 he who *h* his heart falls into trouble
Ro 9: 18 and he *h* whom he wants to harden.

HARDER (HARD)

1Co 15: 10 No, I worked *h* than all of them—
2Co 11: 23 I have worked much *h*, been

HARDSHIP (HARD)

Ro 8: 35 Shall trouble or *h* or persecution
2Ti 2: 3 Endure *h* with us like a good
4: 5 endure *h*, do the work
Heb 12: 7 Endure *h* as discipline; God is

HARDSHIPS (HARD)

Ac 14: 22 go through many *h* to enter
2Co 6: 4 in troubles, *h* and distresses;
12: 10 in insults, in *h*, in persecutions,
Rev 2: 3 and have endured *h* for my name,

HARLOT see PROSTITUTE

HARM (HARMS)

1Ch 16: 22 do my prophets no *h*."
Ps 105: 15 do my prophets no *h*."
121: 6 the sun will not *h* you by day,
Pr 3: 29 not plot *h* against your neighbour,
12: 21 No *h* befalls the righteous,
31: 12 She brings him good, not *h*,
Jer 10: 5 they can do no *h*
29: 11 to prosper you and not to *h* you,
Ro 13: 10 Love does no *h* to its neighbour.
1Co 11: 17 for your meetings do more *h*
1Jn 5: 18 the evil one cannot *h* him.

HARMONY*

Zec 6: 13 there will be *h* between the two.'
Ro 12: 16 Live in *h* with one another.
2Co 6: 15 What *h* is there between Christ
1Pe 3: 8 live in *h* with one another;

HARMS* (HARM)

Pr 8: 36 whoever fails to find me *h* himself;

HARP (HARPS)

Ge 4: 21 the father of all who play the *h*
1Sa 16: 23 David would take his *h* and play.
Ps 33: 2 Praise the LORD with the *h*;
98: 5 with the *h* and the sound of singing
150: 3 praise him with the *h* and lyre,
Rev 5: 8 Each one had a *h* and they were

HARPS (HARP)

Ps 137: 2 we hung our *h*,

HARSH

Pr 15: 1 but a *h* word stirs up anger.
Col 2: 23 and their *h* treatment of the body,
3: 19 and do not be *h* with them.
1Pe 2: 18 but also to those who are *h*.
Jude : 15 of all the *h* words ungodly sinners

HARVEST (HARVESTERS)

Ge 8: 22 seedtime and *h*,
Ex 23: 16 the Feast of *H* with the firstfruits
Dt 16: 15 God will bless you in all your *h*
Pr 10: 5 during *h* is a disgraceful son.
Jer 8: 20 "The *h* is past,
Joel 3: 13 for the *h* is ripe.
Mt 9: 37 *h* is plentiful but the workers are
Lk 10: 2 He told them, "The *h* is plentiful,
Jn 4: 35 at the fields! They are ripe for *h*.
1Co 9: 11 if we reap a material *h* from you?
2Co 9: 10 the *h* of your righteousness.
Gal 6: 9 at the proper time we will reap a *h*
Heb 12: 11 it produces a *h* of righteousness
Jas 3: 18 in peace raise a *h* of righteousness.
Rev 14: 15 for the *h* of the earth is ripe."

HARVESTERS (HARVEST)

Ru 2: 3 to glean in the fields behind the *h*.

HASTE (HASTEN HASTY)

Ex 12: 11 it in *h*; it is the LORD's Passover.
Pr 21: 5 as surely as *h* leads to poverty.
29: 20 Do you see a man who speaks in *h*?

HASTEN (HASTE)

Ps 70: 1 *H*, O God, to save me;
119: 60 I will *h* and not delay

HASTY* (HASTE)

Pr 19: 2 nor to be *h* and miss the way.
Ecc 5: 2 do not be *h* in your heart
1Ti 5: 22 Do not be *h* in the laying

HATE (GOD-HATERS HATED HATES HATING HATRED)

Lev 19: 17 "'Do not *h* your brother
Ps 5: 5 you *h* all who do wrong.
36: 2 too much to detect or *h* his sin.
45: 7 righteousness and *h* wickedness;
97: 10 those who love the LORD *h* evil,
119: 104 therefore I *h* every wrong path.
119: 163 I *h* and abhor falsehood
139: 21 Do I not *h* those who *h* you,
Pr 8: 13 To fear the LORD is to *h* evil;
9: 8 rebuke a mocker or he will *h* you;
13: 5 The righteous *h* what is false,
25: 17 too much of you, and he will *h* you.
29: 10 Bloodthirsty men *h* a man
Ecc 3: 8 a time to love and a time to *h*,
Isa 61: 8 I *h* robbery and iniquity.
Eze 35: 6 Since you did not *h* bloodshed,
Am 5: 15 *H* evil, love good;
Mal 2: 16 "I *h* divorce," says the LORD God
Mt 5: 43 your neighbour and *h* your enemy.'
10: 22 All men will *h* you because of me,
Lk 6: 22 Blessed are you when men *h* you,
6: 27 do good to those who *h* you,
14: 26 does not *h* his father and mother,
Ro 12: 9 *H* what is evil; cling to what is good

HATED (HATE)

Mal 1: 3 loved Jacob, but Esau I have *h*,
Jn 15: 18 keep in mind that it *h* me first.
Ro 9: 13 "Jacob I loved, but Esau I *h*."
Eph 5: 29 no-one ever *h* his own body,
Heb 1: 9 righteousness and *h* wickedness;

HATES (HATE)

Pr 6: 16 There are six things the LORD *h*,
13: 24 He who spares the rod *h* his son,
15: 27 but he who *h* bribes will live.
26: 28 A lying tongue *h* those it hurts,
Jn 3: 20 Everyone who does evil *h* the light,
12: 25 while the man who *h* his life
1Jn 2: 9 *h* his brother is still in the darkness.
4: 20 "I love God," yet *h* his brother,

HATING (HATE)

Jude : 23 *h* even the clothing stained

HATRED (HATE)

Pr 10: 12 *H* stirs up dissension,
15: 17 than a fattened calf with *h*.
Jas 4: 4 with the world is *h* towards God?

HAUGHTY

Pr 6: 17 detestable to him: / *h* eyes,
16: 18 a *h* spirit before a fall.

HAVEN

Ps 107: 30 he guided them to their desired *h*.

HAY

1Co 3: 12 costly stones, wood, *h* or straw,

HEAD (HEADS HOTHEADED)

Ge 3: 15 he will crush your *h*,
Nu 6: 5 no razor may be used on his *h*.
Jdg 16: 17 If my *h* were shaved, my strength
1Sa 9: 2 a *h* taller than any of the others.
2Sa 18: 9 Absalom's *h* got caught in the tree.
Ps 23: 5 You anoint my *h* with oil;
133: 2 is like precious oil poured on the *h*,
Pr 10: 6 Blessings crown the *h*
25: 22 will heap burning coals on his *h*,
Isa 59: 17 and the helmet of salvation on his *h*
Eze 33: 4 his blood will be on his own *h*.
Mt 8: 20 of Man has nowhere to lay his *h*."
Jn 19: 2 crown of thorns and put it on his *h*.
Ro 12: 20 will heap burning coals on his *h*."
1Co 11: 3 and the *h* of Christ is God,
11: 5 her *h* uncovered dishonours her *h*—
12: 21 And the *h* cannot say to the feet,
Eph 1: 22 him to be *h* over everything
5: 23 For the husband is the *h* of the wife
Col 1: 18 And he is the *h* of the body,

2Ti 4: 5 keep your *h* in all situations,
Rev 14: 14 with a crown of gold on his *h*
19: 12 and on his *h* are many crowns.

HEADS (HEAD)

Lev 26: 13 you to walk with *h* held high.
Ps 22: 7 they hurl insults, shaking their *h*:
24: 7 Lift up your *h*, O you gates;
Isa 35: 10 everlasting joy will crown their *h*.
51: 11 everlasting joy will crown their *h*.
Mt 27: 39 shaking their *h* and saying,
Lk 21: 28 stand up and lift up your *h*,
Ac 18: 6 "Your blood be on your own *h*!
Rev 4: 4 and had crowns of gold on their *h*.

HEAL* (HEALED HEALING HEALS)

Nu 12: 13 please *h* her!" The LORD replied
Dt 32: 39 I have wounded and I will *h*,
2Ki 20: 5 and seen your tears; I will *h* you.
20: 8 the sign that the LORD will *h* me
2Ch 7: 14 their sin and will *h* their land.
Job 5: 18 he injures, but his hands also *h*.
Ps 6: 2 *h* me, for my bones are in agony.
41: 4 *h* me, for I have sinned against you
Ecc 3: 3 a time to kill and a time to *h*,
Isa 19: 22 he will strike them and *h* them.
19: 22 respond to their pleas and *h* them.
57: 18 seen his ways, but I will *h* him;
57: 19 "And I will *h* them."
Jer 17: 14 *H* me, O LORD, and I will be
30: 17 and *h* your wounds,'
33: 6 I will *h* my people and will let them
La 2: 13 Who can *h* you?
Hos 5: 13 not able to *h* your sores.
6: 1 but he will *h* us;
7: 1 whenever I would *h* Israel,
14: 4 "I will *h* their waywardness
Na 3: 19 Nothing can *h* your wound;
Zec 11: 16 or seek the young, or *h* the injured,
Mt 8: 7 said to him, "I will go and *h* him."
10: 1 to *h* every disease and sickness.
10: 8 *H* the sick, raise the dead,
12: 10 "Is it lawful to *h* on the Sabbath?"
13: 15 and turn, and I would *h* them.'
17: 16 but they could not *h* him."
Mk 3: 2 if he would *h* him on the Sabbath.
6: 5 on a few sick people and *h* them.
Lk 4: 23 to me: 'Physician, *h* yourself!
5: 17 present for him to *h* the sick.
6: 7 to see if he would *h* on the Sabbath.
7: 3 him to come and *h* his servant,
8: 43 years, but no-one could *h* her.
9: 2 kingdom of God and to *h* the sick.
10: 9 *H* the sick who are there
13: 32 and *h* people today and tomorrow,
14: 3 "Is it lawful to *h* on the Sabbath
Jn 4: 47 begged him to come and *h* his son,
12: 40 nor turn—and I would *h* them."
Ac 4: 30 Stretch out your hand to *h*
28: 27 and turn and I would *h* them.'

HEALED* (HEAL)

Ge 20: 17 to God, and God *h* Abimelech,
Ex 21: 19 and see that he is completely *h*.
Lev 13: 37 hair has grown in it, the itch is *h*.
14: 3 If the person has been *h*
Jos 5: 8 were in camp until they were *h*.
1Sa 6: 3 you will be *h*, and you will know
2Ki 2: 21 LORD says: "I have *h* this water.
2Ch 30: 20 heard Hezekiah and *h* the people.
Ps 30: 2 and you *h* me.
107: 20 He sent forth his word and *h* them;
Isa 6: 10 and turn and be *h*."
53: 5 and by his wounds we are *h*.
Jer 14: 19 us so that we cannot be *h*?
17: 14 Heal me, O LORD, and I will be *h*;
51: 8 perhaps she can be *h*.
51: 9 but she cannot be *h*;
51: 9 "'We would have *h* Babylon,
Eze 34: 4 the weak or *h* the sick
Hos 11: 3 it was I who *h* them.
Mt 4: 24 and the paralytics, and he *h* them.
8: 8 the word, and my servant will be *h*.
8: 13 his servant was *h* at that very hour.
8: 16 with a word and *h* all the sick.
9: 21 If I only touch his cloak, I will be *h*
9: 22 he said, "your faith has *h* you."
9: 22 woman was *h* from that moment.
12: 15 him, and he *h* all their sick,
12: 22 Jesus *h* him, so that he could both
14: 14 on them and *h* their sick.
14: 36 and all who touched him were *h*.
15: 28 And her daughter was *h*
15: 30 laid them at his feet; and he *h* them
17: 18 and he was *h* from that moment.
19: 2 followed him, and he *h* them there.
21: 14 to him at the temple, and he *h* them
Mk 1: 34 and Jesus *h* many who had various
3: 10 For he had *h* many, so that those
5: 23 hands on her so that she will be *h*
5: 28 If I just touch his clothes, I will be *h*
5: 34 "Daughter, your faith has *h* you.
6: 13 people with oil and *h* them.
6: 56 and all who touched him were *h*.
10: 52 said Jesus, "your faith has *h* you."
Lk 4: 40 hands on each one, he *h* them.
5: 15 and to be *h* of their sicknesses.
6: 18 and to be *h* of their diseases.
7: 7 the word, and my servant will be *h*.
8: 47 and how she had been instantly *h*.
8: 48 "Daughter, your faith has *h* you.
8: 50 just believe, and she will be *h*."
9: 11 and *h* those who needed healing.
9: 42 *h* the boy and gave him back
13: 14 Jesus had *h* on the Sabbath,
13: 14 So come and be *h* on those days,
14: 4 he *h* him and sent him away.
17: 15 when he saw he was *h*, came back,
18: 42 your sight; your faith has *h* you."
22: 51 touched the man's ear and *h* him.
Jn 5: 10 said to the man who had been *h*,
5: 13 man who was *h* had no idea who it
Ac 4: 9 and are asked how he was *h*,
4: 10 stands before you *h*.
4: 14 who had been *h* standing there
4: 22 man who was miraculously *h* was
5: 16 evil spirits, and all of them were *h*.
8: 7 paralytics and cripples were *h*.
14: 9 saw that he had faith to be *h*
28: 8 placed his hands on him and *h* him.
Heb 12: 13 may not be disabled, but rather *h*.
Jas 5: 16 for each other so that you may be *h*
1Pe 2: 24 by his wounds you have been *h*.
Rev 13: 3 but the fatal wound had been *h*.
13: 12 whose fatal wound had been *h*.

HEALING* (HEAL)

2Ch 28: 15 food and drink, and *h* balm.
Pr 12: 18 but the tongue of the wise brings *h*.
13: 17 but a trustworthy envoy brings *h*.
15: 4 The tongue that brings *h* is a tree
16: 24 sweet to the soul and *h* to the bones
Isa 58: 8 and your *h* will quickly appear;
Jer 8: 15 for a time of *h*
8: 22 Why then is there no *h*
14: 19 for a time of *h*
30: 12 your injury beyond *h*.
30: 13 no *h* for you.
33: 6 I will bring health and *h* to it;
46: 11 there is no *h* for you.
Eze 30: 21 It has not been bound up for *h*
47: 12 for food and their leaves for *h*."
Mal 4: 2 rise with *h* in its wings.
Mt 4: 23 and *h* every disease and sickness
9: 35 and *h* every disease and sickness.
Lk 6: 19 coming from him and *h* them all.
9: 6 gospel and *h* people everywhere.
9: 11 and healed those who needed *h*.
Jn 7: 23 angry with me for *h* the whole man
Ac 3: 16 him that has given this complete *h*
10: 38 *h* all who were under the power
1Co 12: 9 to another gifts of *h*
12: 28 also those having gifts of *h*,
12: 30 Do all have gifts of *h*? Do all speak
Rev 22: 2 are for the *h* of the nations.

HEALS* (HEAL)

Ex 15: 26 for I am the LORD who *h* you."
Lev 13: 18 a boil on his skin and it *h*,
Ps 103: 3 and *h* all my diseases;
147: 3 He *h* the broken-hearted
Isa 30: 26 and *h* the wounds he inflicted.
Ac 9: 34 said to him, "Jesus Christ *h* you.

HEALTH* (HEALTHIER HEALTHY)

1Sa 25: 6 And good *h* to all that is yours!
25: 6 Good *h* to you and your household
Ps 38: 3 of your wrath there is no *h*
38: 7 there is no *h* in my body.
Pr 3: 8 This will bring *h* to your body
4: 22 and *h* to a man's whole body.
15: 30 and good news gives *h* to the bones
Isa 38: 16 You restored me to *h*
Jer 30: 17 But I will restore you to *h*
33: 6 I will bring *h* and healing to it;
3Jn : 2 I pray that you may enjoy good *h*

HEALTHIER* (HEALTH)

Da 1: 15 end of the ten days they looked *h*

HEALTHY* (HEALTH)

Ge 41: 5 Seven heads of grain, *h* and good,
41: 7 of grain swallowed up the seven *h*,
Ps 73: 4 their bodies are *h* and strong.
Zec 11: 16 or heal the injured, or feed the *h*,
Mt 9: 12 "It is not the *h* who need a doctor,
Mk 2: 17 "It is not the *h* who need a doctor,
Lk 5: 31 "It is not the *h* who need a doctor,

HEAP

Pr 25: 22 you will *h* burning coals
Ro 12: 20 you will *h* burning coals

HEAR (HEARD HEARING HEARS)

Ex 15: 14 The nations will *h* and tremble;
22: 27 I will *h*, for I am compassionate.
Nu 14: 13 Then the Egyptians will *h* about it!
Dt 1: 16 *H* the disputes between your
4: 36 heaven he made you *h* his voice
6: 4 *H*, O Israel: The LORD our God,
19: 20 The rest of the people will *h* of this
31: 13 must *h* it and learn
Jos 7: 9 of the country will *h* about this
1Ki 8: 30 *H* the supplication of your servant
2Ki 19: 16 O LORD, and *h*; open your eyes,
2Ch 7: 14 then will I *h* from heaven
Job 31: 35 ("Oh, that I had someone to *h* me!
Ps 94: 9 he who implanted the ear not *h*?
95: 7 Today, if you *h* his voice,
Ecc 7: 21 or you may *h* your servant cursing
Isa 21: 3 I am staggered by what I *h*,
29: 18 that day the deaf will *h* the words
39: 21 your ears will *h* a voice behind you,
51: 7 *H* me, you who know what is right,
59: 1 nor his ear too dull to *h*.
65: 24 while they are still speaking I will *h*
Jer 5: 21 who have ears but do not *h*:
Eze 33: 7 so *h* the word I speak and give
37: 4 'Dry bones, *h* the word
Mt 11: 5 the deaf *h*, the dead are raised,
11: 15 He who has ears, let him *h*.
13: 17 and to *h* what you *h* but did not *h* it
Mk 12: 29 answered Jesus, "is this: '*H*,
Lk 7: 22 the deaf *h*, the dead are raised,
Jn 8: 47 reason you do not *h* is that you do
Ac 13: 7 he wanted to *h* the word of God.
13: 44 gathered to *h* the word of the Lord.
17: 32 "We want to *h* you again
Ro 2: 13 is not those who *h* the law who are
10: 14 they *h* without someone preaching
2Ti 4: 3 what their itching ears want to *h*.
Heb 3: 7 "Today, if you *h* his voice,
Rev 1: 3 and blessed are those who *h* it

HEARD (HEAR)

Ex 2: 24 God *h* their groaning and he
Dt 4: 32 has anything like it ever been *h* of?
2Sa 7: 22 as we have *h* with our own ears.
Job 42: 5 My ears had *h* of you

Isa 40: 21 Have you not *h*?
40: 28 Have you not *h*?
66: 8 Who has ever *h* of such a thing?
Jer 18: 13 Who has ever *h* anything like this?
Da 10: 12 your words were *h*, and I have
12: 8 I *h*, but I did not understand.
Hab 3: 16 I *h* and my heart pounded,
Mt 5: 21 "You have *h* that it was said
5: 27 "You have *h* that it was said,
5: 33 you have *h* that it was said
5: 38 "You have *h* that it was said,
5: 43 "You have *h* that it was said,
Lk 12: 3 in the dark will be *h* in the daylight,
Jn 8: 26 and what I have *h* from him I tell
Ac 2: 6 because each one *h* them speaking
1Co 2: 9 no ear has *h*,
2Co 12: 4 He *h* inexpressible things,
1Th 2: 13 word of God, which you *h* from us,
2Ti 1: 13 What you *h* from me, keep
Jas 1: 25 not forgetting what he has *h*,
Rev 22: 8 am the one who *h* and saw these

HEARING (HEAR)

Isa 6: 9 Be ever *h*, but never understanding
Mt 13: 14 will be ever *h* but never
Mk 4: 12 ever *h* but never understanding;
Ac 28: 26 will be ever *h* but never
Ro 10: 17 faith comes from *h* the message,
1Co 12: 17 where would the sense of *h* be?

HEARS (HEAR)

Jn 5: 24 whoever *h* my word and believes
1Jn 5: 14 according to his will, he *h* us.
Rev 3: 20 If anyone *h* my voice and opens

HEART (BROKEN-HEARTED FAINT-HEARTED HARD-HEARTED HEART'S HEARTACHE HEARTS KIND-HEARTED SIMPLE-HEARTED STOUT-HEARTED WHOLEHEARTED WHOLEHEARTEDLY)

Ge 6: 5 of his *h* was only evil all the time.
Ex 4: 21 But I will harden his *h*
25: 2 each man whose *h* prompts him
35: 21 and whose *h* moved him came
Lev 19: 17 Do not hate your brother in your *h*.
Dt 4: 9 or let them slip from your *h* as long
4: 29 if you look for him with all your *h*
6: 5 LORD your God with all your *h*
10: 12 LORD your God with all your *h*
11: 13 and to serve him with all your *h*
13: 3 you love him with all your *h*
15: 10 and do so without a grudging *h*;
26: 16 observe them with all your *h*
29: 18 you today whose *h* turns away
30: 2 and obey him with all your *h*
30: 6 you may love him with all your *h*
30: 10 LORD your God with all your *h*
Jos 22: 5 and to serve him with all your *h*
23: 14 You know with all your *h*
1Sa 10: 9 God changed Saul's *h*,
12: 20 serve the LORD with all your *h*.
12: 24 serve him faithfully with all your *h*;
13: 14 sought out a man after his own *h*
14: 7 I am with you *h* and soul."
16: 7 but the LORD looks at the *h*."
17: 32 "Let no-one lose *h* on account
1Ki 2: 4 faithfully before me with all their *h*
3: 9 So give your servant a discerning *h*
3: 12 give you a wise and discerning *h*,
8: 48 back to you with all their *h*
9: 3 and my *h* will always be there.
9: 4 walk before me in integrity of *h*
10: 24 the wisdom God had put in his *h*.
11: 4 and his *h* was not fully devoted
14: 8 and followed me with all his *h*,
15: 14 Asa's *h* was fully committed
2Ki 22: 19 Because your *h* was responsive
23: 3 with all his *h* and all his soul,
1Ch 28: 9 for the LORD searches every *h*
2Ch 6: 38 back to you with all their *h*
7: 16 and my *h* will always be there.
15: 12 of their fathers, with all their *h*
2Ch 15: 17 Asa's *h* was fully committed
17: 6 His *h* was devoted to the ways
22: 9 sought the LORD with all his *h*."
34: 31 with all his *h* and all his soul,
36: 13 stiff-necked and hardened his *h*
Ezr 1: 5 everyone whose *h* God had moved
Ne 4: 6 the people worked with all their *h*.
Job 19: 27 How my *h* yearns within me!
22: 22 and lay up his words in your *h*.
37: 1 "At this my *h* pounds
Ps 9: 1 you, O LORD, with all my *h*;
14: 1 The fool says in his *h*,
16: 9 Therefore my *h* is glad
19: 14 and the meditation of my *h*
20: 4 he give you the desire of your *h*
24: 4 who has clean hands and a pure *h*,
26: 2 examine my *h* and my mind;
37: 4 will give you the desires of your *h*.
37: 31 The law of his God is in his *h*;
44: 21 since he knows the secrets of the *h*
45: 1 My *h* is stirred by a noble theme
51: 10 Create in me a pure *h*, O God,
51: 17 a broken and contrite *h*,
53: 1 The fool says in his *h*,
66: 18 If I had cherished sin in my *h*,
73: 1 to those who are pure in *h*.
73: 26 My flesh and my *h* may fail,
86: 11 give me an undivided *h*,
90: 12 that we may gain a *h* of wisdom.
97: 11 and joy on the upright in *h*.
108: 1 My *h* is steadfast, O God;
109: 22 and my *h* is wounded within me.
111: 1 will extol the LORD with all my *h*
112: 7 his *h* is steadfast, trusting
112: 8 His *h* is secure, he will have no fear
119: 2 and seek him with all their *h*.
119: 10 I seek you with all my *h*;
119: 11 I have hidden your word in my *h*
119: 30 I have set my *h* on your laws.
119: 32 for you have set my *h* free.
119: 34 and obey it with all my *h*.
119: 36 Turn my *h* towards your statutes
119: 58 sought your face with all my *h*;
119: 69 I keep your precepts with all my *h*.
119: 111 they are the joy of my *h*.
119: 112 My *h* is set on keeping your
119: 145 I call with all my *h*; answer me,
125: 4 to those who are upright in *h*.
138: 1 you, O LORD, with all my *h*;
139: 23 Search me, O God, and know my *h*
Pr 2: 2 applying your *h* to understanding,
3: 1 but keep my commands in your *h*,
3: 3 write them on the tablet of your *h*.
3: 5 Trust in the LORD with all your *h*
4: 4 hold of my words with all your *h*;
4: 21 keep them within your *h*;
4: 23 Above all else, guard your *h*,
6: 21 Bind them upon your *h* for ever;
7: 3 write them on the tablet of your *h*.
10: 8 The wise in *h* accept commands,
13: 12 Hope deferred makes the *h* sick,
14: 13 Even in laughter the *h* may ache,
14: 30 A *h* at peace gives life to the body,
15: 13 A happy *h* makes the face cheerful,
15: 15 the cheerful *h* has a continual feast.
15: 28 *h* of the righteous weighs its
15: 30 A cheerful look brings joy to the *h*,
16: 23 A wise man's *h* guides his mouth,
17: 22 A cheerful *h* is good medicine,
20: 9 can say, "I have kept my *h* pure;
22: 11 He who loves a pure *h*
22: 17: apply your *h* to what I teach,
22: 18 when you keep them in your *h*
23: 15 My son, if your *h* is wise,
23: 19 and keep your *h* on the right path.
23: 26 My son, give me your *h*
24: 17 stumbles, do not let your *h* rejoice,
27: 19 so a man's *h* reflects the man.
Ecc 5: 2 do not be hasty in your *h*
8: 5 wise *h* will know the proper time
11: 10 banish anxiety from your *h*
SS 3: 1 I looked for the one my *h* loves;
4: 9 You have stolen my *h*, my sister,
SS 5: 2 I slept but my *h* was awake
5: 4 my *h* began to pound for him.
8: 6 Place me like a seal over your *h*,
Isa 6: 10 Make the *h* of this people calloused
40: 11 and carries them close to his *h*;
57: 15 and to revive the *h* of the contrite.
66: 14 you see this, your *h* will rejoice
Jer 3: 15 give you shepherds after my own *h*,
4: 14 wash the evil from your *h*
9: 26 of Israel is uncircumcised in *h*."
17: 9 The *h* is deceitful above all things
20: 9 is in my *h* like a fire,
24: 7 I will give them a *h* to know me,
29: 13 when you seek me with all your *h*.
32: 39 I will give them singleness of *h*
32: 41 them in this land with all my *h*
51: 46 Do not lose *h* or be afraid
Eze 11: 19 I will give them an undivided *h*
18: 31 and get a new *h* and a new spirit.
36: 26 I will give you a new *h*
44: 7 foreigners uncircumcised in *h*
Da 7: 4 and the *h* of a man was given to it.
Joel 2: 12 "return to me with all your *h*,
2: 13 Rend your *h*
Zep 3: 14 Be glad and rejoice with all your *h*,
Mt 5: 8 Blessed are the pure in *h*,
5: 28 adultery with her in his *h*.
6: 21 treasure is, there your *h* will be
11: 29 for I am gentle and humble in *h*,
12: 34 of the *h* the mouth speaks.
13: 15 For this people's *h* has become
15: 18 out of the mouth come from the *h*,
15: 19 For out of the *h* come evil thoughts
18: 35 forgive your brother from your *h*."
22: 37 the Lord your God with all your *h*
Mk 11: 23 and does not doubt in his *h*
12: 30 the Lord your God with all your *h*
12: 33 To love him with all your *h*,
Lk 2: 19 and pondered them in her *h*.
2: 51 treasured all these things in her *h*.
6: 45 out of the good stored up in his *h*,
6: 45 overflow of his *h* his mouth speaks.
8: 15 for those with a noble and good *h*,
10: 27 the Lord your God with all your *h*
12: 34 treasure is, there your *h* will be
Jn 12: 27 "Now my *h* is troubled,
Ac 1: 24 "Lord, you know everyone's *h*.
2: 37 they were cut to the *h*
4: 32 All the believers were one in *h*
8: 21 your *h* is not right before God.
15: 8 who knows the *h*, showed that he
16: 14 The Lord opened her *h* to respond
28: 27 For this people's *h* has become
Ro 1: 9 with my whole *h* in preaching
2: 29 in circumcision of the *h*,
10: 9 in your *h* that God raised him
10: 10 is with your *h* that you believe
15: 6 with one *h* and mouth you may
1Co 14: 25 the secrets of his *h* will be laid bare.
2Co 2: 4 anguish of *h* and with many tears,
4: 1 this ministry, we do not lose *h*.
4: 16 Therefore we do not lose *h*.
9: 7 give what he has decided in his *h*
Eph 1: 18 eyes of your *h* may be enlightened
5: 19 make music in your *h* to the Lord,
6: 5 and with sincerity of *h*, just
6: 6 doing the will of God from your *h*.
Php 1: 7 since I have you in my *h*; for
Col 2: 2 is that they may be encouraged in *h*
3: 22 but with sincerity of *h*
3: 23 work at it with all your *h*,
1Ti 1: 5 which comes from a pure *h*
3: 1 If anyone sets his *h*
2Ti 2: 22 call on the Lord out of a pure *h*.
Phm : 12 who is my very *h*—back to you.
: 20 in the Lord; refresh my *h* in Christ.
Heb 4: 12 the thoughts and attitudes of the *h*.
1Pe 1: 22 one another deeply, from the *h*.

HEART'S* (HEART)

2Ch 1: 11 "Since this is your *h* desire
Jer 15: 16 they were my joy and my *h* delight,
Eze 24: 25 delight of their eyes, their *h* desire,

Ro 10: 1 my *h* desire and prayer to God

HEARTACHE* (HEART)

Pr 15: 13 but *h* crushes the spirit.

HEARTLESS*

La 4: 3 but my people have become *h*
Ro 1: 31 they are senseless, faithless, *h*,

HEARTS (HEART)

Lev 26: 41 their uncircumcised *h* are humbled
Dt 6: 6 are to be upon your *h*.
10: 16 Circumcise your *h*, therefore,
11: 18 Fix these words of mine in your *h*
30: 6 your God will circumcise your *h*
Jos 11: 20 himself who hardened their *h*
24: 23 and yield your *h* to the LORD,
1Sa 7: 3 to the LORD with all your *h*,
10: 26 valiant men whose *h* God had
2Sa 15: 6 and so he stole the *h* of the men
1Ki 8: 39 for you alone know the *h* of all men
8: 61 your *h* must be fully committed
18: 37 are turning their *h* back again."
1Ch 29: 18 and keep their *h* loyal to you.
2Ch 6: 30 (for you alone know the *h* of men),
11: 16 tribe of Israel who set their *h*
29: 31 all whose *h* were willing brought
Ps 7: 9 who searches minds and *h*,
33: 21 In him our *h* rejoice,
62: 8 pour out your *h* to him,
95: 8 do not harden your *h* as you did
Ecc 3: 11 also set eternity in the *h* of men;
Isa 26: 8 are the desire of our *h*.
29: 13 but their *h* are far from me.
35: 4 say to those with fearful *h*,
51: 7 people who have my law in your *h*:
63: 17 harden our *h* so we do not revere
65: 14 out of the joy of their *h*,
Jer 4: 4 circumcise your *h*,
12: 2 but far from their *h*.
17: 1 on the tablets of their *h*
31: 33 and write it on their *h*.
Mal 4: 6 He will turn the *h* of the fathers
Mt 15: 8 but their *h* are far from me.
Mk 6: 52 the loaves; their *h* were hardened.
7: 6 but their *h* are far from me.
7: 21 out of men's *h*, come evil thoughts,
Lk 1: 17 to turn the *h* of the fathers
16: 15 of men, but God knows your *h*.
24: 32 "Were not our *h* burning within us
Jn 5: 42 not have the love of God in your *h*.
14: 1 "Do not let your *h* be troubled.
14: 27 Do not let your *h* be troubled
Ac 7: 51 with uncircumcised *h* and ears!
11: 23 true to the Lord with all their *h*.
15: 9 for he purified their *h* by faith.
28: 27 understand with their *h*
Ro 1: 21 and their foolish *h* were darkened.
2: 15 of the law are written on their *h*,
5: 5 love into our *h* by the Holy Spirit,
8: 27 who searches our *h* knows
1Co 4: 5 will expose the motives of men's *h*.
2Co 1: 22 put his Spirit in our *h* as a deposit,
3: 2 written in our *h*, known
3: 3 but on tablets of human *h*.
4: 6 shine in our *h* to give us the light
6: 11 and opened wide our *h* to you.
6: 13 to my children—open wide your *h*
7: 2 Make room for us in your *h*.
Gal 4: 6 the Spirit of his Son into our *h*,
Eph 3: 17 dwell in your *h* through faith.
Php 4: 7 will guard your *h* and your minds
Col 3: 1 set your *h* on things above,
3: 15 the peace of Christ rule in your *h*,
3: 16 with gratitude in your *h* to God.
1Th 2: 4 men but God, who tests our *h*.
3: 13 May he strengthen your *h*
2Th 2: 17 encourage your *h* and strengthen
Phm : 7 have refreshed the *h* of the saints.
Heb 3: 8 do not harden your *h*
8: 10 and write them on their *h*.
10: 16 I will put my laws in their *h*,
10: 22 having our *h* sprinkled
Jas 4: 8 purify your *h*, you double-minded.
2Pe 1: 19 the morning star rises in your *h*.
1Jn 3: 20 For God is greater than our *h*,

HEAT

Ps 19: 6 nothing is hidden from its *h*.
2Pe 3: 12 and the elements will melt in the *h*.

HEATHEN see GENTILES, NATIONS

HEAVEN (HEAVENLY HEAVENS HEAVENWARDS)

Ge 14: 19 Creator of *h* and earth.
28: 12 with its top reaching to *h*,
Ex 16: 4 rain down bread from *h* for you.
20: 22 that I have spoken to you from *h*:
Dt 26: 15 from *h*, your holy dwelling-place,
30: 12 "Who will ascend into *h* to get it
1Ki 8: 27 the highest *h*, cannot contain you.
8: 30 Hear from *h*, your dwelling-place,
22: 19 the host of *h* standing round him
2Ki 2: 1 up to *h* in a whirlwind,
19: 15 You have made *h* and earth.
2Ch 7: 14 then will I hear from *h*
Isa 14: 12 How you have fallen from *h*,
66: 1 "*H* is my throne
Da 7: 13 coming with the clouds of *h*.
Mt 3: 2 for the kingdom of *h* is near."
3: 16 At that moment *h* was opened,
4: 17 for the kingdom of *h* is near."
5: 12 because great is your reward in *h*,
5: 19 great in the kingdom of *h*.
6: 9 "'Our Father in *h*,
6: 10 done on earth as it is in *h*.
6: 20 up for yourselves treasures in *h*,
7: 21 Lord,' will enter the kingdom of *h*,
16: 19 bind on earth will be bound in *h*,
18: 3 will never enter the kingdom of *h*.
18: 18 bind on earth will be bound in *h*,
19: 14 the kingdom of *h* belongs to such
19: 21 and you will have treasure in *h*.
19: 23 man to enter the kingdom of *h*.
23: 13 the kingdom of *h* in men's faces.
24: 35 *H* and earth will pass away,
26: 64 and coming on the clouds of *h*."
28: 18 "All authority in *h*
Mk 1: 10 he saw *h* being torn open
10: 21 and you will have treasure in *h*.
13: 31 *H* and earth will pass away,
14: 62 and coming on the clouds of *h*."
16: 19 he was taken up into *h*
Lk 3: 21 *h* was opened and the Holy Spirit
10: 18 saw Satan fall like lightning from *h*.
10: 20 that your names are written in *h*."
12: 33 in *h* that will not be exhausted,
15: 7 in *h* over one sinner who repents
18: 22 and you will have treasure in *h*.
21: 33 *H* and earth will pass away,
24: 51 left them and was taken up into *h*.
Jn 3: 13 No-one has ever gone into *h*
6: 38 down from *h* not to do my will
12: 28 Then a voice came from *h*,
Ac 1: 11 has been taken from you into *h*,
7: 49 the prophet says: "'*H* is my
7: 55 looked up to *h* and saw the glory
9: 3 a light from *h* flashed around him.
26: 19 disobedient to the vision from *h*.
Ro 10: 6 'Who will ascend into *h*?'" (that is,
1Co 15: 47 the earth, the second man from *h*.
2Co 5: 1 an eternal house in *h*, not built
12: 2 ago was caught up to the third *h*.
Eph 1: 10 to bring all things in *h*
Php 2: 10 *h* and on earth and under the earth,
3: 20 But our citizenship is in *h*.
Col 1: 16 things in *h* and on earth, visible
4: 1 that you also have a Master in *h*.
1Th 1: 10 and to wait for his Son from *h*,
4: 16 himself will come down from *h*,
Heb 1: 3 hand of the Majesty in *h*.
8: 5 and shadow of what is in *h*.
9: 24 he entered *h* itself, now to appear
12: 23 whose names are written in *h*.
1Pe 1: 4 spoil or fade—kept in *h* for you,
3: 22 who has gone into *h* and is
2Pe 3: 13 we are looking forward to a new *h*
Rev 5: 13 Then I heard every creature in *h*
11: 19 God's temple in *h* was opened,
12: 7 And there was war in *h*.
15: 5 this I looked and in *h* the temple,
19: 1 of a great multitude in *h* shouting:
19: 11 I saw *h* standing open and there
21: 1 Then I saw a new *h* and a new earth
21: 10 coming down out of *h* from God.

HEAVENLY (HEAVEN)

Ps 8: 5 him a little lower than the *h* beings
2Co 5: 2 to be clothed with our *h* dwelling,
Eph 1: 3 in the *h* realms with every spiritual
1: 20 at his right hand in the *h* realms,
2Ti 4: 18 bring me safely to his *h* kingdom.
Heb 12: 22 to the *h* Jerusalem, the city

HEAVENS (HEAVEN)

Ge 1: 1 In the beginning God created the *h*
11: 4 with a tower that reaches to the *h*,
Dt 33: 26 who rides on the *h* to help you
1Ki 8: 27 The *h*, even the highest heaven,
2Ch 2: 6 since the *h*, even the highest
Ezr 9: 6 and our guilt has reached to the *h*.
Ne 9: 6 You made the *h*, even the highest
Job 11: 8 They are higher than the *h*—
38: 33 Do you know the laws of the *h*?
Ps 8: 3 When I consider your *h*,
19: 1 The *h* declare the glory of God;
33: 6 of the LORD were the *h* made,
57: 5 Be exalted, O God, above the *h*;
102: 25 the *h* are the work of your hands.
103: 11 as high as the *h* are above the earth,
108: 4 is your love, higher than the *h*;
115: 16 The highest *h* belong to the LORD
119: 89 it stands firm in the *h*.
135: 6 in the *h* and on the earth,
139: 8 If I go up to the *h*, you are there;
148: 1 Praise the LORD from the *h*,
Isa 40: 26 Lift your eyes and look to the *h*:
45: 8 "You *h* above, rain
51: 6 Lift up your eyes to the *h*,
55: 9 "As the *h* are higher than the earth,
65: 17 new *h* and a new earth.
Jer 31: 37 if the *h* above can be measured
32: 17 you have made the *h* and the earth
Eze 1: 1 *h* were opened and I saw visions
Da 12: 3 shine like the brightness of the *h*,
Joel 2: 30 I will show wonders in the *h*
Mt 24: 31 from one end of the *h* to the other.
Mk 13: 27 of the earth to the ends of the *h*.
Eph 4: 10 who ascended higher than all the *h*,
Heb 4: 14 priest who has gone through the *h*,
7: 26 from sinners, exalted above the *h*.
2Pe 3: 5 ago by God's word the *h* existed
3: 10 The *h* will disappear with a roar;

HEAVENWARDS (HEAVEN)

Php 3: 14 for which God has called me *h*

HEAVIER (HEAVY)

Pr 27: 3 provocation by a fool is *h* than both

HEAVY (HEAVIER)

1Ki 12: 4 and the *h* yoke he put on us,
Ecc 1: 13 What a *h* burden God has laid
Isa 47: 6 you laid a very *h* yoke.
Mt 23: 4 They tie up *h* loads and put them

HEBREW (HEBREWS)

Ge 14: 13 and reported this to Abram the *H*.
2Ki 18: 26 speak to us in *H* in the hearing
Php 3: 5 tribe of Benjamin, a *H* of Hebrews;

HEBREWS (HEBREW)

Ex 9: 1 of the *H*, says: "Let my people go,
2Co 11: 22 Are they *H*? So am I.

HEBRON

Ge 13: 18 near the great trees of Mamre at *H*,

Ge 23: 2 died at Kiriath Arba (that is, *H*)
Jos 14: 13 and gave him *H* as his inheritance.
20: 7 *H*) in the hill country of Judah.
21: 13 the priest they gave *H* (a city
2Sa 2: 11 king in *H* over the house

HEDGE
Job 1: 10 "Have you not put a *h* around him

HEED (HEEDS)
Ecc 7: 5 It is better to *h* a wise man's rebuke

HEEDS (HEED)
Pr 13: 1 wise son *h* his father's instruction,
13: 18 whoever *h* correction is honoured.
15: 5 whoever *h* correction shows
15: 32 whoever *h* correction gains

HEEL
Ge 3: 15 and you will strike his *h*."

HEIR (INHERIT)
Gal 4: 7 God has made you also an *h*.
Heb 1: 2 whom he appointed *h* of all things,

HEIRS (INHERIT)
Ro 8: 17 then we are *h*—*h* of God
Gal 3: 29 and *h* according to the promise.
Eph 3: 6 gospel the Gentiles are *h* together
1Pe 3: 7 as *h* with you of the gracious gift

HELD (HOLD)
Ex 17: 11 As long as Moses *h* up his hands,
Dt 4: 4 but all of you who *h* fast
2Ki 18: 6 He *h* fast to the LORD
SS 3: 4 I *h* him and would not let him go
Isa 65: 2 All day long I have *h* out my hands
Ro 10: 21 day long I have *h* out my hands
Col 2: 19 and *h* together by its ligaments

HELL*
Mt 5: 22 will be in danger of the fire of *h*.
5: 29 body to be thrown into *h*.
5: 30 for your whole body to go into *h*.
10: 28 destroy both soul and body in *h*.
18: 9 and be thrown into the fire of *h*.
23: 15 as much a son of *h* as you are.
23: 33 you escape being condemned to *h*?
Mk 9: 43 than with two hands to go into *h*,
9: 45 have two feet and be thrown into *h*.
9: 47 two eyes and be thrown into *h*,
Lk 12: 5 has power to throw you into *h*.
16: 23 In *h*, where he was in torment,
Jas 3: 6 and is itself set on fire by *h*.
2Pe 2: 4 but sent them to *h*, putting them

HELMET
Isa 59: 17 and the *h* of salvation on his head;
Eph 6: 17 Take the *h* of salvation
1Th 5: 8 and the hope of salvation as a *h*.

HELP (HELPED HELPER HELPFUL HELPING HELPLESS HELPS)
Ex 23: 5 leave it there; be sure you *h* him
Lev 25: 35 *h* him as you would an alien
Dt 33: 26 who rides on the heavens to *h* you
2Ch 16: 12 even in his illness he did not seek *h*
Ps 18: 6 I cried to my God for *h*.
30: 2 my God, I called to you for *h*
33: 20 he is our *h* and our shield.
46: 1 an ever-present *h* in trouble.
72: 12 the afflicted who have no-one to *h*.
79: 9 *H* us, O God our Saviour,
108: 12 for the *h* of man is worthless.
115: 9 he is their *h* and shield.
121: 1 where does my *h* come from?
Ecc 4: 10 his friend can *h* him up.
Isa 41: 10 I will strengthen you and *h* you;
Jnh 2: 2 depths of the grave I called for *h*,
Mk 9: 24 *h* me overcome my unbelief!"
Lk 11: 46 will not lift one finger to *h* them.
Ac 16: 9 Come over to Macedonia and *h* us
18: 27 he was a great *h* to those who
20: 35 of hard work we must *h* the weak,
26: 22 I have had God's *h* to this very day,
1Co 12: 28 those able to *h* others, those
2Co 9: 2 For I know your eagerness to *h*,
1Ti 5: 16 she should *h* them and not let

HELPED (HELP)
1Sa 7: 12 "Thus far has the LORD *h* us."

HELPER (HELP)
Ge 2: 18 I will make a *h* suitable for him."
Ps 10: 14 you are the *h* of the fatherless.
Heb 13: 6 Lord is my *h*; I will not be afraid.

HELPFUL (HELP)
Eph 4: 29 only what is *h* for building others

HELPING (HELP)
Ac 9: 36 always doing good and *h* the poor.
1Ti 5: 10 *h* those in trouble and devoting

HELPLESS (HELP)
Ps 10: 12 Do not forget the *h*.
Mt 9: 36 because they were harassed and *h*,

HELPS (HELP)
Ro 8: 26 the Spirit *h* us in our weakness.

HEN
Mt 23: 37 as a *h* gathers her chicks
Lk 13: 34 as a *h* gathers her chicks

HERALD
1Ti 2: 7 for this purpose I was appointed a *h*
2Ti 1: 11 of this gospel I was appointed a *h*

HERBS
Ex 12: 8 with bitter *h*, and bread made

HERITAGE (INHERIT)
Ps 61: 5 you have given me the *h*
119: 111 Your statutes are my *h* for ever;
127: 3 Sons are a *h* from the LORD,

HEROD
1. King of Judea who tried to kill Jesus (Mt 2; Lk 1:5).
2. Son of 1. Tetrarch of Galilee who arrested and beheaded John the Baptist (Mt 14:1-12; Mk 6:14-29; Lk 3:1, 19-20; 9:7-9); tried Jesus (Lk 23:6-15).
3. Grandson of 1. King of Judea who killed James (Ac 12:2); arrested Peter (Ac 12:3-19). Death (Ac 12:19-23).

HERODIAS
Wife of Herod the Tetrarch who persuaded her daughter to ask for John the Baptist's head (Mt 14:1-12; Mk 6:14-29).

HEWN
Isa 51: 1 the quarry from which you were *h*;

HEZEKIAH
King of Judah. Restored the temple and worship (2Ch 29-31). Sought the LORD for help against Assyria (2Ki 18-19; 2Ch 32:1-23; Isa 36-37). Illness healed (2Ki 20:1-11; 2Ch 32:24-26; Isa 38). Judged for showing Babylonians his treasures (2Ki 20:12-21; 2Ch 32:31; Isa 39).

HID (HIDE)
Ge 3: 8 and they *h* from the LORD God
Ex 2: 2 she *h* him for three months.
Jos 6: 17 because she *h* the spies we sent.
1Ki 18: 13 I *h* a hundred of the LORD's
2Ch 22: 11 she *h* the child from Athaliah
Isa 54: 8 I *h* my face from you for a moment,
Mt 13: 44 When a man found it, he *h* it again,
25: 25 and *h* your talent in the ground.
Heb 11: 23 By faith Moses' parents *h* him

HIDDEN (HIDE)
1Sa 10: 22 has *h* himself among the baggage."
Job 28: 11 and brings *h* things to light.
Ps 19: 12 Forgive my *h* faults.
78: 2 I will utter things *h* from of old—
119: 11 I have *h* your word in my heart
Pr 2: 4 and search for it as for *h* treasure,
27: 5 rebuke than *h* love.
Isa 59: 2 your sins have *h* his face from you,
Da 2: 22 He reveals deep and *h* things;
Mt 5: 14 A city on a hill cannot be *h*.
10: 26 or *h* that will not be made known.
11: 25 because you have *h* these things
13: 35 I will utter things *h*
13: 44 of heaven is like treasure *h*
Mk 4: 22 For whatever is *h* is meant
Ro 16: 25 of the mystery *h* for long ages past,
1Co 2: 7 a wisdom that has been *h*
Eph 3: 9 for ages past was kept *h* in God,
Col 1: 26 the mystery that has been kept *h*
2: 3 in whom are *h* all the treasures
3: 3 and your life is now *h* with Christ

HIDE (HID HIDDEN HIDING HIDING-PLACE)
Dt 31: 17 I will *h* my face from them,
Ps 17: 8 *h* me in the shadow of your wings
27: 5 he will *h* me in the shelter
143: 9 for I *h* myself in you.
Isa 53: 3 one from whom men *h* their faces

HIDING (HIDE)
Pr 28: 12 to power, men go into *h*.

HIDING-PLACE (HIDE)
Ps 32: 7 You are my *h*

HIGH
Ge 14: 18 He was priest of God Most *H*,
14: 22 God Most *H*, Creator of heaven
Ps 21: 7 the unfailing love of the Most *H*
82: 6 you are all sons of the Most *H*.'
Isa 14: 14 I will make myself like the Most *H*
Da 4: 17 know that the Most *H* is sovereign
Mk 5: 7 Jesus, Son of the Most *H* God?
Heb 7: 1 and priest of God Most *H*.

HIGHWAY
Isa 40: 3 a *h* for our God.

HILL (HILLS)
Ps 24: 3 ascend the *h* of the LORD?
Isa 40: 4 every mountain and *h* made low;
Mt 5: 14 A city on a *h* cannot be hidden.
Lk 3: 5 every mountain and *h* made low.

HILLS (HILL)
1Ki 20: 23 "Their gods are gods of the *h*.
Ps 50: 10 and the cattle on a thousand *h*.
121: 1 I lift up my eyes to the *h*—
Hos 10: 8 and to the *h*, "Fall on us!"
Lk 23: 30 and to the *h*, "Cover us!"'
Rev 17: 9 The seven heads are seven *h*

HINDER (HINDERED HINDERS)
1Sa 14: 6 Nothing can *h* the LORD
Mt 19: 14 come to me, and do not *h* them,
1Co 9: 12 anything rather than *h* the gospel
1Pe 3: 7 so that nothing will *h* your prayers.

HINDERED (HINDER)
Lk 11: 52 and you have *h* those who were

HINDERS (HINDER)
Heb 12: 1 let us throw off everything that *h*

HINT*
Eph 5: 3 even a *h* of sexual immorality,

HIP
Ge 32: 32 socket of Jacob's *h* was touched

HIRAM
King of Tyre; helped David build his palace

(2Sa 5:11-12; 1Ch 14:1); helped Solomon build the temple (1Ki 5; 2Ch 2) and his navy (1Ki 9:10-27; 2Ch 8).

HIRED

Lk 15: 15 and *h* himself out to a citizen
Jn 10: 12 *h* hand is not the shepherd who

HOARDED (HOARDS)

Ecc 5: 13 wealth *h* to the harm of its owner,
Jas 5: 3 You have *h* wealth in the last days.

HOARDS (HOARDED)

Pr 11: 26 People curse the man who *h* grain,

HOLD (HELD HOLDS)

Ex 20: 7 LORD will not *h* anyone guiltless
Lev 19: 13 "'Do not *h* back the wages
Dt 5: 11 LORD will not *h* anyone guiltless
11: 22 in all his ways and to *h* fast to him
13: 4 serve him and *h* fast to him.
30: 20 listen to his voice, and *h* fast to him
Jos 22: 5 to *h* fast to him and to serve him
2Ki 4: 16 "you will *h* a son in your arms."
Ps 18: 16 from on high and took *h* of me;
73: 23 you *h* me by my right hand.
Pr 4: 4 "Lay *h* of my words
Isa 41: 13 who takes *h* of your right hand
54: 2 do not *h* back;
Eze 3: 18 and I will *h* you accountable
3: 20 and I will *h* you accountable
33: 6 I will *h* the watchman accountable
Zec 8: 23 nations will take firm *h* of one Jew
Mk 11: 25 if you *h* anything against anyone,
Jn 20: 17 Jesus said, "Do not *h* on to me,
Php 2: 16 as you *h* out the word of life—
3: 12 but I press on to take *h* of that
Col 1: 17 and in him all things *h* together.
1Th 5: 21 *H* on to the good.
1Ti 6: 12 Take *h* of the eternal life
Heb 10: 23 Let us *h* unswervingly

HOLDS (HOLD)

Pr 10: 19 but he who *h* his tongue is wise.
17: 28 and discerning if he *h* his tongue.

HOLES

Hag 1: 6 to put them in a purse with *h* in it."
Mt 8: 20 "Foxes have *h* and birds

HOLINESS* (HOLY)

Ex 15: 11 majestic in *h*,
Dt 32: 51 because you did not uphold my *h*
1Ch 16: 29 the LORD in the splendour of his *h*.
2Ch 20: 21 him for the splendour of his *h*
Ps 29: 2 in the splendour of his *h*.
89: 35 Once for all, I have sworn by my *h*
93: 5 *h* adorns your house
96: 9 in the splendour of his *h*;
Isa 29: 23 they will acknowledge the *h*
35: 8 it will be called the Way of *H*.
Eze 36: 23 I will show the *h* of my great name,
38: 23 I will show my greatness and my *h*,
Am 4: 2 LORD has sworn by his *h*:
Lk 1: 75 fear in *h* and righteousness
Ro 1: 4 the Spirit of *h* was declared
6: 19 to righteousness leading to *h*.
6: 22 the benefit you reap leads to *h*,
1Co 1: 30 our righteousness, *h*
2Co 1: 12 in the *h* and sincerity that are
7: 1 perfecting *h* out of reverence
Eph 4: 24 God in true righteousness and *h*.
1Ti 2: 2 quiet lives in all godliness and *h*.
2: 15 love and *h* with propriety.
Heb 12: 10 that we may share in his *h*.
12: 14 without *h* no-one will see the Lord.

HOLY (HALLOWED HOLINESS)

Ge 2: 3 the seventh day and made it *h*,
Ex 3: 5 you are standing is *h* ground."
16: 23 a *h* Sabbath to the LORD.
19: 6 kingdom of priests and a *h* nation.'
20: 8 the Sabbath day by keeping it *h*.
26: 33 Place from the Most *H* Place.
26: 33 curtain will separate the *H* Place
28: 36 seal: *H* TO THE LORD.
29: 37 Then the altar will be most *h*,
30: 10 It is most *h* to the LORD."
30: 29 them so they will be most *h*,
31: 13 I am the LORD, who makes you *h*.
40: 9 all its furnishings, and it will be *h*.
Lev 10: 3 I will show myself *h*;
10: 10 must distinguish between the *h*
10: 13 in a *h* place, because it is your share
11: 44 and be *h*, because I am *h*.
11: 45 therefore be *h*, because I am *h*.
19: 2 'Be *h* because I, the LORD your
19: 8 he has desecrated what is *h*
19: 24 the fourth year all its fruit will be *h*,
20: 3 and profaned my *h* name.
20: 7 "'Consecrate yourselves and be *h*,
20: 8 I am the LORD, who makes you *h*.
20: 26 You are to be *h* to me because I,
21: 6 They must be *h* to their God
21: 8 Consider them *h*, because I
22: 9 am the LORD, who makes them *h*.
22: 32 Do not profane my *h* name.
25: 12 For it is a jubilee and is to be *h*
27: 9 given to the LORD becomes *h*.
Nu 4: 15 they must not touch the *h* things
6: 5 He must be *h* until the period
20: 12 as *h* in the sight of the Israelites,
20: 13 and where he showed himself *h*
Dt 5: 12 the Sabbath day by keeping it *h*,
23: 14 Your camp must be *h*,
26: 15 from heaven, your *h* dwelling-place
33: 2 He came with myriads of *h* ones
Jos 5: 15 place where you are standing is *h*."
24: 19 He is a *h* God; he is a jealous God.
1Sa 2: 2 "there is no-one *h* like the LORD
6: 20 of the LORD, this *h* God?
21: 5 even on missions that are not *h*.
2Ki 4: 9 often comes our way is a *h* man
1Ch 16: 10 Glory in his *h* name;
16: 35 may give thanks to your *h* name,
29: 3 I have provided for this *h* temple:
2Ch 30: 27 heaven, his *h* dwelling-place.
Ezr 9: 2 and have mingled the *h* race
Ne 11: 1 the *h* city, while the remaining nine
Job 6: 10 not denied the words of the *H* One.
Ps 2: 6 King on Zion, my *h* hill."
11: 4 The LORD is in his *h* temple;
16: 10 will you let your *H* One see decay.
22: 3 you are enthroned as the *H* One;
24: 3 Who may stand in his *h* place?
30: 4 praise his *h* name.
77: 13 Your ways, O God, are *h*.
78: 54 to the border of his *h* land,
99: 3 he is *h*.
99: 5 he is *h*.
99: 9 for the LORD our God is *h*.
105: 3 Glory in his *h* name;
111: 9 *h* and awesome is his name.
Pr 9: 10 of the *H* One is understanding.
Isa 5: 16 the *h* God will show himself *h*
6: 3 *H*, *h*, *h* is the LORD Almighty;
8: 13 is the one you are to regard as *h*,
29: 23 they will keep my name *h*;
40: 25 who is my equal?" says the *H* One.
43: 3 the *H* One of Israel, your Saviour;
54: 5 *H* One of Israel is your Redeemer;
57: 15 who lives for ever, whose name is *h*:
58: 13 and the LORD's *h* day honourable,
Jer 17: 22 but keep the Sabbath day *h*,
Eze 20: 41 I will show myself *h* among you
22: 26 to my law and profane my *h* things;
28: 25 I will show myself *h* among them
36: 20 nations they profaned my *h* name,
38: 16 when I show myself *h* through you
44: 23 the difference between the *h*
Da 9: 24 prophecy and to anoint the most *h*.
Hab 2: 20 But the LORD is in his *h* temple;
Zec 14: 5 and all the *h* ones with him.
14: 20 On that day *H* TO THE LORD
Mt 24: 15 in the *h* place 'the abomination
Mk 1: 24 the *H* One of God!" "Be quiet!"
Lk 1: 35 the *h* one to be born will be called
1: 49 *h* is his name.
4: 34 the *H* One of God!" "Be quiet!"
Jn 6: 69 and know that you are the *H* One
Ac 2: 27 will you let your *H* One see decay.
13: 35 will not let your *H* One see decay.'
Ro 1: 2 prophets in the *H* Scriptures
7: 12 and the commandment is *h*,
11: 16 if the root is *h*, so are the branches.
12: 1 as living sacrifices, *h* and pleasing
1Co 1: 2 in Christ Jesus and called to be *h*,
7: 14 be unclean, but as it is, they are *h*.
Eph 1: 4 the creation of the world to be *h*
2: 21 and rises to become a *h* temple
3: 5 by the Spirit to God's *h* apostles
5: 3 improper for God's *h* people.
5: 26 up for her to make her *h*,
Col. 1: 22 death to present you *h* in his sight,
1Th 2: 10 and so is God, of how *h*,
3: 13 and *h* in the presence of our God
4: 7 us to be impure, but to live a *h* life.
2Th 1: 10 to be glorified in his *h* people
1Ti 2: 8 to lift up *h* hands in prayer,
2Ti 1: 9 saved us and called us to a *h* life—
2: 21 for noble purposes, made *h*,
3: 15 you have known the *h* Scriptures,
Tit 1: 8 upright, *h* and disciplined.
Heb 2: 11 Both the one who makes men *h*
7: 26 one who is *h*, blameless, pure,
10: 10 we have been made *h*
10: 14 those who are being made *h*.
10: 19 to enter the Most *H* Place
12: 14 in peace with all men and to be *h*;
13: 12 gate to make the people *h*
1Pe 1: 15 But just as he who called you is *h*,
1: 16 is written: "Be *h*, because I am *h*."
2: 5 house to be a *h* priesthood,
2: 9 a royal priesthood, a *h* nation,
3: 5 For this is the way the *h* women
2Pe 3: 11 You ought to live *h* and godly lives
Jude : 14 upon thousands of his *h* ones
Rev 3: 7 are the words of him who is *h*
4: 8 "*H*, *h*, *h* is the Lord God
15: 4 For you alone are *h*.
20: 6 and *h* are those who have part
22: 11 let him who is *h* continue to be *h*."

HOLY SPIRIT see SPIRIT

HOME (HOMES)

Dt 6: 7 Talk about them when you sit at *h*
11: 19 about them when you sit at *h*
20: 5 Let him go *h*, or he may die
25: 5 is to be free to stay at *h*
Ru 1: 11 "Return *h*, my daughters.
2Sa 7: 10 them so that they can have a *h*
1Ch 16: 43 and David returned *h* to bless his
Ps 84: 3 Even the sparrow has found a *h*,
113: 9 settles the barren woman in her *h*
Pr 3: 33 but he blesses the *h* of the righteous
27: 8 is a man who strays from his *h*.
Ecc 12: 5 Then man goes to his eternal *h*
Eze 36: 8 for they will soon come *h*.
Mic 2: 2 They defraud a man of his *h*,
Mt 1: 24 and took Mary *h* as his wife.
13: 57 "Only in his *h* town
Mk 10: 29 "no-one who has left *h* or brothers
Lk 10: 38 named Martha opened her *h*
Jn 14: 23 to him and make our *h* with him.
19: 27 this disciple took her into his *h*.
Ac 16: 15 baptised, she invited us to her *h*.
Tit 2: 5 to be busy at *h*, to be kind,

HOMELESS*

1Co 4: 11 we are brutally treated, we are *h*.

HOMES (HOME)

Ne 4: 14 daughters, your wives and your *h*."
Isa 32: 18 in secure *h*,
Mk 10: 30 as much in this present age (*h*,
1Ti 5: 14 to manage their *h* and to give

HOMOSEXUAL*
1Co 6: 9 male prostitutes nor *h* offenders

HONEST (HONESTY)
Lev 19: 36 Use *h* scales and *h* weights,
Dt 25: 15 and *h* weights and measures,
Job 31: 6 let God weigh me in *h* scales
Pr 12: 17 truthful witness gives *h* testimony,

HONESTY (HONEST)
2Ki 12: 15 they acted with complete *h*.

HONEY (HONEYCOMB)
Ex 3: 8 a land flowing with milk and *h*—
Jdg 14: 8 a swarm of bees and some *h*,
1Sa 14: 26 they saw the *h* oozing out,
Ps 19: 10 than *h* from the comb.
119: 103 sweeter than *h* to my mouth!
Pr 25: 16 If you find *h*, eat just enough—
SS 4: 11 milk and *h* are under your tongue.
Isa 7: 15 and *h* when he knows enough
Eze 3: 3 it tasted as sweet as *h* in my mouth.
Mt 3: 4 His food was locusts and wild *h*.
Rev 10: 9 mouth it will be as sweet as *h*."

HONEYCOMB (HONEY)
SS 4: 11 Your lips drop sweetness as the *h*,
5: 1 I have eaten my *h* and my honey;

HONOUR (HONOURABLE HONOURABLY HONOURED HONOURS)
Ex 20: 12 "*H* your father and your mother,
Nu 20: 12 trust in me enough to *h* me
25: 13 he was zealous for the *h* of his God
Dt 5: 16 "*H* your father and your mother,
Jdg 4: 9 going about this, the *h* will not be
1Sa 2: 8 and has them inherit a throne of *h*.
2: 30 Those who *h* me I will *h*,
1Ch 29: 12 Wealth and *h* come from you;
2Ch 1: 11 or *h*, nor for the death
18: 1 had great wealth and *h*,
Est 6: 6 for the man the king delights to *h*
Ps 8: 5 and crowned him with glory and *h*.
45: 11 *h* him, for he is your lord.
84: 11 the LORD bestows favour and *h*;
Pr 3: 9 *H* the LORD with your wealth,
3: 35 The wise inherit *h*,
15: 33 and humility comes before *h*.
18: 12 but humility comes before *h*.
20: 3 It is to a man's *h* to avoid strife,
25: 27 is it honourable to seek one's own *h*.
Isa 29: 13 and *h* me with their lips.
Jer 33: 9 and *h* before all nations
Mt 13: 57 own house is a prophet without *h*."
15: 4 '*H* your father and mother'
15: 8 These people *h* me with their lips,
19: 19 *h* your father and mother,'
23: 6 they love the place of *h* at banquets
Mk 6: 4 own house is a prophet without *h*."
Lk 14: 8 do not take the place of *h*,
Jn 5: 23 that all may *h* the Son just
7: 18 does so to gain *h* for himself,
12: 26 My Father will *h* the one who
Ro 12: 10 *H* one another above yourselves.
1Co 6: 20 Therefore *h* God with your body.
Eph 6: 2 "*H* your father and mother"—
1Ti 5: 17 well are worthy of double *h*,
Heb 2: 7 you crowned him with glory and *h*
Rev 4: 9 *h* and thanks to him who sits

HONOURABLE (HONOUR)
1Th 4: 4 body in a way that is holy and *h*,

HONOURABLY (HONOUR)
Heb 13: 18 and desire to live *h* in every way.

HONOURED (HONOUR)
Ps 12: 8 when what is vile is *h* among men.
Pr 13: 18 but whoever heeds correction is *h*.
Da 4: 34 I *h* and glorified him who lives
1Co 12: 26 if one part is *h*, every part rejoices
Heb 13: 4 Marriage should be *h* by all,

HONOURS (HONOUR)
Ps 15: 4 but *h* those who fear the LORD,
Pr 14: 31 to the needy *h* God.

HOOF
Ex 10: 26 not a *h* is to be left behind.

HOOKS
Isa 2: 4 and their spears into pruning *h*.
Joel 3: 10 and your pruning *h* into spears.
Mic 4: 3 and their spears into pruning *h*.

HOPE (HOPES)
Job 13: 15 Though he slay me, yet will I *h*
Ps 25: 3 No-one whose *h* is in you
33: 17 A horse is a vain *h* for deliverance;
33: 18 on those whose *h* is
42: 5 Put your *h* in God,
62: 5 my *h* comes from him.
119: 74 for I have put my *h* in your word.
130: 5 and in his word I put my *h*.
130: 7 O Israel, put your *h* in the LORD,
146: 5 whose *h* is in the LORD his God,
147: 11 who put their *h* in his unfailing love
Pr 13: 12 *H* deferred makes the heart sick,
23: 18 There is surely a future *h* for you,
Isa 40: 31 but those who *h* in the LORD
Jer 29: 11 plans to give you *h* and a future.
La 3: 21 and therefore I have *h*:
Zec 9: 12 to your fortress, O prisoners of *h*;
Ro 5: 4 character; and character, *h*.
8: 20 in *h* that the creation itself will be
8: 24 But *h* that is seen is no *h* at all.
8: 25 if we *h* for what we do not yet have,
12: 12 Be joyful in *h*, patient in affliction,
15: 4 of the Scriptures we might have *h*.
15: 13 May the God of *h* fill you
1Co 13: 13 now these three remain: faith, *h*
15: 19 for this life we have *h* in Christ,
Eph 2: 12 without *h* and without God
Col 1: 27 Christ in you, the *h* of glory.
1Th 1: 3 and your endurance inspired by *h*
5: 8 and the *h* of salvation as a helmet.
1Ti 4: 10 that we have put our *h*
6: 17 but to put their *h* in God,
Tit 1: 2 resting on the *h* of eternal life,
2: 13 while we wait for the blessed *h*—
Heb 6: 19 We have this *h* as an anchor
10: 23 unswervingly to the *h* we profess,
11: 1 faith is being sure of what we *h* for
1Jn 3: 3 Everyone who has this *h*

HOPES (HOPE)
1Co 13: 7 always *h*, always perseveres.

HORN (HORNS)
Ex 19: 13 when the ram's *h* sounds a long
27: 2 Make a *h* at each of the four
Da 7: 8 This *h* had eyes like the eyes

HORNS (HORN)
Da 7: 24 ten *h* are ten kings who will come
Rev 5: 6 He had seven *h* and seven eyes,
12: 3 and ten *h* and seven crowns
13: 1 He had ten *h* and seven heads,
17: 3 and had seven heads and ten *h*.

HORRIBLE (HORROR)
Jer 5: 30 "A *h* and shocking thing

HORROR (HORRIBLE)
Jer 2: 12 and shudder with great *h*,"

HORSE
Ps 147: 10 not in the strength of the *h*,
Pr 26: 3 A whip for the *h*, a halter
Zec 1: 8 before me was a man riding a red *h*
Rev 6: 2 and there before me was a white *h*!
6: 4 Come!" Then another *h* came out,
6: 5 and there before me was a black *h*!
6: 8 and there before me was a pale *h*!
19: 11 and there before me was a white *h*,

HOSANNA
Mt 21: 9 "*H* in the highest!"
Mk 11: 9 "*H*!"
Jn 12: 13 "*H*!"

HOSEA
Prophet whose wife and family pictured the unfaithfulness of Israel (Hos 1-3).

HOSHEA (JOSHUA)
1. Original name of Joshua (Nu 13:16).
2. Last king of Israel (2Ki 15: 30; 17:1-6).

HOSPITABLE* (HOSPITALITY)
1Ti 3: 2 self-controlled, respectable, *h*,
Tit 1: 8 Rather he must be *h*, one who loves

HOSPITABLY* (HOSPITALITY)
Ac 28: 7 and for three days entertained us *h*.

HOSPITALITY* (HOSPITABLE HOSPITABLY)
Ro 12: 13 Practise *h*.
16: 23 whose *h* I and the whole church
1Ti 5: 10 as bringing up children, showing *h*,
1Pe 4: 9 Offer *h* to one another
3Jn : 8 therefore to show *h* to such men

HOSTILE (HOSTILITY)
Ro 8: 7 the sinful mind is *h* to God.

HOSTILITY (HOSTILE)
Eph 2: 14 wall of *h*, by abolishing
2: 16 by which he put to death their *h*.

HOT
1Ti 4: 2 have been seared as with a *h* iron.
Rev 3: 15 that you are neither cold nor *h*.

HOT-TEMPERED (TEMPER)
Pr 15: 18 A *h* man stirs up dissension,
19: 19 A *h* man must pay the penalty;
22: 24 Do not make friends with a *h* man,
29: 22 and a *h* one commits many sins.

HOTHEADED (HEAD)
Pr 14: 16 but a fool is *h* and reckless.

HOUR
Ecc 9: 12 knows when his *h* will come:
Mt 6: 27 you by worrying can add a single *h*
Lk 12: 40 the Son of Man will come at an *h*
Jn 12: 23 The *h* has come for the Son of Man
12: 27 for this very reason I came to this *h*

HOUSE (HOUSEHOLD HOUSEHOLDS HOUSES STOREHOUSE)
Ex 12: 22 the door of his *h* until morning.
20: 17 shall not covet your neighbour's *h*.
Nu 12: 7 he is faithful in all my *h*.
Dt 5: 21 desire on your neighbour's *h*
2Sa 7: 11 LORD himself will establish a *h*
1Ch 17: 23 and his *h* be established for ever.
Ne 10: 39 "We will not neglect the *h*
Ps 23: 6 I will dwell in the *h* of the LORD
27: 4 dwell in the *h* of the LORD
69: 9 for zeal for your *h* consumes me,
84: 10 a doorkeeper in the *h* of my God
122: 1 "Let us go to the *h* of the LORD."
127: 1 Unless the LORD builds the *h*,
Pr 7: 27 Her *h* is a highway to the grave,
21: 9 than share a *h* with a quarrelsome
Isa 56: 7 a *h* of prayer for all nations."
Jer 7: 11 Has this *h*, which bears my Name,
18: 2 "Go down to the potter's *h*,
Eze 33: 7 made you a watchman for the *h*
Joel 3: 18 will flow out of the LORD's *h*
Zec 13: 6 given at the *h* of my friends.'
Mt 7: 24 is like a wise man who built his *h*
10: 11 and stay at his *h* until you leave.
12: 29 can anyone enter a strong man's *h*
21: 13 My *h* will be called a *h* of prayer,'
Mk 3: 25 If a *h* is divided against itself,
11: 17 "'My *h* will be called

Lk 6: 48 He is like a man building a *h*,
10: 7 Do not move around from *h* to *h*.
11: 17 a *h* divided against itself will fall.
11: 24 'I will return to the *h* I left.'
15: 8 sweep the *h* and search carefully
19: 9 Today salvation has come to this *h*,
Jn 2: 16 How dare you turn my Father's *h*
2: 17 "Zeal for your *h* will consume me."
12: 3 the *h* was filled with the fragrance
14: 2 In my Father's *h* are many rooms;
Ac 20: 20 you publicly and from *h* to *h*.
Ro 16: 5 the church that meets at their *h*.
Heb 3: 3 the builder of a *h* has greater honour
1Pe 2: 5 built into a spiritual *h* to be a holy

HOUSEHOLD (HOUSE)
Ex 12: 3 lamb for his family, one for each *h*.
Jos 24: 15 my *h*, we will serve the LORD."
Pr 31: 21 it snows, she has no fear for her *h*;
31: 27 over the affairs of her *h*
Mic 7: 6 are the members of his own *h*.
Mt 10: 36 will be the members of his own *h*.'
12: 25 or *h* divided against itself will not
Ac 16: 31 you will be saved—you and your *h*
Eph 2: 19 people and members of God's *h*,
1Ti 3: 12 manage his children and his *h* well.
3: 15 to conduct themselves in God's *h*,

HOUSEHOLDS (HOUSE)
Tit 1: 11 because they are ruining whole *h*

HOUSES (HOUSE)
Ex 12: 27 passed over the *h* of the Israelites
Mt 19: 29 everyone who has left *h* or brothers

HOVERING* (HOVERS)
Ge 1: 2 of God was *h* over the waters.
Isa 31: 5 Like birds *h* overhead,

HOVERS* (HOVERING)
Dt 32: 11 and *h* over its young,

HULDAH*
Prophetess enquired of by Hilkiah for Josiah (2Ki 22; 2Ch 34:14-28).

HUMAN (HUMANITY)
Lev 24: 17 If anyone takes the life of a *h* being,
Isa 52: 14 his form marred beyond *h* likeness
Jn 8: 15 You judge by *h* standards;
Ro 1: 3 as to his *h* nature was a descendant
9: 5 from them is traced the *h* ancestry
1Co 1: 17 not with words of *h* wisdom,
1: 26 of you were wise by *h* standards;
2: 13 not in words taught us by *h* wisdom
2Co 3: 3 of stone but on tablets of *h* hearts.
Gal 3: 3 to attain your goal by *h* effort?
2Pe 2: 18 lustful desires of sinful *h* nature,

HUMANITY* (HUMAN)
Heb 2: 14 he too shared in their *h* so that

HUMBLE (HUMBLED HUMBLES HUMILIATE HUMILIATED HUMILITY)
Nu 12: 3 (Now Moses was a very *h* man,
2Ch 7: 14 will *h* themselves and pray
Ps 18: 27 You save the *h*
25: 9 He guides the *h* in what is right
149: 4 he crowns the *h* with salvation.
Pr 3: 34 but gives grace to the *h*.
Isa 66: 2 he who is *h* and contrite in spirit,
Mt 11: 29 for I am gentle and *h* in heart,
Eph 4: 2 Be completely *h* and gentle;
Jas 4: 6 but gives grace to the *h*."
4: 10 *H* yourselves before the Lord,
1Pe 5: 5 but gives grace to the *h*."
5: 6 *H* yourselves,

HUMBLED (HUMBLE)
Mt 23: 12 whoever exalts himself will be *h*,
Lk 14: 11 who exalts himself will be *h*,
Php 2: 8 he *h* himself

HUMBLES* (HUMBLE)
1Sa 2: 7 he *h* and he exalts.
Isa 26: 5 He *h* those who dwell on high,
Mt 18: 4 whoever *h* himself like this child is
23: 12 whoever *h* himself will be exalted.
Lk 14: 11 he who *h* himself will be exalted."
18: 14 he who *h* himself will be exalted."

HUMILIATE* (HUMBLE)
Pr 25: 7 than for him to *h* you
1Co 11: 22 and *h* those who have nothing?

HUMILIATED (HUMBLE)
Jer 31: 19 I was ashamed and *h*
Lk 14: 9 *h*, you will have to take the least

HUMILITY* (HUMBLE)
Ps 45: 4 of truth, *h* and righteousness;
Pr 11: 2 but with *h* comes wisdom.
15: 33 and *h* comes before honour.
18: 12 but *h* comes before honour.
22: 4 *H* and the fear of the LORD
Zep 2: 3 Seek righteousness, seek *h*;
Ac 20: 19 I served the Lord with great *h*
Php 2: 3 but in *h* consider others better
Col 2: 18 let anyone who delights in false *h*
2: 23 their false *h* and their harsh
3: 12 *h*, gentleness and patience.
Tit 3: 2 and to show true *h* towards all men.
Jas 3: 13 in the *h* that comes from wisdom.
1Pe 5: 5 Clothe yourselves with *h*

HUNG (HANG)
Dt 21: 23 anyone who is *h* on a tree is
Mt 18: 6 him to have a large millstone *h*
Lk 19: 48 all the people *h* on his words.
Gal 3: 13 "Cursed is everyone who is *h*

HUNGER (HUNGRY)
Ne 9: 15 In their *h* you gave them bread
Pr 6: 30 to satisfy his *h* when he is starving.
Mt 5: 6 Blessed are those who *h*
Lk 6: 21 Blessed are you who *h* now,
2Co 6: 5 sleepless nights and *h*; in purity,
11: 27 I have known *h* and thirst
Rev 7: 16 Never again will they *h*;

HUNGRY (HUNGER)
Job 24: 10 carry the sheaves, but still go *h*.
Ps 107: 9 and fills the *h* with good things.
146: 7 and gives food to the *h*.
Pr 19: 15 and the shiftless man goes *h*.
25: 21 If your enemy is *h*, give him food
27: 7 to the *h* even what is bitter tastes
Isa 58: 7 not to share your food with the *h*
58: 10 spend yourselves on behalf of the *h*
Eze 18: 7 but gives his food to the *h*
18: 16 but gives his food to the *h*
Mt 15: 32 I do not want to send them away *h*,
25: 35 For I was *h* and you gave me
25: 42 For I was *h* and you gave me
Lk 1: 53 He has filled the *h* with good things
Jn 6: 35 comes to me will never go *h*,
Ro 12: 20 "If your enemy is *h*, feed him;
1Co 4: 11 To this very hour we go *h*
Php 4: 12 whether well fed or *h*,

HUR
Ex 17: 12 Aaron and *H* held his hands up—

HURL
Mic 7: 19 *h* all our iniquities into the depths

HURT (HURTS)
Ecc 8: 9 it over others to his own *h*.
Mk 16: 18 deadly poison, it will not *h* them
Rev 2: 11 He who overcomes will not be *h*

HURTS* (HURT)
Ps 15: 4 even when it *h*,
Pr 26: 28 A lying tongue hates those it *h*,

HUSBAND (HUSBAND'S HUSBANDS)
Pr 31: 11 Her *h* has full confidence in her
31: 23 Her *h* is respected at the city gate,
31: 28 her *h* also, and he praises her:
Isa 54: 5 For your Maker is your *h*—
Jer 3: 14 the LORD, "for I am your *h*.
3: 20 like a woman unfaithful to her *h*,
Jn 4: 17 "I have no *h*," she replied.
Ro 7: 2 a married woman is bound to her *h*
1Co 7: 2 and each woman her own *h*.
7: 3 The *h* should fulfil his marital duty
7: 10 wife must not separate from her *h*.
7: 11 And a *h* must not divorce his wife.
7: 13 And if a woman has a *h* who is not
7: 14 For the unbelieving *h* has been
7: 39 A woman is bound to her *h* as long
7: 39 But if her *h* dies, she is free
2Co 11: 2 I promised you to one *h*, to Christ,
Gal 4: 27 woman than of her who has a *h*."
Eph 5: 23 For the *h* is the head of the wife
5: 33 and the wife must respect her *h*.
1Ti 3: 2 the *h* of but one wife, temperate,
3: 12 A deacon must be the *h* of
5: 9 has been faithful to her *h*,
Tit 1: 6 An elder must be blameless, the *h*

HUSBANDMAN see GARDENER

HUSBAND'S (HUSBAND)
Dt 25: 5 Her *h* brother shall take her
Pr 12: 4 of noble character is her *h* crown,
1Co 7: 4 the *h* body does not belong

HUSBANDS (HUSBAND)
Eph 5: 22 submit to your *h* as to the Lord.
5: 25 *H*, love your wives, just
5: 28 *h* ought to love their wives
Col 3: 18 submit to your *h*, as is fitting
3: 19 *H*, love your wives and do not be
Tit 2: 4 the younger women to love their *h*
2: 5 and to be subject to their *h*,
1Pe 3: 1 same way be submissive to your *h*
3: 7 *H*, in the same way be considerate

HUSHAI
Wise man of David who frustrated Ahithophel's advice and foiled Absalom's revolt (2Sa 15:32-37; 16:15-17:16; 1Ch 27:33).

HYMN* (HYMNS)
Ps 40: 3 a *h* of praise to our God.
Mt 26: 30 they had sung a *h*, they went out
Mk 14: 26 they had sung a *h*, they went out
1Co 14: 26 everyone has a *h*, or a word

HYMNS* (HYMN)
Ac 16: 25 Silas were praying and singing *h*
Ro 15: 9 I will sing *h* to your name."
Eph 5: 19 to one another with psalms, *h*
Col 3: 16 *h* and spiritual songs with gratitude

HYPOCRISY* (HYPOCRITE HYPOCRITES HYPOCRITICAL)
Mt 23: 28 but on the inside you are full of *h*
Mk 12: 15 we?" But Jesus knew their *h*.
Lk 12: 1 yeast of the Pharisees, which is *h*.
Gal 2: 13 The other Jews joined him in his *h*,
2: 13 by their *h* even Barnabas was led
1Pe 2: 1 *h*, envy, and slander of every kind.

HYPOCRITE* (HYPOCRISY)
Mt 7: 5 You *h*, first take the plank out
Lk 6: 42 You *h*, first take the plank out

HYPOCRITES* (HYPOCRISY)
Ps 26: 4 nor do I consort with *h*;
Mt 6: 2 as the *h* do in the synagogues
6: 5 when you pray, do not be like the *h*
6: 16 do not look sombre as the *h* do,
15: 7 You *h*! Isaiah was right
22: 18 their evil intent, said, "You *h*,
23: 13 of the law and Pharisees, you *h*!

Mt 23: 15 of the law and Pharisees, you *h*!
23: 23 of the law and Pharisees, you *h*!
23: 25 of the law and Pharisees, you *h*!
23: 27 you *h*! You are like whitewashed
23: 29 of the law and Pharisees, you *h*!
24: 51 and assign him a place with the *h*,
Mk 7: 6 when he prophesied about you *h*;
Lk 12: 56 *H*! You know how
13: 15 The Lord answered him, "You *h*!"

HYPOCRITICAL* (HYPOCRISY)

1Ti 4: 2 teaching come through *h* liars,

HYSSOP

Ex 12: 22 Take a bunch of *h*, dip it
Ps 51: 7 with *h*, and I will be clean;
Jn 19: 29 the sponge on a stalk of the *h* plant,

ICHABOD

1Sa 4: 21 She named the boy *I*, saying,

IDLE* (IDLENESS IDLERS)

Dt 32: 47 They are not just *i* words for you—
Job 11: 3 Will your *i* talk reduce men
Ecc 10: 18 if his hands are *i*, the house leaks.
11: 6 at evening let not your hands be *i*,
Isa 58: 13 as you please or speaking *i* words,
Col 2: 18 mind puffs him up with *i* notions.
1Th 5: 14 those who are *i*, encourage
2Th 3: 6 away from every brother who is *i*
3: 7 We were not *i* when we were
3: 11 We hear that some among you are *i*
1Ti 5: 13 they get into the habit of being *i*

IDLENESS* (IDLE)

Pr 31: 27 and does not eat the bread of *i*.

IDLERS* (IDLE)

1Ti 5: 13 And not only do they become *i*,

IDOL (IDOLATER IDOLATERS IDOLATRY IDOLS)

Ex 20: 4 make for yourself an *i* in the form
32: 4 made it into an *i* cast in the shape
Isa 40: 19 As for an *i*, a craftsman casts it,
41: 7 He nails down the *i*
44: 15 he makes an *i* and bows down to it.
44: 17 From the rest he makes a god, his *i*;
Hab 2: 18 "Of what value is an *i*,
1Co 8: 4 We know that an *i* is nothing at all

IDOLATER* (IDOL)

1Co 5: 11 an *i* or a slanderer, a drunkard
Eph 5: 5 greedy person—such a man is an *i*

IDOLATERS (IDOL)

1Co 5: 10 or the greedy and swindlers, or *i*.
6: 9 Neither the sexually immoral nor *i*

IDOLATRY (IDOL)

1Sa 15: 23 and arrogance like the evil of *i*.
1Co 10: 14 my dear friends, flee from *i*.
Gal 5: 20 and debauchery; *i* and witchcraft;
Col 3: 5 evil desires and greed, which is *i*.
1Pe 4: 3 orgies, carousing and detestable *i*.

IDOLS (IDOL)

Dt 32: 16 angered him with their detestable *i*.
Ps 78: 58 aroused his jealousy with their *i*.
Isa 44: 9 All who make *i* are nothing,
Eze 23: 39 sacrificed their children to their *i*,
Ac 15: 20 to abstain from food polluted by *i*,
21: 25 abstain from food sacrificed to *i*,
1Co 8: 1 Now about food sacrificed to *i*:
1Jn 5: 21 children, keep yourselves from *i*.
Rev 2: 14 to sin by eating food sacrificed to *i*

IGNORANT (IGNORE)

1Co 15: 34 for there are some who are *i* of God
Heb 5: 2 to deal gently with those who are *i*
1Pe 2: 15 good you should silence the *i* talk
2Pe 3: 16 which *i* and unstable people distort

IGNORE (IGNORANT IGNORED IGNORES)

Dt 22: 1 do not *i* it but be sure
Ps 9: 12 he does not *i* the cry of the afflicted
Heb 2: 3 if we *i* such a great salvation?

IGNORED (IGNORE)

Hos 4: 6 you have *i* the law of your God,
1Co 14: 38 he ignores this, he himself will be *i*.

IGNORES* (IGNORE)

Pr 10: 17 whoever *i* correction leads others
13: 18 He who *i* discipline comes
15: 32 He who *i* discipline despises
1Co 14: 38 If he *i* this, he himself will be

ILL (ILLNESS)

Mt 4: 24 brought to him all who were *i*

ILL-GOTTEN

Pr 1: 19 the end of all who go after *i* gain;
10: 2 *I* treasures are of no value,

ILL-TEMPERED* (TEMPER)

Pr 21: 19 than with a quarrelsome and *i* wife.

ILL-TREAT (ILL-TREATED)

Ex 22: 21 "Do not *i* an alien or oppress him,
Eze 22: 29 and needy and *i* the alien,
Lk 6: 28 pray for those who *i* you.

ILL-TREATED (ILL-TREAT)

Eze 22: 7 *i* the fatherless and the widow.
Heb 11: 25 to be *i* along with the people
11: 37 destitute, persecuted and *i*—
13: 3 who are *i* as if you yourselves

ILLEGITIMATE

Heb 12: 8 then you are *i* children

ILLNESS (ILL)

2Ki 8: 9 'Will I recover from this *i*?' "
2Ch 16: 12 even in his *i* he did not seek help
Ps 41: 3 and restore him from his bed of *i*.
Isa 38: 9 king of Judah after his *i*

ILLUMINATED*

Rev 18: 1 and the earth was *i* by his splendour.

IMAGE (IMAGES)

Ge 1: 26 "Let us make man in our *i*,
1: 27 So God created man in his own *i*,
9: 6 for in the *i* of God
Dt 27: 15 "Cursed is the man who carves an *i*
Isa 40: 18 What *i* will you compare him to?
Da 3: 1 King Nebuchadnezzar made an *i*
1Co 11: 7 since he is the *i* and glory of God;
2Co 4: 4 glory of Christ, who is the *i* of God.
Col 1: 15 He is the *i* of the invisible God,
3: 10 in knowledge in the *i* of its Creator.
Rev 13: 14 them to set up an *i* in honour

IMAGES (IMAGE)

Ps 97: 7 All who worship *i* are put to shame,
Jer 10: 14 His *i* are a fraud;
Ro 1: 23 of the immortal God for *i* made

IMAGINATION (IMAGINE)

Eze 13: 2 who prophesy out of their own *i*:

IMAGINE (IMAGINATION)

Eph 3: 20 more than all we ask or *i*,

IMITATE (IMITATORS)

1Co 4: 16 Therefore I urge you to *i* me.
Heb 6: 12 but to *i* those who through faith
13: 7 of their way of life and *i* their faith.
3Jn : 11 do not *i* what is evil but what is

IMITATORS* (IMITATE)

Eph 5: 1 Be *i* of God, therefore,
1Th 1: 6 You became *i* of us and of the Lord
2: 14 became *i* of God's churches

IMMANUEL*

Isa 7: 14 birth to a son, and will call him *I*.
8: 8 O *I*!"
Mt 1: 23 and they will call him *I*"—

IMMORAL* (IMMORALITY)

Pr 6: 24 keeping you from the *i* woman,
1Co 5: 9 to associate with sexually *i* people
5: 10 the people of this world who are *i*,
5: 11 but is sexually *i* or greedy,
6: 9 Neither the sexually *i* nor idolaters
Eph 5: 5 No *i*, impure or greedy person—
Heb 12: 16 See that no-one is sexually *i*,
13: 4 the adulterer and all the sexually *i*.
Rev 21: 8 the murderers, the sexually *i*,
22: 15 the sexually *i*, the murderers,

IMMORALITY* (IMMORAL)

Nu 25: 1 in sexual *i* with Moabite women,
Jer 3: 9 Because Israel's *i* mattered so little
Mt 15: 19 murder, adultery, sexual *i*, theft,
Mk 7: 21 sexual *i*, theft, murder, adultery,
Ac 15: 20 from sexual *i*, from the meat
15: 29 animals and from sexual *i*.
21: 25 animals and from sexual *i*."
Ro 13: 13 not in sexual *i* and debauchery,
1Co 5: 1 reported that there is sexual *i*
6: 13 The body is not meant for sexual *i*,
6: 18 Flee from sexual *i*.
7: 2 But since there is so much *i*,
10: 8 We should not commit sexual *i*,
Gal 5: 19 sexual *i*, impurity and debauchery;
Eph 5: 3 must not be even a hint of sexual *i*,
Col 3: 5 sexual *i*, impurity, lust, evil desires
1Th 4: 3 that you should avoid sexual *i*;
Jude : 4 grace of our God into a licence for *i*
: 7 gave themselves up to sexual *i*
Rev 2: 14 and by committing sexual *i*.
2: 20 misleads my servants into sexual *i*
2: 21 given her time to repent of her *i*,
9: 21 their sexual *i* or their thefts.

IMMORTAL* (IMMORTALITY)

Ro 1: 23 glory of the *i* God for images made
1Ti 1: 17 Now to the King eternal, *i*,
6: 16 who alone is *i* and who lives

IMMORTALITY* (IMMORTAL)

Pr 12: 28 along that path is *i*.
Ro 2: 7 honour and *i*, he will give eternal life
1Co 15: 53 and the mortal with *i*.
15: 54 with *i*, then the saying that is
2Ti 1: 10 and *i* to light through the gospel.

IMPARTIAL*

Jas 3: 17 and good fruit, *i* and sincere.

IMPARTS*

Pr 29: 15 The rod of correction *i* wisdom,

IMPERFECT*

1Co 13: 10 perfection comes, the *i* disappears.

IMPERISHABLE

1Co 15: 42 it is raised *i*; it is sown in dishonour,
15: 50 nor does the perishable inherit the *i*
1Pe 1: 23 not of perishable seed, but of *i*,

IMPLANTED*

Ps 94: 9 Does he who *i* the ear not hear?

IMPLORE*

Mal 1: 9 "Now *i* God to be gracious to us.
2Co 5: 20 We *i* you on Christ's behalf:

IMPORTANCE* (IMPORTANT)

1Co 15: 3 passed on to you as of first *i*:

IMPORTANT (IMPORTANCE)

Mt 6: 25 Is not life more *i* than food,
23: 23 have neglected the more *i* matters
Mk 12: 29 "The most *i* one," answered Jesus,

Mk 12:33 as yourself is more *i* than all burnt
Php 1:18 The *i* thing is that in every way,

IMPOSSIBLE
Mt 17:20 Nothing will be *i* for you."
19:26 "With man this is *i*,
Mk 10:27 "With man this is *i*, but not
Lk 1:37 For nothing is *i* with God."
18:27 "What is *i* with men is possible
Ac 2:24 it was *i* for death to keep its hold
Heb 6:4 It is *i* for those who have once been
6:18 things in which it is *i* for God to lie,
10:4 because it is *i* for the blood of bulls
11:6 without faith it is *i* to please God,

IMPOSTORS
2Ti 3:13 and *i* will go from bad to worse,

IMPRESS* (IMPRESSES)
Dt 6:7 *I* them on your children.

IMPRESSES* (IMPRESS)
Pr 17:10 A rebuke *i* a man of discernment

IMPROPER*
Eph 5:3 these are *i* for God's holy people.

IMPURE (IMPURITY)
Ac 10:15 not call anything *i* that God has
Eph 5:5 No immoral, *i* or greedy person—
1Th 2:3 spring from error or *i* motives,
4:7 For God did not call us to be *i*,
Rev 21:27 Nothing *i* will ever enter it,

IMPURITY (IMPURE)
Ro 1:24 hearts to sexual *i* for the degrading
Gal 5:19 sexual immorality, *i*
Eph 4:19 as to indulge in every kind of *i*,
5:3 or of any kind of *i*, or of greed,
Col 3:5 *i*, lust, evil desires and greed,

INCENSE
Ex 30:1 altar of acacia wood for burning *i*.
40:5 Place the gold altar of *i* in front
Ps 141:2 my prayer be set before you like *i*;
Mt 2:11 him with gifts of gold and of *i*
Heb 9:4 which had the golden altar of *i*
Rev 5:8 were holding golden bowls full of *i*,
8:4 The smoke of the *i*, together

INCLINATION (INCLINES)
Ge 6:5 and that every *i* of the thoughts

INCLINES* (INCLINATION)
Ecc 10:2 The heart of the wise *i* to the right,

INCOME
Ecc 5:10 wealth is never satisfied with his *i*.
1Co 16:2 sum of money in keeping with his *i*,

INCOMPARABLE*
Eph 2:7 ages he might show the *i* riches

INCREASE (EVER-INCREASING INCREASED INCREASES INCREASING)
Ge 1:22 "Be fruitful and *i* in number
3:16 "I will greatly *i* your pains
8:17 be fruitful and *i* in number upon it
Ps 62:10 though your riches *i*,
Pr 22:16 oppresses the poor to *i* his wealth
Isa 9:7 Of the *i* of his government
Mt 24:12 Because of the *i* of wickedness,
Lk 17:5 said to the Lord, "*I* our faith!"
Ac 12:24 But the word of God continued to *i*
Ro 5:20 added so that the trespass might *i*.
1Th 3:12 May the Lord make your love *i*

INCREASED (INCREASE)
Ac 6:7 of disciples in Jerusalem *i* rapidly,
Ro 5:20 But where sin *i*, grace *i* all the more

INCREASES (INCREASE)
Pr 24:5 and a man of knowledge *i* strength;

INCREASING (INCREASE)
Ac 6:1 when the number of disciples was *i*,
2Th 1:3 one of you has for each other is *i*.
2Pe 1:8 these qualities in *i* measure,

INCREDIBLE*
Ac 26:8 of you consider it *i* that God raises

INDECENT
Ro 1:27 Men committed *i* acts

INDEPENDENT*
1Co 11:11 however, woman is not *i* of man,
11:11 of man, nor is man *i* of woman.

INDESCRIBABLE*
2Co 9:15 Thanks be to God for his *i* gift!

INDESTRUCTIBLE*
Heb 7:16 on the basis of the power of an *i* life

INDIGNANT
Mk 10:14 When Jesus saw this, he was *i*.

INDISPENSABLE*
1Co 12:22 seem to be weaker are *i*,

INEFFECTIVE*
2Pe 1:8 they will keep you from being *i*

INEXPRESSIBLE*
2Co 12:4 He heard *i* things, things that man
1Pe 1:8 are filled with an *i* and glorious joy,

INFANCY* (INFANTS)
2Ti 3:15 from *i* you have known the holy

INFANTS (INFANCY)
Ps 8:2 From the lips of children and *i*
Mt 21:16 " 'From the lips of children and *i*
1Co 3:1 but as worldly—mere *i* in Christ.
14:20 In regard to evil be *i*,
Eph 4:14 Then we will no longer be *i*,

INFIRMITIES*
Isa 53:4 Surely he took up our *i*
Mt 8:17 "He took up our *i*

INFLAMED
Ro 1:27 were *i* with lust for one another.

INFLUENTIAL*
1Co 1:26 not many were *i*; not many were

INHABITANTS (INHABITED)
Nu 33:55 " 'But if you do not drive out the *i*
Rev 8:13 Woe! Woe to the *i* of the earth,

INHABITED (INHABITANTS)
Isa 45:18 but formed it to be *i*—

INHERIT (CO-HEIRS HEIR HEIRS HERITAGE INHERITANCE)
Dt 1:38 because he will lead Israel to *i* it.
Jos 1:6 people to *i* the land I swore
Ps 37:11 But the meek will *i* the land
37:29 the righteous will *i* the land
Zec 2:12 The LORD will *i* Judah
Mt 5:5 for they will *i* the earth.
19:29 as much and will *i* eternal life.
Mk 10:17 "what must I do to *i* eternal life?"
Lk 10:25 "what must I do to *i* eternal life?"
18:18 what must I do to *i* eternal life?"
1Co 6:9 the wicked will not *i* the kingdom
15:50 blood cannot *i* the kingdom of God
Rev 21:7 He who overcomes will *i* all this,

INHERITANCE (INHERIT)
Lev 20:24 I will give it to you as an *i*,
Dt 4:20 to be the people of his *i*,
10:9 the LORD is their *i*, as the LORD
Jos 14:3 two-and-a-half tribes their *i* east
Ps 16:6 surely I have a delightful *i*.
33:12 the people he chose for his *i*.
136:21 and gave their land as an *i*,
Pr 13:22 A good man leaves an *i*
Mt 25:34 blessed by my Father; take your *i*,
Eph 1:14 who is a deposit guaranteeing our *i*
5:5 has any *i* in the kingdom of Christ
Col 1:12 you to share in the *i* of the saints
3:24 you know that you will receive an *i*
Heb 9:15 receive the promised eternal *i*—
1Pe 1:4 and into an *i* that can never perish,

INIQUITIES (INIQUITY)
Ps 78:38 he forgave their *i*
103:10 or repay us according to our *i*.
Isa 53:5 he was crushed for our *i*;
53:11 and he will bear their *i*.
59:2 But your *i* have separated
Mic 7:19 and hurl all our *i* into the depths

INIQUITY (INIQUITIES)
Ps 25:11 forgive my *i*, though it is great.
32:5 and did not cover up my *i*.
51:2 Wash away all my *i*
51:9 and blot out all my *i*.
Isa 53:6 the *i* of us all.

INJURED
Eze 34:16 will bind up the *i* and strengthen
Zec 11:16 or heal the *i*, or feed the healthy,

INJUSTICE
2Ch 19:7 the LORD our God there is no *i*

INK
2Co 3:3 not with *i* but with the Spirit

INN*
Lk 2:7 there was no room for them in the *i*
10:34 took him to an *i* and took care

INNOCENT
Ex 23:7 do not put an *i* or honest person
Dt 25:1 acquitting the *i* and condemning
Pr 6:17 hands that shed *i* blood,
17:26 It is not good to punish an *i* man,
Mt 10:16 shrewd as snakes and as *i* as doves.
27:4 "for I have betrayed *i* blood."
27:24 I am *i* of this man's blood," he said.
Ac 20:26 declare to you today that I am *i*
Ro 16:19 what is good, and *i* about what is
1Co 4:4 but that does not make me *i*.

INSCRIPTION
Mt 22:20 And whose *i*?" "Caesar's,"
2Ti 2:19 with this *i*: "The Lord knows those

INSIGHT
1Ki 4:29 Solomon wisdom and very great *i*,
Ps 119:99 I have more *i* than all my teachers,
Pr 5:1 listen well to my words of *i*,
21:30 There is no wisdom, no *i*, no plan
Php 1:9 more in knowledge and depth of *i*,
2Ti 2:7 for the Lord will give you *i*

INSOLENT
Ro 1:30 God-haters, *i*, arrogant

INSPIRED*
Hos 9:7 the *i* man a maniac.
1Th 1:3 and your endurance *i* by hope

INSTALLED
Ps 2:6 "I have *i* my King

INSTINCT* (INSTINCTS)
2Pe 2:12 are like brute beasts, creatures of *i*,
Jude :10 things they do understand by *i*,

INSTINCTS* (INSTINCT)
Jude :19 who follow mere natural *i*

INSTITUTED
Ro 13:2 rebelling against what God has *i*,

1Pe 2: 13 to every authority *i* among men:

INSTRUCT (INSTRUCTED INSTRUCTION INSTRUCTIONS INSTRUCTOR)

Ps 32: 8 I will *i* you and teach you
105: 22 to *i* his princes as he pleased
Pr 9: 9 *I* a wise man and he will be wiser
Ro 15: 14 and competent to *i* one another.
1Co 2: 16 that he may *i* him?"
14: 19 to *i* others than ten thousand words
2Ti 2: 25 who oppose him he must gently *i*,

INSTRUCTED (INSTRUCT)

2Ch 26: 5 who *i* him in the fear of God.
Pr 21: 11 a wise man is *i*, he gets knowledge.
Isa 50: 4 LORD has given me an *i* tongue,
Mt 13: 52 who has been *i* about the kingdom
1Co 14: 31 in turn so that everyone may be *i*

INSTRUCTION (INSTRUCT)

Pr 1: 8 Listen, my son, to your father's *i*
4: 1 Listen, my sons, to a father's *i*;
4: 13 Hold on to *i*, do not let it go;
8: 10 Choose my *i* instead of silver,
8: 33 Listen to my *i* and be wise;
13: 1 A wise son heeds his father's *i*,
13: 13 He who scorns *i* will pay for it,
16: 20 Whoever gives heed to *i* prospers,
16: 21 and pleasant words promote *i*.
19: 20 Listen to advice and accept *i*,
23: 12 Apply your heart to *i*
1Co 14: 6 or prophecy or word of *i*?
14: 26 or a word of *i*, a revelation,
Eph 6: 4 up in the training and *i* of the Lord.
1Th 4: 8 he who rejects this *i* does not reject
2Th 3: 14 If anyone does not obey our *i*
1Ti 1: 18 I give you this *i* in keeping
6: 3 to the sound *i* of our Lord Jesus
2Ti 4: 2 with great patience and careful *i*.

INSTRUCTIONS (INSTRUCT)

1Ti 3: 14 I am writing you these *i* so that,

INSTRUCTOR (INSTRUCT)

Gal 6: 6 share all good things with his *i*.

INSTRUMENT* (INSTRUMENTS)

Eze 33: 32 beautiful voice and plays an *i* well,
Ac 9: 15 This man is my chosen *i*
2Ti 2: 21 he will be an *i* for noble purposes,

INSTRUMENTS (INSTRUMENT)

Ro 6: 13 as *i* of wickedness, but rather offer

INSULT (INSULTED INSULTS)

Pr 9: 7 corrects a mocker invites *i*;
12: 16 but a prudent man overlooks an *i*.
Mt 5: 11 Blessed are you when people *i* you,
Lk 6: 22 when they exclude you and *i* you
1Pe 3: 9 evil with evil or *i* with *i*,

INSULTED (INSULT)

Heb 10: 29 and who has *i* the Spirit of grace?
Jas 2: 6 love him? But you have *i* the poor.
1Pe 4: 14 If you are *i* because of the name

INSULTS (INSULT)

Ps 22: 7 they hurl *i*, shaking their heads:
69: 9 the *i* of those who insult you fall
Pr 22: 10 quarrels and *i* are ended.
Mk 15: 29 passed by hurled *i* at him,
Jn 9: 28 Then they hurled *i* at him and said,
Ro 15: 3 "The *i* of those who insult you have
2Co 12: 10 in *i*, in hardships, in persecutions,
1Pe 2: 23 When they hurled their *i* at him,

INTEGRITY*

Dt 9: 5 or your *i* that you are going
1Ki 9: 4 if you walk before me in *i* of heart
1Ch 29: 17 the heart and are pleased with *i*.
Ne 7: 2 because he was a man of *i*
Job 2: 3 And he still maintains his *i*,
2: 9 "Are you still holding on to your *i*?
Job 6: 29 reconsider, for my *i* is at stake.
27: 5 till I die, I will not deny my *i*.
Ps 7: 8 according to my *i*, O Most High.
25: 21 May *i* and uprightness protect me,
41: 12 In my *i* you uphold me
78: 72 David shepherded them with *i*
Pr 10: 9 The man of *i* walks securely,
11: 3 The *i* of the upright guides them,
13: 6 Righteousness guards the man of *i*,
17: 26 or to flog officials for their *i*.
29: 10 Bloodthirsty men hate a man of *i*
Isa 45: 23 my mouth has uttered in all *i*
59: 4 no-one pleads his case with *i*.
Mt 22: 16 "we know you are a man of *i*
Mk 12: 14 we know you are a man of *i*.
Tit 2: 7 your teaching show *i*, seriousness

INTELLIGENCE (INTELLIGENT)

Isa 29: 14 the *i* of the intelligent will vanish."
1Co 1: 19 *i* of the intelligent I will frustrate."

INTELLIGENT (INTELLIGENCE)

Isa 29: 14 the intelligence of the *i* will vanish

INTELLIGIBLE

1Co 14: 19 I would rather speak five *i* words

INTENDED

Ge 50: 20 place of God? You *i* to harm me,

INTENSE

1Th 2: 17 out of our *i* longing we made every
Rev 16: 9 They were seared by the *i* heat

INTERCEDE (INTERCEDES INTERCEDING INTERCESSION INTERCESSOR)

Heb 7: 25 he always lives to *i* for them.

INTERCEDES* (INTERCEDE)

Ro 8: 26 but the Spirit himself *i* for us
8: 27 because the Spirit *i* for the saints

INTERCEDING* (INTERCEDE)

Ro 8: 34 hand of God and is also *i* for us.

INTERCESSION* (INTERCEDE)

Isa 53: 12 and made *i* for the transgressors.
1Ti 2: 1 *i* and thanksgiving be made

INTERCESSOR* (INTERCEDE)

Job 16: 20 My *i* is my friend

INTEREST [1]

Lev 25: 36 Do not take *i* of any kind from him,
Dt 23: 20 You may charge a foreigner *i*,
Mt 25: 27 would have received it back with *i*.

INTEREST [2] (INTERESTS)

Php 2: 20 who takes a genuine *i*

INTERESTS (INTEREST [2])

1Co 7: 34 his wife—and his *i* are divided.
Php 2: 4 only to your own *i*, but also to the *i*
2: 21 everyone looks out for his own *i*,

INTERFERE*

Ezr 6: 7 Do not *i* with the work

INTERMARRY (MARRY)

Dt 7: 3 Do not *i* with them.
Ezr 9: 14 and *i* with the peoples who commit

INTERPRET (INTERPRETATION INTERPRETER INTERPRETS)

Ge 41: 15 "I had a dream, and no-one can *i* it.
Mt 16: 3 you cannot *i* the signs of the times.
1Co 12: 30 Do all *i*? But eagerly desire
14: 13 pray that he may *i* what he says.
14: 27 one at a time, and someone must *i*.

INTERPRETATION (INTERPRET)

1Co 12: 10 and to still another the *i* of tongues.
1Co 14: 26 a revelation, a tongue or an *i*.
2Pe 1: 20 about by the prophet's own *i*.

INTERPRETER (INTERPRET)

1Co 14: 28 If there is no *i*, the speaker should

INTERPRETS (INTERPRET)

1Co 14: 5 he *i*, so that the church may be

INVADED

2Ki 17: 5 king of Assyria *i* the entire land,
24: 1 king of Babylon *i* the land,

INVENT* (INVENTED)

Ro 1: 30 boastful; they *i* ways of doing evil;

INVENTED* (INVENT)

2Pe 1: 16 We did not follow cleverly *i* stories

INVESTIGATED

Lk 1: 3 I myself have carefully *i* everything

INVISIBLE*

Ro 1: 20 of the world God's *i* qualities—
Col 1: 15 He is the image of the *i* God,
1: 16 and on earth, visible and *i*,
1Ti 1: 17 immortal, *i*, the only God,
Heb 11: 27 because he saw him who is *i*.

INVITE (INVITED INVITES)

Mt 22: 9 *i* to the banquet anyone you find.'
25: 38 did we see you a stranger and *i* you
Lk 14: 12 do not *i* your friends, your brothers
14: 13 you give a banquet, *i* the poor,

INVITED (INVITE)

Zep 1: 7 he has consecrated those he has *i*.
Mt 22: 14 For many are *i*, but few are chosen
25: 35 I was a stranger and you *i* me in,
Lk 14: 10 But when you are *i*, take the lowest
Rev 19: 9 'Blessed are those who are *i*

INVITES (INVITE)

Pr 18: 6 and his mouth *i* a beating.
1Co 10: 27 If some unbeliever *i* you to a meal

INVOLVED

2Ti 2: 4 a soldier gets *i* in civilian affairs—

IRON

2Ki 6: 6 threw it there, and made the *i* float.
Ps 2: 9 will rule them with an *i* sceptre;
Pr 27: 17 As *i* sharpens *i*,
Da 2: 33 and thighs of bronze, its legs of *i*,
1Ti 4: 2 have been seared as with a hot *i*.
Rev 2: 27 He will rule them with an *i* sceptre;
12: 5 all the nations with an *i* sceptre.
19: 15 He will rule them with an *i* sceptre

IRRELIGIOUS*

1Ti 1: 9 and sinful, the unholy and *i*;

IRREVOCABLE*

Ro 11: 29 for God's gifts and his call are *i*.

ISAAC

Son of Abraham by Sarah (Ge 17:19; 21:1-7; 1Ch 1:28). Abrahamic covenant perpetuated through (Ge 17:21; 26:2-5). Offered up by Abraham (Ge 22; Heb 11:17-19). Rebekah taken as wife (Ge 24). Inherited Abraham's estate (Ge 25:5). Fathered Esau and Jacob (Ge 25:19-26; 1Ch 1:34). Nearly lost Rebekah to Abimelech (Ge 26:1-11). Covenant with Abimelech (Ge 26:12-31). Tricked into blessing Jacob (Ge 27). Death (Ge 35:27-29). Father of Israel (Ex 3:6; Dt 29:13; Ro 9:10).

ISAIAH

Prophet to Judah (Isa 1:1). Called by the LORD (Isa 6). Announced judgment to Ahaz (Isa 7), deliverance from Assyria to Hezekiah (2Ki 19; Isa 36-37), deliverance from death to Hezekiah

(2Ki 20:1-11; Isa 38). Chronicler of Judah's history (2Ch 26:22; 32:32)

ISCARIOT see JUDAS

ISH-BOSHETH*

Son of Saul who attempted to succeed him as king (2Sa 2:8-4:12; 1Ch 8:33).

ISHMAEL

Son of Abraham by Hagar (Ge 16; 1Ch 1:28). Blessed, but not son of covenant (Ge 17:18-21; Gal 4:21-31). Sent away by Sarah (Ge 21:8-21). Children (Ge 25:12-18; 1Ch 1:29-31). Death (Ge 25:17).

ISLAND

Rev 1: 9 was on the *i* of Patmos
16: 20 Every *i* fled away

ISRAEL (ISRAEL'S ISRAELITE ISRAELITES)

1. Name given to Jacob (see JACOB).
2. Corporate name of Jacob's descendants; often specifically Northern Kingdom.

Ex 28: 11 Engrave the names of the sons of *I*
28: 29 of the sons of *I* over his heart
Nu 24: 17 a sceptre will rise out of *I*.
Dt 6: 4 Hear, O *I*: The LORD our God,
10: 12 O *I*, what does the LORD your
Jos 4: 22 *I* crossed the Jordan on dry ground
Jdg 17: 6 In those days *I* had no king;
Ru 2: 12 of *I*, under whose wings you have
1Sa 3: 20 *I* from Dan to Beersheba
4: 21 "The glory has departed from *I*"—
14: 23 So the LORD rescued *I* that day,
15: 26 has rejected you as king over *I*!"
17: 46 will know that there is a God in *I*.
18: 16 But all *I* and Judah loved David,
2Sa 5: 2 'You will shepherd my people *I*,
5: 3 they anointed David king over *I*.
14: 25 In all *I* there was not a man
1Ki 1: 35 I have appointed him ruler over *I*
10: 9 of the LORD's eternal love for *I*,
18: 17 "Is that you, you troubler of *I*?"
19: 18 Yet I reserve seven thousand in *I*—
2Ki 5: 8 know that there is a prophet in *I*."
1Ch 17: 22 made your people *I* your very own
21: 1 incited David to take a census of *I*.
29: 25 Solomon in the sight of all *I*
2Ch 9: 8 of the love of your God for *I*
Ps 73: 1 Surely God is good to *I*,
81: 8 if you would but listen to me, O *I*!
98: 3 his faithfulness to the house of *I*;
99: 8 you were to *I* a forgiving God,
Isa 11: 12 and gather the exiles of *I*;
27: 6 *I* will bud and blossom
44: 21 O *I*, I will not forget you.
46: 13 my splendour to *I*.
Jer 2: 3 *I* was holy to the LORD,
23: 6 and *I* will live in safety.
31: 2 I will come to give rest to *I*."
31: 10 'He who scattered *I* will gather
31: 31 covenant with the house of *I*
33: 17 sit on the throne of the house of *I*,
Eze 3: 17 you a watchman for the house of *I*;
33: 7 you a watchman for the house of *I*;
34: 2 prophesy against the shepherds of *I*
37: 28 that I the LORD make *I* holy,
39: 23 of *I* went into exile for their sin,
Da 9: 20 my sin and the sin of my people *I*
Hos 11: 1 "When *I* was a child, I loved him,
Am 4: 12 prepare to meet your God, O *I*."
7: 11 and *I* will surely go into exile,
8: 2 "The time is ripe for my people *I*;
9: 14 I will bring back my exiled people *I*
Mic 5: 2 one who will be ruler over *I*,
Zep 3: 13 The remnant of *I* will do no wrong;
Zec 11: 14 brotherhood between Judah and *I*.
Mal 1: 5 even beyond the borders of *I*!'
Mt 2: 6 be the shepherd of my people *I*.'"
10: 6 Go rather to the lost sheep of *I*.
15: 24 only to the lost sheep of *I*."
Mk 12: 29 'Hear, O *I*, the Lord our God,
Lk 22: 30 judging the twelve tribes of *I*.
Ac 1: 6 going to restore the kingdom to *I*?"
9: 15 and before the people of *I*.
Ro 9: 4 of my own race, the people of *I*.
9: 6 all who are descended from *I* are *I*.
9: 31 but *I*, who pursued a law
11: 7 What *I* sought so earnestly it did
11: 26 And so all *I* will be saved,
Gal 6: 16 who follow this rule, even to the *I*
Eph 2: 12 excluded from citizenship in *I*
3: 6 Gentiles are heirs together with *I*,
Heb 8: 8 covenant with the house of *I*
Rev 7: 4 144,000 from all the tribes of *I*.
21: 12 the names of the twelve tribes of *I*.

ISRAEL'S (ISRAEL)

Jdg 10: 16 he could bear *I* misery no longer.
2Sa 23: 1 *I* singer of songs:
Isa 44: 6 *I* King and Redeemer, the LORD
Jer 3: 9 Because *I* immorality mattered
31: 9 because I am *I* father,
Jn 3: 10 "You are *I* teacher," said Jesus,

ISRAELITE (ISRAEL)

Ex 16: 1 The whole *I* community set out
35: 29 All the *I* men and women who
Nu 8: 16 offspring from every *I* woman.
20: 1 the whole *I* community arrived
20: 22 The whole *I* community set out
Jn 1: 47 "Here is a true *I*, in whom there is
Ro 11: 1 I am an *I* myself, a descendant

ISRAELITES (ISRAEL)

Ex 1: 7 the *I* were fruitful and multiplied
2: 23 The *I* groaned in their slavery
3: 9 the cry of the *I* has reached me,
12: 35 The *I* did as Moses instructed
12: 37 The *I* journeyed from Rameses
14: 22 and the *I* went through the sea
16: 12 I have heard the grumbling of the *I*.
16: 35 The *I* ate manna forty years,
24: 17 To the *I* the glory of the LORD
28: 30 decisions for the *I* over his heart
29: 45 Then I will dwell among the *I*
31: 16 The *I* are to observe the Sabbath,
33: 5 "Tell the *I*, 'You are a stiff-necked
39: 42 The *I* had done all the work just
Lev 22: 32 be acknowledged as holy by the *I*.
25: 46 rule over your fellow *I* ruthlessly.
25: 55 for the *I* belong to me as servants.
Nu 2: 32 These are the *I*, counted according
6: 23 'This is how you are to bless the *I*.
9: 2 "Have the *I* celebrate the Passover
9: 17 the *I* set out; wherever the cloud
10: 12 Then the *I* set out from the Desert
14: 2 All the *I* grumbled against Moses
20: 12 as holy in the sight of the *I*,
21: 6 they bit the people and many *I* died
26: 65 had told those *I* they would surely
27: 12 and see the land I have given the *I*.
33: 3 The *I* set out from Rameses
35: 10 "Speak to the *I* and say to them:
Dt 33: 1 on the *I* before his death.
Jos 1: 2 about to give to them—to the *I*.
5: 6 The *I* had moved about
7: 1 the *I* acted unfaithfully in regard
8: 32 There in the presence of the *I*,
18: 1 of the *I* gathered at Shiloh
21: 3 the *I* gave the Levites the following
22: 9 of Manasseh left the *I* at Shiloh
Jdg 2: 11 Then the *I* did evil in the eyes
3: 12 Once again the *I* did evil
4: 1 the *I* once again did evil in the eyes
6: 1 Again the *I* did evil in the eyes
10: 6 Again the *I* did evil in the eyes
13: 1 Again the *I* did evil in the eyes
1Sa 17: 2 Saul and the *I* assembled
1Ki 8: 63 and all the *I* dedicated the temple
9: 22 did not make slaves of any of the *I*;
12: 1 for all the *I* had gone there
12: 17 But as for the *I* who were living
2Ki 17: 24 towns of Samaria to replace the *I*.
1Ch 9: 2 in their own towns were some *I*,
10: 1 fought against Israel; the *I* fled
11: 4 and all the *I* marched to Jerusalem,
2Ch 7: 6 and all the *I* were standing.
Ne 1: 6 the sins we *I*, including myself
Jer 16: 14 who brought the *I* up out of Egypt,'
Hos 1: 10 "Yet the *I* will be like the sand
3: 1 Love her as the LORD loves the *I*,
Am 4: 5 boast about them, you *I*,
Mic 5: 3 return to join the *I*.
Ro 9: 27 the number of the *I* be like the sand
10: 1 for the *I* is that they may be saved.
10: 16 But not all the *I* accepted the good
2Co 11: 22 Are they *I*? So am I.

ISSACHAR

Son of Jacob by Leah (Ge 30:18; 35:23; 1Ch 2:1). Tribe of blessed (Ge 49:14-15; Dt 33:18-19), numbered (Nu 1:29; 26:25), allotted land (Jos 19:17-23; Eze 48:25), assisted Deborah (Jdg 5:15), 12,000 from (Rev 7:7).

ISSUING*

Da 9: 25 From the *i* of the decree to restore

ITALY

Ac 27: 1 decided that we would sail for *I*,
Heb 13: 24 from *I* send you their greetings.

ITCHING*

2Ti 4: 3 to say what their *i* ears want to hear

ITHAMAR

Son of Aaron (Ex 6:23; 1Ch 6:3). Duties at tabernacle (Ex 38:21; Nu 4:21-33; 7:8).

ITTAI

2Sa 15: 19 The king said to *I* the Gittite,

IVORY

1Ki 10: 22 silver and *i*, and apes and baboons.
22: 39 the palace he built and inlaid with *i*

JABBOK

Ge 32: 22 and crossed the ford of the *J*.
Dt 3: 16 and out to the *J* River,

JABESH

1Sa 11: 1 And all the men of *J* said to him,
31: 12 wall of Beth Shan and went to *J*,
1Ch 10: 12 and his sons and brought them to *J*.

JABESH GILEAD

Jdg 21: 8 that no-one from *J* had come to
2Sa 2: 4 the men of *J* who had buried Saul,
1Ch 10: 11 the inhabitants of *J* heard

JACOB

Second son of Isaac, twin of Esau (Ge 26:21-26; 1Ch 1:34). Bought Esau's birthright (Ge 26:29-34); tricked Isaac into blessing him (Ge 27:1-37). Fled to Haran (Ge 28:1-5). Abrahamic covenant perpetuated through (Ge 28:13-15; Mal 1:2). Vision at Bethel (Ge 28:10-22). Served Laban for Rachel and Leah (Ge 29:1-30). Children (Ge 29:31-30:24; 35:16-26; 1Ch 2-9). Flocks increased (Ge 30:25-43). Returned to Canaan (Ge 31). Wrestled with God; name changed to Israel (Ge 32:22-32). Reconciled to Esau (Ge 33). Returned to Bethel (Ge 35:1-15). Favoured Joseph (Ge 37:3). Sent sons to Egypt during famine (Ge 42-43). Settled in Egypt (Ge 46). Blessed Ephraim and Manasseh (Ge 48). Blessed sons (Ge 49:1-28; Heb 11:21). Death (Ge 49:29-33). Burial (Ge 50:1-14).

JAEL*

Woman who killed Canaanite general, Sisera (Jdg 4:17-22; 5:24-27).

JAIR

Judge from Gilead (Jdg 10:3-5).

JAIRUS*

Synagogue ruler whose daughter Jesus raised (Mk 5:22-43; Lk 8:41-56).

JAMES

1. Apostle; brother of John (Mt 4:21-22; 10:2; Mk 3:17; Lk 5:1-10). At transfiguration (Mt 17:1-13; Mk 9:1-13; Lk 9:28-36). Killed by Herod (Ac 12:2).

2. Apostle; son of Alphaeus (Mt 10:3; Mk 3:18; Lk 6:15).

3. Brother of Jesus (Mt 13:55; Mk 6:3; Lk 24:10; Gal 1:19) and Judas (Jude 1). With believers before Pentecost (Ac 1:13). Leader of church at Jerusalem (Ac 12:17; 15; 21:18; Gal 2:9, 12). Author of epistle (Jas 1:1).

JAPHETH

Son of Noah (Ge 5:32; 1Ch 1:4-5). Blessed (Ge 9:18-28). Sons of (Ge 10:2-5).

JAR (JARS)

Ge 24:14 let down your *j* that I may have
1Ki 17:14 'The *j* of flour will not be used up
Jer 19:1 "Go and buy a clay *j* from a potter.
Lk 8:16 hides it in a *j* or puts it under a bed.

JARS (JAR)

Jn 2:6 Nearby stood six stone water *j*,
2Co 4:7 we have this treasure in *j* of clay

JASPER

Ex 28:20 row a chrysolite, an onyx and a *j*.
Eze 28:13 chrysolite, onyx and *j*,
Rev 4:3 sat there had the appearance of *j*
21:19 The first foundation was *j*,

JAVELIN

1Sa 17:45 me with sword and spear and *j*,

JAWBONE

Jdg 15:15 Finding a fresh *j* of a donkey,

JEALOUS (JEALOUSY)

Ex 20:5 the LORD your God, am a *j* God,
34:14 whose name is *J*, is a *j* God.
Dt 4:24 God is a consuming fire, a *j* God.
6:15 is a *j* God and his anger will burn
32:21 They made me *j* by what is no god
Jos 24:19 He is a holy God; he is a *j* God.
Eze 16:38 of my wrath and *j* anger.
16:42 my *j* anger will turn away from you
23:25 I will direct my *j* anger against you,
36:6 in my *j* wrath because you have
Joel 2:18 the LORD will be *j* for his land
Na 1:2 LORD is a *j* and avenging God;
Zep 3:8 consumed by the fire of my *j* anger.
Zec 1:14 I am very *j* for Jerusalem and Zion,
8:2 "I am very *j* for Zion; I am burning
2Co 11:2 I am *j* for you with a godly jealousy

JEALOUSY (JEALOUS)

Ps 79:5 How long will your *j* burn like fire?
Pr 6:34 for *j* arouses a husband's fury,
27:4 but who can stand before *j*?
SS 8:6 its *j* unyielding as the grave.
Zep 1:18 In the fire of his *j*
Zec 8:2 I am burning with *j* for her."
Ro 13:13 debauchery, not in dissension and *j*
1Co 3:3 For since there is *j* and quarrelling
10:22 trying to arouse the Lord's *j*?
2Co 11:2 I am jealous for you with a godly *j*.
12:20 *j*, outbursts of anger, factions,
Gal 5:20 hatred, discord, *j*, fits of rage,

JECONIAH see JEHOIACHIN

JEERS*

Heb 11:36 Some faced *j* and flogging,

JEHOAHAZ

1. Son of Jehu; king of Israel (2Ki 13:1-9).

2. Son of Josiah; king of Judah (2Ki 23:31-34; 2Ch 36:1-4).

JEHOASH

1. See JOASH.

2. Son of Jehoahaz; king of Israel. Defeat of Aram prophesied by Elisha (2Ki 13:10-25). Defeated Amaziah in Jerusalem (2Ki 14:1-16; 2Ch 25:17-24).

JEHOIACHIN

Son of Jehoiakim; king of Judah exiled by Nebuchadnezzar (2Ki 24:8-17; 2Ch 36:8-10; Jer 22:24-30; 24:1). Raised from prisoner status (2Ki 25:27-30; Jer 52:31-34).

JEHOIADA

Priest who sheltered Joash from Athaliah (2Ki 11-12; 2Ch 22:11-24:16).

JEHOIAKIM

Son of Jehoahaz; made king of Judah by Pharaoh Neco (2Ki 23:34-24:6; 2Ch 36:4-8; Jer 22:18-23). Burned scroll of Jeremiah's prophecies (Jer 36).

JEHORAM

1. Son of Jehoshaphat; king of Judah (2Ki 8:16-24). Prophesied against by Elijah; killed by the LORD (2Ch 21).

2. See JORAM.

JEHOSHAPHAT

Son of Asa; king of Judah. Strengthened his kingdom (2Ch 17). Joined with Ahab against Aram (2Ki 22; 2Ch 18). Established judges (2Ch 19). Joined with Joram against Moab (2Ki 3; 2Ch 20).

JEHOVAH see †LORD

JEHU

1. Prophet against Baasha (2Ki 16:1-7).

2. King of Israel. Anointed by Elijah to obliterate house of Ahab (1Ki 19:16-17); anointed by servant of Elisha (2Ki 9:1-13). Killed Joram and Ahaziah (2Ki 9:14-29; 2Ch 22:7-9), Jezebel (2Ki 9:30-37), relatives of Ahab (2Ki 10:1-17), ministers of Baal (2Ki 10:18-29). Death (2Ki 10:30-36).

JEPHTHAH

Judge from Gilead who delivered Israel from Ammon (Jdg 10:6-12:7). Made rash vow concerning his daughter (Jdg 11:30-40).

JEREMIAH

Prophet to Judah (Jer 1:1-3). Called by the LORD (Jer 1). Put in stocks (Jer 20:1-3). Threatened for prophesying (Jer 11:18-23; 26). Opposed by Hananiah (Jer 28). Scroll burned (Jer 36). Imprisoned (Jer 37). Thrown into cistern (Jer 38). Forced to Egypt with those fleeing Babylonians (Jer 43).

JERICHO

Nu 22:1 along the Jordan across from *J*.
Jos 3:16 the people crossed over opposite *J*.
5:10 camped at Gilgal on the plains of *J*,
Lk 10:30 going down from Jerusalem to *J*,
Heb 11:30 By faith the walls of *J* fell,

JEROBOAM

1. Official of Solomon; rebelled to become first king of Israel (1Ki 11:26-40; 12:1-20; 2Ch 10). Idolatry (1Ki 12:25-33); judgment for (1Ki 13-14; 2Ch 13).

2. Son of Jehoash; king of Israel (2Ki 14:23-29).

JERUB-BAAL see GIDEON

JERUSALEM

Jos 10:1 of *J* heard that Joshua had taken Ai
15:8 of the Jebusite city (that is, *J*).
Jdg 1:8 The men of Judah attacked *J* also
1Sa 17:54 head and brought it to *J*,
2Sa 5:5 and in *J* he reigned over all Israel
5:6 and his men marched to *J*
9:13 And Mephibosheth lived in *J*,
11:1 But David remained in *J*.
15:29 took the ark of God back to *J*
24:16 stretched out his hand to destroy *J*,
1Ki 3:1 the LORD, and the wall around *J*.
9:15 the wall of *J*, and Hazor, Megiddo
9:19 whatever he desired to build in *J*,
10:26 cities and also with him in *J*.
10:27 as common in *J* as stones,
11:7 of *J*, Solomon built a high place
11:13 my servant and for the sake of *J*,
11:36 always have a lamp before me in *J*,
11:42 Solomon reigned in *J*
12:27 at the temple of the LORD in *J*,
14:21 and he reigned seventeen years in *J*
14:25 Shishak king of Egypt attacked *J*.
15:2 and he reigned in *J* three years.
15:10 and he reigned in *J* forty-one years.
22:42 he reigned in *J* twenty-five years.
2Ki 8:17 and he reigned in *J* eight years.
8:26 and he reigned in *J* one year.
12:1 and he reigned in *J* forty years.
12:17 Then he turned to attack *J*.
14:2 he reigned in *J* twenty-nine years.
14:13 Then Jehoash went to *J*
15:2 and he reigned in *J* fifty-two years.
15:33 and he reigned in *J* sixteen years.
16:2 and he reigned in *J* sixteen years.
16:5 Israel marched up to fight against *J*
18:2 he reigned in *J* twenty-nine years.
18:17 Lachish to King Hezekiah at *J*.
19:31 For out of *J* will come a remnant,
21:1 and he reigned in *J* fifty-five years.
21:12 going to bring such disaster on *J*
21:19 and he reigned in *J* two years.
22:1 he reigned in *J* thirty-one years.
23:27 and I will reject *J*, the city I chose,
23:31 and he reigned in *J* three months.
23:36 and he reigned in *J* eleven years.
24:8 and he reigned in *J* three months.
24:10 king of Babylon advanced on *J*
24:14 He carried into exile all *J*:
24:18 and he reigned in *J* eleven years.
24:20 anger that all this happened to *J*
25:1 king of Babylon marched against *J*
25:9 royal palace and all the houses of *J*.
1Ch 11:4 and all the Israelites marched to *J*,
21:16 sword in his hand extended over *J*.
2Ch 1:4 he had pitched a tent for it in *J*.
3:1 the LORD in *J* on Mount Moriah,
6:6 now I have chosen *J* for my Name
9:1 she came to *J* to test him
20:15 and all who live in Judah and *J*!
20:27 and *J* returned joyfully to *J*,
29:8 LORD has fallen on Judah and *J*;
36:19 and broke down the wall of *J*;
Ezr 1:2 a temple for him at *J* in Judah.
2:1 to Babylon (they returned to *J*
3:1 people assembled as one man in *J*.
4:12 up to us from you have gone to *J*
4:24 of God in *J* came to a standstill
6:12 or to destroy this temple in *J*.
7:8 Ezra arrived in *J* in the fifth month
9:9 a wall of protection in Judah and *J*.
10:7 for all the exiles to assemble in *J*.
Ne 1:2 the exile, and also about *J*.
1:3 The wall of *J* is broken down,
2:11 to *J*, and after staying there three
2:17 Come, let us rebuild the wall of *J*,
2:20 you have no share in *J* or any claim
3:8 They restored *J* as far as the Broad
4:8 fight against *J* and stir up trouble
11:1 leaders of the people settled in *J*,
12:27 At the dedication of the wall of *J*,
12:43 in *J* could be heard far away.
Ps 51:18 build up the walls of *J*.
79:1 they have reduced *J* to rubble.
122:2 in your gates, O *J*.
122:3 *J* is built like a city
122:6 Pray for the peace of *J*:
125:2 As the mountains surround *J*,
128:5 may you see the prosperity of *J*,

Ps 137: 5 If I forget you, O *J*,
147: 2 The LORD builds up *J*;
147: 12 Extol the LORD, O *J*;
SS 6: 4 lovely as *J*,
Isa 1: 1 and *J* that Isaiah son of Amoz saw
2: 1 saw concerning Judah and *J*:
3: 1 is about to take from *J* and Judah
3: 8 *J* staggers,
4: 3 recorded among the living in *J*.
8: 14 And for the people of *J* he will be
27: 13 LORD on the holy mountain in *J*.
31: 5 the LORD Almighty will shield *J*;
33: 20 your eyes will see *J*,
40: 2 Speak tenderly to *J*,
40: 9 You who bring good tidings to *J*,
52: 1 O *J*, the holy city.
52: 2 rise up, sit enthroned, O *J*.
62: 6 on your walls, O *J*;
62: 7 give him no rest till he establishes *J*
65: 18 for I will create *J* to be a delight
Jer 2: 2 and proclaim in the hearing of *J*:
3: 17 time they will call *J* The Throne
4: 5 and proclaim in *J* and say:
4: 14 O *J*, wash the evil from your heart
5: 1 "Go up and down the streets of *J*,
6: 6 and build siege ramps against *J*.
8: 5 Why does *J* always turn away?
9: 11 "I will make *J* a heap of ruins,
13: 27 Woe to you, O *J*!
23: 14 And among the prophets of *J*
24: 1 into exile from *J* to Babylon
26: 18 *J* will become a heap of rubble,
32: 2 of Babylon was then besieging *J*,
33: 10 the streets of *J* that are deserted,
39: 1 This is how *J* was taken: In
51: 50 and think on *J*."
52: 14 broke down all the walls around *J*.
La 1: 7 *J* remembers all the treasures
Eze 14: 21 send against *J* my four dreadful
16: 2 confront *J* with her detestable
Da 6: 10 the windows opened towards *J*.
9: 2 of *J* would last seventy years.
9: 12 done like what has been done to *J*.
9: 25 and rebuild *J* until the Anointed
Joel 3: 1 restore the fortunes of Judah and *J*,
3: 16 and thunder from *J*;
3: 17 *J* will be holy;
Am 2: 5 will consume the fortresses of *J*."
Ob : 11 and cast lots for *J*,
Mic 1: 5 Is it not *J*?
4: 2 the word of the LORD from *J*.
Zep 3: 16 On that day they will say to *J*,
Zec 1: 14 'I am very jealous for *J* and Zion,
1: 17 comfort Zion and choose *J*.'"
2: 2 He answered me, "To measure *J*,
2: 4 '*J* will be a city without walls
8: 3 I will return to Zion and dwell in *J*.
8: 8 I will bring them back to live in *J*;
8: 15 determined to do good again to *J*
8: 22 powerful nations will come to *J*
9: 9 Shout, Daughter of *J*!
9: 10 and the war-horses from *J*,
12: 3 I will make *J* an immovable rock
12: 10 the inhabitants of *J* a spirit of grace
14: 2 the nations of *J* to fight against it;
14: 8 living water will flow out from *J*,
14: 16 that have attacked *J* will go up
Mt 16: 21 to his disciples that he must go to *J*
20: 18 said to them, "We are going up to *J*
21: 10 When Jesus entered *J*, the whole
23: 37 "O *J*, *J*, you who kill the prophets
Mk 10: 33 "We are going up to *J*," he said,
Lk 2: 22 Mary took him to *J* to present him
2: 41 Every year his parents went to *J*
2: 43 the boy Jesus stayed behind in *J*,
4: 9 The devil led him to *J*
9: 31 about to bring to fulfilment at *J*.
9: 51 Jesus resolutely set out for *J*,
13: 34 die outside *J*! "O *J*, *J*,
18: 31 told them, "We are going up to *J*,
19: 41 As he approached *J* and saw
21: 20 "When you see *J* surrounded
21: 24 *J* will be trampled
Lk 24: 47 name to all nations, beginning at *J*.
Jn 4: 20 where we must worship is in *J*."
Ac 1: 4 this command: "Do not leave *J*,
1: 8 and you will be my witnesses in *J*,
6: 7 of disciples in *J* increased rapidly,
20: 22 by the Spirit, I am going to *J*,
23: 11 As you have testified about me in *J*
Ro 15: 19 So from *J* all the way
Gal 4: 25 corresponds to the present city of *J*
4: 26 But the *J* that is above is free,
Heb 12: 22 to the heavenly *J*, the city
Rev 3: 12 the new *J*, which is coming
21: 2 I saw the Holy City, the new *J*,
21: 10 and showed me the Holy City, *J*,

JESSE

Father of David (Ru 4:17-22; 1Sa 16; 1Ch 2:12-17).

JESUS

LIFE: Genealogy (Mt 1:1-17; Lk 3:21-37). Birth announced (Mt 1:18-25; Lk 1:26-45). Birth (Mt 2:1-12; Lk 2:1-40). Escape to Egypt (Mt 2:13-23). As a boy in the temple (Lk 2:41-52). Baptism (Mt 3:13-17; Mk 1:9-11; Lk 3:21-22; Jn 1:32-34). Temptation (Mt 4:1-11; Mk 1:12-13; Lk 4:1-13). Ministry in Galilee (Mt 4:12-18:35; Mk 1:14-9:50; Lk 4:14-13:9; Jn 1:35-2:11; 4; 6), Transfiguration (Mt 17:1-8; Mk 9:2-8; Lk 9:28-36), on the way to Jerusalem (Mt 19-20; Mk 10; Lk 13:10-19:27), in Jerusalem (Mt 21-25; Mk 11-13; Lk 19:28-21:38; Jn 2:12-3:36; 5; 7-12). Last supper (Mt 26:17-35; Mk 14:12-31; Lk 22:1-38; Jn 13-17). Arrest and trial (Mt 26:36-27:31; Mk 14:43-15:20; Lk 22:39-23:25; Jn 18:1-19:16). Crucifixion (Mt 27:32-66; Mk 15:21-47; Lk 23:26-55; Jn 19:28-42). Resurrection and appearances (Mt 28; Mk 16; Lk 24; Jn 20-21; Ac 1:1-11; 7:56; 9:3-6; 1Co 15:1-8; Rev 1:1-20).

MIRACLES. Healings: official's son (Jn 4:43-54), demoniac in Capernaum (Mk 1:23-26; Lk 4:33-35), Peter's mother-in-law (Mt 8:14-17; Mk 1:29-31; Lk 4:38-39), leper (Mt 8:2-4; Mk 1:40-45; Lk 5:12-16), paralytic (Mt 9:1-8; Mk 2:1-12; Lk 5:17-26), cripple (Jn 5:1-9), shrivelled hand (Mt 12:10-13; Mk 3:1-5; Lk 6:6-11), centurion's servant (Mt 8:5-13; Lk 7:1-10), widow's son raised (Lk 7:11-17), demoniac (Mt 12:22-23; Lk 11:14), Gadarene demoniacs (Mt 8:28-34; Mk 5:1-20; Lk 8:26-39), woman's bleeding and Jairus' daughter (Mt 9:18-26; Mk 5:21-43; Lk 8:40-56), blind man (Mt 9:27-31), mute man (Mt 9:32-33), Canaanite woman's daughter (Mt 15:21-28; Mk 7:24-30), deaf man (Mk 7:31-37), blind man (Mk 8:22-26), demoniac boy (Mt 17:14-18; Mk 9:14-29; Lk 9:37-43), ten lepers (Lk 17:11-19), man born blind (Jn 9:1-7), Lazarus raised (Jn 11), crippled woman (Lk 13:11-17), man with dropsy (Lk 14:1-6), two blind men (Mt 20:29-34; Mk 10:46-52; Lk 18:35-43), Malchus' ear (Lk 22:50-51). Other Miracles: water to wine (Jn 2:1-11), catch of fish (Lk 5:1-11), storm stilled (Mt 8:23-27; Mk 4:37-41; Lk 8:22-25), 5,000 fed (Mt 14:15-21; Mk 6:35-44; Lk 9:10-17; Jn 6:1-14), walking on water (Mt 14:25-33; Mk 6:48-52; Jn 6:15-21), 4,000 fed (Mt 15:32-39; Mk 8:1-9), money from fish (Mt 17:24-27), fig-tree cursed (Mt 21:18-22; Mk 11:12-14), catch of fish (Jn 21:1-14).

MAJOR TEACHING: Sermon on the Mount (Mt 5-7; Lk 6:17-49), to Nicodemus (Jn 3), to Samaritan woman (Jn 4), Bread of Life (Jn 6:22-59), at Feast of Tabernacles (Jn 7-8), woes to Pharisees (Mt 23; Lk 11:37-54), Good Shepherd (Jn 10:1-18), Mt of Olives Discourse (Mt 24-25; Mk 13; Lk 21:5-36), Upper Room Discourse (Jn 13-16).

PARABLES: Sower (Mt 13:3-23; Mk 4:3-25; Lk 8:5-18), seed's growth (Mk 4:26-29), wheat and weeds (Mt 13:24-30, 36-43), mustard seed (Mt 13:31-32; Mk 4:30-32), yeast (Mt 13:33-35; Mk 4:33-34), hidden treasure (Mt 13:44), valuable pearl (Mt 13:45-46), net (Mt 13:47-51), house owner (Mt 13:52), good Samaritan (Lk 10:25-37), unmerciful servant (Mt 18:15-35), lost sheep (Mt 18:10-14; Lk 15:4-7), lost coin (Lk 15:8-10), prodigal son (Lk 15:11-32), dishonest manager (Lk 16:1-13), rich man and Lazarus (Lk 16:19-31), persistent widow (Lk 18:1-8), Pharisee and tax collector (Lk 18:9-14), payment of workers (Mt 20:1-16), tenants and the vineyard (Mt 21:28-46; Mt 12:1-12; Lk 20:9-19), wedding banquet (Mt 22:1-14), faithful servant (Mt 24:45-51), ten virgins (Mt 25:1-13), talents (Mt 25:1-30; Lk 19:12-27).

DISCIPLES see APOSTLES. Call of (Jn 1:35-51; Mt 4:18-22; 9:9; Mk 1:16-20; 2:13-14; Lk 5:1-11, 27-28). Named Apostles (Mk 3:13-19; Lk 6:12-16). Twelve sent out (Mt 10; Mk 6:7-11; Lk 9:1-5). Seventy sent out (Lk 10:1-24). Defection of (Jn 6:60-71; Mt 26:56; Mk 14:50-52). Final commission (Mt 28:16-20; Jn 21:15-23; Ac 1:3-8).

Ac 2: 32 God has raised this *J* to life,
9: 5 "I am *J*, whom you are persecuting
9: 34 said to him, "*J* Christ heals you.
15: 11 of our Lord *J* that we are saved,
16: 31 "Believe in the Lord *J*,
20: 24 the task the Lord *J* has given me—
Ro 3: 24 redemption that came by Christ *J*.
5: 17 life through the one man, *J* Christ.
8: 1 for those who are in Christ *J*,
1Co 1: 7 for our Lord *J* Christ to be revealed
2: 2 except *J* Christ and him crucified.
6: 11 in the name of the Lord *J* Christ
8: 6 and there is but one Lord, *J* Christ,
12: 3 and no-one can say, "*J* is Lord,"
2Co 4: 5 not preach ourselves, but *J* Christ
13: 5 Do you not realise that Christ *J* is
Gal 2: 16 but by faith in *J* Christ.
3: 28 for you are all one in Christ *J*.
5: 6 in Christ *J* neither circumcision
6: 17 bear on my body the marks of *J*.
Eph 1: 5 as his sons through *J* Christ,
2: 10 created in Christ *J*
2: 20 with Christ *J* himself as the chief
Php 1: 6 until the day of Christ *J*.
2: 5 be the same as that of Christ *J*:
2: 10 name of *J* every knee should bow,
Col 3: 17 do it all in the name of the Lord *J*,
1Th 1: 10 whom he raised from the dead—*J*,
4: 14 We believe that *J* died
5: 23 at the coming of our Lord *J* Christ.
2Th 1: 7 when the Lord *J* is revealed
2: 1 the coming of our Lord *J* Christ
1Ti 1: 15 Christ *J* came into the world
2Ti 1: 10 appearing of our Saviour, Christ *J*,
2: 3 us like a good soldier of Christ *J*.
3: 12 life in Christ *J* will be persecuted,
Tit 2: 13 our great God and Saviour, *J* Christ,
Heb 2: 9 But we see *J*, who was made a little
2: 11 So *J* is not ashamed to call them
3: 1 fix your thoughts on *J*, the apostle
3: 3 *J* has been found worthy
4: 14 through the heavens, *J* the Son
6: 20 where *J*, who went before us,
7: 22 *J* has become the guarantee
7: 24 but because *J* lives for ever,
8: 6 But the ministry *J* has received is
12: 2 Let us fix our eyes on *J*, the author
12: 24 to *J* the mediator of a new
1Pe 1: 3 the resurrection of *J* Christ
2Pe 1: 16 and coming of our Lord *J* Christ,
1Jn 1: 7 and the blood of *J*, his Son,
2: 1 *J* Christ, the Righteous One.
2: 6 to live in him must walk as *J* did.
4: 15 anyone acknowledges that *J* is
Rev 1: 1 The revelation of *J* Christ,
22: 16 *J*, have sent my angel
22: 20 Come, Lord *J*.

JETHRO

Father-in-law and adviser of Moses (Ex 3:1; 18). Also known as Reuel (Ex 2:18).

JEW (JEWS JEWS' JUDAISM)

Est 2: 5 of Susa a *J* of the tribe of Benjamin,
Zec 8: 23 of one *J* by the edge of his robe
Ac 21: 39 "I am a *J*, from Tarsus in Cilicia,

Ro 1:16 first for the *J*, then for the Gentile.
2:28 A man is not a *J* if he is only one
10:12 there is no difference between *J*
1Co 9:20 To the Jews I became like a *J*,
Gal 2:14 "You are a *J*, yet you live like
3:28 There is neither *J* nor Greek,
Col 3:11 Here there is no Greek or *J*,

JEWEL (JEWELLERY JEWELS)

Pr 20:15 that speak knowledge are a rare *j*.
SS 4:9 with one *j* of your necklace.
Rev 21:11 that of a very precious *j*,

JEWELLERY (JEWEL)

Ex 35:22 and brought gold *j* of all kinds:
Jer 2:32 Does a maiden forget her *j*,
Eze 16:11 you with *j*: I put bracelets
1Pe 3:3 wearing of gold *j* and fine clothes.

JEWELS (JEWEL)

Isa 54:12 your gates of sparkling *j*,
61:10 as a bride adorns herself with her *j*.
Zec 9:16 like *j* in a crown.

JEWS (JEW)

Ne 4:1 He ridiculed the *J*,
Est 3:13 kill and annihilate all the *J*—
4:14 and deliverance for the *J* will arise
Mt 2:2 who has been born king of the *J*?
27:11 "Are you the king of the *J*?" "Yes,
Jn 4:9 (For *J* do not associate
4:22 for salvation is from the *J*.
19:3 saying, "Hail, O king of the *J*!"
Ac 20:21 I have declared to both *J*
Ro 3:29 Is God the God of *J* only?
9:24 not only from the *J* but
15:27 they owe it to the *J* to share
1Co 1:22 *J* demand miraculous signs
9:20 To the *J* I became like a Jew,
12:13 whether *J* or Greeks, slave or free
Gal 2:8 of Peter as an apostle to the *J*,
Rev 2:9 slander of those who say they are *J*
3:9 claim to be *J* though they are not,

JEWS' (JEW)

Ro 15:27 shared in the *J* spiritual blessings,

JEZEBEL

Sidonian wife of Ahab (1Ki 16:31). Promoted Baal worship (1Ki 16:32-33). Killed prophets of the LORD (1Ki 18:4, 13). Opposed Elijah (1 Ki 19:1-2). Had Naboth killed (1Ki 21). Death prophesied (1Ki 21:17-24). Killed by Jehu (2Ki 9:30-37).

JEZREEL

2Ki 9:36 at *J* dogs will devour Jezebel's flesh
10:7 and sent them to Jehu in *J*.
Jos 1:4 house of Jehu for the massacre at *J*,

JOAB

Nephew of David (1Ch 2:16). Commander of his army (2Sa 8:16). Victorious over Ammon (2Sa 10; 1Ch 19), Rabbah (2Sa 11; 1Ch 20), Jerusalem (1Ch 11:6), Absalom (2Sa 18), Sheba (2Sa 20). Killed Abner (2Sa 3:22-39), Amasa (2Sa 20:1-13). Numbered David's army (2Sa 24; 1Ch 21). Sided with Adonijah (1Ki 1:17, 19). Killed by Benaiah (1Ki 2:5-6, 28-35).

JOASH

Son of Ahaziah; king of Judah. Sheltered from Athaliah by Jehoiada (2 Ki 11; 2Ch 22:10-23:21). Repaired temple (2Ki 12; 2Ch 24).

JOB

Wealthy man from Uz; feared God (Job 1:1-5). Righteousness tested by disaster (Job 1:6-22), personal affliction (Job 2). Maintained innocence in debate with three friends (Job 3-31), Elihu (Job 32-37). Rebuked by the LORD (Job 38-41). Vindicated and restored to greater stature by the LORD (Job 42). Example of righteousness (Eze 14:14, 20).

JOCHEBED*

Mother of Moses and Aaron (Ex 6:20; Nu 26:59).

JOEL

Prophet (Joel 1:1; Ac 2:16).

JOHN

1. Son of Zechariah and Elizabeth (Lk 1). Called the Baptist (Mt 3:1-12; Mk 1:2-8). Witness to Jesus (Mt 3:11-12; Mk 1:7-8; Lk 3:15-18; Jn 1:6-35; 3:27-30; 5:33-36). Doubts about Jesus (Mt 11:2-6; Lk 7:18-23). Arrest (Mt 4:12; Mk 1:14). Execution (Mt 14:1-12; Mk 6:14-29; Lk 9:7-9). Ministry compared to Elijah (Mt 11:7-19; Mk 9:11-13; Lk 7:24-35).

2. Apostle; brother of James (Mt 4:21-22; 10:2; Mk 3:17; Lk 5:1-10). At transfiguration (Mt 17:1-13; Mk 9:1-13; Lk 9:28-36). Desire to be greatest (Mk 10:35-45). Leader of church at Jerusalem (Ac 4:1-3; Gal 2:9). Elder who wrote epistles (2Jn 1; 3Jn 1). Prophet who wrote Revelation (Rev 1:1; 22:8).

3. Cousin of Barnabas, co-worker with Paul, (Ac 12:12-13:13; 15:37), see MARK.

JOIN (JOINED JOINS)

Ne 10:29 all these now *j* their brothers
Pr 23:20 Do not *j* those who drink too much
24:21 and do not *j* with the rebellious,
Jer 3:18 of Judah will *j* the house of Israel,
Eze 37:17 *J* them together into one stick
Da 11:34 who are not sincere will *j* them.
Ro 15:30 to *j* me in my struggle by praying
2Ti 1:8 *j* with me in suffering for the gospel

JOINED (JOIN)

Zec 2:11 "Many nations will be *j*
Mt 19:6 Therefore what God has *j* together,
Mk 10:9 Therefore what God has *j* together,
Ac 1:14 They all *j* together constantly
Eph 2:21 him the whole building is *j* together
4:16 *j* and held together

JOINS (JOIN)

1Co 16:16 and to everyone who *j* in the work,

JOINT (JOINTS)

Ps 22:14 and all my bones are out of *j*.

JOINTS (JOINT)

Heb 4:12 even to dividing soul and spirit, *j*

JOKING*

Ge 19:14 his sons-in-law thought he was *j*.
Pr 26:19 and says, "I was only *j*!"
Eph 5:4 or coarse *j*, which are out of place,

JONAH

Prophet in days of Jeroboam II (2Ki 14:25). Called to Nineveh; fled to Tarshish (Jnh 1:1-3). Cause of storm; thrown into sea (Jnh 1:4-16). Swallowed by fish (Jnh 1:17). Prayer (Jnh 2). Preached to Nineveh (Jnh 3). Attitude reproved by the LORD (Jnh 4). Sign of (Mt 12:39-41; Lk 11:29-32).

JONATHAN

Son of Saul (1Sa 13:16; 1Ch 8:33). Valiant warrior (1Sa 13-14). Relation to David (1Sa 18:1-4; 19-20; 23:16-18). Killed at Gilboa (1Sa 31). Mourned by David (2Sa 1).

JOPPA

Ezr 3:7 logs by sea from Lebanon to *J*,
Jnh 1:3 to *J*, where he found a ship bound
Ac 9:43 Peter stayed in *J* for some time

JORAM

1. Son of Ahab; king of Israel. Fought with Jehoshaphat against Moab (2Ki 3). Killed with Ahaziah by Jehu (2Ki 8:25-29; 9:14-26; 2Ch 22:5-9).

2. See JEHORAM.

JORDAN

Ge 13:10 plain of the *J* was well watered,
Nu 22:1 and camped along the *J*
34:12 boundary will go down along the *J*
Dt 3:27 you are not going to cross this *J*.
Jos 1:2 get ready to cross the *J* River
3:11 go into the *J* ahead of you.
3:17 ground in the middle of the *J*,
4:22 Israel crossed the *J* on dry ground.'
2Ki 2:7 and Elisha had stopped at the *J*.
2:13 and stood on the bank of the *J*.
5:10 wash yourself seven times in the *J*,
6:4 They went to the *J* and began
Ps 114:3 the *J* turned back;
Isa 9:1 along the *J*—The people walking
Jer 12:5 manage in the thickets by the *J*?
Mt 3:6 baptised by him in the *J* River.
4:15 the way to the sea, along the *J*,
Mk 1:9 and was baptised by John in the *J*.

JOSEPH

1. Son of Jacob by Rachel (Ge 30:24; 1Ch 2:2). Favoured by Jacob, hated by brothers (Ge 37:3-4). Dreams (Ge 37:5-11). Sold by brothers (Ge 37:12-36). Served Potiphar; imprisoned by false accusation (Ge 39). Interpreted dreams of Pharaoh's servants (Ge 40), of Pharaoh (Ge 41:4-40). Made greatest in Egypt (Ge 41:41-57). Sold grain to brothers (Ge 42-45). Brought Jacob and sons to Egypt (Ge 46-47). Sons Ephraim and Manasseh blessed (Ge 48). Blessed (Ge 49:22-26; Dt 33:13-17). Death (Ge 50:22-26; Ex 13:19; Heb 11:22). 12,000 from (Rev 7:8).

2. Husband of Mary, mother of Jesus (Mt 1:16-24; 2:13-19; Lk 1:27; 2; Jn 1:45).

3. Disciple from Arimathea, who gave his tomb for Jesus' burial (Mt 27:57-61; Mk 15:43-47; Lk 24:50-52).

4. Original name of Barnabas (Ac 4:36).

JOSHUA (HOSHEA)

1. Son of Nun; name changed from Hoshea (Nu 13:8, 16; 1Ch 7:27). Fought Amalekites under Moses (Ex 17:9-14). Servant of Moses on Sinai (Ex 24:13; 32:17). Spied Canaan (Nu 13). With Caleb, allowed to enter land (Nu 14:6, 30). Succeeded Moses (Dt 1:38; 31:1-18; 33:9).

Charged Israel to conquer Canaan (Jos 1). Crossed Jordan (Jos 3-4). Circumcised sons of wilderness wanderings (Jos 5). Conquered Jericho (Jos 6), Ai (Jos 7-8), five kings at Gibeon (Jos 10:1-28), southern Canaan (Jos 10:29-43), northern Canaan (Jos 11-12). Defeated at Ai (Jos 7). Deceived by Gibeonites (Jos 9). Renewed covenant (Jos 8:30-35; 24:1-27). Divided land among tribes (Jos 13-22). Last words (Jos 23). Death (Jos 24:28-31).

2. High priest during rebuilding of temple (Hag 1-2; Zec 3:1-9; 6:11).

JOSIAH

Son of Amon; king of Judah (2Ki 21:26; 1Ch 3:14). Prophesied (1Ki 13:2). Book of Law discovered during his reign (2Ki 22; 2Ch 34:14-31). Reforms (2Ki 23:1-25; 2Ch 34:1-13; 35:1-19). Killed by Pharaoh Neco (2Ki 23:29-30; 2Ch 35:20-27).

JOTHAM

1. Son of Gideon (Jdg 9).

2. Son of Azariah (Uzziah); king of Judah (2Ki 15:32-38; 2Ch 26:21-27:9).

JOURNEY

Dt 1:33 who went ahead of you on your *j*,
2:7 over your *j* through this vast desert
Jdg 18:6 Your *j* has the LORD's approval."
Ezr 8:21 and ask him for a safe *j* for us
Job 16:22 before I go on the *j* of no return.
Isa 35:8 The unclean will not *j* on it;
Mt 25:14 it will be like a man going on a *j*,
Ro 15:24 to have you assist me on my *j* there

JOY* (ENJOY ENJOYMENT JOYFUL JOYOUS OVERJOYED REJOICE REJOICES REJOICING)

Ge 31: 27 so I could send you away with *j*
Lev 9: 24 shouted for *j* and fell face down.
Dt 16: 15 and your *j* will be complete.
Jdg 9: 19 may Abimelech be your *j*,
1Ch 12: 40 and sheep, for there was *j* in Israel.
16: 27 strength and *j* in his dwelling-place.
16: 33 sing for *j* before the LORD,
29: 17 with *j* how willingly your people
29: 22 drank with great *j* in the presence
2Ch 30: 26 There was great *j* in Jerusalem,
Ezr 3: 12 while many others shouted for *j*.
3: 13 of the shouts of *j* from the sound
6: 16 of the house of God with *j*.
6: 22 with *j* by changing the attitude
6: 22 *j* the Feast of Unleavened Bread,
Ne 8: 10 for the *j* of the LORD is your
8: 12 and to celebrate with great *j*,
8: 17 And their *j* was very great.
12: 43 God had given them great *j*.
Est 8: 16 a time of happiness and *j*,
8: 17 there was *j* and gladness
9: 17 and made it a day of feasting and *j*.
9: 18 and made it a day of feasting and *j*.
9: 19 as a day of *j* and feasting,
9: 22 and *j* and giving presents of food
9: 22 their sorrow was turned into *j*
Job 3: 7 may no shout of *j* be heard in it.
6: 10 my *j* in unrelenting pain—
8: 21 and your lips with shouts of *j*.
9: 25 they fly away without a glimpse of *j*
10: 20 from me so I can have a moment's *j*
20: 5 the *j* of the godless lasts
33: 26 he sees God's face and shouts for *j*;
38: 7 and all the angels shouted for *j*?
Ps 4: 7 have filled my heart with greater *j*
5: 11 let them ever sing for *j*.
16: 11 me with *j* in your presence,
19: 8 giving *j* to the heart.
20: 5 We will shout for *j*
21: 1 How great is his *j* in the victories
21: 6 with the *j* of your presence.
27: 6 will I sacrifice with shouts of *j*;
28: 7 My heart leaps for *j*
30: 11 sackcloth and clothed me with *j*,
33: 3 play skilfully, and shout for *j*.
35: 27 shout for *j* and gladness;
42: 4 with shouts of *j* and thanksgiving
43: 4 to God, my *j* and my delight.
45: 7 by anointing you with the oil of *j*.
45: 15 They are led in with *j* and gladness;
47: 1 shout to God with cries of *j*.
47: 5 God has ascended amid shouts of *j*,
48: 2 the *j* of the whole earth.
51: 8 Let me hear *j* and gladness;
51: 12 to me the *j* of your salvation
65: 8 you call forth songs of *j*.
65: 13 they shout for *j* and sing.
66: 1 Shout with *j* to God, all the earth!
67: 4 the nations be glad and sing for *j*,
71: 23 My lips will shout for *j*
81: 1 Sing for *j* to God our strength;
86: 4 Bring *j* to your servant,
89: 12 Hermon sing for *j* at your name.
90: 14 for *j* and be glad all our days.
92: 4 I sing for *j* at the works
94: 19 your consolation brought *j*
95: 1 let us sing for *j* to the LORD;
96: 12 the trees of the forest will sing for *j*;
97: 11 and *j* on the upright in heart.
98: 4 for *j* to the LORD, all the earth,
98: 6 shout for *j* before the LORD,
98: 8 the mountains sing together for *j*;
100: 1 for *j* to the LORD, all the earth.
105: 43 his chosen ones with shouts of *j*;
106: 5 share in the *j* of your nation
107: 22 and tell of his works with songs of *j*
118: 15 Shouts of *j* and victory
119: 111 they are the *j* of my heart.
126: 2 our tongues with songs of *j*.
126: 3 and we are filled with *j*.
Ps 126: 5 will reap with songs of *j*.
126: 6 will return with songs of *j*,
132: 9 may your saints sing for *j*."
132: 16 and her saints will ever sing for *j*.
137: 3 tormentors demanded songs of *j*;
137: 6 my highest *j*.
149: 5 and sing for *j* on their beds.
Pr 10: 1 A wise son brings *j* to his father,
10: 28 The prospect of the righteous is *j*,
11: 10 wicked perish, there are shouts of *j*.
12: 20 but *j* for those who promote peace.
14: 10 and no-one else can share its *j*.
14: 13 and *j* may end in grief.
15: 20 A wise son brings *j* to his father,
15: 23 A man finds *j* in giving an apt reply
15: 30 A cheerful look brings *j*
17: 21 there is no *j* for the father of a fool.
21: 15 it brings *j* to the righteous
23: 24 of a righteous man has great *j*;
27: 9 incense bring *j* to the heart,
27: 11 my son, and bring *j* to my heart;
29: 3 A man who loves wisdom brings *j*
Ecc 8: 15 Then *j* will accompany him
11: 9 let your heart give you *j* in the days
Isa 9: 3 and increased their *j*;
12: 3 With *j* you will draw water
12: 6 Shout aloud and sing for *j*,
16: 9 shouts of *j* over your ripened fruit
16: 10 *J* and gladness are taken away
22: 13 But see, there is *j* and revelry,
24: 11 all *j* turns to gloom,
24: 14 raise their voices, they shout for *j*;
26: 19 wake up and shout for *j*.
35: 2 will rejoice greatly and shout for *j*.
35: 6 the mute tongue shout for *j*.
35: 10 Gladness and *j* will overtake them,
35: 10 everlasting *j* will crown their heads
42: 11 Let the people of Sela sing for *j*;
44: 23 Sing for *j*, O heavens,
48: 20 Announce this with shouts of *j*
49: 13 Shout for *j*, O heavens;
51: 3 *J* and gladness will be found in her,
51: 11 Gladness and *j* will overtake them,
51: 11 everlasting *j* will crown their heads
52: 8 together they shout for *j*.
52: 9 Burst into songs of *j* together,
54: 1 burst into song, shout for *j*,
55: 12 You will go out in *j*
56: 7 give them *j* in my house of prayer.
58: 14 then you will find your *j*
60: 5 heart will throb and swell with *j*;
60: 15 and the *j* of all generations.
61: 7 and everlasting *j* will be theirs.
65: 14 out of the *j* of their hearts,
65: 18 and its people a *j*.
66: 5 that we may see your *j*!'
Jer 7: 34 will bring an end to the sounds of *j*
15: 16 they were my *j* and my heart's
16: 9 will bring an end to the sounds of *j*
25: 10 banish from them the sounds of *j*
31: 7 "Sing with *j* for Jacob;
31: 12 shout for *j* on the heights of Zion;
31: 13 give them comfort and *j* instead
33: 9 this city will bring me renown, *j*,
33: 11 be heard once more the sounds of *j*
48: 33 *J* and gladness are gone
48: 33 no-one treads them with shouts of *j*
48: 33 they are not shouts of *j*.
51: 48 will shout for *j* over Babylon,
La 2: 15 the *j* of the whole earth?"
5: 15 *J* is gone from our hearts;
Eze 7: 7 not *j*, upon the mountains.
24: 25 their *j* and glory, the delight
Joel 1: 12 Surely the *j* of mankind
1: 16 *j* and gladness
Mt 13: 20 and at once receives it with *j*.
13: 44 in his *j* went and sold all he had
28: 8 afraid yet filled with *j*,
Mk 4: 16 and at once receive it with *j*.
Lk 1: 14 He will be a *j* and delight to you,
1: 44 the baby in my womb leaped for *j*.
1: 58 great mercy, and they shared her *j*.
2: 10 news of great *j* that will be
Lk 6: 23 "Rejoice in that day and leap for *j*,
8: 13 the word with *j* when they hear it,
10: 17 The seventy-two returned with *j*
10: 21 full of *j* through the Holy Spirit,
24: 41 still did not believe it because of *j*
24: 52 returned to Jerusalem with great *j*.
Jn 3: 29 That *j* is mine, and it is now
3: 29 full of *j* when he hears
15: 11 and that your *j* may be complete.
15: 11 this so that my *j* may be in you
16: 20 but your grief will turn to *j*.
16: 21 because of her *j* that a child is born
16: 22 and no-one will take away your *j*.
16: 24 and your *j* will be complete.
17: 13 measure of my *j* within them.
Ac 2: 28 with *j* in your presence.'
8: 8 So there was great *j* in that city.
13: 52 And the disciples were filled with *j*
14: 17 and fills your hearts with *j*."
16: 34 the whole family was filled with *j*,
Ro 14: 17 peace and *j* in the Holy Spirit,
15: 13 the God of hope fill you with all *j*
15: 32 will I may come to you with *j*
16: 19 so I am full of *j* over you;
2Co 1: 24 but we work with you for your *j*,
2: 3 that you would all share my *j*.
7: 4 our troubles my *j* knows no
7: 7 so that my *j* was greater than ever.
8: 2 their overflowing *j* and their
Gal 4: 15 What has happened to all your *j*?
5: 22 *j*, peace, patience, kindness,
Php 1: 4 I always pray with *j*
1: 25 for your progress and *j* in the faith,
1: 26 being with you again your *j*
2: 2 then make my *j* complete
2: 29 him in the Lord with great *j*,
4: 1 and long for, my *j* and crown,
1Th 1: 6 with the *j* given by the Holy Spirit.
2: 19 For what is our hope, our *j*,
2: 20 Indeed, you are our glory and *j*.
3: 9 you in return for all the *j* we have
2Ti 1: 4 so that I may be filled with *j*.
Phm : 7 Your love has given me great *j*
Heb 1: 9 by anointing you with the oil of *j*."
12: 2 for the *j* set before him endured
13: 17 them so that their work will be a *j*,
Jas 1: 2 Consider it pure *j*, my brothers,
4: 9 to mourning and your *j* to gloom.
1Pe 1: 8 with an inexpressible and glorious *j*
1Jn 1: 4 this to make our *j* complete.
2Jn : 4 It has given me great *j* to find some
: 12 so that our *j* may be complete.
3Jn : 3 It gave me great *j* to have some
: 4 I have no greater *j*
Jude : 24 without fault and with great *j*—

JOYFUL* (JOY)

Dt 16: 14 Be *j* at your Feast—you, your sons
1Sa 18: 6 with *j* songs and with tambourines
1Ki 8: 66 *j* and glad in heart
1Ch 15: 16 as singers to sing *j* songs,
2Ch 7: 10 *j* and glad in heart
Ps 68: 3 may they be happy and *j*.
100: 2 come before him with *j* songs.
Ecc 9: 7 and drink your wine with a *j* heart,
Isa 24: 8 the *j* harp is silent.
Jer 31: 4 and go out to dance with the *j*.
Hab 3: 18 I will be *j* in God my Saviour.
Zec 8: 19 and tenth months will become *j*
10: 7 Their children will see it and be *j*;
Ro 12: 12 Be *j* in hope, patient in affliction,
1Th 5: 16 Be *j* always; pray continually;
Heb 12: 22 thousands of angels in *j* assembly,

JOYOUS* (JOY)

Est 8: 15 the city of Susa held a *j* celebration.

JUBILANT

Ps 96: 12 let the fields be *j*, and everything
98: 4 burst into *j* song with music;

JUBILEE

Lev 25: 11 The fiftieth year shall be a *j* for you;

JUDAH (JUDEA)

1. Son of Jacob by Leah (Ge 29:35; 35:23; 1Ch 2:1). Did not want to kill Joseph (Ge 37:26-27). Among Canaanites, fathered Perez by Tamar (Ge 38). Tribe of blessed as ruling tribe (Ge 49:8-12; Dt 33:7), numbered (Nu 1:27; 26:22), allotted land (Jos 15; Eze 48:7), failed to fully possess (Jos 15:63; Jdg 1:1-20).

2. Name used for people and land of Southern Kingdom.

Ru 1: 7 take them back to the land of *J*.
2Sa 2: 4 king over the house of *J*.
Isa 1: 1 The vision concerning *J*
3: 8 *J* is falling;
Jer 13: 19 All *J* will be carried into exile,
30: 3 bring my people Israel and *J* back
Hos 1: 7 I will show love to the house of *J*;
Zec 10: 4 From *J* will come the cornerstone,
Mt 2: 6 least among the rulers of *J*;
Heb 7: 14 that our Lord descended from *J*,
8: 8 and with the house of *J*.
Rev 5: 5 of the tribe of *J*, the Root of David,

JUDAISM (JEW)

Ac 13: 43 devout converts to *J* followed Paul
Gal 1: 13 of my previous way of life in *J*,
1: 14 advancing in *J* beyond many Jews

JUDAS

1. Apostle; son of James (Lk 6:16; Jn 14:22; Ac 1:13). Probably also called Thaddaeus (Mt 10:3; Mk 3:18).

2. Brother of James and Jesus (Mt 13:55; Mk 6:3), also called Jude (Jude 1).

3. Christian prophet (Ac 15:22-32).

4. Apostle, also called Iscariot, who betrayed Jesus (Mt 10:4; 26:14-56; Mk 3:19; 14:10-50; Lk 6:16; 22:3-53; Jn 6:71; 12:4; 13:2-30; 18:2-11). Suicide of (Mt 27:3-5; Ac 1:16-25).

JUDE see JUDAS

JUDEA (JUDAH)

Mt 2: 1 born in Bethlehem in *J*,
24: 16 are in *J* flee to the mountains.
Lk 3: 1 Pontius Pilate was governor of *J*,
Ac 1: 8 and in all *J* and Samaria,
9: 31 Then the church throughout *J*,
1Th 2: 14 imitators of God's churches in *J*,

JUDGE (JUDGED JUDGES JUDGING JUDGMENT JUDGMENTS)

Ge 16: 5 May the LORD *j* between you
18: 25 Will not the *J* of all the earth do
Lev 19: 15 but *j* your neighbour fairly.
Dt 1: 16 between your brothers and *j* fairly,
17: 12 man who shows contempt for the *j*
32: 36 The LORD will *j* his people
Jdg 2: 18 Whenever the LORD raised up a *j*
1Sa 2: 10 the LORD will *j* the ends
3: 13 that I would *j* his family for ever
7: 15 *j* over Israel all the days of his life.
24: 12 May the LORD *j* between you
1Ki 8: 32 *J* between your servants,
1Ch 16: 33 for he comes to *j* the earth.
2Ch 6: 23 *J* between your servants, repaying
19: 7 *J* carefully, for with the LORD our
Job 9: 15 plead with my *J* for mercy.
Ps 7: 8 *J* me, O LORD, according
7: 8 let the LORD *j* the peoples.
7: 11 God is a righteous *j*,
9: 8 He will *j* the world in righteousness
50: 6 for God himself is *j*.
51: 4 and justified when you *j*.
75: 2 it is I who *j* uprightly.
76: 9 when you, O God, rose up to *j*,
82: 8 Rise up, O God, *j* the earth,
94: 2 Rise up, O *J* of the earth;
96: 10 he will *j* the peoples with equity.
96: 13 He will *j* the world in righteousness
98: 9 He will *j* the world in righteousness
110: 6 He will *j* the nations, heaping up
Pr 31: 9 Speak up and *j* fairly;
Isa 2: 4 He will *j* between the nations
3: 13 he rises to *j* the people.
11: 3 He will not *j* by what he sees
33: 22 For the LORD is our *j*,
Jer 11: 20 Almighty, you who *j* righteously
Eze 7: 3 I will *j* you according
7: 27 by their own standards I will *j* them
18: 30 O house of Israel, I will *j* you,
20: 36 so I will *j* you, declares
22: 2 "Son of man, will you *j* her?
34: 17 I will *j* between one sheep
Joel 3: 12 sit to *j* all the nations on every side.
Mic 3: 11 Her leaders *j* for a bribe,
4: 3 He will *j* between many peoples
Mt 7: 1 Do not *j*, or you too will be judged.
Lk 6: 37 "Do not *j*, and you will not be
18: 2 there was a *j* who neither feared
Jn 5: 27 And he has given him authority to *j*
5: 30 By myself I can do nothing; I *j* only
8: 16 But if I do *j*, my decisions are right,
12: 47 For I did not come to *j* the world,
12: 48 There is a *j* for the one who rejects
Ac 10: 42 as *j* of the living and the dead.
17: 31 a day when he will *j* the world
Ro 2: 16 day when God will *j* men's secrets
3: 6 how could God *j* the world?
14: 10 then, why do you *j* your brother?
1Co 4: 3 indeed, I do not even *j* myself.
4: 5 Therefore *j* nothing
6: 2 And if you are to *j* the world,
6: 2 that the saints will *j* the world?
Gal 2: 6 not *j* by external appearance—
Col 2: 16 Therefore do not let anyone *j* you
2Ti 4: 1 who will *j* the living and the dead,
4: 8 which the Lord, the righteous *J*,
Heb 10: 30 "The Lord will *j* his people."
12: 23 come to God, the *j* of all men,
13: 4 for God will *j* the adulterer
Jas 4: 12 There is only one Lawgiver and *J*,
4: 12 who are you to *j* your neighbour?
1Pe 4: 5 to him who is ready to *j* the living
Rev 20: 4 who had been given authority to *j*.

JUDGED (JUDGE)

Mt 7: 1 "Do not judge, or you too will be *j*.
1Co 4: 3 I care very little if I am *j* by you
10: 29 For why should my freedom be *j*
11: 31 But if we *j* ourselves, we would not
14: 24 all that he is a sinner and will be *j*
Jas 3: 1 who teach will be *j* more strictly.
Rev 20: 12 The dead were *j* according

JUDGES (JUDGE)

Jdg 2: 16 Then the LORD raised up *j*,
Job 9: 24 he blindfolds its *j*.
Ps 58: 11 there is a God who *j* the earth."
75: 7 But it is God who *j*:
Pr 29: 14 If a king *j* the poor with fairness,
Jn 5: 22 Moreover, the Father *j* no-one,
1Co 4: 4 It is the Lord who *j* me.
Heb 4: 12 it *j* the thoughts and attitudes
1Pe 1: 17 on a Father who *j* each man's work
2: 23 himself to him who *j* justly.
Rev 19: 11 With justice he *j* and makes war.

JUDGING (JUDGE)

Ps 9: 4 on your throne, *j* righteously.
Pr 24: 23 To show partiality in *j* is not good:
Isa 16: 5 one who in *j* seeks justice
Mt 19: 28 *j* the twelve tribes of Israel.
Jn 7: 24 Stop *j* by mere appearances,

JUDGMENT (JUDGE)

Nu 33: 4 for the LORD had brought *j*
Dt 1: 17 of any man, for *j* belongs to God.
32: 41 and my hand grasps it in *j*,
1Sa 25: 33 May you be blessed for your good *j*
Ps 1: 5 the wicked will not stand in the *j*,
9: 7 he has established his throne for *j*.
76: 8 From heaven you pronounced *j*,
82: 1 he gives *j* among the "gods":
119: 66 Teach me knowledge and good *j*,
143: 2 Do not bring your servant into *j*,
Pr 3: 21 preserve sound *j* and discernment,
6: 32 man who commits adultery lacks *j*;
8: 14 Counsel and sound *j* are mine;
10: 21 but fools die for lack of *j*.
11: 12 man who lacks *j* derides his
12: 11 but he who chases fantasies lacks *j*.
17: 18 A man lacking in *j* strikes hands
18: 1 he defies all sound *j*.
28: 16 A tyrannical ruler lacks *j*,
Ecc 12: 14 God will bring every deed into *j*,
Isa 3: 14 The LORD enters into *j*
28: 6 justice to him who sits in *j*,
53: 8 By oppression and *j*, he was taken
66: 16 the LORD will execute *j*
Jer 2: 35 But I will pass *j* on you
25: 31 he will bring *j* on all mankind
51: 18 when their *j* comes, they will
Eze 11: 10 and I will execute *j* on you
Da 7: 22 pronounced *j* in favour of the saints
Am 7: 4 Sovereign LORD was calling for *j*
Zec 8: 16 and sound *j* in your courts;
Mal 3: 5 "So I will come near to you for *j*.
Mt 5: 21 who murders will be subject to *j*.'
5: 22 with his brother will be subject to *j*.
10: 15 on the day of *j* than for that town.
11: 24 on the day of *j* than for you."
12: 36 have to give account on the day of *j*
12: 41 up at the *j* with this generation
Jn 5: 22 but has entrusted all *j* to the Son,
5: 30 as I hear, and my *j* is just,
7: 24 appearances, and make a right *j*."
8: 26 "I have much to say in *j* of you.
9: 39 "For *j* I have come into this world,
12: 31 Now is the time for *j* on this world;
16: 8 to sin and righteousness and *j*:
16: 11 in regard to *j*, because the prince
Ac 24: 25 self-control and the *j* to come,
Ro 2: 1 you who pass *j* on someone else,
2: 2 Now we know that God's *j*
5: 16 The *j* followed one sin
12: 3 rather think of yourself with sober *j*
14: 10 stand before God's *j* seat.
14: 13 Therefore let us stop passing *j*
1Co 7: 40 In my *j*, she is happier if she stays
11: 29 body of the Lord eats and drinks *j*
2Co 5: 10 appear before the *j* seat of Christ,
2Th 1: 5 is evidence that God's *j* is right,
1Ti 3: 6 fall under the same *j* as the devil.
5: 12 Thus they bring *j* on themselves,
Heb 6: 2 of the dead, and eternal *j*.
9: 27 to die once, and after that to face *j*,
10: 27 but only a fearful expectation of *j*
Jas 2: 13 *j* without mercy will be shown
4: 11 are not keeping it, but sitting in *j*
1Pe 4: 17 For it is time for *j* to begin
2Pe 2: 9 the unrighteous for the day of *j*,
3: 7 being kept for the day of *j*
1Jn 4: 17 have confidence on the day of *j*,
Jude : 6 bound with everlasting chains for *j*
Rev 14: 7 because the hour of his *j* has come.

JUDGMENTS (JUDGE)

Jer 1: 16 I will pronounce my *j* on my people
Da 9: 11 and sworn *j* written in the Law
Hos 6: 5 my *j* flashed like lightning
Ro 11: 33 How unsearchable his *j*,
1Co 2: 15 spiritual man makes *j* about all
Rev 16: 7 true and just are your *j*."

JUG

1Sa 26: 12 and water *j* near Saul's head,
1Ki 17: 12 of flour in a jar and a little oil in a *j*.

JUST* (JUSTICE JUSTIFICATION JUSTIFIED JUSTIFIES JUSTIFY JUSTIFYING JUSTLY)

Ge 18: 19 LORD by doing what is right and *j*,
Dt 32: 4 and all his ways are *j*.

Dt 32: 4 upright and *j* is he.
2Sa 8: 15 doing what was *j* and right
1Ch 18: 14 doing what was *j* and right
2Ch 12: 6 and said, "The LORD is *j*."
Ne 9: 13 and laws that are *j* and right,
9: 33 you have been *j*; you have acted
Job 34: 17 Will you condemn the *j*
35: 2 Elihu said: "Do you think this is *j*?
Ps 37: 28 For the LORD loves the *j*
37: 30 and his tongue speaks what is *j*.
99: 4 what is *j* and right.
111: 7 of his hands are faithful and *j*;
119: 121 I have done what is righteous and *j*;
Pr 1: 3 doing what is right and *j* and fair;
2: 8 for he guards the course of the *j*
2: 9 will understand what is right and *j*
8: 8 All the words of my mouth are *j*;
8: 15 and rulers make laws that are *j*;
12: 5 The plans of the righteous are *j*,
21: 3 To do what is right and *j*
Isa 32: 7 even when the plea of the needy is *j*
58: 2 They ask me for *j* decisions
Jer 4: 2 if in a truthful, *j* and righteous way
22: 3 what the LORD says: Do what is *j*
22: 15 He did what was right and *j*,
23: 5 do what is *j* and right in the land.
33: 15 he will do what is *j* and right
Eze 18: 5 who does what is *j* and right.
18: 19 Since the son has done what is *j*
18: 21 and does what is *j* and right,
18: 25 'The way of the Lord is not *j*.'
18: 27 and does what is *j* and right,
18: 29 'The way of the Lord is not *j*.'
33: 14 and does what is *j* and right—
33: 16 He has done what is *j* and right;
33: 17 But it is their way that is not *j*.
33: 17 'The way of the Lord is not *j*.'
33: 19 and does what is *j* and right,
33: 20 'The way of the Lord is not *j*.'
45: 9 and oppression and do what is *j*
Da 4: 37 does is right and all his ways are *j*.
Jn 5: 30 as I hear, and my judgment is *j*,
Ro 3: 26 as to be *j* and the one who justifies
2Th 1: 6 God is *j*: He will pay back trouble
Heb 2: 2 received its *j* punishment,
1Jn 1: 9 and *j* and will forgive us our sins
Rev 15: 3 *J* and true are your ways,
16: 5 "You are *j* in these judgments,
16: 7 true and *j* are your judgments."
19: 2 for true and *j* are his judgments.

JUSTICE* (JUST)

Ge 49: 16 "Dan will provide *j* for his people
Ex 23: 2 do not pervert *j* by siding
23: 6 "Do not deny *j* to your poor people
Lev 19: 15 " 'Do not pervert *j*; do not show
Dt 16: 19 Do not pervert *j* or show partiality.
16: 20 Follow *j* and *j* alone,
24: 17 the alien or the fatherless of *j*,
27: 19 Cursed is the man who withholds *j*
1Sa 8: 3 accepted bribes and perverted *j*.
2Sa 15: 4 and I would see that he gets *j*."
15: 6 came to the king asking for *j*,
1Ki 3: 11 for discernment in administering *j*,
3: 28 wisdom from God to administer *j*.
7: 7 the Hall of *J*, where he was to judge
10: 9 to maintain *j* and righteousness."
2Ch 9: 8 to maintain *j* and righteousness."
Ezr 7: 25 and judges to administer *j*
Est 1: 13 experts in matters of law and *j*,
Job 8: 3 Does God pervert *j*?
9: 19 matter of *j*, who will summon him?
19: 7 though I call for help, there is no *j*.
27: 2 as God lives, who has denied me *j*,
29: 14 *j* was my robe and my turban.
31: 13 "If I have denied *j*
34: 5 but God denies me *j*.
34: 12 that the Almighty would pervert *j*.
34: 17 Can he who hates *j* govern?
36: 3 I will ascribe *j* to my Maker.
36: 17 *j* have taken hold of you.
37: 23 in his *j* and great righteousness,
Job 40: 8 "Would you discredit my *j*?
Ps 7: 6 Awake, my God; decree *j*.
9: 8 he will govern the peoples with *j*.
9: 16 The LORD is known by his *j*;
11: 7 he loves *j*;
33: 5 LORD loves righteousness and *j*;
36: 6 your *j* like the great deep.
37: 6 *j* of your cause like the noonday
45: 6 a sceptre of *j* will be the sceptre
72: 1 Endow the king with your *j*, O God
72: 2 your afflicted ones with *j*.
89: 14 *j* are the foundation of your throne;
97: 2 *j* are the foundation of his throne.
99: 4 The King is mighty, he loves *j*—
101: 1 I will sing of your love and *j*;
103: 6 and *j* for all the oppressed.
106: 3 Blessed are they who maintain *j*,
112: 5 who conducts his affairs with *j*.
140: 12 I know that the LORD secures *j*
Pr 8: 20 along the paths of *j*,
16: 10 and his mouth should not betray *j*.
17: 23 to pervert the course of *j*.
18: 5 or to deprive the innocent of *j*.
19: 28 A corrupt witness mocks at *j*,
21: 15 When *j* is done, it brings joy
28: 5 Evil men do not understand *j*,
29: 4 By *j* a king gives a country stability
29: 7 The righteous care about *j*
29: 26 from the LORD that man gets *j*.
Ecc 3: 16 place of *j*—wickedness was there.
5: 8 poor oppressed in a district, and *j*
Isa 1: 17 Seek *j*,
1: 21 She once was full of *j*;
1: 27 Zion will be redeemed with *j*,
5: 7 he looked for *j*, but saw bloodshed;
5: 16 Almighty will be exalted by his *j*,
5: 23 but deny *j* to the innocent.
9: 7 it with *j* and righteousness
10: 2 and withhold *j* from the oppressed
11: 4 with *j* he will give decisions
16: 5 one who in judging seeks *j*
28: 6 He will be a spirit of *j*
28: 17 I will make *j* the measuring line
29: 21 deprive the innocent of *j*.
30: 18 For the LORD is a God of *j*.
32: 1 and rulers will rule with *j*.
32: 16 *J* will dwell in the desert
33: 5 with *j* and righteousness.
42: 1 and he will bring *j* to the nations.
42: 3 In faithfulness he will bring forth *j*;
42: 4 till he establishes *j* on earth.
51: 4 my *j* will become a light
51: 5 my arm will bring *j* to the nations.
56: 1 "Maintain *j*
59: 4 No-one calls for *j*;
59: 8 there is no *j* in their paths.
59: 9 So *j* is far from us,
59: 11 We look for *j*, but find none;
59: 14 So *j* is driven back,
59: 15 that there was no *j*.
61: 8 "For I, the LORD, love *j*;
Jer 9: 24 *j* and righteousness on earth,
10: 24 Correct me, LORD, but only with *j*
12: 1 speak with you about your *j*:
21: 12 " 'Administer *j* every morning;
30: 11 I will discipline you but only with *j*;
46: 28 I will discipline you but only with *j*;
La 3: 36 to deprive a man of *j*—
Eze 22: 29 ill-treat the alien, denying them *j*.
34: 16 I will shepherd the flock with *j*.
Hos 2: 19 you in righteousness and *j*,
12: 6 maintain love and *j*,
Am 2: 7 and deny *j* to the oppressed.
5: 7 You who turn *j* into bitterness
5: 12 and you deprive the poor of *j*
5: 15 maintain *j* in the courts.
5: 24 But let *j* roll on like a river,
6: 12 But you have turned *j* into poison
Mic 3: 1 Should you not know *j*,
3: 8 and with *j* and might,
3: 9 who despise *j*
Hab 1: 4 and *j* never prevails.
1: 4 so that *j* is perverted.
Zep 3: 5 by morning he dispenses his *j*,
Zec 7: 9 'Administer true *j*; show mercy
Mal 2: 17 or "Where is the God of *j*?"
3: 5 and deprive aliens of *j*,
Mt 12: 18 he will proclaim *j* to the nations.
12: 20 till he leads *j* to victory.
23: 23 important matters of the law—*j*,
Lk 11: 42 you neglect *j* and the love of God.
18: 3 'Grant me *j* against my adversary.'
18: 5 I will see that she gets *j*,
18: 7 And will not God bring about *j*
18: 8 he will see that they get *j*,
Ac 8: 33 humiliation he was deprived of *j*.
17: 31 with *j* by the man he has appointed.
28: 4 *J* has not allowed him to live."
Ro 3: 25 He did this to demonstrate his *j*,
3: 26 it to demonstrate his *j*
2Co 7: 11 what readiness to see *j* done.
Heb 11: 33 administered *j*, and gained what
Rev 19: 11 With *j* he judges and makes war.

JUSTIFICATION* (JUST)

Eze 16: 52 for you have furnished some *j*
Ro 4: 25 and was raised to life for our *j*.
5: 16 many trespasses and brought *j*.
5: 18 of righteousness was *j* that brings

JUSTIFIED* (JUST)

Ps 51: 4 and *j* when you judge.
Lk 18: 14 rather than the other, went home *j*
Ac 13: 39 from everything you could not be *j*
13: 39 him everyone who believes is *j*
Ro 3: 24 and are *j* freely by his grace
3: 28 For we maintain that a man is *j*
4: 2 If, in fact, Abraham was *j* by works,
5: 1 since we have been *j* through faith,
5: 9 Since we have now been *j*
8: 30 those he called, he also *j*; those he *j*,
10: 10 heart that you believe and are *j*,
1Co 6: 11 you were *j* in the name
Gal 2: 16 in Christ Jesus that we may be *j*
2: 16 observing the law no-one will be *j*.
2: 16 sinners' know that a man is not *j*
2: 17 "If, while we seek to be *j* in Christ,
3: 11 Clearly no-one is *j* before God
3: 24 to Christ that we might be *j* by faith
5: 4 to be *j* by law have been alienated
Tit 3: 7 so that, having been *j* by his grace,
Jas 2: 24 You see that a person is *j*

JUSTIFIES* (JUST)

Ro 3: 26 one who *j* those who have faith
4: 5 but trusts God who *j* the wicked,
8: 33 God has chosen? It is God who *j*.

JUSTIFY* (JUST)

Est 7: 4 such distress would *j* disturbing
Job 40: 8 you condemn me to *j* yourself?
Isa 53: 11 my righteous servant will *j* many,
Lk 10: 29 But he wanted to *j* himself,
16: 15 "You are the ones who *j* yourselves
Ro 3: 30 who will *j* the circumcised by faith
Gal 3: 8 that God would *j* the Gentiles

JUSTIFYING* (JUST)

Job 32: 2 angry with Job for *j* himself rather

JUSTLY* (JUST)

Ps 58: 1 Do you rulers indeed speak *j*?
67: 4 for you rule the peoples *j*
Jer 7: 5 and deal with each other *j*,
Mic 6: 8 To act *j* and to love mercy
Lk 23: 41 We are punished *j*,
1Pe 2: 23 himself to him who judges *j*.

KADESH

Nu 20: 1 of Zin, and they stayed at *K*.
Dt 1: 46 And so you stayed in *K* many days

KADESH BARNEA

Nu 32: 8 I sent them from *K* to look over

KEBAR

Eze 1: 1 among the exiles by the *K* River,

KEDORLAOMER

Ge 14: 17 Abram returned from defeating *K*

KEEP (KEEPER KEEPING KEEPS KEPT)

Ge 31: 49 "May the LORD *k* watch
Ex 15: 26 his commands and *k* all his
20: 6 and *k* my commandments.
Lev 15: 31 You must *k* the Israelites separate
Nu 6: 24 and *k* you;
Dt 4: 2 but *k* the commands of the LORD
6: 17 Be sure to *k* the commands
7: 9 who love him and *k* his commands.
7: 12 your God will *k* his covenant
11: 1 your God and *k* his requirements,
13: 4 *K* his commands and obey him;
30: 10 your God and *k* his commands
30: 16 and to *k* his commands, decrees
Jos 22: 5 careful to *k* the commandment
1Ki 8: 58 and to *k* the commands,
2Ki 17: 19 Judah did not *k* the commands
23: 3 the LORD and *k* his commands,
1Ch 29: 18 and *k* their hearts loyal to you.
2Ch 6: 14 you who *k* your covenant of love
34: 31 the LORD and *k* his commands,
Job 14: 16 but not *k* track of my sin.
Ps 18: 28 You, O LORD, *k* my lamp burning
19: 13 *K* your servant also from wilful
78: 10 they did not *k* God's covenant
119: 2 Blessed are they who *k* his statutes
119: 9 can a young man *k* his way pure?
121: 7 The LORD will *k* you
141: 3 *k* watch over the door of my lips.
Pr 4: 21 *k* them within your heart;
4: 24 *k* corrupt talk far from your lips.
30: 8 *K* falsehood and lies far from me;
Ecc 3: 6 a time to *k* and a time
12: 13 and *k* his commandments,
Isa 26: 3 You will *k* in perfect peace
42: 6 I will *k* you and will make you
58: 13 "If you *k* your feet
Jer 16: 11 forsook me and did not *k* my law.
Eze 20: 19 and be careful to *k* my laws.
Mt 10: 10 for the worker is worth his *k*.
Lk 12: 35 and *k* your lamps burning,
17: 33 tries to *k* his life will lose it,
Jn 10: 24 How long will you *k* us in suspense
12: 25 in this world will *k* it for eternal life
Ac 2: 24 for death to *k* its hold on him.
18: 9 "Do not be afraid; *k* on speaking,
Ro 7: 19 want to do—this I *k* on doing.
12: 11 but *k* your spiritual fervour,
14: 22 you believe about these things *k*
16: 17 *K* away from them.
1Co 1: 8 He will *k* you strong to the end,
2Co 12: 7 To *k* me from becoming conceited
Gal 5: 25 let us *k* in step with the Spirit.
Eph 4: 3 Make every effort to *k* the unity
2Th 3: 6 to *k* away from every brother who
1Ti 5: 22 *K* yourself pure.
2Ti 4: 5 *k* your head in all situations,
Heb 9: 20 God has commanded you to *k*."
13: 5 *K* your lives free from the love
Jas 1: 26 and yet does not *k* a tight rein
2: 8 If you really *k* the royal law found
3: 2 able to *k* his whole body in check.
2Pe 1: 8 will *k* you from being ineffective
Jude : 21 *K* yourselves in God's love
: 24 able to *k* you from falling
Rev 3: 10 also *k* you from the hour
22: 9 of all who *k* the words of this book.

KEEPER (KEEP)

Ge 4: 9 I my brother's *k*?" The LORD

KEEPING (KEEP)

Ex 20: 8 the Sabbath day by *k* it holy.
Dt 5: 12 the Sabbath day by *k* it holy,
13: 18 *k* all his commands that I am
Ps 19: 11 in *k* them there is great reward.
119: 112 My heart is set on *k* your decrees
Pr 15: 3 *k* watch on the wicked
Mt 3: 8 Produce fruit in *k* with repentance.
Lk 2: 8 *k* watch over their flocks at night.
1Co 7: 19 *K* God's commands is what counts.
2Co 8: 5 and then to us in *k* with God's will.
Jas 4: 11 you are not *k* it, but sitting
1Pe 3: 16 and respect, *k* a clear conscience,
2Pe 3: 9 Lord is not slow in *k* his promise,

KEEPS (KEEP)

Ne 1: 5 who *k* his covenant of love
Ps 15: 4 who *k* his oath
Pr 12: 23 A prudent man *k* his knowledge
15: 21 of understanding *k* a straight
17: 28 a fool is thought wise if he *k* silent,
29: 11 a wise man *k* himself under control
Isa 56: 2 who *k* the Sabbath
Da 9: 4 who *k* his covenant of love
Am 5: 13 Therefore the prudent man *k* quiet
Jn 7: 19 Yet not one of you *k* the law.
8: 51 if anyone *k* my word, he will never
1Co 13: 5 is not easily angered, it *k* no record
Jas 2: 10 For whoever *k* the whole law
Rev 22: 7 Blessed is he who *k* the words

KEILAH

1Sa 23: 13 that David had escaped from *K*,

KEPT (KEEP)

Ex 12: 42 Because the LORD *k* vigil that
Dt 7: 8 and *k* the oath he swore
2Ki 18: 6 he *k* the commands the LORD had
Ne 9: 8 You have *k* your promise
Ps 130: 3 If you, O LORD, *k* a record of sins,
Isa 38: 17 In your love you *k* me
Mt 19: 20 these I have *k*," the young man
2Co 11: 9 I have *k* myself from being
2Ti 4: 7 finished the race, I have *k* the faith.
1Pe 1: 4 spoil or fade—*k* in heaven for you,

KEY (KEYS)

Isa 33: 6 the fear of the LORD is the *k*
Rev 20: 1 having the *k* to the Abyss

KEYS* (KEY)

Mt 16: 19 I will give you the *k* of the kingdom
Rev 1: 18 And I hold the *k* of death

KICK*

Ac 26: 14 for you to *k* against the goads.'

KILL (KILLED KILLS)

Ecc 3: 3 a time to *k* and a time to heal,
Mt 10: 28 *k* the body but cannot *k* the soul.
17: 23 They will *k* him, and on the third
Mk 9: 31 will *k* him, and after three days
10: 34 spit on him, flog him and *k* him.

KILLED (KILL)

Ge 4: 8 his brother Abel and *k* him.
Ex 2: 12 he *k* the Egyptian and hid him
13: 15 the LORD *k* every firstborn
Nu 35: 11 who has *k* someone accidentally
1Sa 17: 50 down the Philistine and *k* him.
Ne 9: 26 They *k* your prophets, who had
Hos 6: 5 I *k* you with the words
Lk 11: 48 they *k* the prophets, and you build
Ac 3: 15 You *k* the author of life,

KILLS (KILL)

Ex 21: 12 *k* him shall surely be put to death.
Lev 24: 21 but whoever *k* a man must be put
2Co 3: 6 for the letter *k*, but the Spirit gives

KIND [1] (KINDS)

Ge 1: 24 animals, each according to its *k*."
1Co 15: 35 With what *k* of body will they

KIND [2] (KINDNESS KINDNESSES)

2Ch 10: 7 "If you will be *k* to these people
Ps 86: 5 You are *k* and forgiving, O Lord,
Pr 11: 17 A *k* man benefits himself,
12: 25 but a *k* word cheers him up.
14: 21 blessed is he who is *k* to the needy.
14: 31 whoever is *k* to the needy honours
19: 17 He who is *k* to the poor lends
Da 4: 27 by being *k* to the oppressed.
Lk 6: 35 because he is *k* to the ungrateful
1Co 13: 4 Love is patient, love is *k*.
Eph 4: 32 Be *k* and compassionate
1Th 5: 15 but always try to be *k* to each other
2Ti 2: 24 instead, he must be *k* to everyone,
Tit 2: 5 to be busy at home, to be *k*,

KIND-HEARTED* (HEART)

Pr 11: 16 A *k* woman gains respect,

KINDNESS (KIND [2])

Ge 24: 12 and show *k* to my master Abraham
32: 10 I am unworthy of all the *k*
39: 21 he showed him *k* and granted him
Jdg 8: 35 also failed to show *k* to the family
Ru 2: 20 has not stopped showing his *k*
2Sa 9: 3 to whom I can show God's *k*?"
22: 51 he shows unfailing *k*
Ps 18: 50 he shows unfailing *k*
141: 5 righteous man strike me—it is a *k*;
Isa 54: 8 but with everlasting *k*
Jer 9: 24 I am the LORD, who exercises *k*,
Hos 11: 4 I led them with cords of human *k*,
Ac 14: 17 He has shown *k* by giving you rain
Ro 11: 22 Consider therefore the *k*
2Co 6: 6 understanding, patience and *k*;
Gal 5: 22 peace, patience, *k*, goodness,
Eph 2: 7 expressed in his *k* to us
Col 3: 12 yourselves with compassion, *k*,
Tit 3: 4 But when the *k* and love
2Pe 1: 7 brotherly *k*; and to brotherly *k*,

KINDNESSES* (KIND [2])

Ps 106: 7 did not remember your many *k*,
Isa 63: 7 I will tell of the *k* of the LORD,
63: 7 to his compassion and many *k*.

KINDS (KIND [1])

Ge 1: 12 bearing seed according to their *k*
1Co 12: 4 There are different *k* of gifts,
1Ti 6: 10 of money is a root of all *k* of evil.
1Pe 1: 6 had to suffer grief in all *k* of trials.

KING (KING'S KINGDOM KINGDOMS KINGS)

1. Kings of Judah and Israel: see Saul, David, Solomon.

2. Kings of Judah: see Rehoboam, Abijah, Asa, Jehoshaphat, Jehoram, Ahaziah, Athaliah (Queen), Joash, Amaziah, Azariah (Uzziah), Jotham, Ahaz, Hezekiah, Manasseh, Amon, Josiah, Jehoahaz, Jehoiakim, Jehoiachin, Zedekiah.

3. Kings of Israel: see Jeroboam I, Nadab, Baasha, Elah, Zimri, Tibni, Omri, Ahab, Ahaziah, Joram, Jehu, Jehoahaz, Jehoash, Jeroboam II, Zechariah, Shallum, Menahem, Pekah, Pekahiah, Hoshea.

Ex 1: 8 a new *k*, who did not know about
Dt 17: 14 "Let us set a *k* over us like all
Jdg 17: 6 In those days Israel had no *k*;
1Sa 8: 5 now appoint a *k* to lead us,
11: 15 as *k* in the presence of the LORD.
12: 12 the LORD your God was your *k*.
2Sa 2: 4 and there they anointed David *k*
1Ki 1: 30 Solomon your son shall be *k*
Ps 2: 6 "I have installed my *K*
24: 7 that the *K* of glory may come in.
44: 4 You are my *K* and my God,
47: 7 For God is the *K* of all the earth;
Isa 32: 1 See, a *k* will reign in righteousness
Jer 30: 9 and David their *k*,
Hos 3: 5 their God and David their *k*.
Mic 2: 13 *k* will pass through before them,
Zec 9: 9 See, your *k* comes to you,
Mt 2: 2 is the one who has been born *k*
27: 11 "Are you the *k* of the Jews?" "Yes,
Lk 19: 38 "Blessed is the *k* who comes
23: 3 "Are you the *k* of the Jews?" "Yes,
23: 38 THE *K* OF THE JEWS.
Jn 1: 49 of God; you are the *K* of Israel."

Jn 12:13 "Blessed is the *K* of Israel!"
Ac 17: 7 saying that there is another *k*,
1Ti 1:17 Now to the *K* eternal, immortal,
6:15 the *K* of kings and Lord of lords,
Heb 7: 1 This Melchizedek was *k* of Salem
1Pe 2:13 to the *k*, as the supreme authority,
2:17 of believers, fear God, honour the *k*.
Rev 15: 3 *K* of the ages.
17:14 he is Lord of lords and *K* of kings—
19:16 *K* OF KINGS AND LORD

KING'S (KING)

Pr 21: 1 The *k* heart is in the hand
Ecc 8: 3 in a hurry to leave the *k* presence.

KINGDOM (KING)

Ex 19: 6 you will be for me a *k* of priests
Dt 17:18 When he takes the throne of his *k*,
2Sa 7:12 body, and I will establish his *k*.
1Ki 11:31 to tear the *k* out of Solomon's hand
1Ch 17:11 own sons, and I will establish his *k*.
29:11 Yours, O LORD, is the *k*;
Ps 45: 6 justice will be the sceptre of your *k*.
103:19 and his *k* rules over all.
145:11 They will tell of the glory of your *k*
Eze 29:14 There they will be a lowly *k*.
Da 2:39 "After you, another *k* will rise,
4: 3 His *k* is an eternal *k*;
7:27 His *k* will be an everlasting *k*,
Ob :21 And the *k* will be the LORD's.
Mt 3: 2 Repent, for the *k* of heaven is near
4:17 Repent, for the *k* of heaven is near
4:23 preaching the good news of the *k*,
5: 3 for theirs is the *k* of heaven.
5:10 for theirs is the *k* of heaven.
5:19 great in the *k* of heaven.
5:19 least in the *k* of heaven,
5:20 you will certainly not enter the *k*
6:10 your *k* come,
6:33 But seek first his *k* and his
7:21 Lord,' will enter the *k* of heaven,
8:11 Isaac and Jacob in the *k* of heaven.
8:12 the subjects of the *k* will be thrown
9:35 preaching the good news of the *k*
10: 7 preach this message: 'The *k*
11:11 least in the *k* of heaven is greater
11:12 the *k* of heaven has been forcefully
12:25 "Every *k* divided against itself will
12:26 How then can his *k* stand?
12:28 then the *k* of God has come
13:11 knowledge of the secrets of the *k*
13:19 hears the message about the *k*
13:24 "The *k* of heaven is like a man who
13:31 *k* of heaven is like a mustard seed,
13:33 "The *k* of heaven is like yeast that
13:38 stands for the sons of the *k*.
13:41 of his *k* everything that causes sin
13:43 the sun in the *k* of their Father.
13:44 *k* of heaven is like treasure hidden
13:45 the *k* of heaven is like a merchant
13:47 *k* of heaven is like a net that was let
13:52 has been instructed about the *k*
16:19 the keys of the *k* of heaven;
16:28 the Son of Man coming in his *k*."
18: 1 the greatest in the *k* of heaven?"
18: 3 you will never enter the *k*
18: 4 the greatest in the *k* of heaven.
18:23 the *k* of heaven is like a king who
19:12 because of the *k* of heaven.
19:14 for the *k* of heaven belongs to such
19:23 man to enter the *k* of heaven.
19:24 for a rich man to enter the *k* of God
20: 1 "For the *k* of heaven is like
20:21 the other at your left in your *k*."
21:31 the prostitutes are entering the *k*
21:43 "Therefore I tell you that the *k*
22: 2 "The *k* of heaven is like a king who
23:13 You shut the *k* of heaven
24: 7 rise against nation, and *k* against *k*.
24:14 gospel of the *k* will be preached
25: 1 "At that time the *k*
25:34 the *k* prepared for you
26:29 anew with you in my Father's *k*."
Mk 1:15 "The *k* of God is near.
3:24 If a *k* is divided against itself,
3:24 against itself, that *k* cannot stand.
4:11 "The secret of the *k*
4:26 "This is what the *k* of God is like.
4:30 "What shall we say the *k*
6:23 I will give you, up to half my *k*."
9: 1 before they see the *k* of God come
9:47 better for you to enter the *k* of God
10:14 for the *k* of God belongs to such
10:15 anyone who will not receive the *k*
10:23 for the rich to enter the *k* of God!"
10:24 how hard it is to enter the *k* of God
10:25 for a rich man to enter the *k* of God
11:10 "Blessed is the coming *k*
12:34 "You are not far from the *k* of God
13: 8 rise against nation, and *k* against *k*.
14:25 day when I drink it anew in the *k*
15:43 who was himself waiting for the *k*
Lk 1:33 Jacob for ever; his *k* will never
4:43 of the *k* of God to the other towns
6:20 for yours is the *k* of God.
7:28 in the *k* of God is greater than he."
8: 1 proclaiming the good news of the *k*
8:10 knowledge of the secrets of the *k*
9: 2 out to preach the *k* of God
9:11 spoke to them about the *k* of God,
9:27 before they see the *k* of God."
9:60 you go and proclaim the *k* of God
9:62 fit for service in the *k* of God."
10: 9 'The *k* of God is near you.'
10:11 sure of this: The *k* of God is near.'
11: 2 your *k* come.
11:17 "Any *k* divided against itself will
11:18 himself, how can his *k* stand?
11:20 then the *k* of God has come to you.
12:31 seek his *k*, and these things will be
12:32 has been pleased to give you the *k*.
13:18 "What is the *k* of God like?
13:20 What shall I compare the *k* of God
13:28 all the prophets in the *k* of God,
13:29 places at the feast in the *k* of God.
14:15 eat at the feast in the *k* of God."
16:16 the good news of the *k*
17:20 when the *k* of God would come,
17:20 *k* of God does not come with your
17:21 because the *k* of God is within you
18:16 for the *k* of God belongs to such
18:17 anyone who will not receive the *k*
18:24 for the rich to enter the *k* of God!
18:25 for a rich man to enter the *k* of God
18:29 for the sake of the *k* of God will fail
19:11 and the people thought that the *k*
21:10 rise against nation, and *k* against *k*.
21:31 you know that the *k* of God is near.
22:16 until it finds fulfilment in the *k*
22:18 the vine until the *k* of God comes."
22:29 And I confer on you a *k*, just
22:30 and drink at my table in my *k*
23:42 me when you come into your *k*."
23:51 he was waiting for the *k* of God.
Jn 3: 3 he cannot see the *k* of God."
3: 5 he cannot enter the *k* of God.
18:36 now my *k* is from another place."
18:36 "My *k* is not of this world.
Ac 1: 3 and spoke about the *k* of God.
1: 6 going to restore the *k* to Israel?"
8:12 he preached the good news of the *k*
14:22 hardships to enter the *k* of God,"
19: 8 arguing persuasively about the *k*
20:25 about preaching the *k* will ever see
28:23 and declared to them the *k* of God
28:31 hindrance he preached the *k*
Ro 14:17 For the *k* of God is not a matter
1Co 4:20 For the *k* of God is not a matter
6: 9 the wicked will not inherit the *k*
6:10 swindlers will inherit the *k* of God.
15:24 hands over the *k* to God the Father
15:50 blood cannot inherit the *k* of God,
Gal 5:21 live like this will not inherit the *k*
Eph 2: 2 and of the ruler of the *k* of the air,
5: 5 has any inheritance in the *k*
Col 1:12 of the saints in the *k* of light.
Col 1:13 and brought us into the *k*
4:11 among my fellow-workers for the *k*
1Th 2:12 who calls you into his *k* and glory.
2Th 1: 5 will be counted worthy of the *k*
2Ti 4: 1 in view of his appearing and his *k*,
4:18 bring me safely to his heavenly *k*.
Heb 1: 8 will be the sceptre of your *k*.
12:28 we are receiving a *k* that cannot be
Jas 2: 5 to inherit the *k* he promised those
2Pe 1:11 into the eternal *k* of our Lord
Rev 1: 6 has made us to be a *k* and priests
1: 9 companion in the suffering and *k*
5:10 You have made them to be a *k*
11:15 of the world has become the *k*
11:15 "The *k* of the world has become
12:10 the power and the *k* of our God,
16:10 his *k* was plunged into darkness.
17:12 who have not yet received a *k*,

KINGDOMS (KING)

2Ki 19:15 God over all the *k* of the earth.
19:19 so that all *k* on earth may know
2Ch 20: 6 rule over all the *k* of the nations.
Ps 68:32 Sing to God, O *k* of the earth,
Isa 37:16 God over all the *k* of the earth.
37:20 so that all *k* on earth may know
Eze 29:15 It will be the lowliest of *k*
37:22 or be divided into two *k*.
Da 4:17 Most High is sovereign over the *k*
7:17 great beasts are four *k* that will rise
Zep 3: 8 to gather the *k*

KINGS (KING)

Ps 2: 2 The *k* of the earth take their stand
47: 9 for the *k* of the earth belong to God
68:29 *k* will bring you gifts.
72:11 All *k* will bow down to him
110: 5 he will crush *k* on the day
149: 8 to bind their *k* with fetters,
Pr 16:12 *K* detest wrongdoing,
Isa 24:21 and the *k* on the earth below.
52:15 and *k* will shut their mouths
60:11 their *k* led in triumphal procession.
Da 2:21 he sets up *k* and deposes them.
7:24 ten horns are ten *k* who will come
Lk 21:12 and you will be brought before *k*
1Co 4: 8 You have become *k*—
1Ti 2: 2 for *k* and all those in authority,
6:15 the King of *k* and Lord of lords,
Rev 1: 5 and the ruler of the *k* of the earth.
17:14 he is Lord of lords and King of *k*—
19:16 KING OF *K* AND LORD

KINSMAN-REDEEMER (REDEEM)

Ru 3: 9 over me, since you are a *k*."
4:14 day has not left you without a *k*.

KISS (KISSED KISSES)

Ps 2:12 *K* the Son, lest he be angry
Pr 24:26 is like a *k* on the lips.
SS 1: 2 Let him *k* me
8: 1 I would *k* you,
Lk 22:48 the Son of Man with a *k*?"
Ro 16:16 Greet one another with a holy *k*.
1Co 16:20 Greet one another with a holy *k*.
2Co 13:12 Greet one another with a holy *k*.
1Th 5:26 Greet all the brothers with a holy *k*
1Pe 5:14 Greet one another with a *k* of love.

KISSED (KISS)

Mk 14:45 Judas said, "Rabbi!" and *k* him.
Lk 7:38 *k* them and poured perfume

KISSES* (KISS)

Pr 27: 6 but an enemy multiplies *k*.
SS 1: 2 with the *k* of his mouth—

KNEE (KNEES)

Isa 45:23 Before me every *k* will bow;
Ro 14:11 'Every *k* will bow before me;
Php 2:10 name of Jesus every *k* should bow,

KNEEL (KNELT)

Est 3: 2 But Mordecai would not *k* down
Ps 95: 6 let us *k* before the LORD our
Eph 3: 14 For this reason I *k*

KNEES (KNEE)

1Ki 19: 18 all whose *k* have not bowed
Isa 35: 3 steady the *k* that give way;
Da 6: 10 times a day he got down on his *k*
Lk 5: 8 he fell at Jesus' *k* and said,
Heb 12: 12 your feeble arms and weak *k*.

KNELT* (KNEEL)

1Ki 1: 16 Bathsheba bowed low and *k*
2Ch 6: 13 and then *k* down before the whole
7: 3 they *k* on the pavement
29: 29 everyone present with him *k* down
Est 3: 2 officials at the king's gate *k* down
Mt 8: 2 and *k* before him and said,
9: 18 a ruler came and *k* before him
15: 25 The woman came and *k* before him
17: 14 a man approached Jesus and *k*
27: 29 *k* in front of him and mocked him.
Lk 22: 41 *k* down and prayed, "Father,
Ac 20: 36 he *k* down with all of them
21: 5 there on the beach we *k* to pray.

KNEW (KNOW)

2Ch 33: 13 Manasseh *k* that the LORD is God
Job 23: 3 If only I *k* where to find him;
Pr 24: 12 "But we *k* nothing about this,"
Jer 1: 5 you in the womb I *k* you,
Jnh 4: 2 I *k* that you are a gracious
Mt 7: 23 tell them plainly, 'I never *k* you.
12: 25 Jesus *k* their thoughts
Jn 2: 24 himself to them, for he *k* all men.
14: 7 If you really *k* me, you would know

KNIFE

Ge 22: 10 and took the *k* to slay his son.
Pr 23: 2 and put a *k* to your throat

KNOCK* (KNOCKS)

Mt 7: 7 *k* and the door will be opened
Lk 11: 9 *k* and the door will be opened
Rev 3: 20 I am! I stand at the door and *k*.

KNOCKS (KNOCK)

Mt 7: 8 and to him who *k*, the door will be

KNOW (FOREKNEW FOREKNOWLEDGE KNEW KNOWING KNOWLEDGE KNOWN KNOWS)

Ge 22: 12 Now I *k* that you fear God,
Ex 6: 7 you will *k* that I am the LORD
14: 4 and the Egyptians will *k* that I am
33: 13 teach me your ways so I may *k* you
Dt 7: 9 *K* therefore that the LORD your
18: 21 "How can we *k* when a message
Jos 4: 24 of the earth might *k* that the hand
23: 14 You *k* with all your heart
1Sa 17: 46 the whole world will *k* that there is
1Ki 8: 39 heart (for you alone *k* the hearts
Job 11: 6 *K* this: God has even forgotten
19: 25 I *k* that my Redeemer lives,
42: 3 things too wonderful for me to *k*.
Ps 9: 10 Those who *k* your name will trust
46: 10 "Be still, and *k* that I am God;
100: 3 *K* that the LORD is God.
139: 1 and you *k* me.
139: 23 Search me, O God, and *k* my heart;
145: 12 so that all men may *k*
Pr 27: 1 for you do not *k* what a day may
30: 4 Tell me if you *k*!
Ecc 8: 5 wise heart will *k* the proper time
Isa 29: 15 "Who sees us? Who will *k*?"
40: 21 Do you not *k*?
Jer 6: 15 they do not even *k* how to blush.
22: 16 Is that not what it means to *k* me?"
24: 7 I will give them a heart to *k* me,
31: 34 his brother, saying, '*K* the LORD,'
33: 3 unsearchable things you do not *k*.'
Eze 2: 5 they will *k* that a prophet has been
6: 10 they will *k* that I am the LORD;
Da 11: 32 people who *k* their God will firmly
Mt 6: 3 let your left hand *k* what your right
7: 11 *k* how to give good gifts
9: 6 But so that you may *k* that the Son
22: 29 you do not *k* the Scriptures
24: 42 you do not *k* on what day your
26: 74 "I don't *k* the man!" Immediately
Mk 12: 24 you do not *k* the Scriptures
Lk 1: 4 so that you may *k* the certainty
11: 13 *k* how to give good gifts
12: 48 But the one who does not *k*
13: 25 'I don't *k* you or where you come
21: 31 you *k* that the kingdom of God is
23: 34 for they do not *k* what they are
Jn 1: 26 among you stands one you do not *k*
3: 11 we speak of what we *k*,
4: 22 we worship what we do *k*,
4: 42 and we *k* that this man really is
6: 69 and *k* that you are the Holy One
7: 28 You do not *k* him, but I *k* him
8: 14 for I *k* where I came from
8: 19 "You do not *k* me or my Father,"
8: 32 Then you will *k* the truth,
8: 55 Though you do not *k* him, I *k* him.
9: 25 One thing I do *k*.
10: 4 him because they *k* his voice.
10: 14 I *k* my sheep and my sheep *k* me—
10: 27 I *k* them, and they follow me.
12: 35 the dark does not *k* where he is
13: 17 Now that you *k* these things,
13: 35 All men will *k* that you are my
14: 17 you *k* him, for he lives with you
15: 21 for they do not *k* the One who sent
16: 30 we can see that you *k* all things
17: 3 that they may *k* you, the only true
17: 23 to let the world *k* that you sent me
21: 15 he said, "you *k* that I love you."
21: 24 We *k* that his testimony is true.
Ac 1: 7 "It is not for you to *k* the times
1: 24 "Lord, you *k* everyone's heart.
Ro 3: 17 and the way of peace they do not *k*
6: 3 Or don't you *k* that all
6: 6 For we *k* that our old self was
6: 16 Don't you *k* that when you offer
7: 14 We *k* that the law is spiritual;
7: 18 I *k* that nothing good lives in me,
8: 22 We *k* that the whole creation has
8: 26 We do not *k* what we ought to pray
8: 28 we *k* that in all things God works
1Co 1: 21 through its wisdom did not *k* him,
2: 2 For I resolved to *k* nothing
3: 16 Don't you *k* that you yourselves
5: 6 Don't you *k* that a little yeast
6: 2 Do you not *k* that the saints will
6: 15 Do you not *k* that your bodies are
6: 16 Do you not *k* that he who unites
6: 19 Do you not *k* that your body is
7: 16 How do you *k*, wife, whether you
8: 2 does not yet *k* as he ought to *k*.
9: 13 Don't you *k* that those who work
9: 24 Do you not *k* that
13: 9 For we *k* in part and we prophesy
13: 12 Now I *k* in part; then I shall *k* fully,
15: 58 because you *k* that your labour
2Co 5: 1 we *k* that if the earthly tent we live
5: 11 we *k* what it is to fear the Lord,
8: 9 For you *k* the grace
Gal 1: 11 you to *k*, brothers, that the gospel I
2: 16 not 'Gentile sinners' *k* that a man
Eph 1: 17 so that you may *k* him better.
1: 18 in order that you may *k* the hope
6: 8 you *k* that the Lord will reward
6: 9 since you *k* that he who is both
Php 3: 10 I want to *k* Christ and the power
4: 12 I *k* what it is to be in need,
Col 2: 2 order that they may *k* the mystery
4: 1 because you *k* that you
4: 6 so that you may *k* how
1Th 3: 3 You *k* quite well that we were
5: 2 for you *k* very well that the day
2Th 1: 8 punish those who do not *k* God
1Ti 1: 7 they do not *k* what they are talking
3: 5 (If anyone does not *k* how
3: 15 you will *k* how people ought
2Ti 1: 12 because I *k* whom I have believed,
2: 23 you *k* they produce quarrels.
3: 14 you *k* those from whom you
Heb 8: 11 because they will all *k* me,
11: 8 he did not *k* where he was going.
Jas 1: 3 because you *k* that the testing
3: 1 you *k* that we who teach will be
4: 4 don't you *k* that friendship
4: 14 *k* what will happen tomorrow.
1Pe 1: 18 For you *k* that it was not
2Pe 1: 12 even though you *k* them
1Jn 2: 3 We *k* that we have come
2: 4 The man who says, "I *k* him,"
2: 5 This is how we *k* we are in him:
2: 11 he does not *k* where he is going,
2: 20 and all of you *k* the truth.
2: 29 you *k* that everyone who does
3: 1 not *k* us is that it did not *k* him.
3: 2 But we *k* that when he appears,
3: 10 This is how we *k* who the children
3: 14 We *k* that we have passed
3: 16 This is how we *k* what love is:
3: 19 then is how we *k* that we belong
3: 24 We *k* it by the Spirit he gave us.
4: 8 does not love does not *k* God,
4: 13 We *k* that we live in him
4: 16 so we *k* and rely on the love God
5: 2 This is how we *k* that we love
5: 13 so that you may *k* that you have
5: 15 And if we *k* that he hears us—
5: 18 We *k* that anyone born
5: 20 We *k* also that the Son
Rev 2: 2 I *k* your deeds, your hard work
2: 9 I *k* your afflictions and your
2: 19 I *k* your deeds, your love and faith,
3: 3 you will not *k* at what time I will
3: 15 I *k* your deeds, that you are neither

KNOWING (KNOW)

Ge 3: 5 and you will be like God, *k* good
3: 22 now become like one of us, *k* good
Jn 19: 28 *k* that all was now completed,
Php 3: 8 of *k* Christ Jesus my Lord,
Phm :21 *k* that you will do even more
Heb 13: 2 entertained angels without *k* it.

KNOWLEDGE (KNOW)

Ge 2: 9 the tree of the *k* of good and evil.
2: 17 eat from the tree of the *k* of good
2Ch 1: 10 and *k*, that I may lead this people,
Job 21: 22 "Can anyone teach *k* to God,
38: 2 counsel with words without *k*?
42: 3 obscures my counsel without *k*?'
Ps 19: 2 night after night they display *k*.
73: 11 Does the Most High have *k*?"
94: 10 Does he who teaches man lack *k*?
119: 66 Teach me *k* and good judgment,
139: 6 Such *k* is too wonderful for me,
Pr 1: 4 *k* and discretion to the young—
1: 7 of the LORD is the beginning of *k*,
2: 5 and find the *k* of God.
2: 6 from his mouth come *k*
2: 10 and *k* will be pleasant to your soul.
3: 20 by his *k* the deeps were divided,
8: 10 *k* rather than choice gold,
8: 12 I possess *k* and discretion.
9: 10 *k* of the Holy One is understanding
10: 14 Wise men store up *k*,
12: 1 Whoever loves discipline loves *k*,
12: 23 A prudent man keeps his *k*
13: 16 Every prudent man acts out of *k*,
14: 6 *k* comes easily to the discerning.
15: 7 The lips of the wise spread *k*;
15: 14 The discerning heart seeks *k*,
17: 27 A man of *k* uses words
18: 15 heart of the discerning acquires *k*;
19: 2 to have zeal without *k*,
19: 25 discerning man, and he will gain *k*.
20: 15 lips that speak *k* are a rare jewel.
23: 12 and your ears to words of *k*.

Pr 24: 4 through *k* its rooms are filled
Ecc 7: 12 but the advantage of *k* is this:
Isa 11: 2 the Spirit of *k* and of the fear
11: 9 full of the *k* of the LORD
40: 14 Who was it that taught him *k*
Jer 3: 15 who will lead you with *k*
Hos 4: 6 are destroyed from lack of *k*.
Hab 2: 14 filled with the *k* of the glory
Mal 2: 7 lips of a priest ought to preserve *k*,
Mt 13: 11 The *k* of the secrets of the kingdom
Lk 8: 10 The *k* of the secrets of the kingdom
11: 52 you have taken away the key to *k*.
Ac 18: 24 with a thorough *k* of the Scriptures
Ro 1: 28 worth while to retain the *k* of God,
10: 2 but their zeal is not based on *k*.
11: 33 riches of the wisdom and *k* of God!
1Co 8: 1 *K* puffs up, but love builds up.
8: 11 Christ died, is destroyed by your *k*.
12: 8 to another the message of *k*
13: 2 can fathom all mysteries and all *k*,
13: 8 where there is *k*, it will pass away.
2Co 2: 14 everywhere the fragrance of the *k*
4: 6 light of the *k* of the glory of God
8: 7 in *k*, in complete earnestness
11: 6 a trained speaker, but I do have *k*.
Eph 3: 19 to know this love that surpasses *k*
4: 13 and in the *k* of the Son of God
Php 1: 9 and more in *k* and depth of insight,
Col 1: 9 God to fill you with the *k* of his will
1: 10 every good work, growing in the *k*
2: 3 all the treasures of wisdom and *k*.
3: 10 which is being renewed in *k*
1Ti 2: 4 and to come to a *k* of the truth.
6: 20 ideas of what is falsely called *k*,
Tit 1: 1 and the *k* of the truth that leads
Heb 10: 26 after we have received the *k*
2Pe 1: 5 and to goodness, *k*; and to *k*,
3: 18 grow in the grace and *k* of our Lord

KNOWN (KNOW)

Ex 6: 3 the LORD I did not make myself *k*
Ps 16: 11 You have made *k* to me the path
89: 1 I will make your faithfulness *k*
98: 2 LORD has made his salvation *k*
105: 1 make *k* among the nations what he
119: 168 for all my ways are *k* to you.
Pr 20: 11 Even a child is *k* by his actions,
Isa 12: 4 make *k* among the nations what he
46: 10 *k* the end from the beginning,
61: 9 Their descendants will be *k*
Eze 38: 23 I will make myself *k* in the sight
39: 7 " 'I will make *k* my holy name
Mt 10: 26 or hidden that will not be made *k*.
24: 43 of the house had *k* at what time
Lk 19: 42 had only *k* on this day what would
Jn 15: 15 from my Father I have made *k*
16: 14 from what is mine and making it *k*
17: 26 I have made you *k* to them,
Ac 2: 28 You have made *k* to me the paths
Ro 1: 19 since what may be *k* about God is
3: 21 apart from law, has been made *k*,
9: 22 his wrath and make his power *k*,
11: 34 "Who has *k* the mind of the Lord?
15: 20 the gospel where Christ was not *k*,
16: 26 and made *k* through the prophetic
1Co 2: 16 "For who has *k* the mind
8: 3 But the man who loves God is *k*
13: 12 know fully, even as I am fully *k*.
2Co 3: 2 written on our hearts, *k*
Gal 4: 9 or rather are *k* by God—
Eph 3: 5 which was not made *k* to men
6: 19 will fearlessly make *k* the mystery
2Ti 3: 15 infancy you have *k* the holy
2Pe 2: 21 than to have *k* it and then

KNOWS (KNOW)

1Sa 2: 3 for the LORD is a God who *k*,
Est 4: 14 And who *k* but that you have come
Job 23: 10 But he *k* the way that I take;
Ps 44: 21 since he *k* the secrets of the heart?
94: 11 The LORD *k* the thoughts of man;
103: 14 for he *k* how we are formed,
Ecc 8: 7 Since no man *k* the future,
Ecc 8: 17 Even if a wise man claims he *k*,
9: 12 no man *k* when his hour will come:
Isa 29: 16 "He *k* nothing"?
Jer 9: 24 that he understands and *k* me,
Mt 6: 8 for your Father *k* what you need
11: 27 No-one *k* the Son
24: 36 "No-one *k* about that day or hour,
Lk 12: 47 "That servant who *k* his master's
16: 15 of men, but God *k* your hearts.
Ac 15: 8 who *k* the heart, showed that he
Ro 8: 27 who searches our hearts *k* the mind
1Co 2: 11 who among men *k* the thoughts
8: 2 who thinks he *k* something does
2Ti 2: 19 The Lord *k* those who are his," and
Jas 4: 17 who *k* the good he ought to do
1Jn 4: 6 and whoever *k* God listens to us;
4: 7 born of God and *k* God.

KOHATHITE (KOHATHITES)

Nu 3: 29 The *K* clans were to camp

KORAH

Levite who led rebellion against Moses and Aaron (Nu 16; Jude 11).

KORAZIN

Mt 11: 21 "Woe to you, *K*! Woe to you,

KOHATHITES (KOHATHITE)

Nu 3: 28 The *K* were responsible
4: 15 *K* are to carry those things that are

LABAN

Brother of Rebekah (Ge 24:29), father of Rachel and Leah (Ge 29:16). Received Abraham's servant (Ge 24:29-51). Provided daughters as wives for Jacob in exchange for Jacob's service (Ge 29:1-30). Provided flocks for Jacob's service (Ge 30:25-43). After Jacob's departure, pursued and covenanted with him (Ge 31).

LABOUR (LABOURING)

Ex 1: 11 to oppress them with forced *l*,
20: 9 Six days you shall *l* and do all your
Dt 5: 13 Six days you shall *l* and do all your
Ps 127: 1 its builders *l* in vain.
128: 2 You will eat the fruit of your *l*;
Pr 12: 24 but laziness ends in slave *l*.
Isa 54: 1 you who were never in *l*;
55: 2 and your *l* on what does not satisfy
Mt 6: 28 They do not *l* or spin.
Jn 4: 38 have reaped the benefits of their *l*."
1Co 3: 8 rewarded according to his own *l*.
15: 58 because you know that your *l*
Gal 4: 27 you who have no *l* pains;
Php 2: 16 day of Christ that I did not run or *l*
Rev 14: 13 "they will rest from their *l*,

LABOURING* (LABOUR)

2Th 3: 8 *l* and toiling so that we would not

LACK (LACKED LACKING LACKS)

Ps 34: 9 for those who fear him *l* nothing.
Pr 5: 23 He will die for *l* of discipline,
10: 21 but fools die for *l* of judgment.
11: 14 For *l* of guidance a nation falls,
15: 22 Plans fail for *l* of counsel,
28: 27 to the poor will *l* nothing,
Mk 6: 6 he was amazed at their *l* of faith.
16: 14 he rebuked them for their *l* of faith
Ro 3: 3 Will their *l* of faith nullify God's
1Co 1: 7 you do not *l* any spiritual gift
7: 5 because of your *l* of self-control.
Col 2: 23 *l* any value in restraining sensual

LACKED (LACK)

Dt 2: 7 and you have not *l* anything.
Ne 9: 21 them in the desert; they *l* nothing,
1Co 12: 24 honour to the parts that *l* it,

LACKING (LACK)

Pr 17: 18 A man *l* in judgment strikes hands
Ro 12: 11 Never be *l* in zeal, but keep your
Jas 1: 4 and complete, not *l* anything.

LACKS (LACK)

Pr 6: 32 who commits adultery *l* judgment;
11: 12 man who *l* judgment derides his
12: 11 he who chases fantasies *l* judgment
15: 21 delights a man who *l* judgment,
24: 30 of the man who *l* judgment;
25: 28 is a man who *l* self-control.
28: 16 A tyrannical ruler *l* judgment,
31: 11 and *l* nothing of value.
Eze 34: 8 because my flock *l* a shepherd
Jas 1: 5 any of you *l* wisdom, he should ask

LAID (LAY)

Isa 53: 6 and the LORD has *l* on him
Mk 6: 29 took his body and *l* it in a tomb.
Lk 6: 48 and *l* the foundation on rock.
Ac 6: 6 and *l* their hands on them.
1Co 3: 11 other than the one already *l*,
1Ti 4: 14 body of elders *l* their hands on you.
1Jn 3: 16 Jesus Christ *l* down his life for us.

LAKE

Mt 8: 24 a furious storm came up on the *l*,
14: 25 out to them, walking on the *l*.
Mk 4: 1 into a boat and sat in it out on the *l*,
Lk 8: 33 down the steep bank into the *l*
Jn 6: 25 him on the other side of the *l*,
Rev 19: 20 into the fiery *l* of burning sulphur.
20: 14 The *l* of fire is the second death.

LAMB (LAMB'S LAMBS)

Ge 22: 8 "God himself will provide the *l*
Ex 12: 21 and slaughter the Passover *l*.
Nu 9: 11 are to eat the *l*, together
2Sa 12: 4 he took the ewe *l* that belonged
Isa 11: 6 The wolf will live with the *l*,
53: 7 he was led like a *l* to the slaughter,
Mk 14: 12 to sacrifice the Passover *l*,
Jn 1: 29 *L* of God, who takes away the sin
Ac 8: 32 as a *l* before the shearer is silent,
1Co 5: 7 our Passover *l*, has been sacrificed.
1Pe 1: 19 a *l* without blemish or defect.
Rev 5: 6 Then I saw a *L*, looking
5: 12 "Worthy is the *L*, who was slain,
7: 14 white in the blood of the *L*.
14: 4 They follow the *L* wherever he
15: 3 of God and the song of the *L*:
17: 14 but the *L* will overcome them
19: 9 to the wedding supper of the *L*!' "
21: 23 gives it light, and the *L* is its lamp.

LAMB'S (LAMB)

Rev 21: 27 written in the *L* book of life.

LAMBS (LAMB)

Lk 10: 3 I am sending you out like *l*
Jn 21: 15 Jesus said, "Feed my *l*."

LAME

Isa 33: 23 even the *l* will carry off plunder.
35: 6 Then will the *l* leap like a deer,
Mt 11: 5 The blind receive sight, the *l* walk,
15: 31 the *l* walking and the blind seeing.
Lk 14: 21 the crippled, the blind and the *l*.'

LAMENT

2Sa 1: 17 took up this *l* concerning Saul
Eze 19: 1 Take up a *l* concerning the princes

LAMP (LAMPS LAMPSTAND LAMPSTANDS)

2Sa 22: 29 You are my *l*, O LORD;
Ps 18: 28 You, O LORD, keep my *l* burning;
119: 105 Your word is a *l* to my feet
132: 17 and set up a *l* for my anointed one.
Pr 6: 23 For these commands are a *l*,
20: 27 *l* of the LORD searches the spirit
31: 18 and her *l* does not go out at night.
Mt 6: 22 "The eye is the *l* of the body.
Lk 8: 16 "No-one lights a *l* and hides it
Rev 21: 23 gives it light, and the Lamb is its *l*.
22: 5 They will not need the light of a *l*

LAMPS (LAMP)
Mt 25: 1 be like ten virgins who took their *l*
Lk 12: 35 for service and keep your *l* burning,
Rev 4: 5 the throne, seven *l* were blazing.

LAMPSTAND (LAMP)
Ex 25: 31 "Make a *l* of pure gold
Zec 4: 2 "I see a solid gold *l* with a bowl
4: 11 on the right and the left of the *l*?"
Heb 9: 2 In its first room were the *l*,
Rev 2: 5 and remove your *l* from its place.

LAMPSTANDS (LAMP)
2Ch 4: 7 He made ten gold *l* according
Rev 1: 12 when I turned I saw seven golden *l*,
1: 20 and of the seven golden *l* is this:

LAND (LANDS)
Ge 1: 10 God called the dry ground "*l*",
1: 11 "Let the *l* produce vegetation:
1: 24 "Let the *l* produce living creatures
12: 1 and go to the *l* I will show you.
12: 7 To your offspring I will give this *l*."
13: 15 All the *l* that you see I will give
15: 18 "To your descendants I give this *l*,
50: 24 out of this *l* to the *l* he promised
Ex 3: 8 a *l* flowing with milk and honey—
6: 8 to the *l* I swore with uplifted hand
33: 3 Go up to the *l* flowing with milk
Lev 25: 23 *l* must not be sold permanently,
Nu 14: 8 us into that *l*, a *l* flowing with milk
35: 33 Do not pollute the *l* where you are.
Dt 1: 8 See, I have given you this *l*.
8: 7 God is bringing you into a good *l*—
11: 10 The *l* you are entering to take
28: 21 you from the *l* you are entering
29: 19 will bring disaster on the watered *l*
34: 1 LORD showed him the whole *l*—
Jos 13: 2 "This is the *l* that remains:
14: 4 Levites received no share of the *l*
14: 9 *l* on which your feet have walked
2Sa 21: 14 answered prayer on behalf of the *l*.
2Ki 17: 5 of Assyria invaded the entire *l*,
24: 1 king of Babylon invaded the *l*,
25: 21 into captivity, away from her *l*.
2Ch 7: 14 their sin and will heal their *l*.
7: 20 then I will uproot Israel from my *l*,
36: 21 The *l* enjoyed its Sabbath rests;
Ezr 9: 11 entering to possess is a *l* polluted
Ne 9: 36 in the *l* you gave our forefathers
Ps 37: 11 But the meek will inherit the *l*
37: 29 the righteous will inherit the *l*
136: 21 and gave their *l* as an inheritance,
142: 5 my portion in the *l* of the living."
Pr 2: 21 For the upright will live in the *l*,
12: 11 who works his *l* will have abundant
Isa 6: 13 though a tenth remains in the *l*,
53: 8 cut off from the *l* of the living;
Jer 2: 7 But you came and defiled my *l*
Eze 36: 24 and bring you back into your own *l*.

LANDS (LAND)
Ps 111: 6 giving them the *l* of other nations.
Eze 20: 6 honey, the most beautiful of all *l*.
Zec 10: 9 in distant *l* they will remember me.

LANGUAGE (LANGUAGES)
Ge 11: 1 Now the whole world had one *l*
11: 9 there the LORD confused the *l*
Ps 19: 3 There is no speech or *l*
Jn 8: 44 When he lies, he speaks his native *l*
Ac 2: 6 heard them speaking in his own *l*.
Col 3: 8 slander, and filthy *l* from your lips.
Rev 5: 9 from every tribe and *l* and people
7: 9 every nation, tribe, people and *l*,
14: 6 to every nation, tribe, *l* and people.

LANGUAGES (LANGUAGE)
Zec 8: 23 "In those days ten men from all *l*

LAODICEA
Rev 3: 14 the angel of the church in *L* write:

LAP
Jdg 7: 5 "Separate those who *l* the water

LASHES
Pr 17: 10 more than a hundred *l* a fool.
2Co 11: 24 from the Jews the forty *l* minus one

LAST [1] (LATTER)
2Sa 23: 1 These are the *l* words of David:
Isa 2: 2 and Jerusalem: In the *l* days
41: 4 and with the *l*—I am he."
44: 6 I am the first and I am the *l*;
48: 12 I am the first and I am the *l*.
Hos 3: 5 and to his blessings in the *l* days.
Mic 4: 1 In the *l* days
Mt 19: 30 But many who are first will be *l*,
20: 8 beginning with the *l* ones hired
21: 37 *L* of all, he sent his son to them.
Mk 9: 35 must be the very *l*, and the servant
10: 31 are first will be *l*, and the *l* first."
15: 37 a loud cry, Jesus breathed his *l*.
Jn 6: 40 and I will raise him up at the *l* day."
Ac 2: 17 " 'In the *l* days, God says,
Ro 1: 17 is by faith from first to *l*,
1Co 15: 26 *l* enemy to be destroyed is death.
15: 52 of an eye, at the *l* trumpet.
2Ti 3: 1 will be terrible times in the *l* days.
2Pe 3: 3 in the *l* days scoffers will come,
Jude : 18 "In the *l* times there will be
Rev 1: 17 I am the First and the *L*.
22: 13 the First and the *L*, the Beginning

LAST [2] (LASTING LASTS)
Jn 15: 16 and bear fruit—fruit that will *l*.

LASTING (LAST [2])
Ex 12: 14 to the LORD—a *l* ordinance.
Lev 24: 8 of the Israelites, as a *l* covenant.
Nu 25: 13 have a covenant of a *l* priesthood,
Heb 10: 34 had better and *l* possessions.

LASTS (LAST [2])
Ps 30: 5 For his anger *l* only a moment,
2Co 3: 11 greater is the glory of that which *l*!

LATTER (LAST [1])
Job 42: 12 The LORD blessed the *l* part
Mt 23: 23 You should have practised the *l*,
Php 1: 16 *l* do so in love, knowing that I am

LAUGH (LAUGHED LAUGHS LAUGHTER)
Ps 59: 8 But you, O LORD, *l* at them;
Pr 31: 25 she can *l* at the days to come.
Ecc 3: 4 a time to weep and a time to *l*,
Lk 6: 21 for you will *l*.
6: 25 Woe to you who *l* now,

LAUGHED (LAUGH)
Ge 17: 17 Abraham fell face down; he *l*
18: 12 So Sarah *l* to herself as she thought,

LAUGHS (LAUGH)
Ps 2: 4 The One enthroned in heaven *l*;
37: 13 but the Lord *l* at the wicked,

LAUGHTER (LAUGH)
Ge 21: 6 Sarah said, "God has brought me *l*,
Ps 126: 2 Our mouths were filled with *l*,
Pr 14: 13 Even in *l* the heart may ache,
Jas 4: 9 Change your *l* to mourning

LAVISHED
Eph 1: 8 of God's grace that he *l* on us
1Jn 3: 1 great is the love the Father has *l*

LAW (LAWFUL LAWGIVER LAWS)
Lev 24: 22 are to have the same *l* for the alien
Nu 6: 13 " 'Now this is the *l* for the Nazirite
Dt 1: 5 Moses began to expound this *l*,
6: 25 to obey all this *l* before the LORD
27: 26 of this *l* by carrying them out."
31: 11 you shall read this *l* before them
Dt 31: 26 "Take this Book of the *L*
Jos 1: 7 to obey all the *l* my servant Moses
1: 8 of the *L* depart from your mouth;
22: 5 and the *l* that Moses the servant
2Ki 22: 8 of the *L* in the temple of the LORD
2Ch 6: 16 walk before me according to my *l*,
17: 9 the Book of the *L* of the LORD;
34: 14 of the *L* of the LORD that had
Ezr 7: 6 versed in the *L* of Moses,
Ne 8: 2 Ezra the priest brought the *L*
8: 8 from the Book of the *L* of God,
Ps 1: 2 and on his *l* he meditates day
19: 7 The *l* of the LORD is perfect,
37: 31 The *l* of his God is in his heart;
40: 8 your *l* is within my heart."
119: 18 wonderful things in your *l*.
119: 70 but I delight in your *l*.
119: 72 *l* from your mouth is more precious
119: 77 for your *l* is my delight.
119: 97 Oh, how I love your *l*!
119: 163 but I love your *l*.
119: 165 peace have they who love your *l*,
Pr 28: 9 If anyone turns a deaf ear to the *l*,
29: 18 but blessed is he who keeps the *l*.
Isa 2: 3 The *l* will go out from Zion,
8: 20 To the *l* and to the testimony!
42: 21 to make his *l* great and glorious.
Jer 2: 8 deal with the *l* did not know me;
8: 8 for we have the *l* of the LORD,"
31: 33 "I will put my *l* in their minds
Mic 4: 2 The *l* will go out from Zion,
Hab 1: 7 they are a *l* to themselves
Zec 7: 12 as flint and would not listen to the *l*
Mt 5: 17 that I have come to abolish the *L*
7: 12 sums up the *L* and the Prophets.
22: 36 greatest commandment in the *L*?"
22: 40 All the *L* and the Prophets hang
23: 23 more important matters of the *l*—
Lk 11: 52 "Woe to you experts in the *l*,
16: 17 stroke of a pen to drop out of the *L*.
24: 44 me in the *L* of Moses,
Jn 1: 17 For the *l* was given through Moses;
Ac 13: 39 justified from by the *l* of Moses.
Ro 2: 12 All who sin apart from the *l* will
2: 15 of the *l* are written on their hearts,
2: 20 you have in the *l* the embodiment
2: 25 value if you observe the *l*,
3: 19 we know that whatever the *l* says,
3: 20 in his sight by observing the *l*;
3: 21 apart from *l*, has been made known
3: 28 by faith apart from observing the *l*.
3: 31 Not at all! Rather, we uphold the *l*.
4: 13 It was not through *l* that Abraham
4: 15 worthless, because *l* brings wrath.
4: 16 not only to those who are of the *l*
5: 13 for before the *l* was given,
5: 20 *l* was added so that the trespass
6: 14 because you are not under *l*,
6: 15 we are not under *l* but under grace?
7: 1 that the *l* has authority
7: 4 also died to the *l* through the body
7: 5 aroused by the *l* were at work
7: 6 released from the *l* so that we serve
7: 7 then? Is the *l* sin? Certainly not!
7: 8 For apart from *l*, sin is dead.
7: 12 *l* is holy, and the commandment is
7: 14 We know that the *l* is spiritual;
7: 22 my inner being I delight in God's *l*;
7: 25 in my mind am a slave to God's *l*,
8: 2 because through Christ Jesus the *l*
8: 3 For what the *l* was powerless to do
8: 4 of the *l* might be fully met in us,
8: 7 It does not submit to God's *l*,
9: 4 covenants, the receiving of the *l*,
9: 31 who pursued a *l* of righteousness,
10: 4 Christ is the end of the *l*
13: 8 his fellow-man has fulfilled the *l*.
13: 10 love is the fulfilment of the *l*.
1Co 6: 6 goes to *l* against another—
9: 9 For it is written in the *L* of Moses:
9: 20 the *l* I became like one under the *l*
9: 21 I became like one not having the *l*
15: 56 and the power of sin is the *l*.

Gal 2: 16 justified by observing the *l*,
2: 19 For through the *l* I died to the *l*
3: 2 the Spirit by observing the *l*,
3: 5 you because you observe the *l*,
3: 10 on observing the *l* are under a curse
3: 11 justified before God by the *l*,
3: 13 curse of the *l* by becoming a curse
3: 17 The *l*, introduced 430 years later,
3: 19 then, was the purpose of the *l*?
3: 21 Is the *l*, therefore, opposed
3: 23 we were held prisoners by the *l*,
3: 24 So the *l* was put in charge to lead us
4: 21 you who want to be under the *l*,
5: 3 obligated to obey the whole *l*.
5: 4 justified by *l* have been alienated
5: 14 The entire *l* is summed up
5: 18 by the Spirit, you are not under *l*.
6: 2 and in this way you will fulfil the *l*
Eph 2: 15 flesh the *l* with its commandments
Php 3: 9 of my own that comes from the *l*,
1Ti 1: 8 We know that the *l* is good
Heb 7: 12 there must also be a change of the *l*.
7: 19 (for the *l* made nothing perfect),
10: 1 The *l* is only a shadow
Jas 1: 25 intently into the perfect *l* that gives
2: 8 If you really keep the royal *l* found
2: 10 For whoever keeps the whole *l*
4: 11 or judges him speaks against the *l*
1Jn 3: 4 Everyone who sins breaks the *l*;

LAWFUL (LAW)
Mt 12: 12 Therefore it is *l* to do good

LAWGIVER* (LAW)
Isa 33: 22 the LORD is our *l*,
Jas 4: 12 There is only one *L* and Judge,

LAWLESS (LAWLESSNESS)
2Th 2: 8 And then the *l* one will be revealed
Heb 10: 17 "Their sins and *l* acts

LAWLESSNESS* (LAWLESS)
2Th 2: 3 and the man of *l* is revealed,
2: 7 power of *l* is already at work;
1Jn 3: 4 sins breaks the law; in fact, sin is *l*.

LAWS (LAW)
Ex 21: 1 "These are the *l* you are to set
Lev 25: 18 and be careful to obey my *l*,
Dt 4: 1 and *l* I am about to teach you.
30: 16 decrees and *l*; then you will live
Ps 119: 30 I have set my heart on your *l*.
119: 43 for I have put my hope in your *l*.
119: 120 I stand in awe of your *l*.
119: 164 for your righteous *l*.
119: 175 and may your *l* sustain me.
Eze 36: 27 and be careful to keep my *l*.
Heb 8: 10 I will put my *l* in their minds
10: 16 I will put my *l* in their hearts,

LAWSUITS
Hos 10: 4 therefore *l* spring up
1Co 6: 7 The very fact that you have *l*

LAY (LAID LAYING LAYS)
Ex 29: 10 and his sons shall *l* their hands
Lev 1: 4 He is to *l* his hand on the head
4: 15 the community are to *l* their hands
Nu 8: 10 the Israelites are to *l* their hands
27: 18 whom is the spirit, and *l* your hand
1Sa 26: 9 Who can *l* a hand on the LORD's
Job 1: 12 on the man himself do not *l* a finger
22: 22 and *l* up his words in your heart.
Ecc 10: 4 calmness can *l* great errors to rest.
Isa 28: 16 "See, I *l* a stone in Zion,
Mt 8: 20 of Man has nowhere to *l* his head."
28: 6 Come and see the place where he *l*.
Mk 6: 5 *l* his hands on a few sick people
Lk 9: 58 of Man has nowhere to *l* his head."
Jn 10: 15 and I *l* down my life for the sheep.
10: 18 but I *l* it down of my own accord.
15: 13 that one *l* down his life
Ac 8: 19 on whom I *l* my hands may receive
Ro 9: 33 I *l* in Zion a stone that causes men
1Co 3: 11 no-one can *l* any foundation other
1Pe 2: 6 "See, I *l* a stone in Zion,
1Jn 3: 16 And we ought to *l* down our lives
Rev 4: 10 They *l* their crowns

LAYING (LAY)
Lk 4: 40 and *l* his hands on each one,
Ac 8: 18 at the *l* on of the apostles' hands,
1Ti 5: 22 Do not be hasty in the *l* on of hands
2Ti 1: 6 is in you through the *l*
Heb 6: 1 not *l* again the foundation
6: 2 instruction about baptisms, the *l*

LAYS (LAY)
Jn 10: 11 The good shepherd *l* down his life

LAZARUS
1. Poor man in Jesus' parable (Lk 16:19-31).
2. Brother of Mary and Martha whom Jesus raised from the dead (Jn 11:1-12:19).

LAZINESS* (LAZY)
Pr 12: 24 but *l* ends in slave labour.
19: 15 *L* brings on deep sleep,

LAZY* (LAZINESS)
Ex 5: 8 They are *l*; that is why they are
5: 17 "*L*, that's what you are—*l*!
Pr 10: 4 *L* hands make a man poor,
12: 27 The *l* man does not roast his game,
26: 15 he is too *l* to bring it back
Ecc 10: 18 If a man is *l*, the rafters sag;
Mt 25: 26 replied, 'You wicked, *l* servant!
Tit 1: 12 liars, evil brutes, *l* gluttons."
Heb 6: 12 We do not want you to become *l*,

LEAD (LEADER LEADERS LEADERSHIP LEADS LED)
Ex 15: 13 "In your unfailing love you will *l*
Nu 14: 8 with us, he will *l* us into that land,
Dt 31: 2 and I am no longer able to *l* you.
Jos 1: 6 because you will *l* these people
1Sa 8: 5 now appoint a king to *l* us,
2Ch 1: 10 knowledge, that I may *l* this people
Ps 27: 11 *l* me in a straight path
61: 2 *l* me to the rock that is higher
139: 24 and *l* me in the way everlasting.
143: 10 *l* me on level ground.
Pr 4: 11 and *l* you along straight paths.
Ecc 5: 6 Do not let your mouth *l* you
Isa 11: 6 and a little child will *l* them.
49: 10 and *l* them beside springs of water.
Da 12: 3 those who *l* many to righteousness,
Mt 6: 13 And *l* us not into temptation,
Lk 11: 4 And *l* us not into temptation.'"
Gal 3: 24 So the law was put in charge to *l* us
1Th 4: 11 it your ambition to *l* a quiet life,
1Jn 3: 7 do not let anyone *l* you astray.
Rev 7: 17 he will *l* them to springs

LEADER (LEAD)
1Sa 7: 6 Samuel was *l* of Israel at Mizpah.
10: 1 Has not the LORD anointed you *l*
12: 2 I have been your *l* from my youth
13: 14 and appointed him *l* of his people,

LEADERS (LEAD)
Heb 13: 7 Remember your *l*, who spoke
13: 17 Obey your *l* and submit

LEADERSHIP* (LEAD)
Nu 33: 1 by divisions under the *l* of Moses
Ps 109: 8 may another take his place of *l*.
Ac 1: 20 "'May another take his place of *l*.'
Ro 12: 8 if it is *l*, let him govern diligently;

LEADS (LEAD)
Dt 27: 18 is the man who *l* the blind astray
Ps 23: 2 he *l* me beside quiet waters,
37: 8 do not fret—it *l* only to evil.
68: 6 he *l* forth the prisoners
Pr 2: 18 For her house *l* down to death
10: 17 ignores correction *l* others astray.
14: 23 but mere talk *l* only to poverty.
16: 25 but in the end it *l* to death.
19: 23 The fear of the LORD *l* to life:
20: 7 righteous man *l* a blameless life;
21: 5 as surely as haste *l* to poverty.
Isa 40: 11 he gently *l* those that have young.
Mt 7: 13 and broad is the road that *l*
12: 20 till he *l* justice to victory.
15: 14 If a blind man *l* a blind man,
Jn 10: 3 sheep by name and *l* them out.
Ro 6: 16 which *l* to death, or to obedience,
6: 22 the benefit you reap *l* to holiness,
14: 19 effort to do what *l* to peace
2Co 2: 14 always *l* us in triumphal procession
7: 10 sorrow brings repentance that *l*
Tit 1: 1 of the truth that *l* to godliness—

LEAH
Wife of Jacob (Ge 29:16-30); bore six sons and one daughter (Ge 29:31-30:21; 34:1; 35:23).

LEAN (LEANED)
Pr 3: 5 *l* not on your own understanding;

LEANED (LEAN)
Ge 47: 31 as he *l* on the top of his staff.
Jn 21: 20 (This was the one who had *l* back
Heb 11: 21 as he *l* on the top of his staff.

LEAP (LEAPED LEAPS)
Isa 35: 6 Then will the lame *l* like a deer,
Mal 4: 2 *l* like calves released from the stall.
Lk 6: 23 "Rejoice in that day and *l* for joy,

LEAPED (LEAP)
Lk 1: 41 heard Mary's greeting, the baby *l*

LEAPS (LEAP)
Ps 28: 7 My heart *l* for joy

LEARN (LEARNED LEARNING LEARNS)
Dt 4: 10 so that they may *l* to revere me
5: 1 *L* them and be sure to follow them.
31: 12 and *l* to fear the LORD your God
Ps 119: 7 as I *l* your righteous laws.
Isa 1: 17 *l* to do right!
26: 9 of the world *l* righteousness.
Mt 11: 29 yoke upon you and *l* from me,
Jn 14: 31 world must *l* that I love the Father
1Th 4: 4 that each of you should *l*
1Ti 2: 11 A woman should *l* in quietness
5: 4 these should *l* first of all

LEARNED (LEARN)
Ps 119: 152 Long ago I *l* from your statutes
Mt 11: 25 things from the wise and *l*,
Php 4: 9 Whatever you have *l* or received
4: 11 for I have *l* to be content whatever
2Ti 3: 14 continue in what you have *l*
Heb 5: 8 he *l* obedience from what he

LEARNING (LEARN)
Pr 1: 5 let the wise listen and add to their *l*,
9: 9 man and he will add to his *l*.
Isa 44: 25 who overthrows the *l* of the wise
Jn 7: 15 "How did this man get such *l*
2Ti 3: 7 always *l* but never able

LEARNS (LEARN)
Jn 6: 45 and *l* from him comes to me.

LEATHER
2Ki 1: 8 and a *l* belt round his waist."
Mt 3: 4 and he had a *l* belt round his waist

LEAVES
Ge 3: 7 so they sewed fig *l* together
Eze 47: 12 for food and their *l* for healing."
Rev 22: 2 the *l* of the tree are for the healing

LEBANON
Dt 11: 24 from the desert to *L*,
1Ki 4: 33 from the cedar of *L*

LED (LEAD)
Ex 3: 1 and he *l* the flock to the far side
Dt 8: 2 the LORD your God *l* you all
1Ki 11: 3 and his wives *l* him astray.
2Ch 26: 16 his pride *l* to his downfall.
Ne 13: 26 he was *l* into sin by foreign women.
Ps 68: 18 you *l* captives in your train;
78: 52 he *l* them like sheep
Pr 7: 21 persuasive words she *l* him astray;
20: 1 whoever is *l* astray
Isa 53: 7 he was *l* like a lamb to the slaughter
Jer 11: 19 I had been like a gentle lamb *l*
Am 2: 10 and I *l* you forty years in the desert
Mt 4: 1 Then Jesus was *l* by the Spirit
27: 31 they *l* him away to crucify him.
Lk 4: 1 was *l* by the Spirit in the desert,
Ac 8: 32 "He was *l* like a sheep
Ro 8: 14 those who are *l* by the Spirit
2Co 7: 9 your sorrow *l* you to repentance.
Gal 5: 18 But if you are *l* by the Spirit,
Eph 4: 8 he *l* captives in his train

LEEKS*
Nu 11: 5 melons, *l*, onions and garlic.

LEFT
Dt 28: 14 or to the *l*, following other gods
Jos 1: 7 turn from it to the right or to the *l*,
23: 6 aside to the right or to the *l*.
2Ki 22: 2 aside to the right or to the *l*.
Pr 4: 27 Do not swerve to the right or the *l*;
Isa 30: 21 turn to the right or to the *l*,
Mt 6: 3 do not let your *l* hand know what
25: 33 on his right and the goats on his *l*.

LEGALISTIC*
Php 3: 6 as for *l* righteousness, faultless.

LEGION
Mk 5: 9 "My name is *L*," he replied,

LEND (LENDER LENDS MONEY-LENDER)
Lev 25: 37 You must not *l* him money
Dt 15: 8 freely *l* him whatever he needs.
Ps 37: 26 are always generous and *l* freely;
Eze 18: 8 He does not *l* at usury
Lk 6: 34 if you *l* to those from whom you

LENDER (LEND)
Pr 22: 7 and the borrower is servant to the *l*.
Isa 24: 2 for borrower as for *l*,

LENDS (LEND)
Ps 15: 5 who *l* his money without usury
112: 5 to him who is generous and *l* freely,
Pr 19: 17 to the poor *l* to the LORD,

LENGTH (LONG [1])
Ps 90: 10 The *l* of our days is seventy years—
Pr 10: 27 The fear of the LORD adds *l* to life

LENGTHY* (LONG [1])
Mk 12: 40 and for a show make *l* prayers.
Lk 20: 47 and for a show make *l* prayers.

LEOPARD
Isa 11: 6 the *l* will lie down with the goat,
Da 7: 6 beast, one that looked like a *l*.
Rev 13: 2 The beast I saw resembled a *l*,

LEPROSY (LEPROUS)
Nu 12: 10 towards her and saw that she had *l*;
2Ki 5: 1 was a valiant soldier, but he had *l*.
7: 3 men with *l* at the entrance
2Ch 26: 21 King Uzziah had *l*
Mt 11: 5 those who have *l* are cured,
Lk 17: 12 ten men who had *l* met him.

LEPROUS (LEPROSY)
Ex 4: 6 and when he took it out, it was *l*,

LETTER (LETTERS)
Mt 5: 18 not the smallest *l*, not the least
2Co 3: 2 You yourselves are our *l*, written
3: 6 for the *l* kills, but the Spirit gives
2Th 3: 14 not obey our instruction in this *l*,

LETTERS (LETTER)
2Co 3: 7 which was engraved in *l* on stone,
10: 10 "His *l* are weighty and forceful,
2Pe 3: 16 His *l* contain some things that are

LEVEL
Ps 143: 10 lead me on *l* ground.
Pr 4: 26 Make *l* paths for your feet
Isa 26: 7 The path of the righteous is *l*;
40: 4 the rough ground shall become *l*,
Jer 31: 9 on a *l* path where they will not
Heb 12: 13 "Make *l* paths for your feet,"

LEVI (LEVITE LEVITES LEVITICAL)
1. Son of Jacob by Leah (Ge 29:34; 46:11; 1Ch 2:1). With Simeon avenged rape of Dinah (Ge 34). Tribe of blessed (Ge 49:5-7; Dt 33:8-11), chosen as priests (Nu 3-4), numbered (Nu 3:39; 26:62), allotted cities, but not land (Nu 18; 35; Dt 10:9; Jos 13:14; 21), land (Eze 48:8-22), 12,000 from (Rev 7:7).
2. See MATTHEW.

LEVIATHAN
Job 41: 1 pull in the *l* with a fish-hook
Ps 74: 14 you who crushed the heads of *L*
Isa 27: 1 *L* the gliding serpent,

LEVITE (LEVI)
Dt 26: 12 you shall give it to the *L*, the alien,
Jdg 19: 1 a *L* who lived in a remote area

LEVITES (LEVI)
Nu 1: 53 The *L* are to be responsible
3: 12 "I have taken the *L*
8: 6 "Take the *L* from among the other
18: 21 I give to the *L* all the tithes in Israel
35: 7 must give the *L* forty-eight towns,
2Ch 31: 2 assigned the priests and *L*
Mal 3: 3 he will purify the *L* and refine them

LEVITICAL (LEVI)
Heb 7: 11 attained through the *L* priesthood

LEWDNESS
Mk 7: 22 malice, deceit, *l*, envy, slander,

LIAR* (LIE [2])
Dt 19: 18 and if the witness proves to be a *l*,
Job 34: 6 I am considered a *l*;
Pr 17: 4 *l* pays attention to a malicious
19: 22 better to be poor than a *l*.
30: 6 will rebuke you and prove you a *l*.
Mic 2: 11 If a *l* and deceiver comes and says,
Jn 8: 44 for he is a *l* and the father of lies.
8: 55 I did not, I would be a *l* like you,
Ro 3: 4 Let God be true, and every man a *l*.
1Jn 1: 10 we make him out to be a *l*
2: 4 not do what he commands is a *l*,
2: 22 Who is the *l*? It is the man who
4: 20 yet hates his brother, he is a *l*.
5: 10 God had made him out to be a *l*,

LIARS* (LIE [2])
Ps 63: 11 the mouths of *l* will be silenced.
116: 11 "All men are *l*."
Isa 57: 4 the offspring of *l*?
Mic 6: 12 her people are *l*
1Ti 1: 10 for slave traders and *l* and perjurers
4: 2 come through hypocritical *l*,
Tit 1: 12 "Cretans are always *l*, evil brutes,
Rev 3: 9 though they are not, but are *l*—
21: 8 magic arts, the idolaters and all *l*—

LIBERATED*
Ro 8: 21 that the creation itself will be *l*

LICENCE
Jude : 4 of our God into a *l* for immorality

LICK
Ps 72: 9 and his enemies will *l* the dust.
Isa 49: 23 they will *l* the dust at your feet.
Mic 7: 17 They will *l* dust like a snake,

LIE [1]
Lev 18: 22 " 'Do not *l* with a man
Dt 6: 7 when you *l* down and when you get
25: 2 the judge shall make him *l* down
Ps 4: 8 I will *l* down and sleep in peace,
23: 2 me *l* down in green pastures,
Pr 3: 24 when you *l* down, you will not be
Isa 11: 6 leopard will *l* down with the goat,
Eze 34: 14 they will *l* down in good grazing

LIE [2] (LIAR LIARS LIED LIES LYING)
Lev 19: 11 " 'do not *l*.
Nu 23: 19 God is not a man, that he should *l*,
1Sa 15: 29 the Glory of Israel does not *l*
Ps 89: 35 and I will not *l* to David
Isa 28: 15 for we have made a *l* our refuge
Jer 9: 5 They have taught their tongues to *l*
23: 14 They commit adultery and live a *l*.
Eze 13: 6 are false and their divinations a *l*
Ro 1: 25 exchanged the truth of God for a *l*,
Col 3: 9 Do not *l* to each other
2Th 2: 11 so that they will believe the *l*
Tit 1: 2 which God, who does not *l*,
Heb 6: 18 it is impossible for God to *l*,
1Jn 2: 21 because no *l* comes from the truth.
Rev 14: 5 No *l* was found in their mouths;

LIED* (LIE [2])
Ac 5: 4 You have not *l* to men but to God."

LIES* (LIE [2])
Lev 6: 3 finds lost property and *l* about it,
Ps 5: 6 You destroy those who tell *l*;
10: 7 His mouth is full of curses and *l*
12: 2 Everyone *l* to his neighbour;
34: 13 and your lips from speaking *l*.
58: 3 they are wayward and speak *l*.
144: 8 whose mouths are full of *l*,
Pr 6: 19 a false witness who pours out *l*
12: 17 but a false witness tells *l*.
19: 5 he who pours out *l* will not go free.
19: 9 and he who pours out *l* will perish.
29: 12 If a ruler listens to *l*,
30: 8 Keep falsehood and *l* far from me;
Isa 59: 3 Your lips have spoken *l*,
Jer 5: 31 The prophets prophesy *l*,
9: 3 like a bow, to shoot *l*;
14: 14 "The prophets are prophesying *l*
Hos 11: 12 Ephraim has surrounded me with *l*,
Jn 8: 44 for he is a liar and the father of *l*.

LIFE (LIVE)
Ge 1: 30 everything that has the breath of *l*
2: 7 into his nostrils the breath of *l*,
2: 9 of the garden were the tree of *l*
6: 17 to destroy all *l* under the heavens,
9: 5 for the *l* of his fellow-man.
9: 11 Never again will all *l* be cut
Ex 21: 6 Then he will be his servant for *l*.
21: 23 you are to take *l* for *l*, eye for eye,
23: 26 I will give you a full *l* span.
Lev 17: 14 the *l* of every creature is its blood.
24: 17 " 'If anyone takes the *l*
24: 18 must make restitution—*l* for *l*.
Nu 35: 31 a ransom for the *l* of a murderer,
Dt 4: 42 one of these cities and save his *l*.
12: 23 because the blood is the *l*,
19: 21 Show no pity: *l* for *l*, eye for eye,
30: 15 I set before you today *l*
30: 19 Now choose *l*, so that you
30: 20 For the LORD is your *l*,
32: 39 I put to death and I bring to *l*,
32: 47 words for you—they are your *l*.

1Sa 19: 5 He took his *l* in his hands
Job 2: 6 hands; but you must spare his *l*."
33: 4 of the Almighty gives me *l*.
33: 30 that the light of *l* may shine on him.
Ps 16: 11 known to me the path of *l*;
17: 14 this world whose reward is in this *l*.
23: 6 all the days of my *l*,
27: 1 LORD is the stronghold of my *l*—
34: 12 Whoever of you loves *l*
36: 9 For with you is the fountain of *l*;
39: 4 let me know how fleeting is my *l*.
41: 2 will protect him and preserve his *l*;
49: 7 No man can redeem the *l*
49: 8 the ransom for a *l* is costly,
49: 15 God will redeem my *l*
63: 3 Because your love is better than *l*,
69: 28 they be blotted out of the book of *l*
91: 16 With long *l* will I satisfy him
104: 33 I will sing to the LORD all my *l*;
119: 25 preserve my *l* according to your word
Pr 1: 3 a disciplined and prudent *l*,
3: 2 will prolong your *l* many years
3: 18 of *l* to those who embrace her;
4: 23 for it is the wellspring of *l*.
6: 23 are the way to *l*,
6: 26 adulteress preys upon your very *l*.
7: 23 little knowing it will cost him his *l*.
8: 35 For whoever finds me finds *l*
10: 11 of the righteous is a fountain of *l*,
10: 27 of the LORD adds length to *l*,
11: 30 of the righteous is a tree of *l*,
13: 3 He who guards his lips guards his *l*,
13: 12 but a longing fulfilled is a tree of *l*.
13: 14 of the wise is a fountain of *l*,
14: 27 of the LORD is a fountain of *l*,
15: 4 that brings healing is a tree of *l*,
16: 22 Understanding is a fountain of *l*
19: 3 A man's own folly ruins his *l*,
19: 23 The fear of the LORD leads to *l*:
21: 21 finds *l*, prosperity and honour.
Isa 53: 10 LORD makes his *l* a guilt offering,
53: 11 he will see the light of *l*,
53: 12 he poured out his *l* unto death,
Jer 10: 23 that a man's *l* is not his own;
La 3: 58 you redeemed my *l*.
Eze 18: 27 and right, he will save his *l*.
37: 5 enter you, and you will come to *l*.
Da 12: 2 some to everlasting *l*, others
Jnh 2: 6 you brought my *l* up from the pit,
Mal 2: 5 a covenant of *l* and peace,
Mt 6: 25 Is not *l* more important than food,
7: 14 and narrow the road that leads to *l*,
10: 39 Whoever finds his *l* will lose it,
16: 21 and on the third day be raised to *l*.
16: 25 wants to save his *l* will lose it,
18: 8 better for you to enter *l* maimed
19: 16 thing must I do to get eternal *l*?"
19: 29 as much and will inherit eternal *l*.
20: 28 to give his *l* as a ransom for many."
25: 46 but the righteous to eternal *l*."
Mk 8: 35 but whoever loses his *l* for me
9: 43 better for you to enter *l* maimed
10: 17 "what must I do to inherit eternal *l*
10: 30 and in the age to come, eternal *l*.
10: 45 to give his *l* as a ransom for many."
Lk 6: 9 to save *l* or to destroy it?"
9: 22 and on the third day be raised to *l*."
9: 24 wants to save his *l* will lose it,
12: 15 a man's *l* does not consist
12: 22 do not worry about your *l*,
12: 25 can add a single hour to his *l*?
14: 26 even his own *l*—he cannot be my
17: 33 tries to keep his *l* will lose it,
21: 19 standing firm you will gain *l*.
Jn 1: 4 In him was *l*, and that *l* was
3: 15 believes in him may have eternal *l*.
3: 36 believes in the Son has eternal *l*,
4: 14 of water welling up to eternal *l*."
5: 21 raises the dead and gives them *l*,
5: 24 him who sent me has eternal *l*
5: 26 For as the Father has *l* in himself,
5: 39 that by them you possess eternal *l*.
5: 40 refuse to come to me to have *l*.
Jn 6: 27 for food that endures to eternal *l*,
6: 33 down from heaven and gives *l*
6: 35 Jesus declared, "I am the bread of *l*
6: 40 believes in him shall have eternal *l*,
6: 47 he who believes has everlasting *l*.
6: 48 I am the bread of *l*.
6: 51 give for the *l* of the world."
6: 53 and drink his blood, you have no *l*
6: 63 The Spirit gives *l*; the flesh counts
6: 68 You have the words of eternal *l*.
8: 12 but will have the light of *l*."
10: 10 I have come that they may have *l*,
10: 15 and I lay down my *l* for the sheep.
10: 17 loves me is that I lay down my *l*—
10: 28 I give them eternal *l*, and they shall
11: 25 "I am the resurrection and the *l*.
12: 25 The man who loves his *l* will lose it,
12: 50 his command leads to eternal *l*.
13: 37 I will lay down my *l* for you."
14: 6 am the way and the truth and the *l*.
15: 13 lay down his *l* for his friends.
17: 2 people that he might give eternal *l*
17: 3 Now this is eternal *l*: that they may
20: 31 that by believing you may have *l*
Ac 2: 32 God has raised this Jesus to *l*,
3: 15 You killed the author of *l*,
11: 18 the Gentiles repentance unto *l*."
13: 48 appointed for eternal *l* believed.
Ro 2: 7 immortality, he will give eternal *l*.
4: 25 was raised to *l* for our justification.
5: 10 shall we be saved through his *l*!
5: 18 was justification that brings *l*
5: 21 righteousness to bring eternal *l*
6: 4 the Father, we too may live a new *l*.
6: 13 have been brought from death to *l*;
6: 22 holiness, and the result is eternal *l*.
6: 23 but the gift of God is eternal *l*
8: 6 mind controlled by the Spirit is *l*
8: 11 also give *l* to your mortal bodies
8: 38 convinced that neither death nor *l*,
1Co 15: 19 If only for this *l* we have hope
15: 36 What you sow does not come to *l*
2Co 2: 16 to the other, the fragrance of *l*.
3: 6 letter kills, but the Spirit gives *l*.
4: 10 so that the *l* of Jesus may
5: 4 is mortal may be swallowed up by *l*.
Gal 2: 20 The *l* I live in the body, I live
3: 21 had been given that could impart *l*,
6: 8 from the Spirit will reap eternal *l*.
Eph 4: 1 I urge you to live a *l* worthy
Php 2: 16 as you hold out the word of *l*—
4: 3 whose names are in the book of *l*.
Col 1: 10 order that you may live a *l* worthy
3: 3 your *l* is now hidden with Christ
1Th 4: 12 so that your daily *l* may win
1Ti 1: 16 on him and receive eternal *l*.
4: 8 for both the present *l* and the *l*
4: 12 in *l*, in love, in faith and in purity.
4: 16 Watch your *l* and doctrine closely.
6: 12 Take hold of the eternal *l*
6: 19 hold of the *l* that is truly *l*.
2Ti 1: 9 saved us and called us to a holy *l*—
1: 10 destroyed death and has brought *l*
3: 12 to live a godly *l* in Christ Jesus will
Tit 1: 2 resting on the hope of eternal *l*,
3: 7 heirs having the hope of eternal *l*.
Heb 7: 16 of the power of an indestructible *l*.
Jas 1: 12 crown of *l* that God has promised
3: 13 Let him show it by his good *l*,
1Pe 3: 7 with you of the gracious gift of *l*,
3: 10 "Whoever would love *l*
4: 2 rest of his earthly *l* for evil human
2Pe 1: 3 given us everything we need for *l*
1Jn 1: 1 proclaim concerning the Word of *l*.
2: 25 he promised us—even eternal *l*.
3: 14 we have passed from death to *l*,
3: 16 Jesus Christ laid down his *l* for us.
5: 11 has given us eternal *l*, and this *l* is
5: 20 He is the true God and eternal *l*.
Jude : 21 Christ to bring you to eternal *l*.
Rev 2: 7 the right to eat from the tree of *l*,
2: 8 who died and came to *l* again.
2: 10 and I will give you the crown of *l*.
Rev 3: 5 name from the book of *l*,
13: 8 written in the book of *l* belonging
17: 8 in the book of *l* from the creation
20: 12 was opened, which is the book of *l*.
20: 15 not found written in the book of *l*,
21: 6 from the spring of the water of *l*.
21: 27 written in the Lamb's book of *l*.
22: 1 me the river of the water of *l*,
22: 2 side of the river stood the tree of *l*,
22: 14 may have the right to the tree of *l*
22: 17 take the free gift of the water of *l*.
22: 19 from him his share in the tree of *l*

LIFE-GIVING (GIVE)
Pr 15: 31 He who listens to a *l* rebuke
1Co 15: 45 being"; the last Adam, a *l* spirit.

LIFETIME (LIVE)
Ps 30: 5 but his favour lasts a *l*;
Lk 16: 25 in your *l* you received your good

LIFT (LIFTED LIFTING LIFTS)
Ps 28: 2 as I *l* up my hands
63: 4 in your name I will *l* up my hands.
91: 12 they will *l* you up in their hands,
121: 1 I *l* up my eyes to the hills—
123: 1 I *l* up my eyes to you,
134: 2 *L* up your hands in the sanctuary
143: 8 for to you I *l* up my soul.
Isa 40: 9 *l* up your voice with a shout,
La 2: 19 *L* up your hands to him
3: 41 Let us *l* up our hearts and our
Mt 4: 6 they will *l* you up in their hands,
Lk 21: 28 stand up and *l* up your heads,
1Ti 2: 8 everywhere to *l* up holy hands
Jas 4: 10 the Lord, and he will *l* you up.
1Pe 5: 6 that he may *l* you up in due time.

LIFTED (LIFT)
Ne 8: 6 and all the people *l* their hands
Ps 24: 7 be *l* up, you ancient doors,
40: 2 He *l* me out of the slimy pit,
41: 9 has *l* up his heel against me.
Isa 52: 13 *l* up and highly exalted.
63: 9 he *l* them up and carried them
Jn 3: 14 Moses *l* up the snake in the desert,
8: 28 "When you have *l* up the Son
12: 32 when I am *l* up from the earth,
12: 34 'The Son of Man must be *l* up'?
13: 18 shares my bread has *l* up his heel

LIFTING (LIFT)
Ps 141: 2 may the *l* up of my hands be like

LIFTS (LIFT)
Ps 3: 3 Glorious One, who *l* up my head.
113: 7 and *l* the needy from the ash heap;

LIGHT [1]
Mt 11: 30 yoke is easy and my burden is *l*."

LIGAMENT* (LIGAMENTS)
Eph 4: 16 held together by every supporting *l*

LIGAMENTS* (LIGAMENT)
Col 2: 19 held together by its *l* and sinews,

LIGHT [2] (ENLIGHTENED LIGHTS)
Ge 1: 3 "Let there be *l*," and there was *l*.
Ex 13: 21 in a pillar of fire to give them *l*,
25: 37 it so that they *l* the space in front
2Sa 22: 29 LORD turns my darkness into *l*.
Job 38: 19 "What is the way to the abode of *l*?
Ps 4: 6 Let the *l* of your face shine upon us
18: 28 my God turns my darkness into *l*.
19: 8 giving *l* to the eyes.
27: 1 LORD is my *l* and my salvation—
36: 9 in your *l* we see *l*.
56: 13 God in the *l* of life.
76: 4 You are resplendent with *l*,
89: 15 who walk in the *l* of your presence,
104: 2 He wraps himself in *l*
119: 105 and a *l* for my path.
119: 130 The unfolding of your words gives *l*;

Ps 139: 12 for darkness is as *l* to you.
Pr 4: 18 till the full *l* of day.
Isa 2: 5 let us walk in the *l* of the LORD.
9: 2 have seen a great *l*;
42: 6 and a *l* for the Gentiles,
45: 7 I form the *l* and create darkness,
49: 6 also make you a *l* for the Gentiles,
53: 11 he will see the *l* ⌊of life⌋
60: 1 "Arise, shine, for your *l* has come,
60: 19 LORD will be your everlasting *l*,
Eze 1: 27 and brilliant *l* surrounded him.
Mic 7: 8 the LORD will be my *l*.
Mt 4: 16 have seen a great *l*;
5: 14 "You are the *l* of the world.
5: 15 it gives *l* to everyone in the house.
5: 16 let your *l* shine before men,
6: 22 your whole body will be full of *l*.
17: 2 his clothes became as white as the *l*
24: 29 and the moon will not give its *l*;
Mk 13: 24 and the moon will not give its *l*;
Lk 2: 32 a *l* for revelation to the Gentiles
8: 16 those who come in can see the *l*.
11: 33 those who come in may see the *l*.
Jn 1: 4 and that life was the *l* of men.
1: 5 The *l* shines in the darkness,
1: 7 witness to testify concerning that *l*,
1: 9 The true *l* that gives *l*
3: 19 but men loved darkness instead of *l*
3: 20 Everyone who does evil hates the *l*,
8: 12 he said, "I am the *l* of the world.
9: 5 in the world, I am the *l* of the world
12: 35 Walk while you have the *l*,
12: 46 I have come into the world as a *l*,
Ac 13: 47 " 'I have made you a *l*
Ro 13: 12 darkness and put on the armour of *l*.
2Co 4: 6 made his *l* shine in our hearts
6: 14 Or what fellowship can *l* have
11: 14 masquerades as an angel of *l*.
Eph 5: 8 but now you are *l* in the Lord.
1Th 5: 5 You are all sons of the *l*
1Ti 6: 16 and who lives in unapproachable *l*,
1Pe 2: 9 of darkness into his wonderful *l*.
2Pe 1: 19 as to a *l* shining in a dark place,
1Jn 1: 5 God is *l*; in him there is no
1: 7 But if we walk in the *l*,
2: 9 Anyone who claims to be in the *l*
Rev 21: 23 for the glory of God gives it *l*,
22: 5 for the Lord God will give them *l*.

LIGHTNING
Ex 9: 23 and *l* flashed down to the ground.
20: 18 and *l* and heard the trumpet
Ps 18: 12 with hailstones and bolts of *l*.
Eze 1: 13 it was bright, and *l* flashed out of it.
Da 10: 6 his face like *l*, his eyes like flaming
Mt 24: 27 For as the *l* comes from the east
28: 3 His appearance was like *l*,
Lk 10: 18 "I saw Satan fall like *l* from heaven.
Rev 4: 5 From the throne came flashes of *l*,

LIGHTS (LIGHT [2])
Ge 1: 14 "Let there be *l* in the expanse
Lk 8: 16 No-one *l* a lamp and hides it in a jar

LIKE-MINDED* (MIND)
Php 2: 2 make my joy complete by being *l*,

LIKENESS
Ge 1: 26 man in our image, in our *l*,
Ps 17: 15 I will be satisfied with seeing your *l*
Isa 52: 14 his form marred beyond human *l*—
Ro 8: 3 Son in the *l* of sinful man
8: 29 to be conformed to the *l* of his Son,
2Co 3: 18 his *l* with ever-increasing glory,
Php 2: 7 being made in human *l*.
Jas 3: 9 who have been made in God's *l*.

LILIES (LILY)
Lk 12: 27 "Consider how the *l* grow.

LILY (LILIES)
SS 2: 1 a *l* of the valleys.
2: 2 Like a *l* among thorns

LIMIT
Ps 147: 5 his understanding has no *l*.
Jn 3: 34 him God gives the Spirit without *l*.

LINEN
Lev 16: 4 He is to put on the sacred *l* tunic,
Pr 31: 22 she is clothed in fine *l* and purple.
31: 24 She makes *l* garments
Mk 15: 46 So Joseph bought some *l* cloth,
Jn 20: 6 He saw the strips of *l* lying there,
Rev 15: 6 shining *l* and wore golden sashes
19: 8 Fine *l*, bright and clean,

LINGER
Hab 2: 3 Though it *l*, wait for it;

LION (LION'S LIONS')
Jdg 14: 6 power so that he tore the *l* apart
1Sa 17: 34 When a *l* or a bear came
Isa 11: 7 and the *l* will eat straw like the ox.
65: 25 and the *l* will eat straw like the ox,
Eze 1: 10 right side each had the face of a *l*,
10: 14 the third the face of a *l*,
Da 7: 4 "The first was like a *l*,
1Pe 5: 8 around like a roaring *l* looking
Rev 4: 7 The first living creature was like a *l*
5: 5 See, the *L* of the tribe of Judah,

LION'S (LION)
Ge 49: 9 You are a *l* cub, O Judah;

LIONS' (LION)
Da 6: 7 shall be thrown into the *l* den.

LIPS
Ps 8: 2 From the *l* of children and infants
34: 1 his praise will always be on my *l*.
40: 9 I do not seal my *l*,
63: 3 my *l* will glorify you.
119: 171 May my *l* overflow with praise,
140: 3 the poison of vipers is on their *l*.
141: 3 keep watch over the door of my *l*.
Pr 10: 13 on the *l* of the discerning,
10: 18 who conceals his hatred has lying *l*,
10: 32 *l* of the righteous know what is
12: 22 The LORD detests lying *l*,
13: 3 He who guards his *l* guards his life
14: 7 will not find knowledge on his *l*.
24: 26 is like a kiss on the *l*.
26: 23 are fervent *l* with an evil heart.
27: 2 someone else, and not your own *l*.
Isa 6: 5 For I am a man of unclean *l*,
28: 11 with foreign *l* and strange tongues
29: 13 and honour me with their *l*,
Mal 2: 7 "For the *l* of a priest ought
Mt 15: 8 These people honour me with their *l*
21: 16 " 'From the *l* of children
Lk 4: 22 words that came from his *l*.
Ro 3: 13 "The poison of vipers is on their *l*."
Col 3: 8 and filthy language from your *l*.
Heb 13: 15 the fruit of *l* that confess his name.
1Pe 3: 10 and his *l* from deceitful speech.

LISTEN (LISTENED LISTENING LISTENS)
Dt 18: 15 You must *l* to him.
30: 20 *l* to his voice, and hold fast to him.
1Ki 4: 34 came to *l* to Solomon's wisdom,
2Ki 21: 9 But the people did not *l*.
Pr 1: 5 let the wise *l* and add
Ecc 5: 1 Go near to *l* rather
Eze 2: 5 And whether they *l* or fail to *l*—
Mt 12: 42 earth to *l* to Solomon's wisdom,
Mk 9: 7 *L* to him!" Suddenly,
Jn 10: 27 My sheep *l* to my voice; I know
Ac 3: 22 you must *l* to everything he tells
Jas 1: 19 Everyone should be quick to *l*,
1: 22 Do not merely *l* to the word,
1Jn 4: 6 not from God does not *l* to us.

LISTENED (LISTEN)
Ne 8: 3 And all the people *l* attentively
Isa 66: 4 when I spoke, no-one *l*.
Da 9: 6 We have not *l* to your servants

LISTENING (LISTEN)
1Sa 3: 9 Speak, LORD, for your servant is *l*
Pr 18: 13 He who answers before *l*—
Lk 10: 39 at the Lord's feet *l* to what he said.

LISTENS (LISTEN)
Pr 12: 15 but a wise man *l* to advice.
Lk 10: 16 "He who *l* to you *l*
1Jn 4: 6 and whoever knows God *l* to us;

LIVE (ALIVE LIFE LIFETIME LIVES LIVING)
Ge 3: 22 tree of life and eat, and *l* for ever."
Ex 20: 12 so that you may *l* long
33: 20 for no-one may see me and *l*."
Nu 21: 8 who is bitten can look at it and *l*."
Dt 5: 24 we have seen that a man can *l*
6: 2 as you *l* by keeping all his decrees
8: 3 to teach you that man does not *l*
Job 14: 14 If a man dies, will he *l* again?
Ps 15: 1 Who may *l* on your holy hill?
24: 1 the world, and all who *l* in it;
26: 8 I love the house where you *l*,
119: 175 Let me *l* that I may praise you,
Pr 21: 9 Better to *l* on a corner of the roof
21: 19 Better to *l* in a desert
Ecc 9: 4 a *l* dog is better off than a dead lion
Isa 26: 19 But your dead will *l*;
55: 3 hear me, that your soul may *l*.
Eze 17: 19 LORD says: As surely as I *l*,
20: 11 for the man who obeys them will *l*
37: 3 can these bones *l*?" I said,
Am 5: 6 Seek the LORD and *l*,
Hab 2: 4 but the righteous will *l* by his faith
Zec 2: 11 I will *l* among you and you will
Mt 4: 4 'Man does not *l* on bread alone,
Lk 4: 4 'Man does not *l* on bread alone.' "
Jn 14: 19 Because I *l*, you also will *l*.
Ac 17: 24 does not *l* in temples built by hands
17: 28 'For in him we *l* and move
Ro 1: 17 "The righteous will *l* by faith."
2Co 5: 7 We *l* by faith, not by sight.
6: 16 "I will *l* with them and walk
Gal 2: 20 The life I *l* in the body, I *l* by faith
3: 11 "The righteous will *l* by faith."
5: 25 Since we *l* by the Spirit, let us keep
Eph 4: 17 that you must no longer *l*
Php 1: 21 to *l* is Christ and to die is gain.
Col 1: 10 order that you may *l* a life worthy
1Th 4: 1 we instructed you how to *l* in order
5: 13 *L* in peace with each other.
1Ti 2: 2 that we may *l* peaceful
2Ti 3: 12 who wants to *l* a godly life
Tit 2: 12 and to *l* self-controlled, upright
Heb 10: 38 But my righteous one will *l* by faith
12: 14 Make every effort to *l* in peace
1Pe 1: 17 *l* your lives as strangers here
3: 8 *l* in harmony with one another;

LIVES (LIVE)
Ge 45: 7 and to save your *l* by a great
Job 19: 25 I know that my Redeemer *l*,
Pr 1: 19 it takes away the *l*
Isa 57: 15 he who *l* for ever, whose name is
Da 3: 28 to give up their *l* rather than serve
Jn 14: 17 for he *l* with you and will be in you.
Ro 6: 10 but the life he *l*, he *l* to God.
7: 18 I know that nothing good *l* in me,
8: 9 if the Spirit of God *l* in you.
14: 7 For none of us *l* to himself alone
1Co 3: 16 and that God's Spirit *l* in you?
Gal 2: 20 I no longer live, but Christ *l* in me.
1Th 2: 8 only the gospel of God but our *l*
1Ti 2: 2 quiet *l* in all godliness and holiness.
Tit 2: 12 and godly *l* in this present age,
Heb 7: 24 but because Jesus *l* for ever,
13: 5 Keep your *l* free from the love
1Pe 3: 2 the purity and reverence of your *l*.
2Pe 3: 11 You ought to live holy and godly *l*
1Jn 3: 16 to lay down our *l* for our brothers.
4: 16 Whoever *l* in love *l* in God,

LIVING (LIVE)
Ge 2: 7 and man became a *l* being.

1Sa 17: 26 defy the armies of the *l* God?"
Isa 53: 8 cut off from the land of the *l*;
Jer 2: 13 the spring of *l* water,
Eze 1: 5 what looked like four *l* creatures.
Zec 14: 8 On that day *l* water will flow out
Mt 22: 32 the God of the dead but of the *l*."
Jn 4: 10 he would have given you *l* water."
6: 51 I am the *l* bread that came
7: 38 streams of *l* water will flow
Ro 8: 11 Jesus from the dead is *l* in you,
12: 1 to offer your bodies as *l* sacrifices,
1Co 9: 14 the gospel should receive their *l*
Heb 4: 12 For the word of God is *l* and active.
10: 20 and *l* way opened for us
10: 31 to fall into the hands of the *l* God.
1Pe 1: 23 through the *l* and enduring word
Rev 1: 18 I am the *L* One; I was dead,
4: 6 the throne, were four *l* creatures,
7: 17 to springs of *l* water.

LOAD (LOADS)
Gal 6: 5 for each one should carry his own *l*.

LOADS (LOAD)
Mt 23: 4 They tie up heavy *l* and put them

LOAF (LOAVES)
1Co 10: 17 for we all partake of the one *l*.

LOAVES (LOAF)
Mk 6: 41 Taking the five *l* and the two fish
8: 6 When he had taken the seven *l*
Lk 11: 5 'Friend, lend me three *l* of bread,

LOCKED
Jn 20: 26 the doors were *l*, Jesus came
Gal 3: 23 *l* up until faith should be revealed.

LOCUSTS
Ex 10: 4 I will bring *l* into your country
Joel 2: 25 you for the years the *l* have eaten—
Mt 3: 4 His food was *l* and wild honey.
Rev 9: 3 And out of the smoke *l* came

LOFTY
Ps 139: 6 too *l* for me to attain.
Isa 57: 15 is what the high and *l* One says—

LONELY
Ps 68: 6 God sets the *l* in families,
Lk 5: 16 Jesus often withdrew to *l* places

LONG [1] (LENGTH LENGTHY)
Ex 17: 11 As *l* as Moses held up his hands,
Nu 6: 5 the hair of his head grow *l*.
1Ki 18: 21 "How *l* will you waver
Ps 119: 97 I meditate on it all day *l*.
Mt 25: 5 The bridegroom was a *l* time
Jn 9: 4 As *l* as it is day, we must do
1Co 11: 14 that if a man has *l* hair,
Eph 3: 18 to grasp how wide and *l* and high

LONG [2] (LONGED LONGING LONGINGS LONGS)
Ps 119: 174 I *l* for your salvation, O Lord,
Hos 7: 13 I *l* to redeem them
Am 5: 18 Why do you *l* for the day
Php 1: 8 God can testify how I *l* for all
1Pe 1: 12 Even angels *l* to look

LONGED (LONG [2])
Mt 13: 17 righteous men *l* to see what you see
23: 37 how often I have *l*
Lk 13: 34 how often I have *l*
2Ti 4: 8 to all who have *l* for his appearing.

LONGING* (LONG [2])
Dt 28: 65 with *l*, and a despairing heart.
Job 7: 2 Like a slave *l* for the evening
Ps 119: 20 My soul is consumed with *l*
119: 81 with *l* for your salvation,
119: 131 *l* for your commands.
143: 7 my spirit faints with *l*.

Pr 13: 12 but a *l* fulfilled is a tree of life.
13: 19 A *l* fulfilled is sweet to the soul,
Eze 23: 27 look on these things with *l*
Lk 16: 21 and *l* to eat what fell from the rich
Ro 15: 23 since I have been *l* for many years
2Co 5: 2 *l* to be clothed with our heavenly
7: 7 He told us about your *l* for me,
7: 11 what alarm, what *l*, what concern,
1Th 2: 17 out of our intense *l* we made every
Heb 11: 16 they were *l* for a better country—

LONGINGS* (LONG [2])
Ps 38: 9 All my *l* lie open before you,
112: 10 the *l* of the wicked will come

LONGS* (LONG [2])
Ps 63: 1 my body *l* for you,
Isa 26: 9 in the morning my spirit *l* for you.
30: 18 Yet the LORD *l* to be gracious
Php 2: 26 For he *l* for all of you and is

LOOK (LOOKED LOOKING LOOKS)
Ge 19: 17 "Flee for your lives! Don't *l* back,
Ex 3: 6 because he was afraid to *l* at God.
Nu 21: 8 anyone who is bitten can *l* at it
32: 8 Kadesh Barnea to *l* over the land.
Dt 4: 29 you will find him if you *l* for him
1Sa 16: 7 The LORD does not *l*
Job 31: 1 not to *l* lustfully at a girl.
Ps 34: 5 Those who *l* to him are radiant;
105: 4 *L* to the LORD and his strength;
113: 6 who stoops down to *l*
123: 2 As the eyes of slaves *l* to the hand
Pr 1: 28 they will *l* for me but will not find
4: 25 Let your eyes *l* straight ahead,
15: 30 A cheerful *l* brings joy to the heart,
Isa 17: 7 In that day men will *l*
31: 1 do not *l* to the Holy One of Israel,
40: 26 Lift your eyes and *l* to the heavens:
60: 5 Then you will *l* and be radiant,
Jer 3: 3 Yet you have the brazen *l*
6: 16 "Stand at the crossroads and *l*;
Eze 34: 11 for my sheep and *l* after them.
Hab 1: 13 Your eyes are too pure to *l* on evil;
Zec 12: 10 They will *l* on me, the one they
Mt 18: 10 "See that you do not *l* down on one
18: 12 go to *l* for the one that wandered
23: 27 which *l* beautiful on the outside
Mk 13: 21 '*L*, here is the Christ!' or, '*L*,
Lk 6: 41 "Why do you *l* at the speck
24: 39 *L* at my hands and my feet.
Jn 1: 36 he said, "*L*, the Lamb of God!"
4: 35 open your eyes and *l* at the fields!
19: 37 "They will *l* on the one they have
Ro 14: 10 why do you *l* down on your brother
Php 2: 4 Each of you should *l* not only
1Ti 4: 12 Don't let anyone *l* down on you
Jas 1: 27 to *l* after orphans and widows
1Pe 1: 12 long to *l* into these things.
2Pe 3: 12 as you *l* forward to the day of God

LOOKED (LOOK)
Ge 19: 26 Lot's wife *l* back and she became
Ex 2: 25 So God *l* on the Israelites
1Sa 6: 19 because they had *l* into the ark
SS 3: 1 I *l* for the one my heart loves;
Eze 22: 30 "I *l* for a man among them who
34: 6 and no-one searched or *l* for them.
44: 4 I *l* and saw the glory
Da 7: 9 "As I *l*,
10: 5 I *l* up and there before me was
Hab 3: 6 he *l*, and made the nations tremble.
Mt 25: 36 I was sick and you *l* after me,
Lk 18: 9 and *l* down on everybody else,
22: 61 The Lord turned and *l* straight
1Jn 1: 1 which we have *l* at and our hands

LOOKING (LOOK)
Ps 69: 3 *l* for my God.
119: 82 My eyes fail, *l* for your promise;
119: 123 My eyes fail, *l* for your salvation,
Mk 16: 6 "You are *l* for Jesus the Nazarene,
2Co 10: 7 You are *l* only on the surface

Php 4: 17 Not that I am *l* for a gift,
1Th 2: 6 We were not *l* for praise from men,
2Pe 3: 13 with his promise we are *l* forward
Rev 5: 6 I saw a Lamb, *l* as if it had been

LOOKS (LOOK)
1Sa 16: 7 Man *l* at the outward appearance,
Ezr 8: 22 is on everyone who *l* to him,
Ps 104: 32 He *l* at the earth, and it trembles;
138: 6 on high, he *l* upon the lowly,
Pr 27: 18 he who *l* after his master will be
Eze 34: 12 As a shepherd *l* after his scattered
Mt 5: 28 But I tell you that anyone who *l*
16: 4 and adulterous generation *l*
Lk 9: 62 and *l* back is fit for service
Jn 6: 40 Father's will is that everyone who *l*
12: 45 When he *l* at me, he sees the one
Php 2: 21 For everyone *l* out
Jas 1: 25 But the man who *l* intently

LOOSE
Isa 33: 23 Your rigging hangs *l*:
Mt 16: 19 and whatever you *l* on earth will be
18: 18 and whatever you *l* on earth will be

***LORD (LORD'S LORDED LORDING)**
Ge 18: 27 been so bold as to speak to the *L*,
Ex 15: 17 O *L*, your hands established.
Nu 16: 13 now you also want to *l* it over us?
Dt 10: 17 God of gods and *L* of lords,
Jos 3: 13 the *L* of all the earth—set foot
1Ki 3: 10 *L* was pleased that Solomon had
Ne 4: 14 Remember the *L*, who is great
Job 28: 28 'The fear of the *L*—that is wisdom
Ps 37: 13 but the *L* laughs at the wicked,
38: 22 O *L* my Saviour.
54: 4 the *L* is the one who sustains me.
62: 12 and that you, O *L*, are loving.
69: 6 O *L*, the LORD Almighty;
86: 5 You are forgiving and good, O *L*,
86: 8 gods there is none like you, O *L*;
89: 49 O *L*, where is your former great
110: 1 The LORD says to my *L*:
110: 5 The *L* is at your right hand;
130: 3 O *L*, who could stand?
135: 5 that our *L* is greater than all gods.
136: 3 Give thanks to the *L* of lords:
147: 5 Great is our *L* and mighty in power
Isa 6: 1 I saw the *L* seated on a throne,
Da 2: 47 and the *L* of kings and a revealer
9: 4 "O *L*, the great and awesome God,
9: 7 "*L*, you are righteous,
9: 9 The *L* our God is merciful
9: 19 O *L*, listen! O *L*, forgive! O *L*,
Mt 3: 3 'Prepare the way for the *L*,
4: 7 'Do not put the *L* your God
4: 10 'Worship the *L* your God,
7: 21 "Not everyone who says to me, '*L*,
9: 38 Ask the *L* of the harvest, therefore,
12: 8 Son of Man is *L* of the Sabbath."
20: 25 of the Gentiles *l* it over them,
21: 9 comes in the name of the *L*!"
22: 37 "'Love the *L* your God
22: 44 For he says, "'The *L* said to my *L*:
23: 39 comes in the name of the *L*.'"
Mk 1: 3 'Prepare the way for the *L*,
12: 11 the *L* has done this,
12: 29 the *L* our God, the *L* is one.
12: 30 Love the *L* your God
Lk 2: 9 glory of the *L* shone around them,
6: 5 The Son of Man is *L* of the Sabbath
6: 46 "Why do you call me, '*L*, *L*,'
10: 27 "'Love the *L* your God
11: 1 one of his disciples said to him, "*L*,
24: 34 The *L* has risen and has appeared
Jn 1: 23 'Make straight the way for the *L*.'"
Ac 2: 21 on the name of the *L* will be saved.'
2: 25 "'I saw the *L* always before me.
2: 34 "'The *L* said to my *L*:
8: 16 into the name of the *L* Jesus.
9: 5 "Who are you, *L*?" Saul asked.
10: 36 through Jesus Christ, who is *L*
11: 23 true to the *L* with all their hearts.

*See also †LORD, †LORD's.

Ac 16:31 replied, "Believe in the *L* Jesus,
Ro 4:24 in him who raised Jesus our *L*
5:11 in God through our *L* Jesus Christ,
6:23 life in Christ Jesus our *L*.
8:39 of God that is in Christ Jesus our *L*.
10:9 with your mouth, "Jesus is *L*,"
10:13 on the name of the *L* will be saved
10:16 *L*, who has believed our message?"
11:34 Who has known the mind of the *L*?
12:11 your spiritual fervour, serving the *L*.
13:14 yourselves with the *L* Jesus Christ,
14:4 for the *L* is able to make him stand.
14:8 we live to the *L*; and if we die,
1Co 1:31 Let him who boasts boast in the *L*."
3:5 the *L* has assigned to each his task.
4:5 time; wait till the *L* comes.
6:13 for the *L*, and the *L* for the body.
6:14 By his power God raised the *L*
7:32 affairs—how he can please the *L*.
7:34 to be devoted to the *L* in both body
7:35 in undivided devotion to the *L*.
7:39 but he must belong to the *L*.
8:6 and there is but one *L*, Jesus Christ,
10:9 We should not test the *L*,
11:23 For I received from the *L* what I
12:3 "Jesus is *L*," except by the Holy
15:57 victory through our *L* Jesus Christ.
15:58 fully to the work of the *L*,
16:22 If anyone does not love the *L*—
2Co 1:24 Not that we *l* it over your faith,
2:12 found that the *L* had opened a door
3:17 Now the *L* is the Spirit,
4:5 but Jesus Christ as *L*, and ourselves
5:6 in the body we are away from the *L*
8:5 they gave themselves first to the *L*
8:21 not only in the eyes of the *L* but
10:17 Let him who boasts boast in the *L*."
10:18 but the one whom the *L* commends
13:10 the authority the *L* gave me
Gal 6:14 in the cross of our *L* Jesus Christ,
Eph 4:5 one *L*, one faith, one baptism;
5:8 but now you are light in the *L*.
5:10 and find out what pleases the *L*.
5:19 make music in your heart to the *L*,
5:22 submit to your husbands as to the *L*
6:1 obey your parents in the *L*,
6:7 as if you were serving the *L*,
6:8 know that the *L* will reward
6:10 in the *L* and in his mighty power.
Php 2:11 confess that Jesus Christ is *L*,
3:1 my brothers, rejoice in the *L*!
3:8 of knowing Christ Jesus my *L*,
4:1 you should stand firm in the *L*,
4:4 Rejoice in the *L* always.
4:5 The *L* is near.
Col 1:10 you may live a life worthy of the *L*
2:6 as you received Christ Jesus as *L*,
3:13 Forgive as the *L* forgave you.
3:17 do it all in the name of the *L* Jesus,
3:18 your husbands, as is fitting in the *L*.
3:20 in everything, for this pleases the *L*
3:23 as working for the *L*, not for men,
3:24 It is the *L* Christ you are serving.
3:24 receive an inheritance from the *L*
4:17 work you have received in the *L*."
1Th 3:8 since you are standing firm in the *L*
3:12 May the *L* make your love increase
4:1 and urge you in the *L* Jesus
4:6 The *L* will punish men
4:15 who are left till the coming of the *L*
5:2 day of the *L* will come like a thief
5:23 at the coming of our *L* Jesus Christ.
2Th 1:7 when the *L* Jesus is revealed
1:12 of our *L* Jesus may be glorified
2:1 the coming of our *L* Jesus Christ
2:8 whom the *L* Jesus will overthrow
3:3 *L* is faithful, and he will strengthen
3:5 May the *L* direct your hearts
1Ti 6:15 the King of kings and *L* of lords,
2Ti 1:8 ashamed to testify about our *L*,
2:19 "The *L* knows those who are his,"
4:8 which the *L*, the righteous Judge,
4:17 But the *L* stood at my side
Heb 1:10 O *L*, you laid the foundations
10:30 "The *L* will judge his people."
12:14 holiness no-one will see the *L*.
13:6 *L* is my helper; I will not be afraid.
Jas 3:9 With the tongue we praise our *L*
4:10 Humble yourselves before the *L*,
5:11 The *L* is full of compassion
1Pe 1:25 the word of the *L* stands for ever."
2:3 you have tasted that the *L* is good.
3:12 eyes of the *L* are on the righteous
3:15 in your hearts set apart Christ as *L*.
2Pe 1:11 into the eternal kingdom of our *L*
1:16 and coming of our *L* Jesus Christ,
2:1 the sovereign *L* who bought
2:9 then the *L* knows how
3:9 The *L* is not slow in keeping his
3:18 and knowledge of our *L* and Saviour
Jude :14 the *L* is coming with thousands
Rev 4:8 holy, holy is the *L* God Almighty,
4:11 "You are worthy, our *L* and God,
11:15 has become the kingdom of our *L*
17:14 he is *L* of lords and King of kings—
19:16 KINGS AND *L* OF LORDS.
22:5 for the *L* God will give them light.
22:20 Come, *L* Jesus.

*LORD'S (*LORD)

Lk 1:38 "I am the *L* servant," Mary
Ac 11:21 The *L* hand was with them,
21:14 and said, "The *L* will be done."
1Co 7:32 is concerned about the *L* affairs—
10:26 "The earth is the *L*, and everything
11:26 you proclaim the *L* death
2Co 3:18 faces all reflect the *L* glory,
Eph 5:17 but understand what the *L* will is.
2Ti 2:24 And the *L* servant must not quarrel
Heb 12:5 light of the *L* discipline,
Jas 4:15 you ought to say, "If it is the *L* will,
5:8 because the *L* coming is near..
1Pe 2:13 Submit yourselves for the *L* sake

LORDED (*LORD)

Ne 5:15 Their assistants also *l* it

LORDING (*LORD)

1Pe 5:3 not *l* it over those entrusted to you,

†LORD (†LORD'S)

Ge 2:4 When the *L* God made the earth
2:7 And the *L* God formed man
2:22 Then the *L* God made a woman
3:21 The *L* God made garments of skin
3:23 So the *L* God banished him
4:4 The *L* looked with favour on Abel
4:26 began to call on the name of the *L*.
6:7 So the *L* said, "I will wipe mankind
7:16 Then the *L* shut him in.
9:26 Blessed be the *L*, the God of Shem!
11:9 there the *L* confused the language
12:1 *L* had said to Abram, "Leave your
15:6 Abram believed the *L*,
15:18 On that day the *L* made a covenant
17:1 the *L* appeared to him and said,
18:1 The *L* appeared to Abraham
18:14 Is anything too hard for the *L*?
18:19 way of the *L* by doing what is right
21:1 Now the *L* was gracious to Sarah
22:14 that place "The *L* will provide."
24:1 the *L* had blessed him in every way
26:2 The *L* appeared to Isaac and said,
28:13 There above it stood the *L*,
31:49 "May the *L* keep watch
39:2 The *L* was with Joseph
39:21 in the prison, the *L* was with him;
Ex 3:2 the angel of the *L* appeared to him
4:11 Is it not I, the *L*? Now go;
4:31 heard that the *L* was concerned
6:2 also said to Moses, "I am the *L*.
9:12 the *L* hardened Pharaoh's heart
12:27 'It is the Passover sacrifice to the *L*,
12:43 The *L* said to Moses and Aaron,
13:9 For the *L* brought you out of Egypt
13:21 By day the *L* went ahead of them
14:13 the deliverance the *L* will bring
14:30 That day the *L* saved Israel
15:3 The *L* is a warrior;
15:11 among the gods is like you, O *L*?
15:26 for I am the *L* who heals you."
16:12 know that I am the *L* your God.'"
16:23 day of rest, a holy Sabbath to the *L*.
17:15 and called it The *L* is my Banner.
19:8 will do everything the *L* has said."
19:20 The *L* descended to the top
20:2 "I am the *L* your God, who
20:5 the *L* your God, am a jealous God,
20:7 for the *L* will not hold anyone
20:10 a Sabbath to the *L* your God.
20:11 in six days the *L* made the heavens
20:12 in the land the *L* your God is giving
23:25 Worship the *L* your God,
24:3 "Everything the *L* has said we will
24:12 The *L* said to Moses, "Come up
24:16 and the glory of the *L* settled
25:1 The *L* said to Moses, "Tell
28:36 HOLY TO THE *L*.
30:11 Then the *L* said to Moses,
31:13 so you may know that I am the *L*,
31:18 When the *L* finished speaking
33:11 The *L* would speak to Moses face
33:19 And the *L* said, "I will cause all my
34:1 *L* said to Moses, "Chisel out two
34:6 proclaiming, "The *L*, the *L*,
34:10 awesome is the work that I, the *L*,
34:29 because he had spoken with the *L*.
40:34 glory of the *L* filled the tabernacle.
40:38 So the cloud of the *L* was
Lev 8:36 did everything the *L* commanded
9:23 and the glory of the *L* appeared
10:2 and they died before the *L*.
19:2 'Be holy because I, the *L* your God,
20:8 I am the *L*, who makes you holy.
20:26 to be holy to me because I, the *L*,
23:40 and rejoice before the *L* your God
24:11 the name of the *L* with a curse;
Nu 6:24 Say to them: "'"The *L* bless you
8:5 *L* said to Moses: "Take the Levites
11:1 hardships in the hearing of the *L*,
14:14 O *L*, have been seen face to face,
14:18 you have declared: 'The *L* is slow
14:21 glory of the *L* fills the whole earth,
21:6 Then the *L* sent venomous snakes
22:31 Then the *L* opened Balaam's eyes,
23:12 "Must I not speak what the *L* puts
30:2 When a man makes a vow to the *L*
32:12 followed the *L* wholeheartedly.'
Dt 1:21 and take possession of it as the *L*,
2:7 forty years the *L* your God has
4:29 there you seek the *L* your God,
5:6 And he said: "I am the *L* your God,
5:9 the *L* your God, am a jealous God,
6:4 The *L* our God, the *L* is one.
6:5 Love the *L* your God
6:16 Do not test the *L* your God
6:25 law before the *L* our God,
7:1 When the *L* your God brings you
7:6 holy to the *L* your God.
7:8 But it was because the *L* loved you
7:9 that the *L* your God is God;
7:12 then the *L* your God will keep his
8:5 so the *L* your God disciplines you.
9:10 The *L* gave me two stone tablets
10:12 but to fear the *L* your God,
10:14 To the *L* your God belong
10:17 For the *L* your God is God of gods
10:20 Fear the *L* your God and serve him
10:22 now the *L* your God has made you
11:1 Love the *L* your God and keep his
11:13 to love the *L* your God
16:1 the Passover of the *L* your God,
17:15 the king the *L* your God chooses.
28:1 If you fully obey the *L* your God
28:15 if you do not obey the *L* your God
29:1 covenant the *L* commanded Moses
29:29 things belong to the *L* our God,
30:4 from there the *L* your God will
30:6 *L* your God will circumcise your
30:10 if you obey the *L* your God
30:16 today to love the *L* your God,
30:20 For the *L* is your life, and he will

†This entry represents the translation of the Hebrew name for God, *Yahweh*, always indicated in the NIV by LORD. For Lord, see the concordance entries *LORD and *LORD'S.

Dt 31: 6 for the *L* your God goes with you;
34: 5 of the *L* died there in Moab,
Jos 10: 14 a day when the *L* listened to a man.
22: 5 to love the *L* your God, to walk
23: 11 careful to love the *L* your God.
24: 15 my household, we will serve the *L*
24: 18 We too will serve the *L*,
Jdg 2: 12 They forsook the *L*, the God
Ru 1: 8 May the *L* show kindness to you,
4: 13 And the *L* enabled her to conceive,
1Sa 1: 11 him to the *L* for all the days
1: 15 I was pouring out my soul to the *L*.
1: 28 So now I give him to the *L*.
2: 2 "There is no-one holy like the *L*;
2: 25 but if a man sins against the *L*,
2: 26 in favour with the *L* and with men.
3: 9 *L*, for your servant is listening.'"
3: 19 The *L* was with Samuel
7: 12 "Thus far has the *L* helped us."
9: 17 sight of Saul, the *L* said to him,
11: 15 as king in the presence of the *L*.
12: 18 all the people stood in awe of the *L*
12: 22 his great name the *L* will not reject
12: 24 But be sure to fear the *L*
13: 14 the *L* has sought out a man
14: 6 Nothing can hinder the *L*
15: 22 "Does the *L* delight
16: 13 Spirit of the *L* came upon David
17: 45 you in the name of the *L* Almighty,
2Sa 6: 14 danced before the *L*
7: 22 How great you are, O Sovereign *L*!
8: 6 *L* gave David victory everywhere
12: 7 This is what the *L*, the God
22: 2 "The *L* is my rock, my fortress
22: 29 You are my lamp, O *L*;
22: 31 the word of the *L* is flawless.
1Ki 1: 30 today what I swore to you by the *L*,
2: 3 and observe what the *L* your God
3: 7 O *L* my God, you have made your
5: 5 for the Name of the *L* my God,
5: 12 The *L* gave Solomon wisdom,
8: 11 the glory of the *L* filled his temple.
8: 23 towards heaven and said: "O *L*,
8: 61 fully committed to the *L* our God,
9: 3 The *L* said to him: "I have heard
10: 9 Praise be to the *L* your God,
15: 14 committed to the *L* all his life.
18: 21 If the *L* is God, follow him;
18: 36 "O *L*, God of Abraham, Isaac
18: 39 "The *L*—he is God! The *L*—
21: 23 also concerning Jezebel the *L* says:
2Ki 13: 23 But the *L* was gracious to them
17: 18 So the *L* was very angry with Israel
18: 5 Hezekiah trusted in the *L*,
19: 1 and went into the temple of the *L*.
20: 11 *L* made the shadow go back the ten
21: 12 Therefore this is what the *L*,
22: 2 right in the eyes of the *L*
22: 8 of the Law in the temple of the *L*."
23: 3 to follow the *L* and keep his
23: 21 the Passover to the *L* your God,
23: 25 a king like him who turned to the *L*
24: 2 The *L* sent Babylonian, Aramean,
24: 4 and the *L* was not willing to forgive
1Ch 10: 13 because he was unfaithful to the *L*;
11: 3 with them at Hebron before the *L*,
11: 9 the *L* Almighty was with him.
13: 6 from there the ark of God the *L*, who
16: 8 Give thanks to the *L*, call
16: 11 Look to the *L* and his strength;
16: 14 He is the *L* our God;
16: 23 Sing to the *L*, all the earth;
17: 1 covenant of the *L* is under a tent."
21: 24 take for the *L* what is yours,
22: 5 to be built for the *L* should be
22: 11 build the house of the *L* your God,
22: 13 and laws that the *L* gave Moses
22: 16 Now begin the work, and the *L* be
22: 19 soul to seeking the *L* your God.
25: 7 and skilled in music for the *L*—
28: 9 for the *L* searches every heart
28: 20 for the *L* God, my God, is with you
29: 1 not for man but for the *L* God.
29: 11 O *L*, is the greatness and the power
1Ch 29: 18 O *L*, God of our fathers Abraham,
29: 25 The *L* highly exalted Solomon
2Ch 1: 1 for the *L* his God was with him
5: 13 to give praise and thanks to the *L*.
5: 14 the glory of the *L* filled the temple
6: 16 "Now *L*, God of Israel, keep
6: 41 O *L* God, and come
6: 42 O *L* God, do not reject your
7: 1 the glory of the *L* filled the temple.
7: 12 the *L* appeared to him at night
7: 21 'Why has the *L* done such a thing
9: 8 as king to rule for the *L* your God.
13: 12 do not fight against the *L*,
14: 2 right in the eyes of the *L* his God.
15: 14 to the *L* with loud acclamation,
16: 9 of the *L* range throughout the earth
17: 9 the Book of the Law of the *L*;
18: 13 said, "As surely as the *L* lives,
19: 6 judging for man but for the *L*,
19: 9 wholeheartedly in the fear of the *L*.
20: 15 This is what the *L* says to you:
20: 20 Have faith in the *L* your God
20: 21 appointed men to sing to the *L*
26: 5 As long as he sought the *L*,
26: 16 He was unfaithful to the *L* his God,
29: 30 to praise the *L* with the words
30: 9 for the *L* your God is gracious
31: 20 and faithful before the *L* his God.
32: 8 with us is the *L* our God to help us
34: 14 Law of the *L* that had been given
34: 31 to follow the *L* and keep his
Ezr 3: 10 foundation of the temple of the *L*,
7: 6 for the hand of the *L* his God was
7: 10 observance of the Law of the *L*,
9: 5 hands spread out to the *L* my God
9: 8 the *L* our God has been gracious
9: 15 O *L*, God of Israel, you are
Ne 1: 5 Then I said: "O *L*, God of heaven,
8: 1 which the *L* had commanded
9: 6 You alone are the *L*.
Job 1: 6 to present themselves before the *L*,
1: 21 *L* gave and the *L* has taken away;
38: 1 the *L* answered Job out
42: 9 and the *L* accepted Job's prayer.
42: 12 The *L* blessed the latter part
Ps 1: 2 But his delight is in the law of the *L*
1: 6 For the *L* watches over the way
4: 6 of your face shine upon us, O *L*.
4: 8 for you alone, O *L*,
5: 3 Morning by morning, O *L*,
6: 1 O *L*, do not rebuke me
8: 1 O *L*, our Lord,
9: 9 The *L* is a refuge for the oppressed,
9: 19 Arise, O *L*, let not man triumph;
10: 16 The *L* is King for ever and ever;
12: 6 And the words of the *L* are flawless
16: 5 *L*, you have assigned me my
16: 8 I have set the *L* always before me.
18: 1 I love you, O *L*, my strength.
18: 6 In my distress I called to the *L*;
18: 30 the word of the *L* is flawless.
19: 7 The law of the *L* is perfect,
19: 14 O *L*, my Rock and my Redeemer.
20: 5 May the *L* grant all your requests.
20: 7 in the name of the *L* our God.
22: 8 let the *L* rescue him.
23: 1 The *L* is my shepherd, I shall not
23: 6 I will dwell in the house of the *L*
24: 3 Who may ascend the hill of the *L*?
24: 8 The *L* strong and mighty,
25: 10 All the ways of the *L* are loving
27: 1 The *L* is my light and my salvation
27: 4 to gaze upon the beauty of the *L*
27: 6 I will sing and make music to the *L*.
29: 1 Ascribe to the *L*, O mighty ones,
29: 4 The voice of the *L* is powerful;
30: 4 Sing to the *L*, you saints of his;
31: 5 redeem me, O *L*, the God of truth.
32: 2 whose sin the *L* does not count
33: 1 joyfully to the *L*, you righteous;
33: 6 of the *L* were the heavens made,
33: 12 is the nation whose God is the *L*,
33: 18 But the eyes of the *L* are
34: 1 I will extol the *L* at all times;
Ps 34: 3 Glorify the *L* with me;
34: 4 I sought the *L*, and he answered me
34: 7 The angel of the *L* encamps
34: 8 Taste and see that the *L* is good;
34: 9 Fear the *L*, you his saints,
34: 15 The eyes of the *L* are
34: 18 The *L* is close to the broken-hearted
37: 4 Delight yourself in the *L*
37: 5 Commit your way to the *L*;
39: 4 "Show me, O *L*, my life's end
40: 1 I waited patiently for the *L*;
40: 5 Many, O *L* my God,
46: 8 Come and see the works of the *L*,
47: 2 How awesome is the *L* Most High,
48: 1 Great is the *L*, and most worthy
50: 1 The Mighty One, God, the *L*,
55: 22 Cast your cares on the *L*
59: 8 But you, O *L*, laugh at them;
68: 4 his name is the *L*—
68: 18 O *L* God, might dwell there.
68: 20 from the Sovereign *L* comes escape
69: 31 This will please the *L* more
72: 18 Praise be to the *L* God, the God
75: 8 In the hand of the *L* is a cup
78: 4 the praiseworthy deeds of the *L*,
84: 8 my prayer, O *L* God Almighty;
84: 11 For the *L* God is a sun and shield;
85: 7 Show us your unfailing love, O *L*,
86: 11 Teach me your way, O *L*,
87: 2 the *L* loves the gates of Zion
89: 5 heavens praise your wonders, O *L*,
89: 8 O *L* God Almighty, who is like you
91: 2 I will say of the *L*, "He is my refuge
92: 1 It is good to praise the *L*
92: 4 by your deeds, O *L*;
92: 13 planted in the house of the *L*,
93: 1 The *L* reigns, he is robed in majesty
93: 5 house for endless days, O *L*.
94: 1 O *L*, the God who avenges,
94: 12 is the man you discipline, O *L*,
94: 18 your love, O *L*, supported me.
95: 1 Come, let us sing for joy to the *L*;
95: 3 For the *L* is the great God,
95: 6 let us kneel before the *L* our Maker
96: 1 Sing to the *L* a new song;
96: 5 but the *L* made the heavens.
96: 8 to the *L* the glory due his name;
96: 9 Worship the *L* in the splendour
96: 13 they will sing before the *L*,
97: 1 The *L* reigns, let the earth be glad;
97: 9 O *L*, are the Most High
98: 1 Sing to the *L* a new song,
98: 2 *L* has made his salvation known
98: 4 Shout for joy to the *L*, all the earth,
99: 1 The *L* reigns,
99: 2 Great is the *L* in Zion;
99: 5 Exalt the *L* our God
99: 9 Exalt the *L* our God
100: 1 Shout for joy to the *L*, all the earth.
100: 2 Worship the *L* with gladness;
100: 3 Know that the *L* is God.
100: 5 For the *L* is good and his love
101: 1 to you, O *L*, I will sing praise.
102: 12 But you, O *L*, sit enthroned for ever
103: 1 Praise the *L*, O my soul;
103: 8 The *L* is compassionate
103: 19 The *L* has established his throne
104: 1 O *L* my God, you are very great;
104: 24 How many are your works, O *L*!
104: 33 I will sing to the *L* all my life;
105: 4 Look to the *L* and his strength;
105: 7 He is the *L* our God;
106: 2 proclaim the mighty acts of the *L*
107: 1 Give thanks to the *L*, for he is good
107: 8 to the *L* for his unfailing love
107: 21 to the *L* for his unfailing love
107: 43 and consider the great love of the *L*
108: 3 I will praise you, O *L*,
109: 26 Help me, O *L* my God;
110: 1 The *L* says to my Lord:
110: 4 The *L* has sworn
111: 2 Great are the works of the *L*;
111: 4 *L* is gracious and compassionate.
111: 10 The fear of the *L* is the beginning

Ps 112: 1 Blessed is the man who fears the *L*,
113: 1 Praise, O servants of the *L*,
113: 2 Let the name of the *L* be praised,
113: 4 *L* is exalted over all the nations,
113: 5 Who is like the *L* our God,
115: 1 Not to us, O *L*, not to us
115: 18 it is we who extol the *L*,
116: 12 How can I repay the *L*
116: 15 Precious in the sight of the *L*
117: 1 Praise the *L*, all you nations;
118: 1 Give thanks to the *L*, for he is good
118: 5 In my anguish I cried to the *L*,
118: 8 It is better to take refuge in the *L*
118: 18 The *L* has chastened me severely,
118: 23 the *L* has done this,
118: 24 This is the day the *L* has made;
118: 26 comes in the name of the *L*.
119: 1 to the law of the *L*.
119: 64 with your love, O *L*;
119: 89 Your word, O *L*, is eternal;
119: 126 It is time for you to act, O *L*;
119: 159 O *L*, according to your love.
120: 1 I call on the *L* in my distress,
121: 2 My help comes from the *L*,
121: 5 The *L* watches over you—
121: 8 the *L* will watch over your coming
122: 1 "Let us go to the house of the *L*."
123: 2 so our eyes look to the *L* our God,
124: 1 If the *L* had not been on our side—
124: 8 Our help is in the name of the *L*,
125: 2 so the *L* surrounds his people
126: 3 The *L* has done great things for us,
126: 4 Restore our fortunes, O *L*,
127: 1 Unless the *L* builds the house,
127: 3 Sons are a heritage from the *L*,
128: 1 Blessed are all who fear the *L*,
130: 1 O *L*;/O Lord, hear my voice
130: 3 If you, O *L*, kept a record of sins,
130: 5 I wait for the *L*, my soul waits,
131: 3 O Israel, put your hope in the *L*
132: 1 O *L*, remember David
132: 13 For the *L* has chosen Zion,
133: 3 For there the *L* bestows his
134: 3 May the *L*, the Maker of heaven
135: 4 For the *L* has chosen Jacob
135: 6 The *L* does whatever pleases him,
136: 1 Give thanks to the *L*, for he is good
137: 4 How can we sing the songs of the *L*
138: 1 I will praise you, O *L*,
138: 8 The *L* will fulfil ,his purpose,
139: 1 O *L*, you have searched me
140: 1 Rescue me, O *L*, from evil men;
141: 1 O *L*, I call to you; come quickly
141: 3 Set a guard over my mouth, O *L*;
142: 5 I cry to you, O *L*;
143: 9 Rescue me from my enemies, O *L*,
144: 3 O *L*, what is man that you care
145: 3 Great is the *L* and most worthy
145: 8 *L* is gracious and compassionate,
145: 9 The *L* is good to all;
145: 17 The *L* is righteous in all his ways
145: 18 The *L* is near to all who call on him
146: 5 whose hope is in the *L* his God,
146: 7 The *L* sets prisoners free,
147: 2 The *L* builds up Jerusalem;
147: 7 Sing to the *L* with thanksgiving;
147: 11 *L* delights in those who fear him,
147: 12 Extol the *L*, O Jerusalem;
148: 1 Praise the *L* from the heavens,
148: 7 Praise the *L* from the earth,
149: 4 For the *L* takes delight
150: 1 Praise the *L*.
150: 6 that has breath praise the *L*.
Pr 1: 7 The fear of the *L* is the beginning
1: 29 and did not choose to fear the *L*,
2: 5 will understand the fear of the *L*
2: 6 For the *L* gives wisdom,
3: 5 Trust in the *L* with all your heart
3: 7 fear the *L* and shun evil.
3: 9 Honour the *L* with your wealth,
3: 12 the *L* disciplines those he loves,
3: 19 By wisdom the *L* laid the earth's
5: 21 are in full view of the *L*,
6: 16 There are six things the *L* hates,
Pr 8: 13 To fear the *L* is to hate evil;
9: 10 "The fear of the *L* is the beginning
10: 27 The fear of the *L* adds length to life
11: 1 The *L* abhors dishonest scales,
12: 22 The *L* detests lying lips,
14: 2 whose walk is upright fears the *L*,
14: 26 He who fears the *L* has a secure
14: 27 The fear of the *L* is a fountain
15: 3 The eyes of the *L* are everywhere,
15: 16 Better a little with the fear of the *L*
15: 33 of the *L* teaches a man wisdom,
16: 2 but motives are weighed by the *L*.
16: 3 Commit to the *L* whatever you do,
16: 4 The *L* works out everything
16: 5 The *L* detests all the proud of heart
16: 9 but the *L* determines his steps.
16: 33 but its every decision is from the *L*.
18: 10 The name of the *L* is a strong tower
18: 22 and receives favour from the *L*.
19: 14 but a prudent wife is from the *L*.
19: 17 to the poor lends to the *L*,
19: 23 The fear of the *L* leads to life:
20: 10 the *L* detests them both.
21: 2 but the *L* weighs the heart.
21: 3 to the *L* than sacrifice.
21: 30 that can succeed against the *L*.
21: 31 but victory rests with the *L*.
22: 2 The *L* is the Maker of them all.
22: 23 for the *L* will take up their case
23: 17 for the fear of the *L*.
24: 18 or the *L* will see and disapprove
24: 21 Fear the *L* and the king, my son,
25: 22 and the *L* will reward you.
28: 14 is the man who always fears the *L*,
29: 26 from the *L* that man gets justice.
30: 7 "Two things I ask of you, O *L*;
31: 30 a woman who fears the *L* is
Isa 2: 3 up to the mountain of the *L*,
2: 10 the ground from dread of the *L*
3: 17 the *L* will make their scalps bald."
4: 2 of the *L* will be beautiful
5: 16 the *L* Almighty will be exalted
6: 3 holy, holy is the *L* Almighty;
9: 7 The zeal of the *L* Almighty
11: 2 The Spirit of the *L* will rest on him
11: 9 full of the knowledge of the *L*
12: 2 The *L*, the *L*, is my strength
18: 7 of the Name of the *L* Almighty.
24: 1 the *L* is going to lay waste the earth
25: 1 O *L*, you are my God;
25: 6 this mountain the *L* Almighty will
25: 8 The Sovereign *L* will wipe away
26: 4 Trust in the *L* for ever,
26: 8 *L*, walking in the way of your laws,
26: 13 O *L*, our God, other lords
26: 21 the *L* is coming out of his dwelling
27: 1 the *L* will punish with his sword,
27: 12 In that day the *L* will thresh
28: 5 In that day the *L* Almighty
29: 6 the *L* Almighty will come
29: 15 to hide their plans from the *L*,
30: 18 For the *L* is a God of justice.
30: 26 when the *L* binds up the bruises
30: 27 the Name of the *L* comes from afar
30: 30 The *L* will cause men
33: 2 O *L*, be gracious to us;
33: 6 the fear of the *L* is the key
33: 22 For the *L* is our judge,
34: 2 The *L* is angry with all nations;
35: 2 they will see the glory of the *L*,
35: 10 the ransomed of the *L* will return.
38: 7 to you that the *L* will do what he
40: 3 the way for the *L*;
40: 5 the glory of the *L* will be revealed,
40: 7 the breath of the *L* blows on them.
40: 10 the Sovereign *L* comes with power,
40: 14 Whom did the *L* consult
40: 28 The *L* is the everlasting God,
40: 31 but those who hope in the *L*
41: 14 will help you," declares the *L*,
41: 20 that the hand of the *L* has done this
42: 6 the *L*, have called you
42: 8 "I am the *L*; that is my name!
42: 13 The *L* will march out like a mighty
Isa 42: 21 It pleased the *L*
43: 3 For I am the *L*, your God,
43: 11 I, even I, am the *L*,
44: 6 "This is what the *L* says—
44: 24 I am the *L*,
45: 5 I am the *L*, and there is no other;
45: 7 I, the *L*, do all these things.
45: 21 Was it not I, the *L*?
48: 17 "I am the *L* your God,
50: 4 Sovereign *L* has given me
50: 10 Who among you fears the *L*
51: 1 and who seek the *L*:
51: 11 The ransomed of the *L* will return.
51: 15 the *L* Almighty is his name.
53: 1 the arm of the *L* been revealed?
53: 6 and the *L* has laid on him
53: 10 and the will of the *L* will prosper
54: 5 the *L* Almighty is his name—
55: 6 Seek the *L* while he may be found;
55: 7 to the *L*, and he will have mercy
56: 6 who bind themselves to the *L*
58: 8 of the *L* will be your rear guard.
58: 11 The *L* will guide you always;
59: 1 the arm of the *L* is not too short
60: 1 the glory of the *L* rises upon you.
60: 16 Then you will know that I, the *L*,
60: 20 the *L* will be your everlasting light,
61: 1 Spirit of the Sovereign *L* is on me,
61: 3 a planting of the *L*
61: 10 I delight greatly in the *L*;
61: 11 so the Sovereign *L* will make
62: 4 for the *L* will take delight in you,
63: 7 I will tell of the kindnesses of the *L*,
64: 8 Yet, O *L*, you are our Father.
66: 15 See, the *L* is coming with fire,
Jer 1: 9 Then the *L* reached out his hand
2: 19 when you forsake the *L* your God
3: 25 sinned against the *L* our God,
4: 4 Circumcise yourselves to the *L*,
8: 7 the requirements of the *L*.
9: 24 I am the *L*, who exercises kindness,
10: 6 No-one is like you, O *L*;
10: 10 But the *L* is the true God;
12: 1 You are always righteous, O *L*,
14: 7 O *L*, do something for the sake
14: 20 O *L*, we acknowledge our
16: 15 will say, 'As surely as the *L* lives,
16: 19 O *L*, my strength and my fortress,
17: 7 is the man who trusts in the *L*,
17: 10 "I the *L* search the heart
20: 11 *L* is with me like a mighty warrior;
23: 6 The *L* Our Righteousness.
24: 7 heart to know me, that I am the *L*.
28: 9 as one truly sent by the *L* only
31: 11 For the *L* will ransom Jacob
31: 22 The *L* will create a new thing
31: 34 his brother, saying, 'Know the *L*,'
32: 27 I am the *L*, the God of all mankind.
33: 16 The *L* Our Righteousness.'
36: 6 the words of the *L* that you wrote
40: 3 now the *L* has brought it about;
42: 3 Pray that the *L* your God will tell
42: 4 I will tell you everything the *L* says
42: 6 we will obey the *L* our God,
50: 4 go in tears to seek the *L* their God.
51: 10 " 'The *L* has vindicated us;
51: 56 For the *L* is a God of retribution;
La 3: 24 to myself, "The *L* is my portion;
3: 25 *L* is good to those whose hope is
3: 40 and let us return to the *L*.
Eze 1: 3 the word of the *L* came
1: 28 of the likeness of the glory of the *L*.
4: 14 Sovereign *L*! I have never defiled
10: 4 Then the glory of the *L* rose
15: 7 you will know that I am the *L*.
30: 3 the day of the *L* is near—
36: 23 nations will know that I am the *L*,
37: 4 'Dry bones, hear the word of the *L*!
43: 4 glory of the *L* entered the temple
44: 4 LORD filling the temple of the *L*,
Da 9: 2 to the word of the *L* given
Hos 1: 7 horsemen, but by the *L* their God."
2: 20 and you will acknowledge the *L*.
3: 1 as the *L* loves the Israelites,

Hos 3: 5 They will come trembling to the *L*
6: 1 "Come, let us return to the *L*.
6: 3 Let us acknowledge the *L*;
10: 12 for it is time to seek the *L*,
12: 5 the *L* is his name of renown!
14: 1 O Israel, to the *L* your God.
Joel 1: 1 The word of the *L* that came
1: 15 For the day of the *L* is near;
2: 1 for the day of the *L* is coming.
2: 11 The day of the *L* is great;
2: 13 Return to the *L* your God,
2: 23 rejoice in the *L* your God,
2: 31 the great and dreadful day of the *L*.
2: 32 on the name of the *L* will be saved;
3: 14 For the day of the *L* is near
3: 16 the *L* will be a refuge for his people,
Am 4: 13 the *L* God Almighty is his name.
5: 6 Seek the *L* and live,
5: 15 Perhaps the *L* God Almighty will
5: 18 long for the day of the *L*?
7: 15 *L* took me from tending the flock
8: 12 searching for the word of the *L*,
9: 5 The Lord, the *L* Almighty,
Ob :15 "The day of the *L* is near
Jnh 1: 3 But Jonah ran away from the *L*
1: 4 the *L* sent a great wind on the sea,
1: 17 But the *L* provided a great fish
2: 9 Salvation comes from the *L*."
4: 2 He prayed to the *L*, "O *L*,
4: 6 Then the *L* God provided a vine
Mic 1: 1 The word of the *L* given to Micah
4: 2 up to the mountain of the *L*,
5: 4 flock in the strength of the *L*,
6: 2 For the *L* has a case
6: 8 And what does the *L* require of you
7: 7 as for me, I watch in hope for the *L*,
Na 1: 2 The *L* takes vengeance on his foes
1: 3 The *L* is slow to anger
Hab 2: 14 knowledge of the glory of the *L*,
2: 20 But the *L* is in his holy temple;
3: 2 I stand in awe of your deeds, O *L*.
Zep 1: 1 The word of the *L* that came
1: 7 for the day of the *L* is near.
3: 17 The *L* your God is with you,
Hag 1: 1 the word of the *L* came
1: 8 and be honoured," says the *L*.
2: 23 that day,' declares the *L* Almighty,
Zec 1: 1 the word of the *L* came
1: 17 and the *L* will again comfort Zion
3: 1 standing before the angel of the *L*,
4: 6 by my Spirit,' says the *L* Almighty.
6: 12 and build the temple of the *L*.
8: 21 the *L* and seek the *L* Almighty.
9: 16 The *L* their God will save them
14: 5 Then the *L* my God will come,
14: 9 The *L* will be king
14: 16 the *L* Almighty, and to celebrate
Mal 1: 1 The word of the *L* to Israel
3: 6 "I the *L* do not change.
4: 5 and dreadful day of the *L* comes.

†LORD'S (†LORD)

Ex 4: 14 the *L* anger burned against Moses
12: 11 Eat it in haste; it is the *L* Passover.
34: 34 he entered the *L* presence
Lev 23: 4 "'These are the *L* appointed feasts,
Nu 9: 23 At the *L* command they encamped
14: 41 you disobeying the *L* command?
32: 13 The *L* anger burned against Israel
Dt 6: 18 is right and good in the *L* sight,
10: 13 and to observe the *L* commands
32: 9 For the *L* portion is his people,
Jos 21: 45 Not one of all the *L* good promises
1Sa 24: 10 because he is the *L* anointed.'
1Ki 10: 9 Because of the *L* eternal love
Ps 24: 1 The earth is the *L*, and everything
32: 10 but the *L* unfailing love
89: 1 of the *L* great love for ever;
103: 17 *L* love is with those who fear him,
118: 15 "The *L* right hand has done mighty
Pr 3: 11 do not despise the *L* discipline
19: 21 but it is the *L* purpose that prevails.
Isa 24: 14 west they acclaim the *L* majesty.
30: 9 to listen to the *L* instruction.
Isa 49: 4 Yet what is due to me is in the *L*
53: 10 Yet it was the *L* will to crush him
55: 13 This will be for the *L* renown,
61: 2 to proclaim the year of the *L* favour
62: 3 of splendour in the *L* hand,
Jer 25: 17 So I took the cup from the *L* hand
48: 10 lax in doing the *L* work!
51: 7 was a gold cup in the *L* hand;
La 3: 22 of the *L* great love we are not
Eze 7: 19 them in the day of the *L* wrath.
Joel 3: 18 will flow out of the *L* house
Ob :21 And the kingdom will be the *L*.
Mic 4: 1 of the *L* temple will be established
6: 2 O mountains, the *L* accusation;
Hab 2: 16 from the *L* right hand is coming
Zep 2: 3 sheltered on the day of the *L* anger.

LOSE (LOSES LOSS LOST)

Dt 1: 28 Our brothers have made us *l* heart.
1Sa 17: 32 "Let no-one *l* heart on account
Isa 7: 4 Do not *l* heart because of these two
Mt 10: 39 Whoever finds his life will *l* it,
Lk 9: 25 and yet *l* or forfeit his very self?
Jn 6: 39 that I shall *l* none of all that he has
2Co 4: 1 this ministry, we do not *l* heart.
4: 16 Therefore we do not *l* heart.
Heb 12: 3 will not grow weary and *l* heart.
12: 5 do not *l* heart when he rebukes you
2Jn : 8 that you do not *l* what you have

LOSES (LOSE)

Mt 5: 13 But if the salt *l* its saltiness,
Lk 15: 4 you has a hundred sheep and *l* one
15: 8 has ten silver coins and *l* one.

LOSS (LOSE)

Ro 11: 12 and their *l* means riches
1Co 3: 15 he will suffer *l*; he himself will be
Php 3: 8 I consider everything a *l* compared

LOST (LOSE)

Ps 73: 2 I had nearly *l* my foothold.
Jer 50: 6 "My people have been *l* sheep;
Eze 34: 4 the strays or searched for the *l*.
34: 16 for the *l* and bring back the strays.
Mt 18: 14 any of these little ones should be *l*.
Lk 15: 4 go after the *l* sheep until he finds it?
15: 6 with me; I have found my *l* sheep.'
15: 9 with me; I have found my *l* coin.'
15: 24 is alive again; he was *l* and is found
19: 10 to seek and to save what was *l*."
Php 3: 8 for whose sake I have *l* all things.

LOT [1]

Nephew of Abraham (Ge 11:27; 12:5). Chose to live in Sodom (Ge 13). Rescued from four kings (Ge 14). Rescued from Sodom (Ge 19:1-29; 2Pe 2:7). Fathered Moab and Ammon by his daughters (Ge 19: 30-38).

LOT [2] (LOTS)

Est 3: 7 the *l*) in the presence of Haman
9: 24 the *l*) for their ruin and destruction.
Pr 16: 33 The *l* is cast into the lap,
18: 18 Casting the *l* settles disputes
Ecc 3: 22 his work, because that is his *l*.
Ac 1: 26 Then they cast lots, and the *l* fell

LOTS (LOT [2])

Jos 18: 10 Joshua then cast *l* for them
Ps 22: 18 and cast *l* for my clothing.
Joel 3: 3 They cast *l* for my people
Ob :11 and cast *l* for Jerusalem,
Mt 27: 35 divided up his clothes by casting *l*.
Ac 1: 26 Then they cast *l*, and the lot fell

LOVE* (BELOVED LOVED LOVELY LOVER LOVER'S LOVERS LOVES LOVING LOVING-KINDNESS)

Ge 20: 13 'This is how you can show your *l*
22: 2 your only son Isaac, whom you *l*,
29: 18 Jacob was in *l* with Rachel and said
29: 20 days to him because of his *l* for her.
29: 32 Surely my husband will *l* me now."
Ex 15: 13 "In your unfailing *l* you will lead
20: 6 showing *l* to thousands who *l* me
21: 5 'I *l* my master and my wife
34: 6 abounding in *l* and faithfulness,
34: 7 maintaining *l* to thousands,
Lev 19: 18 but *l* your neighbour as yourself.
19: 34 *L* him as yourself,
Nu 14: 18 abounding in *l* and forgiving sin
14: 19 In accordance with your great *l*,
Dt 5: 10 showing *l* to thousands who *l* me
6: 5 *L* the LORD your God
7: 9 generations of those who *l* him
7: 9 keeping his covenant of *l*
7: 12 God will keep his covenant of *l*
7: 13 He will *l* you and bless you
10: 12 to walk in all his ways, to *l* him,
10: 19 you are to *l* those who are aliens,
11: 1 *L* the LORD your God
Dt 11: 13 to *l* the LORD your God
11: 22 to *l* the LORD your God,
13: 3 you *l* him with all your heart
13: 6 wife you *l*, or your closest friend
19: 9 to *l* the LORD your God
21: 15 the son of the wife he does not *l*,
21: 16 the son of the wife he does not *l*.
30: 6 so that you may *l* him
30: 16 today to *l* the LORD your God,
30: 20 and that you may *l* the LORD your
33: 3 Surely it is you who *l* the people;
Jos 22: 5 to *l* the LORD your God, to walk
23: 11 careful to *l* the LORD your God.
Jdg 5: 31 may they who *l* you be like the sun
14: 16 You hate me! You don't really *l* me
16: 4 he fell in *l* with a woman
16: 15 "How can you say, 'I *l* you,'
1Sa 18: 20 Saul's daughter Michal was in *l*
20: 17 had David reaffirm his oath out of *l*
2Sa 1: 26 Your *l* for me was wonderful,
7: 15 But my *l* will never be taken away
13: 1 son of David fell in *l* with Tamar,
13: 4 said to him, "I'm in *l* with Tamar,
16: 17 "Is this the *l* you show your friend?
19: 6 You *l* those who hate you
19: 6 hate you and hate those who *l* you.
1Ki 3: 3 Solomon showed his *l*
8: 23 you who keep your covenant of *l*
10: 9 of the LORD's eternal *l* for Israel,
11: 2 Solomon held fast to them in *l*.
1Ch 16: 34 his *l* endures for ever.
16: 41 "for his *l* endures for ever."
17: 13 I will never take my *l* away
2Ch 5: 13 his *l* endures for ever."
6: 14 you who keep your covenant of *l*
6: 42 Remember the great *l* promised
7: 3 his *l* endures for ever."
7: 6 saying, "His *l* endures for ever."
9: 8 Because of the *l* of your God
19: 2 and *l* those who hate the LORD?
20: 21 for his *l* endures for ever."
Ezr 3: 11 his *l* to Israel endures for ever."
Ne 1: 5 covenant of *l* with those who *l* him
9: 17 slow to anger and abounding in *l*.
9: 32 who keeps his covenant of *l*,
13: 22 to me according to your great *l*.
Job 15: 34 of those who *l* bribes.
19: 19 those I *l* have turned against me.
37: 13 or to water his earth and show his *l*.
Ps 4: 2 How long will you *l* delusions
5: 11 that those who *l* your name may
6: 4 save me because of your unfailing *l*.
11: 5 wicked and those who *l* violence
13: 5 But I trust in your unfailing *l*;
17: 7 Show the wonder of your great *l*,
18: 1 I *l* you, O LORD, my strength.
21: 7 through the unfailing *l*
23: 6 Surely goodness and *l* will follow
25: 6 O LORD, your great mercy and *l*,
25: 7 according to your *l* remember me,
26: 3 for your *l* is ever before me,
26: 8 I *l* the house where you live,
31: 7 I will be glad and rejoice in your *l*,
31: 16 save me in your unfailing *l*.
31: 21 for he showed his wonderful *l*
31: 23 *L* the LORD, all his saints!

Ps 32: 10 but the LORD's unfailing *l*
33: 5 the earth is full of his unfailing *l*.
33: 18 whose hope is in his unfailing *l*,
33: 22 May your unfailing *l* rest upon us,
36: 5 Your *l*, O LORD, reaches
36: 7 How priceless is your unfailing *l*!
36: 10 Continue your *l* to those who know
40: 10 I do not conceal your *l*
40: 11 may your *l* and your truth always
40: 16 may those who *l* your salvation
42: 8 By day the LORD directs his *l*,
44: 26 of your unfailing *l*.
45: 7 You *l* righteousness and hate
48: 9 we meditate on your unfailing *l*.
51: 1 according to your unfailing *l*;
52: 3 You *l* evil rather than good,
52: 4 You *l* every harmful word,
52: 8 I trust in God's unfailing *l*
57: 3 God sends his *l* and his faithfulness
57: 10 For great is your *l*, reaching
59: 16 in the morning I will sing of your *l*;
60: 5 that those you *l* may be delivered.
61: 7 appoint your *l* and faithfulness
63: 3 Because your *l* is better than life,
66: 20 or withheld his *l* from me!
69: 13 in your great *l*, O God,
69: 16 out of the goodness of your *l*;
69: 36 and those who *l* his name will dwell
70: 4 may those who *l* your salvation
77: 8 Has his unfailing *l* vanished for ever
85: 7 Show us your unfailing *l*, O LORD
85: 10 *L* and faithfulness meet together;
86: 5 abounding in *l* to all who call
86: 13 For great is your *l* towards me;
86: 15 abounding in *l* and faithfulness.
88: 11 Is your *l* declared in the grave,
89: 1 of the LORD's great *l* for ever;
89: 2 declare that your *l* stands firm
89: 14 *l* and faithfulness go before you.
89: 24 My faithful *l* will be with him,
89: 28 I will maintain my *l* to him for ever,
89: 33 but I will not take my *l* from him,
89: 49 where is your former great *l*,
90: 14 with your unfailing *l*,
92: 2 to proclaim your *l* in the morning
94: 18 your *l*, O LORD, supported me.
97: 10 Let those who *l* the LORD hate
98: 3 He has remembered his *l*
100: 5 is good and his *l* endures for ever;
101: 1 I will sing of your *l* and justice;
103: 4 crowns me with *l* and compassion.
103: 8 slow to anger, abounding in *l*.
103: 11 so great is his *l* for those who fear
103: 17 LORD's *l* is with those who fear
106: 1 his *l* endures for ever.
106: 45 and out of his great *l* he relented.
107: 1 his *l* endures for ever.
107: 8 to the LORD for his unfailing *l*
107: 15 to the LORD for his unfailing *l*
107: 21 to the LORD for his unfailing *l*
107: 31 to the LORD for his unfailing *l*
107: 43 consider the great *l* of the LORD.
108: 4 For great is your *l*, higher
108: 6 that those you *l* may be delivered.
109: 21 out of the goodness of your *l*,
109: 26 save me in accordance with your *l*.
115: 1 because of your *l* and faithfulness.
116: 1 I *l* the LORD, for he heard my
117: 2 For great is his *l* towards us,
118: 1 his *l* endures for ever.
118: 2 "His *l* endures for ever."
118: 3 "His *l* endures for ever."
118: 4 "His *l* endures for ever."
118: 29 his *l* endures for ever.
119: 41 May your unfailing *l* come to me,
119: 47 because I *l* them.
119: 48 for your commandments, which I *l*,
119: 64 The earth is filled with your *l*,
119: 76 May your unfailing *l* be my
119: 88 my life according to your *l*,
119: 97 Oh, how I *l* your law!
119: 113 but I *l* your law.
119: 119 therefore I *l* your statutes.
119: 124 your servant according to your *l*

Ps 119: 127 Because I *l* your commands
119: 132 to those who *l* your name.
119: 149 in accordance with your *l*;
119: 159 O LORD, according to your *l*.
119: 159 See how I *l* your precepts;
119: 163 but I *l* your law.
119: 165 peace have they who *l* your law,
119: 167 for I *l* them greatly.
122: 6 "May those who *l* you be secure.
130: 7 for with the LORD is unfailing *l*
136: 1-26 *His* l *endures for ever.*
138: 2 for your *l* and your faithfulness,
138: 8 your *l*, O LORD, endures for ever
143: 8 of your unfailing *l*,
143: 12 In your unfailing *l*, silence my
145: 8 slow to anger and rich in *l*.
145: 20 over all who *l* him,
147: 11 who put their hope in his unfailing *l*
Pr 1: 22 you simple ones *l* your simple
3: 3 Let *l* and faithfulness never leave
4: 6 *l* her, and she will watch over you.
5: 19 you ever be captivated by her *l*.
7: 18 let's drink deep of *l* till morning;
7: 18 let's enjoy ourselves with *l*!
8: 17 I *l* those who *l* me,
8: 21 wealth on those who *l* me
8: 36 all who hate me *l* death."
9: 8 rebuke a wise man and he will *l* you
10: 12 but *l* covers over all wrongs.
14: 22 those who plan what is good find *l*
15: 17 of vegetables where there is *l*
16: 6 Through *l* and faithfulness sin is
17: 9 over an offence promotes *l*,
18: 21 and those who *l* it will eat its fruit.
19: 22 What a man desires is unfailing *l*;
20: 6 claims to have unfailing *l*,
20: 13 Do not *l* sleep or you will grow
20: 28 *L* and faithfulness keep a king safe;
20: 28 through *l* his throne is made secure
21: 21 who pursues righteousness and *l*
27: 5 rebuke than hidden *l*.
Ecc 3: 8 a time to *l* and a time to hate,
9: 1 but no man knows whether *l*
9: 6 Their *l*, their hate
9: 9 life with your wife, whom you *l*,
SS 1: 2 for your *l* is more delightful
1: 3 No wonder the maidens *l* you!
1: 4 we will praise your *l* more
1: 7 you whom I *l*, where you graze
2: 4 and his banner over me is *l*.
2: 5 for I am faint with *l*.
2: 7 Do not arouse or awaken *l*
3: 5 Do not arouse or awaken *l*
4: 10 How delightful is your *l*, my sister,
4: 10 How much more pleasing is your *l*
5: 8 Tell him I am faint with *l*.
7: 6 O *l*, with your delights!
7: 12 there I will give you my *l*.
8: 4 Do not arouse or awaken *l*
8: 6 for *l* is as strong as death,
8: 7 Many waters cannot quench *l*;
8: 7 all the wealth of his house for *l*,
Isa 1: 23 they all *l* bribes
5: 1 I will sing for the one I *l*
16: 5 In *l* a throne will be established;
38: 17 In your *l* you kept me
43: 4 and because I *l* you,
54: 10 yet my unfailing *l* for you will not
55: 3 my faithful *l* promised to David.
56: 6 to *l* the name of the LORD,
56: 10 they *l* to sleep.
57: 8 a pact with those whose beds you *l*,
61: 8 "For I, the LORD, *l* justice;
63: 9 In his *l* and mercy he redeemed
66: 10 all you who *l* her;
Jer 2: 25 I *l* foreign gods,
2: 33 How skilled you are at pursuing *l*!
5: 31 and my people *l* it this way.
12: 7 I will give the one I *l*
14: 10 "They greatly *l* to wander;
16: 5 my *l* and my pity from this people
31: 3 you with an everlasting *l*;
32: 18 You show *l* to thousands
33: 11 his *l* endures for ever."

La 3: 22 of the LORD's great *l* we are not
3: 32 so great is his unfailing *l*.
Eze 16: 8 saw that you were old enough for *l*,
23: 17 of *l*, and in their lust they defiled
33: 32 more than one who sings *l* songs
Da 9: 4 covenant of *l* with all who *l* him
Hos 1: 6 for I will no longer show *l*
1: 7 Yet I will show *l* to the house
2: 4 I will not show my *l* to her children
2: 19 in *l* and compassion.
2: 23 I will show my *l* to the one I called
3: 1 Go, show your *l* to your wife again,
3: 1 and *l* the sacred raisin cakes."
3: 1 *L* her as the LORD loves
4: 1 "There is no faithfulness, no *l*,
4: 18 their rulers dearly *l* shameful ways.
6: 4 Your *l* is like the morning mist,
9: 1 you *l* the wages of a prostitute
9: 15 I will no longer *l* them;
10: 12 reap the fruit of unfailing *l*,
11: 4 with ties of *l*;
12: 6 maintain *l* and justice,
14: 4 and *l* them freely,
Joel 2: 13 slow to anger and abounding in *l*,
Am 4: 5 for this is what you *l* to do,"
5: 15 Hate evil, *l* good;
Jnh 4: 2 slow to anger and abounding in *l*,
Mic 3: 2 you who hate good and *l* evil;
6: 8 To act justly and to *l* mercy
Zep 3: 17 he will quiet you with his *l*,
Zec 8: 17 and do not *l* to swear falsely.
8: 19 Therefore *l* truth and peace."
Mt 3: 17 "This is my Son, whom I *l*;
5: 43 '*L* your neighbour and hate your
5: 44 *L* your enemies and pray
5: 46 you *l* those who *l* you, what reward
6: 5 for they *l* to pray standing
6: 24 he will hate the one and *l* the other,
12: 18 the one I *l*, in whom I delight;
17: 5 "This is my Son, whom I *l*;
19: 19 and '*l* your neighbour as yourself.'"
22: 37 "'*L* the Lord your God
22: 39 '*L* your neighbour as yourself.'
23: 6 they *l* the place of honour
23: 7 they *l* to be greeted
24: 12 the *l* of most will grow cold,
Mk 1: 11 "You are my Son, whom I *l*;
9: 7 "This is my Son, whom I *l*.
12: 30 *L* the Lord your God
12: 31 '*L* your neighbour as yourself.'
12: 33 To *l* him with all your heart,
12: 33 and to *l* your neighbour
Lk 3: 22 "You are my Son, whom I *l*;
6: 27 you who hear me: *L* your enemies,
6: 32 Even 'sinners' *l* those who *l* them.
6: 32 you *l* those who *l* you, what credit
6: 35 *l* your enemies, do good to them,
7: 42 which of them will *l* him more?"
10: 27 and, '*L* your neighbour as yourself
10: 27 "'*L* the Lord your God
11: 42 you neglect justice and the *l* of God
11: 43 you *l* the most important seats
16: 13 he will hate the one and *l* the other,
20: 13 whom I *l*; perhaps they will respect
20: 46 *l* to be greeted in the market-places
Jn 5: 42 I know that you do not have the *l*
8: 42 were your Father, you would *l* me,
11: 3 "Lord, the one you *l* is sick."
13: 1 them the full extent of his *l*.
13: 34 I give you: *L* one another.
13: 34 so you must *l* one another.
13: 35 disciples if you *l* one another."
14: 15 "If you *l* me, you will obey what I
14: 21 I too will *l* him and show myself
14: 23 My Father will *l* him, and we will
14: 24 He who does not *l* me will not obey
14: 31 world must learn that I *l* the Father
15: 9 Now remain in my *l*.
15: 10 commands and remain in his *l*.
15: 10 you will remain in my *l*,
15: 12 *L* each other as I have loved you.
15: 13 Greater *l* has no-one than this,
15: 17 This is my command: *L* each other.
15: 19 to the world, it would *l* you

Jn 17:26 known in order that the *l* you have
21:15 do you truly *l* me more than these
21:15 he said, "you know that I *l* you."
21:16 Yes, Lord, you know that I *l* you."
21:16 do you truly *l* me?" He answered,
21:17 all things; you know that I *l* you."
21:17 "Do you *l* me?" He said, "Lord,
21:17 "Simon son of John, do you *l* me?"
Ro 5:5 because God has poured out his *l*
5:8 God demonstrates his own *l* for us
8:28 for the good of those who *l* him,
8:35 us from the *l* of Christ?
8:39 us from the *l* of God that is
12:9 *L* must be sincere.
12:10 to one another in brotherly *l*.
13:8 continuing debt to *l* one another,
13:9 "*L* your neighbour as yourself."
13:10 Therefore *l* is the fulfilment
13:10 *L* does no harm to its neighbour.
14:15 you are no longer acting in *l*.
15:30 and by the *l* of the Spirit,
16:8 Greet Ampliatus, whom I *l*
1Co 2:9 prepared for those who *l* him"—
4:17 my son whom I *l*, who is faithful
4:21 or in *l* and with a gentle spirit?
8:1 Knowledge puffs up, but *l* builds up
13:1 have not *l*, I am only a resounding
13:2 but have not *l*, I am nothing.
13:3 but have not *l*, I gain nothing.
13:4 *L* is patient, *l* is kind.
13:6 *L* does not delight in evil
13:8 *L* never fails.
13:13 But the greatest of these is *l*.
13:13 three remain: faith, hope and *l*.
14:1 way of *l* and eagerly desire spiritual
16:14 Do everything in *l*.
16:22 If anyone does not *l* the Lord—
16:24 My *l* to all of you in Christ Jesus.
2Co 2:4 to let you know the depth of my *l*
2:8 therefore, to reaffirm your *l* for him
5:14 For Christ's *l* compels us,
6:6 in the Holy Spirit and in sincere *l*;
8:7 complete earnestness and in your *l*
8:8 sincerity of your *l* by comparing it
8:24 show these men the proof of your *l*
11:11 Why? Because I do not *l* you?
12:15 If I *l* you more, will you *l* me less?
13:11 And the God of *l* and peace will be
13:14 of the Lord Jesus Christ, and the *l*
Gal 5:6 is faith expressing itself through *l*.
5:13 rather, serve one another in *l*.
5:14 "*L* your neighbour as yourself."
5:22 But the fruit of the Spirit is *l*, joy,
Eph 1:4 In *l* he predestined us
1:15 and your *l* for all the saints,
2:4 But because of his great *l* for us,
3:17 being rooted and established in *l*,
3:18 and high and deep is the *l* of Christ,
3:19 and to know this *l* that surpasses
4:2 bearing with one another in *l*.
4:15 Instead, speaking the truth in *l*,
4:16 grows and builds itself up in *l*,
5:2 loved children and live a life of *l*,
5:25 *l* your wives, just as Christ loved
5:28 husbands ought to *l* their wives
5:33 each one of you also must *l* his wife
6:23 *l* with faith from God the Father
6:24 Christ with an undying *l*.
6:24 to all who *l* our Lord Jesus Christ
Php 1:9 that your *l* may abound more
1:16 so in *l*, knowing that I am put here
2:1 from his *l*, if any fellowship
2:2 having the same *l*, being one
4:1 you whom I *l* and long for,
Col 1:4 of the *l* you have for all the saints—
1:5 *l* that spring from the hope that is
1:8 also told us of your *l* in the Spirit.
2:2 in heart and united in *l*,
3:14 And over all these virtues put on *l*,
3:19 *l* your wives and do not be harsh
1Th 1:3 your labour prompted by *l*,
3:6 good news about your faith and *l*.
3:12 May the Lord make your *l* increase
1Th 4:9 about brotherly *l* we do not need
4:9 taught by God to *l* each other.
4:10 you do *l* all the brothers
5:8 on faith and *l* as a breastplate,
5:13 them in the highest regard in *l*
2Th 1:3 and the *l* every one of you has
2:10 because they refused to *l* the truth
3:5 direct your hearts into God's *l*
1Ti 1:5 The goal of this command is *l*,
1:14 and *l* that are in Christ Jesus.
2:15 *l* and holiness with propriety.
4:12 in life, in *l*, in faith and in purity.
6:10 For the *l* of money is a root
6:11 faith, *l*, endurance and gentleness.
2Ti 1:7 of power, of *l* and of self-discipline.
1:13 with faith and *l* in Christ Jesus.
2:22 and pursue righteousness, faith, *l*
3:3 unholy, without *l*, unforgiving,
3:10 faith, patience, *l*, endurance,
Tit 2:2 in faith, in *l* and in endurance.
2:4 women to *l* their husbands
3:4 and *l* of God our Saviour appeared,
3:15 Greet those who *l* us in the faith.
Phm :5 and your *l* for all the saints.
:7 Your *l* has given me great joy
:9 yet I appeal to you on the basis of *l*.
Heb 6:10 and the *l* you have shown him
10:24 may spur one another on towards *l*
13:5 free from the *l* of money
Jas 1:12 promised to those who *l* him.
2:5 he promised those who *l* him?
2:8 "*L* your neighbour as yourself,"
1Pe 1:8 you have not seen him, you *l* him;
1:22 the truth so that you have sincere *l*
1:22 *l* one another deeply,
2:17 *L* the brotherhood of believers,
3:8 be sympathetic, *l* as brothers,
3:10 "Whoever would *l* life
4:8 Above all, *l* each other deeply,
4:8 *l* covers over a multitude of sins.
5:14 Greet one another with a kiss of *l*.
2Pe 1:7 and to brotherly kindness, *l*.
1:17 "This is my Son, whom I *l*;
1Jn 2:5 God's *l* is truly made complete
2:15 Do not *l* the world or anything
2:15 the *l* of the Father is not in him.
3:1 How great is the *l* the Father has
3:10 anyone who does not *l* his brother.
3:11 We should *l* one another.
3:14 Anyone who does not *l* remains
3:14 because we *l* our brothers.
3:16 This is how we know what *l* is:
3:17 how can the *l* of God be in him?
3:18 let us not *l* with words or tongue
3:23 to *l* one another as he commanded
4:7 Dear friends, let us *l* one another,
4:7 for *l* comes from God.
4:8 Whoever does not *l* does not know
4:8 not know God, because God is *l*.
4:9 This is how God showed his *l*
4:10 This is *l*: not that we loved God,
4:11 we also ought to *l* one another.
4:12 and his *l* is made complete in us.
4:12 seen God; but if we *l* each other,
4:16 God is *l*.
4:16 Whoever lives in *l* lives in God,
4:16 and rely on the *l* God has for us.
4:17 *l* is made complete among us
4:18 But perfect *l* drives out fear,
4:18 There is no fear in *l*.
4:18 who fears is not made perfect in *l*.
4:19 We *l* because he first loved us.
4:20 If anyone says, "I *l* God,"
4:20 anyone who does not *l* his brother,
4:20 whom he has seen, cannot *l* God,
4:21 loves God must also *l* his brother.
5:2 we know that we *l* the children
5:3 This is *l* for God: to obey his
2Jn :1 whom I *l* in the truth—
:3 will be with us in truth and *l*.
:5 I ask that we *l* one another.
:6 his command is that you walk in *l*.
:6 this is *l*: that we walk in obedience
3Jn :1 To my dear friend Gaius, whom I *l*
:6 have told the church about your *l*.
Jude :2 peace and *l* be yours in abundance.
:12 men are blemishes at your *l* feasts,
:21 Keep yourselves in God's *l*
Rev 2:4 You have forsaken your first *l*.
2:19 I know your deeds, your *l* and faith
3:19 Those whom I *l* I rebuke
12:11 they did not *l* their lives so much

LOVED* (LOVE)

Ge 24:67 she became his wife, and he *l* her;
25:28 *l* Esau, but Rebekah *l* Jacob.
29:30 and he *l* Rachel more than Leah.
29:31 the LORD saw that Leah was not *l*,
29:33 the LORD heard that I am not *l*,
34:3 and he *l* the girl and spoke tenderly
37:3 Now Israel *l* Joseph more than any
37:4 saw that their father *l* him more
Dt 4:37 Because he *l* your forefathers
7:8 But it was because the LORD *l* you
10:15 on your forefathers and *l* them,
1Sa 1:5 a double portion because he *l* her,
18:1 in spirit with David, and he *l* him
18:3 with David because he *l* him
18:16 But all Israel and Judah *l* David,
18:28 that his daughter Michal *l* David,
20:17 because he *l* him as he *l* himself.
2Sa 1:23 in life they were *l* and gracious,
12:24 The LORD *l* him; and
12:25 and because the LORD *l* him,
13:15 hated her more than he had *l* her.
1Ki 11:1 *l* many foreign women
2Ch 11:21 Rehoboam *l* Maacah daughter
26:10 in the fertile lands, for he *l* the soil.
Ne 13:26 He was *l* by his God, and God
Ps 44:3 light of your face, for you *l* them.
47:4 the pride of Jacob, whom he *l*.
78:68 Mount Zion, which he *l*.
88:18 taken my companions and *l* ones
109:17 He *l* to pronounce a curse—
Isa 5:1 My *l* one had a vineyard
Jer 2:2 how as a bride you *l* me
8:2 which they have *l* and served
31:3 "I have *l* you with an everlasting
Eze 16:37 those you *l* as well as those you
Hos 2:1 and of your sisters, 'My *l* one.'
2:23 to the one I called 'Not my *l* one.'
3:1 though she is *l* by another
9:10 became as vile as the thing they *l*.
11:1 "When Israel was a child, I *l* him,
Mal 1:2 "But you ask, 'How have you *l* us?'
1:2 "I have *l* you," says the LORD.
1:2 "Yet I have *l* Jacob, but Esau I
Mk 10:21 Jesus looked at him and *l* him.
12:6 left to send, a son, whom he *l*.
Lk 7:47 been forgiven—for she *l* much.
16:14 The Pharisees, who *l* money,
Jn 3:16 so *l* the world that he gave his one
3:19 but men *l* darkness instead of light
11:5 Jesus *l* Martha and her sister
11:36 "See how he *l* him!" But some
12:43 for they *l* praise from men more
13:1 Having *l* his own who were
13:23 the disciple whom Jesus *l*,
13:34 As I have *l* you, so you must love
14:21 He who loves me will be *l*
14:28 If you *l* me, you would be glad that
15:9 the Father has *l* me, so have I *l* you.
15:12 Love each other as I have *l* you.
16:27 loves you because you have *l* me
17:23 have *l* them even as you have *l* me.
17:24 you *l* me before the creation
19:26 the disciple whom he *l* standing
20:2 one Jesus *l*, and said, "They have
21:7 the disciple whom Jesus *l* said
21:20 whom Jesus *l* was following
Ro 1:7 To all in Rome who are *l* by God
8:37 conquerors through him who *l* us.
9:13 "Jacob I *l*, but Esau I hated."
9:25 her 'my *l* one' who is not my *l* one,"
11:28 they are *l* on account

Gal 2: 20 who *l* me and gave himself for me.
Eph 5: 1 as dearly *l* children and live a life
5: 2 as Christ *l* us and gave himself up
5: 25 just as Christ *l* the church
Col 3: 12 and dearly *l*, clothe yourselves
1Th 1: 4 Brothers *l* by God, we know that
2: 8 We *l* you so much that we were
2Th 2: 13 for you, brothers *l* by the Lord,
2: 16 who *l* us and by his grace gave us
2Ti 4: 10 for Demas, because he *l* this world,
Heb 1: 9 You have *l* righteousness
2Pe 2: 15 who *l* the wages of wickedness.
1Jn 4: 10 This is love: not that we *l* God,
4: 10 but that he *l* us and sent his Son
4: 11 Dear friends, since God so *l* us,
4: 19 We love because he first *l* us.
Jude : 1 who are *l* by God the Father
Rev 3: 9 and acknowledge that I have *l* you.

LOVELY* (LOVE)

Ge 29: 17 but Rachel was *l* in form,
Est 1: 11 and nobles, for she was *l* to look at.
2: 7 was *l* in form and features,
Ps 84: 1 How *l* is your dwelling-place,
SS 1: 5 Dark am I, yet *l*,
2: 14 and your face is *l*.
4: 3 your mouth is *l*.
5: 16 he is altogether *l*.
6: 4 *l* as Jerusalem,
Am 8: 13 *l* young women and strong young
Php 4: 8 whatever is *l*, whatever is

LOVER* (LOVE)

SS 1: 13 My *l* is to me a sachet of myrrh
1: 14 My *l* is to me a cluster
1: 16 How handsome you are, my *l*!
2: 3 is my *l* among the young men.
2: 8 Listen! My *l*!
2: 9 My *l* is like a gazelle or a young
2: 10 My *l* spoke and said to me,
2: 16 My *l* is mine and I am his;
2: 17 turn, my *l*,
4: 16 Let my *l* come into his garden
5: 2 Listen! My *l* is knocking:
5: 4 My *l* thrust his hand
5: 5 I arose to open for my *l*,
5: 6 I opened for my *l*,
5: 6 but my *l* had left; he was gone.
5: 8 if you find my *l*,
5: 10 My *l* is radiant and ruddy,
5: 16 This is my *l*, this my friend,
6: 1 Where has your *l* gone,
6: 1 Which way did your *l* turn,
6: 2 My *l* has gone
6: 3 I am my lover's and my *l* is mine;
7: 9 May the wine go straight to my *l*,
7: 10 I belong to my *l*,
7: 11 my *l*, let us go to the countryside,
7: 13 that I have stored up for you, my *l*.
8: 5 leaning on her *l*?
8: 14 Come away, my *l*,
1Ti 3: 3 not quarrelsome, not a *l* of money.

LOVER'S* (LOVE)

SS 6: 3 I am my *l* and my lover is mine;

LOVERS* (LOVE)

SS 5: 1 drink your fill, O *l*.
Jer 3: 1 as a prostitute with many *l*—
3: 2 the roadside you sat waiting for *l*,
4: 30 Your *l* despise you;
La 1: 2 Among all her *l*
Eze 16: 33 but you give gifts to all your *l*,
16: 36 in your promiscuity with your *l*,
16: 37 I am going to gather all your *l*,
16: 39 Then I will hand you over to your *l*,
16: 41 and you will no longer pay your *l*.
23: 5 she lusted after her *l*, the Assyrians
23: 9 I handed her over to her *l*,
23: 20 There she lusted after her *l*,
23: 22 I will stir up your *l* against you,
Hos 2: 5 She said, 'I will go after my *l*,
2: 7 She will chase after her *l*
2: 10 lewdness before the eyes of her *l*;
Hos 2: 12 she said were her pay from her *l*;
2: 13 and went after her *l*,
8: 9 Ephraim has sold herself to *l*.
2Ti 3: 2 People will be *l* of themselves,
3: 2 *l* of money, boastful, proud,
3: 3 without self-control, brutal, not *l*
3: 4 *l* of pleasure rather than *l* of God—

LOVES* (LOVE)

Ge 44: 20 sons left, and his father *l* him.'
Dt 10: 18 and *l* the alien, giving him food
15: 16 because he *l* you and your family
21: 15 and he *l* one but not the other,
21: 16 son of the wife he *l* in preference
23: 5 because the LORD your God *l* you
28: 54 wife he *l* or his surviving children,
28: 56 will begrudge the husband she *l*
33: 12 and the one the LORD *l* rests
Ru 4: 15 who *l* you and who is better to you
2Ch 2: 11 "Because the LORD *l* his people,
Ps 11: 7 he *l* justice;
33: 5 The LORD *l* righteousness
34: 12 Whoever of you *l* life
37: 28 For the LORD *l* the just
87: 2 the LORD *l* the gates of Zion
91: 14 Because he *l* me," says the LORD,
99: 4 The King is mighty, he *l* justice—
119: 140 and your servant *l* them,
127: 2 for he grants sleep to those he *l*.
146: 8 the LORD *l* the righteous.
Pr 3: 12 the LORD disciplines those he *l*,
12: 1 Whoever *l* discipline *l* knowledge,
13: 24 he who *l* him is careful
15: 9 he *l* those who pursue
17: 17 A friend *l* at all times,
17: 19 He who *l* a quarrel *l* sin;
19: 8 He who gets wisdom *l* his own soul
21: 17 He who *l* pleasure will become
21: 17 whoever *l* wine and oil will never
22: 11 He who *l* a pure heart and whose
29: 3 A man who *l* wisdom brings joy
Ecc 5: 10 Whoever *l* money never has
5: 10 whoever *l* wealth is never satisfied
SS 3: 1 I looked for the one my heart *l*;
3: 2 I will search for the one my heart *l*.
3: 3 "Have you seen the one my heart *l*
3: 4 when I found the one my heart *l*.
Hos 3: 1 as the LORD *l* the Israelites,
10: 11 that *l* to thresh;
12: 7 he *l* to defraud.
Mal 2: 11 the sanctuary the LORD *l*,
Mt 10: 37 anyone who *l* his son or daughter
10: 37 "Anyone who *l* his father
Lk 7: 5 because he *l* our nation
7: 47 has been forgiven little *l* little."
Jn 3: 35 Father *l* the Son and has placed
5: 20 For the Father *l* the Son
10: 17 reason my Father *l* me is that I lay
12: 25 The man who *l* his life will lose it,
14: 21 He who *l* me will be loved
14: 21 obeys them, he is the one who *l* me.
14: 23 Jesus replied, "If anyone *l* me,
16: 27 the Father himself *l* you
Ro 13: 8 for he who *l* his fellow-man has
1Co 8: 3 But the man who *l* God is known
2Co 9: 7 for God *l* a cheerful giver.
Eph 1: 6 has freely given us in the One he *l*.
5: 28 He who *l* his wife *l* himself.
5: 33 must love his wife as he *l* himself,
Col 1: 13 us into the kingdom of the Son he *l*,
Tit 1: 8 one who *l* what is good, who is
Heb 12: 6 the Lord disciplines those he *l*,
1Jn 2: 10 Whoever *l* his brother lives
2: 15 If anyone *l* the world, the love
4: 7 Everyone who *l* has been born
4: 21 Whoever *l* God must also love his
5: 1 who *l* the father *l* his child
3Jn : 9 but Diotrephes, who *l* to be first,
Rev 1: 5 To him who *l* us and has freed us
20: 9 camp of God's people, the city he *l*.
22: 15 and everyone who *l* and practises

LOVING* (LOVE)

Ps 25: 10 All the ways of the LORD are *l*
Ps 59: 10 my *l* God.
59: 17 O God, are my fortress, my *l* God.
62: 12 and that you, O Lord, are *l*.
144: 2 He is my *l* God and my fortress,
145: 13 and *l* towards all he has made.
145: 17 and *l* towards all he has made.
Pr 5: 19 A *l* doe, a graceful deer—
Heb 13: 1 Keep on *l* each other as brothers.
1Jn 5: 2 by *l* God and carrying out his

LOVING-KINDNESS* (LOVE)

Jer 31: 3 I have drawn you with *l*.

LOWER

Ps 8: 5 You made him a little *l*
1Co 11: 7 a sin for me to *l* myself in order
Heb 2: 7 You made him a little *l*

LOWING

1Sa 15: 14 What is this *l* of cattle that I hear?"

LOWLY

Job 5: 11 The *l* he sets on high,
Ps 138: 6 on high, he looks upon the *l*,
Pr 29: 23 but a man of *l* spirit gains honour.
Isa 57: 15 also with him who is contrite and *l*
Eze 21: 26 *l* will be exalted and the exalted
1Co 1: 28 He chose the *l* things of this world

LOYAL

1Ch 29: 18 and keep their hearts *l* to you.
Ps 78: 8 whose hearts were not *l* to God,

LUKE*

Co-worker with Paul (Col 4:14; 2Ti 4:11; Phm 24).

LUKEWARM*

Rev 3: 16 So, because you are *l*—neither hot

LUST (LUSTED LUSTS)

Pr 6: 25 Do not *l* in your heart
Eze 20: 30 and *l* after their vile images?
Col 3: 5 sexual immorality, impurity, *l*,
1Th 4: 5 not in passionate *l* like the heathen,
1Pe 4: 3 in debauchery, *l*, drunkenness,
1Jn 2: 16 the *l* of his eyes and the boasting

LUSTED (LUST)

Eze 23: 5 she *l* after her lovers, the Assyrians

LUSTS* (LUST)

Nu 15: 39 yourselves by going after the *l*
Ro 1: 26 God gave them over to shameful *l*.

LUXURY

Jas 5: 5 You have lived on earth in *l*

LYDIA'S*

Ac 16: 40 went to *L* house, where they met

LYING (LIE [2])

Pr 6: 17 a *l* tongue,
12: 22 The LORD detests *l* lips,
21: 6 A fortune made by a *l* tongue
26: 28 A *l* tongue hates those it hurts,

MACEDONIA

Ac 16: 9 "Come over to *M* and help us."

MAD

Dt 28: 34 The sights you see will drive you *m*

MADE (MAKE)

Ge 1: 7 So God *m* the expanse
1: 16 God *m* two great lights—
1: 16 He also *m* the stars.
1: 25 God *m* the wild animals according
1: 31 God saw all that he had *m*,
2: 22 Then the LORD God *m* a woman
6: 6 was grieved that he had *m* man
9: 6 has God *m* man.
15: 18 that day the LORD *m* a covenant

Ex 20: 11 six days the LORD *m* the heavens
20: 11 the Sabbath day and *m* it holy.
24: 8 the covenant that the LORD has *m*
32: 4 *m* it into an idol cast in the shape
Lev 16: 34 Atonement is to be *m* once a year
Dt 32: 6 who *m* you and formed you?
Jos 24: 25 On that day Joshua *m* a covenant
2Ki 19: 15 You have *m* heaven and earth.
2Ch 2: 12 the God of Israel, who *m* heaven
Ne 9: 6 You *m* the heavens,
9: 10 You *m* a name for yourself,
Ps 33: 6 of the LORD were the heavens *m*,
95: 5 The sea is his, for he *m* it,
96: 5 but the LORD *m* the heavens.
100: 3 It is he who *m* us, and we are his;
118: 24 This is the day the LORD has *m*;
136: 7 who *m* the great lights—
139: 14 I am fearfully and wonderfully *m*;
Ecc 3: 11 He has *m* everything beautiful
Isa 43: 7 whom I formed and *m*."
45: 12 It is I who *m* the earth
45: 18 he who fashioned and *m* the earth,
66: 2 Has not my hand *m* all these things
Jer 10: 12 But God *m* the earth by his power;
27: 5 and outstretched arm I *m* the earth
32: 17 you have *m* the heavens
33: 2 LORD says, he who *m* the earth,
51: 15 "He *m* the earth by his power;
Eze 3: 17 I have *m* you a watchman
33: 7 I have *m* you a watchman
Am 5: 8 (he who *m* the Pleiades and Orion,
Jnh 1: 9 who *m* the sea and the land."
Mk 2: 27 "The Sabbath was *m* for man,
Jn 1: 3 Through him all things were *m*;
Ac 17: 24 "The God who *m* the world
1Co 3: 6 watered it, but God *m* it grow.
Heb 1: 2 through whom he *m* the universe.
Jas 3: 9 who have been *m* in God's likeness
Rev 14: 7 Worship him who *m* the heavens,

MAGDALENE

Lk 8: 2 Mary (called *M*) from whom seven

MAGI

Mt 2: 1 *M* from the east came to Jerusalem

MAGIC (MAGICIANS)

Eze 13: 20 I am against your *m* charms
Rev 21: 8 those who practise *m* arts,
22: 15 those who practise *m* arts,

MAGICIANS (MAGIC)

Ex 7: 11 the Egyptian *m* also did the same
Da 2: 2 So the king summoned the *m*,

MAGNIFICENCE* (MAGNIFICENT)

1Ch 22: 5 for the LORD should be of great *m*

MAGNIFICENT (MAGNIFICENCE)

1Ki 8: 13 I have indeed built a *m* temple
Isa 28: 29 in counsel and *m* in wisdom.
Mk 13: 1 stones! What *m* buildings!"

MAGOG

Eze 38: 2 of the land of *M*, the chief prince
39: 6 I will send fire on *M*
Rev 20: 8 and *M*—to gather them for battle.

MAIDEN (MAIDENS)

Pr 30: 19 and the way of a man with a *m*.
Isa 62: 5 As a young man marries a *m*,
Jer 2: 32 Does a *m* forget her jewellery,

MAIDENS (MAIDEN)

SS 1: 3 No wonder the *m* love you!

MAIMED

Mt 18: 8 It is better for you to enter life *m*

MAINTAIN (MAINTAINING)

Ps 82: 3 *m* the rights of the poor
106: 3 Blessed are they who *m* justice,
Hos 12: 6 *m* love and justice
Am 5: 15 *m* justice in the courts.
Ro 3: 28 For we *m* that a man is justified

MAINTAINING* (MAINTAIN)

Ex 34: 7 faithfulness, *m* love to thousands,

MAJESTIC* (MAJESTY)

Ex 15: 6 was *m* in power.
15: 11 *m* in holiness,
Job 37: 4 he thunders with his *m* voice.
Ps 8: 1 how *m* is your name in all the earth
8: 9 how *m* is your name in all the earth
29: 4 the voice of the LORD is *m*.
68: 15 of Bashan are *m* mountains;
76: 4 more *m* than mountains rich
111: 3 Glorious and *m* are his deeds,
SS 6: 4 *m* as troops with banners.
6: 10 *m* as the stars in procession?
Isa 30: 30 men to hear his *m* voice
Eze 31: 7 It was *m* in beauty,
2Pe 1: 17 came to him from the *M* Glory,

MAJESTY* (MAJESTIC)

Ex 15: 7 In the greatness of your *m*
Dt 5: 24 has shown us his glory and his *m*,
11: 2 his *m*, his mighty hand, his
33: 17 In *m* he is like a firstborn bull;
33: 26 and on the clouds in his *m*.
1Ch 16: 27 Splendour and *m* are before him;
29: 11 and the *m* and the splendour,
Est 1: 4 the splendour and glory of his *m*.
7: 3 if it pleases your *m*, grant me my
Job 37: 22 God comes in awesome *m*.
40: 10 and clothe yourself in honour and *m*
Ps 21: 5 on him splendour and *m*.
45: 3 with splendour and *m*.
45: 4 In your *m* ride forth victoriously
68: 34 whose *m* is over Israel,
93: 1 The LORD reigns, he is robed in *m*
93: 1 the LORD is robed in *m*
96: 6 Splendour and *m* are before him;
104: 1 clothed with splendour and *m*.
110: 3 Arrayed in holy *m*,
145: 5 of the glorious splendour of your *m*,
Isa 2: 10 and the splendour of his *m*!
2: 19 and the splendour of his *m*,
2: 21 and the splendour of his *m*,
24: 14 west they acclaim the LORD's *m*.
26: 10 and regard not the *m* of the LORD.
53: 2 or *m* to attract us to him,
Eze 31: 2 can be compared with you in *m*?
31: 18 with you in splendour and *m*?
Da 4: 30 and for the glory of my *m*?"
Mic 5: 4 in the *m* of the name
Zec 6: 13 and he will be clothed with *m*
Ac 19: 27 will be robbed of her divine *m*."
25: 26 to write to His *M* about him.
2Th 1: 9 and from the *m* of his power
Heb 1: 3 hand of the *M* in heaven.
8: 1 of the throne of the *M* in heaven,
2Pe 1: 16 but we were eye-witnesses of his *m*.
Jude : 25 only God our Saviour be glory, *m*,

MAKE (MADE MAKER MAKERS MAKES MAKING MAN-MADE)

Ge 1: 26 "Let us *m* man in our image,
2: 18 I will *m* a helper suitable for him."
6: 14 *m* yourself an ark of cypress wood;
12: 2 "I will *m* you into a great nation
Ex 22: 3 thief must certainly *m* restitution,
25: 9 *M* this tabernacle and all its
25: 40 See that you *m* them according
Nu 6: 25 the LORD *m* his face shine
2Sa 7: 9 Now I will *m* your name great,
Job 7: 17 "What is man that you *m* so much
Ps 4: 8 *m* me dwell in safety.
20: 4 and *m* all your plans succeed.
108: 1 *m* music with all my soul.
110: 1 hand until I *m* your enemies
119: 165 and nothing can *m* them stumble.
Pr 3: 6 and he will *m* your paths straight.
4: 26 *M* level paths for your feet
20: 18 *M* plans by seeking advice;
Isa 14: 14 I will *m* myself like the Most High
29: 16 "He did not *m* me"?
55: 3 I will *m* an everlasting covenant
61: 8 and *m* an everlasting covenant
Jer 31: 31 "when I will *m* a new covenant
Eze 37: 26 I will *m* a covenant of peace
Mt 3: 3 *m* straight paths for him.'"
28: 19 and *m* disciples of all nations,
Mk 1: 17 "and I will *m* you fishers of men."
Lk 13: 24 "*M* every effort to enter
14: 23 country lanes and *m* them come in,
Ro 14: 19 *m* every effort to do what leads
2Co 5: 9 So we *m* it our goal to please him,
Eph 4: 3 *M* every effort to keep the unity
Col 4: 5 *m* the most of every opportunity.
1Th 4: 11 *M* it your ambition
Heb 4: 11 *m* every effort to enter that rest,
8: 5 it that you *m* everything according
12: 14 *M* every effort to live in peace
2Pe 1: 5 *m* every effort to add
3: 14 *m* every effort to be found spotless,

MAKER* (MAKE)

Job 4: 17 Can a man be more pure than his *M*
9: 9 He is the *M* of the Bear and Orion,
32: 22 my *M* would soon take me away.
35: 10 no-one says, 'Where is God my *M*,
36: 3 I will ascribe justice to my *M*.
40: 19 yet his *M* can approach him
Ps 95: 6 kneel before the LORD our *M*;
115: 15 the *M* of heaven and earth.
121: 2 the *M* of heaven and earth.
124: 8 the *M* of heaven and earth.
134: 3 the *M* of heaven and earth,
146: 6 the *M* of heaven and earth,
149: 2 Let Israel rejoice in their *M*;
Pr 14: 31 poor shows contempt for their *M*,
17: 5 poor shows contempt for their *M*;
22: 2 The LORD is the *M* of them all.
Ecc 11: 5 the *M* of all things.
Isa 17: 7 that day men will look to their *M*
27: 11 so their *M* has no compassion
45: 9 to him who quarrels with his *M*,
45: 11 the Holy One of Israel, and its *M*:
51: 13 that you forget the LORD your *M*,
54: 5 For your *M* is your husband—
Jer 10: 16 for he is the *M* of all things,
51: 19 for he is the *M* of all things,
Hos 8: 14 Israel has forgotten his *M*

MAKERS* (MAKE)

Isa 45: 16 All the *m* of idols will be put

MAKES (MAKE)

Ps 23: 2 *m* me lie down in green pastures,
Pr 13: 12 Hope deferred *m* the heart sick,
1Co 3: 7 but only God, who *m* things grow.

MAKING (MAKE)

Ps 19: 7 *m* wise the simple.
Ecc 12: 12 Of *m* many books there is no end,
Jn 5: 18 *m* himself equal with God.
Eph 5: 16 *m* the most of every opportunity,

MALACHI*

Mal 1: 1 of the LORD to Israel through *M*.

MALE

Ge 1: 27 *m* and female he created them.
Ex 13: 2 to me every firstborn *m*.
Nu 8: 16 the first *m* offspring
Mt 19: 4 the Creator 'made them *m*
Gal 3: 28 slave nor free, *m* nor female,

MALICE (MALICIOUS)

Mk 7: 22 adultery, greed, *m*, deceit,
Ro 1: 29 murder, strife, deceit and *m*.
1Co 5: 8 the yeast of *m* and wickedness,
Eph 4: 31 along with every form of *m*.
Col 3: 8 *m*, slander, and filthy language
1Pe 2: 1 rid yourselves of all *m*

MALICIOUS (MALICE)

Pr 26: 24 A *m* man disguises himself

1Ti 3: 11 not *m* talkers but temperate
6: 4 *m* talk, evil suspicions

MALIGN

Tit 2: 5 so that no-one will *m* the word

MAMMON see MONEY, WEALTH

MAN (MAN'S MANKIND MEN MEN'S WOMAN WOMEN)

Ge 1: 26 "Let us make *m* in our image,
2: 7 God formed the *m* from the dust
2: 8 *m* became a living being
2: 15 God took the *m* and put
2: 18 for the *m* to be alone
2: 20 *m* gave names to all the
2: 23 she was taken out of *m*.
2: 25 *m* and his wife were both
3: 9 God called to the *m*,
3: 22 *m* has now become like
4: 1 I have brought forth a *m*.
6: 3 not contend with *m* for ever,
6: 6 grieved that he had made *m*
9: 6 Whoever sheds the blood of *m*,
Dt 8: 3 *m* does not live on bread
1Sa 13: 14 a *m* after his own heart
15: 29 he is not a *m* that he
16: 7 at the things *m* looks at.
Job 14: 1 *M* born of woman is of few
14: 14 If a *m* dies, will he live
Ps 1: 1 Blessed is the *m* who does
8: 4 what is *m* that you are
32: 2 Blessed is the *m* whose sin
40: 4 Blessed is the *m* who makes
84: 12 blessed is the *m* who trusts
103: 15 As for *m*, his days are
112: 1 Blessed is the *m* who fears
119: 9 can a young *m* keep his
127: 5 Blessed is the *m* whose quiver
144: 3 what is *m* that you care
Pr 3: 13 Blessed is the *m* who finds
9: 9 Instruct a wise *m*
14: 12 that seems right to a *m*,
30: 19 way of a *m* with a maiden.
Isa 53: 3 a *m* of sorrows,
Jer 17: 5 the one who trusts in *m*,
17: 7 blessed is the *m* who trusts
Eze 22: 30 I looked for a *m*
Mt 4: 4 *M* does not live on bread
19: 5 a *m* will leave his father
Mk 8: 36 What good is it for a *m*
Lk 4: 4 '*M* does not live on bread
Ro 5: 12 entered the world through one *m*
1Co 2: 15 spiritual *m* makes judgments
3: 12 If any *m* builds on this
7: 1 good for a *m* not to marry.
7: 2 each *m* should have his own
11: 3 head of every *m* is Christ,
11: 3 head of the woman is *m*
13: 11 When I became a *m*,
15: 21 death came through a *m*,
15: 45 first *m* Adam became a
15: 47 the second *m* from heaven
2Co 12: 2 I know a *m* in Christ
Eph 2: 15 create in himself one new *m*
5: 31 a *m* will leave his father
Php 2: 8 found in appearance as a *m*,
1Ti 2: 5 the *m* Christ Jesus,
2: 11 have authority over a *m*;
2Ti 3: 17 that the *m* of God may be
Heb 2: 6 what is *m* that you are
9: 27 as *m* is destined to die

MAN'S (MAN)

Pr 20: 24 A *m* steps are directed by
Jer 10: 23 a *m* life is not his own;
1Co 1: 25 is wiser than *m* wisdom,

MAN-MADE (MAKE)

Heb 9: 11 perfect tabernacle that is not *m*,
9: 24 not enter a *m* sanctuary that was

MANAGE (MANAGER)

Jer 12: 5 how will you *m* in the thickets
1Ti 3: 4 He must *m* his own family well
3: 12 one wife and must *m* his children
5: 14 to *m* their homes and to give

MANAGER (MANAGE)

Lk 12: 42 Who then is the faithful and wise *m*
16: 1 a rich man whose *m* was accused

MANASSEH

1. Firstborn of Joseph (Ge 41:51; 46:20). Blessed by Jacob but not firstborn (Ge 48). Tribe of blessed (Dt 33:17), numbered (Nu 1:35; 26:34), half allotted land east of Jordan (Nu 32; Jos 13:8-33), half west (Jos 16; Eze 48:4), failed to fully possess (Jos 16:10; Jdg 1:27), 12,000 from (Rev 7:6).

2. Son of Hezekiah; king of Judah (2Ki 21:1-18; 2Ch 33:1-20). Judah exiled for his detestable sins (2Ki 21:10-15). Repentance (2Ch 33:12-19).

MANDRAKES

Ge 30: 14 give me some of your son's *m*."

MANGER

Lk 2: 12 wrapped in cloths and lying in a *m*."

MANIFESTATION*

1Co 12: 7 to each one the *m* of the Spirit is

MANKIND (MAN)

Ge 6: 7 I will wipe *m*, whom I have created
Ps 33: 13 and sees all *m*;
Pr 8: 31 and delighting in *m*.
Ecc 7: 29 God made *m* upright,
Isa 40: 5 and all *m* together will see it.
45: 12 and created *m* upon it.
Jer 32: 27 "I am the LORD, the God of all *m*.
Zec 2: 13 Be still before the LORD, all *m*,
Lk 3: 6 And all *m* will see God's salvation

MANNA

Ex 16: 31 people of Israel called the bread *m*.
Dt 8: 16 He gave you *m* to eat in the desert,
Jn 6: 49 Your forefathers ate the *m*
Rev 2: 17 I will give some of the hidden *m*.

MANNER

1Co 11: 27 in an unworthy *m* will be guilty
Php 1: 27 conduct yourselves in a *m* worthy

MANSIONS*

Ps 49: 14 far from their princely *m*.
Isa 5: 9 the fine *m* left without occupants.
Am 3: 15 and the *m* will be demolished,"
5: 11 though you have built stone *m*,

MARCH

Jos 6: 4 *m* around the city seven times,
Isa 42: 13 LORD will *m* out like a mighty

MARITAL* (MARRY)

Ex 21: 10 of her food, clothing and *m* rights.
Mt 5: 32 except for *m* unfaithfulness,
19: 9 except for *m* unfaithfulness,
1Co 7: 3 husband should fulfil his *m* duty

MARK [1] (MARKS)

Ge 4: 15 Then the LORD put a *m* on Cain
Rev 13: 16 to receive a *m* on his right hand

MARK [2]

Cousin of Barnabas (Col 4:10; 2Ti 4:11; Phm 24; 1Pe 5:13), see JOHN.

MARKET (MARKET-PLACE MARKET-PLACES)

Jn 2: 16 turn my Father's house into a *m*!"

MARKET-PLACE (MARKET)

Lk 7: 32 are like children sitting in the *m*

MARKET-PLACES (MARKET)

Mt 23: 7 they love to be greeted in the *m*

MARKS (MARK [1])

Jn 20: 25 Unless I see the nail *m* in his hands
Gal 6: 17 bear on my body the *m* of Jesus.

MARRED

Isa 52: 14 his form *m* beyond human likeness

MARRIAGE (MARRY)

Mt 22: 30 neither marry nor be given in *m*;
24: 38 marrying and giving in *m*,
Ro 7: 2 she is released from the law of *m*.
Heb 13: 4 by all, and the *m* bed kept pure,

MARRIED (MARRY)

Dt 24: 5 happiness to the wife he has *m*.
Ezr 10: 10 you have *m* foreign women,
Pr 30: 23 an unloved woman who is *m*,
Mt 1: 18 pledged to be *m* to Joseph,
Mk 12: 23 since the seven were *m* to her?"
Ro 7: 2 by law a *m* woman is bound
1Co 7: 27 Are you *m*? Do not seek a divorce.
7: 33 But a *m* man is concerned about
7: 36 They should get *m*.

MARRIES (MARRY)

Mt 5: 32 and anyone who *m* a woman
19: 9 and *m* another woman commits
Lk 16: 18 the man who *m* a divorced woman

MARROW

Heb 4: 12 joints and *m*; it judges the thoughts

MARRY (INTERMARRY MARITAL MARRIAGE MARRIED MARRIES)

Dt 25: 5 brother shall take her and *m* her
Mt 22: 30 resurrection people will neither *m*
1Co 7: 1 It is good for a man not to *m*.
7: 9 control themselves, they should *m*,
7: 28 if you do *m*, you have not sinned;
1Ti 4: 3 They forbid people to *m*
5: 14 So I counsel younger widows to *m*,

MARTHA*

Sister of Mary and Lazarus (Lk 10:38-42; Jn 11; 12:2).

MARVELLED* (MARVELLOUS)

Lk 2: 33 mother *m* at what was said about
2Th 1: 10 and to be *m* at among all those who

MARVELLING* (MARVELLOUS)

Lk 9: 43 While everyone was *m*

MARVELLOUS* (MARVELLED MARVELLING)

1Ch 16: 24 his *m* deeds among all peoples.
Job 37: 5 God's voice thunders in *m* ways;
Ps 71: 17 to this day I declare your *m* deeds.
72: 18 who alone does *m* deeds.
86: 10 For you are great and do *m* deeds;
96: 3 his *m* deeds among all peoples.
98: 1 for he has done *m* things;
118: 23 and it is *m* in our eyes.
Isa 25: 1 you have done *m* things,
Zec 8: 6 but will it seem *m* to me?"
8: 6 "It may seem *m* to the remnant
Mt 21: 42 and it is *m* in our eyes"?
Mk 12: 11 and it is *m* in our eyes'?"
Rev 15: 1 in heaven another great and *m* sign
15: 3 "Great and *m* are your deeds,

MARY

1. Mother of Jesus (Mt 1:16-25; Lk 1:27-56; 2:1-40). With Jesus at temple (Lk 2:41-52), at the wedding in Cana (Jn 2:1-5), questioning his sanity (Mk 3:21), at the cross (Jn 19:25-27). Among disciples after Ascension (Ac 1:14).

2. Magdalene; former demoniac (Lk 8:2). Helped support Jesus' ministry (Lk 8:1-3). At the cross (Mt 27:56; Mk 15:40; Jn 19:25), burial (Mt

27:61; Mk 15:47). Saw angel after resurrection (Mt 28:1-10; Mk 16:1-9; Lk 24:1-12); also Jesus (Jn 20:1-18).

3. Sister of Martha and Lazarus (Jn 11). Washed Jesus' feet (Jn 12:1-8).

MASQUERADES*

2Co 11: 14 for Satan himself *m* as an angel

MASTER (MASTER'S MASTERED MASTERS MASTERY)

Ge 4: 7 to have you, but you must *m* it."
Hos 2: 16 you will no longer call me 'my *m*'.
Mal 1: 6 If I am a *m*, where is the respect
Mt 10: 24 nor a servant above his *m*.
23: 8 for you have only one *M*
24: 46 that servant whose *m* finds him
25: 21 "His *m* replied, 'Well done,
25: 23 "His *m* replied, 'Well done,
Ro 6: 14 For sin shall not be your *m*,
14: 4 To his own *m* he stands or falls.
Col 4: 1 you know that you also have a *M*
2Ti 2: 21 useful to the *M* and prepared

MASTER'S (MASTER)

Mt 25: 21 Come and share your *m* happiness

MASTERED* (MASTER)

1Co 6: 12 but I will not be *m* by anything.
2Pe 2: 19 a slave to whatever has *m* him.

MASTERS (MASTER)

Pr 25: 13 he refreshes the spirit of his *m*.
Mt 6: 24 "No-one can serve two *m*.
Lk 16: 13 "No servant can serve two *m*.
Eph 6: 5 obey your earthly *m* with respect
6: 9 And *m*, treat your slaves
Col 3: 22 obey your earthly *m* in everything;
4: 1 *M*, provide your slaves
1Ti 6: 1 should consider their *m* worthy
6: 2 who have believing *m* are not
Tit 2: 9 subject to their *m* in everything,
1Pe 2: 18 to your *m* with all respect,

MASTERY* (MASTER)

Ro 6: 9 death no longer has *m* over him.

MAT

Mk 2: 9 'Get up, take your *m* and walk'?
Ac 9: 34 Get up and take care of your *m*."

MATCHED*

2Co 8: 11 do it may be *m* by your completion

MATTHEW*

Apostle; former tax collector (Mt 9:19-13; 10:3; Mk 3:18; Lk 6:15; Ac 1:13). Also called Levi (Mk 2:14-17; Lk 5:27-32).

MATTHIAS

Ac 1: 26 the lot fell to *M*; so he was added

MATURE* (MATURITY)

Lk 8: 14 and pleasures, and they do not *m*.
1Co 2: 6 a message of wisdom among the *m*,
Eph 4: 13 of the Son of God and become *m*,
Php 3: 15 of us who are *m* should take such
Col 4: 12 firm in all the will of God, *m*
Heb 5: 14 But solid food is for the *m*,
Jas 1: 4 work so that you may be *m*

MATURITY* (MATURE)

Heb 6: 1 about Christ and go on to *m*,

MEAL

Pr 15: 17 Better a *m* of vegetables where
1Co 10: 27 some unbeliever invites you to a *m*
Heb 12: 16 for a single *m* sold his inheritance

MEANING

Ne 8: 8 and giving the *m* so that the people

MEANINGLESS

Ecc 1: 2 "*M*! *M*!" says the Teacher.
1Ti 1: 6 from these and turned to *m* talk.

MEANS

1Co 9: 22 by all possible *m* I might save some

MEASURE (MEASURED MEASURES)

Ps 71: 15 though I know not its *m*.
Eze 45: 3 In the sacred district, *m*
Zec 2: 2 He answered me, "To *m* Jerusalem
Lk 6: 38 A good *m*, pressed
Eph 3: 19 to the *m* of all the fulness of God.
4: 13 to the whole *m* of the fulness
Rev 11: 1 "Go and *m* the temple of God

MEASURED (MEASURE)

Isa 40: 12 Who has *m* the waters
Jer 31: 37 if the heavens above can be *m*

MEASURES (MEASURE)

Dt 25: 14 Do not have two differing *m*
Pr 20: 10 Differing weights and differing *m*

MEAT

Pr 23: 20 or gorge themselves on *m*,
Ro 14: 6 He who eats *m*, eats to the Lord,
14: 21 It is better not to eat *m*
1Co 8: 13 I will never eat *m* again,
10: 25 *m* market without raising questions

MEDDLER* (MEDDLES)

1Pe 4: 15 kind of criminal, or even as a *m*.

MEDDLES* (MEDDLER)

Pr 26: 17 is a passer-by who *m*

MEDIATOR

1Ti 2: 5 and one *m* between God and men,
Heb 8: 6 of which he is *m* is superior
9: 15 For this reason Christ is the *m*
12: 24 to Jesus the *m* of a new covenant,

MEDICINE*

Pr 17: 22 A cheerful heart is good *m*,

MEDITATE* (MEDITATED MEDITATES MEDITATION)

Ge 24: 63 out to the field one evening to *m*,
Jos 1: 8 from your mouth; *m* on it day
Ps 48: 9 we *m* on your unfailing love.
77: 12 I will *m* on all your works
119: 15 I *m* on your precepts
119: 23 your servant will *m*
119: 27 then I will *m* on your wonders.
119: 48 and I *m* on your decrees.
119: 78 but I will *m* on your precepts.
119: 97 I *m* on it all day long.
119: 99 for I *m* on your statutes.
119: 148 that I may *m* on your promises.
143: 5 I *m* on all your works
145: 5 I will *m* on your wonderful works.

MEDITATED* (MEDITATE)

Ps 39: 3 and as I *m*, the fire burned;

MEDITATES* (MEDITATE)

Ps 1: 2 and on his law he *m* day and night.

MEDITATION* (MEDITATE)

Ps 19: 14 of my mouth and the *m* of my heart
104: 34 May my *m* be pleasing to him,

MEDIUM

Lev 20: 27 "'A man or woman who is a *m*

MEEK* (MEEKNESS)

Ps 37: 11 But the *m* will inherit the land
Zep 3: 12 the *m* and humble,
Mt 5: 5 Blessed are the *m*,

MEEKNESS* (MEEK)

2Co 10: 1 By the *m* and gentleness of Christ,

MEET (MEETING MEETINGS MEETS)

Ps 42: 2 When can I go and *m* with God?
85: 10 Love and faithfulness *m* together;
Am 4: 12 prepare to *m* your God, O Israel."
1Co 11: 34 when you *m* together it may not
1Th 4: 17 them in the clouds to *m* the Lord

MEETING (MEET)

Ex 40: 34 the cloud covered the Tent of *M*,
Heb 10: 25 Let us not give up *m* together,

MEETINGS* (MEET)

1Co 11: 17 for your *m* do more harm

MEETS (MEET)

Heb 7: 26 Such a high priest *m* our need—

MELCHIZEDEK

Ge 14: 18 *M* king of Salem brought out bread
Ps 110: 4 in the order of *M*."
Heb 7: 11 in the order of *M*, not in the order

MELT (MELTS)

2Pe 3: 12 and the elements will *m* in the heat.

MELTS (MELT)

Am 9: 5 he who touches the earth and it *m*,

MEMBER (MEMBERS)

Ro 12: 5 each *m* belongs to all the others.

MEMBERS (MEMBER)

Mic 7: 6 a man's enemies are the *m*
Mt 10: 36 a man's enemies will be the *m*
Ro 7: 23 law at work in the *m* of my body,
12: 4 of us has one body with many *m*,
1Co 6: 15 not know that your bodies are *m*
12: 24 But God has combined the *m*
Eph 3: 6 *m* together of one body,
4: 25 for we are all *m* of one body.
5: 30 for we are *m* of his body.
Col 3: 15 as *m* of one body you were called

MEMORABLE* (MEMORY)

Eze 39: 13 day I am glorified will be a *m* day

MEMORIES* (MEMORY)

1Th 3: 6 us that you always have pleasant *m*

MEMORY (MEMORABLE MEMORIES)

Pr 10: 7 *m* of the righteous will be
Mt 26: 13 she has done will also be told, in *m*

MEN (MAN)

Ge 6: 2 daughters of *m* were beautiful,
6: 4 heroes of old, *m* of renown
Ps 9: 20 nations know they are but *m*.
11: 4 He observes the sons of *m*;
Mt 4: 19 will make you fishers of *m*
5: 16 your light shine before *m*
6: 14 if you forgive *m* when
10: 32 acknowledges me before *m*
12: 31 blasphemy will be forgiven *m*,
12: 36 *m* will have to give account
23: 5 is done for *m* to see:
Mk 7: 7 are but rules taught by *m*.
Lk 6: 22 Blessed are you when *m*
6: 26 Woe to you when all *m*
Jn 1: 4 life was the light of *m*.
2: 24 for he knew all *m*.
3: 19 *m* loved darkness instead
12: 32 will draw all *m* to myself
13: 35 all *m* will know that you
Ac 5: 29 obey God rather than *m*!
Ro 1: 18 wickedness of *m*
1: 27 indecent acts with other *m*,
5: 12 death came to all *m*,
1Co 2: 11 among *m* knows the thoughts
3: 3 acting like mere *m*?
3: 21 no more boasting about *m*!
9: 22 all things to all *m*
13: 1 tongues of *m* and of angels
16: 13 be *m* of courage;

1Co 16: 18 Such *m* deserve recognition.
2Co 5: 11 we try to persuade *m*.
8: 21 but also in the eyes of *m*.
Gal 1: 1 sent not from *m* nor
1: 10 to win approval of *m*, or
Eph 4: 8 and gave gifts to *m*.
1Th 2: 4 as *m* approved by God
2: 13 not as the word of *m*,
1Ti 2: 4 wants all *m* to be saved
2: 6 as a ransom for all *m*—
4: 10 the Saviour of all *m*
5: 2 younger *m* as brothers
2Ti 2: 2 entrust to reliable *m*
Tit 2: 11 has appeared to all *m*.
Heb 5: 1 is selected from among *m*
7: 28 high priests *m* who are weak;
2Pe 1: 21 but *m* spoke from God
Rev 21: 3 dwelling of God is with *m*,

MEN'S (MAN)
2Ki 19: 18 fashioned by *m* hands.
2Ch 32: 19 the work of *m* hands.
1Co 2: 5 not rest on *m* wisdom,

MENAHEM*
King of Israel (2Ki 15:17-22).

MENE
Da 5: 25 that was written: *M*, *M*,

MEPHIBOSHETH
Son of Jonathan shown kindness by David (2Sa 4:4; 9; 21:7). Accused of siding with Absalom (2Sa 16:1-4; 19:24-30).

MERCHANT
Pr 31: 14 She is like the *m* ships,
Mt 13: 45 of heaven is like a *m* looking

MERCIFUL (MERCY)
Dt 4: 31 the LORD your God is a *m* God;
Ne 9: 31 for you are a gracious and *m* God.
Ps 77: 9 Has God forgotten to be *m*?
78: 38 Yet he was *m*;
Jer 3: 12 for I am *m*,' declares the LORD,
Da 9: 9 The Lord our God is *m*
Mt 5: 7 Blessed are the *m*,
Lk 1: 54 remembering to be *m*
6: 36 Be *m*, just as your Father is *m*.
Heb 2: 17 in order that he might become a *m*
Jas 2: 13 to anyone who has not been *m*.
Jude : 22 Be *m* to those who doubt; snatch

MERCY (MERCIFUL)
Ex 33: 19 *m* on whom I will have *m*,
2Sa 24: 14 of the LORD, for his *m* is great;
1Ch 21: 13 for his *m* is very great;
Ne 9: 31 But in your great *m* you did not put
Ps 25: 6 O LORD, your great *m* and love,
28: 6 for he has heard my cry for *m*.
57: 1 Have *m* on me, O God, have *m*
Pr 28: 13 renounces them finds *m*.
Isa 63: 9 and *m* he redeemed them;
Da 9: 18 but because of your great *m*.
Hos 6: 6 for I desire *m*, not sacrifice,
Am 5: 15 LORD God Almighty will have *m*
Mic 6: 8 To act justly and to love *m*
7: 18 but delight to show *m*.
Hab 3: 2 in wrath remember *m*.
Zec 7: 9 show *m* and compassion
Mt 5: 7 for they will be shown *m*.
9: 13 learn what this means: 'I desire *m*,
12: 7 'I desire *m*, not sacrifice,' you
18: 33 Shouldn't you have had *m*
23: 23 justice, *m* and faithfulness.
Lk 1: 50 His *m* extends to those who fear
Ro 9: 15 "I will have *m* on whom I have *m*,
9: 18 Therefore God has *m*
11: 32 so that he may have *m* on them all.
12: 1 brothers, in view of God's *m*,
12: 8 if it is showing *m*, let him do it
Eph 2: 4 who is rich in *m*, made us alive
1Ti 1: 13 I was shown *m* because I acted
1: 16 for that very reason I was shown *m*
Tit 3: 5 we had done, but because of his *m*.
Heb 4: 16 so that we may receive *m*
Jas 2: 13 judgment without *m* will be shown
2: 13 *M* triumphs over judgment!
3: 17 submissive, full of *m* and good fruit
5: 11 full of compassion and *m*.
1Pe 1: 3 In his great *m* he has given us new
2: 10 once you had not received *m*,
Jude : 23 to others show *m*, mixed with fear

MERRY
Lk 12: 19 Take life easy; eat, drink and be *m*

MESHACH
Hebrew exiled to Babylon; name changed from Mishael (Da 1:6-7). Refused defilement by food (Da 1:8-20). Refused to worship idol (Da 3:1-18); saved from furnace (Da 3:19-30).

MESSAGE (MESSENGER)
Isa 53: 1 Who has believed our *m*
Jn 12: 38 "Lord, who has believed our *m*
Ac 5: 20 "and tell the people the full *m*
10: 36 You know the *m* God sent
17: 11 for they received the *m*
Ro 10: 16 who has believed our *m*?"
10: 17 faith comes from hearing the *m*,
1Co 1: 18 For the *m* of the cross is
2: 4 My *m* and my preaching were not
2Co 5: 19 to us the *m* of reconciliation.
2Th 3: 1 pray for us that the *m*
Tit 1: 9 firmly to the trustworthy *m*
Heb 4: 2 the *m* they heard was of no value
1Pe 2: 8 because they disobey the *m*—

MESSENGER (MESSAGE)
Pr 25: 13 is a trustworthy *m*
Mal 3: 1 I will send my *m*, who will prepare
Mt 11: 10 "'I will send my *m* ahead of you,
2Co 12: 7 a *m* of Satan, to torment me.

MESSIAH*
Jn 1: 41 "We have found the *M*" (that is,
4: 25 "I know that *M*" (called Christ) "is

METHUSELAH
Ge 5: 27 Altogether, *M* lived 969 years,

MICAH
1. Idolater from Ephraim (Jdg 17-18).
2. Prophet from Moresheth (Jer 26:18-19; Mic 1:1).

MICAIAH
Prophet of the LORD who spoke against Ahab (1Ki 22:1-28; 2Ch 18:1-27).

MICHAEL
Archangel (Jude 9); warrior in angelic realm, protector of Israel (Da 10:13, 21; 12:1; Rev 12:7).

MICHAL
Daughter of Saul, wife of David (1Sa 14:49; 18:20-28). Warned David of Saul's plot (1Sa 19). Saul gave her to Paltiel (1Sa 25:44); David retrieved her (2Sa 3:13-16). Criticised David for dancing before the ark (2Sa 6:16-23; 1Ch 15:29).

MIDIAN
Ex 2: 15 Pharaoh and went to live in *M*,
Jdg 7: 2 me to deliver *M* into their hands.

MIDWIVES
Ex 1: 17 The *m*, however, feared God

MIGHT (ALMIGHTY MIGHTIER MIGHTY)
Jdg 16: 30 Then he pushed with all his *m*,
2Sa 6: 5 with all their *m* before the LORD,
6: 14 before the LORD with all his *m*,
2Ch 20: 6 Power and *m* are in your hand,
Ps 21: 13 we will sing and praise your *m*.
54: 1 vindicate me by your *m*.
Isa 63: 15 Where are your zeal and your *m*?
Mic 3: 8 and with justice and *m*,
Zec 4: 6 'Not by *m* nor by power,
Col 1: 11 power according to his glorious *m*
1Ti 6: 16 To him be honour and *m* for ever.

MIGHTIER (MIGHT)
Ps 93: 4 *M* than the thunder

MIGHTY (MIGHT)
Ge 49: 24 of the hand of the *M* One of Jacob,
Ex 6: 1 of my *m* hand he will drive them
13: 3 out of it with a *m* hand.
Dt 5: 15 out of there with a *m* hand
7: 8 he brought you out with a *m* hand
10: 17 the great God, *m* and awesome,
34: 12 no-one has ever shown the *m* power
2Sa 1: 19 How the *m* have fallen!
23: 8 the names of David's *m* men:
Ne 9: 32 the great, *m* and awesome God,
Job 36: 5 God is *m*, but does not despise men
Ps 24: 8 The LORD strong and *m*,
45: 3 upon your side, O *m* one;
50: 1 The *M* One, God, the LORD,
62: 7 he is my *m* rock, my refuge.
68: 33 who thunders with *m* voice.
71: 16 proclaim your *m* acts,
77: 12 and consider all your *m* deeds.
77: 15 With your *m* arm you redeemed
89: 8 You are *m*, O LORD,
93: 4 the LORD on high is *m*.
99: 4 The King is *m*, he loves justice—
110: 2 LORD will extend your *m* sceptre
118: 15 right hand has done *m* things!
136: 12 with a *m* hand and outstretched
145: 4 they will tell of your *m* acts.
145: 12 all men may know of your *m* acts
147: 5 Great is our Lord and *m* in power;
SS 8: 6 like a *m* flame.
Isa 9: 6 Wonderful Counsellor, *M* God,
60: 16 your Redeemer, the *M* One
63: 1 *m* to save."
Jer 10: 6 and your name is *m* in power.
20: 11 with me like a *m* warrior;
32: 19 your purposes and *m* are your
Eze 20: 33 I will rule over you with a *m* hand
Zep 3: 17 he is *m* to save.
Mt 26: 64 at the right hand of the *M* One
Eph 1: 19 like the working of his *m* strength,
6: 10 in the Lord and in his *m* power.
1Pe 5: 6 therefore, under God's *m* hand,

MILE*
Mt 5: 41 If someone forces you to go one *m*,

MILK
Ex 3: 8 a land flowing with *m* and honey—
23: 19 a young goat in its mother's *m*.
Pr 30: 33 as churning the *m* produces butter,
Isa 55: 1 Come, buy wine and *m*
1Co 3: 2 I gave you *m*, not solid food,
Heb 5: 12 You need *m*, not solid food!
1Pe 2: 2 babies, crave pure spiritual *m*,

MILLSTONE (STONE)
Lk 17: 2 sea with a *m* tied round his neck

MIND (DOUBLE-MINDED LIKE-MINDED MINDED MINDFUL MINDS)
Nu 23: 19 that he should change his *m*.
Dt 28: 65 LORD will give you an anxious *m*,
1Sa 15: 29 Israel does not lie or change his *m*;
1Ch 28: 9 devotion and with a willing *m*,
2Ch 30: 12 the people to give them unity of *m*
Ps 26: 2 examine my heart and my *m*;
110: 4 and will not change his *m*:
Isa 26: 3 him whose *m* is steadfast,
Jer 17: 10 and examine the *m*,
Mt 22: 37 all your soul and with all your *m*.'
Mk 12: 30 with all your *m* and with all your
Lk 10: 27 your strength and with all your *m*';

Ac 4: 32 believers were one in heart and *m*.
Ro 1: 28 he gave them over to a depraved *m*
7: 25 I myself in my *m* am a slave
8: 6 The *m* of sinful man is death,
8: 7 the sinful *m* is hostile to God.
12: 2 by the renewing of your *m*.
14: 13 make up your *m* not
1Co 1: 10 you may be perfectly united in *m*
2: 9 no *m* has conceived
14: 14 spirit prays, but my *m* is unfruitful.
2Co 13: 11 be of one *m*, live in peace.
Php 3: 19 Their *m* is on earthly things.
Col 2: 18 and his unspiritual *m* puffs him up
1Th 4: 11 to *m* your own business
Heb 7: 21 and will not change his *m*:

MINDED* (MIND)
1Pe 4: 7 be clear *m* and self-controlled

MINDFUL* (MIND)
Ps 8: 4 what is man that you are *m* of him,
Lk 1: 48 God my Saviour, for he has been *m*
Heb 2: 6 What is man that you are *m* of him,

MINDS (MIND)
Dt 11: 18 of mine in your hearts and *m*;
Ps 7: 9 who searches *m* and hearts,
Jer 31: 33 "I will put my law in their *m*
Lk 24: 38 and why do doubts rise in your *m*?
24: 45 Then he opened their *m*
Ro 8: 5 to the sinful nature have their *m* set
2Co 4: 4 god of this age has blinded the *m*
Eph 4: 23 new in the attitude of your *m*;
Col 3: 2 Set your *m* on things above,
Heb 8: 10 I will put my laws in their *m*
10: 16 and I will write them on their *m*."
1Pe 1: 13 prepare your *m* for action;
Rev 2: 23 I am he who searches hearts and *m*,

MINISTER (MINISTERING MINISTERS MINISTRY)
Ps 101: 6 will *m* to me.
1Ti 4: 6 you will be a good *m*

MINISTERING (MINISTER)
Heb 1: 14 Are not all angels *m* spirits sent

MINISTERS (MINISTER)
2Co 3: 6 as *m* of a new covenant—

MINISTRY (MINISTER)
Ac 6: 4 to prayer and the *m* of the word."
Ro 11: 13 I make much of my *m*
2Co 4: 1 God's mercy we have this *m*,
5: 18 gave us the *m* of reconciliation:
6: 3 so that our *m* will not be
Gal 2: 8 who was at work in the *m* of Peter
2Ti 4: 5 discharge all the duties of your *m*.
Heb 8: 6 But the *m* Jesus has received is

MIRACLE* (MIRACLES MIRACULOUS)
Ex 7: 9 'Perform a *m*,' then say to Aaron,
Mk 9: 39 "No-one who does a *m*
Lk 23: 8 hoped to see him perform some *m*.
Jn 7: 21 "I did one *m*, and you are all
Ac 4: 16 they have done an outstanding *m*,

MIRACLES* (MIRACLE)
1Ch 16: 12 his *m*, and the judgments he
Ne 9: 17 to remember the *m* you performed
Job 5: 9 *m* that cannot be counted.
9: 10 *m* that cannot be counted.
Ps 77: 11 I will remember your *m* of long ago
77: 14 You are the God who performs *m*;
78: 12 He did *m* in the sight
105: 5 his *m*, and the judgments he
106: 7 they gave no thought to your *m*;
106: 22 *m* in the land of Ham
Mt 7: 22 out demons and perform many *m*?'
11: 20 most of his *m* had been performed,
11: 21 If the *m* that were performed
Mt 11: 23 If the *m* that were performed
13: 58 And he did not do many *m* there
24: 24 and perform great signs and *m*
Mk 6: 2 does *m*! Isn't this the carpenter?
6: 5 He could not do any *m* there,
13: 22 and *m* to deceive the elect—
Lk 10: 13 For if the *m* that were performed
19: 37 for all the *m* they had seen:
Jn 7: 3 disciples may see the *m* you do.
10: 25 *m* I do in my Father's name speak
10: 32 "I have shown you many great *m*
10: 38 do not believe me, believe the *m*,
14: 11 the evidence of the *m* themselves.
15: 24 But now they have seen these *m*,
Ac 2: 22 accredited by God to you by *m*,
8: 13 by the great signs and *m* he saw.
19: 11 God did extraordinary *m*
Ro 15: 19 by the power of signs and *m*,
1Co 12: 28 third teachers, then workers of *m*,
12: 29 Are all teachers? Do all work *m*?
2Co 12: 12 and *m*—were done among you
Gal 3: 5 work *m* among you because you
2Th 2: 9 in all kinds of counterfeit *m*,
Heb 2: 4 it by signs, wonders and various *m*,

MIRACULOUS (MIRACLE)
Dt 13: 1 and announces to you a *m* sign
Mt 12: 39 generation asks for a *m* sign!
13: 54 this wisdom and these *m* powers?"
Jn 2: 11 This, the first of his *m* signs,
2: 23 people saw the *m* signs he was
3: 2 could perform the *m* signs you are
4: 48 "Unless you people see *m* signs
7: 31 will he do more *m* signs
9: 16 "How can a sinner do such *m* signs
12: 37 Jesus had done all these *m* signs
20: 30 Jesus did many other *m* signs
Ac 2: 43 *m* signs were done by the apostles.
5: 12 apostles performed many *m* signs
1Co 1: 22 Jews demand *m* signs and Greeks
12: 10 to another *m* powers,

MIRE
Ps 40: 2 out of the mud and *m*;
Isa 57: 20 whose waves cast up *m* and mud.

MIRIAM
Sister of Moses and Aaron (Nu 26:59). Led dancing at Red Sea (Ex 15:20-21). Struck with leprosy for criticising Moses (Nu 12). Death (Nu 20:1).

MIRROR
1Co 13: 12 reflection as in a *m*;
Jas 1: 23 a man who looks at his face in a *m*

MISDEEDS*
Ps 99: 8 though you punished their *m*.
Ro 8: 13 put to death the *m* of the body,

MISERY
Ex 3: 7 "I have indeed seen the *m*
Jdg 10: 16 he could bear Israel's *m* no longer.
Hos 5: 15 in their *m* they will earnestly seek
Ro 3: 16 ruin and *m* mark their ways,
Jas 5: 1 of the *m* that is coming upon you.

MISFORTUNE
Ob : 12 brother in the day of his *m*,

MISLEAD (MISLED)
Isa 47: 10 wisdom and knowledge *m* you

MISLED (MISLEAD)
1Co 15: 33 Do not be *m*: "Bad company

MISS (MISSES)
Pr 19: 2 nor to be hasty and *m* the way.

MISSES (MISS)
Heb 12: 15 See to it that no-one *m* the grace

MIST
Hos 6: 4 Your love is like the morning *m*,
Jas 4: 14 You are a *m* that appears for a little

MISUSE* (MISUSES)
Ex 20: 7 "You shall not *m* the name
Dt 5: 11 "You shall not *m* the name
Ps 139: 20 your adversaries *m* your name.

MISUSES* (MISUSE)
Ex 20: 7 anyone guiltless who *m* his name.
Dt 5: 11 anyone guiltless who *m* his name.

MIXED (MIXING)
Da 2: 41 even as you saw iron *m* with clay.

MIXING (MIXED)
Isa 5: 22 and champions at *m* drinks,

MOAB (MOABITESS)
Ge 19: 37 she named him *M*; he is the father
Dt 34: 6 He buried him in *M*, in the valley
Ru 1: 1 live for a while in the country of *M*.
Isa 15: 1 An oracle concerning *M*:
Jer 48: 16 "The fall of *M* is at hand;
Am 2: 1 "For three sins of *M*,

MOABITESS (MOAB)
Ru 1: 22 accompanied by Ruth the *M*,

MOAN
Ps 90: 9 we finish our years with a *m*.

MOCK (MOCKED MOCKER MOCKERS MOCKING MOCKS)
Ps 22: 7 All who see me *m* me;
119: 51 The arrogant *m* me
Pr 1: 26 I will *m* when calamity overtakes
14: 9 Fools *m* at making amends for sin,
Mk 10: 34 who will *m* him and spit on him,

MOCKED (MOCK)
Ps 89: 51 with which they have *m* every step
Mt 27: 29 knelt in front of him and *m* him.
27: 41 of the law and the elders *m* him.
Gal 6: 7 not be deceived: God cannot be *m*.

MOCKER (MOCK)
Pr 9: 7 corrects a *m* invites insult;
9: 12 if you are a *m*, you alone will suffer
20: 1 Wine is a *m* and beer a brawler;
22: 10 Drive out the *m*, and out goes strife

MOCKERS (MOCK)
Ps 1: 1 or sit in the seat of *m*.
Pr 29: 8 *M* stir up a city,

MOCKING (MOCK)
Isa 50: 6 face from *m* and spitting.

MOCKS (MOCK)
Pr 17: 5 He who *m* the poor shows
30: 17 "The eye that *m* a father,

MODEL*
Eze 28: 12 "'You were the *m* of perfection,
1Th 1: 7 And so you became a *m*
2Th 3: 9 to make ourselves a *m* for you

MODESTY*
1Co 12: 23 are treated with special *m*,

MOLECH
Lev 20: 2 of his children to *M* must be put
1Ki 11: 33 and *M* the god of the Ammonites,

MOMENT (MOMENTARY)
Job 20: 5 the joy of the godless lasts but a *m*.
Ps 2: 12 for his wrath can flare up in a *m*.
30: 5 For his anger lasts only a *m*,
Pr 12: 19 but a lying tongue lasts only a *m*.
Isa 54: 7 "For a brief *m* I abandoned you,
66: 8 or a nation be brought forth in a *m*?

Gal 2: 5 We did not give in to them for a *m*,

MOMENTARY* (MOMENT)

2Co 4: 17 and *m* troubles are achieving

MONEY

Pr 13: 11 Dishonest *m* dwindles away,
Ecc 5: 10 Whoever loves *m* never has *m*
Isa 55: 1 and you who have no *m*,
Mt 6: 24 You cannot serve both God and *M*.
27: 5 Judas threw the *m* into the temple
Lk 3: 14 "Don't extort *m* and don't accuse
9: 3 no bread, no *m*, no extra tunic.
16: 13 You cannot serve both God and *M*
Ac 5: 2 part of the *m* for himself,
1Co 16: 2 set aside a sum of *m* in keeping
1Ti 3: 3 not quarrelsome, not a lover of *m*.
6: 10 For the love of *m* is a root
2Ti 3: 2 lovers of *m*, boastful, proud,
Heb 13: 5 free from the love of *m*
1Pe 5: 2 not greedy for *m*, but eager to serve

MONEY-LENDER* (LEND)

Ex 22: 25 not be like a *m*; charge him no
Lk 7: 41 men owed money to a certain *m*.

MONTH (MONTHS)

Ex 12: 2 "This *m* is to be for you the first
Eze 47: 12 Every *m* they will bear,
Rev 22: 2 of fruit, yielding its fruit every *m*.

MONTHS (MONTH)

Gal 4: 10 and *m* and seasons and years!
Rev 11: 2 trample on the holy city for 42 *m*.
13: 5 his authority for forty-two *m*.

MOON

Jos 10: 13 and the *m* stopped,
Ps 8: 3 the *m* and the stars,
74: 16 you established the sun and *m*.
89: 37 be established for ever like the *m*,
104: 19 The *m* marks off the seasons,
121: 6 nor the *m* by night.
136: 9 the *m* and stars to govern the night;
148: 3 Praise him, sun and *m*,
SS 6: 10 fair as the *m*, bright as the sun,
Joel 2: 31 and the *m* to blood
Hab 3: 11 and *m* stood still in the heavens
Mt 24: 29 and the *m* will not give its light;
Ac 2: 20 and the *m* to blood
1Co 15: 41 *m* another and the stars another;
Col 2: 16 a New *M* celebration or a Sabbath
Rev 6: 12 the whole *m* turned blood red,
21: 23 city does not need the sun or the *m*

MORAL*

Jas 1: 21 rid of all *m* filth and the evil that is

MORDECAI

Benjamite exile who raised Esther (Est 2:5-15). Exposed plot to kill Xerxes (Est 2:19-23). Refused to honour Haman (Est 3:1-6; 5:9-14). Charged Esther to foil Haman's plot against the Jews (Est 4). Xerxes forced Haman to honour Mordecai (Est 6). Mordecai exalted (Est 8-10). Established Purim (Est 9:18-32).

MORIAH*

Ge 22: 2 and go to the region of *M*.
2Ch 3: 1 LORD in Jerusalem on Mount *M*,

MORNING

Ge 1: 5 and there was *m*—the first day.
Dt 28: 67 In the *m* you will say, "If only it
2Sa 23: 4 he is like the light of *m* at sunrise
Ps 5: 3 *M* by *m*, O LORD,
Pr 27: 14 blesses his neighbour early in the *m*,
Isa 14: 12 O *m* star, son of the dawn!
La 3: 23 They are new every *m*;
2Pe 1: 19 and the *m* star rises in your hearts.
Rev 2: 28 I will also give him the *m* star.
22: 16 of David, and the bright *M* Star."

MORTAL

Ge 6: 3 for he is *m*; his days will be
Job 10: 4 Do you see as a *m* sees?
Ro 8: 11 also give life to your *m* bodies
1Co 15: 53 and the *m* with immortality.
2Co 5: 4 that what is *m* may be swallowed

MOSES

Levite; brother of Aaron (Ex 6:20; 1Ch 6:3). Put in basket into Nile; discovered and raised by Pharaoh's daughter (Ex 2:1-10). Fled to Midian after killing Egyptian (Ex 2:11-15). Married to Zipporah, fathered Gershom (Ex 2:16-22).

Called by the LORD to deliver Israel (Ex 3-4). Pharaoh's resistance (Ex 5). Ten plagues (Ex 7-11). Passover and Exodus (Ex 12-13). Led Israel through Red Sea (Ex 14). Song of deliverance (Ex 15:1-21). Brought water from rock (Ex 17:1-7). Raised hands to defeat Amalekites (Ex 17:8-16). Delegated judges (Ex 18; Dt 1:9-18).

Received Law at Sinai (Ex 19-23; 25-31; Jn 1:17). Announced Law to Israel (Ex 19:7-8; 24; 35). Broke tablets because of golden calf (Ex 32; Dt 9). Saw glory of the LORD (Ex 33-34). Supervised building of tabernacle (Ex 36-40). Set apart Aaron and priests (Lev 8-9). Numbered tribes (Nu 1-4; 26). Opposed by Aaron and Miriam (Nu 12). Sent spies into Canaan (Nu 13). Announced forty years of wandering for failure to enter land (Nu 14). Opposed by Korah (Nu 16). Forbidden to enter land for striking rock (Nu 20:1-13; Dt 1:37). Lifted bronze snake for healing (Nu 21: 4-9; Jn 3:14). Final address to Israel (Dt 31-33). Succeeded by Joshua (Nu 27:12-23; Dt 34). Death (Dt 34:5-12).

"Law of Moses" (1Ki 2:3; Ezr 3:2; Mk 12:26; Lk 24:44). "Book of Moses" (2Ch 25:12; Ne 13:1). "Song of Moses" (Ex 15:1-21; Rev 15:3). "Prayer of Moses" (Ps 90).

MOTH

Mt 6: 19 where *m* and rust destroy,

MOTHER (GRANDMOTHER MOTHER-IN-LAW MOTHER'S)

Ge 2: 24 and *m* and be united to his wife,
3: 20 because she would become the *m*
Ex 20: 12 "Honour your father and your *m*,
Lev 20: 9 " 'If anyone curses his father or *m*,
Dt 5: 16 "Honour your father and your *m*,
21: 18 who does not obey his father and *m*
27: 16 who dishonours his father or his *m*."
Jdg 5: 7 arose a *m* in Israel.
1Sa 2: 19 Each year his *m* made him a little
Ps 113: 9 as a happy *m* of children.
Pr 10: 1 but a foolish son grief to his *m*.
23: 22 do not despise your *m*
23: 25 May your father and *m* be glad;
29: 15 a child left to itself disgraces his *m*.
30: 17 that scorns obedience to a *m*,
31: 1 an oracle his *m* taught him:
Isa 49: 15 "Can a *m* forget the baby
66: 13 As a *m* comforts her child,
Jer 20: 17 with my *m* as my grave,
Mic 7: 6 a daughter rises up against her *m*,
Mt 10: 35 a daughter against her *m*,
10: 37 or *m* more than me is not worthy
12: 48 He replied, "Who is my *m*,
15: 4 'Honour your father and *m*'
19: 5 and *m* and be united to his wife,
19: 19 honour your father and *m*,'
Mk 7: 10 'Honour your father and *m*,' and,
10: 19 honour your father and *m*.' "
Lk 11: 27 "Blessed is the *m* who gave you
12: 53 daughter and daughter against *m*,
18: 20 honour your father and *m*.' "
Jn 19: 27 to the disciple, "Here is your *m*."
Gal 4: 26 is above is free, and she is our *m*.
Eph 5: 31 and *m* and be united to his wife,
6: 2 "Honour your father and *m*"—
1Th 2: 7 like a *m* caring for her little
2Ti 1: 5 and in your *m* Eunice and,

MOTHER-IN-LAW (MOTHER)

Ru 2: 19 Ruth told her *m* about the one
Mt 10: 35 a daughter-in-law against her *m*—

MOTHER'S (MOTHER)

Job 1: 21 "Naked I came from my *m* womb,
Pr 1: 8 and do not forsake your *m* teaching
Ecc 5: 15 from his *m* womb,
11: 5 the body is formed in a *m* womb,
Jn 3: 4 time into his *m* womb to be born!"

MOTIVE* (MOTIVES)

1Ch 28: 9 and understands every *m*

MOTIVES* (MOTIVE)

Pr 16: 2 but *m* are weighed by the LORD.
1Co 4: 5 will expose the *m* of men's hearts.
Php 1: 18 whether from false *m* or true,
1Th 2: 3 spring from error or impure *m*,
Jas 4: 3 because you ask with wrong *m*,

MOULDED*

Job 10: 9 Remember that you *m* me like clay

MOULDY

Jos 9: 5 of their food supply was dry and *m*.

MOUNT (MOUNTAIN MOUNTAINS MOUNTAINTOPS)

Ps 89: 9 when its waves *m* up, you still them
Isa 14: 13 enthroned on the *m* of assembly,
Eze 28: 14 You were on the holy *m* of God;
Zec 14: 4 stand on the *M* of Olives,

MOUNTAIN (MOUNT)

Ge 22: 14 "On the *m* of the LORD it will be
Ex 24: 18 And he stayed on the *m* forty days
Dt 5: 4 face to face out of the fire on the *m*.
Job 14: 18 "But as a *m* erodes and crumbles
Ps 48: 1 in the city of our God, his holy *m*.
Isa 40: 4 every *m* and hill made low;
Mic 4: 2 Let us go up to the *m* of the LORD,
Mt 4: 8 the devil took him to a very high *m*
17: 20 say to this *m*, 'Move from here
Mk 9: 2 with him and led them up a high *m*,
Lk 3: 5 every *m* and hill made low.
Jn 4: 21 the Father neither on this *m*
2Pe 1: 18 were with him on the sacred *m*.

MOUNTAINS (MOUNT)

Ps 36: 6 righteousness is like the mighty *m*,
46: 2 the *m* fall into the heart of the sea,
90: 2 Before the *m* were born
Isa 52: 7 How beautiful on the *m*
54: 10 Though the *m* be shaken
55: 12 the *m* and hills
Eze 34: 6 My sheep wandered over all the *m*
Mt 24: 16 are in Judea flee to the *m*.
Lk 23: 30 they will say to the *m*, "Fall on us!"
1Co 13: 2 if I have a faith that can move *m*,
Rev 6: 16 They called to the *m* and the rocks,

MOUNTAINTOPS (MOUNT)

Isa 42: 11 let them shout from the *m*.

MOURN (MOURNING MOURNS)

Ecc 3: 4 a time to *m* and a time to dance,
Isa 61: 2 to comfort all who *m*,
Mt 5: 4 Blessed are those who *m*,
Ro 12: 15 *m* with those who *m*.

MOURNING (MOURN)

Isa 61: 3 instead of *m*,
Jer 31: 13 I will turn their *m* into gladness;
Rev 21: 4 There will be no more death or *m*

MOURNS (MOURN)

Zec 12: 10 as one *m* for an only child,

MOUTH (MOUTHS)

Nu 22: 38 only what God puts in my *m*."
Dt 8: 3 comes from the *m* of the LORD.
18: 18 I will put my words in his *m*,

Dt 30: 14 it is in your *m* and in your heart
Jos 1: 8 of the Law depart from your *m*;
2Ki 4: 34 *m* to *m*, eyes to eyes, hands
Ps 10: 7 His *m* is full of curses and lies
17: 3 resolved that my *m* will not sin.
19: 14 May the words of my *m*
37: 30 *m* of the righteous man utters
40: 3 He put a new song in my *m*,
71: 8 My *m* is filled with your praise,
119: 103 sweeter than honey to my *m*!
141: 3 Set a guard over my *m*, O LORD;
Pr 2: 6 and from his *m* come knowledge
4: 24 Put away perversity from your *m*;
10: 11 The *m* of the righteous is a fountain
10: 31 *m* of the righteous brings forth
16: 23 A wise man's heart guides his *m*,
26: 28 and a flattering *m* works ruin.
27: 2 praise you, and not your own *m*;
Ecc 5: 2 Do not be quick with your *m*,
SS 1: 2 with the kisses of his *m*—
5: 16 His *m* is sweetness itself;
Isa 29: 13 come near to me with their *m*
40: 5 For the *m* of the LORD has spoken
45: 23 my *m* has uttered in all integrity
51: 16 I have put my words in your *m*
53: 7 so he did not open his *m*.
55: 11 my word that goes out from my *m*:
59: 21 *m* will not depart from your *m*,
Eze 3: 2 So I opened my *m*, and he gave me
Mal 2: 7 and from his *m* men should seek
Mt 4: 4 comes from the *m* of God.'"
12: 34 overflow of the heart the *m* speaks.
15: 11 into a man's *m* does not make him
15: 18 out of the *m* come from the heart,
Lk 6: 45 overflow of his heart his *m* speaks.
Ro 10: 9 That if you confess with your *m*,
15: 6 and *m* you may glorify the God
1Pe 2: 22 and no deceit was found in his *m*."
Rev 1: 16 and out of his *m* came a sharp
2: 16 them with the sword of my *m*.
3: 16 I am about to spit you out of my *m*.
19: 15 Out of his *m* comes a sharp sword

MOUTHS (MOUTH)
Ps 78: 36 would flatter him with their *m*,
Eze 33: 31 With their *m* they express devotion
Ro 3: 14 "Their *m* are full of cursing
Eph 4: 29 talk come out of your *m*,
Jas 3: 3 bits into the *m* of horses

MOVE (MOVED MOVES)
Dt 19: 14 Do not *m* your neighbour's
Pr 23: 10 Do not *m* an ancient boundary
Ac 17: 28 and *m* and have our being.'
1Co 13: 2 have a faith that can *m* mountains,
15: 58 Let nothing *m* you.

MOVED (MOVE)
Ex 35: 21 and whose heart *m* him came
2Ch 36: 22 the LORD *m* the heart
Ezr 1: 5 everyone whose heart God had *m*
Ps 93: 1 it cannot be *m*.
Jn 11: 33 he was deeply *m* in spirit
Col 1: 23 not *m* from the hope held out

MOVES (MOVE)
Dt 23: 14 For the LORD your God *m* about

MUD (MUDDIED)
Ps 40: 2 out of the *m* and mire;
Isa 57: 20 whose waves cast up mire and *m*.
Jn 9: 6 made some *m* with the saliva,
2Pe 2: 22 back to her wallowing in the *m*."

MUDDIED (MUD)
Pr 25: 26 Like a *m* spring or a polluted well
Eze 32: 13 or *m* by the hoofs of cattle.

MULBERRY*
Lk 17: 6 you can say to this *m* tree,

MULTITUDE (MULTITUDES)
Isa 31: 1 who trust in the *m* of their chariots
Jas 5: 20 and cover over a *m* of sins.
1Pe 4: 8 love covers over a *m* of sins.
Rev 7: 9 me was a great *m* that no-one could
19: 1 of a great *m* in heaven shouting:

MULTITUDES (MULTITUDE)
Ne 9: 6 and the *m* of heaven worship you.
Da 12: 2 *M* who sleep in the dust
Joel 3: 14 *M*, *m* in the valley of decision!

MURDER (MURDERED MURDERER MURDERERS)
Ex 20: 13 "You shall not *m*.
Dt 5: 17 "You shall not *m*.
Pr 28: 17 A man tormented by the guilt of *m*
Mt 5: 21 'Do not *m*, and anyone who
15: 19 *m*, adultery, sexual immorality,
Ro 1: 29 *m*, strife, deceit and malice.
13: 9 "Do not *m*," "Do not steal,"
Jas 2: 11 adultery," also said, "Do not *m*."

MURDERED (MURDER)
Mt 23: 31 of those who *m* the prophets.
Ac 7: 52 now you have betrayed and *m* him
1Jn 3: 12 to the evil one and *m* his brother.

MURDERER (MURDER)
Nu 35: 16 he is a *m*; the *m* shall be put
Jn 8: 44 He was a *m* from the beginning,
1Jn 3: 15 who hates his brother is a *m*,

MURDERERS (MURDER)
1Ti 1: 9 for *m*, for adulterers and perverts,
Rev 21: 8 the *m*, the sexually immoral,
22: 15 the sexually immoral, the *m*,

MUSIC* (MUSICAL MUSICIAN MUSICIANS)
Ge 31: 27 singing to the *m* of tambourines
Jdg 5: 3 I will make *m* to the LORD,
1Ch 6: 31 put in charge of the *m* in the house
6: 32 They ministered with *m*
25: 6 fathers for the *m* of the temple
25: 7 and skilled in *m* for the LORD—
Ne 12: 27 and with the *m* of cymbals,
Job 21: 12 They sing to the *m* of tambourine
Ps 27: 6 and make *m* to the LORD.
33: 2 make *m* to him on the ten-stringed
45: 8 the *m* of the strings makes you glad
57: 7 I will sing and make *m*.
81: 2 Begin the *m*, strike the tambourine,
87: 7 As they make *m* they will sing,
92: 1 and make *m* to your name,
92: 3 to the *m* of the ten-stringed lyre
95: 2 and extol him with *m* and song.
98: 4 burst into jubilant song with *m*;
98: 5 make *m* to the LORD
108: 1 make *m* with all my soul.
144: 9 the ten-stringed lyre I will make *m*
147: 7 make *m* to our God on the harp.
149: 3 make *m* to him with tambourine
Isa 30: 32 will be to the *m* of tambourines
La 5: 14 young men have stopped their *m*.
Eze 26: 13 *m* of your harps will be heard no
Da 3: 5 lyre, harp, pipes and all kinds of *m*,
3: 7 and all kinds of *m*, all the peoples,
3: 10 and all kinds of *m* must fall down
3: 15 lyre, harp, pipes and all kinds of *m*,
Am 5: 23 to the *m* of your harps.
Hab 3: 19 For the director of *m*.
Lk 15: 25 came near the house, he heard *m*
Eph 5: 19 make *m* in your heart to the Lord,
Rev 18: 22 The *m* of harpists and musicians,

MUSICAL* (MUSIC)
1Ch 15: 16 accompanied by *m* instruments:
23: 5 with the *m* instruments I have
2Ch 7: 6 with the LORD's *m* instruments,
23: 13 with *m* instruments were leading
34: 12 skilled in playing *m* instruments—
Ne 12: 36 with *m* instruments prescribed
Am 6: 5 and improvise on *m* instruments.

MUSICIAN* (MUSIC)
1Ch 6: 33 Heman, the *m*, the son of Joel,

MUSICIANS* (MUSIC)
1Ki 10: 12 to make harps and lyres for the *m*.
1Ch 9: 33 Those who were *m*, heads
15: 19 The *m* Heman, Asaph
2Ch 5: 12 All the Levites who were *m*—
9: 11 to make harps and lyres for the *m*.
35: 15 The *m*, the descendants of Asaph,
Ps 68: 25 are the singers, after them the *m*;
Rev 18: 22 The music of harpists and *m*,

MUSTARD
Mt 13: 31 kingdom of heaven is like a *m* seed,
17: 20 you have faith as small as a *m* seed,
Mk 4: 31 It is like a *m* seed, which is

MUTE
Mk 7: 37 the deaf hear and the *m* speak."
1Co 12: 2 and led astray to *m* idols.

MUTILATORS*
Php 3: 2 those men who do evil, those *m*

MUTUAL* (MUTUALLY)
Ro 14: 19 leads to peace and to *m* edification.
1Co 7: 5 by *m* consent and for a time,

MUTUALLY* (MUTUAL)
Ro 1: 12 and I may be *m* encouraged

MUZZLE*
Dt 25: 4 Do not *m* an ox while it is treading
Ps 39: 1 I will put a *m* on my mouth
1Co 9: 9 "Do not *m* an ox while it is
1Ti 5: 18 "Do not *m* the ox while it is

MYRRH
Ps 45: 8 All your robes are fragrant with *m*
SS 1: 13 My lover is to me a sachet of *m*
Mt 2: 11 of gold and of incense and of *m*.
Mk 15: 23 offered him wine mixed with *m*,
Jn 19: 39 Nicodemus brought a mixture of *m*
Rev 18: 13 of incense, *m* and frankincense,

MYSTERIES* (MYSTERY)
Job 11: 7 "Can you fathom the *m* of God?
Da 2: 28 a God in heaven who reveals *m*.
2: 29 of *m* showed you what is going
2: 47 Lord of kings and a revealer of *m*,
1Co 13: 2 can fathom all *m* and all knowledge
14: 2 he utters *m* with his spirit.

MYSTERY* (MYSTERIES)
Da 2: 18 God of heaven concerning this *m*,
2: 19 the night the *m* was revealed
2: 27 to the king the *m* he has asked
2: 30 this *m* has been revealed to me,
2: 47 for you were able to reveal this *m*."
4: 9 and no *m* is too difficult for you.
Ro 11: 25 you to be ignorant of this *m*,
16: 25 to the revelation of the *m* hidden
1Co 15: 51 I tell you a *m*: We will not all sleep,
Eph 1: 9 to us the *m* of his will according
3: 3 the *m* made known to me
3: 4 insight into the *m* of Christ,
3: 6 This *m* is that through the gospel
3: 9 the administration of this *m*,
5: 32 This is a profound *m*—
6: 19 I will fearlessly make known the *m*
Col 1: 26 the *m* that has been kept hidden
1: 27 the glorious riches of this *m*,
2: 2 in order that they may know the *m*
4: 3 so that we may proclaim the *m*
1Ti 3: 16 the *m* of godliness is great:
Rev 1: 20 *m* of the seven stars that you saw
10: 7 the *m* of God will be accomplished,
17: 5 written on her forehead: M
17: 7 explain to you the *m* of the woman

MYTHS*
1Ti 1: 4 nor to devote themselves to *m*
4: 7 Have nothing to do with godless *m*
2Ti 4: 4 from the truth and turn aside to *m*.

Tit 1: 14 will pay no attention to Jewish *m*

NAAMAN

Aramean general whose leprosy was cleansed by Elisha (2Ki 5).

NABAL

Wealthy Carmelite the LORD killed for refusing to help David (1Sa 25). David married Abigail, his widow (1Sa 25:39-42).

NABOTH*

Jezreelite killed by Jezebel for his vineyard (1Ki 21). Ahab's family destroyed for this (1Ki 21:17-24; 2Ki 9:21-37).

NADAB

1. Firstborn of Aaron (Ex 6:23); killed with Abihu for offering unauthorised fire (Lev 10; Nu 3:4).

2. Son of Jeroboam I; king of Israel (1Ki 15:25-32).

NAHUM

Prophet against Nineveh (Na 1:1).

NAIL* (NAILING)

Jn 20: 25 "Unless I see the *n* marks

NAILING* (NAIL)

Ac 2: 23 him to death by *n* him to the cross.
Col 2: 14 he took it away, *n* it to the cross.

NAIVE

Ro 16: 18 they deceive the minds of *n* people.

NAKED

Ge 2: 25 The man and his wife were both *n*,
Job 1: 21 *N* I came from my mother's womb,
Isa 58: 7 when you see the *n*, to clothe him,
2Co 5: 3 are clothed, we will not be found *n*.

NAME (NAMES)

Ge 2: 19 man to see what he would *n* them;
4: 26 to call on the *n* of the LORD.
11: 4 so that we may make a *n*
12: 2 I will make your *n* great,
32: 29 Jacob said, "Please tell me your *n*."
Ex 3: 15 This is my *n* for ever, the *n*
20: 7 "You shall not misuse the *n*
34: 14 for the LORD, whose *n* is Jealous,
Lev 24: 11 Israelite woman blasphemed the *N*
Dt 5: 11 "You shall not misuse the *n*
12: 11 choose as a dwelling for his *N*—
18: 5 minister in the LORD's *n* always.
25: 6 carry on the *n* of the dead brother
28: 58 this glorious and awesome *n*—
Jos 7: 9 do for your own great *n*?"
Jdg 13: 17 "What is your *n*, so that we may
1Sa 12: 22 of his great *n* the LORD will not
2Sa 6: 2 which is called by the *N*, the *n*
7: 9 Now I will make your *n* great,
1Ki 5: 5 will build the temple for my *N*.'
8: 29 you said, 'My *N* shall be there,'
1Ch 17: 8 I will make your *n* like the names
2Ch 7: 14 my people, who are called by my *n*,
Ne 9: 10 You made a *n* for yourself,
Ps 8: 1 how majestic is your *n*
9: 10 Those who know your *n* will trust
20: 7 in the *n* of the LORD our God.
29: 2 to the LORD the glory due his *n*;
34: 3 let us exalt his *n* together.
44: 20 If we had forgotten the *n*
66: 2 Sing the glory of his *n*;
68: 4 Sing to God, sing praise to his *n*,
79: 9 for the glory of your *n*;
96: 8 to the LORD the glory due his *n*;
103: 1 my inmost being, praise his holy *n*.
115: 1 but to your *n* be the glory,
138: 2 your *n* and your word.
145: 1 I will praise your *n* for ever
147: 4 and calls them each by *n*.
Pr 3: 4 you will win favour and a good *n*
18: 10 *n* of the LORD is a strong tower;
22: 1 A good *n* is more desirable
30: 4 What is his *n*, and the *n* of his son?
Ecc 7: 1 A good *n* is better
SS 1: 3 your *n* is like perfume poured out.
Isa 12: 4 thanks to the LORD, call on his *n*;
26: 8 your *n* and renown
40: 26 and calls them each by *n*.
42: 8 "I am the LORD; that is my *n*!
56: 5 I will give them an everlasting *n*
57: 15 who lives for ever, whose *n* is holy:
63: 14 to make for yourself a glorious *n*.
Jer 14: 7 do something for the sake of your *n*
15: 16 for I bear your *n*,
Eze 20: 9 of my *n* I did what would keep it
20: 14 of my *n* I did what would keep it
20: 22 of my *n* I did what would keep it
Da 12: 1 everyone whose *n* is found written
Hos 12: 5 the LORD is his *n* of renown!
Joel 2: 32 on the *n* of the LORD will be saved
Mic 5: 4 in the majesty of the *n*
Zep 3: 9 call on the *n* of the LORD
Zec 6: 12 is the man whose *n* is the Branch,
14: 9 one LORD, and his *n* the only *n*.
Mal 1: 6 priests, who show contempt for my *n*.
Mt 1: 21 and you are to give him the *n* Jesus,
6: 9 hallowed be your *n*,
18: 20 or three come together in my *n*,
24: 5 For many will come in my *n*,
28: 19 them in the *n* of the Father
Mk 9: 41 gives you a cup of water in my *n*
Lk 11: 2 hallowed be your *n*,
Jn 10: 3 He calls his own sheep by *n*
14: 13 I will do whatever you ask in my *n*,
16: 24 asked for anything in my *n*.
Ac 2: 21 on the *n* of the Lord will be saved.'
4: 12 for there is no other *n*
Ro 10: 13 "Everyone who calls on the *n*
Php 2: 9 him the *n* that is above every *n*,
2: 10 at the *n* of Jesus every knee should
Col 3: 17 do it all in the *n* of the Lord Jesus,
Heb 1: 4 as the *n* he has inherited is superior
Jas 5: 14 him with oil in the *n* of the Lord.
1Jn 5: 13 believe in the *n* of the Son of God
Rev 2: 17 stone with a new *n* written on it,
3: 5 I will never blot out his *n*
3: 12 I will also write on him my new *n*.
19: 13 and his *n* is the Word of God.
20: 15 If anyone's *n* was not found written

NAMES (NAME)

Ex 28: 9 engrave on them the *n* of the sons
Lk 10: 20 but rejoice that your *n* are written
Php 4: 3 whose *n* are in the book of life.
Heb 12: 23 whose *n* are written in heaven.
Rev 21: 27 but only those whose *n* are written

NAOMI

Wife of Elimelech, mother-in-law of Ruth (Ru 1:2, 4). Left Bethlehem for Moab during famine (Ru 1:1). Returned a widow, with Ruth (Ru 1:6-22). Advised Ruth to seek marriage with Boaz (Ru 2:17-3:4). Cared for Ruth's son Obed (Ru 4:13-17).

NAPHTALI

Son of Jacob by Bilhah (Ge 30:8; 35:25; 1Ch 2:2). Tribe of blessed (Ge 49:21; Dt 33:23), numbered (Nu 1:43; 26:50), allotted land (Jos 19:32-39; Eze 48:3), failed to fully possess (Jdg 1:33), supported Deborah (Jdg 4:10; 5:18), David (1Ch 12:34), 12,000 from (Rev 7:6).

NARROW

Mt 7: 13 "Enter through the *n* gate.
7: 14 and *n* the road that leads to life,

NATHAN

Prophet and chronicler of Israel's history (1Ch 29:29; 2Ch 9:29). Announced the Davidic covenant (2Sa 7; 1Ch 17). Denounced David's sin with Bathsheba (2Sa 12). Supported Solomon (1Ki 1).

NATHANAEL*

Apostle (Jn 1:45-49; 21:2). Probably also called Bartholomew (Mt 10:3).

NATION (NATIONS)

Ge 12: 2 "I will make you into a great *n*
Ex 19: 6 a kingdom of priests and a holy *n*.'
Dt 4: 7 What other *n* is so great
Jos 5: 8 And after the whole *n* had been
2Sa 7: 23 one *n* on earth that God went out
Ps 33: 12 Blessed is the *n* whose God is
Pr 11: 14 For lack of guidance a *n* falls,
14: 34 Righteousness exalts a *n*,
Isa 2: 4 *N* will not take up sword
26: 2 that the righteous *n* may enter,
60: 12 For the *n* or kingdom that will not
65: 1 To a *n* that did not call on my name
66: 8 a *n* be brought forth in a moment?
Mic 4: 3 *N* will not take up sword
Mt 24: 7 *N* will rise against *n*,
Mk 13: 8 *N* will rise against *n*,
1Pe 2: 9 a royal priesthood, a holy *n*,
Rev 5: 9 and language and people and *n*.
7: 9 from every *n*, tribe, people
14: 6 to every *n*, tribe, language

NATIONS (NATION)

Ge 17: 4 You will be the father of many *n*.
18: 18 and all *n* on earth will be blessed
Ex 19: 5 of all *n* you will be my treasured
Lev 20: 26 apart from the *n* to be my own.
Dt 7: 1 drives out before you many *n*—
15: 6 You will rule over many *n*
Jdg 3: 1 These are the *n* the LORD left
2Ch 20: 6 rule over all the kingdoms of the *n*.
Ne 1: 8 I will scatter you among the *n*,
Ps 2: 1 Why do the *n* conspire
2: 8 I will make the *n* your inheritance,
9: 5 You have rebuked the *n*
22: 28 and he rules over the *n*.
46: 10 I will be exalted among the *n*,
47: 8 God reigns over the *n*;
66: 7 his eyes watch the *n*—
67: 2 your salvation among all *n*.
68: 30 Scatter the *n* who delight in war.
72: 17 All *n* will be blessed through him.
96: 3 Declare his glory among the *n*,
99: 2 he is exalted over all the *n*.
106: 35 but they mingled with the *n*
110: 6 He will judge the *n*, heaping up
113: 4 The LORD is exalted over all the *n*
Isa 2: 2 and all *n* will stream to it.
11: 10 the *n* will rally to him,
12: 4 among the *n* what he has done,
40: 15 Surely the *n* are like a drop
42: 1 and he will bring justice to the *n*.
51: 4 justice will become a light to the *n*.
52: 15 so will he sprinkle many *n*,
56: 7 a house of prayer for all *n*."
60: 3 *N* will come to your light,
66: 18 and gather all *n* and tongues,
Jer 1: 5 you as a prophet to the *n*."
3: 17 and all *n* will gather in Jerusalem
31: 10 "Hear the word of the LORD, O *n*;
33: 9 and honour before all *n*
46: 28 I completely destroy all the *n*
Eze 22: 4 you an object of scorn to the *n*
34: 13 I will bring them out from the *n*
36: 23 *n* will know that I am the LORD,
37: 22 and they will never again be two *n*
39: 21 I will display my glory among the *n*
Hos 7: 8 "Ephraim mixes with the *n*;
Joel 2: 17 a byword among the *n*.
3: 2 I will gather all *n*
Am 9: 12 and all the *n* that bear my name,"
Zep 3: 8 I have decided to assemble the *n*,
Hag 2: 7 and the desired of all *n* will come,
Zec 8: 13 an object of cursing among the *n*,

Zec 8:23 *n* will take firm hold of one Jew
9:10 He will proclaim peace to the *n*.
14:2 I will gather all the *n* to Jerusalem
Mt 12:18 he will proclaim justice to the *n*.
24:9 and you will be hated by all *n*
24:14 whole world as a testimony to all *n*,
25:32 All the *n* will be gathered
28:19 and make disciples of all *n*,
Mk 11:17 a house of prayer for all *n*'?
Ac 4:25 "'Why do the *n* rage
Ro 15:12 who will arise to rule over the *n*;
Gal 3:8 All *n* will be blessed through you."
1Ti 3:16 was preached among the *n*,
Rev 15:4 All *n* will come
21:24 Then *n* will walk by its light,
22:2 are for the healing of the *n*.

NATURAL (NATURE)

Ro 6:19 you are weak in your *n* selves.
1Co 15:44 If there is a *n* body, there is

NATURE (NATURAL)

Ro 1:20 his eternal power and divine *n*—
7:18 lives in me, that is, in my sinful *n*.
8:4 do not live according to the sinful *n*
8:5 to the sinful *n* have their minds set
8:8 by the sinful *n* cannot please God.
13:14 to gratify the desires of the sinful *n*.
Gal 5:13 freedom to indulge the sinful *n*;
5:19 The acts of the sinful *n* are obvious:
5:24 Jesus have crucified the sinful *n*
Php 2:6 Who, being in very *n* God,
Col 3:5 whatever belongs to your earthly *n*
2Pe 1:4 you may participate in the divine *n*

NAZARENE* (NAZARETH)

Mt 2:23 prophets: "He will be called a *N*."
Mk 14:67 "You also were with that *N*, Jesus,"
16:6 "You are looking for Jesus the *N*,
Ac 24:5 He is a ringleader of the *N* sect and

NAZARETH (NAZARENE)

Mt 4:13 Leaving *N*, he went and lived
Lk 4:16 to *N*, where he had been brought
Jn 1:46 "*N*! Can anything good come

NAZIRITE

Nu 6:2 of separation to the LORD as a *N*,
Jdg 13:7 because the boy will be a *N* of God

NEBO

Dt 34:1 Then Moses climbed Mount *N*

NEBUCHADNEZZAR

Babylonian king. Subdued and exiled Judah (2Ki 24-25; 2Ch 36; Jer 39). Dreams interpreted by Daniel (Da 2; 4). Worshipped God (Da 3:28-29; 4:34-37).

NECESSARY*

Ac 1:21 Therefore it is *n* to choose one
Ro 13:5 it is *n* to submit to the authorities,
2Co 9:5 I thought it *n* to urge the brothers
Php 1:24 it is more *n* for you that I remain
2:25 But I think it is *n* to send back
Heb 8:3 and so it was *n* for this one
9:16 it is *n* to prove the death
9:23 It was *n*, then, for the copies

NECK (STIFF-NECKED)

Pr 3:22 an ornament to grace your *n*.
6:21 fasten them around your *n*.
Mt 18:6 a large millstone hung around his *n*

NECO

Pharaoh who killed Josiah (2Ki 23:29-30; 2Ch 35:20-22), deposed Jehoahaz (2Ki 23:33-35; 2Ch 36:3-4).

NEED (NEEDS NEEDY)

1Ki 8:59 Israel according to each day's *n*,
Ps 79:8 for we are in desperate *n*.
116:6 when I was in great *n*, he saved me.
Ps 142:6 for I am in desperate *n*;
Mt 6:8 for your Father knows what you *n*
Lk 15:14 country, and he began to be in *n*.
Ac 2:45 they gave to anyone as he had *n*.
Ro 12:13 with God's people who are in *n*.
1Co 12:21 say to the hand, "I don't *n* you!"
Eph 4:28 something to share with those in *n*.
1Ti 5:3 to those widows who are really in *n*
Heb 4:16 grace to help us in our time of *n*.
1Jn 3:17 sees his brother in *n* but has no pity

NEEDLE

Mt 19:24 go through the eye of a *n*

NEEDS (NEED)

Isa 58:11 he will satisfy your *n*
Php 2:25 sent to take care of my *n*.
4:19 God will meet all your *n* according
Jas 2:16 does nothing about his physical *n*,

NEEDY (NEED)

Dt 15:11 towards the poor and *n* in your land.
1Sa 2:8 and lifts the *n* from the ash heap;
Ps 35:10 and *n* from those who rob them."
69:33 The LORD hears the *n*
72:12 he will deliver the *n* who cry out,
140:12 and upholds the cause of the *n*.
Pr 14:21 blessed is he who is kind to the *n*.
14:31 to the *n* honours God.
22:22 and do not crush the *n* in court,
31:9 defend the rights of the poor and *n*
31:20 and extends her hands to the *n*.
Mt 6:2 "So when you give to the *n*,

NEGLECT* (NEGLECTED)

Dt 12:19 Be careful not to *n* the Levites
14:27 And do not *n* the Levites living
Ezr 4:22 Be careful not to *n* this matter.
Ne 10:39 We will not *n* the house of our God
Est 6:10 Do not *n* anything you have
Ps 119:16 I will not *n* your word.
Lk 11:42 you *n* justice and the love of God.
Ac 6:2 for us to *n* the ministry of the word
1Ti 4:14 Do not *n* your gift, which was

NEGLECTED (NEGLECT)

Mt 23:23 But you have *n* the more important

NEHEMIAH

Cupbearer of Artaxerxes (Ne 2:1); governor of Israel (Ne 8:9). Returned to Jerusalem to rebuild walls (Ne 2-6). With Ezra, re-established worship (Ne 8). Prayer confessing nation's sin (Ne 9). Dedicated wall (Ne 12).

NEIGHBOUR (NEIGHBOUR'S)

Ex 20:16 give false testimony against your *n*.
20:17 or anything that belongs to your *n*
Lev 19:13 Do not defraud your *n* or rob him.
19:17 Rebuke your *n* frankly
19:18 but love your *n* as yourself.
Ps 15:3 who does his *n* no wrong
Pr 3:29 Do not plot harm against your *n*,
11:12 who lacks judgment derides his *n*,
14:21 He who despises his *n* sins,
16:29 A violent man entices his *n*
24:28 against your *n* without cause,
25:18 gives false testimony against his *n*.
27:10 better a *n* near by than a brother far
27:14 If a man loudly blesses his *n*
29:5 Whoever flatters his *n*
Jer 31:34 No longer will a man teach his *n*,
Zec 8:17 do not plot evil against your *n*,
Mt 5:43 Love your *n* and hate your enemy.'
19:19 and 'love your *n* as yourself.'"
Mk 12:31 The second is this: 'Love your *n*
Lk 10:27 and, 'Love your *n* as yourself.'"
10:29 who is my *n*?" In reply Jesus said:
Ro 13:9 "Love your *n* as yourself."
13:10 Love does no harm to its *n*.
15:2 Each of us should please his *n*
Gal 5:14 "Love your *n* as yourself."
Eph 4:25 and speak truthfully to his *n*,
Heb 8:11 No longer will a man teach his *n*,
Jas 2:8 "Love your *n* as yourself,"

NEIGHBOUR'S (NEIGHBOUR)

Ex 20:17 You shall not covet your *n* wife,
Dt 5:21 not set your desire on your *n* house
19:14 not move your *n* boundary stone
27:17 who moves his *n* boundary stone."
Pr 25:17 Seldom set foot in your *n* house—

NESTS

Mt 8:20 and birds of the air have *n*,

NET (NETS)

Pr 1:17 How useless to spread a *n*
Hab 1:15 he catches them in his *n*,
Mt 13:47 of heaven is like a *n* that was let
Jn 21:6 "Throw your *n* on the right side

NETS (NET)

Ps 141:10 Let the wicked fall into their own *n*
Mt 4:20 At once they left their *n*
Lk 5:4 and let down the *n* for a catch."

NEVER-FAILING*

Am 5:24 righteousness like a *n* stream!

NEW

Ps 40:3 He put a *n* song in my mouth,
98:1 Sing to the LORD a *n* song,
Ecc 1:9 there is nothing *n* under the sun.
Isa 42:9 and *n* things I declare;
62:2 you will be called by a *n* name
65:17 *n* heavens and a *n* earth.
66:22 "As the *n* heavens and the *n* earth
Jer 31:31 "when I will make a *n* covenant
La 3:23 They are *n* every morning;
Eze 11:19 undivided heart and put a *n* spirit
18:31 and get a *n* heart and a *n* spirit.
36:26 give you a *n* heart and put a *n* spirit
Zep 3:5 and every *n* day he does not fail,
Mt 9:17 Neither do men pour *n* wine
Mk 16:17 they will speak in *n* tongues;
Lk 5:39 after drinking old wine wants the *n*
22:20 "This cup is the *n* covenant
Jn 13:34 "A *n* commandment I give you:
Ac 5:20 the full message of this *n* life."
Ro 6:4 the Father, we too may live a *n* life.
1Co 5:7 old yeast that you may be a *n* batch
11:25 "This cup is the *n* covenant
2Co 3:6 as ministers of a *n* covenant—
5:17 he is a *n* creation; the old has gone,
Gal 6:15 what counts is a *n* creation.
Eph 4:23 to be made *n* in the attitude
4:24 and to put on the *n* self, created
Col 3:10 and have put on the *n* self,
Heb 8:8 when I will make a *n* covenant
9:15 is the mediator of a *n* covenant,
10:20 by a *n* and living way opened for us
12:24 Jesus the mediator of a *n* covenant,
1Pe 1:3 great mercy he has given us *n* birth
2Pe 3:13 to a *n* heaven and a *n* earth,
1Jn 2:8 Yet I am writing you a *n* command;
Rev 2:17 stone with a *n* name written on it,
3:12 the *n* Jerusalem, which is coming
21:1 I saw a *n* heaven and a *n* earth,

NEWBORN (BEAR [1])

1Pe 2:2 Like *n* babies, crave pure spiritual

NEWS

2Ki 7:9 This is a day of good *n*
Ps 112:7 He will have no fear of bad *n*;
Pr 15:30 good *n* gives health to the bones.
25:25 is good *n* from a distant land.
Isa 52:7 the feet of those who bring good *n*,
61:1 me to preach good *n* to the poor.
Na 1:15 the feet of one who brings good *n*,
Mt 4:23 preaching the good *n*
9:35 preaching the good *n*
11:5 the good *n* is preached to the poor.
Mk 1:15 Repent and believe the good *n*!"

Mk 16: 15 preach the good *n* to all creation.
Lk 1: 19 and to tell you this good *n*.
2: 10 I bring you good *n*
3: 18 and preached the good *n* to them.
4: 43 "I must preach the good *n*
8: 1 proclaiming the good *n*
16: 16 the good *n* of the kingdom
Ac 5: 42 proclaiming the good *n* that Jesus
10: 36 telling the good *n* of peace
14: 7 continued to preach the good *n*.
14: 21 They preached the good *n*
17: 18 preaching the good *n* about Jesus
Ro 10: 15 feet of those who bring good *n*!"

NICODEMUS*

Pharisee who visited Jesus at night (Jn 3). Argued fair treatment of Jesus (Jn 7:50-52). With Joseph, prepared Jesus for burial (Jn 19:38-42).

NIGHT (NIGHT-TIME NIGHTS)

Ge 1: 5 and the darkness he called "*n*".
1: 16 and the lesser light to govern the *n*.
Ex 13: 21 and by *n* in a pillar of fire
Dt 28: 66 filled with dread both *n* and day,
Jos 1: 8 and *n*, so that you may be careful
Job 35: 10 who gives songs in the *n*,
Ps 1: 2 on his law he meditates day and *n*.
19: 2 *n* after *n* they display knowledge.
42: 8 at *n* his song is with me—
63: 6 of you through the watches of the *n*
77: 6 I remembered my songs in the *n*.
90: 4 or like a watch in the *n*.
91: 5 You will not fear the terror of *n*,
119: 148 through the watches of the *n*,
121: 6 nor the moon by *n*.
136: 9 the moon and stars to govern the *n*;
Pr 31: 18 and her lamp does not go out at *n*.
Isa 21: 11 Watchman, what is left of the *n*?"
58: 10 and your *n* will become like
Jer 33: 20 and my covenant with the *n*,
Lk 2: 8 watch over their flocks at *n*.
6: 12 and spent the *n* praying to God.
Jn 3: 2 He came to Jesus at *n* and said,
9: 4 *N* is coming, when no-one can work
1Th 5: 2 Lord will come like a thief in the *n*.
5: 5 We do not belong to the *n*
Rev 21: 25 for there will be no *n* there.

NIGHT-TIME* (NIGHT)

Zec 14: 7 or *n*—a day known to the LORD.

NIGHTS (NIGHT)

Jnh 1: 17 the fish three days and three *n*.
Mt 4: 2 After fasting forty days and forty *n*
12: 40 three *n* in the belly of a huge fish,
2Co 6: 5 in hard work, sleepless *n*

NIMROD

Ge 10: 9 "Like *N*, a mighty hunter

NINEVEH

Jnh 1: 2 "Go to the great city of *N*
Na 1: 1 An oracle concerning *N*.
Mt 12: 41 The men of *N* will stand up

NOAH

Righteous man (Eze 14:14, 20) called to build ark (Ge 6-8; Heb 11:7; 1Pe 3:20; 2Pe 2:5). God's covenant with (Ge 9:1-17). Drunkenness of (Ge 9:18-23). Blessed sons, cursed Canaan (Ge 9:24-27).

NOBLE

Ru 3: 11 you are a woman of *n* character.
Ps 45: 1 My heart is stirred by a *n* theme
Pr 12: 4 of *n* character is her husband's
31: 10 A wife of *n* character who can find?
31: 29 "Many women do *n* things,
Isa 32: 8 But the *n* man makes *n* plans,
Lk 8: 15 good soil stands for those with a *n*
Ro 9: 21 of clay some pottery for *n* purposes
Php 4: 8 whatever is *n*, whatever is right,
2Ti 2: 20 some are for *n* purposes

NOSTRILS

Ge 2: 7 and breathed into his *n* the breath
Ex 15: 8 By the blast of your *n*
Ps 18: 15 at the blast of breath from your *n*.

NOTE

Ac 4: 13 and they took *n* that these men had
Php 3: 17 take *n* of those who live according

NOTHING

2Sa 24: 24 offerings that cost me *n*."
Ne 9: 21 in the desert; they lacked *n*,
Jer 32: 17 *N* is too hard for you
Jn 15: 5 apart from me you can do *n*.

NOURISH

Pr 10: 21 The lips of the righteous *n* many,

NULLIFY

Mt 15: 6 Thus you *n* the word of God
Ro 3: 31 Do we, then, *n* the law by this faith

OATH

Ex 33: 1 up to the land I promised on *o*
Nu 30: 2 or takes an *o* to obligate himself
Dt 6: 18 promised on *o* to your forefathers,
7: 8 and kept the *o* he swore
29: 12 you this day and sealing with an *o*,
Ps 95: 11 So I declared on *o* in my anger,
119: 106 I have taken an *o* and confirmed it,
132: 11 The LORD swore an *o* to David,
Ecc 8: 2 because you took an *o* before God.
Mt 5: 33 'Do not break your *o*, but keep
Heb 7: 20 And it was not without an *o*!

OBADIAH

1. Believer who sheltered 100 prophets from Jezebel (1Ki 18:1-16).
2. Prophet against Edom (Ob 1).

OBEDIENCE* (OBEY)

Ge 49: 10 and the *o* of the nations is his.
Jdg 2: 17 of *o* to the LORD's commands.
1Ch 21: 19 So David went up in *o*
2Ch 31: 21 in *o* to the law and the commands,
Pr 30: 17 that scorns *o* to a mother,
Lk 23: 56 Sabbath in *o* to the commandment.
Ac 21: 24 but that you yourself are living in *o*
Ro 1: 5 to the *o* that comes from faith.
5: 19 also through the *o* of the one man
6: 16 to *o*, which leads to righteousness?
16: 19 Everyone has heard about your *o*,
2Co 9: 13 for the *o* that accompanies your
10: 6 once your *o* is complete.
Phm :21 Confident of your *o*, I write to you,
Heb 5: 8 he learned *o* from what he suffered
1Pe 1: 2 for *o* to Jesus Christ and sprinkling
2Jn :6 that we walk in *o* to his commands.

OBEDIENT* (OBEY)

Dt 30: 17 heart turns away and you are not *o*,
Isa 1: 19 If you are willing and *o*,
Lk 2: 51 with them and was *o* to them.
Ac 6: 7 of priests became *o* to the faith.
2Co 2: 9 if you would stand the test and be *o*
7: 15 he remembers that you were all *o*,
10: 5 thought to make it *o* to Christ.
Php 2: 8 and became *o* to death—
Tit 3: 1 to be *o*, to be ready
1Pe 1: 14 As *o* children, do not conform

OBEY (OBEDIENCE OBEDIENT OBEYED OBEYING OBEYS)

Ex 12: 24 "*O* these instructions as a lasting
19: 5 Now if you *o* me fully and keep my
24: 7 the LORD has said; we will *o*."
Lev 18: 4 You must *o* my laws and be careful
25: 18 and be careful to *o* my laws,
Nu 15: 40 remember to *o* all my commands
Dt 5: 27 We will listen and *o*."
6: 3 careful to *o* so that it may go well
6: 24 us to *o* all these decrees
11: 13 if you faithfully *o* the commands I
12: 28 to *o* all these regulations I am
13: 4 Keep his commands and *o* him;
21: 18 son who does not *o* his father
28: 1 If you fully *o* the LORD your God
28: 15 if you do not *o* the LORD your
30: 2 and *o* him with all your heart
30: 10 if you *o* the LORD your God
30: 14 and in your heart so you may *o* it.
32: 46 children to *o* carefully all the words
Jos 1: 7 to *o* all the law my servant Moses
22: 5 in all his ways, to *o* his commands,
24: 24 the LORD our God and *o* him."
1Sa 15: 22 To *o* is better than sacrifice,
1Ki 8: 61 by his decrees and *o* his commands
2Ki 17: 13 that I commanded your fathers to *o*
2Ch 34: 31 and to *o* the words of the covenant
Ne 1: 5 who love him and *o* his commands,
Ps 103: 18 and remember to *o* his precepts.
103: 20 who *o* his word.
119: 17 I will *o* your word.
119: 34 and *o* it with all my heart.
119: 57 I have promised to *o* your words.
119: 67 but now I *o* your word.
119: 100 for I *o* your precepts.
119: 129 therefore I *o* them.
119: 167 I *o* your statutes,
Pr 5: 13 I would not *o* my teachers
Jer 7: 23 I gave them this command: *O* me,
11: 4 '*O* me and do everything I
11: 7 and again, saying, "*O* me."
42: 6 we will *o* the LORD our God,
Da 9: 4 who love him and *o* his commands,
Mt 8: 27 the winds and the waves *o* him!"
19: 17 to enter life, *o* the commandments
28: 20 to *o* everything I have commanded
Lk 11: 28 hear the word of God and *o* it."
Jn 14: 15 you will *o* what I command.
14: 23 loves me, he will *o* my teaching.
14: 24 not love me will not *o* my teaching.
15: 10 If you *o* my commands, you will
Ac 5: 29 "We must *o* God rather than men!
5: 32 given to those who *o* him."
Ro 2: 13 it is those who *o* the law who will
6: 12 body so that you *o* its evil desires.
6: 16 slaves to the one whom you *o*—
6: 16 yourselves to someone to *o* him
15: 18 in leading the Gentiles to *o* God
16: 26 nations might believe and *o* him—
Gal 5: 3 obligated to *o* the whole law.
Eph 6: 1 *o* your parents in the Lord,
6: 5 *o* your earthly masters with respect
Col 3: 20 *o* your parents in everything,
3: 22 *o* your earthly masters
2Th 3: 14 anyone does not *o* our instruction
1Ti 3: 4 and see that his children *o* him
Heb 5: 9 eternal salvation for all who *o* him
13: 17 *O* your leaders and submit
1Pe 4: 17 for those who do not *o* the gospel
1Jn 3: 24 Those who *o* his commands live
5: 3 love for God: to *o* his commands.
Rev 12: 17 those who *o* God's commandments
14: 12 the saints who *o* God's

OBEYED (OBEY)

Ge 22: 18 blessed, because you have *o* me."
Jos 1: 17 we fully *o* Moses, so we will obey
Ps 119: 4 that are to be fully *o*.
Da 9: 10 we have not *o* the LORD our God
Jnh 3: 3 Jonah *o* the word of the LORD
Mic 5: 15 the nations that have not *o* me."
Jn 15: 10 as I have *o* my Father's commands
15: 20 If they *o* my teaching, they will
17: 6 and they have *o* your word.
Ac 7: 53 through angels but have not *o* it."
Ro 6: 17 you wholeheartedly *o* the form
Php 2: 12 as you have always *o*—not only
Heb 11: 8 *o* and went, even though he did not
1Pe 3: 6 who *o* Abraham and called him her

OBEYING (OBEY)

1Sa 15: 22 as in *o* the voice of the LORD?
Ps 119: 5 steadfast in *o* your decrees!

Gal 5: 7 and kept you from *o* the truth?
1Pe 1: 22 purified yourselves by *o* the truth

OBEYS (OBEY)
Lev 18: 5 for the man who *o* them will live
Pr 19: 16 He who *o* instructions guards his
Eze 20: 11 for the man who *o* them will live
Jn 14: 21 has my commands and *o* them,
Ro 2: 27 and yet *o* the law will condemn you
1Jn 2: 5 if anyone *o* his word, God's love is

OBLIGATED (OBLIGATION)
Ro 1: 14 I am *o* both to Greeks

OBLIGATION (OBLIGATED)
Ro 8: 12 Therefore, brothers, we have an *o*

OBSCENITY*
Eph 5: 4 Nor should there be *o*, foolish talk

OBSCURES*
Job 42: 3 'Who is this that *o* my counsel

OBSERVE (OBSERVING)
Ex 31: 13 'You must *o* my Sabbaths.
Lev 25: 2 the land itself must *o* a sabbath
Dt 4: 6 *O* them carefully, for this will show
5: 12 "*O* the Sabbath day
8: 6 *O* the commands of the LORD
11: 22 If you carefully *o* all these
26: 16 carefully *o* them with all your heart
Ps 37: 37 the blameless, *o* the upright;

OBSERVING (OBSERVE)
Ro 3: 27 principle? On that of *o* the law?
Gal 2: 16 a man is not justified by *o* the law,
3: 2 you receive the Spirit by *o* the law,
3: 10 All who rely on *o* the law are

OBSOLETE
Heb 8: 13 he has made the first one *o*;

OBSTACLE* (OBSTACLES)
Ro 14: 13 or *o* in your brother's way.

OBSTACLES (OBSTACLE)
Ro 16: 17 put *o* in your way that are contrary

OBSTINATE
Isa 65: 2 hands to an *o* people,
Ro 10: 21 to a disobedient and *o* people."

OBTAIN (OBTAINED OBTAINS)
Ro 11: 7 sought so earnestly it did not *o*,
2Ti 2: 10 they too may *o* the salvation that

OBTAINED (OBTAIN)
Ro 9: 30 not pursue righteousness, have *o* it,
Php 3: 12 Not that I have already *o* all this,
Heb 9: 12 having *o* eternal redemption.

OBTAINS* (OBTAIN)
Pr 12: 2 A good man *o* favour

OBVIOUS*
Mt 6: 18 so that it will not be *o*
Gal 5: 19 The acts of the sinful nature are *o*:
1Ti 5: 24 The sins of some men are *o*,
5: 25 In the same way, good deeds are *o*,

OCCASIONS
Eph 6: 18 in the Spirit on all *o* with all kinds

OFFENCE (OFFENCES OFFENDED OFFENDERS OFFENSIVE)
Pr 17: 9 over an *o* promotes love,
19: 11 it is to his glory to overlook an *o*.
Gal 5: 11 In that case the *o* of the cross has

OFFENCES (OFFENCE)
Isa 44: 22 swept away your *o* like a cloud,
59: 12 For our *o* are many in your sight,
Eze 18: 30 Repent! Turn away from all your *o*;
33: 10 "Our *o* and sins weigh us down,

OFFENDED (OFFENCE)
Pr 18: 19 An *o* brother is more unyielding

OFFENDERS* (OFFENCE)
1Co 6: 9 nor homosexual *o* nor thieves

OFFENSIVE (OFFENCE)
Ps 139: 24 See if there is any *o* way in me,

OFFER (OFFERED OFFERING OFFERINGS OFFERS)
Ps 4: 5 *O* right sacrifices
66: 2 *o* him glory and praise!
Ro 6: 13 Do not *o* the parts of your body
12: 1 to *o* your bodies as living sacrifices,
Heb 9: 25 he enter heaven to *o* himself again
13: 15 therefore, let us continually *o*

OFFERED (OFFER)
Isa 50: 6 I *o* my back to those who beat me,
1Co 9: 13 share in what is *o* on the altar?
10: 20 of pagans are *o* to demons,
Heb 7: 27 once for all when he *o* himself.
9: 14 the eternal Spirit *o* himself
11: 4 By faith Abel *o* God a better
11: 17 when God tested him, *o* Isaac
Jas 5: 15 prayer *o* in faith will make the sick

OFFERING (OFFER)
Ge 4: 3 of the soil as an *o* to the LORD.
22: 2 a burnt *o* on one of the mountains I
22: 8 provide the lamb for the burnt *o*,
Ex 29: 24 before the LORD as a wave *o*.
29: 40 fourth of a hin of wine as a drink *o*.
Lev 1: 3 If the *o* is a burnt *o* from the herd,
2: 4 " 'If you bring a grain *o* baked
3: 1 " 'If someone's *o* is a fellowship *o*,
4: 3 a sin *o* for the sin he has committed
5: 15 It is a guilt *o*.
7: 37 ordination *o* and the fellowship *o*,
9: 24 and consumed the burnt *o*
22: 18 to fulfil a vow or as a freewill *o*,
22: 21 a special vow or as a freewill *o*,
1Sa 13: 9 And Saul offered up the burnt *o*.
1Ch 21: 26 from heaven on the altar of burnt *o*.
2Ch 7: 1 and consumed the burnt *o*
Ps 40: 6 Sacrifice and *o* you did not desire,
116: 17 I will sacrifice a thank *o* to you
Isa 53: 10 the LORD makes his life a guilt *o*,
Mt 5: 23 if you are *o* your gift at the altar
Ro 8: 3 likeness of sinful man to be a sin *o*.
Eph 5: 2 as a fragrant *o* and sacrifice to God.
Php 2: 17 I am being poured out like a drink *o*
4: 18 are a fragrant *o*, an acceptable
2Ti 4: 6 being poured out like a drink *o*,
Heb 10: 5 "Sacrifice and *o* you did not desire,
1Pe 2: 5 *o* spiritual sacrifices acceptable

OFFERINGS (OFFER)
1Sa 15: 22 Does the LORD delight in burnt *o*
2Ch 35: 7 and goats for the Passover *o*,
Isa 1: 13 Stop bringing meaningless *o*!
Hos 6: 6 of God rather than burnt *o*.
Mal 3: 8 do we rob you?' "In tithes and *o*.
Mk 12: 33 is more important than all burnt *o*
Heb 10: 8 First he said, "Sacrifices and *o*,

OFFERS (OFFER)
Heb 10: 11 and again he *o* the same sacrifices,

OFFICER (OFFICIALS)
2Ti 2: 4 wants to please his commanding *o*.

OFFICIALS (OFFICER)
Pr 17: 26 or to flog *o* for their integrity.
29: 12 all his *o* become wicked.

OFFSPRING
Ge 3: 15 and between your *o* and hers;
12: 7 "To your *o* I will give this land."
13: 16 I will make your *o* like the dust
26: 4 and through your *o* all nations
28: 14 blessed through you and your *o*.
Ex 13: 2 The first *o* of every womb
Ru 4: 12 Through the *o* the LORD gives
Isa 44: 3 I will pour out my Spirit on your *o*,
53: 10 he will see his *o* and prolong his
Ac 3: 25 'Through your *o* all peoples
17: 28 own poets have said, 'We are his *o*.'
17: 29 "Therefore since we are God's *o*,
Ro 4: 18 said to him, "So shall your *o* be."
9: 8 who are regarded as Abraham's *o*.

OG
Nu 21: 33 *O* king of Bashan and his whole
Ps 136: 20 and *O* king of Bashan—

OIL
Ex 29: 7 Take the anointing *o* and anoint
30: 25 It will be the sacred anointing *o*.
Dt 14: 23 tithe of your grain, new wine and *o*,
1Sa 10: 1 Then Samuel took a flask of *o*
16: 13 So Samuel took the horn of *o*
1Ki 17: 16 and the jug of *o* did not run dry,
2Ki 4: 6 Then the *o* stopped flowing.
Ps 23: 5 You anoint my head with *o*;
45: 7 by anointing you with the *o* of joy.
104: 15 *o* to make his face shine,
133: 2 It is like precious *o* poured
Pr 21: 17 loves wine and *o* will never be
Isa 1: 6 or soothed with *o*.
61: 3 the *o* of gladness
Mt 25: 3 but did not take any *o* with them.
Heb 1: 9 by anointing you with the *o* of joy."

OLIVE (OLIVES)
Ge 8: 11 beak was a freshly plucked *o* leaf!
Jdg 9: 8 said to the *o* tree, 'Be our king.'
Jer 11: 16 LORD called you a thriving *o* tree
Zec 4: 3 Also there are two *o* trees by it,
Ro 11: 17 and you, though a wild *o* shoot,
11: 24 of an *o* tree that is wild by nature,
Rev 11: 4 These are the two *o* trees

OLIVES (OLIVE)
Zec 14: 4 stand on the Mount of *O*,
Mt 24: 3 sitting on the Mount of *O*,
Jas 3: 12 a fig-tree bear *o*, or a grapevine bear

OMEGA*
Rev 1: 8 "I am the Alpha and the *O*,"
21: 6 I am the Alpha and the *O*,
22: 13 I am the Alpha and the *O*,

OMIT*
Jer 26: 2 I command you; do not *o* a word.

OMRI
King of Israel (1Ki 16:21-26).

ONESIMUS*
Col 4: 9 He is coming with *O*, our faithful
Phm : 10 I appeal to you for my son *O*,

ONESIPHORUS*
2Ti 1: 16 mercy to the household of *O*,
4: 19 Aquila and the household of *O*.

ONIONS*
Nu 11: 5 melons, leeks, *o* and garlic.

ONYX
Ex 28: 9 "Take two *o* stones and engrave
28: 20 in the fourth row a chrysolite, an *o*

OPEN-HANDED* (HAND)
Dt 15: 8 Rather be *o* and freely lend him
15: 11 you to be *o* towards your brothers

OPINIONS*
1Ki 18: 21 will you waver between two *o*?
Pr 18: 2 but delights in airing his own *o*.

OPPONENTS (OPPOSE)
Pr 18: 18 and keeps strong *o* apart.

OPPORTUNE (OPPORTUNITY)
Lk 4: 13 he left him until an *o* time.

OPPORTUNITY* (OPPORTUNE)
1Sa 18: 21 "Now you have a second *o*
Jer 46: 17 he has missed his *o*.'
Mt 26: 16 watched for an *o* to hand him over.
Mk 14: 11 So he watched for an *o* to hand him
Lk 22: 6 and watched for an *o* to hand Jesus
Ac 25: 16 and has had an *o* to defend himself
Ro 7: 8 seizing the *o* afforded
7: 11 seizing the *o* afforded
1Co 16: 12 but he will go when he has the *o*.
2Co 5: 12 are giving you an *o* to take pride
11: 12 from under those who want an *o*
Gal 6: 10 as we have *o*, let us do good
Eph 5: 16 making the most of every *o*,
Php 4: 10 but you had no *o* to show it.
Col 4: 5 make the most of every *o*.
1Ti 5: 14 to give the enemy no *o* for slander.
Heb 11: 15 they would have had *o* to return.

OPPOSE (OPPONENTS OPPOSED OPPOSES OPPOSING OPPOSITION)
Ex 23: 22 and will *o* those who *o* you.
1Sa 2: 10 those who *o* the LORD will be
Job 23: 13 he stands alone, and who can *o* him
Ac 11: 17 I to think that I could *o* God!"
2Ti 2: 25 Those who *o* him he must gently
Tit 1: 9 doctrine and refute those who *o* it.
2: 8 so that those who *o* you may be

OPPOSED (OPPOSE)
Gal 2: 11 to Antioch, I *o* him to his face,
3: 21 therefore, *o* to the promises of God

OPPOSES (OPPOSE)
Jas 4: 6 "God *o* the proud
1Pe 5: 5 because, "God *o* the proud

OPPOSING (OPPOSE)
1Ti 6: 20 the *o* ideas of what is falsely called

OPPOSITION (OPPOSE)
Heb 12: 3 Consider him who endured such *o*

OPPRESS (OPPRESSED OPPRESSES OPPRESSION OPPRESSOR)
Ex 1: 11 masters over them to *o* them
22: 21 "Do not ill-treat an alien or *o* him,
Isa 3: 5 People will *o* each other—
Eze 22: 29 they *o* the poor and needy
Da 7: 25 the Most High and *o* his saints
Am 5: 12 You *o* the righteous and take bribes
Zec 7: 10 Do not *o* the widow
Mal 3: 5 who *o* the widows

OPPRESSED (OPPRESS)
Jdg 2: 18 as they groaned under those who *o*
Ps 9: 9 The LORD is a refuge for the *o*,
82: 3 the rights of the poor and *o*.
146: 7 He upholds the cause of the *o*
Pr 16: 19 in spirit and among the *o*
31: 5 and deprive all the *o* of their rights.
Isa 1: 17 encourage the *o*.
53: 7 He was *o* and afflicted,
58: 10 and satisfy the needs of the *o*,
Zec 10: 2 *o* for lack of a shepherd.
Lk 4: 18 to release the *o*,

OPPRESSES (OPPRESS)
Pr 14: 31 He who *o* the poor shows contempt
22: 16 He who *o* the poor
Eze 18: 12 He *o* the poor and needy.

OPPRESSION (OPPRESS)
Ps 12: 5 "Because of the *o* of the weak
72: 14 He will rescue them from *o*
119: 134 Redeem me from the *o* of men,
Isa 53: 8 By *o* and judgment, he was taken
58: 9 "If you do away with the yoke of *o*,

OPPRESSOR (OPPRESS)
Ps 72: 4 he will crush the *o*.
Isa 51: 13 For where is the wrath of the *o*?
Jer 22: 3 hand of his *o* the one who has been

ORDAINED
Ps 8: 2 you have *o* praise
111: 9 he *o* his covenant for ever—
139: 16 All the days *o* for me
Eze 28: 14 for so I *o* you.
Hab 1: 12 you have *o* them to punish.
Mt 21: 16 you have *o* praise'?"

ORDER (ORDERLY ORDERS)
Nu 9: 23 They obeyed the LORD's *o*,
Ps 110: 4 in the *o* of Melchizedek."
Heb 5: 10 priest in the *o* of Melchizedek.
9: 10 until the time of the new *o*.
Rev 21: 4 for the old *o* of things has passed

ORDERLY (ORDER)
1Co 14: 40 done in a fitting and *o* way.
Col 2: 5 and delight to see how *o* you are

ORDERS (ORDER)
Mk 1: 27 He even gives *o* to evil spirits
3: 12 But he gave them strict *o* not
9: 9 Jesus gave them *o* not

ORDINARY
Ac 4: 13 that they were unschooled, *o* men,

ORGIES*
Ro 13: 13 not in *o* and drunkenness,
Gal 5: 21 drunkenness, *o*, and the like.
1Pe 4: 3 *o*, carousing and detestable

ORIGIN (ORIGINATE ORIGINS)
2Pe 1: 21 For prophecy never had its *o*

ORIGINATE* (ORIGIN)
1Co 14: 36 Did the word of God *o* with you?

ORIGINS* (ORIGIN)
Mic 5: 2 whose *o* are from of old,

ORNAMENT* (ORNAMENTED)
Pr 3: 22 an *o* to grace your neck.
25: 12 of gold or an *o* of fine gold

ORNAMENTED (ORNAMENT)
Ge 37: 3 and he made a richly *o* robe for him

ORPHAN* (ORPHANS)
Ex 22: 22 advantage of a widow or an *o*.

ORPHANS (ORPHAN)
Jn 14: 18 will not leave you as *o*; I will come
Jas 1: 27 to look after *o* and widows

OTHNIEL
Nephew of Caleb (Jos 15:15-19; Jdg 1:12-15). Judge who freed Israel from Aram (Jdg 3:7-11).

OUTBURSTS*
2Co 12: 20 jealousy, *o* of anger, factions,

OUTCOME
Heb 13: 7 Consider the *o* of their way of life
1Pe 4: 17 what will the *o* be for those who do

OUTNUMBER
Ps 139: 18 they would *o* the grains of sand.

OUTSIDERS*
Col 4: 5 wise in the way you act towards *o*;
1Th 4: 12 daily life may win the respect of *o*
1Ti 3: 7 also have a good reputation with *o*,

OUTSTANDING
SS 5: 10 *o* among ten thousand.
Ro 13: 8 no debt remain *o*,

OUTSTRETCHED
Ex 6: 6 and will redeem you with an *o* arm
Dt 4: 34 by a mighty hand and an *o* arm,
5: 15 with a mighty hand and an *o* arm.
1Ki 8: 42 your mighty hand and your *o* arm
Ps 136: 12 with a mighty hand and *o* arm;
Jer 27: 5 and *o* arm I made the earth
32: 17 by your great power and *o* arm.
Eze 20: 33 an *o* arm and with outpoured wrath

OUTWEIGHS (WEIGH)
2Co 4: 17 an eternal glory that far *o* them all.

OUTWIT*
2Co 2: 11 in order that Satan might not *o* us.

OVERAWED* (AWE)
Ps 49: 16 Do not be *o* when a man grows rich

OVERBEARING*
Tit 1: 7 not *o*, not quick-tempered,

OVERCAME (OVERCOME)
Rev 3: 21 as I *o* and sat down with my Father
12: 11 They *o* him

OVERCOME (OVERCAME OVERCOMES)
Mt 16: 18 and the gates of Hades will not *o* it.
Mk 9: 24 I do believe; help me *o* my unbelief
Lk 10: 19 to *o* all the power of the enemy;
Jn 16: 33 But take heart! I have *o* the world."
Ro 12: 21 Do not be *o* by evil, but *o* evil
2Pe 2: 20 and are again entangled in it and *o*,
1Jn 2: 13 because you have *o* the evil one.
4: 4 are from God and have *o* them,
5: 4 is the victory that has *o* the world,
Rev 17: 14 but the Lamb will *o* them

OVERCOMES* (OVERCOME)
1Jn 5: 4 born of God *o* the world.
5: 5 Who is it that *o* the world?
Rev 2: 7 To him who *o*, I will give the right
2: 11 He who *o* will not be hurt at all
2: 17 To him who *o*, I will give some
2: 26 To him who *o* and does my will
3: 5 He who *o* will, like them, be
3: 12 Him who *o* I will make a pillar
3: 21 To him who *o*, I will give the right
21: 7 He who *o* will inherit all this,

OVERFLOW (OVERFLOWING OVERFLOWS)
Ps 65: 11 and your carts *o* with abundance.
119: 171 May my lips *o* with praise,
La 1: 16 and my eyes *o* with tears.
Mt 12: 34 out of the *o* of the heart the mouth
Lk 6: 45 out of the *o* of his heart his mouth
Ro 5: 15 Jesus Christ, *o* to the many! Again,
15: 13 so that you may *o* with hope
2Co 4: 15 to *o* to the glory of God.
1Th 3: 12 *o* for each other and for everyone

OVERFLOWING (OVERFLOW)
Pr 3: 10 then your barns will be filled to *o*,
2Co 8: 2 their *o* joy and their extreme
9: 12 *o* in many expressions of thanks
Col 2: 7 as you were taught, and *o*

OVERFLOWS* (OVERFLOW)
Ps 23: 5 my cup *o*.
2Co 1: 5 also through Christ our comfort *o*.

OVERJOYED* (JOY)
Da 6: 23 The king was *o* and gave orders
Mt 2: 10 they saw the star, they were *o*.
Jn 20: 20 The disciples were *o*
Ac 12: 14 she was so *o* she ran back
1Pe 4: 13 so that you may be *o*

OVERLOOK
Pr 19: 11 it is to his glory to *o* an offence.

OVERSEER* (OVERSEERS)
Pr 6: 7 no *o* or ruler,
1Ti 3: 1 anyone sets his heart on being an *o*,
3: 2 Now the *o* must be above reproach,
Tit 1: 7 Since an *o* is entrusted
1Pe 2: 27 returned to the Shepherd and *O*

OVERSEERS* (OVERSEER)
Ac 20: 28 the Holy Spirit has made you *o*.
Php 1: 1 together with the *o* and deacons:
1Pe 5: 2 as *o*—not because you must,

OVERSHADOW* (OVERSHADOWING)
Lk 1: 35 power of the Most High will *o* you.

OVERSHADOWING (OVERSHADOW)
Ex 25: 20 wings spread upwards, *o* the cover
Heb 9: 5 Glory, *o* the atonement cover

OVERTHROW (OVERTHROWS)
2Th 2: 8 whom the Lord Jesus will *o*

OVERTHROWS (OVERTHROW)
Pr 13: 6 but wickedness *o* the sinner.
Isa 44: 25 who *o* the learning of the wise

OVERWHELMED (OVERWHELMING)
2Sa 22: 5 the torrents of destruction *o* me.
1Ki 10: 5 temple of the LORD, she was *o*.
Ps 38: 4 My guilt has *o* me
65: 3 When we were *o* by sins,
Mt 26: 38 "My soul is *o* with sorrow
Mk 7: 37 People were *o* with amazement.
9: 15 they were *o* with wonder
2Co 2: 7 so that he will not be *o*

OVERWHELMING (OVERWHELMED)
Pr 27: 4 Anger is cruel and fury *o*,
Isa 10: 22 *o* and righteous.
28: 15 When an *o* scourge sweeps by,

OWE
Ro 13: 7 If you *o* taxes, pay taxes; if revenue
Phm : 19 to mention that you *o* me your very

OWNER'S (OWNERSHIP)
Isa 1: 3 the donkey his *o* manger,

OWNERSHIP* (OWNER'S)
2Co 1: 22 He anointed us, set his seal of *o*

OX (OXEN)
Dt 25: 4 Do not muzzle an *o*
Isa 11: 7 and the lion will eat straw like the *o*
Eze 1: 10 and on the left the face of an *o*;
Lk 13: 15 of you on the Sabbath untie his *o*
1Co 9: 9 "Do not muzzle an *o*
1Ti 5: 18 "Do not muzzle the *o*
Rev 4: 7 second was like an *o*, the third had

OXEN (OX)
1Ki 19: 20 Elisha then left his *o* and ran
Lk 14: 19 'I have just bought five yoke of *o*,

PAGAN (PAGANS)
Mt 18: 17 as you would a *p* or a tax collector.
Lk 12: 30 For the *p* world runs

PAGANS* (PAGAN)
Isa 2: 6 and clasp hands with *p*.
Mt 5: 47 Do not even *p* do that? Be perfect,
6: 7 do not keep on babbling like *p*,
6: 32 For the *p* run after all these things,
1Co 5: 1 that does not occur even among *p*:
10: 20 but the sacrifices of *p* are offered
12: 2 You know that when you were *p*,
1Pe 2: 12 such good lives among the *p* that,
4: 3 in the past doing what *p* choose
3Jn : 7 receiving no help from the *p*.

PAID (PAY)
Isa 40: 2 that her sin has been *p* for,
Zec 11: 12 So they *p* me thirty pieces of silver.

PAIN (PAINFUL PAINS)
Ge 3: 16 with *p* you will give birth
6: 6 and his heart was filled with *p*.
Job 6: 10 my joy in unrelenting *p*—
33: 19 may be chastened on a bed of *p*
Jer 4: 19 I writhe in *p*.
15: 18 Why is my *p* unending
Mt 4: 24 suffering severe *p*,
Jn 16: 21 woman giving birth to a child has *p*
1Pe 2: 19 up under the *p* of unjust suffering
Rev 21: 4 or mourning or crying or *p*,

PAINFUL (PAIN)
Ge 3: 17 through *p* toil you will eat of it
5: 29 and *p* toil of our hands caused
Job 6: 25 How *p* are honest words!
Eze 28: 24 neighbours who are *p* briers
2Co 2: 1 I would not make another *p* visit
Heb 12: 11 seems pleasant at the time, but *p*.
1Pe 4: 12 at the *p* trial you are suffering,

PAINS (PAIN)
Ge 3: 16 "I will greatly increase your *p*
Mt 24: 8 these are the beginning of birth-*p*.
Ro 8: 22 as in the *p* of childbirth right up
Gal 4: 19 again in the *p* of childbirth
1Th 5: 3 as labour *p* on a pregnant woman,

PAIRS
Ge 7: 8 *P* of clean and unclean animals,

PALACE (PALACES)
2Sa 7: 2 "Here I am, living in a *p* of cedar,
Jer 22: 6 is what the LORD says about the *p*
22: 13 "Woe to him who builds his *p*

PALACES (PALACE)
Mt 11: 8 wear fine clothes are in kings' *p*.
Lk 7: 25 and indulge in luxury are in *p*.

PALE
Isa 29: 22 no longer will their faces grow *p*.
Jer 30: 6 every face turned deathly *p*?
Da 10: 8 my face turned deathly *p*
Rev 6: 8 and there before me was a *p* horse!

PALM (PALMS)
Jn 12: 13 They took *p* branches and went out
Rev 7: 9 and were holding *p* branches

PALMS (PALM)
Isa 49: 16 you on the *p* of my hands;

PAMPERS*
Pr 29: 21 If a man *p* his servant from youth,

PANIC
Dt 20: 3 or give way to *p* before them.
1Sa 14: 15 It was a *p* sent by God.
Eze 7: 7 there is *p*, not joy,
Zec 14: 13 by the LORD with great *p*.

PANTS
Ps 42: 1 As the deer *p* for streams of water,

PARABLES
See also JESUS: Parables
Ps 78: 2 I will open my mouth in *p*,
Mt 13: 35 "I will open my mouth in *p*,
Lk 8: 10 but to others I speak in *p*, so that,

PARADISE*
Lk 23: 43 today you will be with me in *p*."
2Co 12: 4 God knows—was caught up to *P*.
Rev 2: 7 of life, which is in the *p* of God.

PARALYTIC
Mt 9: 2 Some men brought to him a *p*,
Mk 2: 3 bringing to him a *p*, carried by four
Ac 9: 33 a *p* who had been bedridden

PARCHED
Ps 143: 6 my soul thirsts for you like a *p* land.

PARCHMENTS*
2Ti 4: 13 and my scrolls, especially the *p*.

PARDON* (PARDONED PARDONS)
2Ch 30: 18 *p* everyone who sets his heart
Job 7: 21 Why do you not *p* my offences
Isa 55: 7 and to our God, for he will freely *p*.
Joel 3: 21 I will *p*."

PARDONED* (PARDON)
Nu 14: 19 as you have *p* them from the time
Joel 3: 21 bloodguilt, which I have not *p*,

PARDONS* (PARDON)
Mic 7: 18 who *p* sin and forgives

PARENTS
Pr 17: 6 and *p* are the pride of their children
Pr 19: 14 wealth are inherited from *p*,
Mt 10: 21 children will rebel against their *p*
Lk 18: 29 left home or wife or brothers or *p*
21: 16 You will be betrayed by *p*, brothers
Jn 9: 3 Neither this man nor his *p* sinned,"
Ro 1: 30 they disobey their *p*; they are
2Co 12: 14 for their *p*, but *p* for their children.
Eph 6: 1 Children, obey your *p* in the Lord,
Col 3: 20 obey your *p* in everything,
1Ti 5: 4 repaying their *p* and grandparents,
2Ti 3: 2 disobedient to their *p*, ungrateful,

PARTAKE*
1Co 10: 17 for we all *p* of the one loaf.

PARTIAL* (PARTIALITY)
Pr 18: 5 It is not good to be *p* to the wicked

PARTIALITY (PARTIAL)
Lev 19: 15 do not show *p* to the poor
Dt 1: 17 Do not show *p* in judging;
10: 17 who shows no *p* and accepts no
16: 19 Do not pervert justice or show *p*.
2Ch 19: 7 our God there is no injustice or *p*
Job 32: 21 I will show *p* to no-one,
34: 19 who shows no *p* to princes
Pr 24: 23 To show *p* in judging is not good:
Mal 2: 9 have shown *p* in matters of the law
Lk 20: 21 and that you do not show *p*
1Ti 5: 21 keep these instructions without *p*,

PARTICIPANTS (PARTICIPATE)
1Co 10: 20 you to be *p* with demons.

PARTICIPATE (PARTICIPANTS PARTICIPATION)
1Pe 4: 13 rejoice that you *p* in the sufferings
2Pe 1: 4 that through them you may *p*

PARTICIPATION (PARTICIPATE)
1Co 10: 16 is not the bread that we break a *p*

PARTNER (PARTNERS PARTNERSHIP)
Pr 2: 17 who has left the *p* of her youth
Mal 2: 14 though she is your *p*, the wife
1Pe 3: 7 them with respect as the weaker *p*

PARTNERS (PARTNER)
Eph 5: 7 Therefore do not be *p* with them.

PARTNERSHIP* (PARTNER)
Php 1: 5 because of your *p* in the gospel

PASS (PASSED PASSER-BY PASSING)
Ex 12: 13 and when I see the blood, I will *p*
33: 19 goodness to *p* in front of you,
1Ki 9: 8 all who *p* by will be appalled
19: 11 for the LORD is about to *p* by."
Ps 90: 10 for they quickly *p*, and we fly away.
105: 19 till what he foretold came to *p*,
Isa 31: 5 he will '*p* over' it and will rescue it

Isa 43: 2 When you *p* through the waters,
62: 10 *P* through, *p* through the gates!
Jer 22: 8 "People from many nations will *p*
La 1: 12 to you, all you who *p* by?
Da 7: 14 dominion that will not *p* away,
Am 5: 17 for I will *p* through your midst,"
Mt 24: 34 will certainly not *p* away
24: 35 Heaven and earth will *p* away,
Mk 13: 31 Heaven and earth will *p* away,
Lk 21: 33 Heaven and earth will *p* away,
1Co 13: 8 there is knowledge, it will *p* away.
Jas 1: 10 he will *p* away like a wild flower.
1Jn 2: 17 The world and its desires *p* away,

PASSED (PASS)

Ge 15: 17 a blazing torch appeared and *p*
Ex 33: 22 you with my hand until I have *p* by.
2Ch 21: 20 He *p* away, to no-one's regret,
Ps 57: 1 wings until the disaster has *p*.
Lk 10: 32 saw him, *p* by on the other side.
1Co 15: 3 For what I received I *p* on to you
Heb 11: 29 By faith the people *p*

PASSER-BY* (PASS)

Pr 26: 10 is he who hires a fool or any *p*.
26: 17 is a *p* who meddles

PASSING (PASS)

1Co 7: 31 world in its present form is *p* away.
1Jn 2: 8 because the darkness is *p*

PASSION* (PASSIONATE PASSIONS)

Hos 7: 6 Their *p* smoulders all night;
1Co 7: 9 better to marry than to burn with *p*.

PASSIONATE* (PASSION)

1Th 4: 5 not in *p* lust like the heathen,

PASSIONS* (PASSION)

Ro 7: 5 the sinful *p* aroused
Gal 5: 24 crucified the sinful nature with its *p*
Tit 2: 12 to ungodliness and worldly *p*,
3: 3 and enslaved by all kinds of *p*

PASSOVER

Ex 12: 11 Eat it in haste; it is the LORD's *P*.
Nu 9: 2 Have the Israelites celebrate the *P*
Dt 16: 1 celebrate the *P* of the LORD your
Jos 5: 10 the Israelites celebrated the *P*.
2Ki 23: 21 "Celebrate the *P* to the LORD
Ezr 6: 19 the exiles celebrated the *P*.
Mk 14: 12 customary to sacrifice the *P* lamb,
Lk 22: 1 called the *P*, was approaching,
1Co 5: 7 our *P* lamb, has been sacrificed.
Heb 11: 28 he kept the *P* and the sprinkling

PAST

Isa 43: 18 do not dwell on the *p*.
65: 16 For the *p* troubles will be forgotten
Ro 15: 4 in the *p* was written to teach us,
16: 25 the mystery hidden for long ages *p*,
Eph 3: 9 which for ages *p* was kept hidden
Heb 1: 1 In the *p* God spoke

PASTORS*

Eph 4: 11 and some to be *p* and teachers,

PASTURE (PASTURES)

Ps 37: 3 dwell in the land and enjoy safe *p*.
95: 7 and we are the people of his *p*,
100: 3 we are his people, the sheep of his *p*
Jer 50: 7 against the LORD, their true *p*,
Eze 34: 13 I will *p* them on the mountains
Zec 11: 4 "*P* the flock marked for slaughter.
Jn 10: 9 come in and go out, and find *p*.

PASTURES (PASTURE)

Ps 23: 2 He makes me lie down in green *p*,

PATCH

Jer 10: 5 Like a scarecrow in a melon *p*,
Mt 9: 16 No-one sews a *p* of unshrunk cloth

PATH (PATHS)

Ps 16: 11 known to me the *p* of life;
27: 11 lead me in a straight *p*
119: 32 I run in the *p* of your commands,
119: 105 and a light for my *p*.
Pr 2: 9 and fair—every good *p*.
12: 28 along that *p* is immortality.
15: 10 awaits him who leaves the *p*;
15: 19 the *p* of the upright is a highway.
15: 24 The *p* of life leads upwards
21: 16 from the *p* of understanding
Isa 26: 7 The *p* of the righteous is level;
Jer 31: 9 on a level *p* where they will not
Mt 13: 4 fell along the *p*, and the birds came
Lk 1: 79 to guide our feet into the *p* of peace
2Co 6: 3 no stumbling-block in anyone's *p*,

PATHS (PATH)

Ps 23: 3 He guides me in *p* of righteousness
25: 4 teach me your *p*;
Pr 2: 13 who leave the straight *p*
3: 6 and he will make your *p* straight.
4: 11 and lead you along straight *p*.
4: 26 Make level *p* for your feet
5: 21 and he examines all his *p*.
8: 20 along the *p* of justice,
22: 5 In the *p* of the wicked lie thorns
Isa 2: 3 so that we may walk in his *p*."
Jer 6: 16 ask for the ancient *p*,
Mic 4: 2 so that we may walk in his *p*."
Mt 3: 3 make straight *p* for him.'"
Ac 2: 28 to me the *p* of life;
Ro 11: 33 and his *p* beyond tracing out!
Heb 12: 13 "Make level *p* for your feet,"

PATIENCE* (PATIENT)

Pr 19: 11 A man's wisdom gives him *p*;
25: 15 Through *p* a ruler can be persuaded
Ecc 7: 8 and *p* is better than pride.
Isa 7: 13 Is it not enough to try the *p* of men?
7: 13 Will you try the *p* of my God also?
Ro 2: 4 and *p*, not realising that God's
9: 22 bore with great *p* the objects
2Co 6: 6 understanding, *p* and kindness;
Gal 5: 22 joy, peace, *p*, kindness, goodness,
Col 1: 11 may have great endurance and *p*,
3: 12 humility, gentleness and *p*.
1Ti 1: 16 Jesus might display his unlimited *p*
2Ti 3: 10 my purpose, faith, *p*, love,
4: 2 with great *p* and careful instruction
Heb 6: 12 *p* inherit what has been promised.
Jas 5: 10 as an example of *p* in the face
2Pe 3: 15 that our Lord's *p* means salvation,

PATIENT* (PATIENCE PATIENTLY)

Ne 9: 30 For many years you were *p*
Job 6: 11 What prospects, that I should be *p*?
Pr 14: 29 A *p* man has great understanding,
15: 18 but a *p* man calms a quarrel.
16: 32 Better a *p* man than a warrior,
Mt 18: 26 'Be *p* with me,' he begged,
18: 29 'Be *p* with me, and I will pay you
Ro 12: 12 Be joyful in hope, *p* in affliction,
1Co 13: 4 Love is *p*, love is kind.
2Co 1: 6 produces in you *p* endurance
Eph 4: 2 humble and gentle; be *p*,
1Th 5: 14 help the weak, be *p* with everyone.
Jas 5: 7 Be *p*, then, brothers,
5: 7 and how *p* he is for the autumn
5: 8 You too, be *p* and stand firm,
2Pe 3: 9 He is *p* with you, not wanting
Rev 1: 9 *p* endurance that are ours in Jesus,
13: 10 This calls for *p* endurance
14: 12 This calls for *p* endurance

PATIENTLY* (PATIENT)

Ps 37: 7 still before the LORD and wait *p*
40: 1 I waited *p* for the LORD;
Isa 38: 13 I waited *p* till dawn,
Hab 3: 16 Yet I will wait *p* for the day
Ac 26: 3 I beg you to listen to me *p*.
Ro 8: 25 we do not yet have, we wait for it *p*.
Heb 6: 15 after waiting *p*, Abraham received
1Pe 3: 20 ago when God waited *p* in the days
Rev 3: 10 kept my command to endure *p*,

PATTERN

Ex 25: 40 according to the *p* shown you
Ro 5: 14 who was a *p* of the one to come.
12: 2 longer to the *p* of this world,
2Ti 1: 13 keep as the *p* of sound teaching,
Heb 8: 5 according to the *p* shown you

PAUL

Also called Saul (Ac 13:9). Pharisee from Tarsus (Ac 9:11; Php 3:5). Apostle (Gal 1). At stoning of Stephen (Ac 8:1). Persecuted Church (Ac 9:1-2; Gal 1:13). Vision of Jesus on road to Damascus (Ac 9:4-9; 26:12-18). In Arabia (Gal 1:17). Preached in Damascus; escaped death through the wall in a basket (Ac 9:19-25). In Jerusalem; sent back to Tarsus (Ac 9:26-30).

Brought to Antioch by Barnabas (Ac 11:22-26). First missionary journey to Cyprus and Galatia (Ac 13-14). Stoned at Lystra (Ac 14:19-20). At Jerusalem Council (Ac 15). Split with Barnabas over Mark (Ac 15:36-41).

Second missionary journey with Silas (Ac 16-20). Called to Macedonia (Ac 16:6-10). Freed from prison in Philippi (Ac 16:16-40). In Thessalonica (Ac 17:1-9). Speech in Athens (Ac 17:16-33). In Corinth (Ac 18). In Ephesus (Ac 19). Return to Jerusalem (Ac 20). Farewell to Ephesian elders (Ac 20:13-38). Arrival in Jerusalem (Ac 21:1-26). Arrested (Ac 21:27-36). Addressed crowds (Ac 22). Sanhedrin (Ac 23:1-11). Transferred to Caesarea (Ac 23:12-35). Trial before Felix (Ac 24), Festus (Ac 25:1-12). Before Agrippa (Ac 25:13-26:32). Voyage to Rome; shipwreck (Ac 27). Arrival in Rome (Ac 28).

Epistles: Romans, 1 and 2 Corinthians, Galatians, Ephesians, Philippians, Colossians, 1 and 2 Thessalonians, 1 and 2 Timothy, Titus, Philemon.

PAVEMENT

Jn 19: 13 as The Stone *P* (which

PAY (PAID PAYMENT PAYS REPAID REPAY REPAYING)

Lev 26: 43 They will *p* for their sins
Dt 7: 12 If you *p* attention to these laws
Pr 4: 1 *p* attention and gain understanding
4: 20 My son, *p* attention to what I say;
5: 1 My son, *p* attention to my wisdom,
6: 31 if he is caught, he must *p* sevenfold,
19: 19 man must *p* the penalty;
22: 17 *P* attention and listen
24: 29 I'll *p* that man back for what he did
Eze 40: 4 and *p* attention to everything I am
Zec 11: 12 give me my *p*; but if not, keep it."
Mt 20: 2 He agreed to *p* them a denarius
22: 16 you *p* no attention to who they are.
22: 17 Is it right to *p* taxes to Caesar
Lk 3: 14 falsely—be content with your *p*."
19: 8 I will *p* back four times the amount
Ro 13: 6 This is also why you *p* taxes,
2Pe 1: 19 you will do well to *p* attention to it,

PAYMENT (PAY)

Ps 49: 8 no *p* is ever enough—
Php 4: 18 I have received full *p* and

PAYS (PAY)

Pr 17: 13 If a man *p* back evil for good,
1Th 5: 15 sure that nobody *p* back wrong

PEACE (PEACE-LOVING PEACEABLE PEACEFUL PEACEMAKERS)

Lev 26: 6 "'I will grant *p* in the land,
Nu 6: 26 and give you *p*."'
25: 12 him I am making my covenant of *p*
Dt 20: 10 make its people an offer of *p*.

Jdg 3:11 So the land had *p* for forty years,
3:30 and the land had *p* for eighty years.
5:31 Then the land had *p* for forty years.
6:24 and called it "The LORD is *P*."
8:28 the land enjoyed *p* for forty years.
1Sa 7:14 And there was *p* between Israel
2Sa 10:19 they made *p* with the Israelites
1Ki 2:33 may there be the LORD's *p* for ever
22:44 also at *p* with the king of Israel.
2Ki 9:17 come in *p*?' " The horseman rode
1Ch 19:19 they made *p* with David
22:9 and I will grant Israel *p*
2Ch 14:1 and in his days the country was at *p*
20:30 kingdom of Jehoshaphat was at *p*,
Job 3:26 I have no *p*, no quietness;
22:21 to God and be at *p* with him;
Ps 29:11 LORD blesses his people with *p*.
34:14 seek *p* and pursue it.
37:11 and enjoy great *p*.
37:37 there is a future for the man of *p*.
85:10 righteousness and *p* kiss each other
119:165 Great *p* have they who love your
120:7 I am a man of *p*;
122:6 Pray for the *p* of Jerusalem:
147:14 He grants *p* to your borders
Pr 12:20 but joy for those who promote *p*.
14:30 A heart at *p* gives life to the body,
16:7 his enemies live at *p* with him.
17:1 Better a dry crust with *p* and quiet
Ecc 3:8 a time for war and a time for *p*.
Isa 9:6 Everlasting Father, Prince of *P*.
14:7 All the lands are at rest and at *p*;
26:3 You will keep in perfect *p*
32:17 The fruit of righteousness will be *p*;
48:18 your *p* would have been like a river,
48:22 "There is no *p*," says the LORD,
52:7 who proclaim *p*,
53:5 punishment that brought us *p* was
54:10 nor my covenant of *p* be removed,"
55:12 and be led forth in *p*;
57:2 enter into *p*;
57:19 *P*, *p*, to those far and near,"
57:21 "There is no *p*," says my God,
59:8 The way of *p* they do not know;
Jer 6:14 '*P*, *p*,' they say,
8:11 "*P*, *p*," . . . there is no *p*.
30:10 Jacob will again have *p*
46:27 Jacob will again have *p*
Eze 13:10 "*P*," when there is no *p*,
34:25 " 'I will make a covenant of *p*
37:26 I will make a covenant of *p*
Mic 5:5 And he will be their *p*.
Zec 8:19 Therefore love truth and *p*."
9:10 He will proclaim *p* to the nations.
Mal 2:5 a covenant of life and *p*,
2:6 He walked with me in *p*
Mt 10:34 I did not come to bring *p*,
Mk 9:50 and be at *p* with each other."
Lk 1:79 to guide our feet into the path of *p*
2:14 on earth *p* to men on whom his
19:38 "*P* in heaven and glory
Jn 14:27 *P* I leave with you; my *p*
16:33 so that in me you may have *p*.
Ro 1:7 and *p* to you from God our Father
2:10 and *p* for everyone who does good:
5:1 we have *p* with God
8:6 by the Spirit is life and *p*;
12:18 on you, live at *p* with everyone.
14:19 effort to do what leads to *p*
1Co 7:15 God has called us to live in *p*.
14:33 a God of disorder but of *p*.
2Co 13:11 be of one mind, live in *p*.
Gal 5:22 joy, *p*, patience, kindness,
Eph 2:14 he himself is our *p*, who has made
2:15 thus making *p*, and in this one body
2:17 and *p* to those who were near.
6:15 comes from the gospel of *p*.
Php 4:7 the *p* of God, which transcends all
Col 1:20 by making *p* through his blood,
3:15 Let the *p* of Christ rule
3:15 of one body you were called to *p*.
1Th 5:3 While people are saying, "*P*
5:13 Live in *p* with each other.
1Th 5:23 the God of *p*, sanctify you through
2Th 3:16 the Lord of *p* himself give you *p*
2Ti 2:22 righteousness, faith, love and *p*,
Heb 7:2 "king of Salem" means "king of *p*."
12:11 *p* for those who have been trained
12:14 effort to live in *p* with all men
13:20 May the God of *p*, who
1Pe 3:11 he must seek *p* and pursue it.
2Pe 3:14 blameless and at *p* with him.
Rev 6:4 power to take *p* from the earth

PEACE-LOVING (PEACE)
Jas 3:17 then *p*, considerate,

PEACEABLE* (PEACE)
Tit 3:2 to slander no-one, to be *p*

PEACEFUL (PEACE)
1Ti 2:2 that we may live *p* and quiet lives

PEACEMAKERS* (PEACE)
Mt 5:9 Blessed are the *p*,
Jas 3:18 *P* who sow in peace raise a harvest

PEARL* (PEARLS)
Rev 21:21 each gate made of a single *p*.

PEARLS (PEARL)
Mt 7:6 do not throw your *p* to pigs.
13:45 like a merchant looking for fine *p*.
1Ti 2:9 or gold or *p* or expensive clothes,
Rev 21:21 The twelve gates were twelve *p*,

PEDDLE*
2Co 2:17 we do not *p* the word of God

PEG
Jdg 4:21 She drove the *p* through his temple

PEKAH
King of Israel (2Ki 16:25-31; Isa 7:1).

PEKAHIAH*
Son of Menahem; king of Israel (2Ki 16:22-26).

PEN
Ps 45:1 my tongue is the *p*
Mt 5:18 letter, not the least stroke of a *p*,
Jn 10:1 who does not enter the sheep *p*

PENETRATES*
Heb 4:12 it *p* even to dividing soul and spirit,

PENNIES* (PENNY)
Lk 12:6 not five sparrows sold for two *p*?

PENNY* (PENNIES)
Mt 5:26 out until you have paid the last *p*.
10:29 Are not two sparrows sold for a *p*?
Mk 12:42 worth only a fraction of a *p*.
Lk 12:59 out until you have paid the last *p*."

PENTECOST*
Ac 2:1 of *P* came, they were all together
20:16 if possible, by the day of *P*.
1Co 16:8 I will stay on at Ephesus until *P*,

PEOPLE (PEOPLES)
Ge 11:6 as one *p* speaking the same
Ex 5:1 Let my *p* go,
6:7 take you as my own *p*,
8:23 between my *p* and your *p*.
15:13 the *p* you have redeemed.
19:8 The *p* all responded together,
24:3 Moses went and told the *p*
32:1 When the *p* saw that Moses
32:9 they are a stiff-necked *p*.
33:13 this nation is your *p*.
Lev 9:7 for yourself and the *p*:
16:24 the burnt offering for the *p*,
26:12 and you will be my *p*.
Nu 11:11 burden of all these *p* on
Nu 14:11 *p* treat me with contempt?
14:19 forgive the sin of these *p*,
22:5 A *p* has come out of Egypt
Dt 4:6 a wise and understanding *p*.
4:20 the *p* of his inheritance,
5:28 what this *p* said to you.
7:6 a *p* holy to the LORD
26:18 that you are his *p*,
31:7 you must go with this *p*
31:16 these *p* will soon prostitute
32:9 the LORD's portion is his *p*,
32:43 atonement for his land and *p*.
33:29 a *p* saved by the LORD?
Jos 1:6 you will lead this *p*
24:24 the *p* said to Joshua,
Jdg 2:7 *p* served the LORD throughout
Ru 1:16 Your *p* will be my *p*
1Sa 8:7 the *p* are saying to you;
12:22 LORD will not reject his *p*,
2Sa 5:2 will shepherd my *p* Israel
7:10 provide a place for my *p*
1Ki 3:8 among the *p* you have chosen,
8:30 your *p* Israel when they pray
8:56 has given rest to his *p*
18:39 when all the *p* saw this,
2Ki 23:3 all the *p* pledged themselves
1Ch 17:21 to redeem *p* for himself
29:17 how willingly your *p* who are
2Ch 2:11 Because the LORD loves his *p*,
7:5 *p* dedicated the temple
7:14 if my *p*, who are called
30:6 "*P* of Israel, return to
36:16 was aroused against his *p*
Ezr 2:1 These are the *p* of the
3:1 *p* assembled as one man
Ne 1:10 your *p*, whom you redeemed
4:6 *p* worked with all their heart
8:1 *p* assembled as one man
Est 3:6 to destroy all Mordecai's *p*,
Job 12:2 Doubtless you are the *p*,
Ps 29:11 gives strength to his *p*;
33:12 *p* he chose for his inheritance
50:4 that he may judge his *p*
53:6 restores the fortunes of his *p*,
81:13 If my *p* would but listen
94:14 LORD will not reject his *p*;
95:7 we are the *p* of his pasture,
95:10 a *p* whose hearts go astray,
125:2 the LORD surrounds his *p*
135:14 LORD will vindicate his *p*
144:15 *p* whose God is the LORD.
Pr 14:34 sin is a disgrace to any *p*.
29:2 righteous thrive, the *p* rejoice
29:18 the *p* cast off restraint
Isa 1:3 my *p* do not understand.
1:4 a *p* loaded with guilt,
5:13 my *p* will go into exile
6:10 the heart of this *p* calloused;
9:2 the *p* walking in darkness
12:12 will assemble the scattered *p*
19:25 Blessed be Egypt my *p*,
25:8 remove the disgrace of his *p*
29:13 These *p* come near to me
40:1 Comfort, comfort my *p*
40:7 Surely the *p* are grass.
42:6 a covenant for the *p*
49:13 the LORD comforts his *p*
51:4 "Listen to me, my *p*;
52:6 my *p* will know my name;
53:8 for the transgression of my *p*
60:21 will all your *p* be righteous
62:12 will be called the Holy *P*,
65:23 they will be a *p* blessed
Jer 2:11 my *p* have exchanged their
2:13 *p* have committed two sins:
2:32 my *p* have forgotten me,
4:22 My *p* are fools;
5:14 Because the *p* have spoken
5:31 my *p* love it this way
7:16 do not pray for this *p*
18:15 my *p* have forgotten me;
25:7 They will be my *p*,
30:3 I will bring my *p* Israel

Eze 13: 23 I will save my *p* from
36: 8 fruit for my *p* Israel,
36: 28 you will be my *p*,
36: 38 be filled with flocks of *p*.
37: 13 Then you, my *p*, will know
38: 14 *p* Israel are living in safety
39: 7 name among my *p* Israel.
Da 7: 27 saints, the *p* of the Most High.
8: 24 mighty men and the holy *p*
9: 19 your *p* bear your name
9: 24 are decreed for your *p*
9: 26 *p* of the ruler who will come
10: 14 will happen to your *p*
11: 32 *p* who know their God will
12: 1 prince who protects your *p*.
Hos 1: 10 'You are not my *p*,'
2: 23 'You are my *p*';
4: 14 a *p* without understanding
Joel 2: 18 and take pity on his *p*.
3: 16 be a refuge for his *p*,
Am 9: 14 back my exiled *p* Israel;
Mic 6: 2 a case against his *p*;
7: 14 Shepherd your *p* with
Hag 1: 12 remnant of the *p* obeyed
Zec 2: 11 and will become my *p*.
8: 7 I will save my *p*
13: 9 will say, 'They are my *p*,'
Mk 7: 6 *p* honour me with their lips
8: 27 "Who do *p* say I am?"
Lk 1: 17 make ready a *p* prepared
1: 68 and has redeemed his *p*.
2: 10 joy that will be for all the *p*.
21: 23 and wrath against this *p*.
Jn 11: 50 one man die for the *p*
18: 14 if one man died for the *p*.
Ac 15: 14 from the Gentiles a *p*.
18: 10 have many *p* in this city.
Ro 9: 25 will call them 'my *p*.'
11: 1 Did God reject his *p*?
15: 10 O Gentiles, with his *p*."
2Co 6: 16 and they will be my *p*."
Tit 2: 14 a *p* that are his very own,
Heb 2: 17 for the sins of the *p*.
4: 9 a Sabbath-rest for the *p*
5: 3 for the sins of the *p*.
10: 30 Lord will judge his *p*.
11: 25 ill-treated along with the *p*
13: 12 to make the *p* holy
1Pe 2: 9 you are a chosen *p*,
2: 10 Once you were not a *p*,
2: 10 you are the *p* of God;
2Pe 2: 1 false prophets among the *p*,
3: 11 kind of *p* ought you to be?
Rev 18: 4 "Come out of her, my *p*,
21: 3 They will be his *p*,

PEOPLES (PEOPLE)

Ge 17: 16 kings of *p* will come from her
25: 23 two *p* from within you will
27: 29 and *p* bow down to you
28: 3 become a community of *p*.
48: 4 you a community of *p*.
Dt 14: 2 of all the *p* on the face of
28: 10 Then all the *p* on earth
32: 8 set up boundaries for the *p*
Jos 4: 24 all the *p* of the earth might
1Ki 8: 43 all the *p* of the earth may
2Ch 7: 20 of ridicule among all *p*.
Ps 9: 8 he will govern the *p*
67: 5 may all the *p* praise you.
87: 6 in the register of the *p*:
96: 10 he will judge the *p*
Isa 2: 4 settle disputes for many *p*.
17: 12 Oh, the uproar of the *p*—
25: 6 of rich food for all *p*,
34: 1 pay attention, you *p*!
55: 4 him a witness to the *p*,
Jer 10: 3 customs of the *p* are worthless
Da 7: 14 all *p*, nations and men
Mic 4: 1 and *p* will stream to it.
4: 3 will judge between many *p*
5: 7 in the midst of many *p*
Zep 3: 9 purify the lips of the *p*,
Zep 3: 20 among all the *p* of the
Zec 8: 20 Many *p* and the inhabitants
12: 2 all the surrounding *p* reeling.
Rev 10: 11 prophesy again about many *p*,
17: 15 the prostitute sits, are *p*,

PEOR

Nu 25: 3 joined in worshipping the Baal of *P*.
Dt 4: 3 who followed the Baal of *P*,

PERCEIVE (PERCEIVING)

Ps 139: 2 you *p* my thoughts from afar.
Pr 24: 12 not he who weighs the heart *p* it?

PERCEIVING* (PERCEIVE)

Isa 6: 9 be ever seeing, but never *p*.'
Mt 13: 14 you will be ever seeing but never *p*.
Mk 4: 12 may be ever seeing but never *p*,
Ac 28: 26 you will be ever seeing but never *p*

PERFECT* (PERFECTER PERFECTING PERFECTION)

Dt 32: 4 He is the Rock, his works are *p*,
2Sa 22: 31 "As for God, his way is *p*;
22: 33 and makes my way *p*.
Job 36: 4 one *p* in knowledge is with you.
37: 16 of him who is *p* in knowledge?
Ps 18: 30 As for God, his way is *p*;
18: 32 and makes my way *p*.
19: 7 The law of the LORD is *p*,
50: 2 From Zion, *p* in beauty,
64: 6 "We have devised a *p* plan!"
SS 6: 9 but my dove, my *p* one, is unique,
Isa 25: 1 for in *p* faithfulness
26: 3 You will keep in *p* peace
Eze 16: 14 had given you made your beauty *p*,
27: 3 "I am *p* in beauty."
28: 12 full of wisdom and *p* in beauty.
Mt 5: 48 Do not even pagans do that? Be *p*,
5: 48 as your heavenly Father is *p*.
19: 21 answered, "If you want to be *p*,
Ro 12: 2 his good, pleasing and *p* will.
2Co 12: 9 for my power is made *p*
Php 3: 12 or have already been made *p*,
Col 1: 28 so that we may present everyone *p*
3: 14 binds them all together in *p* unity.
Heb 2: 10 the author of their salvation *p*
5: 9 what he suffered and, once made *p*,
7: 19 useless (for the law made nothing *p*
7: 28 who has been made *p* for ever.
9: 11 and more *p* tabernacle that is not
10: 1 make *p* those who draw
10: 14 he has made *p* for ever those who
11: 40 with us would they be made *p*.
12: 23 spirits of righteous men made *p*,
Jas 1: 17 Every good and *p* gift is from above
1: 25 into the *p* law that gives freedom,
3: 2 he is a *p* man, able
1Jn 4: 18 But *p* love drives out fear,
4: 18 The one who fears is not made *p*

PERFECTER* (PERFECT)

Heb 12: 2 the author and *p* of our faith,

PERFECTING* (PERFECT)

2Co 7: 1 *p* holiness out of reverence for God

PERFECTION* (PERFECT)

Ps 119: 96 To all *p* I see a limit;
La 2: 15 the *p* of beauty,
Eze 27: 4 builders brought your beauty to *p*.
27: 11 they brought your beauty to *p*.
28: 12 "'You were the model of *p*,
1Co 13: 10 but when *p* comes, the imperfect
2Co 13: 9 and our prayer is for your *p*.
13: 11 Aim for *p*, listen to my appeal,
Heb 7: 11 If *p* could have been attained

PERFORM (PERFORMED PERFORMS)

Ex 3: 20 with all the wonders that I will *p*
2Sa 7: 23 to *p* great and awesome wonders
Jn 3: 2 no-one could *p* the miraculous

PERFORMED (PERFORM)

Mt 11: 21 If the miracles that were *p*
Jn 10: 41 John never *p* a miraculous

PERFORMS (PERFORM)

Ps 77: 14 You are the God who *p* miracles;

PERFUME

Ecc 7: 1 A good name is better than fine *p*,
SS 1: 3 your name is like *p* poured out.
Mk 14: 3 jar of very expensive *p*,

PERIL

2Co 1: 10 us from such a deadly *p*,

PERISH (PERISHABLE PERISHED PERISHES PERISHING)

Ge 6: 17 Everything on earth will *p*.
Est 4: 16 And if I *p*, I *p*."
Ps 1: 6 but the way of the wicked will *p*.
37: 20 But the wicked will *p*:
73: 27 Those who are far from you will *p*;
102: 26 They will *p*, but you remain;
Pr 11: 10 when the wicked *p*, there are
19: 9 and he who pours out lies will *p*.
21: 28 A false witness will *p*,
28: 28 when the wicked *p*, the righteous
Isa 1: 28 who forsake the LORD will *p*.
29: 14 the wisdom of the wise will *p*,
60: 12 that will not serve you will *p*;
Zec 11: 9 the dying die, and the perishing *p*.
Lk 13: 3 unless you repent, you too will all *p*
13: 5 unless you repent, you too will all *p*
21: 18 But not a hair of your head will *p*.
Jn 3: 16 whoever believes in him shall not *p*
10: 28 eternal life, and they shall never *p*;
Ro 2: 12 apart from the law will also *p* apart
Col 2: 22 These are all destined to *p* with use,
2Th 2: 10 They *p* because they refused
Heb 1: 11 They will *p*, but you remain;
1Pe 1: 4 into an inheritance that can never *p*
2Pe 3: 9 not wanting anyone to *p*,

PERISHABLE (PERISH)

1Co 15: 42 The body that is sown is *p*,
1Pe 1: 18 not with *p* things such
1: 23 not of *p* seed, but of imperishable,

PERISHED (PERISH)

Ps 119: 92 I would have *p* in my affliction.

PERISHES (PERISH)

Job 8: 13 so *p* the hope of the godless.
1Pe 1: 7 which *p* even though refined by fire

PERISHING (PERISH)

1Co 1: 18 foolishness to those who are *p*,
2Co 2: 15 being saved and those who are *p*.
4: 3 it is veiled to those who are *p*.

PERJURERS* (PERJURY)

Mal 3: 5 and *p*, against those who defraud
1Ti 1: 10 for slave traders and liars and *p*—

PERJURY* (PERJURERS)

Jer 7: 9 murder, commit adultery and *p*,

PERMANENT

Heb 7: 24 lives for ever, he has a *p* priesthood.

PERMISSIBLE (PERMIT)

1Co 6: 12 "Everything is *p* for me"—
10: 23 "Everything is *p*"—but not

PERMIT (PERMISSIBLE PERMITTED)

Hos 5: 4 "Their deeds do not *p* them
1Ti 2: 12 I do not *p* a woman to teach

PERMITTED (PERMIT)

Mt 19: 8 Moses *p* you to divorce your wives
2Co 12: 4 things that man is not *p* to tell.

PERSECUTE (PERSECUTED PERSECUTION PERSECUTIONS)

Ps 119: 86 for men *p* me without cause.
Mt 5: 11 *p* you and falsely say all kinds
5: 44 and pray for those who *p* you,
Jn 15: 20 they persecuted me, they will *p* you
Ac 9: 4 why do you *p* me?" "Who are you,
Ro 12: 14 Bless those who *p* you; bless

PERSECUTED (PERSECUTE)

Mt 5: 10 Blessed are those who are *p*
5: 12 same way they *p* the prophets who
Jn 15: 20 If they *p* me, they will persecute
1Co 4: 12 when we are *p*, we endure it;
15: 9 because I *p* the church of God.
2Co 4: 9 in despair; *p*, but not abandoned;
1Th 3: 4 kept telling you that we would be *p*.
2Ti 3: 12 life in Christ Jesus will be *p*,
Heb 11: 37 destitute, *p* and ill-treated—

PERSECUTION (PERSECUTE)

Mt 13: 21 When trouble or *p* comes
Ro 8: 35 or hardship or *p* or famine

PERSECUTIONS (PERSECUTE)

Mk 10: 30 and with them, *p*) and in the age
2Co 12: 10 in hardships, in *p*, in difficulties.
2Th 1: 4 faith in all the *p* and trials you are
2Ti 3: 11 love, endurance, *p*, sufferings—

PERSEVERANCE* (PERSEVERE)

Ro 5: 3 we know that suffering produces *p*;
5: 4 *p*, character; and character, hope.
2Co 12: 12 were done among you with great *p*.
2Th 1: 4 churches we boast about your *p*
3: 5 into God's love and Christ's *p*.
Heb 12: 1 run with *p* the race marked out
Jas 1: 3 the testing of your faith develops *p*.
1: 4 *P* must finish its work
5: 11 You have heard of Job's *p*
2Pe 1: 6 *p*; and to *p*, godliness;
Rev 2: 2 your hard work and your *p*.
2: 19 and faith, your service and *p*,

PERSEVERE* (PERSEVERANCE PERSEVERED PERSEVERES PERSEVERING)

1Ti 4: 16 *P* in them, because if you do,
Heb 10: 36 You need to *p* so that

PERSEVERED* (PERSEVERE)

Heb 11: 27 he *p* because he saw him who is
Jas 5: 11 consider blessed those who have *p*.
Rev 2: 3 You have *p* and have endured

PERSEVERES* (PERSEVERE)

1Co 13: 7 trusts, always hopes, always *p*.
Jas 1: 12 Blessed is the man who *p*

PERSEVERING* (PERSEVERE)

Lk 8: 15 retain it, and by *p* produce a crop.

PERSIANS

Da 6: 15 law of the Medes and *P* no decree

PERSISTENCE*

Ro 2: 7 To those who by *p*

PERSUADE (PERSUADED PERSUASIVE)

Ac 18: 4 trying to *p* Jews and Greeks.
2Co 5: 11 is to fear the Lord, we try to *p* men.

PERSUADED (PERSUADE)

Ro 4: 21 being fully *p* that God had power

PERSUASIVE (PERSUADE)

1Co 2: 4 not with wise and *p* words,

PERVERSION* (PERVERT)

Lev 18: 23 sexual relations with it; that is a *p*.
20: 12 What they have done is a *p*;
Ro 1: 27 the due penalty for their *p*.
Jude : 7 up to sexual immorality and *p*.

PERVERT (PERVERSION PERVERTED PERVERTS)

Ex 23: 2 do not *p* justice by siding
Dt 16: 19 Do not *p* justice or show partiality.
Job 34: 12 that the Almighty would *p* justice.
Pr 17: 23 to *p* the course of justice.
Gal 1: 7 are trying to *p* the gospel of Christ.

PERVERTED (PERVERT)

1Sa 8: 3 and accepted bribes and *p* justice.

PERVERTS* (PERVERT)

1Ti 1: 10 for murderers, for adulterers and *p*,

PESTILENCE (PESTILENCES)

Ps 91: 6 nor the *p* that stalks in the darkness

PESTILENCES (PESTILENCE)

Lk 21: 11 famines and *p* in various places,

PETER

Apostle, brother of Andrew, also called Simon (Mt 10:2; Mk 3:16; Lk 6:14; Ac 1:13), and Cephas (Jn 1:42). Confession of Christ (Mt 16:13-20; Mk 8:27-30; Lk 9:18-27). At transfiguration (Mt 17:1-8; Mk 9:2-8; Lk 9:28-36; 2Pe 1:16-18). Caught fish with coin (Mt 17:24-27). Denial of Jesus predicted (Mt 26:31-35; Mk 14:27-31; Lk 22:31-34; Jn 13:31-38). Denied Jesus (Mt 26:69-75; Mk 14:66-72; Lk 22:54-62; Jn 18: 15-27). Commissioned by Jesus to shepherd his flock (Jn 21:15-23).

Speech at Pentecost (Ac 2). Healed beggar (Ac 3:1-10). Speech at temple (Ac 3:11-26), before Sanhedrin (Ac 4:1-22). In Samaria (Ac 8:14-25). Sent by vision to Cornelius (Ac 10). Announced salvation of Gentiles in Jerusalem (Ac 11; 15). Freed from prison (Ac 12). Inconsistency at Antioch (Gal 2:11-21). At Jerusalem Council (Ac 15).

Epistles: 1-2 Peter.

PETITION (PETITIONS)

1Ch 16: 4 to make *p*, to give thanks,
Php 4: 6 by prayer and *p*, with thanksgiving,

PETITIONS (PETITION)

Heb 5: 7 he offered up prayers and *p*

PHANTOM*

Ps 39: 6 Man is a mere *p* as he goes to

PHARAOH (PHARAOH'S)

Ge 12: 15 her to *P*, and she was taken
41: 14 So *P* sent for Joseph, and he was
Ex 14: 4 glory for myself through *P*
14: 17 And I will gain glory through *P*

PHARAOH'S (PHARAOH)

Ex 7: 3 But I will harden *P* heart, and

PHARISEE (PHARISEES)

Ac 23: 6 brothers, I am a *P*, the son of a *P*.
Php 3: 5 in regard to the law, a *P*; as for zeal,

PHARISEES (PHARISEE)

Mt 5: 20 surpasses that of the *P*
16: 6 guard against the yeast of the *P*
23: 13 of the law and *P*, you hypocrites!
Jn 3: 1 a man of the *P* named Nicodemus,

PHILADELPHIA

Rev 3: 7 the angel of the church in *P* write:

PHILEMON*

Phm : 1 To *P* our dear friend and fellow

PHILIP

1. Apostle (Mt 10:3; Mk 3:18; Lk 6:14; Jn 1:43-48; 14:8; Ac 1:13).
2. Deacon (Ac 6:1-7); evangelist in Samaria (Ac 8:4-25), to Ethiopian (Ac 8:26-40).

PHILIPPI

Ac 16: 12 From there we travelled to *P*,
Php 1: 1 To all the saints in Christ Jesus at *P*

PHILISTINE (PHILISTINES)

Jos 13: 3 of the five *P* rulers in Gaza,
1Sa 14: 1 let's go over to the *P* outpost
17: 26 is this uncircumcised *P* that he
17: 37 me from the hand of this *P*."

PHILISTINES (PHILISTINE)

Jdg 10: 7 them into the hands of the *P*
13: 1 the hands of the *P* for forty years.
16: 5 The rulers of the *P* went to her
1Sa 4: 1 at Ebenezer, and the *P* at Aphek.
5: 8 together all the rulers of the *P*
13: 23 a detachment of *P* had gone out
17: 1 the *P* gathered their forces for war
23: 1 the *P* are fighting against Keilah
27: 1 is to escape to the land of the *P*.
31: 1 Now the *P* fought against Israel;
2Sa 5: 17 When the *P* heard that David had
8: 1 David defeated the *P* and subdued
21: 15 there was a battle between the *P*
2Ki 18: 8 he defeated the *P*, as far as Gaza
Am 1: 8 Ekron till the last of the *P* is dead,"

PHILOSOPHER* (PHILOSOPHY)

1Co 1: 20 Where is the *p* of this age?

PHILOSOPHY* (PHILOSOPHER)

Col 2: 8 through hollow and deceptive *p*,

PHINEHAS

Nu 25: 7 When *P* son of Eleazar, the son
Ps 106: 30 But *P* stood up and intervened,

PHOEBE*

Ro 16: 1 I commend to you our sister *P*,

PHYLACTERIES*

Mt 23: 5 They make their *p* wide

PHYSICAL

Ro 2: 28 merely outward and *p*.
Col 1: 22 by Christ's *p* body through death
1Ti 4: 8 For *p* training is of some value,
Jas 2: 16 but does nothing about his *p* needs,

PICK (PICKED)

Mk 16: 18 they will *p* up snakes

PICKED (PICK)

Lk 14: 7 noticed how the guests *p* the places
Jn 5: 9 he *p* up his mat and walked.

PIECE (PIECES)

Jn 19: 23 woven in one *p* from top to bottom.

PIECES (PIECE)

Ge 15: 17 and passed between the *p*.
Jer 34: 18 and then walked between its *p*.
Zec 11: 12 So they paid me thirty *p* of silver.
Mt 14: 20 of broken *p* that were left over.

PIERCE (PIERCED)

Ex 21: 6 and *p* his ear with an awl.
Pr 12: 18 Reckless words *p* like a sword,
Lk 2: 35 a sword will *p* your own soul too."

PIERCED (PIERCE)

Ps 22: 16 they have *p* my hands and my feet.
40: 6 but my ears you have *p*;
Isa 53: 5 But he was *p* for our transgressions,
Zec 12: 10 look on me, the one they have *p*,
Jn 19: 37 look on the one they have *p*."
Rev 1: 7 even those who *p* him;

PIG'S (PIGS)

Pr 11: 22 Like a gold ring in a *p* snout

PIGEONS

Lev 5: 11 afford two doves or two young *p*,

Lk 2:24 "a pair of doves or two young *p*."

PIGS (PIG'S)

Mt 7:6 do not throw your pearls to *p*.
Mk 5:11 A large herd of *p* was feeding on

PILATE

Governor of Judea. Questioned Jesus (Mt 27:1-26; Mk 15:15; Lk 22:66-23:25; Jn 18:28-19:16); sent him to Herod (Lk 23:6-12); consented to his crucifixion when crowds chose Barabbas (Mt 27:15-26; Mk 15:6-15; Lk 23:13-25; Jn 19:1-10).

PILLAR (PILLARS)

Ge 19:26 and she became a *p* of salt.
Ex 13:21 ahead of them in a *p* of cloud
1Ti 3:15 the *p* and foundation of the truth.
Rev 3:12 who overcomes I will make a *p*

PILLARS (PILLAR)

Gal 2:9 and John, those reputed to be *p*,

PINIONS

Dt 32:11 and carries them on its *p*.

PISGAH

Dt 3:27 Go up to the top of *P* and look west

PIT

Ps 7:15 falls into the *p* he has made.
40:2 He lifted me out of the slimy *p*,
103:4 he redeems my life from the *p*
Pr 23:27 for a prostitute is a deep *p*
26:27 If a man digs a *p*, he will fall into it;
Isa 24:17 Terror and *p* and snare await you,
38:17 me from the *p* of destruction;
Mt 15:14 a blind man, both will fall into a *p*."

PITCH

Ge 6:14 and coat it with *p* inside and out.
Ex 2:3 and coated it with tar and *p*.

PITIED (PITY)

1Co 15:19 we are to be *p* more than all men.

PITY (PITIED)

Ps 72:13 He will take *p* on the weak
Ecc 4:10 But *p* the man who falls
Lk 10:33 when he saw him, he took *p* on him

PLAGUE (PLAGUED PLAGUES)

2Ch 6:28 "When famine or *p* comes
Ps 91:6 nor the *p* that destroys at midday.

PLAGUED* (PLAGUE)

Ps 73:5 they are not *p* by human ills.
73:14 All day long I have been *p*;

PLAGUES (PLAGUE)

Hos 13:14 Where, O death, are your *p*?
Rev 21:9 full of the seven last *p* came
22:18 to him the *p* described in this book.

PLAIN [1]

Isa 40:4 the rugged places a *p*.

PLAIN [2]

Ro 1:19 what may be known about God is *p*

PLAN (PLANNED PLANS)

Ex 26:30 according to the *p* shown you
Job 42:2 no *p* of yours can be thwarted.
Pr 14:22 those who *p* what is good find love
21:30 is no wisdom, no insight, no *p*
Am 3:7 nothing without revealing his *p*
Eph 1:11 predestined according to the *p*

PLANK

Mt 7:3 attention to the *p* in your own eye?
Lk 6:41 attention to the *p* in your own eye?

PLANNED (PLAN)

Ps 40:5 The things you *p* for us
Isa 14:24 "Surely, as I have *p*, so it will be,
23:9 The LORD Almighty *p* it,
46:11 what I have *p*, that will I do.
Heb 11:40 God had *p* something better for us

PLANS (PLAN)

Ps 20:4 and make all your *p* succeed.
33:11 *p* of the LORD stand firm for ever,
Pr 15:22 *P* fail for lack of counsel,
16:3 and your *p* will succeed.
19:21 Many are the *p* in a man's heart,
20:18 Make *p* by seeking advice;
Isa 29:15 to hide their *p* from the LORD,
30:1 those who carry out *p* that are not
32:8 But the noble man makes noble *p*,
2Co 1:17 Or do I make my *p* in a worldly

PLANT (PLANTED PLANTING PLANTS)

Am 9:15 I will *p* Israel in their own land,
Mt 15:13 "Every *p* that my heavenly Father

PLANTED (PLANT)

Ge 2:8 the LORD God had *p* a garden
Ps 1:3 He is like a tree *p* by streams
Jer 17:8 He will be like a tree *p* by the water
Mt 15:13 Father has not *p* will be pulled
21:33 was a landowner who *p* a vineyard.
Lk 13:6 "A man had a fig-tree, *p*
1Co 3:6 I *p* the seed, Apollos watered it,
Jas 1:21 humbly accept the word *p* in you,

PLANTING (PLANT)

Isa 61:3 a *p* of the LORD

PLANTS (PLANT)

Pr 31:16 out of her earnings she *p* a vineyard
1Co 3:7 So neither he who *p* nor he who
9:7 Who *p* a vineyard and does not eat

PLATTER

Mk 6:25 head of John the Baptist on a *p*."

PLAY (PLAYED)

1Sa 16:23 David would take his harp and *p*.
Isa 11:8 The infant will *p* near the hole

PLAYED (PLAY)

Lk 7:32 "'We *p* the flute for you,
1Co 14:7 anyone know what tune is being *p*

PLEA (PLEAD PLEADED PLEADS)

1Ki 8:28 to your servant's prayer and his *p*
Ps 102:17 he will not despise their *p*.
La 3:56 You heard my *p*: "Do not close

PLEAD (PLEA)

Isa 1:17 *p* the case of the widow.

PLEADED (PLEA)

2Co 12:8 Three times I *p* with the Lord

PLEADS (PLEA)

Job 16:21 on behalf of a man he *p* with God

PLEASANT (PLEASE)

Ge 49:15 and how *p* is his land,
Ps 16:6 for me in *p* places;
133:1 How good and *p* it is
135:3 sing praise to his name, for that is *p*
147:1 how *p* and fitting to praise him!
Pr 2:10 knowledge will be *p* to your soul.
3:17 Her ways are *p* ways,
16:21 and *p* words promote instruction.
16:24 *P* words are a honeycomb,
Isa 30:10 Tell us *p* things,
1Th 3:6 that you always have *p* memories
Heb 12:11 No discipline seems *p* at the time,

PLEASANTNESS* (PLEASE)

Pr 27:9 the *p* of one's friend springs

PLEASE (PLEASANT PLEASANTNESS PLEASED PLEASES PLEASING PLEASURE PLEASURES)

Ps 69:31 This will *p* the LORD more
Pr 20:23 and dishonest scales do not *p* him.
Isa 46:10 and I will do all that I *p*.
Jer 6:20 your sacrifices do not *p* me."
27:5 and I give it to anyone I *p*.
Jn 5:30 for I seek not to *p* myself
Ro 8:8 by the sinful nature cannot *p* God.
15:1 of the weak and not to *p* ourselves.
15:2 Each of us should *p* his neighbour
1Co 7:32 affairs—how he can *p* the Lord.
10:33 I try to *p* everybody in every way.
2Co 5:9 So we make it our goal to *p* him,
Gal 1:10 or of God? Or am I trying to *p* men
6:8 the one who sows to *p* the Spirit,
Col 1:10 and may *p* him in every way:
1Th 2:4 We are not trying to *p* men
4:1 how to live in order to *p* God,
2Ti 2:4 wants to *p* his commanding officer.
Tit 2:9 to try to *p* them, not to talk back
Heb 11:6 faith it is impossible to *p* God,

PLEASED (PLEASE)

Dt 28:63 as it *p* the LORD to make you
1Sa 12:22 LORD was *p* to make you his own.
1Ki 3:10 The Lord was *p* that Solomon had
1Ch 29:17 that you test the heart and are *p*
Mic 6:7 Will the LORD be *p*
Mal 1:10 I am not *p* with you," says
Mt 3:17 whom I love; with him I am well *p*
17:5 whom I love; with him I am well *p*.
Mk 1:11 whom I love; with you I am well *p*
Lk 3:22 whom I love; with you I am well *p*
1Co 1:21 God was *p* through the foolishness
Col 1:19 For God was *p* to have all his
Heb 10:6 you were not *p*.
10:8 nor were you *p* with them"
10:38 I will not be *p* with him."
11:5 commended as one who *p* God.
13:16 for with such sacrifices God is *p*.
2Pe 1:17 whom I love; with him I am well *p*

PLEASES (PLEASE)

Job 23:13 He does whatever he *p*.
Ps 115:3 he does whatever *p* him.
135:6 The LORD does whatever *p* him,
Pr 15:8 but the prayer of the upright *p* him.
21:1 it like a watercourse wherever he *p*.
Ecc 2:26 To the man who *p* him, God gives
7:26 man who *p* God will escape her,
Da 4:35 He does as he *p*
Jn 3:8 The wind blows wherever it *p*.
8:29 for I always do what *p* him."
Eph 5:10 truth) and find out what *p* the Lord
Col 3:20 in everything, for this *p* the Lord.
1Ti 2:3 This is good, and *p* God our Saviour,
1Jn 3:22 his commands and do what *p* him.

PLEASING (PLEASE)

Ge 2:9 trees that were *p* to the eye
Lev 1:9 an aroma *p* to the LORD.
Ps 19:14 be *p* in your sight,
104:34 May my meditation be *p* to him,
Pr 15:26 but those of the pure are *p* to him.
16:7 When a man's ways are *p*
SS 1:3 *P* is the fragrance of your perfumes
4:10 How much more *p* is your love
7:6 How beautiful you are and how *p*,
Ro 12:1 *p* to God—which is your spiritual
14:18 Christ in this way is *p* to God
Php 4:18 an acceptable sacrifice, *p* to God.
1Ti 5:4 grandparents, for this is *p* to God.
Heb 13:21 may he work in us what is *p* to him,

PLEASURE (PLEASE)

Ps 5:4 You are not a God who takes *p*
51:16 you do not take *p* in burnt offerings
147:10 His *p* is not in the strength
Pr 10:23 A fool finds *p* in evil conduct,
18:2 A fool finds no *p* in understanding
21:17 He who loves *p* will become poor;

Isa 1: 11 I have no *p*
Jer 6: 10 they find no *p* in it.
Eze 18: 23 Do I take any *p* in the death
18: 32 For I take no *p* in the death
33: 11 I take no *p* in the death
Lk 10: 21 Father, for this was your good *p*.
Eph 1: 5 in accordance with his *p* and will—
1: 9 of his will according to his good *p*,
1Ti 5: 6 the widow who lives for *p* is dead
2Ti 3: 4 lovers of *p* rather than lovers
2Pe 2: 13 Their idea of *p* is to carouse

PLEASURES* (PLEASE)

Ps 16: 11 with eternal *p* at your right hand.
Lk 8: 14 and *p*, and they do not mature.
Tit 3: 3 by all kinds of passions and *p*.
Heb 11: 25 rather than to enjoy the *p* of sin
Jas 4: 3 may spend what you get on your *p*.
2Pe 2: 13 revelling in their *p* while they feast

PLEDGE

Dt 24: 17 take the cloak of the widow as a *p*.
1Pe 3: 21 but the *p* of a good conscience

PLEIADES

Job 38: 31 "Can you bind the beautiful *P*?
Am 5: 8 (he who made the *P* and Orion,

PLENTIFUL (PLENTY)

Mt 9: 37 harvest is *p* but the workers are
Lk 10: 2 harvest is *p*, but the workers are

PLENTY (PLENTIFUL)

2Co 8: 14 the present time your *p* will supply
Php 4: 12 whether living in *p* or in want.

PLOT (PLOTS)

Est 2: 22 Mordecai found out about the *p*
Ps 2: 1 and the peoples *p* in vain?
Pr 3: 29 not *p* harm against your neighbour,
Zec 8: 17 do not *p* evil against your neighbour,
Ac 4: 25 and the peoples *p* in vain?

PLOTS (PLOT)

Pr 6: 14 who *p* evil with deceit in his heart

PLOUGH (PLOUGHMAN PLOUGHSHARES)

Lk 9: 62 "No-one who puts his hand to the *p*

PLOUGHMAN (PLOUGH)

1Co 9: 10 because when the *p* ploughs

PLOUGHSHARES (PLOUGH)

1Sa 13: 20 to the Philistines to have their *p*,
Isa 2: 4 They will beat their swords into *p*
Joel 3: 10 Beat your *p* into swords
Mic 4: 3 They will beat their swords into *p*

PLUCK

Mk 9: 47 your eye causes you to sin, *p* it out.

PLUNDER (PLUNDERED)

Ex 3: 22 And so you will *p* the Egyptians."
Est 3: 13 of Adar, and to *p* their goods.
8: 11 to *p* the property of their enemies.
9: 10 did not lay their hands on the *p*.
Pr 22: 23 and will *p* those who *p* them.
Isa 3: 14 the *p* from the poor is

PLUNDERED (PLUNDER)

Eze 34: 8 lacks a shepherd and so has been *p*

PLUNGE

1Ti 6: 9 and harmful desires that *p* men
1Pe 4: 4 think it strange that you do not *p*

PODS

Lk 15: 16 with the *p* that the pigs were eating,

POINT

Mt 4: 5 on the highest *p* of the temple.
26: 38 with sorrow to the *p* of death.
Jas 2: 10 yet stumbles at just one *p* is guilty
Rev 2: 10 Be faithful, even to the *p* of death,

POISON

Ps 140: 3 the *p* of vipers is on their lips.
Mk 16: 18 and when they drink deadly *p*,
Ro 3: 13 "The *p* of vipers is on their lips."
Jas 3: 8 It is a restless evil, full of deadly *p*.

POLE (POLES)

Nu 21: 8 "Make a snake and put it up on a *p*;
Dt 16: 21 not set up any wooden Asherah *p*

POLES (POLE)

Ex 25: 13 Then make *p* of acacia wood

POLISHED

Isa 49: 2 he made me into a *p* arrow

POLLUTE* (POLLUTED POLLUTES)

Nu 35: 33 "'Do not *p* the land where you are.
Jude : 8 these dreamers *p* their own bodies,

POLLUTED* (POLLUTE)

Ezr 9: 11 entering to possess is a land *p*
Pr 25: 26 Like a muddied spring or a *p* well
Ac 15: 20 to abstain from food *p* by idols,
Jas 1: 27 oneself from being *p* by the world.

POLLUTES* (POLLUTE)

Nu 35: 33 Bloodshed *p* the land,

PONDER (PONDERED)

Ps 64: 9 and *p* what he has done.
119: 95 but I will *p* your statutes.

PONDERED (PONDER)

Ps 111: 2 they are *p* by all who delight
Lk 2: 19 up all these things and *p* them

POOR (POVERTY)

Lev 19: 10 Leave them for the *p* and the alien.
23: 22 Leave them for the *p* and the alien.
27: 8 If anyone making the vow is too *p*
Dt 15: 4 there should be no *p* among you,
15: 7 is a *p* man among your brothers
15: 11 There will always be *p* people
24: 12 If the man is *p*, do not go to sleep
24: 14 advantage of a hired man who is *p*
Job 5: 16 So the *p* have hope,
24: 4 force all the *p* of the land
Ps 14: 6 frustrate the plans of the *p*,
34: 6 This *p* man called, and the LORD
35: 10 You rescue the *p* from those too
40: 17 Yet I am *p* and needy;
68: 10 O God, you provided for the *p*.
82: 3 maintain the rights of the *p*
112: 9 scattered abroad his gifts to the *p*,
113: 7 He raises the *p* from the dust
140: 12 the LORD secures justice for the *p*
Pr 10: 4 Lazy hands make a man *p*,
13: 7 to be *p*, yet has great wealth.
14: 20 The *p* are shunned
14: 31 oppresses the *p* shows contempt
17: 5 who mocks the *p* shows contempt
19: 1 Better a *p* man whose walk is
19: 17 to the *p* lends to the LORD,
19: 22 better to be *p* than a liar.
20: 13 not love sleep or you will grow *p*;
21: 13 to the cry of the *p*,
21: 17 who loves pleasure will become *p*;
22: 2 Rich and *p* have this in common:
22: 9 for he shares his food with the *p*.
22: 22 not exploit the *p* because they are *p*
28: 6 Better a *p* man whose walk is
28: 27 to the *p* will lack nothing,
29: 7 care about justice for the *p*,
31: 9 defend the rights of the *p*
31: 20 She opens her arms to the *p*
Ecc 4: 13 Better a *p* but wise youth
Isa 3: 14 the plunder from the *p* is
10: 2 to deprive the *p* of their rights
14: 30 of the *p* will find pasture,
25: 4 You have been a refuge for the *p*,
32: 7 schemes to destroy the *p* with lies,
61: 1 me to preach good news to the *p*.
Jer 22: 16 He defended the cause of the *p*
Eze 18: 12 He oppresses the *p* and needy.
Am 2: 7 They trample on the heads of the *p*
4: 1 you women who oppress the *p*
5: 11 You trample on the *p*
Zec 7: 10 or the fatherless, the alien or the *p*.
Mt 5: 3 saying: "Blessed are the *p* in spirit,
11: 5 the good news is preached to the *p*.
19: 21 your possessions and give to the *p*,
26: 11 The *p* you will always have
Mk 12: 42 But a *p* widow came and put
14: 7 The *p* you will always have
Lk 4: 18 me to preach good news to the *p*.
6: 20 "Blessed are you who are *p*,
11: 41 is inside ⌊the dish⌋ to the *p*,
14: 13 invite the *p*, the crippled, the lame,
21: 2 also saw a *p* widow put
Jn 12: 8 You will always have the *p*
Ac 9: 36 doing good and helping the *p*.
10: 4 and gifts to the *p* have come up
24: 17 to bring my people gifts for the *p*
Ro 15: 26 for the *p* among the saints
1Co 13: 3 If I give all I possess to the *p*
2Co 6: 10 sorrowful, yet always rejoicing; *p*,
8: 9 yet for your sakes he became *p*,
Gal 2: 10 continue to remember the *p*,
Jas 2: 2 and a *p* man in shabby clothes
2: 5 not God chosen those who are *p*
2: 6 But you have insulted the *p*.

POPULATION*

Pr 14: 28 A large *p* is a king's glory,

PORTION

Nu 18: 29 as the LORD's *p* the best
Dt 32: 9 For the LORD's *p* is his people,
1Sa 1: 5 But to Hannah he gave a double *p*
2Ki 2: 9 "Let me inherit a double *p*
Ps 73: 26 and my *p* for ever.
119: 57 You are my *p*, O LORD;
Isa 53: 12 Therefore I will give him a *p*
Jer 10: 16 He who is the *P* of Jacob is not like
La 3: 24 to myself, "The LORD is my *p*;
Zec 2: 12 LORD will inherit Judah as his *p*

PORTRAIT

Lk 20: 24 Whose *p* and inscription are on it?"

PORTRAYED

Gal 3: 1 very eyes Jesus Christ was clearly *p*

POSITION (POSITIONS)

Ro 12: 16 to associate with people of low *p*.
Jas 1: 9 ought to take pride in his high *p*.
2Pe 3: 17 and fall from your secure *p*.

POSITIONS (POSITION)

2Ch 20: 17 Take up your *p*; stand firm
Jude : 6 the angels who did not keep their *p*

POSSESS (POSSESSED POSSESSING POSSESSION POSSESSIONS)

Nu 33: 53 for I have given you the land to *p*.
Dt 4: 14 you are crossing the Jordan to *p*.
Pr 8: 12 I *p* knowledge and discretion.
Jn 5: 39 that by them you *p* eternal life.

POSSESSED (POSSESS)

Jn 10: 21 the sayings of a man *p* by a demon.

POSSESSING* (POSSESS)

2Co 6: 10 nothing, and yet *p* everything.

POSSESSION (POSSESS)

Ge 15: 7 to give you this land to take *p* of it
Ex 6: 8 I will give it to you as a *p*.
19: 5 nations you will be my treasured *p*.
Nu 13: 30 "We should go up and take *p*
Dt 7: 6 to be his people, his treasured *p*.
Jos 1: 11 take *p* of the land the LORD your

2Sa 22: 4 to the LORD, who is worthy of *p*,
22: 47 The LORD lives! *P* be to my Rock
1Ch 16: 25 is the LORD and most worthy of *p*;
16: 35 that we may glory in your *p*."
23: 5 four thousand are to *p* the LORD
29: 10 "*P* be to you, O LORD,
2Ch 5: 13 they raised their voices in *p*
20: 21 and to *p* him for the splendour
29: 30 to *p* the LORD with the words
Ezr 3: 10 took their places to *p* the LORD,
Ne 9: 5 and *p* the LORD your God,
Ps 8: 2 you have ordained *p*
9: 1 I will *p* you, O LORD,
16: 7 I will *p* the LORD, who counsels
26: 7 proclaiming aloud your *p*
30: 4 *p* his holy name.
33: 1 it is fitting for the upright to *p* him.
34: 1 his *p* will always be on my lips.
40: 3 a hymn of *p* to our God.
42: 5 for I will yet *p* him,
43: 5 for I will yet *p* him,
45: 17 the nations will *p* you for ever
47: 7 sing to him a psalm of *p*.
48: 1 the LORD, and most worthy of *p*,
51: 15 and my mouth will declare your *p*.
56: 4 In God, whose word I *p*,
57: 9 I will *p* you, O Lord,
63: 4 I will *p* you as long as I live,
65: 1 *P* awaits you, O God, in Zion;
66: 2 offer him glory and *p*!
66: 8 *P* our God, O peoples,
68: 19 *P* be to the Lord, to God our Saviour
68: 26 *p* the LORD in the assembly
69: 30 I will *p* God's name in song
69: 34 Let heaven and earth *p* him,
71: 8 My mouth is filled with your *p*,
71: 14 I will *p* you more and more.
71: 22 I will *p* you with the harp
74: 21 the poor and needy *p* your name.
86: 12 I will *p* you, O Lord my God,
89: 5 The heavens *p* your wonders,
92: 1 It is good to *p* the LORD
96: 2 Sing to the LORD, *p* his name;
100: 4 and his courts with *p*;
101: 1 to you, O LORD, I will sing *p*.
102: 18 not yet created may *p* the LORD:
103: 1 *P* the LORD, O my soul;
103: 20 *P* the LORD, you his angels,
104: 1 *P* the LORD, O my soul.
105: 2 Sing to him, sing *p* to him;
106: 1 *P* the LORD.
108: 3 I will *p* you, O LORD,
111: 1 *P* the LORD.
113: 1 *P* the LORD.
117: 1 *P* the LORD, all you nations;
119: 175 Let me live that I may *p* you,
135: 1 *P* the LORD.
135: 20 you who fear him, *p* the LORD.
138: 1 I will *p* you, O LORD,
139: 14 I *p* you because I am fearfully
144: 1 *P* be to the LORD, my Rock,
145: 3 is the LORD and most worthy of *p*;
145: 10 All you have made will *p* you,
145: 21 Let every creature *p* his holy name
146: 1 *P* the LORD, O my soul.
147: 1 how pleasant and fitting to *p* him!
148: 1 *P* the LORD from the heavens,
148: 13 Let them *p* the name of the LORD,
149: 1 his *p* in the assembly of the saints.
149: 6 May the *p* of God be
149: 9 *P* the LORD.
150: 2 *p* him for his surpassing greatness.
150: 6 that has breath *p* the LORD.
Pr 27: 2 Let another *p* you, and not your
27: 21 man is tested by the *p* he receives.
31: 31 let her works bring her *p*
SS 1: 4 we will *p* your love more than wine
Isa 12: 1 "I will *p* you, O LORD.
42: 10 his *p* from the ends of the earth,
61: 3 and a garment of *p*
Jer 33: 9 *p* and honour before all nations
Da 2: 20 "*P* be to the name of God for ever
4: 37 *p* and exalt and glorify the King
Mt 5: 16 and *p* your Father in heaven.
21: 16 you have ordained *p*'?"
Lk 19: 37 to *p* God in loud voices
Jn 5: 44 effort to obtain the *p* that comes
12: 43 for they loved *p* from men more
Ro 2: 29 Such a man's *p* is not from men,
15: 7 in order to bring *p* to God.
2Co 1: 3 *P* be to the God and Father
Eph 1: 3 *P* be to the God and Father
1: 6 to the *p* of his glorious grace,
1: 12 might be for the *p* of his glory.
1: 14 to the *p* of his glory.
1Th 2: 6 We were not looking for *p*
Heb 13: 15 offer to God a sacrifice of *p*—
Jas 3: 9 With the tongue we *p* our Lord
5: 13 happy? Let him sing songs of *p*.
Rev 5: 13 be *p* and honour and glory
7: 12 *P* and glory

PRAISED (PRAISE)

1Ch 29: 10 David *p* the LORD in the presence
Ne 8: 6 Ezra *p* the LORD, the great God;
Job 1: 21 may the name of the LORD be *p*."
Ps 113: 2 Let the name of the LORD be *p*,
Pr 31: 30 who fears the LORD is to be *p*.
Isa 63: 7 the deeds for which he is to be *p*,
Da 2: 19 Then Daniel *p* the God of heaven
4: 34 Then I *p* the Most High; I honoured
Lk 18: 43 the people saw it, they also *p* God.
23: 47 seeing what had happened, *p* God
Ro 9: 5 who is God over all, for ever *p*!
Gal 1: 24 And they *p* God because of me.
1Pe 4: 11 that in all things God may be *p*

PRAISES (PRAISE)

2Sa 22: 50 I will sing *p* to your name.
Ps 18: 49 I will sing *p* to your name.
47: 6 Sing *p* to God, sing *p*;
147: 1 How good it is to sing *p* to our God,
Pr 31: 28 her husband also, and he *p* her:
1Pe 2: 9 that you may declare the *p*

PRAISEWORTHY* (PRAISE)

Ps 78: 4 the *p* deeds of the LORD,
Php 4: 8 if anything is excellent or *p*—

PRAISING (PRAISE)

Lk 2: 13 *p* God and saying, "Glory to God
2: 20 *p* God for all the things they had
Ac 2: 47 *p* God and enjoying the favour
10: 46 speaking in tongues and *p* God.
1Co 14: 16 If you are *p* God with your spirit,

PRAY (PRAYED PRAYER PRAYERS PRAYING PRAYS)

Dt 4: 7 is near us whenever we *p* to him?
1Sa 12: 23 the LORD by failing to *p* for you.
1Ki 8: 30 when they *p* towards this place.
2Ch 7: 14 will humble themselves and *p*
Ezr 6: 10 and *p* for the well-being of the king
Job 42: 8 My servant Job will *p* for you,
Ps 5: 2 for to you I *p*.
32: 6 let everyone who is godly *p*
122: 6 *P* for the peace of Jerusalem:
Jer 29: 7 *P* to the LORD for it,
29: 12 upon me and come and *p* to me,
42: 3 *P* that the LORD your God will
Mt 5: 44 and *p* for those who persecute you,
6: 5 "But when you *p*, do not be like
6: 9 "This is how you should *p*:
14: 23 up into the hills by himself to *p*.
19: 13 hands on them and *p* for them.
26: 36 Sit here while I go over there and *p*
Lk 6: 28 *p* for those who ill-treat you.
11: 1 us to *p*, just as John taught his
18: 1 them that they should always *p*
22: 40 "*P* that you will not fall
Jn 17: 20 I *p* also for those who will believe
Ro 8: 26 do not know what we ought to *p*,
1Co 14: 13 in a tongue should *p* that he may
Eph 1: 18 I *p* also that the eyes
3: 16 I *p* that out of his glorious riches he
6: 18 And *p* in the Spirit on all occasions
Col 1: 10 we *p* this in order that you may live
4: 3 *p* for us, too, that God may open
1Th 5: 17 Be joyful always; *p* continually;
2Th 1: 11 in mind, we constantly *p* for you,
Jas 5: 13 one of you in trouble? He should *p*.
5: 16 *p* for each other so that you may be
1Pe 4: 7 self-controlled so that you can *p*.
Jude : 20 up in your most holy faith and *p*

PRAYED (PRAY)

1Sa 1: 27 I *p* for this child, and the LORD
1Ki 18: 36 Elijah stepped forward and *p*:
19: 4 under it and *p* that he might die.
2Ki 6: 17 And Elisha *p*, "O LORD,
2Ch 30: 18 But Hezekiah *p* for them, saying,
Ne 4: 9 we *p* to our God and posted a guard
Job 42: 10 After Job had *p* for his friends,
Da 6: 10 got down on his knees and *p*,
9: 4 I *p* to the LORD my God
Jnh 2: 1 From inside the fish Jonah *p*
Mt 26: 39 with his face to the ground and *p*,
Mk 1: 35 off to a solitary place, where he *p*.
14: 35 *p* that if possible the hour might
Lk 22: 41 knelt down and *p*, "Father,
Jn 17: 1 he looked towards heaven and *p*:
Ac 4: 31 After they *p*, the place where they
6: 6 who *p* and laid their hands on them
8: 15 they *p* for them that they might
13: 3 So after they had fasted and *p*,

PRAYER (PRAY)

2Ch 30: 27 for their *p* reached heaven,
Ezr 8: 23 about this, and he answered our *p*.
Ps 4: 1 be merciful to me and hear my *p*.
6: 9 the LORD accepts my *p*.
17: 1 Give ear to my *p*—
17: 6 give ear to me and hear my *p*.
65: 2 O you who hear *p*,
66: 20 who has not rejected my *p*
86: 6 Hear my *p*, O LORD;
Pr 15: 8 but the *p* of the upright pleases him
15: 29 but he hears the *p* of the righteous.
Isa 56: 7 a house of *p* for all nations."
Mt 21: 13 house will be called a house of *p*,'
21: 22 receive whatever you ask for in *p*."
Mk 9: 29 This kind can come out only by *p*."
11: 24 whatever you ask for in *p*,
Jn 17: 15 My *p* is not that you take them out
Ac 1: 14 all joined together constantly in *p*,
2: 42 to the breaking of bread and to *p*.
6: 4 and will give our attention to *p*
10: 31 has heard your *p* and remembered
16: 13 expected to find a place of *p*.
Ro 12: 12 patient in affliction, faithful in *p*.
1Co 7: 5 you may devote yourselves to *p*.
2Co 13: 9 and our *p* is for your perfection.
Php 1: 9 this is my *p*: that your love may
4: 6 but in everything, by *p* and petition
Col 4: 2 yourselves to *p*, being watchful
1Ti 2: 8 to lift up holy hands in *p*,
4: 5 by the word of God and *p*.
Jas 5: 15 *p* offered in faith will make the sick
1Pe 3: 12 and his ears are attentive to their *p*,

PRAYERS (PRAY)

1Ch 5: 20 He answered their *p*, because they
Isa 1: 15 even if you offer many *p*,
Mk 12: 40 and for a show make lengthy *p*.
2Co 1: 11 as you help us by your *p*.
Eph 6: 18 on all occasions with all kinds of *p*
1Ti 2: 1 then, first of all, that requests, *p*,
1Pe 3: 7 so that nothing will hinder your *p*.
Rev 5: 8 which are the *p* of the saints.
8: 3 with the *p* of all the saints,

PRAYING (PRAY)

Ge 24: 45 "Before I finished *p* in my heart,
1Sa 1: 12 As she kept on *p* to the LORD,
Mk 11: 25 And when you stand *p*,
Lk 3: 21 as he was *p*, heaven was opened
6: 12 and spent the night *p* to God.
9: 29 As he was *p*, the appearance
Jn 17: 9 I am not *p* for the world,

Ac 9: 11 from Tarsus named Saul, for he is *p*
16: 25 and Silas were *p* and singing hymns
Ro 15: 30 in my struggle by *p* to God for me.
Eph 6: 18 always keep on *p* for all the saints.

PRAYS (PRAY)

1Co 14: 14 my spirit *p*, but my mind is

PREACH (PREACHED PREACHING)

Isa 61: 1 me to *p* good news to the poor.
Mt 10: 7 As you go, *p* this message:
23: 3 they do not practise what they *p*.
Mk 16: 15 and *p* the good news to all creation.
Lk 4: 18 me to *p* good news to the poor.
Ac 9: 20 At once he began to *p*
16: 10 us to *p* the gospel to them.
Ro 1: 15 am so eager to *p* the gospel
10: 15 how can they *p* unless they are sent
15: 20 to *p* the gospel where Christ was
1Co 1: 17 to *p* the gospel—not with words
1: 23 wisdom, but we *p* Christ crucified:
9: 14 that those who *p* the gospel should
9: 16 Woe to me if I do not *p* the gospel!
2Co 4: 5 For we do not *p* ourselves,
10: 16 so that we can *p* the gospel
Gal 1: 8 from heaven should *p* a gospel
2Ti 4: 2 I give you this charge: *P* the Word;

PREACHED (PREACH)

Mt 24: 14 gospel of the kingdom will be *p*
Mk 6: 12 and *p* that people should repent.
13: 10 And the gospel must first be *p*
14: 9 wherever the gospel is *p*
Ac 8: 4 had been scattered *p* the word
28: 31 hindrance he *p* the kingdom
1Co 9: 27 so that after I have *p* to others,
15: 1 you of the gospel I *p* to you,
2Co 11: 4 other than the Jesus we *p*,
Gal 1: 8 other than the one we *p* to you,
Eph 2: 17 *p* peace to you who were far away
Php 1: 18 false motives or true, Christ is *p*.
1Ti 3: 16 was *p* among the nations,
1Pe 1: 25 this is the word that was *p* to you.
3: 19 and *p* to the spirits in prison who

PREACHING (PREACH)

Lk 9: 6 *p* the gospel and healing people
Ac 18: 5 devoted himself exclusively to *p*,
Ro 10: 14 hear without someone *p* to them?
1Co 2: 4 and my *p* were not with wise
9: 18 in *p* the gospel I may offer it free
Gal 1: 9 If anybody is *p* to you a gospel
1Ti 4: 13 the public reading of Scripture, to *p*
5: 17 especially those whose work is *p*

PRECEDE*

1Th 4: 15 will certainly not *p* those who have

PRECEPTS*

Dt 33: 10 He teaches your *p* to Jacob
Ps 19: 8 The *p* of the LORD are right,
103: 18 and remember to obey his *p*.
105: 45 that they might keep his *p*
111: 7 all his *p* are trustworthy.
111: 10 who follow his *p* have good
119: 4 You have laid down *p*
119: 15 I meditate on your *p*
119: 27 understand the teaching of your *p*;
119: 40 How I long for your *p*!
119: 45 for I have sought out your *p*.
119: 56 I obey your *p*.
119: 63 to all who follow your *p*.
119: 69 I keep your *p* with all my heart.
119: 78 but I will meditate on your *p*.
119: 87 but I have not forsaken your *p*.
119: 93 I will never forget your *p*,
119: 94 I have sought out your *p*.
119: 100 for I obey your *p*.
119: 104 I gain understanding from your *p*;
119: 110 but I have not strayed from your *p*.
119: 128 because I consider all your *p* right,
119: 134 that I may obey your *p*.

Ps 119: 141 I do not forget your *p*.
119: 159 See how I love your *p*;
119: 168 I obey your *p* and your statutes,
119: 173 for I have chosen your *p*.

PRECIOUS

Ps 19: 10 They are more *p* than gold,
72: 14 for *p* is their blood in his sight.
116: 15 *P* in the sight of the LORD
119: 72 from your mouth is more *p* to me
139: 17 How *p* to me are your thoughts,
Pr 8: 11 for wisdom is more *p* than rubies,
Isa 28: 16 a *p* cornerstone for a sure
1Pe 1: 19 but with the *p* blood of Christ,
2: 4 but chosen by God and *p* to him—
2: 6 a chosen and *p* cornerstone,
2Pe 1: 1 Christ have received a faith as *p*
1: 4 us his very great and *p* promises,

PREDESTINED* (DESTINY)

Ro 8: 29 *p* to be conformed to the likeness
8: 30 And those he *p*, he also called;
Eph 1: 5 In love he *p* us to be adopted
1: 11 having been *p* according

PREDICTED (PREDICTION)

1Sa 28: 17 The LORD has done what he *p*
Ac 7: 52 killed those who *p* the coming
1Pe 1: 11 when he *p* the sufferings of Christ

PREDICTION* (PREDICTED PREDICTIONS)

Jer 28: 9 only if his *p* comes true."

PREDICTIONS (PREDICTION)

Isa 44: 26 and fulfils the *p* of his messengers,

PREGNANT

Ex 21: 22 who are fighting hit a *p* woman
Mt 24: 19 be in those days for *p* women
1Th 5: 3 as labour pains on a *p* woman.

PREPARE (PREPARED)

Ps 23: 5 You *p* a table before me
Isa 25: 6 the LORD Almighty will *p*
40: 3 "In the desert *p*
Am 4: 12 *p* to meet your God, O Israel."
Mal 3: 1 who will *p* the way before me.
Mt 3: 3 '*P* the way for the Lord,
Jn 14: 2 there to *p* a place for you.
Eph 4: 12 to *p* God's people for works
1Pe 1: 13 Therefore, *p* your minds for action;

PREPARED (PREPARE)

Ex 23: 20 to bring you to the place I have *p*.
Mt 25: 34 the kingdom *p* for you
Ro 9: 22 of his wrath—*p* for destruction?
1Co 2: 9 what God has *p* for those who love
Eph 2: 10 which God *p* in advance for us
2Ti 2: 21 and *p* to do any good work.
4: 2 be *p* in season and out of season;
1Pe 3: 15 Always be *p* to give an answer

PRESCRIBED

Ezr 7: 23 Whatever the God of heaven has *p*,

PRESENCE (PRESENT [1])

Ex 25: 30 Put the bread of the *P* on this table
33: 14 The LORD replied, "My *P* will go
Nu 4: 7 "Over the table of the *P* they are
1Sa 6: 20 in the *p* of the LORD, this
21: 6 of the *P* that had been removed
2Sa 22: 13 Out of the brightness of his *p*
2Ki 17: 23 LORD removed them from his *p*,
23: 27 also from my *p* as I removed Israel,
Ezr 9: 15 one of us can stand in your *p*."
Ps 16: 11 you will fill me with joy in your *p*,
21: 6 with the joy of your *p*.
23: 5 in the *p* of my enemies.
31: 20 the shelter of your *p* you hide them
41: 12 and set me in your *p* for ever.
51: 11 Do not cast me from your *p*
52: 9 in the *p* of your saints.

Ps 89: 15 who walk in the light of your *p*,
90: 8 our secret sins in the light of your *p*
114: 7 O earth, at the *p* of the Lord,
139: 7 Where can I flee from your *p*?
Isa 26: 17 so were we in your *p*, O LORD.
Jer 5: 22 "Should you not tremble in my *p*?
Eze 38: 20 of the earth will tremble at my *p*.
Hos 6: 2 that we may live in his *p*.
Na 1: 5 The earth trembles at his *p*,
Mal 3: 16 in his *p* concerning those who
Ac 2: 28 you will fill me with joy in your *p*.'
1Th 3: 9 have in the *p* of our God
3: 13 and holy in the *p* of our God
2Th 1: 9 and shut out from the *p* of the Lord
Heb 9: 24 now to appear for us in God's *p*.
1Jn 3: 19 rest in his *p* whenever our hearts
Jude : 24 before his glorious *p* without fault

PRESENT [1] (PRESENCE)

Ps 46: 1 an ever *p* help in trouble.
1Co 3: 22 life or death or the *p* or the future—
7: 26 of the *p* crisis, I think that it is good
1Ti 4: 8 holding promise for both the *p* life

PRESENT [2]

2Co 11: 2 so that I might *p* you as a pure
Eph 5: 27 and to *p* her to himself
2Ti 2: 15 Do your best to *p* yourself to God
Jude : 24 and to *p* you before his glorious

PRESERVE

Lk 17: 33 and whoever loses his life will *p* it.

PRESS (PRESSED PRESSURE)

Php 3: 12 but I *p* on to take hold of that
3: 14 I *p* on towards the goal

PRESSED (PRESS)

Lk 6: 38 *p* down, shaken together

PRESSURE (PRESS)

2Co 1: 8 We were under great *p*, far
11: 28 I face daily the *p* of my concern

PREVAILS

1Sa 2: 9 "It is not by strength that one *p*;
Pr 19: 21 but it is the LORD's purpose that *p*

PRICE (PRICELESS)

Job 28: 18 the *p* of wisdom is beyond rubies.
1Co 6: 20 your own; you were bought at a *p*.
7: 23 bought at a *p*; do not become slaves

PRICELESS* (PRICE)

Ps 36: 7 How *p* is your unfailing love!

PRIDE (PROUD)

Pr 8: 13 I hate *p* and arrogance,
11: 2 When *p* comes, then comes
13: 10 *P* only breeds quarrels,
16: 18 *P* goes before destruction,
29: 23 A man's *p* brings him low,
Isa 25: 11 God will bring down their *p*
Da 4: 37 And those who walk in *p* he is able
Am 8: 7 The LORD has sworn by the *P*
2Co 5: 12 giving you an opportunity to take *p*
7: 4 in you; I take great *p* in you.
8: 24 and the reason for our *p* in you,
Gal 6: 4 Then he can take *p* in himself,
Jas 1: 9 ought to take *p* in his high position.

PRIEST (PRIESTHOOD PRIESTLY PRIESTS)

Ge 14: 18 He was *p* of God Most High,
Nu 5: 10 to the *p* will belong to the *p*.'"
2Ch 13: 9 and seven rams may become a *p*
Ps 110: 4 "You are a *p* for ever,
Heb 2: 17 faithful high *p* in service to God,
3: 1 and high *p* whom we confess.
4: 14 have a great high *p* who has gone
4: 15 do not have a high *p* who is unable
5: 6 "You are a *p* for ever,
6: 20 He has become a high *p* for ever,

Heb 7: 3 Son of God he remains a *p* for ever.
7: 15 clear if another *p* like Melchizedek
7: 26 Such a high *p* meets our need—
8: 1 We do have such a high *p*,
10: 11 Day after day every *p* stands
13: 11 The high *p* carries the blood

PRIESTHOOD (PRIEST)

Heb 7: 24 lives for ever, he has a permanent *p*.
1Pe 2: 5 into a spiritual house to be a holy *p*,
2: 9 you are a chosen people, a royal *p*,

PRIESTLY (PRIEST)

Ro 15: 16 to the Gentiles with the *p* duty.

PRIESTS (PRIEST)

Ex 19: 6 you will be for me a kingdom of *p*
Lev 21: 1 "Speak to the *p*, the sons of Aaron,
Eze 42: 13 where the *p* who approach
46: 2 *p* are to sacrifice his burnt offering
Rev 5: 10 to be a kingdom and *p*
20: 6 but they will be *p* of God

PRIME

Isa 38: 10 recovery: I said, "In the *p* of my life

PRINCE (PRINCES PRINCESS)

Isa 9: 6 Everlasting Father, *P* of Peace.
Eze 34: 24 and my servant David will be *p*
37: 25 my servant will be their *p* for ever.
Da 8: 25 stand against the *P* of princes.
Jn 12: 31 now the *p* of this world will be
Ac 5: 31 as *P* and Saviour that he might give

PRINCES (PRINCE)

Ps 118: 9 than to trust in *p*.
148: 11 you *p* and all rulers on earth,
Isa 40: 23 He brings *p* to naught

PRINCESS* (PRINCE)

Ps 45: 13 All glorious is the *p*

PRISCILLA*

Wife of Aquila; co-worker with Paul (Ac 18; Ro 16:3; 1Co 16:19; 2Ti 4:19); instructor of Apollos (Ac 18:24-28).

PRISON (PRISONER PRISONERS)

Ps 66: 11 You brought us into *p*
142: 7 Set me free from my *p*,
Isa 42: 7 to free captives from *p*
Mt 25: 36 I was in *p* and you came to visit me
2Co 11: 23 been in *p* more frequently,
Heb 11: 36 others were chained and put in *p*.
13: 3 Remember those in *p*
1Pe 3: 19 spirits in *p* who disobeyed long ago
Rev 20: 7 Satan will be released from his *p*

PRISONER (PRISON)

Ro 7: 23 and making me a *p* of the law of sin
Gal 3: 22 declares that the whole world is a *p*
Eph 3: 1 the *p* of Christ Jesus for the sake

PRISONERS (PRISON)

Ps 68: 6 he leads forth the *p* with singing;
79: 11 groans of the *p* come before you;
107: 10 *p* suffering in iron chains,
146: 7 The LORD sets *p* free,
Isa 61: 1 and release from darkness for the *p*,
Zec 9: 12 to your fortress, O *p* of hope;
Lk 4: 18 me to proclaim freedom for the *p*
Gal 3: 23 we were held *p* by the law,

PRIVILEGE*

2Co 8: 4 pleaded with us for the *p* of sharing

PRIZE*

1Co 9: 24 Run in such a way as to get the *p*.
9: 24 but only one gets the *p*? Run
9: 27 will not be disqualified for the *p*.
Php 3: 14 on towards the goal to win the *p*
Col 2: 18 of angels disqualify you for the *p*.

PROBE

Job 11: 7 Can you *p* the limits
Ps 17: 3 Though you *p* my heart

PROCEDURE

Ecc 8: 6 For there is a proper time and *p*

PROCESSION

Ps 68: 24 Your *p* has come into view, O God,
118: 27 boughs in hand, join in the festal *p*
1Co 4: 9 on display at the end of the *p*,
2Co 2: 14 us in triumphal *p* in Christ

PROCLAIM (PROCLAIMED PROCLAIMING PROCLAIMS PROCLAMATION)

Ex 33: 19 and I will *p* my name, the LORD,
Lev 25: 10 and *p* liberty throughout the land
Dt 30: 12 and *p* it to us so we may obey it?"
2Sa 1: 20 *p* it not in the streets of Ashkelon,
1Ch 16: 23 *p* his salvation day after day.
Ne 8: 15 and that they should *p* this word
Ps 2: 7 I will *p* the decree of the LORD:
9: 11 *p* among the nations what he has
19: 1 the skies *p* the work of his hands.
22: 31 They will *p* his righteousness
40: 9 I *p* righteousness in the great
50: 6 the heavens *p* his righteousness,
64: 9 they will *p* the works of God
68: 34 *P* the power of God,
71: 16 I will come and *p* your mighty acts,
92: 2 to *p* your love in the morning
96: 2 *p* his salvation day after day.
97: 6 The heavens *p* his righteousness,
106: 2 Who can *p* the mighty acts
118: 17 will *p* what the LORD has done.
145: 6 and I will *p* your great deeds.
Isa 12: 4 and *p* that his name is exalted.
42: 12 and *p* his praise in the islands.
52: 7 who *p* salvation,
61: 1 to *p* freedom for the captives
66: 19 They will *p* my glory
Jer 7: 2 house and there *p* this message:
50: 2 lift up a banner and *p* it;
Hos 5: 9 I *p* what is certain.
Zec 9: 10 He will *p* peace to the nations.
Mt 10: 27 in your ear, *p* from the housetops.
12: 18 and he will *p* justice to the nations.
Lk 4: 18 me to *p* freedom for the prisoners
9: 60 you go and *p* the kingdom of God."
Ac 17: 23 unknown I am going to *p*
20: 27 hesitated to *p* to you the whole will
1Co 11: 26 you *p* the Lord's death
Col 1: 28 We *p* him, admonishing
4: 4 Pray that I may *p* it clearly,
1Jn 1: 1 this we *p* concerning the Word

PROCLAIMED (PROCLAIM)

Ex 9: 16 and that my name might be *p*
34: 5 there with him and *p* his name,
Ps 68: 11 was the company of those who *p* it:
Ro 15: 19 I have fully *p* the gospel of Christ.
Col 1: 23 that has been *p* to every creature
2Ti 4: 17 me the message might be fully *p*

PROCLAIMING (PROCLAIM)

Ps 26: 7 *p* aloud your praise
92: 15 *p*, "The LORD is upright;
Ac 5: 42 and *p* the good news that Jesus is
Ro 10: 8 the word of faith we are *p*:

PROCLAIMS (PROCLAIM)

Dt 18: 22 If what a prophet *p* in the name

PROCLAMATION (PROCLAIM)

Isa 62: 11 The LORD has made *p*

PRODUCE (PRODUCES)

Mt 3: 8 *P* fruit in keeping with repentance.
3: 10 tree that does not *p* good fruit will

PRODUCES (PRODUCE)

Pr 30: 33 so stirring up anger *p* strife."

Ro 5: 3 that suffering *p* perseverance;
Heb 12: 11 it *p* a harvest of righteousness

PROFANE (PROFANED)

Lev 19: 12 and so *p* the name of your God.
22: 32 Do not *p* my holy name.
Mal 2: 10 Why do we *p* the covenant

PROFANED (PROFANE)

Eze 36: 20 the nations they *p* my holy name,

PROFESS*

1Ti 2: 10 for women who *p* to worship God.
Heb 4: 14 let us hold firmly to the faith we *p*.
10: 23 unswervingly to the hope we *p*,

PROFIT (PROFITABLE)

Pr 14: 23 All hard work brings a *p*,
21: 5 The plans of the diligent lead to *p*
Isa 44: 10 which can *p* him nothing?
2Co 2: 17 not peddle the word of God for *p*.
Php 3: 7 was to my *p* I now consider loss

PROFITABLE* (PROFIT)

Pr 3: 14 for she is more *p* than silver
31: 18 She sees that her trading is *p*,
Tit 3: 8 These things are excellent and *p*

PROFOUND

Job 9: 4 His wisdom is *p*, his power is vast.
Ps 92: 5 how *p* your thoughts!
Eph 5: 32 This is a *p* mystery—but I am

PROGRESS

Php 1: 25 continue with all of you for your *p*
1Ti 4: 15 so that everyone may see your *p*.

PROLONG*

Dt 5: 33 *p* your days in the land that you
Ps 85: 5 Will you *p* your anger
Pr 3: 2 for they will *p* your life many years
Isa 53: 10 will see his offspring and *p* his days,
La 4: 22 he will not *p* your exile.

PROMISE (PROMISED PROMISES)

Nu 23: 19 Does he *p* and not fulfil?
Jos 23: 14 Every *p* has been fulfilled;
2Sa 7: 25 keep for ever the *p* you have made
1Ki 8: 20 The LORD has kept the *p* he made
8: 24 You have kept your *p*
Ne 5: 13 man who does not keep this *p*.
9: 8 have kept your *p* because you are
Ps 77: 8 Has his *p* failed for all time?
119: 41 your salvation according to your *p*;
119: 50 Your *p* renews my life.
119: 58 to me according to your *p*.
119: 162 I rejoice in your *p*
Ac 2: 39 The *p* is for you and your children
Ro 4: 13 offspring received the *p* that he
4: 20 unbelief regarding the *p* of God,
Gal 3: 14 that by faith we might receive the *p*
Eph 2: 12 foreigners to the covenants of the *p*
1Ti 4: 8 holding *p* for both the present life
Heb 6: 13 When God made his *p* to Abraham
11: 11 him faithful who had made the *p*.
2Pe 3: 9 Lord is not slow in keeping his *p*,
3: 13 with his *p* we are looking forward

PROMISED (PROMISE)

Ge 21: 1 did for Sarah what he had *p*.
24: 7 who spoke to me and *p* me on oath,
Ex 3: 17 And I have *p* to bring you up out
Nu 10: 29 for the LORD has *p* good things
Dt 15: 6 your God will bless you as he has *p*,
26: 18 his treasured possession as he *p*,
2Sa 7: 28 you have *p* these good things
1Ki 9: 5 I *p* David your father when I said,
2Ch 6: 15 with your mouth you have *p*
Ps 119: 57 I have *p* to obey your words.
Lk 24: 49 to send you what my Father has *p*;
Ac 1: 4 but wait for the gift my Father *p*,

Ac 13: 32 What God *p* our fathers he has
Ro 4: 21 power to do what he had *p*.
Tit 1: 2 *p* before the beginning of time,
Heb 10: 23 for he who *p* is faithful.
10: 36 you will receive what he has *p*.
Jas 1: 12 the crown of life that God has *p*
2: 5 the kingdom he *p* those who love
2Pe 3: 4 "Where is this 'coming' he *p*?
1Jn 2: 25 And this is what he *p* us—

PROMISES (PROMISE)

Jos 21: 45 one of all the LORD's good *p*
23: 14 of all the good *p* the LORD your
1Ki 8: 56 failed of all the good *p* he gave
1Ch 17: 19 and made known all these great *p*.
Ps 85: 8 he *p* peace to his people, his saints
106: 12 Then they believed his *p*
119: 140 Your *p* have been thoroughly
119: 148 that I may meditate on your *p*.
145: 13 The LORD is faithful to all his *p*
Ro 9: 4 the temple worship and the *p*.
2Co 1: 20 matter how many *p* God has made,
7: 1 Since we have these *p*, dear friends,
Heb 8: 6 and it is founded on better *p*.
2Pe 1: 4 us his very great and precious *p*,

PROMOTE (PROMOTES)

Pr 12: 20 but joy for those who *p* peace.
16: 21 and pleasant words *p* instruction.
1Ti 1: 4 These *p* controversies rather

PROMOTES (PROMOTE)

Pr 17: 9 over an offence *p* love,

PROMPTED

1Th 1: 3 your labour *p* by love, and your
2Th 1: 11 and every act *p* by your faith.

PRONOUNCE (PRONOUNCED)

1Ch 23: 13 to *p* blessings in his name for ever.

PRONOUNCED (PRONOUNCE)

1Ch 16: 12 miracles, and the judgments he *p*,

PROOF (PROVE)

Ac 17: 31 He has given *p* of this to all men
2Co 8: 24 Therefore show these men the *p*

PROPER

Ps 104: 27 give them their food at the *p* time.
145: 15 give them their food at the *p* time.
Ecc 5: 18 Then I realised that it is good and *p*
8: 5 the wise heart will know the *p* time
Mt 24: 45 give them their food at the *p* time?
Lk 1: 20 which will come true at their *p* time
1Co 11: 13 Is it *p* for a woman to pray to God
Gal 6: 9 at the *p* time we will reap a harvest
1Ti 2: 6 the testimony given in its *p* time.
1Pe 2: 17 Show *p* respect to everyone:

PROPERTY

Heb 10: 34 the confiscation of your *p*,

PROPHECIES (PROPHESY)

1Co 13: 8 where there are *p*, they will cease;
1Th 5: 20 do not treat *p* with contempt.

PROPHECY (PROPHESY)

Da 9: 24 to seal up vision and *p*
1Co 12: 10 miraculous powers, to another *p*,
13: 2 of *p* and can fathom all mysteries
14: 1 gifts, especially the gift of *p*.
14: 6 or *p* or word of instruction?
14: 22 *p*, however, is for believers,
2Pe 1: 20 you must understand that no *p*
Rev 22: 18 the words of the *p* of this book:

PROPHESIED (PROPHESY)

Nu 11: 25 the Spirit rested on them, they *p*,
1Sa 19: 24 and also *p* in Samuel's presence.
Jn 11: 51 that year he *p* that Jesus would
Ac 19: 6 and they spoke in tongues and *p*.
21: 9 four unmarried daughters who *p*.

PROPHESIES (PROPHESY)

Jer 28: 9 the prophet who *p* peace will be
Eze 12: 27 and he *p* about the distant future.'
1Ch 11: 4 *p* with his head covered dishonours
14: 3 But everyone who *p* speaks to men

PROPHESY (PROPHECIES PROPHECY PROPHESIED PROPHESIES PROPHESYING PROPHET PROPHET'S PROPHETESS PROPHETS)

1Sa 10: 6 and you will *p* with them;
Eze 13: 2 Say to those who *p* out
13: 17 daughters of your people who *p* out
34: 2 *p* against the shepherds of Israel;
37: 4 "*P* to these bones and say to them,
Joel 2: 28 Your sons and daughters will *p*,
Mt 7: 22 Lord, did we not *p* in your name,
Ac 2: 17 Your sons and daughters will *p*,
1Co 13: 9 know in part and we *p* in part,
14: 39 my brothers, be eager to *p*,
Rev 11: 3 and they will *p* for 1,260 days,

PROPHESYING (PROPHESY)

1Ch 25: 1 and Jeduthun for the ministry of *p*,
Ro 12: 6 If a man's gift is *p*, let him use it

PROPHET (PROPHESY)

Ex 7: 1 your brother Aaron will be your *p*.
Nu 12: 6 "When a *p* of the LORD is
Dt 13: 1 If a *p*, or one who foretells
18: 18 up for them a *p* like you
18: 22 If what a *p* proclaims in the name
1Sa 3: 20 that Samuel was attested as a *p*
9: 9 because the *p* of today used
1Ki 1: 8 son of Jehoiada, Nathan the *p*,
18: 36 the *p* Elijah stepped forward
2Ki 5: 8 and he will know that there is a *p*
6: 12 "but Elisha, the *p* who is in Israel,
20: 1 The *p* Isaiah son of Amoz went
2Ch 35: 18 since the days of the *p* Samuel;
36: 12 himself before Jeremiah the *p*,
Ezr 5: 1 Haggai the *p* and Zechariah the *p*,
Eze 2: 5 they will know that a *p* has been
33: 33 they will know that a *p* has been
Hos 9: 7 the *p* is considered a fool,
Am 7: 14 "I was neither a *p* nor a prophet's
Hab 1: 1 that Habakkuk the *p* received.
Hag 1: 1 came through the *p* Haggai
Zec 1: 1 to the *p* Zechariah son of Berekiah,
13: 4 that day every *p* will be ashamed
Mal 4: 5 I will send you the *p* Elijah
Mt 10: 41 Anyone who receives a *p*
11: 9 what did you go out to see? A *p*?
12: 39 except the sign of the *p* Jonah.
Lk 1: 76 will be called a *p* of the Most High;
4: 24 "no *p* is accepted in his home town.
7: 16 A great *p* has appeared among us,"
24: 19 "He was a *p*, powerful in word
Jn 1: 21 "Are you the *P*?" He answered,
Ac 7: 37 'God will send you a *p* like me
21: 10 a *p* named Agabus came
1Co 14: 37 If anybody thinks he is a *p*
Rev 16: 13 and out of the mouth of the false *p*.

PROPHET'S (PROPHESY)

2Pe 1: 20 about by the *p* own interpretation.

PROPHETESS (PROPHESY)

Ex 15: 20 Then Miriam the *p*, Aaron's sister,
Jdg 4: 4 a *p*, the wife of Lappidoth,
Isa 8: 3 I went to the *p*, and she conceived
Lk 2: 36 a *p*, Anna, the daughter of Phanuel,

PROPHETS (PROPHESY)

Nu 11: 29 that all the LORD's people were *p*
1Sa 10: 11 Is Saul also among the *p*?"
28: 6 him by dreams or Urim or *p*.
1Ki 19: 10 put your *p* to death with the sword.
1Ch 16: 22 do my *p* no harm."
Ps 105: 15 do my *p* no harm."
Jer 23: 9 Concerning the *p*:
23: 30 "I am against the *p* who steal
Eze 13: 2 prophesy against the *p*
Mt 5: 17 come to abolish the Law or the *P*;
7: 12 for this sums up the Law and the *P*.
7: 15 "Watch out for false *p*.
22: 40 and the *P* hang on these two
23: 37 you who kill the *p* and stone those
24: 24 false Christs and false *p* will appear
26: 56 of the *p* might be fulfilled."
Lk 10: 24 For I tell you that many *p*
11: 49 'I will send them *p* and apostles,
24: 25 believe all that the *p* have spoken!
24: 44 me in the Law of Moses, the *P*
Ac 3: 24 "Indeed, all the *p* from Samuel on,
10: 43 All the *p* testify about him that
13: 1 the church at Antioch there were *p*
26: 22 nothing beyond what the *p*
28: 23 the Law of Moses and from the *P*.
Ro 1: 2 through his *p* in the Holy
3: 21 to which the Law and the *P* testify.
11: 3 they have killed your *p*
1Co 12: 28 second *p*, third teachers, then
12: 29 Are all *p*? Are all teachers?
14: 32 The spirits of *p* are subject
Eph 2: 20 foundation of the apostles and *p*,
3: 5 Spirit to God's holy apostles and *p*.
4: 11 some to be *p*, some
Heb 1: 1 through the *p* at many times
1Pe 1: 10 Concerning this salvation, the *p*,
2Pe 1: 19 word of the *p* made more certain,
3: 2 spoken in the past by the holy *p*
1Jn 4: 1 because many false *p* have gone out
Rev 11: 10 these two *p* had tormented those
18: 20 Rejoice, saints and apostles and *p*!

PROPITIATION see (atoning) SACRIFICE

PROPORTION

Dt 16: 10 by giving a freewill offering in *p*
16: 17 Each of you must bring a gift in *p*

PROPRIETY*

1Ti 2: 9 with decency and *p*,
2: 15 in faith, love and holiness with *p*.

PROSPECT*

Pr 10: 28 The *p* of the righteous is joy,

PROSPER (PROSPERED PROSPERITY PROSPEROUS PROSPERS)

Dt 5: 33 so that you may live and *p*
28: 63 pleased the LORD to make you *p*
29: 9 that you may *p* in everything you
1Ki 2: 3 so that you may *p* in all you do
Ezr 6: 14 and *p* under the preaching
Pr 11: 10 When the righteous *p*, the city
11: 25 A generous man will *p*;
17: 20 A man of perverse heart does not *p*
28: 13 who conceals his sins does not *p*,
28: 25 he who trusts in the LORD will *p*.
Isa 53: 10 of the LORD will *p* in his hand.
Jer 12: 1 Why does the way of the wicked *p*?

PROSPERED (PROSPER)

Ge 39: 2 was with Joseph and he *p*,
2Ch 14: 7 So they built and *p*.
31: 21 And so he *p*.

PROSPERITY (PROSPER)

Dt 28: 11 will grant you abundant *p*—
30: 15 I set before you today life and *p*,
Job 36: 11 will spend the rest of their days in *p*
Ps 73: 3 when I saw the *p* of the wicked.
122: 9 I will seek your *p*.
128: 2 blessings and *p* will be yours.
Pr 3: 2 and bring you *p*.
13: 21 but *p* is the reward of the righteous.
21: 21 finds life, *p* and honour.
Isa 45: 7 I bring *p* and create disaster;

PROSPEROUS (PROSPER)

Dt 30: 9 your God will make you most *p*

Jos 1: 8 Then you will be *p* and successful.
Job 42: 10 the LORD made him *p* again

PROSPERS (PROSPER)
Ps 1: 3 Whatever he does *p*.
Pr 16: 20 gives heed to instruction *p*,
19: 8 he who cherishes understanding *p*.

PROSTITUTE (PROSTITUTES PROSTITUTION)
Lev 20: 6 and spiritists to *p* himself
Nu 15: 39 and not *p* yourselves by going
Jos 2: 1 the house of a *p* named Rahab
Pr 6: 26 for the *p* reduces you to a loaf
7: 10 like a *p* and with crafty intent.
23: 27 for a *p* is a deep pit
Eze 16: 15 and used your fame to become a *p*.
23: 7 a *p* to all the elite of the Assyrians
Hos 3: 3 you must not be a *p* or be intimate
1Co 6: 15 of Christ and unite them with a *p*?
6: 16 with a *p* is one with her in body?
Rev 17: 1 you the punishment of the great *p*,

PROSTITUTES (PROSTITUTE)
Pr 29: 3 of *p* squanders his wealth.
Mt 21: 31 and the *p* are entering the kingdom
Lk 15: 30 property with *p* comes home,
1Co 6: 9 male *p* nor homosexual offenders

PROSTITUTION (PROSTITUTE)
Eze 16: 16 where you carried on your *p*.
23: 3 engaging in *p* from their youth.
Hos 4: 10 engage in *p* but not increase,

PROSTRATE
Dt 9: 18 again I fell *p* before the LORD
1Ki 18: 39 they fell *p* and cried, "The LORD

PROTECT (PROTECTED PROTECTION PROTECTS)
Dt 23: 14 about in your camp to *p* you
Ps 25: 21 integrity and uprightness *p* me,
32: 7 you will *p* me from trouble
40: 11 your truth always *p* me.
41: 2 The LORD will *p* him
91: 14 I will *p* him, for he acknowledges
140: 1 *p* me from men of violence,
Pr 2: 11 Discretion will *p* you,
4: 6 forsake wisdom, and she will *p* you;
Jn 17: 11 *p* them by the power of your name
17: 15 that you *p* them from the evil one.
2Th 3: 3 and *p* you from the evil one.

PROTECTED (PROTECT)
Jos 24: 17 He *p* us on our entire journey
1Sa 30: 23 He has *p* us and handed
Ps 37: 28 They will be *p* for ever,
Jn 17: 12 I *p* them and kept them safe

PROTECTION (PROTECT)
Ezr 9: 9 he has given us a wall of *p* in Judah
Ps 5: 11 Spread your *p* over them,

PROTECTS (PROTECT)
Ps 116: 6 The LORD *p* the simple-hearted;
Pr 2: 8 and *p* the way of his faithful ones.
1Co 13: 7 It always *p*, always trusts,

PROUD (PRIDE)
Ps 31: 23 but the *p* he pays back in full.
101: 5 has haughty eyes and a *p* heart,
138: 6 but the *p* he knows from afar.
Pr 3: 34 He mocks *p* mockers
16: 5 The LORD detests all the *p*
16: 19 than to share plunder with the *p*.
18: 12 his downfall a man's heart is *p*,
21: 4 Haughty eyes and a *p* heart,
Isa 2: 12 store for all the *p* and lofty,
Ro 12: 16 Do not be *p*, but be willing
1Co 13: 4 it does not boast, it is not *p*.
2Ti 3: 2 lovers of money, boastful, *p*,
Jas 4: 6 "God opposes the *p*
1Pe 5: 5 because, "God opposes the *p*

PROVE (PROOF PROVED PROVING)
Pr 29: 25 Fear of man will *p* to be a snare,
Jn 8: 46 Can any of you *p* me guilty of sin?
Ac 26: 20 *p* their repentance by their deeds.
1Co 4: 2 been given a trust must *p* faithful.

PROVED (PROVE)
Ps 51: 4 so that you are *p* right
Mt 11: 19 wisdom is *p* right by her actions."
Ro 3: 4 "So that you may be *p* right
1Pe 1: 7 may be *p* genuine and may result

PROVIDE (PROVIDED PROVIDES PROVISION)
Ge 22: 8 "God himself will *p* the lamb
22: 14 that place "The LORD will *p*."
Isa 43: 20 because I *p* water in the desert
61: 3 and *p* for those who grieve in Zion
1Co 10: 13 *p* a way out so that you can stand
1Ti 5: 8 If anyone does not *p*
Tit 3: 14 in order that they may *p*

PROVIDED (PROVIDE)
Ps 68: 10 O God, you *p* for the poor.
111: 9 He *p* redemption for his people;
Jnh 1: 17 But the LORD *p* a great fish
4: 6 Then the LORD God *p* a vine
4: 7 dawn the next day God *p* a worm,
4: 8 God *p* a scorching east wind,
Gal 4: 18 to be zealous, *p* the purpose is good
Heb 1: 3 After he had *p* purification for sins,

PROVIDES (PROVIDE)
Ps 111: 5 He *p* food for those who fear him;
Pr 31: 15 she *p* food for her family
Eze 18: 7 and *p* clothing for the naked.
1Ti 6: 17 who richly *p* us with everything
1Pe 4: 11 it with the strength God *p*,

PROVING* (PROVE)
Ac 9: 22 by *p* that Jesus is the Christ.
17: 3 and *p* that the Christ had to suffer
18: 28 *p* from the Scriptures that Jesus

PROVISION (PROVIDE)
Ro 5: 17 who receive God's abundant *p*

PROVOKED
Ecc 7: 9 Do not be quickly *p* in your spirit,
Jer 32: 32 Judah have *p* me by all the evil they

PROWLS
1Pe 5: 8 Your enemy the devil *p*

PRUDENCE* (PRUDENT)
Pr 1: 4 for giving *p* to the simple,
8: 5 You who are simple, gain *p*;
8: 12 "I, wisdom, dwell together with *p*;
15: 5 whoever heeds correction shows *p*.
19: 25 and the simple will learn *p*;

PRUDENT* (PRUDENCE)
Pr 1: 3 acquiring a disciplined and *p* life,
12: 16 but a *p* man overlooks an insult.
12: 23 A *p* man keeps his knowledge
13: 16 Every *p* man acts out of knowledge
14: 8 The wisdom of the *p* is
14: 15 a *p* man gives thought to his steps.
14: 18 the *p* are crowned with knowledge.
19: 14 but a *p* wife is from the LORD.
22: 3 *p* man sees danger and takes
27: 12 The *p* see danger and take refuge,
Jer 49: 7 Has counsel perished from the *p*?
Am 5: 13 Therefore the *p* man keeps quiet

PRUNES
Jn 15: 2 branch that does bear fruit he *p*

PRUNING
Isa 2: 4 and their spears into *p* hooks.
Joel 3: 10 and your *p* hooks into spears.

PSALMS
Eph 5: 19 Speak to one another with *p*,
Col 3: 16 and as you sing *p*, hymns

PUBLICLY
Ac 20: 20 have taught you *p* and from house
1Ti 5: 20 Those who sin are to be rebuked *p*,

PUFFS
1Co 8: 1 Knowledge *p* up, but love builds up

PULLING
2Co 10: 8 building you up rather than *p* you

PUNISH (PUNISHED PUNISHES PUNISHMENT)
Ge 15: 14 But I will *p* the nation they serve
Ex 32: 34 I will *p* them for their sin."
Pr 17: 26 It is not good to *p* an innocent man,
23: 13 if you *p* him with the rod, he will
Isa 13: 11 I will *p* the world for its evil,
Jer 2: 19 Your wickedness will *p* you;
21: 14 I will *p* you as your deeds deserve,
Zep 1: 12 and *p* those who are complacent,
Ac 7: 7 But I will *p* the nation they serve
2Th 1: 8 He will *p* those who do not know
1Pe 2: 14 by him to *p* those who do wrong

PUNISHED (PUNISH)
Ezr 9: 13 you have *p* us less than our sins
Ps 99: 8 though you *p* their misdeeds.
La 3: 39 complain when *p* for his sins?
Mk 12: 40 Such men will be *p* most severely."
Lk 23: 41 the same sentence? We are *p* justly,
2Th 1: 9 be *p* with everlasting destruction
Heb 10: 29 to be *p* who has trampled the Son

PUNISHES (PUNISH)
Heb 12: 6 and he *p* everyone he accepts

PUNISHMENT (PUNISH)
Isa 53: 5 the *p* that brought us peace was
Jer 4: 18 This is your *p*.
Mt 25: 46 Then they will go away to eternal *p*
Lk 12: 48 and does things deserving *p* will be
21: 22 For this is the time of *p*
Ro 13: 4 wrath to bring *p* on the wrongdoer.
Heb 2: 2 disobedience received its just *p*,
2Pe 2: 9 while continuing their *p*.

PURCHASED
Ps 74: 2 Remember the people you *p* of old,
Rev 5: 9 with your blood you *p* men for God

PURE (PURIFICATION PURIFIED PURIFIES PURIFY PURITY)
2Sa 22: 27 to the *p* you show yourself *p*,
Job 14: 4 Who can bring what is *p*
Ps 19: 9 The fear of the LORD is *p*,
24: 4 who has clean hands and a *p* heart,
51: 10 Create in me a *p* heart, O God,
119: 9 can a young man keep his way *p*?
Pr 15: 26 those of the *p* are pleasing to him.
20: 9 can say, "I have kept my heart *p*;
Isa 52: 11 Come out from it and be *p*,
Hab 1: 13 Your eyes are too *p* to look on evil;
Mt 5: 8 Blessed are the *p* in heart,
2Co 11: 2 I might present you as a *p* virgin
Php 4: 8 whatever is *p*, whatever is lovely,
1Ti 1: 5 which comes from a *p* heart
5: 22 Keep yourself *p*.
2Ti 2: 22 call on the Lord out of a *p* heart.
Tit 1: 15 To the *p*, all things are *p*,
2: 5 to be self-controlled and *p*,
Heb 7: 26 blameless, *p*, set apart from sinners
13: 4 and the marriage bed kept *p*,
Jas 1: 27 that God our Father accepts as *p*
3: 17 comes from heaven is first of all *p*;
1Jn 3: 3 him purifies himself, just as he is *p*.

PURGE
Pr 20: 30 and beatings *p* the inmost being.

PURIFICATION (PURE)
Heb 1: 3 After he had provided *p* for sins,

PURIFIED (PURE)
Ac 15: 9 for he *p* their hearts by faith.
1Pe 1: 22 Now that you have *p* yourselves

PURIFIES* (PURE)
1Jn 1: 7 of Jesus, his Son, *p* us from all sin.
3: 3 who has this hope in him *p* himself,

PURIFY (PURE)
Nu 19: 12 He must *p* himself with the water
2Co 7: 1 us *p* ourselves from everything that
Tit 2: 14 to *p* for himself a people that are
Jas 4: 8 you sinners, and *p* your hearts,
1Jn 1: 9 and *p* us from all unrighteousness.

PURIM
Est 9: 26 Therefore these days were called *P*

PURITY* (PURE)
Hos 8: 5 long will they be incapable of *p*?
2Co 6: 6 in *p*, understanding, patience
1Ti 4: 12 in life, in love, in faith and in *p*.
5: 2 as sisters, with absolute *p*.
1Pe 3: 2 when they see the *p* and reverence

PURPLE
Pr 31: 22 she is clothed in fine linen and *p*.
Mk 15: 17 They put a *p* robe on him, then

PURPOSE (PURPOSED PURPOSES)
Ex 9: 16 I have raised you up for this very *p*,
Job 36: 5 he is mighty, and firm in his *p*.
Pr 19: 21 but it is the LORD's *p* that prevails
Isa 46: 10 I say: My *p* will stand,
55: 11 and achieve the *p* for which I sent it
Ac 2: 23 handed over to you by God's set *p*
Ro 8: 28 have been called according to his *p*.
9: 11 in order that God's *p*
9: 17 "I raised you up for this very *p*,
1Co 3: 8 the man who waters have one *p*,
2Co 5: 5 who has made us for this very *p*
Gal 4: 18 be zealous, provided the *p* is good,
Eph 1: 11 in conformity with the *p* of his will,
3: 11 according to his eternal *p* which he
Php 2: 2 love, being one in spirit and *p*.
2: 13 and to act according to his good *p*.
2Ti 1: 9 but because of his own *p* and grace.

PURPOSED (PURPOSE)
Isa 14: 24 and as I have *p*, so it will stand.
14: 27 For the LORD Almighty has *p*,
Eph 1: 9 which he *p* in Christ, to be put

PURPOSES (PURPOSE)
Ps 33: 10 he thwarts the *p* of the peoples.
Jer 23: 20 the *p* of his heart.
32: 19 great are your *p* and mighty are

PURSE (PURSES)
Hag 1: 6 to put them in a *p* with holes in it."
Lk 10: 4 Do not take a *p* or bag or sandals;
22: 36 "But now if you have a *p*, take it,

PURSES (PURSE)
Lk 12: 33 Provide *p* for yourselves that will

PURSUE (PURSUES)
Ps 34: 14 seek peace and *p* it.
Pr 15: 9 he loves those who *p* righteousness
Ro 9: 30 who did not *p* righteousness,
1Ti 6: 11 and *p* righteousness, godliness,
2Ti 2: 22 and *p* righteousness, faith,
1Pe 3: 11 he must seek peace and *p* it.

PURSUES (PURSUE)
Pr 21: 21 He who *p* righteousness and love
28: 1 wicked man flees though no-one *p*,

QUAIL
Ex 16: 13 That evening *q* came and covered
Nu 11: 31 and drove *q* in from the sea.

QUALITIES* (QUALITY)
Da 6: 3 by his exceptional *q* that the king
Ro 1: 20 of the world God's invisible *q*—
2Pe 1: 8 For if you possess these *q*

QUALITY (QUALITIES)
1Co 3: 13 and the fire will test the *q*

QUARREL (QUARRELLING QUARRELS QUARRELSOME)
Pr 15: 18 but a patient man calms a *q*.
17: 14 Starting a *q* is like breaching a dam;
17: 19 He who loves a *q* loves sin;
20: 3 but every fool is quick to *q*.
26: 17 in a *q* not his own.
26: 20 without gossip a *q* dies down.
2Ti 2: 24 And the Lord's servant must not *q*;
Jas 4: 2 You *q* and fight.

QUARRELLING (QUARREL)
1Co 3: 3 For since there is jealousy and *q*
2Ti 2: 14 before God against *q* about words;

QUARRELS (QUARREL)
Pr 13: 10 Pride only breeds *q*,
Isa 45: 9 Woe to him who *q* with his Maker,
1Ti 6: 4 *q* about words that result in envy,
2Ti 2: 23 because you know they produce *q*.
Jas 4: 1 What causes fights and *q*

QUARRELSOME (QUARREL)
Pr 19: 13 a *q* wife is like a constant dripping.
21: 9 than share a house with a *q* wife.
26: 21 so is a *q* man for kindling strife.
1Ti 3: 3 not violent but gentle, not *q*,

QUEEN
1Ki 10: 1 When the *q* of Sheba heard about
2Ch 9: 1 When the *q* of Sheba heard
Mt 12: 42 The *Q* of the South will rise

QUENCH (QUENCHED)
SS 8: 7 Many waters cannot *q* love;

QUENCHED (QUENCH)
Isa 66: 24 nor will their fire be *q*,
Mk 9: 48 and the fire is not *q*.'

QUICKEN see (make) ALIVE, (give) LIFE, RESTORE, REVIVE

QUICK-TEMPERED* (TEMPER)
Pr 14: 17 A *q* man does foolish things,
14: 29 but a *q* man displays folly.
Tit 1: 7 not *q*, not given to much wine,

QUIET (QUIETNESS)
Ps 23: 2 he leads me beside *q* waters,
Pr 17: 1 Better a dry crust with peace and *q*
Ecc 9: 17 The *q* words of the wise are more
Am 5: 13 Therefore the prudent man keeps *q*
Zep 3: 17 he will *q* you with his love,
Lk 19: 40 he replied, "if they keep *q*,
1Th 4: 11 it your ambition to lead a *q* life,
1Ti 2: 2 we may live peaceful and *q* lives
1Pe 3: 4 beauty of a gentle and *q* spirit,

QUIETNESS (QUIET)
Isa 30: 15 in *q* and trust is your strength,
32: 17 the effect of righteousness will be *q*
1Ti 2: 11 A woman should learn in *q*

QUIVER
Ps 127: 5 whose *q* is full of them.

RACE
Ecc 9: 11 The *r* is not to the swift
Ac 20: 24 if only I may finish the *r*
1Co 9: 24 that in a *r* all the runners run,
Gal 2: 2 that I was running or had run my *r*
5: 7 You were running a good *r*.
2Ti 4: 7 I have finished the *r*, I have kept
Heb 12: 1 perseverance the *r* marked out

RACHEL
Daughter of Laban (Ge 29:16); wife of Jacob (Ge 29:28); bore two sons (Ge 30:22-24; 35:16-24; 46:19). Stole Laban's gods (Ge 31:19, 32-5). Death (Ge 35:19-20).

RADIANCE (RADIANT)
Eze 1: 28 so was the *r* around him.
Heb 1: 3 The Son is the *r* of God's glory

RADIANT (RADIANCE)
Ex 34: 29 he was not aware that his face was *r*
Ps 34: 5 Those who look to him are *r*;
SS 5: 10 My lover is *r* and ruddy,
Isa 60: 5 Then you will look and be *r*,
Eph 5: 27 her to himself as a *r* church,

RAGE
Ac 4: 25 "'Why do the nations *r*
Col 3: 8 *r*, malice, slander, and filthy

RAGS
Isa 64: 6 our righteous acts are like filthy *r*;

RAHAB
1. Prostitute of Jericho who hid Israelite spies (Jos 2; 6:22-25; Heb 11:31; Jas 2:25)
2. Mother of Boaz (Mt 1:5).

RAIN (RAINBOW)
Ge 7: 4 from now I will send *r* on the earth
1Ki 17: 1 nor *r* in the next few years
18: 1 and I will send *r* on the land."
Mt 5: 45 and sends *r* on the righteous
Jas 5: 17 it did not *r* on the land for three
Jude : 12 They are clouds without *r*,

RAINBOW (RAIN)
Ge 9: 13 I have set my *r* in the clouds,

RAISE (RISE)
Jn 6: 39 but *r* them up at the last day.
1Co 15: 15 he did not *r* him if in fact the dead

RAISED (RISE)
Isa 52: 13 he will be *r* and lifted up
Mt 17: 23 on the third day he will be *r* to life
Lk 7: 22 the deaf hear, the dead are *r*,
Ac 2: 24 But God *r* him from the dead,
Ro 4: 25 was *r* to life for our justification.
6: 4 as Christ was *r* from the dead
8: 11 And if the Spirit of him who *r* Jesus
10: 9 in your heart that God *r* him
1Co 15: 4 that he was *r* on the third day
15: 20 But Christ has indeed been *r*

RALLY*
Isa 11: 10 the nations will *r* to him,

RAM (RAMS)
Ge 22: 13 there in a thicket he saw a *r* caught
Da 8: 3 before me was a *r* with two horns,

RAMPART*
Ps 91: 4 will be your shield and *r*.

RAMS (RAM)
1Sa 15: 22 to heed is better than the fat of *r*.
Mic 6: 7 pleased with thousands of *r*,

RAN (RUN)
Jnh 1: 3 But Jonah *r* away from the LORD

RANSOM (RANSOMED)
Isa 50: 2 Was my arm too short to *r* you?
Hos 13: 14 "I will *r* them from the power
Mt 20: 28 and to give his life as a *r* for many."
Mk 10: 45 and to give his life as a *r* for many."
1Ti 2: 6 who gave himself as a *r* for all men
Heb 9: 15 as a *r* to set them free

RANSOMED (RANSOM)
Isa 35: 10 and the *r* of the LORD will return.

RARE
Pr 20: 15 that speak knowledge are a *r* jewel.

RAVEN (RAVENS)
Ge 8: 7 made in the ark and sent out a *r*,
Job 38: 41 Who provides food for the *r*

RAVENS (RAVEN)
1Ki 17: 6 The *r* brought him bread
Ps 147: 9 and for the young *r* when they call.
Lk 12: 24 Consider the *r*: They do not sow

READ (READING READS)
Dt 17: 19 he is to *r* it all the days of his life
Jos 8: 34 Joshua *r* all the words of the law—
2Ki 23: 2 He *r* in their hearing all the words
Ne 8: 8 They *r* from the Book of the Law
Jer 36: 6 and *r* to the people from the scroll
2Co 3: 2 known and *r* by everybody.

READING (READ)
1Ti 4: 13 to the public *r* of Scripture,

READS (READ)
Rev 1: 3 Blessed is the one who *r* the words

REAFFIRM
2Co 2: 8 therefore, to *r* your love for him.

REAL* (REALITIES REALITY)
Jn 6: 55 is *r* food and my blood is *r* drink.
1Jn 2: 27 all things and as that anointing is *r*,

REALITIES* (REAL)
Heb 10: 1 are coming—not the *r* themselves.

REALITY* (REAL)
Col 2: 17 the *r*, however, is found in Christ.

REALM (REALMS)
Hab 2: 9 "Woe to him who builds his *r*

REALMS (REALM)
Eph 1: 3 the heavenly *r* with every spiritual
2: 6 in the heavenly *r* in Christ Jesus,

REAP (REAPER REAPS)
Job 4: 8 and those who sow trouble *r* it.
Ps 126: 5 will *r* with songs of joy.
Hos 8: 7 and *r* the whirlwind.
10: 12 *r* the fruit of unfailing love,
Jn 4: 38 you to *r* what you have not worked
Ro 6: 22 the benefit you *r* leads to holiness,
2Co 9: 6 generously will also *r* generously.
Gal 6: 8 from that nature will *r* destruction;

REAPER (REAP)
Jn 4: 36 and the *r* may be glad together.

REAPS (REAP)
Pr 11: 18 who sows righteousness *r* a sure
22: 8 He who sows wickedness *r* trouble,
Gal 6: 7 A man *r* what he sows.

REASON (REASONED)
Ge 2: 24 For this *r* a man will leave his
Isa 1: 18 "Come now, let us *r* together,"
Mt 19: 5 'For this *r* a man will leave his
Jn 12: 27 it was for this very *r* I came
15: 25 'They hated me without *r*.'
1Pe 3: 15 to give the *r* for the hope that you
2Pe 1: 5 For this very *r*, make every effort

REASONED (REASON)
1Co 13: 11 thought like a child, I *r* like a child.

REBEKAH
Sister of Laban, secured as bride for Isaac (Ge 24). Mother of Esau and Jacob (Ge 25:19-26). Taken by Abimelech as sister of Isaac; returned (Ge 26:1-11). Encouraged Jacob to trick Isaac out of blessing (Ge 27:1-17).

REBEL (REBELLED REBELLION REBELS)
Nu 14: 9 Only do not *r* against the LORD.
1Sa 12: 14 and do not *r* against his commands,
Mt 10: 21 children will *r* against their parents

REBELLED (REBEL)
Ps 78: 56 and *r* against the Most High;
Isa 63: 10 Yet they *r*

REBELLION (REBEL)
Ex 34: 7 and forgiving wickedness, *r* and sin
Nu 14: 18 in love and forgiving sin and *r*.
1Sa 15: 23 For *r* is like the sin of divination,
2Th 2: 3 will not come, until the *r* occurs

REBELS (REBEL)
Ro 13: 2 he who *r* against the authority is
1Ti 1: 9 but for lawbreakers and *r*,

REBIRTH* (BEAR [1])
Tit 3: 5 us through the washing of *r*

REBUILD (BUILD)
Ezr 5: 2 set to work to *r* the house of God
Ne 2: 17 let us *r* the wall of Jerusalem,
Ps 102: 16 For the LORD will *r* Zion
Da 9: 25 and *r* Jerusalem until the Anointed
Am 9: 14 they will *r* the ruined cities
Ac 15: 16 Its ruins I will *r*,

REBUILT (BUILD)
Zec 1: 16 and there my house will be *r*.

REBUKE (REBUKED REBUKES REBUKING)
Lev 19: 17 *R* your neighbour frankly
Ps 141: 5 let him *r* me—it is oil on my head.
Pr 3: 11 and do not resent his *r*,
9: 8 *r* a wise man and he will love you.
15: 31 He who listens to a life-giving *r*
17: 10 A *r* impresses a man
19: 25 *r* a discerning man, and he will gain
25: 12 is a wise man's *r* to a listening ear.
27: 5 Better is open *r*
30: 6 or he will *r* you and prove you a liar
Ecc 7: 5 It is better to heed a wise man's *r*
Isa 54: 9 never to *r* you again.
Jer 2: 19 your backsliding will *r* you.
Lk 17: 3 "If your brother sins, *r* him,
1Ti 5: 1 Do not *r* an older man harshly,
2Ti 4: 2 correct, *r* and encourage—
Tit 1: 13 Therefore, *r* them sharply,
2: 15 Encourage and *r* with all authority.
Rev 3: 19 Those whom I love I *r*

REBUKED (REBUKE)
Mk 16: 14 he *r* them for their lack of faith
1Ti 5: 20 Those who sin are to be *r* publicly,

REBUKES (REBUKE)
Job 22: 4 "Is it for your piety that he *r* you
Pr 28: 23 He who *r* a man will
29: 1 remains stiff-necked after many *r*
Heb 12: 5 do not lose heart when he *r* you,

REBUKING (REBUKE)
2Ti 3: 16 *r*, correcting and training

RECEIVE (RECEIVED RECEIVES)
Mt 10: 41 a righteous man will *r* a righteous
Mk 10: 15 anyone who will not *r* the kingdom
Jn 20: 22 and said, "*R* the Holy Spirit.
Ac 1: 8 you will *r* power when the Holy
2: 38 you will *r* the gift of the Holy Spirit
19: 2 "Did you *r* the Holy Spirit
20: 35 'It is more blessed to give than to *r*
1Co 9: 14 the gospel should *r* their living
2Co 6: 17 and I will *r* you."
1Ti 1: 16 believe on him and *r* eternal life.
Jas 1: 7 should not think he will *r* anything
2Pe 1: 11 and you will *r* a rich welcome
1Jn 3: 22 and *r* from him anything we ask,
Rev 4: 11 to *r* glory and honour and power,
5: 12 to *r* power and wealth and wisdom

RECEIVED (RECEIVE)
Mt 6: 2 they have *r* their reward in full.
10: 8 Freely you have *r*, freely give.
Mk 11: 24 believe that you have *r* it,
Jn 1: 12 Yet to all who *r* him,
1: 16 his grace we have all *r* one blessing
Ac 8: 17 and they *r* the Holy Spirit.
10: 47 They have *r* the Holy Spirit just
Ro 8: 15 but you *r* the Spirit of sonship.
1Co 11: 23 For I *r* from the Lord what I
2Co 1: 4 the comfort we ourselves have *r*
Col 2: 6 just as you *r* Christ Jesus as Lord,
1Pe 4: 10 should use whatever gift he has *r*

RECEIVES (RECEIVE)
Pr 18: 22 and *r* favour from the LORD.
27: 21 but man is tested by the praise he *r*.
Mt 7: 8 everyone who asks *r*; he who seeks
10: 40 he who *r* me *r* the one who sent me.
10: 40 "He who *r* you *r* me, and he who
Ac 10: 43 believes in him *r* forgiveness of sins

RECITE
Ps 45: 1 as I *r* my verses for the king;

RECKLESS
Pr 12: 18 *R* words pierce like a sword,
14: 16 but a fool is hotheaded and *r*.

RECKONING
Isa 10: 3 What will you do on the day of *r*,
Hos 9: 7 the days of *r* are at hand.

RECLAIM* (CLAIM)
Isa 11: 11 time to *r* the remnant that is left

RECOGNISE (RECOGNISED RECOGNITION)
Mt 7: 16 By their fruit you will *r* them.
1Jn 4: 2 This is how you can *r* the Spirit
4: 6 This is how we *r* the Spirit of truth

RECOGNISED (RECOGNISE)
Mt 12: 33 for a tree is *r* by its fruit.
Ro 7: 13 in order that sin might be *r* as sin,

RECOGNITION (RECOGNISE)
1Co 16: 18 Such men deserve *r*.
1Ti 5: 3 Give proper *r* to those widows who

RECOMPENSE*
Isa 40: 10 and his *r* accompanies him.
62: 11 and his *r* accompanies him.'"

RECONCILE* (RECONCILED RECONCILIATION RECONCILING)
Ac 7: 26 He tried to *r* them by saying, 'Men,
Eph 2: 16 in this one body to *r* both of them
Col 1: 20 him to *r* to himself all things,

RECONCILED* (RECONCILE)
Mt 5: 24 First go and be *r* to your brother;
Lk 12: 58 try hard to be *r* to him on the way,
Ro 5: 10 how much more, having been *r*,
5: 10 we were *r* to him through the death
1Co 7: 11 or else be *r* to her husband.
2Co 5: 18 who *r* us to himself through Christ
5: 20 you on Christ's behalf: Be *r* to God.
Col 1: 22 he has *r* you by Christ's physical

RECONCILIATION* (RECONCILE)
Ro 5: 11 whom we have now received *r*.
11: 15 For if their rejection is the *r*
2Co 5: 18 and gave us the ministry of *r*:
5: 19 committed to us the message of *r*.

RECONCILING* (RECONCILE)
2Co 5: 19 that God was *r* the world to himself

RECORD (RECORDED)
Ps 130: 3 If you, O LORD, kept a *r* of sins,

RELATIVES
Pr 19: 7 A poor man is shunned by all his *r*
Mk 6: 4 among his *r* and in his own house is
Lk 21: 16 betrayed by parents, brothers, *r*
1Ti 5: 8 If anyone does not provide for his *r*

RELEASE (RELEASED)
Isa 61: 1 and *r* from darkness for the prisoners,
Lk 4: 18 to *r* the oppressed,

RELEASED (RELEASE)
Ro 7: 6 we have been *r* from the law
Rev 20: 7 Satan will be *r* from his prison

RELENTED (RELENTS)
Ex 32: 14 the LORD *r* and did not bring
Ps 106: 45 and out of his great love he *r*.

RELENTS* (RELENTED)
Joel 2: 13 and he *r* from sending calamity.
Jnh 4: 2 a God who *r* from sending calamity

RELIABLE (RELY)
Pr 22: 21 teaching you true and *r* words,
Jn 8: 26 But he who sent me is *r*,
2Ti 2: 2 witnesses entrust to *r* men who will

RELIANCE* (RELY)
Pr 25: 19 is *r* on the unfaithful in times

RELIED (RELY)
2Ch 13: 18 were victorious because they *r*
16: 8 Yet when you *r* on the LORD,
Ps 71: 6 From birth I have *r* on you;

RELIEF
Job 35: 9 they plead for *r* from the arm
Ps 94: 13 you grant him *r* from days
143: 1 come to my *r*.
La 3: 49 without *r*,
3: 56 to my cry for *r*."
2Th 1: 7 and give *r* to you who are troubled,

RELIGION* (RELIGIOUS)
Ac 25: 19 dispute with him about their own *r*
26: 5 to the strictest sect of our *r*,
1Ti 5: 4 all to put their *r* into practice
Jas 1: 26 himself and his *r* is worthless.
1: 27 *R* that God our Father accepts

RELIGIOUS (RELIGION)
Jas 1: 26 If anyone considers himself *r*

RELY (RELIABLE RELIANCE RELIED)
Isa 50: 10 and *r* on his God.
Eze 33: 26 you then possess the land? You *r*
2Co 1: 9 this happened that we might not *r*
Gal 3: 10 All who *r* on observing the law are
1Jn 4: 16 and *r* on the love God has for us.

REMAIN (REMAINS)
Nu 33: 55 allow to *r* will become barbs
Ps 102: 27 But you *r* the same,
Jn 1: 32 from heaven as a dove and *r* on him
15: 4 *R* in me, and I will *r* in you.
15: 7 If you *r* in me and my words
15: 9 Now *r* in my love.
Ro 13: 8 Let no debt *r* outstanding,
1Co 13: 13 And now these three *r*: faith,
2Ti 2: 13 he will *r* faithful,
Heb 1: 11 They will perish, but you *r*;
1Jn 2: 27 just as it has taught you, *r* in him.

REMAINS (REMAIN)
Ps 146: 6 the LORD, who *r* faithful for ever.
Heb 7: 3 Son of God he *r* a priest for ever.

REMEDY
Isa 3: 7 "I have no *r*.

REMEMBER (REMEMBERED REMEMBERS REMEMBRANCE)
Ge 9: 15 I will *r* my covenant between me
Ex 20: 8 "*R* the Sabbath day
33: 13 *R* that this nation is your people."
Dt 5: 15 *R* that you were slaves in Egypt
1Ch 16: 12 *R* the wonders he has done,
Job 36: 24 *R* to extol his work,
Ps 25: 6 *R*, O LORD, your great mercy
63: 6 On my bed I *r* you;
74: 2 *R* the people you purchased of old,
77: 11 I will *r* the deeds of the LORD;
Ecc 12: 1 *R* your Creator
Isa 46: 8 "*R* this, fix it in mind,
Jer 31: 34 and will *r* their sins no more."
Hab 3: 2 in wrath *r* mercy.
Lk 1: 72 and to *r* his holy covenant,
Gal 2: 10 we should continue to *r* the poor,
Php 1: 3 I thank my God every time I *r* you.
2Ti 2: 8 *R* Jesus Christ, raised
Heb 8: 12 and will *r* their sins no more."

REMEMBERED (REMEMBER)
Ex 2: 24 he *r* his covenant with Abraham,
3: 15 am to be *r* from generation
Ps 98: 3 He has *r* his love
106: 45 for their sake he *r* his covenant
111: 4 He has caused his wonders to be *r*;
136: 23 to the One who *r* us
Isa 65: 17 The former things will not be *r*,
Eze 18: 22 offences he has committed will be *r*
33: 13 things he has done will be *r*;

REMEMBERS (REMEMBER)
Ps 103: 14 he *r* that we are dust.
111: 5 he *r* his covenant for ever.
Isa 43: 25 and *r* your sins no more.

REMEMBRANCE (REMEMBER)
Lk 22: 19 given for you; do this in *r* of me."
1Co 11: 24 which is for you; do this in *r* of me
11: 25 whenever you drink it, in *r* of me."

REMIND
Jn 14: 26 will *r* you of everything I have said
2Pe 1: 12 I will always *r* you of these things,

REMNANT
Ezr 9: 8 has been gracious in leaving us a *r*
Isa 11: 11 time to reclaim the *r* that is left
Jer 23: 3 "I myself will gather the *r*
Zec 8: 12 inheritance to the *r* of this people.
Ro 11: 5 the present time there is a *r* chosen

REMOVED
Ps 30: 11 you *r* my sackcloth and clothed me
103: 12 so far has he *r* our transgressions
Jn 20: 1 and saw that the stone had been *r*

REND
Joel 2: 13 *R* your heart

RENEW (RENEWAL RENEWED RENEWING RENEWS)
Ps 51: 10 and *r* a steadfast spirit within me.
Isa 40: 31 will *r* their strength.

RENEWAL (RENEW)
Isa 57: 10 You found *r* of your strength,
Tit 3: 5 of rebirth and *r* by the Holy Spirit,

RENEWED (RENEW)
Ps 103: 5 that my youth is *r* like the eagle's.
2Co 4: 16 yet inwardly we are being *r* day

RENEWING* (RENEW)
Ro 12: 2 transformed by the *r* of your mind.

RENEWS* (RENEW)
Ps 119: 50 Your promise *r* my life.

RENOUNCE (RENOUNCED RENOUNCES)
Da 4: 27 *R* your sins by doing what is right,

RENOUNCED (RENOUNCE)
2Co 4: 2 we have *r* secret and shameful

RENOUNCES (RENOUNCE)
Pr 28: 13 confesses and *r* them finds

RENOWN*
Ge 6: 4 were the heroes of old, men of *r*.
Ps 102: 12 *r* endures through all generations.
135: 13 *r*, O LORD, through all
Isa 26: 8 your name and *r*
55: 13 This will be for the LORD's *r*,
63: 12 to gain for himself everlasting *r*,
Jer 13: 11 to be my people for my *r* and praise
32: 20 have gained the *r* that is still yours.
33: 9 Then this city will bring me *r*, joy,
49: 25 the city of *r* not been abandoned,
Eze 26: 17 How you are destroyed, O city of *r*,
Hos 12: 5 the LORD is his name of *r*!

REPAID (PAY)
Lk 6: 34 to 'sinners,' expecting to be *r* in full
14: 14 you will be *r* at the resurrection
Col 3: 25 Anyone who does wrong will be *r*

REPAY (PAY)
Dt 7: 10 But those who hate him he will *r*
32: 35 It is mine to avenge; I will *r*.
Ru 2: 12 May the LORD *r* you
Ps 103: 10 or *r* us according to our iniquities.
116: 12 How can I *r* the LORD
Jer 25: 14 I will *r* them according
Ro 12: 17 Do not *r* anyone evil for evil.
12: 19 "It is mine to avenge; I will *r*,"
1Pe 3: 9 Do not *r* evil with evil

REPAYING (PAY)
2Ch 6: 23 *r* the guilty by bringing
1Ti 5: 4 so *r* their parents and grandparents

REPEATED
Heb 10: 1 the same sacrifices *r* endlessly year

REPENT (REPENTANCE REPENTED REPENTS)
1Ki 8: 47 *r* and plead with you in the land
Job 36: 10 commands them to *r* of their evil.
42: 6 and *r* in dust and ashes."
Jer 15: 19 "If you *r*, I will restore you
Eze 18: 30 *R*! Turn away from all your
18: 32 *R* and live! "Take up a lament
Mt 3: 2 "*R*, for the kingdom of heaven is
4: 17 "*R*, for the kingdom of heaven is
Mk 6: 12 and preached that people should *r*.
Lk 13: 3 unless you *r*, you too will all perish.
Ac 2: 38 Peter replied, "*R* and be baptised,
3: 19 *R*, then, and turn to God,
17: 30 all people everywhere to *r*.
26: 20 also, I preached that they should *r*
Rev 2: 5 *R* and do the things you did at first.

REPENTANCE (REPENT)
Isa 30: 15 "In *r* and rest is your salvation,
Mt 3: 8 Produce fruit in keeping with *r*.
Mk 1: 4 a baptism of *r* for the forgiveness
Lk 3: 8 Produce fruit in keeping with *r*.
5: 32 call the righteous, but sinners to *r*."
24: 47 and *r* and forgiveness of sins will be
Ac 20: 21 that they must turn to God in *r*
26: 20 and prove their *r* by their deeds.
Ro 2: 4 kindness leads you towards *r*?
2Co 7: 10 Godly sorrow brings *r* that leads
2Pe 3: 9 but everyone to come to *r*.

REPENTED (REPENT)
Mt 11: 21 they would have *r* long ago

REPENTS (REPENT)
Lk 15: 7 in heaven over one sinner who *r*
15: 10 of God over one sinner who *r*."
17: 3 rebuke him, and if he *r*, forgive him

REPORTS
Ex 23: 1 "Do not spread false *r*.

REPOSES*
Pr 14: 33 Wisdom *r* in the heart

REPRESENTATION*
Heb 1: 3 and the exact *r* of his being,

REPROACH
Job 27: 6 my conscience will not *r* me
Isa 51: 7 Do not fear the *r* of men
1Ti 3: 2 Now the overseer must be above *r*,

REPUTATION
1Ti 3: 7 also have a good *r* with outsiders,

REQUESTS
Ps 20: 5 May the LORD grant all your *r*.
Php 4: 6 with thanksgiving, present your *r*

REQUIRE (REQUIRED REQUIRES)
Mic 6: 8 And what does the LORD *r* of you

REQUIRED (REQUIRE)
1Co 4: 2 it is *r* that those who have been
Gal 5: 3 himself be circumcised that he is *r*

REQUIRES (REQUIRE)
1Ki 2: 3 what the LORD your God *r*:
Heb 9: 22 the law *r* that nearly everything be

RESCUE (RESCUED RESCUES)
Ps 22: 8 let the LORD *r* him.
31: 2 come quickly to my *r*;
69: 14 *R* me from the mire,
91: 14 says the LORD, "I will *r* him;
143: 9 *R* me from my enemies, O LORD,
Da 6: 20 been able to *r* you from the lions?"
Ro 7: 24 Who will *r* me from this body
Gal 1: 4 himself for our sins to *r* us
2Pe 2: 9 how to *r* godly men from trials

RESCUED (RESCUE)
Ps 18: 17 He *r* me from my powerful enemy,
Pr 11: 8 The righteous man is *r*
Col 1: 13 For he has *r* us from the dominion

RESCUES (RESCUE)
Da 6: 27 He *r* and he saves;
1Th 1: 10 who *r* us from the coming wrath.

RESENT* (RESENTFUL RESENTS)
Pr 3: 11 and do not *r* his rebuke,

RESENTFUL* (RESENT)
2Ti 2: 24 to everyone, able to teach, not *r*.

RESENTS* (RESENT)
Pr 15: 12 A mocker *r* correction;

RESERVE (RESERVED)
1Ki 19: 18 Yet I *r* seven thousand in Israel—

RESERVED (RESERVE)
Ro 11: 4 "I have *r* for myself seven

RESIST (RESISTED RESISTS)
Da 11: 32 know their God will firmly *r* him.
Mt 5: 39 I tell you, Do not *r* an evil person.
Lk 21: 15 of your adversaries will be able to *r*
Jas 4: 7 *R* the devil, and he will flee
1Pe 5: 9 *R* him, standing firm in the faith,

RESISTED (RESIST)
Job 9: 4 Who has *r* him and come out

RESISTS* (RESIST)
Ro 9: 19 For who *r* his will?" But who are

RESOLVED
Ps 17: 3 I have *r* that my mouth will not sin.
Da 1: 8 But Daniel *r* not to defile himself
1Co 2: 2 For I *r* to know nothing while I was

RESOUNDING*
Ps 150: 5 praise him with *r* cymbals.
1Co 13: 1 I am only a *r* gong or a clanging

RESPECT (RESPECTABLE RESPECTED RESPECTS)
Lev 19: 3 "'Each of you must *r* his mother
19: 32 show *r* for the elderly and revere
Pr 11: 16 A kind-hearted woman gains *r*,
Mal 1: 6 where is the *r* due me?" says
Eph 5: 33 and the wife must *r* her husband.
6: 5 obey your earthly masters with *r*
1Th 4: 12 so that your daily life may win the *r*
5: 12 to *r* those who work hard
1Ti 3: 4 children obey him with proper *r*.
3: 8 are to be men worthy of *r*, sincere,
3: 11 are to be women worthy of *r*,
6: 1 their masters worthy of full *r*,
Tit 2: 2 worthy of *r*, self-controlled,
1Pe 2: 17 Show proper *r* to everyone:
3: 7 them with *r* as the weaker partner
3: 16 But do this with gentleness and *r*,

RESPECTABLE* (RESPECT)
1Ti 3: 2 self-controlled, *r*, hospitable,

RESPECTED (RESPECT)
Pr 31: 23 Her husband is *r* at the city gate,

RESPECTS (RESPECT)
Pr 13: 13 he who *r* a command is rewarded.

RESPLENDENT*
Ps 76: 4 You are *r* with light,
132: 18 but the crown on his head will be *r*

RESPOND
Ps 102: 17 He will *r* to the prayer
Hos 2: 21 "I will *r* to the skies,

RESPONSIBILITY (RESPONSIBLE)
Ac 18: 6 your own heads! I am clear of my *r*.

RESPONSIBLE (RESPONSIBILITY)
Nu 1: 53 The Levites are to be *r* for the care
1Co 7: 24 Brothers, each man, as *r* to God,

REST (RESTED RESTS SABBATH-REST)
Ex 31: 15 the seventh day is a Sabbath of *r*,
33: 14 go with you, and I will give you *r*."
Lev 25: 5 The land is to have a year of *r*.
Dt 31: 16 going to *r* with your fathers,
Jos 14: 15 Then the land had *r* from war.
21: 44 The LORD gave them *r*
1Ki 5: 4 Lord my God has given me *r*
1Ch 22: 9 who will be a man of peace and *r*,
Job 3: 17 and there the weary are at *r*.
Ps 16: 9 my body also will *r* secure,
33: 22 May your unfailing love *r* upon us,
62: 1 My soul finds *r* in God alone;
62: 5 Find *r*, O my soul, in God alone;
90: 17 of the Lord our God *r* upon us;
91: 1 will *r* in the shadow
95: 11 "They shall never enter my *r*."
Pr 6: 10 a little folding of the hands to *r*—
Isa 11: 2 Spirit of the LORD will *r* on him—
11: 10 and his place of *r* will be glorious.
30: 15 "In repentance and *r* is your
32: 18 in undisturbed places of *r*.
57: 20 which cannot *r*,
Jer 6: 16 and you will find *r* for your souls.
47: 6 'how long till you *r*?
Mt 11: 28 and burdened, and I will give you *r*.
2Co 12: 9 so that Christ's power may *r* on me
Heb 3: 11 'They shall never enter my *r*.'"
4: 3 'They shall never enter my *r*.'"
4: 10 for anyone who enters God's *r*
Rev 14: 13 "they will *r* from their labour,

RESTED (REST)
Ge 2: 2 so on the seventh day he *r*
Heb 4: 4 "And on the seventh day God *r*

RESTITUTION
Ex 22: 3 "A thief must certainly make *r*,
Lev 6: 5 He must make *r* in full, add a fifth
Nu 5: 8 the *r* belongs to the LORD

RESTORE (RESTORES)
Ps 51: 12 *R* to me the joy of your salvation
80: 3 *R* us, O God;
126: 4 *R* our fortunes, O LORD,
Jer 31: 18 *R* me, and I will return,
La 5: 21 *R* us to yourself, O LORD,
Da 9: 25 From the issuing of the decree to *r*
Na 2: 2 The LORD will *r* the splendour
Gal 6: 1 are spiritual should *r* him gently.
1Pe 5: 10 will himself *r* you and make you

RESTORES (RESTORE)
Ps 23: 3 he *r* my soul.

RESTRAINED (RESTRAINT)
Ps 78: 38 Time after time he *r* his anger

RESTRAINING (RESTRAINT)
Pr 27: 16 *r* her is like *r* the wind
Col 2: 23 value in *r* sensual indulgence.

RESTRAINT (RESTRAINED RESTRAINING)
Pr 17: 27 of knowledge uses words with *r*,
23: 4 have the wisdom to show *r*.
29: 18 no revelation, the people cast off *r*;

RESTS (REST)
Dt 33: 12 and the one the LORD loves *r*
Pr 19: 23 one *r* content, untouched
Lk 2: 14 to men on whom his favour *r*."

RESULT
Lk 21: 13 This will *r* in your being witnesses
Ro 6: 22 to holiness, and the *r* is eternal life.
11: 31 as a *r* of God's mercy to you.
2Co 3: 3 from Christ, the *r* of our ministry,
2Th 1: 5 as a *r* you will be counted worthy
1Pe 1: 7 may be proved genuine and may *r*

RESURRECTION*
Mt 22: 23 who say there is no *r*, came to him
22: 28 at the *r*, whose wife will she be
22: 30 At the *r* people will neither marry
22: 31 But about the *r* of the dead—
27: 53 and after Jesus' *r* they went
Mk 12: 18 who say there is no *r*, came to him
12: 23 At the *r* whose wife will she be,
Lk 14: 14 repaid at the *r* of the righteous."
20: 27 who say there is no *r*, came to Jesus
20: 33 at the *r* whose wife will she be,
20: 35 in the *r* from the dead will neither
20: 36 since they are children of the *r*.
Jn 11: 24 again in the *r* at the last day."
11: 25 Jesus said to her, "I am the *r*
Ac 1: 22 become a witness with us of his *r*."
2: 31 he spoke of the *r* of the Christ,
4: 2 in Jesus the *r* of the dead.
4: 33 to testify to the *r* of the Lord Jesus,
17: 18 good news about Jesus and the *r*.
17: 32 When they heard about the *r*
23: 6 of my hope in the *r* of the dead."
23: 8 Sadducees say that there is no *r*,
24: 15 that there will be a *r*
24: 21 "It is concerning the *r*
Ro 1: 4 Son of God by his *r* from the dead:
6: 5 also be united with him in his *r*.
1Co 15: 12 some of you say that there is no *r*
15: 13 If there is no *r* of the dead,
15: 21 the *r* of the dead comes
15: 29 if there is no *r*, what will those do
15: 42 So will it be with the *r* of the dead.
Php 3: 10 power of his *r* and the fellowship

Php 3:11 to attain to the *r* from the dead.
2Ti 2:18 say that the *r* has already taken
Heb 6:2 on of hands, the *r* of the dead,
11:35 so that they might gain a better *r*.
1Pe 1:3 hope through the *r* of Jesus Christ
3:21 It saves you by the *r* of Jesus Christ
Rev 20:5 This is the first *r*.
20:6 those who have part in the first *r*.

RETALIATE*

1Pe 2:23 he did not *r*; when he suffered,

RETRIBUTION

Ps 69:22 may it become *r* and a trap.
Jer 51:56 For the LORD is a God of *r*;
Ro 11:9 a stumbling-block and a *r* for them.

RETURN (RETURNED RETURNS)

Ge 3:19 and to dust you will *r*."
2Sa 12:23 go to him, but he will not *r* to me."
2Ch 30:9 If you *r* to the LORD, then you
Ne 1:9 but if you *r* to me and obey my
Job 10:21 joy before I go to the place of no *r*,
16:22 before I go on the journey of no *r*.
22:23 If you *r* to the Almighty, you will
Ps 80:14 *R* to us, O God Almighty!
126:6 will *r* with songs of joy,
Isa 10:21 A remnant will *r*, a remnant
35:10 the ransomed of the LORD will *r*.
55:11 It will not *r* to me empty,
Jer 24:7 for they will *r* to me
31:8 a great throng will *r*.
La 3:40 and let us *r* to the LORD.
Hos 6:1 "Come, let us *r* to the LORD.
12:6 But you must *r* to your God;
14:1 *R*, O Israel, to the LORD your
Joel 2:12 "*r* to me with all your heart,
Zec 1:3 '*R* to me,' declares the LORD
10:9 and they will *r*.

RETURNED (RETURN)

Ps 35:13 When my prayers *r*
Am 4:6 yet you have not *r* to me,"
1Pe 2:25 now you have *r* to the Shepherd

RETURNS (RETURN)

Pr 3:14 and yields better *r* than gold.
Isa 52:8 When the LORD *r* to Zion,
Mt 24:46 finds him doing so when he *r*.

REUBEN

Firstborn of Jacob by Leah (Ge 29:32; 46:8; 1Ch 2:1). Attempted to rescue Joseph (Ge 37:21-30). Lost birthright for sleeping with Bilhah (Ge 35:22; 49:4). Tribe of blessed (Ge 49:3-4; Dt 33:6), numbered (Nu 1:21; 26:7), allotted land east of Jordan (Nu 32; 34:14; Jos 13:15), west (Eze 48:6), failed to help Deborah (Jdg 5:15-16), supported David (1Ch 12:37), 12,000 from (Rev 7:5).

REVEAL (REVEALED REVEALS REVELATION REVELATIONS)

Mt 11:27 to whom the Son chooses to *r* him.
Gal 1:16 was pleased to *r* his Son in me

REVEALED (REVEAL)

Dt 29:29 but the things *r* belong to us
Isa 40:5 the glory of the LORD will be *r*,
43:12 I have *r* and saved and proclaimed
53:1 the arm of the LORD been *r*?
65:1 I *r* myself to those who did not ask
Mt 11:25 and *r* them to little children.
Jn 12:38 the arm of the LORD been *r*?"
17:6 "I have *r* you to those whom you
Ro 1:17 a righteousness from God is *r*,
8:18 with the glory that will be *r* in us.
10:20 I *r* myself to those who did not ask
16:26 but now *r* and made known
1Co 2:10 but God has *r* it to us by his Spirit.
2Th 1:7 happen when the Lord Jesus is *r*
2:3 and the man of lawlessness is *r*,
1Pe 1:7 and honour when Jesus Christ is *r*.
1:20 but was *r* in these last times
4:13 overjoyed when his glory is *r*.

REVEALS* (REVEAL)

Nu 23:3 Whatever he *r* to me I will tell you
Job 12:22 He *r* the deep things of darkness
Da 2:22 He *r* deep and hidden things;
2:28 a God in heaven who *r* mysteries.
Am 4:13 and *r* his thoughts to man,

REVELATION* (REVEAL)

2Sa 7:17 David all the words of this entire *r*.
1Ch 17:15 David all the words of this entire *r*.
Pr 29:18 Where there is no *r*, the people cast
Da 10:1 a *r* was given to Daniel (who was
Hab 2:2 "Write down the *r*
2:3 For the *r* awaits an appointed time;
Lk 2:32 a light for *r* to the Gentiles
Ro 16:25 according to the *r*
1Co 14:6 I bring you some *r* or knowledge
14:26 a *r*, a tongue or an interpretation.
14:30 And if a *r* comes to someone who is
Gal 1:12 I received it by *r* from Jesus Christ.
2:2 I went in response to a *r*
Eph 1:17 you the Spirit of wisdom and *r*,
3:3 mystery made known to me by *r*,
Rev 1:1 *r* of Jesus Christ, which God gave

REVELATIONS* (REVEAL)

2Co 12:1 on to visions and *r* from the Lord.
12:7 of these surpassingly great *r*,

REVELLED* (REVELRY)

Ne 9:25 they *r* in your great goodness.

REVELRY (REVELLED)

Ex 32:6 drink and got up to indulge in *r*.
1Co 10:7 and got up to indulge in pagan *r*."

REVENGE (VENGEANCE)

Lev 19:18 "'Do not seek *r* or bear a grudge
Ro 12:19 Do not take *r*, my friends,

REVERE* (REVERENCE REVERENT REVERING)

Lev 19:32 for the elderly and *r* your God.
Dt 4:10 so that they may learn to *r* me
13:4 must follow, and him you must *r*.
14:23 to *r* the LORD your God always.
17:19 learn to *r* the LORD his God
28:58 and do not *r* this glorious
Job 37:24 Therefore, men *r* him,
Ps 22:23 *R* him, all you descendants
33:8 let all the people of the world *r* him
102:15 of the earth will *r* your glory.
Ecc 3:14 God does it, so men will *r* him.
Isa 25:3 cities of ruthless nations will *r* you.
59:19 of the sun, they will *r* his glory.
63:17 hearts so we do not *r* you?
Jer 10:7 Who should not *r* you,
Hos 10:3 because we did not *r* the LORD.
Mal 4:2 But for you who *r* my name,

REVERENCE (REVERE)

Lev 19:30 and have *r* for my sanctuary.
Ne 5:15 of *r* for God I did not act like that.
Ps 5:7 in *r* will I bow down
Da 6:26 people must fear and *r* the God
2Co 7:1 perfecting holiness out of *r* for God
Eph 5:21 to one another out of *r* for Christ.
Col 3:22 of heart and *r* for the Lord.
1Pe 3:2 when they see the purity and *r*
Rev 11:18 and those who *r* your name,

REVERENT* (REVERE)

Ecc 8:12 with God-fearing men, who are *r*
Tit 2:3 women to be *r* in the way they live,
Heb 5:7 because of his *r* submission.
1Pe 1:17 as strangers here in *r* fear.

REVERING* (REVERE)

Dt 8:6 walking in his ways and *r* him.
Ne 1:11 who delight in *r* your name.

REVERSE*

Isa 43:13 When I act, who can *r* it?"

REVIVE* (REVIVING)

Ps 80:18 *r* us, and we will call on your name.
85:6 Will you not *r* us again,
Isa 57:15 and to *r* the heart of the contrite.
57:15 to *r* the spirit of the lowly
Hos 6:2 After two days he will *r* us;

REVIVING (REVIVE)

Ps 19:7 *r* the soul.

REVOKED

Isa 45:23 a word that will not be *r*:

REWARD (REWARDED REWARDING REWARDS)

Ge 15:1 your very great *r*."
1Sa 24:19 May the LORD *r* you well
Ps 19:11 in keeping them there is great *r*.
62:12 Surely you will *r* each person
127:3 children a *r* from him.
Pr 9:12 are wise, your wisdom will *r* you;
11:18 sows righteousness reaps a sure *r*.
13:21 prosperity is the *r* of the righteous.
19:17 he will *r* him for what he has done.
25:22 and the LORD will *r* you.
31:31 Give her the *r* she has earned,
Isa 40:10 See, his *r* is with him,
49:4 and my *r* is with my God."
61:8 In my faithfulness I will *r* them
62:11 See, his *r* is with him,
Jer 17:10 to *r* a man according to his conduct
32:19 you *r* everyone according
Mt 5:12 because great is your *r* in heaven,
6:1 you will have no *r*
6:5 they have received their *r* in full.
10:41 a prophet will receive a prophet's *r*,
16:27 and then he will *r* each person
Lk 6:23 because great is your *r* in heaven.
6:35 Then your *r* will be great,
1Co 3:14 built survives, he will receive his *r*.
Eph 6:8 know that the Lord will *r* everyone
Col 3:24 an inheritance from the Lord as a *r*.
Heb 11:26 he was looking ahead to his *r*.
Rev 22:12 I am coming soon! My *r* is with me

REWARDED (REWARD)

Ru 2:12 May you be richly *r* by the LORD,
2Sa 22:21 of my hands he has *r* me.
2Ch 15:7 for your work will be *r*."
Ps 18:24 The LORD has *r* me according
Pr 13:13 he who respects a command is *r*.
14:14 and the good man *r* for his.
Jer 31:16 for your work will be *r*,"
1Co 3:8 and each will be *r* according
Heb 10:35 your confidence; it will be richly *r*.
2Jn :8 but that you may be *r* fully.

REWARDING* (REWARD)

Rev 11:18 for *r* your servants the prophets

REWARDS (REWARD)

1Sa 26:23 The LORD *r* every man
Pr 12:14 the work of his hands *r* him.
Heb 11:6 that he *r* those who earnestly seek

RIBS

Ge 2:21 he took one of the man's *r*

RICH (RICHES RICHEST)

Job 34:19 does not favour the *r* over the poor,
Ps 49:16 overawed when a man grows *r*,
145:8 slow to anger and *r* in love.
Pr 21:17 loves wine and oil will never be *r*.
22:2 *R* and poor have this in common:
23:4 Do not wear yourself out to get *r*;

Pr 28: 6 than a *r* man whose ways are
28: 20 to get *r* will not go unpunished.
28: 22 A stingy man is eager to get *r*
Ecc 5: 12 but the abundance of a *r* man
Isa 33: 6 a *r* store of salvation and wisdom
53: 9 and with the *r* in his death,
Jer 9: 23 or the *r* man boast of his riches,
Zec 3: 4 and I will put *r* garments on you."
Mt 19: 23 it is hard for a *r* man
Lk 1: 53 but has sent the *r* away empty.
6: 24 "But woe to you who are *r*,
12: 21 for himself but is not *r* towards God
16: 1 "There was a *r* man whose
21: 1 Jesus saw the *r* putting their gifts
2Co 6: 10 yet making many *r*; having nothing
8: 2 poverty welled up in *r* generosity.
8: 9 he was *r*, yet for your sakes he
9: 11 You will be made *r* in every way
Eph 2: 4 love for us, God, who is *r* in mercy,
1Ti 6: 9 want to get *r* fall into temptation
6: 17 Command those who are *r*
6: 18 to do good, to be *r* in good deeds,
Jas 1: 10 the one who is *r* should take pride
2: 5 the eyes of the world to be *r* in faith
5: 1 you *r* people, weep and wail
Rev 2: 9 and your poverty—yet you are *r*!
3: 18 you can become *r*; and white

RICHES (RICH)

Job 36: 18 that no-one entices you by *r*;
Ps 49: 6 and boast of their great *r*?
49: 12 despite his *r*, does not endure;
62: 10 though your *r* increase,
119: 14 as one rejoices in great *r*.
Pr 3: 16 in her left hand are *r* and honour.
11: 28 Whoever trusts in his *r* will fall,
22: 1 is more desirable than great *r*;
27: 24 for *r* do not endure for ever,
30: 8 give me neither poverty nor *r*,
Isa 10: 3 Where will you leave your *r*?
60: 5 to you the *r* of the nations will
Jer 9: 23 or the rich man boast of his *r*,
Lk 8: 14 *r* and pleasures, and they do not
Ro 9: 23 to make the *r* of his glory known
11: 33 the depth of the *r* of the wisdom
Eph 2: 7 he might show the incomparable *r*
3: 8 to the Gentiles the unsearchable *r*
Col 1: 27 among the Gentiles the glorious *r*
2: 2 so that they may have the full *r*

RICHEST (RICH)

Isa 55: 2 and your soul will delight in the *r*

RID

Ge 21: 10 "Get *r* of that slave woman
1Co 5: 7 Get *r* of the old yeast that you may
Gal 4: 30 "Get *r* of the slave woman

RIDE (RIDER RIDING)

Ps 45: 4 In your majesty *r* forth victoriously

RIDER (RIDE)

Rev 6: 2 was a white horse! Its *r* held a bow,
19: 11 whose *r* is called Faithful and True.

RIDING (RIDE)

Zec 9: 9 gentle and *r* on a donkey,
Mt 21: 5 gentle and *r* on a donkey,

RIGGING

Isa 33: 23 Your *r* hangs loose:

RIGHT [1] (RIGHTS)

Ge 4: 7 But if you do not do what is *r*,
18: 19 of the LORD by doing what is *r*
18: 25 the Judge of all the earth do *r*?"
Ex 15: 26 and do what is *r* in his eyes,
Dt 6: 18 Do what is *r* and good
13: 18 and doing what is *r* in his eyes.
1Sa 12: 23 you the way that is good and *r*.
1Ki 3: 9 to distinguish between *r* and wrong
15: 5 For David had done what was *r*
2Ki 7: 9 to each other, "We're not doing *r*.
Ne 9: 13 and laws that are just and *r*,
Ps 19: 8 The precepts of the LORD are *r*,
25: 9 He guides the humble in what is *r*
33: 4 For the word of the LORD is *r*
51: 4 so that you are proved *r*
106: 3 who constantly do what is *r*.
119: 144 Your statutes are for ever *r*;
Pr 1: 3 doing what is *r* and just and fair;
14: 12 There is a way that seems *r*
18: 17 The first to present his case seems *r*
Ecc 7: 20 who does what is *r* and never sins.
SS 1: 4 How *r* they are to adore you!
Isa 1: 17 learn to do *r*!
7: 15 reject the wrong and choose the *r*.
30: 10 us no more visions of what is *r*!
64: 5 to the help of those who gladly do *r*
Jer 23: 5 and do what is just and *r* in the land
Eze 18: 5 who does what is just and *r*.
18: 21 and does what is just and *r*,
33: 14 and does what is just and *r*—
Hos 14: 9 The ways of the LORD are *r*;
Jn 1: 12 he gave the *r* to become children
Ro 3: 4 "So that you may be proved *r*
9: 21 Does not the potter have the *r*
12: 17 careful to do what is *r* in the eyes
1Co 9: 4 Don't we have the *r* to food
2Co 8: 21 we are taking pains to do what is *r*,
Eph 6: 1 parents in the Lord, for this is *r*.
Php 4: 8 whatever is *r*, whatever is pure,
2Th 3: 13 never tire of doing what is *r*.
Jas 2: 8 as yourself," you are doing *r*.
1Pe 3: 14 if you should suffer for what is *r*,
1Jn 2: 29 who does what is *r* has been born
Rev 2: 7 I will give the *r* to eat from the tree
3: 21 I will give the *r* to sit with me
22: 11 let him who does *r* continue to do *r*

RIGHT [2]

Ge 48: 13 on his left towards Israel's *r* hand,
Ex 15: 6 Your *r* hand, O LORD,
Dt 5: 32 do not turn aside to the *r*
Jos 1: 7 do not turn from it to the *r*
Ps 16: 8 Because he is at my *r* hand,
16: 11 eternal pleasures at your *r* hand.
17: 7 you who save by your *r* hand
18: 35 and your *r* hand sustains me;
44: 3 it was your *r* hand, your arm,
45: 4 let your *r* hand display awesome
63: 8 your *r* hand upholds me.
73: 23 you hold me by my *r* hand.
91: 7 ten thousand at your *r* hand,
98: 1 his *r* hand and his holy arm
110: 1 "Sit at my *r* hand
118: 15 LORD's *r* hand has done mighty
137: 5 may my *r* hand forget ⌊its skill⌋.
139: 10 your *r* hand will hold me fast.
Pr 4: 27 Do not swerve to the *r* or the left;
Isa 30: 21 Whether you turn to the *r*
41: 10 you with my righteous *r* hand.
41: 13 who takes hold of your *r* hand
48: 13 my *r* hand spread out the heavens;
Mt 5: 29 If your *r* eye causes you to sin,
6: 3 know what your *r* hand is doing,
22: 44 "Sit at my *r* hand
25: 33 He will put the sheep on his *r*
Ac 2: 34 "Sit at my *r* hand
7: 55 Jesus standing at the *r* hand of God
Ro 8: 34 is at the *r* hand of God and is
Eph 1: 20 and seated him at his *r* hand
Heb 1: 3 down at the *r* hand of the Majesty

RIGHTEOUS (RIGHTEOUSLY RIGHTEOUSNESS)

Ge 6: 9 Noah was a *r* man blameless
18: 23 "Will you sweep away the *r*
Nu 23: 10 Let me die the death of the *r*,
Ne 9: 8 your promise because you are *r*.
Job 36: 7 He does not take his eyes off the *r*;
Ps 1: 5 nor sinners in the assembly of the *r*.
5: 12 O LORD, you bless the *r*;
Ps 11: 7 For the LORD is *r*,
15: 2 and who does what is *r*,
34: 15 The eyes of the LORD are on the *r*
37: 16 Better the little that the *r* have
37: 21 but the *r* give generously;
37: 25 yet I have never seen the *r* forsaken
37: 30 of the *r* man utters wisdom,
55: 22 he will never let the *r* fall.
64: 10 Let the *r* rejoice in the LORD
68: 3 But may the *r* be glad
112: 4 compassionate and *r* man.
118: 20 through which the *r* may enter.
119: 7 as I learn your *r* laws.
119: 137 *R* are you, O LORD,
140: 13 Surely the *r* will praise your name
143: 2 for no-one living is *r* before you.
145: 17 The LORD is *r* in all his ways
Pr 3: 33 but he blesses the home of the *r*.
4: 18 of the *r* is like the first gleam
10: 7 of the *r* will be a blessing,
10: 11 The mouth of the *r* is a fountain
10: 16 The wages of the *r* bring them life
10: 20 The tongue of the *r* is choice silver,
10: 24 what the *r* desire will be granted.
10: 28 The prospect of the *r* is joy,
10: 32 of the *r* know what is fitting,
11: 23 The desire of the *r* ends only
11: 30 The fruit of the *r* is a tree of life,
12: 10 A *r* man cares for the needs
12: 21 No harm befalls the *r*,
13: 9 The light of the *r* shines brightly,
15: 28 of the *r* weighs its answers,
15: 29 but he hears the prayer of the *r*.
16: 31 it is attained by a *r* life.
18: 10 the *r* run to it and are safe.
20: 7 The *r* man leads a blameless life;
21: 15 justice is done, it brings joy to the *r*
23: 24 The father of a *r* man has great joy;
28: 1 but the *r* are as bold as a lion.
29: 6 but a *r* one can sing and be glad.
29: 7 The *r* care about justice
29: 27 The *r* detest the dishonest;
Ecc 7: 20 There is not a *r* man on earth
Isa 26: 7 The path of the *r* is level;
41: 10 you with my *r* right hand.
45: 21 a *r* God and a Saviour;
53: 11 his knowledge my *r* servant will
64: 6 and all our *r* acts are like filthy rags
Jer 23: 5 up to David a *r* Branch,
Eze 3: 20 when a *r* man turns
18: 5 "Suppose there is a *r* man
18: 20 of the *r* man will be credited
33: 12 The *r* man, if he sins, will not be
Da 9: 18 requests of you because we are *r*,
Hab 2: 4 but the *r* will live by his faith—
Zec 9: 9 *r* and having salvation,
Mal 3: 18 see the distinction between the *r*
Mt 5: 45 rain on the *r* and the unrighteous.
9: 13 For I have not come to call the *r*,
10: 41 and anyone who receives a *r* man
13: 43 Then the *r* will shine like the sun
13: 49 and separate the wicked from the *r*
25: 37 "Then the *r* will answer him, 'Lord,
25: 46 to eternal punishment, but the *r*
Ac 24: 15 will be a resurrection of both the *r*
Ro 1: 17 as it is written: "The *r* will live
2: 5 when his *r* judgment will be
2: 13 the law who will be declared *r*.
3: 10 "There is no-one *r*, not even one;
3: 20 Therefore no-one will be declared *r*
5: 19 one man the many will be made *r*.
Gal 3: 11 because, "The *r* will live by faith."
1Ti 1: 9 law is not made for the *r*
2Ti 4: 8 which the Lord, the *r* Judge,
Tit 3: 5 because of *r* things we had done,
Heb 10: 38 But my *r* one will live by faith.
Jas 5: 16 The prayer of a *r* man is powerful
1Pe 3: 12 the eyes of the Lord are on the *r*
3: 18 the *r* for the unrighteous,
4: 18 "If it is hard for the *r* to be saved,
1Jn 2: 1 defence—Jesus Christ, the *R* One.
3: 7 does what is right is *r*, just as he is *r*.
Rev 19: 8 stands for the *r* acts of the saints.)

RIGHTEOUSLY* (RIGHTEOUS)
Ps 9: 4 on your throne, judging *r*.
Isa 33: 15 He who walks *r*
Jer 11: 20 LORD Almighty, you who judge *r*

RIGHTEOUSNESS (RIGHTEOUS)
Ge 15: 6 and he credited it to him as *r*.
Dt 9: 4 of this land because of my *r*."
1Sa 26: 23 LORD rewards every man for his *r*
1Ki 10: 9 to maintain justice and *r*."
Job 37: 23 great *r*, he does not oppress.
Ps 7: 17 to the LORD because of his *r*
9: 8 He will judge the world in *r*;
17: 15 And I—in *r* I will see your face;
23: 3 He guides me in paths of *r*
33: 5 The LORD loves *r* and justice;
35: 28 My tongue will speak of your *r*
36: 6 Your *r* is like the mighty
37: 6 He will make your *r* shine like
40: 9 I proclaim *r* in the great assembly;
45: 4 on behalf of truth, humility and *r*;
45: 7 You love *r* and hate wickedness;
48: 10 your right hand is filled with *r*.
65: 5 us with awesome deeds of *r*,
71: 2 Rescue me and deliver me in your *r*
71: 15 My mouth will tell of your *r*,
71: 19 Your *r* reaches to the skies, O God,
85: 10 *r* and peace kiss each other.
89: 14 *R* and justice are the foundation
96: 13 He will judge the world in *r*
98: 9 He will judge the world in *r*
103: 6 The LORD works *r*
103: 17 his *r* with their children's children
106: 31 This was credited to him as *r*
111: 3 and his *r* endures for ever.
118: 19 Open for me the gates of *r*;
132: 9 May your priests be clothed with *r*;
145: 7 and joyfully sing of your *r*.
Pr 11: 5 *r* of the blameless makes a straight
11: 18 he who sows *r* reaps a sure reward.
13: 6 *R* guards the man of integrity,
14: 34 *R* exalts a nation,
16: 8 Better a little with *r*
16: 12 a throne is established through *r*.
21: 21 He who pursues *r* and love
Isa 5: 16 will show himself holy by his *r*.
9: 7 it with justice and *r*
11: 4 but with *r* he will judge the needy,
16: 5 and speeds the cause of *r*.
26: 9 the people of the world learn *r*.
32: 17 The fruit of *r* will be peace;
42: 6 "I, the LORD, have called you in *r*;
42: 21 the LORD for the sake of his *r*
45: 8 "You heavens above, rain down *r*;
51: 1 "Listen to me, you who pursue *r*
51: 6 my *r* will never fail.
51: 8 But my *r* will last for ever,
58: 8 then your *r* will go before you,
59: 17 He put on *r* as his breastplate,
61: 10 and arrayed me in a robe of *r*,
63: 1 "It is I, speaking in *r*,
Jer 9: 24 justice and *r* on earth,
23: 6 The LORD Our *R*.
Eze 3: 20 a righteous man turns from his *r*
14: 20 save only themselves by their *r*.
18: 20 The *r* of the righteous man will be
33: 12 *r* of the righteous man will not save
Da 9: 24 to bring in everlasting *r*,
12: 3 and those who lead many to *r*,
Hos 10: 12 Sow for yourselves *r*,
Am 5: 24 *r* like a never-failing stream!
Mic 7: 9 I will see his *r*.
Zep 2: 3 Seek *r*, seek humility;
Mal 4: 2 the sun of *r* will rise with healing
Mt 5: 6 those who hunger and thirst for *r*,
5: 10 who are persecuted because of *r*,
5: 20 unless your *r* surpasses that
6: 1 to do your 'acts of *r*' before men,
6: 33 But seek first his kingdom and his *r*
Jn 16: 8 world of guilt in regard to sin and *r*
Ac 24: 25 Paul discoursed on *r*, self-control
Ro 1: 17 For in the gospel a *r* from God is
3: 5 brings out God's *r* more clearly,
Ro 3: 22 This *r* from God comes
4: 3 and it was credited to him as *r*."
4: 5 wicked, his faith is credited as *r*.
4: 6 man to whom God credits *r* apart
4: 9 faith was credited to him as *r*.
4: 13 through the *r* that comes by faith.
4: 22 why "it was credited to him as *r*."
5: 18 of *r* was justification that brings life
6: 13 body to him as instruments of *r*.
6: 16 or to obedience, which leads to *r*?
6: 18 and have become slaves to *r*.
6: 19 in slavery to *r* leading to holiness.
8: 10 yet your spirit is alive because of *r*.
9: 30 did not pursue *r*, have obtained it,
10: 3 they did not know the *r* that comes
14: 17 but of *r*, peace and joy
1Co 1: 30 our *r*, holiness and redemption.
2Co 3: 9 is the ministry that brings *r*!
5: 21 that in him we might become the *r*
6: 7 with weapons of *r* in the right hand
6: 14 For what do *r* and wickedness have
9: 9 his *r* endures for ever."
Gal 2: 21 for if *r* could be gained
3: 6 and it was credited to him as *r*."
3: 21 then *r* would certainly have come
Eph 4: 24 created to be like God in true *r*
5: 9 *r* and truth) and find out what
6: 14 with the breastplate of *r* in place,
Php 1: 11 filled with the fruit of *r* that comes
3: 6 as for legalistic *r*, faultless.
3: 9 not having a *r* of my own that
1Ti 6: 11 and pursue *r*, godliness, faith, love,
2Ti 2: 22 and pursue *r*, faith, love and peace,
3: 16 correcting and training in *r*,
4: 8 is in store for me the crown of *r*,
Heb 1: 8 and *r* will be the sceptre
5: 13 with the teaching about *r*.
7: 2 his name means "king of *r*";
11: 7 became heir of the *r* that comes
12: 11 it produces a harvest of *r*
Jas 2: 23 and it was credited to him as *r*,"
3: 18 sow in peace raise a harvest of *r*.
1Pe 2: 24 die to sins and live for *r*;
2Pe 2: 21 not to have known the way of *r*,
3: 13 and a new earth, the home of *r*.

RIGHTS (RIGHT [1])
Ps 82: 3 maintain the *r* of the poor
Pr 31: 8 for the *r* of all who are destitute.
Isa 10: 2 to deprive the poor of their *r*
La 3: 35 to deny a man his *r*
Gal 4: 5 that we might receive the full *r*

RING
Pr 11: 22 Like a gold *r* in a pig's snout
Lk 15: 22 Put a *r* on his finger and sandals

RIOTS
2Co 6: 5 imprisonments and *r*; in hard work,

RIPE
Joel 3: 13 for the harvest is *r*.
Am 8: 1 showed me: a basket of *r* fruit.
Jn 4: 35 at the fields! They are *r* for harvest.
Rev 14: 15 for the harvest of the earth is *r*."

RISE (RAISE RAISED RISEN ROSE)
Lev 19: 32 "'*R* in the presence of the aged,
Nu 24: 17 a sceptre will *r* out of Israel.
Isa 26: 19 their bodies will *r*.
Mal 4: 2 of righteousness will *r* with healing
Mt 27: 63 'After three days I will *r* again.'
Mk 8: 31 and after three days *r* again.
Lk 18: 33 On the third day he will *r* again."
Jn 5: 29 those who have done good will *r*
20: 9 had to *r* from the dead.)
Ac 17: 3 had to suffer and *r* from the dead.
1Th 4: 16 and the dead in Christ will *r* first.

RISEN (RISE)
Mt 28: 6 He is not here; he has *r*, just
Mk 16: 6 He has *r*! He is not here.
Lk 24: 34 The Lord has *r* and has appeared

RIVER (RIVERS)
Ps 46: 4 There is a *r* whose streams make
Isa 66: 12 "I will extend peace to her like a *r*,
Eze 47: 12 grow on both banks of the *r*.
Rev 22: 1 Then the angel showed me the *r*

RIVERS (RIVER)
Ps 137: 1 By the *r* of Babylon we sat

ROAD (CROSSROADS ROADS)
Mt 7: 13 and broad is the *r* that leads

ROADS (ROAD)
Lk 3: 5 crooked *r* shall become straight,

ROARING
1Pe 5: 8 prowls around like a *r* lion looking

ROB (ROBBERS ROBBERY ROBS)
Mal 3: 8 "Will a man *r* God? Yet you *r* me.

ROBBERS (ROB)
Jer 7: 11 become a den of *r* to you?
Mk 15: 27 They crucified two *r* with him,
Lk 19: 46 but you have made it 'a den of *r*.'"
Jn 10: 8 came before me were thieves and *r*,

ROBBERY (ROB)
Isa 61: 8 I hate *r* and iniquity.

ROBE (ROBED ROBES)
Ge 37: 3 and he made a richly ornamented *r*
Isa 6: 1 the train of his *r* filled the temple.
61: 10 arrayed me in a *r* of righteousness,
Rev 6: 11 each of them was given a white *r*,

ROBED (ROBE)
Ps 93: 1 the LORD is *r* in majesty
Isa 63: 1 Who is this, *r* in splendour,

ROBES (ROBE)
Ps 45: 8 All your *r* are fragrant with myrrh
Rev 7: 13 "Those in white *r*—who are they,

ROBS* (ROB)
Pr 19: 26 He who *r* his father and drives out
28: 24 He who *r* his father or mother

ROCK
Ge 49: 24 of the Shepherd, the *R* of Israel,
Ex 17: 6 Strike the *r*, and water will come
Nu 20: 8 Speak to that *r* before their eyes
Dt 32: 4 He is the *R*, his works are perfect,
32: 13 him with honey from the *r*,
2Sa 22: 2 "The LORD is my *r*, my fortress
Ps 18: 2 The LORD is my *r*, my fortress
19: 14 O LORD, my *R* and my Redeemer
40: 2 he set my feet on a *r*
61: 2 lead me to the *r* that is higher
92: 15 he is my *R*, and there is no
Isa 26: 4 the LORD, is the *R* eternal.
51: 1 to the *r* from which you were cut
Da 2: 34 you were watching, a *r* was cut out,
Mt 7: 24 man who built his house on the *r*.
16: 18 and on this *r* I will build my church
Ro 9: 33 and a *r* that makes them fall,
1Co 10: 4 the spiritual *r* that accompanied
1Pe 2: 8 and a *r* that makes them fall."

ROD (RODS)
2Sa 7: 14 I will punish him with the *r* of men,
Ps 23: 4 your *r* and your staff,
Pr 13: 24 He who spares the *r* hates his son,
22: 15 the *r* of discipline will drive it far
23: 13 if you punish him with the *r*,
29: 15 *r* of correction imparts wisdom,
Isa 11: 4 the earth with the *r* of his mouth;

RODS (ROD)
2Co 11: 25 Three times I was beaten with *r*,

ROLL (ROLLED)
Mk 16: 3 "Who will *r* the stone away

ROLLED (ROLL)

Lk 24: 2 They found the stone *r* away

ROMAN

Ac 16: 37 even though we are *R* citizens,
22: 25 you to flog a *R* citizen who hasn't

ROOF

2Ki 19: 26 like grass sprouting on the *r*,
Isa 37: 27 like grass sprouting on the *r*,
Pr 21: 9 Better to live on a corner of the *r*

ROOM (ROOMS)

Mt 6: 6 When you pray, go into your *r*,
Mk 14: 15 He will show you a large upper *r*,
Lk 2: 7 there was no *r* for them in the inn.
Jn 8: 37 because you have no *r* for my word
21: 25 the whole world would not have *r*
2Co 7: 2 Make *r* for us in your hearts.

ROOMS (ROOM)

Jn 14: 2 In my Father's house are many *r*;

ROOT (ROOTED ROOTS)

Isa 11: 10 In that day the *R* of Jesse will stand
53: 2 and like a *r* out of dry ground.
Mt 3: 10 already at the *r* of the trees,
13: 21 But since he has no *r*, he lasts only
Ro 11: 16 if the *r* is holy, so are the branches.
15: 12 "The *r* of Jesse will spring up,
1Ti 6: 10 of money is a *r* of all kinds of evil.
Rev 5: 5 the *R* of David, has triumphed.
22: 16 I am the *R* and the Offspring

ROOTED (ROOT)

Eph 3: 17 being *r* and established in love,

ROOTS (ROOT)

Isa 11: 1 from his *r* a Branch will bear fruit.

ROSE [1]

SS 2: 1 I am a *r* of Sharon,

ROSE [2] (RISE)

1Th 4: 14 believe that Jesus died and *r* again

ROTS

Pr 14: 30 but envy *r* the bones.

ROUGH

Isa 42: 16 and make the *r* places smooth.
Lk 3: 5 the *r* ways smooth.

ROUND

Ecc 1: 6 *r* and *r* it goes,

ROYAL

Ps 45: 9 at your right hand is the *r* bride
Da 1: 8 not to defile himself with the *r* food
Jas 2: 8 If you really keep the *r* law found
1Pe 2: 9 a *r* priesthood, a holy nation,

RUBBISH*

Php 3: 8 I consider them *r*, that I may gain

RUBIES

Job 28: 18 the price of wisdom is beyond *r*.
Pr 3: 15 She is more precious than *r*;
8: 11 for wisdom is more precious than *r*,
31: 10 She is worth far more than *r*.

RUDDER*

Jas 3: 4 by a very small *r* wherever the pilot

RUDDY

1Sa 16: 12 He was *r*, with a fine appearance
SS 5: 10 My lover is radiant and *r*,

RUDE*

1Co 13: 5 It is not *r*, it is not self-seeking,

RUIN (RUINED RUINING RUINS)

Pr 10: 8 but a chattering fool comes to *r*.
10: 10 and a chattering fool comes to *r*.
10: 14 but the mouth of a fool invites *r*.
10: 29 but it is the *r* of those who do evil.
18: 24 many companions may come to *r*,
19: 13 A foolish son is his father's *r*,
26: 28 and a flattering mouth works *r*.
SS 2: 15 that *r* the vineyards,
Eze 21: 27 A *r*! A *r*! I will make it a *r*!
1Ti 6: 9 desires that plunge men into *r*

RUINED (RUIN)

Isa 6: 5 "I am *r*! For I am a man
Mt 9: 17 and the wineskins will be *r*.
12: 25 divided against itself will be *r*,

RUINING* (RUIN)

Tit 1: 11 they are *r* whole households

RUINS (RUIN)

Pr 19: 3 A man's own folly *r* his life,
Ecc 4: 5 and *r* himself.
2Ti 2: 14 and only *r* those who listen.

RULE (RULER RULERS RULES)

Ge 1: 26 let them *r* over the fish of the sea
3: 16 and he will *r* over you."
Jdg 8: 22 said to Gideon, "*R* over us—
1Sa 12: 12 'No, we want a king to *r* over us'—
Ps 2: 9 You will *r* them with an iron
67: 4 for you *r* the peoples justly
119: 133 let no sin *r* over me.
Pr 17: 2 A wise servant will *r*
Isa 28: 10 *r* on *r*, *r* on *r*;
Eze 20: 33 I will *r* over you with a mighty
Zec 6: 13 and will sit and *r* on his throne.
9: 10 His *r* will extend from sea to sea
Ro 13: 9 are summed up in this one *r*:
15: 12 arise to *r* over the nations;
1Co 7: 17 This is the *r* I lay down in all
Gal 6: 16 and mercy to all who follow this *r*,
Eph 1: 21 far above all *r* and authority,
Col 3: 15 the peace of Christ *r* in your hearts.
2Th 3: 10 we gave you this *r*: "If a man will
Rev 2: 27 He will *r* them with an iron sceptre;
12: 5 who will *r* all the nations
19: 15 He will *r* them with an iron sceptre

RULER (RULE)

Ps 8: 6 You made him *r* over the works
Pr 19: 6 Many curry favour with a *r*,
23: 1 When you sit to dine with a *r*,
25: 15 Through patience a *r* can be
29: 26 Many seek an audience with a *r*,
Isa 60: 17 and righteousness your *r*.
Da 9: 25 the *r*, comes, there will be seven
Mic 5: 2 one who will be *r* over Israel,
Mt 2: 6 for out of you will come a *r*
Eph 2: 2 of the *r* of the kingdom of the air,
1Ti 6: 15 God, the blessed and only *R*,
Rev 1: 5 and the *r* of the kings of the earth.

RULERS (RULE)

Ps 2: 2 and the *r* gather together
119: 161 *R* persecute me without cause,
119: 23 Though *r* sit together and slander
Isa 40: 23 reduces the *r* of this world
Da 7: 27 and all *r* will worship and obey him
Mt 20: 25 "You know that the *r*
Ac 13: 27 and their *r* did not recognise Jesus,
Ro 13: 3 For *r* hold no terror
1Co 2: 6 of this age or of the *r* of this age,
Eph 3: 10 should be made known to the *r*
6: 12 the *r*, against the authorities,
Col 1: 16 or powers or *r* or authorities;

RULES (RULE)

Nu 15: 15 is to have the same *r* for you
2Sa 23: 3 when he *r* in the fear of God,
Ps 22: 28 and he *r* over the nations.
66: 7 He *r* for ever by his power,
103: 19 and his kingdom *r* over all,
Isa 29: 13 is made up only of *r* taught by men.
40: 10 and his arm *r* for him.
Mt 15: 9 their teachings are but *r* taught
Lk 22: 26 one who *r* like the one who serves.
2Ti 2: 5 he competes according to the *r*.

RUMOURS

Jer 51: 46 afraid when *r* are heard in the land;
Mt 24: 6 You will hear of wars and *r* of wars,

RUN (RAN RUNNERS RUNNING RUNS)

Ps 19: 5 champion rejoicing to *r* his course.
Pr 4: 12 when you *r*, you will not stumble.
18: 10 the righteous *r* to it and are safe.
Isa 10: 3 To whom will you *r* for help?
40: 31 they will *r* and not grow weary,
Joel 3: 18 ravines of Judah will *r* with water.
Hab 2: 2 so that a herald may *r* with it.
1Co 9: 24 *R* in such a way as to get the prize.
Gal 2: 2 that I was running or had *r* my race
Php 2: 16 on the day of Christ that I did not *r*
Heb 12: 1 let us *r* with perseverance the race

RUNNERS* (RUN)

1Co 9: 24 that in a race all the *r* run,

RUNNING (RUN)

Ps 133: 2 *r* down on Aaron's beard,
Lk 17: 23 Do not go *r* off after them.
1Co 9: 26 I do not run like a man *r* aimlessly;
Gal 5: 7 You were *r* a good race.

RUNS (RUN)

Jn 10: 12 he abandons the sheep and *r* away.

RUSH

Pr 1: 16 for their feet *r* into sin,
6: 18 feet that are quick to *r* into evil,
Isa 59: 7 Their feet *r* into sin;

RUST

Mt 6: 19 where moth and *r* destroy,

RUTH*

Moabitess; widow who went to Bethlehem with mother-in-law Naomi (Ru 1). Gleaned in field of Boaz; shown favour (Ru 2). Proposed marriage to Boaz (Ru 3). Married (Ru 4:1-12); bore Obed, ancestor of David (Ru 4:13-22), Jesus (Mt 1:5).

RUTHLESS

Pr 11: 16 but *r* men gain only wealth.
Ro 1: 31 are senseless, faithless, heartless, *r*.

SABBATH (SABBATHS)

Ex 20: 8 "Remember the *S* day
31: 14 " 'Observe the *S*, because it is holy
Lev 25: 2 the land itself must observe a *s*
Dt 5: 12 "Observe the *S* day
Isa 56: 2 keeps the *S* without desecrating it,
56: 6 all who keep the *S*
58: 13 if you call the *S* a delight
Jer 17: 21 not to carry a load on the *S* day
Mt 12: 1 through the cornfields on the *S*.
Lk 13: 10 On a *S* Jesus was teaching in one
Col 2: 16 a New Moon celebration or a *S* day

SABBATH-REST* (REST)

Heb 4: 9 then, a *S* for the people of God;

SABBATHS (SABBATH)

2Ch 2: 4 evening and on *S* and New Moons
Eze 20: 12 Also I gave them my *S*

SACKCLOTH

Ps 30: 11 you removed my *s* and clothed me
Da 9: 3 in fasting, and in *s* and ashes.
Mt 11: 21 would have repented long ago in *s*

SACRED

Lev 23: 2 are to proclaim as *s* assemblies.
Mt 7: 6 "Do not give dogs what is *s*;
Ro 14: 5 One man considers one day more *s*
1Co 3: 17 for God's temple is *s*, and you are

2Pe 1: 18 were with him on the *s* mountain.
2: 21 on the *s* command that was

SACRIFICE (SACRIFICED SACRIFICES)

Ge 22: 2 *S* him there as a burnt offering
Ex 12: 27 'It is the Passover *s* to the LORD,
1Sa 15: 22 To obey is better than *s*,
1Ki 18: 38 the LORD fell and burned up the *s*,
1Ch 21: 24 or *s* a burnt offering that costs me
Ps 40: 6 *S* and offering you did not desire,
50: 14 *S* thank-offerings to God,
51: 16 You do not delight in *s*,
54: 6 I will *s* a freewill offering to you;
107: 22 Let them *s* thank-offerings
141: 2 of my hands be like the evening *s*.
Pr 15: 8 The LORD detests the *s*
21: 3 to the LORD than *s*.
Da 9: 27 that 'seven' he will put an end to *s*
12: 11 time that the daily *s* is abolished
Hos 6: 6 For I desire mercy, not *s*,
Mt 9: 13 this means: 'I desire mercy, not *s*.'
Ro 3: 25 God presented him as a *s*
Eph 5: 2 as a fragrant offering and *s* to God.
Php 4: 18 an acceptable *s*, pleasing to God.
Heb 9: 26 away with sin by the *s* of himself.
10: 5 "*S* and offering you did not desire,
10: 10 holy through the *s* of the body
10: 14 by one *s* he has made perfect
10: 18 there is no longer any *s* for sin.
11: 4 faith Abel offered God a better *s*
13: 15 offer to God a *s* of praise—
1Jn 2: 2 He is the atoning *s* for our sins,
4: 10 as an atoning *s* for our sins.

SACRIFICED (SACRIFICE)

Ac 15: 29 are to abstain from food *s* to idols,
1Co 5: 7 our Passover lamb, has been *s*.
8: 1 Now about food *s* to idols:
Heb 7: 27 He *s* for their sins once for all
9: 28 so Christ was *s* once

SACRIFICES (SACRIFICE)

Ps 51: 17 The *s* of God are a broken spirit;
Mk 12: 33 than all burnt offerings and *s*."
Ro 12: 1 to offer your bodies as living *s*,
Heb 9: 23 with better *s* than these.
13: 16 for with such *s* God is pleased.
1Pe 2: 5 offering spiritual *s* acceptable

SAD

Lk 18: 23 he heard this, he became very *s*,

SADDUCEES

Mt 16: 6 the yeast of the Pharisees and *S*."
Mk 12: 18 *S*, who say there is no resurrection,
Ac 23: 8 *S* say that there is no resurrection,

SAFE (SAVE)

Ps 27: 5 he will keep me *s* in his dwelling;
37: 3 in the land and enjoy *s* pasture.
Pr 18: 10 the righteous run to it and are *s*.
28: 26 he who walks in wisdom is kept *s*.
29: 25 in the LORD is kept *s*.
Jer 12: 5 If you stumble in *s* country,
Jn 17: 12 kept them *s* by that name you gave
1Ti 2: 15 But women will be kept *s*
1Jn 5: 18 born of God keeps him *s*,

SAFETY (SAVE)

Ps 4: 8 make me dwell in *s*.
Hos 2: 18 so that all may lie down in *s*.
1Th 5: 3 people are saying, "Peace and *s*,"

SAINTS

1Sa 2: 9 He will guard the feet of his *s*,
Ps 16: 3 As for the *s* who are in the land,
30: 4 Sing to the LORD, you *s* of his:
31: 23 Love the LORD, all his *s*!
34: 9 Fear the LORD, you his *s*,
116: 15 is the death of his *s*.
149: 1 his praise in the assembly of the *s*.
149: 5 Let the *s* rejoice in this honour
Da 7: 18 the *s* of the Most High will receive
Ro 8: 27 intercedes for the *s* in accordance
1Co 6: 2 not know that the *s* will judge
Eph 1: 15 Jesus and your love for all the *s*,
1: 18 of his glorious inheritance in the *s*,
6: 18 always keep on praying for all the *s*
Phm : 7 have refreshed the hearts of the *s*.
Rev 5: 8 which are the prayers of the *s*.
19: 8 for the righteous acts of the *s*.)

SAKE (SAKES)

1Sa 12: 22 For the *s* of his great name
Ps 23: 3 righteousness for his name's *s*.
44: 22 Yet for your *s* we face death all day
106: 8 Yet he saved them for his name's *s*,
Isa 42: 21 for the *s* of his righteousness
43: 25 your transgressions, for my own *s*,
48: 9 For my own name's *s* I delay my
48: 11 For my own *s*, for my own *s*,
Jer 14: 7 for the *s* of your name.
14: 21 for the *s* of your name do not
Eze 20: 9 But for the *s* of my name I did what
20: 14 But for the *s* of my name I did what
20: 22 and for the *s* of my name I did what
36: 22 but for the *s* of my holy name,
Da 9: 17 For your *s*, O Lord, look with favour
Mt 10: 39 life for my *s* will find it.
19: 29 for my *s* will receive a hundred
1Co 9: 23 I do all this for the *s* of the gospel,
2Co 12: 10 for Christ's *s*, I delight
Php 3: 7 loss for the *s* of Christ.
Heb 11: 26 He regarded disgrace for the *s*
1Pe 2: 13 for the Lord's *s* to every authority
3Jn : 7 was for the *s* of the Name that they

SAKES* (SAKE)

2Co 8: 9 yet for your *s* he became poor,

SALEM

Ge 14: 18 king of *S* brought out bread
Heb 7: 2 "king of *S*" means "king of peace".

SALT

Ge 19: 26 and she became a pillar of *s*.
Nu 18: 19 covenant of *s* before the LORD
Mt 5: 13 "You are the *s* of the earth.
Col 4: 6 with *s*, so that you may know how
Jas 3: 11 *s* water flow from the same spring?

SALVATION* (SAVE)

Ex 15: 2 he has become my *s*.
2Sa 22: 3 my shield and the horn of my *s*.
23: 5 Will he not bring to fruition my *s*
1Ch 16: 23 proclaim his *s* day after day.
2Ch 6: 41 O LORD God, be clothed with *s*,
Ps 9: 14 and there rejoice in your *s*.
13: 5 my heart rejoices in your *s*.
14: 7 that *s* for Israel would come out
18: 2 is my shield and the horn of my *s*,
27: 1 The LORD is my light and my *s*—
28: 8 a fortress of *s* for his anointed one.
35: 3 "I am your *s*."
35: 9 and delight in his *s*.
37: 39 The *s* of the righteous comes
40: 10 I speak of your faithfulness and *s*.
40: 16 those who love your *s* always say,
50: 23 way so that I may show him the *s*
51: 12 Restore to me the joy of your *s*
53: 6 that *s* for Israel would come out
62: 1 my *s* comes from him.
62: 2 He alone is my rock and my *s*;
62: 6 He alone is my rock and my *s*;
62: 7 My *s* and my honour depend
67: 2 your *s* among all nations.
69: 13 answer me with your sure *s*.
69: 27 do not let them share in your *s*.
69: 29 may your *s*, O God, protect me.
70: 4 those who love your *s* always say,
71: 15 of your *s* all day long,
74: 12 you bring *s* upon the earth.
85: 7 and grant us your *s*.
85: 9 Surely his *s* is near those who fear
Ps 91: 16 and show him my *s*."
95: 1 to the Rock of our *s*.
96: 2 proclaim his *s* day after day.
98: 1 have worked *s* for him.
98: 2 The LORD has made his *s* known
98: 3 the *s* of our God.
116: 13 I will lift up the cup of *s*
118: 14 he has become my *s*.
118: 21 you have become my *s*.
119: 41 your *s* according to your promise;
119: 81 with longing for your *s*,
119: 123 My eyes fail, looking for your *s*,
119: 155 *S* is far from the wicked,
119: 166 I wait for your *s*, O LORD,
119: 174 I long for your *s*, O LORD,
132: 16 I will clothe her priests with *s*,
149: 4 he crowns the humble with *s*.
Isa 12: 2 Surely God is my *s*;
12: 2 he has become my *s*."
12: 3 from the wells of *s*.
25: 9 let us rejoice and be glad in his *s*."
26: 1 God makes *s*
26: 18 We have not brought *s* to the earth;
30: 15 "In repentance and rest is your *s*,
33: 2 our *s* in time of distress.
33: 6 a rich store of *s* and wisdom
45: 8 let *s* spring up,
45: 17 the LORD with an everlasting *s*;
46: 13 I will grant *s* to Zion,
46: 13 and my *s* will not be delayed.
49: 6 that you may bring my *s*
49: 8 and in the day of *s* I will help you;
51: 5 my *s* is on the way,
51: 6 But my *s* will last for ever,
51: 8 my *s* through all generations."
52: 7 who proclaim *s*,
52: 10 the *s* of our God.
56: 1 for my *s* is close at hand
59: 16 so his own arm worked *s* for him,
59: 17 and the helmet of *s* on his head;
60: 18 but you will call your walls *S*
61: 10 me with garments of *s*
62: 1 her *s* like a blazing torch.
63: 5 so my own arm worked *s* for me,
Jer 3: 23 is the *s* of Israel.
La 3: 26 quietly for the *s* of the LORD.
Jnh 2: 9 *S* comes from the LORD."
Zec 9: 9 righteous and having *s*,
Lk 1: 69 He has raised up a horn of *s* for us
1: 71 of long ago), *s* from our enemies
1: 77 give his people the knowledge of *s*
2: 30 For my eyes have seen your *s*,
3: 6 And all mankind will see God's *s*
19: 9 "Today *s* has come to this house,
Jn 4: 22 for *s* is from the Jews.
Ac 4: 12 *S* is found in no-one else,
13: 26 message of *s* has been sent.
13: 47 that you may bring *s* to the ends
28: 28 to know that God's *s* has been sent
Ro 1: 16 for the *s* of everyone who believes:
11: 11 *s* has come to the Gentiles
13: 11 because our *s* is nearer now
2Co 1: 6 it is for your comfort and *s*;
6: 2 and in the day of *s* I helped you."
6: 2 of God's favour, now is the day of *s*.
7: 10 brings repentance that leads to *s*
Eph 1: 13 word of truth, the gospel of your *s*.
6: 17 Take the helmet of *s* and the sword
Php 2: 12 to work out your *s* with fear
1Th 5: 8 and the hope of *s* as a helmet.
5: 9 to receive *s* through our Lord Jesus
2Ti 2: 10 they too may obtain the *s* that is
3: 15 wise for *s* through faith
Tit 2: 11 of God that brings *s* has appeared
Heb 1: 14 to serve those who will inherit *s*?
2: 3 This *s*, which was first announced
2: 3 escape if we ignore such a great *s*?
2: 10 of their *s* perfect through suffering.
5: 9 of eternal *s* for all who obey him
6: 9 case—things that accompany *s*.
9: 28 to bring *s* to those who are waiting
1Pe 1: 5 the coming of the *s* that is ready
1: 9 of your faith, the *s* of your souls.

1Pe 1: 10 Concerning this *s*, the prophets,
2: 2 by it you may grow up in your *s*,
2Pe 3: 15 that our Lord's patience means *s*,
Jude : 3 to write to you about the *s* we share
Rev 7: 10 "*S* belongs to our God,
12: 10 have come the *s* and the power
19: 1 *S* and glory and power belong

SAMARIA (SAMARITAN)
1Ki 16: 24 He bought the hill of *S*
2Ki 17: 6 the king of Assyria captured *S*
Jn 4: 4 Now he had to go through *S*.
4: 5 came to a town in *S* called Sychar,

SAMARITAN (SAMARIA)
Lk 10: 33 But a *S*, as he travelled, came where
17: 16 and thanked him—and he was a *S*.
Jn 4: 7 When a *S* woman came

SAMSON
Danite judge. Birth promised (Jdg 13). Married to Philistine, but wife given away (Jdg 14). Vengeance on Philistines (Jdg 15). Betrayed by Delilah (Jdg 16:1-22). Death (Jdg 16:23-31). Feats of strength: killed lion (Jdg 14:6), 30 Philistines (Jdg 14:19), 1,000 Philistines with jaw-bone (Jdg 15:13-17), carried off gates of Gaza (Jdg 16:3), pushed down temple of Dagon (Jdg 16:25-30).

SAMUEL
Ephraimite judge and prophet (Heb 11:32). Birth prayed for (1Sa 1:10-18). Dedicated to temple by Hannah (1Sa 1:21-28). Raised by Eli (1Sa 2:11, 18-26). Called as prophet (1Sa 3). Led Israel to victory over Philistines (1Sa 7). Asked by Israel for a king (1Sa 8). Anointed Saul as king (1Sa 9-10). Farewell speech (1Sa 12). Rebuked Saul for sacrifice (1Sa 13). Announced rejection of Saul (2Sa 15). Anointed David as king (1Sa 16). Protected David from Saul (1Sa 19:18-24). Death (1Sa 25:1). Returned from dead to condemn Saul (1Sa 28).

SANBALLAT
Led opposition to Nehemiah's rebuilding of Jerusalem (Ne 2:10, 19; 4; 6).

SANCTIFIED* (SANCTIFY)
Jn 17: 19 that they too may be truly *s*.
Ac 20: 32 among all those who are *s*.
26: 18 among those who are *s* by faith
Ro 15: 16 to God, *s* by the Holy Spirit.
1Co 1: 2 to those *s* in Christ Jesus
6: 11 But you were washed, you were *s*,
7: 14 and the unbelieving wife has been *s*
7: 14 the unbelieving husband has been *s*
1Th 4: 3 God's will that you should be *s*:
Heb 10: 29 blood of the covenant that *s* him,

SANCTIFY* (SANCTIFIED SANCTIFYING)
Jn 17: 17 *S* them by the truth; your word is
17: 19 For them I *s* myself, that they too
1Th 5: 23 *s* you through and through.
Heb 9: 13 are ceremonially unclean *s* them

SANCTIFYING* (SANCTIFY)
2Th 2: 13 through the *s* work of the Spirit
1Pe 1: 2 through the *s* work of the Spirit,

SANCTUARY
Ex 25: 8 "Then have them make a *s* for me,
Lev 19: 30 and have reverence for my *s*.
Ps 15: 1 LORD, who may dwell in your *s*?
63: 2 I have seen you in the *s*
68: 24 of my God and King into the *s*.
68: 35 are awesome, O God, in your *s*;
73: 17 me till I entered the *s* of God;
102: 19 looked down from his *s* on high,
134: 2 Lift up your hands in the *s*
150: 1 Praise God in his *s*;
Eze 37: 26 I will put my *s* among them for ever
41: 1 the man brought me to the outer *s*
Da 9: 26 will destroy the city and the *s*.
Heb 6: 19 It enters the inner *s*
8: 2 in the *s*, the true tabernacle set up
8: 5 They serve at a *s* that is a copy
9: 24 enter a man-made *s* that was only

SAND
Ge 22: 17 and as the *s* on the seashore.
Mt 7: 26 man who built his house on *s*.

SANDAL (SANDALS)
Ru 4: 7 one party took off his *s*

SANDALS (SANDAL)
Ex 3: 5 off your *s*, for the place where you
Dt 25: 9 take off one of his *s*, spit in his face
Jos 5: 15 off your *s*, for the place where you
Mt 3: 11 whose *s* I am not fit to carry.

SANG (SING)
Ex 15: 1 and the Israelites *s* this song
15: 21 Miriam *s* to them:
Nu 21: 17 Then Israel *s* this song:
Jdg 5: 1 Barak son of Abinoam *s* this song:
1Sa 18: 7 As they danced, they *s*:
2Sa 22: 1 David *s* to the LORD the words
2Ch 5: 13 in praise to the LORD and *s*:
29: 30 So they *s* praises with gladness
Ezr 3: 11 thanksgiving they *s* to the LORD:
Job 38: 7 while the morning stars *s* together
Ps 106: 12 and *s* his praise.
Rev 5: 9 And they *s* a new song:
5: 12 In a loud voice they *s*:
14: 3 they *s* a new song before the throne
15: 3 and *s* the song of Moses the servant

SAP
Ro 11: 17 share in the nourishing *s*

SAPPHIRA*
Ac 5: 1 together with his wife *S*,

SARAH
Wife of Abraham, originally named Sarai; barren (Ge 11:29-31; 1Pe 3:6). Taken by Pharaoh as Abraham's sister; returned (Ge 12:10-20). Gave Hagar to Abraham; sent her away in pregnancy (Ge 16). Name changed; Isaac promised (Ge 17:15-21; 18:10-15; Heb 11:11). Taken by Abimelech as Abraham's sister; returned (Ge 20). Isaac born; Hagar and Ishmael sent away (Ge 21:1-21; Gal 4:21-31). Death (Ge 23).

SARDIS
Rev 3: 1 the angel of the church in *S* write:

SASH (SASHES)
Rev 1: 13 with a golden *s* around his chest.

SASHES (SASH)
Rev 15: 6 wore golden *s* around their chests.

SAT (SIT)
Ps 137: 1 By the rivers of Babylon we *s*
Mk 16: 19 and he *s* at the right hand of God.
Lk 10: 39 who *s* at the Lord's feet listening
Heb 1: 3 he *s* down at the right hand
8: 1 who *s* down at the right hand
10: 12 he *s* down at the right hand of God.
12: 2 and *s* down at the right hand

SATAN
Job 1: 6 and *S* also came with them.
Zec 3: 2 said to *S*, "The LORD rebuke you,
Mt 12: 26 If *S* drives out *S*, he is divided
16: 23 *S*! You are a stumbling-block to me
Mk 4: 15 *S* comes and takes away the word
Lk 10: 18 "I saw *S* fall like lightning
22: 3 *S* entered Judas, called Iscariot,
Ro 16: 20 The God of peace will soon crush *S*
1Co 5: 5 is present, hand this man over to *S*,
2Co 11: 14 for *S* himself masquerades
12: 7 a messenger of *S*, to torment me.
1Ti 1: 20 handed over to *S* to be taught not
Rev 12: 9 serpent called the devil or *S*,
20: 2 or *S*, and bound him for a thousand
20: 7 *S* will be released from his prison

SATISFIED (SATISFY)
Ps 17: 15 I will be *s* with seeing your likeness
22: 26 The poor will eat and be *s*;
63: 5 My soul will be *s* as with the richest
104: 28 they are *s* with good things.
105: 40 *s* them with the bread of heaven.
Pr 13: 4 the desires of the diligent are fully *s*
30: 15 are three things that are never *s*,
Ecc 5: 10 whoever loves wealth is never *s*
Isa 53: 11 he will see the light ⌞of life⌟ and be *s*
Mt 14: 20 They all ate and were *s*,
Lk 6: 21 for you will be *s*.

SATISFIES* (SATISFY)
Ps 103: 5 He *s* my desires with good things,
107: 9 for he *s* the thirsty
147: 14 and *s* you with the finest of wheat.

SATISFY (SATISFIED SATISFIES)
Ps 90: 14 *S* us in the morning
145: 16 *s* the desires of every living thing.
Pr 5: 19 may her breasts *s* you always,
Isa 55: 2 and your labour on what does not *s*?
58: 10 and *s* the needs of the oppressed,

SAUL
1. Benjamite; anointed by Samuel as first king of Israel (1Sa 9-10). Defeated Ammonites (1Sa 11). Rebuked for offering sacrifice (1Sa 13:1-15). Defeated Philistines (1Sa 14). Rejected as king for failing to annihilate Amalekites (1Sa 15). Soothed from evil spirit by David (1Sa 16:14-23). Sent David against Goliath (1Sa 17). Jealousy and attempted murder of David (1Sa 18:1-11). Gave David Michal as wife (1Sa 18:12-30). Second attempt to kill David (1Sa 19). Anger at Jonathan (1Sa 20:26-34). Pursued David: killed priests at Nob (1Sa 22), went to Keilah and Ziph (1Sa 23), life spared by David at En Gedi (1Sa 24) and in his tent (1Sa 26). Rebuked by Samuel's spirit for consulting witch at Endor (1Sa 28). Wounded by Philistines; took his own life (1Sa 31; 1Ch 10). Lamented by David (2Sa 1:17-27). Children (1Sa 14:49-51; 1Ch 8).
2. See PAUL

SAVAGE
Ac 20: 29 *s* wolves will come in among you

SAVE (SAFE SAFETY SALVATION SAVED SAVES SAVIOUR)
Ge 45: 5 to *s* lives that God sent me ahead
1Ch 16: 35 Cry out, "*S* us, O God our Saviour;
Job 40: 14 that your own right hand can *s* you.
Ps 17: 7 you who *s* by your right hand
18: 27 You *s* the humble
28: 9 *S* your people and bless your
31: 16 *s* me in your unfailing love.
69: 35 for God will *s* Zion
71: 2 turn your ear to me and *s* me.
72: 13 and *s* the needy from death.
89: 48 or *s* himself from the power
91: 3 Surely he will *s* you
109: 31 to *s* his life from those who
146: 3 in mortal men, who cannot *s*.
Pr 2: 16 will *s* you also from the adulteress,
Isa 35: 4 he will come to *s* you."
38: 20 The LORD will *s* me,
46: 7 it cannot *s* him from his troubles.
59: 1 of the LORD is not too short to *s*.
63: 1 mighty to *s*."
Jer 17: 14 *s* me and I will be saved,
Eze 3: 18 ways in order to *s* his life,
7: 19 able to *s* them in the day
14: 14 they could *s* only themselves
33: 12 of the righteous man will not *s* him

Eze 34: 22 I will *s* my flock, and they will no
Da 3: 17 the God we serve is able to *s* us
Hos 1: 7 and I will *s* them—not by bow,
Zep 1: 18 will be able to *s* them
3: 17 he is mighty to *s*.
Zec 8: 7 "I will *s* my people
Mt 1: 21 he will *s* his people from their sins
16: 25 wants to *s* his life will lose it,
Lk 19: 10 to seek and to *s* what was lost."
Jn 3: 17 but to *s* the world through him.
12: 47 come to judge the world, but to *s* it.
Ro 11: 14 people to envy and *s* some of them.
1Co 7: 16 whether you will *s* your husband?
1Ti 1: 15 came into the world to *s* sinners—
Heb 7: 25 to *s* completely those who come
Jas 5: 20 of his way will *s* him from death
Jude : 23 others from the fire and *s* them;

SAVED (SAVE)

Ps 22: 5 They cried to you and were *s*;
33: 16 No king is *s* by the size of his army;
34: 6 he *s* him out of all his troubles.
106: 21 They forgot the God who *s* them,
116: 6 when I was in great need, he *s* me.
Isa 25: 9 we trusted in him, and he *s* us.
45: 22 "Turn to me and be *s*,
64: 5 How then can we be *s*?
Jer 4: 14 from your heart and be *s*.
8: 20 and we are not *s*."
Eze 3: 19 but you will have *s* yourself.
33: 5 warning, he would have *s* himself.
Joel 2: 32 on the name of the LORD will be *s*;
Mt 10: 22 firm to the end will be *s*.
24: 13 firm to the end will be *s*.
Mk 13: 13 firm to the end will be *s*.
16: 16 believes and is baptised will be *s*,
Jn 10: 9 enters through me will be *s*.
Ac 2: 21 on the name of the Lord will be *s*.'
2: 47 daily those who were being *s*.
4: 12 to men by which we must be *s*."
15: 11 of our Lord Jesus that we are *s*,
16: 30 do to be *s*?" They replied,
Ro 5: 9 how much more shall we be *s*
9: 27 only the remnant will be *s*.
10: 1 the Israelites is that they may be *s*.
10: 9 him from the dead, you will be *s*.
10: 13 on the name of the Lord will be *s*."
11: 26 so all Israel will be *s*, as it is written:
1Co 1: 18 to us who are being *s* it is the power
3: 15 will suffer loss; he himself will be *s*,
5: 5 his spirit *s* on the day of the Lord.
10: 33 of many, so that they may be *s*.
15: 2 By this gospel you are *s*,
Eph 2: 5 it is by grace you have been *s*.
2: 8 For it is by grace you have been *s*,
2Th 2: 13 you to be *s* through the sanctifying
1Ti 2: 4 who wants all men to be *s*
2Ti 1: 9 who has *s* us and called us
Tit 3: 5 He *s* us through the washing
Heb 10: 39 but of those who believe and are *s*.

SAVES (SAVE)

Ps 7: 10 who *s* the upright in heart.
68: 20 Our God is a God who *s*;
145: 19 he hears their cry and *s* them.
1Pe 3: 21 It *s* you by the resurrection

SAVIOUR* (SAVE)

Dt 32: 15 and rejected the Rock his *S*.
2Sa 22: 3 stronghold, my refuge and my *s*—
22: 47 Exalted be God, the Rock, my *S*!
1Ch 16: 35 Cry out, "Save us, O God our *S*;
Ps 18: 46 Exalted be God my *S*!
24: 5 and vindication from God his *S*.
25: 5 for you are God my *S*,
27: 9 O God my *S*.
38: 22 O Lord my *S*.
42: 5 my *S* and
42: 11 my *S* and my God.
43: 5 my *S* and my God.
65: 5 O God our *S*,
68: 19 Praise be to the Lord, to God our *S*,
79: 9 Help us, O God our *S*,
Ps 85: 4 Restore us again, O God our *S*,
89: 26 My God, the Rock my *S*.'
Isa 17: 10 You have forgotten God your *S*;
19: 20 he will send them a *s* and defender,
43: 3 the Holy One of Israel, your *S*;
43: 11 and apart from me there is no *s*.
45: 15 O God and *S* of Israel.
45: 21 a righteous God and a *S*;
49: 26 that I, the LORD, am your *S*,
60: 16 know that I, the LORD, am your *S*,
62: 11 'See, your *S* comes!
63: 8 and so he became their *S*.
Jer 14: 8 its *S* in times of distress,
Hos 13: 4 no *S* except me.
Mic 7: 7 I wait for God my *S*;
Hab 3: 18 I will be joyful in God my *S*.
Lk 1: 47 and my spirit rejoices in God my *S*,
2: 11 of David a *S* has been born to you;
Jn 4: 42 know that this man really is the *S*
Ac 5: 31 *S* that he might give repentance
13: 23 God has brought to Israel the *S*
Eph 5: 23 his body, of which he is the *S*.
Php 3: 20 we eagerly await a *S* from there,
1Ti 1: 1 by the command of God our *S*
2: 3 This is good, and pleases God our *S*
4: 10 who is the *S* of all men,
2Ti 1: 10 through the appearing of our *S*,
Tit 1: 3 me by the command of God our *S*,
1: 4 the Father and Christ Jesus our *S*.
2: 10 about God our *S* attractive.
2: 13 appearing of our great God and *S*,
3: 4 and love of God our *S* appeared,
3: 6 through Jesus Christ our *S*,
2Pe 1: 1 *S* Jesus Christ have received a faith
1: 11 eternal kingdom of our Lord and *S*
2: 20 and *S* Jesus Christ and are again
3: 2 and *S* through your apostles.
3: 18 and knowledge of our Lord and *S*
1Jn 4: 14 Son to be the *S* of the world.
Jude : 25 to the only God our *S* be glory,

SCALE

Ps 18: 29 with my God I can *s* a wall.

SCALES [1]

Lev 11: 9 may eat any that have fins and *s*.

SCALES [2]

Lev 19: 36 Use honest *s* and honest weights,
Pr 11: 1 The LORD abhors dishonest *s*,
Da 5: 27 You have been weighed on the *s*
Rev 6: 5 Its rider was holding a pair of *s*

SCAPEGOAT (GOAT)

Lev 16: 10 by sending it into the desert as a *s*.

SCARECROW*

Jer 10: 5 Like a *s* in a melon patch,

SCARLET

Jos 2: 21 she tied the *s* cord in the window.
Isa 1: 18 "Though your sins are like *s*,
Mt 27: 28 They stripped him and put a *s* robe

SCATTER (SCATTERED SCATTERS)

Dt 4: 27 The LORD will *s* you
Ne 1: 8 I will *s* you among the nations,
Jer 9: 16 I will *s* them among nations that
30: 11 the nations among which I *s* you,
Zec 10: 9 I *s* them among the peoples,

SCATTERED (SCATTER)

Isa 11: 12 he will assemble the *s* people
Jer 31: 10 "He who *s* Israel will gather them
Zec 2: 6 "for I have *s* you to the four winds
13: 7 and the sheep will be *s*,
Mt 26: 31 and the sheep of the flock will be *s*.'
Jn 11: 52 but also for the *s* children of God,
Ac 8: 4 who had been *s* preached the word
Jas 1: 1 To the twelve tribes *s*
1Pe 1: 1 *s* throughout Pontus, Galatia,

SCATTERS (SCATTER)

Mt 12: 30 he who does not gather with me *s*.

SCEPTRE

Ge 49: 10 The *s* will not depart from Judah,
Nu 24: 17 a *s* will rise out of Israel.
Ps 2: 9 You will rule them with an iron *s*;
45: 6 a *s* of justice will be the *s*
Heb 1: 8 and righteousness will be the *s*
Rev 2: 27 'He will rule them with an iron *s*;
12: 5 rule all the nations with an iron *s*.
19: 15 "He will rule them with an iron *s*."

SCHEMES

Pr 6: 18 a heart that devises wicked *s*,
24: 9 The *s* of folly are sin,
2Co 2: 11 For we are not unaware of his *s*.
Eph 6: 11 stand against the devil's *s*.

SCHOLAR*

1Co 1: 20 Where is the *s*? Where is

SCOFFERS

2Pe 3: 3 that in the last days *s* will come,

SCORN (SCORNED SCORNING SCORNS)

Ps 69: 7 For I endure *s* for your sake,
69: 20 *S* has broken my heart
89: 41 he has become the *s*
109: 25 I am an object of *s* to my accusers;
119: 22 Remove from me *s* and contempt,
Mic 6: 16 you will bear the *s* of the nations."

SCORNED (SCORN)

Ps 22: 6 *s* by men and despised

SCORNING (SCORN)

Heb 12: 2 him endured the cross, *s* its shame,

SCORNS (SCORN)

Pr 13: 13 He who *s* instruction will pay for it,
30: 17 that *s* obedience to a mother,

SCORPION

Lk 11: 12 will give him a *s*? If you then,
Rev 9: 5 sting of a *s* when it strikes a man.

SCOUNDREL

Pr 6: 12 A *s* and villain,

SCRIPTURE (SCRIPTURES)

Jn 2: 22 Then they believed the *S*
7: 42 Does not the *S* say that the Christ
10: 35 and the *S* cannot be broken—
Ac 8: 32 was reading this passage of *S*:
1Ti 4: 13 yourself to the public reading of *S*,
2Ti 3: 16 All *S* is God-breathed
2Pe 1: 20 that no prophecy of *S* came about

SCRIPTURES (SCRIPTURE)

Mt 22: 29 because you do not know the *S*
Lk 24: 27 said in all the *S* concerning himself.
24: 45 so they could understand the *S*.
Jn 5: 39 These are the *S* that testify about
Ac 17: 11 examined the *S* every day to see
2Ti 3: 15 you have known the holy *S*,
2Pe 3: 16 as they do the other *S*,

SCROLL

Ps 40: 7 it is written about me in the *s*.
Isa 34: 4 and the sky rolled up like a *s*;
Eze 3: 1 eat what is before you, eat this *s*;
Heb 10: 7 it is written about me in the *s*—
Rev 6: 14 The sky receded like a *s*, rolling up,
10: 8 take the *s* that lies open in the hand

SCUM

1Co 4: 13 this moment we have become the *s*

SEA (SEASHORE)

Ex 14: 16 go through the *s* on dry ground.

Dt 30: 13 "Who will cross the s to get it
1Ki 7: 23 He made the S of cast metal,
Job 11: 9 and wider than the s.
Ps 93: 4 mightier than the breakers of the s
95: 5 The s is his, for he made it,
Ecc 1: 7 All streams flow into the s,
Isa 57: 20 the wicked are like the tossing s,
Jnh 1: 4 LORD sent a great wind on the s,
Mic 7: 19 iniquities into the depths of the s.
Hab 2: 14 as the waters cover the s.
Zec 9: 10 His rule will extend from s to s
Mt 18: 6 drowned in the depths of the s.
1Co 10: 1 that they all passed through the s.
Jas 1: 6 who doubts is like a wave of the s,
Jude : 13 They are wild waves of the s,
Rev 10: 2 He planted his right foot on the s
13: 1 I saw a beast coming out of the s.
20: 13 The s gave up the dead that were
21: 1 and there was no longer any s.

SEAL (SEALED SEALS)

Ps 40: 9 I do not s my lips,
SS 8: 6 Place me like a s over your heart,
Da 12: 4 and s the words of the scroll
Jn 6: 27 God the Father has placed his s
1Co 9: 2 For you are the s of my apostleship
2Co 1: 22 set his s of ownership on us,
Eph 1: 13 you were marked in him with a s,
Rev 6: 3 the Lamb opened the second s,
6: 5 When the Lamb opened the third s,
6: 7 the Lamb opened the fourth s,
6: 9 When he opened the fifth s,
6: 12 I watched as he opened the sixth s.
8: 1 When he opened the seventh s,
9: 4 people who did not have the s
22: 10 "Do not s up the words

SEALED (SEAL)

Eph 4: 30 with whom you were s for the day
2Ti 2: 19 solid foundation stands firm, s
Rev 5: 1 on both sides and s with seven seals

SEALS (SEAL)

Rev 5: 2 "Who is worthy to break the s
6: 1 opened the first of the seven s.

SEAMLESS*

Jn 19: 23 This garment was s, woven

SEARCH (SEARCHED SEARCHES SEARCHING)

Ps 4: 4 s your hearts and be silent.
139: 23 S me, O God, and know my heart;
Pr 2: 4 and s for it as for hidden treasure,
25: 2 to s out a matter is the glory
SS 3: 2 I will s for the one my heart loves.
Jer 17: 10 "I the LORD s the heart
Eze 34: 11 I myself will s for my sheep
34: 16 I will s for the lost and bring back
Lk 15: 8 and s carefully until she finds it?

SEARCHED (SEARCH)

Ps 139: 1 O LORD, you have s me
Ecc 12: 10 The Teacher s to find just the right
1Pe 1: 10 s intently and with the greatest

SEARCHES (SEARCH)

1Ch 28: 9 for the LORD s every heart
Ps 7: 9 who s minds and hearts,
Pr 11: 27 but evil comes to him who s for it.
20: 27 The lamp of the LORD s the spirit
Ro 8: 27 And he who s our hearts knows
1Co 2: 10 The Spirit s all things,
Rev 2: 23 will know that I am he who s hearts

SEARCHING (SEARCH)

Jdg 5: 15 there was much s of heart.
Am 8: 12 s for the word of the LORD,

SEARED

1Ti 4: 2 whose consciences have been s

SEASHORE (SEA)

Jos 11: 4 as numerous as the sand on the s.
1Ki 4: 29 as measureless as the sand on the s.

SEASON (SEASONS)

Lev 26: 4 I will send you rain in its s,
Ps 1: 3 which yields its fruit in s
2Ti 4: 2 be prepared in s and out of s;

SEASONED*

Col 4: 6 full of grace, s with salt,

SEASONS (SEASON)

Ge 1: 14 signs to mark s and days and years,
Gal 4: 10 and months and s and years!

SEAT (SEATED SEATS)

Ps 1: 1 or sit in the s of mockers.
Pr 31: 23 where he takes his s
Da 7: 9 and the Ancient of Days took his s.
Lk 14: 9 say to you, 'Give this man your s.'
2Co 5: 10 before the judgment s of Christ,

SEATED (SEAT)

Ps 47: 8 God is s on his holy throne.
Isa 6: 1 I saw the Lord s on a throne,
Lk 22: 69 of Man will be s at the right hand
Eph 1: 20 and s him at his right hand
2: 6 and s us with him in the heavenly
Col 3: 1 where Christ is s at the right hand
Rev 14: 14 s on the cloud was one "like a son
20: 11 white throne and him who was s

SEATS (SEAT)

Lk 11: 43 you love the most important s

SECLUSION*

Lk 1: 24 and for five months remained in s.

SECRET (SECRETLY SECRETS)

Dt 29: 29 The s things belong
Jdg 16: 6 Tell me the s of your great strength
Ps 90: 8 our s sins in the light
139: 15 when I was made in the s place.
Pr 11: 13 but a trustworthy man keeps a s.
21: 14 A gift given in s soothes anger,
Jer 23: 24 Can anyone hide in s places
Mt 6: 4 so that your giving may be in s.
6: 18 who sees what is done in s,
Mk 4: 11 "The s of the kingdom
1Co 2: 7 No, we speak of God's s wisdom,
4: 1 entrusted with the s things of God.
2Co 4: 2 we have renounced s and shameful
Eph 5: 12 what the disobedient do in s.
Php 4: 12 I have learned the s

SECRETLY (SECRET)

2Pe 2: 1 They will s introduce destructive
Jude : 4 about long ago have s slipped

SECRETS (SECRET)

Ps 44: 21 since he knows the s of the heart?
Ro 2: 16 day when God will judge men's s
1Co 14: 25 the s of his heart will be laid bare.
Rev 2: 24 Satan's so-called deep s (I will not

SECURE (SECURITY)

Dt 33: 12 beloved of the LORD rest s in him,
Ps 16: 5 you have made my lot s.
16: 9 my body also will rest s,
112: 8 His heart is s, he will have no fear;
Pr 14: 26 fears the LORD has a s fortress,
Heb 6: 19 an anchor for the soul, firm and s.
2Pe 3: 17 and fall from your s position.

SECURITY (SECURE)

Job 31: 24 or said to pure gold, 'You are my s,'

SEED (SEEDS SEEDTIME)

Ge 1: 11 on the land that bear fruit with s
Isa 55: 10 so that it yields s for the sower
Mt 13: 3 "A farmer went out to sow his s.
13: 31 of heaven is like a mustard s,
17: 20 have faith as small as a mustard s,
Lk 8: 11 of the parable: The s is the word
1Co 3: 6 I planted the s, Apollos watered it,
2Co 9: 10 he who supplies s to the sower
Gal 3: 29 then you are Abraham's s,
1Pe 1: 23 not of perishable s,
1Jn 3: 9 because God's s remains in him;

SEEDS (SEED)

Jn 12: 24 But if it dies, it produces many s.
Gal 3: 16 Scripture does not say "and to s,"

SEEDTIME* (SEED)

Ge 8: 22 s and harvest,

SEEK (SEEKING SEEKS SELF-SEEKING SOUGHT)

Lev 19: 18 Do not s revenge or bear a grudge
Dt 4: 29 if from there you s the LORD your
1Ki 22: 5 "First s the counsel of the LORD."
1Ch 28: 9 If you s him, he will be found
2Ch 7: 14 themselves and pray and s my face
15: 2 If you s him, he will be found
Ps 34: 10 those who s the LORD lack no
105: 3 of those who s the LORD rejoice.
105: 4 s his face always.
119: 2 and s him with all their heart.
119: 10 I s you with all my heart;
119: 176 S your servant,
Pr 8: 17 and those who s me find me.
18: 15 the ears of the wise s it out.
25: 27 is it honourable to s one's own honour
28: 5 those who s the LORD understand
Isa 55: 6 S the LORD while he may be
65: 1 found by those who did not s me.
Jer 29: 13 You will s me and find me
Hos 10: 12 for it is time to s the LORD,
Am 5: 4 "S me and live;
Zep 2: 3 S the LORD, all you humble
Mt 6: 33 But s first his kingdom
7: 7 and it will be given to you; s
Lk 12: 31 s his kingdom, and these things will
19: 10 For the Son of Man came to s
Jn 5: 30 for I s not to please myself
Ro 10: 20 found by those who did not s me;
1Co 7: 27 you married? Do not s a divorce.
10: 24 Nobody should s his own good,
Heb 11: 6 rewards those who earnestly s him.
1Pe 3: 11 he must s peace and pursue it.

SEEKING (SEEK)

2Ch 30: 19 who sets his heart on s God—
Pr 20: 18 Make plans by s advice;
Mal 3: 1 the Lord you are s will come
Jn 8: 50 I am not s glory for myself;
1Co 10: 33 For I am not s my own good

SEEKS (SEEK)

Pr 11: 27 He who s good finds good will,
Mt 7: 8 he who s finds; and to him who
Jn 4: 23 the kind of worshippers the Father s.
Ro 3: 11 no-one who s God.

SEER

1Sa 9: 9 of today used to be called a s.)

SELF-CONTROL* (CONTROL)

Pr 25: 28 is a man who lacks s.
Ac 24: 25 s and the judgment to come,
1Co 7: 5 you because of your lack of s.
Gal 5: 23 faithfulness, gentleness and s.
2Ti 3: 3 slanderous, without s, brutal,
2Pe 1: 6 and to knowledge, s; and to s,

SELF-CONTROLLED* (CONTROL)

1Th 5: 6 are asleep, but let us be alert and s.
5: 8 let us be s, putting on faith and love
1Ti 3: 2 s, respectable, hospitable,
Tit 1: 8 who is s, upright, holy
2: 2 worthy of respect, s, and sound
2: 5 to be s and pure, to be busy at home
2: 6 encourage the young men to be s.
2: 12 to live s, upright and godly lives

1Pe 1: 13 prepare your minds for action; be *s*;
4: 7 and *s* so that you can pray.
5: 8 Be *s* and alert.

SELF-DISCIPLINE* (DISCIPLINE)
2Ti 1: 7 a spirit of power, of love and of *s*.

SELF-INDULGENCE*
Mt 23: 25 inside they are full of greed and *s*.
Jas 5: 5 lived on earth in luxury and *s*.

SELF-SEEKING* (SEEK)
Ro 2: 8 But for those who are *s*
1Co 13: 5 it is not *s*, it is not easily angered,

SELFISH*
Ps 119: 36 and not towards *s* gain.
Pr 18: 1 An unfriendly man pursues *s* ends;
Gal 5: 20 fits of rage, *s* ambition, dissensions,
Php 1: 17 preach Christ out of *s* ambition,
2: 3 Do nothing out of *s* ambition
Jas 3: 14 and *s* ambition in your hearts,
3: 16 you have envy and *s* ambition,

SELL (SELLING SELLS SOLD)
Ge 25: 31 "First *s* me your birthright."
Mk 10: 21 *s* everything you have
Rev 13: 17 or *s* unless he had the mark,

SELLING (SELL)
Lk 17: 28 buying and *s*, planting and building

SELLS (SELL)
Pr 31: 24 makes linen garments and *s* them,

SEND (SENDING SENDS SENT)
Ps 43: 3 *S* forth your light and your truth,
Isa 6: 8 *S* me!" He said, "Go and tell this
Mal 3: 1 "See, I will *s* my messenger,
Mt 9: 38 to *s* out workers into his harvest
24: 31 And he will *s* his angels
Mk 1: 2 I will *s* my messenger ahead of you,
Lk 20: 13 I will *s* my son, whom I love;
Jn 3: 17 For God did not *s* his Son
16: 7 but if I go, I will *s* him to you.
1Co 1: 17 For Christ did not *s* me to baptise,

SENDING (SEND)
Mt 10: 16 "I am *s* you out like sheep
Jn 20: 21 Father has sent me, I am *s* you."
Ro 8: 3 God did by *s* his own Son

SENDS (SEND)
Ps 57: 3 God *s* his love and his faithfulness.

SENNACHERIB
Assyrian king whose siege of Jerusalem was overthrown by the LORD following prayer of Hezekiah and Isaiah (2Ki 18:13-19:37; 2Ch 32:1-21; Isa 36-37).

SENSES*
Lk 15: 17 "When he came to his *s*, he said,
1Co 15: 34 Come back to your *s* as you ought,
2Ti 2: 26 and that they will come to their *s*

SENSITIVITY*
Eph 4: 19 Having lost all *s*, they have given

SENSUAL* (SENSUALITY)
Col 2: 23 value in restraining *s* indulgence.
1Ti 5: 11 For when their *s* desires overcome

SENSUALITY* (SENSUAL)
Eph 4: 19 have given themselves over to *s*

SENT (SEND)
Ex 3: 14 to the Israelites: 'I AM has *s* me
Isa 55: 11 achieve the purpose for which I *s* it.
61: 1 He has *s* me to bind up
Jer 28: 9 as one truly *s* by the LORD only
Mt 10: 40 me receives the one who *s* me.
Mk 6: 7 he *s* them out two by two
Lk 4: 18 He has *s* me to proclaim freedom
9: 2 and he *s* them out to preach
10: 16 rejects me rejects him who *s* me."
Jn 1: 6 There came a man who was *s*
4: 34 "is to do the will of him who *s* me
5: 24 believes him who *s* me has eternal
8: 16 I stand with the Father who *s* me.
9: 4 must do the work of him who *s* me.
16: 5 "Now I am going to him who *s* me,
17: 3 and Jesus Christ, whom you have *s*.
17: 18 As you *s* me into the world,
20: 21 As the Father has *s* me, I am
Ro 10: 15 can they preach unless they are *s*?
Gal 4: 4 God *s* his Son, born of a woman,
1Jn 4: 10 but that he loved us and *s* his Son

SENTENCE
2Co 1: 9 in our hearts we felt the *s* of death.

SEPARATE (SEPARATED SEPARATES SEPARATION)
Mt 19: 6 has joined together, let man not *s*."
Ro 8: 35 Who shall *s* us from the love
1Co 7: 10 wife must not *s* from her husband.
2Co 6: 17 and be *s*, says the Lord.
Eph 2: 12 at that time you were *s* from Christ,

SEPARATED (SEPARATE)
Isa 59: 2 But your iniquities have *s*
Eph 4: 18 in their understanding and *s*

SEPARATES (SEPARATE)
Pr 16: 28 and a gossip *s* close friends.
17: 9 repeats the matter *s* close friends.
Mt 25: 32 as a shepherd *s* the sheep

SEPARATION (SEPARATE)
Nu 6: 2 a vow of *s* to the LORD

SERAPHS*
Isa 6: 2 Above him were *s*, each
6: 6 Then one of the *s* flew to me

SERIOUSNESS*
Tit 2: 7 *s* and soundness of speech that

SERPENT (SERPENT'S)
Ge 3: 1 the *s* was more crafty than any
Isa 27: 1 Leviathan the coiling *s*;
Rev 12: 9 that ancient *s* called the devil
20: 2 that ancient *s*, who is the devil,

SERPENT'S (SERPENT)
2Co 11: 3 Eve was deceived by the *s* cunning,

SERVANT (SERVANTS)
Ex 14: 31 trust in him and in Moses his *s*.
21: 2 "If you buy a Hebrew *s*, he is
1Sa 3: 10 "Speak, for your *s* is listening."
2Sa 7: 19 the future of the house of your *s*.
1Ki 20: 40 While your *s* was busy here
Job 1: 8 "Have you considered my *s* Job?
Ps 19: 11 By them is your *s* warned;
19: 13 Keep your *s* also from wilful sins;
31: 16 Let your face shine on your *s*;
89: 3 I have sworn to David my *s*,
Pr 14: 35 A king delights in a wise *s*,
17: 2 wise *s* will rule over a disgraceful
22: 7 and the borrower is *s* to the lender.
31: 15 and portions for her *s* girls.
Isa 41: 8 "But you, O Israel, my *s*,
49: 3 He said to me, "You are my *s*,
53: 11 my righteous *s* will justify
Zec 3: 8 going to bring my *s*, the Branch.
Mal 1: 6 his father, and a *s* his master.
Mt 8: 13 his *s* was healed at that very hour.
20: 26 great among you must be your *s*,
24: 45 Who then is the faithful and wise *s*,
25: 21 'Well done, good and faithful *s*!
Lk 1: 38 I am the Lord's *s*," Mary answered.
16: 13 "No *s* can serve two masters.
Jn 12: 26 and where I am, my *s* also will be.
Ro 1: 1 a *s* of Christ Jesus, called
13: 4 For he is God's *s* to do you good.
Php 2: 7 taking the very nature of a *s*,
Col 1: 23 of which I, Paul, have become a *s*.
2Ti 2: 24 And the Lord's *s* must not quarrel;

SERVANTS (SERVANT)
Lev 25: 55 for the Israelites belong to me as *s*.
2Ki 17: 13 to you through my *s* the prophets."
Ezr 5: 11 "We are the *s* of the God of heaven
Ps 34: 22 The LORD redeems his *s*;
103: 21 you his *s* who do his will.
104: 4 flames of fire his *s*.
Isa 44: 26 who carries out the words of his *s*
65: 8 so will I do on behalf of my *s*;
65: 13 my *s* will drink,
Lk 17: 10 should say, 'We are unworthy *s*;
Jn 15: 15 longer call you *s*, because a servant
Ro 13: 6 for the authorities are God's *s*,
1Co 3: 5 And what is Paul? Only *s*,
Heb 1: 7 his *s* flames of fire."

SERVE (SERVED SERVES SERVICE SERVING)
Dt 10: 12 to *s* the LORD your God
11: 13 and to *s* him with all your heart
13: 4 *s* him and hold fast to him.
28: 47 you did not *s* the LORD your
Jos 22: 5 and to *s* him with all your heart
24: 15 this day whom you will *s*,
24: 18 We too will *s* the LORD,
1Sa 7: 3 to the LORD and *s* him only,
12: 20 but *s* the LORD with all your heart
12: 24 *s* him faithfully with all your heart;
2Ch 19: 9 "You must *s* faithfully
Job 36: 11 If they obey and *s* him,
Ps 2: 11 *S* the LORD with fear
Da 3: 17 the God we *s* is able to save us
Mt 4: 10 Lord your God, and *s* him only.'"
6: 24 "No-one can *s* two masters.
20: 28 but to *s*, and to give his life
Ro 12: 7 If it is serving, let him *s*;
Gal 5: 13 rather, *s* one another in love.
Eph 6: 7 *S* wholeheartedly,
1Ti 6: 2 they are to *s* them even better,
Heb 9: 14 so that we may *s* the living God!
1Pe 4: 10 gift he has received to *s* others,
5: 2 greedy for money, but eager to *s*;
Rev 5: 10 kingdom and priests to *s* our God,

SERVED (SERVE)
Mt 20: 28 Son of Man did not come to be *s*,
Jn 12: 2 Martha *s*, while Lazarus was
Ac 17: 25 And he is not *s* by human hands,
Ro 1: 25 and *s* created things rather
1Ti 3: 13 Those who have *s* well gain

SERVES (SERVE)
Lk 22: 26 one who rules like the one who *s*.
22: 27 But I am among you as one who *s*.
Jn 12: 26 Whoever *s* me must follow me;
Ro 14: 18 because anyone who *s* Christ
1Pe 4: 11 If anyone *s*, he should do it

SERVICE (SERVE)
Lk 9: 62 fit for *s* in the kingdom
12: 35 "Be dressed ready for *s*
Ro 15: 17 in Christ Jesus in my *s* to God.
1Co 12: 5 There are different kinds of *s*,
16: 15 themselves to the *s* of the saints.
2Co 9: 12 This *s* that you perform is not only
Eph 4: 12 God's people for works of *s*,
Rev 2: 19 and faith, your *s* and perseverance,

SERVING (SERVE)
Jos 24: 15 if *s* the LORD seems undesirable
2Ch 12: 8 learn the difference between *s* me
Ro 12: 7 If it is *s*, let him serve;
12: 11 your spiritual fervour, *s* the Lord.
16: 18 people are not *s* our Lord Christ,
Eph 6: 7 as if you were *s* the Lord, not men,
Col 3: 24 It is the Lord Christ you are *s*.
2Ti 2: 4 No-one *s* as a soldier gets involved

SETH
Ge 4: 25 birth to a son and named him *S*,

SETTLE
Mt 5: 25 "*S* matters quickly
2Th 3: 12 in the Lord Jesus Christ to *s* down

SEVEN (SEVENS SEVENTH)
Ge 7: 2 Take with you *s* of every kind
Jos 6: 4 march around the city *s* times,
1Ki 19: 18 Yet I reserve *s* thousand in Israel—
Pr 6: 16 *s* that are detestable to him:
24: 16 a righteous man falls *s* times,
Isa 4: 1 In that day *s* women
Da 9: 25 comes, there will be *s* 'sevens',
Mt 18: 21 Up to *s* times?" Jesus answered,
Lk 11: 26 takes *s* other spirits more wicked
Ro 11: 4 for myself *s* thousand who have not
Rev 1: 4 To the *s* churches in the province
6: 1 opened the first of the *s* seals.
8: 2 and to them were given *s* trumpets.
10: 4 And when the *s* thunders spoke,
15: 7 to the *s* angels *s* golden bowls filled

SEVENS* (SEVEN)
Da 9: 24 "Seventy '*s*' are decreed
9: 25 will be seven '*s*', and sixty-two '*s*'.
9: 26 the sixty-two '*s*', the Anointed

SEVENTH (SEVEN)
Ge 2: 2 By the *s* day God had finished
Ex 20: 10 but the *s* day is a Sabbath
23: 11 but during the *s* year let the land lie
23: 12 but on the *s* day do not work,
Heb 4: 4 "And on the *s* day God rested

SEVERE
2Co 8: 2 Out of the most *s* trial, their
1Th 1: 6 of the Lord; in spite of *s* suffering,

SEWED (SEWS)
Ge 3: 7 so they *s* fig leaves together

SEWS (SEWED)
Mt 9: 16 No-one *s* a patch of unshrunk cloth

SEXUAL (SEXUALLY)
Ex 22: 19 "Anyone who has *s* relations
Lev 18: 6 relative to have *s* relations.
18: 7 father by having *s* relations
18: 20 *s* relations with your neighbour's
Mt 15: 19 murder, adultery, *s* immorality,
Ac 15: 20 by idols, from *s* immorality,
1Co 5: 1 reported that there is *s* immorality
6: 13 body is not meant for *s* immorality,
6: 18 Flee from *s* immorality.
10: 8 should not commit *s* immorality,
2Co 12: 21 *s* sin and debauchery
Gal 5: 19 *s* immorality, impurity
Eph 5: 3 even a hint of *s* immorality,
Col 3: 5 *s* immorality, impurity, lust,
1Th 4: 3 that you should avoid *s* immorality

SEXUALLY (SEXUAL)
1Co 5: 9 to associate with *s* immoral people
6: 9 Neither the *s* immoral nor idolaters
6: 18 he who sins *s* sins against his own
Heb 12: 16 See that no-one is *s* immoral,
13: 4 the adulterer and all the *s* immoral.
Rev 21: 8 the murderers, the *s* immoral,

SHADE
Ps 121: 5 the LORD is your *s*
Isa 25: 4 and a *s* from the heat.

SHADOW
Ps 17: 8 hide me in the *s* of your wings
23: 4 through the valley of the *s* of death,
36: 7 find refuge in the *s* of your wings.
91: 1 will rest in the *s* of the Almighty.
Isa 51: 16 covered you with the *s* of my hand
Col 2: 17 These are a *s* of the things that
Heb 8: 5 and *s* of what is in heaven.
10: 1 The law is only a *s*

SHADRACH
Hebrew exiled to Babylon; name changed from Hananiah (Da 1:6-7). Refused defilement by food (Da 1:8-20). Refused to worship idol (Da 3:1-18); saved from furnace (Da 3:19-30).

SHAKE (SHAKEN SHAKING)
Ps 64: 8 all who see them will *s* their heads
99: 1 let the earth *s*.
Hag 2: 6 I will once more *s* the heavens
Heb 12: 26 "Once more I will *s* not only

SHAKEN (SHAKE)
Ps 16: 8 I will not be *s*.
30: 6 "I will never be *s*."
62: 2 he is my fortress, I will never be *s*.
112: 6 Surely he will never be *s*;
Isa 54: 10 Though the mountains be *s*
Mt 24: 29 and the heavenly bodies will be *s*.'
Lk 6: 38 *s* together and running over,
Ac 2: 25 I will not be *s*.
Heb 12: 27 that what cannot be *s* may remain.

SHAKING* (SHAKE)
Ps 22: 7 they hurl insults, *s* their heads:
Mt 27: 39 insults at him, *s* their heads
Mk 15: 29 *s* their heads and saying, "So!

SHALLUM
King of Israel (2Ki 15:10-16).

SHAME (ASHAMED SHAMED SHAMEFUL)
Ps 25: 3 will ever be put to *s*,
34: 5 their faces are never covered with *s*
69: 6 not be put to *s* because of me,
Pr 13: 18 discipline comes to poverty and *s*,
18: 13 that is his folly and his *s*.
Jer 8: 9 The wise will be put to *s*;
8: 12 No, they have no *s* at all;
Ro 9: 33 trusts in him will never be put to *s*."
10: 11 trusts in him will never be put to *s*."
1Co 1: 27 things of the world to *s* the wise;
Heb 12: 2 endured the cross, scorning its *s*,

SHAMED (SHAME)
Jer 10: 14 every goldsmith is *s* by his idols.
Joel 2: 26 never again will my people be *s*.

SHAMEFUL (SHAME)
2Co 4: 2 have renounced secret and *s* ways;
2Pe 2: 2 Many will follow their *s* ways
Rev 21: 27 nor will anyone who does what is *s*

SHAMGAR
Judge; killed 600 Philistines (Jdg 3:31).

SHAPE (SHAPES SHAPING)
Job 38: 14 The earth takes *s* like clay

SHAPES (SHAPE)
Isa 44: 10 Who *s* a god and casts an idol,

SHAPING (SHAPE)
Jer 18: 4 the pot he was *s* from the clay was

SHARE (SHARED SHARERS SHARES SHARING)
Ge 21: 10 that slave woman's son will never *s*
Lev 19: 17 frankly so you will not *s* in his guilt.
Dt 10: 9 That is why the Levites have no *s*
1Sa 30: 24 All will *s* alike."
Eze 18: 20 The son will not *s* the guilt
Mt 25: 21 and *s* your master's happiness!'
Lk 3: 11 "The man with two tunics should *s*
Ro 8: 17 if indeed we *s* in his sufferings
12: 13 *S* with God's people who are
2Co 1: 7 as you *s* in our sufferings,
Gal 4: 30 the slave woman's son will never *s*
6: 6 in the word must *s* all good things
Eph 4: 28 something to *s* with those in need.
Col 1: 12 you to *s* in the inheritance
2Th 2: 14 that you might *s* in the glory
1Ti 5: 22 and do not *s* in the sins of others.
6: 18 and to be generous and willing to *s*.
2Ti 2: 6 the first to receive a *s* of the crops.
Heb 12: 10 that we may *s* in his holiness.
13: 16 to do good and to *s* with others,
Rev 22: 19 from him his *s* in the tree of life

SHARED (SHARE)
Ps 41: 9 he who *s* my bread,
Ac 4: 32 but they *s* everything they had.
Heb 2: 14 he too *s* in their humanity so that

SHARERS* (SHARE)
Eph 3: 6 and *s* together in the promise

SHARES (SHARE)
Pr 22: 9 for he *s* his food with the poor.
Jn 13: 18 'He who *s* my bread has lifted up

SHARING (SHARE)
1Co 9: 10 so in the hope of *s* in the harvest.
2Co 9: 13 for your generosity in *s* with them
Php 3: 10 the fellowship of *s* in his sufferings,
Phm : 6 you may be active in *s* your faith,

SHARON
SS 2: 1 I am a rose of *S*,

SHARP (SHARPENED SHARPENS SHARPER)
Pr 5: 4 *s* as a double-edged sword.
Isa 5: 28 Their arrows are *s*,
Rev 1: 16 came a *s* double-edged sword.
19: 15 Out of his mouth comes a *s* sword

SHARPENED (SHARP)
Eze 21: 9 *s* and polished—

SHARPENS* (SHARP)
Pr 27: 17 As iron *s* iron,
27: 17 so one man *s* another.

SHARPER* (SHARP)
Heb 4: 12 *S* than any double-edged sword,

SHATTER (SHATTERED SHATTERS)
Jer 51: 20 with you I *s* nations,

SHATTERED (SHATTER)
1Sa 2: 10 who oppose the LORD will be *s*.
Job 16: 12 All was well with me, but he *s* me;
17: 11 days have passed, my plans are *s*,
Ecc 12: 6 before the pitcher is *s* at the spring,

SHATTERS (SHATTER)
Ps 46: 9 he breaks the bow and *s* the spear,

SHAVED
Jdg 16: 17 my head were *s*, my strength would
1Co 11: 5 it is just as though her head were *s*.

SHEAF (SHEAVES)
Lev 23: 11 is to wave the *s* before the LORD

SHEARER* (SHEARERS)
Ac 8: 32 and as a lamb before the *s* is silent,

SHEARERS (SHEARER)
Isa 53: 7 and as a sheep before her *s* is silent,

SHEAVES (SHEAF)
Ge 37: 7 while your *s* gathered around mine
Ps 126: 6 carrying *s* with him.

SHEBA
1. Benjamite who rebelled against David (2Sa 20).
2. See QUEEN.

SHECHEM
1. Raped Jacob's daughter Dinah; killed by Simeon and Levi (Ge 34).
2. City where Joshua renewed the covenant (Jos 24).

SHED (SHEDDING SHEDS)
Ge 9: 6 by man shall his blood be *s*;
Pr 6: 17 hands that *s* innocent blood,
Ro 3: 15 "Their feet are swift to *s* blood;
Col 1: 20 through his blood, *s* on the cross.

SHEDDING (SHED)
Heb 9: 22 without the *s* of blood there is no

SHEDS (SHED)
Ge 9: 6 "Whoever *s* the blood of man,

SHEEP (SHEEP'S SHEEPSKINS)
Nu 27: 17 LORD's people will not be like *s*
Dt 17: 1 a *s* that has any defect or flaw in it,
1Sa 15: 14 "What then is this bleating of *s*
Ps 44: 22 we are considered as *s*
78: 52 led them like *s* through the desert.
100: 3 we are his people, the *s*
119: 176 I have strayed like a lost *s*.
SS 4: 2 teeth are like a flock of *s* just shorn,
Isa 53: 6 We all, like *s*, have gone astray,
53: 7 as a *s* before her shearers is silent,
Jer 50: 6 "My people have been lost *s*;
Eze 34: 11 I myself will search for my *s*
Zec 13: 7 and the *s* will be scattered,
Mt 9: 36 helpless, like *s* without a shepherd.
10: 16 "I am sending you out like *s*
12: 11 "If any of you has a *s* and it falls
18: 13 he is happier about that one *s*
25: 32 as a shepherd separates the *s*
Jn 10: 1 man who does not enter the *s* pen
10: 3 He calls his own *s* by name
10: 7 the truth, I am the gate for the *s*.
10: 15 and I lay down my life for the *s*.
10: 27 My *s* listen to my voice; I know
21: 17 Jesus said, "Feed my *s*.
1Pe 2: 25 For you were like *s* going astray,

SHEEP'S* (SHEEP)
Mt 7: 15 They come to you in *s* clothing,

SHEEPSKINS* (SHEEP)
Heb 11: 37 They went about in *s* and goatskins

SHEKEL
Ex 30: 13 This half *s* is an offering

SHELTER
Ps 27: 5 me in the *s* of his tabernacle
31: 20 In the *s* of your presence you hide
55: 8 I would hurry to my place of *s*,
61: 4 take refuge in the *s* of your wings.
91: 1 in the *s* of the Most High
Ecc 7: 12 Wisdom is a *s*
Isa 4: 6 It will be a *s* and shade
25: 4 a *s* from the storm
32: 2 Each man will be like a *s*
58: 7 the poor wanderer with *s*—

SHEM
Son of Noah (Ge 5:32; 6:10). Blessed (Ge 9:26). Descendants (Ge 10:21-31; 11:10-32).

SHEPHERD (SHEPHERDS)
Ge 48: 15 the God who has been my *S*
49: 24 because of the *S*, the Rock of Israel
Nu 27: 17 will not be like sheep without a *s*."
2Sa 7: 7 commanded to *s* my people Israel,
1Ki 22: 17 on the hills like sheep without a *s*,
Ps 23: 1 LORD is my *s*, I shall not be in want.
28: 9 be their *s* and carry them for ever.
80: 1 Hear us, O *S* of Israel,
Isa 40: 11 He tends his flock like a *s*:
Jer 31: 10 will watch over his flock like a *s*.'
Eze 34: 5 scattered because there was no *s*,
34: 12 As a *s* looks after his scattered
Zec 11: 9 and said, "I will not be your *s*.
11: 17 "Woe to the worthless *s*,
13: 7 "Strike the *s*,
Mt 2: 6 who will be the *s* of my people
9: 36 and helpless, like sheep without a *s*.
26: 31 "'I will strike the *s*,
Jn 10: 11 The good *s* lays down his life
10: 14 "I am the good *s*; I know my sheep
10: 16 there shall be one flock and one *s*.
Heb 13: 20 that great *S* of the sheep, equip you
1Pe 5: 4 And when the Chief *S* appears,
Rev 7: 17 of the throne will be their *s*;

SHEPHERDS (SHEPHERD)
Jer 23: 1 "Woe to the *s* who are destroying
50: 6 their *s* have led them astray
Eze 34: 2 prophesy against the *s* of Israel;
Lk 2: 8 there were *s* living out in the fields
Ac 20: 28 Be *s* of the church of God,
1Pe 5: 2 Be *s* of God's flock that is
Jude : 12 *s* who feed only themselves.

SHIBBOLETH*
Jdg 12: 6 No," they said, "All right, say '*S*'."

SHIELD (SHIELDED SHIELDS)
Ge 15: 1 I am your *s*,
2Sa 22: 3 my *s* and the horn of my salvation.
22: 36 You give me your *s* of victory;
Ps 3: 3 But you are a *s* around me,
5: 12 with your favour as with a *s*.
7: 10 My *s* is God Most High,
18: 2 He is my *s* and the horn
28: 7 LORD is my strength and my *s*;
33: 20 he is our help and our *s*.
84: 11 For the LORD God is a sun and *s*;
91: 4 his faithfulness will be your *s*
115: 9 he is their help and *s*.
119: 114 You are my refuge and my *s*;
144: 2 my *s*, in whom I take refuge,
Pr 2: 7 he is a *s* to those whose walk is
30: 5 he is a *s* to those who take refuge
Eph 6: 16 to all this, take up the *s* of faith,

SHIELDED (SHIELD)
1Pe 1: 5 through faith are *s* by God's power

SHIELDS (SHIELD)
Dt 33: 12 for he *s* him all day long,

SHIFTLESS*
Pr 19: 15 and the *s* man goes hungry.

SHIMEI
Cursed David (2Sa 16:5-14); spared (2Sa 19:16-23). Killed by Solomon (1Ki 2:8-9, 36-46).

SHINE (SHINES SHINING SHONE)
Nu 6: 25 the LORD make his face *s*
Job 33: 30 that the light of life may *s* on him.
Ps 4: 6 Let the light of your face *s* upon us,
37: 6 make your righteousness *s* like
67: 1 and make his face *s* upon us; *Selah*
80: 1 between the cherubim, *s* forth
118: 27 and he has made his light *s* upon us.
Isa 60: 1 "Arise, *s*, for your light has come,
Da 12: 3 are wise will *s* like the brightness
Mt 5: 16 let your light *s* before men,
13: 43 the righteous will *s* like the sun
2Co 4: 6 made his light *s* in our hearts
Eph 5: 14 and Christ will *s* on you."
Php 2: 15 in which you *s* like stars

SHINES (SHINE)
Ps 50: 2 God *s* forth.
Pr 13: 9 The light of the righteous *s* brightly
Jn 1: 5 The light *s* in the darkness,

SHINING (SHINE)
Pr 4: 18 *s* ever brighter till the full light
2Pe 1: 19 as to a light *s* in a dark place,
Rev 1: 16 His face was like the sun *s*

SHIPS
Pr 31: 14 She is like the merchant *s*,

SHIPWRECKED*
2Co 11: 25 I was stoned, three times I was *s*,
1Ti 1: 19 and so have *s* their faith.

SHISHAK
1Ki 14: 25 *S* king of Egypt attacked Jerusalem
2Ch 12: 2 *S* king of Egypt attacked Jerusalem

SHOCKING*
Jer 5: 30 "A horrible and *s* thing

SHONE (SHINE)
Mt 17: 2 His face *s* like the sun,
Lk 2: 9 glory of the Lord *s* around them,
Rev 21: 11 It *s* with the glory of God,

SHOOT
Isa 53: 2 up before him like a tender *s*,
Ro 11: 17 and you, though a wild olive *s*,

SHORE
Lk 5: 3 asked him to put out a little from *s*.

SHORT (SHORTENED)
Nu 11: 23 "Is the LORD's arm too *s*?
Isa 50: 2 Was my arm too *s* to ransom you?
59: 1 of the LORD is not too *s* to save,
Mt 24: 22 If those days had not been cut *s*,
Ro 3: 23 and fall *s* of the glory of God,
1Co 7: 29 brothers, is that the time is *s*.
Heb 4: 1 of you be found to have fallen *s* of it
Rev 20: 3 he must be set free for a *s* time.

SHORTENED (SHORT)
Mt 24: 22 of the elect those days will be *s*.

SHOULDER (SHOULDERS)
Zep 3: 9 and serve him *s* to *s*.

SHOULDERS (SHOULDER)
Dt 33: 12 LORD loves rests between his *s*."
Isa 9: 6 and the government will be on his *s*
Lk 15: 5 he joyfully puts it on his *s*

SHOUT (SHOUTED)
Ps 47: 1 *s* to God with cries of joy.
66: 1 *S* with joy to God, all the earth!
95: 1 let us *s* aloud to the Rock
98: 4 *S* for joy to the LORD, all the earth
100: 1 *S* for joy to the LORD, all the earth
Isa 12: 6 *S* aloud and sing for joy, people
26: 19 wake up and *s* for joy.
35: 6 the mute tongue *s* for joy.
40: 9 lift up your voice with a *s*,
42: 2 He will not *s* or cry out,
44: 23 *s* aloud, O earth beneath.
54: 1 burst into song, *s* for joy,
Zec 9: 9 *S*, Daughter of Jerusalem!

SHOUTED (SHOUT)
Job 38: 7 and all the angels *s* for joy?

SHOW (SHOWED)
Ex 18: 20 and *s* them the way to live
33: 18 Moses said, "Now *s* me your glory
2Sa 22: 26 the faithful you *s* yourself faithful,
1Ki 2: 2 "So be strong, *s* yourself a man,
Ps 17: 7 *S* the wonder of your great love,
25: 4 *S* me your ways, O LORD,
39: 4 "*S* me, O LORD, my life's end
85: 7 *S* us your unfailing love, O LORD,
143: 8 *S* me the way I should go,
Pr 23: 4 have the wisdom to *s* restraint.
SS 2: 14 *s* me your face,
Isa 5: 16 the holy God will *s* himself holy
30: 18 he rises to *s* you compassion.
Eze 28: 25 I will *s* myself holy among them
Joel 2: 30 I will *s* wonders in the heavens
Zec 7: 9 *s* mercy and compassion
Ac 2: 19 I will *s* wonders in the heaven
10: 34 it is that God does not *s* favouritism
1Co 12: 31 now I will *s* you the most excellent
Eph 2: 7 ages he might *s* the incomparable
Tit 2: 7 In your teaching *s* integrity,
Jas 2: 18 I will *s* you my faith by what I do.
Jude : 23 to others *s* mercy, mixed with fear

SHOWED (SHOW)
1Ki 3: 3 Solomon *s* his love for the LORD
Lk 24: 40 he *s* them his hands and feet.
1Jn 4: 9 This is how God *s* his love

SHOWERS
Eze 34: 26 in season; there will be *s* of blessing
Hos 10: 12 and *s* righteousness on you.

SHREWD
2Sa 22: 27 to the crooked you show yourself *s*.
Mt 10: 16 Therefore be as *s* as snakes and

SHRINK (SHRINKS)
Heb 10: 39 But we are not of those who *s* back

SHRINKS* (SHRINK)
Heb 10: 38 And if he *s* back,

SHRIVEL
Isa 64: 6 we all *s* up like a leaf,

SHUDDER
Eze 32: 10 and their kings will *s* with horror

SHUHITE
Job 2: 11 Bildad the *S* and Zophar

SHUN* (SHUNS)
Job 28: 28 and to *s* evil is understanding.'"
Pr 3: 7 fear the LORD and *s* evil.

SHUNS (SHUN)
Job 1: 8 a man who fears God and *s* evil."
Pr 14: 16 man fears the LORD and *s* evil,

SHUT
Ge 7: 16 Then the LORD *s* him in.
Isa 22: 22 what he opens no-one can *s*,
60: 11 they will never be *s*, day or night,
Da 6: 22 and he *s* the mouths of the lions.
Heb 11: 33 who *s* the mouths of lions,
Rev 3: 7 no-one can *s*; and what he shuts,
21: 25 On no day will its gates ever be *s*,

SICK (SICKNESS)
Pr 13: 12 Hope deferred makes the heart *s*,
Eze 34: 4 or healed the *s* or bound up
Mt 9: 12 who need a doctor, but the *s*.
10: 8 Heal the *s*, raise the dead, cleanse
25: 36 I was *s* and you looked after me,
1Co 11: 30 many among you are weak and *s*,
Jas 5: 14 of you *s*? He should call the elders

SICK-BED* (BED)
Ps 41: 3 LORD will sustain him on his *s*

SICKLE
Joel 3: 13 Swing the *s*,
Rev 14: 14 gold on his head and a sharp *s*

SICKNESS (SICK)
Mt 4: 23 and healing every disease and *s*

SIDE (SIDES)
Ps 91: 7 A thousand may fall at your *s*,
124: 1 If the LORD had not been on our *s*
Jn 18: 37 Everyone on the *s* of truth listens
20: 20 he showed them his hands and *s*.
2Ti 4: 17 But the Lord stood at my *s*
Heb 10: 33 at other times you stood *s* by *s*

SIDES (SIDE)
Nu 33: 55 in your eyes and thorns in your *s*.

SIFT
Lk 22: 31 Satan has asked to *s* you as wheat.

SIGHING
Isa 35: 10 and sorrow and *s* will flee away.

SIGHT
Ps 51: 4 and done what is evil in your *s*,
90: 4 For a thousand years in your *s*
116: 15 Precious in the *s* of the LORD
Pr 3: 4 in the *s* of God and man.
Mt 11: 5 The blind receive *s*, the lame walk,
Ac 4: 19 right in God's *s* to obey you rather
1Co 3: 19 this world is foolishness in God's *s*.
2Co 5: 7 We live by faith, not by *s*.
1Pe 3: 4 which is of great worth in God's *s*.

SIGN (SIGNS)
Ge 9: 12 "This is the *s* of the covenant I am
17: 11 and it will be the *s* of the covenant
Isa 7: 14 the Lord himself will give you a *s*:
55: 13 for an everlasting *s*,
Eze 20: 12 I gave them my Sabbaths as a *s*
Mt 12: 38 to see a miraculous *s* from you."
24: 3 what will be the *s* of your coming
24: 30 "At that time the *s* of the Son
Lk 2: 12 This will be a *s* to you: You will
11: 29 It asks for a miraculous *s*,
Ro 4: 11 he received the *s* of circumcision,
1Co 11: 10 to have a *s* of authority on her head
14: 22 are a *s*, not for believers

SIGNS (SIGN)
Ge 1: 14 let them serve as *s* to mark seasons
Ps 78: 43 day he displayed his miraculous *s*
105: 27 They performed his miraculous *s*
Da 6: 27 he performs *s* and wonders
Mt 24: 24 and perform great *s* and miracles
Mk 16: 17 these *s* will accompany those who
Jn 3: 2 perform the miraculous *s* you are
20: 30 Jesus did many other miraculous *s*
Ac 2: 19 and *s* on the earth below,
1Co 1: 22 Jews demand miraculous *s*
2Co 12: 12 *s*, wonders and miracles—
2Th 2: 9 *s* and wonders, and in every sort

SIHON
Nu 21: 21 to say to *S* king of the Amorites:
Ps 136: 19 *S* king of the Amorites

SILAS*
Prophet (Ac 15:22-32); co-worker with Paul on second missionary journey (Ac 16-18; 2Co 1:19). Co-writer with Paul (1Th 1:1; 2Th 1:1); Peter (1Pe 5:12).

SILENCE (SILENCED SILENT)
1Pe 2: 15 good you should *s* the ignorant talk
Rev 8: 1 there was *s* in heaven

SILENCED (SILENCE)
Ro 3: 19 so that every mouth may be *s*
Tit 1: 11 They must be *s*, because they are

SILENT (SILENCE)
Est 4: 14 For if you remain *s* at this time,
Ps 30: 12 to you and not be *s*.
32: 3 When I kept *s*,
39: 2 But when I was *s* and still,
Pr 17: 28 a fool is thought wise if he keeps *s*,
Ecc 3: 7 a time to be *s* and a time to speak,
Isa 53: 7 as a sheep before her shearers is *s*,
62: 1 For Zion's sake I will not keep *s*,
Hab 2: 20 let all the earth be *s* before him."
Ac 8: 32 and as a lamb before the shearer is *s*
1Co 14: 34 women should remain *s*
1Ti 2: 12 over a man; she must be *s*.

SILVER
Ps 12: 6 like *s* refined in a furnace of clay,
66: 10 you refined us like *s*.
Pr 2: 4 and if you look for it as for *s*
3: 14 for she is more profitable than *s*
8: 10 Choose my instruction instead of *s*,
22: 1 to be esteemed is better than *s*
25: 4 Remove the dross from the *s*,
25: 11 is like apples of gold in settings of *s*.
Isa 48: 10 I have refined you, though not as *s*;
Eze 22: 18 They are but the dross of *s*.
Da 2: 32 its chest and arms of *s*, its belly
Hag 2: 8 'The *s* is mine and the gold is mine,'
Zec 13: 9 I will refine them like *s*
Ac 3: 6 Peter said, "*S* or gold I do not have,
1Co 3: 12 *s*, costly stones, wood, hay or straw
1Pe 1: 18 not with perishable things such as *s*

SILVERSMITH
Ac 19: 24 A *s* named Demetrius, who made

SIMEON
Son of Jacob by Leah (Ge 29:33; 35:23; 1Ch 2:1). With Levi killed Shechem for rape of Dinah (Ge 34:25-29). Held hostage by Joseph in Egypt (Ge 42:24-43:23). Tribe of blessed (Ge 49:5-7), numbered (Nu 1:23; 26:14), allotted land (Jos 19:1-9; Eze 48:24), 12,000 from (Rev 7:7).

SIMON
1. See PETER.
2. Apostle, called the Zealot (Mt 10:4; Mk 3:18; Lk 6:15; Ac 1:13).
3. Samaritan sorcerer (Ac 8:9-24).

SIMPLE
Ps 19: 7 making wise the *s*.
119: 130 it gives understanding to the *s*.
Pr 8: 5 You who are *s*, gain prudence;
14: 15 A *s* man believes anything,

SIMPLE-HEARTED* (HEART)
Ps 116: 6 The LORD protects the *s*;

SIN (SINFUL SINNED SINNER SINNERS SINNING SINS)
Ge 4: 7 *s* is crouching at your door;
Ex 32: 32 please forgive their *s*—but if not,
Nu 5: 7 and must confess the *s* he has
32: 23 be sure that your *s* will find you
Dt 24: 16 each is to die for his own *s*.
1Sa 12: 23 it from me that I should *s*
15: 23 For rebellion is like the *s*
1Ki 8: 46 for there is no-one who does not *s*
2Ch 7: 14 and will forgive their *s* and will heal
Job 1: 22 Job did not *s* by charging God
Ps 4: 4 In your anger do not *s*;
17: 3 resolved that my mouth will not *s*.
32: 2 whose *s* the LORD does not count
32: 5 Then I acknowledged my *s* to you
36: 2 too much to detect or hate his *s*.
38: 18 I am troubled by my *s*.
39: 1 and keep my tongue from *s*;
51: 2 and cleanse me from my *s*.
66: 18 If I had cherished *s* in my heart,
119: 11 that I might not *s* against you.
119: 133 let no *s* rule over me.
Pr 5: 22 the cords of his *s* hold him fast.
10: 19 words are many, *s* is not absent,
14: 9 Fools mock at making amends for *s*
16: 6 faithfulness *s* is atoned for;
17: 19 He who loves a quarrel loves *s*;
20: 9 I am clean and without *s*"?
Isa 3: 9 they parade their *s* like Sodom;
6: 7 is taken away and your *s* atoned
64: 5 But when we continued to *s*
Jer 31: 30 everyone will die for his own *s*;
Eze 3: 18 that wicked man will die for his *s*,
18: 26 his righteousness and commits *s*,
33: 8 that wicked man will die for his *s*,
Am 4: 4 "Go to Bethel and *s*;
Mic 6: 7 of my body for the *s* of my soul?
7: 18 who pardons *s* and forgives
Zec 3: 4 "See, I have taken away your *s*,
Mt 18: 6 little ones who believe in me to *s*,
Mk 3: 29 he is guilty of an eternal *s*."
9: 43 If your hand causes you to *s*,
Lk 17: 1 people to *s* are bound to come,
Jn 1: 29 who takes away the *s* of the world!
Jn 8: 7 "If any one of you is without *s*,
8: 34 everyone who sins is a slave to *s*.
8: 46 Can any of you prove me guilty of *s*
Ro 2: 12 All who *s* apart from the law will
5: 12 as *s* entered the world

Ro 5: 20 where *s* increased, grace increased
6: 2 By no means! We died to *s*;
6: 11 count yourselves dead to *s*
6: 14 For *s* shall not be your master,
6: 23 For the wages of *s* is death,
7: 7 I would not have known what *s* was
7: 25 sinful nature a slave to the law of *s*.
14: 23 that does not come from faith is *s*.
1Co 8: 12 When you *s* against your brothers
15: 56 The sting of death is *s*,
2Co 5: 21 God made him who had no *s* to be *s*
Gal 6: 1 if someone is caught in a *s*,
1Ti 5: 20 Those who *s* are to be rebuked
Heb 4: 15 just as we are—yet was without *s*.
9: 26 to do away with *s* by the sacrifice
11: 25 the pleasures of *s* for a short time.
12: 1 and the *s* that so easily entangles,
Jas 1: 15 it gives birth to *s*; and *s*,
1Pe 2: 22 "He committed no *s*,
1Jn 1: 7 his Son, purifies us from all *s*.
1: 8 If we claim to be without *s*,
2: 1 But if anybody does *s*, we have one
3: 4 in fact, *s* is lawlessness.
3: 5 And in him is no *s*.
3: 6 No-one who continues to *s* has
3: 9 born of God will continue to *s*,
5: 16 There is a *s* that leads to death.
5: 17 All wrongdoing is *s*, and there is *s*
5: 18 born of God does not continue to *s*;

SINAI

Ex 19: 20 descended to the top of Mount *S*
31: 18 speaking to Moses on Mount *S*,
Ps 68: 17 from *S* into his sanctuary.

SINCERE* (SINCERITY)

Da 11: 34 many who are not *s* will join them.
Ac 2: 46 ate together with glad and *s* hearts,
Ro 12: 9 Love must be *s*.
2Co 6: 6 in the Holy Spirit and in *s* love;
11: 3 somehow be led astray from your *s*
1Ti 1: 5 a good conscience and a *s* faith.
3: 8 *s*, not indulging in much wine,
2Ti 1: 5 have been reminded of your *s* faith,
Heb 10: 22 near to God with a *s* heart
Jas 3: 17 and good fruit, impartial and *s*.
1Pe 1: 22 the truth so that you have *s* love

SINCERITY* (SINCERE)

1Co 5: 8 bread without yeast, the bread of *s*
2Co 1: 12 in the holiness and *s* that are
2: 17 speak before God with *s*,
8: 8 but I want to test the *s* of your love
Eph 6: 5 and with *s* of heart, just
Col 3: 22 but with *s* of heart and reverence

SINFUL (SIN)

Ps 51: 5 *s* at birth, *s* from the time
Lk 5: 8 from me, Lord; I am a *s* man!"
Ro 7: 5 we were controlled by the *s* nature,
7: 18 lives in me, that is, in my *s* nature.
7: 25 but in the *s* nature a slave to the law
8: 3 Son in the likeness of *s* man
8: 4 not live according to the *s* nature
8: 7 the *s* mind is hostile to God.
8: 8 by the *s* nature cannot please God.
8: 9 are controlled not by the *s* nature
8: 13 if you live according to the *s* nature
13: 14 to gratify the desires of the *s* nature
1Co 5: 5 so that the *s* nature may be
Gal 5: 13 freedom to indulge the *s* nature;
5: 16 gratify the desires of the *s* nature.
5: 19 The acts of the *s* nature are obvious
5: 24 Jesus have crucified the *s* nature
6: 8 sows to please his *s* nature,
Col 2: 11 in the putting off of the *s* nature,
Heb 3: 12 brothers, that none of you has a *s*,
1Pe 2: 11 abstain from *s* desires, which war
1Jn 3: 8 He who does what is *s* is

SING (SANG SINGER SINGING SINGS SONG SONGS SUNG)

Ex 15: 1 "I will *s* to the LORD,
Ps 5: 11 let them ever *s* for joy.
13: 6 I will *s* to the LORD,
30: 4 *s* to the LORD, you saints of his;
33: 1 *S* joyfully to the LORD, you
47: 6 *S* praises to God, *s* praises;
57: 7 I will *s* and make music.
59: 16 But I will *s* of your strength,
63: 7 I *s* in the shadow of your wings.
66: 2 *S* the glory of his name;
89: 1 I will *s* of the LORD's great love
95: 1 Come, let us *s* for joy to the LORD
96: 1 *S* to the LORD a new song;
98: 1 *S* to the LORD a new song,
101: 1 I will *s* of your love and justice;
108: 1 I will *s* and make music
137: 3 "*S* us one of the songs of Zion!"
147: 1 is to *s* praises to our God,
149: 1 *S* to the LORD a new song,
Isa 54: 1 "*S*, O barren woman,
1Co 14: 15 also pray with my mind; I will *s*
Eph 5: 19 *S* and make music in your heart
Col 3: 16 and as you *s* psalms, hymns
Jas 5: 13 Is anyone happy? Let him *s* songs

SINGER* (SING)

2Sa 23: 1 Israel's *s* of songs:

SINGING (SING)

Ps 63: 5 with *s* lips my mouth will praise
68: 6 he leads forth the prisoners with *s*;
98: 5 with the harp and the sound of *s*,
Isa 35: 10 They will enter Zion with *s*;
Zep 3: 17 he will rejoice over you with *s*."
Ac 16: 25 Silas were praying and *s* hymns
Rev 5: 13 on the sea, and all that is in them, *s*:

SINGLE

Ex 23: 29 I will not drive them out in a *s* year,
Mt 6: 27 you by worrying can add a *s* hour
Gal 5: 14 law is summed up in a *s* command:

SINGS (SING)

Eze 33: 32 more than one who *s* love songs

SINNED (SIN)

Lev 5: 5 confess in what way he has *s*
1Sa 15: 24 Then Saul said to Samuel, "I have *s*
2Sa 12: 13 "I have *s* against the LORD."
24: 10 I have *s* greatly in what I have done
2Ch 6: 37 'We have *s*, we have done wrong
Job 1: 5 "Perhaps my children have *s*
33: 27 'I *s*, and perverted what was right,
Ps 51: 4 Against you, you only, have I *s*
Jer 2: 35 because you say, 'I have not *s*.'
14: 20 we have indeed *s* against you.
Da 9: 5 we have *s* and done wrong.
Mic 7: 9 Because I have *s* against him,
Mt 27: 4 "I have *s*," he said,
Lk 15: 18 I have *s* against heaven
Ro 3: 23 for all have *s* and fall short
5: 12 all *s*—for before the law was given,
2Pe 2: 4 did not spare angels when they *s*,
1Jn 1: 10 claim we have not *s*, we make him

SINNER (SIN)

Ps 51: 5 Surely I have been a *s* from birth,
Ecc 9: 18 but one *s* destroys much good.
Lk 15: 7 in heaven over one *s* who repents
18: 13 'God, have mercy on me, a *s*.'
1Co 14: 24 convinced by all that he is a *s*
Jas 5: 20 Whoever turns a *s* from the error
1Pe 4: 18 become of the ungodly and the *s*?"

SINNERS (SIN)

Ps 1: 1 or stand in the way of *s*
37: 38 But all *s* will be destroyed;
Pr 1: 10 My son, if *s* entice you,
23: 17 Do not let your heart envy *s*,
Mt 9: 13 come to call the righteous, but *s*."
Ro 5: 8 While we were still *s*, Christ died
Gal 2: 17 evident that we ourselves are *s*,
1Ti 1: 15 came into the world to save *s*—
Heb 7: 26 set apart from *s*, exalted

SINNING (SIN)

Ex 20: 20 be with you to keep you from *s*."
1Co 15: 34 stop *s*; for there are some who are
Heb 10: 26 If we deliberately keep on *s*
1Jn 3: 6 No-one who lives in him keeps on *s*
3: 9 go on *s*, because he has been born

SINS (SIN)

Lev 5: 1 "'If a person *s* because he does not
16: 30 you will be clean from all your *s*.
26: 40 "'But if they will confess their *s*
Nu 15: 30 "'But anyone who *s* defiantly,
1Sa 2: 25 If a man *s* against another man,
2Ki 14: 6 each is to die for his own *s*."
Ezr 9: 6 our *s* are higher than our heads
9: 13 less than our *s* have deserved
Ps 19: 13 your servant also from wilful *s*;
32: 1 whose *s* are covered.
51: 9 Hide your face from my *s*
79: 9 deliver us and forgive our *s*
85: 2 and covered all their *s*.
103: 3 He forgives all my *s*
103: 10 does not treat us as our *s* deserve
130: 3 O LORD, kept a record of *s*,
Pr 14: 21 He who despises his neighbour *s*,
28: 13 who conceals his *s* does not
29: 22 one commits many *s*.
Ecc 7: 20 who does what is right and never *s*.
Isa 1: 18 "Though your *s* are like scarlet,
38: 17 you have put all my *s*
43: 25 and remembers your *s* no more.
59: 2 your *s* have hidden his face
64: 6 like the wind our *s* sweep us away.
Jer 31: 34 and will remember their *s* no more
La 3: 39 complain when punished for his *s*?
Eze 18: 4 soul who *s* is the one who will die.
33: 10 Our offences and *s* weigh us down,
36: 33 day I cleanse you from all your *s*,
Hos 14: 1 Your *s* have been your downfall!
Mt 1: 21 he will save his people from their *s*
6: 15 if you do not forgive men their *s*,
9: 6 authority on earth to forgive *s* . . ."
18: 15 "If your brother *s* against you,
26: 28 for many for the forgiveness of *s*.
Lk 5: 24 authority on earth to forgive *s* . . ."
11: 4 Forgive us our *s*,
17: 3 "If your brother *s*, rebuke him,
Jn 8: 24 you will indeed die in your *s*."
20: 23 If you forgive anyone his *s*,
Ac 2: 38 for the forgiveness of your *s*.
3: 19 so that your *s* may be wiped out,
10: 43 forgiveness of *s* through his name."
22: 16 be baptised and wash your *s* away,
26: 18 they may receive forgiveness of *s*
Ro 4: 7 whose *s* are covered.
4: 25 delivered over to death for our *s*
1Co 15: 3 died for our *s* according
2Co 5: 19 not counting men's *s* against them.
Gal 1: 4 himself for our *s* to rescue us
Eph 2: 1 dead in your transgressions and *s*,
Col 2: 13 us all our *s*, having cancelled
1Ti 5: 22 and do not share in the *s* of others.
Heb 1: 3 he had provided purification for *s*,
2: 17 atonement for the *s* of the people.
7: 27 He sacrificed for their *s* once for all
8: 12 and will remember their *s* no more
9: 28 to take away the *s* of many people;
10: 4 of bulls and goats to take away *s*.
10: 12 for all time one sacrifice for *s*,
10: 26 of the truth, no sacrifice for *s* is left,
Jas 4: 17 ought to do and doesn't do it, *s*.
5: 16 Therefore confess your *s*
5: 20 and cover over a multitude of *s*.
1Pe 2: 24 He himself bore our *s* in his body
3: 18 For Christ died for *s* once for all,
4: 8 love covers over a multitude of *s*.
1Jn 1: 9 If we confess our *s*, he is faithful
2: 2 He is the atoning sacrifice for our *s*,
3: 5 so that he might take away our *s*.
4: 10 as an atoning sacrifice for our *s*.
Rev 1: 5 has freed us from our *s* by his blood

SISERA
Jdg 4: 2 The commander of his army was *S*,
5: 26 She struck *S*, she crushed his head,

SISTER (SISTERS)
Lev 18: 9 have sexual relations with your *s*,
Mk 3: 35 does God's will is my brother and *s*

SISTERS (SISTER)
Mt 19: 29 or brothers or *s* or father or mother
1Ti 5: 2 as *s*, with absolute purity.

SIT (SAT SITS SITTING)
Dt 6: 7 them when you *s* at home
1Ki 8: 25 fail to have a man to *s* before me
Ps 1: 1 or *s* in the seat of mockers.
26: 5 and refuse to *s* with the wicked.
80: 1 you who *s* enthroned
110: 1 "*S* at my right hand
139: 2 You know when I *s* and when I rise
SS 2: 3 I delight to *s* in his shade,
Isa 16: 5 in faithfulness a man will *s* on it—
Mic 4: 4 Every man will *s* under his own
Mt 20: 23 to *s* at my right or left is not for me
22: 44 "*S* at my right hand
Lk 22: 30 in my kingdom and *s* on thrones,
Heb 1: 13 "*S* at my right hand
Rev 3: 21 right to *s* with me on my throne,

SITS (SIT)
Ps 99: 1 *s* enthroned between the cherubim,
Isa 40: 22 He *s* enthroned above the circle
Mt 19: 28 of Man *s* on his glorious throne,
Rev 4: 9 thanks to him who *s* on the throne

SITTING (SIT)
Est 2: 19 Mordecai was *s* at the king's gate.
Mt 26: 64 the Son of Man *s* at the right hand
Rev 4: 2 in heaven with someone *s* on it.

SITUATION (SITUATIONS)
1Co 7: 24 remain in the *s* God called him
Php 4: 12 of being content in any and every *s*,

SITUATIONS* (SITUATION)
2Ti 4: 5 head in all *s*, endure hardship,

SKIES (SKY)
Ps 19: 1 the *s* proclaim the work
71: 19 Your righteousness reaches to the *s*
108: 4 your faithfulness reaches to the *s*.

SKILFUL (SKILL)
Ps 45: 1 my tongue is the pen of a *s* writer.
78: 72 with *s* hands he led them.

SKILL (SKILFUL SKILLED)
Ps 137: 5 may my right hand forget ⌊its *s*⌋
Ecc 10: 10 but *s* will bring success.

SKILLED (SKILL)
Pr 22: 29 Do you see a man *s* in his work?

SKIN (SKINS)
Job 19: 20 with only the *s* of my teeth.
19: 26 And after my *s* has been destroyed,
Jer 13: 23 Can the Ethiopian change his *s*

SKINS (SKIN)
Ex 25: 5 ram *s* dyed red and hides
Lk 5: 37 the new wine will burst the *s*,

SKULL
Mt 27: 33 (which means The Place of the *S*).

SKY (SKIES)
Ge 1: 8 God called the expanse "*s*".
Pr 30: 19 the way of an eagle in the *s*,
Isa 34: 4 and the *s* rolled up like a scroll;
Jer 33: 22 stars of the *s* and as measureless
Mt 24: 29 the stars will fall from the *s*,
24: 30 coming on the clouds of the *s*,
Rev 20: 11 Earth and *s* fled from his presence,

SLACK*
Pr 18: 9 One who is *s* in his work

SLAIN (SLAY)
1Sa 18: 7 "Saul has *s* his thousands,
Eze 37: 9 into these *s*, that they may live.'"
Rev 5: 6 as if it had been *s*, standing
5: 12 "Worthy is the Lamb, who was *s*,
6: 9 the souls of those who had been *s*

SLANDER (SLANDERED SLANDERER SLANDERERS SLANDEROUS)
Lev 19: 16 "'Do not go about spreading *s*
Ps 15: 3 and has no *s* on his tongue,
Pr 10: 18 and whoever spreads *s* is a fool.
2Co 12: 20 outbursts of anger, factions, *s*,
Eph 4: 31 rage and anger, brawling and *s*,
1Ti 5: 14 the enemy no opportunity for *s*.
Tit 3: 2 to *s* no-one, to be peaceable
1Pe 3: 16 in Christ may be ashamed of their *s*
2Pe 2: 10 afraid to *s* celestial beings;

SLANDERED (SLANDER)
1Co 4: 13 when we are *s*, we answer kindly.

SLANDERER (SLANDER)
1Co 5: 11 an idolater or a *s*, a drunkard

SLANDERERS (SLANDER)
Ro 1: 30 They are gossips, *s*, God-haters,
1Co 6: 10 nor the greedy nor drunkards nor *s*
Tit 2: 3 not to be *s* or addicted

SLANDEROUS (SLANDER)
2Ti 3: 3 unforgiving, *s*, without self-control
2Pe 2: 11 do not bring *s* accusations

SLAUGHTER (SLAUGHTERED)
Isa 53: 7 he was led like a lamb to the *s*,
Jer 11: 19 been like a gentle lamb led to the *s*;
Ac 8: 32 "He was led like a sheep to the *s*,

SLAUGHTERED (SLAUGHTER)
Ps 44: 22 we are considered as sheep to be *s*.
Ro 8: 36 we are considered as sheep to be *s*

SLAVE (ENSLAVED SLAVERY SLAVES)
Ge 21: 10 "Get rid of that *s* woman
Mt 20: 27 wants to be first must be your *s*—
Jn 8: 34 everyone who sins is a *s* to sin.
Ro 7: 14 I am unspiritual, sold as a *s* to sin.
1Co 7: 21 Were you a *s* when you were called
12: 13 whether Jews or Greeks, *s* or free
Gal 3: 28 *s* nor free, male nor female,
4: 7 So you are no longer a *s*, but a son;
4: 30 Get rid of the *s* woman and her son
Col 3: 11 barbarian, Scythian, *s* or free,
1Ti 1: 10 for *s* traders and liars and perjurers
Phm : 16 no longer as a *s*, but better than a *s*,
2Pe 2: 19 a man is a *s* to whatever has

SLAVERY (SLAVE)
Ex 2: 23 The Israelites groaned in their *s*
Ro 6: 19 parts of your body in *s* to impurity
Gal 4: 3 were in *s* under the basic principles
1Ti 6: 1 of *s* should consider their masters

SLAVES (SLAVE)
Ps 123: 2 As the eyes of *s* look to the hand
Ecc 10: 7 I have seen *s* on horseback,
Ro 6: 6 that we should no longer be *s* to sin
6: 16 you are *s* to sin, which leads
6: 22 and have become *s* to God,
Gal 2: 4 in Christ Jesus and to make us *s*.
4: 8 you were *s* to those who
Eph 6: 5 *S*, obey your earthly masters
Col 3: 22 *S*, obey your earthly masters
4: 1 provide your *s* with what is right
Tit 2: 9 Teach *s* to be subject

SLAY (SLAIN)
Job 13: 15 Though he *s* me, yet will I hope

SLEEP (ASLEEP SLEEPER SLEEPING SLEEPS)
Ge 2: 21 the man to fall into a deep *s*;
15: 12 Abram fell into a deep *s*,
28: 11 it under his head and lay down to *s*.
Ps 4: 8 I will lie down and *s* in peace,
121: 4 will neither slumber nor *s*.
127: 2 for he grants *s* to those he loves.
Pr 6: 9 When will you get up from your *s*?
Ecc 5: 12 The *s* of a labourer is sweet,
1Co 15: 51 We will not all *s*, but we will all be
1Th 5: 7 For those who *s*, *s* at night,

SLEEPER (SLEEP)
Eph 5: 14 "Wake up, O *s*,

SLEEPING (SLEEP)
Mk 13: 36 suddenly, do not let him find you *s*.

SLEEPLESS*
2Co 6: 5 in hard work, *s* nights and hunger;

SLEEPS (SLEEP)
Pr 10: 5 he who *s* during harvest is

SLIMY
Ps 40: 2 He lifted me out of the *s* pit,

SLING
1Sa 17: 50 over the Philistine with a *s*

SLIP (SLIPPING)
Dt 4: 9 let them *s* from your heart as long
Ps 121: 3 He will not let your foot *s*—

SLIPPING (SLIP)
Ps 66: 9 and kept our feet from *s*.

SLOW
Ex 34: 6 and gracious God, *s* to anger,
Jas 1: 19 *s* to speak and *s* to become angry,
2Pe 3: 9 The Lord is not *s* in keeping his

SLUGGARD
Pr 6: 6 Go to the ant, you *s*;
13: 4 The *s* craves and gets nothing,
20: 4 A *s* does not plough in season;
26: 15 The *s* buries his hand in the dish;

SLUMBER
Ps 121: 3 he who watches over you will not *s*;
Pr 6: 10 A little sleep, a little *s*,
Ro 13: 11 for you to wake up from your *s*,

SLUR
Ps 15: 3 and casts no *s* on his fellow-man,

SMELL
Ecc 10: 1 As dead flies give perfume a bad *s*,
2Co 2: 16 To the one we are the *s* of death;

SMITTEN
Isa 53: 4 *s* by him, and afflicted.

SMOKE
Ex 19: 18 Mount Sinai was covered with *s*,
Ps 104: 32 touches the mountains, and they *s*.
Isa 6: 4 and the temple was filled with *s*.
Joel 2: 30 blood and fire and billows of *s*.
Ac 2: 19 blood and fire and billows of *s*.
Rev 15: 8 filled with *s* from the glory

SMYRNA
Rev 2: 8 the angel of the church in *S* write:

SNAKE (SNAKES)
Nu 21: 8 "Make a *s* and put it up on a pole;
Pr 23: 32 In the end it bites like a *s*
Jn 3: 14 Moses lifted up the *s* in the desert,

SNAKES (SNAKE)
Mt 10: 16 as shrewd as *s* and as innocent

Mk 16:18 they will pick up *s* with their hands;

SNARE (ENSNARE ENSNARED SNARED)

Dt 7:16 for that will be a *s* to you.
Ps 69:22 before them become a *s*;
91:3 from the fowler's *s*
Pr 29:25 Fear of man will prove to be a *s*,
Ro 11:9 "May their table become a *s*

SNARED (SNARE)

Pr 3:26 will keep your foot from being *s*.

SNATCH

Jn 10:28 no-one can *s* them out of my hand.
Jude :23 *s* others from the fire and save

SNOUT

Pr 11:22 Like a gold ring in a pig's *s*

SNOW

Ps 51:7 and I will be whiter than *s*.
Isa 1:18 they shall be as white as *s*;

SNUFF (SNUFFED)

Isa 42:3 a smouldering wick he will not *s* out.
Mt 12:20 a smouldering wick he will not *s* out,

SNUFFED (SNUFF)

Pr 13:9 but the lamp of the wicked is *s* out.

SOAP

Mal 3:2 a refiner's fire or a launderer's *s*.

SOAR (SOARED)

Isa 40:31 They will *s* on wings like eagles;

SOARED (SOAR)

2Sa 22:11 he *s* on the wings of the wind.

SOBER

Ro 12:3 think of yourself with *s* judgment,

SODOM

Ge 13:12 and pitched his tents near *S*.
19:24 rained down burning sulphur on *S*
Isa 1:9 we would have become like *S*,
Lk 10:12 on that day for *S* than for that town
Ro 9:29 we would have become like *S*,
Rev 11:8 which is figuratively called *S*

SOIL

Ge 4:2 kept flocks, and Cain worked the *s*.
Mt 13:23 on good *s* is the man who hears

SOLD (SELL)

1Ki 21:25 who *s* himself to do evil in the eyes
Mt 10:29 Are not two sparrows *s* for a penny
13:44 then in his joy went and *s* all he had
Ro 7:14 I am unspiritual, *s* as a slave to sin.

SOLDIER

1Co 9:7 as a *s* at his own expense?
2Ti 2:3 with us like a good *s* of Christ Jesus

SOLE

Dt 28:65 place for the *s* of your foot.
Isa 1:6 From the *s* of your foot to the top

SOLID

2Ti 2:19 God's *s* foundation stands firm,
Heb 5:12 You need milk, not *s* food!

SOLOMON

Son of David by Bathsheba; king of Judah (2Sa 12:24; 1Ch 3:5, 10). Appointed king by David (1Ki 1); adversaries Adonijah, Joab, Shimei killed by Benaiah (1Ki 2). Asked for wisdom (1Ki 3; 2Ch 1). Judged between two prostitutes (1Ki 3:16-28). Built temple (1Ki 5-7; 2Ch 2-5); prayer of dedication (1Ki 8; 2Ch 6). Visited by Queen of Sheba (1Ki 9; 2Ch 9). Wives turned his heart from God (1Ki 11:1-13). Jeroboam rebelled against (1Ki 11:26-40). Death (1Ki 11:41-43; 2Ch 9:29-31).

Proverbs of (1Ki 4:32; Pr 1:1; 10:1; 25:1); psalms of (Ps 72; 127); song of (SS 1:1).

SON (SONS SONSHIP)

Ge 17:19 your wife Sarah will bear you a *s*,
21:10 rid of that slave woman and her *s*,
22:2 "Take your *s*, your only *s* Isaac,
Ex 11:5 Every firstborn *s* in Egypt will die,
Dt 1:31 father carries his *s*, all the way you
6:20 In the future, when your *s* asks you,
8:5 as a man disciplines his *s*,
21:18 rebellious *s* who does not obey his
2Sa 7:14 be his father, and he will be my *s*.
1Ki 3:20 and put her dead *s* by my breast.
Ps 2:7 He said to me, "You are my *S*;
2:12 Kiss the *S*, lest he be angry
8:4 the *s* of man that you care for him?
Pr 3:12 as a father the *s* he delights in.
6:20 My *s*, keep your father's
10:1 A wise *s* brings joy to his father,
13:24 He who spares the rod hates his *s*,
29:17 Discipline your *s*, and he will give
Isa 7:14 with child and will give birth to a *s*,
Eze 18:20 The *s* will not share the guilt
Da 3:25 the fourth looks like a *s* of the gods
7:13 before me was one like a *s* of man,
Hos 11:1 and out of Egypt I called my *s*.
Am 7:14 neither a prophet nor a prophet's *s*,
Mt 1:1 of Jesus Christ the *s* of David,
1:21 She will give birth to a *s*,
2:15 "Out of Egypt I called my *s*."
3:17 "This is my *S*, whom I love;
4:3 "If you are the *S* of God, tell these
8:20 but the *S* of Man has nowhere
11:27 No-one knows the *S* except the Father,
12:8 For the *S* of Man is Lord
12:32 a word against the *S* of Man will be
12:40 so the *S* of Man will be three days
13:41 *S* of Man will send out his angels,
13:55 "Isn't this the carpenter's *s*?
14:33 "Truly you are the *S* of God."
16:16 "You are the Christ, the *S*
16:27 For the *S* of Man is going to come
17:5 "This is my *S*, whom I love;
19:28 when the *S* of Man sits
20:18 and the *S* of Man will be betrayed
20:28 as the *S* of Man did not come
21:9 "Hosanna to the *S* of David!"
22:42 Whose *s* is he?" "The *s* of David,"
24:27 so will be the coming of the *S*
24:30 They will see the *S* of Man coming
24:44 the *S* of Man will come at an hour
25:31 "When the *S* of Man comes
26:63 if you are the Christ, the *S* of God."
27:54 "Surely he was the *S* of God!"
28:19 and of the *S* and of the Holy Spirit,
Mk 1:11 "You are my *S*, whom I love;
2:28 So the *S* of Man is Lord
8:38 the *S* of Man will be ashamed
9:7 "This is my *S*, whom I love.
10:45 even the *S* of Man did not come
13:32 not the *S*, but only the Father.
14:62 you will see the *S* of Man sitting
Lk 1:32 and will be called the *S*
2:7 she gave birth to her firstborn, a *s*.
3:22 "You are my *S*, whom I love;
9:35 This is my *S*, whom I have chosen;
9:58 but the *S* of Man has nowhere
12:8 the *S* of Man will also acknowledge
15:20 he ran to his *s*, threw his arms
18:8 when the *S* of Man comes,
18:31 written by the prophets about the *S*
19:10 For the *S* of Man came to seek
Jn 1:14 the glory of the one and only ⌊*S*⌋,
1:34 I testify that this is the *S* of God."
3:14 so the *S* of Man must be lifted up,
3:16 that he gave his one and only *S*,
3:36 believes in the *S* has eternal life,
5:19 the *S* can do nothing by himself;
6:40 is that everyone who looks to the *S*
11:4 so that God's *S* may be glorified
17:1 Glorify your *S*, that your *S* may
Ac 7:56 and the *S* of Man standing
13:33 "'You are my *S*;
Ro 1:4 with power to be the *S* of God
5:10 to him through the death of his *S*,
8:3 did by sending his own *S*
8:29 conformed to the likeness of his *S*,
8:32 He who did not spare his own *S*,
1Co 15:28 then the *S* himself will be made
Gal 2:20 I live by faith in the *S* of God,
4:4 God sent his *S*, born of a woman,
4:30 rid of the slave woman and her *s*,
1Th 1:10 and to wait for his *S* from heaven,
Heb 1:2 days he has spoken to us by his *S*,
1:5 "You are my *S*;
2:6 the *s* of man that you care for him?
4:14 Jesus the *S* of God, let us hold
5:5 "You are my *S*;
7:28 appointed the *S*, who has been
10:29 punished who has trampled the *S*
12:6 everyone he accepts as a *s*."
2Pe 1:17 saying, "This is my *S*, whom I love;
1Jn 1:3 is with the Father and with his *S*,
1:7 his *S*, purifies us from all sin.
2:23 whoever acknowledges the *S* has
3:8 reason the *S* of God appeared was
4:9 only *S* into the world that we might
4:14 that the Father has sent his *S*
5:5 he who believes that Jesus is the *S*
5:11 eternal life, and this life is in his *S*.
Rev 1:13 lampstands was someone "like a *s*
14:14 on the cloud was one "like a *s*

SONG (SING)

Ex 15:2 LORD is my strength and my *s*;
Ps 40:3 He put a new *s* in my mouth,
69:30 I will praise God's name in *s*
96:1 Sing to the LORD a new *s*;
98:4 burst into jubilant *s* with music;
119:54 Your decrees are the theme of my *s*
149:1 Sing to the LORD a new *s*,
Isa 49:13 burst into *s*, O mountains!
55:12 will burst into *s* before you,
Rev 5:9 And they sang a new *s*:
15:3 and sang the *s* of Moses the servant

SONGS (SING)

2Sa 23:1 Israel's singer of *s*;
Job 35:10 who gives *s* in the night,
Ps 100:2 come before him with joyful *s*.
126:6 will return with *s* of joy,
137:3 "Sing us one of the *s* of Zion!"
Eph 5:19 with psalms, hymns and spiritual *s*.
Jas 5:13 Is anyone happy? Let him sing *s*

SONS (SON)

Ge 6:2 the *s* of God saw that the daughters
10:20 the *s* of Ham by their clans
Ru 4:15 who is better to you than seven *s*,
Ps 127:3 *S* are a heritage from the LORD,
132:12 if your *s* keep my covenant
Hos 1:10 they will be called '*s*
Joel 2:28 Your *s* and daughters will prophesy
Mt 5:9 for they will be called *s* of God.
Lk 6:35 and you will be *s* of the Most High,
Jn 12:36 so that you may become *s* of light."
Ro 8:14 by the Spirit of God are *s* of God.
9:26 they will be called '*s*
2Co 6:18 and you will be my *s* and daughters
Gal 3:26 You are all *s* of God through faith
4:5 we might receive the full rights of *s*.
4:6 Because you are *s*, God sent
Heb 12:7 discipline; God is treating you as *s*.

SONSHIP* (SON)

Ro 8:15 but you received the Spirit of *s*.

SORCERY

Lev 19:26 "'Do not practise divination or *s*.

SORROW (SORROWS)

Ps 6:7 My eyes grow weak with *s*;

Ps 116: 3 I was overcome by trouble and *s*.
Isa 60: 20 and your days of *s* will end.
Jer 31: 12 and they will *s* no more.
Ro 9: 2 I have great *s* and unceasing
2Co 7: 10 Godly *s* brings repentance that

SORROWS (SORROW)
Isa 53: 3 a man of *s*, and familiar

SOUGHT (SEEK)
2Ch 26: 5 As long as he *s* the LORD,
31: 21 he *s* his God and worked
Ps 34: 4 I *s* the LORD, and he answered me
119: 58 I have *s* your face with all my heart;

SOUL (SOULS)
Dt 6: 5 with all your *s* and with all your
10: 12 all your heart and with all your *s*,
30: 6 all your heart and with all your *s*,
Jos 22: 5 with all your heart and all your *s*."
2Ki 23: 25 and with all his *s* and with all his
Ps 23: 3 he restores my *s*.
63: 8 my *s* clings to you
34: 2 My *s* will boast in the LORD;
42: 1 so my *s* pants for you, O God.
42: 11 Why are you downcast, O my *s*?
62: 5 Find rest, O my *s*, in God alone;
94: 19 consolation brought joy to my *s*.
103: 1 Praise the LORD, O my *s*;
Pr 13: 19 A longing fulfilled is sweet to the *s*,
16: 24 sweet to the *s* and healing
22: 5 he who guards his *s* stays far
Isa 55: 2 your *s* will delight in the richest
La 3: 20 and my *s* is downcast within me.
Eze 18: 4 For every living *s* belongs to me,
Mt 10: 28 kill the body but cannot kill the *s*.
16: 26 yet forfeits his *s*? Or what can
22: 37 with all your *s* and with all your
Heb 4: 12 even to dividing *s* and spirit,
3Jn : 2 even as your *s* is getting along well.

SOULS (SOUL)
Pr 11: 30 and he who wins *s* is wise.
Jer 6: 16 and you will find rest for your *s*.
Mt 11: 29 and you will find rest for your *s*.

SOUND [1] (FINE-SOUNDING)
Ge 3: 8 and his wife heard the *s*
Eze 3: 12 I heard behind me a loud rumbling *s*
Jn 3: 8 You hear its *s*, but you cannot tell
Ac 2: 2 Suddenly a *s* like the blowing
1Co 14: 8 if the trumpet does not *s* a clear call
15: 52 the trumpet will *s*, the dead will

SOUND [2]
Pr 3: 21 preserve *s* judgment
1Ti 1: 10 to the *s* doctrine that conforms
2Ti 4: 3 men will not put up with *s* doctrine
Tit 1: 9 can encourage others by *s* doctrine
2: 1 is in accord with *s* doctrine.

SOUR
Eze 18: 2 "'The fathers eat *s* grapes,

SOURCE
Heb 5: 9 became the *s* of eternal salvation

SOVEREIGN (SOVEREIGNTY)
Ge 15: 2 But Abram said, "O *S* LORD,
2Sa 7: 18 O *S* LORD, and what is my family,
Ps 71: 16 your mighty acts, O *S* LORD;
Isa 25: 8 *S* LORD will wipe away the tears
40: 10 the *S* LORD comes with power,
50: 4 *S* LORD has given me
61: 1 The Spirit of the *S* LORD is on me,
61: 11 so the *S* LORD will make
Jer 32: 17 to the LORD: "Ah, *S* LORD,
Eze 12: 28 fulfilled, declares the *S* LORD.'"
Da 4: 25 that the Most High is *s*
2Pe 2: 1 denying the *s* Lord who bought
Jude : 4 and deny Jesus Christ our only *S*

SOVEREIGNTY (SOVEREIGN)
Da 7: 27 Then the *s*, power and greatness

SOW [1] (SOWER SOWN SOWS)
Job 4: 8 and those who *s* trouble reap it.
Ps 126: 5 Those who *s* in tears
Hos 8: 7 "They *s* the wind
10: 12 *S* for yourselves righteousness,
Mt 6: 26 they do not *s* or reap or store away
13: 3 "A farmer went out to *s* his seed.
1Co 15: 36 What you *s* does not come to life
Jas 3: 18 Peacemakers who *s*

SOW [2]
2Pe 2: 22 and, "A *s* that is washed goes back

SOWER (SOW [1])
Isa 55: 10 so that it yields seed for the *s*
Mt 13: 18 to what the parable of the *s* means:
Jn 4: 36 so that the *s* and the reaper may be
2Co 9: 10 Now he who supplies seed to the *s*

SOWN (SOW [1])
Mt 13: 8 sixty or thirty times what was *s*.
Mk 4: 15 along the path, where the word is *s*.
1Co 15: 42 The body that is *s* is perishable,

SOWS (SOW [1])
Pr 11: 18 he who *s* righteousness reaps a sure
22: 8 He who *s* wickedness reaps trouble
2Co 9: 6 Whoever *s* sparingly will
Gal 6: 7 A man reaps what he *s*.

SPARE (SPARES SPARING)
Est 7: 3 *s* my people—this is my request.
Ro 8: 32 He who did not *s* his own Son,
11: 21 natural branches, he will not *s* you
2Pe 2: 4 For if God did not *s* angels
2: 5 if he did not *s* the ancient world

SPARES (SPARE)
Pr 13: 24 He who *s* the rod hates his son,

SPARING (SPARE)
Pr 21: 26 but the righteous give without *s*.

SPARKLE
Zec 9: 16 They will *s* in his land

SPARROW (SPARROWS)
Ps 84: 3 Even the *s* has found a home,

SPARROWS (SPARROW)
Mt 10: 29 Are not two *s* sold for a penny?

SPAT
Mt 27: 30 They *s* on him, and took the staff

SPEAR (SPEARS)
1Sa 19: 10 as Saul drove the *s* into the wall.
Ps 46: 9 breaks the bow and shatters the *s*,

SPEARS (SPEAR)
Isa 2: 4 and their *s* into pruning hooks.
Joel 3: 10 and your pruning hooks into *s*.
Mic 4: 3 and their *s* into pruning hooks.

SPECIAL
Jas 2: 3 If you show *s* attention

SPECK
Mt 7: 3 look at the *s* of sawdust

SPECTACLE
1Co 4: 9 We have been made a *s*
Col 2: 15 he made a public *s* of them,

SPEECH
Ps 19: 3 There is no *s* or language
Pr 22: 11 pure heart and whose *s* is gracious
2Co 8: 7 in faith, in *s*, in knowledge,
1Ti 4: 12 set an example for the believers in *s*

SPEND (SPENT)
Pr 31: 3 do not *s* your strength on women,
Isa 55: 2 Why *s* money on what is not bread,
2Co 12: 15 So I will very gladly *s*

SPENT (SPEND)
Mk 5: 26 many doctors and had *s* all she had,
Lk 6: 12 and *s* the night praying to God.
15: 14 After he had *s* everything,

SPIN
Mt 6: 28 They do not labour or *s*.

SPIRIT (SPIRIT'S SPIRITS SPIRITUAL SPIRITUALLY)
Ge 1: 2 and the S of God was hovering
6: 3 "My *S* will not contend
Ex 31: 3 I have filled him with the *S* of God,
Nu 11: 25 and put the *S* on the seventy elders.
Dt 34: 9 filled with the *s* of wisdom
Jdg 6: 34 Then the *S* of the LORD came
11: 29 Then the *S* of the LORD came
13: 25 and the *S* of the LORD began
1Sa 10: 10 the *S* of God came upon him
16: 13 day on the *S* of the LORD came
16: 14 the *S* of the LORD had departed
2Sa 23: 2 "The *S* of the LORD spoke
2Ki 2: 9 inherit a double portion of your *s*,"
Ne 9: 20 You gave your good *S*
9: 30 By your *S* you admonished them
Job 33: 4 The *S* of God has made me;
Ps 31: 5 Into your hands I commit my *s*;
34: 18 saves those who are crushed in *s*.
51: 10 and renew a steadfast *s* within me.
51: 11 or take your Holy *S* from me.
51: 17 sacrifices of God are a broken *s*;
106: 33 rebelled against the *S* of God,
139: 7 Where can I go from your *S*?
143: 10 may your good *S*
Isa 11: 2 The *S* of the LORD will rest
30: 1 an alliance, but not by my *S*,
32: 15 till the *S* is poured upon us
44: 3 I will pour out my *S*
57: 15 him who is contrite and lowly in *s*,
61: 1 The *S* of the Sovereign LORD is
63: 10 and grieved his Holy *S*.
Eze 11: 19 an undivided heart and put a new *s*
13: 3 prophets who follow their own *s*
36: 26 you a new heart and put a new *s*
Da 4: 8 and the *s* of the holy gods is in him
Joel 2: 28 I will pour out my *S* on all people.
Zec 4: 6 but by my *S*,' says the LORD
Mt 1: 18 to be with child through the Holy *S*
3: 11 will baptise you with the Holy *S*
3: 16 he saw the *S* of God descending
4: 1 led by the *S* into the desert
5: 3 saying: "Blessed are the poor in *s*,
10: 20 but the *S* of your Father speaking
12: 31 against the *S* will not be forgiven.
26: 41 *s* is willing, but the body is weak."
28: 19 and of the Son and of the Holy *S*,
Mk 1: 8 he will baptise you with the Holy *S*
Lk 1: 35 "The Holy *S* will come upon you,
1: 80 child grew and became strong in *s*;
3: 16 will baptise you with the Holy *S*
4: 18 "The *S* of the Lord is on me,
11: 13 Father in heaven give the Holy *S*
23: 46 into your hands I commit my *s*."
Jn 1: 33 who will baptise with the Holy *S*.'
3: 5 a man is born of water and the *S*,
4: 24 God is *s*, and his worshippers must
6: 63 The *S* gives life; the flesh counts
7: 39 Up to that time the *S* had not been
14: 26 But the Counsellor, the Holy *S*,
16: 13 But when he, the *S* of truth, comes,
20: 22 and said, "Receive the Holy *S*.
Ac 1: 5 will be baptised with the Holy *S*."
1: 8 when the Holy *S* comes on you;
2: 4 of them were filled with the Holy *S*
2: 17 I will pour out my *S* on all people.
2: 38 will receive the gift of the Holy *S*.
4: 31 they were all filled with the Holy *S*

Ac 5: 3 that you have lied to the Holy *S*
6: 3 who are known to be full of the *S*
8: 15 that they might receive the Holy *S*,
9: 17 and be filled with the Holy *S*."
11: 16 will be baptised with the Holy *S*.'
13: 2 and fasting, the Holy *S* said,
19: 2 "Did you receive the Holy *S*
Ro 8: 4 nature but according to the *S*.
8: 5 set on what the *S* desires.
8: 9 And if anyone does not have the *S*
8: 13 but if by the *S* you put
8: 16 The *S* himself testifies
8: 23 who have the first fruits of the *S*,
8: 26 the *S* helps us in our weakness.
1Co 2: 10 God has revealed it to us by his *S*.
2: 14 man without the *S* does not accept
5: 3 present, I am with you in *s*.
6: 19 body is a temple of the Holy *S*,
12: 13 baptised by one *S* into one body—
2Co 1: 22 and put his *S* in our hearts
3: 3 but with the *S* of the living God,
3: 6 the letter kills, but the *S* gives life.
3: 17 Now the Lord is the *S*,
5: 5 and has given us the *S* as a deposit,
7: 1 that contaminates body and *s*,
Gal 3: 2 Did you receive the *S*
5: 16 by the *S*, and you will not gratify
5: 22 But the fruit of the *S* is love, joy,
5: 25 let us keep in step with the *S*.
6: 8 from the *S* will reap eternal life.
Eph 1: 13 with a seal, the promised Holy *S*,
2: 22 in which God lives by his *S*.
4: 4 There is one body and one *S*—
4: 30 do not grieve the Holy *S* of God,
5: 18 Instead, be filled with the *S*.
6: 17 of salvation and the sword of the *S*,
Php 2: 2 being one in *s* and purpose.
1Th 5: 23 May your whole *s*, soul
2Th 2: 13 the sanctifying work of the *S*
1Ti 3: 16 was vindicated by the *S*,
2Ti 1: 7 For God did not give us a *s*
Heb 2: 4 of the Holy *S* distributed according
4: 12 even to dividing soul and *s*,
10: 29 and who has insulted the *S* of grace
1Pe 3: 4 beauty of a gentle and quiet *s*,
2Pe 1: 21 carried along by the Holy *S*.
1Jn 3: 24 We know it by the *S* he gave us.
4: 1 Dear friends, do not believe every *s*
4: 13 because he has given us of his *S*.
Jude :20 holy faith and pray in the Holy *S*.
Rev 2: 7 let him hear what the *S* says

SPIRIT'S* (SPIRIT)

1Co 2: 4 a demonstration of the *S* power,
1Th 5: 19 not put out the *S* fire; do not treat

SPIRITS (SPIRIT)

1Co 12: 10 the ability to distinguish between *s*,
14: 32 The *s* of prophets are subject
1Jn 4: 1 test the *s* to see whether they are

SPIRITUAL (SPIRIT)

Ro 12: 1 to God—this is your *s* act of
12: 11 but keep your *s* fervour, serving
1Co 2: 13 expressing *s* truths in *s* words.
3: 1 I could not address you as *s* but
12: 1 Now about *s* gifts, brothers,
14: 1 of love and eagerly desire *s* gifts,
15: 44 a natural body, it is raised a *s* body.
Gal 6: 1 you who are *s* should restore him
Eph 1: 3 with every *s* blessing in Christ.
5: 19 with psalms, hymns and *s* songs.
6: 12 and against the *s* forces of evil
1Pe 2: 2 newborn babies, crave pure *s* milk,
2: 5 are being built into a *s* house

SPIRITUALLY (SPIRIT)

1Co 2: 14 because they are *s* discerned.

SPIT

Rev 3: 16 I am about to *s* you out

SPLENDOUR

1Ch 16: 29 the LORD in the *s* of his holiness.
29: 11 the glory and the majesty and the *s*,
Job 37: 22 of the north he comes in golden *s*;
Ps 29: 2 in the *s* of his holiness.
45: 3 clothe yourself with *s* and majesty.
96: 6 *S* and majesty are before him;
96: 9 in the *s* of his holiness;
104: 1 you are clothed with *s* and majesty.
145: 5 of the glorious *s* of your majesty,
145: 12 and the glorious *s* of your kingdom.
148: 13 his *s* is above the earth
Pr 4: 9 and present you with a crown of *s*."
16: 31 Grey hair is a crown of *s*;
20: 29 grey hair the *s* of the old.
Isa 55: 5 for he has endowed you with *s*."
60: 21 for the display of my *s*.
61: 3 the LORD for the display of his *s*.
63: 1 Who is this, robed in *s*,
Hab 3: 4 His *s* was like the sunrise;
Mt 6: 29 in all his *s* was dressed like one
Lk 9: 31 appeared in glorious *s*, talking
2Th 2: 8 and destroy by the *s* of his coming.

SPOIL (SPOILS)

Ps 119: 162 like one who finds great *s*.

SPOILS (SPOIL)

Isa 53: 12 he will divide the *s* with the strong,
Jn 6: 27 Do not work for food that *s*,

SPONTANEOUS*

Phm :14 so that any favour you do will be *s*

SPOTLESS

2Pe 3: 14 make every effort to be found *s*,

SPOTS (SPOTTED)

Jer 13: 23 or the leopard its *s*?

SPOTTED (SPOTS)

Ge 30: 32 and every *s* or speckled goat.

SPREAD (SPREADING SPREADS)

Ps 78: 19 "Can God *s* a table in the desert?
Ac 6: 7 So the word of God *s*.
12: 24 of God continued to increase and *s*.
13: 49 of the Lord *s* through the whole
19: 20 the word of the Lord *s* widely
2Th 3: 1 message of the Lord may *s* rapidly

SPREADING (SPREAD)

Pr 29: 5 is *s* a net for his feet.
1Th 3: 2 God's fellow-worker in *s* the gospel

SPREADS (SPREAD)

Pr 10: 18 and whoever *s* slander is a fool.

SPRING (SPRINGS WELLSPRING)

Jer 2: 13 the *s* of living water,
Jn 4: 14 in him a *s* of water welling up
Jas 3: 12 can a salt *s* produce fresh water.

SPRINGS (SPRING)

2Pe 2: 17 These men are *s* without water

SPRINKLE (SPRINKLED SPRINKLING)

Lev 16: 14 and with his finger *s* it on the front

SPRINKLED (SPRINKLE)

Heb 10: 22 having our hearts *s* to cleanse us

SPRINKLING (SPRINKLE)

1Pe 1: 2 to Jesus Christ and *s* by his blood:

SPROUT

Pr 23: 5 for they will surely *s* wings
Jer 33: 15 I will make a righteous Branch *s*

SPUR*

Heb 10: 24 how we may *s* one another

SPURNS*

Pr 15: 5 A fool *s* his father's discipline,

SPY

Gal 2: 4 ranks to *s* on the freedom we have

SQUANDERED (SQUANDERS)

Lk 15: 13 there *s* his wealth in wild living.

SQUANDERS* (SQUANDERED)

Pr 29: 3 of prostitutes *s* his wealth.

SQUARE

Rev 21: 16 The city was laid out like a *s*,

STABILITY*

Pr 29: 4 By justice a king gives a country *s*,

STAFF

Ge 49: 10 the ruler's *s* from between his feet,
Ex 7: 12 Aaron's *s* swallowed up their staffs.
Nu 17: 6 and Aaron's *s* was among them.
Ps 23: 4 your rod and your *s*,
Heb 9: 4 Aaron's *s* that had budded,

STAIN (STAINED)

Eph 5: 27 without *s* or wrinkle or any other

STAINED (STAIN)

Isa 63: 1 with his garments *s* crimson?

STAKES

Isa 54: 2 strengthen your *s*.

STAND (STANDING STANDS STOOD)

Ex 14: 13 *S* firm and you will see
Jos 10: 12 "O sun, *s* still over Gibeon,
2Ch 20: 17 *s* firm and see the deliverance
Job 19: 25 in the end he will *s* upon the earth.
Ps 1: 1 or *s* in the way of sinners
1: 5 Therefore the wicked will not *s*
24: 3 Who may *s* in his holy place?
33: 11 of the LORD *s* firm for ever,
40: 2 and gave me a firm place to *s*.
76: 7 Who can *s* before you
93: 5 Your statutes *s* firm;
119: 120 I *s* in awe of your laws.
130: 3 O Lord, who could *s*?
Ecc 5: 7 Therefore *s* in awe of God.
Isa 7: 9 If you do not *s* firm in your faith,
29: 23 will *s* in awe of the God of Israel.
Eze 22: 30 *s* before me in the gap on behalf
Hab 3: 2 I *s* in awe of your deeds, O LORD.
Zec 14: 4 On that day his feet will *s*
Mal 3: 2 Who can *s* when he appears?
Mt 12: 25 divided against itself will not *s*.
Ro 14: 4 for the Lord is able to make him *s*.
14: 10 we will all *s* before God's judgment
1Co 10: 13 out so that you can *s* up under it.
15: 58 Therefore, my dear brothers, *s* firm
16: 13 Be on your guard; *s* firm in the faith
Gal 5: 1 *S* firm, then, and do not let
Eph 6: 14 *S* firm then, with the belt
2Th 2: 15 *s* firm and hold to the teachings we
Jas 5: 8 You too, be patient and *s* firm,
Rev 3: 20 Here I am! I *s* at the door

STANDING (STAND)

Ex 3: 5 where you are *s* is holy ground."
Jos 5: 15 the place where you are *s* is holy."
Ru 2: 1 a man of *s*, whose name was Boaz.
4: 11 May you have *s* in Ephrathah
Lk 21: 19 By *s* firm you will save yourselves.
1Ti 3: 13 have served well gain an excellent *s*
1Pe 5: 9 Resist him, *s* firm in the faith,

STANDS (STAND)

Ps 89: 2 that your love *s* firm for ever,
119: 89 it *s* firm in the heavens.
Pr 12: 7 the house of the righteous *s* firm.
Isa 40: 8 but the word of our God *s* for ever."
Mt 10: 22 but he who *s* firm to the end will be
2Ti 2: 19 God's solid foundation *s* firm,
1Pe 1: 25 but the word of the Lord *s* for ever

STAR (STARS)
Nu 24: 17 A *s* will come out of Jacob;
Isa 14: 12 O morning *s*, son of the dawn!
Mt 2: 2 We saw his *s* in the east
2Pe 1: 19 the morning *s* rises in your hearts.
Rev 2: 28 I will also give him the morning *s*.
22: 16 and the bright Morning *S*."

STARS (STAR)
Ge 1: 16 He also made the *s*.
Job 38: 7 while the morning *s* sang together
Da 12: 3 like the *s* for ever and ever.
Php 2: 15 in which you shine like *s*

STATURE
1Sa 2: 26 boy Samuel continued to grow in *s*
Lk 2: 52 And Jesus grew in wisdom and *s*,

STATUTES
Ps 19: 7 *s* of the LORD are trustworthy,
93: 5 Your *s* stand firm;
119: 2 Blessed are they who keep his *s*
119: 14 I rejoice in following your *s*
119: 24 Your *s* are my delight;
119: 36 Turn my heart towards your *s*
119: 99 for I meditate on your *s*.
119: 111 Your *s* are my heritage for ever;
119: 125 that I may understand your *s*.
119: 129 Your *s* are wonderful;
119: 138 The *s* you have laid
119: 152 Long ago I learned from your *s*
119: 167 I obey your *s*,

STEADFAST*
Ps 51: 10 and renew a *s* spirit within me.
57: 7 My heart is *s*, O God,
57: 7 my heart is *s*;
108: 1 My heart is *s*, O God;
111: 8 They are *s* for ever and ever,
112: 7 his heart is *s*, trusting in the LORD
119: 5 Oh, that my ways were *s*
Isa 26: 3 him whose mind is *s*,
1Pe 5: 10 and make you strong, firm and *s*.

STEADY
Isa 35: 3 *s* the knees that give way;

STEAL (STOLEN)
Ex 20: 15 "You shall not *s*.
Lev 19: 11 " 'Do not *s*.
Dt 5: 19 "You shall not *s*.
Mt 19: 18 do not *s*, do not give false
Ro 13: 9 "Do not *s*," "Do not covet,"
Eph 4: 28 has been stealing must *s* no longer,

STEP (FOOTSTEPS STEPS)
Job 34: 21 he sees their every *s*.
Gal 5: 25 let us keep in *s* with the Spirit.

STEPHEN
Deacon (Ac 6:5). Arrested (Ac 6:8-15). Speech to Sanhedrin (Ac 7). Stoned (Ac 7:54-60; 22:20).

STEPS (STEP)
Ps 37: 23 whose *s* he has made firm;
Pr 14: 15 prudent man gives thought to his *s*.
16: 9 but the LORD determines his *s*.
20: 24 A man's *s* are directed
Jer 10: 23 it is not for man to direct his *s*.
1Pe 2: 21 that you should follow in his *s*.

STERN (STERNNESS)
Pr 15: 10 *S* discipline awaits him who leaves

STERNNESS* (STERN)
Ro 11: 22 and *s* of God: *s* to those who fell,

STICKS
Pr 18: 24 there is a friend who *s* closer

STIFF-NECKED (NECK)
Ex 34: 9 Although this is a *s* people,
Pr 29: 1 A man who remains *s*

STILL
Jos 10: 13 So the sun stood *s*,
Ps 37: 7 Be *s* before the LORD
46: 10 "Be *s*, and know that I am God;
89: 9 its waves mount up, you *s* them.
Zec 2: 13 Be *s* before the LORD, all mankind
Mk 4: 39 said to the waves, "Quiet! Be *s*!"

STIMULATE*
2Pe 3: 1 as reminders to *s* you

STING
1Co 15: 55 Where, O death, is your *s*?"

STINGY
Pr 28: 22 A *s* man is eager to get rich

STIRRED (STIRS)
Ps 45: 1 My heart is *s* by a noble theme

STIRS (STIRRED)
Pr 6: 19 and a man who *s* up dissension
10: 12 Hatred *s* up dissension,
15: 1 but a harsh word *s* up anger.
15: 18 hot-tempered man *s* up dissension,
16: 28 A perverse man *s* up dissension,
28: 25 A greedy man *s* up dissension,
29: 22 An angry man *s* up dissension,

STOLEN (STEAL)
Lev 6: 4 he must return what he has *s*
SS 4: 9 You have *s* my heart, my sister,

STOMACH
1Co 6: 13 Food for the *s* and the *s* for food"—
Php 3: 19 their god is their *s*, and their glory

STONE (CAPSTONE CORNERSTONE MILLSTONE STONED STONES)
Ex 24: 4 set up twelve *s* pillars representing
28: 10 on one *s* and the remaining six
34: 1 "Chisel out two *s* tablets like
Dt 4: 13 then wrote them on two *s* tablets.
19: 14 your neighbour's boundary *s* set up
1Sa 17: 50 the Philistine with a sling and a *s*;
Ps 91: 12 will not strike your foot against a *s*.
118: 22 The *s* the builders rejected
Pr 22: 28 not move an ancient boundary *s*
Isa 8: 14 a *s* that causes men to stumble
28: 16 "See, I lay a *s* in Zion,
Eze 11: 19 remove from them their heart of *s*
36: 26 remove from you your heart of *s*
Mt 7: 9 will give him a *s*? Or if he asks
21: 42 " 'The *s* the builders rejected
24: 2 not one *s* here will be left
Mk 16: 3 "Who will roll the *s* away
Lk 4: 3 tell this *s* to become bread."
Jn 8: 7 the first to throw a *s* at her."
Ac 4: 11 " 'the *s* you builders rejected,
Ro 9: 32 stumbled over the "stumbling-*s*."
2Co 3: 3 not on tablets of *s* but on tablets
1Pe 2: 6 "See, I lay a *s* in Zion,
Rev 2: 17 also give him a white *s*

STONED (STONE)
2Co 11: 25 once I was *s*, three times I was
Heb 11: 37 They were *s*; they were sawed

STONES (STONE)
Ex 28: 21 are to be twelve *s*, one for each
Jos 4: 3 to take up twelve *s* from the middle
1Sa 17: 40 chose five smooth *s*
Mt 3: 9 out of these *s* God can raise up
1Co 3: 12 silver, costly *s*, wood, hay or straw,
1Pe 2: 5 also, like living *s*, are being built

STOOD (STAND)
Jos 10: 13 So the sun *s* still,
Lk 22: 28 You are those who have *s* by me
2Ti 4: 17 But the Lord *s* at my side
Jas 1: 12 because when he has *s* the test,

STOOP (STOOPS)
2Sa 22: 36 you *s* down to make me great.

STOOPS (STOOP)
Ps 113: 6 who *s* down to look

STOP
Job 37: 14 *s* and consider God's wonders.
Isa 1: 13 *S* bringing meaningless offerings!
1: 16 *S* doing wrong,
2: 22 *S* trusting in man,
Jer 32: 40 I will never *s* doing good to them,
Mk 9: 39 "Do not *s* him," Jesus said.
Jn 6: 43 "*S* grumbling among yourselves,"
7: 24 *S* judging by mere appearances,
20: 27 *S* doubting and believe."
Ro 14: 13 Therefore let us *s* passing judgment
1Co 14: 20 Brothers, *s* thinking like children.

STORE (STORED)
Pr 2: 1 and *s* up my commands within you,
7: 1 and *s* up my commands within you.
10: 14 Wise men *s* up knowledge,
Isa 33: 6 a rich *s* of salvation and wisdom
Mt 6: 19 not *s* up for yourselves treasures
6: 26 or reap or *s* away in barns,
2Ti 4: 8 Now there is in *s* for me the crown

STORED (STORE)
Lk 6: 45 out of the good *s* up in his heart,
Col 1: 5 from the hope that is *s* up for you

STOREHOUSE (HOUSE)
Mal 3: 10 Bring the whole tithe into the *s*,

STORIES*
2Pe 1: 16 did not follow cleverly invented *s*
2: 3 you with *s* they have made up.

STORM
Job 38: 1 LORD answered Job out of the *s*.
Ps 107: 29 He stilled the *s* to a whisper;
Lk 8: 24 the *s* subsided, and all was calm.

STOUT-HEARTED* (HEART)
Ps 138: 3 you made me bold and *s*.

STRAIGHT
Ps 27: 11 lead me in a *s* path
107: 7 He led them by a *s* way
Pr 2: 13 who leave the *s* paths
3: 6 and he will make your paths *s*.
4: 11 and lead you along *s* paths.
4: 25 Let your eyes look *s* ahead,
11: 5 of the blameless makes a *s* way
15: 21 of understanding keeps a *s* course.
Isa 40: 3 make *s* in the wilderness
Mt 3: 3 make *s* paths for him.' "
Jn 1: 23 'Make *s* the way for the Lord.' "
2Pe 2: 15 They have left the *s* way

STRAIN (STRAINING)
Mt 23: 24 You *s* out a gnat but swallow

STRAINING (STRAIN)
Php 3: 13 and *s* towards what is ahead,

STRANGE (STRANGER STRANGERS)
Isa 28: 11 with foreign lips and *s* tongues
1Co 14: 21 "Through men of *s* tongues
1Pe 4: 4 They think it *s* that you do not

STRANGER (STRANGE)
Ps 119: 19 I am a *s* on earth;
Mt 25: 35 I was a *s* and you invited me in,
Jn 10: 5 But they will never follow a *s*;

STRANGERS (STRANGE)
Heb 13: 2 Do not forget to entertain *s*,
1Pe 2: 11 as aliens and *s* in the world,

STRAW
Isa 11: 7 and the lion will eat *s* like the ox.
1Co 3: 12 silver, costly stones, wood, hay or *s*

STRAYED (STRAYS)
Ps 119: 176 I have *s* like a lost sheep.
Jer 31: 19 After I *s*,

STRAYS (STRAYED)
Pr 21: 16 A man who *s* from the path
Eze 34: 16 for the lost and bring back the *s*.

STREAM (STREAMS)
Am 5: 24 righteousness like a never-failing *s*!

STREAMS (STREAM)
Ps 1: 3 He is like a tree planted by *s*
46: 4 is a river whose *s* make glad
Ecc 1: 7 All *s* flow into the sea,
Jn 7: 38 *s* of living water will flow

STREET
Mt 6: 5 on the *s* corners to be seen by men.
22: 9 Go to the *s* corners and invite
Rev 21: 21 The *s* of the city was of pure gold,

STRENGTH (STRONG)
Ex 15: 2 The LORD is my *s* and my song;
Dt 4: 37 by his Presence and his great *s*,
6: 5 all your soul and with all your *s*.
Jdg 16: 15 told me the secret of your great *s*."
2Sa 22: 33 It is God who arms me with *s*
2Ki 23: 25 with all his soul and with all his *s*,
1Ch 16: 11 Look to the LORD and his *s*;
16: 28 ascribe to the LORD glory and *s*,
29: 12 In your hands are *s* and power
Ne 8: 10 for the joy of the LORD is your *s*."
Ps 18: 1 I love you, O LORD, my *s*.
21: 13 Be exalted, O LORD, in your *s*;
28: 7 The LORD is my *s* and my shield;
29: 11 The LORD gives *s* to his people;
33: 16 no warrior escapes by his great *s*.
46: 1 God is our refuge and *s*,
59: 17 O my *S*, I sing praise to you;
65: 6 having armed yourself with *s*,
73: 26 but God is the *s* of my heart
84: 5 Blessed are those whose *s* is in you,
96: 7 ascribe to the LORD glory and *s*.
105: 4 Look to the LORD and his *s*;
118: 14 The LORD is my *s* and my song;
147: 10 not in the *s* of the horse,
Pr 24: 5 a man of knowledge increases *s*;
30: 25 Ants are creatures of little *s*,
Isa 12: 2 the LORD, is my *s* and my song;
31: 1 and in the great *s* of their horsemen
40: 26 of his great power and mighty *s*,
40: 31 will renew their *s*.
63: 1 forward in the greatness of his *s*?
Jer 9: 23 or the strong man boast of his *s*
Mic 5: 4 flock in the *s* of the LORD,
Hab 3: 19 The Sovereign LORD is my *s*;
Mk 12: 30 all your mind and with all your *s*.'
1Co 1: 25 of God is stronger than man's *s*.
Eph 1: 19 is like the working of his mighty *s*,
Php 4: 13 through him who gives me *s*.
Heb 11: 34 whose weakness was turned to *s*;
1Pe 4: 11 it with the *s* God provides,

STRENGTHEN (STRONG)
2Ch 16: 9 to *s* those whose hearts are fully
Ps 119: 28 *s* me according to your word.
Isa 35: 3 *S* the feeble hands,
41: 10 I will *s* you and help you;
Lk 22: 32 have turned back, *s* your brothers."
Eph 3: 16 of his glorious riches he may *s* you
1Th 3: 13 May he *s* your hearts
2Th 2: 17 and *s* you in every good deed
Heb 12: 12 *s* your feeble arms and weak knees.

STRENGTHENED (STRONG)
Col 1: 11 being *s* with all power according
Heb 13: 9 good for our hearts to be *s* by grace,

STRENGTHENING (STRONG)
1Co 14: 26 done for the *s* of the church.

STRETCHES
Ps 104: 2 he *s* out the heavens like a tent

STRICKEN (STRIKE)
Isa 53: 8 of my people he was *s*.

STRICT
1Co 9: 25 in the games goes into *s* training.

STRIFE (STRIVE)
Pr 17: 1 than a house full of feasting, with *s*.
20: 3 It is to a man's honour to avoid *s*,
22: 10 out the mocker, and out goes *s*;
30: 33 so stirring up anger produces *s*."

STRIKE (STRIKES STROKE)
Ge 3: 15 and you will *s* his heel."
Zec 13: 7 "*S* the shepherd,
Mt 4: 6 so that you will not *s* your foot
26: 31 "'I will *s* the shepherd,

STRIKES (STRIKE)
Mt 5: 39 If someone *s* you on the right

STRIPS
Jn 20: 5 in at the *s* of linen lying there

STRIVE* (STRIFE)
Ac 24: 16 I *s* always to keep my conscience
1Ti 4: 10 (and for this we labour and *s*),

STROKE (STRIKE)
Mt 5: 18 the smallest letter, not the least *s*

STRONG (STRENGTH STRENGTHEN STRENGTHENED STRENGTHENING STRONGER)
Dt 3: 24 your greatness and your *s* hand.
31: 6 Be *s* and courageous.
Jos 1: 6 "Be *s* and courageous,
Jdg 5: 21 March on, my soul; be *s*!
2Sa 10: 12 Be *s* and let us fight bravely
1Ki 2: 2 "So be *s*, show yourself a man,
1Ch 28: 20 "Be *s* and courageous,
2Ch 32: 7 them with these words: "Be *s*
Ps 24: 8 The LORD *s* and mighty,
31: 2 a *s* fortress to save me.
62: 11 that you, O God, are *s*,
Pr 18: 10 The name of the LORD is a *s* tower
31: 17 her arms are *s* for her tasks.
Ecc 9: 11 or the battle to the *s*,
SS 8: 6 for love is as *s* as death,
Isa 35: 4 "Be *s*, do not fear;
53: 12 he will divide the spoils with the *s*,
Jer 9: 23 or the *s* man boast of his strength
50: 34 Yet their Redeemer is *s*;
Hag 2: 4 Be *s*, all you people of the land,'
Mt 12: 29 can anyone enter a *s* man's house
Lk 2: 40 And the child grew and became *s*;
Ro 15: 1 We who are *s* ought to bear
1Co 1: 8 He will keep you *s* to the end,
1: 27 things of the world to shame the *s*.
16: 13 in the faith; be men of courage; be *s*
2Co 12: 10 For when I am weak, then I am *s*.
Eph 6: 10 be *s* in the Lord and in his mighty
2Ti 2: 1 be *s* in the grace that is
1Pe 5: 10 restore you and make you *s*,

STRONGER (STRONG)
Dt 4: 38 before you nations greater and *s*
1Co 1: 25 of God is *s* than man's strength.

STRONGHOLD (STRONGHOLDS)
2Sa 22: 3 He is my *s*, my refuge and my
Ps 9: 9 a *s* in times of trouble.
18: 2 the horn of my salvation, my *s*.
27: 1 The LORD is the *s* of my life—
144: 2 my *s* and my deliverer,

STRONGHOLDS (STRONGHOLD)
Zep 3: 6 their *s* are demolished.
2Co 10: 4 have divine power to demolish *s*.

STRUGGLE (STRUGGLED STRUGGLING)
Ro 15: 30 me in my *s* by praying to God
Eph 6: 12 For our *s* is not against flesh
Heb 12: 4 In your *s* against sin, you have not

STRUGGLED (STRUGGLE)
Ge 32: 28 because you have *s* with God

STRUGGLING* (STRUGGLE)
Col 1: 29 To this end I labour, *s*
2: 1 to know how much I am *s* for you

STUDENT (STUDY)
Mt 10: 24 "A *s* is not above his teacher,

STUDY (STUDENT)
Ezr 7: 10 Ezra had devoted himself to the *s*
Ecc 12: 12 and much *s* wearies the body.
Jn 5: 39 You diligently *s* the Scriptures

STUMBLE (STUMBLES STUMBLING)
Ps 37: 24 though he *s*, he will not fall,
119: 165 and nothing can make them *s*.
Pr 3: 23 and your foot will not *s*;
Isa 8: 14 a stone that causes men to *s*
Jer 13: 16 before your feet *s*
31: 9 a level path where they will not *s*,
Eze 7: 19 for it has made them *s* into sin.
Hos 14: 9 but the rebellious *s* in them.
Mal 2: 8 teaching have caused many to *s*;
Jn 11: 9 A man who walks by day will not *s*,
Ro 9: 33 in Zion a stone that causes men to *s*
14: 20 that causes someone else to *s*.
1Co 10: 32 Do not cause anyone to *s*,
Jas 3: 2 We all *s* in many ways.
1Pe 2: 8 and, "A stone that causes men to *s*
1Jn 2: 10 nothing in him to make him *s*.

STUMBLES (STUMBLE)
Pr 24: 17 when he *s*, do not let your heart
Jn 11: 10 is when he walks by night that he *s*,
Jas 2: 10 and yet *s* at just one point is guilty

STUMBLING (STUMBLE)
Ps 56: 13 and my feet from *s*,

STUMBLING-BLOCK
Lev 19: 14 put a *s* in front of the blind,
Mt 16: 23 Satan! You are a *s* to me;
Ro 11: 9 a *s* and a retribution for them
14: 13 up your mind not to put any *s*
1Co 1: 23 a *s* to Jews and foolishness
8: 9 freedom does not become a *s*
2Co 6: 3 We put no *s* in anyone's path,

STUMBLING-STONE
Ro 9: 32 They stumbled over the "*s*".

STUMP
Isa 6: 13 so the holy seed will be the *s*
11: 1 up from the *s* of Jesse;

STUPID
Pr 12: 1 but he who hates correction is *s*.
2Ti 2: 23 to do with foolish and *s* arguments,

STUPOR
Ro 11: 8 "God gave them a spirit of *s*,

SUBDUE (SUBDUED)
Ge 1: 28 in number; fill the earth and *s* it.

SUBDUED (SUBDUE)
Jos 10: 40 So Joshua *s* the whole region,
Ps 47: 3 He *s* nations under us,

SUBJECT (SUBJECTED)
Mt 5: 22 angry with his brother will be *s*
1Co 14: 32 of prophets are *s* to the control

1Co 15: 28 then the Son himself will be made *s*
Tit 2: 5 and to be *s* to their husbands,
2: 9 slaves to be *s* to their masters
3: 1 Remind the people to be *s* to rulers

SUBJECTED (SUBJECT)
Ro 8: 20 For the creation was *s*

SUBMISSION (SUBMIT)
1Co 14: 34 but must be in *s*, as the Law says.
1Ti 2: 11 learn in quietness and full *s*.

SUBMISSIVE (SUBMIT)
Jas 3: 17 then peace-loving, considerate, *s*,
1Pe 3: 1 in the same way be *s*
5: 5 in the same way be *s*

SUBMIT (SUBMISSION SUBMISSIVE SUBMITS)
Ro 13: 1 Everyone must *s* himself
13: 5 necessary to *s* to the authorities,
1Co 16: 16 to *s* to such as these
Eph 5: 21 *S* to one another out of reverence
Col 3: 18 Wives, *s* to your husbands,
Heb 12: 9 How much more should we *s*
13: 17 Obey your leaders and *s*
Jas 4: 7 *S* yourselves, then, to God.
1Pe 2: 18 *s* yourselves to your masters

SUBMITS* (SUBMIT)
Eph 5: 24 Now as the church *s* to Christ,

SUBTRACT*
Dt 4: 2 what I command you and do not *s*

SUCCEED (SUCCESS SUCCESSFUL)
Ps 20: 4 and make all your plans *s*.
Pr 15: 22 but with many advisers they *s*.
16: 3 and your plans will *s*.
21: 30 that can *s* against the LORD.

SUCCESS (SUCCEED)
Ge 39: 23 and gave him *s* in whatever he did.
1Sa 18: 14 In everything he did he had great *s*,
1Ch 12: 18 *S*, *s* to you, and *s*
22: 13 you will have *s* if you are careful
2Ch 26: 5 the LORD, God gave him *s*.
Ecc 10: 10 but skill will bring *s*.

SUCCESSFUL (SUCCEED)
Jos 1: 7 that you may be *s* wherever you go.
2Ki 18: 7 he was *s* in whatever he undertook.
2Ch 20: 20 in his prophets and you will be *s*."

SUFFER (SUFFERED SUFFERING SUFFERINGS SUFFERS)
Job 36: 15 those who *s* he delivers
Isa 53: 10 to crush him and cause him to *s*,
Mk 8: 31 the Son of Man must *s* many things
Lk 24: 26 the Christ have to *s* these things
24: 46 The Christ will *s* and rise
2Co 1: 6 of the same sufferings we *s*.
Php 1: 29 to *s* for him, since you are going
Heb 9: 26 would have had to *s* many times
1Pe 3: 17 to *s* for doing good
4: 16 However, if you *s* as a Christian,

SUFFERED (SUFFER)
Heb 2: 9 and honour because he *s* death,
2: 18 Because he himself *s*
1Pe 2: 21 Christ *s* for you, leaving you
4: 1 he who has *s* in his body is done

SUFFERING (SUFFER)
Job 36: 15 who suffer he delivers in their *s*;
Ps 22: 24 the *s* of the afflicted one;
Isa 53: 3 of sorrows, and familiar with *s*.
53: 11 After the *s* of his soul,
La 1: 12 Is any *s* like my *s*
Ac 5: 41 worthy of *s* disgrace for the Name.
Ro 5: 3 know that *s* produces
2Ti 1: 8 But join with me in *s* for the gospel,
Heb 2: 10 of their salvation perfect through *s*.
Heb 13: 3 as if you yourselves were *s*.
1Pe 4: 12 at the painful trial you are *s*,

SUFFERINGS (SUFFER)
Ro 5: 3 but we also rejoice in our *s*,
8: 17 share in his *s* in order that we may
8: 18 that our present *s* are not worth
2Co 1: 5 as the *s* of Christ flow
Php 3: 10 the fellowship of sharing in his *s*,
1Pe 4: 13 rejoice that you participate in the *s*
5: 9 are undergoing the same kind of *s*.

SUFFERS (SUFFER)
Pr 13: 20 but a companion of fools *s* harm.
1Co 12: 26 If one part *s*, every part *s* with it;

SUFFICIENT
2Co 12: 9 said to me, "My grace is *s* for you,

SUITABLE
Ge 2: 18 I will make a helper *s* for him."

SUMMED* (SUMS)
Ro 13: 9 there may be, are *s* up
Gal 5: 14 The entire law is *s* up

SUMMONS
Ps 50: 1 speaks and *s* the earth
Isa 45: 3 God of Israel, who *s* you by name.

SUMS* (SUMMED)
Mt 7: 12 for this *s* up the Law

SUN (SUNRISE)
Jos 10: 13 So the *s* stood still,
Jdg 5: 31 may they who love you be like the *s*
Ps 84: 11 For the LORD God is a *s*
121: 6 the *s* will not harm you by day,
136: 8 the *s* to govern the day,
Ecc 1: 9 there is nothing new under the *s*.
Isa 60: 19 The *s* will no more be your light
Mal 4: 2 the *s* of righteousness will rise
Mt 5: 45 He causes his *s* to rise on the evil
13: 43 the righteous will shine like the *s*
17: 2 His face shone like the *s*,
Lk 23: 45 for the *s* stopped shining.
Eph 4: 26 Do not let the *s* go
Rev 1: 16 His face was like the *s* shining
21: 23 The city does not need the *s*

SUNG (SING)
Mt 26: 30 When they had *s* a hymn, they

SUNRISE (SUN)
2Sa 23: 4 he is like the light of morning at *s*
Hab 3: 4 His splendour was like the *s*;

SUPERIOR
Heb 1: 4 he became as much *s* to the angels
8: 6 ministry Jesus has received is as *s*.

SUPERVISION
Gal 3: 25 longer under the *s* of the law.

SUPPER
Lk 22: 20 after the *s* he took the cup, saying,
1Co 11: 25 after *s* he took the cup,
Rev 19: 9 to the wedding *s* of the Lamb!' "

SUPPLIED (SUPPLY)
Ac 20: 34 of mine have *s* my own needs
Php 4: 18 and even more; I am amply *s*,

SUPPLY (SUPPLIED SUPPLYING)
2Co 8: 14 your plenty will *s* what they need,
1Th 3: 10 and *s* what is lacking in your faith.

SUPPLYING* (SUPPLY)
2Co 9: 12 you perform is not only *s* the needs

SUPPORT (SUPPORTED SUPPORTING)
Ps 18: 18 but the LORD was my *s*.
Ro 11: 18 consider this: You do not *s* the root
1Co 9: 12 If others have this right of *s*

SUPPORTED (SUPPORT)
Ps 94: 18 your love, O LORD, *s* me.
Col 2: 19 *s* and held together by its ligaments

SUPPORTING (SUPPORT)
Eph 4: 16 held together by every *s* ligament,

SUPPRESS*
Ro 1: 18 wickedness of men who *s* the truth

SUPREMACY* (SUPREME)
Col 1: 18 in everything he might have the *s*.

SUPREME (SUPREMACY)
Pr 4: 7 Wisdom is *s*; therefore get wisdom.

SURE
Nu 28: 31 Be *s* the animals are without defect
32: 23 you may be *s* that your sin will find
Dt 6: 17 Be *s* to keep the commands
14: 22 Be *s* to set aside a tenth
29: 18 make *s* there is no root
Jos 23: 13 then you may be *s* that the LORD
1Sa 12: 24 But be *s* to fear the LORD
Ps 19: 9 The ordinances of the LORD are *s*
132: 11 a *s* oath that he will not revoke:
Pr 27: 23 Be *s* you know the condition
Isa 28: 16 cornerstone for a *s* foundation;
Eph 5: 5 of this you can be *s*: No immoral,
Heb 11: 1 faith is being *s* of what we hope for
2Pe 1: 10 to make your calling and election *s*.

SURFACE
2Co 10: 7 You are looking only on the *s*

SURPASS* (SURPASSED SURPASSES SURPASSING)
Pr 31: 29 but you *s* them all."

SURPASSED* (SURPASS)
Jn 1: 15 'He who comes after me has *s* me
1: 30 man who comes after me has *s* me

SURPASSES* (SURPASS)
Pr 8: 19 what I yield *s* choice silver.
Mt 5: 20 unless your righteousness *s* that
Eph 3: 19 to know this love that *s* knowledge

SURPASSING* (SURPASS)
Ps 150: 2 praise him for his *s* greatness.
2Co 3: 10 in comparison with the *s* glory.
9: 14 of the *s* grace God has given you.
Php 3: 8 the *s* greatness of knowing Christ

SURPRISE (SURPRISED)
1Th 5: 4 that this day should *s* you like

SURPRISED (SURPRISE)
1Pe 4: 12 do not be *s* at the painful trial you
1Jn 3: 13 Do not be *s*, my brothers,

SURRENDER
1Co 13: 3 and *s* my body to the flames,

SURROUND (SURROUNDED SURROUNDS)
Ps 5: 12 you *s* them with your favour
32: 7 and *s* me with songs of deliverance.
89: 7 awesome than all who *s* him.
125: 2 As the mountains *s* Jerusalem,
Jer 31: 22 a woman will *s* a man."

SURROUNDED (SURROUND)
Heb 12: 1 since we are *s* by such a great cloud

SURROUNDS* (SURROUND)
Ps 32: 10 *s* the man who trusts in him.
89: 8 and your faithfulness *s* you.
125: 2 so the LORD *s* his people

SUSA
Ezr 4: 9 and Babylon, the Elamites of *S*,

Ne 1: 1 while I was in the citadel of *S*,

SUSPENDS*

Job 26: 7 he *s* the earth over nothing.

SUSPICIONS*

1Ti 6: 4 evil *s* and constant friction

SUSTAIN (SUSTAINING SUSTAINS)

Ps 55: 22 and he will *s* you;
Isa 46: 4 I am he, I am he who will *s* you.

SUSTAINING* (SUSTAIN)

Heb 1: 3 *s* all things by his powerful word.

SUSTAINS (SUSTAIN)

Ps 18: 35 and your right hand *s* me;
146: 9 and *s* the fatherless and the widow,
147: 6 The LORD *s* the humble
Isa 50: 4 to know the word that *s* the weary.

SWALLOW (SWALLOWED)

Isa 25: 8 he will *s* up death for ever.
Jnh 1: 17 provided a great fish to *s* Jonah,
Mt 23: 24 You strain out a gnat but *s* a camel.

SWALLOWED (SWALLOW)

1Co 15: 54 "Death has been *s* up in victory."
2Co 5: 4 so that what is mortal may be *s* up

SWAYED

Mt 11: 7 A reed *s* by the wind? If not,
22: 16 You aren't *s* by men, because you
2Ti 3: 6 are *s* by all kinds of evil desires,

SWEAR (SWORE SWORN)

Lev 19: 12 " 'Do not *s* falsely by my name
Ps 24: 4 or *s* by what is false.
Isa 45: 23 by me every tongue will *s*.
Mt 5: 34 Do not *s* at all: either by heaven,
Jas 5: 12 Above all, my brothers, do not *s*—

SWEAT*

Ge 3: 19 By the *s* of your brow
Lk 22: 44 his *s* was like drops of blood falling

SWEET (SWEETER SWEETNESS)

Job 20: 12 "Though evil is *s* in his mouth
Ps 119: 103 How *s* are your promises
Pr 9: 17 "Stolen water is *s*;
13: 19 A longing fulfilled is *s* to the soul,
16: 24 *s* to the soul and healing
20: 17 by fraud tastes *s* to a man,
24: 14 also that wisdom is *s* to your soul;
Ecc 5: 12 The sleep of a labourer is *s*,
Isa 5: 20 and *s* for bitter.
Eze 3: 3 it tasted as *s* as honey in my mouth.
Rev 10: 10 It tasted as *s* as honey in my mouth

SWEETER (SWEET)

Pr 19: 10 they are *s* than honey,
119: 103 *s* than honey to my mouth!

SWEETNESS* (SWEET)

SS 4: 11 Your lips drop *s* as the honeycomb,
5: 16 His mouth is *s* itself;

SWEPT

Mt 12: 44 finds the house unoccupied, *s* clean

SWERVE*

Pr 4: 5 do not forget my words or *s*
4: 27 Do not *s* to the right or the left;

SWIFT

Pr 1: 16 they are *s* to shed blood.
Ecc 9: 11 The race is not to the *s*
Isa 59: 7 they are *s* to shed innocent blood.
Ro 3: 15 "Their feet are *s* to shed blood;
2Pe 2: 1 bringing *s* destruction

SWINDLER* (SWINDLERS)

1Co 5: 11 or a slanderer, a drunkard or a *s*.

SWINDLERS* (SWINDLER)

1Co 5: 10 or the greedy and *s*, or idolaters.
6: 10 *s* will inherit the kingdom of God.

SWORD (SWORDS)

Ge 3: 24 and a flaming *s* flashing back
Dt 32: 41 when I sharpen my flashing *s*
Jos 5: 13 of him with a drawn *s* in his hand
1Sa 17: 45 "You come against me with *s*
17: 47 here will know that it is not by *s*
31: 4 so Saul took his own *s* and fell on it.
2Sa 12: 10 therefore, the *s* will never depart
Ps 44: 6 my *s* does not bring me victory;
45: 3 Gird your *s* upon your side,
Pr 12: 18 Reckless words pierce like a *s*,
Isa 2: 4 Nation will not take up *s*
Mic 4: 3 Nation will not take up *s*
Mt 10: 34 come to bring peace, but a *s*.
26: 52 all who draw the *s* will die by the *s*.
Lk 2: 35 a *s* will pierce your own soul too."
Ro 13: 4 for he does not bear the *s*
Eph 6: 17 of salvation and the *s* of the Spirit,
Heb 4: 12 Sharper than any double-edged *s*,
Rev 1: 16 came a sharp double-edged *s*.
19: 15 Out of his mouth comes a sharp *s*

SWORDS (SWORD)

Ps 64: 3 who sharpen their tongues like *s*
Isa 2: 4 They will beat their *s*
Joel 3: 10 Beat your ploughshares into *s*

SWORE (SWEAR)

Heb 6: 13 for him to swear by, he *s* by himself

SWORN (SWEAR)

Ps 110: 4 The LORD has *s*
Eze 20: 42 the land I had *s* with uplifted hand
Heb 7: 21 "The Lord has *s*

SYCAMORE-FIG (FIG)

Am 7: 14 and I also took care of *s* trees.
Lk 19: 4 and climbed a *s* tree to see him,

SYMBOLISES*

1Pe 3: 21 this water *s* baptism that now saves

SYMPATHETIC* (SYMPATHY)

1Pe 3: 8 in harmony with one another; be *s*,

SYMPATHISED* (SYMPATHY)

Heb 10: 34 You *s* with those in prison

SYMPATHY (SYMPATHETIC SYMPATHISED)

Ps 69: 20 I looked for *s*, but there was none,

SYNAGOGUE

Lk 4: 16 the Sabbath day he went into the *s*,
Ac 17: 2 custom was, Paul went into the *s*,

TABERNACLE (TABERNACLES)

Ex 40: 34 the glory of the LORD filled the *t*.
Heb 8: 2 the true *t* set up by the Lord,
9: 11 and more perfect *t* that is not
9: 21 sprinkled with the blood both the *t*
Rev 15: 5 that is, the *t* of Testimony,

TABERNACLES (TABERNACLE)

Lev 23: 34 the LORD's Feast of *T* begins,
Dt 16: 16 Feast of Weeks and the Feast of *T*.
Zec 14: 16 and to celebrate the Feast of *T*.

TABLE (TABLES)

Ex 25: 23 "Make a *t* of acacia wood—
Ps 23: 5 You prepare a *t* before me

TABLES (TABLE)

Jn 2: 15 money-changers and overturned their *t*.
Ac 6: 2 word of God in order to wait on *t*.

TABLET (TABLETS)

Pr 3: 3 write them on the *t* of your heart.
7: 3 write them on the *t* of your heart.

TABLETS (TABLET)

Ex 31: 18 he gave him the two *t*
Dt 10: 5 and put the *t* in the ark I had made,
2Co 3: 3 not on *t* of stone but on *t*

TAKE (TAKEN TAKES TAKING TOOK)

Ge 15: 7 land to *t* possession of it."
22: 17 Your descendants will *t* possession
Ex 3: 5 "*T* off your sandals,
21: 23 you are to *t* life for life, eye for eye,
22: 22 "Do not *t* advantage of a widow
Lev 10: 17 given to you to *t* away the guilt
25: 14 do not *t* advantage of each other.
Nu 13: 30 and *t* possession of the land,
Dt 1: 8 and *t* possession of the land that
12: 32 do not add to it or *t* away from it.
31: 26 "*T* this Book of the Law
1Sa 8: 11 He will *t* your sons and make them
1Ch 17: 13 I will never *t* my love away
Job 23: 10 But he knows the way that I *t*;
Ps 2: 12 Blessed are all who *t* refuge in him.
25: 18 and *t* away all my sins.
27: 14 be strong and *t* heart
31: 24 Be strong and *t* heart,
49: 17 for he will *t* nothing with him
51: 11 or *t* your Holy Spirit from me.
73: 24 afterwards you will *t* me into glory.
118: 8 It is better to *t* refuge in the LORD
Pr 22: 23 for the LORD will *t* up their case
Isa 62: 4 for the LORD will *t* delight in you,
Eze 3: 10 and *t* to heart all the words I speak
33: 11 I *t* no pleasure in the death
Mt 10: 38 anyone who does not *t* his cross
11: 29 *T* my yoke upon you and learn
16: 24 deny himself and *t* up his cross
26: 26 saying, "*T* and eat; this is my body
Mk 14: 36 *T* this cup from me.
1Ti 6: 12 *T* hold of the eternal life

TAKEN (TAKE)

Ge 2: 23 for she was *t* out of man."
Lev 6: 4 must return what he has stolen or *t*
Nu 8: 16 I have *t* them as my own in place
19: 3 it is to be *t* outside the camp
Ecc 3: 14 added to it and nothing *t* from it.
Isa 6: 7 your guilt is *t* away and your sin
Zec 3: 4 "See, I have *t* away your sin,
Mt 13: 12 even what he has will be *t* from him
24: 40 one will be *t* and the other left.
26: 39 may this cup be *t* from me.
Mk 16: 19 he was *t* up into heaven
Ac 1: 9 he was *t* up before their very eyes,
Ro 5: 13 But sin is not *t* into account
1Ti 3: 16 was *t* up in glory.

TAKES (TAKE)

1Ki 20: 11 should not boast like one who *t* it
Ps 5: 4 You are not a God who *t* pleasure
34: 8 blessed is the man who *t* refuge
Lk 6: 30 and if anyone *t* what belongs to you
Jn 1: 29 who *t* away the sin of the world!
10: 18 No-one *t* it from me, but I lay it
Rev 22: 19 And if anyone *t* words away

TAKING (TAKE)

Ac 15: 14 by *t* from the Gentiles a people
Php 2: 7 *t* the very nature of a servant,

TALENT

Mt 25: 15 to another one *t*, each according

TALES*

1Ti 4: 7 with godless myths and old wives' *t*

TALL

1Sa 17: 4 He was over nine feet *t*.
1Ch 11: 23 who was seven and a half feet *t*.

TAMAR

1. Wife of Judah's sons Er and Onan (Ge 38:1-10). Tricked Judah into fathering children when he refused her his third son (Ge 38:11-30).

2. Daughter of David, raped by Amnon (2Sa 13).

TAMBOURINE
Ps 150: 4 praise him with *t* and dancing,

TAME* (TAMED)
Jas 3: 8 but no man can *t* the tongue.

TAMED* (TAME)
Jas 3: 7 the sea are being *t* and have been *t*

TARSHISH
Jnh 1: 3 from the LORD and headed for *T*.

TARSUS
Ac 9: 11 ask for a man from *T* named Saul,

TASK (TASKS)
1Ch 29: 1 The *t* is great, because this palatial
Mk 13: 34 each with his assigned *t*,
Ac 20: 24 complete the *t* the Lord Jesus has
1Co 3: 5 the Lord has assigned to each his *t*.
2Co 2: 16 And who is equal to such a *t*?
1Ti 3: 1 an overseer, he desires a noble *t*.

TASKS (TASK)
Pr 31: 17 her arms are strong for her *t*.

TASTE (TASTED TASTY)
Ps 34: 8 *T* and see that the LORD is good;
119: 103 sweet are your words to my *t*,
Pr 24: 13 from the comb is sweet to your *t*.
SS 2: 3 and his fruit is sweet to my *t*.
Col 2: 21 Do not *t*! Do not touch!"?
Heb 2: 9 the grace of God he might *t* death

TASTED (TASTE)
Eze 3: 3 it *t* as sweet as honey in my mouth.
1Pe 2: 3 now that you have *t* that the Lord
Rev 10: 10 It *t* as sweet as honey in my mouth,

TASTY (TASTE)
Ge 27: 4 Prepare me the kind of *t* food I like

TATTOO*
Lev 19: 28 or put *t* marks on yourselves.

TAUGHT (TEACH)
1Ki 4: 33 He also *t* about animals and birds,
2Ki 17: 28 *t* them how to worship the LORD.
2Ch 17: 9 They *t* throughout Judah,
Ps 119: 102 for you yourself have *t* me.
Pr 4: 4 he *t* me and said,
31: 1 an oracle his mother *t* him:
Isa 29: 13 is made up only of rules *t* by men.
50: 4 ear to listen like one being *t*.
Mt 7: 29 he *t* as one who had authority,
15: 9 their teachings are but rules *t*
Lk 4: 15 He *t* in their synagogues,
Ac 20: 20 have *t* you publicly and from house
1Co 2: 13 but in words *t* by the Spirit,
Gal 1: 12 nor was I *t* it; rather, I received it
1Ti 1: 20 to Satan to be *t* not to blaspheme.
1Jn 2: 27 just as it has *t* you, remain in him.

TAX (TAXES)
Mt 11: 19 a friend of *t* collectors and "sinners
17: 24 of the two-drachma *t* came to Peter

TAXES (TAX)
Mt 22: 17 Is it right to pay *t* to Caesar or not
Ro 13: 7 If you owe *t*, pay *t*; if revenue,

TEACH (TAUGHT TEACHER TEACHERS TEACHES TEACHING TEACHINGS)
Ex 4: 12 and will *t* you what to say."
18: 20 *T* them the decrees and laws,
33: 13 *t* me your ways so I may know you
Lev 10: 11 and you must *t* the Israelites all
Dt 4: 9 *T* them to your children
6: 1 me to *t* you to observe
8: 3 to *t* you that man does not live
11: 19 *T* them to your children, talking
1Sa 12: 23 I will *t* you the way that is good
1Ki 8: 36 *T* them the right way to live,
Job 12: 7 ask the animals, and they will *t* you
Ps 32: 8 *t* you in the way you should go;
34: 11 I will *t* you the fear of the LORD.
51: 13 I will *t* transgressors your ways,
78: 5 forefathers to *t* their children,
90: 12 *T* us to number our days aright,
119: 33 *T* me, O LORD, to follow your
143: 10 *T* me to do your will,
Pr 9: 9 *t* a righteous man and he will add
Jer 31: 34 No longer will a man *t* his neighbour
Mic 4: 2 He will *t* us his ways,
Lk 11: 1 said to him, "Lord, *t* us to pray,
12: 12 for the Holy Spirit will *t* you
Jn 14: 26 will *t* you all things and will remind
Ro 2: 21 who *t* others, do you not *t* yourself?
15: 4 in the past was written to *t* us,
1Ti 2: 12 I do not permit a woman to *t*
3: 2 respectable, hospitable, able to *t*,
2Ti 2: 2 also be qualified to *t* others.
2: 24 kind to everyone, able to *t*,
Tit 2: 1 You must *t* what is in accord
2: 15 then, are the things you should *t*.
Heb 8: 11 No longer will a man *t* his neighbour
Jas 3: 1 know that we who *t* will be judged
1Jn 2: 27 you do not need anyone to *t* you.

TEACHER (TEACH)
Ecc 1: 1 The words of the *T*, son of David,
Mt 10: 24 "A student is not above his *t*,
13: 52 "Therefore every *t*
23: 10 Nor are you to be called '*t*',
Lk 6: 40 A student is not above his *t*,
Jn 3: 2 we know you are a *t* who has come
13: 14 and *T*, have washed your feet,

TEACHERS (TEACH)
Ps 119: 99 I have more insight than all my *t*,
Pr 5: 13 I would not obey my *t*
Lk 20: 46 "Beware of the *t* of the law.
1Co 12: 28 third *t*, then workers of miracles,
Eph 4: 11 and some to be pastors and *t*,
2Ti 4: 3 around them a great number of *t*
Heb 5: 12 by this time you ought to be *t*,
Jas 3: 1 of you should presume to be *t*,
2Pe 2: 1 as there will be false *t* among you.

TEACHES (TEACH)
Ps 25: 9 and *t* them his way.
94: 10 Does he who *t* man lack
Pr 15: 33 of the LORD *t* a man wisdom,
Isa 48: 17 who *t* you what is best for you,
Mt 5: 19 *t* these commands will be called
1Ti 6: 3 If anyone *t* false doctrines
Tit 2: 12 It *t* us to say "No" to ungodliness
1Jn 2: 27 his anointing *t* you about all things

TEACHING (TEACH)
Ezr 7: 10 to *t* its decrees and laws in Israel.
Pr 1: 8 and do not forsake your mother's *t*.
3: 1 My son, do not forget my *t*,
6: 23 this *t* is a light,
Mt 28: 20 *t* them to obey everything I have
Jn 7: 17 whether my *t* comes from God or
8: 31 to my *t*, you are really my disciples.
14: 23 loves me, he will obey my *t*.
Ac 2: 42 themselves to the apostles' *t*
Ro 12: 7 let him serve; if it is *t*, let him teach;
Eph 4: 14 and there by every wind of *t*
2Th 3: 6 to the *t* you received from us.
1Ti 4: 13 of Scripture, to preaching and to *t*.
5: 17 whose work is preaching and *t*.
6: 3 Lord Jesus Christ and to godly *t*,
2Ti 3: 16 is God-breathed and is useful for *t*,
Tit 1: 11 by *t* things they ought not
2: 7 In your *t* show integrity,
Heb 5: 13 with the *t* about righteousness.
2Jn : 9 and does not continue in the *t*

TEACHINGS (TEACH)
Pr 7: 2 guard my *t* as the apple of your eye.
2Th 2: 15 hold to the *t* we passed on to you,
Heb 6: 1 leave the elementary *t* about Christ

TEAR (TEARS)
Rev 7: 17 God will wipe away every *t*
21: 4 He will wipe every *t*

TEARS (TEAR)
Ps 126: 5 Those who sow in *t*
Isa 25: 8 LORD will wipe away the *t*
Jer 31: 16 and your eyes from *t*,
50: 4 in *t* to seek the LORD their God.
Lk 7: 38 she began to wet his feet with her *t*.
2Co 2: 4 anguish of heart and with many *t*,
Php 3: 18 and now say again even with *t*,

TEETH (TOOTH)
Job 19: 20 with only the skin of my *t*.
Ps 35: 16 they gnashed their *t* at me.
Jer 31: 29 and the children's *t* are set on edge
Mt 8: 12 will be weeping and gnashing of *t*."

TEMPER (EVEN-TEMPERED HOT-TEMPERED ILL-TEMPERED QUICK-TEMPERED)
Pr 16: 32 a man who controls his *t*

TEMPERANCE see SELF-CONTROL

TEMPERATE*
1Ti 3: 2 *t*, self-controlled, respectable,
3: 11 not malicious talkers but *t*
Tit 2: 2 Teach the older men to be *t*,

TEMPEST
Ps 50: 3 and around him a *t* rages.
55: 8 far from the *t* and storm."

TEMPLE (TEMPLES)
1Ki 6: 1 began to build the *t* of the LORD.
6: 38 the *t* was finished in all its details
8: 10 the cloud filled the *t* of the LORD.
8: 27 How much less this *t* I have built!
2Ch 36: 19 They set fire to God's *t*
36: 23 me to build a *t* for him at Jerusalem
Ezr 6: 14 finished building the *t* according
Ps 27: 4 and to seek him in his *t*.
Isa 6: 1 and the train of his robe filled the *t*.
Eze 10: 4 cloud filled the *t*, and the court was
43: 4 glory of the LORD entered the *t*
Hab 2: 20 But the LORD is in his holy *t*;
Mt 12: 6 that one greater than the *t* is here.
26: 61 'I am able to destroy the *t* of God
27: 51 of the *t* was torn in two from top
Lk 21: 5 about how the *t* was adorned
Jn 2: 14 In the *t* courts he found men selling
1Co 3: 16 that you yourselves are God's *t*
6: 19 you not know that your body is a *t*
2Co 6: 16 For we are the *t* of the living God.
Rev 21: 22 I did not see a *t* in the city,

TEMPLES (TEMPLE)
Ac 17: 24 does not live in *t* built by hands.

TEMPORARY
2Co 4: 18 what is seen is *t*, but what is unseen

TEMPT* (TEMPTATION TEMPTED TEMPTER TEMPTING)
1Co 7: 5 again so that Satan will not *t* you
Jas 1: 13 does he *t* anyone; but each one is

TEMPTATION* (TEMPT)
Mt 6: 13 And lead us not into *t*,
26: 41 pray so that you will not fall into *t*.
Mk 14: 38 pray so that you will not fall into *t*.
Lk 11: 4 And lead us not into *t*.'"
22: 40 "Pray that you will not fall into *t*."
22: 46 pray so that you will not fall into *t*
1Co 10: 13 No *t* has seized you except what is
1Ti 6: 9 want to get rich fall into *t*

TEMPTED* (TEMPT)
Mk 4: 1 into the desert to be *t* by the devil.
1: 13 was in the desert forty days, being *t*

Lk 4: 2 for forty days he was *t* by the devil.
1Co 10: 13 But when you are *t*, he will
10: 13 he will not let you be *t*
Gal 6: 1 yourself, or you also may be *t*.
1Th 3: 5 way the tempter might have *t* you
Heb 2: 18 able to help those who are being *t*.
2: 18 he himself suffered when he was *t*,
4: 15 but we have one who has been *t*
Jas 1: 13 For God cannot be *t* by evil,
1: 13 When *t*, no-one should say,
1: 14 each one is *t* when, by his own evil

TEMPTER* (TEMPT)
Mt 4: 3 The *t* came to him and said,
1Th 3: 5 some way the *t* might have

TEMPTING* (TEMPT)
Lk 4: 13 the devil had finished all this *t*,
Jas 1: 13 no-one should say, "God is *t* me."

TEN (TENTH TITHE TITHES)
Ex 34: 28 covenant—the *T* Commandments.
Lev 26: 8 of you will chase *t* thousand,
Dt 4: 13 covenant, the *T* Commandments,
10: 4 The *T* Commandments he had
Ps 91: 7 *t* thousand at your right hand,
Da 7: 24 *t* horns are *t* kings who will come
Mt 25: 1 will be like *t* virgins who took
25: 28 it to the one who has the *t* talents.
Lk 15: 8 suppose a woman has *t* silver coins
Rev 12: 3 and *t* horns and seven crowns

TENANTS
Mt 21: 34 servants to the *t* to collect his fruit.

TEND
Jer 23: 2 to the shepherds who *t* my people:
Eze 34: 14 I will *t* them in a good pasture,

TENDERNESS*
Isa 63: 15 Your *t* and compassion are
Php 2: 1 fellowship with the Spirit, if any *t*

TENT (TENTMAKER TENTS)
Ex 27: 21 In the *T* of Meeting,
40: 2 "Set up the tabernacle, the *T*
Isa 54: 2 "Enlarge the place of your *t*,
2Co 5: 1 that if the earthly *t* we live
2Pe 1: 13 as long as I live in the *t* of this body,

TENTH (TEN)
Ge 14: 20 Abram gave him a *t* of everything.
Nu 18: 26 you must present a *t* of that tithe
Dt 14: 22 Be sure to set aside a *t*
1Sa 8: 15 He will take a *t* of your grain
Lk 11: 42 you give God a *t* of your mint,
18: 12 I fast twice a week and give a *t*
Heb 7: 4 patriarch Abraham gave him a *t*

TENTMAKER* (TENT)
Ac 18: 3 and because he was a *t* as they were

TENTS (TENT)
Ge 13: 12 and pitched his *t* near Sodom.
Ps 84: 10 than dwell in the *t* of the wicked.

TERAH
Ge 11: 31 *T* took his son Abram, his

TERRIBLE (TERROR)
2Ti 3: 1 There will be *t* times

TERRIFIED (TERROR)
Dt 7: 21 Do not be *t* by them,
20: 3 do not be *t* or give way to panic
Ps 90: 7 and *t* by your indignation.
Mt 14: 26 walking on the lake, they were *t*.
17: 6 they fell face down to the ground, *t*.
27: 54 they were *t*, and exclaimed,
Mk 4: 41 They were *t* and asked each other,

TERRIFYING (TERROR)
Heb 12: 21 The sight was so *t* that Moses said,

TERRITORY
2Co 10: 16 done in another man's *t*.

TERROR (TERRIBLE TERRIFIED TERRIFYING)
Dt 2: 25 very day I will begin to put the *t*
28: 67 of the *t* that will fill your hearts
Job 9: 34 so that his *t* would frighten me no
Ps 91: 5 You will not fear the *t* of night,
Pr 21: 15 but *t* to evildoers.
Isa 13: 8 *T* will seize them,
24: 17 *T* and pit and snare await you,
51: 13 live in constant *t* every day
54: 14 *T* will be far removed;
Lk 21: 26 Men will faint from *t*, apprehensive
Ro 13: 3 For rulers hold no *t*

TEST (TESTED TESTING TESTS)
Dt 6: 16 Do not *t* the LORD your God
Jdg 3: 1 to *t* all those Israelites who had not
1Ki 10: 1 came to *t* him with hard questions.
1Ch 29: 17 that you *t* the heart and are pleased
Ps 26: 2 *T* me, O LORD, and try me,
78: 18 They wilfully put God to the *t*
106: 14 wasteland they put God to the *t*.
139: 23 *t* me and know my anxious
Jer 11: 20 and *t* the heart and mind,
Lk 4: 12 put the Lord your God to the *t*.'"
Ac 5: 9 How could you agree to *t* the Spirit
Ro 12: 2 Then you will be able to *t*
1Co 3: 13 and the fire will *t* the quality
10: 9 We should not *t* the Lord,
2Co 13: 5 unless, of course, you fail the *t*?
1Th 5: 21 *T* everything.
Jas 1: 12 because when he has stood the *t*,
1Jn 4: 1 *t* the spirits to see whether they are

TESTAMENT see COVENANT

TESTED (TEST)
Ge 22: 1 Some time later God *t* Abraham.
Job 23: 10 when he has *t* me, I will come forth
34: 36 that Job might be *t* to the utmost
Ps 66: 10 For you, O God, *t* us;
Pr 27: 21 man is *t* by the praise he receives.
Isa 28: 16 a *t* stone,
48: 10 I have *t* you in the furnace
1Ti 3: 10 They must first be *t*; and then
Heb 11: 17 By faith Abraham, when God *t* him

TESTIFIES (TESTIFY)
Jn 5: 32 There is another who *t* in my favour,
Ro 8: 16 The Spirit himself *t*

TESTIFY (TESTIFIES TESTIMONY)
Pr 24: 28 Do not *t* against your neighbour
Jn 1: 7 a witness to *t* concerning that light,
1: 34 and I *t* that this is the Son of God."
5: 39 are the Scriptures that *t* about me,
7: 7 because I *t* that what it does is evil.
15: 26 he will *t* about me; but you
Ac 4: 33 continued to *t* to the resurrection
10: 43 All the prophets *t* about him that
2Ti 1: 8 ashamed to *t* about our Lord,
1Jn 4: 14 *t* that the Father has sent his Son
5: 7 For there are three that *t*: the Spirit

TESTIMONY (TESTIFY)
Ex 20: 16 "You shall not give false *t*
31: 18 gave him the two tablets of the *T*,
Nu 35: 30 only on the *t* of witnesses.
Dt 19: 18 giving false *t* against his brother,
Pr 12: 17 A truthful witness gives honest *t*,
Isa 8: 20 and to the *t*! If they do not speak
Mt 15: 19 sexual immorality, theft, false *t*,
24: 14 preached in the whole world as a *t*
Lk 18: 20 not give false *t*, honour your father
Jn 2: 25 He did not need man's *t* about man
21: 24 We know that his *t* is true.
1Jn 5: 9 but God's *t* is greater because it is
Rev 12: 11 and by the word of their *t*;

TESTING (TEST)
Lk 8: 13 but in the time of *t* they fall away.
Heb 3: 8 during the time of *t* in the desert,
Jas 1: 3 because you know that the *t*

TESTS (TEST)
Pr 17: 3 but the LORD *t* the heart.
1Th 2: 4 but God, who *t* our hearts.

THADDAEUS
Apostle (Mt 10:3; Mk 3:18); probably also known as Judas son of James (Lk 6:16; Ac 1:13).

THANK (THANKFUL THANKFULNESS THANKS THANKSGIVING)
Php 1: 3 I *t* my God every time I remember
1Th 3: 9 How can we *t* God enough for you

THANKFUL (THANK)
Col 3: 15 And be *t*.
Heb 12: 28 let us be *t*, and so worship God

THANKFULNESS (THANK)
1Co 10: 30 If I take part in the meal with *t*,
Col 2: 7 taught, and overflowing with *t*.

THANKS (THANK)
1Ch 16: 8 Give *t* to the LORD, call
Ne 12: 31 assigned two large choirs to give *t*.
Ps 7: 17 I will give *t* to the LORD
28: 7 and I will give *t* to him in song.
30: 12 my God, I will give you *t* for ever.
35: 18 I will give you *t* in the great
75: 1 we give *t*, for your Name is near;
100: 4 give *t* to him and praise his name.
107: 1 Give *t* to the LORD, for he is good;
118: 28 are my God, and I will give you *t*;
136: 1 Give *t* to the LORD, for he is good.
Ro 1: 21 as God nor gave *t* to him,
1Co 11: 24 when he had given *t*, he broke it
15: 57 *t* be to God! He gives us the victory
2Co 2: 14 *t* be to God, who always leads us
9: 15 *T* be to God for his indescribable
1Th 5: 18 give *t* in all circumstances,
Rev 4: 9 and *t* to him who sits on the throne

THANKSGIVING (THANK)
Ps 95: 2 Let us come before him with *t*
100: 4 Enter his gates with *t*
1Co 10: 16 cup of *t* for which we give thanks
Php 4: 6 by prayer and petition, with *t*,
1Ti 4: 3 created to be received with *t*

THEFT (THIEF)
Mt 15: 19 sexual immorality, *t*, false

THEFTS* (THIEF)
Rev 9: 21 their sexual immorality or their *t*.

THEME*
Ps 45: 1 My heart is stirred by a noble *t*
119: 54 Your decrees are the *t* of my song

THIEF (THEFT THEFTS THIEVES)
Ex 22: 3 A *t* must certainly make restitution
Pr 6: 30 Men do not despise a *t* if he steals
Lk 12: 39 at what hour the *t* was coming,
1Th 5: 2 day of the Lord will come like a *t*
1Pe 4: 15 or *t* or any other kind of criminal,
Rev 16: 15 I come like a *t*! Blessed is he who

THIEVES (THIEF)
Mt 6: 19 and where *t* break in and steal.
Jn 10: 8 who ever came before me were *t*
1Co 6: 10 nor homosexual offenders nor *t*

THINK (THINKING THOUGHT THOUGHTS)
Ps 63: 6 I *t* of you through the watches
Isa 44: 19 No-one stops to *t*,
Mt 22: 42 "What do you *t* about the Christ?
Ro 12: 3 Do not *t* of yourself more highly
Php 4: 8 praiseworthy—*t* about such things

THINKING (THINK)
Pr 23: 7 who is always *t* about the cost.
1Co 14: 20 Brothers, stop *t* like children.
2Pe 3: 1 to stimulate you to wholesome *t*.

THIRST (THIRSTS THIRSTY)
Ps 69: 21 and gave me vinegar for my *t*.
Mt 5: 6 Blessed are those who hunger and *t*
Jn 4: 14 the water I give him will never *t*.
2Co 11: 27 I have known hunger and *t*
Rev 7: 16 never again will they *t*.

THIRSTS (THIRST)
Ps 42: 2 My soul *t* for God,

THIRSTY (THIRST)
Ps 107: 9 for he satisfies the *t*
Pr 25: 21 if he is *t*, give him water to drink.
Isa 55: 1 "Come, all you who are *t*,
Mt 25: 35 I was *t* and you gave me something
Jn 7: 37 "If anyone is *t*, let him come to me
Ro 12: 20 if he is *t*, give him something
Rev 21: 6 To him who is *t* I will give to drink
22: 17 Whoever is *t*, let him come;

THOMAS
Apostle (Mt 10:3; Mk 3:18; Lk 6:15; Jn 11:16; 14:5; 21:2; Ac 1:13). Doubted resurrection (Jn 20:24-28).

THONGS
Mk 1: 7 *t* of whose sandals I am not worthy

THORN (THORNBUSHES THORNS)
2Co 12: 7 there was given me a *t* in my flesh,

THORNBUSHES (THORN)
Lk 6: 44 People do not pick figs from *t*,

THORNS (THORN)
Ge 3: 18 It will produce *t* and thistles
Nu 33: 55 in your eyes and *t* in your sides.
Mt 13: 7 fell among *t*, which grew up
27: 29 and then twisted together a crown of *t*
Heb 6: 8 But land that produces *t*

THOUGHT (THINK)
Pr 14: 15 a prudent man gives *t* to his steps.
21: 29 an upright man gives *t* to his ways.
1Co 13: 11 I talked like a child, I *t* like a child,

THOUGHTS (THINK)
1Ch 28: 9 every motive behind the *t*.
Ps 94: 11 The LORD knows the *t* of man;
139: 23 test me and know my anxious *t*.
Isa 55: 8 "For my *t* are not your *t*,
Mt 15: 19 For out of the heart come evil *t*,
1Co 2: 11 among men knows the *t* of a man
Heb 4: 12 it judges the *t* and attitudes

THREE
Ge 6: 10 Noah had *t* sons: Shem, Ham
Ex 23: 14 "*T* times a year you are
Dt 19: 15 the testimony of two or *t* witnesses.
2Sa 23: 8 a Tahkemonite, was chief of the *T*;
Pr 30: 15 "There are *t* things that are never
30: 18 "There are *t* things that are too
30: 21 "Under *t* things the earth trembles,
30: 29 "There are *t* things that are stately
Ecc 4: 12 of *t* strands is not quickly broken.
Da 3: 24 "Wasn't it *t* men that we tied up
Am 1: 3 "For *t* sins of Damascus,
Jnh 1: 17 inside the fish *t* days and *t* nights.
Mt 12: 40 so the Son of Man will be *t* days
12: 40 *t* nights in the belly of a huge fish,
12: 40 *t* nights in the heart of the earth.
17: 4 I will put up *t* shelters—one
18: 20 or *t* come together in my name,
26: 34 you will disown me *t* times."
26: 75 you will disown me *t* times."
27: 63 'After *t* days I will rise again.'
Mk 8: 31 and after *t* days rise again.
9: 5 Let us put up *t* shelters—one
14: 30 yourself will disown me *t* times."
Jn 2: 19 and I will raise it again in *t* days."
1Co 13: 13 And now these *t* remain: faith,
14: 27 or at the most *t*—should speak,
2Co 13: 1 testimony of two or *t* witnesses."
1Jn 5: 7 For there are *t* that testify:

THRESHER* (THRESHING-FLOOR)
1Co 9: 10 ploughman ploughs and the *t* threshes,

THRESHING-FLOOR (THRESHER)
Ru 3: 6 So she went down to the *t*
2Sa 24: 18 an altar to the LORD on the *t*
Lk 3: 17 is in his hand to clear his *t*

THREW (THROW)
Da 6: 16 and *t* him into the lions' den.
Jnh 1: 15 took Jonah and *t* him overboard,

THRIVE
Pr 29: 2 When the righteous *t*, the people

THROAT (THROATS)
Ps 5: 9 Their *t* is an open grave;
Pr 23: 2 and put a knife to your *t*

THROATS (THROAT)
Ro 3: 13 "Their *t* are open graves;

THROB*
Isa 60: 5 your heart will *t* and swell with joy;

THRONE (ENTHRONED ENTHRONES THRONES)
2Sa 7: 16 your *t* will be established for ever
1Ch 17: 12 and I will establish his *t* for ever.
Ps 11: 4 the LORD is on his heavenly *t*.
45: 6 Your *t*, O God, will last for ever
47: 8 God is seated on his holy *t*.
89: 14 justice are the foundation of your *t*;
Isa 6: 1 I saw the Lord seated on a *t*,
66: 1 "Heaven is my *t*
Eze 28: 2 I sit on the *t* of a god
Da 7: 9 His *t* was flaming with fire,
Mt 19: 28 Son of Man sits on his glorious *t*,
Ac 7: 49 prophet says: "'Heaven is my *t*,
Heb 1: 8 "Your *t*, O God, will last for ever
4: 16 Let us then approach the *t* of grace
12: 2 at the right hand of the *t* of God.
Rev 3: 21 sat down with my Father on his *t*.
3: 21 the right to sit with me on my *t*,
4: 2 there before me was a *t* in heaven
4: 10 They lay their crowns before the *t*
20: 11 Then I saw a great white *t*
22: 3 *t* of God and of the Lamb will be

THRONES (THRONE)
Mt 19: 28 me will also sit on twelve *t*,
Rev 4: 4 throne were twenty-four other *t*,

THROW (THREW)
Jn 8: 7 the first to *t* a stone at her."
Heb 10: 35 So do not *t* away your confidence;
12: 1 Let us *t* off everything that hinders

THUNDER (THUNDERS)
Ps 93: 4 Mightier than the *t*
Mk 3: 17 which means Sons of *T*); Andrew,

THUNDERS (THUNDER)
Job 37: 5 God's voice *t* in marvellous ways;
Ps 29: 3 the God of glory *t*,
Rev 10: 3 the voices of the seven *t* spoke.

THWART* (THWARTED)
Isa 14: 27 has purposed, and who can *t* him?

THWARTED (THWART)
Job 42: 2 no plan of yours can be *t*.

THYATIRA
Rev 2: 18 the angel of the church in *T* write:

TIBNI
King of Israel (1Ki 16:21-22).

TIDINGS
Isa 40: 9 You who bring good *t* to Jerusalem
52: 7 who bring good *t*,

TIES
Hos 11: 4 with *t* of love;
Mt 12: 29 unless he first *t* up the strong man?

TIGHT*
Jas 1: 26 and yet does not keep a *t* rein

TIGHT-FISTED*
Dt 15: 7 or *t* towards your poor brother.

TIME (TIMES)
Est 4: 14 come to royal position for such a *t*
Ecc 3: 1 There is a *t* for everything,
8: 5 wise heart will know the proper *t*
Da 7: 25 to him for a *t*, times and half a *t*.
12: 7 "It will be for a *t*, times and half a *t*.
Hos 10: 12 for it is *t* to seek the LORD,
Jn 2: 4 Jesus replied, "My *t* has not yet
17: 1 prayed: "Father, the *t* has come.
Ro 9: 9 "At the appointed *t* I will return,
13: 11 understanding the present *t*.
1Co 7: 29 brothers, is that the *t* is short.
2Co 6: 2 now is the *t* of God's favour,
2Ti 1: 9 Jesus before the beginning of *t*,
Tit 1: 2 promised before the beginning of *t*,
Heb 9: 28 and he will appear a second *t*,
10: 12 for all *t* one sacrifice for sins,
1Pe 4: 17 For it is *t* for judgment to begin

TIMES (TIME)
Ps 9: 9 a stronghold in *t* of trouble.
31: 15 My *t* are in your hands;
62: 8 Trust in him at all *t*, O people;
Pr 17: 17 A friend loves at all *t*,
Isa 46: 10 from ancient *t*, what is still to come
Am 5: 13 for the *t* are evil.
Mt 16: 3 cannot interpret the signs of the *t*.
18: 21 how many *t* shall I forgive my
Ac 1: 7 "It is not for you to know the *t*
Rev 12: 14 *t* and half a time, out

TIMID (TIMIDITY)
1Th 5: 14 encourage the *t*, help the weak,

TIMIDITY* (TIMID)
2Ti 1: 7 For God did not give us a spirit of *t*

TIMOTHY
Believer from Lystra (Ac 16:1). Joined Paul on second missionary journey (Ac 16-20). Sent to settle problems at Corinth (1Co 4:17; 16:10). Led church at Ephesus (1Ti 1:3). Co-writer with Paul (1Th 1:1; 2Th 1:1; Phm 1).

TIP
Job 33: 2 my words are on the *t* of my tongue

TIRE (TIRED)
2Th 3: 13 never *t* of doing what is right.

TIRED (TIRE)
Ex 17: 12 When Moses' hands grew *t*,
Isa 40: 28 He will not grow *t* or weary,

TITHE (TEN)
Lev 27: 30 "'A *t* of everything from the land,
Dt 12: 17 eat in your own towns the *t*
Mal 3: 10 the whole *t* into the storehouse,

TITHES (TEN)
Nu 18: 21 give to the Levites all the *t* in Israel
Mal 3: 8 'How do we rob you?' "In *t*

TITUS*

Gentile co-worker of Paul (Gal 2:1-3; 2Ti 4:10); sent to Corinth (2Co 2:13; 7-8; 12:18), Crete (Tit 1:4-5).

TODAY

Ps 2: 7 *t* I have become your Father.
95: 7 *T*, if you hear his voice,
Mt 6: 11 Give us *t* our daily bread.
Lk 2: 11 *T* in the town of David a Saviour has
23: 43 *t* you will be with me in paradise."
Ac 13: 33 *t* I have become your Father.'
Heb 1: 5 *t* I have become your Father"?
3: 7 "*T*, if you hear his voice,
3: 13 daily, as long as it is called *T*,
5: 5 *t* I have become your Father."
13: 8 Christ is the same yesterday and *t*

TOIL (TOILED TOILING)

Ge 3: 17 through painful *t* you will eat of it

TOILED (TOIL)

2Co 11: 27 and *t* and have often gone

TOILING (TOIL)

2Th 3: 8 *t* so that we would not be a burden

TOLERANCE* (TOLERATE)

Ro 2: 4 for the riches of his kindness, *t*,

TOLERATE (TOLERANCE)

Hab 1: 13 you cannot *t* wrong.
Rev 2: 2 that you cannot *t* wicked men,

TOMB

Mt 27: 65 make the *t* as secure as you know
Lk 24: 2 the stone rolled away from the *t*,

TOMORROW

Pr 27: 1 Do not boast about *t*,
Isa 22: 13 "for *t* we die!"
Mt 6: 34 Therefore do not worry about *t*,
1Co 15: 32 for *t* we die."
Jas 4: 13 "Today or *t* we will go to this

TONGUE (TONGUES)

Ex 4: 10 I am slow of speech and *t*."
Job 33: 2 my words are on the tip of my *t*.
Ps 5: 9 with their *t* they speak deceit.
34: 13 keep your *t* from evil
37: 30 and his *t* speaks what is just.
39: 1 and keep my *t* from sin;
51: 14 my *t* will sing of your righteousness
52: 4 O you deceitful *t*!
71: 24 My *t* will tell of your righteous acts
119: 172 May my *t* sing of your word,
137: 6 May my *t* cling to the roof
139: 4 Before a word is on my *t*
Pr 6: 17 a lying *t*,
10: 19 but he who holds his *t* is wise.
12: 18 but the *t* of the wise brings healing.
15: 4 The *t* that brings healing is a tree
17: 20 he whose *t* is deceitful falls
21: 23 He who guards his mouth and his *t*
25: 15 and a gentle *t* can break a bone.
26: 28 A lying *t* hates those it hurts,
28: 23 than he who has a flattering *t*.
31: 26 and faithful instruction is on her *t*.
SS 4: 11 milk and honey are under your *t*.
Isa 32: 4 and the stammering *t* will be fluent
45: 23 by me every *t* will swear.
50: 4 has given me an instructed *t*,
59: 3 and your *t* mutters wicked things.
Lk 16: 24 of his finger in water and cool my *t*,
Ro 14: 11 every *t* will confess to God.'"
1Co 14: 2 speaks in a *t* does not speak to men
14: 4 He who speaks in a *t* edifies himself
14: 9 intelligible words with your *t*,
14: 13 in a *t* should pray that he may
14: 19 than ten thousand words in a *t*.
14: 26 revelation, a *t* or an interpretation.
14: 27 If anyone speaks in a *t*, two—
Php 2: 11 every *t* confess that Jesus Christ is
Jas 1: 26 does not keep a tight rein on his *t*,
3: 5 Likewise the *t* is a small part
3: 8 but no man can tame the *t*.
1Jn 3: 18 or *t* but with actions and in truth.

TONGUES (TONGUE)

Ps 12: 4 "We will triumph with our *t*;
126: 2 our *t* with songs of joy.
Isa 28: 11 with foreign lips and strange *t*
66: 18 and gather all nations and *t*,
Jer 23: 31 the prophets who wag their own *t*
Mk 16: 17 in new *t*; they will pick up snakes
Ac 2: 3 to be *t* of fire that separated
2: 4 and began to speak in other *t*
10: 46 For they heard them speaking in *t*
19: 6 and they spoke in *t* and prophesied
Ro 3: 13 their *t* practise deceit."
1Co 12: 10 still another the interpretation of *t*.
12: 28 speaking in different kinds of *t*.
12: 30 Do all speak in *t*? Do all interpret?
13: 1 If I speak in the *t* of men
13: 8 where there are *t*, they will be
14: 5 greater than one who speaks in *t*,
14: 18 speak in *t* more than all of you.
14: 21 "Through men of strange *t*
14: 39 and do not forbid speaking in *t*.

TOOK (TAKE)

Isa 53: 4 Surely he *t* up our infirmities
Mt 8: 17 "He *t* up our infirmities
26: 26 they were eating, Jesus *t* bread,
26: 27 Then he *t* the cup, gave thanks
1Co 11: 23 the night he was betrayed, *t* bread,
11: 25 after supper he *t* the cup, saying,
Php 3: 12 for which Christ Jesus *t* hold of me.

TOOTH (TEETH)

Ex 21: 24 eye for eye, *t* for *t*, hand for hand,
Mt 5: 38 "Eye for eye, and *t* for *t*."

TOP

Dt 28: 13 you will always be at the *t*,
Isa 1: 6 of your foot to the *t* of your head
Mt 27: 51 torn in two from *t* to bottom.

TORMENT (TORMENTED TORMENTORS)

Lk 16: 28 also come to this place of *t*.'
2Co 12: 7 a messenger of Satan, to *t* me.

TORMENTED (TORMENT)

Rev 20: 10 They will be *t* day and night

TORMENTORS (TORMENT)

Ps 137: 3 our *t* demanded songs of joy;

TORN

Gal 4: 15 you would have *t* out your eyes
Php 1: 23 I do not know! I am *t*

TORTURED*

Heb 11: 35 Others were *t* and refused

TOSSED (TOSSING)

Eph 4: 14 *t* back and forth by the waves,
Jas 1: 6 of the sea, blown and *t* by the wind.

TOSSING (TOSSED)

Isa 57: 20 But the wicked are like the *t* sea,

TOUCH (TOUCHED TOUCHES)

Ge 3: 3 you must not *t* it, or you will die.'"
Ex 19: 12 go up the mountain or *t* the foot
Ps 105: 15 "Do not *t* my anointed ones;
Mt 9: 21 If I only *t* his cloak, I will be healed
Lk 18: 15 babies to Jesus to have him *t* them.
24: 39 It is I myself! *T* me and see;
2Co 6: 17 *T* no unclean thing,
Col 2: 21 Do not taste! Do not *t*!"?

TOUCHED (TOUCH)

1Sa 10: 26 men whose hearts God had *t*.
Isa 6: 7 With it he *t* my mouth and said,
Mt 14: 36 and all who *t* him were healed.
Lk 8: 45 "Who *t* me?" Jesus asked.
1Jn 1: 1 looked at and our hands have *t*—

TOUCHES (TOUCH)

Ex 19: 12 Whoever *t* the mountain shall
Zec 2: 8 for whoever *t* you *t* the apple

TOWER

Ge 11: 4 with a *t* that reaches to the heavens
Pr 18: 10 of the LORD is a strong *t*;

TOWN (TOWNS)

Mt 2: 23 and lived in a *t* called Nazareth.
Lk 4: 24 prophet is accepted in his home *t*.

TOWNS (TOWN)

Nu 35: 2 to give the Levites *t* to live
35: 15 These six *t* will be a place of refuge
Jer 11: 13 as many gods as you have *t*,
Mt 9: 35 Jesus went through all the *t*

TRACING*

Ro 11: 33 and his paths beyond *t* out!

TRACK

Job 14: 16 but not keep *t* of my sin.

TRADERS (TRADING)

1Ti 1: 10 for slave *t* and liars and perjurers—

TRADING (TRADERS)

1Ki 10: 22 The king had a fleet of *t* ships at sea
Pr 31: 18 She sees that her *t* is profitable,

TRADITION (TRADITIONS)

Mt 15: 2 "Why do your disciples break the *t*
15: 6 word of God for the sake of your *t*.
Mk 7: 13 by your *t* that you have handed
Col 2: 8 which depends on human *t*

TRADITIONS (TRADITION)

Mk 7: 8 are holding on to the *t* of men."
Gal 1: 14 zealous for the *t* of my fathers.

TRAIL

1Ti 5: 24 the sins of others *t* behind them.

TRAIN [1]*

Ps 68: 18 you led captives in your *t*;
Isa 6: 1 the *t* of his robe filled the temple.
Eph 4: 8 he led captives in his *t*.

TRAIN [2]* (TRAINED TRAINING)

Pr 22: 6 *T* a child in the way he should go,
Isa 2: 4 nor will they *t* for war any more.
Mic 4: 3 nor will they *t* for war any more.
1Ti 4: 7 rather, *t* yourself to be godly.
Tit 2: 4 they can *t* the younger women

TRAINED (TRAIN [2])

Lk 6: 40 everyone who is fully *t* will be like
Ac 22: 3 Under Gamaliel I was thoroughly *t*
2Co 11: 6 I may not be a *t* speaker,
Heb 5: 14 by constant use have *t* themselves
12: 11 for those who have been *t* by it.

TRAINING* (TRAIN [2])

1Co 9: 25 in the games goes into strict *t*.
Eph 6: 4 up in the *t* and instruction
1Ti 4: 8 For physical *t* is of some value,
2Ti 3: 16 correcting and *t* in righteousness,

TRAITOR (TRAITORS)

Lk 6: 16 and Judas Iscariot, who became a *t*.
Jn 18: 5 Judas the *t* was standing there

TRAITORS (TRAITOR)

Ps 59: 5 show no mercy to wicked *t*.

TRAMPLE (TRAMPLED)

Joel 3: 13 Come, *t* the grapes,
Am 2: 7 They *t* on the heads of the poor
5: 11 You *t* on the poor

Am 8: 4 Hear this, you who *t* the needy
Mt 7: 6 they may *t* them under their feet,
Lk 10: 19 I have given you authority to *t*

TRAMPLED (TRAMPLE)

Isa 63: 6 I *t* the nations in my anger;
Lk 21: 24 Jerusalem will be *t*
Heb 10: 29 to be punished who has *t* the Son
Rev 14: 20 They were *t* in the winepress

TRANCE*

Ac 10: 10 was being prepared, he fell into a *t*.
11: 5 and in a *t* I saw a vision.
22: 17 into a *t* and saw the Lord speaking.

TRANQUILLITY*

Ecc 4: 6 Better one handful with *t*

TRANSACTIONS*

Ru 4: 7 method of legalising *t* in Israel.)

TRANSCENDS*

Php 4: 7 which *t* all understanding,

TRANSFIGURED*

Mt 17: 2 There he was *t* before them.
Mk 9: 2 There he was *t* before them.

TRANSFORM* (TRANSFORMED)

Php 3: 21 will *t* our lowly bodies

TRANSFORMED (TRANSFORM)

Ro 12: 2 be *t* by the renewing of your mind.
2Co 3: 18 are being *t* into his likeness

TRANSGRESSED* (TRANSGRESSION)

Da 9: 11 All Israel has *t* your law

TRANSGRESSION* (TRANSGRESSED TRANSGRESSIONS TRANSGRESSORS)

Ps 19: 13 innocent of great *t*.
Isa 53: 8 for the *t* of my people he was
Da 9: 24 and your holy city to finish *t*,
Mic 1: 5 All this is because of Jacob's *t*,
1: 5 What is Jacob's *t*?
3: 8 to declare to Jacob his *t*,
6: 7 Shall I offer my firstborn for my *t*.
7: 18 who pardons sin and forgives the *t*
Ro 4: 15 where there is no law there is no *t*.
11: 11 Rather, because of their *t*,
11: 12 if their *t* means riches for the world

TRANSGRESSIONS* (TRANSGRESSION)

Ps 32: 1 whose *t* are forgiven,
32: 5 my *t* to the LORD"—
39: 8 Save me from all my *t*;
51: 1 blot out my *t*.
51: 3 For I know my *t*,
65: 3 you forgave our *t*.
103: 12 so far has he removed our *t* from us
Isa 43: 25 your *t*, for my own sake,
50: 1 of your *t* your mother was sent
53: 5 But he was pierced for our *t*,
Mic 1: 13 for the *t* of Israel
Ro 4: 7 whose *t* are forgiven,
Gal 3: 19 because of *t* until the Seed to whom
Eph 2: 1 you were dead in your *t* and sins,
2: 5 even when we were dead in *t*—

TRANSGRESSORS* (TRANSGRESSION)

Ps 51: 13 Then I will teach *t* your ways,
Isa 53: 12 and made intercession for the *t*.
53: 12 and was numbered with the *t*.
Lk 22: 37 'And he was numbered with the *t*';

TRAP (TRAPPED TRAPS)

Ps 69: 22 may it become retribution and a *t*.
Pr 20: 25 a *t* for a man to dedicate something
28: 10 will fall into his own *t*,
Isa 8: 14 a *t* and a snare.
Mt 22: 15 and laid plans to *t* him in his words.
Lk 21: 34 close on you unexpectedly like a *t*.
Ro 11: 9 their table become a snare and a *t*.
1Ti 3: 7 into disgrace and into the devil's *t*.
6: 9 and a *t* and into many foolish
2Ti 2: 26 and escape from the *t* of the devil,

TRAPPED (TRAP)

Pr 6: 2 if you have been *t* by what you said
12: 13 An evil man is *t* by his sinful talk,

TRAPS (TRAP)

Jos 23: 13 they will become snares and *t*
La 4: 20 was caught in their *t*.

TRAVEL (TRAVELLER)

Pr 4: 15 Avoid it, do not *t* on it;
Mt 23: 15 You *t* over land and sea

TRAVELLER (TRAVEL)

Job 31: 32 door was always open to the *t*—
Jer 14: 8 like a *t* who stays only a night?

TREACHEROUS (TREACHERY)

Ps 25: 3 who are *t* without excuse.
2Ti 3: 4 not lovers of the good, *t*, rash,

TREACHERY (TREACHEROUS)

Isa 59: 13 rebellion and *t* against the LORD,

TREAD (TREADING TREADS)

Ps 91: 13 You will *t* upon the lion

TREADING (TREAD)

Dt 25: 4 an ox while it is *t* out the grain.
1Co 9: 9 an ox while it is *t* out the grain."
1Ti 5: 18 the ox while it is *t* out the grain,"

TREADS (TREAD)

Rev 19: 15 He *t* the winepress of the fury

TREASURE (TREASURED TREASURES TREASURY)

Pr 2: 4 and search for it as for hidden *t*,
Isa 33: 6 of the LORD is the key to this *t*.
Mt 6: 21 For where your *t* is, there your
13: 44 of heaven is like *t* hidden in a field.
Lk 12: 33 a *t* in heaven that will not be
2Co 4: 7 But we have this *t* in jars of clay
1Ti 6: 19 In this way they will lay up *t*

TREASURED (TREASURE)

Ex 19: 5 you will be my *t* possession.
Dt 7: 6 to be his people, his *t* possession.
26: 18 his *t* possession as he promised,
Job 23: 12 I have *t* the words
Mal 3: 17 when I make up my *t* possession.
Lk 2: 19 But Mary *t* up all these things
2: 51 But his mother *t* all these things

TREASURES (TREASURE)

1Ch 29: 3 my God I now give my personal *t*
Pr 10: 2 Ill-gotten *t* are of no value,
Mt 6: 19 up for yourselves *t* on earth,
13: 52 out of his storeroom new *t*
Col 2: 3 in whom are hidden all the *t*
Heb 11: 26 of greater value than the *t* of Egypt,

TREASURY (TREASURE)

Mk 12: 43 more into the *t* than all the others.

TREAT (TREATED TREATING TREATMENT)

Lev 22: 2 sons to *t* with respect the sacred
Ps 103: 10 he does not *t* us as our sins deserve
Mt 18: 17 *t* him as you would a pagan
18: 35 my heavenly Father will *t* each
Eph 6: 9 *t* your slaves in the same way.
1Th 5: 20 do not *t* prophecies with contempt.
1Ti 5: 1 *T* younger men as brothers,
1Pe 3: 7 and *t* them with respect

TREATED (TREAT)

Lev 19: 34 The alien living with you must be *t*
25: 40 He is to be *t* as a hired worker
1Sa 24: 17 "You have *t* me well, but I have
Heb 10: 29 who has *t* as an unholy thing

TREATING (TREAT)

Ge 18: 25 *t* the righteous and the wicked
Heb 12: 7 as discipline; God is *t* you as sons.

TREATMENT (TREAT)

Col 2: 23 and their harsh *t* of the body,

TREATY

Ex 34: 12 not to make a *t* with those who live
Dt 7: 2 Make no *t* with them, and show

TREE (FIG-TREE TREES)

Ge 2: 9 and the *t* of the knowledge of good
2: 9 of the garden were the *t* of life
Dt 21: 23 hung on a *t* is under God's curse.
2Sa 18: 9 Absalom's head got caught in the *t*.
1Ki 14: 23 and under every spreading *t*.
Ps 1: 3 He is like a *t* planted by streams
52: 8 But I am like an olive *t*
92: 12 righteous will flourish like a palm *t*,
Pr 3: 18 She is a *t* of life to those who
11: 30 of the righteous is a *t* of life,
Isa 65: 22 For as the days of a *t*,
Jer 17: 8 He will be like a *t* planted
Eze 17: 24 I the LORD bring down the tall *t*
Da 4: 10 before me stood a *t* in the middle
Mt 3: 10 every *t* that does not produce good
12: 33 for a *t* is recognised by its fruit.
Lk 19: 4 climbed a sycamore-fig *t* to see him
Ac 5: 30 killed by hanging him on a *t*.
Ro 11: 24 be grafted into their own olive *t*!
Gal 3: 13 is everyone who is hung on a *t*."
1Pe 2: 24 sins in his body on the *t*,
Rev 2: 7 the right to eat from the *t* of life,
22: 2 side of the river stood the *t* of life,
22: 14 they may have the right to the *t*
22: 19 from him his share in the *t* of life

TREES (TREE)

Jdg 9: 8 One day the *t* went out
Ps 96: 12 Then all the *t* of the forest will sing
Isa 55: 12 and all the *t* of the field
Mt 3: 10 The axe is already at the root of the *t*
Mk 8: 24 they look like *t* walking around."
Jude : 12 autumn *t*, without fruit

TREMBLE (TREMBLED TREMBLES TREMBLING)

Ex 15: 14 The nations will hear and *t*;
1Ch 16: 30 *T* before him, all the earth!
Ps 114: 7 *T*, O earth, at the presence
Jer 5: 22 "Should you not *t* in my presence?
Eze 38: 20 of the earth will *t* at my presence.
Joel 2: 1 Let all who live in the land *t*,
Hab 3: 6 he looked, and made the nations *t*.

TREMBLED (TREMBLE)

Ex 19: 16 Everyone in the camp *t*.
20: 18 in smoke, they *t* with fear.
2Sa 22: 8 "The earth *t* and quaked,
Ac 7: 32 Moses *t* with fear and did not dare

TREMBLES (TREMBLE)

Ps 97: 4 the earth sees and *t*.
104: 32 He looks at the earth, and it *t*;
Isa 66: 2 and *t* at my word.
Jer 10: 10 When he is angry, the earth *t*;
Na 1: 5 The earth *t* at his presence,

TREMBLING (TREMBLE)

Ps 2: 11 and rejoice with *t*.
Da 10: 10 set me *t* on my hands and knees.
Php 2: 12 out your salvation with fear and *t*,
Heb 12: 21 terrifying that Moses said, "I am *t*

TRESPASS* (TRESPASSES)

Ro 5: 15 But the gift is not like the *t*.
5: 15 died by the *t* of the one man,
5: 17 For if, by the *t* of the one man,
5: 18 result of one *t* was condemnation

Ro 5: 20 added so that the *t* might increase.

TRESPASSES* (TRESPASS)

Ro 5: 16 but the gift followed many *t*

TRIAL (TRIALS)

Ps 37: 33 condemned when brought to *t*.
Mk 13: 11 you are arrested and brought to *t*,
2Co 8: 2 most severe *t*, their overflowing
Jas 1: 12 is the man who perseveres under *t*,
1Pe 4: 12 at the painful *t* you are suffering,
Rev 3: 10 you from the hour of *t* that is going

TRIALS* (TRIAL)

Dt 7: 19 saw with your own eyes the great *t*,
29: 3 own eyes you saw those great *t*,
Lk 22: 28 who have stood by me in my *t*.
1Th 3: 3 one would be unsettled by these *t*.
2Th 1: 4 the persecutions and *t* you are
Jas 1: 2 whenever you face *t* of many kinds,
1Pe 1: 6 had to suffer grief in all kinds of *t*.
2Pe 2: 9 how to rescue godly men from *t*

TRIBE (HALF-TRIBE TRIBES)

Heb 7: 13 no-one from that *t* has ever served
Rev 5: 5 See, the Lion of the *t* of Judah,
5: 9 God from every *t* and language
11: 9 men from every people, *t*,
14: 6 to every nation, *t*, language

TRIBES (TRIBE)

Ge 49: 28 All these are the twelve *t* of Israel,
Mt 19: 28 judging the twelve *t* of Israel.

TRIBULATION*

Rev 7: 14 who have come out of the great *t*;

TRICKERY*

Ac 13: 10 full of all kinds of deceit and *t*.
2Co 12: 16 fellow that I am, I caught you by *t*!

TRIED (TRY)

Ps 73: 16 When I *t* to understand all this,
95: 9 where your fathers tested and *t* me,
Heb 3: 9 where your fathers tested and *t* me

TRIES (TRY)

Lk 17: 33 Whoever *t* to keep his life will lose

TRIMMED

Mt 25: 7 virgins woke up and *t* their lamps.

TRIUMPH (TRIUMPHAL TRIUMPHED TRIUMPHING TRIUMPHS)

Ps 25: 2 nor let my enemies *t* over me.
54: 7 my eyes have looked in *t*
112: 8 in the end he will look in *t*
118: 7 I will look in *t* on my enemies.
Pr 28: 12 When the righteous *t*, there is great
Isa 42: 13 and will *t* over his enemies.

TRIUMPHAL* (TRIUMPH)

Isa 60: 11 their kings led in *t* procession.
2Co 2: 14 us in *t* procession in Christ

TRIUMPHED (TRIUMPH)

Rev 5: 5 of Judah, the Root of David, has *t*.

TRIUMPHING* (TRIUMPH)

Col 2: 15 of them, *t* over them by the cross.

TRIUMPHS* (TRIUMPH)

Jas 2: 13 Mercy *t* over judgment! What

TROUBLE (TROUBLED TROUBLES)

Ge 41: 51 God has made me forget all my *t*
Jos 7: 25 Why have you brought this *t* on us?
Job 2: 10 good from God, and not *t*?"
5: 7 Yet man is born to *t*
14: 1 is of few days and full of *t*.
42: 11 him over all the *t* the LORD had
Ps 7: 14 conceives *t* gives birth
7: 16 The *t* he causes recoils on himself;
9: 9 a stronghold in times of *t*.
10: 14 But you, O God, do see *t* and grief;
22: 11 for *t* is near
27: 5 For in the day of *t*
32: 7 you will protect me from *t*
37: 39 he is their stronghold in time of *t*.
41: 1 LORD delivers him in times of *t*.
46: 1 an ever-present help in *t*.
50: 15 and call upon me in the day of *t*;
59: 16 my refuge in times of *t*.
66: 14 spoke when I was in *t*.
86: 7 In the day of my *t* I will call to you,
91: 15 I will be with him in *t*,
107: 6 to the LORD in their *t*,
107: 13 they cried to the LORD in their *t*,
116: 3 I was overcome by *t* and sorrow.
119: 143 *T* and distress have come upon me,
138: 7 Though I walk in the midst of *t*,
143: 11 righteousness, bring me out of *t*.
Pr 11: 8 righteous man is rescued from *t*,
11: 17 a cruel man brings *t* on himself.
11: 29 He who brings *t* on his family will
12: 13 but a righteous man escapes *t*.
12: 21 but the wicked have their fill of *t*.
15: 27 A greedy man brings *t* to his family
19: 23 one rests content, untouched by *t*.
22: 8 He who sows wickedness reaps *t*,
24: 10 If you falter in times of *t*,
25: 19 on the unfaithful in times of *t*.
28: 14 he who hardens his heart falls into *t*
Jer 30: 7 It will be a time of *t* for Jacob,
Na 1: 7 a refuge in times of *t*.
Zep 1: 15 a day of *t* and ruin,
Mt 6: 34 Each day has enough *t* of its own.
13: 21 When *t* or persecution comes
Jn 16: 33 In this world you will have *t*.
Ro 8: 35 Shall *t* or hardship or persecution
2Co 1: 4 those in any *t* with the comfort we
2Th 1: 6 *t* to those who *t* you
Jas 5: 13 one of you in *t*? He should pray.

TROUBLED (TROUBLE)

Ps 38: 18 I am *t* by my sin.
Isa 38: 14 I am *t*; O Lord, come to my aid!"
Mk 14: 33 began to be deeply distressed and *t*.
Jn 14: 1 "Do not let your hearts be *t*.
14: 27 Do not let your hearts be *t*
2Th 1: 7 and give relief to you who are *t*,

TROUBLES (TROUBLE)

Ps 34: 6 he saved him out of all his *t*.
34: 17 he delivers them from all their *t*.
34: 19 A righteous man may have many *t*,
40: 12 For *t* without number surround me
54: 7 he has delivered me from all my *t*,
1Co 7: 28 those who marry will face many *t*
2Co 1: 4 who comforts us in all our *t*,
4: 17 and momentary *t* are achieving
6: 4 in *t*, hardships and distresses;
7: 4 in all our *t* my joy knows no bounds
Php 4: 14 good of you to share in my *t*.

TRUE (TRUTH)

Nu 11: 23 not what I say will come *t* for you."
12: 7 this is not *t* of my servant Moses;
Dt 18: 22 does not take place or come *t*,
Jos 23: 15 of the LORD your God has come *t*
1Sa 9: 6 and everything he says comes *t*.
1Ki 10: 6 and your wisdom is *t*.
2Ch 6: 17 your servant David come *t*.
15: 3 was without the *t* God,
Ps 33: 4 of the LORD is right and *t*;
119: 142 and your law is *t*.
119: 151 and all your commands are *t*.
119: 160 All your words are *t*;
Pr 8: 7 My mouth speaks what is *t*,
22: 21 teaching you *t* and reliable words,
Jer 10: 10 But the LORD is the *t* God;
28: 9 only if his prediction comes *t*."
Eze 33: 33 "When all this comes *t*—
Lk 16: 11 who will trust you with *t* riches?
Jn 1: 9 The *t* light that gives light
4: 23 when the *t* worshippers will worship
6: 32 Father who gives you the *t* bread
7: 28 on my own, but he who sent me is *t*
15: 1 "I am the *t* vine and my Father is
17: 3 the only *t* God, and Jesus Christ,
19: 35 testimony, and his testimony is *t*.
21: 24 We know that his testimony is *t*.
Ac 10: 34 "I now realise how *t* it is that God
11: 23 all to remain *t* to the Lord
14: 22 them to remain *t* to the faith.
17: 11 day to see if what Paul said was *t*.
Ro 3: 4 Let God be *t*, and every man a liar.
Php 4: 8 whatever is *t*, whatever is noble,
1Jn 2: 8 and the *t* light is already shining.
5: 20 He is the *t* God and eternal life.
Rev 19: 9 "These are the *t* words of God."
22: 6 These words are trustworthy and *t*.

TRUMPET (TRUMPETS)

Isa 27: 13 And in that day a great *t* will sound
Eze 33: 5 Since he heard the sound of the *t*
Zec 9: 14 Sovereign LORD will sound the *t*;
Mt 24: 31 send his angels with a loud *t* call,
1Co 14: 8 if the *t* does not sound a clear call,
15: 52 For the *t* will sound, the dead will
1Th 4: 16 and with the *t* call of God,
Rev 8: 7 The first angel sounded his *t*,

TRUMPETS (TRUMPET)

Jdg 7: 19 They blew their *t* and broke the jars
Rev 8: 2 and to them were given seven *t*.

TRUST* (ENTRUST ENTRUSTED TRUSTED TRUSTFULLY TRUSTING TRUSTS TRUSTWORTHY)

Ex 14: 31 put their *t* in him and in Moses his
19: 9 and will always put their *t* in you."
Nu 20: 12 "Because you did not *t*
Dt 1: 32 you did not *t* in the LORD your
9: 23 You did not *t* him or obey him.
28: 52 walls in which you *t* fall down.
Jdg 11: 20 did not *t* Israel to pass
2Ki 17: 14 who did not *t* in the LORD their
18: 30 to *t* in the LORD when he says,
1Ch 9: 22 to their positions of *t* by David
Job 4: 18 If God places no *t* in his servants,
15: 15 If God places no *t* in his holy ones,
31: 24 "If I have put my *t* in gold
39: 12 Can you *t* him to bring
Ps 4: 5 and *t* in the LORD.
9: 10 Those who know your name will *t*
13: 5 But I *t* in your unfailing love;
20: 7 Some *t* in chariots and some
20: 7 we *t* in the name of the LORD our
22: 4 In you our fathers put their *t*;
22: 9 you made me *t* in you
25: 2 I lift up my soul; in you I *t*,
31: 6 I *t* in the LORD.
31: 14 But I *t* in you, O LORD;
33: 21 for we *t* in his holy name.
37: 3 *T* in the LORD and do good;
37: 5 *t* in him and he will do this:
40: 3 and put their *t* in the LORD.
40: 4 who makes the LORD his *t*,
44: 6 I do not *t* in my bow,
49: 6 those who *t* in their wealth
49: 13 of those who *t* in themselves,
52: 8 I *t* in God's unfailing love
55: 23 But as for me, I *t* in you.
56: 3 I will *t* in you.
56: 4 in God I *t*; I will not be afraid.
56: 11 in God I *t*; I will not be afraid.
62: 8 *T* in him at all times, O people;
62: 10 Do not *t* in extortion
78: 7 Then they would put their *t* in God
78: 22 or *t* in his deliverance.
91: 2 my God, in whom I *t*."
115: 8 and so will all who *t* in them.
115: 9 O house of Israel, *t* in the LORD—
115: 10 O house of Aaron, *t* in the LORD
115: 11 You who fear him, *t* in the LORD

Ps 118: 8 than to *t* in man.
118: 9 than to *t* in princes.
119: 42 for I *t* in your word.
125: 1 Those who *t* in the LORD are like
135: 18 and so will all who *t* in them.
143: 8 for I have put my *t* in you.
146: 3 Do not put your *t* in princes,
Pr 3: 5 *T* in the LORD with all your heart
21: 22 the stronghold in which they *t*.
22: 19 So that your *t* may be in the LORD
Isa 8: 17 I will put my *t* in him.
12: 2 I will *t* and not be afraid.
26: 4 *T* in the LORD for ever,
30: 15 in quietness and *t* is your strength,
31: 1 who *t* in the multitude
36: 15 to *t* in the LORD when he says,
42: 17 But those who *t* in idols,
50: 10 *t* in the name of the LORD
Jer 2: 37 LORD has rejected those you *t*;
5: 17 the fortified cities in which you *t*.
7: 4 Do not *t* in deceptive words
7: 14 the temple you *t* in, the place I gave
9: 4 do not *t* your brothers.
12: 6 Do not *t* them,
28: 15 you have persuaded this nation to *t*
39: 18 you *t* in me, declares the LORD.'"
48: 7 Since you *t* in your deeds
49: 4 you *t* in your riches and say,
49: 11 Your widows too can *t* in me."
Mic 7: 5 Do not *t* a neighbour;
Na 1: 7 He cares for those who *t* in him,
Zep 3: 2 She does not *t* in the LORD,
3: 12 who *t* in the name of the LORD.
Lk 16: 11 who will *t* you with true riches?
Jn 12: 36 Put your *t* in the light
14: 1 *T* in God; *t* also in me.
Ac 14: 23 Lord in whom they had put their *t*.
Ro 15: 13 you with all joy and peace as you *t*
1Co 4: 2 been given a *t* must prove faithful.
9: 17 discharging the *t* committed
2Co 13: 6 I *t* that you will discover that we
Heb 2: 13 "I will put my *t* in him."

TRUSTED* (TRUST)

1Sa 27: 12 Achish *t* David and said to himself,
2Ki 18: 5 Hezekiah *t* in the LORD, the God
1Ch 5: 20 their prayers, because they *t*
Job 12: 20 He silences the lips of *t* advisers
Ps 5: 9 from their mouth can be *t*;
22: 4 they *t* and you delivered them.
22: 5 in you they *t* and were not
26: 1 I have *t* in the LORD
41: 9 Even my close friend, whom I *t*,
52: 7 but *t* in his great wealth
Isa 20: 5 Those who *t* in Cush and boasted
25: 9 This is the LORD, we *t* in him;
25: 9 we *t* in him, and he saved us.
47: 10 You have *t* in your wickedness
Jer 13: 25 and *t* in false gods.
38: 22 those *t* friends of yours.
48: 13 ashamed when they *t* in Bethel.
Eze 16: 15 "'But you *t* in your beauty
Da 3: 28 They *t* in him and defied the king's
6: 23 because he had *t* in his God.
Lk 11: 22 the armour in which the man *t*
16: 10 *t* with very little can also be *t*
Ac 12: 20 a *t* personal servant of the king,
Tit 2: 10 but to show that they can be fully *t*,
3: 8 so that those who have *t*

TRUSTFULLY* (TRUST)

Pr 3: 29 who lives *t* near you.

TRUSTING* (TRUST)

Job 15: 31 by *t* what is worthless,
Ps 112: 7 his heart is steadfast, *t*
Isa 2: 22 Stop *t* in man,
Jer 7: 8 you are *t* in deceptive words that

TRUSTS* (TRUST)

Job 8: 14 What he *t* in is fragile;
Ps 21: 7 For the king *t* in the LORD;
22: 8 "He *t* in the LORD;
28: 7 my heart *t* in him, and I am helped.
32: 10 surrounds the man who *t* in him.
84: 12 blessed is the man who *t* in you.
86: 2 who *t* in you.
Pr 11: 28 Whoever *t* in his riches will fall,
16: 20 blessed is he who *t* in the LORD.
28: 25 he who *t* in the LORD will prosper.
28: 26 He who *t* in himself is a fool,
29: 25 whoever *t* in the LORD is kept safe
Isa 26: 3 because he *t* in you.
28: 16 one who *t* will never be dismayed.
Jer 17: 5 "Cursed is the one who *t* in man,
17: 7 blessed is the man who *t*
Eze 33: 13 but then he *t* in his righteousness
Hab 2: 18 For he who makes it *t*
Mt 27: 43 He *t* in God.
Ro 4: 5 but *t* God who justifies the wicked,
9: 33 one who *t* in him will never be put
10: 11 "Anyone who *t* in him will never
1Co 13: 7 always protects, always *t*,
1Pe 2: 6 and the one who *t* in him

TRUSTWORTHY* (TRUST)

Ex 18: 21 *t* men who hate dishonest gain—
2Sa 7: 28 you are God! Your words are *t*,
Ne 13: 13 these men were considered *t*.
Ps 19: 7 The statutes of the LORD are *t*,
111: 7 all his precepts are *t*.
119: 86 All your commands are *t*;
119: 138 they are fully *t*.
Pr 11: 13 but a *t* man keeps a secret.
13: 17 but a *t* envoy brings healing.
25: 13 is a *t* messenger to those who send
Da 2: 45 and the interpretation is *t*."
6: 4 he was *t* and neither corrupt
Lk 16: 11 So if you have not been *t*
16: 12 And if you have not been *t*
19: 17 'Because you have been *t*
1Co 7: 25 one who by the Lord's mercy is *t*.
1Ti 1: 15 Here is a *t* saying that deserves full
3: 1 Here is a *t* saying: If anyone sets his
3: 11 but temperate and *t* in everything.
4: 9 This is a *t* saying that deserves full
2Ti 2: 11 Here is a *t* saying:
Tit 1: 9 must hold firmly to the *t* message
3: 8 This is a *t* saying.
Rev 21: 5 for these words are *t* and true."
22: 6 "These words are *t* and true.

TRUTH* (TRUE TRUTHFUL TRUTHFULNESS TRUTHS)

Ge 42: 16 tested to see if you are telling the *t*.
1Ki 17: 24 LORD from your mouth is the *t*."
22: 16 the *t* in the name of the LORD?"
2Ch 18: 15 the *t* in the name of the LORD?"
Ps 15: 2 who speaks the *t* from his heart
25: 5 guide me in your *t* and teach me,
26: 3 and I walk continually in your *t*.
31: 5 redeem me, O LORD, the God of *t*
40: 10 do not conceal your love and your *t*
40: 11 your *t* always protect me.
43: 3 Send forth your light and your *t*,
45: 4 victoriously on behalf of *t*, humility
51: 6 Surely you desire *t*
52: 3 than speaking the *t*.
86: 11 and I will walk in your *t*;
96: 13 and the peoples in his *t*.
119: 30 I have chosen the way of *t*;
119: 43 of *t* from my mouth,
145: 18 to all who call on him in *t*.
Pr 16: 13 they value a man who speaks the *t*.
23: 23 Buy the *t* and do not sell it;
Isa 45: 19 I, the LORD, speak the *t*;
48: 1 but not in *t* or righteousness—
59: 14 *t* has stumbled in the streets,
59: 15 *T* is nowhere to be found,
65: 16 will do so by the God of *t*;
65: 16 will swear by the God of *t*.
Jer 5: 1 who deals honestly and seeks the *t*,
5: 3 do not your eyes look for *t*?
Jer 7: 28 *T* has perished; it has vanished
9: 3 it is not by *t*
9: 5 and no-one speaks the *t*.
26: 15 for in *t* the LORD has sent me
Da 8: 12 and *t* was thrown to the ground.
9: 13 and giving attention to your *t*.
10: 21 what is written in the Book of *T*.
11: 2 "Now then, I tell you the *t*:
Am 5: 10 and despise him who tells the *t*.
Zec 8: 3 will be called The City of *T*,
8: 16 are to do: Speak the *t* to each other.
8: 19 Therefore love *t* and peace."
Mt 5: 18 I tell you the *t*, until heaven
5: 26 I tell you the *t*, you will not get out
6: 2 I tell you the *t*, they have received
6: 5 I tell you the *t*, they have received
6: 16 I tell you the *t*, they have received
8: 10 "I tell you the *t*, I have not found
10: 15 I tell you the *t*, it will be more
10: 23 I tell you the *t*, you will not finish
10: 42 I tell you the *t*, he will certainly not
11: 11 I tell you the *t*: Among those born
13: 17 For I tell you the *t*, many prophets
16: 28 I tell you the *t*, some who are
17: 20 I tell you the *t*, if you have faith
18: 3 And he said: "I tell you the *t*,
18: 13 And if he finds it, I tell you the *t*,
18: 18 "I tell you the *t*, whatever you bind
19: 23 to his disciples, "I tell you the *t*,
19: 28 "I tell you the *t*, at the renewal
21: 21 Jesus replied, "I tell you the *t*,
21: 31 Jesus said to them, "I tell you the *t*,
22: 16 of God in accordance with the *t*.
23: 36 I tell you the *t*, all this will come
24: 2 "I tell you the *t*, not one stone here
24: 34 I tell you the *t*, this generation will
24: 47 I tell you the *t*, he will put him
25: 12 "I tell you the *t*, I don't know you.'
25: 40 The King will reply, 'I tell you the *t*
25: 45 "He will reply, 'I tell you the *t*,
26: 13 tell you the *t*, wherever this gospel
26: 21 "I tell you the *t*, one
26: 34 "I tell you the *t*," Jesus answered,
Mk 3: 28 I tell you the *t*, all the sins
5: 33 with fear, told him the whole *t*.
8: 12 I tell you the *t*, no sign will be given
9: 1 he said to them, "I tell you the *t*,
9: 41 I tell you the *t*, anyone who gives
10: 15 I tell you the *t*, anyone who will not
10: 29 "I tell you the *t*," Jesus replied,
11: 23 "I tell you the *t*, if anyone says
12: 14 of God in accordance with the *t*.
12: 43 Jesus said, "I tell you the *t*,
13: 30 I tell you the *t*, this generation will
14: 9 I tell you the *t*, wherever the gospel
14: 18 "I tell you the *t*, one
14: 25 "I tell you the *t*, I will not drink
14: 30 "I tell you the *t*," Jesus answered,
Lk 4: 24 "I tell you the *t*," he continued,
9: 27 I tell you the *t*, some who are
12: 37 I tell you the *t*, he will dress himself
12: 44 I tell you the *t*, he will put him
18: 17 I tell you the *t*, anyone who will not
18: 29 "I tell you the *t*," Jesus said to them,
20: 21 of God in accordance with the *t*.
21: 3 "I tell you the *t*," he said, "this
21: 32 tell you the *t*, this generation will
23: 43 answered him, "I tell you the *t*,
Jn 1: 14 from the Father, full of grace and *t*.
1: 17 and *t* came through Jesus Christ.
1: 51 "I tell you the *t*, you shall see
3: 3 "I tell you the *t*, unless a man is
3: 5 Jesus answered, "I tell you the *t*,
3: 11 I tell you the *t*, we speak
3: 21 But whoever lives by the *t* comes
4: 23 worship the Father in spirit and *t*,
4: 24 must worship in spirit and in *t*."
5: 19 "I tell you the *t*, the Son can do
5: 24 "I tell you the *t*, whoever hears my
5: 25 I tell you the *t*, a time is coming
5: 33 and he has testified to the *t*.
6: 26 "I tell you the *t*, you are looking
6: 32 Jesus said to them, "I tell you the *t*,

Jn 6: 47 I tell you the *t*, he who believes has
6: 53 Jesus said to them, "I tell you the *t*,
7: 18 the one who sent him is a man of *t*;
8: 32 Then you will know the *t*,
8: 32 and the *t* will set you free."
8: 34 Jesus replied, "I tell you the *t*,
8: 40 who has told you the *t* that I heard
8: 44 to the *t*, for there is no *t* in him.
8: 45 I tell the *t*, you do not believe me!
8: 46 I am telling the *t*, why don't you
8: 51 I tell you the *t*, if a man keeps my
8: 58 "I tell you the *t*," Jesus answered,
10: 1 "I tell you the *t*, the man who does
10: 7 "I tell you the *t*, I am the gate
12: 24 I tell you the *t*, unless a grain
13: 16 I tell you the *t*, no servant is greater
13: 20 tell you the *t*, whoever accepts
13: 21 "I tell you the *t*, one of you is going
13: 38 I tell you the *t*, before the cock
14: 6 I am the way and the *t* and the life.
14: 12 I tell you the *t*, anyone who has
14: 17 with you for ever—the Spirit of *t*.
15: 26 the Spirit of *t* who goes out
16: 7 But I tell you the *t*: It is
16: 13 But when he, the Spirit of *t*, comes,
16: 13 comes, he will guide you into all *t*.
16: 20 I tell you the *t*, you will weep
16: 23 I tell you the *t*, my Father will give
17: 17 them by the *t*; your word is *t*.
18: 23 if I spoke the *t*, why did you strike
18: 37 into the world, to testify to the *t*.
18: 37 on the side of *t* listens to me."
18: 38 "What is *t*?" Pilate asked.
19: 35 He knows that he tells the *t*,
21: 18 I tell you the *t*, when you were
Ac 20: 30 and distort the *t* in order
21: 24 everybody will know there is no *t*
21: 34 commander could not get at the *t*
24: 8 able to learn the *t* about all these
28: 25 "The Holy Spirit spoke the *t*
Ro 1: 18 of men who suppress the *t*
1: 25 They exchanged the *t* of God
2: 2 who do such things is based on *t*.
2: 8 who reject the *t* and follow evil,
2: 20 embodiment of knowledge and *t*—
9: 1 I speak the *t* in Christ—I am not
15: 8 of the Jews on behalf of God's *t*,
1Co 5: 8 the bread of sincerity and *t*.
13: 6 in evil but rejoices with the *t*.
2Co 4: 2 setting forth the *t* plainly we
11: 10 As surely as the *t* of Christ is in me,
12: 6 because I would be speaking the *t*.
13: 8 against the *t*, but only for the *t*.
Gal 2: 5 so that the *t* of the gospel might
2: 14 in line with the *t* of the gospel,
4: 16 enemy by telling you the *t*?
5: 7 and kept you from obeying the *t*?
Eph 1: 13 when you heard the word of *t*,
4: 15 Instead, speaking the *t* in love,
4: 21 him in accordance with the *t* that is
5: 9 and *t*) and find out what pleases
6: 14 with the belt of *t* buckled
Col 1: 5 heard about in the word of *t*.
1: 6 understood God's grace in all its *t*.
2Th 2: 10 because they refused to love the *t*
2: 12 who have not believed the *t*
2: 13 and through belief in the *t*.
1Ti 2: 4 to come to a knowledge of the *t*.
2: 7 I am telling the *t*, I am not lying—
3: 15 the pillar and foundation of the *t*.
4: 3 who believe and who know the *t*.
6: 5 who have been robbed of the *t*
2Ti 2: 15 correctly handles the word of *t*.
2: 18 have wandered away from the *t*.
2: 25 them to a knowledge of the *t*,
3: 7 never able to acknowledge the *t*.
3: 8 so also these men oppose the *t*—
4: 4 will turn their ears away from the *t*
Tit 1: 1 the knowledge of the *t* that leads
1: 14 of those who reject the *t*.
Heb 10: 26 received the knowledge of the *t*,
Jas 1: 18 birth through the word of *t*,
3: 14 do not boast about it or deny the *t*.
Jas 5: 19 of you should wander from the *t*
1Pe 1: 22 by obeying the *t* so that you have
2Pe 1: 12 established in the *t* you now have.
2: 2 the way of *t* into disrepute.
1Jn 1: 6 we lie and do not live by the *t*.
1: 8 deceive ourselves and the *t* is not
2: 4 commands is a liar, and the *t* is not
2: 8 its *t* is seen in him and you,
2: 20 and all of you know the *t*.
2: 21 because no lie comes from the *t*.
2: 21 because you do not know the *t*,
3: 18 or tongue but with actions and in *t*.
3: 19 we know that we belong to the *t*,
4: 6 is how we recognise the Spirit of *t*
5: 6 testifies, because the Spirit is the *t*.
2Jn : 1 whom I love in the *t*—
: 2 who know the *t*—because of the *t*,
: 3 will be with us in *t* and love.
: 4 of your children walking in the *t*,
3Jn : 1 friend Gaius, whom I love in the *t*.
: 3 how you continue to walk in the *t*.
: 3 tell about your faithfulness to the *t*
: 4 my children are walking in the *t*.
: 8 we may work together for the *t*.
: 12 everyone—and even by the *t* itself.

TRUTHFUL* (TRUTH)

Pr 12: 17 A *t* witness gives honest testimony,
12: 19 *T* lips endure for ever,
12: 22 but he delights in men who are *t*.
14: 5 A *t* witness does not deceive,
14: 25 A *t* witness saves lives,
Jer 4: 2 and if in a *t*, just and righteous way
Jn 3: 33 it has certified that God is *t*.
2Co 6: 7 in *t* speech and in the power

TRUTHFULNESS* (TRUTH)

Ro 3: 7 "If my falsehood enhances God's *t*

TRUTHS* (TRUTH)

1Co 2: 13 expressing spiritual *t*
1Ti 3: 9 hold of the deep *t* of the faith
4: 6 brought up in the *t* of the faith
Heb 5: 12 to teach you the elementary *t*

TRY (TRIED TRIES TRYING)

Ps 26: 2 Test me, O LORD, and *t* me,
Isa 7: 13 enough to *t* the patience of men?
Lk 12: 58 *t* hard to be reconciled to him
13: 24 will *t* to enter and will not be able
1Co 10: 33 even as I *t* to please everybody
14: 12 *t* to excel in gifts that build up
2Co 5: 11 is to fear the Lord, we *t*
1Th 5: 15 always *t* to be kind to each other
Tit 2: 9 to *t* to please them, not to talk back

TRYING (TRY)

2Co 5: 12 We are not *t* to commend ourselves
Gal 1: 10 If I were still *t* to please men,
1Th 2: 4 We are not *t* to please men but God
1Pe 1: 11 *t* to find out the time
1Jn 2: 26 things to you about those who are *t*

TUMOURS

1Sa 5: 6 them and afflicted them with *t*.

TUNE

1Co 14: 7 anyone know what *t* is being

TUNIC (TUNICS)

Lk 6: 29 do not stop him from taking your *t*.

TUNICS (TUNIC)

Lk 3: 11 "The man with two *t* should share

TURMOIL

Ps 65: 7 and the *t* of the nations.
Pr 15: 16 than great wealth with *t*.

TURN (TURNED TURNING TURNS)

Ex 32: 12 *T* from your fierce anger; relent
Nu 32: 15 If you *t* away from following him,
Dt 5: 32 do not *t* aside to the right
Dt 28: 14 Do not *t* aside from any
30: 10 and *t* to the LORD your God
Jos 1: 7 do not *t* from it to the right
1Ki 8: 58 May he *t* our hearts to him,
2Ch 7: 14 and *t* from their wicked ways,
30: 9 He will not *t* his face from you
Job 33: 30 to *t* back his soul from the pit,
Ps 28: 1 do not *t* a deaf ear to me.
34: 14 *T* from evil and do good;
51: 13 and sinners will *t* back to you.
78: 6 they in *t* would tell their children.
119: 36 *T* my heart towards your statutes
119: 132 *T* to me and have mercy on me,
Pr 22: 6 when he is old he will not *t* from it.
Isa 17: 7 *t* their eyes to the Holy One
28: 6 to those who *t* back the battle
29: 16 You *t* things upside down,
30: 21 Whether you *t* to the right
45: 22 "*T* to me and be saved,
55: 7 Let him *t* to the LORD,
Jer 31: 13 I will *t* their mourning
Eze 33: 9 if you do warn the wicked man to *t*
33: 11 *T*! *T* from your evil ways!
Jnh 3: 9 and with compassion *t*
Mal 4: 6 He will *t* the hearts of the fathers
Mt 5: 39 you on the right cheek, *t*
10: 35 For I have come to *t*
Lk 1: 17 to *t* the hearts of the fathers
Jn 12: 40 nor *t*—and I would heal them."
16: 20 but your grief will *t* to joy.
Ac 3: 19 Repent, then, and *t* to God,
26: 18 and *t* them from darkness to light,
1Co 14: 31 For you can all prophesy in *t*
15: 23 But each in his own *t*; Christ,
1Ti 6: 20 *T* away from godless chatter
1Pe 3: 11 He must *t* from evil and do good;

TURNED (TURN)

Dt 23: 5 *t* the curse into a blessing for you,
1Ki 11: 4 his wives *t* his heart
2Ch 15: 4 But in their distress they *t*
Est 9: 1 but now the tables were *t*
9: 22 when their sorrow was *t* into joy
Ps 14: 3 All have *t* aside,
30: 11 You *t* my wailing into dancing;
40: 1 he *t* to me and heard my cry.
Isa 9: 12 for all this, his anger is not *t* away,
53: 6 each of us has *t* to his own way;
Hos 7: 8 Ephraim is a flat cake not *t* over.
Joel 2: 31 The sun will be *t* to darkness
Lk 22: 32 And when you have *t* back,
Ro 3: 12 All have *t* away,

TURNING (TURN)

2Ki 21: 13 wiping it and *t* it upside down.
Pr 2: 2 *t* your ear to wisdom
14: 27 *t* a man from the snares of death.

TURNS (TURN)

2Sa 22: 29 the LORD *t* my darkness into light
Pr 15: 1 A gentle answer *t* away wrath,
Isa 44: 25 and *t* it into nonsense,
Jas 5: 20 Whoever *t* a sinner from the error

TWELVE

Ge 35: 22 Jacob had *t* sons: The sons of Leah:
49: 28 All these are the *t* tribes of Israel,
Mt 10: 1 He called his *t* disciples to him
Lk 9: 17 the disciples picked up *t* basketfuls
Rev 21: 12 the names of the *t* tribes of Israel.
21: 14 of the *t* apostles of the Lamb.

TWIN (TWINS)

Ge 25: 24 there were *t* boys in her womb.

TWINKLING*

1Co 15: 52 in a flash, in the *t* of an eye,

TWINS (TWIN)

Ro 9: 11 before the *t* were born

TWISTING* (TWISTS)

Pr 30: 33 and as *t* the nose produces blood,

TWISTS (TWISTING)
Ex 23: 8 and *t* the words of the righteous.

TYRANNICAL*
Pr 28: 16 A *t* ruler lacks judgment,

TYRE
Eze 28: 12 a lament concerning the king of *T*
Mt 11: 22 it will be more bearable for *T*

UNAPPROACHABLE*
1Ti 6: 16 immortal and who lives in *u* light,

UNASHAMED*
1Jn 2: 28 and *u* before him at his coming.

UNBELIEF* (UNBELIEVER UNBELIEVERS UNBELIEVING)
Mk 9: 24 help me overcome my *u*!"
Ro 4: 20 through *u* regarding the promise
11: 20 they were broken off because of *u*,
11: 23 And if they do not persist in *u*,
1Ti 1: 13 because I acted in ignorance and *u*.
Heb 3: 19 able to enter, because of their *u*.

UNBELIEVER* (UNBELIEF)
1Co 7: 15 But if the *u* leaves, let him do so.
10: 27 If some *u* invites you to a meal
14: 24 if an *u* or someone who does not
2Co 6: 15 have in common with an *u*?
1Ti 5: 8 the faith and is worse than an *u*.

UNBELIEVERS* (UNBELIEF)
Lk 12: 46 and assign him a place with the *u*.
Ro 15: 31 rescued from the *u* in Judea
1Co 6: 6 another—and this in front of *u*!
14: 22 however, is for believers, not for *u*.
14: 22 not for believers but for *u*;
14: 23 do not understand or some *u* come
2Co 4: 4 this age has blinded the minds of *u*,
6: 14 Do not be yoked together with *u*.

UNBELIEVING* (UNBELIEF)
Mt 17: 17 "O *u* and perverse generation,"
Mk 9: 19 "O *u* generation," Jesus replied,
Lk 9: 41 "O *u* and perverse generation,"
1Co 7: 14 For the *u* husband has been
7: 14 and the *u* wife has been sanctified
Heb 3: 12 *u* heart that turns away
Rev 21: 8 But the cowardly, the *u*, the vile,

UNBLEMISHED*
Heb 9: 14 the eternal Spirit offered himself *u*

UNCEASING
Ro 9: 2 and *u* anguish in my heart.

UNCERTAIN*
1Ti 6: 17 which is so *u*, but to put their hope

UNCHANGEABLE* (UNCHANGING)
Heb 6: 18 by two *u* things in which it is

UNCHANGING* (UNCHANGEABLE)
Heb 6: 17 wanted to make the *u* nature

UNCIRCUMCISED
Lev 26: 41 when their *u* hearts are humbled
1Sa 17: 26 Who is this *u* Philistine that he
Jer 9: 26 house of Israel is *u* in heart."
Ac 7: 51 stiff-necked people, with *u* hearts
Ro 4: 11 had by faith while he was still *u*.
1Co 7: 18 Was a man *u* when he was called?
Col 3: 11 circumcised or *u*, barbarian,

UNCIRCUMCISION
1Co 7: 19 is nothing and *u* is nothing.
Gal 5: 6 neither circumcision nor *u* has any

UNCLEAN
Ge 7: 2 and two of every kind of *u* animal,
Lev 10: 10 between the *u* and the clean,
11: 4 it is ceremonially *u* for you.
Isa 6: 5 ruined! For I am a man of *u* lips,
52: 11 Touch no *u* thing!
Mt 15: 11 mouth does not make him '*u*',
Ac 10: 14 never eaten anything impure or *u*."
Ro 14: 14 fully convinced that no food is *u*
2Co 6: 17 Touch no *u* thing,

UNCLOTHED*
2Co 5: 4 because we do not wish to be *u*

UNCONCERNED*
Eze 16: 49 were arrogant, overfed and *u*;

UNCOVERED
Ru 3: 7 Ruth approached quietly, *u* his feet
1Co 11: 5 with her head *u* dishonours her head
11: 13 to pray to God with her head *u*?
Heb 4: 13 Everything is *u* and laid bare

UNDERGOES* (UNDERGOING)
Heb 12: 8 (and everyone *u* discipline),

UNDERGOING* (UNDERGOES)
1Pe 5: 9 the world are *u* the same kind

UNDERSTAND (UNDERSTANDING UNDERSTANDS UNDERSTOOD)
Ne 8: 8 the people could *u* what was being
Job 38: 4 Tell me, if you *u*.
42: 3 Surely I spoke of things I did not *u*,
Ps 14: 2 men to see if there are any who *u*,
73: 16 When I tried to *u* all this,
119: 27 Let me *u* the teaching
119: 125 that I may *u* your statutes.
Pr 2: 5 then you will *u* the fear
2: 9 Then you will *u* what is right
30: 18 four that I do not *u*:
Ecc 7: 25 to *u* the stupidity of wickedness
11: 5 so you cannot *u* the work of God,
Isa 6: 10 *u* with their hearts,
44: 18 know nothing, they *u* nothing;
52: 15 they have not heard, they will *u*.
Jer 17: 9 Who can *u* it?
31: 19 after I came to *u*,
Da 9: 25 and *u* this: From the issuing
Hos 14: 9 Who is discerning? He will *u* them.
Mt 13: 15 *u* with their hearts
24: 15 Daniel—let the reader *u*—
Lk 24: 45 so they could *u* the Scriptures.
Ac 8: 30 "Do you *u* what you are reading?"
Ro 7: 15 I do not *u* what I do.
15: 21 those who have not heard will *u*."
1Co 2: 12 that we may *u* what God has freely
2: 14 and he cannot *u* them,
14: 16 those who do not *u* say "Amen"
Eph 5: 17 but *u* what the Lord's will is.
Heb 11: 3 By faith we *u* that the universe was
2Pe 1: 20 you must *u* that no prophecy
3: 3 you must *u* that in the last days
3: 16 some things that are hard to *u*,

UNDERSTANDING (UNDERSTAND)
1Ki 4: 29 and a breadth of *u* as measureless
Job 12: 12 Does not long life bring *u*?
28: 12 Where does *u* dwell?
28: 28 and to shun evil is *u*.'"
32: 8 of the Almighty, that gives him *u*.
36: 26 How great is God—beyond our *u*!
37: 5 he does great things beyond our *u*.
Ps 111: 10 follow his precepts have good *u*.
119: 34 Give me *u*, and I will keep your law
119: 100 I have more *u* than the elders,
119: 104 I gain *u* from your precepts;
119: 130 it gives *u* to the simple.
136: 5 who by his *u* made the heavens,
147: 5 his *u* has no limit.
Pr 2: 2 and applying your heart to *u*,
2: 6 his mouth come knowledge and *u*.
3: 5 and lean not on your own *u*;
3: 13 the man who gains *u*,
4: 5 Get wisdom, get *u*;
4: 7 Though it cost all you have, get *u*.
7: 4 and call *u* your kinsman;
9: 10 knowledge of the Holy One is *u*.
10: 23 but a man of *u* delights in wisdom.
11: 12 but a man of *u* holds his tongue.
14: 29 A patient man has great *u*,
15: 21 a man of *u* keeps a straight course.
15: 32 whoever heeds correction gains *u*.
16: 16 to choose *u* rather than silver!
16: 22 *U* is a fountain of life
17: 27 and a man of *u* is even-tempered.
18: 2 A fool finds no pleasure in *u*
19: 8 he who cherishes *u* prospers.
20: 5 but a man of *u* draws them out.
23: 23 get wisdom, discipline and *u*.
Isa 11: 2 the Spirit of wisdom and of *u*,
40: 28 and his *u* no-one can fathom.
56: 11 They are shepherds who lack *u*;
Jer 3: 15 you with knowledge and *u*.
10: 12 stretched out the heavens by his *u*.
Da 5: 12 a keen mind and knowledge and *u*,
10: 12 that you set your mind to gain *u*
Hos 4: 11 which take away the *u*
Mk 4: 12 and ever hearing but never *u*;
12: 33 with all your *u* and with all your
Lk 2: 47 who heard him was amazed at his *u*
2Co 6: 6 in purity, *u*, patience and kindness;
Eph 1: 8 on us with all wisdom and *u*.
Php 4: 7 of God, which transcends all *u*,
Col 1: 9 through all spiritual wisdom and *u*.
2: 2 have the full riches of complete *u*,
1Jn 5: 20 God has come and has given us *u*,

UNDERSTANDS (UNDERSTAND)
1Ch 28: 9 and *u* every motive
Jer 9: 24 that he *u* and knows me,
Mt 13: 23 man who hears the word and *u* it.
Ro 3: 11 there is no-one who *u*,
1Ti 6: 4 he is conceited and *u* nothing.

UNDERSTOOD (UNDERSTAND)
Ne 8: 12 they now *u* the words that had
Ps 73: 17 then I *u* their final destiny.
Isa 40: 13 Who has *u* the mind of the LORD,
40: 21 Have you not *u* since the earth was
Jn 1: 5 but the darkness has not *u* it.
Ro 1: 20 being *u* from what has been made,

UNDESIRABLE*
Jos 24: 15 But if serving the LORD seems *u*

UNDIVIDED*
1Ch 12: 33 to help David with *u* loyalty—
Ps 86: 11 give me an *u* heart,
Eze 11: 19 I will give them an *u* heart
1Co 7: 35 way in *u* devotion to the Lord.

UNDOING
Pr 18: 7 A fool's mouth is his *u*,

UNDYING*
Eph 6: 24 Lord Jesus Christ with an *u* love.

UNEQUALLED*
Mt 24: 21 *u* from the beginning of the world
Mk 13: 19 of distress *u* from the beginning,

UNFADING*
1Pe 3: 4 the *u* beauty of a gentle

UNFAILING*
Ex 15: 13 "In your *u* love you will lead
1Sa 20: 14 But show me *u* kindness like that
2Sa 22: 51 he shows *u* kindness
Ps 6: 4 save me because of your *u* love.
13: 5 But I trust in your *u* love;
18: 50 he shows *u* kindness
21: 7 through the *u* love
31: 16 save me in your *u* love.
32: 10 but the LORD's *u* love
33: 5 the earth is full of his *u* love.
33: 18 those whose hope is in his *u* love,
33: 22 May your *u* love rest upon us,
36: 7 How priceless is your *u* love!

Ps 44: 26 redeem us because of your *u* love.
48: 9 we meditate on your *u* love.
51: 1 according to your *u* love;
52: 8 I trust in God's *u* love
77: 8 Has his *u* love vanished for ever?
85: 7 Show us your *u* love, O LORD,
90: 14 in the morning with your *u* love,
107: 8 thanks to the LORD for his *u* love
107: 15 thanks to the LORD for his *u* love
107: 21 to the LORD for his *u* love
107: 31 to the LORD for his *u* love
119: 41 May your *u* love come to me,
119: 76 May your *u* love be my comfort,
130: 7 for with the LORD is *u* love
143: 8 bring me word of your *u* love,
143: 12 In your *u* love, silence my enemies;
147: 11 who put their hope in his *u* love.
Pr 19: 22 What a man desires is *u* love;
20: 6 Many a man claims to have *u* love,
Isa 54: 10 yet my *u* love for you will not be
La 3: 32 so great is his *u* love.
Hos 10: 12 reap the fruit of *u* love,

UNFAITHFUL (UNFAITHFULNESS)
Lev 6: 2 is *u* to the LORD by deceiving his
Nu 5: 6 and so is *u* to the LORD,
1Ch 10: 13 because he was *u* to the LORD;
Pr 11: 6 the *u* are trapped by evil desires.
13: 2 the *u* have a craving for violence.
13: 15 but the way of the *u* is hard.
22: 12 but he frustrates the words of the *u*.
23: 28 and multiplies the *u* among men.
25: 19 is reliance on the *u* in times
Jer 3: 20 But like a woman *u* to her husband,

UNFAITHFULNESS (UNFAITHFUL)
1Ch 9: 1 to Babylon because of their *u*.
Mt 5: 32 except for marital *u*, causes her
19: 9 for marital *u*, and marries another

UNFIT*
Tit 1: 16 and *u* for doing anything good.

UNFORGIVING*
2Ti 3: 3 unholy, without love, *u*, slanderous

UNFRIENDLY*
Pr 18: 1 An *u* man pursues selfish ends;

UNFRUITFUL
1Co 14: 14 my spirit prays, but my mind is *u*.

UNGODLINESS (UNGODLY)
Tit 2: 12 It teaches us to say "No" to *u*

UNGODLY (UNGODLINESS)
Ro 5: 6 powerless, Christ died for the *u*.
1Ti 1: 9 the *u* and sinful, the unholy
2Ti 2: 16 in it will become more and more *u*.
2Pe 2: 6 of what is going to happen to the *u*;
Jude : 15 and to convict all the *u*

UNGRATEFUL*
Lk 6: 35 he is kind to the *u* and wicked.
2Ti 3: 2 disobedient to their parents, *u*,

UNHOLY*
1Ti 1: 9 and sinful, the *u* and irreligious;
2Ti 3: 2 ungrateful, *u*, without love,
Heb 10: 29 as an *u* thing the blood

UNINTENTIONALLY
Lev 4: 2 'When anyone sins *u* and does
Nu 15: 22 " 'Now if you *u* fail to keep any
Dt 4: 42 flee if he had *u* killed his neighbour

UNIT
1Co 12: 12 body is a *u*, though it is made up

UNITE (UNITED UNITY)
1Co 6: 15 and *u* them with a prostitute?

UNITED (UNITE)
Ge 2: 24 and mother and be *u* to his wife,
Mt 19: 5 and mother and be *u* to his wife,
Ro 6: 5 If we have been *u* with him
Eph 5: 31 and mother and be *u* to his wife,
Php 2: 1 from being *u* with Christ,
Col 2: 2 encouraged in heart and *u* in love,

UNITY* (UNITE)
2Ch 30: 12 the people to give them *u* of mind
Ps 133: 1 is when brothers live together in *u*!
Jn 17: 23 May they be brought to complete *u*
Ro 15: 5 a spirit of *u* among yourselves
Eph 4: 3 effort to keep the *u* of the Spirit
4: 13 up until we all reach *u* in the faith
Col 3: 14 them all together in perfect *u*.

UNIVERSE*
1Co 4: 9 made a spectacle to the whole *u*,
Eph 4: 10 in order to fill the whole *u*.)
Php 2: 15 which you shine like stars in the *u*
Heb 1: 2 and through whom he made the *u*.
11: 3 understand that the *u* was formed

UNJUST
Ro 3: 5 That God is *u* in bringing his wrath
9: 14 What then shall we say? Is God *u*?
1Pe 2: 19 up under the pain of *u* suffering

UNKNOWN
Ac 17: 23 TO AN *U* GOD.

UNLEAVENED
Ex 12: 17 "Celebrate the Feast of *U* Bread,
Dt 16: 16 at the Feast of *U* Bread, the Feast

UNLIMITED*
1Ti 1: 16 Jesus might display his *u* patience

UNLOVED
Pr 30: 23 an *u* woman who is married,

UNMARRIED
1Co 7: 8 It is good for them to stay *u*,
7: 27 Are you *u*? Do not look for a wife.
7: 32 An *u* man is concerned about

UNPLOUGHED
Ex 23: 11 the seventh year let the land lie *u*
Hos 10: 12 and break up your *u* ground;

UNPRODUCTIVE
Tit 3: 14 necessities and not live *u* lives.
2Pe 1: 8 and *u* in your knowledge

UNPROFITABLE
Tit 3: 9 because these are *u* and useless.

UNPUNISHED
Ex 34: 7 Yet he does not leave the guilty *u*;
Pr 6: 29 no-one who touches her will go *u*.
11: 21 of this: The wicked will not go *u*,
19: 5 A false witness will not go *u*,

UNQUENCHABLE
Lk 3: 17 he will burn up the chaff with *u* fire

UNREPENTANT*
Ro 2: 5 stubbornness and your *u* heart,

UNRIGHTEOUS*
Zep 3: 5 yet the *u* know no shame.
Mt 5: 45 rain on the righteous and the *u*.
1Pe 3: 18 the righteous for the *u*, to bring you
2Pe 2: 9 and to hold the *u* for the day

UNSEARCHABLE
Ro 11: 33 How *u* his judgments,
Eph 3: 8 preach to the Gentiles the *u* riches

UNSEEN*
Mt 6: 6 and pray to your Father, who is *u*.
6: 18 who is *u*; and your Father,
2Co 4: 18 on what is seen, but on what is *u*.
4: 18 temporary, but what is *u* is eternal.

UNSETTLED*
1Th 3: 3 so that no-one would be *u*
2Th 2: 2 not to become easily *u*

UNSHRUNK
Mt 9: 16 patch of *u* cloth on an old garment,

UNSPIRITUAL*
Ro 7: 14 but I am *u*, sold as a slave to sin.
Col 2: 18 and his *u* mind puffs him up
Jas 3: 15 down from heaven but is earthly, *u*,

UNSTABLE*
Jas 1: 8 he is a double-minded man, *u*
2Pe 2: 14 they seduce the *u*; they are experts
3: 16 ignorant and *u* people distort,

UNTHINKABLE*
Job 34: 12 It is *u* that God would do wrong,

UNTIE
Mk 1: 7 worthy to stoop down and *u*.
Lk 13: 15 each of you on the Sabbath *u* his ox

UNVEILED*
2Co 3: 18 with *u* faces all reflect the Lord's

UNWHOLESOME*
Eph 4: 29 Do not let any *u* talk come out

UNWISE
Eph 5: 15 how you live—not as *u* but as wise,

UNWORTHY*
Ge 32: 10 I am *u* of all the kindness
Job 40: 4 "I am *u*—how can I reply to you?
Lk 17: 10 should say, 'We are *u* servants;
1Co 11: 27 Lord in an *u* manner will be guilty

UPHOLD (UPHOLDS)
Isa 41: 10 I will *u* you with my righteous right
Ro 3: 31 Not at all! Rather, we *u* the law.

UPHOLDS* (UPHOLD)
Ps 37: 17 but the LORD *u* the righteous.
37: 24 for the LORD *u* him with his hand.
63: 8 your right hand *u* me.
140: 12 and *u* the cause of the needy.
145: 14 The LORD *u* all those who fall
146: 7 He *u* the cause of the oppressed

UPRIGHT
Dt 32: 4 *u* and just is he.
Job 1: 1 This man was blameless and *u*;
Ps 7: 10 who saves the *u* in heart.
11: 7 *u* men will see his face.
25: 8 Good and *u* is the LORD;
33: 1 it is fitting for the *u* to praise him.
64: 10 let all the *u* in heart praise him!
92: 15 proclaiming, "The LORD is *u*;
97: 11 and joy on the *u* in heart.
119: 7 I will praise you with an *u* heart
Pr 2: 7 He holds victory in store for the *u*,
3: 32 but takes the *u* into his confidence.
14: 2 whose walk is *u* fears the LORD,
15: 8 but the prayer of the *u* pleases him.
21: 29 an *u* man gives thought to his ways.
Isa 26: 7 O *u* One, you make the way
Tit 1: 8 who is self-controlled, *u*, holy
2: 12 *u* and godly lives in this present

UPROOTED
Dt 28: 63 You will be *u* from the land you are
Jer 31: 40 The city will never again be *u*
Jude : 12 without fruit and *u*—twice dead.

UPSET
Lk 10: 41 are worried and *u* about many

URIAH

Hittite husband of Bathsheba, killed by David's order (2Sa 11).

USEFUL

Eph 4:28 doing something *u*
2Ti 2:21 *u* to the Master and prepared
3:16 Scripture is God-breathed and is *u*
Phm :11 now he has become *u* both to you

USELESS

1Co 15:14 our preaching is *u*
Tit 3:9 these are unprofitable and *u*.
Phm :11 Formerly he was *u* to you,
Heb 7:18 *u* (for the law made nothing perfect
Jas 2:20 faith without deeds is *u*?

USURY

Ne 5:10 But let the exacting of *u* stop!
Ps 15:5 who lends his money without *u*

UTMOST

Job 34:36 that Job might be tested to the *u*

UTTER (UTTERS)

Ps 78:2 I will *u* things hidden from of old—
Mt 13:35 I will *u* things hidden

UTTERS (UTTER)

1Co 14:2 he *u* mysteries with his spirit.

UZZIAH

Son of Amaziah; king of Judah also known as Azariah (2Ki 15:1-7; 1Ch 6:24; 2Ch 26). Struck with leprosy because of pride (2Ch 26:16-23).

VAIN

Ps 33:17 A horse is a *v* hope for deliverance;
73:13 in *v* have I kept my heart pure;
127:1 its builders labour in *v*.
Isa 65:23 They will not toil in *v*
1Co 15:2 Otherwise, you have believed in *v*.
15:58 labour in the Lord is not in *v*.
2Co 6:1 not to receive God's grace in *v*.
Gal 2:2 running or had run my race in *v*.

VALIANT

1Sa 10:26 by *v* men whose hearts God had

VALID

Jn 8:14 my own behalf, my testimony is *v*,

VALLEY (VALLEYS)

Ps 23:4 walk through the *v* of the shadow
Isa 40:4 Every *v* shall be raised up,
Joel 3:14 multitudes in the *v* of decision!

VALLEYS (VALLEY)

SS 2:1 a lily of the *v*.

VALUABLE (VALUE)

Lk 12:24 And how much more *v* you are

VALUE (VALUABLE VALUED)

Lev 27:3 set the *v* of a male between the ages
Pr 16:13 they *v* a man who speaks with truth.
31:11 and lacks nothing of *v*.
Mt 13:46 When he found one of great *v*,
1Ti 4:8 For physical training is of some *v*,
Heb 11:26 as of greater *v* than the treasures

VALUED (VALUE)

Lk 16:15 What is highly *v* among men is

VANISHES

Jas 4:14 appears for a little while and then *v*.

VASHTI*

Queen of Persia replaced by Esther (Est 1-2).

VAST

Ge 2:1 completed in all their *v* array.
Dt 1:19 of the Amorites through all that *v*
Dt 8:15 He led you through the *v*
Ps 139:17 How *v* is the sum of them!

VEGETABLES

Pr 15:17 of *v* where there is love
Ro 14:2 whose faith is weak, eats only *v*.

VEIL

Ex 34:33 to them, he put a *v* over his face.
2Co 3:14 for to this day the same *v* remains

VENGEANCE (AVENGE AVENGER AVENGES AVENGING REVENGE)

Nu 31:3 to carry out the LORD's *v* on them
Isa 34:8 For the LORD has a day of *v*,
Na 1:2 The LORD takes *v* on his foes

VERDICT

Jn 3:19 This is the *v*; Light has come

VICTOR'S* (VICTORY)

2Ti 2:5 he does not receive the *v* crown

VICTORIES* (VICTORY)

2Sa 22:51 He gives his king great *v*;
Ps 18:50 He gives his king great *v*;
21:1 great is his joy in the *v* you give!
21:5 Through the *v* you gave, his glory is
44:4 who decrees *v* for Jacob.

VICTORIOUS (VICTORY)

Ps 20:5 for joy when you are *v*

VICTORIOUSLY* (VICTORY)

Ps 45:4 In your majesty ride forth *v*

VICTORY (VICTOR'S VICTORIES VICTORIOUS VICTORIOUSLY)

2Sa 8:6 gave David *v* everywhere he
Ps 44:6 my sword does not bring me *v*;
60:12 With God we will gain the *v*,
129:2 they have not gained the *v* over me.
Pr 11:14 but many advisers make *v* sure.
1Co 15:54 "Death has been swallowed up in *v*
15:57 He gives us the *v* through our Lord
1Jn 5:4 This is the *v* that has overcome

VIEW

Pr 5:21 are in full *v* of the LORD,
2Ti 4:1 and in *v* of his appearing

VILLAGE

Mk 6:6 went around teaching from *v* to *v*.

VINDICATED (VINDICATION)

Job 13:18 I know I will be *v*.
1Ti 3:16 was *v* by the Spirit,

VINDICATION (VINDICATED)

Ps 24:5 and *v* from God his Saviour.

VINE (VINEYARD)

Ps 128:3 Your wife will be like a fruitful *v*
Isa 36:16 one of you will eat from his own *v*
Jnh 4:6 Jonah was very happy about the *v*.
Jn 15:1 "I am the true *v* and my Father is

VINEGAR

Pr 10:26 As *v* to the teeth and smoke
Mk 15:36 filled a sponge with wine *v*,

VINEYARD (VINE)

1Ki 21:1 an incident involving a *v* belonging
Pr 31:16 out of her earnings she plants a *v*.
SS 1:6 my own *v* I have neglected.
Isa 5:1 My loved one had a *v*
1Co 9:7 Who plants a *v* and does not eat

VIOLATION

Heb 2:2 every *v* and disobedience received

VIOLENCE (VIOLENT)

Ge 6:11 in God's sight and was full of *v*.
Isa 53:9 though he had done no *v*,
60:18 No longer will *v* be heard
Eze 45:9 Give up your *v* and oppression
Joel 3:19 of *v* done to the people of Judah,
Jnh 3:8 give up their evil ways and their *v*.

VIOLENT (VIOLENCE)

Eze 18:10 "Suppose he has a *v* son, who sheds
1Ti 1:13 and a persecutor and a *v* man,
3:3 not *v* but gentle, not quarrelsome,
Tit 1:7 not *v*, not pursuing dishonest gain.

VIPERS

Ps 140:3 the poison of *v* is on their lips.
Lk 3:7 "You brood of *v*! Who warned you
Ro 3:13 "The poison of *v* is on their lips."

VIRGIN (VIRGINS)

Dt 22:15 shall bring proof that she was a *v*
Isa 7:14 The *v* will be with child
Mt 1:23 "The *v* will be with child
Lk 1:34 I am a *v*?" The angel answered,
2Co 11:2 that I might present you as a pure *v*

VIRGINS (VIRGIN)

Mt 25:1 will be like ten *v* who took their
1Co 7:25 Now about *v*: I have no command

VIRTUES*

Col 3:14 And over all these *v* put on love,

VISIBLE

Eph 5:13 exposed by the light becomes *v*,
Col 1:16 and on earth, *v* and invisible,

VISION (VISIONS)

Da 9:24 to seal up *v* and prophecy
Ac 26:19 disobedient to the *v* from heaven.

VISIONS (VISION)

Nu 12:6 I reveal myself to him in *v*,
Joel 2:28 your young men will see *v*.
Ac 2:17 your young men will see *v*,

VOICE

Dt 30:20 listen to his *v*, and hold fast to him.
1Sa 15:22 as in obeying the *v* of the LORD?
Job 40:9 and can your *v* thunder like his?
Ps 19:4 Their *v* goes out into all the earth,
29:3 The *v* of the LORD is
66:19 and heard my *v* in prayer.
95:7 Today, if you hear his *v*,
Pr 8:1 Does not understanding raise her *v*
Isa 30:21 your ears will hear a *v* behind you,
40:3 A *v* of one calling:
Mk 1:3 "a *v* of one calling in the desert,
Jn 5:28 are in their graves will hear his *v*
10:3 and the sheep listen to his *v*.
Ro 10:18 "Their *v* has gone out
Heb 3:7 "Today, if you hear his *v*,
Rev 3:20 If anyone hears my *v* and opens

VOMIT

Lev 18:28 it will *v* you out as it vomited out
Pr 26:11 As a dog returns to its *v*,
2Pe 2:22 "A dog returns to its *v*," and,

VOW (VOWS)

Nu 6:2 a *v* of separation to the LORD
30:2 When a man makes a *v*
Jdg 11:30 Jephthah made a *v* to the LORD:

VOWS (VOW)

Ps 116:14 I will fulfil my *v* to the LORD
Pr 20:25 and only later to consider his *v*.

VULTURES

Mt 24:28 is a carcass, there the *v* will gather.

WAGE (WAGES WAGING)
2Co 10: 3 we do not *w* war as the world does.

WAGES (WAGE)
Mal 3: 5 who defraud labourers of their *w*,
Lk 10: 7 for the worker deserves his *w*.
Ro 4: 4 his *w* are not credited to him
6: 23 For the *w* of sin is death,
1Ti 5: 18 and "The worker deserves his *w*."

WAGING (WAGE)
Ro 7: 23 *w* war against the law of my mind

WAILING
Ps 30: 11 You turned my *w* into dancing;

WAIST
2Ki 1: 8 and a leather belt round his *w*."
Mt 3: 4 he had a leather belt round his *w*."

WAIT (AWAITS WAITED WAITING WAITS)
Ps 27: 14 *W* for the LORD;
130: 5 I *w* for the LORD, my soul waits,
Isa 30: 18 Blessed are all who *w* for him!
Ac 1: 4 *w* for the gift my Father promised,
Ro 8: 23 as we *w* eagerly for our adoption
1Th 1: 10 and to *w* for his Son from heaven,
Tit 2: 13 while we *w* for the blessed hope—

WAITED (WAIT)
Ps 40: 1 I *w* patiently for the LORD;

WAITING (WAIT)
Heb 9: 28 to those who are *w* for him.

WAITS (WAIT)
Ro 8: 19 creation *w* in eager expectation

WAKE (AWAKE WAKENS)
Eph 5: 14 "*W* up, O sleeper,

WAKENS* (WAKE)
Isa 50: 4 He *w* me morning by morning,
50: 4 *w* my ear to listen like one being

WALK (WALKED WALKING WALKS)
Lev 26: 12 I will *w* among you and be your
Dt 5: 33 *W* in all the way that the LORD
6: 7 and when you *w* along the road,
10: 12 to *w* in all his ways, to love him,
11: 19 and when you *w* along the road,
11: 22 to *w* in all his ways and to hold fast
26: 17 and that you will *w* in his ways,
Jos 22: 5 to *w* in all his ways,
Ps 1: 1 who does not *w* in the counsel
15: 2 He whose *w* is blameless
23: 4 Even though I *w*
84: 11 from those whose *w* is blameless.
89: 15 who *w* in the light of your presence
119: 45 I will *w* about in freedom,
Pr 4: 12 When you *w*, your steps will not be
6: 22 When you *w*, they will guide you;
Isa 2: 3 so that we may *w* in his paths."
2: 5 let us *w* in the light of the LORD.
30: 21 saying, "This is the way; *w* in it."
40: 31 they will *w* and not be faint.
57: 2 Those who *w* uprightly
Jer 6: 16 ask where the good way is, and *w*
Da 4: 37 And those who *w* in pride he is able
Am 3: 3 Do two *w* together
Mic 4: 5 All the nations may *w*
6: 8 and to *w* humbly with your God.
Mk 2: 9 'Get up, take your mat and *w*'?
Jn 8: 12 Whoever follows me will never *w*
1Jn 1: 6 with him yet *w* in the darkness,
1: 7 But if we *w* in the light,
2Jn : 6 his command is that you *w* in love.

WALKED (WALK)
Ge 5: 24 Enoch *w* with God; then he was no
Jos 14: 9 which your feet have *w* will be your
Mt 14: 29 and *w* on the water to Jesus.

WALKING (WALK)
1Ki 3: 3 love for the LORD by *w* according
Da 3: 25 I see four men *w* around in the fire,
2Jn : 4 of your children *w* in the truth,

WALKS (WALK)
Pr 10: 9 The man of integrity *w* securely,
13: 20 He who *w* with the wise grows wise
Isa 33: 15 He who *w* righteously
Jn 11: 9 A man who *w* by day will not

WALL (WALLS)
Jos 6: 20 *w* collapsed; so every man charged
Ne 2: 17 let us rebuild the *w* of Jerusalem,
Eph 2: 14 the dividing *w* of hostility,
Rev 21: 12 It had a great, high *w*

WALLOWING
2Pe 2: 22 back to her *w* in the mud."

WALLS (WALL)
Isa 58: 12 be called Repairer of Broken *W*,
60: 18 but you will call your *w* Salvation
Heb 11: 30 By faith the *w* of Jericho fell,

WANDER (WANDERED)
Nu 32: 13 he made them *w* in the desert forty
Jas 5: 19 one of you should *w* from the truth

WANDERED (WANDER)
Eze 34: 6 My sheep *w* over all the mountains
Mt 18: 12 go to look for the one that *w* off?
1Ti 6: 10 have *w* from the faith and pierced
2Ti 2: 18 who have *w* away from the truth.

WANT (WANTED WANTING WANTS)
1Sa 8: 19 "We *w* a king over us.
Mt 19: 21 Jesus answered, "If you *w*
Lk 19: 14 'We don't *w* this man to be our king
Ro 7: 15 For what I *w* to do I do not do,
13: 3 Do you *w* to be free from fear
2Co 12: 14 what I *w* is not your possessions
Php 3: 10 I *w* to know Christ and the power

WANTED (WANT)
1Co 12: 18 of them, just as he *w* them to be.
Heb 6: 17 Because God *w* to make

WANTING (WANT)
Da 5: 27 weighed on the scales and found *w*.
2Pe 3: 9 with you, not *w* anyone to perish,

WANTS (WANT)
Mt 5: 42 from the one who *w* to borrow
20: 26 whoever *w* to become great
Mk 8: 35 For whoever *w* to save his life will
10: 43 whoever *w* to become great
Ro 9: 18 he hardens whom he *w* to harden.
1Ti 2: 4 who *w* all men to be saved
1Pe 5: 2 you are willing, as God *w* you to be;

WAR (WARRIOR WARS)
Jos 11: 23 Then the land had rest from *w*,
1Sa 15: 18 make *w* on them until you have
Ps 68: 30 the nations who delight in *w*.
120: 7 but when I speak, they are for *w*.
144: 1 who trains my hands for *w*,
Isa 2: 4 nor will they train for *w* any more.
Da 9: 26 *W* will continue until the end,
Ro 7: 23 waging *w* against the law
2Co 10: 3 we do not wage *w* as the world does
1Pe 2: 11 which *w* against your soul.
Rev 12: 7 And there was *w* in heaven.
19: 11 With justice he judges and makes *w*

WARN* (WARNED WARNING WARNINGS)
Ex 19: 21 *w* the people so they do not force
Nu 24: 14 let me *w* you of what this people
1Sa 8: 9 but *w* them solemnly and let them
1Ki 2: 42 swear by the LORD and *w* you,
2Ch 19: 10 you are to *w* them not to sin
Ps 81: 8 O my people, and I will *w* you—
Jer 42: 19 I *w* you today that you made a fatal
Eze 3: 18 and you do not *w* him or speak out
3: 19 But if you do *w* the wicked man
3: 20 Since you did not *w* him, he will die
3: 21 if you do *w* the righteous man not
33: 3 blows the trumpet to *w* the people,
33: 6 blow the trumpet to *w* the people
33: 9 if you do *w* the wicked man to turn
Lk 16: 28 Let him *w* them, so that they will
Ac 4: 17 we must *w* these men
1Co 4: 14 but to *w* you, as my dear children.
Gal 5: 21 I *w* you, as I did before, that those
1Th 5: 14 brothers, *w* those who are idle,
2Th 3: 15 an enemy, but *w* him as a brother.
2Ti 2: 14 *W* them before God
Tit 3: 10 and then *w* him a second time.
3: 10 *W* a divisive person once,
Rev 22: 18 I *w* everyone who hears the words

WARNED (WARN)
2Ki 17: 13 The LORD *w* Israel and Judah
Ps 19: 11 By them is your servant *w*;
Jer 22: 21 I *w* you when you felt secure,
Mt 3: 7 Who *w* you to flee
1Th 4: 6 have already told you and *w* you.
Heb 11: 7 when *w* about things not yet seen,
12: 25 they refused him who *w* them

WARNING (WARN)
Jer 6: 8 Take *w*, O Jerusalem,
1Ti 5: 20 so that the others may take *w*.

WARNINGS (WARN)
1Co 10: 11 and were written down as *w* for us,

WARRIOR (WAR)
Ex 15: 3 The LORD is a *w*;
1Ch 28: 3 you are a *w* and have shed blood.'
Pr 16: 32 Better a patient man than a *w*,

WARS (WAR)
Ps 46: 9 He makes *w* cease to the ends
Mt 24: 6 You will hear of *w* and rumours of *w*,

WASH (WASHED WASHING)
Ps 51: 7 *w* me, and I will be whiter
Jer 4: 14 *w* the evil from your heart
Jn 13: 5 and began to *w* his disciples' feet,
Ac 22: 16 be baptised and *w* your sins away,
Jas 4: 8 *W* your hands, you sinners,
Rev 22: 14 Blessed are those who *w* their robes

WASHED (WASH)
Ps 73: 13 in vain have I *w* my hands
1Co 6: 11 you were *w*, you were sanctified,
Heb 10: 22 and having our bodies *w*
2Pe 2: 22 and, "A sow that is *w* goes back
Rev 7: 14 they have *w* their robes

WASHING (WASH)
Eph 5: 26 cleansing her by the *w* with water
1Ti 5: 10 showing hospitality, *w* the feet
Tit 3: 5 us through the *w* of rebirth

WASTED (WASTING)
Jn 6: 12 Let nothing be *w*."

WASTING (WASTED)
2Co 4: 16 Though outwardly we are *w* away,

WATCH (WATCHER WATCHES WATCHING WATCHMAN)
Ge 31: 49 "May the LORD keep *w*
Ps 90: 4 or like a *w* in the night.
141: 3 keep *w* over the door of my lips.
Pr 4: 6 love her, and she will *w* over you.
6: 22 when you sleep, they will *w*
Jer 31: 10 will *w* over his flock like a shepherd
Mic 7: 7 I *w* in hope for the LORD,
Mt 24: 42 "Therefore keep *w*, because you do
26: 41 *W* and pray so that you will not fall
Mk 13: 35 "Therefore keep *w* because you do
Lk 2: 8 keeping *w* over their flocks at night

1Ti 4: 16 *W* your life and doctrine closely.
Heb 13: 17 They keep *w* over you

WATCHER* (WATCH)

Job 7: 20 O *w* of men?

WATCHES* (WATCH)

Nu 19: 5 While he *w*, the heifer is
Job 24: 15 The eye of the adulterer *w* for dusk;
Ps 1: 6 For the LORD *w* over the way
33: 14 from his dwelling-place he *w*
63: 6 of you through the *w* of the night.
119: 148 through the *w* of the night,
121: 3 he who *w* over you will not slumber
121: 4 indeed, he who *w* over Israel
121: 5 The LORD *w* over you—
127: 1 Unless the LORD *w* over the city,
145: 20 LORD *w* over all who love him,
146: 9 The LORD *w* over the alien
Pr 31: 27 She *w* over the affairs
Ecc 11: 4 Whoever *w* the wind will not plant;
La 2: 19 as the *w* of the night begin;
4: 16 he no longer *w* over them.

WATCHING (WATCH)

Lk 12: 37 whose master finds them *w*

WATCHMAN (WATCH)

Eze 3: 17 I have made you a *w* for the house
33: 6 but I will hold the *w* accountable

WATER (WATERED WATERING WATERS WELL-WATERED)

Ex 7: 20 all the *w* was changed into blood.
17: 1 but there was no *w* for the people
Nu 20: 2 there was no *w* for the community,
Ps 1: 3 like a tree planted by streams of *w*,
22: 14 I am poured out like *w*,
42: 1 As the deer pants for streams of *w*,
Pr 25: 21 if he is thirsty, give him *w* to drink.
Isa 12: 3 With joy you will draw *w*
30: 20 of adversity and the *w* of affliction,
32: 2 like streams of *w* in the desert
49: 10 and lead them beside springs of *w*.
Jer 2: 13 broken cisterns that cannot hold *w*.
17: 8 will be like a tree planted by the *w*
31: 9 I will lead them beside streams of *w*
Eze 36: 25 I will sprinkle clean *w* on you,
Zec 14: 8 On that day living *w* will flow out
Mt 14: 29 and walked on the *w* to Jesus.
Mk 9: 41 anyone who gives you a cup of *w*
Lk 5: 4 to Simon, "Put out into deep *w*,
Jn 3: 5 a man is born of *w* and the Spirit,
4: 10 he would have given you living *w*."
7: 38 streams of living *w* will flow
Eph 5: 26 washing with *w* through the word,
Heb 10: 22 our bodies washed with pure *w*.
1Pe 3: 21 this *w* symbolises baptism that now
2Pe 2: 17 These men are springs without *w*
1Jn 5: 6 This is the one who came by *w*
5: 6 come by *w* only, but by *w*
5: 8 the Spirit, the *w* and the blood;
Rev 7: 17 to springs of living *w*.
21: 6 cost from the spring of the *w* of life.

WATERED (WATER)

1Co 3: 6 I planted the seed, Apollos *w* it,

WATERING (WATER)

Isa 55: 10 it without *w* the earth

WATERS (WATER)

Ps 23: 2 he leads me beside quiet *w*,
Ecc 11: 1 Cast your bread upon the *w*,
SS 8: 7 Many *w* cannot quench love;
Isa 11: 9 as the *w* cover the sea.
43: 2 When you pass through the *w*,
55: 1 come to the *w*;
58: 11 like a spring whose *w* never fail.
Hab 2: 14 as the *w* cover the sea.
1Co 3: 7 plants nor he who *w* is anything,

WAVE (WAVES)

Lev 23: 11 He is to *w* the sheaf
Jas 1: 6 he who doubts is like a *w* of the sea,

WAVER*

1Ki 18: 21 "How long will you *w*
Ro 4: 20 Yet he did not *w* through unbelief

WAVES (WAVE)

Isa 57: 20 whose *w* cast up mire and mud.
Mt 8: 27 Even the winds and the *w* obey him
Eph 4: 14 tossed back and forth by the *w*,

WAY (WAYS)

Ex 13: 21 of cloud to guide them on their *w*
18: 20 and show them the *w* to live
Dt 1: 33 to show you the *w* you should go.
32: 6 Is this the *w* you repay the LORD,
1Sa 12: 23 I will teach you the *w* that is good
2Sa 22: 31 "As for God, his *w* is perfect;
1Ki 8: 23 wholeheartedly in your *w*,
8: 36 Teach them the right *w* to live,
Job 23: 10 But he knows the *w* that I take;
Ps 1: 1 or stand in the *w* of sinners
32: 8 teach you in the *w* you should go;
37: 5 Commit your *w* to the LORD;
86: 11 Teach me your *w*, O LORD,
119: 9 can a young man keep his *w* pure?
139: 24 See if there is any offensive *w* in me
Pr 4: 11 I guide you in the *w* of wisdom
12: 15 The *w* of a fool seems right to him,
14: 12 There is a *w* that seems right
16: 17 he who guards his *w* guards his life
19: 2 nor to be hasty and miss the *w*.
22: 6 Train a child in the *w* he should go,
30: 19 and the *w* of a man with a maiden.
Isa 30: 21 saying, "This is the *w*; walk in it."
35: 8 it will be called the *W* of Holiness.
40: 3 the *w* for the LORD;
48: 17 you in the *w* you should go.
53: 6 each of us has turned to his own *w*;
55: 7 Let the wicked forsake his *w*
Jer 5: 31 and my people love it this *w*.
Mal 3: 1 who will prepare the *w* before me.
Mt 3: 3 'Prepare the *w* for the Lord,
Lk 7: 27 who will prepare your *w* before you
Jn 14: 6 "I am the *w* and the truth
Ac 1: 11 in the same *w* you have seen him go
9: 2 any there who belonged to the *W*,
24: 14 of the *W*, which they call a sect.
1Co 10: 13 also provide a *w* out so that you can
12: 31 will show you the most excellent *w*.
14: 1 Follow the *w* of love and eagerly
Col 1: 10 and may please him in every *w*:
Tit 2: 10 that in every *w* they will make
Heb 4: 15 who has been tempted in every *w*,
9: 8 was showing by this that the *w*
10: 20 and living *w* opened for us
13: 18 desire to live honourably in every *w*.

WAYS (WAY)

Ex 33: 13 teach me your *w* so I may know
Dt 10: 12 to walk in all his *w*, to love him,
26: 17 and that you will walk in his *w*,
30: 16 in his *w*, and to keep his commands
32: 4 and all his *w* are just.
Jos 22: 5 in all his *w*, to obey his commands,
2Ch 11: 17 walking in the *w* of David
Job 34: 21 "His eyes are on the *w* of men;
Ps 25: 4 Show me your *w*, O LORD,
25: 10 All the *w* of the LORD are loving
37: 7 fret when men succeed in their *w*,
51: 13 I will teach transgressors your *w*,
77: 13 Your *w*, O God, are holy.
119: 59 I have considered my *w*
139: 3 you are familiar with all my *w*.
145: 17 The LORD is righteous in all his *w*
Pr 3: 6 in all your *w* acknowledge him,
4: 26 and take only *w* that are firm.
5: 21 For a man's *w* are in full view
16: 2 All a man's *w* seem innocent
16: 7 When a man's *w* are pleasing
Isa 2: 3 He will teach us his *w*,
55: 8 neither are your *w* my *w*,"
Eze 28: 15 You were blameless in your *w*
33: 8 out to dissuade him from his *w*,
Hos 14: 9 The *w* of the LORD are right;
Ro 1: 30 they invent *w* of doing evil;
Jas 3: 2 We all stumble in many *w*.

WEAK (WEAKER WEAKNESS WEAKNESSES)

Ps 41: 1 is he who has regard for the *w*;
72: 13 He will take pity on the *w*
82: 3 Defend the cause of the *w*
Eze 34: 4 You have not strengthened the *w*
Mt 26: 41 spirit is willing, but the body is *w*."
Ac 20: 35 of hard work we must help the *w*,
Ro 14: 1 Accept him whose faith is *w*,
15: 1 to bear with the failings of the *w*
1Co 1: 27 God chose the *w* things
8: 9 become a stumbling-block to the *w*.
9: 22 To the *w* I became *w*, to win the *w*.
11: 30 That is why many among you are *w*
2Co 12: 10 For when I am *w*, then I am strong.
1Th 5: 14 help the *w*, be patient
Heb 12: 12 your feeble arms and *w* knees.

WEAK-WILLED (WILL)

2Ti 3: 6 and gain control over *w* women,

WEAKER* (WEAK)

2Sa 3: 1 the house of Saul grew *w* and *w*.
1Co 12: 22 seem to be *w* are indispensable,
1Pe 3: 7 them with respect as the *w* partner

WEAKNESS* (WEAK)

La 1: 6 in *w* they have fled
Ro 8: 26 the Spirit helps us in our *w*.
1Co 1: 25 and the *w* of God is stronger
2: 3 I came to you in *w* and fear,
15: 43 it is sown in *w*, it is raised in power;
2Co 11: 30 boast of the things that show my *w*.
12: 9 for my power is made perfect in *w*
13: 4 he was crucified in *w*, yet he lives
Heb 5: 2 since he himself is subject to *w*.
11: 34 whose *w* was turned to strength;

WEAKNESSES* (WEAK)

2Co 12: 5 about myself, except about my *w*.
12: 9 all the more gladly about my *w*,
12: 10 I delight in *w*, in insults,
Heb 4: 15 unable to sympathise with our *w*,

WEALTH

Dt 8: 18 gives you the ability to produce *w*,
2Ch 1: 11 and you have not asked for *w*,
Ps 39: 6 he heaps up *w*, not knowing who
Pr 3: 9 Honour the LORD with your *w*,
10: 4 but diligent hands bring *w*.
11: 4 *W* is worthless in the day of wrath,
13: 7 to be poor, yet has great *w*.
15: 16 than great *w* with turmoil.
22: 4 bring *w* and honour and life.
Ecc 5: 10 whoever loves *w* is never satisfied
5: 13 *w* hoarded to the harm of its owner,
SS 8: 7 all the *w* of his house for love,
Mt 13: 22 and the deceitfulness of *w* choke it,
Mk 10: 22 away sad, because he had great *w*.
12: 44 They all gave out of their *w*; but she
Lk 15: 13 and there squandered his *w*
1Ti 6: 17 nor to put their hope in *w*,
Jas 5: 2 Your *w* has rotted, and moths have
5: 3 You have hoarded *w*

WEAPON (WEAPONS)

Ne 4: 17 work with one hand and held a *w*

WEAPONS (WEAPON)

Ecc 9: 18 Wisdom is better than *w* of war,
2Co 6: 7 with *w* of righteousness
10: 4 The *w* we fight with are not

WEAR (WEARING)

Dt 8: 4 Your clothes did not *w* out
22: 5 nor a man *w* women's clothing,
Ps 102: 26 they will all *w* out like a garment.

Pr 23: 4 Do not *w* yourself out to get rich;
Isa 51: 6 the earth will *w* out like a garment
Heb 1: 11 they will all *w* out like a garment.
Rev 3: 18 and white clothes to *w*,

WEARIES (WEARY)
Ecc 12: 12 and much study *w* the body.

WEARING (WEAR)
Jn 19: 5 When Jesus came out *w* the crown
Jas 2: 3 attention to the man *w* fine clothes
1Pe 3: 3 as braided hair and the *w*
Rev 7: 9 They were *w* white robes

WEARY (WEARIES)
Isa 40: 28 He will not grow tired or *w*,
40: 31 they will run and not grow *w*,
50: 4 know the word that sustains the *w*.
Mt 11: 28 all you who are *w* and burdened,
Gal 6: 9 Let us not become *w* in doing good,
Heb 12: 3 so that you will not grow *w*
Rev 2: 3 my name, and have not grown *w*.

WEDDING
Mt 22: 11 who was not wearing *w* clothes.
Rev 19: 7 For the *w* of the Lamb has come,

WEEDS
Mt 13: 25 and sowed *w* among the wheat,

WEEK
Mt 28: 1 at dawn on the first day of the *w*,
1Co 16: 2 On the first day of every *w*,

WEEP (WEEPING WEPT)
Ecc 3: 4 a time to *w* and a time to laugh,
Lk 6: 21 Blessed are you who *w* now,
23: 28 *w* for yourselves and for your

WEEPING (WEEP)
Ps 30: 5 *w* may remain for a night,
126: 6 He who goes out *w*,
Jer 31: 15 Rachel *w* for her children
Mt 2: 18 Rachel *w* for her children
8: 12 where there will be *w* and gnashing

WEIGH (OUTWEIGHS WEIGHED WEIGHS WEIGHTIER WEIGHTS)
1Co 14: 29 others should *w* carefully what is

WEIGHED (WEIGH)
Job 28: 15 nor can its price be *w* in silver.
Da 5: 27 You have been *w* on the scales
Lk 21: 34 or your hearts will be *w*

WEIGHS (WEIGH)
Pr 12: 25 An anxious heart *w* a man down,
15: 28 of the righteous *w* its answers,
21: 2 but the LORD *w* the heart.
24: 12 not he who *w* the heart perceive

WEIGHTIER* (WEIGH)
Jn 5: 36 "I have testimony *w* than that

WEIGHTS (WEIGH)
Lev 19: 36 Use honest scales and honest *w*,
Dt 25: 13 Do not have two differing *w*
Pr 11: 1 but accurate *w* are his delight.

WELCOME (WELCOMES)
Mk 9: 37 welcomes me does not *w* me
2Pe 1: 11 and you will receive a rich *w*

WELCOMES (WELCOME)
Mt 18: 5 whoever *w* a little child like this
2Jn : 11 Anyone who *w* him shares

WELL [1] (WELLED WELLING WELLS)
Lk 14: 5 falls into a *w* on the Sabbath day,

WELL [2]
Mt 15: 31 crippled made *w*, the lame walking
Lk 17: 19 your faith has made you *w*."
Jas 5: 15 in faith will make the sick person *w*

WELL-WATERED (WATER)
Isa 58: 11 You will be like a *w* garden,

WELLED* (WELL [1])
2Co 8: 2 and their extreme poverty *w* up

WELLING* (WELL [1])
Jn 4: 14 of water *w* up to eternal life."

WELLS (WELL [1])
Isa 12: 3 from the *w* of salvation.

WELLSPRING *(SPRING)
Pr 4: 23 for it is the *w* of life.

WEPT (WEEP)
Ps 137: 1 of Babylon we sat and *w*
Lk 22: 62 And he went outside and *w* bitterly
Jn 11: 35 Jesus *w*.

WEST
Ps 103: 12 as far as the east is from the *w*,
107: 3 from east and *w*, from north

WHEAT
Mt 3: 12 gathering the *w* into his barn
13: 25 and sowed weeds among the *w*,
Lk 22: 31 Satan has asked to sift you as *w*.
Jn 12: 24 a grain of *w* falls to the ground

WHEELS
Eze 1: 16 appearance and structure of the *w*:

WHIRLWIND (WIND)
2Ki 2: 1 to take Elijah up to heaven in a *w*,
Hos 8: 7 and reap the *w*.
Na 1: 3 His way is in the *w* and the storm,

WHISPER (WHISPERED)
1Ki 19: 12 And after the fire came a gentle *w*.
Job 26: 14 how faint the *w* we hear of him!
Ps 107: 29 He stilled the storm to a *w*;

WHISPERED (WHISPER)
Mt 10: 27 speak in the daylight; what is *w*

WHITE (WHITER)
Isa 1: 18 they shall be as *w* as snow;
Da 7: 9 His clothing was as *w* as snow;
7: 9 the hair of his head was *w* like wool
Mt 28: 3 and his clothes were *w* as snow.
Rev 1: 14 hair were *w* like wool, as *w* as snow,
3: 4 dressed in *w*, for they are worthy.
6: 2 and there before me was a *w* horse!
7: 13 "These in *w* robes—who are they,
19: 11 and there before me was a *w* horse,
20: 11 Then I saw a great *w* throne

WHITER (WHITE)
Ps 51: 7 and I will be *w* than snow.

WHOLE
Ge 1: 29 plant on the face of the *w* earth
2: 6 and watered the *w* surface
11: 1 Now the *w* world had one language
Ex 12: 47 The *w* community
19: 5 Although the *w* earth is mine,
Lev 16: 17 and the *w* community of Israel.
Nu 14: 21 of the LORD fills the *w* earth,
32: 13 until the *w* generation
Dt 13: 16 *w* burnt offering to the LORD your
19: 8 gives you the *w* land he promised
Jos 2: 3 come to spy out the *w* land."
1Sa 1: 28 For his *w* life he will be given
17: 46 the *w* world will know that there is
1Ki 10: 24 The *w* world sought audience
2Ki 21: 8 and will keep the *w* Law that my
Ps 72: 19 may the *w* earth be filled
Pr 4: 22 and health to a man's *w* body.
8: 31 rejoicing in his *w* world
Ecc 12: 13 for this is the *w* duty of man.
Isa 1: 5 Your *w* head is injured,
6: 3 the *w* earth is full of his glory."
14: 26 plan determined for the *w* world;
Eze 34: 6 were scattered over the *w* earth,
37: 11 these bones are the *w* house
Da 2: 35 mountain and filled the *w* earth.
Zep 1: 18 the *w* world will be consumed,
Zec 14: 9 will be king over the *w* earth.
Mal 3: 10 the *w* tithe into the storehouse,
Mt 5: 29 than for your *w* body to be thrown
6: 22 your *w* body will be full of light.
16: 26 for a man if he gains the *w* world,
24: 14 will be preached in the *w* world
Lk 21: 35 live on the face of the *w* earth.
Jn 12: 19 Look how the *w* world has gone
13: 10 to wash his feet; his *w* body is clean
21: 25 the *w* world would not have room
Ac 17: 26 they should inhabit the *w* earth;
20: 27 proclaim to you the *w* will of God.
Ro 1: 9 whom I serve with my *w* heart
3: 19 and the *w* world held accountable
8: 22 know that the *w* creation has been
1Co 4: 9 made a spectacle to the *w* universe,
12: 17 If the *w* body were an ear,
Gal 3: 22 declares that the *w* world is
5: 3 obligated to obey the *w* law.
Eph 4: 10 in order to fill the *w* universe.)
4: 13 attaining to the *w* measure
1Th 5: 23 May your *w* spirit, soul
Jas 2: 10 For whoever keeps the *w* law
1Jn 2: 2 but also for the sins of the *w* world.
Rev 3: 10 going to come upon the *w* world

WHOLEHEARTED* (HEART)
2Ki 20: 3 you faithfully and with *w* devotion
1Ch 28: 9 and serve him with *w* devotion
29: 19 my son Solomon the *w* devotion
Isa 38: 3 you faithfully and with *w* devotion

WHOLEHEARTEDLY* (HEART)
Nu 14: 24 a different spirit and follows me *w*,
32: 11 they have not followed me *w*,
32: 12 for they followed the LORD *w*.'
Dt 1: 36 because he followed the LORD *w*
Jos 14: 8 followed the LORD my God *w*.
14: 9 followed the LORD my God *w*.'
14: 14 the LORD, the God of Israel, *w*.
1Ki 8: 23 with your servants who continue *w*
1Ch 29: 9 for they had given freely and *w*
2Ch 6: 14 with your servants who continue *w*
15: 15 oath because they had sworn it *w*.
19: 9 and *w* in the fear of the LORD.
25: 2 in the eyes of the LORD, but not *w*
31: 21 he sought his God and worked *w*.
Ro 6: 17 you *w* obeyed the form of teaching
Eph 6: 7 Serve *w*, as if you were serving

WHOLESOME*
2Ki 2: 22 And the water has remained *w*
2Pe 3: 1 to stimulate you to *w* thinking.

WICK
Isa 42: 3 a smouldering *w* he will not snuff out
Mt 12: 20 a smouldering *w* he will not snuff out

WICKED (WICKEDNESS)
Ge 13: 13 Now the men of Sodom were *w*
39: 9 How then could I do such a *w* thing
Ex 23: 1 Do not help a *w* man
Nu 14: 35 things to this whole *w* community,
Dt 15: 9 not to harbour this *w* thought:
Jdg 19: 22 some of the *w* men
1Sa 2: 12 Eli's sons were *w* men; they had no
15: 18 completely destroy those *w* people,
25: 17 He is such a *w* man that no-one can
2Sa 13: 12 in Israel! Don't do this *w* thing.
2Ki 17: 11 They did *w* things that provoked
2Ch 7: 14 and turn from their *w* ways,
19: 2 "Should you help the *w*
Ne 13: 17 "What is this *w* thing you are doing
Ps 1: 1 walk in the counsel of the *w*
1: 5 Therefore the *w* will not stand
7: 9 to an end the violence of the *w*

Ps 10: 13 Why does the *w* man revile God?
11: 5 the *w* and those who love violence
12: 8 The *w* freely strut about
26: 5 and refuse to sit with the *w*.
32: 10 Many are the woes of the *w*,
36: 1 concerning the sinfulness of the *w*:
37: 13 but the LORD laughs at the *w*,
49: 5 when *w* deceivers surround me—
50: 16 But to the *w*, God says:
58: 3 Even from birth the *w* go astray;
73: 3 when I saw the prosperity of the *w*.
82: 2 and show partiality to the *w*? *Selah*
112: 10 the longings of the *w* will come
119: 61 Though the *w* bind me with ropes,
119: 155 Salvation is far from the *w*,
140: 8 do not grant the *w* their desires,
141: 10 Let the *w* fall into their own nets,
146: 9 but he frustrates the ways of the *w*.
Pr 2: 12 you from the ways of *w* men,
4: 14 Do not set foot on the path of the *w*
6: 18 a heart that devises *w* schemes,
9: 7 whoever rebukes a *w* man incurs
10: 20 the heart of the *w* is of little value.
10: 28 the hopes of the *w* come to nothing
11: 5 *w* are brought down by their own
11: 10 when the *w* perish, there are shouts
11: 21 The *w* will not go unpunished,
12: 5 but the advice of the *w* is deceitful.
12: 10 the kindest acts of the *w* are cruel.
14: 19 the *w* at the gates of the righteous.
15: 3 keeping watch on the *w*
15: 26 detests the thoughts of the *w*,
21: 10 The *w* man craves evil;
21: 29 A *w* man puts up a bold front,
28: 1 *w* man flees though no-one pursues,
28: 4 who forsake the law praise the *w*,
29: 7 but the *w* have no such concern.
29: 16 When the *w* thrive, so does sin,
29: 27 the *w* detest the upright.
Isa 11: 4 breath of his lips he will slay the *w*.
13: 11 the *w* for their sins.
26: 10 Though grace is shown to the *w*,
48: 22 says the LORD, "for the *w*."
53: 9 He was assigned a grave with the *w*
55: 7 Let the *w* forsake his way
57: 20 But the *w* are like the tossing sea,
Jer 35: 15 of you must turn from your *w* ways
Eze 3: 18 that *w* man will die for his sin,
13: 22 you encouraged the *w* not to turn
14: 7 and puts a *w* stumbling-block
18: 21 "But if a *w* man turns away
18: 23 pleasure in the death of the *w*?
21: 25 " 'O profane and *w* prince of Israel,
33: 8 When I say to the *w*, 'O *w* man,
33: 11 pleasure in the death of the *w*,
33: 14 to the *w* man, 'You will surely die,'
33: 19 And if a *w* man turns away
Da 12: 10 but the *w* will continue to be *w*.
Mt 12: 39 *w* and adulterous generation asks
12: 45 be with this *w* generation."
12: 45 with it seven other spirits more *w*
Lk 6: 35 he is kind to the ungrateful and *w*.
Ac 2: 23 and you, with the help of *w* men,
Ro 4: 5 but trusts God who justifies the *w*,
1Co 5: 13 "Expel the *w* man from among you
6: 9 not know that the *w* will not inherit
Rev 2: 2 that you cannot tolerate *w* men,

WICKEDNESS (WICKED)

Ge 6: 5 The LORD saw how great man's *w*
Ex 34: 7 and forgiving *w*, rebellion and sin.
Lev 16: 21 and confess over it all the *w*
19: 29 to prostitution and be filled with *w*.
Dt 9: 4 it is on account of the *w*
Ne 9: 2 and confessed their sins and the *w*
Ps 45: 7 You love righteousness and hate *w*;
92: 15 he is my Rock, and there is no *w*
Pr 13: 6 but *w* overthrows the sinner.
Jer 3: 2 land with your prostitution and *w*.
8: 6 No-one repents of his *w*,
14: 20 O LORD, we acknowledge our *w*
Eze 18: 20 the *w* of the wicked will be charged
28: 15 created till *w* was found in you.
33: 19 wicked man turns away from his *w*
Da 4: 27 and your *w* by being kind
9: 24 to atone for *w*, to bring
Jnh 1: 2 its *w* has come up before me."
Mt 24: 12 Because of the increase of *w*,
Lk 11: 39 inside you are full of greed and *w*.
Ac 1: 18 (With the reward he got for his *w*,
Ro 1: 18 who suppress the truth by their *w*,
1Co 5: 8 the yeast of malice and *w*,
2Co 6: 14 what do righteousness and *w* have
2Ti 2: 19 of the Lord must turn away from *w*
Tit 2: 14 for us to redeem us from all *w*
Heb 1: 9 loved righteousness and hated *w*;
8: 12 For I will forgive their *w*
2Pe 2: 15 who loved the wages of *w*.

WIDE

Ps 81: 10 Open *w* your mouth and I will fill it
Isa 54: 2 stretch your tent curtains *w*,
Mt 7: 13 For *w* is the gate and broad is
2Co 6: 13 my children—open *w* your hearts
Eph 3: 18 to grasp how *w* and long and high

WIDOW (WIDOWS)

Ex 22: 22 "Do not take advantage of a *w*
Dt 10: 18 cause of the fatherless and the *w*,
Ps 146: 9 sustains the fatherless and the *w*,
Isa 1: 17 plead the case of the *w*.
Lk 21: 2 saw a poor *w* put in two very small
1Ti 5: 4 But if a *w* has children

WIDOWS (WIDOW)

Ps 68: 5 to the fatherless, a defender of *w*,
Ac 6: 1 their *w* were being overlooked
1Co 7: 8 to the unmarried and the *w* I say:
1Ti 5: 3 to those *w* who are really
Jas 1: 27 look after orphans and *w*

WIFE (WIVES WIVES')

Ge 2: 24 and mother and be united to his *w*,
19: 26 But Lot's *w* looked back
24: 67 she became his *w*, and he loved her;
Ex 20: 17 shall not covet your neighbour's *w*,
Lev 20: 10 adultery with another man's *w*—
Dt 5: 21 shall not covet your neighbour's *w*.
24: 5 happiness to the *w* he has married.
Ru 4: 13 took Ruth and she became his *w*.
Pr 5: 18 in the *w* of your youth.
12: 4 *w* of noble character is her
18: 22 He who finds a *w* finds what is
19: 13 quarrelsome *w* is like a constant
31: 10 *w* of noble character who can find?
Hos 1: 2 take to yourself an adulterous *w*
Mal 2: 14 the witness between you and the *w*
Mt 1: 20 to take Mary home as your *w*,
19: 3 for a man to divorce his *w* for any
Lk 17: 32 Remember Lot's *w*! Whoever tries
18: 29 or *w* or brothers or parents
1Co 7: 2 each man should have his own *w*,
7: 33 how he can please his *w*—
Eph 5: 23 the husband is the head of the *w*
5: 33 must love his *w* as he loves himself,
1Ti 3: 2 husband of but one *w*, temperate,
Rev 21: 9 I will show you the bride, the *w*

WILD

Ge 1: 25 God made the *w* animals according
8: 1 Noah and all the *w* animals
Lk 15: 13 squandered his wealth in *w* living.
Ro 11: 17 and you, though a *w* olive shoot,

WILFUL (WILL)

Pr 19: 13 Keep your servant also from *w* sins;

WILL (WEAK-WILLED WILFUL WILLING WILLINGNESS)

Ps 40: 8 I desire to do your *w*, O my God;
143: 10 Teach me to do your *w*,
Isa 53: 10 Yet it was the LORD's *w*
Mt 6: 10 your *w* be done
7: 21 who does the *w* of my Father
10: 29 apart from the *w* of your Father.
12: 50 does the *w* of my Father
26: 39 Yet not as I *w*, but as you *w*."
26: 42 I drink it, may your *w* be done."
Jn 6: 38 but to do the *w* of him who sent me.
7: 17 If anyone chooses to do God's *w*,
Ac 20: 27 to you the whole *w* of God.
Ro 12: 2 and approve what God's *w* is—
1Co 7: 37 but has control over his own *w*,
Eph 5: 17 understand what the Lord's *w* is.
Php 2: 13 for it is God who works in you to *w*
1Th 4: 3 God's *w* that you should be sanctified:
5: 18 for this is God's *w* for you
2Ti 2: 26 has taken them captive to do his *w*.
Heb 2: 4 distributed according to his *w*.
9: 16 In the case of a *w*, it is necessary
10: 7 I have come to do your *w*, O God
13: 21 everything good for doing his *w*,
Jas 4: 15 "If it is the Lord's *w*,
1Pe 3: 17 It is better, if it is God's *w*,
4: 2 but rather for the *w* of God.
2Pe 1: 21 never had its origin in the *w*
1Jn 5: 14 we ask anything according to his *w*,
Rev 4: 11 and by your *w* they were created

WILLING (WILL)

1Ch 28: 9 devotion and with a *w* mind,
29: 5 who is *w* to consecrate himself
Ps 51: 12 grant me a *w* spirit, to sustain me.
Da 3: 28 were *w* to give up their lives rather
Mt 18: 14 Father in heaven is not *w* that any
23: 37 her wings, but you were not *w*.
26: 41 The spirit is *w*, but the body is weak
1Ti 6: 18 and to be generous and *w* to share.
1Pe 5: 2 but because you are *w*,

WILLINGNESS* (WILL)

2Co 8: 11 so that your eager *w*
8: 12 For if the *w* is there, the gift is

WIN (WINS WON)

1Co 9: 19 myself a slave to everyone, to *w*
Php 3: 14 on towards the goal to *w* the prize
1Th 4: 12 your daily life may *w* the respect

WIND (WHIRLWIND WINDS)

Ps 1: 4 that the *w* blows away.
Ecc 2: 11 meaningless, a chasing after the *w*;
Hos 8: 7 "They sow the *w*
Mk 4: 41 Even the *w* and the waves obey
Jn 3: 8 The *w* blows wherever it pleases.
Eph 4: 14 and there by every *w* of teaching
Jas 1: 6 blown and tossed by the *w*.

WINDOW

Jos 2: 21 she tied the scarlet cord in the *w*.
Ac 20: 9 in a *w* was a young man named
2Co 11: 33 in a basket from a *w* in the wall

WINDS (WIND)

Ps 104: 4 He makes *w* his messengers,
Mt 24: 31 gather his elect from the four *w*,
Heb 1: 7 "He makes his angels *w*,

WINE

Ps 104: 15 *w* that gladdens the heart of man,
Pr 20: 1 *W* is a mocker and beer a brawler;
23: 20 join those who drink too much *w*
23: 31 Do not gaze at *w* when it is red,
31: 6 *w* to those who are in anguish;
SS 1: 2 your love is more delightful than *w*.
Isa 28: 7 And these also stagger from *w*
55: 1 Come, buy *w* and milk
Mt 9: 17 Neither do men pour new *w*
Lk 23: 36 They offered him *w* vinegar
Jn 2: 3 When the *w* was gone, Jesus'
Ro 14: 21 not to eat meat or drink *w*
Eph 5: 18 on *w*, which leads to debauchery.
1Ti 5: 23 a little *w* because of your stomach
Rev 16: 19 with the *w* of the fury of his wrath.

WINEPRESS

Isa 63: 2 like those of one treading the *w*?
Rev 19: 15 He treads the *w* of the fury

WINESKINS
Mt 9: 17 do men pour new wine into old *w*.

WINGS
Ex 19: 4 and how I carried you on eagles' *w*
Ru 2: 12 under whose *w* you have come
Ps 17: 8 hide me in the shadow of your *w*
91: 4 under his *w* you will find refuge;
Isa 6: 2 him were seraphs, each with six *w*:
40: 31 They will soar on *w* like eagles;
Eze 1: 6 of them had four faces and four *w*.
Zec 5: 9 in their *w*! They had *w* like those
Mal 4: 2 rise with healing in its *w*.
Lk 13: 34 hen gathers her chicks under her *w*,
Rev 4: 8 the four living creatures had six *w*

WINS (WIN)
Pr 11: 30 and he who *w* souls is wise.

WINTER
Mk 13: 18 that this will not take place in *w*,

WIPE (WIPED)
Isa 25: 8 The Sovereign LORD will *w* away
Rev 7: 17 God will *w* away every tear
21: 4 He will *w* every tear

WIPED (WIPE)
Lk 7: 38 Then she *w* them with her hair,
Ac 3: 19 so that your sins may be *w* out,

WISDOM (WISE)
Ge 3: 6 and also desirable for gaining *w*,
1Ki 4: 29 God gave Solomon *w* and very
2Ch 1: 10 Give me *w* and knowledge,
Ps 51: 6 you teach me *w* in the inmost place
111: 10 of the LORD is the beginning of *w*;
Pr 2: 6 For the LORD gives *w*,
3: 13 Blessed is the man who finds *w*,
4: 7 *W* is supreme; therefore get
8: 11 for *w* is more precious than rubies,
11: 2 but with humility comes *w*.
13: 10 *w* is found in those who take advice
23: 23 get *w*, discipline and understanding
29: 3 A man who loves *w* brings joy
29: 15 The rod of correction imparts *w*,
31: 26 She speaks with *w*,
Isa 11: 2 Spirit of *w* and of understanding,
28: 29 in counsel and magnificent in *w*.
Jer 10: 12 he founded the world by his *w*
Mic 6: 9 and to fear your name is *w*—
Mt 11: 19 But *w* is proved right by her actions
Lk 2: 52 And Jesus grew in *w* and stature,
Ac 6: 3 known to be full of the Spirit and *w*.
Ro 11: 33 the depth of the riches of the *w*
1Co 1: 17 not with words of human *w*,
1: 30 who has become for us *w* from God
12: 8 through the Spirit the message of *w*
Eph 1: 17 may give you the Spirit of *w*
Col 2: 3 are hidden all the treasures of *w*
2: 23 indeed have an appearance of *w*,
Jas 1: 5 of you lacks *w*, he should ask God,
3: 13 in the humility that comes from *w*.
Rev 5: 12 and wealth and *w* and strength

WISE (WISDOM WISER)
1Ki 3: 12 give you a *w* and discerning heart,
Job 5: 13 He catches the *w* in their craftiness
Ps 19: 7 making *w* the simple.
Pr 3: 7 Do not be *w* in your own eyes;
9: 8 rebuke a *w* man and he will love
10: 1 A *w* son brings joy to his father,
11: 30 and he who wins souls is *w*.
13: 1 A *w* son heeds his father's
13: 20 He who walks with the *w* grows *w*,
16: 23 A *w* man's heart guides his mouth,
17: 28 Even a fool is thought *w*
Ecc 9: 17 The quiet words of the *w* are more
Jer 9: 23 "Let not the *w* man boast
Eze 28: 6 "'Because you think you are *w*,
Da 2: 21 He gives wisdom to the *w*
Da 12: 3 Those who are *w* will shine like
Mt 11: 25 hidden these things from the *w*
25: 2 them were foolish and five were *w*.
1Co 1: 19 I will destroy the wisdom of the *w*;
1: 27 things of the world to shame the *w*;
3: 19 He catches the *w* in their craftiness
Eph 5: 15 but as *w*, making the most
2Ti 3: 15 able to make you *w* for salvation
Jas 3: 13 Who is *w* and understanding

WISER (WISE)
Pr 9: 9 a wise man and he will be *w* still;
1Co 1: 25 of God is *w* than man's wisdom,

WISH (WISHES)
Jn 15: 7 ask whatever you *w*, and it will be
Ro 9: 3 For I could *w* that I myself were
Rev 3: 15 I *w* you were either one

WISHES (WISH)
Rev 22: 17 let him come; and whoever *w*,

WITCHCRAFT
Dt 18: 10 engages in *w*, or casts spells,
Gal 5: 20 idolatry and *w*; hatred, discord,

WITHDREW
Lk 5: 16 But Jesus often *w* to lonely places

WITHER (WITHERS)
Ps 1: 3 and whose leaf does not *w*.
37: 19 In times of disaster they will not *w*;

WITHERS (WITHER)
Isa 40: 7 The grass *w* and the flowers fall,
1Pe 1: 24 the grass *w* and the flowers fall,

WITHHELD (WITHHOLD)
Ge 22: 12 you have not *w* from me your son,

WITHHOLD (WITHHELD WITHHOLDS)
Ps 84: 11 no good things does he *w*
Pr 23: 13 Do not *w* discipline from a child;

WITHHOLDS (WITHHOLD)
Dt 27: 19 "Cursed is the man who *w* justice

WITNESS (EYE-WITNESSES WITNESSES)
Pr 12: 17 truthful *w* gives honest testimony,
19: 9 A false *w* will not go unpunished,
Jn 1: 8 he came only as a *w* to the light.

WITNESSES (WITNESS)
Dt 19: 15 by the testimony of two or three *w*.
Mt 18: 16 by the testimony of two or three *w*.'
Ac 1: 8 and you will be my *w* in Jerusalem,

WIVES (WIFE)
Eph 5: 22 *W*, submit to your husbands
5: 25 love your *w*, just as Christ loved
1Pe 3: 1 talk by the behaviour of their *w*,

WIVES' (WIFE)
1Ti 4: 7 with godless myths and old *w* tales

WOE
Isa 6: 5 "*W* to me!" I cried.
Eze 34: 2 *W* to the shepherds
Mt 18: 7 *W* to the world
23: 13 "*W* to you, teachers of the law
Jude : 11 *W* to them! They have taken

WOLF (WOLVES)
Isa 65: 25 *w* and the lamb will feed together,

WOLVES (WOLF)
Mt 10: 16 you out like sheep among *w*.

WOMAN (MAN)
Ge 2: 22 God made a *w* from
2: 23 she shall be called '*w*,'
3: 6 *w* saw that the fruit
3: 12 The *w* you put here with
3: 15 between you and the *w*,
3: 16 To the *w* he said,
12: 11 a beautiful *w* you are.
20: 3 because of the *w* you have
24: 5 if the *w* is unwilling
Ex 2: 1 married a Levite *w*
3: 22 Every *w* is to ask her
21: 10 If he marries another *w*
21: 22 hit a pregnant *w*
Lev 12: 2 *w* who becomes pregnant
15: 19 *w* has her regular flow
15: 25 a *w* has a discharge
18: 17 sexual relations with both a *w*
20: 13 as one lies with a *w*,
Nu 5: 29 when a *w* goes astray
30: 3 young *w* still living in
30: 9 by a widow or divorced *w*
30: 10 *w* living with her husband
Dt 20: 7 become pledged to a *w*
21: 11 the captives a beautiful *w*
22: 5 *w* must not wear men's
22: 13 married this *w* but when
Jdg 4: 9 hand Sisera over to a *w*.
13: 6 the *w* went to her husband
14: 2 have seen a Philistine *w*
16: 4 he fell in love with a *w*
20: 4 husband of the murdered *w*
Ru 3: 11 a *w* of noble character
1Sa 1: 15 a *w* who is deeply troubled
25: 3 intelligent and beautiful *w*,
28: 7 a *w* who is a medium,
2Sa 11: 2 he saw a *w* bathing
13: 17 "Get this *w* out of here
14: 2 had a wise *w* brought
20: 16 a wise *w* called from
1Ki 3: 18 this *w* also had a baby.
17: 24 the *w* said to Elijah,
2Ki 4: 8 a well-to-do *w* was there,
8: 1 Elisha had said to the *w*
9: 34 "Take care of that cursed *w*,"
Job 14: 1 Man born of *w* is of few
Pr 11: 16 A kind-hearted *w* gains respect,
11: 22 a beautiful *w* who shows no
14: 1 a wise *w* builds her house,
30: 23 unloved *w* who is married,
31: 30 a *w* who fears the LORD
Isa 54: 1 O barren *w*, you who never
Mt 5: 28 looks at a *w* lustfully
9: 20 a *w* who had been subject
15: 28 *W* you have great faith!
26: 7 a *w* came to him with
Mk 5: 25 a *w* was there who had
7: 25 a *w* whose little daughter
Lk 7: 39 what kind of a *w* she is
10: 38 a *w* named Martha opened
13: 12 "*W*, you are set free
15: 8 suppose a *w* has ten silver
Jn 2: 4 *w*, why do you involve
4: 7 a Samaritan *w* came
8: 3 a *w* caught in adultery.
19: 26 *w*, here is your son,"
20: 15 *W*, 'he said, "why are you crying?
Ac 9: 40 Turning towards the dead *w*,
16: 14 was a *w* named Lydia,
Ro 7: 2 a married *w* is bound to
1Co 7: 2 each *w* her own husband
7: 15 a believing man or *w* is
7: 34 an unmarried *w* or virgin
7: 39 *w* is bound to her husband
11: 3 the head of the *w* is man,
11: 7 the *w* is the glory of man
11: 13 a *w* to pray to God with
Gal 4: 4 his Son, born of a *w*,
4: 31 not children of the slave *w*,
1Ti 2: 11 A *w* should learn in
5: 16 any *w* who is a believer
Rev 2: 20 You tolerate that *w* Jezebel,
12: 1 a *w* clothed with the sun
12: 13 he pursued the *w* who had
17: 3 a *w* sitting on a scarlet

WOMB

Job 1:21 Naked I came from my mother's *w*,
Ps 139:13 in my mother's *w*.
Pr 31:2 "O my son, O son of my *w*,
Jer 1:5 you in the *w* I knew you,
Lk 1:44 the baby in my *w* leaped for joy.
Jn 3:4 into his mother's *w* to be born!"

WOMEN (MAN)

Mt 11:11 among those born of *w*,
28:5 The angel said to the *w*,
Mk 15:41 Many other *w* who had come
Lk 1:42 Blessed are you among *w*,
8:2 also some *w* who had been
23:27 *w* who mourned and wailed
24:11 they did not believe the *w*,
Ac 1:14 along with the *w* and Mary
16:13 speak to the *w* who had
17:4 not a few prominent *w*.
Ro 1:26 *w* exchanged natural relations
1Co 14:34 *w* should remain silent in
Php 4:3 help these *w* who have
1Ti 2:9 want *w* to dress modestly
5:2 older *w* as mothers,
Tit 2:3 teach the older *w* to be
2:4 train the younger *w* to love
Heb 11:35 *W* received back their dead
1Pe 3:5 the holy *w* of the past

WON (WIN)

1Pe 3:1 they may be *w* over without words

WONDER (WONDERFUL WONDERS)

Ps 17:7 Show the *w* of your great love,
SS 1:3 No *w* the maidens love you!

WONDERFUL* (WONDER)

2Sa 1:26 Your love for me was *w*,
1:26 more *w* than that of women.
1Ch 16:9 tell of all his *w* acts.
Job 42:3 things too *w* for me to know.
Ps 26:7 and telling of all your *w* deeds.
31:21 for he showed his *w* love to me
75:1 men tell of your *w* deeds.
105:2 tell of all his *w* acts.
107:8 and his *w* deeds for men,
107:15 and his *w* deeds for men,
107:21 and his *w* deeds for men.
107:24 his *w* deeds in the deep.
107:31 and his *w* deeds for men.
119:18 *w* things in your law.
119:129 Your statutes are *w*;
131:1 or things too *w* for me.
139:6 Such knowledge is too *w* for me,
139:14 your works are *w*,
145:5 I will meditate on your *w* works.
Isa 9:6 *W* Counsellor, Mighty God,
28:29 *w* in counsel and magnificent
Mt 21:15 of the law saw the *w* things he did
Lk 13:17 with all the *w* things he was doing.
1Pe 2:9 out of darkness into his *w* light.

WONDERS (WONDER)

Ex 3:20 with all the *w* that I will perform
Dt 10:21 and awesome *w* you saw
2Sa 7:23 awesome *w* by driving out nations
Job 37:14 stop and consider God's *w*.
Ps 9:1 I will tell of all your *w*.
89:5 The heavens praise your *w*,
119:27 then I will meditate on your *w*.
Joel 2:30 I will show *w* in the heavens
Ac 2:11 we hear them declaring the *w*
2:19 I will show *w* in the heaven above
5:12 many miraculous signs and *w*
2Co 12:12 that mark an apostle—signs, *w*
2Th 2:9 and *w*, and in every sort
Heb 2:4 also testified to it by signs, *w*

WOOD

Isa 44:19 Shall I bow down to a block of *w*?"
1Co 3:12 costly stones, *w*, hay or straw,

WOOL

Pr 31:13 She selects *w* and flax
Isa 1:18 they shall be like *w*.
Da 7:9 hair of his head was white like *w*.
Rev 1:14 and hair were white like *w*,

WORD (BYWORD WORDS)

Nu 30:2 he must not break his *w*
Dt 8:3 but on every *w* that comes
2Sa 22:31 the *w* of the LORD is flawless.
Ps 56:4 In God, whose *w* I praise,
119:9 By living according to your *w*.
119:11 I have hidden your *w* in my heart
119:105 Your *w* is a lamp to my feet
Pr 12:25 but a kind *w* cheers him up.
15:1 but a harsh *w* stirs up anger.
25:11 A *w* aptly spoken
30:5 "Every *w* of God is flawless;
Isa 55:11 so is my *w* that goes out
Jer 23:29 "Is not my *w* like fire," declares
Mt 4:4 but on every *w* that comes
12:36 for every careless *w* they have
15:6 Thus you nullify the *w* of God
Mk 4:14 parable? The farmer sows the *w*.
Jn 1:1 was the *W*, and the *W* was
1:14 The *W* became flesh and made
17:17 them by the truth; your *w* is truth.
Ac 6:4 and the ministry of the *w*."
2Co 2:17 we do not peddle the *w* of God
4:2 nor do we distort the *w* of God.
Eph 6:17 of the Spirit, which is the *w* of God.
Php 2:16 as you hold out the *w* of life—
Col 3:16 Let the *w* of Christ dwell
2Ti 2:15 and who correctly handles the *w*
Heb 4:12 For the *w* of God is living
Jas 1:22 Do not merely listen to the *w*,
2Pe 1:19 And we have the *w* of the prophets

WORDS

Dt 11:18 Fix these *w* of mine in your hearts
Ps 12:6 the *w* of the LORD are flawless,
119:103 How sweet are your *w* to my taste,
119:130 The unfolding of your *w* gives light,
119:160 All your *w* are true;
Pr 2:1 My son, if you accept my *w*
10:19 When *w* are many, sin is not absent
16:24 Pleasant *w* are a honeycomb,
30:6 Do not add to his *w*,
Ecc 12:11 The *w* of the wise are like goads,
Jer 15:16 When your *w* came, I ate them;
Mt 24:35 but my *w* will never pass away.
Lk 6:47 and hears my *w* and puts them
Jn 6:68 You have the *w* of eternal life.
15:7 in me and my *w* remain in you,
1Co 2:13 but in *w* taught by the Spirit,
14:19 rather speak five intelligible *w*
Rev 22:19 And if anyone takes *w* away

WORK (FELLOW-WORKERS WORKED WORKER WORKERS WORKING WORKMAN WORKMANSHIP WORKS)

Ge 2:2 day he rested from all his *w*.
Ex 23:12 "Six days do your *w*,
Nu 8:11 ready to do the *w* of the LORD.
Dt 5:14 On it you shall not do any *w*,
Ps 19:1 the skies proclaim the *w*
Pr 8:22 me at the beginning of his *w*,
Ecc 5:19 his lot and be happy in his *w*—
Jer 48:10 lax in doing the LORD's *w*!
Mt 20:1 to hire men to *w* in his vineyard.
Jn 6:27 Do not *w* for food that spoils,
9:4 we must do the *w* of him who sent
Ac 13:2 for the *w* to which I have called
1Co 3:13 test the quality of each man's *w*.
4:12 We *w* hard with our own hands.
Eph 4:16 up in love, as each part does its *w*.
Php 1:6 that he who began a good *w*
2:12 continue to *w* out your salvation
Col 3:23 Whatever you do, *w* at it
1Th 4:11 and to *w* with your hands,
5:12 to respect those who *w* hard
2Th 3:10 If a man will not *w*, he shall not eat
2Ti 3:17 equipped for every good *w*.
Heb 6:10 he will not forget your *w*
2Jn :11 him shares in his wicked *w*.
3Jn :8 men so that we may *w* together

WORKED (WORK)

1Co 15:10 No, I *w* harder than all of them—
2Th 3:8 On the contrary, we *w* night

WORKER (WORK)

Lk 10:7 for the *w* deserves his wages.
1Ti 5:18 and "The *w* deserves his wages."

WORKERS (WORK)

Mt 9:37 is plentiful but the *w* are few.

WORKING (WORK)

Col 3:23 as *w* for the Lord, not for men,

WORKMAN (WORK)

2Ti 2:15 a *w* who does not need

WORKMANSHIP* (WORK)

Eph 2:10 For we are God's *w*, created

WORKS (WORK)

Ps 66:5 how awesome his *w* on man's behalf
145:6 of the power of your awesome *w*,
Pr 31:31 let her *w* bring her praise
Ro 4:2 in fact, Abraham was justified by *w*
8:28 in all things God *w* for the good
Eph 2:9 not by *w*, so that no-one can boast.
4:12 to prepare God's people for *w*

WORLD (WORLDLY)

Ps 9:8 He will judge the *w*
50:12 for the *w* is mine, and all that is in it
96:13 He will judge the *w*
Pr 8:23 before the *w* began.
Isa 13:11 I will punish the *w* for its evil,
Zep 1:18 the whole *w* will be consumed,
Mt 5:14 "You are the light of the *w*.
16:26 for a man if he gains the whole *w*,
Mk 16:15 into all the *w* and preach the good
Jn 1:29 who takes away the sin of the *w*!
3:16 so loved the *w* that he gave his one
8:12 he said, "I am the light of the *w*.
15:19 As it is, you do not belong to the *w*,
16:33 In this *w* you will have trouble.
17:5 had with you before the *w* began.
17:14 not of the *w* any more than I am
18:36 "My kingdom is not of this *w*.
Ac 17:24 "The God who made the *w*
Ro 3:19 and the whole *w* held accountable
10:18 their words to the ends of the *w*."
1Co 1:27 things of the *w* to shame the strong.
3:19 the wisdom of this *w* is foolishness
6:2 that the saints will judge the *w*?
2Co 5:19 that God was reconciling the *w*
10:3 For though we live in the *w*,
1Ti 6:7 For we brought nothing into the *w*,
Heb 11:38 the *w* was not worthy of them.
Jas 2:5 poor in the eyes of the *w* to be rich
4:4 with the *w* is hatred towards God?
1Pe 1:20 before the creation of the *w*,
1Jn 2:2 but also for the sins of the whole *w*.
2:15 not love the *w* or anything in the *w*.
5:4 born of God overcomes the *w*.
Rev 13:8 slain from the creation of the *w*.

WORLDLY (WORLD)

1Co 3:1 address you as spiritual but as *w*—
Tit 2:12 to ungodliness and *w* passions,

WORM

Mk 9:48 "'their *w* does not die,

WORRY (WORRYING)

Mt 6: 25 I tell you, do not *w* about your life,
10: 19 do not *w* about what to say

WORRYING (WORRY)

Mt 6: 27 of you by *w* can add a single hour

WORSHIP (WORSHIPPED WORSHIPS)

Jos 22: 27 that we will *w* the LORD
2Ki 17: 36 arm, is the one you must *w*.
1Ch 16: 29 *w* the LORD in the splendour
Ps 95: 6 Come, let us bow down in *w*,
100: 2 *W* the LORD with gladness;
Zec 14: 17 up to Jerusalem to *w* the King,
Mt 2: 2 and have come to *w* him."
4: 9 "if you will bow down and *w* me."
Jn 4: 24 and his worshippers must *w* in spirit
Ro 12: 1 this is your spiritual act of *w*.
Heb 10: 1 perfect those who draw near to *w*.

WORSHIPPED (WORSHIP)

2Ch 29: 30 and bowed their heads and *w*.
Mt 28: 9 clasped his feet and *w* him.

WORSHIPS (WORSHIP)

Isa 44: 15 But he also fashions a god and *w* it;

WORTH (WORTHY)

Job 28: 13 Man does not comprehend its *w*;
Pr 31: 10 She is *w* far more than rubies.
Mt 10: 31 are *w* more than many sparrows.
Ro 8: 18 sufferings are not *w* comparing
1Pe 1: 7 of greater *w* than gold,
3: 4 which is of great *w* in God's sight.

WORTHLESS

Pr 11: 4 Wealth is *w* in the day of wrath,
Jas 1: 26 himself and his religion is *w*.

WORTHY (WORTH)

1Ch 16: 25 For great is the LORD and most *w*
Mt 10: 37 more than me is not *w* of me;
Lk 15: 19 I am no longer *w* to be called your
Eph 4: 1 to live a life *w* of the calling you
Php 1: 27 in a manner *w* of the gospel
Col 1: 10 in order that you may live a life *w*
1Ti 3: 8 are to be men *w* of respect, sincere,
Heb 3: 3 Jesus has been found *w*
3Jn : 6 on their way in a manner *w* of God.
Rev 5: 2 "Who is *w* to break the seals

WOUND (WOUNDS)

1Co 8: 12 and *w* their weak conscience,

WOUNDS (WOUND)

Pr 27: 6 *w* from a friend can be trusted,
Isa 53: 5 and by his *w* we are healed.
Zec 13: 6 'What are these *w* on your body?'
1Pe 2: 24 by his *w* you have been healed.

WRAPS

Ps 104: 2 He *w* himself in light

WRATH

2Ch 36: 16 scoffed at his prophets, until the *w*
Ps 2: 5 and terrifies them in his *w*, saying,
76: 10 Surely your *w* against men brings
Pr 15: 1 A gentle answer turns away *w*,
Isa 13: 13 at the *w* of the LORD Almighty,
51: 17 the cup of his *w*,
Jer 25: 15 filled with the wine of my *w*
Eze 5: 13 my *w* against them will subside,
20: 8 So I said I would pour out my *w*
Am 1: 3 I will not turn back ⌊my *w*⌋.
Na 1: 2 maintains his *w* against his enemies
Zep 1: 15 That day will be a day of *w*,
Jn 3: 36 for God's *w* remains on him."
Ro 1: 18 The *w* of God is being revealed
2: 5 you are storing up *w*
5: 9 saved from God's *w* through him!
9: 22 choosing to show his *w*
1Th 5: 9 God did not appoint us to suffer *w*
Rev 6: 16 and from the *w* of the Lamb!
19: 15 the fury of the *w* of God Almighty.

WRESTLED

Ge 32: 24 and a man *w* with him till daybreak

WRITE (WRITER WRITING WRITTEN WROTE)

Dt 6: 9 *W* them on the door-frames
10: 2 I will *w* on the tablets the words
Pr 7: 3 *w* them on the tablet of your heart.
Jer 31: 33 and *w* it on their hearts.
Heb 8: 10 and *w* them on their hearts.
Rev 3: 12 I will also *w* on him my new name.

WRITER* (WRITE)

Ps 45: 1 my tongue is the pen of a skilful *w*.

WRITING (WRITE)

1Co 14: 37 him acknowledge that what I am *w*

WRITTEN (WRITE)

Dt 28: 58 which are *w* in this book,
Jos 1: 8 careful to do everything *w* in it.
23: 6 to obey all that is *w* in the Book
Ps 40: 7 it is *w* about me in the scroll.
Da 12: 1 everyone whose name is found *w*
Mal 3: 16 A scroll of remembrance was *w*
Lk 10: 20 but rejoice that your names are *w*
24: 44 must be fulfilled that is *w* about me
Jn 20: 31 these are *w* that you may believe
21: 25 for the books that would be *w*.
Ro 2: 15 of the law are *w* on their hearts,
1Co 4: 6 "Do not go beyond what is *w*."
10: 11 as examples and were *w* down
2Co 3: 3 *w* not with ink but with the Spirit
Col 2: 14 having cancelled the *w* code,
Heb 10: 7 it is *w* about me in the scroll—
12: 23 whose names are *w* in heaven.
Rev 21: 27 but only those whose names are *w*

WRONG (WRONGDOING WRONGED WRONGS)

Ex 23: 2 Do not follow the crowd in doing *w*
Nu 5: 7 must make full restitution for his *w*,
Dt 32: 4 A faithful God who does no *w*,
Job 34: 12 unthinkable that God would do *w*,
Ps 5: 5 you hate all who do *w*.
Gal 2: 11 to his face, because he was in the *w*.
1Th 5: 15 that nobody pays back *w* for *w*,

WRONGDOING (WRONG)

Job 1: 22 sin by charging God with *w*.
1Jn 5: 17 All *w* is sin, and there is sin that

WRONGED (WRONG)

1Co 6: 7 not rather be *w*? Why not rather

WRONGS (WRONG)

Pr 10: 12 but love covers over all *w*.
1Co 13: 5 angered, it keeps no record of *w*.

WROTE (WRITE)

Ex 34: 28 And he *w* on the tablets the words
Jn 5: 46 for he *w* about me.
8: 8 down and *w* on the ground.

XERXES

King of Persia, husband of Esther. Deposed Vashti; replaced her with Esther (Est 1-2). Sealed Haman's edict to annihilate the Jews (Est 3). Received Esther without having called her (Est 5:1-8). Honoured Mordecai (Est 6). Hanged Haman (Est 7). Issued edict allowing Jews to defend themselves (Est 8). Exalted Mordecai (Est 8:1-2, 15; 9:4; 10).

YEAR (YEARS)

Ex 34: 23 Three times a *y* all your men are
Lev 16: 34 to be made once a *y* for all the sins
Lev 25: 4 But in the seventh *y* the land is
25: 11 The fiftieth *y* shall be a jubilee
Heb 10: 1 repeated endlessly *y* after *y*,

YEARS (YEAR)

Ge 1: 14 to mark seasons and days and *y*,
Ex 12: 40 lived in Egypt was 430 *y*.
16: 35 The Israelites ate manna forty *y*,
Job 36: 26 of his *y* is past finding out.
Ps 90: 4 For a thousand *y* in your sight
90: 10 The length of our days is seventy *y*
Pr 3: 2 they will prolong your life many *y*
Lk 3: 23 Jesus himself was about thirty *y* old
2Pe 3: 8 the Lord a day is like a thousand *y*,
Rev 20: 2 and bound him for a thousand *y*.

YEAST

Ex 12: 15 are to eat bread made without *y*.
Mt 16: 6 guard against the *y* of the Pharisees
1Co 5: 6 you know that a little *y* works

YESTERDAY

Heb 13: 8 Jesus Christ is the same *y*

YOKE (YOKED)

1Ki 12: 4 and the heavy *y* he put on us,
Mt 11: 29 Take my *y* upon you and learn
Gal 5: 1 be burdened again by a *y*

YOKED (YOKE)

2Co 6: 14 Do not be *y* together

YOUNG (YOUNGER YOUTH)

2Ch 10: 14 he followed the advice of the *y* men
Ps 37: 25 I was *y* and now I am old,
119: 9 How can a *y* man keep his way
Pr 20: 29 The glory of *y* men is their strength
Isa 40: 11 he gently leads those that have *y*.
Joel 2: 28 your *y* men will see visions.
Ac 2: 17 your *y* men will see visions,
7: 58 at the feet of a *y* man named Saul.
1Ti 4: 12 down on you because you are *y*,
Tit 2: 6 encourage the *y* men
1Pe 5: 5 *Y* men, in the same way be
1Jn 2: 13 I write to you, *y* men,

YOUNGER (YOUNG)

1Ti 5: 1 Treat *y* men as brothers, older
Tit 2: 4 Then they can train the *y* women

YOUTH (YOUNG)

Ps 103: 5 so that my *y* is renewed like
Ecc 12: 1 Creator in the days of your *y*,
2Ti 2: 22 Flee the evil desires of *y*,

ZACCHAEUS

Lk 19: 2 A man was there by the name of *Z*;

ZEAL (ZEALOUS)

Ps 69: 9 for *z* for your house consumes me,
Pr 19: 2 to have *z* without knowledge,
Isa 59: 17 and wrapped himself in *z*
Jn 2: 17 "*Z* for your house will consume me
Ro 10: 2 their *z* is not based on knowledge.
12: 11 Never be lacking in *z*,

ZEALOUS (ZEAL)

Nu 25: 13 he was *z* for the honour of his God
Pr 23: 17 always be *z* for the fear
Eze 39: 25 and I will be *z* for my holy name.
Gal 4: 18 fine to be *z*, provided the purpose is

ZEBULUN

Son of Jacob by Leah (Ge 30:20; 35:23; 1Ch 2:1). Tribe of blessed (Ge 49:13; Dt 33:18-19), numbered (Nu 1:31; 26:27), allotted land (Jos 19:10-16; Eze 48:26), failed to fully possess (Jdg 1:30), supported Deborah (Jdg 4:6-10; 5:14, 18), David (1Ch 12:33), 12,000 from (Rev 7:8).

ZECHARIAH

1. Son of Jeroboam II; king of Israel (2Ki 15:8-12).

2. Post-exilic prophet who encouraged rebuilding of temple (Ezr 5:1; 6:14; Zec 1:1).

ZEDEKIAH

1. False prophet (1Ki 22:11-24; 2Ch 18:10-23).
2. Mattaniah, son of Josiah (1Ch 3:15), made king of Judah by Nebuchadnezzar (2Ki 24:17-25:7; 2Ch 36:10-14; Jer 37-39; 52:1-11).

ZEPHANIAH

Prophet; descendant of Hezekiah (Zep 1:1).

ZERUBBABEL

Descendant of David (1Ch 3:19; Mt 1:3). Led return from exile (Ezr 2:2; Ne 7:7). Governor of Israel; helped rebuild altar and temple (Ezr 3; Hag 1-2; Zec 4).

ZILPAH

Servant of Leah, mother of Jacob's sons Gad and Asher (Ge 30:9-12; 35:26, 46:16-18).

ZIMRI

King of Israel (1Ki 16:9-20).

ZION

2Sa 5: 7 David captured the fortress of *Z*,
Ps 2: 6 King on *Z*, my holy hill."
9: 11 to the LORD, enthroned in *Z*;
74: 2 Mount *Z*, where you dwelt.
87: 2 the LORD loves the gates of *Z*
102: 13 and have compassion on *Z*,
137: 3 "Sing us one of the songs of *Z*!"
Isa 2: 3 The law will go out from *Z*,
28: 16 "See, I lay a stone in *Z*,
51: 11 They will enter *Z* with singing;
52: 8 When the LORD returns to *Z*,
Jer 50: 5 They will ask the way to *Z*
Joel 3: 21 The LORD dwells in *Z*!
Am 6: 1 to you who are complacent in *Z*,
Mic 4: 2 The law will go out from *Z*,
Zec 9: 9 Rejoice greatly, O Daughter of *Z*!
Ro 9: 33 I lay in *Z* a stone that causes men
11: 26 "The deliverer will come from *Z*;
Heb 12: 22 But you have come to Mount *Z*,
Rev 14: 1 standing on Mount *Z*,

ZIPPORAH*

Daughter of Reuel; wife of Moses (Ex 2:21-22; 4:20-26; 18:1-6).

ZOPHAR

One of Job's friends (Job 11; 20).

INDEX TO MAPS

Many places in the Bible were known by different names at different times or in different languages. Alternative names are given in brackets after the main entries. Place names for which the geographical locations are uncertain are followed by a question mark.

Each place name in the index is followed by a map number and a letter. On the map referred to, the letter can be found at the top of the map frame. The place can be found vertically below the letter.